GARDNER'S

ART

THROUGH THE

AGES

ELEVENTH EDITION

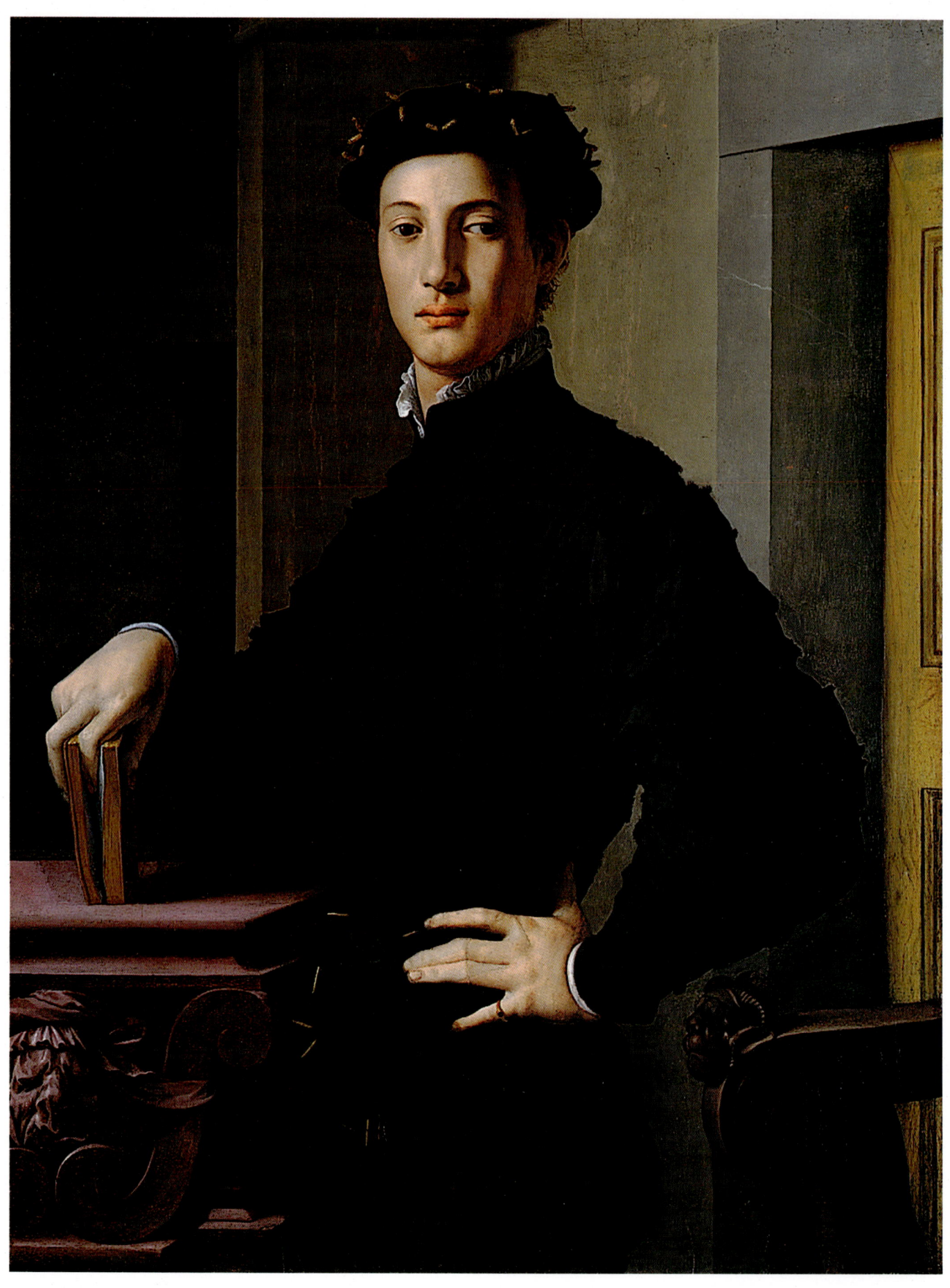

BRONZINO, *Portrait of a Young Man,* ca. 1530s. Oil on wood, approx. 3′ 1½″ × 2′ 5½″. Metropolitan Museum of Art, H. O. Havemeyer Collection. Bequest of Mrs. H. O. Havemeyer, 1929 (29.100.16). Photograph copyright © 1990, Metropolitan Museum of Art.

GARDNER'S
ART
THROUGH THE
AGES

ELEVENTH EDITION

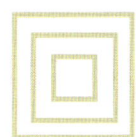

FRED S. KLEINER

CHRISTIN J. MAMIYA

RICHARD G. TANSEY

HARCOURT COLLEGE PUBLISHERS

Fort Worth   Philadelphia   San Diego   New York   Orlando   Austin   San Antonio
Toronto   Montreal   London   Sydney   Tokyo

PUBLISHER Earl McPeek
EXECUTIVE EDITOR David Tatom
ACQUISITIONS EDITOR John R. Swanson
MARKET STRATEGIST Steve Drummond
DEVELOPMENTAL EDITOR Stacey Sims
PROJECT EDITOR Kathryn M. Stewart
ART DIRECTOR Linda Beaupré
PRODUCTION MANAGER Diane Gray

Cover image: BRONZINO, *Portrait of a Young Man* (detail), ca. 1530s. Oil on wood, approx. 3′ 1 1/2″ × 2′ 5 1/2″. Metropolitan Museum of Art, H. O. Havemeyer Collection. Bequest of Mrs. H. O. Havemeyer, 1929 (29.100.16). Photograph copyright © 1990, Metropolitan Museum of Art.

ISBN: 0-15-508315-5
Library of Congress Catalog Card Number: 00-103800

Address for Domestic Orders
Harcourt College Publishers, 6277 Sea Harbor Drive, Orlando, FL 32887-6777
800-782-4479

Address for International Orders
International Customer Service
Harcourt, Inc., 6277 Sea Harbor Drive, Orlando, FL 32887-6777
407-345-3800
(fax) 407-345-4060
(e-mail) hbintl@harcourt.com

Address for Editorial Correspondence
Harcourt College Publishers, 301 Commerce Street, Suite 3700, Fort Worth, TX 76102

Web Site Address
http://www.harcourtcollege.com

Harcourt College Publishers will provide complimentary supplements or supplement packages to those adopters qualified under our adoption policy. Please contact your sales representative to learn how you qualify. If as an adopter or potential user you receive supplements you do not need, please return them to your sales representative or send them to: Attn: Returns Department, Troy Warehouse, 465 South Lincoln Drive, Troy, MO 63379.

Printed in the United States of America

0 1 2 3 4 5 6 7 8 9 048 9 8 7 6 5 4 3 2 1

Harcourt College Publishers

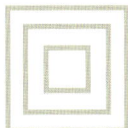

IN MEMORIAM

Richard G. Tansey

WE NOTE WITH DEEP SORROW the death of our good friend and esteemed colleague Richard G. Tansey.

Through six previous editions of *Art through the Ages* he probably introduced more students to the discipline

of art history than any other author or teacher, establishing himself as one of the greatest art-historical

educators of the twentieth century. While we mourn his passing, we celebrate his life, remembering his

keen intellect, wide learning, sharp wit, and unfailing generosity. With the publication of this new edition

his influence will endure in another century, indeed in another millennium.

We dedicate the eleventh edition of *Art through the Ages* to him.

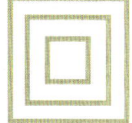

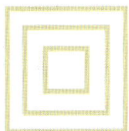

PREFACE

THE CLASSIC FOR A NEW AGE

HELEN GARDNER'S VISION In the mid 1920s, Helen Gardner had a vision—to provide students with a textbook that would introduce them to the artistic legacy of not only Europe and the United States, but of the entire globe. In 1926, Harcourt Brace and Company published that vision—Helen Gardner's *Art through the Ages.* For seventy-five years, from just before the introduction of the Model A automobile through the computer revolution and the dawn of a new millennium, Helen Gardner's book has been the most widely read introduction to the history of art in the English language. At the beginning of the twenty-first century, to mark the seventy-fifth anniversary of the initial publication, Harcourt College Publishers offers the eleventh edition of *Gardner's Art through the Ages,* the classic for a new age.

The fundamental belief that guided Helen Gardner, and one that we share, is that the history of art is essential to a liberal education. The study of art history has as its aim the appreciation and understanding of works of high aesthetic quality and historical significance produced throughout the world and across thousands of years of human history. We think that the most effective way to tell the story of art through the ages, especially for those who are studying art history for the first time, is to organize the vast array of artistic monuments according to the civilizations that produced them and to consider each work in roughly chronological order. Not only has this approach stood the test of time, but it is the most appropriate for narrating the *history* of art. We believe that the enormous variation in the form and meaning of paintings, sculptures, buildings, and other artworks is largely the result of the constantly changing historical, social, economic, religious, and cultural context in which artists and architects worked. A historically based narrative is therefore best suited for a global history of art.

NEW AUTHOR TEAM A new team of authors has revised every chapter of Helen Gardner's pioneering work, rewriting many chapters almost in their entirety. Fred S. Kleiner, Professor of Art History and Archaeology at Boston University and former Editor-in-Chief of the *American Journal of Archaeology,* worked with Richard G. Tansey on the tenth edition. Although Professor Tansey passed away before his work on the eleventh edition could begin, his contributions to *Art through the Ages* over the last thirty years are evident on every page and they remain an enduring legacy. His name appropriately remains on the title page of this book. Christin J. Mamiya, Professor of Art History at the University of Nebraska—Lincoln, joins the author team with this new edition. Professor Mamiya, whose special research interests include Pop art, has revised all of the chapters on modern and contemporary art, in addition to updating and revising the coverage of Renaissance and Baroque art. Professor Kleiner has reworked the chapters on ancient art that he contributed to the tenth edition and has revised all the chapters on the Middle Ages.

FEATURES OF THE ELEVENTH EDITION

REORGANIZATION The eleventh edition of *Art through the Ages* is the most extensively reviewed in the book's history and maintains the Gardner reputation of being the authoritative and up-to-date choice for introducing students to the history of art. We have, however, made many changes to this classic work. As before, the book is available both in a one-volume clothbound and a two-volume paperback edition, but we have divided the history of art into thirty-four chapters, six more than in the tenth edition. A reevaluation of the treatment of the art and architecture of the eighteenth and nineteenth centuries led us to reorganize those chapters. With the collaboration of four contributing authors, we have also rethought our coverage of Asian, African, Oceanic, and pre-Columbian art. Robert L. Brown (University of California—Los Angeles), Virginia E. Miller (Univeristy of Illinois—Chicago), and Quitman Eugene Phillips (University of Wisconsin—Madison) revised the chapters on India and Southeast Asia; the native arts of the Americas; and China, Korea, and Japan, respectively. George Corbin (Lehman College of the City University of New York) revised the chapter on Africa first contributed by Herbert Cole in the tenth edition, expanding and updating the material to meet the requirements of the new edition. He also revised the coverage of Oceanic art, which now has a chapter of its own. For the first time we devote two chapters each to India, China and Korea, Japan, Africa, and the native arts of the Americas. The chapters on early Asian art follow that on Greece. Discussion of the ancient arts of the Americas and Africa follow the chapters on Byzantium and Islam. We treat later developments in Asian art after the chapter on seventeenth- and eighteenth-century Europe, and the later arts of the Americas, Oceania, and Africa after the discussion of the rise of modernism in the West.

This new organization has allowed us to interweave the narrative of the western and non-European traditions more effectively and to present a global history of art that highlights the interactions between geographically distant and culturally distinct societies. An important additional advantage of the new scheme is that in the two-volume paperbound version of this book, chapters on Asian, African, and pre-Columbian art and architecture now appear in both volumes and can be covered in both semesters of a two-semester course.

TRADITION AND INNOVATION The new author team has also revised the eleventh edition to reflect the latest art historical research emphases, while maintaining the traditional strengths that have made all the previous editions of *Art through the Ages* so successful. While sustaining attention to style, chronology, iconography, and technique, we pay greater attention than ever before to function and context. We consider artworks with a view toward their purpose and meaning in the society that produced them at the time at which they were produced. We also address the very important role of patronage in the production of art and examine the role of the individuals or groups who paid the artists and influenced the shape the monuments took. We give greater attention to the role of women and women artists in societies worldwide over time. Throughout, we have aimed to integrate the historical, political, and social context of art and architecture with the artistic and intellectual aspects. Consequently, we now often treat painting, sculpture, architecture, and the so-called minor arts together, highlighting how they all reflect the conventions and aspirations of a common culture, rather than treating them as separate and distinct media.

ENHANCED ILLUSTRATION PROGRAM The eleventh edition of Helen Gardner's classic text contains more illustrations, more illustrations in color, and more full-page illustrations than any previous edition. More than fourteen hundred photographs, plans, and drawings appear in the book, including more than sixty-five full-page photos (at least one in every chapter). Over sixty-eight percent of the photographs are in color—the highest percentage of color illustrations in any art history survey textbook. Harcourt College Publishers has printed these photographs using a five-color production process and high-quality paper.

NEW MONUMENTS Throughout the eleventh edition, we have also introduced dozens of new monuments. We have tried in our choice of artworks and buildings to reflect the increasingly wide range of interests of scholars today, while not rejecting the traditional list of "great" works or the very notion of a "canon." Recent discoveries, such as the world's oldest paintings, in the Chauvet Cave in France, are illustrated, as are recently cleaned works, like Leonardo da Vinci's *Last Supper* in Milan, Italy. The expanded selection of works encompasses every artistic medium and almost every era and culture. Some are famous works that have never appeared before in *Art through the Ages.* Many, however, are rarely illustrated works of high artistic and historical interest that significantly enrich the character of the traditional art history survey—for example, the costly vestments worn by Byzantine patriarchs and Ottoman emperors.

NEW BOXED ESSAYS To include important background information and other material designed to enhance understanding, every chapter of *Art through the Ages* now features boxed discussions focusing on selected themes and issues in the history of art. The boxes allow us to maintain a clear narrative thread throughout the text while providing students with concise information about terminology, technique, and iconography; an appreciation of the cultural and historical context of art and architecture; and an introduction to some of the major scholarly and ethical controversies of the new millennium. We present these short essays in six broad categories.

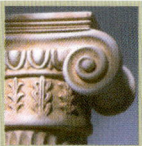

Architectural Basics provide students with a sound foundation for the understanding of all discussions of architecture. These discussions are concise primers, with drawings and diagrams of the major aspects of design and construction. The information included is essential to an understanding of architectural technology and terminology. The boxes address questions of how and why various forms developed, the problems architects confronted, and the solutions they used to resolve them. Topics discussed include how the Egyptians built the pyramids, the orders of classical architecture, the revolutionary nature of Roman concrete construction, the origin and development of the Islamic mosque, and the construction of Gothic cathedrals.

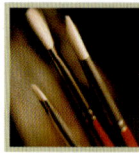

Materials and Techniques essays explain the various media artists employed from prehistoric to modern times. Since materials and techniques often influence the character of works of art, these discussions also contain essential information on why many monuments look the way they do. Hollow-casting bronze statues, fresco painting, Chinese silk, Andean weaving, Islamic tilework, embroidery and tapestry, woodblock prints, and perspective are among the many subjects treated.

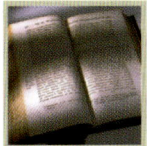

Written Sources present and discuss key historical documents illuminating important monuments of art and architecture and the careers of some of the world's leading artists, architects, and patrons. The passages we quote permit voices from the past to speak directly to the reader, providing vivid and unique insights into the creation of artworks in all media. Examples include Saint Bernard of Clairvaux's treatise on sculpture in medieval churches, Sinan the Great's commentary on the mosque he built for Selim II, Vasari's biographies of Renaissance artists, as well as texts that bring the past to life, such as eyewitness accounts of the volcanic eruption that buried Roman Pompeii and of the fire that destroyed Canterbury Cathedral in medieval England.

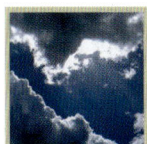

Religion and Mythology boxes introduce students to the principal elements of the world's great religions, past and present, and to the representation of religious and mythological themes in painting and sculpture of all periods and places. These discussions of belief systems and iconography give readers a richer understanding of some of the greatest artworks ever created. The topics include the gods and goddesses of Egypt, Mesopotamia, Greece, and Rome; the life of Jesus in art; Buddha and Buddhism; Muhammad and Islam; and Aztec religion.

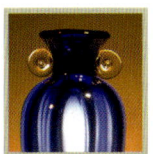

Art and Society essays treat the historical, social, political, cultural, and religious context of art and architecture. In some instances, specific monuments are the basis for a discussion of broader themes, as when we use the Hegeso stele to serve as the springboard for an exploration of the role of women in ancient Greek society. In other cases, we discuss how people's evaluation today of artworks can differ from those of the society that produced them, as when we examine the problems created by the contemporary market for undocumented archeological finds. Other subjects include Egyptian mummification, the art of freed Roman slaves, the Mesoamerican ballgame, the shifting fortunes of Vincent van Gogh, Japanese court culture, and Native American artists.

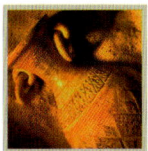

Art in the News boxes present accounts of the latest archeological finds and discussions of current controversies in the history of art. Among the discoveries and issues we highlight are the excavation of the tomb of the sons of the pharaoh Ramses and the restoration of Michelangelo's frescoes in the Sistine Chapel.

SPECIAL VOLUME TWO REVIEW MATERIAL Since many students taking the second half of a year-long introductory art history survey course will only have the second volume of the paperbound edition of *Art through the Ages,* we have provided a new feature not found in any other textbook currently available: a special set of Volume II boxes on *Art and Society before 1300*. These discussions immediately follow the Preface and Introduction to Volume II and provide concise primers on religion and mythology and on architectural terminology and construction methods in the ancient and medieval worlds—information that is essential for under-

standing the history of art after 1300, both in the West and the East. The subjects of these special boxes are the Gods and Goddesses of Mount Olympus; the Life of Jesus in Art; Buddhism and Buddhist Iconography; Classical Architecture; and Medieval Churches.

MAPS AND TIMELINES The eleventh edition of *Art through the Ages* includes new or revised maps and timelines at the beginning of every chapter. We have taken great care to make sure that every site discussed in the text appears on our maps. These maps vary widely in both geographical and chronological scope. Some focus on a small region or even a single city, while others encompass a vast territory and occasionally bridge two or more continents. Several maps plot the art-producing sites of a given area over hundreds, even thousands, of years. In every instance, our aim has been to provide readers with maps that will easily allow them to locate the places where works of art originated or were found and where buildings were erected. To this end we have regularly placed the names of modern nations on maps of the territories of past civilizations. The maps, therefore, are pedagogical tools and do not constitute a historical atlas. A historical timeline does, however, accompany each map. At the top is a time rule and the names of historical periods. The central zone features thumbnail photographs of significant monuments in chronological order. The third zone lists important historical figures and major political, cultural, and religious events.

LANGUAGE, GLOSSARY, BIBLIOGRAPHY A group of college students has carefully read many chapters of the revised text of the eleventh edition to assure ease of comprehension and liveliness of expression. The new author team has also provided more frequent headings and subheadings in the text to act as guides for both initial reading and subsequent reviewing for examinations. In addition, in order to aid our readers in mastering the vocabulary of art history, we have italicized and defined all art historical terms and other unfamiliar words at their first occurrence in the text—and at later occurrences too, whenever the term has not been used again for several chapters. Definitions of all terms introduced in the text appear once more in the Glossary at the back of the book, which, for the first time, includes pronunciations. We have also included a pronunciation guide to artists' names, a refined and revised version of that popular feature of the tenth edition. *Art through the Ages* also has a comprehensive bibliography of books in English, including both general works and a chapter-by-chapter list of more focused studies.

PHOTO CAPTIONS The captions to our more than 1400 illustrations contain a wealth of information, including the name of the artist or architect, if known; the formal title (printed in italics), if assigned, description of the work, or name of the building; the findspot or place of production of the object or location of the building; the date; the material or materials used; the size; and the present location if the work is in a museum or private collection. We urge readers to pay attention to the scales provided on all plans and to all dimensions given in the captions. The objects we illustrate vary enormously in size, from colossal sculptures carved into mountain cliffs and paintings that cover entire walls or ceilings to tiny figurines, coins, and jewelry that one can hold in the hand. Note too the location of the monuments discussed. Although many buildings and museums may be in cities or countries that a reader may never visit, others are likely to be close to home. Nothing can substitute for walking through a building, standing in the presence of a statue, or inspecting the brushwork of a painting close up. Consequently, we have made a special effort to illustrate artworks in geographically wide-ranging public collections.

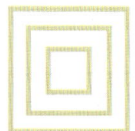

ACKNOWLEDGMENTS

A work as extensive as a global history of art could not be undertaken or completed without the counsel of experts in all areas of world art. For contributions to the eleventh edition in the form of extended critiques of the tenth edition or of the penultimate drafts of the eleventh edition chapters, as well as other assistance of various sorts, we wish to thank Trudi Abram, California State University—Northridge; Catherine Asher, University of Minnesota; Frederick Asher, University of Minnesota; Paul Bahn; Barbara Barletta, University of Florida; Marina Belozerskaya, Radcliffe Institute for Advanced Study; Roberta Bernstein, State University of New York—Albany; Jonathan Best, Wesleyan University; Philip Betancourt, Temple University; Alan Birnholz, State University of New York—Buffalo; Robert Bianchi; Barbara Blackmun, San Diego Mesa College; Ann Marie Bouche, Princeton University; Arthur Bourgeois, Governors State University; Celeste Brusati, University of Michigan; Kathleen Burke-Kelly, Glendale Community College; Walter B. Cahn, Yale University; Anne-Marie Carr, Southern Methodist University; Derrick Cartwright, Musée d'Art Américain—Giverny; Hipolito Chacon, University of Montana; Pramrod Chandra, Harvard University; Michael Charlesworth, University of Texas—Austin; Petra Chu, Seton Hall University; John Clarke, University of Texas—Austin; Adam Cohen, University of California—Berkeley; Jadviga de Costa Nunes, Muhlenburg College; Jeffrey Collins, University of Washington; Joan Coutu, University of Waterloo; Tom Cummins, University of Chicago; Kathy Curnow, Cleveland State University; Anthony Cutler, Pennsylvania State University; Nancy DeGrummond, Florida State University; Walter Denny, University of Massachusetts—Amherst; Marilyn Dunn, Loyola University; Susan Erickson, University of Michigan—Dearborn; Kate Ezra, Columbia College; Betsy Fahlman, Arizona State University; Claire Farago, University of Colorado—Boulder; James Farmer, Virginia Commonwealth University; Peter Fergusson, Wellesley College; Phyllis Floyd, Michigan State University; Mitchell Frank, University of Toronto; Vivien Fryd, Vanderbilt University; Christopher Fulton, Southern Methodist University; Mark Graham, Auburn University; Anthony Gully, Arizona State University; Peter Bacon Hales, University of Illinois—Chicago; Catherine Harding; University of Victoria; Mary Beth Heston, College of Charleston; Jeanne Hokin, Arizona State University; Jeffrey Hughes, Webster University; Susan Huntington, Ohio State University; Carol Ivory, Washington State University; dele jegede, Indiana State University; Amelia Jones, University of California—Riverside; Christy Junkerman, San Jose State University; Deborah Kahn, Boston University; Richard Karberg, Cuyahoga Community College—East Campus; Karl Kilinski, Southern Methodist University; Joni L. Kinsey, University of Iowa; Phyllis Kozlowski, Moraine Valley Community College; David Ludley, Clayton College State University; Rita Parham McCaslin; Sheila McTighe, Columbia University; Patricia Mainardi, City University of New York; Joanne Mannell-Noel, Montana State University; Lynn R. Matteson, University of Southern California; Mark Meadow, University of California—Santa Barbara; Walter Melion, Johns Hopkins University; Arline Meyer, Ohio State University; Anne Mochon, University of Masschusetts—Amherst; Larry Nees, University of Delaware; Mary Pardo, University of North Carolina—Chapel Hill; Robert S. Petersen, Eastern Illinois University; Robert Poor, University of Minnesota; JoAnn Quillman, Louisiana State University; Nancy Ramage, Ithaca College; Ingrida Raudzens, Salem State College; Louise Rice, Duke University; Howard Risatti, Virginia Commonwealth University; Lilien F. Robinson, George Washington University; Mark Rose, *Archaeology Magazine;* Patricia Rose, Florida State University; Christopher D. Roy, The University of Iowa; John Russell, Massachusetts College of Art; Ray Silverman, Michigan State University; Jeffrey Smith, University of Texas—Austin; Jack Spalding, Fordham University; Kristine Stiles, Duke University; Melinda Takeuchi, Stanford University; Roberta Tarbell, Rutgers University—Camden campus; Elizabeth ten Grotenhuis, Boston University; Jan Newstrom Thompson, San Jose State University; Thomas Toone, Utah State University; Bailey Van Hook, Virginia Polytechnic Institute and State University; Richard Vinograd, Stanford University; Deborah Waite, University of Hawaii; Josephine Withers, University of Maryland; Marcilene Wittmer, University of Miami; Mimi Yiengpruksawan, Yale University; and Paul Zimansky, Boston University. Innumerable other instructors and students have also sent us helpful reactions, comments, and suggestions for ways to improve the book. We are grateful for their interest and their insights.

Among those at Harcourt College Publishers who worked with us to make the new edition of *Art through the Ages* the best ever are the president, Ted Buchholz; senior vice president, editorial, Chris Klein; vice president, publisher, Earl McPeek; executive editor, David Tatom; acquisitions editor, John Swanson; technology specialists, Diane Drexler and Sarah Davis Packard; our developmental editors, Helen Triller, Stacey Sims, and Michelle Vardeman; our copy editor, Kay Kaylor; our senior vice president of production, Tim Frelick; senior project editor, Kathryn Stewart; our photo editors,

Carrie Ward, Susan Holtz, and Elsa Peterson, all under the in-house supervision of Shirley Webster; our assistant manager of art and design, senior art director, Linda Beaupré; our senior production manager, Diane Gray, and our manager of manufacturing, Lisa Kelly. We are also grateful to the marketing staff for their dedication to making the book successful: Roland Hernandez, senior vice president, marketing; Pat Murphree, executive product manager for marketing avenues; Steve Drummond, executive market strategist; Laura Brennan, market strategist; Mekelle Douglas, marketing coordinator; and Van Strength and Laura Lashley of the Marketing Intelligence Group. Recognition and thanks are also due to our proofreader, Carolyn Crabtree and our indexer, Linda Webster. We take special pleasure in thanking Helen Triller, who has been associated with *Art through the Ages* since the ninth edition. Only those who have worked with Helen on a daily basis can appreciate how important her efforts, expertise, and experience have been to the continuing success of this book.

Among family and friends who have provided various kinds of support, we single out Luraine Tansey, whose contributions to several editions have been chronicled in successive prefaces, and Alex Kleiner, who, to our amazement and delight, was always able to figure out how to make compatible the several different software programs and hardware systems the six authors and many editors used during the preparation of a very long and complex manuscript. We also owe a deep debt of gratitude to our colleagues at Boston University and the University of Nebraska—Lincoln, and to the thousands of students and the scores of teaching fellows in our art history courses over many years in Boston and Lincoln, and at the University of Virginia and Yale University. From them we have learned much that has helped determine the form and content of the eleventh edition.

Fred S. Kleiner
Christin J. Mamiya

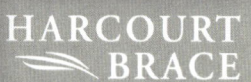
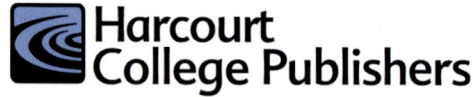

GARDNER'S

ART

THROUGH THE

AGES

ELEVENTH EDITION

ANCILLARY PACKAGE

IN ADDITION TO THE WEALTH OF FEATURES IN THE ELEVENTH EDITION OF *Art through the Ages,* A VARIETY OF ANCILLARIES ARE AVAILABLE TO COMPLEMENT THE TEXTBOOK. CONTACT HARCOURT COLLEGE PUBLISHERS FOR INFORMATION ON HOW TO OBTAIN THESE ITEMS.

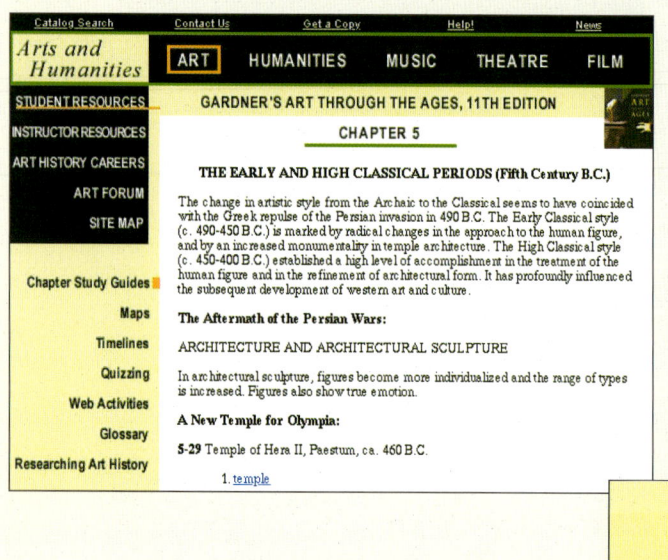

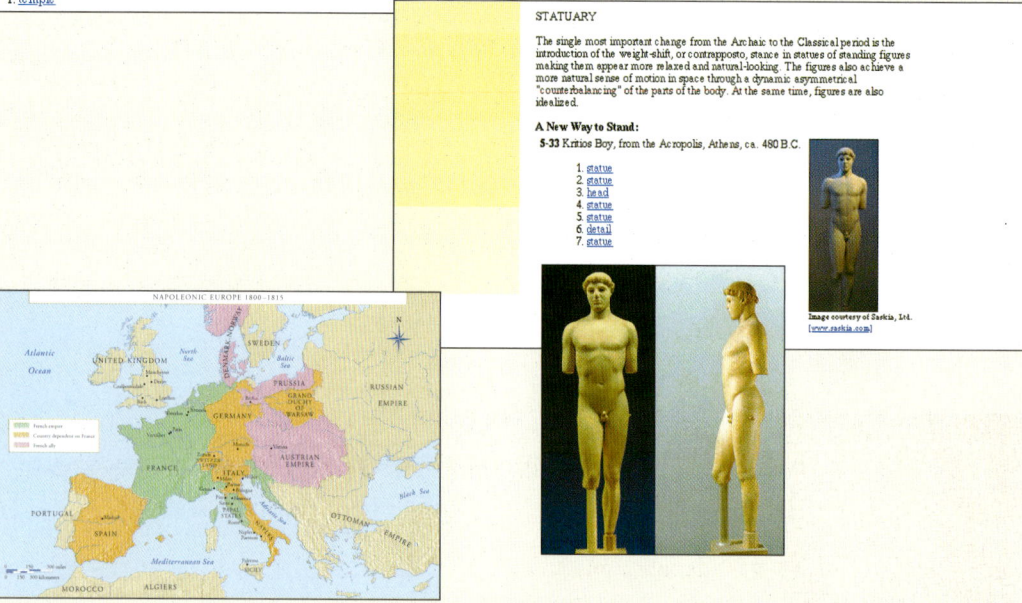

WEB SITE Readers are urged to venture beyond the printed page and explore *Art through the Ages* on the Internet at **http://www.harcourtcollege.com/arts/gardner.** This unique resource provides a collection of hundreds of additional images of the works discussed, timelines that chart developments across cultures and over longer periods of time, tips for researching art history on the Internet, and a teaching assistant's guide. It also includes a pronunciation guide, a glossary, self-assessment quizzes, and links to hundreds of other useful sites, all continuously updated. In addition, the thirty-six maps presented in the book have been prepared in an electronic format for access on the Web site.

ONLINE COURSE MATERIALS For the first time, a text-specific online course is also available for adoption with *Gardner's Art through the Ages*. Prepared by Linda Scalera Woodward and Deborah Ellington of North Harris College, the course includes chapter-by-chapter learning modules with assignments, discussion questions, Web links and activities, and self-tests. Harcourt College Publishers also offers a variety of other options for WebCT or other course management tool use from free access to a blank WebCT template or basic online testing to customized course creation using materials provided by the instructor.

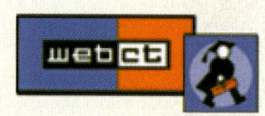

SLIDE SETS Harcourt College Publishers has assembled three new slide sets for use with the eleventh edition of *Gardner's Art through the Ages*. A full set of 300 images, available in separate parts for Volume I and Volume II, is composed of slides not offered with the tenth edition. Approximately twenty-five percent of the slides illustrate artworks and buildings new to the eleventh edition. A second set contains 50 slides exclusively of works discussed for the first time in the new edition, and a final set of 100 slides consists of plans, sections, diagrams, and maps directly from the textbook.

HARCOURT VIDEO AND CD-ROM ART LIBRARY This extensive library of videos and CD-ROMs contains selections from every era along with a variety of media including architecture and photography. Videos and CD-ROMs are available covering civilizations from around the globe. Examples include *The Caves of Altamira; The Body of Christ in Art; Ancient Treasures: Imperial Art of China;* and *Bauhaus: The Face of the 20th Century.*

GREAT ARTISTS CD-ROM This CD-ROM focuses on eight major artists—William Blake, El Greco, Leonardo da Vinci, Pablo Picasso, Rembrandt, Vincent van Gogh, J.M.W. Turner, and Jean-Antoine Watteau. It includes 1,000 full-color images, 20 minutes of video, biographies of the artists, 500,000 words of descriptive text, 100 music and video clips, an examination of the artists' materials and methods.

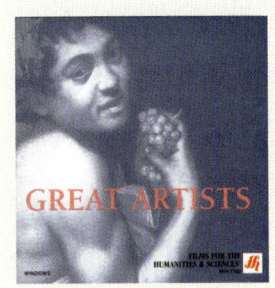

PRINT ANCILLARIES A comprehensive package of teaching and study aids accompanies the eleventh edition of *Gardner's Art through the Ages.* The *Study Guide* by Kathleen Cohen (San Jose State University) contains chapter-by-chapter drills on the identification of styles, terms, iconography, major art movements, geographical locations, time periods, and specific philosophical, religious, and historical movements as they relate to particular works of art examined in the textbook. Self-quizzes and discussion questions enable students to evaluate their grasp of the material. Lilla Sweatt (San Diego State University) is the author of the *Instructor's Manual,* which includes sample lecture topics for each chapter, a testbank of questions in formats ranging from matching to essay, studio projects, and lists of resources. A computerized testbank, consisting of questions from the Instructor's Manual, has been created for textbook users. An Internet guide, *Art H.I.T.S. on the Web* is also available with the book. It provides a general introduction to using the World Wide Web and covers Web browsers, search engines, the creation of personal homepages, and presents guidelines for conducting art historical research online as well as for navigating the Gardner Web site.

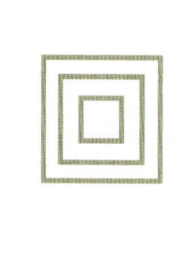

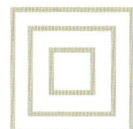

CONTENTS IN BRIEF

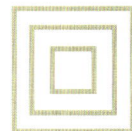

CONTENTS

Chapter 23

Chapter 24

Chapter 25

Chapter 26

CHAPTER 27

FROM THE SHOGUNS TO THE PRESENT: THE ART OF LATER JAPAN 817

CHAPTER 28

THE ENLIGHTENMENT AND ITS LEGACY: NEOCLASSICISM THROUGH THE MID-NINETEENTH CENTURY 835

CHAPTER 29

THE RISE OF MODERNISM: THE LATER NINETEENTH CENTURY 889

CHAPTER 34

CHAPTER 34

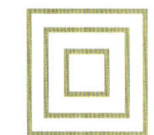

GARDNER'S
ART
THROUGH THE
AGES

ELEVENTH EDITION

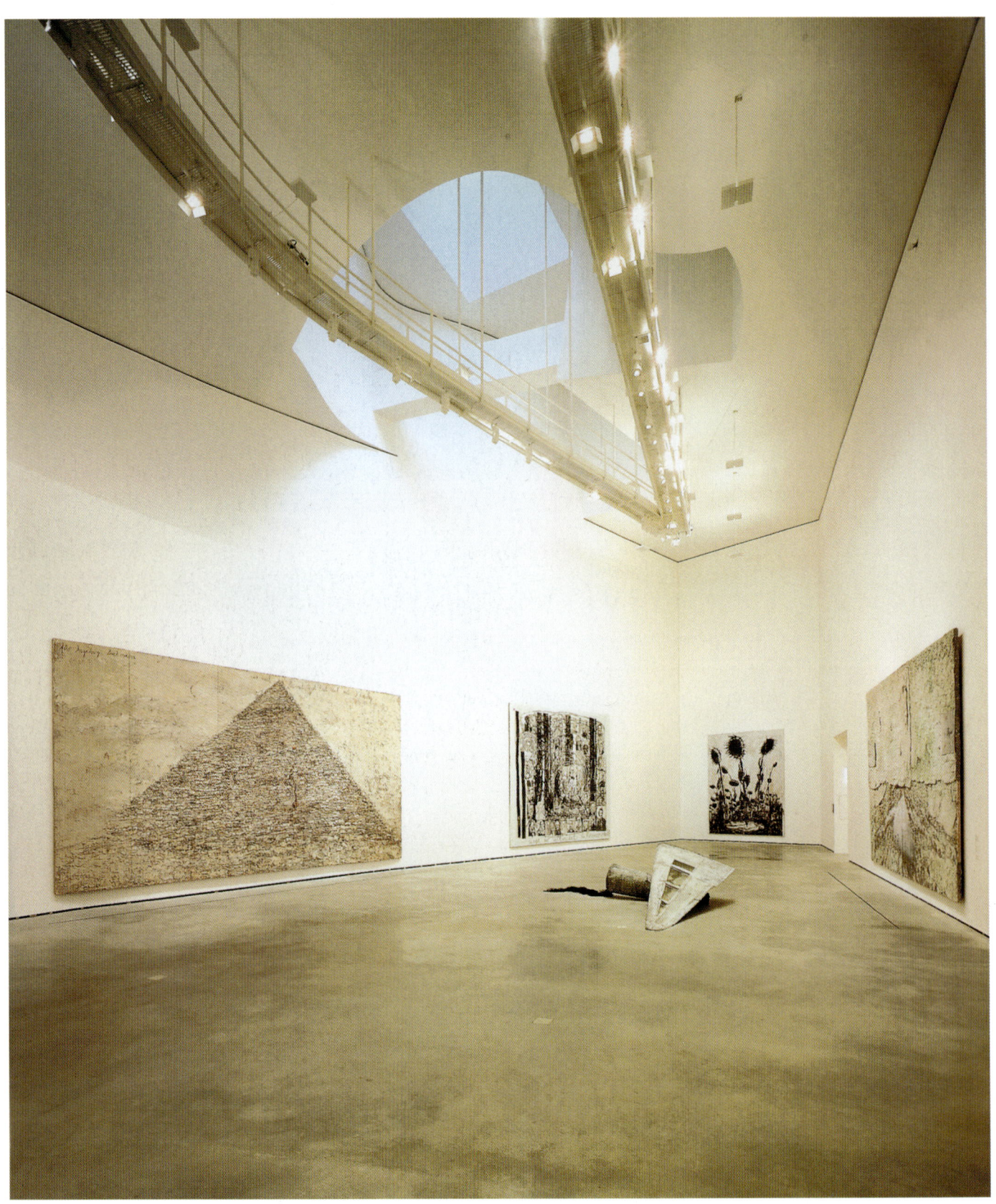

Intro-1 FRANK GEHRY, interior of Guggenheim Museum, Bilbao, Spain, 1997.

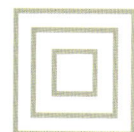

INTRODUCTION

THE SUBJECTS AND VOCABULARY

OF ART HISTORY

ART, HISTORY, AND THE HISTORY OF ART

PEOPLE DO NOT OFTEN JUXTAPOSE THE terms *art* and *history*. They tend to think of history as the record and interpretation of past human actions, particularly social and political actions. Most think of art, quite correctly, as part of the present—as objects people can see and touch. People cannot, of course, see or touch history's vanished human events. But a visible and tangible artwork is a kind of persisting event. One or more artists made it at a certain time and in a specific place, even if no one now knows just who, when, where, or why. Although created in the past, an artwork continues to exist in the present, long surviving its times. The first painters and sculptors died thirty thousand years ago, but their works remain, some of them exhibited in glass cases in museums built only a few years ago.

Modern museum visitors can admire these relics of the remote past and the countless other objects humankind has produced over the millennia without any knowledge of the circumstances that led to the creation of those works. An object's beauty or sheer size can impress people, the artist's virtuosity in the handling of ordinary or costly materials can dazzle them, or the subject depicted can move them. Viewers can react to what they see, interpret the work in the light of their own experience, and judge it a success or a failure. These are all valid responses to a work of art. But the enjoyment and appreciation of artworks in museum settings (FIG. **Intro-1**) are relatively recent phenomena, as is the creation of artworks solely for museum-going audiences to view.

Today, it is common for artists to work in private studios and to create paintings, sculptures, and other objects commercial art galleries will offer for sale. Usually, someone the artist has never met will purchase the artwork and display it in a setting the artist has never seen. But although this is not a new phenomenon in the history of art—an ancient potter decorating a vase for sale at a village market stall also probably did not know who would buy the pot or where it would be housed—it is not at all typical. In fact, it is exceptional. Artists created a high percentage of the paintings, sculptures, and other objects exhibited in museums today for specific patrons and settings and to fulfill a specific purpose. Often, no one knows the original contexts of those artworks. Although people may appreciate the visual and tactile qualities of these objects, they cannot understand why they were made or why they look the way they do without knowing the circumstances of their creation. *Art appreciation* does not require a knowledge of the historical context of an artwork (or a building). *Art history* does.

Thus, a central aim of art historians is to determine the original context of artworks. They seek to achieve a full understanding not only of why these "persisting events" of human history look the way they do but also why the artistic "events" happened at all. What unique set of circumstances gave rise to the erection of a particular building or led a specific patron to commission an individual artist to fashion a singular artwork for a certain place? The study of history is therefore vital to art history. And art history is often very important to the study of history. Art objects and buildings are historical documents that can shed light on the peoples who made them and on the times of their creation in a way other historical documents cannot. Furthermore, artists and architects can affect history by reinforcing or challenging cultural values and practices through the objects they create and the structures they build. Thus, the history of art and architecture is inseparable from the study of history, although the two disciplines are not the same. In the following pages, we outline some of the distinctive subjects art historians address and the kinds of questions they ask, and explain some of the basic terminology art historians use when answering their questions. Armed with this arsenal of questions and words, the reader will be ready to explore the multifaceted world of art through the ages.

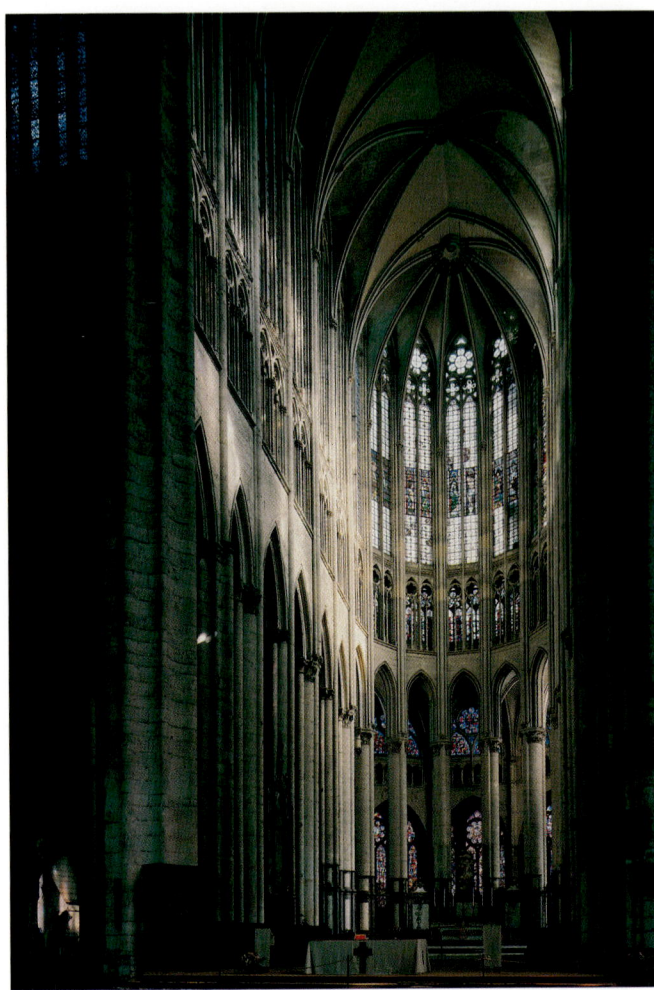

Intro-2   Choir of Beauvais Cathedral, Beauvais, France, rebuilt after 1284.

ART HISTORY IN THE TWENTY-FIRST CENTURY

Art historians study the visual and tangible objects humans make and the structures humans build. They traditionally have classified such works as architecture, sculpture, the pictorial arts (painting, drawing, printmaking, and photography), and the craft arts, or arts of design. The craft arts comprise utilitarian objects, such as ceramic and metal wares, textiles, jewelry, and similar accessories of ordinary living. Artists of every age have blurred the boundaries between these categories, but this is especially true today, when *multimedia* works abound.

From the earliest Greco-Roman art critics on, scholars have studied objects that their makers consciously manufactured as "artworks" and to which the artists assigned formal titles. But today's art historians also study a vast number of objects whose creators and owners almost certainly did not consider artworks. Few ancient Romans, for example, would have regarded a coin bearing their emperor's portrait as anything but money. Today, an art museum may exhibit that coin, and scholars may subject it to the same kind of art historical analysis as a portrait by an acclaimed Renaissance or modern sculptor or painter.

The range of objects art historians study is constantly expanding and now includes, for example, computer-generated images, whereas in the past almost anything produced using a machine would not have been regarded as "art." Most people still consider the performing arts—music, drama, and dance—as outside art history's realm because these arts are temporal, rather than spatial and static, media. But, recently, even this distinction between "fine art" and performance art has become blurred. Art historians, however, generally ask the same kinds of questions about what they study, whether they employ a restrictive or an expansive definition of art.

The Questions Art Historians Ask

HOW OLD IS IT?   Before art historians can construct a history of art, they must be sure they know the date of each work they study. Thus, an indispensable subject of art historical inquiry is *chronology*, the dating of art objects and buildings. If researchers cannot determine a monument's age, they cannot place the work in its historical context. Art historians have developed many ways to establish, or at least approximate, the date of an artwork.

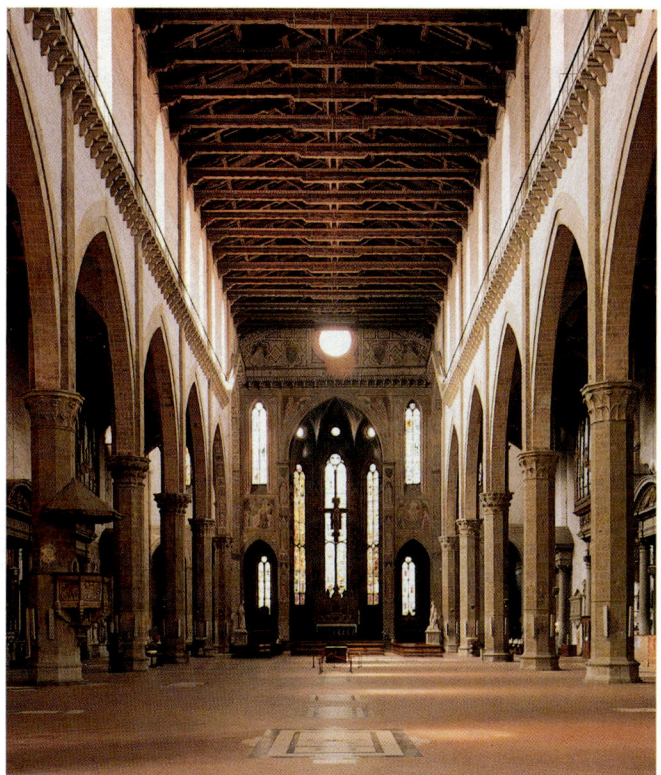

Intro-3 Interior of Santa Croce, Florence, Italy, begun 1294.

Physical evidence often reliably indicates an object's age. The material used for a statue or painting—bronze, plastic, or oil-based pigment, to name only a few—may not have been invented before a certain time, indicating the earliest possible date someone could have fashioned the work. Or artists may have ceased using certain materials—such as specific kinds of inks and papers for drawings and prints—at a known time, providing the latest possible dates for objects made of such materials. Sometimes the material (or the manufacturing technique) of an object or a building can establish a very precise date for an artwork or a building. Studying tree rings, for instance, usually can determine within a narrow range the date of a wood statue or a timber roof beam.

Documentary evidence also can help pinpoint the date of an object or building when a dated written document mentions the work. For example, official records may note when church officials commissioned a new altarpiece—and how much they paid to which artist.

Visual evidence, too, can play a significant role in dating an artwork. A painter might have depicted an identifiable person or a kind of hairstyle, clothing, or furniture fashionable only at a certain time. If so, the art historian can assign a more accurate date to that painting.

Stylistic evidence is also very important. The analysis of *style*—an artist's distinctive manner of producing an object, the way a work looks—is the art historian's special sphere. Unfortunately, because it is a subjective assessment, stylistic evidence is by far the most unreliable chronological criterion.

Still, art historians sometimes find style a very useful tool for establishing chronology.

WHAT IS ITS STYLE? Defining artistic style is one of the key elements of art historical inquiry, although the analysis of artworks solely in terms of style no longer dominates the field the way it once did. Art historians speak of several different kinds of artistic styles.

Period style refers to the characteristic artistic manner of a specific time, usually within a distinct culture, such as "Archaic Greek" or "Early Italian Renaissance." But many periods do not display any stylistic unity at all. How would historians define the artistic style of the 1990s in North America? Far too many crosscurrents existed in that decade for anyone to describe a period style of the late twentieth century—even in a single city such as New York.

Regional style is the term art historians use to describe variations in style tied to geography. Like an object's date, its *provenance,* or place of origin, can significantly determine its character. Very often two artworks from the same place made centuries apart are more similar than contemporaneous works from two different regions. To cite one example, usually only an expert can distinguish between an Egyptian statue carved in 2500 B.C. and one made in 500 B.C. But no one would mistake an Egyptian statue of 500 B.C. for a Greek or Olmec (Mexican) one of the same date.

Considerable variations in a given area's style are possible, however, even during a single historical period. In late medieval Europe during the so-called Gothic age, French architecture differed significantly from Italian architecture. The interiors of Beauvais Cathedral (FIG. **Intro-2**) and Santa Croce in Florence (FIG. **Intro-3**) typify the architectural styles of France and Italy, respectively, at the end of the thirteenth century. The rebuilding of the choir of Beauvais Cathedral began in 1284. Construction commenced on Santa Croce only ten years later. Both structures employ the characteristic Gothic pointed arch, yet they contrast strikingly. The French church has towering stone vaults and large expanses of stained-glass windows, while the Italian building has a low timber roof and small, widely separated windows. Because the two contemporaneous churches served similar purposes, regional style mainly explains their differing appearance.

Personal style, the distinctive manner of individual artists or architects, often decisively explains stylistic discrepancies among monuments of the same time and place. In 1930 the American painter GEORGIA O'KEEFFE produced a series of paintings of flowering plants. One of them was *Jack-in-the-Pulpit IV* (FIG. **Intro-4**), a sharply focused close-up view of petals and leaves. O'Keeffe captured the growing plant's slow, controlled motion while converting the organic form into a powerful abstract composition of lines, shapes, and colors (see our discussion of art historical vocabulary in the next section). Only a year later, another American artist, BEN SHAHN, painted *The Passion of Sacco and Vanzetti* (FIG. **Intro-5**), a stinging commentary on social injustice inspired by the trial and execution of two Italian anarchists, Nicola Sacco and Bartolomeo Vanzetti. Many people believed Sacco and Vanzetti had been unjustly convicted of killing two men in a holdup in 1920. Shahn's painting compresses time in a symbolic representation of the trial and its aftermath. The

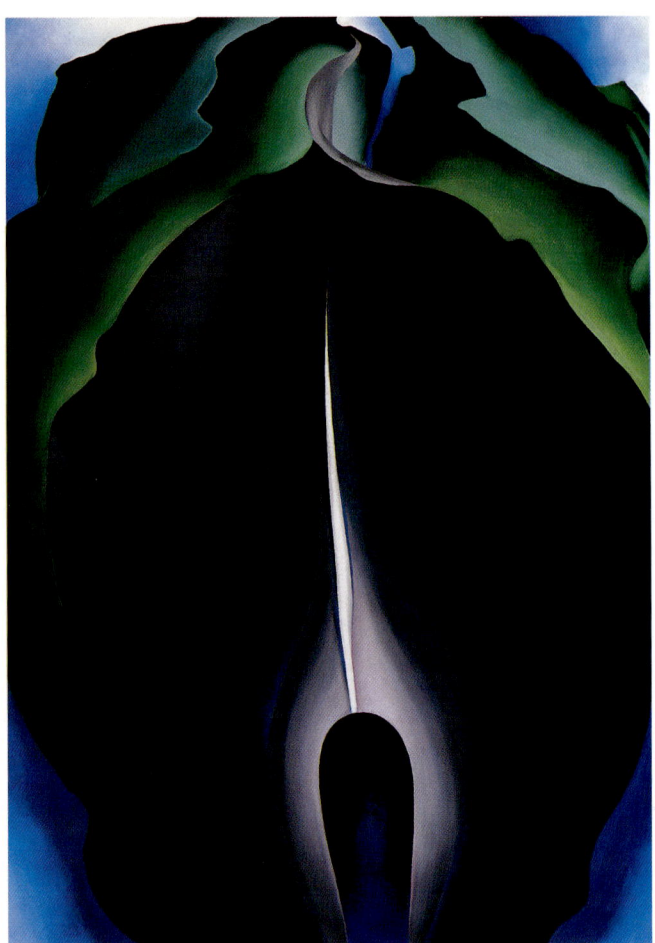

Intro-4 GEORGIA O'KEEFFE, *Jack-in-the-Pulpit IV*, 1930. Oil on canvas, 3′ 4″ × 2′ 6″. Formerly in the collection of Georgia O'Keeffe.

no subject, not even a setting. But when artists represent people, places, or actions, viewers must identify these aspects to achieve complete understanding of the works. Art historians traditionally separate pictorial subjects into various categories, such as religious, historical, mythological, *genre* (daily life), portraiture, *landscape* (a depiction of a place), *still life* (an arrangement of inanimate objects), and their numerous subdivisions and combinations.

Iconography—literally, the "writing of images"—refers both to the *content,* or subject of an artwork, and to the study of content in art. By extension, it also includes the study of *symbols,* images that stand for other images or encapsulate ideas. In Christian art, two intersecting lines of unequal length or a simple geometric cross can serve as an emblem of the religion as a whole, symbolizing the cross of Jesus Christ's crucifixion. A symbol also can be a familiar object the artist

two executed men lie in their coffins. Presiding over them are the three members of the commission (headed by a college president wearing academic cap and gown) who declared the original trial fair and cleared the way for the executions. Behind, on the wall of a columned government building, hangs the framed portrait of the judge who pronounced the initial sentence. Personal style, not period or regional style, sets Shahn's canvas apart from O'Keeffe's. The contrast is extreme here because of the very different subjects the artists chose. But when two artists depict the same subject, the results also can vary widely. The *way* O'Keeffe painted flowers and the *way* Shahn painted faces are distinctive and unlike the styles of their contemporaries. (See the "Who Made It?" discussion on page xxxviii.)

The different kinds of artistic styles are not mutually exclusive. For example, an artist's personal style may change dramatically during a long career. Art historians then must distinguish among the different period styles of a particular artist, such as the "Blue Period" and the "Cubist Period" of the prolific twentieth-century artist Pablo Picasso.

WHAT IS ITS SUBJECT? Another major concern of art historians is, of course, subject matter, encompassing the story, or *narrative;* the scene presented; the action's time and place; the persons involved; and the environment and its details. Some artworks, such as modern abstract paintings, have

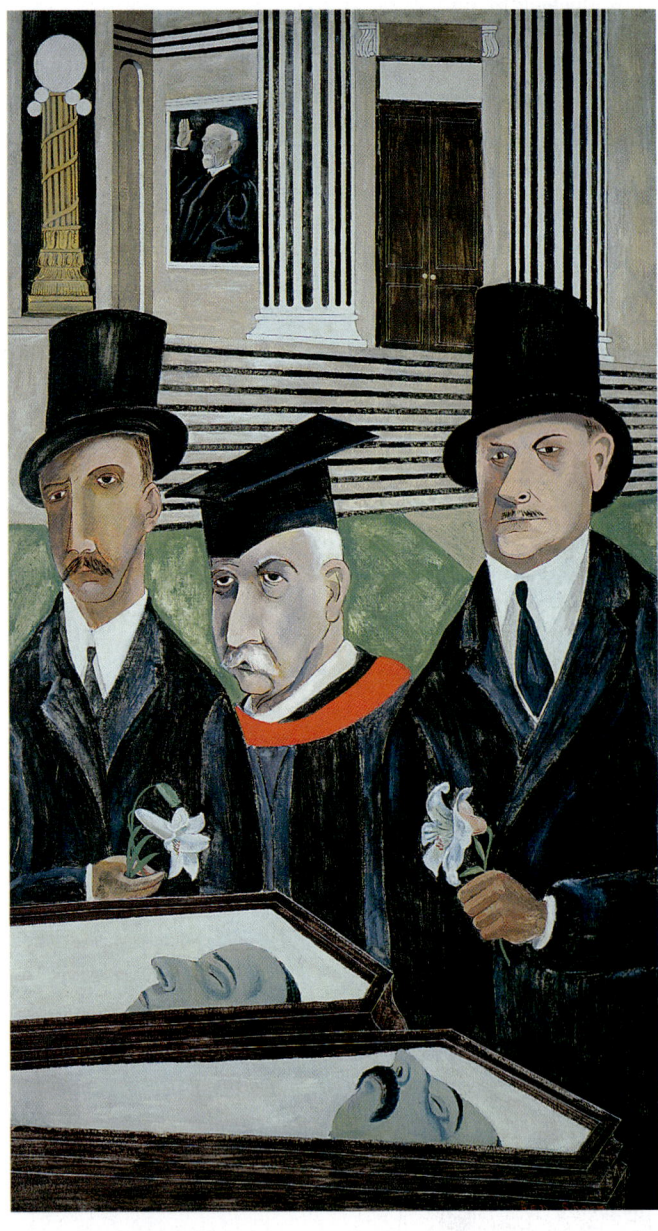

Intro-5 BEN SHAHN, *The Passion of Sacco and Vanzetti*, 1931–1932. Tempera on canvas, 7′ ½″ × 4′. Whitney Museum of American Art, New York (gift of Edith and Milton Lowenthal in memory of Juliana Force).

imbued with greater meaning. A balance or scale, for example, may symbolize justice or the weighing of souls on Judgment Day (FIG. **Intro-6**).

Artists also may depict figures with unique *attributes* identifying them. The Greek god Apollo (FIG. **Intro-7**), an archer, almost always carries a bow and quiver of arrows. In Asian art, the Buddha (FIG. **Intro-8**) has an *urna* (a coil of hair between the brows sometimes shown as a dot), an *ushnisha* (bump on top of the skull), and elongated earlobes as distinguishing marks. In Christian art, Saint Peter—and only Peter—carries the keys to the kingdom of Heaven.

Throughout the history of art, artists also used *personifications*—abstract ideas codified in bodily form. Worldwide, people visualize Liberty as a robed woman with a torch because of the fame of the colossal statue set up in New York

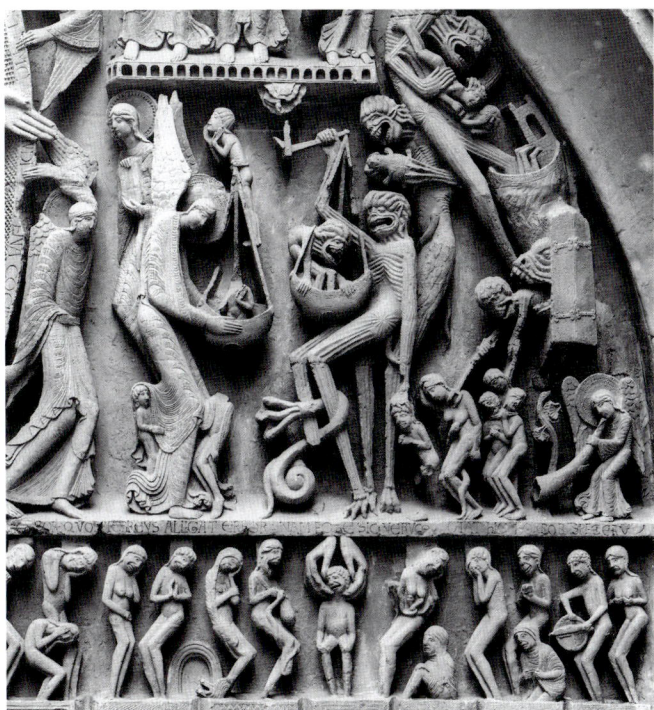

Intro-6   The weighing of souls, detail of west tympanum of Saint-Lazare, Autun, France, ca. 1130.

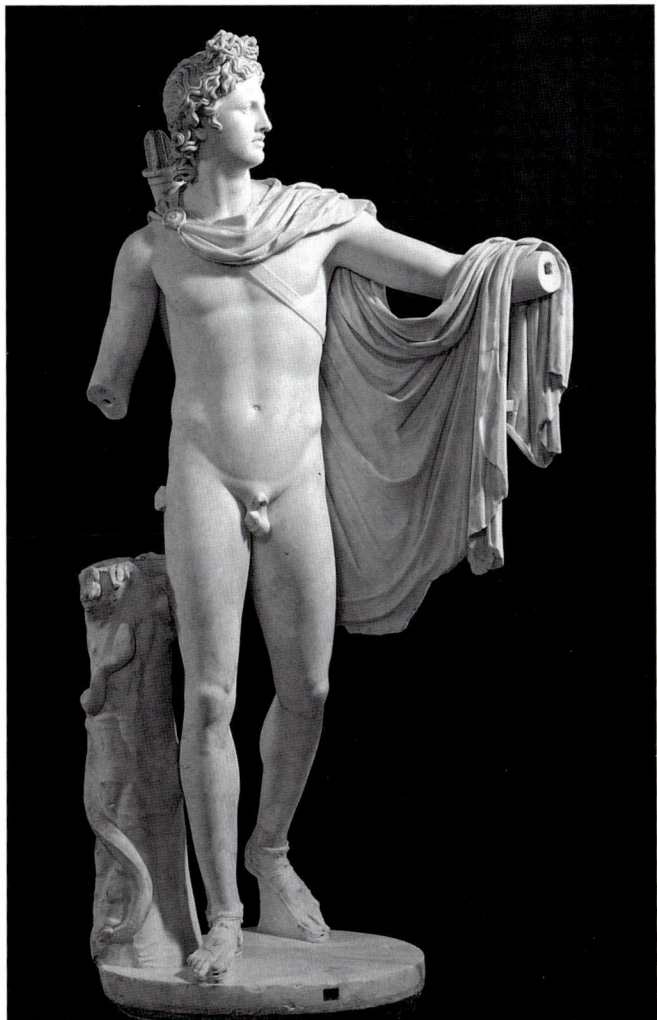

Intro-7   *Apollo Belvedere,* Roman copy or variation of a Greek statue of the mid-fourth century B.C. Marble, approx. 7′ 4″ high. Vatican Museums, Rome.

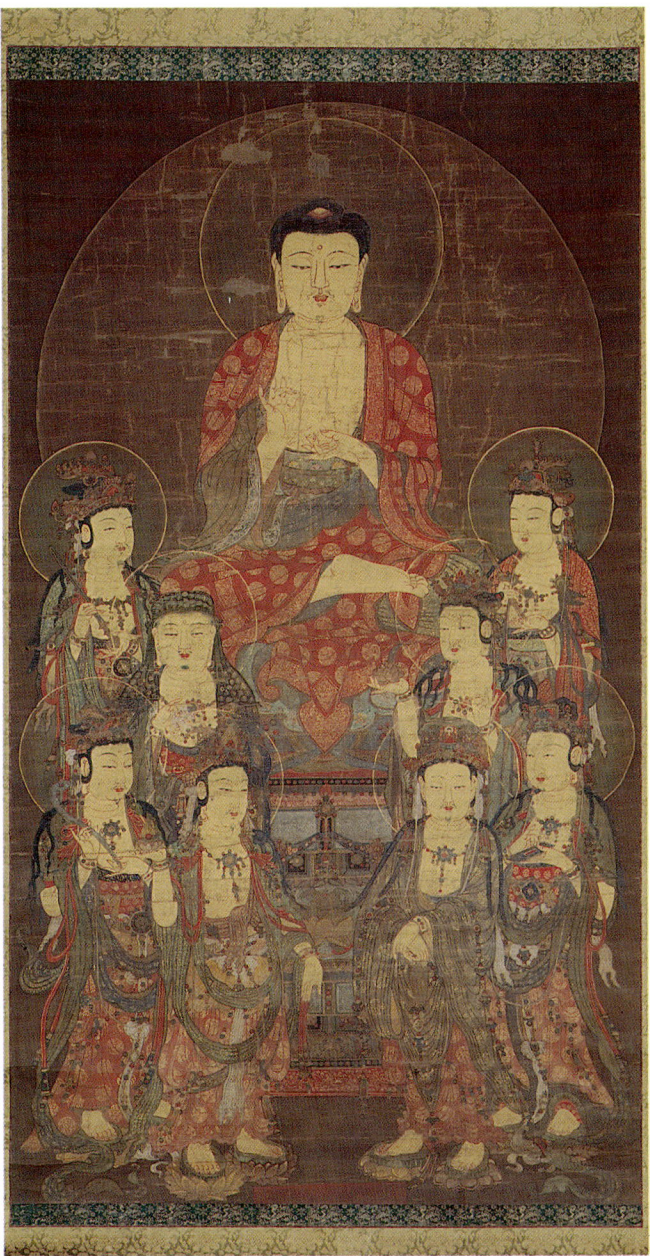

Intro-8   Buddha Amitabha and eight great Bodhisattvas (hanging scroll), Koryo dynasty, from Korea, fourteenth century. Ink, colors, and gold on silk, approx. 4′ 11½″ × 2′ 11″. Asian Art Museum of San Francisco, San Francisco (Avery Brundage Collection).

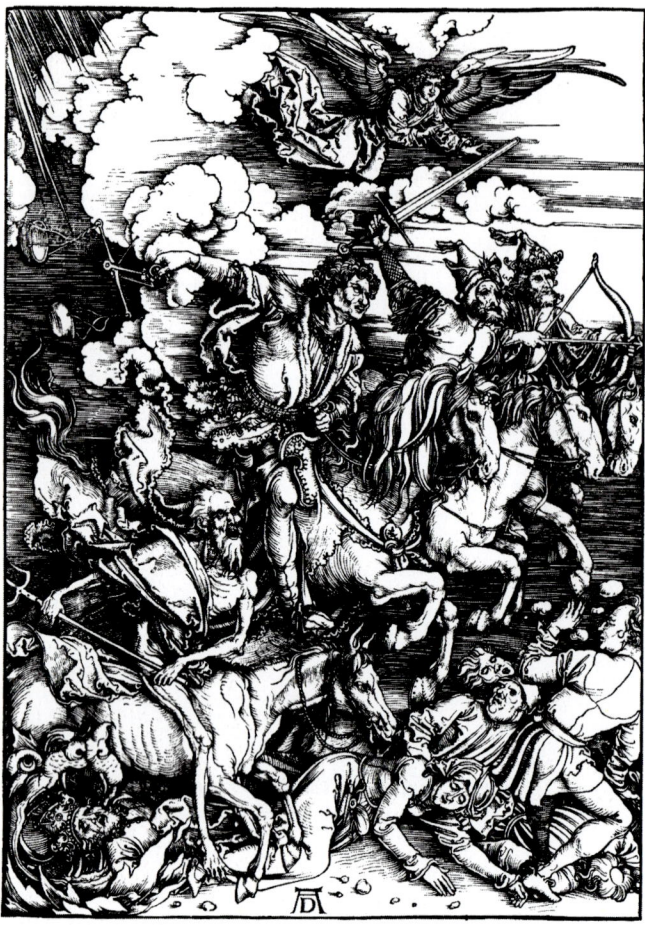

Intro-9   ALBRECHT DÜRER, *The Four Horsemen of the Apocalypse,* ca. 1498. Woodcut, approx. 1′ 3¼″ × 11″. Metropolitan Museum of Art, New York (gift of Junius S. Morgan, 1919).

City's harbor in the nineteenth century. *The Four Horsemen of the Apocalypse* (FIG. **Intro-9**) is a terrifying late-fifteenth-century depiction of the fateful day at the end of time when, according to the Bible's last book, Death, Famine, War, and Pestilence will cut down the human race. The artist, AL-BRECHT DÜRER, personified Death as an emaciated old man with a pitchfork. Dürer's Famine swings the scales that will weigh human souls (compare FIG. Intro-6), War wields a sword, and Pestilence draws a bow.

Even without considering style and without knowing a work's maker, informed viewers can determine much about the work's period and provenance by iconographical and subject analysis alone. In *The Passion of Sacco and Vanzetti* (FIG. Intro-5), for example, the two coffins, the trio headed by an academic, and the robed judge in the background are all pictorial clues revealing the painting's subject. The work's date must be after the trial and execution, probably while the event was still newsworthy. And because the two men's deaths caused the greatest outrage in the United States, the painter/social critic was probably American.

WHO MADE IT?   If Ben Shahn had not signed his painting of Sacco and Vanzetti, an art historian could still assign, or *attribute,* the work to him based on knowledge of the artist's personal style. Although signing (and dating) works is quite common (but by no means universal) today, in the his-

tory of art countless works exist whose artists remain unknown. Since personal style can play a large role in determining an artwork's character, art historians often try to attribute anonymous works to known artists. Sometimes they attempt to assemble a group of works all thought to be by the same person, even though none of the objects in the group is the known work of an artist with a recorded name. Art historians thus reconstruct the careers of people such as "the Andokides Painter," the anonymous ancient Greek artist who painted the vases the potter Andokides produced. Scholars attribute works based on internal evidence, such as the distinctive way an artist draws or carves drapery folds, earlobes, or flowers. It requires a keen, highly trained eye and long experience to become a *connoisseur,* an expert in assigning artworks to "the hand" of one artist rather than another. Attribution is, of course, subjective and ever open to doubt. At present, for example, international debate rages over attributions to the famous Dutch painter Rembrandt.

Sometimes a group of artists works in the same style at the same time and place. Art historians designate such a group as a *school.* "School" does not mean an educational institution. The term only connotes chronological, stylistic, and geographic similarity. Art historians speak, for example, of the Dutch school of the seventeenth century and, within it, of subschools such as those of the cities of Haarlem, Utrecht, and Leyden.

WHO PAID FOR IT?   The interest many art historians show in attribution reflects their conviction that the identity of an artwork's maker is the major reason the object looks the way that it does. For them, personal style is of paramount importance. But in many times and places artists had little to say about what form their work would take. They toiled in obscurity, doing the bidding of their *patrons,* those who paid them to make individual works or employed them on a continuing basis. The role of patrons in dictating the content and shaping the form of artworks is also an important subject of art historical inquiry.

In the art of portraiture, to name only one category of painting and sculpture, the patron has often played a dominant role in deciding how the artist represented the subject, whether the patron or another person, such as a spouse, son, or mother. Many Egyptian pharaohs and some Roman emperors, for example, insisted artists depict them with unlined faces and perfect youthful bodies no matter how old they were when portrayed. In these cases, the state employed the sculptors and painters, and the artists had no choice but to depict their patrons in the officially approved manner. This is why Augustus, who lived to age seventy-six, looks so young in his portraits (FIG. **Intro-10**). Although Roman emperor for more than forty years, Augustus demanded artists always represent him as a young, godlike head of state.

All modes of artistic production reveal the impact of patronage. Learned monks provided the themes for the sculptural decoration of medieval church portals. Renaissance princes and popes dictated the subjects, sizes, and materials of artworks destined, sometimes, for buildings constructed according to their specifications. An art historian could make a very long list along these lines, and it would indicate that throughout the history of art, patrons have had diverse tastes

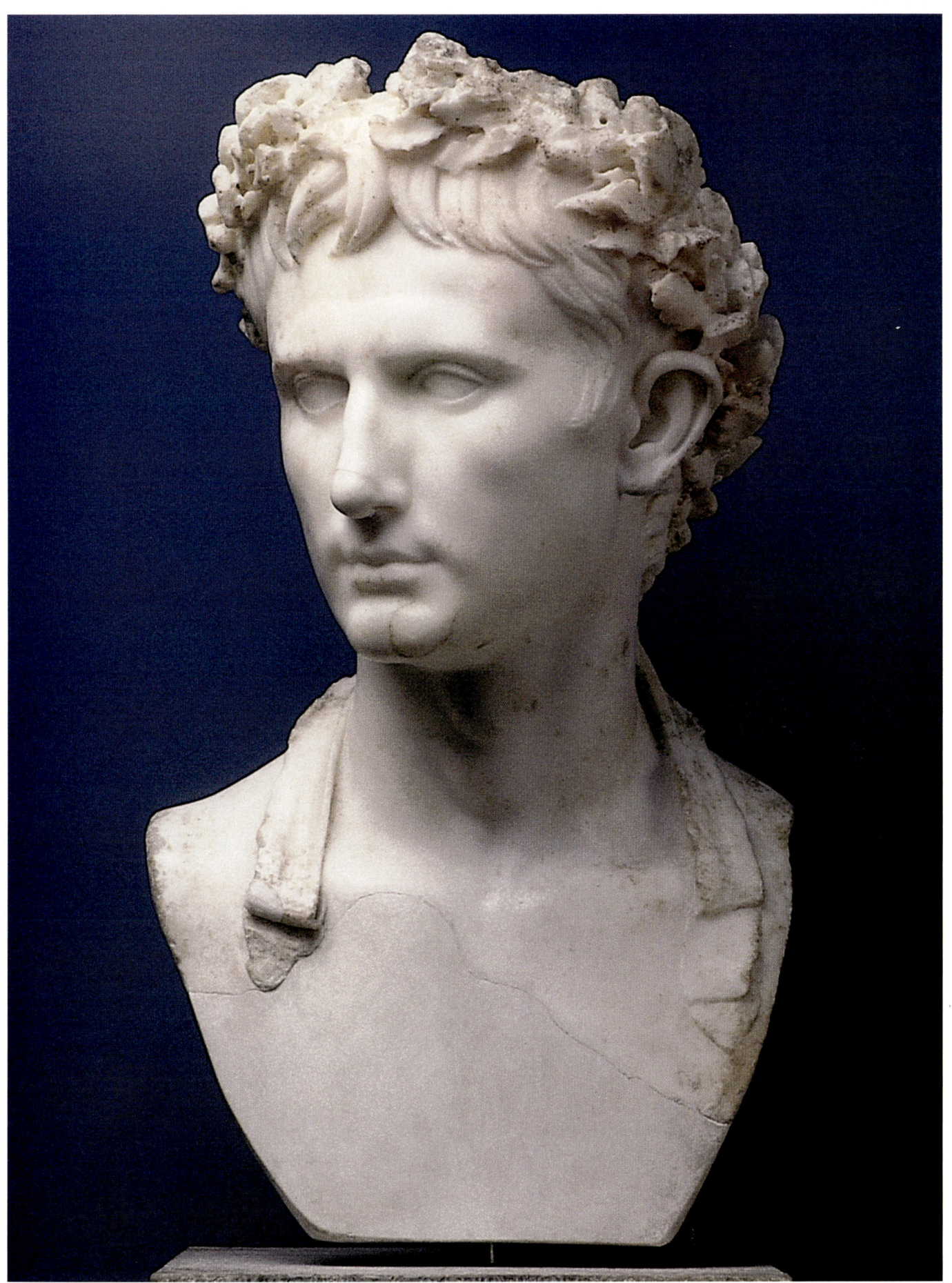

Intro-10 Augustus wearing *corona civica* (civic crown), early first century A.D. Marble, approx. 1′ 5″ high. Glyptothek, Munich.

and needs and demanded different kinds of art. Whenever a patron contracts an artist or architect to paint, sculpt, or build in a prescribed manner, personal style often becomes a very minor factor in how the painting, statue, or building looks. In such cases, knowing the patron's identity reveals more to art historians than does the identity of the artist or school. The portrait of Augustus illustrated here was the work of a virtuoso sculptor, a master wielder of hammer and chisel. But scores of similar portraits of that emperor exist today. They differ in quality but not in kind from this one. The patron, not the artist, determined the character of such artworks. Augustus's public image never varied.

The Words Art Historians Use

Like all specialists, art historians have their own specialized vocabulary. That vocabulary consists of hundreds of words, but certain basic terms are indispensable for describing artworks and buildings of any time and place, and we use those terms throughout this book. They make up the essential vocabulary of *formal analysis,* the visual analysis of artistic form. We define the most important of these art historical terms here. For a much longer list, consult the Glossary in this book's end material.

FORM AND COMPOSITION   *Form* refers to an object's shape and structure, either in two dimensions (for example, a figure painted on a canvas) or in three dimensions (such as a statue carved from a marble block). Two forms may take the same shape but may differ in their color, texture, and other qualities. *Composition* refers to how an artist organizes (composes) forms in an artwork, either by placing shapes on a flat surface or arranging forms in space.

MATERIAL AND TECHNIQUE   To create art forms, artists shape *materials* (pigment, clay, marble, gold, and many more) with *tools* (pens, brushes, chisels, and so forth). Each of the materials and tools available has its own potentialities and limitations. Part of all artists' creative activity is to select the medium and instrument most suitable to the artists' purpose—or to pioneer the use of new media and tools, such as bronze and concrete in antiquity and cameras and computers in modern times. The processes artists employ, such as applying paint to canvas with a brush, and the distinctive, personal ways they handle materials constitute their *technique.* Form, material, and technique interrelate and are central to analyzing any work of art.

LINE   *Line* is one of the most important elements defining an artwork's shape or form. A line can be understood as the path of a point moving in space, an invisible line of sight or a visual *axis.* But, more commonly, artists and architects make a line concrete by drawing (or chiseling) it on a *plane,* a flat and two-dimensional surface. A line may be very thin, wirelike, and delicate, it may be thick and heavy, or it may alternate quickly from broad to narrow, the strokes jagged or the outline broken. When a continuous line defines an object's outer shape, art historians call it a *contour* line.

One can observe all of these line qualities in Dürer's *Four Horsemen of the Apocalypse* (FIG. Intro-9). Contour lines define

the basic shapes of clouds, human and animal limbs, and weapons. Within the forms, series of short broken lines create shadows and textures. An overall pattern of long parallel strokes suggests the dark sky on the frightening day when the world is about to end.

COLOR   Light reveals all colors. *Light* in the world of the painter and other artists differs from natural light. Natural light, or sunlight, is whole or *additive* light. As the sum of all the wavelengths composing the visible *spectrum,* it may be disassembled or fragmented into the spectral band's individual colors. The painter's light in art—the light reflected from pigments and objects—is *subtractive* light. Paint pigments produce their individual colors by reflecting a segment of the spectrum while absorbing all the rest. "Green" pigment, for example, subtracts or absorbs all the light in the spectrum except that seen as green, which it reflects to the eyes.

Hue is the property giving a color its name. Although the spectrum colors merge into each other, artists usually conceive of their hues as distinct from one another. Color has two basic variables—the apparent amount of light reflected and the apparent purity. A change in one must produce a change in the other. Some terms for these variables are *value* or *tonality* (the degree of lightness or darkness) and *intensity* or *saturation* (the purity of a color, its brightness or dullness).

A *color triangle* (FIG. **Intro-11**) clearly shows the relationships among the six main colors. Red, yellow, and blue, the *primary colors,* are the vertexes of the large triangle. Orange, green, and purple, the *secondary colors* resulting from mixing pairs of primaries, lie between them. Colors opposite each other in the spectrum—red and green, purple and yellow, and orange and blue here—are *complementary colors.* They "complement," or complete, each other, one absorbing colors the other reflects. When painters mix complementaries in the right proportions, a neutral tone or gray (theoretically, black) results.

TEXTURE   *Texture* is the quality of a surface (such as rough or shiny) that light reveals. Art historians distinguish between *actual* textures, or the surface's tactile quality, and *represented* textures, as when painters depict an object as hav-

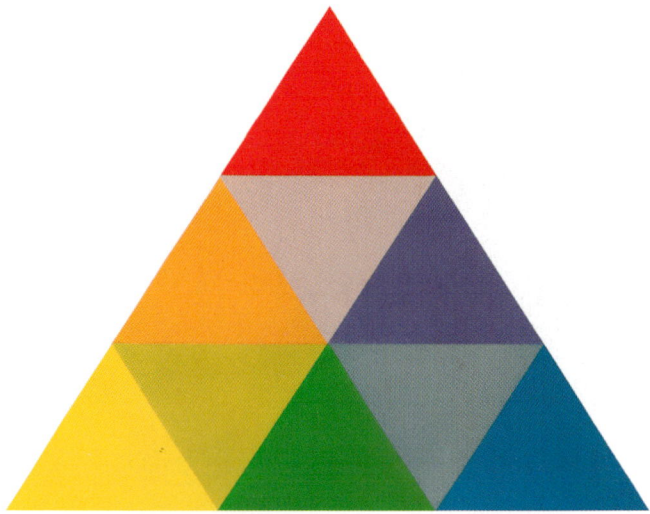

Intro-11   Color triangle developed by Josef Albers and Sewell Sillman. Yale University Art Gallery, New Haven.

ing a certain texture, even though the paint is the actual texture. Sometimes artists combine different materials of different textures on a single surface, juxtaposing paint with pieces of wood, newspaper, fabric, and so forth. Art historians refer to this *mixed-media* technique as *collage.* Texture is, of course, a key determinant of any sculpture's character. People's first impulse is usually to handle a piece of sculpture—even though museum signs often warn "Do not touch!" Sculptors plan for this natural human response, using surfaces varying in texture from rugged coarseness to polished smoothness. Textures are often intrinsic to a material, influencing the type of stone, wood, plastic, clay, or metal sculptors select.

SPACE, MASS, AND VOLUME   *Space* is the bounded or boundless "container" of objects. For art historians, space can be *actual,* the three-dimensional space occupied by a statue or a vase or contained within a room or courtyard. Or it can be *illusionistic,* as when painters depict an image (or illusion) of the three-dimensional spatial world onto a two-dimensional surface.

Mass and *volume* describe three-dimensional space. In both architecture and sculpture, mass is the bulk, density, and weight of matter in space. Yet the mass need not be solid. It can be the exterior form of enclosed space. "Mass" can apply to a solid Egyptian pyramid or wooden statue, to a church, synagogue, or mosque—architectural shells enclosing sometimes vast spaces—and to a hollow metal statue or baked clay pot. Volume is the space that mass organizes, divides, or encloses. It may be a building's interior spaces, the intervals between a structure's masses, or the amount of space occupied by three-dimensional objects such as sculpture, pottery, or furniture. Volume and mass describe both the exterior and interior forms of a work of art—the forms of the matter of which it is composed and the spaces immediately around the work and interacting with it.

PERSPECTIVE AND FORESHORTENING   *Perspective* is one of the most important pictorial devices for organizing forms in space. Throughout history, artists have used various types of perspective to create an illusion of depth or space on a two-dimensional surface. The French painter CLAUDE LORRAIN employed several perspectival devices in *Embarkation of the Queen of Sheba* (FIG. **Intro-12**), a painting of a biblical episode set in a seventeenth-century European harbor

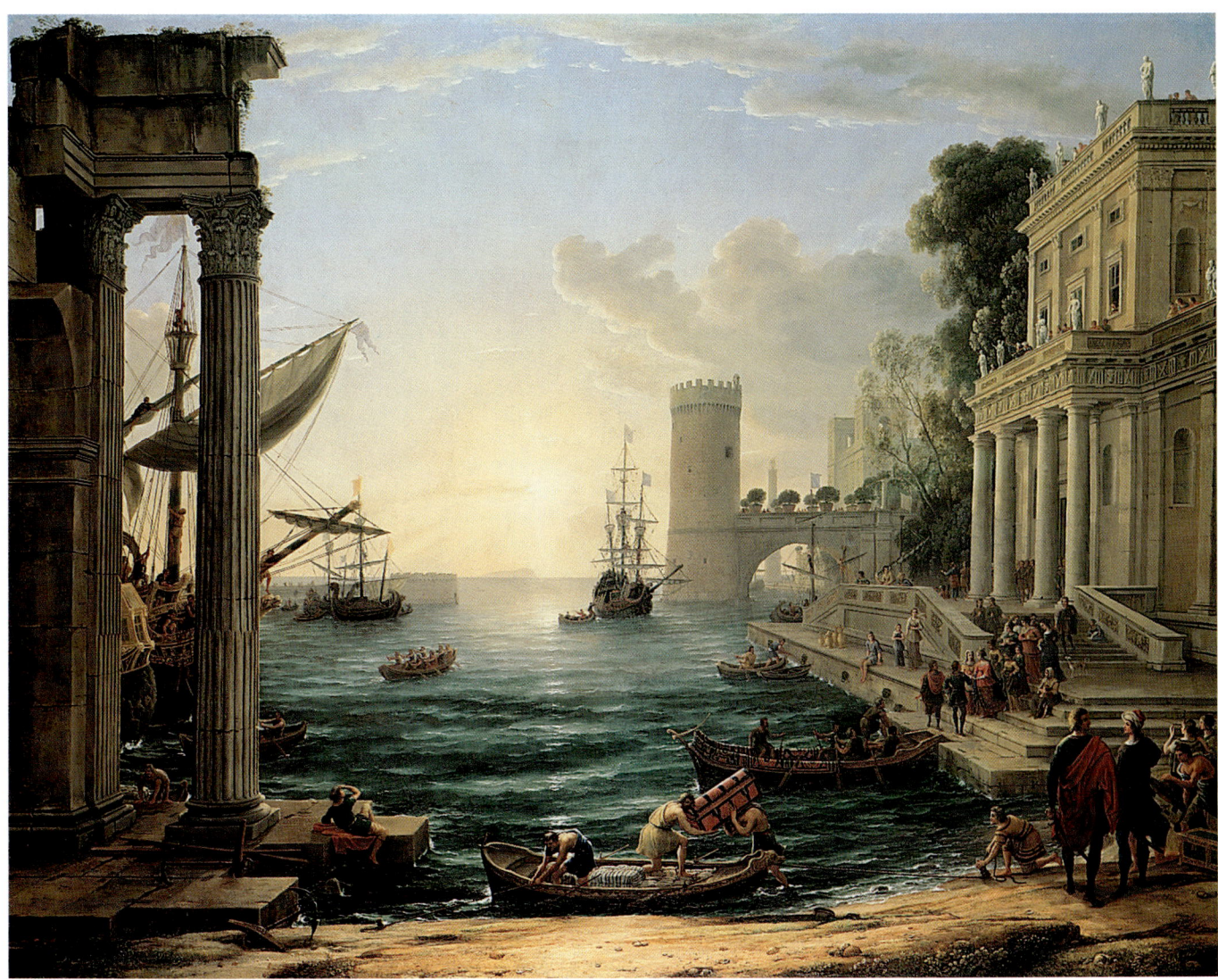

Intro-12 CLAUDE LORRAIN, *Embarkation of the Queen of Sheba,* 1648. Oil on canvas, approx. 4′ 10″ × 6′ 4″. National Gallery, London.

with a Roman ruin in the left foreground. For example, the figures and boats on the shoreline are much larger than those in the distance. Decreasing an object's size makes it appear farther away from viewers. Also, the top and bottom of the port building at the painting's right side are not parallel horizontal lines, as they are in an actual building. Instead, the lines converge beyond the structure, leading viewers' eyes toward the hazy, indistinct sun on the horizon. These perspectival devices—the reduction of figure size, the convergence of diagonal lines, and the blurring of distant forms—have been familiar features of Western art since the ancient Greeks. But it is important to note at the outset that all kinds of perspective are only pictorial conventions, even when one or more types of perspective may be so common in a given culture that they are accepted as "natural" or "true" means of representing the natural world.

In *Red Plum Blossoms* (FIG. **Intro-13**) a Japanese landscape painting, OGATA KORIN used none of these Western perspective conventions. He showed the plum tree as seen from a position on the ground, while viewers look down on the stream from above. Less concerned with locating the tree and stream in space than with composing shapes on a surface, the painter played the water's gently swelling curves against the jagged contours of the branches and trunk. Neither the French nor the Japanese painting can be said to "correctly" project what viewers "in fact" see. One painting is not a "better" picture of the world than the other. The artists simply approached the problem of picture-making differently.

Artists also represent single figures in space in varying ways. When PETER PAUL RUBENS painted *Lion Hunt* (FIG. **Intro-14**) in the early seventeenth century, he used *foreshortening* for all the hunters and animals, that is, he represented their bodies at angles to the picture plane. When in life one views a figure at an angle, the body appears to contract as it extends back in space. Foreshortening is a kind of perspective. It produces the illusion that one part of the body is farther away than another, even though all the forms are on the same surface. Especially noteworthy in *Lion Hunt* are the gray horse at the left, seen from behind with the bottom of its left rear hoof facing viewers and most of its head hidden by its rider's shield, and the fallen hunter at the canvas's lower right corner, whose barely visible legs and feet recede into the distance.

The artist who carved the portrait of the ancient Egyptian official Hesire (FIG. **Intro-15**) did not employ foreshortening. That artist's purpose was to present the various human body parts as clearly as possible, without overlapping. The lower part of Hesire's body is in profile to give the most complete view of the legs, with both the heels and toes of the foot visible. The frontal torso, however, allows viewers to see its full shape, including both shoulders, equal in size, as in na-

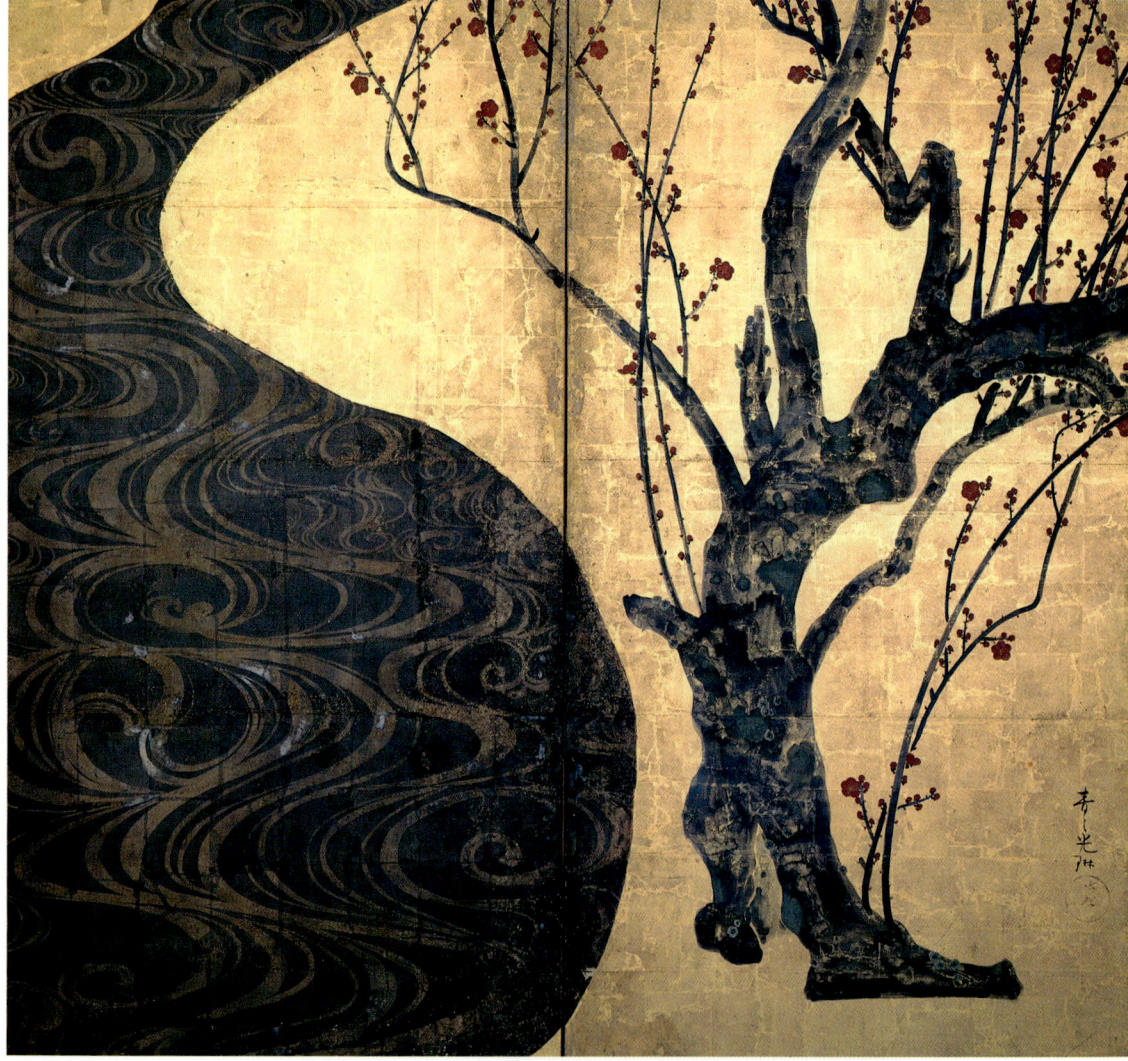

Intro-13 OGATA KO-RIN, *Red Plum Blossoms,* Edo period, ca. 1710–1716. One of a pair of twofold screens. Ink, color, and gold leaf on paper, 5′ 1⅝″ × 5′ 7⅞″. Museum of Art, Atami.

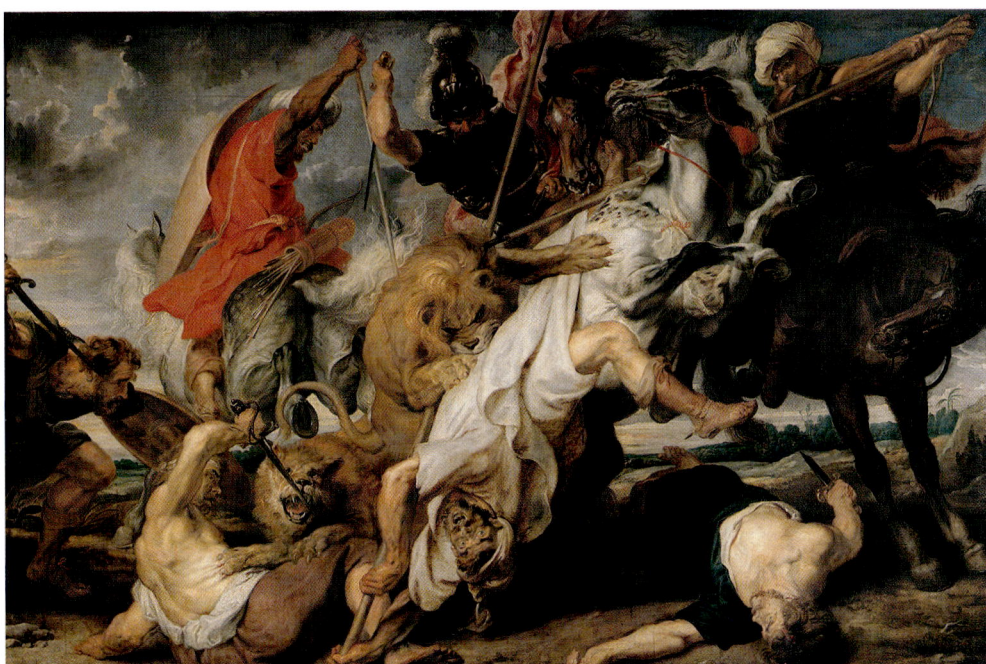

Intro-14 PETER PAUL RUBENS, *Lion Hunt,* 1617–1618. Oil on canvas, approx. 8′ 2″ × 12′ 5″. Alte Pinakothek, Munich.

ture. (Compare the shoulders of the hunter on the gray horse or those of the fallen hunter in *Lion Hunt*'s left foreground.) The result, an "unnatural" ninety-degree twist at the waist, provides a precise picture of human body parts. Rubens and the ancient sculptor used very different means of depicting forms in space. Once again, neither is the "correct" manner.

PROPORTION AND SCALE *Proportion* concerns the relationships (in terms of size) of the parts of persons, buildings, or objects. "Correct proportions" may be judged intuitively ("that statue's head seems the right size for the body"). Or proportion may be formalized as a mathematical relationship between the size of one part of an artwork or building and the other parts within the work. Proportion in art implies using a *module,* or basic unit of measure. When an artist or architect uses a formal system of proportions, all parts of a building, body, or other entity will be fractions or multiples of the module. A module might be a column's diameter, the height of a human head, or any other component whose dimensions can be multiplied or divided to determine the size of the work's other parts.

In certain times and places, artists have formulated *canons,* or systems, of "correct" or "ideal" proportions for representing human figures, constituent parts of buildings, and so forth. In ancient Greece, many sculptors formulated canons of proportions so strict and all-encompassing that they calculated the size of every body part in advance, even the fingers and toes, according to mathematical ratios (FIG. Intro-7). The ideal of human beauty the Greeks created based on "correct" proportions influenced the work of countless later artists in the Western world and endures to this day. Proportional systems can differ sharply from period to period, culture to culture, and artist to artist. Part of the task art history students face is to perceive and adjust to these differences.

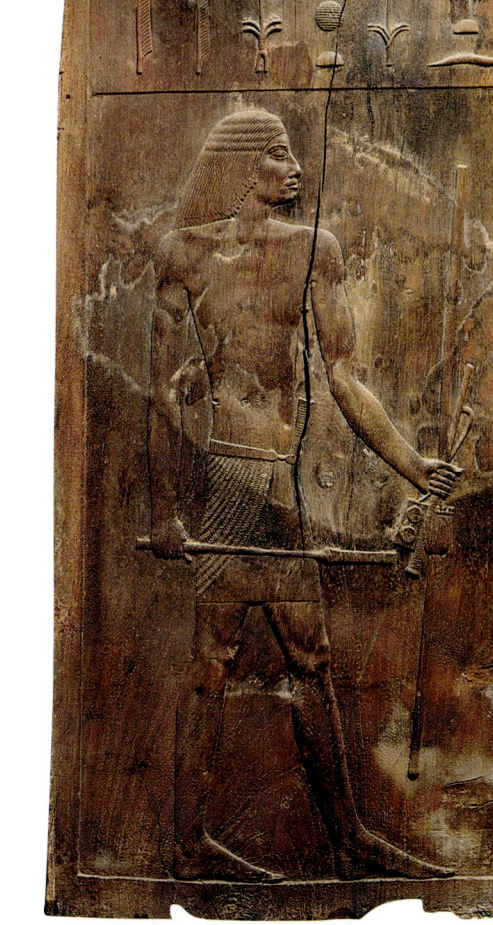

Intro-15 Hesire, from his tomb at Saqqara, Egypt, Dynasty III, ca. 2650 B.C. Wood, approx. 3′ 9″ high. Egyptian Museum, Cairo.

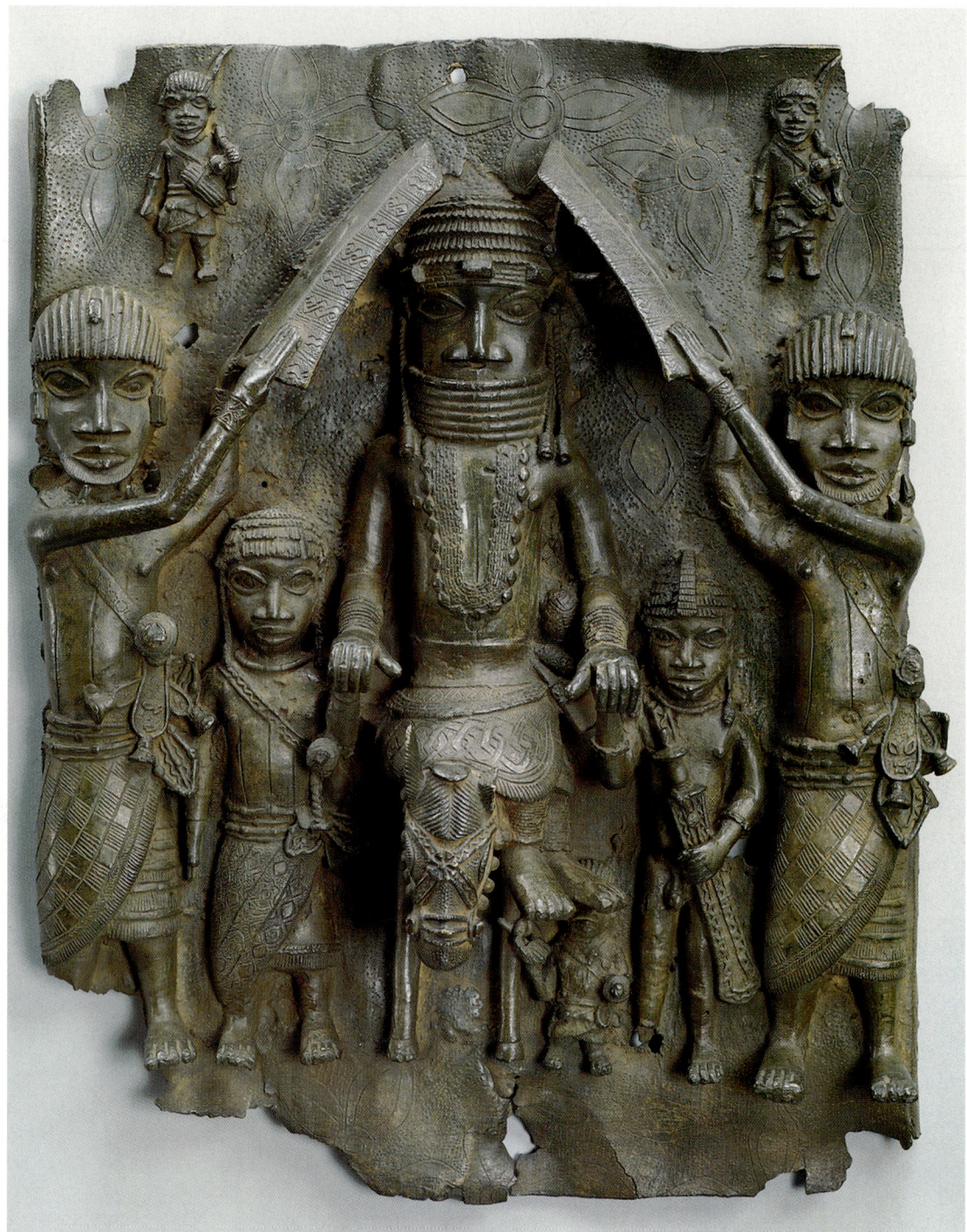

Intro-16   King on horseback with attendants, from Benin, Nigeria, ca. 1550–1680. Bronze, 1′ 7½″ high. Metropolitan Museum of Art, New York (Michael C. Rockefeller Memorial Collection, gift of Nelson A. Rockefeller).

In fact, many artists have used *disproportion* and distortion deliberately for expressive effect. In the medieval French depiction of the weighing of souls on Judgment Day (FIG. Intro-6), the devilish figure yanking down on the scale has distorted facial features and stretched, lined limbs with animal-like paws for feet. Disproportion and distortion make him appear "inhuman," precisely as the sculptor intended.

In other cases, artists have used disproportion to focus attention on one body part (often the head) or to single out a group member (usually the leader). These intentional "unnatural" discrepancies in proportion constitute what art historians call *hierarchy of scale,* the enlarging of elements considered the most important. On a bronze plaque from Benin, Nigeria (FIG. **Intro-16**), the sculptor enlarged all the heads for emphasis and also varied the size of each figure according to its social status. Central, largest, and therefore most important is the Benin king, mounted on horseback. The horse has been a symbol of power and wealth in many societies from prehistory to the present. That the Benin king is disproportionately larger than his horse, contrary to nature, further aggrandizes him. Two large attendants fan the king. Other figures of smaller size and status at the Benin court stand on the king's left and right and in the plaque's upper corners. One tiny figure next to the horse is almost hidden from view beneath the king's feet.

CARVING AND CASTING   Sculptural technique falls into two basic categories, *subtractive* and *additive. Carving* is a

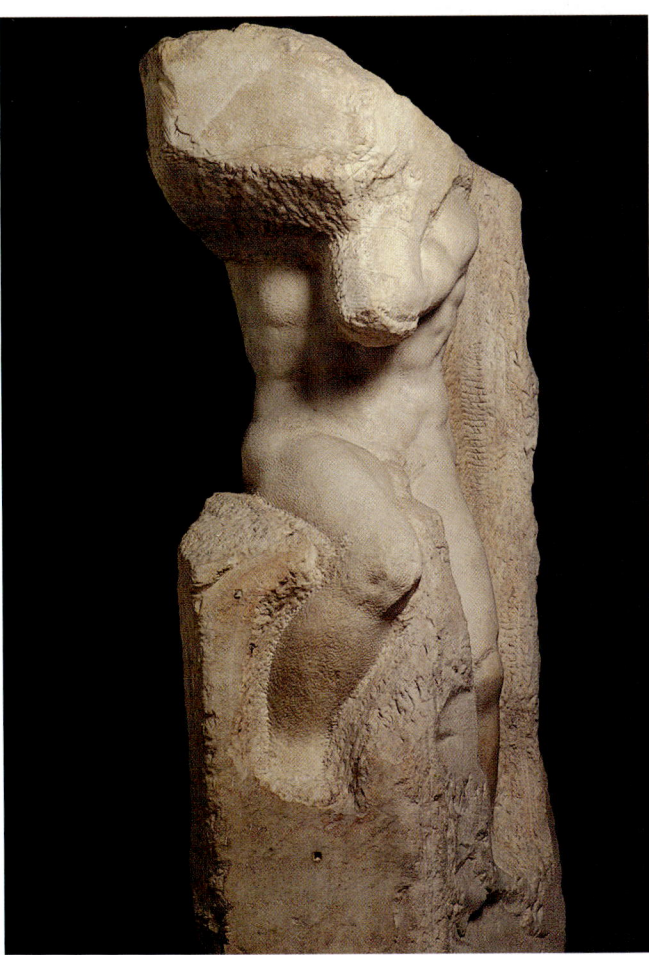

Intro-17   MICHELANGELO, unfinished captive, 1527–1528. Marble, 8′ 7½″ high. Accademia, Florence.

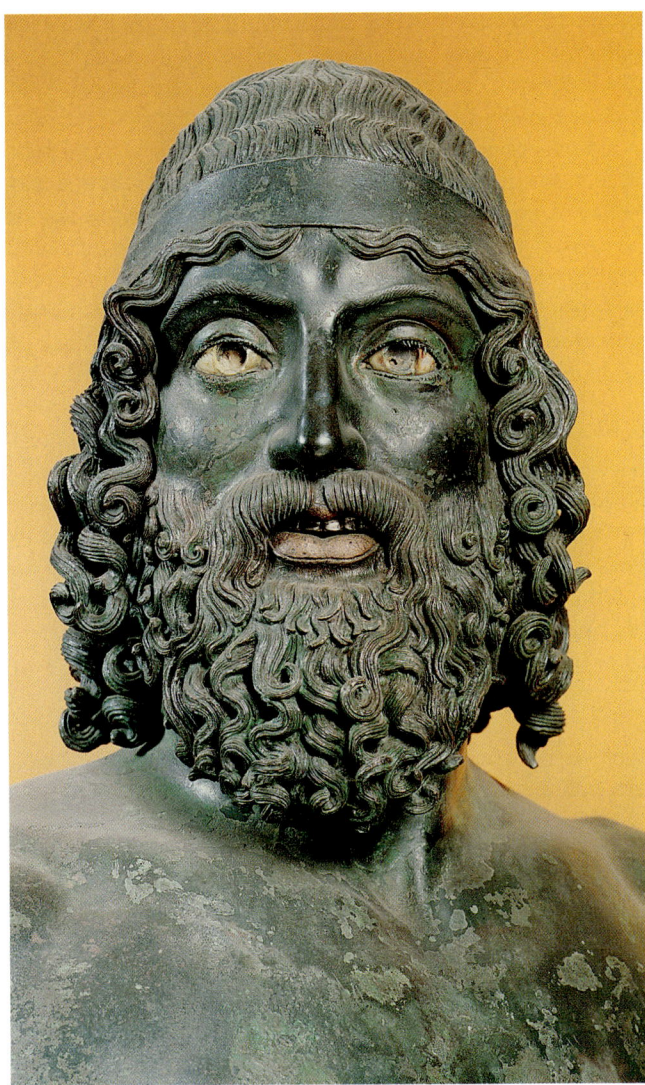

Intro-18   Head of a warrior, detail of a statue from the sea off Riace, Italy, ca. 460–450 B.C. Bronze, statue approx. 6′ 6″ high. Archeological Museum, Reggio Calabria.

subtractive technique. The final form is a reduction of the original mass of a block of stone, a piece of wood, or another material. Wooden statues were once tree trunks, and stone statues began as blocks pried from mountains. In an unfinished sixteenth-century marble statue of a bound slave (FIG. **Intro-17**) by MICHELANGELO, the stone block's original shape is still visible. Michelangelo thought of sculpture as a process of "liberating" the statue within the block. All sculptors of stone or wood cut away (subtract) "excess material." When they finish, they "leave behind" the statue—in our example, a twisting nude male form whose head Michelangelo never freed from the stone block.

In additive sculpture, the artist builds up the forms, usually in clay around a framework, or *armature.* Or a sculptor may fashion a *mold,* a hollow form for shaping, or *casting,* a fluid substance such as bronze. The ancient Greek sculptor who made the bronze statue of a warrior found in the sea near Riace, Italy, cast the head (FIG. **Intro-18**), limbs, torso, hands, and feet in separate molds and then *welded* them (joined them by heating). Finally, the artist added features, such as the pupils of the eyes (now missing), in other materials. The warrior's teeth are silver and his lower lip is copper.

RELIEF SCULPTURE   Statues that exist independent of any architectural frame or setting and that viewers can walk around are *freestanding* sculptures, or sculptures "in the round," whether the piece was carved (FIG. Intro-7) or cast

(FIG. Intro-18). In *relief sculptures,* the subjects project from the background but remain part of it. In *high relief* sculpture, the images project boldly. In some cases, such as the weighing-of-souls relief at Autun (FIG. Intro-6), the relief is so high that not only do the forms cast shadows on the background, but some parts are actually in the round. The scale's arms are fully detached from the background in places—which explains why some pieces broke off centuries ago. In *low relief,* or *bas-relief,* such as the wooden relief of Hesire (FIG. Intro-15), the projection is slight. In a variation of both techniques, *sunken relief,* the sculptor cuts the design into the surface so that the image's highest projecting parts are no higher than the surface itself. Relief sculpture, like sculpture in the round, can be produced either by carving or casting. The plaque from Benin (FIG. Intro-16) is a good example of bronze-casting in high relief. Artists also can make reliefs by hammering a sheet of metal from behind, pushing the subject out from the background in a technique called *repoussé.*

ARCHITECTURAL DRAWINGS   Buildings are groupings of enclosed spaces and enclosing masses. People experience architecture both visually and by moving through and around it, so they perceive architectural space and mass together. These spaces and masses can be represented graphically in several ways, including as plans, sections, elevations, and cutaway drawings.

A *plan,* essentially a map of a floor, shows the placement of a structure's masses and, therefore, the spaces they bound and enclose. A *section,* like a vertical plan, depicts the placement of the masses as if the building were cut through along a plane. Drawings showing a theoretical slice across a structure's width are *lateral sections.* Those cutting through a building's length are *longitudinal sections.* Illustrated here is the plan and half of the lateral section of Bourges Cathedral (FIG. **Intro-19**), a French Gothic church similar in character to Beauvais Cathedral (FIG. Intro-2). The plan shows not only the building's shape and the location of the piers dividing the aisles and supporting the vaults above but also the pattern of the crisscrossing vault *ribs.* The lateral section shows both the main area of the church and the vaults below the floor.

Other types of architectural drawings appear throughout this book. An *elevation* drawing is a head-on view of an external or internal wall. A *cutaway* combines an exterior view with an interior view of part of a building in a single drawing.

This overview of the art historian's vocabulary is not exhaustive, nor have artists used only painting, drawing, sculpture, and architecture as media over the millennia. Ceramics, jewelry, textiles, photography, and computer art are just some of the numerous other arts. All of them involve highly specialized techniques described in distinct vocabularies. These are considered and defined where they arise in the text.

Art History and Other Disciplines

By its very nature, the work of art historians intersects with that of others in many fields of knowledge, not only in the humanities but also in the social and natural sciences. To "do their job" well today, art historians regularly must go beyond the boundaries of what the public and even professional art historians of previous generations traditionally have considered the specialized discipline of art history. Art historical research in the twenty-first century is frequently *interdisciplinary* in nature. To cite one example, in an effort to unlock the secrets of a particular statue, an art historian might conduct archival research hoping to uncover new documents shedding light on who paid for the work and why, who made it and when, where it originally stood, how its contemporaries viewed it, and a host of other questions. Realizing, however, that the authors of the written documents often were not objective recorders of fact but observers with their own biases and agendas, the art historian may also use methodologies developed in fields such as literary criticism, philosophy, sociology, and gender studies to weigh the evidence the documents provide.

At other times, rather than attempting to master many disciplines at once, art historians band together with other specialists in *multidisciplinary* inquiries. Art historians might call in chemists to date an artwork based on the composition of the materials used or might ask geologists to determine which quarry furnished the stone for a particular statue. X-ray technicians might be enlisted in an attempt to establish whether or not a painting is a forgery. Of course, art historians often

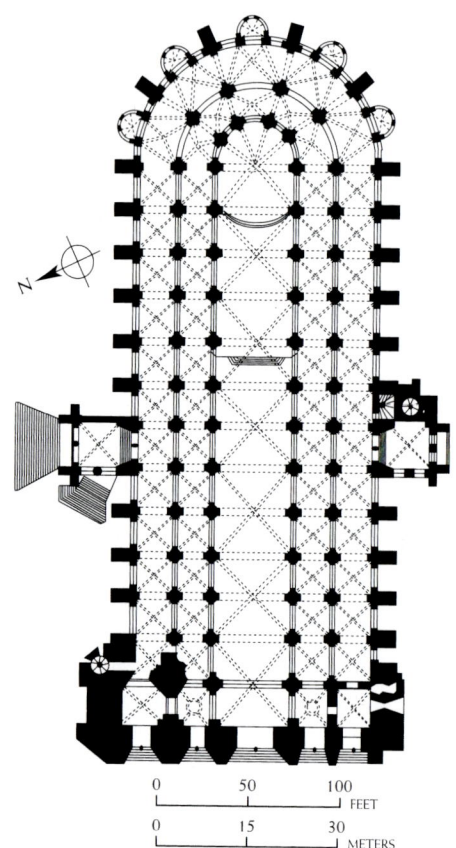

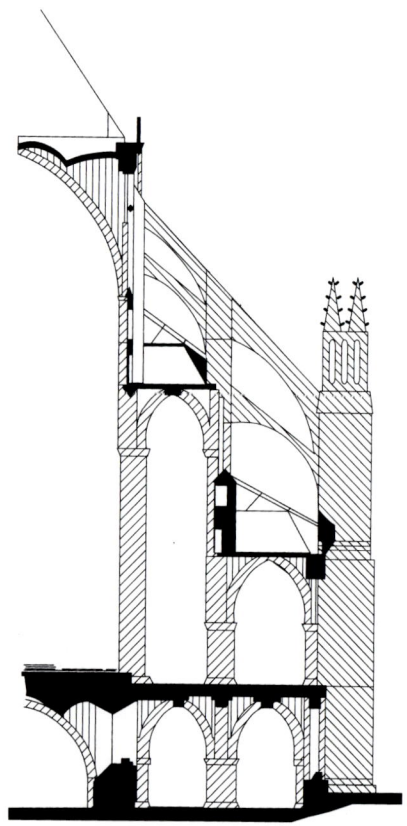

Intro-19 Plan *(left)* and lateral section *(right)* of Bourges Cathedral, Bourges, France, 1195–1255.

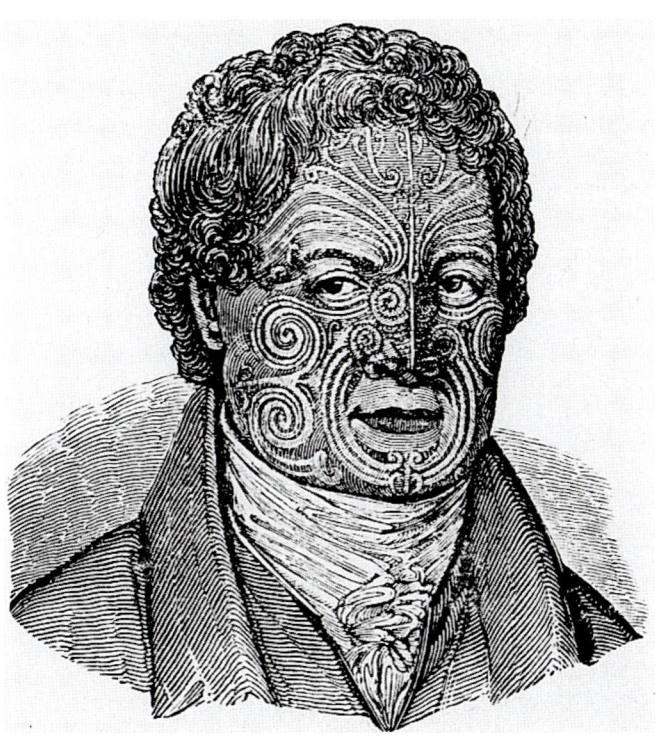 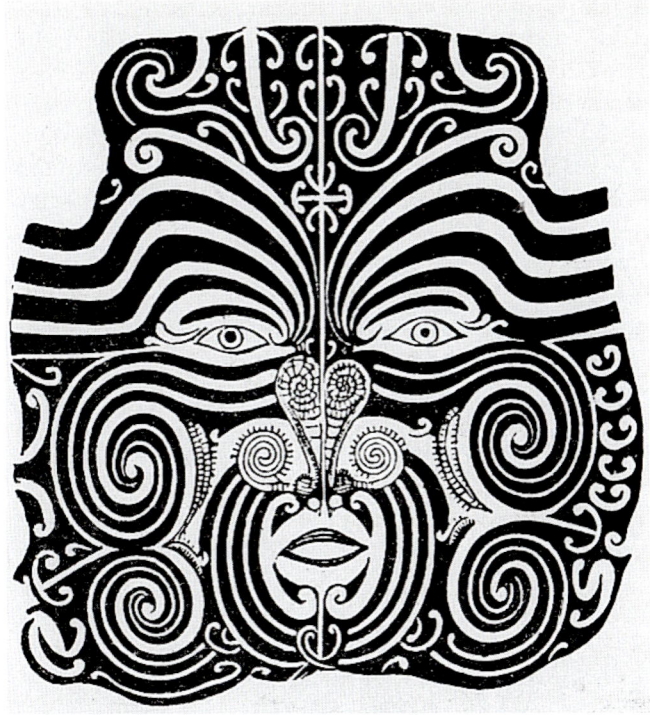

Intro-20 JOHN SYLVESTER *(left)* and TE PEHI KUPE *(right)*, portraits of Maori chief Te Pehi Kupe, 1826. From *The Childhood of Man,* by Leo Frobenius (New York: J. B. Lippincott, 1909).

contribute their expertise to the solution of problems in other disciplines. A historian, for example, might ask an art historian to determine—based on style, material, iconography, and other criteria—if any of the portraits of a certain king were made after his death. That would help establish the ruler's continuing prestige during his successors' reigns. (Some portraits of Augustus, FIG. Intro-10, the Roman Empire's founder, postdate his death by decades, even centuries.)

DIFFERENT WAYS OF SEEING

The history of art can be a history of artists and their works, of styles and stylistic change, of materials and techniques, of images and themes and their meanings, and of contexts and cultures and patrons. The best art historians analyze artworks from many viewpoints. But no art historian (or scholar in any other field!), no matter how broad-minded in approach and no matter how experienced, can be truly objective. Like artists, art historians are members of a society, participants in its culture. How can scholars (and museum visitors and travelers to foreign locales) comprehend cultures unlike their own? They can try to reconstruct the original cultural contexts of artworks, but they are bound to be limited by their distance from the thought patterns of the cultures they study and by the obstructions to understanding their own thought patterns raise—the assumptions, presuppositions, and prejudices peculiar to their own culture. Art historians may reconstruct a distorted picture of the past because of culture-bound blindness.

A single instance underscores how differently people of diverse cultures view the world and how various ways of seeing can cause sharp differences in how artists depict the world.

We illustrate two contemporaneous portraits of a nineteenth-century Maori chieftain side by side (FIG. **Intro-20**)—one by an Englishman, JOHN SYLVESTER, and the other by the New Zealand chieftain himself, TE PEHI KUPE. Both reproduce the chieftain's facial tattooing. The European artist included the head and shoulders and underplayed the tattooing. The tattoo pattern is one aspect of the likeness among many, no more or less important than the fact the chieftain is dressed like a European. Sylvester also recorded his subject's momentary glance toward the right and the play of light on his hair, fleeting aspects that have nothing to do with the figure's identity.

By contrast, Te Pehi Kupe's self-portrait—made during a trip to Liverpool, England, to obtain European arms to take back to New Zealand—is not a picture of a man situated in space and bathed in light. Rather, it is the chieftain's statement of the supreme importance of the design that symbolizes his rank among his people. Remarkably, Te Pehi Kupe created the tattoo patterns from memory, without the aid of a mirror. The splendidly composed insignia, presented as a flat design separated from the body and even from the head, is Te Pehi Kupe's image of himself. Only by understanding the cultural context of each portrait can viewers hope to understand why either looks the way it does.

As noted at the outset, the study of the context of artworks and buildings is one of the central aims of art history. Our purpose in writing *Art through the Ages* is to present a history of art and architecture that will help readers understand not only the subjects, styles, and techniques of paintings, sculptures, buildings, and other art forms created in all parts of the world for thirty millennia but also their cultural and historical contexts. That story now begins.

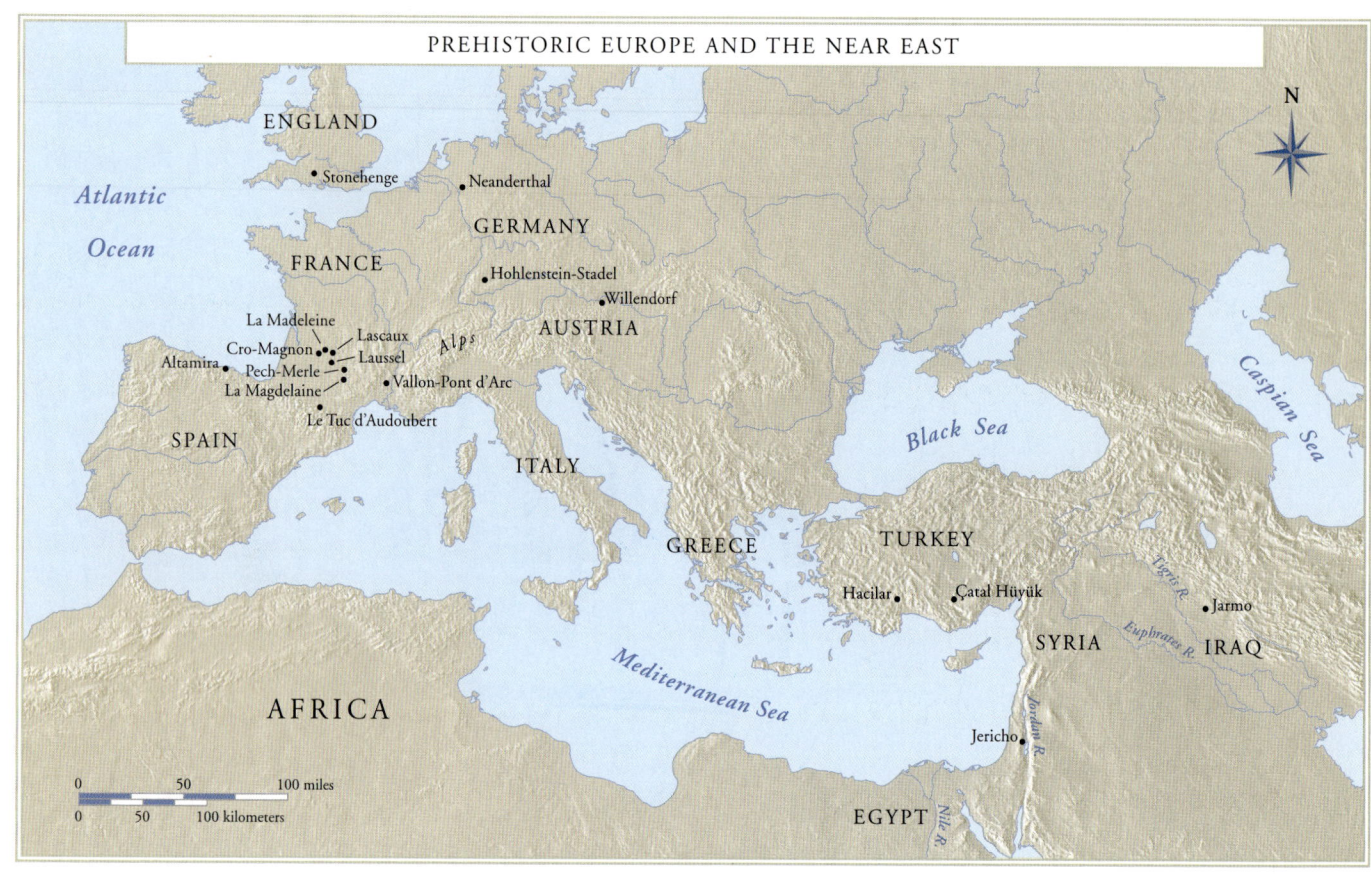

PREHISTORIC EUROPE AND THE NEAR EAST

ENGLAND

Atlantic Ocean

• Stonehenge

• Neanderthal

GERMANY

FRANCE

• Hohlenstein-Stadel

• Willendorf

AUSTRIA

La Madeleine
Cro-Magnon • Lascaux
• Laussel
Altamira • Pech-Merle
La Magdelaine
• Vallon-Pont d'Arc
Le Tuc d'Audoubert

Alps

SPAIN

ITALY

GREECE

Black Sea

Caspian Sea

TURKEY

Hacilar •
• Çatal Hüyük

Tigris R.

• Jarmo

Euphrates R.

SYRIA

IRAQ

Mediterranean Sea

Jordan R.

Jericho •

AFRICA

EGYPT

Nile R.

N

0   50   100 miles
0   50   100 kilometers

| 35,000 B.C. | 25,000 B.C. | 15,000 B.C. | 12,000 B.C. |

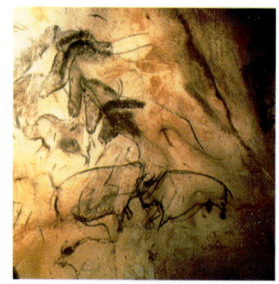

Chauvet Cave
Vallon-Pont-d'Arc
ca. 30,000–28,000 B.C.

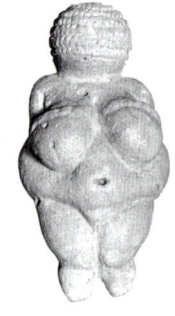

Venus of Willendorf
ca. 28,000–25,000 B.C.

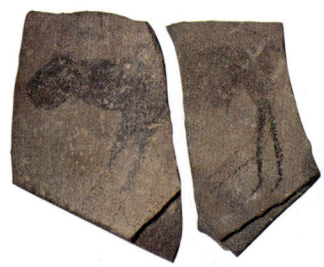

Painted plaque
Apollo 11 Cave, Namibia
ca. 23,000 B.C.

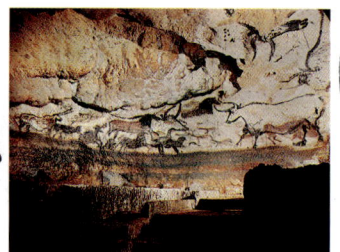

Hall of the Bulls, Lascaux
ca. 15,000–13,000 B.C.

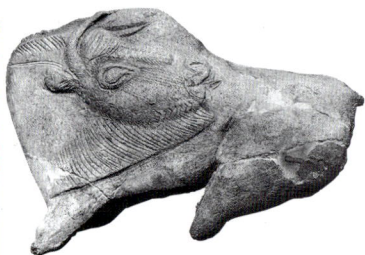

Bison with turned head
La Madeleine
ca. 12,000 B.C.

Neanderthal era, ca. 35,000 B.C.

Emergence of Cro-Magnons, ca. 32,000 B.C.

First Paleolithic paintings and sculptures, ca. 30,000 B.C.

THE BIRTH OF ART

AFRICA, EUROPE, AND THE NEAR EAST

IN THE STONE AGE

7000 B.C.	6000 B.C.	4000 B.C.	2000 B.C.

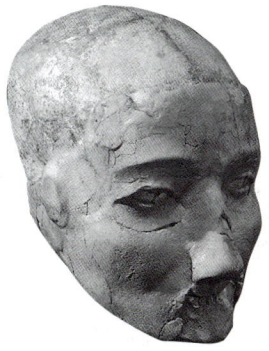

Human skull with restored features, Jericho ca. 7000–6000 B.C.

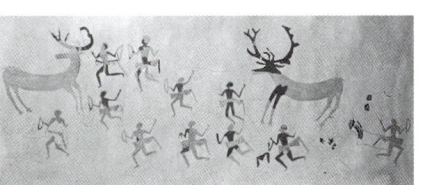

Deer hunt mural, Çatal Hüyük ca. 5750 B.C.

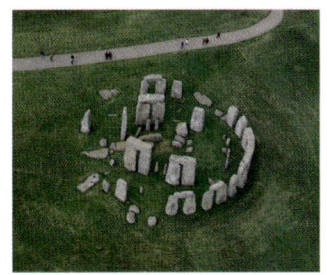

Stonehenge, Salisbury Plain ca. 2550–1600 B.C.

Final recession of ice and onset of temperate climate, ca. 9000 B.C.

Earliest farming communities, ca. 7000 B.C.

Neolithic begins in Europe, ca. 4000 B.C.

Neolithic begins in the Near East, ca. 8000 B.C.

WHAT IS ART?

OUT OF AFRICA   Humankind seems to have originated in Africa in the very remote past. From that great continent also comes the earliest evidence of human recognition of abstract images in the natural environment, if not the first examples of what people generally call "art." In 1925, explorers of a cave at Makapansgat in South Africa (see map, Chapter 15, page 414) discovered bones of *Australopithecus,* a predecessor of modern humans who lived some three million years ago. Associated with the bones was a waterworn reddish brown jasperite pebble (FIG. **1-1**) that bears an uncanny resemblance to a human face. The nearest known source of this variety of ironstone is twenty miles away from the cave. One of the early humans who took refuge in the rock shelter at Makapansgat must have noticed the pebble in a streambed and, awestruck by the "face" on the stone, brought it back for safekeeping.

Is the Makapansgat pebble art? In modern times, many artists have created works people universally consider art by removing objects from their normal contexts, altering them, and then labeling them. In 1917, for example, Marcel Duchamp took a ceramic urinal, set it on its side, called it *Fountain* (see FIG. 33-41), and declared his "ready-made" worthy of exhibition among more conventional artworks. But the artistic environment of the past century cannot be projected into the remote past. For art historians to declare a found object such as the Makapansgat pebble an "artwork," it must have been modified by human intervention beyond mere selection—and it was not. In fact, evidence indicates that not until three million years later, around 30,000 B.C., did humans *intentionally manufacture* sculptures and paintings. That is when the story of art through the ages really begins.

PALEOLITHIC ART

Africa

The several millennia following 30,000 B.C. saw a powerful outburst of artistic creativity. The artworks produced range from simple shell necklaces to human and animal forms in ivory, clay, and stone to monumental paintings, engravings, and relief sculptures covering the huge wall surfaces of caves. Scholars attribute this breakthrough to the emergence of Cro-Magnon peoples (named after a site in France), who replaced Neanderthals (a German site) during the Old Stone Age. These peoples of the *Paleolithic* (from the Greek *paleo,* "old," and *lithos,* "stone") period took the remarkable steps that transformed humankind from makers of simple stone tools to artists. The Cro-Magnons seem to have been the first to go beyond the *recognition* of human and animal forms in the natural environment to the *representation* (literally, the presenting again—in different and substitute form—of something observed) of humans and animals. The immensity of this achievement cannot be exaggerated.

PAINTED ANIMALS OF GREAT ANTIQUITY Some of the earliest paintings yet discovered come from Africa, and, like the treasured pebble in the form of a face found at Makapansgat, the oldest African paintings were portable objects. Between 1969 and 1972, scientists work-

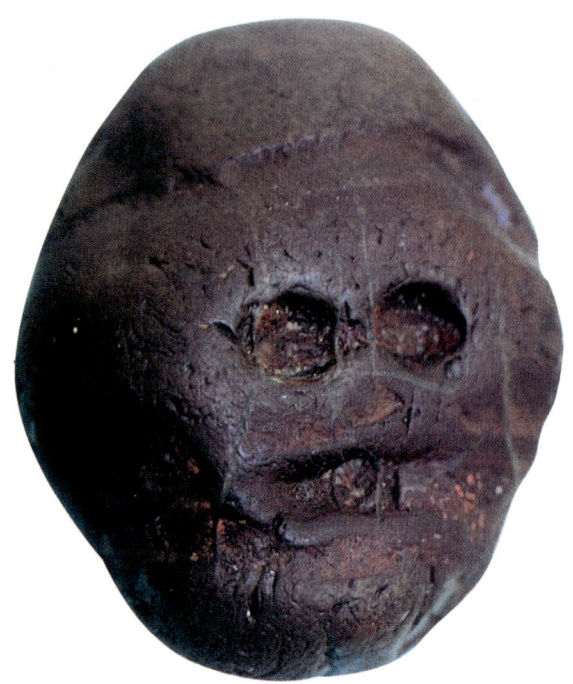

1-1   Waterworn pebble resembling a human face, from Makapansgat, South Africa, ca. 3,000,000 B.C. Reddish brown jasperite, approx. $2\frac{3}{8}''$ wide.

ing in the Apollo 11 Cave in Namibia (see map, Chapter 15, page 414) found seven fragments of stone plaques with paint on them, including four or five recognizable images of animals. In most cases, including the example we illustrate (FIG. **1-2**), the species is uncertain, but the forms are always carefully rendered. One plaque depicts a striped beast, possibly a zebra. The charcoal used to sketch the Namibian animals has been dated to around 23,000 B.C.

Like every artist in every age in every medium, the painter of the Apollo 11 plaque had to answer two questions before beginning work: *What* shall be my subject? *How* shall I represent it? In Paleolithic art, the almost universal answer to the first question was an animal—bison, mammoth, ibex, and horse were most common. In fact, Paleolithic painters and sculptors depicted humans infrequently and men almost never. In equally stark contrast to today's world, Paleolithic artists also

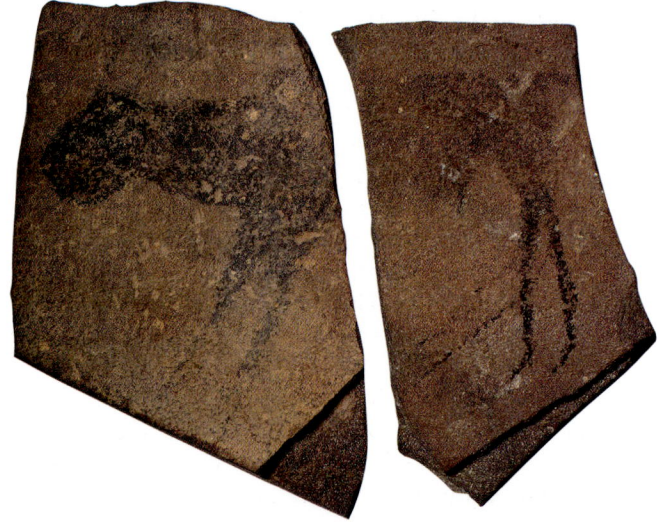

1-2   Animal facing left, from the Apollo 11 Cave, Namibia, ca. 23,000 B.C. Charcoal on stone, approx. $5'' \times 4\frac{1}{4}''$. State Museum of Namibia, Windhoek.

agreed on the best answer to the second question. Virtually every animal in every Paleolithic, *Mesolithic* (Middle Stone Age), and *Neolithic* (New Stone Age) painting was presented in the same manner—in strict profile. The profile was the only view of an animal wherein the head, body, tail, and all four legs can be seen. A frontal view would have concealed most of the body, and a three-quarter view would not have shown either the front or side fully. Only the profile view is completely informative about the animal's shape, and this is why the Stone Age painter always chose it. A very long time passed before artists placed any premium on "variety" or "originality," either in subject choice or in representational manner. These are quite modern notions in the history of art. The aim of the earliest painters was to create a convincing image of the subject, a kind of pictorial definition of the animal capturing its very essence, and only the profile view met their needs.

Western Europe

THE FIRST SCULPTURES IN EUROPE   Even older than the Namibian painted plaques are some of the first sculptures and paintings of western Europe, although examples of still greater antiquity may yet be found in Africa, bridging the gap between the Makapansgat pebble and the Apollo 11 painted plaques. One of the earliest sculptures discovered to date is an extraordinary ivory statuette (FIG. **1-3**), which may be as old as 30,000 B.C., from a cave at Hohlenstein-Stadel in Germany. Carved out of mammoth ivory and nearly a foot tall—a truly huge image for its era—the statuette represents something that existed only in the vivid imagination of the unknown artist who conceived it. It is a human (whether male or female is debated) with a feline head.

Such composite creatures with animal heads and human bodies (and vice versa) were common in the art of the ancient Near East and Egypt (compare, for example, FIGS. 2-10 and 3-39). In those civilizations, surviving texts usually allow historians to name the figures and describe their role in contemporary religion and mythology. But for Stone Age representations, no one knows what the artists had in mind. The animal-headed humans of Paleolithic art sometimes have been called sorcerers and described as magicians wearing masks. Similarly, Paleolithic human-headed animals have been interpreted as humans dressed up as animals. In the absence of any Stone Age written explanations—this is a time before writing, before (or *pre*-) history—researchers only can speculate on the purpose and function of a statuette such as that from Hohlenstein-Stadel.

Art historians are certain, however, that such statuettes were important to those who created and revered them, because manufacturing an ivory figure, especially one a foot tall, was a very difficult process. First, a tusk had to be removed from the dead animal by cutting into the ivory where it joined the head. The artist then cut the tusk to the desired size and rubbed it into its approximate final shape with sandstone. Finally, the sculptor used a sharp stone blade to carve the body, limbs, and head, and a stone *burin* (a pointed engraving tool) to *incise* (scratch) lines into the surfaces, as on the Hohlenstein-Stadel creature's arms. All this probably required at least several days of skilled work.

WOMEN IN PALEOLITHIC ART   The composite feline-human from Germany is exceptional for the Stone Age.

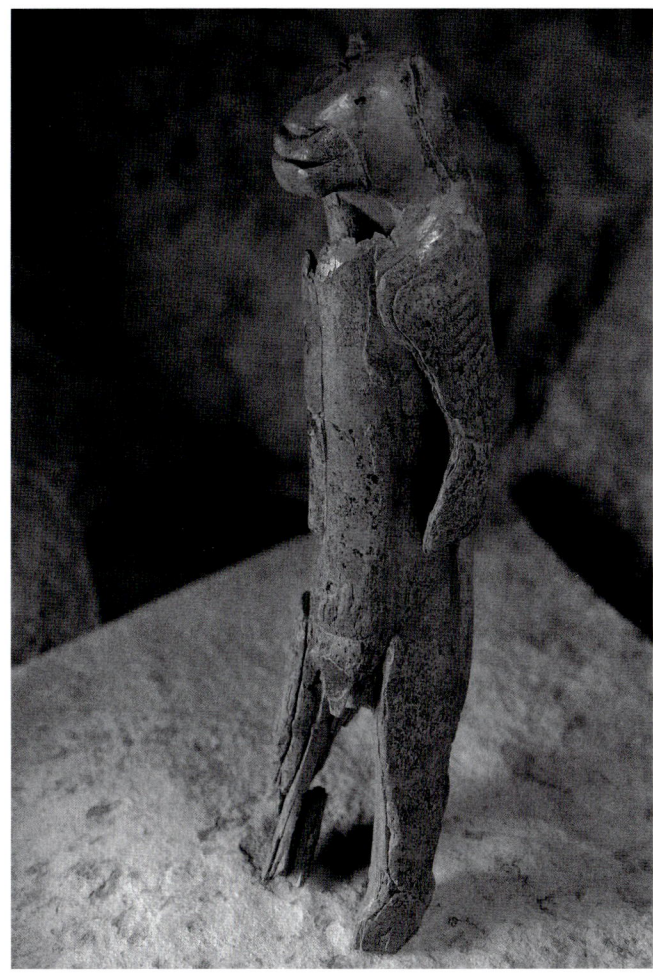

1-3   Human with feline head, from Hohlenstein-Stadel, Germany, ca. 30,000–28,000 B.C. Mammoth ivory, $11\frac{5}{8}''$ high. Ulmer Museum, Ulm.

The vast majority of prehistoric sculptures depict either animals or humans. In the earliest art, humankind consists almost exclusively of women as opposed to men, and the artists almost invariably showed them nude, although scholars generally assume that in life both women and men wore garments covering parts of their bodies. When archeologists first discovered Paleolithic statuettes of women, they dubbed them "Venuses," after the Greco-Roman goddess of beauty and love, whom artists usually depicted nude (see FIG. 5-60). The nickname is inappropriate and misleading. Not only does no evidence exist for named gods and goddesses in human form during the Old Stone Age, but also it is doubtful these figurines represented deities of any kind.

One of the oldest and the most famous of the prehistoric female figures is the tiny (only slightly more than four inches tall) limestone figurine of a woman that long has been known as the *Venus of Willendorf* (FIG. **1-4**) after its findspot in Austria. Its cluster of almost ball-like shapes is unusual, the result in part of the artist's response to the natural shape of the stone selected for carving. The anatomical exaggeration has suggested to many that this and similar statuettes served as fertility images. But other Paleolithic stone women of far more slender proportions exist, and the meaning of these images is as elusive as everything else about Paleolithic art. Yet the preponderance of female over male figures in the Old Stone Age seems to indicate a preoccupation with women, whose child-bearing capabilities insured the survival of the species.

Hohlenstein-Stadel figures were sculpted *in the round* (that is, they are *freestanding* objects). The Laussel woman is one of the earliest *relief sculptures* known. The artist employed a stone chisel to cut into the relatively flat surface of a large rock and create an image that projects from its background.

Today the Laussel relief is exhibited in a museum, divorced from its original context, a detached piece of what once was a much more imposing monument. When the relief was discovered, the Laussel woman (who is about $1\frac{1}{2}$ feet tall, much larger than the Willendorf statuette) was part of a great stone block that measured about 140 cubic feet. The carved block stood in the open air in front of a Paleolithic rock shelter. Such shelters were a common type of dwelling for early humans, along with huts and the mouths of caves. The Laussel relief is one of many examples of open-air art in the Old Stone Age. The popular notions that early humans dwelled exclusively in caves and that all Paleolithic art comes from mysterious dark caverns are false.

After the Laussel sculptor chiseled out the female form and etched the details with a sharp burin, red ocher was applied to the body. (The same color is also preserved on parts of the *Venus of Willendorf*.) Contrary to modern misconceptions about ancient art, artists frequently painted stone sculptures in antiquity, not only in prehistoric times and in the ancient Near East and Egypt but in the Greco-Roman era as well. The Laussel woman has the same bulbous forms as the earlier Willendorf figurine, with a similar exaggeration of the breasts, abdomen, and hips. The head is once again featureless, but the arms have

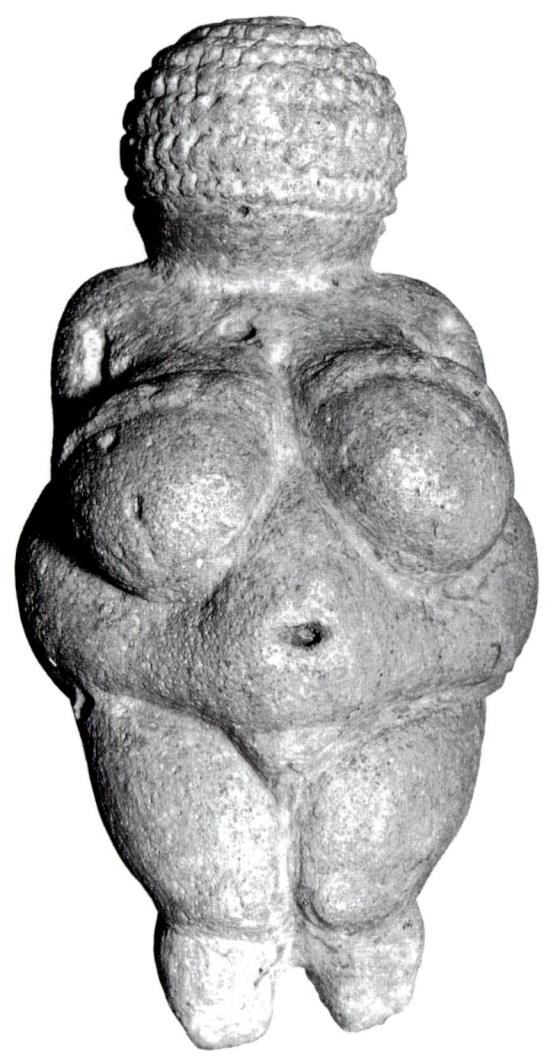

1-4   Nude woman *(Venus of Willendorf)*, from Willendorf, Austria, ca. 28,000–25,000 B.C. Limestone, approx. $4\frac{1}{4}''$ high. Naturhistorisches Museum, Vienna.

One thing at least is clear. The *Venus of Willendorf* sculptor did not aim for naturalism in shape and proportion. As with most Paleolithic figures, the sculptor did not carve any facial features. Here the artist suggested only a mass of curly hair or, as some researchers have recently argued, a hat woven from plant fibers—evidence for the art of textile manufacture at a very early date. In either case, the emphasis is on female fertility. The breasts of the Willendorf woman are enormous, far larger than the tiny forearms and hands that rest upon them, and the middle of the body bulges out even more than it does in actual pregnancies. The artist also took pains to scratch into the stone the outline of the pubic triangle. Sculptors often omitted this detail in other early figurines, leading some scholars to question the nature of these figures as fertility images. Whatever the purpose of such statuettes, the artists' intent seems not to have been to represent a specific woman but womanhood.

A ROCK SHELTER IN FRANCE   Because precision in dating is impossible for the Paleolithic era, art historians usually can be no more specific than assigning a range of several thousand years to each artifact. But probably later in date than the *Venus of Willendorf* is another female figure (FIG. **1-5**), from Laussel in France. The Willendorf and

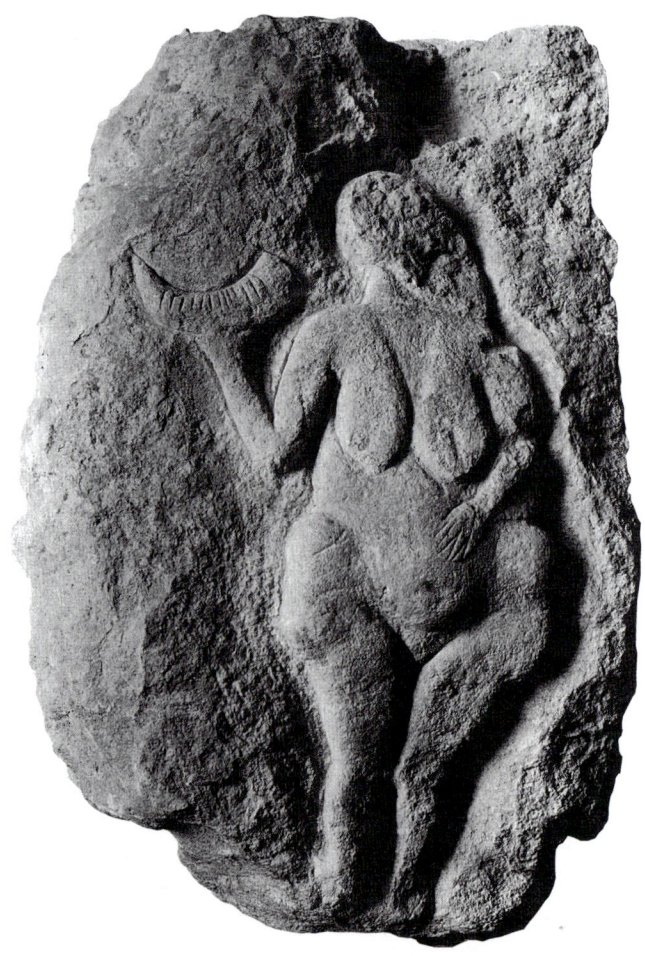

1-5   Woman holding a bison horn, from Laussel, Dordogne, France, ca. 25,000–20,000 B.C. Painted limestone, approx. $1'6''$ high. Musée d'Aquitaine, Bordeaux.

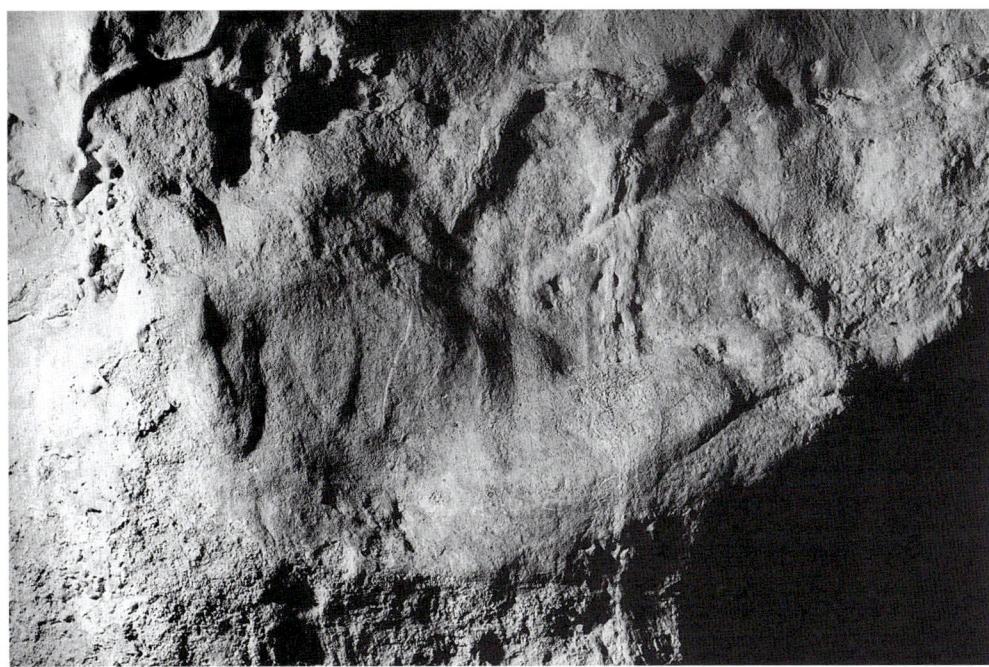

1-6 Reclining woman, rock-cut relief, La Magdelaine cave, Tarn, France, ca. 12,000 B.C. Approx. half life-size.

taken on greater importance. The left arm rests on the pregnant midsection and draws attention to it, and the raised right hand holds a bison horn. The meaning of the horn is debated.

WOMEN AND BISON IN FRENCH CAVES   Relief sculptures of nude women also adorned the walls of caves. Some of the most remarkable are the rock-cut reliefs, about half life-size, found in a cave at La Magdelaine in France. We illustrate one of the reliefs here (FIG. **1-6**). This sculpture is typical of many Paleolithic reliefs in that the artist used the natural contours of the stone wall as the basis for the representation. Old Stone Age artists frequently and skillfully used the caves' naturally irregular surfaces—the projections, recessions, fissures, and ridges—to help give the illusion of real

presence to their forms. Once an appropriate rock formation was selected, the sculptor then accentuated the outlines and added internal details to the figure with a stone chisel. The La Magdelaine woman reclines with extended arms and her left leg crossed over her right one. She lacks a head, but the sculptor carefully delineated her large breasts and pubic triangle.

Other Paleolithic artists created reliefs by building up forms out of clay rather than by cutting into stone blocks or stone walls. Sometime twelve thousand to seventeen thousand years ago in the low-ceilinged circular space at the end of a succession of cave chambers at Le Tuc d'Audoubert, a master sculptor modeled a pair of bison in clay against a large, irregular freestanding rock (FIG. **1-7**). The two bison, like the much older painted animal from the Apollo 11 Cave in Namibia (FIG. 1-2),

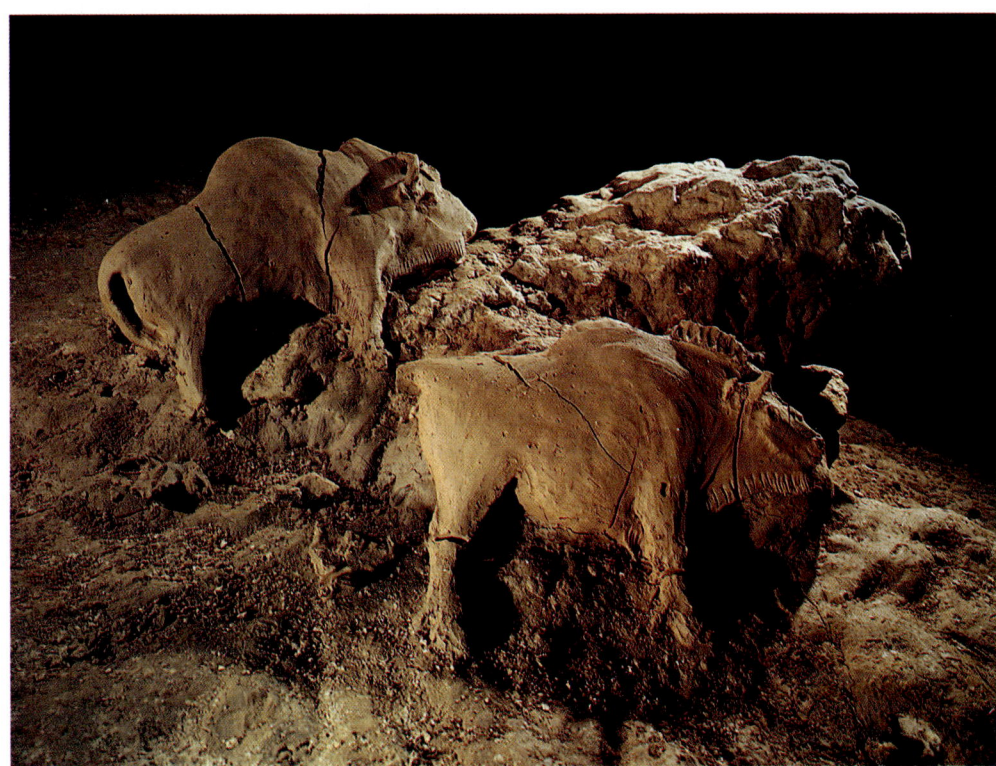

1-7 Two bison, reliefs in cave at Le Tuc d'Audoubert, Ariège, France, ca. 15,000–10,000 B.C. Clay, each approx. 2′ long.

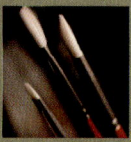

Paleolithic Cave Painting

The caves of Altamira (FIG. 1-9), Lascaux (FIGS. 1-11 and 1-13), and other sites in prehistoric Europe had served as underground water channels, a few hundred to several thousand feet long. They are often choked, sometimes almost impassably, by deposits, such as stalactites and stalagmites. Far inside these caverns, well removed from the cave mouths early humans sometimes chose for habitation, hunter-artists painted pictures on the dark walls. For light, they used tiny stone lamps filled with marrow or fat, with a wick, perhaps, of moss. For drawing, they used chunks of red and yellow ocher. For painting, they ground these same ochers into powders they blew onto the walls or mixed with some medium, such as animal fat, before applying. Recent analyses of the pigments used show they comprise many different minerals mixed according to different recipes, attesting to a technical sophistication surprising at so early a date.

Large flat stones served as the painters' palettes. The artists made brushes from reeds or bristles and used a blowpipe of reeds or hollow bones to trace outlines of figures and to put pigments on out-of-reach surfaces. Lascaux has recesses cut into the rock walls seven or more feet above the floor that once probably anchored a scaffolding that supported a platform made of saplings lashed together. This permitted the painters access to the upper surfaces of the caves.

Despite the difficulty of the work, modern attempts at replicating the techniques of Paleolithic painting have demonstrated that skilled artists could cover large surfaces with images in less than a day.

---

are in strict profile. Each is about two feet long. They are among the largest Paleolithic sculptures known. The sculptor brought the clay from another chamber in the cave complex and modeled it by hand into the overall shape of the animals. The artist then smoothed the surfaces with a spatula-like tool and finally engraved the eyes, nostrils, mouths, and manes with a stone burin. The cracks in the two animals resulted from the drying process and probably appeared within days of the sculptures' completion.

AN ANTLER BECOMES A BISON As already noted, artists fashioned ivory mammoth tusks into human and animal forms from very early times (FIG. 1-3). Prehistoric sculptors also used antlers as a sculptural medium, even though it meant the artists were forced to work on a very small scale. Although only four inches long, one of the finest sculptures of the Paleolithic era is a carved reindeer antler representing a bison (FIG. **1-8**). It was found at La Madeleine in France. As at Le Tuc d'Audoubert, the sculptor incised lines into the surface of this bison's mane with a sharp point. But here the engraving is much more detailed and extends to the horns, eye, ear, nostrils,

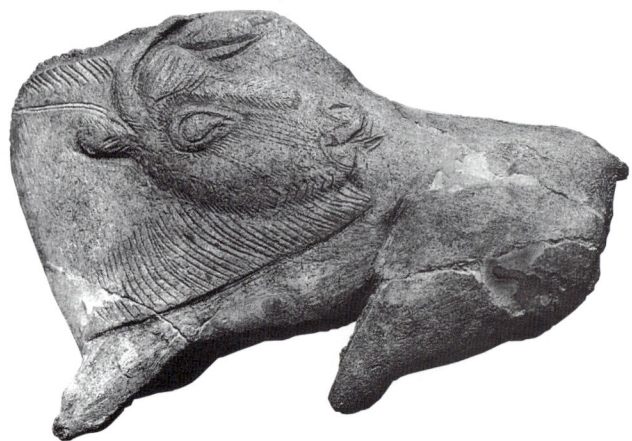

1-8 Bison with turned head, from La Madeleine, Dordogne, France, ca. 12,000 B.C. Reindeer horn, approx. 4″ long. Musée des Antiquités Nationales, Saint-Germain-en-Laye.

mouth, and the hair on the face. Especially interesting is the artist's decision to represent the bison with the head turned. The small size of the reindeer horn fragment may have been the motivation for this space-saving device. Whatever the reason, it is noteworthy that the sculptor turned the neck a full 180 degrees to maintain the strict profile Paleolithic artists insisted on for the sake of clarity and completeness, both in sculpture and in painting.

A LITTLE GIRL DISCOVERS PAINTINGS IN A CAVE The works examined here thus far, whether portable or fixed to rocky outcroppings or cave walls, are all small. They are dwarfed by the "herds" of painted animals that roam the cave walls of southern France and northern Spain, where some of the most spectacular prehistoric art has been discovered. The first examples of cave paintings were found accidentally by an amateur archeologist in 1879 at Altamira, Spain. Don Marcelino Sanz de Sautuola was exploring on his estate a cave where he had already found specimens of flint and carved bone. His little daughter Maria was with him when they reached a chamber some eighty-five feet from the cave's entrance. Because it was dark and the ceiling of the debris-filled cavern was only a few inches above the father's head, the child was the first to discern, from her lower vantage point, the shadowy forms of painted beasts on the cave roof (FIG. **1-9**, a detail of a much larger painting approximately sixty feet long).

Sanz de Sautuola was certain the bison painted on the Altamira ceiling dated back to prehistoric times. Professional archeologists, however, doubted the authenticity of these works, and at the Lisbon Congress on Prehistoric Archeology in 1880, they officially dismissed the paintings as forgeries. But by the close of the century, other caves had been discovered with painted walls partially covered by mineral deposits that would have taken thousands of years to accumulate. Skeptics were finally persuaded that the first paintings were of an age far more remote than they had ever dreamed. Examples of Paleolithic painting now have been found at more than two hundred sites (see "Paleolithic Cave Painting," above). Art historians still regard painted caves as rare

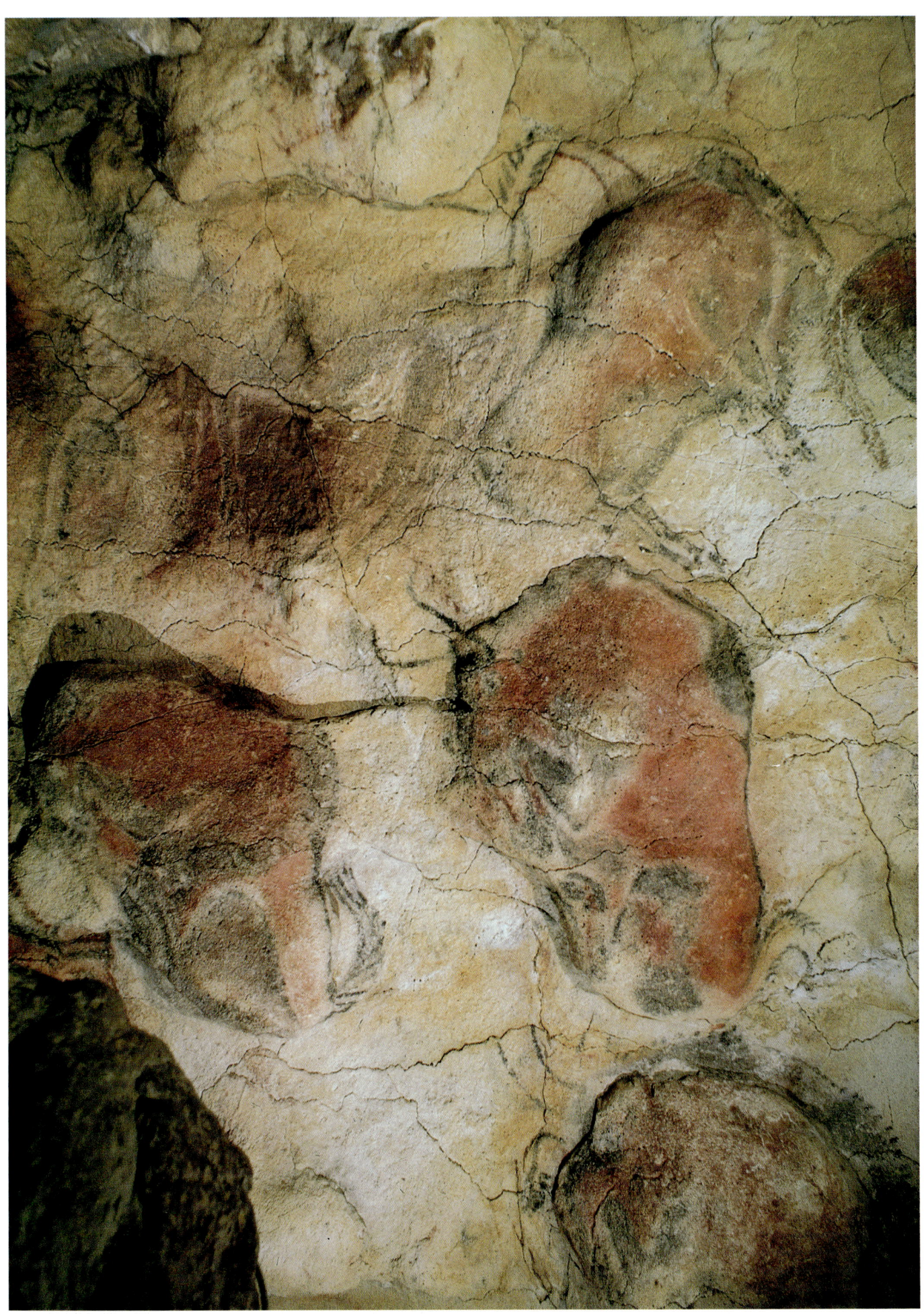

1-9 Bison, detail of a painted ceiling in the Altamira cave, Santander, Spain, ca. 12,000–11,000 B.C. Each bison approx. 8′ long.

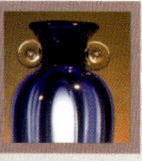

Animals and Magic in the Old Stone Age

From the moment in 1879 that cave paintings were discovered at Altamira (FIG. 1-9), scholars have wondered why the hunter-artists of the Old Stone Age decided to cover the walls of dark caverns with animal images. Various answers have been given, including that they were mere decoration, but this theory cannot explain the narrow range of subjects or the inaccessibility of many of the paintings. In fact, the remoteness and difficulty of access of many of the cave painting sites and the fact they appear to have been used for centuries are precisely what have led many scholars to suggest that the prehistoric hunters attributed magical properties to the images they painted. According to this argument, by confining animals to the surfaces of their cave walls, the artists believed they were bringing the beasts under their control. Some have even hypothesized that rituals or dances were performed in front of the images and that these rites served to improve the hunters' luck. Still others have stated that the painted animals may have served as teaching tools to instruct new hunters about the character of the various species they would encounter or even to serve as targets for spears!

By contrast, some scholars have argued that the magical purpose of the paintings was not to facilitate the *destruction*

of bison and other species. Instead, they believe prehistoric painters created animal images to assure the *survival* of the herds Paleolithic peoples depended on for their food supply and for their clothing. A central problem for both the hunting-magic and food-creation theories is that the animals that seem to have been diet staples of Old Stone Age peoples are not those most frequently portrayed. At Altamira, for example, faunal remains show that red deer, not bison, were eaten.

Other scholars have sought to reconstruct an elaborate mythology based on the cave paintings, suggesting that Paleolithic humans believed they had animal ancestors. Still others have equated certain species with men and others with women and also found sexual symbolism in the abstract signs that sometimes accompany the images. Almost all of these theories have been discredited over time, and art historians must admit that no one knows the intent of these paintings. In fact, a single explanation for all Paleolithic murals, even paintings similar in subject, style, and *composition* (how the motifs are arranged on the surface), is unlikely to apply universally. For now, the paintings remain an enigma.

---

occurrences, though, because the images in them, even if they number in the hundreds, were created over a period of some twenty thousand years.

The bison at Altamira were painted in Spain thirteen thousand to fourteen thousand years ago, but the artist approached the problem of representing an animal in essentially the same way as the painter of the stone plaque from Namibia (FIG. 1-2), who worked more than ten thousand years earlier. Every one of the Altamira bison is in profile, whether alive and standing or curled up on the ground (probably dead, although this is disputed). To maintain the profile in the latter case, the artist had to adopt a viewpoint above the animal, looking down, rather than the view a person standing on the ground would have.

Art historians often refer to the Altamira animals as a *group* of bison, but that is very likely a misnomer. The several bison in our illustration do not stand on a common *ground line* (a painted or carved baseline on which figures appear to stand in paintings and reliefs), nor do they share a common orientation. They seem almost to float above viewers' heads, like clouds in the sky. And the dead(?) bison are seen in an "aerial view," while the others are seen from a position on the ground. The painting has no setting, no background, no indication of place. The Paleolithic painter was not at all concerned with *where* the animals were or with how they related to one another, if at all. Instead, several *separate* images of a bison adorn the ceiling, perhaps painted at different times, and each is as complete and informative as possible—even if their meaning remains a mystery (see "Animals and Magic in the Old Stone Age," above).

THE BIRTH OF WRITING? That the paintings did have meaning to the Paleolithic peoples who made and ob-

served them cannot, however, be doubted. In fact, signs consisting of checks, dots, squares, or other arrangements of lines often accompany the pictures of animals. Several observers have seen a primitive writing form in these representations of nonliving things, but the signs, too, may have had some other significance. Some look like traps and arrows and, according to the hunting-magic theory, may have been drawn to insure success in capturing or killing animals with these devices. At Pech-Merle in France, the "spotted horses" painted on the cave wall (FIG. **1-10**) may not have spots. Some scholars have argued that the "spots," which appear both within and without the horses' outlines, are painted rocks thrown at the animals.

Representations of human hands also are common. Those around the Pech-Merle horses, and the majority of painted hands at other sites, are "negative," that is, the artist placed one hand against the wall and then painted or blew pigment around it. Occasionally, the artist dipped a hand in paint and then pressed it against the wall, leaving a "positive" imprint. These handprints, too, must have had a purpose. Some scholars have considered them "signatures" of cult or community members or, less likely, of individual artists.

The mural paintings at Pech-Merle also allow some insight into the reason certain subjects may have been chosen for a specific location. One of the horses (at the right in our illustration) may have been inspired by the rock formation in the wall surface resembling a horse's head and neck. Like the reclining woman at La Magdelaine (FIG. 1-6), the Pech-Merle representations may have been created after someone noticed a resemblance between a chance configuration in nature and an animal or person. The artists then "finished" the perceived forms by accentuating the outlines with stone tools, as at La Magdelaine, or by the addition of color, as at Pech-Merle. Art histori-

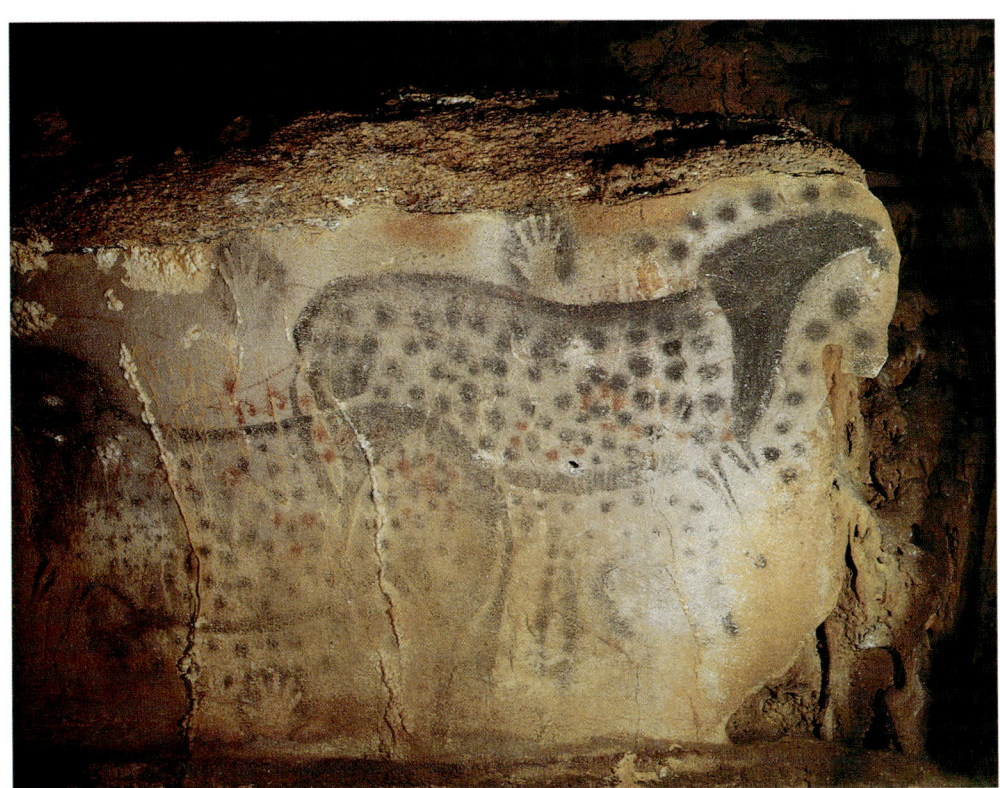

1-10 Spotted horses and negative hand imprints, wall painting in the cave at Pech-Merle, Lot, France, ca. 22,000 B.C. Approx. 11′ 2″ long.

ans also have observed that nearly all horses and hands are painted on concave surfaces, while bison and cattle appear almost exclusively on convex surfaces. What this signifies has yet to be determined.

THE "RUNNING OF THE BULLS" AT LASCAUX
Perhaps the best known Paleolithic caves are those at Lascaux, near Montignac, France, which are extensively decorated. Many of the painted chambers are characteristically hundreds of feet from the entrance. The first chamber one encounters, although even it is far removed from the daylight, is the so-called Hall of the Bulls (FIG. **1-11**). It is also the most magnificent. Not all of the animals depicted are bulls, despite the

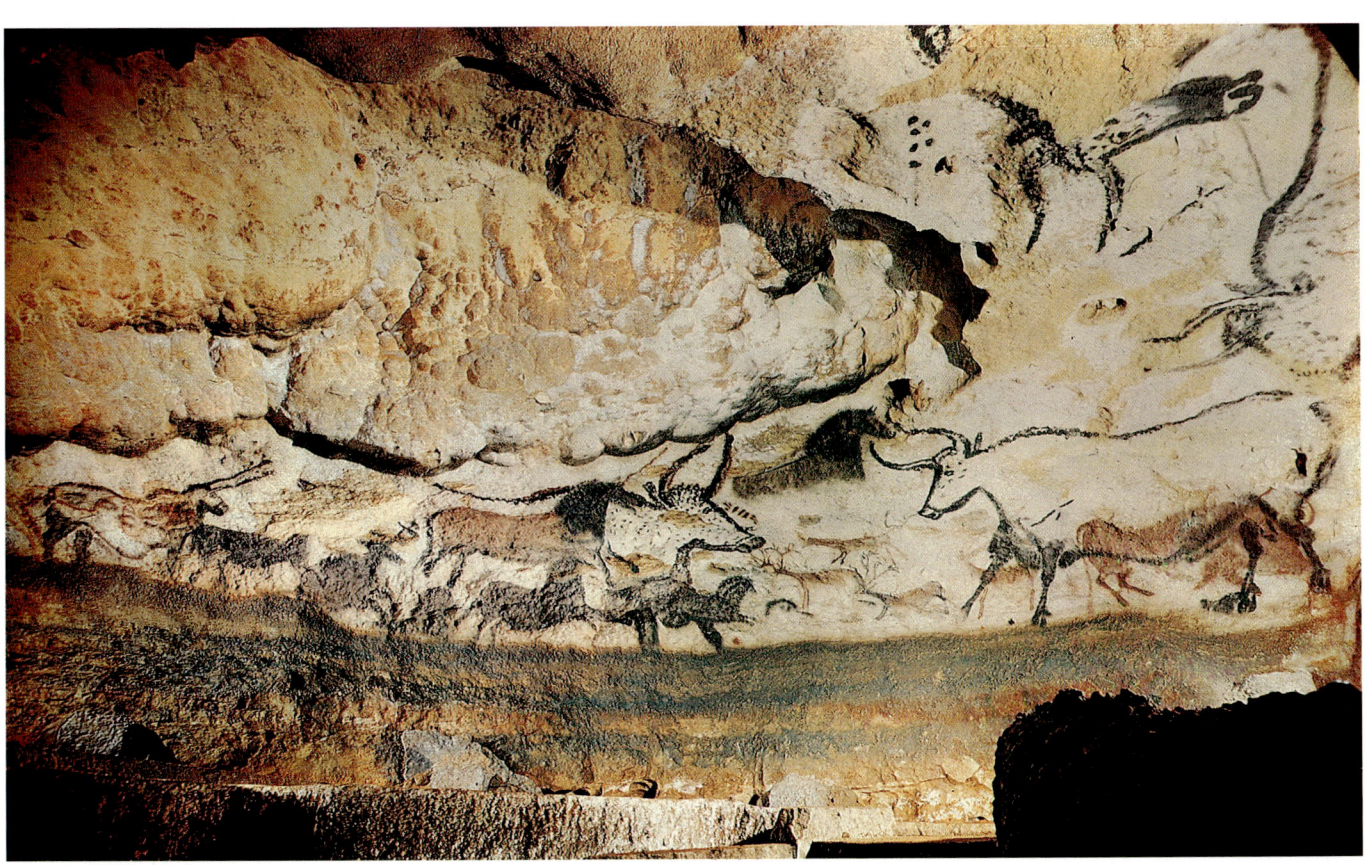

1-11   Hall of the Bulls (left wall), Lascaux, Dordogne, France, ca. 15,000–13,000 B.C. Largest bull approx. 11′ 6″ long.

1-12 Aurochs, horses, and rhinoceroses, wall painting in Chauvet Cave, Vallon-Pont-d'Arc, Ardèche, France, ca. 30,000–28,000 B.C. Approx. half life-size.

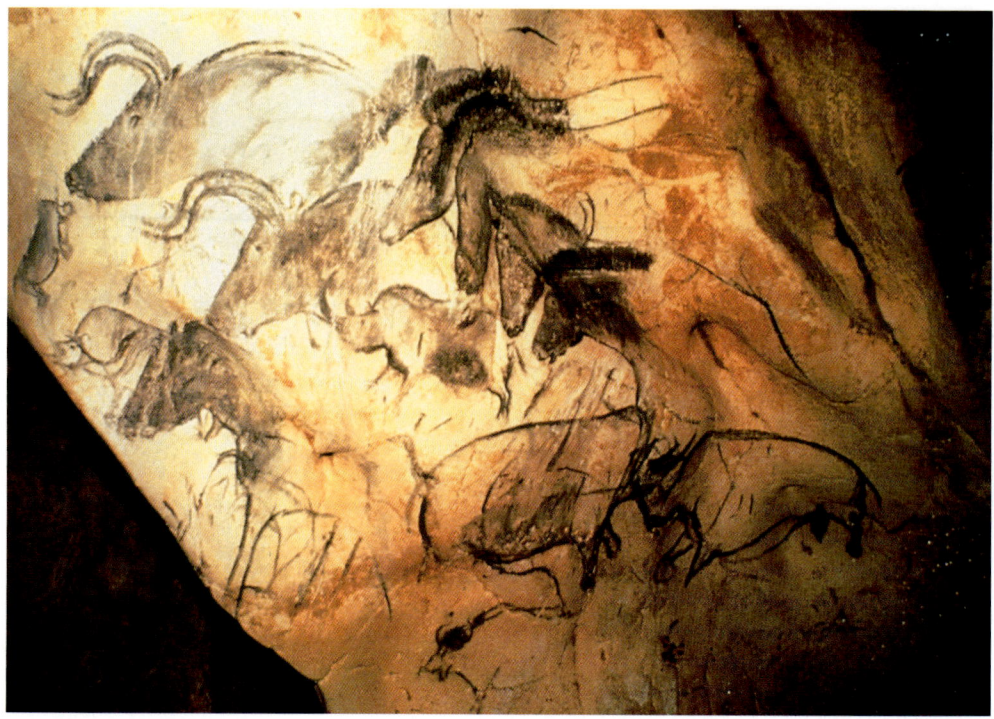

modern nickname of the great circular gallery, and the several species depicted vary in size. Many are represented using colored silhouettes, as in the cave at Altamira (FIG. 1-9) and on the Namibian plaque (FIG. 1-2). Others—such as the great bull at the right in our illustration—were created by outline alone, as were the Pech-Merle horses (FIG. 1-10). On the walls of the Lascaux cave one sees, side by side, the two basic approaches to drawing and painting found repeatedly in the history of art. (Compare, for example, the Greek techniques of *black-figure* [silhouette] and *red-figure* [outline] painting a dozen millennia later in FIG. 5-20.) These differences in style and technique alone suggest that the animals in the Hall of the Bulls were painted at different times, and the modern impression of a rapidly moving herd of beasts was probably not the artists' intent. In any case, the "herd" consists of several different kinds of animals of various sizes moving in different directions.

Another feature of the Lascaux paintings deserves attention. The bulls there show a convention of representing horns that has been called *twisted perspective,* because viewers see the heads in profile but the horns from the front. Thus, the artist's approach is not strictly or consistently *optical* (seen from a fixed viewpoint). Rather, the approach is *descriptive* of the fact cattle have two horns. Two horns are part of the concept "bull." In strict optical-perspective profile, only one horn would be visible, but to paint the animal in that way would, as it were, amount to an incomplete definition of it. This kind of twisted perspective was the norm in prehistoric painting, but it was not universal. In fact, the recent discovery of the world's earliest datable paintings in the Chauvet Cave (FIG. **1-12**) at Vallon-Pont-d'Arc in France, where the painters represented horns in a more natural way, has caused art historians to rethink many of the assumptions they had made about Paleolithic art (see "The World's Oldest Paintings," page 11).

PALEOLITHIC NARRATIVE ART? Perhaps the most perplexing painting in all the Paleolithic caves is the one deep in the well shaft at Lascaux (FIG. **1-13**), where man (as opposed to woman) makes one of his earliest appearances in prehistoric painting. At the left is a rhinoceros, rendered with all the skilled attention to animal detail customarily seen in cave art. Beneath its tail are two rows of three dots of uncertain significance. At the right is a bison, more crudely painted, but the artist quite successfully suggested the bristling rage of the animal, whose bowels are hanging from it in a heavy coil. Between the two beasts is a bird-faced (masked?) man (compare the feline-headed human from Hohlenstein-Stadel, FIG. 1-3) with outstretched arms and hands with only four fingers. The artist depicted the man with far less care and detail than the animals, but made his gender explicit by the prominent penis. Perhaps the painter did not have to strive for a realistic portrayal because the community had no need to create humans for magical or other purposes. The position of the man is also ambiguous. Is he wounded or dead or merely tilted back and unharmed? Do the staff(?) with the bird on top and the spear belong to him? Is it he or the rhinoceros who has gravely wounded the bison—or neither? Which animal, if either, has knocked the man down, if indeed he is on the ground? Are these three images related at all? Art historians can be sure of nothing, but if the painter placed these figures beside each other to tell a story, then this is evidence for the creation of complex *narrative* compositions involving humans and animals at a much earlier date than anyone had imagined only a few generations ago. Yet it is important to remember that even if a story was intended, very few people would have been able to "read" it. The painting, in a deep shaft, is very difficult to reach and could have been viewed only in the flickering light of a primitive lamp.

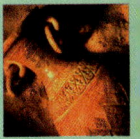

The World's Oldest Paintings

One of the most spectacular archeological finds of the past century came to light in December 1994 at Vallon-Pont-d'Arc, France, and was announced at a dramatic press conference in Paris on January 18, 1995. The next day, people around the world were startled when they picked up their morning newspapers or turned on their televisions and saw a sampling of pictures of extraordinary Paleolithic cave paintings. Unlike some other recent "finds" of prehistoric art that proved to be forgeries, the paintings in the Chauvet Cave (named after the leader of the exploration team, Jean-Marie Chauvet) seemed to be authentic. But no one, including Chauvet and his colleagues, guessed at the time of their discovery that direct *radiocarbon dating* (a measure of the rate of degeneration of carbon 14 in organic materials) of the paintings would establish that the murals in the cave were more than fifteen thousand years older than those at Altamira (FIG. 1-9). The Chauvet Cave paintings are, in fact, the oldest yet found anywhere, datable around 30,000–28,000 B.C. They have caused scholars to reevaluate the scheme of "stylistic development" from simple to more complex forms that had been nearly universally accepted for decades.

Chauvet and his team have written a moving account of their exploration of the cave. When they encountered the painted wall we illustrate here (FIG. 1-12), this is how they reacted: "There was a moment of ecstasy. . . . Jean-Marie . . . was stammering. Christian [Hillaire] was uttering exclamations of amazement. When Eliette [Brunel Deschamps] and [her daughter] Carole rushed over, they overflowed with joy and emotion in their turn. . . . These were minutes of indescribable madness."[1]

Many species of animals appear on the cave walls, including several ferocious animals that were never part of the Paleolithic human diet, such as lions and bears. Bears, in fact, hibernated in the cave and more than fifty bear skulls are still there. When the bears resided in the cave, it was a dangerous place for anyone to venture into.

Several of the paintings Chauvet's team discovered occupy a special place in the history of art. In the Chauvet Cave, many thousands of years before Lascaux (FIG. 1-11), the horns of the aurochs (extinct long-horned wild oxen) are shown naturalistically, one behind the other, not in the twisted perspective thought to be universally characteristic of Paleolithic art. And the aurochs and horses, although presented in the standard profile view, are incomplete, violating the "rule" that Paleolithic painters always sketched complete forms. Moreover, the two rhinoceroses at the lower right of our illustration appear to confront each other, suggesting to some observers that a narrative was intended, another "first" in either painting or sculpture.

Much research remains to be conducted in the Chauvet Cave, and more paintings have been discovered as work has progressed. But it is already obvious that the assumption that Paleolithic art "evolved" from primitive to more sophisticated representations is wrong. In time, other widely accepted theories probably also will be proven false. This is the frustration—and the excitement—of studying the art of an age so remote that almost nothing remains and almost every new find causes art historians to reevaluate what had previously been taken for granted.

[1] Jean-Marie Chauvet et al., *Dawn of Art: The Chauvet Cave* (New York: Harry N. Abrams, 1996), 48–50.

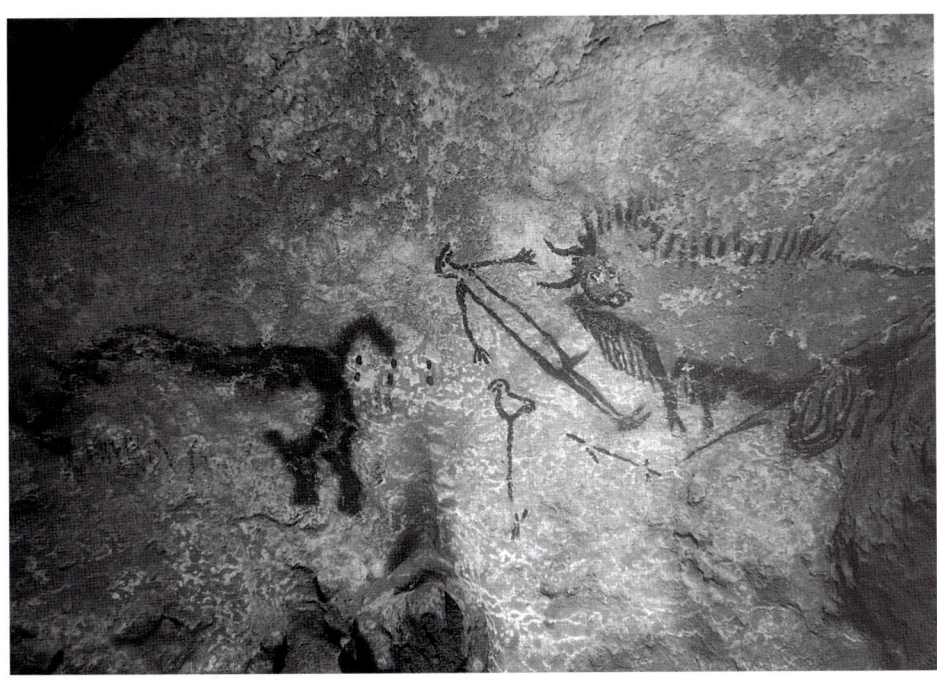

1-13 Rhinoceros, wounded man, and disemboweled bison, painting in the well, Lascaux, Dordogne, France, ca. 15,000–13,000 B.C. Bison approx. 3′ 8″ long.

NEOLITHIC ART

THE ICE RECEDES   Around 9000 B.C., the ice that covered much of northern Europe during the Paleolithic period melted as the climate grew warmer. The reindeer migrated north, and the woolly mammoth and rhinoceros disappeared. The Paleolithic gave way to a transitional period, the Mesolithic, when Europe became climatically, geographically, and biologically much as it is today. Then, for several thousand years at different times in different parts of the globe, a great new age, the Neolithic, dawned.

In a supreme intellectual feat, Paleolithic peoples had learned to abstract their world by making pictures of it. By capturing and holding its image, they may have hoped to control it. In the Neolithic period, human beings took a giant stride toward the actual, concrete control of their environment by settling in fixed abodes and domesticating plants and animals. Their food supply assured, many groups changed from hunters to herders, to farmers, and finally to townspeople. Wandering hunters settled down to organized community living in villages surrounded by cultivated fields.

The conventional division of prehistory into the Paleolithic, Mesolithic, and Neolithic periods is based on the development of stone implements. However, a different kind of distinction may be made between an age of food gathering and an age of food production. In this scheme, the Paleolithic period corresponds roughly to the age of food gathering, and the Mesolithic period, the last phase of that age, is marked by intensified food gathering and the taming of the dog. In the Neolithic period, agriculture and stock raising became humankind's major food sources. The transition to the Neolithic occurred first in the ancient Near East.

Ancient Near East

THE DAWN OF CIVILIZATION   At one time, researchers proposed that the area known today as the Middle East, the ancient Near East, dried out into desert and semidesert climates after the last retreat of the glaciers. They suggested that this compelled the inhabitants to move to the fertile valleys of the Nile River in Egypt and the Tigris and Euphrates Rivers in Mesopotamia (parts of modern Syria and Iraq). This view is no longer tenable in light of archeological and ecological findings. The oldest settled communities were found not in the river valleys but in the grassy uplands bordering them. These regions provided the necessary preconditions for the development of agriculture. Species of native plants, such as wild wheat and barley, were plentiful, as were herds of animals (goats, sheep, and pigs) that could be domesticated. Sufficient rain occurred for the raising of crops. Only after village farming life was well developed did settlers, attracted by the greater fertility of the soil and perhaps also by the need to find more land for their rapidly growing populations, move into the river valleys and deltas. There, in addition to systematic agriculture, Neolithic societies originated government, law, and formal religion, as well as writing, measurement and calculation, weaving, metalworking, and pottery.

Based on the information known today, these innovations appear to have occurred first in Mesopotamia and then spread to northern Syria, Anatolia (Turkey), and Egypt at an early

date. Village farming communities such as Jarmo in Iraq and Çatal Hüyük in southern Anatolia date back to the mid-seventh millennium B.C. The remarkable fortified town of Jericho, before whose walls the biblical Joshua appeared thousands of years later, is even older. Archeologists are constantly uncovering surprises, and the discovery and exploration of new sites each year is compelling them to revise their views about the emergence of Neolithic civilization. But two sites known for some time, Jericho on the Jordan River and Çatal Hüyük in Anatolia, offer a reasonably representative picture of the rapid and exciting transformation of human society— and of art—during the Neolithic period.

A STONE TOWER TEN THOUSAND YEARS OLD   By 7000 B.C., agriculture was well established in at least three Near Eastern regions: ancient Palestine, Iran, and Anatolia. Although no remains of domestic cereals have been found that can be dated before 7000 B.C., the advanced state of agriculture at that time presupposes a long development. Indeed, the very existence of a town such as Jericho gives strong support to this assumption. The site of Jericho—a plateau in the Jordan River valley with an unfailing spring—was occupied by a small village as early as the ninth millennium B.C. This village underwent spectacular development around 8000 B.C., when a new Neolithic town covering about ten acres was built. Its mud-brick houses sat on round or oval stone foundations and had roofs of branches covered with earth.

As the town's wealth grew and powerful neighbors established themselves, the need for protection resulted in the first known permanent stone fortifications. By approximately 7500 B.C., the town, estimated to have had a population of more than two thousand people, was surrounded by a wide rock-cut ditch and a five-foot-thick wall. Into this wall, which has been preserved to a height of almost thirteen feet, was built a great circular stone tower (FIG. **1-14**),

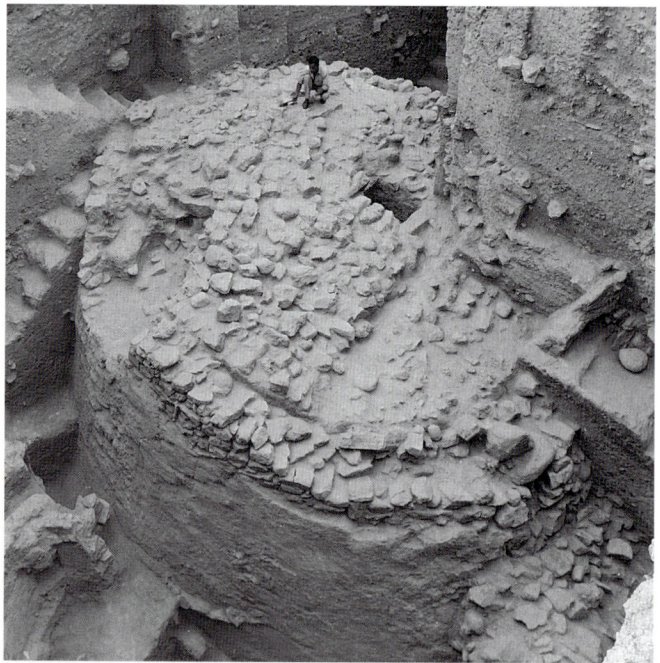

1-14   Great stone tower built into the settlement wall, Jericho, ca. 8000–7000 B.C.

twenty-eight feet high. Almost thirty-three feet in diameter at the base, the tower has an inner stairway leading to its summit. Not enough of the site has been excavated to determine whether this tower was solitary or one of several similar towers that formed a complete defense system. In either case, a structure such as this, built with only the most primitive kinds of stone tools, was certainly a tremendous technological achievement. It constitutes the beginning of a long history of monumental architecture, which leads from this stone tower in Neolithic Jericho to today's hundred-story skyscrapers of steel, concrete, and glass.

SKULLS WITH RESTORED FACES Around 7000 B.C., the original inhabitants abandoned the Jericho site, but new settlers arrived in the early seventh millennium. They built rectangular mud-brick houses on stone foundations and carefully plastered and painted their floors and walls. Several of the excavated buildings seem to have served as shrines, and the settlers fashioned statuettes of women or goddesses and of animals. Most unusual is a group of human skulls whose features artists "reconstructed" in plaster (FIG. **1-15**). Subtly modeled, with inlaid seashells for eyes and painted hair (including a painted mustache preserved on one specimen), their appearance is strikingly lifelike. The features depicted should, however, be regarded as typical rather than a record of specific faces. The Jericho skulls are not portraits in the modern sense of accurate individual likenesses.

Because the skulls were not only detached from the bodies and given new faces, but also were buried separately, the people of Neolithic Jericho must have attached special sig-

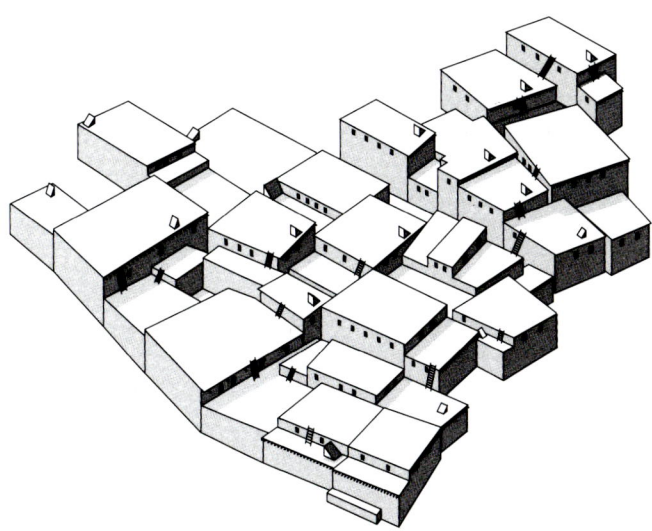

1-16 Schematic reconstruction drawing of a section of Level VI, Çatal Hüyük, Turkey, ca. 6000–5900 B.C. (after J. Mellaart).

nificance to the heads. Some scholars think they attest to belief in an afterlife following the body's death. Whatever their purpose, by their size alone the Jericho heads are distinguished from Paleolithic figurines such as the tiny *Venus of Willendorf* (FIG. 1-4) and even the foot-tall ivory statuette from Hohlenstein-Stadel (FIG. 1-3). They mark the beginning of monumental sculpture in the ancient Near East.

A NEOLITHIC TOWN WITH NO STREETS Remarkable discoveries also have been made in Anatolia. Excavations at Hacilar, Çatal Hüyük, and elsewhere have shown that the central Anatolian plateau was the site of a flourishing Neolithic culture between 7000 and 5000 B.C. Twelve successive building levels excavated at Çatal Hüyük between 1961 and 1965 have been dated between 6500 and 5700 B.C. On a single site, it is possible to retrace, in an unbroken sequence, the evolution of a Neolithic culture over a period of eight hundred years. (Only one of thirty-two acres had been explored before the recent resumption of excavations. The new project promises to expand and perhaps revise the current picture of Neolithic life.)

The source of Çatal Hüyük's wealth was trade, especially in obsidian, a glasslike volcanic stone easily chipped into fine cutting edges and highly valued by Neolithic toolmakers and weapon makers. Along with Jericho, Çatal Hüyük seems to have been one of the first experiments in urban living. The regularity of its plan suggests that the town was built according to some predetermined scheme. A peculiar feature is the settlement's complete lack of streets (FIG. **1-16**); the houses adjoin one another and have no doors. Openings just below the roofs provided access to the interiors. The openings also served as chimneys to ventilate the hearth in the combination living room/kitchen that formed the house's core. Impractical as such an arrangement may appear today, it did offer some advantages. The attached buildings were more stable than freestanding structures and, at the limits of the town site, formed a perimeter wall well suited to defense against human or natural forces. Thus, if enemies managed to breach the exterior wall, they would find themselves not inside the town but above the houses with the defenders waiting there on the roof.

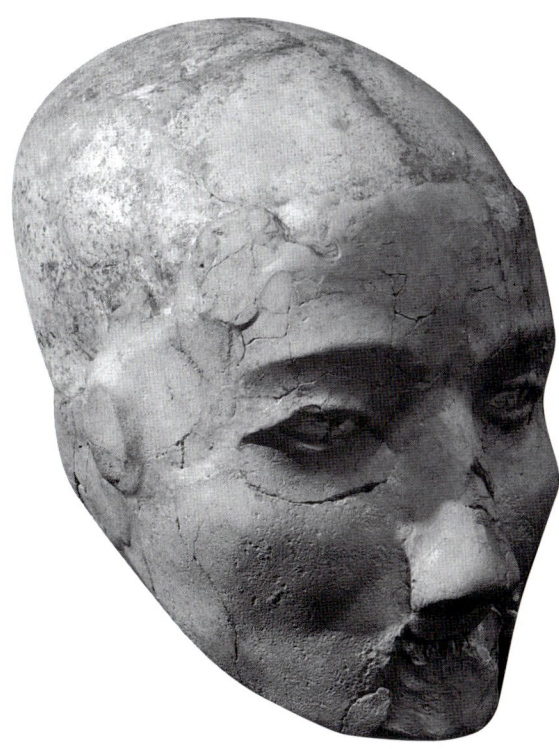

1-15 Human skull with restored features, Jericho, ca. 7000–6000 B.C. Features molded in plaster, painted, and inlaid with shell. Archeological Museum, Amman.

The houses, constructed of mud brick strengthened by sturdy timber frames, varied in size but were of a standard plan. Walls and floors were plastered and painted, and platforms along walls served as sites for sleeping, working, and eating. The dead were buried beneath the floors. A great number of shrines have been found intermingled with standard houses. Varying with the different building levels, the average ratio in the excavated portion of the town is very high, about one shrine to every three houses. Their numbers suggest the important role these shrines played in the life of Çatal Hüyük's inhabitants.

The shrines are distinguished from the house structures by the greater richness of their interior decoration, which consisted of wall paintings, plaster reliefs, animal heads, and *bucrania* (bovine skulls). Bulls' horns, widely thought to be symbols of masculine potency, adorn most shrines, sometimes in considerable numbers. In some rooms they are displayed next to plaster breasts, symbols of female fertility, projecting from the walls. Statuettes of stone or *terracotta* (baked clay) also have been found in considerable numbers at Çatal Hüyük. Most are quite small (two to eight inches high) and primarily depict female figures. Only a few reach twelve inches.

HUNTING DEER IN NEOLITHIC TURKEY

Although at Çatal Hüyük animal husbandry was well established, hunting continued to play an important part in the early Neolithic economy. The importance of hunting as a food source (until about 5700 B.C.) is reflected also in wall paintings, where, in the older shrines, hunting scenes predominate. In style and concept, however, the deer hunt mural at Çatal Hüyük (FIG. **1-17**) is worlds apart from the wall paintings the hunter-artists of Paleolithic times produced. Perhaps what is most strikingly new about the Çatal Hüyük painting and others like it is the regular appearance of the human figure—not only singly but also in large, coherent groups with a wide variety of poses, subjects, and settings. As noted earlier, humans were unusual in Paleolithic cave paintings, and pictorial narratives have almost never been found. Even the "hunting scene" in the well at Lascaux (FIG. 1-13) is doubtful as a narrative. In Neolithic paintings, human themes and concerns and action scenes with humans dominating animals are central.

In the Çatal Hüyük hunt, the group of hunters—and no one doubts it is, indeed, an organized hunting party, not a series of individual figures—shows a tense exaggeration of movement and a rhythmic repetition of basic shapes customary for the era. The painter took care to distinguish important descriptive details—for example, bows, arrows, and garments—and the heads have clearly defined noses, mouths, chins, and hair. The Neolithic painter placed all the heads in profile for the same reason Paleolithic artists universally chose the profile view for representations of animals. Only the side view of the human head shows all its shapes clearly. However, the Neolithic artist presents the torsos from the front—again, the most informative viewpoint—while the profile view is the choice for the legs and arms. This *composite view* of the human body is quite artificial because the human body cannot make an abrupt ninety-degree shift at the hips. But it is very descriptive of what a human body is—as opposed to what it looks like from a particular viewpoint. The composite view is another manifestation of the twisted perspective of Paleolithic paintings that combined a frontal view of an animal's two horns with a profile view of the head (FIGS. 1-11 and 1-13). Artists overwhelmingly preferred the composite view of the human body for millennia, until the Greeks suddenly and definitively rejected it at the dawn of the Classical age, around 500 B.C. (see Chapter 5).

The technique of painting also changed dramatically since Paleolithic times. The pigments were applied with a brush to a white background of dry plaster. The careful preparation of the wall surface is in striking contrast to the direct application of pigment to the rock face. This was a significant step toward the modern notion of an easel painting with a frame that defines its limits.

THE FIRST LANDSCAPE?

More remarkable still is a painting in one of the older shrines at Çatal Hüyük (FIG. **1-18**) that generally has been acclaimed as the world's first *landscape* (a picture of a natural setting in its own right, without any narrative content). As such, it remained unique for thousands of years. According to radiocarbon dating, the painting was executed around 6150 B.C. In the foreground is a town, with rectangular houses neatly laid out side by side, probably representing Çatal Hüyük itself. Behind the town appears a mountain with two peaks. Art historians think the dots and lines issuing from the higher of the two cones represent a volcanic eruption. They have identified the mountain as the ten thousand six hundred-foot Hasan Dağ. It is located within view of Çatal Hüyük and is the only twin-peaked volcano in central Anatolia. Because the painting appears on a shrine wall, the conjectured volcanic eruption very likely had some religious meaning, but the mural does not necessarily depict a specific historic event. If, however, the Çatal Hüyük painting relates a story, even a recurring one, then it cannot be considered a pure landscape. Nonetheless, this mural is the first depiction of a place devoid of both humans and animals.

The rich finds at Çatal Hüyük give the impression of a prosperous and well-ordered society that practiced a great variety of arts and crafts. In addition to painting and sculpture,

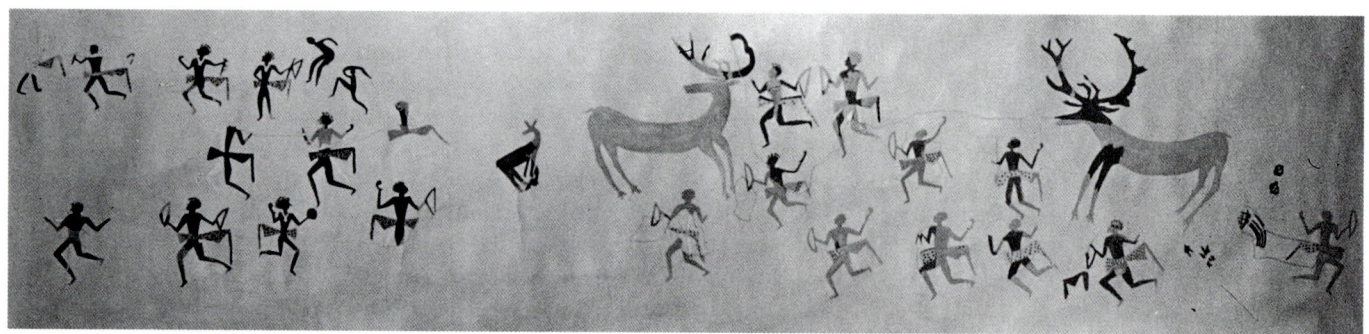

1-17 Deer hunt, detail of a copy of a wall painting from Level III, Çatal Hüyük, Turkey, ca. 5750 B.C.

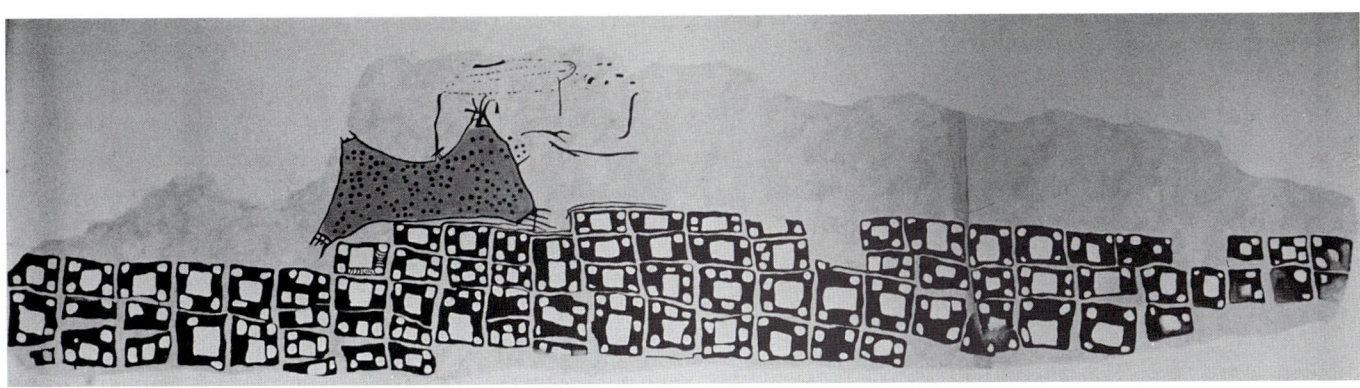

1-18   Landscape with volcanic eruption(?), detail of a copy of a wall painting from Level VII, Çatal Hüyük, Turkey, ca. 6150 B.C.

weaving and pottery were well established, and even the art of smelting copper and lead in small quantities was known before 6000 B.C. The conversion to an agricultural economy appears to have been completed by about 5700 B.C.

Western Europe

A NEOLITHIC ASTRONOMICAL OBSERVATORY In western Europe, where Paleolithic paintings and sculptures abound, no comparably developed towns of the time of Çatal Hüyük have been found. However, in succeeding millennia, perhaps as early as 4000 B.C., the local Neolithic populations in several areas developed a monumental architecture employing massive rough-cut stones. The very dimensions of the stones, some as high as seventeen feet and weighing as much as fifty tons, have prompted historians to call them *megaliths* (great stones) and to designate the culture that produced them *megalithic*.

Sometimes these huge stones were arranged in a circle known as a *cromlech* or *henge*, often surrounded by a ditch. The most imposing today is Stonehenge (FIG. **1-19**) on the Salisbury Plain in southern England. Stonehenge is a complex of rough-cut sarsen (a form of sandstone) stones and smaller "bluestones" (various volcanic rocks). Outermost is a ring, almost one hundred feet in diameter, of large monoliths of sarsen stones capped by *lintels* (a

stone "beam" used to span an opening; see FIG. 4-18). Next is a ring of bluestones, which, in turn, encircle a horseshoe (open end facing east) of *trilithons* (three-stone constructions)—five lintel-topped pairs of the largest sarsens, each weighing forty-five to fifty tons. Standing apart and to the east (outside our photograph at the lower right corner) is the "heel-stone," which, for a person looking outward from the center of the complex, would have marked the point where the sun rose at the midsummer solstice.

Stonehenge probably was built in several phases in the centuries before and after 2000 B.C. It seems to have been a kind of astronomical observatory. The mysterious structures were believed in the Middle Ages to have been the work of the magician Merlin of the King Arthur legend, who spirited them from Ireland. Most archeologists now consider Stonehenge a remarkably accurate solar calendar. This achievement is testimony to the rapidly developing intellectual powers of Neolithic humans as well as to their capacity for heroic physical effort.

Impressive as this *prehistoric* achievement is even today, by 2000 B.C. the peoples occupying the Mesopotamian plain between the Tigris and Euphrates Rivers had been erecting multichambered temples on huge platforms for at least a millennium. In the fertile valley of the Nile in Egypt, the great stone pyramids of the pharaohs were already five hundred or more years old when Stonehenge was erected. We now turn to those civilizations, with their written records and *historical* personalities.

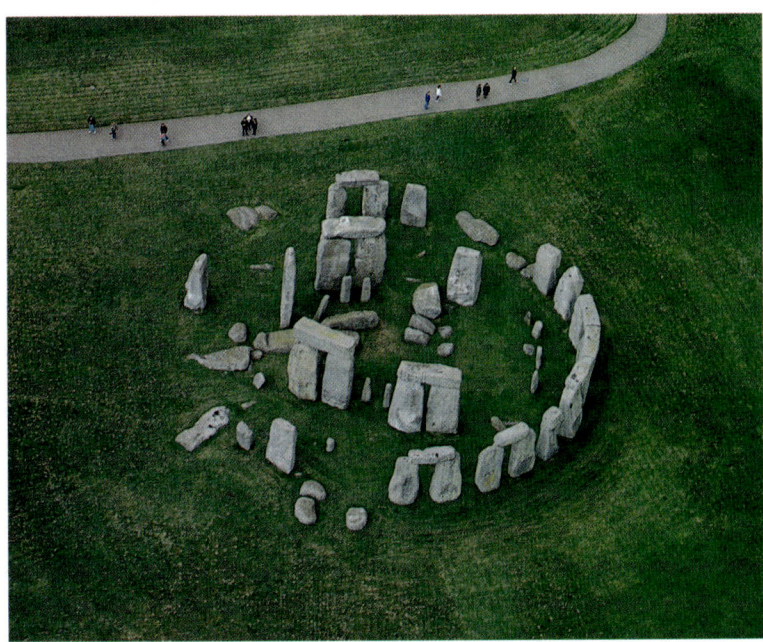

1-19   Stonehenge, Salisbury Plain, Wiltshire, England, aerial view, ca. 2550–1600 B.C. Circle is 97' diameter; trilithons approx. 24' high.

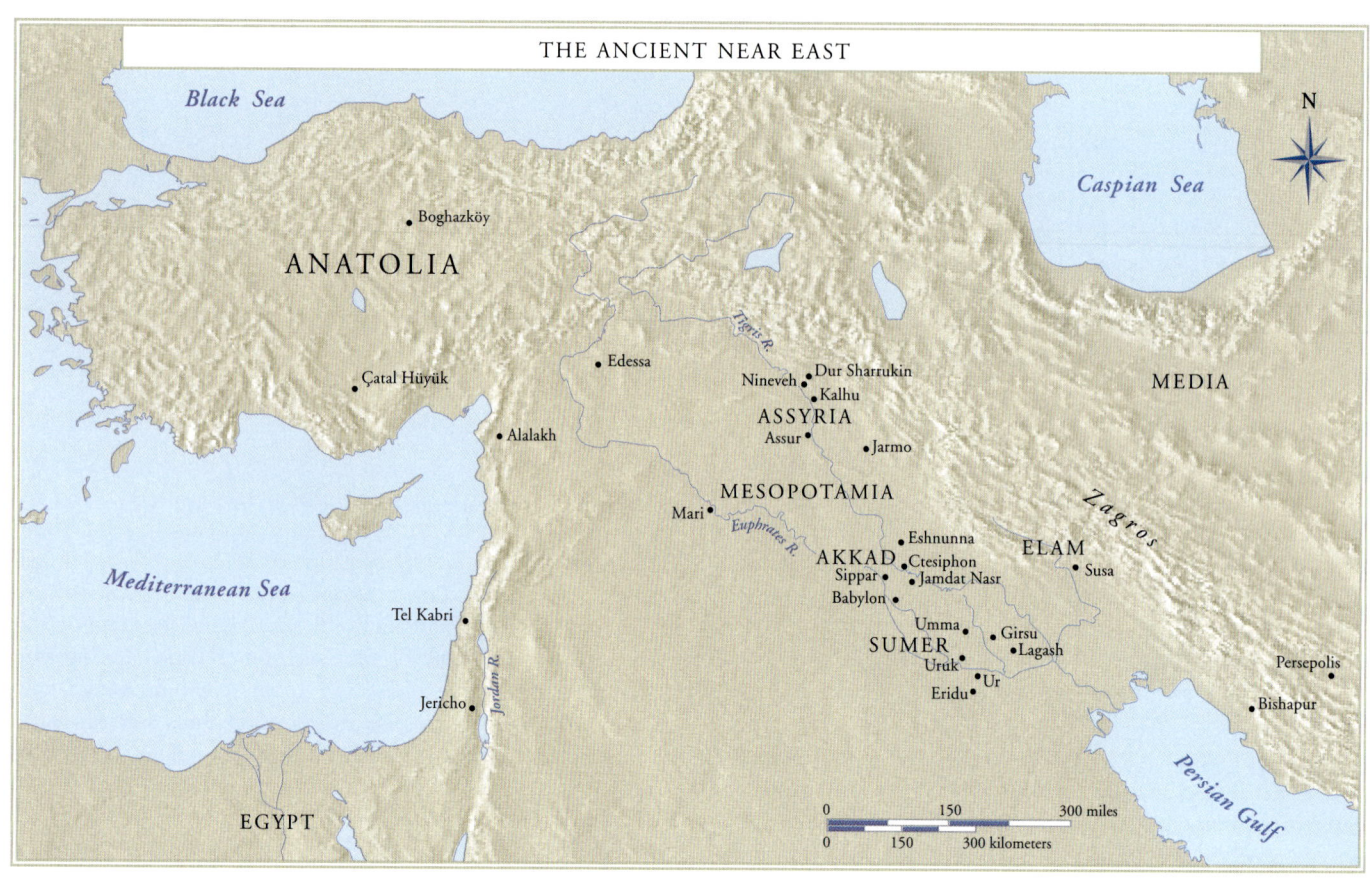

THE ANCIENT NEAR EAST

Black Sea

Caspian Sea

N

Boghazköy

ANATOLIA

MEDIA

Çatal Hüyük

Edessa

Tigris R.

Nineveh • Dur Sharrukin
Kalhu
ASSYRIA
Assur • Jarmo

Alalakh

MESOPOTAMIA

Mari •
Euphrates R.

Zagros

Eshnunna
AKKAD • Ctesiphon
Sippar • Jamdat Nasr
Babylon •

ELAM

• Susa

Mediterranean Sea

Tel Kabri

Jordan R.

Umma •
SUMER • Girsu
Uruk • Lagash
Eridu • Ur

Persepolis

• Bishapur

Jericho

Persian Gulf

EGYPT

0   150   300 miles
0   150   300 kilometers

3500 B.C.	3100 B.C.	2900 B.C.	2300 B.C.	2150 B.C.	2000 B.C.	1800 B.C.	1600 B.C.	
URUK		JAMDAT NASR	EARLY DYNASTIC (SUMERIAN)	AKKADIAN DYNASTY	THIRD DYNASTY OF UR (NEO-SUMERIAN)		OLD BABYLONIAN	KASSITES AND MITANNI (MESOPOTAMIA)
								HITTITES (ANATOLIA)
								MIDDLE ELAMITE PERIOD (IRAN)

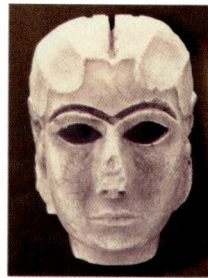

Female head (Inanna?)
from Uruk
ca. 3200–3000 B.C.

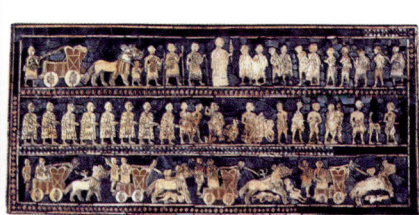

Standard of Ur
ca. 2600 B.C.

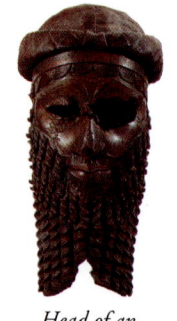

Head of an
Akkadian ruler, from Nineveh
ca. 2250–2200 B.C.

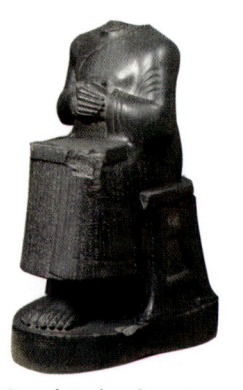

Seated Gudea, from Girsu
ca. 2100 B.C.

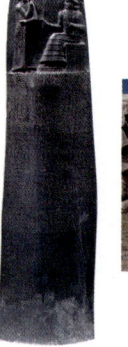

Stele of
Hammurabi
ca. 1780 B.C.

Lion Gate, Boghazköy
ca. 1400 B.C.

Invention of the wheel

Development of writing and the
beginnings of recorded history

Flowering of independent city-states

Sargon of Akkad, ca. 2300 B.C.

Naram-Sin, r. ca. 2254–2218 B.C.

Guti invasion, ca. 2150 B.C.

Gudea of Lagash, ca. 2100 B.C.

Hammurabi, r. ca. 1792–1750 B.C.

Sack of Babylon by Hittites,
ca. 1595 B.C.

2

THE RISE OF CIVILIZATION

THE ART OF THE ANCIENT NEAR EAST

1000 B.C.	900 B.C.		612 B.C.		538 B.C.		330 B.C.	A.D. 224		636
		Assyrian Empire	Neo-Babylonian Empire		Achaemenid Persian Empire			Greco-Roman	Sasanian Dynasty	

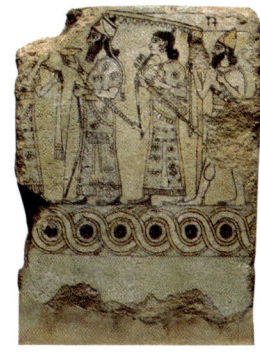

Ashurnasirpal II and attendants
from Kalhu, ca. 875–860 B.C.

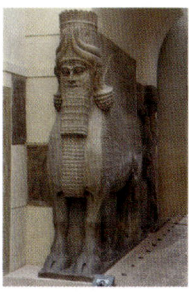

Lamassu
Citadel of Sargon II
Dur Sharrukin
ca. 720–705 B.C.

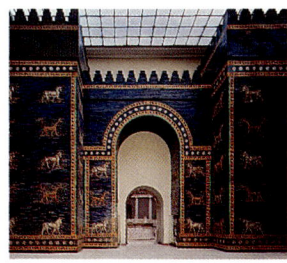

Ishtar Gate
Babylon, ca. 575 B.C.

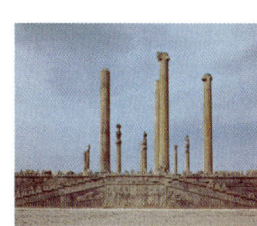

Palace, Persepolis
ca. 521–465 B.C.

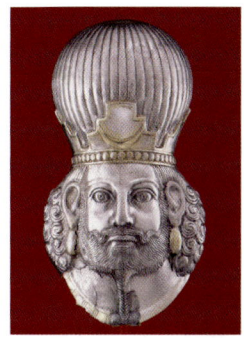

Head of Shapur II(?)
ca. A.D. 350

Darius I, r. 522–486 B.C.

Xerxes, r. 486–465 B.C.

Final defeat of Persians
by the Arabs, A.D. 642

Ashurnasirpal II, r. 883–859 B.C.

Sargon II, r. 721–705 B.C.

Ashurbanipal, r. 668–627 B.C.

Nebuchadnezzar II, r. 604–562 B.C.

Battle of Issus, 331 B.C.

Death of Alexander the Great, 323 B.C.

Augustus, first emperor of Rome, r. 27 B.C.–A.D. 14

Defeat of Valerian by Shapur I, A.D. 260

THE LAND BETWEEN THE RIVERS

When humans first gave up the dangerous and uncertain life of the hunter and gatherer for the more predictable and stable life of the farmer and herder, the change in human society was so astounding, so fundamental, that it justly has been called the Neolithic Revolution. This revolutionary change in the nature of daily life first occurred in Mesopotamia—a Greek word that means "the land between the [Tigris and Euphrates] rivers." Mesopotamia is at the core of the region often called the Fertile Crescent, a land mass that forms a huge arc from the mountainous border between Turkey and Syria through Iraq to Iran's Zagros Mountain range. There humankind first learned how to use the wheel and the plow, how to control floods and construct irrigation canals. The land became an oasis—and the presumed setting for the biblical Garden of Eden.

THE ANCIENT NEAR EAST REDISCOVERED

As the region that gave birth to three of the world's great modern faiths—Judaism, Christianity, and Islam—the Near East long has been of interest to history and religion students. But not until the nineteenth century did systematic excavation open the world's eyes to the extraordinary art and architecture of the ancient Mesopotamians. The great museums of Europe quickly began to fill their galleries with stone reliefs depicting warfare and hunting (FIGS. 2-22, 2-24, and 2-25) and with colossal statues of monstrous human-headed bulls (FIG. 2-21) from the palaces of the Assyrians, rulers of a northern Mesopotamian empire during the ninth to the seventh centuries B.C. In the treasure-hunting spirit of the era, Austen Henry Layard, one of the pioneers of Near Eastern archeology, had specific instructions from the British Museum. He was to obtain as many well-preserved artworks as he could while spending the least possible amount of time and money doing so. Interest heightened with each new discovery, and North American museums also began to collect Near Eastern art.

Nothing that emerged from the Mesopotamian soil attracted as much attention as the treasures Leonard Woolley discovered in the 1920s at the Royal Cemetery at Ur in southern Mesopotamia. The interest in the unearthing of lavish third-millennium B.C. Sumerian burials rivaled the public fascination with the 1922 discovery of the Egyptian boy-king Tutankhamen's tomb (see FIGS. 3-36 to 3-38). The Ur cemetery was filled with gold objects, jewelry, artworks, and musical instruments (FIGS. 2-8 to 2-11). Europe's royalty and elite frequently visited the site. One of the visitors was the mystery writer Agatha Christie, who later married one of the British archeologists working at Ur. Her 1936 *Murder in Mesopotamia* centers on an excavation in Iraq. The discovery of the treasures of ancient Ur put the Sumerians once again in a prominent position on the world stage. They had been absent for four thousand years.

SUMERIAN ART

THE INVENTION OF WRITING   The Sumerians

were the people who transformed the vast, flat lower valley between the Tigris and Euphrates into the Fertile Crescent of the ancient world. Sparsely inhabited before the Sumerians, this area is now southern Iraq. In the fourth millennium B.C., the Sumerians established the first great urban communities and developed the earliest known writing system. The oldest written documents were records of administrative acts and commercial transactions, but the Sumerians also produced great literature. The most famous Sumerian work, the *Epic of Gilgamesh,* antedates Homer's *Iliad* and *Odyssey* by some fifteen hundred years.

At first, around 3400–3200 B.C., the Sumerians made inventories of cattle, food, and other items by scratching *pictographs* (simplified pictures standing for words) into soft clay with a sharp tool, or *stylus.* The clay plaques hardened into breakable, yet nearly indestructible, tablets, accounting for the existence today of thousands of documents dating back nearly five millennia. The Sumerians wrote their pictorial signs from the top down and arranged them in boxes they read from right to left. By 3000–2900 B.C., they had further simplified the pictographic signs by reducing them to a group of wedge-shaped *(cuneiform)* signs. This marked the beginning of writing, as historians strictly define it. By 2600 B.C., cuneiform texts were sophisticated enough to express complex grammatical constructions.

The Sumerian language does not belong to any of the major linguistic groups of antiquity, yet historians do not doubt the Sumerians were a major force in the spread of civilization. Their influence extended widely from southern Mesopotamia, eastward to the Iranian plateau, northward to Assyria, and westward to Syria. Thousands of cuneiform tablets testify to the far-flung network of Sumerian contacts made throughout the ancient Near East. Trade was essential for the Sumerians, because despite their land's fertility, it was poor in such vital natural resources as metal, stone, and wood.

THE FIRST CITY-STATES AND THEIR GODS

Ancient Sumer was not a unified nation but was made up of a dozen or so independent *city-states,* and each was thought to be under the protection of a different one of the Mesopotamian gods (see "The Gods and Goddesses of Mesopotamia," page 19). The Sumerian rulers were the gods' representatives on earth and the stewards of their earthly treasure. The rulers and priests directed all communal activities, including canal construction, crop collection, and food distribution to those who were not farmers. The development of agriculture to the point where only a portion of the population had to produce food made possible such an organization of the labor force. Some members of the community could specialize in activities such as manufacturing, trade, and administration. This type of labor specialization is the hallmark of the first complex urban societies. In the city-states of ancient Sumer, activities that once had been individually initiated became institutionalized for the first time. The community, rather than the family, assumed functions such as defense against enemies and against the caprices of nature. The city-states gained permanent identities as discrete communities ruled by a single person or a council chosen from among the leading families. The city-state was one of the great Sumerian inventions.

The Sumerian city plan reflected the local god's central role in the daily life of the city-state's occupants. The god's temple formed the city's monumental nucleus. It was not only the focus of local religious practice but also served as an administra-

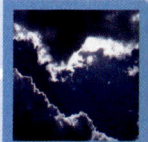

The Gods and Goddesses of Mesopotamia

The Sumerians and their successors in the ancient Near East worshiped numerous deities, mostly nature gods. We list some of the most important of these gods and goddesses here, including all those discussed in this chapter.

Anu Anu, the chief deity of the Sumerians, was the god of the sky and of the city of Uruk, where the ruins of one of the earliest Sumerian temples (FIGS. 2-1 and 2-2) still may be seen.

Enlil Enlil, Anu's son, was the lord of the winds and the earth. He eventually replaced his father as king of the gods.

Inanna Inanna was the Sumerian goddess of love and war. Later known as *Ishtar,* she is the most important female deity in all periods of Mesopotamian history. A sanctuary dedicated to Inanna was constructed at Uruk at a very early date. Amid the ruins, excavators have uncovered fourth-millennium B.C. statues and reliefs (FIGS. 2-3 and 2-4) connected with her worship. Whether or not the goddess herself was represented in human form at that time is uncertain. Inanna/Ishtar is unmistakably depicted with her sacred lion in a mural painting in the eighteenth-century B.C. palace of Zimri-Lim at Mari (FIG. 2-17).

Nanna Nanna, the moon god, also known as *Sin,* was the chief deity of Ur, where his most important shrine was located.

Utu Utu, god of the sun, known later as *Shamash,* was especially revered at Sippar. On a Babylonian stele of ca. 1780 B.C., King Hammurabi presents his law code to Shamash, who is depicted with flames radiating from his shoulders (FIG. 2-16).

Marduk, Nabu, and Adad Marduk was the chief god of the Babylonians. His son Nabu was the god of writing and wisdom. Adad was the Babylonian god of storms. Nabu's dragon and Adad's sacred bull are depicted on the sixth-century B.C. Ishtar Gate at Babylon (FIG. 2-26).

Ningirsu Ningirsu was the local god of Lagash and Girsu. His name means "lord of Girsu." Eannatum, one of the early rulers of Lagash, defeated an enemy army with the god's assistance and commemorated Ningirsu's role in the victory on the so-called *Stele of the Vultures* (FIG. 2-7) of ca. 2600–2500 B.C. Gudea (FIG. 2-15), one of Eannatum's Neo-Sumerian successors, built a great temple about 2100 B.C. in honor of Ningirsu after the god instructed him to do so in a dream.

Ashur Ashur, the local deity of Assur, the city that took his name, became the king of the Assyrian gods. He sometimes is identified with Enlil.

---

tive and economic center. It was indeed the domain of the god, whom the Sumerians regarded as a great and rich holder of lands and herds, as well as the city-state's protector. The vast temple complex, a kind of city within a city, thus had both religious and secular functions. A temple staff of priests and scribes carried on official business, looking after both the god's and the ruler's possessions.

A MUD-BRICK TOWER TO THE SKY The outstanding preserved example of early Sumerian temple architecture is the five-thousand-year-old White Temple (FIG. **2-1**) at Uruk, the home of the legendary king and hero Gilgamesh. Usually only the foundations of early Mesopotamian temples still can be recognized. The White Temple is a rare exception. Sumerian builders did not have access to stone quarries and instead formed mud bricks for the superstructures of their temples and other buildings. Almost all these structures have eroded over the course of time. The fragile nature of the building materials did not, however, prevent the Sumerians from erecting towering works such as the Uruk temple several centuries before the Egyptians built their stone pyramids. This says a great deal about the Sumerian desire to provide monumental settings for the worship of their deities.

Enough of the Uruk complex remains to permit a fairly reliable reconstruction drawing (FIG. **2-2**). The temple (whose whitewashed walls lend it its modern nickname) stands on top of a high stepped platform, or *ziggurat,* forty feet above

street level in the city center. A stairway (FIG. 2-1) leads to the top but does not end in front of any of the temple doorways, necessitating two or three angular changes in direction. This "bent-axis" approach is the standard arrangement for Sumerian temples, a striking contrast to the linear approach the Egyptians preferred for their temples and tombs (see Chapter 3).

Like other Sumerian temples, the corners of the White Temple are oriented to the cardinal points of the compass. The building, probably dedicated to Anu, the sky god, is of modest proportions (sixty-one by sixteen feet). By design, it did not accommodate large throngs of worshipers but only a select few, the priests and perhaps the leading community members. The temple has several chambers. The central hall, or *cella,* was set aside for the divinity and housed a stepped altar. The Sumerians referred to their temples as "waiting rooms," a reflection of their belief that the deity would descend from the heavens to appear before the priests in the cella. How or if the Uruk temple was roofed is uncertain.

The Sumerian idea that the gods reside above the world of humans is central to most of the world's religions. Moses ascended Mount Sinai to receive the Ten Commandments from the Hebrew God, and the Greeks placed the home of their gods and goddesses on Mount Olympus. The elevated placement of Mesopotamian temples on giant platforms reaching to the sky is consistent with this widespread religious concept. Eroded ziggurats still dominate most of the ruined cities of

2-1   White Temple and ziggurat, Uruk (modern Warka), Iraq, ca. 3200–3000 B.C.

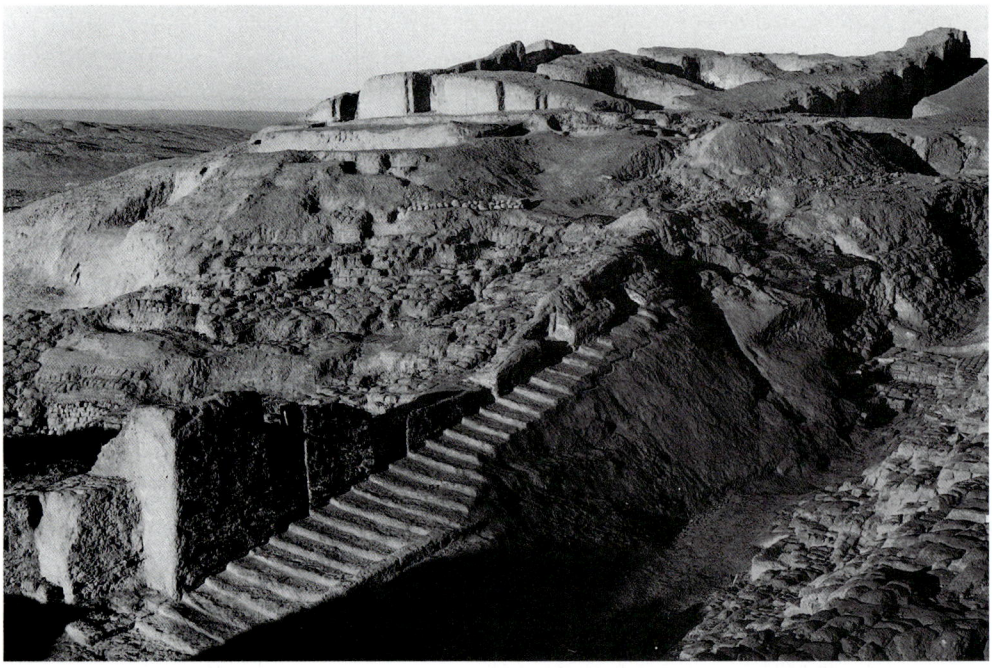

Sumer. The loftiness of the great temple platforms made a profound impression on the peoples of the ancient Near East. The tallest ziggurat of all—at Babylon—was about two hundred and seventy feet high. Known to the Hebrews as the Tower of Babel, it became the centerpiece of a biblical story about the insolent pride of humans (see "Babylon: City of Wonders," page 37).

SCULPTURE IN MARBLE AND GOLD   The White Temple at Uruk towers over all other vestiges of that ancient city, but a fragmentary white marble female head (FIG. 2-3) is also an extraordinary achievement at so early a date. The head is actually only a face with a flat back. Although found in the sacred precinct of the goddess Inanna, the subject is unknown. Many have suggested that it is an image of Inanna, but a mortal woman, perhaps a priestess, may be portrayed. Unlike the life-size Neolithic plastered and painted skulls from Jericho (see FIG. 1-15), human hands fashioned the entire Uruk face. The stone had to be imported and was too costly to use for the full statue. The marble face has drilled holes for attachment to a head and body, probably of wood.

The sculptor refined the features of the goddess or woman. The bright coloration of the eyes, brows, and hair, however, likely overshadowed the soft modeling of the cheeks and mouth. The deep groove at the top anchored a wig, probably made of gold leaf. The hair strands engraved in the metal fell in waves over the forehead and sides of the head. Colored

shell or stone filled the deep recesses for the eyebrows and the large eyes. Often the present condition of an artwork can be very misleading, and the Uruk head is a dramatic example. Its original appearance would have been much more vibrant than the pure white fragment archeologists uncovered.

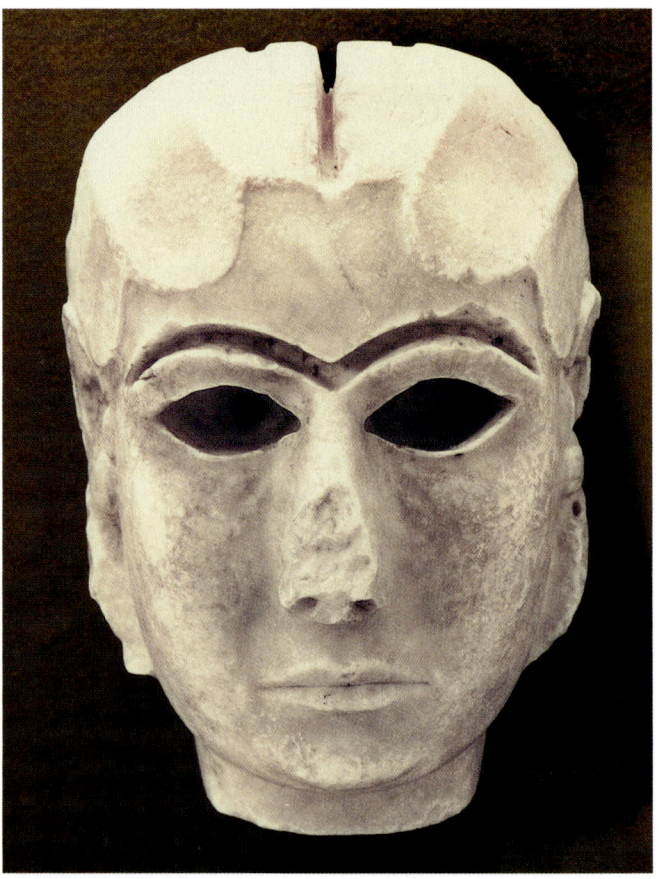

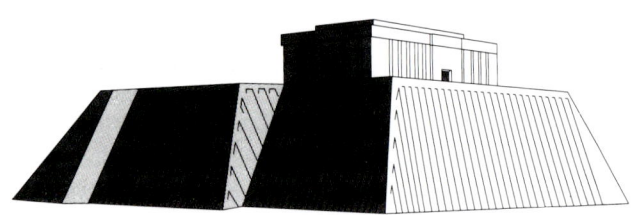

2-2   Reconstruction drawing of the White Temple and ziggurat, Uruk (modern Warka), Iraq, ca. 3200–3000 B.C. (after S. E. Piggott).

2-3   Female head (Inanna?), from Uruk (modern Warka), Iraq, ca. 3200–3000 B.C. Marble, approx. 8″ high. Iraq Museum, Baghdad.

GIFTS FOR A GODDESS The Sumerians, pioneers in so many areas, also may have been the first to use pictures to tell coherent stories. Sumerian narrative art goes far beyond the Stone Age artists' tentative efforts at storytelling. The so-called *Warka Vase* (FIG. **2-4**) from Uruk (modern Warka) is the first great work of narrative relief sculpture known. Found within the Inanna temple complex, it depicts a religious festival in the goddess's honor. The sculptor divided the vase's reliefs into three bands (also called *registers* or *friezes*). The lowest shows sheep and rams above barley and flax and a wavy line representing water. These are the staple commodities of the Sumerian economy. Their inclusion on the vase indicates that Inanna had blessed Uruk's inhabitants with good crops and increased herds. The animals on the *Warka Vase* are in strict profile, consistent with an approach to representation that was then some twenty-five thousand years old. But the organization of the animals (and plants and humans) in a reg-

ister and standing on a *ground line* (the horizontal base of the composition) is new. It marks a significant break with the haphazard figure placement in earlier art. The register format for telling a story was to have a very long future. In fact, artists still employ registers today in modified form in comic books.

A procession of naked men occupies the central band of the stone vase. The men carry baskets and jars overflowing with earth's abundance. They will present their bounty to the goddess as a *votive offering* (gift of gratitude to a deity usually made in fulfillment of a vow) and will deposit it in her temple. The spacing of each figure involves no overlapping. The Uruk men, like the prehistoric deer hunters at Çatal Hüyük (see FIG. 1-17), are a composite of frontal and profile views, with large staring frontal eyes in profile heads. The artist indicated those human bodily parts necessary to communicate the human form and avoided positions, attitudes, or views that would conceal the characterizing parts. For example, if the figures were in strict profile, an arm and perhaps a leg would be hidden. The body would appear to have only half its breadth. And the eye would not "read" as an eye at all, because it would not have its distinctive flat oval shape. Art historians call this characteristic early approach to representation "conceptual," as opposed to "optical," because artists who used it did not record the immediate, fleeting aspect of figures. Instead, they rendered the human body's distinguishing and fixed properties. The fundamental forms of figures and the artist's knowledge of them, not their accidental appearance, directed the artist's hand and dictated the artist's selection of the composite view as the best way to represent the human body.

In the uppermost (and tallest) band is a female figure (not visible in our photograph) with a tall horned headdress. Whether she is Inanna or her priestess is not known. In the portion shown in FIG. 2-4, the food offerings already have been deposited in Inanna's shrine. (The goat and lion are actually animal-shaped vessels—note the spouts on their backs.) An attendant assists an only partially preserved larger figure (at the far right) who is usually, if ambiguously, referred to as a "priest-king" because similar figures appear in other Sumerian artworks as leaders in both religious and secular contexts. On the *Warka Vase,* the attendant carries the leader's broad tasseled belt like a train. The greater height of the "priest-king" indicates his greater importance, a convention called *hierarchy of scale.* Some scholars interpret the scene as a symbolic marriage between the "priest-king" and the goddess, insuring her continued goodwill—and reaffirming the leader's exalted position in society.

STATUETTES OF PERPETUAL WORSHIPERS Further insight into Sumerian religious beliefs and rituals comes from a cache of gypsum statuettes inlaid with shell and black limestone (FIG. **2-5**). The figures were reverently buried beneath the floor of a temple at Eshnunna (modern Tell Asmar) when the structure was remodeled. They range in size from well under a foot to about thirty inches tall. The differing heights of the men and women represented may correspond to their relative importance in the community. All of the figures represent mortals, rather than deities, with their hands folded in front of their chests in a gesture of prayer. Many also hold the small beakers the Sumerians used in religious rites. Hundreds of such goblets have been found in the

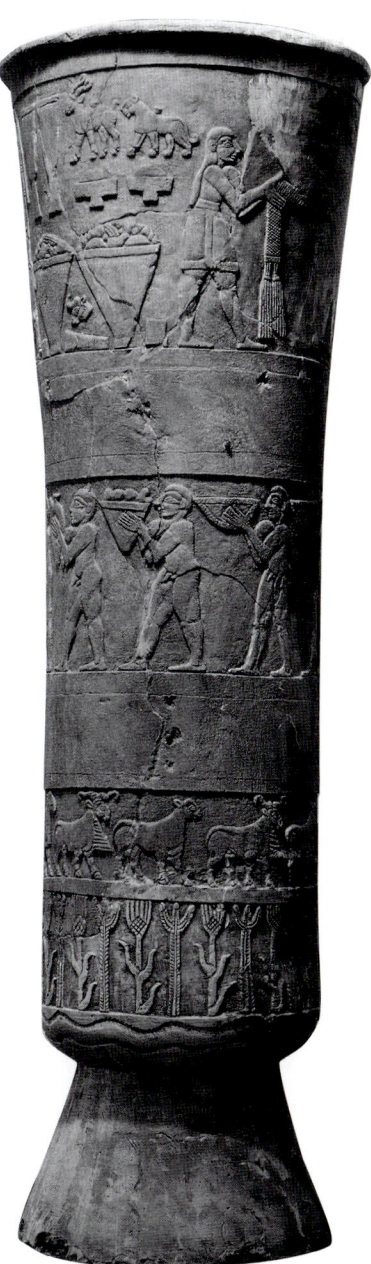

2-4 Presentation of offerings to Inanna *(Warka Vase),* from Uruk, Iraq, ca. 3200–3000 B.C. Alabaster, 3' $\frac{1}{4}$" high. Iraq Museum, Baghdad.

2-5   Statuettes of worshipers, from the Square Temple at Eshnunna (modern Tell Asmar), Iraq, ca. 2700 B.C. Gypsum inlaid with shell and black limestone, tallest figure approx. 2′ 6″ high. Iraq Museum, Baghdad, and Oriental Institute, University of Chicago.

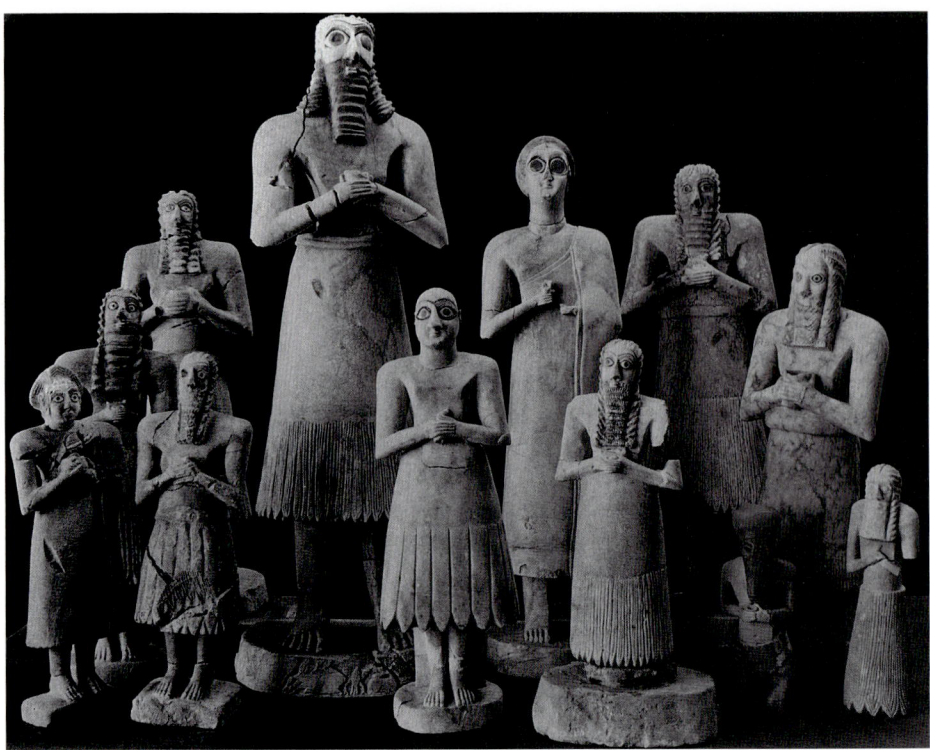

temple complex at Eshnunna. The men wear belts and fringed skirts. Most have beards and shoulder-length hair. The women wear long robes, with the right shoulder bare. Similar figurines from other sites bear inscriptions giving such information as the name of the donor and the god or even specific prayers to the deity on the owner's behalf. With their heads tilted upward, they wait in the Sumerian "waiting room" for the divinity to appear.

The sculptors of the Eshnunna statuettes employed simple forms, primarily cones and cylinders, for the figures. The statuettes are not portraits in the strict sense of the word, but the sculptors did distinguish physical types. At least one child was portrayed—next to the tallest of the female figures are the remains of two small legs (not visible in the group photo). Most striking is the disproportionate relationship between the oversized eyes and the tiny hands. Scholars have explained the exaggeration of the eye size in various ways. But because the purpose of these votive figures was to offer constant prayers to the gods on their donors' behalf, the open-eyed stares most likely symbolize the eternal wakefulness necessary to fulfill their duty.

Another group of Sumerian votive statuettes comes from the Temple of Ishtar at Mari. Of particular interest is the figure of Urnanshe (FIG. **2-6**), identified by an inscription. His eyes—inlaid with shell and *lapis lazuli* (a rich azure-blue stone imported from Afghanistan)—are unwavering in their intense gaze. Like the other figures in the group, Urnanshe is bare chested, wears a tufted fleece skirt, and holds his arms (now broken) in front of his chest in a gesture of prayer. But he sits on a cushion with legs crossed, and he is beardless, with long straight hair that reaches to the waist, suggesting that he was a *eunuch* (castrated male). Urnanshe was neither priest nor ruler but the official singer at the Mari court. Another, very fragmentary, statuette portrays Urnanshe with a stringed instrument, that is, in his role as musician and singer at religious ceremonies. His statuettes attest that he stands ever ready to serve the goddess as well as his ruler.

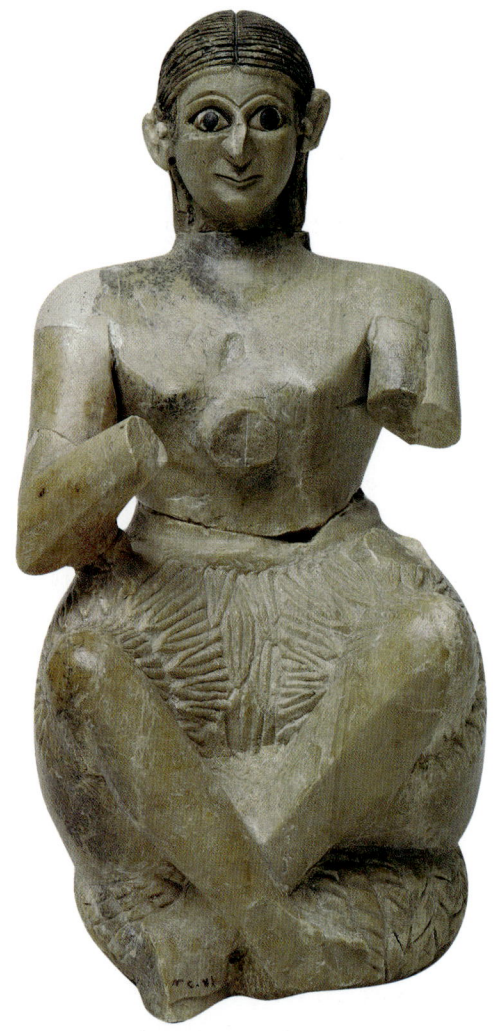

2-6   Seated statuette of Urnanshe, from the Ishtar temple at Mari (modern Tell Hariri), Syria, ca. 2600–2500 B.C. Gypsum inlaid with shell and lapis lazuli, 10 $\frac{1}{4}$″ high. National Museum, Damascus.

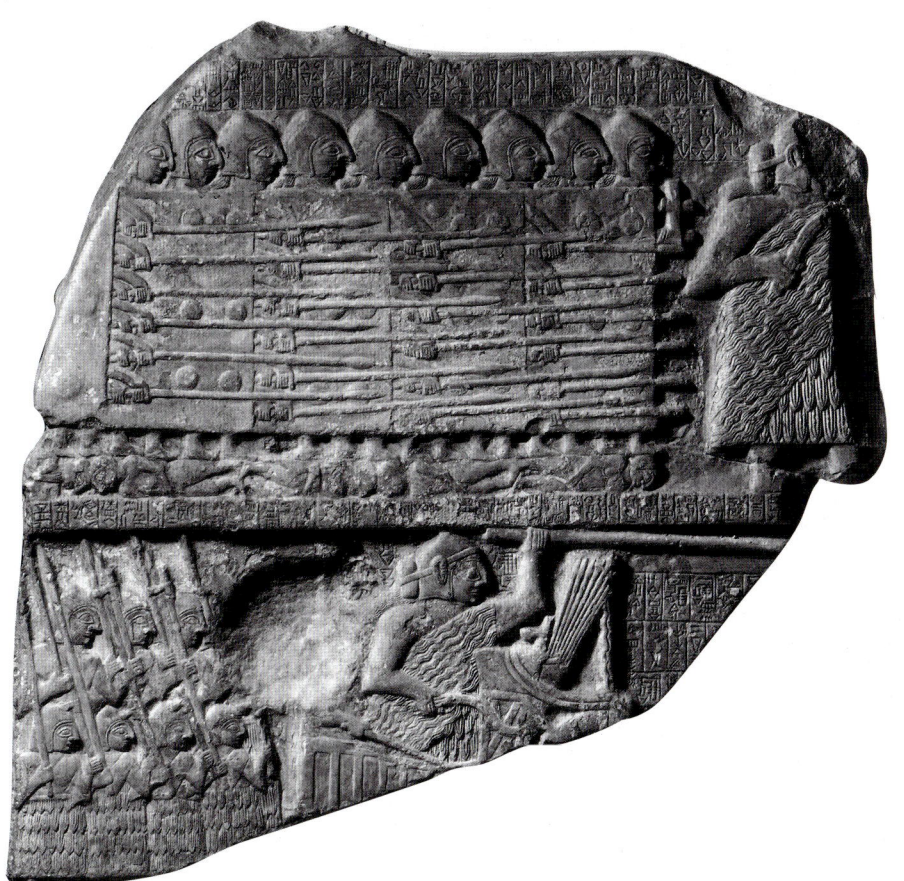

2-7   Fragment of the victory stele of Eannatum *(Stele of the Vultures)*, from Girsu (modern Telloh), Syria, ca. 2600–2500 B.C. Limestone, full stele approx. 5′ 11″ high. Louvre, Paris.

VICTORY AND VULTURES   The city-states of ancient Sumer were often at war with one another, and warfare is the theme of the so-called *Stele of the Vultures* (FIG. **2-7**) from Girsu. A *stele* is a carved stone slab erected to commemorate a historical event or, in some other cultures, to mark a grave (see FIG. 5-55). The Girsu stele presents, in fact, a labeled historical narrative. (It is not, however, the first historical representation in the history of art. That honor belongs—at the moment—to an Egyptian relief, FIG. 3-2, carved more than three centuries earlier.) Although the *Stele of the Vultures* is fragmentary, cuneiform inscriptions almost everywhere on the monument reveal that it celebrates the victory of Eannatum, the *ensi* (ruler; king?) of Lagash, over the neighboring city-state of Umma. The stele has reliefs on both sides and takes its nickname from a fragment with a gruesome scene of vultures carrying off the severed heads and arms of the defeated enemy soldiers. Another fragment shows the giant figure of the local god Ningirsu holding tiny enemies in a net and beating one of them on the head with a mace.

Our illustration depicts Eannatum leading an infantry battalion into battle (above) and attacking from a war chariot (below). The foot soldiers are protected behind a wall of shields and trample naked enemies as they advance. (The fragment showing vultures devouring corpses belongs just to the right in the same register.) Both on foot and in a chariot, Eannatum is larger than anyone else, except Ningirsu on the other side of the stele. He is shown as the fearless general who paves the way for his army. Lives were lost, however, and Eannatum himself was wounded in the campaign. But the outcome was never in doubt because Ningirsu fought with the men of Lagash.

Despite its fragmentary state, the *Stele of the Vultures* is an extraordinary document, not only as a very early effort to record historical events in relief but also for the insight it yields about Sumerian society. Through both words and pictures, it provides information about warfare techniques and the special nature of the Sumerian ruler. Eannatum was greater in stature than other men, and Ningirsu watched over him. According to the text, the ensi was born from the god Enlil's semen, implanted in the womb by Ningirsu. When Eannatum was wounded in battle, it says, the god shed tears for him. He was a divinely chosen ruler who presided over all aspects of his city-state, both in war and in peace. This also seems to have been the role of the ensi in the other Sumerian city-states.

WAR AND PEACE   The spoils of war as well as success in farming and trade brought considerable wealth to some of the city-states of ancient Sumer. Nowhere is this clearer than in the so-called Royal Cemetery at Ur, the city that was home to the biblical Abraham. In the third millennium B.C., the leading families of Ur buried their dead in vaulted chambers beneath the earth. Scholars still debate whether these deceased were true kings and queens or simply aristocrats and priests, but they were laid to rest in regal fashion. Archeologists exploring the Ur cemetery uncovered gold helmets and daggers with handles of lapis lazuli, golden beakers and bowls, jewelry of gold and lapis, musical instruments, chariots, and other luxurious items in the graves. A retinue of musicians, servants, charioteers, and soldiers accompanied the "kings and queens" into the afterlife, giving their own lives when their rulers died.

2-8(a)   War side of the *Standard of Ur*, from Tomb 779, Royal Cemetery, Ur (modern Tell Muqayyar), Iraq, ca. 2600 B.C. Wood inlaid with shell, lapis lazuli, and red limestone, approx. 8″ × 1′ 7″. British Museum, London.

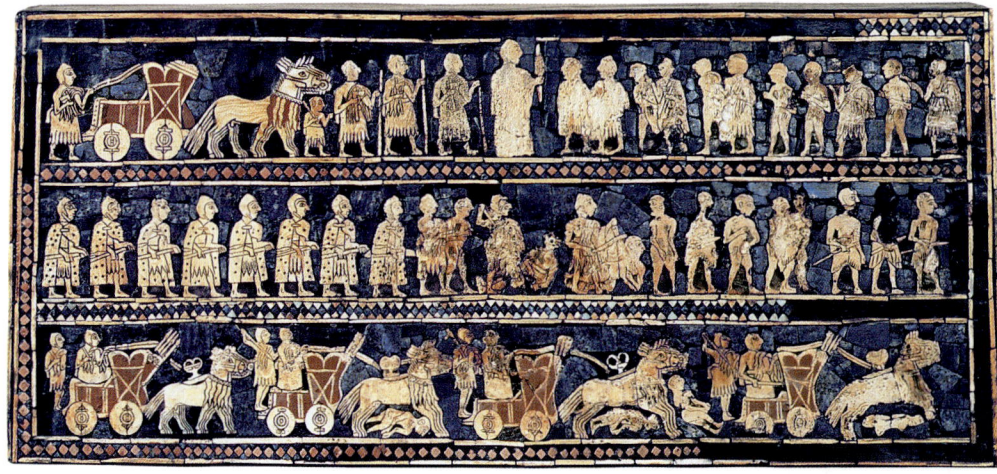

Not the costliest object found in the "royal" graves, but probably the most significant from the viewpoint of the history of art, is the so-called *Standard of Ur* (FIG. **2-8**). This rectangular box of uncertain function has sloping sides inlaid with shell, lapis lazuli, and red limestone. The excavator, Leonard Woolley, thought the object was originally mounted on a pole and considered it a kind of military standard—hence its nickname. The two long sides of the box have been designated as the "war side" and "peace side," but they may represent the first and second parts of a single narrative. Each is divided into three horizontal bands. The narrative reads from left to right and bottom to top. On the war side, four ass-drawn four-wheeled war chariots mow down enemies, whose bodies appear on the ground in front of and beneath the animals. The gait of the asses accelerates along the band from left to right. Above, a file of foot soldiers gathers up and leads away captured foes. In the uppermost register, soldiers present bound captives (who have been stripped naked to degrade them) to a kinglike figure, who has stepped out of his chariot. His central place in the composition and his greater stature set him apart from all the other figures. Note how his head breaks through the border at the top.

In the lowest band on the peace side, men carry provisions, possibly war booty, on their backs. Above, attendants bring animals, perhaps also spoils of war, and fish for the great banquet depicted in the uppermost register. There, seated dignitaries and a larger-than-life "king" (third from the left) feast, while a lyre player and singer (at the far right, with long straight hair—like Urnanshe, FIG. 2-6) entertain the group. Art historians have interpreted the scene both as a victory celebration and as a banquet in connection with cult ritual. The two are not necessarily incompatible. The absence of an inscription prevents connecting the scenes with a specific event or person, but the *Standard of Ur* undoubtedly depicts figures from the period. The story told in the six registers is another early example of historical narrative.

MUSIC IN THE AFTERLIFE   From the "King's Grave" at Ur comes a splendid lyre (FIG. **2-9**) that, in its restored state, resembles the instrument depicted in the feast scene on the *Standard of Ur*. A magnificent bull's head, fashioned of gold leaf over a wooden core with hair, beard, and details of lapis lazuli, caps the instrument's sound box. The sound box itself (FIG. **2-10**) also features bearded, but here human-headed, bulls in the uppermost of its four inlaid panels. Such

imaginary composite creatures are commonplace in the art of the ancient Near East and Egypt. The man-headed lion known as the Great Sphinx of Gizeh (see FIG. 3-11) is undoubtedly the most famous example. On the Ur lyre, a heroic figure embraces the two man-bulls in a *heraldic composition* (symmetrical around a central figure). His body and that of the scorpion-man in the lowest panel are in composite view. The animals are, equally characteristically, solely in profile:

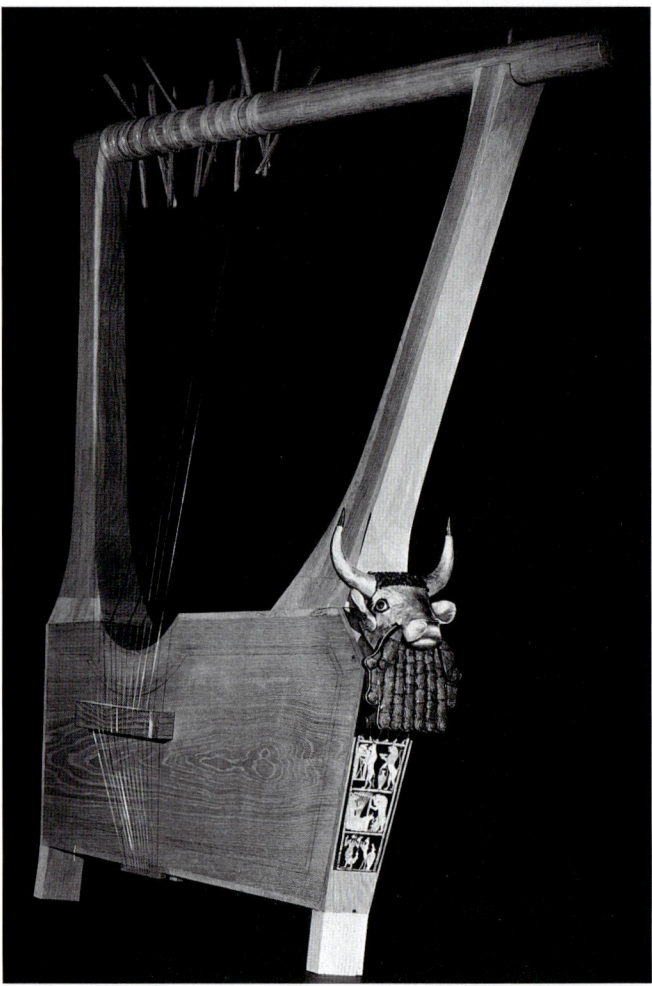

2-9   Bull-headed lyre (restored) from Tomb 789 ("King's Grave"), Royal Cemetery, Ur (modern Tell Muqayyar), Iraq, ca. 2600 B.C. Gold leaf and lapis lazuli over a wooden core, approx. 5′ 5″ high. University Museum, University of Pennsylvania, Philadelphia.

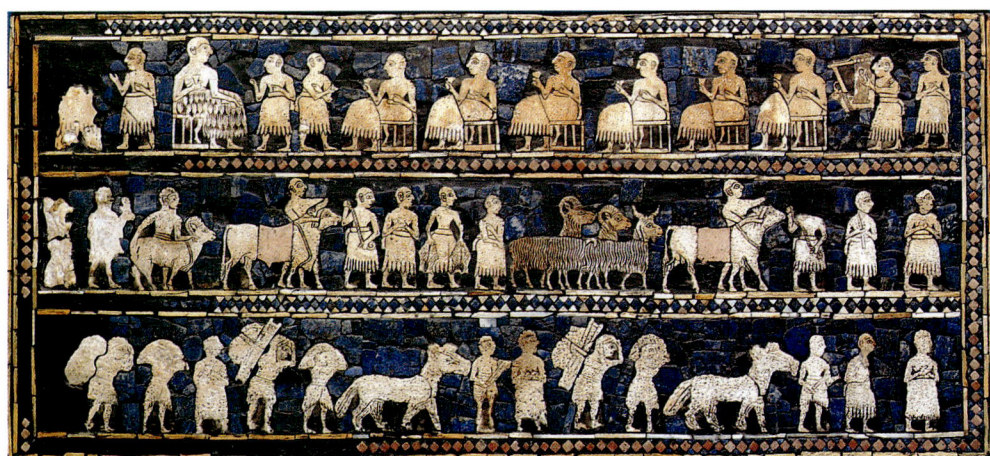

2-8(b) Peace side of the *Standard of Ur,* from Tomb 779, Royal Cemetery, Ur (modern Tell Muqayyar), Iraq, ca. 2600 B.C. Wood inlaid with shell, lapis lazuli, and red limestone, approx. 8″ × 1′ 7″. British Museum, London.

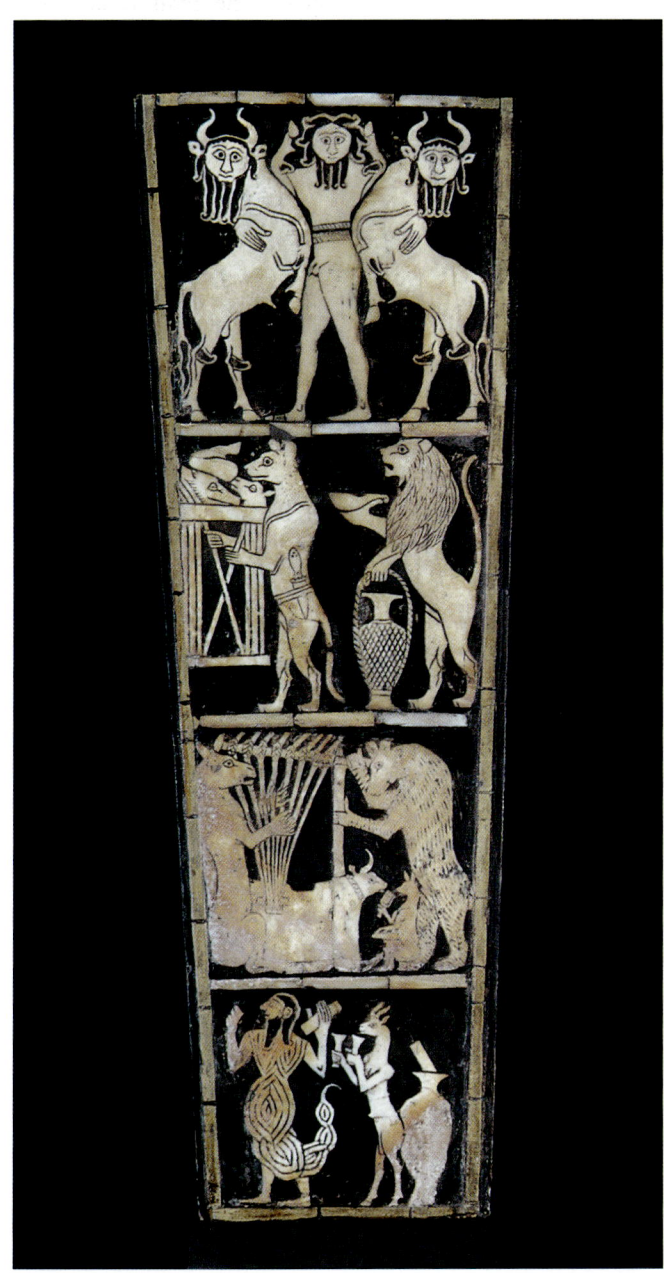

2-10 Soundbox of the lyre from Tomb 789, Royal Cemetery, Ur (modern Tell Muqayyar), Iraq, ca. 2600 B.C. Wood with inlaid gold, lapis lazuli, and shell, approx. 1′ high. University Museum, University of Pennsylvania, Philadelphia.

the dog wearing a dagger and carrying a laden table, the lion bringing in the beverage service, the ass playing the lyre, the jackal playing the zither, the bear steadying the lyre (or perhaps dancing), and the gazelle bearing goblets. The banquet animals almost seem to be burlesquing the kind of regal feast reproduced on the *Standard of Ur*'s peace side. The meaning of the sound box scenes is unclear. Some scholars have suggested, for example, that the creatures inhabit the land of the dead and that the narrative has a funerary significance. In any event, the Ur lyre's sound box is a very early specimen of the recurring theme in both literature and art of animals acting as people. Later examples include Aesop's fables in ancient Greece, medieval bestiaries, and Walt Disney's cartoon animal actors.

ART IN MINIATURE ON CYLINDER SEALS A banquet is also the subject of a *cylinder seal* (FIG. **2-11**) found in the tomb of "Queen" Pu-abi and inscribed with her name. (Many historians prefer to designate her more conservatively and ambiguously as "Lady" Pu-abi.) The seal is typical of the period, consisting of a cylindrical piece of stone engraved to produce a raised impression when rolled over clay (see "Mesopotamian Cylinder Seals," page 26). In the upper zone, a man and a woman, probably Pu-abi, sit and drink from beakers, attended by servants. Below, male attendants serve two more seated men. Even in miniature and in a medium very different from that of the *Standard of Ur,* the Sumerian artist employed the same figure types and followed the same compositional rules. All the figures are in composite views with large frontal eyes in profile heads, and the seated dignitaries are once again larger in scale to underscore their elevated position in the social hierarchy.

AKKADIAN, NEO-SUMERIAN, BABYLONIAN, AND HITTITE ART

THE FIRST NEAR EASTERN KINGS In 2334 B.C., the loosely linked group of cities known as Sumer came under the domination of a great ruler, Sargon of Akkad. The specific site of the city of Akkad has yet to be located but was in the vicinity of Babylon. The Akkadians were Semitic in origin, that is, they were a Near Eastern people who spoke a language

MATERIALS AND TECHNIQUES

Mesopotamian Cylinder Seals

Cylinder seals have been unearthed in great numbers at sites throughout Mesopotamia. Generally made of stone—the favorite materials were carnelian, jasper, lapis lazuli, and agate—seals of ivory, glass, and other materials also survive. As the name implies, the seals are cylindrical. Most have a hole drilled lengthwise through the center of the cylinder so that they could be strung and worn around the neck or suspended from the wrist. Cylinder seals were prized possessions, signifying high positions in society, and they frequently were buried with the dead.

Their primary function, however, was not to serve as items of adornment. With this device, the Sumerians (and later peoples of the Near East) sealed and identified their documents and protected storage jars and doors against unauthorized opening. The oldest seals were found with some of the world's earliest written records and served to ratify the accuracy of administrative accounts. Seals and writing developed together in ancient Sumer. Some seals, in fact, bear long cuneiform inscriptions and record the names and titles of rulers, bureaucrats, and deities. Although sealing is increasingly rare, the tradition lives on today whenever a letter is sealed with a lump of wax and then stamped with a monogram or other identifying mark. Customs officials often still seal packages and sacks with official stamps when goods cross national borders.

In the ancient Near East, cylinder seals were decorated with incised designs, producing a raised pattern when the seal was rolled over soft clay. We illustrate a seal from the Royal Cemetery at Ur and a modern impression made from it (FIG. 2-11). Note how cracks in the stone cylinder become raised lines in the impression and how the engraved figures, chairs, and cuneiform characters appear in relief. Continuous rolling of the seal over a clay strip results in a repeating design, as our illustration also demonstrates at the edges.

The miniature reliefs the seals produce are a priceless source of information about Mesopotamian religion and society. Without them, archeologists would know much less about how Mesopotamians dressed and dined; what their shrines looked like; how they depicted their gods, rulers, and mythological figures; and how they fought wars. Clay seal impressions excavated in architectural contexts shed a welcome light on the administration and organization of Mesopotamian city-states. Cylinder seals are also an invaluable resource for art historians, providing them with thousands of examples of Mesopotamian relief sculpture spread over roughly three thousand years.

---

related to Hebrew and Arabic. Their language—Akkadian—was entirely different from the language of Sumer, but they used the Sumerians' cuneiform characters for their written documents. Under Sargon (whose name means "true king") and his followers, the Akkadians introduced a new concept of royal power based on unswerving loyalty to the king rather than to the city-state. During the rule of Sargon's grandson, Naram-Sin (r. 2254–2218 B.C.), governors of cities were considered mere servants of the king, who, in turn, called himself "King of the Four Quarters"—in effect, ruler of the earth, akin to a god.

IMPERIAL MAJESTY IN COPPER   A magnificent copper head of an Akkadian king found at Nineveh (FIG. 2-12) embodies this new concept of absolute monarchy. The harm the head suffered was due to its status as a political artwork. The head is all that survives of a statue that was knocked over in antiquity, perhaps by an enemy of the Akkadians. But the damage to the portrait was not due solely to the statue's toppling. Vandals gouged out the eyes, once inlaid with precious or semiprecious stones. They also broke off the lower part of the beard and mutilated the ears. Nonetheless, the king's majestic serenity, dignity, and authority are evident.

2-11 Banquet scene, cylinder seal *(left)* and its modern impression *(right),* from the tomb of Pu-abi (tomb 800), Royal Cemetery, Ur (modern Tell Muqayyar), Iraq, ca. 2600 B.C. Lapis lazuli, approx. 2″ high. British Museum, London.

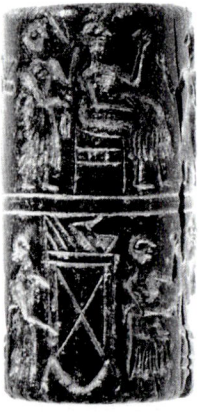
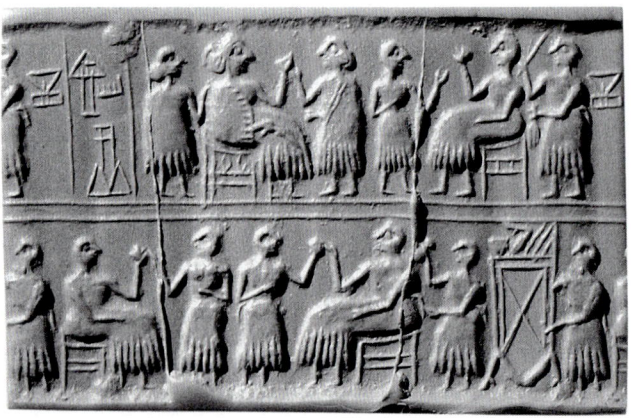

honor of Naram-Sin and once by an Elamite king who had captured Sippar in 1157 B.C. and taken the stele as booty back to Susa, where it was found. On the stele, the grandson of Sargon leads his victorious army up the slopes of a wooded mountain. His routed enemies fall, flee, die, or beg for mercy. The king stands alone, far taller than his men, treading on the bodies of two of the fallen Lullubi. He wears the horned helmet—the first time a king appears as a god in Mesopotamian art—and at least three favorable stars (the stele is damaged at the top and broken at the bottom) shine on his triumph.

By storming the mountain, Naram-Sin seems also to be scaling the ladder to the heavens, the same conceit that lies behind the great ziggurat towers of the ancient Near East. His troops march up the mountain behind him in orderly files, suggesting the discipline and organization of the king's forces.

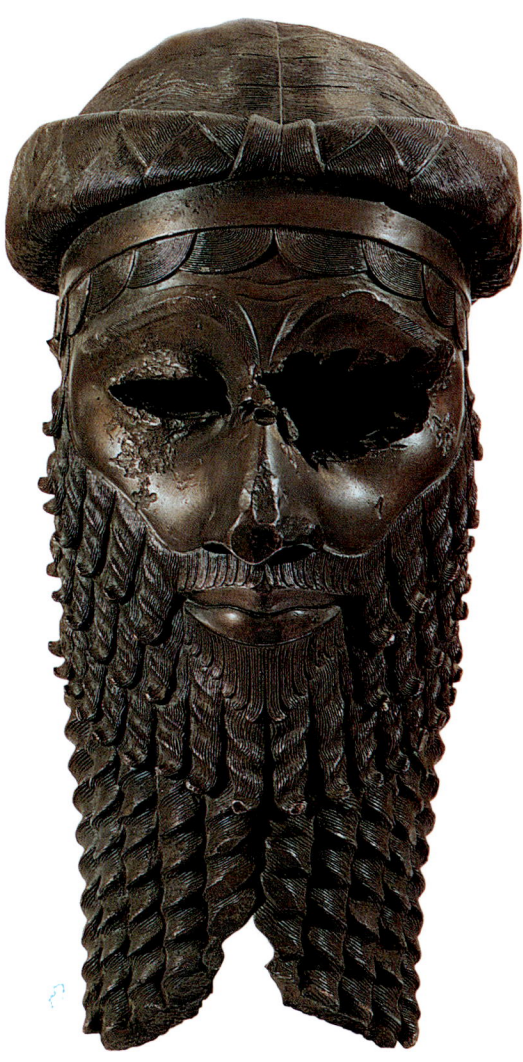

2-12   Head of an Akkadian ruler, from Nineveh (modern Kuyunjik), Iraq, ca. 2250–2200 B.C. Copper, 1′ 2⅜″ high. Iraq Museum, Baghdad.

So, too, is the masterful way the sculptor balanced naturalism and abstract patterning. The artist carefully observed and recorded the man's distinctive features—the profile of the nose and the long, curly beard. The sculptor brilliantly communicated the differing textures of flesh and hair—even the contrasting textures of the mustache, beard, and the braided hair on the top of the head. The coiffure's triangles, lozenges, and overlapping disks of hair and the great arching eyebrows that give such character to the portrait reveal that the artist was also sensitive to formal pattern.

No less remarkable is the fact this is a life-size, hollow-cast metal sculpture (see "Hollow-Casting Life-Size Bronze Statues," Chapter 5, page 124), one of the earliest known. The head demonstrates the artisan's sophisticated skill in casting and polishing copper and in engraving the details. The portrait is the first great extant monumental work of hollow-cast sculpture, but it would have been a superb achievement at any date.

A GOD-KING CRUSHES AN ENEMY The godlike sovereignty the kings of Akkad claimed is also evident in the victory stele (FIG. **2-13**) Naram-Sin set up at Sippar. The stele commemorates his defeat of the Lullubi, a people of the Iranian mountains to the east. It is inscribed twice, once in

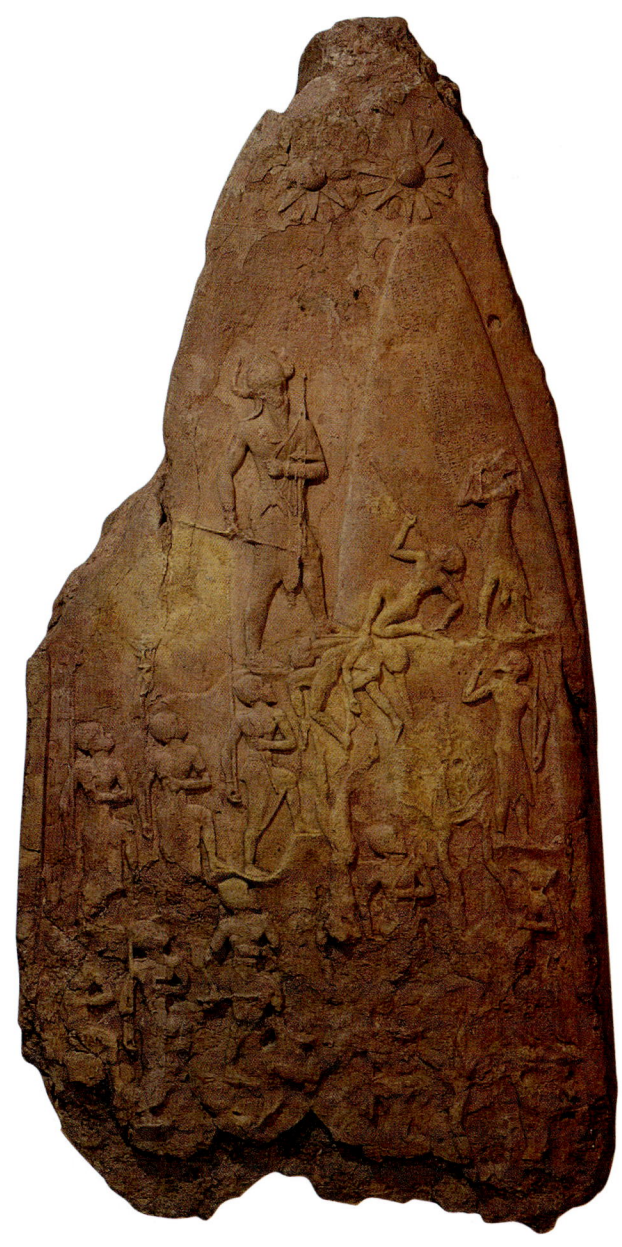

2-13   Victory stele of Naram-Sin, from Susa, Iran, 2254–2218 B.C. Pink sandstone, approx. 6′ 7″ high. Louvre, Paris.

RELIGION AND MYTHOLOGY

The Piety of Gudea

One of the central figures of the Neo-Sumerian age was Gudea, ensi of Lagash ca. 2100 B.C. Nearly two dozen portraits of him survive, carved in diorite and polished to a brilliant finish. Gudea's statues all stood in temples where they could render perpetual service to the gods and intercede with the divine powers on his behalf. Although a powerful ruler, Gudea rejected the regal trappings of Sargon of Akkad and his successors in favor of a return to the Sumerian votive tradition of the statuettes from Eshnunna and Mari (FIGS. 2-5 and 2-6). Like the earlier examples, some of Gudea's statues are inscribed with messages to the gods of Sumer. One from Girsu says, "I am the shepherd loved by my king [Ningirsu, the god of Girsu]; may my life be prolonged." Another, also from Girsu, as if in answer to the first, says, "Gudea, the builder of the temple, has been given life."

In fact, Gudea, at great cost, built or rebuilt all the temples where he placed his statues. One characteristic portrait (FIG. 2-15) depicts the pious ruler of Lagash seated with his hands clasped in front of him in a gesture of prayer. As in his other portraits, Gudea has a muscular physique with well-developed arms, and he wears a long garment that leaves his right shoulder bare. The head is unfortunately lost, but the statue is of

unique interest because Gudea has a temple plan drawn on a tablet on his lap. The ruler buried accounts of his building enterprises in the temple foundations. The surviving texts describe how the sites were prepared and purified, the materials obtained, and the completed temples dedicated. They also record Gudea's dreams of the gods asking him to erect temples in their honor, promising him prosperity if he fulfilled his duty. In one of these dreams, Ningirsu addresses Gudea:

> When, O faithful shepherd Gudea, thou shalt have started work for me on Erinnu, my royal abode [Ningirsu's new temple], I will call up in heaven a humid wind. It shall bring the abundance from on high. . . . All the great fields will bear for thee; dykes and canals will swell for thee; . . . good weight of wool will be given in thy time.[1]

In our statue, Gudea presents Ningirsu with his plan for the god's new temple. And when the structure was completed and his people enjoyed good harvests and their flocks were plentiful, they knew it was the result of Gudea's piety.

[1] Thorkild Jacobsen, trans., *The Art and Architecture of the Ancient Orient,* by Henri Frankfort, 4th ed. (New Haven: Yale University Press, 1970), 98.

The enemy, by contrast, is in disarray, depicted in a great variety of postures—one falls headlong down the mountainside. The sculptor adhered to older conventions in many details, especially by portraying the king and his soldiers in composite views. Note, too, the frontal placement of Naram-Sin's two-horned helmet on his profile head. But, in other respects, this work shows daring innovation. Here, the sculptor created the first landscape in Near Eastern art since the Çatal Hüyük mural (see FIG. 1-18) and set the figures on successive tiers within that landscape. This was a bold rejection of the stan-

dard means of telling a story in a series of horizontal registers, the compositional formula that was the rule not only in earlier Mesopotamian art but also in Egyptian art.

THE RESURGENCE OF SUMER   A raid by mountain people, the Guti, brought Akkadian power to an end. The Guti dominated life in central and lower Mesopotamia until the cities of Sumer united in response to the alien presence and established a Neo-Sumerian state ruled by the kings of Ur. This age saw the construction of one of the greatest ziggurats

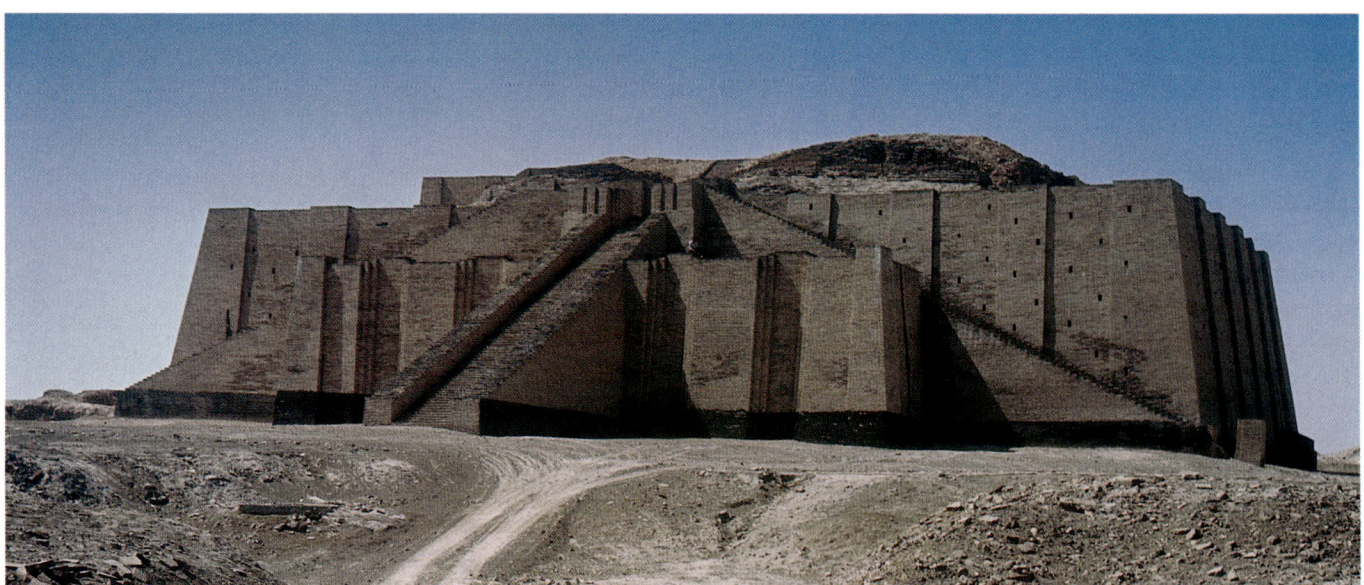

2-14   Ziggurat (northeastern facade with restored stairs), Ur (modern Tell Muqayyar), Iraq, ca. 2100 B.C.

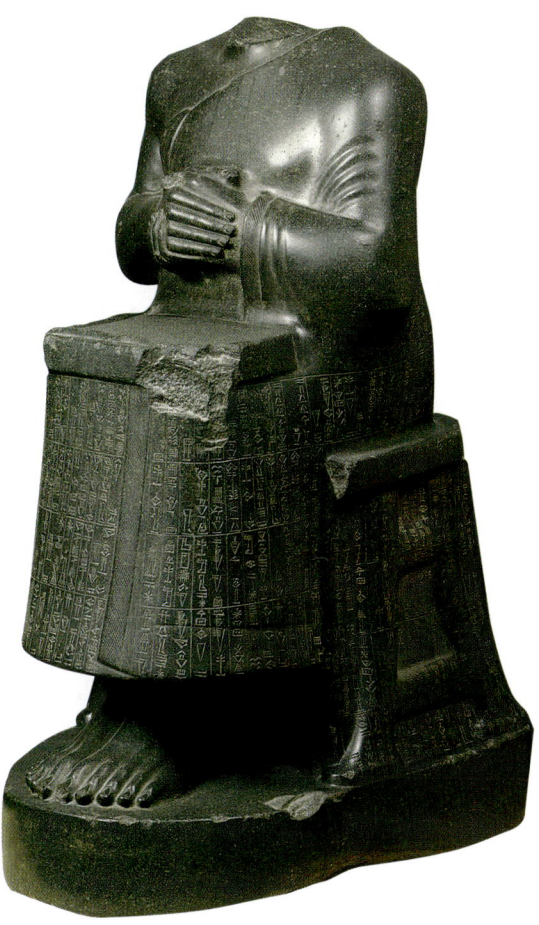

2-15 Seated statue of Gudea holding temple plan, from Girsu (modern Telloh), Iraq, ca. 2100 B.C. Diorite, approx. 2′ 5″ high. Louvre, Paris.

in Mesopotamia, that at Ur (FIG. **2-14**). It was built about a millennium later than the ziggurat at Uruk (FIGS. 2-1 and 2-2) and is much larger. The base is a solid mass of mud brick fifty feet high. The builders used baked bricks laid in *bitumen,* an asphaltlike substance, for the facing of the entire monument. Three ramplike stairways of a hundred steps each converge on a tower-flanked gateway. From there another flight of steps probably led to the temple proper, which does not survive, even in part.

GUDEA'S DIORITE PORTRAITS The most conspicuous preserved sculptural monuments of the Neo-Sumerian age portray the ensi of Lagash, Gudea. About twenty statues of Gudea survive, showing him seated or standing, hands tightly clasped, head shaven, sometimes wearing a woolen brimmed hat, and always dressed in a long garment that leaves one shoulder and arm exposed (FIG. **2-15**). Gudea was zealous in granting the gods their due, and the numerous statues he commissioned are an enduring testimony to his piety (see "The Piety of Gudea," page 28)—and also to his wealth and pride. All his portraits are of diorite, a rare and costly dark stone that had to be imported. Diorite is also extremely hard and difficult to carve. The prestige of the material—which in turn lent prestige to Gudea's portraits—is evident from an inscription on one of Gudea's statues: "This statue has not been made from silver nor from lapis lazuli, nor from copper nor from lead, nor yet from bronze; it is made of diorite."

HAMMURABI AND THE RISE OF BABYLON
The resurgence of Sumer was short lived under the kings of what historians refer to as the Third Dynasty of Ur. The last of those kings fell from the attacks of the Elamites, who ruled the territory east of the Tigris River. The following two centuries witnessed the reemergence of the traditional Mesopotamian political pattern of several independent city-states existing side by side. Until Babylon's most powerful king, Hammurabi (r. 1792–1750 B.C.), reestablished a centralized government that ruled southern Mesopotamia, Babylon was one of these city-states. Perhaps the most renowned king in Mesopotamian history, Hammurabi was famous for his conquests. But he is best known today for his law code, which prescribed penalties for everything from adultery and murder to the cutting down of a neighbor's trees (see "Hammurabi's Law Code," page 30).

The code is inscribed on a tall black-basalt stele (FIG. **2-16**) that was carried off as booty to Susa in 1157 B.C., together

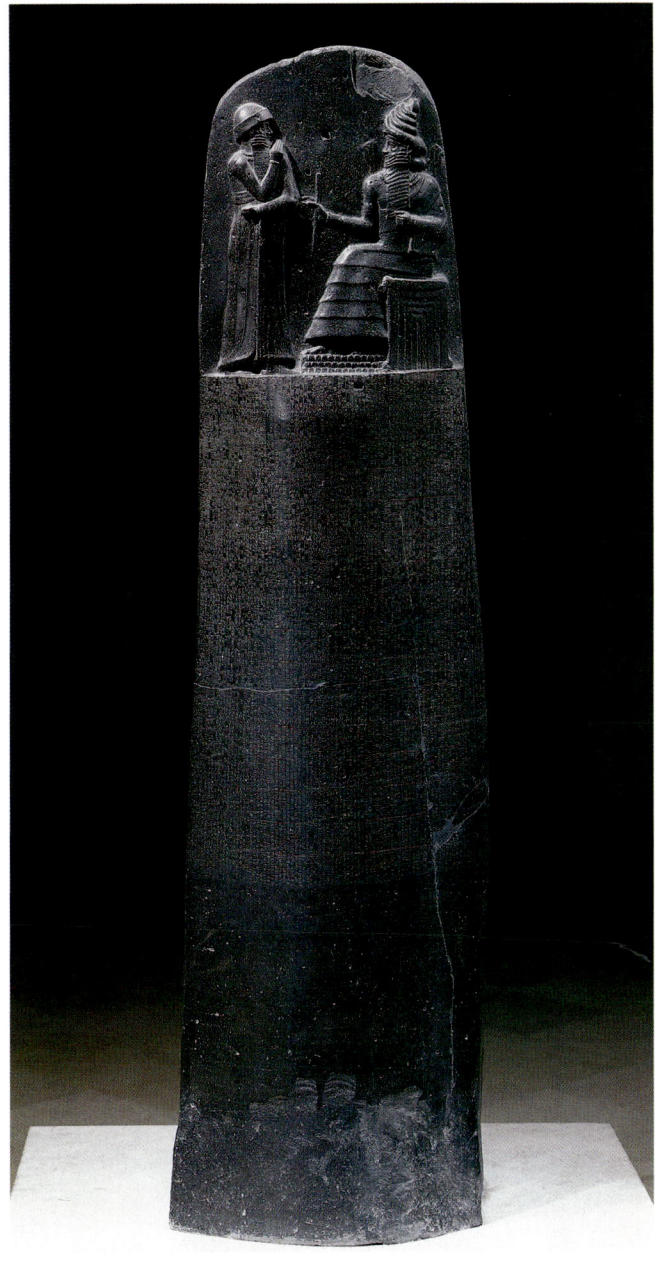

2-16 Stele with law code of Hammurabi, from Susa, Iran, ca. 1780 B.C. Basalt, approx. 7′ 4″ high. Louvre, Paris.

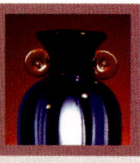

ART AND SOCIETY

Hammurabi's Law Code

In the early eighteenth century B.C., King Hammurabi of Babylon formulated a comprehensive law code for his people. At the time, parts of Europe were still in the Stone Age (see FIG. 1-19). And even in Greece, it was not until more than a thousand years later that Draco provided Athens with its first written set of laws. Hammurabi was following the tradition his Sumerian predecessors established. Two similar earlier law codes survive in part, but Hammurabi's laws are the only ones known in great detail, thanks to the chance survival of a tall and narrow stele depicting Hammurabi receiving the measuring rod and line from the god Shamash (FIG. 2-16). The rod and line symbolize the authority to measure people's lives, that is, to render judgments. The sculptor thus informed viewers that Hammurabi had the god-given authority to enforce the laws spelled out on the stele. The judicial code, written in Akkadian, was inscribed in thirty-five hundred lines of cuneiform characters. Hammurabi's laws governed all aspects of Babylonian life, from commerce and property to murder and theft to marital fidelity, inheritances, and the treatment of slaves.

We list only a small sample of the infractions described and the penalties imposed (which vary with the person's standing in society).

If a man puts out the eye of another man, his eye shall be put out.
If he kills a man's slave, he shall pay one-third of a mina.
If someone steals property from a temple, he will be put to death, as will the person who receives the stolen goods.
If a man rents his boat and the boat is wrecked, the renter shall replace the boat with another.
If a married woman dies before bearing any sons, her dowry shall be repaid to her father, but if she gave birth to sons, the dowry shall belong to them.
If a man's wife is caught in bed with another man, both will be tied up and thrown in the water.

---

with the Naram-Sin stele (FIG. 2-13). At the top is a relief depicting Hammurabi in the presence of the flame-shouldered sun god, Shamash. The king raises his hand in respect. The god bestows on Hammurabi the authority to rule and to enforce the laws.

The sculptor depicted Shamash in the familiar convention of combined front and side views, but with two important exceptions. His great headdress with its four pairs of horns is in true profile so that only four, not all eight, of the horns are visible. And the artist seems to have tentatively explored the notion of *foreshortening*—a device for suggesting depth by representing a figure or object at an angle, rather than frontally or in profile. The god's beard is a series of diagonal rather than horizontal lines, suggesting its recession from the picture plane.

ISHTAR GRANTS POWER TO A NEW KING While Hammurabi ruled Babylon, King Zimri-Lim (r. 1779–1757 B.C.) controlled the Sumerian city-state of Mari. Zimri-Lim constructed a huge palace complex at Mari, but in 1757 B.C. Hammurabi led an army into the city and destroyed the royal residence. Fortunately, some of the extremely fragile paintings on plaster that adorned the mudbrick palace walls survive. They provide a rare opportunity to study the art of mural painting in Mesopotamia.

The painting we reproduce (FIG. **2-17**) adorned one wall of the palace's main courtyard near the entrance to the throne room suite. At the center, the painter represented the *investiture* of Zimri-Lim, the granting of his right to rule, by the goddess Ishtar. The king approaches Ishtar with his right arm raised in greeting and respect, just as Hammurabi appeared before Shamash (FIG. 2-16). The goddess has one foot on her sacred lion and hands Zimri-Lim the emblems of power, the

rod and line. A god and two other goddesses witness the ceremony. Below, two more goddesses display vases from which plants grow and streams of life-giving water flow. Fish swim freely in the current. The general theme is a venerable one. The gods grant royal authority to their chosen kings and prosperity to their people.

As on Hammurabi's stele, the horned crowns the deities wear are in profile, although the painter showed no interest in foreshortening. In fact, such experiments are very uncommon. Like the bold abandonment of the register format in favor of a tiered landscape on the Naram-Sin stele (FIG. 2-13), innovations in representational modes were exceptional in early eras of the history of art. These occasional departures from the norm testify to the creativity and brilliance of the ancient Near Eastern artists.

A HITTITE FORTRESS IN TURKEY The Babylonian Empire was toppled in the face of an onslaught by the Hittites, an Anatolian people who conquered and sacked Babylon around 1595 B.C. They then retired to their homeland, leaving Babylon in the hands of the Kassites. Remains of the strongly fortified capital city of the Hittites still may be seen near the modern Turkish village of Boghazköy. Constructed of large blocks of heavy stone—a striking contrast to the brick architecture of Mesopotamia—the walls and towers of the Hittites effectively protected them from attack. Still symbolically guarding the gateway to the Boghazköy citadel (FIG. **2-18**) are two huge (seven-foot-high) lions. Their simply carved forequarters project from massive stone blocks on either side of the entrance. These Hittite guardian beasts are early examples of a theme that was to be echoed on many Near Eastern gates. Notable are those of Assyria (FIG. 2-21), one of the greatest empires of the ancient world, and

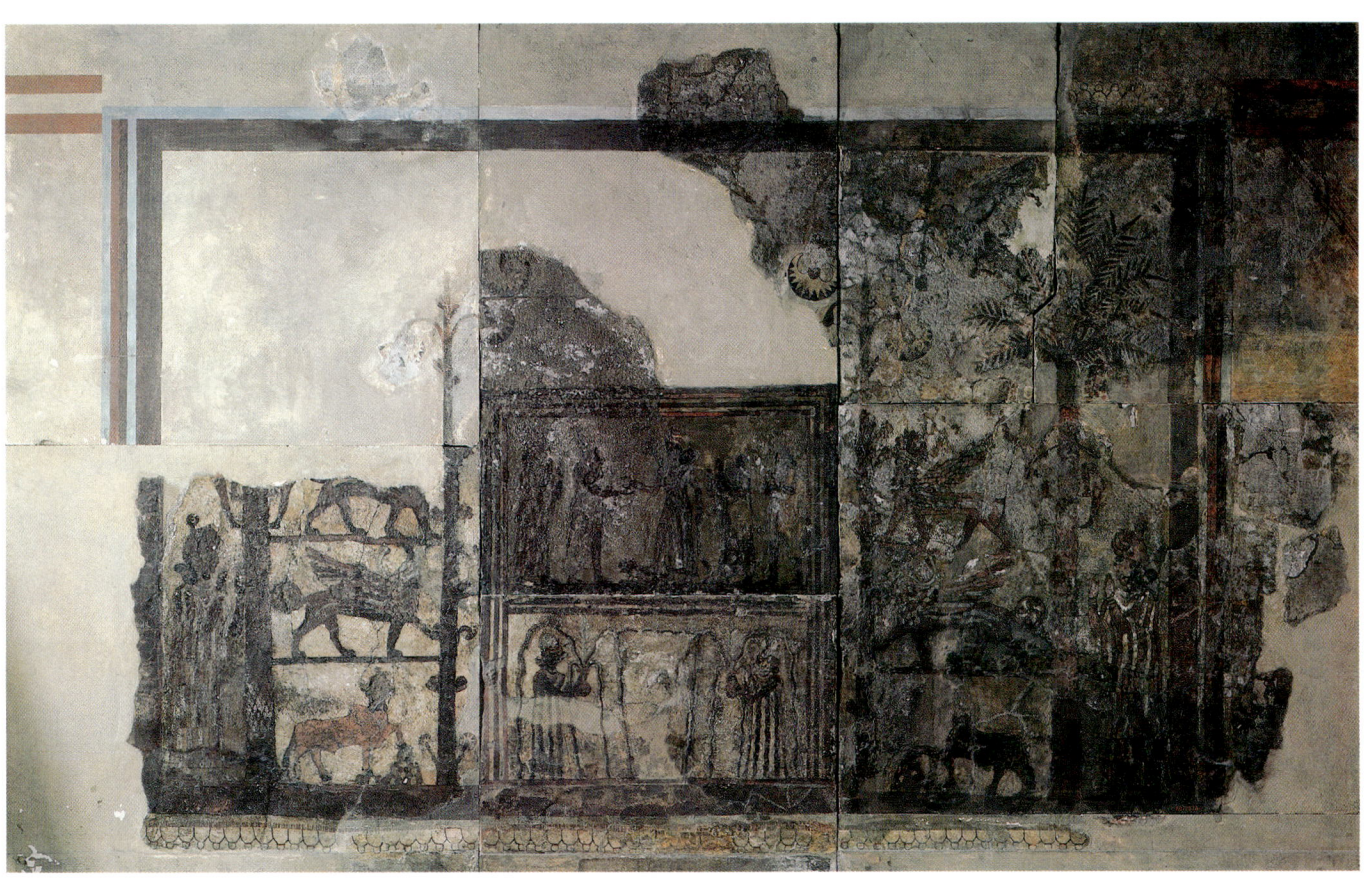

2-17   Investiture of Zimri-Lim, mural painting from Court 106 of the palace at Mari (modern Tell Hariri), Syria, ca. 1775–1760 B.C. Louvre, Paris.

of the reborn Babylon (FIG. 2-26) in the first millennium B.C. But the idea of protecting a city, palace, temple, or tomb from evil by placing wild beasts or fantastic monsters before an entranceway was not unique to the Near Eastern world. Examples abound in Egypt, Greece, Italy, and elsewhere.

ELAMITE AND ASSYRIAN ART

THE RISE OF SUSA   To the east of Sumer, Akkad, and Babylon, in what is western Iran today, a civilization flourished that historians refer to by the biblical name Elam.

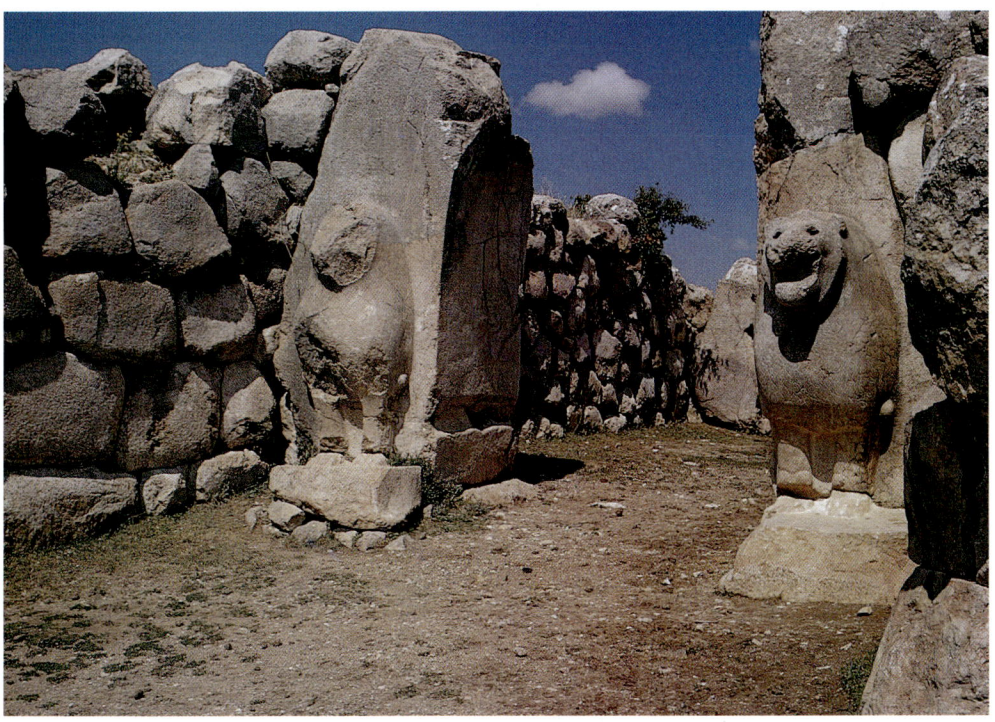

2-18   Lion Gate, Boghazköy, Turkey, ca. 1400 B.C. Limestone, lions approx. 7′ high.

During the second half of the second millennium B.C., Elam reached the height of its political and military power. At this time Elam was strong enough to plunder Babylonia and to carry off the stelae of Naram-Sin and Hammurabi (FIGS. 2-13 and 2-16) and reerect them at its capital city, Susa. The Assyrian king Ashurbanipal finally destroyed the empire of Elam in 641 B.C. when he sacked Susa. The city would rise again to great importance under the Achaemenid Persian Empire.

AN IMMOVABLE PORTRAIT OF A QUEEN

From the ruins of Susa came the life-size bronze-and-copper statue of Queen Napir-Asu (FIG. 2-19), wife of one of the most powerful Elamite kings, Untash-Napirisha. The statue weighs 3,760 pounds even in its fragmentary and mutilated state, because the sculptor, incredibly, cast the statue with a solid bronze core inside a hollow-cast copper shell. The bronze core increased the cost of the statue enormously, but the queen wished her portrait to be a permanent, immovable votive offering in the temple where it was found. In fact, the

Elamite inscription on the queen's skirt explicitly asks the gods to protect the statue:

> He who would seize my statue, who would smash it, who would destroy its inscription, who would erase my name, may he be smitten by the curse of [the gods], that his name shall become extinct, that his offspring be barren. . . . This is Napir-Asu's offering.[1]

The statue thus falls within the votive tradition going back to the third millennium B.C. and the figurines from Eshnunna and Mari (FIGS. 2-5 and 2-6). In the Elamite statue of Queen Napir-Asu, the Mesopotamian instinct for cylindrical volume is again evident. The portrait's tight silhouette, strict frontality, and firmly crossed hands held close to the body are all enduring characteristics common to the Sumerian statuettes. Yet within these rigid conventions of form and pose, the Elamite artist managed to create refinements that must have come from close observation. The sculptor conveyed the feminine softness of arm and bust, the grace and elegance of the long-fingered hands, the supple and quiet bend of the wrist, the ring and bracelets, and the gown's patterned fabric. The figure presents the ideal in queenly deportment, with just a touch of modesty to lessen the conventional pose's severity. The loss of the head is especially unfortunate.

THE FORTRESS-PALACES OF THE ASSYRIANS

During the first half of the first millennium B.C., a fearsome resurgent force in the Near East, the Assyrians, vanquished the various warfaring peoples that succeeded the Babylonians and Hittites. The Assyrians took their name from Assur, the city on the Tigris River in northern Iraq named for the god Ashur. At the height of their power, the Assyrians ruled an empire that extended from the Tigris to the Nile Rivers and from the Persian Gulf to Asia Minor. Their palaces have been excavated in large part, yielding not only their plans but also statues, mural paintings, and the most extensive series of narrative reliefs in the ancient Near East.

The unfinished royal citadel of King Sargon II (r. 721–705 B.C.) of Assyria built at Dur Sharrukin (FIG. 2-20) reveals in its ambitious layout the confidence of the Assyrian kings in their all-conquering might. Its strong defensive walls also reflect a society ever fearful of attack during a period of almost constant warfare. The city measures about a square mile in area. The palace, elevated on a mound fifty feet high, covered some twenty-five acres and had more than two hundred courtyards and rooms. As our reconstruction drawing shows, although the palace complex layout had a basic symmetry, the plan is rambling. It embraced a collection of timber-roofed rectangular rooms and halls grouped around square and rectangular courts. Behind the main courtyard, whose sides each measured three hundred feet, were the residential quarters of the king, who received foreign emissaries in the long, high, brightly painted throne room. All visitors entered from another large courtyard, where giant figures of the king and his courtiers lined the walls.

Sargon II regarded his city and palace as an expression of his grandeur. The Assyrians cultivated an image of themselves as merciless to anyone who dared oppose them, although they were forgiving to those who submitted to their will. Sargon, for example, wrote in an inscription, "I built a city with [the labors of] the peoples subdued by my hand, whom Ashur, Nabu, and Marduk had caused to lay themselves at

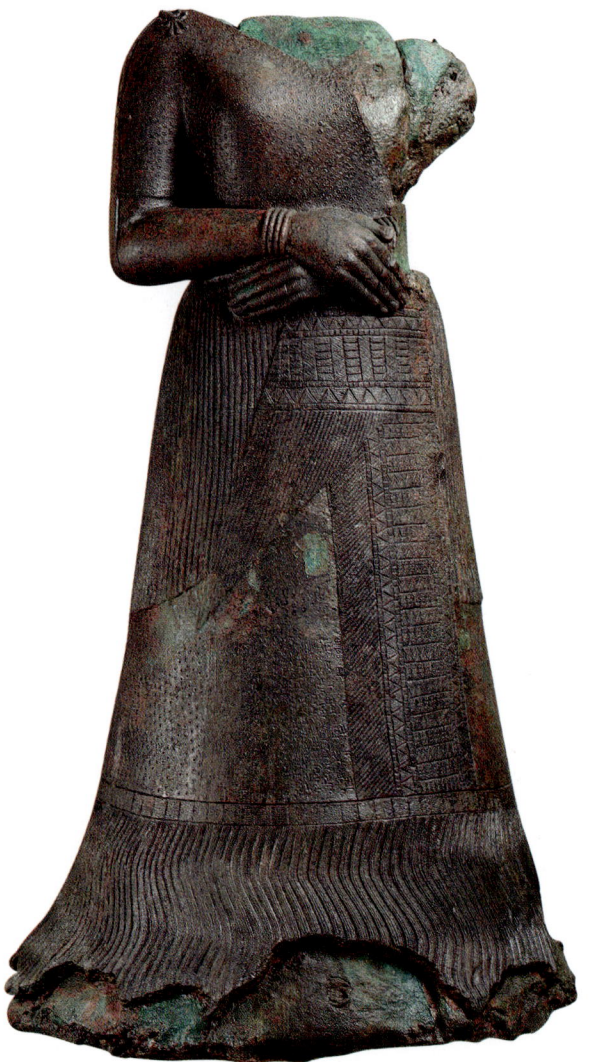

2-19   Statue of Queen Napir-Asu, from Susa, Iran, ca. 1350–1300 B.C. Bronze and copper, 4′ 2¾″ high. Louvre, Paris.

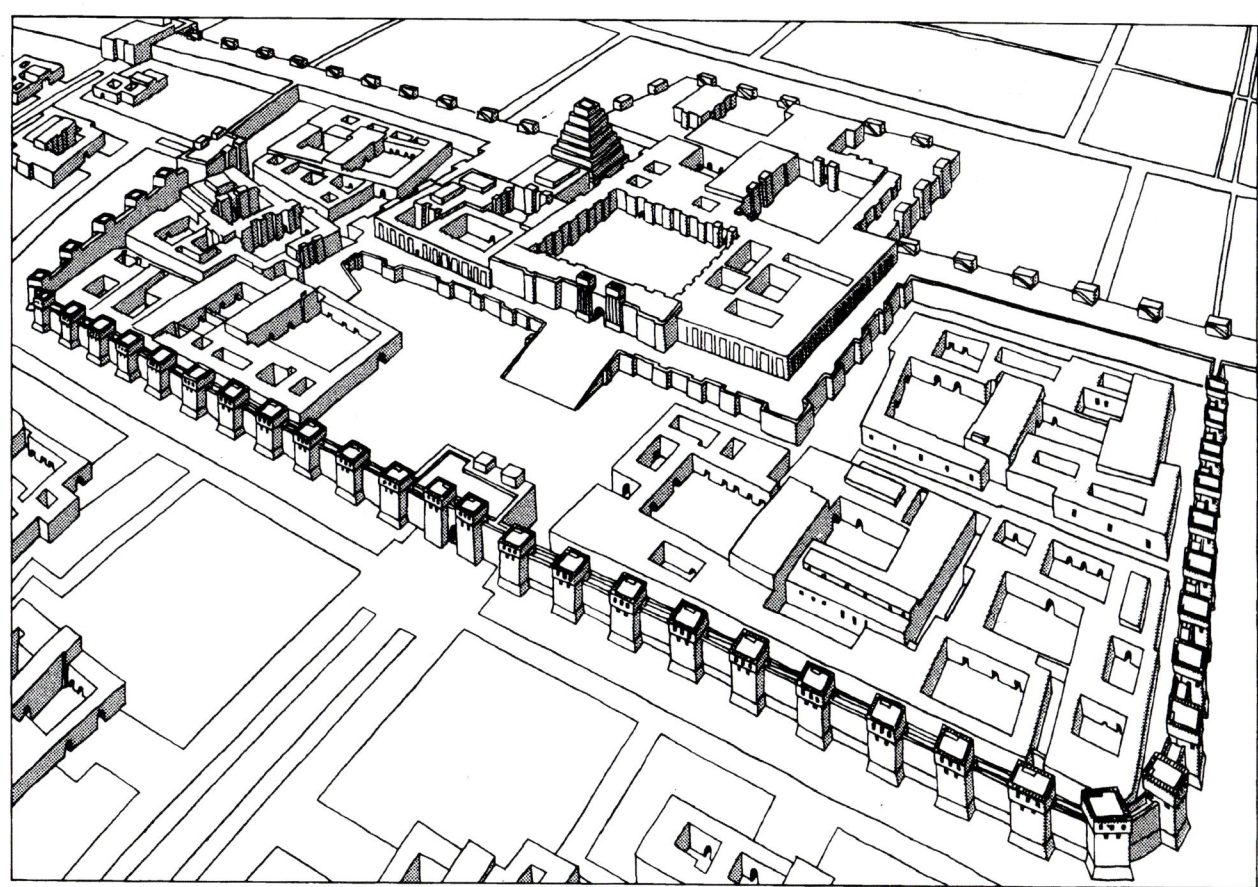

2-20   Reconstruction drawing of the citadel of Sargon II, Dur Sharrukin (modern Khorsabad), Iraq, ca. 720–705 B.C. (after Charles Altman).

my feet and bear my yoke." And in another text, he proclaimed, "Sargon, King of the World, has built a city. Dur Sharrukin he has named it. A peerless palace he has built within it."

In addition to the complex of courtyards, throne room, state chambers, service quarters, and guard rooms that made up the palace, the citadel included a great ziggurat and six sanctuaries for six different gods. The ziggurat at Dur Sharrukin may have had as many as seven stories. Four remain, each eighteen feet high and painted a different color. A continuous ramp spiraled around the building from its base to the temple at its summit. Here, the legacy of the Sumerian bent-axis approach may be seen more than two millennia after the erection of the White Temple on the ziggurat at Uruk (FIG. 2-1).

SARGON'S MONSTROUS GUARDIANS   Guarding the gate to Sargon's palace were colossal limestone monsters (FIG. 2-21), probably called *lamassu* by the Assyrians. These winged, man-headed bulls served to ward off the king's enemies, visible and invisible. The task of moving and installing such immense stone sculptures was so daunting that several reliefs in the palace of Sargon's successor celebrate the feat, showing scores of men dragging lamassu figures with the aid of ropes and sledges.

The Assyrian lamassu sculptures are partly in the round, but the sculptor nonetheless conceived them as high reliefs on adjacent sides of a corner. They combine the front view of the animal at rest with the side view of it in motion.

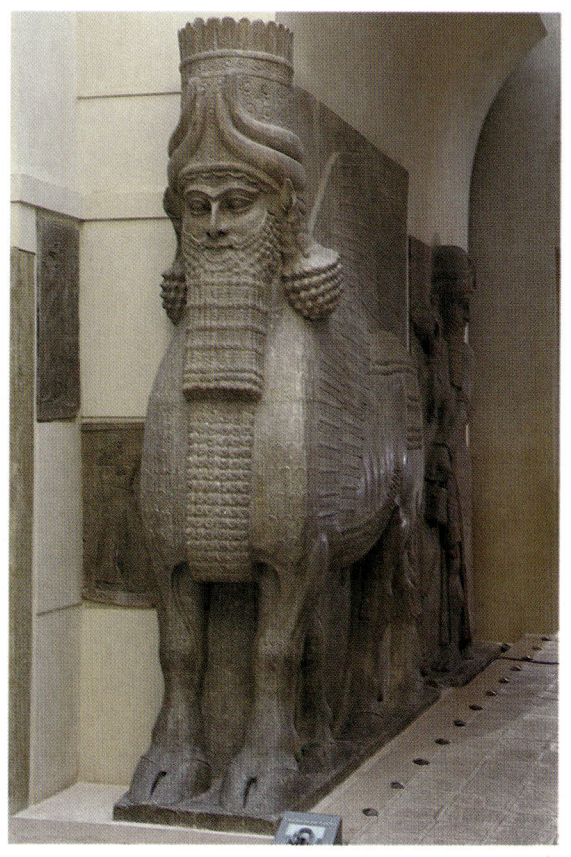

2-21   Lamassu (winged, human-headed bull), from the citadel of Sargon II, Dur Sharrukin (modern Khorsabad), Iraq, ca. 720–705 B.C. Limestone, approx. 13′ 10″ high. Louvre, Paris.

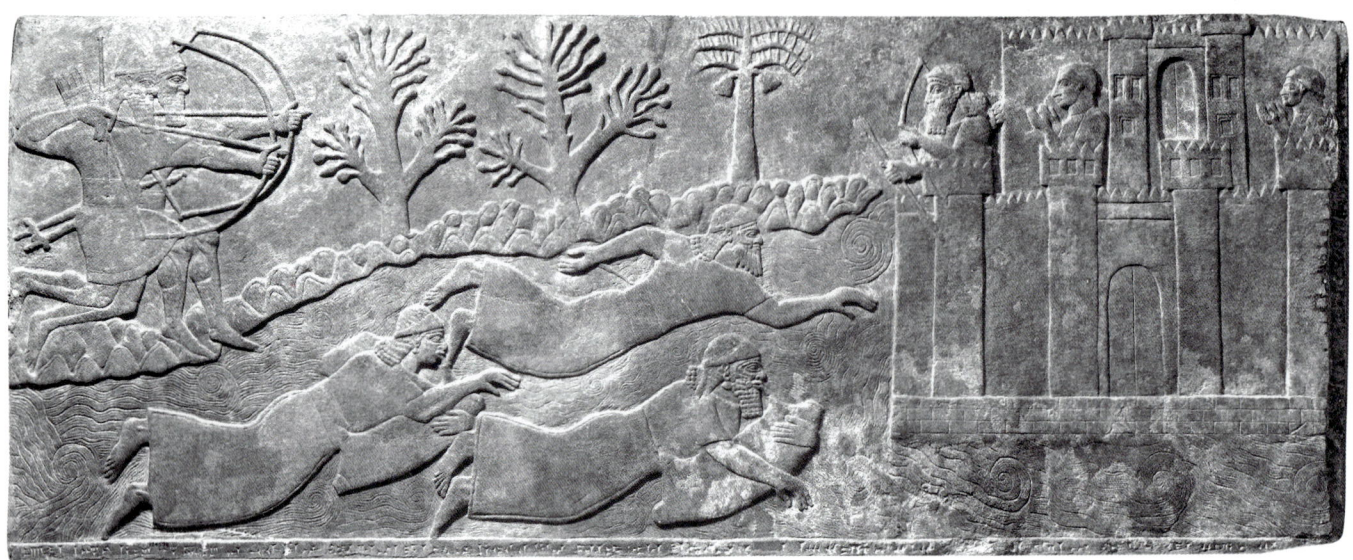

2-22   Assyrian archers pursuing enemies, relief from the Northwest Palace of Ashurnasirpal II, Kalhu (modern Nimrud), Iraq, ca. 875–860 B.C. Gypsum, 2′ 10⅝″ high. British Museum, London.

Seeking to present a complete picture of the lamassu from both the front and the side, the sculptor gave the monster five legs (two seen from the front, four seen from the side). The three-quarter view the modern photographer chose would not have been favored in antiquity. This sculpture, then, is yet another case of early artists providing a "conceptual" picture of an animal or person and of all its important parts, as opposed to an "optical" view of the lamassu as it actually would stand in space.

CHRONICLES OF GREAT DEEDS   The Assyrian kings expected their greatness to be recorded in unmistakably exact forms in their palaces. To this end, they commissioned sculptors to produce extensive series of narrative reliefs exalting royal power and piety and recording not only battlefield victories but also the slaying of wild animals. (The Assyrians, like many other societies before and after, regarded prowess in hunting as a manly virtue on a par with success in warfare.) The narrative reliefs of military campaigns and hunting covering Assyrian palace walls have precedents only in Egypt, but in a very different format (see Chapter 3). The degree of documentary detail in the Assyrian reliefs is without parallel in the ancient Near East, even in such narratives as those on the *Stele of the Vultures* (FIG. 2-7) and the *Standard of Ur* (FIG. 2-8). Archeologists have found nothing else comparable made before the Roman Empire (see Chapter 10).

One of the most extensive—and earliest—examples of a cycle of historical narrative reliefs comes from the palace of Ashurnasirpal II (r. 883–859 B.C.) at Kalhu. (The Assyrian kings frequently incorporated Ashur's name into their own.) Throughout the palace, painted gypsum reliefs sheathed the lower parts of the mud-brick walls below brightly colored plaster. Rich textiles on the floors contributed to the luxurious ambience. Every relief celebrated the king and bore an inscription naming Ashurnasirpal and describing his accomplishments.

The example we illustrate (FIG. **2-22**) probably depicts an episode that occurred in 878 B.C. when Ashurnasirpal drove his enemy's forces into the Euphrates River. In the relief, two Assyrian archers shoot arrows at the fleeing foe. Three enemy soldiers are in the water. One swims with an arrow in his back. The other two attempt to float to safety by inflating animal skins. Their destination is a fort where their compatriots await them. The artist showed the fort as if it were in the middle of the river, but it must, of course, have been on land, perhaps at some distance from where the escapees entered the water. The artist's purpose was to tell the story clearly and economically. In art, distances can be compressed and the human actors enlarged so that they stand out from their environment. (Literally interpreted, the defenders of the fort are too tall to walk through its archway.) The sculptor also combined different viewpoints in the same frame, just as the figures are composites of frontal and profile views. Viewers see the river from above while observing the men, trees, and fort from the side. The artist also made other adjustments for clarity. So as not to hide the archers' faces, the sculptor depicted their bowstrings in front of their bodies but behind their heads. The men will snare their own heads in their bows when they launch their arrows! All these liberties with optical reality result, however, in a vivid and easily legible retelling of a decisive moment in the king's victorious campaign. This was the artist's primary goal.

ASSYRIAN COURT RITUAL   The Assyrian palace reliefs frequently portrayed the king and his retinue in ceremonial roles or paying homage to the gods. The subjects court sculptors depicted also occupied the painters in the king's employ. Unfortunately, Assyrian paintings, because of their fragile nature, are much rarer today than stone reliefs. A fine example of the painter's art is the *glazed* (painted and then kiln fired to fuse the color with the baked clay) brick from Ashurnasirpal II's Kalhu palace (FIG. **2-23**). It shows the king, taller than everyone else as befits his rank, delicately holding a cup. With it, he will make a *libation* (ritual pouring of liquid) in honor of the protective gods. The artist rendered the figures in outline, lavishing much attention on the patterns of the rich fabrics they wear. The king and the

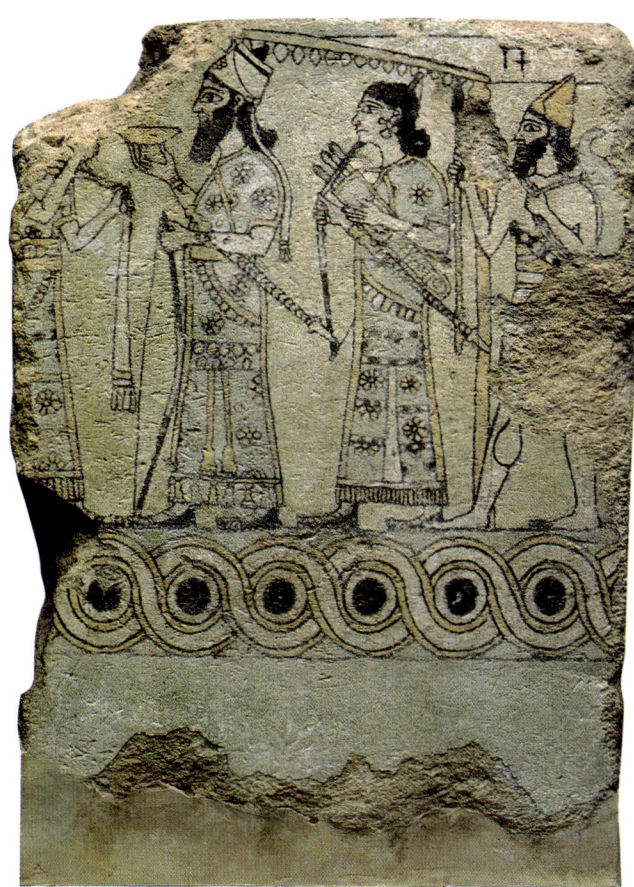

2-23 Ashurnasirpal II with attendants and soldier, from his palace at Kalhu, Iraq, ca. 875–860 B.C. Glazed brick, 11¾″ high. British Museum, London.

attendant behind him are in consistent profile view, but the rule of showing the eye from the front in a profile head still held. Painted scenes such as this hint at what the Assyrian stone reliefs might have looked like with their original paint intact.

NOBLE ANIMAL ADVERSARIES   Two centuries later, sculptors carved hunting reliefs for the Nineveh palace of the conqueror of Elamite Susa, Ashurbanipal (r. 668–627 B.C.). The hunt did not take place in the wild but in a controlled environment, assuring the king's safety and success. In the relief illustrated here (FIG. 2-24), lions released from cages in a large enclosed arena charge the king, who, in his chariot and with his attendants protecting his blind sides, shoots down the enraged animals. The king, menaced by the savage spring of a lion at his back, escapes harm by the quick action of two of his spearmen. They ward off the beast but do not kill it. Only the great king had that privilege. Behind his chariot lies a pathetic trail of dead and dying animals, pierced by what appears to be far more arrows than needed to kill them. A dying lioness (FIG. 2-25), blood streaming from her wounds, drags her hindquarters, paralyzed by arrows that have pierced her spine. The artist ruthlessly depicted the straining muscles, the swelling veins, the muzzle's wrinkled skin, and the flattened ears. Modern sympathies make this scene of carnage a kind of heroic tragedy, with the lions as protagonists. It is unlikely, however, that the king's artists had any intention other than to glorify their ruler by showing the king of men pitting himself against and conquering the king of beasts repeatedly. Depicting Ashurbanipal's beastly foes as possessing not merely strength but courage and nobility as well served to make the king's accomplishments that much grander.

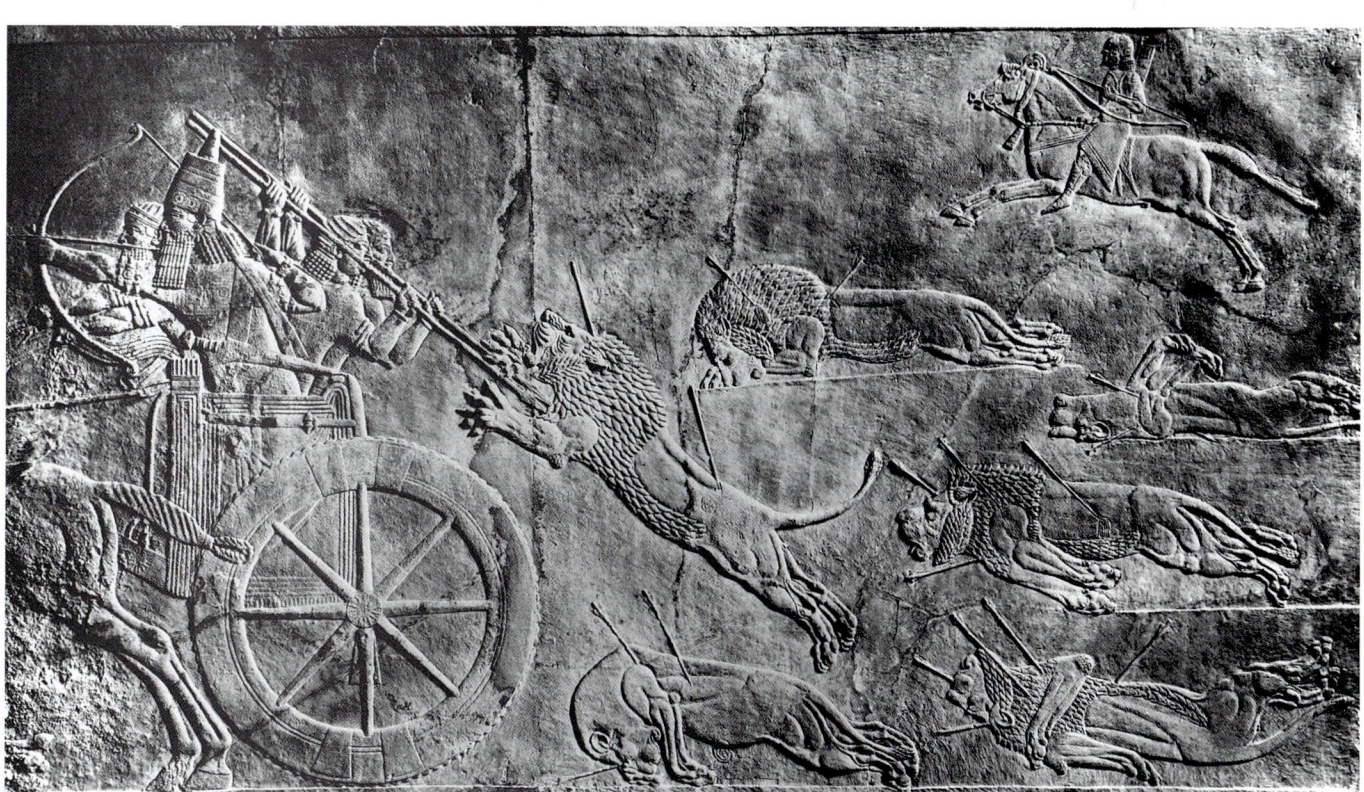

2-24   Ashurbanipal hunting lions, relief from the North Palace of Ashurbanipal, Nineveh (modern Kuyunjik), Iraq, ca. 645–640 B.C. Gypsum, approx. 5′ high. British Museum, London.

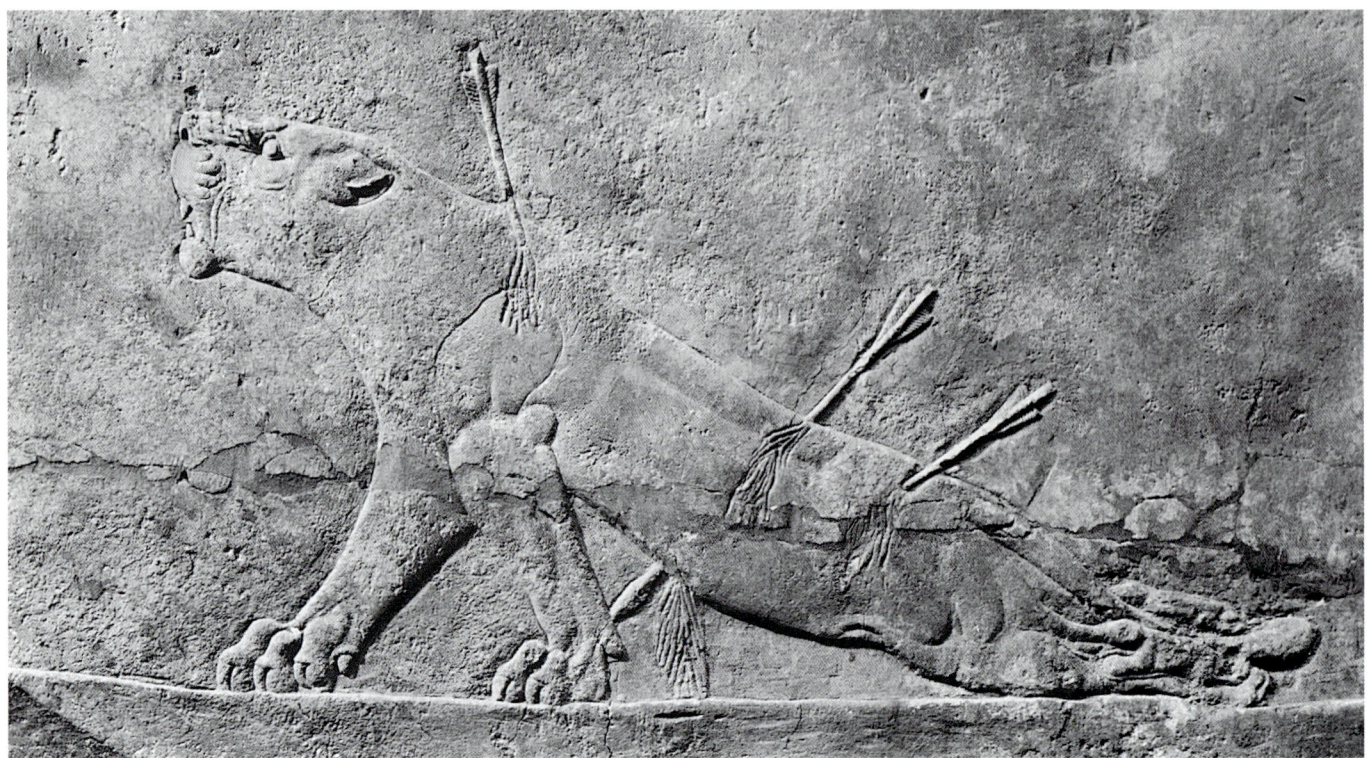

2-25 Dying lioness, detail of a relief from the palace of Ashurbanipal, Nineveh (modern Kuyunjik), Iraq, ca. 645–640 B.C. Gypsum, figure approx. 1′ 4″ high. British Museum, London.

2-26 Ishtar Gate (restored), Babylon, Iraq, ca. 575 B.C. Glazed brick. Staatliche Museen, Berlin.

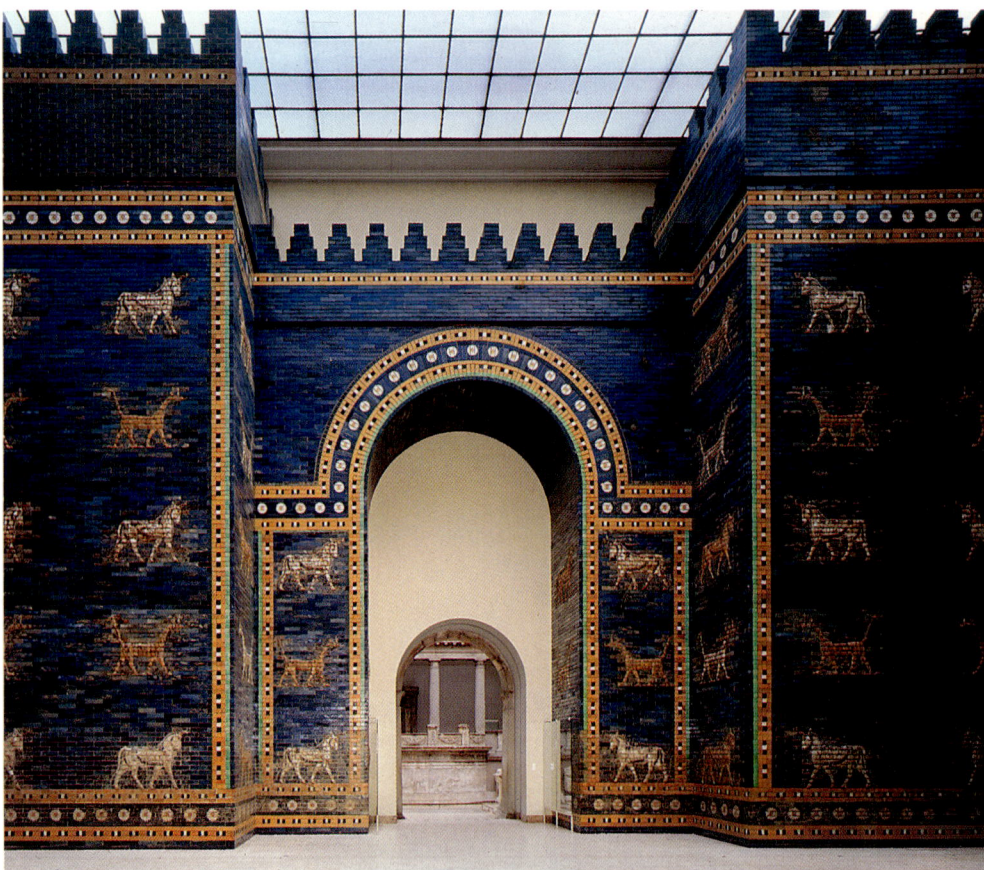

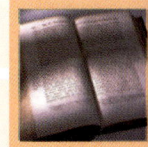

Babylon
City of Wonders

The uncontested list of the Seven Wonders of the ancient world was not codified until the sixteenth century. But already in the second century B.C. a roster of seven must-see monuments—including six of the seven later Wonders—was recorded by Antipater of Sidon, a Greek poet. All of the ancient Wonders were of colossal size and constructed at great expense. Three of them were of great antiquity: the pyramids of Gizeh (see FIG. 3-8), which Antipater described as "man-made mountains," and "the hanging gardens" and "walls of impregnable Babylon."

Babylon was the only site on Antipater's list that could boast two Wonders. Later list makers preferred to distribute the Seven Wonders among seven different cities. Most of these Wonders date to Greek times—the Temple of Artemis at Ephesus, with its sixty-foot-tall columns; Phidias's colossal gold-and-ivory statue of Zeus at Olympia; the grandiose tomb of Mausolus (the "Mausoleum") at Halikarnassos; the Colossus of Rhodes, a bronze statue of the sun god one hundred and ten feet tall; and the three-story lighthouse at Alexandria, perhaps the tallest building in the ancient world. The pyramids are the oldest and the Babylonian gardens the only Wonder in the category of "landscape architecture."

Several ancient texts describe the Babylonian gardens. We quote part of the account of Quintus Curtius Rufus from his history of Alexander the Great written in the mid-first century A.D.:

On the top of the citadel are the hanging gardens, a wonder celebrated in the tales of the Greeks. . . . Columns of stone were set up to sustain the whole work, and on these was laid a floor of squared blocks, strong enough to hold the earth which is thrown upon it to a great depth, as well as the water with which they irrigate the soil; and the structure supports trees of such great size that the thickness of

their trunks equals a measure of eight cubits [about twelve feet]. They tower to a height of fifty feet, and they yield as much fruit as if they were growing in their native soil. . . . To those who look upon [the trees] from a distance, real woods seem to be overhanging their native mountains.[1]

Not qualifying as a Wonder, but in some ways no less impressive, was Babylon's Marduk ziggurat, the biblical Tower of Babel. According to the Bible, God was angered by humankind's arrogant desire to build a tower to Heaven. The Lord put an end to it by causing the workers to speak different languages, preventing them from communicating with one another. The fifth-century B.C. Greek historian Herodotus describes the Babylonian temple complex:

In the middle of the sanctuary [of Marduk] has been built a solid tower . . . which supports another tower, which in turn supports another, and so on: there are eight towers in all. A stairway has been constructed to wind its way up the outside of all the towers; halfway up the stairway there is a shelter with benches to rest on, where people making the ascent can sit and catch their breath. In the last tower there is a huge temple. The temple contains a large couch, which is adorned with fine coverings and has a golden table standing beside it, but there are no statues at all standing there. . . . [The Babylonians] say that the god comes in person to the temple [compare the Sumerian notion of the temple as a "waiting room"] and rests on the couch; I do not believe this story myself.[2]

[1] John C. Rolfe, trans., *Quintus Curtius I* (Cambridge: Harvard University Press, 1971), 337–39.

[2] Robin Waterfield, trans., *Herodotus: The Histories* (New York: Oxford University Press, 1998), 79–80.

NEO-BABYLONIAN AND ACHAEMENID PERSIAN ART

The Assyrian Empire was never very secure, and most of its kings had to fight revolts in large sections of the Near East. Assyria's conquest of Elam in the seventh century B.C. and frequent rebellions in Babylonia apparently overextended its resources. During the last years of Ashurbanipal's reign, the empire began to disintegrate. Under his successors, it collapsed from the simultaneous onslaught of the Medes from the east and the resurgent Babylonians from the south. Babylonian kings held sway over the former Assyrian Empire until the Persian conquest.

NEBUCHADNEZZAR'S WONDROUS BABYLON
The most renowned of the Neo-Babylonian kings was

Nebuchadnezzar II (r. 604–562 B.C.), whose exploits the biblical Book of Daniel recounts. Nebuchadnezzar restored Babylon to its rank as one of the great cities of antiquity. The city's famous "hanging gardens" were counted among the Seven Wonders of the ancient world, and its enormous ziggurat was immortalized in the Bible as the Tower of Babel (see "Babylon: City of Wonders," above).

Nebuchadnezzar's Babylon was a mud-brick city, but dazzling blue-glazed bricks faced the most important monuments. Some of the buildings, such as the Ishtar Gate (FIG. 2-26), with its imposing arched opening flanked by towers, featured glazed bricks with molded reliefs of animals, real and imaginary. Glazed bricks had been used earlier (FIG. 2-23), but the surface of the bricks, even of those with figures, was flat. On the surfaces of the Ishtar Gate, laboriously reassembled in Berlin, are the alternating profile figures of the dragon of Marduk and the bull of Adad. Lining the processional way leading up to the gate were reliefs of Ishtar's sacred lion, glazed in yellow, brown, and red against a blue ground. The Babylonian glazes were opaque and hard. Each brick had to be molded and glazed separately, then set in proper sequence on the wall.

THE TRIUMPH OF PERSIA   Although Nebuchadnezzar, the biblical Daniel's "King of Kings," had boasted that "I caused a mighty wall to circumscribe Babylon . . . so that the enemy who would do evil would not threaten," Cyrus of Persia (r. 559–529 B.C.) captured his city in the sixth century B.C. Cyrus, who may have been descended from an Elamite line, was the founder of the Achaemenid dynasty and traced his ancestry back to a mythical King Achaemenes. Babylon was but one of the Persians' conquests. Egypt fell to them in 525 B.C., and by 480 B.C. the Persian Empire was the largest the world had yet known, extending from the Indus River in southeastern Asia to the Danube River in northeastern Europe. Only the successful Greek resistance in the fifth century B.C. prevented Persia from embracing southeastern Europe as well (see Chapter 5). The Achaemenid line ended with the death of Darius III in 330 B.C., after his defeat at the hands of Alexander the Great (see FIG. 5-69).

PERSIAN GRANDEUR AT PERSEPOLIS   The most important source of knowledge about Persian architecture is the palace at Persepolis (FIG. 2-27), built between 521 and 465 B.C. by Darius I (r. 522–486 B.C.) and Xerxes (r. 486–465 B.C.), successors of Cyrus. Situated on a high plateau, the heavily fortified palace stood on a wide platform overlooking the plain. Alexander the Great razed the palace in

a gesture symbolizing the destruction of Persian imperial power. Some say it was an act of revenge for the Persian sack of the Athenian acropolis in the early fifth century B.C. But even the ruins of the palace complex are impressive.

The dominant structure was a vast columned hall, sixty feet high and more than two hundred feet square. Standing on its own rock-cut podium, this huge royal audience hall, or *apadana,* contained thirty-six colossal columns. The approach to the apadana led through a monumental gateway flanked by Assyrian-inspired colossal man-headed winged bulls. Broad ceremonial stairways provided access to the royal audience hall. Reliefs still decorate the walls of the terrace and staircases. They represent processions of royal guards, Persian nobles and dignitaries, and representatives from twenty-three subject nations bringing the king tribute. Every one of the emissaries wears his national costume and carries a typical regional gift for the conqueror.

Traces of color found on similar monuments at other Persian sites suggest that the Persepolis reliefs were painted, and the original effect must have been even more striking than it is today. Still, the absence of color makes it easier to appreciate the highly refined sculptural style. The cutting of the stone is technically superb, with subtly modeled surfaces and crisply chiseled details. Although the reliefs may have been inspired by those in Assyrian palaces, they are different in style. The forms are more rounded and project more from the background. Some of the details, notably the treatment of drapery folds, echo forms characteristic of Archaic Greek sculpture, and Greek influence seems to be one of the ingredients of Achaemenid style.

The impact of Egyptian and Near Eastern art on Greek art of the previous century was so strong that art historians

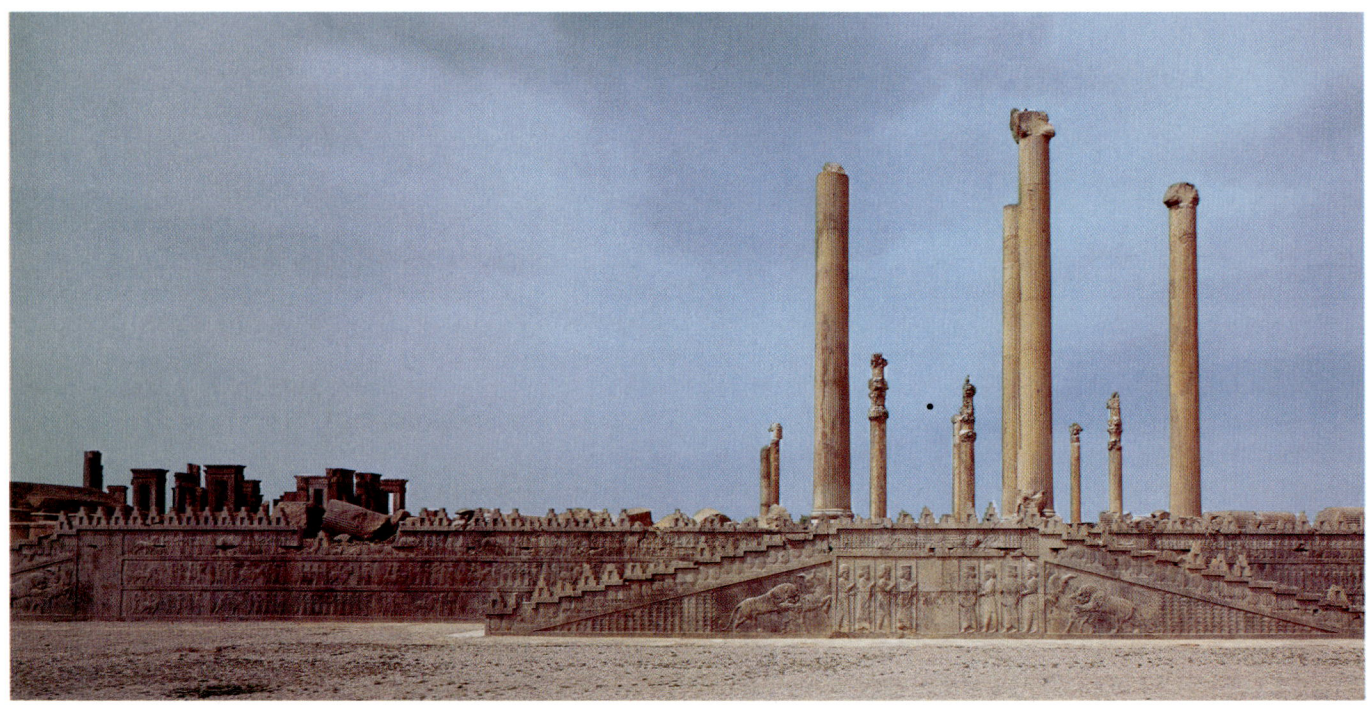

2-27   Royal audience hall *(apadana)* and stairway, palace of Darius I and Xerxes I, Persepolis, Iran, ca. 521–465 B.C.

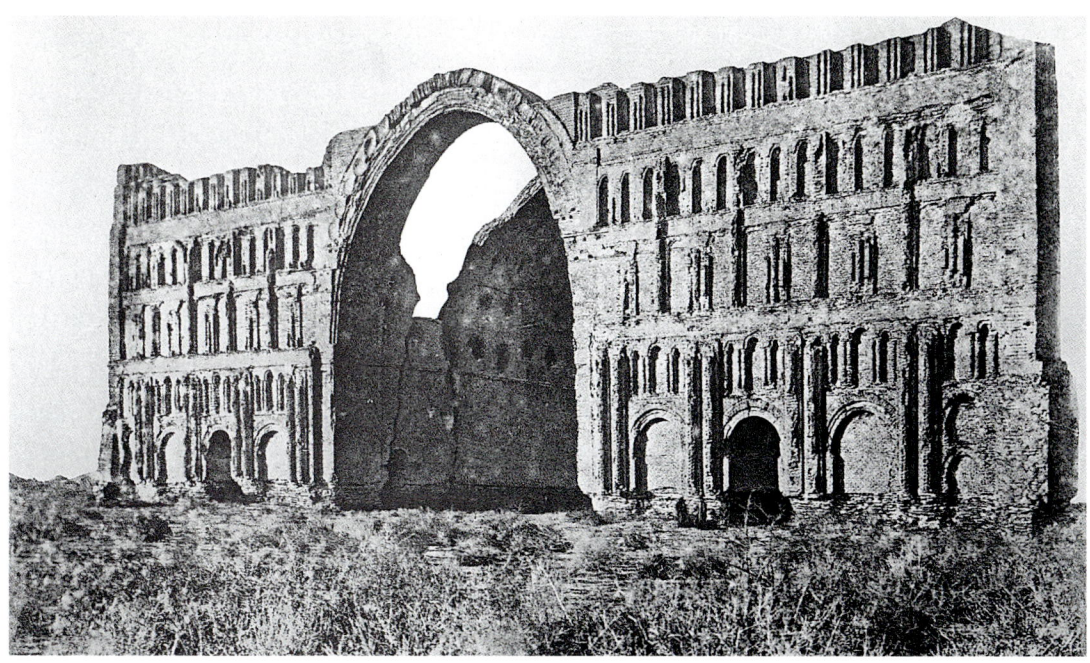

2-28   Palace of Shapur I, Ctesiphon, Iraq, ca. A.D. 250.

commonly apply the term "Orientalizing" to this period of Greek art (see Chapter 5). The detection of Greek elements in late sixth- and early fifth-century B.C. Persian art testifies to the active exchange of ideas and artists among all the Mediterranean and Near Eastern civilizations at this date. A building inscription at Susa, for example, names Ionian Greeks, Medes (who occupied the land north of Persia), Egyptians, and Babylonians among those who built and decorated the palace. Under the single-minded direction of its Persian masters, this heterogeneous workforce, with a widely varied cultural and artistic background, created a new and coherent style that perfectly suited the expression of Persian imperial ambitions.

NEAR EASTERN ART AFTER ALEXANDER

THE NEW PERSIAN EMPIRE   With the conquest of Persia by Alexander the Great in 330 B.C., ancient Near Eastern history becomes part of Greek and Roman history. In the third century A.D., however, a new power rose up in Persia to challenge the Romans and sought to force them out of Asia. The new rulers called themselves Sasanians. They traced their lineage to a legendary figure named Sasan, said to be a direct descendant of the Achaemenid kings. Their New Persian Empire was founded in A.D. 224, when the first Sasanian king, Artaxerxes I (r. 211–241), defeated the Parthians (another of Rome's eastern enemies).

A SOARING AUDIENCE HALL   The son and successor of Artaxerxes, Shapur I (r. 241–272), succeeded in further extending Sasanian territory. He also erected a great

palace at Ctesiphon, the capital his father had established near modern Baghdad in Iraq. Shapur's palace is today in a ruined state, but our photograph (FIG. 2-28), taken before an 1880 earthquake caused the collapse of the facade's right-hand portion, gives a good idea of its character. The palace's central feature was the monumental *iwan,* or brick audience hall, covered by a *barrel vault* (in effect, a deep arch over an oblong space) that came almost to a point some thirty yards above the ground. The facade to the left and right of the iwan was divided into a series of horizontal bands made up of *blind arcades,* a series of arches without actual openings, applied as wall decoration. A thousand years later, Islamic architects looked at Shapur's palace and especially its soaring iwan and established it as the standard for judging their own engineering feats (see Chapter 13).

SASANIAN SPLENDOR   A silver head (FIG. 2-29), thought by many to portray Shapur II (r. 310–379), suggests the splendor of Sasanian court life. It testifies not only to the wealth of the Sasanian dynasty but also to the superb skills of its court artists. The head is slightly under life-size. The sculptor employed the *repoussé* technique, that is, hammered the shape from a single sheet of metal and pushed the features out from behind. The artist then engraved the details into the silver surface to give form and texture to the hair and beard and to lend the eyes an almost hypnotic stare. Selected portions have mercury gilding to give the metal an even richer look and to add color to the portrait. In this work, an unknown sculptor captured the essence of imperial majesty.

A REVERSAL OF FORTUNES   So powerful was the Sasanian army that in A.D. 260 Shapur I even succeeded in capturing the Roman emperor Valerian near Edessa (in

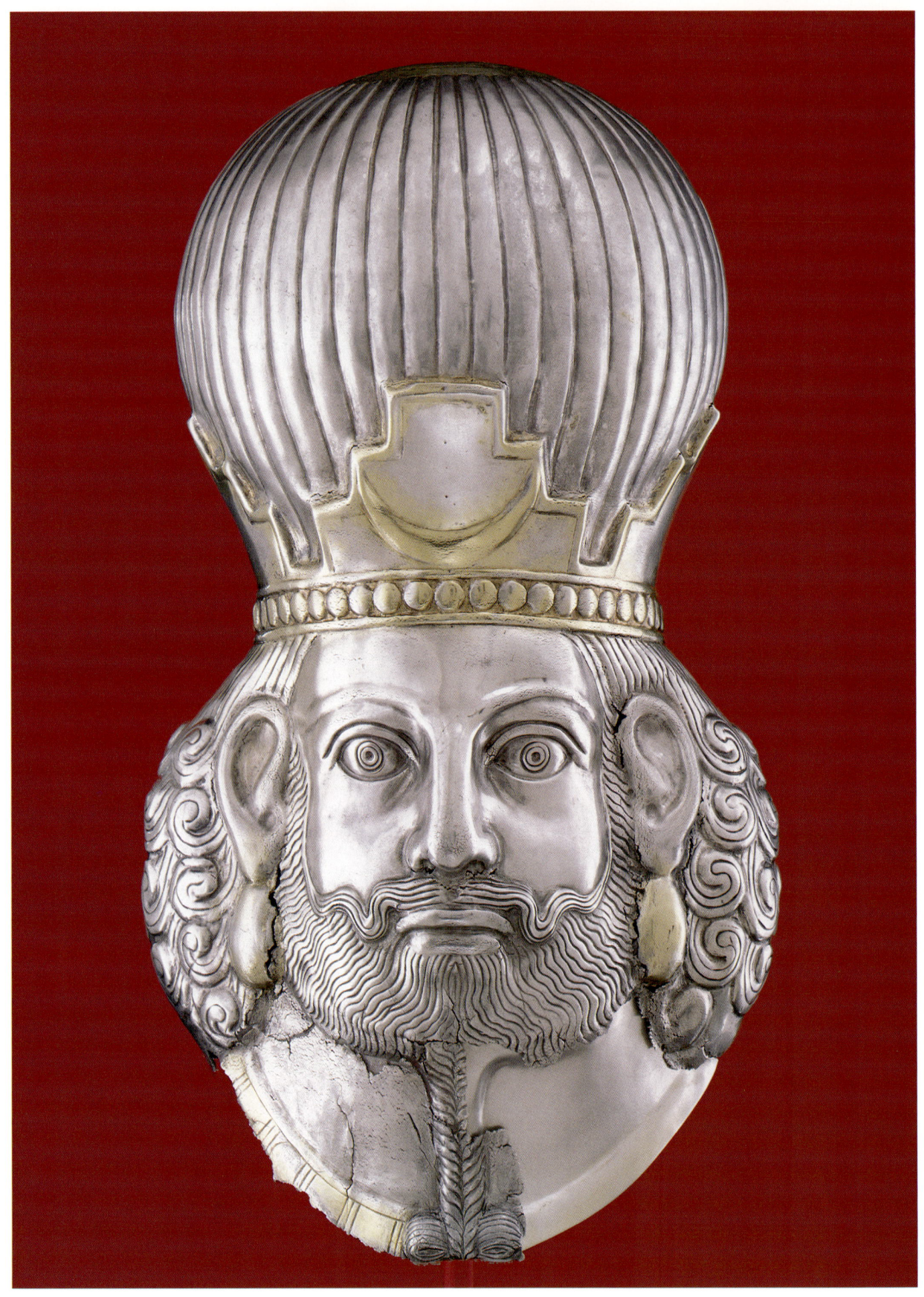

2-29 Head of a Sasanian king (Shapur II?), ca. A.D. 350. Silver with mercury gilding, 1′ 3¾″ high. Metropolitan Museum of Art, New York.

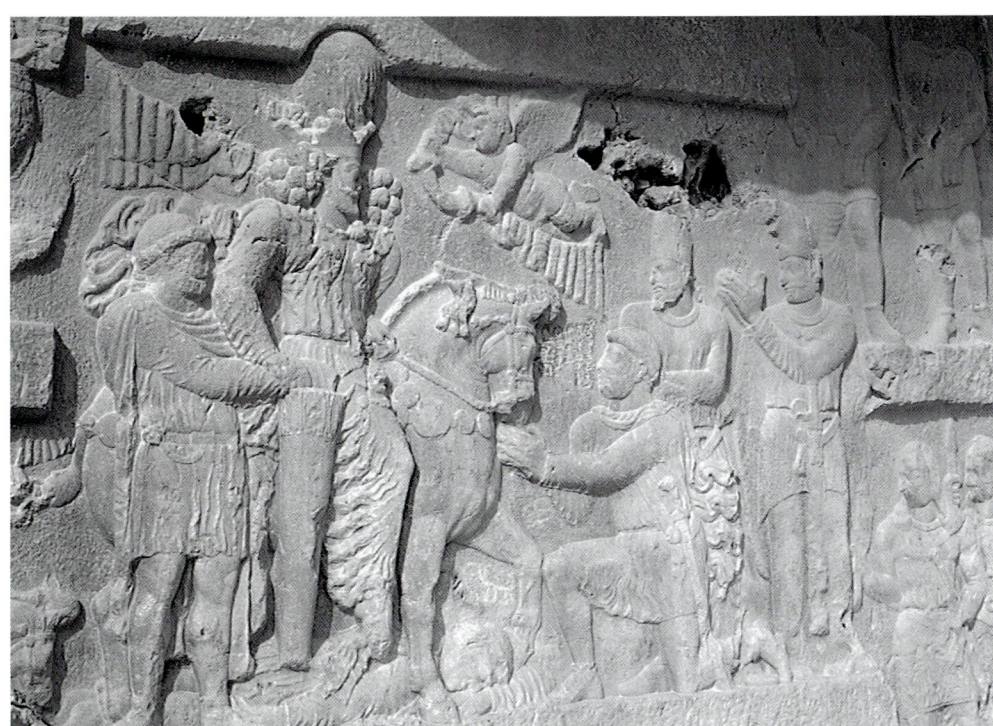

2-30 Triumph of Shapur I over Valerian, rock-cut relief, Bishapur, Iran, ca. A.D. 260.

modern Turkey). His victory over Valerian was so significant an event that Shapur commemorated it in a series of rock-cut reliefs in the cliffs of Bishapur in Iran, far from the site of his triumph. We illustrate a detail of one of the Bishapur reliefs (FIG. **2-30**). Shapur appears larger than life, riding in from the left and wearing the same distinctive tall Sasanian crown the king in the silver portrait wears. The crown breaks through the relief's border and draws the viewer's attention to the king. A Roman soldier's crumpled body lies between the legs of the Sasanian's horse—a time-honored motif (compare the *Standard of Ur,* FIG. 2-8). Here the sculptor probably meant to personify the entire Roman army. At the right, attendants lead in Valerian, who kneels before Shapur and begs for mercy. Above, a *putto*-like

(cherub or childlike) figure borrowed from the repertory of Greco-Roman art hovers above the king and brings him a victory garland. Similar scenes of kneeling enemies before triumphant generals are commonplace in Roman art—but at Bishapur the roles are reversed. This appropriation of Roman compositional patterns and motifs in a relief celebrating the Sasanian defeat of the Romans adds another, ironic, level of meaning to the political message in stone.

The New Persian Empire endured more than four hundred years, until the Arabs drove the Sasanians out of Mesopotamia in 636, just four years after the death of Muhammad, the prophet and founder of Islam. Thereafter, the greatest artists and architects of Mesopotamia worked in the service of Islam. We shall describe their achievements in Chapter 13.

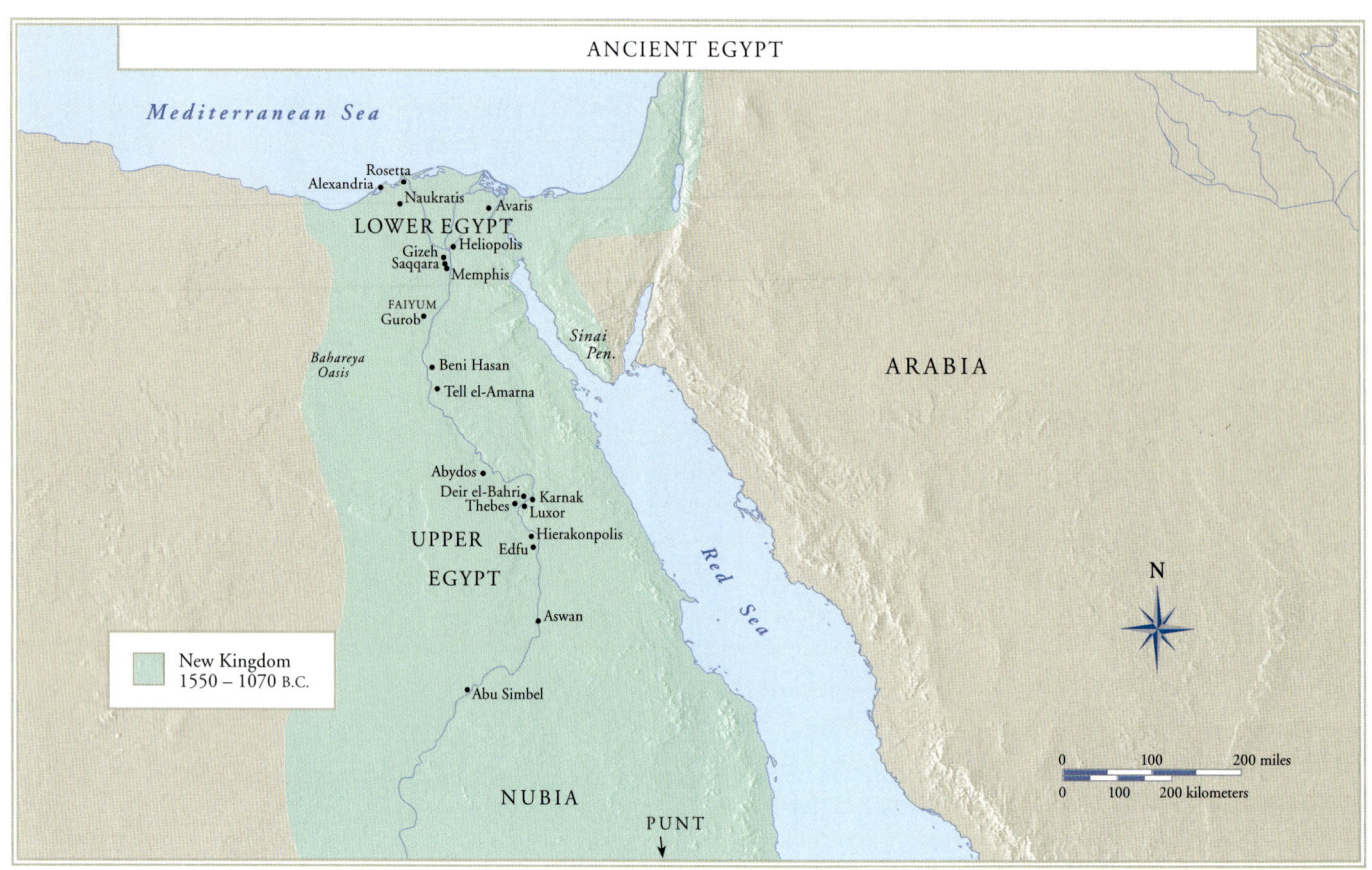

ANCIENT EGYPT

Mediterranean Sea

Rosetta
Alexandria • Naukratis
• Avaris
LOWER EGYPT
• Heliopolis
Gizeh
Saqqara • Memphis
FAIYUM
Gurob•
Bahareya Oasis
• Beni Hasan
• Tell el-Amarna
Sinai Pen.
ARABIA
Abydos •
Deir el-Bahri
Thebes • Karnak
Luxor
• Hierakonpolis
Edfu •
UPPER EGYPT
Red Sea
• Aswan
N
•Abu Simbel

New Kingdom
1550 – 1070 B.C.

NUBIA
PUNT

0   100   200 miles
0   100   200 kilometers

2920 B.C.	2575 B.C.		2134 B.C.	2040 B.C.	1640 B.C.
PREDYNASTIC	EARLY DYNASTIC (DYNASTIES I–III)	OLD KINGDOM (DYNASTIES IV–VIII)		MIDDLE KINGDOM (DYNASTIES XI–XIV)	

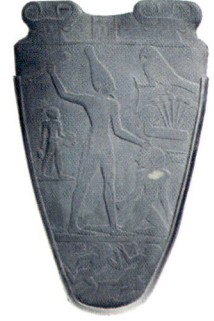

Palette of King Narmer
ca. 3000–2920 B.C.

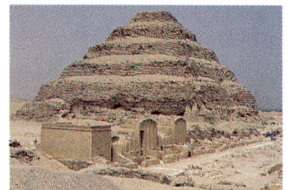

Stepped Pyramid of Djoser
Saqqara
ca. 2630–2611 B.C.

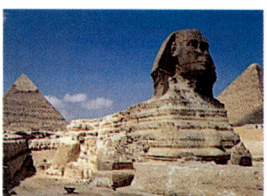

Great Sphinx and Pyramid
of Khafre, Gizeh
ca. 2520–2494 B.C.

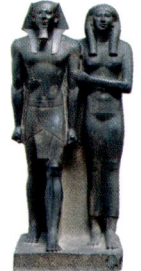

Menkaure and
Khamerernebty
ca. 2490–2472 B.C.

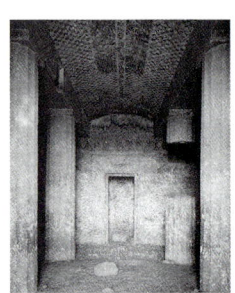

Tomb of Amenemhet
Beni Hasan
ca. 1950–1900 B.C.

Union of Upper and Lower
Egypt, ca. 3000–2920 B.C.

Imhotep, first recorded name
of an artist, ca. 2625 B.C.

Sneferu, first pharaoh of the Old
Kingdom, r. 2575–2551 B.C.

Khufu, Khafre, and Menkaure,
builders of the Great Pyramids,
ca. 2551–2472 B.C.

First Intermediate Period,
2134–2040 B.C.

Second
Intermediate
Period,
1640–1550 B.C.

Reunification of Egypt
under Mentuhotep I, 2040 B.C.

3

PHARAOHS AND THE AFTERLIFE

THE ART OF ANCIENT EGYPT

1550 B.C.		1070 B.C.	712 B.C.	332 B.C.	30 B.C.
NEW KINGDOM (DYNASTIES XVIII–XX)			LATE PERIOD (DYNASTIES XXV–XXXI)	GREEK (PTOLEMAIC)	ROMAN

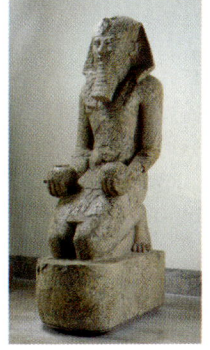

Hatshepsut with
offering jars
ca. 1473–1458 B.C.

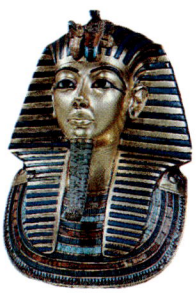

Death mask of
Tutankhamen
ca. 1323 B.C.

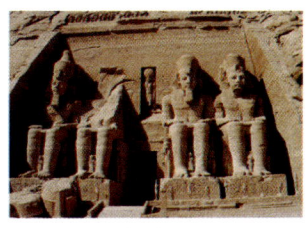

Temple of Ramses II
Abu Simbel
ca. 1290–1224 B.C.

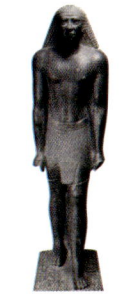

Mentuemhet
ca. 650 B.C.

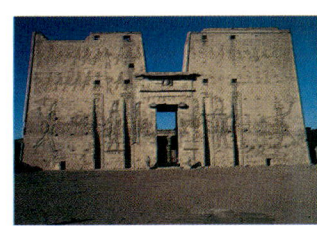

Temple of Horus
Edfu
ca. 237–47 B.C.

Ahmose I defeats the Hyksos, 1550 B.C.

Hatshepsut, r. 1473–1458 B.C.

Akhenaton and the Amarna period, 1353–1335 B.C.

Tutankhamen, r. 1333–1323 B.C.

Ramses II, r. 1290–1224 B.C.

Third Intermediate Period, 1070–712 B.C.

Persia conquers Egypt, 525 B.C.

Alexander the Great conquers Persia
and Egypt, 332 B.C.

Ptolemy I, r. 304–284 B.C.

Egypt
becomes
a Roman
province,
30 B.C.

THE LAND OF THE NILE

THE WONDERS OF EGYPT Nearly twenty-five hundred years ago, the Greek historian Herodotus wrote, "Concerning Egypt itself I shall extend my remarks to a great length, because there is no country that possesses so many wonders, nor any that has such a number of works that defy description."[1] Even today, many would agree with this assessment. The ancient Egyptians left to the world a profusion of imposing monuments dating across three millennia. From the cliffs of the Libyan and Arabian Deserts they cut giant blocks of stone, the imperishable material that symbolized the timelessness of their world. The Egyptians then erected grand stone temples to their immortal gods (see "The Gods and Goddesses of Egypt," page 45), set up countless statues of their equally immortal god-kings, and built thousands of tombs to serve as eternal houses of the dead (see "Mummification and the Afterlife," page 46). The solemn and ageless art of the Egyptians expresses the unchanging order that, for them, was divinely established.

The backbone of Egypt was, and still is, the Nile River, which supported all life in that ancient land. Even more than the Tigris and the Euphrates Rivers of Mesopotamia, the Nile, by virtue of its presence, defined the cultures that developed along its banks. Originating deep in Africa, the world's longest river descends through many waterfalls over cliffs to sea level in Egypt, where, in annual flood, it deposits rich soil brought thousands of miles from the African hills. Hemmed in by the narrow valley, which reaches a width of only about twelve miles in its widest parts, the Nile flows through regions that may not have a single drop of rainfall in a decade. Yet crops thrive from the fertilizing silt. In ancient times game also was abundant. The great river that made life possible entered the Egyptians' consciousness as a symbol of life and of the endless cycles of natural processes.

In the time of the *pharaohs,* the ancient Egyptian kings, the land of the Nile consisted of marshes dotted with island ridges. What is now arid desert valley was grassy parkland well suited for hunting and for grazing cattle. Amphibious animals swarmed in the marshes and were hunted through tall forests of papyrus and rushes (FIGS. 3-16 and 3-30). Egypt's fertility was famous. When Egypt became a province of the Roman Empire after Queen Cleopatra's death (r. 51–30 B.C.), it was the granary of the Mediterranean world.

THE BIRTH OF EGYPTOLOGY In the Middle Ages, Egypt's reputation as an ancient land of wonders and mystery lived on. Until the late eighteenth century, people regarded its undeciphered writing and exotic monuments as treasures of occult wisdom, locked away from any but those initiated in the mystic arts. Scholars knew something of Egypt's history from references in the Old Testament, from Herodotus and other Greco-Roman authors, and from preserved portions of a history of Egypt an Egyptian high priest named Manetho wrote in Greek in the third century B.C. Manetho described the succession of pharaohs, dividing them into the still-useful groups called *dynasties,* but his chronology is inaccurate, and the absolute dates of the pharaohs are still debated. The chronologies scholars have proposed for the earliest Egyptian dynasties can vary by as much as two centuries. Exact years cannot be assigned to the reigns of individual pharaohs until 664 B.C. (Dynasty XXVI).[2]

At the end of the eighteenth century, when Europeans rediscovered Egypt, the land of the Nile became the first subject of archeological exploration. In 1799, Napoleon Bonaparte, on a military expedition to Egypt, took with him a small troop of scholars, linguists, antiquarians, and artists. The chance discovery of the famed *Rosetta Stone,* now in the British Museum, gave the eager scholars a key to deciphering Egyptian *hieroglyphic* writing. The stone bears an inscription in three sections: one in Greek, which was easily read; one in *demotic* (Late Egyptian); and one in formal hieroglyphic. Scholars at once suspected that the text was the same in all three sections and that, using Greek as the key, they could decipher the other two sections. More than two decades later, after many false starts, a young linguist, Jean-François Champollion, deduced that the hieroglyphs were not simply pictographs. He proposed that they were the signs of a once-spoken language whose traces survived in Coptic, the later language of Christian Egypt. Champollion's feat established him as a giant in the new field of *Egyptology.*

THE PREDYNASTIC AND EARLY DYNASTIC PERIODS

Painting and Sculpture

THE OLDEST EGYPTIAN ART The Predynastic, or prehistoric, beginnings of Egyptian civilization are chronologically vague. But tantalizing remains from around 3500 B.C. attest to the existence of a sophisticated civilization on the banks of the Nile. A wall painting from the late Predynastic period (FIG. **3-1**), found in a tomb at Hierakonpolis, represents what seems to be, at least in part, a funerary scene with people, animals, and large boats. The stick figures and their apparently random arrangement recall the Neolithic painted hunters of Çatal Hüyük (see FIG. 1-17). The boats, symbolic of the journey down the river of life and death, are painted white. They carry cargo of uncertain significance. Also depicted are a heraldic grouping of two animals flanking a human figure (at the lower center) and a man striking three prisoners with a mace (lower left). The heraldic group, a compositional type usually associated with Mesopotamian art (see FIG. 2-10), suggests that influences from Mesopotamia not only had reached Egypt by this time but also already had made the thousand-mile journey up the Nile. The second group, however, is characteristically Egyptian, and the motif was to have a long history in Egyptian painting and sculpture alike.

THE UNIFICATION OF THE TWO EGYPTS In Predynastic times, Egypt was divided geographically and politically into Upper Egypt (the southern, upstream part of the Nile Valley), which was dry, rocky, and culturally rustic, and Lower (northern) Egypt, which was opulent, urban, and populous. The ancient Egyptians began the history of their kingdom with the unification of the two lands. Until recently, this was thought to have occurred during the rule of the First Dynasty pharaoh Menes, identified by many scholars with King Narmer. Narmer's image and name appear on both sides of a ceremonial *palette* (stone slab with a circular depression) found at Hierakonpolis. The palette is one of

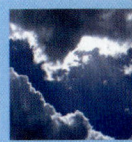

The Gods and Goddesses of Egypt

The Egyptian worldview was distinct from that of their neighbors in the ancient Mediterranean and Near Eastern worlds. Egyptians believed that before the beginning of time the primeval waters, called *Nun,* existed alone in the darkness. At the moment of creation, a mound rose out of the limitless waters—just as muddy mounds emerge from the Nile after the annual flood recedes. On this mound the creator god appeared and brought light to the world. In later times, the mound was formalized as a pyramidal stone called the *ben-ben* supporting the supreme god, the sun god, variously worshiped under the name of *Re, Amen,* or *Aton.*

The supreme god also created the first of the other gods and goddesses of Egypt. According to one version of the myth, the creator masturbated and produced *Shu* and *Tefnut,* the primary male and female forces in the universe. They coupled to give birth to *Geb* (Earth) and *Nut* (Sky), who bore Osiris, Seth, Isis, and Nephthys. The eldest, *Osiris* (FIG. 3-39), was the god of order and was revered as the king who brought civilization to Egypt. His brother *Seth* was his evil opposite, the god of chaos. Seth murdered Osiris and cut him into pieces, which he scattered across Egypt. *Isis* (FIG. 3-39), the sister and consort of Osiris, succeeded in collecting Osiris's body parts and with her powerful magic brought him back to life. *Nephthys* (FIG. 3-39), Seth's wife, helped her. With Isis,

the resurrected Osiris fathered a son, *Horus,* who avenged his father's death and displaced Seth as king of Egypt. Osiris then became the lord of the underworld. Horus is represented in art either as a falcon, considered the noblest bird of the sky, or as a falcon-headed man (FIGS. 3-2, 3-12, 3-28, and 3-39). All Egyptian pharaohs were identified with Horus while alive and with Osiris after they died.

Other Egyptian deities included *Mut,* the consort of the sun god Amen, and *Khonsu,* the moon god, who was their son. *Thoth,* another lunar deity and the god of knowledge and writing, appears in art as an ibis, a baboon, or an ibis-headed man crowned with the crescent moon and the moon disk (FIG. 3-39). When Seth tore out Horus's falcon-eye (*wedjat*), Thoth restored it. He, too, was associated with rebirth and the afterlife. *Hathor,* the daughter of Re, was a divine mother of the pharaoh, nourishing him with her milk. She appears in Egyptian art as a cow-headed woman or as a woman with a cow's horns (FIGS. 3-2 and 3-28). *Anubis,* a jackal or jackal-headed deity, was the god of mummification and the weigher of hearts in the underworld (FIG. 3-39). *Maat,* daughter of Re, was the goddess of truth and justice. Her feather was used to measure the weight of the deceased's heart to determine if the *ka* (life force) would be blessed in the afterlife.

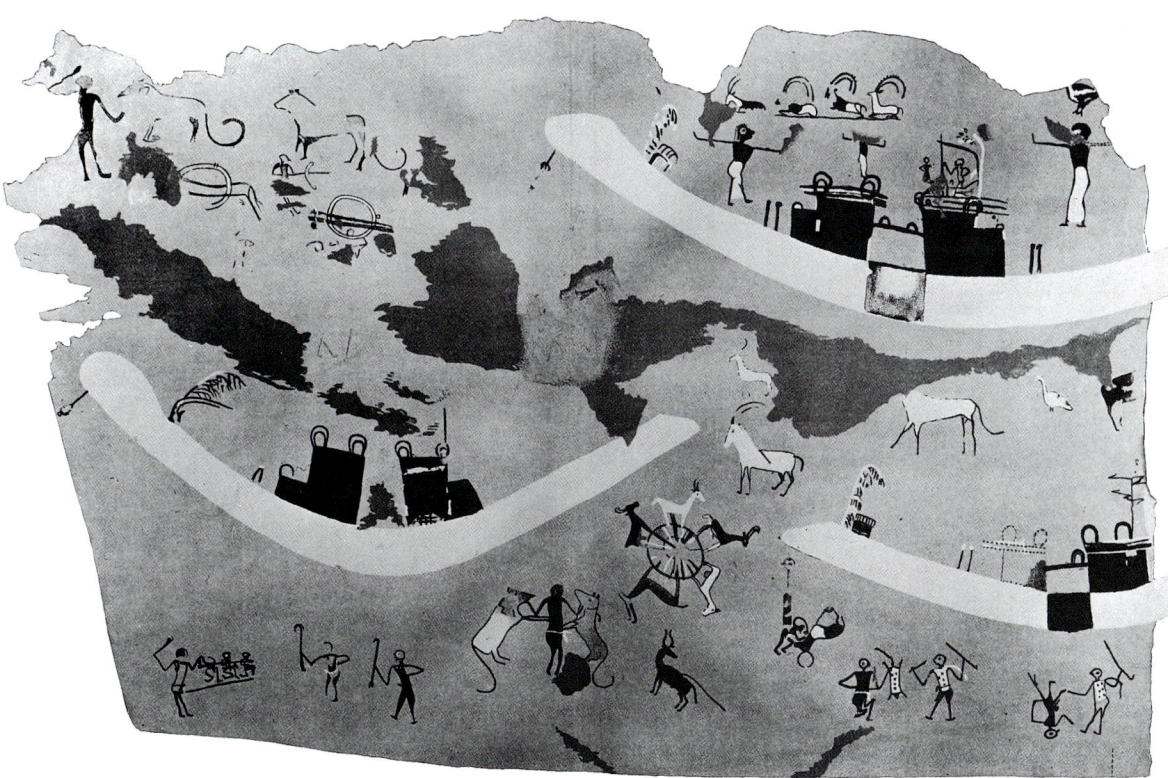

3-1 People, boats, and animals, detail of a watercolor copy of a wall painting from Tomb 100 at Hierakonpolis, Egypt, Predynastic, ca. 3500–3200 B.C. Egyptian Museum, Cairo.

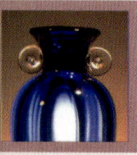

Mummification and the Afterlife

The Egyptians did not make the sharp distinction between body and soul that is basic to many religions. Rather, they believed that, from birth, a person was accompanied by a kind of other self, the *ka* or life force, which, on the death of the fleshly body, could inhabit the corpse and live on. For the ka to live securely, however, the dead body had to remain as nearly intact as possible. To insure that it did, the Egyptians developed the technique of embalming *(mummification)* to a high art. Their success is evident in numerous well-preserved mummies of kings, princes, and others of noble birth, as well as those of some common persons. The practice endured for thousands of years. In 1996, for example, archeologists discovered an unplundered Roman-period cemetery at Bahareya Oasis containing hundreds of mummies. Systematic excavation began in 1999 and will probably continue for a decade, so rich was the find.

The embalming process was said to have been invented by the god Anubis to preserve the body of the murdered Osiris (see "The Gods and Goddesses of Egypt," page 45). Embalming was first practiced systematically during the Fourth Dynasty, and the process generally lasted seventy days. The first step was the surgical removal of the lungs, liver, stomach, and intestines through an incision in the left flank. The Egyptians believed these organs were most subject to decay. The organs were individually wrapped and placed in four containers known as *Canopic jars* for eventual deposit in the burial chamber with the corpse. (The jars take their name from the mythical Canopus, a Greek sailor who died and was subsequently worshiped in Egypt in the form of a jar.) The brain was extracted through the nostrils and discarded. The Egyptians did not attach any special significance to the brain. But they left in place the heart, necessary for life and regarded as the seat of intelligence.

Next, the body was treated for forty days with natron, a naturally occurring salt compound that dehydrated the body.

Then the corpse was filled with resin-soaked linens, and the embalming incision was closed and covered with a representation of the wedjat eye of Horus, a powerful *amulet* (a device to ward off evil and promote rebirth). Finally, the body was treated with lotions and resins and then wrapped tightly with hundreds of yards of linen bandages to maintain its shape. The Egyptians often placed other amulets within the bandages or on the corpse. The most important were heart *scarabs* (gems in the shape of beetles). Spells written on them assured that the heart would be returned to its owner if it was ever lost. A scroll copy of the *Book of the Dead* (FIG. 3-39) frequently was placed between the legs of the deceased. It contained some two hundred spells intended to protect the mummy and the ka in the afterlife. The mummies of the wealthy had their faces covered with funerary masks (FIG. 3-37). When Egypt became part of the Roman Empire, painted portraits were often substituted (see FIG. 10-63).

Preserving the deceased's body by mummification was only the first requirement for immortality. Food and drink also had to be provided, as did clothing, utensils, and furniture. Nothing that had been enjoyed on earth was to be lacking. Statuettes called *ushabtis* (answerers) also were placed in the tomb. These figurines performed any labor required of the deceased in the afterlife, answering whenever his or her name was called.

Images of the deceased, sculpted in the round and placed in shallow recesses, also were set up in the tomb. They were meant to guarantee the permanence of the person's identity by providing substitute dwelling places for the ka in case the mummy disintegrated. Wall paintings and reliefs recorded, with great animation and detail, the recurring round of human activities. The Egyptians hoped and expected that the images and inventory of life, collected and set up within the tomb's protective stone walls, would insure immortality.

---

the earliest *historical* (versus prehistorical) artworks preserved (FIG. **3-2**). Although it is no longer regarded as commemorating the foundation of the first of Egypt's thirty-one dynasties around 2920 B.C. (the last ended in 332 B.C.), it does record the unification of Upper and Lower Egypt into the "Kingdom of the Two Lands" at the very end of the Predynastic period.

The *Palette of King Narmer* is an elaborate, formalized version of a utilitarian object commonly used in the Predynastic period. Egyptians prepared eye makeup on such tablets for protecting their eyes against irritation and the sun's glare. The *Palette* is important not only as a document marking the transition from the prehistorical to the historical period in ancient Egypt but also as a kind of early blueprint of the formula for

figure representation that characterized Egyptian art for three thousand years.

On the back of the palette, the king, wearing the high, white, bowling-pin-shaped crown of Upper Egypt and accompanied by an official who carries his sandals, is shown slaying an enemy. The motif closely resembles the group at the lower left of the Hierakonpolis mural (FIG. 3-1) and became the standard pictorial formula signifying the inevitable triumph of the Egyptian god-kings. A falcon with human arms at the top right of Narmer's palette is the symbol of Horus, the king's protector. It faces Narmer and takes captive a man-headed hieroglyph with a papyrus plant growing from it that stands for the land of Lower Egypt. Below the king are two fallen enemies. Two heads of Hathor, a goddess favorably disposed to

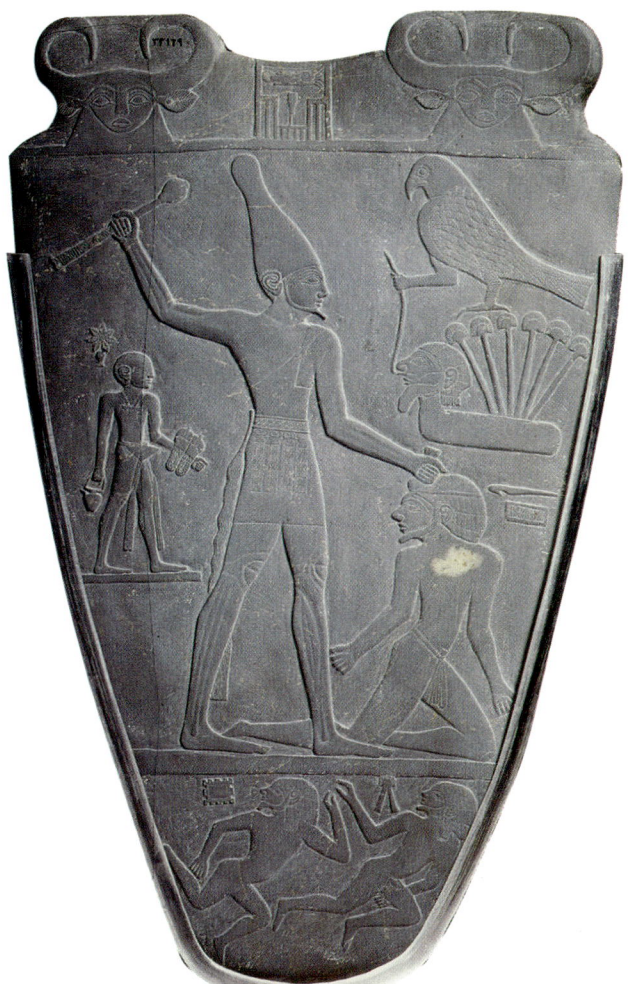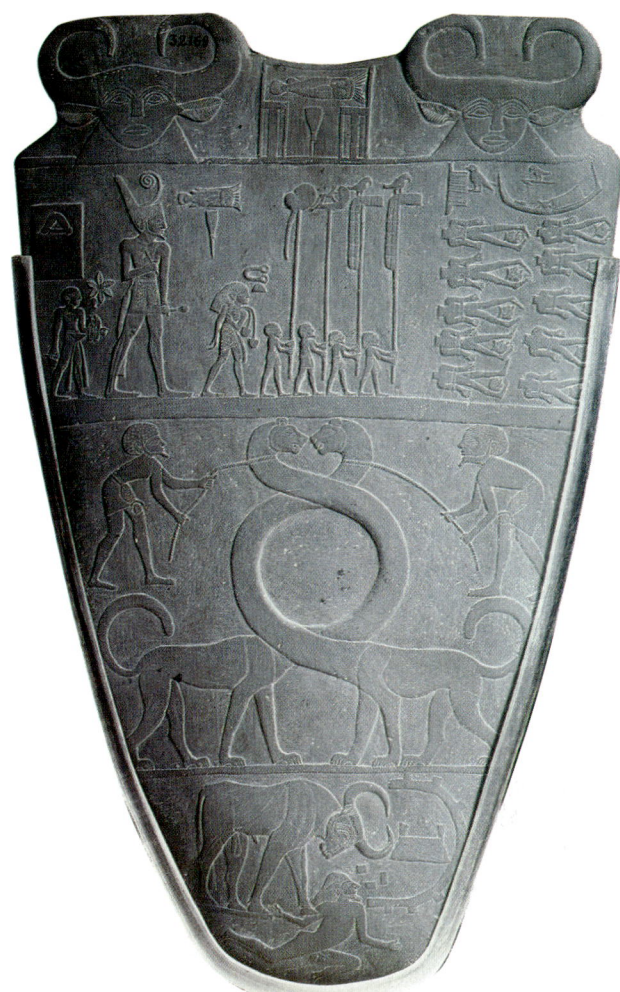

3-2   *Palette of King Narmer* (*left,* back; *right,* front), from Hierakonpolis, Egypt, Predynastic, ca. 3000–2920 B.C. Slate, approx. 2′ 1″ high. Egyptian Museum, Cairo.

Narmer and shown as a cow with a woman's face, are at the top of the palette. Between the Hathor heads is the hieroglyph giving Narmer's name within a frame representing the royal palace, making Narmer's palette the earliest existing labeled work of historical art.

THE PORTRAYAL OF DIVINE KINGS   On the front of the palette, the elongated necks of two felines form the circular depression that would have held eye makeup in an ordinary palette not made for display. The intertwined necks of the animals may be another pictorial reference to Egypt's unification. In the uppermost register, Narmer, wearing the red cobra crown of Lower Egypt, reviews the beheaded bodies of the enemy. The dead are seen from above, like the bison lying on the ground on the Altamira cave's ceiling (see FIG. 1-9). The artist depicted each body with its severed head neatly placed between its legs. By virtue of his superior rank, the king, on both sides of the palette, performs his ritual task alone and towers over his own men and the enemy. The king's superhuman strength is symbolized in the lowest band by a great bull knocking down a rebellious city whose fortress walls also are seen in an "aerial view." Specific historical narrative is not the artist's goal in this work. What is im-

portant is the characterization of the king as a deified figure, isolated from and larger than all ordinary men and solely responsible for the triumph over the enemy. Here, at the very beginning of Egyptian history, is evidence of the Egyptian convention of thought, of art, and of state policy that established kings as divine and proclaimed that their prestige was one with the prestige of the gods.

The figure of Narmer on both sides reveals the stereotype of kingly transcendence that, with several slight variations, was repeated, with few exceptions, in subsequent representations of all Egyptian rulers. The artist's portrayal of the king combined profile views of his head, legs, and arms with front views of his eye and torso. As noted in Chapters 1 and 2, this composite view of the human figure also characterized Mesopotamian art and even some Stone Age paintings. Although the human figure's proportions changed, the method of its representation became a standard for all later Egyptian art. The *Palette of King Narmer* established the basic laws that governed art along the Nile for thousands of years. In the Hierakonpolis painting (FIG. 3-1), the artist scattered the figures across the wall more or less haphazardly. On Narmer's palette, the sculptor subdivided the surface into bands and inserted the pictorial elements into their organized setting in a neat and orderly way. The horizontal lines separating the registers also define the ground supporting the figures, a mode of representation that persisted in hundreds of acres of Egyptian wall paintings and reliefs. This was also the preferred mode for narrative art in the ancient Near East (see Chapter 2).

Architecture

ART AND THE AFTERLIFE　Narmer's palette is exceptional among surviving Egyptian artworks because it is commemorative rather than funerary in nature. Far more typical is the Predynastic mural from Hierakonpolis (FIG. 3-1), the earliest known representative of a long tradition of building and decorating the tombs of pharaohs and other important members of Egyptian society. In fact, Egyptian tombs provide the principal, if not the exclusive, evidence for the historical reconstruction of Egyptian civilization. Herodotus described the Egyptians as "religious to excess," and their concern for immortality amounted to near obsession. The overall preoccupation in this life was to insure safety and happiness in the next life. The majority of monuments the Egyptians left behind were dedicated to this preoccupation (see "Mummification and the Afterlife," page 46).

The standard tomb type in early Egypt was the *mastaba* (FIG. **3-3**). The mastaba (Arabic for "bench") was a rectangular brick or stone structure with sloping sides erected over an underground tomb chamber. A shaft connected the burial chamber with the outside, providing the ka with access to the tomb. The form probably was developed from earth or stone mounds that had covered even earlier tombs.

Although mastabas originally housed single burials, as in our example (FIG. 3-3), during the latter part of the Old Kingdom they were used for multiple family burials and became increasingly complex. The central underground chamber was surrounded by storage rooms and compartments whose number and size increased with time until the area covered far surpassed that of the tomb chamber. Built into the superstructure, or sometimes attached to the outside of its eastern face, was the funerary chapel, which contained a statue of the deceased in a small concealed chamber called the *serdab*. The chapel's interior walls and the ancillary rooms were decorated with colored relief carvings and paintings of scenes from daily life intended to magically provide the deceased with food and entertainment.

THE FIRST PYRAMID　One of the most renowned figures in Egyptian history is IMHOTEP, the royal builder for King Djoser (r. 2630–2611 B.C.) of the Third Dynasty. Imhotep was a man of legendary powers who served as the pharaoh's chancellor and high priest of the sun god Re, as well as architect. He is the first known artist of recorded history. After his death, Imhotep was revered as a god. Imhotep designed the Stepped Pyramid (FIG. **3-4**) of Djoser at Saqqara, the ancient *necropolis* (Greek for "city of the dead") for Memphis, the capital city Menes founded. Built before 2600 B.C., the pyramid is one of the oldest stone structures in Egypt and the first monumental royal tomb.

Begun as a large mastaba with each of its faces oriented toward one of the cardinal points of the compass, Djoser's tomb was enlarged at least twice before taking on its final shape.

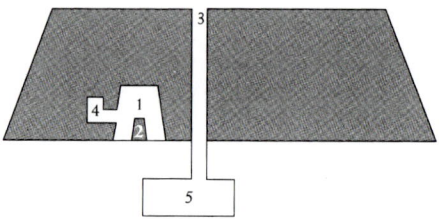

1. Chapel
2. False door
3. Shaft into burial chamber
4. Serdab (chamber for statue of deceased)
5. Burial chamber

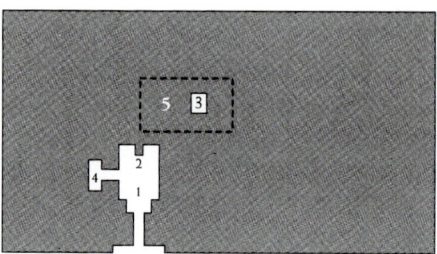

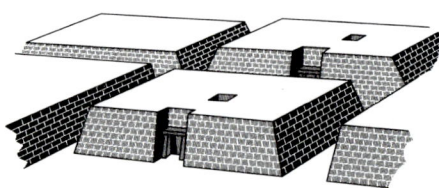

3-3　Section *(top)*, plan *(middle)*, and restored view *(bottom)* of typical Egyptian mastaba tombs.

About two hundred feet high, the Stepped Pyramid seems to be composed of a series of mastabas of diminishing size, stacked one on top of another to form a structure that resembles the great ziggurats of Mesopotamia (see FIG. 2-14). Unlike the ziggurats, however, the pyramid Imhotep designed for Djoser is a tomb, not a temple platform, and its dual function was to protect the mummified king and his possessions and to symbolize, by its gigantic presence, his absolute and godlike power. Beneath the pyramid is a network of underground galleries resembling a palace. It was to be Djoser's new home in the afterlife.

Befitting the god-king's majesty, Djoser's pyramid stands near the center of an immense (thirty-seven-acre) rectangular enclosure surrounded by a monumental (thirty-four-foot-high and five thousand four hundred-foot-long) wall of white limestone (FIG. **3-5**). The huge precinct with its protective walls and tightly regulated access stands in sharp contrast to the roughly contemporary Sumerian Royal Cemetery at Ur, where no barriers kept people away from the burial area. Nor did the Mesopotamian cemetery have a temple for the worship of the deified dead. At Saqqara, a funerary temple stands against the northern face of Djoser's pyramid (no. 2 on the plan). Priests performed daily rituals at the temple in celebration of the divine pharaoh.

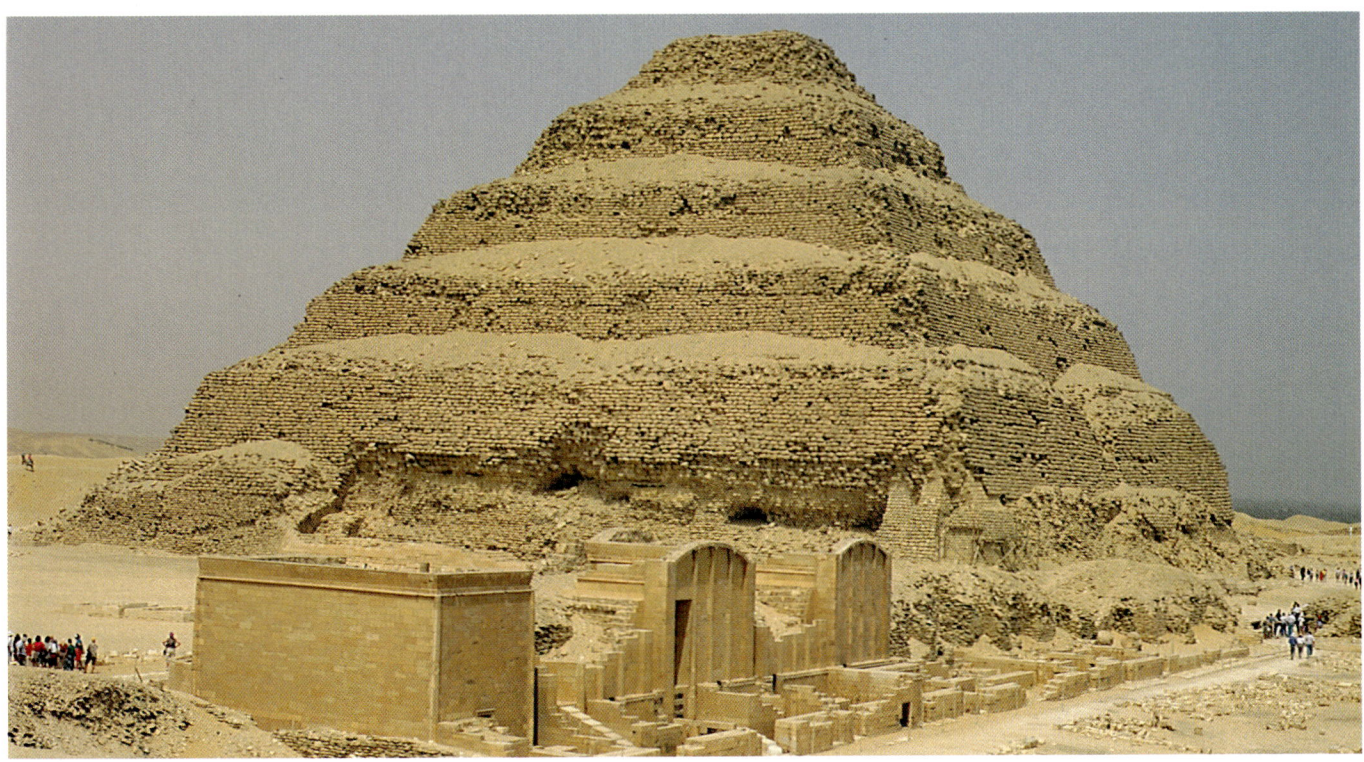

3-4 IMHOTEP, Stepped Pyramid and mortuary precinct of Djoser, Saqqara, Egypt, Dynasty III, ca. 2630–2611 B.C.

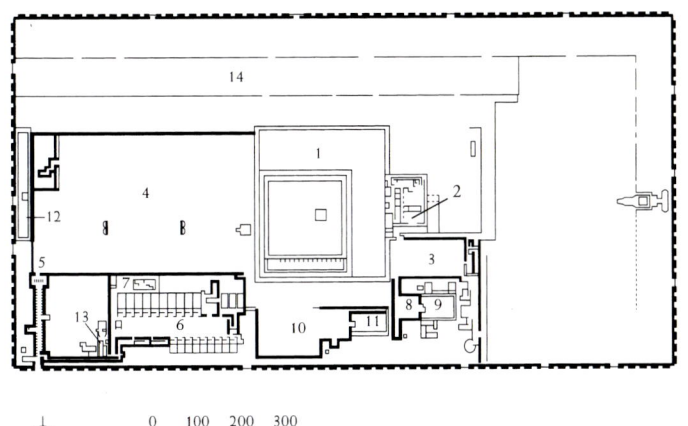

1. Stepped pyramid derived from square-plan mastaba
2. Funerary temple of Djoser
3. Court with serdab
4. Large court with altar and two B-shaped stones
5. Entrance portico
6. Heb-Sed court flanked by sham chapels
7. Small temple
8. Court before North Palace
9. North Palace
10. Court before South Palace
11. South Palace
12. South tomb
13. Royal Pavilion
14. Magazines

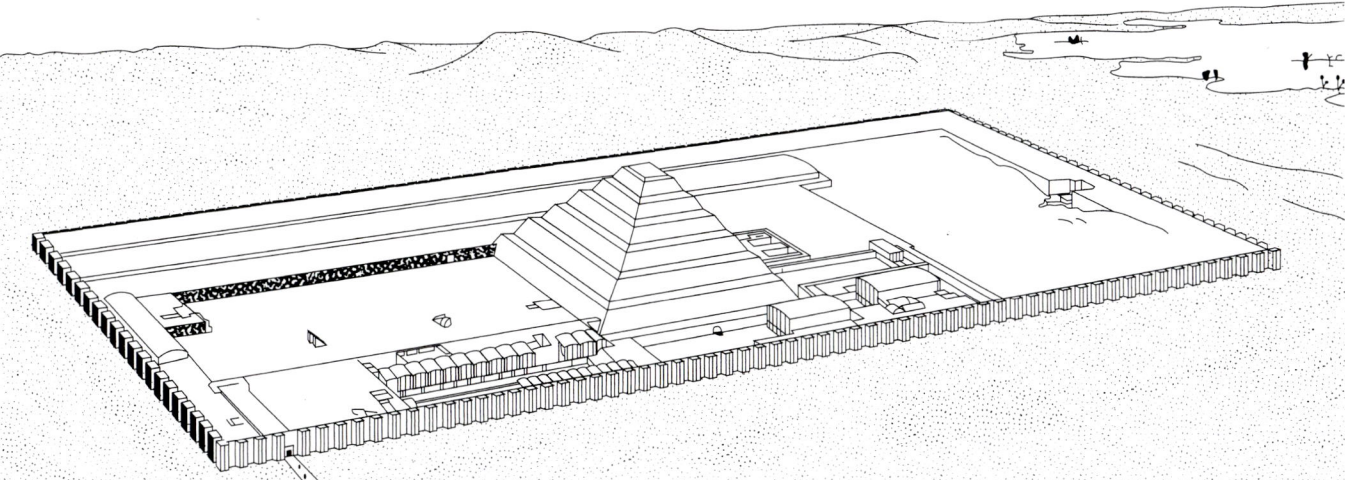

3-5 IMHOTEP, restored plan *(top)* and view *(bottom)* of the mortuary precinct of Djoser, Saqqara, Egypt, Dynasty III, ca. 2630–2611 B.C.

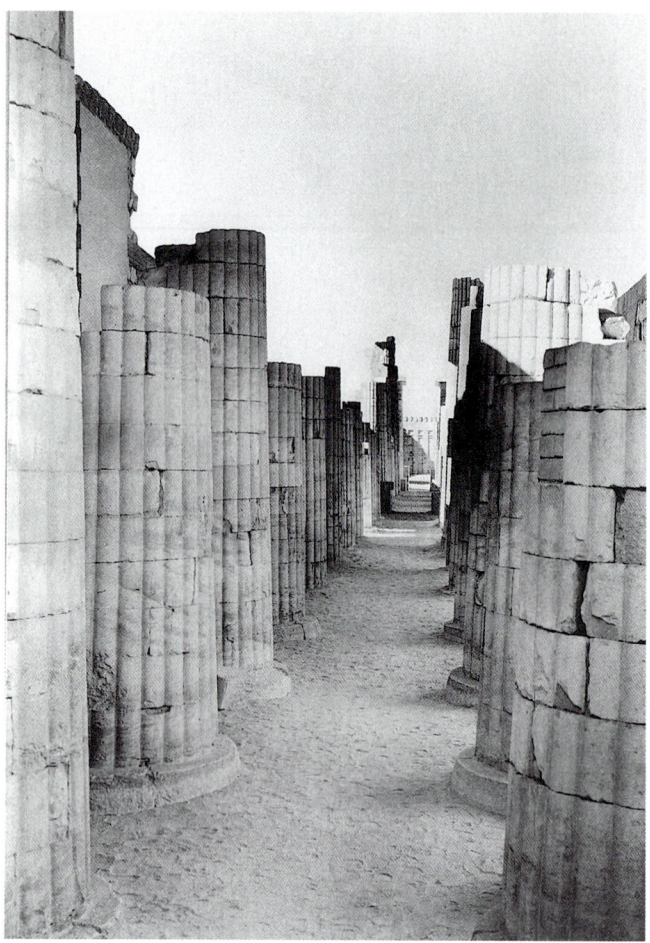

3-6   Imhotep, columnar entrance corridor to the mortuary precinct of Djoser, Saqqara, Egypt, Dynasty III, ca. 2630–2611 B.C.

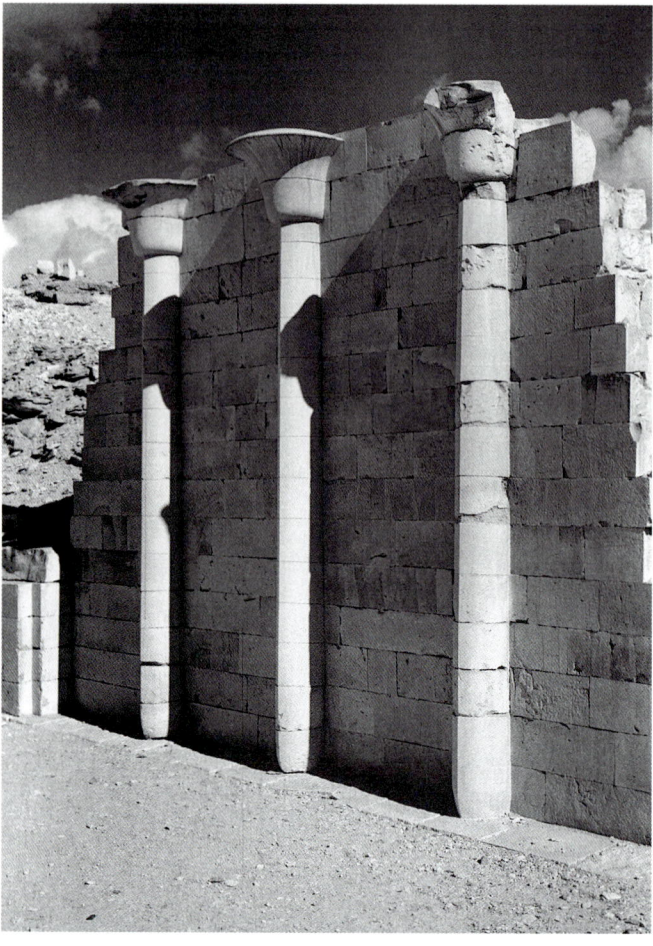

3-7   Imhotep, facade of the North Palace of the mortuary precinct of Djoser, Saqqara, Egypt, Dynasty III, ca. 2630–2611 B.C.

Djoser's funerary temple was but one of many buildings arranged around several courts. Most of the others were dummy structures with stone walls enclosing fills of rubble, sand, or gravel (no. 6 on the plan). The buildings imitated in stone masonry various types of temporary structures made of plant stems and mats erected in Upper and Lower Egypt to celebrate the Jubilee Festival. This event perpetually reaffirmed the royal existence in the hereafter.

The translation into stone of structural forms previously made out of plants may be seen in the long entrance corridor to Djoser's funerary precinct (FIG. **3-6**). There, columns that resemble bundles of reeds project from short spur walls on either side of the once-roofed and dark passageway. A person walking through it would have emerged suddenly into a large courtyard and the brilliant light of the Egyptian sun. To the right, the visitor would have seen the gleaming focus of the entire complex, Djoser's pyramid.

The columns flanking the pathway into Djoser's precinct resemble later Greek columns. Architectural historians have little doubt today that the buildings of ancient Egypt had a profound impact on the designers of the first Greek stone columnar temples (see Chapter 5). The upper parts of the Saqqara entrance portico columns are not preserved, but

those of Djoser's North Palace (FIG. **3-7**; no. 9 in FIG. 3-5) still stand. They end in *capitals* ("heads") that take the form of the papyrus blossoms of Lower Egypt. The column shafts resemble papyrus stalks. The later Greek columns also terminate in capitals, although the Greek capitals take a very different form. Greek column shafts are also generally freestanding, but all the columns in the Saqqara complex are *engaged* (attached) to walls. The Egyptian builders seemed not to have realized the full structural potential of stone columns. Still, this is the first appearance of stone columns in the history of architecture. Imhotep's greatest achievement as an architect was to translate the impermanent building types of prehistoric Egypt into lasting stone.

THE OLD KINGDOM

The Old Kingdom is the first of the three great periods of Egyptian history, called the Old, Middle, and New Kingdoms, respectively. Many Egyptologists now begin the Old Kingdom with the first pharaoh of the Fourth Dynasty, Sneferu (r. 2575–2551 B.C.), although the traditional division of Kingdoms places Djoser and the Third Dynasty in the Old Kingdom. It ended with the demise of the Eighth Dynasty around 2134 B.C. During the Old Kingdom, Egyptian sculptors, painters, and architects codified the modes of representation and methods of construction that would become the rule in the land of the Nile for more than two thousand years.

Architecture

THE GREAT PYRAMIDS AND THE SUN GOD RE

The Egyptians always buried their dead on the west side of the Nile, where the sun sets. At Gizeh, near modern Cairo but on the west side of the river, stand the three pyramids (FIG. **3-8**) of the Fourth Dynasty pharaohs Khufu (r. 2551–2528 B.C.), Khafre (r. 2520–2494 B.C.), and Menkaure (r. 2490–2472 B.C.). Built in the course of about seventy-five years, the Great Pyramids of Gizeh are the oldest of the Seven Wonders of the ancient world (see "Babylon: City of Wonders," Chapter 2, page 37).

The Gizeh pyramids represent the culmination of an architectural evolution that began with the mastaba. The pyramid form did not evolve out of necessity. Kings could have gone on indefinitely stacking mastabas to make their weighty tombs. Rather, scholars have suggested that the kings of the Third Dynasty came under the influence of Heliopolis, a city not far from their royal residence at Memphis. Heliopolis was the seat of the powerful cult of Re, the sun god, whose emblem was a pyramidal stone, the *ben-ben* (see "The Gods and Goddesses of Egypt," page 45). By the Fourth Dynasty, the pharaohs considered themselves the sons of Re and his incarnation on earth. For the pharaohs, it would have been only a small step from their belief that the spirit and power of Re resided in the pyramidal *ben-ben* to the belief that their divine spirits and bodies would be similarly preserved within pyramidal tombs.

Is the pyramid form, then, an invention inspired by a religious demand, rather than the result of a formal evolution? Although interesting, this question is beyond the scope of this book. Of more concern are the remarkable features of the Great Pyramids. Of the three Fourth Dynasty pyramids at

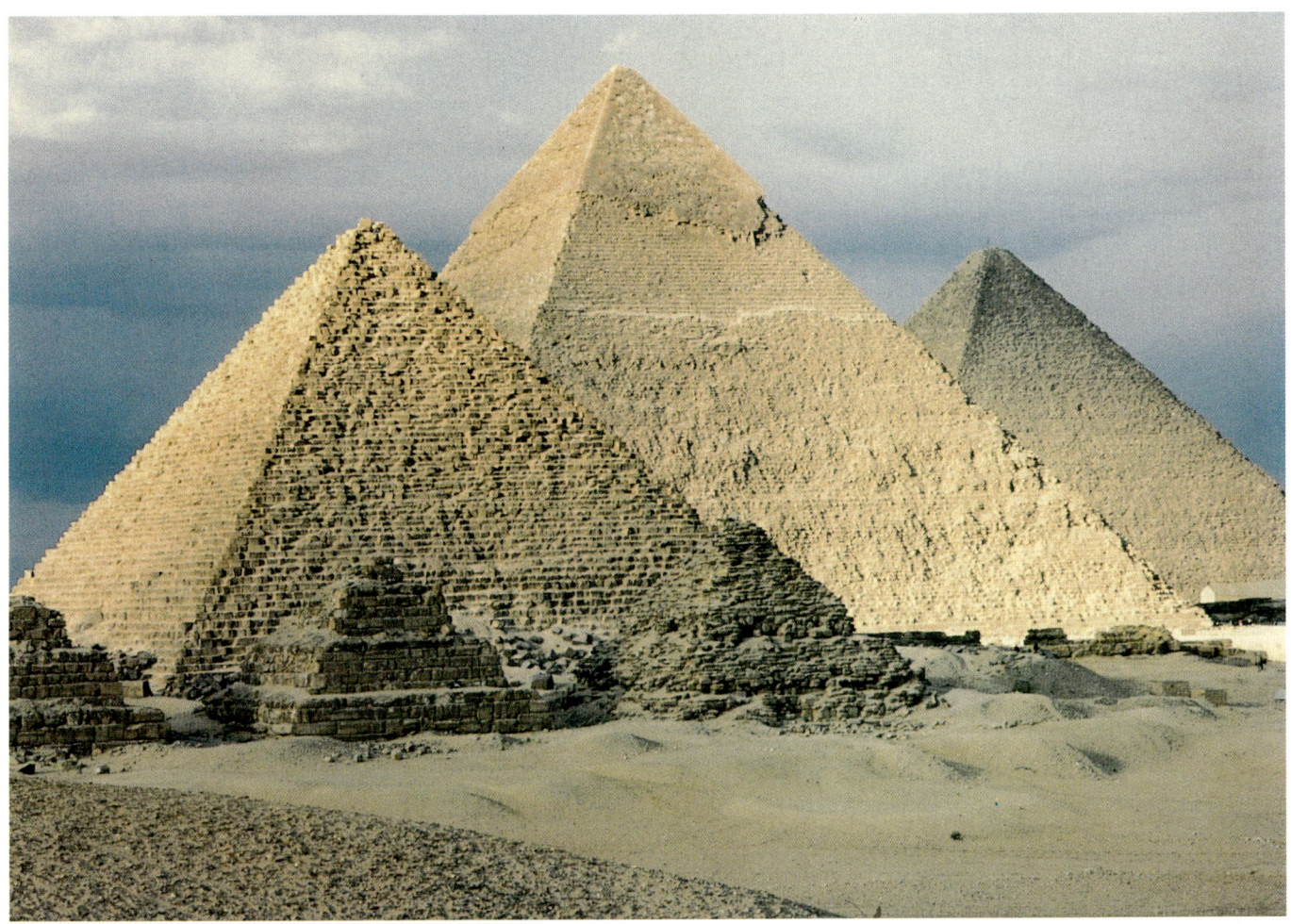

3-8 Great Pyramids, Gizeh, Egypt, Dynasty IV. *From left:* Pyramids of Menkaure, ca. 2490–2472 B.C.; Khafre, ca. 2520–2494 B.C.; and Khufu, ca. 2551–2528 B.C.

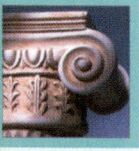

ARCHITECTURAL BASICS

Building the Great Pyramids

The three Great Pyramids of Khufu, Khafre, and Menkaure at Gizeh (FIG. 3-8) are the oldest of the Seven Wonders of the ancient world (see "Babylon: City of Wonders," Chapter 2, page 37). The prerequisites for membership in this elite club were colossal size and enormous cost, and the Gizeh pyramids testify to the wealth and pretensions of the Fourth Dynasty pharaohs. But they also attest to Egyptian builders' mastery of stone masonry and to their ability to mobilize, direct, house, and feed a huge workforce engaged in one of the most labor-intensive enterprises ever undertaken.

Like all building projects of this type, the process of erecting the pyramids began with the quarrying of stone, in this case the limestone of the eastern Nile cliffs. Teams of skilled workers had to cut into the cliff faces and remove large blocks of roughly equal size using stone or copper chisels and wooden mallets and wedges. Often, the artisans had to cut deep tunnels into the mountainsides to find high-quality stone free of cracks and other flaws. To remove a block, the workers cut channels on all sides and partly underneath. Then they pried the stones free from the bedrock with wooden levers.

After workers liberated the stones from the cliffs, the rough blocks had to be transported to the building site and *dressed* (shaped to the exact dimensions required, with smooth faces for a perfect fit). Small blocks could be carried on a man's shoulders or on the back of a donkey, but the massive blocks used to construct the Great Pyramids were moved using wooden rollers and sleds. They then were loaded onto boats and floated across the Nile during the seasonal floods. Once

across, the blocks had to be dragged further overland to the tomb site. The artisans dressed the blocks by chiseling and pounding the surfaces and, in the last stage, by rubbing and grinding the surfaces with fine polishing stones. This kind of construction, where carefully cut and regularly shaped blocks of stone are piled in successive rows, or *courses,* is called *ashlar masonry.*

To set the ashlar blocks in place, workers erected great rubble ramps against the core of the pyramid. Their size and slope were adjusted as work progressed and the tomb grew in height. Scholars still debate whether the Egyptians used simple linear ramps inclined at a right angle to one face of the pyramid or zigzag or spiral ramps akin to staircases. Linear ramps would have had the advantage of simplicity and would have left three sides of the pyramid unobstructed. But zigzag ramps placed against one side of the structure or spiral ramps winding around the pyramid would have greatly reduced the slope of the incline and would have made the dragging of the blocks easier. Some scholars have also suggested a combination of straight and spiral ramps. Ropes, pulleys, and levers were used both to lift and to lower the stones, guiding each block into its designated place. Finally, the pyramid was surfaced with a casing of pearly white limestone, cut so precisely that the eye could scarcely detect the joints. A few casing stones still can be seen in the cap that covers the Pyramid of Khafre (FIGS. 3-8, center, and 3-11). They are all that remain after many centuries of people stripping the pyramids to supply limestone for the Islamic builders of Cairo.

Gizeh, that of the pharoah Khufu (FIG. **3-9**) is the oldest and largest. Except for the galleries and burial chamber, it is an almost solid mass of limestone masonry (see "Building the Great Pyramids," above)—a stone mountain built on the same principle as the Stepped Pyramid of King Djoser (FIG. 3-4). In our section drawing of Khufu's tomb, the dotted lines at the base of the structure (no. 2 in FIG. 3-9) indicate the path ancient grave robbers cut into the pyramid. Unable to locate the carefully sealed and hidden entrance, they started some forty feet above the base and tunneled into the structure until they intercepted the ascending corridor. Many royal tombs were plundered almost as soon as the funeral ceremonies had ended. The very conspicuousness of a pyramid was an invitation to looting. The successors of the Old Kingdom pyramid builders had learned this hard lesson. They built few pyramids, and those were relatively small and inconspicuous.

The immensity of the Gizeh pyramids and that of Khufu in particular is indicated by some dimensions. At the base, the length of one side of Khufu's tomb is approximately 775 feet, and its area is some thirteen acres. Its present height is about

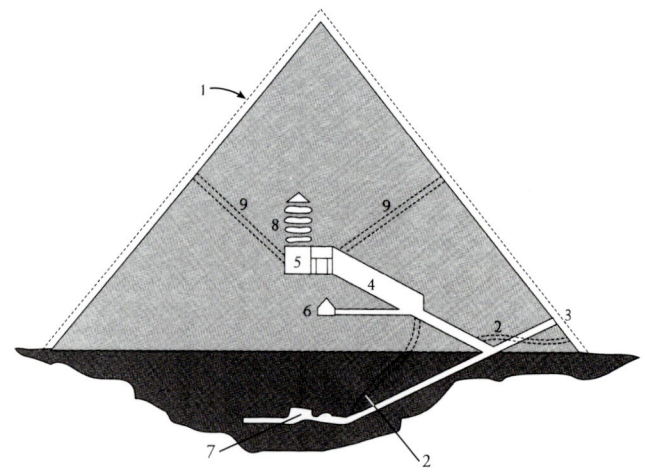

1. Silhouette with original facing stone
2. Thieves' tunnels
3. Entrance
4. Grand gallery
5. King's chamber
6. So-called queen's chamber
7. False tomb chamber
8. Relieving blocks
9. Airshafts(?)

3-9 Section of the Pyramid of Khufu, Gizeh, Egypt.

four hundred and fifty feet (originally four hundred and eighty feet). The structure contains roughly 2.3 million blocks of stone, each weighing an average of two and one-half tons. Napoleon's scholars calculated that the blocks in the three Great Pyramids were sufficient to build a wall one foot wide and ten feet high around France.

The art of the pyramids is inherent not only in their huge size and successful engineering but also in their formal design. Their proportions and immense dignity are consistent with their funerary and religious functions and well adapted to their geographic setting. As with Djoser's Stepped Pyramid, the four sides of each of the Great Pyramids are oriented to the cardinal points of the compass. The simple mass of these monuments dominates the flat landscape to the horizon. But the funerary temples associated with the three Gizeh pyramids are not placed on the north side, facing the stars of the northern sky, as was Djoser's temple. The temples sit on the east side, facing the rising sun and underscoring their connection with Re.

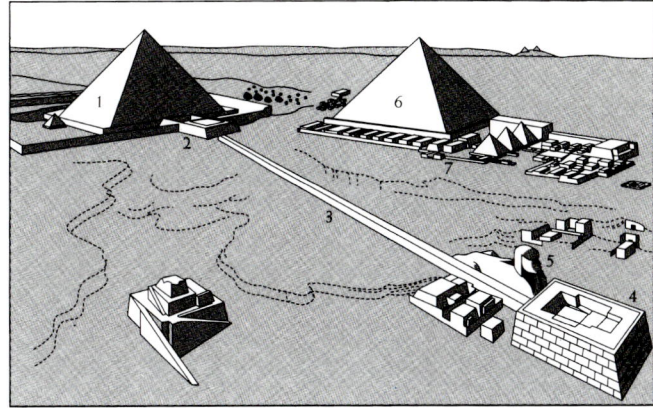

1. Pyramid of Khafre
2. Mortuary temple
3. Covered causeway
4. Valley temple
5. Great Sphinx
6. Pyramid of Khufu
7. Pyramids of the royal family and mastabas of nobles

3-10   Reconstruction drawing of the Dynasty IV Pyramids of Khafre, ca. 2520–2494 B.C., and Khufu, ca. 2551–2528 B.C., Gizeh, Egypt.

KHAFRE'S TEMPLE AND GUARDIAN SPHINX
From the remains surrounding the Pyramid of Khafre at Gizeh, archeologists have been able to reconstruct an entire funerary complex (FIG. **3-10**). The complex included the pyramid itself with the pharaoh's burial chamber; the *mortuary temple* (temple for the worship of the dead), adjoining the pyramid on the east side, where offerings were made, cere-monies performed, and cloth, food, and ceremonial vessels stored; the covered *causeway* (raised path) leading down to the valley; and the *valley temple* (vestibule), of the causeway.

Beside the causeway and dominating the temple of Khafre rises the Great Sphinx (FIG. **3-11**). Carved from a spur of

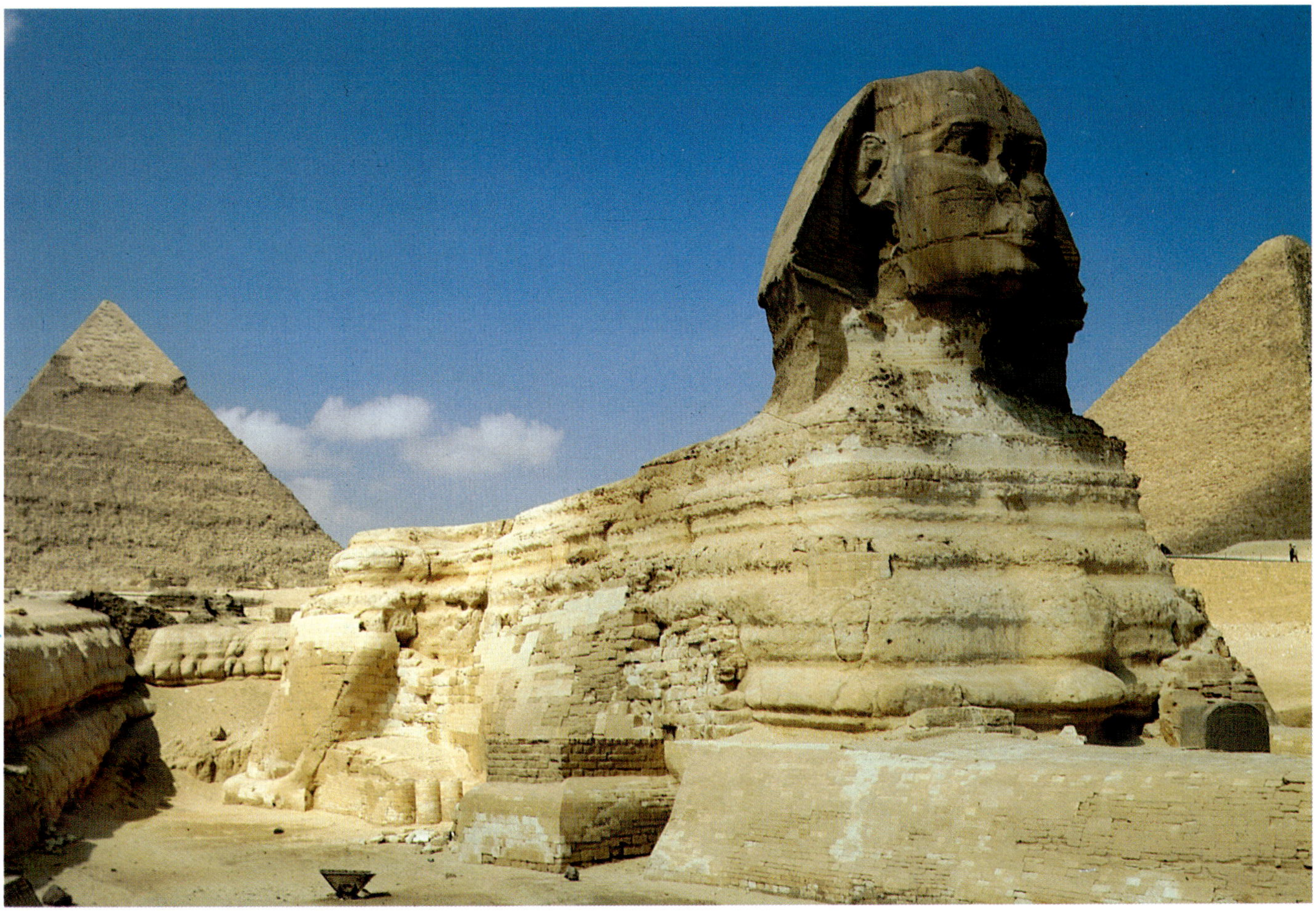

3-11   Great Sphinx (with Pyramid of Khafre in the background at left), Gizeh, Egypt, Dynasty IV, ca. 2520–2494 B.C. Sandstone, approx. 65′ high, 240′ long.

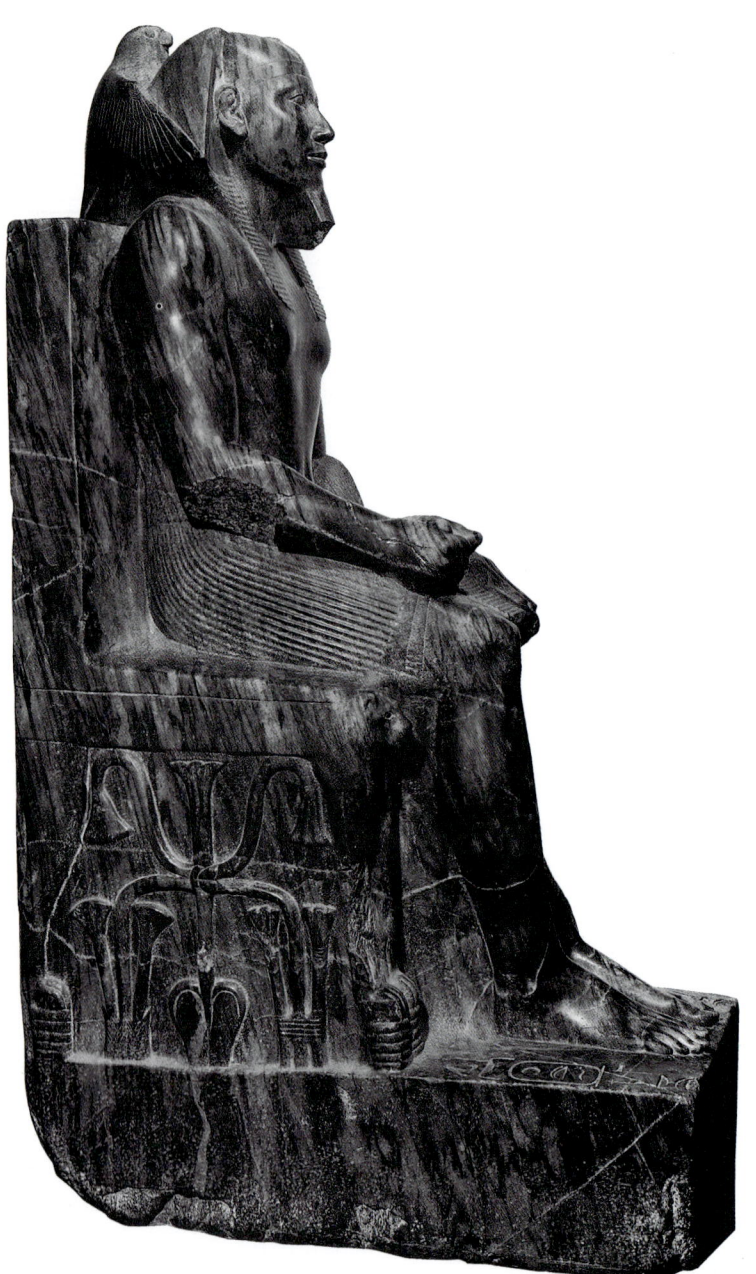
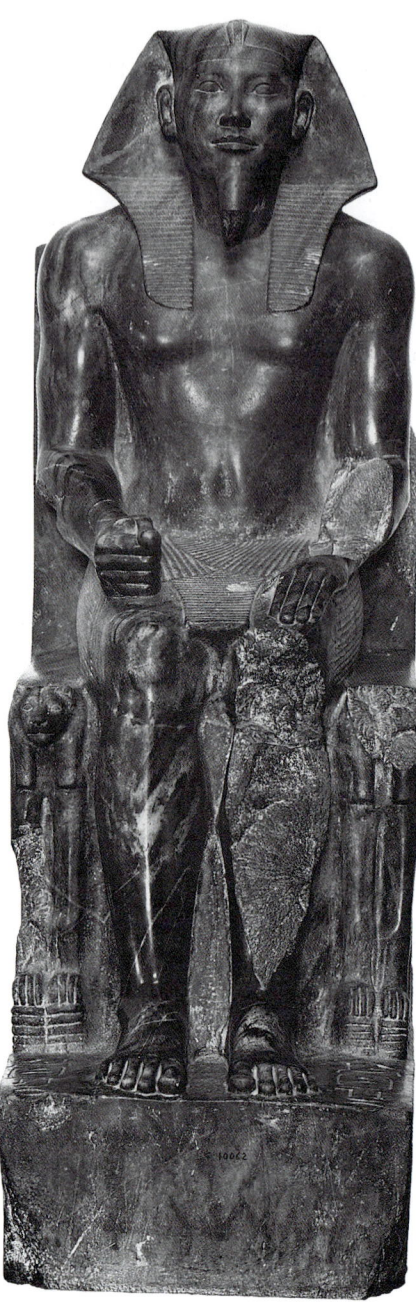

3-12   Khafre (right side and front), from Gizeh, Egypt, Dynasty IV, ca. 2520–2494 B.C. Diorite, approx. 5′ 6″ high. Egyptian Museum, Cairo.

rock, it commemorated the pharaoh and served as an immovable, eternal silent guardian of his tomb. Its role was like that of the later Near Eastern lions and lamassu (see FIGS. 2-18 and 2-21) that stood watch at the entrances to the palaces of their kings. At Gizeh, the rock was cut so that the immense figure of the Sphinx (a *sphinx* is a lion with a human head), adjacent to the valley temple's west front, gives visitors coming from the east the illusion that it rests on a great pedestal. The colossal statue is probably an image of Khafre. It imbues the god-king with the awesome strength and authority of the king of beasts.

Sculpture

STATUES TO SERVE FOR ETERNITY   As already noted, in Egyptian tombs statues fulfilled an important function. Sculptors created images of the deceased to serve as

abodes for the ka should the mummies be destroyed. For this reason, an interest in portrait sculpture developed early in Egypt. Thus, too, permanence of style and material was essential. Although sculptors used wood, clay, and other materials, mostly for images of those not of the royal or noble classes, their primary material was stone.

The seated statue of Khafre (FIG. **3-12**) is one of a series of similar statues carved for the pharaoh's valley temple near the Great Sphinx (FIG. 3-10, no. 4). The stone is diorite, an exceptionally hard dark stone brought seven hundred miles down the Nile from royal quarries in the south. (The Neo-Sumerian ruler Gudea [see FIG. 2-15] so admired diorite that he imported it to faraway Girsu.) Khafre's statues are the only organic forms in his temple. They contrast with the structure's geometrically severe flat-planed red granite posts and lintels devoid of decoration. The king wears a simple kilt and sits rigidly upright on a throne formed of two stylized lions' bodies. Intertwined lotus and papyrus plants—symbol of the united Egypt—are carved between the throne's legs. The falcon-god Horus extends his protective wings to shelter Khafre's head, indicating the pharaoh's divine status. Khafre has the royal fake beard fastened to his chin and wears the royal linen *nemes* headdress with the *uraeus* cobra of kingship on the front. The headdress covers his forehead and falls in pleated folds over his shoulders. (The head of the Great Sphinx is similarly attired but does not have the ceremonial beard.) As befitting a divinity, Khafre is shown with a well-developed, flawless body and a perfect face. The Egyptians considered ideal proportions appropriate for representing imposing majesty, and artists used them quite independently of reality. This generalized anatomy persisted in Egyptian statuary even into the period following Alexander the Great's conquest of Egypt, regardless of the actual age and physique of the pharaoh portrayed.

The seated king is permeated with serenity, reflecting the enduring power of the pharaoh and of kingship in general. The sculptor created this effect, common to Egyptian royal statues, in part by giving the figure great compactness and solidity, with few projecting, breakable parts. The form manifests the purpose: to last for eternity. Khafre's body is attached to the unarticulated slab that forms the back of the king's throne. His arms are held close to the torso and thighs, and his legs are close together and connected to the chair by the stone the artist chose not to remove. The pose is frontal, rigid, and *bilaterally symmetrical* (the same on either side of an axis, in this case the vertical axis). The sculptor suppressed all movement and with it the notion of time.

This repeatable scheme arranges the bodily parts so that they are presented in a totally frontal projection or entirely in profile. The sculptor produced the statue by first drawing the front, back, and two profile views of the pharaoh on the four vertical faces of the stone block. Next, apprentices chiseled away the excess stone on each side, working inward until the planes met at right angles. Finally, the master sculpted the parts of Khafre's body, the falcon, and so forth. The finishing was done by *abrasion* (rubbing or grinding the surface). This *subtractive* method of creating the pharaoh's portrait accounts in large part for the blocklike look of the standard Egyptian statue. Nevertheless, many sculptors, both ancient and modern, have transformed stone blocks into dynamic, twisting human forms (compare FIG. 5-85). Khafre's eternal stillness is a deliberate aesthetic choice.

AN EMOTIONLESS ROYAL EMBRACE The seated statue is one of only a small number of basic formulaic types the sculptors of the Old Kingdom employed to represent the human figure. Another is the image of a person or deity standing, either alone or in groups. Superb examples of the standing type are the joined portrait statues of Menkaure and his queen, Khamerernebty (FIG. 3-13), which once stood in the valley temple of Menkaure's pyramid complex at Gizeh. Here, too, the statues remain wedded to the stone block from which they were carved, and the sculptor used conventional postures to suggest the timeless nature of these eternal substitute homes for the ka. Menkaure's pose, which is duplicated in countless other Egyptian statues, is rigidly frontal with the

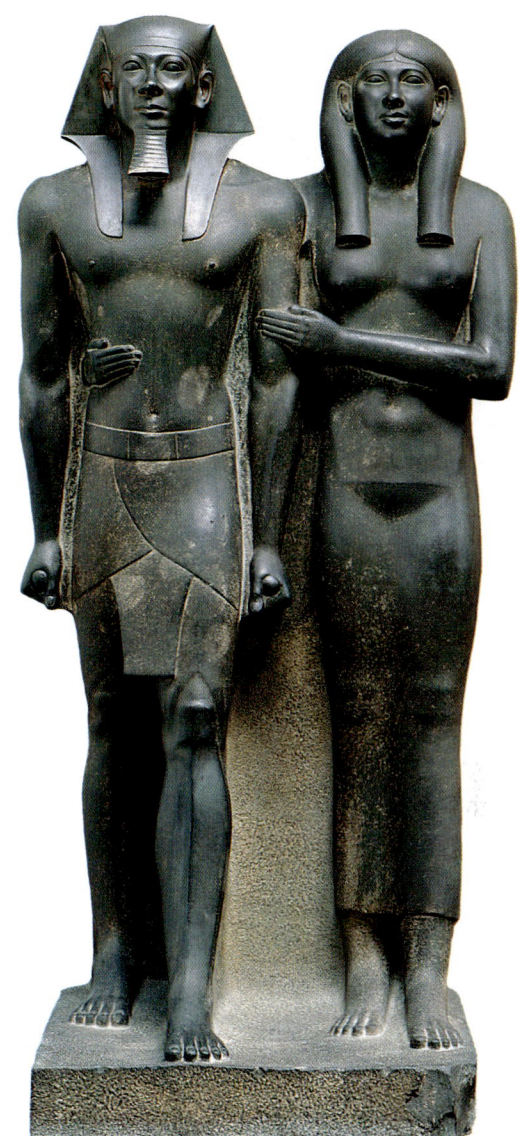

3-13 Menkaure and Khamerernebty, from Gizeh, Egypt, Dynasty IV, ca. 2490–2472 B.C. Slate, approx. 4' 6½" high. Museum of Fine Arts, Boston.

arms hanging straight down and close to his well-built body. His hands are clenched into fists with the thumbs forward. His left leg is slightly advanced, but no shift occurs in the angle of the hips to correspond to the uneven distribution of weight. Khamerernebty stands in a similar position. Her right arm, however, circles around her husband's waist, and her left hand gently rests on his left arm. This frozen stereotypical gesture indicates their marital status. The husband and wife show no other sign of affection or emotion and look not at each other but out into space.

PAINTED STATUES AND EGYPTIAN REALISM The timeless quality of the portraits of Khafre, Menkaure, and Khamerernebty is enhanced by the absence of any color but that of the dark natural stone selected for the statues. Many other Egyptian portrait statues, however, were painted, including the striking image of a Fifth Dynasty seated scribe

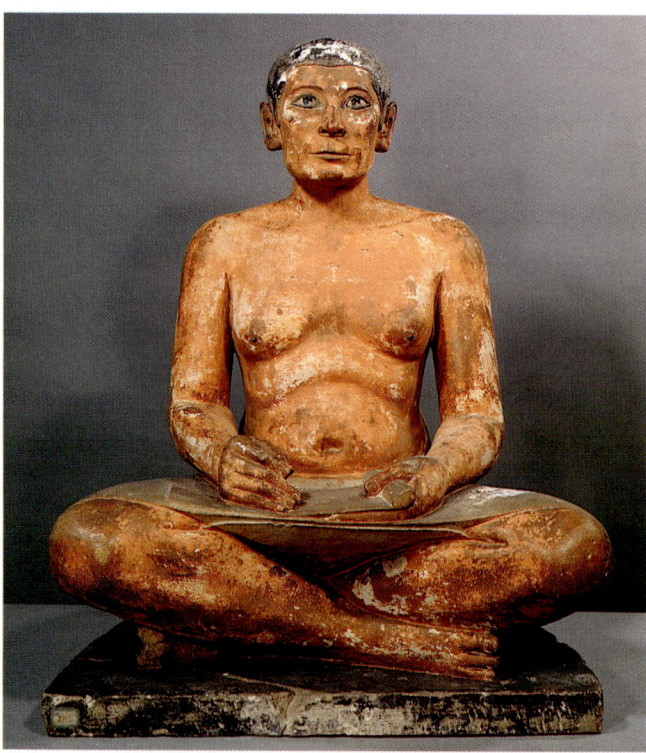

3-14   Seated scribe (Kay?), from his mastaba at Saqqara, Egypt, Dynasty V, ca. 2450–2350 B.C. Painted limestone, approx. 1′ 9″ high. Louvre, Paris.

sometimes identified as Kay (FIG. **3-14**). Despite the stiff upright posture and the frontality of head and body, the color lends a lifelike quality to the statue. But one might argue that this is detrimental to the portrait's success, inasmuch as the color detracts from the statue's role as a timeless image of the deceased placed in his mastaba.

The head displays an extraordinary sensitivity. The sculptor conveyed the personality of a sharply intelligent and alert individual with a penetration and sympathy seldom achieved at such an early date. The scribe sits directly on the ground, not on a throne nor even on a chair. Although he occupied a position of honor in a largely illiterate society, the scribe is a much lower figure in the Egyptian hierarchy than the pharaoh, whose divinity makes him superhuman. In the history of art, especially portraiture, it is almost a rule that as a human subject's importance decreases, formality is relaxed and realism is increased. It is telling that the scribe is shown with sagging chest muscles and a protruding belly. Such signs of age would have been disrespectful and wholly inappropriate in a "portrait" of an Egyptian god-king. The royal statues are never accurate likenesses but are idealized images that proclaim the godlike nature of the divine kings and queens. Their purpose was not to record individual facial features or even the true shapes of bodies. But the scribe's statue is also not a true portrait. Rather, it is a composite of conventional types. In fact, the face's sunken cheeks are difficult to reconcile with the flabby body. Nonetheless, these realistic touches were unthinkable in a pharaonic statue.

A PORTRAIT IN WOOD AND ROCK CRYSTAL   A second portrait illustrating this rule of relaxed formality and increased realism is the Fifth Dynasty wooden statue of an official named Ka-Aper (FIG. **3-15**). Like the statue of the seated scribe, Ka-Aper's portrait comes from the deceased's

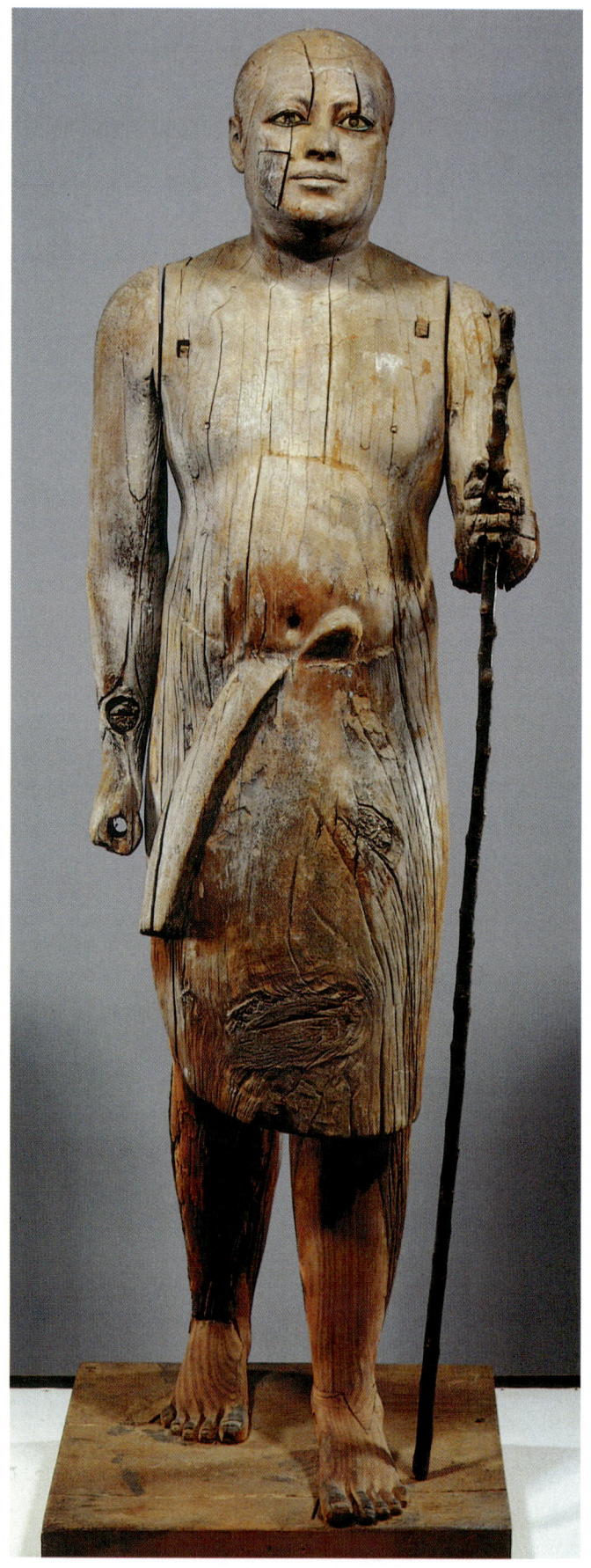

3-15   Ka-Aper, from his mastaba at Saqqara, Egypt, Dynasty V, ca. 2450–2350 B.C. Wood, approx. 3′ 7″ high. Egyptian Museum, Cairo.

simple brick mastaba at Saqqara. Ka-Aper's face is also startlingly alive, an effect the eyes of rock crystal heighten.

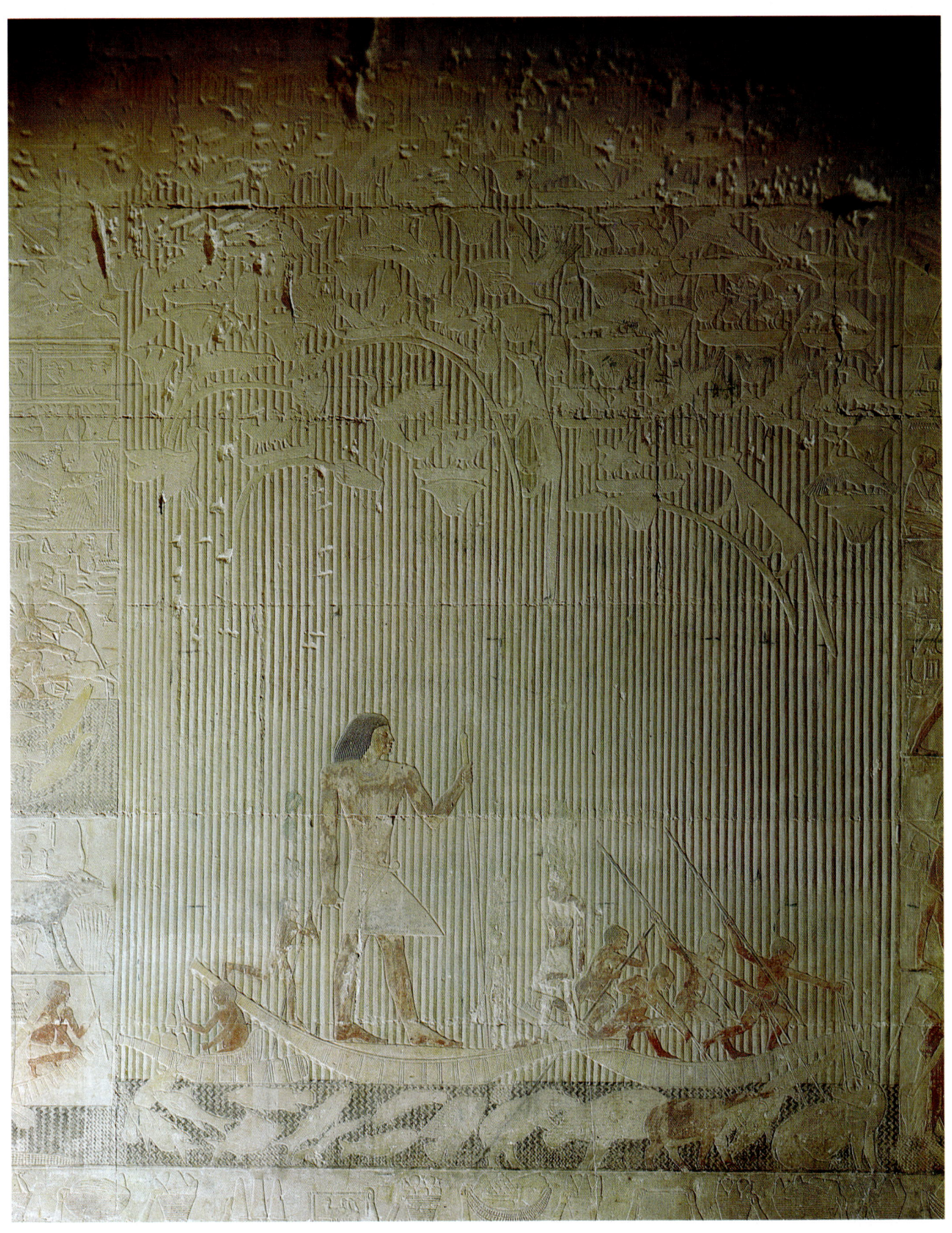

3-16 Ti watching a hippopotamus hunt, relief in the mastaba of Ti, Saqqara, Egypt, Dynasty V, ca. 2450–2350 B.C. Painted limestone, hunting scene approx. 4′ high.

The figure stands erect in the conventional frontal pose used for pharaonic portraits, with the left leg advanced. He is shown with the badges of his rank—a tall walking stick (restored) in his left hand and a baton (missing) in his right. Ka-Aper's paunchy physique is in even greater contrast than the scribe's to the idealized proportions used to portray Khafre and Menkaure. He was, after all, only a minor official. The statue somewhat retains the shape of the tree trunk from which the sculptor fashioned it (the arms were carved separately and pegged onto the body). Because the statue has no back slab, it seems to stand more freely than the stone images of Menkaure and Khamerernebty. The artist, however, had no more interest in portraying motion than had the sculptor of those royal images in stone. Actually, the work is only the wood core that the sculptor originally covered with painted plaster, a common procedure when soft or unattractive woods were used.

HUNTING AND FARMING IN THE AFTERLIFE
In Egyptian tombs, the deceased were not represented exclusively in freestanding statuary. Artists also depicted many individuals in relief sculpture and in mural painting, sometimes alone—as on the wooden panel of Hesire discussed in the Introduction (FIG. Intro-15)—and sometimes in a narrative context. The scenes in painted limestone relief (FIGS. **3-16** and **3-17**) that decorate the walls of the mastaba of Ti at Saqqara typify the subjects Old Kingdom patrons favored for the adornment of their final resting places. Ti was an official of the Fifth Dynasty. Depictions of agriculture and hunting fill his tomb. These activities represented the fundamental human concern with nature and were associated with the provisioning of the ka in the hereafter. But they also had powerful symbolic overtones. In ancient Egypt, success in the hunt, for example, was a metaphor for the triumph over the forces of evil.

On one wall (FIG. 3-16), Ti, his men, and his boats move slowly through the marshes, hunting hippopotami and birds in a dense growth of towering papyrus. The reedy stems of the plants are delineated with repeated fine grooves that fan out gracefully at the top into a commotion of frightened birds and stalking foxes. The water beneath the boats, signified by a pattern of wavy lines, is crowded with hippopotami and fish. Ti's men seem frantically busy with their spears, while Ti, depicted twice their size, stands aloof. The basic conventions of Egyptian figure representation used half a millennium earlier in the *Palette of King Narmer* (FIG. 3-2) are seen again here. As on the Predynastic palette and the portrait relief of Hesire (see FIG. Intro-15), the artist used the *conceptual* rather than the *optical* approach, representing what was known to be true of the subject, instead of a random view of it, and showing its

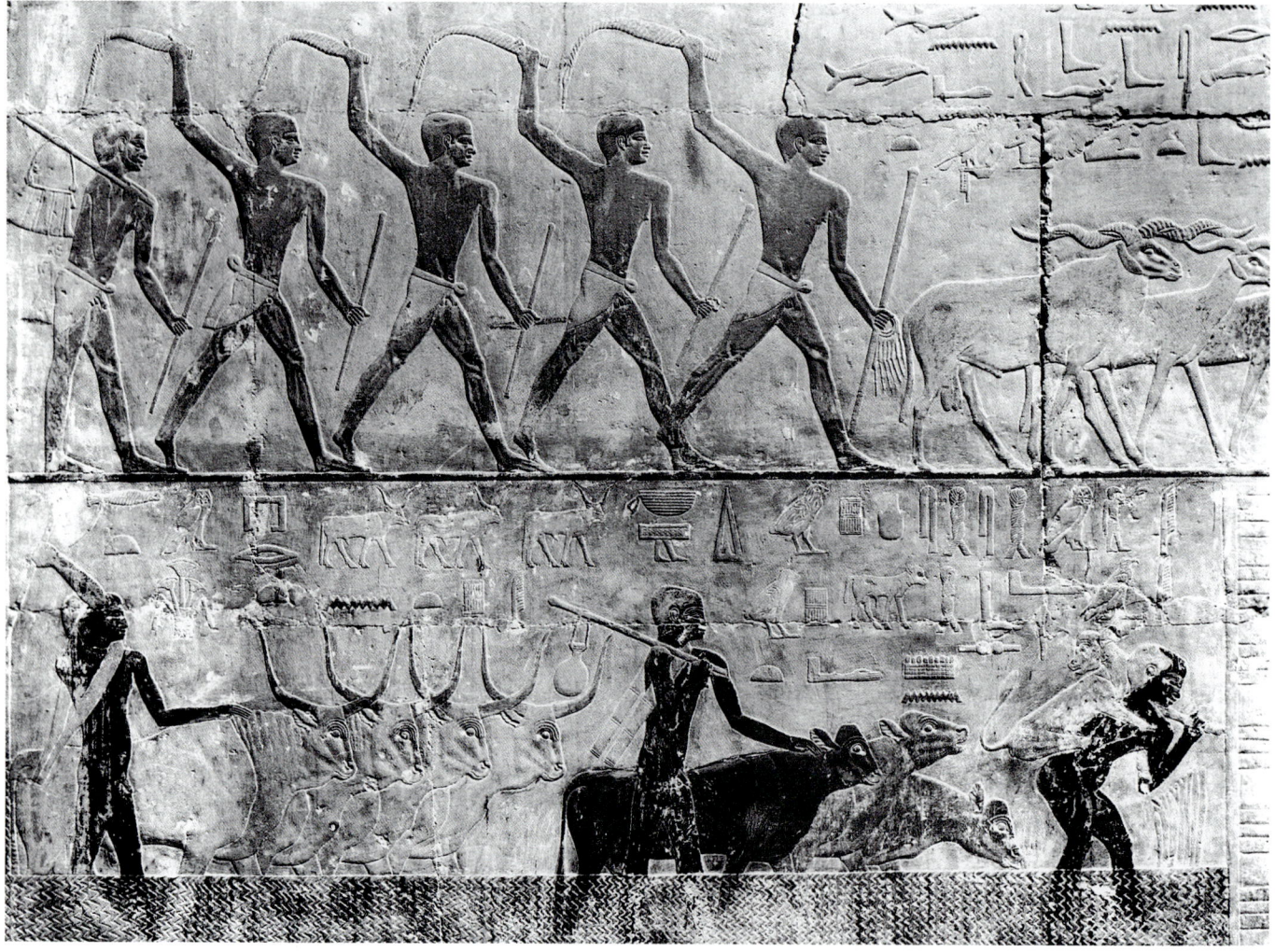

3-17 Goats treading seed and cattle fording a canal, reliefs in the mastaba of Ti, Saqqara, Egypt, Dynasty V, ca. 2450–2350 B.C. Painted limestone.

most characteristic parts at right angles to the line of vision. This conceptual approach expressed a feeling for the constant and changeless aspect of things and was well suited for Egyptian funerary art. Ti's outsize proportions bespeak his rank. His conventional pose contrasts with the realistically rendered activities of his tiny servants and with the naturalistically carved and painted birds and animals among the papyrus buds. Ti's immobility suggests that he is not an actor in the hunt. He does not *do* anything. He simply *is,* a figure apart from time and an impassive observer of life, like his ka.

The idealized and stiff image of Ti is typical of Egyptian relief sculpture. Egyptian artists regularly ignored the endless variations in body types of real human beings. Painters and sculptors did not sketch their subjects from life but applied a strict *canon,* or system of proportions, to the human figure. They first drew a grid on the wall. Then they placed various human bodily parts at specific points on the network of squares. The height of a figure, for example, was a fixed number of squares, and the head, shoulders, waist, knees, and other bodily parts also had a predetermined size and place within the scheme. This approach to design lasted for thousands of years. Specific proportions might vary from workshop to workshop or change over time, but the principle of the canon persisted.

On another wall of Ti's mastaba, the artist represented goats treading in seeds and cattle fording a canal in the Nile in two registers (FIG. 3-17). Ti is absent, and all the men and animals participate in the narrative. Despite the sculptor's repeated use of similar poses for most of the human and animal figures, the reliefs are full of anecdotal details. Especially charming is the group at the lower right of our illustration. A youth, depicted in a complex unconventional posture, carries a calf on his back. The animal, not a little afraid, turns its head back a full 180 degrees (compare the Paleolithic bison in FIG. 1-8) to seek reassurance from its mother, who returns the calf's gaze. Scenes such as this demonstrate that Egyptian artists could be close observers of daily life. The absence of the anecdotal (that is, of the time bound) from their representations of the deceased both in relief and in the round was a deliberate choice. Their primary purpose was to suggest the deceased's eternal existence in the afterlife, not to portray nature. Once again, the scenes may be interpreted on a symbolic, as well as a literal, level. The fording of the Nile was a metaphor for the deceased's passage from life to the hereafter.

THE MIDDLE KINGDOM

The art of the Old Kingdom is the classic art of Egypt in that the conventions its artists established remained the basis of Egyptian art through three millennia. But the political history of ancient Egypt was not nearly as stable. About 2150 B.C., the Egyptians challenged the pharaohs' power, and for more than a century the land was in a state of civil unrest and near anarchy. But in 2040 B.C. the pharaoh of Upper Egypt, Mentuhotep I (r. 2061–2010 B.C.), managed to unite Egypt again under the rule of a single king and established the so-called Middle Kingdom (Dynasties XI–XIV).

TOMBS TO WARD OFF THIEVES   During the Middle Kingdom, the Egyptians continued to build pyramids but on a much smaller scale than in the Old Kingdom. Because it had become apparent that size was no defense against tomb robbers, builders next attempted to thwart thieves with intricate and ingenious interior layouts. Entrances were hidden and screened from the secret tomb chamber by various types of sliding doors and by a series of passages that turned and doubled back on themselves at various levels like labyrinths. Because the Middle Kingdom pyramids were less massive than their Old Kingdom predecessors, they were built either entirely of brick or as stone frameworks filled with brick or rubble.

What the pyramids lost in size and mass during the Middle Kingdom, however, was partly gained back by the increased size of the *sarcophagi* (literally "flesh eaters") inside the tombs that contained the mummified remains of the dead. These granite coffins were extremely large and heavy. Designed like small tomb chambers and weighing up to one hundred fifty tons, they were intended to foil potential robbers by their very bulk and mass.

MOUNTAINSIDES FASHIONED INTO TOMBS   New forms of tombs also were introduced during the Middle Kingdom. Among the most characteristic remains of the period are the rock-cut tombs at Beni Hasan (FIG. **3-18**), south of Memphis. One of the best preserved is the Twelfth Dynasty tomb of Khnumhotep, who boasted in an inscription of its elaborateness, saying that its doors were of cedar seven cubits (about twenty feet) high. Expressing the characteristic Egyptian attitude toward the last resting place, he added:

> My chief nobility was: I executed a cliff-tomb, for a man should imitate that which his father does. My father made for himself a house of the ka in the town of Menofret, of good stone of Ayan, in order to perpetuate his name forever and establish it eternally.

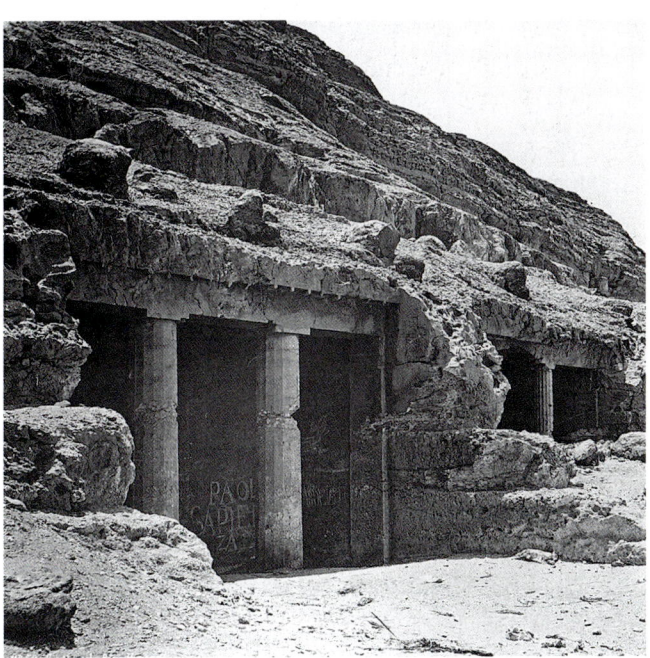

3-18 Rock-cut tombs, Beni Hasan, Egypt, Dynasty XII, ca. 1950–1900 B.C.

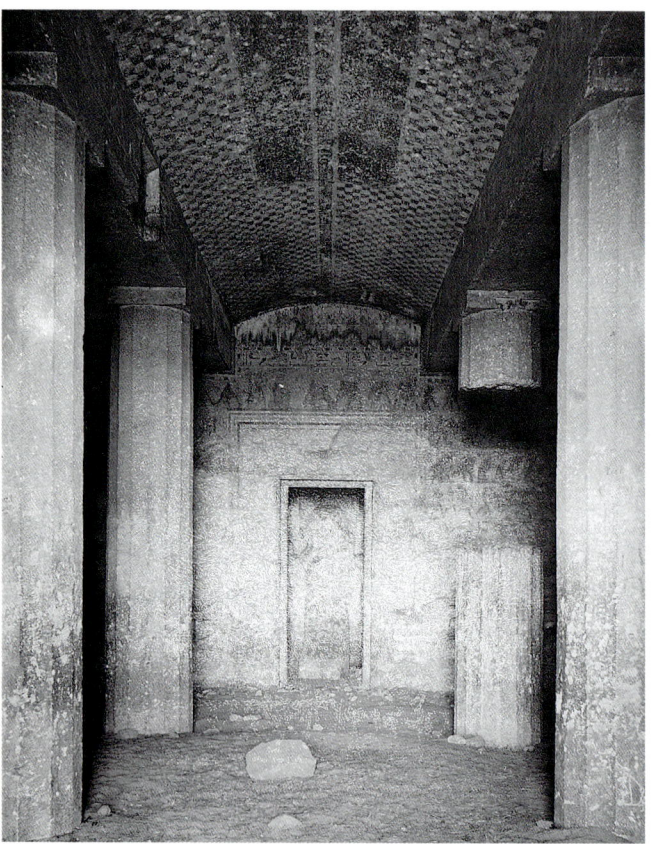

3-19 Interior hall of the rock-cut tomb of Amenemhet, Beni Hasan, Egypt, Dynasty XII, ca. 1950–1900 B.C.

The rock-cut tombs of the Middle Kingdom largely replaced the Old Kingdom mastabas. Hollowed out of the cliffs at remote sites, these tombs often were fronted by a shallow columnar vestibule (porch), which led into a columned hall and then into a sacred chamber. In the hall of the Twelfth Dynasty rock-cut tomb of Amenemhet (FIG. 3-19), the columns serve no supporting function because, like the porch columns, they are continuous parts of the rock fabric. (Note the broken column in the rear suspended from the ceiling like a stalactite.) The column shafts are *fluted* with vertical channels in a manner similar to later Greek columns. Fluted Egyptian columns were first used by Imhotep during the Third Dynasty. Archeologists believe fluting derived from the *dressing,* or smoothing of the surfaces, of softwood trunks with the rounded cutting edge of the adze. Fluted stone columns are yet another case of Egyptians translating perishable natural forms into permanent architecture. Artists decorated the tomb walls with paintings and painted reliefs, as in former times, and the subjects were much the same.

THE NEW KINGDOM

EGYPT AT ITS HEIGHT Like its predecessor, the Middle Kingdom disintegrated, and power passed to the Hyksos, or shepherd kings, who descended on Egypt from the Syrian and Mesopotamian uplands. They brought with them a new and influential culture and that practical animal, the horse. Their innovations in weaponry and war tech-

niques ironically contributed to their own overthrow by native Egyptian kings of the Seventeenth Dynasty around 1600–1550 B.C. Ahmose I (r. 1550–1525 B.C.), final conqueror of the Hyksos and first king of the Eighteenth Dynasty, ushered in the New Kingdom, the most brilliant period in Egypt's long history.

At this time, Egypt extended its borders by conquest from the Euphrates River in the east deep into Nubia (the Sudan) to the south. Visiting embassies and new and profitable trade with Asia and the Aegean Islands widened foreign contact (see "Minoan Paintings Discovered in Egypt," Chapter 4, page 84). The booty Egyptians took in wars and the tribute they exacted from subjected peoples made possible the development of a new capital—Thebes, in Upper Egypt, south of the Predynastic royal cemetery at Abydos. It became a great and luxurious metropolis with magnificent palaces, tombs, and temples along both banks of the Nile.

Architecture

A TEMPLE FOR A DIVINE QUEEN If the most impressive monuments of the Old Kingdom are its pyramids, those of the New Kingdom are its grandiose temples, often built to honor pharaohs and queens, as well as gods. Great pharaonic mortuary temples arose along the Nile near Thebes. These shrines provided the rulers with a place for worshiping their patron gods during their lifetimes and then served as temples in their own honor after their death. The temples were elaborate and luxuriously decorated, befitting both the pharaohs and the gods.

The most majestic of these royal mortuary temples, at Deir el-Bahri (FIG. 3-20), was constructed for the female pharaoh Hatshepsut, one of the most remarkable women of the ancient world (see "Hatshepsut: The Woman Who Would Be King," page 61). The temple is the work of SENMUT, Hatshepsut's chancellor, architect-engineer, and possible lover. Modeled in part on the neighboring Middle Kingdom temple of Mentuhotep II (at the far left in FIG. 3-20), Hatshepsut's temple rises from the valley floor in three colonnaded terraces connected by ramps. It is remarkable how visually well suited the structure is to its natural setting. The long horizontals and verticals of the colonnades and their rhythm of light and dark repeat the pattern of the limestone cliffs above. The colonnade pillars, which are either simply rectangular or *chamfered* (beveled, or flattened at the edges) into sixteen sides, are well proportioned and rhythmically spaced.

In Hatshepsut's day, the terraces were not the barren places they are now but gardens with frankincense trees and rare plants the pharaoh brought from the faraway "land of Punt" on the Red Sea. Her expedition to Punt figures prominently in the poorly preserved but once brightly painted low reliefs that cover many of the complex's walls. In addition to great deeds, the reliefs also represent Hatshepsut's coronation and divine birth. She was said to be the daughter of the god Amen-Re, whose sanctuary was situated on the temple's uppermost level. The painted reliefs of Hatshepsut's mortuary temple constitute the first great pictorial tribute to a woman's achievements in the history of art.

A WOMAN PORTRAYED AS A MAN As many as two hundred statues in the round depicting Hatshepsut in various

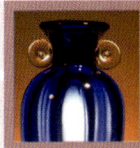

ART AND SOCIETY

Hatshepsut
The Woman Who Would Be King

In 1479 B.C., Thutmose II, the fourth pharaoh of the Eighteenth Dynasty (r. 1492–1479 B.C.), died. His principal wife (and half sister), Queen Hatshepsut (r. 1473–1458 B.C.), had not given birth to any sons who survived, so the title of king went to the twelve-year-old Thutmose III, son of Thutmose II by a minor wife. (Egyptian pharaohs had extensive harems.) Hatshepsut was named regent for the boy king. Within a few years, however, the queen announced that had she not been a woman, as the daughter of Thutmose I she rightfully would be king. She proclaimed herself pharaoh and insisted that Thutmose I had actually chosen her as his successor during his lifetime. Indeed, in one of the reliefs decorating Hatshepsut's enormous funerary complex (FIG. 3-20), Thutmose I crowns his daughter as king in the presence of the Egyptian gods.

Hatshepsut was the first great female monarch whose name was recorded. (In the Twelfth Dynasty, Sobekneferu had been crowned king of Egypt, but she reigned as pharaoh for only a few years.) Hatshepsut boasted of having made the "Two Lands to labor with bowed back for her," and for two decades she ruled what was then the most powerful and prosperous empire in the world.

Hatshepsut commissioned numerous building projects, and sculptors produced portraits of the female pharaoh in great numbers for display in those complexes. Many of Hatshepsut's portraits were destroyed after her death at the order of the resentful Thutmose III (r. 1458–1425 B.C.), whose elevation to sole kingship was delayed for two decades when his stepmother declared herself pharaoh. In her surviving portraits, Hatshepsut uniformly wears the costume of the male pharaohs, with royal headdress and kilt, and in some cases even a false ceremonial beard (FIG. 3-21). Many inscriptions refer to Hatshepsut as "*His* Majesty"! In other statues, however, Hatshepsut has delicate features, a slender frame, and breasts, leaving no doubt that the pharaoh also was represented as a woman.

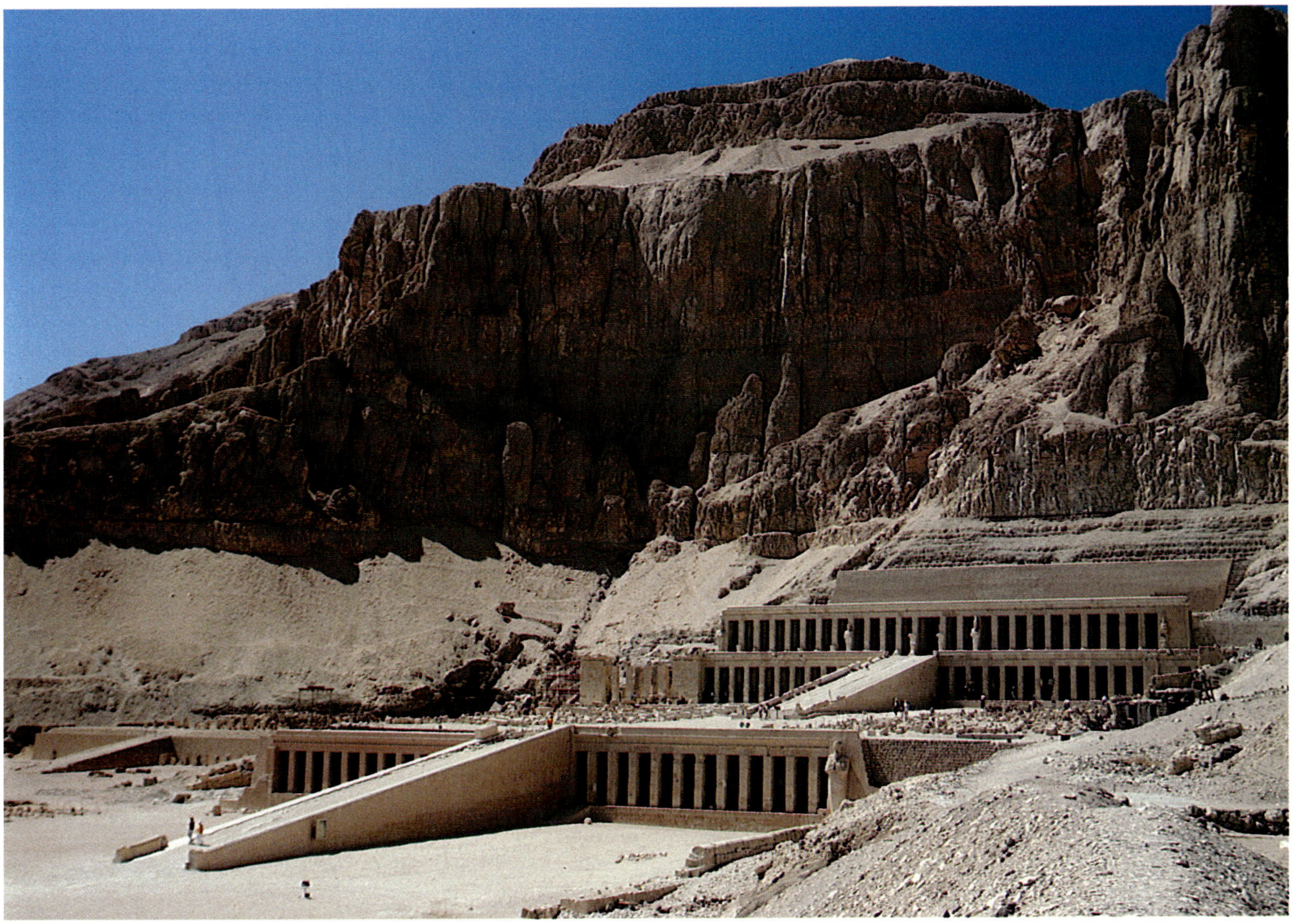

3-20 SENMUT, mortuary temple of Hatshepsut (with the Middle Kingdom mortuary temple of Mentuhotep II at left), Deir el-Bahri, Egypt, Dynasty XVIII, ca. 1473–1458 B.C.

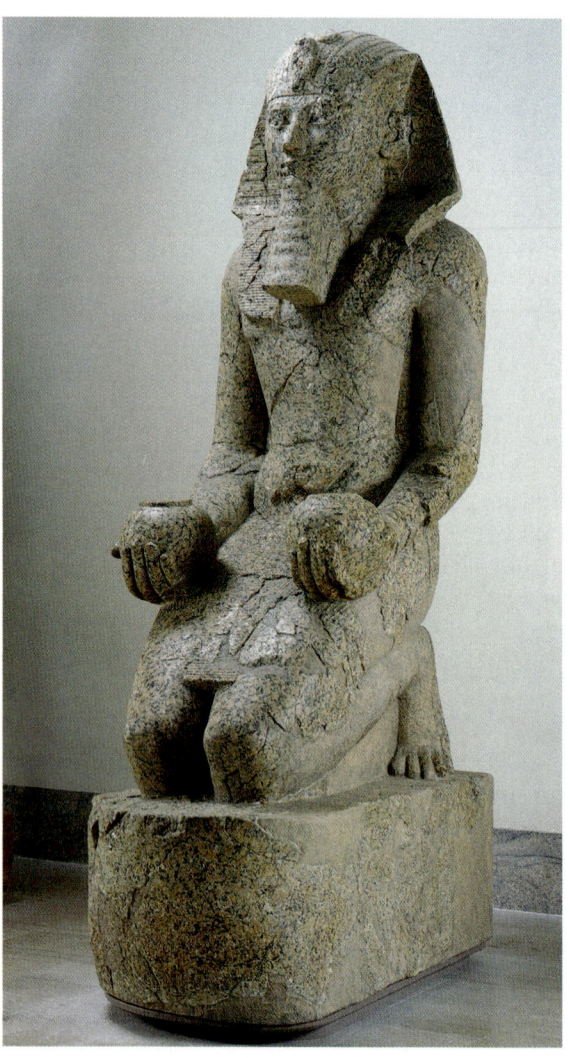

3-21 Hatshepsut with offering jars, from the upper court of her mortuary temple, Deir el-Bahri, Egypt, ca. 1473–1458 B.C. Red granite, approx. 8′ 6″ high. Metropolitan Museum of Art, New York.

COLOSSI CARVED OUT OF A CLIFF Hatshepsut's mortuary temple never fails to impress visitors by its sheer size, and this is no less true of the immense rock-cut temple of Ramses II (r. 1290–1224 B.C.) at Abu Simbel (FIG. **3-22**). Ramses was Egypt's last great warrior pharaoh, and he ruled for two-thirds of a century, an extraordinary accomplishment in an era when life expectancy was far less than it is today. Although Ramses was buried in a tomb in the Valley of the Kings at Thebes, his temple was built far up the Nile. The whole monument was moved in 1968 to save it from submersion in the Aswan High Dam reservoir.

The pharaoh, proud of his many campaigns to restore the empire, proclaimed his greatness by placing four colossal images of himself on the temple facade. The portraits are almost eight times as large as Hatshepsut's kneeling statues and almost a dozen times an ancient Egyptian's height, even though the pharaoh is seated. Spectacular as they are, the rock-cut statues nonetheless lack the refinement of earlier periods, because much was sacrificed to overwhelming size. This is a characteristic of colossal statuary of every period and every place.

The grand scale was carried out in the interior also (FIG. **3-23**), where giant (thirty-two-foot) figures of the king, carved as one with the pillars, face each other across the narrow corridor. The pillars, carved from the cliff like the pharaoh's facade portraits, have no load-bearing function. In this respect, they resemble the columns in the tombs at Beni Hasan (FIG. 3-19). The statue-column, in its male (*atlantid*) or female (*caryatid*) variants, reappears throughout the history of art. Often, as here, the human figure is attached to a column or pier (for example, FIGS. 18-6 and 18-16). At other times the figure replaces the architectural member and forms the sole source of support (see FIG. 5-52).

Ramses, like the other pharaohs, had many wives and he fathered scores of sons. North of his own temple, Ramses ordered the construction of a grand temple for his principal wife, Nefertari. Huge rock-cut statues—four standing images of the king and two of the queen—also dominated that temple's facade. For his sons, Ramses constructed a separate grand tomb underground. The rediscovery of that huge subterranean complex was one of the past century's major archeological finds (see "The Tomb of the Sons of Ramses II," page 63).

IMMENSE NEW KINGDOM PYLON TEMPLES Distinct from the mortuary temples built during the New Kingdom are the edifices built to honor one or more of the gods. Successive kings often added to them until they reached gigantic size. The temple of Amen-Re at Karnak (FIG. **3-24**), for example, was largely the work of the Eighteenth Dynasty pharaohs, including Thutmose I and III and Hatshepsut, but Ramses II (Nineteenth Dynasty) and others also contributed sections. Chapels were added to the complex as late as the Twenty-Sixth Dynasty. An artificial sacred lake near the Karnak temple (not included on our plan) is a reference to the primeval waters before creation. The temple rises from the earth as the original sacred mound rose from the waters at the beginning of time.

The New Kingdom *pylon temples* all had similar plans. (The name derives from the simple and massive gateway, or pylon, with sloping walls, as in FIG. 3-28.) A typical pylon temple like that at Karnak is bilaterally symmetrical along a single axis that runs from an approaching avenue through a

guises complemented the extensive relief program. Unfortunately, the jealous and revengeful Thutmose III removed or shattered them after her death. On the lowest terrace, to either side of the processional way, Hatshepsut was repeatedly portrayed as a sphinx. On the uppermost level, the female pharaoh was represented standing, seated, and in the form of a mummy. At least eight colossal kneeling statues in red granite lined the way to the entrance of the Amen-Re sanctuary.

Our example (FIG. **3-21**) suffered the same fate as most of Hatshepsut's portraits. After it was smashed, the pieces were thrown in a dump. The statue has been skillfully reassembled from the recovered fragments. Hatshepsut holds a globular offering jar in each hand as she takes part in a ritual in honor of the sun god. (A king kneeled only before a god, never a mortal.) She wears the royal male nemes headdress (compare FIGS. 3-11 to 3-13) and the pharaoh's ceremonial beard. The agents of Thutmose III hacked off the uraeus cobra that once adorned the front of the headdress. The figure is also anatomically male, although other surviving portraits of Hatshepsut represent her with a woman's breasts. The male imagery is, however, consistent with the queen's formal assumption of the title of king and with the many inscriptions that address her as a man.

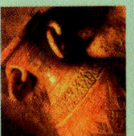

The Tomb of the Sons of Ramses II

In 1825, James Burton, a British explorer, uncovered the entrance and a few chambers of a royal tomb in the Valley of the Kings at Thebes. (The narrow valley across the Nile from Karnak and Luxor was so named because it contains the tombs of numerous New Kingdom pharaohs.) In an age when archeological excavation was little more than treasure hunting, archeologists never fully investigated the tomb (KV5) because no precious objects were found when it was opened. Almost a century later, in 1902, Howard Carter, who later discovered Tutankhamen's tomb, made a probe into KV5, but he, too, concluded that the site was unpromising and abandoned work there. Later archeologists ignored the tomb, and its location was forgotten until an American team led by Kent R. Weeks found KV5 anew in 1987. It wasn't until 1995, however, that the tomb's immense size and unique character were revealed.

KV5 is the largest tomb ever found in the Valley of the Kings and may have been the largest in Egypt. No other Theban tomb has more than thirty chambers—a half dozen is typical—but this tomb has scores of rooms, and it is still only partially excavated. The chambers open onto several long corridors leading out of a central hall, fifty meters square, filled with sixteen stone pillars. Inscriptions inside the tomb leave no doubt that this was the burial place of the sons of the great Nineteenth Dynasty pharaoh Ramses II. Paintings and reliefs depicting Ramses and his royal sons with the major deities of Egypt—Osiris, Hathor, Horus, Thoth, and Isis—decorate the tomb walls.

KV5, unfortunately, was robbed within a half century of its construction. The culprit was identified, a workman named Kenena, son of Ruta. But the excavators found material the thief left behind, including a statue of Osiris, god of the afterlife, in a niche at the end of a long corridor. Weeks's team also discovered a number of small mummy-shaped statuettes called *ushabtis,* which served as servants of the royal sons for eternity. What they have not found are the royal burials themselves. The excavators have postulated that dozens more rooms—the actual burial chambers—may yet be discovered on a lower level. No one knows if Kenena or other thieves removed the presumed treasures buried with the pharaoh's sons or whether they remain to be uncovered. Work by Weeks and his colleagues is likely to continue for decades. Readers can keep posted on the progress of the excavations at the following Web site:

www.KV5.com

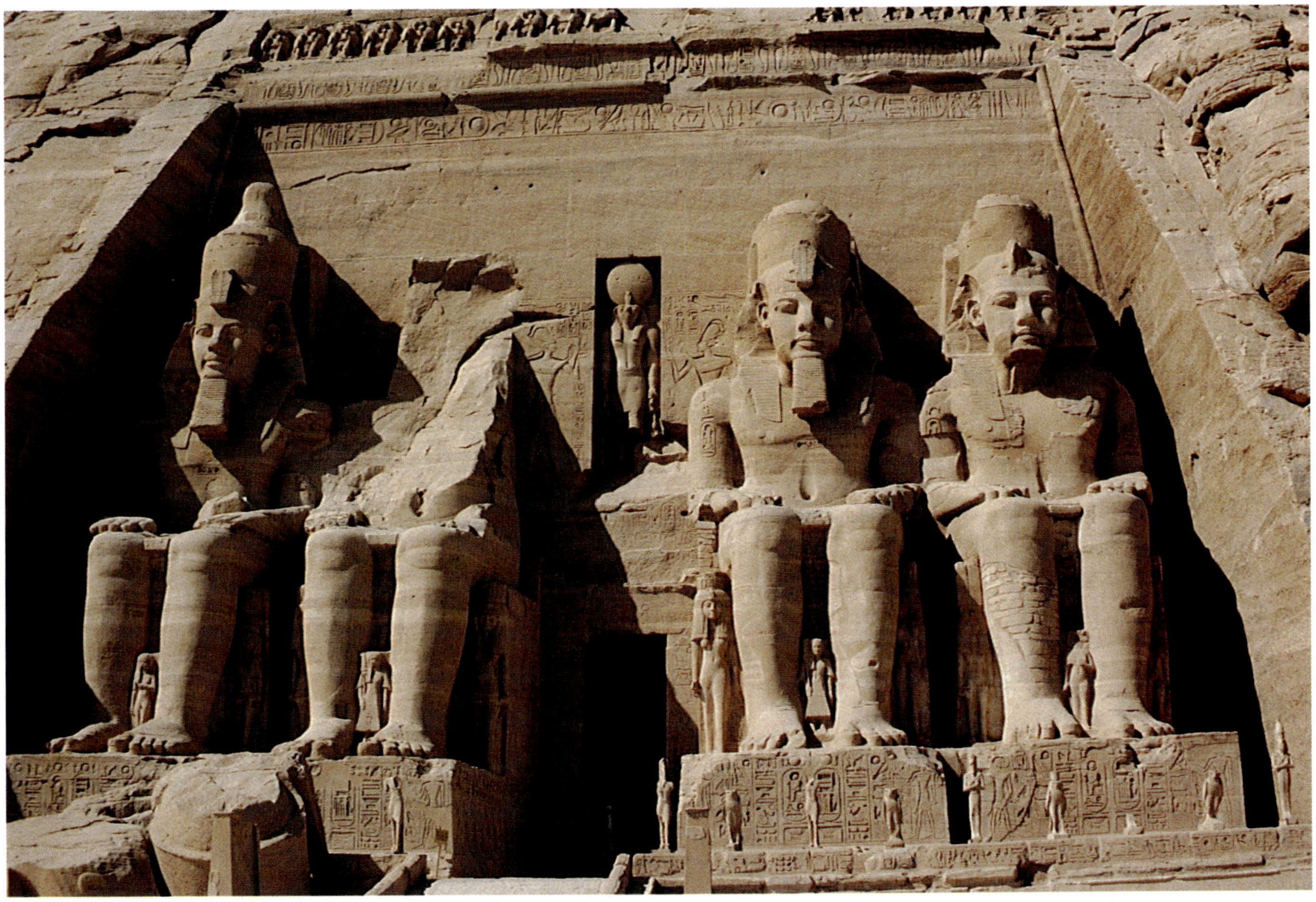

![Temple of Ramses II, Abu Simbel]

3-22   Temple of Ramses II, Abu Simbel (now relocated), Egypt, Dynasty XIX, ca. 1290–1224 B.C. Colossi approx. 65′ high.

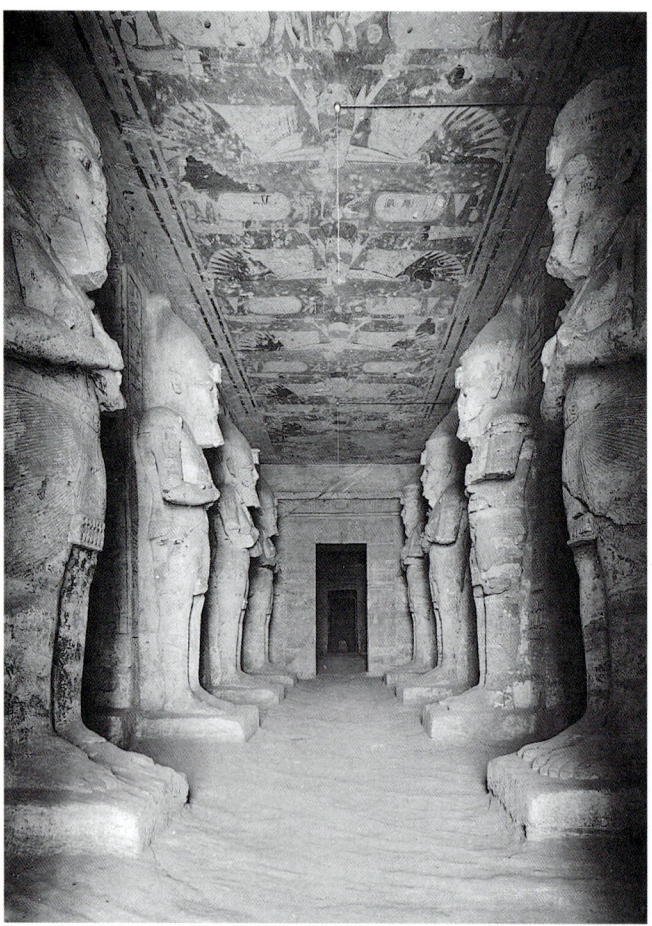

3-23 Interior of the temple of Ramses II, Abu Simbel (now relocated), Egypt, Dynasty XIX, ca. 1290–1224 B.C. Pillar statues approx. 32′ high.

colonnaded court and hall into a dimly lit sanctuary. This Egyptian temple plan evolved from ritualistic requirements. Only the pharaohs and the priests could enter the sanctuary. A chosen few were admitted to the great columnar hall. The majority of the people were allowed only as far as the open court, and a high mud-brick wall shut off the site from the outside world. The conservative Egyptians did not deviate from this basic plan for hundreds of years. In fact, the New

Kingdom pylon temple plan's central feature—a narrow axial passageway through the complex—had characterized Egyptian architecture since the Old Kingdom. Axial corridors are also the approaches to the great pyramids of Gizeh (FIG. 3-10) and to the multilevel mortuary temple of Hatshepsut at Deir el-Bahri (FIG. 3-20).

The dominating feature of the statuary-lined approach to a New Kingdom temple was the monumental facade of the pylon, which was routinely covered with reliefs glorifying Egypt's rulers. Inside was an open court with columns on two or more sides, followed by a hall between the court and sanctuary, its long axis placed at right angles to the entire building complex's corridor. This *hypostyle* hall (one with a roof supported by columns) was crowded with massive columns and roofed by stone slabs carried on lintels. The lintels rested on *impost blocks* (stones with the shape of shortened, inverted pyramids) resting on giant capitals. In the hypostyle hall at Karnak (FIGS. **3-25** and **3-26**), the central columns are sixty-six feet high, and the capitals are twenty-two feet in diameter at the top, large enough to hold one hundred people. The Egyptians, who used no cement, depended on the weight of the huge stone blocks to hold the columns in place.

In the Amen-Re temple at Karnak and in many other Egyptian hypostyle halls, the builders made the central rows of columns higher than those at the sides. Raising the roof's central section created a *clerestory.* Openings in the clerestory permitted light to filter into the interior. This method of construction appeared in primitive form as early as the Old Kingdom in the valley temple of the Pyramid of Khafre. Evidently an Egyptian innovation, its significance hardly can be overstated. Before the invention of the lightbulb, illuminating a building's interior was always a challenge for architects. The clerestory played a key role, for example, in Roman basilica and medieval church design and has remained an important architectural feature down to the present.

NEW KINGDOM COLUMNS In the hypostyle hall at Karnak, the columns are indispensable structurally, unlike the rock-cut columns of the tombs at Beni Hasan (FIG. 3-19) and Abu Simbel (FIG. 3-23). But their function as vertical supports is almost hidden by horizontal bands of painted *sunken*

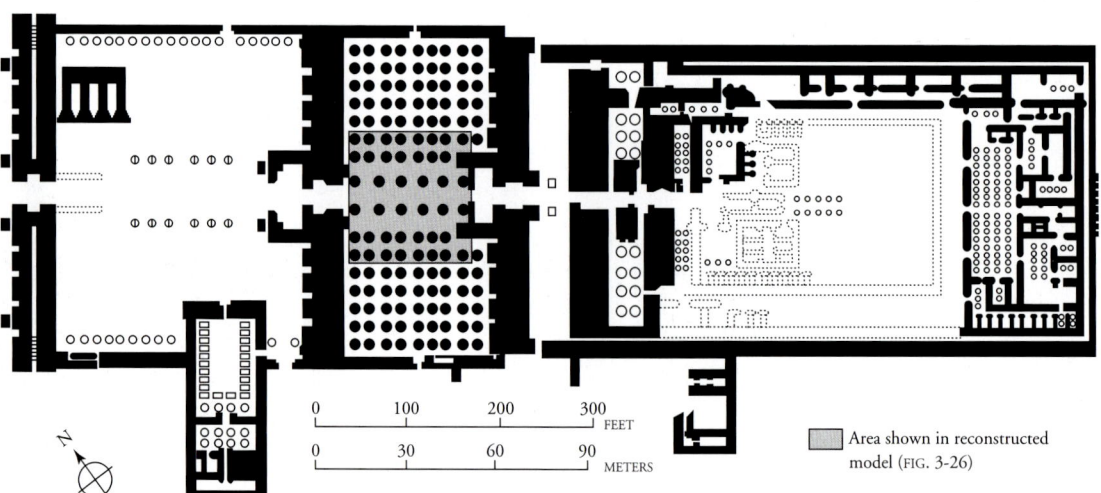

3-24 Plan of the temple of Amen-Re, Karnak, Egypt, begun fifteenth century B.C. (after Sir Bannister Fletcher). The shaded area in the hypostyle hall corresponds to the model in FIG. 3-26.

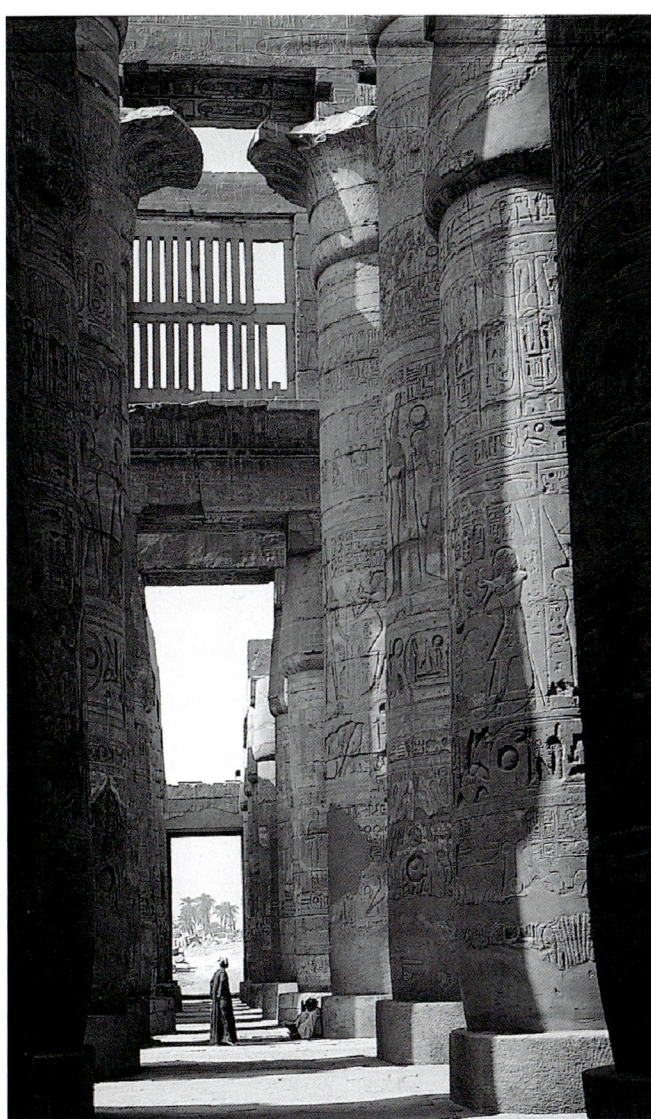

3-25 Hypostyle hall, temple of Amen-Re, Karnak, Egypt, Dynasty XIX, ca. 1290–1224 B.C.

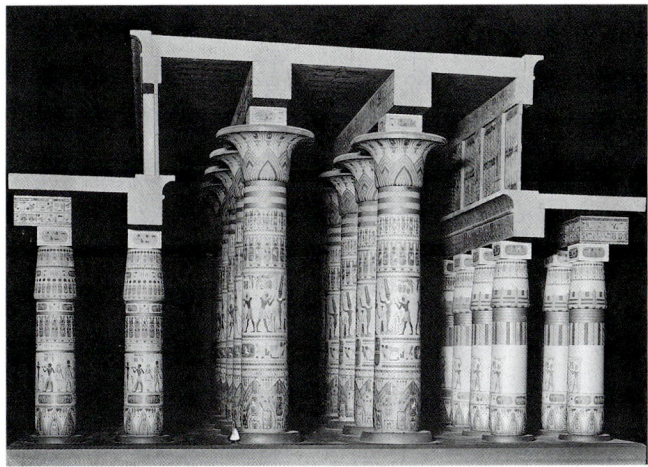

3-26 Model of hypostyle hall, temple of Amen-Re, Karnak, Egypt, Dynasty XIX, ca. 1290–1224 B.C. Metropolitan Museum of Art, New York. (Levi Hale Willard Bequest, 1890).

relief sculpture. To create such reliefs, sculptors chisel deep outlines below the stone's surface, rather than cutting back the stone around the figures to make the figures project from the surface. Sunken reliefs preserve the contours of the columns they adorn. Otherwise, the Karnak columns would have had an irregular, wavy profile. But despite this effort to maintain sharp architectural lines, the overwhelming of the surfaces with reliefs suggests that the architects' intention was not to emphasize the columns' functional role. Instead, they used columns as image- and message-bearing surfaces. Most builders, however, even in ancient Egypt, emphasized the column's vertical lines and structural function by freeing the shaft's surfaces from all ornament. The Karnak columns are exceptional in the history of architecture.

Typical New Kingdom columns can be found in the courts and colonnades of the Temple of Amen-Mut-Khonsu at Luxor (FIG. **3-27**). Egyptian columns appear to have originated from an early building technique that used firmly bound sheaves of reeds and swamp plants as roof supports in

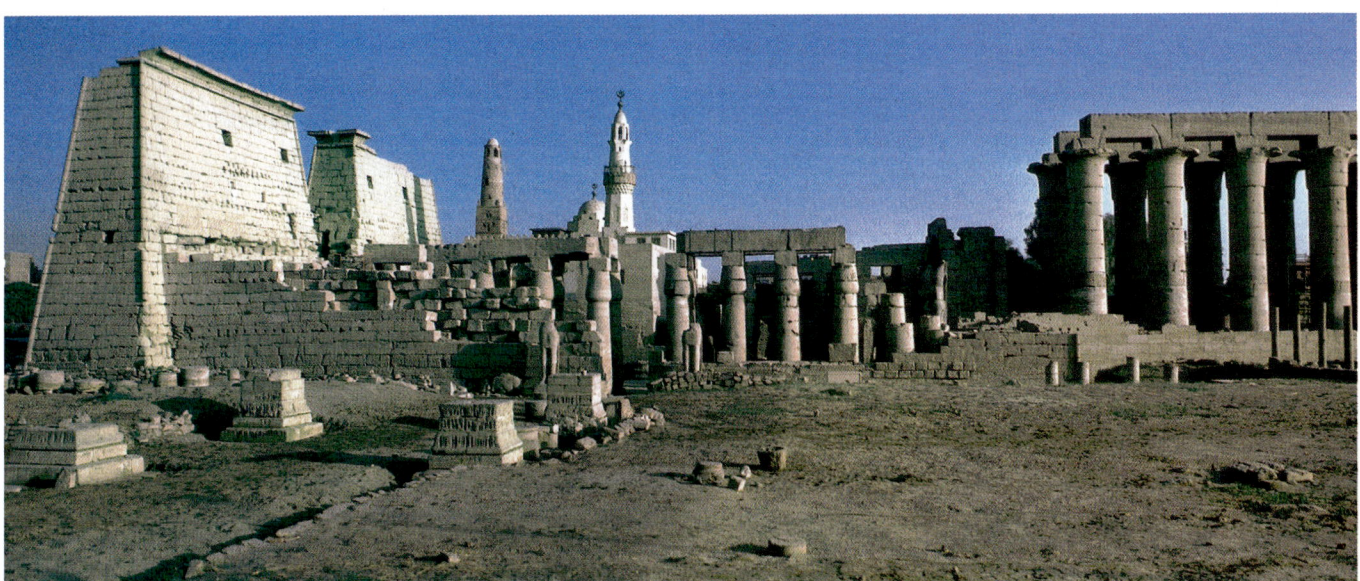

3-27 Temple of Amen-Mut-Khonsu, Luxor, Egypt. *Left:* pylon and court of Ramses II, Dynasty XIX, ca. 1290–1224 B.C.; *right:* colonnaded court of Amenhotep III, Dynasty XVIII, ca. 1390–1353 B.C.

3-28 Temple of Horus, Edfu, Egypt, ca. 237–47 B.C.

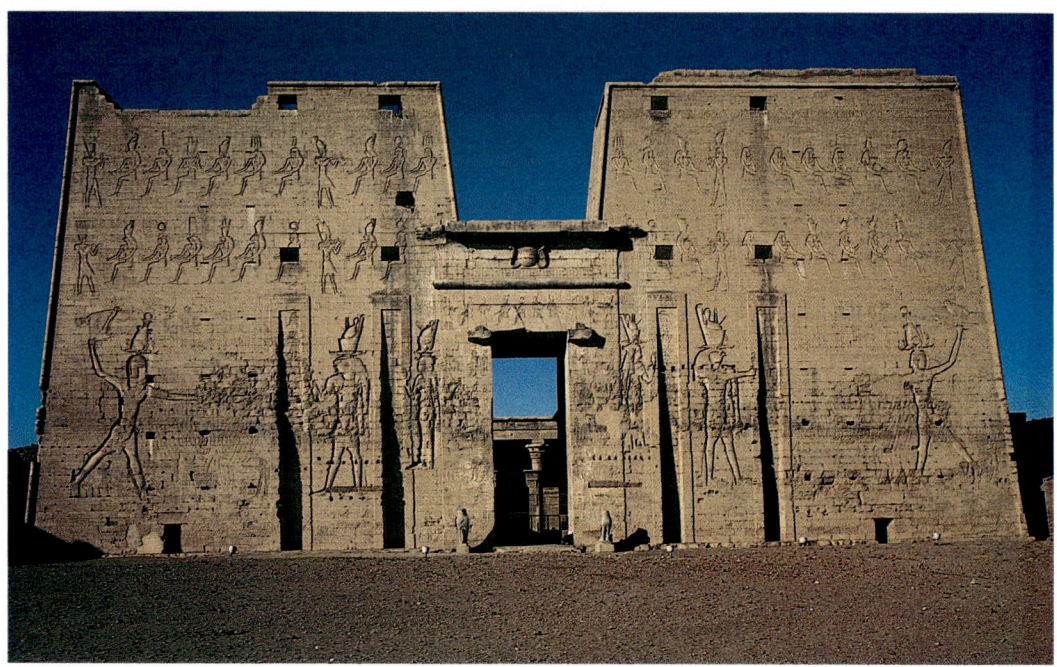

adobe structures. Imhotep first translated such early and relatively impermanent building methods into stone (FIGS. 3-6 and 3-7). Evidence of their swamp-plant origin is still seen in the columns at Karnak and Luxor, which have bud-cluster or bell-shaped capitals resembling lotus or papyrus (the plants of Upper and Lower Egypt).

Egyptian traditions once formulated tended to have very long lives, in architecture as in the other arts. The pylon temple of Horus at Edfu (FIG. **3-28**), built during the third, second, and first centuries B.C., still follows the basic scheme architects worked out more than a thousand years before. The great entrance pylon at Edfu is especially impressive. The broad surface of its massive facade, with its sloping walls, is broken only by the doorway with its overshadowing cornice, moldings at the top and sides, by deep channels to hold great flagstaffs, and by sunken reliefs. The reliefs depict Horus and Hathor witnessing an oversized King Ptolemy XIII (r. 51–47 B.C.) smiting undersized enemies. It is a striking monument to the persistence of Egyptian architectural and sculptural types.

Sculpture and Painting

The patterns the Old Kingdom masters set continued to dominate statuary production in the Nile Valley even under the Roman emperors. Hatshepsut's funerary complex, for example, was bedecked with statues of the female pharaoh that conformed to types established long before, including the standing and seated portrait and the reclining sphinx. The bilateral symmetry of all the poses and the frozen action were unvarying features even when new motifs were introduced.

BLOCK STATUES   Extremely popular during the Middle and New Kingdoms were *block statues*. In these works the idea that the ka could find an eternal home in the cubic stone image of the deceased was expressed in an even more

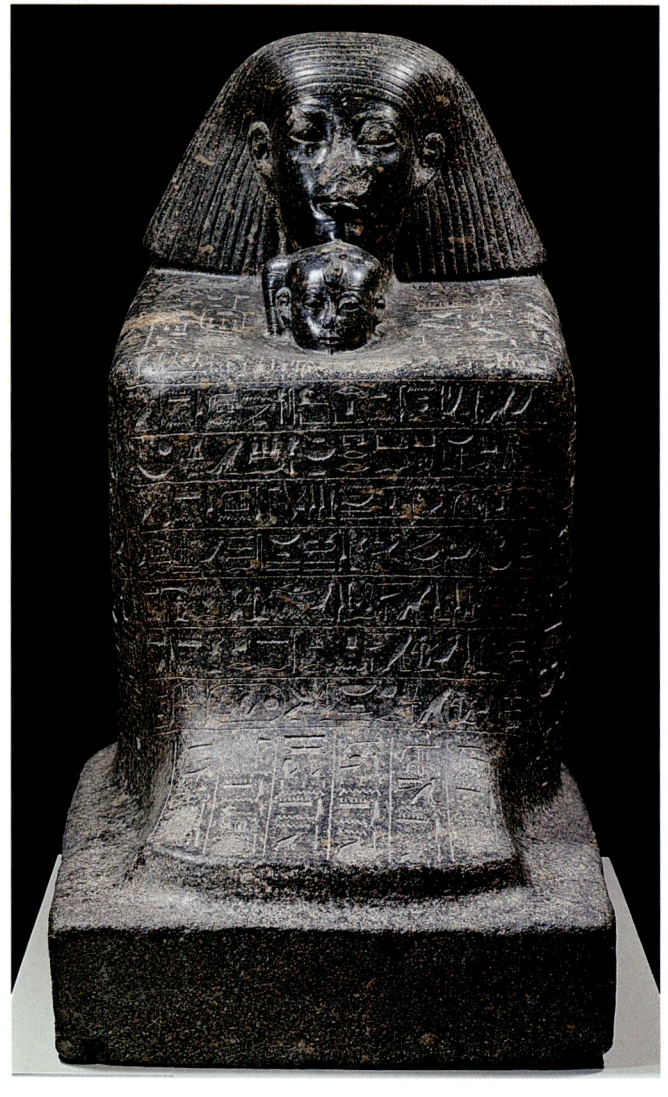

3-29 Senmut with Princess Nefrua, from Thebes, Egypt, Dynasty XVIII, ca. 1470–1460 B.C. Granite, approx. 3′ $\frac{1}{2}$″ high. Ägyptisches Museum, Berlin.

radical simplification of form than was common in Old Kingdom statuary. A fine example of this genre is the block statue of Senmut and Princess Nefrua (FIG. **3-29**). Hatshepsut's chancellor holds the pharaoh's daughter by Thutmose II in his "lap" and envelops the girl in his cloak. The streamlined design concentrates attention on the heads and treats the two bodies as a single cubic block, given over to inscriptions. The polished stone shape has its own simple beauty. With surfaces turning subtly about smoothly rounded corners, it is another expression of the Egyptian fondness for volume enclosed by flat, unambiguous planes. The work—one of many surviving statues depicting Senmut with Hatshepsut's daughter—is also a reflection of the power of Egypt's female ruler. The frequent depiction of Senmut with Nefrua was meant to enhance Senmut's stature through his association with the princess (he was her tutor) and, by implication, with Hatshepsut herself. Toward the end of her reign, however, Hatshepsut believed Senmut had become too powerful, and she had him removed.

A PAINTED TOMB AT THEBES The long life of Egyptian artistic formulas also can be seen in New Kingdom painting. In the Eighteenth-Dynasty Theban tomb of Nebamun, the deceased nobleman, whose official titles were "scribe and counter of grain," is shown standing in his boat, flushing birds from a papyrus swamp (FIG. **3-30**).

The hieroglyphic text beneath his left arm says that Nebamun is enjoying recreation in his eternal afterlife. In contrast to the static pose of Ti watching others hunt hippopotami (FIG. 3-16), Nebamun is shown striding forward and vigorously swinging his throwing stick. In his right hand, he holds three birds he has caught. A wild cat, impossibly perched on a papyrus stem just in front of and below him, has caught two more in her claws and is holding the wings of a third in her teeth. Nebamun is accompanied on this hunt by his wife and daughter, who are holding the lotuses they have gathered. The artist scaled down their figures in proportion to their rank. Save for the participation of the deceased and his family in the hunt, formally and conceptually this New Kingdom fowling scene differs little from the hippopotamus hunt in the Old Kingdom tomb of Ti. The painter used the usual conventions to represent the water and the human figures. Cat, fish, and birds, like the Saqqara animals, show a naturalism based on careful observation.

The technique is also that employed in Old Kingdom tombs: *fresco secco* (dry fresco), whereby artists let the plaster dry before painting on it. This procedure, in contrast to true fresco painting on wet plaster (see "Fresco Painting," Chapter 19, page 543), lends itself to slow and meticulous work. It allows the trained professional to express an exact knowledge of the subject.

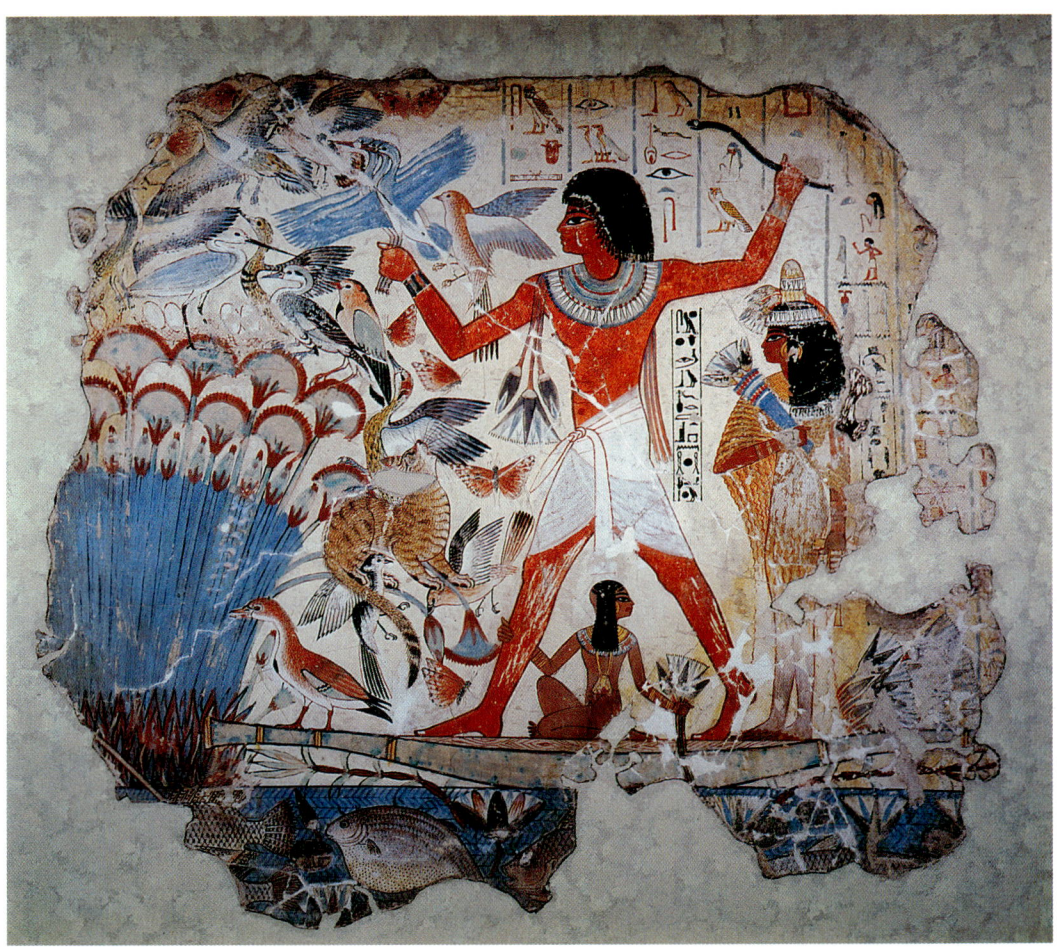

3-30 Fowling scene, from the tomb of Nebamun, Thebes, Egypt, Dynasty XVIII, ca. 1400–1350 B.C. Fresco on dry plaster, approx. 2′ 8″ high. British Museum, London.

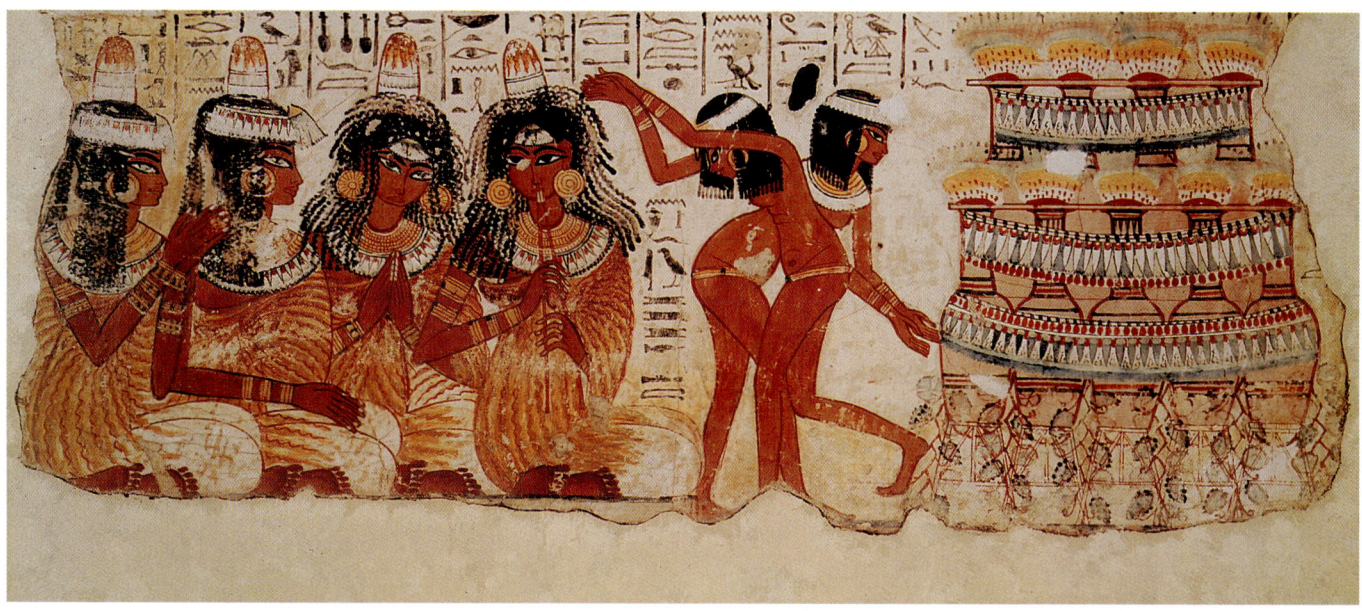

3-31 Musicians and dancers, detail of a fresco from the tomb of Nebamun, Thebes, Egypt, Dynasty XVIII, ca. 1400–1350 B.C. Fragment approx. 1′ × 2′ 3″. British Museum, London.

Another fresco fragment from Nebamun's tomb shows four noblewomen watching and apparently participating in a musicale and dance where two nimble and almost nude dancing girls perform at a banquet (FIG. **3-31**). When Nebamun was buried, his family must have eaten the customary ceremonial meal at his tomb. They would have returned one day each year to partake in a commemorative banquet for the living to commune with the dead. This fresco represents just such a funerary feast, with an ample supply of wine jars at the right. It also shows that New Kingdom artists did not always adhere to the old standards for figural representation. The overlapping of the dancers' figures, their facing in opposite directions, and their rather complicated gyrations were carefully and accurately observed and executed, and the result is also a pleasing intertwined motif. The profile view of the dancers is consistent with their lesser importance than the others in the Egyptian hierarchy. The composite view is still reserved for Nebamun and his family. Of the four seated women, the artist represented the two at the left conventionally, but the other two face the observer in what is a rarely attempted frontal pose. They clap and beat time to the dance, while one of them plays the reeds. The artist took careful note of the soles of their feet as they sat cross-legged and suggested the movement of the women's heads by the loose arrangement of their hair strands. This informality constituted a relaxation of the Old Kingdom's stiff representational rules.

The frescoes in Nebamun's tomb testify to the luxurious life of the Egyptian nobility, filled with good food and drink, fine musicians, lithe dancers, and leisure time to hunt and fish in the marshes. But, as in the earlier tomb of Ti, the scenes should be read both literally and allegorically. Although Nebamun is shown enjoying himself in the afterlife, the artist symbolically asked viewers to recall how he got there. Hunting scenes reminded Egyptians of Horus, the son of Osiris, hunting down his father's murderer, Seth, the god of disorder, thus assuring a happy existence for Nebamun. And music and dance were sacred to Hathor, who aided the

dead in their passage to the other world. The sensual women at the banquet are a reference to fertility, rebirth, and regeneration—the conquest of death that made the afterlife possible.

Akhenaton and the Amarna Period

A RELIGIOUS REVOLUTION Not long after Nebamun was laid to rest in his tomb at Thebes, a short but violent upheaval occurred in Egyptian society and in Egyptian art—the only major break in the continuity of their long tradition. In the mid-fourteenth century B.C., the pharaoh Amenhotep IV, later known as Akhenaton (r. 1353–1335 B.C.), abandoned the worship of most of the Egyptian gods in favor of Aton, the universal and only god, identified with the sun disk. He blotted out the name of Amen from all inscriptions and even from his own name and that of his father, Amenhotep III. He emptied the great temples, enraged the priests, and moved his capital downriver from Thebes to a site named for Aton and now called Tell el-Amarna, where he built his own city and shrines. The pharaoh claimed for himself the new and universal god, making himself both the son and sole prophet of Aton. To him alone could the god make revelation. Moreover, in stark contrast to earlier practice, Akhenaton's god was represented neither in animal nor in human form but simply as the sun disk emitting life-giving rays.

A NEW APPROACH TO REPRESENTATION After Akhenaton's death, his new city was largely abandoned, and traditional religion triumphed. But during the brief heretical episode, profound changes occurred in Egyptian art. A colossal statue of Akhenaton from Karnak (FIG. **3-32**), toppled and buried after his death, retains the standard frontal pose of canonical pharaonic portraits. But the effeminate body, with its curving contours, and the long full-lipped face, heavy-lidded eyes, and dreaming ex-

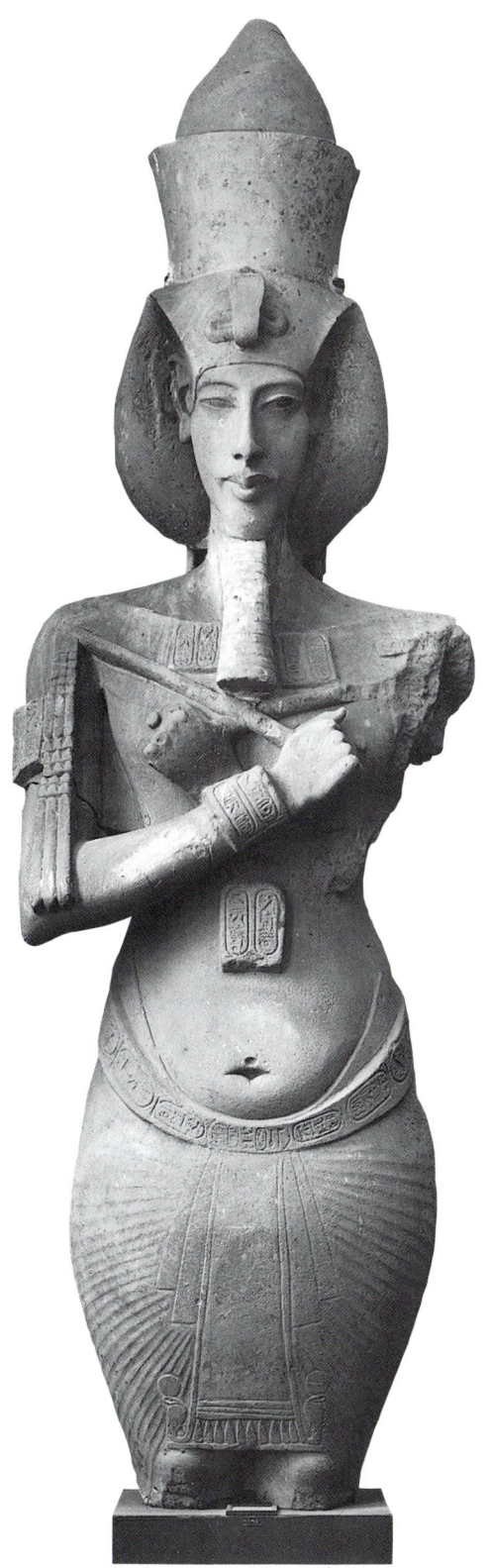

rians think that Akhenaton's portrait is a deliberate artistic reaction against the established style, paralleling the suppression of traditional religion. They argue that Akhenaton's artists tried to formulate a new androgynous image of the pharaoh as the manifestation of Aton, the sexless sun disk. But no consensus exists other than that the style was revolutionary and short lived.

PORTRAITS OF TWO QUEENS The famous painted limestone bust of Akhenaton's queen, Nefertiti (FIG. **3-33**), exhibits a similar expression of entranced musing and an almost mannered sensitivity and delicacy of curving contour. The piece was found in the workshop of the queen's official sculptor, THUTMOSE, and is a deliberately unfinished model very likely by the master's own hand. The left eye socket still lacks the inlaid eyeball, making the portrait a kind of before-and-after demonstration piece. With this elegant bust, Thutmose may have been alluding to a heavy flower on its slender stalk by exaggerating the weight of the crowned head and the length of the almost serpentine neck. Readers might think of those modern descendants of Nefertiti (her name means "The Beautiful One Is Here")—models in fashion magazines, with

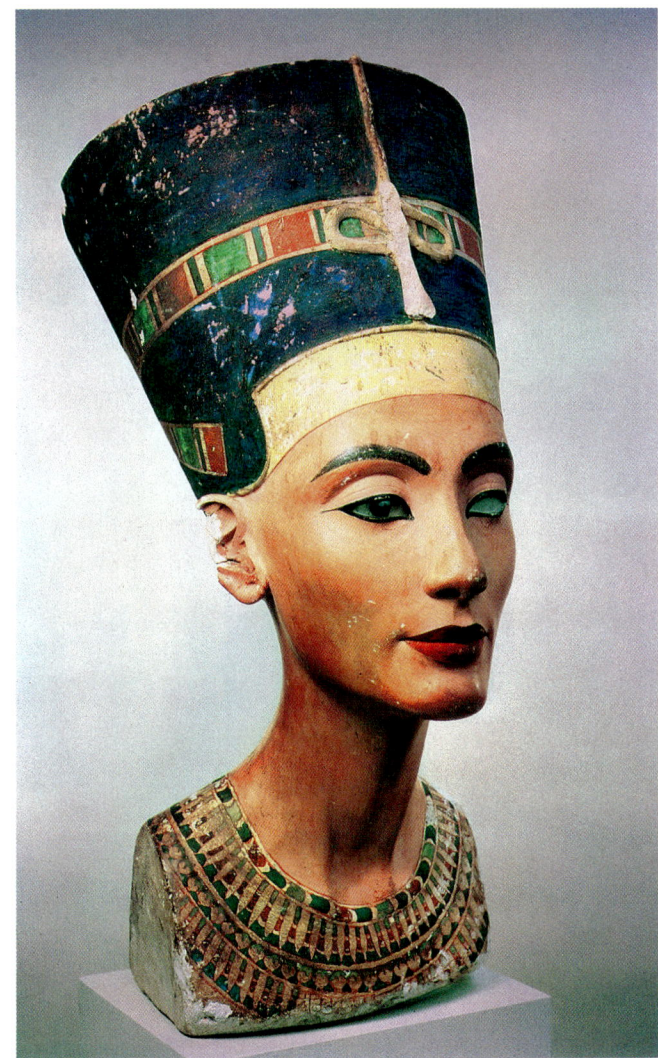

3-32 Akhenaton, from the temple of Amen-Re, Karnak, Egypt, Dynasty XVIII, ca. 1353–1335 B.C. Sandstone, approx. 13′ high. Egyptian Museum, Cairo.

pression are a far cry indeed from the heroically proportioned figures of Akhenaton's predecessors (compare FIG. 3-13). Akhenaton's body is curiously misshapen, with weak arms, a narrow waist, protruding belly, wide hips, and fatty thighs. Modern doctors have tried to explain his physique by a variety of illnesses. They cannot agree on a diagnosis, and their premise—that the statue is an accurate depiction of a physical deformity—is probably faulty. Some art histo-

3-33 THUTMOSE, Nefertiti, from Tell el-Amarna, Egypt, Dynasty XVIII, ca. 1353–1335 B.C. Painted limestone, approx. 1′ 8″ high. Ägyptisches Museum, Berlin.

their gaunt, swaying frames; masklike faces; and enormous shadowed eyes. As modern mannerism shapes living models to its dictates, so the sculptors of Tell el-Amarna may have adjusted their subjects' actual likenesses to their standard of spiritual beauty.

A moving portrait of old age is preserved in the miniature head of Queen Tiye (FIG. **3-34**), mother of Akhenaton. Tiye was the chief wife of Amenhotep III and a commoner by birth. The pharaoh seems to have married her for love rather than for political reasons. The portrait illustrated here was fashioned during her son's reign and was found at Gurob with other objects connected with the funerary cult of Amenhotep III. The beautiful black queen (the Egyptians were a people of mixed race and frequently married other Africans) is shown as an older woman with lines and furrows, consistent with the new relaxation of artistic rules in the Amarna age. The head was carved in yew wood, the heavy-lidded slanting eyes are inlaid with alabaster and ebony, the lips are painted red, and the preserved earring is of gold and lapis lazuli. The present headcloth

is of plaster and linen with small blue beads; it covers what was originally a silver-foil headdress. A gold band still adorns the forehead. The luxurious materials were worthy of a beloved queen.

AN INTIMATE LOOK AT A ROYAL COUPLE
During the last three years of his reign, Akhenaton's co-regent was his half brother, Smenkhkare. A relief from Tell el-Amarna (FIG. **3-35**) may show Smenkhkare and his wife Meritaten in an informal, even intimate, pose that contrasts strongly with the traditional formality in representations of exalted persons. Undulating curves replace rigid lines, and Smenkhkare's pose has no known precedent. The prince leans casually on his staff, one leg at ease, in an attitude that indicates the sculptor's knowledge of the flexible shift of body masses, a principle not fully demonstrated until the fifth century B.C. in Greece. This quite realistic detail accompanies others that show a freer expression of what the artist observed. These include details of costume and departures from the tra-

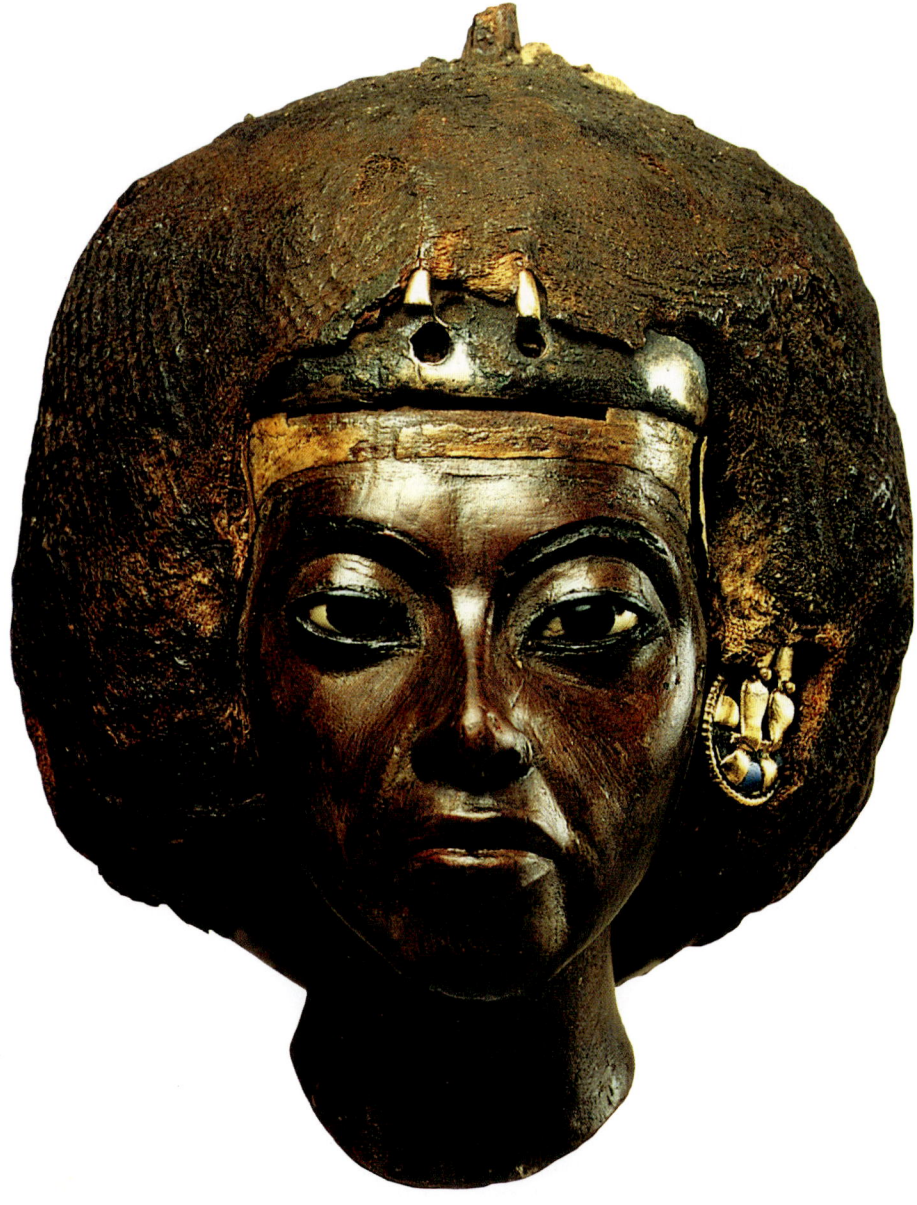

3-34   Tiye, from Gurob, Egypt, Dynasty XVIII, ca. 1353–1335 B.C. Wood, with gold, silver, alabaster, and lapis lazuli, approx. $3\frac{3}{4}''$ high. Ägyptisches Museum, Berlin.

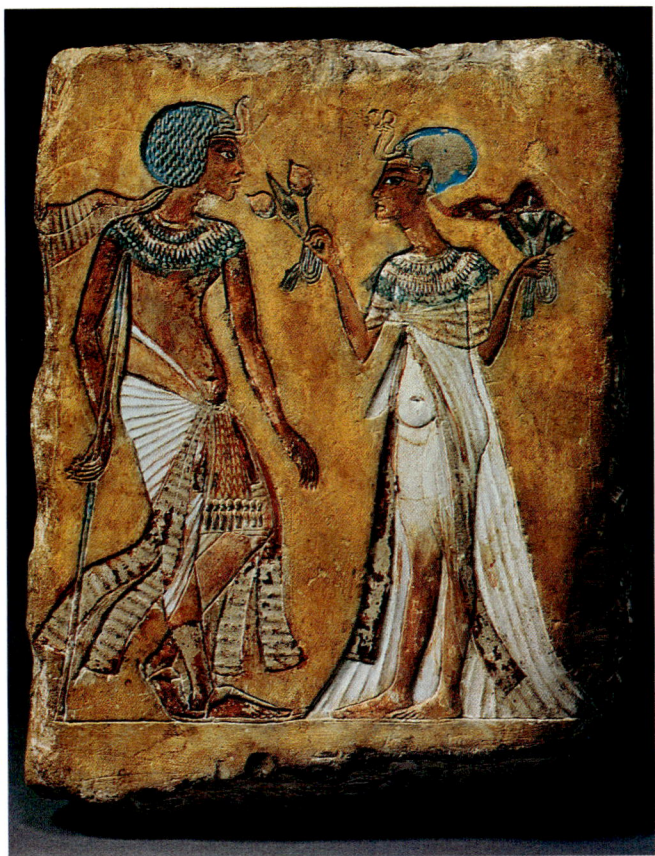

3-35 Smenkhkare and Meritaten(?), from Tell el-Amarna, Egypt, Dynasty XVIII, ca. 1335 B.C. Painted limestone relief, approx. $9\frac{1}{2}''$ high. Ägyptisches Museum, Berlin.

ditional formality, such as the elongated neck and head of Meritaten and the prominent bellies that characterize figures of the Amarna school. The political and religious revolution under Akhenaton was matched by an equally radical upheaval in relief sculpture and painting, as well as in statuary.

The Tomb of Tutankhamen and the Post-Amarna Period

The pharaohs who followed Akhenaton reestablished the cult and priesthood of Amen and restored the temples and the inscriptions. The gigantic temple complexes at Karnak and Luxor (FIGS. 3-25 to 3-27) already examined were dedicated to the renewed worship of the Theban god Amen. When Akhenaton's religious revolution was undone, artists, too, soon returned to the old conservative manner.

TREASURES OF A BOY KING The legacy of the Amarna style may be seen, however, in the fabulously rich art and artifacts found in the largely unplundered tomb of Tutankhamen (r. 1333–1323 B.C.), who was probably Akhenaton's son by a minor wife. Tutankhamen ruled for a decade and died at age eighteen. The treasures of his tomb, which include sculpture, furniture, jewelry, and accessories of all sorts, were uncovered in 1922. The adventure of their discovery

gained world renown not only for their excavator, Howard Carter, but also for the boy king. Tutankhamen was a very minor figure in Egyptian history. The public remembers him today solely because of the chance survival of his tomb's furnishings.

The principal monument in the collection is the enshrined body of the pharaoh himself. The royal mummy reposed in the innermost of three coffins, nested one within the other. The innermost coffin (FIG. **3-36**) was the most luxurious of the three. Made of beaten gold (about a quarter ton of it) and inlaid with such semiprecious stones as lapis lazuli, turquoise,

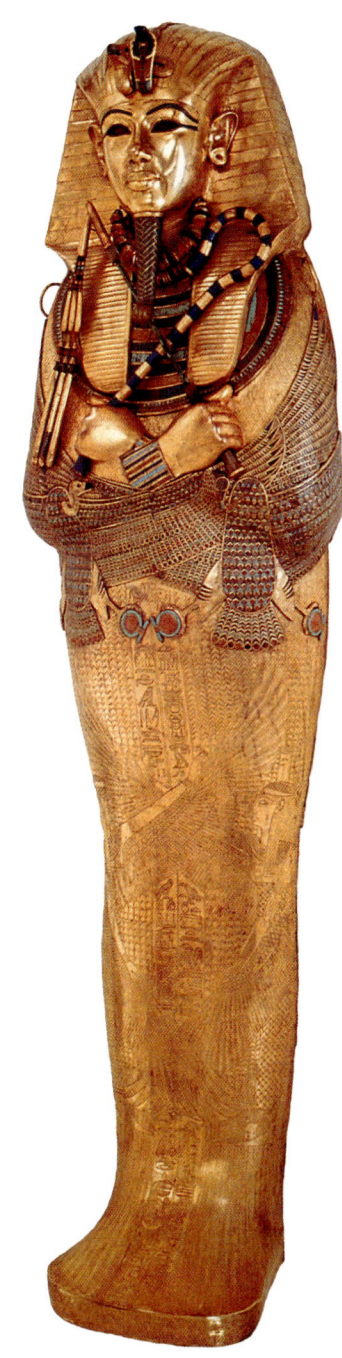

3-36 Innermost coffin of Tutankhamen, from his tomb at Thebes, Egypt, Dynasty XVIII, ca. 1323 B.C. Gold with inlay of enamel and semiprecious stones, approx. 6' 1" long. Egyptian Museum, Cairo.

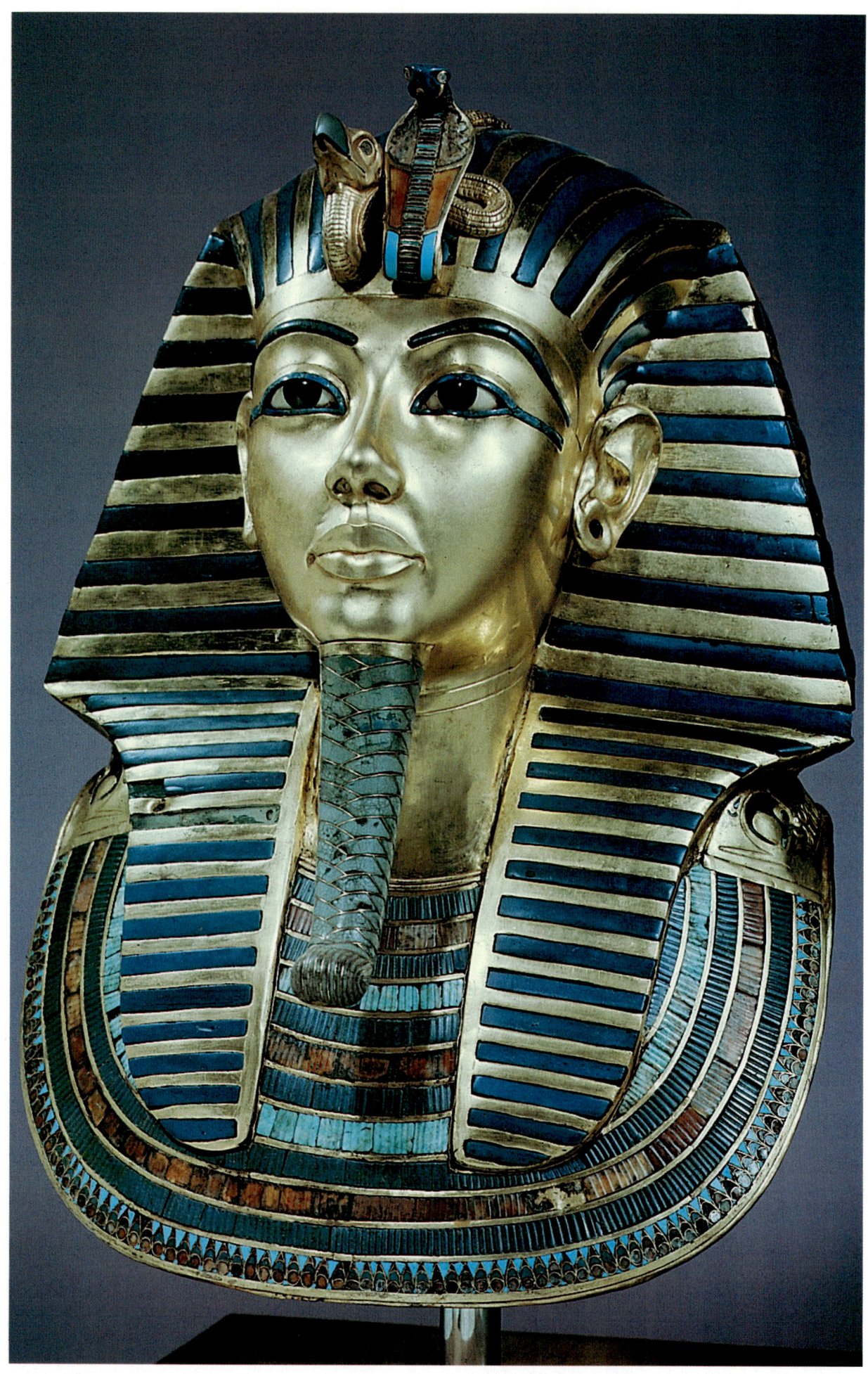

3-37 Death mask of Tutankhamen, from the innermost coffin in his tomb at Thebes, Egypt, Dynasty XVIII, ca. 1323 B.C. Gold with inlay of semiprecious stones, $1'9\frac{1}{4}''$ high. Egyptian Museum, Cairo.

and carnelian, it is a supreme monument to the sculptor's and goldsmith's crafts. The portrait mask (FIG. 3-37), which covered the king's face, is also made of gold with inlaid semiprecious stones. It is a sensitive portrayal of the serene adolescent king dressed in his official regalia, including the nemes headdress and false beard. The general effects of the mask and of the tomb treasures as a whole are of grandeur and richness expressive of Egyptian power, pride, and affluence. One can scarcely imagine what kinds of luxury goods were buried with the truly important pharaohs.

TUTANKHAMEN AS WORLD CONQUEROR Although Tutankhamen probably was considered too young to fight, his position as king required that he be represented as a conqueror. He is shown as such in the panels of a painted chest (FIG. **3-38**) deposited in his tomb. The lid panel shows the king as a successful hunter pursuing droves of fleeing animals in the desert, and the side panel shows him as a great warrior. Together, the two panels are a double advertisement of royal power comparable to the later reliefs adorning Assyrian

palaces (see FIGS. 2-22 and 2-24). From a war chariot drawn by spirited, plumed horses, Tutankhamen, shown larger than all other figures on the chest, draws his bow against a cluster of bearded Asian enemies, who fall in confusion before him. He slays the enemy, like game, in great numbers. Behind Tutankhamen are three tiers of undersized war chariots, which serve to magnify the king's figure and to increase the count of his warriors. The themes are traditional, but the fluid, curvilinear forms are features reminiscent of the Amarna style. So are the artist's dynamic compositions, with their emphasis on movement and action. This emphasis is seen in the disposition of the hunted, overthrown animals and enemy, who, freed of conventional ground lines, race wildly across the panels.

OSIRIS AND THE *BOOK OF THE DEAD* Tutankhamen's mummy case (FIG. 3-36) shows the boy king in the guise of Osiris, god of the dead and king of the underworld, as well as giver of eternal life. The ritual of the cult of Osiris is recorded in collections of spells and prayers that comprise the so-called *Book of the Dead*. Illustrated papyrus

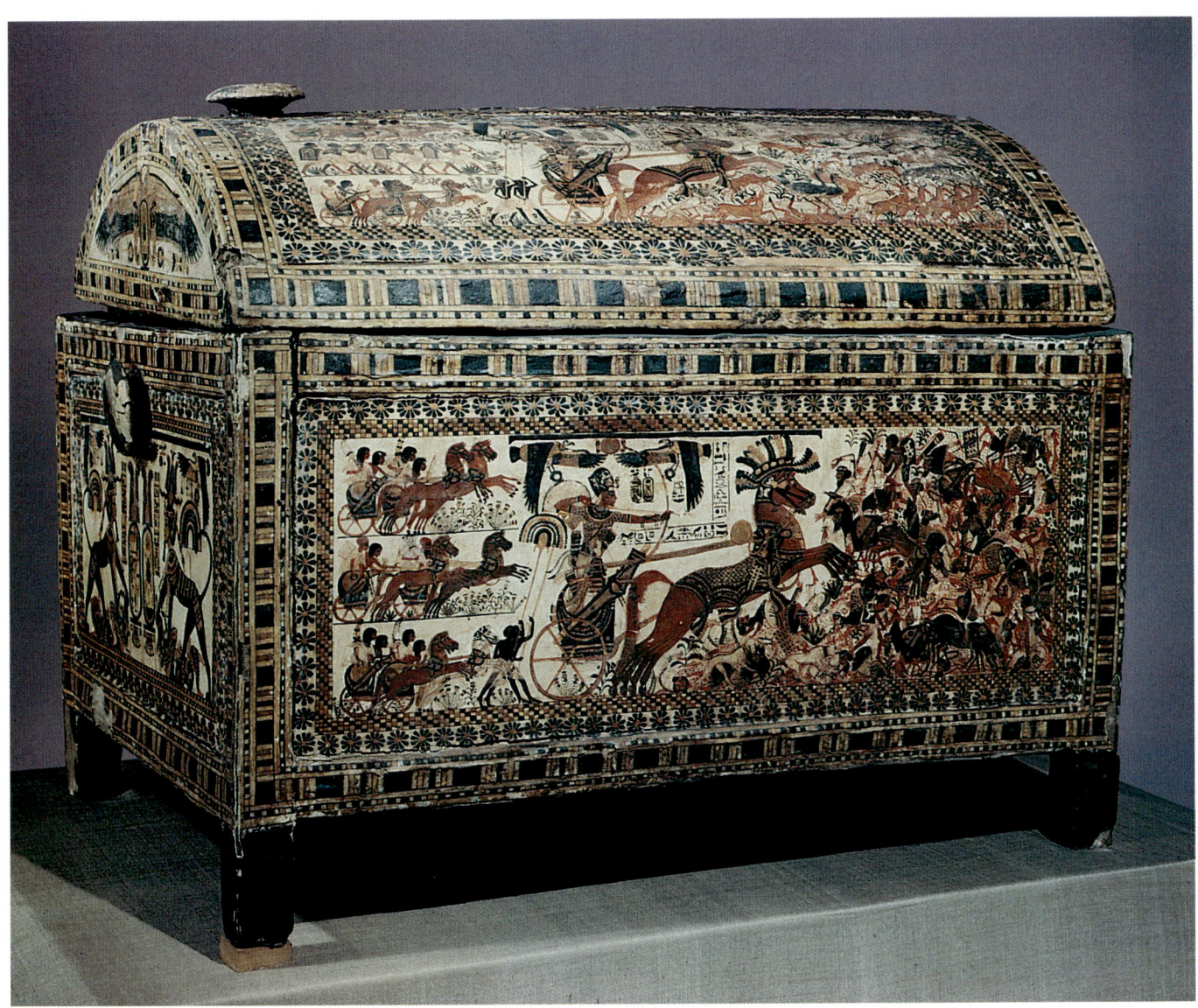

3-38   Painted chest, from the Tomb of Tutankhamen, Thebes, Egypt, ca. 1333–1323 B.C. Wood, approx. 1′ 8″ long. Egyptian Museum, Cairo.

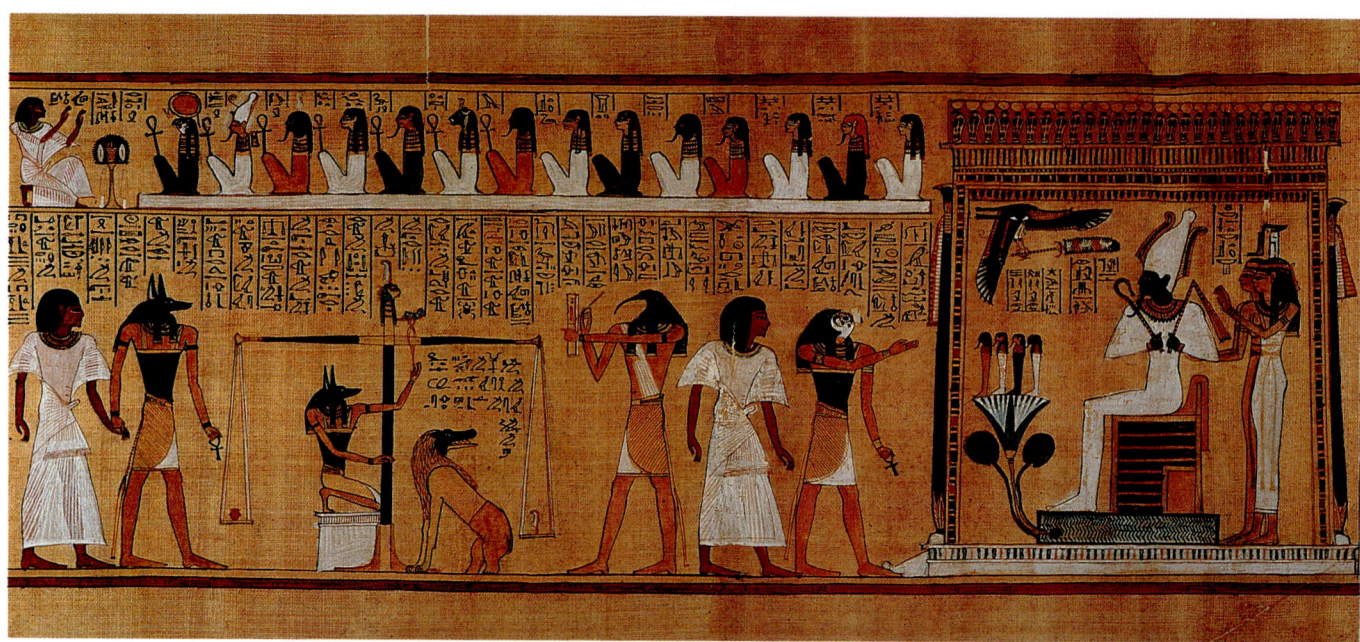

3-39 Last judgment of Hu-Nefer, from his tomb at Thebes, Egypt, Dynasty XIX, ca. 1290–1280 B.C. Painted papyrus scroll, approx. 1′ 6″ high. British Museum, London.

scrolls, some as long as seventy feet, containing these texts were the essential equipment of the tombs of well-to-do persons. The scroll of Hu-Nefer, the royal scribe and steward of the pharaoh Seti I, was found in his tomb in the Theban necropolis. Our illustration (FIG. **3-39**) represents the final judgment of the deceased. At the left, Anubis, the jackal-headed god of embalming, leads Hu-Nefer into the hall of judgment. The god then adjusts the scales to weigh the dead man's heart against the feather of the goddess Maat, protectress of truth and right. A hybrid monster, Ammit, half hippopotamus and half lion, the devourer of the sinful, awaits the decision of the scales. If the weighing had been unfavorable to the deceased, the monster would have eaten his heart on the spot. The ibis-headed god Thoth records the proceedings. Above, the gods of the Egyptian pantheon are arranged as witnesses, while Hu-Nefer kneels in adoration before them. Having been justified by the scales, Hu-Nefer is brought by Osiris's son, the falcon-headed Horus, into the presence of the green-faced Osiris and his sisters Isis and Nephthys to receive the award of eternal life.

THE LATE PERIOD

THE TRIUMPH OF TRADITION   In Hu-Nefer's scroll, the figures have all the formality of stance, shape, and attitude of Old Kingdom art. Abstract figures and hieroglyphs alike are aligned rigidly. Nothing here was painted in the flexible, curvilinear style suggestive of movement that was evident in the art of Amarna and Tutankhamen. The return to conser-

vatism was complete. So, in essence, it remained through the last centuries of ancient Egyptian figural art. During this time, Egypt lost the commanding role it once had played in the ancient Near East. The empire dwindled away, and foreign powers invaded, occupied, and ruled the land, until it was taken over by Alexander the Great of Macedon and his Greek successors and, eventually, by the emperors of Rome.

A portrait statue of Mentuemhet (FIG. **3-40**), a rich and powerful man who was Mayor of Thebes and Fourth Priest of Amen during the Twenty-Sixth Dynasty in the seventh century B.C., easily could be mistaken for an Old Kingdom work. The venerable formulas, conventions, and details of representation are all here in summary. The rigidity of the stance, the frontality, and the spareness of silhouette with arms at the side and left leg advanced all recall Old Kingdom statuary (compare FIG. 3-13). Only the double wig, characteristic of the New Kingdom, and the realism of the head, with its rough and almost brutal characterization, differentiate the work from that of the earlier age.

The Late Period pharaohs deliberately referred back to the art of Egypt's classical phase to give their royal image authority. Religious and political motives only partly explain this deliberate archaism, however. As noted throughout this chapter, conservatism was an Egyptian character trait, perhaps the principal trait. The ancient Egyptians' resistance to significant change for almost three millennia is one of the marvels of the history of art. It testifies to the invention of a pictorial style that proved so satisfactory that it endured in Egypt, while everywhere else in the ancient Mediterranean, stylistic change was the only common denominator.

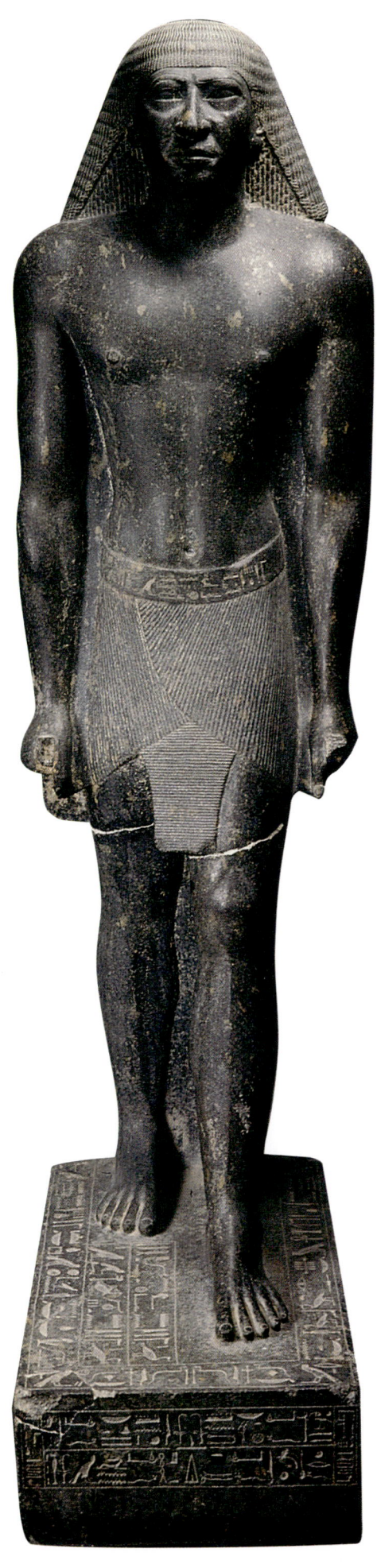

3-40 Mentuemhet, from Karnak, Egypt, Dynasty XXVI, ca. 650 B.C. Granite, approx. 4′ 5″ high. Egyptian Museum, Cairo.

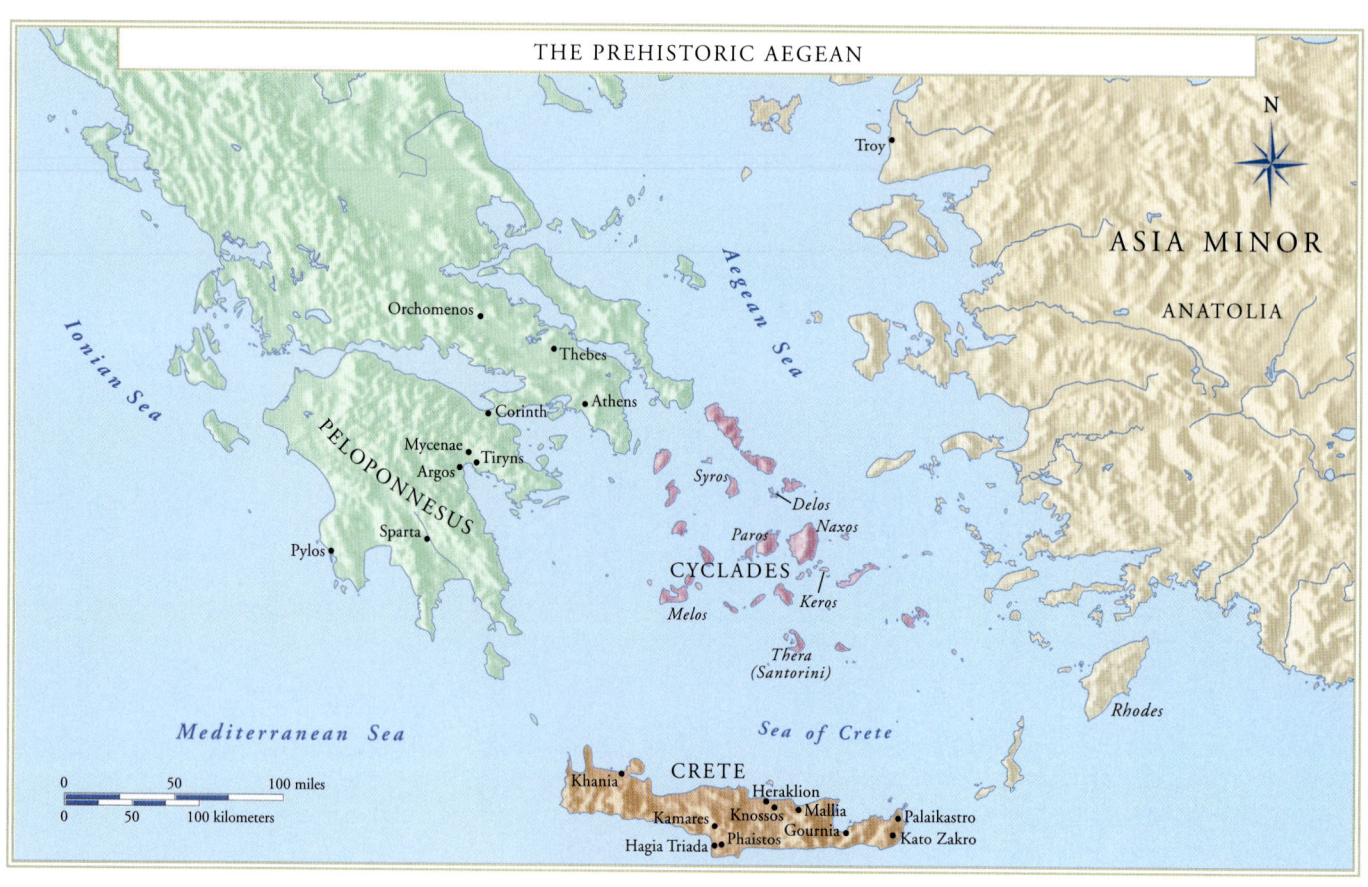

THE PREHISTORIC AEGEAN

	3000 B.C.	2000 B.C.	1700 B.C.	1600 B.C.
CYCLADES	EARLY CYCLADIC	MIDDLE CYCLADIC	LATE CYCLADIC	
CRETE	EARLY MINOAN	MIDDLE MINOAN	LATE MINOAN	
MAINLAND GREECE	EARLY HELLADIC	MIDDLE HELLADIC	LATE HELLADIC (MYCENAEAN)	

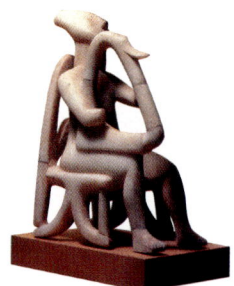

Cycladic lyre player
Keros, ca. 2700–2500 B.C.

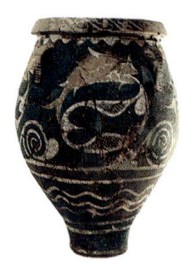

Kamares Ware jar
Phaistos, ca. 1800–1700 B.C.

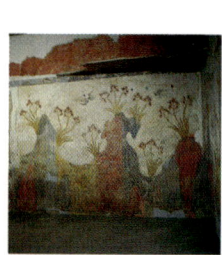

Spring Fresco
Akrotiri, ca. 1650 B.C.

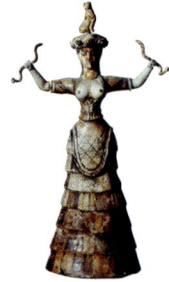

Snake Goddess
Knossos, ca. 1600 B.C.

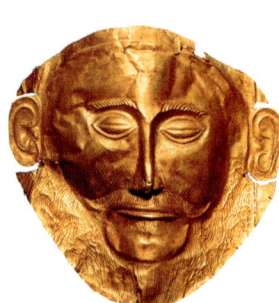

Gold funerary mask
Mycenae, ca. 1600–1500 B.C.

Old Palace period on Crete, ca. 2000–1700 B.C.

Linear A script developed, ca. 1700–1600 B.C.

New Palace period on Crete, ca. 1700–1400 B.C.

Theran eruption, ca. 1628 B.C.

4

MINOS AND THE HEROES OF HOMER

THE ART OF THE PREHISTORIC AEGEAN

1500 B.C.	1400 B.C.	1300 B.C.	1200 B.C.
			SUB-MINOAN
			SUB-MYCENAEAN

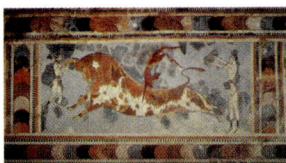

Toreador Fresco
Knossos, ca. 1450–1400 B.C.

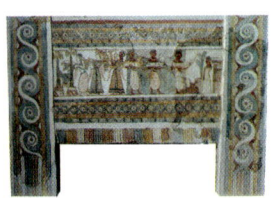

Hagia Triada sarcophagus
ca. 1450–1400 B.C.

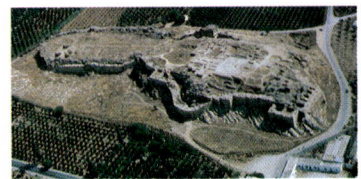

Citadel, Tiryns
ca. 1400–1200 B.C.

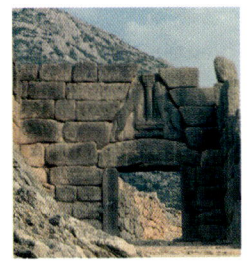

Lion Gate, Mycenae
ca. 1300–1250 B.C.

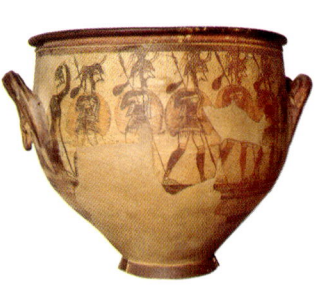

Warrior Vase
Mycenae, ca. 1200 B.C.

Mycenaeans at Knossos, ca. 1450–1400 B.C.

Linear B script developed, ca. 1400–1300 B.C.

Post-palatial period on Crete, ca. 1400–1200 B.C.

Destruction of
Mycenaean palaces,
ca. 1200 B.C.

THE PREHISTORIC AEGEAN REDISCOVERED

HOMER'S TROY

Clan after clan poured out from the ships and huts onto the plain . . . innumerable as the leaves and blossoms in their season . . . the Athenians . . . the men of Argos and Tiryns of the Great Walls . . . troops from the great stronghold of Mycenae, from wealthy Corinth . . . from Knossos . . . Phaistos . . . and the other troops that had their homes in Crete of the Hundred Towns.[1]

So Homer describes in the *Iliad* the might and splendor of the Greek armies poised before the walls of Troy. The Greeks had come to seek revenge against Paris, the Trojan prince who had abducted Helen, wife of King Menelaus of Sparta.

Many consider the *Iliad*, composed around 750 B.C., to be the finest epic poem ever written. It is unquestionably the first great work of Greek literature. Until about 1870, however, Homer's tale was regarded as pure fiction, and scholars discounted the bard as a historian, attributing the profusion of names and places in his writings to the rich abundance of his imagination. The prehistory of Greece remained shadowy and lost, historians believed, in an impenetrable world of myth.

That scholars had done less than justice to the truth of Homer's account was proved by a German amateur archeologist. Between 1870 and his death twenty years later, Heinrich Schliemann uncovered some of the very cities of the heroes Homer celebrated: Troy, Mycenae, and Tiryns. In 1870, Schliemann began work at Hissarlik on the northwestern coast of Turkey, which a British archeologist, Frank Calvert, had postulated was the site of Homer's Troy. Schliemann dug into a vast *tell*, or mound, and found a number of fortified cities built on the remains of one another. One of them had been destroyed by fire in the thirteenth century B.C. This, scholars now generally agree, was the Troy of King Priam and his son Paris, celebrated by Homer some five hundred years later.

Schliemann continued his excavations at Mycenae on the Greek mainland, where, he believed, King Agamemnon, Menelaus's brother, had once ruled. Here his finds were even more startling. A massive fortress-palace; elaborate tombs; and quantities of gold jewelry and ornaments, cups, and inlaid weapons revealed a magnificent civilization far older than the famous vestiges of Classical Greece that had always remained visible in Athens and elsewhere. Further discoveries proved that Mycenae had not been the only center of this fabulous civilization.

KING MINOS'S CRETE
The lesson of Schliemann's success in pursuing hunches based on the careful reading of ancient literature was not lost on his successors. Another Greek legend told of King Minos of Knossos on the island of Crete, who had exacted from Athens a tribute of youths and maidens to be fed to the Minotaur, a creature half bull and half man housed in a vast labyrinth. Might this story, too, be based on fact? In 1900, an Englishman, Arthur Evans, began work at Knossos. A short time later he uncovered a palace that did indeed resemble a maze. Evans named the people who had erected it the Minoans, after their mythological king. His initial findings were augmented quickly by additional excavations at Phaistos, Hagia Triada, and other sites, including Gournia, which was explored between 1901 and 1904 by an American archeologist, Harriet Boyd Hawes, one of the first women to direct a major excavation.

More recently, important Minoan remains have been excavated at many other locations on Crete, and contemporary sites have been discovered on other islands in the Aegean, most notably on Santorini (ancient Thera). Art historians now have an array of buildings, paintings, and, to a lesser extent, sculptures that attests to the wealth and sophistication of the people who lived in that once obscure heroic age celebrated in later Greek mythology.

AEGEAN ARCHEOLOGY TODAY Less glamorous than the palaces and works of art, but arguably more important for the understanding of Aegean society, are the many documents archeologists have discovered written in scripts dubbed Linear A and Linear B. The progress made during the past several decades in the deciphering of these texts has provided a welcome corrective to the romanticism that characterized the work of Schliemann and Evans. Scholars have begun to reconstruct Aegean civilization by referring to contemporary records of mundane transactions and not just to Homer's heroic account.

Historians now also know that humans inhabited Greece as far back as the Lower Paleolithic period and that village life was firmly established in Greece in Neolithic times. But the heyday of the ancient Aegean was not until the second millennium B.C., well after the emergence of the river valley civilizations of Egypt and Mesopotamia. Close contact existed at various times between the peoples of the Aegean and the Near East and Egypt, but each civilization manifested an originality of its own.

The Aegean civilizations have long held a special interest for students of the later history of Western art, because they were the direct forerunners of the first truly European civilization, that of Greece. But the art and architecture of the ancient Near East and Egypt also played a major role in the early development of Greek art. And it is also well to remember that the Minoans and Mycenaeans were not Greeks, did not speak Greek, and did not worship Greek gods, even though they inhabited a part of the Mediterranean today incorporated in the modern nation of Greece.

AEGEAN GEOGRAPHY AND AEGEAN ART The sea-dominated geography of the Aegean contrasts sharply with that of the Near East, as does its temperate climate. The situation of Crete and the Aegean Islands at the commercial crossroads of the ancient Mediterranean had a major effect on their prosperity. The sea also provided a natural defense against the frequent and often disruptive invasions that checker the histories of land-bound civilizations such as those of Mesopotamia.

Historians, art historians, and archeologists alike divide the prehistoric Aegean into three geographic areas, and each has a distinctive artistic identity. *Cycladic* art is the art of the Cycladic Islands (those that *circle* around Delos), as well as of the adjacent islands in the Aegean, excluding Crete. *Minoan* art encompasses the art of Crete. *Helladic* art is the art of the Greek mainland (*Hellas* in Greek). Each area is subdivided chronologically into early, middle, and late periods, with the art of the Late Helladic period designated *Mycenaean* after Agamemnon's great citadel of Mycenae.

CYCLADIC ART

"MODERN" SCULPTURE CA. 2500 B.C.   Marble was abundantly available in the superb quarries of the Aegean Islands, especially on Naxos and Paros. These same quarries later supplied the master sculptors of classical Greece and Rome with fine marble blocks for monumental statues. But nothing surviving from the classical era is quite like the marble statuettes (FIGS. **4-1** and **4-2**) that date from the Early Cycladic period. These sculptures are much revered today (see "Archeology, Art History, and the Art Market," page 81) because of their striking abstract forms, which call to mind the simple and sleek shapes of some twentieth-century statues (see FIGS. 33-17 and 33-72).

Most of the Cycladic sculptures, like many of their Stone Age predecessors in the Aegean, the Near East, and western Europe (see FIG. 1-4), represent nude women with their arms folded across their abdomens. They vary in height from a few inches to almost life-size. Our example (FIG. 4-1) is about a foot and a half tall and comes from a grave on the island of Syros. The statuette typifies many of these figures. It is almost flat, and the human body is rendered in a highly schematized manner. Large simple triangles dominate the form. Note the shape of the head and the body, which tapers from exceptionally broad shoulders to tiny feet, as well as, of course, the incised triangular pubis. The feet are too fragile to support the figurine. If these sculptures were primarily funerary offerings, as archeologists believe they were, they must have been placed on their backs in the graves—lying down, like the deceased themselves. Whether they represent those buried with the statuettes or fertility figures or goddesses is still debated. As in all such images, the sculptor took pains to emphasize the breasts as well as the pubic area. In the Syros statuette a slight swelling of the belly may suggest pregnancy.

Traces of paint found on some of the Cycladic figurines indicate that at least parts of these sculptures were colored. The now almost featureless faces would have had painted eyes and mouths in addition to the sculptured noses. Red and blue necklaces and bracelets, as well as painted dots on the cheeks, characterize a number of the surviving figurines.

A MUSICIAN PLAYS FOR ALL ETERNITY   Male figures also occur in the Cycladic repertoire. The most elaborate of these take the form of seated musicians, such as the lyre player from Keros (FIG. 4-2). Wedged between the echoing shapes of chair and instrument, he may be playing for the deceased in the afterlife, although, again, the meaning of these statuettes remains elusive. The harpist reflects the same preference for simple geometric shapes and large flat planes as the female figures. Still, the artist showed a keen interest in recording the elegant shape of what must have been a prized possession: the harp with its duck-bill or swan-head ornament at the apex of its sound box.

In one instance figurines of both a musician and a reclining woman were placed in a woman's grave. This suggests that the lyre players are not images of dead men, but it does not prove that the female figurines represent dead women. The man might be entertaining the deceased herself, not her image. The musicians also could portray a deity, a forerunner of the Greek god Apollo, whose instrument was the lyre and whose sacred animal was the swan. Given the absence of written documents in Greece at this date, as in prehistoric western Europe and the Near East, art historians cannot be sure of the meaning of many artworks. Some Cycladic figurines have been found in settlements rather than cemeteries, and it is likely, in fact, that the same form took on different meanings in different contexts.

MINOAN ART

Architecture

A PALACE CULTURE EMERGES   During the third millennium B.C., both on the Aegean Islands and on the Greek mainland, most settlements were small and consisted only of simple buildings. Only rarely were the dead buried with costly offerings such as the Cycladic statuettes examined in the previous section. The opening centuries of the second millennium (the Middle Minoan period on Crete) are marked, in contrast, by the construction of palaces to house

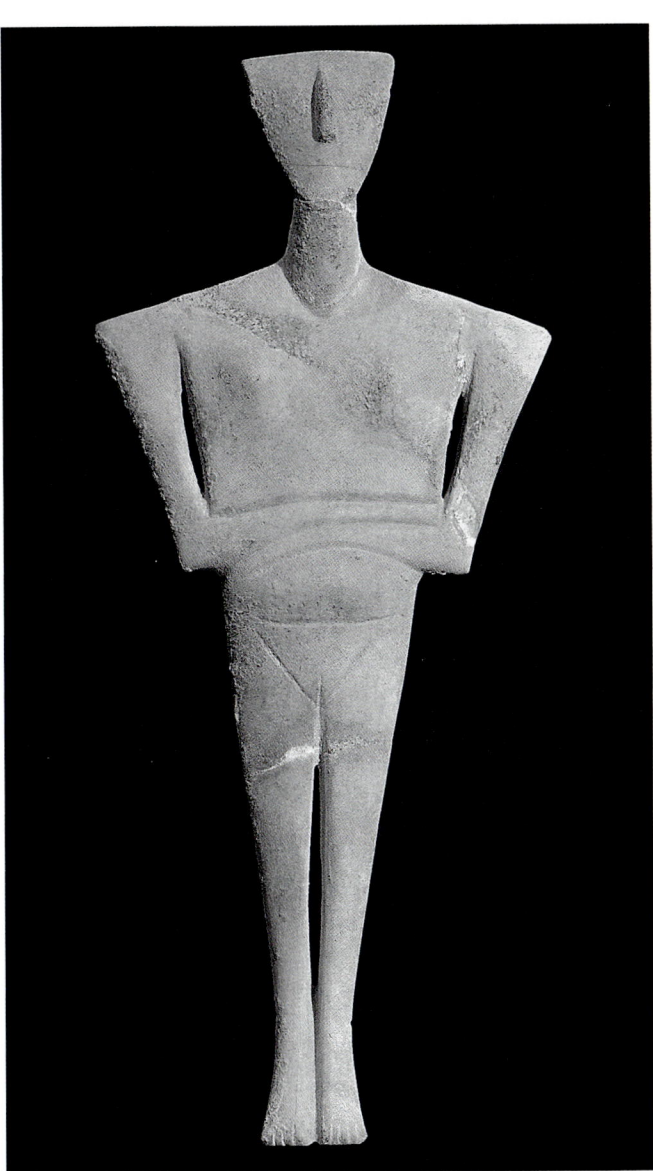

4-1   Figurine of a woman, from Syros (Cyclades), Greece, ca. 2500–2300 B.C. Marble, approx. 1′ 6″ high. National Archeological Museum, Athens.

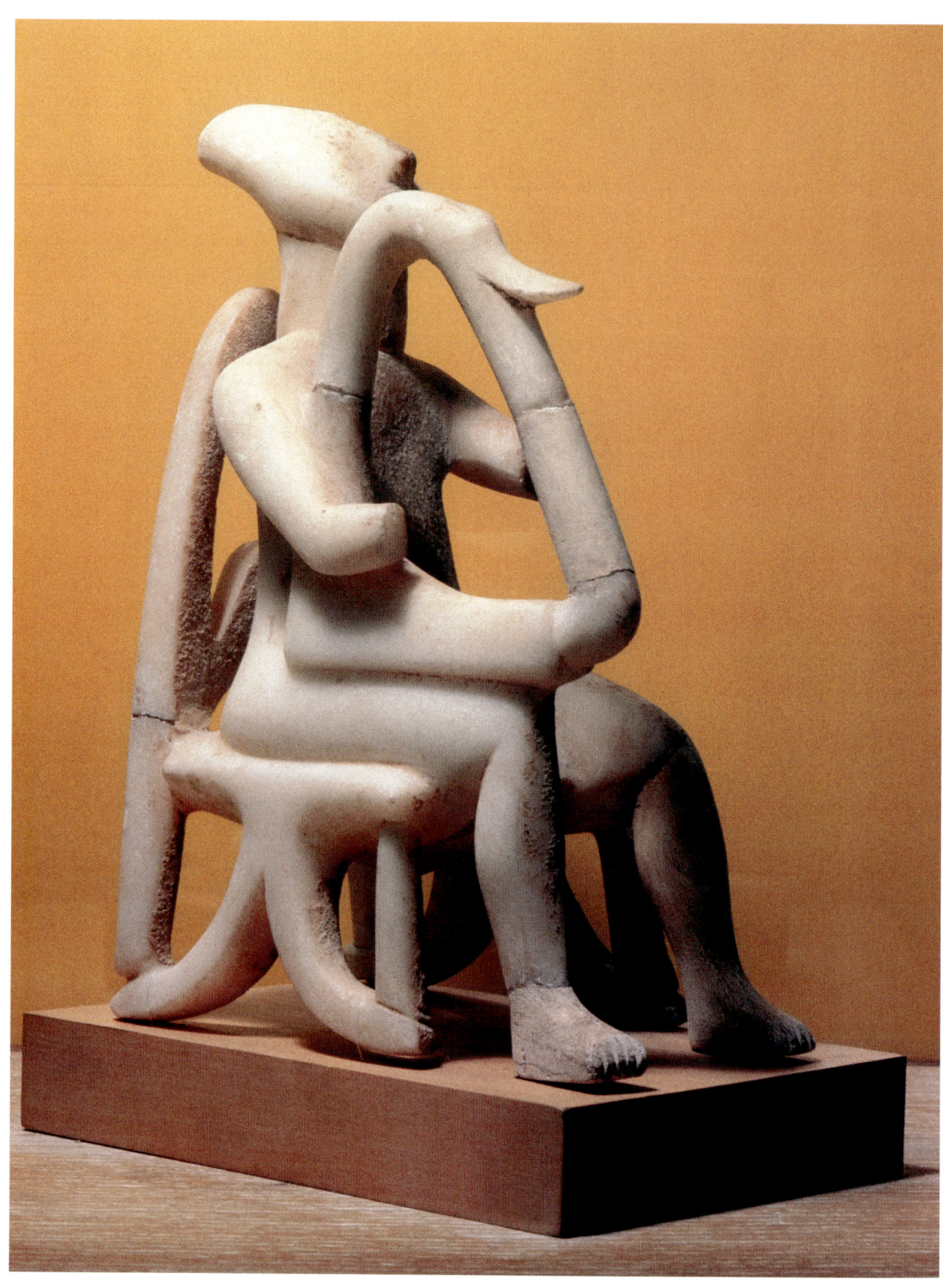

4-2 Male lyre player, from Keros (Cyclades), Greece, ca. 2700–2500 B.C. Marble, approx. 9″ high. National Archeological Museum, Athens.

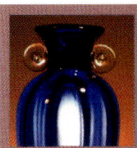

ART AND SOCIETY

Archeology, Art History, and the Art Market

One way the ancient world is fundamentally different from the world today is that ancient art is largely anonymous and undated. No equivalent exists in antiquity for the systematic signing and dating of artworks commonplace in the contemporary world. That is why the role of archeology in the study of ancient art is so important. Only the scientific excavation of ancient monuments can establish their context. Exquisite and strikingly "modern" sculptures such as the marble Cycladic figurines we illustrate (FIGS. 4-1 and 4-2) may be appreciated as masterpieces when displayed in splendid isolation in glass cases in museums or private homes. But to understand the role these or any other artworks played in ancient society—in many cases, even to determine the date and place of origin of an object—the art historian must know where the piece was uncovered. Only when the context of an artwork is known can one go beyond an appreciation of its formal qualities and begin to analyze its place in art history—and in the society that produced it.

The extraordinary popularity of Cycladic figurines in recent decades has had unfortunate consequences. Clandestine treasure hunters, anxious to meet the insatiable demands of modern collectors, have plundered many sites and smuggled their finds out of Greece to sell to the highest bidder on the international art market. Entire prehistoric cemeteries and towns have been destroyed because of the high esteem now held for these sculptures. Two British scholars recently calculated that only about ten percent of the known Cycladic marble statuettes come from secure archeological contexts. Many of the rest are probably forgeries, produced mostly after World War II when developments in modern art fostered a new appreciation of these abstract renditions of human anatomy and created a boom in demand for "Cycladica" among collectors. For some categories of Cycladic sculptures—those of unusual type or size—not a single piece with a documented provenance exists. Those groups may be inventions of twentieth-century artisans designed to fetch even higher prices due to their rarity. Consequently, most of the conclusions art historians have drawn about chronology, attribution to different workshops, range of types, and how the figurines were used are purely speculative. The importance of the information the original contexts would have provided cannot be underestimated. That information is, however, probably never recoverable.

---

kings, priestesses, and their retinues. This first, or Old Palace, period came to an abrupt end around 1700 B.C., when these grand structures were destroyed, probably by an earthquake. Rebuilding began sometime after 1700 B.C., and the ensuing New Palace (Late Minoan) period is the golden age of Crete, an era when the first great Western civilization emerged.

The rebuilt palaces were large, comfortable, and handsome, with ample staircases and courtyards for pageants, ceremonies, and games. They also had storerooms, offices, and shrines that permitted these huge complexes to serve as the key administrative, commercial, and religious centers of Minoan life, as well as royal residences. Archeologists have uncovered their ruins, along with rich treasures of art and artifacts that document the power and prosperity of Minoan civilization. The principal palace sites on Crete are at Knossos, Phaistos, Mallia, Kato Zakro, and Khania. All of the palaces were laid out along similar lines.

THE LABYRINTH OF THE MINOTAUR The largest of the palaces, at Knossos (FIGS. **4-3** and **4-4**), was the legendary home of King Minos. Here the hero Theseus was said to have battled with and defeated the bull-man Minotaur. According to legend, Theseus found his way out of the mazelike palace complex only with the aid of Minos's daughter Ariadne, who had given him a spindle of thread to mark his path through the labyrinth and then safely out again. In fact, the English word *labyrinth* derives from the intricate plan and scores of rooms of the Knossos palace. *Labrys* means "double ax" in Greek, and it is a recurring motif in the Minoan palace, referring to sacrificial slaughter. The *labyrinth* was the "House of the Double Axes," where the Minotaur dwelled.

Our aerial view (FIG. 4-3) reveals that the Knossos palace was a rambling structure built against the upper slopes and across the top of a low hill that rises from a fertile plain. All around the palace proper were mansions and villas, presumably belonging to high officials in the service of the royal house. The great rectangular court (no. 4 in FIG. 4-4), with the palace units grouped around it, had been leveled in the time of the old palace. The manner of the grouping of buildings suggests that the new palace was carefully planned, with the court as the major organizing element.

A secondary organization of the palace plan involves two long corridors. On the west side of the court, a north-south corridor (no. 6) separates official and ceremonial rooms from the magazines (no. 8), where wine, grain, oil, and honey were stored in large jars. On the east side of the court, a smaller east-west corridor (no. 14) separates the living quarters and reception rooms (to the south) from the workers' and servants' quarters (to the north). At the northwest corner of the palace is a theater-like area (no. 5) with steps on two sides that may have served as seats. This form is a possible forerunner of the later Greek theater (see FIG. 5-70). Its purpose is unknown, but it is a feature paralleled in the Phaistos palace.

The grand courtyard is the focus of many Cretan palaces, and, despite the complexity of the plans, these palaces seem to be variations of a common layout. The buildings were well constructed, with thick walls composed of rough, unshaped fieldstones imbedded in clay. Ashlar masonry was used at

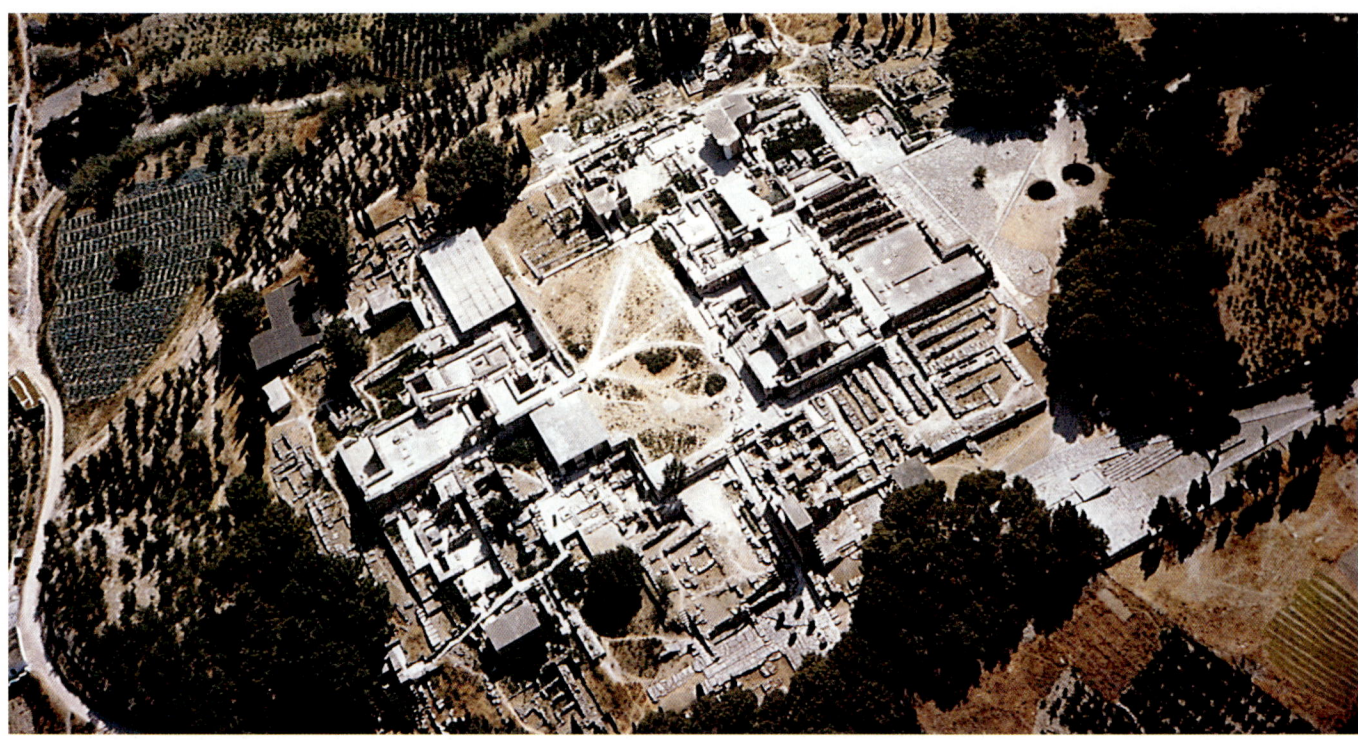

4-3   Aerial view of the palace at Knossos (Crete), Greece, ca. 1700–1400 B.C.

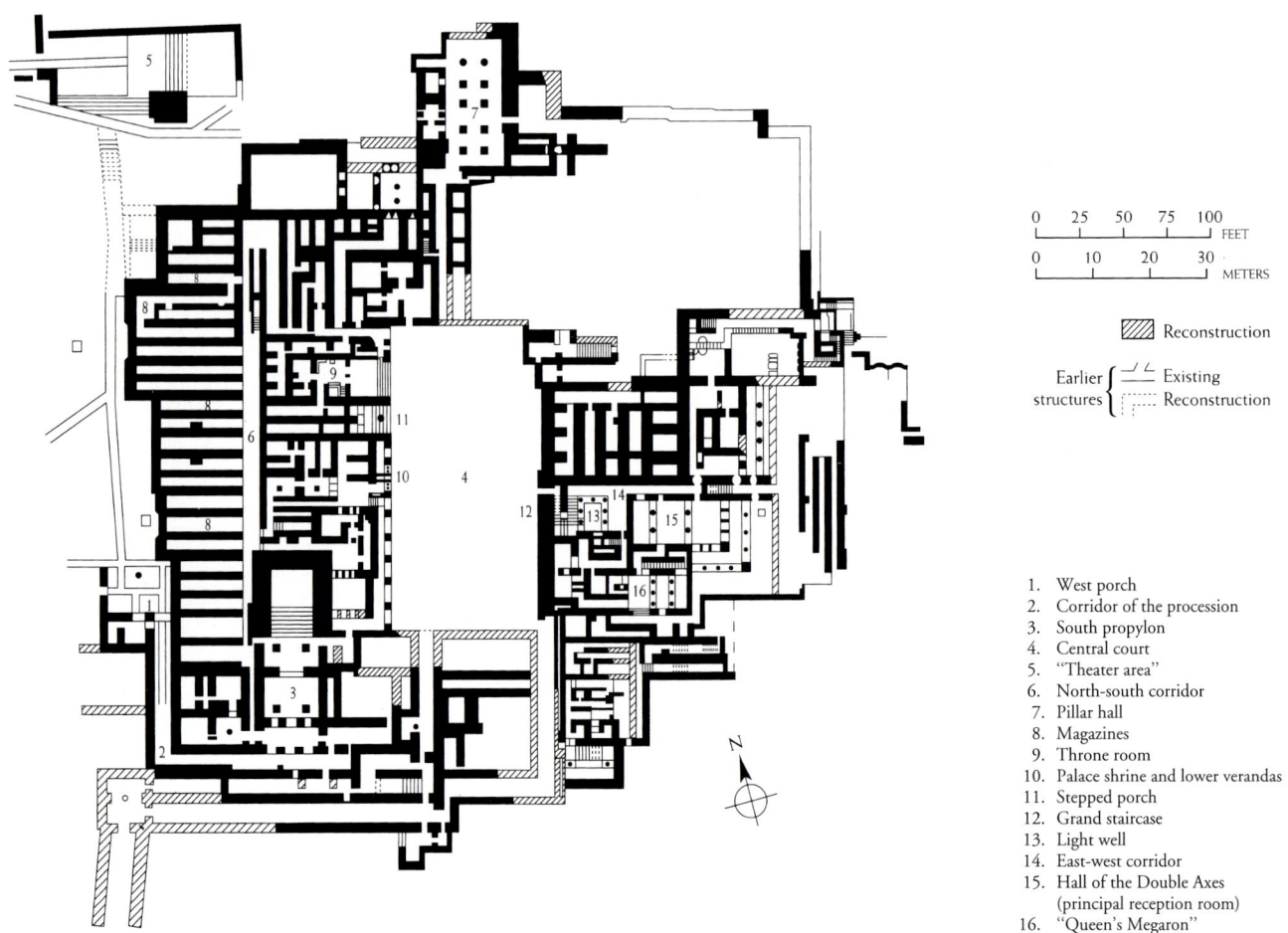

0   25   50   75   100
⊢—————————⊣ FEET

0   10   20   30
⊢—————————⊣ METERS

▨ Reconstruction

Earlier ⎰ ⌐⌐ Existing
structures ⎱ ┈┈ Reconstruction

1. West porch
2. Corridor of the procession
3. South propylon
4. Central court
5. "Theater area"
6. North-south corridor
7. Pillar hall
8. Magazines
9. Throne room
10. Palace shrine and lower verandas
11. Stepped porch
12. Grand staircase
13. Light well
14. East-west corridor
15. Hall of the Double Axes
    (principal reception room)
16. "Queen's Megaron"

4-4   Plan of the palace at Knossos (Crete), Greece, ca. 1700–1400 B.C.

From a ceremonial scene of uncertain significance comes the famous fragment (FIG. **4-6**) dubbed *La Parisienne (The Parisian Woman)* on its discovery because of the elegant dress, elaborate coiffure, and full rouged lips of the young woman (perhaps a priestess or even a goddess) depicted in the fresco. Although the representation is still convention bound (note especially the oversized frontal eye in the profile head), the charm and freshness of the mural are undeniable. The painting method used is appropriate to the lively spirit of the Minoans. Unlike the Egyptians, who painted in *fresco secco* (dry fresco), the Minoans used a *true (wet) fresco* method (see "Fresco Painting," Chapter 19, page 543), which required rapid execution and great skill in achieving quick, almost impressionistic effects. The spirit of *La Parisienne* is in large part from the verve of the artist's hand. The simple, light delicacy of the technique exactly matches the vivacity of the subject.

Liveliness and spontaneity also characterize the so-called *Toreador Fresco* (FIG. **4-7**) from the palace at Knossos. Although here, too, only fragments of the full composition have been recovered (the dark patches are original; the rest is a modern restoration), they are extraordinary in their depiction of the dangerous Minoan ceremony of bull-leaping (see "Minoan Paintings Discovered in Egypt," page 84). Despite the modern nickname of the fresco, Minoan bull games were unlike Spanish bullfights. No weapons were used, and the bull was left unharmed, unless it was sacrificed after the games concluded.

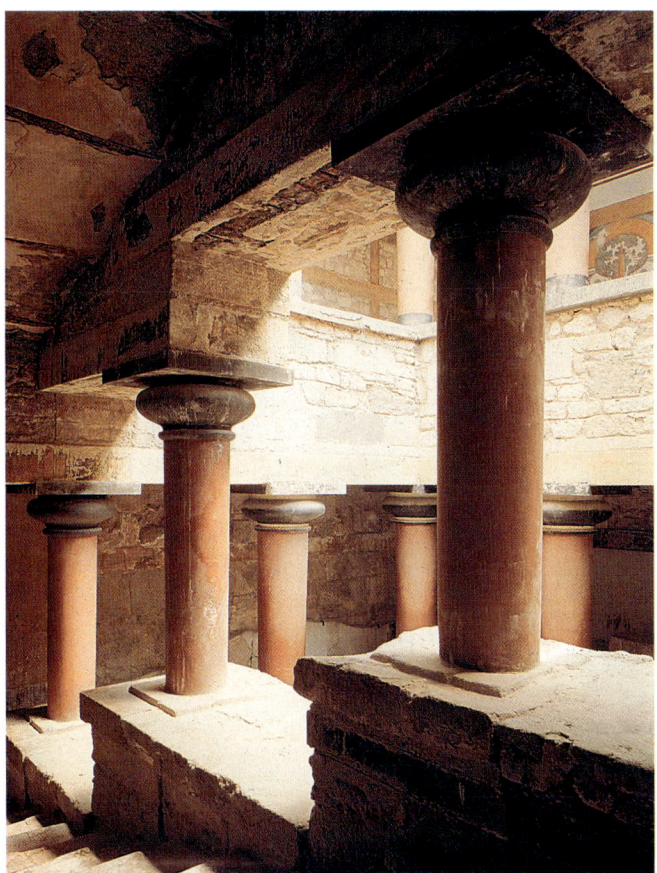

4-5 Stairwell in the residential quarter of the palace at Knossos (Crete), Greece, ca. 1700–1400 B.C.

building corners and around door and window openings. The Minoans also gave thought to such questions as drainage. A remarkably efficient system of terracotta pipes underlies the palace. The bathrooms and toilets in the residential quarter were luxuries at the time.

The Knossos palace was complex not only in plan but also in elevation. It had as many as three stories around the central court and even more on the south and east sides where the terrain sloped off sharply. Interior staircases built around light and air wells (FIG. **4-5**) provided necessary illumination and ventilation. Painted Minoan columns, originally fashioned of wood but restored in stone, are characterized by their bulbous, cushionlike capitals, which resemble those of the later Greek Doric order (see "Doric and Ionic Temples," Chapter 5, page 112), and by their distinctive shape. The shafts taper from a wide top to a narrower base—the opposite of both Egyptian and later Greek columns.

Painting

FRESCOES FIT FOR A KING AND QUEEN
Mural paintings liberally adorn the palace at Knossos, one of its most striking aspects. The rough fabric of the rubble walls was often coated with a fine white lime plaster and painted with frescoes, which, together with the red shafts and black capitals of the wooden columns, must have provided an extraordinarily rich effect. The frescoes depict many aspects of Minoan life (bull-leaping, processions, and ceremonies) and of nature (birds, animals, flowers, and marine life).

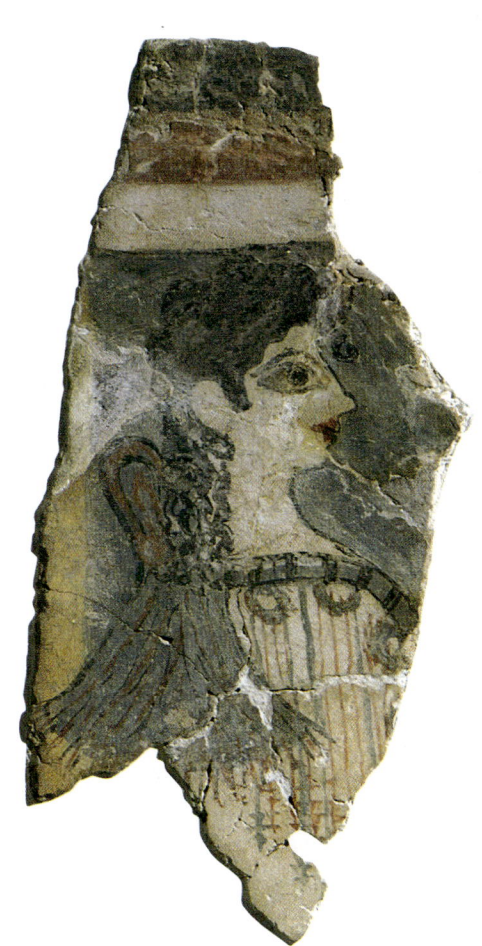

4-6 Minoan woman or goddess *(La Parisienne)*, from the palace at Knossos (Crete), Greece, ca. 1450–1400 B.C. Fragment of a fresco, approx. 10″ high. Archeological Museum, Herakleion.

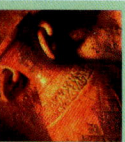

ART IN THE NEWS

Minoan Paintings Discovered in Egypt

Knowledge of ancient art and architecture grows daily as archeologists uncover new paintings, sculptures, pots, and other objects, as well as remains of previously unknown buildings. Archeologists infrequently, however, make a truly astounding discovery, but that is what happened when, in the 1980s, an Austrian expedition to Tell el-Daba in the eastern Nile Delta explored a huge palace of the sixteenth century B.C.

Tell el-Daba, ancient Avaris (see map, Chapter 3, page 42), was the capital city of the Hyksos. Until they were driven out around 1530 B.C. by Ahmose, founder of the New Kingdom, the Hyksos ruled the land of the Nile. The palatial complex the Austrians discovered was either built by Ahmose at the beginning of the Eighteenth Dynasty or under the last Hyksos pharaoh and destroyed by Ahmose. The archeologists uncovered the unexpected: pumice from the eruption of the Theran volcano (see "A Volcano Erupts, and the History of Art Is Revised," page 87) and thousands of fragments of Aegean wall paintings.

The most impressive of the Avaris murals depicts bull-leapers seen against a maze background that many believe is a topographical reference to the Minoan palace at Knossos. It is certain that not only is the subject of the painting Aegean but also the costumes, style, and technique—primarily true fresco on lime plaster. No one doubts that Aegean rather than Egyptian artists decorated the palace. One possible explanation for the Avaris paintings is that Ahmose or one of the last Hyksos kings of Egypt married an Aegean princess and that Aegean artists were brought at her request to the Nile to adorn the walls of her new home.

Whatever the final answer to this new archeological and historical riddle, the excavations at Tell el-Daba have demonstrated that contacts between Egypt and the Aegean world were not confined to trade and politics. In fact, painted walls and floors of Aegean style, technique, and subject also have been discovered in recent years in a Canaanite palace at Tel Kabri in northern Israel. Similar finds had been made much earlier at Alalakh in Syria (see map, Chapter 2, page 16, for both sites). Together these startling discoveries provide evidence for a rich international exchange of artists and ideas in the Mediterranean world at the middle of the second millennium B.C. Art historians can no longer study the great civilizations of Egypt, the Near East, and the Aegean in isolation.

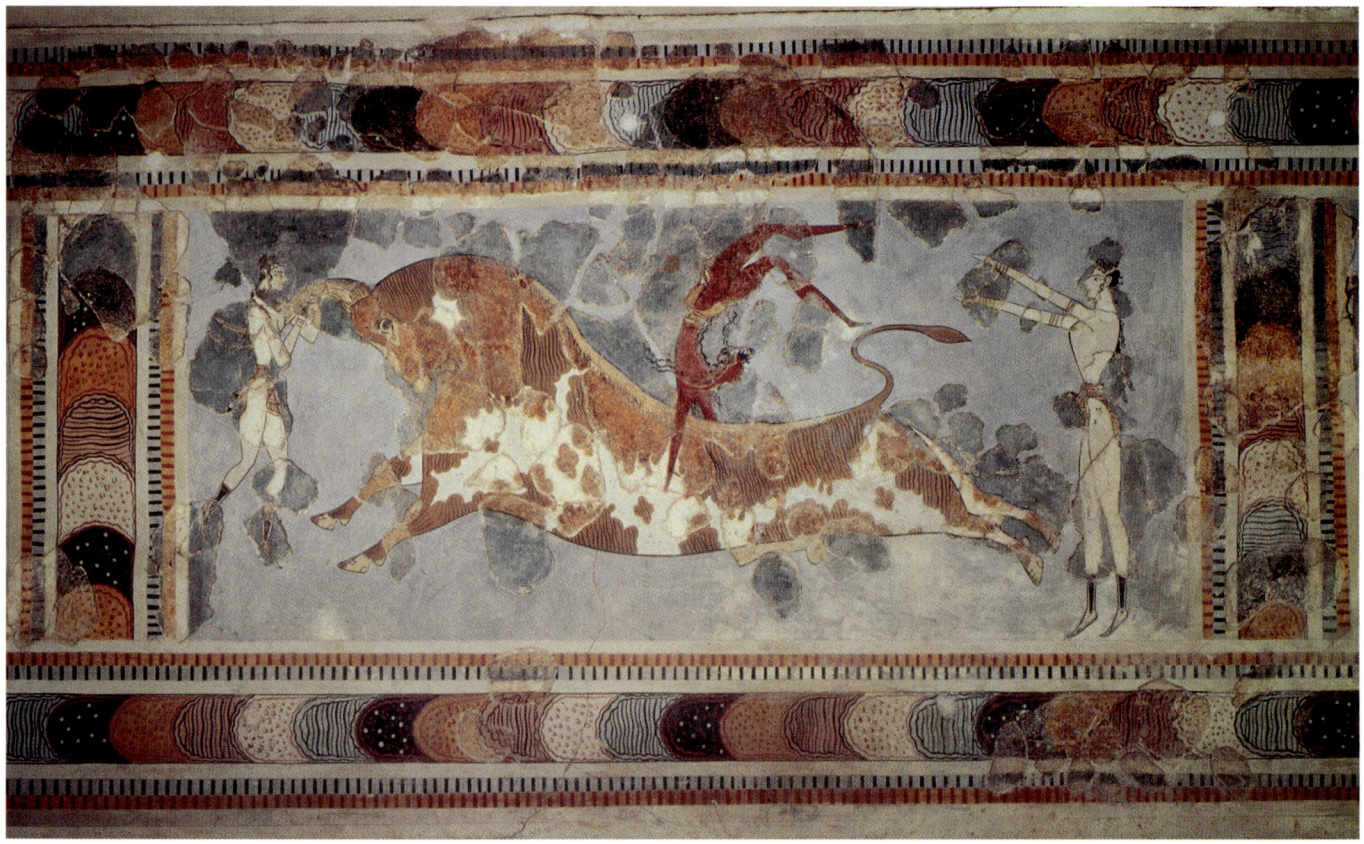

4-7   Bull-leaping *(Toreador Fresco)*, from the palace at Knossos (Crete), Greece, ca. 1450–1400 B.C. Approx. 2′ 8″ high, including border. Archeological Museum, Herakleion.

In the Knossos painting, the young women (with fair skin) and the youth (with dark skin) are depicted according to the widely accepted ancient convention for distinguishing male and female. The young man is shown in the air, having, it seems, grasped the bull's horns and somersaulted over its back in a perilous and extremely difficult acrobatic maneuver. The powerful charge of the bull is brilliantly suggested by the elongation of the animal's shape and the sweeping lines that form a funnel of energy, beginning at the very narrow hindquarters of the bull and culminating in its large sharp horns and galloping forelegs. The human figures also have stylized shapes, with typically Minoan pinched waists, and are highly animated. Although the profile pose with the full-view eye was a familiar convention in Egypt and Mesopotamia, the elegance of the Cretan figures, with their long, curly hair and proud and self-confident bearing distinguishes them from all other early figure styles. The angularity of the figures seen in Egyptian wall paintings is modified by the curving Minoan line that suggests the elasticity of the living and moving being.

FRESCOES BURIED BY A VOLCANO   The Minoan figure style also may be seen in the fresco of a young fisherman (FIG. 4-8) who holds his abundant catch in both hands. The painting is remarkable as a very early monumental study of the nude male figure, a subject that preoccupied later Greek artists for centuries. The fresco is not, however, from Knossos or even from Crete. It was uncovered much more recently in the excavations of Akrotiri on the volcanic island of Santorini (ancient Thera) in the Cyclades, some sixty miles north of Crete. In the Late Cycladic period, Thera was artistically, and possibly also politically, within the Minoan orbit. The extremely well-preserved mural paintings from Akrotiri are invaluable additions to the fragmentary and frequently misrestored frescoes from Crete. The excellent preservation of the Theran paintings is due to an enormous seismic explosion on Santorini that buried Akrotiri in volcanic pumice and ash, making it a kind of Pompeii of the prehistoric Aegean (see "A Volcano Erupts, and the History of Art Is Revised," page 87).

The Akrotiri frescoes decorated the walls of houses, not the walls of a great palace such as that at Knossos, and therefore the number of painted walls from the site is especially impressive. Another fresco from the same room of the same house as that of the fisherman is much smaller but filled with dozens of figures, ships, and buildings. This *Miniature Ships Fresco,* as it has been called, formed a frieze about seventeen inches high at the top of at least three walls of the room. In our detail of the fresco (FIG. 4-9), a great fleet sails between two ports, perhaps taking part in a sea festival or perhaps engaged in a naval campaign that calls to mind Homer's much later catalog of ships in the *Iliad.* Such a detailed representation of the movement of ships and people from port to port does not appear again until the Column of the Roman emperor Trajan (see FIG. 10-42) almost two millennia later. The details of ship design and sailing are carefully observed in the fresco, as if it were painted by one who knew ships well. Just as closely studied are the placements and poses of sailors, rowers, and passengers.

Little of the conventional stereotyping and repetition that appears in such representations throughout the history of art is evident in the Akrotiri fresco. Instead, the arrangement of

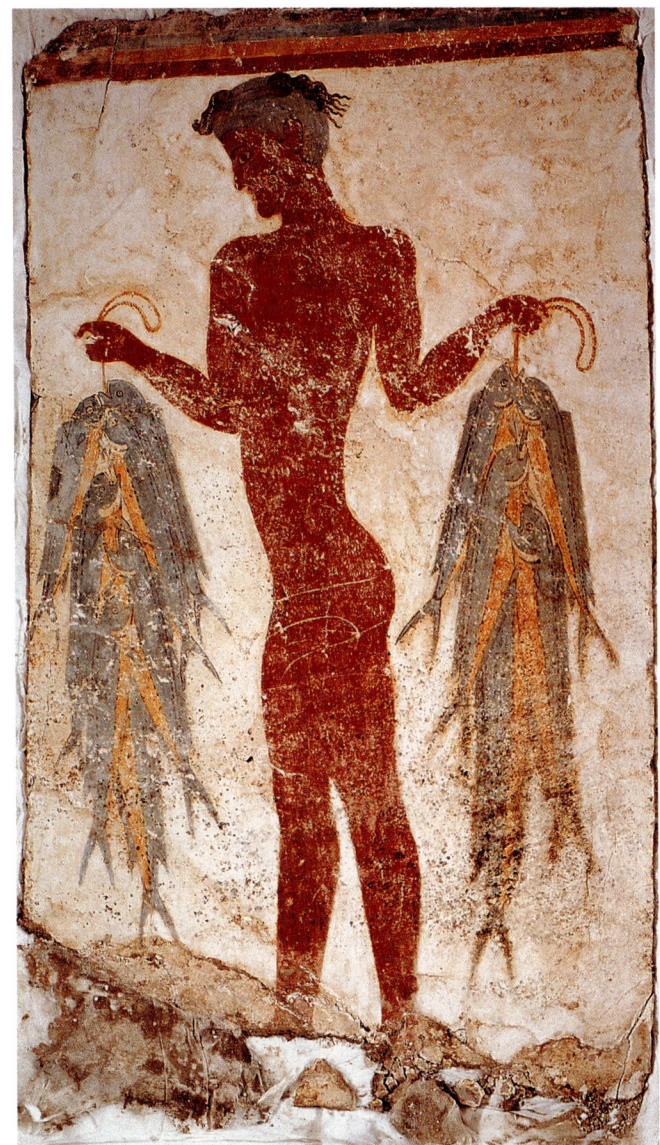

4-8   Young fisherman with his catch, detail of a fresco in Room 5, West House, Akrotiri, Thera (Cyclades), Greece, ca. 1650 B.C. Approx. 4′ 5″ high. National Archeological Museum, Athens.

figures and poses varies significantly according to each person's role—steering, tending to the sail, rowing, or simply sitting and conversing. Dolphins frolic about the ships, and on the left shore (FIG. 4-9, upper left) a lion pursues fleeing deer. The ports—the one at the left encircled by a river represented as arching above it—show quays, houses, and streets occupied by a variety of people attentive to the coming and going of the ships. The whole composition has an openness and lightness that suggest the freedom of movement of a people born to the sea.

THE CELEBRATION OF NATURE   The almost perfectly preserved mural paintings (FIG. 4–10) of another room from Akrotiri capture especially well the freshness and vitality of this vision of the Aegean world. In *Spring Fresco,* nature itself is the sole subject, although the artist's aim was not to render the rocky island terrain realistically but, rather, to capture the landscape's essence and to express joy in the splendid

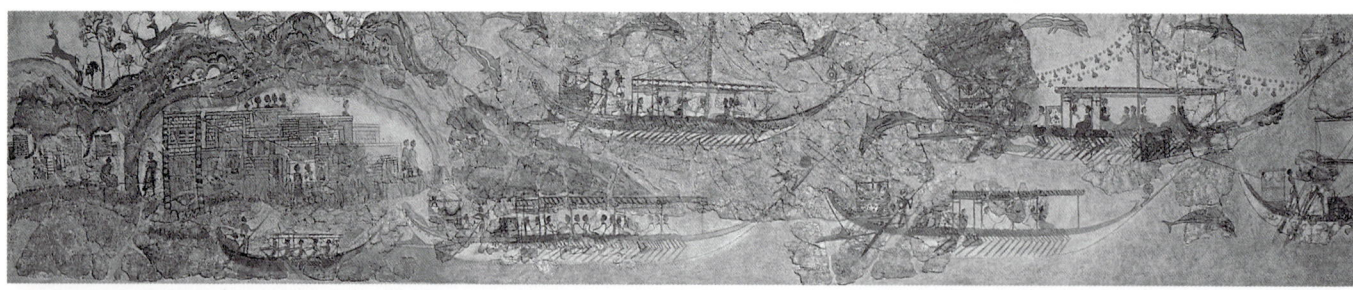

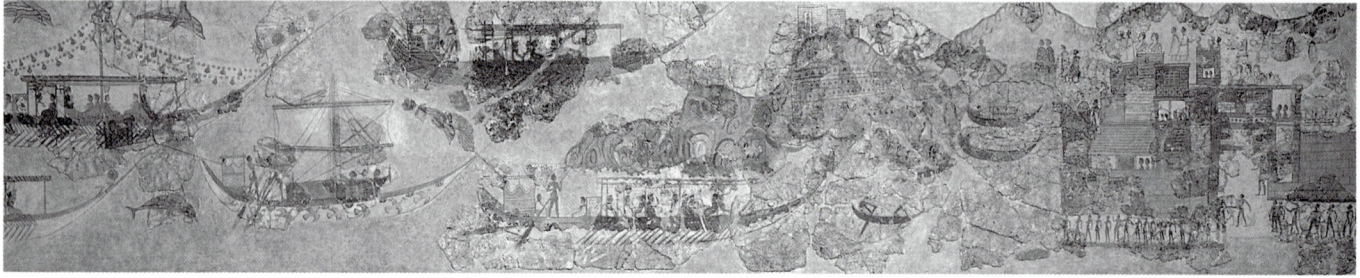

4-9   Flotilla, detail of *Miniature Ships Fresco,* from Room 5, West House, Akrotiri, Thera (Cyclades), Greece, ca. 1650 B.C. Approx. 1′ 5″ high. National Archeological Museum, Athens.

surroundings. The irrationally undulating and vividly colored rocks, the graceful lilies swaying in the cool island breezes, and the darting swallows express the vigor of growth, the delicacy of flowering, and the lightness of birdsong and flight. In the lyrical language of curving line, the artist celebrated the rhythms of spring. This is the first known example of a pure landscape painting, one that not only has no humans but also has no narrative element (compare FIG. 1-18). The *Spring Fresco* represents the polar opposite of the first efforts at mural painting in the caves of Paleolithic Europe, where animals (and occasionally humans) appeared as isolated figures without any indication of setting.

SEA LIFE ON MINOAN POTTERY   The love of nature manifested itself in Crete on the surfaces of painted vases

even before the period of the new palaces. During the Middle Minoan period, Cretan potters fashioned sophisticated shapes using newly introduced potters' wheels and decorated their vases in a distinctive and fully polychromatic style. These Kamares Ware vessels, named for the cave on the slope of Mount Ida where they were first discovered, have been found in quantity at Phaistos and Knossos. On our example (FIG. **4-11**), as on other Kamares vases, creamy white and reddish-brown decoration is set against a rich black ground. The central motif is a great leaping fish—a forerunner of the diving dolphins of Late Minoan and Late Cycladic murals—and perhaps a fishnet surrounded by a host of curvilinear abstract patterns including waves and spirals. The swirling lines evoke life in the sea, and both the abstract and the natural forms are beautifully adjusted to and integrated with the shape of the vessel.

4-10   Landscape with swallows *(Spring Fresco),* from Room Delta 2, Akrotiri, Thera (Cyclades), Greece, ca. 1650 B.C. Approx. 7′ 6″ high. National Archeological Museum, Athens.

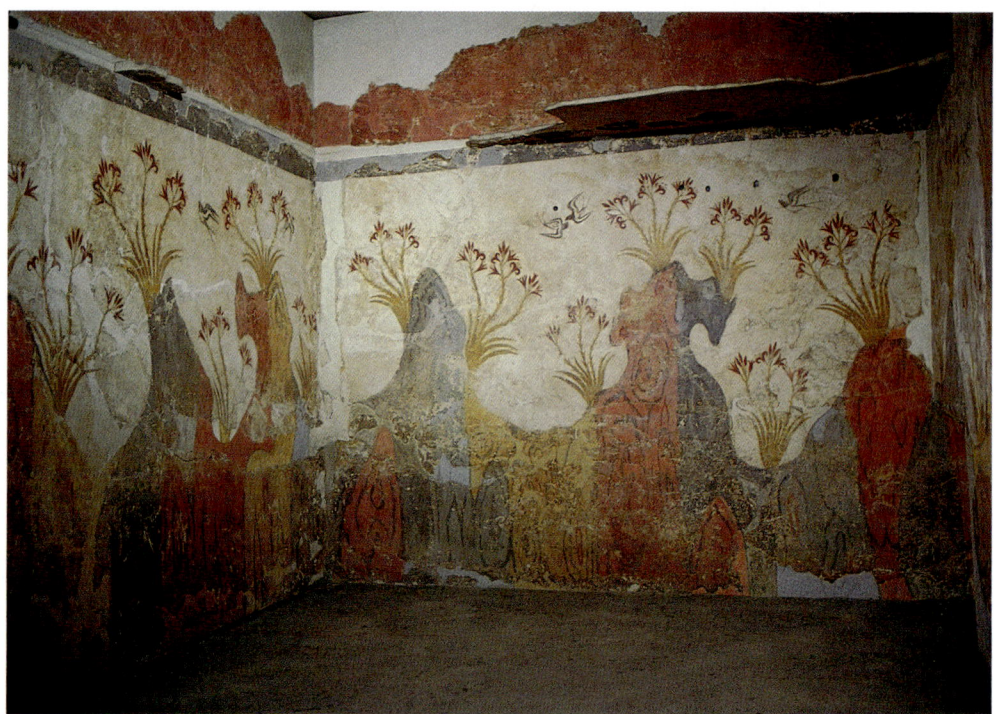

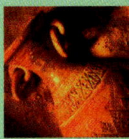

A Volcano Erupts, and the History of Art Is Revised

Today, ships bound for the beautiful Greek island of Santorini, with its picture-postcard white houses, churches, shops, and restaurants, weigh anchor in a bay beneath steep, crescent-shaped cliffs. Until about 20,000 B.C., however, ancient Thera had a roughly circular shape and gentler slopes. Then, suddenly, a volcanic eruption blew out the center of the island, leaving behind the moon-shaped main island and several lesser islands grouped around a bay that roughly corresponds to the shape of the gigantic ancient volcano. The volcano erupted again, thousands of years later, during the zenith of Aegean civilization.

Then, the site of Akrotiri, which Greek excavators gradually are uncovering, was buried by a pumice layer more than a yard deep in some areas and by an even larger volume of volcanic ash (*tephra*) that often exceeds five yards in depth, even after nearly forty centuries of erosion. Whole rooms were filled with tephra, and the walls of some houses were pelted with boulders the volcano spewed forth. Closer to the volcano's cone, the tephra is almost sixty yards deep in places. In fact, the eruption's force was so powerful that ash was blown by the wind and pumice carried by the sea currents throughout the ancient Mediterranean, not only to Crete, Rhodes, and Cyprus but also as far away as Anatolia, Egypt (see "Minoan Paintings Discovered in Egypt," page 84), Syria, and Israel.

Until recently, most scholars embraced the theory Spyridon Marinatos, an eminent Greek archeologist, formulated that the otherwise unexplained demise of Minoan civilization on Crete around 1500 B.C. was the by-product of the volcanic eruption on Thera. According to Marinatos, devastating famine followed the rain of ash that fell on Crete. This view has been reevaluated in the light of new evidence. Archeologists now know that after the eruption, life went on in Crete, if not on Thera. At one Cretan site Theran pumice was collected in conical cups and placed on a monumental stairway, possibly as a votive offering. Archeologists and other scientists, working closely in an impressive and most welcome interdisciplinary research effort, have pinpointed the date of a major climatic event as 1628 B.C. They have studied tree rings at sites in Europe and in North America for evidence of retarded growth and have examined ice cores in Greenland for peak acidity layers. Both kinds of evidence testify to a significant disruption in weather patterns in that year. Today most—but not all—scholars believe the cause of this disruption was the cataclysmic volcanic eruption on Thera.

The revised date of the Theran eruption has profound consequences for the chronology of Aegean art. All the Theran paintings illustrated here (FIGS. 4-8 to 4-10) are now thought to be at least one hundred fifty years older than they were considered not long ago. They predate by many decades the great frescoes from the Knossos palace (FIGS. 4-6 and 4-7). The discovery has implications for the dating of art objects from other areas as well because of the important interconnections between the Aegean, Egypt, and the Near East during the second millennium B.C.

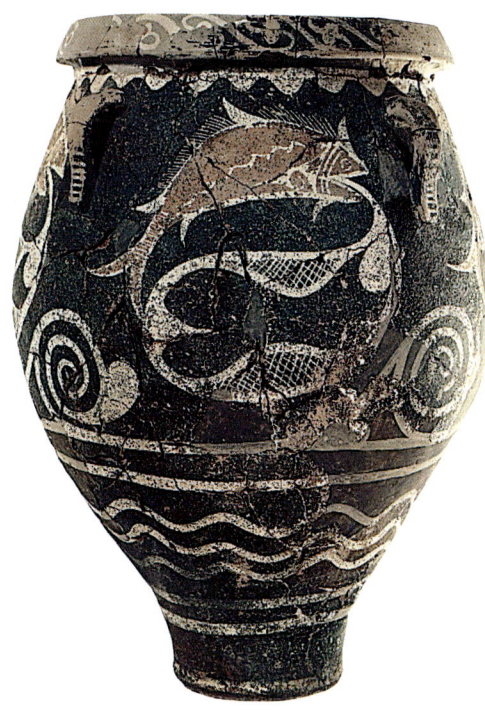

4-11 Kamares Ware jar, from Phaistos (Crete), Greece, ca. 1800–1700 B.C. Approx. 1′ 8″ high. Archeological Museum, Herakleion.

The sea and the creatures that inhabit it also inspired the Late Minoan Marine Style octopus jar (FIG. **4-12**) from Palaikastro, which is contemporary with the new palaces at Knossos and elsewhere. The tentacles of the octopus reach out over the vessel's curving surfaces, embracing the piece and emphasizing its volume. This is a masterful realization of the relationship between the vessel's decoration and its shape, always a problem for the ceramicist. This later vase differs markedly from its Kamares Ware predecessor in color. Not only is the octopus jar more muted in tone, but the Late Minoan artist also reversed the earlier scheme and placed dark silhouettes on a light ground. This remained the norm for about a millennium in Greece, until about 530 B.C. when, albeit in a very different form, light figures on a dark ground emerged once again as the preferred manner (see FIG. 5-20).

MINOAN FUNERARY RITUALS Midway in size and complexity between the decorated clay vessels and the monumental frescoes of Crete and Thera are the paintings on a Late Minoan limestone sarcophagus (FIG. **4-13**) found at Hagia Triada on the southern coast of Crete. The paintings are closely related in technique, color scheme, and figure style to contemporary palace frescoes, but the subject is foreign to the

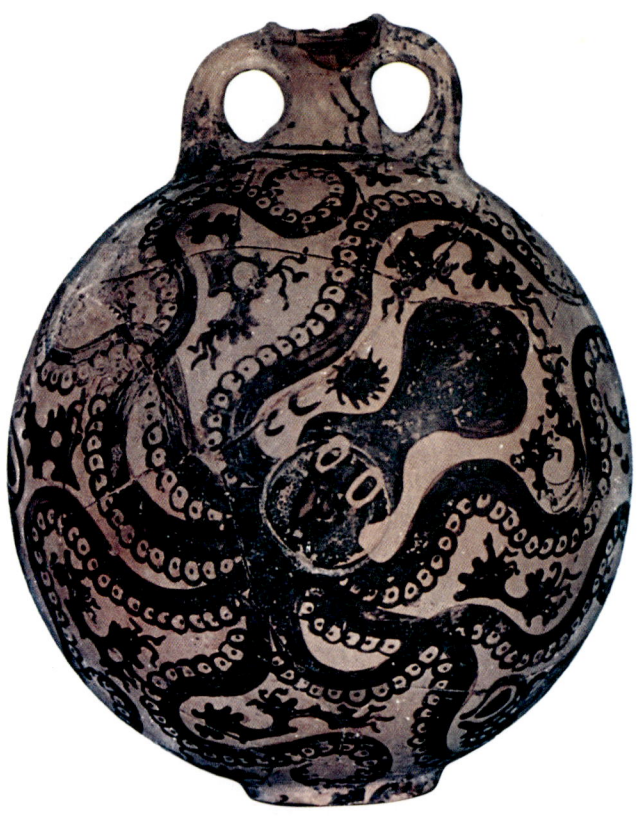

4-12 Marine Style octopus jar, from Palaikastro (Crete), Greece, ca. 1500 B.C. Approx. 11″ high. Archeological Museum, Herakleion.

palace repertoire. Befitting the function of the sarcophagus as a burial container, the paintings illustrate the funerary rites in honor of the dead. They provide welcome information about Minoan religion, which still remains obscure despite a century of excavation on Crete. At the right the dead man appears upright in front of his own tomb, like the New Testament's raised Lazarus in medieval art, and watches as three men (note their dark flesh tone) bring offerings to him.

At the left, two light-skinned women carry vessels and pour a libation to the deceased while a male musician plays a lyre. The musician immediately brings to mind the Early Cycladic statuettes of lyre players (FIG. 4-2) deposited in tombs, which may indicate some continuity in funerary customs and beliefs from the Early to the Late Bronze Age in the Aegean.

Sculpture

JOYFUL FARMERS   Also from Hagia Triada is the so-called *Harvester Vase* (FIG. **4-14**), probably the finest surviving example of Minoan relief sculpture. Only the upper half of the egg-shaped body and neck of the vessel are preserved. Missing are the lower parts of the harvesters (or, as some think, sowers) and the ground on which they stand. Formulaic scenes of sowing and harvesting were staples of Egyptian funerary art (see FIG. 3-17), but the Minoan artist shunned static repetition in favor of a composition that bursts with the energy of its individually characterized figures. The relief shows a riotous crowd singing and shouting as they go to or return from the fields with the forward movement and lusty exuberance of the youths vividly expressed.

Although most of the figures conform to the age-old convention of combined profile and frontal views, one figure (near the center of our illustration) is singled out from his companions. He shakes a rattle to beat time, and the artist depicted him in full profile with his lungs so inflated with air that his ribs show. This is one of the first instances in the history of art of a sculptor showing a keen interest in the underlying muscular and skeletal structure of the human body. This is not a pictogram for humans, but a painstaking study of human anatomy, a remarkable achievement, especially given the size of the *Harvester Vase*, barely five inches at its greatest diameter. Equally noteworthy is how the sculptor recorded the tension and relaxation of facial muscles with astonishing exactitude. This degree of animation of the human face is without precedent in ancient art.

4-13 Sarcophagus, from Hagia Triada (Crete), Greece, ca. 1450–1400 B.C. Painted limestone, approx. 4′ 6″ long. Archeological Museum, Herakleion.

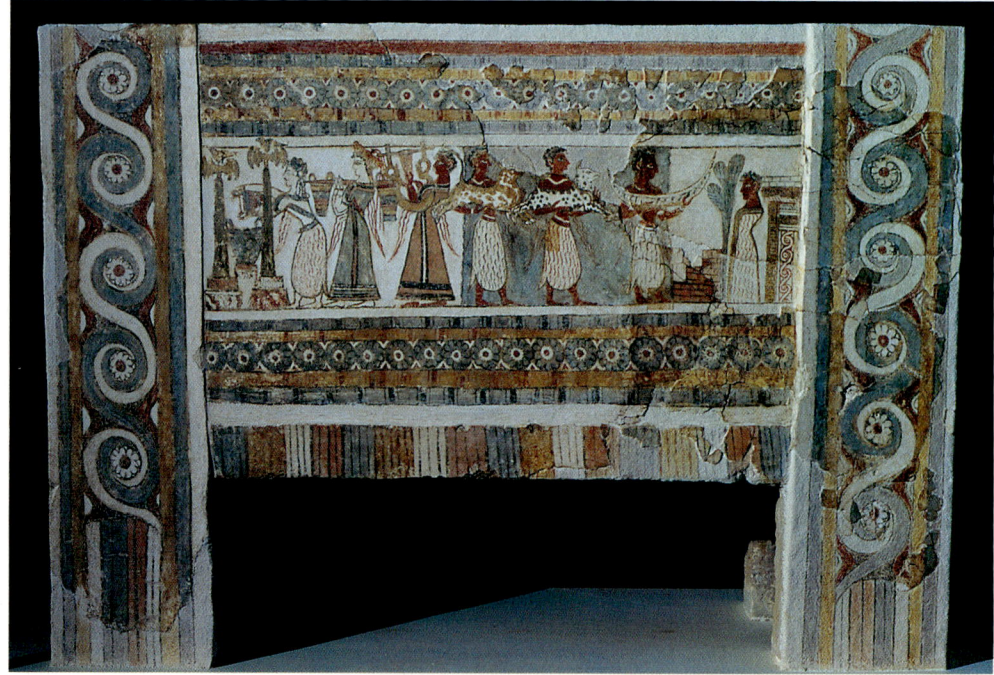

SNAKE GODDESS OR PRIESTESS? Unlike Mesopotamia and Egypt, Minoan Crete had no temples nor any monumental statues of gods, kings, or monsters, although large wooden images may once have existed. What remains of Minoan sculpture in the round is small in scale, such as the so-called *Snake Goddess* (FIG. **4-15**) from the palace at Knossos. It is one of several similar figurines some scholars believe may represent mortal attendants rather than a deity, although the prominently exposed breasts suggest that these figurines stand in the long line of prehistoric fertility images usually considered divinities. (The woman depicted in the Knossos statuette not only holds snakes in her hands but also supports a leopardlike feline peacefully on her head. This implied power over the animal world also seems appropriate for a deity.) The frontality of the figure is reminiscent of Egyptian and Near Eastern statuary, but the costume is clearly Minoan. The open bodice and flounced skirt worn by Minoan women are frequently depicted in Minoan art. If the statuette represents a goddess, as seems more likely, then it is yet another example of human beings fashioning their gods in their own images.

Scholars dispute the circumstances ending the Minoan civilization, although they now widely believe Mycenaeans had already moved onto Crete and established themselves at Knossos at the end of the New Palace period. From the palace at

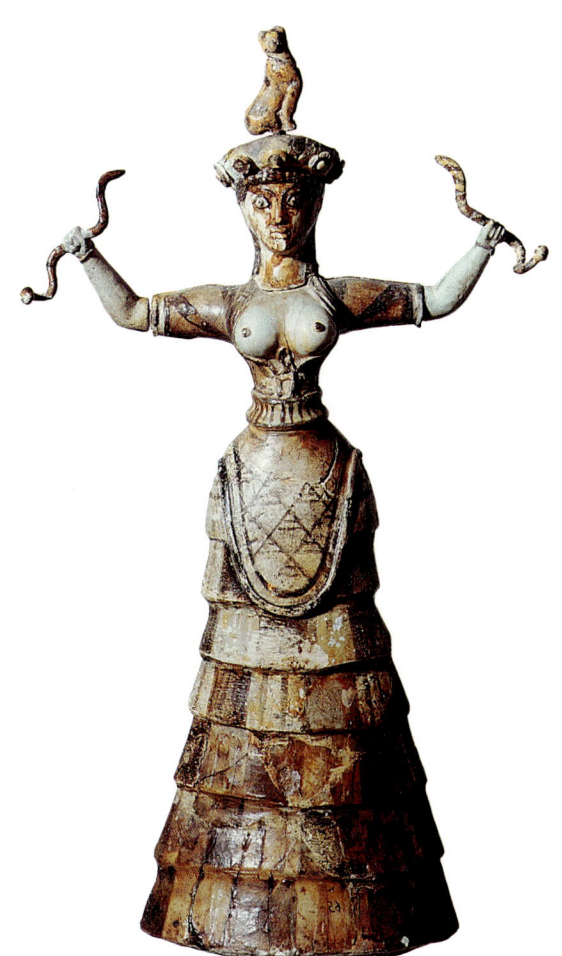

4-15 *Snake Goddess*, from the palace at Knossos (Crete), Greece, ca. 1600 B.C. Faience, approx. 1′ 1½″ high. Archeological Museum, Herakleion.

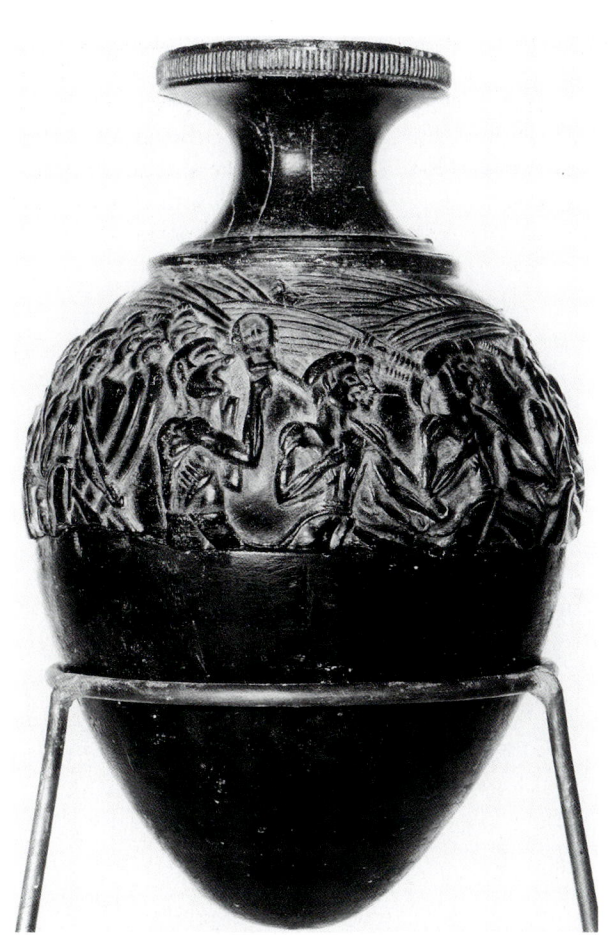

4-14 *Harvester Vase*, from Hagia Triada (Crete), Greece, ca. 1500 B.C. Steatite, greatest diameter approx. 5″. Archeological Museum, Herakleion.

Knossos, these intruders appear to have ruled the island for at least half a century, perhaps much longer. Parts of the palace continued to be occupied until its final destruction around 1200 B.C., but its importance as a cultural center faded soon after 1400 B.C., as the focus of Aegean civilization shifted to the Greek mainland.

MYCENAEAN (LATE HELLADIC) ART

HOMER'S MYCENAEANS The origins of the Mycenaean culture are still debated. The only certainty is the presence of these forerunners of the Greeks on the mainland about the time the old palaces were built on Crete—that is, about the beginning of the second millennium B.C. Doubtless these people were influenced by Crete even then, and some believe the mainland was a Minoan economic dependency for a long time. In any case, Mycenaean power developed on the mainland in the days of the new palaces on Crete, and by 1500 B.C. a distinctive Mycenaean culture was flourishing in Greece. Several centuries later, Homer described Mycenae as "rich in gold." The dramatic discoveries of Schliemann and his successors have fully justified this characterization, even if today's archeologists no longer view the Mycenaeans solely through the heroic eyes of Homer.

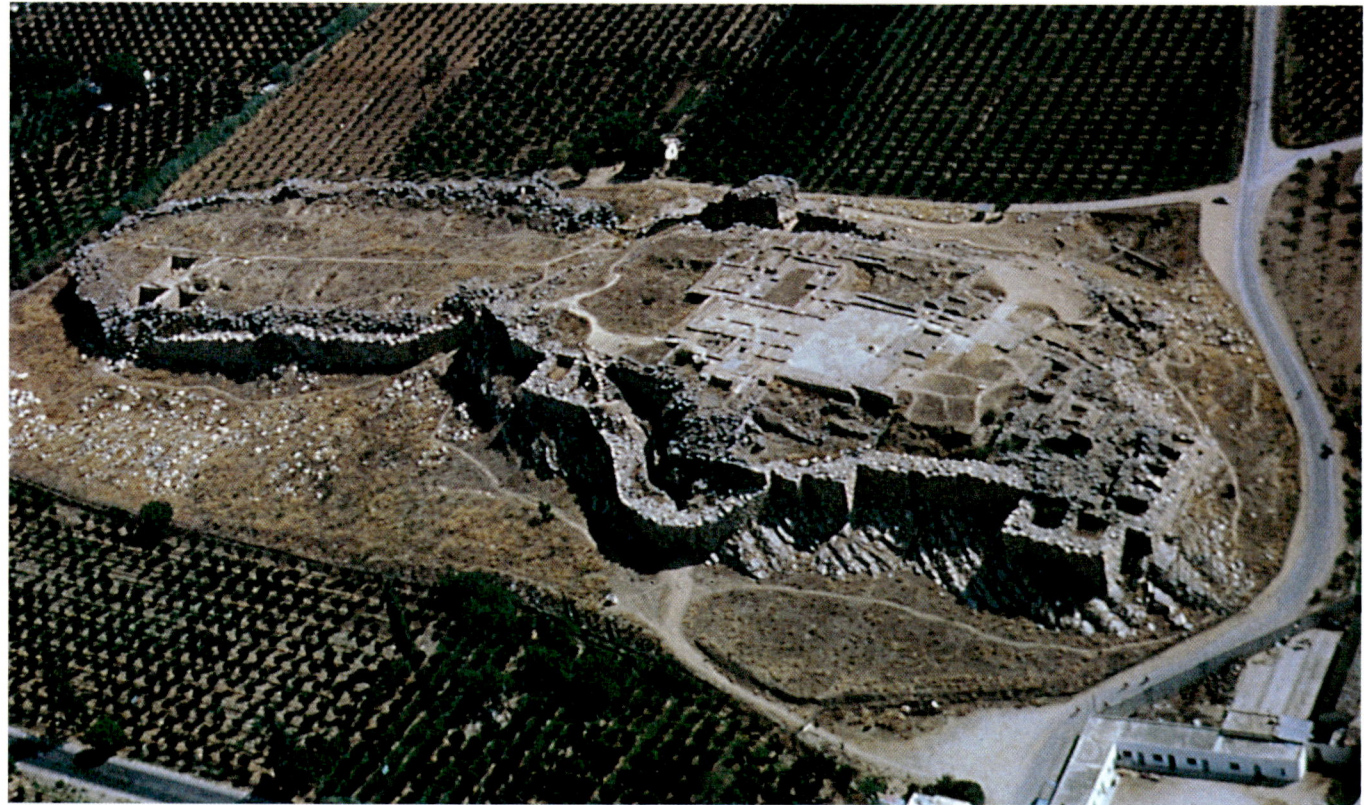

4-16   Aerial view of the citadel at Tiryns, Greece, ca. 1400–1200 B.C.

Architecture

The destruction of the Cretan palaces left the mainland culture supreme. Although this Late Helladic civilization has come to be called Mycenaean, Mycenae was but one of several large citadels. Mycenaean remains also have been uncovered at Tiryns, Orchomenos, Pylos, and elsewhere, and Mycenaean fortification walls have even been found on the Acropolis of Athens. The best-preserved and most impressive Mycenaean remains are those of the fortified palaces at Tiryns and Mycenae. Both were built beginning about 1400 B.C. and burned (along with all the others) between 1250 and 1200 B.C., when the Mycenaeans seem to have been overrun by northern invaders or to have fallen victim to internal warfare.

A CITADEL GIANTS BUILT   Homer knew the citadel of Tiryns (FIGS. **4-16** and **4-17**), located about ten miles from Mycenae, as Tiryns of the Great Walls. In the second century A.D., when Pausanias, author of an invaluable guidebook to Greece, visited the site, he marveled at the towering fortifications and considered the walls of Tiryns as spectacular as the pyramids of Egypt. Indeed, the Greeks of the historical age believed mere humans could not have erected such edifices and instead attributed the construction of the great Mycenaean citadels to the mythical *Cyclopes*, a one-eyed race of giants. Historians still refer to the huge roughly cut stone blocks forming the massive fortification walls of Tiryns and other Mycenaean sites as *Cyclopean masonry.*

The heavy walls of Tiryns and other Mycenaean palaces contrast sharply with the open Cretan palaces and clearly reveal their defensive character. Those of Tiryns average about twenty feet in thickness and in one section house a long

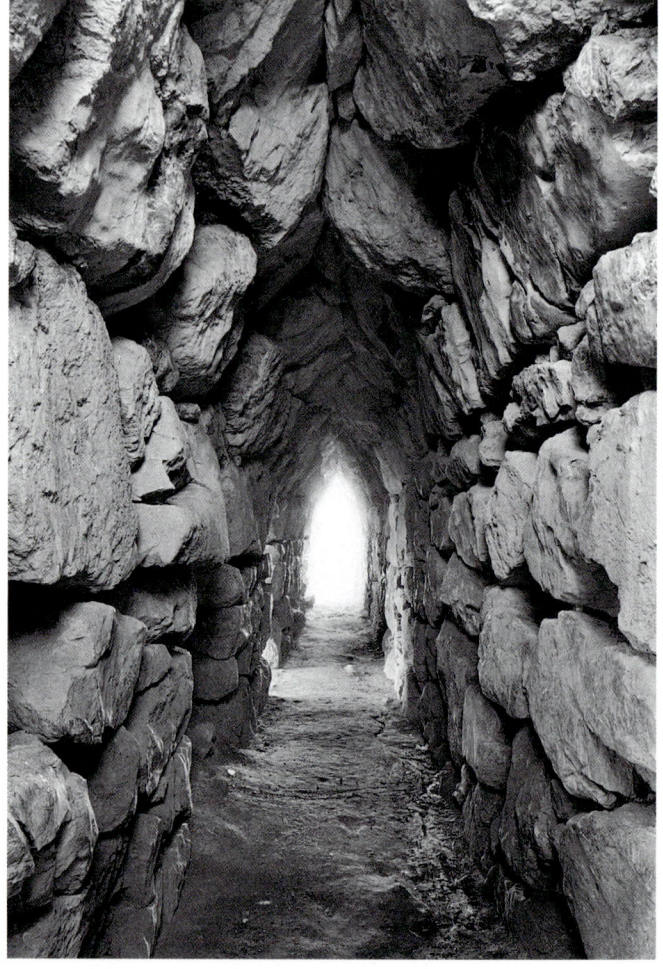

4-17   Corbeled gallery in the walls of the citadel, Tiryns, Greece, ca. 1400–1200 B.C.

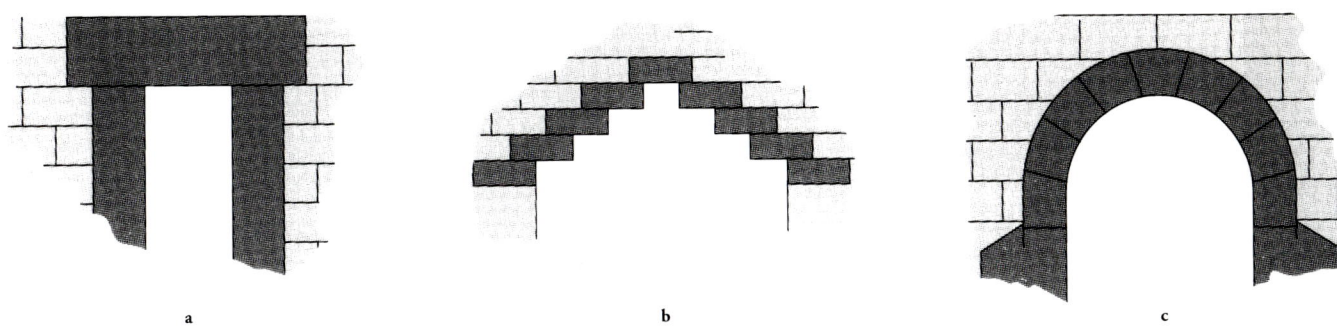

4-18   Three methods of spanning a passageway: (*a*) post and lintel, (*b*) corbeled arch, (*c*) arch.

gallery (FIG. 4-17) covered by a *corbeled vault* (FIG. **4-18***b*). Here the large irregular Cyclopean blocks were piled in horizontal courses and then cantilevered inward until the two walls met in a pointed arch. No mortar was used, and the vault is held in place only by the weight of the blocks (often several tons each), by the smaller stones used as wedges, and by the clay that fills some of the empty spaces. This primitive but effective vaulting scheme possesses an earthy dynamism and is very impressive in its crude monumentality. It is easy to see how a later age came to believe that the uncouth Cyclopes were responsible for these massive but unsophisticated fortifications.

Would-be attackers at Tiryns were compelled to approach the palace within the walls (FIG. 4-19) via a long ramp that forced the (usually right-handed) soldiers to expose their unshielded sides to the Mycenaean defenders above. Then—if

they got that far—they had to pass through a series of narrow gates that also could be defended easily. Inside, at Tiryns as elsewhere, the most important element in the palace plan was the *megaron,* or reception hall, of the king. The main room of the megaron had a throne against the right wall and a central hearth bordered by four Minoan-style wooden columns serving as supports for the roof. The throne room was preceded by a vestibule with a columnar facade. A variation of this plan later formed the core of some of the earliest Greek temple plans. This fact suggests some architectural continuity during the so-called Dark Ages that followed the collapse of Mycenaean civilization.

THE HOME OF THE CONQUERORS OF TROY
The severity of these fortress-palaces was relieved by frescoes, as in the Cretan palaces, and, at Agamemnon's Mycenae at least, by monumental architectural sculpture. The Lion Gate (FIG. **4-20**) is the outer gateway of the stronghold at Mycenae. It is protected on the left by a wall built on a natural rock outcropping and on the right by a projecting bastion of large blocks. Any approaching enemies would have had to enter this twenty-foot-wide channel and face Mycenaean defenders above them on both sides. The gate itself is formed of two great monoliths capped with a huge lintel (FIG. 4-18*a*). Above the lintel, the masonry courses form a corbeled arch (FIG. 4-18*b*), leaving an opening that lightens the weight the lintel carries. This *relieving triangle* is filled with a great limestone slab where two lions carved in high relief stand on the sides of a Minoan-type column. They rest their forepaws on the two altars under the column. The whole design admirably fills its triangular space, harmonizing in dignity, strength, and scale with the massive stones that form the walls and gate. Similar groups appear in miniature on Cretan seals, but the idea of placing monstrous guardian figures at the entrances to palaces, tombs, and sacred places has its origin in Egypt and the Near East (compare, for example, the Great Sphinx of Gizeh, FIG. 3-11, and the later lion and lamassu gates of Assyria, FIGS. 2-18 and 2-21). In fact, at Mycenae the animals' heads were fashioned separately and are lost. It is possible that the "lions" were actually composite beasts in the Eastern tradition, perhaps sphinxes.

A TOMB BENEATH A MOUND   The Lion Gate at Mycenae and the towering fortification wall circuit of which it formed a part were constructed at about the presumed date of the Trojan War. At that time wealthy Mycenaeans were laid to rest outside the citadel walls in beehive-shaped tombs (*tholoi;*

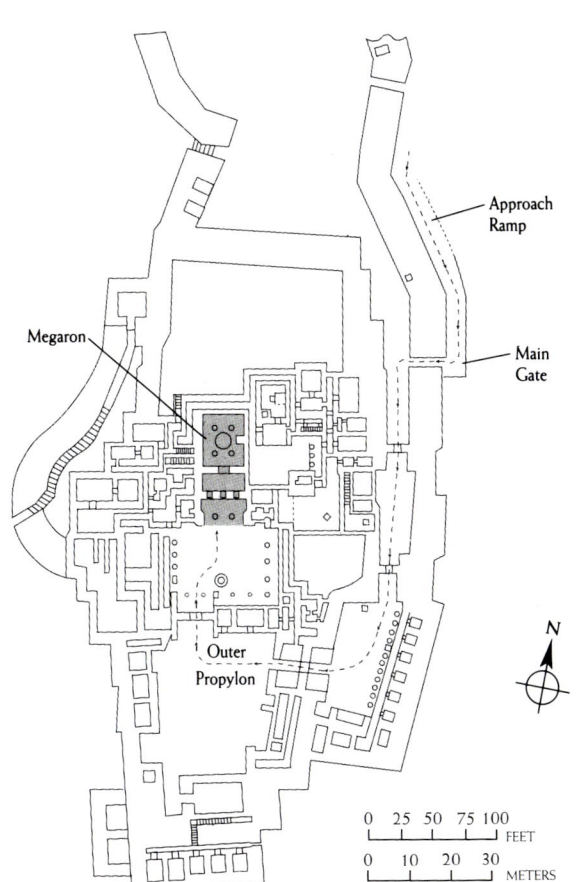

4-19   Plan of the palace and southern part of the citadel, Tiryns, Greece, ca. 1400–1200 B.C.

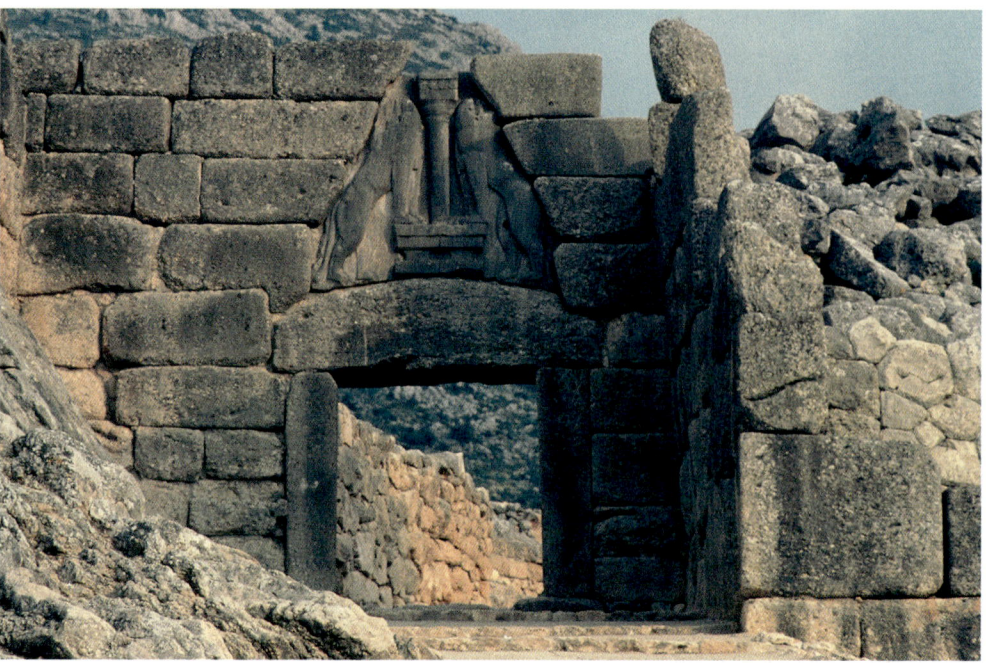

4-20 Lion Gate, Mycenae, Greece, ca. 1300–1250 B.C. Limestone, relief panel approx. 9′ 6″ high.

singular, *tholos)* covered by enormous earthen mounds. The best preserved of these is the so-called Treasury of Atreus (FIG. **4-21**), which already in antiquity was mistakenly believed to be the repository of the treasure of Atreus, father of Agamemnon and Menelaus. Approached by a long passageway *(dromos)*, the tomb chamber was entered through a doorway surmounted by a relieving triangle similar to that employed in the roughly contemporary Lion Gate. The tholos is composed of a series of stone corbeled courses laid on a circular base and ending in a lofty dome (FIG. **4-22**). The vault probably was built using rough-hewn blocks. After they were set in place, the stonemasons had to finish the surfaces with great precision to conform to both the horizontal and vertical curves of the wall. The principle involved is no different from that of the corbeled gallery of Tiryns (FIG. 4-17). But the problem of constructing a complete dome is much more complicated, and the execution of the vault in the Treasury of Atreus is much more sophisticated than that of the vaulted gallery at Tiryns. About forty-three feet high, this is the largest known vaulted space without interior supports in all antiquity until the Roman Pantheon (see FIG. 10-50), a building constructed almost fifteen hundred years later using a new technology—concrete construction—unknown to the Mycenaeans.

Metalwork, Sculpture, and Painting

TREASURES OF REVERED KINGS The Treasury of Atreus had been thoroughly looted long before its modern rediscovery, but spectacular grave goods have been found elsewhere at Mycenae. Just inside the Lion Gate, but predating it by some three centuries, Schliemann came across what archeologists now designate as Grave Circle A. Here, at a site protected within the circuit of the later walls, Schliemann excavated six deep shafts that had served as tombs for kings and their families. The dead were laid to rest on the floors of these shaft graves with masks covering their faces, recalling the Egyptian funerary practice doubtless familiar to the Mycenaeans. Women were buried with their jewelry and men with their weapons and golden cups.

Among the most spectacular of Schliemann's finds is the beaten *(repoussé)* gold mask illustrated here (FIG. **4-23**), one of several from the royal burial complex. It often has been compared to the fabulous gold mummy mask of Tutankhamen

4-21 Cutaway view of the Treasury of Atreus, Mycenae, Greece, ca. 1300–1250 B.C.

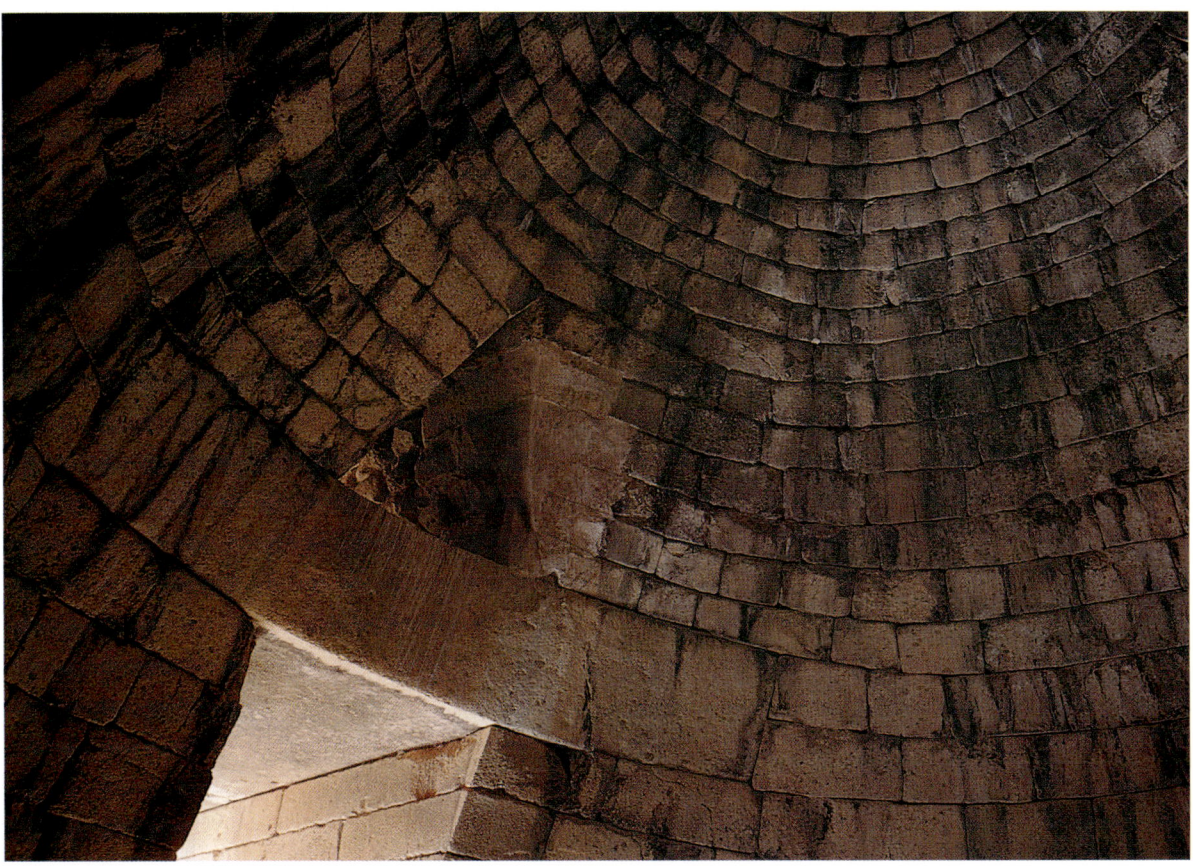

4-22   Vault of the tholos of the Treasury of Atreus, Mycenae, Greece, ca. 1300–1250 B.C. Approx. 43′ high.

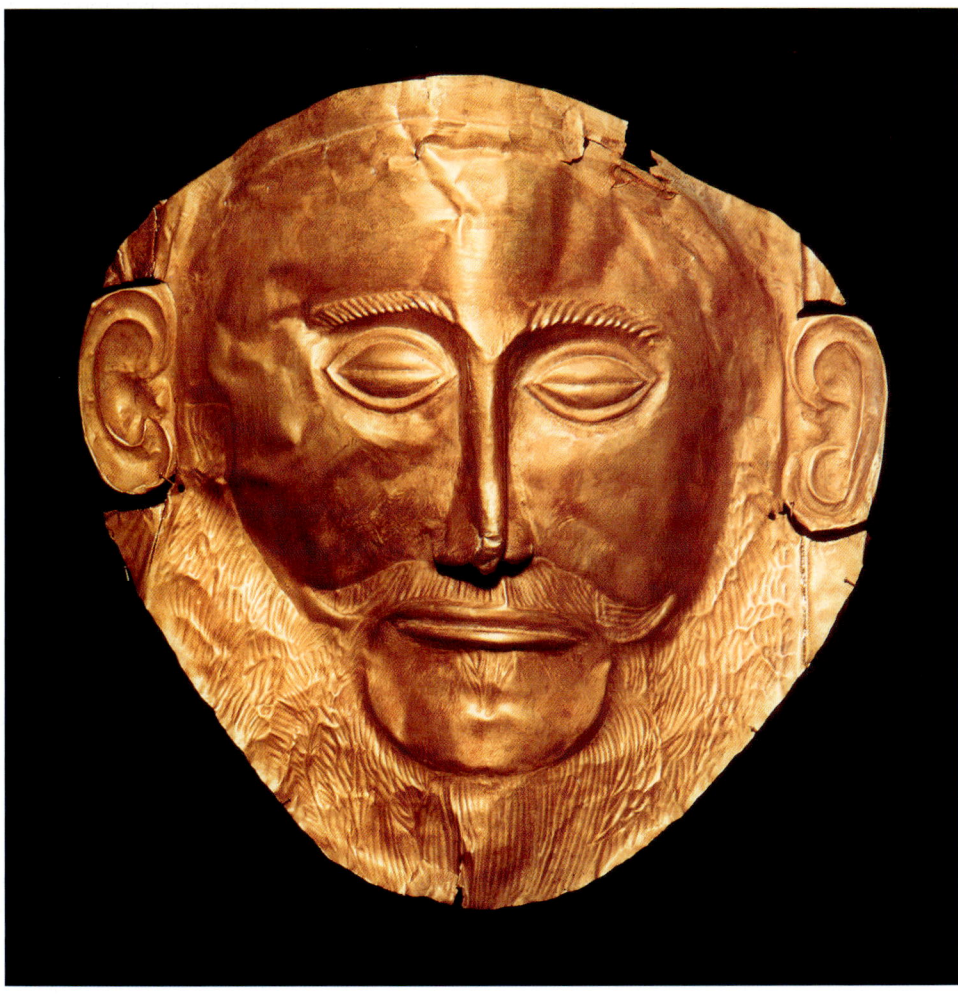

4-23   Funerary mask, from Grave Circle A, Mycenae, Greece, ca. 1600–1500 B.C. Beaten gold, approx. 1′ high. National Archeological Museum, Athens.

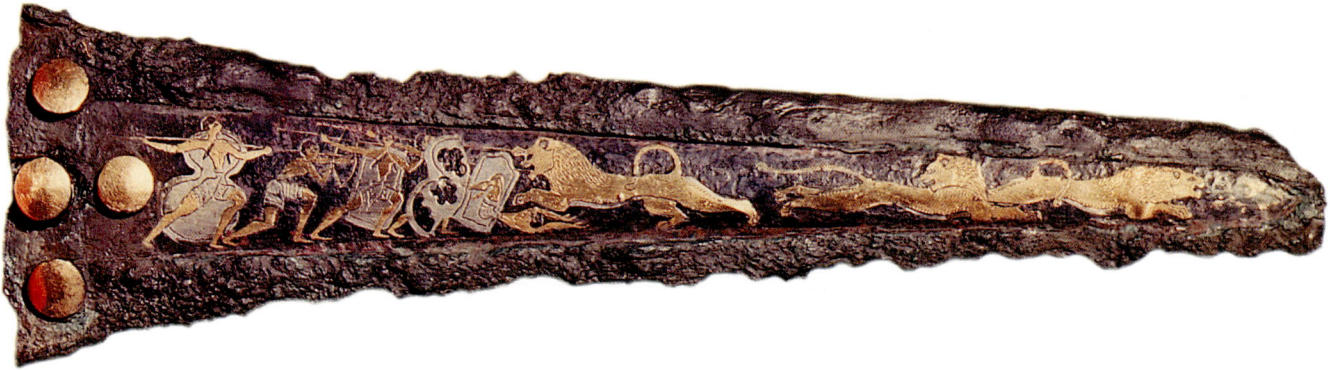

4-24 Inlaid dagger blade with lion hunt, from Grave Circle A, Mycenae, Greece, ca. 1600–1500 B.C. Bronze, inlaid with gold, silver, and niello, approx. 9″ long. National Archeological Museum, Athens.

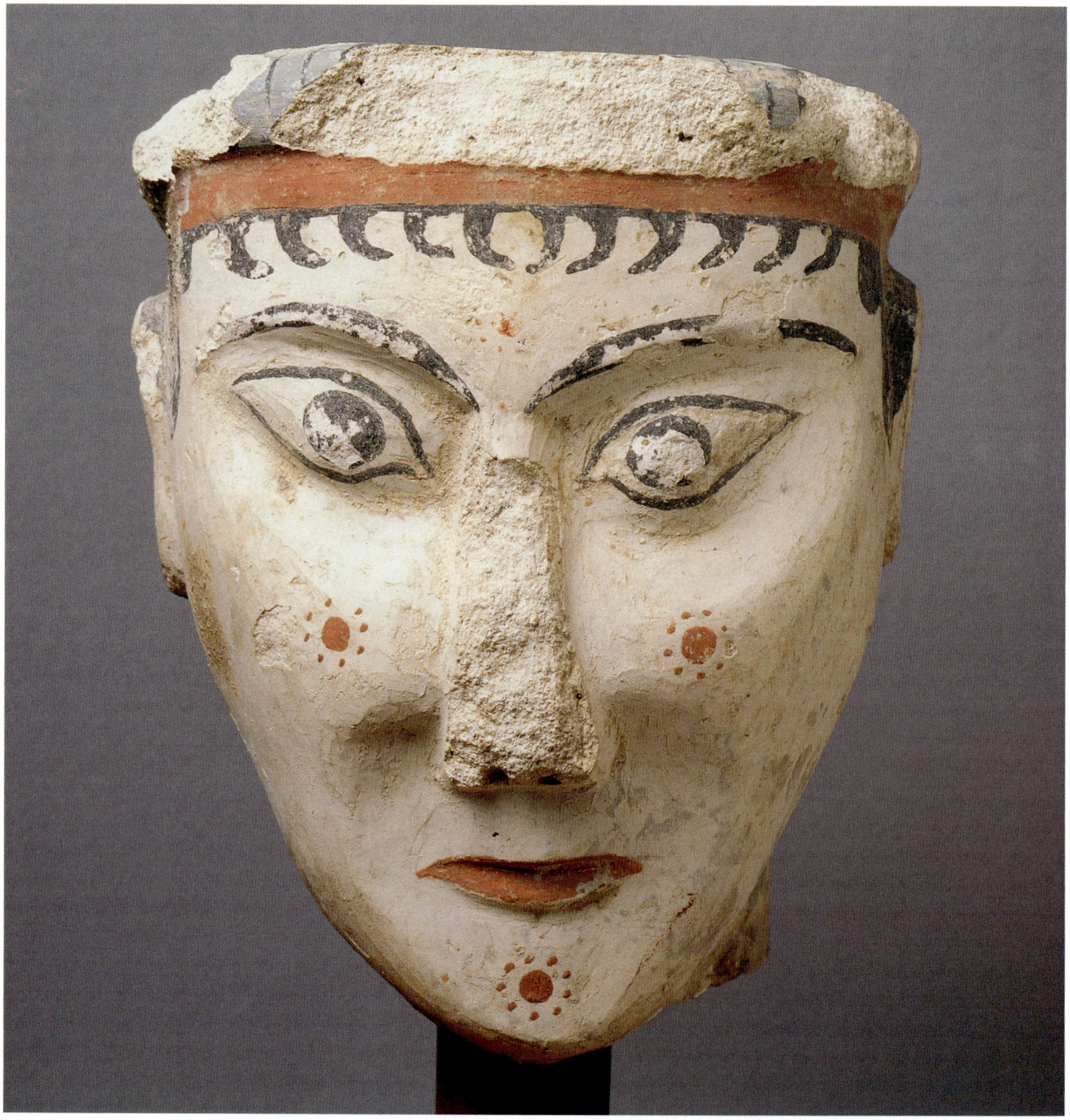

4-25 Head of a sphinx(?), from Mycenae, Greece, ca. 1300–1250 B.C. Painted plaster, approx. $6\frac{1}{2}$″ high. National Archeological Museum, Athens.

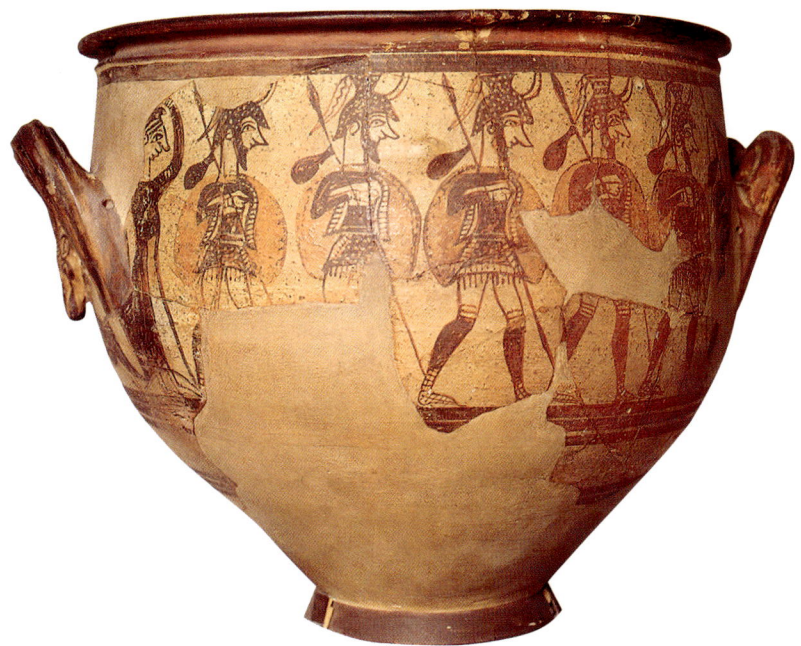

4-26 *Warrior Vase*, from Mycenae, Greece, ca. 1200 B.C. Approx. 1′ 4″ high. National Archeological Museum, Athens.

(see FIG. 3-37). The treatment of the human face is, of course, more primitive in the Mycenaean mask. But this was one of the first known attempts in Greece to render the human face at life-size, whereas Tutankhamen's mask stands in a venerable line of monumental Egyptian sculptures going back more than a millennium. It is not known whether the Mycenaean masks were intended as portraits, but different physical types were recorded with care. Youthful faces as well as mature ones were depicted. Our example, with its full beard, must portray a mature man, perhaps a king—although not Agamemnon, as Schliemann wished. If Agamemnon was a real king, he lived some three hundred years after this mask was fashioned. Clearly the Mycenaeans were "rich in gold" long before Homer's heroes fought at Troy.

Also found in Grave Circle A were several magnificent bronze dagger blades inlaid with gold, silver, and *niello* (a black metallic alloy), again attesting to the wealth of the Mycenaean kings, as well as to their warlike nature. The largest and most elaborate of the group (FIG. **4-24**) is decorated with a scene of four hunters attacking a lion that has struck down a fifth hunter, while two other lions flee. The slim-waisted, long-haired figures are Minoan in style, but the subject is borrowed from the repertoire of the ancient Near East. It is likely a Minoan metalworker made the dagger for a Mycenaean patron who admired Minoan art but had different tastes in subject matter than his Cretan counterparts.

A MYCENAEAN SPHINX? Monumental figural art is very rare on the Greek mainland, as on Crete, other than the Minoan-style paintings that once adorned the walls of Mycenaean palaces. The triangular relief of the Lion Gate at Mycenae is exceptional, as is the painted plaster head (FIG. **4-25**) of a woman, goddess, or, perhaps, sphinx found just outside the citadel of Mycenae. The white flesh tone indicates the head is female. The hair and eyes are painted dark blue, almost black, while the lips, ears, and headband are red. The artist decorated the cheeks and chin with red circles surrounded by a ring of red dots, recalling the facial paint or tattoos recorded on Early Cycladic figurines of women. The large staring eyes give the face a menacing, if not terrifying, expression appropriate for a guardian figure such as a sphinx.

Were it not for this head and one or two other exceptional pieces, art historians might have concluded, wrongly, that the Mycenaeans had no monumental freestanding statuary—a reminder that it is always dangerous to generalize from the fragmentary remains of an ancient civilization. Nonetheless, life-size Aegean statuary must have been rare. After the collapse of Mycenaean civilization and for the next several hundred years, no attempts at monumental statuary are evident until, after the waning of the Dark Ages, Greek sculptors were exposed to the great sculptural tradition of Egypt.

WARRIORS MARCH TO BATTLE One art that did continue throughout the period after the downfall of the Mycenaean palaces was vase painting. One of the latest examples of Bronze Age painting is the *krater* (bowl for mixing wine and water) from Mycenae commonly called the *Warrior Vase* (FIG. **4-26**) after its prominent frieze of soldiers marching off to war. At the left a woman bids farewell to the column of heavily armed warriors moving away from her. The painting on this vase has no indication of setting and lacks the landscape elements that characterized earlier Minoan and Mycenaean art. All the soldiers also repeat the same pattern, a far cry from the variety and anecdotal detail of the lively procession of the Minoan *Harvester Vase* (FIG. 4-14).

This simplification of narrative is paralleled in other painted vases by the increasingly schematic and abstract treatment of marine life. The octopus, for example, eventually became a stylized motif composed of concentric circles and spirals that are almost unrecognizable as a sea creature. By Homer's time, the heyday of Aegean civilization was but a distant memory, and the men and women of Crete and Mycenae—Minos and Ariadne, Agamemnon and Helen—had assumed the stature of heroes of a lost golden age.

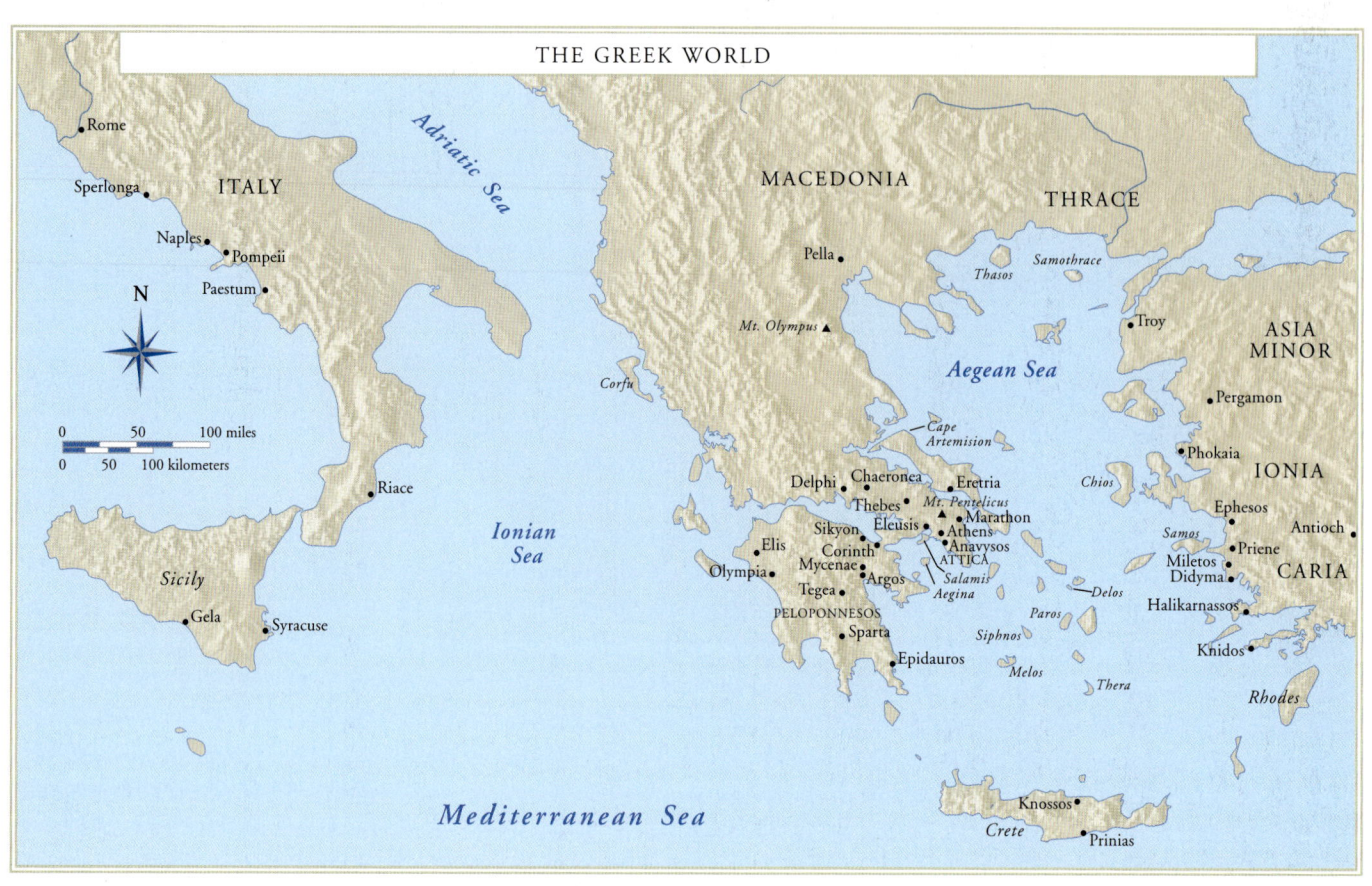

THE GREEK WORLD

Adriatic Sea

Rome
Sperlonga
ITALY
Naples • Pompeii
Paestum

N

0   50   100 miles
0 50 100 kilometers

Riace

Ionian Sea

Sicily

Gela
Syracuse

MACEDONIA

Pella

Thasos   *Samothrace*

THRACE

Mt. Olympus ▲

Corfu

Cape Artemision

Delphi • Chaeronea • Eretria
Thebes • *Mt. Pentelicus* ▲
Sikyon • Eleusis • Marathon
Elis • Corinth • Athens
Olympia • Mycenae • Anavysos
ATTICA
Tegea • Argos • *Salamis*
Aegina
PELOPONNESOS
Sparta
Epidauros

Aegean Sea

Troy

ASIA MINOR

• Pergamon

• Phokaia   IONIA

Chios   Ephesos
            Antioch
Samos Miletos • Priene
        Didyma   CARIA
Halikarnassos

Delos

Paros

Siphnos   Knidos

Melos   *Thera*

Rhodes

Mediterranean Sea

Knossos
Crete   Prinias

900 B.C.	700 B.C.	600 B.C.	500 B.C.
GEOMETRIC	ORIENTALIZING	ARCHAIC	

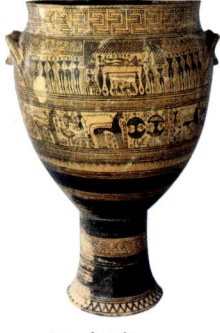

*Dipylon krater
ca. 740 B.C.*

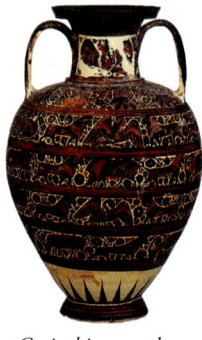

*Corinthian amphora
ca. 625–600 B.C.*

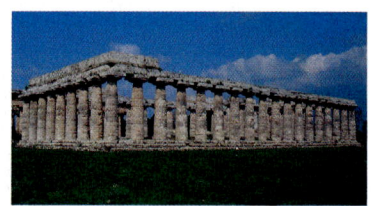

*Temple of Hera I
Paestum, ca. 550 B.C.*

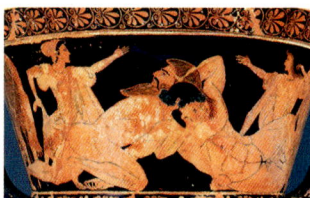

*Euphronios, Herakles wrestling
Antaios, ca. 510 B.C.*

First Olympic Games, 776 B.C.

Homer, fl. ca. 750–700 B.C.

Greek trading post established at Naukratis,
Egypt, ca. 650–630 B.C.

Draco formulates first written
law code for Athens, 621 B.C.

Sappho, fl. ca. 600 B.C.

Aeschylus, 525–456 B.C.

Democratic reforms of
Kleisthenes, 507 B.C.

5

GODS, HEROES, AND ATHLETES

THE ART OF ANCIENT GREECE

480 B.C.	450 B.C.	400 B.C.	323 B.C.	31 B.C.
EARLY CLASSICAL (SEVERE)	HIGH CLASSICAL	LATE CLASSICAL	HELLENISTIC	

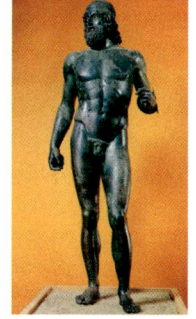

Riace warrior
ca. 460–450 B.C.

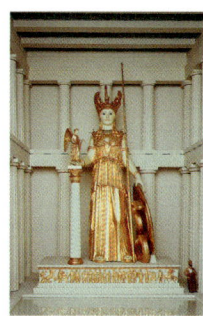

Phidias
Athena Parthenos
ca. 438 B.C.

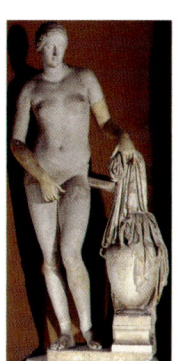

Praxiteles
Aphrodite of Knidos
ca. 350–340 B.C.

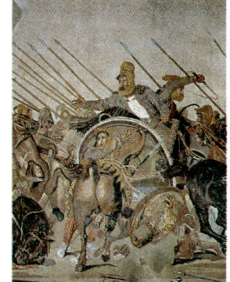

Philoxenos of Eretria
Battle of Issus
ca. 310 B.C.

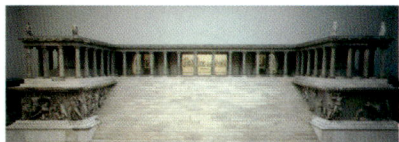

Altar of Zeus
Pergamon
ca. 175 B.C.

Persian Wars, 499–479 B.C.

Sophocles, 496–406 B.C.

Pericles, 490–429 B.C.

Herodotus, ca. 485–425 B.C.

Euripides, 485–406 B.C.

Sack of Athenian Acropolis by Persians, 480 B.C.

Socrates, 469–399 B.C.

Delian League treasury transferred to Athens, 454 B.C.

Peloponnesian War, 431–404 B.C.

Plato, 429–347 B.C.

Aristotle, 384–322 B.C.

Battle of Issus, 333 B.C.

Alexander the Great, r. 336–323 B.C.

Roman conquest of Greece, 146 B.C.

Attalos III wills Pergamene kingdom to Rome, 133 B.C.

Sack of Athens by Sulla, 86 B.C.

Battle of Actium, 31 B.C.

GREEK HUMANISM

"For we are lovers of the beautiful, yet simple in our tastes, and we cultivate the mind without loss of manliness. . . . [We are] the school of Hellas."[1] In the fifth century B.C., the golden age of Athens, the historian Thucydides quoted Pericles, the leader of the Athenians, making this assertion in praise of his fellow citizens, comparing their open, democratic society with the closed barracks state of their rivals, the Spartans. But Pericles might have been speaking in general of Greek culture and its ideal of humanistic education and life. For the Greeks, humanity was what mattered, and humans were, in the words of the philosopher Protagoras, the "measure of all things." This humanistic worldview led the Greeks to create the concept of democracy (rule by the *demos*, the people) and to make seminal contributions in the fields of art, literature, and science. The Greek exaltation of humanity and honoring of the individual are so completely part of the modern Western habits of mind that most people are scarcely aware that these ideas originated in the minds of the Greeks.

GODS AND HUMANS IN GREECE   Even the gods of the Greeks (see "The Gods and Goddesses of Mount Olympus," page 99), in marked contrast to the divinities of the Near East, assumed human forms whose grandeur and nobility were not free from human frailty. Indeed, unlike the gods of Egypt and Mesopotamia, the Greek deities differed from human beings only in that they were immortal. It has been said the Greeks made their gods into humans and their humans into gods. Humans, becoming the measure of all things, in turn must represent, if all things in their perfection are beautiful, the unchanging standard of the best. Creating the perfect individual became the Greek ideal.

The Greeks, or *Hellenes,* as they called themselves, appear to have been the product of an intermingling of Aegean peoples and Indo-European invaders. They never formed a single nation but instead established independent city-states or *poleis* (singular, *polis*). The Dorians of the north, who many believe brought an end to Mycenaean civilization, settled in the Peloponnesos. Across the Aegean, the western coast of Asia Minor (modern Turkey) was settled by the Ionians, whose origin is disputed. Some say they were forced out of Greece by the northern invaders and sailed from Athens to Asia Minor. Others hold that the Ionians developed in Asia Minor itself between the eleventh and eighth centuries B.C. out of a mixed stock of settlers. Whatever the origins of the various regional populations, political development differed from polis to polis, although a pattern emerged. Rule was first by kings, then by nobles, and then by tyrants who seized personal power. At last, in Athens, twenty-five hundred years ago, the tyrants were overthrown and democracy was established.

OLYMPIA, HELLAS, AND ATHENS   In 776 B.C., the separate Greek-speaking states held their first ceremonial games in common at Olympia. The later Greeks calculated their chronology from these first Olympic Games—the first *Olympiad.* From then on, despite their differences and rivalries, the Greeks regarded themselves as citizens of *Hellas,* distinct from the surrounding "barbarians" who did not speak Greek. The enterprising Hellenes, greatly aided by their indented coasts and island stepping-stones, became a trading and colonizing people who enlarged the geographic and cultural boundaries of Hellas. In fact, today the best preserved of all the grand temples the Greeks erected are found not in Greece proper but in their western colonies in Italy.

Nonetheless, Athens, the capital of Greece today, has justifiably become the symbol of ancient Greek culture. Many of the finest products of Greek civilization were created there. Athens is where the great plays of Aeschylus, Sophocles, and Euripides were performed. And there, in the city's marketplace *(agora),* covered colonnades *(stoas),* and gymnasiums *(palestras),* Socrates engaged his fellow citizens in philosophical argument and Plato formulated his prescription for the ideal form of government in the *Republic.* The rich intellectual life of ancient Athens was complemented by a strong interest in physical exercise, which played a large role in education, as well as in daily life. The Athenian aim of achieving a balance of intellectual and physical discipline, an ideal of humanistic education, is well expressed in the familiar phrase "a sound mind in a sound body."

GREEK ART AND CULTURE REASSESSED   The distinctiveness and originality of Greek contributions to art, science, and politics should not, however, obscure the enormous debt Greek civilization owed to the earlier great cultures of Egypt and the Near East. Scholars today increasingly recognize this debt, and the ancient Greeks themselves readily acknowledged borrowing ideas, motifs, conventions, and skills from these older civilizations.

Nor should a high estimation of Greek art and culture blind historians to the realities of Hellenic life and society. The uncritical admiration in the eighteenth and nineteenth centuries of anything Greek has undergone sharp revision in our time. Many modern artists have rejected Greek standards (the late-nineteenth-century French painter Paul Gauguin called Greek art "a lie!"). Even Athenian "democracy" was a political reality for only one segment of the demos. Slavery was regarded as natural, even beneficial, and was a universal institution among the Greeks. Aristotle, the eminent philosopher who tutored Alexander the Great, declared at the beginning of his *Politics:* "It is clear that some are free by nature, and others are slaves."[2] And Greek women were in no way the equals of Greek men. Women normally remained secluded in their homes, emerging usually only for weddings, funerals, and religious festivals. They played little part in public or political life. Despite the fame of the poet Sappho, only a handful of female artists' names are known, and none of their works survive. The existence of slavery and the exclusion of women from public life are both reflected in Greek art. On many occasions freeborn men and women appear with their slaves in monumental sculpture. The symposium (attended only by men and prostitutes) is a popular subject on painted vases.

Although the Greeks invented and passed on to future generations the concept and practice of democracy, most Greek states, even those constituted as democracies, were dominated by wellborn white males, and the most admired virtues were not wisdom and justice but statecraft and military valor. Greek men were educated in the values of Homer's heroes and in the athletic exercises of the palestra. War among the city-states was chronic and often atrocious. Fighting among themselves and incapable of unification, the Greeks eventually fell victim to Macedon's autocracy and Rome's imperialism.

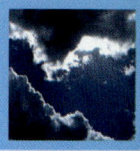

The Gods and Goddesses of Mount Olympus

The names of scores of Greek gods and goddesses appear already in Homer's epic tales of the war against Troy *(Iliad)* and of the adventures of the Greek hero Odysseus on his long and tortuous journey home *(Odyssey)*. Even more are enumerated in the poems of Hesiod, especially his *Theogony (Geneaology of the Gods)* composed around 700 B.C.

The Greek deities most often represented in art are all ultimately the offspring of the two key elements of the Greek universe, Earth *(Gaia/Ge;* we give the names in Greek/Latin form) and Heaven *(Ouranos/Uranus)*. Earth and Heaven mated to produce twelve Titans, including Ocean *(Okeanos/Oceanus)* and his youngest brother *Kronos (Saturn)*. Kronos castrated his father in order to rule in his place, married his sister *Rhea*, and then swallowed all his children as they were born, lest one of them seek in turn to usurp him (see FIG. 28-40). When *Zeus (Jupiter)* was born, Rhea deceived Kronos by feeding him a stone wrapped in clothes in place of the infant. After growing to manhood, Zeus forced Kronos to vomit up Zeus's siblings. Together they overthrew their father and the other Titans and ruled the world from their home on Mount Olympus, Greece's highest peak.

This cruel and bloody tale of the origin of the Greek gods has parallels in Near Eastern mythology and is clearly pre-Greek in origin, one of many Greek borrowings from the Orient. The Greek version of the creation myth, however, appears infrequently in painting and sculpture. Instead the later twelve *Olympian gods and goddesses*, the chief deities of Greece, figure most prominently in art—not only in Greek, Etruscan, and Roman times but also in the Middle Ages, the Renaissance, and down to the present.

THE OLYMPIAN GODS
(AND THEIR ROMAN EQUIVALENTS)

Zeus (Jupiter) King of the gods, Zeus (see FIGS. 5-36 and 29-42) ruled the sky and allotted the sea to Poseidon and the Underworld to Hades. His weapon was the thunderbolt, and with it he led the other gods to victory over the Giants (FIGS. 5-17 and 5-79), who had challenged the Olympians for control of the world.

Hera (Juno) Wife and sister of Zeus, Hera was the goddess of marriage and was often angered by Zeus's many love affairs. Her favorite cities were Mycenae, Sparta, and Argos, and she aided the Greeks in their war against the Trojans.

Poseidon (Neptune) Zeus's brother, Poseidon (see FIGS. 10-62 and 23-17) was one of the three sons of Kronos and Rhea and was lord of the sea. He controlled waves, storms, and earthquakes with his three-pronged pitchfork *(trident)*.

Hestia (Vesta) Daughter of Kronos and Rhea and sister of Zeus, Poseidon, and Hera, Hestia was goddess of the hearth. In Rome, Vesta had an ancient shrine with a sacred fire in the Roman Forum. Her six *Vestal Virgins* were the most important priestesses of the state, drawn only from aristocratic families.

Demeter (Ceres) Third sister of Zeus, Demeter was the goddess of grain and agriculture. She taught humans how to sow and plow. The English word *cereal* derives from *Ceres*.

Ares (Mars) God of war, Ares was the son of Zeus and Hera and the lover of Aphrodite. In the *Iliad* he took the side of the Trojans. Mars, father of the twin founders of Rome, *Romulus* and *Remus* (see FIG. 9-10), looms much larger in Roman mythology and religion than Ares does in Greek.

Athena (Minerva) Goddess of wisdom and warfare, Athena (FIGS. 5-32, 5-44, and 5-79) was a virgin (*parthenos* in Greek) born not from the womb of a woman but from the head of her father, Zeus. Her city was Athens, and her greatest temple was the Parthenon (FIG. 5-42).

Hephaistos (Vulcan) God of fire and of metalworking, Hephaistos fashioned the armor Achilles wore in battle against Troy. He also provided Zeus his scepter and Poseidon his trident and was the "surgeon" who split open Zeus's head when Athena was born. In some accounts, Hephaistos is the son of Hera without a male partner. In others, he is the son of Hera and Zeus. Born lame and, uncharacteristically for a god, ugly, his wife Aphrodite was unfaithful to him.

Apollo (Apollo) God of light and music and a great archer, Apollo (see FIGS. Intro-7, 5-3, 5-57, and 24-63) was the son of Zeus with *Leto/Latona*, daughter of one of the Titans. His epithet *Phoibos* means "radiant," and the young, beautiful Apollo is sometimes identified with the Sun *(Helios/Sol)*.

Artemis (Diana) Sister of Apollo, Artemis (see FIGS. 5-57 and 22-46) was goddess of the hunt and of wild animals. As Apollo's twin, she was occasionally regarded as the Moon *(Selene/Luna)*.

Aphrodite (Venus) Daughter of Zeus and *Dione* (daughter of Okeanos and one of the *nymphs*—the goddesses of springs, caves, and woods), Aphrodite (FIGS. 5-60 and 5-83) was the goddess of love and beauty. In one version of her myth, she was born from the foam *(aphros* in Greek) of the sea (see FIG. 21-27). She was the mother of Eros by Ares and of the Trojan hero *Aeneas* by *Anchises*. Julius Caesar and Augustus traced their lineage to Venus through Aeneas.

Hermes (Mercury) Son of Zeus and another nymph, Hermes (FIGS. 5-58 and 5-62) was the fleet-footed messenger of the gods and possessed winged sandals. He was also the guide of travelers, including the dead journeying to the Underworld, and he carried the *caduceus,* a magical herald's rod entwined by serpents, and wore a traveler's hat, often also shown with wings.

Equal in stature to the Olympians was *Hades (Pluto)*, one of the children of Kronos who fought with his brothers against the Titans but who never resided on Mount Olympus. Hades was the lord of the Underworld and god of the dead.

Other important Greek gods and goddesses are *Dionysos (Bacchus,* see FIG. 22-37), the god of wine and the son of Zeus and a mortal woman; *Eros (Amor* or *Cupid)* (see FIGS. 5-48, 5-84, 22-43, and 24-85), the winged child god of love and the son of Aphrodite and Ares; and *Asklepios (Aesculapius),* son of Apollo and a mortal woman, the Greek god of healing, whose serpent-entwined staff is the emblem of modern medicine.

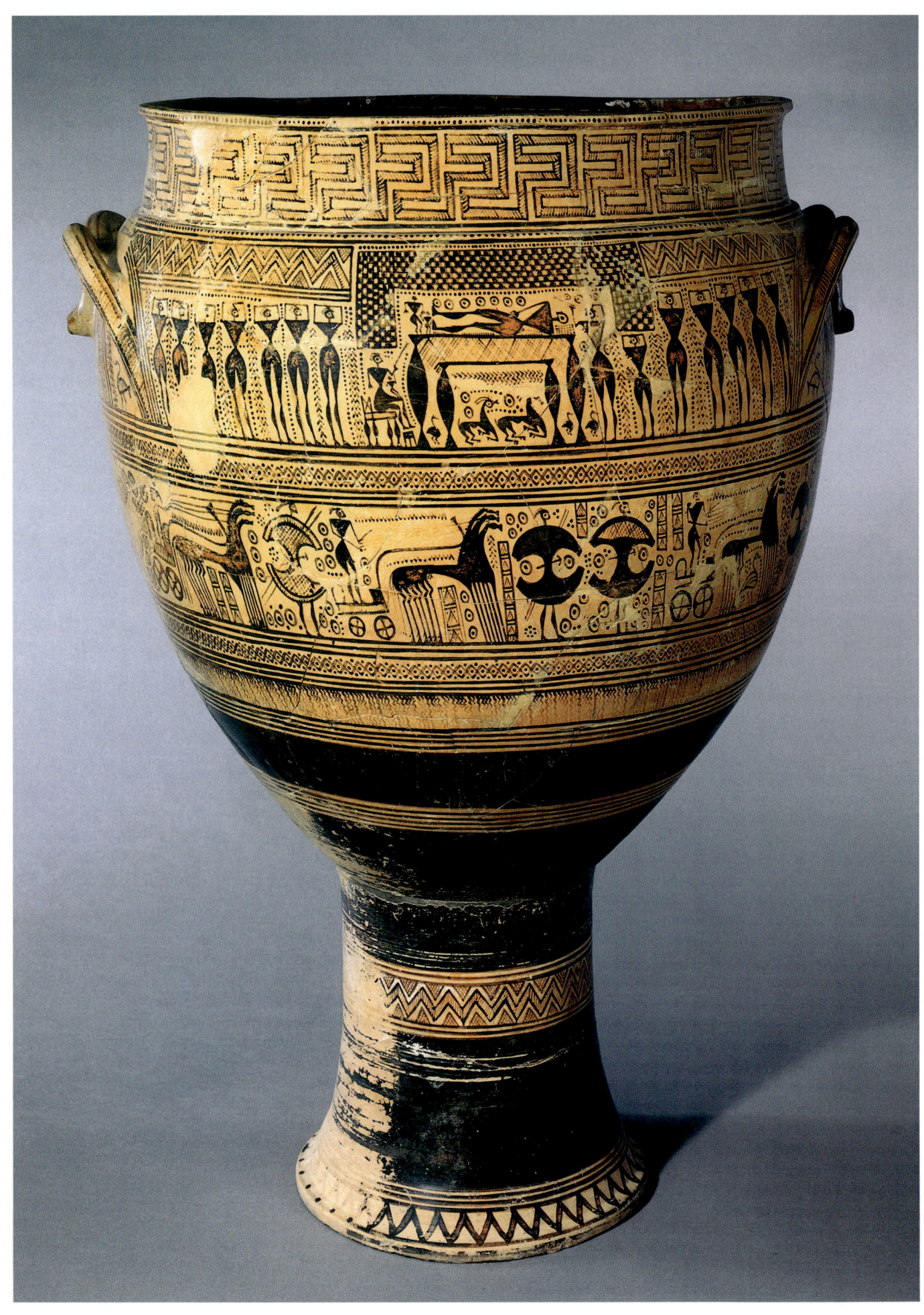

5-1 Geometric krater, from the Dipylon cemetery, Athens, Greece, ca. 740 B.C. Approx. 3′ 4½″ high. Metropolitan Museum of Art, New York, (Rogers Fund).

THE GEOMETRIC AND ORIENTALIZING PERIODS (NINTH–SEVENTH CENTURIES B.C.)

EMERGENCE FROM THE DARK AGE   The destruction of the Mycenaean palaces was accompanied by the disintegration of the Bronze Age social order. The disappearance of powerful kings and their retinues led to the loss of the knowledge of how to cut masonry, to construct citadels and tombs, to paint frescoes, and to sculpt in stone. Even the arts of reading and writing were forgotten. The succeeding centuries, sometimes called the Dark Age of Greece, were characterized by depopulation, poverty, and an almost total loss of contact with the outside world.

Only in the eighth century B.C. did economic conditions improve and the population begin to grow again. This era was in its own way a heroic age, a time when the poleis of Classical Greece took shape; when the Greeks broke out of their isolation and once again began to trade with cities both in the east and the west; when Homer's epic poems, formerly memorized and passed down from bard to bard, were recorded in written form; and when the Olympic Games were established.

Geometric Art

THE HUMAN FIGURE RETURNS TO ART   Also during the eighth century the human figure returned to Greek art—not, of course, in monumental statuary, which was exceedingly rare even in Bronze Age Greece, but painted on the surfaces of ceramic pots, which continued to be manufactured after the fall of Mycenae and even throughout the Dark Age.

One of the earliest examples is a huge *krater* (FIG. **5-1**), or mixing bowl, that marked the grave of an Athenian man buried around 740 B.C. At well over a yard tall, this remarkable vase is a considerable technical achievement and testifies both to the potter's skill and to the wealth and position of the deceased's family in the community. The bottom of the great vessel is open, perhaps to permit visitors to the grave to pour libations in honor of the dead, perhaps simply to provide a drain for rainwater, or both. The artist covered much of the surface with precisely painted abstract angular motifs, especially the *meander,* or key, pattern, in horizontal bands of varying height. Most early Greek vases were decorated exclusively with such motifs. The nature of the ornament has led art historians to designate this formative period of Greek art as *Geometric.* The earliest examples of the Geometric style date to the ninth century B.C.

On our krater the artist reserved the widest part of the vase for two bands of human figures and horse-drawn chariots, rather than for abstract ornament. Befitting the vase's function as a grave marker, the scenes depict the mourning for a man laid out on his bier and the grand chariot procession in his honor. In the upper band, the shroud, raised to reveal the corpse, is an abstract checkerboard-like backdrop, and the funerary couch has only two legs because the artist had no interest in suggesting depth or representing space. The human figures and the furniture are as two-dimensional as the geometric shapes elsewhere on the vessel. The painter filled every empty surface with circles and M-shaped ornament, further negating

any sense that the mourners inhabit open space. The figures are silhouettes constructed of triangular (frontal) torsos with attached profile arms, legs, and heads (with a single large frontal eye in the center!), following the age-old convention. The painter distinguished male from female. The deceased's penis grows out of one of his thighs. The mourning women, who tear their hair out in grief, have breasts emerging beneath their armpits. In both cases the artist was concerned with specifying gender, not with anatomical accuracy. Below, the chariots are accompanied by warriors drawn as though they are walking shields, and, in the old conceptual manner, both wheels of the chariots are shown. The horses have the correct number of heads and legs but seem to share a common body, negating any sense of depth. Despite the highly stylized and conventional manner of representation, this vessel marks a significant turning point in the history of Greek art. Not only was the human figure reintroduced into the painter's repertoire, but also the art of storytelling was resuscitated.

A HERO BATTLES A MONSTER   Similar schematic figures also appeared in the round at this date, but only at very small scale. One of the most impressive surviving Geometric sculptures is a small solid-cast bronze group (FIG. **5-2**) of a hero, probably Herakles (see "Herakles: Greatest of Greek Heroes," page 103), battling a *centaur* (a mythological beast that was part man, part horse), possibly Nessos, the centaur who had volunteered to carry the hero's bride across a river and then assaulted her. Whether or not the hero is Herakles

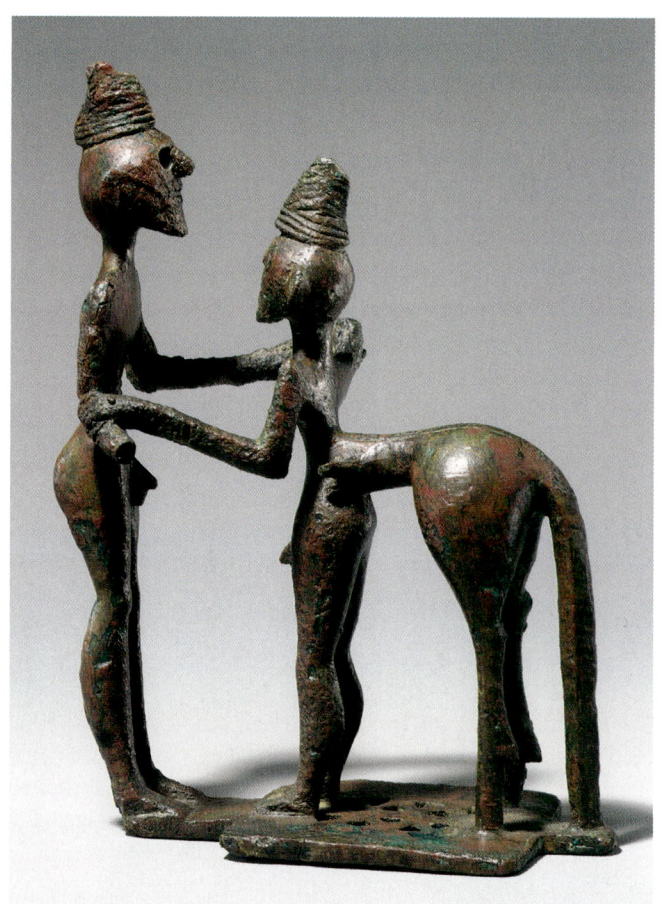

5-2   Hero and centaur (Herakles and Nessos?), ca. 750–730 B.C. Bronze, approx. $4\frac{1}{2}''$ high. Metropolitan Museum of Art, New York, (gift of J. Pierpont).

and the centaur is Nessos, the mythological nature of the group is certain. The repertoire of the Geometric artist was not limited to scenes inspired by daily life (and death).

Composite monsters were enormously popular in the ancient Near East and Egypt (see Chapters 2 and 3), and renewed contact with foreign cultures may have inspired such figures in Geometric Greece. The centaur is, however, a purely Greek invention—and one that posed a problem for the artist, who had, of course, never seen such a creature. The Geometric centaur was conceived as a man in front and a horse in back, a rather unhappy and unconvincing configuration that results in the forelegs belonging to a different species than the hindlegs. In our example, the figure of the hero and the human part of the centaur were rendered in a similar fashion. Both are bearded and wear helmets, but (contradictory to nature) the man is larger than the horse, probably to suggest that he will be the victor. Like other Geometric male figures, both painted and sculptured, this hero is nude, in contrast to the Near Eastern statuettes that might have inspired such Greek works. Here, at the very beginning of Greek figural art, one can recognize the Hellenic instinct for the natural beauty of the human figure, which is reflected by the fact Greek athletes exercised without their clothes and even competed nude in the Olympic Games from very early times.

Orientalizing Art

AN OFFERING TO APOLLO   One of the masterworks of the early seventh century B.C. is the *Mantiklos Apollo* (FIG. **5-3**), a small bronze statuette dedicated to Apollo at Thebes by an otherwise unknown man named Mantiklos. With characteristic pride in the ability to write, the sculptor (or another) scratched into the thighs of the figure a message from the dedicator to the deity: "Mantiklos dedicated me as a tithe to the far-shooting Lord of the Silver Bow; you, Phoibos [Apollo], might give some pleasing favor in return." Because the Greeks conceived their gods in human form, one cannot be sure whether the figure was meant to represent the youthful Apollo or Mantiklos (or neither). But if the left hand at one time held a bow, then the statuette is certainly an image of the deity. In any case, the purpose of the votive offering is clear. Equally apparent is the increased interest Greek artists at this time had in reproducing details of human anatomy, such as the long hair framing the unnaturally elongated neck, and the pectoral and abdominal muscles, which define the stylized triangular torso. The triangular face has eye sockets that were once inlaid, and the head may have had a separately fashioned helmet on it.

THE GREEKS LOOK EASTWARD   The *Mantiklos Apollo* was created when the pace and scope of Greek trade and colonization had accelerated and when Greek artists were exposed more than ever before to Eastern artworks, especially small portable objects such as Syrian ivory carvings. The closer contact had a profound effect on the development of Greek art. Indeed, so many motifs borrowed from or inspired by Egyptian and Near Eastern art entered the Greek pictorial vocabulary at this time that historians have dubbed the seventh century B.C. the *Orientalizing* period.

An elaborate Corinthian *amphora* (FIG. **5-4**), or two-handled storage jar, typifies the new Greek fascination with the Orient. In a series of bands recalling the organization of Geometric painted vases, animals such as the native boar appear beside exotic lions and panthers and composite creatures inspired by Eastern monsters such as the sphinx and lamassu—in this instance the *siren* (part bird, part woman) prominently displayed on the amphora's neck.

The appeal of such vases was not due solely to their Orientalizing animal friezes but also to a new ceramic technique the Corinthians invented, which art historians call *black-figure* painting (see "Greek Vase Painting," page 104). The black-figure painter first put down black silhouettes on the clay surface, as in Geometric times, but then used a sharp, pointed instrument to incise linear details within the forms,

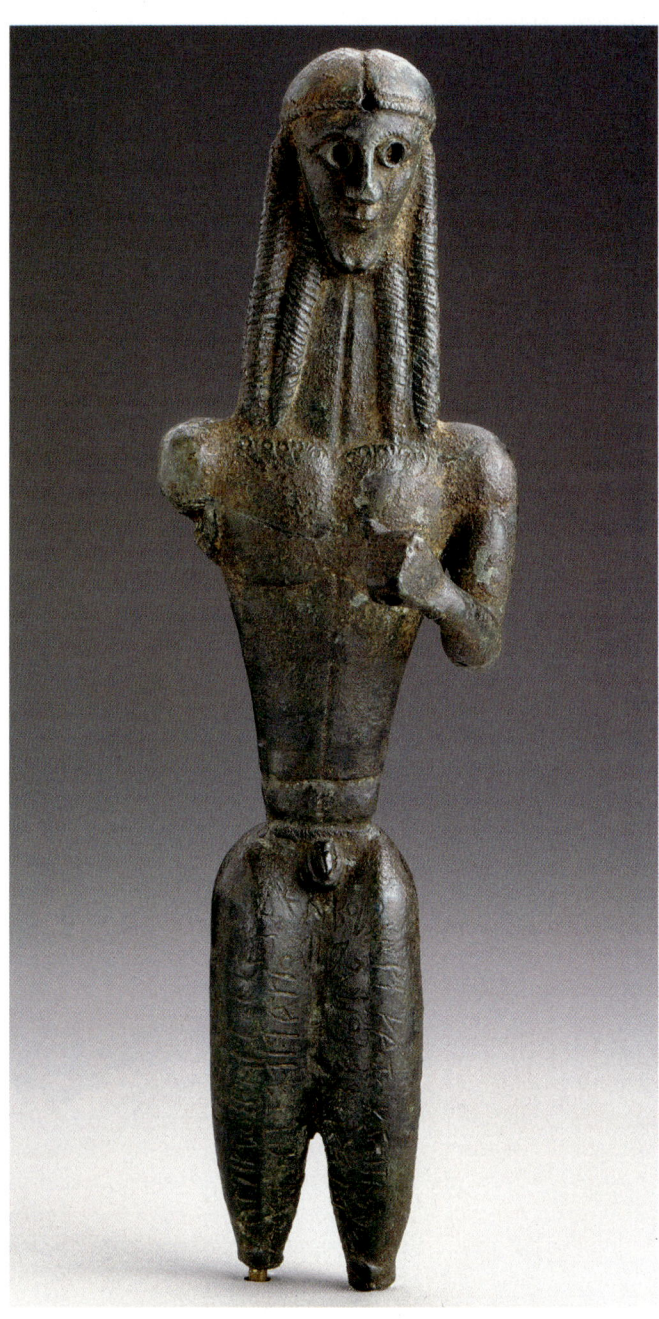

5-3   *Mantiklos Apollo,* statuette of a youth dedicated by Mantiklos to Apollo, from Thebes, Greece, ca. 700–680 B.C. Bronze, approx. 8″ high. Museum of Fine Arts, Boston.

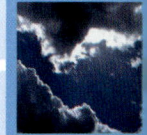

Herakles
Greatest of Greek Heroes

Greek heroes were a class of mortals intermediate between ordinary humans and the immortal gods. Most often the children of gods, some were great warriors, such as those who fought at Troy and were celebrated in Homer's epic poems. Others went from one fabulous adventure to another, ridding the world of monsters and generally benefiting humankind. Many heroes were worshiped after their deaths, and the greatest of them were honored with shrines, especially in the cities most closely associated with them. For example, the bones of Theseus, king of Athens and victor over the Minotaur who inhabited the labyrinthine palace at Knossos (see FIGS. 4-3 to 4-5), were transferred to Athens around 475 B.C. from Skyros, where Theseus had been killed, and deposited in his sanctuary near the city center.

The greatest of all the Greek heroes was *Herakles* (the Roman *Hercules*), born in Thebes and the son of Zeus and Alkmene, a mortal woman. Zeus's wife Hera hated Herakles and sent two serpents to attack him in his cradle, but the infant strangled them. Later, Hera caused the hero to go mad and to kill his wife and children. As punishment he was condemned to perform twelve great labors. In the first, he defeated the legendary lion of Nemea and ever after wore its pelt. The lion's skin and his weapon, a club, are Herakles' distinctive attributes (FIGS. 5-63 and 5-66). His last task was to obtain the golden apples Gaia gave to Hera at her marriage (FIG. 5-32). They grew from a tree in the garden of the Hesperides at the farthest western edge of the Ocean and a dragon guarded them. After completion of the twelve, seemingly impossible, tasks, Herakles was awarded immortality. Athena, who had watched over him carefully throughout his life and assisted him in performing the labors, introduced him into the realm of the gods on Mount Olympus. According to legend, it was Herakles who established the quadrennial Olympic Games.

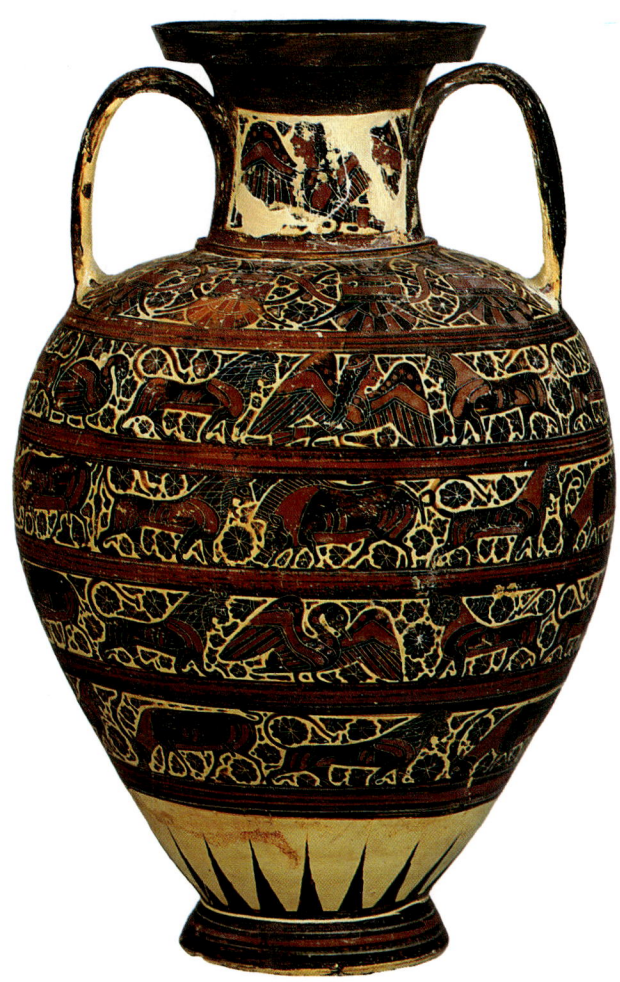

usually adding highlights in purplish red or white over the black figures before firing the vessel. The combination of the weighty black silhouettes with the delicate detailing and the bright polychrome overlay proved to be irresistible, and Athenian painters soon copied the technique from the Corinthians.

THE FIRST GREEK STONE TEMPLES The foundation of the Greek trading colony of Naukratis in Egypt (see map, Chapter 3, page 42) before 630 B.C. brought the Greeks into direct contact with the monumental stone architecture of the Egyptians. Not long after that the first stone buildings since the fall of the Mycenaean kingdoms began to be constructed in Greece. At Prinias on Crete, for example, a stone temple, called Temple A (FIG. 5-5), was built around 625 B.C. to honor an unknown deity. Although the inspiration for the structure came from the East, the form resembles that of a typical Mycenaean megaron, such as that at Tiryns (see FIG. 4-19), with a hearth or sacrificial pit flanked by two columns

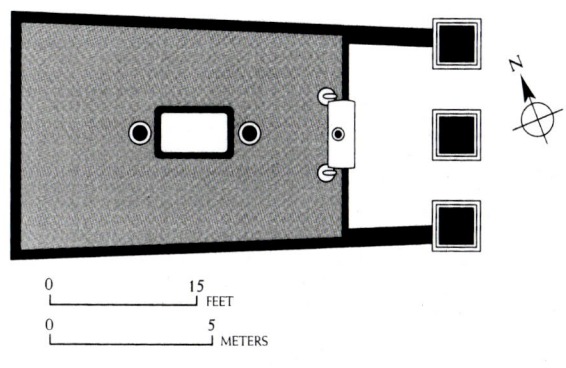

5-4 Corinthian black-figure amphora with animal friezes, from Rhodes, Greece, ca. 625–600 B.C. Approx. 1′ 2″ high. British Museum, London.

5-5 Plan of Temple A, Prinias, Greece, ca. 625 B.C.

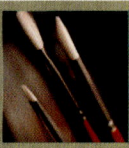

MATERIALS AND TECHNIQUES

Greek Vase Painting

The techniques Greek ceramicists used to shape and decorate fine vases required a great deal of skill, acquired over many years as apprentices in the workshops of master potters. During the Archaic and Classical periods, when the art of vase painting was at its zenith in Greece, both potters and painters frequently signed their work. These signatures reveal the pride of the artists. They also might have functioned as "brand names" for a large export market. The products of the workshops in Corinth and Athens in particular were much prized and have been found all over the Mediterranean world. The Corinthian amphora illustrated here (FIG. 5-4) was found on Rhodes, an island at the opposite side of the Aegean from mainland Corinth. Athenian *(Attic)* vases were staples in Etruscan tombs in Italy, and all but one of our examples (FIGS. 5-18 to 5-23, 5-57, and 5-58) came from an Etruscan site. Other painted Attic pots have been found as far apart as France, Russia, and the Sudan.

The first step in manufacturing a Greek vase was to remove any impurities found in the natural clay and then to knead it, like dough, to remove air bubbles and make it flexible. The Greeks used dozens of different kinds and shapes of pots, and most were fashioned in several parts. The vessel's body was formed by placing the clay on a rotating horizontal wheel. While an apprentice turned the wheel by hand, the potter pulled up the clay with the fingers until the desired shape was achieved. The handles were shaped separately and attached to the vase body by applying *slip* (liquefied clay) to the joints.

Then a specialist, the painter, was called in, although many potters decorated their own work. (Today most people tend to regard painters as more elevated artists than potters, but in Greece the potters owned the shops and employed the painters.) The "pigment" the painter applied to the clay surface is customarily referred to as *glaze,* but the black areas on Greek pots are neither pigment nor glaze but a slip of finely sifted clay that originally was of the same rich red orange color as the clay of the pot. In the three-phase firing process Greek potters used, the first *(oxidizing)* phase turned both pot and slip red. During the second *(reducing)* phase, the oxygen supply into the kiln was shut off, and both pot and slip turned black. In the final *(reoxidizing)* phase, the pot's coarser material reabsorbed oxygen and became red again, while the smoother, silica-laden slip did not and remained black. After long experiment, Greek potters developed a velvety jet-black "glaze" of this kind, produced in kilns heated to temperatures as high as 950 degrees Celsius (about 1742 degrees Fahrenheit). The firing process was the same whether the painter worked in black-figure or in red-figure. In fact, sometimes both manners were used on the same vase (FIG. 5-20).

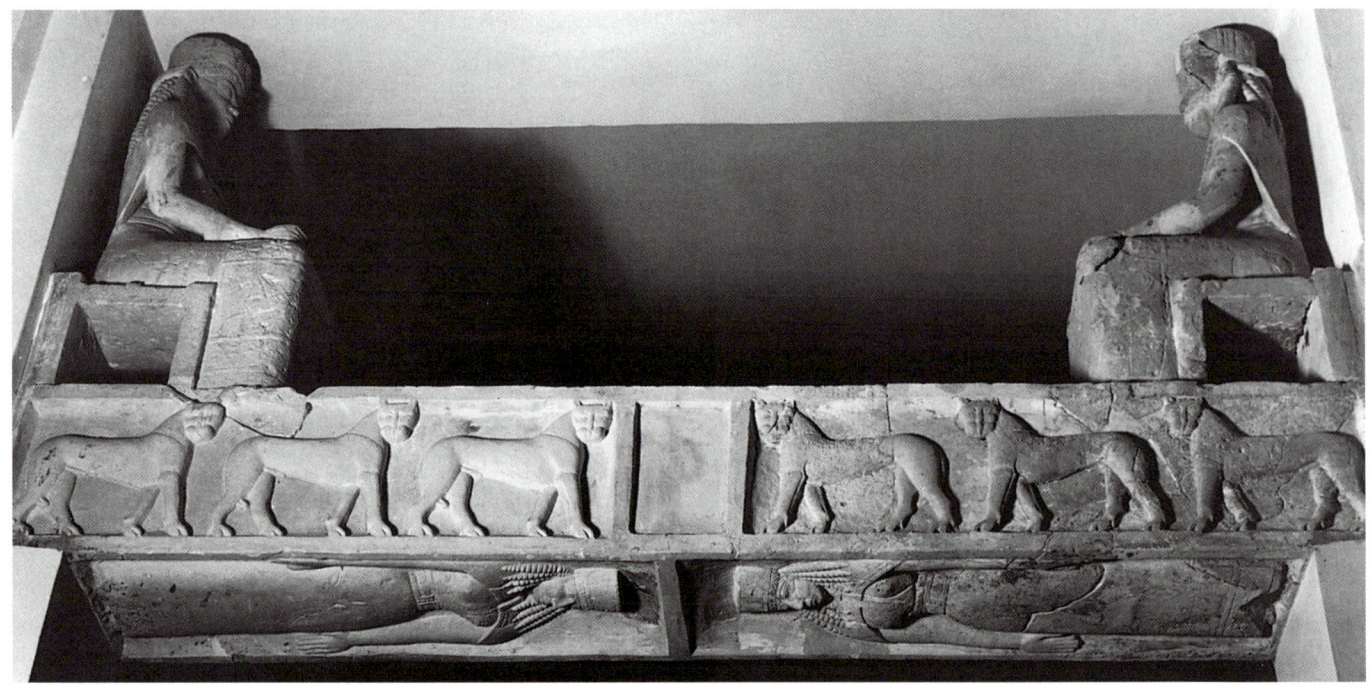

5-6   Lintel of Temple A, Prinias, Greece, ca. 625 B.C. Limestone, approx. 2′ 9″ high; seated goddesses approx. 2′ 8″ high. Archeological Museum, Herakleion.

in the cella. The facade consisted of three great piers; the roof was probably flat.

Above the doorway of the Prinias temple was a huge limestone lintel (FIG. 5-6), surmounted by confronting statues of seated women, probably goddesses, wearing tall headdresses and capes. Two other similarly dressed, but standing, goddesses are carved in relief on the underside of the block, visible to those entering the temple. On the face of the lintel is a frieze of Orientalizing panthers with frontal heads—the same motif as that on the contemporary Corinthian black-figure amphora (FIG. 5-4). Temple A at Prinias is the earliest known example of a Greek temple with sculptured decoration.

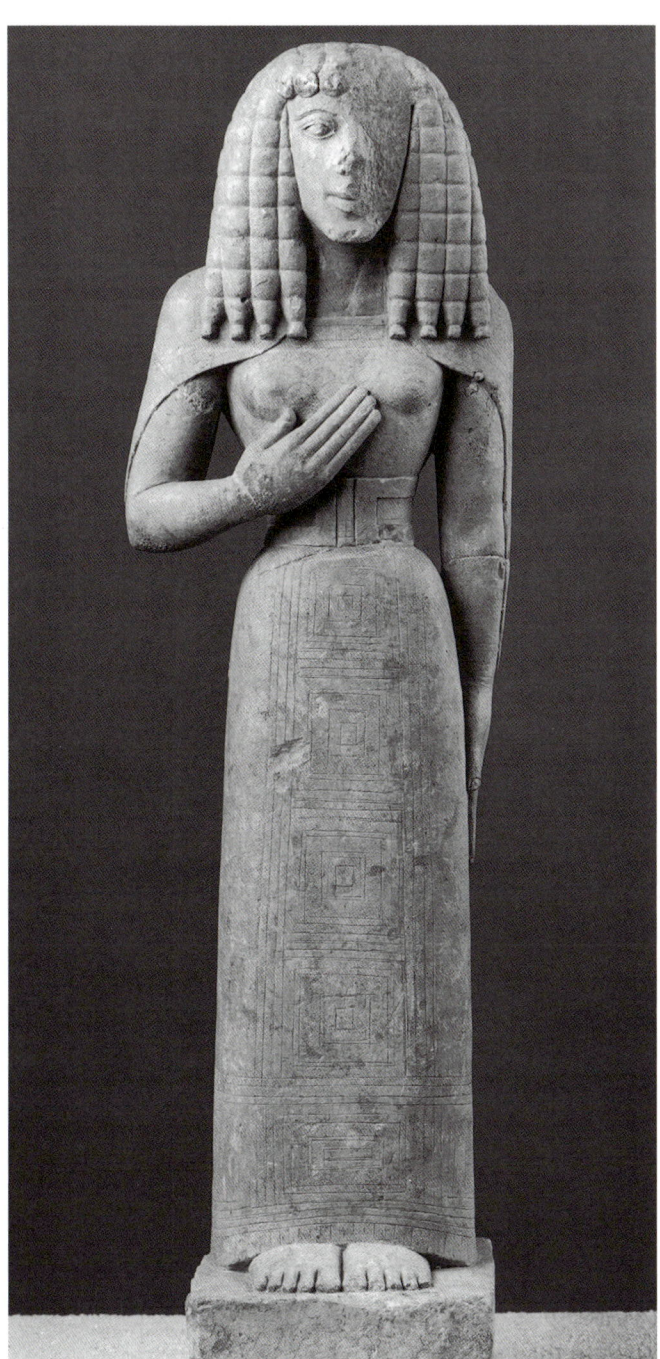

5-7 *Lady of Auxerre*, statue of a goddess or kore, ca. 650–625 B.C. Limestone, approx. 2' 1½" high. Louvre, Paris.

GODDESS OR WOMAN? Somewhat earlier and probably also originally from Crete is a limestone statuette of a goddess or maiden (*kore*; plural, *korai*) popularly known as the *Lady of Auxerre* (FIG. 5-7) after the French town that is her oldest recorded provenance. As with the figure dedicated by Mantiklos, it is uncertain whether the young woman is a mortal or a deity. She wears a long skirt and a cape, as do the Prinias women, but the Auxerre maiden has no headdress, and the right hand placed across the chest is probably a gesture of prayer, indicating that this is a kore. The style is, however, comparable. Characteristic is the triangular flat-topped head framed by long strands of hair that form complementary triangles to that of the face. Also typical are the small belted waist and a fondness for pattern: Note the almost Geometric treatment of the long skirt with its incised concentric squares, once brightly painted. Despite its monumental quality, the statue is only a little more than two feet tall—smaller than the seated goddesses of the Prinias lintel but much larger than the bronze statuettes of the era.

DAEDALUS, MASTER OF ALL ARTS The *Lady of Auxerre* is the masterpiece of a style usually referred to as *Daedalic,* after the legendary artist DAEDALUS, whose name means "the skillful one." In addition to having been a great sculptor, Daedalus was said to have built the labyrinth in Crete to house the Minotaur and also to have designed a temple at Memphis in Egypt (see map, Chapter 3, page 42). The historical Greeks attributed to him almost all the great achievements in early sculpture and architecture before the names of artists and architects were recorded. The story that Daedalus worked in Egypt reflects the enormous impact of Egyptian art and architecture on the Greeks of the aptly named Orientalizing age, as well as on their offspring in the succeeding Archaic period.

THE ARCHAIC PERIOD (SIXTH CENTURY B.C.)

Statuary

GREEK KOUROI AND EGYPTIAN STATUES According to one Greek writer, Daedalus used the same compositional patterns for his statues as the Egyptians used for their own, and the first truly monumental stone statues of the Greeks follow very closely the canonical Egyptian format. A life-size marble *kouros* ("youth;" plural, *kouroi*) in New York (FIG. 5-8) emulates the stance of Egyptian statues—for example, the portrait of Mentuemhet (see FIG. 3-40) carved only a half century before the Greek statue. In both cases the figure is rigidly frontal with the left foot advanced slightly. The arms are held beside the body, and the fists are clenched with the thumbs forward. This kouros even served a funerary purpose. It is said to have stood over a grave in the countryside somewhere near Athens. Such statues replaced the huge vases (FIG. 5-1) of Geometric times as the preferred form of grave marker in the sixth century B.C. They also were used as votive offerings in sanctuaries. (At one time it was thought that all kouroi were images of Apollo.) The kouros type, because of its generic quality, could be employed in several different contexts.

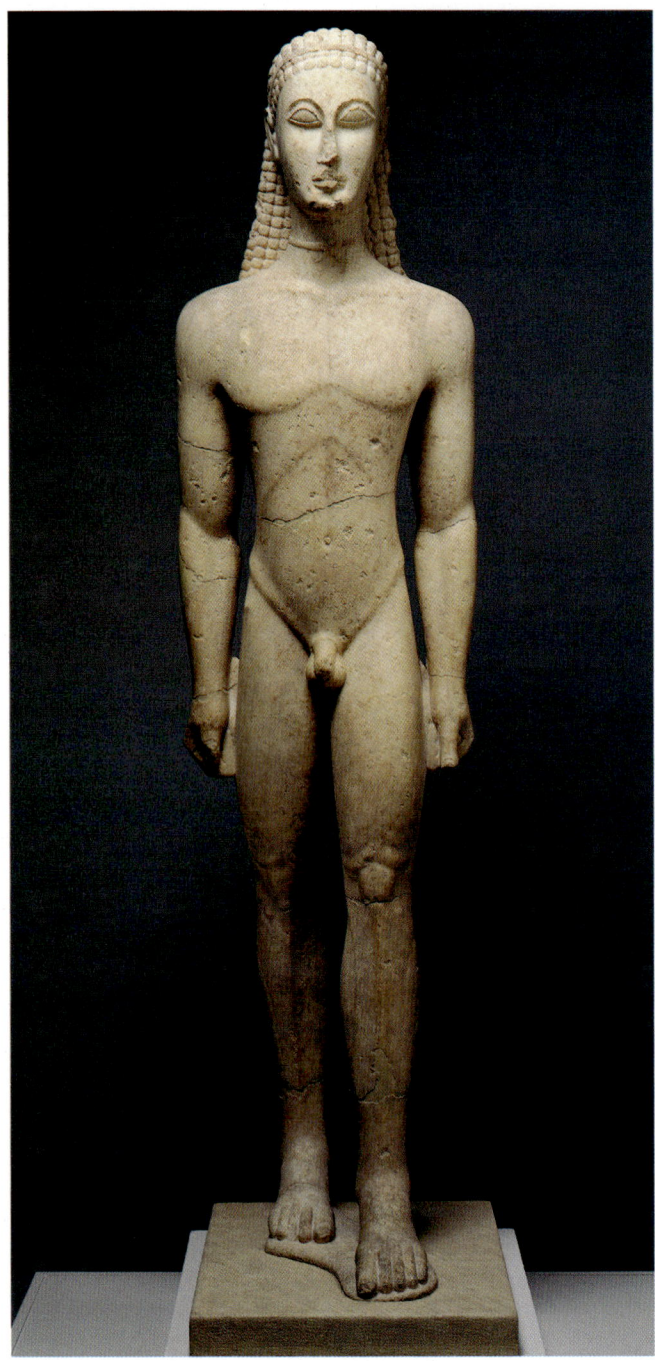

5-8   Kouros, ca. 600 B.C. Marble, approx. 6' ½" high. Metropolitan Museum of Art, New York.

Despite the adherence to Egyptian prototypes, Greek kouros statues differ from their Oriental brethren in two important ways. First, they were liberated from their original stone block. The Egyptian obsession with permanence was alien to the Greeks, who were preoccupied with finding ways to represent motion rather than stability in their sculptured figures. Second, the kouroi are nude, and, in the absence of attributes, the monumental marble statues, like the tiny bronze dedicated by Mantiklos (FIG. 5-3), are formally indistinguishable from Greek images of deities with their perfect bodies exposed for all to see.

The New York kouros shares many traits with Greek Orientalizing works such as the *Mantiklos Apollo* and the *Lady of*

Auxerre, especially the triangular shape of head and hair and the flatness of the face. Eyes, nose, and mouth all sit on the front of the head, ears were placed on the sides, and the long hair forms a flat backdrop behind the head. In every instance one sees the result of the sculptor's having drawn these features on four independent sides of the marble block, following the same workshop procedure used in Egypt for millennia. The New York kouros also has the slim waist of earlier Greek statues, and the same love of pattern may be discerned. The pointed arch of the rib cage, for example, echoes the V-shaped ridge of the hips, which suggests but does not accurately reproduce the rounded flesh and muscle of the human body.

A SMILING CALF BEARER   A generation later than the New York kouros is the statue of a *moschophoros,* or calf bearer (FIG. 5-9), found on the Athenian Acropolis in frag-

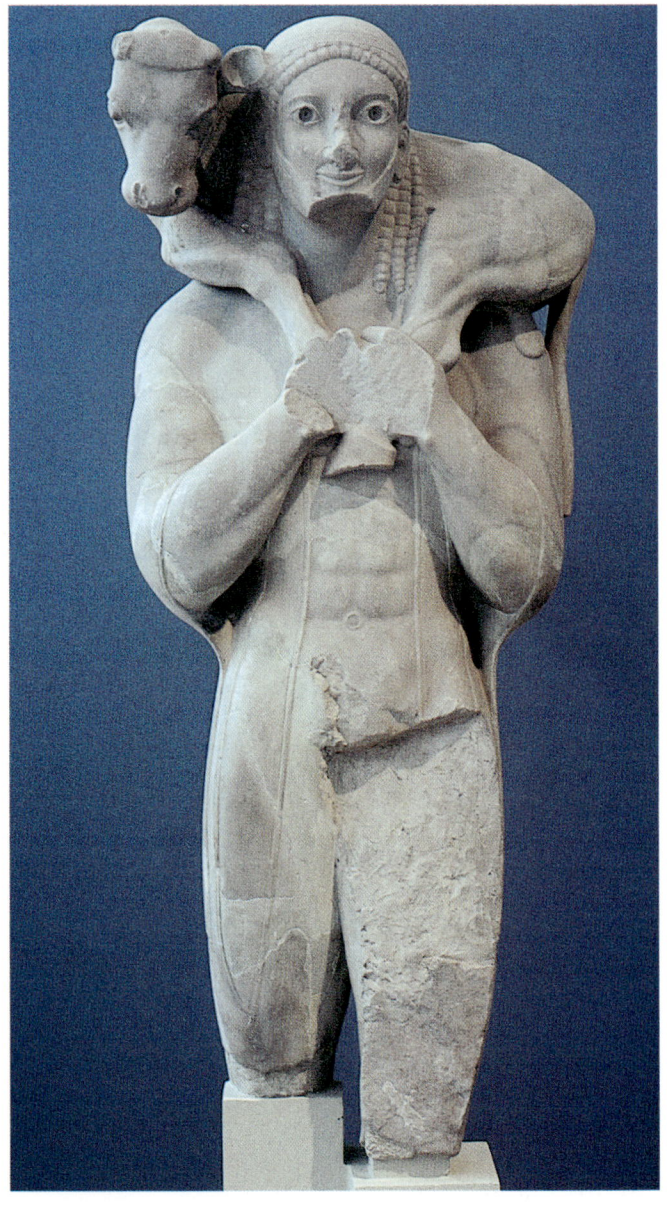

5-9   Calf Bearer (*Moschophoros*), dedicated by Rhonbos on the Acropolis, Athens, Greece, ca. 560 B.C. Marble, restored height approx. 5' 5". Acropolis Museum, Athens.

ments. Its inscribed base (not visible in our photograph) states that a man whose name has been reconstructed as Rhonbos dedicated the statue. Rhonbos is almost certainly the calf bearer himself bringing an offering to Athena in thanksgiving for his prosperity. He stands in the left-foot-forward manner of the kouroi, but he is bearded and therefore no longer a youth. He wears a thin cloak (which once was set off from the otherwise nude body by paint). No one dressed in such a manner in ancient Athens. The sculptor adhered to the artistic convention of male nudity and attributed to the calf bearer the noble perfection such nudity suggests while also indicating that this mature gentleman is clothed, as any respectable citizen would be in such a context. The Archaic sculptor's love of pattern was paramount once again in the way the difficult problem of representing man and animal together was tackled. The calf's legs and the moschophoros's arms form a bold X that unites the two bodies both physically and formally.

The calf bearer's face differs markedly from those of earlier Greek statues (and those of Egypt and the Near East also) in one notable way: The man smiles—or seems to. From this time on, Archaic Greek statues always smile, even in the most inappropriate contexts (see, for example, FIG. 5-27, where a dying warrior with an arrow in his chest grins broadly at the spectator!). This so-called *Archaic smile* has been variously interpreted, but it is not to be taken literally. Rather, the smile seems to be the Archaic sculptor's way of indicating that the person portrayed is alive. By adopting such a convention, the Greek artist signaled a very different intention from any Egyptian counterpart.

A STATUE FOR A HERO'S GRAVE Sometime around 530 B.C. a young man named Kroisos died a hero's death in battle, and his grave at Anavysos, not far from Athens, was marked by a kouros statue (FIG. **5-10**). The inscribed base invites visitors to "stay and mourn at the tomb of dead Kroisos, whom raging Ares destroyed one day as he fought in the foremost ranks." The statue, with its distinctive Archaic smile, is no more a portrait of a specific youth than is the New York kouros. But two generations later, the Greek sculptor greatly refined the type and, without rejecting the Egyptian stance, rendered the human body in a far more naturalistic manner. The head is no longer too large for the body, and the face is more rounded, with swelling cheeks replacing the flat planes of the earlier work. The long hair does not form a stiff backdrop to the head but falls naturally over the back. Rounded hips replace the V-shaped ridges of the New York kouros.

The original paint survives in part on the Kroisos statue, enhancing the sense of life. All Greek stone statues were painted. The modern notion that classical statuary was pure white is mistaken. The Greeks did not, however, color their statues garishly. The flesh was left in the natural color of the stone, which was waxed and polished, while eyes, lips, hair, and drapery were painted in *encaustic* (see "Iaia of Cyzicus and the Art of Encaustic Painting," Chapter 10, page 289). In this technique the pigment was mixed with wax and applied to the surface while hot.

KORAI FROM THE SACK OF THE ACROPOLIS A stylistic "sister" to the Anavysos kouros is the statue of a kore wearing a *peplos* (FIG. **5-11**), a simple, long, woolen belted garment that gives the female figure a columnar appearance. Traces of paint are preserved here also. As with the Kroisos statue, this kore was covered by earth for more than two millennia, protecting the painted surface from the destructive effects of exposure to the atmosphere and to bad weather. The *Peplos Kore,* as she is known, was, like the earlier statue of the calf bearer (FIG. 5-9), thrown down by the Persians during their sack of the Acropolis in 480 B.C. (discussed later) and shortly thereafter buried by the Athenians themselves. Before that time, she stood as a votive offering in Athena's sanctuary. Her missing left arm was extended, a break from the frontal compression of the arms at the sides in

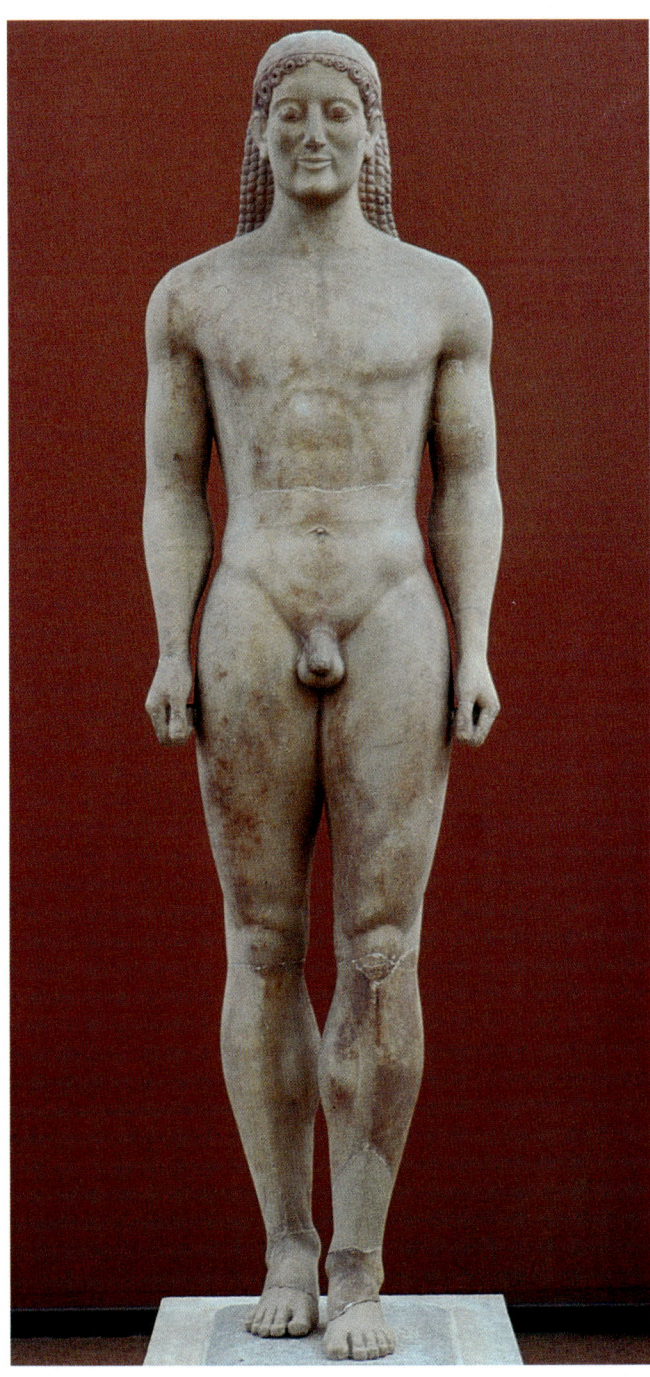

5-10 Kroisos, from Anavysos, Greece, ca. 530 B.C. Marble, approx. 6' 4" high. National Archeological Museum, Athens.

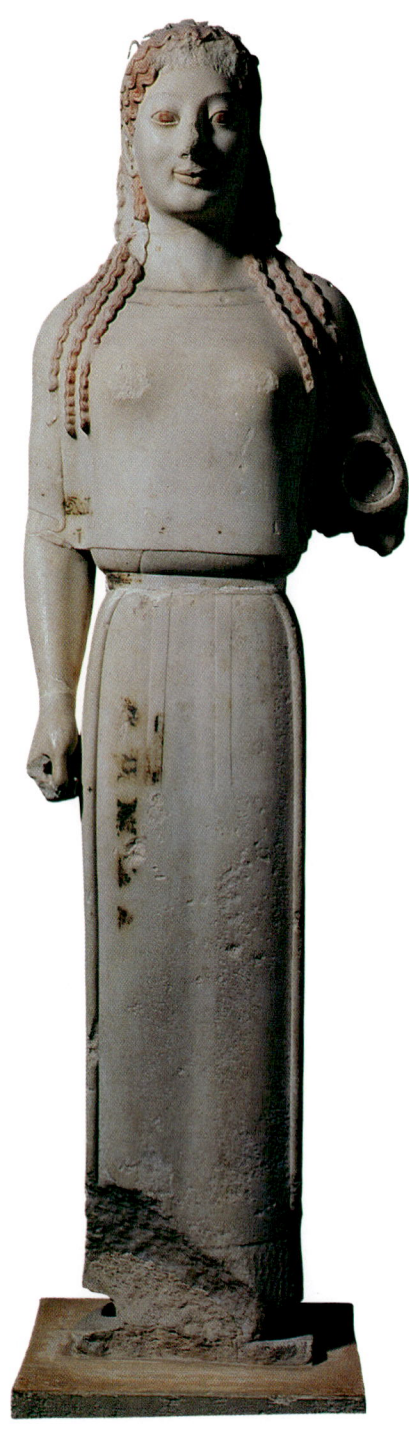

Ionian *chiton,* worn in conjunction with a heavier *himation* (mantle), was the garment of choice for fashionable women. Archaic sculptors delighted in rendering the intricate patterns created by the cascading folds of thin, soft material, as may be seen in another kore (FIG. **5-12**) buried on the Acropolis after the Persian destruction. In this statue the asymmetry of the folds greatly relieves the stiff frontality of the body and makes the figure appear much more lifelike than contemporary kouroi. The sculptor achieved added variety by showing the kore grasping part of her chiton in her left hand (unfortunately broken off) to lift it off the ground as she takes a step forward. This is the equivalent of the advanced left foot of the kouroi and is standard for statues of korai. Despite the varied surface treatment of brightly colored garments on the korai, the kore postures are as fixed as those of their male counterparts.

5-11   *Peplos Kore,* from the Acropolis, Athens, Greece, ca. 530 B.C. Marble, approx. 4′ high. Acropolis Museum, Athens.

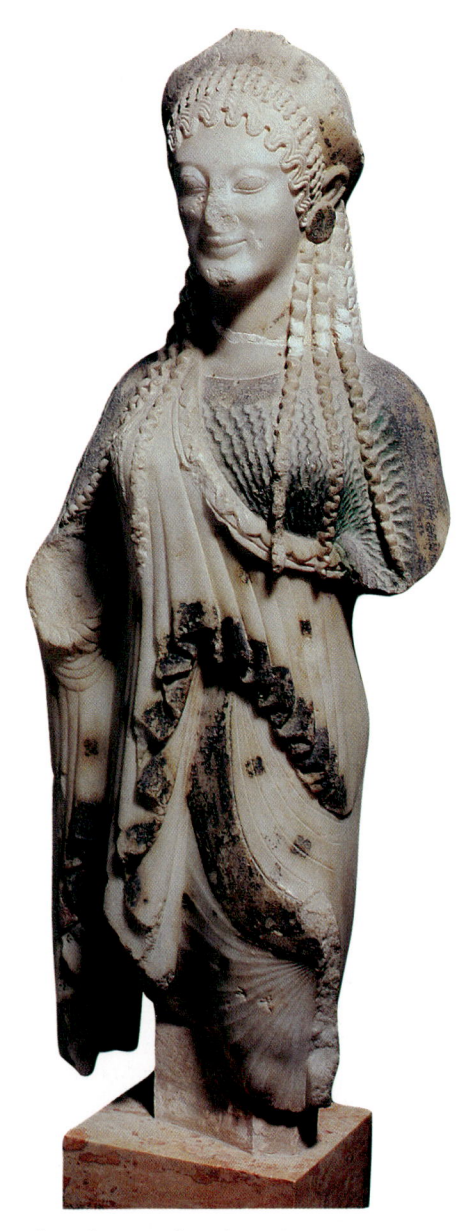

Egyptian statues. She once held in her hand an attribute that would identify the figure as a maiden or, as some have suggested, a goddess, perhaps Athena herself. Whatever her identity, the contrast with the *Lady of Auxerre* (FIG. 5-7) is striking. Although in both cases the drapery conceals the entire body save for head, arms, and feet, the later sculptor rendered the soft female form much more naturally, sharply differentiating it from the hard muscular body of the kouros.

The *Peplos Kore* is one of the latest peplos-clad dedications on the Acropolis. By the later sixth century, the light linen

5-12   Kore, from the Acropolis, Athens, Greece, ca. 510 B.C. Marble, approx. 1′ 9½″ high. Acropolis Museum, Athens.

Architecture and Architectural Sculpture

THE CANONICAL TEMPLE TAKES SHAPE Already, in the Orientalizing seventh century B.C., at Prinias, the Greeks had built a stone temple embellished with stone sculptures (FIGS. 5-5 and 5-6). But despite the contemporary Daedalic style of its statues and reliefs, the Cretan temple resembled the megaron of a Mycenaean palace more than anything Greek traders had seen in their travels overseas. In the Archaic age of the sixth century, with the model of Egyptian columnar halls such as that at Karnak (see FIG. 3-25) before them, Greek architects began to build the gable-roofed columnar stone temples that have been more influential on the later history of architecture in the Western world than any other building type ever devised.

Greek architecture and its Roman and Renaissance descendants and hybrids are almost as familiar as modern architecture. The so-called Greek revival European architects instituted in the late eighteenth century led to a wide diffusion of the Greek architectural style. Official public buildings (courthouses, banks, city halls, legislative chambers), designed for impressive formality, especially imitated classical architecture. The ancient Greeks were industrious builders, even though their homes were unpretentious places, they had no monarchs to house royally until Hellenistic times, and they performed religious rites in the open. Their temples were not places the faithful gathered in to worship a deity, as they are for most of the world's modern religions. The altar lay outside the temple at the east end, facing the rising sun, and the temple proper was a shrine for that grandest of all votive offerings to the deities, the cult statue. Both in its early and mature manifestations, the Greek temple was the house of the god or goddess, not of his or her followers.

Figural sculpture played a major role in the exterior program of the Greek temple from early times, partly to embellish the god's shrine, partly to tell something about the deity symbolized within, and partly to serve as a votive offering. But the building itself, with its finely carved capitals and moldings, also was conceived as sculpture, abstract in form and possessing the power of sculpture to evoke human responses. The commanding importance of the sculptured temple, its inspiring function in public life, was emphasized in its elevated site, often on a hill above the city (*acropolis* means "high city"). As Aristotle stipulated: "The site should be a spot seen far and wide, which gives due elevation to virtue and towers over the neighborhood."[3]

Many of the earliest Greek temples do not survive because they were made of wood and mud brick. Pausanias, who wrote an invaluable guidebook to Greece in the second century A.D., noted that in the even-then ancient Temple of Hera at Olympia, one oak column was still in place. The others had been replaced by stone columns. Archaic and later Greek temples were, however, built of more permanent materials—limestone, in many cases, and, where it was available, marble, which was more impressive (and more expensive). In Greece proper, if not in its western colonies, marble was readily at hand. Bluish white stone came from Hymettus, just east of Athens. Glittering white stone particularly adapted for carving was brought from Pentelicus, northeast of the city. And

from the Aegean Islands, Paros in particular, marble of varying quantities and qualities was supplied.

In its canonical plan the Greek temple (see "Doric and Ionic Temples," page 112) still discloses a close affinity with the Mycenaean megaron (see FIG. 4-19), and, even in its most elaborate form, it retains the latter structure's basic simplicity. In all cases, the Greek scheme's remarkable order, compactness, and symmetry strike the eye first, reflecting the Greeks' sense of proportion and their effort to achieve ideal forms in terms of regular numerical relationships and geometric rules. Whether the plan is simple or more complex, no fundamental change occurs in the nature of the units or of their grouping. Classical Greek architecture, like classical music, has a simple core theme with a series of complex, but always quite intelligible, variations developed from it.

The Greeks' insistence on proportional order guided their experiments with the proportions of temple plans. The earliest temples tended to be long and narrow, with the proportion of the ends to the sides roughly expressible as 1:3. From the sixth century on, plans approached but rarely had a proportion of exactly 1:2. Classical temples tended to be a little longer than twice their width. Proportion in architecture and sculpture, and harmony in music, were much the same to the Greek mind and reflected and embodied the cosmic order (see "Polykleitos's Prescription for the Perfect Statue," page 126).

Sculptural ornament was concentrated on the upper part of the building, in the frieze and pediments. Architectural sculpture, like freestanding statuary, was painted and usually was placed only in the building parts that had no structural function. This is true particularly of the Doric order, where decorative sculpture appears only in the metope and pediment "voids." Ionic builders, less severe in this respect as well, were willing to decorate the entire frieze and sometimes even the lower column drums. Occasionally, they replaced their columns with female figures (*caryatids*; FIGS. 5-16 and 5-52). By using color, the designer could bring out more clearly the relationships of the structural parts, soften the stone's glitter at specific points, and provide a background to set off the figures.

Although color was used for emphasis and to relieve what might have seemed too bare a simplicity, Greek architecture primarily depended on clarity and balance. To the Greeks, it was unthinkable to use surfaces in the way the Egyptians used their gigantic columns—as fields for complicated ornamentation (see FIG. 3-25). The history of Greek temple architecture is the history of Greek architects' unflagging efforts to find the most satisfactory (that is, what they believed were perfect) proportions for each part of the building and for the structure as a whole.

A TEMPLE FOR HERA IN ITALY The prime example of early Greek efforts at Doric temple design is the unusually well-preserved Archaic temple (FIG. **5-13**) erected around 550 B.C. at Paestum (Greek Poseidonia), south of Naples in Italy. The entire peripteral colonnade of this huge (eighty feet by one hundred seventy feet) building is still standing, but most of the entablature, including the frieze, pediment, and all of the roof, has vanished. Called the "Basilica"

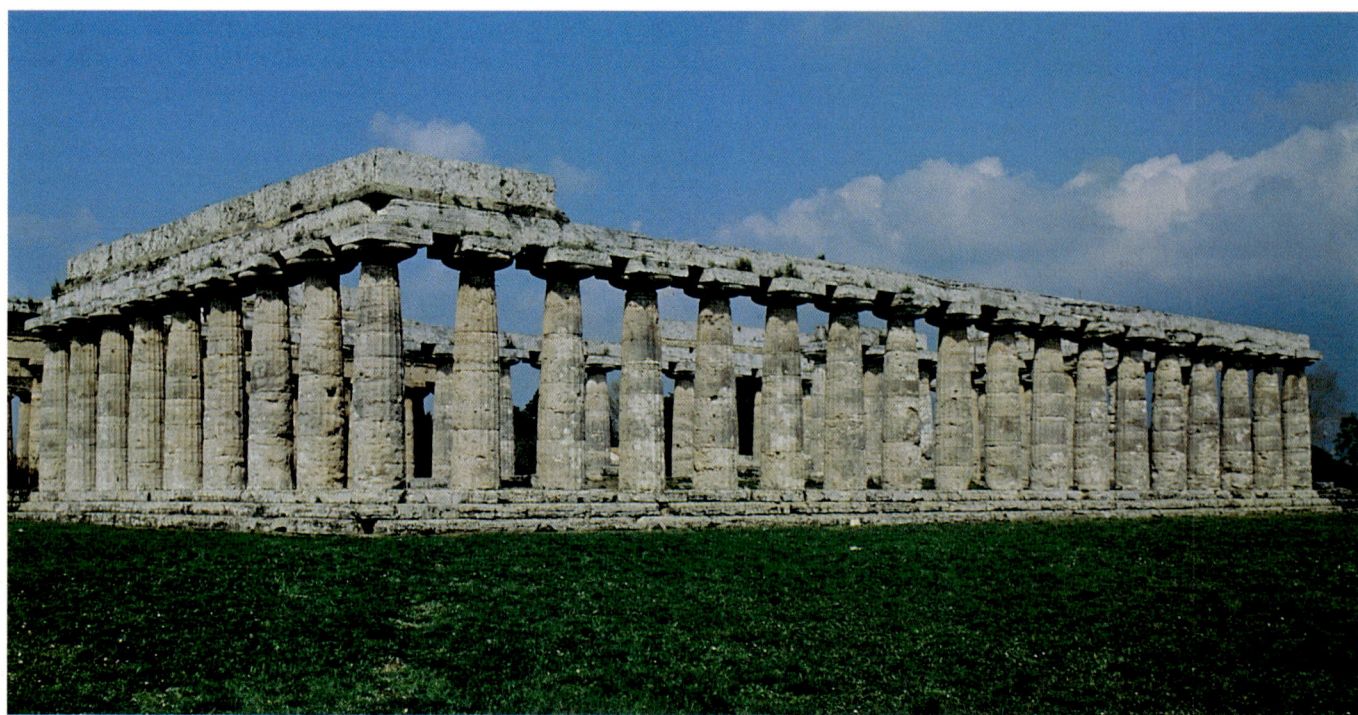

5-13 Temple of Hera I ("Basilica"), Paestum, Italy, ca. 550 B.C.

after the Roman columnar hall building type that early investigators felt it resembled, the structure is now known to be a temple dedicated to Hera. Scholars refer to it as the Temple of Hera I to distinguish it from the later Temple of Hera II (FIG. 5-29), which stands nearby.

The misnomer is partly due to the building's plan (FIG. **5-14**), which differs from that of most other Greek temples. The unusual feature, found only in early Archaic temples, is the central row of columns that divides the cella into two aisles. Placing columns underneath the *ridgepole* (the timber beam running the length of the building below the peak of the gabled roof) might seem the logical way to provide inte-

rior support for the roof structure. But it resulted in several disadvantages. Among these was that this interior arrangement allowed no place for a central statue of the deity to whom the temple was dedicated. Also, the peripteral colonnade, in order to correspond with the interior, had to have an odd number of columns (nine in this case) across the building's facade. At Paestum, three columns were also set in antis instead of the canonical two, which in turn ruled out a central doorway for viewing the statue. However, eighteen columns on each side of the Hera I temple resulted in a simple 1:2 ratio of facade and flank columns.

The temple's elevation is characterized by heavy, closely spaced columns with a pronounced swelling *(entasis)* at the middle of the shafts, giving the columns a profile akin to that of a cigar. The shafts are topped by large, bulky, pancakelike Doric capitals, which seem compressed by the overbearing weight of the entablature. If the temple's immense roof were preserved, these columns would seem even more compressed, squatting beneath what must have been a high and massive entablature. The columns and capitals thus express in a vivid manner their weight-bearing function. One structural reason, perhaps, for the heaviness of the design and the narrowness of the spans between the columns might be that the Archaic builders were afraid thinner and more widely spaced columns would result in the superstructure's collapse. In later Doric temples, the columns were placed farther apart, and the forms were gradually refined. The shafts became more slender, the entasis subtler, the capitals smaller, and the entablature lighter. The Greek architects were seeking the ideal proportional relationship among the parts of their buildings. The sculptors of Archaic kouroi and korai were grappling with similar problems contemporaneously. Architecture and sculpture developed in a parallel manner in the sixth century.

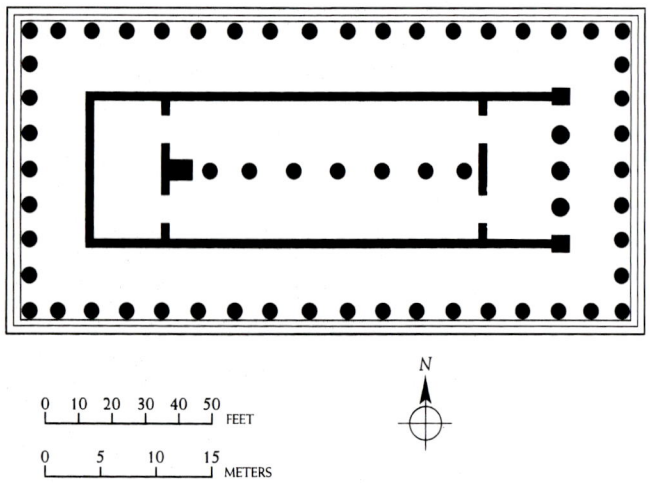

0 10 20 30 40 50 FEET

0 5 10 15 METERS

N

5-14 Plan of the Temple of Hera I, Paestum, Italy, ca. 550 B.C.

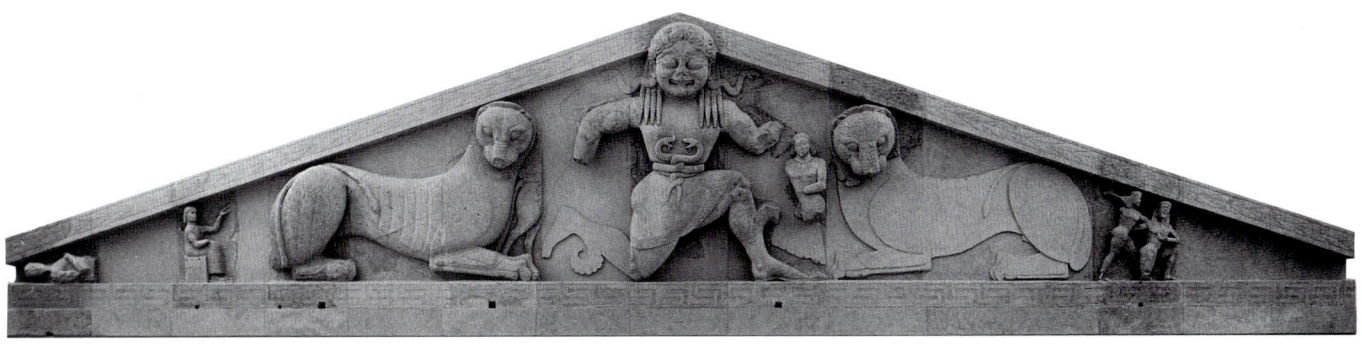

5-15 West pediment from the Temple of Artemis, Corfu, Greece, ca. 600–580 B.C. Limestone, greatest height approx. 9′ 4″. Archeological Museum, Corfu.

A HUGE ISLAND TEMPLE Architects and sculptors were also frequently called on to work together, as at Corfu (ancient Corcyra), where a great Doric temple dedicated to Artemis was constructed early in the sixth century B.C. Corfu is an island off the western coast of Greece and was an important stop on the trade route between the mainland and the Greek settlements in Italy. Prosperity made possible the erection of one of the earliest stone peripteral temples in Greece, one also lavishly embellished with sculpture. The metopes were decorated with reliefs (unfortunately very fragmentary today), and both pediments were filled with huge sculptures (more than nine feet high at the center). The pediments on both ends of the temple appear to have been decorated in an identical manner. The west pediment (FIG. **5-15**) is better preserved.

Designing figural decoration for a pediment was never an easy task because of its awkward triangular shape. Central figures needed to be of great size. By contrast, as the pediment tapered toward the corners, the available area became increasingly cramped. The central figure at Corfu is the *gorgon* Medusa, a demon with a woman's body and bird wings. Medusa also had a hideous face and snake hair, and anyone who gazed at her was turned into stone. She is shown in the conventional Archaic bent-leg, bent-arm, pinwheel-like posture that signifies running or, for a winged creature, flying. To her left and right are two great felines. Together they serve as temple guardians, repulsing all enemies from the sanctuary of the goddess. Similar panthers stand sentinel on the lintel of the seventh-century temple at Prinias (FIG. 5-6). The Corfu felines are in the tradition of the guardian lions of the citadel gate at Mycenae (see FIG. 4-20) and of the sphinx and lamassu figures that stood guard at the entrances to tombs and palaces in Egypt (see FIG. 3-11) and the ancient Near East (see FIGS. 2-18 and 2-21). The triad of Medusa and the felines recalls as well the herald ichuman-beast compositions of Mesopotamia (see FIG. 2-10). The Corfu figures are, in short, still further examples of the Orientalizing manner in early Greek sculpture.

Between Medusa and the great beasts are two small figures—the human Chrysaor at her left and the winged horse Pegasus at her right. Chrysaor and Pegasus are Medusa's children. According to legend, they sprang from her head when it was severed by the sword of the Greek hero Perseus. Their presence here on either side of the living Medusa is therefore a chronological impossibility. The Archaic artist was not interested in telling a coherent story but in identifying the central figure by depicting her offspring. Narration was, however, the purpose of the much smaller groups situated in the pediment corners. To the viewer's right is Zeus, brandishing his thunderbolt and slaying a kneeling giant. In the extreme corner was a dead giant. The *gigantomachy* (battle of gods and giants) was a popular theme in Greek art from Archaic through Hellenistic times and was a metaphor for the triumph of reason and order over chaos. In the pediment's left corner is one of the Trojan War's climactic events. Achilles' son Neoptolemos kills the enthroned King Priam. The fallen figure to the left of this group may be a dead Trojan.

The master responsible for the Corfu pediments was a pioneer, and the composition shows all the signs of experimentation. The lack of narrative unity in the Corfu pediment and the extraordinary scale diversity of the figures eventually gave way to pedimental designs with figures all acting out a single event and appearing the same size. But the Corfu designer already had shown the way. That sculptor realized, for example, that the area beneath the raking cornice could be filled with gods and heroes of similar size if a combination of standing, leaning, kneeling, seated, and prostrate figures were employed in the composition. And the Corfu master discovered that animals could be very useful space fillers because, unlike humans, they have one end taller than the other.

GODS AND GIANTS STRUGGLE AT DELPHI The sixth century B.C. also saw the erection of grandiose Ionic temples on the Aegean Islands and the west coast of Asia Minor. The gem of Archaic Ionic architecture and architectural sculpture is, however, not a temple but a treasury (FIG. **5-16**) the city of Siphnos erected in the Sanctuary of Apollo at Delphi. Greek *treasuries* were small buildings set up for the safe storage of votive offerings. At Delphi many poleis expressed their civic pride by erecting these templelike, but nonperipteral, structures. Athens built one with Doric columns in the porch and sculptured metopes in the frieze. The Siphnians equally characteristically employed the Ionic order for their Delphic treasury. The building was made possible by the wealth from the island's gold and silver mines. In the porch, where one would expect to find fluted Ionic columns, far more elaborate caryatids were employed instead. Caryatids are rare, even in Ionic architecture, but they are unknown in Doric architecture, where they would have been discordant

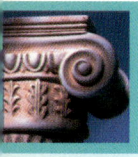

ARCHITECTURAL BASICS

Doric and Ionic Temples

The *plan* and *elevation* of Greek temples varied with date, geography, and the requirements of individual projects, but all canonical Greek temples have common defining elements that set them apart from both the religious edifices of other civilizations and other kinds of Greek buildings.

Plan   The temple core was the *naos* or *cella*, a room with no windows that usually housed the cult statue of the deity. It was preceded by a porch, or *pronaos,* often with two columns between the extended walls (columns *in antis,* that is, between the *antae*). A smaller second room might be placed behind the cella, but in its classical form, the Greek temple had a porch at the rear *(opisthodomos)* set against the blank back wall of the cella. The purpose was not functional but decorative, satisfying the Greek passion for balance and symmetry. A colonnade could be placed across the front of the temple (*prostyle;* FIG. 5-50), across both front and back (*amphiprostyle;* FIG. 5-53), or, more commonly, all around the cella and its porch(es) to form a *peristyle,* as in our diagram (compare FIGS. 5-13 and 5-14). Single *(peripteral)* colonnades are the norm, but double *(dipteral)* colonnades were features of especially elaborate temples (FIG. 5-74).

Elevation   The elevation of a Greek temple is described in terms of the platform, the colonnade, and the superstructure *(entablature).* In the Archaic period, two basic systems evolved for articulating the three units. These are the so-called *orders* of Greek architecture. The orders are differentiated both in the nature of the details and in the relative proportions of the parts. The names of the orders are derived from the Greek regions where they were most commonly employed. The *Doric* was formulated on the mainland and remained the preferred manner there and in the western colonies of the Greeks. The *Ionic* was the order of choice in the Aegean Islands and on the western coast of Asia Minor. The geographical distinctions are by no means absolute. The Ionic order was, for example, often used in Athens (where, according to some, the Athenians were considered Ionians who never migrated).

In both orders, the columns rest on the *stylobate,* the uppermost course of the platform. Metal *clamp*s held together the stone blocks in each horizontal course, while metal *dowels* joined vertically the blocks of different courses. The columns have two or three parts, depending on the order: the *shaft,* which is marked with vertical channels *(flutes);* the *capital;* and, in the Ionic order, the *base.* Greek column shafts, in contrast to their Minoan and Mycenaean forebears, taper gradually from bottom to top. They usually are composed of separate *drums* joined by metal dowels to prevent turning as well as shifting, although instances of *monolithic* (single-piece) columns are known. In the Doric order, the top of the shaft is marked with one or several horizontal lines *(necking)* that furnish the transition to the capital. The capital has two elements. The lower of them (the *echinus*) varies with the order. In the Doric, it is convex and cushionlike, similar to the echinus of Minoan (see FIG. 4-5) and Mycenaean (see FIG. 4-20) capitals. In the Ionic, it is small and supports a bolster ending in scrolllike spirals (the *volutes*). The upper element, present in both orders, is a flat, square block (the *abacus*) that provides the immediate support for the entablature.

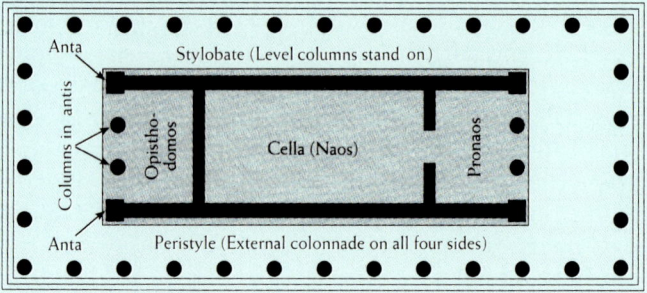

elements in that much more severe order. The Siphnian statue-columns resemble contemporary korai dressed in Ionian chitons and himations (FIG. 5-12).

Another Ionic feature of the Siphnian Treasury is the continuous sculptured frieze on all four sides of the building. The north frieze represents the popular theme of the gigantomachy, but it is a much more detailed rendition than that in the corner of the Corfu pediment. In the section reproduced here (FIG. **5-17**), Apollo and Artemis pursue a fleeing giant at the right, while behind them one of the lions pulling a goddess's chariot attacks a giant and bites into his midsection. The crowded composition was originally enlivened by paint (painted labels identified the various protagonists), and some figures had metal weapons. The effect must have been dazzling. On one of the shields the sculptor inscribed his name (unfortunately lost), a clear indication of pride in accomplishment.

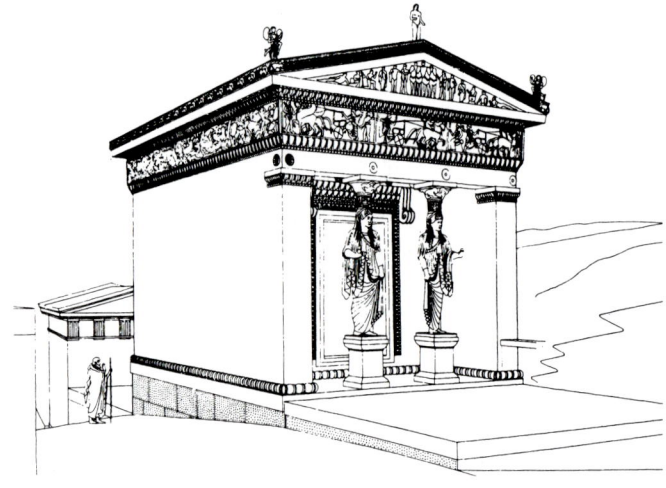

5-16   Reconstruction drawing of the Siphnian Treasury, Delphi, Greece, ca. 530 B.C.

The entablature has three parts: the *architrave* or *epistyle*, the main weight-bearing and weight-distributing element; the *frieze;* and the *cornice*, a molded horizontal projection that together with two sloping *(raking)* cornices forms a triangle that enframes the *pediment*. In the Ionic order, the architrave is usually subdivided into three horizontal bands *(fasciae)*. In the Doric order, the frieze is subdivided into *triglyphs* and *metopes,* while in the Ionic the frieze is left open to provide a continuous field for relief sculpture.

Many of the Doric components seem to be translations into stone of an earlier timber architecture. The frieze division into triglyphs and metopes, for example, can be explained best as a stone version of what was originally carpentry. The triglyphs most likely are derived from the ends of crossbeams that rested on the main horizontal support, the architrave. The metopes then would correspond to the voids between the beam ends in the original wooden structure.

The Doric order is massive in appearance, its sturdy columns firmly planted on the stylobate. Compared with the weighty and severe Doric, the Ionic order seems light, airy, and much more decorative. Its columns are more slender and rise from molded bases. The Doric flutes meet in sharp ridges *(arrises)*, but the Ionic ridges are flat *(fillets)*. The most obvious differences between the two orders are, of course, in the capitals—the Doric, severely plain, and the Ionic, highly ornamental.

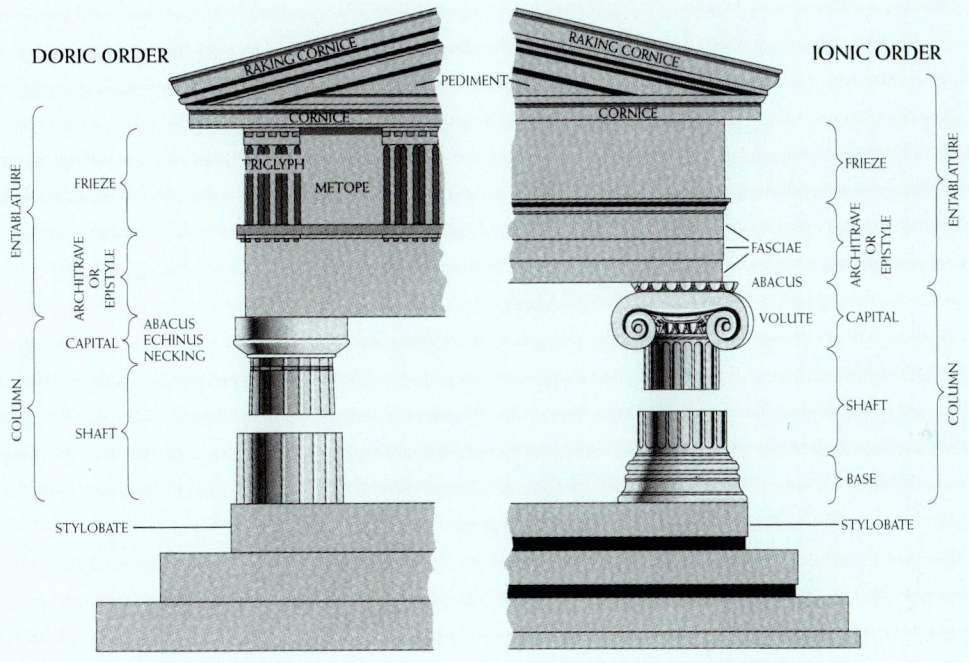

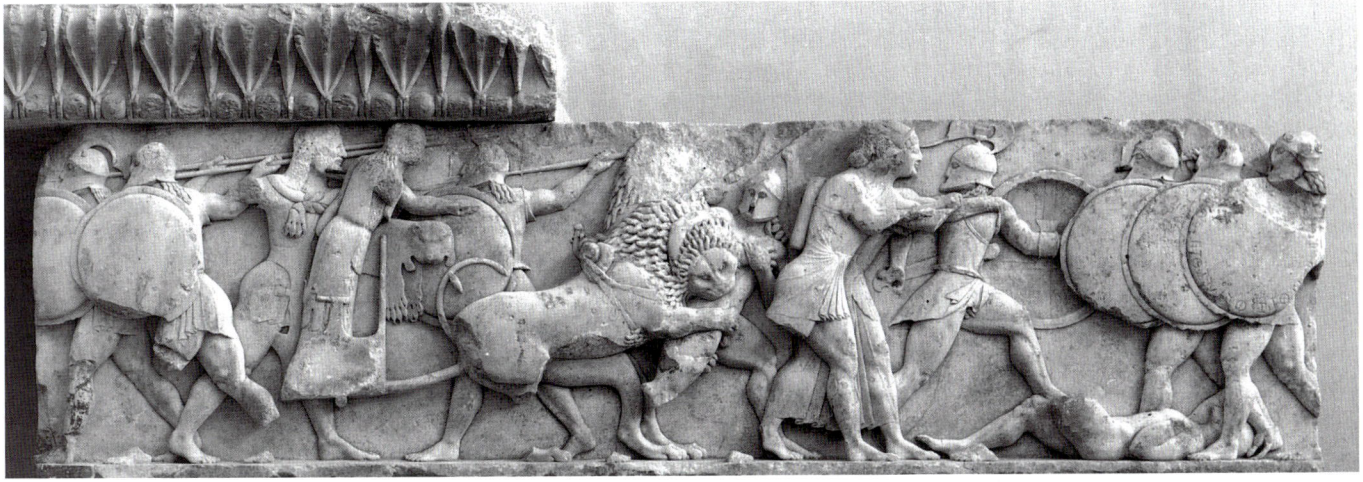

5-17   Gigantomachy, detail of the north frieze of the Siphnian Treasury, Delphi, Greece, ca. 530 B.C. Marble, approx. 2′ 1″ high. Archeological Museum, Delphi.

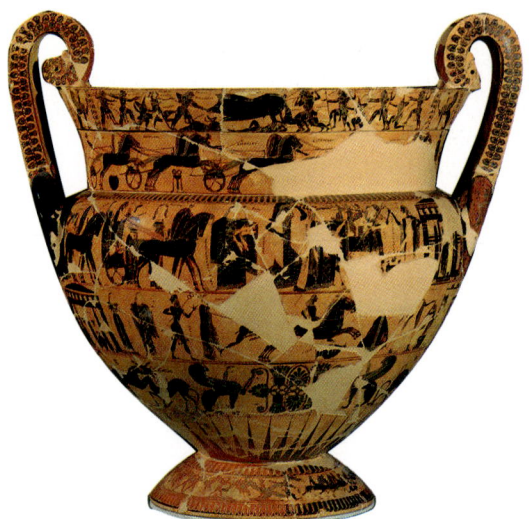
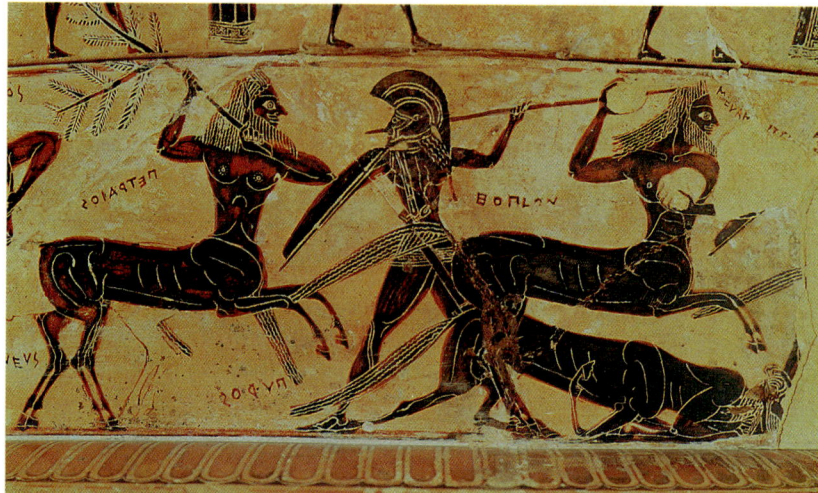

5-18 KLEITIAS and ERGOTIMOS, *François Vase* (Attic black-figure volute krater), from Chiusi, Italy, ca. 570 B.C. General view *(left)* and detail of centauromachy on other side of vase *(right)*. Approx. 2′ 2″ high. Museo Archeologico, Florence.

Vase Painting

ARTISTS' SIGNATURES   Labeled figures and artists' signatures also appear on Archaic painted vases. The masterpiece of this stage of Greek vase painting is the *François Vase* (FIG. **5-18**), named for the excavator who uncovered it (in an enormous number of fragments) in an Etruscan tomb at Chiusi in Italy (see map, Chapter 9, page 230), where it had been imported from Athens. This is in itself a testimony to the esteem held for Athenian potters and painters at this time. In fact, having learned the black-figure technique from the Corinthians, the Athenians had by now taken over the export market for fine painted ceramics.

The *François Vase* (a new kind of krater with volute-shaped handles probably inspired by costly metal prototypes) is signed by both its painter ("Kleitias painted me") and potter ("Ergotimos made me"). In fact, each signed twice! It has more than two hundred figures in six registers. Labels abound, naming humans and animals alike, even some inanimate objects. Only one of the bands was given over to the Orientalizing repertoire of animals and sphinxes. The rest constitute a selective encyclopedia of Greek mythology, focusing on the exploits of Peleus and his son Achilles, the great hero of Homer's *Iliad,* and of Theseus, the legendary king of Athens.

In the detail shown here, Lapiths (a northern Greek tribe) and centaurs battle *(centauromachy)* after a wedding celebration where the man-beasts, who were invited guests, got drunk and attempted to abduct the Lapith maidens and young boys. Theseus, also on the guest list, was prominent among the centaurs' Greek adversaries. Kleitias did not fill the space between his figures with decorative ornament, as did his Geometric predecessors (FIG. 5-1). But his heroes conform to the age-old composite type (profile heads with frontal eyes, frontal torsos, and profile legs and arms). His centaurs are much more believable than their Geometric counterparts (FIG. 5-2). The man-horse combination is top/bottom rather than front/back. The lower (horse) portion has four legs of uniform type, and the upper part of the monster is fully human. In characteristic fashion, the animal section of the cen-

taur is shown in strict profile, while the human head and torso are a composite of frontal and profile views. (Kleitias used a consistent profile for the more adventurous detail of the collapsed centaur at the right.)

EXEKIAS, MASTER OF BLACK-FIGURE   The acknowledged master of the black-figure technique was an Athenian named EXEKIAS, whose vases were not only widely exported but copied as well. Perhaps his greatest work is an amphora (FIG. **5-19**), found in an Etruscan tomb at Vulci (see map, Chapter 9, page 230), that Exekias signed as both painter and potter. He did not divide the surface into a series of horizontal bands. Instead, a single large framed panel is peopled by figures of monumental stature. At the left is Achilles, fully armed. He plays a dice game with his comrade Ajax. Out of the lips of Achilles comes the word *tesara* (four); Ajax calls out *tria* (three). Ajax has taken off his helmet, but both men hold their spears. Their shields are nearby, and each man is ready for action at a moment's notice. It is a classic case of "the calm before the storm." The moment Exekias chose to depict is the antithesis of the Archaic penchant for dramatic action. The gravity and tension that will characterize much Classical Greek art of the next century, but are absent in Archaic art, already may be seen here.

Exekias has no equal as a black-figure painter. That may be seen in such details as the extraordinarily intricate engraving of the patterns on the heroes' cloaks (highlighted with delicate touches of white) and in the brilliant composition. The arch formed by the backs of the two warriors echoes the shape of the rounded shoulders of the amphora. The vessel's shape is echoed again in the void between the heads and spears of Achilles and Ajax. Exekias also used the spears to lead the viewer's eyes toward the thrown dice, where the heroes' eyes are fixed. Of course, those eyes do not really look down at the table but stare out from the profile heads in the old manner. For all his brilliance, Exekias was still wedded to many of the old conventions. Real innovation in figure drawing would have to await the invention of a new ceramic painting technique of greater versatility than black-figure, with its dark silhouettes and incised details.

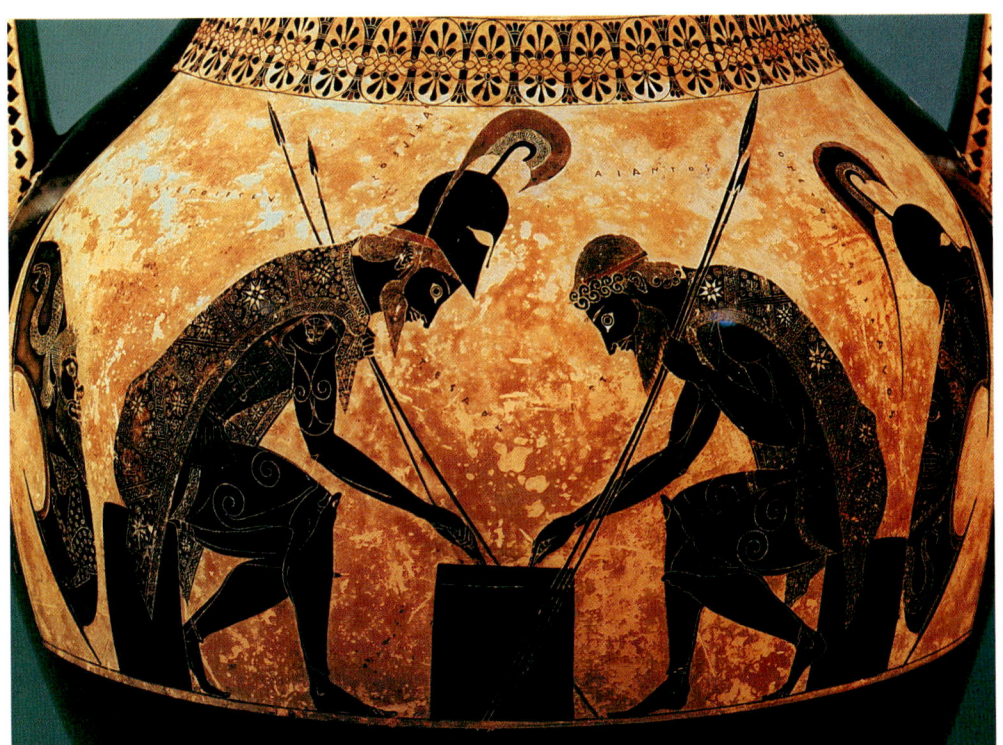

5-19 EXEKIAS, Achilles and Ajax playing a dice game (detail from an Athenian black-figure amphora), from Vulci, Italy, ca. 540–530 B.C. Whole vessel approx. 2′ high. Vatican Museums, Rome.

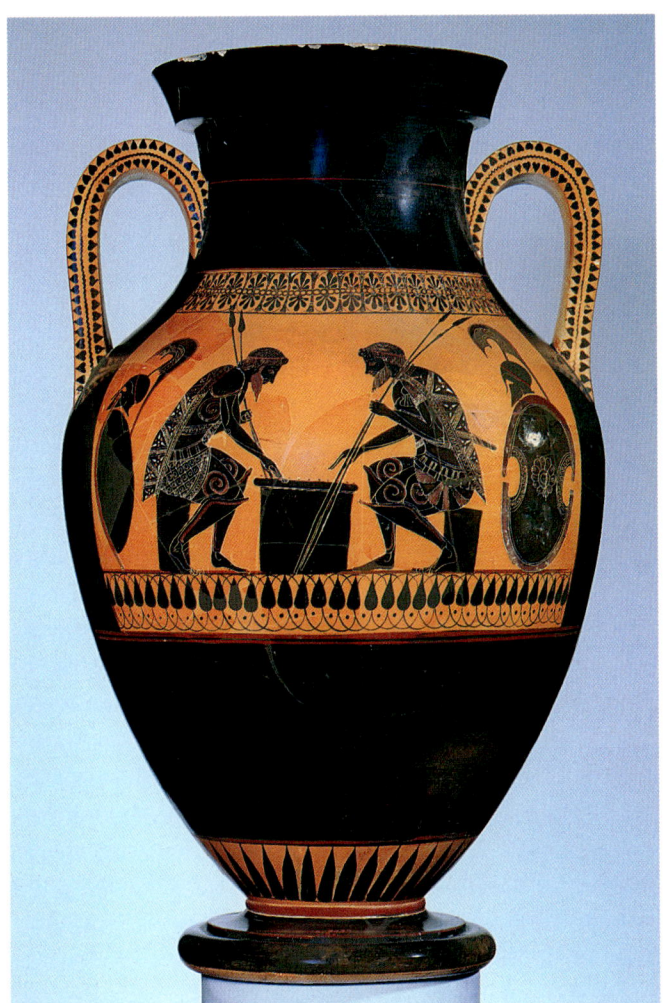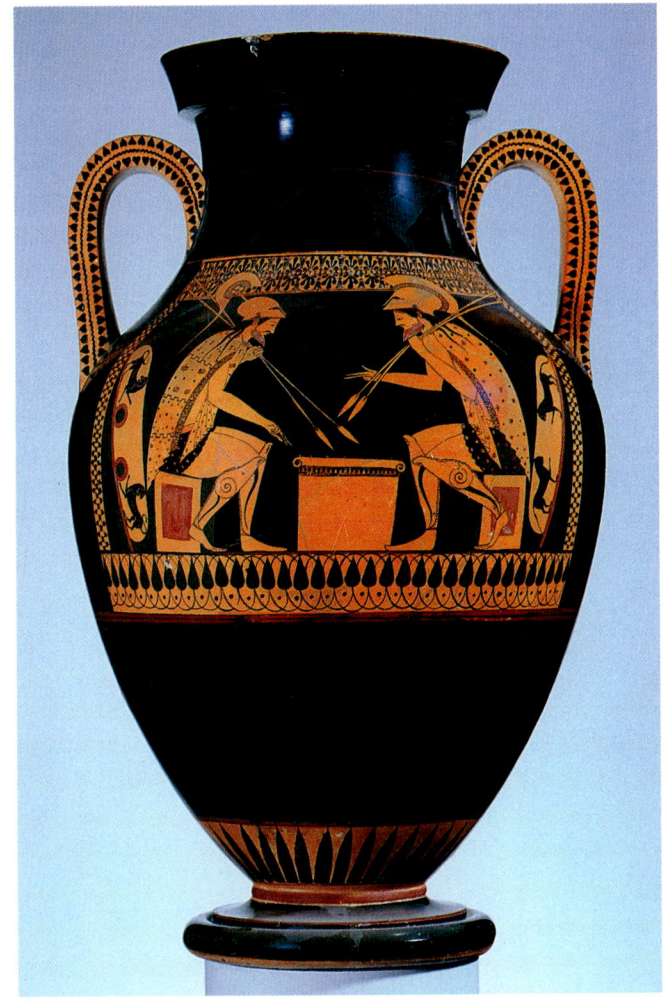

5-20 ANDOKIDES PAINTER, Achilles and Ajax playing a dice game (Attic bilingual amphora), from Orvieto, Italy, ca. 525–520 B.C. Black-figure side *(left)* and red-figure side *(right)*. Approx. 1′ 9″ high. Museum of Fine Arts, Boston.

"BILINGUAL" PAINTING   The birth of this new technique came around 530 B.C., and the person responsible is known as the ANDOKIDES PAINTER, that is, the anonymous painter who decorated the vases signed by the potter Andokides. The differences between the two techniques can best be studied on a series of experimental vases with the same composition painted on both sides, once in black-figure and once in the new technique, *red-figure*. Such vases, nicknamed *bilingual vases,* were produced only for a short time. An especially interesting example is the amphora, now in Boston, by the Andokides Painter (FIG. **5-20**), which features copies of the Achilles and Ajax panel of the bilingual painter's teacher, Exekias.

Neither in black-figure nor red-figure did the Andokides Painter capture the intensity of the model, and the treatment of details is decidedly inferior. Yet the new red-figure technique has obvious advantages over the old black-figure manner. Red-figure is the opposite of black-figure. What was previously black is now red and vice versa. The artist still employs the same black glaze. But instead of using the glaze to create the silhouettes of figures, the painter outlines the figures and then colors the background black. The red clay is reserved for the figures themselves. Interior details are then drawn with the soft brush in place of the stiff metal graver. And the artist can vary the glaze thickness, building it up to give relief to hair curls or diluting it to create brown shades, thereby expanding the chromatic range of the Greek vase painter's craft. The Andokides Painter—many think he was

the potter Andokides himself—did not yet appreciate the full potential of his own invention. But he created a technique that, in the hands of other, more skilled artists, helped revolutionize the art of drawing.

EUPHRONIOS, MASTER OF RED-FIGURE   One of these younger and more adventurous painters was EUPHRONIOS, whose krater depicting the struggle between Herakles and Antaios (FIG. **5-21**) reveals the exciting possibilities of the new red-figure technique. Antaios was a Libyan giant, a son of Earth, and he derived his power from contact with the ground. To defeat him, Herakles had to lift him up into the air and strangle him while no part of the giant's body touched the earth. But Euphronios did not represent the moment of Herakles' triumph. The two wrestle on the ground, and Antaios still possesses enormous strength. Nonetheless, Herakles has the upper hand. The giant's face is a mask of pain. His eyes roll and his teeth are bared. His right arm is paralyzed, with the fingers limp. Euphronios used diluted glaze to show Antaios's unkempt golden brown hair—intentionally contrasted with the neat coiffure and carefully trimmed beard of the emotionless Greek hero.

The artist also used thinned glaze to delineate the muscles of both figures. But Euphronios was interested not only in rendering human anatomy convincingly. He also wished to show that his figures occupy space. The conventional composite posture for the human figure, which communicates so well the specific parts of the human body, was deliberately rejected

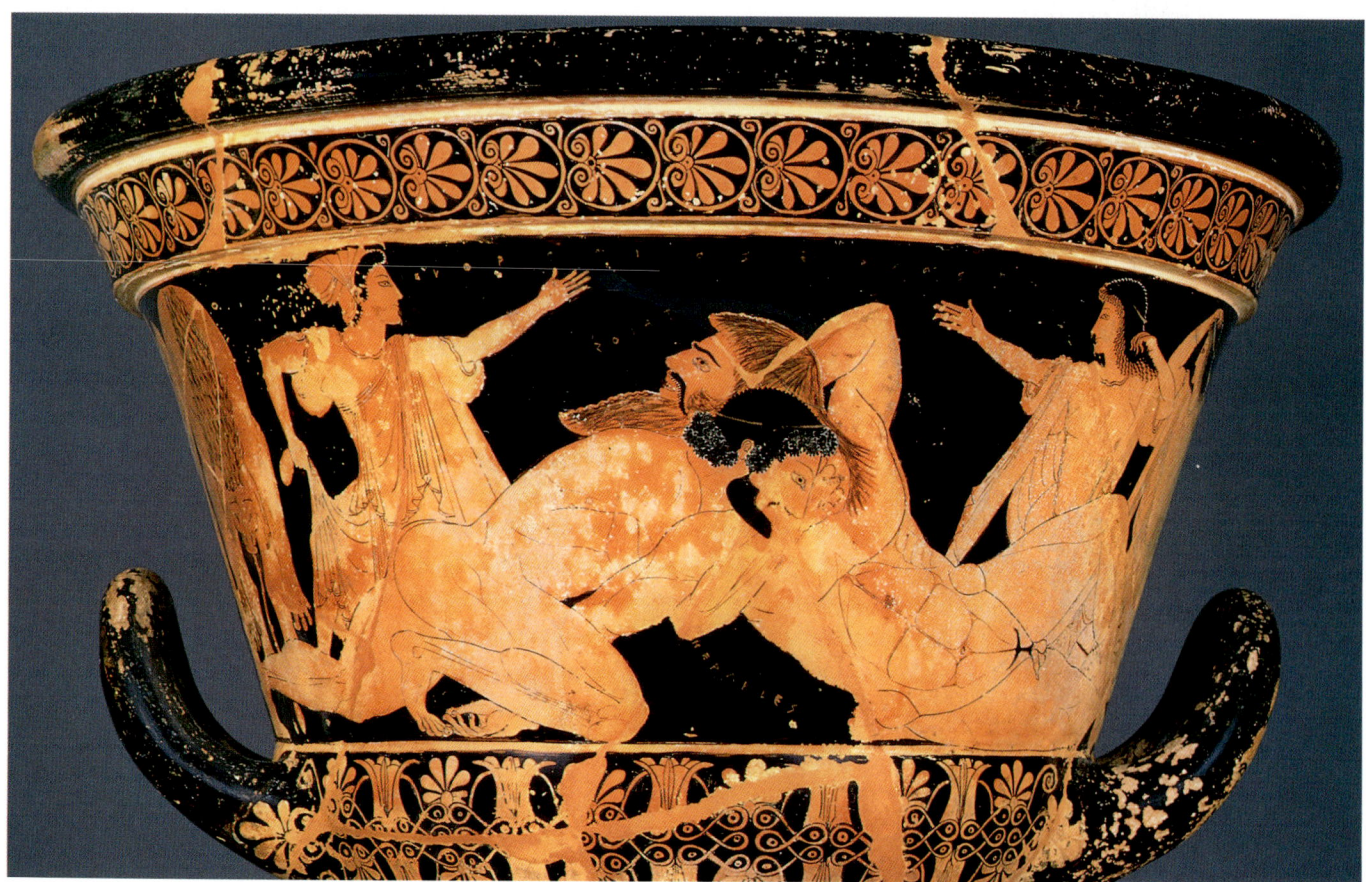

5-21   EUPHRONIOS, Herakles wrestling Antaios (detail of an Attic red-figure calyx krater), from Cerveteri, Italy, ca. 510 B.C. Whole vessel approx. 1′ 7″ high. Louvre, Paris.

as Euphronios attempted to reproduce how a particular human body is *seen*. He presented, for example, the right thigh of Antaios from the front. The lower leg disappears behind the giant, and one glimpses only part of the right foot. The viewer must make the connection between the upper leg and the foot in the mind. Euphronios did not paint a two-dimensional panel filled with figures in stereotypical postures, as his Archaic and pre-Greek predecessors always did. His panel is a window onto a mythological world with protagonists occupying three-dimensional space. This was a revolutionary new conception of what a picture was supposed to be.

THE RIVALS OF EUPHRONIOS   A preoccupation with the art of drawing per se may be seen in a remarkable amphora (FIG. **5-22**) painted by EUTHYMIDES, a contemporary and competitor of Euphronios. The subject is appropriate for a wine storage jar—three tipsy revelers. But the theme was little more than an excuse for the artist to experiment with the representation of unusual positions of the human form. It is no coincidence that the bodies do not overlap, for each is an independent figure study. Euthymides rejected the conventional frontal and profile composite views. Instead, he

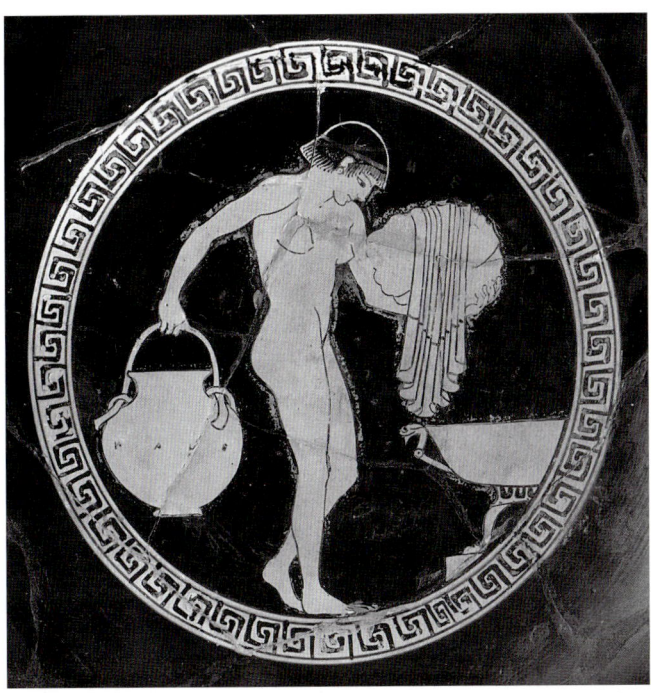

5-23   ONESIMOS, Girl preparing to bathe (interior of an Attic red-figure kylix), from Chiusi, Italy, ca. 490 B.C. Tondo approx. 6″ in diameter. Musées Royaux, Brussels.

painted torsos that are not two-dimensional surface patterns but are *foreshortened,* that is, drawn in a three-quarter view. Most remarkable is the central figure, who is shown from the rear with a twisting spinal column and buttocks in three-quarter view. Earlier artists had no interest in attempting such postures because they are not only incomplete but also do not show the "main" side of the human body. But for Euthymides the challenge of drawing the figure from such an unusual viewpoint was a reward in itself. With understandable pride he proclaimed his achievement by adding to the formulaic signature "Euthymides painted me" the phrase "as never Euphronios [could do]!"

Interest in the foreshortening of the human figure soon extended to studies of nude women, as on the interior of a *kylix* (drinking cup) ONESIMOS painted (FIG. **5-23**). The representation is remarkable not only for the successful foreshortening of the girl's torso and breasts, seen in three-quarter view, but also for its subject. This is neither mythology nor a scene of wealthy noblemen partying. This is a servant girl, not the lady of the house, who has removed her clothes to bathe. Such a genre scene, not to mention female nudity, would never have been portrayed publicly in monumental painting or sculpture of this time. Only in the private sphere was such a subject acceptable.

Aegina and the Transition to the Classical Period

EVOLUTION AND REVOLUTION   The years just before and after 500 B.C. were also a time of dynamic transition in architecture and architectural sculpture. Some of the changes were evolutionary in nature, others revolutionary.

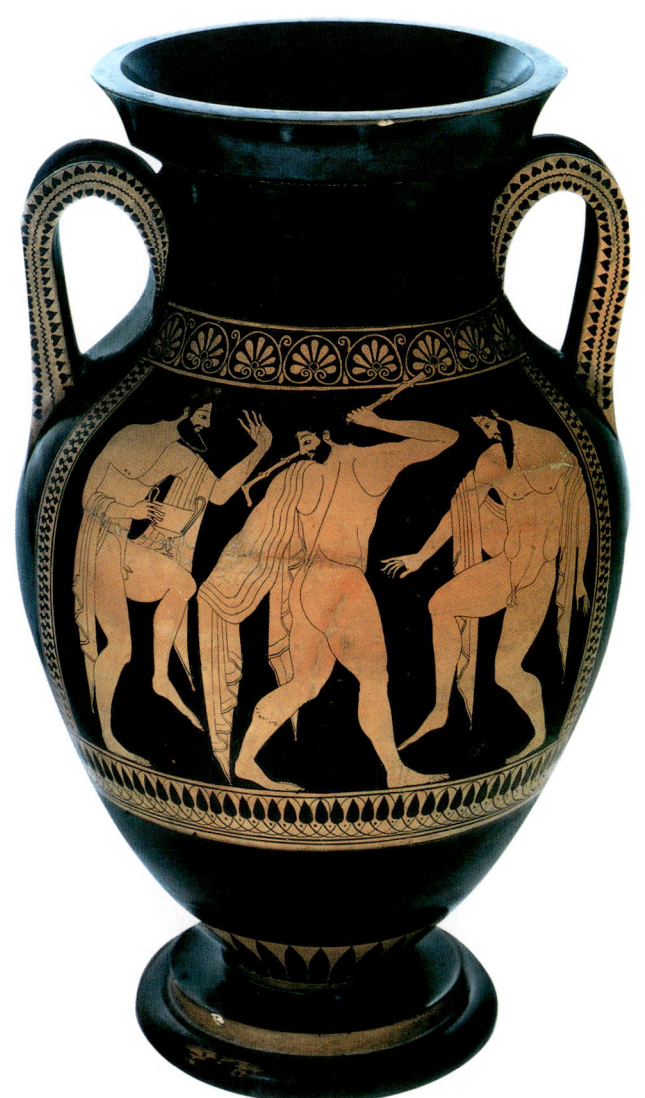

5-22   EUTHYMIDES, Three revelers (Attic red-figure amphora), from Vulci, Italy, ca. 510 B.C. Approx. 2′ high. Staatliche Antikensammlungen, Munich.

Both kinds are evident in the Temple of Aphaia at Aegina (FIG. **5-24**). The temple sits on a prominent ridge with dramatic views out to the sea. The colonnade is forty-five feet by ninety-five feet and consists of six Doric columns on the facade and twelve on the flanks. This is a much more compact structure than the impressive but ungainly Archaic Temple of Hera I at Paestum (FIG. 5-13), even though the ratio of width to length is similar. Doric architects had learned a great deal in the half century that elapsed. The columns of the Aegina temple are more widely spaced and more slender. The capitals create a smooth transition from the vertical shafts below to the horizontal architrave above. Gone are the Archaic flattened echinuses and bulging shafts of the Paestum columns.

5-24 Temple of Aphaia, Aegina, Greece, ca. 500–490 B.C.

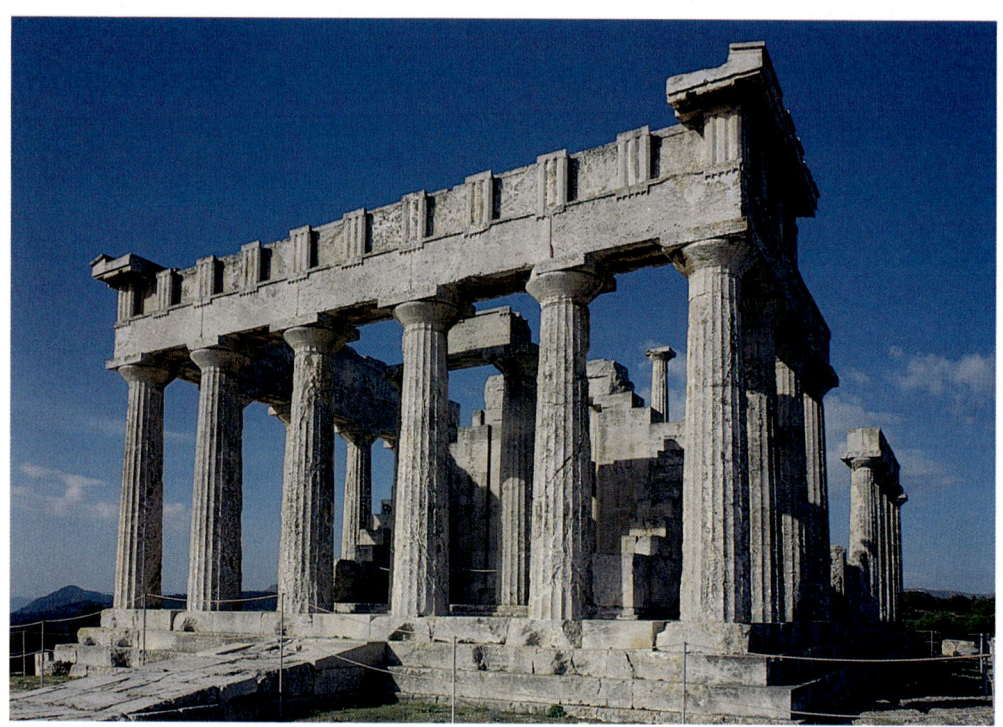

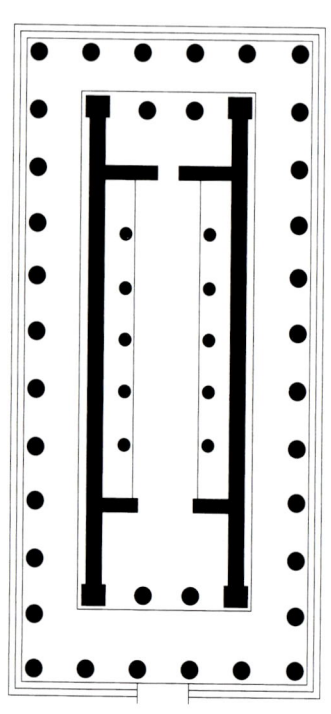
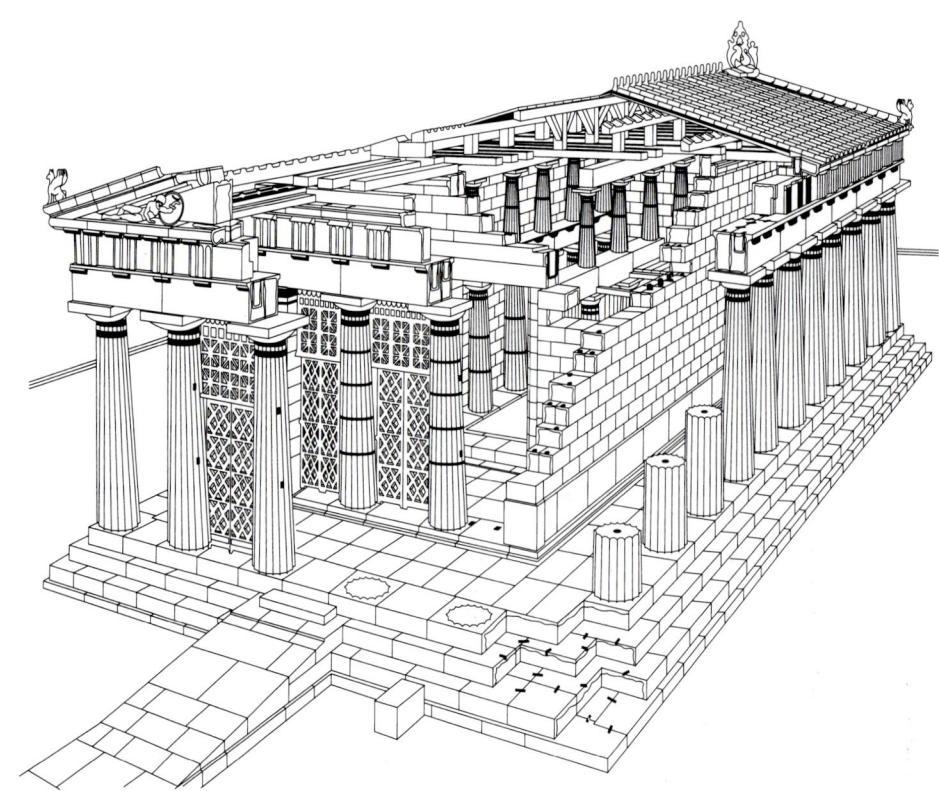

5-25 Plan *(left)* and restored cutaway view *(right)* of the Temple of Aphaia, Aegina, Greece, ca. 500–490 B.C.

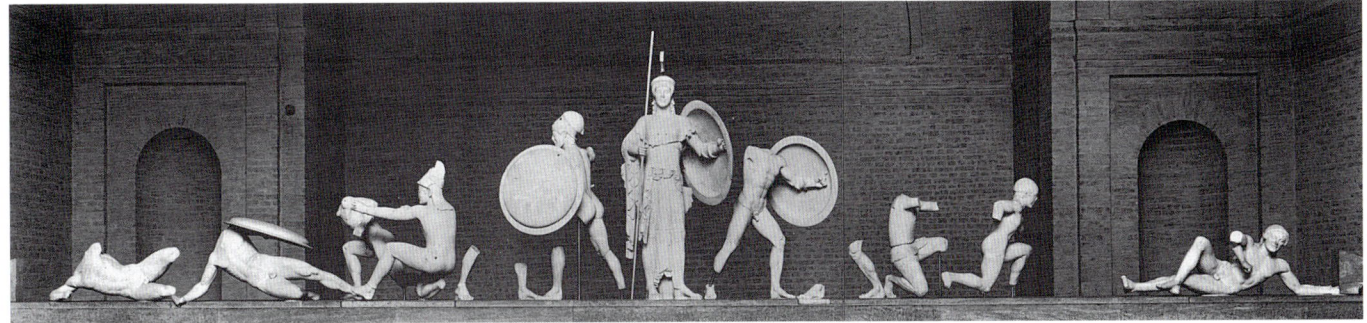

5-26 West pediment of the Temple of Aphaia, Aegina, Greece, ca. 500-490 B.C. Marble, approx. 5′ 8″ high at center. Glyptothek, Munich.

The temple plan and internal elevation (FIG. **5-25**) also were refined. In place of a single row of columns down the cella's center is a double colonnade—and each row has two stories. This arrangement allowed the placement of a statue on the central axis and also gave those gathered in front of the building an unobstructed view through the pair of columns in the pronaos.

Both pediments were filled with life-size statuary (FIG. **5-26**), and the same subject and similar compositions were employed. The theme was the battle of Greeks and Trojans, with Athena at the center of the bloody combat. She is larger than all the other figures because she is superhuman, but the mortal heroes are all carved at the same scale, regardless of their position in the pediment. Unlike the experimental design at Corfu (FIG. **5-15**), the Aegina pediments feature a unified theme and consistent size. The latter was achieved by using the whole gamut of bodily postures from upright (Athena) to leaning, falling, kneeling, and lying (Greeks and Trojans).

ARCHAISM YIELDS TO CLASSICISM The sculptures of the Aegina pediments were set in place when the temple was completed around 490 B.C. But the pedimental statues at the eastern end were damaged and replaced with a new group a decade or two later. It is very instructive to compare the earlier and later figures. The west pediment's dying warrior (FIG. **5-27**) was still conceived in the Archaic mode. His torso is rigidly frontal, and he looks out directly at the spectator. In fact, he smiles at us, in spite of the bronze arrow (now missing) that punctures his chest. He is like a mannequin in a store window whose arms and legs have been arranged by someone else for effective display. The viewer has no sense whatsoever of a thinking and feeling human being. The later east pediment's comparable figure (FIG. **5-28**) is radically different. Not only is his posture more natural and more complex, with the torso placed at an angle to the viewer—he is on a par with the painted figures of Euphronios and Euthymides—but he also reacts to his wound as a

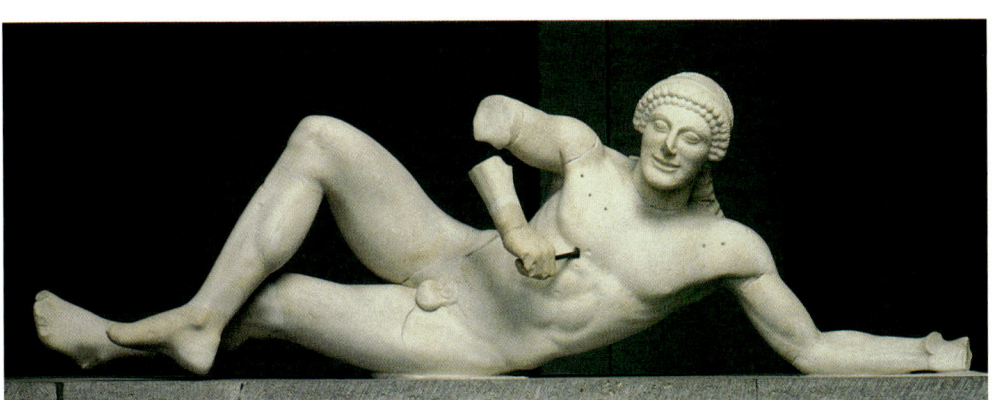

5-27 Dying warrior, from the west pediment of the Temple of Aphaia, Aegina, Greece, ca. 500–490 B.C. Marble, approx. 5′ 2$\frac{1}{2}$″ long. Glyptothek, Munich.

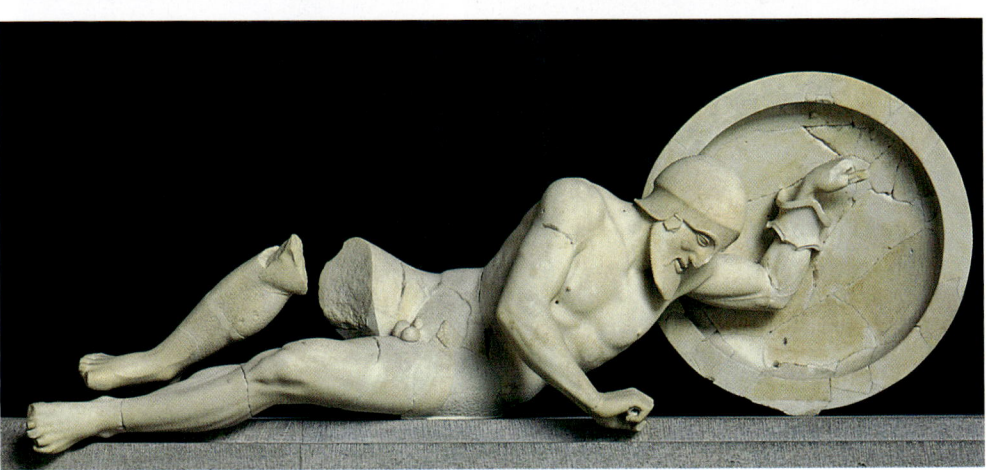

5-28 Dying warrior, from the east pediment of the Temple of Aphaia, Aegina, Greece, ca. 490–480 B.C. Marble, approx. 6′ 1″ long. Glyptothek, Munich.

flesh-and-blood human would. He knows that death is inevitable, but he still struggles to rise once again, using his shield for support. And he does not look out at the spectator. He is concerned with his pain, not with the spectator. Only a decade, perhaps two, separates the two statues, but they belong to different eras. The later warrior is not a creation of the Archaic world, when sculptors imposed anatomical patterns (and smiles) on statues from without. This statue belongs to the Classical world, where statues move as humans move and possess the self-consciousness of real men and women. This was a radical change in the conception of what a statue was meant to be. In sculpture, as in painting, the Classical revolution had occurred.

THE EARLY AND HIGH CLASSICAL PERIODS (FIFTH CENTURY B.C.)

THE AFTERMATH OF THE PERSIAN WARS Art historians reckon the beginning of the Classical* age from a historical event, the defeat of the Persian invaders of Greece by the allied Hellenic city-states. Shortly after Athens was occupied and sacked in 480 B.C., the Greeks won a decisive naval victory over the Persians at Salamis. It had been a difficult war, and at times it had seemed as though Greece would be swallowed up by Asia and the Persian king Xerxes would rule over all. When the Greek city Miletos was destroyed in 494 B.C., the Persians killed the male inhabitants and sold the women and children into slavery. The close escape of the Greeks from domination by Asian "barbarians" nurtured a sense of Hellenic identity so strong that from then on the history of European civilization would be distinct from the civilization of Asia, even though they continued to interact.

Typical of the time were the views of the great dramatist Aeschylus, who celebrated, in his *Oresteia,* the triumph of reason and law over barbarous crimes, blood feuds, and mad vengeance. Himself a veteran of the epic battle of Marathon, Aeschylus repudiated in majestic verse all the slavish and inhuman traits of nature that the Greeks at that time of crisis associated with the Persians.

The decades following the removal of the Persian threat are universally considered the high point of Greek civilization. This is the era of the dramatists Sophocles and Euripides, as well as Aeschylus, the historian Herodotus, the statesman Pericles, the philosopher Socrates, and many of the most famous Greek architects, sculptors, and painters.

Architecture and Architectural Sculpture

A NEW TEMPLE FOR OLYMPIA The first great monument of Classical art and architecture is the Temple of Zeus at Olympia, site of the quadrennial Olympic Games. The temple was begun about 470 B.C. and was probably completed by 457 B.C. The architect was LIBON OF ELIS. Today the structure is in ruins, its picturesque tumbled column drums an eloquent reminder of the effect of the passage of time on even the grandest monuments humans have built. Students of art history can get a good idea of its original appearance, however, by looking at a slightly later Doric temple modeled closely on the Olympian shrine of Zeus—the second Temple of Hera at Paestum (FIG. **5-29**). The plans and elevations of both temples follow the pattern of the Temple of Aphaia at Aegina (FIG. 5-25): an even number of columns (six) on the short ends, two columns in antis, and two rows of columns in two stories inside the cella. But the Temple of Zeus was more lavishly decorated than even the Aphaia temple. Statues not only filled both pediments, but also the six metopes of the Doric frieze of the pronaos and the matching six of the opisthodomos were adorned with reliefs.

*Note: In *Art through the Ages* the adjective "Classical," with uppercase *C,* refers specifically to the Classical period of ancient Greece, 480–323 B.C. Lowercase "classical" refers to Greco-Roman antiquity in general, that is, the period treated in Chapters 5, 6, and 10.

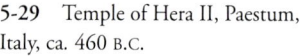
5-29   Temple of Hera II, Paestum, Italy, ca. 460 B.C.

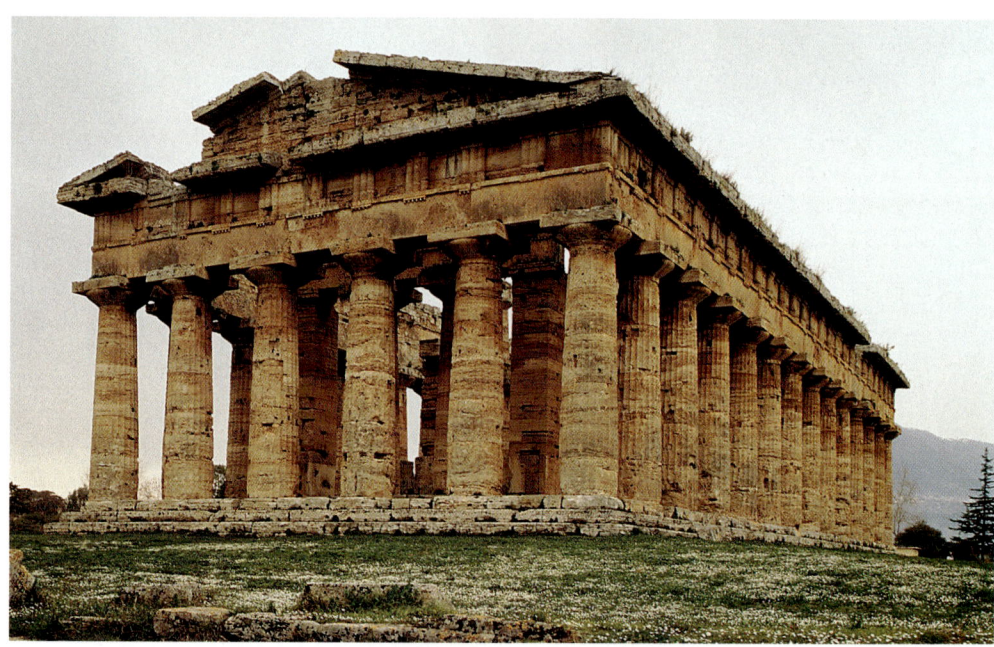

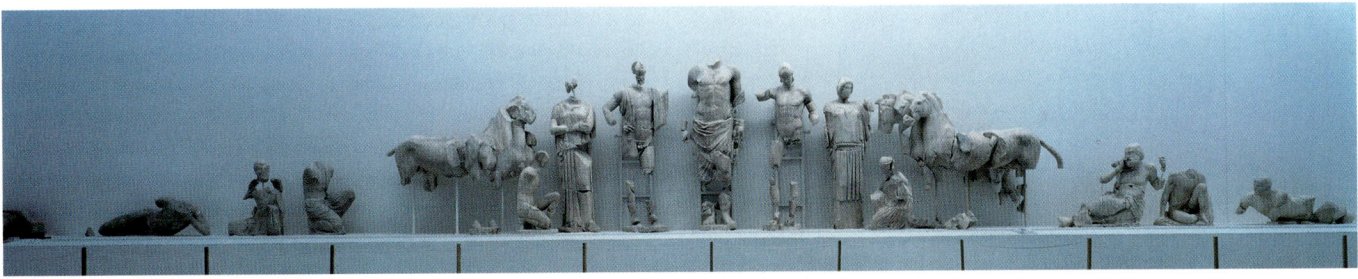

5-30   East pediment from the Temple of Zeus, Olympia, Greece, ca. 470–456 B.C. Marble, approx. 87′ wide. Archeological Museum, Olympia.

TREACHERY IN A CHARIOT RACE   The subject of the Temple of Zeus's east pediment (FIG. **5-30**) had deep local significance: the chariot race between Pelops (from whom the Peloponnesos takes its name) and King Oinomaos. The story is a sinister one. Oinomaos had one daughter, Hippodameia, and it was foretold that he would die if she married. Consequently, Oinomaos challenged any suitor who wished to make Hippodameia his bride to a chariot race from Olympia to Corinth. If the suitor won, he also won the hand of the king's daughter. But if he lost, he was killed. The outcome of each race was predetermined, because Oinomaos possessed divine horses his father Ares gave him. Many suitors had been killed, and to insure his victory Pelops resorted to bribing the king's groom Myrtilos to rig the royal chariot so that it would collapse during the race. Oinomaos was killed and Pelops won his bride, but he drowned Myrtilos rather than pay his debt to him. Before he died Myrtilos brought a curse on Pelops and his descendants. This curse led to the murder of Pelops's son Atreus and to events that figure prominently in some of the great Greek tragedies of the day, the three plays known collectively as Aeschylus's *Oresteia:* the sacrifice by Atreus's son Agamemnon of his daughter Iphigeneia; the slaying of Agamemnon by Aegisthus, lover of Agamemnon's wife Clytaemnestra; and the murder of Aegisthus and Clytaemnestra by Orestes, the son of Agamemnon and Clytaemnestra.

The pedimental statues (which faced toward the starting point of all Olympic chariot races) are, in fact, posed like actors on a stage—Zeus in the center, Oinomaos and his wife on one side, Pelops and Hippodameia on the other, and their respective chariots to each side. All are quiet; the horrible events known to every spectator have yet to occur. Only one man reacts—a seer (FIG. **5-31**) who knows the future. He is a remarkable figure. Unlike the gods, heroes, and noble youths and maidens who are the almost exclusive subjects of Archaic and Classical Greek statuary, this seer is a rare depiction of old age. He has a balding, wrinkled head and sagging musculature—and a horrified expression on his face. This is a true show of emotion, unlike the stereotypical "Archaic smile," without precedent in earlier Greek sculpture and not a regular feature of Greek art until the Hellenistic age.

THE TWELVE LABORS OF HERAKLES   The metopes of the Zeus temple are also thematically connected with the site, for they depict the twelve labors of Herakles (see "Herakles: Greatest of Greek Heroes," page 103), the legendary founder of the Olympic Games. In the metope illustrated here (FIG. **5-32**), Herakles holds up the sky (with the aid of the goddess Athena—and a cushion) in place of Atlas, who had undertaken the dangerous journey to fetch the golden apples of the Hesperides for the hero. The load soon will be transferred back to Atlas, but now each of the very high relief figures in the metope stands quietly with the same serene dignity as the statues in the Olympia pediment.

In both attitude and dress (simple Doric peplos for the women), all the Olympia figures display a severity that contrasts sharply with the smiling and elaborately clad figures of the Late Archaic period. Many art historians call this Early Classical phase of Greek art the "Severe Style."

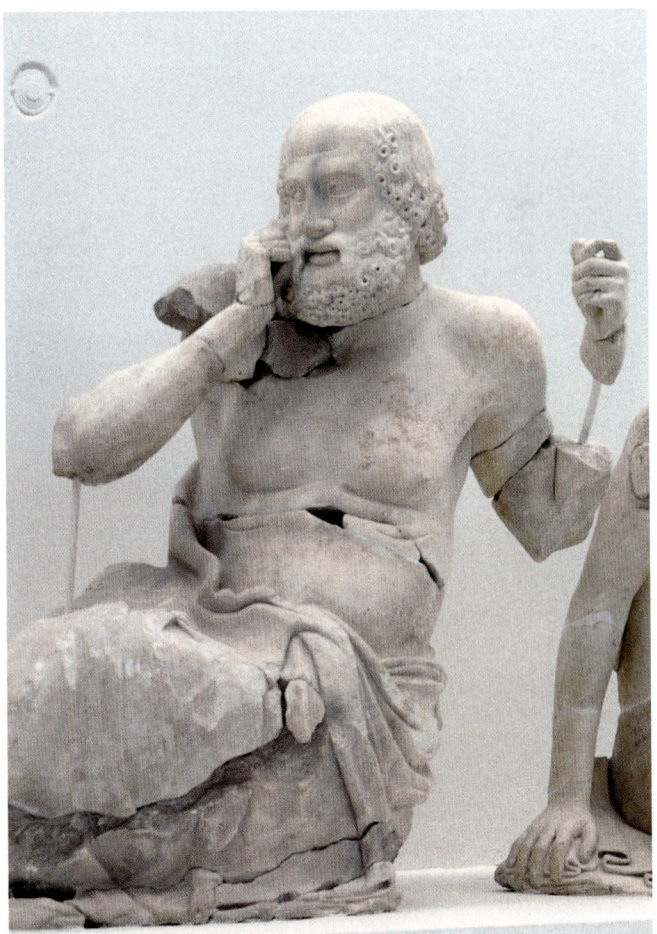

5-31   Seer, from the east pediment of the Temple of Zeus, Olympia, Greece, ca. 470–456 B.C. Marble, approx. 4′ 6″ high. Archeological Museum, Olympia.

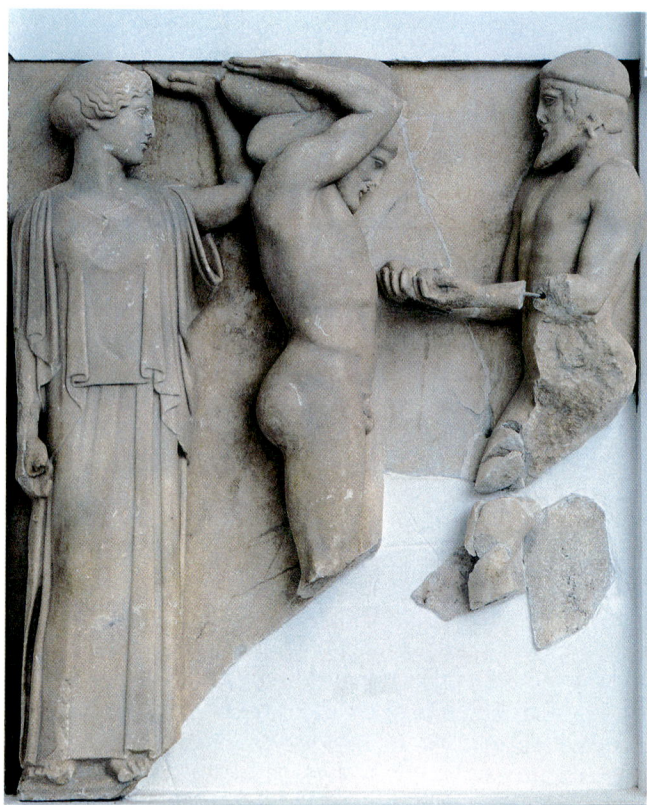

5-32 Athena, Herakles, and Atlas with the apples of the Hesperides, metope from the Temple of Zeus, Olympia, Greece, ca. 470–456 B.C. Marble, approx. 5′ 3″ high. Archeological Museum, Olympia.

Statuary

A NEW WAY TO STAND The Early Classical style is also characterized by a final break from the rigid and unnatural Egyptian-inspired pose of the Archaic *kouroi*. This change may be seen in the postures of the Olympia figures and in the somewhat earlier statue from the Athenian Acropolis known as the *Kritios Boy* (FIG. **5-33**) because it was once thought to have been carved by the sculptor KRITIOS. For the first time, a sculptor was concerned not simply with representing the body but with portraying how a human being (as opposed to a stone image) actually stands. Real people do not stand in the stiff-legged pose of the kouroi and korai or their Egyptian predecessors. Humans shift their weight and the position of the main bodily parts around the vertical, but flexible, axis of the spine. When humans move, the body's elastic musculoskeletal structure dictates a harmonious, smooth motion of all its elements. The sculptor of the *Kritios Boy* was among the first to grasp this fact and to represent it in statuary. The youth has a slight dip to the right hip, indicating the shifting of weight onto his left leg. His right leg is bent, at ease. Even his head turns slightly to the right, breaking the unwritten rule of frontality dictating the form of virtually all earlier statues. This weight shift, which art historians describe as *contrapposto* (counterbalance), separates Classical from Archaic Greek statuary. When it reappeared, after a long absence, in the sculpture of the later Middle Ages and the Renaissance, it was an unmistakable sign of renewed interest in Classical art.

BRONZE STATUES RESCUED FROM THE SEA The innovations of the *Kritios Boy* were carried even further in the bronze statue of a warrior (FIG. **5-34**) found in the sea near Riace at the "toe" of the Italian "boot." It is one of a pair of statues found in the cargo of a ship that sank in antiquity on its way from Greece probably to Rome, where Greek sculpture was much admired. These statues, now known as the *Riace Bronzes,* were discovered accidentally by a diver. Although they had to undergo several years of cleaning and restoration after nearly two millennia of submersion in salt

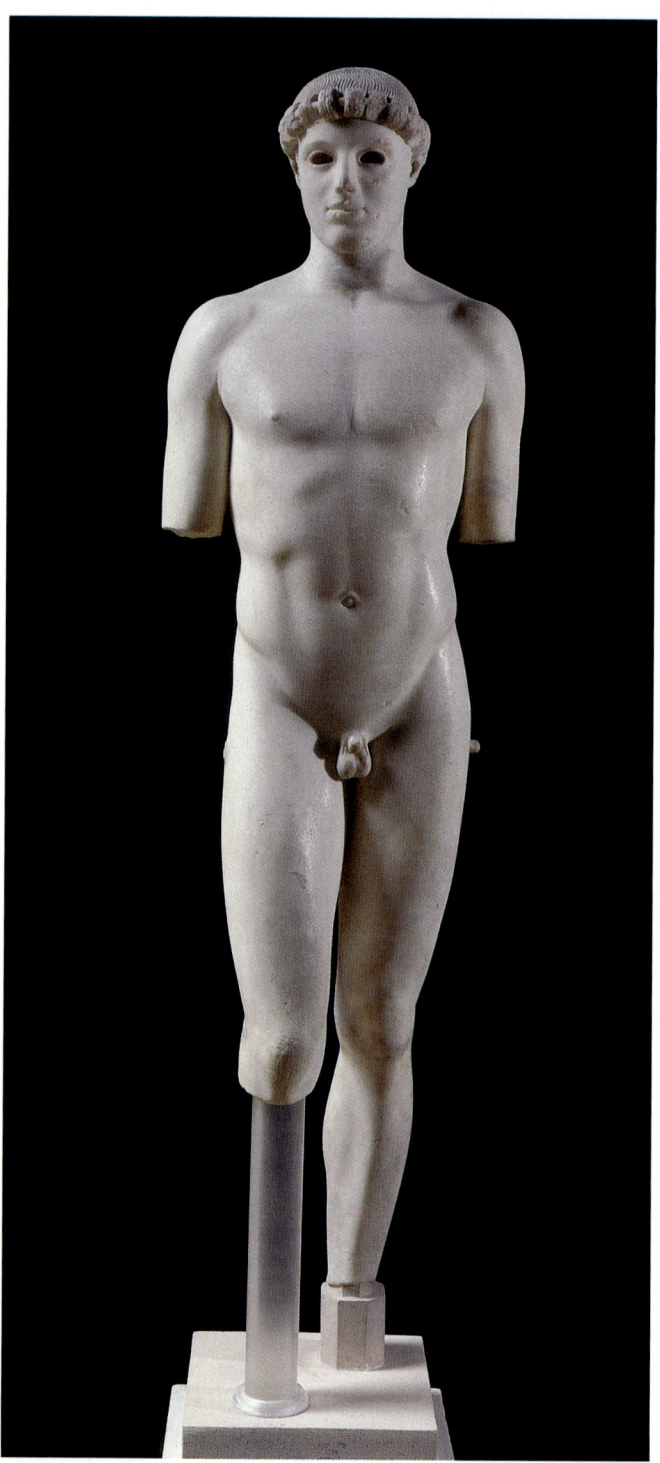

5-33 *Kritios Boy,* from the Acropolis, Athens, Greece, ca. 480 B.C. Marble, approx. 2′ 10″ high. Acropolis Museum, Athens.

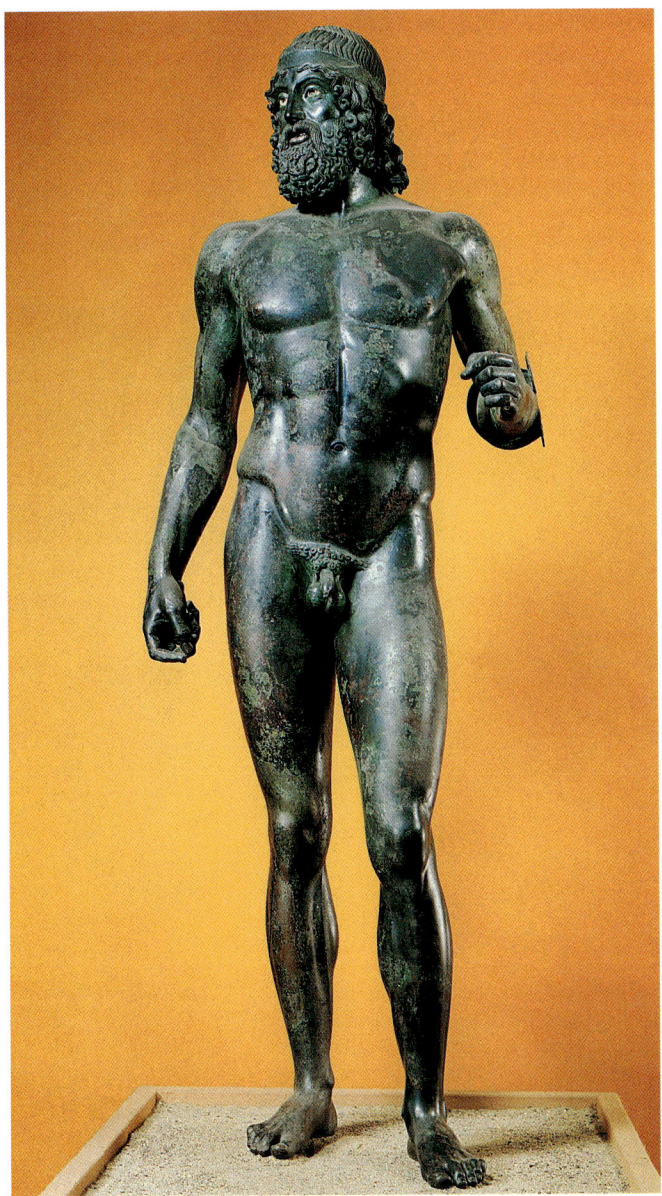

5-34 Warrior, from the sea off Riace, Italy, ca. 460–450 B.C. Bronze, approx. 6′ 6″ high. Archeological Museum, Reggio Calabria.

the turn of the head and feet in opposite directions as well as a slight twist at the waist are in keeping with the Severe Style. The moment chosen for depiction is not during the frenetic race but after, when the driver quietly and modestly holds his horses still in the winner's circle. He grasps the reins in his outstretched right hand (the lower left arm, cast separately, is missing), and he wears the standard charioteer's garment, girdled high and held in at the shoulders and the back to keep it from flapping. The folds emphasize both the verticality and calm of the figure and recall the flutes of a Greek column. A band inlaid with silver is tied around the head and confines the hair. The eyes are made of glass paste and shaded by delicate bronze lashes.

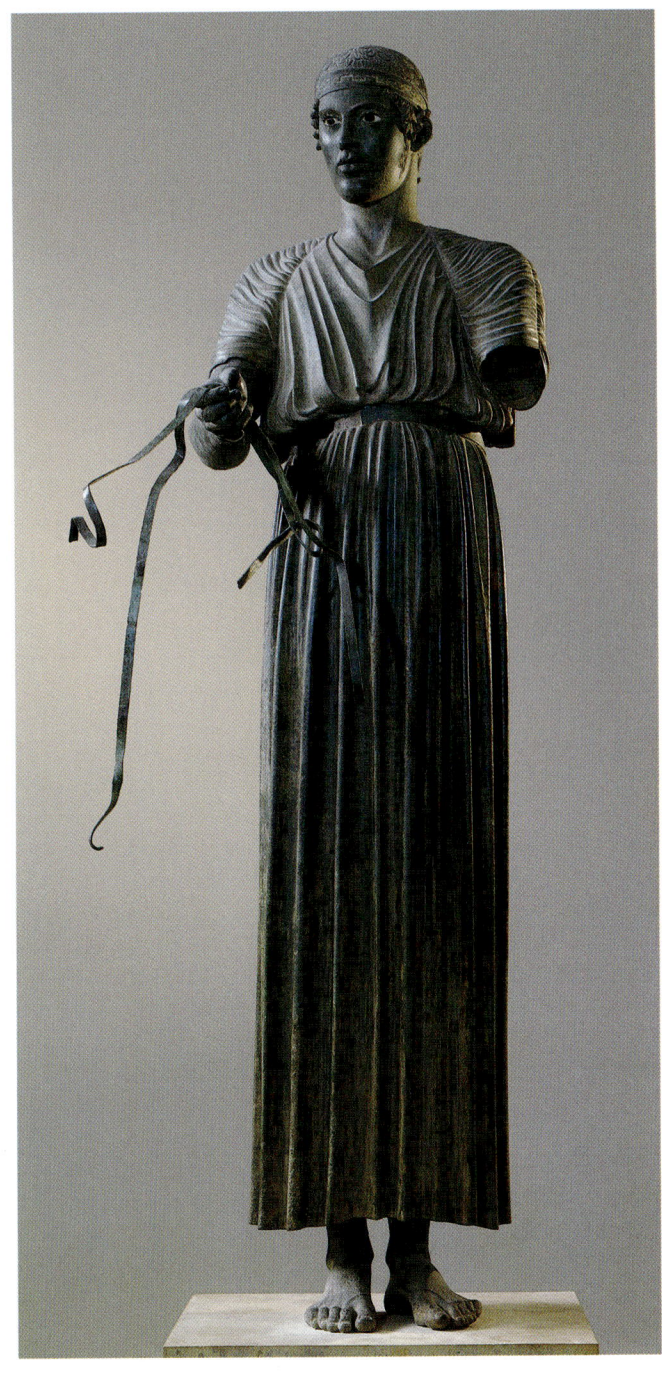

5-35 Charioteer, from a group dedicated by Polyzalos of Gela in the Sanctuary of Apollo, Delphi, Greece, ca. 470 B.C. Bronze, approx. 5′ 11″ high. Archeological Museum, Delphi.

water, they are nearly intact. The statue shown here lacks only its shield, spear, and wreath. It is a masterpiece of hollow-casting (see "Hollow-Casting Life-Size Bronze Statues," page 124), with inlaid eyes, silver teeth and eyelashes, and copper lips and nipples (see FIG. Intro-18). The weight shift is more pronounced than in the *Kritios Boy*. The warrior's head turns more forcefully to the right, his shoulders tilt, his hips swing more markedly, and his arms are freed from the body. Archaic frontality and rigidity gave way to natural motion in space.

A QUIET VICTOR AND A THUNDERING GOD

The high technical quality of the Riace warrior is equaled in another bronze statue (FIG. **5-35**) set up a decade or two earlier to commemorate the victory of the tyrant Polyzalos of Gela (Sicily) in a chariot race at Delphi. The statue is almost all that remains of an enormous group composed of Polyzalos's driver, the chariot, the team of horses, and a young groom. The charioteer stands in an almost Archaic pose, but

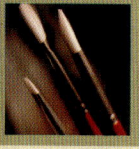

Hollow-Casting Life-Size Bronze Statues

Monumental bronze statues such as the Riace warrior (FIG. 5-34), the Delphi charioteer (FIG. 5-35), and the Artemision god (FIG. 5-36) required great technical skill to produce. They could not be manufactured using a single simple mold, as were small-scale Geometric and Archaic figures (FIGS. 5-2 and 5-3). Weight, cost, and the tendency of large masses of bronze to distort when cooling made life-size castings in solid bronze impractical, if not impossible. Instead, large statues were hollow-cast by the *cire perdue* (lost-wax) method. The lost-wax process entailed several steps and had to be repeated many times, because monumental statues were typically cast in parts—head, arms, hands, torso, and so forth.

First, the sculptor fashioned a full-size *clay model* of the intended statue. Then a clay *master mold* was made around the model and removed in sections. When dry, the various pieces of the master mold were put back together for each separate bodily part. Next, a layer of beeswax was applied to the inside of each mold. When the wax cooled, the mold was removed, and the sculptor was left with a hollow *wax model* in the shape of the original clay model. The artist could then correct or refine details, for example, engrave fingernails on the wax hands or individual locks of hair on the head.

In the next stage, a final clay mold (*investment*) was applied to the exterior of the wax model, and a liquid clay core was poured inside the hollow wax. Metal pins (*chaplets*) then were driven through the new mold to connect the investment with the clay core (*a*). Now the wax was melted out ("lost") and molten bronze poured into the mold in its place (*b*). When the bronze hardened and assumed the shape of the wax

model, the investment and as much of the core as possible were removed, and the casting process was complete. Finally, the individually cast pieces were fitted together and soldered, surface imperfections and joins smoothed, eyes inlaid, teeth and eyelashes added, attributes such as spears and wreaths provided, and so forth. Such statues were costly to make and much prized.

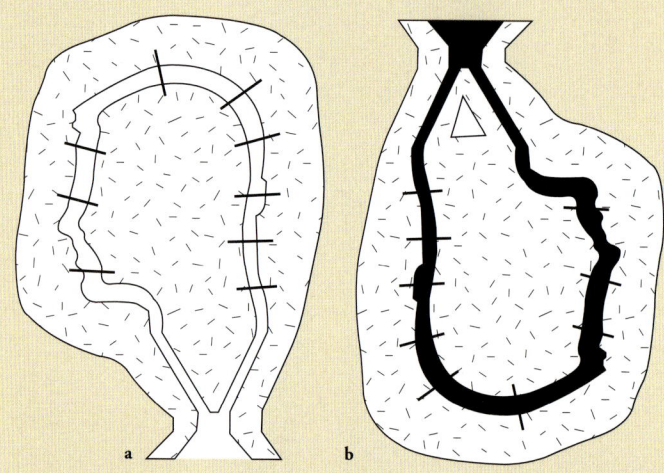

Two stages of the lost-wax method of bronzecasting (after S. A. Hemingway[1]): (*a*) clay mold (investment), wax model, and clay core connected by chaplets; (*b*) wax melted out and molten bronze poured into the mold.

[1] Sean A. Hemingway, *How Bronze Statues Were Made in Classical Antiquity* (Cambridge, Mass.: Harvard University Art Museums, 1996), 4.

The male human form in motion is, by contrast, the subject of another Early Classical bronze statue (FIG. 5-36), which, like the Riace warrior, divers found in an ancient shipwreck, this time off the coast of Greece itself at Cape Artemision. The bearded god once hurled a weapon held in his right hand, probably a thunderbolt, in which case he is Zeus. A less likely suggestion is that this is Poseidon with his trident. The pose could be employed equally well for a javelin thrower. Both arms are boldly extended, and the right heel is raised off the ground, underscoring the lightness and stability of hollow-cast monumental statues.

A GREEK STATUE FOR A ROMAN PATRON A bronze statue similar to the Artemision Zeus was the renowned *Diskobolos (Discus Thrower)* by MYRON (FIG. **5-37**), which is known only through marble copies made in Roman times. Even when the original was removed from Greece, as were the Riace and Artemision bronzes, only one community or individual could own it. Demand so far exceeded the supply that a veritable industry was born to meet the Roman call for Greek statuary to display in public places and private villas alike. The copies usually were made in less costly marble. The change in medium resulted in a different surface appearance. In most

cases, the copyist also had to add an intrusive tree trunk to support the great weight of the stone statue and struts between arms and body to strengthen weak points. The copies rarely approach the quality of the originals, and the Roman sculptors sometimes took liberties with their models to conform to their own tastes and needs. Occasionally, for example, a mirror image of the original was created for a specific setting. Nevertheless, the copies are indispensable today. Without them it would be impossible to reconstruct the history of Greek sculpture after the Archaic period.

Myron's *Discus Thrower* is a vigorous action statue, like the Artemision Zeus, but it is composed in an almost Archaic manner, with profile limbs and a nearly frontal chest, suggesting the tension of a coiled spring. Like the arm of a pendulum clock, the right arm of the *Diskobolos* has reached the apex of its arc but has not yet begun to swing down again. Myron froze the action and arranged the body and limbs so that two intersecting arcs were formed, creating the impression of a tightly stretched bow a moment before the string is released. This tension is not, however, mirrored in the athlete's face, which remains expressionless. Once again, as in the later of the two warrior statues from the Aegina pediments (FIG. 5-28), the head is turned away from the spectator. In

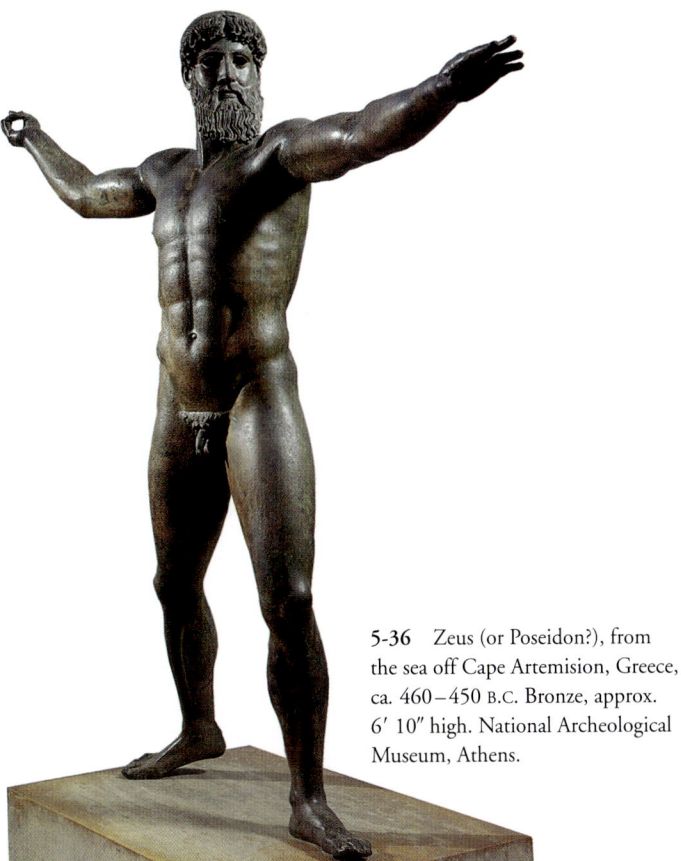

5-36   Zeus (or Poseidon?), from the sea off Cape Artemision, Greece, ca. 460–450 B.C. Bronze, approx. 6' 10" high. National Archeological Museum, Athens.

contrast to Archaic athlete statues, the Classical *Diskobolos* does not perform for the spectator but concentrates on the task at hand.

THE QUEST FOR IDEAL FORM   One of the most frequently copied Greek statues was the *Doryphoros (Spear Bearer)* by POLYKLEITOS, a work that epitomizes the intellectual rigor of Classical statuary design. The original is lost. We illustrate a marble copy (FIG. **5-38**) that stood in a palestra at Pompeii, where it served as a model for Roman athletes. The *Doryphoros* is the embodiment of Polykleitos's vision of the ideal statue of a nude male athlete or warrior. In fact, it was made as a demonstration piece to accompany a treatise on the subject. *Spear Bearer* is but a modern

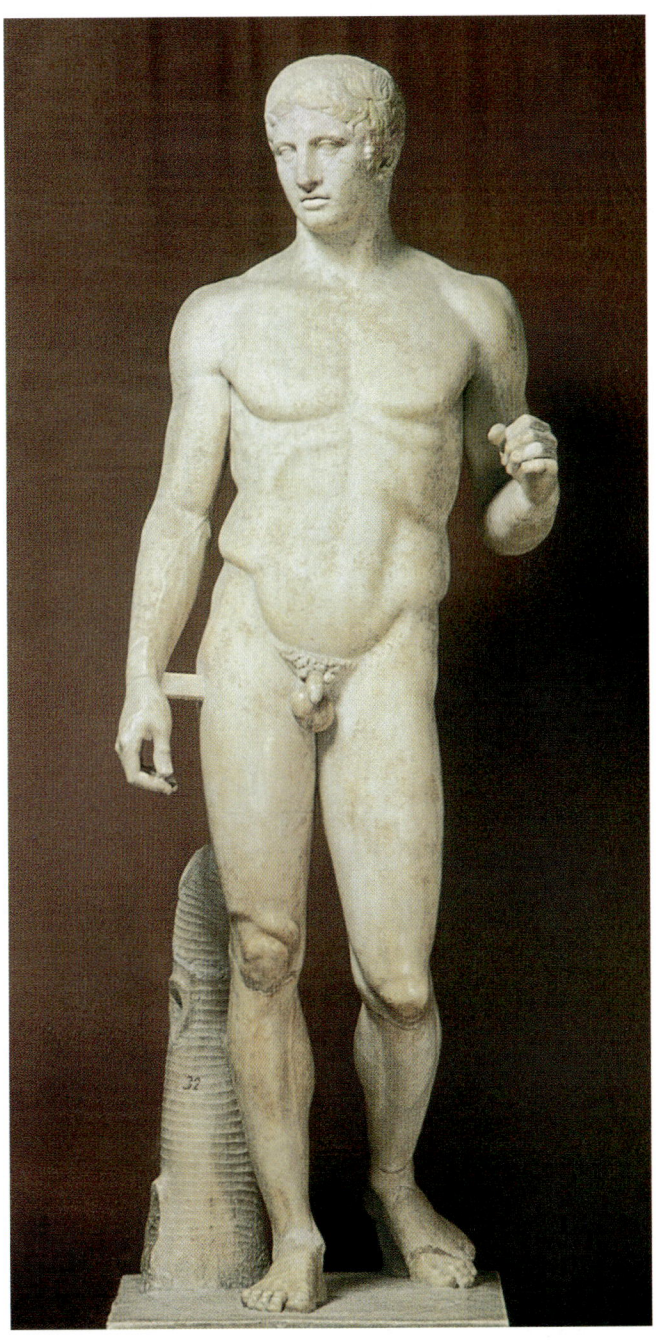

5-38   POLYKLEITOS, *Doryphoros (Spear Bearer)*. Roman marble copy from Pompeii, Italy, after a bronze original of ca. 450–440 B.C., 6' 11" high. Museo Nazionale, Naples.

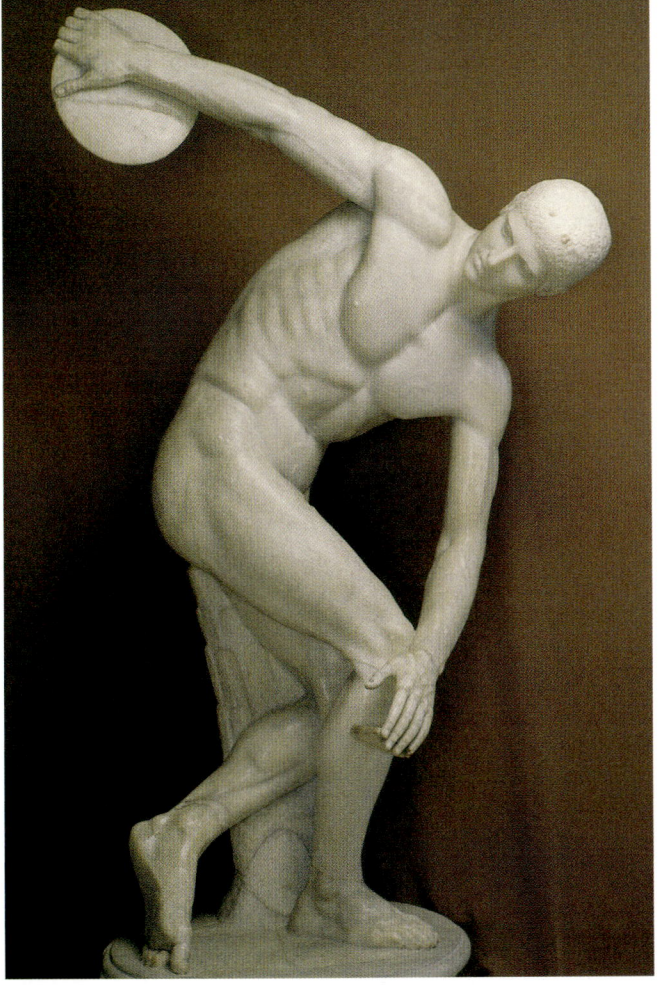

5-37   MYRON, *Diskobolos (Discus Thrower)*. Roman marble copy after a bronze original of ca. 450 B.C., 5' 1" high. Museo Nazionale Romano, Rome.

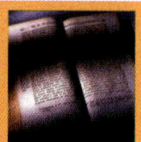

Polykleitos's Prescription for the Perfect Statue

One of the most influential philosophers of the ancient world was Pythagoras of Samos, who lived during the latter part of the sixth century B.C. A famous geometric theorem still bears his name. Pythagoras also is said to have discovered that harmonic chords in music are produced on the strings of a lyre at regular intervals that may be expressed as ratios of whole numbers—2:1, 3:2, 4:3. He and his followers, the Pythagoreans, believed more generally that underlying harmonic proportions could be found in all of nature, determining the form of the cosmos as well as of things on earth, and that beauty resided in harmonious numerical ratios.

By this reasoning, a perfect statue would be one constructed according to an all-encompassing mathematical formula. In the mid-fifth century B.C., the sculptor Polykleitos of Argos set out to make just such a statue (FIG. 5-38). He recorded the principles he followed and the proportions he used in a treatise titled the *Canon*. His treatise is unfortunately lost, but Galen, a physician who lived during the second century A.D., summarized the sculptor's philosophy as follows: "[Beauty arises from] the commensurability [*symmetria*] of the parts, that is to say, of finger to finger, and of all the fingers to the palm and the wrist, and of these to the forearm, and of the forearm to the upper arm, and of all the other parts to each other, as they are set forth in the *Canon* of

Polykleitos. . . . [The sculptor] supported his treatise [by making] a statue according to [its] tenets, and he called the statue, like the treatise, the *Canon*." This is why Pliny the Elder, writing in the first century A.D., maintained that Polykleitos, "alone of men is deemed to have rendered art itself [that is, the theoretical basis of art] in a work of art."[1]

Polykleitos's belief that a successful statue resulted from the precise application of abstract principles is reflected in an anecdote (probably a later invention) the Roman historian Aelian told:

Polykleitos made two statues at the same time, one which would be pleasing to the crowd and the other according to the principles of his art. In accordance with the opinion of each person who came into his workshop, he altered something and changed its form, submitting to the advice of each. Then he put both statues on display. The one was marvelled at by everyone, and the other was laughed at. Thereupon Polykleitos said, "But the one that you find fault with, you made yourselves; while the one that you marvel at, I made."[2]

[1] J. J. Pollitt, trans., *The Art of Ancient Greece: Sources and Documents* (New York: Cambridge University Press, 1990), 75.

[2] Ibid., 79.

---

descriptive epithet for the statue. The name assigned to it by Poly-kleitos was *Canon* (see "Polykleitos's Prescription for the Perfect Statue," above).

The *Doryphoros* is the culmination of the evolution in Greek statuary from the Archaic kouros to the *Kritios Boy* to the Riace warrior. The contrapposto is more pronounced than ever before in a standing statue, but Polykleitos was not content with simply rendering a figure that stands naturally. His aim was to impose order on human movement, to make it "beautiful," to "perfect" it. He achieved this through a system of *chiastic,* or cross, balance. What appears at first to be a casually natural pose is, in fact, the result of an extremely complex and subtle organization of the figure's various parts. Note, for instance, how the supporting leg's function is echoed by the straight-hanging arm to provide the figure's right side with the columnar stability needed to anchor the left side's dynamically flexed limbs. If read anatomically, however, the tensed and relaxed limbs may be seen to oppose each other diagonally. That is, the right arm and the left leg are relaxed, and the tensed supporting leg is opposed by the flexed arm, which held a spear. In like manner, the head turns to the right while the hips twist slightly to the left. And although the *Doryphoros* seems to take a step forward, he does not move. This dynamic asymmetrical balance, this motion while at rest, and the resulting harmony of opposites are the essence of the Polykleitan style.

The Athenian Acropolis

ATHENIAN VICTORY AND TYRANNY While Polykleitos was formulating his *Canon* in Argos, the Athenians, under the leadership of Pericles, were at work on one of the most ambitious building projects ever undertaken, the reconstruction of the Acropolis after the Persian sack of 480 B.C. Athens, despite the damage it suffered at the hands of the army of Xerxes, emerged from the war with enormous power and prestige. The Athenian commander Themistocles had decisively defeated the Persian navy off the island of Salamis, southwest of Athens, and forced it to retreat to Asia.

In 478 B.C., in the aftermath of the Persians' expulsion from the Aegean, the Greeks formed an alliance for mutual protection against any renewed threat from the Orient. The new confederacy came to be known as the Delian League, because its headquarters were on the sacred island of Delos, midway between the Greek mainland and the coast of Asia Minor. Although at the outset each league member had an equal vote, Athens was "first among equals," providing the allied fleet commander and determining which cities were to furnish ships and which were instead to pay an annual tribute to the treasury at Delos. Continued fighting against the Persians kept the alliance intact, but Athens gradually assumed a dominant role. In 454 B.C. the Delian treasury was transferred to Athens, ostensibly for security reasons. Pericles, who was only in his teens when the Persians laid waste to the Acropolis, was by midcentury the recognized leader of the Athenians, and he succeeded in converting the alliance into an Athenian empire. Tribute continued to be paid, but the surplus reserves were not expended for the common good of the allied Greek states. Rather, they were expropriated to pay the enormous cost of executing Pericles' grand plan to embellish the Acropolis of Athens.

The reaction of the allies—in reality the subjects of Athens—was predictable. Plutarch, who wrote a biography of Pericles in the early second century A.D., indicated the wrath the Greek victims of Athenian tyranny felt by recording the protest voiced against Pericles' decision even in the Athenian assembly. Greece, Pericles' enemies said, had been dealt "a terrible, wanton insult" when Athens used the funds contributed out of necessity for a common war effort to "gild and embellish itself with images and extravagant temples, like some pretentious woman decked out with precious stones."[4] This is important to keep in mind when examining those great and universally admired buildings erected on the Acropolis in accordance with Pericles' vision of his polis reborn from the ashes of the Persian sack. They are *not*, as some would wish people to believe, the glorious fruits of Athenian democracy but are instead the by-products of tyranny and the abuse of power. Too often art and architectural historians do not ask

how a monument was financed. The answer can be very revealing—and very embarrassing.

THE "OLYMPIAN PERICLES" A number of Roman copies are preserved of a famous bronze portrait statue of Pericles fashioned by KRESILAS, who was born on Crete but who worked in Athens. The portrait was set up on the Acropolis, probably immediately after the leader's death in 429 B.C., and depicted Pericles in heroic nudity. The statue must have resembled that of the Riace warrior (FIG. 5-34) but with the helmet of a *strategos* (general), the position Pericles was elected to fifteen times. The copies, in marble, only reproduce the head. Ours (FIG. **5-39**) is a *herm* (a bust on a square pillar) inscribed "Pericles, son of Xanthippos, the Athenian." Pericles was said to have had an abnormally elongated skull, and Kresilas recorded this feature (while also concealing it) by providing a glimpse through the helmet's eye slots of the hair at the top of the head. This, together with the unblemished features of Pericles' Classically aloof face and, no doubt, his body's perfect physique, led Pliny to assert that Kresilas had the ability to make noble men appear even more noble in their portraits. In fact, he referred to Kresilas's "portrait"—it is not a portrait at all in the modern sense of an individual's likeness—of the Athenian statesman as "the Olympian Pericles," for in this image Pericles appeared almost godlike.[5]

PERICLES' ACROPOLIS, THEN AND NOW The centerpiece of Pericles' great building program on the Acropolis (FIGS. **5-40** and **5-41**) was the Parthenon, or the Temple of Athena Parthenos, erected in the remarkably short period between 447 and 438 B.C. (Work on the great temple's ambitious sculptural ornamentation continued until 432 B.C.) As soon as the Parthenon was completed, construction commenced on a grand new gateway to the Acropolis from the west (the only accessible side of the natural plateau), the Propylaia (FIG. 5-41). Begun in 437 B.C., it was left unfinished in 431 B.C. at the outbreak of the Peloponnesian War between Athens and Sparta. Two later temples, the Erechtheion and the Temple of Athena Nike (FIG. 5-41), built after Pericles' death, were probably also part of the original design. The greatest Athenian architects and sculptors of the Classical period focused their attention on the construction and decoration of these four buildings. More human creative genius concentrated on the Periclean Acropolis than in any other place or time in the history of Western civilization.

That these buildings exist at all today is something of a miracle. The Parthenon, for example, was converted into a Byzantine church and later a Catholic church in the Middle Ages and then, after the Ottoman conquest of Greece, into an Islamic mosque. Each time the building was remodeled for a different religion, it was modified structurally. The colossal statue of Athena inside was removed early on, and the churches had a great curved *apse* at the east end housing the altar, while the mosque had a *minaret* tower used to call the faithful to prayer. In 1687, the Venetians besieged the Acropolis, which at that time was in Turkish hands. One of their rockets scored a direct hit on the ammunition depot the Turks had installed in part of the Parthenon. The resultant explosion blew out the building's center. To make matters worse, the Venetians subsequently tried to remove some of the statues from the Parthenon's pediments. In more than one case,

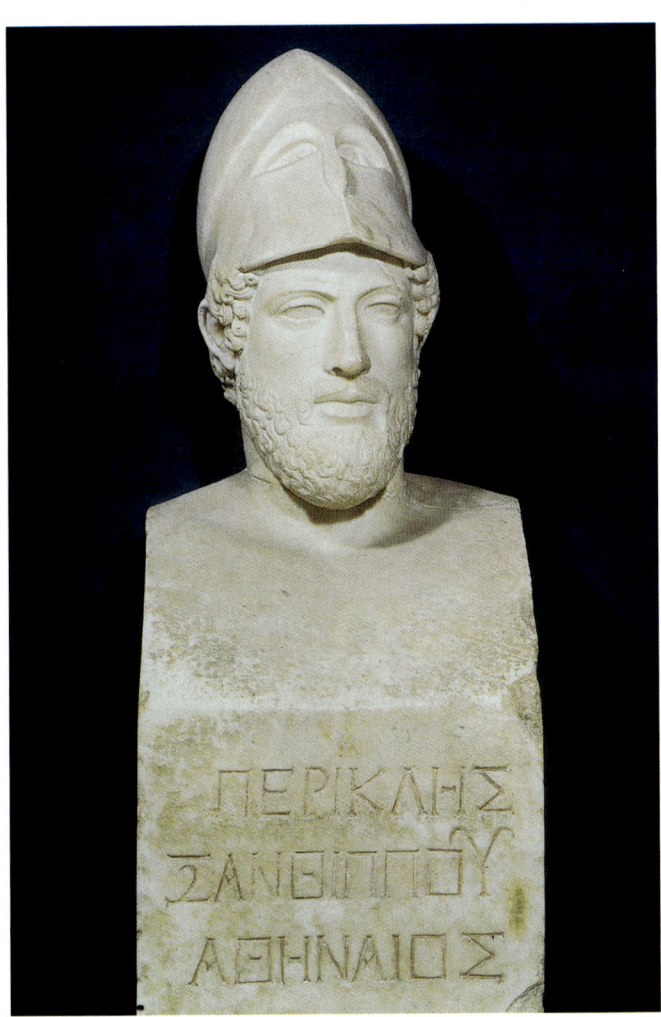

5-39 KRESILAS, Pericles. Roman marble herm copy after a bronze original of ca. 429 B.C., approx. 6' high. Vatican Museums, Rome.

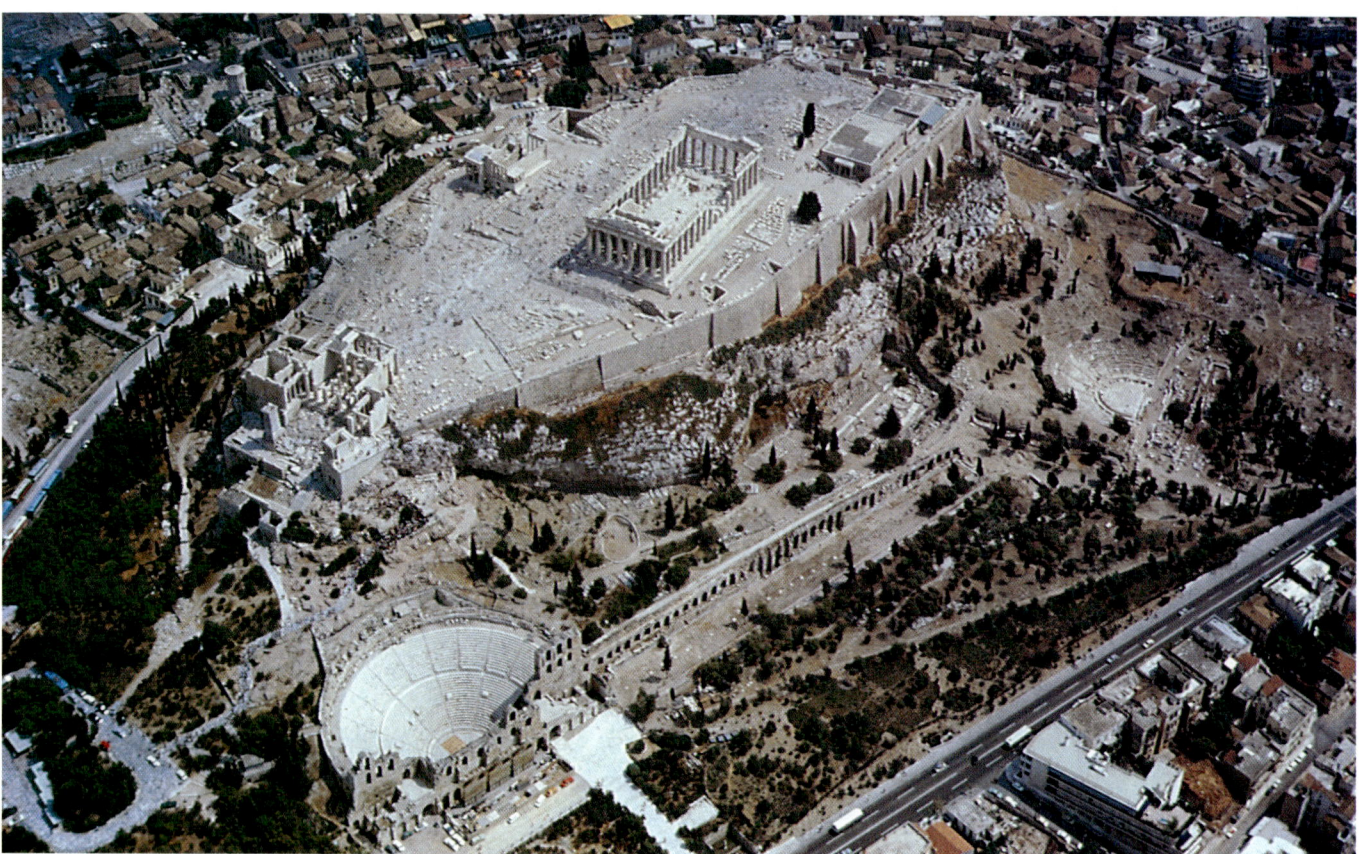

5-40   Aerial view of the Acropolis, Athens, Greece.

statues were dropped and smashed on the ground. Today, a uniquely modern blight threatens the Parthenon and the other buildings of the Periclean age. The corrosive emissions of factories and automobiles are decomposing the ancient marbles. A great campaign has been under way for some time to protect the columns and walls from further deterioration. What little original sculpture remained *in situ* when modern restoration began was transferred to the Acropolis Museum's climate-controlled rooms.

Despite the ravages of time and humanity, most of the Parthenon's peripteral colonnade (FIG. **5-42**) is still standing (or has been reerected), and art historians know a great deal about the building and its sculptural program. The architects were IKTINOS and KALLIKRATES. The statue of Athena (FIG. 5-44) was the work of PHIDIAS, who was also the overseer of the temple's sculptural decoration. In fact, Plutarch claims that Phidias was in charge of the entire Periclean Acropolis project.

MATHEMATICS AND THE IDEAL TEMPLE   Just as the contemporary *Doryphoros* by Polykleitos may be seen as the culmination of nearly two centuries of searching for the ideal proportions of the various human bodily parts, so, too, the Parthenon may be viewed as the ideal solution to the Greek architect's quest for perfect proportions in Doric temple design. Its well-spaced columns, with their slender shafts, and the capitals, with their straight-sided conical echinuses, are the ultimate refinement of the bulging and squat Doric columns and compressed capitals of the Archaic Hera temple at Paestum (FIG. 5-13). The Parthenon architects and the *Doryphoros* sculptor were kindred spirits in their belief that beautiful proportions resulted from strict adherence to harmonious numerical ratios, whether they were designing a temple more than two hundred feet long or a life-size statue

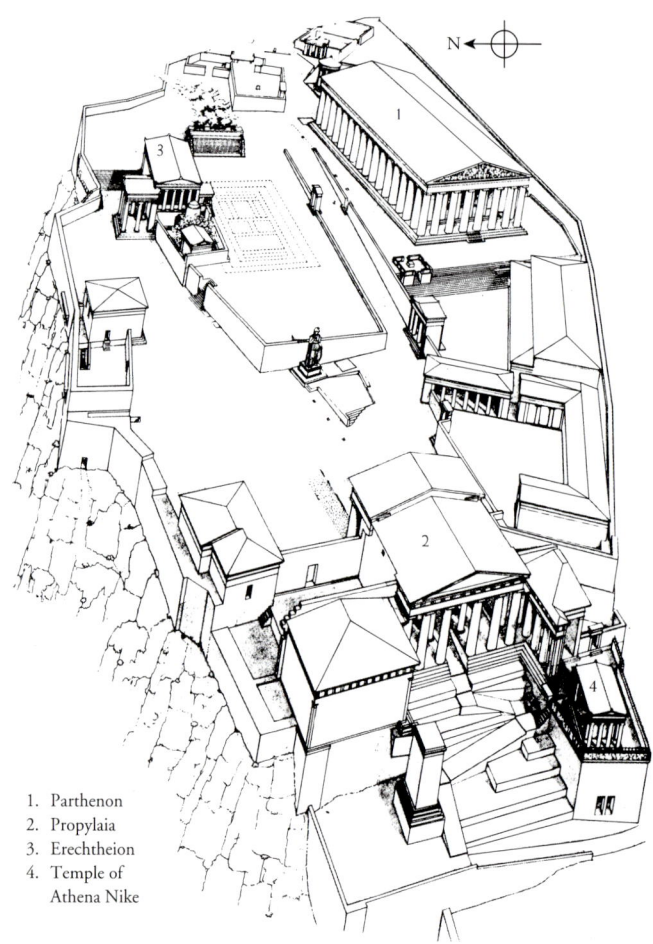

1. Parthenon
2. Propylaia
3. Erechtheion
4. Temple of Athena Nike

5-41   Restored view of the Acropolis, Athens, Greece, seen from the northwest (G. P. Stevens).

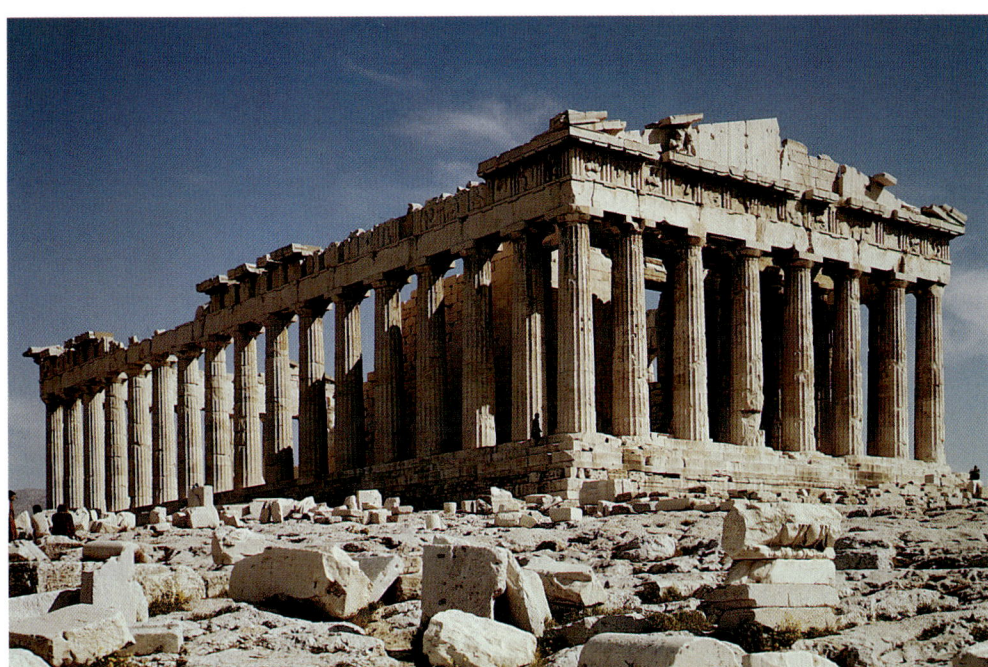

5-42 IKTINOS and KALLIKRATES, Parthenon, the Temple of Athena Parthenos (view from the northwest), Acropolis, Athens, Greece, 447–438 B.C.

of a nude man. For the Parthenon, the controlling ratio for the *symmetria* of the parts may be expressed algebraically as $x = 2y + 1$, where x is the larger number and y is the smaller number. Thus, for example, the temple's short ends have eight columns and the long sides have seventeen: $17 = (2 \times 8) + 1$. The stylobate's ratio of length to width is 9:4 ($9 = [2 \times 4] + 1$), and this ratio also characterizes the cella's proportion of length to width, the distance between the centers of two adjacent column drums (the *interaxial*) in proportion to the columns' diameter, and so forth.

The Parthenon's harmonious design and the mathematical precision of the sizes of its constituent elements tend to obscure the fact this temple, as actually constructed, is quite irregular in shape. Throughout the building are pronounced deviations from the strictly horizontal and vertical lines assumed to be the basis of all Greek post-and-lintel structures. The stylobate, for example, curves upward at the center on both the sides and the facade, forming a kind of shallow dome, and this curvature is carried up into the entablature. Moreover, the peristyle columns lean inward slightly. Those at the corners have a diagonal inclination and are also about two inches thicker than the rest. If their lines were continued, they would meet about one and one-half miles above the temple. These deviations from the norm meant that virtually every Parthenon block and drum had to be carved according to the special set of specifications its unique place in the structure dictated.

This was obviously a daunting task, and a reason must have existed for these so-called refinements in the Parthenon. Some modern observers note, for example, how the curving of horizontal lines and the tilting of vertical ones create a dynamic balance in the building—a kind of architectural contrapposto—and give it a greater sense of life. The oldest recorded explanation, however, may be the correct one. Vitruvius, a Roman architect of the late first century B.C. who claims to have had access to the treatise on the Parthenon Iktinos wrote—again note the kinship with the *Canon* of Polykleitos—maintains that these adjustments were made to compensate for optical illusions. Vitruvius states, for example,

that if a stylobate is laid out on a level surface, it will appear to sag at the center and that the corner columns of a building should be thicker since they are surrounded by light and would otherwise appear thinner than their neighbors.

The Parthenon is "irregular" in other ways as well. One of the ironies of this most famous of all Doric temples is that it is "contaminated" by Ionic elements (FIG. **5-43**). Although the cella had a two-story Doric colonnade around Phidias's Athena statue, the back room (which housed the goddess's treasury and the tribute collected from the Delian League) had four tall and slender Ionic columns as sole supports for the superstructure. And while the temple's exterior had a canonical Doric frieze, the inner frieze that ran around the top of the cella wall was Ionic. Perhaps this fusion of Doric and Ionic elements reflects the Athenians' belief that the Ionians of the Cycladic Islands and Asia Minor were descended from Athenian settlers and were therefore their kin. Or it may be Pericles and Iktinos's way of suggesting that Athens was the leader of *all* the Greeks. In any case, a mix of Doric and Ionic features characterizes the fifth-century buildings of the Acropolis as a whole.

LORD ELGIN'S MARBLES The costly decision to incorporate two sculptured friezes in the Parthenon's design is symptomatic. This Pentelic-marble temple was more lavishly decorated than any Greek temple before it, Doric or Ionic (FIG. 5-43). Every one of the ninety-two Doric metopes was decorated with relief sculpture. So, too, was every inch of the five hundred twenty-four-foot-long Ionic frieze. The pediments were filled with dozens of larger-than-life-size statues. Most of the Parthenon's reliefs and statues are today exhibited in a special gallery in the British Museum in London, where they are known popularly as the "Elgin Marbles." Between 1801 and 1803, while Greece was still under Turkish rule, Lord Elgin, the British ambassador to the Ottoman court at Istanbul, was permitted to dismantle many of the Parthenon sculptures and to ship the best-preserved ones to England. He eventually sold them to the British government at a great financial loss to himself. Although he often has been accused of

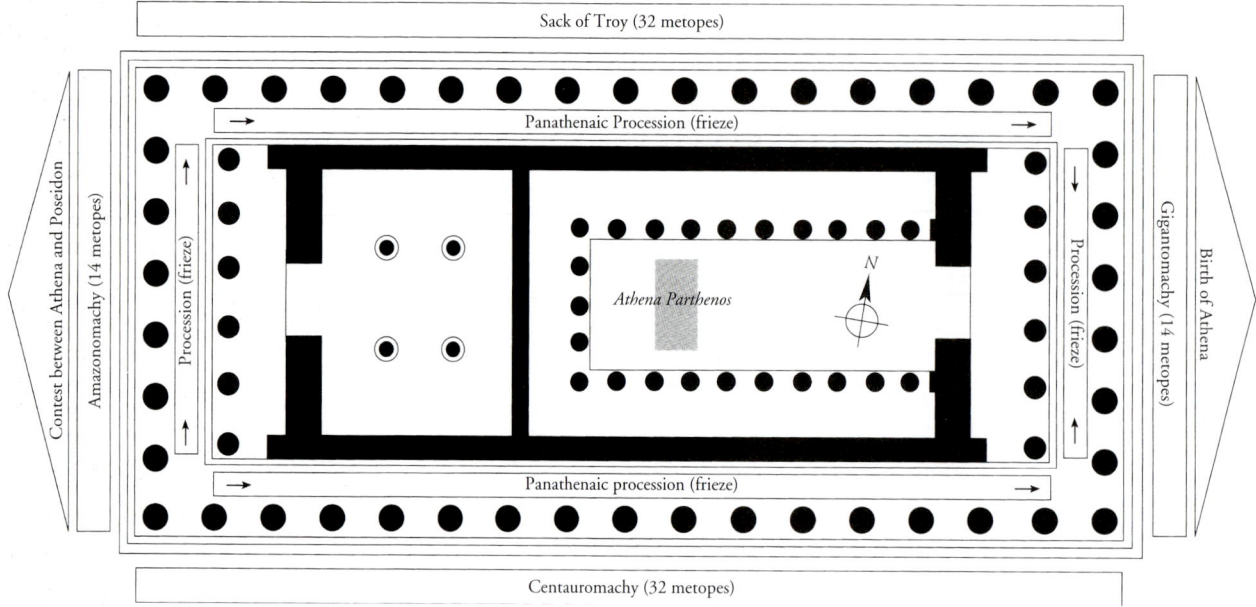

Sack of Troy (32 metopes)

Panathenaic Procession (frieze)

Contest between Athena and Poseidon

Amazonomachy (14 metopes)

Procession (frieze)

Athena Parthenos

N

Procession (frieze)

Gigantomachy (14 metopes)

Birth of Athena

Panathenaic procession (frieze)

Centauromachy (32 metopes)

5-43   Plan of the Parthenon, Acropolis, Athens, Greece, with diagram of sculptural program (after A. Stewart), 447–432 B.C.

"stealing" Greece's cultural heritage (the Greek government has long sought the return of the Elgin Marbles to Athens), Lord Elgin must be credited with saving the sculptures from almost certain ruin if they had been left at the site.

PHIDIAS'S GOLD AND IVORY ATHENA   One statue that even Elgin could not recover was Phidias's *Athena Parthenos,* the Virgin, which had been destroyed long before the nineteenth century. Art historians know a great deal about it, however, from descriptions by Greek and Latin authors and from Roman copies. A model in Toronto (FIG. **5-44**) gives a good idea of its appearance and setting. It was a *chryselephantine* statue, that is, fashioned of gold and ivory, the latter used for Athena's exposed flesh. Phidias's statue stood thirty-eight feet tall, and to a large extent the Parthenon was designed around it. To accommodate its huge size, the cella had to be wider than usual. This, in turn, dictated the width of the eight-column facade at a time when six columns were the norm, as at Aegina (FIGS. 5-24 and 5-25).

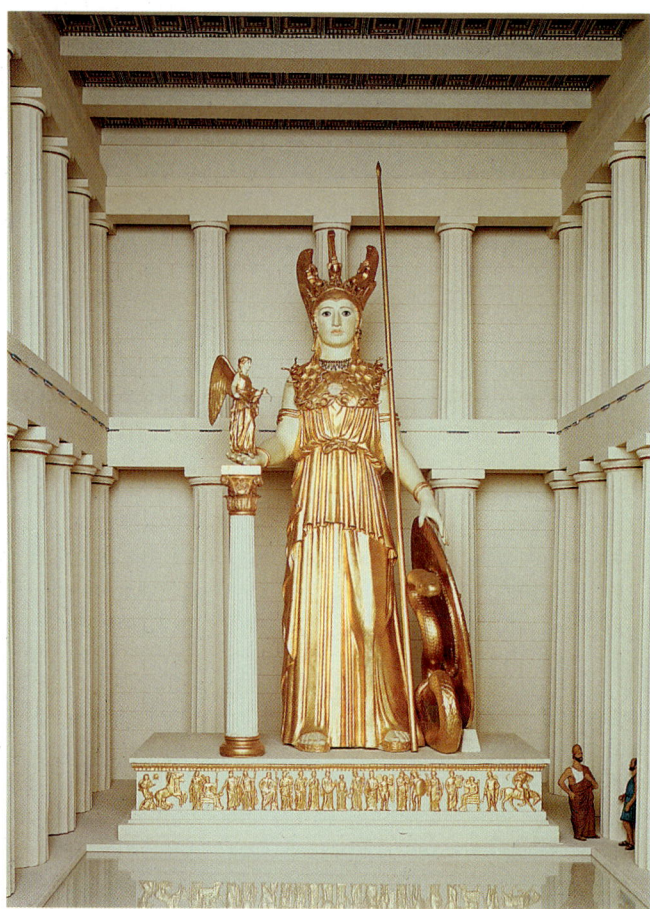

5-44   PHIDIAS, *Athena Parthenos,* in the cella of the Parthenon, Acropolis, Athens, Greece, ca. 438 B.C. Model of the lost statue which was approx. 38' tall. Royal Ontario Museum, Toronto.

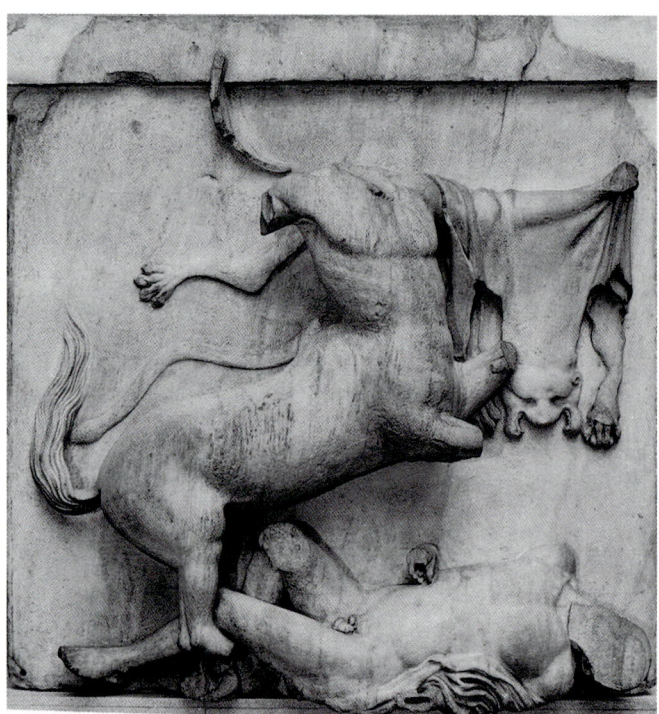

5-45   Lapith versus centaur, metope from the south side of the Parthenon, Acropolis, Athens, Greece, ca. 447–438 B.C. Marble, approx. 4' 8" high. British Museum, London.

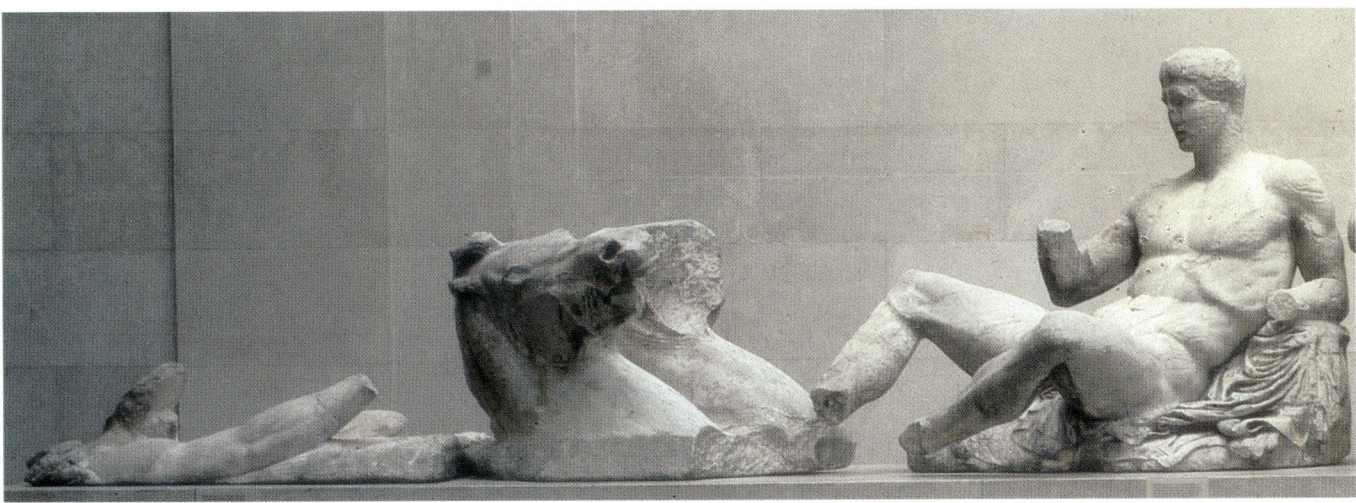

5-46   Helios and his horses, and Dionysos (Herakles?), from the east pediment of the Parthenon, Acropolis, Athens, Greece, ca. 438–432 B.C. Marble, greatest height approx. 4′ 3″. British Museum, London.

Athena was fully armed with shield, spear, and helmet and held Nike (the winged female personification of Victory) in her extended right hand. No one doubts that this Nike referred to the victory of 479 B.C. The memory of the Persian sack of the Acropolis was still vivid, and the Athenians were intensely conscious that by driving back the Persians, they were saving their civilization from the Oriental "barbarians" who had committed atrocities at Miletos. In fact, the *Athena Parthenos* had multiple allusions to the Persian defeat. On the thick soles of Athena's sandals was a representation of a centauromachy. Her shield's exterior was emblazoned with high reliefs depicting the battle of Greeks and Amazons *(Amazonomachy)* when Theseus drove the Amazons out of Athens. And a gigantomachy was painted on the shield's interior. Each of these mythological contests was a metaphor for the triumph of order over chaos, of civilization over barbarism, and of Athens over Persia.

GODS AND HEROES ON THE PARTHENON
These same themes were taken up again in the Parthenon's Doric metopes (FIG. 5-43). The best-preserved metopes are those of the south side, which depicted the battle of Lapiths and centaurs, a combat in which Theseus of Athens played a major role. On one extraordinary slab (FIG. 5-45), a triumphant centaur rises up on its hind legs, exulting over the crumpled body of the Greek it has defeated. The relief is so high that parts are fully in the round; some have broken off. The sculptor knew how to distinguish the vibrant, powerful

form of the living beast from the lifeless corpse on the ground. In other metopes the Greeks have the upper hand, but the full set suggests the battle was a difficult one against a dangerous enemy and that losses as well as victories occurred. The same was true of the war against the Persians.

The subjects of the two pediments were especially appropriate for a temple that celebrated not only Athena but also the Athenians. At the east the birth of Athena was depicted, while at the west was the contest between Athena and Poseidon to determine which one would become the city's patron deity. Athena won, giving her name to the polis and its citizens. It is significant that in the story and in the pediment the Athenians are the judges of the relative merits of the two gods. Here one sees the same arrogance that led to the use of Delian League funds to adorn the Acropolis.

The center of the east pediment was damaged when the apse was added to the Parthenon at the time of its conversion into a church. What remains are the spectators to the left and the right who witnessed Athena's birth on Mount Olympus. At the far left are the head and arms of Helios (the Sun) and his chariot horses rising from the pediment floor (FIG. 5-46). Next to them is a powerful male figure usually identified as Dionysos or possibly Herakles, who entered the realm of the gods on completion of his twelve labors. At the right are three goddesses, probably Hestia, Dione, and Aphrodite (FIG. 5-47), and either Selene (the Moon) or Nyx (Night) and more horses, this time sinking

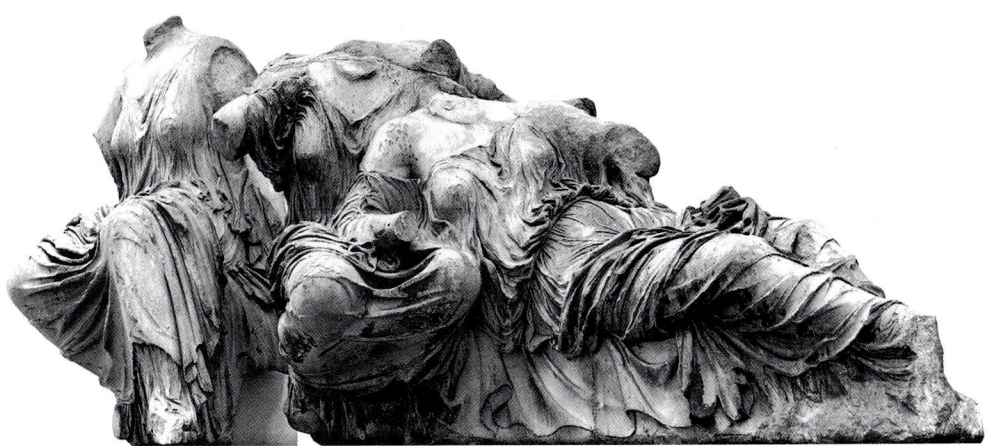

5-47   Three goddesses (Hestia, Dione, and Aphrodite?), from the east pediment of the Parthenon, Acropolis, Athens, Greece, ca. 438–432 B.C. Marble, greatest height approx. 4′ 5″. British Museum, London.

5-48 Details of the Panathenaic Festival procession frieze, from the Parthenon, Acropolis, Athens, Greece, ca. 447–438 B.C. Marble, approx. 3′ 6″ high. Horsemen of north frieze *(top)*, British Museum, London; seated gods and goddesses (Poseidon, Apollo, Artemis, Aphrodite, and Eros) of east frieze *(center)*, Acropolis Museum, Athens; and elders and maidens of east frieze *(bottom)*, Louvre, Paris.

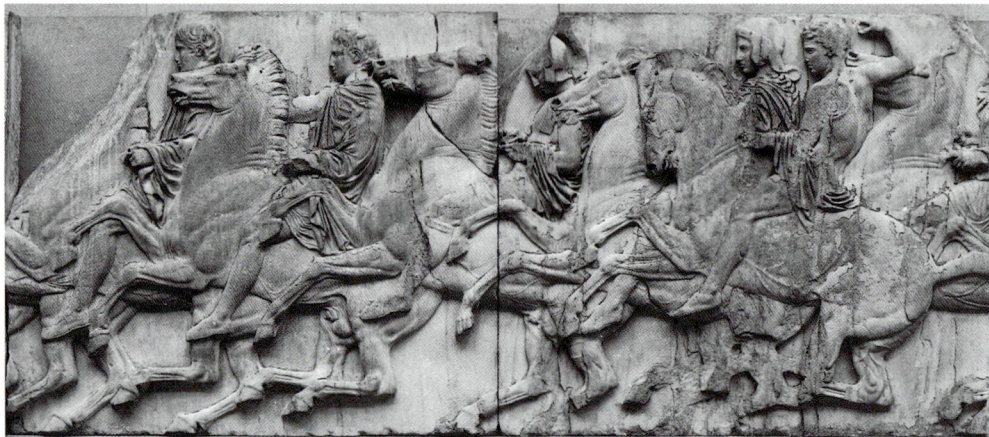

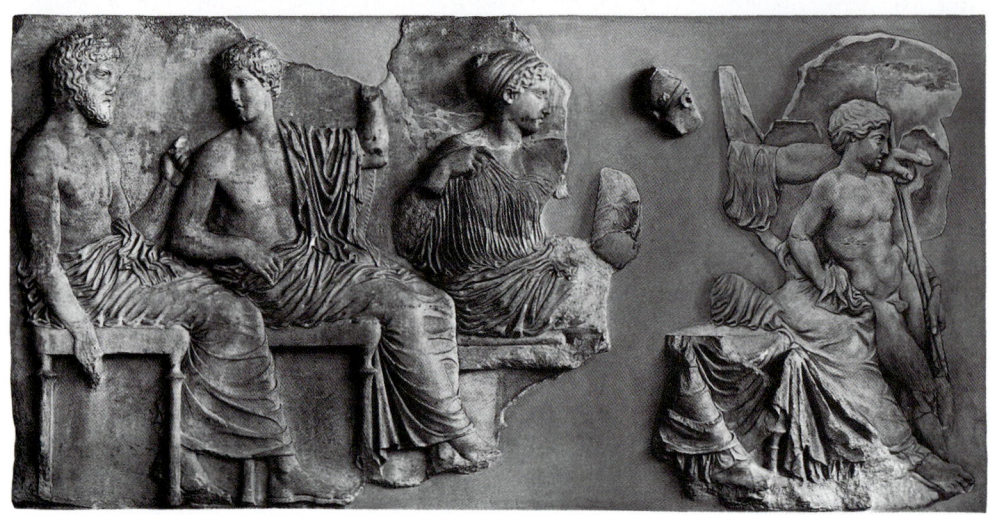

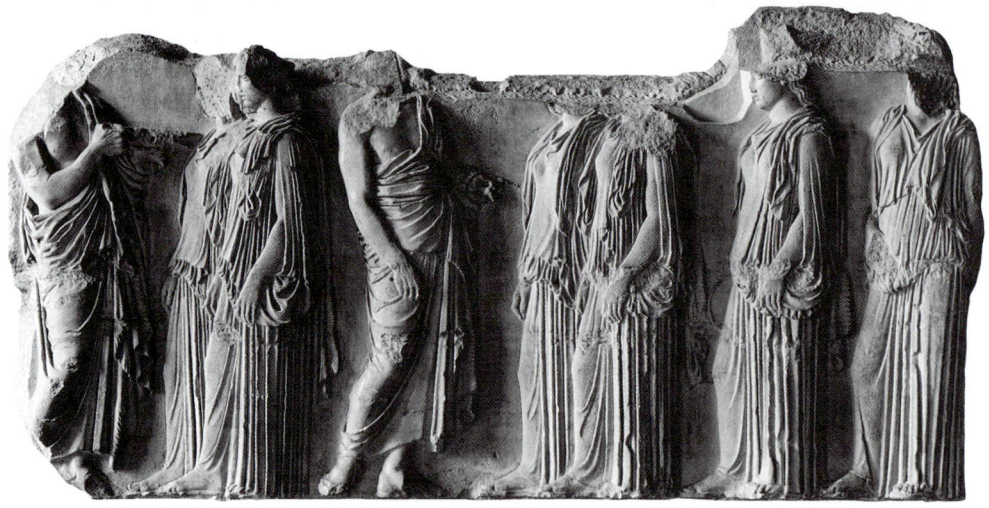

below the pediment's floor. Phidias, who designed the composition even if his assistants executed it, discovered an entirely new way to deal with the awkward triangular frame of the pediment. Its bottom line is the horizon line, and charioteers and their horses move through it effortlessly. The individual figures, even the animals, are brilliantly characterized. The horses of the Sun, at the beginning of the day, are energetic. Those of the Moon or Night, having labored until dawn, are weary.

The reclining figures fill the space beneath the raking cornice beautifully. Dionysos/Herakles and Aphrodite in the lap of her mother Dione are monumental Olympian presences yet totally relaxed organic forms. The sculptors fully under-

stood not only the surface appearance of human anatomy, both male and female, but also the mechanics of how muscles and bones beneath the flesh and garments make the body move. The Phidian school also mastered the rendition of clothed forms. In the Dione-Aphrodite group, the thin and heavy folds of the garments alternately reveal and conceal the main and lesser bodily masses while swirling in a compositional tide that subtly unifies the two figures. The articulation and integration of the bodies produce a wonderful variation of surface and play of light and shade. Not only are the bodies fluidly related to each other, but they are related to the draperies as well, although the latter, once painted, remain distinct from the bodily forms.

ATHENIANS ON ATHENA'S TEMPLE   In many ways the most remarkable part of the Parthenon's sculptural program is the inner Ionic frieze (FIG. **5-48**). Scholars still debate the frieze's subject, but most agree that what is represented is the Panathenaic Festival procession that took place every four years in Athens. If this identification is correct, the Athenians judged themselves fit for inclusion in the temple's sculptural decoration. It is another example of the extraordinarily high opinion the Athenians had of their own worth.

The procession began in the *agora* (marketplace) and ended on the Acropolis, where a new peplos was placed on an ancient wooden statue of Athena. That statue (probably similar in general appearance to the *Lady of Auxerre*, FIG. 5-7) was housed in the Archaic temple the Persians razed. The statue had been removed from the Acropolis before the Persian attack for security reasons, and eventually it was installed in the Erechtheion (FIG. 5-51, no. 1). On the Parthenon frieze the procession began on the west, that is, at the temple's rear, the side one first reached after emerging from the gateway to the Acropolis. It then proceeded in parallel lines down the long north and south sides of the building and ended at the center of the east frieze, over the doorway to the cella housing Phidias's statue. It is noteworthy that the upper part of the relief was higher than the lower part so that the more distant and more shaded upper zone was as legible from the ground as the lower part of the frieze. This was another instance of taking optical effects into consideration in the Parthenon's design.

The frieze vividly communicates the procession's acceleration and deceleration. At the outset, on the west side, marshals gather and youths mount their horses. On the north (FIG. 5-48, top) and south, the momentum picks up as the cavalcade moves from the lower town to the Acropolis, accompanied by chariots, musicians, jar carriers, and animals destined for sacrifice. On the east, seated gods and goddesses (FIG. 5-48, center), the invited guests, watch the procession slow almost to a halt (FIG. 5-48, bottom) as it nears its goal at the shrine of Athena's ancient wooden idol. Most remarkable of all is the role assigned to the Olympian deities. They do not take part in the festival or determine its outcome but are merely spectators. Aphrodite, in fact, extends her left arm to draw her son Eros's attention to the Athenians, just as today a parent at a parade would point out important people to a child. And the Athenian people *were* important—self-important one might say. They were the masters of an empire, and in Pericles' famous funeral oration he painted a picture of Athens that elevated its citizens almost to the stature of gods. The Parthenon celebrated the greatness of Athens and the Athenians as much as it honored Athena.

PROPYLAIA: GATEWAY TO THE ACROPOLIS   Even before all the sculpture was in place on the Parthenon, work began on a new monumental entrance to the Acropolis, the Propylaia (FIG. **5-49**). The architect entrusted with this important commission was MNESIKLES. The site was a difficult one, on a steep slope, but Mnesikles succeeded in disguising the change in ground level by splitting the building into eastern and western sections (FIG. 5-41), each one resembling a Doric temple facade. Practical considerations dictated that the space between the central pair of columns on each side be enlarged. This was the path the chariots and animals of the Panathenaic Festival procession took, and they required a wide ramped causeway. To either side of the central ramp were stairs for pedestrian traffic. Inside, tall, slender Ionic columns supported the split-level roof. Once again an Athenian architect mixed the two orders on the Acropolis. But as with the Parthenon, the Doric order was used for the stately exterior and the Ionic only for the interior. It would have been considered unseemly at this date to combine different kinds of columns on one facade. Later Greek architects were not as reticent (FIG. 5-77).

Mnesikles' full plan for the Propylaia was never executed because of a change in the fortunes of Athens after the outbreak of the Peloponnesian War in 431 B.C. Of the side wings that were part of the original project, only the northwest one was completed. That wing is of special importance in the history of art. In Roman times it housed a *pinakotheke* (picture

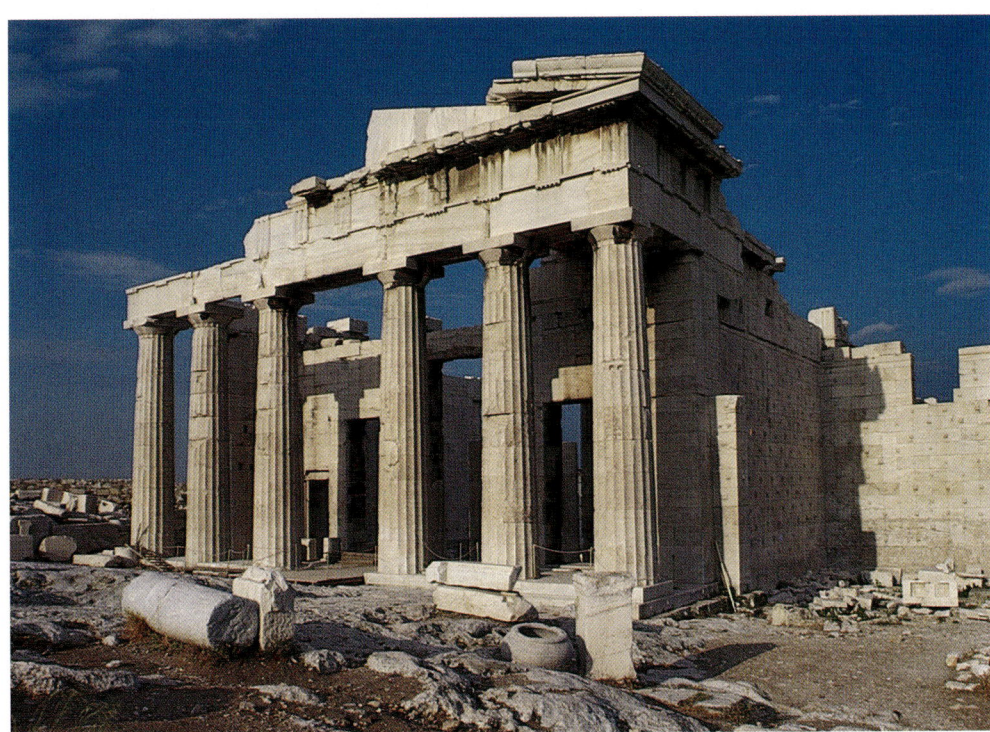

5-49 MNESIKLES, Propylaia (view from the northeast), Acropolis, Athens, Greece, 437–432 B.C.

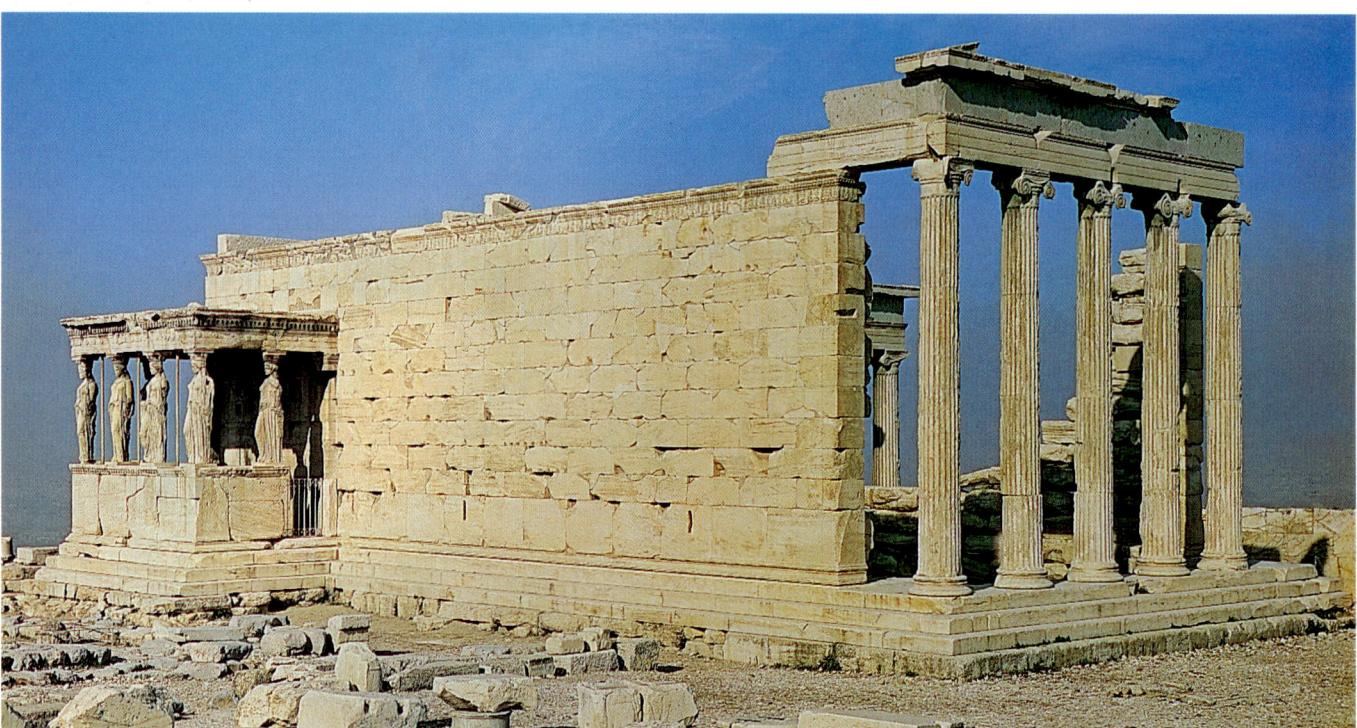

5-50   Erechtheion (view from the southeast), Acropolis, Athens, Greece, ca. 421–405 B.C.

gallery). In it were displayed paintings on wooden panels by some of the major artists of the fifth century B.C. It is uncertain whether or not this was the wing's original function. But if it was, the Propylaia's pinakotheke is the first recorded structure built for the specific purpose of displaying artworks and it is the forerunner of modern museums.

ERECHTHEION: SHRINE OF GODS AND KINGS

In 421 B.C. work finally began on the temple that was to replace the Archaic Athena temple the Persians had razed. The new structure, the Erechtheion (FIG. **5-50**), built to the north of the old temple's remains, was, however, to be a multiple shrine. It honored Athena and housed the ancient wooden image of the goddess that was the Panathenaic Festival procession's goal. But it also incorporated shrines to a host of other gods and demigods who loomed large in the city's legendary past. Among these were Erechtheus, an early king of Athens, during whose reign the ancient wooden idol of Athena was said to have fallen from the heavens, and Kekrops, another king of Athens, who served as judge of the contest between Athena and Poseidon. In fact, the site chosen for the new temple was the very spot where that contest occurred. Poseidon had staked his claim to Athens by striking the Acropolis rock with his trident and producing a salt-water spring. The imprint of his trident remained for Athenians of the historical period to see (FIG. **5-51**). Nearby, Athena had miraculously caused an olive tree to grow. This tree still stood as a constant reminder of her victory over Poseidon.

The asymmetrical plan of the Ionic Erechtheion is unique for a Greek temple and the antithesis of the simple and harmoniously balanced plan of the Doric Parthenon across the way. Its irregular form reflected the need to incorporate the tomb of Kekrops and other preexisting shrines, the trident mark, and the olive tree into a single complex. The unknown architect responsible for the building also had to struggle with the problem of uneven terrain. The area could not be made level by ter-

racing because that would disturb the ancient sacred sites. As a result, the Erechtheion not only has four sides of very different character, but each side also rests on a different ground level.

Perhaps to compensate for the awkward character of the building as a whole, great care was taken with the Erechtheion's decorative details. The frieze, for example, was given special treatment. The stone chosen was the dark-blue limestone of Eleusis to contrast with the white Pentelic marble of the walls and columns. White relief figures were attached to this dark ground; fragments are now in the Acropolis Museum. The effect was much like that of modern Neoclassical Wedgwood pottery, which, through Roman intermediaries, is ultimately based on the Erechtheion frieze.

1. Shrine housing wooden image of Athena
2. Athena's olive tree
3. Poseidon's trident mark
4. Ruins of Archaic temple

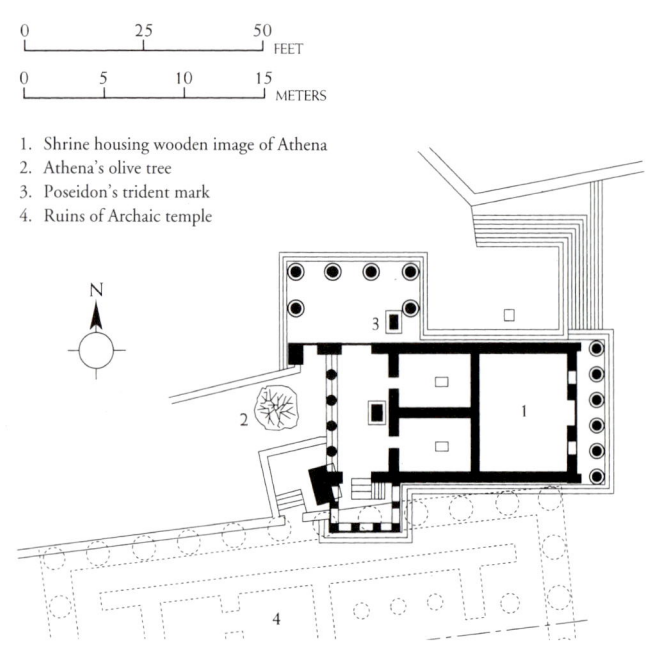

5-51   Plan of the Erechtheion, Acropolis, Athens, Greece, ca. 421–405 B.C.

5-52 Caryatid from the south porch of the Erechtheion, Acropolis, Athens, Greece, ca. 421–405 B.C. Marble, 7′ 7″ high. British Museum, London.

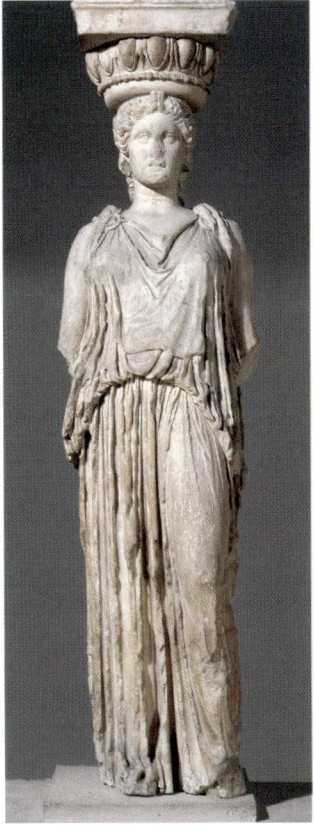

Other details of the Erechtheion's ornament were also much emulated, both in antiquity and in later times. But the temple's most striking and famous feature is its south porch, where caryatids (FIGS. 5-50 and 5-52) replaced Ionic columns, as they did a century earlier on the Ionic Siphnian Treasury at Delphi (FIG. 5-16). The Delphi caryatids resemble Archaic korai, and their Classical counterparts equally characteristically look like Phidian-era statues. Although they exhibit the weight shift that was standard for the fifth century, the role of the caryatids as architectural supports for the unusual flat roof is underscored by the vertical flutelike drapery folds concealing their stiff, weight-bearing legs. The Classical architect-sculptor successfully balanced the dual and contradictory

functions of these female statue-columns. The figures have enough rigidity to suggest the structural column and just the degree of flexibility needed to suggest the living body.

ATHENA, BRINGER OF VICTORY Another Ionic building on the Athenian Acropolis is the little Temple of Athena Nike (FIG. 5-53), designed by Kallikrates, who worked with Iktinos on the Parthenon (and perhaps was responsible for the Ionic elements of that Doric temple). The temple is amphiprostyle with four columns on both the east and west facades. It stands on what used to be a Mycenaean bastion near the Propylaia and greets all visitors entering Athena's great sanctuary. As on the Parthenon, reference was made here to the victory over the Persians—and not just in the temple's name. Part of its frieze is devoted to a representation of the decisive battle at Marathon that turned the tide against the Persians—a human event, as in the Parthenon's Panathenaic Festival procession frieze. But now a specific occasion was chronicled, not a recurring event anonymous citizens acted out.

Around the building, at the bastion's edge, a parapet was built about 410 B.C. and decorated with exquisite reliefs. The balustrade's theme matched that of the temple proper—Nike (Victory). Her image was repeated dozens of times, always in different attitudes, sometimes erecting trophies bedecked with Persian spoils and sometimes bringing forward sacrificial bulls to Athena. The most beautiful of the reliefs (FIG. 5-54) shows

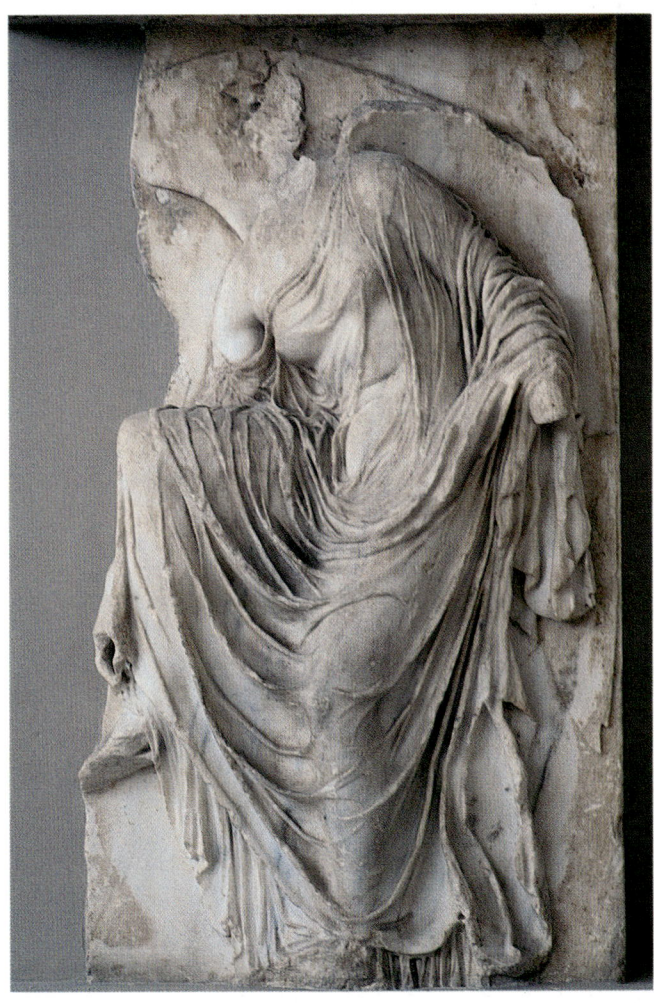

5-54 Nike adjusting her sandal, from the south side of the parapet of the Temple of Athena Nike, Acropolis, Athens, Greece, ca. 410 B.C. Marble, approx. 3′ 6″ high. Acropolis Museum, Athens.

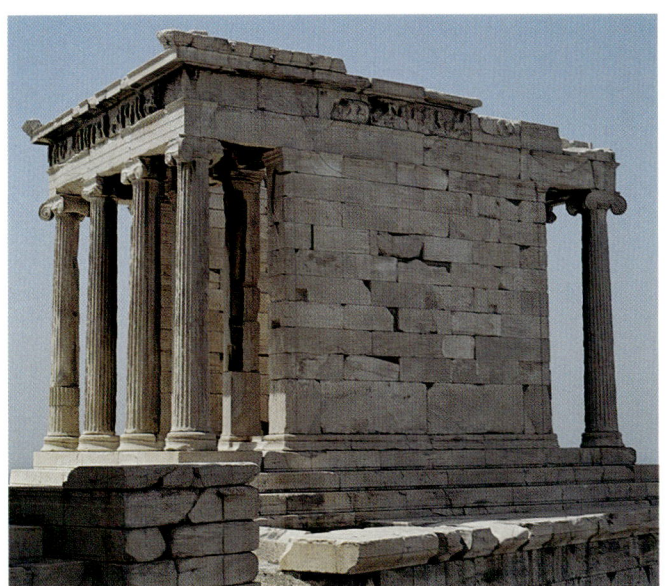

5-53 KALLIKRATES, Temple of Athena Nike (view from the northeast), Acropolis, Athens, Greece, ca. 427–424 B.C.

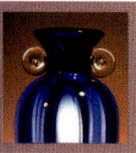

A Greek Woman in Her Father's Home
The Hegeso Stele

In Geometric times huge amphoras and kraters (FIG. 5-1) marked the graves of wealthy Athenians. In the Archaic period, kouroi (FIGS. 5-8 and 5-10) and, to a lesser extent, korai were placed over Greek burials, as were grave stelae ornamented with relief depictions of the deceased. The grave stele of Hegeso (FIG. 5-55) is in this tradition. It was erected at the end of the fifth or beginning of the fourth century B.C. to commemorate the death of Hegeso, daughter of Proxenos, whose names are inscribed on the cornice of the pediment that crowns the stele. Antae at left and right complete the architectural framework.

Hegeso is the well-dressed woman seated on an elegant chair (with footstool). She examines a piece of jewelry (once rendered in paint, not now visible) she has selected from a box a servant girl brings to her. The maid's simple ungirt chiton contrasts sharply with the more elaborate attire of her mistress. The garments of both women reveal the bodily forms beneath them. The faces are serene, without a trace of sadness. Indeed, both mistress and maid are shown in a characteristic shared moment out of daily life. Only the epitaph reveals that Hegeso is the one who has departed.

The simplicity of the scene on the Hegeso stele is, however, deceptive. This is not merely a bittersweet scene of tranquil domestic life before an untimely death. The setting itself is significant — the secluded women's quarters of a Greek house, from which Hegeso rarely would have emerged. Contemporary grave stelae of men regularly show them in the public domain, as warriors. And the servant girl is not so much the faithful companion of the deceased in life as she is Hegeso's possession, like the jewelry box. The slave girl may look solicitously at her mistress, but Hegeso has eyes only for her ornaments. Both slave and jewelry attest to the wealth of Hegeso's father, unseen but prominently cited in the epitaph. (It is noteworthy that the mother's name is not mentioned.) Indeed, even the jewelry box carries a deeper significance, for it probably represents the dowry Proxenos would have provided to his daughter's husband when she left her father's home to enter her husband's home. In ancient Greece's patriarchal society, the dominant position of men is manifest even when only women are depicted.

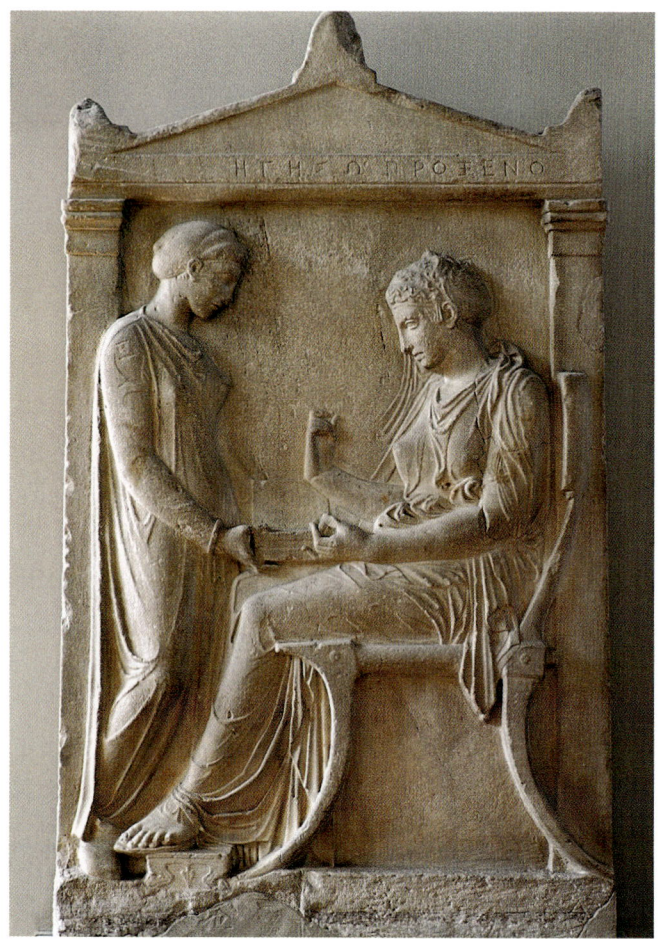

5-55　Grave stele of Hegeso, from the Dipylon cemetery, Athens, Greece, ca. 400 B.C. Marble, 5′ 2″ high. National Archeological Museum, Athens.

Nike adjusting her sandal — an awkward posture rendered elegant and graceful by an anonymous master sculptor. The artist carried the style of the Parthenon pediments (see FIG. 5-47) even further and created a figure whose garments cling so tightly to the body that they seem almost transparent, as if drenched with water. The sculptor was, however, interested in much more than revealing the supple beauty of the young female body. The drapery folds form intricate linear patterns unrelated to the body's anatomical structure and have a life of their own as abstract designs. Deep carving produced pockets of shade to contrast with the polished marble surface and enhance the design's ornamental beauty.

Although the decoration for the great building projects on the Acropolis must have occupied most of the finest sculptors of Athens in the second half of the fifth century B.C., other commissions were available in the city, notably in the Dipylon cemetery. There, around 400 B.C., a beautiful and touching grave stele (FIG. **5-55**) in the style of the Temple of Athena Nike parapet reliefs was set up in memory of a woman named Hegeso. Its subject — a young woman in her home, attended by her maid (see "A Greek Woman in Her Father's Home: The Hegeso Stele," above) — and its composition have close parallels in contemporary vase painting.

Painting

POLYCHROMY IN VASE PAINTING　Art historians know from ancient accounts that in the Classical period some of the most renowned artists were the painters of monumental wooden panels displayed in public buildings, both secular and religious. Such works are, by nature, perishable,

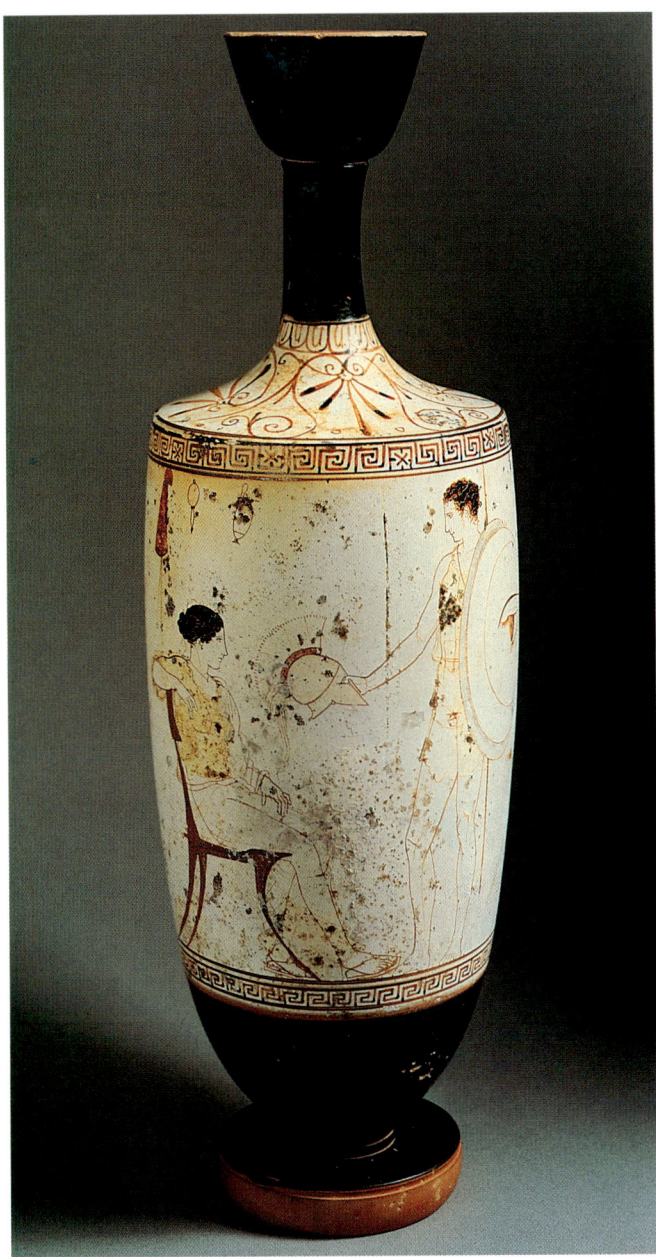

5-56 ACHILLES PAINTER, *Warrior taking leave of his wife* (Attic white-ground lekythos), from Eretria, Greece, ca. 440 B.C. Approx. 1′ 5″ high. National Archeological Museum, Athens.

and, unfortunately, all of the great panels of the masters are lost. Nonetheless, one can get some idea of the polychrome nature of those panel paintings by studying Greek vases such as the *lekythos* (flask containing perfumed oil) painted by the so-called ACHILLES PAINTER (FIG. **5-56**) about 440 B.C. The artist here employed the *white-ground* technique, which takes its name from the chalky-white slip used to provide a background for the painted figures. Experiments with white-ground painting date back to the Andokides Painter, but the method became popular only toward the middle of the fifth century B.C.

White-ground is essentially a variation of the red-figure technique. The pot was first covered with a slip of very fine white clay, then black glaze was applied to outline the figures, and diluted brown, purple, red, and white were used to color them. Other colors—for example, the yellow chosen for the garments of both figures on our lekythos—also could be employed, but these had to be applied after firing because the

Greeks did not know how to make them withstand the kiln's heat. Despite the white-ground technique's obvious attractions, the impermanence of the expanded range of colors discouraged its use for everyday vessels, such as drinking cups and kraters. In fact, the full polychrome possibilities of white-ground painting were explored almost exclusively on lekythoi, which were commonly placed in Greek graves as offerings to the deceased. For such vessels designed for short-term use, the white-ground technique's fragile nature was of little concern.

The Achilles Painter's lekythos is decorated with a scene appropriate for its funerary purpose. A youthful warrior takes leave of his wife. The red scarf, mirror, and jug hanging on the wall behind the woman indicate that the setting is the interior of their home. The motif of the seated woman is strikingly similar to that of Hegeso on her grave (FIG. 5-55), but here the woman is the survivor. It is her husband, preparing to go to war with helmet, shield, and spear, who will depart, never to return. On his shield is a huge painted eye, roughly life-size. Greek shields often were decorated with devices such as the horrific face of Medusa, intended to ward off evil spirits and frighten the enemy. This eye undoubtedly was meant to recall this venerable tradition, but it was little more than an excuse for the Achilles Painter to display superior drawing skills. Since the late sixth century B.C., Greek painters had abandoned the Archaic habit of placing frontal eyes on profile faces and attempted to render the eyes in profile. The Achilles Painter's mastery of this difficult problem in foreshortening is on exhibit here.

POLYGNOTOS'S REVOLUTIONARY PAINTINGS

The leading painter of the first half of the fifth century B.C. was POLYGNOTOS OF THASOS, whose works adorned important buildings both in Athens and Delphi. One of these was the pinakotheke of Mnesikles' Propylaia, but the most famous was a portico in the Athenian marketplace that came to be called the Stoa Poikile (Painted Stoa). Descriptions of Polygnotos's paintings make clear that he introduced a revolutionary compositional style, rejecting the scheme used on all the Greek vases examined thus far. Before Polygnotos, figures were situated on a common ground line at the bottom of the picture plane, whether they appeared in horizontal bands or single panels. Polygnotos placed his figures on different levels, staggered in tiers in the manner of Ashurbanipal's lion hunt relief (see FIG. 2-24) of two centuries before. He also incorporated landscape elements into his paintings, making his pictures true "windows onto the world" and not simply surface designs peopled with foreshortened figures. The abandonment of a single ground line by Polygnotos and his followers was as momentous a break from the past as was the rejection of frontality in statuary by Early Classical Greek sculptors.

THE MASSACRE OF NIOBE'S CHILDREN

One can visualize Polygnotos's compositions by looking at a red-figure krater (FIG. 5-57) painted around the middle of the fifth century B.C. by the NIOBID PAINTER. The painter, whose vases are unsigned, was given this modern nickname from this krater, where one side is devoted to the massacre of the Niobids, the children of Niobe, by Apollo and Artemis. Niobe, who had at least a dozen children, had boasted that she was

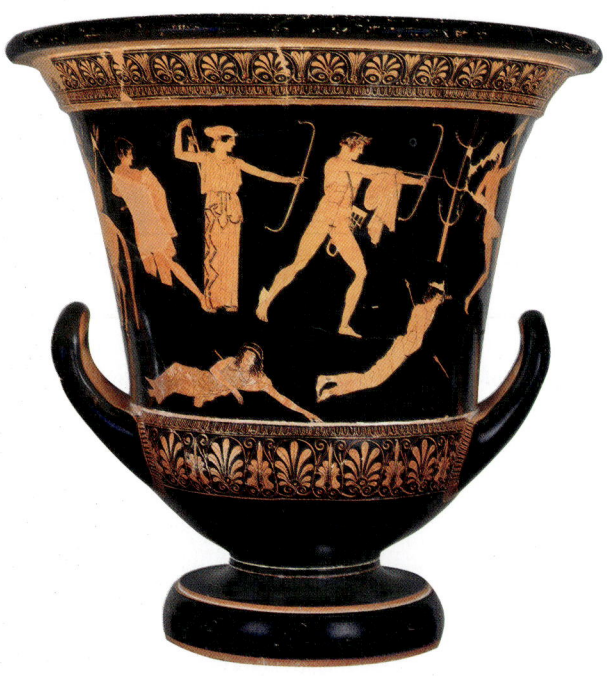

5-57   Niobid Painter, Artemis and Apollo slaying the children of Niobe (Attic red-figure calyx krater), from Orvieto, Italy, ca. 450 B.C. Approx. 1' 9" high. Louvre, Paris.

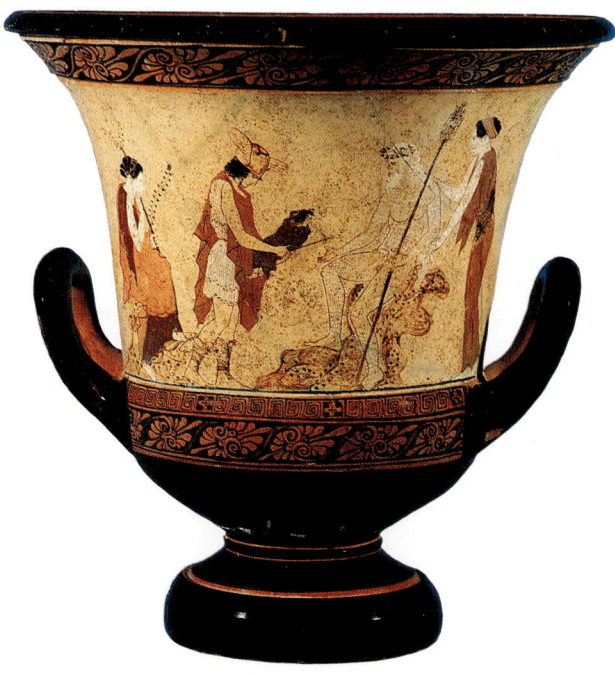

5-58   Phiale Painter, Hermes bringing the infant Dionysos to Papposilenos (Attic white-ground calyx krater), from Vulci, Italy, ca. 440–435 B.C. Approx. 1' 2" high. Vatican Museums, Rome.

superior to the goddess Leto, who had only two offspring, Apollo and Artemis. To punish her *hubris* (arrogance) and teach the lesson that no mortal could be superior to a god or goddess, Leto sent her two children to slay all of Niobe's many sons and daughters. On the Niobid Painter's krater, the horrible slaughter occurs in a schematic landscape setting of rocks and trees. The figures are disposed on several levels, and they actively interact with their setting. One slain son, for example, not only has fallen upon a rocky outcropping, but he also is partially hidden by it. His face was drawn in a three-quarter view, something that even Euphronios and Euthymides had not attempted.

WHITE-GROUND LANDSCAPE PAINTING Further insight into the appearance of monumental panel painting of the fifth century B.C. comes from a white-ground krater (FIG. 5-58) by the so-called PHIALE PAINTER. The subject is Hermes handing over his half brother, the infant Dionysos, to Papposilenos ("grandpa-satyr"). The other figures represent the nymphs in the shady glens of Nysa, where Zeus had sent Dionysos, one of his numerous natural sons, to be raised, safe from the possible wrath of his wife Hera. Unlike the decorators of funerary lekythoi, the Phiale Painter used for this krater only colors that could survive the Greek kiln's heat— reds, brown, purple, and a special snowy white reserved for

5-59   Youth diving, painted ceiling of the Tomb of the Diver, Paestum, Italy, ca. 480 B.C. Approx. 3' 4" high. Museo Archeologico Nazionale, Paestum.

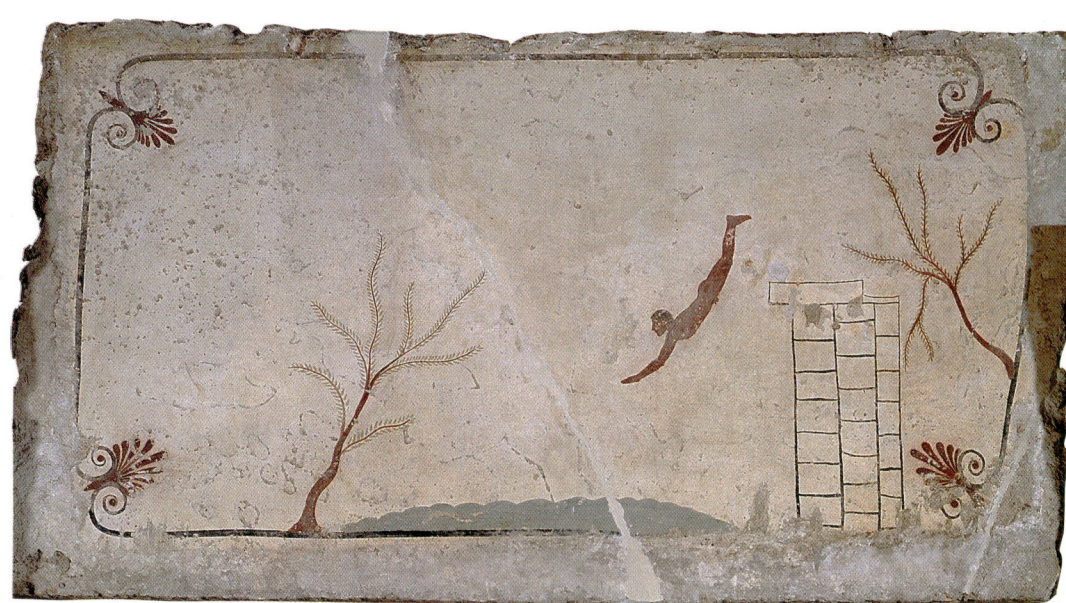

the flesh of the nymphs and for such details as the hair, beard, and shaggy body of Papposilenos. The use of diluted brown wash to color and shade the rocks may reflect the coloration of Polygnotos's landscapes. This vase and the Niobid krater together provide art historians with a shadowy idea of the character and magnificence of Polygnotos's great paintings.

A PLUNGE INTO THE NETHERWORLD Although all of the panel paintings of the masters were lost long ago, some Greek mural paintings are preserved today. A fine early example is in the so-called Tomb of the Diver at Paestum in southern Italy. The four walls of this small, coffinlike tomb are decorated with banquet scenes such as appear regularly on Greek vases. On the tomb's ceiling (FIG. **5-59**), a youth dives from a stone platform into a body of water. The scene most likely symbolizes the plunge from this life into the next. Trees resembling those of the Niobid krater are included within the decorative frame. The theme has no parallels on extant Greek vases, but it appears on an Etruscan tomb wall of the late sixth century B.C. (see FIG. 9-9). The Greek painter of the Tomb of the Diver seems to have been as aware of developments in Etruscan painting in Italy as of the work of contemporaries in mainland Greece.

THE LATE CLASSICAL PERIOD (FOURTH CENTURY B.C.)

POLITICAL UPHEAVAL AND ARTISTIC CHANGE The Peloponnesian War, which began in 431 B.C., ended in 404 B.C. with the complete defeat of a plague-weakened Athens and left Greece drained of its strength. The victor, Sparta, and then Thebes undertook the leadership of Greece, both unsuccessfully. In the middle of the fourth century B.C., a threat from without caused the rival Greek states to put aside their animosities and unite for their common defense, as they had earlier against the Persians. But at the battle of Chaeronea in 338 B.C., the Greek cities suffered a devastating loss and had to relinquish their independence to Philip II, king of Macedon. Philip was assassinated in 336 B.C. and his son, Alexander III, better known simply as Alexander the Great, succeeded him. In the decade before his death in 323 B.C., Alexander led a powerful army on an extraordinary campaign that overthrew the Persian Empire (the ultimate revenge for the Persian invasion of Greece in the early fifth century B.C.), wrested control of Egypt, and even reached India.

The fourth century B.C. was thus a time of political upheaval in Greece, and the chaos had a profound impact on the psyche of the Greeks and on the art they produced. In the fifth century B.C., Greeks had generally believed that rational human beings could impose order on their environment, create "perfect" statues such as the *Canon* of Polykleitos, and discover the "correct" mathematical formulas for constructing temples such as the Parthenon. The Parthenon frieze celebrated the Athenians as a community of citizens with shared values. The Peloponnesian War and the fourth century B.C.'s unceasing strife brought an end to the fifth century B.C.'s serene idealism. Disillusionment and alienation followed. Greek thought and Greek art began to focus more on the individual and on the real world of appearances rather than on the community and the ideal world of perfect beings and perfect buildings.

Sculpture

THE HUMANIZATION OF GREEK SCULPTURE The new humanizing approach to art is immediately apparent in the work of PRAXITELES, one of the great masters of the fourth century B.C. Praxiteles did not reject the themes the sculptors of the High Classical period favored. His Olympian gods and goddesses retained their superhuman beauty, but in his hands they lost some of their solemn grandeur and took on a worldly sensuousness.

Nowhere is this new spirit plainer than in the statue of Aphrodite that Praxiteles made for the Knidians (FIG. **5-60**).

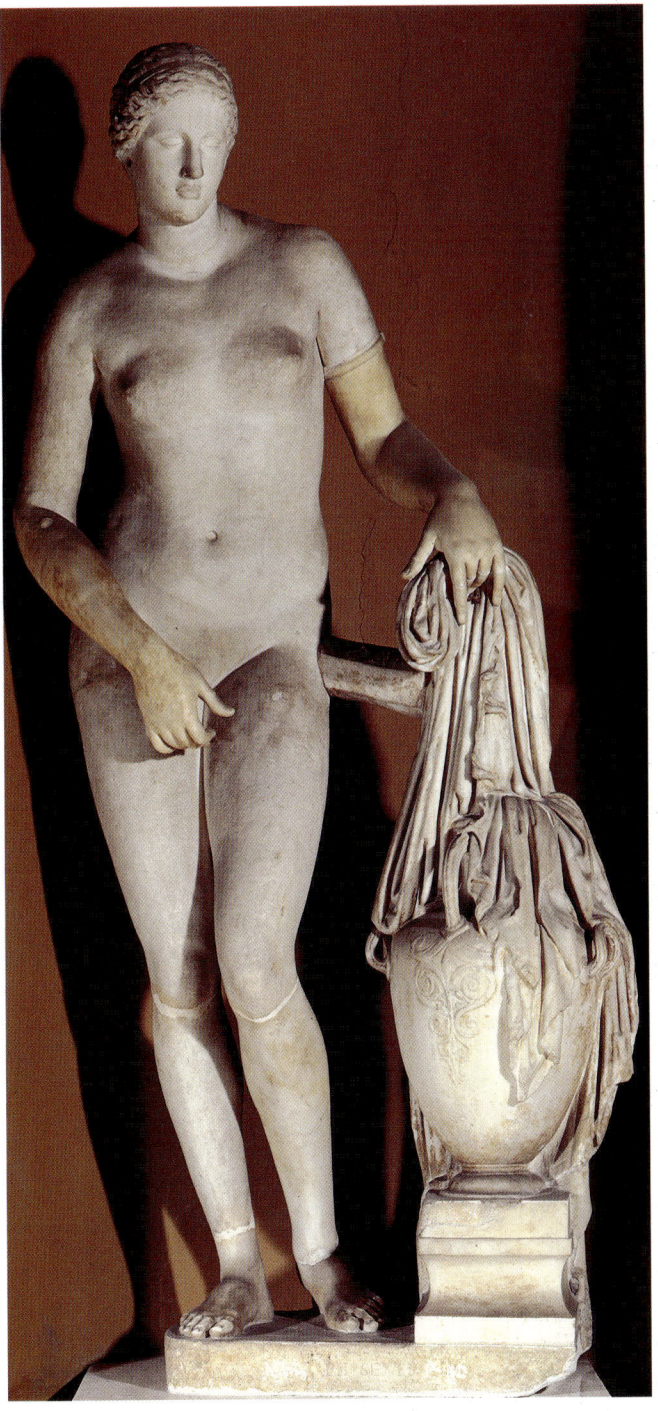

5-60 PRAXITELES, *Aphrodite of Knidos*. Roman marble copy after an original of ca. 350–340 B.C. Approx. 6′ 8″ high. Vatican Museums, Rome.

The lost original, carved from Parian marble, is known only through copies made for the Romans, but Pliny considered it "superior to all the works, not only of Praxiteles, but indeed in the whole world." It made Knidos famous, and many people sailed there just to see the statue in its round temple (compare FIG. 5-71), where "it was possible to view the image of the goddess from every side." According to Pliny, some visitors were "overcome with love for the statue."[6]

The *Aphrodite of Knidos* caused such a sensation in its time because Praxiteles took the unprecedented step of representing the goddess of love completely nude. Female nudity was exceedingly rare in earlier Greek art and had been confined almost exclusively to paintings on vases designed for household use, such as the kylix of Onesimos (FIG. 5-23) discussed earlier. The women so depicted also tended to be courtesans or slave girls, not noblewomen or goddesses, and no one had dared fashion for a temple a statue of a goddess without her clothes. Moreover, Praxiteles' Aphrodite is not a cold and remote image. In fact, the goddess engages in a trivial act out of everyday life. She has removed her garment, draped it over a large *hydria* (water pitcher), and is about to step into the bath. The motif is strikingly similar to that Onesimos painted.

DEWY EYES AND SENSUOUS LANGUOR Although shocking in its day, the *Aphrodite of Knidos* is not openly erotic (the goddess modestly shields her pelvis with her right hand), but she is quite sensuous. Lucian, writing in the second century A.D., noted that she has a "welcoming look" and a "slight smile" and that Praxiteles was renowned for his ability to transform marble into soft and radiant flesh. Lucian mentions, for example, the "dewy quality of Aphrodite's eyes."[7] Unfortunately, the rather mechanical Roman copies do not capture the quality of Praxiteles' modeling of the stone, but one can imagine the "look" of the *Aphrodite of Knidos* from original works by sculptors who emulated the master's manner.

One of the finest of these is the head of a woman from Chios (FIG. **5-61**) that was once set into a draped statue. This sculptor wielded the chisel in the Praxitelean manner, suggesting the softness of the young girl's face and the "dewy" gaze of the eyes. The sharp outlining of precisely measured bodily parts that characterized the work of Polykleitos and his contemporaries has given way to a smooth flow of flesh from forehead to chin and to a very human sensuousness. In the statues of Praxiteles and his followers, the deities of Mount Olympus still possess a beauty mortals can aspire to, although not achieve, but they are no longer awesome and remote. The Greek gods stepped off their fifth-century B.C. pedestals and entered the fourth-century B.C. world of human experience.

The Praxitelean manner also may be seen in a statue once thought to be by the hand of the master himself but now generally considered a copy of the very highest quality. The statue of Hermes and the infant Dionysos (FIG. **5-62**) found in the Temple of Hera at Olympia brings to the realm of monumental statuary the theme the Phiale Painter had chosen for a white-ground krater (FIG. 5-58) a century earlier. Hermes has stopped to rest in a forest on his journey to Nysa to entrust the upbringing of Dionysos to Papposilenos and the nymphs. Hermes leans on a tree trunk (here it is an integral part of the

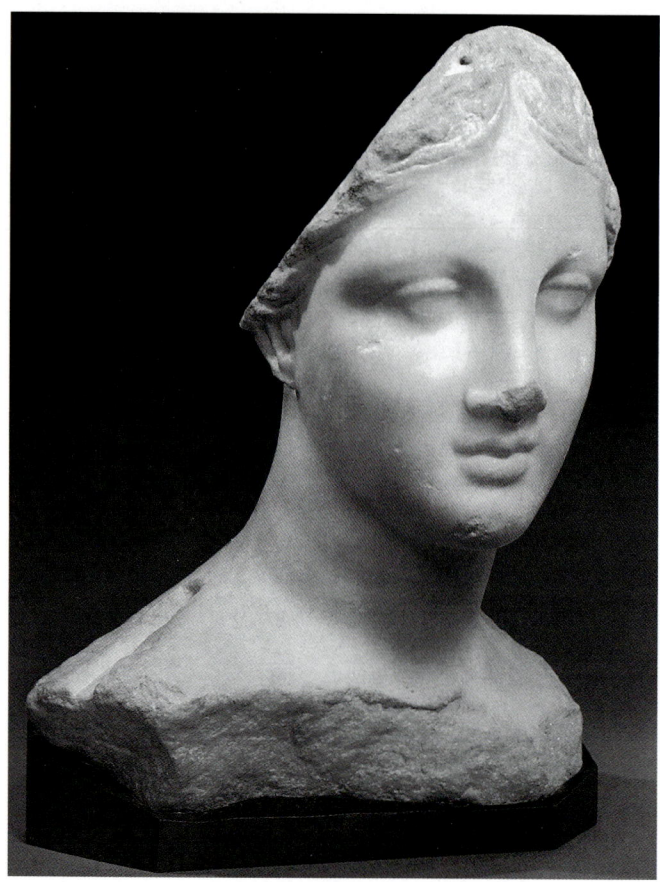

5-61 Head of a woman, from Chios, Greece, ca. 320–300 B.C. Marble, approx. 1′ 2″ high. Museum of Fine Arts, Boston.

composition and not the copyist's addition), and his slender body forms a sinuous, shallow S-curve that is the hallmark of many of Praxiteles' statues. He looks off dreamily into space while he dangles a bunch of grapes (now missing) as a temptation for the infant who is to become the Greek god of the vine. This is the kind of tender and very human interaction between an adult and a child that one encounters frequently in real life but that had been absent from Greek statuary before the fourth century B.C.

The superb quality of the carving is faithful to the Praxitelean original. The modeling is deliberately smooth and subtle, producing soft shadows that follow the planes as they flow almost imperceptibly one into another. The delicacy of the marble head's features stand in sharp contrast to the metallic precision of Polykleitos's bronze *Doryphoros* (FIG. 5-38). Even the *Spear Bearer's* locks of hair were subjected to the fifth-century B.C. sculptor's laws of symmetry and do not violate the skull's perfect curve. One need only compare these two statues to see how broad a change in artistic attitude and intent took place from the mid-fifth to the mid-fourth century B.C. Sensuous languor and an order of beauty that appeals more to the eye than to the mind replaced majestic strength and rationalizing design.

THE PASSIONATE STYLE OF SKOPAS In the Archaic period and throughout most of the Early and High Classical periods, Greek sculptors generally shared common

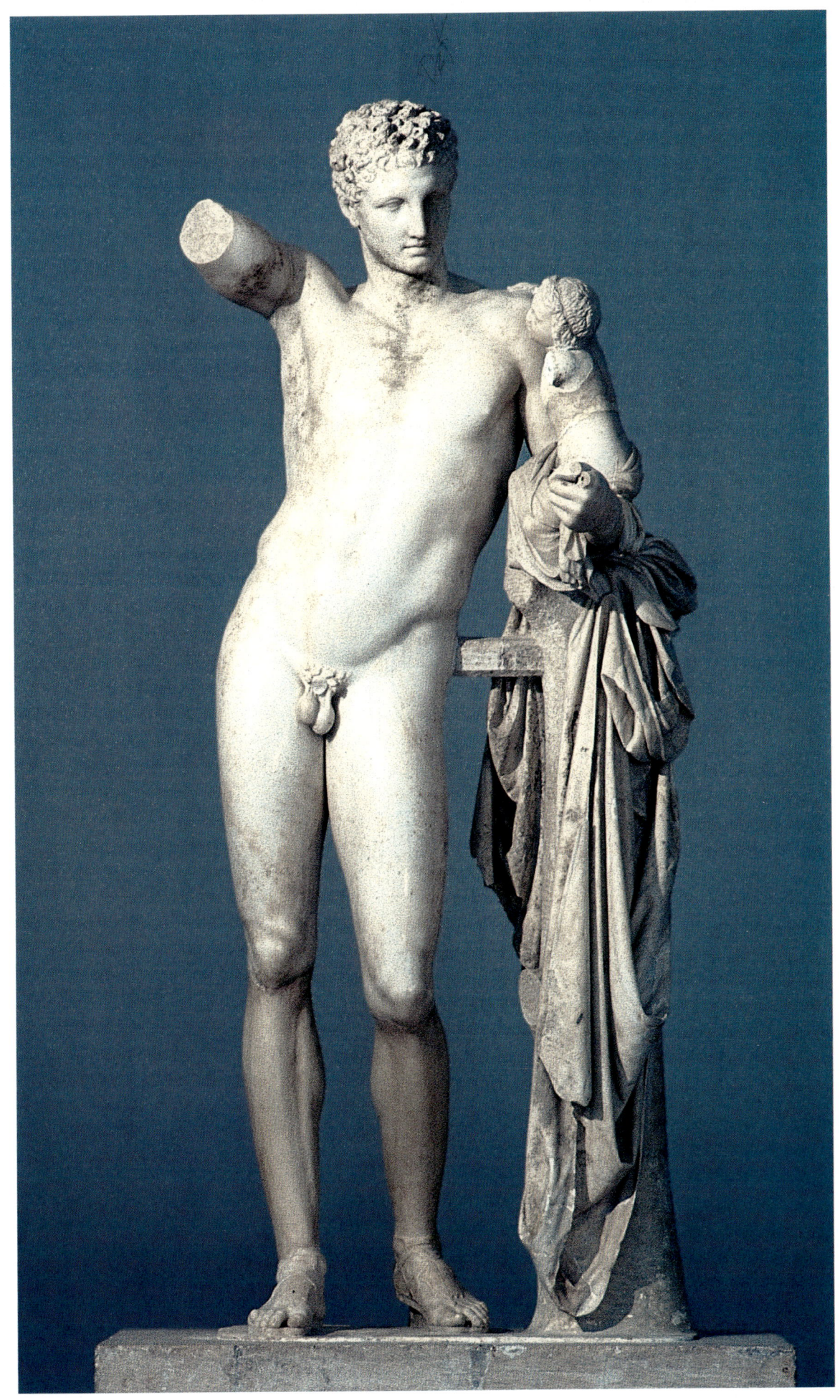

5-62 PRAXITELES, Hermes and the infant Dionysos, from the Temple of Hera, Olympia, Greece. Marble copy after an original of ca. 340 B.C., approx. 7′ 1″ high. Archeological Museum, Olympia.

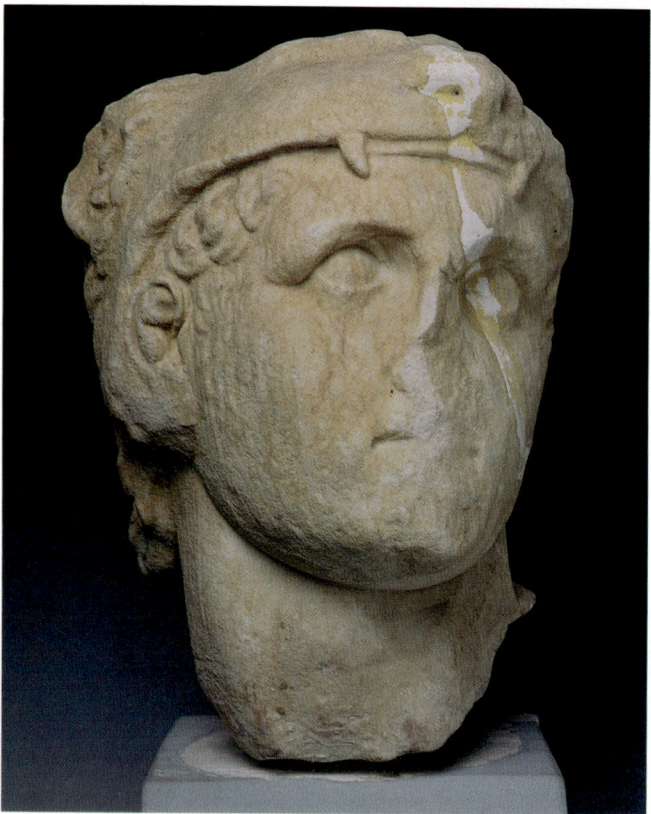

5-63 Head of Herakles or Telephos, from the west pediment of the Temple of Athena Alea, Tegea, Greece, ca. 340 B.C. Marble, approx. 1′ ½″ high. (Stolen from) Archeological Museum, Tegea.

goals, but in the Late Classical period of the fourth century B.C., distinctive individual styles emerged. The dreamy, beautiful divinities of Praxiteles had enormous appeal, and, as the head of the woman from Chios (FIG. 5-61) attests, the master had many followers. But other master sculptors pursued very different interests. One of these was SKOPAS OF PAROS, and although his work reflects the general trend toward the humanization of the Greek gods and heroes, his style is marked by intense emotionalism.

Skopas was an architect as well as a sculptor. He designed the Temple of Athena Alea at Tegea. Fragments of the pedimental statues from that temple are preserved, and they epitomize his approach to sculpture, even if they are not by his own hand. One of the heads (FIG. 5-63) portrays a hero wearing a lion-skin headdress. It must be either Herakles or his son Telephos, whose battle with Achilles was the west pediment's subject. The head, like others from the Tegea pediments, is highly dramatic. The hero's head takes an abrupt turn, and his facial expression shows great psychological tension. His large eyes are set deeply into his head. Fleshy overhanging brows create deep shadows. His lips are slightly parted. The passionate face reveals an anguished soul within. Skopas's work broke with the Classical tradition of benign, serene features and prefigured later Hellenistic depictions of unbridled emotion.

An unprecedented psychological intensity also may be seen in a grave stele (FIG. 5-64) found near the Ilissos River in Athens that incorporates the innovations of Skopas. The stele was originally set into an architectural frame similar to that of the earlier Hegeso stele (FIG. 5-55). A comparison between

the two works is very telling. In the Ilissos stele the relief is much higher, with parts of the figures carved fully in the round. But the major difference is the pronounced change in mood. The later work makes a clear distinction between the living and the dead, and depicts overt mourning. The deceased is a young hunter whose features recall those of Skopas's Tegean heroes. At his feet a small boy, either his servant or perhaps a younger brother, sobs openly. The hunter's dog also droops its head in sorrow. Beside the youth an old man, undoubtedly his father, leans on a walking stick and, in a gesture reminiscent of that of the seer at Olympia (FIG. 5-31), ponders the irony of fate that has taken the life of his powerful son and preserved him in his frail old age. Most remarkable of all, the hunter himself looks out at the viewer, inviting sympathy, and creating an emotional bridge between the spectator and the artwork that is inconceivable in the art of the High Classical period.

THE ATHLETES AND HEROES OF LYSIPPOS

The third great Late Classical sculptor, LYSIPPOS OF SIKYON, was so renowned he was selected by Alexander the Great to create his official portrait. (Alexander could afford to employ the best. The Macedonian kingdom enjoyed vast wealth. King Philip hired the leading thinker of his age, Aristotle, as the young Alexander's tutor!)

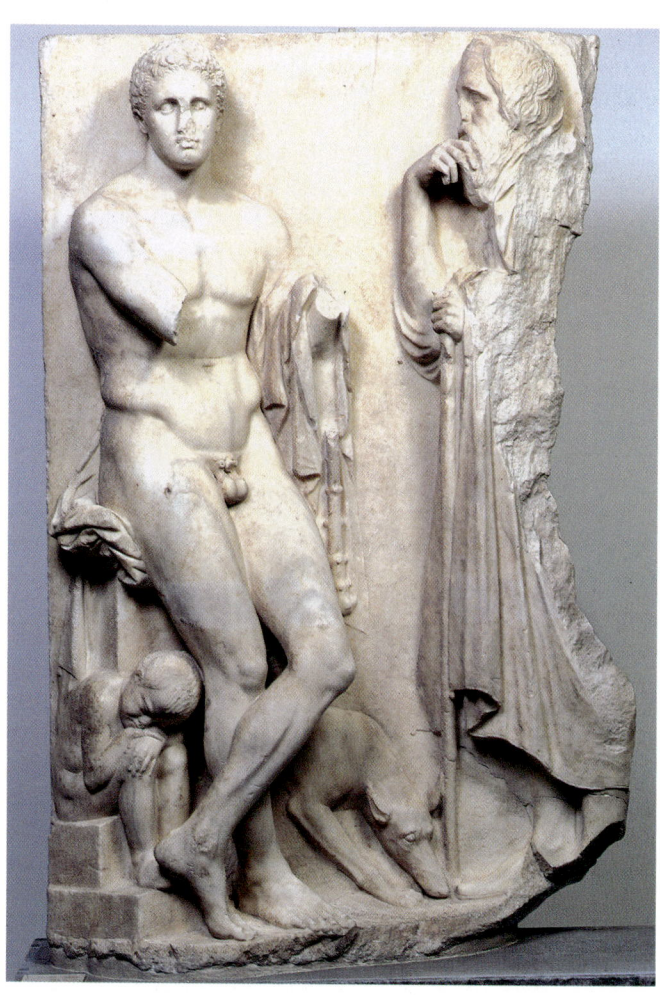

5-64 Grave stele of a young hunter, found near the Ilissos River, Athens, Greece, ca. 340–330 B.C. Marble, approx. 5′ 6″ high. National Archeological Museum, Athens.

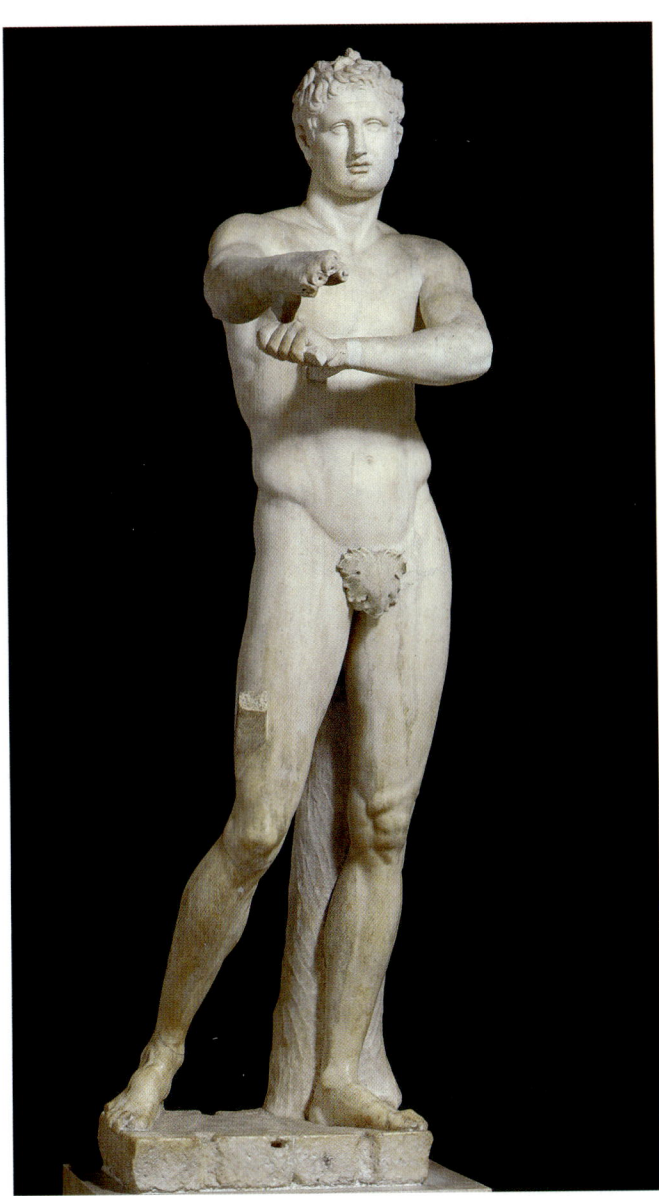

5-65 LYSIPPOS, *Apoxyomenos (Scraper)*. Roman marble copy after a bronze original of ca. 330 B.C., approx. 6′ 9″ high. Vatican Museums, Rome.

Lysippos introduced a new canon of proportions making the bodies more slender than those of Polykleitos—whose own canon continued to exert enormous influence—and the heads roughly one-eighth the height of the body rather than one-seventh, as in the previous century. The new proportions may be seen in one of Lysippos's most famous works, a bronze statue of an *Apoxyomenos* (an athlete scraping oil from his body after exercising), known, as usual, only from Roman copies in marble (FIG. **5-65**). A comparison with Polykleitos's *Doryphoros* (FIG. 5-38) reveals more than a change in physique. A nervous energy runs through the *Apoxyomenos* that one seeks in vain in the balanced form of the *Doryphoros*. The *strigil* (scraper) is about to reach the end of the right arm, and at any moment it will be switched to the other hand so that the left arm can be scraped. The weight will shift at the same time and the positions of the legs will be reversed. Lysippos also began to break down the dominance of the frontal view in statuary and encouraged the observer to look at his athlete from multiple angles. The *Apoxyomenos* breaks out of the shallow rectangular box that defined the boundaries of

earlier statues by boldly thrusting his right arm forward. To comprehend the action, the observer must move to the side and view the work at a three-quarter angle or in full profile.

To grasp the full meaning of another of Lysippos's works, a colossal statue depicting a weary Herakles (FIG. **5-66**), the viewer must walk around it. Once again, the original is lost. The most impressive of the surviving marble copies is nearly twice life-size and was exhibited in the Baths of the emperor Caracalla in Rome (see FIGS. 10-67 and 10-68). Like the marble copy of Polykleitos's *Doryphoros* from the Roman palestra at Pompeii (FIG. 5-38), Lysippos's muscle-bound Greek hero provided inspiration for Romans who came to the baths to exercise. (The statue is signed by the copyist, GLYKON OF ATHENS. Lysippos's name is not mentioned. The educated Roman public did not need a label to identify the famous work.) In the hands of Lysippos, however, the exaggerated muscular development of Herakles is poignantly ironic, for the sculptor depicted the strongman as so weary that he must lean on his club for support. Without that prop Herakles would topple

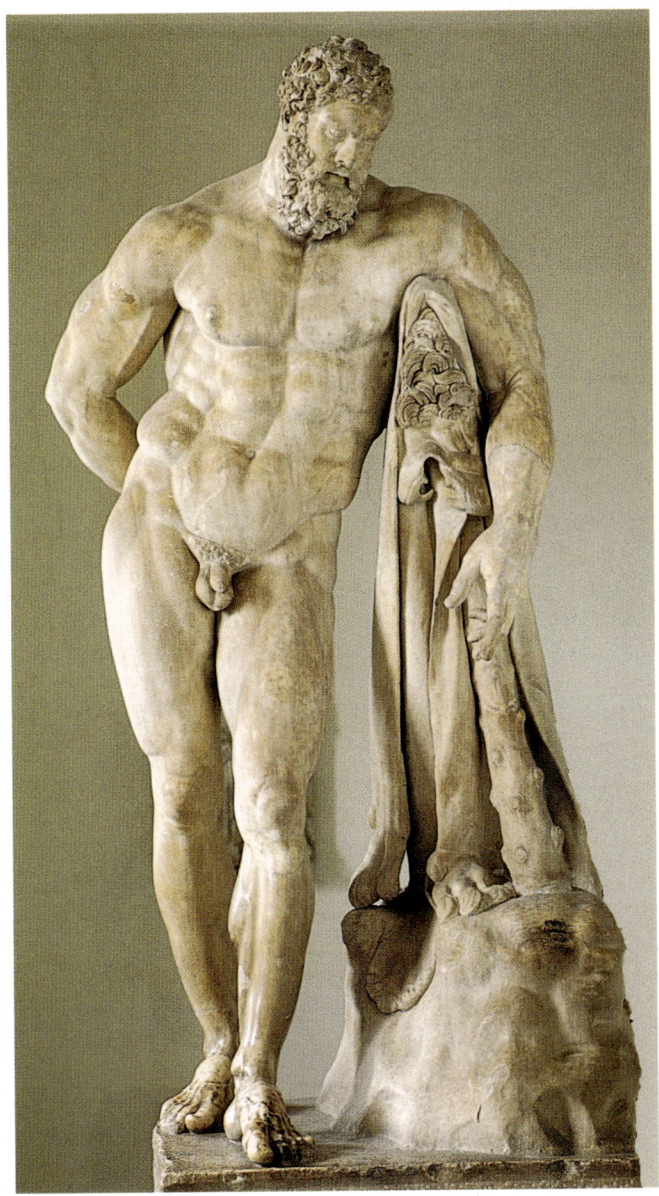

5-66 LYSIPPOS, Weary Herakles *(Farnese Herakles)*. Roman marble copy from Rome, Italy, signed by GLYKON OF ATHENS, after a bronze original of ca. 320 B.C. Approx. 10′ 5″ high. Museo Nazionale, Naples.

over. Lysippos and other fourth-century B.C. artists rejected stability and balance as worthy goals for statuary. Herakles holds the golden apples of the Hesperides in his right hand behind his back—unseen unless one walks around the statue. Lysippos's subject is thus the same as that of the metope of the Early Classical Temple of Zeus at Olympia (FIG. 5-32), but the fourth-century B.C. Herakles is no longer serene. Instead of expressing joy, or at least satisfaction, at having completed one of the impossible twelve labors (see "Herakles: Greatest of Greek Heroes," page 103), he is almost dejected. Exhausted by his physical efforts, he can think only of his pain and weariness, not of the reward of immortality that awaits him. Lysippos's portrayal of Herakles in this statue is perhaps the most eloquent testimony yet to Late Classical sculptors' interest in humanizing the great gods and heroes of the Greeks. In this respect, despite their divergent styles, Praxiteles, Skopas, and Lysippos followed a common path.

Alexander the Great and Macedonian Court Art

ALEXANDER AS EPIC HERO Alexander the Great's favorite book was the *Iliad,* and his own life was very much like an epic saga, full of heroic battles, exotic places, and unceasing drama. Alexander was a man of singular character, an inspired leader with boundless energy and an almost fool-

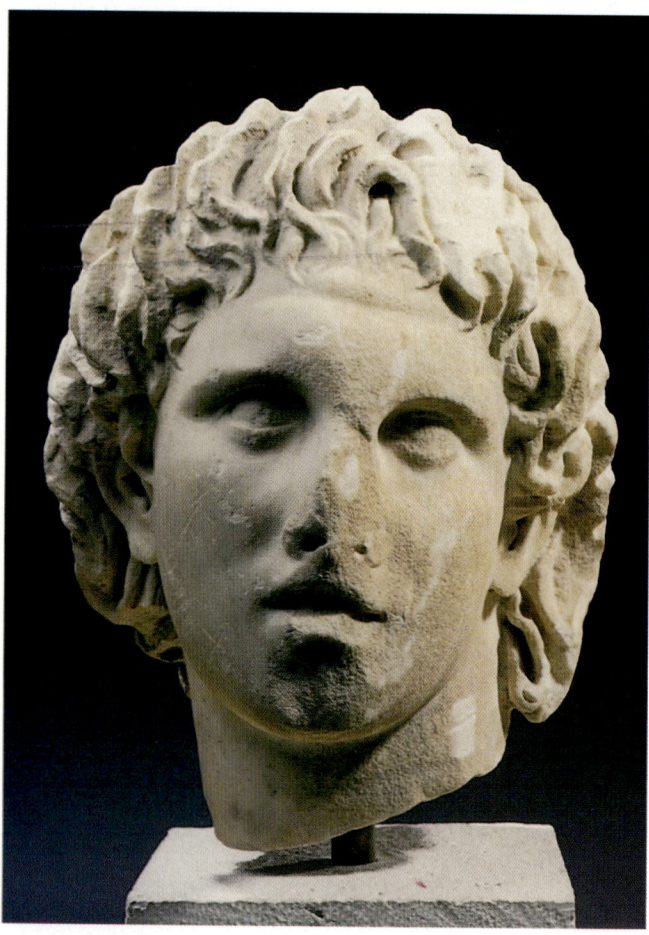

5-67 Head of Alexander the Great, from Pella, Greece, ca. 200–150 B.C. Marble, approx. 1′ high. Archeological Museum, Pella.

hardy courage. He regularly personally led his army into battle on the back of Bucephalus, the wild and mighty steed only he could tame and ride.

Ancient sources reveal that Alexander believed that only Lysippos had captured his essence in a portrait, and that is why only he was authorized to sculpt the king's image. Lysippos's most famous portrait of the Macedonian king was a full-length heroically nude bronze statue of Alexander holding a lance and turning his head toward the sky. Plutarch reported that on the base was inscribed an epigram stating the statue depicted Alexander gazing at Zeus and proclaiming, "I place the earth under my sway; you, O Zeus, keep Olympus." Plutarch further stated that the portrait was characterized by "leonine" hair and a "melting glance."[8]

The Lysippan original is lost, and because Alexander was portrayed so many times for centuries after his death, it is very difficult to determine which of the many surviving images is most faithful to the fourth-century B.C. portrait. A leading candidate is a second-century B.C. marble head (FIG. 5-67) from Pella, the capital of Macedonia and Alexander's birthplace. It has the sharp turn of the head and thick mane of hair that were key ingredients of Lysippos's portrait. The sculptor's treatment of the features also is consistent with the style of the later fourth century B.C. The deep-set eyes and parted lips recall the manner of Skopas, and the delicate handling of the flesh brings to mind the faces of Praxitelean statues. Although not a copy, this head very likely approximates the young king's official portrait and provides insight not only into Alexander's personality but also into the art of Lysippos.

OPULENCE AT THE MACEDONIAN COURT Alexander's palace has not been excavated, but one can form an idea of the sumptuousness of life at the Macedonian court from the costly objects found in Macedonian graves and from the abundance of mosaics (see "Mosaics," Chapter 11, page 314) uncovered at Pella in the homes of the wealthy. The Pella mosaics are *pebble mosaics.* The floors are formed of small stones of various colors collected from beaches and riverbanks and set into a thick coat of cement. The finest yet to come to light (FIG. 5-68) has a stag hunt as its *emblema* (central framed panel), bordered in turn by an intricate floral pattern and a stylized wave motif (not shown in our detail). The artist signed his work in the same manner as proud Greek vase painters and potters did "GNOSIS made it." This is the earliest mosaicist's signature known, and its prominence in the design undoubtedly attests to the artist's reputation. The house owner wanted guests to know that Gnosis himself, and not an imitator, had laid this floor.

Gnosis's stag hunt, with its light figures against a dark ground, has much in common with red-figure painting. In the pebble mosaic, however, most of the contour lines and some of the interior details are defined by thin strips of lead or terracotta, while the interior volumes are suggested by subtle gradations of yellow, brown, and red, as well as black, white, and gray pebbles. The musculature of the hunters, and even their billowing cloaks and the animals' bodies, are modeled by shading. Such use of light and dark to suggest volume is rarely seen on Greek painted vases, although examples do exist. Monumental painters, however, commonly used shading. The Greek term for shading was *skiagraphia* (literally,

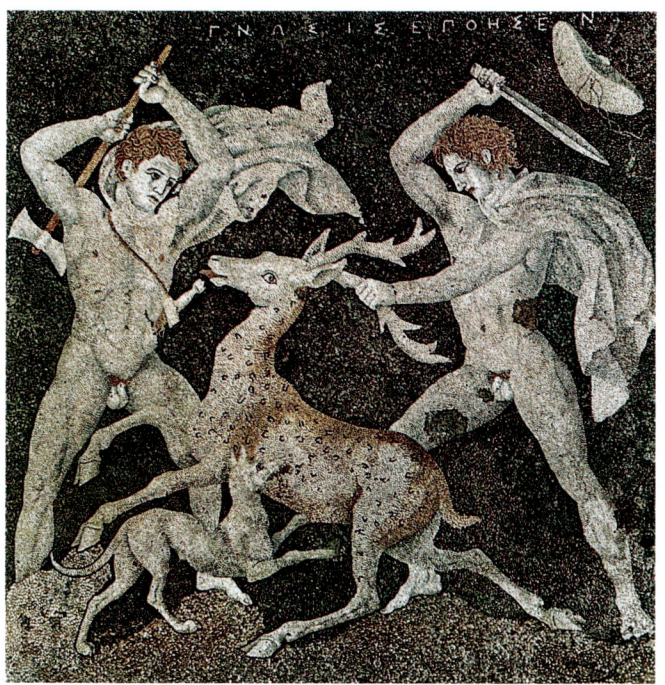

5-68 GNOSIS, Stag hunt, from Pella, Greece, ca. 300 B.C. Pebble mosaic, figural panel 10′ 2″ high. Archeological Museum, Pella.

shadow painting), and it was said to have been invented by an Athenian painter of the fifth century B.C. named APOLLO-DOROS. Gnosis's emblema, with its sparse landscape setting, probably reflects contemporary panel painting.

THE PERSIAN KING FLEES FROM ALEXANDER

An even better idea of monumental painting during Alexander's time may be gleaned from a mosaic that decorated the floor of one room of a lavishly appointed Roman house at Pompeii. In the *Alexander Mosaic* (FIG. **5-69**), *tesserae* (tiny stones or pieces of glass cut to the desired size and shape) were employed instead of pebbles (see "Mosaics," Chapter 11, page 314). The subject is a great battle between Alexander the Great and the Persian king Darius III, probably the battle of Issus in southeastern Turkey, when Darius fled the battlefield in his chariot in humiliating defeat. The mosaic dates to the late second or early first century B.C. It is widely believed to be a reasonably faithful copy of a famous panel painting of ca. 310 B.C. that PHILOXENOS OF ERETRIA made for King Cassander, one of Alexander's successors.

Philoxenos's painting is notable for its technical mastery of problems that had long fascinated Greek painters. The rearing horse in front of Darius's chariot, for example, is seen in a three-quarter rear view that even Euthymides would have marveled at. The subtle modulation of the horse's rump through shading in browns and yellows is precisely what Gnosis was striving to imitate in his pebble mosaic. Other details are even more impressive. The Persian to the right of the rearing horse has fallen to the ground and raises, backwards, a dropped Macedonian shield to protect himself from being trampled. Philoxenos recorded the reflection of the man's terrified face on the shield's polished surface. Everywhere men, animals, and weapons cast shadows on the ground. Philoxenos and other Classical painters' interest in the reflection of insubstantial light on a shiny surface, and in the

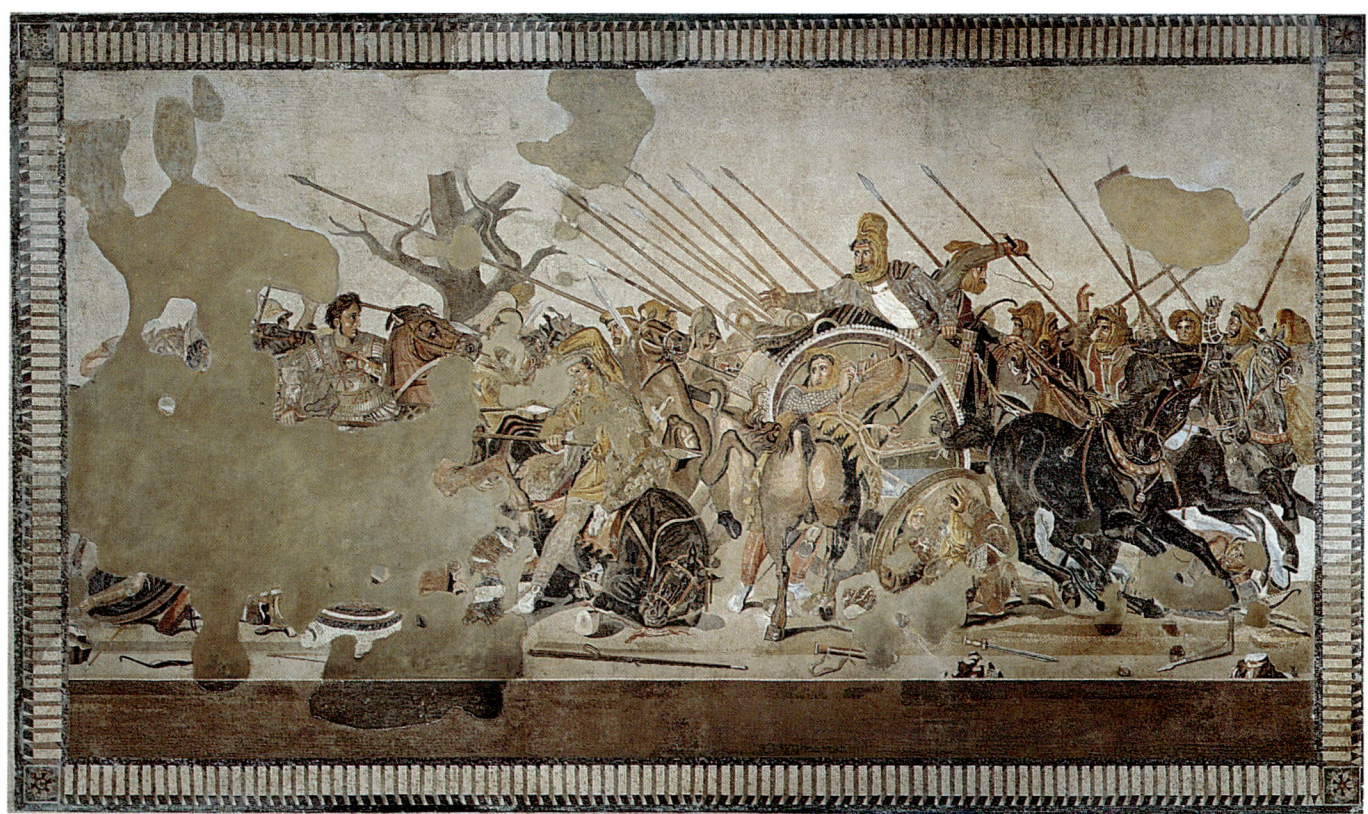

5-69 PHILOXENOS OF ERETRIA, *Battle of Issus,* ca. 310 B.C. Roman copy (the *Alexander Mosaic*) from the House of the Faun, Pompeii, Italy, late second or early first century B.C. Tessera mosaic, approx. 8′ 10″ × 16′ 9″. Museo Nazionale, Naples.

absence of light (shadows), was far removed from earlier painters' preoccupation with the clear presentation of weighty figures seen against a blank background. The Greek painter here truly opened a window into a world filled not only with figures, trees, and sky but also with light. This Classical Greek notion of what a painting should be characterizes most of the history of art in the Western world from the Renaissance on.

Most impressive about the *Battle of Issus*, however, is not the virtuoso details but the psychological intensity of the drama unfolding before the viewer's eyes. Alexander is on horseback leading his army into battle, recklessly one might say, without even a helmet to protect him. He drives his spear through one of Darius's trusted "Immortals," who were sworn to guard the king's life, while the Persian's horse collapses beneath him. The Macedonian king is only a few yards away from Darius, and Alexander directs his gaze at the Persian king, not at the man impaled on his now-useless spear. Darius has called for retreat. In fact, his charioteer is already whipping the horses and speeding the king to safety. Before he escapes, Darius looks back at Alexander and in a pathetic gesture reaches out toward his brash foe. But the victory has slipped out of his hands. Pliny says Philoxenos's painting of the battle between Alexander and Darius was "inferior to none."[9] It is easy to see how he reached that conclusion.

Architecture

A WONDROUS MAUSOLEUM   Five of the Seven Wonders of the ancient world were Greek (see "Babylon: City of Wonders," Chapter 2, page 37), but only one Greek Wonder was a tomb. The tomb built at Halikarnassos for Mausolos, the ruler of Caria in Asia Minor from 377 to 353 B.C., was the only funerary monument the ancients considered worthy

of comparison with the pyramids of Egypt (see FIG. 3-8), the solitary Egyptian Wonder. The tomb was erected by Mausolos's wife, Artemisia, and she employed some of the leading sculptors of the day, Skopas among them, to decorate it.

Mausolos's tomb was dismantled long ago, but ancient descriptions permit a reconstruction of the building in general terms. The multistory structure consisted of a high stepped podium, an Ionic colonnade, and a pyramidal roof capped by a colossal marble group of Mausolos in a four-horse chariot. The height of the tomb, including the chariot, was one hundred forty feet. Its fame was so great that already in Roman times *mausoleum* had become a generic term for any grandiose funerary monument. But the tomb, famous as it was, was only one of the triumphs of Greek architects in the fourth century B.C.

THE GREEK THEATER   In ancient Greece, plays were not performed repeatedly over months or years as they are today, but only once, during sacred festivals. Greek drama was closely associated with religious rites and was not pure entertainment. At Athens, for example, the great tragedies of Aeschylus, Sophocles, and Euripides were performed in the fifth century B.C. at the Dionysos festival in the theater dedicated to the god on the southern slope of the Acropolis (FIG. 5-40, far right). The finest theater in Greece, however, is at Epidauros (FIG. **5-70**). It was constructed shortly after Alexander the Great was born. The architect was POLYKLEITOS THE YOUNGER, possibly a nephew of the great fifth-century sculptor. His theater is still used for performances of ancient Greek dramas to the delight of tourists and natives alike.

The precursor of the formal Greek theater was a place where ancient rites, songs, and dances were performed. This circular piece of earth with a hard and level surface later be-

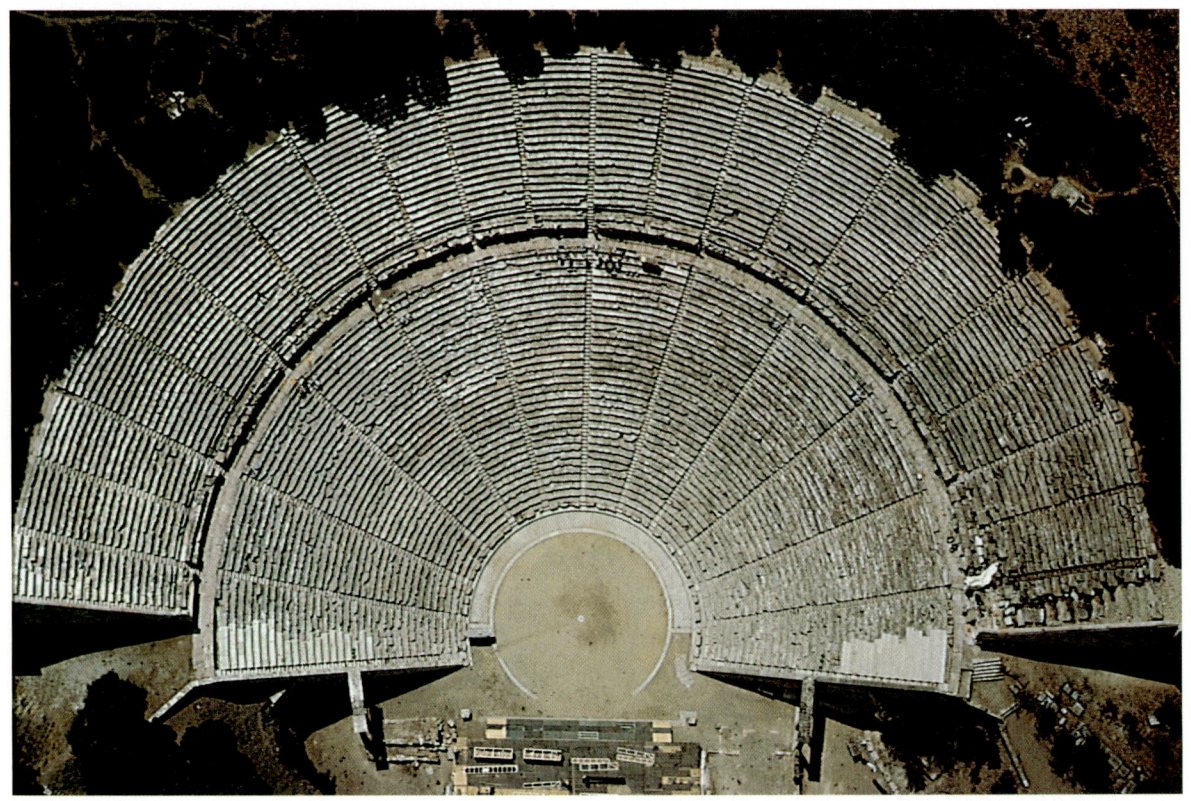

5-70   POLYKLEITOS THE YOUNGER, Theater, Epidauros, Greece, ca. 350 B.C.

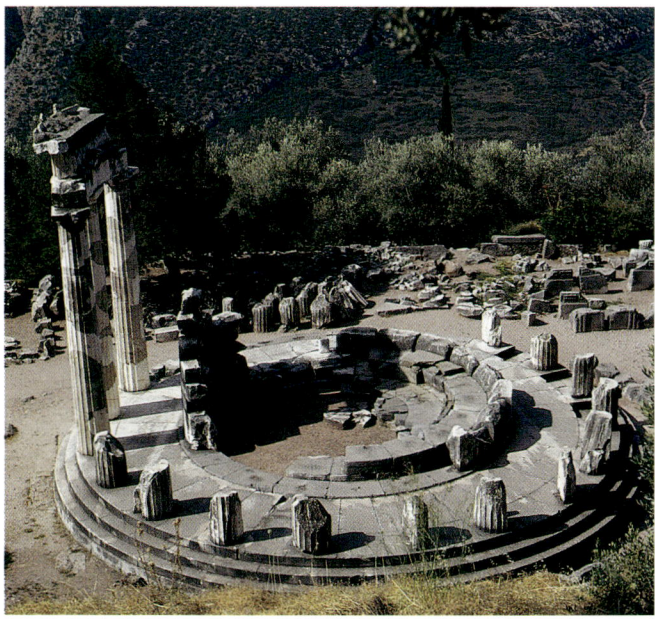

5-71 THEODOROS OF PHOKAIA, Tholos, Delphi, Greece, ca. 375 B.C.

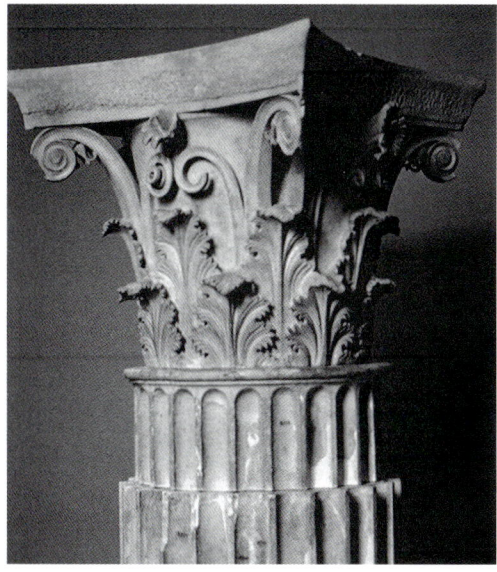

5-72 POLYKLEITOS THE YOUNGER, Corinthian capital, from the tholos, Epidauros, Greece, ca. 350 B.C. Archeological Museum, Epidauros.

came the orchestra of the theater. *Orchestra* literally means *dancing place*. The actors and the chorus performed there, and at Epidauros an altar to Dionysos stood at the center of the circle. The spectators sat on a slope overlooking the orchestra—the *theatron,* or *place for seeing*. When the Greek theater took architectural shape, the auditorium (*cavea,* Latin for *hollow place, cavity*) was always situated on a hillside. The cavea at Epidauros, composed of wedge-shaped sections (*cunei,* singular *cuneus*) of stone benches separated by stairs, is somewhat greater than a semicircle in plan. The auditorium is three hundred and eighty-seven feet in diameter, and its fifty-five rows of seats accommodated about twelve thousand spectators. They entered the theater via a passageway between the seating area and the scene building *(skene),* which housed dressing rooms for the actors and also formed a backdrop for the plays. The design is quite simple but perfectly suited to its function. Even in antiquity Polykleitos the Younger's theater was renowned for the harmony of its proportions. Although spectators sitting in some of the seats in the Epidauros theater would have had a poor view of the skene, all had unobstructed views of the orchestra. Because of the open-air cavea's excellent acoustics, everyone could hear the actors and chorus.

CORINTHIAN CAPITALS The theater at Epidauros is situated some five hundred yards southeast of the sanctuary of Asklepios, and Polykleitos the Younger worked there as well. He was the architect of the *tholos,* the circular shrine that probably housed the healing god's sacred snakes. That building lies in ruins today, its architectural fragments removed to the local museum, but one can get an approximate idea of its original appearance by looking at the somewhat earlier and partially reconstructed tholos at Delphi (FIG. **5-71**) designed by THEODOROS OF PHOKAIA. Both tholoi had an exterior colonnade of Doric columns. Within, however, both the Delphi and Epidauros columns (FIG. **5-72**) were crowned by *Corinthian capitals* (see "The Corinthian Capital," page 148), an innovation of the second half of the fifth century B.C.

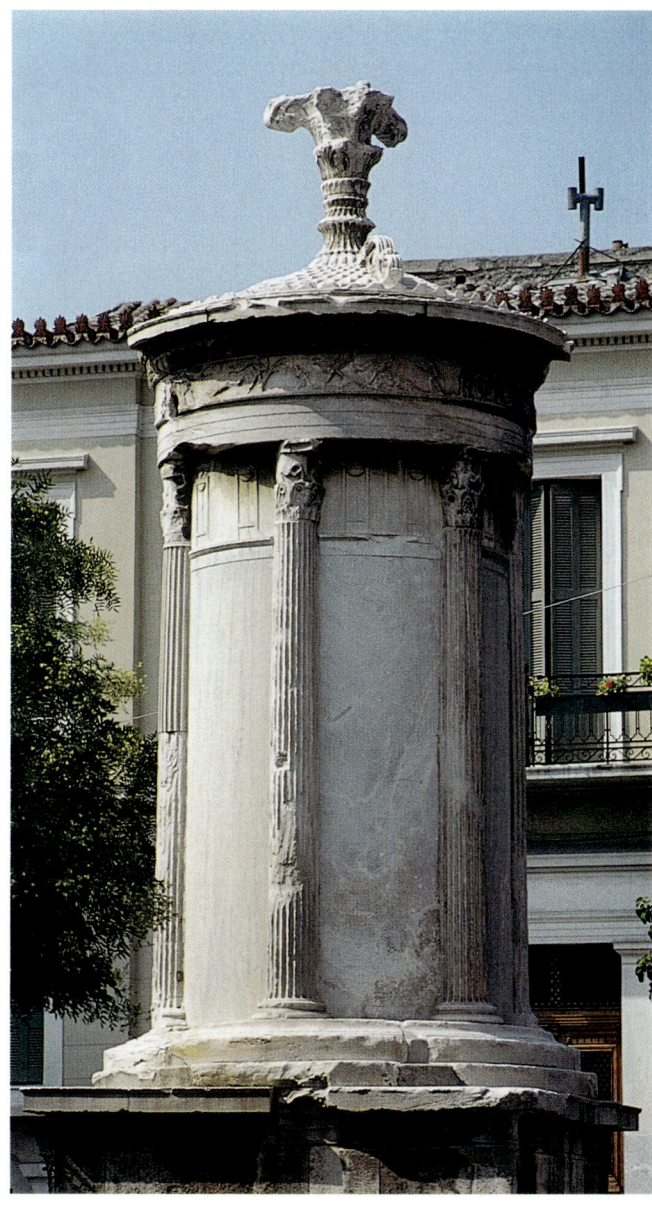

5-73 Choragic Monument of Lysikrates, Athens, Greece, 334 B.C.

The Corinthian Capital

The *Corinthian capital* (FIG. 5-72) is more ornate than either the Doric or Ionic (see "Doric and Ionic Temples," page 112). It consists of a double row of acanthus leaves, from which tendrils and flowers emerge, wrapped around a bell-shaped echinus. Although this capital often is cited as the Corinthian order's distinguishing feature, strictly speaking, no Corinthian order exists. The new capital type was simply substituted for the volute capital in the Ionic order.

The Corinthian capital was invented during the second half of the fifth century B.C. by the sculptor KALLIMACHOS. Vitruvius recorded the circumstances that supposedly led to its creation:

> A maiden who was a citizen of Corinth . . . died. After her funeral, her nurse collected the goblets in which the maiden had taken delight while she was alive, and after putting them together in a basket, she took them to the grave monument and put them on top of it. In order that they should remain in place for a long time, she covered them with a tile. Now it happened that this basket was placed over the root of an acanthus. As time went on the acanthus root, pressed down in the middle by the weight, sent forth, when it was about springtime, leaves and stalks; its stalks growing up along the sides of the basket and being pressed out from the angles because of the weight of the tile, were forced to form volute-like curves at their extremities. At this point, Kallimachos happened to be going by and noticed the basket with this gentle growth of leaves around it. Delighted with the order and the novelty of the form, he made columns using it as his model and established a canon of proportions for it.[1]

Kallimachos worked on the Acropolis. He made the golden lamp that stood beside the ancient wooden statue of Athena in the Erechtheion. Many scholars believe that a Corinthian column supported the outstretched right hand of the Phidian *Athena Parthenos* (FIG. 5-44) because some of the lost statue's Roman copies have such a column. In any case, the earliest preserved Corinthian capital dates to the time of Kallimachos. The new type became enormously popular in later Greek and especially Roman times, not only because of its ornate character, but also because it eliminated certain problems of both the Doric and Ionic orders.

The Ionic capital, unlike the Doric, has two distinct profiles—the front and back (with the volutes) and the sides. The volutes always faced outward on a Greek temple, but architects met with a vexing problem at the corners of their buildings, which had two adjacent "fronts." They solved the problem by placing volutes on both outer faces of the corner capitals (as on the Erechtheion, FIG. 5-50, and the Temple of Athena Nike, FIG. 5-53), but the solution was an awkward one.

Doric design rules also presented problems for Greek architects at the corners of buildings. The Doric frieze was organized according to three supposedly inflexible rules: (1) A triglyph must be exactly over the center of each column; (2) a triglyph must be over the center of each intercolumniation; and (3) triglyphs at the corners of the frieze must meet so that no space is left over. But the rules are contradictory. If the corner triglyphs must meet, then they cannot be placed over the center of the corner column (see, for example, the Doric temples at Aegina and Paestum and the Parthenon in Athens, FIGS. 5-24, 5-29, and 5-42).

The Corinthian capital eliminated both problems. Because the capital's four sides have a similar appearance, corner Corinthian capitals do not have to be modified, as do corner Ionic capitals. And because the Ionic frieze is used for the Corinthian "order," architects do not have to contend with metopes or triglyphs.

[1] J. J. Pollitt, trans., *The Art of Ancient Greece: Sources and Documents* (New York: Cambridge University Press, 1990), 193–94.

Consistent with the extremely conservative nature of Greek temple design, architects did not readily embrace the Corinthian capital. Until the second century B.C., Corinthian capitals were employed, as at Delphi and Epidauros, only for the interiors of sacred buildings. The earliest instance of a Corinthian capital on the exterior of a Greek building is the Choragic Monument of Lysikrates (FIG. **5-73**), which is not really a building at all. Lysikrates had sponsored a chorus in a theatrical contest in 334 B.C., and, after he won, he erected a monument to commemorate his victory. The monument consists of a cylindrical drum resembling a tholos on a rectangular base. Engaged Corinthian columns adorn the drum of Lysikrates' monument, and a huge Corinthian capital sits on top of the roof. The freestanding capital once supported the victor's prize, a bronze tripod.

THE HELLENISTIC PERIOD (323–31 B.C.)

THE GREEK WORLD AFTER ALEXANDER Alexander the Great's conquest of India, the Near East, and Egypt (where the Macedonian king was buried) ushered in a new cultural age that historians and art historians alike call *Hellenistic*. The Hellenistic period is traditionally reckoned from the death of Alexander in 323 B.C. and lasted nearly three centuries, until 31 B.C., when Queen Cleopatra of Egypt and her Roman consort Mark Antony were decisively defeated at the battle of Actium by Antony's rival Augustus. A year later, Augustus made Egypt a province of the Roman Empire. It is said that when Alexander was on his deathbed, his generals, greedy for the lands their young leader had conquered, asked, "To which one of us do you leave your empire?" He supposedly answered, "To the strongest."[10] Although probably a later invention, this exchange points out the near inevitability of what followed—the division of Alexander's far-flung empire among his Greek generals and their subsequent naturalization among those they subjugated.

The cultural centers of the Hellenistic period were the court cities of the Greek kings—Antioch in Syria, Alexandria in Egypt, Pergamon in Asia Minor, and others. An international culture united the Hellenistic world, and its language was Greek. Hellenistic kings became enormously rich on the spoils of the East, priding themselves on their libraries, art collections, scientific enterprises, and skills as critics and connoisseurs, as well as on the learned men they could assemble at their courts. The world of the small, austere, and heroic city-state passed away, as did the power and prestige of its center, Athens. A world, or cosmopolitan ("citizen of the world," in Greek), civilization, much like today's, replaced it.

Architecture

NEW ARCHITECTS BREAK OLD RULES Hellenistic culture's greater variety, complexity, and sophistication called for an architecture on an imperial scale and of wide diversity, something far beyond the requirements of the Classical polis, even beyond that of Athens at the height of its power. Building activity shifted from the old centers on the Greek mainland to the opulent cities of the Hellenistic monarchs in Asia Minor—sites more central to the Hellenistic world.

Great scale, a theatrical surprise element, and a willingness to break the rules of canonical temple design characterize one of the Hellenistic period's most ambitious temple projects, the Temple of Apollo at Didyma (FIG. **5-74**). The Hellenistic temple was built to replace the Archaic temple at the site the Persians had burned down in 494 B.C. when they sacked nearby Miletos. Construction began in 313 B.C. according to the design of two architects who were natives of the area, PAIONIOS OF EPHESOS and DAPHNIS OF MILETOS. So vast was the undertaking, however, that work on the temple continued off and on for more than five hundred years—and still the project was never completed.

The temple was dipteral in plan and had an unusually broad facade of ten huge Ionic columns almost sixty-five feet tall. The sides had twenty-one columns, consistent with the Classical formula for perfect proportions used for the Parthenon—$(2 \times 10) + 1$—but nothing else about the design is Classical. One anomaly immediately apparent to anyone who approached the building was that it had no pediment and no roof—it was *hypaethral,* or open to the sky. And the grand doorway to what should be the temple's cella was elevated nearly five feet off the ground so that it could not be entered. The explanation for these peculiarities is that the doorway served rather as a kind of stage where the oracle of Apollo could be announced to those assembled in front of the temple. The unroofed dipteral colonnade was really only an elaborate frame for a central courtyard that housed a small prostyle shrine that protected a statue of Apollo. Entrance to the interior court was through two smaller doorways to the left and right of the great portal and down two narrow vaulted tunnels that could accommodate only a single file of people. From these dark and mysterious lateral passageways worshipers emerged into the clear light of the courtyard, which contained a sacred spring and was planted with laurel trees in honor of Apollo. Opposite Apollo's inner temple, a stairway some fifty feet wide rose majestically toward three portals leading into the oracular room that also opened onto the front of the temple. This complex spatial planning marks a sharp departure from Classical Greek architecture, which stressed a building's exterior almost as a work of sculpture and left its interior relatively undeveloped.

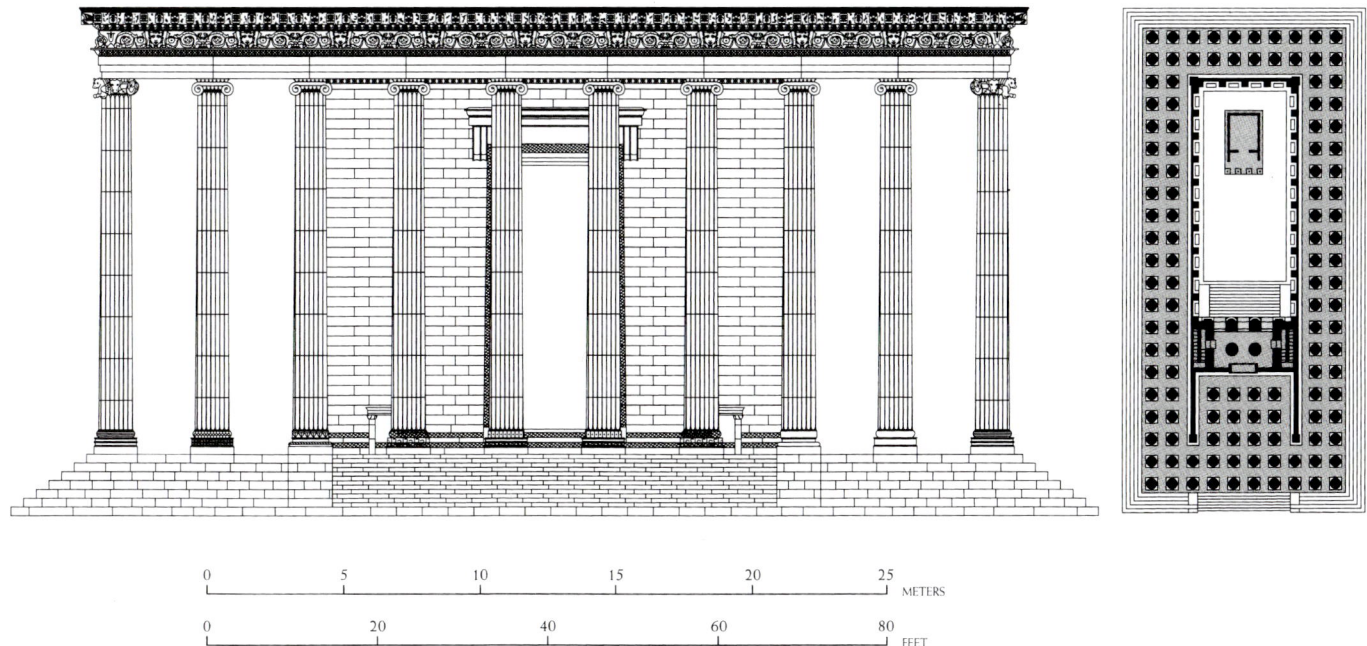

0   5   10   15   20   25   METERS

0   20   40   60   80   FEET

5-74   PAIONIOS OF EPHESOS and DAPHNIS OF MILETOS, Temple of Apollo, Didyma, Turkey, begun 313 B.C. Restored view of facade *(left)* and plan *(right).*

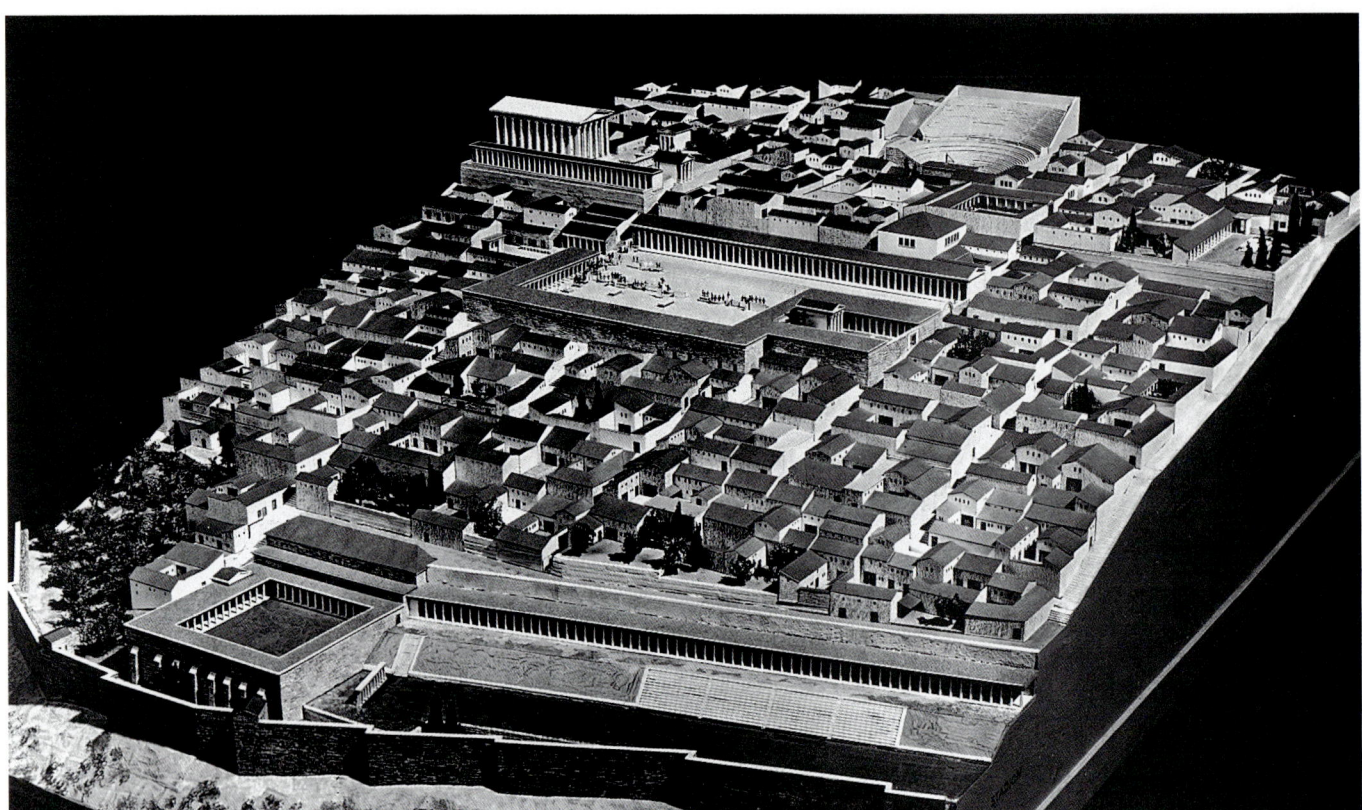

5-75   Model of the city of Priene, Turkey, fourth century B.C. and later. Staatliche Museen, Berlin.

THE IDEAL GREEK CITY   When the Persians were finally expelled from the Greek poleis of Asia Minor in 479 B.C., the cities were in near ruin. Reconstruction of Miletos began after 466 B.C., according to a plan laid out by HIPPODAMOS OF MILETOS, whom Aristotle singled out as the father of rational city planning. Hippodamos imposed a strict grid plan on the site, regardless of the terrain, so that all streets would meet at right angles. Such *orthogonal* planning actually predates Hippodamos, not only in Archaic Greece but also in the ancient Near East and Egypt. But Hippodamos was so famous that his name has ever since been synonymous with such urban plans. The so-called *Hippodamian plan* also designated separate quarters for public, private, and religious functions. A "Hippodamian city" was logically, as well as regularly, planned. This desire to impose order on nature and to assign a proper place in the whole to each of the city's constituent parts was very much in keeping with the philosophical tenets of the fifth century B.C. Hippodamos's formula for the ideal city was another manifestation of the same outlook that produced Polykleitos's *Canon* for the human body and Iktinos's treatise on the Parthenon.

An excellent example of Hippodamian planning is the city of Priene (FIG. **5-75**), also in Asia Minor. The city, laid out during the fourth century B.C., had fewer than five thousand inhabitants. (Hippodamos thought ten thousand was the ideal number.) It was situated on sloping ground, so many of the narrow north-south streets were little more than long stairways. Uniformly sized city blocks were nonetheless imposed on the irregular terrain. The central *agora* (marketplace) was allotted six blocks. More than one unit also was reserved for major structures such as the Temple of Athena and the theater.

LIFE IN A GREEK HOME   As in any city, ancient or modern, houses occupied most of the area within Priene's walls, rather than civic or religious buildings. Information about the homes of ordinary citizens is scanty, in part because archeologists have been more interested in uncovering grand edifices, such as temples and theaters, and in part because ancient authors usually described only exceptional buildings, not common dwellings. The unpretentious Priene houses (for example, FIG. **5-76**) were typical of later Greek times. They are

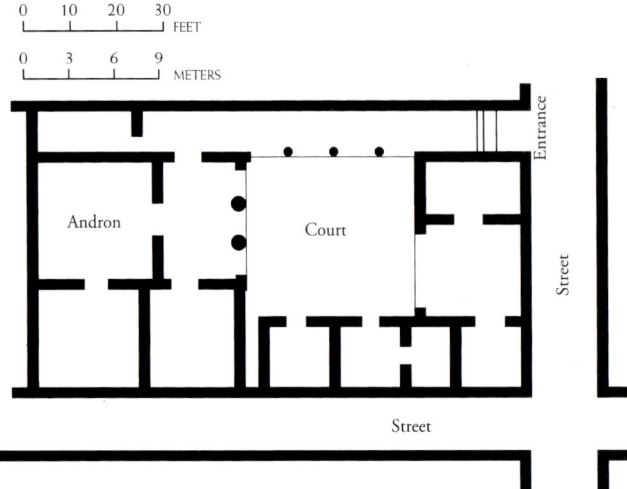

5-76   Plan of House XXXII, Priene, Turkey, fourth century B.C.

rectangular in plan and fit neatly into the Hippodamian grid, but internally they were not laid out symmetrically. A single entrance from the street led to a modest central court, the largest room in the house, surrounded by several smaller roofed units. In the wealthiest homes the courtyard was framed by a peristyle and paved with a pebble mosaic. The house illustrated here has columns (of differing dimensions) on only two sides of the court. Exterior windows were rare, because most houses shared walls with their neighbors, and the court provided welcome light and air to the interior. These courtyards also allowed the collection of rainwater, stored in underground cisterns and used for drinking, cooking, and washing. In most houses a dining room (andron) opened onto the court (or onto an anteroom that in turn opened onto the court, as in our example) and was furnished with couches so that the man of the house and his male guests could recline while eating. A kitchen would not be far away. Bedrooms also might open onto the court, but, when a second floor existed, they were normally located upstairs.

PHILOSOPHERS AND STOAS   The heart of Priene was its agora, bordered by *stoas*. These covered colonnades, which often housed shops and civic offices, were ideal vehicles for shaping urban spaces, and they were staples of Hellenistic cities. Even the agora of Athens, an ancient city notable for its haphazard, unplanned development, was eventually framed to the east and south by stoas placed at right angles to one another. These new *porticos* joined the famous Classical Painted Stoa (see page 137), where the Hellenistic philosopher Zeno and his successors taught. The *Stoic* school of Greek philosophy took its name from that building.

The finest of the new Athenian stoas was the Stoa of Attalos II (FIG. 5-77), a gift to the city by a grateful alumnus, the king of Pergamon (r. 159–138 B.C.), who had studied at

Athens in his youth. The stoa was meticulously reconstructed under the direction of the American School of Classical Studies at Athens and today has a second life as a museum housing more than six decades of finds from the Athenian agora, as well as the American excavation team's offices. The stoa has two stories, each with twenty-one shops opening onto the colonnade. The facade columns are Doric on the ground level and Ionic on the second story. Such mixing of the two orders on a single facade had occurred even in the Late Classical period. But it became increasingly common in the Hellenistic period, when respect for the old rules of Greek architecture was greatly diminished and a desire for variety and decorative effects often prevailed. Practical considerations also governed the form of the Stoa of Attalos. The columns are far more widely spaced than in Greek temple architecture, to allow for easy access. And the builders left the lower third of every Doric column shaft unfluted to guard against damage from constant traffic.

Pergamon

The kingdom of Attalos II (r. 158–138 B.C.) was one of those born in the early third century B.C. after the breakup of Alexander's empire. Founded by Philetairos, the Pergamene kingdom embraced almost all of western and southern Asia Minor. Upon the death in 133 B.C. of the last of its kings, Attalos III (r. 138–133 B.C.), the kingdom was bequeathed to Rome, which by then was the greatest power in the Mediterranean world. The Attalids enjoyed immense wealth, and much of it was expended on embellishing their capital city of Pergamon, especially its acropolis. Located there were the royal palace, an arsenal and barracks, a great library and theater, an agora, and the sacred precincts of Athena and Zeus.

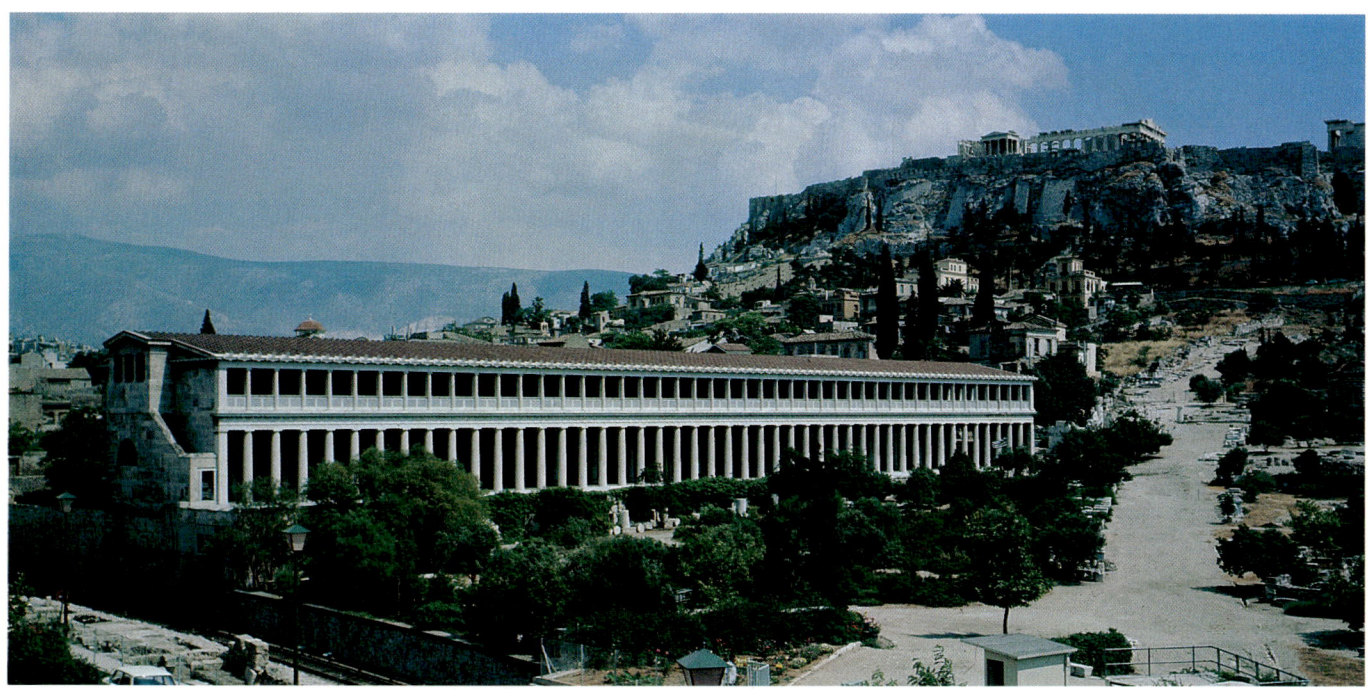

5-77   Stoa of Attalos II, Agora, Athens, Greece, ca. 150 B.C. (Acropolis in the background).

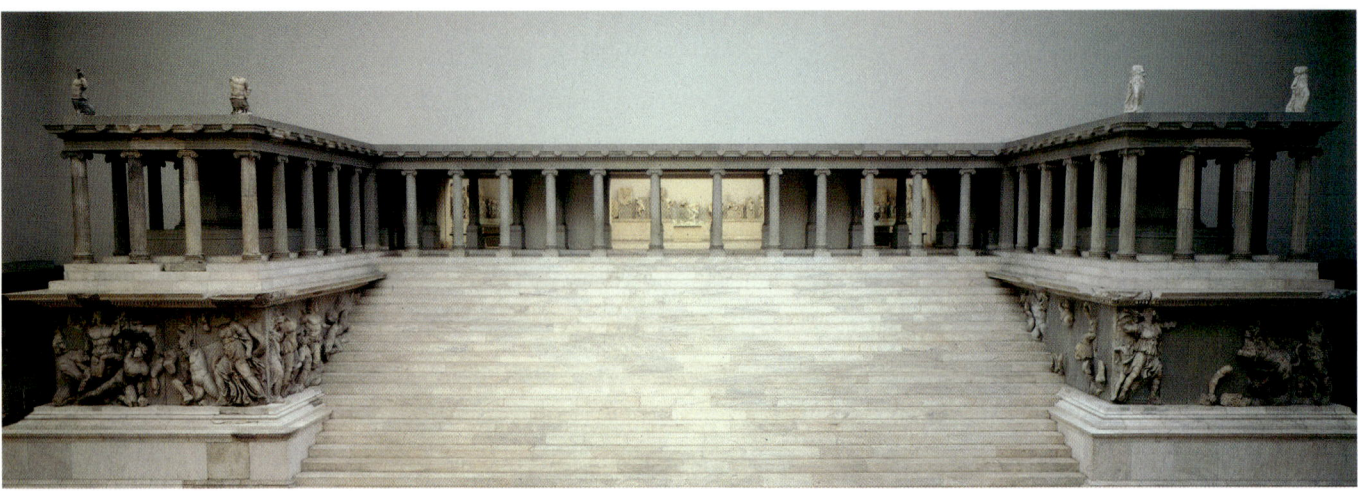

5-78   Reconstructed west front of the Altar of Zeus, from Pergamon, Turkey, ca. 175 B.C. Staatliche Museen, Berlin.

AN EPIC STRUGGLE FOR THE COSMOS   The Altar of Zeus, erected on the Pergamene acropolis about 175 B.C., is the most famous of all Hellenistic sculptural ensembles. The monument's west front (FIG. **5-78**) has been reconstructed in Berlin. The altar proper was on an elevated platform and framed by an Ionic stoalike colonnade with projecting wings on either side of a broad central staircase. All around the platform was a sculptured frieze almost four hundred feet long populated by some one hundred larger-than-life-size figures (FIG. **5-79**). The subject is the battle of Zeus and the gods against the giants. It is the most extensive representation Greek artists ever attempted of that epic conflict for control of the world. A similar subject appeared on the shield of Phidias's *Athena Parthenos* and on some of the metopes of the Parthenon, where the Athenians wished to draw a parallel between the defeat of the giants and the defeat of the Persians.

In the third century B.C., King Attalos I (r. 241–197 B.C.) had successfully turned back an invasion by the Gauls in Asia Minor. The gigantomachy of the Altar of Zeus alluded to the Pergamene victory over those barbarians.

A deliberate connection was also made with Athens, whose earlier defeat of the Persians was by then legendary, and with the Parthenon, which already was recognized as a Classical monument—in both senses of the word. The figure of Athena, for example, who grabs the hair of the giant Alkyoneos as Nike flies in to crown her (FIG. 5-79), is a quotation of the Athena from the Parthenon's east pediment. Zeus himself (not illustrated) was based on the Poseidon of the west pediment. But the Pergamene frieze is not a dry series of borrowed motifs. On the contrary, its tumultuous narrative has an emotional intensity that has no parallel to earlier monuments. The battle rages everywhere, even up and down the

5-79   Athena battling Alkyoneos, detail of the gigantomachy frieze, from the Altar of Zeus, Pergamon, Turkey. Marble, approx. 7′ 6″ high. Staatliche Museen, Berlin.

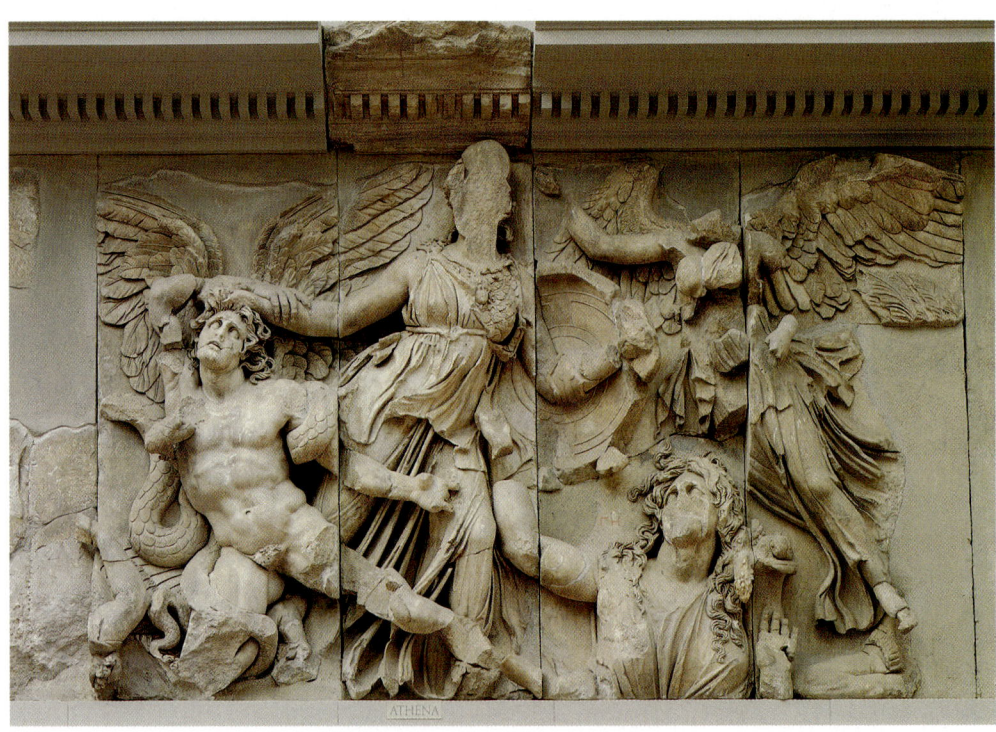

5-80 EPIGONOS(?), *Gallic chieftain killing himself and his wife.* Roman marble copy after a bronze original from Pergamon, Turkey, ca. 230–220 B.C. Approx. 6′ 11″ high. Museo Nazionale Romano—Palazzo Altemps, Rome.

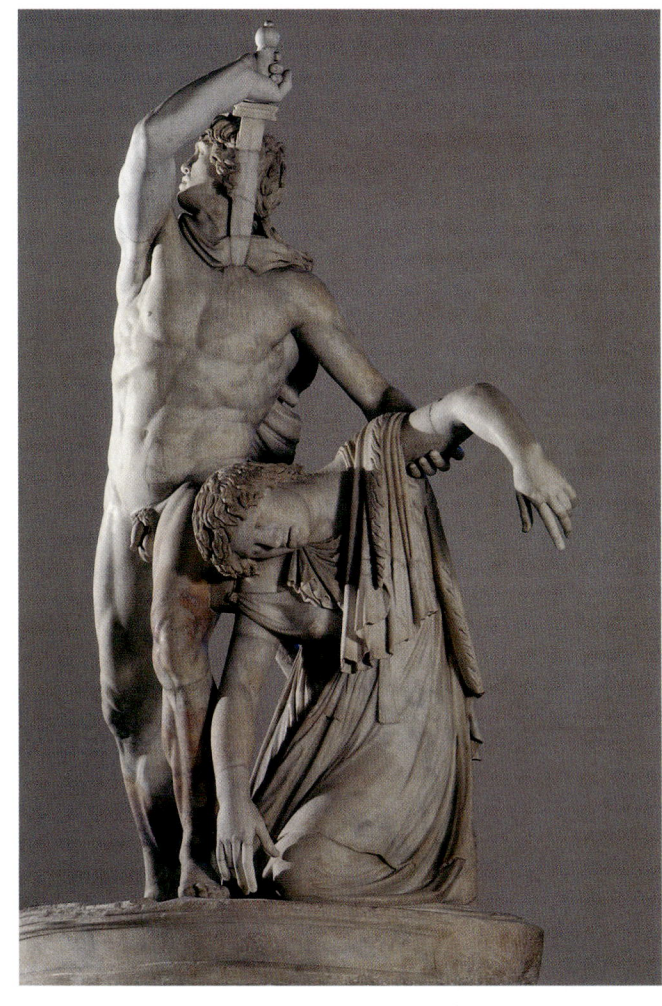

very steps one must ascend to reach Zeus's altar (FIG. 5-78). Violent movement, swirling draperies, and vivid depictions of death and suffering are the norm. Wounded figures writhe in pain, and their faces reveal their anguish. When Zeus hurls his thunderbolt, one can almost hear the thunderclap. Deep carving creates dark shadows. The figures project from the background like bursts of light. These features have been justly termed "baroque" and reappear in seventeenth-century European sculpture (see Chapter 24). One can hardly imagine a greater contrast than between the Pergamene gigantomachy frieze and that of the Archaic Siphnian Treasury at Delphi (FIG. 5-17).

A NOBLE DEATH FOR BARBARIC FOES On the Altar of Zeus, the victory of Attalos I over the Gauls was presented in mythological disguise. In an earlier statuary group set up on Pergamon's acropolis, the defeat of the barbarians was explicitly represented. Roman copies of some of these figures survive (FIGS. **5-80** and **5-81**). The sculptor carefully

5-81 EPIGONOS(?), *Dying Gaul.* Roman marble copy after a bronze original from Pergamon, Turkey, ca. 230–220 B.C., approx. 3′ $\frac{1}{2}$″ high. Museo Capitolino, Rome.

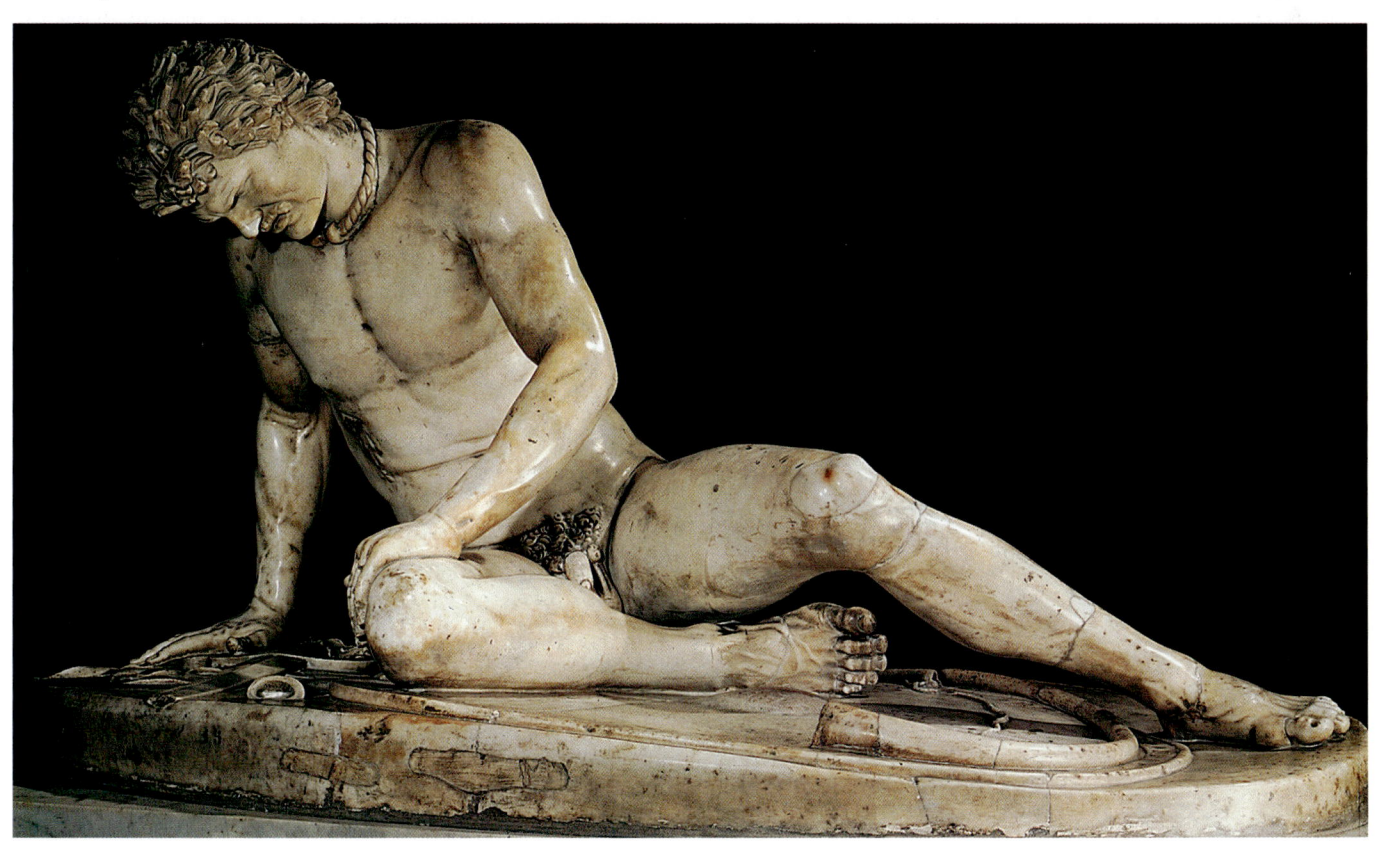

studied and reproduced the distinctive features of the foreign Gauls, most notably their long, bushy hair and mustaches and the *torques* (neck bands) they frequently wore. The Pergamene victors were apparently not included in the group. The viewer saw only their foes and their noble and moving response to defeat.

In what was probably the Attalid group's centerpiece (FIG. 5-80), a heroic Gallic chieftain defiantly drives a sword into his own chest just below the collarbone, preferring suicide to surrender. He already has taken the life of his wife, who, if captured, would have been sold as a slave. In the best Lysippan tradition, the group only can be fully appreciated by walking around it. From one side the observer sees the Gaul's intensely expressive face, from another his powerful body, and from a third the woman's limp and almost lifeless body. The man's twisting posture, the almost theatrical gestures, and the suicidal act's emotional intensity are hallmarks of the Pergamene "baroque" style and were closely paralleled in the later frieze of Zeus's altar.

The third Gaul from this group is a trumpeter who collapses upon his large oval shield as blood pours out of the gash in his chest (FIG. 5-81). He stares at the ground with a pained expression on his face. The Hellenistic figure is reminiscent of the dying warrior from the east pediment of the Temple of Aphaia at Aegina (FIG. 5-28), but the suffering Gaul's pathos and drama are far more pronounced. As in the suicide group and the gigantomachy frieze, the male musculature was rendered in an exaggerated manner. Note the chest's tautness and the left leg's bulging veins—implying that the unseen Attalid hero who has struck down this noble and savage foe must have been an extraordinary man. If this figure is the *tubicen* (trumpeter) Pliny mentioned as the work of the Pergamene master EPIGONOS, then Epigonos may be the sculptor of the entire group and the creator of the dynamic Hellenistic baroque style.

Sculpture

VICTORY IN A FOUNTAIN   One of the masterpieces of the Hellenistic baroque style was not created for the Attalid kings but was set up in the Sanctuary of the Great Gods on Samothrace. The *Nike of Samothrace* (FIG. **5-82**) has just alighted on a Greek warship's prow. Her missing right arm was once raised high to crown the naval victor—just like Nike places a wreath on Athena on the Altar of Zeus (FIG. 5-79). But the Pergamene relief figure seems calm by comparison. The Samothracian Nike's wings still beat, and the wind sweeps her drapery. Her himation bunches in thick folds around her right leg, and her chiton is pulled tightly across her abdomen and left leg. The statue's theatrical effect was amplified by its setting. The war galley was displayed in the upper basin of a two-tiered fountain. In the lower basin were large boulders. The fountain's flowing water created the illusion of rushing waves dashing up against the ship. The statue's reflection in the shimmering water below accentuated the sense of lightness and movement. The sound of splashing water added an aural dimension to the visual drama. Art and nature were here combined in one of the most successful sculptures ever fashioned. In the *Nike of Samothrace* and other works in the Hellenistic baroque manner, the Polykleitan con-

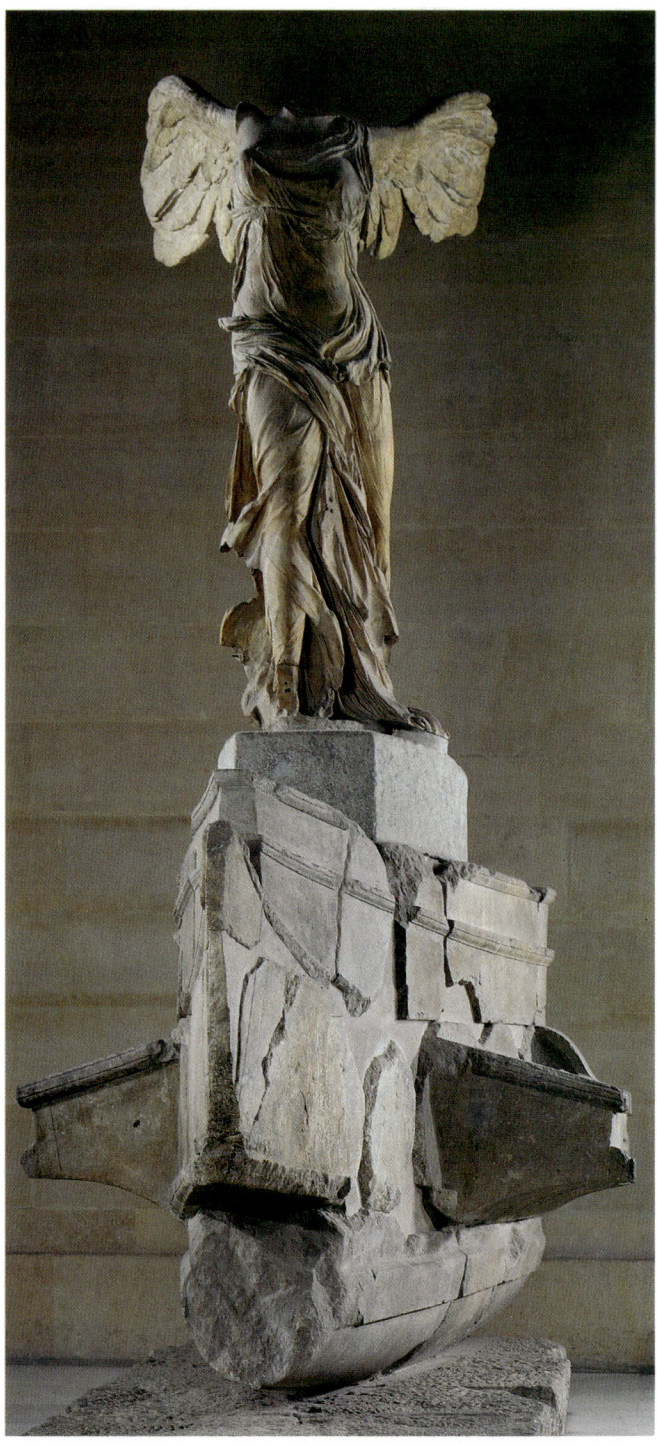

5-82   Nike alighting on a warship (*Nike of Samothrace*) from Samothrace, Greece, ca. 190 B.C. Marble, figure approx. 8′ 1″ high. Louvre, Paris.

ception of a statue as an ideally proportioned, self-contained entity on a bare pedestal was resoundingly rejected. The Hellenistic statues interact with their environment and appear as living, breathing, and intensely emotive human (or divine) presences.

HELLENISTIC EROTICISM   Bold steps in redefining the nature of Greek statuary had already been taken in the fourth century B.C. in different ways by Praxiteles, Skopas, and Lysippos. Their distinctive styles continued to influence sculptors throughout the Hellenistic period. The undressing of Aphrodite by Praxiteles, for example, became the norm,

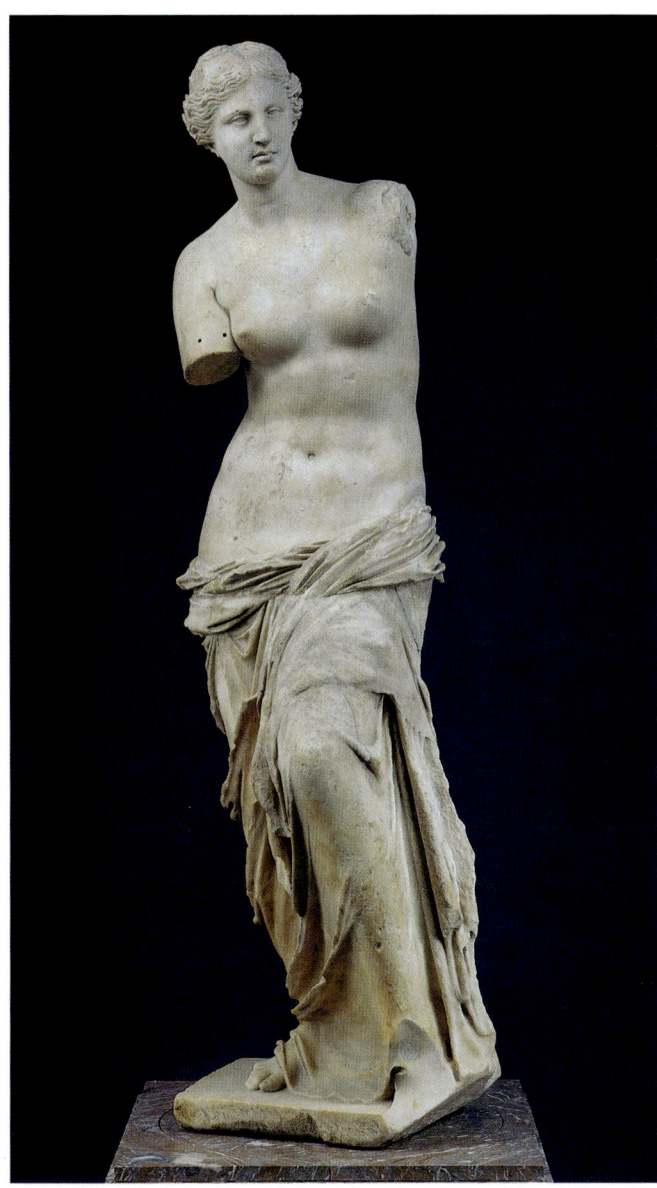

5-83 ALEXANDROS OF ANTIOCH-ON-THE-MEANDER, Aphrodite (*Venus de Milo*), from Melos, Greece, ca. 150–125 B.C. Marble, approx. 6′ 7″ high. Louvre, Paris.

but Hellenistic sculptors went beyond the Late Classical master and openly explored the nude female form's eroticism. The famous *Venus de Milo* (FIG. **5-83**) is a larger-than-life-size marble statue of Aphrodite found on Melos together with its inscribed base (now lost) signed by the sculptor, ALEXANDROS OF ANTIOCH-ON-THE-MEANDER. In this statue the goddess of love is more modestly draped than the *Aphrodite of Knidos* (FIG. 5-60) but more overtly sexual. Her left hand (separately preserved) holds the apple Paris awarded her when he judged her as the most beautiful goddess of all. Her right hand may have lightly grasped the edge of her drapery near the left hip in a halfhearted attempt to keep it from slipping farther down her body. The sculptor intentionally designed the work to tease the spectator. By so doing he imbued his partially draped Aphrodite with a sexuality that is not present in Praxiteles' entirely nude image of the goddess.

The *Aphrodite of Knidos* was directly quoted in an even more playful and irreverent statue of the goddess (FIG. **5-84**) found on Delos. Here, Aphrodite resists the lecherous ad-

vances of the semihuman, semigoat Pan, the Greek god of the woods. She defends herself with one of her sandals, while her loyal son Eros flies in to grab one of Pan's horns in an attempt to protect his mother from an unspeakable fate. One may wonder about the taste of Dionysios of Berytos (Beirut), who paid to have this statue erected in a businessmen's clubhouse—especially since both Aphrodite and Eros are portrayed as almost laughing—but such groups were commonplace in Hellenistic times. The combination of eroticism and parody of earlier Greek masterpieces was apparently irresistible. These whimsical Hellenistic groups are a far cry from the solemn depictions of the deities of Mount Olympus produced during Classical times.

Also different from earlier periods is the way Eros was represented. In the Hellenistic age he was shown as the pudgy infant Cupid as portrayed in innumerable later artworks, while in earlier Greek art he was depicted as an adolescent (FIG. 5-48, center). In the history of art, babies are all too frequently rendered as miniature adults—often with adult personalities to match their mature bodies. Hellenistic sculptors knew how to reproduce the soft forms of infants and how to portray the spirit of young children in memorable statues.

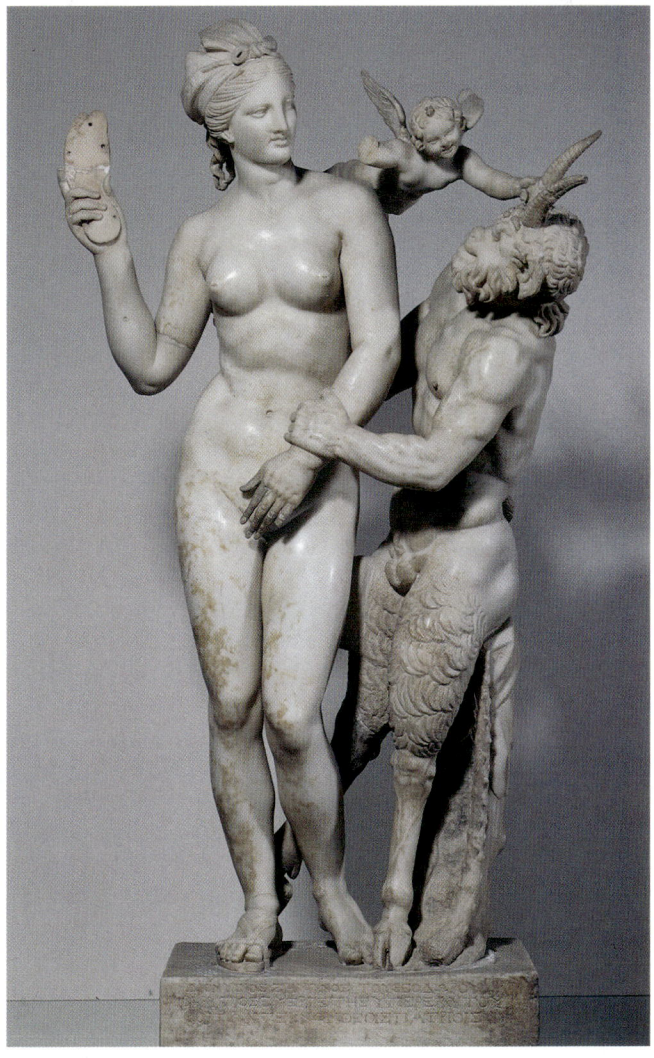

5-84 Aphrodite, Eros, and Pan, from Delos, Greece, ca. 100 B.C. Marble, 4′ 4″ high. National Archeological Museum, Athens.

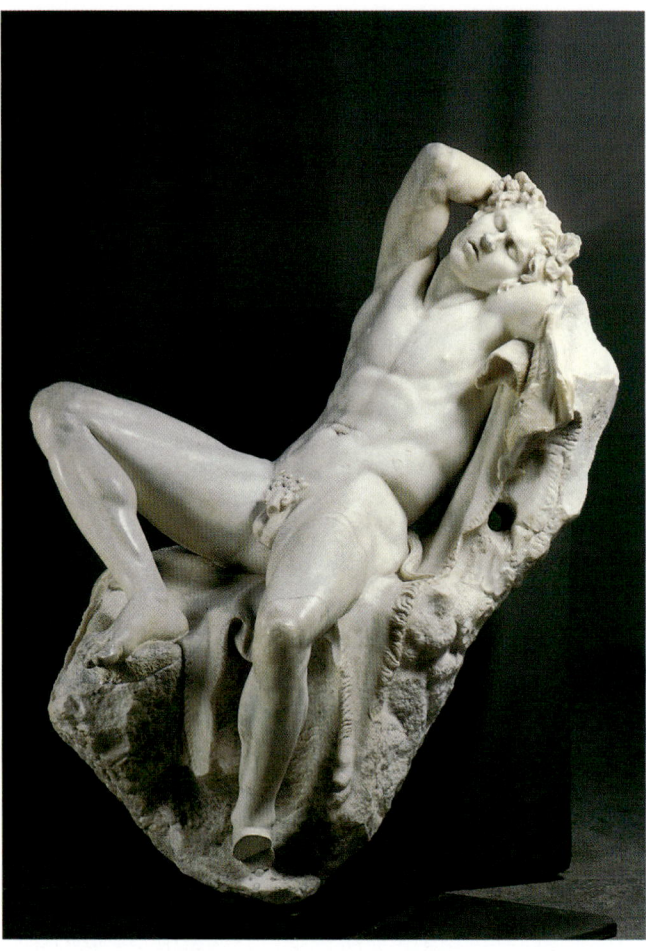

5-85   Sleeping satyr (*Barberini Faun*), from Rome, Italy, ca. 230–200 B.C. Marble, approx. 7′ 1″ high. Glyptothek, Munich.

SLEEP AND INTOXICATION   Archaic statues smile at their viewers, and even when Classical statues look away from the viewer they are always awake and alert. Hellenistic sculptors often portrayed sleep. The suspension of consciousness and the entrance into the fantasy world of dreams—the antithesis of the Classical ideals of rationality and discipline—had great appeal to them. A prime example of this newfound interest is a statue of a drunken, restlessly sleeping satyr known as the *Barberini Faun* (FIG. **5-85**). The statue was found in Rome in the seventeenth century and restored (not entirely accurately) by Gianlorenzo Bernini, the great Italian Baroque sculptor (see Chapter 24). Bernini no doubt felt this dynamic statue in the Pergamene manner was the work of a kindred spirit. The satyr, a follower of Dionysos, has consumed too much wine and has thrown down his panther skin upon a convenient rock and then fallen into a disturbed, intoxicated sleep. His brows are furrowed, and one can almost hear him snore.

Eroticism also comes to the fore in this statue. Although men had been represented naked in Greek art for hundreds of years, Archaic kouroi and Classical athletes and gods do not exude sexuality. Sensuality surfaced in the works of Praxiteles in the fourth century B.C. But the dreamy and supremely beautiful Hermes playfully dangling grapes before the infant Dionysos (FIG. 5-62) has nothing of the blatant sexuality of the *Barberini Faun,* whose wantonly spread

legs focus attention on his genitals. Homosexuality was common in the man's world of ancient Greece. (In Plato's *Symposium,* Alcibiades refers to Socrates' almost superhuman ability to resist seduction.) It is not surprising that when Hellenistic sculptors began to explore the human body's sexuality, they turned their attention to both men and women.

A HUMILIATED, BATTERED BOXER   Although Hellenistic sculptors tackled an expanded range of subjects, they did not abandon such traditional themes as the Greek athlete. But they often rendered the old subjects in novel ways. This is certainly true of the magnificent bronze statue of a seated boxer (FIG. **5-86**), a Hellenistic original found in Rome and perhaps at one time part of a group. The boxer is not a victorious young athlete with a perfect face and body but a heavily battered, defeated veteran whose upward gaze may have been directed at the man who had just beaten him. Too many punches from powerful hands wrapped in leather thongs—Greek boxers did not use the modern sport's cushioned gloves—have distorted the boxer's face. His nose is broken, as are his teeth. He has smashed "cauliflower ears." Inlaid copper blood drips from the cuts on his forehead, nose, and cheeks. How different is this rendition of a powerful bearded man from that of the noble warrior from Riace (see FIGS. 5-34 and Intro-18) of the Early Classical period! The Hellenistic sculptor appealed not to the intellect but to the emotions

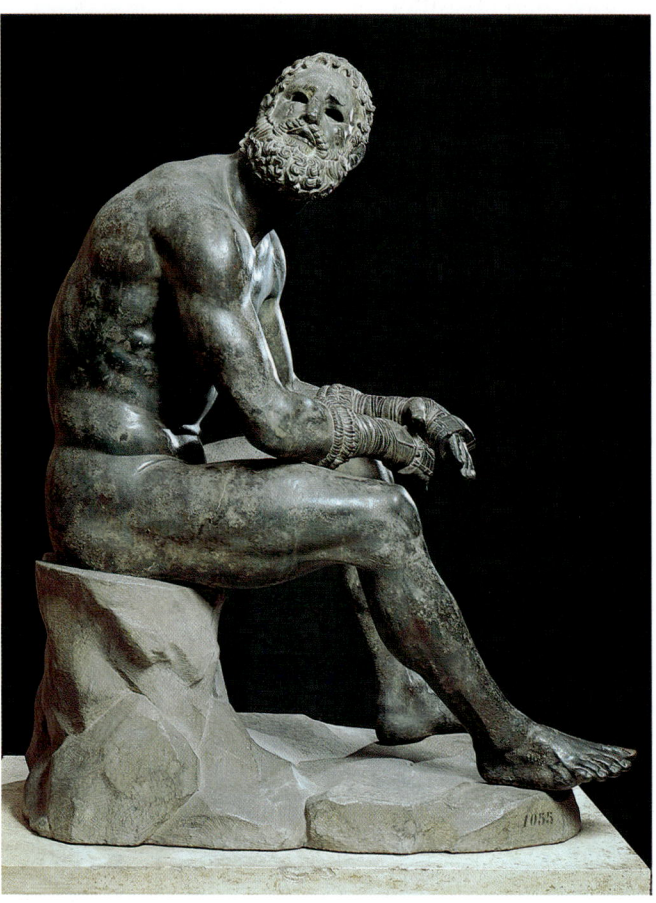

5-86   Seated boxer, from Rome, Italy, ca. 100–50 B.C. Bronze, approx. 4′ 2½″ high. Museo Nazionale Romano, Rome.

when striving to evoke compassion for the pounded hulk of a once-mighty fighter.

THE AGED AND THE UGLY The realistic bent of much of Hellenistic sculpture—the very opposite of the Classical period's idealism—is evident above all in a series of statues of old men and women from the lowest rungs of the social order. Shepherds, fishermen, and drunken beggars are common—the kinds of people who were pictured earlier on red-figure vases but never before were thought worthy of monumental statuary. One of the finest preserved statues of this type (FIG. **5-87**) depicts a haggard old woman bringing chickens and a basket of fruits and vegetables to sell in the market. Her face is wrinkled, her body is bent with age, and her spirit is broken by a lifetime of poverty. She carries on because she must, not because she derives any pleasure from life. Art historians do not know the purpose of such statues, but they attest to an interest in social realism absent in earlier Greek statuary.

Statues of the aged and the ugly are, of course, the polar opposites of the images of the young and the beautiful that dominated Greek art until the Hellenistic age, but they are consistent with the period's changed character. The Hellenistic world was a cosmopolitan place, and the highborn could not help but encounter the poor and a growing number of foreigners (non-Greek "barbarians") on a daily basis. Hellenistic art reflects this different social climate in the depiction of a much wider variety of physical types, including different ethnic types. We already have discussed the sensitive portrayal of Gallic warriors with their shaggy hair, strange mustaches, and golden torques (FIGS. 5-80 and 5-81). Africans, Scythians, and others, formerly only the occasional subject of vase painters, also entered the realm of monumental sculpture in Hellenistic art.

A GREAT ORATOR'S PORTRAIT These sculptures of foreigners and the urban poor, however realistic, are not portraits. Rather, they are sensitive studies of physical types. But the growing interest in the individual beginning in the Late Classical period did lead in the Hellenistic era to the production of true likenesses of specific persons. In fact, one of the great achievements of Hellenistic artists was the redefinition of portraiture. In the Classical period Kresilas was admired for having made the noble Pericles appear even nobler in his portrait (FIG. 5-39). But in Hellenistic times sculptors sought not only to record the actual appearance of their subjects in bronze and stone but also to capture the essence of their personalities in likenesses that were at once accurate and moving.

One of the earliest of these, perhaps the finest of the Hellenistic age and frequently copied in Roman times, was a bronze portrait statue of Demosthenes (FIG. **5-88**) by POLYEUKTOS. The original was set up in the Athenian agora in 280 B.C., forty-two years after the great orator's death. Demosthenes was a frail man and in his youth even suffered from a speech impediment, but he had enormous courage and great moral conviction. A veteran of the disastrous battle against Philip II at Chaeronea, he repeatedly tried to rally opposition to Macedonian imperialism, both before and after Alexander's death. In the end, when it was

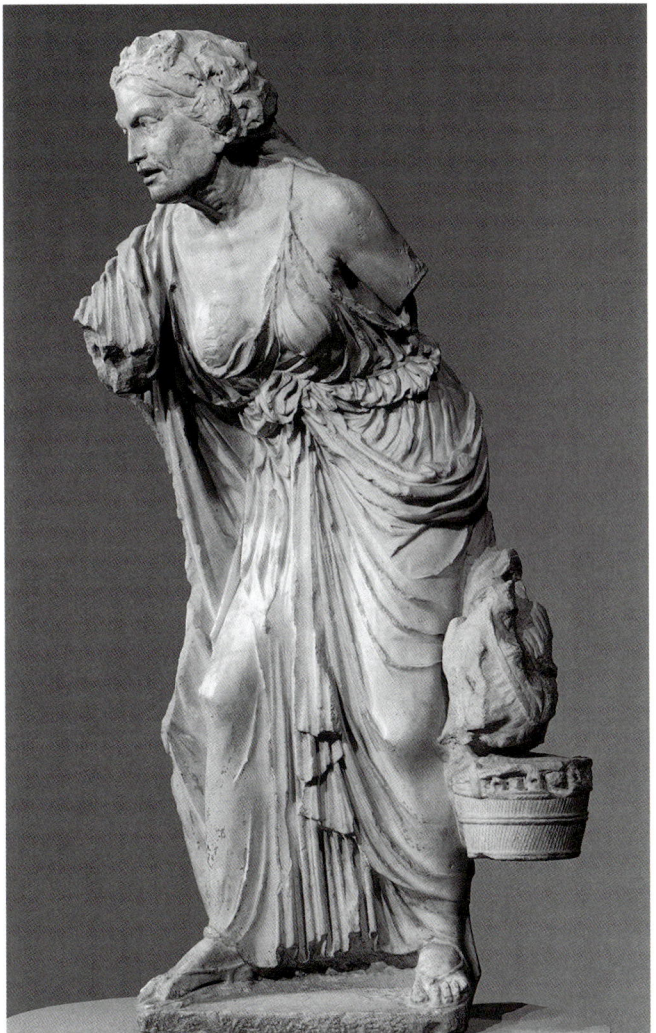

5-87 Old market woman, ca. 150–100 B.C. Marble, approx. $4'\frac{1}{2}''$ high. Metropolitan Museum of Art, New York.

clear the Macedonians would capture him, he took his own life by drinking poison.

Polyeuktos rejected Kresilas and Lysippos's notions of the purpose of portraiture and did not attempt to portray a supremely confident leader with a magnificent physique. His Demosthenes has an aged and slightly stooped body. Demosthenes clasps his hands nervously in front of him as he looks downward, deep in thought. His face is lined, his hair is receding, and his expression is one of great sadness. Whatever physical discomfort Demosthenes felt is here joined by an inner pain, his deep sorrow over the tragic demise of democracy at the hands of the Macedonian conquerors.

Hellenistic Art under Roman Patronage

In the opening years of the second century B.C., the Roman general Flaminius defeated the Macedonian army and declared the old poleis of Classical Greece as free once again. They never, however, regained their former glory. Athens, for example, sided with King Mithridates VI of Pontus (r. 120–63 B.C.) in his war against Rome and was crushed by the general Sulla in 86 B.C. Thereafter, it retained some of its earlier prestige as a

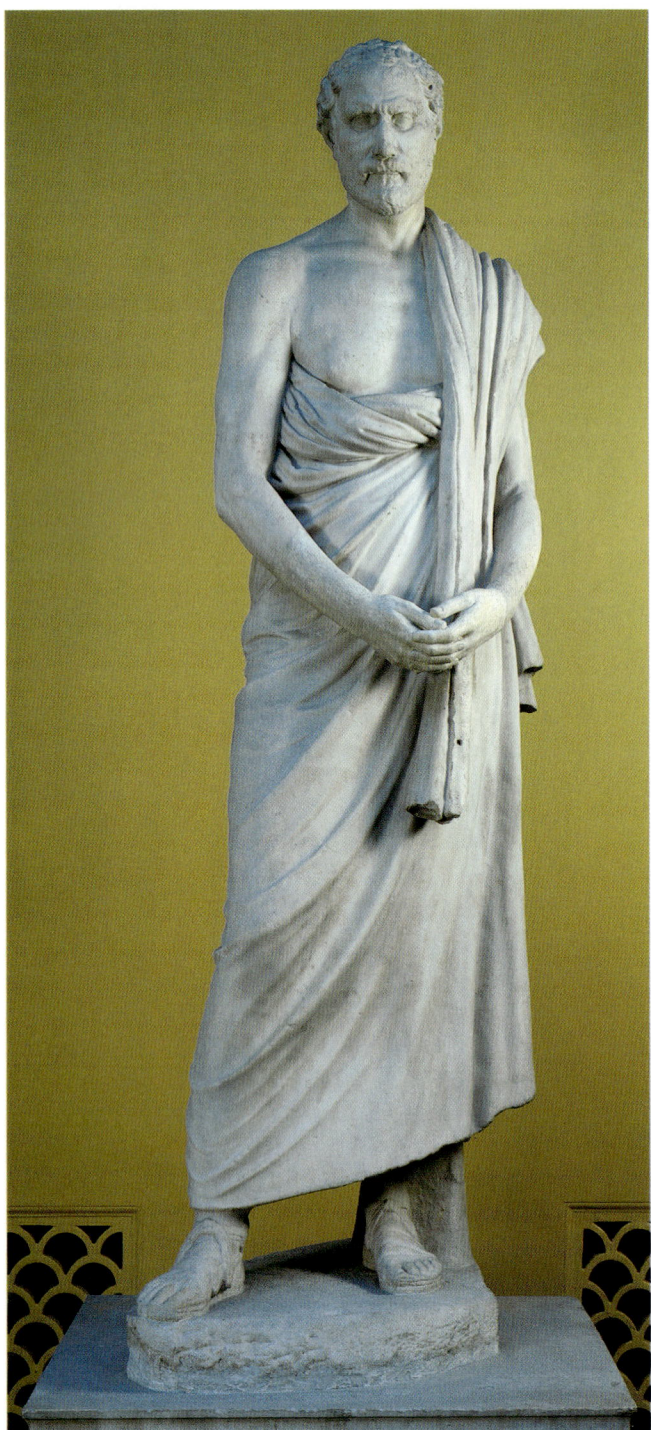

5-88   POLYEUKTOS, Demosthenes. Roman marble copy after a bronze original of ca. 280 B.C. 6′ 7½″ high. Ny Carlsberg Glyptotek, Copenhagen.

center of culture and learning, but politically Athens was just another city incorporated into the ever-expanding Roman Empire. Greek artists, however, continued to be in great demand, not only to furnish the Romans with an endless stream of copies of Classical and Hellenistic masterpieces but also to create new statues *à la grecque* for Roman patrons.

GREEK MYTHOLOGY, ROMAN STATUARY   One such work is the famous group of the Trojan priest Laocoön and his sons (FIG. **5-89**), which was discovered in Rome in 1506 in the presence of the great Italian Renaissance artist

Michelangelo. The marble group, long believed an original of the second century B.C., was found in the remains of the emperor Titus's (r. A.D. 79–81) palace, exactly where Pliny had seen it more than fourteen centuries before. Pliny attributed the statue to three Rhodian sculptors—ATHANADOROS, HAGESANDROS, and POLYDOROS—who are now generally thought to have worked in the early first century A.D. They probably based their group on a Hellenistic masterpiece depicting Laocoön and only one son. Their variation on the original adds the son at Laocoön's left (note the greater compositional integration of the two other figures) to conform with the Roman poet Vergil's account in the *Aeneid*. Vergil vividly described the strangling of Laocoön and his *two* sons by sea serpents while sacrificing at an altar. The gods who favored the Greeks in the war against Troy had sent the serpents to punish Laocoön, who had tried to warn his compatriots about the danger of bringing the Greeks' Wooden Horse within the walls of their city.

In Vergil's graphic account, Laocoön suffered in terrible agony, and the torment of the priest and his sons is communicated in a spectacular fashion in the marble group. The three Trojans writhe in pain as they struggle to free themselves from the death grip of the serpents. One bites into Laocoön's left hip as the priest lets out a ferocious cry. The serpent-entwined figures recall the suffering giants of the great frieze of the Altar of Zeus at Pergamon, and Laocoön himself is strikingly similar to Alkyoneos (FIG. 5-79), Athena's opponent. In fact, many scholars believe that a Pergamene statue of the second century B.C. was the inspiration for the three Rhodian sculptors.

HOMERIC THEMES IN A ROMAN GROTTO   That the work seen by Pliny and displayed in the Vatican Museums today was made for Romans rather than Greeks was confirmed in 1957 by the discovery of fragments of several Hellenistic-style groups illustrating scenes from Homer's *Odyssey*. These fragments were found in a grotto that served as the picturesque summer banquet hall of the seaside villa of the Roman emperor Tiberius (r. A.D. 14–37) at Sperlonga, some sixty miles south of Rome. One of these groups—depicting the monster Scylla attacking Odysseus's ship—is signed by the same three sculptors Pliny cited as the Laocoön group's creators. Another of the groups, installed around a central pool in the grotto, depicted the blinding of the Cyclops Polyphemos by Odysseus and his comrades, an incident also set in a cave in the Homeric epic. The head of Odysseus (FIG. **5-90**) from this theatrical group is one of the finest sculptures of antiquity. The hero's cap can barely contain his swirling locks of hair. Even Odysseus's beard seems to be swept up in the moment's emotional intensity. The parted lips and the deep shadows produced by sharp undercutting add drama to the head, which must have been attached to an agitated body.

At Tiberius's villa in Sperlonga and in Titus's palace in Rome, the baroque school of Hellenistic sculpture lived on long after Greece ceased to be a political force. When Rome inherited the Pergamene kingdom from the last of the Attalids in 133 B.C., it also became heir to the Hellenistic world's artistic legacy. What Rome adopted from Greece it passed on to the medieval and modern worlds. If Greece was peculiarly the inventor of the European spirit, Rome was its propagator and amplifier.

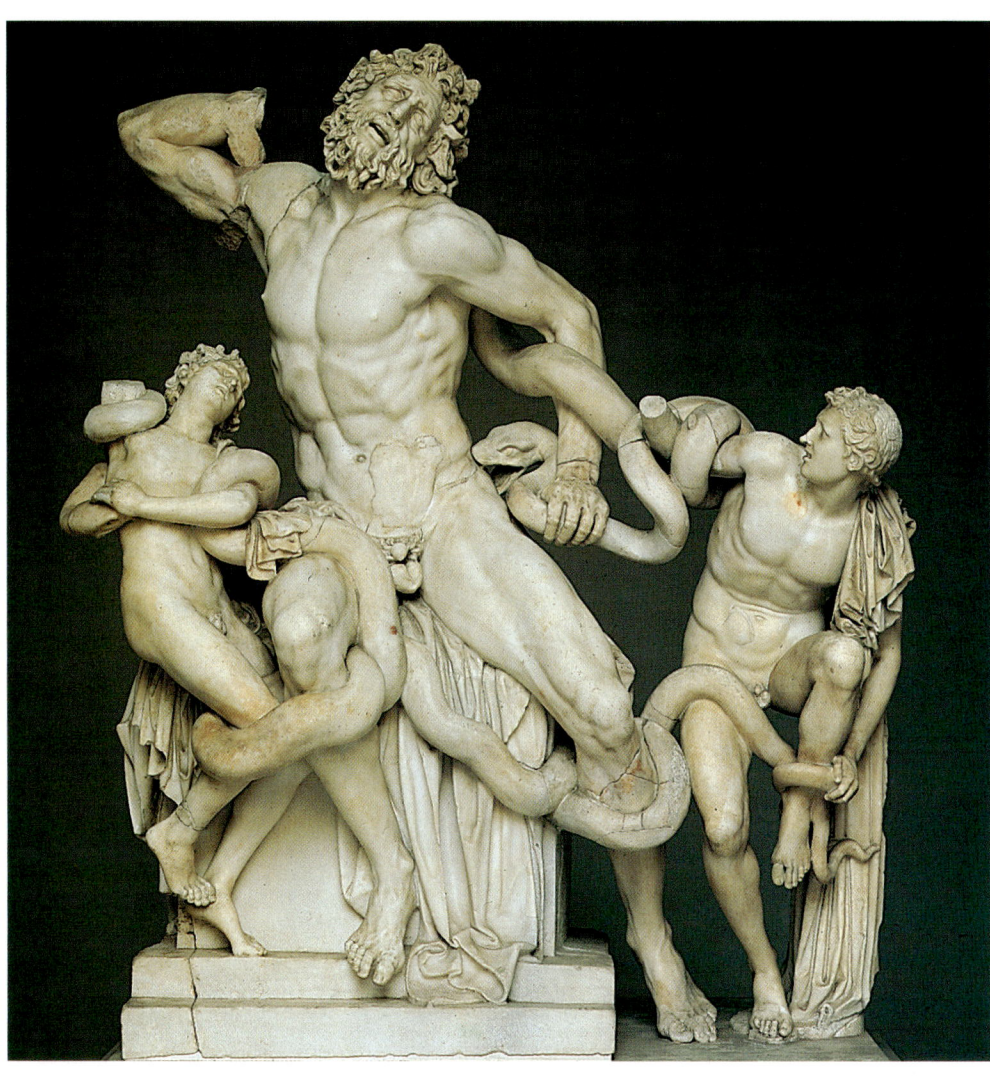

5-89 ATHANADOROS, HAGESANDROS, and POLYDOROS OF RHODES, Laocoön and his sons, from Titus's palace, Rome, Italy, early first century A.D. Marble, approx. 7′ 10½″ high. Vatican Museums, Rome.

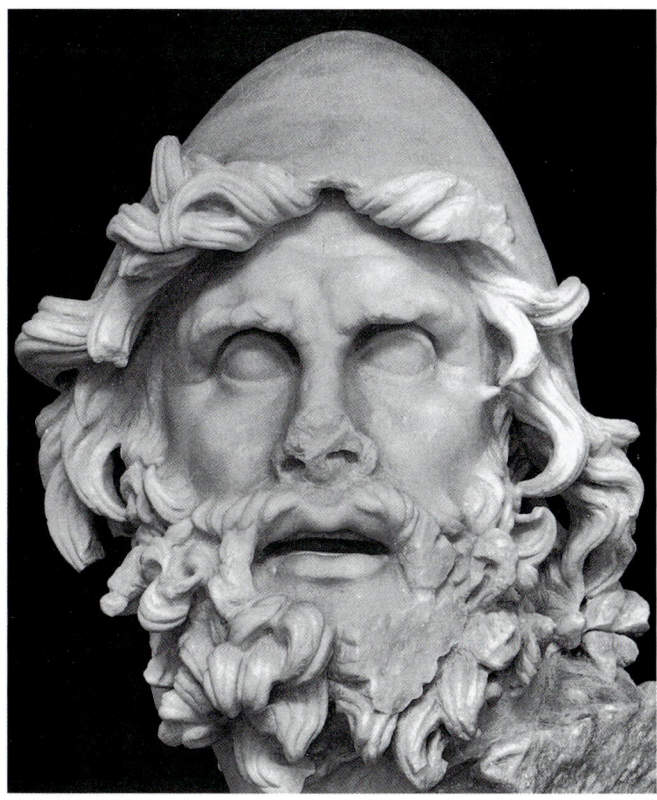

5-90 ATHANADOROS, HAGESANDROS, and POLYDOROS OF RHODES, Head of Odysseus, from Tiberius's villa, Sperlonga, Italy, early first century A.D. Marble, approx. 2′ 1″ high. Museo Archeologico, Sperlonga.

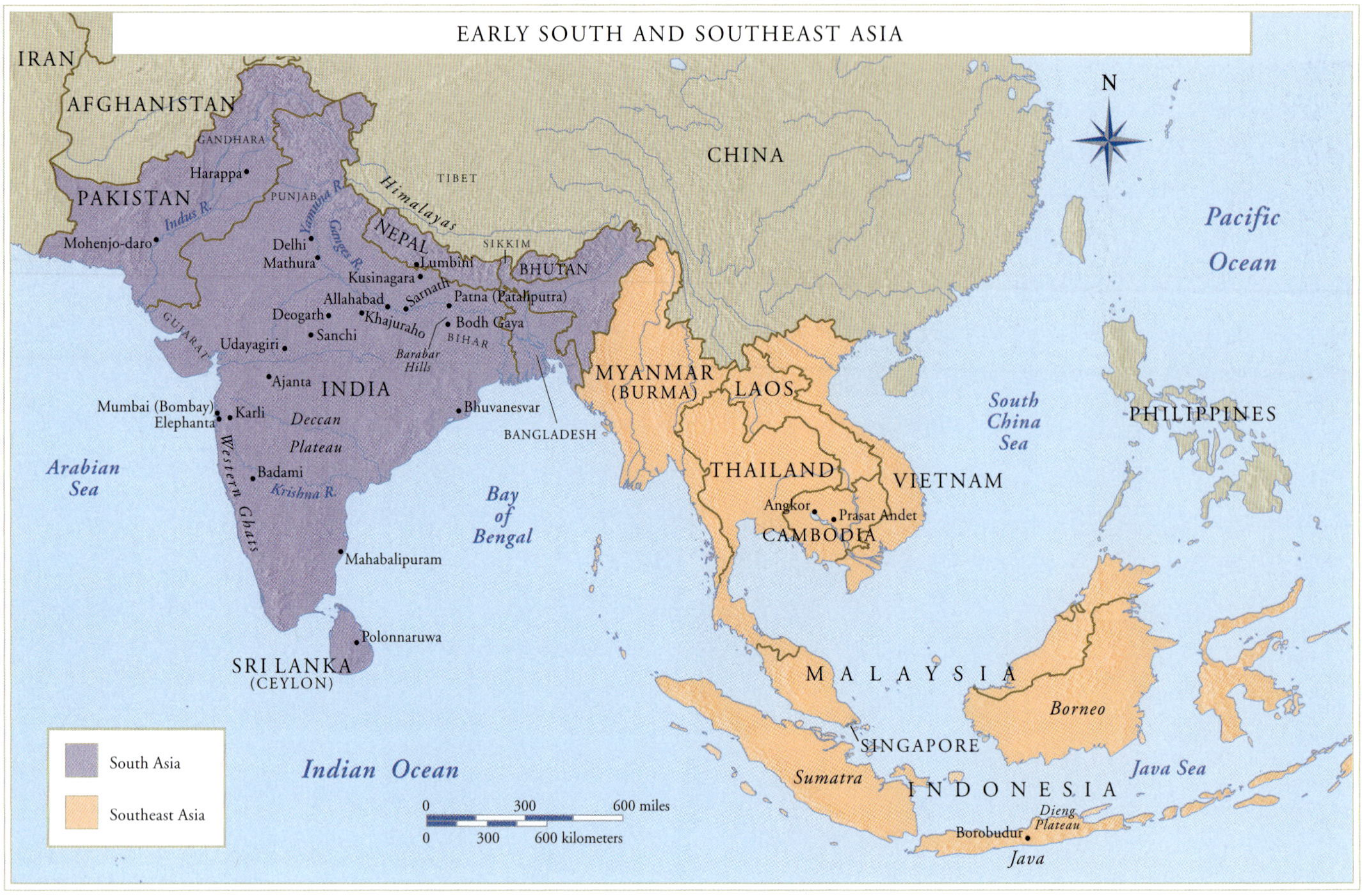

EARLY SOUTH AND SOUTHEAST ASIA

IRAN
AFGHANISTAN
GANDHARA
Harappa
PAKISTAN
PUNJAB
Mohenjo-daro
Indus R.
Delhi
Mathura
Yamuna R.
Himalayas
TIBET
CHINA
Ganges R.
NEPAL
Kusinagara
Lumbini
Allahabad
Sarnath
SIKKIM
BHUTAN
Deogarh
Khajuraho
Patna (Pataliputra)
Bodh Gaya
Sanchi
BIHAR
Udayagiri
Barabar
Hills
BANGLADESH
MYANMAR
(BURMA)
LAOS
Ajanta
INDIA
Bhuvanesvar
Mumbai (Bombay)
Karli
Deccan
Elephanta
Plateau
Western Ghats
THAILAND
VIETNAM
South
China
Sea
PHILIPPINES
Arabian
Sea
Badami
Krishna R.
Bay
of
Bengal
Angkor
Prasat Andet
CAMBODIA
Mahabalipuram
N
Pacific
Ocean
Polonnaruwa
SRI LANKA
(CEYLON)
Indian Ocean
MALAYSIA
SINGAPORE
Borneo
Sumatra
INDONESIA
Java Sea
Dieng
Plateau
Borobudur
Java

South Asia
Southeast Asia

0 300 600 miles
0 300 600 kilometers

	2500 B.C.	1700 B.C.	1000 B.C.	500 B.C.	300 B.C.	185 B.C.	A.D. 1	300
INDIA AND PAKISTAN	URBAN PHASE INDUS CIVILIZATION	VILLAGE PHASE INDUS CIVILIZATION			MAURYA DYNASTY		KUSHAN DYNASTY (NORTHERN INDIA)	
SOUTHEAST ASIA (JAVA AND CAMBODIA)				PRE-ANGKOR KINGDOMS (TO A.D. 802)				

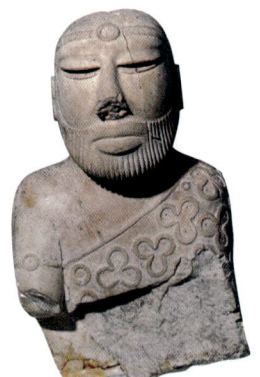

Priest-king(?)
Mohenjo-daro, Pakistan
ca. 2500–1700 B.C.

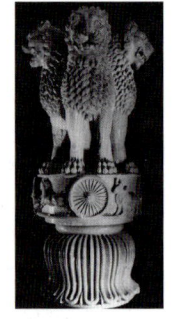

Lion capital, Sarnath, India
third century B.C.

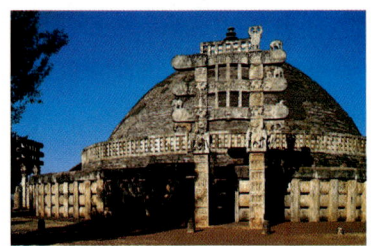

Great Stupa, Sanchi, India
completed first century A.D.

Early Phase Indus Civilization, 5500–2500 B.C.

Ongoing trade between Near East and Indus Valley,
Pakistan, 2500–1700 B.C.

Aryan peoples in Punjab compose
Vedic texts, Vedas, ca. 1500 B.C.

Upanishads, composed in opposition to Vedic texts, 800–500 B.C.

Sakyamuni Buddha's death, ca. 400 B.C.

Alexander the Great reaches Indus River, Pakistan, 327 B.C.

Maurya dynasty's Ashoka (r. 272–231 B.C.)
establishes rule by moral law

Buddhist and Hindu deities first depicted in
human form, first century B.C.–first century A.D.

PATHS TO ENLIGHTENMENT

THE ANCIENT ART OF SOUTH AND

SOUTHEAST ASIA

300	400	500	600	700	800	900	1000	1200	1300
GUPTA DYNASTY (NORTHERN INDIA)			LATER HINDU AND BUDDHIST DYNASTIES (NORTHERN INDIA)						
	CHALUKYA DYNASTY (TO 1000; CENTRAL INDIA)			CHANDELLA DYNASTY* (CENTRAL INDIA)					
	PALLAVA DYNASTY †(TO 900; SOUTHERN INDIA)			CHOLA DYNASTY (SOUTHERN INDIA)					
	CENTRAL JAVA KINGDOMS (TO 1000)		ANGKOR KINGDOMS						

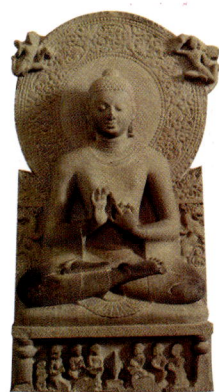

*Seated Buddha
Sarnath, India
fifth century*

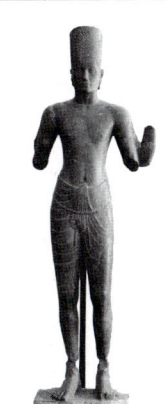

*Harihara, Prasat Andet
Cambodia, seventh century*

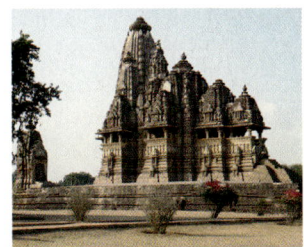

*Visvanatha Temple, Khajuraho
India, ca. 1000*

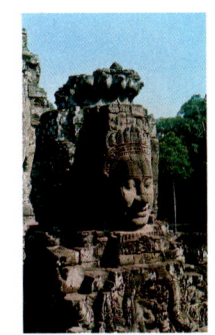

*Bayon, Angkor Thom
Cambodia, twelfth–thirteenth century*

Muslim incursions in South Asia begin, eighth century

Muslim sultanate in Delhi, 1206

Explicit sexual images first appear in Hinduism, ca. ninth century

Jayavarman II (r. 802–850) founds Angkor Dynasty, 802

Note: In view of unreliable written histories for India, specific dates for dynasties are sometimes speculative.

* Chandella dynasty predated its earliest known art and continued beyond the temple construction phase noted here.

† First securely dated Pallava art dates to the sixth century, although historical references refer to the Pallavas earlier.

The South Asian subcontinent, a vast geographic area, includes not only India but also the modern countries of Pakistan, Afghanistan, Nepal, Tibet, Bangladesh, and the island nation of Sri Lanka. Tremendous linguistic and cultural differences among its inhabitants mirror the region's geographic diversity. The people of India speak more than twenty different major languages. Those spoken in the north belong to the Indo-European language family, while those in the south form a completely separate linguistic family called Dravidian. India's art and architecture, produced over some five millennia, are also multicultural. Yet, the material created shares certain themes and characteristics, allowing its organization into categories for comparative discussion. Certainly, the most important attribute is religion. Religious uses and meanings characterize many of the surviving sculptures, paintings, and buildings in India. This chapter discusses the art and architecture of India and Southeast Asia from their beginnings until the thirteenth century. During that time, the two religions of greatest importance were Buddhism and Hinduism.

INDIA AND PAKISTAN

Indus Valley Civilization

In the third millennium B.C., long before the advent of Buddhism and Hinduism, one of the world's earliest important civilizations appeared in South Asia. The Indus Valley civilization spread over a wide geographic area along the Indus River in present-day Pakistan and extended into India as far south as Gujarat and east almost to Delhi. Several large cities, notably Harappa and Mohenjo-daro, attest to a remarkable urban phase for this civilization dating to ca. 2500–1700 B.C. These cities featured streets oriented to compass points, multistoried houses built of brick, and private bathing rooms with elaborate public drainage systems. One intriguing characteristic of the Indus civilization is that archeologists have not yet identified any surviving structures as either temples or palaces. This attribute marks a sharp contrast to the elaborate temple-and-palace architecture of the contemporaneous civilizations of Mesopotamia and Egypt (see Chapters 2 and 3), despite trade between the Indus culture and the ancient Near East.

Archeologists have uncovered a fair number of Indus objects to the west, including discoveries in Bahrain and on the Arabian Peninsula, but have found very few Near Eastern objects at Indus sites. Thus, it appears the Indus civilization traded durable manufactured goods, such as jewelry and stone seals, for nondurable items, perhaps textiles, that have disappeared from the archeological record. Internal trade, also of great importance for the Indus civilization, is one of the explanations for the remarkable cultural consistency among Indus sites.

PRIEST, KING, OR GOD? For such a long-lived civilization, archeologists have discovered surprisingly little art in the Indus Valley, and all of the objects found are small. Sculpture in stone and copper includes only about a dozen examples, the most impressive being the so-called priest-king (FIG. 6-1). This steatite (a soft local soapstone) sculpture, excavated at Mohenjo-daro, shows a bearded man wearing a headband with a central circular emblem, matched by a similar arm-

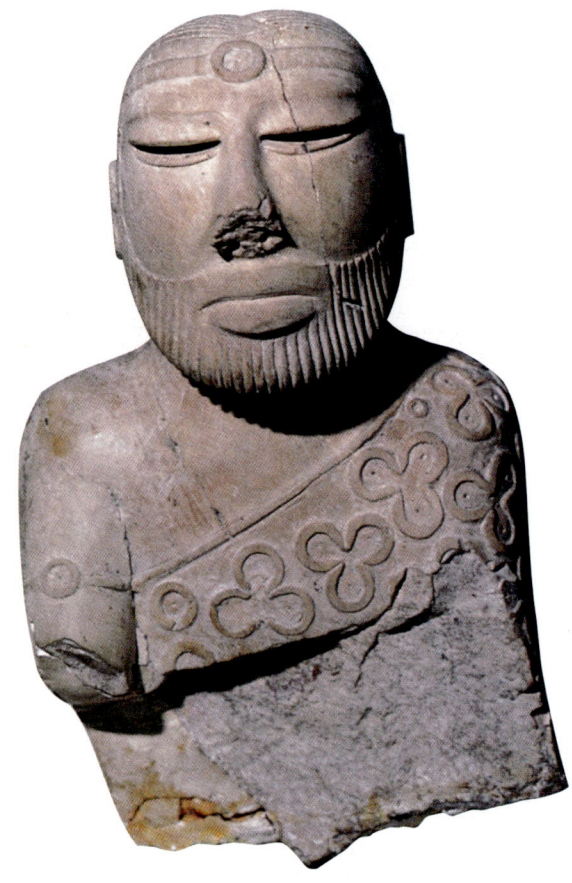

6-1   Priest-king(?), from Mohenjo-daro, Pakistan, ca. 2500–1700 B.C. Steatite, $6\frac{7}{8}''$ high. National Museum of Pakistan, Karachi.

band. A robe decorated with *trefoil* (a cloverlike ornament or symbol with stylized leaves in groups of three) designs covers his left shoulder and goes under his right arm. These designs, as well as the circles of the head- and armbands, originally held colored paste and shell inlays, as did the eyes. The individual depicted has not been identified, although he is clearly an important figure, perhaps a priest, king, or deity.

INDUS SEALS The most common Indus art objects are the so-called seals. Some twenty-five hundred steatite seals with incised designs have been found. They are similar in many ways to the cylinder seals found at contemporaneous sites in Mesopotamia (see "Mesopotamian Cylinder Seals," Chapter 2, page 26). Three impressions taken from typical seal types appear in our illustration (FIG. 6-2). Each seal measures only one or two inches square and has an animal or tiny narrative carved on its face, along with an as yet untranslated pictographic script. On the back, a boss (circular knob) with a hole permitted insertion of a string. As in the ancient Near East, the Indus peoples sometimes used the seals to make impressions on clay, apparently for securing trade goods wrapped in textiles. Most show no wear, however, so people probably also wore the "seals" on their bodies as a sign of identification or badge of office.

The animals most frequently represented on the seals are male bovines, including the humped zebu (FIG. 6-2, left), as well as such wild animals as the rhinoceros (FIG. 6-2, center) and tiger. Some of the narrative seals appear to show that the Indus peoples worshiped trees, as both Buddhists and Hindus later did. Many scholars have suggested that religious and rit-

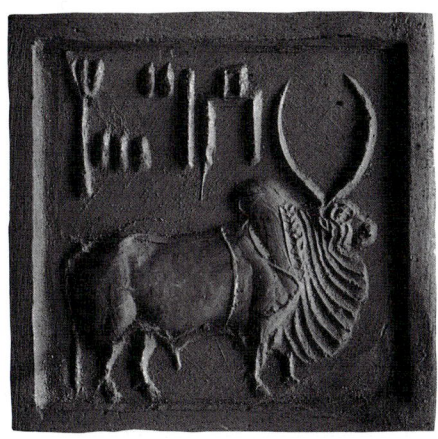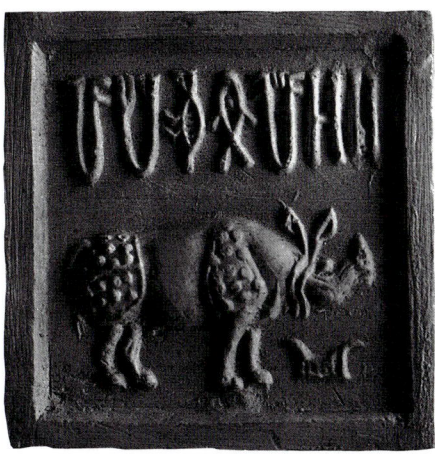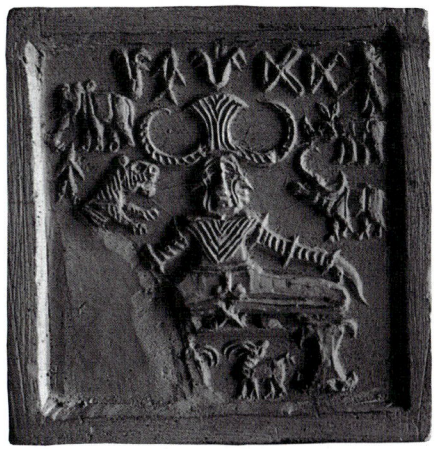

6-2 Seal impressions, from Mohenjo-daro, Pakistan, ca. 2500–1700 B.C. Seals, steatite, each approx. $1\frac{3}{8}'' \times 1\frac{3}{8}''$ square. National Museum, New Delhi.

ual continuities existed between the Indus civilization and later Indian culture.

A BUFFALO MAN IN A YOGIC POSTURE The most famous of the seals depicts a seated male figure with water buffalo horns (FIG. 6-2, right). The figure's folded legs and his arms resting on the knees suggest a yogic posture, a method for controlling the body and calming the mind used in later Indian religions (compare FIG. 6-14). Yogic postures include many seated, standing, walking, and lying positions. The seal figure assumes a very difficult position with the legs folded under the body so that the heels press together. Although most scholars reject the identification of this seal's figure as a prototype of the Hindu god Shiva, the yogic posture argues that this important Indian religious practice began as early as the Indus civilization.

Aryan Culture

By around 1700 B.C., the urban phase of the Indus civilization had ended. Sculptures, seals, and script all disappeared from production, and the culture returned to one of village life. Very little art survives from the next thousand years, presumably because people used such perishable materials as wood, leather, and cloth. But religious foundations laid during this period defined most later Indian art.

ARYAN PRIESTS AND GODS The earliest language yet identified in South Asia is Sanskrit, the language spoken by the Aryans, a mobile herding people who lived in the Punjab, an area of northwestern India. Scholars do not know for certain whether these people originated in the Punjab or migrated from other areas. However, many researchers no longer accept the view that the Aryans invaded the Punjab, and most have concluded these residents represented a mix of peoples and languages.

Around 1500 B.C., the Aryans composed in Sanskrit the first of four Vedic texts, the Rig-Veda (*veda* means "knowledge"). Each Veda is a compilation of religious learning. The Rig-Veda, a book of hymns meant for priests (called Brahmins) to chant or sing, gives a very different picture of religious life than scholars can glean from earlier Indus archeological finds. The Aryan religion centered on sacrifice, the

ritual enactment of often highly intricate and lengthy ceremonies officiated over by the Brahmin priests. The priests placed materials, such as milk and *soma* (the sacrificial brew), into a fire *(Agni)* that took the sacrifices to the gods in the heavens. If the priests performed the rituals accurately, the gods fulfilled the prayers of those who sponsored the sacrifices. These gods, primarily male, included Indra, Varuna, and Surya, gods associated, respectively, with the rains, the ocean, and the sun. It appears the Aryans did not make images of these deities.

The Rise of Buddhism, Jainism, and Hinduism

SAMSARA, KARMA, MOKSHA, AND NIRVANA The Aryans lived far from the Indus heartland. The new urban phase of Indian civilization, beginning around the sixth century B.C., appeared even farther south, in the Ganges River valley. Here, from 800 B.C. to 500 B.C., religious thinkers composed a variety of reactions against the Vedic rituals in texts called the Upanishads. Among their innovative ideas were *samsara, karma,* and *moksha* (or *nirvana*). Samsara is the belief individuals are born again after death in an almost endless round of rebirths. The type of rebirth can vary. One can be reborn as a human being, an animal, or even a god. A person also can be reborn in a hell. An individual's past actions (karma), either good or bad—recorded without a deity's judgment—determine the nature of future rebirths. The ultimate goal of a person's religious life is to stop the round of rebirths by achieving an ending of all existence, called either moksha (for Hindus) or nirvana (for Buddhists).

BUDDHISM, HINDUISM, AND JAINISM As typical of Indian religions, multiple paths can lead to fulfillment of this goal. One of the greatest Indian religious thinkers, the Buddha, advocated the path of *asceticism,* or self-discipline and self-denial (see "Buddhism and Buddhist Iconography," page 164). The Buddha was not the only religious thinker advocating asceticism as the means to end rebirth. Mahavira, a contemporary of the Buddha, believed in an even more rigorously ascetic system. Because the Indians considered Mahavira a *jina,* or saint, scholars call the religion he founded Jainism in English. The Hindus also support the ascetic path with a

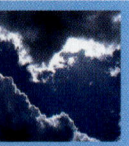

RELIGION AND MYTHOLOGY

Buddhism and Buddhist Iconography

The Buddha, or the Enlightened One, is the title given to Siddhartha Gautama, who also is called Sakyamuni, or the Wise Man of the Sakya Clan. The birth and death dates of this individual, the historical Buddha, are uncertain (different Buddhist sects give different dates). Current scholarship, however, places the Buddha's death around 400 B.C. Written down only many centuries after he died, the Buddha's life story records he was a minor Indian king's son destined to become either a great world conqueror or a great religious leader. He chose the latter. After living in opulence, he abandoned his wife and secular destiny to find enlightenment while meditating (in the yogic tradition) under a Bodhi Tree at Bodh Gaya in eastern India.

THE FOUR NOBLE TRUTHS

The Buddha's insight was that life is pain *(dukha)*, including repeated death with each rebirth. Karmic actions of any kind—motivated by desire for love, children, food, power, or things—cause rebirth. The Buddha proposed a way *(marga* or *path)* to stop desire. This insight, formulated as the Four Noble Truths, stipulated that (1) everything is pain; (2) the origin of pain is desire; (3) the extinction of desire is nirvana; and (4) following the path or way the Buddha discovered leads to the ending of pain. In the Buddha's view, usually a person had to become a monk or nun and cultivate specific virtues to achieve nirvana. Some Buddhist sects believe people can attain nirvana within a single lifetime, while others feel it is virtually impossible even after multiple rebirths. At any rate, the Buddha's system is a monastic organization, and most Buddhist art in India is monastic. Laypeople support the monks where Buddhism thrives—giving them all they need to live, including food, clothing, and shelter—and in doing so create merit (or good karma) for their own better rebirth. Ironically, Buddhism died out almost completely in India by about the thirteenth century.

BUDDHISM OUTSIDE INDIA

The Buddha's teachings changed and developed over time and as they spread from India throughout Asia. One general change came with the development of the Mahayana (great vehicle) doctrines during the early centuries of the Christian era. Although formulated for other purposes, the Mahayana doctrines afforded laypeople new ways to achieve spiritual goals. For example, *bodhisattvas* (enlightened beings; see FIGS. 6-12, 7-13, 8-7, 8-8, and FIG. Intro-8), special virtuous Mahayana deities, help people earn merit. Mahayana Buddhists worship the bodhisattvas independently of the Buddha. It is Mahayana Buddhism that spread to China, Korea, and Japan.

Yet another general shift in Buddhism, the development of Tantric teachings, involves secret or esoteric practices. Tantric Buddhism is also important in East Asia and exists today in Tibet as well. One of the earliest forms of Buddhism, Theravada, continues in Sri Lanka and most of mainland South-

east Asia. A Buddha who acquired special importance in East Asia, Amitabha, Buddha of the West (see FIGS. 7-14, 8-8, and 8-15), told followers he could grant salvation through entrance to his Pure Land paradise. Pure Land teachings maintain that people have no hope of attaining enlightenment on their own because of the corruption of their times. They can obtain rebirth in a heavenly realm, however, simply by faith in Amitabha's promise of salvation.

THE BUDDHA IN ART

The earliest Buddhist artists, although often depicting complex narrative scenes, did not show the Buddha in human form. Instead, they used symbols such as the wheel or the tree to suggest his presence. When artists began depicting the Buddha in human form around the first centuries B.C. and A.D., it was as a monk meditating (see FIGS. 6-13, 7-8, and 25-8) or teaching (FIG. 6-15). But they distinguished the Buddha from monks and bodhisattvas by *lakshanas,* bodily attributes or characteristics indicating the Buddha's superhuman nature. These distinguishing marks include an *urna,* or curl of hair between the eyebrows shown as a dot, and a *ushnisha,* a cranial bump shown as hair on the earliest images (FIGS. 6-13 and 6-14) but later as an actual part of the head (see FIG. Intro-8 and FIG. 6-15).

Episodes from the Buddha's life and death are among the most popular subjects in all Buddhist artistic traditions. No single text provides the complete or authoritative narrative of his life. Thus, numerous versions and variations exist, allowing for a rich artistic repertory. Some of the most popular scenes in Buddhist art, the Buddha's birth, enlightenment, first sermon, and death, took place at different locations (Lumbini, Bodh Gaya, Sarnath, and Kusinagara, now Kushinagar, respectively). Illustrations in this chapter depict three of these events. The enlightenment at Bodh Gaya entails several different phases, but most paintings and sculptures present the Buddha seated in meditation (FIGS. 6-13, 7-8, and 25-8) or touching the earth under the Bodhi Tree (see FIG. 7-28).

Depictions of the first sermon show the Buddha teaching, his hands held together in front of his body to indicate the turning of the Wheel of the Law (FIGS. 6-15 and 6-28). A symbolic hand gesture, or *mudra,* also can indicate concepts such as meditation or reassurance. The Buddha set this Wheel rolling with his first sermon, and the Wheel marks with its track the geographic extent of his teaching. Often, artists depicted the Wheel of the Law as an actual wheel flanked by deer, a reference to the Deer Park at Sarnath (FIG. 6-15, on the base below the Buddha). Finally, in scenes of his death *(parinirvana)*, artists portrayed the Buddha as lying down (FIG. 6-26).

Indian Buddhists erected monasteries and monuments at all four sites of these key events. Monks and lay pilgrims from throughout the Buddhist world continue to visit these places today.

tradition of wandering, homeless ascetics. But Hinduism (discussed in more detail later; see "Hinduism and Hindu Iconography," page 173) differs from both Buddhism and Jainism in not having a human founder. Indeed, no simple definition of Hinduism is possible, as it is highly individualistic. Hinduism and Buddhism both developed in the late centuries B.C. and early centuries A.D. Unlike the practitioners of the Aryan religion these religions displaced, followers of both Hinduism and Buddhism made and used images of their gods in worship.

Maurya Art and Architecture

Many artistic innovations began during the Maurya dynasty (fourth to second centuries B.C.), including the use of stone, a medium not used for the preceding eighteen hundred years of the Vedic and Upanishadic periods. The dynasty's most famous king, Ashoka (r. 272–231 B.C.), ruled almost all of present-day India, a geographic area not matched in size again until the modern nation of India formed in 1947, after it won independence from Britain. Ashoka's capital was Pataliputra (modern Patna in Bihar state). Today, his palace there lies largely in ruins, but an early visitor to Pataliputra left a glowing description of it. Megasthenes, the ambassador at the Maurya court from the Greek king Seleucus Nicator (ruler of Persia and Babylon at the end of the fourth and the beginning of the third centuries B.C.), detailed the attributes of the Maurya capital. Megasthenes described a walled city with sixty-four gates and five hundred seventy towers, as well as gardens, fishponds, and pillared buildings.

ASHOKA'S PILLARS AND MORAL LAW   To rule his vast domains, Ashoka created a unique form of government, rule by *dharma,* or moral law, based largely on the Buddha's teaching (also called dharma). Ashoka had his moral laws inscribed on rocks and tall stone pillars throughout his kingdom in a variety of languages and scripts. The freestanding pillars, usually made of one enormous piece of stone, stood forty feet tall above ground, with another twenty feet buried in the earth. Sculptors placed an elaborate capital, also carved from a single block of stone, above each pillar. The famous lion capital originally topping a pillar at Sarnath (FIG. **6-3**), where the Buddha gave his first sermon, features two pairs of back-to-back lions at the top. They stand on a round abacus decorated with four wheels and four animals carved in relief above a lotus-form capital. The lions once carried a stone wheel, whose fragments still exist, on their backs. The wheel referred to the Buddha's Wheel of the Law but also indicated Ashoka's stature as a *chakravartin,* a universal king whose war chariot marked his secular kingdom with its wheels.

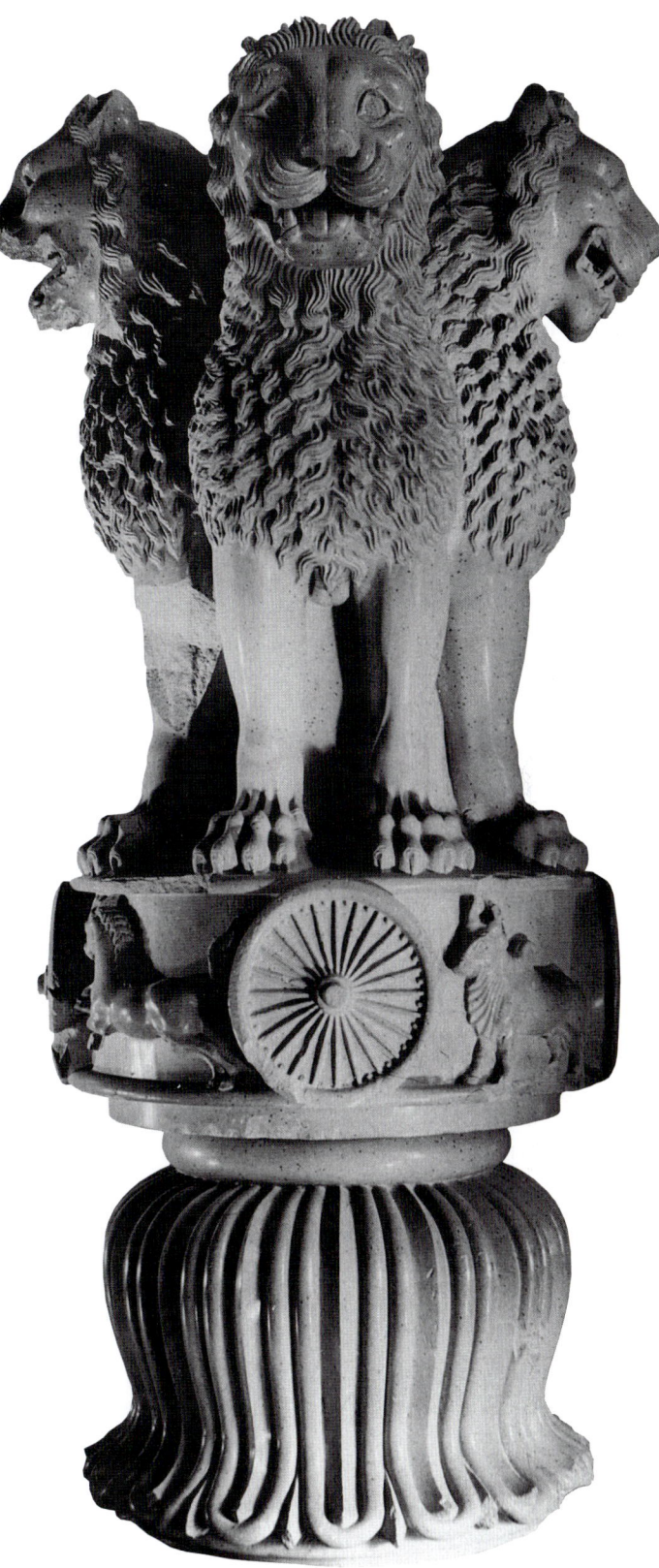

6-3   Lion capital of column erected by Emperor Ashoka (r. 272–231 B.C.), from Sarnath, India. Polished sandstone, 8′ high. Archeological Museum, Sarnath.

THE ROCK-CUT CAVES OF THE AJIVIKAS   Ashoka supported other religious groups as well as the Buddhists, and sponsored the earliest rock-cut caves for a now-extinct ascetic group, the Ajivikas. One of these caves, the Lomas Rishi, contains a room excavated into the rock with a carved curved wall at one end that copies the shape of a

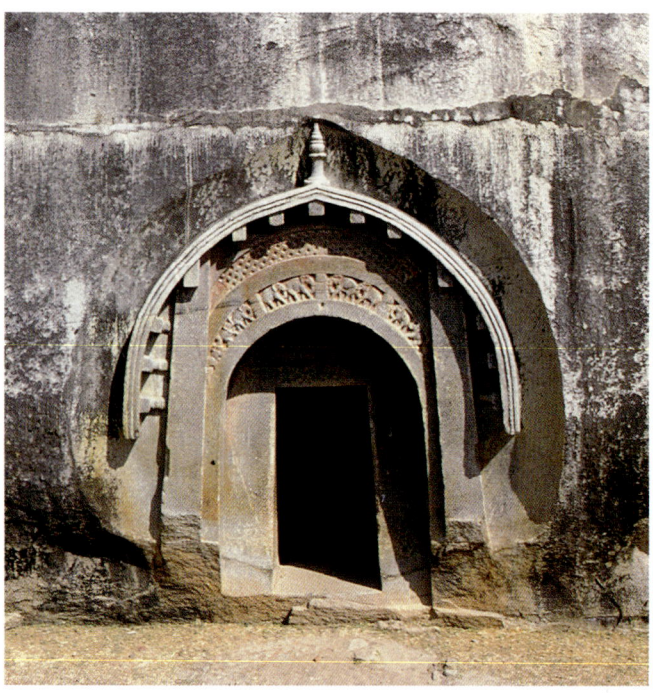

6-4 Entrance to the Lomas Rishi cave, Barabar Hills, India, mid-third century B.C.

Buddhist Art and Architecture

After the fall of the Maurya dynasty around the beginning of the second century B.C., a variety of dynasties ruled India, controlling various geographic areas over time but in constant cycles of expansion and collapse. Although art historians often classify Indian art according to dynastic names, time and place, not dynasties, determined artistic styles. Kings in India sponsored the erection of monuments and image making, but the rulers usually did not determine the style of the buildings or art objects. The artists produced art in the traditions they had learned, traditions determined by the times and by where the artists lived. Nor did religion shape artistic styles. The same artists produced both Buddhist and Hindu art in similar styles. More early Buddhist than Hindu art (particularly until the first century A.D.) has survived in India, because the Buddhists constructed large monastic institutions with durable materials such as stone and brick. The Hindus at this time tended to worship in their homes and at small shrines, using wooden images set up under trees.

THE GREAT STUPA AT SANCHI Sanchi, a Buddhist monastery founded during Ashoka's reign, existed for more than a thousand years. It consists of many buildings constructed over the centuries, including *viharas* (celled structures where monks lived), *stupas* (hemispherical monuments enshrining the relics of the Buddha and other important monks), *chaityas* (buildings with rounded, or apsidal, ends for housing stupas), and temples for sheltering images.

Stupas come in many sizes, from tiny handheld objects to huge structures, such as the Great Stupa at Sanchi (FIGS. **6-5** and **6-6**). The Great Stupa in its present form dates from ca. 50 B.C. to A.D. 50. The dome, solid and filled with earth and rubble, stands fifty feet high with a double stairway on the south side leading to an upper-level walkway. Although nineteenth-century excavators did not find any relics in the earthen dome, archeologists assume the builders did bury relics inside this stupa.

free-standing thatched hut. A carved facade around the cave's door (FIG. **6-4**) mimics contemporaneous bent-wood architecture. A brief inscription at the site states that Ashoka gave one of the caves to shelter the Ajivika monks from the monsoon rains. Both Buddhists and Hindus in India used rock-cut architecture extensively until about the tenth century. The horseshoe shape of the Lomas Rishi's facade decoration became one of the most common motifs in all later Indian architecture (FIG. 6-11). This particular example at Lomas Richi has a pointed top, although many other variations of the form are also common.

6-5 Great Stupa, Sanchi, India, first century B.C. to first century A.D.

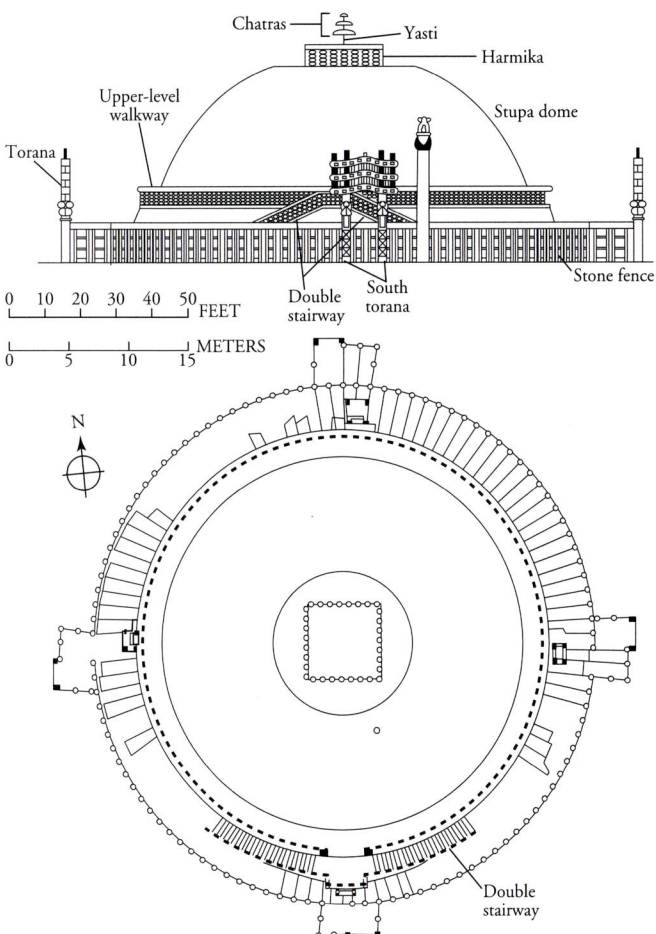

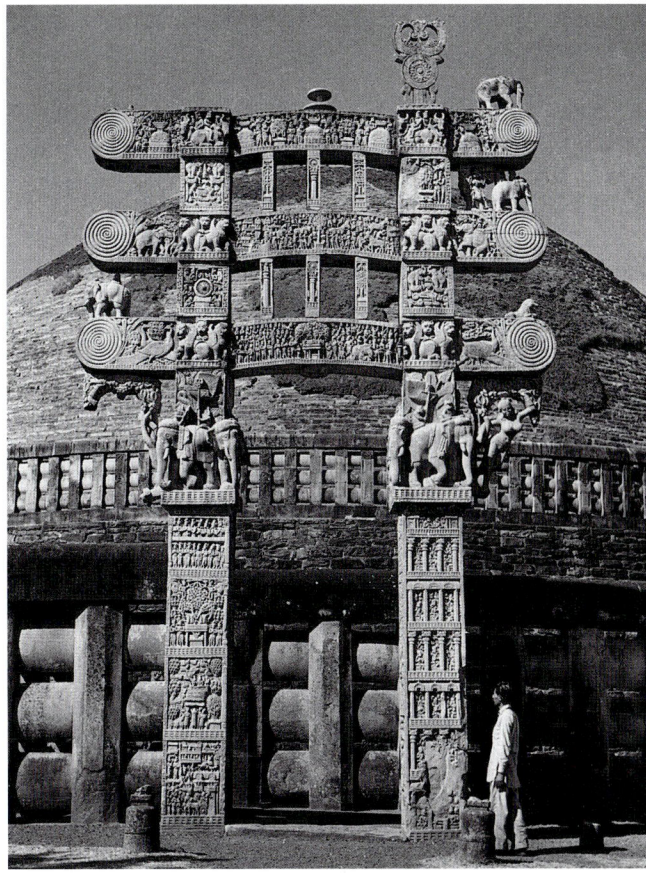

6-7   Eastern gateway, Great Stupa, Sanchi, India, first century B.C. to first century A.D.

6-6   Exterior diagram and plan of Great Stupa, Sanchi, India, first century B.C. to first century A.D.

Several architectural features of the stupa have symbolic meanings, transforming it into a model of the cosmos. The stupa itself (FIG. 6-6) symbolically represents the world mountain, with the cardinal points marked by gateways, or *toranas.* The *harmika,* positioned atop the stupa dome, is a stone fence or railing that encloses a square area representing one of the Buddhist heavens. At the harmika's center, a *yasti,* or pole, symbolizes the axis of the universe. Three stone disks, or *chatras,* assigned various meanings, crown the yasti. The yasti rises from the mountain-dome and passes through the harmika, thus uniting this world with the paradise above. Enclosing the entire structure is a stone fence, nine to eleven feet tall, its toranas (FIG. 6-7) covered with elaborate relief carvings.

Buddhists worship a stupa by *circumambulation,* walking around it in a clockwise direction so that the body's right side faces the monument. Using a fence or railing to mark off a sacred place or object is common in India, and worshipers of the Great Stupa could enter through a gateway and walk on the lower circumambulation path and then climb the stairs to circumambulate at the second level. Carved onto the different parts of the Great Stupa, more than six hundred brief inscriptions show that the donations of hundreds of individuals made the monument's construction possible. The vast majority of them common laypeople, monks, and nuns, they hoped to accrue merit for future rebirths with their gifts.

THE BUDDHA'S PAST LIVES   The reliefs on the four toranas at Sanchi, such as the eastern gateway (FIGS. **6-7** and **6-8**), depict not only the Buddha's life story but also the stories of his past lives *(jatakas).* In Buddhist belief, everyone has

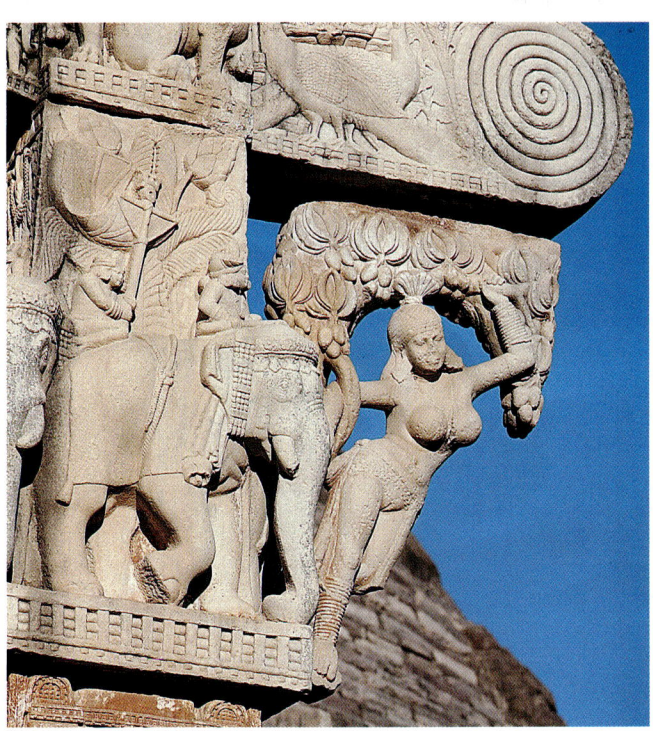

6-8   Yakshi, detail of eastern gateway (FIG. 6-7), Great Stupa, Sanchi, India, first century B.C. to first century A.D.

had innumerable past lives, including Siddhartha. During Siddhartha's past lives, as recorded in the jatakas, he accumulated sufficient merit to achieve enlightenment and become the Buddha. In the life stories recounted in the Great Stupa reliefs, however, the Buddha never appears as a human being. Instead, the artists indicated his presence by using symbols—the form of a wheel, for example. Scholars do not know precisely why early artists avoided portraying the Buddha in human form, but the first such depictions of him appeared around the time of the carving of the Sanchi gateways.

EROTIC ART IN A MONASTERY   Also not clear is the reason an image such as the well-known eastern gateway *yakshi* (FIG. 6-8), an essentially nude and highly erotic female, appears on a monument found within a monastic complex housing celibate monks. Such yakshis, which people worshiped throughout India, are local goddesses associated with fertility and vegetation. It is likely their incorporation into Buddhist monuments stemmed from their popularity with devotees. In the example at Sanchi, the yakshi reaches up to hold onto the mango tree branch above her while pressing her left foot against the trunk, an action intended to bring the tree to flower. Buddhists later adopted this pose, with its rich associations of fertility and abundance, for representing the

Buddha's mother, Maya, giving birth. Thus, the Buddhists adopted pan-Indian symbolism, such as the woman under the tree, to create their own Buddhist iconography.

A MONASTIC HALL CUT OUT OF ROCK Other Buddhist monasteries from the last century B.C. and the first and second centuries A.D. feature viharas (for the monks to sleep in) and chaitya halls (for worship of the stupa) carved out of living rock. The chaitya halls, apsidal structures with pillared *ambulatories* (walking paths), allow worshipers to circumambulate the stupa placed at the back of the hall. The chaitya hall at Karli (FIGS. **6-9** to **6-11**), built around A.D. 100 in the Western Ghats (a chain of mountains) near Bombay (present-day Mumbai), is nearly forty-five feet high and one hundred twenty-five feet long. It surpasses in size and grandeur even the rock-cut chamber of the temple of the great Egyptian pharaoh Ramses II (see FIG. 3-23). Inside, the builders affixed curved wooden beams to the rock ceiling in imitation of small wooden models, even though the beams perform no architectural function here. Elaborate capitals atop the rock-cut pillars depict men and women riding on elephants.

A large horseshoe-shaped window dominates the Karli hall's impressive facade. Images of paired men and women

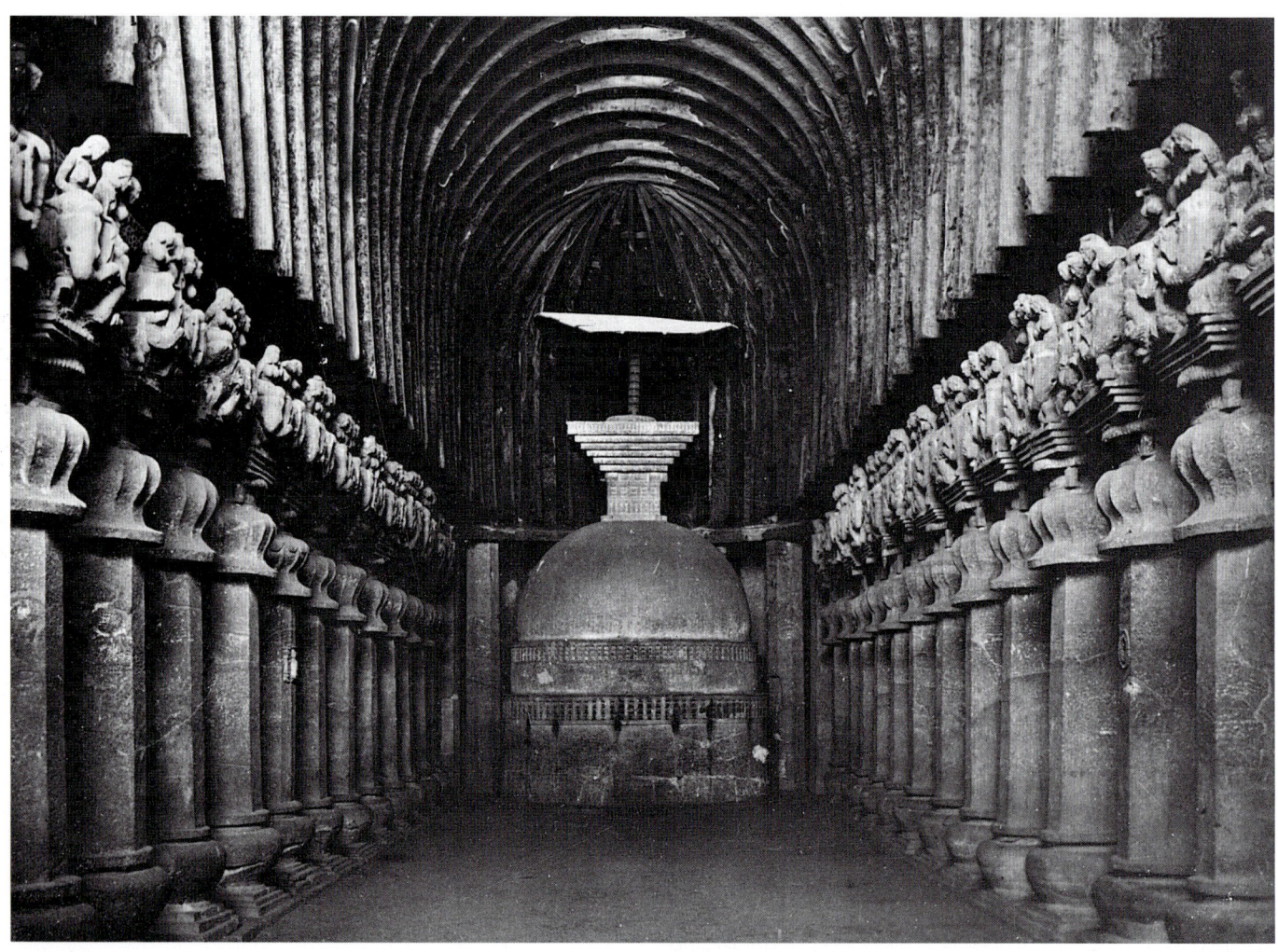

6-9   Interior of chaitya hall, Karli, India, ca. 100.

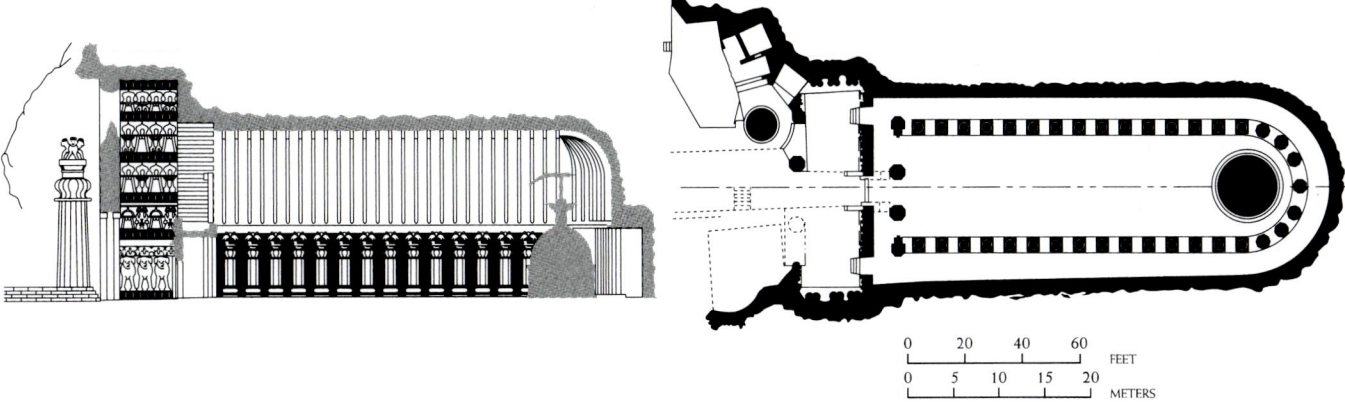

6-10 Section *(left)* and plan *(right)* of chaitya hall, Karli, India, ca. 100.

flank the central doorway. The sculptor inventively placed the couple in our example (FIG. 6-11) in the awkward space of the facade's characteristically horseshoe-shaped false windows.

THE PAINTED CAVES OF AJANTA Buddhist rock-cut architecture appears to have gone out of favor after Karli, only to be revived suddenly some three hundred fifty years later. Several caves at Ajanta, northeast of Bombay, date to the earlier period, but during the second half of the fifth century, a burst of activity at the site produced more than twenty new caves. One reason for their importance is that they retain much of their painted wall decoration. Art historians assume India had a rich painting tradition in ancient times, but because early Indian artists often used perishable materials, such as palm leaf and wood, and because of the tropical climate in much of India, nearly all early Indian painting has been lost. At Ajanta, however, paintings cover the walls, pillars, and ceilings of some of the caves.

The central male individual in one painting (FIG. **6-12**) is a bodhisattva, one of a pair flanking the entrance to the Buddha shrine at the rear center of one of the Ajanta caves. With long, dark hair hanging down below a jeweled crown, he stands holding a lotus flower in his right hand and surrounded by male and female attendants. His face shows great compassion as he gazes downward at the actual worshipers passing through the shrine entrance on their way to the monumental rock-cut Buddha image housed in a cell at the back of the cave. The Ajanta caves provide a tantalizing glimpse of early Indian painting. Significant later examples of paintings in India are rare before the thirteenth century (see Chapter 25).

GANDHARA AND GRECO-ROMAN ART At some point during the first century B.C. or A.D., Indian artists began to depict the Buddha in human form. These images appeared at this time for at least two different reasons. One may be that human Buddha images were not part of the early Indian tradition. Peoples of the Indus and the Vedic periods did not make icons of their chief gods. From the Mauryan period up until the first century B.C., only human images of lesser local gods and goddesses, such as the yakshi depicted on Sanchi's eastern gateway (FIG. 6-8), occur. An additional reason may be the concept of *bhakti* as a path to the deity, which arose in both Buddhist and Hindu thought during the first centuries B.C. and A.D. Bhakti is loving devotion to a particular deity, demonstrated by giving gifts such as food, songs, and flowers to the deity's images. Such gift giving may have stimulated representations of the gods in humanlike forms.

Although researchers cannot pin down an exact place and date for the invention of such Buddha images, they do agree

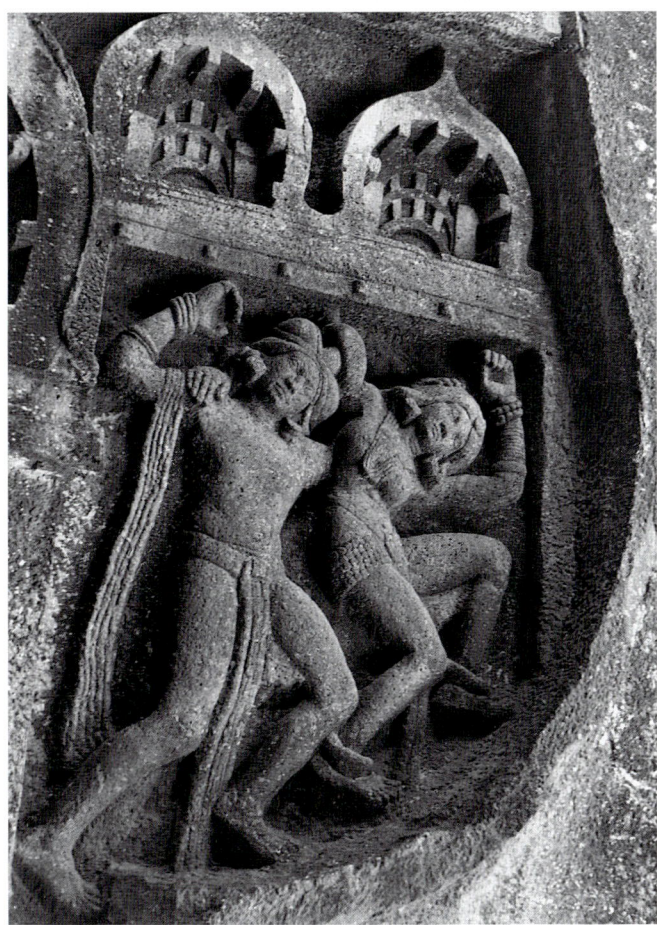

6-11 Loving couple, chaitya hall entrance, Karli, India, ca. 100.

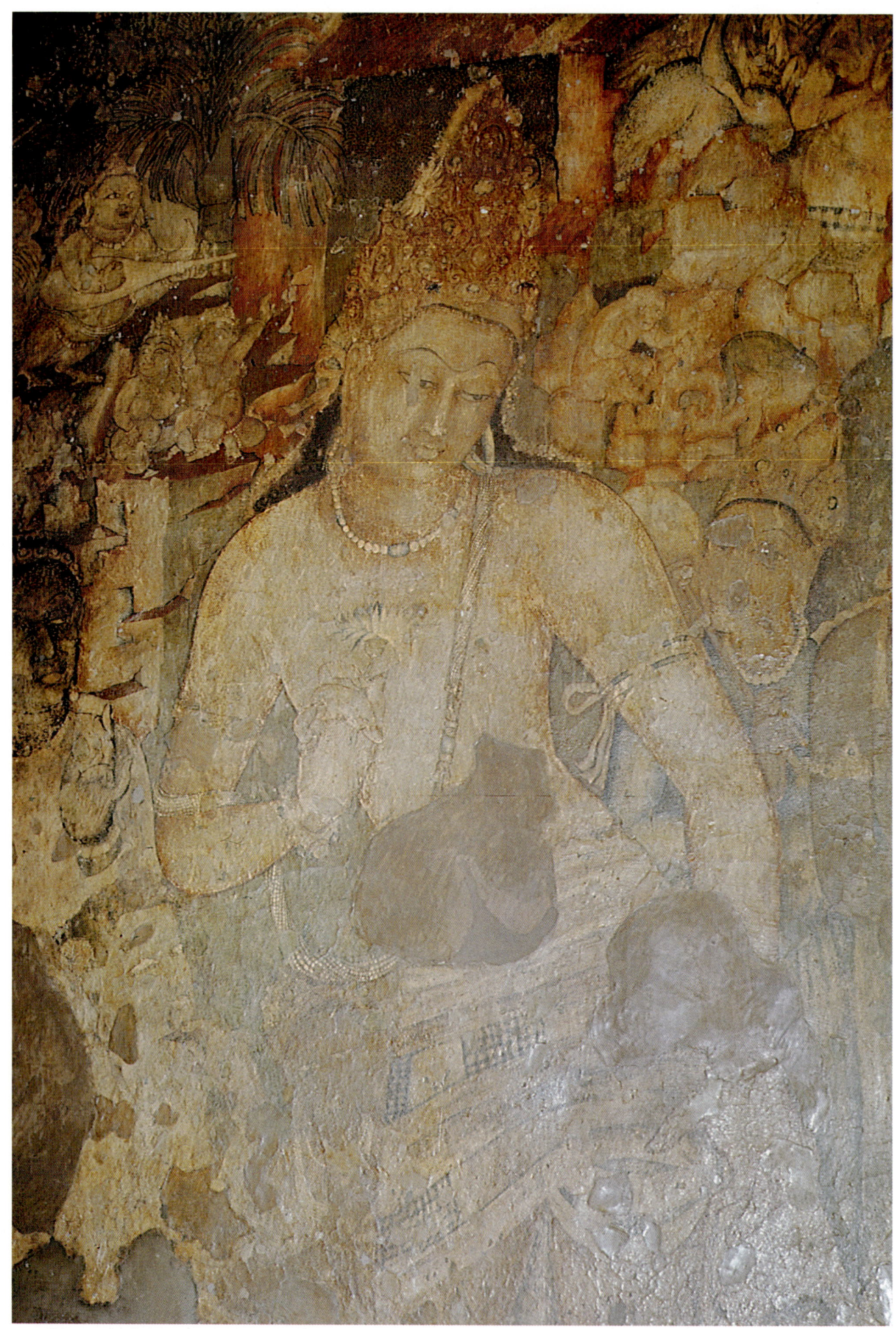

6-12 Bodhisattva, wall fresco in Cave I, Ajanta, India, ca. 450–500.

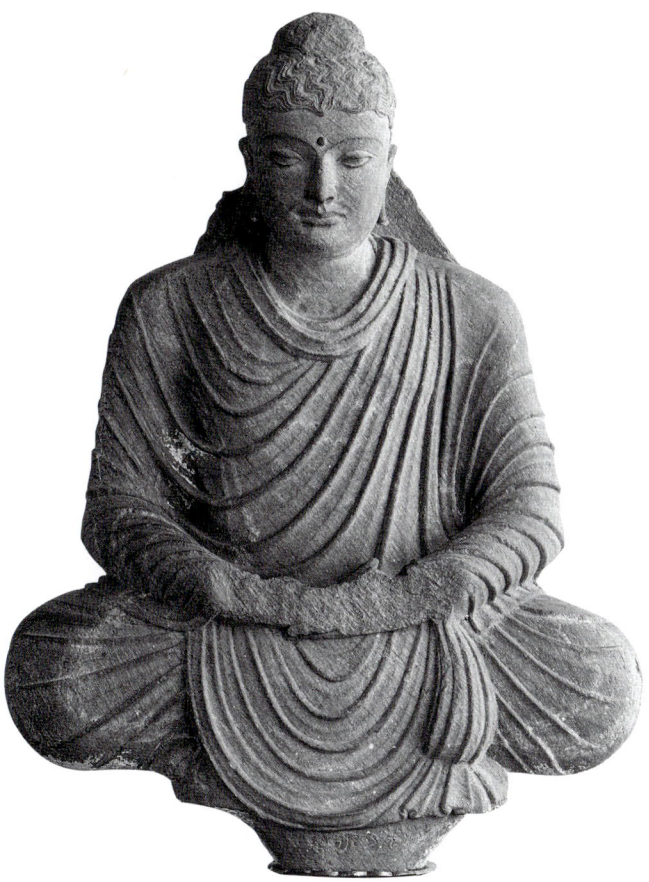

6-13 Seated Buddha, from Gandhara, Pakistan, ca. second to third century. Stone (black schist), 2' 4 3/4" high. Yale University Art Gallery, New Haven.

that, once created, these images became very popular. Among the earliest are those represented by two sculptural styles, one that developed in Gandhara and one at Mathura. Both Gandhara, an area largely in Pakistan today, and Mathura, a city about ninety miles south of Delhi, were important parts of the Kushan empire that ruled much of northern South Asia during the first three centuries A.D.

The Gandhara style (FIG. **6-13**) is, surprisingly, Greco-Roman in character. Gandhara was part of a widespread region of Hellenistic culture and art that stretched across reaches of modern Iran, Russia, Afghanistan, and Pakistan, a legacy of Alexander's incursions in these regions in the fourth century B.C. (see Chapter 5). When Gandharan artists sought models for their Buddha sculptures, they turned to material they were already familiar with—images of deities such as Apollo (see FIG. Intro-7). Thus, they depicted the Buddha with similarly wavy hair, topped by a bun tied with a ribbon. Masking the body underneath, the Buddha's heavy robe emphasizes the elaborate design of the folds, in the Hellenistic-Roman tradition (see FIG. 10-72).

BUDDHIST IMAGERY IN MATHURA Mathura Buddha images (FIG. **6-14**), in contrast, relate more clearly to human images in the Indian tradition—*yakshas,* the male equivalents of the yakshis. Indian artists represented yakshas as bulky, powerful males with broad shoulders and open,

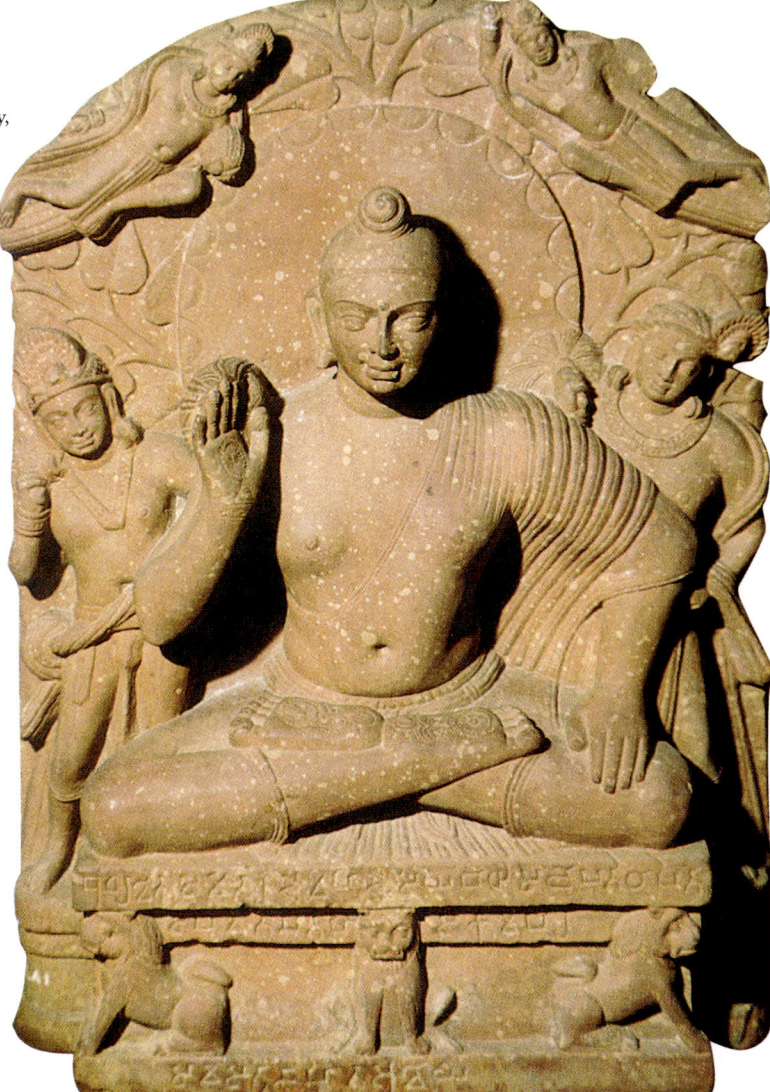

6-14 Seated Buddha, from Mathura, India, second century. Red sandstone, 2' 3 1/2" high. Archeological Museum, Muttra.

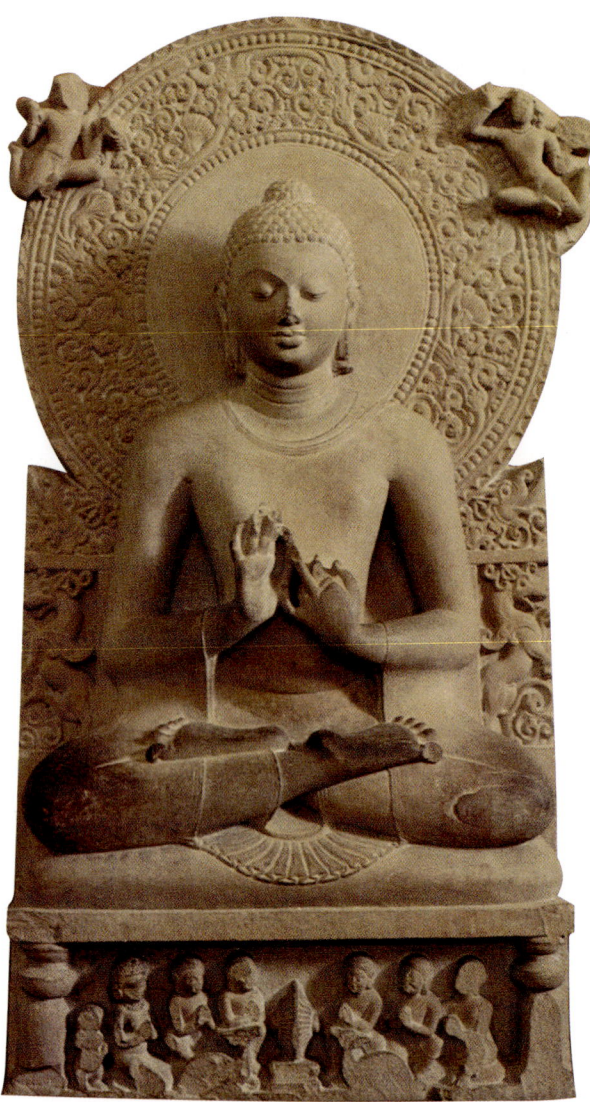

6-15 Seated Buddha preaching first sermon, from Sarnath, India, fifth century. Sandstone, 5′ 3″ high. Archeological Museum, Sarnath.

staring eyes. The Mathura Buddha images retain these characteristics but wear a monk's robe and sit in a yogic posture with the right hand raised palm-out in a gesture indicating to worshipers they need have no fear. The robe appears almost transparent, revealing the thick, full body beneath.

THE TEACHING BUDDHA OF SARNATH The Gandhara Buddha style (FIG. 6-13) had little impact on India's later art, although in China it served as the model for the earliest Chinese Buddha images (see FIG. 7-8). The Mathura-style image, in contrast, was the source for much of later Buddhist sculpture, developing at Sarnath in the fifth century as one of the most important image styles. The Sarnath Buddha (FIG. **6-15**) retains the clinging robe of the earlier Mathura image, revealing a body with a softened build. The Buddha's eyes are downcast, and he holds his hands in front of his body in the Wheel-turning gesture (compare FIG. 6-28), preaching his first sermon, indicated by the tiny Wheel of the Law seen on its edge below the figure. Flanking the Wheel, two now partially broken deer symbolize the Deer Park at Sarnath, where the Buddha delivered his first sermon.

Hindu Art and Architecture

Buddhists and Hindus practiced their religions side by side in India, often at the same site (Mathura, for example). Buddhism and Hinduism are not one-god religions, such as Judaism, Christianity, and Islam. Instead, Buddhists and Hindus approach the spiritual through many gods and varying paths, which permits mutually tolerated differences. Although Hindus worship a multitude of different deities, Vishnu (FIG. 6-16), Shiva (FIGS. 6-17, 6-18, and 6-25), and Devi (or "the Goddess") are the most popular and important (see "Hinduism and Hindu Iconography," page 173).

VISHNU RESCUES THE EARTH The Hindus began to construct cave temples long after the Buddhists did. The earliest, at Udayagiri near Sanchi, constructed ca. A.D. 400, some six hundred years after the first Buddhist examples. Yet, within a century, the Hindu cave temples had reached great size and complexity. Even the earliest Udayagiri caves, although architecturally simple and small, contain monumental relief sculptures showing an already fully developed religious iconography—sometimes with political overtones (see "Myth and History in Indian Sculpture," page 174). The Boar Avatar of Vishnu (sometimes identified as Varaha, using the Sanskrit word for *boar*), carved in a shallow niche of rock at Udayagiri (FIG. **6-16**), stands about thirteen feet tall. The

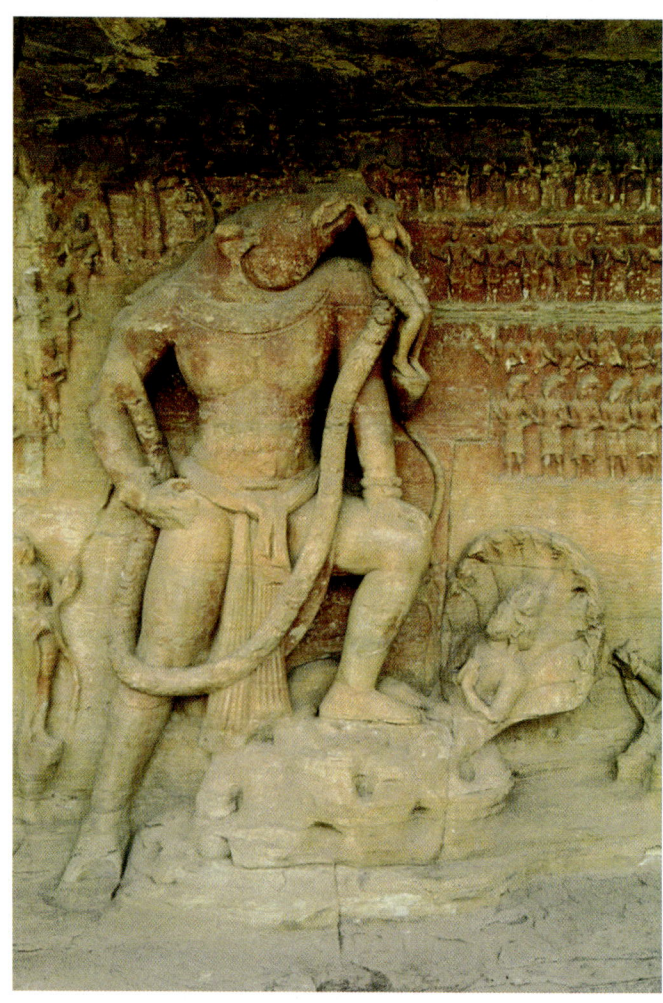

6-16 Boar Avatar of Vishnu, Cave V, Udayagiri, India, ca. 400. Vishnu 12′ 8″ high.

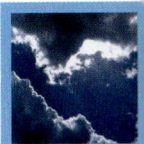

Hinduism and Hindu Iconography

Hinduism has no simple definition. Indeed, the term creates such controversy that Indians have turned to their law courts in an attempt to determine a definition. The actual practices and beliefs of Hindus vary tremendously, with many paths leading to spiritual goals. The three most important Hindu deities, Shiva, Vishnu, and Devi, all have various forms, and Hindus also worship many other gods. The earliest humanlike Hindu images appeared at the same time as the first Buddha images in human form.

Shiva often takes the form of a *linga* (a phallus or cosmic pillar), which artists have represented in a highly abstracted geometric form since about the sixth century. But Shiva also appears in human form in Hindu art, frequently with multiple arms (FIGS. 6-17 and 6-25) and heads (FIG. 6-18).

The many forms Vishnu assumes include *avatars,* manifestations of the deity incarnated in some visible form while performing a sacred function on earth. In these instances, Vishnu descends to earth to protect it from demons. As the Boar Avatar (FIG. 6-16), for example, he saves the earth from floods.

Devi (or the Goddess) assumes multiple forms, too—both benevolent and destructive. Sometimes linked to the male gods Shiva and Vishnu as consort, she also appears alone when worshiped as the supreme deity.

The stationary images of deities in Hindu temples are often made of stone. Hindus periodically remove movable images, often of bronze, from the temple, particularly during festivals to enable many worshipers to take *darshan* (seeing the deity and being seen by the deity) at one time. In temples dedicated to Shiva, the permanent form is the linga, displayed in the *garbha griha* (womb chamber) or inner sanctuary (FIG. 6-22), where priests attend to the deity.

The Shiva Nataraja (FIG. 6-25) is a movable image, but it would not appear in worship as it does in an art history book. Rather, when Hindus worship the Shiva Nataraja, they dress the image, cover it with jewels, and garland it with flowers. The only bronze part visible is the face, marked with colored powders and scented pastes. Considered the embodiment of the deity, the image is not a symbol of the god but the god itself. All must treat the god/image as a living being. Worship of the deity involves taking care of him as if he were an honored person. Bathed, clothed, given foods to eat, and taken for outings, the image also receives such gifts as songs, lights (lit oil lamps), good smells (incense), and flowers—all things he can enjoy through the senses. The food given to the god is particularly important, as he eats the "essence," leaving the remainder for the worshiper. The food is then *prasada* (grace), sacred because it came in contact with the divine. In an especially religious household, the deity resides as an image and receives the food for each meal before the family eats. When the god resides in a temple, it is then the duty of the priests to feed, clothe, and take care of him.

avatar has a human body and a boar's head. Vishnu assumed this form when he rescued the earth, here personified as a female who clings to the boar's tusk, from a flood. Vishnu stands with one foot resting on the coils of a snake king (identified by the multiple hoods behind his human head), who represents the conquered flood waters. Rows of gods and ascetics form lines to witness the event.

A MANY-ARMED DANCING SHIVA   In the sixth century, under the Chalukya kings, Hindu artists carved a series of reliefs in caves at Badami in the Deccan, a plateau area between northern and southern India. One relief (FIG. **6-17**) shows Shiva in the *lalita* or "charming" pose, which he assumes to seduce his consort Parvati. As he dances, his multiple arms swing rhythmically in an arc. Some of the hands hold objects, and others form prescribed *mudras* (symbolic gestures). At the right, a drummer accompanies the dance, while Shiva's son, the elephant-headed Ganesha, tentatively mimics his father. Nandi, Shiva's bull mount, stands at the left.

Artists often represented Hindu deities as part human and part animal (FIG. 6-16) or as figures with multiple body parts (FIG. 6-17). Because these are images of gods, not of human beings, they should not be judged by a standard of human anatomical accuracy. Indeed, these composite and multi-limbed forms indicate that the subjects are not human but more-than-human gods. The Western standard of naturalistic depiction of gods in human form, set by the Greeks

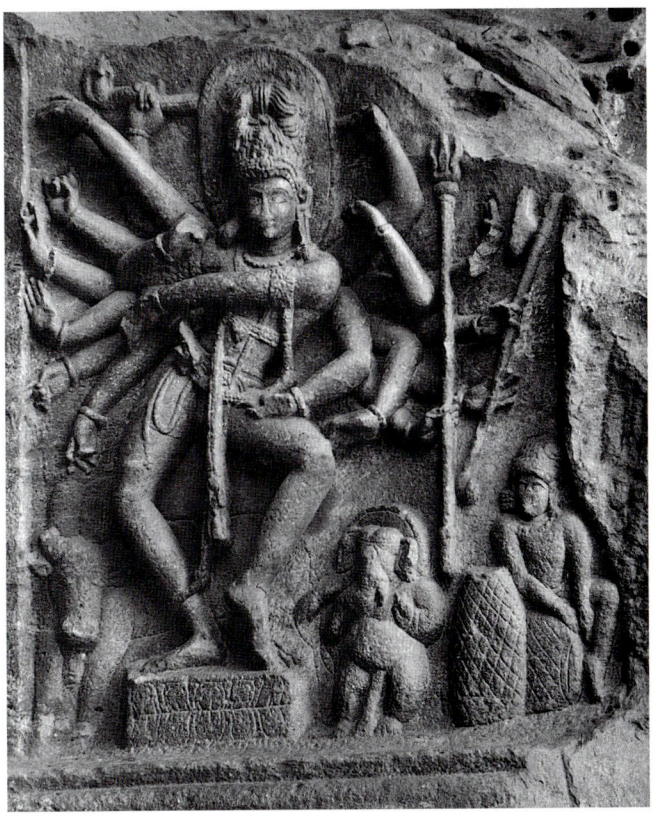

6-17   Dancing Shiva, relief in cave temple, Badami, India, sixth century.

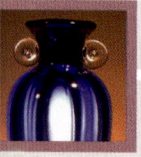

Myth and History in Indian Sculpture

The story of Vishnu's Avatar Varaha rescuing the earth from the flood waters, depicted in the monumental relief at Udayagiri (FIG. 6-16), is a myth, an imaginary or legendary tale. Scholars often contrast mythological narratives with historical ones—that is, narratives based on actual events and personalities. By this definition, mythology, not history, is the almost exclusive subject of early Indian art. Even depictions of the Buddha's life (FIG. 6-15) can be considered mythic, because the artistic representations, as well as the textual narratives of his life, are so far removed from the historical Buddha's lifetime and so filled with the miraculous that it is difficult to label them as historical.

Although in many cultures myth and history can be clearly differentiated, the distinction was much more ambiguous in ancient India. People used the stories of the deities, the myths, as a way of seeing and understanding their world. They interpreted their own actions and lives (that is, "history") in terms of those of the deities (that is, "myth"). This explains in part why it is so difficult to find historical scenes in ancient Indian art.

In the ancient Near East and Egypt, rulers frequently commemorated their victories and other great deeds in stone reliefs (see Chapters 2 and 3), a practice which reached a high point in the ancient world in Roman art (see Chapter 10). But such overtly political artworks featuring historical events and persons appear rarely in ancient Indian art. When Indian kings and powerful elites sponsored religious art, they expected their patronage to gain them merit for future rebirths. But some of their monuments also commemorated contemporary events, such as victories in war. Rather than depicting themselves and the actual events, however, they placed themselves by analogy into a relationship with the deity. Thus, mythic reliefs can have hidden political meaning.

The patron of the Udayagiri Varaha relief, a local king, gave honor in an inscription to Chandragupta II (r. 376–412), the king of the Guptas, the most important and powerful Indian dynasty at the time. The relief's creators apparently dedicated the work to Chandragupta.

Chandragupta consolidated most of northern India into his empire by defeating the last of a group of kings who had ruled that region of India for hundreds of years. At Udayagiri, Varaha's victory in saving the earth parallels Chandragupta's victories. The local king wanted viewers (including perhaps Chandragupta, since inscriptions indicate he actually visited the site) to see Chandragupta as saving his kingdom by ridding it of its enemies much in the way Varaha saved the earth. Certain pictorial clues in the relief reinforce this interpretation. For example, on each side of the niche streams of water (identified by female personifications) meet to form a single stream. The two streams represent the Ganges and Yamuna Rivers, which merge at Allahabad to form the single mighty Ganges that ultimately empties into the ocean in the Bay of Bengal. Allahabad was the capital of the Gupta dynasty. The relief suggests that just as the two great northern rivers unite at Chandragupta's capital, the king united the north under his rule. Thus, the artist clothed contemporary events in mythological guise, as the ancient Greeks frequently did (see Chapter 5).

(see Chapter 5), does not apply to Indian images. Indian artists did not intend to portray accurate anatomy.

SHIVA WITH THREE FACES

A third Hindu cave site, just off the coast of Bombay, is on Elephanta, an island named by early Portuguese colonizers who found a life-size stone elephant sculpture there. Perhaps the most impressive of the Elephanta reliefs is a seventeen-foot-high image of Shiva as Mahadeva (FIG. **6-18**), the "Great God" or Lord of Lords, set deep within the cave in a niche once closed off with wooden doors. Two stone door guardians with dwarf attendants flank the niche. Mahadeva appears to emerge out of the dark of the cave as worshipers' eyes become accustomed to the darkness. This image of Shiva has three faces, which show different aspects of the deity. The central face expresses Shiva's quiet, balanced demeanor. The face's clean planes contrast with the richness of the piled hair encrusted with jewels. The two side faces differ significantly. That on the right is female, with framing hair curls. The left face is a grimacing male with a curling mustache who wears a cobra as an earring. The female (Uma) indicates the creative aspect of Shiva, while the fierce male (Bhairava) represents Shiva's destructive side. Shiva holds these two opposing forces in check, and the central face expresses their balance. The cyclic destruction and creation of the universe, which the side faces also symbolize, is part of Indian notions of time, matched by the cyclic pattern of death and rebirth (samsara) and further symbolized by Shiva as Lord of the Dance (FIG. 6-25).

VISHNU'S TOWER TEMPLE AT DEOGARH

Although the Hindus excavated many striking cave temples out of living rock (unquarried stone), temples constructed of stone blocks became more important in Hinduism. As with the caves, the Hindus initially built rather small and simple temples but with a fully developed iconography. The Vishnu Temple at Deogarh (FIG. **6-19**) in north central India, erected in the early sixth century, is among the first Hindu temples constructed with stone blocks. (The Hindus built temples in wood, thatch, and mud earlier and continued to do so even after the introduction of stone masonry.) A simple square

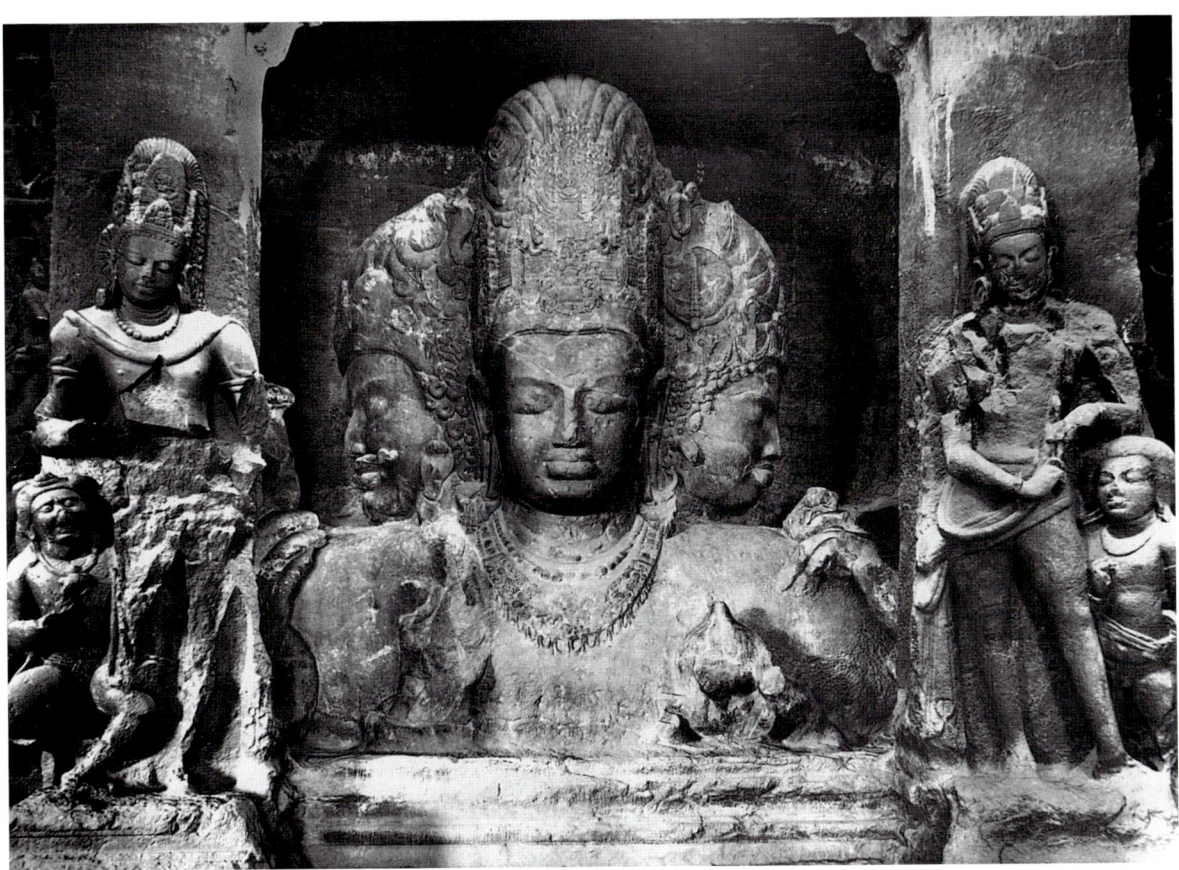

6-18   Shiva as Mahadeva in rock-cut temple, Elephanta, India, sixth century. Shiva 17' high.

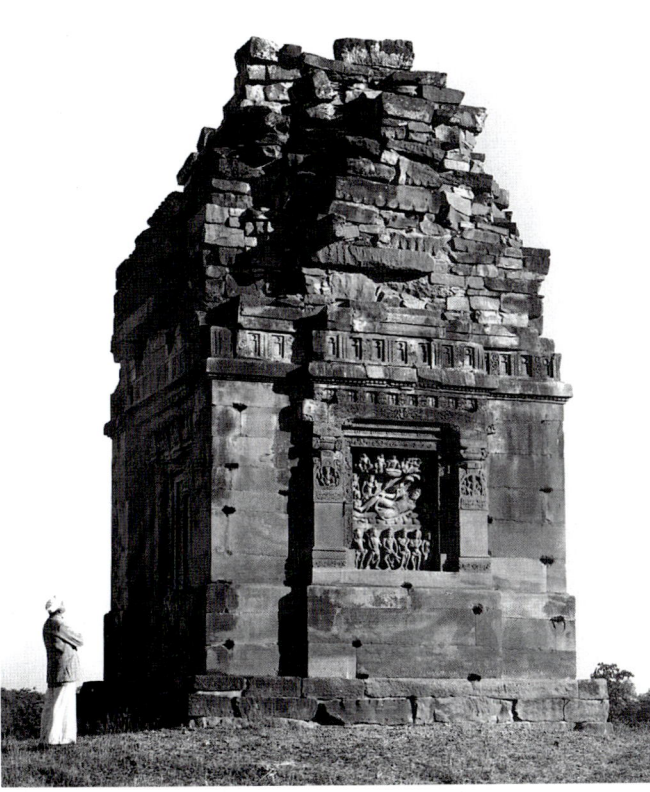

6-19   Vishnu Temple (side view), Deogarh, India, early sixth century.

building on a *plinth* (base) of earth, it has an elaborately decorated doorway at the front and a relief in a niche on each of the other three sides. A small shrine once stood at each corner of the plinth. The temple culminates in a tower (poorly preserved). Inside is a single now-empty room.

Many of the standard elements of later Hindu temple design already appear in the Deogarh temple. Decoration emphasizes the doorway and niches. Much like the guardian figures flanking the niche at Elephanta, sculpted guardians protect both the doorway and the niches at Deogarh, because these are transition areas between the sacred interior and the dangerous outside. Hindus believe Vishnu manifests himself in doorways and niches such as those on the Deogarh temple. That is, he takes a visible form for the benefit of worshipers in a setting accessible to many at once, unlike the small garbha griha or inner sanctuary, where only a small group of priests attends the deity. In much the same way, the three-headed Shiva at Elephanta can be understood as the god manifesting himself in the niche, emerging out of the very mountain where the Elephanta cave was carved. These manifestation places are areas of transition for worshipers and the deity to meet.

THE HINDU TEMPLE AS MOUNTAIN   The earliest Hindu temples, such as the Vishnu Temple at Deogarh, usually featured towers. Over time, as temple plans became more complex, the builders constructed higher, more elaborate towers. The towers played an important symbolic role in

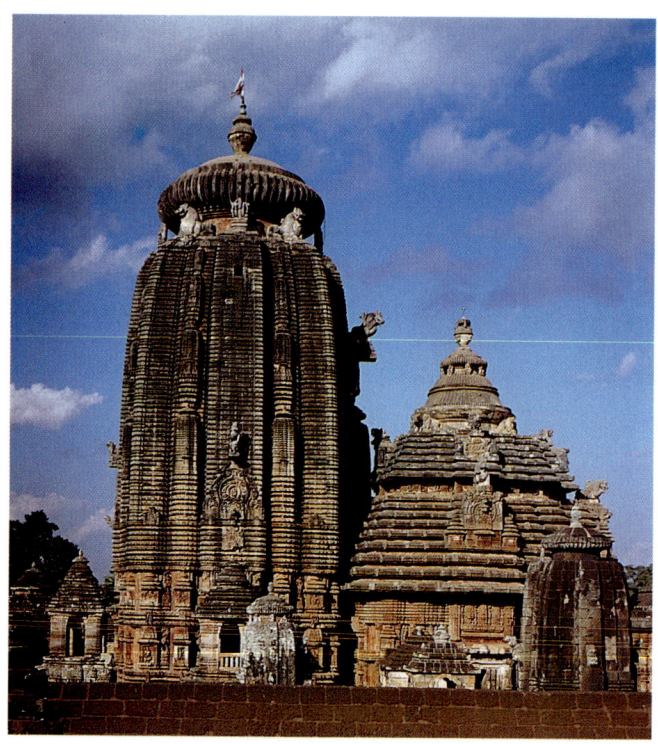

6-20   Lingaraja Temple, Bhuvanesvar, India, ca. eleventh to twelfth century.

Linga) at Bhuvanesvar (FIG. **6-20**) in northeastern India dates from the eleventh to twelfth century. The tallest tower here rises some two hundred feet, although the construction method simply overlaps masonry courses. Relief forms replicating the tower's general shape, but in miniature, decorate the structure's spire in numerous repetitions. Carved lions support the crowning member at the top. Various porches and halls lead from the eastern entrance to the temple's inner sanctuary. A multitude of subsidiary shrines surrounds the structure.

The Visvanatha Temple at Khajuraho (FIGS. **6-21** and **6-22**) in northern India is one of more than twenty large and elaborate temples at that site. Visvanatha is another of the many names for Shiva and means "Lord of the Universe." Erected ca. 1000 and dedicated in 1002 by kings of the Chandella dynasty, the temple structure has four towers of different heights, each rising higher than the preceding one with the tallest tower at the rear, in much the same way the foothills of the Himalayas rise to meet their highest peak.

The mountain symbolism applies to interior temple design at Khajuraho as well. As at Bhuvanesvar, porches and *mandapas* (pillared halls; FIG. 6-22) were added to the simple sanctuary of earlier temples. Steps lead to a small open porch that connects to the first of two mandapas that stand in front of the garbha griha. Aligned in a row, each of the four components (porch, each mandapa, and the garbha griha) supports its own tower. At the back, under the tallest of the exterior towers, the usually small and dark inner sanctuary chamber, like a cave, houses the most important manifestation or form of the deity. Thus, temples such as the Visvanatha symbolize constructed mountains with caves, comparable to the actual

the design of Hindu temples. Hindus thought of the temple tower as a mountain peak and of the temple's garbha griha as the cavelike space within the mountain that serves as the deity's home. The highly complex Lingaraja Temple (Royal

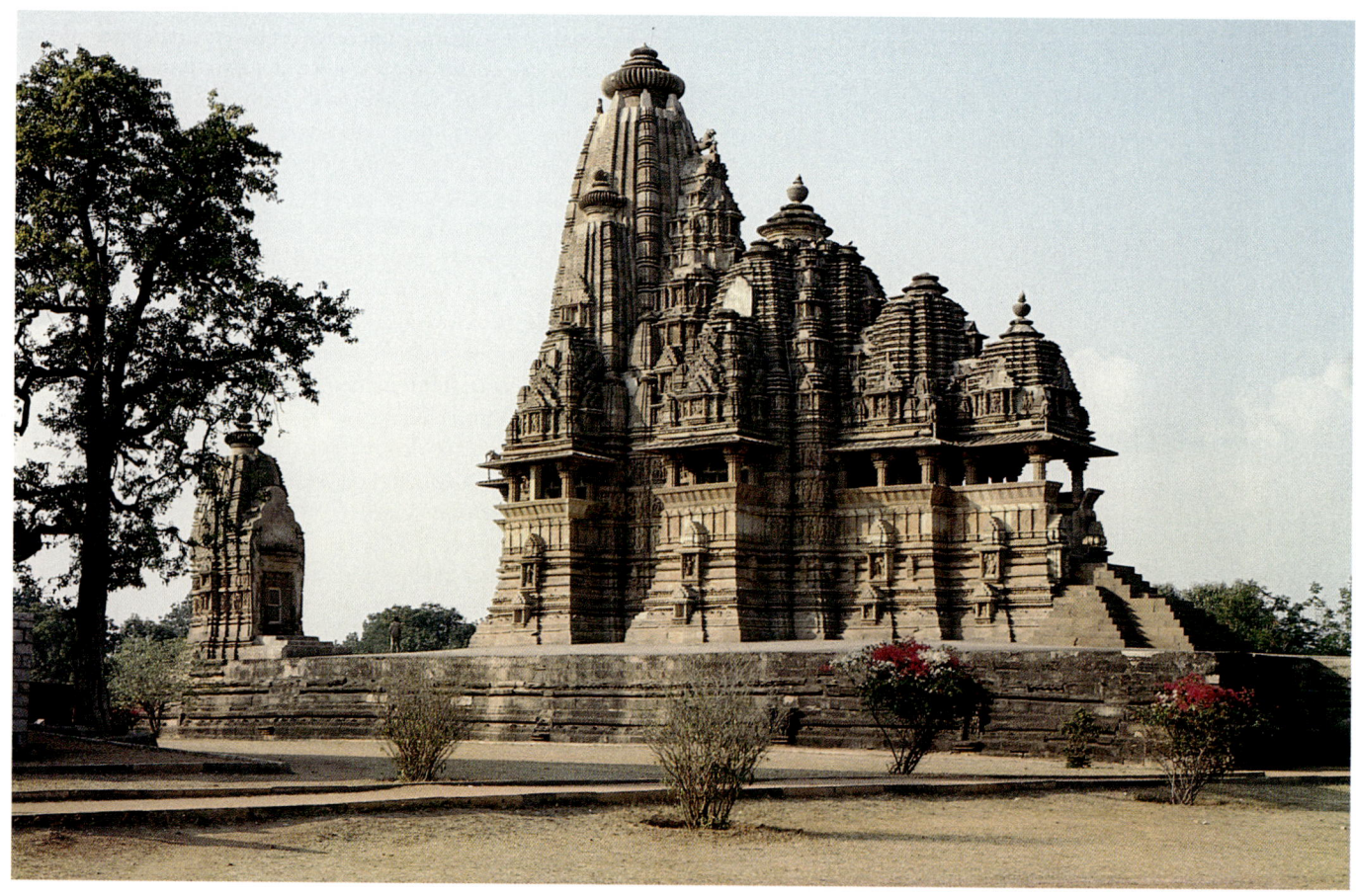

6-21   Visvanatha Temple, Khajuraho, India, ca. 1000.

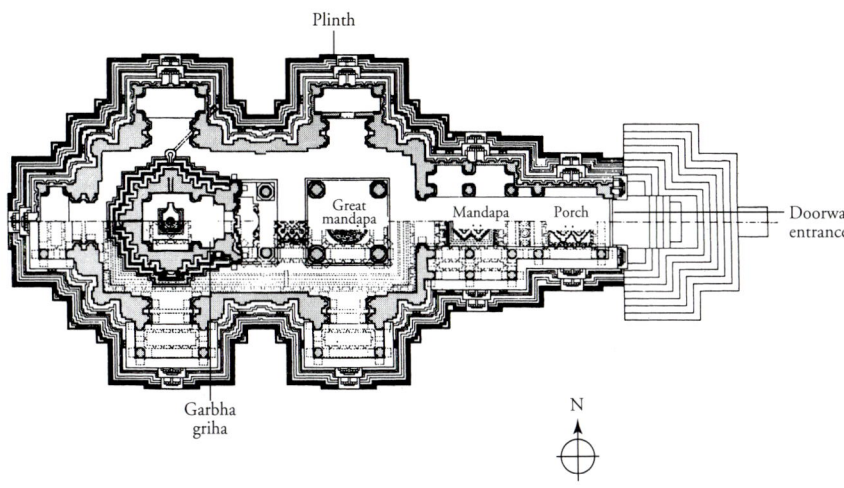

cave temples at Elephanta and other Indian sites. In both cases, the god lives within the cave and takes various forms, manifested in sculpture for worshipers. In Hindu temples constructed of stone blocks (rather than rock cut) joined without mortar, the exterior reliefs are the focus of worship. As in Greek temples (see Chapter 5), the interiors of Indian temples are usually too small and cramped for congregational worship.

REGIONAL STYLES IN TEMPLE DESIGN   The mountain and cave symbolism is not overt in the early Deogarh Temple (FIG. 6-19), but it has the door decoration, exterior niche reliefs, garbha griha, and tower. Thus, the Deogarh tower, although badly damaged, is an early example of the northern Indian type characterizing the large and highly complex temples at Bhuvanesvar and Khajuraho. The northern Indian towers have a beehive shape with compressed stories topped by a large flat disk with ribbed edges *(amalaka)*.

As with sculptural styles, architectural styles in India vary from region to region. Although the arrangement of a tower over a garbha griha entered through a series of pillared halls and porches is standard, the floor plans, sizes, and ornamentation of these units vary greatly. For example, a high wall surrounds the Lingaraja Temple at Bhuvanesvar (FIG. 6-20), while the Visvanatha Temple at Khajuraho (FIGS. 6-21 and 6-22), like other temples the Chandella kings built, sits on a high plinth. These two distinct treatments separate sacred temples from secular space. In addition, the Lingaraja interior is plain, while relief carvings fill the Visvanatha Temple interior.

SEXUAL IMAGERY AT KHAJURAHO   The profusion of carving on the interiors of the Khajuraho temples matches that found on their exteriors (FIG. **6-23**). Ornamental designs cover large areas of the exteriors, while figural reliefs decorate other parts. Scholars can identify few of the figures, numbering in the hundreds, by name, although some are clearly deities such as Shiva, Ganesha, and Vishnu. Most appear human. Pairs of men and women depicted in these reliefs often embrace and sometimes engage in other more

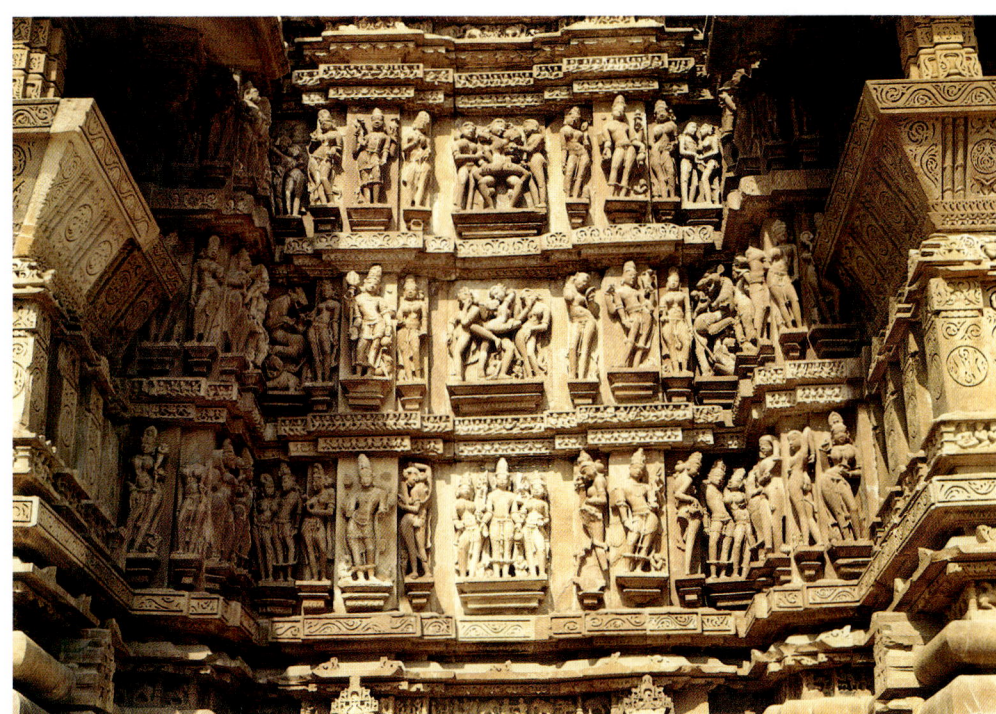

6-23   Sculptures on temple wall, Visvanatha Temple, Khajuraho, India, ca. 1000.

overtly sexual behaviors. The use of amorous couples as a decorative motif, indicating spiritual favor and prosperity, goes back in India to the earliest architectural traditions, both Hindu and Buddhist (FIG. 6-11). Sexuality is a common element in Indian religious symbolism. The mostly nude female under the tree on the eastern gateway at Sanchi (FIG. 6-8) indicates this trait characterized Indian art for centuries.

One explanation appearing to fit some of the sexually explicit images at Khajuraho relates to Tantric practices, rituals that include highly controlled sexual exercises as means to gain spiritual power. Chandella court members practiced Tantric Hinduism, but such an explanation cannot account for all of the images. Despite scholars' ongoing efforts, no one yet fully understands the meaning of the explicit sexual imagery at Khajuraho.

TEMPLES CARVED OUT OF HUGE BOULDERS
In addition to cave temples and masonry temples, Indian architects created a third type of monument—temples carved out of rocky outcroppings (*rathas,* from a word meaning "chariot"), although few examples exist. Rather than excavate a cave, which has an entrance facade but no human-cut exterior structure (FIG. 6-10), Indian architects carved the entire rock, including the temple's exterior. Kings of the Pallava dynasty constructed several such monolithic temples (FIG. **6-24**)

at Mahabalipuram, south of Madras on the Bay of Bengal. Sculpted out of granite boulders that jut out from the sand, they date to the seventh century. The largest of the rathas illustrated (in the foreground), dedicated to Shiva, boasts the typical southern-Indian-style tower resembling a stepped pyramid. The tower ascends in pronounced tiers of cornices decorated with miniature shrines. The lower walls include carved columns and figures of deities inside niches. The ratha to its right, dedicated to Vishnu, has a rectangular plan and a rounded roof, while the next ratha is a smaller example of the southern Indian type. At the end of the row sits a very small temple modeled on a thatched hut and dedicated to Durga, a fierce form of the Goddess. The two largest temples remain unfinished, perhaps because the architect felt that cutting away any more of the rock would collapse the structures under the weight of the stone on top.

SHIVA, LORD OF THE DANCE
In southern India, particularly under the Chola dynasty, which rose to power in 846, artists cast portable representations of deities in solid bronze, some of them large and very heavy. An example of these portable statues (FIG. **6-25**; the holes on the base held poles for carrying the image) represents Shiva performing one of his many cosmic dances. (In another dance described earlier, depicted in the stone relief at Badami, FIG. 6-17, Shiva dances to impress and seduce his wife Parvati.) Here, the

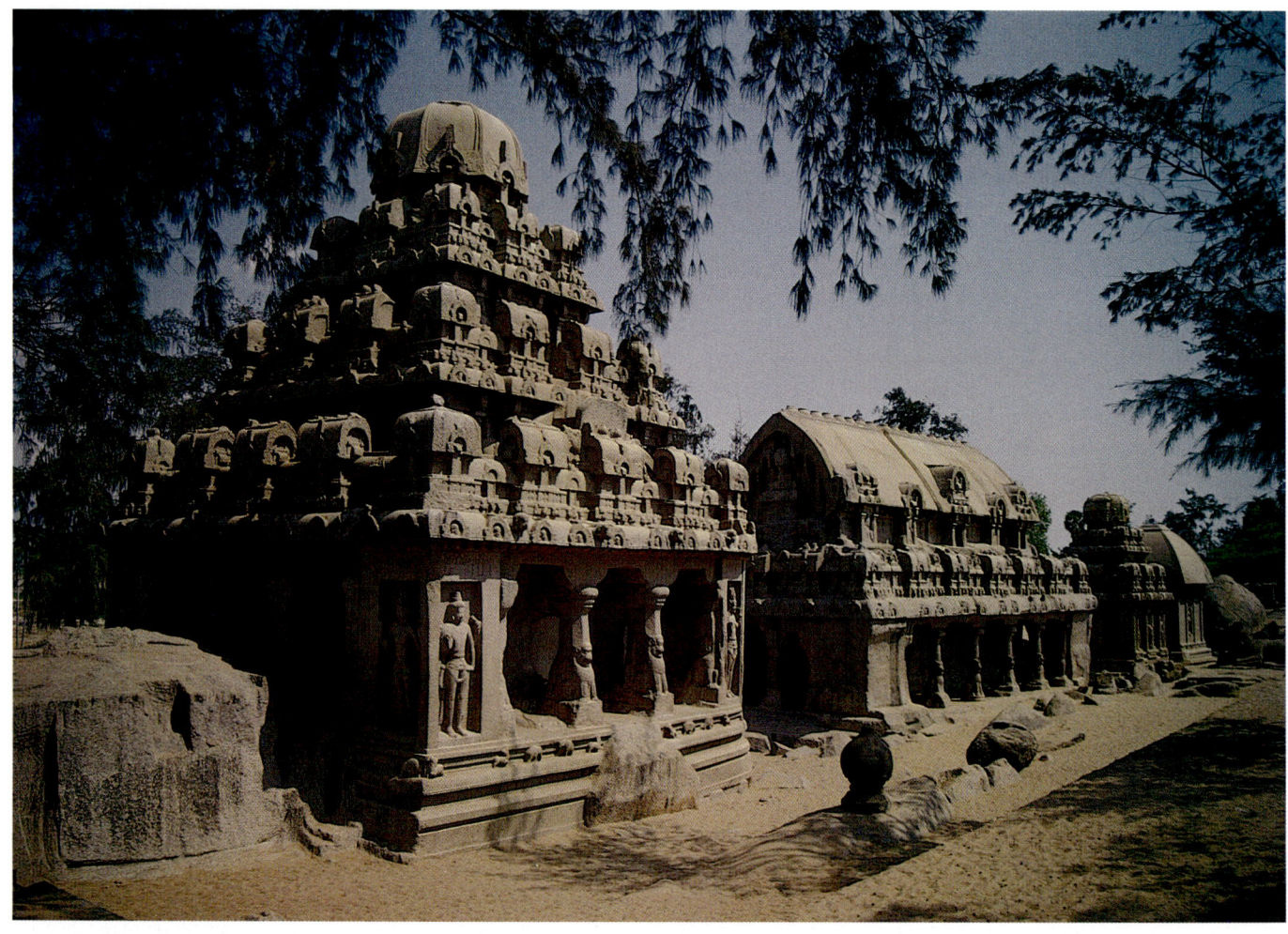

6-24   Rock-cut temples, Mahabalipuram, India, seventh century.

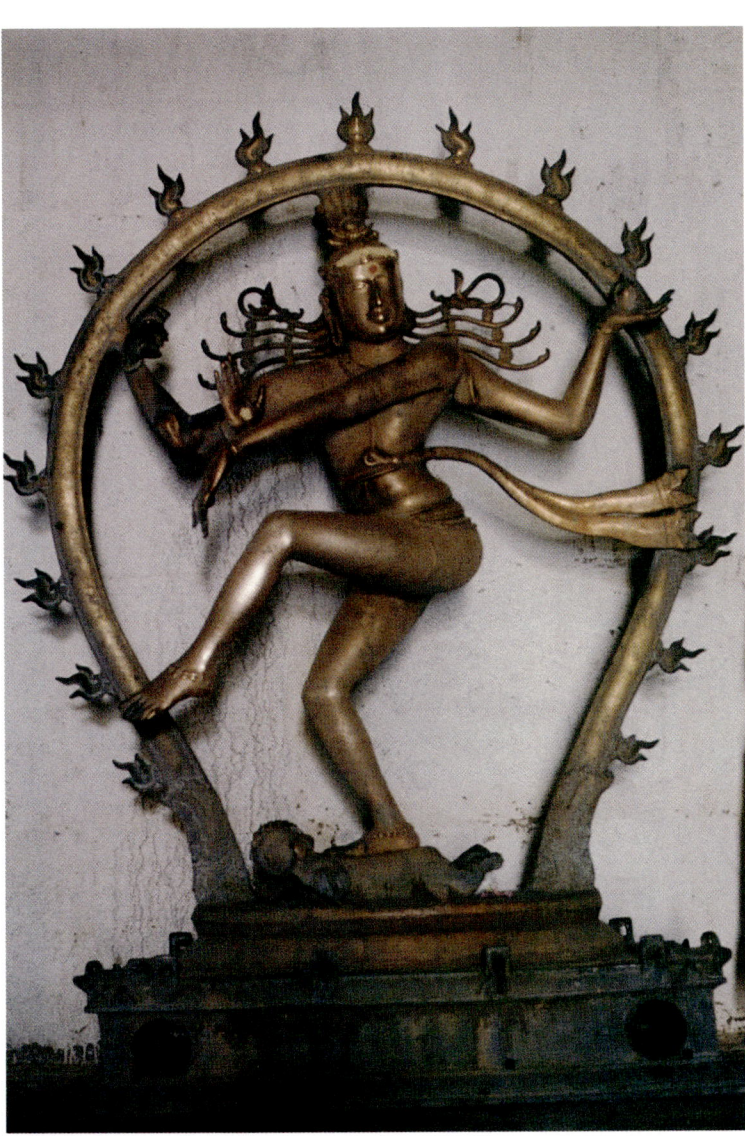

6-25 Shiva as Nataraja, bronze in the Naltunai Isvaram Temple, Punjai, India, ca. 1000.

bronze Shiva dances as Nataraja (Lord of the Dance) by spinning on one leg atop a dwarf representing ignorance, which Shiva stamps out as he dances. Shiva extends all four arms, two of them touching the flaming *nimbus* (light of glory) encircling him. These two upper hands also hold a small drum (at right) and a flame (at left). Shiva creates the universe to the drumbeat's rhythm, while the small fire represents destruction. His lower left hand points to his upraised foot, indicating the foot as the place where devotees can find refuge and enlightenment. Shiva's lower right hand, raised in the fear-not gesture, tells worshipers to come forward without fear. As Shiva spins, his matted hair comes loose and spreads like a fan on both sides of his head.

The Chola dynasty ended in the thirteenth century, a time of political, religious, and cultural change in India. At this point, Buddhism survived in only some areas of India. It soon died out completely there, although the late form of northern Indian Buddhism continued in Tibet and Nepal. At the same time, Islam, present in India as early as the ninth century, spread rapidly over northern India (see Chapter 13). Hindu and Islamic art assumed preeminent roles in India after the thirteenth century (see Chapter 25).

SOUTHEAST ASIA

Southeast Asia is an enormous geographic region of great cultural, ethnic, and linguistic diversity. It includes the modern nations of Myanmar (Burma), Thailand, Laos, Cambodia, Vietnam, Malaysia, and Indonesia, as well as the prosperous city-state of Singapore. For many years, scholars considered the area merely an extension of Indian and Chinese civilizations. Today, however, they recognize Southeast Asian art as one of the most important of the world's artistic traditions.

Sri Lanka

THE EARLY SPREAD OF BUDDHISM   Sri Lanka (formerly Ceylon) is an island located at the very tip of the Indian subcontinent. Its pertinence in a discussion of Southeast Asian art stems from its role as a fountainhead of Southeast Asian Theravada Buddhism. Theravada Buddhism, the oldest form of Buddhism, stressing worship of the historical Buddha, began to dominate Burma, Thailand, Laos, and Cambodia in about the thirteenth century. Buddhism arrived in Sri Lanka

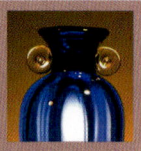

Indianization

Visitors to Borobudur in Indonesia (FIG. 6-27) and Angkor Wat in Cambodia (FIG. 6-31) immediately recognize the imagery of Indian art at those sites. In an effort to explain the Indian character of such Southeast Asian monuments, scholars of earlier generations hypothesized that Indian artists constructed and decorated Borobudur and Angkor, indicating colonization of Southeast Asia by Indians. Today, researchers have concluded that such colonization did not occur. In fact, they believe India never dominated these areas of Southeast Asia politically and did not even send military expeditions to them. The cultural transfer during the first millennium A.D. was peaceful and nonimperialistic. It appears to have developed almost as a by-product of trade.

In the early centuries A.D., extensive trade took place among Rome, India, and China, their ships passing Southeast Asia on the monsoon winds. The tribal chieftains of Southeast Asia quickly saw an opportunity to participate, mainly with their own forest products, such as aromatic woods, bird feathers, and spices. Accompanying trade from India were the already complex religions of Buddhism and Hinduism, a written language (Sanskrit), law texts, and images of the gods. The Southeast Asian chiefs initially used the transferred elements as a sort of "cultural vocabulary" to compete with one another and to participate in an Indian world. But the Southeast Asian peoples soon modified the Indian cultural material, including the art, to make it their own, and with astounding results.

as early as the Maurya period (third century B.C.). With the demise of Buddhism in India in about the thirteenth century, Sri Lanka now has the longest-lived Buddhist tradition in the world. The island, however, also has its own rich artistic tradition, one constantly in contact with that of India.

The recumbent stone Buddha image at Gal Vihara near Polonnaruwa (FIG. **6-26**) measures forty-six feet long and serves as an example of the monumental "sleeping Buddhas" popular in Southeast Asia. Although such reclining Buddha images can be interpreted as representing the Buddha's death (*parinirvana*), worshipers who adhere to Theravadin tradition

tend to interpret them as depictions of the Buddha in meditation while lying down.

Java

Both Hinduism and Buddhism came to Southeast Asia from India (see "Indianization," above). This situation differs from that in China, Korea, and Japan, where only the Buddhist tradition was of any importance in their ancient history (see Chapters 7 and 8). On the island of Java, part of the modern nation of Indonesia, the period from the eighth to the

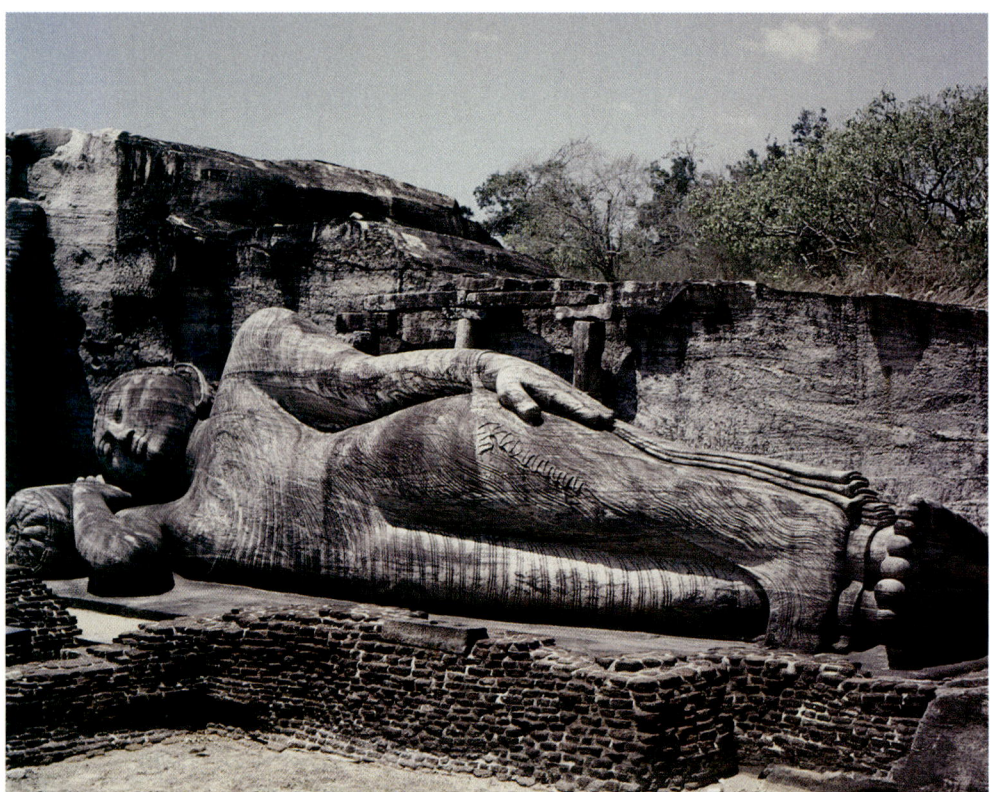

6-26 Buddha, Gal Vihara, Sri Lanka, eleventh to twelfth century. Stone, whole figure 46′ long.

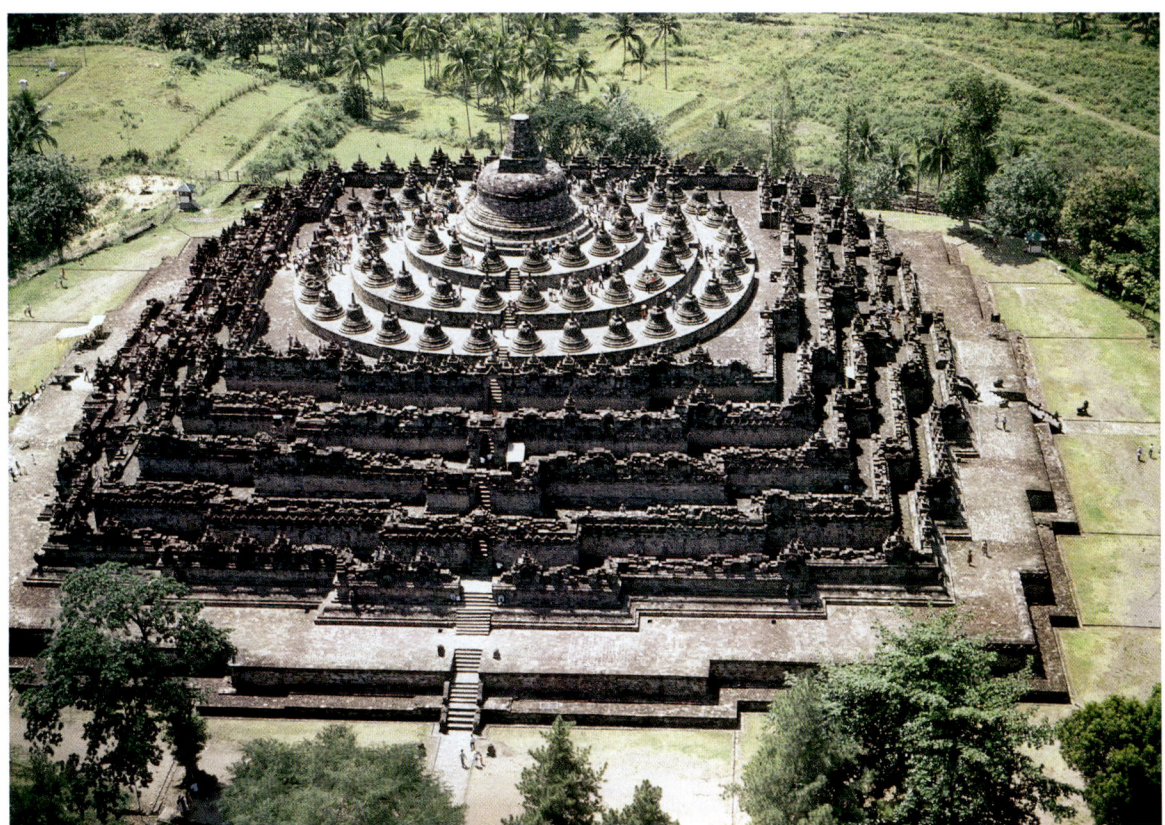

6-27 Stupa, Borobudur, Java, Indonesia, ca. 800.

tenth centuries witnessed the erection of both Hindu and Buddhist monuments. Borobudur (FIGS. **6-27** and **6-28**), a Buddhist monument unique in both form and meaning, is one of the most impressive. Its relationships to Indian art, texts, and Buddhism are clear, yet nothing comparable exists in India.

BUDDHISM ON A COSMIC MOUNTAIN Borobudur is a cosmic mountain on earth, decorated with stupas, Buddha images, and hundreds of relief carvings. Built over a small hill in steps or terraces accessed by four directional stairways, the structure contains literally millions of blocks of volcanic stone. At some point during its construction, the heavy stones caused part of the hill to collapse, requiring the builders to shore up the original foundation with an enormous wall of stone serving as a wide platform. Four square terraces and three circular ones lead to a closed stupa at the top. A *parapet* (wall) flanking each square terrace permits worshipers walking on the terrace to see only the sky. The parapet also prevents people below from seeing those above on higher terraces. Relief carvings cover both the parapet side and the monument side of the path used by worshipers. The architect positioned seventy-two hollow and perforated stupas along the three top circular terraces, each stupa containing a life-size stone image of the Buddha performing the Wheel-turning gesture (FIG. 6-28). Other Buddha images in niches facing out along the top of each parapet perform various other hand gestures.

Extremely large, Borobudur measures about four hundred feet per side at the base and about ninety-eight feet tall. More than five hundred life-size Buddha images, at least a thousand relief panels, and some fifteen hundred stupas of various sizes decorate the massive monument. Worshipers circumambulated the monument, beginning on the lowest terrace and moving

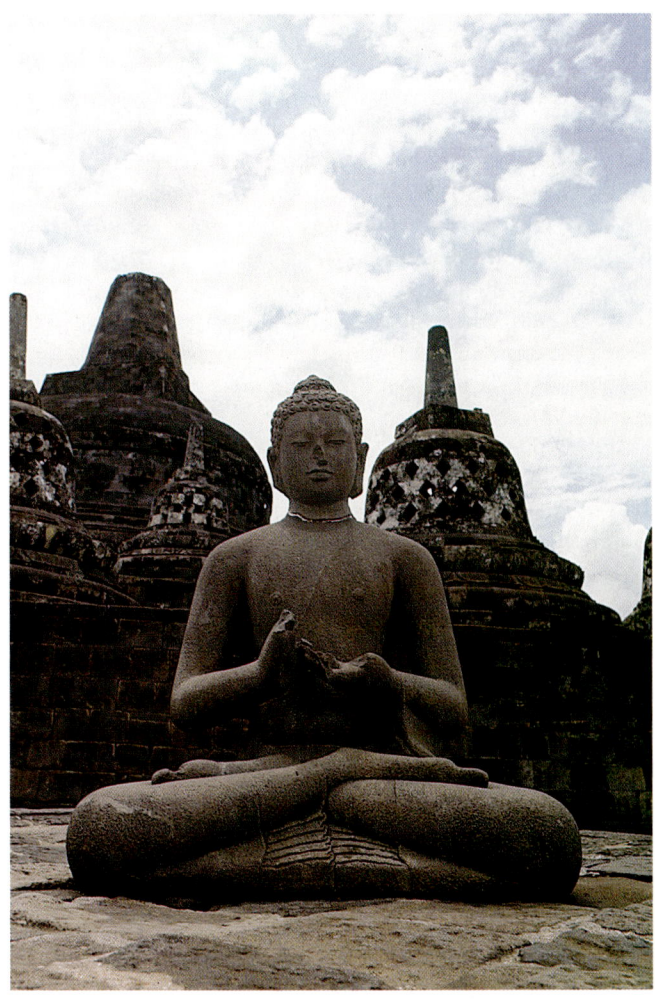

6-28 Buddha in Wheel-turning gesture, once inside perforated stupa, upper circular terrace, Great Stupa, Borobudur, Java, Indonesia, ninth century.

up, terrace by terrace, toward the central stupa at the top. They visually encountered the Buddha and his teachings in the form of numerous images and extensive relief carvings as they progressed. The complex organization of the images and the topics of the reliefs indicate the builder intended worshipers to progress through ever more advanced stages of understanding.

Although scholars cannot give a simple interpretation to such a magnificent conception, they continue to work to unravel the monument's significance. The construction date of about A.D. 800 makes this, in terms of Indian influence, an early monument. Borobudur's sophistication, complexity, and originality, however, underline how completely Southeast Asians absorbed, rethought, and reformulated Indian-related religion and art.

Cambodia

In 802, at about the same time the Javanese built Borobudur, the Khmer King Jayavarman II (r. 802–850) founded the Angkor dynasty, which ruled Cambodia for the next four hundred years and sponsored the construction of hundreds of monuments. For at least two hundred years before the founding of Angkor, the Khmer (the predominant ethnic group in Cambodia) produced Indian-related sculpture of exceptional quality. Images of Vishnu were particularly important during the pre-Angkorian period.

A HALF-VISHNU, HALF-SHIVA STATUE   The Harihara from Prasat Andet (FIG. **6-29**) shows Vishnu in his manifestation as half Shiva and half Vishnu (the meaning of *harihara*). The division is vertical, the left side (facing the image) Shiva and the right side Vishnu. The miter-shaped headgear reflects the division most clearly. The Shiva half, embellished with the winding ascetic's locks, contrasts with the kingly Vishnu's plain miter. The halves originally also were distinguished by the now-lost attributes held in the four hands, but otherwise the artist barely differentiated the sides.

The sculpture's broken arms and ankles indicate the vulnerability of a more-than-life-size stone image carved in the round. Unlike almost all stone sculpture in India, carved in relief on slabs or steles, Khmer artists chose to carve their images in the round, placing weight on the ankles and arms extended into space. The Khmer sculptors intended viewers to see their statues from all sides in the statues' positions at the center of the garbha grihas of brick temples.

ANGKORIAN TEMPLE MOUNTAINS   The Khmer kings worked for more than four centuries on the construction of the site of Angkor in Cambodia. These kings of the Angkor dynasty built temples of brick, but they also used stone to produce enormous monuments, including Angkor Wat (FIGS. **6-30** and 6-31) and the nearby Bayon (FIGS. 6-34 and 6-35). The temples at Angkor include two major types—temple mountains and temples dedicated to an individual Khmer king's ancestors. The temple mountains, with the major deity residing in the top central shrine, were reserved for worship by the King and the elite. Angkor Wat and the Bayon are both temple mountains, monuments whose purpose was to associate the king with his personal de-

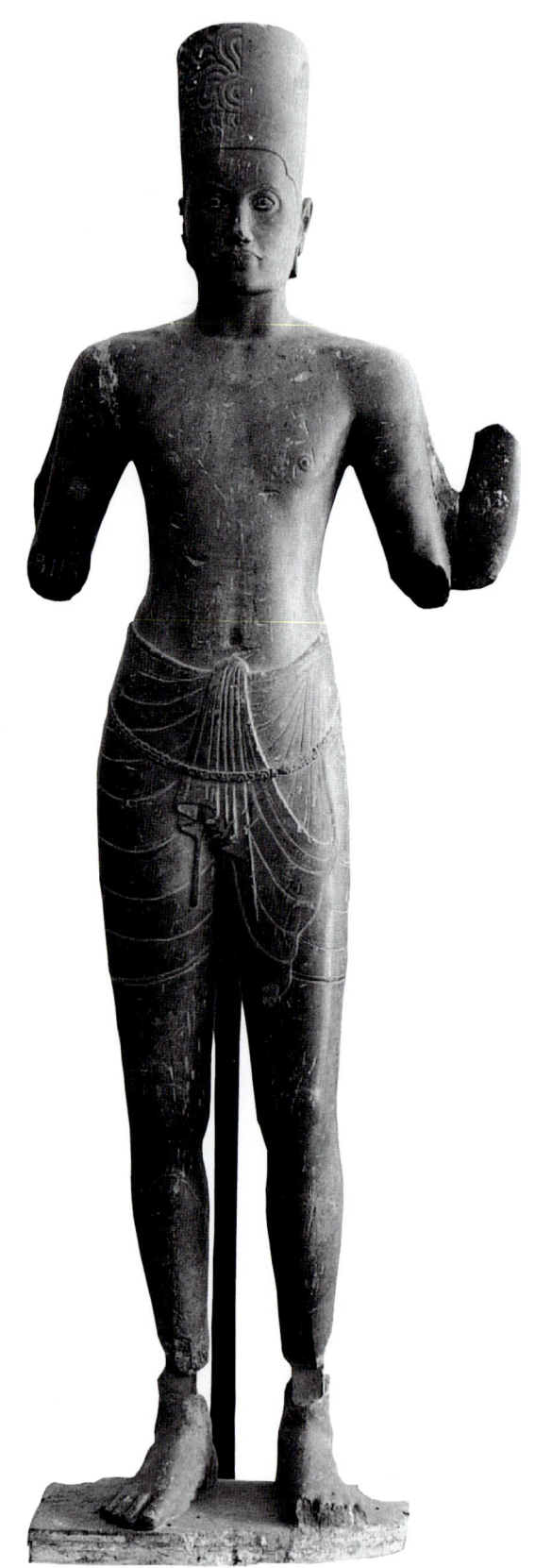

6-29   Harihara, from Prasat Andet, Cambodia, seventh century. Stone, 6′ 3″ high. National Museum, Phnom Penh.

ity (see "Khmer Kingship," page 183). These two temples, however, are unusual in the context of the Angkor kingly tradition, as the kings dedicated Angkor Wat to Vishnu and the Bayon to the Buddha. For hundreds of years before the construction of these two temples, the Khmer kings associated themselves with aspects of Shiva.

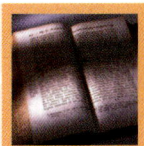

Khmer Kingship

The kings of Angkor were exceedingly powerful, and almost all of the art and architecture surviving at Angkor Wat from hundreds of years of building at the site attest to that fact. The Angkor kings not only displayed their power through lofty monuments, elaborate art programs, and ritual splendor, but they also used the monuments and art to generate power initially. Each king built a temple mountain and installed his personal god—Shiva, Vishnu, or the Buddha—on top. He named the image/god with part of his own royal name, implying that the king was a part or portion of the god. When the king died, the Khmer believed the god reabsorbed him, because he had been the earthly portion of the god during his lifetime, so they worshiped the king's image posthumously as the god. This concept of the king approaches an actual deification of the human ruler, familiar in many other societies, such as ancient Egypt (see Chapter 3).

At the end of the thirteenth century, a Chinese official, Zhou Daguan, visited Angkor and recorded what he saw. He described the spectacle when the Khmer king left his palace in Angkor Thom (see plan of Angkor, FIG. 6-30). The entourage began with "young girls of the palace, three to five hundred in number, who wear floral material and flowers in their hair and hold candles in their hands . . . ; even in broad daylight their candles are lit. Then come girls of the palace carrying gold and silver utensils and a whole series of ornaments." After many other groups—including ministers, princes, concubines, wives, and guards—the king came, "standing on an elephant and holding the precious sword in his hand. The tusks of the elephant are sheathed in gold. There are more than twenty white parasols flecked with gold, with handles of gold. . . . Those who see the king must prostrate themselves and touch the ground in front of them."[1] The Khmer king surrounded himself at all times with symbols of his power and glory, placing himself godlike as separate from his people, using displays of art, wealth, and splendor.

[1] G. Coedes, *The Indianized States of Southeast Asia* (Honolulu: East-West Center, 1968), 216.

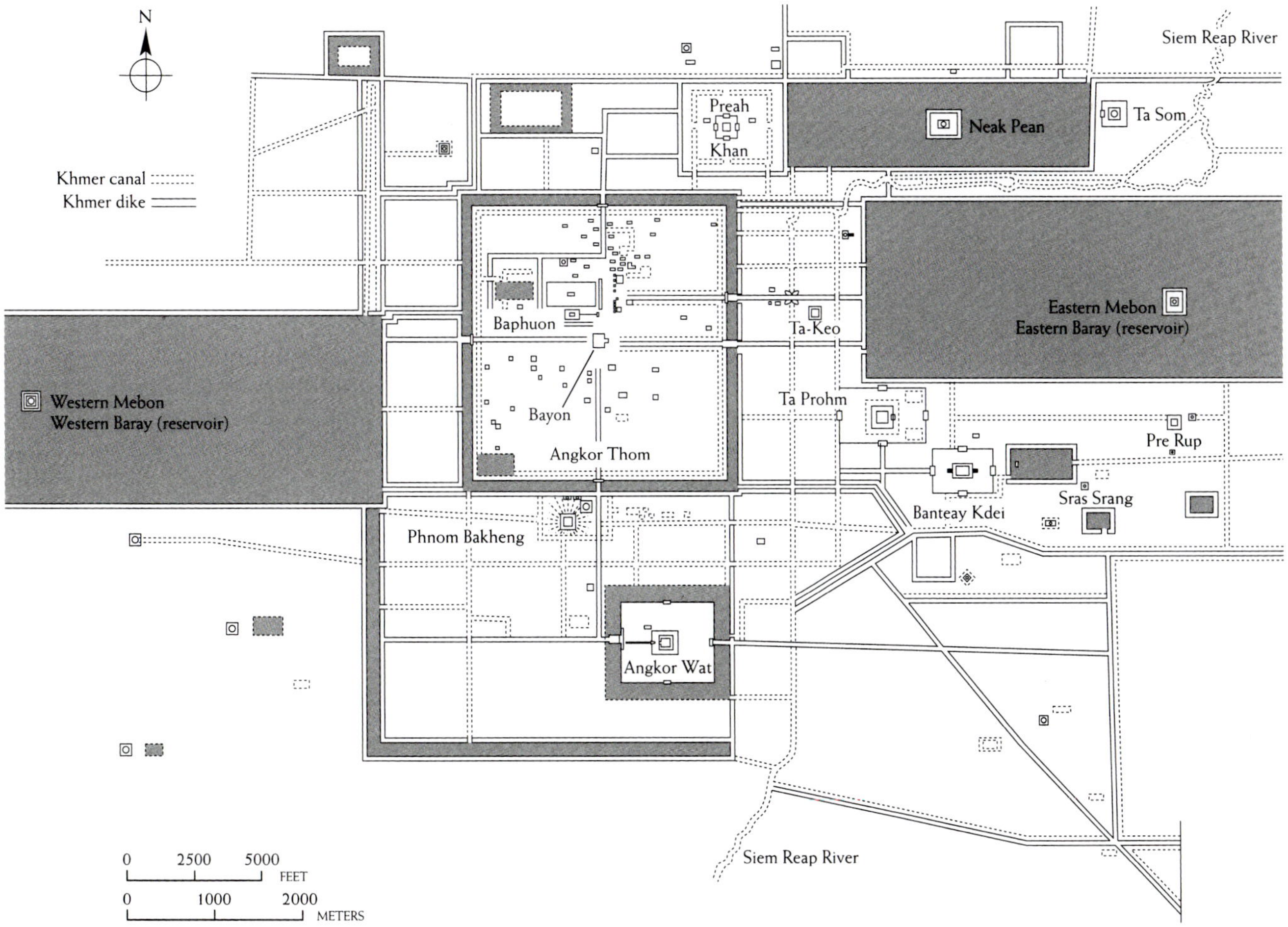

6-30 Overall plan of Angkor site, Cambodia, during the twelfth and thirteenth centuries.

6-31 Angkor Wat, Angkor, Cambodia, twelfth century.

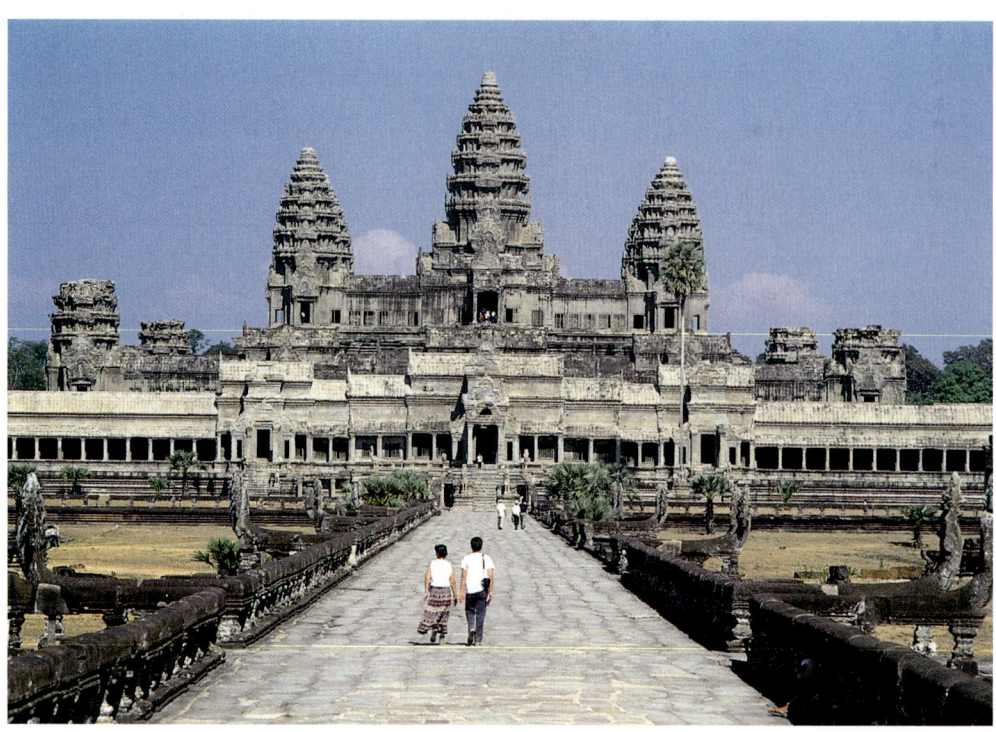

The plan of Angkor (FIG. 6-30) shows the location of Angkor Wat and the Bayon. Angkor Wat, constructed to the south of most of the buildings at Angkor, consists of a temple positioned at the center of a huge rectangle of land delineated by a moat measuring about four thousand nine hundred twenty by four thousand two hundred sixty feet. The Bayon is at the center of another much larger moated and walled area called Angkor Thom in the heart of Angkor. The Khmer kings also built several enormous reservoirs *(barays)* at the site. Scholars continue to debate the use and purpose of the extensive hydraulics at Angkor, but religious and cosmological meanings clearly played a significant role.

A KHMER ROYAL PORTRAIT Suryavarman II (r. 1113–1150) built Angkor Wat (FIGS. **6-31** and **6-32**), which rises, like other temple mountains, in pyramid-like steps,

each level punctuated by tower shrines connected with covered galleries. On the inner wall of the lowest gallery, reliefs depict the king holding court (FIG. 6-32). Suryavarman II sits on an elaborate wooden throne, its bronze legs rising as cobra heads *(nagas)*. Kneeling retainers surround the king, holding a forest of umbrellas and fans as emblems of his rank.

A BRONZE VISHNU ON AN ISLAND Khmer craftspeople were masters of bronze casting. The bronze fragment portraying Vishnu lying on the cosmic ocean (FIG. **6-33**), recovered from the Mebon temple on an island in the Western Baray (FIG. 6-30), is more than eight feet long. In complete form, at well over twenty feet long, it was among the largest bronzes of antiquity. Originally, gold and silver inlays and jewels embellished the image, and it wore a separate miter on

6-32 King Suryavarman II holding court, lowest gallery, south side, Angkor Wat, Angkor, Cambodia, twelfth century. Stone.

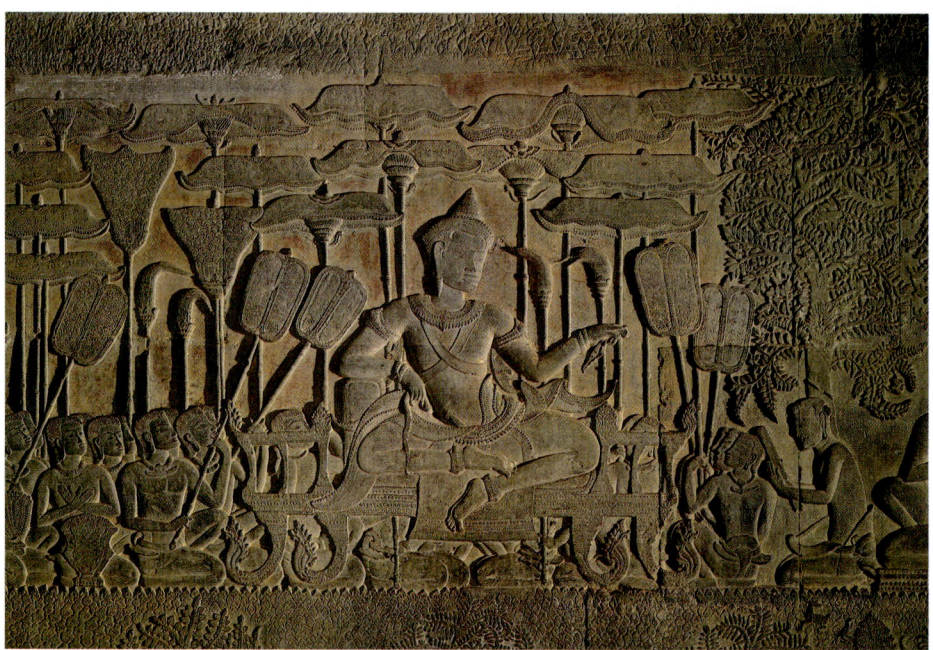

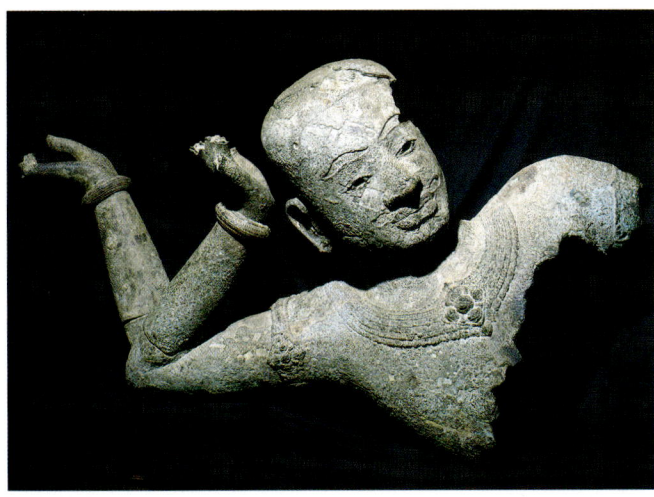

6-33 Vishnu lying on the cosmic ocean, from Mebon temple on island in Western Baray, Angkor, Cambodia, eleventh century. Bronze, 8′ long.

its head. The sleeping Vishnu reproduces the myth of the creation of the universe. The story tells of Vishnu lying on the cosmic ocean, usually represented by a snake but here also literally indicated by the waters of Western Mebon. In the myth, a lotus stem grows from Vishnu's navel, its flower supporting Brahma, the creator god. It appears the bronze Vishnu had a waterspout emerging from his navel, indicating his ability not only to protect the earth and create Brahma and Shiva but also to create the waters.

THE BAYON'S GIANT FACES Jayavarman VII (r. 1181–1219) ruled over much of mainland Southeast Asia and built more during his reign than all of the Khmer kings preceding him in four hundred years. His most important temple, the Bayon, is a complicated and still enigmatic monument constructed with unique circular terraces surmounted by towers carved with huge faces (FIGS. **6-34** and **6-35**). Jayavarman

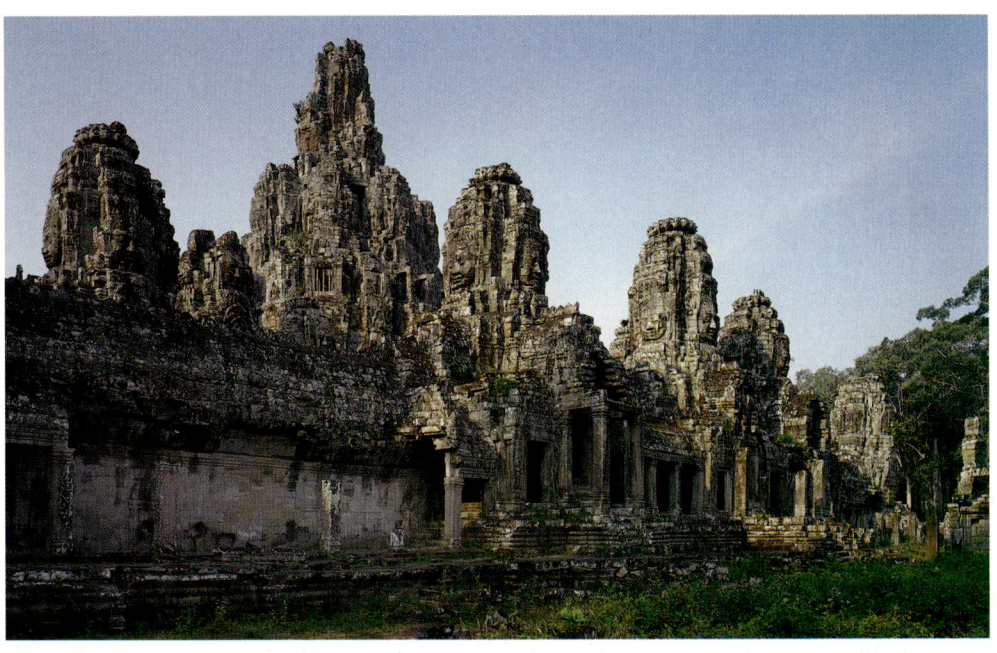

6-34 Tower of the Bayon, Angkor Thom, Cambodia, twelfth to thirteenth century.

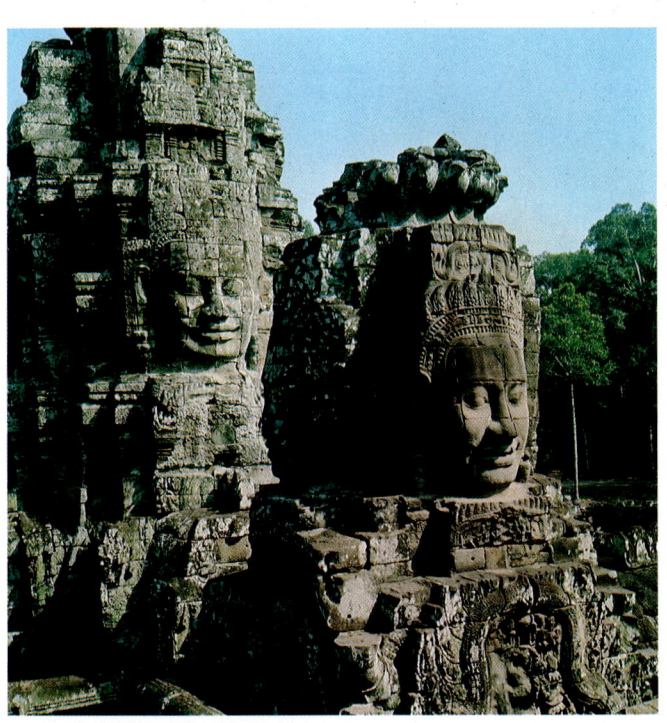

turned to Buddhism from the Hinduism the earlier Khmer rulers embraced. The faces on the Bayon towers perhaps portray a bodhisattva, intended to indicate the watchful compassion emanating in all directions from the capital. Other researchers have proposed that the faces depict Jayavarman or various other deities. Jayavarman's great experiment in religion and art was short lived, but it also marked the point of change in Southeast Asia when Theravada Buddhism began to dominate most of the mainland. Chapter 25 chronicles this important development.

During the first to fourth centuries A.D., Buddhism also traveled to other parts of Asia—to China, Korea, and Japan. Although the artistic traditions in these countries differ greatly from one another, they share, along with the Southeast Asian countries, a tradition of Buddhist art and an ultimate tie with India. Chapters 7 and 8 trace the changes Buddhist art underwent in East Asia, along with the region's other rich artistic traditions.

6-35 Tower of the Bayon, Angkor Thom, Cambodia, twelfth to thirteenth century.

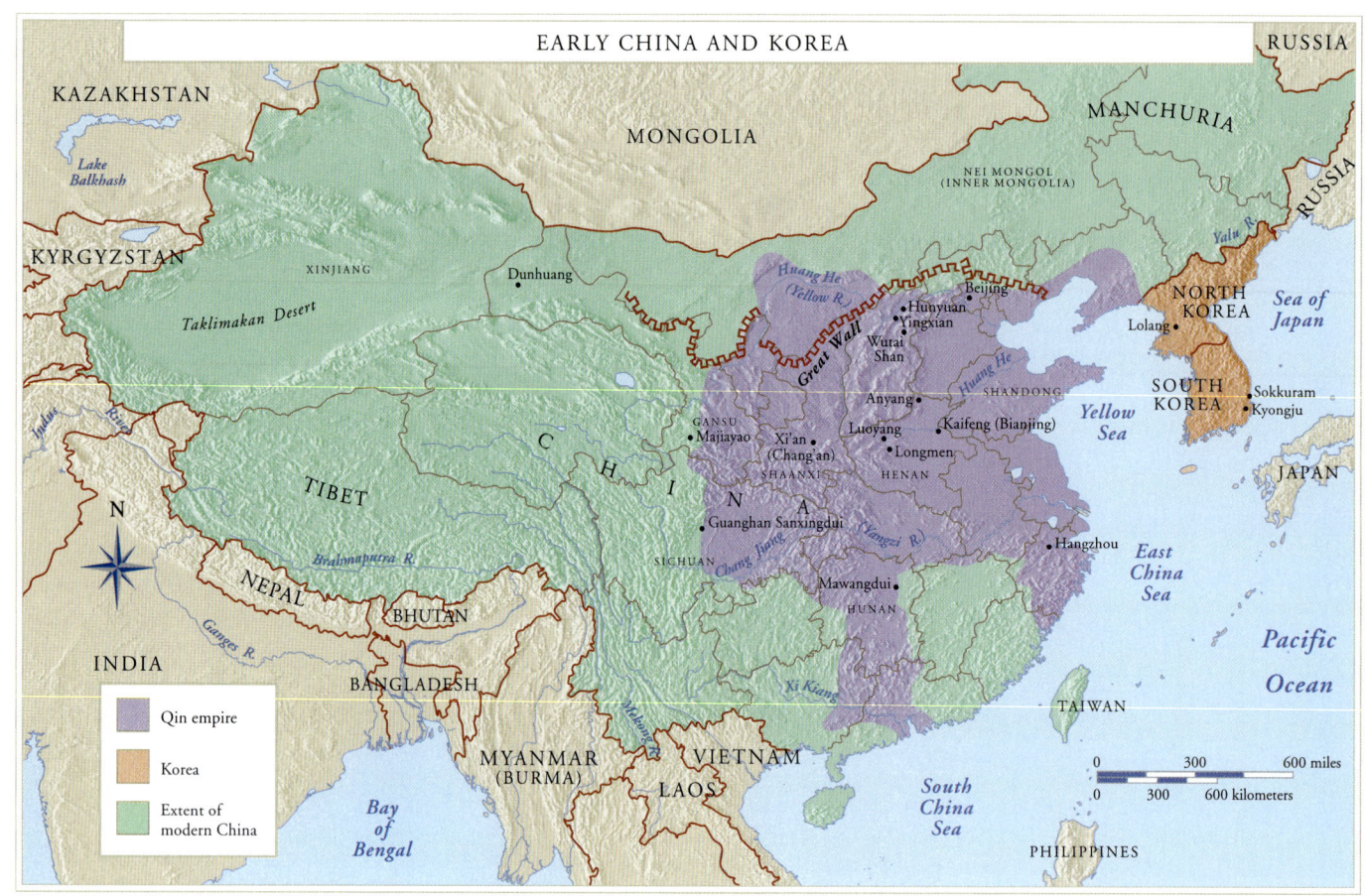

EARLY CHINA AND KOREA

RUSSIA

KAZAKHSTAN

MONGOLIA

MANCHURIA

Lake Balkhash

KYRGYZSTAN

XINJIANG

Taklimakan Desert

Dunhuang

NEI MONGOL (INNER MONGOLIA)

RUSSIA

Yalu R.

Huang He (Yellow R.)

Great Wall

Beijing

Hunyuan
Yingxian

Wutai Shan

NORTH KOREA

Lolang

Sea of Japan

TIBET

C H I N A

GANSU
Majiayao

Huang He

SHANDONG

Anyang

Luoyang
Longmen

Kaifeng (Bianjing)

Yellow Sea

SOUTH KOREA

Sokkuram

Kyongju

Xi'an (Chang'an)

SHAANXI

HENAN

JAPAN

Brahmaputra R.

Guanghan Sanxingdui

Chang Jiang (Yangzi R.)

SICHUAN

Hangzhou

East China Sea

NEPAL

Ganges R.

BHUTAN

Mawangdui

HUNAN

Pacific Ocean

INDIA

BANGLADESH

Xi Kiang

TAIWAN

Qin empire

Korea

Extent of modern China

MYANMAR (BURMA)

LAOS

VIETNAM

Bay of Bengal

Mekong R.

South China Sea

PHILIPPINES

0   300   600 miles
0   300   600 kilometers

	3000 B.C.		1500 B.C.	1050 B.C.		400 B.C.	221 B.C.	206 B.C.		A.D. 220	589
CHINA	NEOLITHIC		SHANG	ZHOU*			QIN	HAN		PERIOD OF DISUNITY†	
KOREA	POTTERY-PRODUCING CULTURES							THREE KINGDOMS			

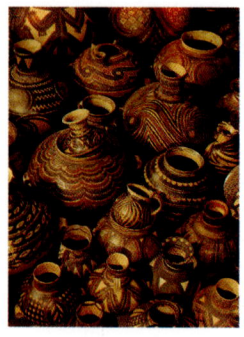

Majiayao vases
3000–2500 B.C.

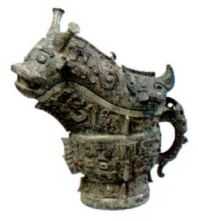

Gong, twelfth
or eleventh century B.C.

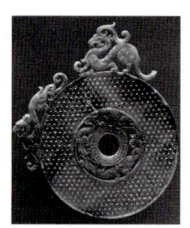

Bi (disk)
fourth–third century B.C.

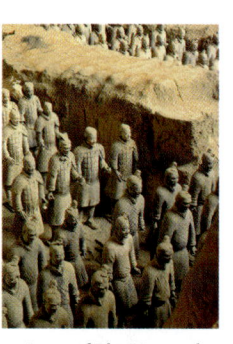

Army of Shi Huangdi
Shaanxi Province, China
ca. 210 B.C.

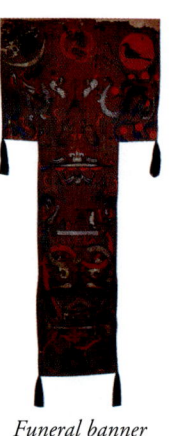

Funeral banner
ca. 168 B.C.

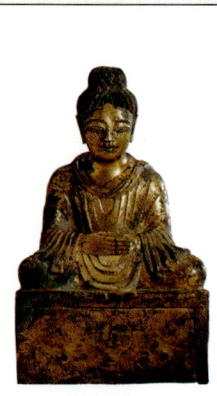

Sakyamuni
Buddha, 338

First evidence of Chinese script, ca. 1400–1200 B.C.

Life of Confucius, ca. 551–479 B.C.

First coins, ca. 500 B.C.

China establishes outposts in
northern Korea, 108 B.C.

Invention of paper, ca. 100 B.C.–100 A.D.

First written evidence of Buddhist
images in China, 193

Buddhism arrives in Korea, 372

Growth of Pure Land sects, 400–500

Xie He, "Six Laws" of painting, ca. 500

* The Warring States period (475–221 B.C.) occurred during this time span also.

† Various short-lived or regional dynasties also developed within the periods
indicated here for major dynasties; mentioned in the text are the Xin, Jin, Zhau,
and Liao, as well as the Northern Wei.

7

DAOISM, CONFUCIANISM, AND BUDDHISM

THE ART OF EARLY CHINA AND KOREA

581	618	688	907	918	960	1000	1127
SUI	TANG		FIVE DYNASTIES	NORTHERN SONG		SOUTHERN SONG	
		GREAT SILLA (TO 935)		KORYO PERIOD			

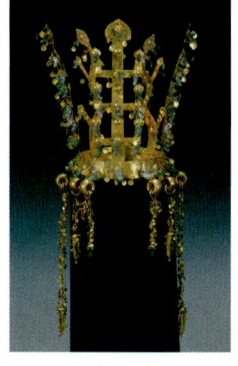 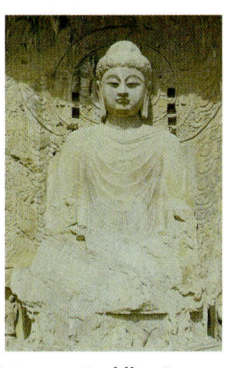 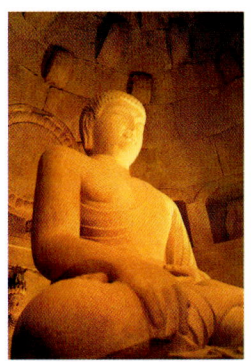 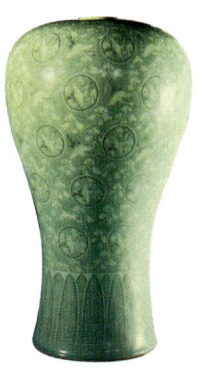 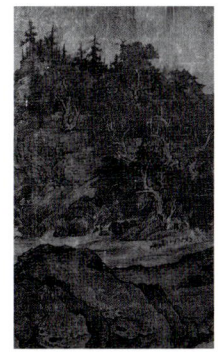 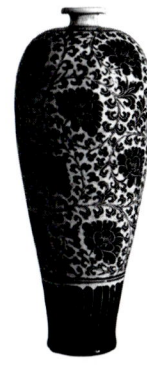

Golden crown
Korea, fifth–sixth century

Vairocana Buddha, Longmen Caves, Luoyang China ca. 670–680

Sakyamuni Buddha Sokkuram, Korea, eighth century

Maebyong vase Korea, ca. 918–1000

Fan Kuan, Travelers among Mountains and Streams early eleventh century

Meiping vase thirteenth century

Earliest cave at Dunhuang, 538–953

Daoist canon distributed by imperial order, 749

Beginnings of woodblock printing, ca. 750

Temporary persecution of Buddhism, 845–847

The new Koryo kingdom founded, 918

Chan Buddhism begins to flourish, ca. 1200

Mongols invade Korea, 1231

The Koryo state ends, 1392

CHINA

A VAST AND ANCIENT LAND   China has the unique distinction as the only continuing civilization originating in the ancient world. Vast and varied both topographically and climatically, China's landscape includes sandy plains, mighty rivers, towering mountains, and fertile farmlands. Northern China has a dry and moderate-to-cold climate, whereas southern China is moist and tropical. The nation is also ethnically diverse. Over the centuries, the Chinese took control of areas inhabited originally by non-Chinese people, including Tibetans, the Turkic peoples of Xinjiang (formerly Chinese Turkestan), the Mongols (of Inner Mongolia), the Manchus (of Manchuria), and the Koreans (north of the Yalu River).

China's spoken language varies so much that speakers of its various dialects do not understand one another. However, the written language long has been widely intelligible, permitting people thousands of miles apart to share literary, philosophic, and religious traditions. Distinct regional art styles appeared in China, flourishing especially in the early eras and during times of political fragmentation, but a broad cultural unity also permitted an easy flow of artistic forms and ideas throughout China.

Neolithic China

BORN ON THE YELLOW RIVER   China traces its beginnings to the basin of the Huang He, the Yellow River. In this respect, Chinese civilization resembles other great civilizations that developed in areas adjacent to major rivers—the Tigris and Euphrates in Mesopotamia, the Nile in Egypt, and the Indus and Ganges in India (see Chapters 2, 3, and 6). The Chinese archeological record, extraordinarily rich, goes back to Neolithic settlements of around 5000 B.C. New discoveries in recent years have expanded the early record enormously. Archeologists have discovered thousands of Neolithic and later sites and have excavated hundreds of them. Their investigations have revealed a complex aggregation of cultures that, despite a limited technology, produced impressive artworks, especially from jade and clay.

CHINA'S EARLY MASTER POTTERS   Even before the invention of the potter's wheel in the fourth millennium B.C., Chinese artists produced high-quality ceramic wares in great variety. Metal had not yet been discovered, and the domestication of animals was in a rudimentary stage, yet the mastery of potter's clay was astonishingly sophisticated in China. The Yangshao culture, among many situated along the

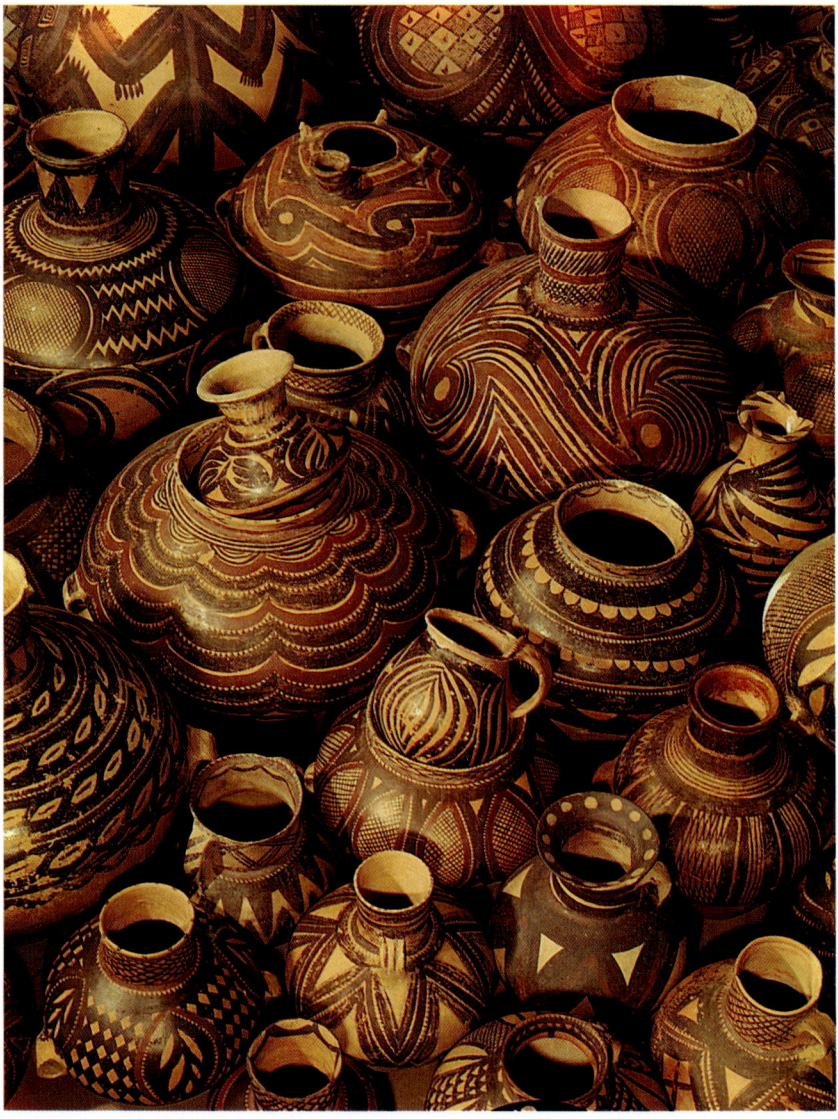

7-1   Neolithic vases, Majiayao culture, from Gansu Province, China, 3000–2500 B.C. Earthenware.

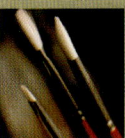

Chinese Earthenwares and Stonewares

China has no rival in the combined length and richness of its ceramic history. Beginning with the makers of the earliest pots in prehistoric villages, ancient Chinese potters showed a flair for shaping carefully prepared and kneaded clay into diverse, often dramatic and elegant vessel forms. Chinese artists continue to produce many of these forms today, inspiring potters around the world.

Until Chinese potters developed true *porcelains* (extremely fine, hard white ceramics; see Chapter 26) in about A.D. 1300, they produced only two types of clay vessels or objects—earthenwares and stonewares. For both types, potters used clays colored by mineral impurities, especially iron compounds ranging from yellow to dark reddish brown.

The clay bodies of *earthenwares* (FIG. 7-1), fired at low temperatures in open pits or simple kilns, remain soft and porous or only partially fused, thus allowing liquids to seep through. Chinese artists also used the low-fire technique to produce terracotta sculptures, even life-size figures of humans and animals (FIG. 7-5). Over time, Chinese potters developed kilns allowing them to fire their clay vessels at much higher temperatures—more than two thousand degrees Fahrenheit. Such temperatures produce *stonewares,* named for their stonelike hardness and density.

Potters in China excelled at the various techniques commonly used to decorate earthenwares and stonewares. Most of these decorative methods depend on changes occurring in the kiln to chemical compounds found in the clay as natural impurities or added to its surface by the artist (see "Greek Vase Painting," Chapter 5, page 104). When fired, many compounds change color dramatically, depending on the conditions in the kiln. For example, if little oxygen remains in a hot kiln, iron oxide (rust) turns either gray or black, while an abundance of oxygen produces a reddish hue.

Potters also can decorate vessels simply by painting their surfaces with ground minerals, such as iron oxides, suspended in water. In one of the oldest decorative techniques, however, potters apply slip (a mixture of clay and water like a fine, thin mud)—by painting, pouring, or dipping—to a clay body not yet fully dry. The natural variety of clay colors can produce a broad, if not bright, palette for decorators, as seen in the Neolithic Majiayao vessels (FIG. 7-1). But potters often also add compounds such as iron oxide to the slip to change or intensify the colors. After vessels have partially dried, potters might incise shapes and lines through the slip down to the clay body to produce designs such as those often seen in later Chinese stonewares (FIG. 7-26).

The slip technique compares with that used by Archaic Greek black-figure painters (see FIGS. 5-4, 5-18, and 5-19). Chinese artists sometimes inlaid designs, too, carving them into plain vessel surfaces and then filling them with slip or soft clay of a contrasting color. Such techniques spread throughout eastern Asia (FIG. 7-29).

To produce a hard, glassy surface after firing, potters coated plain or decorated vessels with a glaze, a finely ground mixture of minerals. Clear or highly translucent glazes best reveal decorated surfaces, while more opaque, richly colored glazes (FIG. 7-18) serve as primary decoration.

Yellow River's middle and upper reaches, was especially prolific in fine *earthenware* pottery (see "Chinese Earthenwares and Stonewares," above) for many centuries. In the third millennium B.C., the potters of Majiayao, in Gansu Province, produced particularly striking vessels (FIG. **7-1**) whose sides swell outward into robust forms with smoothly rounded contours. Decoration in red and brown on a cream-colored ground in a variety of geometric motifs—stripes, spirals, zigzags, and netlike patterns—complements their harmonious proportions. The multiplicity of forms suggests the vessels served a wide variety of functions and attests to the diversified needs of this industrious Neolithic community.

Shang Dynasty (ca. 1500–1050 B.C.)

Traditional Chinese histories trace the origins of China deep into the mythological past. However, until about 221 B.C., many smaller states, even in China's central regions, divided its territory. The earliest traditional dynasty confirmed by archeology is the Shang (ca. 1500–1050 B.C.), whose kings ruled from a series of royal capitals in the Yellow River valley and vied for power and territory with the rulers of neighboring states.

ROYAL BURIALS AT ANYANG In 1928, excavations at Anyang in northern China brought to light not only one of the last Shang capitals but also evidence of the dynasty's earlier development. Findings revealed a warlike, highly stratified society. Walls of pounded earth protected Shang cities. Servants, captives, and even teams of charioteers with chariots and horses accompanied Shang kings to their tombs, a practice noted earlier with regard to the Royal Cemetery at Ur (see Chapter 2). The excavated tomb furnishings include weapons and a great wealth of objects in jade, ivory, lacquer, gold, silver, and bronze. Archeologists also discovered numerous inscribed bones and turtle shells once used for divination. The diviners sought answers to inquiries about many topics, including military strategy, royal tours of inspection, aid from ancestors, childbirth, and the meaning of dreams. The script on these objects was basically pictographic but sufficiently developed to express abstract ideas. These fragmentary records have provided information about Shang kings and their affairs.

SHANG BRONZE-CASTING Shang dynasty artists perfected the casting of elaborate bronze vessels in piece molds. Many of these vessels served as containers for ritual offerings in divination ceremonies. The Shang bronzeworkers began the process by producing a solid clay model of the desired object and allowing it to dry to durable hardness. Then they pressed damp clay around it to form a mold that hardened but remained somewhat flexible. At that point, they carefully cut the mold in pieces and removed the mold from the model. Next, the artists shaved the model to reduce its size to form a core for the piece mold. They then reassembled the mold around the model using bronze spacers to preserve a space between the model and the mold—a space equivalent to the layer of wax in the lost-wax method (see "Hollow-Casting Life Size Bronze Statues," Chapter 5, page 124). The Shang bronze casters then added a final clay layer on the outside to hold everything together, leaving open ducts for pouring molten bronze into the space between the model and the mold and for gases to escape. Once the mold had cooled, they broke it apart, removed the new bronze vessel, and cleaned and polished it. Shang bronzes show a skill in casting rivaling that of any other ancient civilization and indicating a long developmental period for achieving such mastery. The great numbers of cast-bronze vessels strongly suggest well-organized workshops, but no records provide a clear picture of such matters or of the place the artists held in their society. Bronze-casting may have been a hereditary occupation.

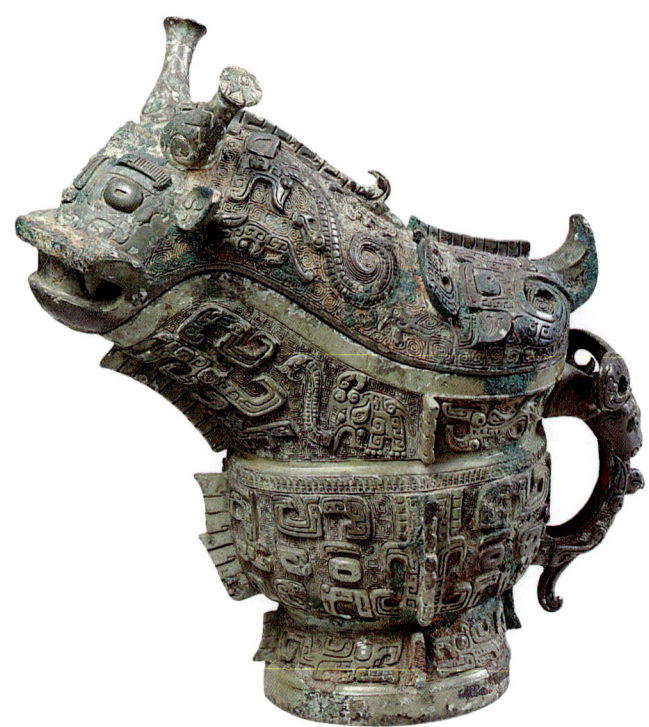

7-2 Gong of animal forms, from Anyang, China, Shang dynasty, twelfth or eleventh century B.C. Bronze, $6\frac{1}{2}''$ high. Asian Art Museum of San Francisco, San Francisco (Avery Brundage Collection).

GONGS IN ANIMAL FORMS Shang bronzes held wine, water, grain, or meat for sacrificial rites. Each vessel's shape matched its intended purpose. Motifs of animal forms were major decorative elements for Shang objects, especially bronzes. They ranged from mere suggestions of animal forms emerging out of linear patterns to identifiable representations of specific creatures. Often, distinct motifs stand out against a background of round or squared spirals ending in hooks. Sometimes these motifs also cover the figures. A major motif is an animal divided in half lengthwise, with the two halves spread out on the vessel body in a bilaterally symmetrical design. The head's two halves, meeting in the center, often also can be read as a complete frontal animal mask with partial bodies at both sides. Such design complexity occurs frequently on Shang vessels, with motifs simultaneously suggesting body parts and independent creatures.

One of the most dramatic Shang vessel forms from Anyang is the *gong*, or covered libation vessel. In the particularly intricate decoration of the gong we illustrate (FIG. **7-2**), the multiple designs and their fields of background spirals integrate so closely with the vessel's form that they are not merely an external embellishment but an integral part of the sculptural whole. Some motifs on the vessel's side may represent the eyes of a tiger and the horns of a ram. (On other Shang vessels, the eyes may be those of a sheep and the horns those of a bull, water buffalo, or deer.) A horned animal forms the front of the lid, and at the rear is a horned head with a bird's beak. Another horned head appears on the handle. Fish, birds, elephants, rabbits, and more abstract composite creatures swarm over the surface against a background of spirals. No broad agreement exists as to the meaning of these animal motifs, but they may represent specific religious concepts. For example,

an animal or bird in the mouth of another animal may signify generation. Or the images may reflect the early Chinese attitude toward the powers of nature and the forces ordering the cosmos. Thus, although the functions of Shang vessels have been determined according to the vessels' shapes, the precise meaning and function of the decor remain uncertain.

AN ANCIENT STATUE OF UNPARALLELED SIZE More recent excavations in other regions of China have greatly expanded historical understanding of this early period. They suggest that, even as Anyang flourished, so did other major centers with distinct aesthetic traditions. For example, in 1986, pits at Guanghan Sanxingdui, in Sichuan Province, yielded objects in gold, bronze, jade, and clay of types never before discovered. The most dramatic find, a bronze statue (FIG. **7-3**) more than eight feet tall, matches anything from Anyang in masterful casting technique. A stylized human figure stands on a thin platform supported by four legs formed of fantastic animal heads with horns and trunklike snouts. These, in turn, rest on a thick, heavy square base. The statue as a whole tapers gently as it rises, and the figure gradually becomes rounder. Just below the neck, great arms branch dramatically outward, ending in oversized hands that once must have encircled another element of the work. Representations of the human figure on this scale in this period are otherwise unknown. A version of Shang surface decoration, with its squared spirals and hook-pointed curves, complements the somewhat abstract rendering of the body and clothing. The figure's facial features suggest a humanized version of the animal mask seen in other bronzes.

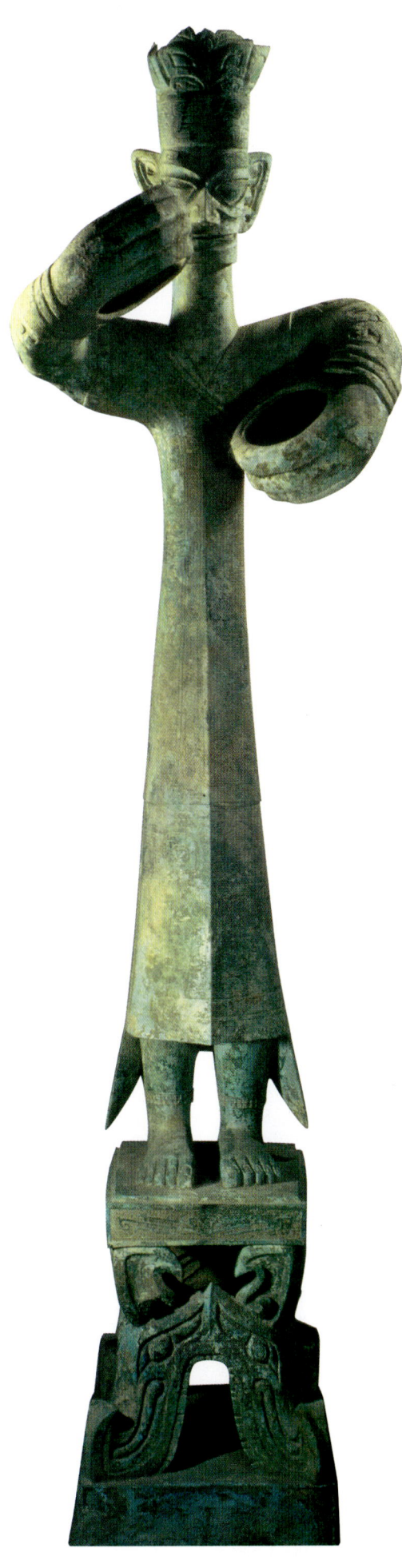

7-3 Standing figure, from Guanghan Sanxingdui, China, Shang dynasty, ca. 1200 B.C. Bronze, 8′ 5″ high, including base. China Cultural Relics Promotional Center, Beijing.

Zhou Dynasty (ca. 1050–256 B.C.)

POLITICAL AND ARTISTIC TRANSITION
Around 1050 B.C., the Zhou, whose dynasty endured until 256 B.C., overthrew the Shang kingdom. The very earliest Zhou art is nearly indistinguishable from that of the Shang, and some artists probably worked for both dynasties. Within a generation, however, changes in vessel shapes already had occurred, and by the fourth century B.C. Zhou bronzes featured entirely new designs—scenes of hunting, religious rites, and magic practices. These may relate to the subjects and compositions of lost paintings mentioned in Zhou literature. Other materials favored in the late Zhou period were jade and *lacquer,* a varnishlike substance made from the sap of the Asiatic sumac and used to decorate wood and other organic materials (see FIG. 26-4). Zhou artists produced objects in great quantity to satisfy the elaborate demands of ostentatious feudal courts vying with one another in lavish display. Bronzes inlaid with gold and silver were popular, as were mirrors highly polished on one side and decorated with a variety of motifs on the other. The mirrors, distributed widely, have even been found among the treasures discovered in Japanese tombs.

JADE'S BEAUTY AND PRESTIGE   The carving of jade jewelry and ritual objects for burial with the dead, beginning in Neolithic times, reached a peak of technical perfection during the Zhou dynasty. Among the most common finds in tombs of the period are *bi* disks, which may have symbolized the circle of heaven. One example (FIG. 7-4), carved in nephrite, like other Chinese jades made before the eighteenth century, features stylized dragons. Nephrite polishes to a more lustrous, slightly buttery finish, while jadeite, the stone preferred in later times, is quite glassy. Both stones come in colors other than the well-known green and are tough, hard, and heavy, as well as beautiful. In China, such qualities became

metaphors for the fortitude and moral perfection of superior persons. Jade also became such an important symbol of rank that later, in the Han dynasty, some rulers were buried in jade bodysuits. Working jade involves laborious sawing, drilling, grinding, and polishing, rather than carving or chipping. Jade sculpture demanded great skill and patience from Zhou artists working with simple hand tools. The intricate *piercework* (carving extending entirely through objects) on the dragons along the outer edge and on the elegant forms surrounding the disk's center testifies to the Zhou craftsperson's mastery of the material. The Chinese thought dragons flew between heaven and earth and brought rain, so these animals long have been symbols of good fortune in eastern Asia. They also symbolized rulers' power to mediate between heaven and earth.

Qin Dynasty (221–206 B.C.)

SHI HUANGDI AND CHINA'S GREAT WALL
From the late Zhou to the founding of the Qin dynasty, China endured more than two centuries of political and social turmoil during what historians have dubbed the Warring States period (475–221 B.C.). The late Zhou dynasty technically ended in 256, when the line of kings completely failed. The Warring States period began when the dynasty lost its power over most of the territory it ruled. Thus, the periods overlap somewhat. This was also a time of intellectual and artistic upheaval, when conflicting schools of philosophy, including Legalism, Daoism, and Confucianism, emerged (see "Daoism and Confucianism," page 193).

The political chaos of the Zhou dynasty's last few hundred years ceased temporarily when the powerful armies of the ruler of the state of Qin conquered all rival states. Qin's ruler took the name Cheng, but he is known to history primarily by his title, Shi Huangdi, the First Emperor of China, and between 221 and 210 B.C. he controlled an area equal to about half of modern China, far more than any of the Kings before him. During his reign, he ordered the linkage of active fortifications along his realm's northern border to form the famous Great Wall. The wall defended China against the fierce nomadic peoples of the north, especially the Huns, who eventually made their way to eastern Europe. By sometimes brutal methods, Shi Huangdi consolidated rule through a centralized bureaucracy and adopted a standardized written language, weights and measures, and coinage. He also repressed schools of thought other than legalism, which had emerged during the Warring States period and espoused absolute obedience to the state's authority and advocated strict laws and punishments. Chinese historians long have condemned Shi Huangdi, but the empire he founded set the stage for the greatly admired Han dynasty and all else thereafter.

ARCHEOLOGISTS UNCOVER AN ARMY   In 1974, excavations started at the site of the immense burial mound of the First Emperor of Qin in Shaanxi Province. For its construction, the ruler conscripted many thousands of laborers and had the tomb filled with treasure—a task that continued after his death. The mound itself remains unexcavated, but pits uncovered around it have revealed an astonishing collection of artifacts, establishing this site as one of the past century's greatest archeological discoveries. Excavators have found more than six thousand life-size terracotta figures of soldiers and horses (FIG. 7-5)—and more recently, bronze horses and

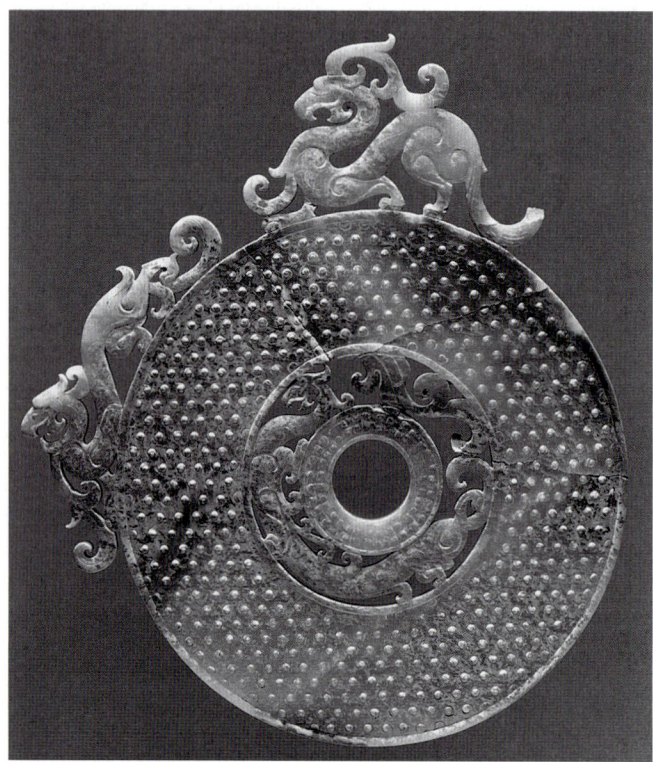

7-4   Bi (disk), late Zhou dynasty, fourth to third century B.C. Nephrite, $6\frac{1}{2}''$ in diameter. Nelson-Atkins Museum, Kansas City.

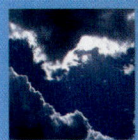

Daoism and Confucianism

Daoism and Confucianism developed during the Warring States period in the fifth through the third centuries B.C., when political turbulence led to social unrest. Daoism and Confucianism embrace both philosophical systems and religions. Religious Daoism, actually rather distinct from its philosophical counterpart, emerged in part out of ancient folk beliefs, and believers adapted many of Buddhism's ritual forms and trappings. These included elaborate ceremonies, brightly colored icons, and lavish temples. Religious Confucianists embraced and developed traditional rites, especially those dedicated to venerating ancestors, great teachers, and heroic leaders. Their practices, too, borrowed from Buddhism, particularly their emphasis on sacred biography, images, and religious ceremonies.

Philosophical Daoism emerged out of the metaphysical teachings attributed to Laozi (604?–531? B.C.) and Zhuangzi (370?–301? B.C.). Daoist philosophy stresses submission to a universal path, or principle, called the Dao, whose features cannot be described but only suggested through analogies. For example, the Dao is said to be like water, always yielding but eventually wearing away the hard stone that does not yield. For Daoists, strength comes from flexibility and nonstruggle. Daoism stresses an intuitive awareness—nurtured by harmonious contact with nature and fellowship with like-minded individuals—over careful reasoning. Historically, Daoist principles encouraged retreat from ordinary society, rather than constructive moral engagement. They emphasized personal development and producing and appreciating personal expressions in poetry and painting.

Confucius (551–479 B.C.) was born in the state of Lu (roughly modern Shandong Province) to an aristocratic family who had fallen on hard times. From an early age, he showed a strong interest in the rites and ceremonies that helped unite people into an orderly society. As he grew older, he developed a deep concern for the suffering the civil conflict of his day caused. Thus, he adopted a philosophy he hoped would lead to order and stability. Confucius stressed empathy for suffering, morality, ceremony, and virtuous social practices based on respect for hierarchical relationships, such as those between parent and child and ruler and subject. He believed that the "superior person, or gentleman," would be a model of such character and behavior.

Confucius spent much of his adult life trying to find rulers willing to apply his teachings, but he died in disappointment. However, he and his follower Mencius (371?–289? B.C.), who helped develop and spread his ideas, had a profound impact upon Chinese thought and social practice. Chinese traditions of venerating deceased ancestors and outstanding leaders encouraged Confucianism's development as a religion as well as a philosophic tradition. Eventually, Emperor Wu Di (r. 140–87 B.C.) of the Han dynasty established Confucianism as the state's official doctrine. Thereafter, it became the primary subject of the civil service exams required for admission into and advancement within government service.

"Confucian" and "Daoist" are broad, imprecise terms scholars often use to distinguish aspects of Chinese culture stressing social responsibility and order (Confucian) from those emphasizing cultivation of individuals, often in reclusion (Daoist). But the two traditions are frequently difficult to separate in art. For example, a landscape painting may seem to depict the ideal places of retreat for Daoists, but its sense of order and structure also may convey Confucian ideals of cosmic order as the model for humanity.

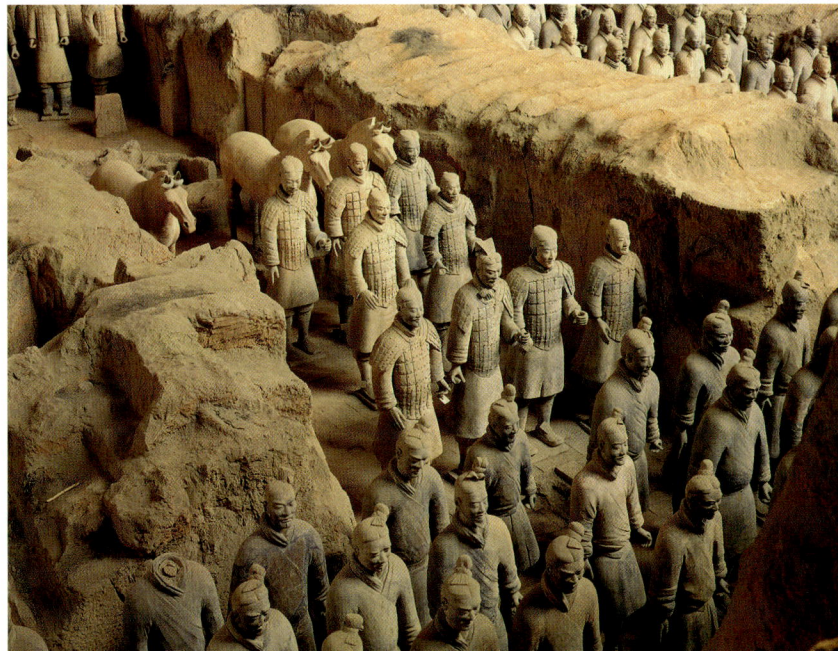

7-5   Army of Emperor Shi Huangdi in pits next to burial mound, Shaanxi Province, China, Qin dynasty, ca. 210 B.C. Painted terracotta, average figure 5′ 10$\frac{7}{8}$″ high.

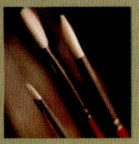

Silk and the Silk Road

Silk is the finest natural fabric ever produced. It comes from the cocoons of caterpillars called silkworms, raised in China since the third millennium B.C., and the basic procedures probably have not changed much in five thousand years. Farmers today still raise silkworms from eggs, which they place in trays kept in rooms with carefully controlled temperature and humidity levels. The farmers also must grow mulberry trees or purchase the leaves, the silkworms' only food source. Eventually, the silkworms form cocoons out of very fine filaments they extrude as liquids from their bodies. The filaments soon solidify with exposure to air. Before the transformed caterpillars emerge as moths and badly damage the silk, the farmers kill them with steam or high heat. They soften the cocoons in hot water and unwind the filaments onto a reel. The filaments are so fine that workers generally unwind those from five to ten cocoons together to bond into a single strand while still soft and sticky. Later, they twist several strands together to form a thicker yarn and then weave the yarn on a loom to produce silk cloth. Both the yarn and the cloth can be dyed. Workers additionally decorate the cloth by weaving threads of different colors together in special patterns (*brocades*) or by stitching in threads of different colors (*embroidery*). Many east Asian artists painted directly on plain silk (FIGS. 7-6, 7-9, 7-16, 7-19, and 7-23, and 7-24).

Greatly admired throughout most of Asia, Chinese silk and the secrets of its production gradually spread throughout the ancient world. The Romans knew of silk as early as the second century B.C. and treasured it for garments and hangings. Silk came to the Romans along the ancient fabled Silk Road, actually two major and several minor caravan tracts linking China and the Mediterranean world. The western part, between the Mediterranean region and India, developed first, due largely to the difficult geographic conditions to India's northeast. In central Asia, the caravans had to skirt the Taklimakan Desert, one of the most inhospitable environments on earth, as well as climb high, dangerous mountain passes. Very few traders actually traveled the entire route. Along the way, goods usually passed through the hands of people from many lands, who often only dimly understood the ultimate origins and destinations of what they traded. The Roman passion for silk ultimately led to the modern name for the caravan tracts, but silk was far from the only product traded along the way. Gold, ivory, exotic animals, and all manner of other merchandise precious enough to warrant the risks passed along the Silk Road. Ideas moved along these trade routes as well. Travelers on the Silk Road brought Buddhism to China from India in the first century A.D.

Upheavals in the East associated with the Tang dynasty's end in A.D. 906 and with the rise of Islam in the Middle East (see Chapter 13) caused a long interruption in trade along the Silk Road. Not until the Venetian Marco Polo's time in the thirteenth century did Europeans reopen it.

---

impressions of chariots. Replicating the emperor's invincible hosts, they served as the immortal imperial bodyguard deployed in trenches outside what researchers believe is a vast underground funerary palace (as yet unexcavated) designed to match the fabulous palace the emperor occupied in life. The historian Sima Qian (136–85 B.C.) described both palaces, but scholars did not take his account seriously until these statues came to light.

Originally in vivid color, the emperor's troops stood in long ranks and files, as if lined up for battle. The terracotta army included cavalry, chariots, archers, lancers, and hand-to-hand fighters. The style of the Qin warriors blends formalism—simplicity of volume and contour, rigidity, and frontality—with sharp realism of detail. Set poses repeat with little or no variation, as if produced from a single mold, but the figures exhibit subtle differences in details of facial features, coiffures, and equipment. Such individualization made the army seem more real and, like the funerary palace, offered the deceased emperor continuity in his passage from this world to the next.

Han Dynasty (206 B.C.–A.D. 220)

Soon after Shi Huangdi's death, the people who had suffered under his reign revolted and founded the Han dynasty in 206 B.C. The Han emperors, ruling China for four centuries, created a new, but equally powerful, centralized government and extended China's southern and western boundaries. Chinese armies penetrated far into Xinjiang and even began to trade indirectly with distant Rome via the fabled Silk Road (see "Silk and the Silk Road," above).

PAINTED SILK IN A NOBLEWOMAN'S TOMB In 1972, archeologists excavated a striking example of Han painting on silk (FIG. **7-6**) in a tomb at Mawangdui in Hunan Province in southern China. The tomb belonged to the wife of the Marquis of Dai. Scholars have not yet determined the function of this T-shaped silk painting, but it may have been used in the funeral ceremonies preceding the woman's burial. Marked by rigorous symmetry and stylized forms, the silk's pictorial field attends less to accurate portrayal than to presenting an iconography of uncertain meaning. Art historians generally agree that the area within the cross at the top of the T represents heaven, most of the vertical section the human realm, and the very bottom the underworld. In the heavenly realm, dragons and immortal beings cavort between and below two orbs—the red sun and its symbol, the raven, on the right and the silvery moon and its symbol, the toad, on the left. Below, the standing figure on the first white platform near the vertical section's center, probably the Marquise of Dai herself, awaits her ascent to heaven, where she can attain im-

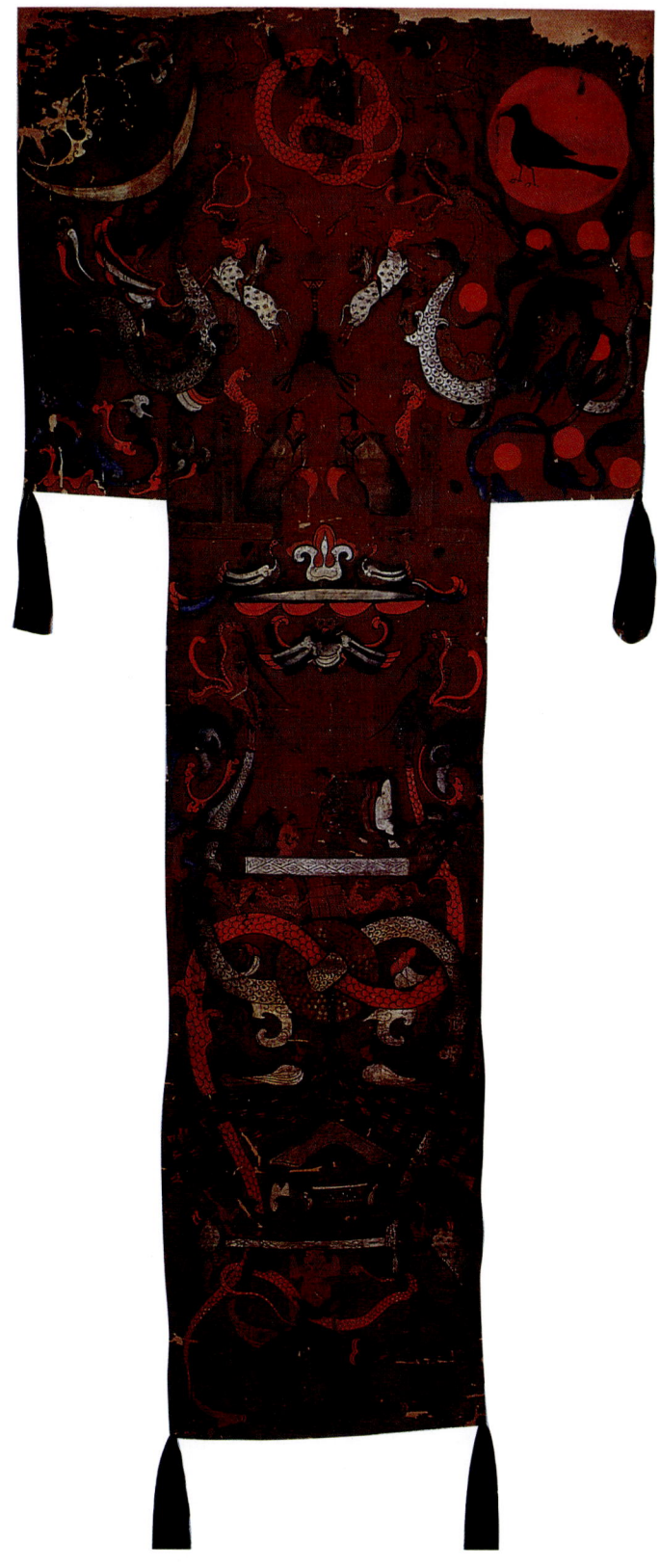

7-6 Funeral banner, from Tomb 1 (tomb of Dai), Mawangdui, China, Western Han dynasty, ca. 168 B.C. Painted silk, 6′ 8¾″ × 3′ ¼″. Hunan Provincial Museum, Changsha.

mortality. Nearer the bottom, the artist depicted the Marquise's funeral. Between these two sections, positions a form resembling a bi disk with two intertwining dragons (compare FIG. 7-4). Their tails reach down to the underworld and their heads point to heaven, unifying the whole composition.

Producing lavish funerary objects such as this funeral banner, performing costly and complex funeral rites, and regularly making offerings to ancestors provide dramatic evidence of how important the ideal of continuity through ancestor veneration has been over time in Chinese life.

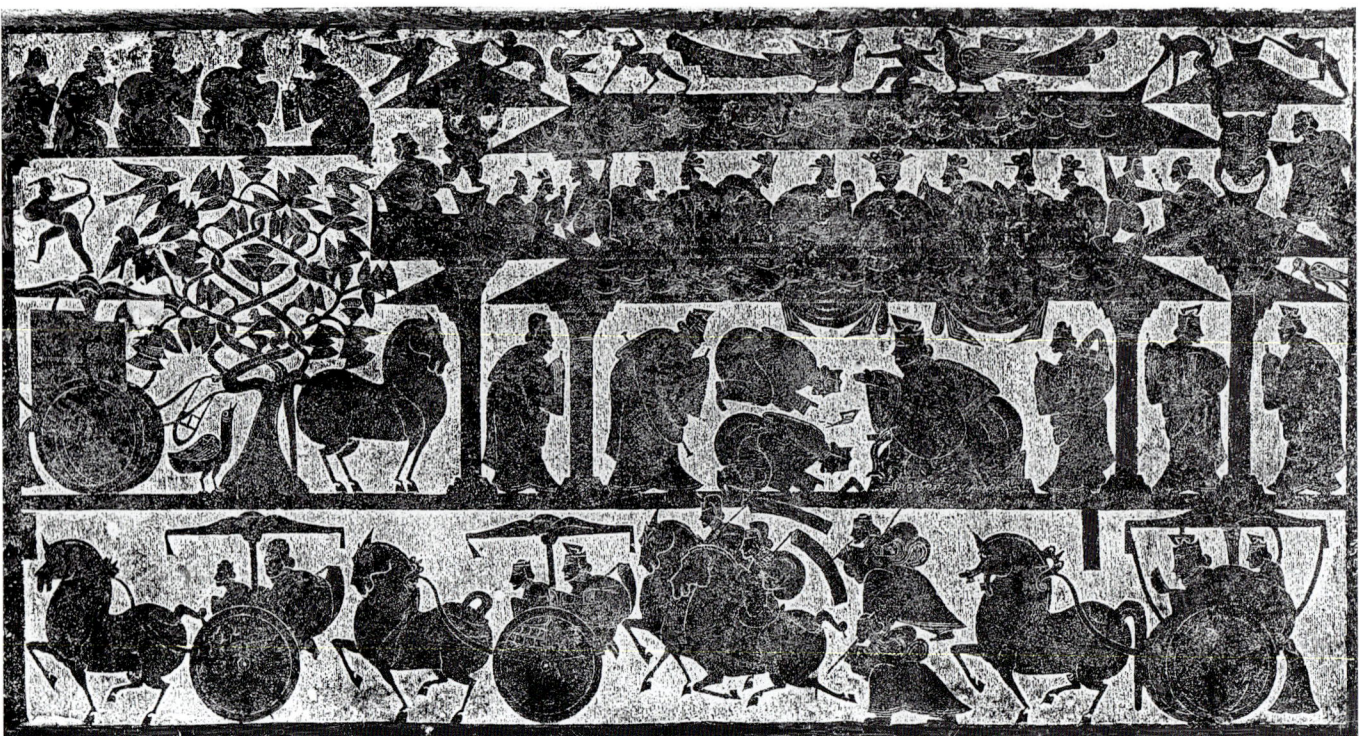

7-7   Mythological scenes, Wu family shrine, Shandong Province, China, late Han dynasty, A.D. 147–168. Rubbing of a stone relief, approx. 5′ long.

YI SAVES THE EARTH   Among the major information sources about Han pictorial style are the reliefs (FIG. 7-7) at the Wu family shrines in the northeastern Shandong Province, datable between A.D. 147 and 168. Dedicated to deceased male family members, the shrines consist of three walls covered by a pitched roof, but they are not large enough to enter. On the exterior slabs of the walls, scenes from history and folklore combine to suggest the dead ancestor's virtues. The slab shown here includes, at the left, a depiction of the archer-hero Yi saving the earth from scorching by shooting down the nine extra suns, represented as crows in the Fusang tree. (The small orbs below the sun on the Mawangdui banner probably allude to the same story.) The inclusion of the archer's story suggests the deceased's reverence for the past and perhaps implies his own courage.

The story on each relief unfolds in registers, as do those in the ancient Near East, Egypt, and early Greece. Images of flat polished stone stand out against an equally flat, though roughly textured, ground. The curved figures relate to one another by the linear rhythms of their contours. Buildings and trees indicate a setting, but the perspective devices of contemporaneous painting and relief sculpture in the classical world are absent. The artist suggested distance by placing one adjacent figure above another, although some chariot wheels do overlap. Important individuals are larger than their subordinates. Most interesting are the trees, highly stylized as masses of intertwined branches bearing isolated overlarge leaves. Yet within this schematic form, a variation via a twisted branch or broken bough shows how the designer's generalization derived from observing specific trees. It also illustrates how a detail in one element can individualize the whole. This subtle relationship between the specific and the abstract became one of the most important attributes of later Chinese painting.

Period of Disunity (220–589)

BUDDHISM REACHES CHINA   For three and a half centuries, from 220 to 589, civil strife divided China into competing states. Scholars variously refer to this era as the Period of Disunity or the period of the Six Dynasties or of the Northern and Southern Dynasties. Buddhism (see "Buddhism and Buddhist Iconography," Chapter 6, page 164) had reached China in the first century A.D., although its first adherents were non-Chinese on the outskirts of the Han empire. Certain practices shared with Daoism, such as withdrawal from ordinary society, helped Buddhism gain an initial foothold among the Chinese. But Buddhism's promise of hope beyond this world's troubles of existence earned it an ever broader audience during the upheavals of the Period of Disunity. In addition, the fully developed Buddhist system of thought attracted intellectuals. Buddhism never fully displaced Confucianism and Daoism, but it did prosper throughout China for centuries and had a profound effect on the further development of the religious forms of those two native traditions.

Pilgrims and missionaries making the hazardous trip along the desert trade routes of central Asia that formed the Silk Road's eastern portion brought Buddhist art to China. Most of the Buddhist art surviving in China from the fourth and fifth centuries originated in the northern states, which non-Chinese peoples ruled. An important early Chinese Buddhist image is the gilded bronze statuette of Sakyamuni Buddha (the historical Buddha; FIG. 7-8), dated by inscription to the year 338. In both style and iconography, this Buddha resembles the prototype conceived and developed at Gandhara, Pakistan (see FIG. 6-13). The Chinese figure recalls its presumed Gandharan models in the flat, relieflike handling of the robe's heavy concentric folds, the ushnisha (cranial bump)

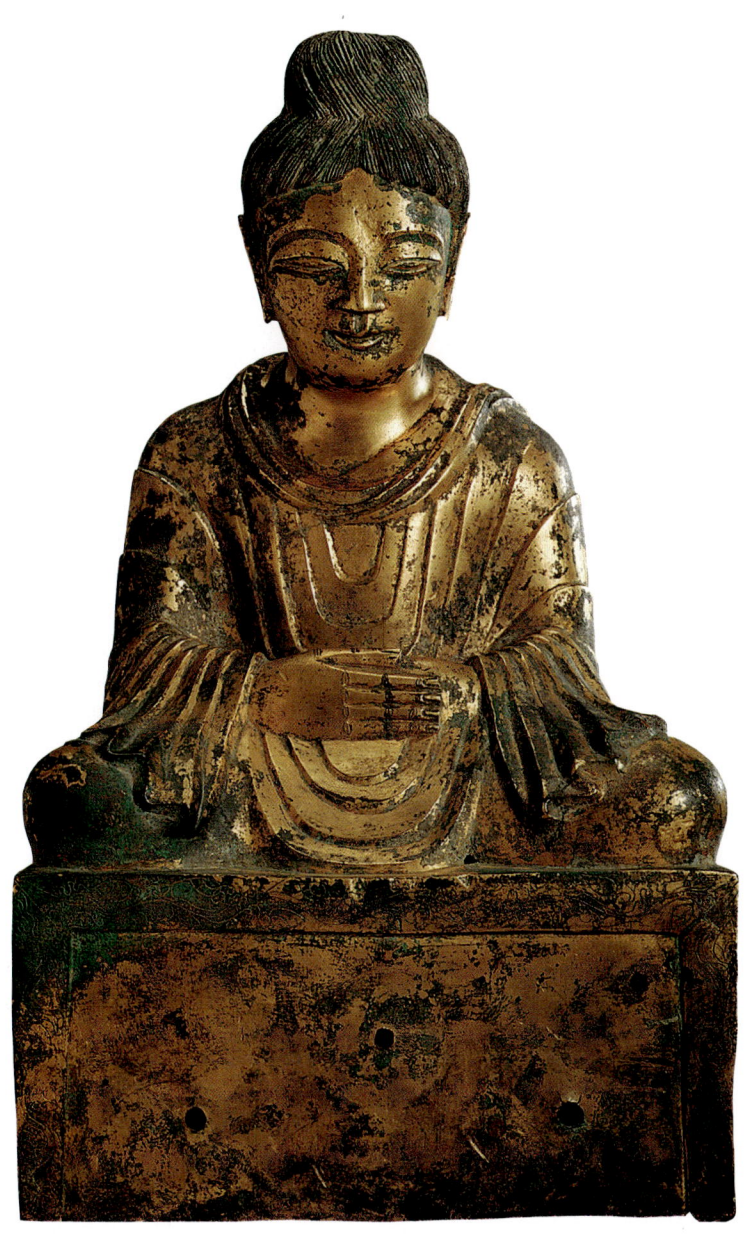

7-8   Sakyamuni Buddha, late Zhau dynasty, Period of Disunity, 338. Gilded bronze, 1' 3 1/2" high, 9 5/8" wide. Asian Art Museum of San Francisco, San Francisco (Avery Brundage Collection).

on the head, and the cross-legged position. So new were the icon and its meaning, however, that the Chinese sculptor incorrectly represented the canonical meditation gesture. Here, the Buddha clasps his hands across his stomach. They should be turned palms upward, with thumbs barely touching in front of the torso (see FIG. 6-13).

By the early sixth century, a thinner and more stylized image of the Buddha had emerged in India. These changes in formal approach spread throughout eastern Asia, as an early-seventh-century bronze from Japan (see FIG. 8-6) indicates. The Chinese, too, produced more graceful, slender figures. As Buddhism flourished in China, so did Chinese Buddhist art, especially in great cave complexes built in the Indian fashion (FIG. 6-12). Even before Buddhism's arrival in China, Mahayana and later teachings in southern and central Asia had developed an expanded group of deities. These gods appeared in the Chinese caves, along with the Buddhas.

CHINESE PAINTING   Buddhist imagery did not hold exclusive sway in this period, however. Secular arts and objects related to Confucian and Daoist practices and beliefs also flour-

ished. Rulers sought calligraphers and painters to lend distinction to their courts. Several distinctive materials and formats characterize Chinese painting (and by extension painting throughout eastern Asia). The basic requirements are the same as for writing—a round tapered brush, soot-based ink, and a support (surface for painting), usually silk or paper. In some paintings (FIG. 7-25), figural outlines reveal the characteristic Chinese line that elastically widens and narrows to convey not only outline but depth and mass as well. In other works (FIG. 7-16), *iron-wire lines* (thin, unmodulated lines with a suggestion of tensile strength, which are often seen in Buddhist figure painting) define the figures. The Chinese also used richly colored minerals as pigments, finely ground and suspended in a gluey medium, and watery washes of mineral and vegetable dyes.

The formats of Chinese paintings not on walls tend to be more personal and intimate than often common in the West. Artists glued some pictures to silk scrolls for vertical display (unrolled) on appropriate occasions. Other paintings were mounted on long, narrow scrolls viewers unrolled horizontally, section by section. Painters attached still others to fans and to paper leaves in albums.

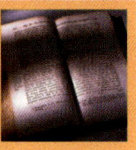

Xie He's Six Laws

China has a long and rich history of scholarship on painting, preserved today in copies of texts from as far back as the fourth century and in citations to even earlier sources. Few of the first texts on painting survive, but later authors often quoted them, preserving the texts for posterity. China's early invention of printing led to an even greater dispersion of such texts. (Printing was used widely in China by the second century A.D.; it is extremely difficult to set even a rough date for its invention there.) Thus, educated Chinese painters and their clients could steep themselves in a rich art historical tradition.

Perhaps the most famous subject of later commentary is a set of six laws of painting Xie He (active early sixth century) formulated. Scholars still debate the precise meaning of his now cryptic laws formed of only four Chinese characters each. Loosely translated, they read:

1. Animation through spirit resonance
2. Bone method in the use of the brush
3. Fidelity to the object in depiction
4. Conforming to type in applying colors
5. Appropriate planning in placement
6. Transmission by copying ancient models

Interpreting these laws in connection with actual paintings, however difficult, offers valuable insights into what the Chinese valued in painting. The simplest laws to understand are the third, fourth, and fifth, because they show painters' concern for accuracy in rendering forms and colors and for care in composition, concerns common in many cultures. However, separating form and color into different laws gives written expression to some of the distinctive features of painting in China and the rest of eastern Asia. Generally, Chinese painters did not use gradations of color when modeling three-dimensional form. Many paintings are brushed-ink drawings with flat applications of thick pigments, washes of color, or both, sometimes supplemented with simple streaks of shading along edges, such as drapery folds (for example, see FIGS. 7-6, 7-14, and 7-16).

Also noteworthy is the order of the laws, suggesting Chinese painters' primary concern—to convey the vital spirit of their subjects and their own sensitivity to that spirit. Next in importance was the handling of the brush, the careful placement of strokes, especially of ink. Although applying these two laws directly to specific paintings is difficult, Gu Kaizhi's figurative paintings (FIG. 7-9) and others' later landscape paintings (FIG. 7-19) certainly suggest values in painting quite distinct from Western values. The forms of such paintings do not conform to simple visual reality, and their textures result from careful handling of the inked brush, a key element in the training of Chinese painters.

The sixth law also speaks to a standard Chinese painting practice—copying. Chinese painters trained by copying their teachers' and other painters' works. In addition, artists often copied famous paintings as sources of forms and ideas for their own works. Gu Kaizhi's scroll (FIG. 7-9) may, in fact, be a copy of another painting of his era. Many renowned Chinese painters consciously painted works in the manner of famous predecessors. Change and individual development occurred in constant reference to the past, the artists always preserving some elements of it.

The horizontal scroll, or *handscroll,* has a long history as a major format for painting in eastern Asia and was frequently used to present illustrated religious texts. These scrolls, sometimes exceeding fifty feet in length, were unrolled to the left and rerolled from the right, with only a small section exposed. Priests and other teachers often placed large-scale instructional scrolls on special stands and presented them to a small audience. Other scrolls were more intimate in scale and best viewed by only one or two people at a time. In later periods, the horizontal scroll also developed as a format for painting continuous landscapes. Art historians have compared the organization of these paintings to a symphony because of how motifs reappear and moods vary in the different sections. Due to the unrolling/rerolling process, appreciation of the landscape scroll involves memory, as well as vision, and the format encourages leisurely contemplation.

LADY FENG'S HEROISM The painter and essayist Gu Kaizhi (ca. 344–406) is one of the few individual artists from the Period of Disunity to whom art historians have been able to attribute extant paintings with confidence. Gu won respect as a calligrapher and was a friend of important members of the imperial court. A horizontal scroll attributed to Gu Kaizhi, called *Admonitions of the Instructress to the Court Ladies,* contains painted scenes between passages of explanatory text. One of the sections (FIG. **7-9**) depicts a well-known act of heroism, the Lady Feng saving her emperor's life by placing herself between him and an attacking bear. Gu set his figures against a blank background and provided only a minimal setting for the scene. The figures' fluid poses and fluttering drapery ribbons, in concert with individualized facial expressions, convey a clear quality of animation. This style accords well with painting ideals expressed in texts of the time, when representing inner vitality and spirit took precedence over reproducing surface appearances (see "Xie He's Six Laws," above).

Early Chinese Architecture

FLEXIBLE SUPPORT AND MULTIPLE COLORS Chinese architecture did not display dramatic changes in style over the centuries, although striking new forms, such as the pagoda (FIGS. 7-21 and 7-22), developed to serve Buddhist

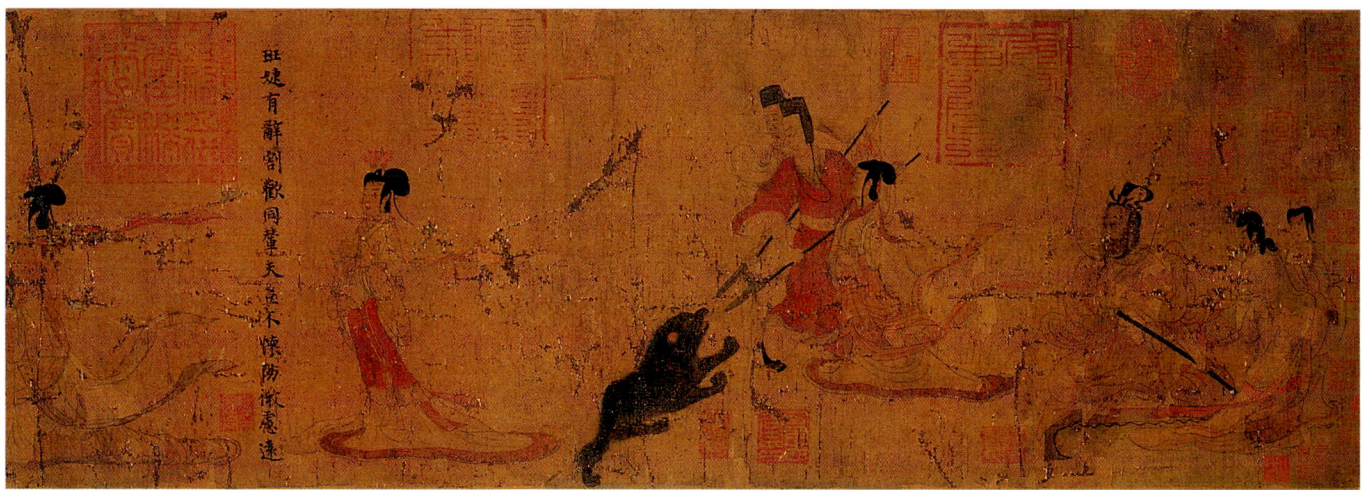

7-9 Attributed to GU KAIZHI, *Lady Feng and the Bear*, detail of *Admonitions of the Instructress to the Court Ladies*, Period of Disunity, late fourth century. Handscroll, ink and colors on silk, $9\frac{3}{4}'' \times 11'\ 4\frac{1}{2}''$. British Museum, London.

needs. As in many other ancient cultures, the Chinese used wood to construct their earliest buildings, and those structures do not survive. However, scholars believe that many of the features giving East Asian architecture its specific character—for example, the roof's curving silhouette—may go back to Zhou times. Even the simple buildings depicted on Han stone carvings (FIG. 7-7) reveal a style and a method of construction long basic to China. This lasting characteristic is an ingenious and flexible support system employing columns, beams, and brackets (see "Chinese Construction Methods and Principles," page 200).

The essentials of a Chinese building consist of a rectangular hall covered by a pitched roof with projecting eaves supported by wooden columns and brackets. The walls serve no weight-bearing function but act only as screening elements. The colors of Chinese buildings, predominantly red, black, yellow, and white, are also distinctive. Chinese timber architecture is customarily multicolored throughout, save for certain parts left in natural color, such as white marble

balustrades (a row of vaselike supports with a railing) or roof crests. The builders usually painted the screen walls and the columns red. Chinese designers often chose dazzling combinations of colors and elaborate patterns (FIG. 7-10) for the beams, brackets, eaves, rafters, and ceilings. The builders painted or lacquered the surfaces to protect the timber from rot and wood parasites, as well as to produce an arresting aesthetic, even spiritual, effect.

THE PRECARIOUS TEMPLE OF HUNYUAN A small temple occupying an almost impossible mountainside site at Hunyuan reveals the technical expertise of Chinese architects. The Xuankong Si, or Hanging Temple (FIG. 7-11), built during the Northern Wei dynasty (386–534), seems to hover in the air in front of a huge cliff about to overwhelm it. The building's light, fragile fabric stands in startling contrast to the brutal mass of stone it seems to defy. Though later masonry foundations lend it support at the base, the original builders erected the structure literally from the top down. They fashioned the separate parts beforehand, lifted them to the top of the cliff, and then lowered the architectural pieces, along with

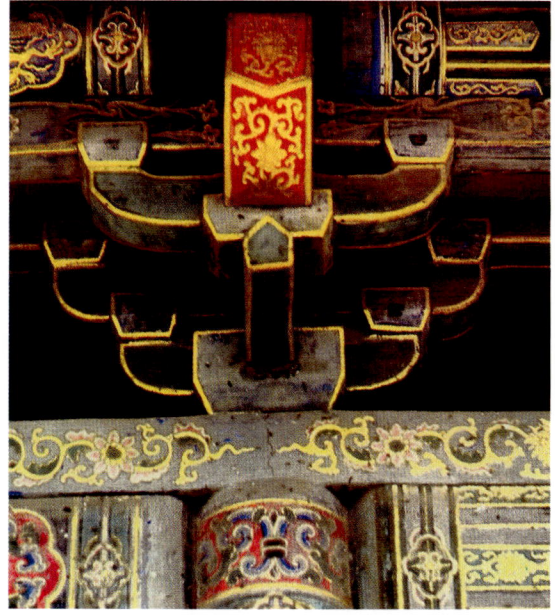

7-10 Console bracket cluster supporting eaves of a bell tower, China.

7-11 Xuankong Si (Hanging Temple), Hunyuan, China, Northern Wei dynasty, 386–534. Reconstructed during the Ming dynasty, 1368–1644.

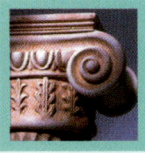

ARCHITECTURAL BASICS

Chinese Construction Methods and Principles

It is a curious paradox that the architecture of China, the oldest continuing civilization in the world, should be represented by few surviving buildings older than the ninth century. China's conservatism would seem to have made preservation of its ancient monuments one of its first cares. Yet the very flexibility of its construction methods made conservation of individual structures less vital. Buildings easily could be dismantled, moved to another site, or simply replaced. And, unlike bronzes, paintings, and so forth, the Chinese did not consider buildings antiquities of intrinsic "artistic" value, and they obviously could not be preserved in collections. Wars, fires, and earthquakes took tremendous tolls on them. Moreover, many Buddhist temples were destroyed during persecutions. More important than the survival of individual buildings was the survival of the tradition of building.

In Chinese architecture, the builders laid *beams* (no. 1 in our diagram) between columns, decreasing the length of the beams as the structure rose. The beams supported vertical *struts* (no. 2), which in turn supported higher beams and eventually the *purlins* (no. 3) running the length of the building and carrying the roof's sloping *rafters* (no. 4). Unlike the rigid elements of the triangular trussed timber roof common in the West and familiar in North American home construction, the varying lengths of the Chinese structure's cross beams and the variously placed purlins could produce roof lines of different shapes. In addition, the interlocking clusters of brackets could *cantilever* (support with brackets) the roof to allow for broad overhang of the *eaves* (no. 5). Multiplication of the *bays* (compartments) formed by column-beam-bracket construction could extend the building's length to any dimen-sion desired. The proportions of the structural elements could be fixed into modules, allowing for standardization of parts. This made rapid construction of a building possible. The workers fit the parts together without using any adhesive substance, such as mortar or glue. Delicately joined as the parts were, they still could carry easily the heavy tiled roofs of the great Chinese temples and halls (FIGS. 7-15 and 7-22).

The Chinese considered the choice of site for a building a cultivated art. The architect diligently calculated the north-south and east-west axes when situating a building, giving careful thought to the landscape environment for both practical and spiritual reasons. The Chinese favored southern and southeastern orientations for the somewhat milder climatic conditions and for assistance in generating vegetation—the life-giving sun against the deadly northern chill. In conformity with the Chinese belief in *fengshui* (wind and water), water must stop the breath of life, which is scattered by wind. Thus architects must adjust the forces of wind and water when orienting buildings. In the layout of building complexes, the seclusion of the units and the spaces of the enclosure express the conservation of breath. The plans are often symmetrical, the buildings facing each other on both sides of a central axis. The axis functions as a path and visual perspective seen through gateways, towers, halls, and courtyards in a sequence of primarily perpendicular units along it. The qualities of symmetry, regularity, uniformity, and secludedness in the layout, not only of halls and temple complexes but also of whole cities, powerfully express the Chinese respect for tradition and order.

---

the workers who assembled them while suspended from the cliff. The column-beam-bracket system, braced against the rock face, took advantage of the cliff's resistance to stabilize the stresses. This remarkable structure, though often restored, has withstood numerous earthquakes. The current structure, rebuilt during the Ming dynasty (1368–1644), shows later enhancements. In particular, the decora]tive function of color and the ornamental exaggeration of the turned-up eaves became more conspicuous in later centuries. The Hanging Temple then took on the dramatically horned or winged silhouette distinguishing later Chinese rooflines.

Tang Dynasty (618–906)

CHINA REUNIFIED The emperors of the short-lived Sui dynasty (581–618) succeeded in reuniting China and prepared the way for the brilliant Tang dynasty (618–906). Under the Tang emperors, China entered a period of unequaled magnificence. Chinese armies marched across central Asia, prompting an influx of foreign peoples, wealth, and ideas. Arab traders, Nestorian Christians (members of a sect originating in western Asia), and other travelers journeyed to the Tang's cosmopolitan capital at Chang'an (modern Xi'an), and the Chinese, in turn, ventured westward. The Tang rulers embellished their empire with extravagant wooden structures, but all have disappeared due to intentional and unintentional destruction by fire. Judging from records, however, the Tang buildings were colorfully painted and of colossal size, possessing furnishings of great luxury and elaborate gold, silver, and bronze ornaments.

A ROCK-CUT COSMIC BUDDHA In its first century, the new dynasty continued to support Buddhism and to sponsor great monuments for Buddhist worshipers. One of the most spectacular is the colossal rock-cut figure of Vairocana Buddha (FIG. **7-12**), the personification of the cosmos, carved out of a cliff in the great Longmen Cave complex near Luoyang between 670 and 680. Work at Longmen had begun almost two centuries earlier, during the Period of Disunity, under the rulers of the Tuoba Wei. The one thousand three hundred fifty-two caves, ninety-seven thousand statues, three thousand six hundred inscriptions, and seven hundred eighty-five carved niches at Longmen provide some notion of the powerful attraction of Buddhism to the Chinese.

Chinese raised beam
construction (after L.
Liu).

1. Beam
2. Strut
3. Purlin
4. Rafter
5. Eaves

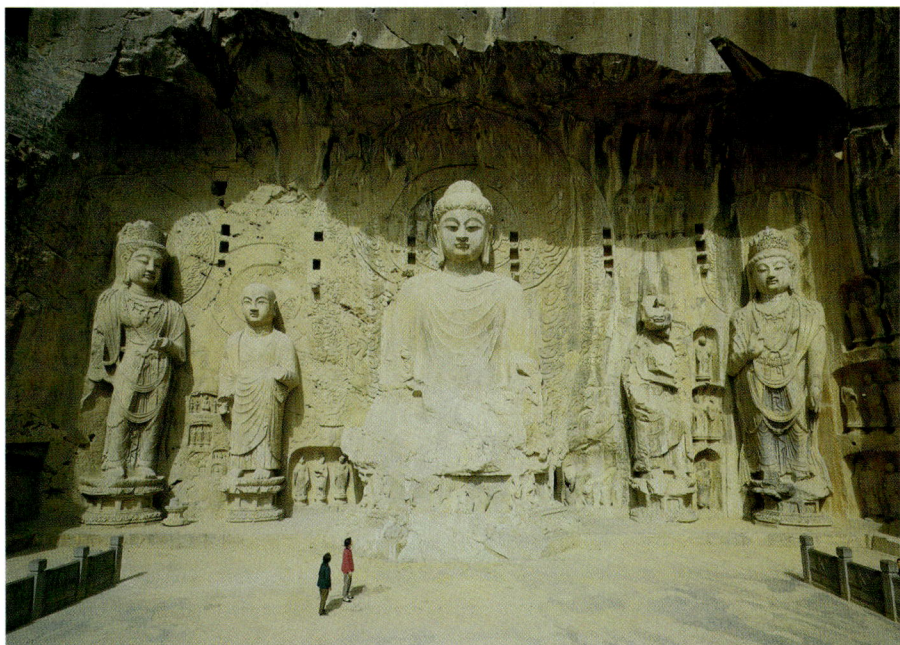

7-12 Vairocana Buddha, Longmen Caves,
Luoyang, China, Tang dynasty, ca. 670–680.
Natural rock, 50′ high.

The Vairocana Buddha presides over an infinite number of worlds, each with its Buddha, symbolized in his throne's lotus petals. In serene majesty, flanked by Buddhas and bodhisattvas, the Longmen Buddha overwhelms visitors to the site. An almost geometric regularity of contour and smoothness of planes emphasizes the massive figure's volume. The folds of his robes fall in a few concentric arcs. The sculptor suppressed surface detail in the interest of monumental simplicity and dignity. The detailed and deeply channeled drapery of the bodhisattvas at the extreme left and right makes a telling contrast with the carving of Vairocana.

A SINUOUS BODHISATTVA By the end of the seventh century, Buddhist sculpture in China had changed dramatically, influenced by the fluid, sensual style of Buddhist sculpture in India (see FIG. 6-15). Fleshiness increased and drapery began to cling, as if wet, against the body. A marble statue of a bodhisattva (FIG. **7-13**) exemplifies the early Tang style admirably, drawing heavily on Indian prototypes. The figure's hip-tilted pose and revealing drapery accentuate its sinuous beauty, in the Indian tradition. Still, the crisp precision of the carving and the figure's robustness mark the work as Tang Chinese. The swaying pose suggests that this bodhisattva was one of the attendants in a Buddha triad. A *Buddha triad* is a group of three statues with a central Buddha flanked on each side by an attendant bodhisattva. Bodhisattvas had strong appeal in eastern Asia as compassionate beings ready to achieve Buddhahood but dedicated to humanity's salvation. Some received direct worship and became the main subjects of sculpture and painting.

THE BUDDHA OF THE WEST AT DUNHUANG The westward expansion of the Tang Empire increased the importance of Dunhuang, the westernmost gateway to China on the Silk Road. Dunhuang long had been a wealthy, cosmopolitan trade center; a Buddhist pilgrimage destination; and home to thriving communities of Buddhist monks and nuns of varied ethnicity, as well as to adherents of other religions. More than three hundred sanctuaries cut into the soft rock of the cliffs near Dunhuang, known as the Mogao Buddhist caves, contain walls decorated with paintings. Images of painted unfired clay and stucco also adorn the chambers. The site was dedicated in 366, but the earliest extant caves date to the late fifth century. By the eighth century, wealthy donors sponsored larger and more elaborately decorated caves.

Paradise of Amitabha (FIG. **7-14**), on the wall of one of the Dunhuang caves, shows how the splendor of the age and religious teachings could come together in a powerful image. Buddhist Pure Land sects, especially those centered on Amitabha, Buddha of the West, had captured the popular imagination in the Period of Disunity under the Six Dynasties and continued to flourish during the Tang dynasty. Pure Land teachings asserted that individuals had no hope of attaining enlightenment through their own power because of the corruption of the age. Instead, they could obtain rebirth in a realm free from corruption simply through faith in Amitabha's promise of salvation. Richly detailed, brilliantly colored pictures steeped in the Tang dynasty's opulence, such as this one, greatly aided worshipers in gaining faith by visual-

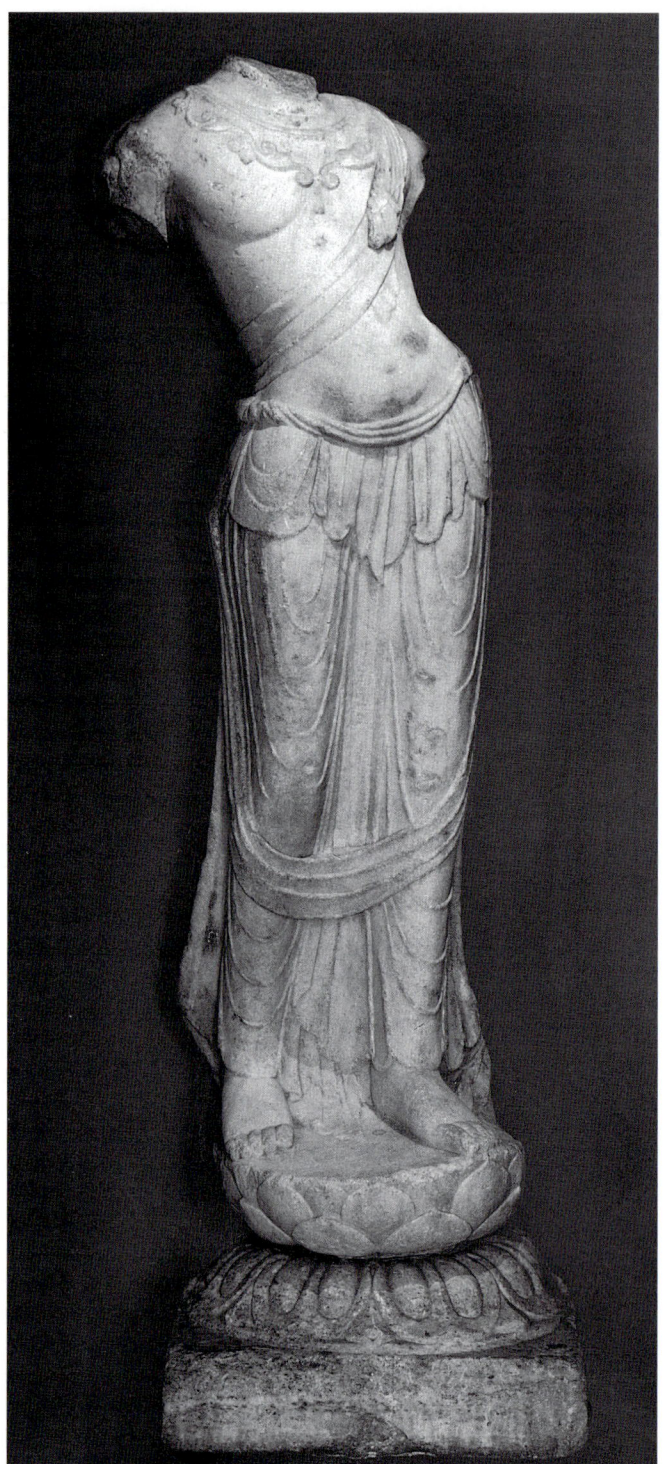

7-13   Bodhisattva, early Tang dynasty, seventh to eighth century. Marble. Charles Uht Collection, New York.

izing the wonders of such a paradise. Amitabha sits in the center of a raised platform, his principal bodhisattvas and lesser divine attendants surrounding him. Before them a celestial dance takes place. The scene's splendor coincides with textual descriptions of Amitabha's Pure Land but with a particularly Chinese visualization. Everything occurs within a setting of Tang-style palace architecture, symmetrically arranged and highly ornate.

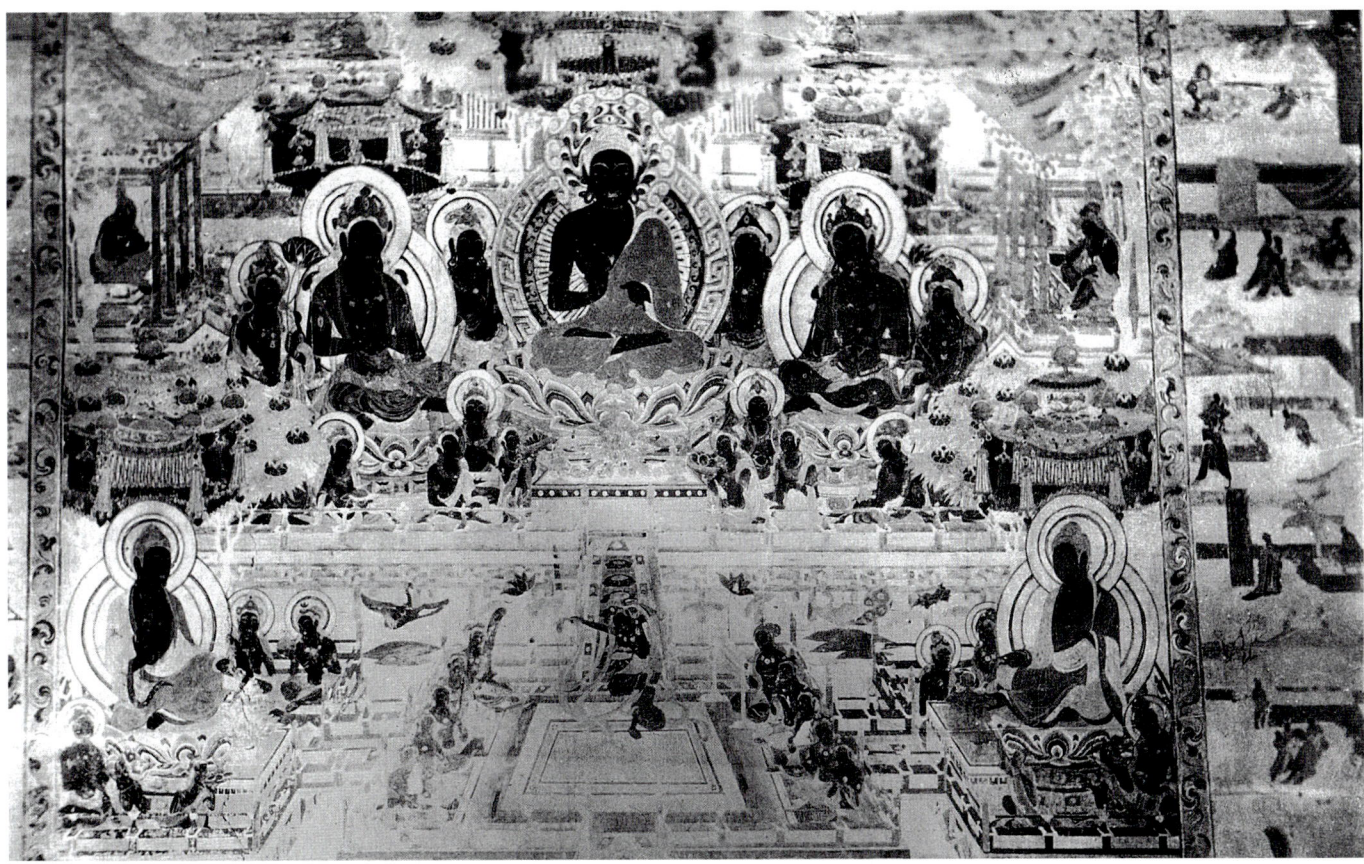

7-14   *Paradise of Amitabha*, Cave 139A, Dunhuang, China, Tang dynasty, ninth century. Wall painting.

THE CHANGING ROLE OF CHINESE ARTISTS

The social circumstances and roles of ancient Chinese artists varied greatly over time and according to specific occupation, but some very general patterns by the time of the Tang dynasty emerge from the historical record. By the seventh century, the great majority of artists served the needs and met the demands of clients ranging from kings to local noblewomen to Buddhist institutions. They often worked under close supervision and also tended to serve collectively. The number of extant Shang (FIG. 7-2) and Zhou bronzes alone suggests the existence of early well-organized workshops. Members may have inherited their occupations, as in later periods. Certainly, workshops (their members locked into their positions as the state's slaves) decorated and furnished great imperial building projects of the Qin and succeeding dynasties. The artists who created the great works at Longmen Caves inherited their occupations, served in workshops, and, until about mid-sixth century, were the state's slaves, unable to accept private commissions without permission.

By the Tang dynasty, however, even artists in the great workshops that carved and painted the Buddhist cave temples had achieved more independent status, although various rulers still sometimes compelled their labor as a form of taxation. Such workshops surely had leaders, but historians know almost nothing about them. A real sense of specific artistic identity only emerges in major records related to calligraphers and to painters such as Gu Kaizhi (FIG. 7-9), who were all men. Scholars know very little about artists in other fields or about women's contributions.

TANG TEMPLES   A cutaway cross-section and perspective drawing (FIG. **7-15**) of one of the oldest surviving Buddhist temples in China, the Foguang Si near Mount Wutai (Wutai Shan) in northern China, shows the realization of Tang architectural ideals in temples. A complex grid of beams and purlins, and a thicket of interlocking brackets, supports the overhang of the eaves—some fourteen feet out from the column faces—as well as the timbered and tiled roof. China's timber technology reached early maturity in this masterpiece of Tang dynasty architecture.

For all its successes, Buddhism never replaced native Chinese religions, and the Buddhist practice of removing people from their families and from public service to enter monastic

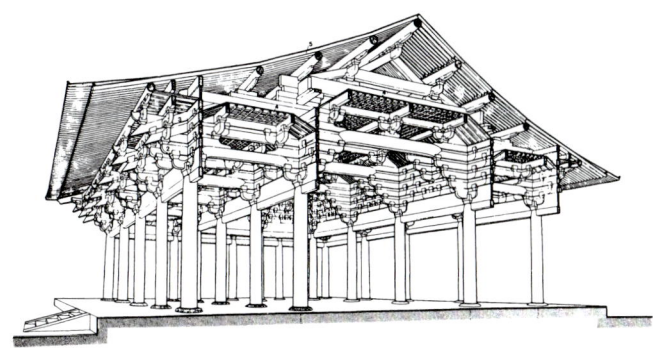

7-15   Schematic cross-section and perspective drawing of Chinese beam-bracketing construction, Foguang Si temple, Wutai Shan, China, Tang dynasty, ca. 857 (after L. Liu).

7-16 Attributed to YAN LIBEN, Tang emperor and attendants, detail of *The Thirteen Emperors*, Tang dynasty, ca. 650. Handscroll, ink and colors on silk, 1′ 8¼″ ×1′ 5½″. Museum of Fine Arts, Boston (Denman Waldo Ross Collection).

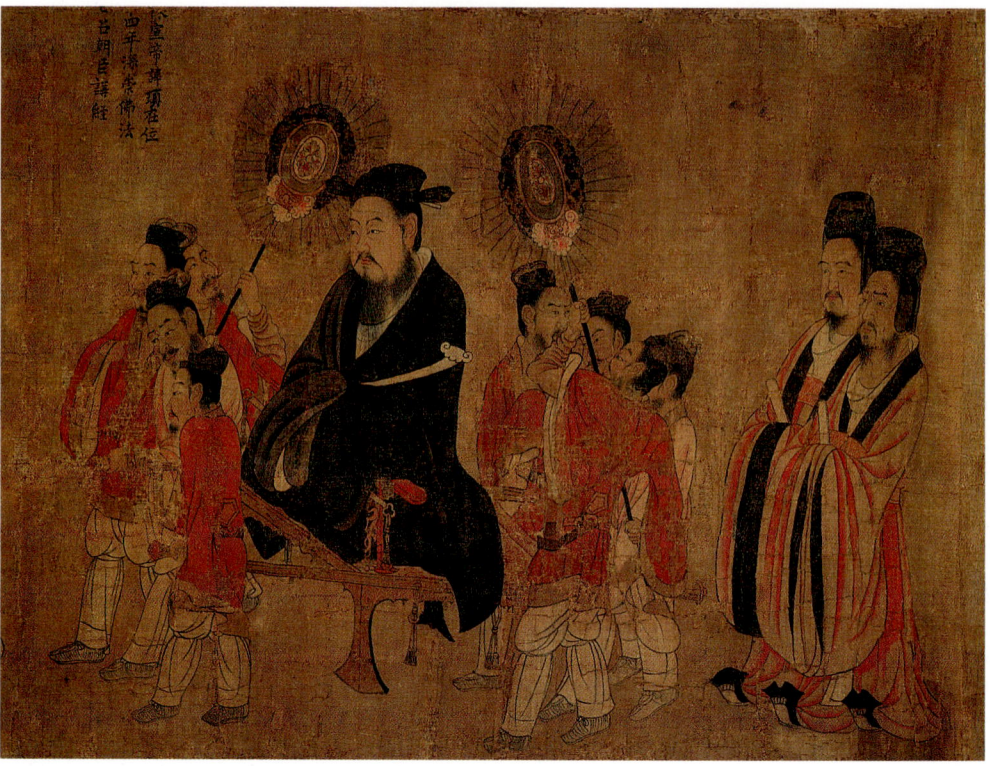

communities conflicted deeply with Confucian values. In 845, the emperor Wuzong instituted a major persecution, destroying four thousand six hundred Buddhist temples and forty thousand shrines and forcing the return of two hundred sixty thousand five hundred monks and nuns to lay life. These policies did not affect Dunhuang, then under Tibetan rule, so it preserves much lost elsewhere, although its painting styles do not fully reflect those of central China. Scholars today also look to survivals of art and architecture in Korea and Japan made during periods of these countries' closest cultural intercourse with China to help fill in the gaps in the visual record.

ART AT THE TANG COURT Chang'an, the Tang capital, was perhaps the greatest city in the world during the seventh and eighth centuries. A brilliant tradition of figurative painting developed at the Tang court that, in its variety and balance, reflected the Tang emperors' worldliness and self-assurance. Indeed, many art historians regard the early Tang dynasty as the golden age of Chinese figurative painting. Glowing accounts by Chinese poets and critics survive, although only a few examples of the paintings remain.

In perfect accord with descriptions of the robust Tang style are the unrestored portions of *The Thirteen Emperors* (FIG. **7-16,** detail), a masterpiece of line drawing and colored washes. YAN LIBEN (d. 673), believed to have been the artist, was a celebrated seventh-century Tang painter and statesman. In the work, each emperor stands or sits in an undefined space, his eminence clearly indicated by his great size relative to his attendants. Simple shading in the faces and the robes gives the figures an added semblance of volume and presence. As a whole, the portrait series offers a pageant of majesty exalting the Tang emperors' power and dignity.

A PRINCESS'S PAINTED TOMB Wall paintings in the tomb of the Tang princess Yongtai permit an analysis of court painting styles unobscured by problems of authenticity and reconstruction. Within the tomb, built in 706 near Chang'an, the figures of palace ladies (FIG. **7-17**) appear as if on a shallow stage. The artist did not provide any indications of background or setting, but intervals between the two rows and the figures' grouping in an oval suggest a consistent ground plane. The women assume a variety of poses, seen in full-face and in three-quarter views, from the front or the back. The device of paired figures facing into and out of the

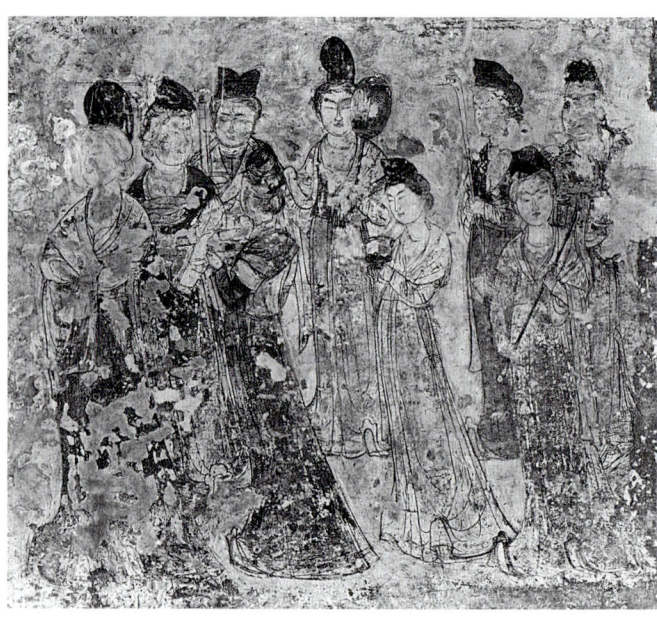

7-17   Palace ladies, in the tomb of Princess Yongtai, near Chang'an (Xi'an), Tang dynasty, 706. Wall painting.

space of the picture in a near mirror image appears often in paintings of this period and effectively creates depth. Thick, even contour lines describe full-volumed faces and suggest solid forms beneath the drapery, all with the utmost economy. This simplicity of form and line, along with the measured cadence of the poses, results in an air of monumental dignity befitting a daughter of the Tang ruling house.

By the eighth century, China had become an international cultural center, integrating concepts and forms from farther west and affecting developments to the south and east. In particular, Tang artists and craftspeople taught visitors from Korea and Japan, and some even traveled abroad. Thus, fair approximations of the Tang artists' elegant approach to figurative painting, dominated by sweeping brush lines, began to appear elsewhere in eastern Asia (see FIG. 8-8).

GLAZED EARTHENWARE SCULPTURE Tang potters also achieved renown, producing fine wares for ostentatious display. They covered their vessels with colorful lead glazes and invented robust shapes with clearly defined parts—base, body, and neck. Earlier potters often had imitated bronze models, but the Tang artists derived their vessel forms more directly from the clay's plastic character and techniques such as wheel-throwing. Tang ceramicists also produced thousands of earthenware figures of people, domesticated animals, and fantastic creatures for burial in tombs. The depiction of such diverse figures as Greek acrobats and Semitic traders indicates the cosmopolitanism of Tang China. The artists painted some figurines with colored slips and decorated others, such as the spirited, handsomely adorned Neighing Horse (FIG. 7-18), with colorful lead glazes that ran in dramatic streams down the objects' sides when fired.

The horse's popularity as a Chinese art subject reflects the importance the emperors placed on the quality of their stables. More than seven hundred thousand studs in the Tang kingdom attested to their significance for the dynasty's military success and glory. The breed represented here is powerful

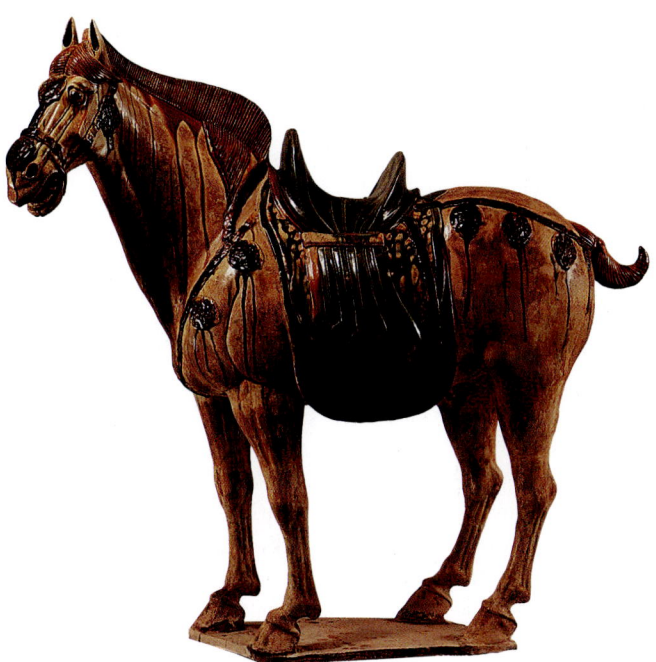

7-18 Neighing Horse, Tang dynasty, eighth to ninth century. Glazed earthenware, 1′ 8″ high. Victoria and Albert Museum, London.

in build. Its beautifully arched neck terminates in a small, elegant head. Richly harnessed and saddled, the horse testifies to its rider's nobility. During the period of Tang power, representing horses in painting and ceramics was a special genre, on equal footing with figural composition and landscape.

Northern Song Dynasty (960–1127)

The last century of Tang rule witnessed the empire's gradual disintegration. When the dynasty finally fell in 906, China once more experienced the ravages of civil war. Conflicting claims between rival states went unresolved until the Song dynasty consolidated the country once again, ruling China from their court at Bianjing (modern Kaifeng in Henan Province). During the interim of internal strife known as the Five Dynasties (907–960), the styles and techniques of painting monumental landscapes evolved rapidly, reaching a peak in the Northern Song period, though figurative painting continued, often as copies of Tang work.

IMAGINARY JOURNEYS IN PAINTED REALMS Landscape painting flourished even before the Tang dynasty. Daoist nature cults and a new appreciation of landscape themes in poetry provided the stimulus for the early development of landscape painting. Indeed, throughout history, landscape painting played a much more important role in China than in the West because landscapes had significance far beyond being sites of human action in great narratives. According to prevailing theory in China, landscapes should evoke both humanity's ideal harmonious relationship with the order of the cosmos and nature's potential to transform the human spirit. The ideal practiced in life meant wandering among streams and mountains, and a shifting, rather than fixed, perspective in painting suggested such a viewing process.

Early descriptive texts on landscape painting by painters and commentators from as early as the fourth century A.D. had a profound impact on Chinese artists in succeeding centuries. Such texts indicate that even then Chinese artists appreciated the almost magical potential of landscape painting to re-create and organize the human experience of nature or to transport viewers to imaginary realms. When the painter ZONG BING (373–443), for example, became too old to continue his mountain wanderings, he re-created favorite landscapes on the walls of his studio so that he could take imaginary journeys. Of the representational power of painting, Zong wrote:

> Nowadays, when I spread out my silk to catch the distant scene, even the form of the Kunlun [Mountain] may be captured within a square inch of space; a vertical stroke of three inches equals a height of several thousand feet. . . . By such means as this, the beauty of the Song and Hua Mountains and the very soul of the Xuanpin [Dark Spirit of the Universe] may all be embraced within a single picture.[1]

Another fifth-century painter, Wang Wei, elaborated on the re-creative potential of landscape painting:

> I unroll a picture and examine it, and reveal mountains and seas unfamiliar to me. The wind scatters in the verdant forests, the torrent overflows in bubbling foam. Ah, how could this be achieved merely by the skillful use of hands and fingers? The spirit must also exercise control over it. For this is the essence of painting.[2]

7-19   Fan Kuan, *Travelers among Mountains and Streams*, Northern Song dynasty, early eleventh century. Hanging scroll, ink and colors on silk, 6′ 9″ × 2′ 5″. National Palace Museum, Taipei.

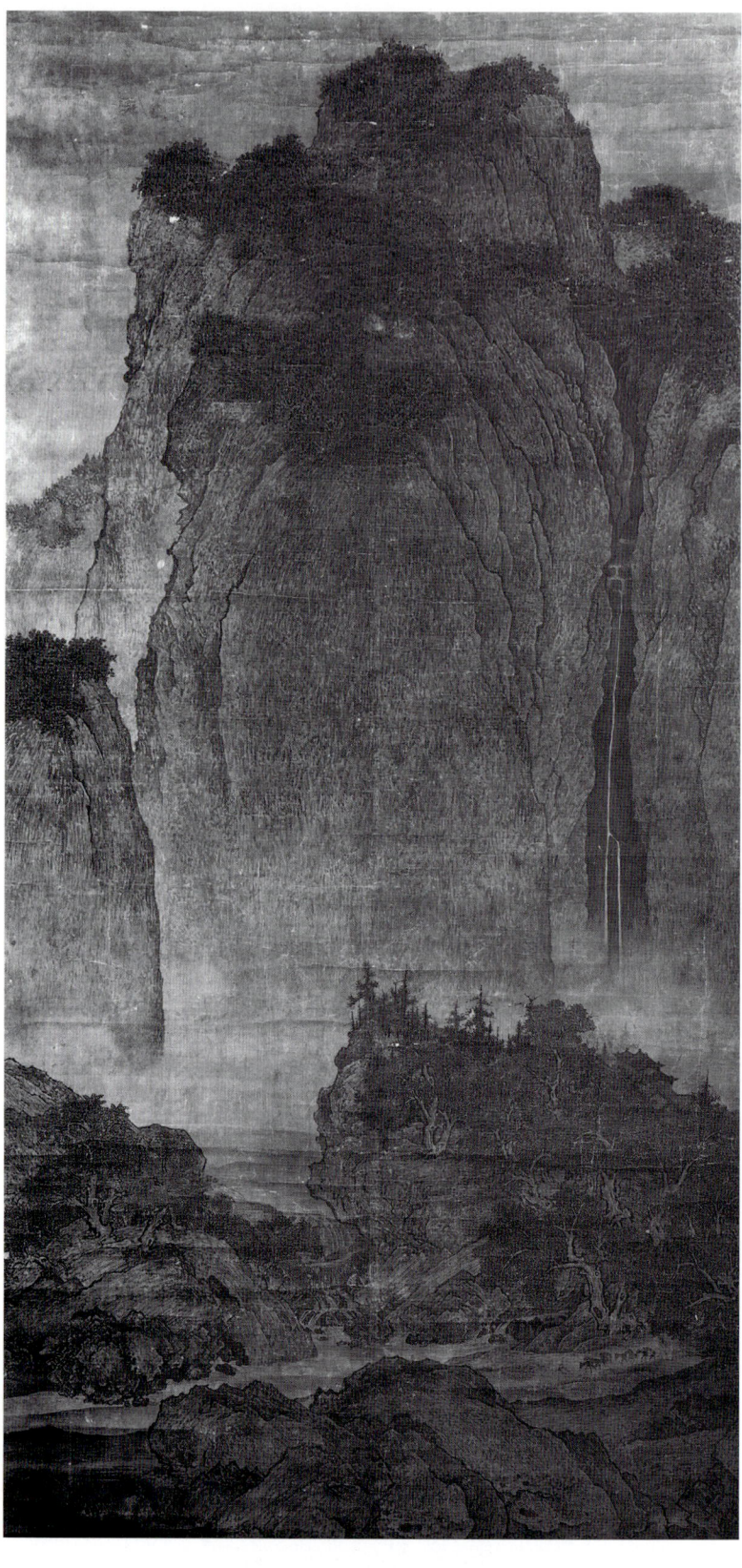

Travelers among Mountains and Streams (FIG. **7-19**), painted by Fan Kuan in the early eleventh century, stands out as a masterpiece of landscape painting. It incorporates the ideals Zong Bing and Wang Wei espoused and illustrates the basic ideals of Chinese painting theory. The picture presents a vertical landscape of massive mountains rising from the distance. The overwhelming natural forms dwarf the human and animal figures, which the artist reduced to minute proportions. Paths and bridges in the middle region vanish, only to reappear and lead spectators on a journey through the landscape—a journey facilitated by shifting perspective points. Fan depicted some elements directly from the side and others obliquely from the top. To appreciate such landscapes fully, viewers must focus not only on the outlines but also on intricate details and on the character of each brush stroke. Numerous "texture strokes" help model massive forms and convey a sense of tactile surfaces. Here, they are small, pale brush marks the Chinese call "raindrop strokes."

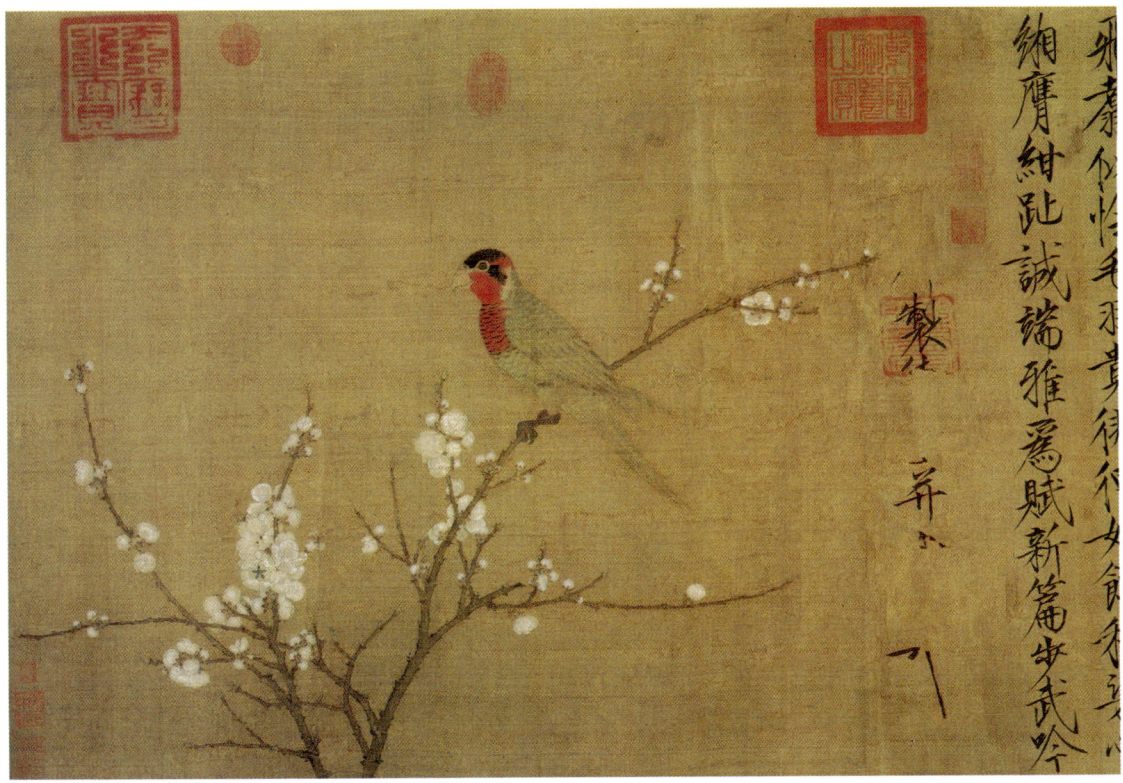

7-20 SONG HUIZONG, *The Five-Color Parakeet*, Northern Song dynasty, ca. 1100–1125. Hanging scroll, ink and color on silk, 1′ 8⅞″ high. Museum of Fine Arts, Boston.

THE EMPEROR WHO PAINTED BIRDS The Song imperial court employed painters, gathering them into official government bureaus that art historians sometimes refer to collectively as the Imperial Painting Academy. Illustrating lines of poetry by painting served frequently as an examination for entrance into the academy. In general, the court painters produced sophisticated and often brightly colored works, according to the emperors' tastes. Treasured albums held fans these master artists painted. The emperor SONG HUIZONG (1082–1135; r. 1100–1125), an avid art collector and patron, was also an important painter, especially renowned for his meticulous pictures of birds. *The Five-Color*

Parakeet (FIG. **7-20**) bears a poem and signature the emperor handwrote. With little regard for animating his subject, Song rendered almost every feather and plum-blossom petal in sharp, precise lines. The emperor's calligraphy, highly elegant and precise but with dynamic flourishes, enhances the silk painting's beauty.

CHINESE PAGODAS During the Northern Song period, the Liao dynasty briefly ruled part of China. In 1056, the Liao rulers built the great Foguang Si Pagoda at Yingxian (FIGS. **7-21** and 7-22). The *pagoda*, or tower, the building

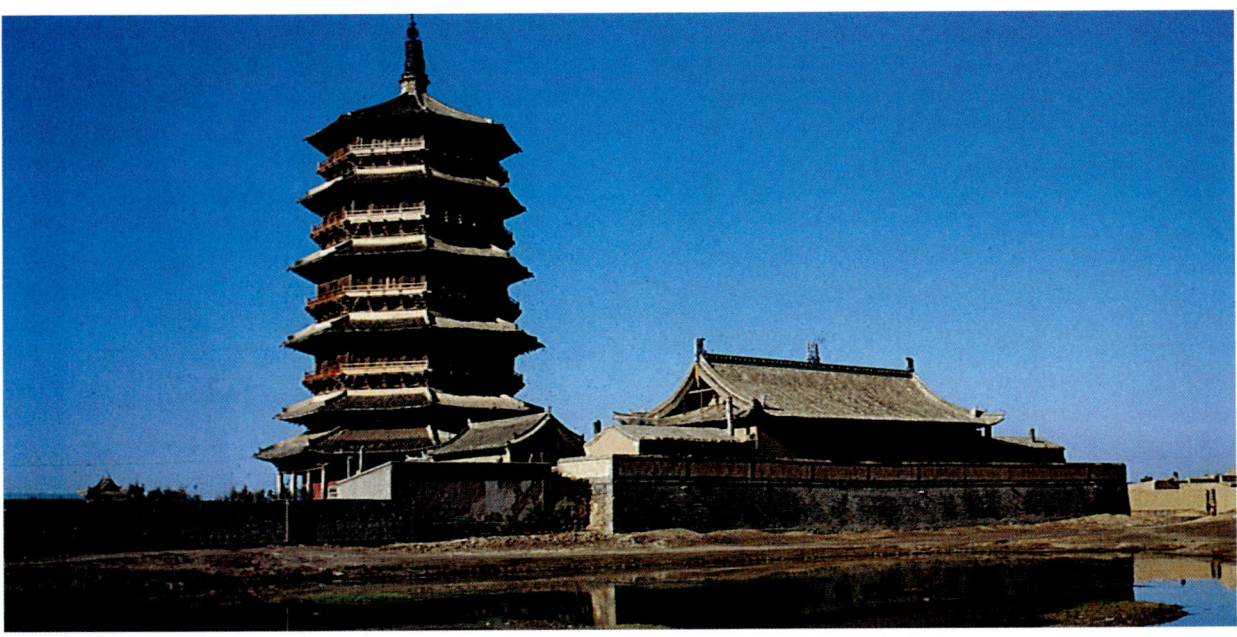

7-21 Foguang Si Pagoda, Yingxian, China, Liao dynasty, 1056.

type most often associated with Buddhism in China and other parts of eastern Asia, is the most eye-catching feature of a temple complex. It somewhat resembles the tall tower form of certain Indian temples (see FIG. 6-20) and its distant ancestor is the Indian stupa (see FIG. 6-5). Like stupas, many early pagodas housed relics and provided a focus for devotion to the Buddha as teacher and to those transmitting the faith. Later pagodas served other functions, such as housing sacred images. The Chinese and Koreans built both stone and brick pagodas, but wooden pagodas were also common and became the standard in Japan.

The Foguang Si Pagoda is two hundred sixteen feet tall and made entirely of wood. As is common with pagodas in other materials, this one is octagonal in plan, although wooden structures more commonly had square plans. Otherwise, its construction is typical. Sixty giant four-tiered bracket clusters carry the floor beams and projecting eaves of the five main stories. The main stories alternate with windowless mezzanines with cantilevered balconies, forming an elevation of nine stories altogether. Along with the open veranda on the ground level and the soaring pinnacle, the balconies visually lighten the building's mass. Our cross-section (FIG. 7-22) shows the symmetrical placement of statues of the Buddha, the colossal scale of the ground-floor statue, and the bewildering intricacy of the beam-and-bracket system at its most ingenious.

Southern Song Dynasty (1127–1279)

In 1127, due to conquests in the north by the Ruzhen, a seminomadic people who had formed an extensive empire, the Song emperors moved China's capital to the southeast. From then until 1279, the Southern Song court lived out its days amid the tranquil beauty of the city of Hangzhou. Neo-Confucianism, a blend of traditional Chinese thought and selected Buddhist concepts, became the leading philosophy. Accordingly, orthodox Buddhism declined. Buddhist art, however, continued to develop both in the north, where the Ruzhen rulers had established themselves as the Jin dynasty (1115–1234), and in the south. Buddhist sculpture in the Southern Song period added grace and elegance to the Tang style. Like secular paintings, many artworks associated with Chan (*Zen* in Japanese; a meditative school of Buddhism) engaged traditional Chinese notions of intimacy between the human spirit and nature.

TWO SPHERES OF BEING   A painting by ZHOU JICHANG, representing *arhats* giving alms to beggars (FIG. 7-23), expresses this new relationship in Buddhism. Arhats are the Buddha's enlightened disciples who have achieved freedom from rebirth (nirvana) by suppression of all desire for earthly things. More than in earlier paintings, in this work the artist placed the figures in a carefully delineated landscape. He arranged the foreground, middle ground, and background vertically to clarify their positions relative to one another and to the beggars. The arhats move with slow dignity in a plane above the ragged wretches who scramble miserably for the alms their serene benefactors throw down. The extreme differ-

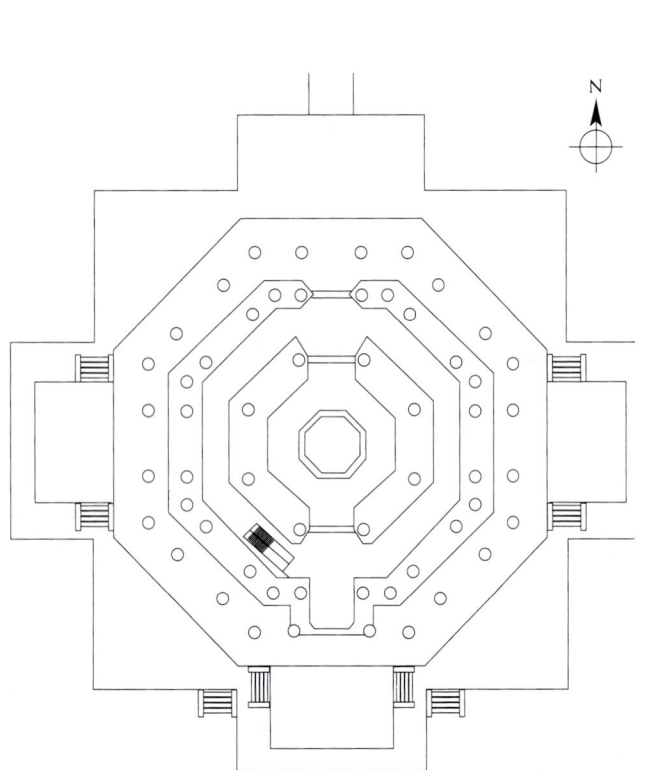
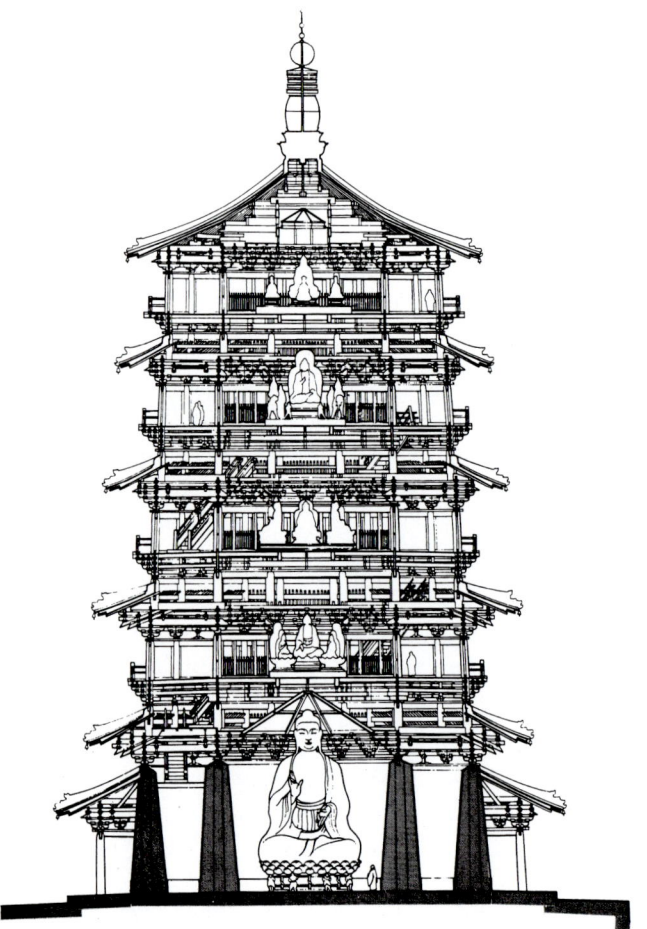

7-22   Plan and cross-section of Foguang Si Pagoda, Yingxian, China, Liao dynasty, 1056 (after L. Liu).

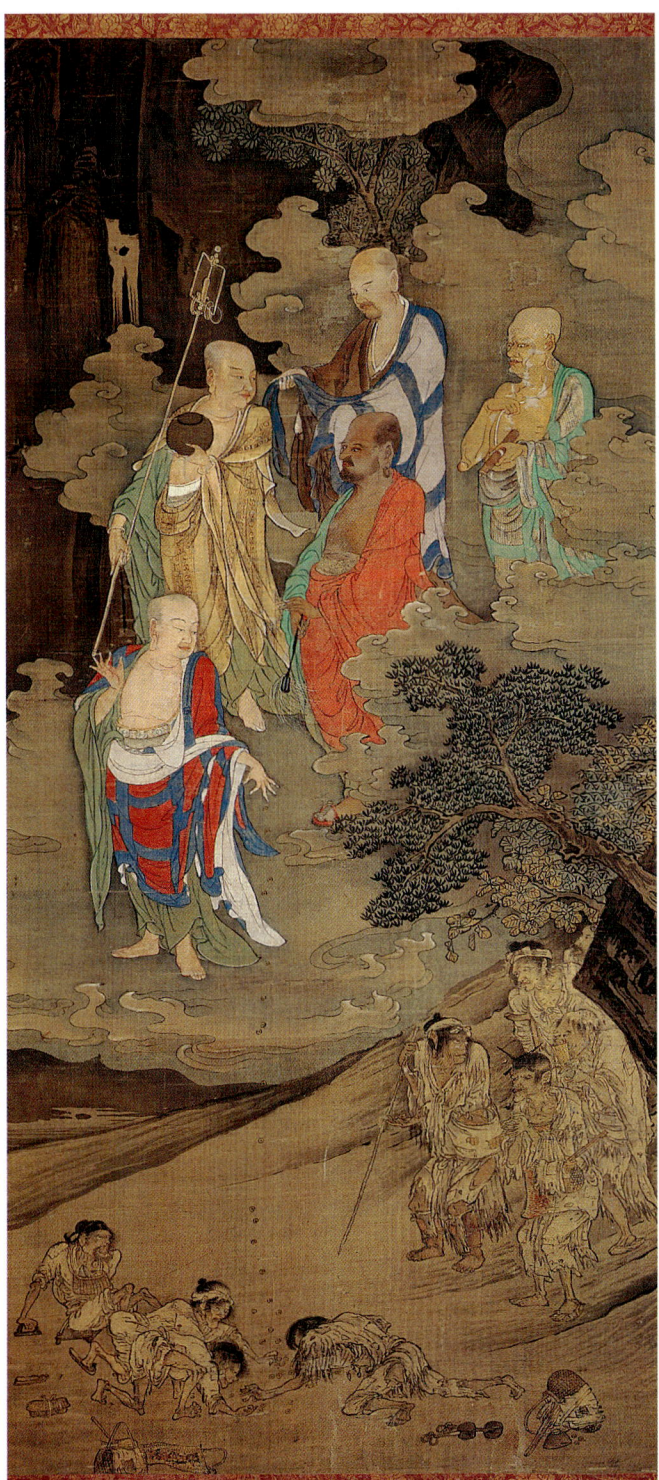

7-23 ZHOU JICHANG, *Arhats Giving Alms to Beggars,* Southern Song dynasty, 1178. Ink and colors on silk, 3′ 8″ × 1′ 9″. Museum of Fine Arts, Boston, General Funds.

MISTY MOUNTAINS AND INFINITE SPACE A landscape can take over the composition entirely in Chinese painting, diminishing or eliminating figures altogether, as in the earlier Northern Song painting (FIG. 7-19). Many Southern Song paintings also feature landscape as a very great presence. Artists adopted a more-or-less conventional system for arranging the landscape elements. A typical Southern Song landscape is basically asymmetrical and composed on a diagonal. It consists of three parts—the foreground weighted in one corner, the middle distance, and the far distance. A field of mist often separates these parts from one another. The painter generally marked the foreground by a rock, which, by its position, emphasizes the distance of the other parts. The middle distance may include a flat cliff or may be given over entirely to mist or water. In the far distance, mountain peaks, usually tinted in pale blue, suggest the infinity of space. The whole composition illustrates how the Song artists used great voids to hold solid masses in equilibrium. The technique is one of China's unique contributions to the art of painting. To this basic composition, which has many variations, the painter frequently added a scholar meditating under a gnarled pine tree and accompanied by an attendant. Such paintings suggest ideals of peace and unity with nature and the Confusian, Daoist, or Buddhist cosmos.

The chief painters in the Southern Song court style were MA YUAN (ca. 1160–1225) and XIA GUI (active ca. 1195–1224). Ma was a master of suggestion, as demonstrated by a small fan-shaped album leaf, *Bare Willows and Distant Mountains* (FIG. **7-24**), a picture of tranquility conveyed in a few sensitively balanced and half-seen shapes. The misty atmosphere, placement of near foreground motifs in one corner, and tall, elegant trees with visible roots are all typical elements in both Ma and Xia's paintings. The

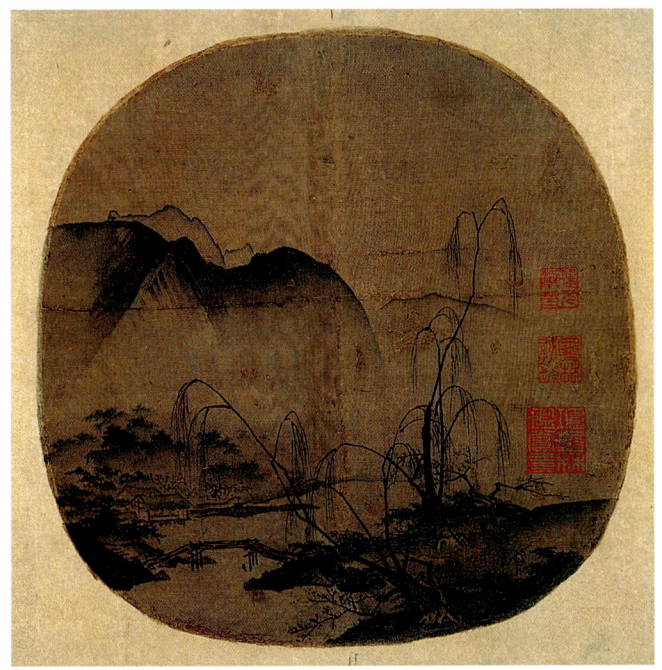

7-24 MA YUAN, *Bare Willows and Distant Mountains,* Southern Song dynasty, thirteenth century. Album leaf, ink and colors on silk, $9\frac{1}{2}$″ × $9\frac{1}{2}$″. Museum of Fine Arts, Boston.

ence in deportment between the two groups distinguishes their status, as do their contrasting features. The arhats' vividly colored attire, flowing draperies, and quiet gestures set them off from the dirt-colored and jagged shapes of the people physically and spiritually beneath them. The landscape's composition—the cloudy platform and lofty peaks of the arhats and the desertlike setting of the beggars—also sharply distinguishes the two spheres of being.

triangular form on the mountain also contains the broad "axe-cut" strokes they preferred. The Ma-Xia style set many standards for later professional painters, in Korea and Japan, as well as in China, who favored bolder treatments over the gentle softness of these two artists.

CHAN BUDDHISM AND ART   As orthodox Buddhism lost ground under the Song, the new school of Chan Buddhism gradually gained importance, until it was second only to Neo-Confucianism. The Chan sect traced its semi-legendary origins through a series of patriarchs (the founder and early leaders, joined in a master–pupil lineage). The first patriarch was Bodhidharma, a legendary sixth-century Indian missionary, who performed such feats as crossing a river on a reed to carry the messages of Chan across China. By the time of the Sixth Chan Patriarch, Huineng, who lived during the early Tang period, the religious forms and practices of the school were already well established. Although Chan monks adapted many of the rituals and ceremonies of other sects over the course of time, the Chan ideal was that followers of Chan teachings would repudiate texts, ritual, and charms as instruments of enlightenment. Their focus was to be instead on the cultivation of the mind or spirit of the individual in order to break through the illusions of ordinary reality, especially by means of meditation. In Chan thought, the means of enlightenment lie within the individual, and direct personal experience with some ultimate reality is the necessary step to its achievement. Meditation is a critical practice. In fact, the word "Chan" is a translation of the Sanskrit word for meditation, and Bodhidharma was said to have meditated so long in a cave that his arms and legs withered away. In practice, the Chan monk or pupil seeks direct personal experience with some ultimate reality through meditation. That breakthrough to Chan enlightenment has often been conceived of as a sudden, almost spontaneous act. These beliefs shaped a new art as they developed in China.

CHAN INFLUENCE IN INK PAINTING   LIANG KAI (ca. 1140–1210) was a master of an abbreviated, expressive style of ink painting that found great favor among Chan monks in China, Korea, and Japan. He served in the Painting Academy of the imperial court in Hangzhou, and his early works include poetic landscapes typical of the Southern Song. Later in life, he left the court to become a Chan monk and concentrated on figure painting. Surviving works attributed to him include two lively, sketchy pictures of the Sixth Patriarch, Huineng. In one, the patriarch tears up a Buddhist sutra in an expression of the Chan rejection of traditional teachings and emphasis on meditation and personal spiritual development. In the other (FIG. 7-25), he crouches as he chops bamboo. The performance of even such mundane tasks had the potential to become spiritual exercises. More specifically, this scene represents the patriarch's "Chan moment," when the sound of the blade striking the bamboo resonates within his spiritually attuned mind to propel him through the final doorway to enlightenment. The scruffy, caricature-like representation of the revered figure suggests that Huineng's mind is not burdened by worldly matters, such as physical appearance or signs of social status. However, Liang Kai utilized a variety of brushstrokes in the execution of this deceptively simple picture. Most are pale and wet, ranging from the fine lines of

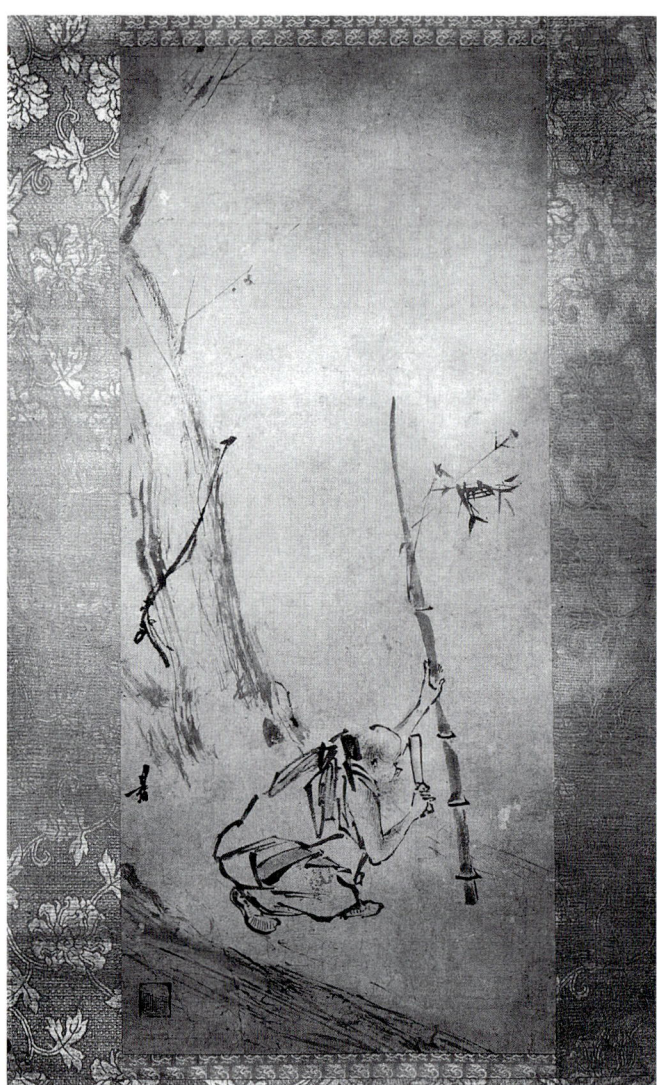

7-25   LIANG KAI *The Sixth Chan Patriarch Chopping Bamboo,* Southern Song dynasty, thirteenth century. Hanging scroll, ink on paper, 2′ 5¼″ high. Tokyo National Museum.

Huineng's beard to the broad texture strokes of the tree. A few darker strokes, which define the vine growing around the tree and the patriarch's clothing, offer visual accents in the painting. This kind of quick and seemingly casual execution of paintings has traditionally been interpreted as a sign of a painter's ability to produce compelling pictures spontaneously as a result of superior training and character, or, in the Chan setting, progress toward enlightenment. Chan and its arts eventually spread to Korea and Japan; in Japan, where it is called Zen, it had an especially extensive, long-term impact on the arts and remains an important sect of Buddhism there today (see Chapter 8).

CIZHOU CERAMICS   Northern and Southern Song artists also produced superb ceramics. Some reflect their patrons' interests in antiquities and imitate the powerful forms of the Shang and Zhou bronzes. However, Song ceramics more commonly had elegant shapes with fluid silhouettes. Many featured monochrome glazes, such as the famous celadon wares, also produced in Korea (FIG. 7-29), but a quite different kind of pottery, loosely classed as Cizhou, emerged in northern China. The example shown (FIG. **7-26**) is a vase of the high-shouldered shape known as *meiping*. Chinese potters developed the subtle techniques of *sgrafitto,* incising the design through a colored slip, during the Northern Song period. They achieved the intricate black-and-white design here by cutting through a black slip (see "Chinese Earthenwares and Stonewares," page 189). The tightly twining vine and flower petal motifs on this vase closely embrace the vessel in a perfect accommodation of surface design to vase shape.

Ancient Chinese culture laid the critical foundations for later East Asian civilization, including that in Korea and Japan. It provided a system of writing; fundamental tenets and ideals in philosophy and religion; numerous basic technologies; standard aesthetic principles; and the formats, materials, basic forms, and subjects of art and architecture. All of these contributions had attained a high level of development well before Christ's birth on the western side of Asia and many diminished dramatically in importance only in the past century. Chinese transformations of Buddhist forms and thought in the early centuries A.D. added another profound component to east Asian civilization. Without question, the cultural debt of later eastern Asia to early China is extremely large. But evoking, even revering, China's past did not prevent reinterpreting its past as part of a dynamic process of cultural and artistic evolution. The next section traces this reinterpretative process in neighboring Korea.

KOREA

Korea, a small peninsula of the Chinese-Manchurian mainland, faces the islands of Japan. Korea's location made it susceptible to attacks from both directions, and, frequently throughout its long history, these attacks have politically destabilized it. Ethnically, the Koreans are related to the peoples of eastern Siberia and Mongolia, as well as to the Japanese. In the early centuries, the Koreans used Chinese characters to write Korean words, but the Korean language later acquired its own phonetic alphabet. Korean art, although unmistakably derived from Chinese models, is not merely derivative but has, like Korean civilization, a discernible native identity. Furthermore, it frequently mediated the cultural developments passing from the continent into Japan.

Pottery-producing cultures appeared on the peninsula in the Neolithic period between five thousand and three thousand years ago, and bronze work dates back to at least 600 B.C. Historians believe that Chinese refugees, fleeing from dynastic wars, settled in northern Korea as early as the twelfth century B.C. Much later, about 100 B.C., during the Han dynasty, the Chinese established a colony in Korea, Lolang, for centuries an important commercial center. Native kingdoms—Koguryo, Paekche, and Silla—arose in different regions of the peninsula. The centuries of their contemporaneous reigns are known as the Three Kingdoms period (ca. 57 B.C.–A.D. 688). The art of these three states laid the foundation for many of the later developments on the peninsula. Paekche continued a strong pottery tradition, lagging somewhat behind the others in metalwork because of poor mineral resources. The other two kingdoms, in contrast, not only produced fine pottery, but excelled at metalworking as well.

GOLD CROWNS IN SILLA TOMBS Gold has been valued around the world from earliest times for its beauty and resistance to corrosion. Exposure to air, heat. moisture, and most solvents does not affect it. Ancient artists frequently cast gold and other metals, but they also forged them into different shapes by hammering, pulling, twisting, cutting, and punching them. Unlike hard metals, such as iron, gold is naturally soft and easy to forge when only slightly heated. Even early artists could beat it into thin sheets or draw it out into fine wires for cutting and shaping. Tombs of the Silla kingdom have yielded spectacular artifacts, such as gold crowns, revealing the wealth

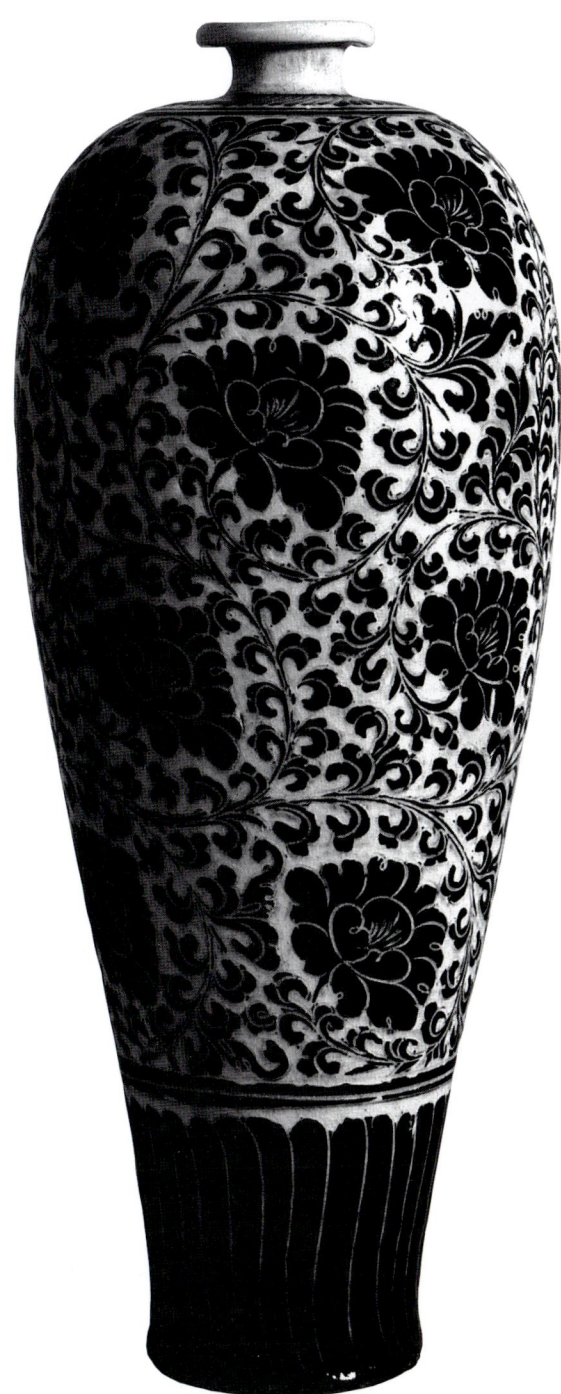

7-26 Meiping vase, Song dynasty, thirteenth century. Stoneware, Cizhou type, with sgraffito decoration, 1′ 7½″ high, 7¾″ wide. Asian Art Museum of San Francisco, San Francisco (Avery Brundage Collection).

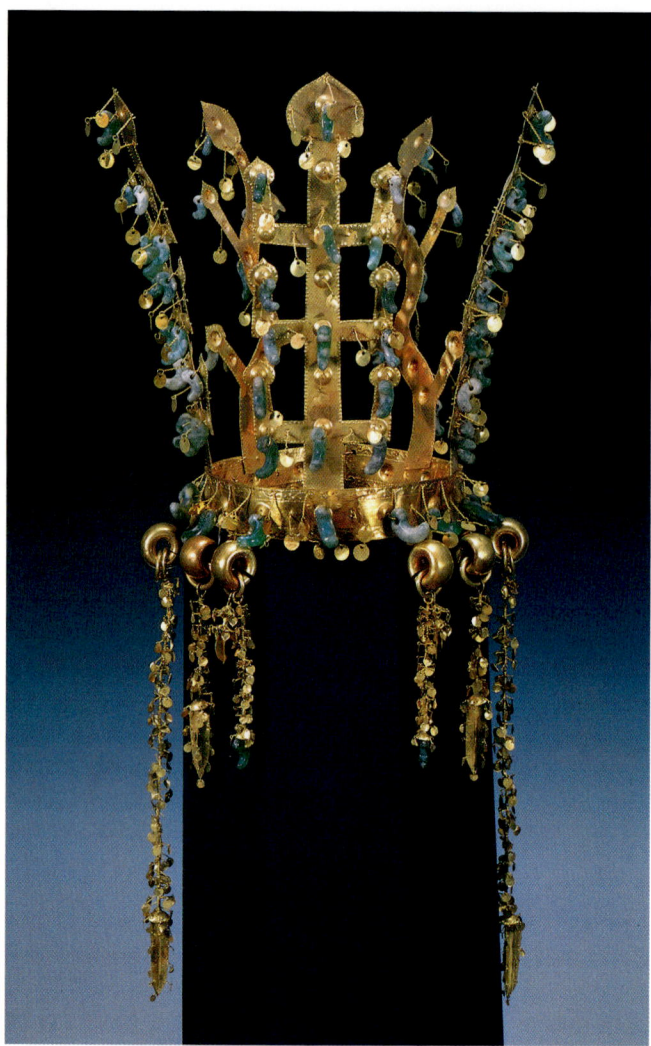

7-27   Crown, from north mound of Tomb 98 at Hwangnamdong, near Kyongju, Korea, Silla kingdom, fifth to sixth century. Gold, 10 ¾″ high. Kyongju National Museum, Kyongju.

and power of the rulers of the three kingdoms. The crown from a tomb at Hwangnamdong (FIG. **7-27**), dated to the fifth or sixth century A.D., attests to the high quality of artisanship among Silla artists. They cut the crown's major elements, the band and the uprights, as well as the myriad spangles adorning them, from sheet gold and embossed these along the edges. Gold rivets and wires secure the whole, as do the comma-shaped pieces of jade further embellishing the crown. Archeologists interpret the uprights as stylized tree and antler forms believed to symbolize life and supernatural power. These magnificent crowns have no counterparts in China, relating instead to Siberian forms.

BUDDHIST ART AND THE THREE KINGDOMS

In A.D. 372, in the Paekche kingdom, Buddhism arrived in Korea from China. Many small gilt bronze statues, very close in style to those produced in China, attest to Buddhism's spread. Korea, in turn, helped spread Buddhism and Buddhist art to Japan, and Japanese works (see FIG. 8-6) reflecting the forms of China and Korea display that continuity.

Aided by China's emperor, the Silla Kingdom conquered the Koguryo and the Paekche kingdoms and unified Korea as Great Silla. Korea's golden age is the era of Great Silla

(688–935), contemporary with the Tang dynasty's brilliant culture in China. The Silla rulers looked upon Buddhism not only as a religion, but also as a protective force. They sponsored the building of temples of magnificent scale in and around their capital of Kyongju to be places of worship and to serve as a supernatural defense against external threats. Unfortunately, none of these monuments survived Korea's turbulent history. However, near the summit of Mount Toham, just east of the city, the splendid granite cave at Sokkuram, with its reliefs and freestanding figures, has survived as the greatest cultural treasure of the period. Scant surviving records suggest that the monument was built under the supervision of Kim Tae-song (the family name appears first), a member of the royal family who served as prime minister. He initiated construction in 742, the year after he resigned his government post, and died in 774 before the project was completed. The records also suggest that Kim intended Sokkuram to honor his parents in his previous life. Certainly the scale of Sokkuram, which is too small for a place of congregation, and its high aesthetic standard support the idea that it was a private chapel for royalty.

The main *rotunda* (circular area under a dome) of the cave measures only about twenty-one feet in diameter. Despite its modest size, the Sokkuram cave project required substantial resources. Unlike some Buddhist caves, the interior wall surfaces and sculpture were not cut from native stone in the

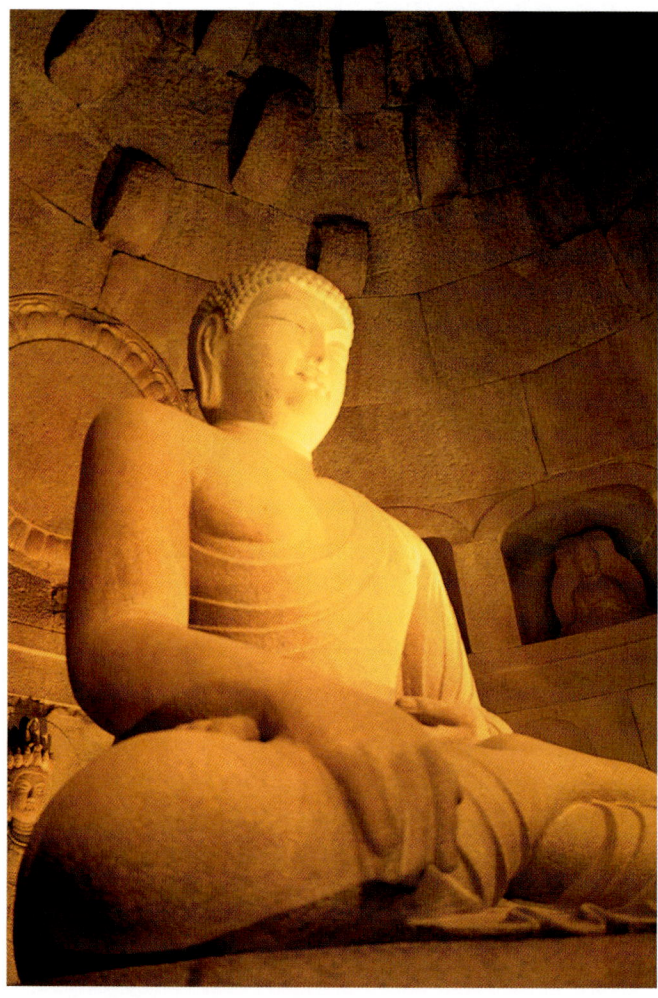

7-28   Sakyamuni Buddha, at entrance to rock chapel, Sokkuram, Korea, Great Silla, eighth century. Granite, about 11′ high.

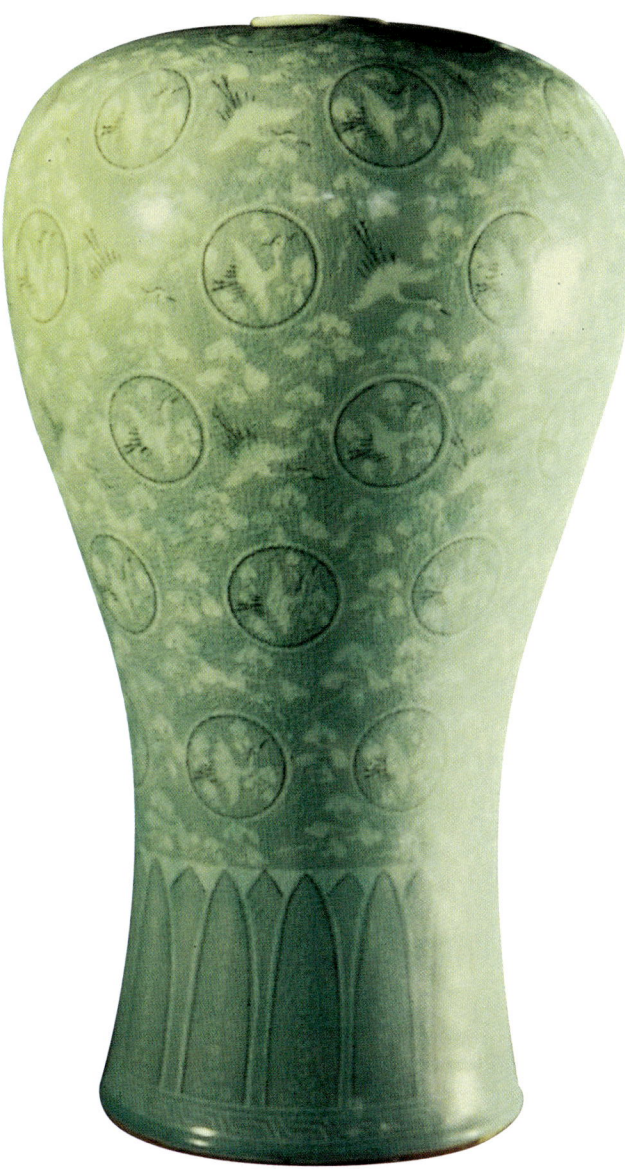

7-29 Maebyong vase, Koryo period, ca. 918–1000. Celadon with inlaid decoration, 1′ 4$\frac{1}{2}$″ tall. Kansong Art Museum, Seoul.

process of excavation. Instead, workers assembled hundreds of granite pieces of various shapes and sizes, attaching them with stone rivets instead of mortar. Sculpted images of bodhisattvas, arhats, and ancient Indian gods line the lower zone of the wall. Above, ten niches contain miniature statues of seated bohhisattvas and believers. All of these figures face inward toward the eleven-foot-tall statue of Sakyamuni (FIG. **7-28**), the historical Buddha, which dominates the chamber as it sits slightly back from center and faces the entrance. Carved from a single block of granite, the image represents the Buddha as he touched the earth to call it to witness the realization of his enlightenment. Although remote in time and place from the Sarnath Buddha in India (see FIG. 6-15), this

majestic image remains faithful to its iconographic prototype. More immediately, the Korean statue draws on the robust, round-faced figures of Tang China (FIG. 7-12), and its drapery is a more schematic version of the fluid type found in Tang sculpture. However, the figure has a distinctly broad-shouldered dignity combined with harmonious proportions that are without close precedents.

CELADON WARE Though Buddhism was the established religion of Korea, Confucianism, introduced from China during the Silla era, increasingly shaped social and political conventions. In the ninth century, the three old kingdoms began to reemerge as distinct political entities, and by 935 the Koryo (from Koguryo) dominated for the next three centuries. The Great Silla and Koryo kingdoms overlap slightly (the period ca. 918–935) because both kingdoms existed as these shifts in power occurred. In 1231, the Mongols, who had invaded China, pushed into Korea, beginning a war lasting thirty years. In the end, the Koryo had to submit to forming an alliance with the invaders.

Koryo potters in the twelfth century produced the famous Korean *celadon* wares, admired worldwide. Highly translucent iron-pigmented glazes, fired in an oxygen-deprived kiln to become gray, pale blue, pale green, or brownish olive, characterize celadon wares. Incised or engraved designs in the vessel alter the glaze's thickness to produce elegant tonal variations.

A vase in the shape known as *maebyong* in Korean (FIG. **7-29**; *meiping* in Chinese, FIG. 7-26) probably dates to early in the Koryo period (ca. 918–1000), as evidenced by its simplicity compared with the elaborateness of later celadon design. The artist incised delicate motifs of flying cranes—some flying down and others, in *roundels* (circular motifs), flying up—into the clay's surface and then filled the grooves with white and colored slip. Next, the potter covered the incised areas with the celadon green glaze. Variation in the spacing of the motifs shows the potter's sure sense of the dynamic relationship between ornamentation and ceramic volume.

As noted earlier, ancient Korean art clearly took shape within the larger framework of an East Asian cultural sphere dominated by China. However, sometimes in very subtle ways apparent only to specialists and sometimes in more pronounced ones obvious to anyone, Korea's art and culture also developed distinctively, as Chapter 26 documents.

Ancient China was to later eastern Asia what both Greece and Rome were to Europe. China's achievements in virtually every field, including writing, literature, technology, philosophy, religion, and art, spread beyond even the boundaries of the vast empire it sometimes controlled. Although Buddhism began in India, the Chinese adaptations and transformations of its teachings, religious practice, and artistic forms were those that endured and spread farther east. Chapters 8, 26, and 27 reveal the importance of early Chinese models to the art of both early and later Japan and of later China and Korea while recognizing each area's own distinct history.

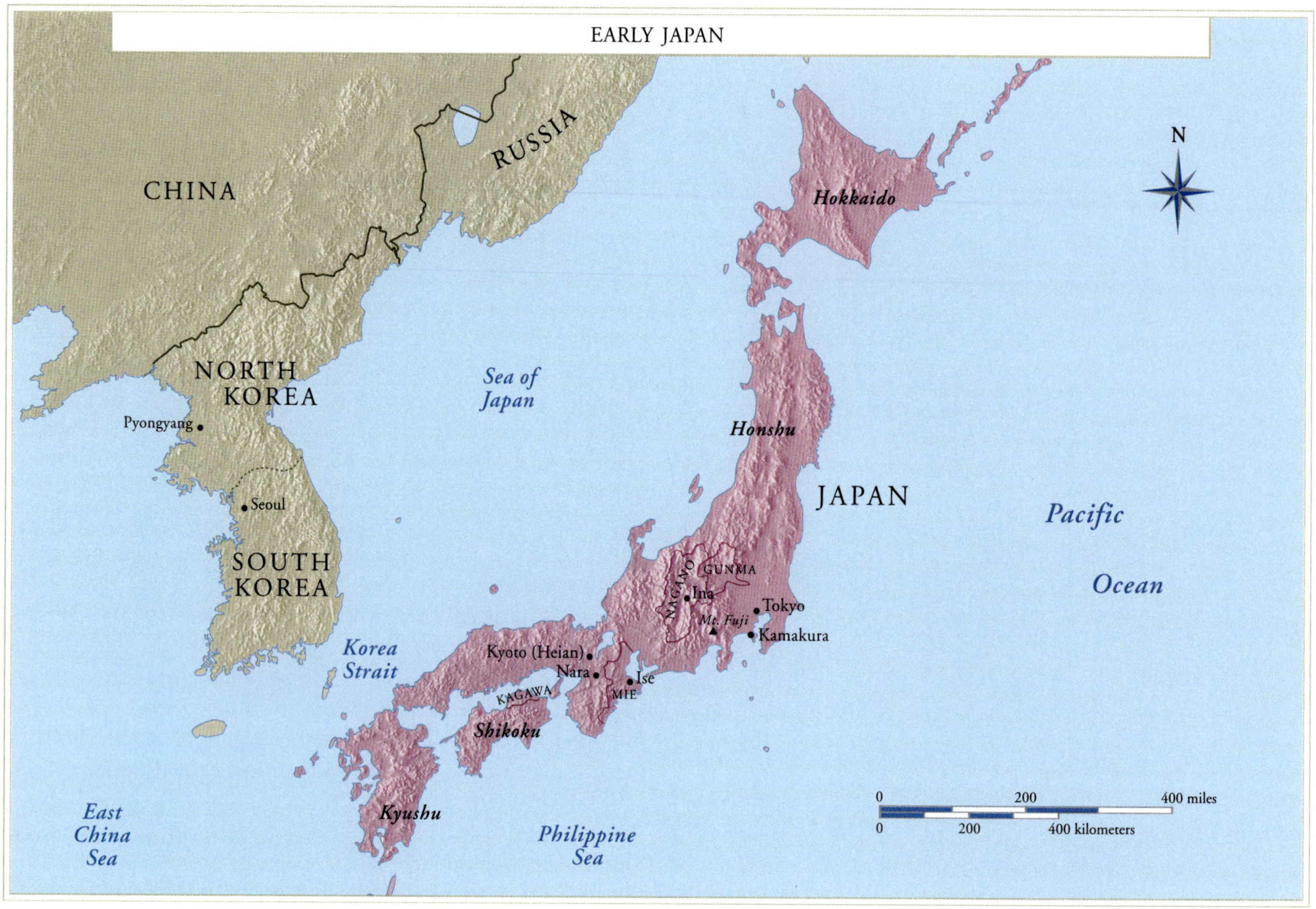

CHINA

RUSSIA

N

NORTH KOREA

Pyongyang •

Sea of Japan

Hokkaido

Honshu

• Seoul

SOUTH KOREA

JAPAN

Pacific Ocean

Korea Strait

NAGANO GUNMA
• Ina
Kyoto (Heian) • *Mt. Fuji* • Tokyo
Nara • • Kamakura
KAGAWA • Ise
MIE

East China Sea

Shikoku

Kyushu

Philippine Sea

| 0 | 200 | 400 miles |
| 0 | 200 | 400 kilometers |

10,500 B.C.	2500 B.C.	1500 B.C.	300 B.C.	A.D. 100	300	552	645
JOMON	MIDDLE JOMON		YAYOI		KOFUN	ASUKA	HAKUHO

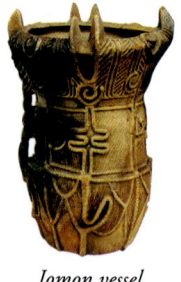

*Jomon vessel
2500–1500 B.C.*

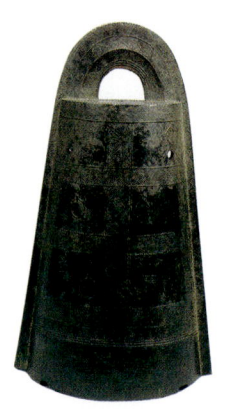

*Dotaku
100–300*

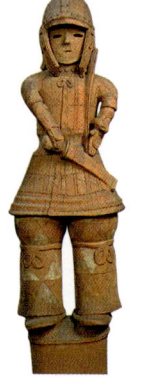

*Haniwa warrior figure
fifth–mid-sixth century*

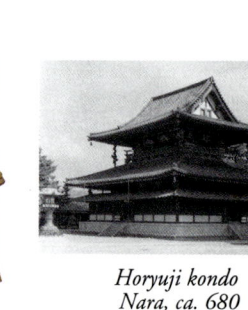

*Horyuji kondo
Nara, ca. 680*

Hunting and fishing

Rice growing and metalworking

Emergence of imperial family

Buddhism officially introduced, 552

SACRED STATUES
AND SECULAR
SCROLLS

THE ART OF EARLY JAPAN

710	794	1185	1332
Nara	Heian	Kamakura	

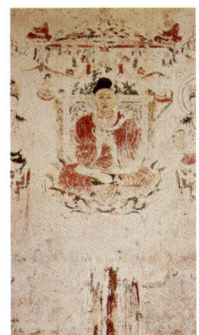

Amida triad
Horyuji, Nara, ca. 710

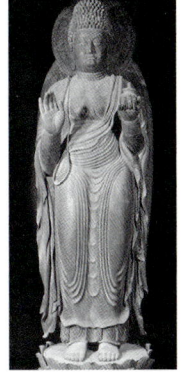

Standing Yakushi
Jingoji, Kyoto, ca. 793

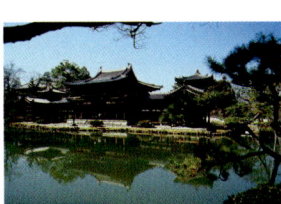

Phoenix Hall
Byodoin, Uji, 1053

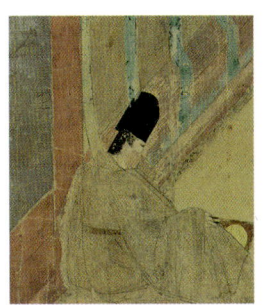

Tale of Genji
to mid-twelfth century

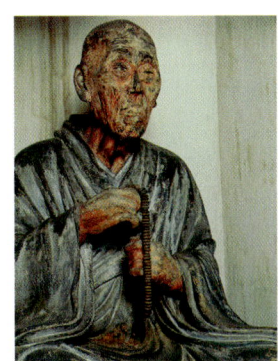

Shunjobo Chogen
Todaiji, Nara
early thirteenth century

Transfer of capital to Nara, 710

Transfer of capital to Heian (Kyoto), 794

New sects of Esoteric Buddhism
introduced, ca. 805

Suspension of diplomatic relations
with China, 894

Pure Land Buddhist teachings gain
importance, from tenth century

Warrior clans rise in power, twelfth century

Kamakura shogunate established, 1185

Popular Pure Land sects
emerge, thirteenth century

The Japanese archipelago consists of four main islands and hundreds of smaller ones, a surprising number of them inhabited. Two major distinct population groups lived on the islands by earliest historical times. The great majority of Japan's inhabitants trace their ancestry to one of these two early groups and consider Japan to have been culturally homogeneous throughout its history. Nevertheless, regional differences and the cultural effects of both immigration and imported ideas long have given Japanese art and culture a varied and dynamic character. In early centuries, the islands' mountainous terrain made travel and communication difficult. This tended to produce strong regional variations in dialect, cuisine, and local customs, persisting to some degree even now. Meanwhile, immigration from the Asian continent's eastern edge, the source of Japan's original population, never really has ceased, helping Japan participate in the cultural developments of eastern Asia. All in all, Japan's close proximity to the continent has allowed the island country to reap tremendous benefits, while the sea has helped protect it from outright invasions. But Japanese culture also has had sufficient opportunity to evolve in its own directions, particularly in times of diminished contact with the outside world.

JAPAN BEFORE BUDDHISM

Jomon Period (ca. 10,500–300 B.C.)

POTTERY BEFORE FARMING   Japan's earliest distinctive culture is the Jomon, named after the cord *(jo)* markings *(mon)* decorating many of its earthenware vessels. The Jomon people were hunter-gatherers, but the richness of their natural environment enabled them to live surprisingly settled existences. Their villages consisted of pit dwellings—shallow round excavations with raised earthen rims and thatched roofs. Escaping the nomadic existence of many early hunter-gatherers permitted the Jomon people to develop ceramic technology well before agriculture. In fact, archeologists have dated some ceramic sherds found in Japan to before 10,000 B.C.—older than the sherds from any other area of the world.

In addition to rope markings, incised lines and applied coils of clay adorned Jomon pottery surfaces. The most impressive examples come from the Middle Jomon period (2500–1500 B.C.). Much of the population then lived in the mountainous inland region, where local variations in ceramic form and surface treatment flourished. However, all Jomon potters shared a highly developed feeling for modeled, rather than painted, ceramic ornament. Jomon pottery displays such a wealth of coils, striped incisions, and sometimes quasi-figural motifs that the sculptural treatment in certain instances even jeopardizes the vessel's basic functionality. Jomon vessels served a wide variety of purposes, from storage to cooking to bone burial. Some of the most elaborate pots may have served ceremonial functions.

A dramatic example from Miyanomae in Nagano Prefecture (a prefecture is a district with a governor; FIG. **8-1**) shows a characteristically deep and intricate surface modeling and a partially sculpted rim. Jomon pottery contrasts strikingly with China's most celebrated Neolithic earthenwares (see FIG. 7-1) in that the Japanese vessels are extremely thick and heavy. The

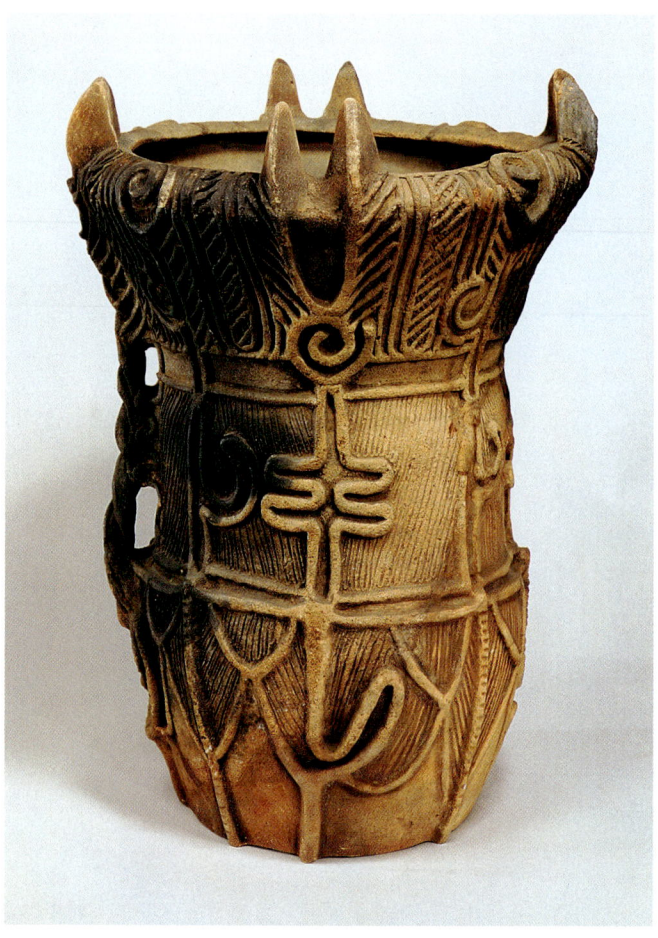

8-1   Vessel, from Miyanomae, Nagano Prefecture, Japan, Middle Jomon period, 2500–1500 B.C. Earthenware, 1′ 11$\frac{2}{3}$″ × 1′ 1$\frac{1}{4}$″. Tokyo National Museum, Tokyo.

harder, thinner, and lighter Neolithic Chinese earthenware emphasizes basic ceramic form and painted decoration.

Yayoi (ca. 300 B.C.–A.D. 300) and Kofun (ca. A.D. 330–552) Periods

Jomon culture gradually gave way to Yayoi beginning around 300 B.C. in Kyushu, the southernmost of the main Japanese islands. Increased interaction with and immigration from Korea brought dramatic social and technological transformations. People continued to live in pit dwellings, but their villages grew in size and developed fortifications, indicating a perceived need for defense. Toward the end of this period, near A.D. 300, Chinese visitors noted that Japan had walled towns, many small kingdoms, and a highly stratified social structure. Wet-rice agriculture provided the social and economic foundations for such development.

JAPANESE BRONZES AND HAN CHINA   Less sculptural and sometimes polychromed pottery, bronze-casting, and loom weaving help characterize the Yayoi period as a time of tremendous change in material culture as well. Among the most intriguing objects Yayoi artisans produced are the *dotaku*, or bells, treasured ceremonial bronzes based on Han Chinese bell forms but not functional as musical instruments. Cast in clay molds, these bronzes generally featured

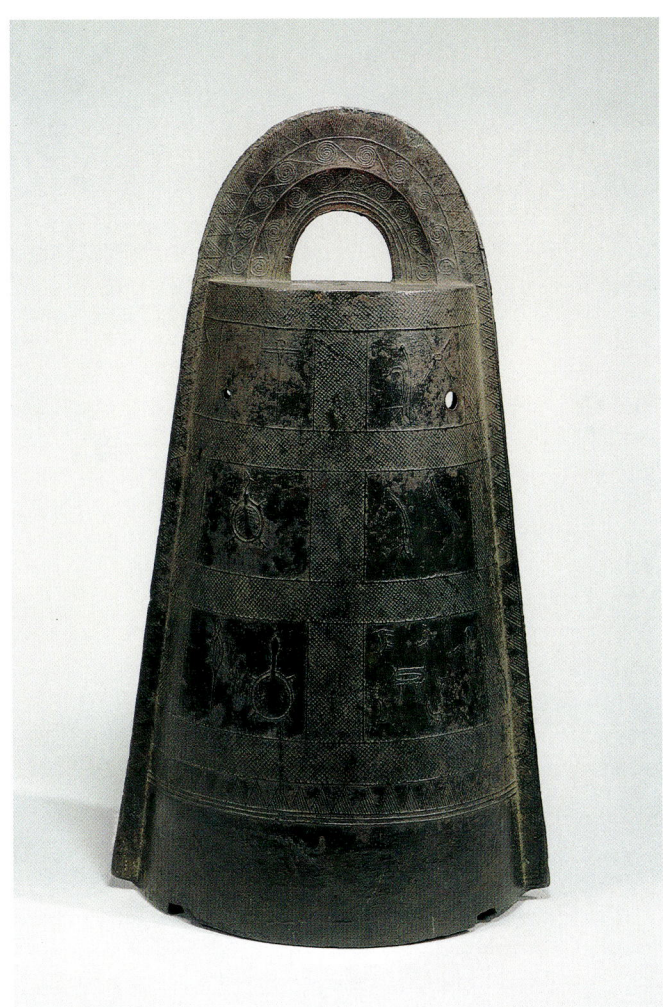

8-2 *Dotaku* (bell) with incised figural motifs, from Kagawa Prefecture, Japan, Late Yayoi period, A.D. 100–300. Bronze, 1′ 4⅞″ high. Tokyo National Museum, Tokyo.

raised decoration. On a few, including the one shown here (FIG. **8-2**) from Kagawa Prefecture, the ornament consists of simple line drawings whose exact meanings scholars still debate. Whatever their meaning, the dotaku engravings are the earliest surviving examples of pictorial art in Japan. The cranes and tortoises, ancient Chinese symbols of longevity, on the bell forms suggest some awareness of Chinese belief systems.

TREASURE-FILLED BURIAL MOUNDS Historians named the succeeding Kofun period (*ko* means "old"; *fun* means "tomb") after the great *tumuli* (pit graves covered by sometimes enormous mounds) that had begun to appear in the third century. These grew dramatically in number and scale in the fourth century, signaling the rise of grand political leaders. The tumuli recall earlier Jomon practices of abandoning the dead on sacred mountains. Important symbolic objects buried with the deceased include examples of items that later became Japanese imperial house regalia—mirrors, swords, and comma-shaped jewels. Numerous bronze mirrors came from China, but the tombs' forms and many of the goods suggest even closer connections with Korea. For example, the comma-shaped jewels closely resemble those found on

Korean Silla crowns (see FIG. 7-27), whose simpler gilt bronze counterparts lay in the Japanese tombs.

CYLINDER-STATUES FOR THE DEAD In association with the great Japanese tumuli, researchers also discovered a very distinctive native element in the earthenware *haniwa,* such as the one from Gunma Prefecture (FIG. **8-3**), placed on and around the pit grave mounds. Compared to the terracotta soldiers and horses buried with the Qin emperor in Shaanxi Province, China (see FIG. 7-5), these statues appear deceptively whimsical as variations on a cylindrical theme (*haniwa* means "clay circle"). Yet haniwa sculptors skillfully adapted the basic clay cylinder into a host of forms, from abstract shapes to objects, animals (such as deer, bears, horses, and monkeys), and human figures familiar in Japanese society at that time—warriors, women nursing babies, shamans, and so forth. These artists altered the shapes of the cylinders,

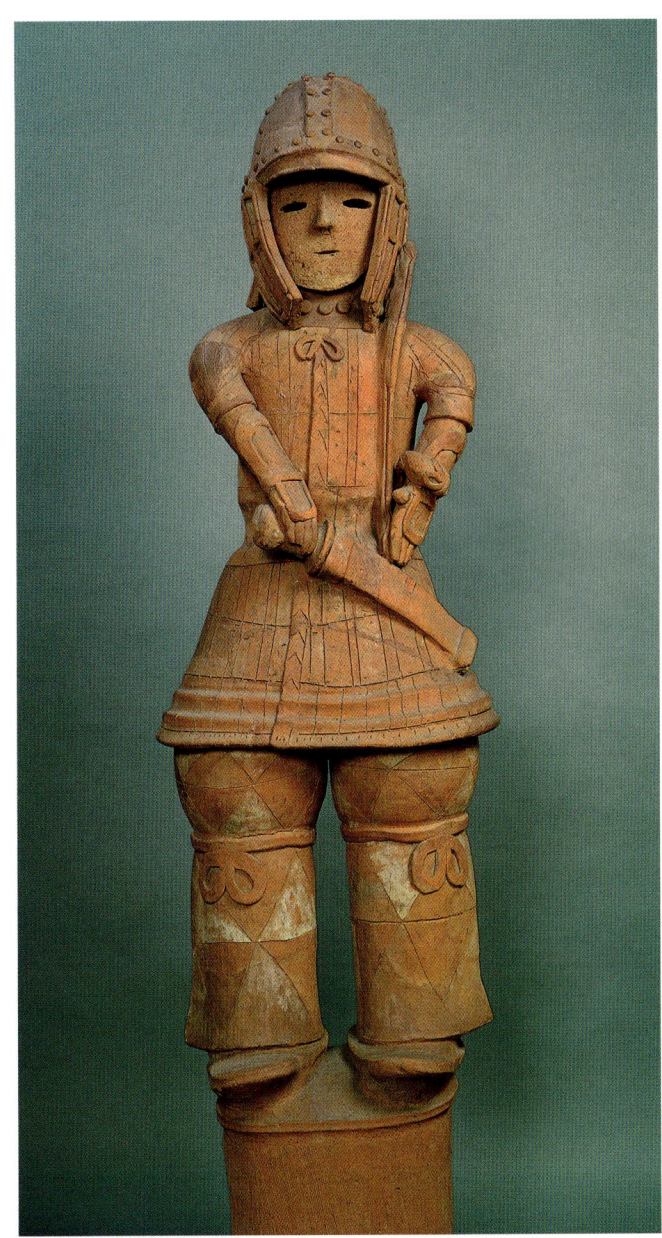

8-3 *Haniwa* (cylindrical) warrior figure, from Gunma Prefecture, Japan, late Kofun period, fifth to mid-sixth century. Low-fired clay, 4′ 1¼″ high. Aikawa Archaeological Museum, Aikawa.

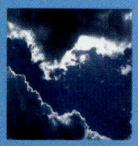

RELIGION AND MYTHOLOGY

Pre-Buddhist Beliefs and Rituals in Japan

The early beliefs and practices of pre-Buddhist Japan, which form a part of the belief system later called Shinto ("Way of the Gods"), did not derive from the teachings of any individual founding figure or distinct leader. Formal scriptures, in the strict sense, do not exist for these beliefs and practices either. Shintoism developed hand in hand with Japanese society. With the advent of agriculture in the Yayoi period, a variety of religious beliefs and practices arose. These included agricultural rites surrounding planting and harvesting and *shamanism*, the belief a priest, or shaman, can influence the ancestral spirits, gods, and demons who produce good and evil. Villagers venerated and prayed to a multitude of local, sometimes specialized, deities or spirits called *kami*. The early Japanese believed kami existed in mountains, waterfalls, and other impressive features and aspects of nature, as well as in charismatic people. When Buddhism arrived in Japan from the mainland in the sixth century, Shinto practices changed under its influence. Before then, painted or carved images of Shinto deities did not exist.

During the Yayoi period, mastery of farming led to larger villages, increased social stratification, division of labor, and conflict with neighbors. Many precious objects used for ceremonial purposes, such as the bronze dotaku (FIG. 8-2), indicated the wealth and power of a community and its leader. Conquests of nearby territories produced small states, which grew rapidly in the Kofun period. The leaders of one of the Kofun states gained power over a particularly large territory, and their line continues unbroken today as the Japanese imperial successors. (In Japan, "emperor" is a conventional term of respect rather than a characterization of the Japanese ruler's authority over great territories.)

The basic societal unit during the Kofun period was the clan, a local group claiming a common ancestor. Each clan had its own protector kami, to whom members offered prayers in the spring for successful planting and in the fall for good harvests. Clan members built shrines made up of several buildings, such as the one at Ise (FIG. 8-4), for kami. Priests made offerings of grains and fruits at these shrines and prayed on behalf of the clans. Ordinary people might hold festivals in the vicinity but could not actually enter the shrine's sacred buildings and sanctuaries, or smaller shrines. Rituals of divination, water purification, and ceremonial purification at the shrines became popular. Visitors to the shrine area had to wash before entering in a ritual of spiritual and physical cleansing.

Purity was such a critical aspect of Japanese religious beliefs that people would abandon buildings and even settlements if negative events, such as poor harvests, suggested spiritual defilement. Even the early imperial court moved several times to newly built towns to escape impurity and the trouble it caused. Such purification concepts are also the basis for the cyclical rebuilding of the sanctuaries at grand shrines. The actual buildings of the inner shrine at Ise, for example, have been rebuilt every twenty years—at least sixty-one times—with few interruptions. Such rebuilding rids the sacred site of physical and spiritual impurities that otherwise might accumulate. During rebuilding, the old structure remains standing until the architects erect an exact duplicate next to it. In this way, the Japanese have preserved ancient forms with great precision.

---

emblazoned them with applied ornaments, punched out and drew forth forms, and then painted the haniwa. The Kofun Japanese set these simple sculptures in curving rows around the burial chambers on the exterior of the mounds. The variety of figure types suggests not a protective army such as that guarding the Qin tomb but figures that may have served as a spiritual barrier protecting both the living and the dead from contamination.

AMATERASU'S ANCIENT SHRINE   The Kofun shrine of the sun goddess, Amaterasu, at Ise (FIG. **8-4**) in Mie Prefecture, built initially during the fifth century and rebuilt every twenty years since then, is the greatest of all Shinto monuments (see "Pre-Buddhist Beliefs and Rituals in Japan," above). Shrine architecture varies tremendously in Japan. Researchers believe that the Ise shrine preserves some of the very earliest designs. The ultimate source of the main sanctuary's form appears to be early granaries, sometimes represented on bronze mirrors or as clay haniwa. Granaries were among the

most important buildings in Japan's early agrarian society, so architects probably imitated the basic granary forms when designing palaces and shrines. Although not every aspect of the Ise shrine is equally ancient, the inner shrine's three main structures convey some sense of Japanese architecture before Buddhism arrived and before the introduction of more elaborately constructed and adorned buildings.

Aside from the thatched roofs and some metallic decorations, the sole construction material at Ise is wood, fitted together in a *mortise-and-tenon* system, the wallboards slipped into slots in the pillars. Two massive freestanding posts (once great cypress trunks), one at each end of the building, support most of the weight of the *ridgepole*, the beam at the roof's crest. The golden-hued cypress columns and planks contrast in color and texture with the white gravel covering the sacred grounds. The thatched roof contains several aesthetic nuances. The builders browned the thatch by a smoking process and sewed it into bundles. Then they carefully laid it in layers that gradually decrease in number from the eaves to the ridgepole.

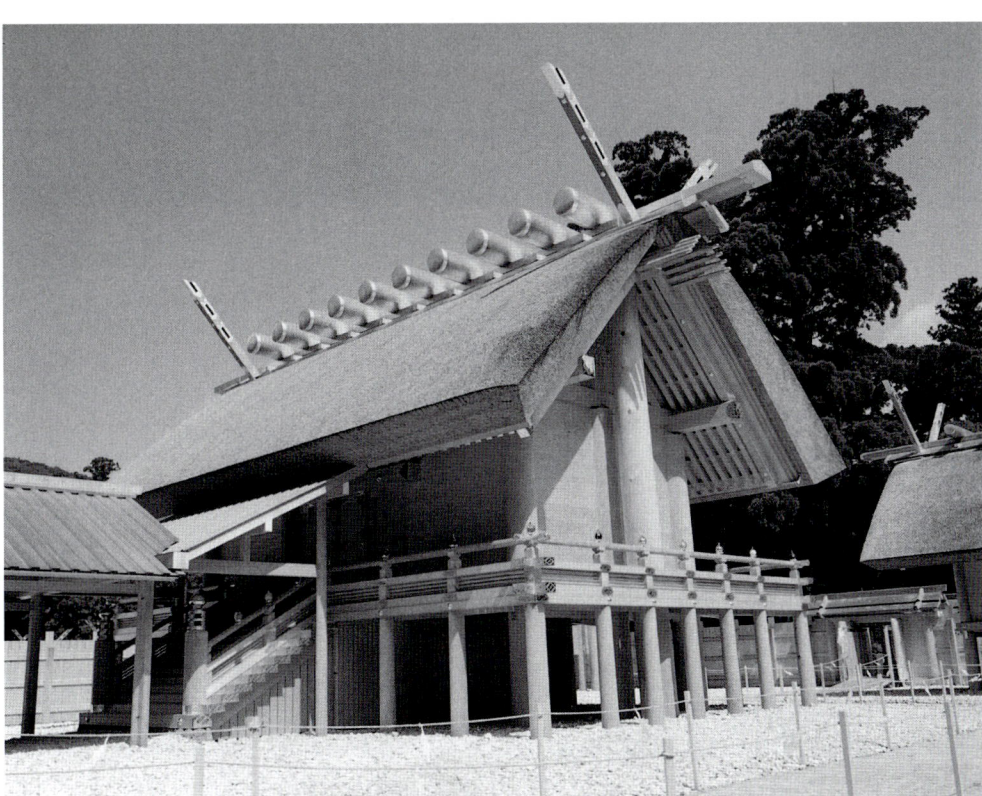

8-4 Main hall, Ise shrine, Ise, Mie Prefecture, Japan, as rebuilt in 1973.

Next, the workers sheared the entire surface smooth to produce a gently changing contour. Finally, they further enhanced the roofline by adding decorative elements that once had a structural function—the *chigi*, or crosspieces, at the gables and cylindrical wooden weights placed at right angles across the ridgepole. The shrine, in its setting, expresses purity and dignity, effectively emphasized by the extreme simplicity of the precisely planned proportions, textures, and architectural forms.

BUDDHIST JAPAN

Asuka (552–645), Hakuho (645–710), and Nara (710–794) Periods

ASUKA JAPAN AND CHINA   In A.D. 552, according to traditional interpretation, the ruler of Paekche, one of Korea's Three Kingdoms (see Chapter 7), sent Japan's ruler a gilded bronze figure of the Buddha and *sutras* (Buddhist scriptures) translated into Chinese, the written language of eastern Asia then. This event marked the beginning of the Asuka period, when Japan's ruling elite firmly established major elements of continental culture that had been gradually filtering into Japan. These cultural components included Chinese writing, Confucianism (see "Daoism and Confucianism," Chapter 7, page 193), and Buddhism (see "Buddhism and Buddhist Iconography," Chapter 6, page 164). The Japanese court, ruling from a series of capitals south of modern Kyoto, increasingly adopted the Chinese court's forms and rites. In 710, the Japanese finally established what they meant as a permanent capital at Nara. City planners laid out the new capital on a symmetrical grid closely modeled on the plan of the Chinese capital of Chang'an. However, Nara remained the capital only until 794.

For half a century after 552, Buddhism met with opposition, but at the end of that time, the new religion was established firmly in Japan. Shinto beliefs and practices continued to have significance, especially as agricultural rituals and imperial court rites. As time passed, Shinto deities even gained new identities as local manifestations of Buddhist deities.

In the arts allied to Buddhist practices, Japan followed Korean and Chinese prototypes very closely, especially in the Asuka, Hakuho, and Nara periods. In fact, early Buddhist architects in Japan adhered so closely to mainland standards (although generally with a considerable time lag) that surviving Japanese temples have helped greatly in the reconstruction of what was almost completely lost on the continent. Buddhist temples served as monasteries as well, because they were homes to monks or nuns and were really building complexes rather than individual structures.

BUDDHIST ARCHITECTURE: PAGODAS   In the early Buddhist period, one of the most important building types was the pagoda. Early Japanese examples tended to be simpler than the very elaborate Chinese version, such as the much later Foguang Si (see FIGS. 7-21 and 7-22), and square in plan with a single pillar rising through the center to the top. Like Indian stupas, pagodas were great reliquaries. Under the main pillar, a stone chamber housed relics of important teachers, celebrating the Buddhist faith's historical transmission through the generations.

THE WORLD'S OLDEST WOODEN BUILDING   The main building in a Japanese Buddhist temple complex, the image hall, housed the major sculptural icons and provided a site of worship and prayer. At Horyuji, outside Nara, an important surviving early temple complex, the image hall (FIG. **8-5**) is known as the *kondo* (Golden Hall). The Horyuji kondo dates from around 680, making it the oldest surviving wooden building in the world. Although periodically repaired and somewhat altered (the covered porch is an eighth-century addition; the upper railing dates to the seventeenth century), the structure retains its graceful but muscular forms beneath the additions. The main pillars (not visible in our illustration) decrease in diameter from bottom to top, as in classical architecture. The tapering made an effective transition between the more delicate brackets above and the columns' stout muscularity, but such tapering was a short-lived feature in Japan. Also somewhat masked by the added porch is the harmonious diminishing from the first to the second story. Following Chinese models, the builders used ceramic tiles as roofing material, rather than the thatching of earlier Japanese structures.

AN EARLY BUDDHA TRIAD IN BRONZE Wood was the mainstay of Buddhist sculpture throughout Japanese history, but bronze also held a significant place. In addition, artists of the Nara period made some surviving works from unfired clay or by using a special lacquer process, both forms supported by a wooden *armature* (framework). Among the earliest extant examples of Japanese Buddhist sculpture is a bronze Buddha triad (FIG. **8-6**). Rescued from a temple destroyed by fire in the seventh century, it became one of the main images in the Horyuji kondo. The central figure in the triad is Shaka (the Indian/Chinese Sakyamuni), the historical Buddha. Behind the main image, a flaming *mandorla* (an almond-shaped nimbus) bears small figures of other Buddhas. The sculptor, TORI BUSSHI (*busshi* means "maker of Buddhist images"), was a descendant of a Chinese immigrant. Tori's Buddha triad dates to 623 but reflects the style of the early to mid-sixth century in China and Korea. He elongated the heads and gave greater attention to the drapery's elegantly stylized folds than to rendering the physical substance of the bodies or their garments with naturalistic modeling.

THE HEALING BUDDHA OF YAKUSHIJI Within little more than half a century, however, Japan had begun to leave behind the Asuka period's style in favor of new ideas and forms coming out of Tang China and Korea. More direct relations with China also narrowed the time gap between developments there and their transfer to Japan. In the Yakushi

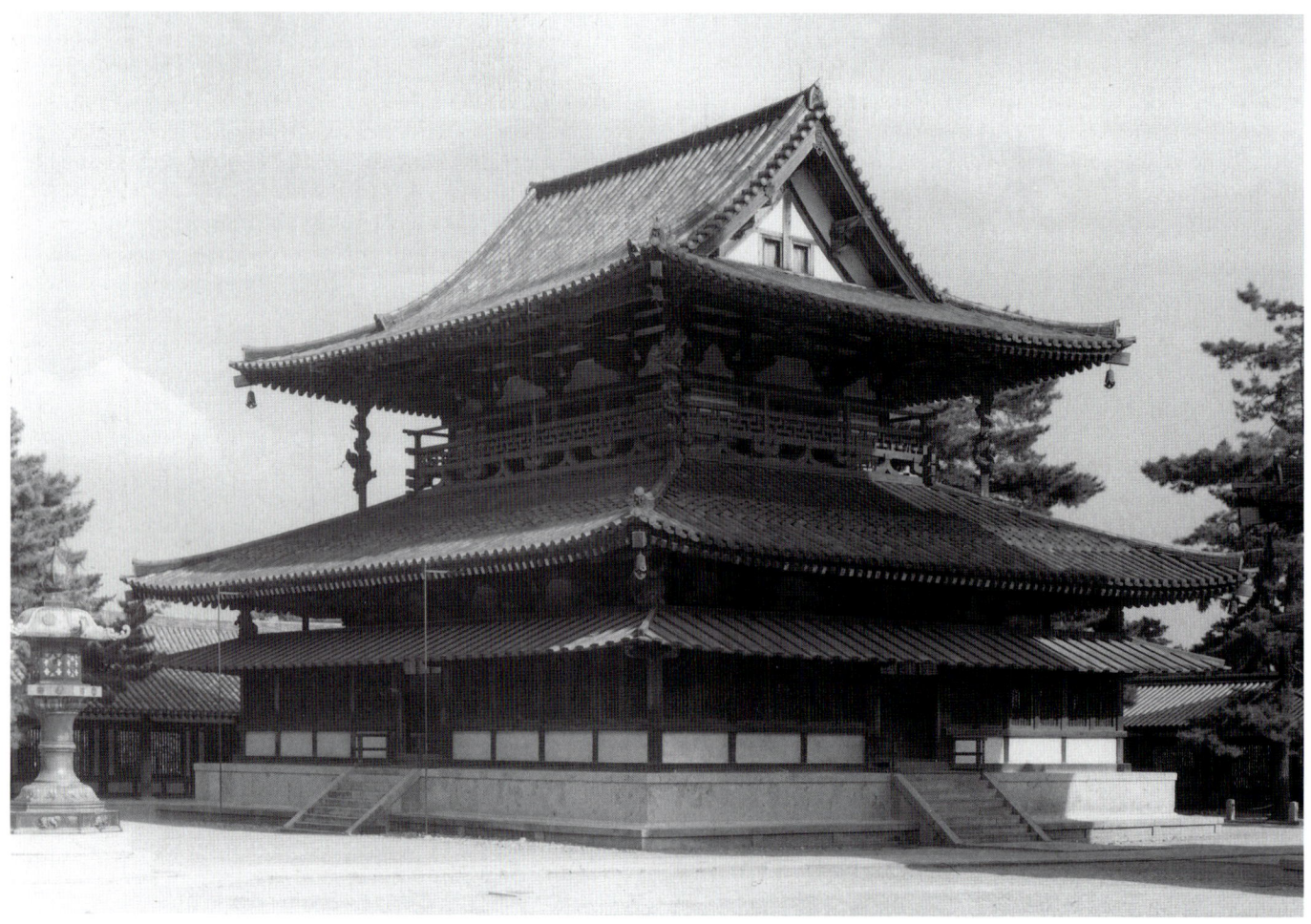

8-5 Horyuji *kondo* (Golden Hall), Nara, Japan, Hakuho period, ca. 680.

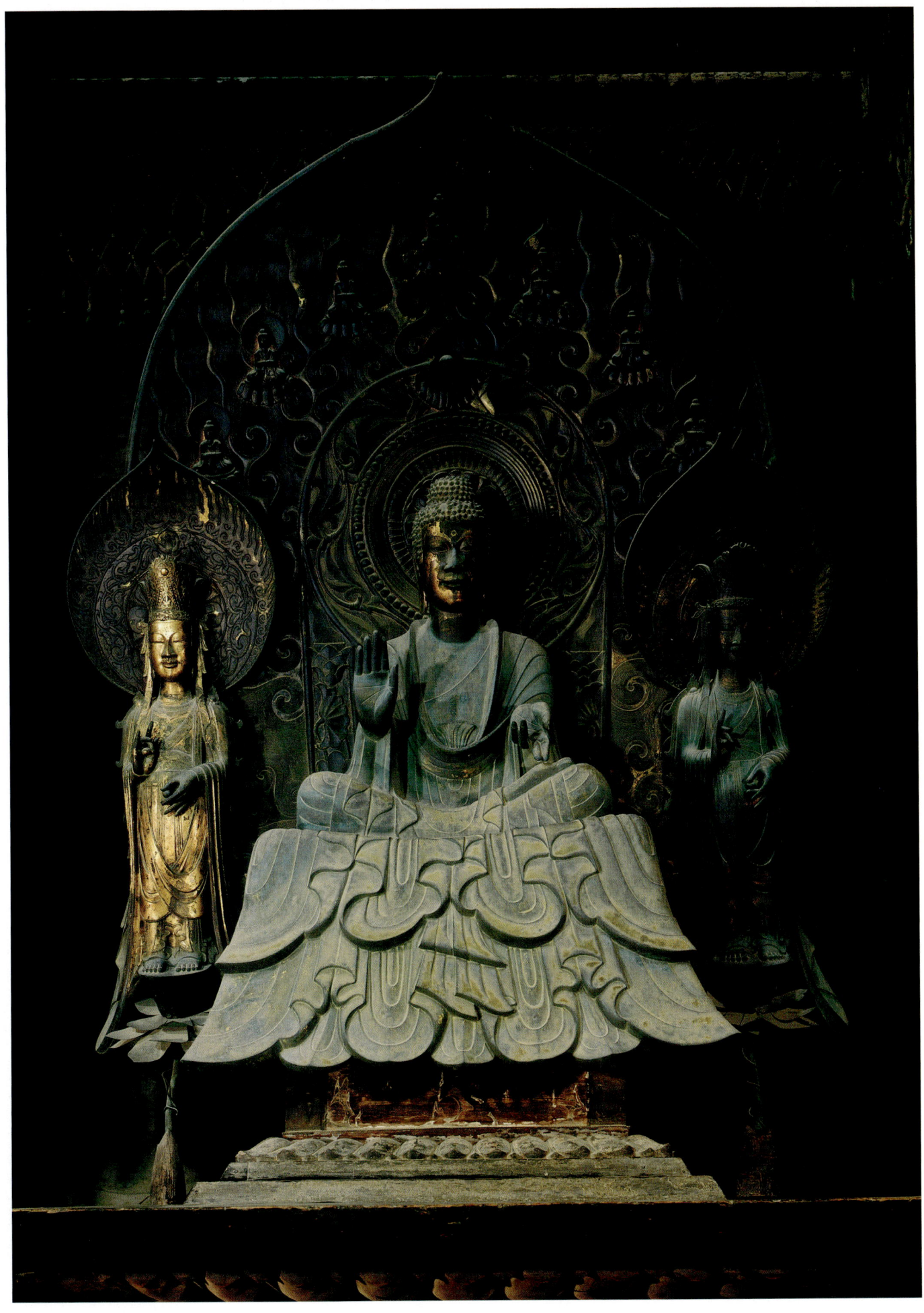

8-6 TORI BUSSHI, Shaka triad, Horyuji kondo, Nara, Japan, Asuka period, 623. Bronze, 5′ 9½″ high.

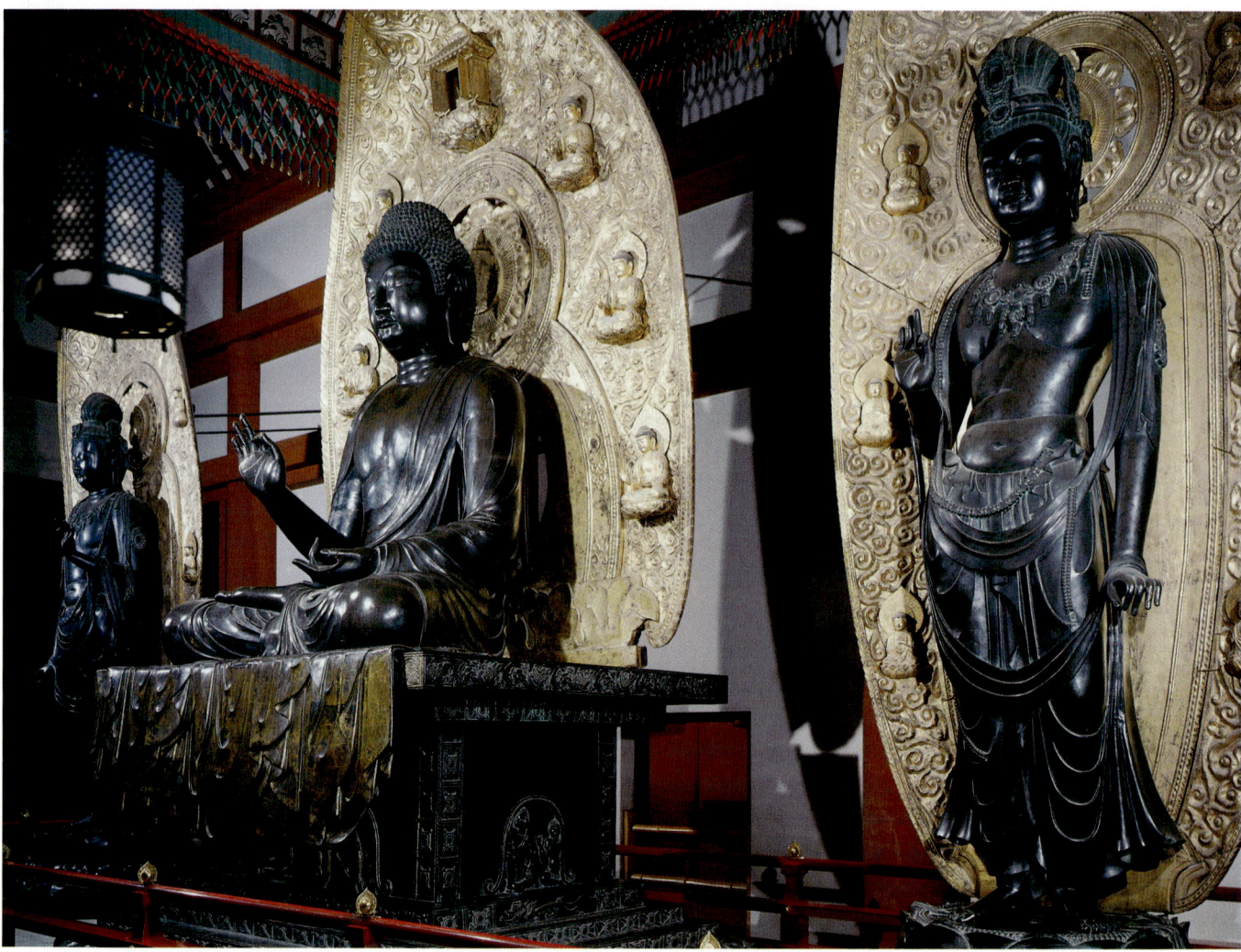

8-7   Yakushi triad, Yakushiji kondo, Nara, Japan, Hakuho period, late seventh or early eighth century. Bronze, central figure 8′ 4″ high.

(Bhaisajyaguru, the Healing Buddha) triad (FIG. **8-7**) in the kondo at the Yakushiji temple of the late seventh century in Nara, the sculptor favored greater anatomical definition and shape-revealing drapery over the dramatic stylizations of the Horyuji statues. The attendant bodhisattvas, especially, reveal the long stylistic trail back through China (see FIG. 7-13) to the sensuous fleshiness of Indian sculpture (see FIG. 6-15). The dark, lustrous surface of the statues—caused by the unusual composition of the cast bronze—makes the figures stand out strikingly from their golden mandorlas.

THE PAINTED WALLS OF HORYUJI Until a disastrous fire in 1949, the interior walls of the Golden Hall at Horyuji preserved some of the finest examples of Buddhist wall painting in eastern Asia, executed around 710, the beginning of the Nara period. The only record of them consists of color photographs. The most important paintings depicted the Buddhas of the four directions. Like the others, Amitabha (Amida in Japanese), the Buddha of the West (FIG. **8-8**), sits enthroned in his Pure Land, attended by bodhisattvas. The exclusive worship of Amida later became a major trend in Japanese Buddhism, and much grander depictions of his paradise appeared, resembling that at Dunhuang in China (see FIG. 7-14). Here, however, the representation is

simple and iconic. Although executed on a dry wall, the painting process involved familiar fresco techniques, such as transferring designs from paper to wall by punching holes in the paper and pushing colored powder through the perforations. As with the Buddha triad at Yakushiji, the mature Tang style, with its echoes of Indian sensuality, survives in this work. The fluid brush lines, thoroughly east Asian, give the figures their substance and life. Such lines belong to a particular type, often seen in Buddhist painting, termed *iron wire* because they are thin and unmodulated with a suggestion of tensile strength. Also, as in many other Buddhist paintings, the lines are red instead of black. The identity of the painters of these pictures is unknown, but some scholars have suggested they were Chinese or Korean rather than Japanese.

THE COSMIC BUDDHA AND THE EMPEROR During the Nara period, the imperial court sponsored the construction in Nara of the largest wooden building in the world, the Golden Hall at the Todaiji temple, later destroyed and significantly altered in rebuilding. Also known as the Great Buddha Hall, it housed a fifty-three-foot bronze image of the Cosmic Buddha, Vairocana (Roshana in Japanese), inspired by colossal stone statues of this type in China (see FIG. 7-12). However, Todaiji and its Buddha played a special role

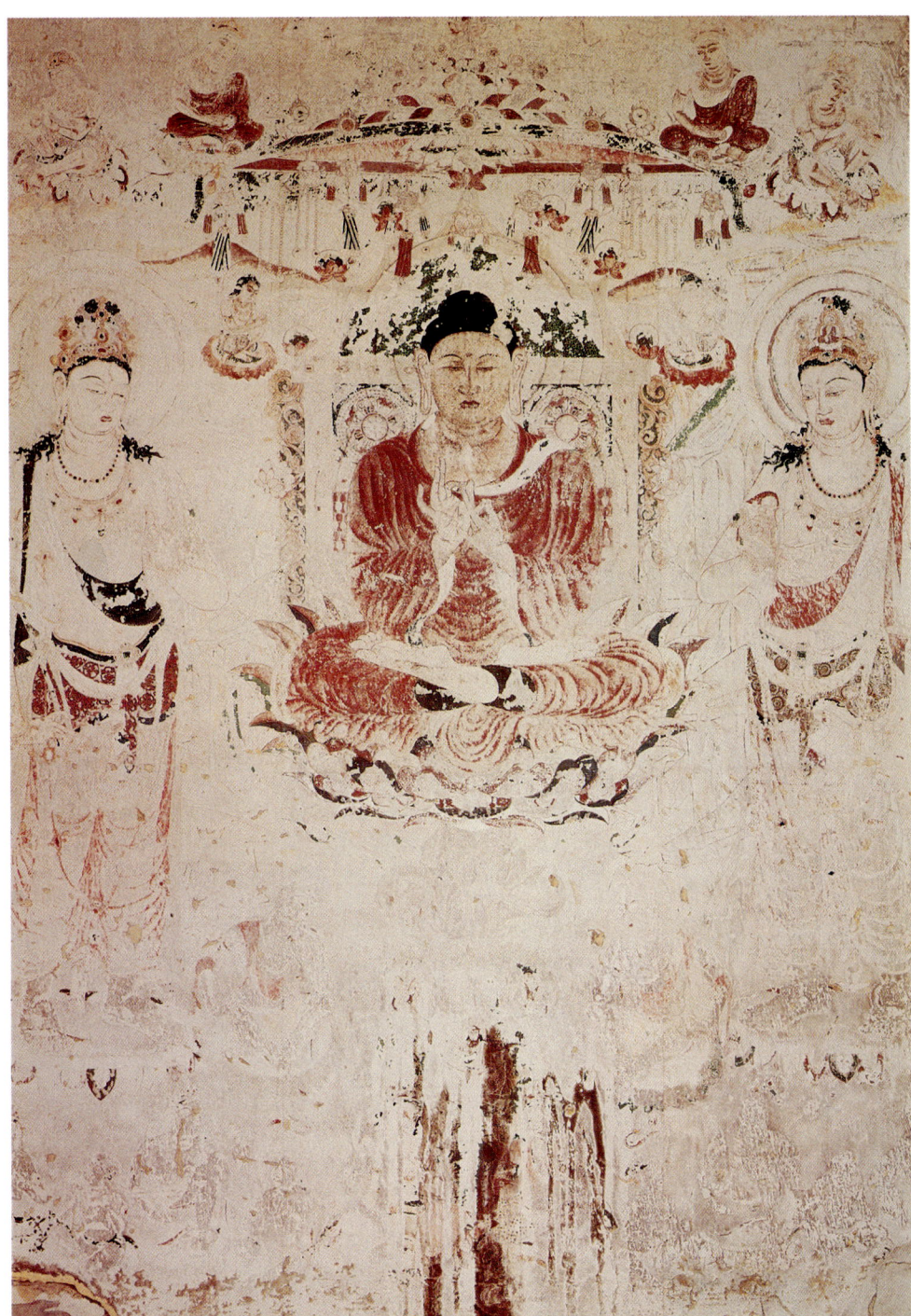

8-8 Amida triad, wall painting (damaged), from Horyuji kondo, Nara, Japan, Hakuho period, ca. 710. Ink and colors, 10′ 3″ × 8′ 6″. Horyuji Treasure House, Nara.

at this juncture in Japanese history. Todaiji was closely linked to the authority of the Japanese imperial throne, and its construction even required signs of the blessing of the Shinto sun goddess, the imperial family's mythical ancestor. The temple served as the administrative center of a network of branch temples built in every province, and the Cosmic Buddha functioned as ideologically similar to the emperor. The consolidation of imperial authority and thorough penetration of Buddhism throughout the country thus went hand in hand. The treasures donated to Todaiji serve today as almost a museum of eighth-century pan-Asian culture. Many of the temple's sculptures are Japanese examples of the finest Tang Chinese art forms.

Heian Period (794–1185)

In 794, possibly to escape the power of the Buddhist priests in Nara, the imperial house moved its capital north to what became its home until modern times. Originally called Heian, it is known today as Kyoto, still one of the great cities of the world for art and culture. In the early Heian period, Japan maintained fairly close ties with China, but from the middle of the ninth century on, relations between Japan and China deteriorated so rapidly that, by that century's end, court-sponsored contacts had ceased. Although never actually isolated, Japanese culture, especially at court, turned much more inward than it had in the preceding few centuries.

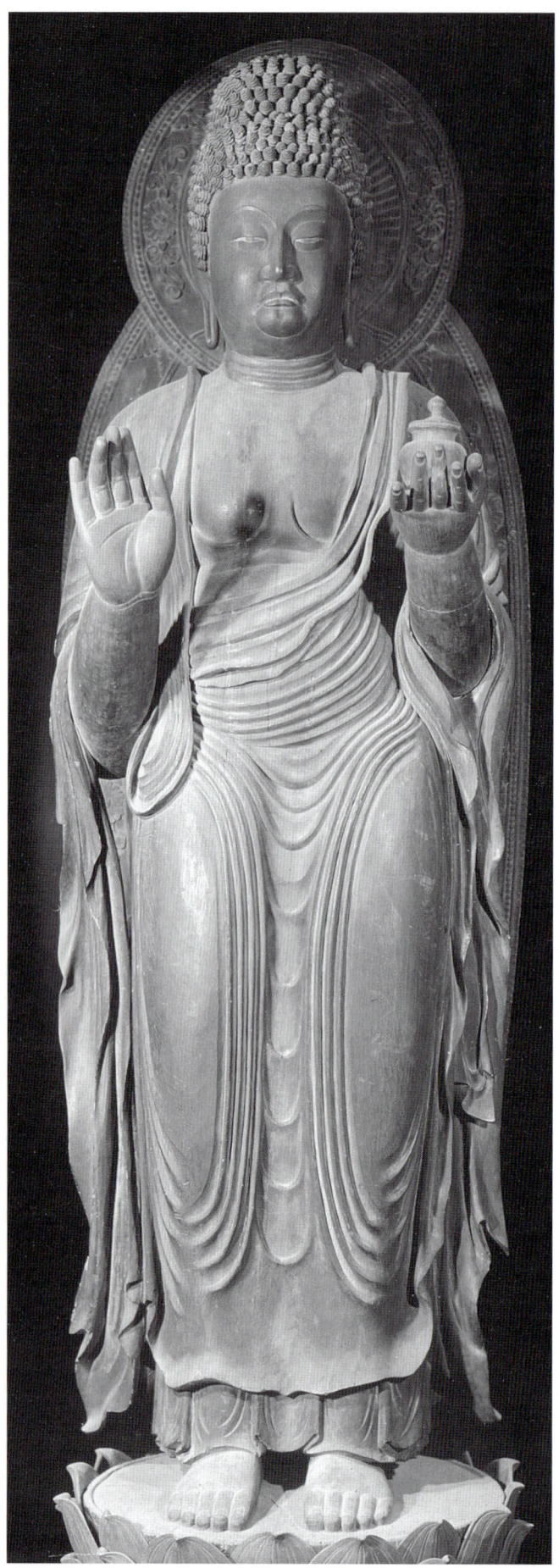

8-9 Standing Yakushi, Jingoji, Kyoto, Japan, Early Heian period, ca. 793. Cypress wood with traces of paint, 5′ 7″ high.

THE CYPRESS BUDDHA OF JINGOJI Distinctive Buddhist images, such as the standing Yakushi (FIG. **8-9**) at the Jingoji temple in Kyoto, survive from the early Heian period. The sculptor carved the statue from a single block of cypress wood, except for the protruding appendages. After the ninth century, artists fashioned large statues from multiple blocks joined together. The second method made carving easier and lessened the dangers of cracking. The Jingoji statue, with stylized drapery folds delineating its massive volumes, reveals a retreat from the naturalism of the eighth century. However, the figure maintains some of the sensuality of the late-seventh- and eighth-century statues to complement its heavy dignity. The narrow, even drapery folds define the swelling forms of the chest, stomach, and thighs. Full lids, nose, and lips lend a sensual gravity to the face.

THE FLOATING PHOENIX HALL OF UJI In the early Heian period, Japanese monks traveled to China and brought back the teachings of various Buddhist sects, especially the Esoteric ones. Esoteric Buddhism embraced a great number of deities, including figures adapted from Hinduism (see "Hinduism and Hindu Iconography," Chapter 6, page 173), Buddhas, and bodhisattvas. Esoteric teachings emphasized rigorous training and study to attain advancement toward enlightenment in this life. However, during the Heian period, belief in the vow of Amida, the Buddha of the West, to save believers through rebirth in his Pure Land also gained great prominence among the Japanese aristocracy. The most important surviving monument in Japan related to Pure Land beliefs is the Phoenix Hall of the Byodoin (FIG. **8-10**), a temple built for Fujiwara Yorimichi (r. 990–1074) on the grounds of his summer villa at Uji. Dedicated in 1053, the Phoenix Hall houses a wooden statue of Amida carved from multiple joined blocks, the dominant approach to wooden sculpture by this time. The building's elaborate winged form evokes images of the Buddha's palace in his Pure Land, as depicted in east Asian paintings (see FIG. 7-14) based on the design of great Chinese palaces. By placing only light pillars on the exterior, elevating the wings, and situating the whole on a reflective pond, the Phoenix Hall builders suggested the floating weightlessness of a celestial architecture. The building's name derives from its overall birdlike shape and from two bronze phoenixes decorating the ridgepole ends. In eastern Asia, these birds were not symbols of rebirth, as in the West, but instead represented imperial might, sometimes associated especially with the empress. The Fujiwara family's authority derived primarily from the marriage of daughters to the imperial line.

TALE OF GENJI Japan's most admired literary classic is *Tale of Genji* (see "Japanese Literature and Court Culture," page 225). Artists probably began producing illustrated copies of this novel soon after its writing in the early eleventh century, but the oldest extant examples are fragments from a deluxe set of early-twelfth-century handscrolls. From textual and physical evidence, scholars have suggested the set originally consisted of about ten handscrolls produced by about five teams of artisans. Each team consisted of a nobleman talented in calligraphy, a chief painter, and assistants. The script is primarily *hiragana,* a sound-based

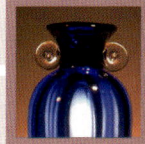

Japanese Literature and Court Culture

During the Nara and Heian periods (710–1185), the Japanese imperial court developed as the center of an elite culture. Both men and women produced literature, paintings, calligraphy, and decorative arts critics generally consider "classical" today. Heian court members, especially those from the great Fujiwara clan dominating the court for a century and a half, compiled the first great anthologies of Japanese poetry and wrote Japan's most influential secular prose.

Japanese poetry and related painting and decorative art emphasize human sentiments intertwined with responses to nature, seasonality, and a body of standard metaphors and symbols. For example, the full moon, flying geese, crying deer, and certain plants symbolize autumn, which in turn evokes somber emotions, fading love, and dying. Such concrete but evocative images frequently appear in paintings.

Even in secular prose, the characters generally speak in poetic form. Exchanging poems was a common Japanese social practice and a frequent preoccupation of lovers.

A lady-in-waiting to an early-eleventh-century empress wrote the best-known and longest-admired work of literature in Japan, *Tale of Genji*. Known as Lady Murasaki, the author is one of many important Heian women writers, including especially diarists and poets. Generally considered the world's oldest full novel, *Tale of Genji* tells of the life and loves of Prince Genji and, after his death, of his heirs. The novel and much of Japanese literature consistently display a sensitivity to the sadness in the world caused by the transience of love and life. Illustrated scrolls of *Tale of Genji* (FIG. 8-11) rely on key poetic motifs and careful compositions to convey such feelings.

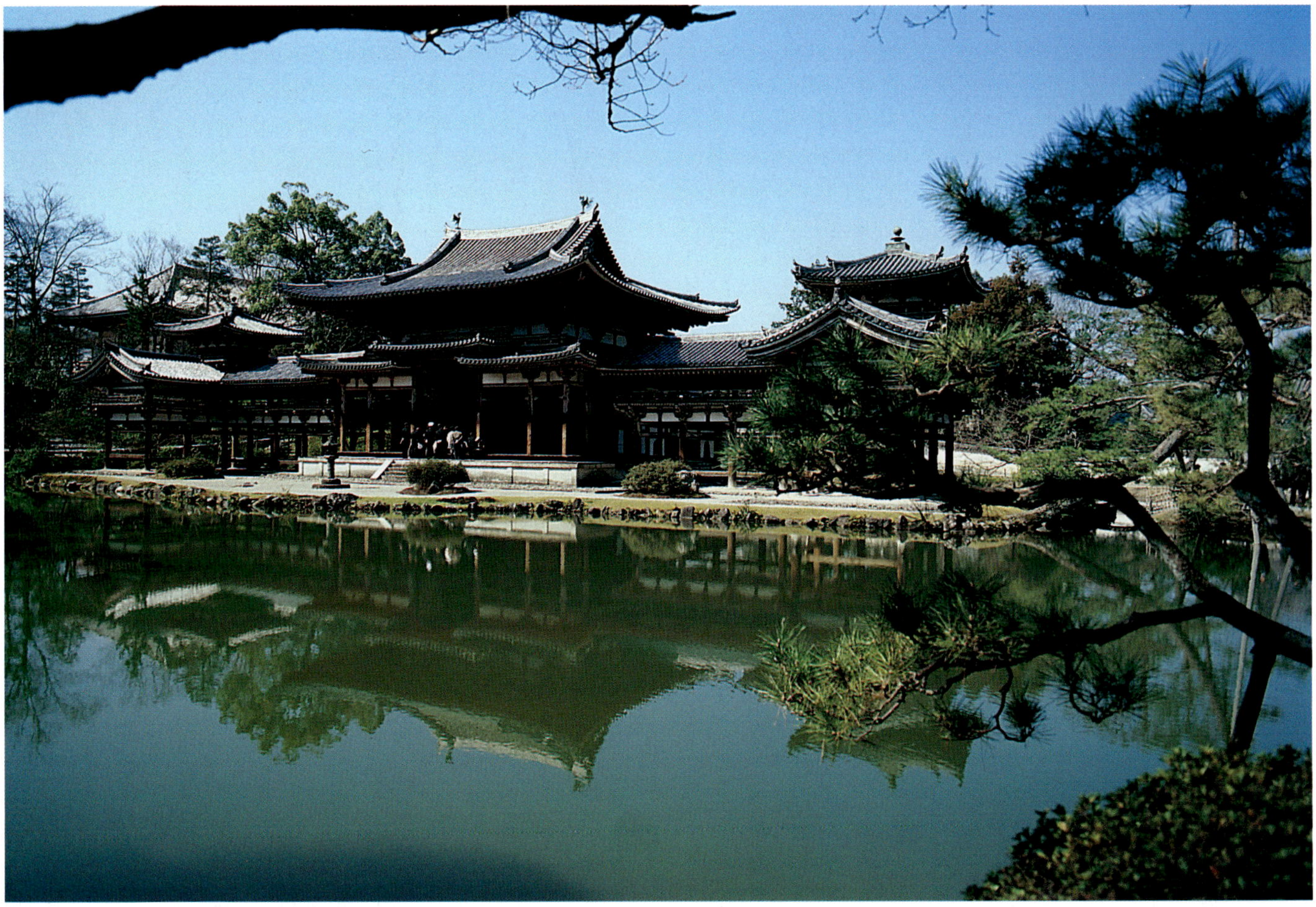

8-10   Phoenix Hall, Byodoin, Uji, Japan, Heian period, 1053.

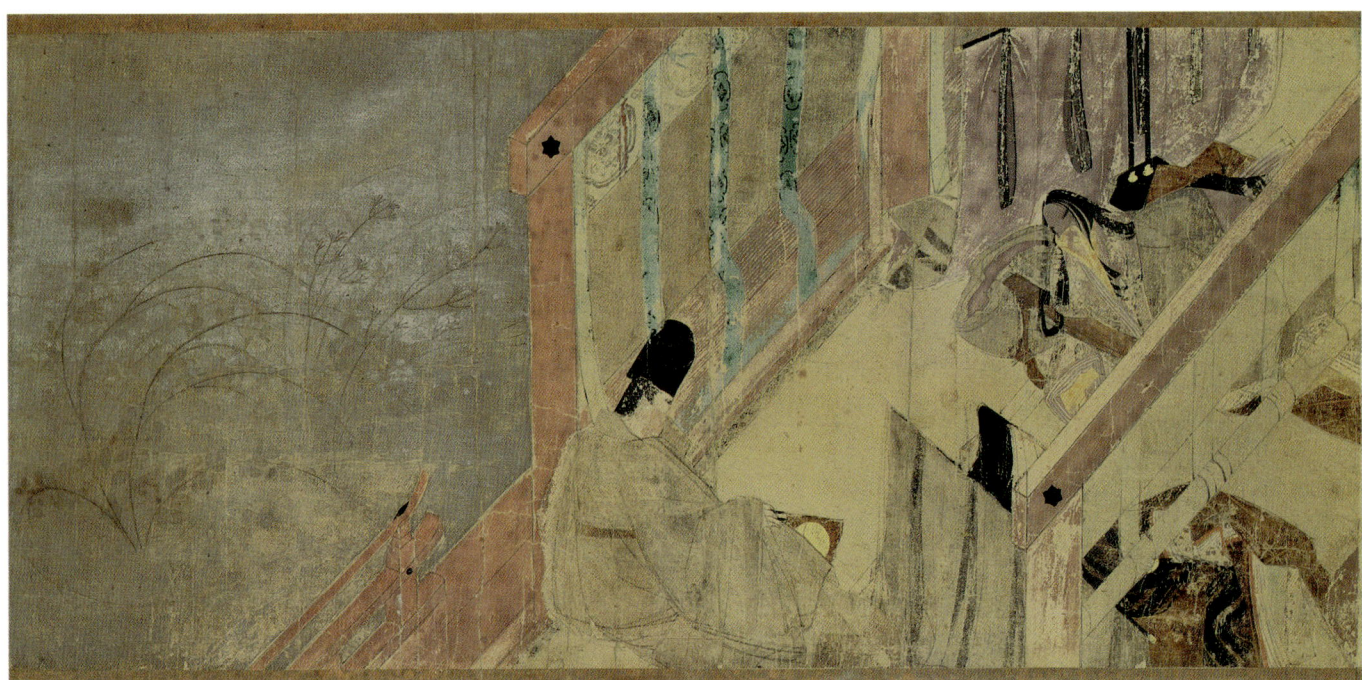

8-11   Scene from Minori chapter, *Tale of Genji*, late Heian period, first half of twelfth century. Handscroll, ink and color on paper, 8 5/8″ high. Goto Art Museum, Tokyo.

writing system developed in Japan from Chinese characters. Hiragana originally served the needs of women, who were not taught Chinese, but it became the primary script for Japanese court poetry. In these handscrolls, pictures alternate with text, as in Gu Kaizhi's *Admonitions* scrolls (see FIG. 7-9). However, the Japanese work focuses on emotionally charged moments in per-

sonal relationships, rather than lessons in exemplary behavior. In the scene illustrated here (FIG. **8-11**), for example, Genji meets with his greatest love, Murasaki (the name given to the novel's otherwise anonymous author), near the time of her death. The bush-clover in the garden identifies the season as Autumn, the season associated with the fading of life and love.

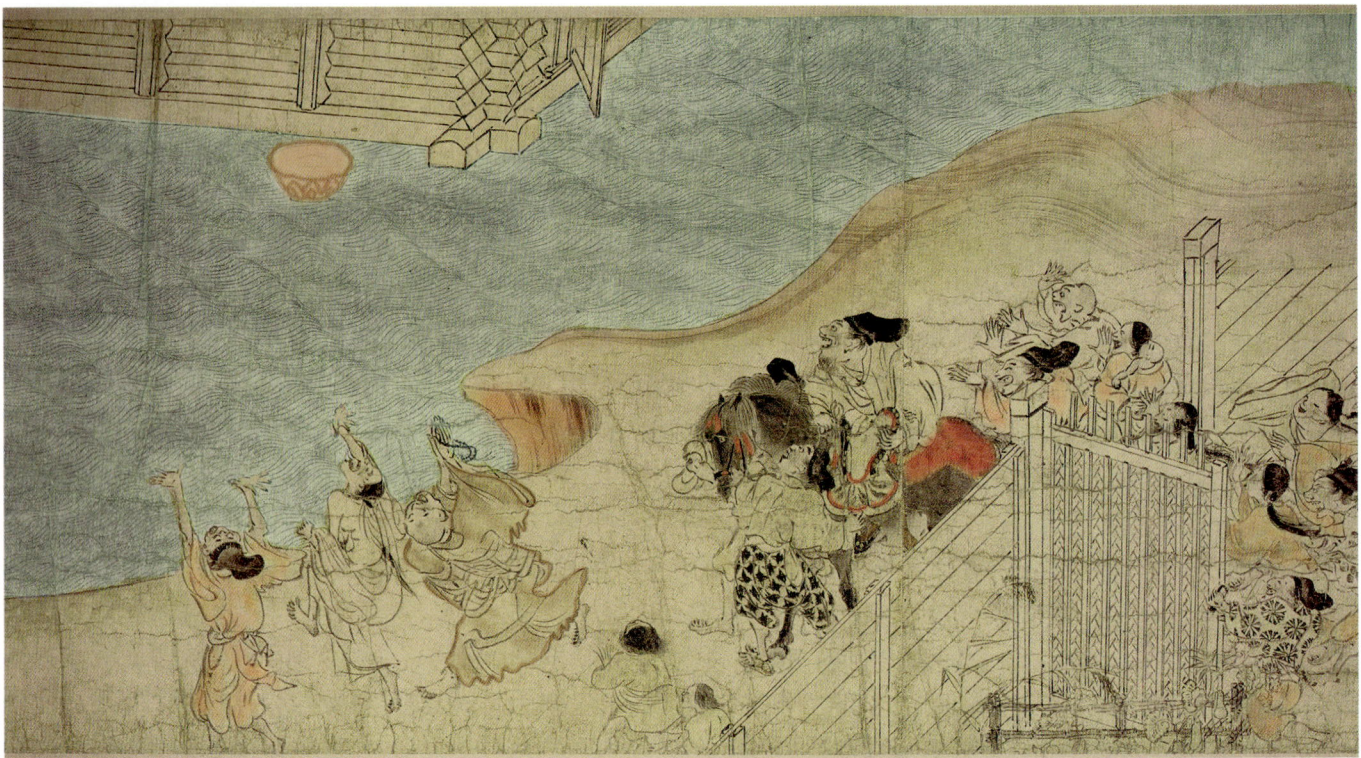

8-12   Detail of *The Flying Storehouse*, from *The Legends of Mount Shigi*, late Heian period, late twelfth century. Handscroll, ink and colors on paper, 1′ 1/2″ high. Chogosonshiji, Nara.

Here, a radically upturned ground plane and strong diagonal lines primarily convey the suggestive, rather than illusionistic, spatial representation. Although this implies an elevated viewpoint, the painter omitted roofs and ceilings to allow a privileged view of the emotionally charged moments typically represented in the interiors. Artists typically represented such moments in the interiors. Flat fields of unshaded color emphasize the painting's two-dimensional character, but rich patterns in the textiles and architectural ornament give a feeling of sumptuousness. The human figures appear constructed of stiff layers of contrasting fabrics, and the artist simplified and generalized the aristocratic faces, using a technique called "line for eye and hook for nose." This lack of individualization may reflect societal restrictions on looking directly on exalted persons, or it may have served to ease viewers' identification with a character in the story. Heian aristocrats tended to participate quite actively in painting and poetry composition, and it is easy to imagine an illustration moving a court member to take on a character's role and write a suitable poem. Several formal features of the *Genji* illustrations—native subjects, bright mineral pigments, lack of emphasis on strong brushwork, and general flatness—were later considered typical of *yamato-e* (native-style painting). In the early Heian period before this example was made, however, yamato-e probably referred only to subject matter.

THE LEGENDS OF MOUNT SHIGI Painted at the end of the Heian period, *The Legends of Mount Shigi* (FIG. 8-12) represents a different facet of narrative handscroll painting. The stories belong to a genre of pious Buddhist tales devoted to miraculous events involving saintly individuals. Unlike the *Genji* scrolls, short segments of text and pictures do not alternate. Instead, the painters took advantage of the scroll format to present several scenes in a long stretch of unbroken setting. For example, the first scroll shows the same travelers at several stages of their journey through a continuous landscape. This sort of pictorial narration does not survive in China, if it ever existed there.

The *Mount Shigi* scrolls illustrate three miracles associated with a Buddhist monk named Myoren. The first relates the story of the flying storehouse and depicts Myoren's begging bowl lifting the rice-filled storehouse of a wealthy landowner and carrying it off to the monk's hut in the mountains (FIG. 8-12). The painter depicted the gaping landowner, his attendants, and several onlookers in various poses—some grimacing, others gesticulating wildly and scurrying about in frantic astonishment. The artist exaggerated each feature of the painted figures, in striking contrast to the *Genji* scroll figures. In handscroll paintings, only the lower classes generally displayed their feelings or became subjects of humorous caricature.

Kamakura Period (1185–1332)

In the late twelfth century, a series of civil wars between rival warrior families led to the Japanese imperial court's end as a major political and social force. The victors, headed by the Minamoto family, established their *shogunate* (military government) at Kamakura. The imperial court remained in Kyoto as the theoretical source of political authority but without actual power. During the Kamakura period, more frequent and positive contact with China brought with it an appreciation for more recent cultural developments there, ranging from new architectural styles to Zen Buddhism.

A MOVING PORTRAIT OF AN AGED PRIEST Rebuilding in Nara, necessitated by the destructive battles that helped bring the Minamoto to power, presented an early opportunity for architectural experimentation. A leading figure in planning and directing the reconstruction efforts was the priest Shunjobo Chogen (1121–1206), who had made three trips to China between 1166 and 1176. After learning about contemporary Chinese architecture, he oversaw the rebuilding of Todaiji and associated projects under the Minamoto's patronage. His portrait statue (FIG. 8-13) is one of the most striking examples of the high level of naturalism prevalent in the early Kamakura period. Characterized by finely painted details, a powerful rendering of aging signs, and the inclusion of such personal attributes as prayer beads, the statue of Chogen exhibits the carving skill and style of the Kei school of sculptors (see "Japanese Artists, Workshops, and Patrons," page 228). The Kei school traced its lineage to a famous sculptor of the mid-eleventh century. Its works display fine Heian carving techniques combined with an increased concern for natural volume and detail learned from studying surviving Nara period works and works imported from Song China.

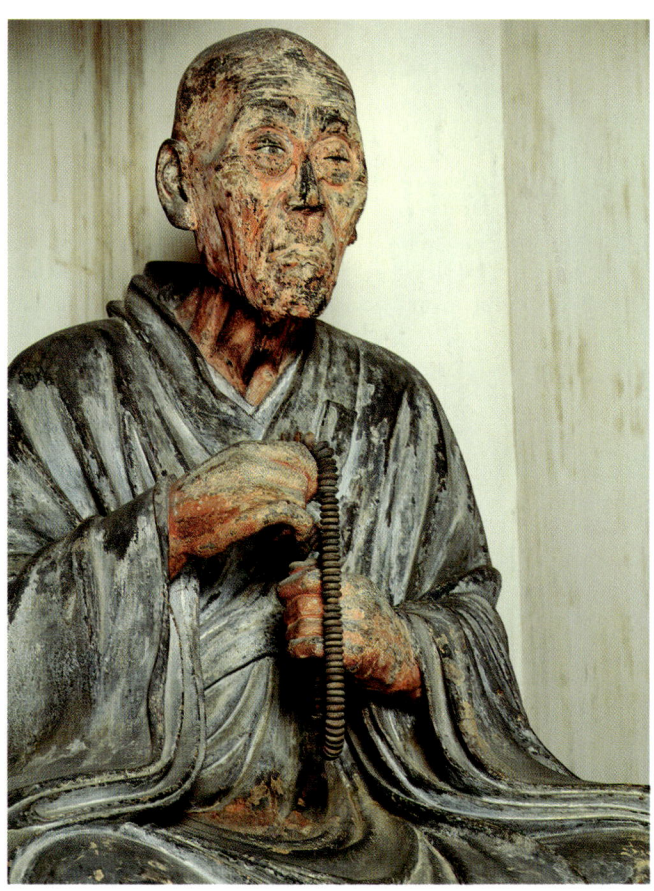

8-13 The priest Shunjobo Chogen, Todaiji, Nara, Japan, Kamakura period, early thirteenth century. Painted cypress wood, 2′ 8⅜″ high.

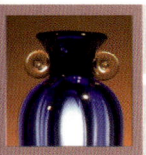

Japanese Artists, Workshops, and Patrons

Until recent times, hierarchically organized male workshops produced most Japanese art. For large projects, some clients assigned an intermediary to oversee the work. Until the late Heian period, major commissions came almost exclusively from the imperial court or the great temples. As warrior families began to gain wealth and power, they, too, extended great commissions—in many cases closely following the aristocrats' precedents in subject and style.

Family-run workshops often created works such as the portrait statue of Chogen (FIG. 8-13), as well as paintings and most other art forms. Many of the master's main assistants and apprentices were relatives. Outsiders of considerable skill sometimes joined workshops, often through marriage. The eldest son most often inherited the master's position, after rigorous training in the necessary skills from a very young age. Therefore, one meaning of the term "school of art" in Japan is a network of workshops tracing their origins back to the same master, a kind of artistic clan. Inside the workshops, the master and senior assistants handled the most important production stages, but those of lower rank helped with the more routine work.

By the Heian period, artists organized in official court bureaus at the imperial palace also cooperated in producing artworks. The most famous of these bureaus created paintings.

Teams of court painters, led by the bureau director, produced pictures such as the scenes in the *Tale of Genji* handscrolls (FIG. 8-11). This system remained vital into the Kamakura period and well beyond. Under the direction of a patron or the patron's representative, the master painter laid out the picture by brushing in the initial outlines and contours. Under his direction, more junior painters applied the colors. Then the master completed the picture by brushing in fresh contours and details such as facial features. Very junior assistants and apprentices assisted in the process by preparing paper, ink, and pigments. Unlike mastership in hereditarily run workshops, competition among several families determined control of the Court Painting Bureau during the Heian and Kamakura periods.

Not all paintings at court came from the Painting Bureau. One aristocratic family of modest court rank became famous for its portraits. Amateur painting was also common among aristocrats of all ranks. As in poetry composition and calligraphy, aristocrats frequently held elegant competitions in painting. Such activities involved both women and men. In fact, court ladies probably played a significant role in developing the painting style seen in the *Genji* scrolls, and a few participated in public projects.

THE BURNING OF THE SANJO PALACE All the painting types flourishing in the Heian period continued to prosper in the Kamakura period. A striking example of narrative handscroll painting is *The Burning of the Sanjo Palace* (FIG. **8-14**), a fragment of a work illustrating some of the battles in the civil wars at the end of the Heian period. Here, viewers see the drama unfold in swift and violent staccato brushwork and vivid flashes of color. At the beginning of the scroll (read from right to left), the eyes focus first on a mass of figures rushing toward a blazing building (not shown here)—

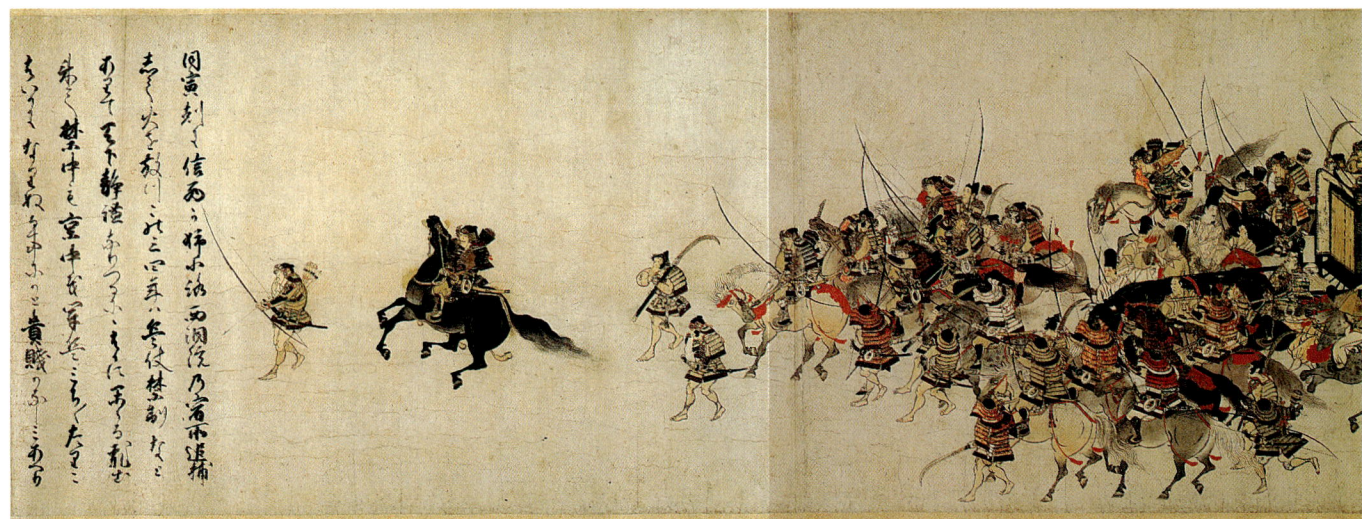

8-14 Detail of *The Burning of the Sanjo Palace,* Kamakura period, thirteenth century. Handscroll, ink and colors on paper, 1′ 4¼″ high; complete scroll, 22′ 10″ long. Museum of Fine Arts, Boston (Fenollosa-Weld Collection).

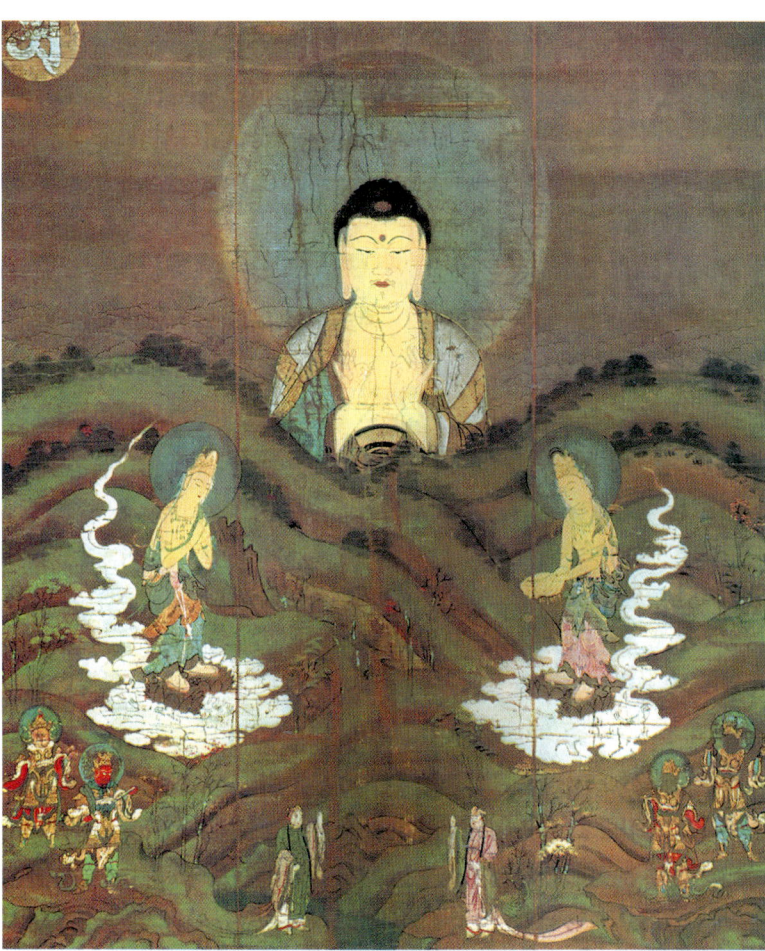

the painting's crescendo—and then move at a slowed pace through swarms of soldiers, horses, and bullock carts. Finally, a warrior on a rearing horse arrests viewers' gaze. The horse and rider, however, serve as a "deceptive cadence" (false ending). They are merely a prelude to the single figure of an archer, who picks up and completes the soldiers' mass movement, drawing the turbulent narrative to a quiet close.

AMIDA DESCENDS TO SAVE THE DEAD   Buddhism and Buddhist painting remained vital in the Kamakura period. Evangelical monks spread Pure Land beliefs throughout Japan to people from all levels of society, and new Pure Land sects emerged that the lower ranks of society, including peasants, found especially appealing. But elite patrons continued to commission major Pure Land artworks. Pure Land beliefs in Japan stressed the grace of Amida, who, if called on, hastened to believers at the moment of death and conveyed their souls to his Pure Land. Pictures of this scene often hung in the presence of a dying person, who recited Amida's name to insure salvation.

One dramatic version of the scene, which scholars call the "speedy descent," depicts Amida and his host rushing on clouds down a mountainside. The composition provides a powerful image of Amida's dedication to humanity's salvation. In the less dramatic but equally powerful *Amida Descending over the Mountains* (FIG. **8-15**), a gigantic Amida appears to move directly toward viewers. His two main attendant bodhisattvas already made the passage. The grand frontal presen-

tation of Amida gives the painting an iconic quality even as the bodhisattvas' movement maintains the narrative of his descent. Particularly striking in this painting is the way in which Amida's halo resembles a rising moon, an image long admired in Japan for its spiritual beauty.

Striking transformations mark the long history of Japanese art as the country's population received, responded to, and developed new forms and ideas from continental eastern Asia. Early metalwork, Buddhist architecture, and the basic painting formats and media, to name only a few examples, readily reveal Japan's close ties to the continent. However, from earliest times, Japan maintained distinctive aesthetic ideals and preferences. For instance, the dynamic forms of Jomon pottery and haniwa figures suggest the early Japanese derived a deep pleasure from allowing the colors and textures of their raw materials to remain vital in the final objects. This tendency may not have been exclusive to Japanese art and certainly did not dominate in later centuries, but it did remain a vital part of Japan's aesthetic heritage, helping determine what people accepted from the continent and how they adapted it. In the end, however, the most distinctive feature of Japanese art is its great variety. This reflects the people's capacity to embrace radically different aesthetics simultaneously, appreciating their separate contributions to a richly diverse material culture. Chapter 27 shows how this cultural flexibility continued after several decades of upheaval, the Kamakura rulers' downfall in the early fourteenth century (1332), and the establishment of a new shogunate by the end of the century.

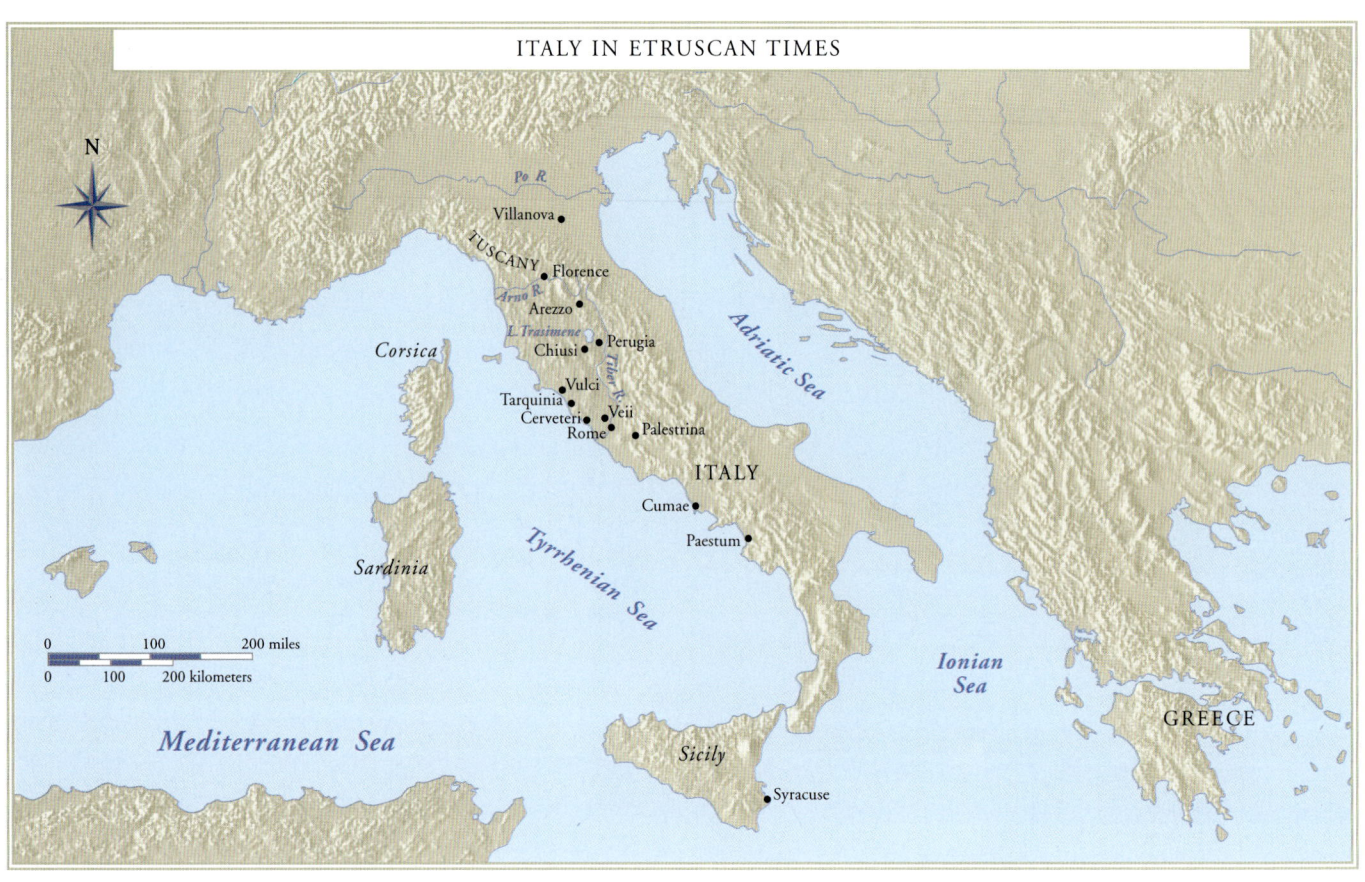

ITALY IN ETRUSCAN TIMES

Po R.

Villanova

TUSCANY

Florence

Arno R.

Arezzo

L. Trasimene

Chiusi • Perugia

Corsica

Vulci

Tarquinia • *Tiber R.*

Cerveteri • Veii

Rome • Palestrina

Adriatic Sea

ITALY

Cumae •

Paestum

Sardinia

Tyrrhenian Sea

Ionian Sea

GREECE

Mediterranean Sea

Sicily

Syracuse •

0   100   200 miles
0   100   200 kilometers

900 B.C.	700 B.C.	600 B.C.	480 B.C.
VILLANOVAN	ORIENTALIZING	ARCHAIC	CLASSICAL

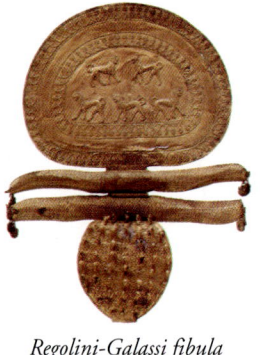

Regolini-Galassi fibula
Cerveteri, ca. 650–640 B.C.

Apulu, Veii
ca. 510–500 B.C.

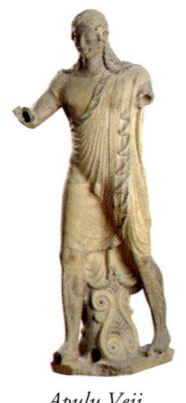

Tomb of the Leopards
Tarquinia, ca. 480–470 B.C.

Greek colonization of southern Italy and Sicily begins, mid-eighth century B.C.

Founding of Rome, 753 B.C.

Tarquinius Priscus, first Etruscan king of Rome, 616 B.C.

Expulsion of Etruscan kings from Rome, 509 B.C.

Etruscan naval defeat by the Greeks at Cumae, 474 B.C.

9

ITALY BEFORE THE ROMANS

THE ART OF THE ETRUSCANS

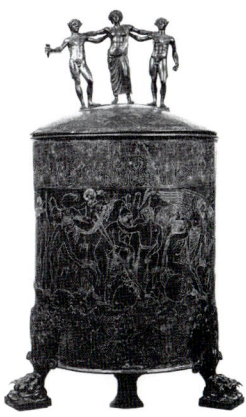

Ficoroni Cista
late fourth century B.C.

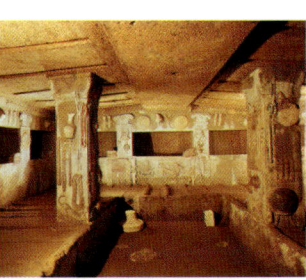

Tomb of the Reliefs
Cerveteri, third century B.C.

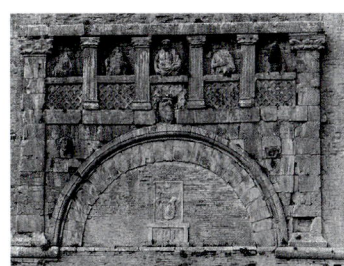

Porta Marzia
Perugia, second century B.C.

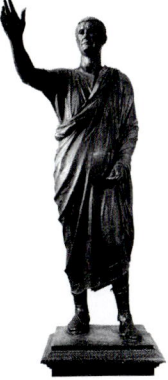

Aule Metele (Arringatore)
early first century B.C.

WHO WERE THE ETRUSCANS?

"The Etruscans, as everyone knows, were the people who occupied the middle of Italy in early Roman days, and whom the Romans, in their usual neighbourly fashion, wiped out entirely." So opens D. H. Lawrence's witty and sensitive *Etruscan Places* (1929), one of the earliest modern essays that highly values Etruscan art and treats it as much more than a debased form of the art of the contemporary city-states of Greece and southern Italy. ("Most people despise everything B.C. that isn't Greek, for the good reason that it ought to be Greek if it isn't," Lawrence goes on to say!) Today it is no longer necessary to argue the importance and originality of Etruscan art. Deeply influenced by, yet different from, Greek art, Etruscan sculpture, painting, and architecture not only provided the models for early Roman art and architecture but also had an impact on the art of the Greek colonies in Italy.

The heartland of the Etruscans was the territory between the Arno and Tiber Rivers of central Italy. The lush green hills still bear their name—Tuscany, the land of the people the Romans called *Tusci,* the region centered on Florence, birthplace of Renaissance art. So do the blue waters that splash up against the Italian peninsula's western coastline, for the Greeks referred to the Etruscans as *Tyrrhenians* and gave their name to the sea off Tuscany. The origin of the Tusci people—the enduring "mystery of the Etruscans"—is, however, not clear at all. Their language, although written in a Greek-derived script and extant in inscriptions that are still in large part obscure, is unrelated to the Indo-European linguistic family. Ancient historians, as fascinated by the puzzle as are modern scholars, generally felt that the Etruscans emigrated from the east. Herodotus specifically declared that they came from Lydia in Asia Minor and were led by King Tyrsenos—hence their Greek name. But Dionysius of Halicarnassus, a Greek author of the end of the first century B.C., maintained that the Tusci were native Italians. And some modern researchers have theorized that the Etruscans came into Italy from the north.

All of these theories are current today, and no doubt some truth exists in all of them. The Etruscan people of historical times were very likely the result of a gradual fusion of native and immigrant populations. This mixing of peoples occurred between the end of the Bronze Age and the so-called Villanovan era (named after an important northern Italian site and comparable to the Geometric period in Greece). At that time the Etruscans emerged as a people with a culture related to but distinct from those of other Italic peoples and from the civilizations of Greece and the Orient.

During the eighth and seventh centuries B.C., the Etruscans, as highly skilled seafarers, enriched themselves through trade abroad. By the sixth century B.C., they controlled most of northern and central Italy from such strongholds as Tarquinia (ancient Tarquinii), Cerveteri (Caere), Vulci, and Veii. But these cities never united to form a state, so it is improper to speak of an Etruscan "nation" or "kingdom," only of *Etruria,* the territory occupied by the Etruscans. The cities coexisted, flourishing or fading independently. Any semblance of unity among them was based primarily on common linguistic ties and religious beliefs and practices. This lack of political cohesion eventually made the Etruscans relatively easy prey for Lawrence's Roman aggressors.

EARLY ETRUSCAN ART

Orientalizing Art

The great mineral wealth of Etruria—iron, tin, copper, and silver were all successfully mined in antiquity—transformed Etruscan society during the seventh century B.C. The modest Villanovan villages and their agriculturally based economies gave way to prosperous cities engaged in international commerce. Cities such as Cerveteri, blessed with rich mines, could acquire foreign goods, and Etruscan aristocrats quickly developed a taste for luxury items incorporating Eastern motifs. To satisfy the demand, local artisans, inspired by imported goods, produced magnificent items for both homes and tombs. As in Greece at the same time, art historians speak of an Orientalizing period of Etruscan art followed by an Archaic period. And, as in Greece, the local products cannot be mistaken for the foreign models.

A BEJEWELED WOMAN'S TOMB   About the middle of the seventh century B.C., a wealthy Etruscan family stocked the so-called Regolini-Galassi Tomb (named for its excavators) at Cerveteri with bronze cauldrons and gold jewelry of Etruscan manufacture and Orientalizing style. The most spectacular of the many luxurious objects in the tomb is a golden *fibula* (clasp or safety pin; FIG. **9-1**) of unique shape used to fasten a woman's gown at the shoulder. The giant fibula is in the Italic tradition, but the five lions that walk across the gold surface were borrowed from the Orient. The technique, also emulating Eastern imports, is masterful, combining hammered relief *(repoussé)* and *granulation* (the fusing of tiny metal balls, or *granules,* to a metal surface). The Regolini-Galassi fibula equals or exceeds in quality anything that might have served as a model.

The jewelry from the Regolini-Galassi Tomb also includes a golden *pectoral* that covered the deceased woman's chest and two gold circlets that may be earrings, although they are large enough to be bracelets. Such a taste for ostentatious display is frequently the hallmark of newly acquired wealth, and this was certainly the case in seventh-century Etruria.

Archaic Art and Architecture

TEMPLES FOR THE ETRUSCAN GODS   Etruscan artists looking eastward for inspiration were also greatly impressed by the art and architecture of Greece. But however eager they may have been to emulate Greek works, the distinctive Etruscan temperament always manifested itself. The vast majority of Archaic Etruscan artworks depart markedly from their prototypes. This is especially true of religious architecture, where the design of Etruscan temples superficially owes much to Greece but where the differences far outweigh the similarities. Because of the materials Etruscan architects employed, usually only the foundations of Etruscan temples have survived. These are nonetheless sufficient to reveal the plans of the edifices, and the archeological record is supplemented by the Roman architect Vitruvius's account of Etruscan temple design in his treatise on classical architecture written near the end of the first century B.C.

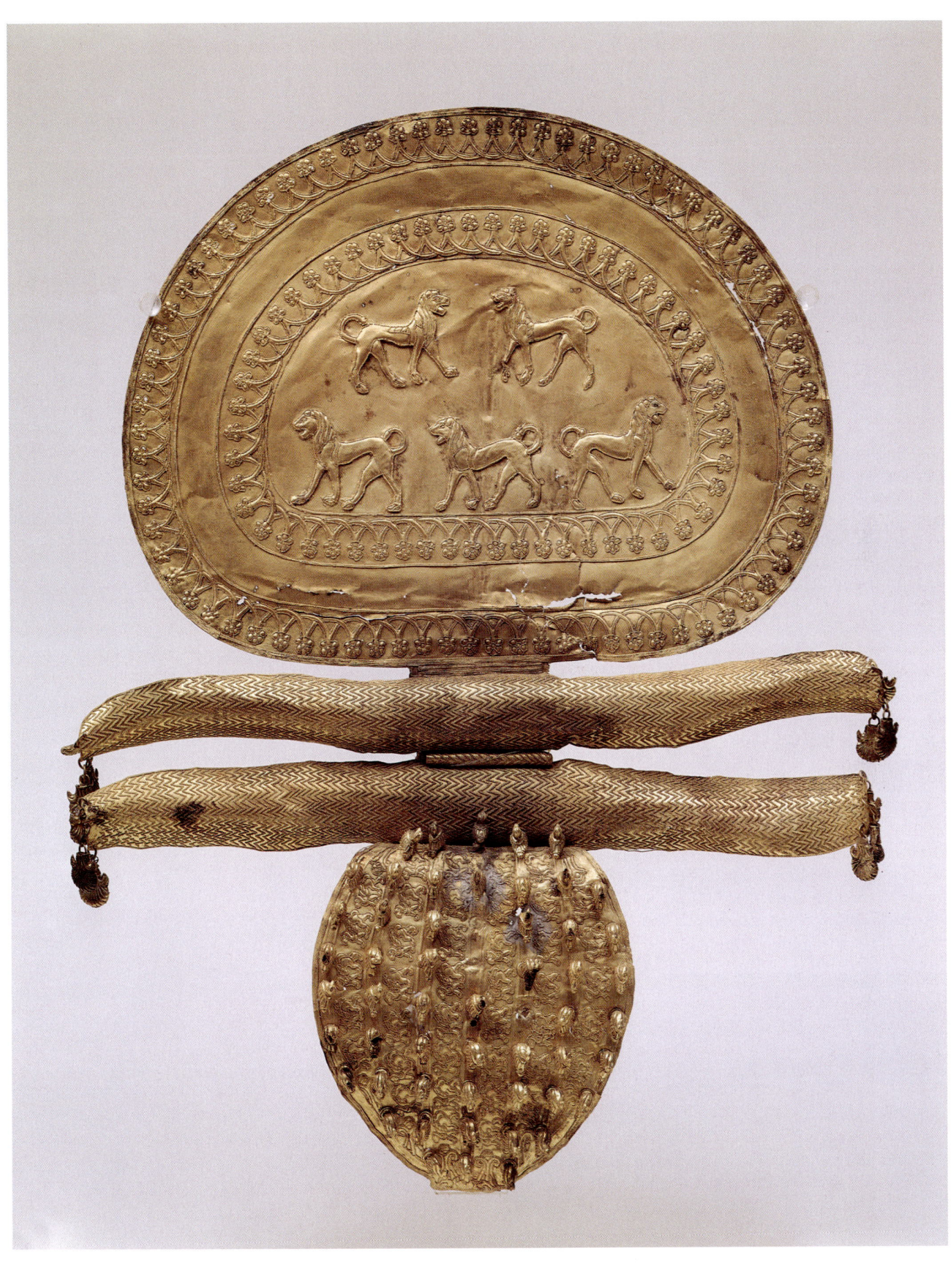

9-1 Fibula with Orientalizing lions, from the Regolini-Galassi Tomb, Cerveteri, Italy, ca. 650–640 B.C. Gold, approx. 1' $\frac{1}{2}$" high. Vatican Museums, Rome.

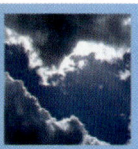

Etruscan Counterparts of Greco-Roman Gods and Heroes

Etruscan	*Greek*	*Roman*
Tinia	Zeus	Jupiter
Uni	Hera	Juno
Menrva	Athena	Minerva
Apulu	Apollo	Apollo
Artumes	Artemis	Diana
Hercle	Herakles	Hercules

The typical Archaic Etruscan temple (FIG. **9-2**) resembles the Greek gable-roofed temple, but it was constructed not of stone but of wood and sun-dried brick with terracotta decoration. Entrance was possible only via a narrow staircase at the center of the front of the temple, which sat on a high podium. Columns also were restricted to the building's front, creating a deep porch that occupied roughly half of the podium, setting off one side of the structure as the main side. This was contrary to Greek practice, where the temple's front and rear were indistinguishable and where steps accompanied the peripteral colonnades on all sides. (It is also one of the important features of Etruscan temple design the Romans retained; see Chapter 10.) The Etruscan temple was not meant to be seen as a sculptural mass from the outside and from all directions, as the Greek temple was, but instead was intended to function primarily as an ornate home for grand statues of Etruscan gods. It was a place of shelter, protected by its roof's wide overhang.

Etruscan temples differed in other ways from those of Greece. Etruscan (or *Tuscan*) columns resembled Greek Doric columns, but they were made of wood, were unfluted, and had bases. Because of the lightness of the superstructure they had to support, Etruscan columns were, as a rule, much more widely spaced than Greek columns. Unlike their Greek counterparts, Etruscan temples frequently had three cellas—one

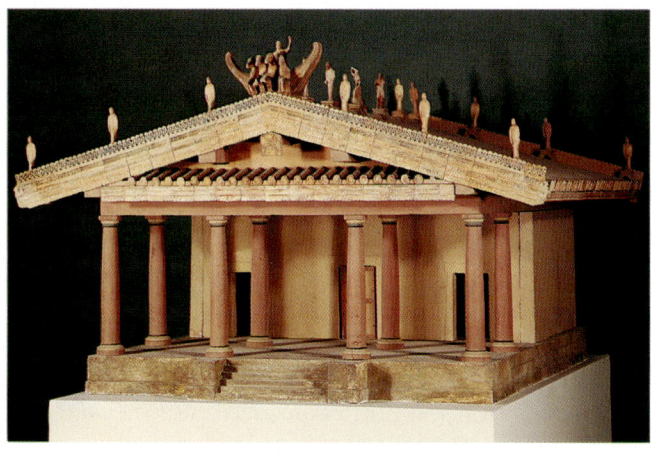

9-2 Model of a typical Etruscan temple of the sixth century B.C., as described by Vitruvius. Istituto di Etruscologia e di Antichità Italiche, Università di Roma, Rome.

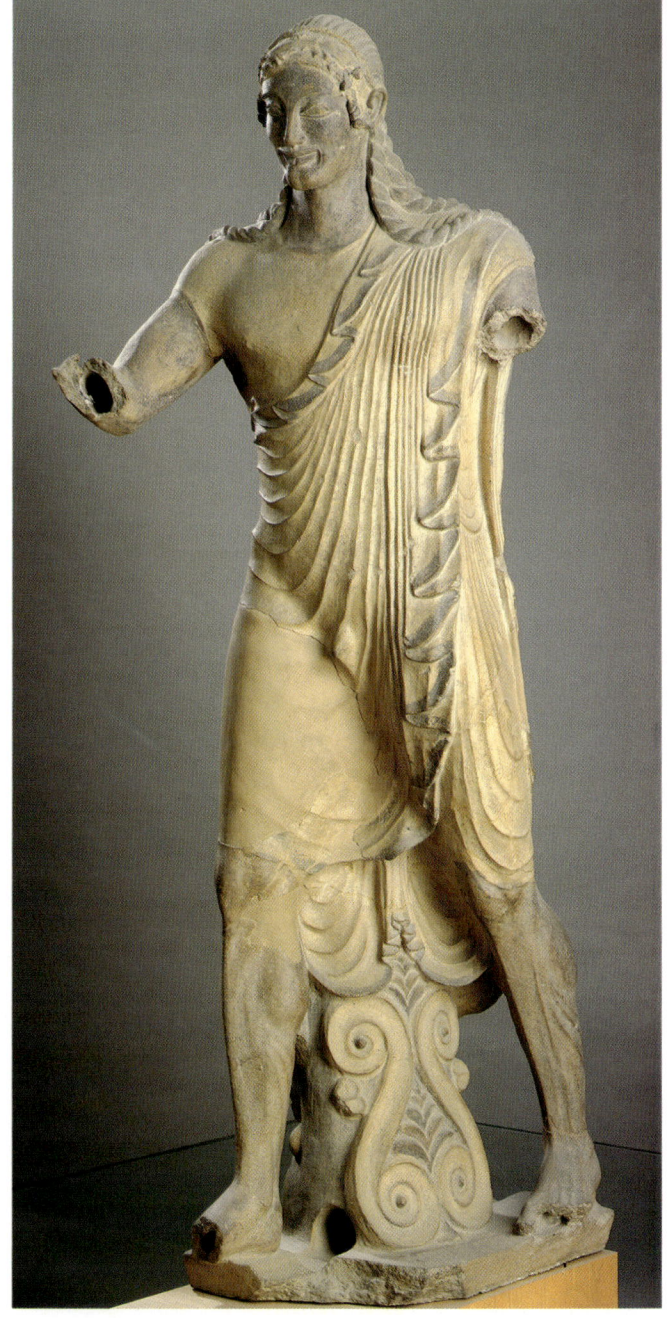

9-3 Apulu (Apollo), from the roof of the Portonaccio Temple, Veii, Italy, ca. 510–500 B.C. Painted terracotta, approx. 5′ 11″ high. Museo Nazionale di Villa Giulia, Rome.

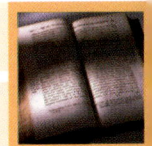

Etruscan Artists in Rome

In 616 B.C., according to the traditional chronology, Tarquinius Priscus of Tarquinia became Rome's first Etruscan king. He ruled for almost forty years. His grandson, Tarquinius Superbus ("the Arrogant"), was Rome's last king, driven out in 509 B.C. by Romans outraged by his tyrannical behavior. Before his expulsion, however, Tarquinius Superbus embarked on a grand program to embellish the modest city of huts Romulus had presided over two centuries before.

The king's most ambitious undertaking was the erection of a magnificent temple on the Capitoline Hill for the joint worship of Jupiter, Juno, and Minerva. For this great commission, he summoned architects, sculptors, and workers from all over Etruria. Rome's first great religious shrine was Etruscan in patronage, in manufacture, and in form. The architect's name is unknown, but several sources preserve the identity of the Etruscan sculptor brought in to adorn the temple. His name was Vulca of Veii. Pliny the Elder describes his works as "the finest images of deities of that era . . . more admired than gold."[1] The Romans entrusted Vulca with making the statue of Jupiter that stood in the central of the Capitoline temple's three cellas. He also fashioned the enormous terracotta statuary group of Jupiter in a four-horse chariot placed on the temple's roof at the highest point directly over the facade's center. The fame of Vulca's red-faced (painted terracotta) portrayal of

Jupiter was so great that Roman generals would paint their faces red in emulation of his Jupiter when they paraded in triumph through Rome after a battlefield victory. (One can get an approximate idea of the appearance of this early Jupiter temple and of Vulca's roof statue from the model reproduced in FIG. 9-2.)

One story told about Vulca's chariot group underscores both its tremendous size and the reverent awe later generations held for it. Terracotta statuary normally condenses and contracts in the furnace as the clay's moisture evaporates in the heating process. Vulca's statue swelled instead, and it only could be removed from the furnace by dismantling its walls and lifting off its roof.[2]

Vulca is the only Etruscan artist named by any ancient writer, but the signatures of other Etruscan artists appear on surviving artworks. One of these is Novios Plautios, who also worked in Rome, although a few centuries later (see FIG. 9-12). By then the Etruscan kings of Rome were a distant memory and the Romans had captured Veii and annexed its territory.

[1] Pliny, *Natural History*, 35.157.

[2] Plutarch, *Life of Poplicola,* 13.

---

for each of their chief gods, Tinia, Uni, and Menrva (see "Etruscan Counterparts of Greco-Roman Gods and Heroes," page 234). And pedimental statuary was exceedingly rare in Etruria. Narrative statuary—in terracotta instead of stone—normally was placed on the peaks of Etruscan temple roofs.

AN EPIC CONTEST ON A ROOFTOP The finest of these rooftop statues to survive today is the life-size image of Apulu (FIG. **9-3**), a brilliant example of the energy and excitement that characterizes Archaic Etruscan art in general. The statue comes from a temple in the Portonaccio sanctuary at Veii. It is but one of a group of at least four painted terracotta figures that adorned the top of the temple's roof. The god confronts Hercle for possession of the Ceryneian hind, a wondrous beast with golden horns that was sacred to Apulu's sister Artumes. The bright paint and the rippling folds of Apulu's garment call to mind the Ionian korai of the Acropolis (see FIG. 5-12). But this vital figure's extraordinary force, huge swelling contours, plunging motion, gesticulating arms, fanlike calf muscles, and animated face are distinctly Etruscan. Some scholars have attributed the Apulu to VULCA OF VEII, the most famous Etruscan sculptor of the time (see "Etruscan Artists in Rome," above). The statue's discovery in 1916 was instrumental in prompting a reevaluation of the originality of Etruscan art.

DINING IN THE AFTERLIFE Although life-size terracotta statuary was known in Greece, this medium was especially favored in Etruria. Another magnificent example of Archaic Etruscan terracotta sculpture is the sarcophagus in the form of a husband and wife reclining on a banqueting couch (FIG. **9-4**) from a tomb in the Cerveteri necropolis. The work was cast in four sections and then joined. It had no parallel in Greece, which, at this date, had no monumental tombs to house such sarcophagi. The Greeks buried their dead in simple graves marked by a stele or a statue. Moreover, although banquets were commonly depicted on Greek vases (which, by the late sixth century B.C., the Etruscans imported in great quantities and regularly deposited in their tombs), only men dined at Greek symposia. The image of a husband and wife sharing the same banqueting couch is uniquely Etruscan (see "The 'Audacity' of Etruscan Women," page 236).

The man and woman on the Cerveteri sarcophagus are as animated as the Apulu of Veii (FIG. **9-3**), even though they are at rest. They are the antithesis of the stiff and formal figures encountered in Egyptian tomb sculptures (compare the portraits of Menkaure and Khamerernebty from Gizeh, FIG. 3-13). Also typically Etruscan, and in striking contrast to contemporary Greek statues with their emphasis on proportion and balance, is how the Cerveteri sculptor rendered the upper and lower parts of each body. The legs were only summarily modeled, and the transition to the torso at the waist is

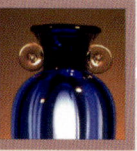

The "Audacity" of Etruscan Women

At the instigation of the emperor Augustus at the end of the first century B.C., Titus Livy wrote a history of Rome from its legendary founding in 753 B.C. to his own day. In the first book of his great work, Livy recounted the tale of Tullia, daughter of Servius Tullius, an Etruscan king of Rome in the sixth century B.C. The princess had married the less ambitious of two brothers of the royal Tarquinius family, while her sister had married the bolder of the two princes. Together, Tullia and her brother-in-law, Tarquinius Superbus, arranged for the murder of their spouses. They then married each other and plotted the overthrow and death of Tullia's father. After the king's murder, Tullia ostentatiously drove her carriage over her father's corpse, spraying herself with his blood. (The Roman road where the evil deed occurred is still called the Street of Infamy.) Livy, while condemning Tullia's actions, nonetheless placed them in the context of the famous "audacity" of Etruscan women.

The independent spirit and relative freedom women enjoyed in Etruscan society similarly horrified (and threatened) other Greco-Roman male authors. The stories the fourth-century B.C. Greek historian Theopompus heard about the debauchery of Etruscan women appalled him. Etruscan women epitomized immorality for Theopompus, but much of what he reported is untrue. Etruscan women did not, for example, exercise naked alongside Etruscan men. But archeological evidence confirms the accuracy of at least one of his "slurs": Etruscan women did attend banquets and recline with their husbands on a common couch (FIGS. 9-4 and 9-8). Aristotle also remarked on this custom. It was so foreign to the Greeks that it both shocked and frightened them. Only men, boys, slave girls, and prostitutes attended Greek symposia. The wives remained at home, excluded from most aspects of public life. In Etruscan Italy, in striking contrast to contemporary Greece, women also regularly attended sporting events with men. This, too, is well documented in paintings and reliefs.

Etruscan inscriptions also reflect the higher status of women in Etruria than in Greece. They often give the names of both the father and mother of the person commemorated (FIG. 9-15), a practice unheard of in Greece (witness the grave stele of "Hegeso, daughter of Proxenos," FIG. 5-55). Etruscan women, moreover, retained their own names and could legally own property independent of their husbands. The frequent inscriptions on Etruscan mirrors and other toilet items (FIG. 9-12) buried with women seem to attest to a high degree of female literacy as well.

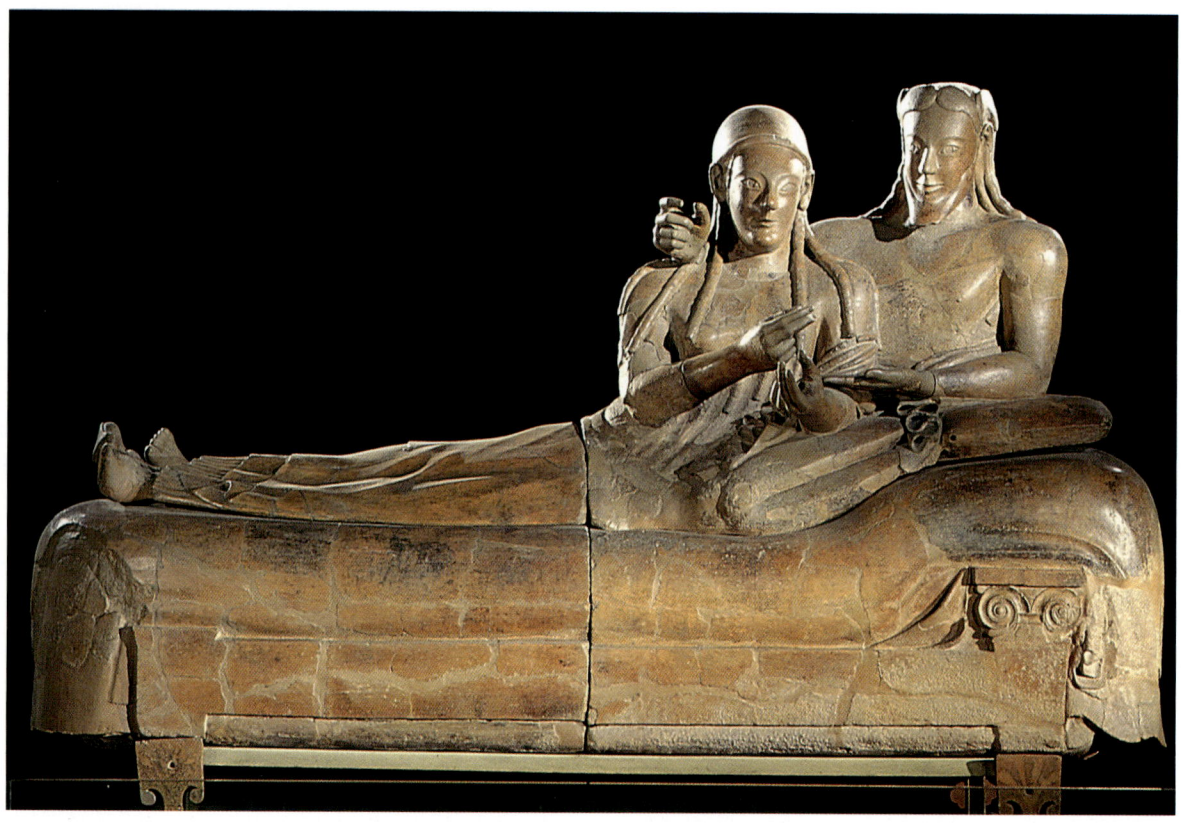

9-4   Sarcophagus with reclining couple, from Cerveteri, Italy, ca. 520 B.C. Painted terracotta, approx. 3′ 9½″ high. Museo Nazionale di Villa Giulia, Rome.

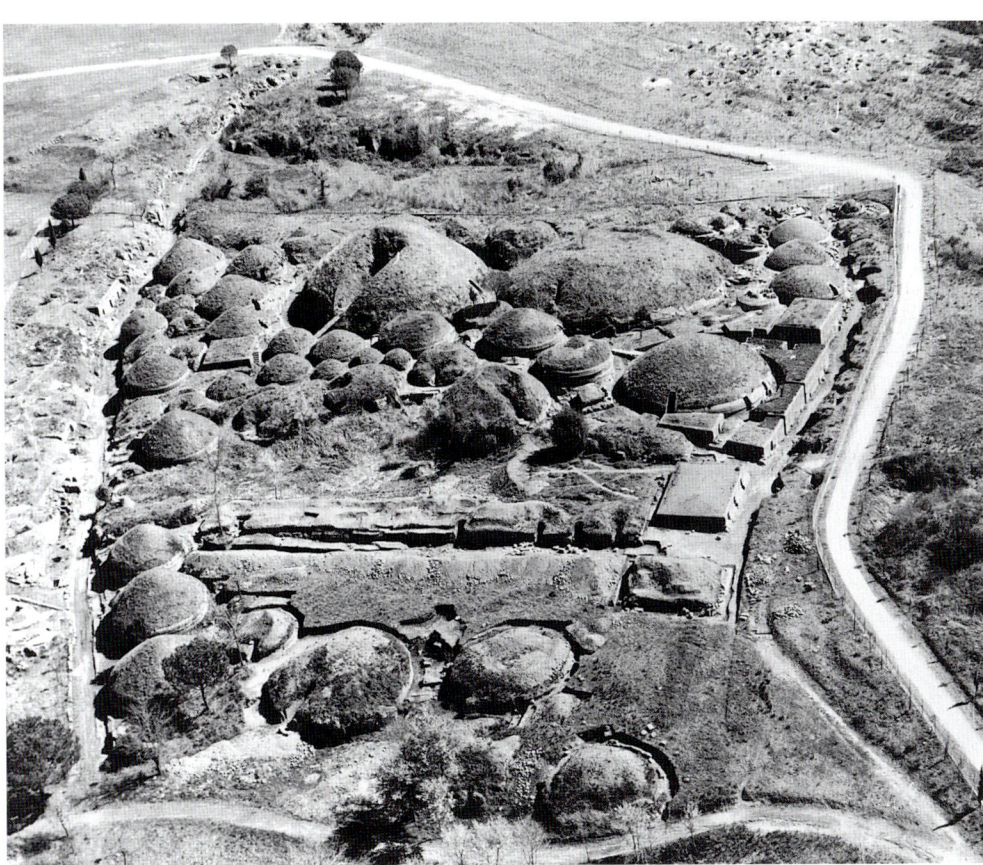

9-5   Aerial view of Banditaccia necropolis, Cerveteri, Italy, seventh to second centuries B.C.

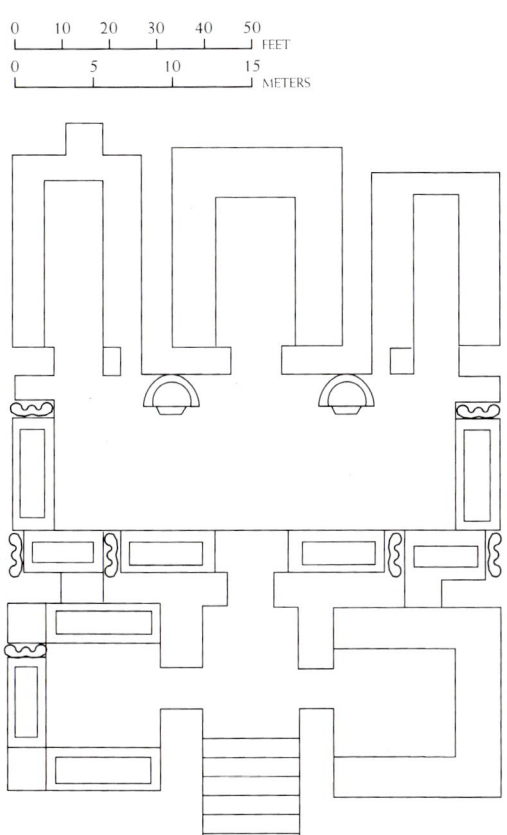

9-6   Plan of the Tomb of the Shields and Chairs, Cerveteri, Italy, second half of the sixth century B.C.

unnatural. The Etruscan artist's interest focused on the upper half of the figures, especially on the vibrant faces and gesticulating arms. Gestures are still an important ingredient of Italian conversation today, and the Cerveteri banqueters and the Veii Apulu speak to viewers in a way Greek statues of similar date, with their closed contours and calm demeanor, never do.

HOUSES FOR THE DEAD   The exact findspot of the Cerveteri sarcophagus is not known, but the kind of tomb that housed such sarcophagi is well documented. The typical tomb at Cerveteri and in other Etruscan cemeteries took the form of a mound, or *tumulus* (plural *tumuli;* FIG. 9-5), not unlike the Mycenaean Treasury of Atreus (see FIG. 4-21). But whereas the Mycenaean tholos tomb was constructed of masonry blocks and then covered by an earthen mound, each Etruscan tumulus covered one or more subterranean multichambered tombs cut out of the dark local limestone called *tufa*. These burial mounds sometimes reached colossal size with diameters in excess of one hundred and thirty feet. They were arranged in cemeteries in an orderly manner along a network of streets and produced the effect of veritable cities of the dead (which is the literal meaning of the Greek word *necropolis*), always located some distance from the cities of the living.

The underground tomb chambers cut into the rock resembled the houses of the living. In the plan of the sixth-century B.C. Tomb of the Shields and Chairs at Cerveteri (FIG. 9-6), for example, the central entrance and the smaller chambers opening onto a large central space mirror the axial sequence of rooms in actual Etruscan houses of the time. (The plan is also similar to that of early Roman houses, which, like Roman

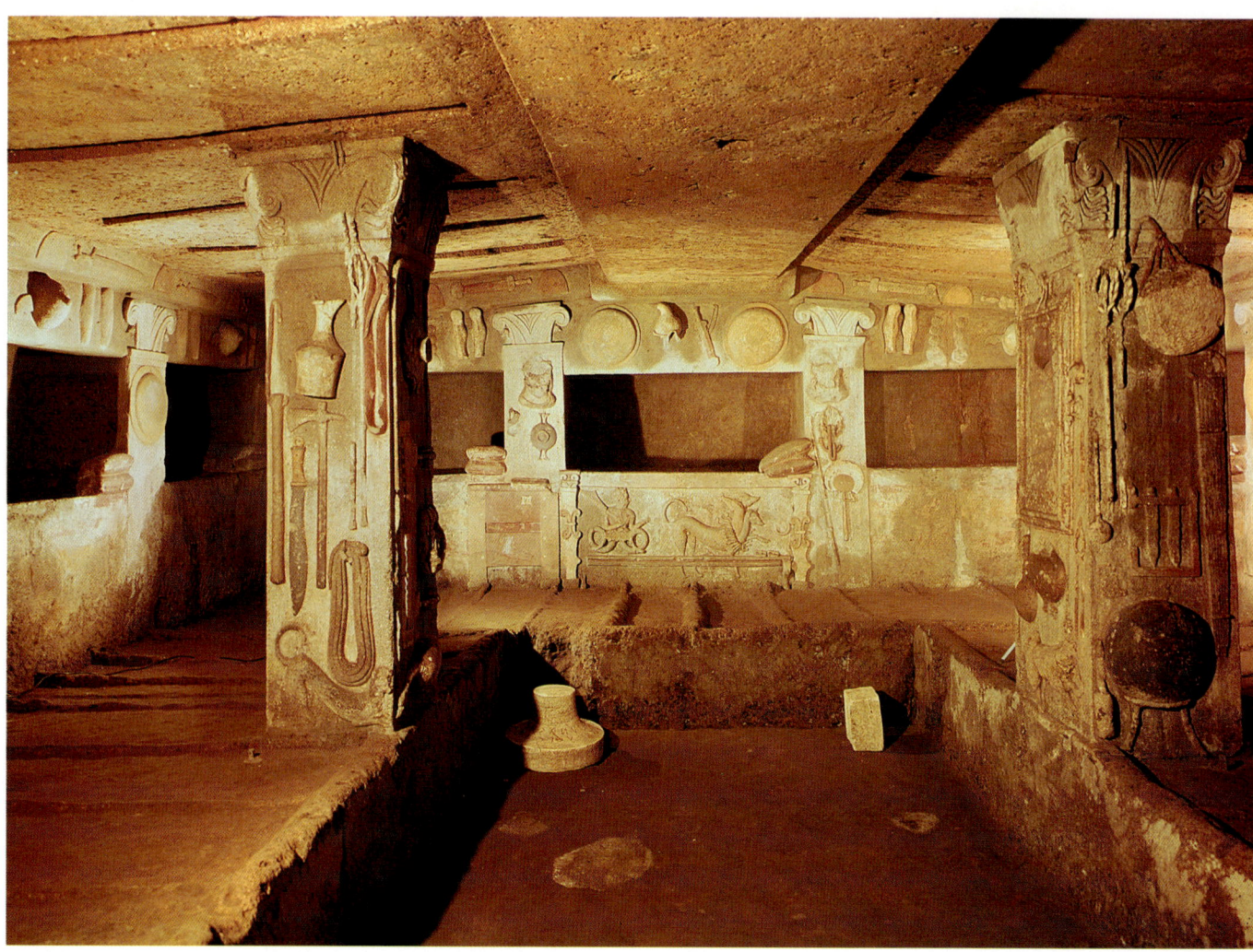

9-7   Interior of the Tomb of the Reliefs, Cerveteri, Italy, third century B.C.

temples, show the deep influence of Etruscan design; see "The Roman House," Chapter 10, page 255.) The effect of a domestic interior was enhanced by cutting out of the rock a series of beds and grand armchairs with curved backs and footstools (clearly visible on the plan), as well as ceiling beams, framed doorways, and even windows. The technique recalls that of the rock-cut Egyptian tombs at Beni Hasan (see FIG. 3-19). One cannot help but notice the very different values of the Etruscans, whose temples no longer stand because they were constructed of wood and mud brick but whose grand subterranean tombs are as permanent as the bedrock itself, versus the Greeks, who employed stone for the shrines of their gods but only rarely built monumental tombs for their dead.

The most elaborate of the Cerveteri underground tombs, in decoration if not in plan, is the so-called Tomb of the Reliefs (FIG. 9-7). Like the much earlier Tomb of the Shields and Chairs, it accommodated several generations of a single family. The walls and piers of this tomb were, as usual, gouged out of the tufa bedrock, but in this instance brightly painted stucco reliefs covered the stone. The stools, mirrors, drinking cups, pitchers, and knives effectively suggest a domestic context, underscoring the connection between Etruscan houses of the dead and those of the living.

A TOMB GUARDED BY PAINTED LEOPARDS
Large underground burial chambers hewn out of the natural

rock were also the norm at Tarquinia. But tumuli do not cover the Tarquinian tombs, and the interiors do not have carvings imitating the appearance of Etruscan houses. In some cases, however, paintings decorate the tomb chamber walls. Painted tombs are statistically rare, the privilege of only the wealthiest Etruscan families. Nevertheless, archeologists have discovered so many at Tarquinia since they began to use periscopes to explore tomb contents from the surface before considering time-consuming and costly excavation that art historians have an almost unbroken record of monumental painting in Etruria from Archaic to Hellenistic times.

A characteristic example dating to the early fifth century B.C. is the Tomb of the Leopards (FIG. 9-8), named for the beasts that guard the painted chamber's interior from their perch within the rear wall pediment. They are reminiscent of the panthers on each side of Medusa in the pediment of the Archaic Greek Temple of Artemis at Corfu (see FIG. 5-15). But mythological figures, whether Greek or Etruscan, are uncommon in Tarquinian murals, and the Tomb of the Leopards has none. Instead, banqueting couples (the men with dark skin, the women with light skin in conformity with the age-old convention) adorn the walls—painted versions of the terracotta sarcophagus from Cerveteri (FIG. 9-4). Pitcher- and cupbearers serve them, and musicians playing double pipes and the seven-stringed lyre entertain them. The banquet takes place in the open air or perhaps in a tent set up for the occasion. In characteristic Etruscan fashion,

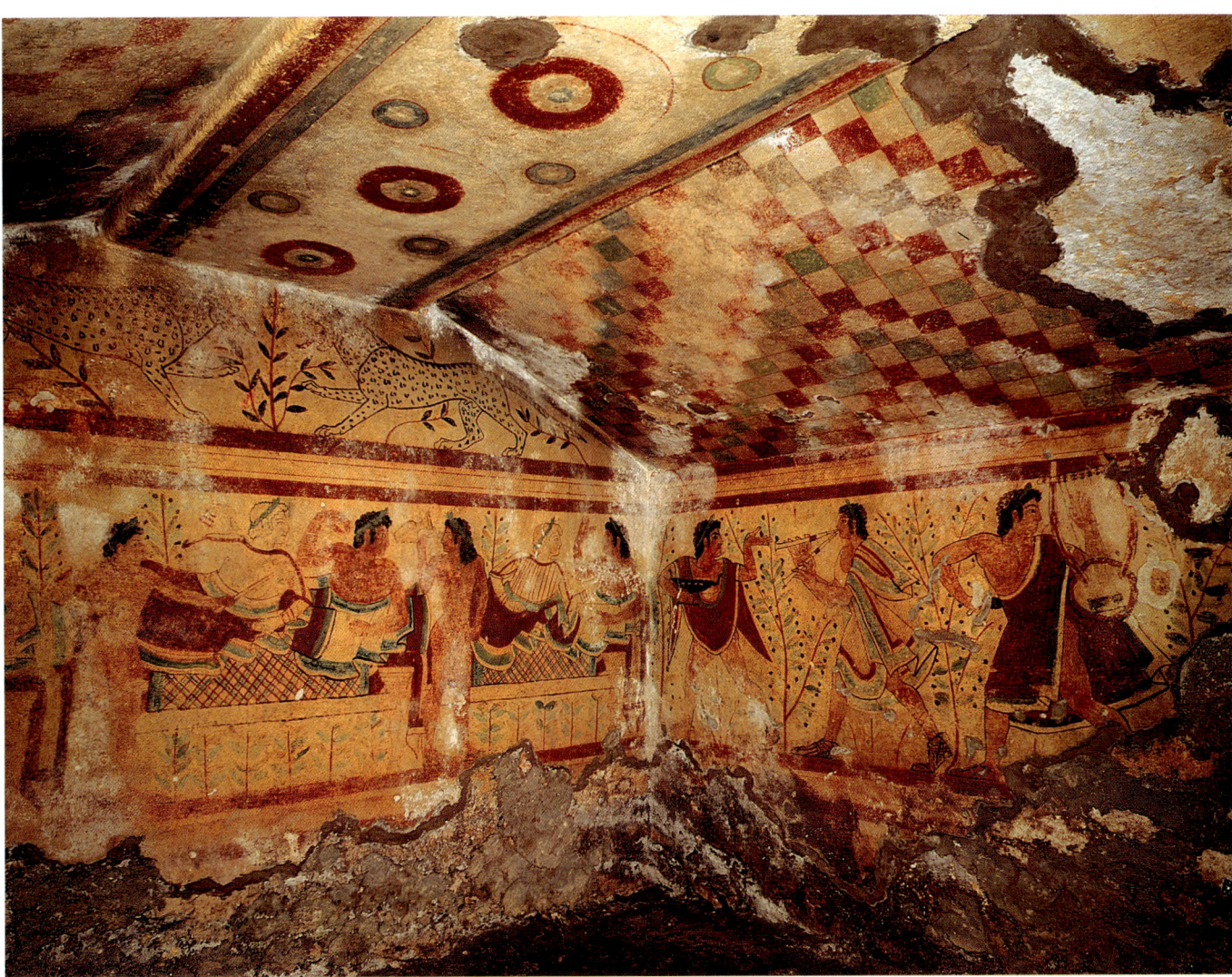

9-8   Banqueters and musicians, detail of mural paintings in the Tomb of the Leopards, Tarquinia, Italy, ca. 480–470 B.C.

the banqueters, servants, and entertainers all make exaggerated gestures with unnaturally enlarged hands. The man on the couch at the far right on the rear wall holds up an egg, the symbol of regeneration. The tone is joyful, a celebration of life, food, wine, music, and dance, rather than a somber contemplation of death.

ETRUSCAN LANDSCAPES   In stylistic terms the Etruscan figures are comparable to those on sixth-century Greek vases before Late Archaic painters became preoccupied with the problem of foreshortening. Etruscan painters may be considered somewhat backward in this respect, but in other ways they seem to have outpaced their counterparts in Greece, especially in their interest in rendering nature. In the Tomb of the Leopards, the landscape is but a few trees and shrubs placed between the entertainers (and leopards) and behind the banqueting couches. But elsewhere the natural environment was the chief interest of the Tarquinian painter.

Scenes of Etruscans enjoying the pleasures of nature decorate all the walls of the main chamber of the aptly named Tomb of Hunting and Fishing at Tarquinia. In our detail (FIG. **9-9**), a youth dives off a rocky promontory, while others fish from a boat. On another wall youthful hunters aim their slingshots at brightly painted birds. The scenes of hunting and fishing recall the painted reliefs in the Old Kingdom Egyptian Tomb of Ti (see FIG. 3-16) and the mural paintings from the New Kingdom Tomb of Nebamun (see FIG. 3-30) and may indicate knowledge of this Egyptian funerary tradition. The multicolored rocks may be compared to those of the Aegean *Spring Fresco* from Thera (see FIG. 4-10), but art historians know of nothing similar in contemporary Greek art save the Tomb of the Diver at Paestum (see FIG. 5-59). The latter is, however, exceptional and from a Greek tomb in *Italy* about a half century *later* than the Tarquinian tomb. In fact, it is likely the Paestum composition emulated older Etruscan designs, undermining the now outdated art historical judgment that Etruscan art was merely derivative and that Etruscan artists never set the standard for Greek artists.

LATER ETRUSCAN ART

The fifth century B.C. was a golden age in Greece but not in Etruria. In 509 B.C., the Romans expelled the last of their Etruscan kings, Tarquinius Superbus (see "Etruscan Artists in Rome," page 235), replacing the monarchy with a republican form of government. In 474 B.C., an alliance of Cumaean Greeks and Hieron I of Syracuse (on Sicily) defeated the Etruscan fleet off Cumae, effectively ending Etruscan dominance of the seas and with it Etruscan prosperity. These events had important consequences in the world of art and architecture. The number of Etruscan tombs, for example, decreased sharply, and the quality of the furnishings declined markedly.

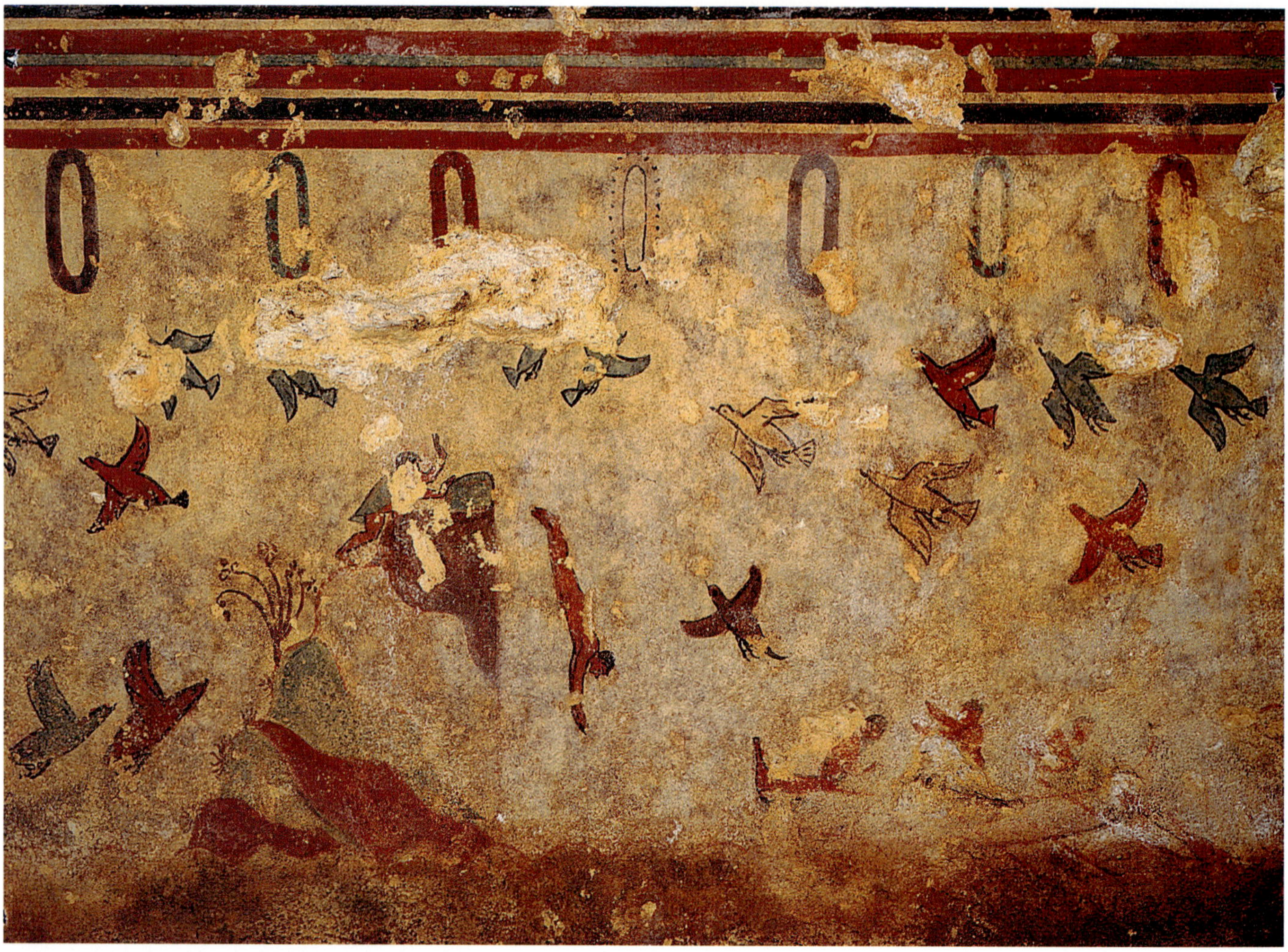

9-9 Diving and fishing, detail of mural paintings in the Tomb of Hunting and Fishing, Tarquinia, Italy, ca. 530–520 B.C.

No longer were tumuli filled with golden jewelry and imported Greek vases or mural paintings of the first rank. But Etruscan art did not cease. Indeed, in the areas Etruscan artists excelled in, especially the casting of statues in bronze and terracotta, they continued to produce impressive works, even if fewer in number.

Classical Art

MYTHICAL ETRUSCAN ANIMALS   The best-known of these later Etruscan statues—one of the most memorable portrayals of an animal in the history of world art—is the *Capitoline Wolf* (FIG. **9-10**). The statue is a somewhat larger-than-life-size hollow-cast bronze portrayal of the she-wolf that, according to ancient legend, nursed Romulus and Remus after they were abandoned as infants. When the twins grew to adulthood, they quarreled and Romulus killed his brother. Romulus founded Rome on April 21, 753 B.C. on the Palatine Hill and became the city's king. The statue of the she-wolf seems to have been made, however, for the new Roman Republic after the expulsion of Tarquinius Superbus. It became the new state's totem. The appropriately defiant image has remained the emblem of Rome to this day.

The *Capitoline Wolf* is not, however, a work of Roman art, which had not yet developed a distinct identity, but the product of an Etruscan workshop. (The suckling infants are

additions of Renaissance date and are probably the work of Antonio Pollaiuolo.) The vitality noted in the human figure in Etruscan art is here concentrated in the tense, watchful animal body of the she-wolf, with her spare flanks, gaunt ribs, and taut, powerful legs. The lowered neck and head, alert ears, glaring eyes, and ferocious muzzle capture the psychic intensity of the fierce and protective beast as danger ap-

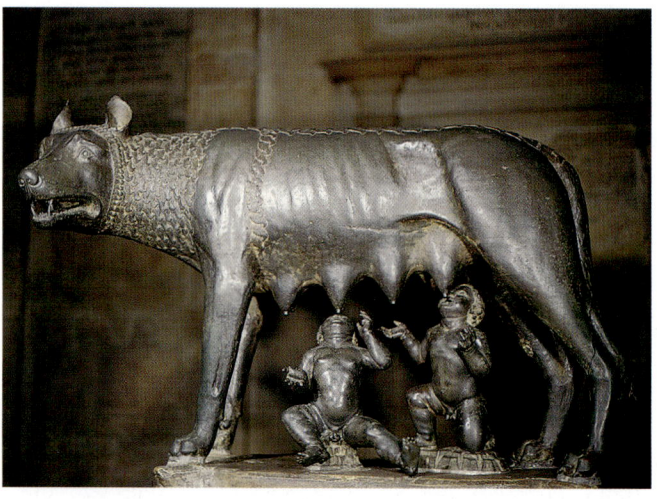

9-10 *Capitoline Wolf,* from Rome, Italy, ca. 500–480 B.C. Bronze, approx. 2′ 7½″ high. Palazzo dei Conservatori, Rome.

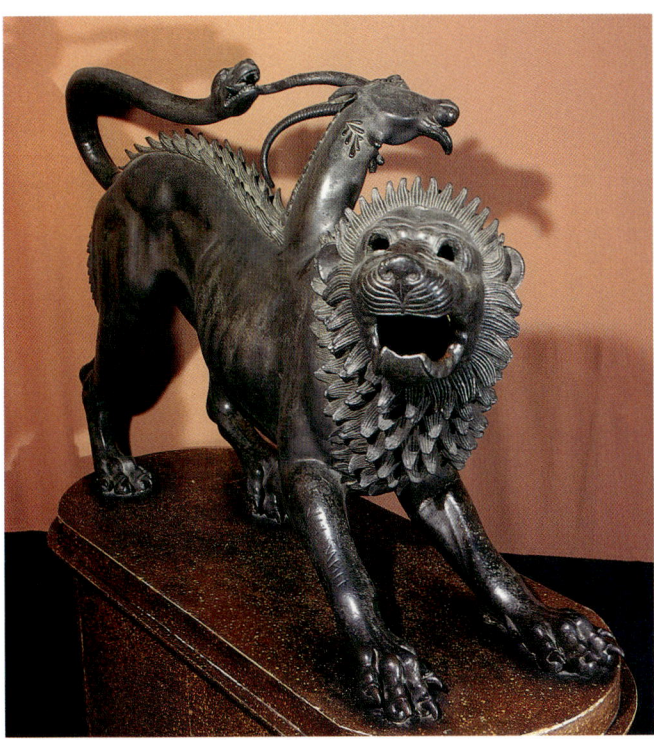

9-11 *Chimera of Arezzo,* from Arezzo, Italy, first half of fourth century B.C. Bronze, approx. 2′ 7½″ high. Museo Archeologico Nazionale, Florence.

proaches. Not even the great animal reliefs of Assyria (see FIG. 2-25) match, much less surpass, this profound rendering of animal temper.

Another masterpiece of Etruscan animal sculpture, found in 1553 and greatly admired during the Renaissance, is the bronze *Chimera of Arezzo* (FIG. **9-11**), which dates about a century later than the *Capitoline Wolf.* The chimera is a monster of Greek invention with a lion's head and body and a serpent's tail. A second head, that of a goat, grows out of the lion's left side and bears the wound inflicted by the Greek hero Bellerophon, who hunted and slew the composite beast. As rendered by the Etruscan sculptor, the chimera, although injured and bleeding, is nowhere near defeated. Like the earlier she-wolf statue, the chimera's muscles are stretched tightly over its rib cage. It prepares to attack, and a ferocious cry emanates from its open jaws. Some scholars have postulated that the statue was part of a group that originally included Bellerophon, but the chimera could have just as well stood alone. The menacing gaze upward toward an unseen adversary need not have been answered. In this respect, too, the chimera is in the tradition of the guardian nurse of Romulus and Remus.

Etruscan Art and the Rise of Rome

ROME OVERWHELMS ETRURIA At about the time the *Chimera of Arezzo* was fashioned, Rome began to appropriate Etrus-can territory. Veii fell to the Romans in 396 B.C., after a terrible ten-year siege. Peace was concluded with Tarquinia in 351 B.C., but by the beginning of the next century, Tarquinia, too, was annexed by Rome, and Cerveteri was conquered in 273 B.C. Rome's growing power in central Italy is indicated indirectly by the engraved inscription on the

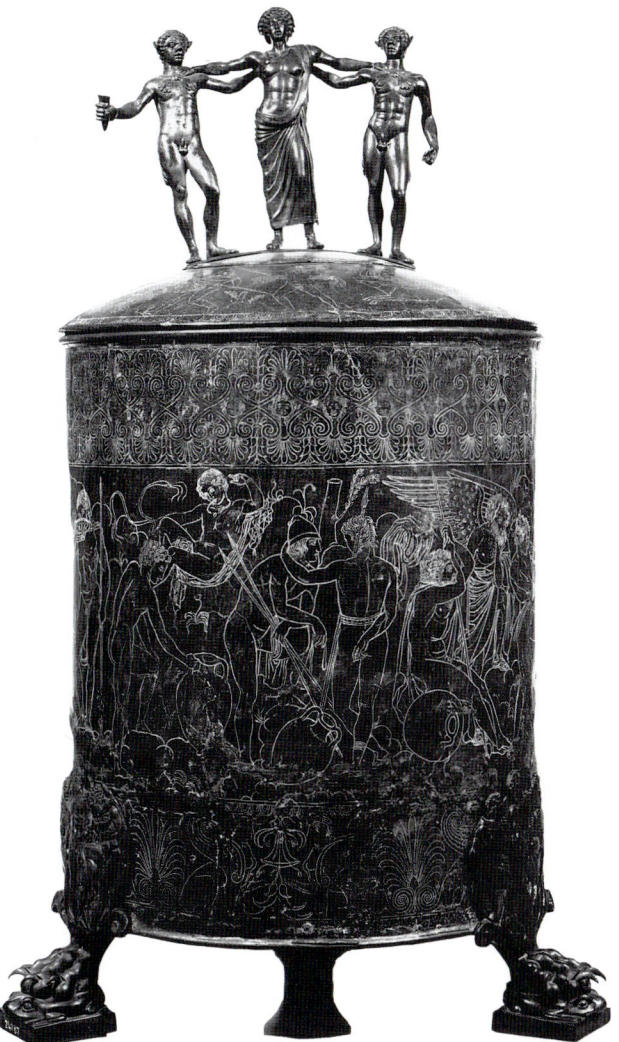

9-12 NOVIOS PLAUTIOS, *Ficoroni Cista,* from Palestrina, Italy, late fourth century B.C. Bronze, approx. 2′ 6″ high. Museo Nazionale di Villa Giulia, Rome.

Ficoroni Cista (FIG. **9-12**). Etruscan artists produced such *cistae* (cylindrical containers for a woman's toilet articles), made of sheet bronze with cast handles and feet and elaborately engraved bodies, in large numbers from the fourth century B.C. forward. Together with engraved bronze mirrors, they were popular gifts for both the living and the dead. The Etruscan bronze cista industry centered in Palestrina (ancient Praeneste), where the *Ficoroni Cista* was found. The inscription on the cista's handle states that Dindia Macolnia, a local noblewoman, deposited the bronze container in her daughter's tomb and that the artist was one NOVIOS PLAUTIOS. According to the inscription, his workshop was not in Palestrina but in Rome, which by this date was becoming an important Italian cultural, as well as political, center.

The engraved frieze of the *Ficoroni Cista* depicts an episode from the Greek story of the expedition of the Argonauts in search of the Golden Fleece. Scholars generally agree that the composition is an adaptation of a lost Greek panel painting, perhaps one on display in Rome—another testimony to the burgeoning wealth and prestige of the city once ruled by Etruscan kings. The Greek source for Novios Plautios's engraving is evident in the figures seen entirely from behind or in three-quarter view, and in the placement of the protagonists on several levels in the Polygnotan manner (see FIG. 5-57).

9-13 *Porta Marzia,* Perugia, Italy, second century B.C.

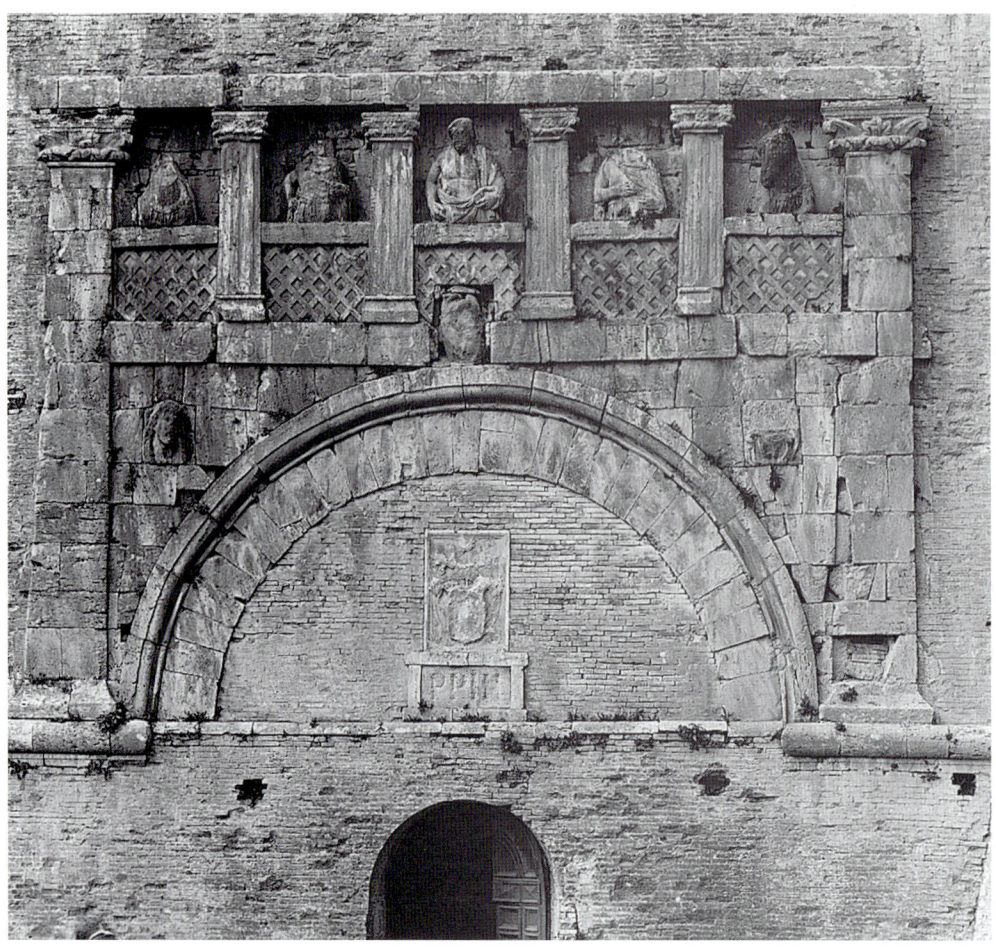

9-14 Sarcophagus of Lars Pulena, from Tarquinia, Italy, early second century B.C. Tufa, approx. 6′ 6″ long. Museo Archeologico Nazionale, Tarquinia.

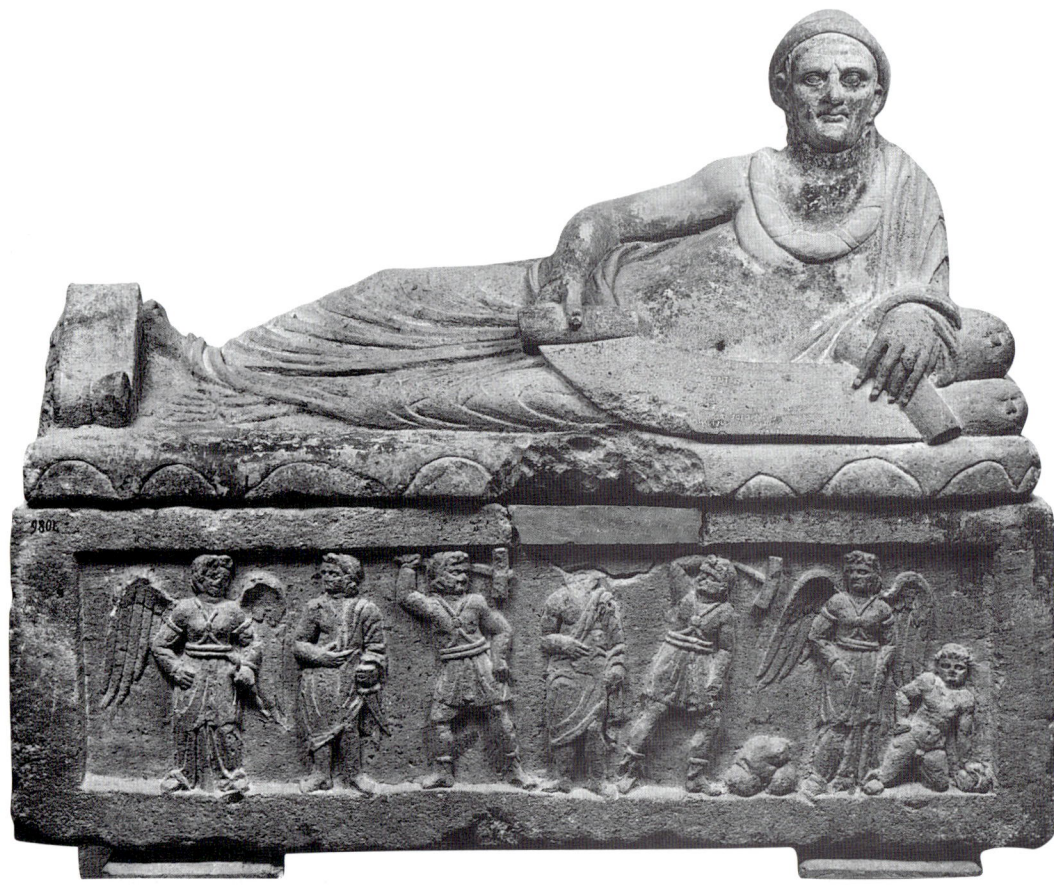

THE GATE OF MARS In the third century B.C., the Etruscan city of Perugia (ancient Perusia) formed an alliance with Rome and was spared the destruction Veii, Cerveteri, and other Etruscan towns suffered. Portions of Perugia's ancient walls are still standing, as are some of its gates. One of these, the so-called *Porta Marzia* (Gate of Mars), was dismantled by the Renaissance architect Antonio da Sangallo, but the gate's upper part is preserved, imbedded in a later wall (FIG. 9-13). The *arcuated* opening is formed by a series of trapezoidal stone *voussoirs* held in place by pressing against each other (compare FIG. 4-18c). Such arches were built earlier in Greece as well as in Mesopotamia (see FIG. 2-26), but Italy, first under the Etruscans and later under the Romans, is where arcuated gateways and freestanding ("triumphal") arches became a major architectural type.

The *Porta Marzia* typifies the Etruscan adaptation of Greek motifs by using Hellenic-inspired pilasters to frame the rounded opening. Arches bracketed by engaged columns or pilasters have a long and distinguished history in Roman and later times. In the *Porta Marzia,* sculptured half-figures of Jupiter and his sons Castor and Pollux and their steeds look out from between the fluted pilasters. The divine twins had appeared miraculously on a battlefield in 484 B.C. to turn the tide in favor of the Romans. The presence of these three deities at the *Porta Marzia's* apex already may reflect the new Roman practice of erecting triumphal arches crowned by gilded bronze statues.

TORMENT IN THE UNDERWORLD In Hellenistic Etruria the descendants of the magnificent Archaic terracotta sarcophagus from Cerveteri (FIG. 9-4) were made of local stone and were carved rather than cast. The leading production center was Tarquinia, and that is where the sarcophagus of Lars Pulena (FIG. 9-14) was fashioned early in the second century B.C. and placed in his family's tomb. The deceased is shown in a reclining position, but he is not at a festive banquet, and his wife is not present. His expression is somber, a far cry from the smiling, confident faces of the Archaic era when Etruria enjoyed its greatest prosperity. Similar heads—realistic but generic types, not true portraits—are found on all later Etruscan sarcophagi and in tomb paintings. They are symptomatic of the economic and political decline of the once-mighty Etruscan city-states.

Also attesting to a gloomy assessment of the future is the theme chosen for the coffin proper. The deceased is shown in the underworld, attacked by two *Charuns* (Etruscan death demons) swinging lethal hammers. Above, on the lid, Lars Pulena exhibits a partially unfurled scroll inscribed with the record of his life's accomplishments. Lacking confidence in a happy afterlife, he dwells instead on the past.

THE END OF THE ETRUSCANS In striking contrast, the portrait of Aule Metele (FIG. 9-15) is a supremely self-confident image. He is portrayed as a magistrate raising his arm to address an assembly—hence his modern nickname *Arringatore (Orator).* The life-size bronze statue was discovered in 1566 near Lake Trasimene and is yet another Etruscan masterpiece known to Italian Renaissance sculptors. The statue of the orator proves that Etruscan artists continued to be experts at bronze-casting long after the heyday of Etruscan prosperity.

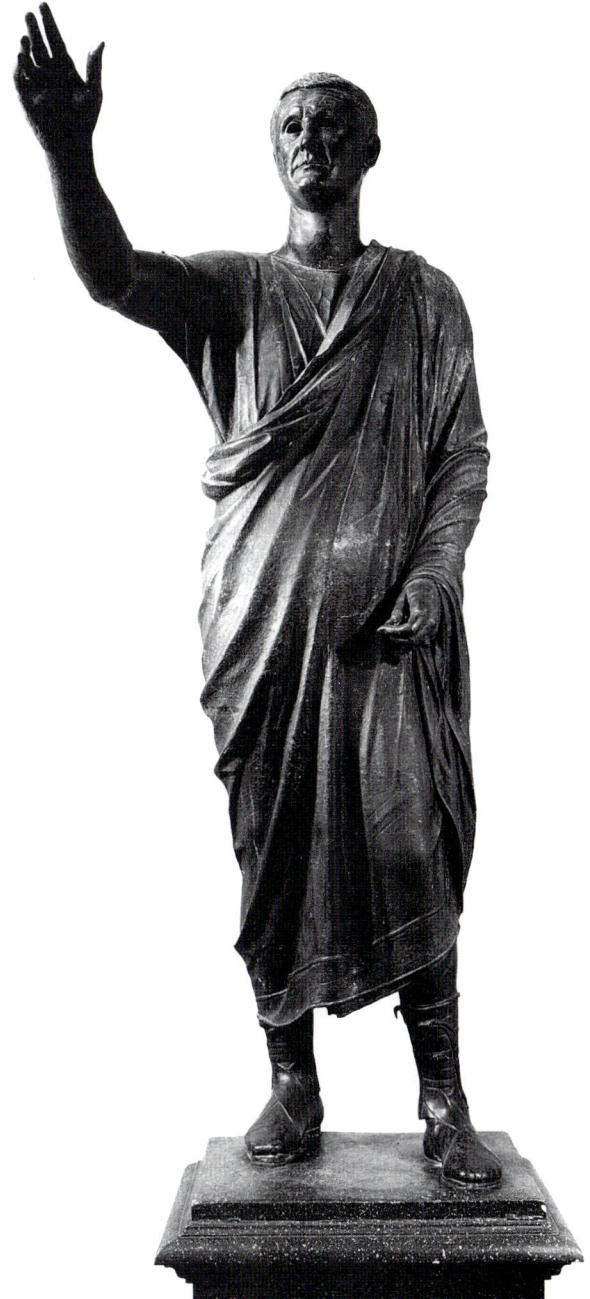

9-15 Aule Metele *(Arringatore, Orator),* from Sanguineto, near Lake Trasimene, Italy, early first century B.C. Bronze, approx. 5′ 7″ high. Museo Archeologico Nazionale, Florence.

The *Arringatore* was most likely produced at about the time that Roman hegemony over the Etruscans became total. The so-called Social War of the early first century B.C. ended in 89 B.C. with the conferring of Roman citizenship on all of Italy's inhabitants. In fact, Aule Metele—his Etruscan name and his father and mother's names are inscribed on his garment's hem—wears the short toga and high laced boots of a Roman magistrate. His head, with its close-cropped hair and signs of age in the face, resembles portraits produced in Rome at the time. This orator is Etruscan in name only. If the origin of the Etruscans remains debatable, the question of their demise has a ready answer. Aule Metele and his compatriots became Romans, and Etruscan art became Roman art.

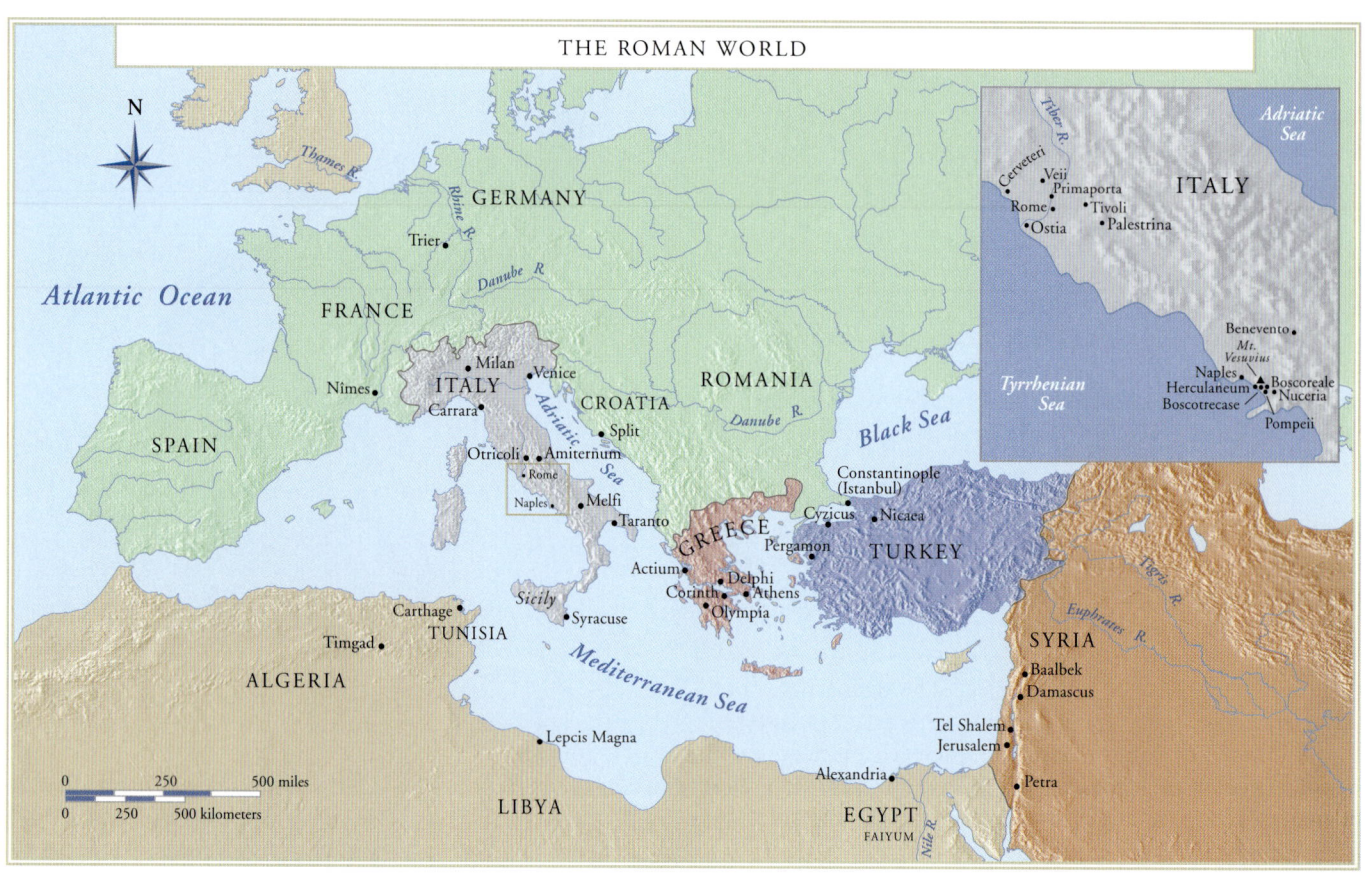

THE ROMAN WORLD

Adriatic Sea

ITALY

Cerveteri • Veii • Primaporta
Rome • Tivoli
Ostia • Palestrina

Tyrrhenian Sea

Benevento •
Mt. Vesuvius
Naples • Boscoreale
Herculaneum • Nuceria
Boscotrecase
Pompeii

Atlantic Ocean

Thames R.

GERMANY

Rhine R.

Trier

Danube R.

FRANCE

Nîmes

SPAIN

Milan
ITALY • Venice
Carrara

Adriatic Sea

CROATIA

Split

ROMANIA

Danube R.

Black Sea

Constantinople (Istanbul)

Otricoli • Amiternum
Rome
Naples • Melfi
Taranto

GREECE

Actium
Corinth • Delphi
Olympia • Athens

Pergamon

Cyzicus • Nicaea

TURKEY

Tigris R.

Euphrates R.

SYRIA

Baalbek
Damascus

Sicily
Syracuse

Carthage

TUNISIA

Timgad

ALGERIA

Mediterranean Sea

Lepcis Magna

Tel Shalem
Jerusalem

Petra

Alexandria

LIBYA

EGYPT
FAIYUM

Nile R.

N

0   250   500 miles
0   250   500 kilometers

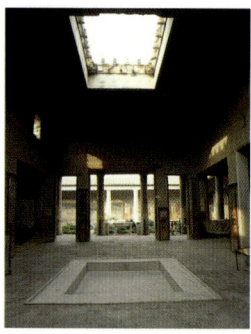

House of the Vettii, Pompeii second century B.C.

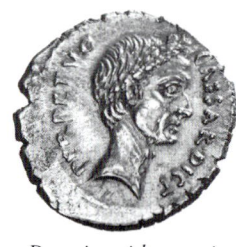

Denarius with portrait of Julius Caesar, 44 B.C.

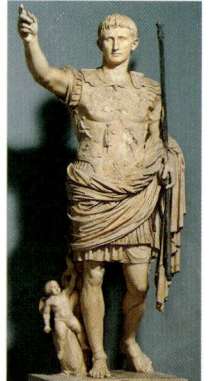

Portrait of Augustus from Primaporta, ca. 20 B.C.

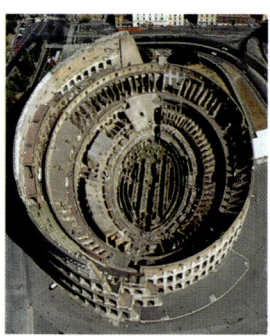

Colosseum, Rome ca. A.D. 70–80

Foundation of Rome by Romulus, 753 B.C.

Expulsion of Etruscan kings from Rome, 509 B.C.

Marcellus brings spoils of Syracuse to Rome, 211 B.C.

Roman conquest of Greece, 146 B.C.

Rome inherits kingdom of Pergamon, 133 B.C.

Foundation of Roman colony at Pompeii, 80 B.C.

Assassination of Julius Caesar, 44 B.C.

Battle of Actium, 31 B.C.

Augustus, r. 27 B.C.–A.D. 14

Vitruvius, *The Ten Books of Architecture*, ca. 25 B.C.

Vergil, 70–19 B.C.

Julio-Claudians, r. 14–68

Flavians, r. 69–96

Eruption of Mount Vesuvius, A.D. 79

10

FROM SEVEN HILLS TO THREE CONTINENTS

THE ART OF ANCIENT ROME

96		192		337
HIGH EMPIRE		LATE EMPIRE		

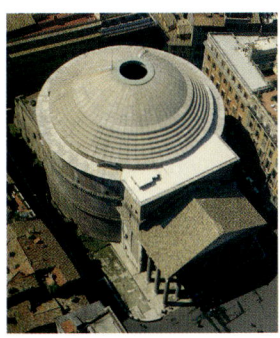

Pantheon, Rome
A.D. 118–125

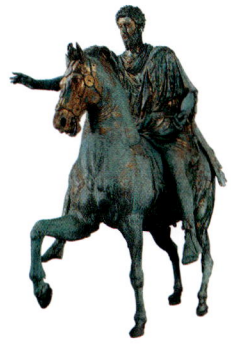

Equestrian statue
of Marcus Aurelius
ca. A.D. 175

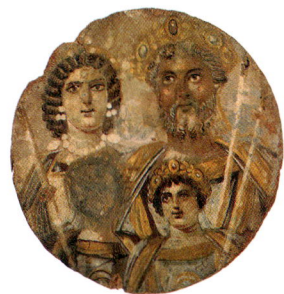

Painted portrait of
the Severan family
ca. A.D. 200

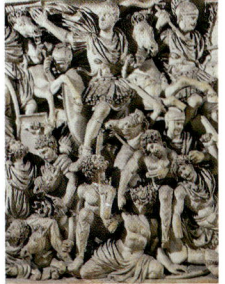

Ludovisi Battle
Sarcophagus
ca. A.D. 250–260

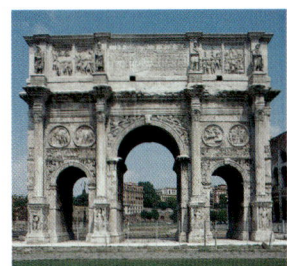

Arch of Constantine
Rome, A.D. 312–315

Trajan, r. 98–117

Hadrian, r. 117–138

Antonines, r. 138–192

Severans, r. 193–235

Soldier emperors, r. 235–284

Diocletian, r. 284–305

Constantine, r. 306–337

Edict of Milan, 313

Dedication of
Constantinople, 330

THE MIGHTY EMPIRE OF ROME

With the rise and triumph of Rome, a single government ruled, for the first time in human history, from the Tigris and Euphrates to the Thames and beyond, from the Rhine and Danube to the Nile. Within the Roman Empire's borders lived people of numerous races, religions, tongues, traditions, and cultures: Britons and Gauls, Greeks and Egyptians, Africans and Syrians, and Jews and Christians, to name only a very few. Of all the ancient civilizations, only the Roman approximates today's world in its multicultural character. Indeed, the Roman world is the bridge—in politics, the arts, and religion—between the ancient and the medieval and modern Western worlds.

ROMAN ART AND THE MODERN WORLD Roman monuments of art and architecture can be found throughout the vast territory the Romans governed and are the most conspicuous and numerous of all the remains of ancient civilization. An extraordinary number of these are part of the fabric of modern life and are not merely ruins that spark the curiosity of tourists, students, and scholars. In Rome, western Europe, Greece, the Middle East, and Africa today, Roman temples and basilicas have an afterlife as churches. The powerful concrete vaults of Roman theaters, baths, circuses, sanctuaries, and office buildings form the cores of modern houses, stores, restaurants, factories, and museums. Bullfights, sports events, operas, and rock concerts occur in Roman arenas and baths. Roman aqueducts continue to supply water to some modern towns. Ships dock in what were once Roman ports, and western Europe's highway system still closely follows the routes of Roman roads.

Even in North America, where no Roman remains exist save for the statues, paintings, mosaics, and other artworks imported by private collectors and museum curators, modern versions of famous Roman buildings such as the Pantheon (FIG. 10-48) may be found in cities and on college campuses. And Roman civilization lives on in the Western world in concepts of law and government, in languages, in calendars—even in the coins used daily. Indeed, Roman art speaks to contemporary Western viewers in a language almost everyone can readily understand. Its diversity and eclecticism foreshadowed the modern world. The Roman use of art, especially portraits and historical relief sculptures, to manipulate public opinion is similar to the carefully crafted imagery of contemporary political campaigns. And the Roman mastery of concrete construction began an architectural revolution still felt today.

FROM VILLAGE TO WORLD CAPITAL The far-flung Roman Empire centered on the city on the Tiber River that, according to legend, Romulus founded as a modest village of huts on April 21, 753 B.C. Nine hundred years later, Rome was the capital of the greatest empire the world had ever known, an empire with some fifty thousand miles of sea routes and expertly engineered highways for travel and commerce. Within its boundaries stood marble and concrete temples, theaters, baths, basilicas, arches, and palaces. Roman walls and ceilings were adorned with paintings and stucco reliefs, the floors covered with marble slabs and mosaics, and the niches and colonnades filled with statues. The imperial city of the second century A.D. awed foreign kings and even later Roman rulers. The historian Ammianus Marcellinus reported that when the emperor Constantius visited Rome in A.D. 357 and entered the Forum of Trajan (FIG. 10-41), he "stopped in his tracks, astonished" and marveled at the Forum's opulence and size, "which cannot be described by words and could never again be attempted by mortal men."[1]

THE REPUBLIC

KINGS, SENATORS, AND CONSULS Our story, however, begins long before Roman art and architecture embodied the imperial ideal of the Roman state, at a time when that "state" encompassed no territory beyond one of its famous seven hills. The Rome of Romulus in the eighth century B.C. comprised only small huts of wood, wattle, and daub, clustered together on the Palatine Hill overlooking what was then uninhabited marshland. In the Archaic period, as discussed in Chapter 9, Rome was essentially an Etruscan city, both politically and culturally. Its greatest shrine, the Temple of Jupiter Optimus Maximus (Best and Greatest) on the Capitoline Hill, was built by an Etruscan king, designed by an Etruscan architect, made of wood and mud brick in the Etruscan manner, and decorated with an Etruscan sculptor's terracotta statuary (see "Etruscan Artists in Rome," Chapter 9, page 235). Rome's earliest monumental art thus was, in all respects, Etruscan art.

In 509 B.C., Tarquinius Superbus, the last of Rome's Etruscan kings, was thrown out and constitutional government was established (see "An Outline of Roman History," page 247). The new Roman Republic vested power mainly in a *senate* (literally, "a council of elders, *senior* citizens") and in two elected *consuls*. Under extraordinary circumstances a *dictator* could be appointed for a specified time and a specific purpose, such as commanding the army during a crisis. All leaders came originally from among the wealthy landowners, or *patricians*, but later also from the *plebeian* class of small farmers, merchants, and freed slaves. Before long, the descendants of Romulus conquered Rome's neighbors one by one: the Etruscans and the Gauls to the north, the Samnites and the Greek colonists to the south. Even the Carthaginians of North Africa, who under Hannibal's dynamic leadership had annihilated some of Rome's legions and almost brought down the Republic, fell before the might of Roman armies.

THE CRAZE FOR GREEK ART For art historians, 211 B.C. was a turning point. An ambitious Roman general made a decision then that had a profound impact on Rome's character. Breaking with precedent, Marcellus, conqueror of the fabulously wealthy Sicilian Greek city of Syracuse, brought back to Rome not only the usual spoils of war—captured arms and armor, gold and silver coins, and the like—but also the city's artistic patrimony. Thus began, in the words of the historian Livy, "the craze for works of Greek art."[2] According to the biographer Plutarch, the Romans, "who had hitherto been accustomed only to fighting or farming," now began "affecting urbane opinions about the arts and about artists, even to the point of wasting the better part of a day on such things."[3] Ships filled with plundered Greek statues and paintings became a frequent sight in the harbor of Ostia at the mouth of the Tiber River.

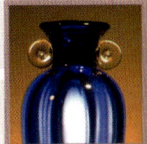

ART AND SOCIETY

An Outline of Roman History

MONARCHY (753–509 B.C.)

In the monarchy period, Latin and Etruscan kings reigned, beginning with Romulus and ending with Tarquinius Superbus (exact dates of rule unreliable).

REPUBLIC (509–27 B.C.)

The Republic lasted from the expulsion of Tarquinius Superbus until the bestowing of the title of Augustus on Octavian, the grandnephew of Julius Caesar and victor over Mark Antony in the Civil War that ended the Republic. Some major figures were:

Marcellus, b. 268(?) B.C., d. 208 B.C., consul
Marius, b. 157 B.C., d. 86 B.C., consul
Sulla, b. 138 B.C., d. 79 B.C., consul and dictator
Pompey, b. 106 B.C., d. 48 B.C., consul
Julius Caesar, b. 100 B.C., d. 44 B.C., consul and dictator
Mark Antony, b. 83 B.C., d. 30 B.C., consul

EARLY EMPIRE (27 B.C.–A.D. 96)

The Early Empire began with the rule of Augustus and his Julio-Claudian successors and continued until the end of the Flavian dynasty. Selected emperors and their dates of rule (with names of the most influential empresses in parentheses) are listed in chronological order:

Augustus (Livia), r. 27 B.C.–A.D. 14
Tiberius, r. 14–37
Caligula, r. 37–41
Claudius (Agrippina the Younger), r. 41–54
Nero, r. 54–68

Vespasian, r. 69–79
Titus, r. 79–81
Domitian, r. 81–96

HIGH EMPIRE (A.D. 96–192)

The High Empire began with the rule of Nerva and the Spanish emperors, Trajan and Hadrian, and ended with the last emperor of the Antonine dynasty. The emperors (and empresses) of this period were:

Nerva, r. 96–98
Trajan (Plotina), r. 98–117
Hadrian (Sabina), r. 117–138
Antoninus Pius (Faustina the Elder), r. 138–161
Marcus Aurelius (Faustina the Younger), r. 161–180
Lucius Verus, coemperor, r. 161–169
Commodus, r. 180–192

LATE EMPIRE (A.D. 192–337)

The Late Empire began with the Severan dynasty and included the soldier emperors of the third century, the tetrarchs, and Constantine, the first Christian emperor. Selected emperors (and empresses) were:

Septimius Severus (Julia Domna), r. 193–211
Caracalla (Plautilla), r. 211–217
Severus Alexander, r. 222–235
Trajan Decius, r. 249–251
Trebonianus Gallus, r. 251–253
Diocletian, r. 284–305
Constantine I, r. 306–337

Exposure to Greek sculpture and painting and to the splendid marble temples of the Greek gods increased as the Romans expanded their conquests beyond Italy to Greece itself, which became a Roman province in 146 B.C., and, after 133 B.C., when the last Attalid king of Pergamon willed his kingdom to Rome (see Chapter 5). Nevertheless, although the Romans developed a virtually insatiable taste for Greek "antiques," their own monuments were not slavish imitations of Greek masterpieces. The Etruscan basis of Roman art and architecture was never forgotten, and the statues and buildings of the Roman Republic are highly eclectic, drawing on both Greek and Etruscan traditions. The resultant mix, however, is distinctly Roman.

Architecture

A HARBOR GOD'S ECLECTIC TEMPLE A superb example of Roman eclecticism is the little temple on the east bank of the Tiber known as the Temple of "Fortuna Virilis"

(FIG. **10-1**), actually the Temple of Portunus, the Roman god of harbors. In plan it follows the Etruscan pattern. The high podium is accessible only at the front, with its wide flight of steps. Freestanding columns are confined to the deep porch. But the structure is built of stone (local tufa and travertine), overlaid originally with stucco in imitation of the gleaming white marble temples of the Greeks. The columns are not Tuscan but Ionic, complete with flutes and bases. Moreover, in an effort to approximate a peripteral Greek temple—while maintaining the basic Etruscan plan—the architect added a series of engaged Ionic half-columns around the cella's sides and back. The result was a *pseudoperipteral* temple, and, although it combines Etruscan and Greek elements, the design is uniquely Roman.

A ROUND TEMPLE ON A CLIFF The Romans' admiration for the Greek temples they encountered in their conquests also led to the importation of the round, or tholos temple type, a form unknown in Etruscan architecture, into

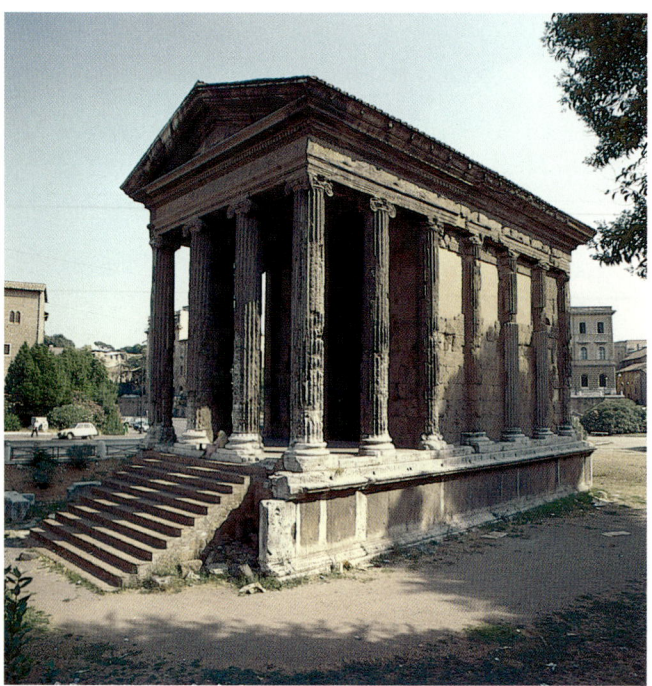

10-1 Temple of "Fortuna Virilis" (Temple of Portunus), Rome, Italy, ca. 75 B.C.

Republican Italy. At Tivoli (ancient Tibur), east of Rome, a Greek-inspired temple with a circular plan—variously known as the Temple of "the Sibyl" or of "Vesta" (FIG. **10-2**)—was erected early in the first century B.C. on a dramatic site overlooking a deep gorge. The travertine columns are Corinthian, and the frieze is carved (with garlands held up by oxen heads),

also in emulation of Greek models. But the high podium can be reached only via a narrow stairway leading to the cella door. This arrangement introduced an axial alignment not found in Greek tholoi (see FIG. 5-71), where, as in Greek rectangular temples (for example, FIG. 5-29), steps continue all around the structure. Also in contrast with Greek practice, the cella wall was constructed not of masonry blocks but of a new material of recent invention: concrete (see "The Roman Architectural Revolution: Concrete Construction," page 249).

CONCRETE TRANSFORMS A HILLSIDE The most impressive and innovative use of concrete during the Republic was in the Sanctuary of Fortuna Primigenia (FIG. **10-3**), constructed in the late second century B.C. on a hillside at Palestrina (ancient Praeneste, formerly an Etruscan city). The great size of the sanctuary, spread out over several terraces leading up to a tholos at the peak of an ascending triangle, reflected the Republican taste for colossal Hellenistic designs. The means of construction, however, was distinctly Roman.

The builder used concrete barrel vaults of enormous strength to support the imposing terraces and to cover the great ramps leading to the grand central staircase, as well as to give shape to the shops aligned on two consecutive levels. In this way, the unknown architect transformed the entire hillside into a grandiose complex symbolic of Roman power. This subjection of nature to human will and rational order was the first full-blown manifestation of the Roman imperial spirit. It contrasted with the more restrained Greek practice of simply crowning a hill with sacred buildings, as opposed to converting the hill itself into architecture.

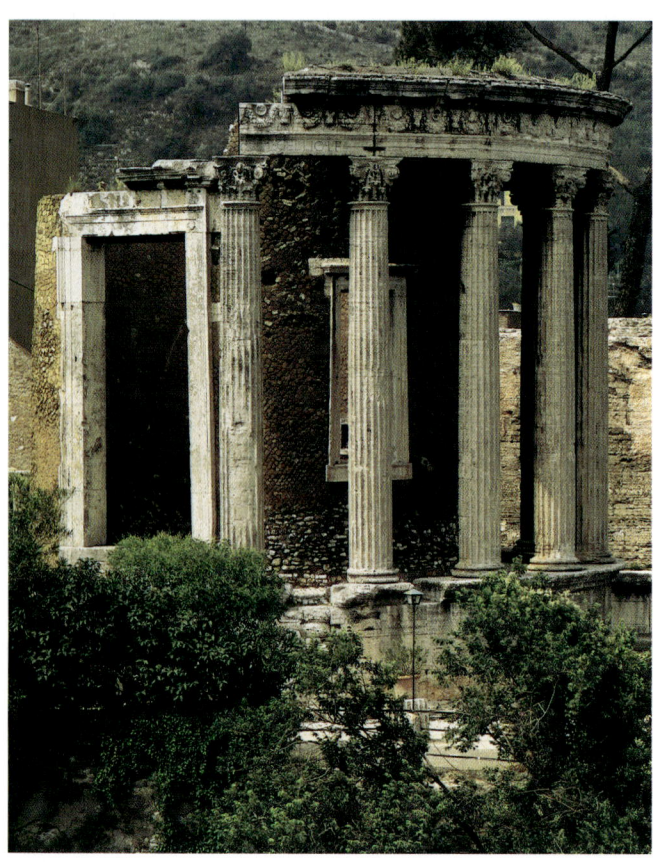

10-2 Temple of "the Sibyl" or of "Vesta," Tivoli, Italy, early first century B.C.

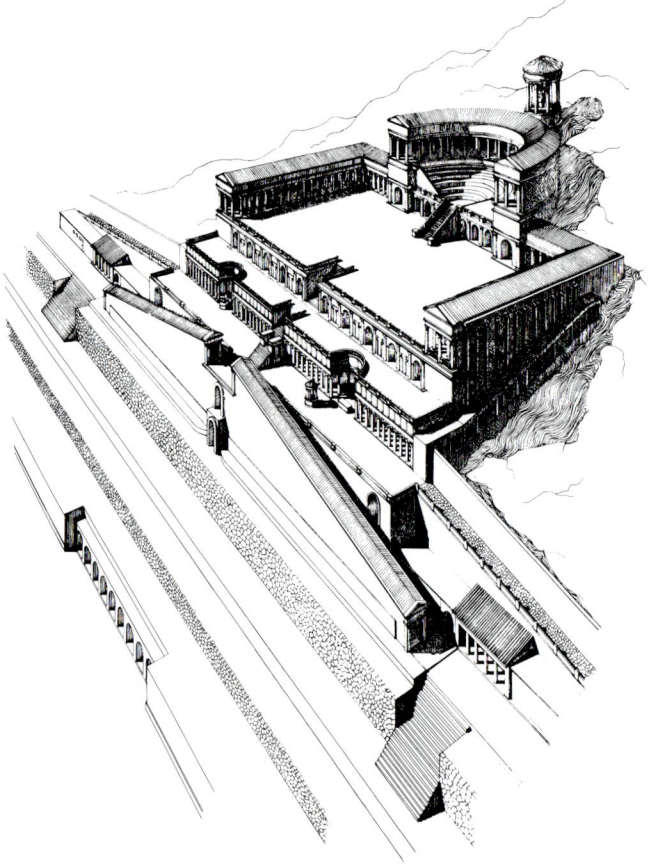

10-3 Reconstruction drawing of the Sanctuary of Fortuna Primigenia, Palestrina, Italy, late second century B.C.

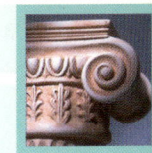

The Roman Architectural Revolution
Concrete Construction

The history of Roman architecture would be very different if the Romans had been content to use the same building materials as the Greeks, Etruscans, and ancient Near Eastern peoples. Instead, the Romans developed concrete construction, causing a revolution in architectural design. Roman *concrete* was made from a changing recipe of lime mortar, volcanic sand, water, and small stones (*caementa,* from which the English word *cement* is derived). The mixture was placed in wooden frames and left to dry and to bond with a brick or stone facing. When the concrete completely dried, the builders removed the wooden molds, leaving behind a solid mass of great strength, though rough in appearance. Afterward, the rough concrete was often covered with stucco or even sheathed with marble *revetment* (facing). Despite this lengthy procedure, concrete walls were much less costly to construct than walls of imported Greek marble or even local tufa and travertine.

The advantages of concrete, however, go well beyond cost. It is possible to fashion concrete shapes that masonry construction cannot achieve, especially huge vaulted and domed rooms without internal supports. The Romans came to prefer these over the Greek and Etruscan post-and-lintel structures. Concrete enabled Roman builders to think of architecture in radical new ways. Roman concrete architecture became an architecture of space rather than of sheer mass.

To cover and give shape to these new "spatial envelopes," the Romans employed a variety of vaulting systems. The most common types were:

Barrel Vaults Also called the *tunnel vault,* the barrel vault is an extension of a simple arch, creating a semicylindrical ceiling over parallel walls. Such vaults were constructed both before and after the Romans using traditional ashlar masonry (see, for example, FIGS. 2-26, 17-3, and 17-34), but those vaults are less stable than concrete barrel vaults. If any of the blocks of a cut-stone vault come loose, the whole may collapse. Also, masonry barrel vaults only can be illuminated by light entering at either end of the tunnel. In concrete barrel vaults, by contrast, windows can be placed at any point, because once the concrete hardens, it forms a seamless sheet of "artificial stone" that may be punctured almost at will. Whether made of stone or concrete, barrel vaults require *buttressing* (lateral support) of the walls below the vaults to counteract their downward and outward thrust.

Groin Vaults Groin or *cross vaults* are formed by the intersection at right angles of two barrel vaults of equal size. Besides appearing lighter than the barrel vault, the groin vault needs less buttressing. The barrel vault's thrust is concentrated along the entire length of the supporting wall. The groin vault's thrust, however, is concentrated along the groins, and buttressing is needed only at the points where the groins meet the vault's vertical supports. The system leaves the covered area open, permitting light to enter. Groin vaults, like barrel vaults, can be built using stone blocks—but with the same structural limitations when compared to concrete vaulting.

When a series of groin vaults covers an interior hall, as in our diagram and in FIGS. 10-44, 10-68, and 10-79, the open lateral arches of the vaults form the equivalent of a clerestory of a traditional timber-roofed structure (for example, see FIG. 11-8). Such a *fenestrated* sequence of groin vaults has a major advantage over wooden clerestories. Concrete vaults are relatively fireproof, always an important consideration given that fires were common occurrences (see "The Burning of Canterbury Cathedral," Chapter 17, page 455).

Hemispherical Domes The largest domed space in the ancient world for more than a millennium was the corbeled, beehive-shaped tholos of the Treasury of Atreus at Mycenae (see FIGS. 4-21 and 4-22). The Romans were able to surpass the Mycenaeans by using concrete to construct hemispherical domes, which usually rested on concrete cylindrical *drums.* If a barrel vault is described as a round arch extended in a line, then a hemispherical dome may be described as a round arch rotated around the full circumference of a circle. Masonry domes (compare FIG. 10-73), like masonry vaults, cannot accommodate windows without threatening their stability. Concrete domes can be opened up even at their apex with a circular "eye" *(oculus),* as in our diagram and FIGS. 10-33, 10-49, and 10-50, allowing much-needed light to reach the vast spaces beneath.

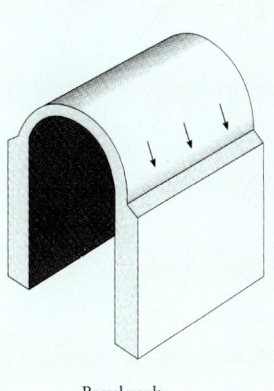

Barrel vault

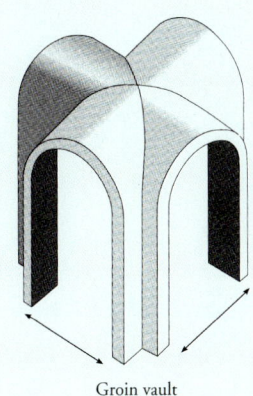

Groin vault

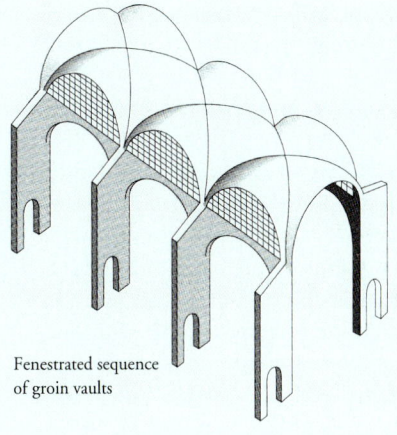

Fenestrated sequence of groin vaults

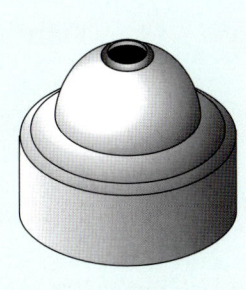

Hemispherical dome with oculus

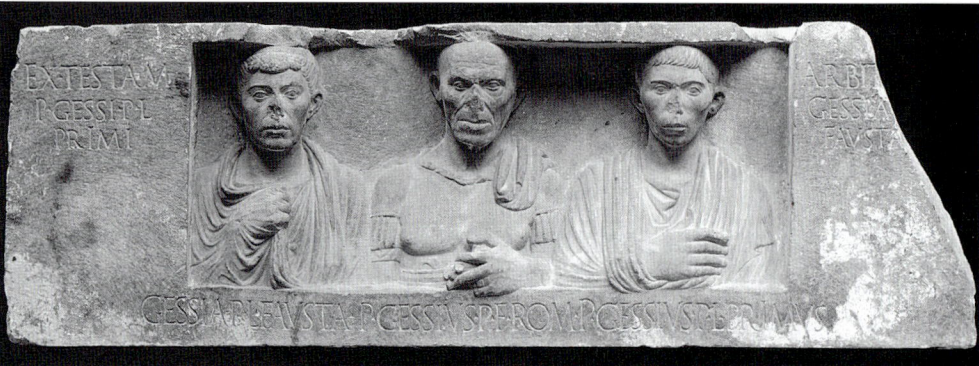

10-4   Funerary relief with portraits of the Gessii, from Rome(?), Italy, ca. 30 B.C. Marble, approx. 2′ 1½″ high. Museum of Fine Arts, Boston (Archibald Cary Coolidge Fund).

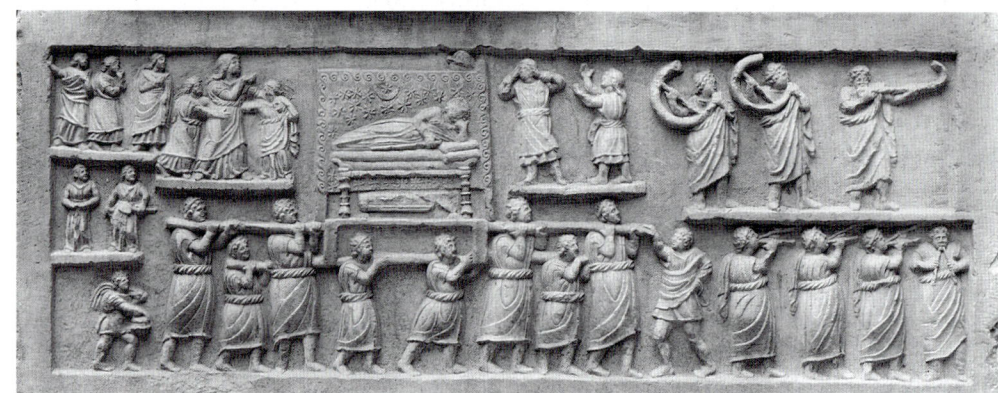

10-5   Relief with funerary procession, from Amiternum, Italy, second half of first century B.C. Limestone, approx. 2′ 2″ high. Museo Nazionale d'Abruzzo, L'Aquila.

Sculpture

THE SOCIAL CONTEXT OF PORTRAITS   The patrons of the Roman Republic's great temples and sanctuaries were in almost all cases men from old and distinguished families, often victorious generals who used the spoils of war to finance public works. These aristocratic patricians were fiercely proud of their lineage. They kept likenesses *(imagines)* of their ancestors in wooden cupboards in their homes and paraded them at the funerals of prominent relatives. (Marius, a renowned Republican general who lacked a long and distinguished genealogy, was ridiculed by contemporary Roman patricians as a man who had no ancestral imagines in his home.)

The surviving sculptural portraits of prominent Roman Republican figures, which are uniformly literal reproductions of individual faces, must be seen in this social context. Although their style derives to some degree from Hellenistic and Etruscan, and perhaps even Ptolemaic Egyptian, portraits, Republican portraits are one way the patrician class celebrated its elevated status. Slaves and former slaves could not possess such portraits, because, under Roman law, their parents and grandparents were not people but property. Yet when freed slaves died, they often ordered portraits for their tombs (FIGS. **10-4** and **10-5**)—in a style that contrasts sharply with that favored by freeborn patricians (see "Art for Former Slaves," page 251).

The subjects of Republican patrician portraits are almost exclusively men (and to a lesser extent women) of advanced age, for generally these elders held the power in the state. These patricians did not ask sculptors to make them appear nobler than they were, as Kresilas portrayed Pericles (see FIG. 5-39). Instead, they requested accurate records of their distinctive features, in the tradition of the treasured household imagines.

One of the most striking of these so-called *veristic* (superrealistic) portraits is the head of an unidentified patrician (FIG. **10-6**) found near Otricoli. The sculptor painstakingly recorded each

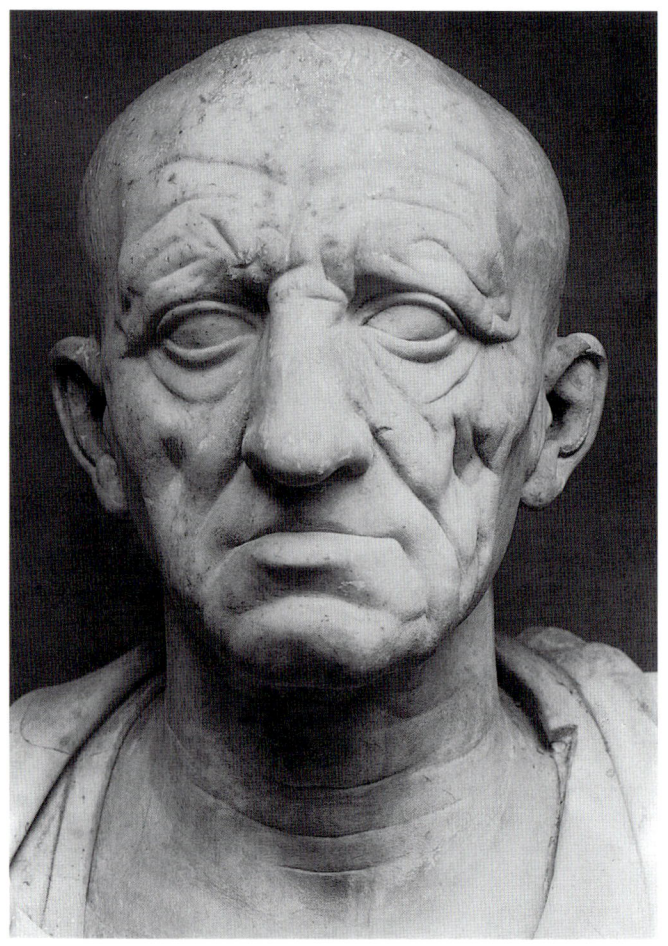

10-6   Head of a Roman patrician, from Otricoli, Italy, ca. 75–50 B.C. Marble, approx. 1′ 2″ high. Museo Torlonia, Rome.

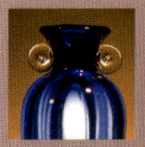

Art for Former Slaves

Historians and art historians alike tend to focus on the lives and monuments of famous individuals, but some of the most interesting remains of ancient Roman civilization are the artworks commissioned by ordinary people, especially former slaves, or *freedmen* and *freedwomen*. Slavery was common in the Roman world, and it is estimated that Italy at the end of the Republic had some two million slaves, or roughly one slave for every three citizens. The very rich might own hundreds of slaves, but slaves could be found in all but the most impoverished households. The practice was so much a part of Roman society that even slaves often became slave owners when their former masters freed them.

The most noteworthy of all the artworks Roman freed slaves paid for are the stone reliefs that regularly adorned their tomb facades. One interesting example (FIG. 10-4) depicts three people, all named Gessius. At the left is Gessia Fausta and at the right Gessius Primus. Both are the freed slaves of Publius Gessius, the freeborn citizen in the center shown wearing a general's *cuirass* (breastplate) and portrayed in the standard Republican superrealistic fashion (FIGS. 10-6 to 10-8). As slaves this couple had no legal standing; they were the property of Publius Gessius. After they were freed, however, in the eyes of the law the ex-slaves became people. These stern frontal portraits proclaim their new status as legal members of Roman society—and their gratitude to Publius Gessius for granting them that status.

As was the custom, the two ex-slaves bear their patron's name, but whether they are sister and brother, wife and husband, or unrelated is unclear. The relief's inscriptions explicitly state that the monument was paid for with funds provided by the will of Gessius Primus and that the work was directed by Gessia Fausta, the only survivor of the three. The relief thus depicts the living and the dead side by side, indistinguishable except by the accompanying message. This theme is common in Roman art (compare FIGS. 10-46 and 10-57) and proclaims that death does not break bonds formed in life.

More rarely, freed slaves commissioned tomb reliefs that were narrative in character. A relief from Amiternum (FIG. 10-5) depicts the cortege in honor of the deceased, complete with musicians, professional female mourners who pull their hair in a display of feigned grief, and the deceased's wife and children. The deceased is laid out on a bier with a canopy as a backdrop, much like the figures on Greek Geometric vases (see FIG. 5-1). Here, however, the dead man surprisingly props himself up as if still alive, surveying his own funeral. This may be an effigy, like the reclining figures on the lids of Etruscan sarcophagi (see FIGS. 9-4 and 9-14), rather than the deceased himself.

Compositionally, the relief is also not what one would expect. Mourners and musicians stand on floating ground lines, as if on "magic carpets." They are not to be viewed as suspended in space, however, but as situated behind the front row of pallbearers and musicians. This sculptor, in striking contrast to the (usually Greek) artists the patrician aristocracy employed, had little regard for the rules of classical art. Overlapping was studiously avoided, and the figures were placed wherever they fit, so long as they were clearly visible. This approach to making pictures was characteristic of pre-classical art but it had been out of favor for several centuries. One looks in vain for similar compositions in the art commissioned by the consuls and senators of the Roman Republic. In ancient Rome's cosmopolitan world, as today, stylistic tastes often were tied to a person's political and social status.

---

rise and fall, each bulge and fold, of the facial surface, like a mapmaker who did not want to miss the slightest detail of surface change. The result was a blunt record of the man's features and a statement about his personality: serious, experienced, determined—virtues that were much admired during the Republic.

AN OLD HEAD ON A YOUNG BODY The portrait from Otricoli is in bust form. The Romans believed the head alone was enough to constitute a portrait. The Greeks, by contrast, believed that head and body were inseparable parts of an integral whole, so their portraits were always full length (see FIG. 5-88). In fact, in Republican portraiture veristic heads were often, although incongruently, placed on bodies to which they could not possibly belong.

Such is the case in the portrait of a general (FIG. **10-7**) found at the Sanctuary of Hercules at Tivoli. A typically stern and lined Republican head sits atop a powerful, youthful body. The sculptor modeled the portrait on the statues of heroically nude Greek youths the Romans admired so much—although this patron's modesty dictated that a mantle shield the genitals. By the general's side, and acting as a prop for the heavy marble statue, is a cuirass, an emblem of his rank. This curious and discordant image nonetheless conveys several messages. The portrait head preserves the patron's appearance, consistent with old Republican values; the cuirass declares he is a military officer; and the Greek-inspired body type proclaims he is a hero. As different as this statue is from the pseudoperipteral Temple of "Fortuna Virilis" (FIG. 10-1), both combine native and imported elements and reveal the eclectic nature of Republican art and architecture.

JULIUS CAESAR BREAKS THE RULES Beginning early in the first century B.C., the Roman desire to advertise distinguished ancestry led to the placement of portraits of illustrious forebears on Republican coins. These ancestral portraits supplanted the earlier Roman tradition (based on Greek convention) of using images of divinities on coins. No Roman, however, dared to place his own likeness on a coin until 44 B.C., when Julius Caesar, shortly before his assassination on the Ides of March, issued coins featuring his portrait and his newly acquired title, *dictator perpetuus* (dictator for life). The *denarius* (the standard Roman silver coin, from which the word *penny* ultimately derives) illustrated here

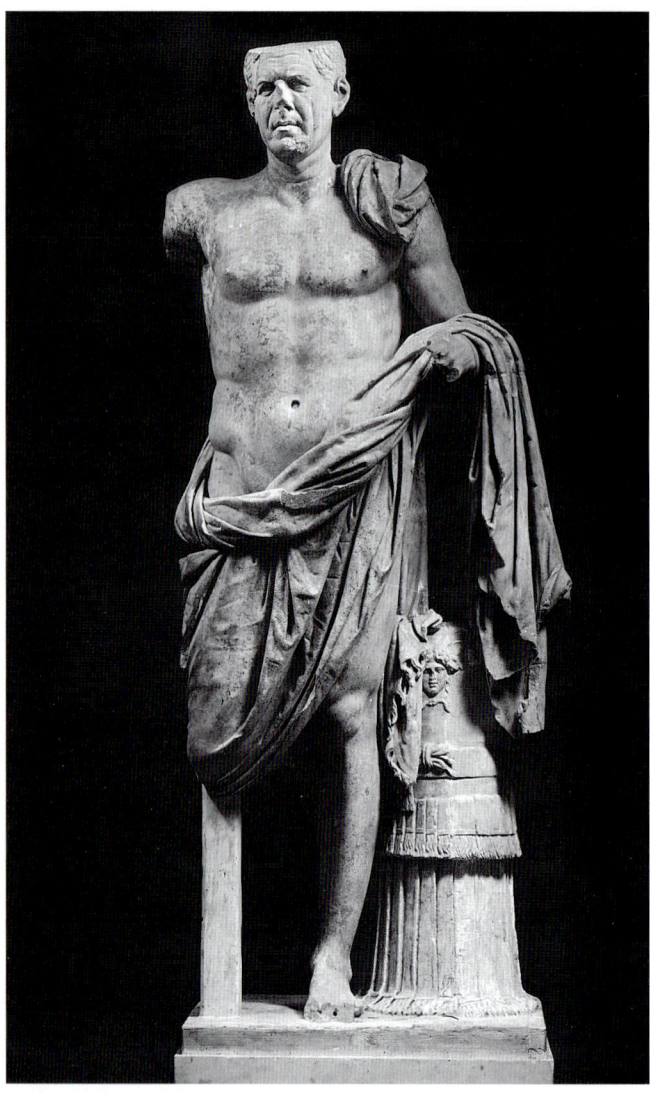

10-7   Portrait of a Roman general, from the Sanctuary of Hercules, Tivoli, Italy, ca. 75–50 B.C. Marble, approx. 6′ 2″ high. Museo Nazionale Romano-Palazzo Massimo alle Terme, Rome.

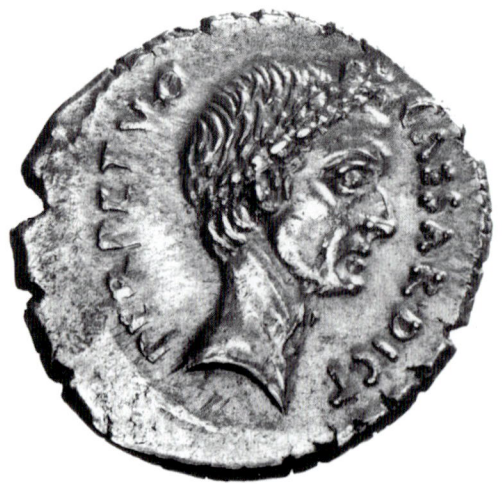

10-8   Denarius with portrait of Julius Caesar, 44 B.C. Silver, diameter approx. $\frac{3}{4}$″. American Numismatic Society, New York.

"Rising from the Ashes: The Excavation of Herculaneum and Pompeii," Chapter 28, page 849). Their remains, still being excavated, permit a reconstruction of the art and life of a Roman town of the Late Republic and Early Empire with a completeness far beyond that possible at any other archeological site.

OSCANS, SAMNITES, AND ROMANS   Pompeii was first settled by the Oscans, one of the many Italic tribes that occupied Italy during the heyday of the Etruscans. It was taken over toward the end of the fifth century B.C. by the Samnites, who, under the influence of their Greek neighbors, greatly expanded the original town and gave monumental shape to the city center. Pompeii fought with other Italian cities on the losing side against Rome in the Social War, and in 80 B.C. Sulla founded a new Roman colony on the site, with Latin as its official language. The colony's population had grown to between ten and twenty thousand when, in February A.D. 62, an earthquake shook the city, causing extensive damage. When Mount Vesuvius erupted seventeen years later, repairs were still in progress.

AN ARCHEOLOGICAL PARK   Walking through Pompeii today is an experience that cannot be approximated anywhere else. The streets, with their heavy flagstone pavements and sidewalks, are still there, as are the stepping stones that enabled pedestrians to cross the streets without having to step in puddles. Ingeniously, the city planners placed these stones in such a way that they could be straddled by vehicle wheels so that supplies could be brought to the shops, taverns, and bakeries. Tourists still can visit the impressive concrete-vaulted rooms of Pompeii's public baths and sit in the seats of its open-air theater and indoor concert hall, even walk among the tombs outside the city's walls. The sights include private homes with magnificently painted walls and pleasant gardens. Some still have their kitchen utensils in place. Pompeii has been called the living city of the dead for good reason.

records Caesar's aging face and receding hairline (FIG. **10-8**) in conformity with the Republican veristic tradition. But placing the likeness of a living person on a coin violated all the norms of Republican propriety. Henceforth, Roman coins, which circulated throughout the vast territories under Roman control, would be used to mold public opinion in favor of the ruler by announcing his achievements both real and fictional.

POMPEII AND THE CITIES OF VESUVIUS

BURIED BY A VOLCANO   On August 24, A.D. 79, Mount Vesuvius, a long-dormant volcano whose fertile slopes were covered with vineyards during the Late Republic and Early Empire, suddenly erupted, burying many prosperous towns around the Bay of Naples (the ancient Greek city of Neapolis), among them Pompeii (see "An Eyewitness Account of the Eruption of Mount Vesuvius," page 253). This catastrophe for the inhabitants of the Vesuvian cities became a boon for archeologists and art historians. When the buried cities were first explored in the eighteenth century, they had been undisturbed for nearly seventeen hundred years (see

Architecture

THE HEART OF POMPEII   The center of civic life in any Roman town was its *forum,* or public square, usually located at the city's geographic center at the intersection of the main north-south street, the *cardo,* and the main east-west avenue, the *decumanus* (FIG. 10-40). The forum, however, gen-

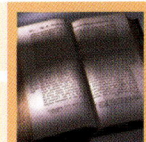

An Eyewitness Account of the Eruption of Mount Vesuvius

Pliny the Elder, whose *Natural History* is one of the most important sources for Greek art history, was among those who tried to rescue others from danger when Mount Vesuvius erupted. He was overcome by fumes the volcano spewed forth, and died. His nephew, Pliny the Younger, a government official under Trajan, left an account of the eruption and his uncle's demise:

> [The volcanic cloud's] general appearance can best be expressed as being like a pine . . . for it rose to a great height on a sort of trunk and then split off into branches. . . . Sometimes it looked white, sometimes blotched and dirty, according to the amount of soil and ashes it carried with it. . . . The buildings were now shaking with vi-

olent shocks, and seemed to be swaying to and fro as if they were torn from their foundations. Outside, on the other hand, there was the danger of falling pumice-stones, even though these were light and porous. . . . Elsewhere there was daylight, [but around Vesuvius, people] were still in darkness, blacker and denser than any night that ever was. . . . When daylight returned on the 26th—two days after the last day [my uncle] had been seen—his body was found intact and uninjured, still fully clothed and looking more like sleep than death.[1]

[1] Betty Radice, trans., *Pliny the Younger: Letters and Panegyricus,* vol. 2 (Cambridge, Mass.: Harvard University Press, 1969), 427–33.

---

erally was closed to all but pedestrian traffic. Pompeii's forum (FIGS. **10-9** and **10-10**) lies in the southwest corner of the expanded Roman city but at the heart of the original town. The forum took on monumental form in the second century B.C. when the Samnites erected two-story colonnades inspired by Hellenistic architecture on three sides of the long and narrow plaza. At the north end they constructed a Temple of Jupiter. When Pompeii became a Roman colony in 80 B.C., the Romans converted the temple into a *Capitolium*—a triple shrine of Jupiter, Juno, and Minerva. (For the Roman gods and goddesses and their Greek equivalents, see "The Gods and Goddesses of Mount Olympus," Chapter 5, page 99.) The temple

is of standard Republican type, constructed of tufa covered with fine white stucco and combining an Etruscan plan with Corinthian columns. It faces into the civic square, dominating the area. This is very different from the siting of Greek temples (see FIGS. 5-40 and 5-41), which stood in isolation and could be approached and viewed from all sides, like colossal statues on giant stepped pedestals. The Roman forum, like the Etrusco-Roman temple, has a chief side, a focus of attention.

The area within the porticoes of the forum at Pompeii was empty, except for statues commemorating local dignitaries and, later, Roman emperors. This is where daily commerce was conducted and festivities held. All around the square, behind the

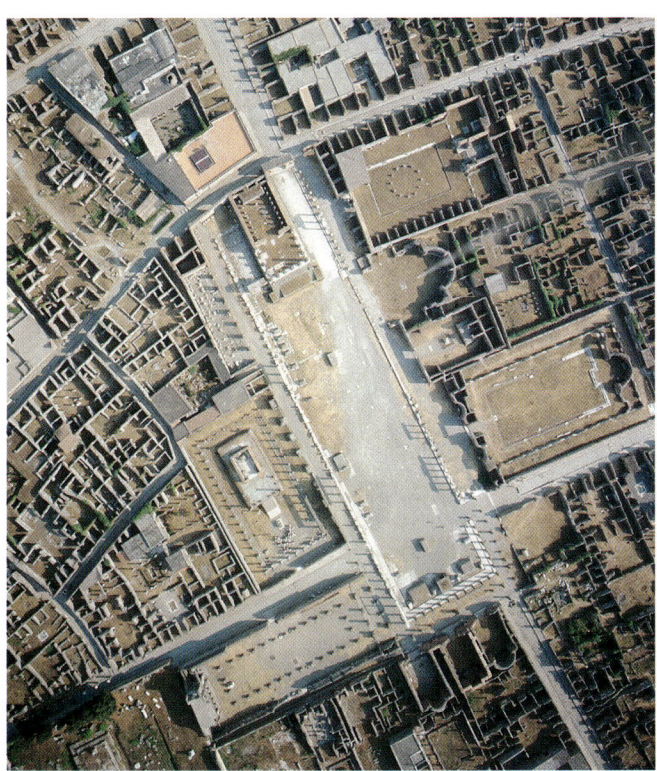

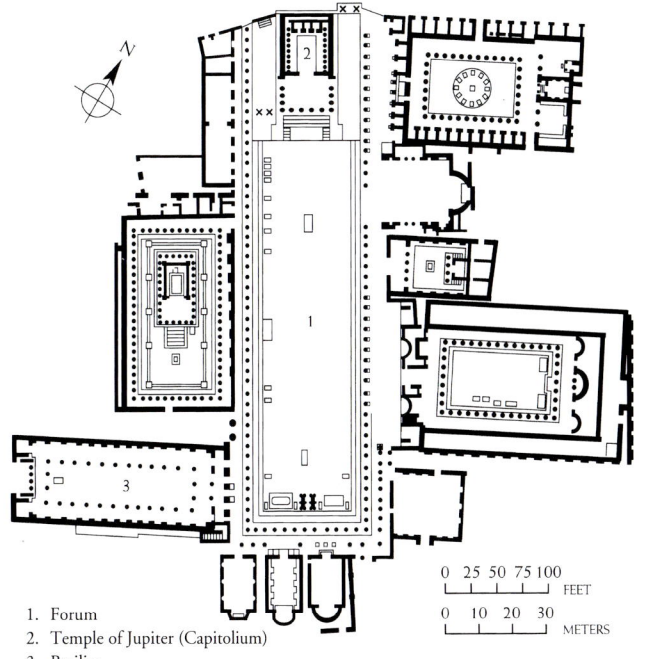

1. Forum
2. Temple of Jupiter (Capitolium)
3. Basilica

0 25 50 75 100 FEET
0 10 20 30 METERS

10-9 Aerial view of the forum, Pompeii, Italy, second century B.C. and later.

10-10 Plan of the forum, Pompeii, Italy, second century B.C. and later.

10-11   Aerial view of the amphitheater, Pompeii, Italy, ca. 80 B.C.

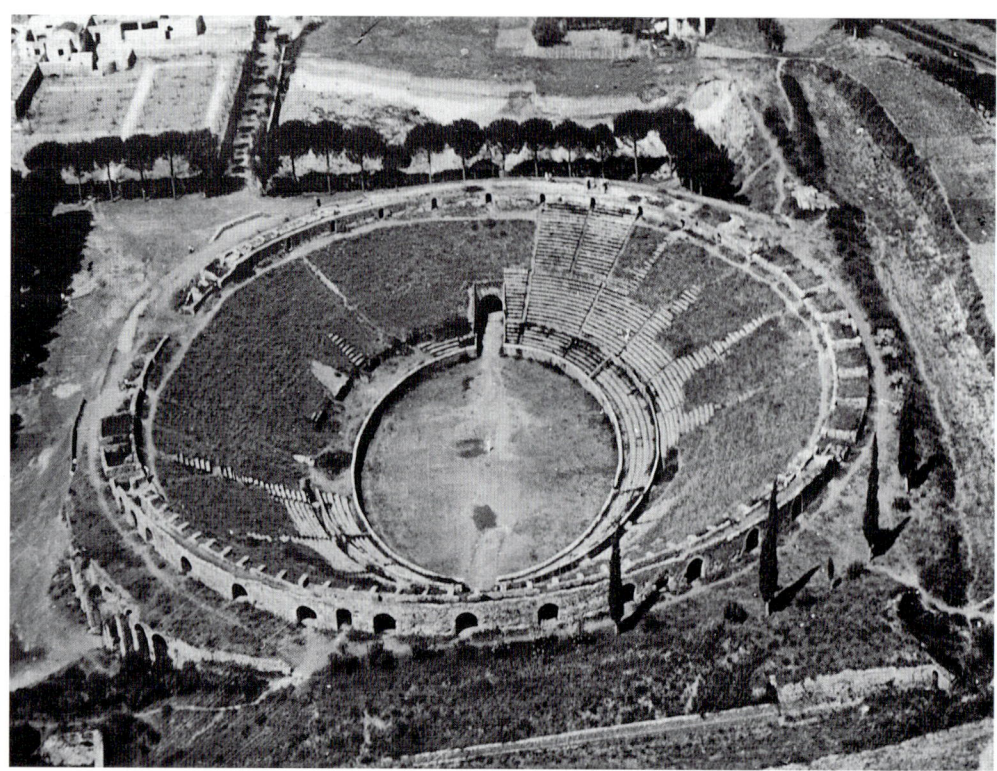

colonnades, were secular and religious structures, including the town's administrative offices. Most noteworthy is the *basilica* at the southwest corner, the earliest well-preserved building of its kind. Constructed during the late second century B.C., the basilica housed the law court of Pompeii and also was used for other official purposes. In plan (FIG. 10-10) it resembles the forum itself: long and narrow, with two stories of internal columns dividing the space into a central *nave* and flanking *aisles*. This scheme had a long afterlife in architectural history and will be familiar to anyone who has ever entered a Christian church.

A HOME FOR GLADIATORS   The forum was an oasis in the heart of Pompeii—an open, airy plaza. Throughout the rest of the city, every square foot of land was developed. At the southeastern end of town, immediately after the Roman colony was founded in 80 B.C., Pompeii's new citizens erected a large amphitheater (FIG. **10-11**). It is the earliest such structure known and could seat some twenty thousand spectators—more than the entire population of the town a century and a half after it was built! The word *amphitheater* means "double theater," and the Roman structures closely resemble two Greek theaters put together, although the Greeks never built amphitheaters. Greek theaters were placed on natural hillsides (see FIGS. 5-40 and 5-70), but supporting an amphitheater's continuous elliptical cavea required building an artificial mountain—and only concrete, unknown to the Greeks, was capable of such a job. In the Pompeii amphitheater a series of radially disposed concrete barrel vaults forms a giant retaining wall that holds up the earthen mound and stone seats. Barrel vaults also form the tunnels leading to the arena, the central area where bloody gladiatorial combats and other boisterous events occurred. (*Arena* is Latin for "sand," which soaked up the contestants' blood.) The Roman amphitheater stands in sharp contrast, both architecturally

and functionally, to the Greek theater, home of refined performances of comedies and tragedies.

A painting (FIG. **10-12**) on the wall of a Pompeian house records an unfortunate incident that occurred in the amphitheater in A.D. 59. A brawl broke out between the Pompeians and their neighbors, the Nucerians, during a contest

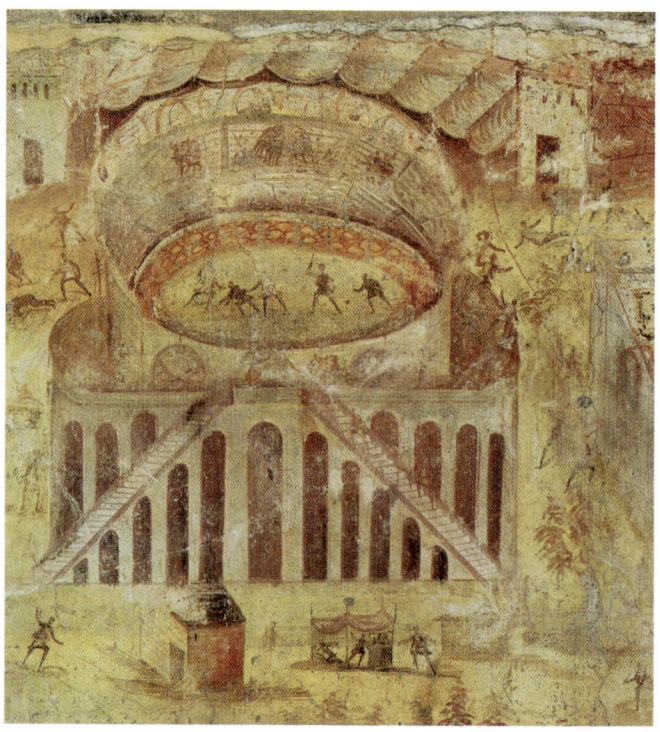

10-12   Brawl in the Pompeii amphitheater, wall painting from House I,3,23, Pompeii, Italy, ca. A.D. 60–79. Approx. 5' 7" × 6' 1". Museo Nazionale, Naples.

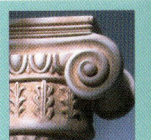

The Roman House

The Roman house was more than just a place to live. It played an important role in Roman societal rituals. In the Roman world individuals were frequently bound to others in a patron-client relationship whereby a wealthier, better-educated, and more powerful *patronus* would protect the interests of a *cliens,* sometimes large numbers of them. The standing of a patron in Roman society often was measured by clientele size. Being seen in public accompanied by a crowd of clients was a badge of honor. In this system, a plebeian might be bound to a patrician, a freed slave to a former owner, or even one patrician to another. Regardless of rank, all clients were obligated to support their patron in political campaigns and to perform specific services on request, as well as to call on and salute the patron at the patron's home.

A client calling on a patron would enter the typical Roman *domus* (private house) through a narrow foyer (*fauces,* the "throat" of the house), which led to a large central reception area, the *atrium.* The rooms flanking the fauces could open inward, as in our diagram, or outward, in which case they were rented out as shops. The roof over the atrium was partially open to the sky, not only to admit light but also to channel rainwater into a basin *(impluvium)* below. The water could be stored in cisterns for household use. Opening onto the atrium was a series of small bedrooms called *cubicula* (cubicles). At the back were the patron's *tablinum* or "home office," a dining room *(triclinium),* a kitchen, and sometimes a small garden.

Endless variations of the same basic plan exist, dictated by the owner's personal taste and means, the nature of the land plot, and so forth, but all Roman houses of this type were inward-looking in nature. The design shut off the street's noise and dust, and all internal activity was focused on the brightly illuminated atrium at the center of the residence. This basic module (only the front half of the typical house in our diagram) resembles the plan of the typical Etruscan house as reflected in the Tomb of the Shields and Chairs (see FIG. 9-6) and other tombs at Cerveteri. Thus few doubt that the early Roman house, like the early Roman temple, grew out of the Etruscan tradition.

During the second century B.C., when Roman architects were beginning to build stone temples with Greek columns, the Roman house also took on Greek airs. A peristyle garden was added behind the Etruscan-style house, providing a second internal illumination source as well as a pleasant setting for meals served in a summer triclinium. The axial symmetry of the plan meant that on entering the fauces of the house, a visitor could be greeted by a vista through the atrium directly into the peristyle garden (as in FIG. 10-13), which often boasted a fountain or pool, marble statuary, mural paintings, and mosaic floors.

Such houses were not, of course, the norm. While they were typical of Pompeii and other towns, they were very rare in large cities such as Rome, where the masses lived instead in multistory apartment houses, discussed later (FIG. 10-53).

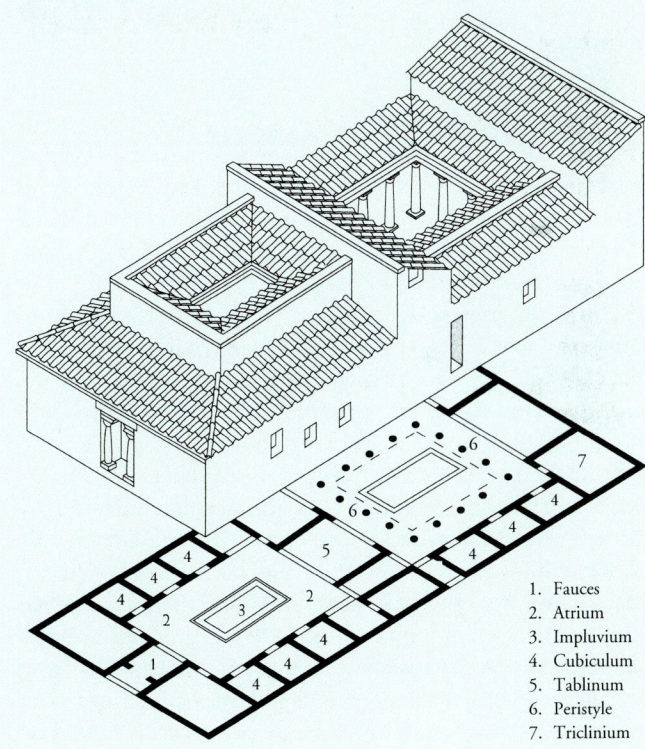

1. Fauces
2. Atrium
3. Impluvium
4. Cubiculum
5. Tablinum
6. Peristyle
7. Triclinium

between the two towns. The fighting left many seriously wounded and led to a decade-long prohibition against such events. The painting shows the cloth awning *(velarium)* that could be rolled down from the top of the cavea to shield spectators from either sun or rain. It also features the distinctive external double staircases (not visible in FIG. 10-11) that enabled large numbers of people to enter and exit the cavea in an orderly fashion.

HOUSES FOR PATRICIANS AND EX-SLAVES At Pompeii, as in modern cities and towns, private homes occupied most of the area. The evidence from Pompeii regarding Roman domestic architecture (see "The Roman House," above) is unparalleled anywhere else and is the most precious by-product of the catastrophic volcanic eruption of A.D. 79. One of the best preserved houses at Pompeii, partially rebuilt and an obligatory stop on every tourist's

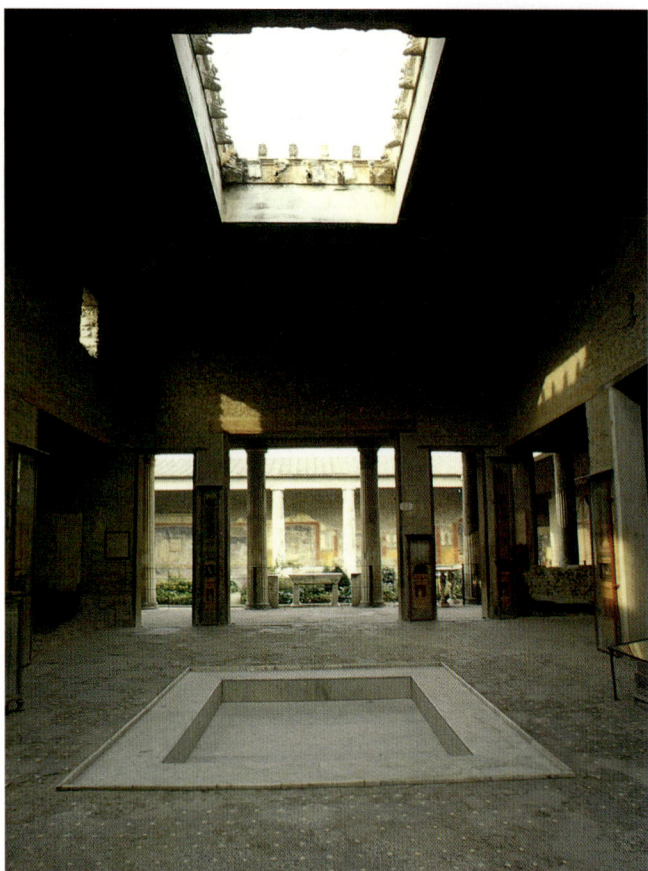

10-13   Atrium of the House of the Vettii, Pompeii, Italy, second century B.C., rebuilt A.D. 62–79.

itinerary today, is the House of the Vettii (FIG. **10-13**), an old Pompeian house remodeled and repainted after the earthquake of A.D. 62. Our photograph was taken in the *fauces*. It shows the *impluvium* in the center of the *atrium*, the opening in the roof above, and, in the background, the *peristyle* garden with its marble tables and splendid mural paintings dating to the last years of the Vesuvian city. At that time, the house was owned by two brothers, Aulus Vettius Restitutus and Aulus Vettius Conviva, probably freedmen who had made their fortune as merchants. Their wealth enabled them to purchase and furnish the kind of fashionable town house that in an earlier era would have been owned only by patricians.

One such house, a luxurious Pompeian mansion of the second century B.C., the so-called House of the Faun, epitomizes Livy's "craze for things Greek" that characterized much of Republican art and architecture. The house was named after the Hellenistic-style bronze statue that stood in one of its two atriums. Its walls were covered with First Style murals of Greek type (see page 257), and on the floor of a room opening onto one of two peristyles, excavators found the mosaic of Alexander the Great battling Darius of Persia (see FIG. 5-69), a copy of a fourth-century B.C. Greek panel painting.

Painting

PAINTED WALLS EVERYWHERE   The houses and villas around Mount Vesuvius have yielded a treasure trove of mural paintings, the most complete record of the changing fashions in interior decoration found anywhere in the entire ancient world. The sheer quantity of these paintings tells a great deal about both the prosperity and the tastes of the times. How many homes today, even of the very wealthy, have custom-painted frescoes in nearly every room?

In the early years of exploration at Pompeii and nearby Herculaneum, excavators focused almost exclusively on the figural panels that formed part of the overall mural designs, especially those depicting Greek heroes and famous myths. These were cut out of the walls and transferred to the Naples Archeological Museum. (The painting of the brawl in the amphitheater, FIG. 10-12, suffered this fate.) In time, more enlightened archeologists put an end to the practice of cutting pieces out of the walls, and gave serious attention finally to the mural designs as a whole. Toward the end of the nineteenth century, August Mau, a German art historian, divided the various mural painting schemes into four so-called Pompeian Styles, numbered by their chronological order. Mau's

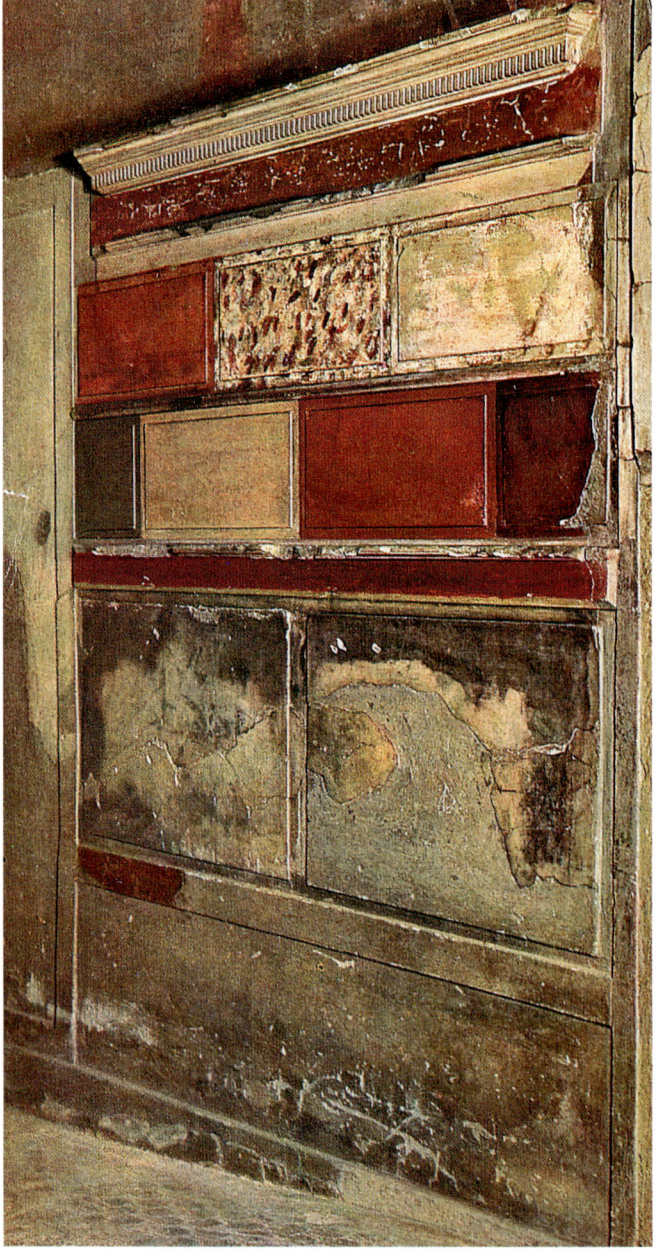

10-14   First Style wall painting in the fauces of the Samnite House, Herculaneum, Italy, late second century B.C.

classification system, although later refined and modified in detail, still serves as the basis for the study of Roman painting.

THE FIRST STYLE AND GREEK PAINTING The *First Style* also has been called the Masonry Style because the decorator's aim was to imitate costly marble panels using painted stucco relief. In the fauces (FIG. **10-14**) of the Samnite House at Herculaneum, the visitor is greeted at the doorway with the illusion of walls constructed, or at least faced, with marbles imported from quarries all over the Mediterranean. This approach to wall decoration is comparable to the modern practice, employed in private libraries and corporate meeting rooms alike, of using cheaper manufactured materials to approximate the look and shape of genuine wood paneling. The practice is not, however, uniquely Pompeian or Roman. First Style walls are well documented in the Greek world from the late fourth century B.C. on. The use of the First Style in Roman houses of the late second and early first centuries B.C. is yet another example of the Hellenization of Republican architecture.

The finest examples of First Style painting, such as those in the Samnite House, create a stunning illusion of actual marble veneers. (For walls revetted with real marble slabs, see FIGS. 10-50 and 17-15.) Roman wall paintings were true frescoes (see "Fresco Painting," Chapter 19, page 543), with the colors applied while the plaster was still damp, but the surface bril-liance was achieved by painstaking preparation of the wall. The plaster, mixed with marble dust if the patron could afford it, was laid on in several layers with a smooth trowel. The dried, painted surface was then polished to a marblelike finish.

THE TRIUMPH OF ILLUSIONISM The First Style never went completely out of fashion, but after 80 B.C. a new approach to mural design became more popular. The *Second Style* is in most respects the antithesis of the First Style. Some scholars have argued that the Second Style also has precedents in Greece, but most believe it is a Roman invention. Certainly, the Second Style evolved in Italy and was popular until around 15 B.C., when the Third Style was introduced. Second Style painters aimed not to create the illusion of an elegant marble wall, as First Style painters sought to do. Rather, they wanted to dissolve a room's confining walls and replace them with the illusion of an imaginary three-dimensional world. They did this purely pictorially. The First Style's modeled stucco panels gave way to the Second Style's flat wall surfaces.

DIONYSIAC MYSTERIES AT POMPEII An early example of the new style is the room that gives its name to the Villa of the Mysteries at Pompeii (FIG. **10-15**). This chamber was probably used to celebrate, in private, the rites of the

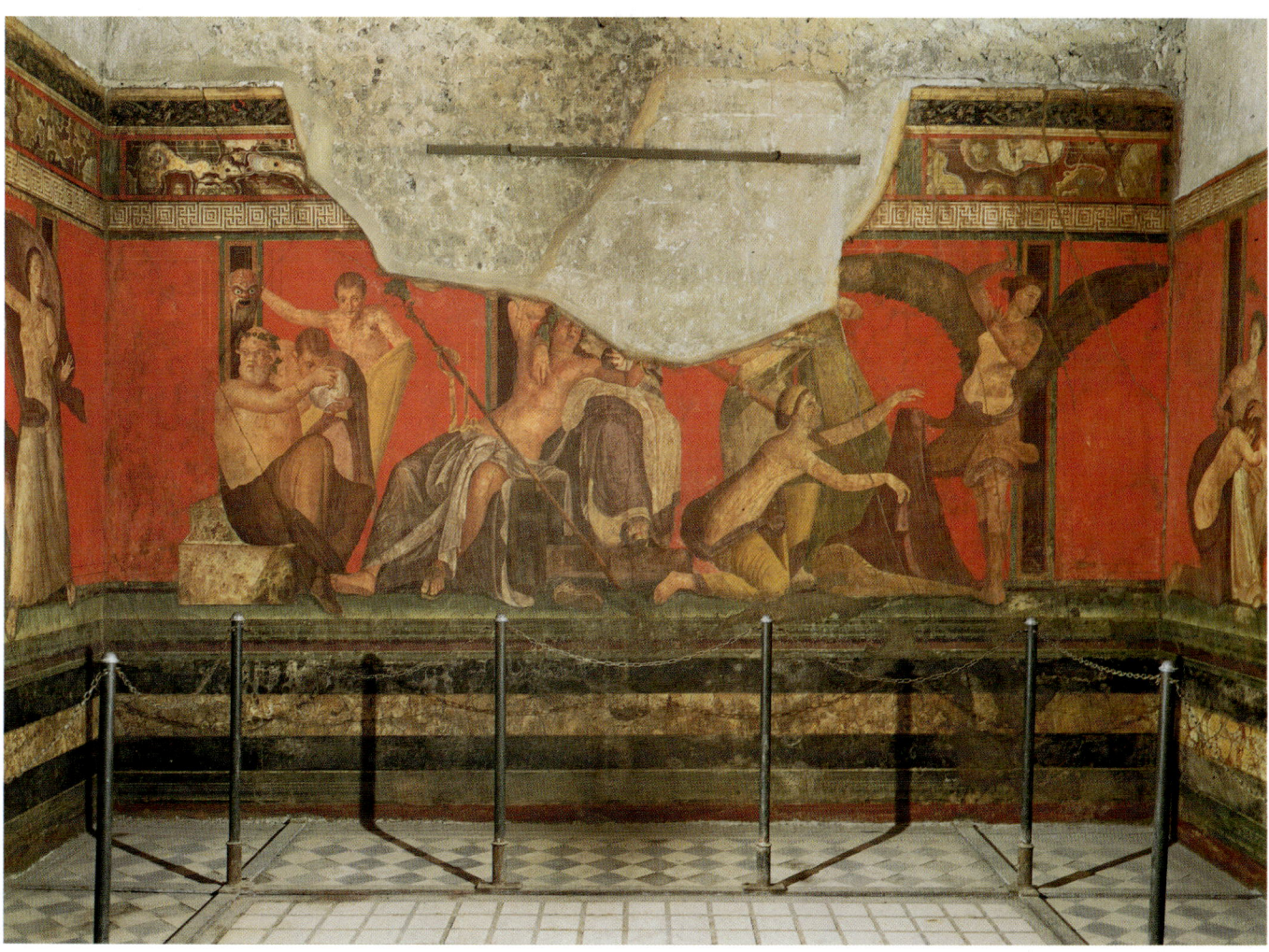

10-15 Dionysiac mystery frieze, Second Style wall paintings in Room 5 of the Villa of the Mysteries, Pompeii, Italy, ca. 60–50 B.C. Frieze approx. 5′ 4″ high.

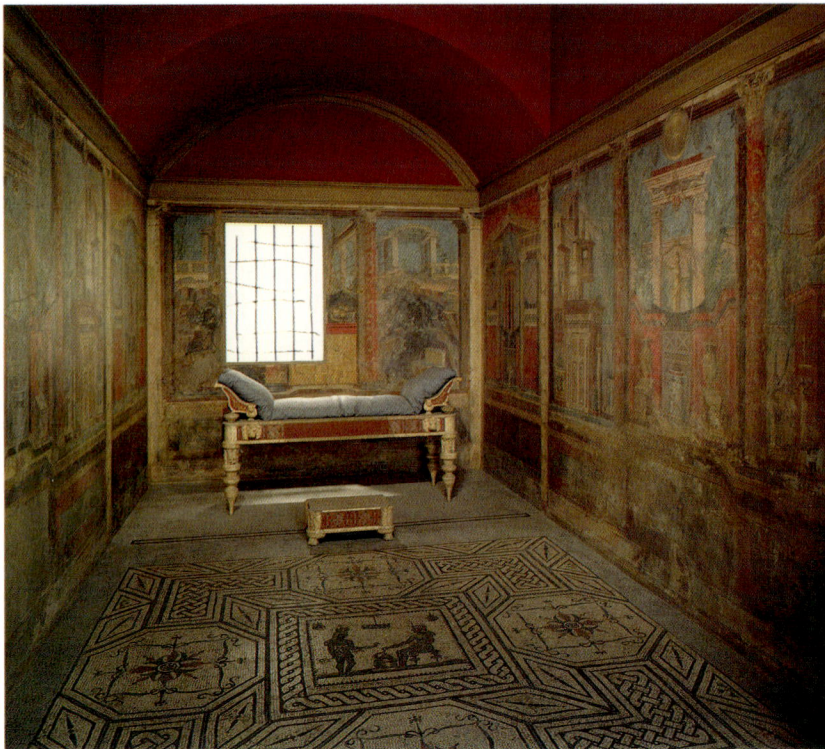 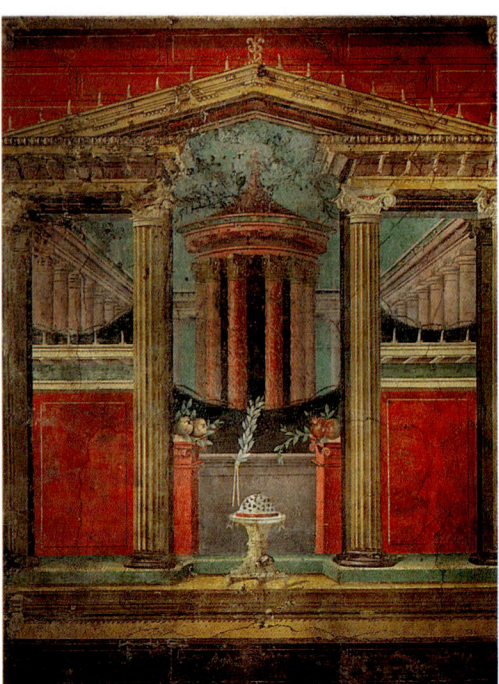

10-16   Second Style wall paintings (general view and detail of tholos) from Cubiculum M of the Villa of Publius Fannius Synistor, Boscoreale, Italy, ca. 50–40 B.C. Approx. 8′ 9″ high. Metropolitan Museum of Art, New York.

Greek god Dionysos (Roman Bacchus). Dionysos was the focus of an unofficial mystery religion popular in Italy at this time among women. The precise nature of the Dionysiac rites is unknown, but the figural cycle in this room, illustrating mortals (all female save for one boy) interacting with mythological figures, is thought to provide some evidence for the cult's initiation rites. In these rites young women, emulating Ariadne, daughter of King Minos (see Chapter 4), were united in marriage with Dionysos.

The backdrop for the nearly life-size figures is a series of painted panels imitating marble revetment, just as in the First Style but without the modeling in relief. In front of this marble wall (but actually on the same two-dimensional surface), the painter created the illusion of a shallow ledge on which the human and divine actors move around the room. Especially striking is how some of the figures interact across the corners of the room. Note, for example, the seminude winged woman at the far right of the rear wall who lashes out with her whip across the space of the room at a kneeling woman with a bare back (the initiate and bride-to-be of Dionysos) on the left end of the right wall. Nothing comparable to this room existed in Hellenistic Greece. Despite the presence of Dionysos, satyrs, and other figures from Greek mythology, this is a Roman design.

10-17   Gardenscape, Second Style wall painting, from the Villa of Livia, Primaporta, Italy, ca. 30–20 B.C. Approx. 6′ 7″ high. Museo Nazionale Romano-Palazzo Massimo alle Terme, Rome.

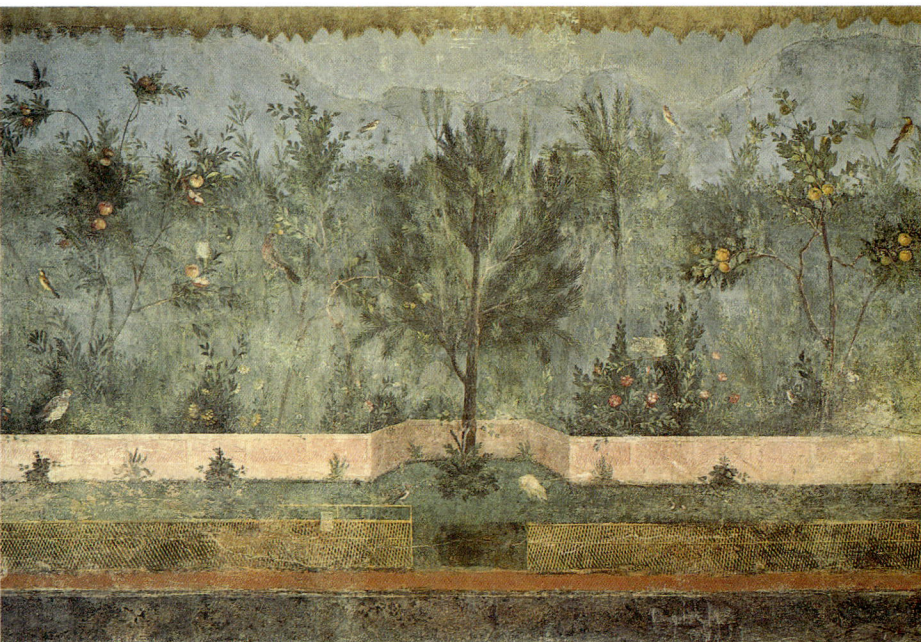

PERSPECTIVE PAINTING IN ANTIQUITY In the early Second Style Dionysiac mystery frieze, the spatial illusionism is confined to the painted platform that projects into the room. But in mature Second Style designs, painters created a three-dimensional setting that also extends beyond the wall. A prime example is a cubiculum (FIG. **10-16**) from the Villa of Publius Fannius Synistor at Boscoreale, near Pompeii, decorated between 50 and 40 B.C. The frescoes were removed soon after their discovery, and today they are part of a reconstructed Roman bedroom in the Metropolitan Museum of Art in New York City. All around the room the Second Style painter opened up the walls with vistas of Italian towns and sacred sanctuaries. Painted doors and gates invite the viewer to walk through the wall into the world the painter created.

Although the Boscoreale painter was inconsistent in applying it, this Roman artist demonstrated a knowledge of *linear (single vanishing-point) perspective*, often incorrectly said to be an innovation of Italian Renaissance artists (see "Depicting Objects in Space: Perspectival Systems in the Early Renaissance," Chapter 21, page 594). In this kind of perspective, all the receding lines in a composition converge on a single point along the painting's central axis to show depth and distance. Ancient writers state that Greek painters of the fifth century B.C. first used linear perspective for the design of Athenian stage sets (hence its Greek name, *skenographia* or *scene painting*). It was most successfully employed in the Boscoreale cubiculum in the far corners, where a low gate leads to a peristyle framing a tholos temple (see detail). Single-vanishing-point perspective was used more consistently and on an even grander scale in the somewhat later Room of the Masks in what was probably the house of the emperor Augustus on the Palatine Hill in Rome. Artists used it less successfully in numerous other Pompeian houses. Linear perspective was a favored tool of Second Style painters seeking to transform the usually windowless walls of Roman houses into "picture-window" vistas that expanded the apparent space of the rooms.

AN EMPRESS'S PAINTED GARDEN The ultimate example of a Second Style picture-window wall was found in the Villa of Livia, wife of the emperor Augustus, at Primaporta, just north of Rome. There, a vaulted, partly underground room was decorated on all sides with lush gardenscapes (FIG. **10-17**). The painter dispensed with the wall entirely, even as a framing element for the landscape. The only architectural element is the flimsy fence of the garden itself. To suggest recession, the painter mastered another kind of perspective, *atmospheric perspective,* indicating depth by the increasingly blurred appearance of objects in the distance. At Livia's villa, the fence, trees, and birds in the foreground are precisely painted, while the details of the dense foliage in the background are indistinct. Among the wall paintings examined so far, only the landscape fresco from Thera (see FIG. 4-10) offers a similar wraparound view of nature. But the Aegean fresco's white sky and red, yellow, and blue rock formations do not create a successful illusion of a world filled with air and light just a few steps away.

THIRD STYLE ELEGANCE AND FANTASY Livia's magnificent verdant gardenscape is the polar opposite of First Style designs, which reinforce, rather than deny, the heavy presence of confining walls with modulated surfaces re-

10-18 Detail of a Third Style wall painting, from Cubiculum 15 of the Villa of Agrippa Postumus, Boscotrecase, Italy, ca. 10 B.C. Approx. 7′ 8″ high. Metropolitan Museum of Art, New York.

producing marble panels. But tastes changed rapidly in the Roman world, as in society today, and not long after the Primaporta villa walls were decorated with gardenscapes, Roman patrons began to favor mural designs that reasserted the primacy of the wall surface. In the *Third Style* of Pompeian painting, artists no longer attempted to replace the walls with three-dimensional worlds of their own creation. Nor did they seek to imitate the appearance of the marble walls of Hellenistic kings. Instead they decorated the walls of their Roman patrons' homes with delicate linear fantasies sketched on predominantly *monochromatic* (one-color) backgrounds.

One of the earliest examples of the new style is a room in the Villa of Agrippa Postumus at Boscotrecase (FIG. **10-18**),

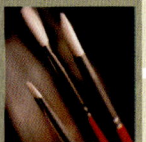

The Roman Illustrated Book

The hundreds of paintings uncovered in the cities Mount Vesuvius buried give the false impression that the history of Roman painting is well documented and that art historians can trace its development decade by decade. But Pompeii, Herculaneum, and the other towns around the Bay of Naples have yielded only frescoes. As in Greece, no Roman paintings on wooden panels have been discovered, save for the special case of Roman Egypt (FIGS. 10-63 and 10-64). Nor has anyone found any of the grand tableaus of battles and beseiged cities that were exhibited in Roman triumphal processions and then displayed in public buildings to perpetuate the memory of a general's great achievements on the state's behalf.

Also apparently lost are virtually all illustrated Roman books, although art historians know they once existed in great numbers. The oldest preserved painted manuscript, itself very incomplete, is the *Vatican Vergil*, which dates from the early fifth century A.D. It originally contained more than

two hundred pictures illustrating all of Vergil's works. Today only fifty painted *folios* (pages) of the *Aeneid* and *Georgics* survive.

On the page illustrated here (FIG. 10-19) is a section of text from the *Georgics*. There, Vergil recounts his visit to a modest farm near Tarentum (Taranto, in southern Italy). The farm belongs to an old man from Corycus in Asia Minor. In the framed painted panel at the bottom of the page, the old farmer is seated at the left. His rustic farmhouse is in the background, rendered in a three-quarter view. The farmer speaks about the pleasures of the simple life in the country and on his methods of gardening. His audience is two laborers and, at the far right, Vergil himself in the guise of a farmhand. The style is reminiscent of Pompeian landscapes, with quick touches that suggest space and atmosphere. In fact, the heavy, dark frame has close parallels in the late Pompeian styles of mural painting (FIG. 10-20).

near Pompeii, also a property the imperial family owned. The villa was probably painted just before 10 B.C. Nowhere does the artist use illusionistic painting to penetrate the wall. In place of the stately columns of the Second Style are insubstantial and impossibly thin *colonnettes* supporting featherweight canopies barely reminiscent of pediments. In the center of this delicate and elegant architectural frame is a tiny floating landscape painted directly on the jet-black ground. It is hard to imagine a sharper contrast with the panoramic gardenscape at Livia's villa. On other Third Style walls, landscapes and mythological scenes appear in frames, like modern canvas paintings hung on walls. Never could these framed panels be mistaken for windows opening onto a world beyond the room.

ROMAN PAINTING AND LATIN POETRY Despite the differences in style, the landscapes of the Primaporta and Boscotrecase villas reveal a love of country life and idealization of nature that also appears in the pastoral poetry of Vergil, a contemporary of Livia and Augustus. Horace, another renowned Augustan poet, also proclaimed in one of his odes the satisfaction afforded the city dweller by a villa in the countryside, where life is beautiful, simple, and natural, in contrast with the urban greed for gold and power. A fifth-century A.D. illustrated manuscript of Vergil's verse (FIG. **10-19**) is in the Vatican Library today. It not only contains Vergil's pastoral poems, but provides invaluable evidence about the nature of Roman illustrated books (see "The Roman Illustrated Book," above).

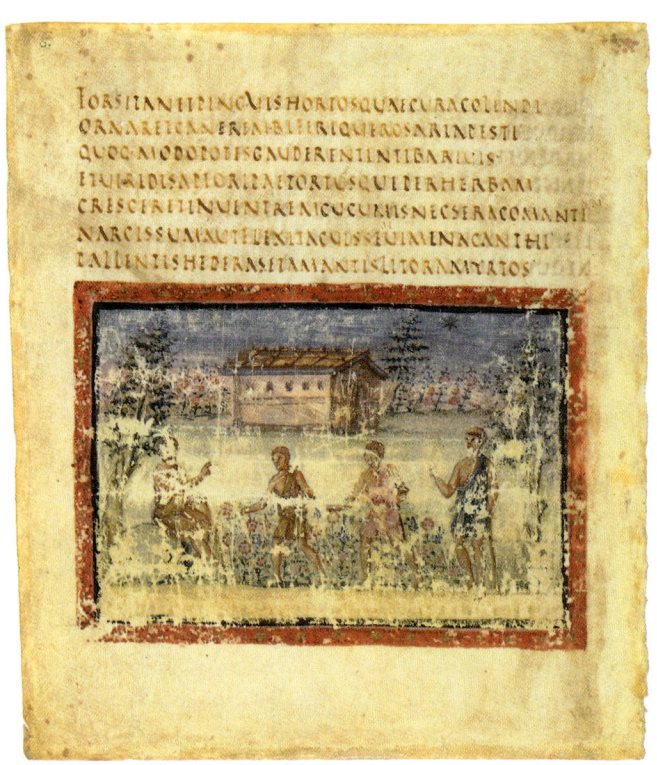

10-19 The old farmer of Corycus, folio 7 verso, from the *Vatican Vergil*, ca. A.D. 400–420. Tempera on parchment, approx. $1\frac{1}{2}$" × 1'. Biblioteca Apostolica Vaticana, Rome.

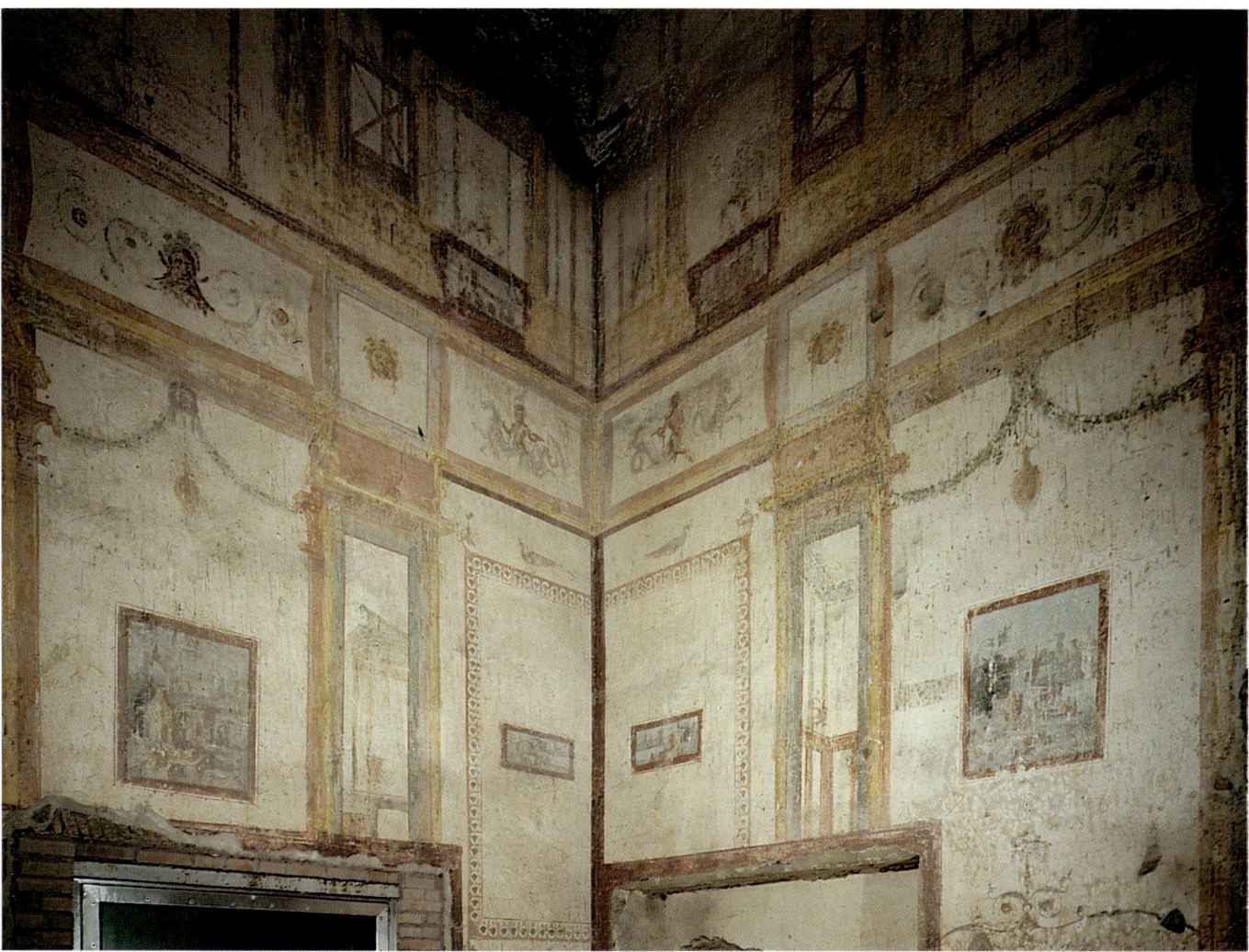

10-20 Fourth Style wall paintings in Room 78 of the *Domus Aurea* of Nero, Rome, Italy, A.D. 64–68.

NERO AND THE FOURTH STYLE In the *Fourth Style,* a taste for illusionism returned once again. This style became popular around the time of the Pompeian earthquake of A.D. 62, and it was the preferred manner of mural decoration when the town was buried in volcanic ash in 79. The earliest examples display a kinship with the Third Style, such as Room 78 (FIG. **10-20**) in the emperor Nero's fabulous *Domus Aurea,* or Golden House, in Rome (see "An Imperial Pleasure Palace: The Golden House of Nero," page 270). All the walls are an austere creamy white. In some areas the artist painted sea creatures, birds, and other motifs directly on the monochromatic background, much like the landscape in the Boscotrecase villa (FIG. 10-18). Landscapes appear here also—as framed paintings in the center of each large white subdivision of the wall. But views through the wall are also part of the design, although the Fourth Style architectural vistas are irrational fantasies. Viewers do not look out on cityscapes or round temples set in peristyles, but at fragments of buildings—columns supporting half-pediments, double stories of columns supporting nothing at all—painted on the same white ground as the rest of the wall. In the Fourth Style, architecture became just another motif in the painter's ornamental repertoire.

PAINTING ON THE EVE OF THE ERUPTION The latest Fourth Style walls conform to the same design principles, but the painters rejected the quiet elegance of the Third Style and early Fourth Style in favor of crowded and confused compositions and sometimes garish color combinations. The Ixion Room (FIG. **10-21**) of the House of the Vettii at Pompeii was decorated in this manner just before the eruption of Mount Vesuvius. The room served as a triclinium in the house remodeled by the Vettius brothers after the earthquake. It opened onto the peristyle seen in the background of FIG. 10-13.

The decor of the dining room is a kind of résumé of all the previous styles, another instance of the eclecticism noted earlier as characteristic of Roman art in general. The lowest zone, for example, is one of the most successful imitations anywhere of costly multicolored imported marbles, despite the fact the illusion is created without recourse to relief, as in the First Style. The large white panels in the corners of the room, with their delicate floral frames and floating central motifs, would fit naturally into the most elegant Third Style design. Unmistakably Fourth Style, however, are the fragmentary architectural vistas of the central and upper zones of the Ixion Room

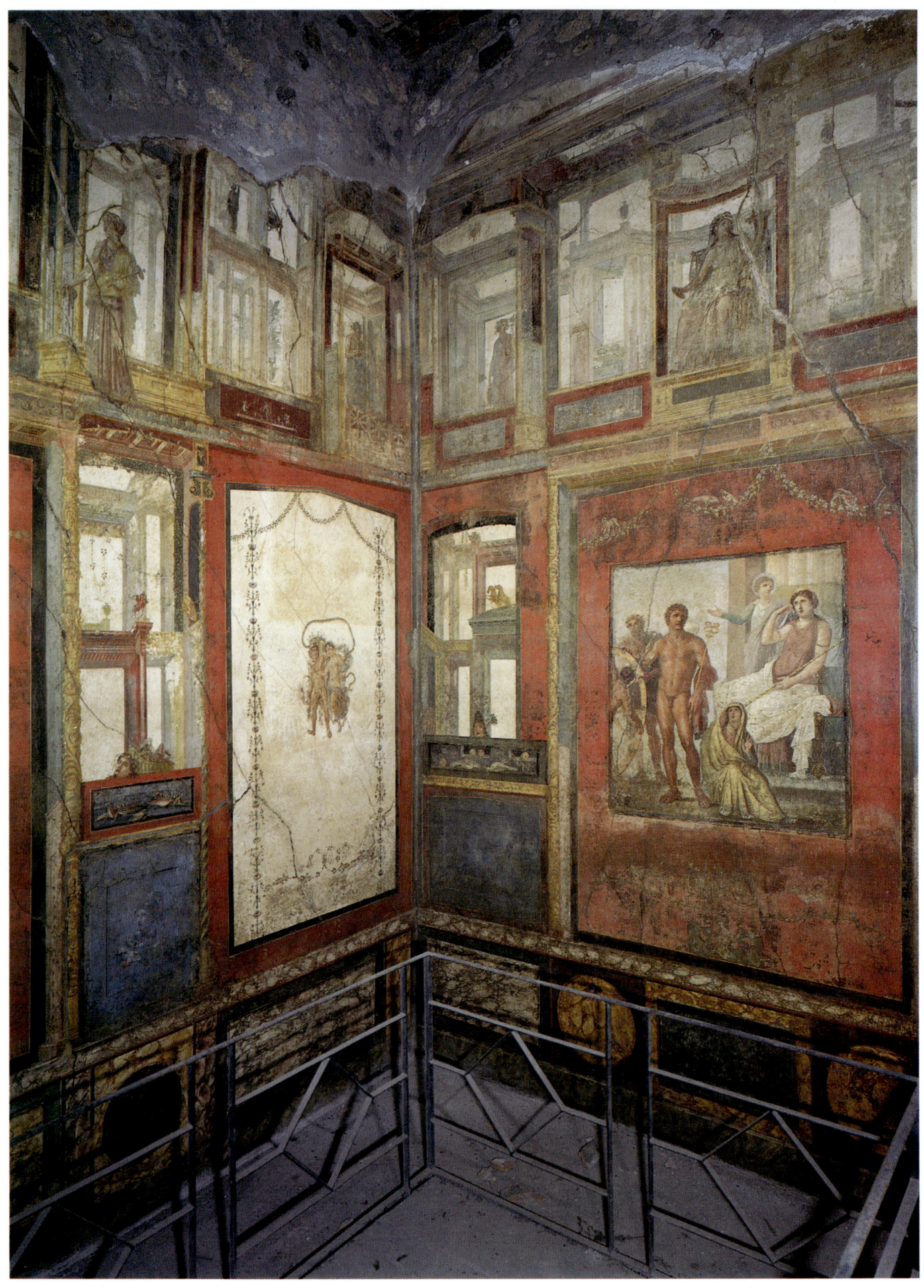

10-21 Fourth Style wall paintings in the Ixion Room (Triclinium P) of the House of the Vettii, Pompeii, Italy, ca. A.D. 70–79.

walls. They are unrelated to one another, do not constitute a unified cityscape beyond the wall, and are peopled with figures that would tumble into the room if they took a single step forward.

GREEK MYTHS ON ROMAN WALLS   The Ixion Room takes its nickname from the mythological panel painting at the center of the rear wall (FIG. 10-21). Ixion had attempted to seduce Hera, and Zeus punished him by binding him to a perpetually spinning wheel. The panels on the two side walls also have Greek myths as subjects. The Ixion Room may be likened to a small private art gallery with paintings decorating the walls, as in many modern homes. Scholars long have believed that these and the many other mythological paintings on Third and Fourth Style walls were based on lost Greek panels, although few, if any, can be described as true copies of "Old Masters." These paintings attest to the Romans' continuing admiration for Greek artworks three centuries after Marcellus brought the treasures of Syracuse to Rome.

Mythological figures were on occasion also the subject of Roman mosaics. The House of Neptune and Amphitrite at Herculaneum takes its name from the mosaic shown here (FIG. **10-22**). Statuesque images of the sea god Neptune and his wife Amphitrite, set into an elaborate niche, appropriately preside over the running water of the fountain in the courtyard in front of them. In the ancient world, mosaics were usually confined to floors (as was the *Battle of Issus,* FIG. 5-69), where the tesserae formed a durable as well as decorative surface. In Roman times, however, mosaics also decorated walls and even ceilings, foreshadowing the extensive use of wall and vault mosaics in the Middle Ages (see "Mosaics," Chapter 11, page 314).

The subjects chosen for Roman wall paintings and mosaics were diverse. Although mythological themes were immensely popular, a vast range of other subjects also has been documented. As noted, landscape paintings frequently appear on

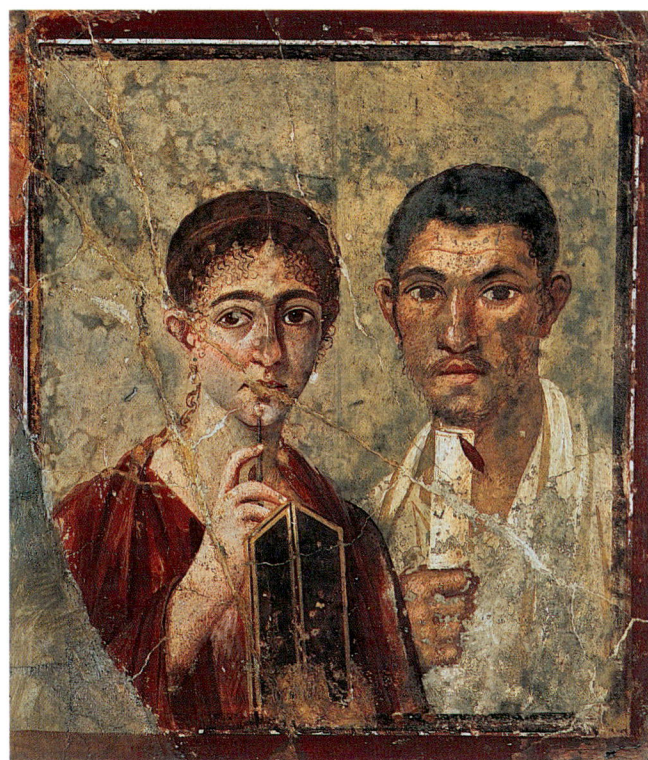

10-23   Portrait of a husband and wife, wall painting from House VII,2,6, Pompeii, Italy, ca. A.D. 70–79. Approx. 1′ 11″ × 1′ 8½″. Museo Nazionale, Naples.

Second, Third, and Fourth Style walls. Paintings and mosaics depicting scenes from history include the *Battle of Issus* mosaic and the mural painting of the brawl in the amphitheater of Pompeii (FIG. 10-12).

PRETENTIOUS PRIVATE PORTRAITS   Given the Roman custom of keeping *imagines* of illustrious ancestors in atriums, it is not surprising that painted portraits have been found on the walls of some Pompeian houses. Almost all were cut out of the walls on discovery and brought to Naples, where they hang in the Archeological Museum as if they were independent panels in the tradition of later portraits on canvas. One must go to Naples to see the portrait of a husband and wife illustrated here (FIG. **10-23**), but originally it formed part of a Fourth Style wall of an *exedra* (recessed area) opening onto the atrium of a Pompeian house. The man holds a scroll and the woman a stylus and a wax writing tablet, standard attributes in Roman marriage portraits. They suggest the fine education of those depicted—even if, as was sometimes true, the individuals were uneducated or even illiterate. Such portraits were thus the Roman equivalent of modern wedding photographs of the bride and groom posing in rented formal garments never worn by them before or afterward. By contrast, the heads are not standard types but sensitive studies of the man and woman's individual faces. This is another instance of a realistic portrait placed on a conventional figure type, a recurring phenomenon in Roman portraiture (see "Role-Playing in Roman Portraiture," page 266) first encountered here in the statue of the Republican general found at Tivoli (FIG. 10-7).

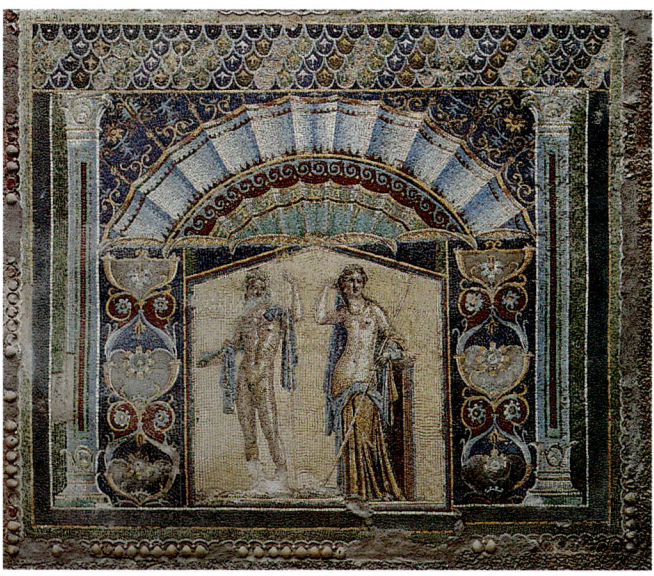

10-22   Neptune and Amphitrite, wall mosaic in the summer triclinium of the House of Neptune and Amphitrite, Herculaneum, Italy, ca. A.D. 62–79.

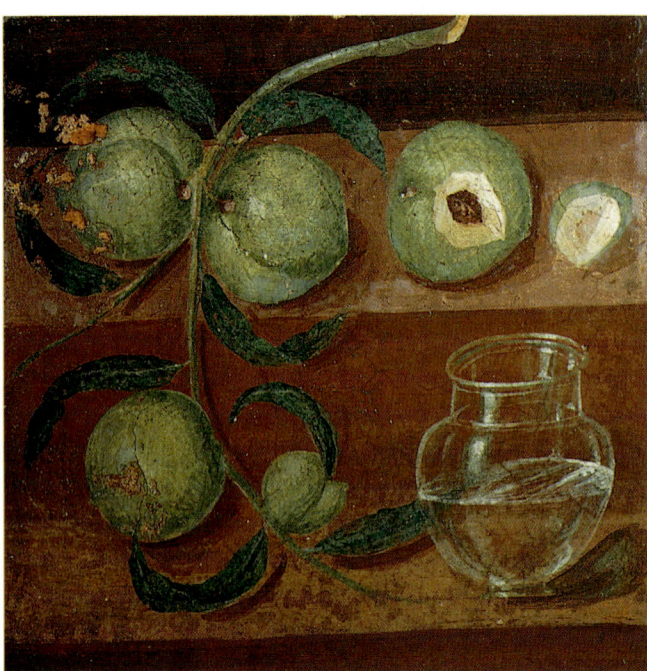

10-24   Still life with peaches, detail of a Fourth Style wall painting, from Herculaneum, Italy, ca. A.D. 62–79. Approx. 1′ 2″ × 1′ 1½″. Museo Nazionale, Naples.

PAINTING THE INANIMATE   Roman painters' interest in the likenesses of individual people was matched by their concern for recording the appearance of everyday objects. This explains the frequent inclusion of still-life paintings in the mural schemes of the Second, Third, and Fourth Styles. A still life with peaches and a carafe, a detail of a painted wall from Herculaneum (FIG. **10-24**), demonstrates that Roman painters sought to create illusionistic effects when depicting small objects, as well as architecture and landscape. Here, the method used involves light and shade with scrupulous attention to shadows and to highlights. Undoubtedly, the artist worked directly from an arrangement made specifically for this painting. The fruit, the stem and leaves, and the glass jar were set out on shelves to give the illusion of the casual, almost accidental, relationship of objects in a cupboard.

Art historians have not found evidence of anything like these Roman studies of food and other inanimate objects until the Dutch still lifes of the seventeenth and eighteenth centuries (see FIG. 24-54). The Roman murals are not as exact in drawing, perspective, or rendering of light and shade as the Dutch canvases. Still, the illusion created here marks the furthest advance by ancient painters in representational technique. The artist seemed to understand that the look of things is a function of light. The goal was to paint light as one would strive to paint the touchable object that reflects and absorbs it.

THE EARLY EMPIRE

ANTONY AND CLEOPATRA VANQUISHED   The murder of Julius Caesar on the Ides of March, 44 B.C., plunged the Roman world into a bloody civil war. The fighting lasted thirteen years and ended only when Octavian (bet-

ter known as Augustus), Caesar's grandnephew and adopted son, crushed the naval forces of Mark Antony and Queen Cleopatra of Egypt at Actium in northwestern Greece. Antony and Cleopatra committed suicide, and in 30 B.C. Egypt, once the ancient world's wealthiest and most powerful kingdom, became another province in the ever-expanding Roman Empire.

Historians reckon the passage from the old Roman Republic to the new Roman Empire from the day in 27 B.C. when the Senate conferred the majestic title of Augustus (r. 27 B.C.–A.D. 14) on Octavian. The Empire was ostensibly a continuation of the Republic, with the same constitutional offices, but in fact Augustus, who was recognized as *princeps* (first citizen), occupied all the key positions. He was consul and *imperator* (commander in chief, from which comes the word *emperor*) and even, after 12 B.C., *pontifex maximus* (chief priest of the state religion). These offices gave Augustus control of all aspects of Roman public life.

THE PAX ROMANA   With powerful armies keeping order on the empire's frontiers and no opposition at home, Augustus brought peace and prosperity to a war-weary Mediterranean world. Known in his own day as the *Pax Augusta* (Augustan Peace), the peace Augustus established prevailed for two centuries. It came to be called simply the *Pax Romana*. During this time the emperors commissioned a huge number of public works throughout the Empire: roads, bridges, forums, temples, basilicas, theaters, amphitheaters, market halls, and bathing complexes, all on an unprecedented scale. And people everywhere were reminded of the source of this beneficence by the erection of imperial portraits and by arches covered with reliefs recounting the emperor's great deeds. These portraits and reliefs often presented a picture of the emperor and his achievements that bore little resemblance to historical fact. Their purpose, however, was not to provide an objective record but to mold public opinion. The Roman emperors and the artists they employed have had few equals in the effective use of art and architecture for propagandistic ends.

Augustus and the Julio-Claudians (27 B.C.–A.D. 68)

THE SON OF A GOD RULES ROME   When Octavian inherited Caesar's fortune in 44 B.C., he was not yet nineteen years old. When he vanquished Antony and Cleopatra at Actium in 31 B.C. and became undisputed master of the Mediterranean world, he had not reached his thirty-second birthday. The rule by elders that had characterized the Roman Republic for nearly half a millennium came to an abrupt end. Suddenly Roman portraitists were called on to produce images of a *youthful* head of state. But Augustus was more than merely young. Caesar had been made a god after his death, and Augustus, while never claiming to be a god himself, widely advertised himself as the son of a god. His portraits—produced in great numbers by anonymous artists the state paid—were designed to present the image of a godlike leader, a superior being who, miraculously, never aged. Although Augustus lived until A.D. 14, even official portraits made near the end of his life continued to show manner of the orator Aule Metele (see FIG. 9-15). Although the head is that of an individual and not a nameless athlete, its overall shape, the sharp ridges of the brows, and the tight cap of layered hair emulate the Polykleitan style. Current events are referred to on Augustus's cuirass, which depicts the return of captured Roman military standards by the Parthians. The Cupid at his feet serves a very different purpose. Caesar's family, the Julians, traced their ancestry back to Venus, and the inclusion of Venus's son was an unsubtle reminder of Augustus's divine descent. Every facet of the Primaporta statue was designed to carry a political message.

A NEVER-AGING EMPRESS A portrait bust of Livia (FIG. **10-26**) shows that the imperial women of the Augustan age shared the emperor's eternal youthfulness. Although she sports the latest Roman coiffure, with the hair rolled over the forehead and knotted at the nape of the neck, Livia's blemishless skin and sharply defined features derive from images of Classical Greek goddesses. Livia outlived Augustus by fifteen years, dying at age eighty-seven. In her portraits, the coiffure changed with the introduction of each new fashion, but her face remained ever young, as befitted her exalted position in the Roman state.

THE AUGUSTAN PEACE COMMEMORATED On Livia's birthday in 9 B.C., Augustus dedicated the Ara Pacis Augustae (Altar of Augustan Peace), the monument

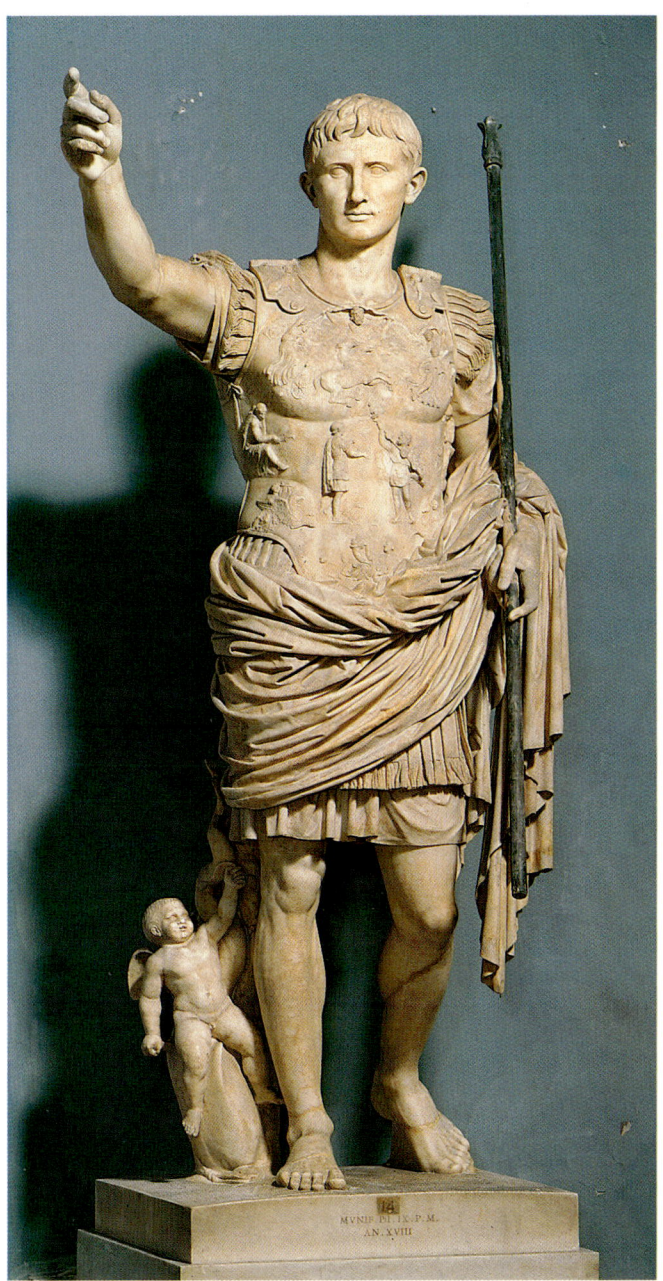

10-25 Portrait of Augustus as general, from Primaporta, Italy, copy of a bronze original of ca. 20 B.C. Marble, 6′ 8″ high. Vatican Museums, Rome.

him as a handsome youth (see FIG. Intro-10). Such a notion may seem ridiculous today, when television, the internet, magazines, and newspapers portray world leaders as they truly appear, but in antiquity few people had actually seen the emperor. His official image was all most knew. It therefore could be manipulated at will.

The models for Augustus's idealized portraits cannot be found in the veristic likenesses of the Roman Republic. Rather, Classical Greek art inspired the emperor's sculptors. The portrait statue of Augustus (FIG. **10-25**) found at his wife Livia's villa at Primaporta depicts the emperor as general. (Others portray him in different roles. See "Role-Playing in Roman Portraiture," page 266.) It is based closely on Polykleitos's *Doryphoros* (see FIG. 5-38). Here, however, the emperor addresses his troops with his right arm extended in the

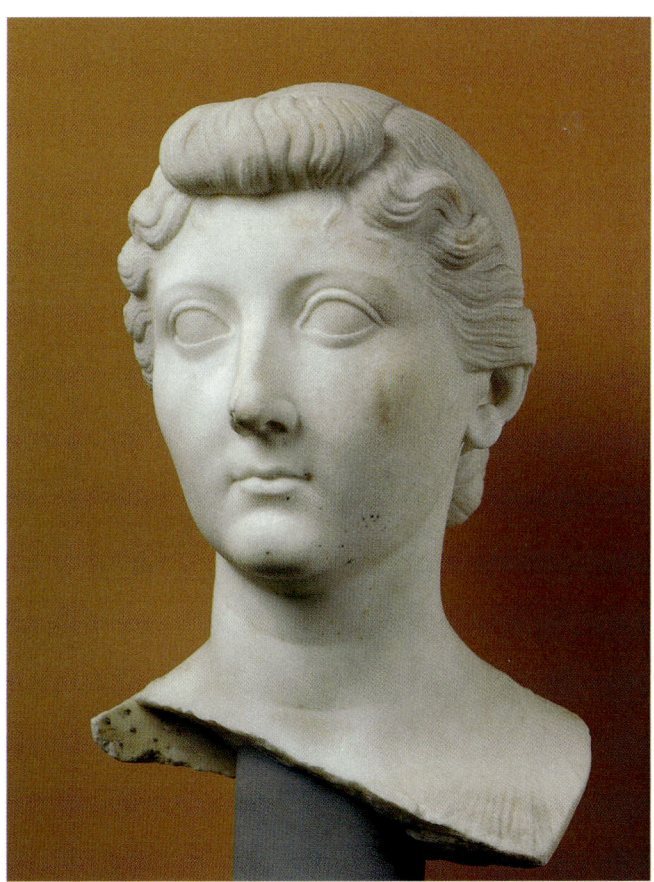

10-26 Portrait bust of Livia, from Faiyum, Egypt, early first century A.D. Marble, approx. 1′1½″ high. Ny Carlsberg Glyptotek, Copenhagen.

ART AND SOCIETY

Role-Playing in Roman Portraiture

In every town throughout the vast Roman Empire, portraits of the emperors and empresses and their families were displayed—in forums, basilicas, baths, and markets; in front of temples; atop triumphal arches—anywhere a statue could be placed. The statue heads varied little from Britain to Syria. All were replicas of official images, either imported or scrupulously copied by local artists. But the portrait heads were placed on many types of bodies. The type chosen depended on the position the person held in Roman society or the various fictitious guises imperial family members assumed. Portraits of Augustus, for example, show him not only as armed general (FIG. 10-25) but also as recipient of the civic crown for saving the lives of fellow citizens (see FIG. Intro-10), veiled priest, toga-clad magistrate, traveling commander on horseback, heroically nude warrior, and various Roman gods, including Jupiter, Apollo, and Mercury.

Such role-playing was not confined to emperors and princes but extended to their wives, daughters, sisters, and mothers. Statues of Livia (FIG. 10-26) portray her as many goddesses, including Ceres, Juno, Venus, and Vesta. She also appears as the personification of Health, Justice, and Piety. In fact, it was common for imperial women to appear on Roman coins not only as goddesses but also as embodiments of feminine virtue. Faustina the Younger, for example, the wife of Marcus Aurelius and mother of thirteen children, appears as Venus and Fecundity, among many other roles. Julia Domna (FIG. 10-64), Septimius Severus's wife, is Juno, Venus, Peace, and Victory in her portraits.

Ordinary citizens also engaged in role-playing. Some assumed literary pretensions, as in the portrait painting of a Pompeian husband and wife discussed earlier (FIG. 10-23). Others equated themselves with Greek heroes (FIG. 10-61) or Roman deities (FIG. 10-62) on their coffins. The common people followed the lead of the emperors and empresses.

---

celebrating his most important achievement, the establishment of peace. The altar (FIG. **10-27**) was reconstructed during the Fascist era in Italy in connection with the two thousandth anniversary of Augustus's birth, when Mussolini was seeking to build and head a modern Roman Empire. The altar stands within an almost square wall enclosure adorned with acanthus tendrils in the lower zone and figural reliefs in the upper zone. Four panels on the east and west ends depict carefully selected mythological subjects, including (at the right in our photograph) a relief of Aeneas making a sacrifice. Aeneas was the son of Venus and one of Augustus's forefathers. The connection between the emperor and Aeneas was a key element of Augustus's political ideology for his new golden age. It is no coincidence that the *Aeneid* was written during the rule of Augustus. Vergil's epic poem glorified the young emperor by celebrating the founder of the Julian line.

A second panel (FIG. **10-28**), on the other end of the altar enclosure, depicts a seated matron with two animated babies on her lap. Her identity has been much disputed. She is usually called Tellus (Mother Earth), although some have called her Pax (Peace), Ceres (goddess of grain), or even Venus. Whatever her name, she epitomizes the fruits of the Pax Augusta. All around her the bountiful earth is in bloom, and animals of different species live peacefully side by side. Personifications of refreshing breezes (note their windblown drapery) flank her. One rides a bird, the other a sea creature. Earth, sky, and water were all incorporated into this picture of peace and fertility in the Augustan cosmos.

Processions of the imperial family and other important dignitaries appear on the long north and south sides of the Ara Pacis (FIG. **10-29**). The parallel friezes of the Ara Pacis were clearly inspired to some degree by the Panathenaic procession frieze of the Parthenon (see FIG. 5-48, bottom). This was another instance of Augustan artists using Classical Greek

models. Augustus sought to present his new order as a golden age like that of Athens under Pericles in the middle of the fifth century B.C. The emulation of Classical models thus made a political statement, as well as an artistic one.

Even so, the Roman procession is very different in character from the Greek. On the Parthenon, anonymous figures act out an event that recurred every four years. The frieze stands for *all* Panathenaic Festival processions. The Ara Pacis depicts a specific event—probably the inaugural ceremony of 13 B.C. when work on the altar began—and recognizable contemporary figures. Among those portrayed are children, who restlessly tug on their elders' garments and talk to one another when they should be quiet on a solemn occasion—in short, children who act like children, and not like miniature adults as they frequently do in the history of art. Their presence lends a great deal of charm to the procession, but that is not why children were included on the Ara Pacis when they had never before appeared on any Greek or Roman state monument. Augustus was concerned about a decline in the birthrate among the Roman nobility, and he enacted a series of laws designed to promote marriage, marital fidelity, and raising children. The portrayal of men with their families on the Altar of Peace was intended as a moral exemplar. Once again, the emperor used art to further his own political and social agenda.

ROME BECOMES A MARBLE CITY Augustus's most ambitious project in the capital was the construction of a new forum with a Temple of Mars facing into a rectangular plaza flanked by porticoes. The temple and colonnades were made of white marble from Carrara (ancient Luna), the same source the great sculptors of the Italian Renaissance used. Prior to the opening of these quarries in the second half of the first century B.C., marble had to be imported at great cost from abroad, and it was used sparingly. The ready availability

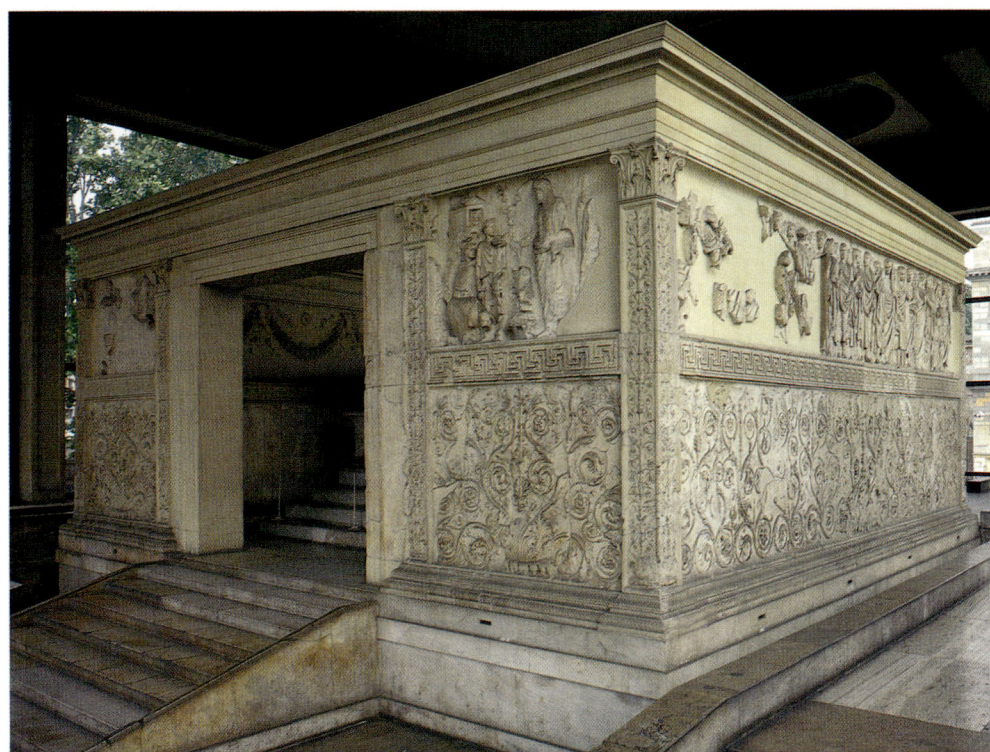

10-27 Ara Pacis Augustae (view from the southwest), Rome, Italy, 13–9 B.C.

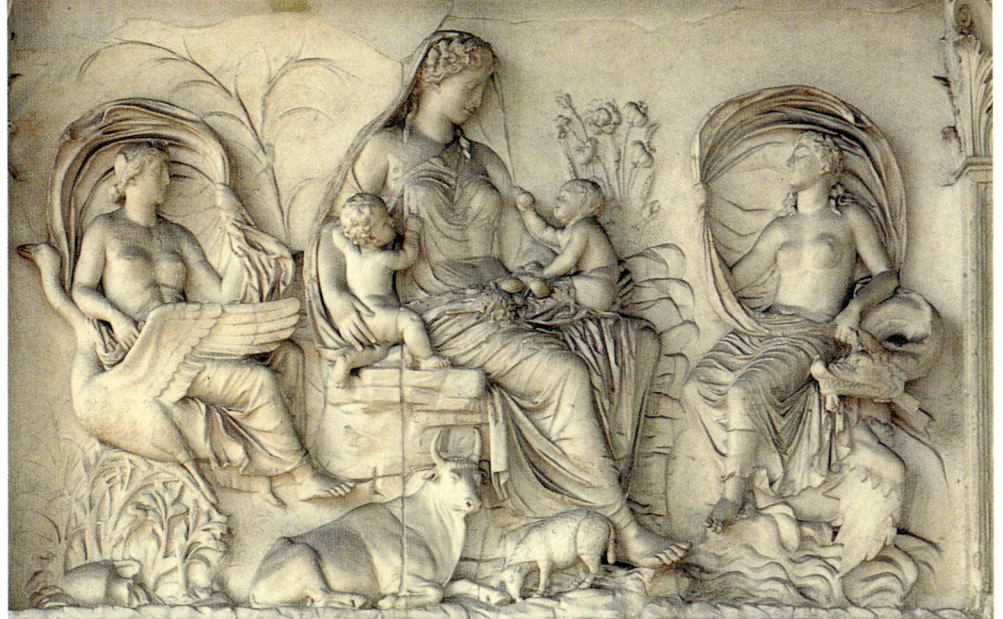

10-28 Female personification (Tellus?), panel from the east facade of the Ara Pacis Augustae, Rome, Italy, 13–9 B.C. Marble, approx. 5′ 3″ high.

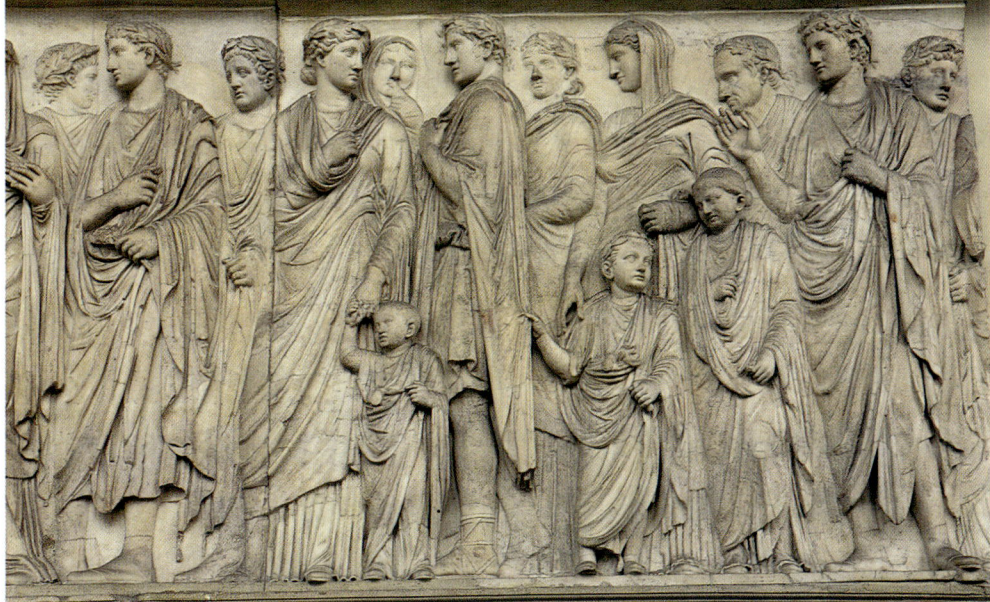

10-29 Procession of the imperial family, detail of the south frieze of the Ara Pacis Augustae, Rome, Italy, 13–9 B.C. Marble, approx. 5′ 3″ high.

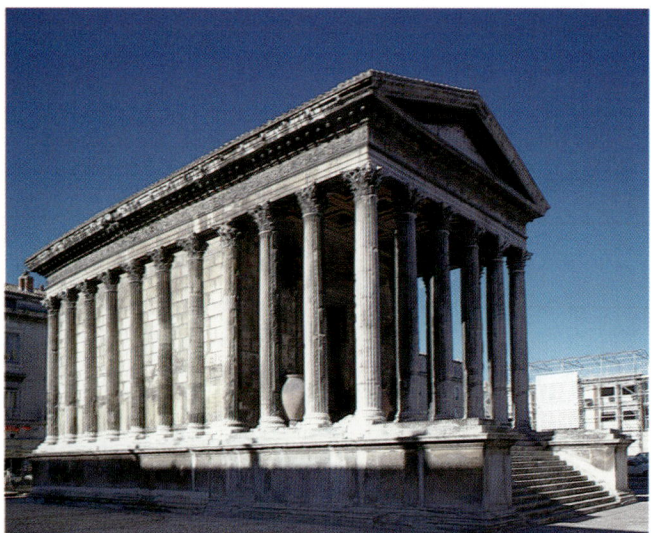

10-30   Maison Carrée, Nîmes, France, ca. A.D. 1–10.

of Italian marble under Augustus made possible the emperor's famous boast that he had found Rome a city of brick and transformed it into a city of marble.

The extensive use of Carrara marble for public monuments (including the Ara Pacis) must be seen as part of Augustus's larger program to make his city the equal of Periclean Athens. In fact, the Forum of Augustus incorporated several explicit references to Classical Athens and to the Acropolis in particular, most notably copies of the caryatids of the Erechtheion (see FIG. 5-52) in the upper story of the porticoes. Roman history also was evoked. The porticoes contained dozens of portrait statues, including images of all the major figures of the Julian family going back to Aeneas. Augustus's forum became a kind of public atrium filled with *imagines*. His family history thus became part of the Roman

state's official history. The Forum of Augustus and those of his successors did serve a practical function by providing alternative areas to the old and overcrowded Republican Forum Romanum for the conduct of state business. Yet they also gave the emperors the opportunity to present their own version of history to the Roman people.

ROMAN GAUL AND THOMAS JEFFERSON   The Forum of Augustus is in ruins today, but the conservative Neo-Classical Augustan style it epitomizes may be seen in an exceptionally well-preserved temple at Nîmes (ancient Nemausus) in southern France (ancient Gaul). The so-called Maison Carrée (FIG. **10-30**) dates to the opening years of the first century A.D. Larger than the Temple of "Fortuna Virilis" in Rome (FIG. 10-1), this Corinthian pseudoperipteral temple was patterned on the Temple of Mars in the Forum of Augustus. In fact, many scholars believe that some of the artisans who worked on the Roman temple went immediately afterward to Nîmes to work on the Maison Carrée.

Vitruvius, whose treatise, *The Ten Books of Architecture,* dedicated to Augustus, became the bible of Renaissance architects, preferred the classicizing architectural style of the Maison Carrée and the Forum of Augustus to the newer Roman vaulted concrete technology. The Maison Carrée was also much admired by Thomas Jefferson, who used it as the model for the State Capitol in Richmond, Virginia, which he designed.

THE FRUITS OF THE PAX ROMANA   An earlier Augustan project at Nîmes was the construction of the great aqueduct-bridge known today as the Pont-du-Gard (FIG. **10-31**). Throughout the far-flung territories Rome administered, millions of individuals depended on the government for food distribution, water supply and sanitation, and police and firefighters. Second only to food provision, an adequate water supply for the urban population was the most pressing need.

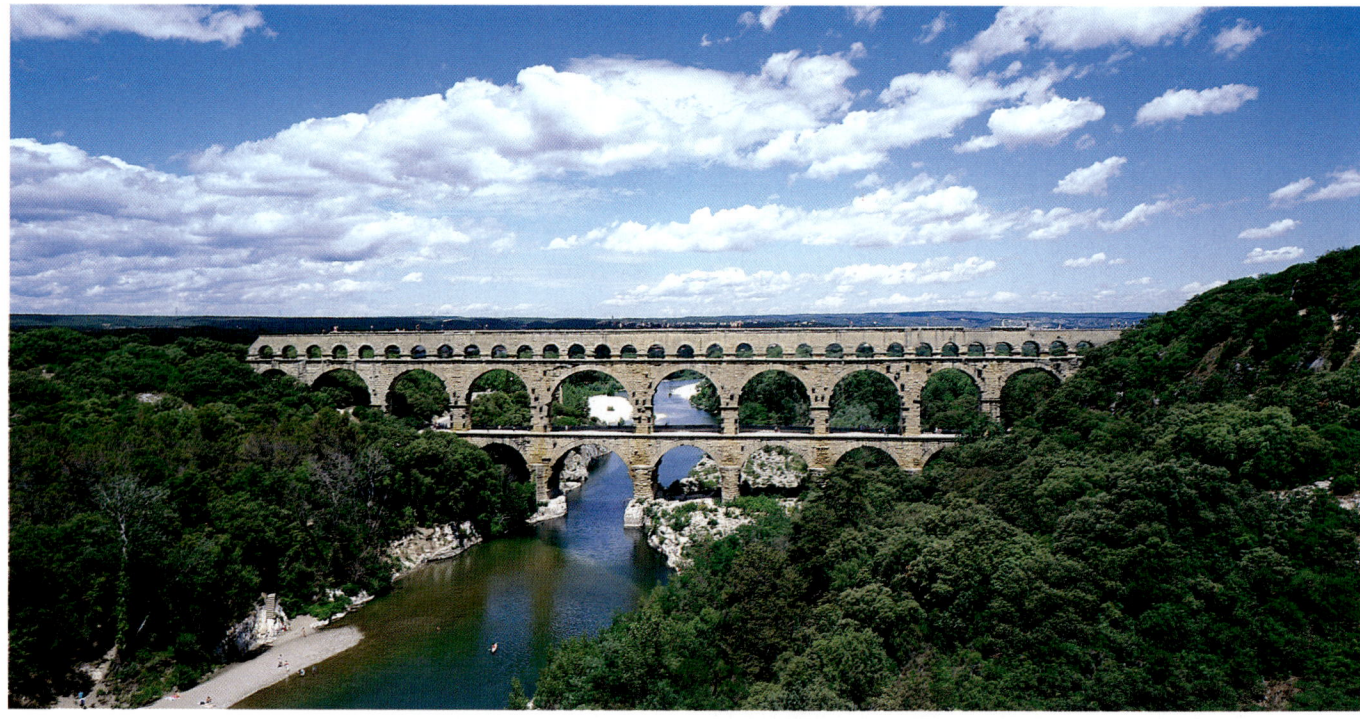

10-31   Pont-du-Gard, Nîmes, France, ca. 16 B.C.

As early as the fourth century B.C., the Romans built aqueducts to carry water from mountain sources to their city on the Tiber River. As Rome's power spread through the Mediterranean world, aqueducts, roads, and bridges were constructed to serve colonies everywhere in the empire.

The Pont-du-Gard demonstrates the skill of Rome's engineers. The aqueduct provided about one hundred gallons of water a day for each inhabitant of Nîmes from a source some thirty miles away. The water was carried over the considerable distance by gravity flow, which required channels built with a continuous gradual decline over the entire route from source to city. The Pont-du-Gard three-story bridge was erected to maintain the height of the water channel where the water crossed the Gard River. Each large arch spans some eighty-two feet and is constructed of uncemented blocks weighing up to two tons each. The bridge's uppermost level consists of a row of smaller arches, three above each of the large openings below. They carry the water channel itself. Their quickened rhythm and the harmonious proportional relationship between the larger and smaller arches reveal that the Roman engineer had a keen aesthetic, as well as practical, sense.

CLAUDIAN RUSTICATION Many aqueducts were required to meet the demand for water in the capital. Under the emperor Claudius (r. A.D. 41–54), a grandiose gate, the Porta Maggiore (FIG. **10-32**), was constructed at the point where two of Rome's water lines (and two intercity trunk roads) converged. Its huge *attic* (uppermost story) bears a wordy dedicatory inscription that conceals the conduits of both aqueducts, one above the other. The gate is the outstanding example of the Roman *rusticated* (rough) masonry style. Instead of using the precisely shaped blocks Hellenic and Augustan architects favored, the designer of the Porta Maggiore combined smooth and rusticated surfaces. These created an exciting, if eccentric, facade with crisply carved

pediments resting on engaged columns composed of rusticated drums. Later architects closely studied the Porta Maggiore, and it profoundly influenced the facade designs of some Renaissance palaces.

NERO'S ARCHITECTURAL REVOLUTION   In A.D. 64, when Nero, stepson and successor of Claudius, was emperor (r. A.D. 54–68), a great fire destroyed large sections of Rome. Afterward, the city was rebuilt in accordance with a new code that required greater fireproofing, resulting in the widespread use of concrete, which was both cheap and fire resistant. Increased use gave Roman architects the opportunity to explore the possibilities the still relatively new material opened up.

After the great fire, Nero asked SEVERUS and CELER, two brilliant architect-engineers, to build a grand imperial palace on a huge confiscated plot of fire-ravaged land near the Forum Romanum (see "An Imperial Pleasure Palace: The Golden House of Nero," page 270). The excavated portion of Nero's *Domus Aurea* contains many rooms of uncertain purpose. Their walls are brick-faced concrete, and concrete vaults cover most rooms. The more important rooms seem to have been located on the southern side, where they faced the villa's artificial lake. Traces of rich decorations, with marble paneling and painted and gilded stucco, have been found in some rooms, while others are adorned with frescoes (FIG. 10-20) in the latest style. Structurally, these chambers are unremarkable. One octagonal hall (drawn in FIG. 10-33), however, stands apart from the rest and testifies to Severus and Celer's entirely new approach to concrete architecture.

The ceiling of the octagonal room is a dome that modulates from an eight-sided to a hemispherical form as it rises toward the oculus. Radiating outward from the five inner sides (the other three, directly or indirectly, face the outside) are smaller, rectangular rooms, covered by concrete vaults.

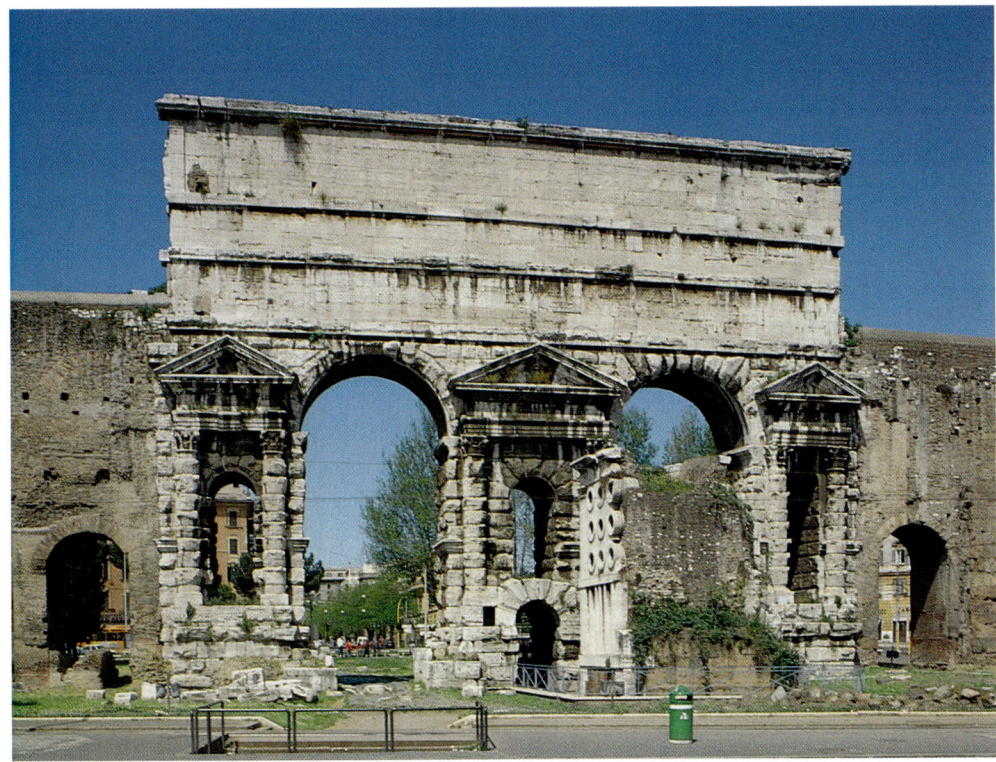

10-32 Porta Maggiore, Rome, Italy, ca. A.D. 50.

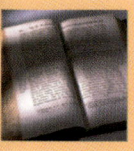

An Imperial Pleasure Palace
The Golden House of Nero

Nero's *Domus Aurea,* or Golden House, was a vast and notoriously extravagant country villa in the heart of Rome. The second-century A.D. Roman biographer Suetonius described it vividly:

> The entrance-hall was large enough to contain a huge statue [of Nero in the guise of Sol, the sun god], 120 feet high; and the pillared arcade ran for a whole mile. An enormous pool, like a sea, was surrounded by buildings made to resemble cities, and by a landscape garden consisting of ploughed fields, vineyards, pastures, and woodlands—where every variety of domestic and wild animal roamed about. Parts of the house were overlaid with gold and studded with precious stones and mother-of-pearl. All the dining-rooms had ceilings of fretted ivory, the panels of which could slide back and let a rain of flowers, or of perfume from hidden sprinklers, shower upon [Nero's] guests. The main dining-room was circular, and its roof revolved, day and night, in time with the sky. Sea water, or sulphur water, was always on tap in the baths. When the palace had been decorated throughout in this lavish style, Nero dedicated it, and condescended to remark: "Good, now I can at last begin to live like a human being!"[1]

Suetonius's description is a welcome reminder that the Roman ruins tourists flock to see are but a dim reflection of the magnificence of the original structures. Only in rare instances, such as the Pantheon, with its marble-revetted walls and floors (FIG. 10-50), can visitors experience anything approaching the architects' intended effects. Even there much of the marble paneling is of later date and the gilded bronze is missing from the dome.

[1] Robert Graves, trans., *Suetonius: The Twelve Caesars* (New York: Penguin, 1957; illustrated edition, 1980), 197–98.

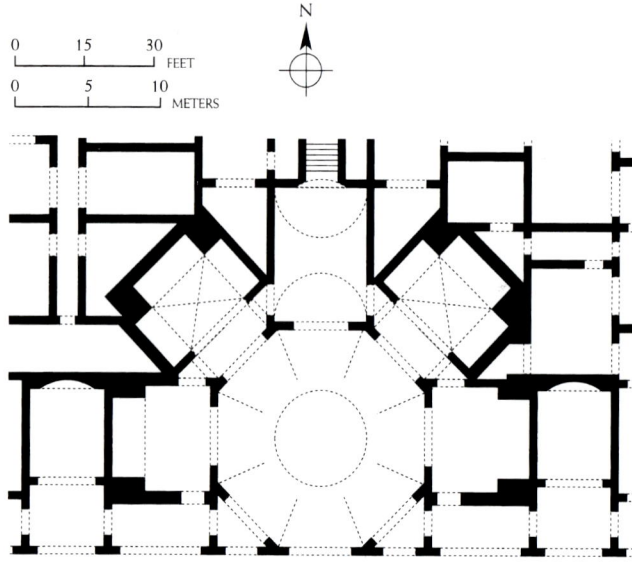

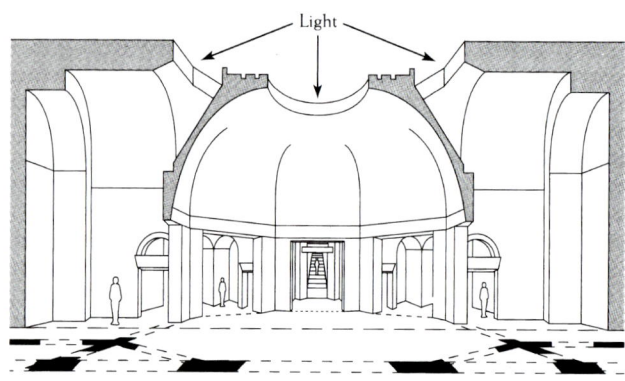

10-33 SEVERUS and CELER, plan *(above)* and section *(below)* of the octagonal hall of the *Domus Aurea* of Nero, Rome, Italy, A.D. 64–68.

These satellite rooms were enlivened by decorative recesses. The middle one contained a waterfall. The architects ingeniously lit the rooms by leaving spaces between their vaulted ceilings and the central dome's exterior. But the most significant aspect of the design is that here, for the first time, the architects appear to have thought of the walls and vaults not as limiting space but as shaping it.

Today, the octagonal hall is deprived of its marble and stucco incrustation, and the concrete shell stands bare, but this serves to focus the visitor's attention on the design's spatial complexity. When one walks through the rooms, one sees that the central domed octagon is defined not by walls but by eight angled piers. The wide square openings between the piers are so large that the rooms beyond look like extensions of the central hall. The grouping of spatial units of different sizes and proportions under a variety of vaults creates a dynamic three-dimensional composition that is both complex and unified. The Neronian architects were not only inventive but also progressive in their recognition of the malleable nature of concrete, a material not limited to the rectilinear forms of traditional post-and-lintel construction.

The Flavians (A.D. 69–96)

Because of his outrageous behavior, Nero was forced to commit suicide in A.D. 68, bringing the Julio-Claudian dynasty to an end. A year of renewed civil strife followed. The man who emerged triumphant in this brief but bloody conflict was Vespasian (r. A.D. 69–79), a general who had served under Claudius and Nero. Vespasian, whose family name was Flavius, had two sons, Titus (r. A.D. 79–81) and Domitian (r. A.D. 81–96). The Flavian dynasty ruled Rome for more than a quarter century.

A TRIUMPH OF ROMAN ENGINEERING   The Flavians left their mark on the capital in many ways, not the least being the construction of the Colosseum (FIG. **10-34**), the monument that, for most people, still represents Rome more than any other building. In the past it was identified so closely with Rome and its empire that in the early Middle Ages there was a saying, "While stands the Colosseum, Rome shall stand; when falls the Colosseum, Rome shall fall; and when Rome falls—the World."[4] The Flavian Amphitheater, as it was known in its own day, was one of Vespasian's first undertakings after becoming emperor. The decision to build the Colosseum was very shrewd politically. The site chosen was the artificial lake on the grounds of Nero's *Domus Aurea,* which was drained for the purpose. By building the new amphitheater there, Vespasian reclaimed for the public the land Nero had confiscated for his private pleasure and provided Romans with the largest arena for gladiatorial combats and other lavish spectacles that had ever been constructed. The Colosseum takes its name, however, not from its size—it could hold more than fifty thousand spectators—but from its location beside the Colossus of Nero, the huge statue of the emperor portrayed as the sun, at the entrance to his urban villa.

Vespasian, who died in A.D. 79, did not live to see the Colosseum in use. The amphitheater was completed in 80 and formally dedicated by Titus. To mark the opening, games were held for one hundred days, at extravagant cost but to the people's delight. The highlight was the flooding of the arena to stage a complete naval battle with more than three thousand participants. Later emperors would compete to see who could put on the most elaborate spectacles, and over the years many thousands of lives were lost in the gladiatorial and animal combats staged in the amphitheater. Many of those who died were Christians, and the Colosseum has never quite outlived its infamy in this respect.

The Colosseum, like the much earlier amphitheater at Pompeii (FIG. 10-11), could not have been built without concrete. The enormous oval seating area is held up by a complex system of corridors covered by concrete barrel vaults. This concrete "skeleton" reveals itself today to anyone who enters the amphitheater. In the centuries following the fall of Rome, the Colosseum served as a convenient quarry for ready-made building materials. Almost all its marble seats were hauled away, exposing the network of vaults below. Hidden in antiquity but visible today are the arena substructures, where were located the waiting rooms for the gladiators, animal cages, and machinery for raising and lowering stage sets as well as animals and humans. Cleverly designed lifting devices brought beasts from their dark dens into the arena's violent light. Above the seats a great velarium, as at Pompeii, once shielded the spectators. It was held up by giant wooden poles affixed to the Colosseum's facade.

The exterior travertine shell is approximately 160 feet high, the height of a modern sixteen-story building. Seventy-six numbered entrances led to the seating area. The relationship of these openings to the tiers of seats within was carefully thought out and resembles that seen in modern sports stadiums. The exterior's decor, however, had nothing to do with

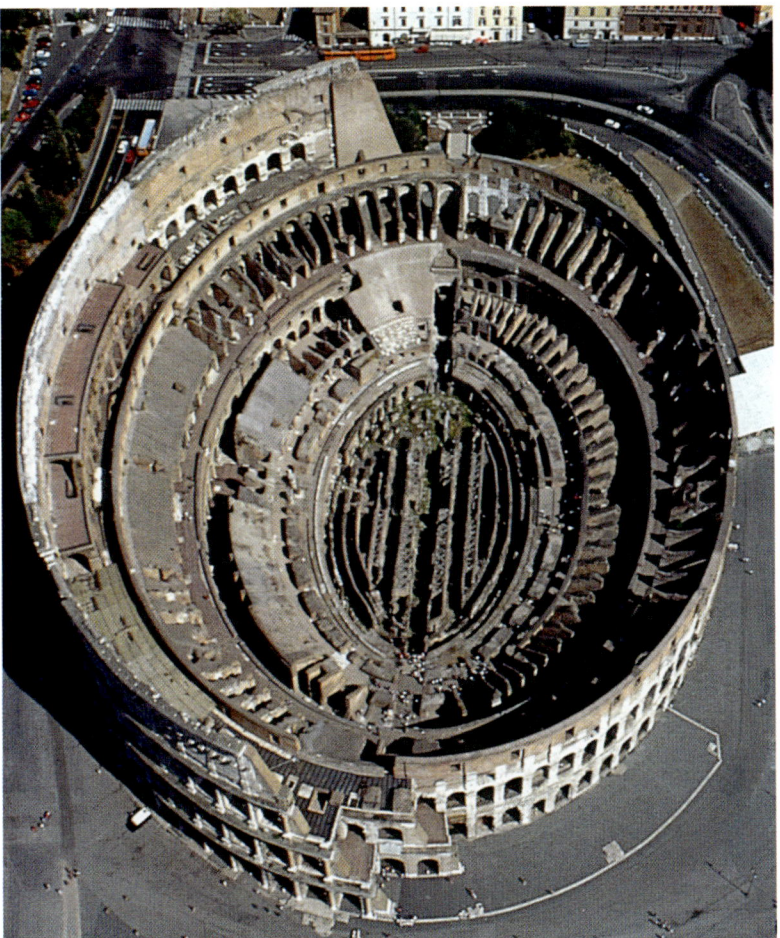

10-34   Aerial view of the Colosseum, Rome, Italy, ca. A.D. 70–80.

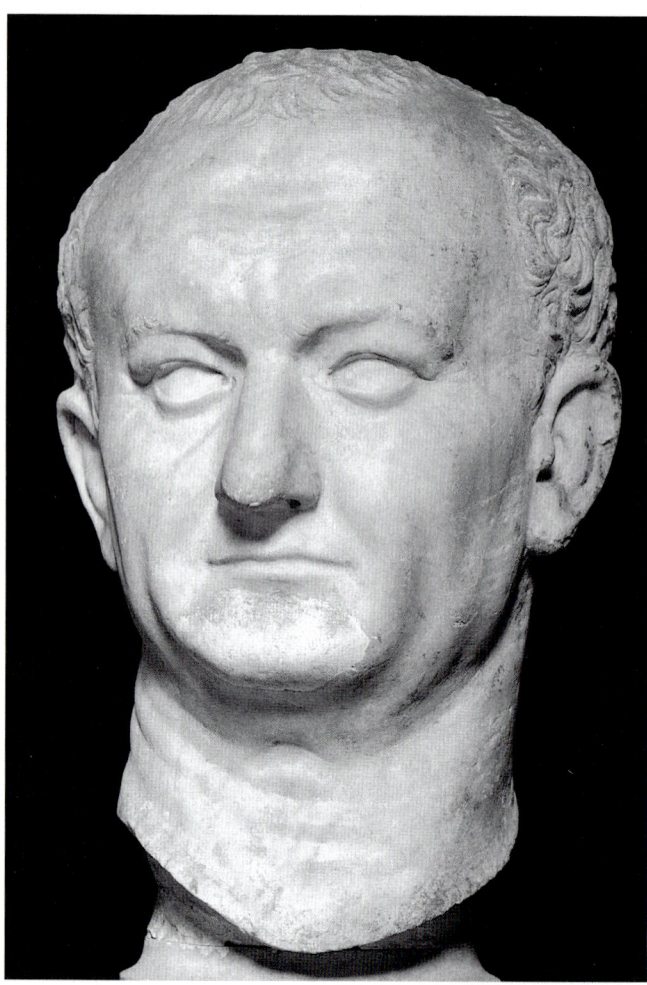

10-35 Portrait of Vespasian, from Ostia, Italy, ca. A.D. 69–79. Marble, approx. 1' 4" high. Museo Nazionale Romano-Palazzo Massimo alle Terme, Rome.

VESPASIAN AND THE REVIVAL OF VERISM

Vespasian was an unpretentious career army officer who desired to distance himself from Nero's extravagant misrule. His portraits (FIG. **10-35**) reflect his much simpler tastes. They also made an important political statement. Breaking with the tradition Augustus established of depicting the Roman emperor as an eternally youthful god on earth, Vespasian's sculptors resuscitated the veristic tradition of the Republic, possibly at his specific direction. Although not as brutally descriptive as many Republican likenesses, Vespasian's portraits frankly recorded his receding hairline and aging leathery skin—proclaiming that his values were different from Nero's.

AN ELEGANT FLAVIAN WOMAN

Flavian portraits of people of all ages exist, in contrast to Republican times, when only elders were deemed worthy of depiction. A portrait bust of a young woman (FIG. **10-36**), probably a Flavian princess, is a case in point. The portrait is notable for its elegance and delicacy and for the virtuoso way the sculptor rendered the differing textures of hair and flesh. The elaborate Flavian coiffure, with its corkscrew curls punched out by skilled hands using a drill instead of a chisel, creates a dense mass of light and shadow set off boldly from the softly modeled and highly polished skin of the face and swanlike neck. The drill played an increasing role in Roman sculpture in succeeding periods and in time was used even for portraits of men, when much longer hair and full beards were fashionable.

function. The facade is divided into four bands, with large arched openings piercing the lower three. Ornamental Greek orders frame the arches in the standard Roman sequence for multistoried buildings: Tuscan Doric, Ionic, and then Corinthian from the ground up. This sequence is based on the proportions of the orders, with the Tuscan viewed as capable of supporting the heaviest load. The uppermost story is circled with Corinthian pilasters (and between them the brackets for the poles that held up the velarium over the cavea).

The framing of the openings in the Colosseum's facade by engaged columns and a lintel is a variation of the scheme used on the Etruscan *Porta Marzia* at Perugia (see FIG. 9-13). The Romans commonly used this scheme from Late Republican times on. Like the pseudoperipteral temple, which is an eclectic mix of Greek orders and Etruscan plan, this way of decorating a building's facade combined Greek orders with an architectural form foreign to Greek post-and-lintel architecture, namely the arch. Revived in the Italian Renaissance, the motif had a long, illustrious history in classical architecture. The Roman practice of framing an arch with an applied Greek order had no structural purpose, but it added variety to a monotonous surface. It also unified a multistoried facade by casting a net of verticals and horizontals over it.

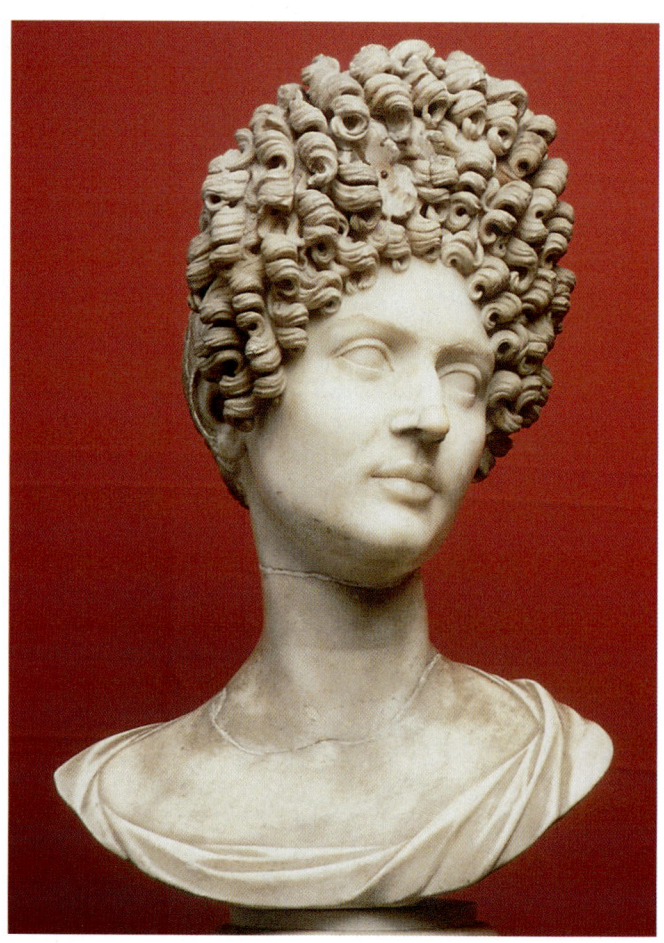

10-36 Portrait bust of a Flavian woman, from Rome, Italy, ca. A.D. 90. Marble, approx. 2' 1" high. Museo Capitolino, Rome.

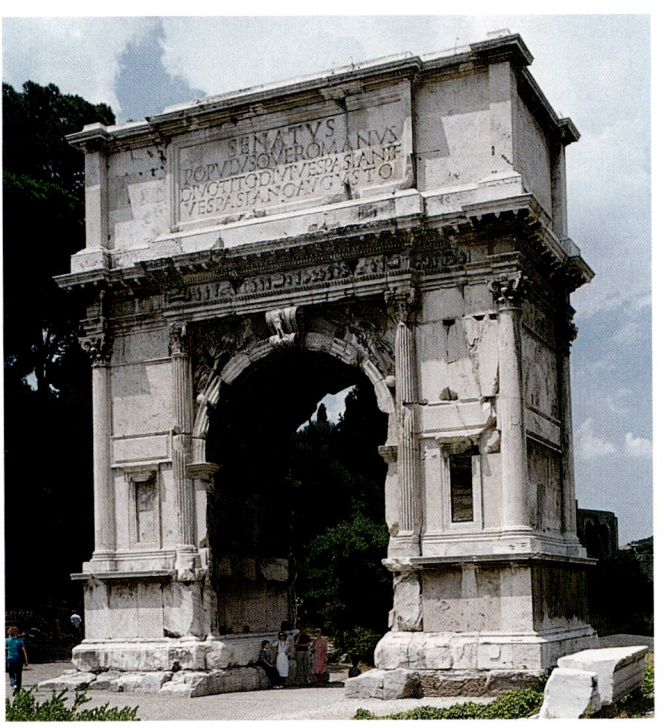

A NEW ARCH FOR A NEW GOD   When Vespasian's older son, Titus, died in A.D. 81, only two years after becoming emperor, his younger brother, Domitian, succeeded him. Domitian erected an arch (FIGS. **10-37** to **10-39**) in Titus's honor on the Sacred Way leading into the Republican Forum Romanum. This type of arch, the so-called *triumphal arch*, has a long history in Roman art and architecture, beginning in the second century B.C. and continuing even into the era of Christian Roman emperors. The term is something of a misnomer, however, because Roman arches celebrated more than just military victories. Such freestanding arches, usually crowned by gilded bronze statues, commemorated a wide variety of events, ranging from victories abroad to the building of roads and bridges at home.

The Arch of Titus is typical of the early triumphal arch and consists of one passageway only. As on the Colosseum, engaged columns frame the arcuate opening, but their capitals are the *Composite* type, an ornate combination of Ionic volutes and Corinthian acanthus leaves that became popular at about the same time as the Fourth Style in Roman painting. Reliefs depicting personified Victories (winged women, as in Greek art) fill the *spandrels*, the area between the arch's

10-37   Arch of Titus, Rome, Italy, after A.D. 81.

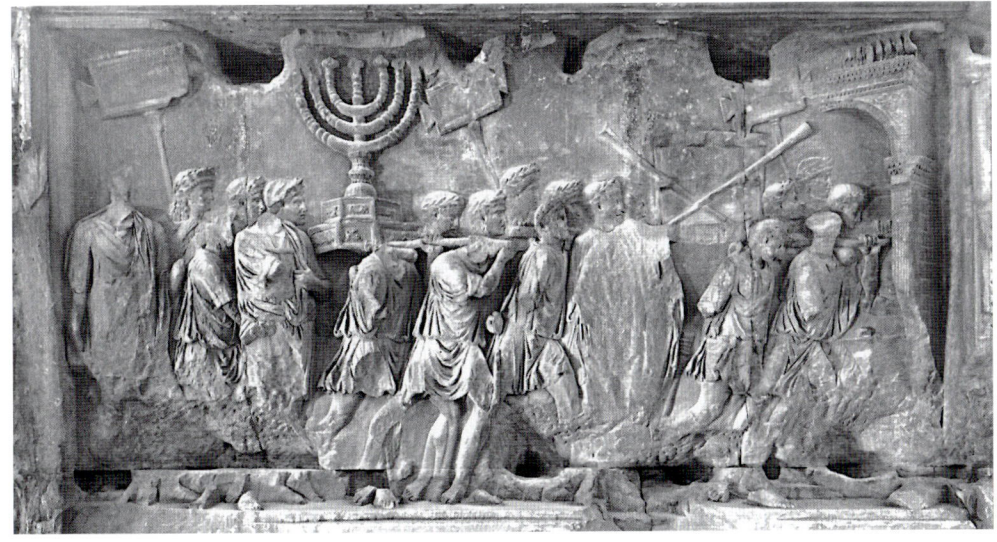

10-38   Spoils of Jerusalem, relief panel from the Arch of Titus, Rome, Italy, after A.D. 81. Marble, approx. 7′ 10″ high.

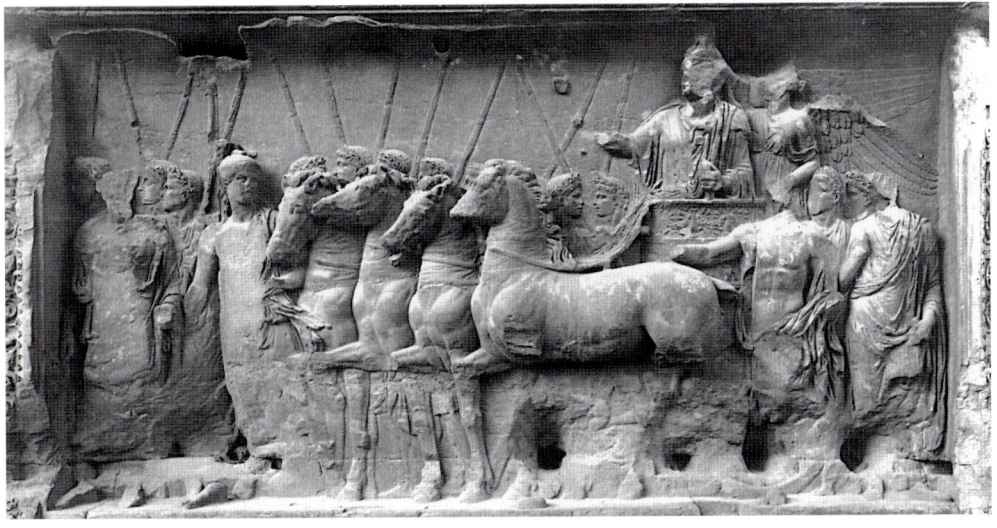

10-39   Triumph of Titus, relief panel from the Arch of Titus, Rome, Italy, after A.D. 81. Marble, approx. 7′ 10″ high.

curve and the framing columns and entablature. A dedicatory inscription stating that the arch was set up to honor the god Titus, son of the god Vespasian, dominates the attic. (Roman emperors normally were proclaimed gods after they died, unless they ran afoul of the Senate; then they were damned. The statues of those who suffered *damnatio memoriae* were torn down and their names were erased from public inscriptions. This was Nero's fate.)

THE SPOILS OF JERUSALEM Inside the passageway of the Arch of Titus are two great relief panels. They represent the triumphal parade of Titus down the Sacred Way after his return from the conquest of Judaea at the end of the Jewish Wars in A.D. 70. One of the reliefs (FIG. 10-38) depicts Roman soldiers carrying the spoils—including the sacred seven-branched candelabrum, the *menorah*—from the Temple in Jerusalem. Despite considerable damage to the relief, the illusion of movement is convincing. The parade moves forward from the left background into the center foreground and disappears through the obliquely placed arch in the right background. The energy and swing of the column of soldiers suggest a rapid march. The sculptor rejected the classicizing low relief of the Ara Pacis (FIG. 10-29) in favor of extremely deep carving, which produces strong shadows. The heads of the forward figures have broken off because they stood free from the block. Their high relief emphasized their different placement in space from the heads in low relief, which are intact. The play of light and shade across the protruding foreground and receding background figures quickens the sense of movement.

The panel on the other side of the passageway (FIG. 10-39) shows Titus in his triumphal chariot. The seeming historical accuracy of the spoils panel—it closely corresponds to the contemporary description of Titus's triumph by the Jewish historian Josephus—gave way in this panel to allegory. Victory rides with Titus in the four-horse chariot and places a wreath on his head. Below her is a bare-chested youth who is probably a personification of Honor (*Honos*). A female personification of Valor (*Virtus*) leads the horses. These allegorical figures transform the relief from a record of Titus's battlefield success into a celebration of imperial virtues. Such an intermingling of divine and human figures occurs on the Villa of the Mysteries frieze at Pompeii (FIG. 10-15), but this was the first known instance of divine beings interacting with humans on an official Roman historical relief. (On the Ara Pacis, FIG. 10-27, Aeneas and "Tellus" appear in separate framed panels and were carefully segregated from the procession of living Romans.) It is well to remember, however, that the Arch of Titus was erected after his death and that its reliefs were carved when Titus was already a god. Soon afterward this kind of interaction between mortals and immortals became a staple of Roman narrative relief sculpture, even on monuments honoring a living emperor.

THE HIGH EMPIRE

THE ROMAN EMPIRE AT ITS PEAK In the second century A.D., under Trajan, Hadrian, and the Antonines, the Roman Empire reached its greatest geographic extent and the height of its power. Rome's might was unchallenged in the Western world, although the Germanic peoples in Europe, the Berbers in Africa, and the Parthians and Persians in the Near East constantly applied pressure. Within the empire's secure boundaries, the Pax Romana meant unprecedented prosperity for all who came under Roman rule.

Trajan (A.D. 98–117)

THE FIRST SPANISH EMPEROR Domitian's extravagant lifestyle and ego resembled Nero's. He demanded to be addressed as *dominus et deus* (lord and god), angering the senators. When he was assassinated in A.D. 96, the Senate chose the elderly Nerva, one of its own, as emperor. Nerva ruled for only sixteen months, but before he died he established a pattern of succession that lasted for almost a century. He adopted Trajan, a capable and popular general to whom he was unrelated by blood. A Spaniard by birth, Trajan was the first non-Italian to become emperor of Rome. Under Trajan, Roman armies brought Roman rule to ever more distant areas, and the imperial government took on ever greater responsibility for its people's welfare by instituting a number of farsighted social programs. Trajan was so popular he was granted the title *Optimus* (the Best), an epithet he shared with Jupiter (who was said to have instructed Nerva to choose Trajan as his successor). In late antiquity Augustus, the founder of the Roman Empire, and Trajan became the yardsticks for success. The goal of new emperors was to be *felicior Augusto, melior Traiano* (luckier than Augustus, better than Trajan).

A NEW COLONY IN AFRICA In A.D. 100 Trajan founded a new colony for army veterans at Timgad, ancient Thamugadi (FIG. **10-40**), in what is today Algeria. Timgad

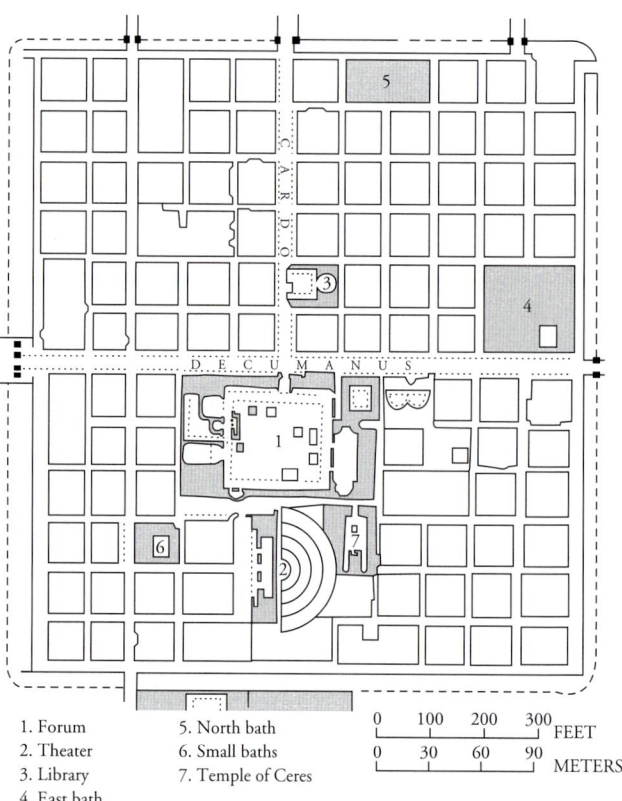

1. Forum   5. North bath
2. Theater   6. Small baths
3. Library   7. Temple of Ceres
4. East bath

0   100   200   300 FEET
0   30   60   90 METERS

10-40   Plan of Timgad (Thamugadi), Algeria, founded A.D. 100.

was built along a major road one hundred miles from the sea. Like other colonies, it became the physical embodiment of Roman authority and civilization for the local population and served as a key to the Romanization of the provinces. The town was planned with great precision, its design resembling that of a Roman military encampment or *castrum*. (Scholars still debate which came first. The castrum may have been based on the layout of Roman colonies.) Unlike the sprawling unplanned cities of Rome and Pompeii, Timgad is a square divided into equal quarters by its two main streets, the *cardo* and the *decumanus*. They cross at right angles and are bordered by colonnades. Monumental gates in the colony's original walls mark the ends of the two avenues. The forum is located at the point where the streets intersect. The quarters are subdivided into square blocks, and the forum and public buildings, such as the theater and baths, occupy areas sized as multiples of these blocks. The Roman plan is a modification of the Hippodamian plan of Greek cities (see FIG. 5-75), though more rigidly ordered.

The fact that most of these colonial settlements were laid out in the same manner, regardless of whether they were in North Africa, Mesopotamia, or England, expresses concretely the unity and centralized power of the Roman Empire at its height. But, even the Romans could not regulate human behavior completely. As the population of Timgad grew sevenfold and burst through the Trajanic settlement walls, rational planning was ignored, and the city and its streets branched out haphazardly.

ROME'S GREATEST FORUM Trajan's major building project in Rome was a huge new forum (FIG. **10-41**), roughly twice the size of the forum Augustus built a century before—even if the enormous market complex next to the forum is excluded. The new forum glorified Trajan's victories in his two wars against the Dacians (who lived in what is now Romania), and was paid for with the spoils of those campaigns. The architect was APOLLODORUS OF DAMASCUS, Trajan's chief military engineer during the Dacian wars, who had constructed a world-famous bridge across the Danube River. Apollodorus's plan incorporated the main features of most early forums (FIG. 10-10), except that a huge basilica, not a temple, dominated the colonnaded open square. The temple (completed after the emperor's death and dedicated to the newest god in the Roman pantheon, Trajan himself) was set instead behind the basilica. It stood at the rear end of the forum in its own courtyard, with two libraries and a giant commemorative column, the Column of Trajan (FIG. 10-42).

One entered Trajan's forum through an impressive gateway resembling a triumphal arch, complete with an attic statuary group of Trajan driving a six-horse chariot while Victory crowns him. Inside the forum were other reminders of Trajan's military prowess. A larger-than-life-size gilded-bronze equestrian statue of the emperor stood at the center of the great court in front of the basilica. Statues of bound Dacians stood above the columns of the forum porticoes.

The Basilica Ulpia (Trajan's family name was Ulpius) was a much larger and far more ornate version of the basilica in the forum of Pompeii(FIG. 10-10). As shown in the model (FIG. 10-41), it had *apses,* or semicircular recesses, on each short end. The nave was flanked by two aisles on each side. In contrast to the Pompeian basilica and later Christian churches, the entrances were on the long side facing the forum. The

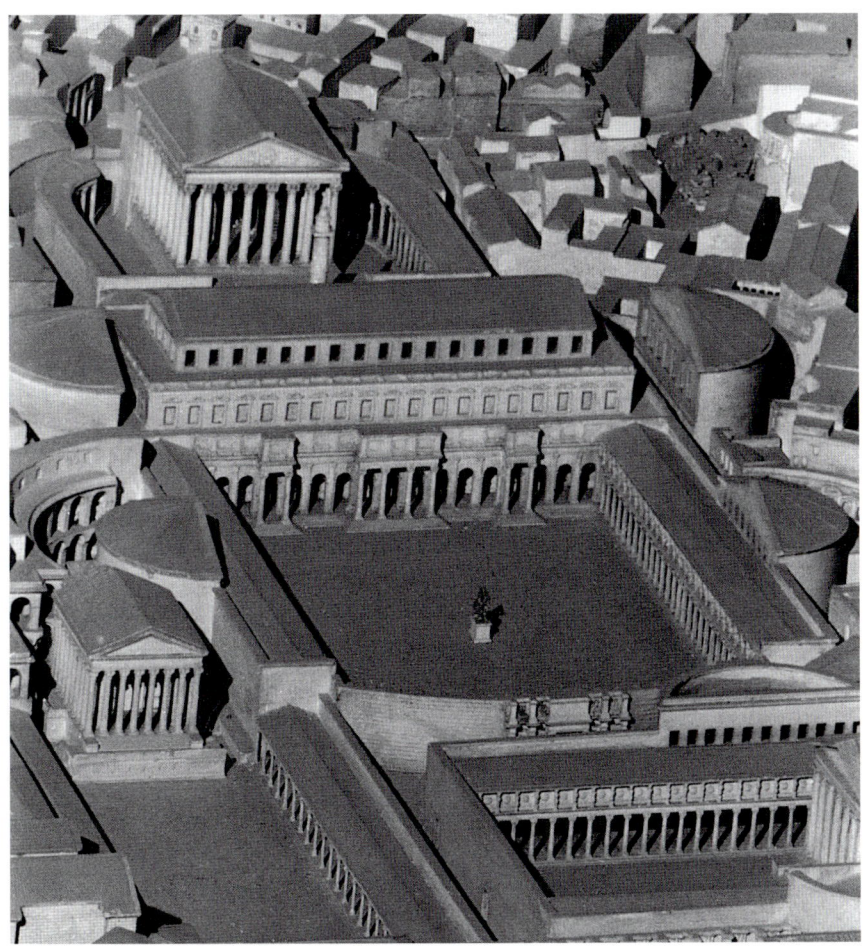

10-41 APOLLODORUS OF DAMASCUS, model of Forum of Trajan, Rome, Italy, dedicated A.D. 112. Museo della Civiltà Romana, Rome.

building was vast: about four hundred feet long (without the apses) and two hundred feet wide. Light entered through *clerestory* windows, made possible by elevating the timber-roofed nave above the colonnaded aisles. In the Republican basilica at Pompeii, light reached the nave only indirectly through aisle windows. The clerestory (used millennia before at Karnak in Egypt, see FIGS. 3-25 and 3-26) was a much better solution. Early Christian architects embraced this feature of the Basilica Ulpia for the design of the first churches (see FIGS. 11-8 and 11-16).

THE COLUMN AND TOMB OF TRAJAN   The Column of Trajan (FIG. **10-42**) was probably also the brainchild of Apollodorus of Damascus. The idea of covering the shaft of a colossal freestanding column with a continuous spiral narrative frieze seems to have been invented here, but it was often copied. As late as the nineteenth century, a column inspired by the Column of Trajan was erected in the Place Vendôme in Paris in commemoration of the victories of Napoleon. The type even appeared in Christian settings with reliefs illustrating the life of Christ (see FIG. 16-26).

Trajan's Column is one hundred twenty-eight feet high. Coins indicate that it was once crowned by a heroically nude statue of the emperor. Trajan's portrait was lost in the Middle Ages, and in the sixteenth century a statue of Saint Peter replaced it. The square base, decorated with captured Dacian arms and armor, served as Trajan's mausoleum. His ashes and those of his wife, Plotina, were placed inside it in golden urns.

The six hundred twenty-five-foot band that winds around the column has been likened to an illustrated scroll of the type housed in the neighboring libraries (and held by Lars Pulena on his sarcophagus, see FIG. 9-14). The reliefs depict Trajan's two successful campaigns against the Dacians. The story is told in more than one hundred and fifty episodes in which some twenty-five hundred figures appear. The band increases in width as it winds to the top of the column, so that it is easier to see the upper portions. Throughout, the relief is very low so as not to distort the contours of the shaft. Legibility was enhanced in antiquity by paint, but it still would have been very difficult for anyone to follow the narrative from beginning to end.

Much of the spiral frieze is given over to easily recognizable compositions like those found on coin reverses and on historical relief panels: Trajan addressing his troops, sacrificing to the gods, and so on. The narrative is not a reliable chronological account of the Dacian Wars, as was once thought. The general character of the campaigns was nonetheless accurately recorded. Notably, battle scenes take up only about a quarter of the frieze. As is true of modern military operations, the Romans spent more time constructing forts, transporting men and equipment, and preparing for battle than fighting. The focus is always on the emperor, who appears again and again in the frieze, but the enemy is not belittled. The Romans won because of their superior organization and more powerful army, not because they were inherently superior beings.

SHOPPING IN IMPERIAL ROME   On the Quirinal Hill overlooking the forum, Apollodorus built the Markets of Trajan (FIG. **10-43**) to house both shops and administrative offices. The transformation of a natural slope into a multilevel

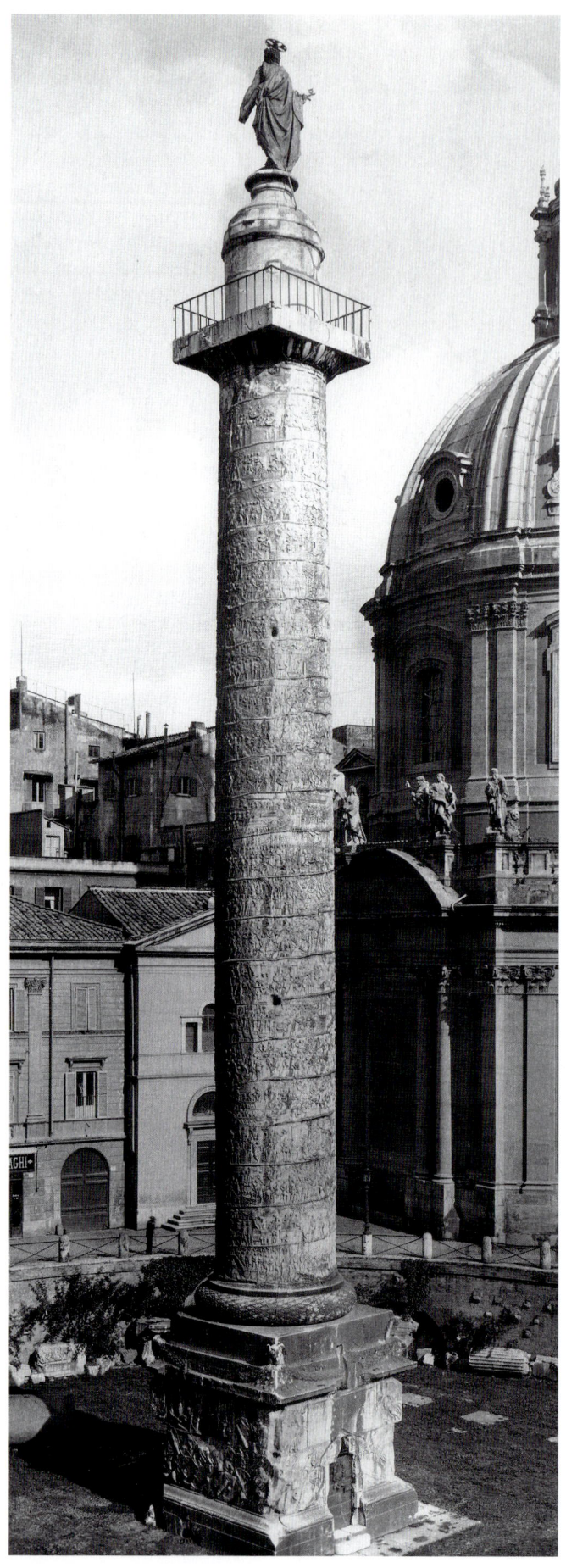

10-42 Column of Trajan, Forum of Trajan, Rome, Italy, dedicated A.D. 112.

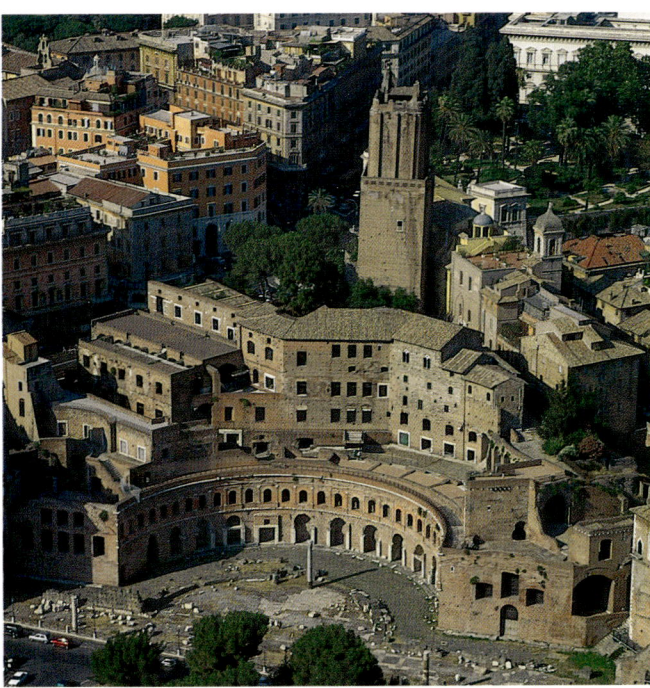

10-43 APOLLODORUS OF DAMASCUS, aerial view of Markets of Trajan, Rome, Italy, ca. A.D. 100–112.

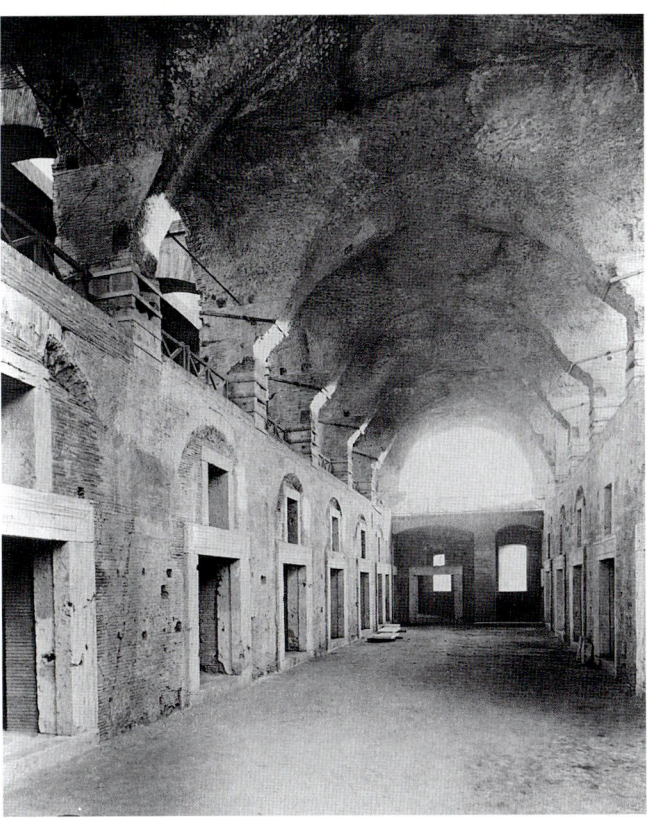

10-44 APOLLODORUS OF DAMASCUS, interior of the great hall, Markets of Trajan, Rome, Italy, ca. A.D. 100–112.

complex was possible here, as earlier at Palestrina (FIG. 10-3), only by using concrete. Trajan's architect was a master of this modern medium as well as of the traditional stone-and-timber post-and-lintel architecture of the forum below.

The basic unit was the *taberna,* a single-room shop covered by a barrel vault. Each taberna had a wide doorway, usually with a window above it that allowed light to enter a wooden inner attic used for storage. The shops were on several levels. They opened either onto a hemispherical facade winding around one of the great exedras of Trajan's forum, onto a paved street farther up the hill, or onto a great indoor market hall (FIG. **10-44**) resembling a modern shopping mall. The hall housed two floors of shops, with the upper shops set back on each side and lit by skylights. Light from the same sources reached the ground-floor shops through arcuate openings beneath the great umbrella-like groin vaults covering the hall (see "The Roman Architectural Revolution: Concrete Construction," page 249).

THE TRIUMPHAL ARCH AS BILLBOARD In A.D. 109 a new road, the Via Traiana, was opened in southern Italy. Several years later a great arch honoring Trajan (FIG. **10-45**) was built at the point where the road entered Benevento (ancient Beneventum). Architecturally, the Arch of Trajan at Benevento is almost identical to Titus's arch on the Sacred Way in Rome (FIG. 10-37), but relief panels cover both facades of the Trajanic arch, giving it a billboardlike function. Every inch of the surface was used to advertise the emperor's achievements. In one panel, he enters Rome after a successful military campaign. In another, he distributes largess to needy children. In still others, he was portrayed as the founder of colonies for army veterans and as the builder of a new port at Ostia, Rome's harbor at the mouth of the Tiber. The reliefs present Trajan as the guarantor of peace and security in the empire, the benefactor of the poor, and the patron of soldiers and merchants alike. In short, the emperor was "all things to all people."

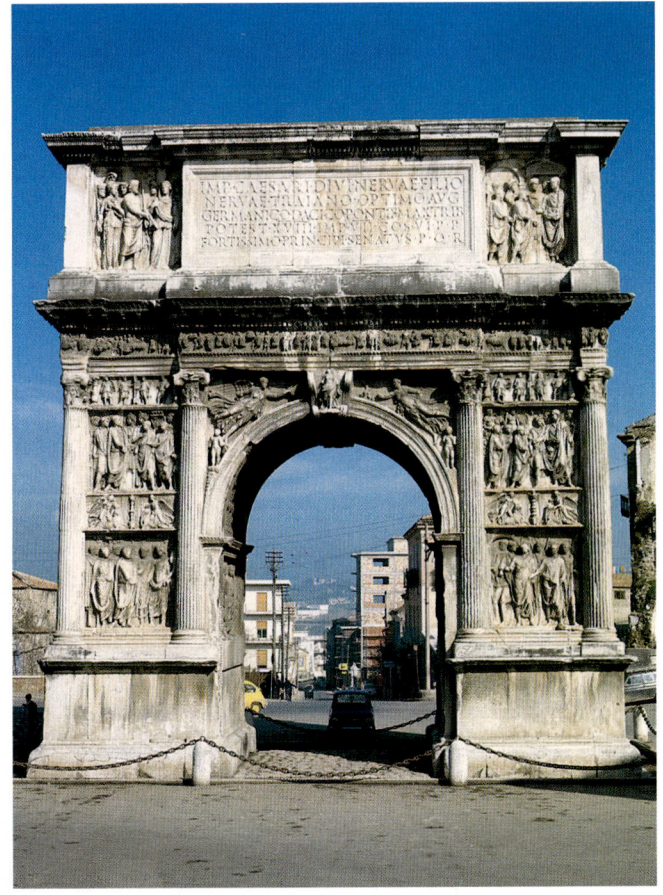

10-45 Arch of Trajan, Benevento, Italy, ca. A.D. 114–118.

10-46 Funerary relief of a circus official, from Ostia, Italy, ca. A.D. 110–130. Marble, approx. 1′ 8″ high. Vatican Museums, Rome.

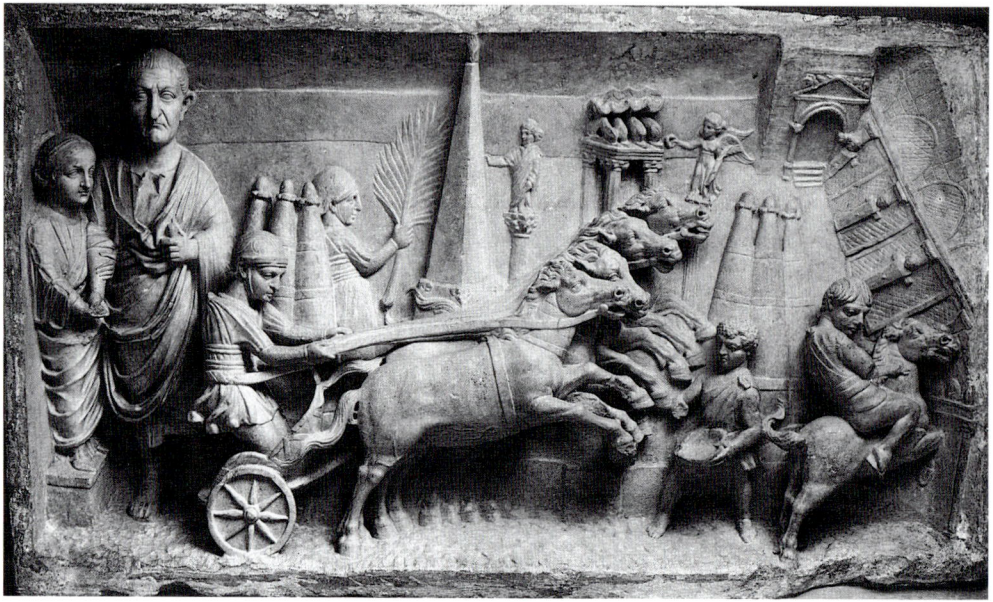

In several of the panels, Trajan freely intermingles with divinities, and on the arch's attic (which may have been completed after his death and deification) Jupiter hands his thunderbolt to the emperor, awarding him dominion over the earth. Such scenes, depicting the "first citizen" of Rome as a divinely sanctioned ruler in the company of the gods, henceforth became the norm, not the exception, in official Roman art.

RACES IN THE CIRCUS MAXIMUS   One of Trajan's other benefactions to the Roman people was the restoration of the Circus Maximus, where the world's best horse teams competed in chariot races. A relief that once decorated a circus official's tomb (FIG. **10-46**) gives a partial view of the refurbished racecourse. The relief is not a product of one of the emperor's official sculptural workshops, and it illustrates once again how different the art produced for Rome's huge working class was from the art the state and old aristocratic families commissioned.

The relief shows the Circus Maximus in distorted perspective. Only one team of horses races around the central island, but the charioteer is shown twice, once driving the horses and a second time holding the palm branch of victory. This is an example of *continuous narration;* that is, the same figure appears more than once in the same space at different stages of a story. This is not the first instance of continuous narration, but few earlier examples exist and only much later did this way of telling a story in pictures become common. (The emperor's appearance in different settings in the Column of Trajan's frieze is not an example of continuous narration.)

In fact, the charioteer may appear a third time within the same relief, for he may be, later in life, the toga-clad official who appears at the panel's left end. There the recently deceased official clasps hands with his wife. (The handshake between man and woman is a symbol of marriage in Roman art.) She is of smaller stature (and less important than her husband in this context, for it is *his* career in the circus commemorated on *his* tomb), and she is shown standing on a base. The base indicates that she is not a living person but a statue. The handshake between man and statue is the plebeian

artist's shorthand way of saying the wife died before the husband, that her death had not broken their marriage bond, and that, because the husband has now died, the two will be reunited in the afterlife. The rules of classical design, which still guided the Roman state's artists, were ignored here, as in the funerary relief from Amiternum (FIG. 10-5), also made for a nonelite patron. Before long, however, some of these nonclassical elements appeared in official art as well.

Hadrian (A.D. 117–138)

A GREEK BEARD FOR A ROMAN EMPEROR   Hadrian, Trajan's chosen successor and fellow Spaniard, was a connoisseur and lover of all the arts, as well as an author and architect. He traveled widely as emperor, often in the Greek East. Everywhere he went, statues and arches were set up in his honor. More portraits of Hadrian exist today than of any other emperor except Augustus. Hadrian, who was forty-one years old at the time of Trajan's death and who ruled for more than two decades, is always depicted in his portraits as a mature adult who never ages.

A fine example is the fragmentary bronze statue of the emperor wearing a cuirass (FIG. **10-47**) found at Tel Shalem, Israel, several miles south of the ancient city of Scythopolis. The portrait probably was erected toward the end of Hadrian's lifetime, when Rome put down a second Jewish revolt and Judaea was reorganized as a new province called Syria Palaestina. Hadrian's portraits more closely resemble Kresilas's portrait of Pericles (see FIG. 5-39) than those of any Roman emperor before him, and no one doubts that his likenesses were inspired by Classical Greek statuary. The idealizing official portraits of Augustus also were inspired by fifth-century B.C. statues, but the prototypes were images of athletes. The models for Hadrian's artists were statues of mature Greek men. Hadrian himself wore a beard—a habit that, in its Roman context, must be viewed as a Greek affectation. Beards then became the norm for all subsequent Roman emperors for more than a century and a half.

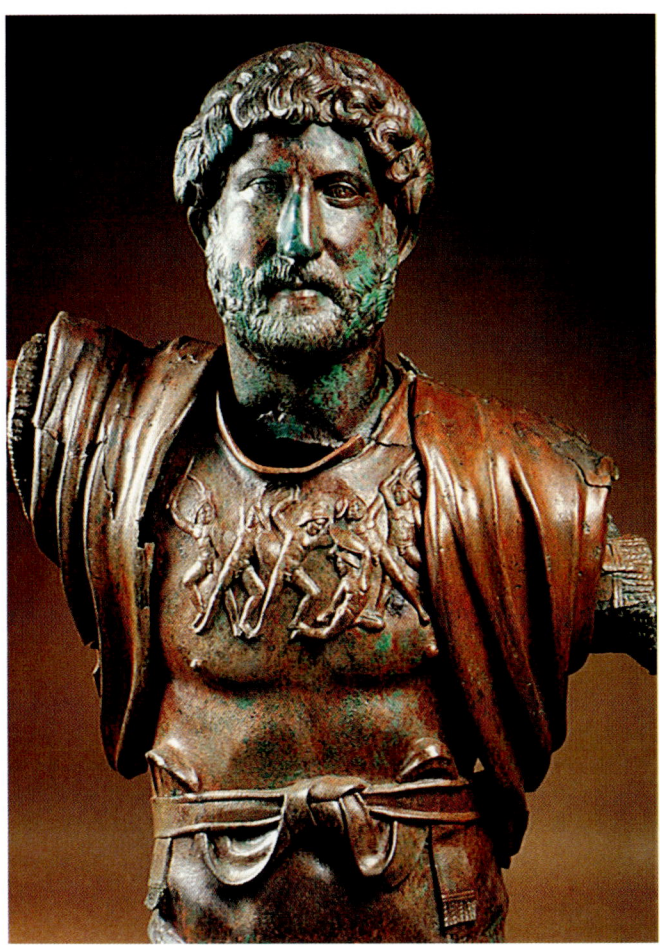

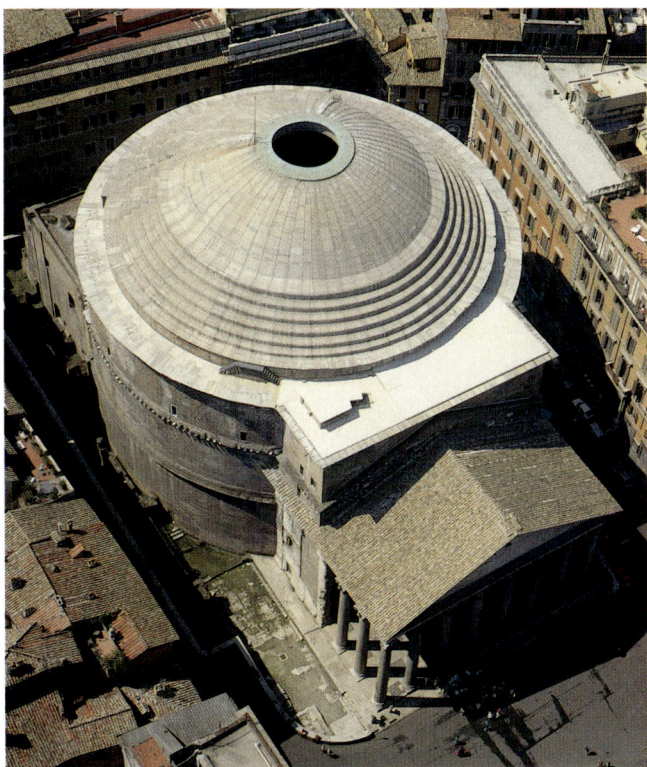

10-48   Aerial view of the Pantheon, Rome, Italy, A.D. 118–125.

10-47   Portrait bust of Hadrian as general, from Tel Shalem, Israel, ca. A.D. 130–138. Bronze, approx. 2′ 11″ high. Israel Museum, Jerusalem.

THE PANTHEON, TEMPLE FOR ALL GODS
Soon after Hadrian became emperor, work began on the Pantheon (FIG. **10-48**), the temple of all the gods, one of the best-preserved buildings of antiquity. It also has been one of the most influential designs in architectural history. The Pantheon reveals the full potential of concrete, both as a building material and as a means for shaping architectural space. The temple originally was approached from a columnar courtyard, and, like temples in Roman forums, stood at one narrow end of the enclosure. Its facade of eight Corinthian columns—almost all that could be seen from ground level in antiquity—

was a bow to tradition. Everything else about the Pantheon is revolutionary. Behind the columnar porch is an immense concrete cylinder covered by a huge hemispherical dome one hundred forty-two feet in diameter. The dome's top is also one hundred forty-two feet from the floor (FIG. **10-49**). The design is thus based on the intersection of two circles (one horizontal, the other vertical) so that the interior space could be imagined as the orb of the earth and the dome as the vault of the heavens.

If the Pantheon's design is simplicity itself, executing that design took all the ingenuity of Hadrian's engineers. The cylindrical drum was built up level by level using concrete of varied composition. Extremely hard and durable basalt was used in the mix for the foundations, and the "recipe" was gradually modified until, at the top, featherweight pumice replaced stones to lighten the load. The dome's thickness also decreases as it nears the *oculus*, the circular opening thirty feet in diameter that is the only light source for the

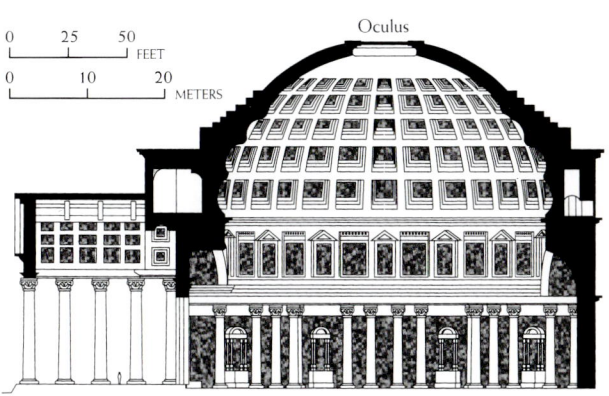

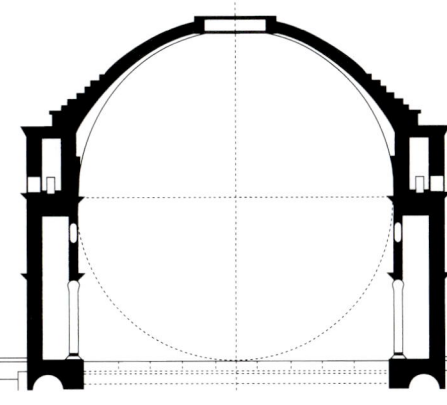

10-49   Longitudinal and lateral sections of the Pantheon, Rome, Italy, A.D. 118–125.

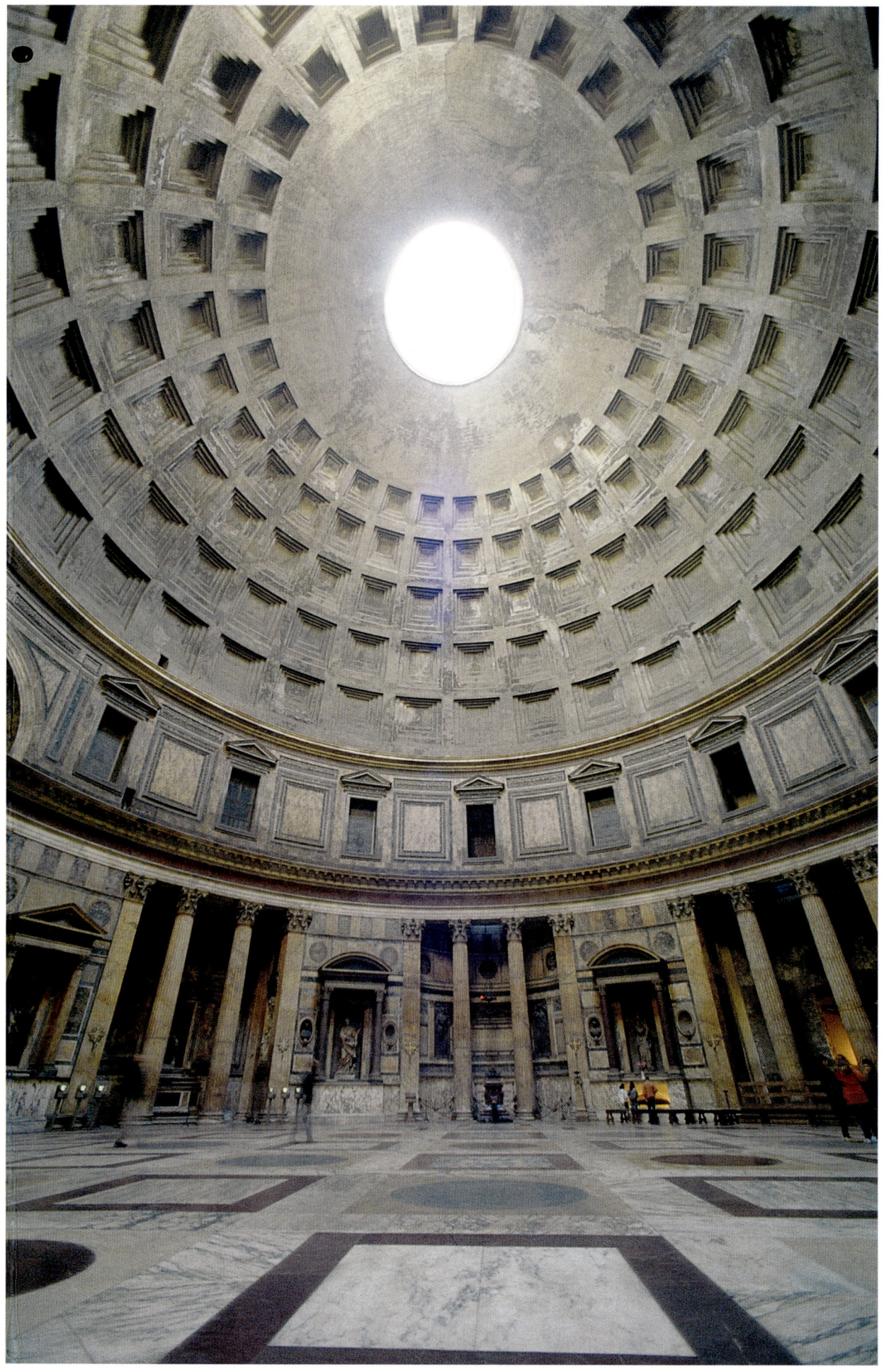

10-50   Interior of the Pantheon, Rome, Italy, A.D. 118–125.

interior (FIG. **10-50**). The dome's weight was lessened, without weakening its structure, through the use of *coffers* (sunken decorative panels). These further reduced the dome's mass and also provided a handsome pattern of squares within the vast circle. Renaissance drawings suggest that each coffer once had a glistening gilded-bronze rosette at its center, enhancing the dome's symbolism as the starry heavens.

Below the dome much of the original marble veneer of the walls, niches, and floor has survived (FIG. 10-50). In the Pantheon visitors can get a sense, as almost nowhere else, of how magnificent the interiors of Roman concrete buildings could be. But despite the luxurious skin of the Pantheon's interior, on first entering the structure one senses not the weight of the enclosing walls but the space they enclose. In pre-Roman architecture, the form of the enclosed space was determined by the placement of the solids, which did not so much shape space as interrupt it. Roman architects were the first to conceive of architecture in terms of units of space that could be shaped by the enclosures. The Pantheon's interior is a single unified, self-sufficient whole, uninterrupted by supporting solids. It encloses visitors without imprisoning them, opening through the oculus to the drifting clouds, the blue sky, the sun, and the gods. In this space, the architect used light not just to illuminate the darkness but to create drama and underscore the interior shape's symbolism. On a sunny day, the light that passes through the oculus forms a circular beam, a disk of light that moves across the coffered dome in the course of the day as the sun moves across the sky itself. Escaping from the noise and torrid heat of a Roman summer day into the Pantheon's cool, calm, and mystical immensity is an experience almost impossible to describe and one that should not be missed.

A WELL-TRAVELED EMPEROR'S RETREAT Although some have suggested that Hadrian himself was the architect of the Pantheon, the amateur builder does not deserve credit for the design. Hadrian was, however, deeply involved with the construction of his own villa at Tivoli, where building activity seems never to have ceased until the emperor's death.

One of the latest projects on the vast estate was the construction of a pool and an artificial grotto, called the *Canopus* and *Serapeum* (FIG. **10-51**), respectively. They commemorated the emperor's trip to Egypt, where he visited a famous temple of the god Serapis on a canal called the Canopus. Nothing about the design, however, derives from Egyptian architecture. The grotto at the end of the pool is made of concrete and has an unusual pumpkin-shaped dome of a type Hadrian designed himself (see "Hadrian: Emperor and Architect," page 282). Yet, in keeping with the persistent eclecticism of Roman art and architecture, the pool was lined with marble copies of famous Greek statues, as one would expect from a lover of Greek art. There is also a Corinthian colonnade at the curved end of the pool, but it is of a type unknown in Classical Greek architecture. Not only does the colonnade lack a superstructure, but it has *arcuated,* as opposed to traditional Greek horizontal, lintels between alternating pairs of columns. This kind of simultaneous respect for Greek architecture—elsewhere on the grounds is a replica of the Temple of Aphrodite at Knidos—and willingness to break Greek design rules typifies much Roman architecture of the High and Late Empire.

A BAROQUE TOMB IN A MOUNTAIN An even more extreme example of what many have called Roman "baroque" architecture (because of the striking parallels with

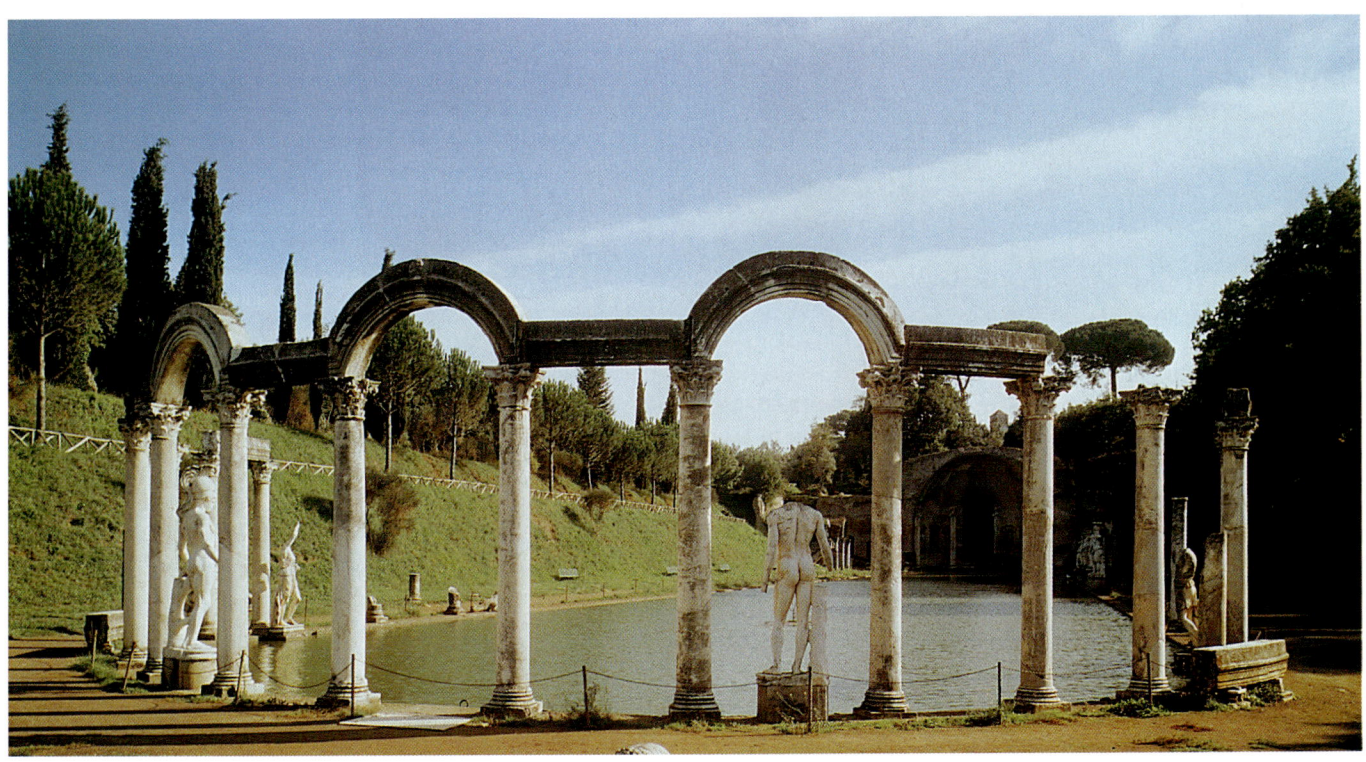

10-51   *Canopus* and *Serapeum,* Hadrian's Villa, Tivoli, Italy, ca. A.D. 130–138.

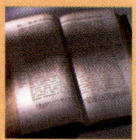

Hadrian
Emperor and Architect

Dio Cassius, a third-century A.D. senator who wrote a history of Rome from its foundation to his own day, recounted a revealing anecdote about Hadrian and Apollodorus of Damascus, architect of the Forum of Trajan (FIG. 10-41):

> Hadrian first drove into exile and then put to death the architect Apollodorus who had carried out several of Trajan's building projects. . . . When Trajan was at one time consulting with Apollodorus about a certain problem connected with his buildings, the architect said to Hadrian, who had interrupted them with some advice, "Go away and draw your pumpkins. You know nothing about these problems." For it so happened that Hadrian was at that time priding himself on some sort of drawing. When he became emperor he remembered this insult and refused to put up with Apollodorus's outspokenness. He sent him [his own] plan for the temple of Venus and Roma, in order to demonstrate that it was possible for a great work to be conceived without his [Apollodorus's] help, and asked him if he thought the building was well designed. Apollodorus sent a [very critical] reply. . . . [The emperor did not] attempt to restrain his anger or hide his pain; on the contrary, he had the man slain.[1]

The story says a great deal both about the absolute power Roman emperors wielded and about how seriously Hadrian took his architectural designs. But perhaps the most interesting detail is the description of Hadrian's drawings of "pumpkins." These must have been drawings of concrete domes like the one in the *Serapeum* at Hadrian's Tivoli villa (FIG. 10-51). Such vaults were too adventurous for Apollodorus, or at least for a public building in Trajanic Rome, and Hadrian had to try them out later at home at his own expense.

[1] J. J. Pollitt, trans., *The Art of Rome, c. 753 B.C.–A.D. 337: Sources and Documents* (New York: Cambridge University Press, 1983), 175–76.

---

seventeenth-century Italian buildings) is the second-century A.D. tomb nicknamed Al-Khazneh, the "Treasury" (FIG. **10-52**), at Petra in modern Jordan. It is one of the most elaborate of many tomb facades cut into the sheer rock faces of the local rose-colored mountains. As at Hadrian's villa, classical architectural elements are used here in a purely ornamental fashion and with a studied disregard for classical rules.

The Treasury's facade is more than one hundred and thirty feet high and consists of two stories. The lower story resembles a temple facade with six columns, but the columns are unevenly spaced and the pediment is only wide enough to cover the central four columns. On the upper level, a temple-within-a-temple is set on top of the lower temple. Here the facade and roof split in half to make room for a central tholoslike cylinder, which contrasts sharply with the rectangles and triangles of the rest of the design. On both levels, the rhythmic alternation of deep projection and indentation creates dynamic patterns of light and shade. At Petra, as at Tivoli, the vocabulary of Greek architecture was maintained, but the syntax is new and distinctively Roman. In fact, the design recalls some of the architectural fantasies painted on the walls of Roman houses—for example, the tholos seen through columns surmounted by a broken pediment in the Second Style cubiculum from Boscoreale (FIG. 10-16).

Ostia

THE CROWDED LIFE OF THE CITY   The average Roman, of course, did not own a luxurious country villa and was not buried in a grand tomb. Ninety percent of Rome's population of close to one million lived in multistory apartment blocks (*insulae*). After the great fire of A.D. 64, these were built of brick-faced concrete. The rents were not cheap, since the law of supply and demand in real estate was just as valid in antiquity as it is today. Juvenal, a Roman satirist of the early second century A.D., commented that people willing to give up chariot races and the other diversions Rome had to offer could purchase a fine home in the countryside "for a year's rent in a dark hovel" in a city so noisy that "the sick die mostly from lack of sleep."[5]

10-52   Al-Khazneh ("Treasury"), Petra, Jordan, second century A.D.

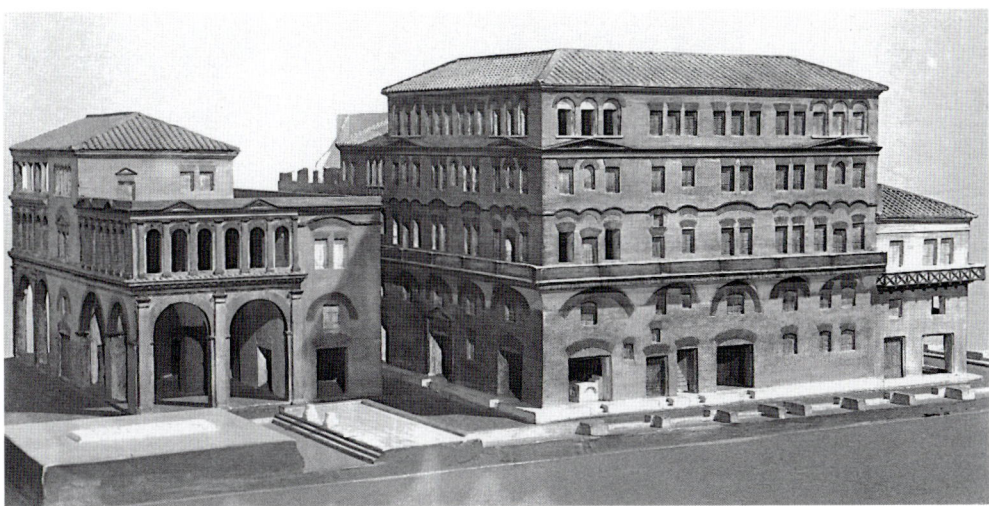

10-53 Model of an insula, Ostia, Italy, second century A.D. Museo della Civiltà Romana, Rome.

Conditions were much the same for the inhabitants of Ostia, Rome's harbor city. After its new port opened under Trajan, Ostia's prosperity increased dramatically and so did its population. A burst of building activity began under Trajan and continued under Hadrian and throughout the second century A.D. Many multistory second-century *insulae* (FIG. **10-53**) have been preserved at Ostia. Shops occupied the ground floors. Above were up to four floors of apartments. Although many of the insula apartments were large, they had neither the space nor the light of the typical Pompeian private *domus* (see "The Roman House," page 255). In place of peristyles, the insulae of Ostia and Rome had only narrow light wells or small courtyards. Consequently, instead of looking inward, large numbers of glass windows faced the city's noisy streets. Only deluxe apartments had private toilets. Others shared latrines, often on a different floor than the apartment. Still, these insulae were quite similar to modern apartment houses, which also sometimes have shops on the ground floor.

Another strikingly modern feature of these multifamily residences is their brick facades, which were not concealed by stucco or marble veneers. When a classical motif was desired, brick pilasters or engaged columns could be added, but the brick was always left exposed. Ostia and Rome have many examples of apartment houses, warehouses, and tombs with intricate moldings and contrasting colors of brick. In the second century A.D., brick came to be appreciated as attractive in its own right.

PAINTED VAULTS AND MOSAIC PAVEMENTS Although the decoration of Ostian insulae tended to be more modest than that of the private houses of Pompeii, the finer apartments had mosaic floors and painted walls and ceilings. The painted groin vaults of Ostia are of special interest, because few painted ceilings are preserved in the cities buried by the eruption of Mount Vesuvius, and they are rarely of the vaulted type. Room IV (FIG. **10-54**) in the aptly named Insula of the Painted Vaults is typical of painted ceiling design of the second and third centuries A.D. Such designs appear both in

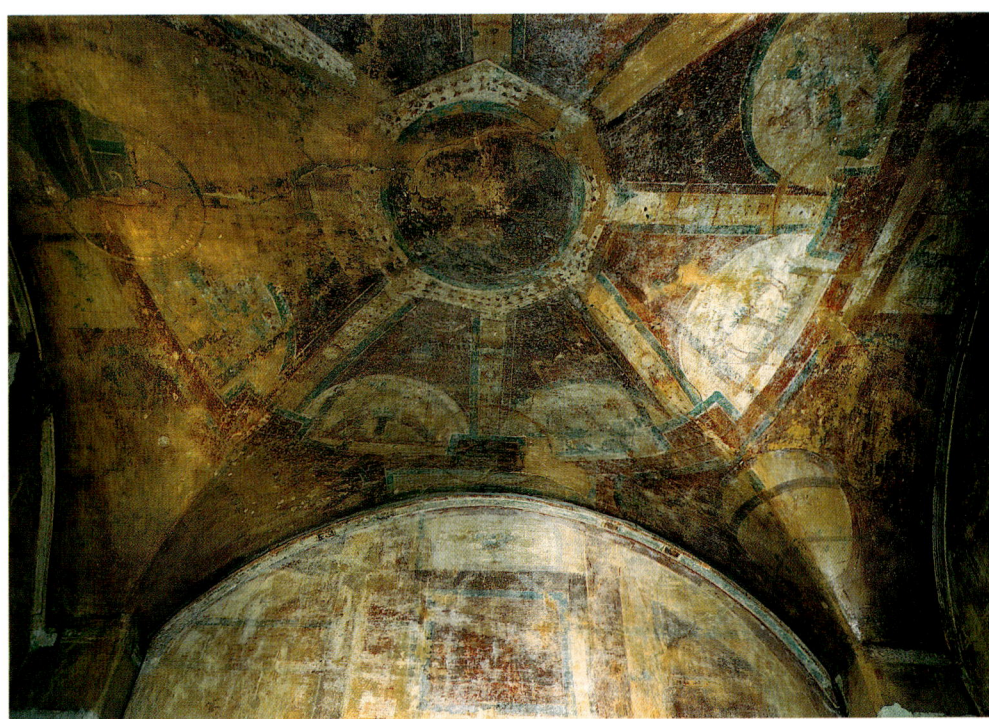

10-54 Ceiling and wall paintings in Room IV of the Insula of the Painted Vaults, Ostia, Italy, early third century A.D.

10-55 Neptune and creatures of the sea, floor mosaic in the Baths of Neptune, Ostia, Italy, ca. A.D. 140.

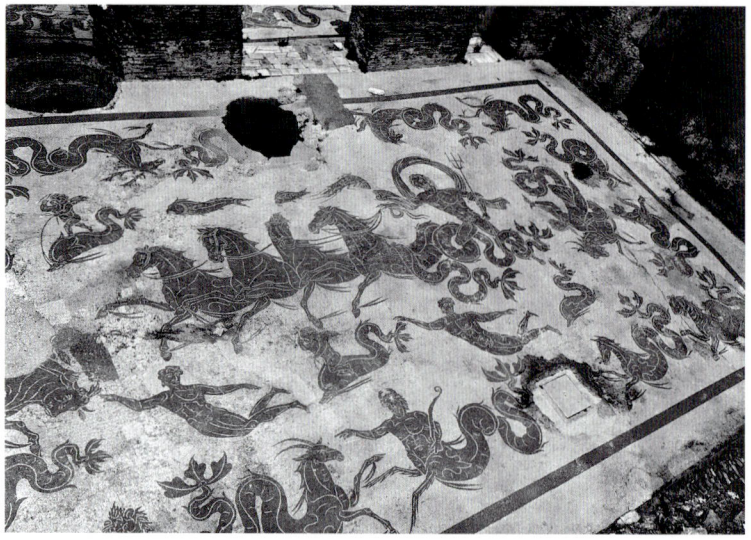

urban buildings and in the underground Christian catacombs (see FIG. 11-3). The groin vault was treated as if it were a dome, with a central oculus-like medallion surrounded by eight wedge-shaped segments resembling wheel spokes. In each segment is a white lunette with delicate paintings of birds and flowers, motifs also common earlier at Pompeii.

The most popular choice for elegant pavements at Ostia in both private and public edifices was the black-and-white mosaic. One of the largest and best preserved examples is in the so-called Baths of Neptune, named for the grand mosaic floor (FIG. **10-55**) with four seahorses pulling the Roman god of the sea across the waves. Neptune needs no chariot to support him as he speeds along, his mantle blowing in the strong wind. All about the god are other sea denizens, positioned so that regardless of which side a visitor enters the room, some figures appear right side up. The artist rejected the complex polychrome modeling of figures seen in Pompeian mosaics such as the *Battle of Issus* (see FIG. 5-69) and used simple black silhouettes enlivened by white interior lines. Roman black-and-white mosaics were conceived as surface decorations and not as three-dimensional windows and thus were especially appropriate for floors.

TOMBS OF WORKING MEN AND WOMEN Ostian tombs of the second century A.D. were usually constructed of brick-faced concrete, and the facades of these houses of the dead resembled those of the contemporary insulae of the living. These were normally communal tombs, not the final resting places of the very wealthy. Many of them were adorned with small painted terracotta plaques immortalizing the activities of middle-class merchants and professional people. We illustrate two of these plaques (FIG. **10-56**). One depicts a young man selling vegetables from behind a counter (which has been tilted forward so that the observer can see the produce clearly). The other shows a midwife delivering a baby. Because she looks out at the viewer rather than at what she is doing and because almost all these reliefs focus on the livelihoods of the deceased, it is likely the relief commemorates the midwife rather than the mother. Scenes of working men and women such as these appear on Roman funerary reliefs all over western Europe. Centuries later they may have served as the models for some medieval illustrations of the "labors of the months." They were as much, or more, a part

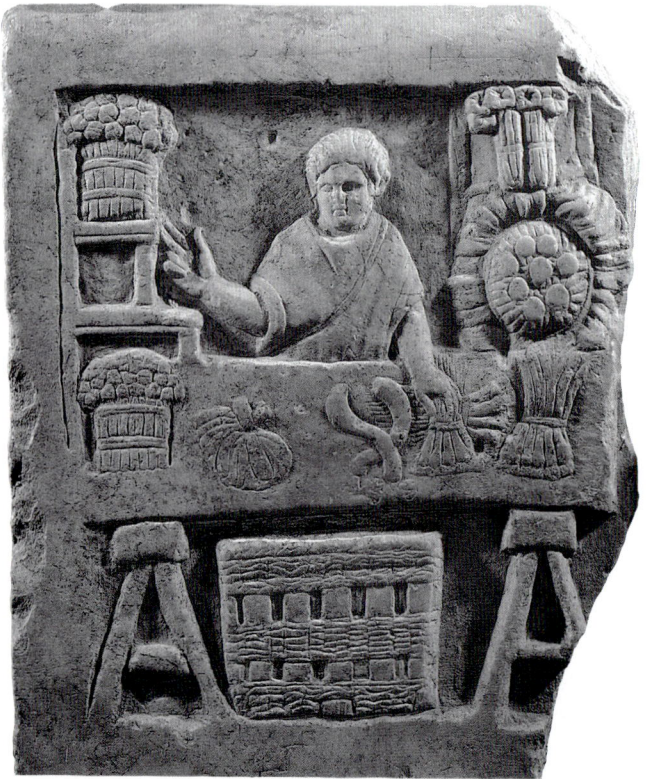

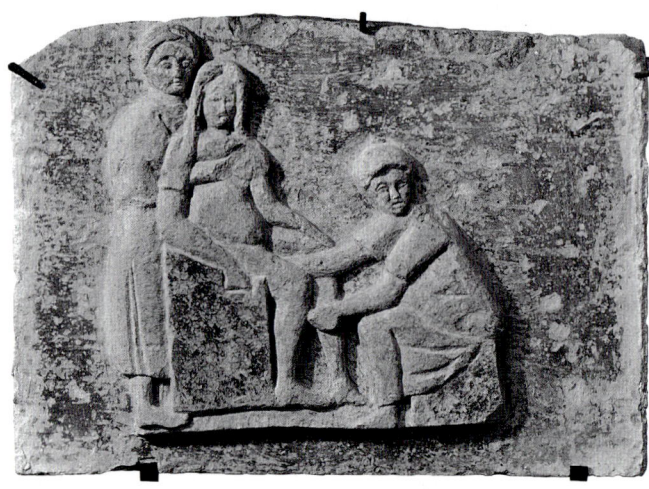

10-56 Funerary reliefs of a vegetable vendor *(left)* and a midwife *(right)*, from Ostia, Italy, second half of second century A.D. Painted terracotta, approx. 1′ 5″ and 11″ high, respectively. Museo Ostiense, Ostia.

of the classical legacy to the later history of art as the monuments Roman emperors commissioned, which until recently were the exclusive interest of art historians.

The Antonines (A.D. 138–192)

SUCCESSION BY ADOPTION   Early in A.D. 138, Hadrian adopted the fifty-one-year-old Antoninus Pius (r. A.D. 138–161). At the same time, he required that Antoninus adopt Marcus Aurelius (r. A.D. 161–180) and Lucius Verus (r. A.D. 161–169), thereby assuring a peaceful succession for at least another generation. When Hadrian died later in the year, he was proclaimed a god, and Antoninus Pius be-

came emperor. Antoninus ruled the Roman world with distinction for twenty-three years. After his death and deification, Marcus Aurelius and Lucius Verus became the Roman Empire's first coemperors.

CLASSICAL AND NON-CLASSICAL   Shortly after Antoninus Pius's death, Marcus and Lucius erected a memorial column in his honor. This column's pedestal has a dedicatory inscription on one side, and a relief illustrating the *apotheosis* (ascent to the heavens) of Antoninus and his wife Faustina the Elder on the opposite side (FIG. **10-57**). On the adjacent sides are two identical representations of the *decursio,* or ritual circling of the imperial funerary pyre (FIG. **10-58**).

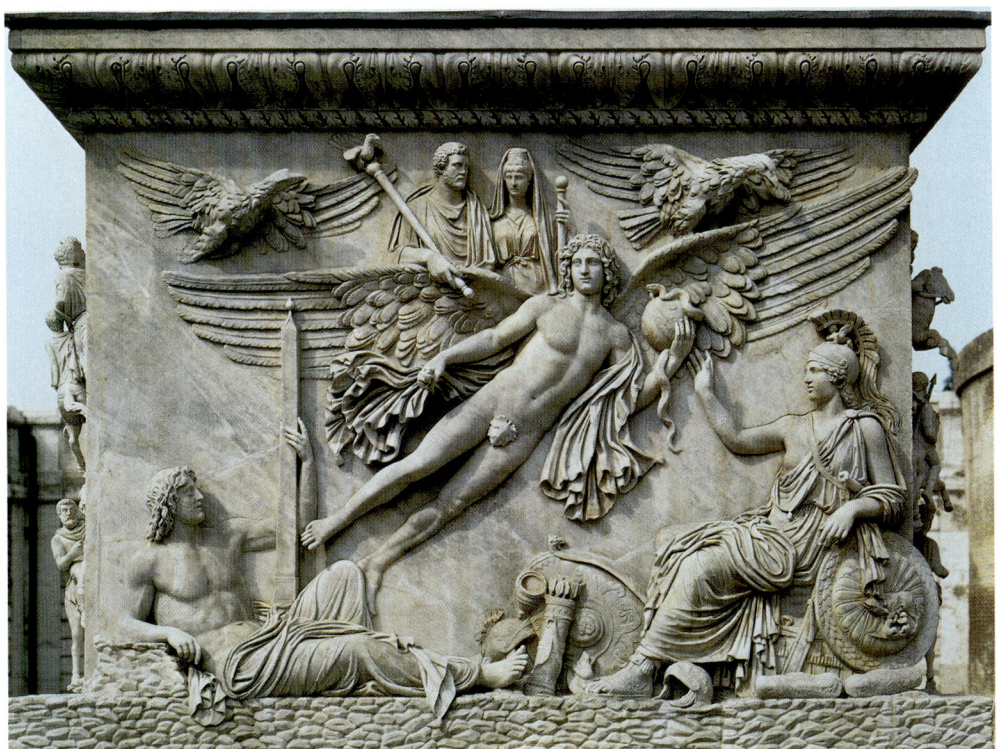

10-57   Apotheosis of Antoninus Pius and Faustina, pedestal of the Column of Antoninus Pius, Rome, Italy, ca. A.D. 161. Marble, approx. 8′ 1½″ high. Vatican Museums, Rome.

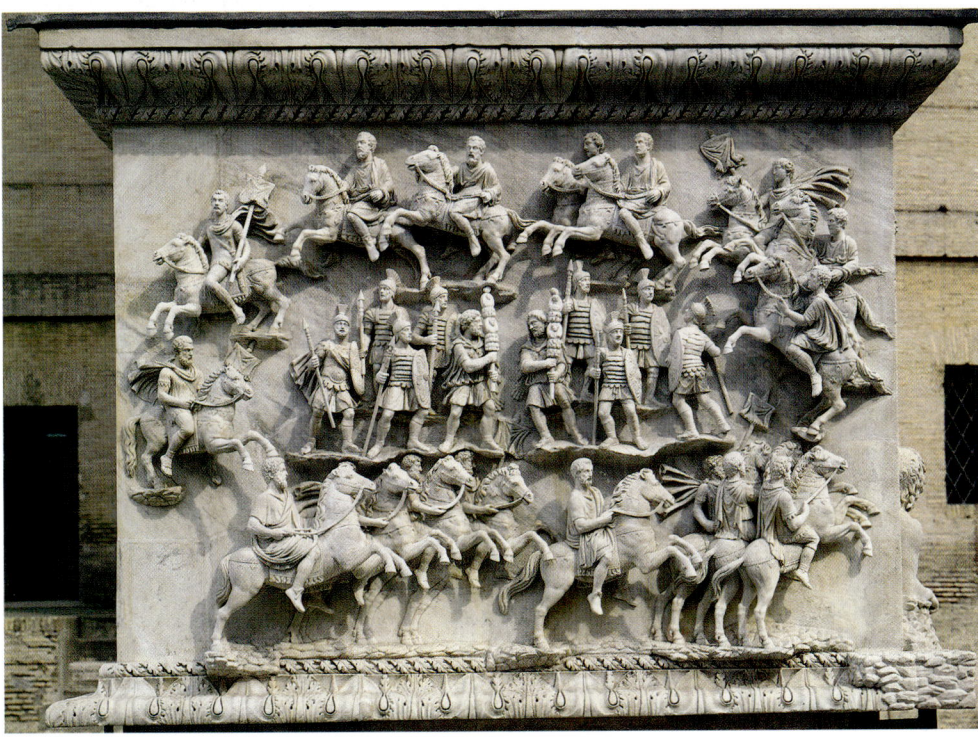

10-58   Decursio, pedestal of the Column of Antoninus Pius, Rome, Italy, ca. A.D. 161. Marble, approx. 8′ 1½″ high. Vatican Museums, Rome.

The two figural compositions are very different. The apotheosis relief remains firmly in the classical tradition with its elegant, well-proportioned figures, personifications, and single ground line corresponding to the panel's lower edge. The Campus Martius (Field of Mars), personified as a youth holding the Egyptian obelisk that stood in that area of Rome, reclines at the lower left corner. Roma (Rome personified) leans on a shield decorated with the she-wolf suckling Romulus and Remus (compare FIG. 9-10). Roma bids farewell to the couple being lifted into the realm of the gods on the wings of a personification of uncertain identity. All this is familiar from earlier scenes of apotheosis. New to the imperial repertoire, however, was the fusion of time the joint apotheosis represents. Faustina had died twenty years before Antoninus Pius. By depicting the two as ascending together, the artist wished to suggest that Antoninus had been faithful to his wife for two decades and that now they would be reunited in the afterlife. This notion had been employed before in the funerary reliefs of freed slaves and the middle class (FIG. 10-46) but had never been used in an elite context.

The decursio reliefs break even more strongly with classical convention. The figures are much stockier than those in the apotheosis relief, and the panel was not conceived as a window onto the world. The ground is the whole surface of the relief, and marching soldiers and galloping horses alike are shown on floating patches of earth. This, too, had not occurred before in imperial art, only in plebeian art (FIG. 10-5). After centuries of following classical design rules, elite Roman artists and patrons finally became dissatisfied with them. When seeking a new direction, they adopted some of the nonclassical conventions of the art of the lower classes.

DISQUIETING ANTONINE PORTRAITS   Another break with the past occurred in the official portraits of Marcus Aurelius, although the pompous trappings of imperial iconography were retained. In the sixteenth century, Pope Paul III selected a larger-than-life-size gilded-bronze equestrian statue of the emperor Marcus Aurelius (FIG. **10-59**) as the centerpiece for Michelangelo's new design for the Capitoline Hill in Rome (see FIGS. 22-26 and 22-27). The statue inspired many Renaissance sculptors to portray their patrons on horseback (see FIGS. 21-32 and 21-33). Recently removed from its Renaissance site and painstakingly restored, the portrait owed its preservation throughout the Middle Ages to the fact it was mistakenly thought to portray Constantine, the first Christian emperor of Rome. Most ancient bronze statues were melted down for their metal value, because they were regarded as impious images from the pagan world. Even today, after centuries of new finds, only a very few bronze equestrian statues are known. The type was, however, often used for imperial portraits—an equestrian statue of Trajan stood in the middle of his forum (FIG. 10-41). Perhaps more than any other statuary type, the equestrian portrait expresses the Roman emperor's majesty and authority.

In this portrait, Marcus possesses a superhuman grandeur and is much larger than any normal human would be in relation to his horse. He stretches out his right arm in a gesture that is both a greeting and an offer of clemency. Some evidence suggests that an enemy once cowered beneath the horse's raised right foreleg begging Marcus for mercy. The

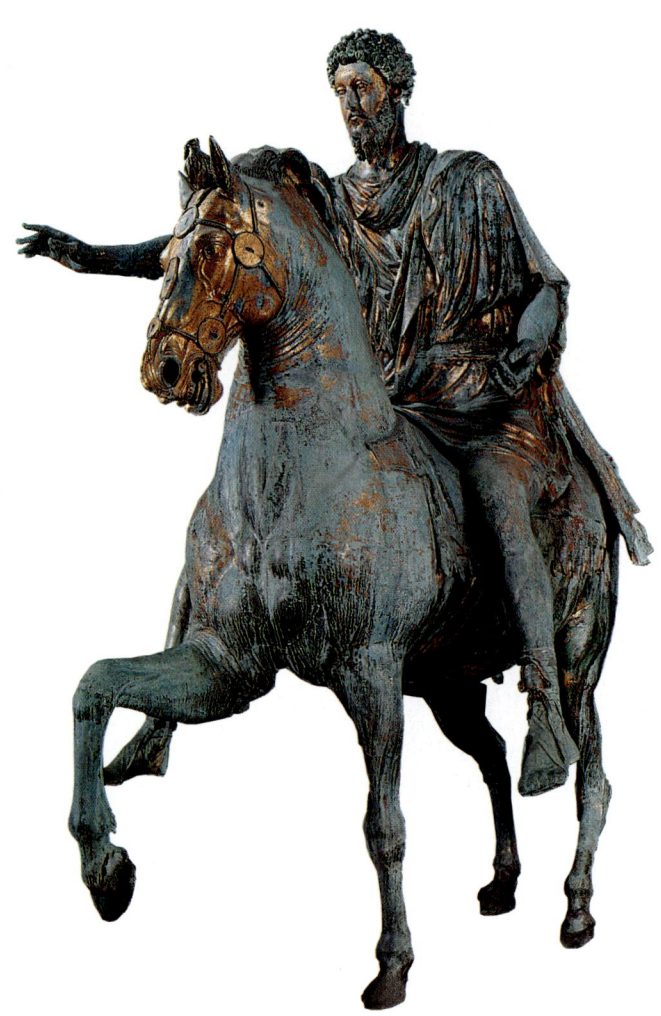

10-59   Equestrian statue of Marcus Aurelius, from Rome, Italy, ca. A.D. 175. Bronze, approx. 11′ 6″ high. Musei Capitolini, Rome.

statue conveys the awesome power of the godlike Roman emperor as ruler of the whole world.

This message of supreme confidence is not, however, conveyed by the statue's portrait head or by the late portraits of the emperor in marble, such as the one illustrated (FIG. **10-60**). The latter is a detail of a panel from a lost arch that probably resembled Trajan's arch at Benevento (FIG. 10-45). The emperor rides in a triumphal chariot, and, like Titus before him (FIG. 10-39), Victory crowns him. The Antonine sculptor, in keeping with contemporary practice, used a drill to render the emperor's long hair and beard and even to accentuate the pupils of his eyes, creating bold patterns of light and shadow across his face. A chisel was used to carve the lines in Marcus's forehead and the deep ridges running from his nostrils to the corners of his mouth.

Portraits of aged emperors were not new (FIG. 10-35), but Marcus's were the first ones where a Roman emperor appears weary, saddened, and even worried. For the first time, the strain of constant warfare on the frontiers and the burden of ruling a worldwide empire show in the emperor's face. The Antonine sculptor ventured beyond Republican verism. The ruler's character, his thoughts, and his soul were exposed for all to see, as Marcus revealed them himself in his *Meditations,* a deeply moving philosophical treatise setting forth the em-

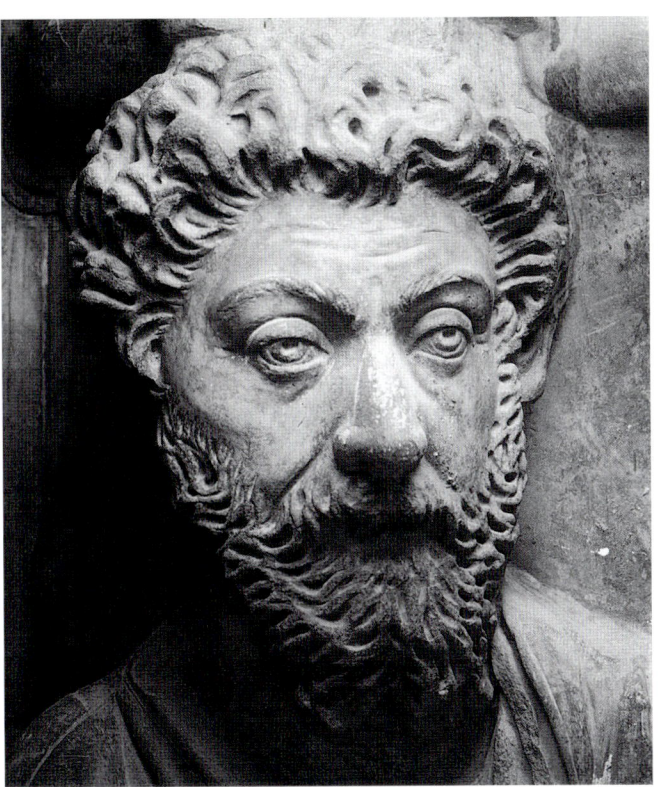

10-60 Portrait of Marcus Aurelius, detail of a relief from a lost arch, Rome, Italy, ca. A.D. 175–180. Marble, approx. life-size. Palazzo dei Conservatori, Rome.

peror's personal worldview. This was a major turning point in the history of ancient art, and, coming as it did when the classical style was being challenged in relief sculpture (FIG. 10-58), it marked the beginning of the end of classical art's domination in the Greco-Roman world.

CREMATION GIVES WAY TO BURIAL Other profound changes also were taking place in Roman art and society at this time. Beginning under Trajan and Hadrian and especially during the rule of the Antonines, Romans began to favor burial over cremation. This reversal of funerary practices may reflect the influence of Christianity and other Eastern religions, whose adherents believed in an afterlife for the human body. Although the emperors themselves continued to be cremated in the traditional Roman manner, many private citizens opted for burial. Thus they required larger containers for their remains than the ash urns that were the norm until the second century A.D. This in turn led to a sudden demand for sarcophagi, which are more similar to modern coffins than any other ancient type of burial container.

ORESTES ON ROMAN SARCOPHAGI Greek mythology was one of the most popular subjects for the decoration of these sarcophagi. In many cases, especially in the late second and third centuries A.D., the Greek heroes and heroines were given the portrait features of the deceased Roman men and women in the marble coffins. These private patrons were following the model of imperial portraiture, where emperors and empresses frequently masqueraded as gods and goddesses and heroes and heroines (see "Role-Playing in Roman Portraiture," page 266). An early example of the type (although it lacks any portraits) is the sarcophagus (FIG. 10-61) now in Cleveland, one of many decorated with the story of the tragic Greek hero Orestes. All the examples of this type use the same basic continuous-narrative composition. Orestes appears several times: slaying his mother Clytaemnestra and her lover Aegisthus to avenge their murder of his father Agamemnon, taking refuge at Apollo's sanctuary at Delphi (symbolized by the god's tripod at the right), and so forth.

The repetition of sarcophagus compositions indicates that sculptors had access to pattern books. In fact, sarcophagus production was a major industry during the High and Late Empire. Several important regional manufacturing centers existed. The sarcophagi produced in the Latin West, such as the Cleveland Orestes sarcophagus, differ in format from those made in the Greek-speaking East. Western sarcophagi have reliefs only on the front and sides, because they were placed in floor-level niches inside Roman tombs. Eastern sarcophagi have reliefs on

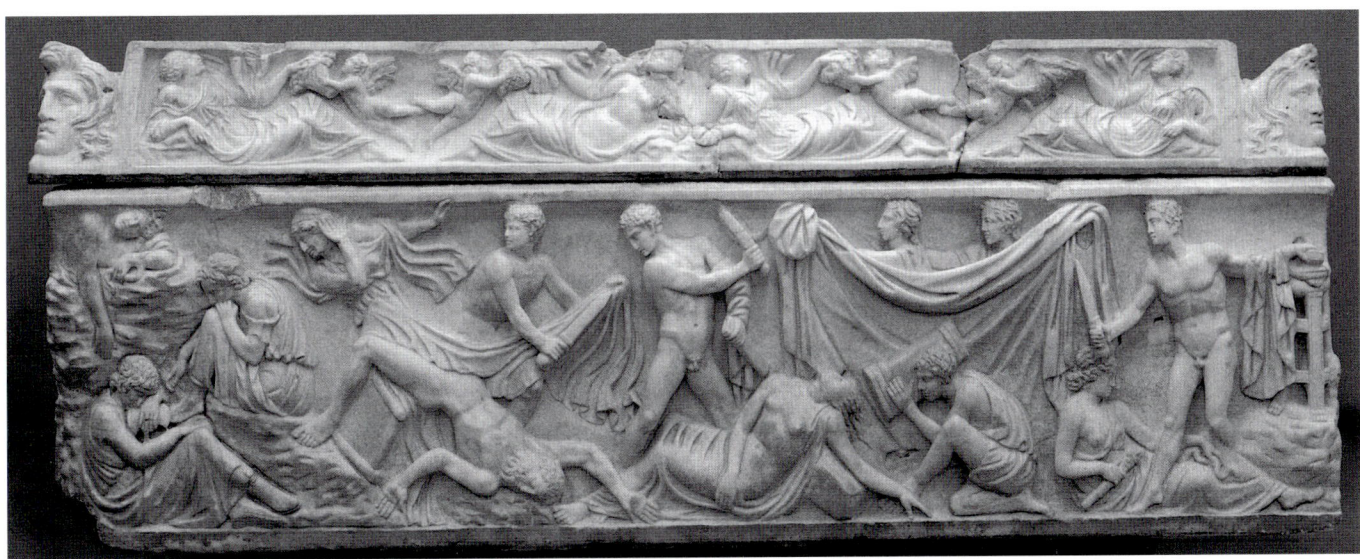

10-61 Sarcophagus with the myth of Orestes, ca. A.D. 140–150. Marble, 2′ 7½″ high. Cleveland Museum of Art, Cleveland.

10-62 Asiatic sarcophagus with *kline* portrait of a woman, from Melfi, Italy, ca. A.D. 165–170. Marble, approx. 5′ 7″ high. Museo Nazionale del Melfese, Melfi.

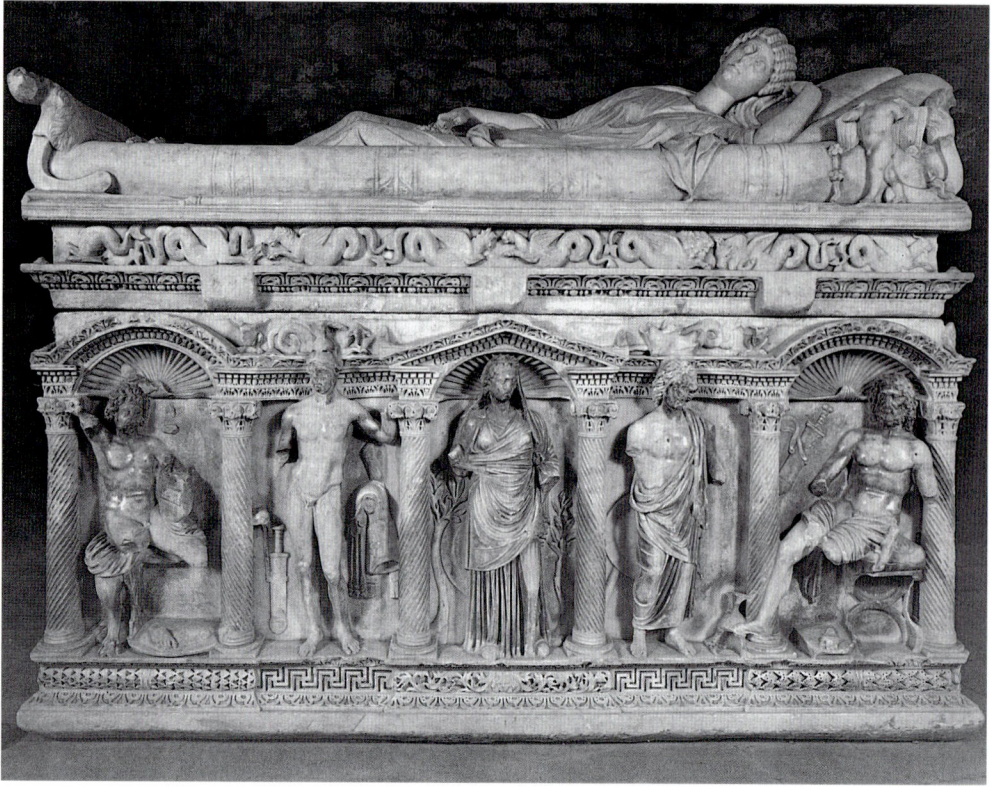

all four sides and stood in the center of the burial chamber. This contrast parallels the essential difference between the Etrusco-Roman and the Greek temple: The former was set against the wall of a forum or sanctuary and approached from the front, while the latter could be reached (and viewed) from every side.

A MORTAL VENUS'S COFFIN An elaborate example of a sarcophagus of the Eastern type (FIG. **10-62**) comes from Melfi in southern Italy. It was manufactured, however, in Asia Minor and attests to the vibrant export market for such luxury items in Antonine times. The decoration of all four sides of the marble box with statuesque images of Greek gods and heroes in architectural frames is distinctively Asiatic. But the lid portrait, which carries on the tradition of Etruscan sarcophagi (see FIGS. 9-4 and 9-14), is also a feature of the most expensive Western Roman coffins. Here the deceased, a woman, reclines on a *kline* (bed). With her are her faithful little dog (only its forepaws remain at the left end of the lid) and Cupid (at the right). The winged infant god mournfully holds a downturned torch, a reference to the death of a woman whose beauty rivaled that of his mother, Venus (who appears in one of the niches on the back of the sarcophagus).

MUMMY PORTRAITS IN ROMAN EGYPT In Egypt, burial had been practiced for millennia. Even after the Kingdom of the Nile was reduced to a Roman province in 30 B.C., Egyptians continued to bury their dead in mummy cases. In Roman times, however, painted portraits on wood replaced the traditional stylized portrait masks (see "Iaia of Cyzicus and the Art of Encaustic Painting," page 289). Hundreds of these mummy portraits have been preserved in the cemeteries of the Faiyum district. One of them (FIG. **10-63**)

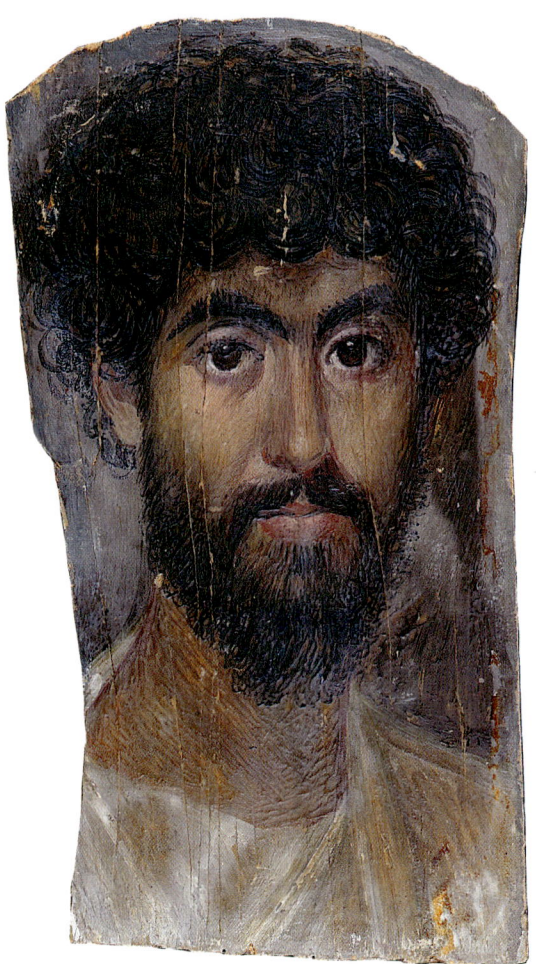

10-63 Mummy portrait of a man, from Faiyum, Egypt, ca. A.D. 160–170. Encaustic on wood, approx. 1′ 2″ high. Albright-Knox Art Gallery, Buffalo (Charles Clifton Fund).

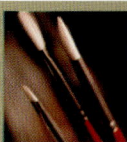

Iaia of Cyzicus and the Art of Encaustic Painting

The names of very few Roman artists are known. Those that are tend to be names of artists and architects who directed major imperial building projects (Severus and Celer, *Domus Aurea;* Apollodorus of Damascus, Forum of Trajan), worked on a gigantic scale (Zenodorus, Colossus of Nero), or made precious objects for famous patrons (Dioscurides, gem cutter for Augustus).

An interesting exception to this rule is IAIA OF CYZICUS. Pliny reported the following about this renowned painter from Asia Minor who worked in Italy during the Republic:

> Iaia of Cyzicus, who remained a virgin all her life, painted at Rome during the time when M. Varro [116–27 B.C.] was a youth, both with a brush and with a cestrum on ivory, specializing mainly in portraits of women; she also painted a large panel in Naples representing an old woman and a portrait of herself done with a mirror. Her hand was quicker than that of any other painter, and her artistry was of such high quality that she commanded much higher prices than the most celebrated painters of the same period.[1]

The *cestrum* Pliny mentioned is a small spatula used in *encaustic* painting, a technique of mixing colors with hot wax and then applying them to the surface. Pliny knew of encaustic paintings of considerable antiquity, including those of Polygnotos of Thasos, a famous fifth-century B.C. Greek painter (see Chapter 5, page 137). The best evidence for the technique comes, however, from Roman Egypt, where mummies were routinely furnished with portraits painted with encaustic on wooden panels (FIG. 10-63).

Artists applied encaustic to marble as well as to wood. According to Pliny, when Praxiteles was asked which one of his statues he preferred, the fourth-century B.C. Greek artist, perhaps the ancient world's greatest marble sculptor, replied: "Those that Nikias painted." This anecdote underscores the importance of coloration in ancient statuary.

[1] J. J. Pollitt, trans., *The Art of Rome, c. 753 B.C.–A.D. 337: Sources and Documents* (New York: Cambridge University Press, 1983), 87.

depicts a man who, following the lead of Marcus Aurelius, has long curly hair and a full beard. Such portraits, which mostly date to the second and third centuries A.D., were probably painted while the subjects were still alive. Art historians use them to trace the evolution of portrait painting after Mount Vesuvius erupted in A.D. 79 (compare FIG. 10-23). Our example is of high quality. Note the refined use of the brush and spatula, soft and delicate modeling, and sensitive portrayal of the calm demeanor of its thoughtful subject.

The Western and Eastern Roman sarcophagi and the mummy cases of Roman Egypt all served the same purpose, despite their differing shape and character. In an empire as vast as Rome's, regional differences are to be expected. As will be discussed later, geography also played a major role in the Middle Ages, when Western and Eastern Christian art differed sharply.

THE LATE EMPIRE

A CIVILIZATION IN TRANSITION By the time of Marcus Aurelius, two centuries after Augustus established the Pax Romana, Roman power was beginning to erode. It was more and more difficult to keep order on the frontiers, and even within the empire the authority of Rome was being challenged. Marcus's son Commodus (r. A.D. 180–192), who succeeded his father, was assassinated, bringing the Antonine dynasty to an end. The economy was in decline, and the efficient imperial bureaucracy was disintegrating. Even the official state religion was losing ground to Eastern cults, Christianity among them, which were beginning to gain large

numbers of converts. The Late Empire was a civilization in transition, a pivotal era in world history, during which the pagan ancient world was gradually transformed into the Christian Middle Ages.

The Severans (A.D. 193–235)

AN AFRICAN RULES THE EMPIRE Civil conflict followed Commodus's death. When it ended, an African-born general named Septimius Severus (r. A.D. 193–211) was master of the Roman world. The new emperor, anxious to establish his legitimacy, adopted himself into the Antonine dynasty, proclaiming himself as Marcus Aurelius's son. It is not surprising, then, that official portraits of Septimius Severus depict him with the long hair and beard of his Antonine "father"—whatever his actual appearance may have been. Many portraits in marble and bronze exist today of the African emperor and of his wife, Julia Domna, the daughter of a Syrian priest, and their two sons, Caracalla and Geta. But only one painted portrait of the family has been found. In fact, the portrait (FIG. **10-64**), discovered in Egypt and painted in *tempera* (pigments in egg yolk) on wood (as were many of the mummy portraits from Faiyum), is the only surviving painted likeness of any Roman emperor. Such portraits, however, must have been quite common all over the empire. Their perishable nature explains their almost total loss.

The Severan family portrait is of special interest for two reasons beyond its mere survival. The emperor's hair is tinged

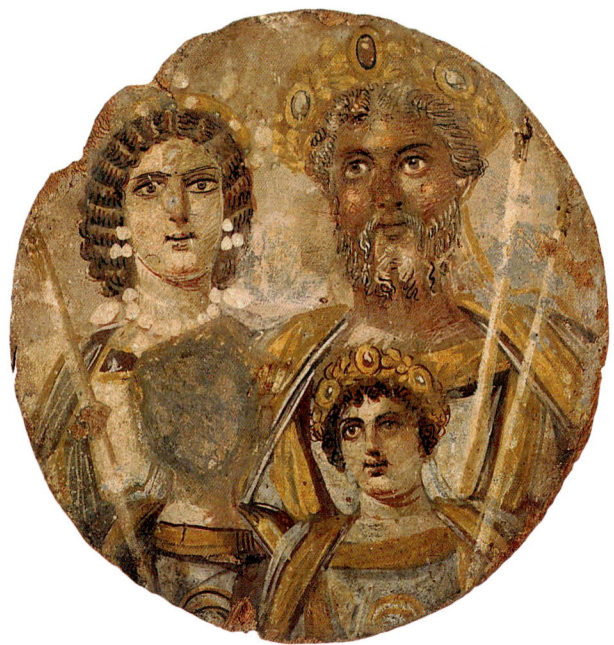

10-64   Painted portrait of Septimius Severus and his family, from Egypt, ca. A.D. 200. Tempera on wood, approx. 1′ 2″ diameter. Staatliche Museen, Berlin.

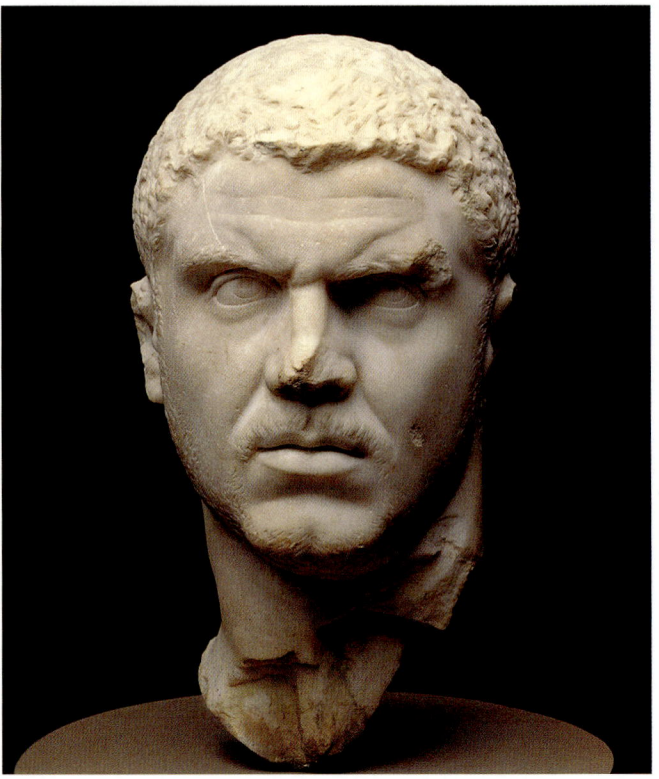

10-65   Portrait of Caracalla, ca. A.D. 211–217. Marble, approx. 1′ 2″ high. Metropolitan Museum of Art, New York.

with gray, suggesting that his marble portraits—which, like all marble sculptures in antiquity, were painted—also may have revealed his advancing age in this way. (The same was very likely true of the marble likenesses of the old and tired Marcus Aurelius.) The group portrait is also notable because the face of the emperor's younger son, Geta, was erased. When Caracalla succeeded his father as emperor, he had his brother murdered and his memory damned. (Caracalla also ordered the death of his own wife, Plautilla.) The painted *tondo* (circular format) portrait from Egypt is an eloquent testimony to that *damnatio memoriae* and to the long arm of Roman authority. This kind of defacement of a political rival's portrait is not new. As noted earlier, for example, Thutmose III of Egypt destroyed the portraits of Hatshepsut after her death (see FIG. 3-21). But the Romans employed damnatio memoriae as a political tool more often and more systematically than any other civilization.

A PORTRAIT OF A RUTHLESS EMPEROR   The ruthless character of Caracalla (r. A.D. 211–217) was captured in his portraits. The marble head shown here (FIG. **10-65**) was typical. The sculptor suggested the texture of Caracalla's short hair and close-cropped beard with incisions into the marble surface. Most remarkable, however, is the moving characterization of the emperor's suspicious nature, a further development from the groundbreaking introspection of the portraits of Marcus Aurelius. Caracalla's brow is knotted, and he abruptly turns his head over his left shoulder, as if he suspects danger from behind. The emperor had reason to be fearful. He was felled by an assassin's dagger in the sixth year of his rule. Assassination would become the fate of many Roman emperors during the turbulent third century A.D.

10-66   Chariot procession of Septimius Severus, relief from the Arch of Septimius Severus, Lepcis Magna, Libya, A.D. 203. Marble, approx. 5′ 6″ high. Castle Museum, Tripoli.

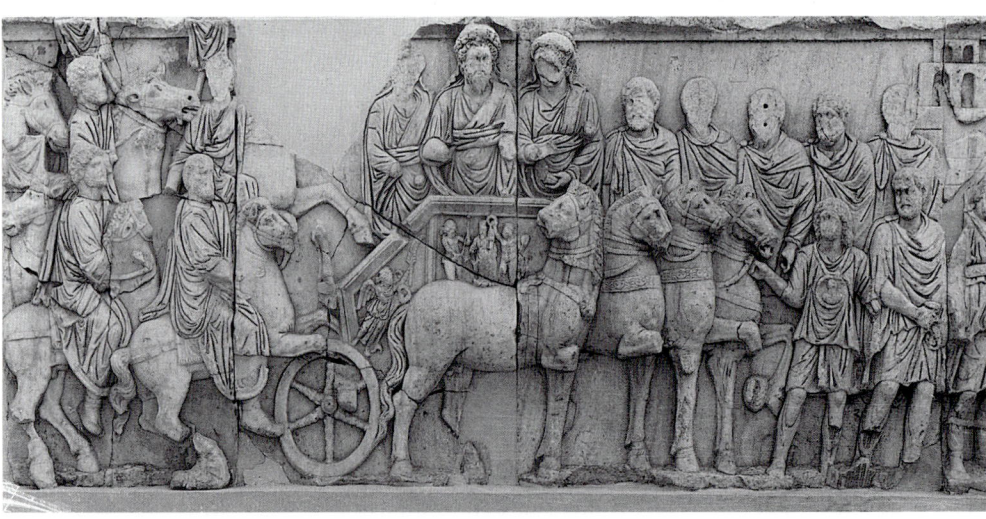

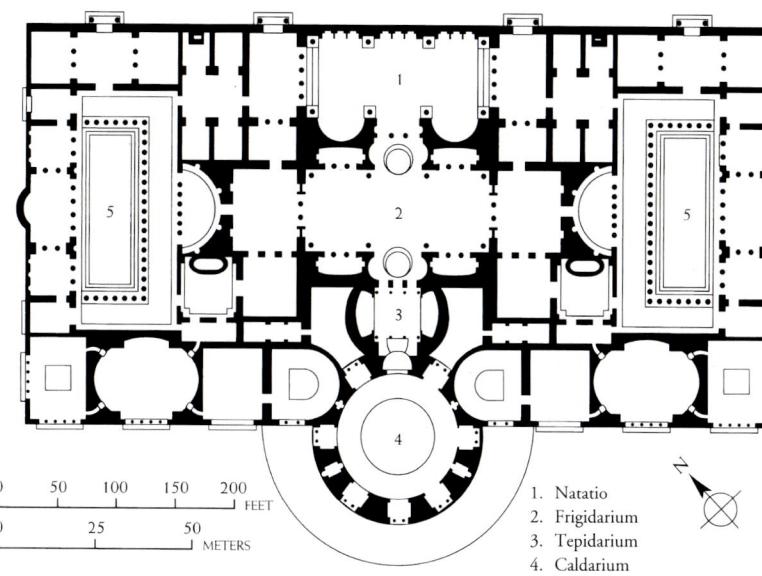

10-67 Plan of the central section of the Baths of Caracalla, Rome, Italy, A.D. 212–216. The bathing, swimming, and exercise areas were surrounded by landscaped gardens, lecture halls, and other rooms, all enclosed within a great concrete perimeter wall.

1. Natatio
2. Frigidarium
3. Tepidarium
4. Caldarium
5. Palaestra

THE NONCLASSICAL STYLE TAKES ROOT The hometown of the Severans was Lepcis Magna, on the coast of what is now Libya. In the late second and early third centuries A.D., imperial funds were used to construct a modern harbor there, as well as a new forum, basilica, arch, and other monuments. The Arch of Septimius Severus, erected in 203 at the intersection of two major streets, had friezes on the attic on all four sides. One of these (FIG. **10-66**) shows the chariot procession of Septimius and his two sons. Unlike the triumph panel from the Arch of Titus in Rome (FIG. 10-39), this relief gives no sense of rushing motion. Rather, it has a stately stillness. The chariot and the horsemen behind it are moving forward, but the emperor and his sons are detached from the procession and face the viewer. Also different is how the figures in the second row have no connection with the ground and are elevated above the heads of those in the first row so that they can be seen more clearly.

Both the frontality and the floating figures were new to official Roman art in Antonine and Severan times, but both appeared long before in the private art of freed slaves (compare FIGS. 10-4 and 10-5). Once embraced by sculptors in the emperor's employ, these non-classical elements had a long afterlife, appearing in medieval art in frontal images of Christ and the saints. As is often true in the history of art, this period of social, political, and economic upheaval was accompanied by the emergence of a new aesthetic.

A GIGANTIC ROMAN HEALTH SPA The Severans were also active builders in the capital. The Baths of Caracalla in Rome (FIGS. **10-67** and **10-68**) were the greatest in a long line of bathing and recreational complexes erected with imperial funds to win the public's favor. Made of brick-faced concrete and covered by enormous vaults springing from thick walls up to one hundred and forty feet high, Caracalla's baths covered an area of almost fifty acres. They dwarfed the typical baths of cities and towns such as Ostia and Pompeii and even Rome itself. The design was symmetrical along a central axis, facilitating the Roman custom of taking sequential plunges in cold-, warm-, and hot-water baths in, respectively, the *frigidarium*, *tepidarium*, and *caldarium*.

The caldarium of Caracalla's baths was a circular chamber so large that today it seats hundreds of spectators at open-air performances of Italian operas. Its dome was almost as large as the Pantheon's (FIG. 10-50), and the concrete drum that supported it was much taller. Our reconstruction of the frigidarium (FIG. 10-68), which was also the central hall of the baths, shows not only the scale of the architecture and the way light entered through fenestrated groin vaults but also how lavishly

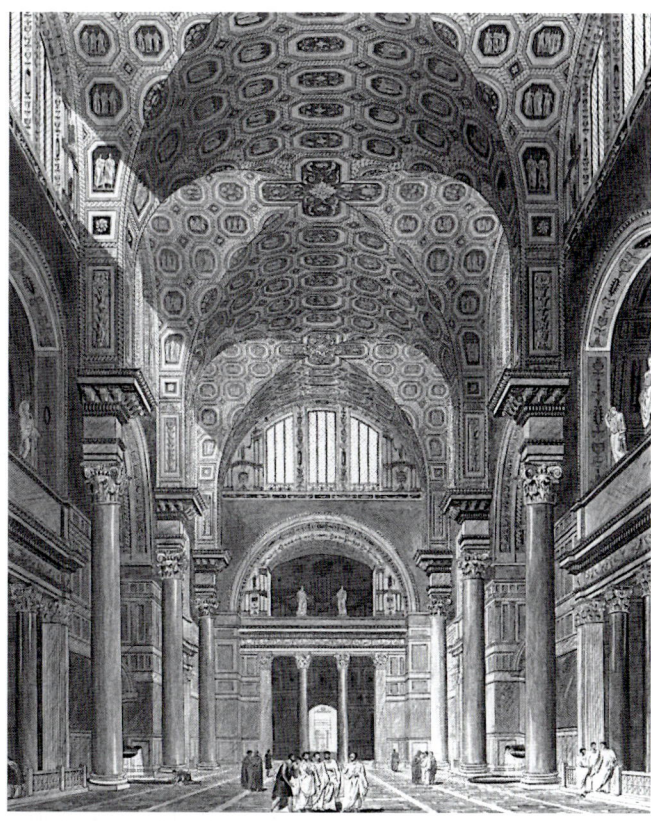

10-68 Reconstruction drawing of the central hall (*frigidarium*) of the Baths of Caracalla, Rome, Italy, A.D. 212–216.

the rooms were decorated. Stuccoed vaults, mosaic floors (both black-and-white and polychrome), marble-faced walls, and colossal statuary were found throughout the complex. Although the vaults themselves collapsed long ago, many of the mosaics and statues are preserved. Among these is the $10\frac{1}{2}$-foot-tall copy of Lysippos's Herakles (see FIG. 5-66), whose muscular body may have inspired Romans of the third century A.D. to exercise vigorously.

Caracalla's baths also had landscaped gardens, lecture halls, libraries, colonnaded exercise courts *(palaestrae)*, and a giant swimming pool *(natatio).* Archeologists estimate that up to sixteen hundred bathers at a time could enjoy this Roman equivalent of a modern health spa. A branch of one of the city's major aqueducts supplied water, and furnaces circulated hot air through hollow floors and walls throughout the complex.

The Soldier Emperors (A.D. 235–284)

MURDER AND CIVIL WAR   The Severan dynasty ended when Severus Alexander (r. A.D. 222–235) was murdered. The next half century was a stormy one. One general after another was declared emperor by his troops, only to be murdered by another general a few years or even a few months later. (In the year 238, two coemperors the Senate chose were dragged from the imperial palace and murdered in

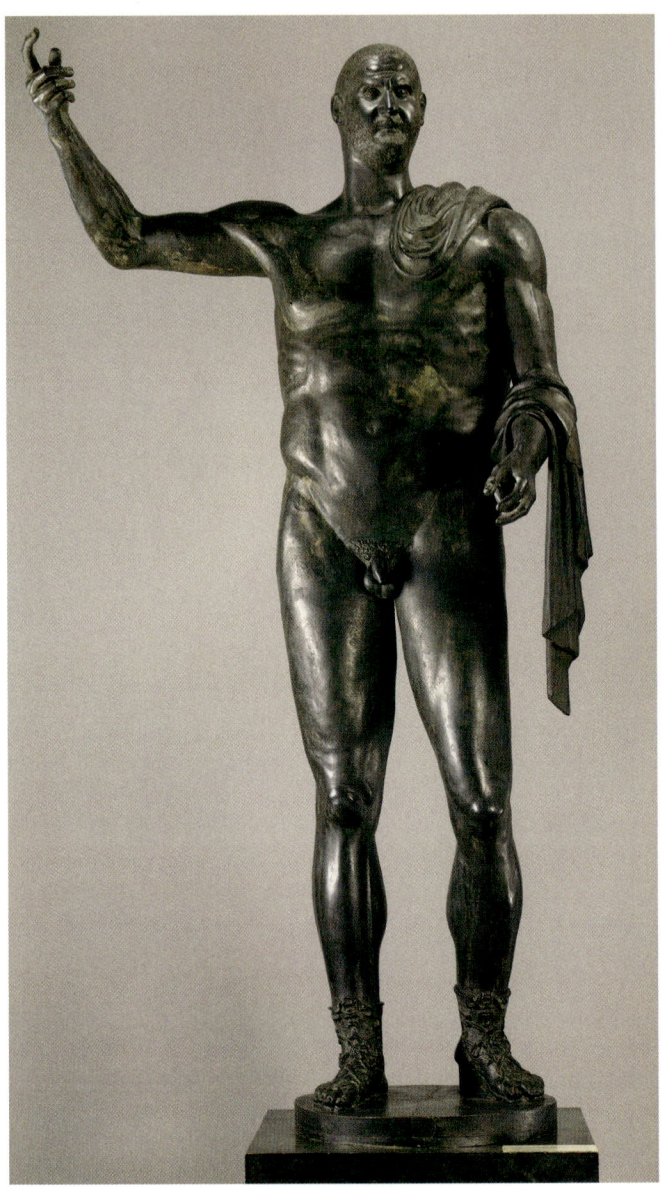

10-70   Heroic portrait of Trebonianus Gallus, from Rome, Italy, A.D. 251–253. Bronze, approx. 7' 11" high. Metropolitan Museum of Art, New York (Rogers Fund).

public after only three months in office.) In these unstable times, no emperor could begin ambitious architectural projects. The only significant building activity in Rome during the "soldier emperors" era occurred under Aurelian (r. A.D. 270–275). He constructed a new defensive wall circuit for the capital—a military necessity and a poignant commentary on the decay of Roman power.

SOUL PORTRAITS OF SOLDIER EMPERORS   If architects went hungry in third-century Rome, sculptors and engravers had much to do. Great quantities of coins (in debased metal) were produced so that the troops could be paid with money stamped with the current emperor's portrait and not with that of his predecessor or rival. Each new ruler set up portrait statues and busts everywhere to assert his authority.

The sculptured portraits of the third century A.D. are among the most moving ever produced. Following the lead of the sculptors of the Marcus Aurelius and Caracalla portraits,

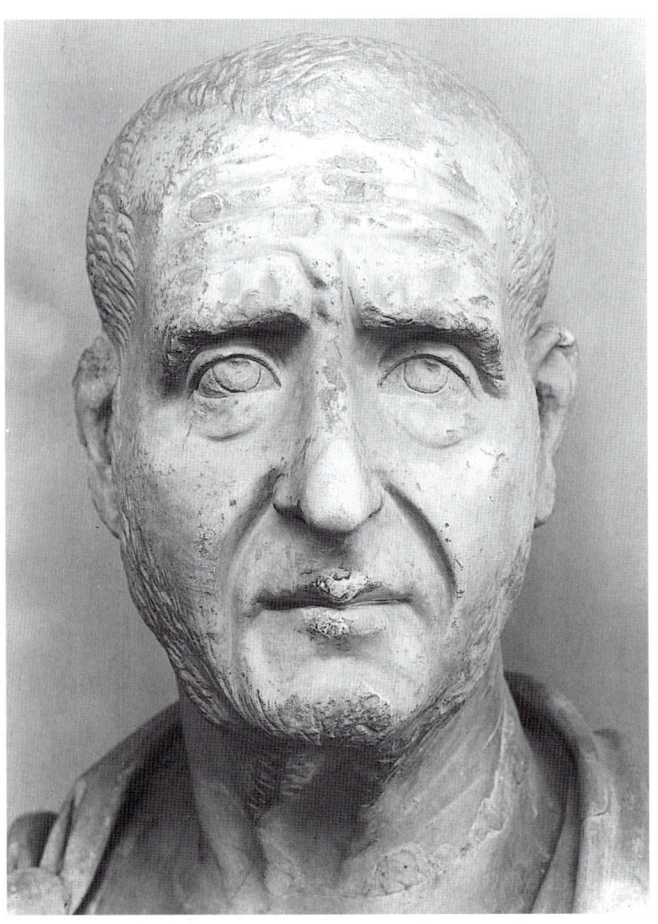

10-69   Portrait bust of Trajan Decius, A.D. 249–251. Marble, approx. 2' 7" high. Museo Capitolino, Rome.

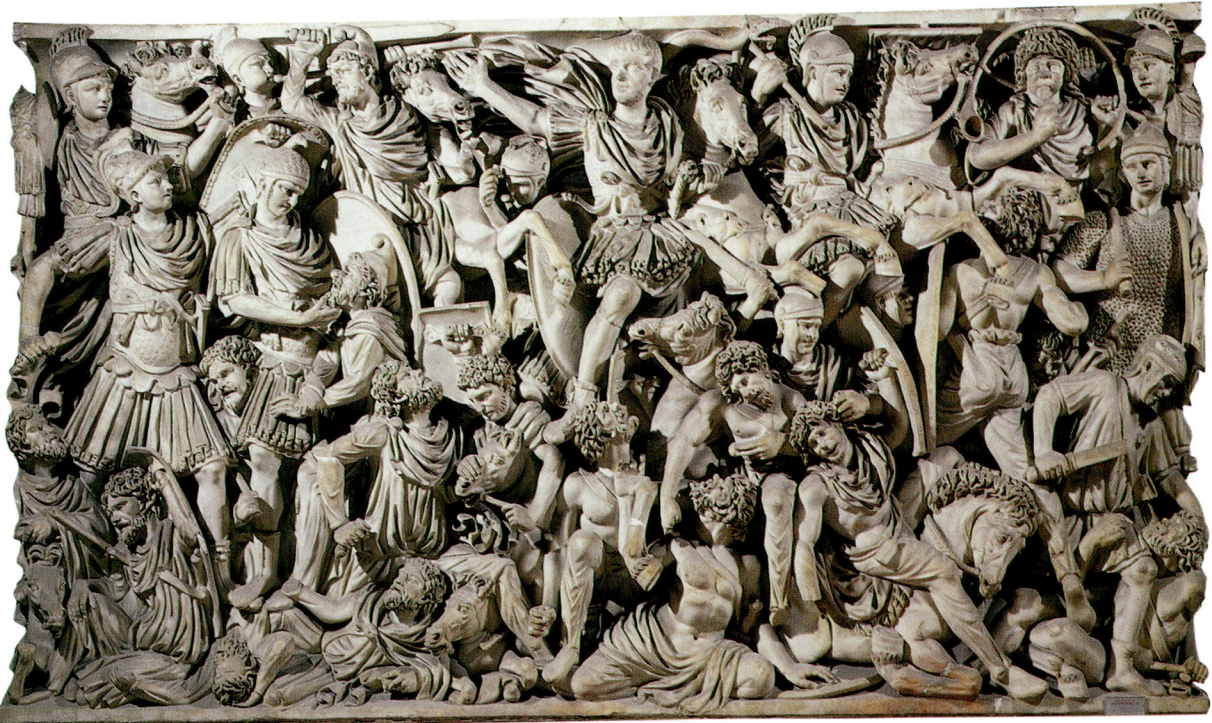

10-71   Battle of Romans and barbarians *(Ludovisi Battle Sarcophagus)*, from Rome, Italy, ca. A.D. 250–260. Marble, approx. 5′ high. Museo Nazionale Romano-Palazzo Altemps, Rome.

artists fashioned likenesses of the soldier emperors that are as notable for their emotional content as they are for their technical virtuosity. Trajan Decius (r. 249–251), for example, whose brief reign is best known for persecution of Christians, was portrayed as an old man with bags under his eyes and a sad expression (FIG. **10-69**). In his eyes, which glance away nervously rather than engage viewers directly, is the anxiety of a man who knows he can do little to restore order to an out-of-control world. The sculptor modeled the marble as if it were pliant clay, compressing the sides of the head at the level of the eyes, etching the hair and beard into the stone, and chiseling the deep lines in the forehead and around the mouth. The portrait reveals the anguished soul of the man—and of the times.

Decius's successor was Trebonianus Gallus (r. A.D. 251–253), another short-lived emperor. A larger-than-life-size bronze portrait (FIG. **10-70**) exists of Trebonianus appearing in heroic nudity, as had so many emperors and generals before him. His physique is not, however, that of the strong but graceful Greek athletes Augustus and his successors admired so much. Instead, his is a wrestler's body with massive legs and a swollen trunk. The heavyset body dwarfs his head, with its nervous expression. In this portrait, the Greek ideal of the keen mind in the harmoniously proportioned body gave way to an image of brute force, an image well suited to the era of the soldier emperors.

BARBARIANS AND PHILOSOPHERS   By the third century, burial of the dead had become so widespread that even the imperial family was practicing it in place of cremation. Sarcophagi were more popular than ever. An unusually large sarcophagus (FIG. **10-71**), discovered in Rome in 1621 and purchased by Cardinal Ludovisi, is decorated on the front with a chaotic scene of battle between Romans and one of their northern foes, probably the Goths. The writhing and highly emotive figures were spread evenly across the entire relief, with no illusion of space behind them. This piling of figures was an even more extreme rejection of classical perspective than using floating ground lines on the pedestal of the Column of Antoninus Pius (FIG. 10-58). It underscores the increasing dissatisfaction Late Roman artists felt with the classical style.

Within this dense mass of intertwined bodies, the central horseman stands out vividly. He is bareheaded and thrusts out his open right hand to demonstrate that he holds no weapon. Several scholars have identified him as one of the sons of Trajan Decius. In an age when the Roman army was far from invincible and Roman emperors were constantly felled by other Romans, the young general on the sarcophagus is boasting that he is a fearless commander assured of victory. His self-assurance may stem from his having embraced one of the increasingly popular Oriental mystery religions. On the youth's forehead is carved the emblem of Mithras, the Persian god of light, truth, and victory over death, many of whose shrines have been found at Rome and Ostia.

The insecurity of the times led many Romans to seek solace in philosophy. On many third-century sarcophagi, the deceased assumes the role of the learned intellectual. (Others continued to masquerade as Greek heroes or Roman generals.) One especially large example (FIG. **10-72**) depicts an enthroned Roman philosopher holding a scroll. He is flanked by two standing women (also with portrait features). In the background are other philosophers, students of the central deceased teacher. This type of sarcophagus became very popular for Christian burials, where the wise-man motif was used not only to portray the deceased (see FIG. 11-4) but also Christ flanked by his apostles (see FIG. 11-5). Frontal three-part

10-72 Sarcophagus of a philosopher, ca. A.D. 270–280. Marble, approx. 4′ 11″ high. Vatican Museums, Rome.

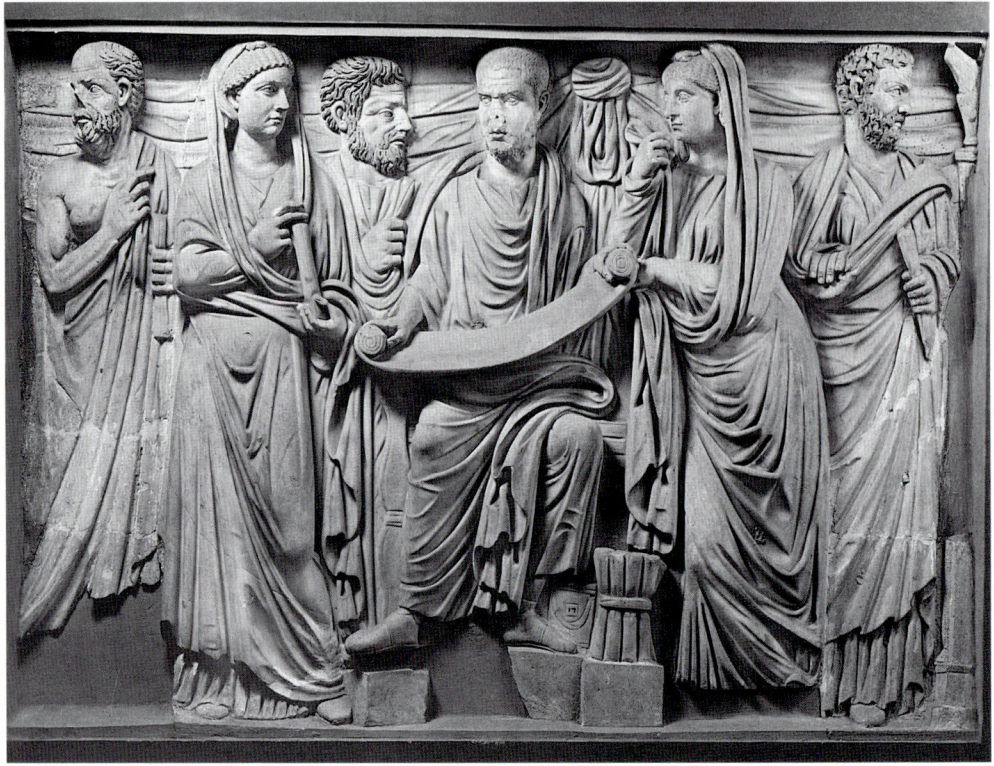

compositions, such as on this sarcophagus and on the Severan arch at Lepcis Magna (FIG. 10-66), are also quite common in Early Christian art (see FIGS. 11-5 and 11-17).

A CRITIQUE OF THE PANTHEON The decline in respect for classical art also can be seen in architecture. At Baalbek (ancient Heliopolis) in modern Lebanon, the architect of the Temple of Venus (FIG. **10-73**), following in the "baroque" tradition of the Treasury at Petra (FIG. 10-52), ignored almost every rule of classical design. Although made of stone, the third-century building, with its circular domed cella set behind a gabled columnar facade, was in many ways a critique of the concrete Pantheon (FIG. 10-48), which by then had achieved the status of a "classic." The platform of the Baalbek temple was

scalloped all around the cella. The columns—the only known instance of *five*-sided Corinthian capitals with corresponding pentagonal bases—also supported a scalloped entablature (which served to buttress the shallow stone dome). These concave forms and those of the niches in the cella walls played off against the cella's convex shape. Even the "traditional" facade of the Baalbek temple was eccentric. The unknown architect inserted an arch within the triangular pediment.

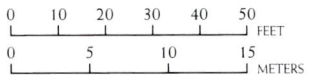

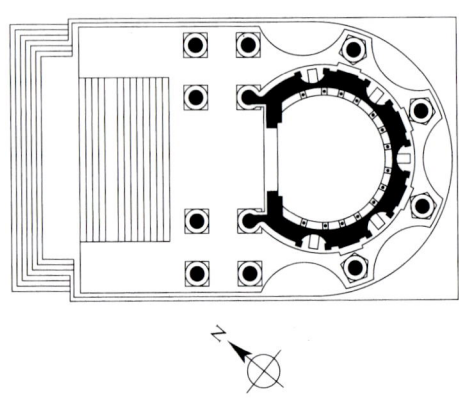

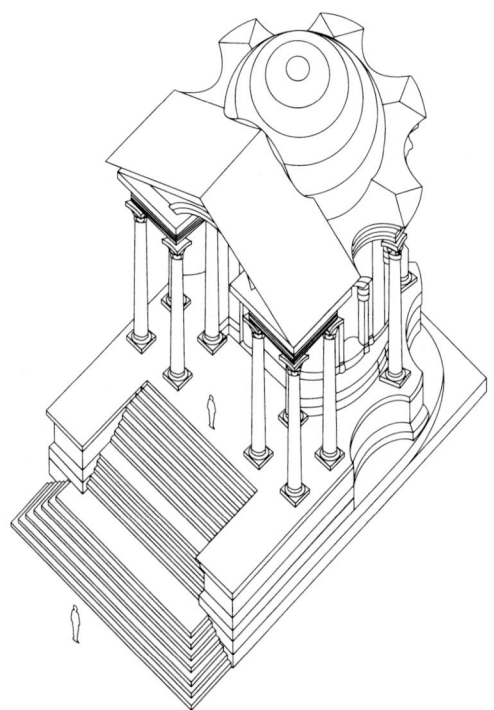

10-73 Plan and reconstruction drawing of the Temple of Venus, Baalbek, Lebanon, third century A.D.

Diocletian and the Tetrarchy (A.D. 284–306)

POWER SHARED AND ORDER RESTORED   In an attempt to restore order to the Roman Empire, Diocletian (r. A.D. 284–305), who was proclaimed emperor by his troops, decided to share power with his potential rivals. In 293, he established the *tetrarchy* (rule by four) and adopted the title of Augustus of the East. The other three tetrarchs were a corresponding Augustus of the West, and Eastern and Western Caesars (whose allegiance to the two Augusti was cemented by marriage to their daughters). Together, the four emperors ruled without strife until Diocletian retired in 305. Without his leadership, the new tetrarchs began fighting among themselves, and the tetrarchic form of government collapsed. The division of the Roman Empire into eastern and western spheres survived, however. It persisted throughout the Middle Ages, setting the Latin West apart from the Byzantine East.

INDIVIDUALITY LOST   The four tetrarchs often were portrayed together, both on coins and in the round. Artists did not try to capture their individual appearances and personalities but sought instead to represent the nature of the tetrarchy itself—that is, to portray four equal partners in power. In the two pairs of *porphyry* (purple marble) portraits of the tetrarchs shown here (FIG. **10-74**), it is impossible to name the rulers. Each of the four emperors has lost his identity as an individual and was subsumed into the larger entity of the tetrarchy. All the tetrarchs are identically clad in cuirass and cloak. Each grasps a sheathed sword in the left hand. With their right arms they embrace one another in an overt display of concord. The figures, like those on the decursio relief of the Column of Antoninus Pius (FIG. 10-58), have large cubical heads on squat bodies. The drapery is schematic and the bodies are shapeless. The faces are emotionless masks, as alike as freehand carving can achieve. In this group portrait, carved eight centuries after Greek sculptors first freed the human form from the formal rigidity of the Egyptian-inspired kouros stance, the human figure was once again conceived in iconic terms. Idealism, naturalism, individuality, and personality now belonged to the past.

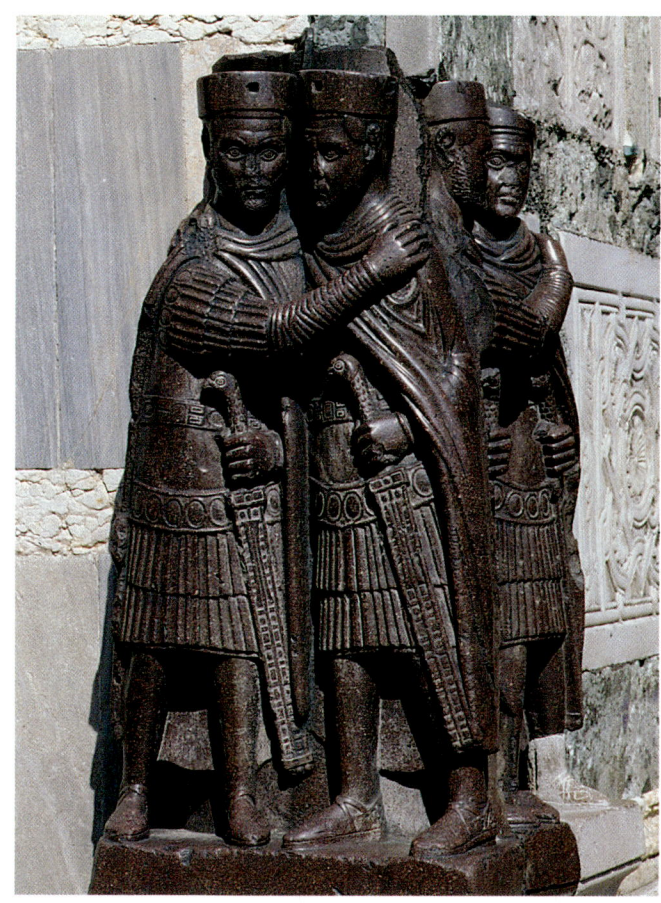

10-74   Portraits of the four tetrarchs, ca. A.D. 305. Porphyry, approx. 4′ 3″ high. Saint Mark's, Venice.

A FORTIFIED IMPERIAL PALACE   When Diocletian abdicated in 305, he returned to Dalmatia (roughly the area of the former Yugoslavia), where he was born. There he built a palace (FIG. **10-75**) for himself at Split, near ancient Salona on the Adriatic coast in Croatia. Just as Aurelian had felt it necessary to girdle Rome with fortress walls, Diocletian instructed his architects to provide him with a well-fortified suburban palace. The complex, which covers about ten acres,

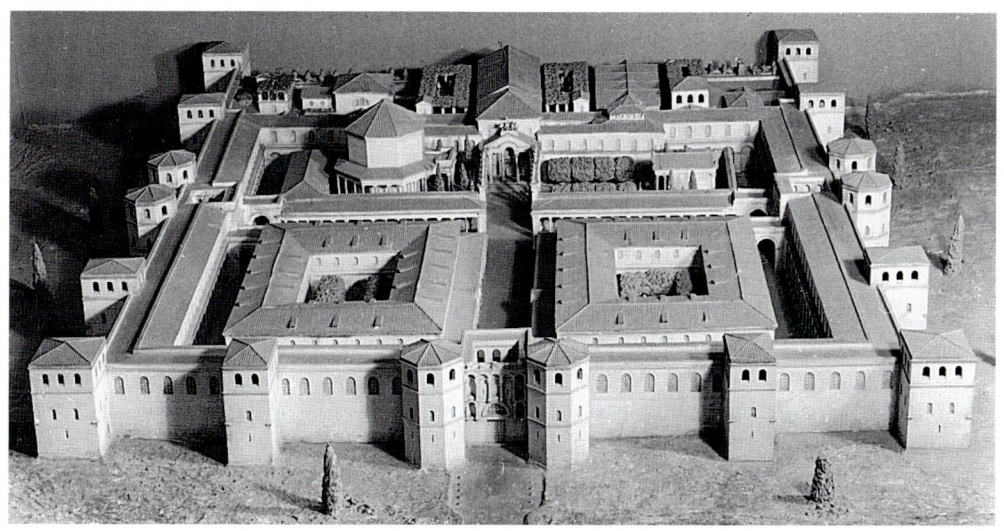

10-75   Model of the Palace of Diocletian, Split, Croatia, ca. A.D. 300–305. Museo della Civiltà Romana, Rome.

was laid out like a Roman castrum, complete with watchtowers flanking the gates. It gave the emperor a sense of security in the most insecure of times.

Within the high walls, two avenues (comparable to the cardo and decumanus in a provincial colony such as Timgad, FIG. 10-40) intersected at the palace's center. Where a city's forum would have been situated, Diocletian's palace had a colonnaded court leading to the entrance to the imperial residence. If admitted to the emperor's private quarters, a visitor passed through a templelike facade with an arch within its pediment, as in the Temple of Venus at Baalbek (FIG. 10-73). This motif's formal purpose was undoubtedly to emphasize the design's central axis, but symbolically it became the "gable of glorification" Diocletian appeared under before those who gathered in the court to pay homage to him. On one side of the court was a Temple of Jupiter; on the other side, Diocletian's mausoleum (left rear in FIG. 10-75), which towered above all the other structures in the complex. The emperor's huge domed tomb was a type that would become very popular in Early Christian times not only for mausoleums but eventually also for churches, especially in the Byzantine East. It is, in fact, used as a church today.

Constantine (A.D. 306–337)

CONSTANTINE AND CHRISTIANITY The short-lived concord among the tetrarchs that ended with Diocletian's abdication was followed by an all-too-familiar period of conflict that ended two decades later with the restoration of one-man rule. The eventual victor was Constantine I ("the Great"), son of Constantius Chlorus, Diocletian's Caesar of the West. After the death of his father, Constantine invaded Italy in 312.

At a battle at the Milvian Bridge at the gateway to Rome, he defeated and killed his chief rival, Maxentius. Constantine attributed his victory to the aid of the Christian god. In 313, he and Licinius, Constantine's coemperor in the East, issued the Edict of Milan, ending the persecution of Christians.

In time, Constantine and Licinius became foes, and in 324 Constantine defeated and executed Licinius near Byzantium (modern Istanbul, Turkey). Constantine was now unchallenged ruler of the whole Roman Empire. Shortly after the death of Licinius, he founded a "New Rome" on the site of Byzantium and named it Constantinople ("City of Constantine"). A year later, in 325, at the Council of Nicaea, Christianity became de facto the official religion of the Roman Empire. From this point on, paganism declined rapidly. Constantinople was dedicated on May 11, 330, "by the commandment of God," and in succeeding decades many Christian churches were erected there. Constantine himself was baptized on his deathbed in 337. For many scholars, the transfer of the seat of power from Rome to Constantinople and the recognition of Christianity mark the beginning of the Middle Ages.

Constantinian art is a mirror of this transition from the classical to the medieval world. In Rome, for example, Constantine was a builder in the grand tradition of the emperors of the first, second, and early third centuries, erecting public baths, a basilica on the Sacred Way leading into the Roman Forum, and a triumphal arch. But he was also the patron of the city's first churches, including Saint Peter's (see FIG. 11-7).

A NEW ARCH WITH OLD RELIEFS After his decisive victory at the Milvian Bridge, Constantine erected a great triple-passageway arch (FIG. **10-76**) in the shadow of the

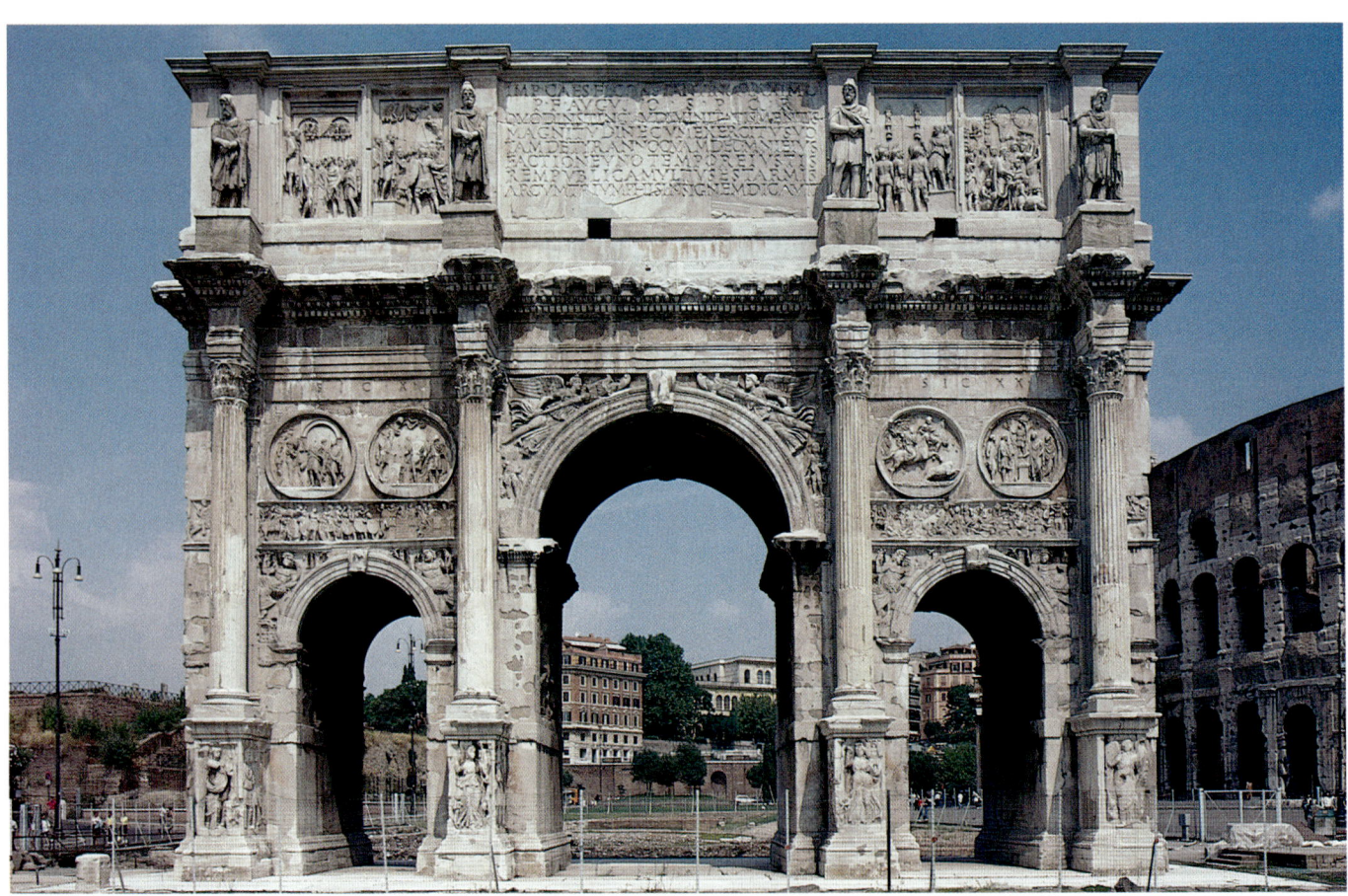

10-76 Arch of Constantine, Rome, Italy, A.D. 312–315 (south side).

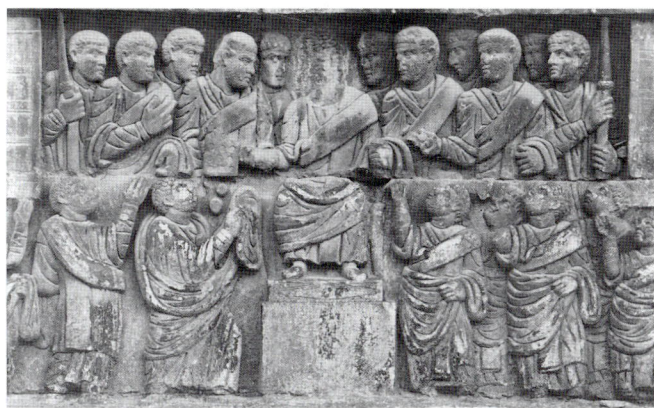

10-77 Distribution of largess, detail of the north frieze of the Arch of Constantine, Rome, Italy, A.D. 312–315. Marble, approx. 3′ 4″ high.

Colosseum to commemorate his defeat of Maxentius. The arch was the largest erected in Rome since the end of the Severan dynasty nearly a century before. Much of the sculptural decoration, however, was taken from earlier monuments of Trajan, Hadrian, and Marcus Aurelius. The columns also date to an earlier era. Sculptors refashioned the second-century reliefs to honor Constantine by recutting the heads of the earlier emperors with the features of the new ruler. They also added labels to the old reliefs, such as *Fundator Quietus* (bringer of peace) and *Liberator Urbis* (liberator of the city), references to the downfall of Maxentius and the end of civil war.

The reuse of statues and reliefs by the Constantinian artists has often been cited as evidence of a decline in creativity and technical skill in the waning years of the pagan Roman Empire. Although such a judgment is in large part deserved, it ignores the fact the reused sculptures were carefully selected to associate Constantine with the "good emperors" of the second century. That message is underscored in one of the new Constantinian reliefs above the arch's lateral passageways. It shows Constantine on the speaker's platform in the Roman Forum, flanked by statues of Hadrian and Marcus Aurelius.

In another Constantinian relief (FIG. **10-77**), the emperor is shown with attendants and distributing largess to grateful citizens who approach him from right and left. Constantine is a frontal and majestic presence, elevated on a throne above the recipients of his munificence. The figures are squat in proportion, like the tetrarchs (FIG. 10-74). They do not move according to any classical principle of naturalistic movement but, rather, with the mechanical and repeated stances and gestures of puppets. The relief is very shallow, the forms were not fully modeled, and the details were incised. The heads were not distinguished from one another. The sculptor depicted a crowd, not a group of individuals. (Constantine's head, which was carved separately and set into the relief, has been lost.) The frieze is less a narrative of action than a picture of actors frozen in time so that the viewer can distinguish instantly the all-important imperial donor (at the center on a throne) from his attendants (to the left and right above) and the recipients of the largess (below and of smaller stature).

This approach to pictorial narrative was once characterized as a "decline of form," and when judged by classical art standards, it was. But the composition's rigid formality, determined by the rank of those portrayed, was consistent with a new set of values. It soon became the preferred mode, sup-

planting the classical notion that a picture is a window onto a world of anecdotal action. Comparing this Constantinian relief with a painted Byzantine icon of the sixth century A.D. (see FIG. 12-15) reveals that the new compositional principles are those of the Middle Ages. They were very different from, but not necessarily "better" or "worse" than, those of classical antiquity. The Arch of Constantine was the quintessential monument of its era, exhibiting a respect for the classical past in its reuse of second-century sculptures while rejecting the norms of classical design in its frieze, paving the way for the iconic art of the Middle Ages.

A COLOSSUS IN A COLOSSAL BASILICA After his victory over Maxentius, Constantine's official portraits broke with tetrarchic tradition as well as with the style of the soldier emperors and resuscitated the Augustan image of an eternally youthful head of state. The head illustrated (FIG. **10-78**) is the most impressive by far of Constantine's preserved portraits. It is eight and one-half feet high, one of several marble fragments of a colossal thirty-foot-tall enthroned statue of the emperor that was composed of a brick core, a wooden torso covered with bronze, and a head and limbs of marble. Constantine's artist modeled the seminude seated portrait on Roman images of Jupiter. The emperor held an orb (possibly surmounted by the cross of Christ), the symbol of global power, in his extended left hand. The nervous glance of third-century portraits is absent, replaced by a frontal mask with enormous eyes set into the broad and simple planes of the head. The emperor's personality is lost in the immense

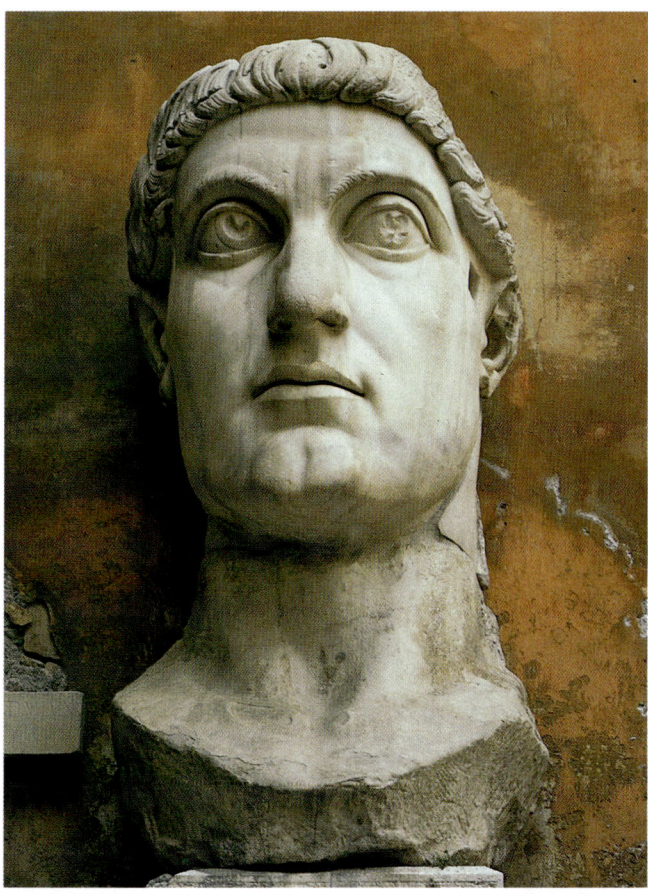

10-78 Portrait of Constantine, from the Basilica Nova, Rome, Italy, ca. A.D. 315–330. Marble, approx. 8′ 6″ high. Palazzo dei Conservatori, Rome.

10-79   Reconstruction drawing of the Basilica Nova (Basilica of Constantine), Rome, Italy, ca. A.D. 306–312.

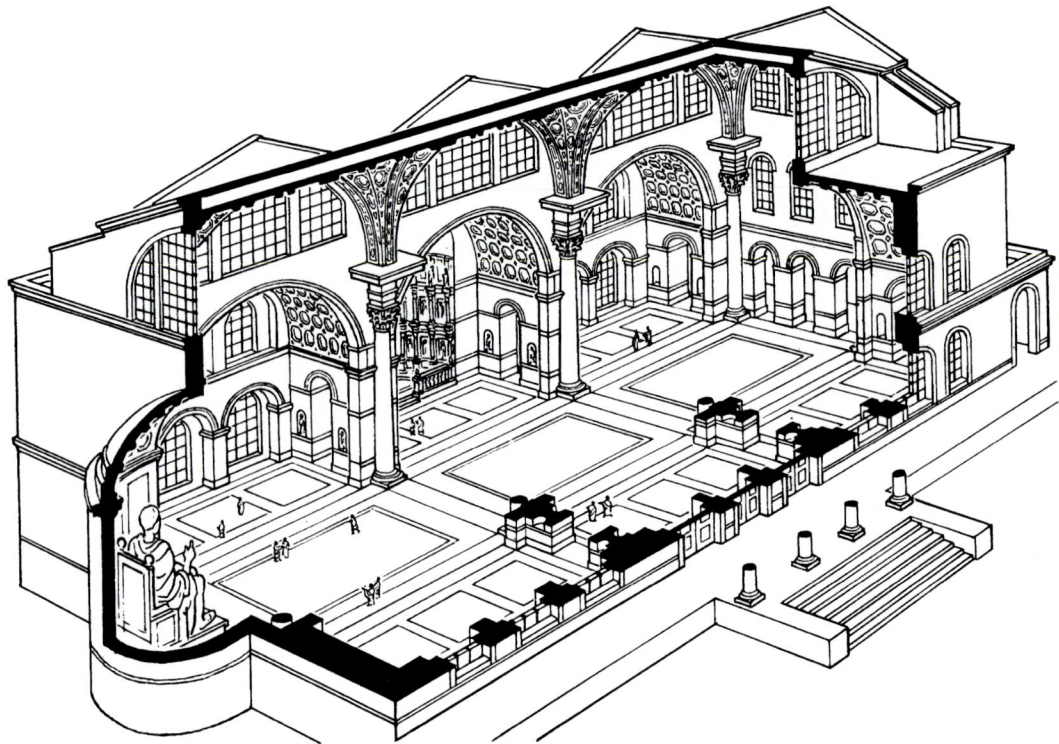

image of eternal authority. The colossal size, the likening of the emperor to Jupiter, the eyes directed at no person or thing of this world—all combine to produce a formula of overwhelming power appropriate to Constantine's exalted position as absolute ruler. To find an image of comparable grandeur and authority, one must go back more than fifteen hundred years to the colossal rock-cut portraits of the Egyptian pharaoh Ramses II (see FIG. 3-22).

Constantine's gigantic portrait sat in the western apse of the Basilica Nova in Rome (FIG. **10-79**), the huge new basilica Maxentius had begun on a site not far from the Arch of Titus. Constantine completed the project after his rival's death. From its position in the apse, the emperor's image dominated the basilica's interior in much the same way enthroned statues of Greco-Roman divinities loomed over awestruck mortals who entered the cellas of pagan temples.

The Basilica Nova ruins never fail to impress tourists with their size and mass. The original structure was three hundred feet long and two hundred fifteen feet wide. Brick-faced concrete walls twenty feet thick supported coffered barrel vaults in the aisles. These vaults also buttressed the groin vaults of the nave, which was one hundred fifteen feet high. The walls and floors were richly marbled and stuccoed and could be readily admired by those who came to the basilica to conduct business, because the groin vaults permitted ample light to enter the nave directly. Our reconstruction (FIG. 10-79) effectively suggests the immensity of the interior, where the great vaults dwarf not only humans but also even the emperor's colossal portrait. The drawing also clearly reveals the fenestration of the groin vaults, a lighting system akin to the clerestory of a traditional stone-and-timber basilica. The lessons learned in the design and construction of buildings such as Trajan's great market hall (FIG. 10-43) and the Baths of Caracalla (FIG. 10-68) were applied here to the Roman basilica.

Although one could argue that the Basilica Nova was the ideal solution to the problem of basilica design with its spacious, well-lit interior and economical, fire-resistant concrete frame, it became the exception rather than the rule. The traditional basilica form exemplified by Trajan's Basilica Ulpia in Rome (FIG. 10-41) remained the norm for centuries.

CONSTANTINE'S GERMAN AUDIENCE HALL

At Trier (ancient Augusta Treverorum) on the Moselle River in Germany, the imperial seat of Constantius Chlorus as Caesar of the West, Constantine built a new palace complex. It included a basilica-like audience hall or Aula Palatina (FIGS. **10-80** and **10-81**) of traditional form and materials. The Trier basilica measures about one hundred ninety feet long and ninety-five feet wide. Its austere brick exterior (FIG. 10-80), with boldly projecting vertical buttresses creating a pattern of alternating voids and solids, characterized much later Roman—and Early Christian—architecture. The building's verticality originally was lessened by horizontal timber galleries, which permitted the servicing of the windows. The brick wall was stuccoed in grayish white. The growing taste for large windows was due to the increasing use of lead-framed panes of window glass. These enabled late Roman builders to give life and movement to blank exterior surfaces.

Inside (FIG. 10-81), the audience hall was also very simple. Its flat, wooden, coffered ceiling is some ninety-five feet above the floor. The interior has no aisles, just a wide space with two stories of large windows that provide ample light. At the narrow north end, the main hall is divided from the semicircular apse (which also has a flat ceiling) by a so-called *triumphal arch*. The Aula Palatina's interior is quite severe, although the arch and apse originally were covered with marble veneer and mosaics to provide a magnificent environment for the enthroned emperor. The design of both the interior and exterior was closely paralleled in many Early Christian basilicas (for example, see FIG. 11-8). The Aula Palatina itself was later converted into a Christian church.

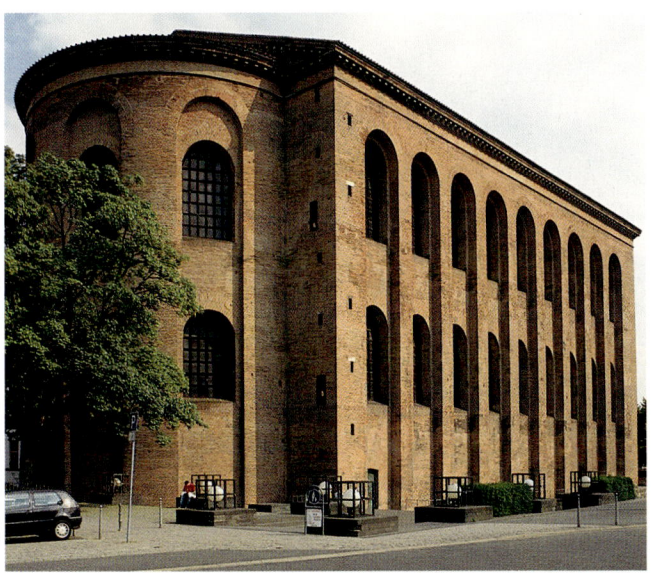

10-80   Aula Palatina (Basilica), Trier, Germany, early fourth century A.D. (exterior).

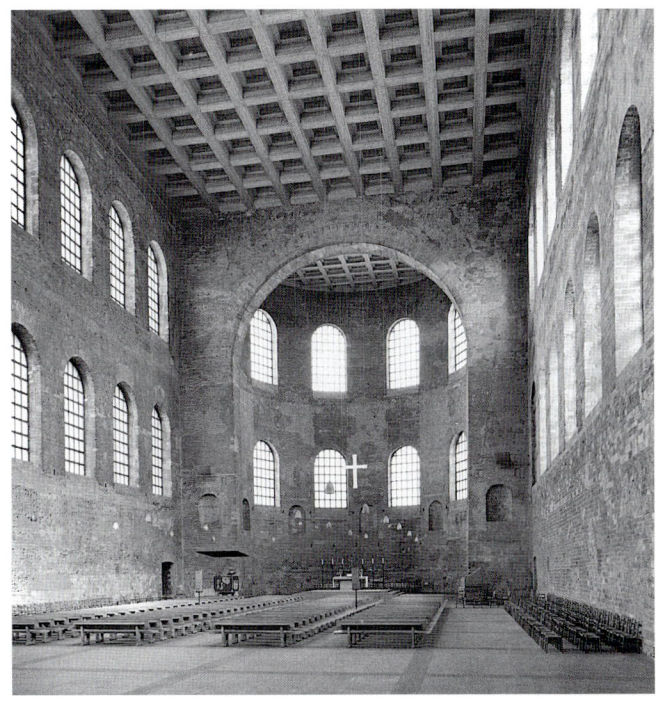

10-81   Aula Palatina, Trier, Germany, early fourth century A.D. (interior).

PORTRAITS THAT ARE NOT LIKENESSES We close our survey of ancient Roman art with two portraits of Constantine stamped on Roman coins. These images reveal both the essential character of Roman imperial portraiture and the special nature of Constantinian art. The first (FIG. **10-82,** left) was struck shortly after the death of Constantine's father, when Constantine was in his early twenties and his position was still insecure. Here, in his official portrait, he appears considerably older, because he adopted the imagery of the tetrarchs. Indeed, were it not for the accompanying label identifying this Caesar as Constantine, it would be impossible to know who was portrayed.

Eight years later, after the defeat of Maxentius and the issuance of the Edict of Milan, Constantine's portrait (FIG. 10-82, right) was transformed. Clean shaven and looking his actual thirty years of age, the unchallenged Augustus of the West rejected the mature tetrarchic "look" in favor of youth. Eternal youthfulness henceforth characterized all the emperor's portraits until his death more than two decades later (compare FIG. 10-78). These two coins should dispel any uncertainty about the often fictive nature of imperial portraiture and the ability of Roman emperors to choose any official image that suited their needs.

CLASSICAL AND MEDIEVAL The later portrait is also an eloquent testimony to the dual nature of Constantinian rule. The emperor appears in his important role as *imperator* (general), dressed in armor, wearing an ornate helmet, and carrying a shield bearing the enduring emblem of the Roman state—the she-wolf nursing Romulus and Remus (compare FIG. 9-10 and Roma's shield in FIG. 10-57). Yet he does not carry the scepter of the pagan Roman emperor. Rather, he holds a cross crowned by an orb. And at the crest of his helmet, at the front, just below the grand plume, is a disk containing the *Christogram,* the monogram made up of *chi* and *rho,* the initial letters of Christ's name in Greek (compare the shield one of the soldiers holds in FIG. 12-10). Constantine was at once portrayed as Roman emperor and as a soldier in the army of the Lord. The coin, like Constantinian art in general, belonged both to the classical and to the medieval world.

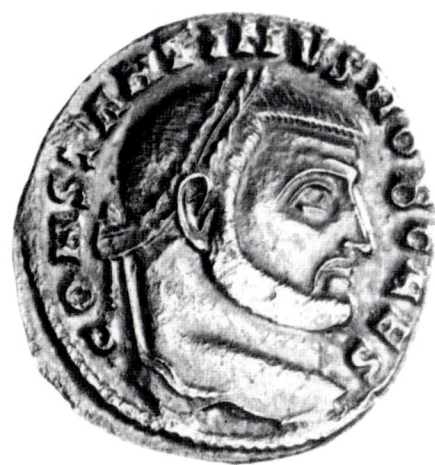

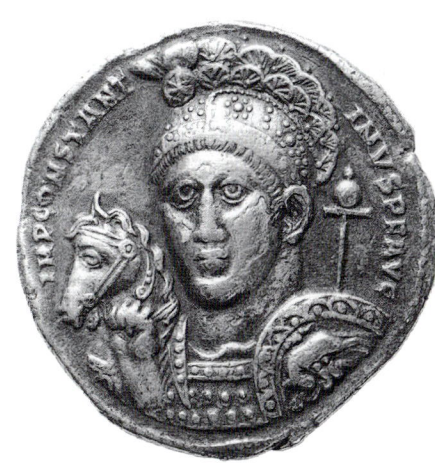

10-82   Coins with portraits of Constantine. Nummus *(left),* A.D. 307. Billon, diameter approx. 1″. American Numismatic Society, New York. Medallion *(right),* ca. A.D. 315. Silver. Staatliche Münzsammlung, Munich.

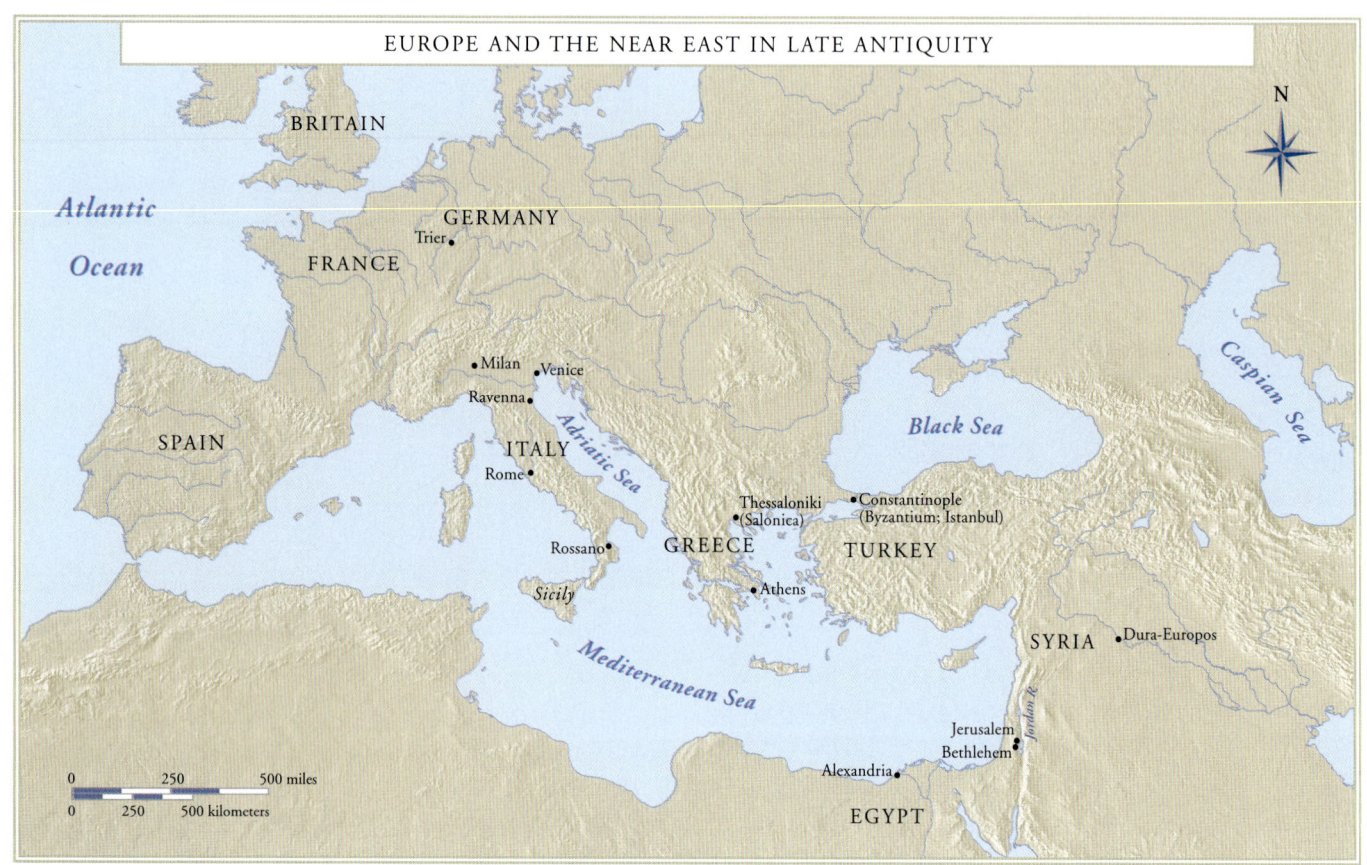

EUROPE AND THE NEAR EAST IN LATE ANTIQUITY

BRITAIN

Atlantic Ocean

GERMANY
Trier•

FRANCE

SPAIN

•Milan •Venice
Ravenna•

ITALY
Rome•

Adriatic Sea

Rossano•

Sicily

Thessaloniki
(Salónica)

GREECE

•Athens

•Constantinople
(Byzantium; Istanbul)

TURKEY

Black Sea

Caspian Sea

SYRIA •Dura-Europos

Jerusalem•
Bethlehem•

Mediterranean Sea

Alexandria•

EGYPT

N

0   250   500 miles
0   250   500 kilometers

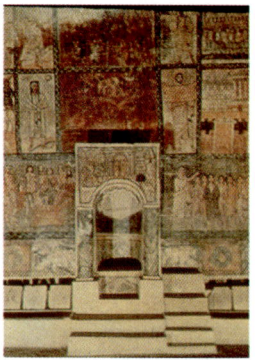

Synagogue, Dura-Europos
ca. 245–256

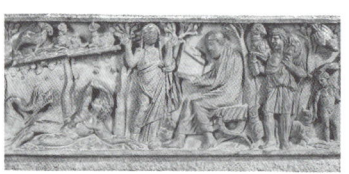

Santa Maria Antiqua
sarcophagus, ca. 270

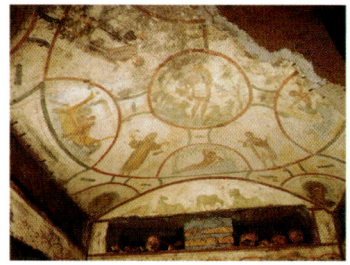

Catacomb of Saints Peter
and Marcellinus, Rome
early fourth century

Crucifixion of Christ, 29

Persecution of the Christians under Trajan Decius, 249–251

Persecution of the Christians under
Diocletian, 303–305

Constantine, r. 306–337

Edict of Milan, 313

Foundation of
Constantinople, 324

PAGANS, CHRISTIANS, AND JEWS

THE ART OF LATE ANTIQUITY

337		476	493	526
SUCCESSORS OF CONSTANTINE		ODOACER	THEODORIC	

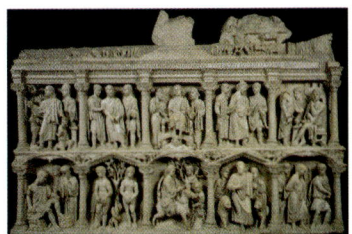

*Sarcophagus of
Junius Bassus, ca. 359*

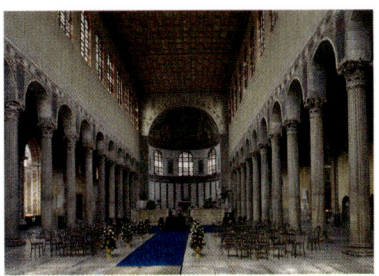

*Santa Sabina
Rome, 422–432*

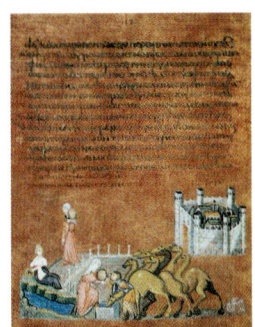

*Vienna Genesis
early sixth century*

Theodosius I, r. 379–395

Christianity proclaimed state religion of Roman Empire, 380

Theodosius prohibits pagan worship, 391

Honorius, r. 395–423

Honorius moves capital to Ravenna, 404

Fall of Rome to Alaric, 410

Romulus Augustus, last Roman emperor, r. 475–476

Fall of Ravenna to Odoacer, 476

Theodoric at Ravenna, 493–526

THE WORLD OF LATE ANTIQUITY

The Roman Empire was home to an extraordinarily diverse population. In Rome alone on any given day, someone walking through the city's various quarters would have encountered people of an astonishing range of social, ethnic, racial, linguistic, and religious backgrounds. And the multicultural character of Roman society became only more pronounced as the empire grew. The previous chapter focused on the rich legacy of art and architecture bequeathed by the *pagan* Roman world. But during the Late Roman Empire a rapidly growing number of people rejected the emperors' polytheism (belief in multiple gods) in favor of the worship of a single all-powerful god. This chapter addresses the Jewish and Christian art produced under Roman rule. These Late Roman sculptures, paintings, mosaics, and buildings occupy a special place in our account of art through the ages because they formed the foundation of the art and architecture of the Middle Ages.

PAGANS, JEWS, AND CHRISTIANS The powerful religious crosscurrents of late antiquity may be seen in microcosm in a distant outpost of the Roman Empire on a promontory overlooking the Euphrates River in Syria. Called Europos by the Greeks and Dura by the Romans, the town probably was founded shortly after the death of Alexander the Great by one of his successors. By the end of the second century B.C., Dura-Europos was in the hands of the Parthians. The city was captured by Trajan in 115 but reverted to Parthian control shortly thereafter.* In 165, under Marcus

---
*Note: From this point on, all dates are A.D. unless otherwise indicated.

Aurelius, the Romans retook Dura and placed a permanent garrison there. Dura-Europos fell in 256 to Rome's new enemy in the East, the Sasanians, heirs to the Parthian Empire (see Chapter 2). The Sasanian victory at Dura is an important fixed point in the chronology of late antiquity because the fortified town's population was evacuated and Dura's buildings were left largely intact. This "Pompeii of the desert" has revealed the remains of more than a dozen different cult buildings, including many shrines of the polytheistic religions of the classical and Near Eastern worlds. But the excavators also discovered worship places for the monotheistic creeds of Judaism and Christianity, even though neither were approved religions in the Roman state.

BIBLICAL PAINTINGS ON SYNAGOGUE WALLS The synagogue at Dura-Europos is remarkable not only for its very existence in a Roman garrison town but also for its extensive cycle of mural paintings (FIG. **11-1**) depicting biblical themes. The building, originally a private house with a central courtyard, was converted into a synagogue during the latter part of the second century. The paintings seem to defy the Bible's Second Commandment prohibiting the making of graven images and surprised scholars when they were first reported. It is now apparent that although the Jews of the Roman Empire did not worship idols as did their pagan contemporaries, biblical stories not only appeared on the painted walls of synagogues such as that at Dura-Europos but also in painted manuscripts. God (YHWH, or Yahweh in the Old Testament), however, never appears in the synagogue paintings or in the illustrated Bibles, except as a hand emerging from the top of the framed panels.

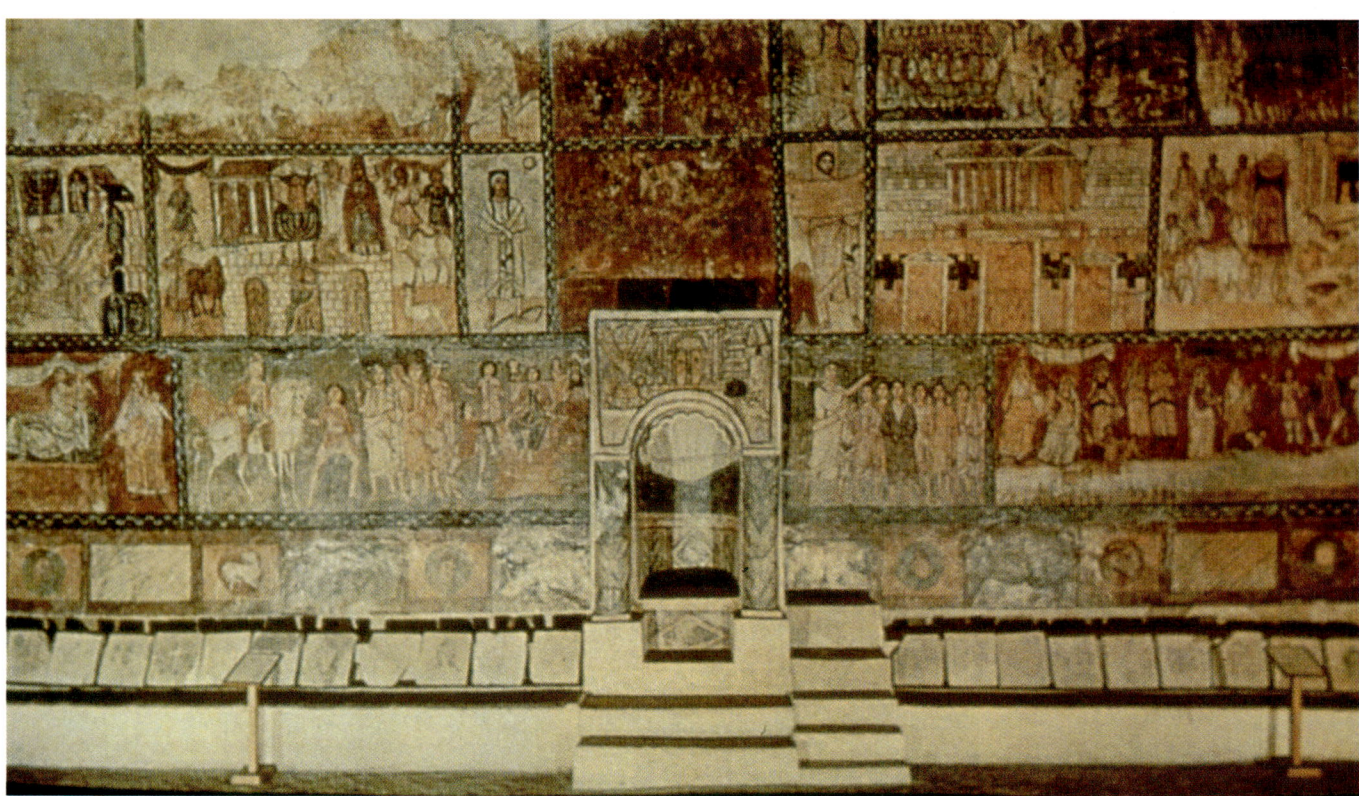

11-1   Interior of the synagogue at Dura-Europos, Syria, with wall-paintings of Old Testament themes, ca. 245–256. Tempera on plaster. National Museum, Damascus.

The style of the Dura murals is also instructive. Even when the subject is a narrative theme, the compositions are devoid of action. The artists tell the stories through stylized gestures, and the figures, which have expressionless features and lack both volume and shadow, tend to stand in frontal rows. This is especially true of the painting just to the right of the niche that housed the sacred Jewish *Torah* (the scroll containing the *Pentateuch,* the first five books of the Hebrew Scriptures). The prophet Samuel is anointing David as the future king of Israel, while his six older brothers look on. The painter drew attention to Samuel by depicting him larger than all the rest. David and his brothers are emotionless and almost disembodied spiritual presences. Their bodies do not even have enough feet! David, however, is distinguished from his brothers by the purple toga he wears. Purple was the color associated with the Roman emperor, and the imperial toga was borrowed here to signify David's royalty. The Dura painting style was characteristic also of much pagan art during the third and fourth centuries. Compare the Dura compositions with the friezes of the earlier Arch of Septimius Severus at Lepcis Magna (FIG. 10-66) and the later Arch of Constantine in Rome (FIG. 10-77). This new Late Antique style characterized much of the art of the Byzantine Empire (see FIGS. 12-10 and 12-11).

BAPTISM IN A SECONDHAND HOUSE The Christian community house at Dura-Europos (FIG. **11-2**) was also a remodeled private residence with a central courtyard. Its meeting hall (created by breaking down the partition between two rooms on the court's south side) could accommodate no more than about seventy people at a time. It had a raised platform at one end where the congregation leader sat or stood. Another room, on the opposite side of the courtyard, had a canopy-covered font for baptismal rites, the all-important ceremony initiating a new convert into the Christian community. Upstairs a communal dining room may have existed for the celebration of the *Eucharist,* when the faithful partook of the bread and wine symbolic of the body and blood of Christ (see "The Life of Jesus in Art," pages 308–309).

Although the baptistery had mural paintings (poorly preserved), the place where Christians gathered to worship at Dura, as elsewhere in the Roman Empire, was a modest secondhand house, in striking contrast to the grand temples of the Roman gods. Without the sanction of the state, Christian communities remained small in number and often attracted the most impoverished classes of society. They found the promise of an afterlife where rich and poor were judged on equal terms especially appealing. Nonetheless, Diocletian was so concerned by the growing popularity of Christianity in the Roman army ranks that he ordered a fresh round of persecutions in 303 to 305, a half century after the last great persecutions under Trajan Decius. The Romans hated the Christians because of their alien beliefs—that their god had been incarnated in the body of a man and that the death and Resurrection of the god-man Christ made possible the salvation and redemption of all. But they also hated them because they refused to pay even token homage to the Roman state's official gods. As Christianity's appeal grew, so, too, did the Roman state's fear of weakening imperial authority. Persecution ended only when the Roman emperor Constantine, after defeating Maxentius at the Milvian Bridge in Rome, came to believe that the Christian god was the source of his power rather than

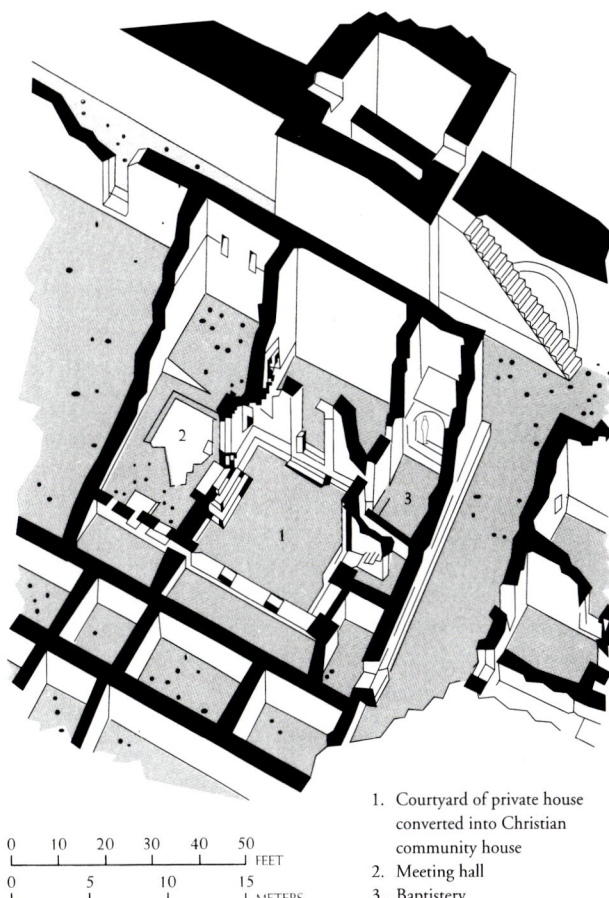

1. Courtyard of private house converted into Christian community house
2. Meeting hall
3. Baptistery

11-2 Reconstruction of the Christian community house at Dura-Europos, Syria, ca. 240–256.

a threat to it (see Chapter 10). A year after that victory, the Edict of Milan brought an end to the official mistreatment of Christians.

THE CATACOMBS
AND FUNERARY ART

THE CHRISTIAN "HOLLOWS" OF ROME Very little is known about the art of the first Christians. When we speak of "Early Christian art," we mean the earliest preserved works with Christian subjects, not the art of Christians at the time of Jesus. The most significant Early Christian monuments in Rome are the least conspicuous; they are entirely underground. These *catacombs* are vast subterranean networks of *galleries,* or passageways, and chambers designed as cemeteries for burying the Christian dead, many of them sainted martyrs. To a much lesser extent, the catacombs also housed the graves of Jews and others. The builders tunneled the catacombs out of the tufa bedrock, much like the Etruscans created the underground tomb chambers in the necropolis at Cerveteri (see FIG. 9-7). The catacombs are less elaborate than the Etruscan tombs, but much more extensive. The name derives from the Latin *ad catacumbas,* which means "in the hollows." The catacombs in Rome (others exist elsewhere) comprise galleries estimated to run for sixty to ninety miles—and additional catacombs may be discovered yet. From the second through the fourth centuries, these catacombs were in constant use. As many as four million bodies may have been buried in them.

In accordance with Roman custom, Christians had to be buried outside a city's walls on private property, usually purchased by a *confraternity,* or association, of Christian families pooling funds. Each of the catacombs was initially of modest extent. First, the builders dug a gallery three to four feet wide around the perimeter of the burial ground at a convenient level below the surface. In the walls of these galleries, they cut openings to receive the bodies of the dead. These openings, called *loculi,* were placed one above another, like shelves. Often, the Christians carved small rooms out of the rock, called *cubicula* (as in Roman houses of the living), to serve as mortuary chapels. Once the original perimeter galleries were full of loculi and cubicula, they cut other galleries at right angles to them. This process continued as long as lateral space permitted. They then dug lower levels connected by staircases. Some catacomb systems extended as deep as five levels. When adjacent burial areas belonged to members of the same Christian confraternity, or by gift or purchase fell into the same hands, the owners opened passageways between the respective cemeteries. The galleries thus spread laterally and gradually acquired a vast extent. After Christianity received official approval, the catacombs fell into disuse except as holy places—monuments to the great martyrs visited by the pious, who could worship in the churches often built directly above the catacombs.

Painting

FRESCOES ON THE DOME OF HEAVEN

The frescoes that decorated many cubicula were Roman in style but Christian in subject. The ceiling organization of a cubiculum in the Catacomb of Saints Peter and Marcellinus in Rome (FIG. **11-3**), for example, is similar to the vaulted-ceiling designs in many Roman houses and tombs. Compare the century-earlier frescoed vault in the Insula of the Painted Vaults at Ostia (see FIG. 10-54). In the catacomb, the polygonal frame of the Ostian spoked-wheel design became a large circle, akin to the Dome of Heaven, and inscribed within is the symbol of the Christian faith, the cross. The cross's arms terminate in four *lunettes* (semicircular frames), which also find parallels in the Ostian composition.

The lunettes contain the key episodes from the Old Testament story of Jonah. The sailors throw him from his ship on the left. He emerges on the right from the "whale" (the Greek word is *ketos,* or sea dragon, and that is how the artist represented the monstrous marine creature that swallowed Jonah). And, safe on land at the bottom, Jonah contemplates the miracle of his salvation and the mercy of God. Jonah was a popular figure in Early Christian painting and sculpture, especially in funerary contexts. The Christians honored him as a *prefiguration* (prophetic forerunner) of Christ, who rose from death as Jonah had been delivered from the belly of the ketos, also after three days. (Old Testament miracles prefiguring

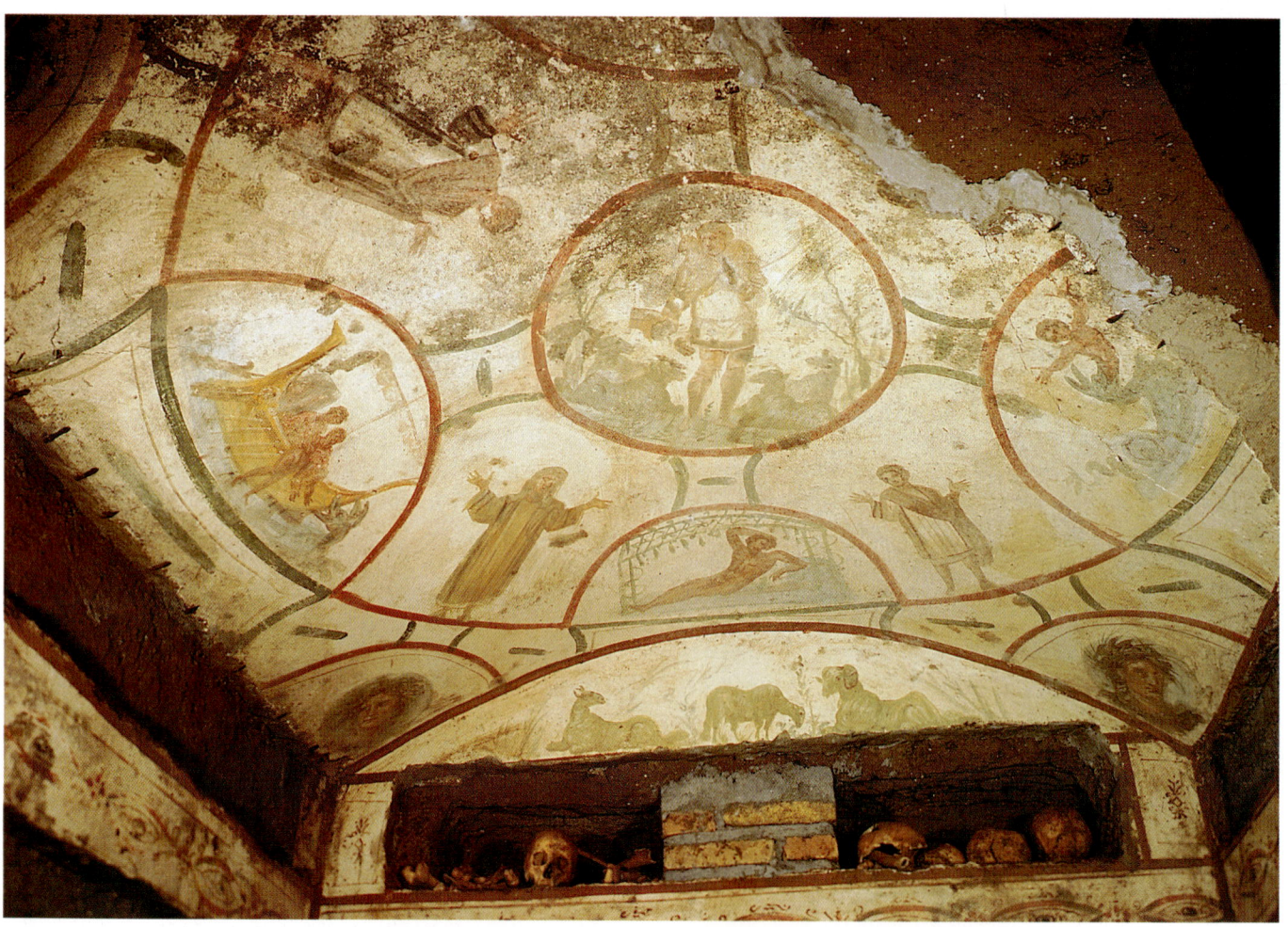

11-3   The Good Shepherd, the story of Jonah, and orants, painted ceiling of a cubiculum in the Catacomb of Saints Peter and Marcellinus, Rome, Italy, early fourth century.

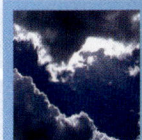

Jewish Subjects in Christian Art

From the beginning, the Old Testament played an important role in Christian life and Christian art, in part because Jesus was a Jew and so many of the first Christians were converted Jews, but also because Christians came to view many of the persons and events of the Old Testament as prefigurations of New Testament persons and events. Christ himself established the pattern for this kind of biblical interpretation when he compared Jonah's spending three days in the belly of the sea monster (usually translated as "whale" in English) to the comparable time he would be entombed in the earth before his Resurrection (Matt. 12:40). In the fourth century Saint Augustine (354–430) confirmed the validity of this approach to the Old Testament when he stated that "the New Testament is hidden in the Old; the Old is clarified by the New."[1]

Thus the Old Testament figured prominently in Early Christian art in all media. Biblical tales of Jewish faith and salvation were especially common in funerary contexts but appeared also in churches and on household objects. The most popular Old Testament stories in Early Christian art are listed here.

Adam and Eve (FIG. 11-5) Eve, the first woman, tempted by a serpent, ate the forbidden fruit of the tree of knowledge. She also fed some to Adam, the first man. As punishment, God expelled Adam and Eve from Paradise. This "Original Sin" ultimately led to Christ's sacrifice on the cross so that all humankind could be saved. Christian theologians often consider Christ the new Adam and his mother, Mary, the new Eve.

Abraham and the Three Angels (see FIGS. 12-8 and 12-34) Sarah, wife of Abraham, the father of the Hebrew nation, was ninety years old and childless when three angels visited Abraham. They announced that Sarah would bear a son, and she later miraculously gave birth to Isaac. Christians believe the Old Testament angels symbolized the Holy Trinity.

Sacrifice of Isaac (FIGS. 11-5 and 12-8) God instructed Abraham to sacrifice Isaac, his only son, as proof of his faith. When it became clear Abraham would obey, the Lord sent an angel to restrain him and provided a ram for sacrifice in Isaac's place. Christians view this episode as a prefiguration of the sacrifice of God's only son, Jesus.

Jonah (FIGS. 11-3 and 11-4) Jonah, an Old Testament prophet, had disobeyed God's command. In his wrath, the Lord caused a storm while Jonah was at sea. Jonah asked the sailors to throw him overboard, and the storm subsided. A sea dragon then swallowed Jonah, but God answered his prayers, and the monster spat out Jonah after three days and nights, foretelling Christ's Resurrection.

Daniel (FIG. 11-5) Daniel, one of the most important Jewish prophets, violated a Persian decree against prayer and the Persians threw him into a den of lions. God sent an angel to shut the lions' mouths, and Daniel emerged unharmed. Like Jonah's story, this is an Old Testament salvation tale, a precursor of Christ's triumph over death.

[1] Augustine, *City of God*, XVI.26.

Christ's Resurrection abound in the catacombs and in Early Christian art in general; see "Jewish Subjects in Christian Art," above.)

A YOUTHFUL CHRIST AND HIS SHEEP A man, a woman, and at least one child occupy the compartments between the Jonah lunettes. They are *orants* (praying figures), raising their arms in the ancient attitude of prayer. Together they make up a cross-section of the Christian family seeking a heavenly afterlife. The cross's central medallion shows Christ as the Good Shepherd, whose powers of salvation are underscored by his juxtaposition with Jonah's story. The motif can be traced back to Archaic Greek art (see FIG. 5-9), but there the pagan calf bearer offered his sheep in sacrifice to Athena. In Early Christian art, Christ is the youthful and loyal protector of the Christian flock, who said to his disciples, "I am the good shepherd; the good shepherd gives his life for the sheep" (John 10:11). In the Christian motif, the sheep on Christ's shoulders is one of the lost sheep he has retrieved, symbolizing a sinner who has strayed and been rescued.

Prior to Constantine, artists almost invariably represented Christ either as the Good Shepherd or as a young teacher. Only after Christianity became the Roman Empire's official religion did Christ take on in art such imperial attributes as the halo, the purple robe, and the throne, which denoted rulership. Eventually artists depicted Christ with the beard of a mature adult, which has been the standard form for centuries, supplanting Early Christian art's youthful imagery.

The style of the catacomb painters was most often a quick, sketchy impressionism that compares unfavorably with the best Roman frescoes. The vast majority of people buried in the catacombs could not afford to employ the best artists. The catacombs were, moreover, very unpromising places for mural decoration. Decomposing corpses spoiled the air, the humidity was excessive, and the lighting (provided largely by oil lamps) was entirely unfit for elaborate compositions or painstaking execution. It is therefore no wonder that painters often completed their frescoes hastily and that the results frequently were of mediocre quality.

Sculpture

COFFINS FOR THE CHRISTIAN FAITHFUL All Christians rejected cremation, and the wealthiest Christian faithful, like their pagan contemporaries, favored impressive marble sarcophagi. Many of these coffins have survived in the catacombs and elsewhere. As expected, the most

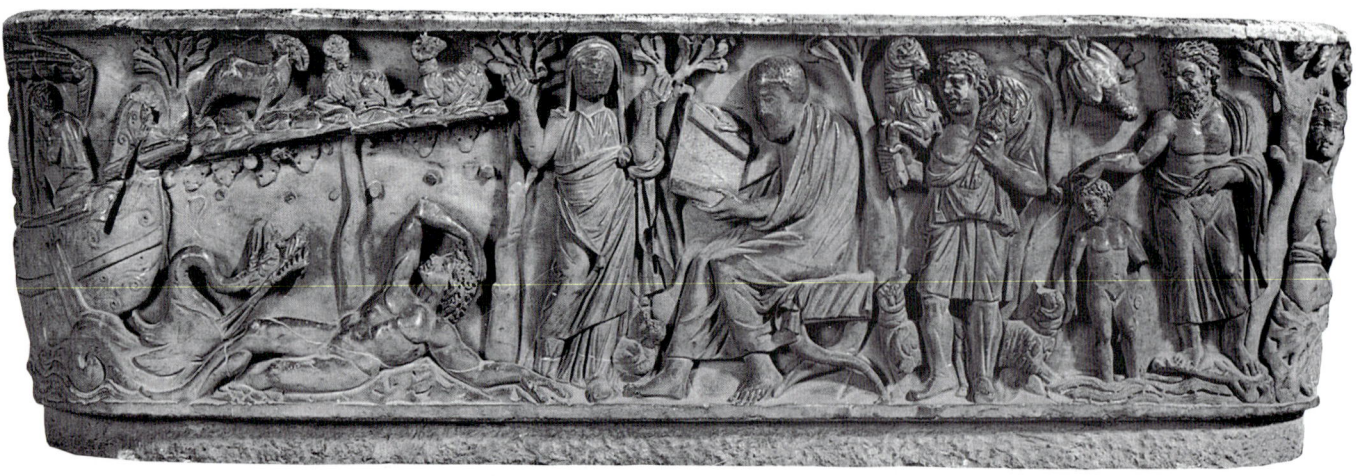

11-4 Sarcophagus with philosopher, orant, and Old and New Testament scenes, Santa Maria Antiqua, Rome, Italy, ca. 270. Marble, 1′ 11¼″ × 7 ′2″.

common themes painted on the walls and vaults of the Roman subterranean cemeteries were also the subjects that appeared on Early Christian sarcophagi. Often, the decoration of the marble coffins was a collection of significant Christian themes, just as on the painted ceiling in the Catacomb of Saints Peter and Marcellinus (FIG. 11-3).

On the front of a sarcophagus (FIG. **11-4**) in Santa Maria Antiqua in Rome, the story of Jonah takes up the left third. At the center is an orant and a seated philosopher, the latter a motif borrowed directly from contemporary pagan sarcophagi (see FIG. 10-72). The heads of both the praying

woman and the seated man reading from a scroll are unfinished. Roman workshops often produced sarcophagi before knowing who would purchase them. The sculptors added the portraits at the time of burial, if they added them at all. This practice underscores the universal appeal of the themes chosen. At the right are two different, yet linked, representations of Jesus—as the Good Shepherd and as a child receiving baptism in the Jordan River, though he really was baptized at age thirty (see "The Life of Jesus in Art," pages 308–309). The sculptor suggested the future ministry of the baptized Jesus by turning the child's head toward the Good

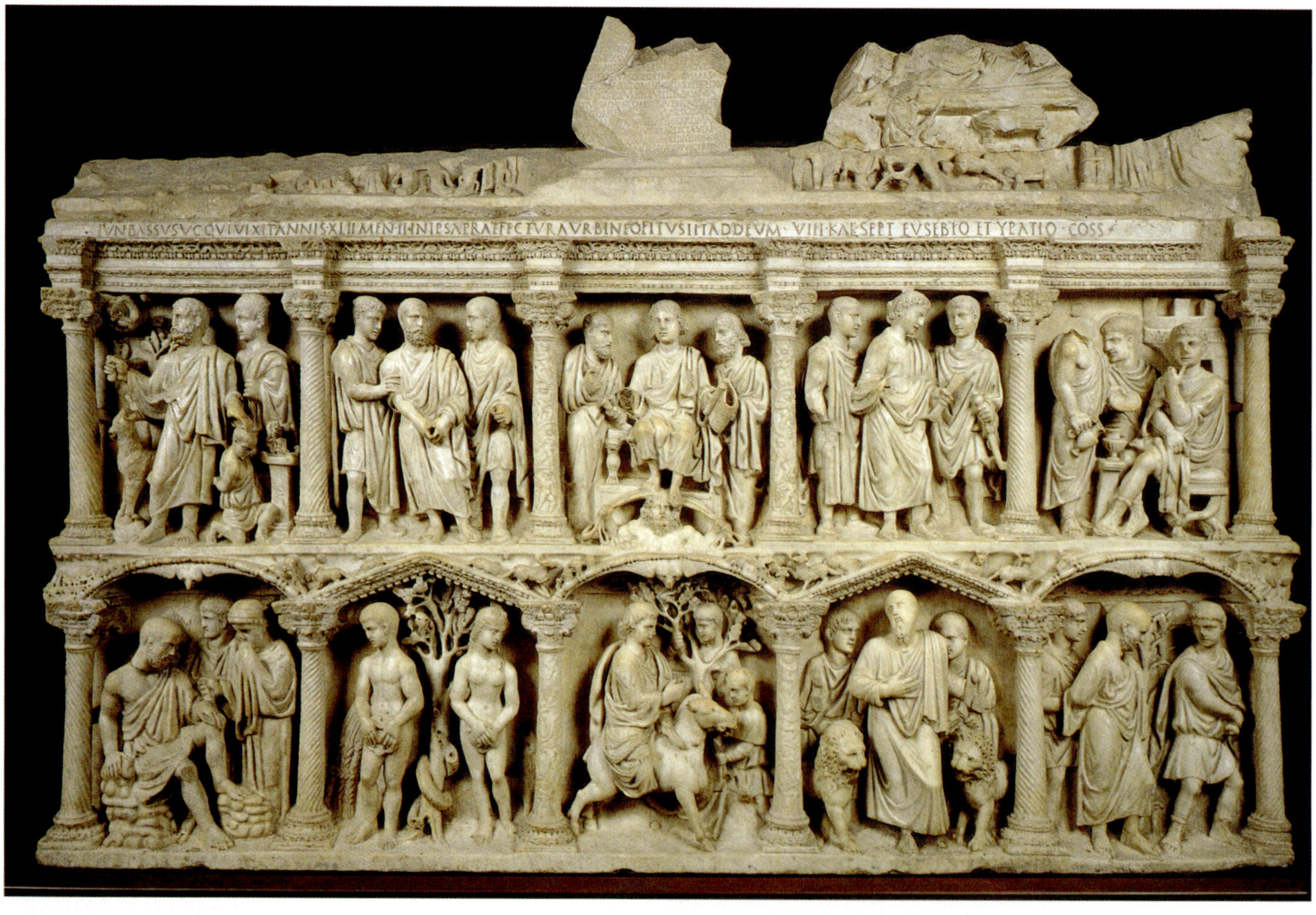

11-5 Sarcophagus of Junius Bassus, from Rome, Italy, ca. 359. Marble, 3′ 10½″ × 8′. Museo Storico del Tesoro della Basilica di San Pietro, Rome.

Shepherd and by placing his right hand on one of the sheep. Baptism was especially significant in the early centuries of Christianity because so many adults were converted to the new faith in this manner.

A CONVERTED CHRISTIAN'S SARCOPHAGUS
One of the Christian converts was the city prefect of Rome, Junius Bassus, who, according to the inscription on his sarcophagus (FIG. 11-5), was baptized just before his death in 359. The sarcophagus, decorated only on the front in the western Roman manner, is divided into two registers of five compartments, each framed by columns in the tradition of Asiatic sarcophagi (see FIG. 10-62). In contrast to the Santa Maria Antiqua sarcophagus, the deceased does not appear on the body of the coffin. Instead, stories from the Old and New Testaments fill the ten niches. Christ has pride of place and appears in the central compartment of each register: as a youthful teacher enthroned between his chief apostles, Saints Peter and Paul (above), and triumphantly entering Jerusalem on a horselike donkey (below). Both compositions owe a great deal to Roman imperial imagery. In the upper zone, Christ, like an enthroned pagan emperor, sits above a personification of the sky god holding a billowing mantle over his head, indicating that Christ is ruler of the universe. The scene below closely follows the pattern of Roman emperors entering cities on horseback. Appropriately, the scene of Christ's heavenly triumph is situated above that of his earthly triumph.

The Old Testament scenes on the Junius Bassus sarcophagus were chosen for their significance in the early Christian Church. Adam and Eve, for example, are in the second niche from the left on the lower level. Their original sin of eating the apple in the Garden of Eden ultimately necessitated Christ's sacrifice for the salvation of humankind. To the right of the entry into Jerusalem is Daniel, unscathed by flanking lions, saved by his faith. At the upper left, Abraham is about to sacrifice Isaac. Christians believe that this Old Testament story was a parable for God's sacrifice of his own son, Jesus.

The Crucifixion itself, however, does not appear on the Junius Bassus sarcophagus. Indeed, the subject was very rare in Early Christian art, and unknown prior to the fifth century. Christ's divinity and exemplary life as teacher and miracle worker, not his suffering and death at the hands of the Romans, were emphasized. The sarcophagus sculptor, however, alluded to the Crucifixion in the scenes in the two compartments at the upper right depicting Jesus being led before Pontius Pilate for judgment. The Romans condemned Jesus to death but he triumphantly overcame it. Junius Bassus and other Christians, whether they were converts from paganism or from Judaism, hoped for a similar salvation.

AN "IDOL" OF CHRIST Apart from the reliefs on privately commissioned sarcophagi, monumental sculpture became increasingly uncommon in the fourth century. Portrait statues of Roman emperors and other officials continued to be erected, and statues of pagan gods and mythological figures were still made, but their numbers decreased sharply. In his *Apologia*, Justin Martyr, a second-century philosopher who converted to Christianity and was mindful of the Second Commandment's admonition to shun graven images, accused

the pagans of worshiping statues as gods. Christians tended to suspect the freestanding statue, linking it with the false gods of the pagans, so Early Christian houses of worship had no "cult statues." Nor did the first churches have any equivalent of the pedimental statues and relief friezes of Greco-Roman temples.

The Greco-Roman experience, however, was still a living part of the Mediterranean mentality, and many Christians like Junius Bassus were recent converts from paganism who retained some of their classical values. This may account for those rare instances of Early Christian "idols," such as the marble statuette of Christ enthroned shown here (FIG. 11-6). Less than three feet tall, the sculpture is contemporary with or somewhat later than, and a freestanding version of, the youthful Christ between Saints Peter and Paul on the Junius Bassus sarcophagus (FIG. 11-5). As on the relief, Christ's head is that of a long-haired Apollo-like youth, but the statuary type was one employed for bearded Roman philosophers of advanced age. The remarkably young teacher wears the Roman tunic, toga, and sandals, and holds an unopened scroll in his left

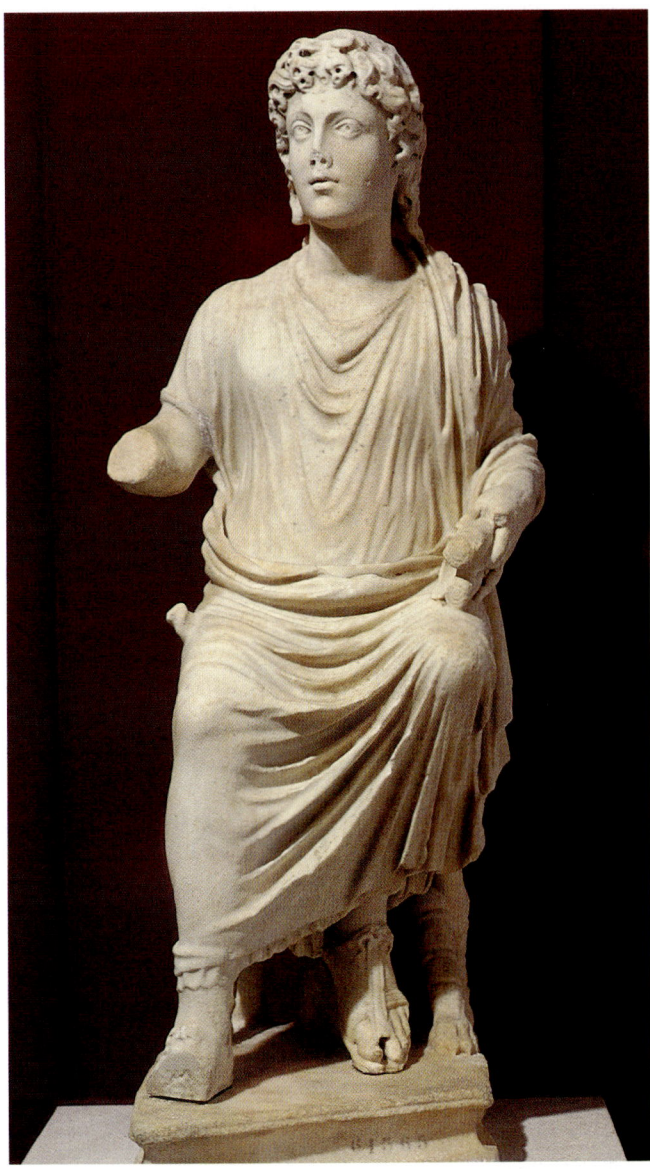

11-6 Christ enthroned, ca. 350–375. Marble, approx. 2' 4½" high. Museo Nazionale Romano, Rome.

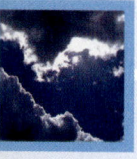

The Life of Jesus in Art

Christians believe that Jesus of Nazareth was the son of God, the *Messiah* (Savior, *Christ*) of the Jews prophesied in the Old Testament. His life, from his miraculous birth from the womb of a virgin mother through his preaching and miracle working to his execution by the Romans and subsequent ascent to heaven, has been the subject of countless artworks from Roman times through the present day. The primary literary sources for these representations are the Gospels of the New Testament attributed to the four Evangelists, Saints Matthew, Mark, Luke, and John; later apocryphal works; and commentaries on these texts by medieval theologians.

The life of Jesus dominated the subject matter of Christian art to a far greater extent than Greco-Roman religion and mythology ever did classical art. Whereas images of athletes, portraits of statesmen and philosophers, narratives of war and peace, genre scenes, and other secular subjects were staples of the classical tradition, Christian iconography held a near monopoly in the art of the Western world in the Middle Ages.

Although many of the events of Jesus' life were rarely or never depicted during certain periods, the cycle as a whole has been one of the most frequent subjects of Western art, even after the revival of classical and secular themes in the Renaissance. Thus it is useful to summarize the entire cycle here in one place, giving selected references to illustrations of the various episodes, from late antiquity to the seventeenth century. We describe the events as they usually appear in the artworks.

INCARNATION AND CHILDHOOD

The first "cycle" of the life of Jesus consists of the events of his conception, birth, infancy, and childhood.

Annunciation to Mary (see FIGS. 12-33, 19-18, and 21-38)   The archangel Gabriel announces to the Virgin Mary that she will miraculously conceive and give birth to God's son Jesus. God's presence at the *Incarnation* is sometimes indicated by a dove, the symbol of the *Holy Spirit*, the third "person" of the *Trinity* with God the Father and Jesus.

Visitation (see FIG. 18-24)   The pregnant Mary visits Elizabeth, her older cousin, who is pregnant with the future Saint John the Baptist. Elizabeth is the first to recognize that the baby Mary is bearing is the Son of God, and they rejoice.

Nativity (see FIGS. 19-3 and 19-4), *Annunciation to the Shepherds* (see FIG. 16-28), and *Adoration of the Shepherds* (see FIG. 24-57) Jesus is born at night in Bethlehem and placed in a basket. Mary and her husband Joseph marvel at the newborn in a stable or, in Byzantine art, in a cave. An angel announces the birth of the Savior to shepherds in the field, who rush to Bethlehem to adore the child.

Adoration of the Magi (see FIG. 21-10)   A bright star alerts three wise men *(magi)* in the East that the King of the Jews has been born. They travel twelve days to find the *Holy Family* and present precious gifts to the infant Jesus.

Presentation in the Temple   In accordance with Jewish tradition, Mary and Joseph bring their first-born son to the temple in Jerusalem, where the aged Simeon, whom God said would not die until he had seen the Messiah, recognizes Jesus as the prophesied Savior of humankind.

Massacre of the Innocents and *Flight into Egypt*   King Herod, fearful that a rival king has been born, orders the massacre of all infants in Bethlehem, but an angel warns the Holy Family and they escape to Egypt.

Dispute in the Temple   Joseph and Mary travel to Jerusalem for the feast of *Passover* (the celebration of the release of the Jews from bondage to the pharaohs of Egypt). Jesus, only twelve years old at the time, engages in learned debate with astonished Jewish scholars in the temple, foretelling his ministry.

PUBLIC MINISTRY

The public ministry cycle comprises the teachings of Jesus and the miracles he performed.

Baptism (FIG. 11-4)   The beginning of Jesus' public ministry is marked by his baptism at age thirty by John the Baptist in the Jordan River, where the dove of the Holy Spirit appears and God's voice is heard proclaiming Jesus as his son.

Calling of Matthew (see FIG. 24-19)   Jesus summons Matthew, a tax collector, to follow him, and Matthew becomes one of his twelve *disciples,* or *apostles* (from the Greek for "messenger"), and later the author of one of the four Gospels.

Miracles   In the course of his teaching and travels, Jesus performs many miracles, revealing his divine nature. These include acts of healing and the raising of the dead, the turning of water into wine, walking on water and calming storms, and the creation of wondrous quantities of food. In the miracle of loaves and fishes (FIG. 11-17), for example, Jesus transforms a few loaves of bread and a handful of fishes into enough food to feed several thousand people.

Delivery of the Keys to Peter (see FIG. 21-42)   The fisherman Peter was one of the first Jesus summoned as a disciple. Jesus chooses Peter as his successor, the rock *(petra)* on which his church will be built, and symbolically delivers to Peter the keys to the kingdom of heaven.

Transfiguration (see FIG. 12-13)   Jesus scales a high mountain and, in the presence of Peter and two other disciples, James and John the Evangelist, is transformed into radiant light. God, speaking from a cloud, discloses that Jesus is his son.

Cleansing of the Temple   Jesus returns to Jerusalem, where he finds money changers and merchants conducting business in the temple. He rebukes them and drives them out of the sacred precinct.

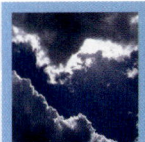

The Life of Jesus in Art *(continued)*

PASSION

The Passion (from Latin *passio*, "suffering") cycle includes the episodes leading to Jesus' death, Resurrection, and ascent to heaven.

Entry into Jerusalem (FIG. 11-5) On the Sunday before his Crucifixion (Palm Sunday), Jesus rides triumphantly into Jerusalem on a donkey, accompanied by disciples. He is greeted enthusiastically by crowds of people who place palm fronds in his path.

Last Supper (see FIGS. 20-8, 21-39, 22-3, 22-52, and 23-4) and *Washing of the Disciples' Feet* In Jerusalem, Jesus celebrates Passover with his disciples. During this Last Supper, Jesus foretells his imminent betrayal, arrest, and death and invites the disciples to remember him when they eat bread (symbol of his body) and drink wine (his blood). This ritual became the celebration of *Mass (Eucharist)* in the Christian Church. At the same meal, Jesus sets an example of humility for his apostles by washing their feet.

Agony in the Garden Jesus goes to the Mount of Olives in the Garden of Gethsemane, where he struggles to overcome his human fear of death by praying for divine strength. The apostles who accompanied him there fall asleep despite his request that they stay awake with him while he prays.

Betrayal and Arrest (see FIG. 19-17) One of the disciples, Judas Iscariot, agrees to betray Jesus to the Jewish authorities in return for thirty pieces of silver. Judas identifies Jesus to the soldiers by kissing him, and Jesus is arrested. Later, a remorseful Judas hangs himself from a tree (FIG. 11-21).

Trials of Jesus (FIGS. 11-5 and 11-20) and *Denial of Peter* Jesus is brought before Caiaphas, the Jewish high priest, and is interrogated about his claim to be the Messiah. Meanwhile, the disciple Peter thrice denies knowing Jesus, as Jesus predicted he would. Jesus is then brought before the Roman governor of Judea, Pontius Pilate, on the charge of treason because he had proclaimed himself as King of the Jews. Pilate asks the crowd to choose between freeing Jesus or Barabbas, a murderer. The people choose Barabbas, and the judge condemns Jesus to death. Pilate washes his hands, symbolically relieving himself of responsibility for the mob's decision.

Flagellation and *Mocking* The Roman soldiers who hold Jesus captive whip (flagellate) him and mock him by dressing him as King of the Jews and placing a crown of thorns on his head.

Carrying of the Cross, Raising of the Cross, (see FIG. 24-34) and *Crucifixion* (see FIGS. 11-21, 12-20, 16-16, and 16-27) The Romans force Jesus to carry the cross on which he will be crucified from Jerusalem to Mount Calvary (Golgotha, the "place of the skull," where Adam was buried). He falls three times and gets stripped along the way. Soldiers erect the cross and nail his hands and feet to it. Jesus' mother, John the Evangelist, and Mary Magdalene mourn at the foot of the cross, while soldiers torment Jesus. One of them (the centurion Longinus) stabs his side with a spear. After suffering great pain, Jesus dies. The Crucifixion occurred on a Friday and Christians celebrate the day each year as Good Friday.

Deposition (see FIGS. 20-6 and 22-41), *Lamentation* (see FIGS. 12-27 and 19-9), and *Entombment* (see FIG. 17-33) Two disciples, Joseph of Arimathea and Nicodemus, remove Jesus' body from the cross (the Deposition); sometimes those present at the Crucifixion look on. They take Jesus to the tomb Joseph had purchased for himself, and Joseph, Nicodemus, the Virgin Mary, Saint John the Evangelist, and Mary Magdalene mourn over the dead Jesus (the Lamentation). (When in art the isolated figure of the Virgin Mary cradles her dead son in her lap, it is called a *Pietà* [Italian for *pity;* see FIGS. 18-53 and 20-19]). In portrayals of the Entombment, his followers lower Jesus into a sarcophagus in the tomb.

Descent into Limbo (see FIGS. 12-23 and 12-31) During the three days he spends in the tomb, Jesus, no longer a mortal human but now the divine Christ, descends into Hell, or Limbo, and triumphantly frees the souls of the righteous, including Adam, Eve, Moses, David, Solomon, and John the Baptist. In Byzantine art, this episode is often labeled *Anastasis* (*Resurrection* in Greek), although it refers to events preceding Christ's emergence from the tomb and reappearance on earth.

Resurrection (see FIG. 21-52) and *Three Marys at the Tomb* On the third day (Easter Sunday), Christ rises from the dead and leaves the tomb while the guards outside are sleeping. The Virgin Mary, Mary Magdalene, and Mary, the mother of James, visit the tomb, find it empty, and learn from an angel that Christ has been resurrected.

Noli Me Tangere, Supper at Emmaus, and *Doubting of Thomas* During the forty days between Christ's Resurrection and his ascent to heaven, he appears on several occasions to his followers. Christ warns Mary Magdalene, weeping at his tomb, with the words "Don't touch me" (*Noli me tangere* in Latin), but he tells her to inform the apostles of his return. At Emmaus he eats supper with two of his astonished disciples. Later, Thomas, who cannot believe that Christ has risen, is invited to touch the wound in his side that he received at his Crucifixion.

Ascension (see FIGS. 12-14 and 17-26) On the fortieth day, on the Mount of Olives, with his mother and apostles as witnesses, Christ gloriously ascends to heaven in a cloud.

hand. The piece is unique and, unfortunately, of unknown provenance, so art historians only can speculate about its original context and function. Several third- and fourth-century marble statuettes of Christ as the Good Shepherd and of Jonah also survive, but they, too, are exceptional. Monumental sculpture of Christian character was not significant in the history of art until the twelfth century (Chapter 17).

ARCHITECTURE AND MOSAICS

THE FRUITS OF IMPERIAL PATRONAGE Although some Christian ceremonies were held in the catacombs, regular services took place in private community houses of the type found at Dura-Europos (FIG. 11-2). Once Christianity achieved imperial sanction under Constantine, an urgent need suddenly arose to construct churches. The new buildings had to meet the Christian liturgy's require-

ments, provide a suitably monumental setting for the celebration of the Christian faith, and accommodate the rapidly growing numbers of worshipers.

Constantine was convinced the Christian god had guided him to victory over Maxentius, and in lifelong gratitude he protected and advanced Christianity throughout the empire, as well as in the obstinately pagan capital city of Rome. As emperor, he was, of course, obliged to safeguard the ancient Roman religion, traditions, and monuments, and, as noted in Chapter 10, he was (for his time) a builder on a grand scale in the heart of the city. But eager to provide buildings to house the Christian rituals and venerated burial places, especially the memorials of founding saints, Constantine also was the first major patron of Christian architecture. He constructed elaborate basilicas, memorials, and mausoleums not only in Rome (see "Constantine's Gifts to the Churches of Rome," page 311) but also in Constantinople, his "New Rome" in the East; and at sites sacred to Christianity, most notably Bethlehem, the birthplace of Jesus; and Jerusalem, the site of his crucifixion.

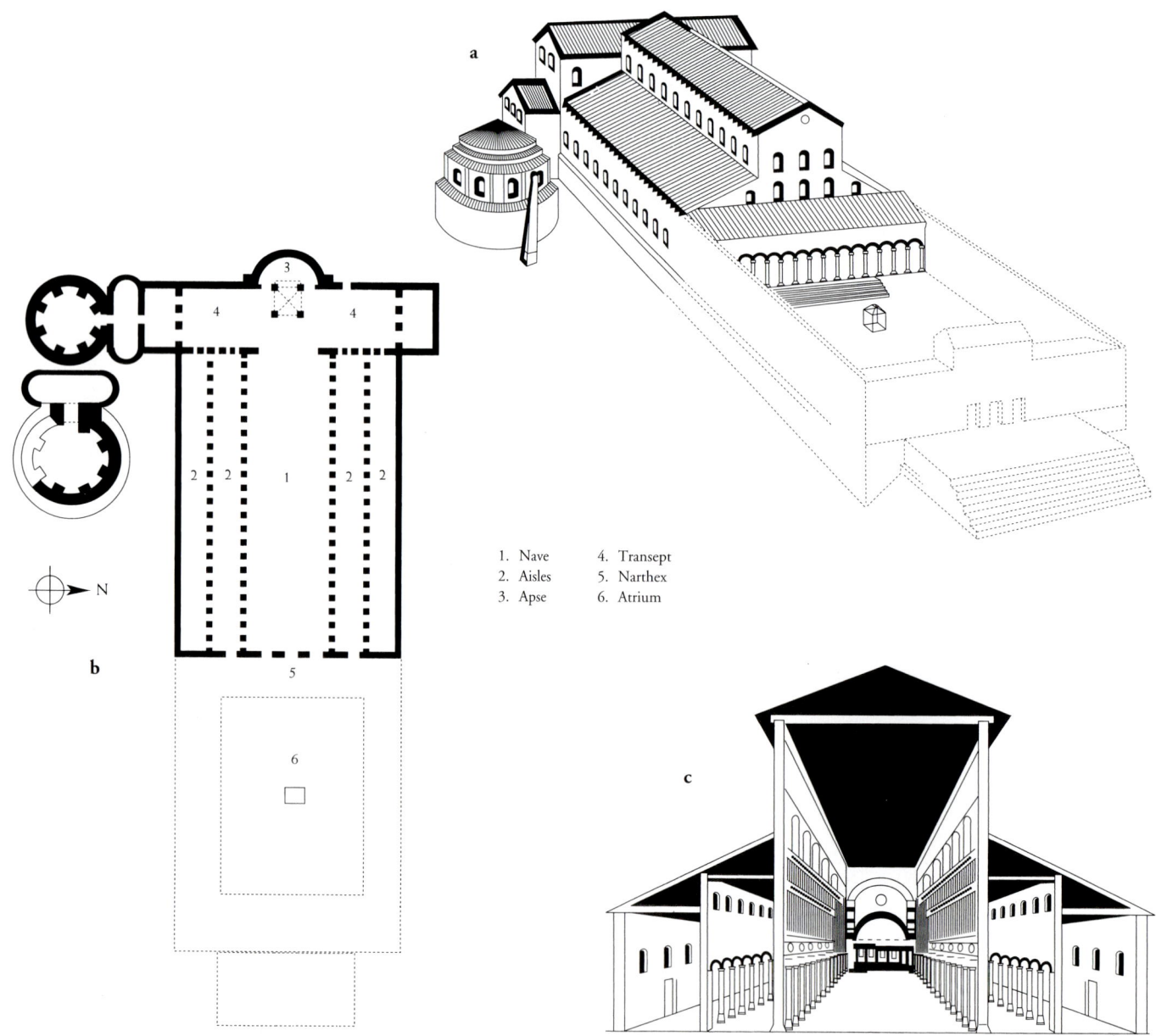

1. Nave
2. Aisles
3. Apse
4. Transept
5. Narthex
6. Atrium

11-7 Restored view (*a*), plan (*b*), and section (*c*) of Old Saint Peter's, Rome, Italy, begun ca. 320. (The restoration of the forecourt is conjectural.)

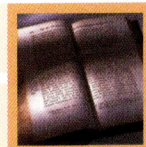

Constantine's Gifts to the Churches of Rome

Constantine the Great was the first emperor to sponsor the construction of churches in Rome. His generosity went well beyond providing land and erecting edifices. It extended to outfitting the interiors with costly altars, chandeliers, candlesticks, pitchers, goblets, and plates fashioned of gold and silver and sometimes embellished with jewels. The *Book of the Popes,* compiled by an anonymous sixth-century author, provides a vivid picture of the emperor's abundance, enumerating Constantine's donations to Old Saint Peter's (FIG. 11-7) and to the great basilica of Saint John Lateran, the cathedral of Rome adjacent to the emperor's palace. The highlight of the very long list of gifts to the Lateran basilica is

> a ciborium [a *baldacchino,* or domical canopy over an altar, supported by four columns] of hammered silver, which has upon the front the Saviour seated upon a chair, in height 5 feet, weighing 120 lbs., and also the 12 apostles, who weigh each 90 lbs., and are 5 feet in height and wear crowns of purest silver; further, on the back, looking toward the apse are the Saviour seated upon a throne in

height 5 feet, of purest silver, weighing 150 lbs., and 4 angels of silver, which weigh each 105 lbs. and are 5 feet in height and have jewels from Alabanda in their eyes and carry spears; the ciborium itself weighs 2025 lbs. of wrought silver; a vaulted ceiling of purest gold; and a lamp of purest gold, which hangs beneath the ciborium, with 50 dolphins of purest gold, weighing each 50 lbs., and chains which weigh 25 lbs.[1]

The description of the silver statues of Christ, the apostles, and angels are especially interesting. They are symptomatic of the triumph of classical taste and tradition over the Christian reluctance to fashion "idols." The marble statuette of Christ already discussed (FIG. 11-6) also may have been made for a patron like Constantine, but of lesser means, who was born a pagan and embraced Christianity only late in life.

[1] Caecilia Davis-Weyer, trans., *Early Medieval Art, 300–1150: Sources and Documents* (Englewood Cliffs, N.J.: Prentice-Hall, 1971), 41.

Rome

CONSTANTINE HONORS SAINT PETER Constantine's dual role as both Roman emperor and champion of the Christian faith was reflected in his decision to locate the new churches of Rome on the city's outskirts to avoid any confrontation between Christian and pagan ideologies. The greatest of Constantine's churches in Rome was Old Saint Peter's (FIG. **11-7**), probably begun as early as 319. The Constantinian structure eventually was replaced by the grand present-day church (see FIG. 24-4), one of the masterpieces of Italian Renaissance and Baroque architecture. Old Saint Peter's stood on the western side of the Tiber River on the spot where Constantine and Pope Sylvester believed Peter, the first apostle and founder of the Roman Christian community, had been buried. Excavations in the Roman cemetery beneath the church have in fact revealed a second-century memorial erected in honor of the early Christian martyr at his reputed grave. The great Constantinian church, capable of housing three to four thousand worshipers at one time, was raised, at immense cost, upon a terrace over the ancient cemetery on the irregular slope of the Vatican Hill. It enshrined one of the most hallowed sites in Christendom, second only to the Holy Sepulcher in Jerusalem, the site of Christ's Resurrection. The project also fulfilled the figurative words of Christ himself, when he said, "Thou art Peter, and upon this rock (in Greek, *petra*) I will build my church" (Matt. 16:18). Peter was Rome's first bishop and also the head of the long line of popes that extends to the present.

BASILICAS BECOME CHURCHES The plan and elevation of Old Saint Peter's resemble those of Roman basilicas and audience halls, such as the Basilica Ulpia in the Forum of

Trajan (FIG. 10-41) and the Aula Palatina at Trier (see FIGS. 10-80 and 10-81), rather than the design of any Greco-Roman temple. The Christians, understandably, did not want their houses of worship to mimic the form of pagan shrines, but practical considerations also contributed to their shunning the pagan temple type. The Greco-Roman temple housed only the cult statue of the deity. All rituals took place outside at open-air altars. The classical temple, therefore, could have been adapted only with great difficulty as a building that accommodated large numbers of people within it. The Roman basilica, in contrast, was ideally suited as a place for congregation, and Early Christian architects eagerly embraced it.

Like Roman basilicas, Old Saint Peter's (FIG. 11-7) had a wide central *nave* (three hundred feet long) flanked by *aisles* and ending in an *apse.* It was preceded by an open colonnaded courtyard, very much like the forum proper in the Forum of Trajan but called an *atrium* like the central room in a private house. Worshipers entered the basilica through a *narthex,* or vestibule. When they emerged in the nave, they had an unobstructed view of the altar in the apse, framed by the so-called *triumphal arch* dividing the nave from the area around the altar. A special feature of the Constantinian church was the transverse aisle, or *transept,* an area perpendicular to the nave between the nave and apse. It housed the relics of Saint Peter that hordes of pilgrims came to see. (*Relics* are the body parts, clothing, or any object associated with a saint or Christ himself; see "Pilgrimages and the Cult of Relics," Chapter 17, page 457.) The transept became a standard element of church design in the West only much later, when it also took on, with the nave and apse, the symbolism of the Christian cross.

INSIDE AN EARLY CHRISTIAN BASILICA Unlike pagan temples but comparable to most Roman basilicas and audience halls, Old Saint Peter's was not adorned with lavish exterior sculptures. Its brick walls were as austere as those of the Aula Palatina at Trier (see FIG. 10-80). Inside, however, were frescoes and mosaics, marble columns (taken from pagan buildings, as was customary at the time), grandiose chandeliers, and gold and silver vessels on jeweled altar cloths for use in the Mass. A huge marble baldacchino supported by spiral columns marked the spot of Saint Peter's tomb beneath the *crossing* of the nave and the transept. The Early Christian basilica may be likened to the ideal Christian, with a somber and plain exterior and a glowing and beautiful soul within.

One can get some idea of the character of the timber-roofed, five-aisled interior of Old Saint Peter's by comparing our section drawing (FIG. 11-7) with the photograph of the interior of Santa Sabina in Rome (FIG. **11-8**). Santa Sabina, built a century later, is a basilican church of much more modest proportions, but it still retains its Early Christian character. The Corinthian columns of Santa Sabina's nave produce a steady rhythm that focuses all attention on the apse within its "triumphal arch," which frames the altar and contains seats for the clergy. In a pagan basilica, the apse was where the enthroned statue of the emperor was displayed, as in the Basilica Nova in Rome (see FIG. 10-79). The seat of episcopal authority thus supplanted the pagan basilica's secular throne. (The word *cathedral* is derived from the Latin *cathedra,* the bishop's chair.) In Santa Sabina, as in Old Saint Peter's, the nave is drenched with light from the clerestory windows piercing the thin upper wall beneath the timber roof. The same light would have illuminated the frescoes and mosaics that commonly adorned the nave, triumphal arch, and apse of Early Christian churches. Outside, Santa Sabina has plain brick walls. They resemble quite closely the exterior of Trier's Aula Palatina (FIG. 10-80).

FROM MAUSOLEUM TO CHURCH The rectangular basilican church design was long the favorite of the Western Christian world, but Early Christian architects also adopted another classical architectural type: the *central-plan* building. The type is so named because the building's parts are of equal or almost equal dimensions around the center. Roman central-plan buildings were usually round or polygonal domed structures. Byzantine architects developed this form to monumental proportions and amplified its theme in numerous ingenious variations. In the West, the central plan was used generally for structures adjacent to the main basilicas, such as mausoleums, baptisteries, and private chapels, rather than for actual churches, as in the East (see Chapter 12).

A highly refined example of the central-plan design is Santa Costanza in Rome (FIGS. **11-9** and **11-10**), built in the mid-fourth century as the mausoleum for Constantia, the emperor Constantine's daughter. It contained her monumental porphyry sarcophagus, which is now in the Vatican Museums. The mausoleum, later converted into a church, stood next to the basilican church of Saint Agnes, whose tomb was in a nearby catacomb. Santa Costanza has antecedents that can be traced back to the beehive tombs of the Mycenaeans (see FIGS. 4-21 and 4-22), but its immediate predecessors were the domed structures of the Romans, such as the Pantheon (see FIGS. 10-48 to 10-50) and especially imperial mausolea such as Diocletian's at Split (see FIG. 10-75). At Santa Costanza, the interior design of the pagan Roman buildings was modified to accommodate an *ambulatory,* a ringlike barrel-vaulted corridor separated from the central domed cylinder by a dozen pairs of columns. (Twelve is the number of Christ's apostles, and twelve pairs of columns were also a feature of Constantine's centrally planned Anastasis Rotunda in Jerusalem.) It is as if the nave of the Early Christian basilica with its clerestory wall were bent around a circle, the ambulatory corresponding to the basilican aisles.

A PORTRAIT IN A MOSAIC VINEYARD Like Early Christian basilicas, Santa Costanza has a severe brick exterior. Its interior was once adorned with mosaics, although most are lost. Old and New Testament themes ap-

11-8 Interior of Santa Sabina, Rome, Italy, 422–432.

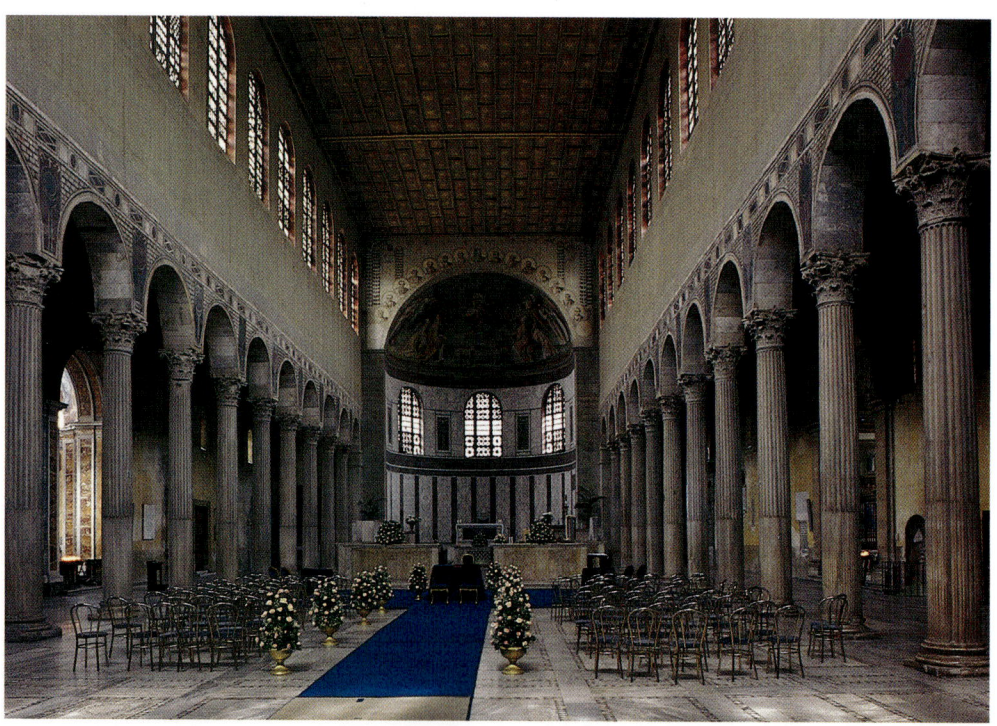

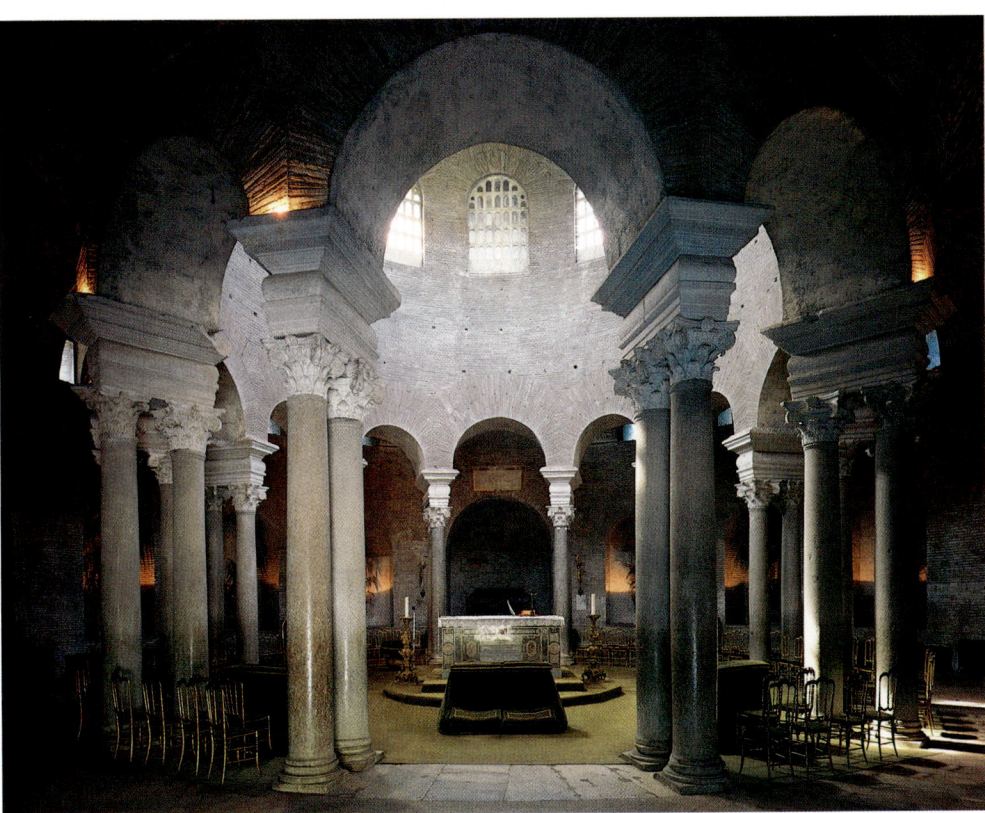

11-9 Interior of Santa Costanza, Rome, Italy, ca. 337–351.

peared side by side, as in the catacombs and on Early Christian sarcophagi. But Santa Costanza also had an abundance of pagan imagery, appropriate for the tomb of an emperor's daughter. In our detail of a mosaic in the ambulatory vault (FIG. 11-11), a portrait bust of Constantia is at the center of a rich vine scroll inhabited by putti and birds. Scenes of putti harvesting grapes and producing wine, echoing the decoration of Constantia's sarcophagus (not shown), surround the portrait.

The surviving mosaics of Santa Costanza, despite their pagan themes, are a reminder of how important a role mosaic decoration played in the interiors of Early Christian buildings (see "Mosaics," page 314). When, under Constantine, Christianity suddenly became a public and official religion in Rome, not only were new buildings required to house the faithful, but wholesale decoration programs for the churches also became necessary. To advertise the new faith in all its diverse aspects—its dogma, scriptural narrative, and symbolism—and to instruct and edify believers, acres of walls in dozens of new churches had to be filled in the style and medium that would carry the message most effectively.

CHRIST AS SUN GOD The earliest known mosaic of explicitly Christian content is the late-third-century vault mosaic (FIG. 11-12) in a small Christian mausoleum not far from Saint Peter's tomb in the Roman cemetery beneath Old Saint Peter's. It depicts Christ in the guise of a familiar pagan deity, Sol Invictus (in Greek, Helios), the Invincible Sun, driving the sun chariot through the golden heavens. All about Christ are vines, as in Constantia's mausoleum (FIG. 11-11). He holds an orb in his left hand, characterizing him as ruler of the universe, another borrowing from the pagan repertory of Roman imperial art. But viewers could easily distinguish the Christian charioteer from the pagan Sol by the halo around his head: The rays suggest the pattern of a cross. This is a far more grandiose

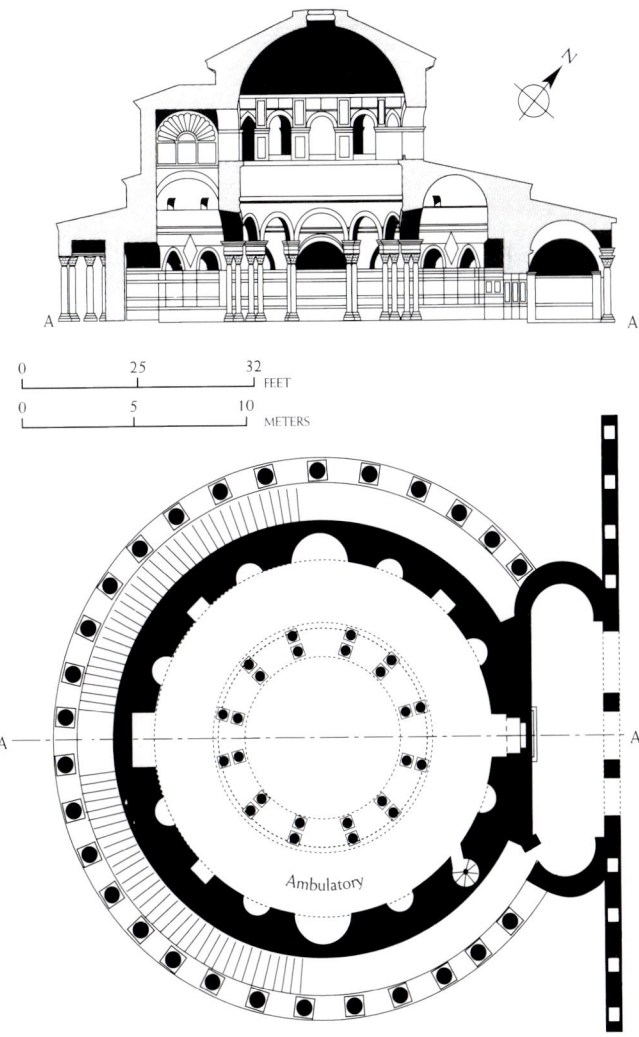

11-10 Longitudinal section (*top*) and plan (*bottom*) of Santa Costanza, Rome, Italy, ca. 337–351.

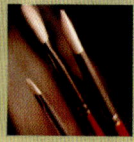

MATERIALS AND TECHNIQUES

Mosaics

As an art form, mosaic had a rather simple and utilitarian beginning, seemingly invented primarily to provide an inexpensive and durable flooring. Originally, small beach pebbles were set, unaltered from their natural form and color, into a thick coat of cement. Artisans soon discovered, however, that the stones could be arranged in decorative patterns. At first, these *pebble mosaics* were uncomplicated and were confined to geometric shapes. Generally, the artists used only black and white stones. Examples of this type, dating back to the eighth century B.C., have been found at Gordion in Asia Minor. Eventually, artists arranged the stones to form more complex pictorial designs, and by the fourth century B.C. the technique had developed to a high sophistication level. Mosaicists depicted elaborate figural scenes using a broad range of colors—yellow, brown, and red in addition to black, white, and gray—and shaded the figures, clothing, and setting to suggest volume. Thin strips of lead provided linear definition (see FIG. 5-68).

By the middle of the third century B.C., artists had invented a new kind of mosaic that permitted the best mosaicists to create designs that more closely approximated true paintings. The new technique employed *tesserae* (Latin for "cubes" or "dice"). These tiny cut stones gave the artist much greater flexibility because their size and shape could be adjusted at will, eliminating the need for lead strips to indicate contours and interior details. Much more gradual gradations of color also became possible, and mosaicists finally could aspire to rival the achievements of panel painters (see FIG. 5-69).

In Early Christian mosaics, sparkling tesserae of reflective glass, as opposed to the opaque marble tesserae the Romans preferred, almost immediately became the standard vehicle of expression. Mosaics particularly suited the flat, thin-walled surfaces of the new basilicas, becoming a durable, tangible part of the wall—a kind of architectural tapestry. The mosaics caught the light flooding through the clerestories in vibrant reflection, producing abrupt effects and contrasts and sharp concentrations of color that could focus attention on a composition's central, most relevant features. Mosaics worked in the Early Christian manner were not intended for the subtle tonal changes a naturalistic painter's approach would require. Color was *placed*, not blended. Bright, hard, glittering texture, set within a rigorously simplified pattern, became the rule. For mosaics situated high on the wall, far above the observer's head, the painstaking use of tiny tesserae seen in Roman floor mosaics became meaningless. Early Christian mosaics, designed to be seen from a distance, employed larger stones. The larger tesserae were also set unevenly so that their surfaces could catch and reflect the light. Artists favored simple designs for optimal legibility. For several centuries, mosaic, in the service of Christian theology, was the medium of some of the supreme masterpieces of medieval art.

11-11   Detail of vault mosaic in the ambulatory of Santa Costanza, Rome, Italy, ca. 337–351.

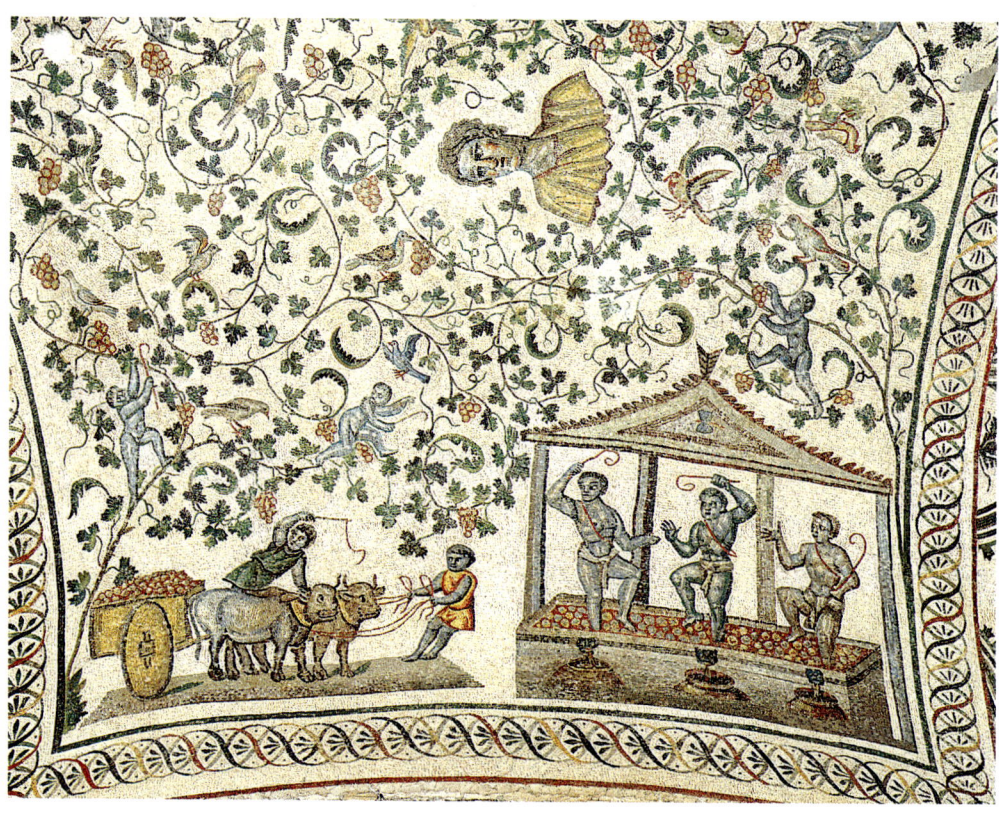

conception of Christ than the role of Good Shepherd and a fitting theme for the vaulted ceiling above the deceased. Christ does appear, however, as the caretaker of the Christian flock below, on the west wall of the tomb. On the east wall, in typical Early Christian fashion, is the story of Jonah.

ABRAHAM AND LOT IN A CHURCH NAVE   Old Testament themes are the focus of the extensive fifth-century mosaic cycle in the nave of the basilican church of Santa Maria Maggiore in Rome. A characteristic panel of great dramatic power represents the parting of Abraham and his nephew Lot (FIG. **11-13**), as set forth in Genesis, the Bible's opening book. Agreeing to disagree, Lot leads his family and followers to the right, toward the city of Sodom, while Abraham heads for Canaan, moving toward a building (perhaps symbolizing the Christian Church) on the left. Lot's is the evil choice, and the instruments of the evil (his two daughters) are in front of him. The figure of the yet unborn Isaac, the instrument of good (and, as noted earlier, a prefiguration of Christ), stands before his father, Abraham.

The cleavage of the two groups is emphatic, and each group was represented by a shorthand device that could be called a "head cluster," which had precedents in antiquity and had a long history in Christian art. The figures turn from each other in a sharp dialogue of glance and gesture. The wide eyes, turned in their sockets; the broad gestures of enlarged hands; and the opposed movements of the groups all may remind viewers of a silent, expressive chorus that comments on the drama's action only with their hands and bodies. Thus, the complex action of Roman art stiffened into the medieval art of simplified motion, which has great power to communicate without ambiguity.

The artist's placing of the panel's figures in the foreground and disinterest in defining the spatial setting also foreshadowed the

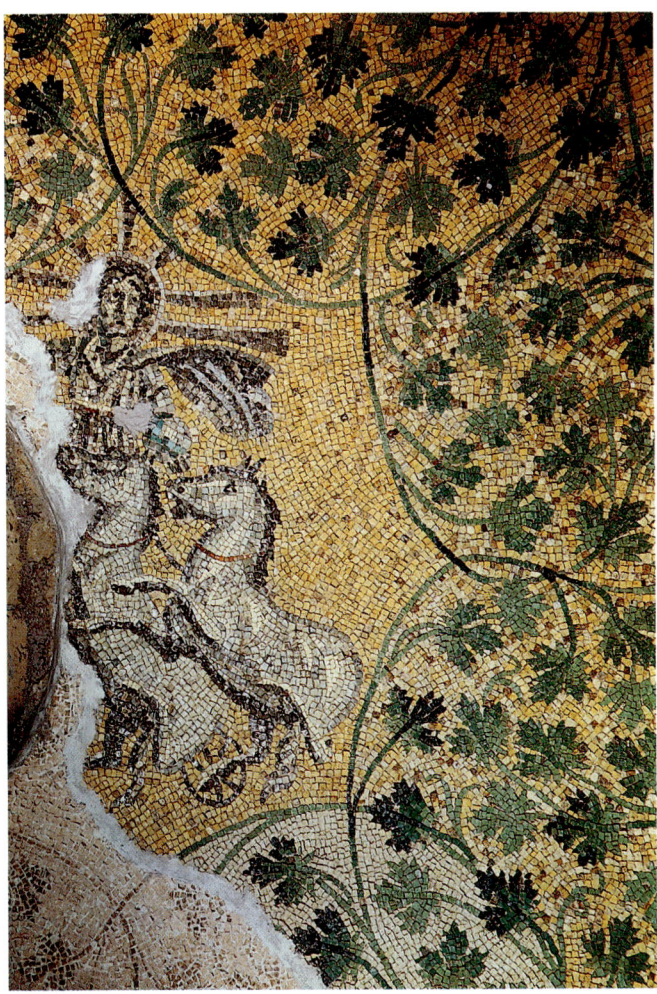

11-12   Christ as Sol Invictus, detail of a vault mosaic in the Mausoleum of the Julii, Rome, Italy, late third century.

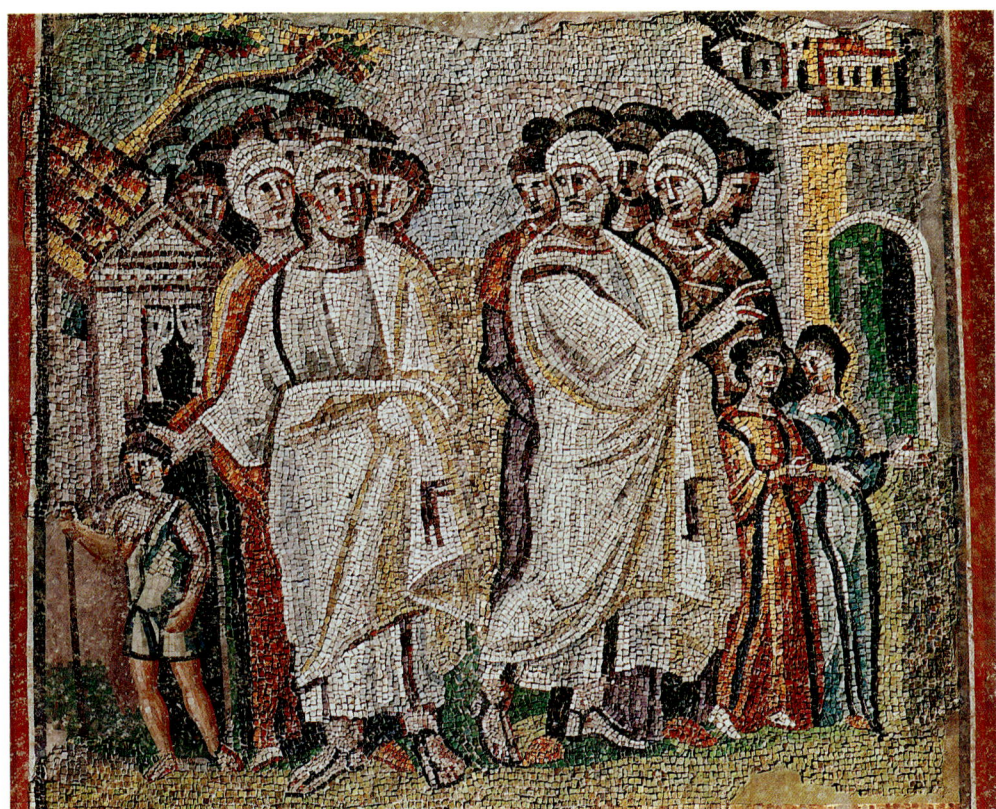

11-13   The parting of Lot and Abraham, mosaic in the nave of Santa Maria Maggiore, Rome, Italy, 432–440.

character of later Christian art. The background town and building are symbolic, rather than descriptive. But within this relatively abstract setting, the figures themselves loom with massive solidity. They cast shadows and were modeled in dark and light to give them the three-dimensional appearance that testified to the artist's heritage of Roman pictorial illusionism. Another century had to pass before Western Christian artists portrayed figures entirely as flat images, rather than as plastic bodies.

Ravenna

NEW CAPITALS FOR A CRUMBLING EMPIRE In the decades following the foundation in 324 of Constantinople, the New Rome in the East, and the death of Constantine in 337, the pace of Christianization of the Roman Empire quickened. In 380 the emperor Theodosius I issued an edict finally establishing Christianity as the state religion. In 391 he enacted a ban against pagan worship. In 394 the Olympic Games, the enduring symbol of the classical world and its values, were abolished. Theodosius died in 395, and imperial power passed to his two sons, Arcadius, who became Emperor of the East, and Honorius, Emperor of the West. The problems that plagued the last pagan emperors, most notably the threat of invasion from the north, did not, however, disappear with the conversion to Christianity.

In 404, when the Visigoths, under their king, Alaric, threatened to overrun Italy from the northwest, Honorius moved the capital of his crumbling empire from Milan to Ravenna, an ancient Roman city (perhaps founded by the Etruscans) near Italy's Adriatic coast, some eighty miles south of Venice. There, in a city surrounded by swamps and thus easily defended, his imperial authority survived the fall of Rome to Alaric in 410. Honorius died in 423, and the reins of government were taken by his half sister, Galla Placidia, whom the Visigoths had captured in Rome in 410. Galla Placidia had married a Visigothic chieftain before returning to Ravenna and the Romans after the chieftain's death six years later. In 476 Ravenna fell to Odoacer, the first Germanic king of Italy, who was overthrown in turn by Theodoric, king of the Ostrogoths, who established his capital at Ravenna in 493. The subsequent history of the city belongs with that of the Byzantine Empire (see Chapter 12).

AN EMPRESS'S MOSAIC-CLAD MAUSOLEUM The so-called Mausoleum of Galla Placidia in Ravenna (FIG. **11-14**) is a rather small *cruciform* (cross-shaped) structure with a dome-covered crossing and barrel-vaulted arms. Dedicated to Saint Lawrence, it was built shortly after 425, almost a quarter century before Galla Placidia's death in 450. The building also housed the sarcophagi of Honorius and Galla Placidia and thus served the double function of imperial mausoleum and martyr's chapel. Originally the building adjoined the narthex of the now greatly altered palace-church of Santa Croce (Holy Cross), which was also cruciform in plan. Although the mausoleum's plan is that of a Latin cross, the cross arms are very short and appear as little more than apselike extensions of a square. The emphasis is on the tall dome-covered crossing. The mausoleum is in essence a central-plan structure. Yet, this small, unassuming building also represents one of the earliest successful fusions of the two basic early church plans, the *longitudinal* (basilican) and the central. It introduced, on a small scale, a building type that had a long his-

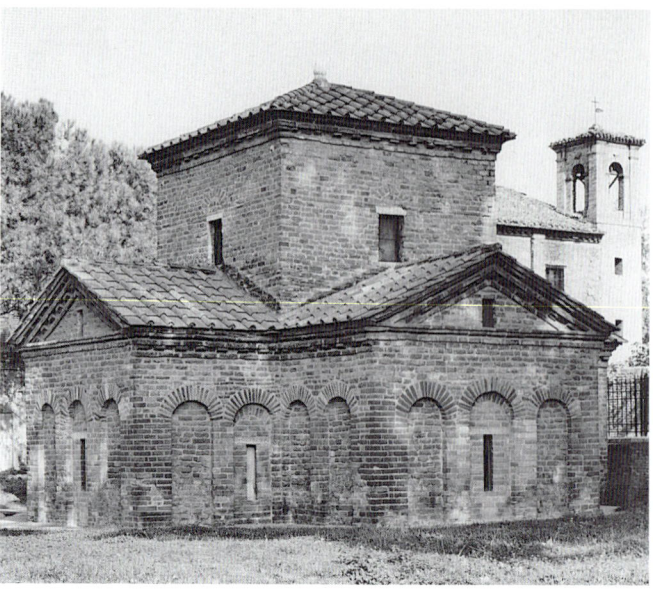

11-14   Mausoleum of Galla Placidia, Ravenna, Italy, ca. 425.

tory in Christian architecture: the basilican plan with a domed crossing.

The mausoleum's unadorned brick shell encloses one of the richest mosaic ensembles in Early Christian art. Mosaics cover every square inch of the interior surfaces above the marble-faced walls. Garlands and decorative medallions resembling snowflakes on a dark blue ground adorn the barrel vaults of the nave and cross arms. The dome has a large golden cross set against a star-studded sky. Representations of saints and apostles cover the other surfaces.

Christ as Good Shepherd is the subject of the lunette above the entrance (FIG. **11-15**). No earlier version of the Good Shepherd is as regal as this one. Instead of carrying a lamb on his shoulders, Jesus sits among his flock, haloed and robed in gold and purple. To his left and right, the sheep are distributed evenly in groups of three. But their arrangement is rather loose and informal, and they occupy a carefully described landscape that extends from foreground to background beneath a blue sky. All the forms have three-dimensional bulk and cast shadows. In short, the panel is full of Greco-Roman illusionistic devices. The mosaicist was still deeply rooted in the classical tradition. Some fifty years later, this artist's successors in Ravenna worked in a much more abstract and formal manner.

THEODORIC'S PALACE-CHURCH Around 504, soon after Theodoric settled in Ravenna, he ordered the construction of his own palace-church, a three-aisled basilica dedicated to the Savior. In the ninth century, the relics of Saint Apollinaris were transferred to this church. The building was rededicated and has been known since that time as Sant'Apollinare Nuovo. The rich mosaic decorations of the interior nave walls (FIG. **11-16**) are in three zones. Only the upper two date from Theodoric's time. Old Testament patriarchs and prophets stand between the clerestory windows. Above them, scenes from Christ's life alternate with decorative panels.

The mosaic depicting the miracle of the loaves and fishes (FIG. **11-17**) illustrates well the stylistic change that occurred since the decoration of the Mausoleum of Galla Placidia. Jesus, beardless, in the imperial dress of gold and purple, and

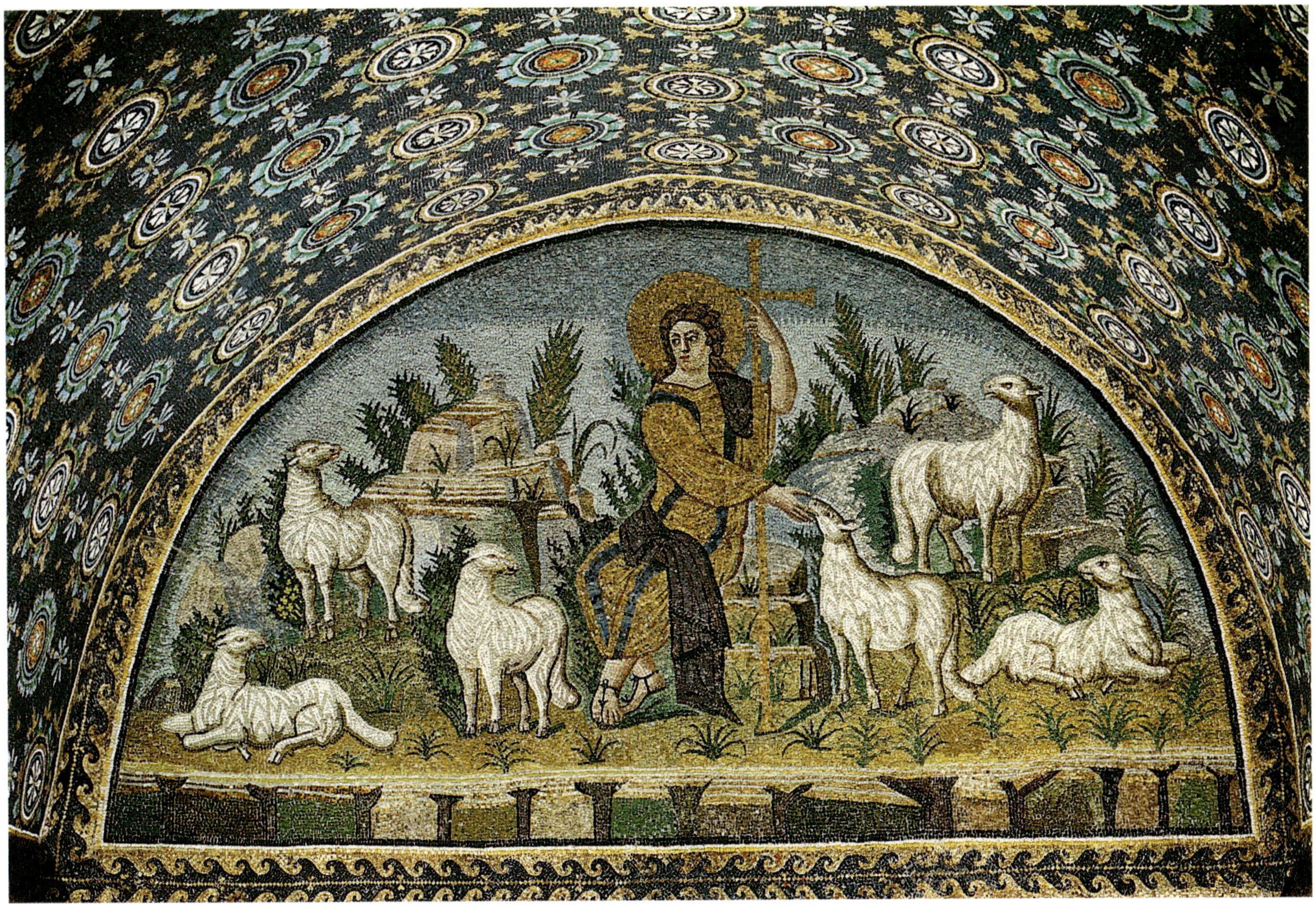

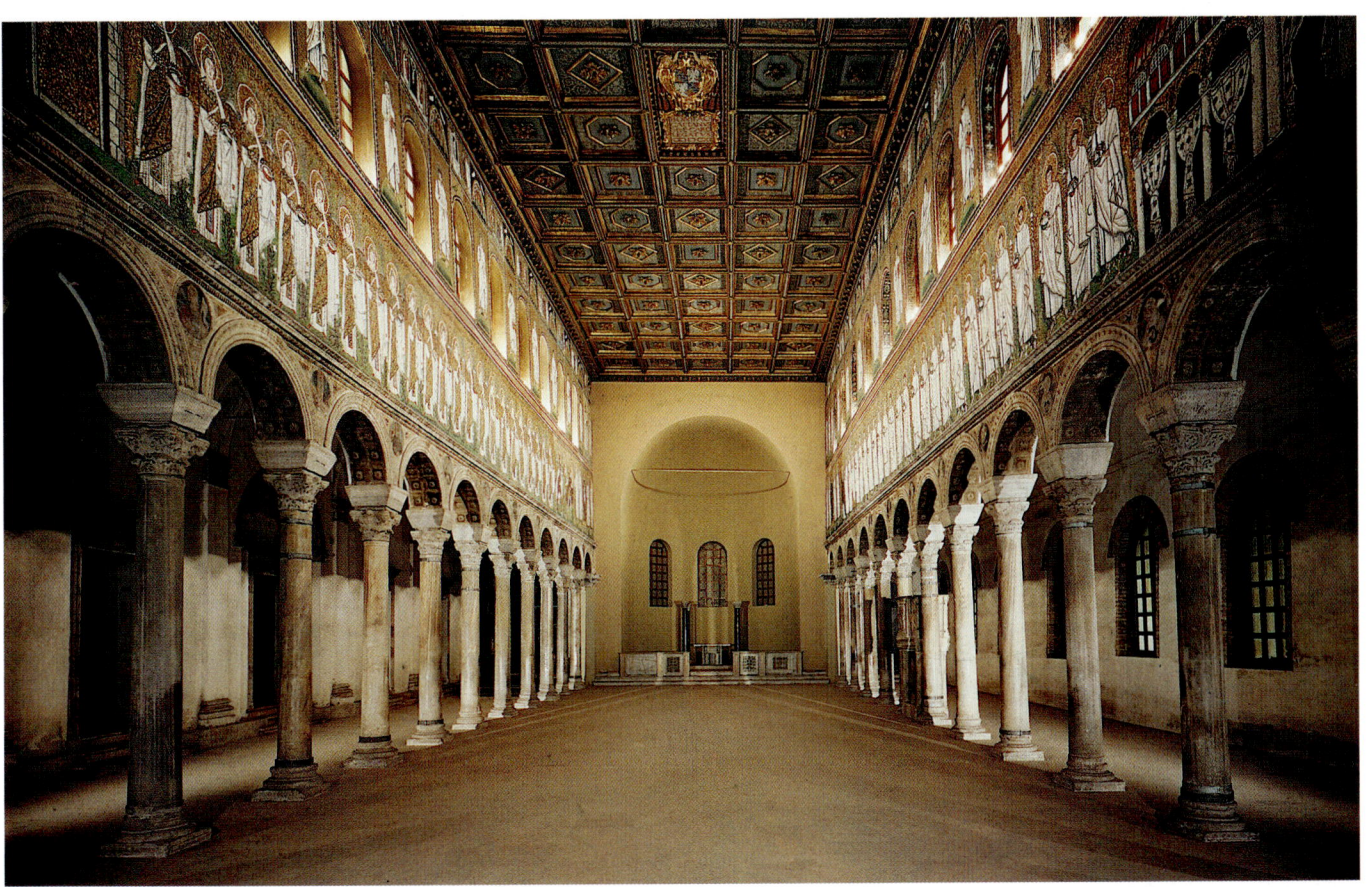

11-15 Christ as the Good Shepherd, mosaic from the entrance wall of the Mausoleum of Galla Placidia, Ravenna, Italy, ca. 425.

11-16 Interior of Sant'Apollinare Nuovo, Ravenna, Italy, dedicated 504.

11-17   Miracle of the loaves and fishes, mosaic from the top register of the nave wall (above the clerestory windows) of Sant'Apollinare Nuovo, Ravenna, Italy, ca. 504.

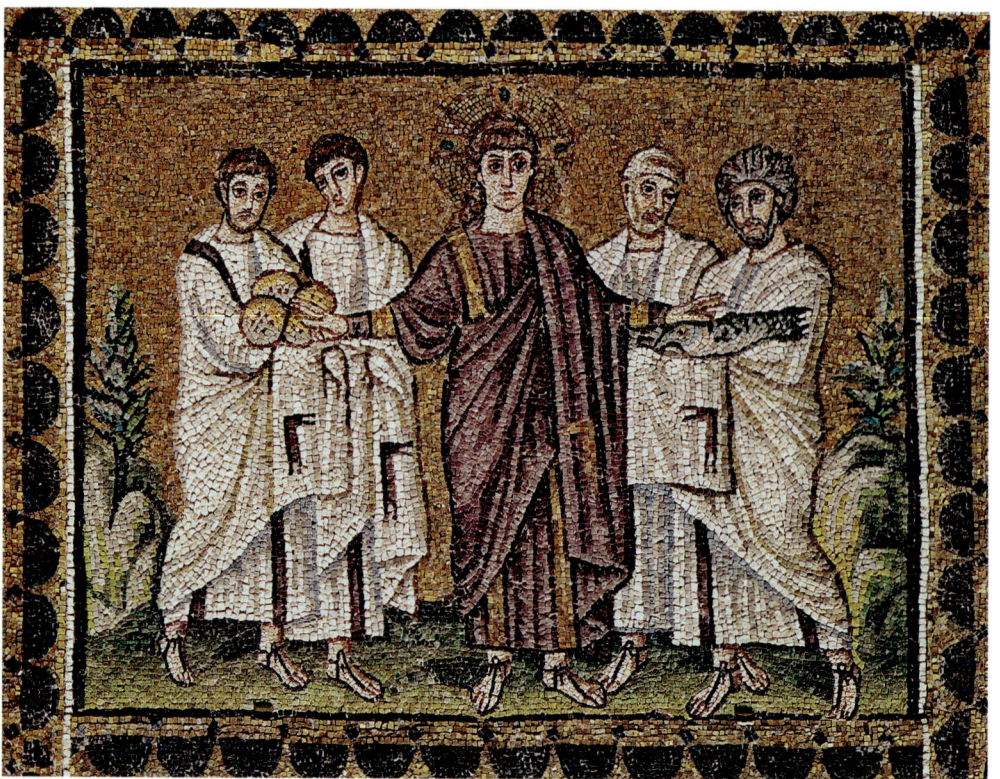

now distinguished by the cross-inscribed *nimbus* (halo) that signifies his divinity, faces directly toward the viewer. With extended arms he directs his disciples to distribute to the great crowd the miraculously increased supply of bread and fish he has produced. The artist made no attempt to supply details of the event. The emphasis is instead on the holy character of it, the spiritual fact that Jesus is performing a miracle by the power of his divinity. The fact of the miracle takes it

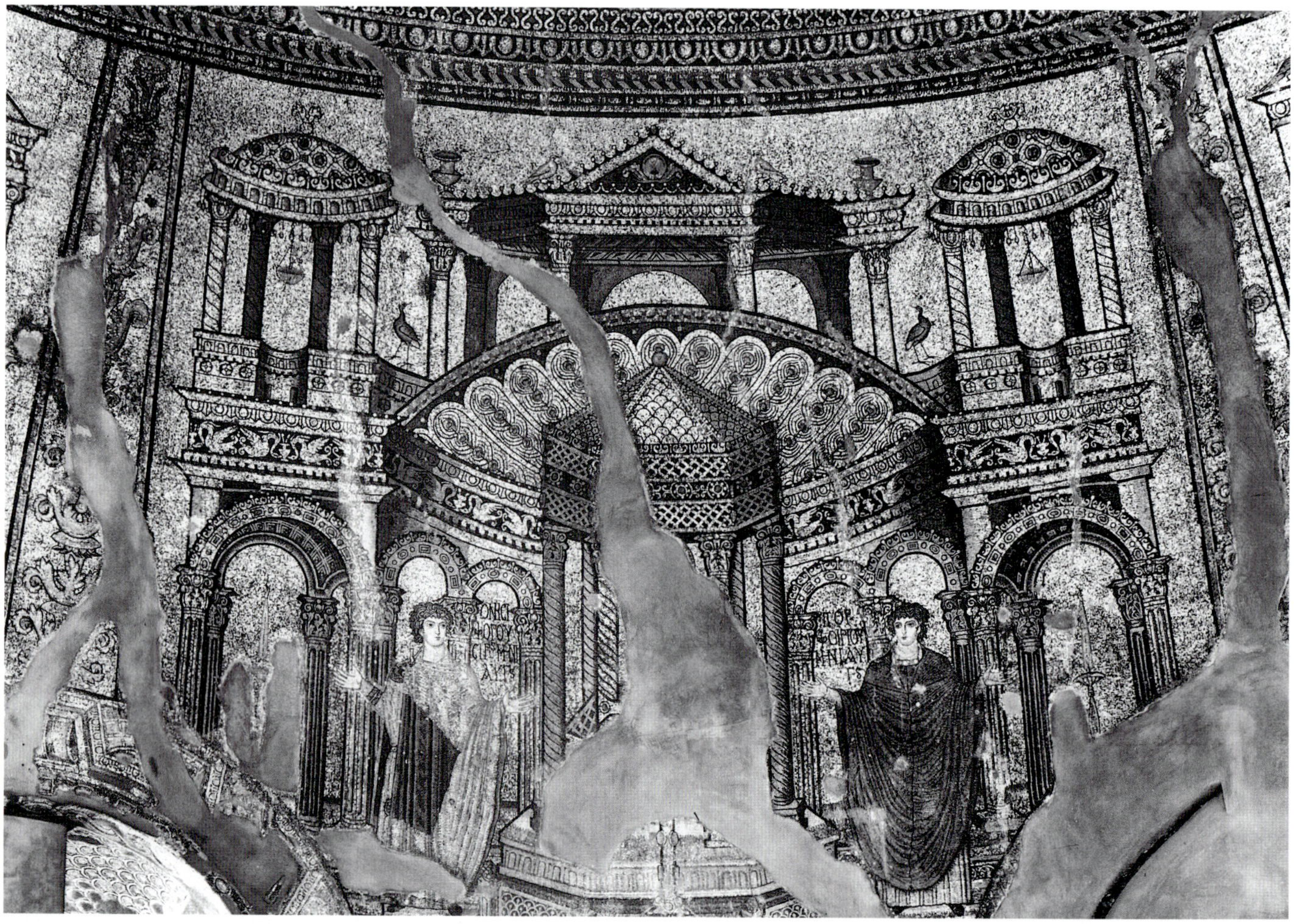

11-18   Saints Onesiphorus and Porphyrius, detail of the dome mosaic, Church of Saint George, Thessaloniki, Greece, ca. 390–450.

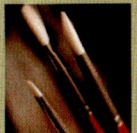

Medieval Manuscript Illumination

Rare as medieval books are, they are far more numerous than their ancient predecessors (see "The Roman Illustrated Book," Chapter 10, page 260). The dissemination of manuscripts, as well as their preservation, was aided greatly by an important invention in the Early Imperial period, the codex. The *codex* is much like a modern book, composed of separate leaves *(folios)* enclosed within a cover and bound together at one side. The new format superseded the long manuscript scroll *(rotulus)* the Egyptians, Greeks, Etruscans, and Romans used. (The Etruscan magistrate Lars Pulena, FIG. 9-14; the philosophers on Roman and Early Christian sarcophagi, FIGS. 10-72 and 11-4; and Christ himself in his role as teacher, FIGS. 11-5 and 11-6, all hold rotuli in their hands.) Much more durable *vellum* (calfskin) and *parchment* (lambskin), which provided better surfaces for painting, also replaced the comparatively brittle papyrus used for ancient scrolls. As a result, luxuriousness of ornament became more and more typical of sacred books in the Middle Ages, and at times the material beauty of the pages and their illustrations overwhelm or usurp the spiritual beauty of the text. Art historians refer to the luxurious painted books produced before the invention of the printing press as *illuminated manuscripts,* from the Latin *illuminare,* meaning "to adorn, ornament, or brighten."

Such books were costly to produce and involved many steps. Numerous artisans performed very specialized tasks, beginning with the curing and cutting (and sometimes the dying) of the animal skin, followed by the sketching of lines to guide the scribe and to set aside spaces for illumination, the lettering of the text, the addition of paintings, and finally the binding of the pages and attachment of covers, buckles, and clasps. The covers could be even more sumptuous than the book itself. Many covers survive that are fashioned of gold and decorated with jewels, ivory carvings, and repoussé reliefs (see FIGS. 16-15 and 16-16).

---

out of the world of time and of incident. The presence of almighty power, not anecdotal narrative, is the important aspect of this scene. The mosaicist told the story with the least number of figures necessary to make its meaning explicit. The artist aligned the figures laterally, moved them close to the foreground, and placed them in a shallow picture box cut off by a golden screen close behind their backs. The landscape setting, which the artist who worked for Galla Placidia so explicitly described, is here merely a few rocks and bushes that enclose the figure group like parentheses. The blue sky of the physical world has given way to the otherworldly splendor of heavenly gold, the standard background color from this point on. Remnants of Roman illusionism appear only in the handling of the individual figures, which still cast shadows and retain some of their former volume. But the shadows of the drapery folds already are only narrow bars. Soon afterward, they disappeared in Christian art.

SAINTS IN A CITY NOT OF THIS WORLD In the eastern Roman Empire, the pace of stylistic change was even more rapid. Many of the features of the Sant'Apollinare Nuovo mosaic may be seen, in more advanced form and created perhaps as much as a century earlier, in the mosaics of the dome of the Church of Saint George at Thessaloniki (Salonica) in northern Greece. The church, of the central-plan type, was originally built around 300 as the mausoleum of Galerius, the tetrarchic Caesar of the East under Diocletian. Its conversion into a church sometime between 390 and 450 (the date is a matter of scholarly controversy) thus parallels the history of the mausoleum of Constantine's daughter, which became Santa Costanza (FIGS. 11-9 to 11-11).

Only part of the mosaic decoration of the Church of Saint George is preserved. The detail we illustrate here (FIG. **11-18**) comes from the lower of two bands of mosaics, which had eight panels. Seven are fairly well preserved. In each one, two saints with their arms raised in prayer stand before two-story architectural fantasies that resemble Roman mural paintings (see FIG. 10-16) and the facades of the rock-cut tombs of Petra (see FIG. 10-52). In this respect, the Thessaloniki mosaics are more closely tied to the classical past than are those of Sant'Apollinare Nuovo. Yet figures and architecture alike have lost almost all substance, and it is increasingly difficult to imagine, for example, rounded torsos and limbs beneath the flat, curtainlike garments worn by Saints Onesiphorus and Porphyrius. A new aesthetic took hold here, one quite foreign to classical art, with its worldly themes, naturalism, perspective illusionism, modeling in light and shade, and proportionality. The formality of the poses and the solemn, priestly demeanor of the Thessaloniki figures, as well as the ethereal golden background, became prominent features of Byzantine art (see Chapter 12). The Saint George dome mosaic seems to have completed the change from the naturalistic images of the pagan floor mosaic, which are literally under the feet and of this world, to the floating images of a celestial world high above the Christian's wondering gaze.

LUXURY ARTS

Illuminated Manuscripts

THE FIRST ILLUSTRATED BIBLES The designers of the Old and New Testament narrative cycles in Santa Maria Maggiore (FIG. 11-13) and Sant'Apollinare Nuovo (FIG. 11-17) must have drawn on a long tradition of pictures in manuscripts that began in pharaonic Egypt (see FIG. 3-39). Richly illustrated texts with Greek, Roman, Hebrew, and Christian themes must have been readily available to the Early Christian

11-19 Rebecca and Eliezer at the well, folio 7 recto of the *Vienna Genesis,* early sixth century. Tempera, gold, and silver on purple vellum, approx. $1'\frac{1}{4}'' \times 9\frac{1}{4}''$. Österreichische Nationalbibliothek, Vienna.

mosaicists. The earliest well-preserved painted manuscript containing biblical scenes is the *Vienna Genesis* (FIG. **11-19**), so called because of its present location. The pages are sumptuous—fine calfskin dyed with rich purple, the same dye used to give imperial cloth its distinctive color, and the text is silver ink (see "Medieval Manuscript Illumination," page 319).

The *Vienna Genesis* represents the somewhat uneasy transition from the scroll to the *codex*, from the old roll format, which favored continuous narrative, to the new bound book, with its series of individual pictures on separate leaves. The *Vienna Genesis* still employs the continuity of a frieze in a scroll, with two or more episodes of a story painted within a single frame. The page we reproduce illustrates the story of Rebecca and Eliezer in the Book of Genesis (24:15–61). When Isaac, Abraham's son, was forty years old, his parents sent their servant Eliezer to find a wife for him. Eliezer chose Rebecca because when he stopped at a well, she was the first woman to draw water for him and his camels. The *Vienna Genesis* scene shows Rebecca at the left, in the first episode of the story, leaving the city of Nahor to fetch water from the well. In the second episode, she gives water to Eliezer and his ten camels, while one already laps water from the well.

The artist painted Nahor as a walled city seen from above, in the manner of the cityscapes on the Santa Maria Maggiore mosaics (FIG. 11-13), which maintained Roman pictorial conventions in widespread use in painting, mosaic, and relief sculpture (for example, on the Column of Trajan, FIG. 10-42). Rebecca walks to the well along the colonnaded avenue of a Roman city. A seminude female personification of a spring is the source of the well water. These are further reminders of the persistence of classical motifs and stylistic modes in Early Christian art. The painter presented the action with all possible simplicity but included convincing touches, such as the drinking camel and Rebecca bracing herself with her raised left foot on the well's rim as she tips up her jug for Eliezer. The figures appear as silhouetted against a blank landscape except for the miniature city and the road to the well. Everything necessary for bare narrative is present and nothing else.

A PURPLE GOSPEL BOOK Closely related to the *Vienna Genesis* is another early-sixth-century manuscript, the *Rossano Gospels*, the earliest preserved illuminated book that contains illustrations of the New Testament. By this time a canon of New Testament iconography had been fairly well established. Like the *Vienna Genesis*, the text of the *Rossano Gospels* is in silver on purple vellum. The Rossano artist, however, attempted with considerable success to harmonize the colors with the purple ground.

The subject of our illustration (FIG. **11-20**), presented with vivid gestures, is the appearance of Jesus before Pilate, who asks the Jews to choose between Jesus and Barabbas (Matt. 27:2–26). In the fashion of continuous narrative, the story's separate episodes appear in the same frame, but without repeating any of the protagonists. The figures are on two levels separated by a simple ground line. In the upper level, Pilate presides over the tribunal. He sits on an elevated dais, following a long-established pattern in Roman art (compare Constantine in the distribution-of-largess frieze on the Arch of Constantine, FIG. 10-77). The people form an arch around Pilate and demand the death of Jesus, while a court scribe records the proceedings. Jesus (here a bearded adult, as soon became the norm for medieval and later depictions of Christ) and the bound Barabbas appear in the lower level. The painter explicitly labeled Barabbas to avoid any possible confusion so that the picture would be as readable as the text. The haloed Christ and Pilate on his magistrate's dais, flanked by painted imperial portraits, needed no further identification.

Ivory Carving

CHRIST CRUCIFIED AND JUDAS HANGED A century before the pages of the *Rossano Gospels* were illuminated with scenes from the Passion cycle, a Roman or northern Italian sculptor produced a series of panels for an ivory casket dramatically recounting the suffering and triumph of Christ. Ivory carving (see "Ivory Carving in Antiquity and the Early Middle Ages," page 322) was another luxury art much admired in the Early Christian period, and these plaques, now in the British Museum, are among the finest known. The narrative on the box begins with Pilate washing his hands, Jesus carrying the cross on the road to Calvary, and the denial of Peter, all compressed into a single panel. The plaque we illustrate (FIG. **11-21**) is the next in the sequence and shows, at the left, Judas hanging from a tree with his open bag of silver dumped on the ground beneath his feet. The Crucifixion is at the right. The Virgin Mary and Joseph of Arimathea are to the left of the cross. On the other side Longinus thrusts his

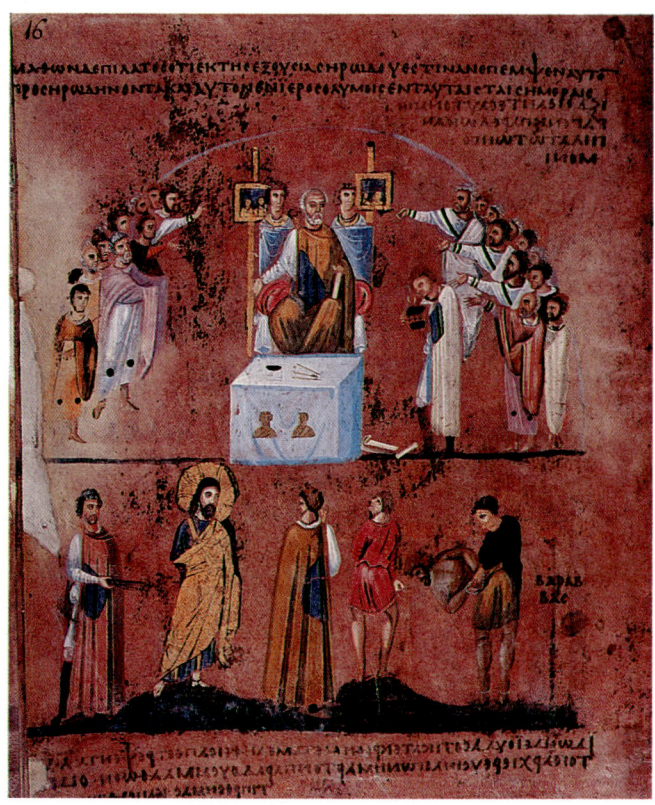

11-20 Christ before Pilate, folio 8 verso of the *Rossano Gospels,* early sixth century. Tempera on purple vellum, approx. 11″ × 10¼″. Diocesan Museum, Archepiscopal Palace, Rossano.

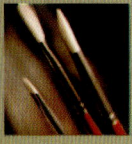

MATERIALS AND TECHNIQUES

Ivory Carving in Antiquity and the Early Middle Ages

Ivory has been prized since the earliest times, when the tusks of Ice Age European mammoths were fashioned into pendants, beads, and other items for bodily adornment, and, occasionally, statuettes (see FIG. 1-3). The primary ivory sources in the historical period are the elephants of India and especially Africa, where the species is larger than the Asian counterpart and the tusks longer, heavier, and of finer grain. African elephant tusks five to six feet in length and weighing ten pounds are common, but tusks of male elephants can be ten feet long or more and weigh well over one hundred pounds. Carved ivories are familiar, if precious, finds at Mesopotamian and Egyptian sites, and ivory objects were manufactured and coveted in the prehistoric Aegean and throughout the classical world. Most frequently employed then for household objects, small votive offerings, and gifts to the deceased, ivory also could be used for grandiose statues such as Phidias's *Athena Parthenos* (see FIG. 5-44).

In the Greco-Roman world, people admired ivory both for its beauty and because of its exotic origin. Elephant tusks were costly imports and Roman generals proudly displayed them in triumphal processions when they paraded the spoils of war before the people. (In FIG. 12-1 a barbarian brings tribute to a Byzantine emperor in the form of an ivory tusk.) Adding to the expense of the material itself was the fact that only highly skilled artisans were capable of working in ivory. The tusks were very hard and of irregular shape, and the ivory workers needed a full toolbox of saws, chisels, knives, files, and gravers close at hand to cut the tusks into blocks for statuettes or thin plaques decorated with relief figures and ornament.

In the late antique and early medieval world, ivory was employed most frequently for book covers (see FIG. 16-15), caskets and chests (FIG. 11-21), and diptychs (see FIGS. 11-22 and 12-2). A *diptych* is a pair of hinged tablets, usually of wood, with a wax layer on the inner sides for writing letters and other documents. (The court scribe recording Jesus' trial in the *Rossano Gospels,* FIG. 11-20, and the woman in a painted portrait from Pompeii, FIG. 10-23, both hold wooden diptychs.) Diptychs fashioned out of ivory generally were created for ceremonial and official purposes: for example, to announce the election of a consul or a marriage between two wealthy families or to commemorate the death of an elevated member of society.

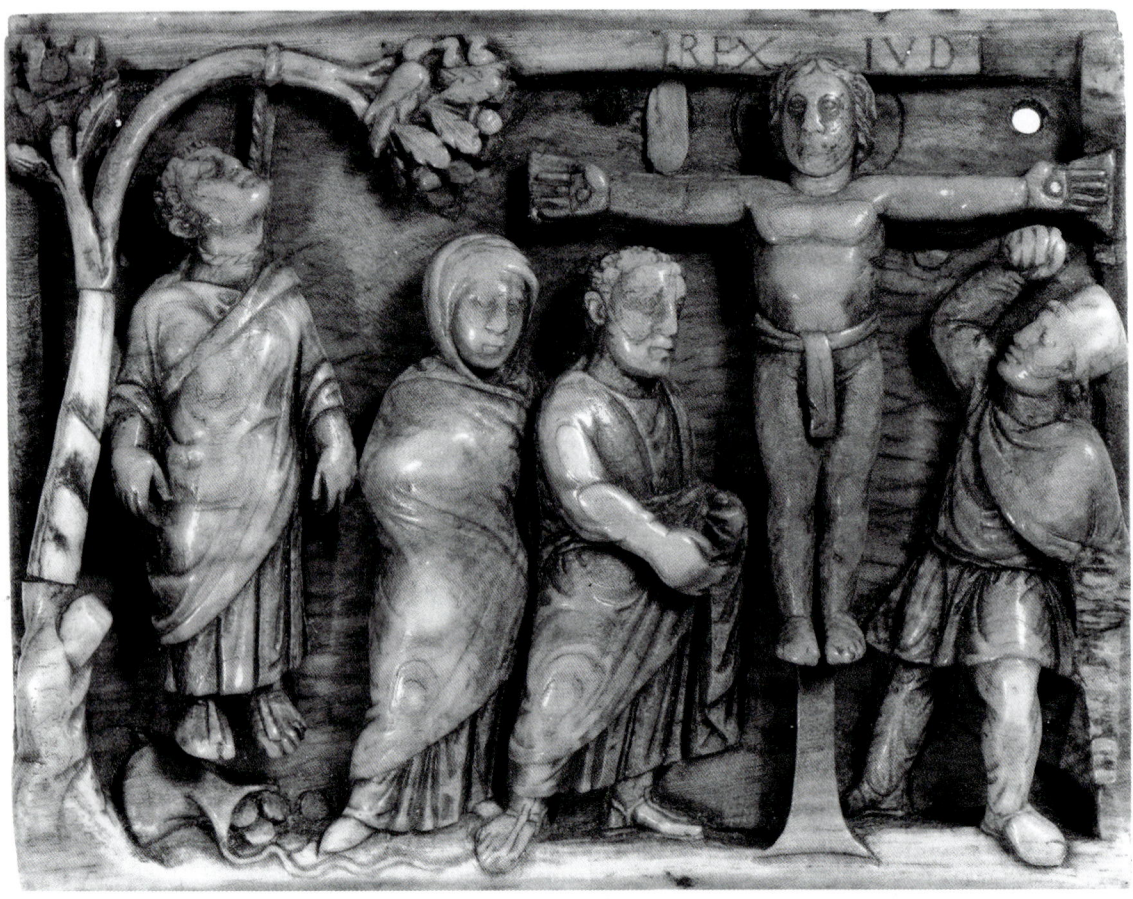

11-21   Suicide of Judas and Crucifixion of Christ, plaque from a casket, ca. 420. Ivory, $3'' \times 3\frac{7}{8}''$. British Museum, London.

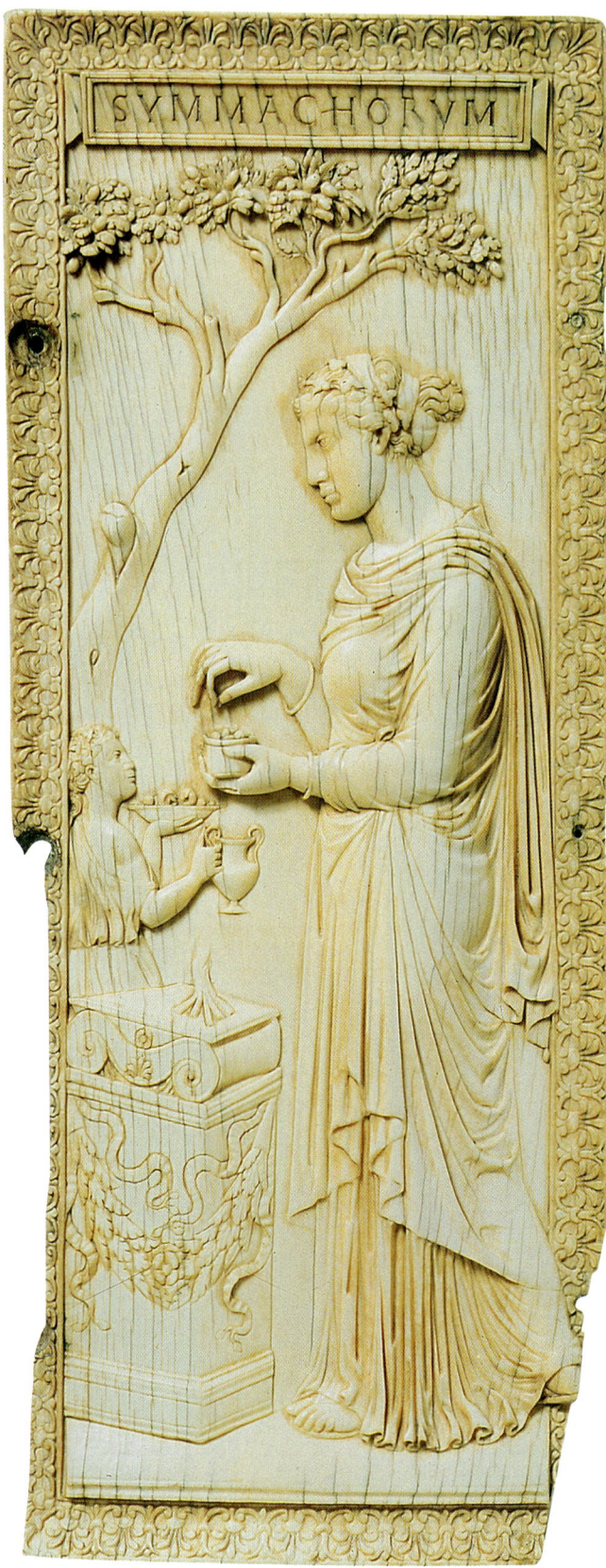

11-22 Priestess celebrating the rites of Bacchus, right leaf of the Diptych of the Nicomachi and the Symmachi, ca. 400. Ivory, $11\frac{3}{4}'' \times 5\frac{1}{2}''$. Victoria and Albert Museum, London.

the wound of the risen Christ. The series is one of the oldest cycles of Passion scenes preserved today. The artist who fashioned the casket helped establish the iconographical types maintained for a millennium for narratives of Christ's life.

On the London ivories, Jesus appears once again as a beardless youth. In the Crucifixion (FIG. 11-21), the earliest known rendition of the subject in the history of art, he exhibits a superhuman imperviousness to pain. The Savior is a muscular, nearly nude, heroic figure who appears virtually weightless. He does not *hang* from the cross; he is *displayed* on it, a divine being who has conquered death. The striking contrast between the powerful frontal unsuffering Jesus on the cross and the limp hanging body of his betrayer with his snapped neck is very effective, both visually and symbolically.

THE ENDURING PAGAN GODS It is important to remember that although after Constantine all the most important architectural projects in Italy were Christian in character, not everyone converted to the new religion, even after Theodosius closed all temples and banned all pagan cults in 391. An ivory plaque (FIG. **11-22**), probably produced in Rome around 400, strikingly exhibits the endurance of pagan themes and patrons and of the classical style. The ivory, one of a pair of leaves of a diptych, commemorates either the marriage of members of two powerful Roman families of the senatorial class, the Nicomachi and the Symmachi, or the passing within a decade of two prominent male members of the two families. Whether their purpose was to celebrate the living or the dead, the Nicomachi and the Symmachi here ostentatiously reaffirmed their faith in the old pagan gods. Certainly, they favored the aesthetic ideals of the classical past, as exemplified by such works as the stately processional friezes of the Greek Parthenon (see FIG. 5-48) and the Roman Ara Pacis (see FIG. 10-29).

The leaf we reproduce, inscribed "of the Symmachi," represents a pagan priestess in front of Jupiter's sacred oak tree. She wears ivy in her hair and seems to be celebrating the rites of both Bacchus and Jupiter at an open-air altar, although scholars dispute the identity of the divinities honored. The other diptych panel, inscribed "of the Nicomachi," shows a priestess honoring Ceres and Cybele. On both panels, the precise yet fluent and graceful line; the easy, gliding poses; and the mood of spiritual serenity reveal an artist who practiced within a still-vital classical tradition that idealized human beauty as its central focus.

The great senatorial magnates of Rome, who resisted the empirewide imposition of the Christian faith at the end of the fourth century probably deliberately sustained the classical tradition. Despite the great changes that had occurred in art during the later third and fourth centuries, classical values lived on. Many artists had turned away from Greco-Roman naturalism to something archaic, abstract, and bluntly expressive—as seen even in official imperial commissions such as the portraits of the tetrarchs (see FIG. 10-74) and the frieze of the Arch of Constantine (see FIG. 10-77). But for other artists and patrons, classical art was still the standard for measuring success. The classical tradition was never fully extinguished in the Middle Ages. It survived in intermittent revivals, renovations, and restorations side by side and in contrast with the opposing, nonclassicizing medieval styles. The rise of classical art to dominance in the Renaissance will be one of the signs of the end of the medieval world.

spear into the side of the "King of the Jews" (*REX IVD* is inscribed above Jesus' head). The two remaining panels show two Marys and two soldiers at the open doors of a tomb with an empty coffin within and the doubting Thomas touching

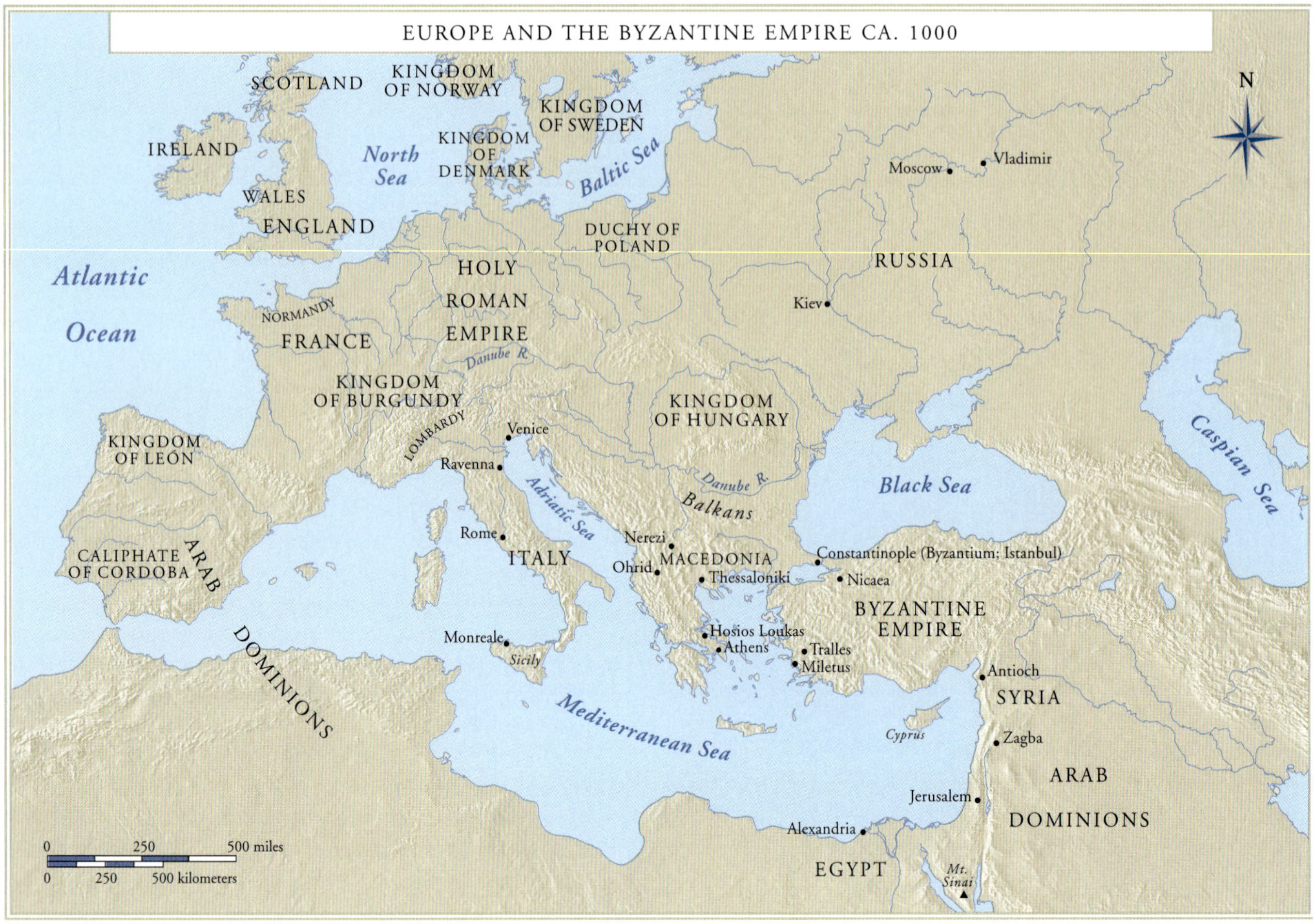

EUROPE AND THE BYZANTINE EMPIRE CA. 1000

SCOTLAND
KINGDOM OF NORWAY
IRELAND
KINGDOM OF SWEDEN
WALES
KINGDOM OF DENMARK
ENGLAND
North Sea
Baltic Sea
Moscow • Vladimir
DUCHY OF POLAND
RUSSIA
Atlantic Ocean
HOLY ROMAN EMPIRE
NORMANDY
FRANCE
Danube R.
Kiev
KINGDOM OF BURGUNDY
KINGDOM OF HUNGARY
Caspian Sea
LOMBARDY
Venice
KINGDOM OF LEÓN
Ravenna
Danube R.
Black Sea
Adriatic Sea
Balkans
CALIPHATE OF CORDOBA
ARAB DOMINIONS
Rome
Nerezi
Constantinople (Byzantium; Istanbul)
ITALY
Ohrid
MACEDONIA
Nicaea
Monreale
Thessaloniki
BYZANTINE EMPIRE
Sicily
Hosios Loukas
Athens
Tralles
Miletus
Antioch
SYRIA
Mediterranean Sea
Cyprus
Zagba
Jerusalem
ARAB DOMINIONS
Alexandria
EGYPT
Mt. Sinai

N

0   250   500 miles
0   250   500 kilometers

527			726	843	
Early Byzantine			Iconoclasm	Middle Byzantine	

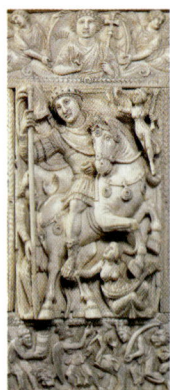

Barberini Ivory mid-sixth century

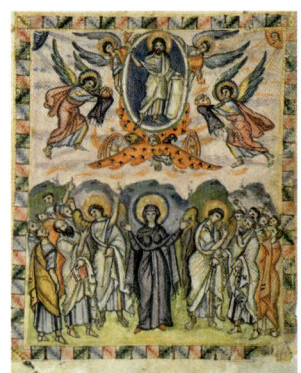

Rabbula Gospels, 586

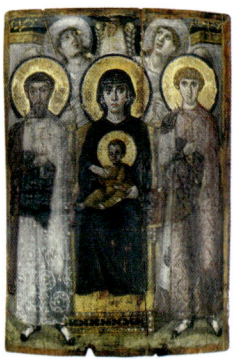

Virgin and Child icon Mount Sinai sixth–seventh century

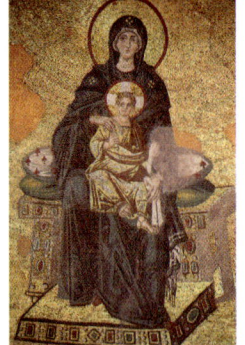

Apse mosaic, Hagia Sophia Constantinople, 867

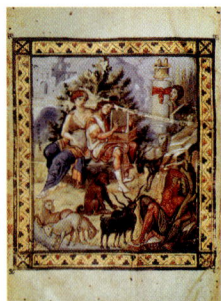

Paris Psalter, ca. 950–970

Fall of Ravenna to Odoacer; end of Western Roman Empire, 476

Heraclius defeats Persians, 627

Restoration of images, 843

Justinian the Great, r. 527–565

Arabs besiege Constantinople, 717–718

Basil I, r. 867–886, founder of Macedonian dynasty

Nika riots in Constantinople, 532

Leo III prohibits image making, 726

Belisarius captures Ravenna, 539

Ravenna falls to the Lombards, 751

Turks convert to Islam, ninth–tenth century

ROME IN THE EAST

THE ART OF BYZANTIUM

1000	1204	1453

LATE BYZANTINE

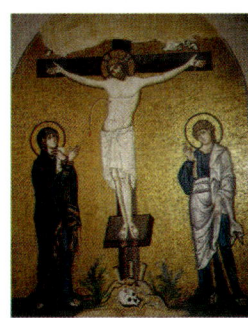

*Crucifixion mosaic
Church of the Dormition
Daphni, ca. 1090–1100*

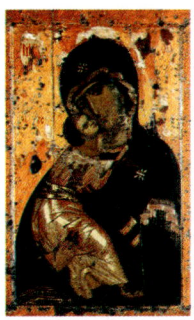

*Vladimir Virgin
late eleventh–
early twelfth century*

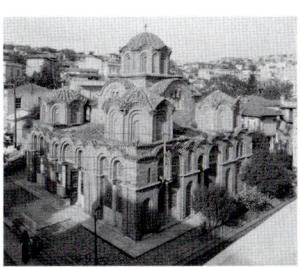

*Church of Saint Catherine
Thessaloniki, ca. 1280*

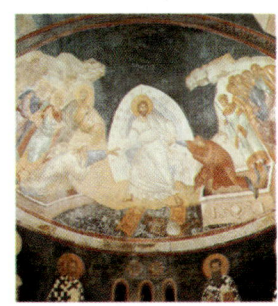

*Anastasis, Church of Christ
in Chora, Constantinople
ca. 1310–1320*

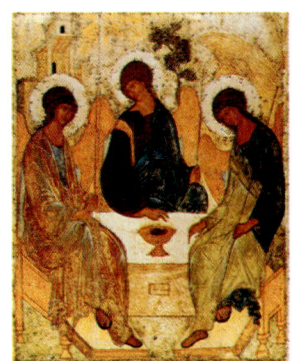

*Andrei Rublyev
Trinity icon, ca. 1410*

Basil II, r. 980–1001, revival of Byzantine power

Schism between Byzantine and Roman churches, 1054

Norman conquest of Sicily, 1060–1092

Seljuk Turks capture Byzantine Asia Minor, 1073

First Crusade, 1095–1099

Fourth Crusade and the Frankish conquest, 1202–1204

Michael VIII Palaeologus recaptures
Constantinople from the Franks, 1261

Ottoman Turks
capture Constantinople;
end of Byzantine
Empire, 1453

BYZANTIUM: THE NEW ROME

THE EASTERN CHRISTIAN EMPIRE When Constantine I founded a "New Rome" in the East in 324 on the site of the ancient Greek city of Byzantium and called it Constantinople in honor of himself, he legitimately could claim to be ruler of a united Roman Empire. In the fifth century, however, that empire, by then officially a Christian state, fell apart. An Emperor of the West ruled from Ravenna and an Emperor of the East ruled from Constantinople. Though not formally codified, the division of the Roman Empire became permanent. Centralized government disintegrated in the western half and was replaced by warring kingdoms that, during the Middle Ages, formed the foundations of the modern western European nations. The eastern half of the Roman Empire, only loosely connected by religion to the west, and with only minor territorial holdings there, had a long and complex history of its own. Centered at New Rome, the Eastern Christian Empire remained a cultural and political entity for a millennium, until the last of a long list of Eastern Roman emperors, ironically named Constantine XI, died at Constantinople in 1453, vainly defending it against the Ottoman Turks.

Historians call that Eastern Christian Roman Empire "Byzantium," after its capital city's original name, and use the term *Byzantine* to identify whatever pertains to Byzantium—its territory, its history, and its culture. The Byzantine emperors, however, did not use these terms to define themselves. They called their empire "Rome" *(Romania)* and themselves "Romans" *(Romaioi).* Though they spoke Greek and not Latin, the Eastern Roman emperors never relinquished their claim as the legitimate successors to the ancient Roman emperors. Nevertheless, *Byzantium* and *Byzantine,* though inexact terms, have become in modern times the accepted designations for the Eastern Roman Empire, and we shall use them here.

Byzantium preserved its identity throughout alternating periods of good rule and misrule, stability and instability, expansion and contraction, and victory and defeat. When its shrinking borders reduced it to a mere fragment of the once mighty Byzantine Empire, when it became only a small medieval Greek kingdom, an enclave around the city of Constantinople, it still was stubbornly "Rome." As such, it had resisted successive assaults of Sasanian Persians, Arabs, Russians, Serbs, Normans, Franks, Venetians, and others, until it finally was overcome by the surging power of the Ottoman Turks. During the long course of its history, Byzantium was the Christian buffer against the expansion of Islam into central and northern Europe, and its cultural influence was felt repeatedly in Europe throughout the Middle Ages. Byzantium Christianized the Slavic peoples of the Balkans and of Russia, giving them its Orthodox religion and alphabet, its literary culture, and its art and architecture. Byzantium's collapse in 1453 brought the Ottoman Empire into Europe as far as the Danube River, but the effect of Constantinople's fall was felt even further to the west. The westward flight of Byzantine scholars from the Rome of the East introduced the study of classical Greek to Italy and helped inspire there the new consciousness of antiquity that historians call the Renaissance.

THE THEOCRATIC STATE Constantine recognized Christianity at the beginning of the fourth century, Theodosius established it as the Roman Empire's official religion at the end of the fourth century, and Justinian, in the sixth century, proclaimed it New Rome's only *lawful* religion. By that time it was not simply the Christian religion but the *Orthodox* Christian doctrine that the Byzantine emperor asserted as the only permissible faith for his subjects. This Orthodox Christianity was *trinitarian.* Its central article of faith was the trinity of Father, Son, and Holy Spirit (as stated in Roman Catholic, Protestant, and Eastern Orthodox creeds today). All other versions of Christianity were called heresies, especially the *Arian,* which denied the equality of the three aspects of the Trinity, and the *Monophysite,* which denied the duality of the divine and human natures in Jesus Christ. Justinian considered it his first duty not only to stamp out the few surviving pagan cults but also to crush all those who professed any Christian doctrine other than the Orthodox.

The Byzantine emperors were believed to be the earthly vicars of Jesus Christ, whose imperial will was God's will. They alone exercised all temporal and spiritual authority. As sole executives for church and state, the emperors shared power with neither senate nor church council. As theocrats they reigned supreme, combining the functions of both pope and caesar, which the Western Christian world would keep strictly separate. The Byzantine emperors' exalted and godlike position made them quasi-divine. Their church was simply an extension of the imperial court, and the imperial court, with its hierarchies of lesser and greater functionaries converging upward to the throne, was an image of the Kingdom of Heaven.

In practice, the Byzantine emperors' attempt to make real the ideal of absolute political and religious unity was a failure. They ruled over peoples of great ethnic, religious, cultural, and linguistic diversity, with varying histories and institutions—Armenians, Syrians, Egyptians, Palestinians, Jews, and Arabs, as well as Greeks, Italians, Germans, Slavs, and many others. Many of these were heretical Christians, and Byzantine efforts to force Orthodoxy on them in the interest of political and doctrinal unity led to bitter resistance, especially in Monophysite Egypt and Syria. When Islam made its way into the Byzantine Empire in the seventh century, the disaffected peoples of these provinces gave it ready support. While religious intolerance lost the great Eastern provinces, the same rigid Orthodoxy also eventually severed its last ties to the Latin Christianity of the West.

A THRICE GLORIOUS EMPIRE The Byzantine Empire's unity, fragmented from invasions by hostile peoples and hostile creeds, also was regularly disrupted by events at home: palace intrigues, conspiracies and betrayals, bureaucratic corruption, violent religious controversy, civil commotions, rebellions, and assassinations. Yet with characteristic resilience, Byzantium, in three periods of revived energy, recovered from dismal defeats, disunity, and stagnation. At those times intelligent, able, and successful rulers in war and peace guided the state. Under them Byzantium prospered and its culture flourished. These were the periods when the unique stylistic features of Byzantine art and architecture were shaped and refined.

Art historians divide the history of Byzantine art into the three periods of its greatest glory, sometimes referred to as "golden ages." The first, *Early Byzantine,* extends from the age of the emperor Justinian (r. 527–565) to the onset of *Iconoclasm* (the destruction of images used in religious worship)

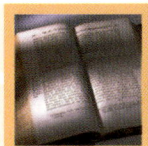

The Emperors of New Rome

Byzantine art is generally, and properly, considered to belong to the Middle Ages rather than to the ancient world, but the emperors of Byzantium, New Rome, considered themselves the direct successors of the emperors of Old Rome. Although the official state religion was Christianity and all pagan cults were suppressed, the political imagery of Byzantine art displays a striking continuity between ancient Rome and medieval Byzantium. Artists continued to portray emperors sitting on thrones holding the orb of the earth in their hands, battling foes while riding on mighty horses, and receiving tribute from defeated enemies. Official portraits continued to be set up in great numbers throughout the territories Byzantium controlled. But, as was true of the classical world, much of imperial Byzantine statuary is forever lost. However, some of the lost portraits of the Byzantine emperors can be visualized from miniature versions of them on ivory reliefs such as the *Barberini Ivory* (FIG. 12-1) and from descriptions in surviving texts.

One especially impressive portrait in the Roman imperial tradition, melted down long ago, depicted the emperor Justinian on horseback atop a grandiose column. Cast in glittering bronze, like the equestrian statue of Marcus Aurelius (see FIG. 10-59), set up nearly four hundred years earlier, it attested to the continuity between the art of Old and New Rome, where pompous imperial images were commonly displayed at the apex of freestanding columns. (Compare FIG. 10-42, where a statue of Saint Peter has replaced a lost statue of the emperor Trajan.) Procopius, the sixth-century historian who chronicled Justinian's wars and who wrote, at the emperor's behest, a treatise on his ambitious building program, described the equestrian portrait:

> Finest bronze, cast into panels and wreaths, encompasses the stones [of the column] on all sides, both binding them securely together and covering them with adornment. . . . This bronze is in color softer than pure gold, while in value it does not fall much short of an equal weight of silver. At the summit of the column stands a huge bronze horse turned towards the east, a most noteworthy sight. . . . Upon this horse is mounted a bronze image of the Emperor like a colossus. . . . He wears a cuirass in heroic fashion and his head is covered with a helmet . . . and a kind of radiance flashes forth from there. . . . He gazes towards the rising sun, steering his course, I suppose, against the Persians. In his left hand he holds a globe, by which the sculptor has signified that the whole earth and sea were subject to him, yet he carries neither sword nor spear nor any other weapon, but a cross surmounts his globe, by virtue of which alone he has won the kingship and victory in war. Stretching forth his right hand towards the regions of the East and spreading out his fingers, he commands the barbarians that dwell there to remain at home and not to advance any further. [1]

Statues such as this are the missing links in an imperial tradition that never really died and that lived on also in the Holy Roman Empire of the Western medieval world (see FIG. 16-11) and in the Renaissance (see FIGS. 21-32 and 21-33).

[1] Cyril Mango, trans., *The Art of the Byzantine Empire, 312–1453: Sources and Documents* (Englewood Cliffs, NJ: Prentice-Hall, 1972), 110–11.

under Leo III in 726. The *Middle Byzantine* period begins with the renunciation of Iconoclasm in 843 and ends with the western Crusaders' occupation of Constantinople in 1204. *Late Byzantine* corresponds to a third golden age in the fourteenth and early fifteenth centuries after the Byzantines recaptured Constantinople in 1261 until its final loss in 1453 to the Ottoman Turks and the conversion of many Christian churches to Islamic mosques.

EARLY BYZANTINE ART (527–726)

THE GOLDEN AGE OF JUSTINIAN The reign of Justinian and his politically astute consort, the Empress Theodora, marks the end of the Late Roman Empire and the beginning of the Byzantine Empire. At this time Byzantine art emerged as a recognizably novel and distinctive style, leaving behind the uncertainties and hesitations of Early Christian artistic experiment. Though still revealing its sources in late antique art, it definitively expressed, with a new independence and power of invention, the unique character of the Eastern Christian culture centered at Constantinople.

Under Justinian, the Roman Empire's power and extent were briefly restored. Justinian's generals, Belisarius and Narses, drove the German Ostrogoths out of Italy, expelled the German Vandals from the African provinces, beat back the Bulgars on the northern frontier, and held the Sasanian Persians at bay on the eastern borders. At home, a dangerous rebellion of political/religious factions in the city was put down, and Orthodoxy triumphed over the Monophysite heresy. In Constantinople alone Justinian built or restored more than thirty churches of the Orthodox faith, and his activities as builder extended throughout the Byzantine Empire. The historian of his reign, Procopius, declared that the emperor's ambitious building program was an obsession that cost his subjects dearly in taxation. But his grand monuments defined the Byzantine style in architecture forever after. Justinian also supervised the codification of Roman law in a great work known as the *Corpus Juris Civilis (Code of Civil Law)*, which became the foundation of the law systems of many modern European nations. Justinian could claim, with considerable justification, to have revived the glory of "Old Rome" in New Rome (see "The Emperors of New Rome," above).

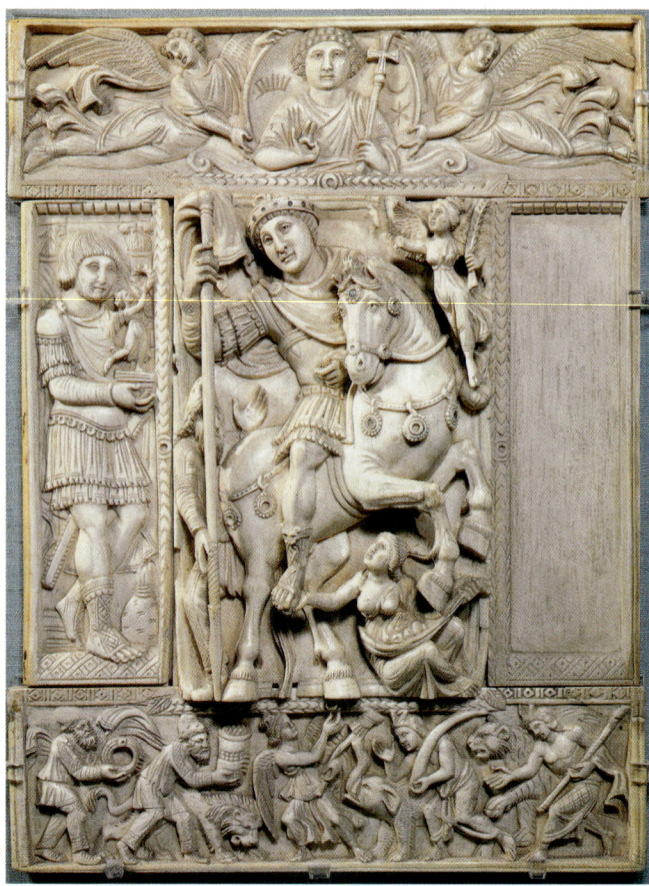

12-1 Justinian as world conqueror, left leaf of a diptych *(Barberini Ivory)*, mid-sixth century. Ivory, 1′ 1½″ × 10½″. Louvre, Paris.

Luxury Arts

JUSTINIAN THE CONQUEROR The triumphant image of Justinian's New Rome was set forth for all to see on an ivory plaque known today as the *Barberini Ivory* (FIG. **12-1**). Carved in five parts (one is lost), the *Barberini Ivory* shows at the center an emperor, usually identified as Justinian, riding triumphantly on a rearing horse, while a startled, half-hidden barbarian recoils in fear behind him. The dynamic twisting postures of both horse and rider and the motif of the spear-thrusting equestrian emperor are survivals of the pagan Roman Empire, as are the personifications of bountiful Earth (below the horse) and palm-bearing Victory (flying in to crown the conqueror). Also borrowed from pagan art are the tribute-bearing and clemency-seeking barbarians at the bottom of the plaque. They are juxtaposed with a lion, elephant, and tiger, exotic animals native to Africa and Asia, sites of Justinianic conquest. At the left, a Roman soldier carries a statuette of another Victory, reinforcing the central panel's message.

The source of the emperor's strength, however, comes not from his earthly armies but from God. The uppermost panel depicts two angels holding aloft a youthful image of Christ carrying a cross in his left hand. Christ blesses Justinian with a gesture of his right hand, indicating approval of Justinian's rule. Still conceived in the language of classical art, the *Barberini Ivory* announced Byzantium's theocratic state.

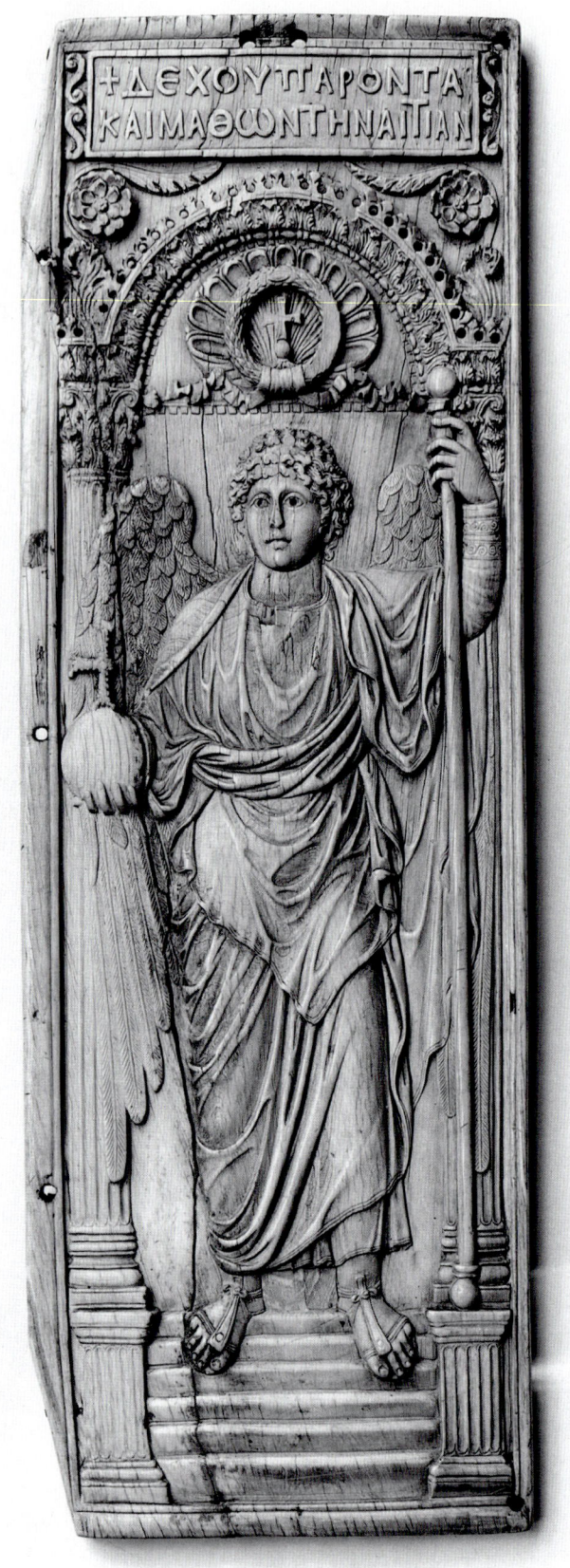

12-2 Saint Michael the Archangel, right leaf of a diptych, early sixth century. Ivory, approx. 1′ 5″ × 5½″. British Museum, London.

VICTORY BECOMES AN ARCHANGEL Another ivory panel (FIG. **12-2**), created somewhat earlier than the *Barberini Ivory* and likewise carved in the Eastern Christian Empire, perhaps in Constantinople, offers still further evidence of classical art's persistence. The panel, depicting Saint

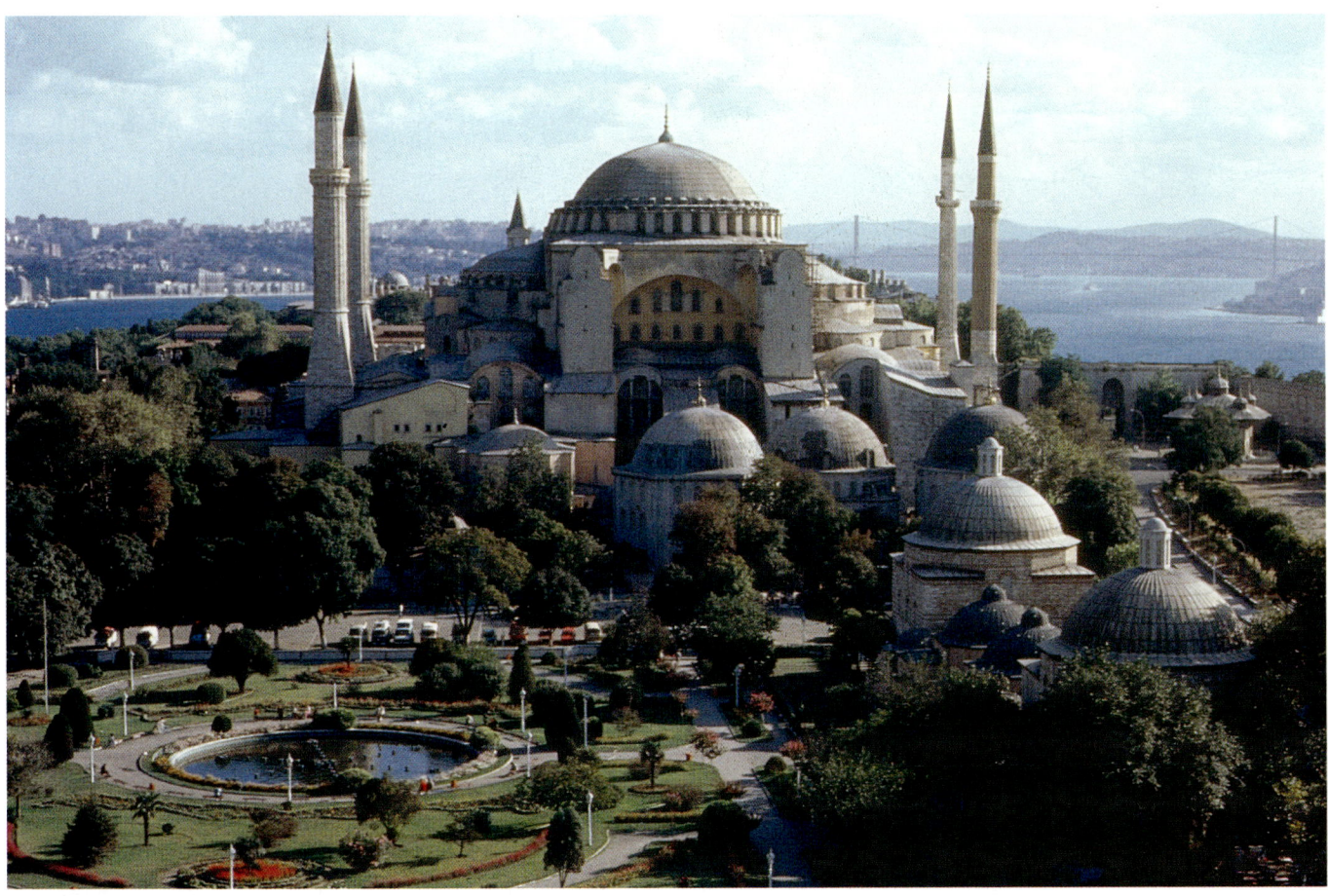

12-3 ANTHEMIUS OF TRALLES and ISIDORUS OF MILETUS, Hagia Sophia, Constantinople (Istanbul), Turkey, 532–537.

Michael the Archangel, is all that is preserved of what was once a hinged diptych in the Early Christian tradition. The prototype of Michael must have been a pagan winged Victory, although Victory was personified as a woman in Greco-Roman art. Instead of carrying the palm branch of victory, as does the Victory on the *Barberini Ivory,* Michael holds forth an orb surmounted by a cross, the symbol of Christianity's triumph. He may have been offering it to a Byzantine emperor depicted on the missing diptych leaf. The flowing classical drapery, the delicately incised wings, and the facial type and coiffure are also of the pre-Christian tradition.

Nonetheless, significant divergences—misinterpretations of or lack of concern for the rules of naturalistic representation—occur here. Subtle ambiguities in the figure's relationship to its architectural setting include such details as the feet hovering above the steps without any real relationship to them and the placement of the upper body, wings, and arms in front of the column shafts while the lower body is behind the column bases at the top of the receding staircase. These details, of course, have little to do with the angel's striking beauty, but they do signify the emergence of a new aesthetic that characterized Byzantine art for centuries. Rejecting the goal of most classical artists to render the three-dimensional world in convincing and consistent fashion and to people that world with fully modeled figures firmly rooted on the ground, the Byzantine artist introduced uncertainties in the spatial setting and rendered figures that seem more to float than to stand.

Architecture and Mosaics

BYZANTIUM'S GREATEST CHURCH The sense of weightlessness, of miraculous suspension in midair, is also characteristic of the most important monument of early Byzantine art, albeit in a very different way. Hagia Sophia (FIG. **12-3**), the church of Holy Wisdom, was built in Constantinople for Justinian by ANTHEMIUS OF TRALLES and ISIDORUS OF MILETUS between 532 and 537. It is Byzantium's grandest building and one of the supreme accomplishments of world architecture. Its dimensions are formidable for any structure not made of steel. In plan (FIG. **12-4**), it is about two hundred seventy feet long and two hundred forty feet wide. The dome is one hundred eight feet in diameter, and its crown rises some one hundred eighty feet above the pavement. (The first dome collapsed in 558 and was replaced by the present one, greater in height and more stable.) In scale, Hagia Sophia rivals the architectural wonders of pagan and Christian Rome: the Pantheon, the Baths of Caracalla, and the Basilica of Constantine. In exterior view, the great dome dominates the structure, but the building's present external aspects are much changed from their original appearance. Huge buttresses were added to the Justinianic design, and four towering Turkish minarets were constructed after the Ottoman conquest of 1453, when Hagia Sophia became an Islamic mosque. The building was secularized in the twentieth century and is now a museum.

12-4 ANTHEMIUS OF TRALLES and ISIDORUS OF MILETUS, longitudinal section and plan of Hagia Sophia, Constantinople (Istanbul), Turkey, 532–537 (after drawings by Van Nice and Antoniades).

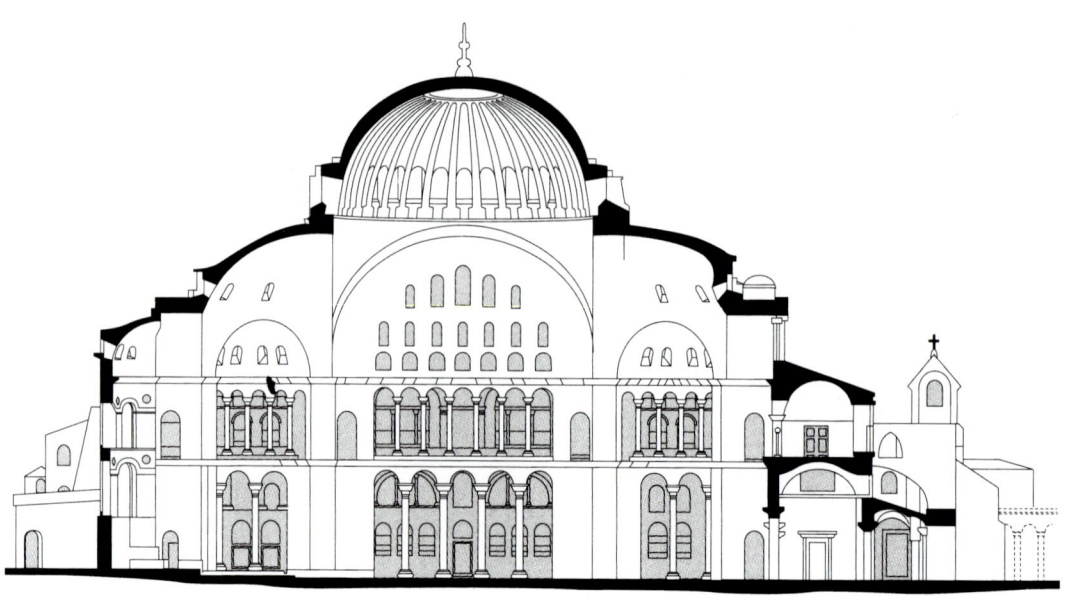

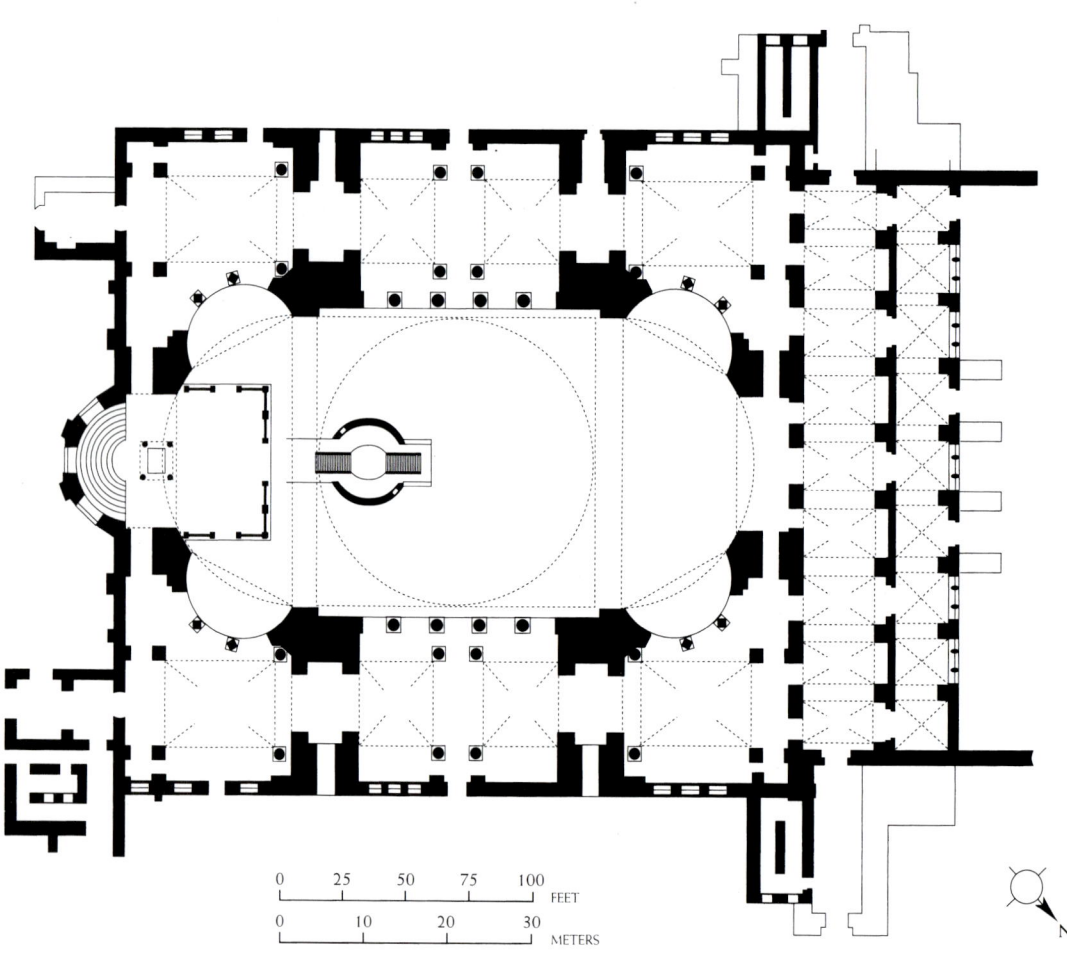

The characteristic Byzantine plainness and unpretentious-ness of the exterior (which, in this case, also disguise the great scale) scarcely prepare visitors for the building's interior (FIG. **12-5**), which was once richly appointed. A contemporaneous poet and member of Justinian's court, Paulus Silentiarius, recorded his impressions of Hagia Sophia. His words allow readers to visualize the original magnificence of the interior, whose walls and floors were clad with colored stones from all over the known world:

Who . . . shall sing the marble meadows gathered upon the mighty walls and spreading pavement. . . . [There is stone] from the green

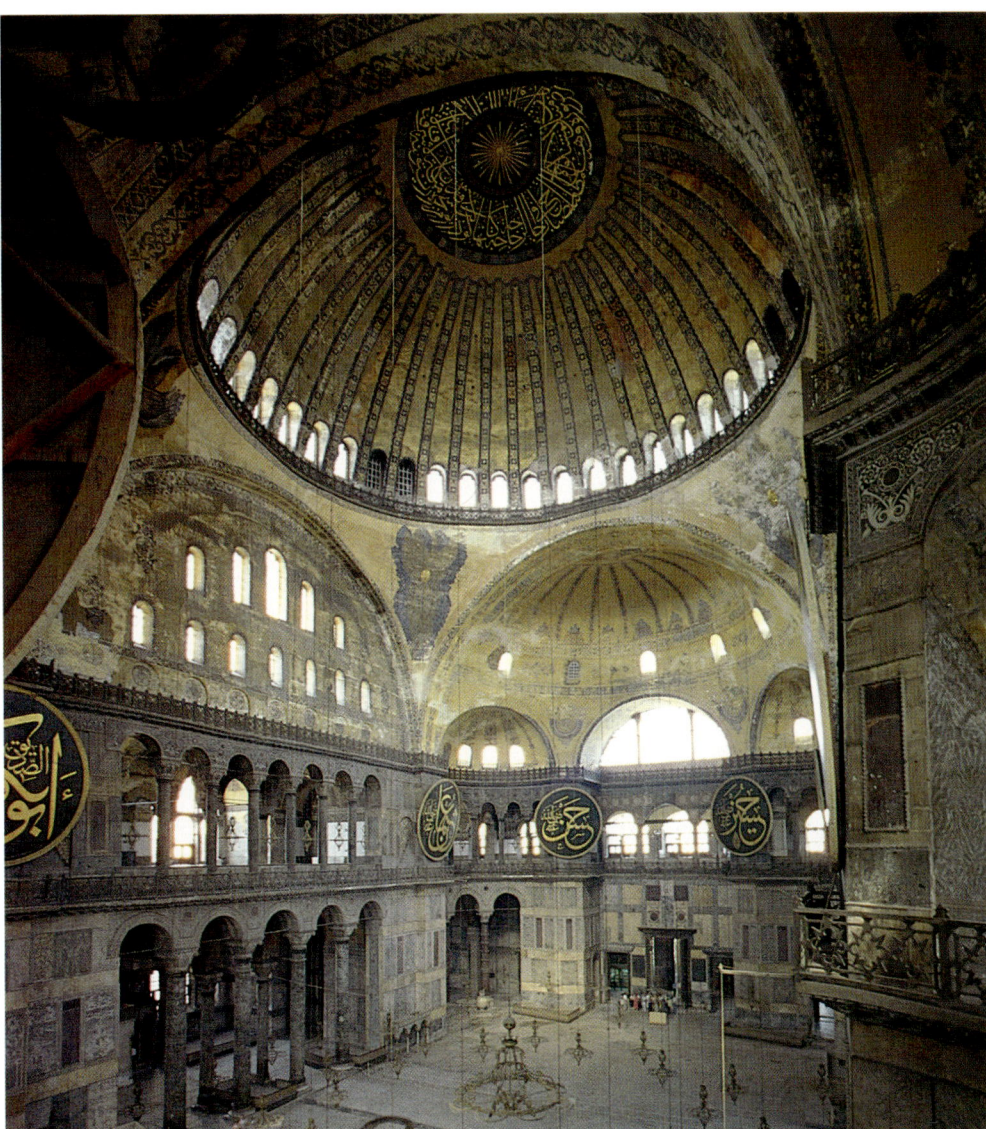

12-5 ANTHEMIUS OF TRALLES and ISIDORUS OF MILETUS, interior of Hagia Sophia, Constantinople (Istanbul), Turkey, 532–537.

flanks of Carystus [and] the speckled Phrygian stone, sometimes rosy mixed with white, sometimes gleaming with purple and silver flowers. There is a wealth of porphyry stone, too, besprinkled with little bright stars. . . . You may see the bright green stone of Laconia and the glittering marble with wavy veins found in the deep gullies of the Iasian peaks, exhibiting slanting streaks of blood-red and livid white; the pale yellow with swirling red from the Lydian headland; the glittering crocus-like golden stone [of Libya]; . . . glittering [Celtic] black [with] here and there an abundance of milk; the pale onyx with glint of precious metal; and [Thessalian marble] in parts vivid green not unlike emerald. . . . It has spots resembling snow next to flashes of black so that in one stone various beauties mingle.[1]

THE MYSTICISM OF LIGHT   What distinguishes Hagia Sophia from the equally lavishly revetted and paved interiors of Roman buildings such as the Pantheon (see FIG. 10-50) is the special mystical quality of the light that floods the interior (FIG. 12-5). The soaring canopy-like dome that dominates the inside as well as the outside of the church rides on a halo of light from windows in the dome's base. Visitors to Hagia Sophia from Justinian's time to today have been struck by the light within the church and its effect on the human spirit. The forty windows at the dome's base create the peculiar illusion that the dome is resting on the light that pours through them. The historian Procopius observed that the dome looked as if it were suspended by "a golden chain from Heaven." Said he: "You might say that the space is not illuminated by the sun from the outside, but that the radiance is generated within, so great an abundance of light bathes this shrine all around."[2]

The poet Paulus compared the dome to "the firmament which rests on air" and described the vaulting as covered with "gilded tesserae from which a glittering stream of golden rays pours abundantly and strikes men's eyes with irresistible force. It is as if one were gazing at the midday sun in spring."[3] Thus, Hagia Sophia has a vastness of space shot through with light and a central dome that *appears* to be supported by the light it admits. Light is the mystic element—light that glitters in the mosaics, shines forth from the marbles, and pervades and defines spaces that, in themselves, seem to escape definition. Light seems to dissolve material substance and transform it into an abstract spiritual vision. Pseudo-Diony-

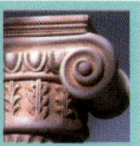

ARCHITECTURAL BASICS

Pendentives and Squinches

Perhaps the most characteristic feature of Byzantine architecture is the placement of a dome, which is circular at its base, over a square, as in the Justinianic church of Hagia Sophia (FIGS. 12-3 to 12-5) and countless later structures (for example, FIGS. 12-19 and 12-22). Two structural devices that are the hallmark of Byzantine engineering made this feat possible: *pendentives* and *squinches*.

In pendentive construction (from the Latin *pendere,* "to hang") a dome rests on what is, in effect, a second, larger dome. The top portion and four segments around the rim of the larger dome are omitted so that four curved triangles, or pendentives, are formed. The pendentives join to form a ring and four arches whose planes bound a square. The dome's weight is thus transferred through the pendentives and arches to the four piers from which the arches spring, instead of to the walls. The first use of pendentives on a monumental scale was in Hagia Sophia in the mid-sixth century, although Near Eastern architects had experimented with them earlier. In Roman and Early Christian central-plan buildings, such as the Pantheon (see FIG. 10-50) and Santa Costanza (see FIGS. 11-9 and 11-10), the domes spring directly from the circular top of a cylinder (see "The Roman Architectural Revolution: Concrete Construction," Chapter 10, page 249).

The pendentive system is a dynamic solution to the problem of setting a round dome over a square or rectangular

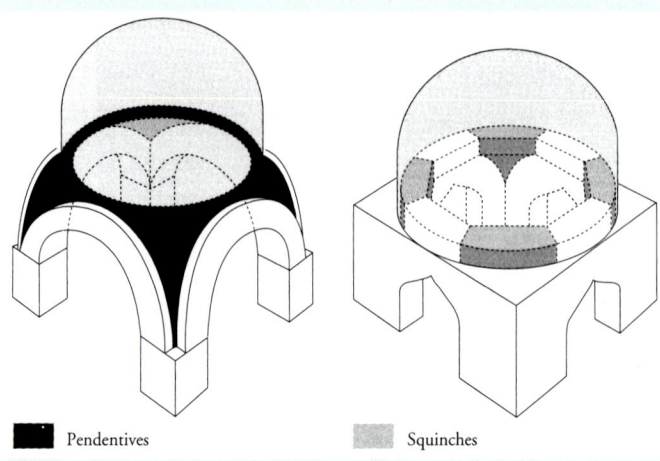

◼ Pendentives   ▨ Squinches

Domes on pendentives *(left)* and squinches *(right).*

space, making possible a union of centralized and longitudinal or basilican structures. A similar effect can be achieved using squinches—arches, corbels, or lintels—that bridge the corners of the supporting walls and form an octagon inscribed within a square. To achieve even greater height, a builder can rest a dome on a cylindrical drum that in turn rests on either pendentives or squinches, but the principle of supporting a dome over a square is the same.

sius, perhaps the most influential mystic philosopher of the age, wrote in *The Divine Names:* "Light comes from the Good and . . . light is the visual image of God." [4]

How was this illusion of a floating "dome of Heaven" achieved? Justinian's architects used *pendentives* (see "Pendentives and Squinches" above) to transfer the weight from the great dome to the piers beneath, rather than to the walls. With pendentives, not only could the space beneath the dome be unobstructed but the walls themselves could be pierced by scores of windows. This created the impression of a dome suspended above, not held up by, walls mortals built. Experts *today* can explain the technical virtuosity of Anthemius and Isidorus, but it remained a mystery to their contemporaries. Procopius communicated the sense of wonderment experienced by those who entered Justinian's great church: "No matter how much they concentrate their attention on this and that, and examine everything with contracted eyebrows, they are unable to understand the craftsmanship and always depart from there amazed by the perplexing spectacle." [5]

THE DOMED BASILICA By placing a hemispherical dome on a square base instead of on a circular base, as in the Pantheon, Anthemius and Isidorus succeeded in fusing two previously independent and seemingly mutually exclusive architectural traditions: the vertically oriented central-plan

building and the longitudinally oriented basilica. Hagia Sophia is, in essence, a domed basilica (FIGS. 12-4 and 12-5) —a uniquely successful conclusion to several centuries of experimentation in Christian church architecture. However, the thrusts of the pendentive construction at Hagia Sophia made other elements necessary: huge wall piers to the north and south and, to the east and west, half-domes, whose thrusts descend, in turn, into still smaller domes covering columned niches that give a curving flow to the design.

The diverse vistas and screenlike ornamented surfaces mask the structural lines. The arcades of the nave and galleries have no real structural function. Like the walls they pierce, they are only part of a fragile "fill" between the huge piers. Structurally, although Hagia Sophia may seem Roman in its great scale and majesty, it does not have Roman organization of its masses. The very fact the "walls" in Hagia Sophia are actually concealed (and barely adequate) piers indicates that the architects sought Roman monumentality as an *effect* and did not design the building according to Roman principles. Using brick in place of concrete marked a further departure from Roman practice and characterizes Byzantine architecture as a distinctive structural style. Hagia Sophia's eight great supporting piers are ashlar masonry, but the screen walls are brick, as are the vaults of the aisles and galleries and the dome and semicircular half-domes known as *conches.*

BYZANTINE LITURGY AND THE EMPEROR The ingenious design of Hagia Sophia provided the illumination and the setting for the solemn liturgy of the Orthodox faith. The large windows along the great dome's rim poured light down upon the interior's jeweled splendor, where priests staged the sacred spectacle. Sung by clerical choirs, the Orthodox equivalent of the Latin Mass celebrated the sacrament of the Eucharist at the altar in the apsidal sanctuary, in spiritual reenactment of Jesus' Crucifixion. Processions of chanting priests, accompanying the patriarch (bishop) of Constantinople, moved slowly to and from the sanctuary and the vast nave. The gorgeous array of their vestments (compare FIG. 12-35) rivaled the interior's polychrome marbles, metals, and mosaics, all glowing in shafts of light from the dome.

The nave of Hagia Sophia, as in all Byzantine churches, was reserved for the clergy not the congregation. The laity, segregated by sex, were confined to the shadows of the aisles and galleries, restrained in most places by marble parapets. The complex spatial arrangement allowed only partial views of the brilliant ceremony. The emperor alone was privileged to enter the sanctuary. When he participated with the patriarch in the liturgical drama, his rule was again sanctified and his person exalted. Church and state were symbolically made one, as in fact they were. The church building was then the earthly image of the court of Heaven, its light the image of God and God's holy wisdom.

At Hagia Sophia, the intricate logic of Greek theology, the ambitious scale of Rome, the vaulting tradition of the Near East, and the mysticism of Eastern Christianity combined to create a monument that is at once a summation of antiquity and a positive assertion of the triumph of Christian faith.

RAVENNA, BYZANTIUM'S SACRED FORTRESS In 493, Theodoric, the Ostrogoths' greatest king, chose the Italian city of Ravenna as the capital of his kingdom, which encompassed much of the Balkans and all of Italy (see Chapter 11). During the short history of Theodoric's unfortunate successors, the importance of the city declined. But in 539, the Byzantine general Belisarius conquered Ravenna for his emperor, Justinian, and led the city into the third and most important stage of its history. Reunited with the Eastern Empire, Ravenna remained the "sacred fortress" of Byzantium, a Byzantine foothold in Italy for two hundred years, until its conquest first by the Lombards and then by the Franks.

Ravenna enjoyed its greatest cultural and economic prosperity during Justinian's reign, at a time when repeated sieges, conquests, and sackings threatened the "eternal city" of Rome with complete extinction. As the seat of Byzantine dominion in Italy, ruled by Byzantine governors, or *exarchs,* Ravenna and its culture became an extension of Constantinople. Its art, miraculously preserved today despite heavy bombing during World War II, even more than that of the Byzantine capital (where relatively little outside of architecture has survived), clearly reveals the transition from the Early Christian to the Byzantine style.

SAN VITALE, MARTYR'S SHRINE San Vitale (FIGS. **12-6** to **12-9**), dedicated by Bishop Maximianus in 547 in honor of Saint Vitalis, who was martyred at Ravenna in the second century, is the most spectacular building in Ravenna. The church is an unforgettable experience for all who have entered it and marveled at its intricate design and magnificent golden mosaics. Construction of San Vitale began under Bishop Ecclesius shortly after Theodoric's death in 526. Julianus Argentarius (Julian the banker) provided the enormous sum of 26,000 gold *solidi* (weighing in excess of three hundred fifty pounds) required to proceed with the work. The church is unlike any of the other Early Christian churches of Ravenna. Indeed, it is unlike any other church in Italy. Although it has a traditional plain exterior and a polygonal apse, San Vitale is not a basilica. It is centrally

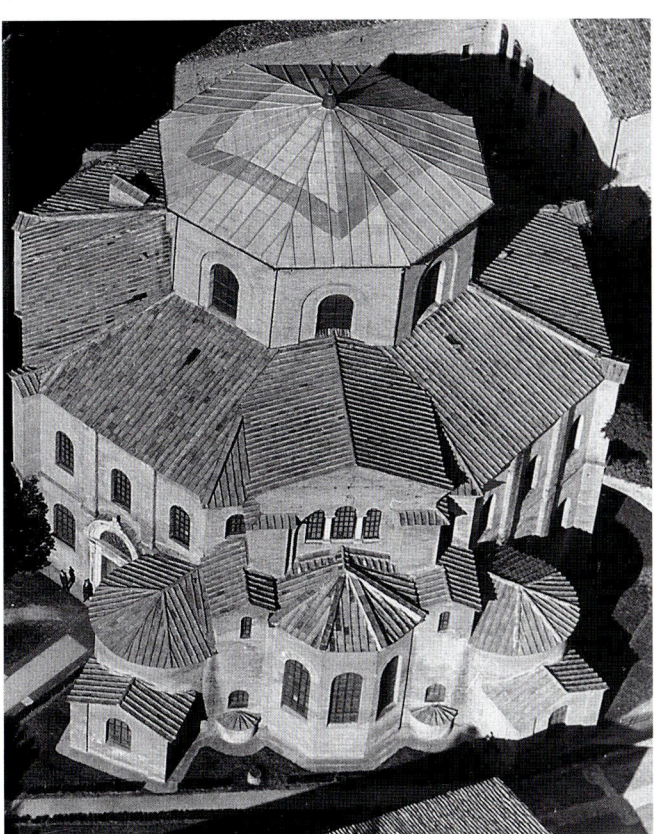

12-6 Aerial view of San Vitale, Ravenna, Italy, 526–547.

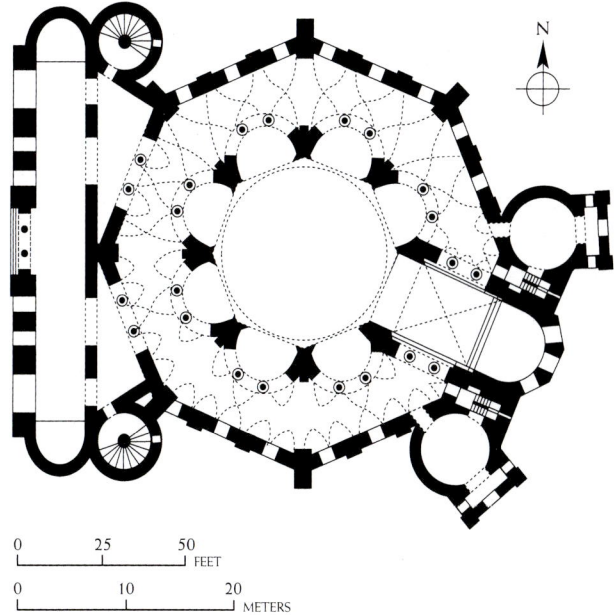

12-7 Plan of San Vitale, Ravenna, Italy, 526–547.

planned, like Justinian's churches in Constantinople, and it seems, in fact, to have been loosely modeled on the earlier Church of Saints Sergius and Bacchus there.

The design features two concentric octagons. The dome-covered inner octagon rises above the surrounding octagon to provide the interior with clerestory lighting (FIG. 12-6). The central space is defined by eight large piers that alternate with curved, columned niches, pushing outward into the surrounding ambulatory (FIG. 12-8) and creating, on the plan (FIG. 12-7), an intricate eight-leafed design. These niches effect a close integration between inner and outer spaces that, otherwise, would have existed simply side by side as independent units. A cross-vaulted choir (FIG. 12-9) preceding the apse interrupts the ambulatory and gives the plan some axial stability. This effect is weakened, however, by the unsymmetrical placement of the narthex (FIG. 12-7), whose odd angle never has been explained fully. (The atrium, which no longer exists, may have paralleled a street that ran in the same direction as the angle of the narthex.) The ambulatory has a second story, the gallery (FIG. 12-8), which was reserved for women and is a typical element of Byzantine churches.

San Vitale's intricate plan and elevation combine to produce an effect of great complexity. The exterior's octagonal regularity is not readily apparent inside. A rich diversity of ever-changing perspectives greets visitors walking through the building (FIGS. 12-8 and 12-9). Arches looping over arches, curving and flattened spaces, and wall and vault shapes seem to change constantly with the viewer's position. Light filtered through alabaster-paned windows plays over the glittering mosaics and glowing marbles that cover the building's complex surfaces, producing a sumptuous effect.

CHURCH AND STATE UNITED   The mosaics that decorate San Vitale's choir and apse (FIG. 12-9), like the building itself, must be regarded as one of the climactic achievements of Byzantine art. Completed less than a decade after the Ostrogoths surrendered Ravenna, the apse and choir decorations proclaim the triumph of Justinian and of the Orthodox faith. The sanctuary's multiple panels form a unified composition, whose theme is the holy ratification of the emperor's right to rule.

In the apse vault, the Second Coming was represented. Christ, youthful in the Early Christian tradition, holds a scroll with seven seals (Rev. 5:1) and sits on the orb of the world. The four rivers of Paradise flow beneath him, and rainbow-hued clouds float above. Christ extends a golden wreath of victory to Vitalis, the patron saint of the church, introduced here by an angel. At Christ's left, another angel introduces Bishop Ecclesius, in whose time the church foundations were

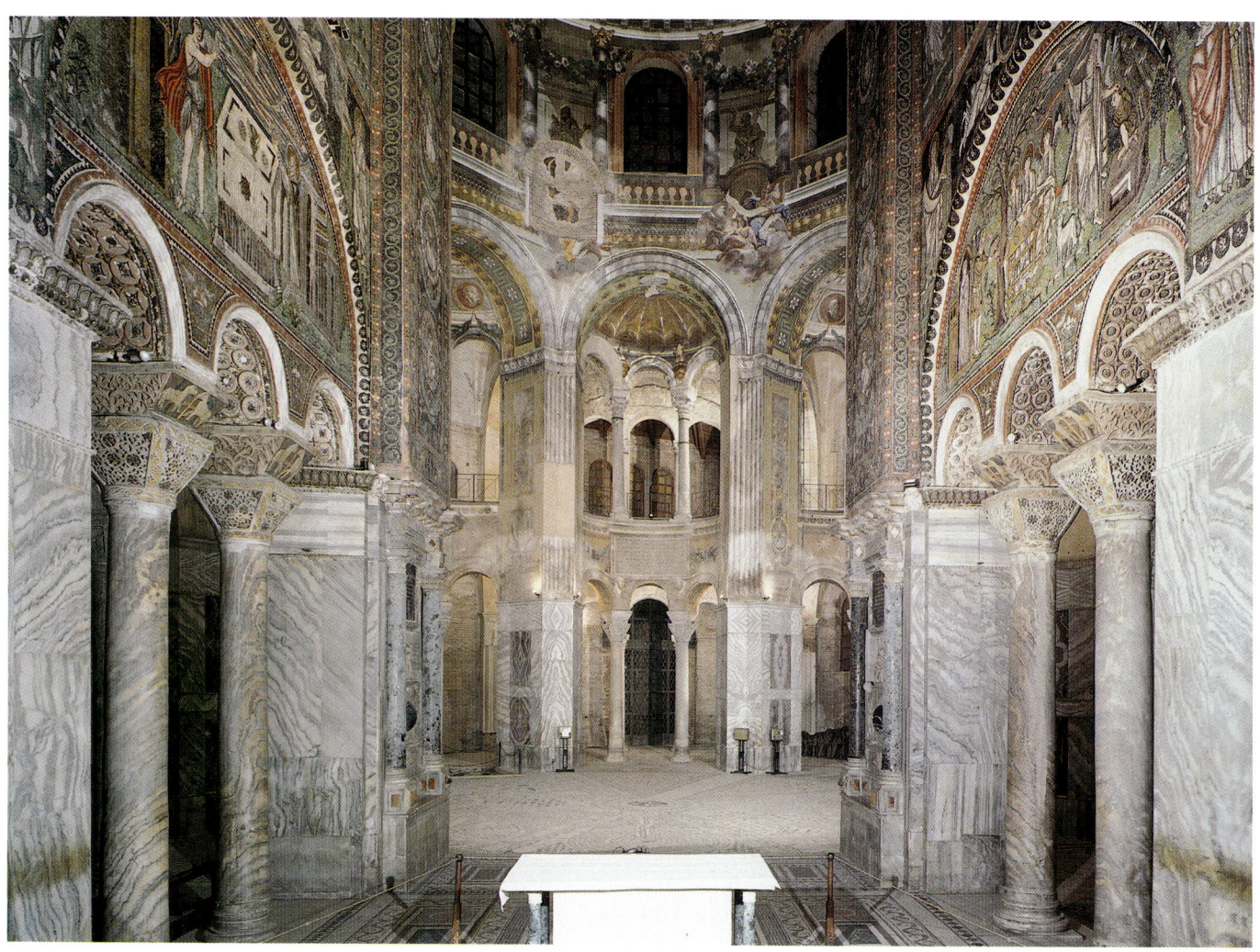

12-8   Interior of San Vitale (view from the apse into the choir), Ravenna, Italy, 526–547.

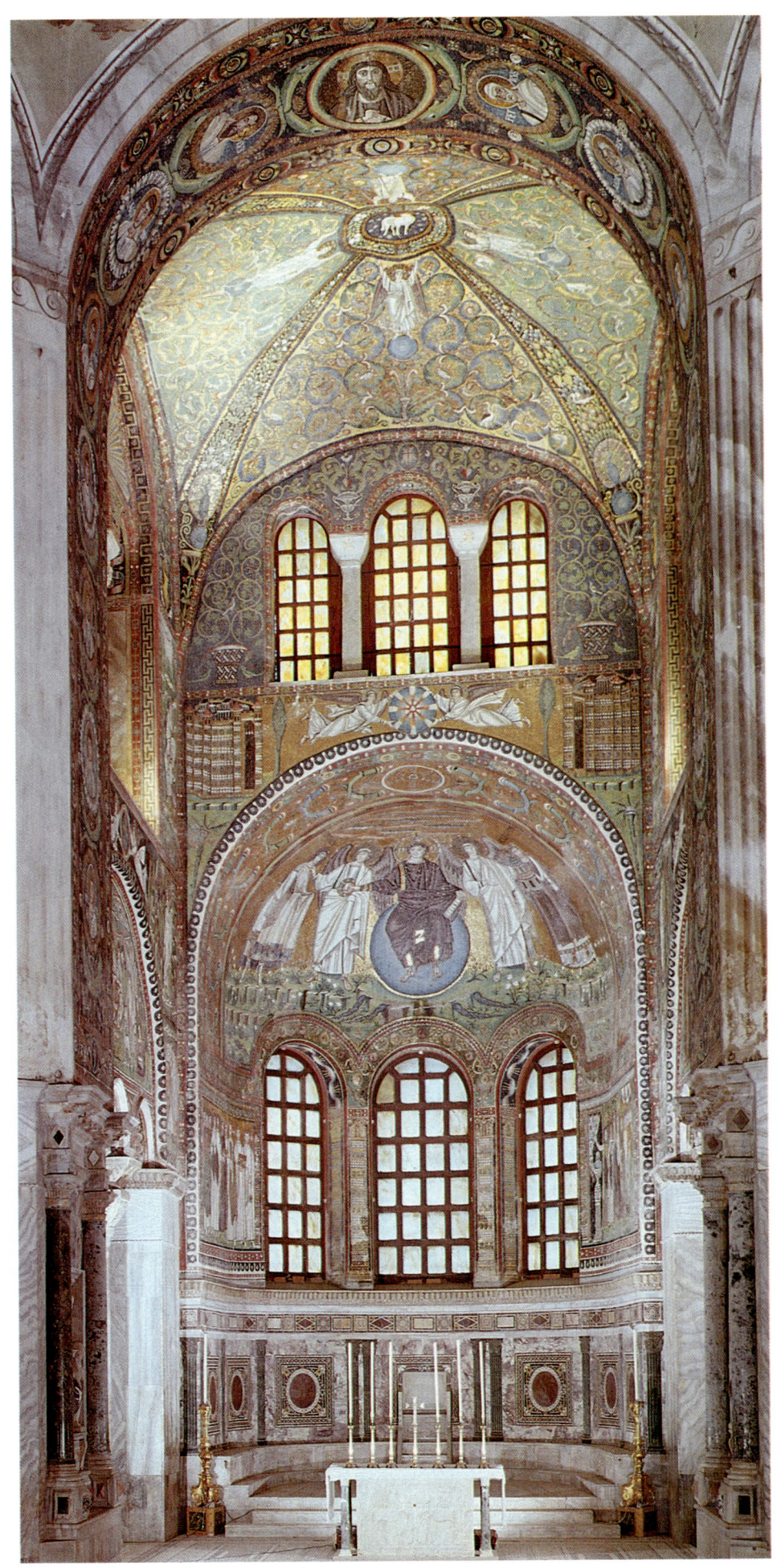

12-9 Choir and apse of San Vitale with mosaic of Christ between two angels, Saint Vitalis, and Bishop Ecclesius, Ravenna, Italy, 526–547.

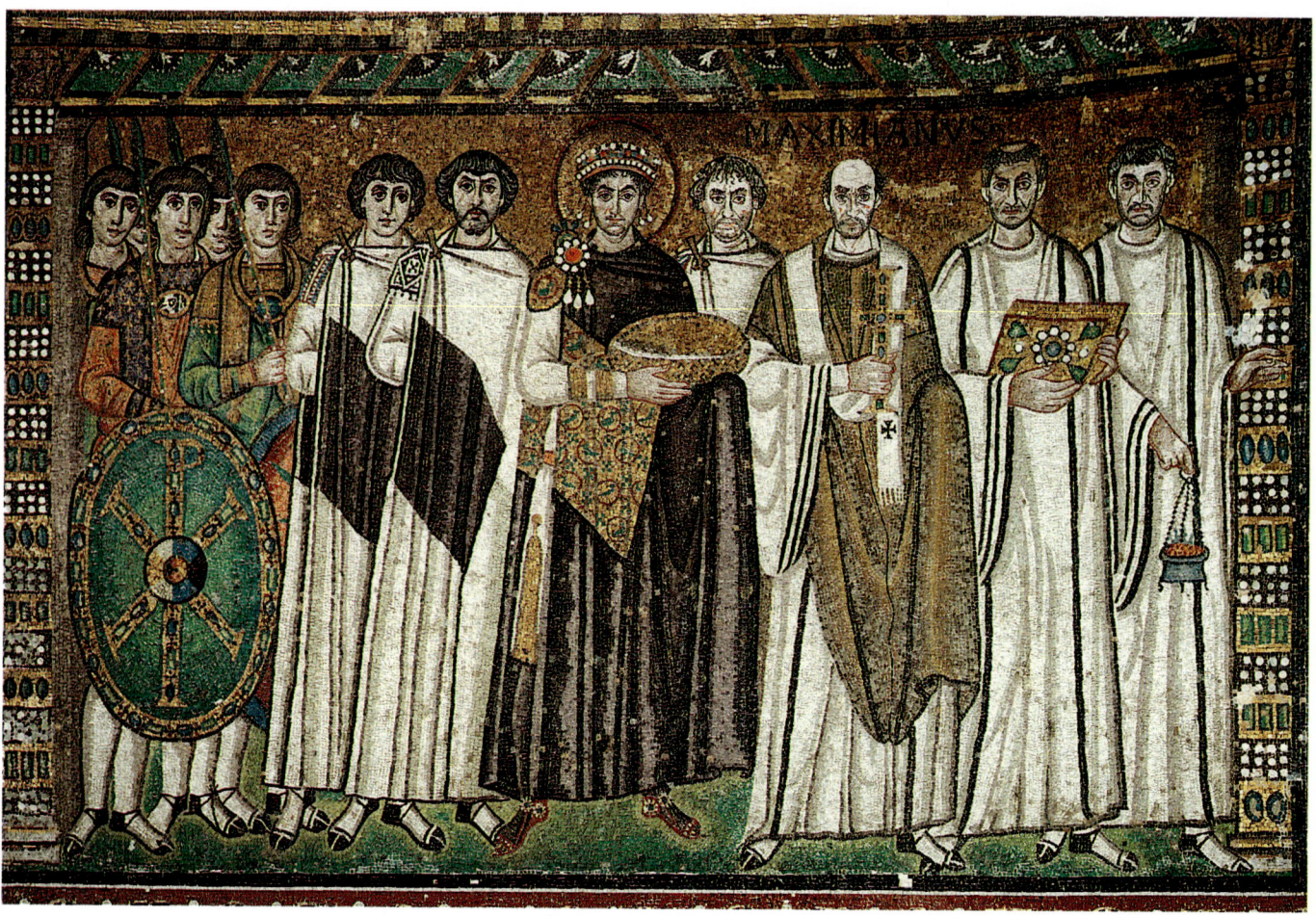

12-10   Justinian, Bishop Maximianus, and attendants, mosaic from the north wall of the apse, San Vitale, Ravenna, Italy, ca. 547.

laid. Ecclesius offers a model of San Vitale to Christ. The arrangement recalls Christ's prophecy of the last days of the world: "And then shall they see the Son of Man coming in the clouds with great power and glory. And then shall he send his angels, and shall gather together his elect from the four winds, from the uttermost part of Heaven" (Mark 13:26–27).

The wreath Christ extends to Saint Vitalis also is extended to Justinian, for he appears, on the Savior's right side, in the dependent mosaic (FIG. 12-10) on the choir wall just below and to the left of the apse mosaic. Thus, these rites confirmed and sanctified his rule, combining (as was typical of such expressions of the Byzantine imperial ideal) the political and the religious into one, as noted earlier. The laws of the Eastern Church and the laws of the state, united in the laws of God, were manifest in the person of the emperor and in his God-given right.

Justinian's counterpart on the opposite wall of the apse is his empress, Theodora (FIG. 12-11), one of the most remarkable women of the Middle Ages (see "Theodora: A Most Unusual Empress," page 338). The monarchs are accompanied by their retinues in a depiction of the offertory procession (the part of the liturgy when the bread and wine of the Eucharist are brought forward and presented). Both processions move into the apse, Justinian proceeding from left to right and Theodora from right to left. Justinian, represented as a priest-king, carries a *paten* (large golden bowl) containing the bread, and Theodora carries the golden cup with the wine.

Images and symbols covering the entire sanctuary express the single idea of Christ's redemption of humanity and the reenactment of it in the Eucharist. To the left of the Justinian mosaic (at the right in FIG. 12-8), for example, the lunette mosaic over the two columns of the choir depicts Abraham and the three angels and the sacrifice of Isaac, prefigurations of the Trinity and of the Crucifixion, respectively. The etiquette and protocol of the imperial court fuse in the imperial mosaics with the ritual of the liturgy of the Orthodox Church. The positions of the figures are all-important. They express the formulas of precedence and rank. In his mosaic, Justinian is at the center, and he is distinguished from the dignitaries who accompany him not only by the imperial purple he wears but also by his halo, an indication of his godlike status. At his left (at right in the mosaic) is Bishop Maximianus, the man responsible for San Vitale's completion. The mosaicist stressed the bishop's importance by labeling his figure with the only identifying inscription in the composition. Some have identified the figure behind and between Justinian and Maximianus as Julius Argentarius, the church's benefactor.

The artist divided the figures into three groups: the emperor and his staff (standing for the imperial administration); the clergy; and the army, bearing a shield with the *chi-rho* monogram of Christ. Each group has a leader whose feet precede (by one foot overlapping) the feet of those who follow. The positions of Justinian and Maximianus are curiously am-

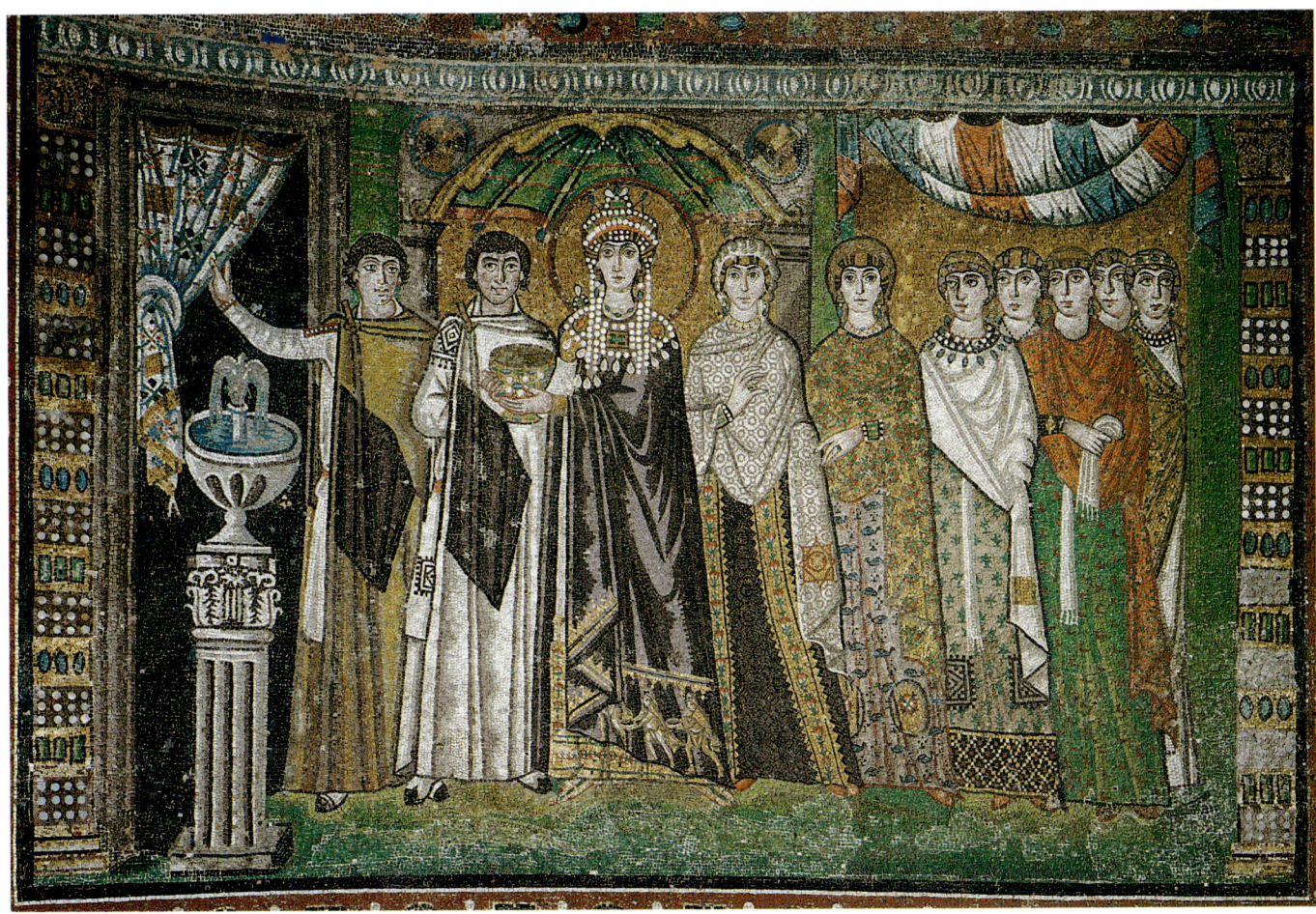

12-11 Theodora and attendants, mosaic from the south wall of the apse, San Vitale, Ravenna, Italy, ca. 547.

biguous. Although the emperor appears to be slightly behind the bishop, the sacred vessel he carries overlaps the bishop's arm. Thus, symbolized by place and gesture, the imperial and churchly powers are in balance. Justinian's paten holding the Eucharist bread, Maximianus's cross, and the attendant clerics' book and censer produce a slow forward movement that strikingly modifies the scene's rigid formality. No background is indicated. The artist expected the observer to understand the procession as taking place in this very sanctuary. Thus, the emperor appears forever as a participant in the sacred rites and as the proprietor of this royal church, the very symbol of his rule of the Western Empire.

THE NEW BYZANTINE AESTHETIC The procession at San Vitale recalls but contrasts with that of Augustus and his entourage on the Ara Pacis (see FIG. 10-29), erected more than half a millennium earlier in Rome. There the fully modeled marble figures have their feet planted firmly on the ground and talk among themselves, unaware of the viewer's presence. Two boys tug on the garments of their elders, while a woman comforts a child by placing her hand on his head. All is anecdote, all very human and of this world, even if the figures themselves conform to a classical ideal of beauty that cannot be achieved. The frontal figures of the Byzantine mosaic, however, hover before viewers, weightless and speechless. Their positions in space are as uncertain as that of Saint Michael on the ivory diptych examined earlier (FIG. 12-2).

Tall, spare, angular, and elegant, the figures have lost the rather squat proportions characteristic of much Early Christian work. The gorgeous draperies fall straight, stiff, and thin from the narrow shoulders. The organic body has dematerialized, and, except for the heads, some of which seem to be true portraits, viewers see a procession of solemn spirits gliding silently in the presence of the sacrament. In this mosaic, the Byzantine world's new aesthetic is revealed. It is very different from that of the classical world but equally compelling. Blue sky has given way to heavenly gold, and matter and material values are disparaged. Byzantine art is an art without solid bodies or cast shadows, with blank golden spaces, and with the perspective of Paradise, which is nowhere and everywhere.

THEODORA IN RAVENNA The portraits of the empress Theodora and her entourage (FIG. 12-11) exhibit the same stylistic traits, but they are represented within a definite architecture, perhaps the narthex of San Vitale. The empress stands in state beneath an imperial canopy, waiting to follow the emperor's procession. An attendant beckons her to pass through the curtained doorway. The fact she is outside the sanctuary in a courtyard with a fountain and only about to enter attests that, in the ceremonial protocol, her rank was not quite equal to her consort's. But the very presence of Theodora at San Vitale is significant. Neither she nor Justinian ever visited Ravenna. Their participation in the liturgy at

Theodora
A Most Unusual Empress

Theodora, wife of Justinian and empress of Byzantium, was not born into an aristocratic family. Her father, who died when she was a child, was the "keeper of bears" for one of the circus *factions* (teams, distinguished by color) at Constantinople. His responsibility was to prepare these animals for bear fights, bear hunts, and acrobatic performances involving bears in a long tradition rooted in ancient Rome. Theodora's mother was an actress, and after the death of her father the young Theodora took up the same career. Acting was not a profession the highborn held in esteem. At Byzantium, actresses often doubled as prostitutes, and the beautiful Theodora was no exception. In fact, actresses were so low on the Byzantine social ladder that the law prohibited senators from marrying them.

Justinian met Theodora when he was about forty years old, she only twenty-five. She became his mistress, but before they could wed, as they did in 525, ignoring all the social norms of the day, Justinian's uncle, the emperor Justin, first had to rewrite the law against senatorial marriages to actresses to permit wedlock with an *ex*-actress. When Justin died in April 527, Justinian was crowned emperor by the patriarch of Con-

stantinople, and Theodora became empress of Byzantium, capping what can be fairly described as one of the most remarkable and improbable "success stories" of any age. By all accounts, even of those openly hostile to the imperial couple, Justinian and Theodora remained faithful to each other for the rest of their lives.

It was not Theodora's beauty alone that attracted Justinian. John the Lydian, a civil servant at Constantinople at the time, described her as "surpassing in intelligence all men who ever lived." As her husband's trusted adviser, she repaid him for elevating her from poverty and disgrace to riches and prestige. During the Nika revolt in Constantinople in 532, when all of her husband's ministers counseled flight from the city, Theodora, by the sheer force of her personality, persuaded Justinian and his generals to hold their ground. The revolt was suppressed.

Byzantine artists immortalized the strong-willed and beautiful Theodora on the mosaic-clad walls of the apse of San Vitale at Ravenna (FIG. 12-11), where she appears as the near equal of her husband.

San Vitale is pictorial fiction. Justinian was represented because he was the head of the Byzantine state, and by his presence he exerted his authority over his territories in Italy. But Theodora's portrayal is more surprising and testifies to her unique position in Justinian's court. Theodora's prominent role in the mosaic program of San Vitale is proof of the power she wielded at Constantinople and, by extension, at Ravenna. In fact, the representation of the Three Magi on the border of her robe suggests she belongs in the elevated company of the three monarchs who approached the newborn Jesus bearing gifts.

THE UNBROKEN BASILICAN TRADITION The Justinianic period in Ravenna closes with the Church of Sant'Apollinare in Classe, a few miles from the city. Here, until the ninth century (when it was transferred to Ravenna), rested the body of Saint Apollinaris, who suffered his martyrdom in Classe, Ravenna's port. The building itself is Early Christian in type, a three-aisled basilica with a plan quite similar to that of Theodoric's palace-church dedicated to the same saint in Ravenna (see FIG. 11-16). As in the earlier church, the building's outside is plain and unadorned, but the interior is decorated with sumptuous mosaics, although in this case they are confined to the triumphal arch and the apse behind it (FIG. **12-12**).

The mosaic decorating the semivault above the apse probably was completed by 549, when the church was dedicated. It shows, against a gold ground, a large medallion with a jeweled cross (symbol of the transfigured Christ). This may represent

the cross Constantine erected on the hill of Calvary to commemorate the martyrdom of Jesus. Visible just above the cross is the hand of God. On either side of the medallion, in the clouds, appear the figures of Moses and Elijah, who appeared before Christ during his Transfiguration. Below these two figures are three sheep, the three disciples who accompanied Christ to the foot of the Mount of the Transfiguration. Beneath, amid green fields with trees, flowers, and birds, stands the church's patron saint, Apollinaris. He is portrayed in the Early Christian manner as an orant with uplifted arms. Accompanying him are twelve sheep, perhaps representing the Christian congregation under the protection of Saint Apollinaris, and forming, as they march in regular file across the apse, a wonderfully decorative base.

On the face of the triumphal arch above, the image of Christ in a medallion appears in the rainbow-streaked heavens, flanked by the four symbolic creatures of the visions of Ezekiel and the Book of Revelation. They stand for the Four Evangelists: the angel for Matthew, the lion for Mark, the ox for Luke, and the eagle for John. (This is not the first appearance of these symbols, which recur throughout medieval art.) The twelve lambs immediately below, issuing from the cities of Bethlehem and Jerusalem, are the Twelve Apostles. The two palms of Paradise in the narrow spandrels of the arch, and the two archangels below them, complete the iconographical program.

BYZANTINE STYLE AND CHRISTIAN DOGMA Comparison of the Early Byzantine Sant'Apollinare in Classe mosaic with the Galla Placidia mosaic (see FIG. 11-15) from

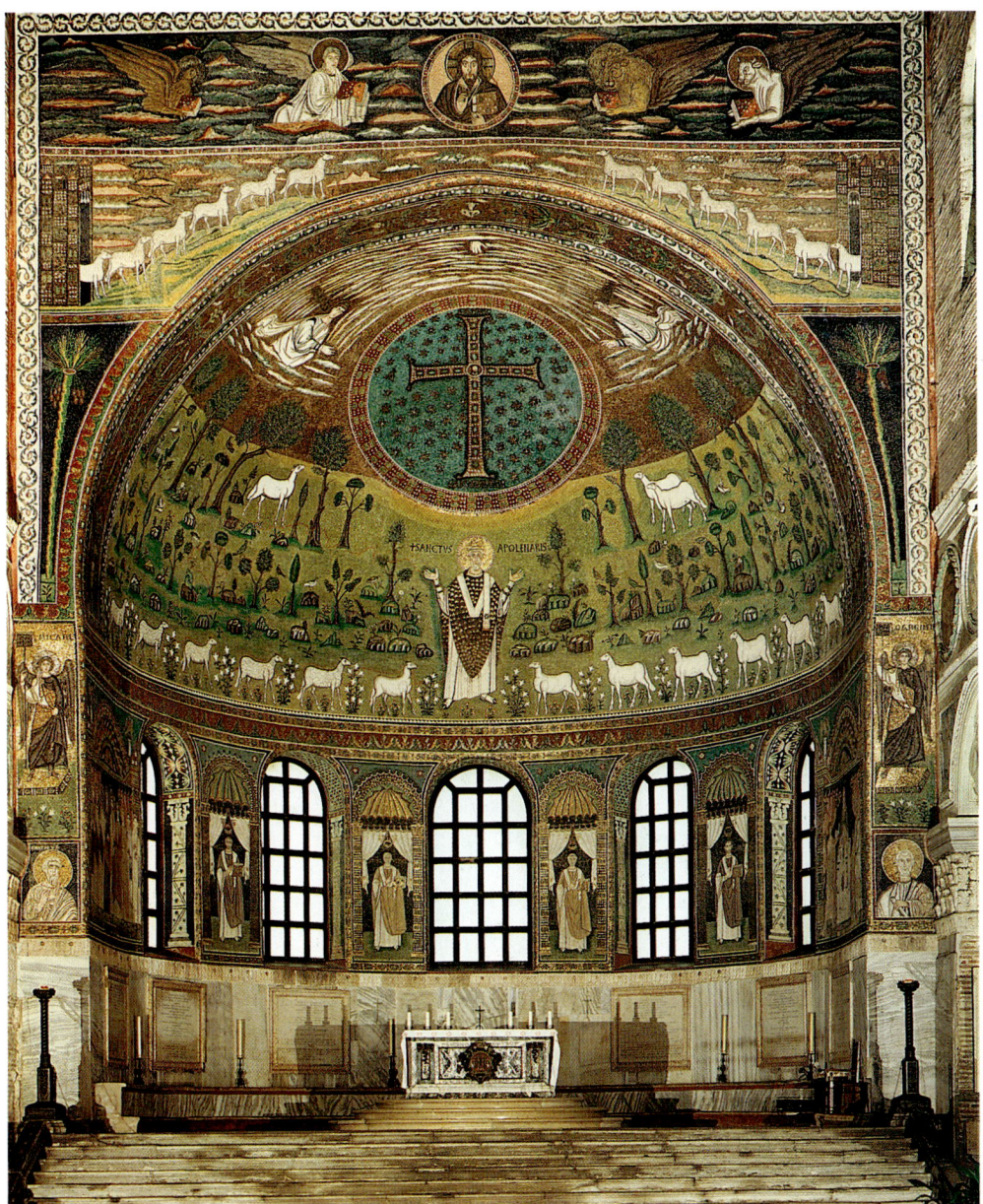

12-12 Saint Apollinaris amid sheep, apse mosaic, Sant'Apollinare in Classe, Ravenna, Italy, ca. 533–549.

the Early Christian period at Ravenna shows how the style and artists' approach to the subject changed during the course of a century. Both mosaics portray a human figure and some sheep in a landscape. But in Classe, in the mid-sixth century, the artist did not try to re-create a segment of the physical world, telling the story instead in terms of flat symbols, lined up side by side. The mosaicist carefully avoided overlapping in what must have been an intentional effort to omit all reference to the three-dimensional space of the material world and physical reality. Shapes have lost the volume seen in the earlier mosaic and instead are flat silhouettes with linear details. The effect is that of an extremely rich, flat tapestry design without illusionistic devices. This new Byzantine style became the ideal vehicle for conveying the extremely complex symbolism of the fully developed Christian dogma.

The Sant'Apollinare in Classe apse mosaic, for example, has much more meaning than first meets the eye. The Transfiguration of Christ—here, into the cross—symbolizes not only his own death, with its redeeming consequences, but also the death of his martyrs (in this case, Saint Apollinaris). The

lamb, also a symbol of martyrdom, appropriately represents the martyred apostles. The whole scene expands above the altar, where the priests celebrated the sacrament of the Eucharist—the miraculous recurrence of the supreme redemptive act. The very altars of Christian churches were, from early times, sanctified by the bones and relics of martyrs (see "Pilgrimages and the Cult of Relics," Chapter 17, page 457). Thus, the mystery and the martyrdom were joined in one concept: The death of the martyr, in imitation of Christ, is a triumph over death that leads to eternal life. The images above the altar present a kind of inspiring vision to the eyes of believers. The way of the martyr is open to them, and the reward of eternal life is within their reach. The organization of the symbolism and the images is hieratic, and the graphic message must have been delivered to the faithful with overwhelming force. Looming above their eyes is the apparition of a great mystery, ordered to make perfectly simple and clear that humankind's duty is to seek salvation. The anonymous artist, working under the direction of the priests, made sure that the devout could read the pictorial message as easily as an

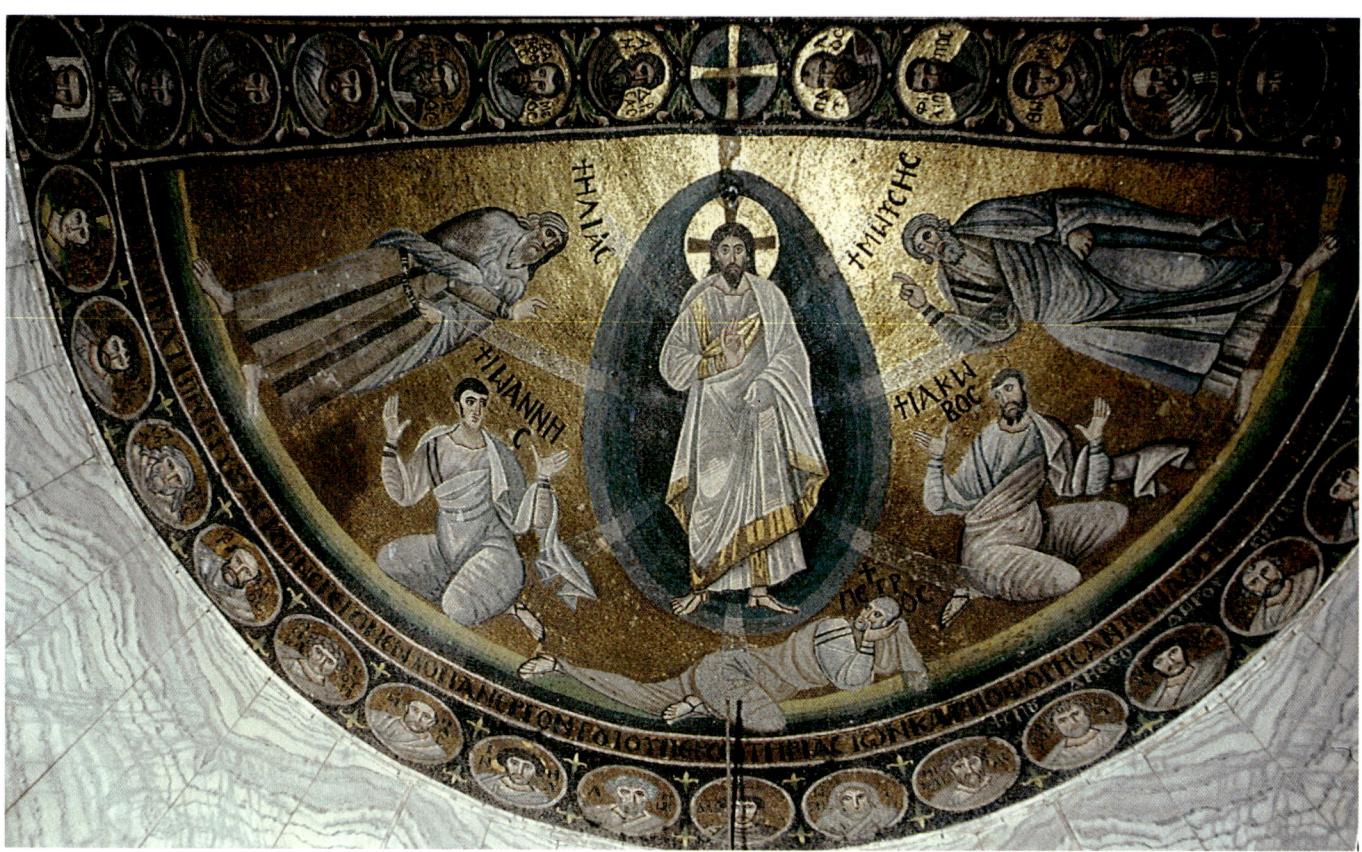

12-13   *Transfiguration of Jesus,* apse mosaic, Church of the Virgin, monastery of Saint Catherine, Mount Sinai, Egypt, ca. 565.

inscription—in fact, more easily, for many of the faithful were illiterate.

BYZANTIUM IN EGYPT   During Justinian's reign, almost continuous building took place, not only in Constantinople and Ravenna but also all over the Byzantine Empire. At Mount Sinai in Egypt, Justinian's builders began work on a major new walled monastery, now called Saint Catherine's, at about the time the mosaicists in Ravenna were completing their pictorial programs for San Vitale and Sant'Apollinare in Classe. The monastic movement began in Egypt in the third century and spread rapidly to Palestine and Syria in the East and as far as Ireland in the West. It began as a migration to the wilderness by those who sought a more spiritual way of life, far from the burdens, distractions, and temptations of town and city. In desert places these refuge seekers lived austerely as hermits, in contemplative isolation, cultivating the soul's perfection. So many thousands fled the cities that the authorities became alarmed—noting the effect on the tax base, military recruitment, and business in general.

By the fifth century, the numbers of these monks were so great that confusion and conflict called for regulation. Individuals were brought together to live according to a rule within a common enclosure, a community under the direction of an abbot (see "Medieval Monasteries and Benedictine Rule," Chapter 16, page 443). The monks typically lived in a walled monastery, an architectural complex that included the monks' residence (an alignment of single cells), a *refectory* (dining hall), a kitchen, storage and service quarters, a guest house for pil-

grims, and, of course, an *oratory* or monastery church (see FIG. 16-20).

Justinian built the fortress monastery at Mount Sinai between 548 and 565 and dedicated its church to the Virgin Mary. In the mid-fifth century, Mary had been officially recognized by the Orthodox Church as the Mother of God (*Theotokos,* "bearer of God" in Greek), putting to rest a controversy about the divine nature of Christ. The new monastery's location was chosen because it was at the foot of the mountain where Moses was believed to have received the Ten Commandments from God and where God first spoke to the Hebrew prophet from a burning bush. Mount Sinai had been an important pilgrimage destination since the fourth century, and Justinian's fortress was intended to protect not only the hermit-monks but also the lay pilgrims during their visits.

The apse mosaic (FIG. **12-13**) in the monastery church at Mount Sinai probably dates to 565, the year of the building's completion, or very shortly thereafter. The subject is the Transfiguration. Jesus appears in a deep-blue egg-shaped *mandorla,* or "glory," flanked by the Old Testament prophets Elijah and Moses. (Other mosaics in the church depict Moses receiving the Law and standing before the burning bush.) At Christ's feet are the disciples John, Peter, and James. Portrait busts of saints and prophets in medallions frame the whole scene. The artist stressed the intense whiteness of Jesus' transfigured, spiritualized form, from which rays stream down on the disciples. The stately figures of Elijah and Moses and the static frontality of Jesus set off the frantic terror and astonishment of the gesticulating dis-

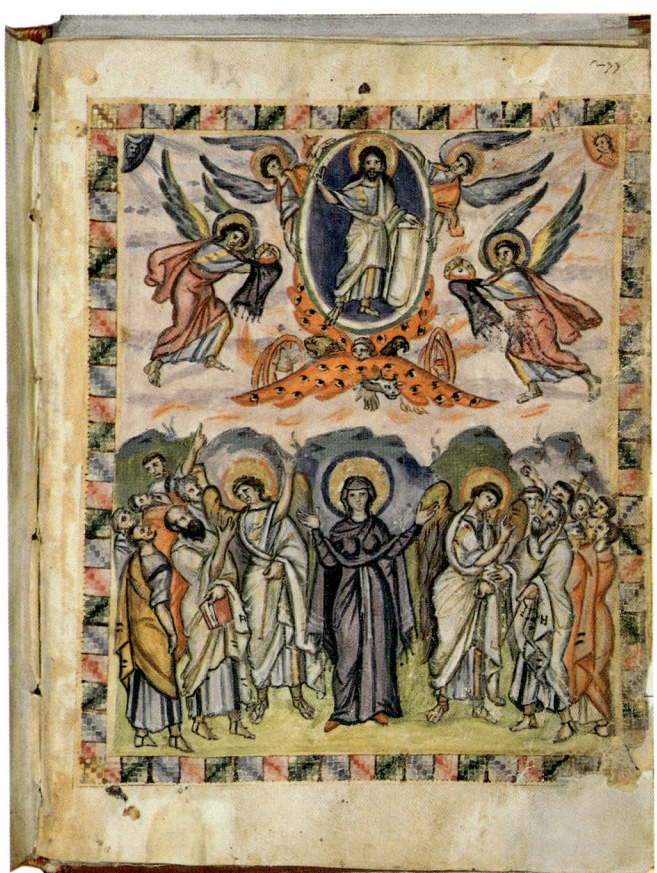

12-14 Ascension of Christ, folio 13 verso of the *Rabbula Gospels,* from Zagba, Syria, 586. Approx. 1′ 1″ × 10½″. Biblioteca Medicea-Laurenziana, Florence.

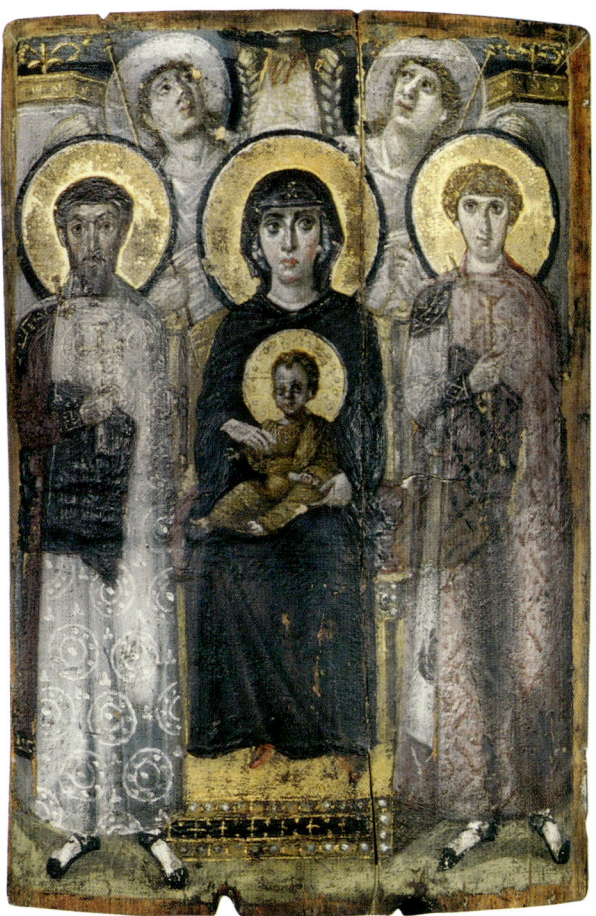

12-15 Virgin (Theotokos) and Child between Saints Theodore and George, icon, sixth or early seventh century. Encaustic on wood, 2′ 3″ × 1′ 7⅜″. Monastery of Saint Catherine, Mount Sinai, Egypt.

ciples. This effectively contrasts the eternal composure of heavenly beings with the distraught responses of the earthbound.

The artist swept away all traces of landscape or architectural setting for a depthless field of gold, fixing the figures and their labels in isolation from one another. A rainbow band of colors graduating from yellow to blue bounds the golden field at its base. The figures are ambiguously related to this multicolor ground line. Sometimes they are placed behind it; sometimes they overlap it. The bodies cast no shadows, even though supernatural light streams over them. This is a world of mystical vision, where all substance that might suggest the passage of time or motion through physical space was subtracted so that the devout can contemplate the eternal and motionless world of religious truth.

Painting

BYZANTIUM IN SYRIA One of the essential truths of Christianity is the belief that following his Crucifixion and entombment, Christ rose from the dead after three days and, on the fortieth day, ascended from the Mount of Olives to Heaven. The Ascension is the subject of a full-page painting (FIG. **12-14**) in a manuscript known as the *Rabbula Gospels.* Written in Syriac by the monk Rabbula at the monastery of Saint John the Evangelist at Zagba in Syria, it dates to the year 586. The composition shows Christ (bearded, as became

the norm in Byzantine art) in a mandorla borne aloft by angels, while his mother, other angels, and various apostles look on. The artist set the figures into a mosaic-like frame, and many think a mural painting or mosaic in a Byzantine church somewhere in the Eastern Empire was the model for the Rabbula Ascension.

The account of Christ's Ascension is not part of the accompanying text of the *Rabbula Gospels* but is borrowed from the Book of Acts. And even Acts omits mention of the Virgin's presence at the miraculous event. Here, however, the Theotokos occupies a very prominent position, central and directly beneath Christ. It is an early example of the prominent role the Mother of God played in later medieval art, both in the East and in the West. Frontal, with a nimbus, and posed as an orant, Mary stands apart from the commotion all about her and looks out at the viewer. Other details also depart from the standard texts. Christ, for example, does not rise in a cloud but in a mandorla above a fiery winged chariot carrying the symbols of the Four Evangelists. This page is not therefore an *illustration* of the Gospels but an independent *illumination* presenting one of the central tenets of Christian faith. Similar compositions appear on pilgrims' flasks from Palestine that were souvenir items reproducing important monuments visited. They reinforce the theory that the *Rabbula Gospels* Ascension was based on a lost painting or mosaic in a major church.

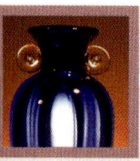

ART AND SOCIETY

Icons and Iconoclasm

Icons ("images" in Greek) are small portable panel paintings depicting Christ, the Virgin, or saints (or a combination of all three, as in FIG. 12-15). Icons survive from as early as the fourth century. From the sixth century on, they became enormously popular in Byzantine worship, both public and private. In Early Christian art the sacred personages of Christianity were often depicted, but in Byzantine icons the focus of attention narrowed to the representation of a particular saint or saints. In Byzantium, Christians considered icons a personal, intimate, and indispensable medium for spiritual transaction with holy figures. Some icons came to be regarded as wonder-working, and believers ascribed miracles and healing powers to them (see FIG. 12-29).

Icons, however, were by no means universally accepted. From the very beginning, many Christians were deeply suspicious of the practice of imaging the divine, whether on portable panels, on the walls of churches, or especially as statues that reminded them of pagan idols. The opponents of Christian figural art had in mind the Old Testament prohibition of images as given by the Lord to Moses in the Second Commandment: "Thou shalt not make unto thee any graven image or any likeness of anything that is in heaven above, or that is in the earth beneath, or that is in the water under the earth. Thou shalt not bow down thyself to them, nor serve them" (Exod. 20:4, 5).

When, early in the fourth century, Constantia, sister of the emperor Constantine, requested an image of Christ from Eusebius, the first great historian of the Christian Church, he rebuked her, referring to the Second Commandment:

> Can it be that you have forgotten that passage in which God lays down the law that no likeness should be made of what is in heaven or in the earth beneath? . . . Are not such things banished and excluded from churches all over the world, and is it not common knowledge that such practices are not permitted to us . . . lest we appear, like idol worshipers, to carry our God around in an image?[1]

Opposition to icons became especially strong in the eighth century, when the faithful often knelt before them in prayer to seek protection or a cure for illness. Icon worship was easy to confuse with idol worship, and this brought about an imperial ban on *all* sacred images. The term for this destruction of holy pictures is *iconoclasm*. The *iconoclasts* (breakers of images) and the *iconophiles* (lovers of images) became bitter and irreconcilable enemies. The anguish of the latter can be read in a graphic description of the deeds of the iconoclasts, written in about 754:

> In every village and town one could witness the weeping and lamentation of the pious, whereas, on the part of the impious, [one saw] sacred things trodden upon, [liturgical] vessels turned to other use, churches scraped down and smeared with ashes because they contained holy images. And wherever there were venerable images of Christ or the Mother of God or the saints, these were consigned to the flames or were gouged out or smeared over.[2]

The consequences of iconoclasm for the history of Byzantine art are difficult to overstate. For more than a century not only did the portrayal of Christ, the Virgin, and the saints cease, but the iconoclasts also systematically destroyed countless works from the early centuries of Christendom. Knowledge of Byzantine art before the revival of image making in the ninth century is therefore very fragmentary. Writing a history of Early Byzantine art presents a great challenge to art historians.

[1]Cyril Mango, trans., *The Art of the Byzantine Empire, 312–1453: Sources and Documents* (Englewood Cliffs, N.J.: Prentice-Hall, 1972), 17–18.

[2]Ibid., 152.

ICONS FOR THE DEVOUT Gospel books such as the *Rabbula Gospels* played an important role in monastic religious life. So, too, did icons, although few early examples survive because of the wholesale destruction of images *(Iconoclasm)* that occurred in the eighth century (see "Icons and Iconoclasm," above). Some of the finest early icons come from Saint Catherine's monastery at Mount Sinai. The one we illustrate (FIG. **12-15**) was painted in encaustic on wood, continuing a tradition of panel painting in Egypt that, like so much else in the Byzantine world, goes back to the Roman Empire (see FIG. 10-63). The Sinai icon represents the enthroned Theotokos and Child with Saints Theodore and George. Behind them, two angels look upward to a shaft of light where the hand of God appears. This format, with minimal variations, remained typical of the compositional features of Byzantine icons for centuries. The foreground figures are strictly frontal and have a solemn demeanor. Background details are few and suppressed. The forward plane of the picture dominates; space is squeezed out. It is a perfect example of Byzantine hieratic style, the mode of grave decorum that suits liturgical ritual. Traces of Greco-Roman illusionism remain in the Virgin's rather personalized features and in her sideways glance, and distant echoes of Hellenistic art endure in the posing of the angels' heads. But the painter rendered the two guardian saints in the new Byzantine manner, especially Saint Theodore, whose piercing eyes command the viewer to witness and revere the miraculous apparition of the Theotokos.

ICONOCLASM (726–843)

BYZANTIUM IN CRISIS The preservation of the Early Byzantine icons at the Mount Sinai monastery is fortuitous but ironic, for opposition to icon worship was especially prominent in the Monophysite provinces of Syria and Egypt. And there, in the seventh century, a series of calamities erupted, indirectly causing the imperial ban on images. The Sasanid Persians, chronically at war with Rome, swept into the eastern provinces early in the seventh century. Between 611 and 617 they captured the great cities of Antioch, Jerusalem, and Alexandria. Hardly had the Byzantine emperor Heraclius pressed them back and defeated them in 627 when a new and overwhelming power appeared unexpectedly on the stage of history. The Arabs, under the banner of the new Islamic religion, conquered not only Byzantium's eastern provinces but also Persia itself, replacing Sasanian Persia in the age-old balance of power with the Christian West. In a few years the Arabs were launching attacks on Constantinople, and Byzantium was fighting for its life.

These were catastrophic years for the Eastern Roman Empire. They terminated once and for all the long story of imperial Rome, closed the Early Byzantine period, and inaugurated the medieval era of Byzantine history. Almost two-thirds of the Byzantine Empire's territory was lost—many cities and much of its population, wealth, and material resources. The shock of these events persuaded the emperor Leo III (r. 717–741) that God had punished the Christian Roman Empire for its idolatrous worship of icons by setting upon it the merciless armies of the infidel. In 726 he formally prohibited the use of images, and for more than a century Byzantine artists produced little new religious figurative art. In place of images, the iconoclasts used symbolic forms already familiar in Early Christian art—the cross (recall the one that crowns the great mosaic of the apse at Sant'Apollinare in Classe, FIG. 12-12), the vacant Throne of Heaven, the cabinet with the scriptural scrolls, and so forth. Stylized floral, animal, and architectural motifs provided decorative fill. In this last respect, iconoclastic art much resembled the contemporaneous *aniconic* (nonimage) art of Islam (see Chapter 13).

MIDDLE BYZANTINE ART (843–1204)

THE RETURN OF THE IMAGE MAKERS In the ninth century, a powerful reaction against iconoclasm set in. The destruction of images was condemned as a heresy, and restoration of the images began in 843. Shortly thereafter, under a new line of emperors, the Macedonian dynasty, art, literature, and learning sprang to life once again. In this great renovation, as historians have called it, Byzantine culture recovered something of its ancient Hellenistic sources and accommodated them to the forms inherited from the Justinianic age.

Basil I (r. 867–886), head of the new dynasty, thought of himself as the restorer of the Roman Empire. He denounced as usurpers the Frankish Carolingian monarchs of the West (see Chapter 16) who, since 800, had claimed the title "Roman Empire" for their realm. Basil bluntly reminded their emissary that the only true emperor of Rome reigned in Constantinople. They were not Roman emperors but merely "kings of the Germans." Iconoclasm had forced Byzantine artists westward, where doubtless they found employment at the courts of these Germanic kings. They strongly influenced the character of western European art. But under Basil and his successors, mural painters, mosaicists, book illuminators, ivory carvers, and metalworkers once again received commissions aplenty.

Architecture and Mosaics

UNDOING ICONOCLASM Basil I and his successors undertook the laborious and costly task of refurbishing the churches the iconoclasts defaced and neglected, Hagia Sophia first among them. There, in 867, the Macedonian dynasty dedicated a new mosaic in the apse depicting the enthroned Virgin with the Christ Child in her lap (FIG. **12-16**). In the vast space beneath the dome of the great church, the figures look undersized, but the seated Theotokos is actually more than sixteen feet tall. An accompanying inscription, now fragmentary, announced that "pious emperors" (the Macedonians) had commissioned the mosaic to replace one the "impostors" (the iconoclasts) had destroyed.

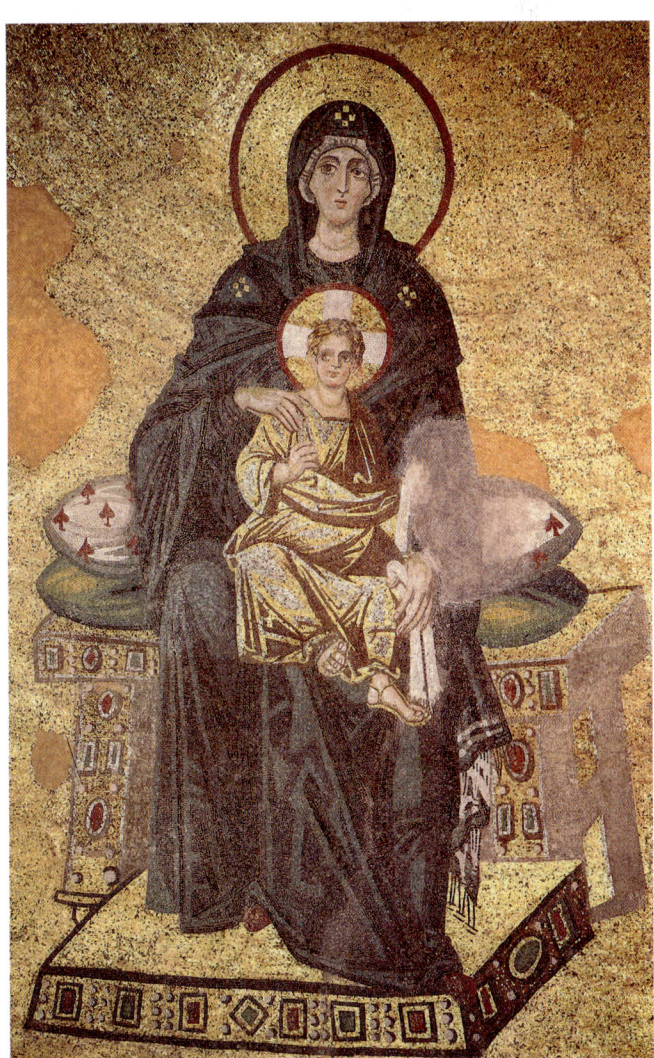

12-16 Virgin (Theotokos) and Child enthroned, apse mosaic, Hagia Sophia, Constantinople (Istanbul), Turkey, dedicated 867.

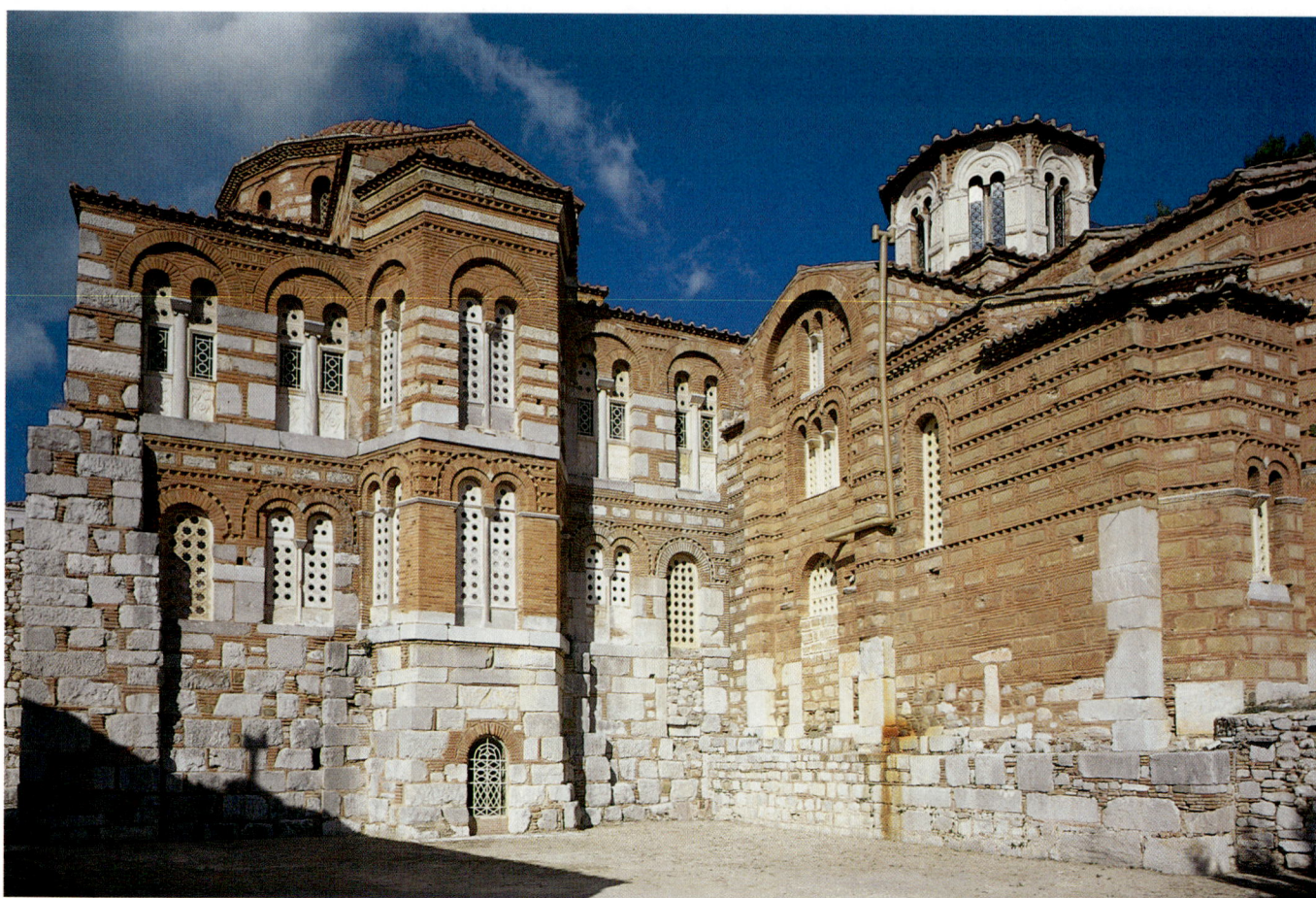

12-17   Monastery churches at Hosios Loukas, Greece (view from the east). Katholikon *(left),* first quarter of eleventh century, and Church of the Theotokos *(right),* tenth century.

The original mosaic's subject is uncertain, but the ninth-century work echoes the style and composition of the Early Byzantine Mount Sinai icon of the Theotokos, Christ, and saints (FIG. 12-15). Here, the strict frontality of Mother and (much older) Child is alleviated by the angular placement of the throne and footstool. The mosaicist rendered the furnishings in a perspective that, although imperfect, recalls once more the Greco-Roman roots of Byzantine art. The treatment of the folds of Christ's robes is, by contrast, even more schematic and flatter than in earlier mosaics. These seemingly contradictory stylistic features are not uncommon in Byzantine paintings and mosaics. Most significant about the images in the Hagia Sophia apse is their very existence. The iconophiles had triumphed over the iconoclasts.

NEW CHURCHES FOR THE OLD FAITH   Although the new emperors did not wait very long to redecorate the churches of their predecessors, they undertook little new church construction in the decades following the renunciation of iconoclasm in 843. But in the tenth century and through the twelfth, a number of monastic churches arose that are the flowers of Middle Byzantine architecture. They feature a brilliant series of variations on the domed central plan. From the exterior, the typical later Byzantine church building is a domed cube, with the dome rising above the square on a kind of cylinder or drum. The churches are small, vertical, high shouldered, and, unlike earlier Byzantine buildings, have exte-

rior wall surfaces with vivid decorative patterns, probably reflecting the impact of Islamic architecture.

The monastery Church of the Theotokos (FIGS. **12-17**, right, and **12-18**, top) at Hosios Loukas (Saint Luke) in

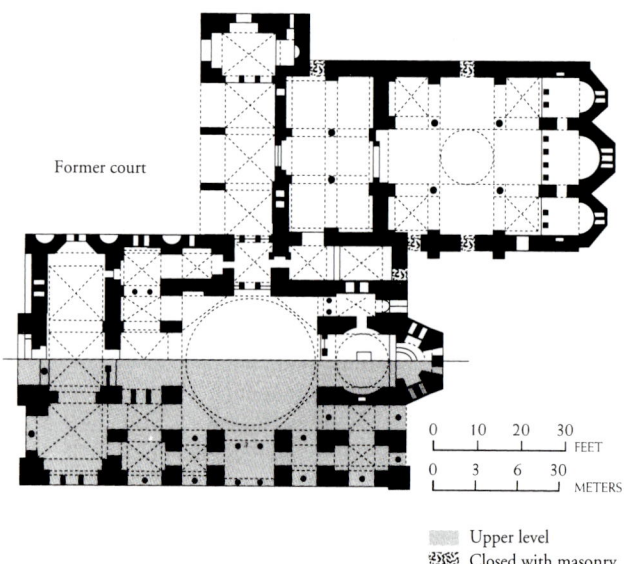

12-18   Plans of Church of the Theotokos *(top)* and Katholikon *(bottom),* Hosios Loukas, Greece, first quarter of eleventh century.

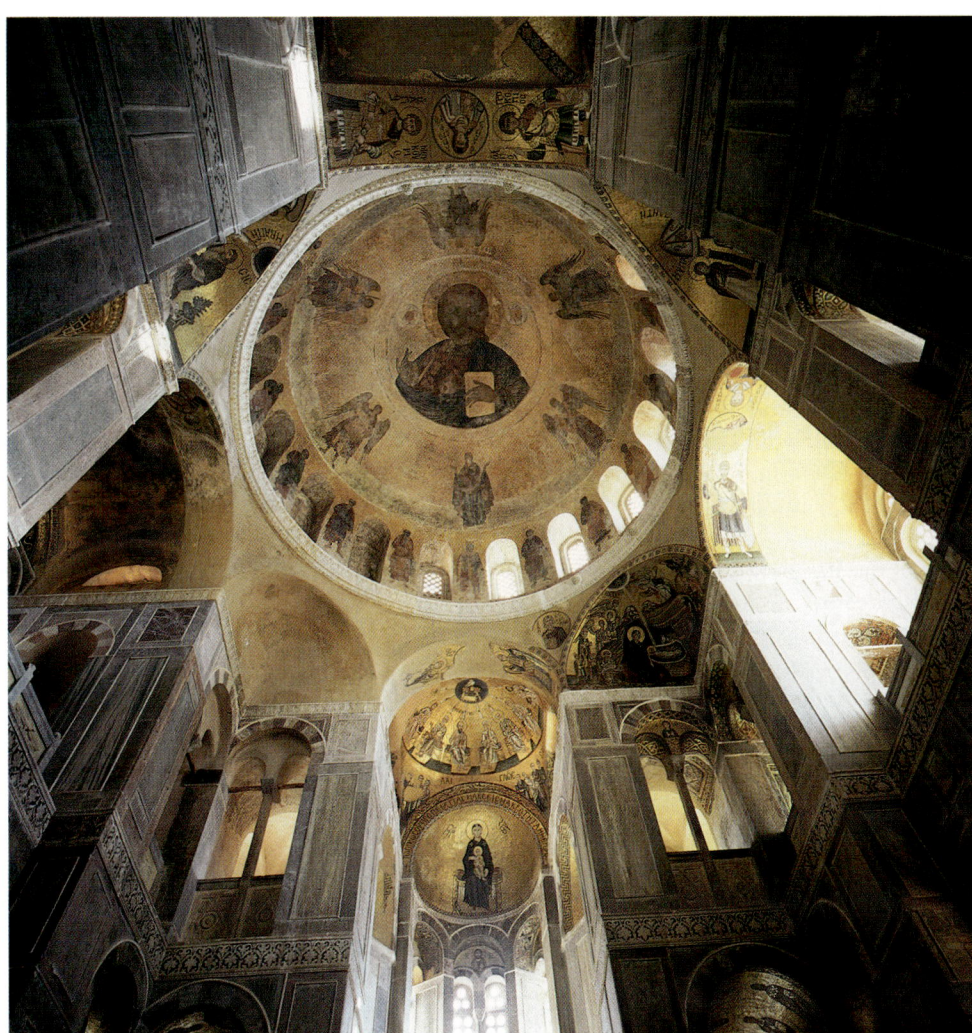

12-19 Interior of Katholikon (view facing east), Hosios Loukas, Greece, first quarter of eleventh century.

Greece, not far from the ancient sanctuary of Apollo at Delphi, dates to the tenth century. One of two churches at the site, it is an outstanding example of church design during this Second Golden Age of Byzantine art and architecture. Light stones framed by dark red bricks—the so-called *cloisonné* technique, a term borrowed from enamel work (see "Cloisonné," Chapter 16, page 429)—make up the walls. The interplay of arcuated windows, projecting apses, and varying roof lines further enhances this surface dynamism. The plan (FIG. 12-18) shows the form of a domed cross in square with four equal-length, vaulted cross arms (the Greek cross). The dome rests on pendentives. Around this unit, and by the duplication of it, Byzantine architects developed bewilderingly involved spaces.

In the adjacent, larger Katholikon (FIGS. 12-17, left, and 12-18, bottom), built in the early eleventh century, the architect placed a dome over an octagon inscribed within a square. The octagon was formed by squinches, which, as noted earlier (see "Pendentives and Squinches," page 332), play the same role as pendentives in making the transition from a square base to a round dome but create a different visual effect on the interior (FIG. 12-19). This arrangement departs from the older designs, such as Santa Costanza's circular plan (see FIG. 11-10), San Vitale's octagonal plan (FIG. 12-7), and Hagia Sophia's dome on pendentives rising from a square (FIG. 12-4). The

Katholikon's complex core lies within two rectangles, the outermost one forming the exterior walls. Thus, in plan from the center out, a circle-octagon-square-oblong series exhibits an intricate interrelationship that is at once complex and unified.

The interior elevation of the Katholikon reflects its involved plan. Like earlier Byzantine buildings, the church creates a mystery out of space, surface, light, and dark. High and narrow, it forces one's gaze to rise and revolve. The eye is drawn upward toward the dome, but much can distract it in the interplay of flat walls and concave recesses; wide and narrow openings; groin and barrel vaults; single, double, and triple windows; and illuminated and dark spaces. Middle Byzantine architects seem to have aimed for the creation of complex interior spaces that issue into multiple domes in the upper levels. From the exterior, this spatial complexity produces spectacular combinations of round forms that develop dramatically shifting perspectives.

A SECOND GOLDEN AGE FOR MOSAICS Most of the original mosaic decoration of the Hosios Loukas Katholikon does not survive, but at Daphni, near Athens, the mosaics produced during Byzantium's Second Golden Age fared much better. In the monastery Church of the Dormition (from the Latin for *sleep,* referring to the ascension

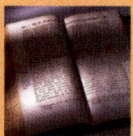

Eulalios
Painter of Christ

Most of the art of Byzantium, and of the Middle Ages in general, is anonymous. The names of the architect-engineers of Justinian's great sixth-century church of Holy Wisdom in Constantinople (FIG. 12-3) are known. But the mosaicist who adorned its apse (FIG. 12-16) in the ninth century is nameless, even though the homily the patriarch Photius delivered for the building's dedication in 867 survives. The scribe Rabbula signed the *Gospels* he wrote in Syriac in 586, but the identity of the painter of its full-page miniatures (FIG. 12-14) is unknown.

Medieval authors, however, did record the name of Eulalios, a painter who worked in the twelfth century. So great was his fame that more than one writer notes his name and describes his paintings. Eulalios's most important commission was the decoration of the dome of the Church of the Holy Apostles in Constantinople with an image of Christ as Pantocrator. Nicephorus Callistus, an early-fourteenth-century poet, historian, and author of saints' lives, was so struck by Eulalios's portrayal of Christ that he speculated the painter had actually seen the Pantocrator:

> Either Christ himself came down from heaven and showed the exact traits of his face to [the painter] or else the famous Eulalios mounted up to the very skies to paint with his skilled hand Christ's exact appearance.[1]

Nicholas Mesarites, who visited the Church of the Holy Apostles around the year 1200, left a more precise description of Eulalios's Christ:

> [The dome] exhibits an image of the God-man Christ looking down, as it were, from the rim of heaven towards the floor of the church and everything that is in it. . . . His head is in proportion to his body that is represented down to the navel, his eyes are joyful and welcoming to those who are not reproached by their conscience, but to those who are condemned by their own judgment, they are wrathful and hostile. . . . The right hand blesses those who walk a straight path, while it admonishes those who do not and, as it were, checks them and turns them back from their disorderly course. The left hand, with its fingers spread as far apart as possible, supports the Gospel.[2]

It is easy to visualize Eulalios's Pantocrator by comparing Nicholas Mesarites' description with surviving representations of the same theme: for example, the painted dome of the Katholikon at Hosios Loukas (FIG. 12-19), the mosaic dome of the Church of the Dormition at Daphni, and even the apse of the Cathedral at Monreale (FIG. 12-24) in faraway Sicily. All conform to the same basic iconographic type—an image of the stern judge of human worth who strikes fear into all who will come before him.

[1] Cyril Mango, trans., *The Art of the Byzantine Empire, 312–1453: Sources and Documents* (Englewood Cliffs, N.J.: Prentice-Hall, 1972), 231–32.

[2] Ibid., 232.

of the Virgin Mary to Heaven at the moment of her death), the main elements of the late-eleventh-century pictorial program are intact, although the mosaics were restored in the nineteenth century. Gazing down from on high in the central dome is the fearsome image of Christ as *Pantocrator* (literally "ruler of all" in Greek but usually applied to Christ in his role as Last Judge of humankind). It is similar in general appearance to the painting in the dome of the Hosios Loukas Katholikon (FIG. 12-19), which replaced an earlier mosaic. The theme was a common one in churches throughout the Byzantine Empire. The most famous Pantocrator of all was the work of EULALIOS, who decorated the dome of the Church of the Holy Apostles in Constantinople (see "Eulalios: Painter of Christ," above).

On one of the walls below the Daphni dome, beneath the barrel vault of one arm of the Greek cross, an unknown artist depicted Christ's Crucifixion (FIG. **12-20**) in a pictorial style characteristic of the post-iconoclastic Middle Byzantine period. It is a subtle blend of the painterly, Hellenistic style and the later more abstract and formalistic Byzantine style. The Byzantine artist fully assimilated classicism's simplicity, dig-

nity, and grace into a perfect synthesis with Byzantine piety and pathos. The figures have regained the classical organic structure to a surprising degree, particularly compared to figures from the Justinianic period (compare FIGS. 12-9 and 12-10). The style is a masterful adaptation of classical statuesque qualities to the linear Byzantine style.

The Virgin and Saint John flank the crucified Christ. A skull at the foot of the cross indicates Golgotha, the "place of skulls." Nothing else was needed to set the scene. In quiet sorrow and resignation, Mary and John point to Christ as if to indicate the cross's meaning. Symmetry and closed space combine to produce an effect of the motionless and unchanging aspect of the deepest mystery of the Christian religion. The timeless presence is, as it were, beheld in unbroken silence. The picture is not a narrative of the historical event of the Crucifixion, the approach taken by the carver of the Early Christian ivory panel (see FIG. 11-21) examined in the previous chapter. Nor is Christ a triumphant, beardless youth, oblivious to pain and defiant of the laws of gravity. Rather, he has a tilted head and sagging body, and blood spurts from the wound Longinus inflicted on him, although he is not overtly

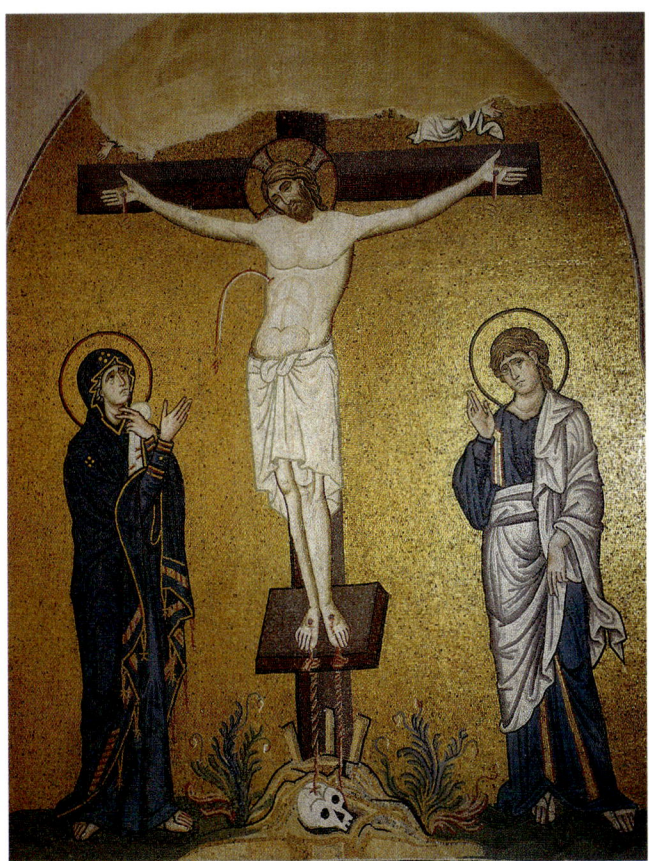

12-20 Crucifixion, mosaic in the Church of the Dormition, Daphni, Greece, ca. 1090–1100.

the four equal arms of the Greek cross. At Saint Mark's the architect elaborated the domes on the exterior, covering them with swelling, wooden, helmetlike forms sheathed in gilded copper. These forms protect the inner masonry domes and contribute to the exuberant composition.

Saint Mark's served both as a martyrium and a palace chapel. In the twelfth century it became the cathedral of Venice. Because of its importance to the city, the doges repeatedly remodeled the eleventh-century structure, and today it is disguised on its lower levels by Romanesque and Gothic additions.

CHRIST TRAMPLES SATAN The interior of Saint Mark's (FIG. **12-22**) is, like its plan, Byzantine in effect. Light enters through a row of windows at the bases of all five domes, vividly illuminating a rich cycle of mosaics. Both Byzantine and local artists worked on Saint Mark's mosaics over the course of two centuries. Recent cleaning and restoration on a grand scale have returned the mosaics to their original splendor. It is now possible to experience to the fullest the radiance of mosaic (some forty thousand square feet of it) as it covers, like a gold-brocaded and figured fabric, all the walls, arches, vaults, and domes.

In the vast central dome, eighty feet above the floor and forty-two feet in diameter, Christ reigns in the company of the Four Evangelists, the Virgin Mary, and personifications of Christian virtues. The great arch framing the church crossing bears a narrative of the Crucifixion and Resurrection of Christ and of his liberation from death of the Old Testament

in pain. The Virgin and John point to the figure on the cross as if to a devotional object, sacramental in itself, that the monks are to view in silent contemplation.

VENICE AND BYZANTIUM The revival on a grand scale of church building, featuring vast stretches of mosaic-covered walls, was not confined to the Greek-speaking Byzantine East in the tenth to twelfth centuries. A resurgence of religious architecture and of the mosaicist's art also occurred in areas of the former Western Roman Empire where the ties with Constantinople were the strongest. In the Early Byzantine period, Venice, about eighty miles north of Ravenna on the eastern coast of Italy, was a dependency of that Byzantine stronghold. When the Lombards wrested control of most of northern Italy from Constantinople and Ravenna fell in 751, Venice became an independent power. Its *doges* (dukes) enriched themselves and the city through seaborn commerce, serving as the crucial link between Byzantium and the West.

Venice had long possessed the relics of Saint Mark, and the doges constructed the first Venetian church dedicated to the evangelist in the ninth century. Fire destroyed that church in 976. They then built a second church on the site, but a grandiose new shrine begun in 1063 replaced it. The third Saint Mark's (FIG. **12-21**), like its two predecessors, was modeled on the Church of the Holy Apostles at Constantinople, built in Justinian's time. The Constantinopolitan church no longer exists, but its key elements were a cruciform plan with a central dome over the crossing and four other domes over

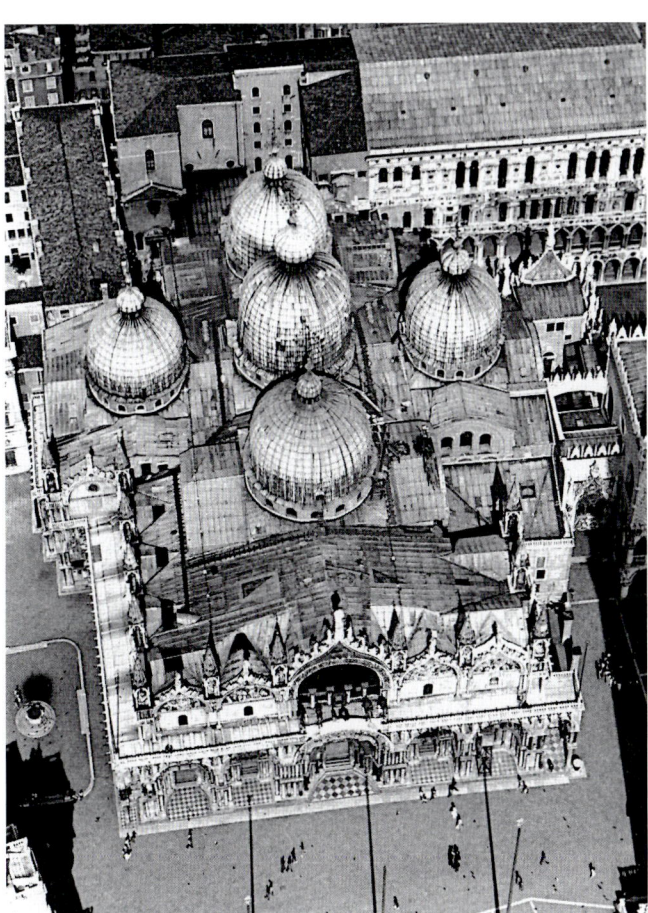

12-21 Aerial view of Saint Mark's, Venice, Italy, begun 1063.

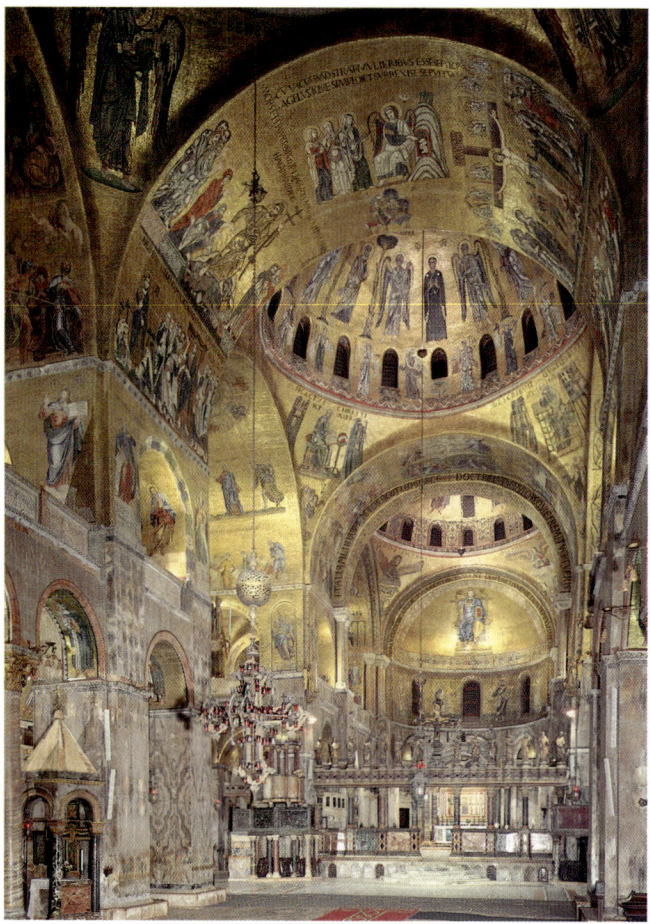

12-22   Interior of Saint Mark's (view facing east), Venice, Italy, begun 1063.

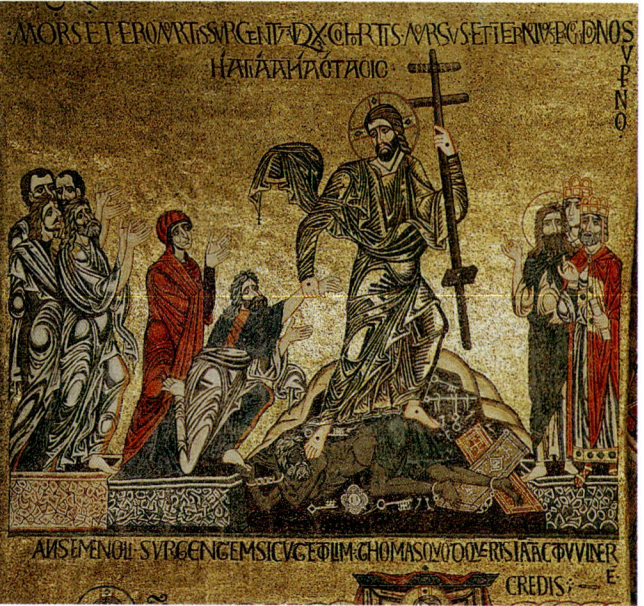

12-23   *Anastasis*, mosaic from the west vault of Saint Mark's, Venice, Italy, ca. 1180.

worthies. The *Anastasis* mosaic (FIG. **12-23**) is one of the most originally interpretive, powerfully expressive, and unforgettable scenes in all of Byzantine art. Between his death and Resurrection, Christ, bearing his cross, has descended into Limbo, where he tramples Satan and receives the supplication of the faithful at the left and the witness of Saint John the Baptist and the prophets at the right. He has come to liberate the righteous who had died before his coming.

The composition is boldly asymmetrical. Below an explanatory label in both Latin and Greek, the off-center giant figure of Christ dominates the mosaic by the strength and span of his stride, the direction and intensity of his glance, and the imperious firmness of his seizure of Adam's hand, the focus of the whole design. The hands of Eve and the other Old Testament figures make a pathetic chorus of begging gestures converging to the saving hand of Christ. Swirling draperies leap and spin. The agitated poses and gestures form jagged silhouettes against a featureless golden ground. The insubstantial figures appear weightless and project from their flat field no more than the elegant Latin and Greek letters above them. Nothing here reflects on the world of matter, of solids, of light and shade, of perspective space. This is a masterpiece of emotional, as well as hieratic, abstraction, revealing the mysteries of the Christian Church. The iconography is Byzantine, but the mosaics are the work not of a Byzantine Greek but of a Venetian master, an outstanding member of the great school of mosaicists that flourished at Saint Mark's in the twelfth and thirteenth centuries.

A ROYAL CHURCH IN SICILY   Venetian success was matched in the western Mediterranean by the Normans who, having driven the Arabs from Sicily, set up a powerful kingdom there, whose resources matched Venice's. Though they were the enemies of Byzantium, the Normans, like the Venetians, assimilated Byzantine culture and even employed Byzantine artisans. In their Sicilian kingdom, the mosaics of the great basilican church of Monreale, not far from Palermo, are striking evidence of Byzantium's presence. They rival those of Saint Mark's not only in quality but also in their extent. One scholar has estimated that more than one hundred million glass and stone tesserae were required for the Monreale mosaics.

These mosaics were paid for by the Norman king William II, who is portrayed twice, continuing the theme of royal presence and patronage of the much earlier Ravenna portraits of Justinian and Theodora at San Vitale (FIGS. 12-10 and 12-11). In one panel, William, clearly labeled, unlike Justinian or his consort, stands next to the enthroned Christ, who places his hand upon William's crown. In the second, the king kneels before the Virgin and presents her with a model of the Monreale church, a role that at San Vitale Bishop Ecclesius played (FIG. 12-9), rather than the emperor or empress. As in the Ravenna church, the mosaic program commemorates both the piety and power of the ruler who reigns with divine authority.

The apse mosaics (FIG. **12-24**) are especially impressive. The image of Christ as Pantocrator, as ruler and judge of heaven and earth, looms menacingly in the vault, a colossal allusion to William's kingly power and a challenge to all who would dispute the royal right. In Byzantium proper, the Pantocrator's image usually appears in the main dome of centralized churches such as those at Daphni and Hosios Loukas (FIG. 12-19), but the Greek churches are monastic churches and they were not built for the glorification of monarchs. Monreale, moreover, is a basilica—longitudinally planned in the Western tradition. The semidome of the apse, the only

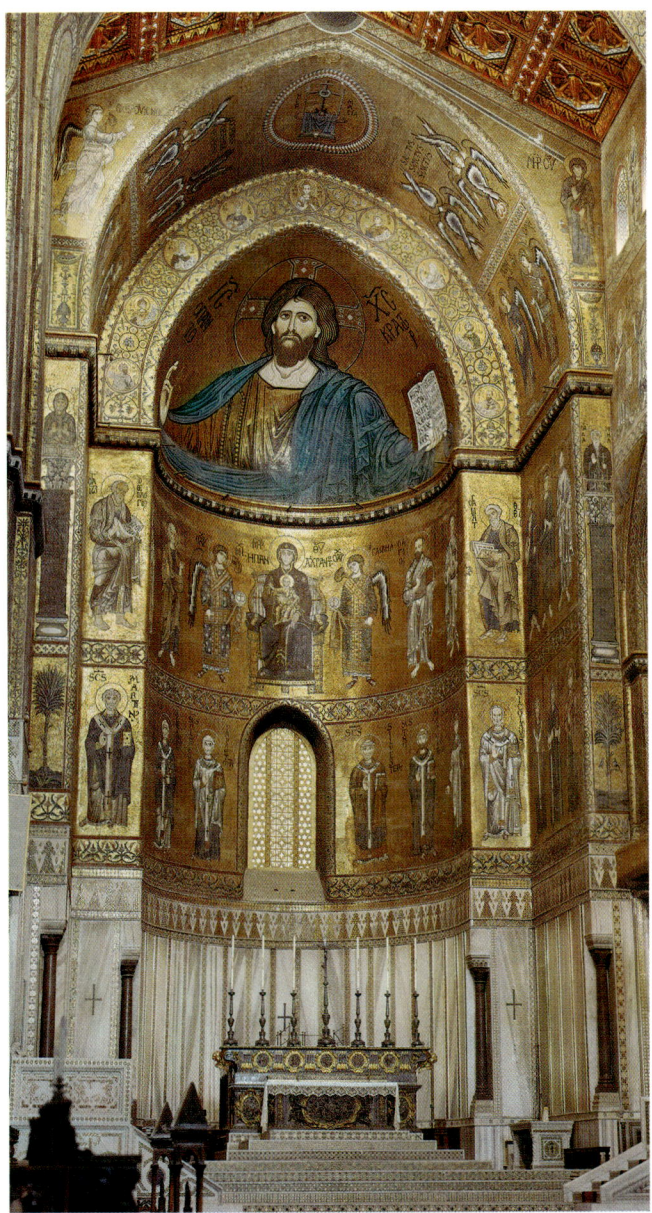

12-24 Pantocrator, Theotokos and Child, angels, and saints, apse mosaic in the cathedral at Monreale, Italy, ca. 1180–1190.

vault in the building and its architectural focus, was the most conspicuous place for the vast image with its politically propagandistic overtones. Below the Pantocrator in rank and dignity, the enthroned Theotokos is flanked by archangels and the Twelve Apostles symmetrically arranged in balanced groups. Lower on the wall (and less elevated in the hierarchy) are popes, bishops, and other saints. The artists observed the stern formalities of style characteristic of Byzantine hieraticism here, far from Constantinople. The Monreale mosaics testify to the stature of Byzantium and of Byzantine art in medieval Italy.

Luxury Arts

EMPRESS IRENE AND SAINT MARK'S The wealth and pretensions of the Venetian dukes and the Norman kings of Sicily are revealed not only by their ambitious building programs with their acres of mosaic-covered walls, vaults, and

domes but also by the sometimes extravagant furnishings of their churches. In 976, the Venetian doge Pietro Orseolo ordered from Constantinople a set of gold-and-enamel plaques nailed on wood for the second church of Saint Mark in Venice. In 1105, under Doge Ordelafo Falier, the plaques were refashioned into a *pala* (altarpiece, or panel placed behind and over the altar) that was again augmented in 1209 with booty from the Crusaders' sack of Constantinople. The altarpiece was modified once more in 1345. In its final form the Venetian *Pala d'Oro (Golden Pala)* reflects contemporaneous (Gothic) taste in Italy and unites plaques of several different periods featuring narrative scenes from Christ's life and dozens of saints, angels, prophets, and temporal rulers in golden niches surrounded by jewels of many different hues.

Among the figures added in 1105 was Doge Falier and the Byzantine Emperor Alexius I Comnenus (r. 1081–1118) and his wife, the Empress Irene (FIG. **12-25**). The regally attired and haloed gold-and-enamel Irene is a frontal, wafer-thin, weightless figure, a stylistic cousin to the mosaic saints and apostles of Monreale, despite the enormous differences in scale and technique. The presence of Alexius and Irene have suggested to some scholars that the *Pala d'Oro* in its 1105 form was an imperial gift to the Venetian church.

The pendant portraits of the Constantinopolitan rulers carried on a tradition of inserting haloed royal images into church programs that went back to the Early Byzantine

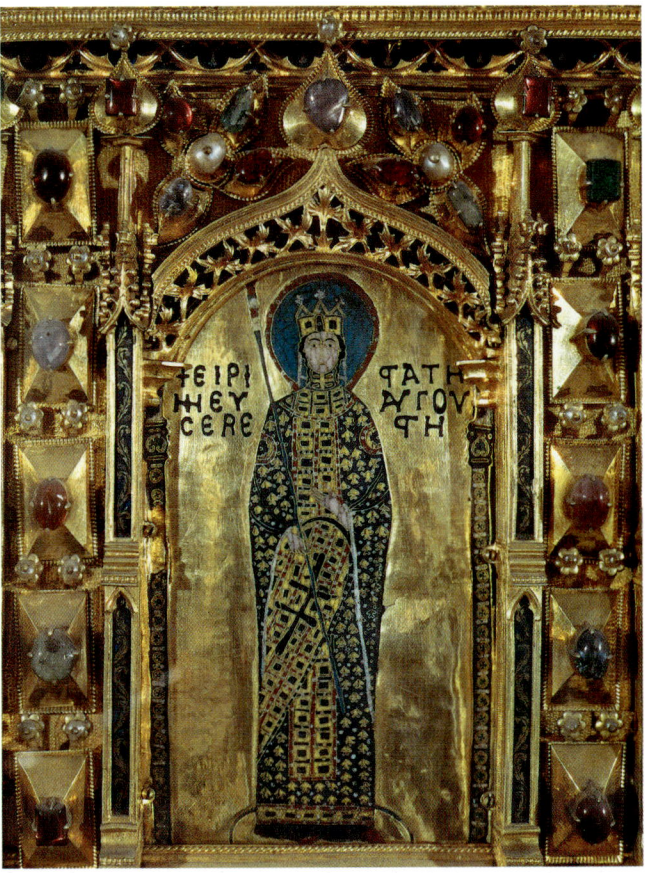

12-25 Empress Irene, detail of the *Pala d'Oro*, Saint Mark's, Venice, Italy, ca. 1105. Gold cloisonné inlaid with precious stones, detail approx. $7'' \times 4\frac{1}{2}''$.

period (FIGS. 12-10 and 12-11). They are reminders once again of the important role the Byzantine empresses played in both life and art and of the commercial, political, and artistic exchanges between Italy and Byzantium in the twelfth century.

DIPTYCH TO TRIPTYCH   Costly carved ivories also were produced in large numbers in the Middle Byzantine period, but after iconoclasm the three-part *triptych* replaced the earlier diptych as the standard format for ivory panels. One of the premier examples of this type is the *Harbaville Triptych* (FIG. **12-26**), a portable shrine with hinged wings that was used for private devotion. Such triptychs were very popular—among those who could afford such luxurious items—and they often replaced icons for use in personal prayer. Carved on the wings of the *Harbaville Triptych*, both front and back, are four pairs of full-length figures and two pairs of medallions depicting saints, mostly bishops but including four military saints on the front. A cross dominates the central panel on the back (not illustrated). On the front is a scene of *Deesis*. Saint John the Baptist and the Theotokos appear as intercessors, praying on behalf of the viewer to the enthroned Savior. Below them are five apostles.

The hieratic formality and solemnity associated with Byzantine art, visible in the mosaics of Ravenna and Monreale and in the *Pala d'Oro* enamel plaques, yielded here to a softer, more fluent technique. They may lack true classical contrapposto, but the looser stances of the figures (most stand on bases, like freestanding statues) and three-quarter views of many of the heads relieve the hard austerity of the customary frontal pose. This more natural classicizing spirit was a second, equally important, stylistic current of the Middle Byzantine period. It also surfaced in mural painting and book illumination.

Painting

BYZANTIUM IN THE BALKANS   When the emperors lifted the ban against religious images and again encouraged religious painting at Constantinople, the impact was felt far and wide. The style varied from region to region, as expected, but a renewed enthusiasm for picturing the key New Testament figures and events was universal.

In 1164, at Nerezi in Macedonia, Byzantine painters embellished the church of Saint Pantaleimon with murals of great emotional power. One of these represents the Lamentation over the dead Christ (FIG. **12-27**). It is an image of passionate grief. The artist captured Christ's friends in attitudes, expressions, and gestures of quite human bereavement. Mary presses her cheek against her dead son's face while Saint John clings to Christ's left hand. Saint Peter and the disciple Nicodemus kneel at his feet. Above, swooning angels hover in a blue sky above a hilly landscape—a striking contrast to the abstract golden world of the mosaics favored for church walls elsewhere in the Byzantine Empire. The artist strove to make utterly convincing an emotionally charged realization of the theme by staging the Gospel story in a more natural setting and peopling it with fully modeled actors. This alternate representational mode, no less Byzantine than the hieratic style of Ravenna or the poignant melancholy of Daphni, found a ready reception in late medieval Italy (compare FIGS. 12-33 and 19-9).

DAVID AS GRECO-ROMAN HARPIST   Another example of this classicizing style is a page from a book of the Psalms of David. The so-called *Paris Psalter* (FIG. **12-28**) reasserts the artistic values of the classical past with astonishing authority. Art historians believe the manuscript dates from

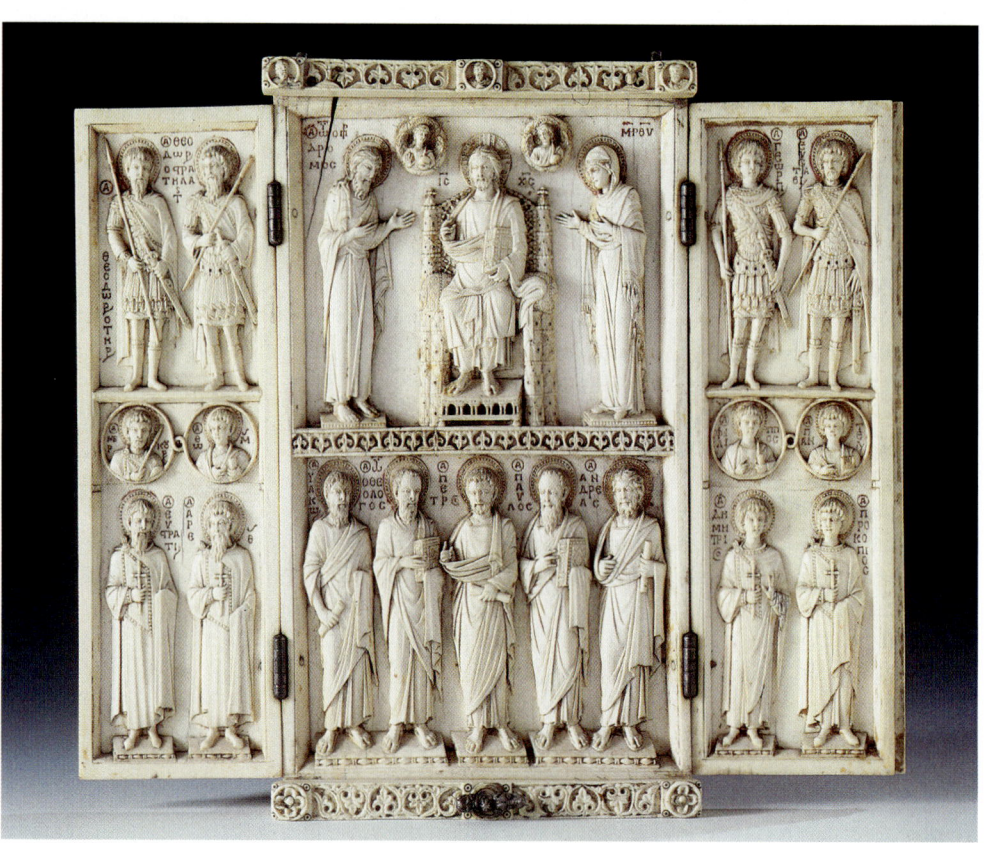

12-26   Christ enthroned with saints *(Harbaville Triptych)*, ca. 950. Ivory, central panel 9½″ × 5½″. Louvre, Paris.

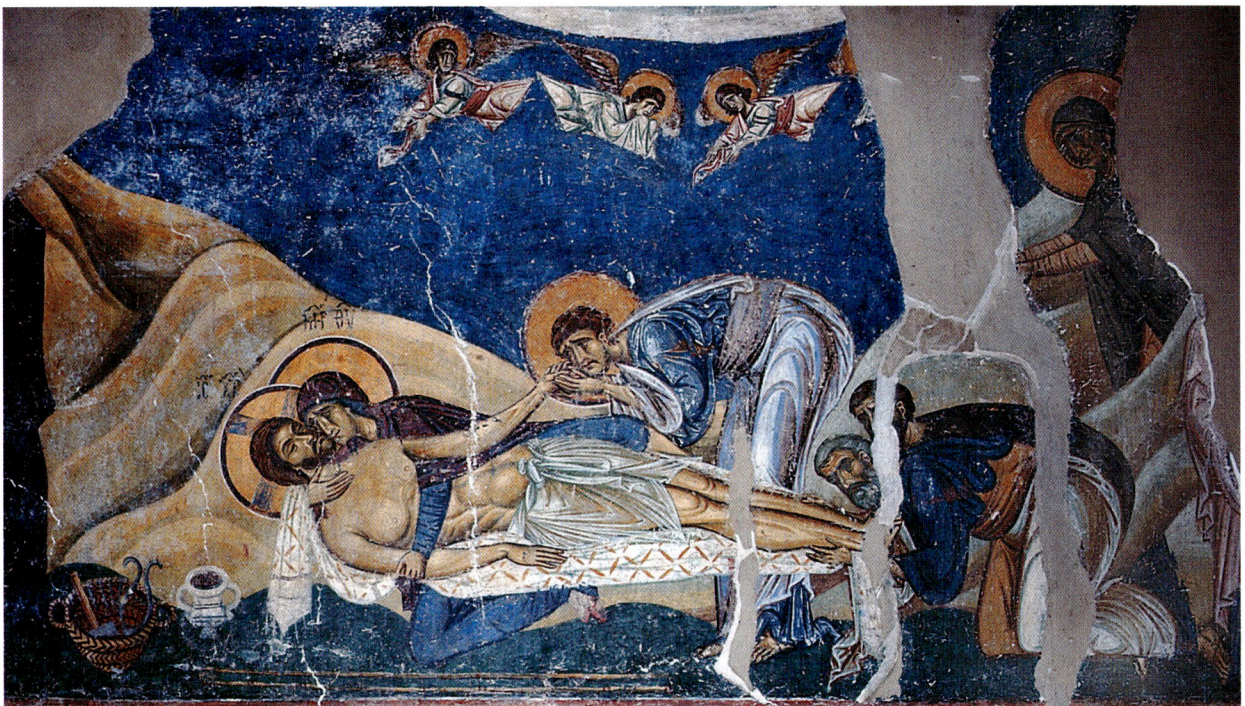

12-27 *Lamentation over the Dead Christ,* wall painting, Saint Pantaleimon, Nerezi, Macedonia, 1164.

the mid-tenth century—the so-called "Macedonian Renaissance," a time of enthusiastic and careful study of ancient Greece's language and literature and of humanistic reverence for the classical past. It was only natural that in art inspiration should be drawn once again from the Hellenistic naturalism of the pre-Christian Mediterranean world.

David, the psalmist, surrounded by sheep, goats, and his faithful dog, plays his harp in a rocky landscape with a town in the background. Similar settings appeared frequently in Pompeian murals. Befitting an ancient depiction of Orpheus, the Greek hero who could charm even inanimate objects with his music, allegorical figures accompany the Old Testament harpist. Melody looks over his shoulder, while Echo peers from behind a column. A reclining male figure points to an inscription that identifies him as representing the mountain of Bethlehem. These allegorical figures do not appear in the Bible. They are the stock population of Greco-Roman painting. Apparently, the artist had seen a work from late antiquity or perhaps earlier and partly translated it into a Byzantine pictorial idiom. In works such as this, Byzantine artists kept the classical style alive in the Middle Ages.

A MIRACLE-WORKING RUSSIAN ICON Nothing in Middle Byzantine art better demonstrates the rejection of the iconoclastic viewpoint than the painted icon's return to prominence. After the restoration of images, such icons multiplied by the thousands to meet public and private demand. In the eleventh century, the clergy began to display icons in hieratic order (Christ, the Theotokos, John the Baptist, and then other saints, as on the *Harbaville Triptych*) in tiers on the *templon,* the columnar screen separating the sanctuary from the main body of a Byzantine church.

One example, the renowned *Vladimir Virgin* (FIG. **12-29**), is a masterpiece of its kind. Descended from works such as the Mount Sinai icon (FIG. 12-15), the *Vladimir Virgin* clearly

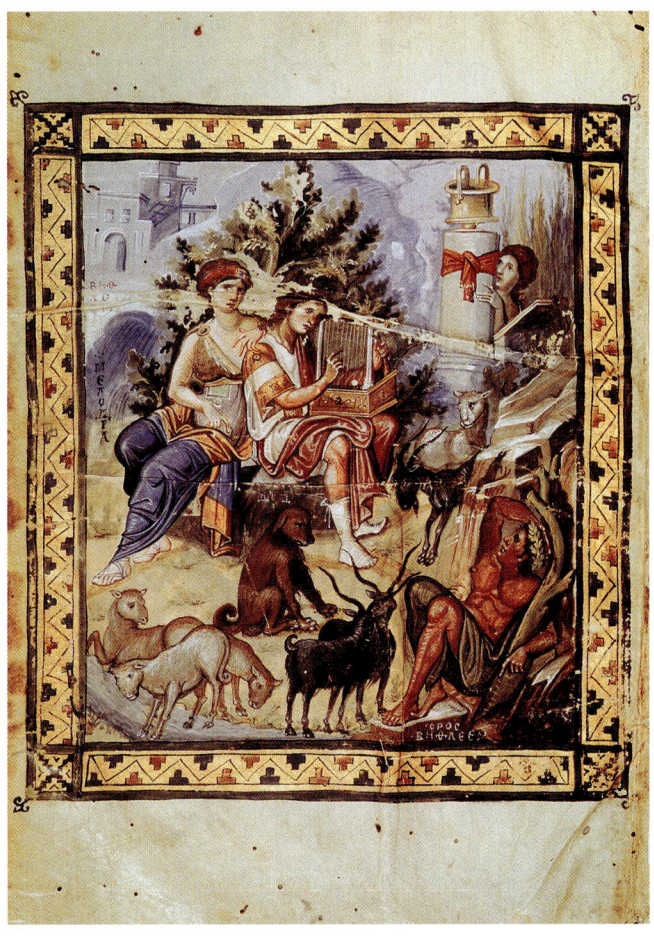

12-28 David composing the Psalms, folio 1 verso of the *Paris Psalter,* ca. 950–970. Tempera on vellum, 1′ 2⅛″ × 10¼″. Bibliothèque Nationale, Paris.

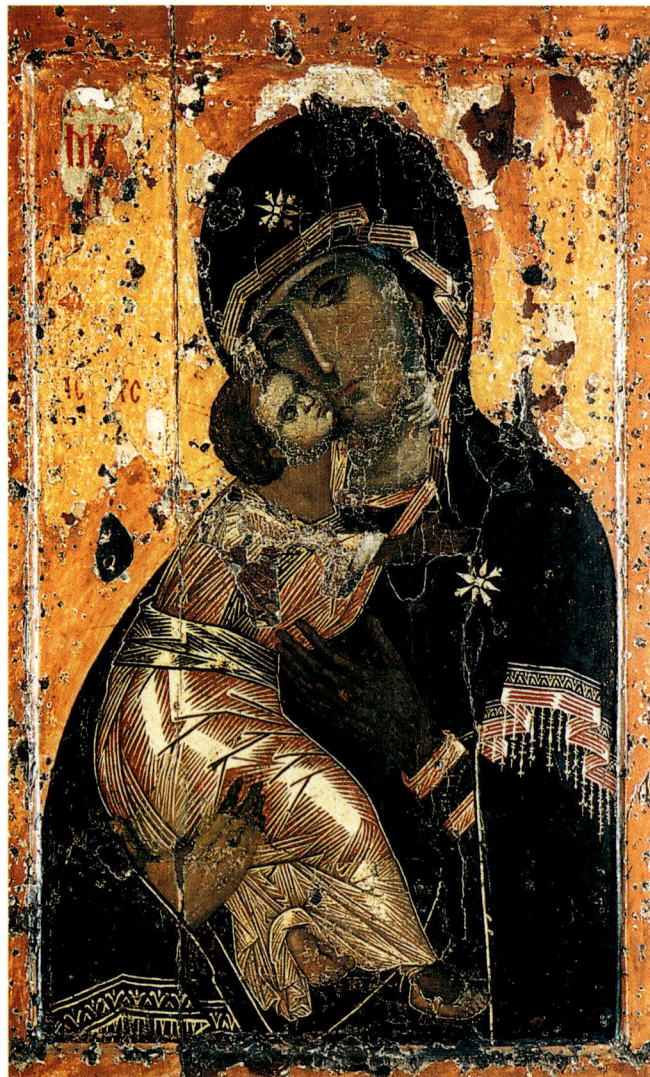

12-29 Virgin (Theotokos) and Child, icon *(Vladimir Virgin)*, late eleventh to early twelfth century. Tempera on wood, original panel approx. 2′ 6½″ × 1′ 9″. Tretyakov Gallery, Moscow.

reveals the stylized abstraction that centuries of working and reworking the conventional image had wrought. Painted by an artist in Byzantium, the characteristic traits of the Byzantine icon of the Virgin and Child are all present: the sharp sidewise inclination of the Virgin's head to meet the tightly embraced Christ Child; the long, straight nose and small mouth; the golden rays in the infant's drapery; the decorative sweep of the unbroken contour that encloses the two figures; the flat silhouette against the golden ground; and the deep pathos of the Virgin's expression as she contemplates the future sacrifice of her son.

The icon of Vladimir, like most icons, has seen hard service. Placed before or above altars in churches or private chapels, incense and the smoke from candles that burned before or below it blackened its surface. It was frequently repainted, often by inferior artists, and only the faces show the original surface. First painted in the late eleventh or early twelfth century, it was exported to Vladimir in Russia—hence its name—and then, as a wonder-working image, was taken in 1395 to Moscow to protect that city from the Mongols. As the especially sacred picture of their country, the Rus-

sians believed it saved the city of Kazan from later Tartar invasions and all of Russia from the Poles in the seventeenth century. It is a historical symbol of Byzantium's religious and cultural mission to the Slavic world.

LATE BYZANTINE ART (1204–1453)

THE SACK OF CONSTANTINOPLE   When rule passed from the Macedonian to the Comnenian dynasty in the later eleventh and the twelfth centuries, three events of fateful significance changed Byzantium's fortunes for the worse. The Seljuk Turks conquered most of Anatolia. The Byzantine Orthodox Church broke finally with the Church of Rome. And the Crusades brought the Latins (a generic term for the peoples of the West) into Byzantine lands on their way to fight for the Cross against the Saracens (Muslims) in the Holy Land (see "The Crusades," Chapter 17, page 473).

Crusaders had passed through Constantinople many times en route to "smite the infidel" and had marveled at its wealth and magnificence. Envy, greed, religious fanaticism (the Latins called the Greeks "heretics"), and even ethnic enmity motivated the Crusaders when, during the Fourth Crusade in 1203 and 1204, the Venetians persuaded them to divert their expedition against the Muslims in Palestine and to attack Constantinople instead. They took the city and atrociously sacked it in a manner so horrible as to be remembered by Greek peoples to this day. Nicetas Choniates, a contemporaneous historian, expressed the feelings of the Byzantines toward the Crusaders: "The accursed Latins would plunder our wealth and wipe out our race. . . . Between us there can be only an unbridgeable gulf of hatred. . . . They bear the Cross of Christ on their shoulders, but even the Saracens are kinder." [6]

The Latins set up kingdoms within Byzantium, notably in Constantinople itself. What remained of Byzantium was split into three small states. The Palaeologans ruled one of these, the kingdom of Nicaea. In 1261, Michael VIII Palaeologus (r. 1259–1282) succeeded in recapturing Constantinople. But his empire was no more than a fragment, and even that disintegrated during the next two centuries. Isolated from the Christian West by Muslim conquests in the Balkans and besieged by Muslim Turks to the east, Byzantium sought help from the West. It was not forthcoming. In 1453, the Ottoman Turks, then a formidable power, captured Constantinople and brought to an end the long history of Byzantium (see Chapter 13). But despite the state's grim political condition under the Palaeologan dynasty, the arts flourished well into the fourteenth century.

Architecture

A MULTIPLICATION OF DOMES   Late Byzantine architecture did not depart radically from the characteristic plans and elevations of Middle Byzantine architecture. But the number of domes and drums increased, and their groupings became more and more dramatic. Elevations became narrower and steeper. Wall and drum arcades were more deeply cut back into overlapping arches. The eaves curved rhythmically and varied brick patterns ornamented the external walls.

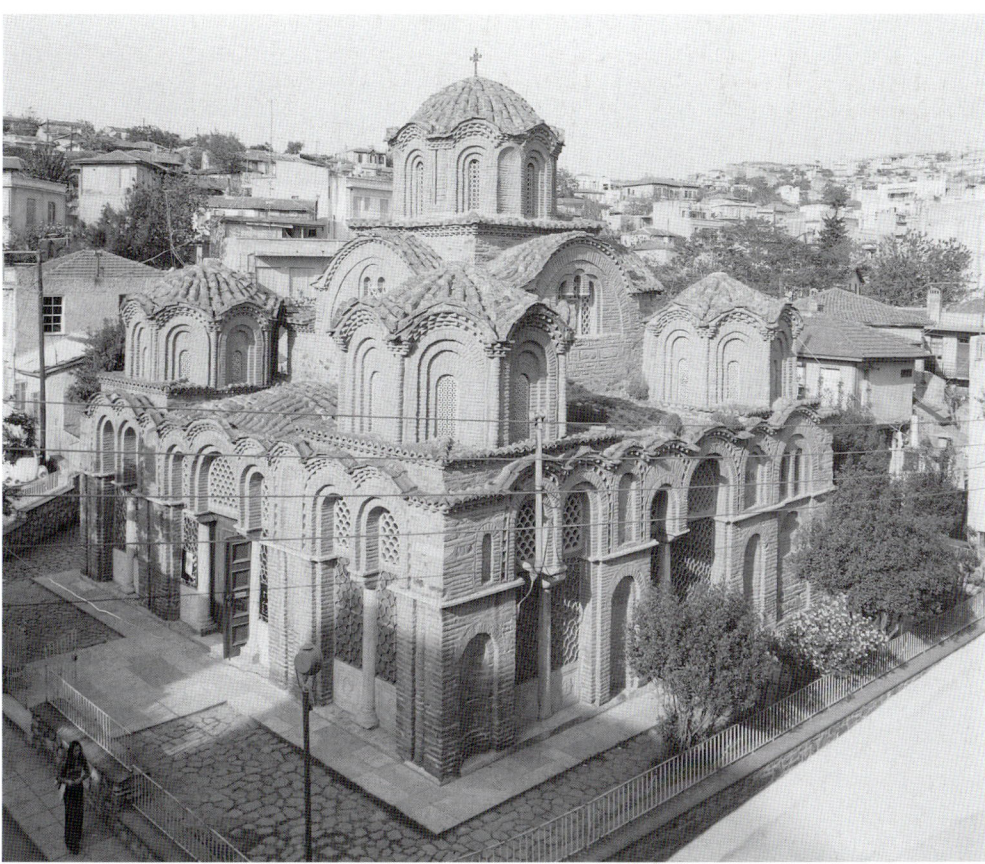

12-30 Church of Saint Catherine, Thessaloniki, Greece, ca. 1280.

The church of Saint Catherine in Thessaloniki (FIG. **12-30**), second city to Constantinople in rank, shows all these Palaeologan variations on the grand stylistic theme of Middle Byzantine architecture. The plan is an inscribed cross with a central dome and four additional domes at the corners. On the exterior these appear as *cupolas,* drums with shallow caps, the central drum rising a level above the others. Thus the church has a vertical gradation from a rectilinear base to the superstructure's cylindrical volumes, culminating in the dominant central unit. Wall and drum arcades are grouped rhythmically in alternating pairs and triads. Lively patternings face and punctuate the enframements of arches and niches and the scalloped eaves. The intricate harmonizing by alternation and repetition of walls and openings and of verticals, half-circles, and cylinders produces a lively rhythm. The complexity of surfaces and details characteristic of earlier Byzantine building interiors broke out to the exterior in Late Byzantine architecture.

Painting

RESURRECTION AND REDEMPTION A new burst of creative energy also enlivened Late Byzantine painting. Artists produced masterpieces of mural and icon painting rivaling those of the earlier periods. A fresco (FIG. **12-31**) in the apse of the *parekklesion* (side chapel, in this instance a funerary chapel) of the Church of Christ in Chora (now the Kariye Museum, formerly the Kariye Camii mosque) in Constantinople is another striking version of the Anastasis theme, represented earlier at Saint Mark's in Venice (FIG. 12-23). Here,

the Anastasis is central to a cycle of pictures portraying the themes of human mortality and redemption by Christ and of the intercession of the Virgin, both appropriate for a funerary chapel.

As in the version in Saint Mark's, Christ, trampling Satan and all the locks and keys of his prison house of Hell, raises Adam and Eve from their tombs. Looking on are John the Baptist, King David, and King Solomon on the left. And on the right are the righteous of the Old Dispensation (led by Saint Stephen, first of the martyrs of the New Dispensation). Comparison with the Saint Mark's version, however, reveals sharp differences in composition, expression, and figure style. Christ does not carry the cross and he appears in a luminous mandorla. Formal symmetry has returned, with Christ at the center, his pose and gaze essentially frontal and his hands, free of the cross, reaching out equally to Adam and Eve. Instead of the rough, tormented angularities of the Saint Mark's mosaic, the action is swift and smooth. All tension is erased, the supple motions executed with the grace of a ballet. The figures float and levitate in a spiritual atmosphere, spaceless and without material mass or shadow-casting volume. This same smoothness and lightness can be seen in the modeling of the figures and the subtly nuanced coloration. The jagged abstractions of drapery found in the Saint Mark's figures are gone in a return to the fluent delineation of drapery characteristic of the long tradition of classical illusionism.

ART FOR A SPIRITUAL WORLD It is useful here to compare the Anastasis of the Kariye not only with that of Saint Mark's but also with the Transfiguration mosaic of Saint

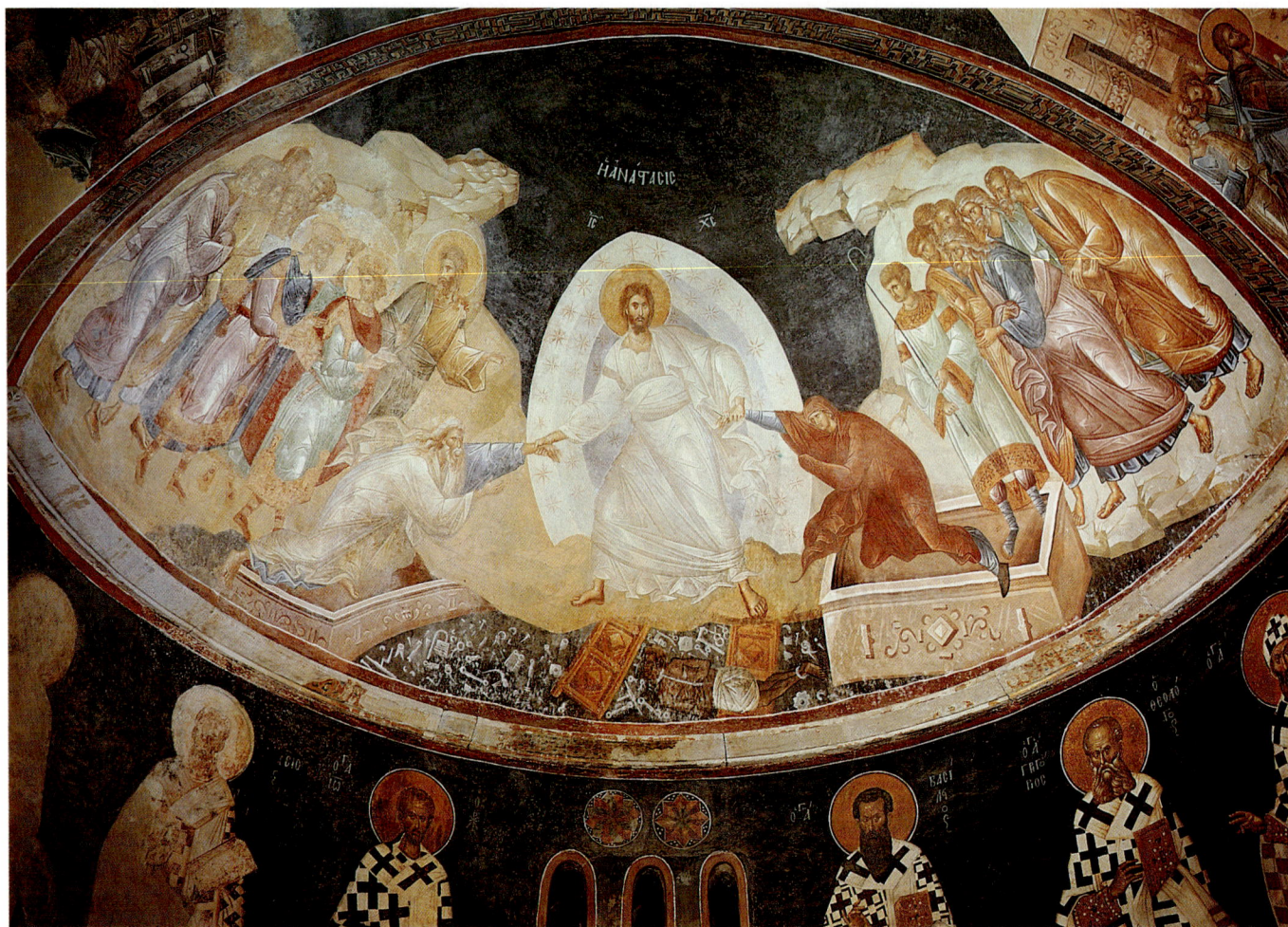

12-31   *Anastasis,* apse fresco in the *parekklesion* of the Church of Christ in Chora (now the Kariye Museum), Constantinople (Istanbul), Turkey, ca. 1310–1320.

Catherine's at Mount Sinai (FIG. 12-13). This comparison sets side by side outstanding works from the three great periods of Byzantine art. Despite obvious differences of individual style and expression, all three display an essential conservatism that determined the iconography, composition, figural and facial types, bodily attitudes, and the rendering of space and volume, as well as the human form and its drapery. Throughout its history, Byzantine art looked back to its antecedents, Greco-Roman illusionism as transformed in the age of Justinian. Like their Orthodox religion, Byzantine artists were suspicious of any real innovation, especially that imported from outside the Byzantine cultural sphere. They drew their images from a persistent and conventionalized vision of a spiritual world unsusceptible to change. Byzantine art was not concerned with the systematic observation of material nature as the source of its imaging of the eternal.

Byzantine spirituality was perhaps most intensely felt in icon painting. In the Late Byzantine period the Early Byzantine low chancel screen separating the church sanctuary from its main area developed into an *iconostasis* (icon stand), a high screen with doors. As its name implies, the iconostasis supported tiers of painted devotional images, which began to be produced again in large numbers, both in Constantinople and throughout the diminished Byzantine Empire.

An outstanding example, notable for the lavish use of finely etched silver foil to frame the tempera figure of Christ as Savior of Souls (FIG. **12-32**), dates to the beginning of the fourteenth century. It comes from the church of Saint Clement at Ohrid in Macedonia, where many Late Byzantine icons imported from the capital have been preserved. The Ohrid Christ, consistent with Byzantine art's conservative nature, adhered to an iconographical and stylistic tradition that went back to the earliest icons from the monastery at Mount Sinai. The artist chose not only the standard presentation of the Savior holding a bejeweled Bible in his left hand while he blesses the faithful with his right hand, but also painted the image in the eclectic style familiar to Byzantium. Note especially the juxtaposition of Christ's fully modeled head and neck, which reveal the Byzantine painter's Greco-Roman heritage, with the schematic linear folds of Christ's garment, which do not envelop the figure but rather seem to be placed in front of it.

A PARADE OF ICONS   In the Late Byzantine period, icons often were painted on two sides because they were intended to be carried in processions. When they were deposited in the church, they were not mounted on the iconostasis but were exhibited on stands so that worshipers could

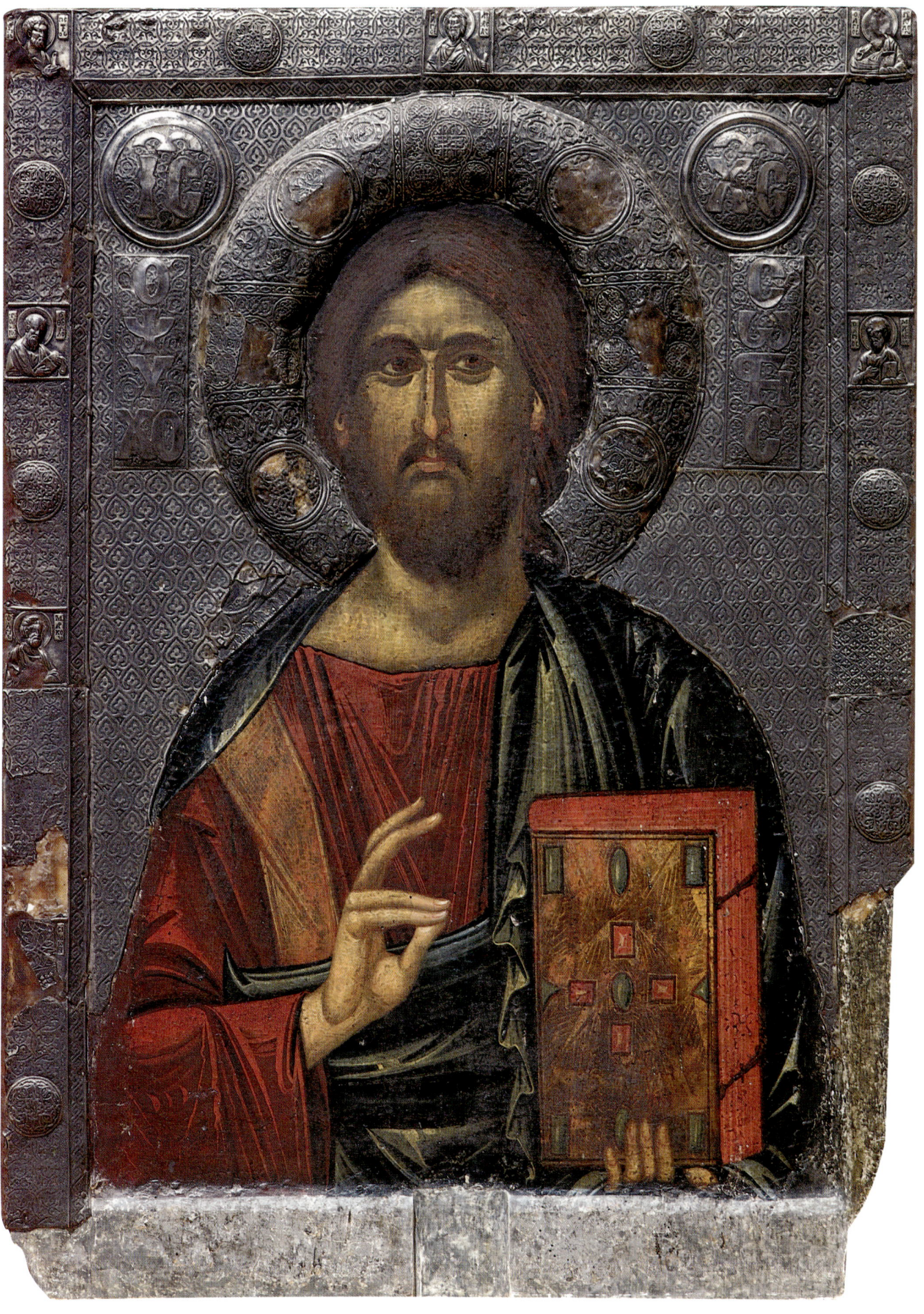

12-32 *Christ as Savior of Souls*, icon from the church of Saint Clement, Ohrid, Macedonia, early fourteenth century. Tempera, linen, and silver on wood, 3′ $\frac{1}{4}$″ × 2′ 2$\frac{1}{2}$″. Icon Gallery of Saint Clement, Ohrid.

view them from both sides. The Ohrid icon of Christ has a painting of the Crucifixion on its reverse. Another double icon from Saint Clement's, also imported from Constantinople, represents the Virgin on the front as Christ's counterpart as Savior of Souls. The Annunciation (FIG. **12-33**) is the subject of the reverse. With a commanding gesture of heavenly authority, the angel Gabriel announces to Mary that she is to be the Mother of God. She responds with a simple gesture conveying both astonishment and acceptance. The gestures and attitudes of the figures are again conventional. Like the highly simplified architectural props, they have a long history in Byzantine art. The tall, elegant figure of the angel, the smooth rhythm of its striding motion, and the delineation and modeling of the drapery reveal its close stylistic kinship to the Christ figure of the Kariye mural (FIG. 12-31). Both exemplify the high artistic achievement of metropolitan Constantinople's narrative art in the Palaeologan revival.

A MASTER ICON PAINTER IN RUSSIA   In Russia, icon painting flourished for centuries, extending the life of the style well beyond the collapse of the Byzantine Empire in 1453. Russian paintings usually had strong patterns, firm lines, and intense contrasting colors. All served to heighten the legibility of the icons in the wavering candlelight and clouds of incense that worshipers encountered in church interiors. For many art historians, Russian painting reached a cli-

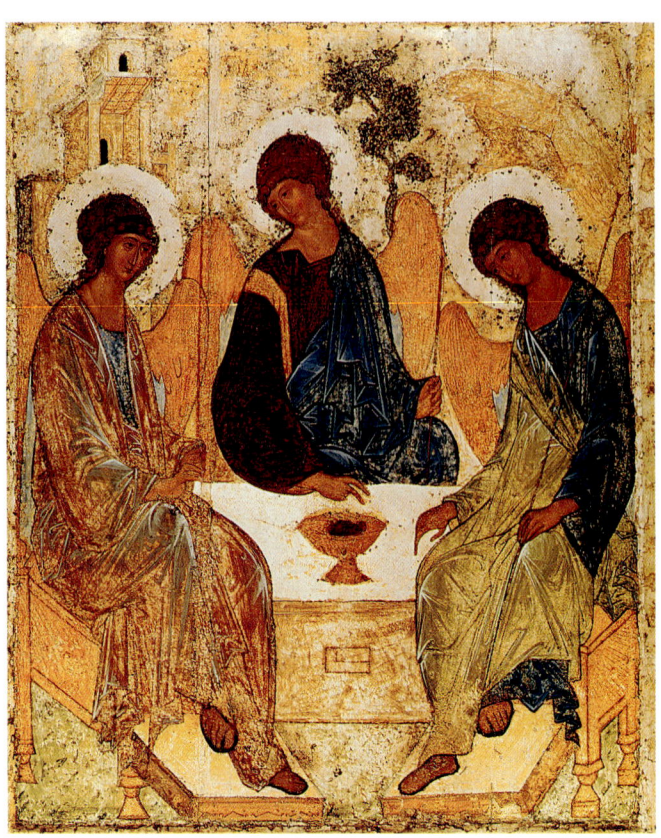

12-34   ANDREI RUBLYEV, Three angels (Old Testament Trinity), ca. 1410. Tempera on wood, 4′ 8″ × 3 ′9″. Tretyakov Gallery, Moscow.

max in the work of ANDREI RUBLYEV (ca. 1370–1430). His rendition of the three Old Testament angels who appeared to Abraham (FIG. **12-34**) is a work of great spiritual power, as well as an unsurpassed example of subtle line in union with intensely vivid color. These angels were interpreted in Christian thought as a prefiguration of the Holy Trinity after Christ's incarnation. Here they sit about a table, each framed with a halo and sweeping wings, three nearly identical figures distinguished only by their garment colors. The light linear play of the draperies sets off the tranquil demeanor of the figures. Color defines the forms and becomes more intense by the juxtaposition of complementary hues. The intense blue and green folds of the central figure's cloak, for example, stand out starkly against the deep-red robe and the gilded orange of the wings. In the figure on the left, the highlights of the orange cloak are an opalescent blue green. The unmodulated saturation, brilliance, and purity of the color harmonies were the hallmark of Rublyev's style.

Luxury Arts

GOD AND EMPEROR ON PRIESTLY ROBES   In Byzantium, other arts also played an indispensable part in the ensemble of a church interior—the carvings and rich metalwork of the iconostasis, serving to frame icons that themselves often were ornamented with precious metals and jewels; the finely wrought, gleaming candlesticks and candelabra; the illuminated books bound in gold or ivory and inlaid with jewels and enamels; and the crosses, croziers, sacred vessels, and processional banners. Each, with its great richness of texture and color, contributed to the total ambience of the Byzantine

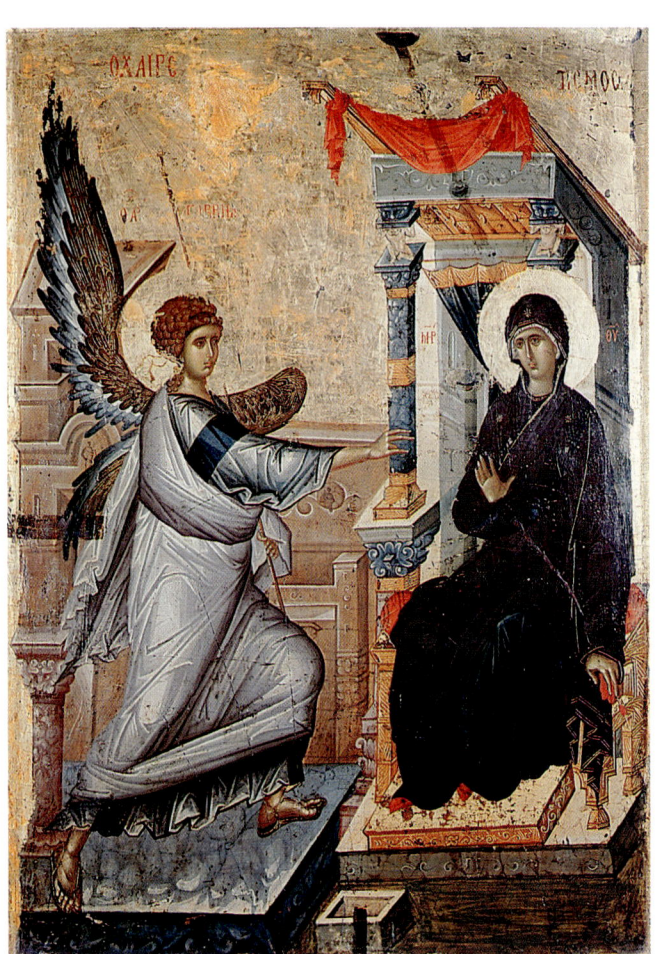

12-33   Annunciation, reverse of two-sided icon from the church of Saint Clement, Ohrid, Macedonia, early fourteenth century. Tempera and linen on wood, 3′ $\frac{1}{4}$″ × 2′ 2$\frac{3}{4}$″. Icon Gallery of Saint Clement, Ohrid.

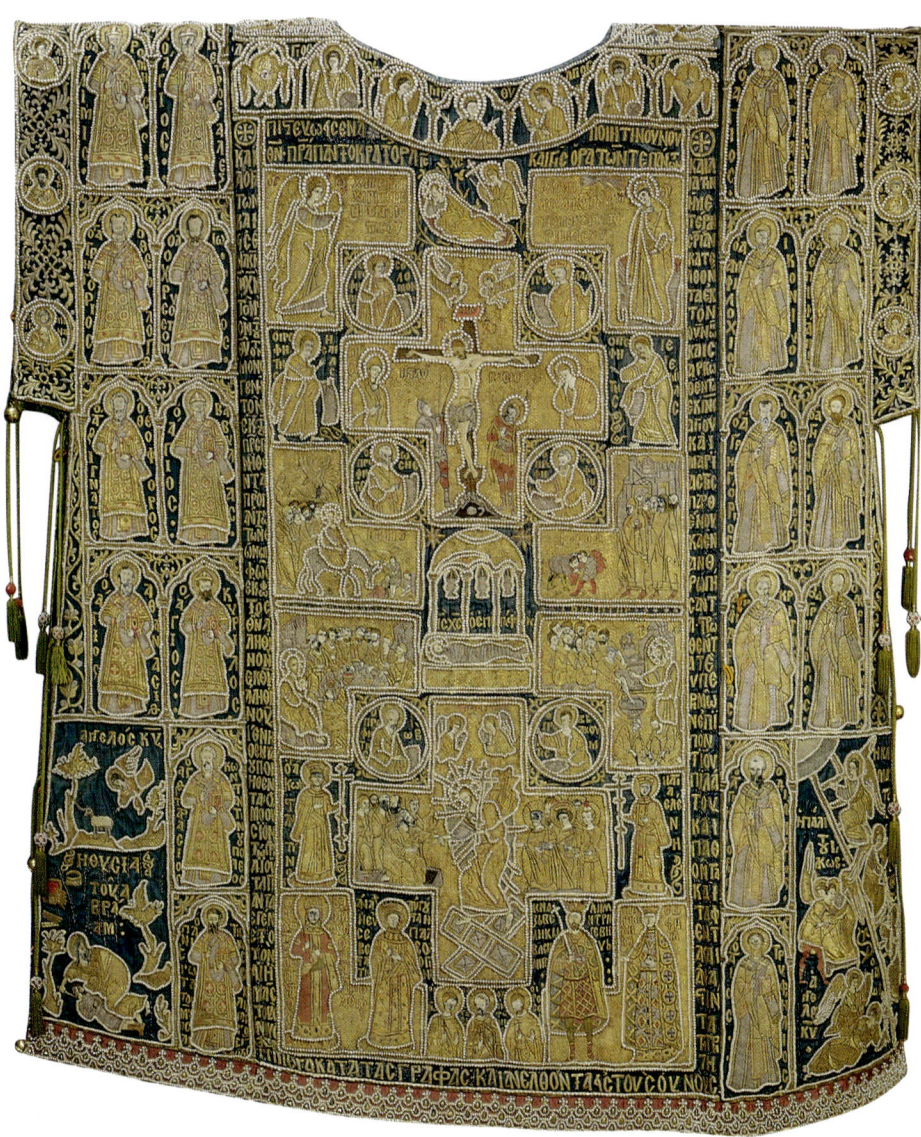

12-35 Large sakkos of Photius, ca. 1417. Satin embroidered with gold and silver thread and silk with pearl ornament, approx. 4'5" long. Kremlin Armory, Moscow.

church. And amid these opulent inanimate treasures, the solemn clergy celebrated the liturgy of the Orthodox faith in magnificent embroidered and bejeweled robes, adding further to the visual feast.

Fortunately some of these vestments have been reverently preserved through centuries of political and social upheaval in Russia. One of them is the so-called "large *sakkos*" (a magnificent "small sakkos" also exists) or tunic (FIG. **12-35**) of Photius, the early-fifteenth-century Metropolitan (Orthodox bishop) of Russia. It can represent here this whole branch of the "minor arts" and remind readers of how incomplete the story of art through the ages would be if the narrative were confined to monumental works of painting, sculpture, and architecture.

Photius's satin sakkos is embroidered with gold and silver thread and colored silks outlined with pearls. Dozens of religious and secular figures appear in a dazzling array of rectilinear, L-shaped, cruciform, and circular frames. The Crucifixion dominates the center of the front, while below is the Anastasis. All around are various Orthodox Church feasts and figures of saints, as well as Old Testament scenes, including the sacrifice of Abraham, linked with the Crucifixion here as it was in Early Christian times. Also portrayed are the Grand Prince of Moscow, Vasily Dimitrievich, and his wife Sophia Vitovtovna

(labeled in Russian), as well as the future emperor John VIII Palaeologus (r. 1425–1448) and his wife Anna Vasilyevna (named in Greek). Beside John is Photius, "Metropolitan of Kiev and all Russia." Needleworkers most likely embroidered the sakkos between the time of John's marriage in 1416 and Anna Vasilyevna's death in 1418. The couple probably sent the sakkos to Photius as a gift. In fifteenth-century Russia, as in sixth-century Ravenna, the rulers of Byzantium, as the vicars of God on earth, joined the clergy in celebration of the liturgy of the Christian Church.

THE THIRD ROME A third of a century after Photius first donned his sakkos, Constantinople fell to the Ottoman Turks, never to be recovered. With the passing of Byzantium, Russia became the self-appointed heir and the defender of Christendom against the infidel. The court of the tsar (the word is derived from *caesar*) declared: "Because the Old Rome has fallen, and because the Second Rome, which is Constantinople, is now in the hands of the godless Turks, thy kingdom, O pious Tsar, is the Third Rome. . . . Two Romes have fallen, but the Third stands, and there shall be no more."[7] Rome, Byzantium, Russia—the worlds of the caesars of Old Rome, New Rome, and Third Rome were a continuum, where artistic change was slow and the old ways never really died.

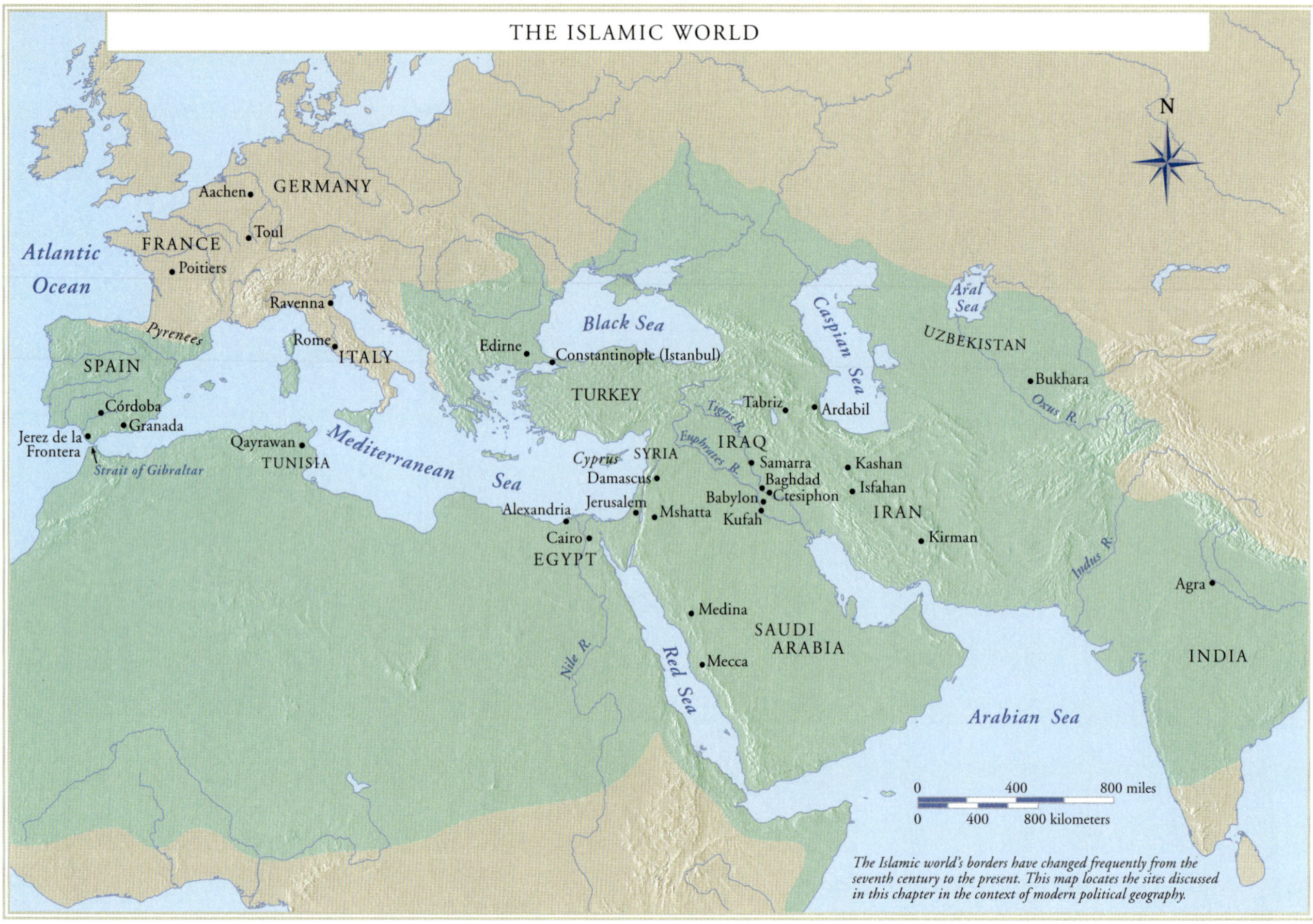

THE ISLAMIC WORLD

The Islamic world's borders have changed frequently from the seventh century to the present. This map locates the sites discussed in this chapter in the context of modern political geography.

	600	700	800	900	1000
SYRIA AND IRAQ		UMAYYAD CALIPHATE	ABBASID CALIPHATE		
SPAIN			UMAYYAD CALIPHATE		
IRAN AND CENTRAL ASIA			SAMANID DYNASTY		
EGYPT				FATIMID DYNASTY	
TURKEY					
INDIA					

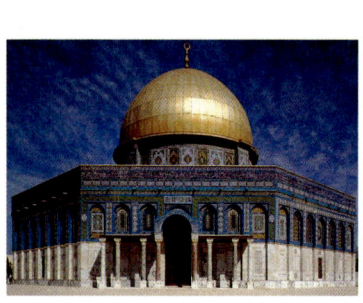

Dome of the Rock
Jerusalem, 687–692

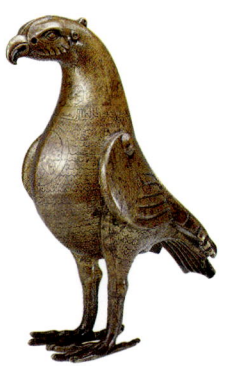

Sulayman
Bird ewer, 796

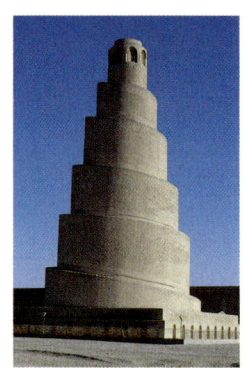

Malwiya minaret
Samarra, 848–852

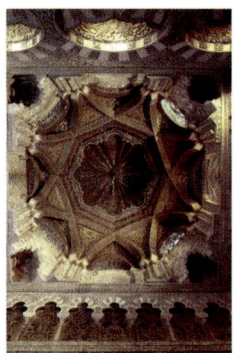

Mihrab dome, Great Mosque
Córdoba, 961–965

Birth of Muhammad in Mecca, ca. 570

Muhammad's first revelation, 610

Muhammad's flight to Mecca (Hijra), 622

Death of Muhammad in Medina, 632

Muslims capture Jerusalem, 638

Muslim conquest of Lower Egypt, 642

Umayyad caliphate established, 661

Muslim armies enter Spain, 711

Charles Martel defeats Muslims at Poitiers, 732

Abbasid caliphate established, 750

Umayyad caliphate established in Spain, 756

Abbasids found Baghdad, 762

Samanid dynasty established in Transoxiana, 819

Fatimid dynasty established in Egypt, 909

Fatamids found Cairo, 969

Fall of Umayyad caliphate in Spain, 1031

13

MUHAMMAD AND THE MUSLIMS

ISLAMIC ART

1100	1200	1300	1400	1500	1600

NASRID DYNASTY

SELJUK DYNASTY

TIMURID DYNASTY

SAFAVID DYNASTY

MAMLUK DYNASTY

OTTOMAN EMPIRE

MUGHAL DYNASTY

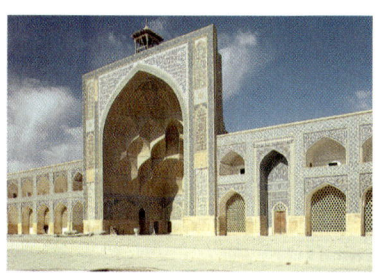

*Great Mosque, Isfahan
begun late eleventh century*

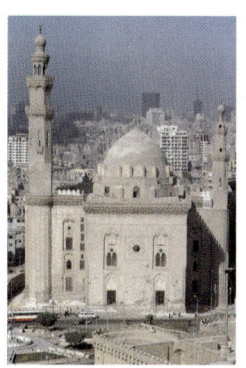

*Mausoleum of Sultan Hasan
Cairo, begun 1356*

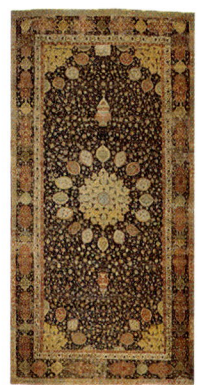

*Maqsud of Kashan
Ardabil carpet, 1540*

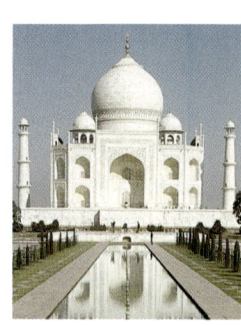

*Taj Mahal
Agra, 1632–1647*

Seljuk dynasty established in Iran, 1038

First Crusade captures Jerusalem, 1099

Nasrid dynasty established at Granada, 1230

Mamluk dynasty established in Egypt, 1250

Mongols sack Baghdad, 1258

Ottoman Empire founded, 1281

Ottomans capture Constantinople, 1453

Fall of Granada to the Christians, 1492

Safavid dynasty established in Iran, 1501

Mughal dynasty established in India, 1526

Ottomans capture Baghdad, 1534

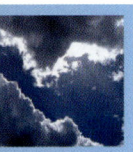

RELIGION AND MYTHOLOGY

Muhammad and Islam

Muhammad, founder of Islam and revered as its Prophet, was a native of Mecca on the west coast of Arabia. Born around 570 into a family that traced its roots to Ishmael, the son of the Hebrew prophet Abraham, Muhammad was a merchant in the great Arabian caravan trade. Critical of the polytheistic religion of his fellow Arabs, he was inspired to prophecy. Muhammad preached a religion of the one and only god, Allah, whose revelations he received beginning in 610 and for the rest of his life. Believers in Islam, who yield their will to Allah's will and have professed so, are *Muslims*. Opposition to Muhammad's message among the Arabs was strong enough to prompt the Prophet and his growing number of followers to flee from Mecca to a desert oasis eventually called Medina ("City of the Prophet"). Islam dates its beginnings from this flight in 622, known as the *Hijra* (emigration). (Muslims date events beginning with the Hijra in the same way Christians reckon events from Christ's birth and the Romans before them began their calendar with Rome's founding by Romulus in 753 B.C. The Muslim year is, however, a 354-day year of twelve lunar months, and dates cannot be converted by simply adding 622 to Christian-era dates.) Barely eight years later, in 630, Muhammad returned to Mecca with ten thousand soldiers. He took control of the city, converted the population to Islam, and destroyed all the idols. But he preserved as the Muslim world's symbolic center the small cubical building that had housed the idols, the *Kaaba* (from the Arabic for "cube"). The Arabs associated the Kaaba with the era of Abraham and Ishmael, the common ancestors of Jews and Arabs. Muhammad died in Medina in 632.

The essential meaning of Islam is acceptance of and submission to Allah's will. It broadly includes living according to the rules laid down in the collected revelations communicated through Muhammad during his lifetime. These are recorded in the Quran (Koran), Islam's sacred book, codified by the Muslim ruler Uthman (r. 644–656). *Quran* means "recitations"—a reference to the archangel Gabriel's instructions to Muhammad in 610 to "recite in the name of Allah." The Quran is composed of one hundred fourteen *surahs* (chapters) divided into verses.

The profession of faith in Allah is the first of five obligations binding all Muslims. In addition, the faithful must pray five times daily, facing in Mecca's direction; give alms to the poor; fast during the month of Ramadan; and once in a lifetime—if possible—make a pilgrimage to Mecca. Muslims are guided not only by the revelations in the Quran but also by Muhammad's example. The *Sunna,* collections of the Prophet's moral sayings and anecdotes of his exemplary deeds, are supplemental to the Quran, offering guidance to the faithful on ethical problems of everyday life. The reward for the Muslim faithful is Paradise.

Islam has much in common with Judaism and Christianity. Its adherents think of it as a continuation, completion, and in some sense a reformation of those other great monotheisms. In addition to the belief in one god, Islam incorporates many of the Old Testament teachings, with their sober ethical standards and hatred of idol worship, and those of the New Testament Gospels. Adam, Abraham, Moses, and Jesus are acknowledged as the prophetic predecessors of Muhammad, the final and greatest of the prophets before Allah's coming. Muhammad did not claim to be divine, as did Jesus, and he did not perform miracles. Rather, he was God's messenger, the purifier and perfecter of the common faith of Jews, Christians, and Muslims in one God. Islam also differs from Judaism and Christianity in its simpler organization. Muslims worship God directly, without a hierarchy of rabbis, priests, or saints acting as intermediaries.

In Islam, as Muhammad defined it, religious and secular authority were united even more completely than in Byzantium. Muhammad established a new social order, replacing the Arabs' old decentralized tribal one. In this he was influenced, no doubt, by the examples of the emperors and kings reigning in the lands his people would conquer. He took complete charge of his community's temporal, as well as spiritual, affairs. After Muhammad's death the *caliphs* (from the Arabic for "successor") continued this practice of uniting religious and political leadership in one ruler. But Muslims are divided over the legitimacy of temporal authority. The *Shiites* believe that only the descendants of the Prophet through his daughter Fatima, his only child, and her husband Ali are qualified for the highest political and religious leadership in Islam. The *Sunnites* recognize the legitimacy of the first caliphs, who were followers of Muhammad but not descended from him, and endorse either an elective or a dynastic principle of Islamic leadership.

THE RISE OF ISLAM

OUT OF ARABIA The religion of *Islam* (an Arabic word meaning "submission to God") arose among the peoples of the Arabian peninsula early in the seventh century (see "Muhammad and Islam," above). A distinctive and compelling Islamic tradition of art and architecture quickly followed. The Arabs were nomadic herders and caravan merchants traversing, from ancient times, the wastes and oases of the vast Arabian desert and settling and controlling its coasts. When Islam arose, the Arabs were peripheral to the Byzantine and Persian empires. Yet within little more than a century, the Mediterranean, once ringed and ruled by Byzantium, had become an Islamic lake. And the armies of Islam had conquered the Middle East, long the seat of Persian dominance and influence.

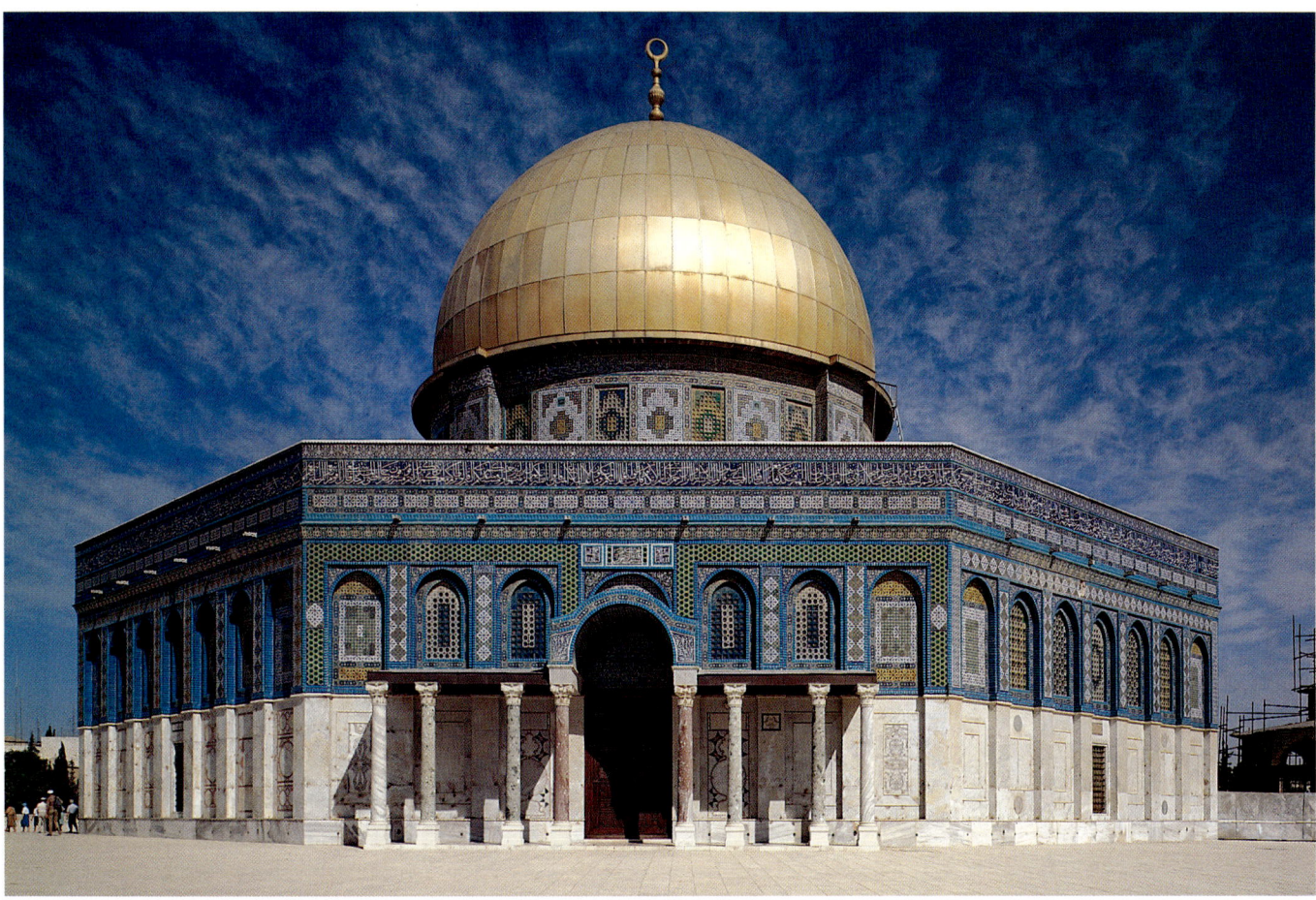

13-1 Dome of the Rock, Jerusalem, 687–692.

The swiftness of the Islamic advance is among the wonders of world history. By 640, Muslim warriors had conquered Syria, Palestine, and Iraq in the name of Islam. In 642, the Byzantine army abandoned Alexandria, marking the Muslim conquest of Lower (northern) Egypt. In 651, Iran was conquered, bringing more than four hundred years of Sasanian rule to an end (see Chapter 2). By 710, all of North Africa had been overrun, and a Muslim army crossed the Strait of Gibraltar into Spain. A victory at Jerez de la Frontera in southern Spain in 711 seemed to open all of western Europe to the Muslims. By 732, they had advanced north to Poitiers in France, where an army of Franks under Charles Martel, the grandfather of Charlemagne, opposed them successfully (see Chapter 16). Although Muslim forces continued to conduct raids in France, they could not extend their control beyond the Pyrenees along the French-Spanish border. But in Spain, the Islamic rulers of Córdoba flourished until 1031, and not until 1492 did Islamic influence and power in the Iberian Peninsula end. That year the Muslims of Granada fell to King Ferdinand and Queen Isabella, the sponsors of Columbus's voyage to the New World. Arab power prevailed in North Africa, the *Maghrib* or Arabic West. In the East, the Muslims reached the Indus River by 751, and only in Anatolia could stubborn Byzantine resistance slow their advance. Relentless Muslim pressure against the shrinking Byzantine Empire eventually caused its collapse in 1453, when the Ottoman Turks conquered Constantinople (see Chapter 12).

The irresistible and far-ranging sweep of Islam from Arabia to India to North Africa and Spain was not due to military might alone. That the initial conquests had effects that endured for centuries can be explained only by the nature of Islamic faith and its appeal to millions of converts. Islam remains today one of the world's great religions, with adherents on all continents. And the sophistication of its civilization has had a profound impact around the globe. Arabic translations of Aristotle and other Greek writers of antiquity were studied eagerly by Christian scholars in the West during the twelfth and thirteenth centuries (see Chapter 18). Arabic love lyrics and poetic descriptions of nature inspired the early French troubadours. Arab scholars laid the foundations of arithmetic and algebra, and their contributions to astronomy, medicine, and the natural sciences have made a lasting impression in the Western world.

EARLY ISLAMIC ART

During the early centuries of Islamic history, the Muslim world's political and cultural center was the Fertile Crescent of ancient Mesopotamia. This crescent-shaped area of cultivable land was strewn with impressive ruins of earlier cultures, from the Sumerians to the Sasanians (see Chapter 2). The caliphs of Damascus (capital of modern Syria) or Baghdad (capital of Iraq) appointed provincial governors to rule the vast territories the Arabs conquered. These governors eventually gained

13-2   Interior of the Dome of the Rock, Jerusalem, 687–692.

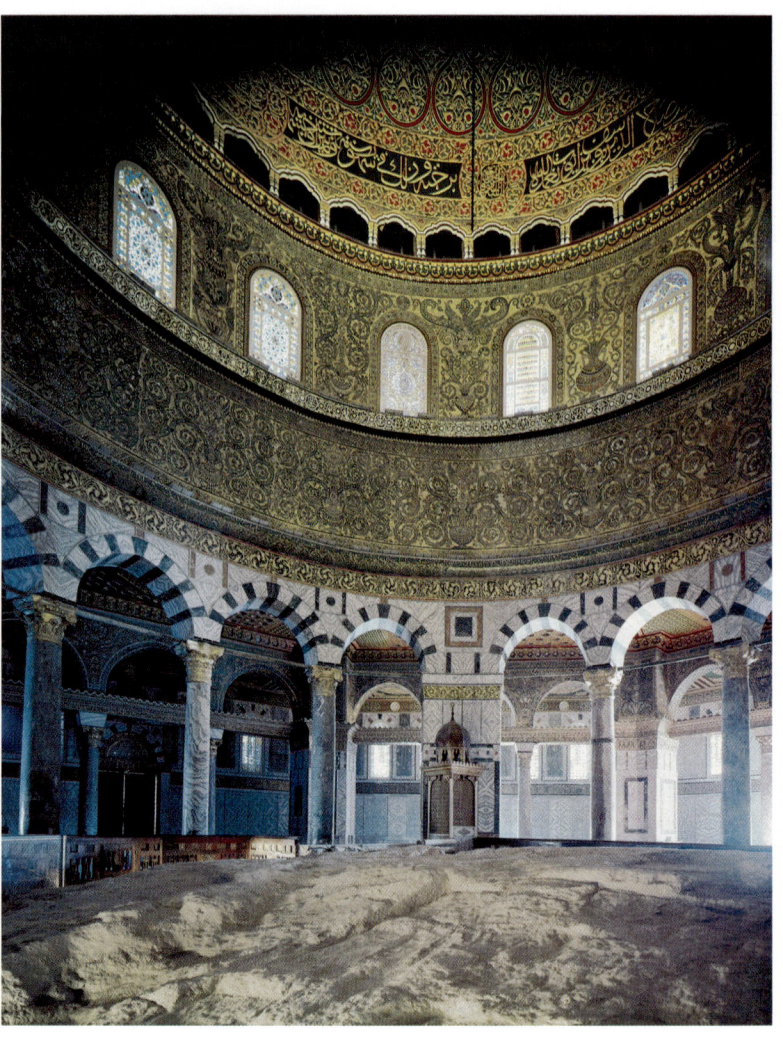

relative independence by setting up dynasties in various territories and provinces: the Umayyads in Syria (661–749) and in Spain (756–1031); the Abbasids in Iraq (749–1258, largely nominal after 945); the Fatimids in Egypt (909–1171); and so on. Despite the Quran's strictures against sumptuousness and attention to worldly pleasures, Islamic rulers often surrounded themselves with luxuries commensurate with their enormous wealth and power. And, like other potentates before and after, they were builders on a grand scale.

Architecture

THE TRIUMPH OF ISLAM IN JERUSALEM   The first great achievement of Islamic architecture is in Jerusalem, which the Muslims had taken from the Byzantines in 638. The Dome of the Rock (FIG. 13-1) was erected by the Umayyad caliph Abd al-Malik (r. 685–705) between 687 and 692. The structure is a monumental sanctuary, an architectural tribute to Islam's triumph. It houses the rock (FIG. 13-2) from which Muslims believe Muhammad ascended to Heaven during a nocturnal journey recalled in Surah 17 of the Quran. The sanctuary was erected on the traditional site of Adam's burial, of Abraham's preparation for Isaac's sacrifice, and of the Temple of Solomon the Romans destroyed in 70. The Dome of the Rock marked the coming of Islam to the city

that had been, and still is, sacred to both Jews and Christians. The structure rises from a huge platform known as the Noble Enclosure. Even today it dominates the skyline of the holy city.

As Islam took much of its teaching from Judaism and Christianity, so its architects and artists borrowed and transformed design, construction, and ornamentation principles that had been long applied in, and were still current in, Byzantium and the Middle East. The Dome of the Rock is a domed octagon resembling San Vitale in Ravenna (see FIG. 12-6) in its basic design. In all likelihood, it was inspired by a neighboring Christian monument, the rotunda of the Holy Sepulchre, which Constantine the Great began in the fourth century. This rotunda bore a family resemblance to the roughly contemporary mausoleum of Constantine's daughter, now Santa Costanza in Rome (see FIGS. 11-9 and 11-10). The Dome of the Rock is a member of the same extended family. Its double-shelled wooden dome, however, some sixty feet across and seventy-five feet high, so dominates the elevation as to reduce the octagon to function merely as its base. This soaring, majestic unit creates a decidedly more commanding effect than that of late Roman and Byzantine domical structures (for example, FIGS. 11-10 and 12-3). The silhouettes of those domes are comparatively insignificant when seen from the outside. The dominating domed cupola characterized Islamic architecture thereafter and, with the later minaret, still identifies it worldwide.

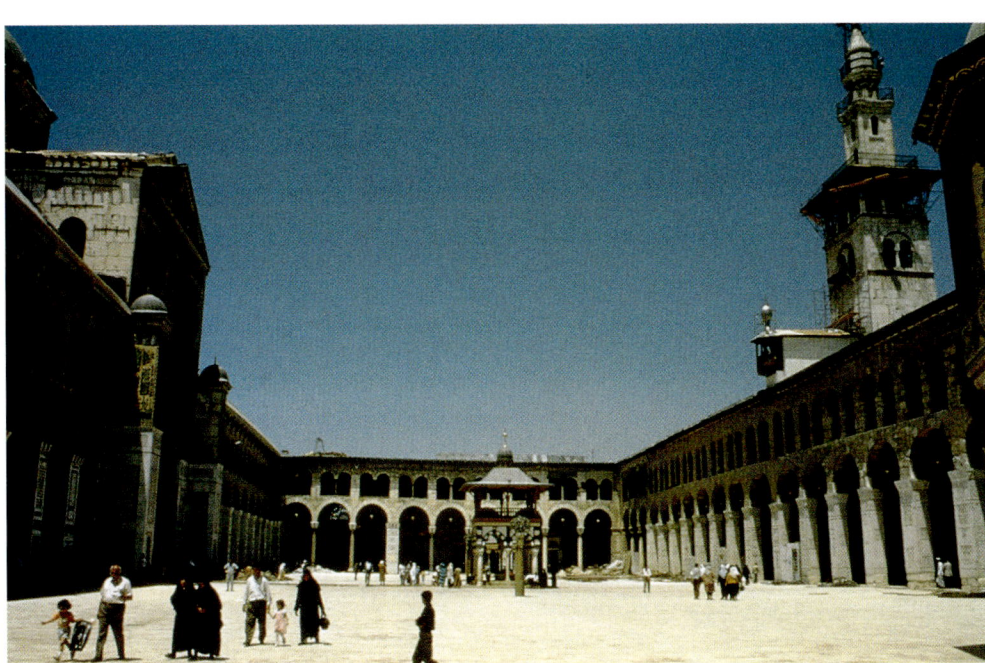

13-3 Great Mosque, Damascus, Syria, 706–715.

The building's exterior has been much restored. Sixteenth-century and later tiling now replaces the original mosaic. Yet the vivid, colorful patterning that wraps the walls like a textile is typical of Islamic ornamentation. It contrasts markedly with Byzantine brickwork and Greco-Roman sculptured profiling and carved decoration. The interior's rich mosaic ornament (FIG. 13-2) has been preserved. From it one can imagine how the exterior walls originally appeared. Islamic practice does not significantly distinguish interior and exterior decor. The splendor of infinitely various surfaces is given to public gaze both within and outside buildings.

A NEW MOSQUE FOR A NEW CAPITAL The Umayyads transferred their capital from Mecca to Damascus in 661. There, Abd al-Malik's son, the caliph al-Walid (r. 705–715), built an imposing new mosque for the expanding Muslim population where a Byzantine church (formerly a Roman temple) stood. The Umayyads destroyed the church, but they used the Roman precinct walls as a foundation for their own construction. Like the Dome of the Rock, the Great Mosque of Damascus (FIG. 13-3) owes much to the architecture of the Greco-Roman and Early Christian East. The courtyard is bounded by pier arcades reminiscent of Roman aqueducts, and it is constructed of masonry blocks, columns, and capitals salvaged from the Roman and Early Christian structures al-Walid demolished to make way for his mosque. The minarets, two at the southern corners and one at the northern side of the enclosure—the earliest in the Islamic world—are modifications of the preexisting Roman square towers. The grand prayer hall (on the left in our photograph) is on the south side of the courtyard (facing Mecca). Its main entrance is distinguished by a facade with a pediment and arches that recall classical and Byzantine models, respectively. The facade faces into the courtyard, like a Roman forum temple (see FIGS. 10-9 and 10-10), a plan that was maintained throughout the long history of Islamic mosque architecture. The Damascus mosque synthesizes elements received from other cultures into a novel architectural unity, which includes the distinctive Islamic elements of mihrab, mihrab dome, minbar, and minaret (see "The Islamic Mosque," page 364).

An extensive cycle of mosaics covers the walls of the Great Mosque. In our example (FIG. 13-4), a conch shell niche "supports" an arcaded pavilion with a flowering rooftop flanked by structures shown in classical perspective. Like the architectural design, the mosaics owe much to Roman, Early Christian, and Byzantine art (compare FIGS. 10-22 and 11-18). Indeed, some evidence indicates that the Great Mosque mosaics are the work of Byzantine mosaicists.

13-4 Detail of a mosaic in the courtyard arcade of the Great Mosque, Damascus, Syria, 706–715.

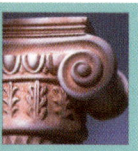

The Islamic Mosque

Muslim religious architecture is closely related to Muslim prayer, an obligation laid down in the Quran for all Muslims. Prayer as a private act requires neither prescribed ceremony nor a special locale. Only the *qibla*—the direction (toward Mecca) Muslims face while praying—is important. But prayer also became a communal act when the first Muslim community established a simple ritual for it. To celebrate the Muslim sabbath, which occurs on Friday, the community convened once a week for the Friday noonday prayer, probably in the Prophet's house in Medina. The main feature of Muhammad's house was a large square court with two *zullahs*, or shaded areas, along the north and south sides. These zullahs consisted of thatched roofs supported by rows of palm trunks. The southern zullah, wider and supported by a double row of trunks, indicated the qibla. During these communal gatherings, the *imam*, or leader of collective worship, standing on a stepped pulpit known as a *minbar* near the qibla wall, pronounced the *khutba*, a speech that included both a sermon and a profession of the community's allegiance to its leader. The minbar thus represents secular authority even as it serves its function in worship.

These features became standard in the Islamic *mosque* (from Arabic *masjid*, a place for bowing down), where the faithful gathered for the five daily prayers. The *masjid-i jami*, or Friday mosque (also referred to as the congregational or great mosque), was ideally large enough to accommodate a community's entire population for the Friday noonday prayer and khutba. A very important feature both of ordinary mosques and of Friday mosques is the *mihrab*, a semicircular niche usually set into the qibla wall (FIG. 13-9). Often a dome over the bay in front of it signalized its position (FIGS. 13-3, 13-9, and 13-14). The niche was a familiar Greco-Roman architectural feature, generally enclosing a statue. But for Islamic architecture, its origin, purpose, and meaning are still

debated. Some scholars believe the mihrab originally may have honored the place where the Prophet stood in his house at Medina when he led the communal prayers. It thus would have been a revered religious memorial. The mihrab also may have symbolized a gateway into Paradise.

In some mosques, the mihrab is preceded by a screened area called the *maqsura*, an area generally reserved for the ruler or his representative. It can be quite elaborate in form (FIG. 13-13). Many mosques, including the very early Great Mosque at Damascus (FIG. 13-3), also have one or more *minarets* (FIGS. 13-3, 13-10, and 13-21), towers for the *muezzin* (crier) to call the faithful to prayer. Early mosques are generally characterized by *hypostyle halls*, prayer halls with roofs supported by a multitude of columns (FIGS. 13-9 and 13-12). Later variations of the early mosque formulation include mosques with four *iwans* (vaulted rectangular recesses), one on each side of the courtyard (FIG. 13-24), and central-plan mosques with a single large dome-covered interior space (FIGS. 13-21 to 13-23), as in Byzantine churches (see Chapter 12).

The mosque's origin is still in dispute, although one prototype may well have been the Prophet's house in Medina. Once the Muslims had firmly established themselves in their conquered territories, they began to build on a large scale, impelled, perhaps, by a desire to create such visible evidence of their power as would surpass in size and splendor that of their non-Islamic predecessors. Today, mosques continue to be erected throughout the world. Despite many variations in design and detail (an adobe-and-wood mosque in Mali, FIG. 15-7, is discussed later in the context of African art) and the employment of modern building techniques and materials unknown in Muhammad's day, the Islamic mosque's essential features are unchanged. All mosques, wherever they are built and whatever their plan, are oriented toward Mecca, and the faithful pray facing the mihrab in the qibla wall.

Characteristically, temples, clusters of houses, trees, and rivers compose the pictorial fields, bounded by stylized vegetal design, familiar in Roman, Early Christian, and Byzantine ornament. No zoomorphic forms, human or animal, appear either in the pictorial or ornamental spaces. This is true of all the mosaics in the Great Mosque as well as the mosaics in the earlier Dome of the Rock (FIG. 13-2). Islamic tradition prohibits the representation of fauna of any kind in sacred places. The world shown in the Damascus mosaics, suspended miragelike in a featureless field of gold, is explained in accompanying inscriptions as an image of Paradise. Many passages from the Quran describe the gorgeous places of Paradise awaiting the faithful—gardens, groves of trees, flowing streams, and "lofty chambers." Indeed, the abundant luxurious images and ornament, floating free of all human reference, create a vision of Paradise appealing to the spiritually oriented imagination, whatever its religion.

AN UMAYYAD DESERT PALACE The Umayyad rulers of Damascus constructed numerous palatial residences throughout the vast territories they governed. The rural palaces were not merely idyllic residences removed from the congestion, noise, and disease of the cities. They seem to have served as nuclei for the agricultural development of conquered territories and possibly as hunting lodges. In addition, the Islamic palaces were symbols of authority over conquered and inherited lands, as well as expressions of their owners' newly acquired wealth.

One of the most impressive Umayyad palaces, despite the fact it was never completed, is at Mshatta in the Jordanian desert (FIGS. **13-5** to **13-7**). Its plan (FIG. 13-5) resembles that of Diocletian's palace at Split (see FIG. 10-75), which in turn reflects the layout of a Roman fortified camp. The high walls of the Mshatta palace incorporate twenty-five towers but lack parapet walkways for patrolling guards. The walls, nonethe-

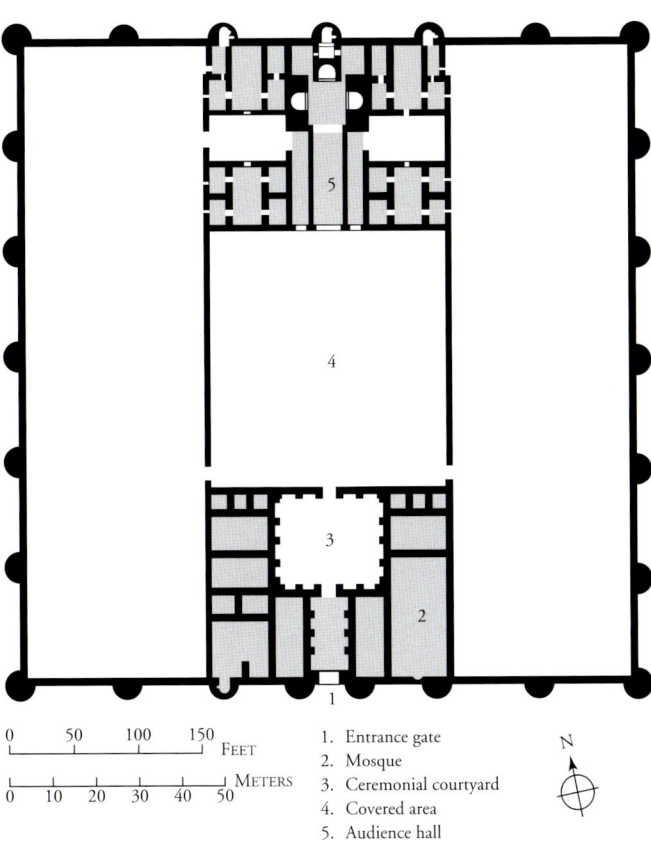

13-5 Plan of the Umayyad palace, Mshatta, Jordan, ca. 740–750 (after Alberto Berengo Gardin).

0   50   100   150 FEET

0   10   20   30   40   50 METERS

N

1. Entrance gate
2. Mosque
3. Ceremonial courtyard
4. Covered area
5. Audience hall

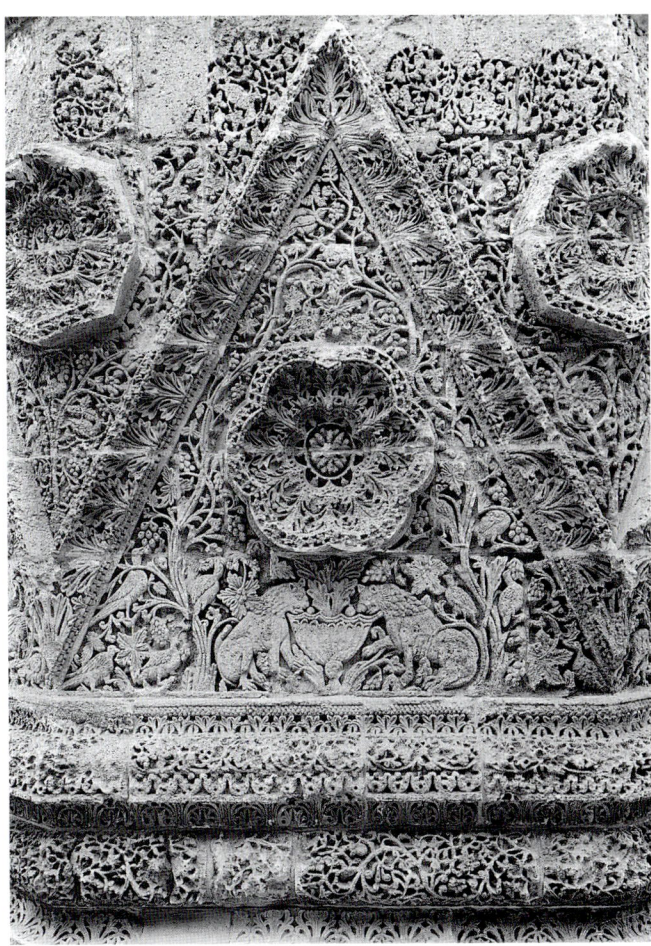

13-6 Detail of the frieze of the Umayyad palace, Mshatta, Jordan, ca. 740–750. Limestone, 16′ 7″ high. Museum für Islamische Kunst, Staatliche Museen, Berlin.

less, offered safety from marauding nomadic tribes and provided privacy for the caliph and his entourage. Visitors entered the palace through a large portal on the south side (FIG. 13-7). To the right was a mosque (the plan shows the mihrab niche in the qibla wall), a necessary element of any isolated palace complex so that the rulers and their guests could fulfill their obligation to pray five times a day. The mosque was sep-

arated from the palace's residential wing and official audience hall by a small open ceremonial courtyard and a large covered area. Most Umayyad palaces also were provided with fairly elaborate bathing facilities that displayed technical features, such as heating systems, adopted from Roman baths. Just as

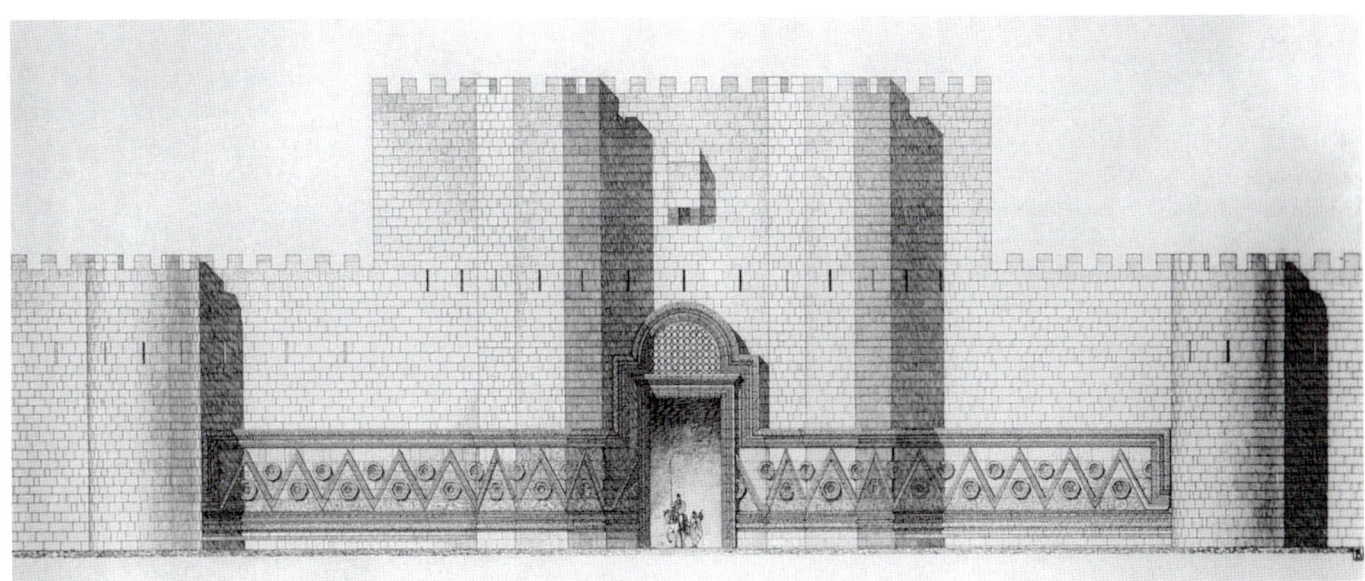

13-7 Reconstruction drawing of the facade of the Umayyed palace, Mshatta, Jordan, ca. 740–750 (after Schulz).

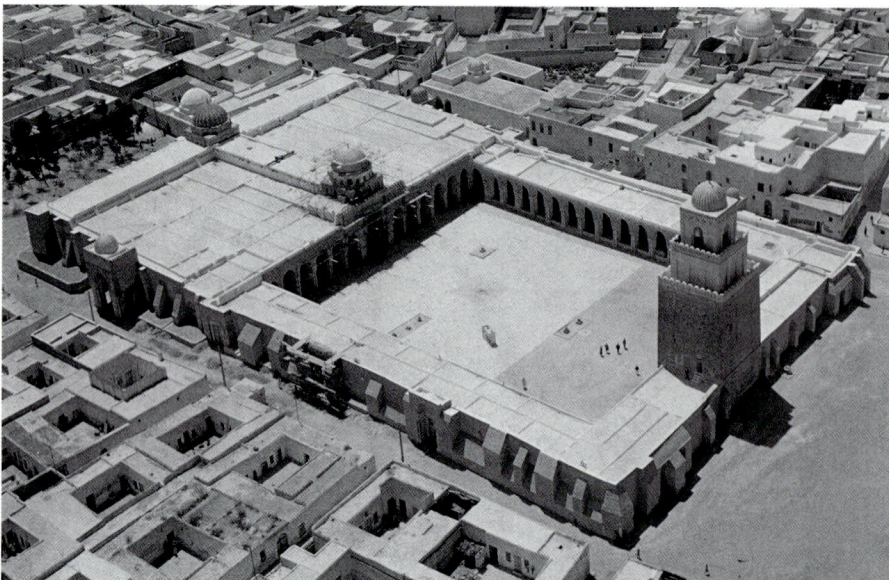

13-8   Aerial view of Great Mosque, Qayrawan, Tunisia, ca. 836–875.

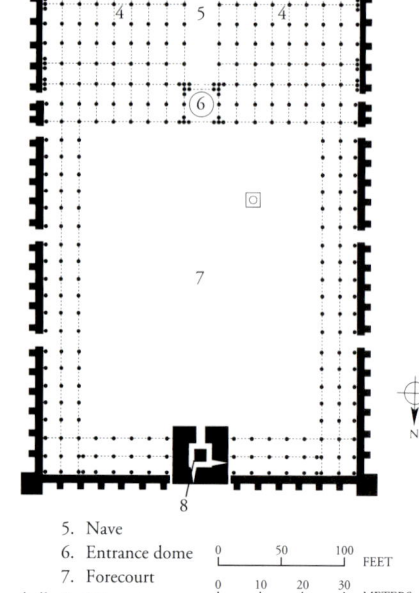

1. Qibla wall   5. Nave
2. Mihrab   6. Entrance dome
3. Mihrab dome   7. Forecourt
4. Hypostyle prayer hall 8. Minaret

13-9   Plan of the Great Mosque, Qayrawan, Tunisia, ca. 836–875.

under the Roman Empire, these baths probably served more than merely hygienic purposes. Indeed, in several Umayyad desert palaces, excavators have uncovered in the baths paintings and sculptures of hunting and other secular themes, including depictions of dancing women—themes traditionally associated with royalty in the Near East. Large halls frequently attached to many of these baths seem to have been used as places of entertainment, as was the case in Roman times. Thus, the bath-spa-social center, a characteristic amenity of Roman urban culture that died out in the Christian world, survived in Islamic culture.

The architectural ornamentation of many of the early Islamic palaces was confined to simply molded stucco and decorative brickwork, but at Mshatta the facade (FIG. 13-7) is enlivened by a richly carved stone frieze. The long band is more than sixteen feet high. Our detail (FIG. 13-6) shows one of a series of triangles framed by elaborately carved moldings. Each triangle contains a large rosette that projects from a field densely covered with curvilinear, vegetal designs. No two triangles were treated the same way, and animal figures appear in some of them. Similar compositions of birds, felines, and vegetal scrolls can be found in Roman, Byzantine, and Sasanian art. The Mshatta frieze, however, has no animal figures to the right of the entrance portal—that is, on the part of the facade corresponding to the mosque's qibla wall.

THE ABBASIDS' ROUND CITY OF PEACE   In 750, after years of civil war, the Abbasids, who claimed descent from Abbas, an uncle of Muhammad, overthrew the Umayyad caliphs. The new rulers moved the capital from Damascus to a site in Iraq near the old Sasanian capital of Ctesiphon (see FIG. 2-28). There the caliph al-Mansur (r. 754–775) established a new capital, Baghdad, which he called Madina al-salam, the City of Peace. The city was laid out in 762 at a time astrologers determined as favorable. It was round in plan, about a mile and a half in diameter. The shape signified that the new capital was the center of the uni-

verse. At the city's center was the caliph's palace, oriented to the four compass points.

For almost three hundred years Baghdad was the hub of Arab power and of a brilliant Islamic culture. The Abbasid caliphs were renowned throughout the world and even established diplomatic relations with Charlemagne at Aachen in Germany. The Abbasids lavished their wealth on art, literature, and science and were responsible for the translation of numerous Greek texts that otherwise would have been lost. Many of these works were introduced to the medieval West through their Arabic versions.

A HYPOSTYLE MOSQUE IN TUNISIA   Of all the variations in mosque plans, the hypostyle mosque most closely reflects the mosque's supposed origin, Muhammad's house in Medina (see "The Islamic Mosque," page 364). One of the finest hypostyle mosques, still in use today, is the mid-eighth-century Great Mosque at Qayrawan (FIGS. **13-8** and **13-9**) in Abbasid Tunisia. The precinct takes the form of a slightly askew parallelogram of huge scale, some four hundred fifty feet by two hundred sixty feet. Built of stone, its walls have sturdy buttresses, square in profile. The arcaded forecourt is entered through a massive minaret not quite in line with the two domes that fix the axis of the hypostyle prayer hall. The first dome is over the entrance bay. The second, more elaborate one is over the bay that fronts the mihrab set into the qibla wall. The axis is defined by a raised nave flanked by eight columned aisles on either side, space for a large congregation. The nave that connects the entrance dome with the mihrab dome intersects with another nave at right angles to it, running the length of the qibla wall. The resultant T-shaped space provides a plan organization and focus often missing from the rambling hypostyle mosque scheme. Inside,

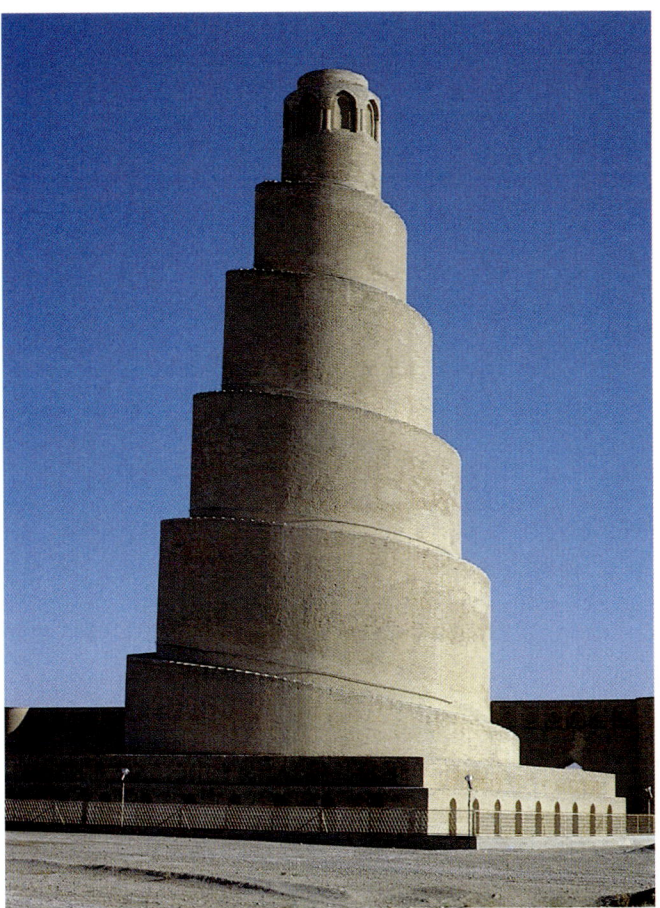

13-10 *Malwiya* minaret of the Great Mosque, Samarra, Iraq, 848–852.

to the right of the mihrab, is the original carved wooden minbar of 862, the oldest known.

THE SPIRAL MINARET OF SAMARRA The three-story minaret of the Qayrawan mosque is square in plan and believed to be a near copy of a Roman lighthouse, but minarets can take a variety of forms. Perhaps the most striking and novel is that of the immense (more than forty-five thousand square yards) Great Mosque at Samarra, the largest mosque in the world. It was erected by the Abbasid caliph al-Mutawakkil (r. 847–861) between 848 and 852. Known as the *Malwiya* ("snail shell" in Arabic) minaret (FIG. **13-10**) and more than 165 feet tall, it now stands alone but originally was linked to the mosque by a bridge. The brick tower is distinguished by its spiral ramp, which increases in slope from bottom to top. Many have compared its form to the ziggurats of ancient Mesopotamia (see FIGS. 2-2 and 2-14), but those rectilinear stepped platforms bear very little resemblance to the Samarran minaret. Some later European depictions of the biblical Tower of Babel (Babylon's ziggurat; see "Babylon: City of Wonders," Chapter 2, page 37) were, however, inspired by the *Malwiya* minaret.

MEMORIALIZING THE DEAD The eastern realms of the Abbasid empire were overseen by dynasties of governors who exercised considerable independence while recognizing the ultimate authority of the Baghdad caliphs. One of these dynasties, the Samanids (r. 819–1005), presided over the eastern frontier beyond the Oxus River (Transoxiana) on the

border with India. In the early tenth century, they erected an imposing domed brick mausoleum at Bukhara in modern Uzbekistan (FIG. **13-11**). Monumental tombs were virtually unknown in the early Islamic period. Muhammad had been opposed to elaborate burials and instructed his followers to bury him in a simple unmarked grave. In time, however, the Prophet's resting place in Medina was enclosed by a wooden screen and covered by a dome. By the ninth century, Abbasid caliphs were laid to rest in dynastic mausoleums.

The Samanid mausoleum at Bukhara is one of the earliest preserved tombs in the Islamic world. It is constructed of baked bricks and takes the form of a cube with slightly sloping sides capped by a dome. The builders painstakingly shaped the bricks to create a vivid and varied surface pattern. Some of the bricks form engaged columns at the corners. A brick *blind arcade* (a series of arches in relief, with blocked openings) runs around all four sides. Inside, the walls are as elaborate as the exterior. The brick dome rests on eight arcuated brick squinches (see "Pendentives and Squinches," Chapter 12, page 332) framed by engaged *colonnettes* (small columns). The dome-on-cube form had a long and distinguished future in Islamic funerary architecture.

THE SPLENDOR OF UMAYYAD CÓRDOBA In 750, only one Umayyad notable, Abd-al-Rahman I, escaped the Abbasid massacre of his clan in Syria. He fled to Spain, where, as noted earlier, the Arabs had overthrown the Christian kingdom of the Visigoths in 711. The Arab military governors of the peninsula accepted the fugitive as their overlord, and he founded the Spanish Umayyad dynasty, which lasted for almost three centuries. The capital of the Spanish Umayyads was Córdoba, which became the center of a brilliant culture rivaling that of the Abbasids at Baghdad and exerting major influence on the civilization of the Christian West.

The jewel of the capital at Córdoba was its Great Mosque, begun in 784 and enlarged several times during the ninth and

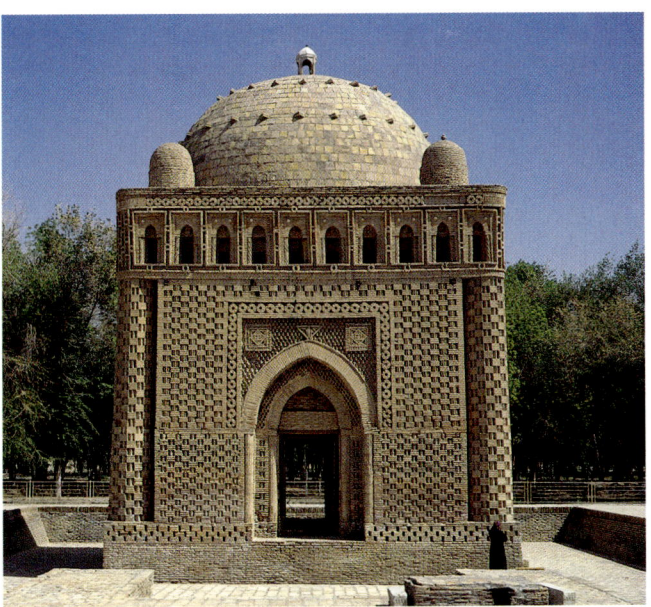

13-11 Mausoleum of the Samanids, Bukhara, Uzbekistan, early tenth century.

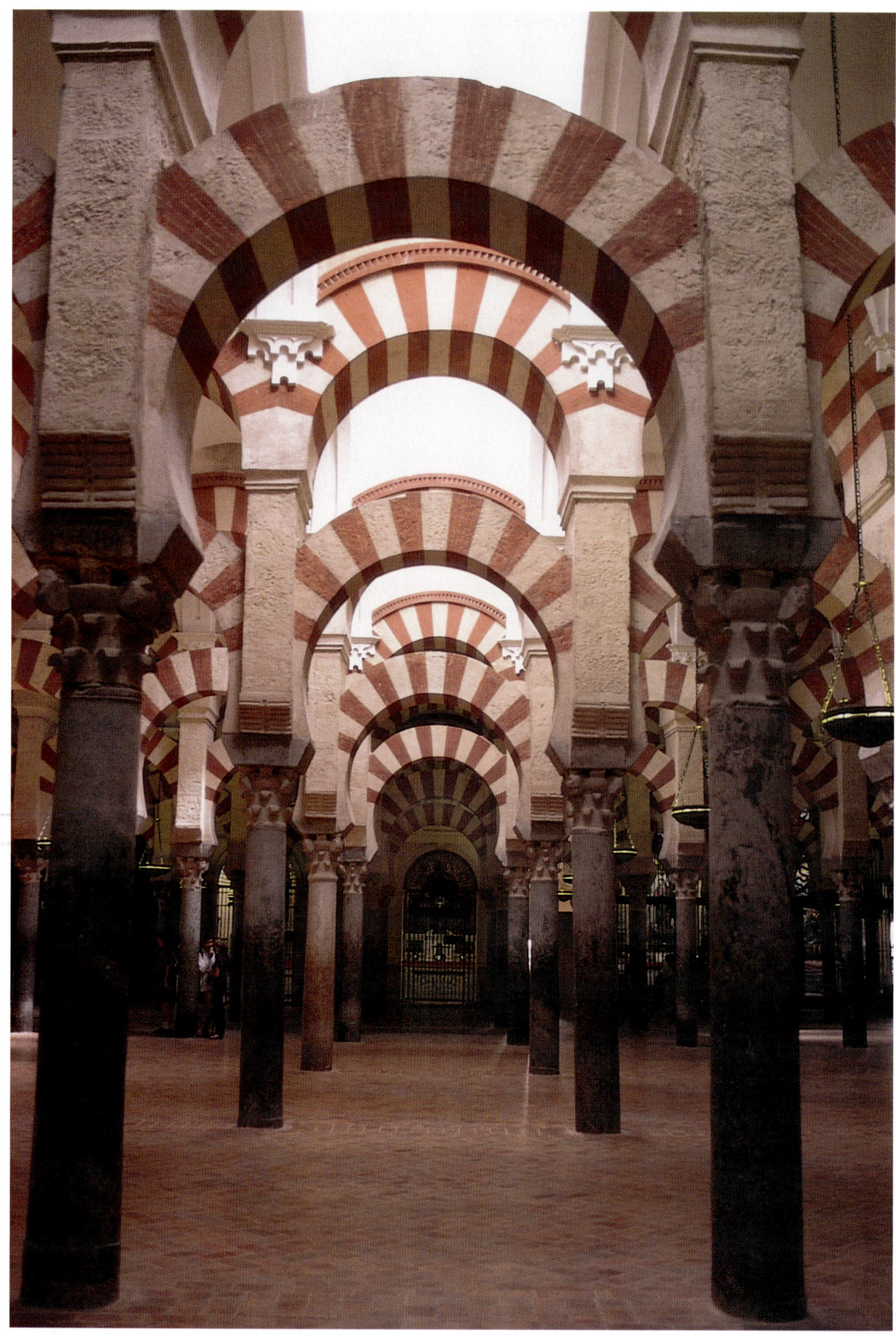

13-12 Prayer hall of the Great Mosque, Córdoba, Spain, eighth to tenth centuries.

tenth centuries. It eventually became the largest mosque in the Islamic West. The additions followed the original style and arrangement of columns and arches, and the builders maintained a striking stylistic unity for the entire building. The hypostyle prayer hall (FIG. **13-12)** has thirty-six piers and five hundred fourteen columns topped by a unique system of double-tiered arches that carried a wooden roof (now replaced by vaults). The lower arches are horseshoe shaped, a form perhaps adapted from earlier Near Eastern architecture or of Visigothic origin. The horseshoe arch quickly became closely associated with Muslim architecture. Visually, these arches seem to billow out like sails blown by the wind, and they contribute greatly to the light and airy effect of the mosque's interior.

The caliph al-Hakam II (r. 961–976) undertook major renovations to the Córdoba mosque. His builders expanded the prayer hall and added a series of domes. They also erected the elaborate screened maqsura (FIG. **13-13**), with its highly decorative multilobed arches, a variation on the two-tiered system of arches in the prayer hall. The area was reserved for the caliph and was connected to his palace by a corridor in the qibla wall. Early Islamic buildings had wooden roofs, and the experiments with arch forms were motivated less by structural necessity than by a desire to create rich and varied abstract patterns. In Córdoba's maqsura the builders further enhanced the magnificent effect of the complex arches by sheathing the walls with marbles and mosaics. The mosaicists and even the tesserae were brought to Spain from Constantinople by al-Hakam II.

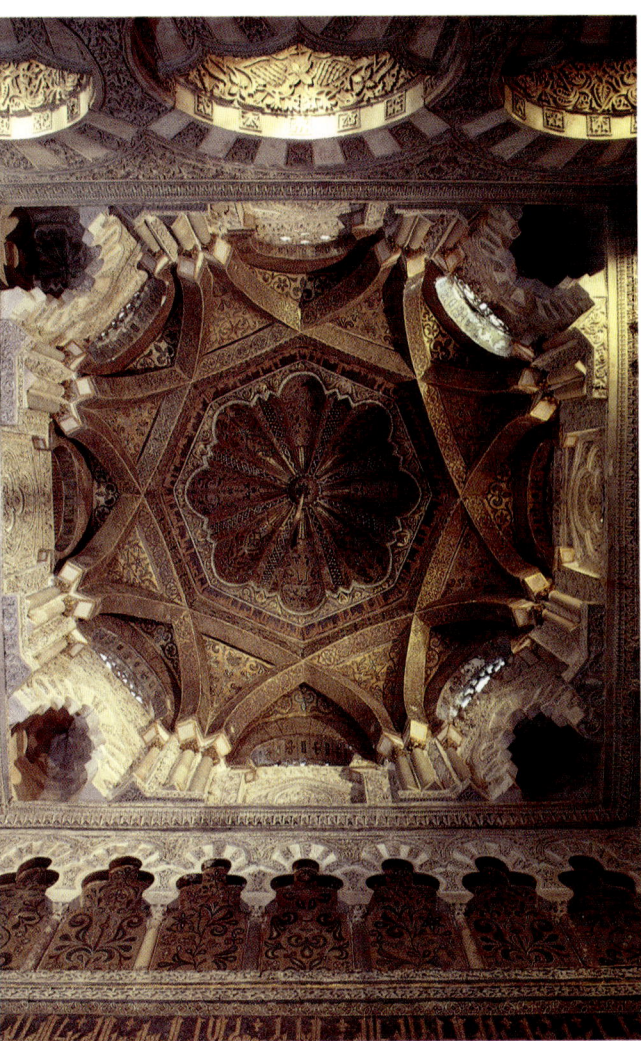

13-14 Dome in front of the mihrab of the Great Mosque, Córdoba, Spain, 961–965.

The same desire for decorative effect inspired the design of the dome that covers the area in front of the mihrab (FIG. **13-14**), one of the four domes built during the tenth century to emphasize the axis leading to the mihrab. The dome rests on an octagonal base of arcuated squinches and is crisscrossed by ribs that form an intricate pattern centered on two squares set at forty-five-degree angles to each other. The mosaic-clad surfaces are the work of the same Byzantine artists responsible for the maqsura's decoration.

Luxury Arts

ISLAMIC DESIGN In the mosaics at Córdoba, as elsewhere in the Islamic world, most of the design elements are based on plant motifs, which are sometimes intermingled with abstract geometric shapes and, in secular settings, with animal figures. But the natural forms often are so stylized that they are lost in the purely decorative tracery of the tendrils, leaves, and stalks. These *arabesques,* as they are often called because they are so characteristic of Islamic ("Arab") art, form a pattern that covers an entire surface, whether that of a small utensil or the wall

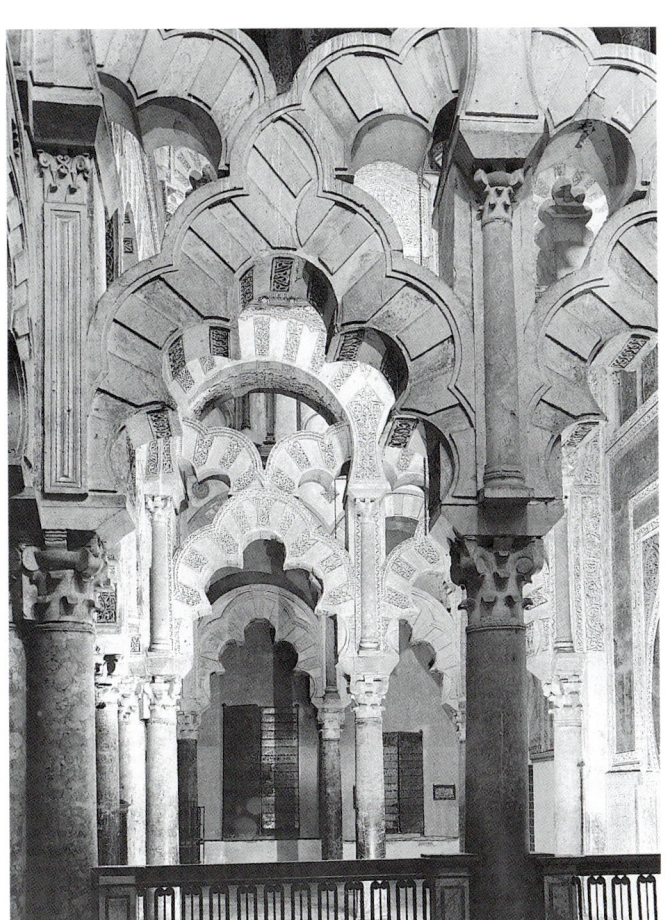

13-13 Maqsura of the Great Mosque, Córdoba, Spain, 961–965.

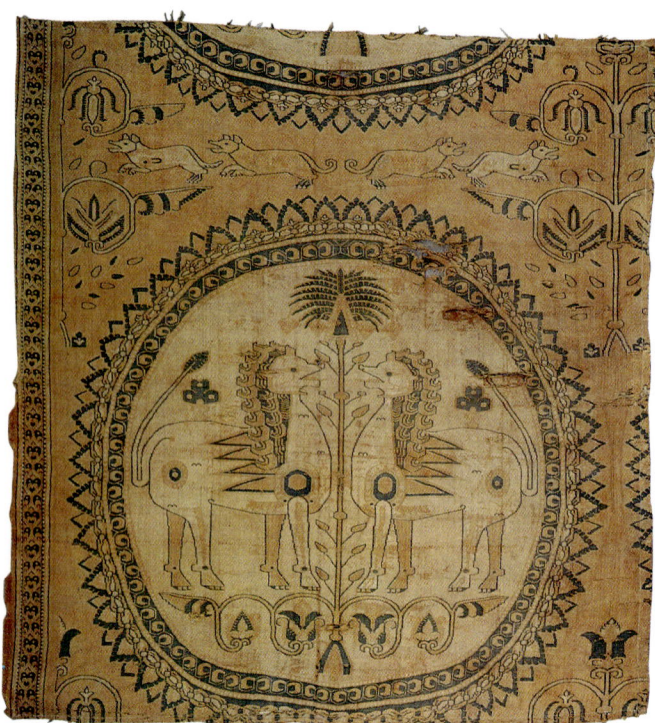

13-15 Confronting lions and palm tree, fragment of a textile from Zandana, Uzbekistan, eighth century. Silk compound twill, 2′ 11″ × 2′ 9½″. Musée Historique de Lorraine, Nancy.

of a building. In all periods of Islamic art, the relationship of one form to another has been more important than the design's totality. The patterns have had no function but to decorate.

This ornamental system offers a potential for unlimited growth, as it permits extension of the designs in any desired direction. Most characteristic, perhaps, is the design's independence of its carrier. Neither its size (within limits) nor its forms are dictated by anything but the design itself. This arbitrariness imparts a certain quality of impermanence to Islamic design, a quality that may reflect the Muslim taste for readily movable furnishings, such as rugs and hangings. Wood is scarce in most of the Islamic world, and the kind of furniture used in the West—beds, tables, and chairs—is rarely found in Muslim structures. Architectural spaces, therefore, are not defined by the type of furniture placed in them. A room's function (eating or sleeping, for example) can change simply by rearranging the carpets and cushions.

ISLAMIC SILK IN A FRENCH CATHEDRAL
Silk textiles and wool carpets are among the glories of Islamic art. Unfortunately, because of their fragile nature and the heavy wear carpets endure, early Islamic textiles are rare today and often fragmentary. Silk thread was also very expensive. Produced by silkworms, which only can flourish in certain temperate regions, silk textiles were manufactured first in China in the third millennium B.C. They were shipped over what came to be called the Silk Road through Asia to the Middle East and Europe (see "Silk and the Silk Road," Chapter 7, page 194).

One of the earliest Islamic silks (FIG. **13-15**) is found today in Nancy, France. Unfortunately, it is fragmentary and its colors,

once rich blues, greens, and oranges, faded long ago. The silk survives because it is associated with the relics of Saint Amon housed in Toul Cathedral. The precious fabric may have been used to wrap the treasures when they were transported to France in 820. It probably dates to the eighth century and comes from Zandana near Bukhara. The design consists of repeated medallions with confronting lions flanking a palm tree. Other animals scamper across the silk between the roundels. Such zoomorphic motifs are foreign to the decorative vocabulary of mosque architecture, but they could be found in Muslim households—even in Muhammad's in Medina. The Prophet, however, was said to have objected to curtains decorated with figures and permitted only cushions adorned with animals or birds.

A SIGNED ZOOMORPHIC EWER The furnishings of Islamic palaces and mosques reflected a love of sumptuous materials and rich decorative patterns. Metal, wood, glass, and ivory were artfully worked into a great variety of objects for the mosque or home. Colored glass was used with striking effect in mosque lamps. Ornate ceramics of high quality were produced in large numbers. Basins, ewers, jewel cases, writing

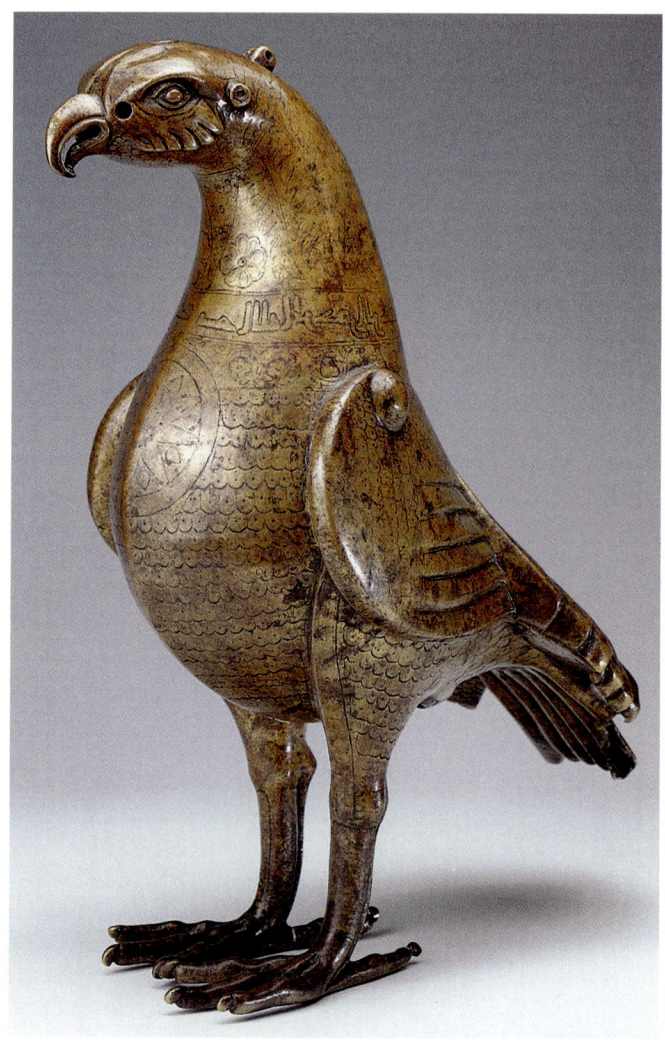

13-16 SULAYMAN, Ewer in the form of a bird, 796. Brass with silver and copper inlay, 1′ 3″ high. Hermitage, Saint Petersburg.

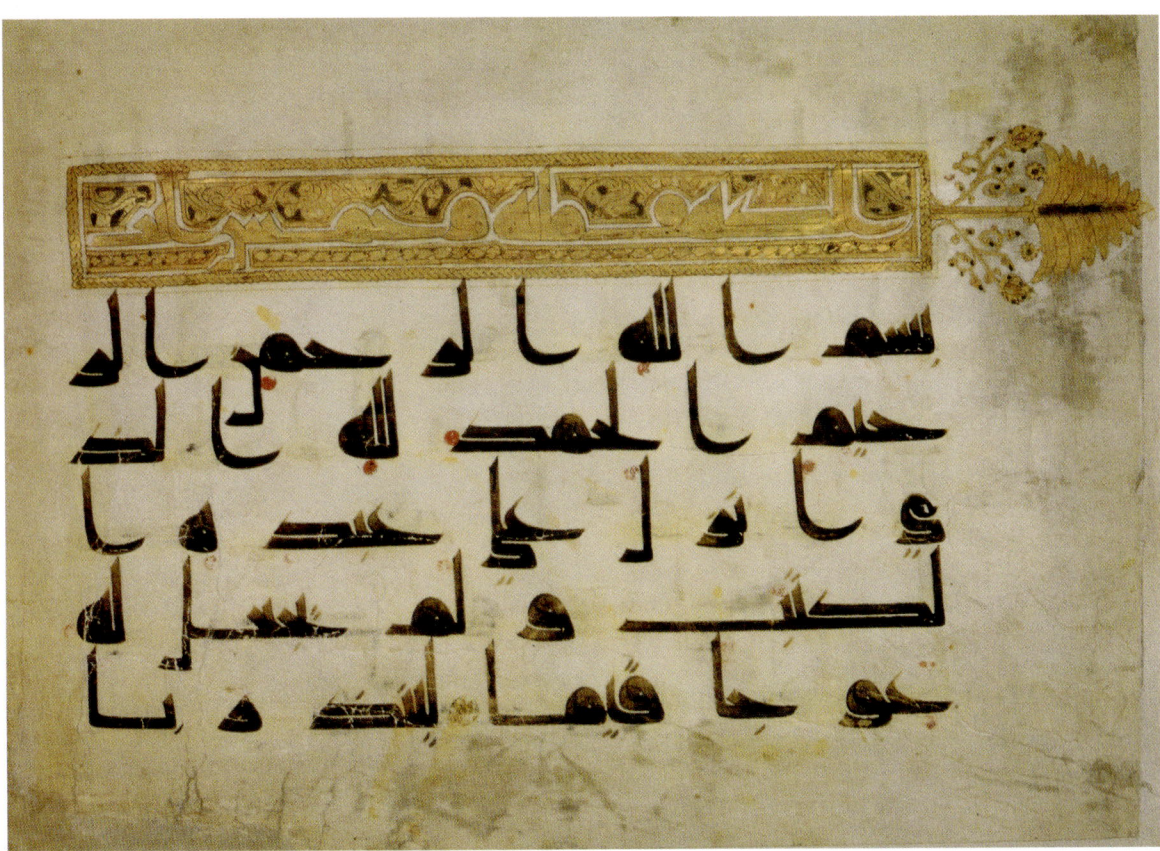

13-17 Quran page with beginning of surah 18, *al-Kahf (The Cave),* ninth or early tenth century. Ink and gold on vellum, $7\frac{1}{4}'' \times 10\frac{1}{4}''$. Chester Beatty Library and Oriental Art Gallery, Dublin.

boxes, and other decorative items were made of bronze or brass, engraved, and inlaid with silver.

One of the most striking examples of the metalworker's art is the cast brass ewer in the form of a bird (FIG. **13-16**) signed by SULAYMAN and dated 796. (The place of origin also was inscribed but is illegible today.) Some fifteen inches tall, the ewer is nothing less than a freestanding statuette. But its utilitarian purpose meant Sulayman did not have to fear accusations of fashioning an idol—the holes between the eyes and beak function as a spout. The decoration on the body, which bears traces of silver and copper inlay, takes a variety of forms. In places, the etched lines seem to suggest natural feathers, but the rosettes on the neck, the large medallions on the breast, and the inscribed collar have no basis in anatomy. Similar motifs can be found in Islamic textiles, pottery, and architectural tiles. The ready adaptability of motifs to various scales and to various techniques again illustrates both the flexibility of Islamic design and its relative independence from its carrier.

THE ART OF THE QURAN In the Islamic world, the art of *calligraphy,* ornamental writing, was more revered even than the art of textiles. The faithful wanted to reproduce the Quran's sacred words in as beautiful a script as human hands could contrive. And these words were displayed not only on the fragile pages of books but also on the walls of buildings. Quotations from the Quran appear, for example, in a mosaic band above the outer ring of columns inside the Dome of the Rock (FIG. 13-2). The practice of calligraphy was itself a holy task and required long and arduous training. The scribe had

to possess exceptional spiritual refinement. An ancient Arabic proverb proclaims, "Purity of writing is purity of soul." Only in China does calligraphy hold so supreme a position among the arts (see "Inscriptions on Chinese Paintings," Chapter 26, page 805).

Arabic script predates Islam. It is written from right to left with certain characters connected by a baseline. Although the chief Islamic book, the sacred Quran, was codified in the mid-seventh century, the earliest preserved Qurans date to the eighth century. Quran pages were either bound into books or stored as loose sheets in boxes. Most of the early examples are written in the script form called *Kufic,* after the city of Kufah, one of the renowned centers of Arabic calligraphy. Kufic script is quite angular, with the uprights forming almost right angles with the baseline. As with Hebrew and other Semitic languages, the usual practice was to write in consonants only. But to facilitate recitation of the Quran, scribes often indicated vowels by red or yellow symbols above or below the line.

All of these features can be seen on a ninth-century or early tenth-century page (FIG. 13-17) in Dublin that carries the heading and opening lines of surah 18 of the Quran. Five text lines in black ink with red vowels appear below a decorative band incorporating the chapter title in gold and ending in a palm-tree *finial* (a crowning ornament). This approach to page design has parallels at the extreme northwestern corner of the then-known world—in the early medieval manuscripts of the British Isles, where text and ornament are similarly united (see FIG. 16-7). But the stylized human and animal forms that populate those Christian books never appear in Qurans.

LATER ISLAMIC ART

Architecture

THE LAST ISLAMIC STRONGHOLD IN SPAIN
In the early years of the eleventh century, the Umayyad caliphs' power in Spain unraveled, and their palaces fell prey to Berber soldiers from North Africa. The Berbers ruled southern Spain for several generations but could not resist the pressure of Christian forces from the north. Córdoba fell to the Christians in 1236. From then until the final Christian triumph in 1492, the Nasrids, an Arab dynasty that established its capital at Granada, ruled the remaining Muslim territories in Spain.

On a rocky spur at Granada, the Nasrids constructed a huge palace-fortress called the Alhambra ("the Red" in Arabic) because of the rose color of the stone used for its walls and twenty-three towers. By the end of the fourteenth century, the complex, a veritable city with a population of some forty thousand Muslims, included at least a half dozen royal residences. Only two of these fared well over the centuries. They present a vivid picture of court life in Islamic Spain before the final Christian conquest. Paradoxically, the two palaces owe their preservation to their Christian conquerors, who maintained a few of the buildings as trophies commemorating the expulsion of the Muslims.

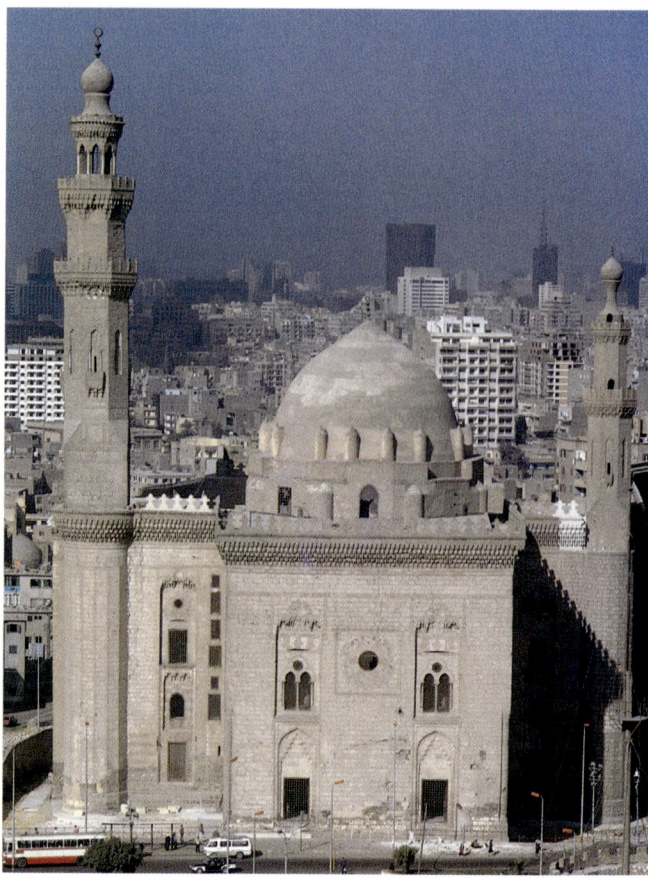

13-19 Madrasa-mosque-mausoleum complex of Sultan Hasan (view from the south with the mausoleum in the foreground), Cairo, Egypt, begun 1356.

PARADISE AND THE DOME OF HEAVEN   One of those palaces is the Palace of the Lions, named for the courtyard fountain with marble lions carrying its water basin on their backs. It is an unusual instance of freestanding stone sculpture in the Islamic world. The palace was the residence of Muhammad V (r. 1354–1391), and its courtyards, lush gardens, and luxurious carpets and other furnishings were designed to conjure the image of Paradise. The complex is noteworthy also for its elaborate stucco ceilings and walls, which never fail to impress visitors.

We reproduce a view of the ceiling of the so-called Hall of the Two Sisters (FIG. **13-18**) in the Palace of the Lions. The dome of the square room rests on an octagonal drum supported by squinches and pierced by eight pairs of windows, but its structure is difficult to discern because of the intricate surface decoration. The ceiling is covered with some five thousand *muqarnas* ("stalactites")—tier after tier of nichelike prismatic forms that seem aimed at denying the structure's solidity. The muqarnas ceiling was intended to catch and reflect sunlight. The lofty vault in this hall and others in the palace were meant to symbolize the dome of heaven. The flickering light and shadows create the effect of a starry sky as the sun's rays move from window to window during the day. To underscore the symbolism, the palace walls were inscribed with verses by the court poet Ibn Zamrak, who compares the Alhambra's lacelike muqarnas ceilings to "the heavenly spheres whose orbits revolve."

THE SLAVE SULTANS OF EGYPT   In the mid-thirteenth century, the Mongols from east-central Asia conquered much of the eastern Islamic world. The center of Is-

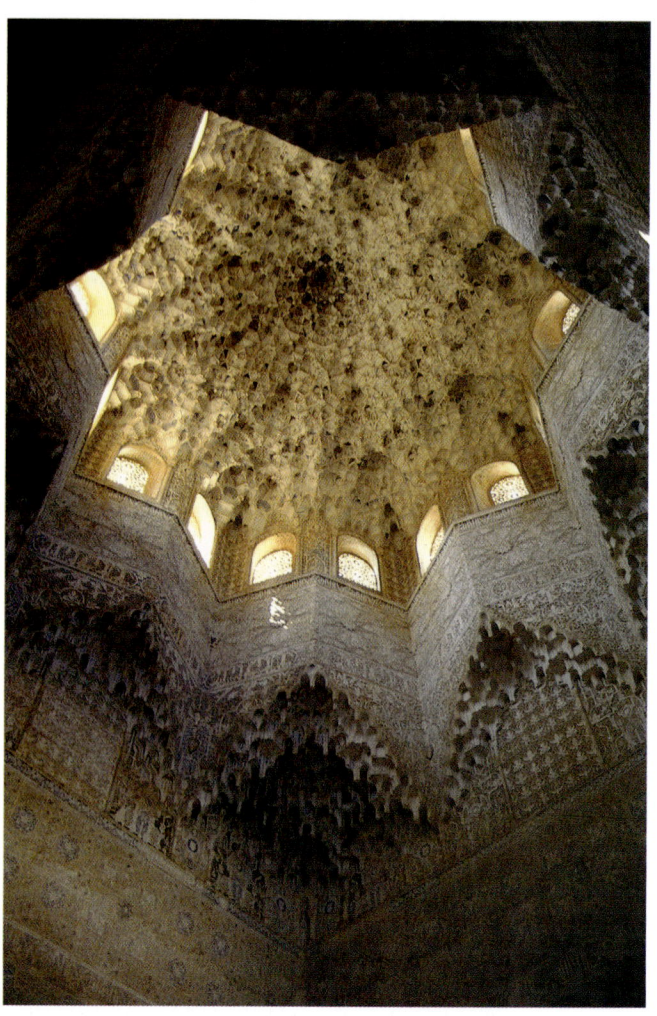

13-18 Muqarnas dome, Hall of the Two Sisters, Alhambra palace, Granada, Spain, 1354–1391.

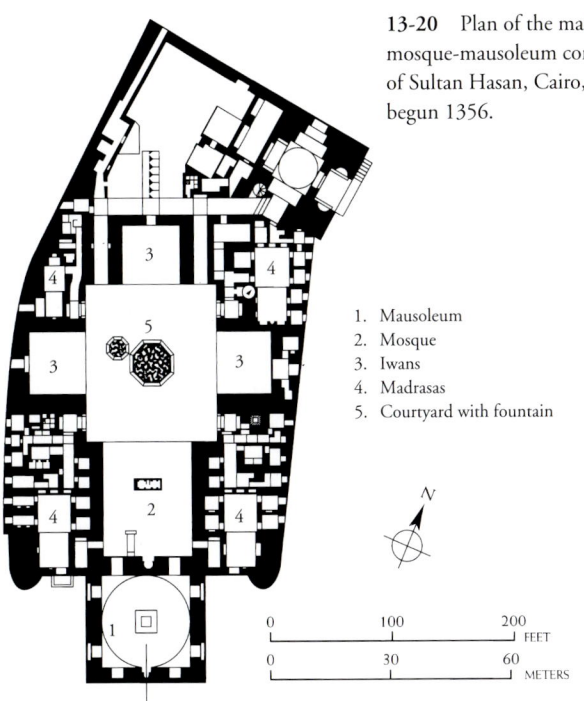

13-20 Plan of the madrasa-mosque-mausoleum complex of Sultan Hasan, Cairo, Egypt, begun 1356.

1. Mausoleum
2. Mosque
3. Iwans
4. Madrasas
5. Courtyard with fountain

```
0        100       200
|---------|---------| FEET
0        30        60
|---------|---------| METERS
```

lamic power moved from Baghdad to Egypt. The lords of Egypt at the time were former Turkish slaves (*mamluks* in Arabic) who converted to Islam. The capital of the Mamluk *sultans* (rulers) was Cairo, which became the largest Muslim city of the late Middle Ages. The Mamluks were ambitious builders, and Sultan Hasan, although not an important figure in Islamic history, was the greatest of all. He ruled briefly as a child and was deposed but regained the sultanate from 1354 until 1361, when he was assassinated.

Hasan's major building project in Cairo was a huge madrasa complex (FIGS. **13-19** and **13-20**) on a plot of land about eight thousand square yards in area. The *madrasa* ("place of study" in Arabic) is a later Islamic institution, a theological college devoted to the teaching of orthodox Sunni Islamic law. Hasan's complex was so large that it housed not only four such colleges for the study of the four major schools of Islamic law but also a mosque, mausoleum, orphanage, and hospital, as well as shops and baths. Like all Islamic building complexes incorporating religious, educational, and charitable functions, this one was supported by a *waqf*, or endowment. Hasan's waqf consisted of various rental properties. The income from these paid the salaries of attendants and faculty, provided furnishings and supplies such as oil for the lamps or free food for the poor, and supported scholarships for needy students.

The grandiose structure has a large central courtyard with a monumental fountain in the center and four *iwans* (rectangular vaulted recesses) opening onto it, a design used earlier for Iranian mosques (FIG. 13-24). In each corner of the main courtyard (FIG. 13-20), between the iwans, is a madrasa with its own courtyard and four or five stories of rooms for the students. The largest iwan in the complex, on the southeastern side, served as a mosque. Contemporaries believed the soaring vault that covered the iwan-mosque was taller than the arch of the Sasanian palace at Ctesiphon (see FIG. 2-28), which was then one of the most admired engineering feats in the world. Behind the qibla wall stands the sultan's mausoleum, a gigantic version of the Samanid mausoleum at Bukhara (FIG.

13-11). The siting of the dome-covered cube south of the mosque was carefully calculated. The prayers of the faithful facing the mihrab and Mecca, therefore, were directed toward Hasan's tomb. (Only the sultan's two sons are actually buried there. Hasan's body was not returned when he was killed.)

The exterior walls of the complex are crowned by a muqarnas cornice, and the mihrab in the mosque and the walls of Hasan's mausoleum are covered with marble plaques of several colors. But the complex as a whole is relatively austere, characterized by its massiveness and geometric clarity. It presents a striking contrast to the filigreed elegance of the contemporary Alhambra, and testifies to the diversity of regional styles within the Islamic world, especially after the end of the Umayyad and Abbasid dynasties.

THE OTTOMANS COME TO POWER During the ninth and tenth centuries, the Turkic people, of central Asian origin, had been converted to Islam. They moved into Iran and the Near East in the eleventh century, and by 1055 the Seljuk Turkish dynasty had built an extensive, although short-lived, empire that stretched from India to western Anatolia. By the end of the twelfth century, this empire had broken up into regional states, and in the early thirteenth century it came under the sway of the Mongols, led by Genghis Khan. After the Seljuks fell, several local dynasties established themselves in Anatolia, among them the Ottomans, founded by Osman I (r. 1290–1326). Under Osman's successors, the Ottoman state expanded for a period of two and a half centuries throughout vast areas of Asia, Europe, and North Africa to become, by the middle of the fifteenth century, one of the great world powers.

The Ottoman emperors were lavish patrons of architecture. Ottoman builders developed a new type of mosque with a square prayer hall covered by a dome as its core. In fact, the dome-covered square, which had been a dominant form in Iran and was employed for the early-tenth-century mausoleum at Bukhara (FIG. 13-11), became the nucleus of all Ottoman architecture. The combination had an appealing geometric clarity. At first used singly, the domed units came to be used in multiples, a turning point in Ottoman architecture. The resultant Ottoman style is geometric and formalistic, rather than ornamental.

After the Ottoman Turks conquered Constantinople (which they renamed Istanbul) in 1453, they firmly established their architectural code. The new lords of Constantinople were impressed by Hagia Sophia (see FIGS. 12-3 to 12-5), which, in some respects, conformed to their own ideals. They converted the Byzantine church into an Islamic mosque with minarets. But the longitudinal orientation of Hagia Sophia's interior never satisfied Ottoman builders, and Anatolian development moved instead toward the central-plan mosque.

SINAN AND THE CENTRAL-PLAN MOSQUE The first examples of the central-plan mosque were built in the 1520s, eclipsed later only by the works of the most famous Ottoman architect, SINAN (ca. 1491–1588). A contemporary of Michelangelo and with equal aspirations to immortality, Sinan perfected the Ottoman architectural style. By his time, the basic domed unit was universally used. It could be multiplied, enlarged, or contracted as needed, and almost any number of units could be used together. Thus, the typical Ottoman

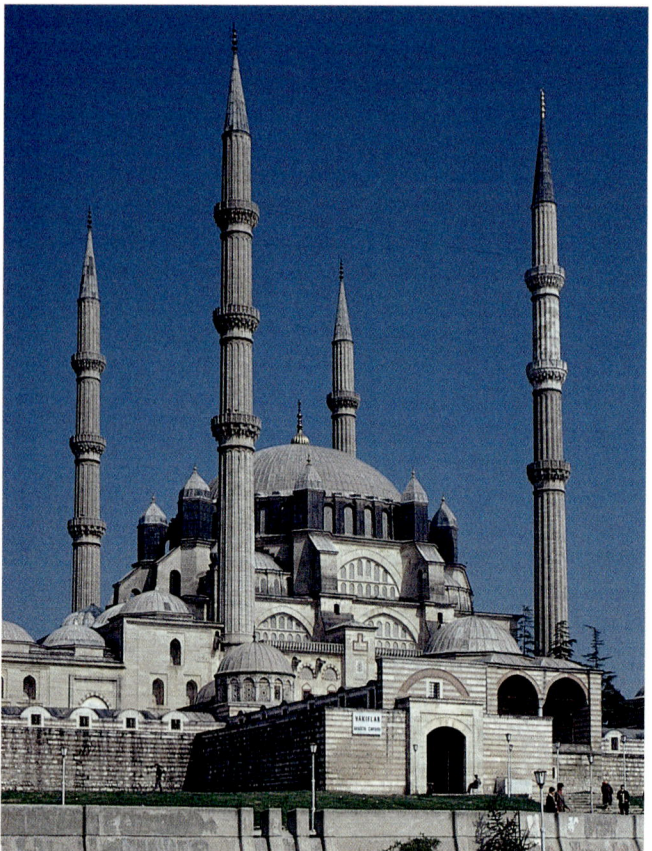

13-21   SINAN, Mosque of Selim II, Edirne, Turkey, 1568–1575.

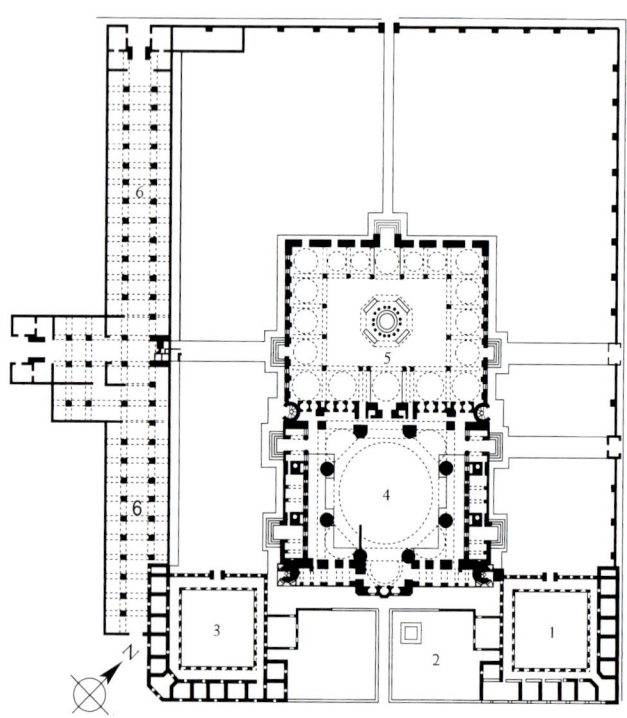

1. Madrasa
2. Cemetery
3. Darül-Kurra (house for the readers of the Quran)
4. Mosque
5. Avlu (courtyard forming summer extension of mosque)
6. Arasta (covered market)

0	250	500
		FEET

0	75	150
		METERS

13-22   SINAN, plan of the Mosque of Selim II, Edirne, Turkey, 1568–1575.

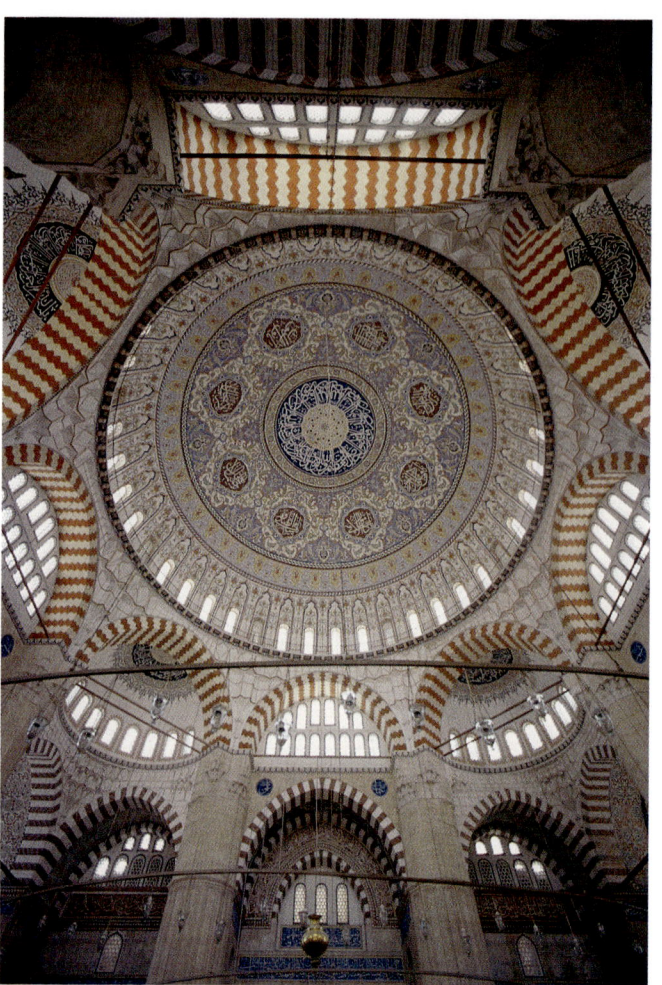

13-23   SINAN, interior of the Mosque of Selim II, Edirne, Turkey, 1568–1575.

building of Sinan's time was a creative assemblage of domical units and artfully juxtaposed geometric spaces. Builders usually erected domes with an extravagant margin of structural safety that since has served them well in earthquake-prone Istanbul and other Ottoman cities. (The sound construction of the Ottoman mosques was vividly demonstrated in August 1999 when a powerful earthquake centered sixty-five miles east of Istanbul toppled hundreds of modern buildings and killed thousands of people but caused no damage to the centuries-old mosques.) Working within this architectural tradition, Sinan searched for solutions to the problems of unifying the additive elements and of creating a monumental centralized space with harmonious proportions.

Sinan's efforts to overcome the limitations of a segmented interior found their ultimate expression in the Mosque of Selim II at Edirne (FIGS. **13-21** to **13-23**), which had been the Ottoman Empire's capital from 1367 to 1472 and remained the imperial residence. There Sinan created a structure that made the mihrab visible from almost any spot in the mosque. The massive dome, effectively set off by four slender pencil-shaped minarets (each more than two hundred feet high, among the tallest ever constructed), dominates the city's skyline (FIG. 13-21). Various dependent structures were placed around the mosque. Most important Ottoman mosques had numerous annexes, including libraries and schools, hospices, baths, soup kitchens for the poor, markets, and hospitals, as well as a cemetery containing the mausoleum of the sultan responsible for building the mosque (compare Hasan's complex

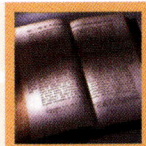

WRITTEN SOURCES

Sinan the Great, the Mosque of Selim II, and Hagia Sophia

Sinan (ca. 1491–1588), called "Sinan the Great," was in fact the greatest Ottoman architect. Born in Anatolia to a Christian family, he was recruited for service in the Ottoman government, converted to Islam, and was trained in engineering and the art of building while in the Ottoman army. His talent was quickly recognized, and he was entrusted with increasing responsibility until, in 1538, he was appointed the chief court architect for Suleyman the Magnificent (r. 1520–1566), a generous patron of art and architecture. Hundreds of building projects, both sacred and secular, have been attributed to Sinan, although he could not have been involved with all that bear his name.

The capstone of Sinan's distinguished career was the mosque (FIGS. 13-21 to 13-23) he designed when he was almost eighty years old for Suleyman's son, Selim II (r. 1566–1574), at Edirne, site of the Ottoman imperial residence. Sa'i Mustafa Çelebi, Sinan's biographer, recorded the architect's achievement in his own words:

> Sultan Selim Khan ordered the erection of a mosque in Edirne. . . . His humble servant [I, Sinan] prepared for him a drawing depicting,

on a dominating site in the city, four minarets on the four corners of a dome. . . . Those who consider themselves architects among Christians say that in the realm of Islam no dome can equal that of the Hagia Sophia; they claim that no Muslim architect would be able to build such a large dome. In this mosque, with the help of God and the support of Sultan Selim Khan, I erected a dome six cubits higher and four cubits wider than the dome of the Hagia Sophia.[1]

Sinan's dome is, in fact, higher than Hagia Sophia's (see FIGS. 12-3 to 12-5) when measured from its base, but its crown is not as far above the pavement as that of the dome of Justinian's church. Nonetheless, Sinan's feat was universally acclaimed as a triumph, and the Mosque of Selim II was considered proof that the Ottomans finally had surpassed the greatest achievement of the Christian emperors of Byzantium in the realm of architecture.

[1]Aptullah Kuran, *Sinan: The Grand Old Master of Ottoman Architecture* (Washington, D.C.: Institute of Turkish Studies, 1987), 168–69.

---

in Cairo, FIG. 13-20). These utilitarian buildings were grouped around the mosque and axially aligned with it if possible. More generally, they were adjusted to their natural site and linked with the central building by planted shrubs and trees.

The Edirne mosque is preceded by a rectangular court covering an area equal to that of the building (FIG. 13-22). Porticoes formed by domed squares surround the courtyard. Behind it, the building rises majestically to its climactic dome, whose height surpasses that of Hagia Sophia (see "Sinan the Great, the Mosque of Selim II, and Hagia Sophia," above). But it is the organization of this mosque's interior space (FIG. 13-23) that reveals the genius of its builder. The mihrab is recessed into an apselike alcove deep enough to permit window illumination from three sides, making the brilliantly colored tile panels of its lower walls sparkle as if with their own glowing light. The plan of the main hall is an ingenious fusion of an octagon with the dome-covered square. The octagon, formed by the eight massive dome supports, is pierced by the four half-dome-covered corners of the square. The result is a fluid interpenetration of several geometric volumes that represents the culminating solution to Sinan's lifelong search for a monumental unified interior space. Sinan's forms are clear and legible, like mathematical equations. Height, width, and masses are related to one another in a simple but effective ratio of 1:2. The building is generally regarded as the climax of Ottoman architecture. Sinan proudly proclaimed it his masterpiece.

IRANIAN MOSQUES SHEATHED WITH TILES

The Mosque of Selim II at Edirne was erected during a single building campaign under the direction of a single master architect, but many other major Islamic architectural projects

were built or remodeled over several centuries. A case in point is the Great Mosque at Isfahan (FIG. **13-24**) in Iran. The earliest mosque on the site, of the hypostyle type, was constructed in the eighth century during the caliphate of the Abbasids. But the present edifice was begun in the eleventh century by Sultan Malik Shah I (r. 1072–1092), whose capital was at Isfahan. The later mosque consists of a large courtyard bordered by a two-story arcade on each side. As in the fourteenth-century complex of Sultan Hasan in Cairo (FIG. 13-20), four iwans open onto the courtyard, one at the center of each side. The southwestern iwan leads into a dome-covered room in front of the mihrab. It functioned as a maqsura reserved for the sultan and his attendants. It is uncertain whether this plan, with four iwans and a dome before the mihrab, was employed for the first time in the Great Mosque at Isfahan, but it became standard in Iranian mosque design. In four-iwan mosques the qibla iwan is always the largest. Its size (and the dome that often accompanied it) immediately indicated to worshipers the proper direction for prayer.

We illustrate the Isfahan mosque's northwestern iwan, whose soaring pointed arch frames a tile-sheathed muqarnas vault. The muqarnas ceiling probably was installed in the fourteenth century, and the ceramic-tile revetment on the walls and vault is the work of the seventeenth-century Safavid rulers of Iran. The use of glazed tiles has a long history in the Middle East. Even in ancient Mesopotamia, gates and walls were sometimes covered with colorful baked bricks (see FIGS. 2-23 and 2-26). In the Islamic world, the art of ceramic tilework reached its peak in the sixteenth and seventeenth centuries in Turkey and Iran (see "Islamic Tilework," page 377). Employed as a veneer over a brick core, tiles could sheathe entire buildings, including domes and minarets.

13-24   Courtyard of the Great Mosque, Isfahan, Iran, eleventh to seventeenth centuries.

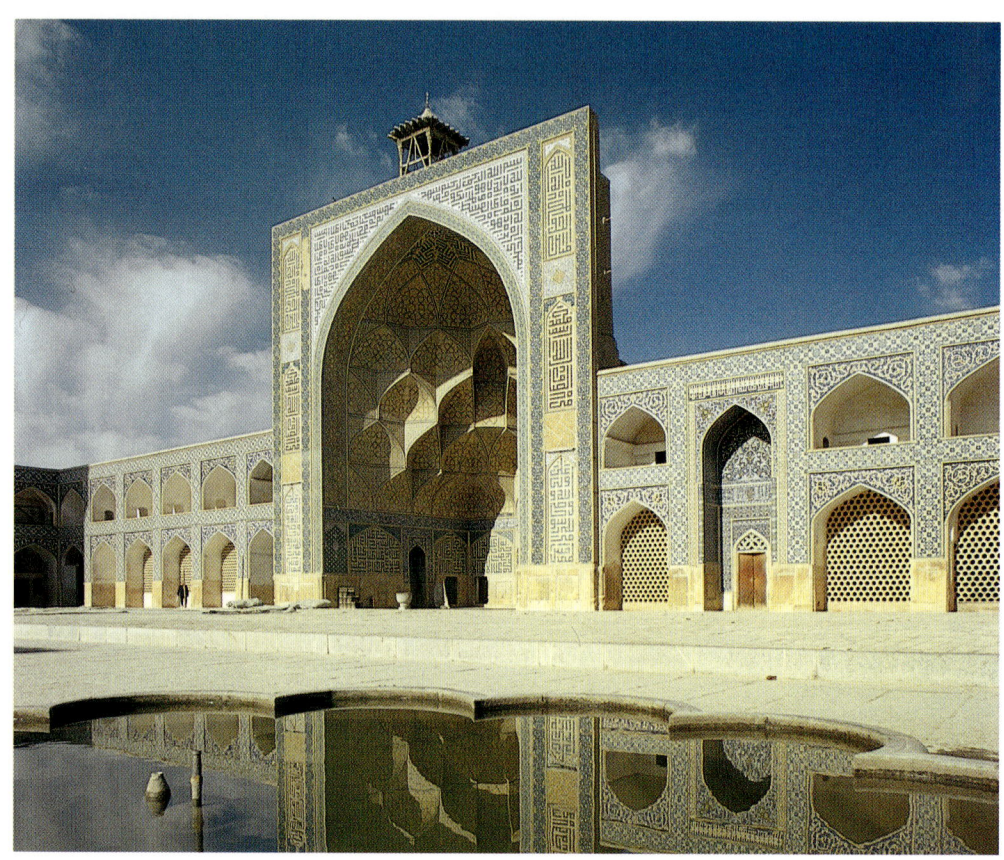

13-25   Dome of the Shah Mosque, Isfahan, Iran, 1611–1638.

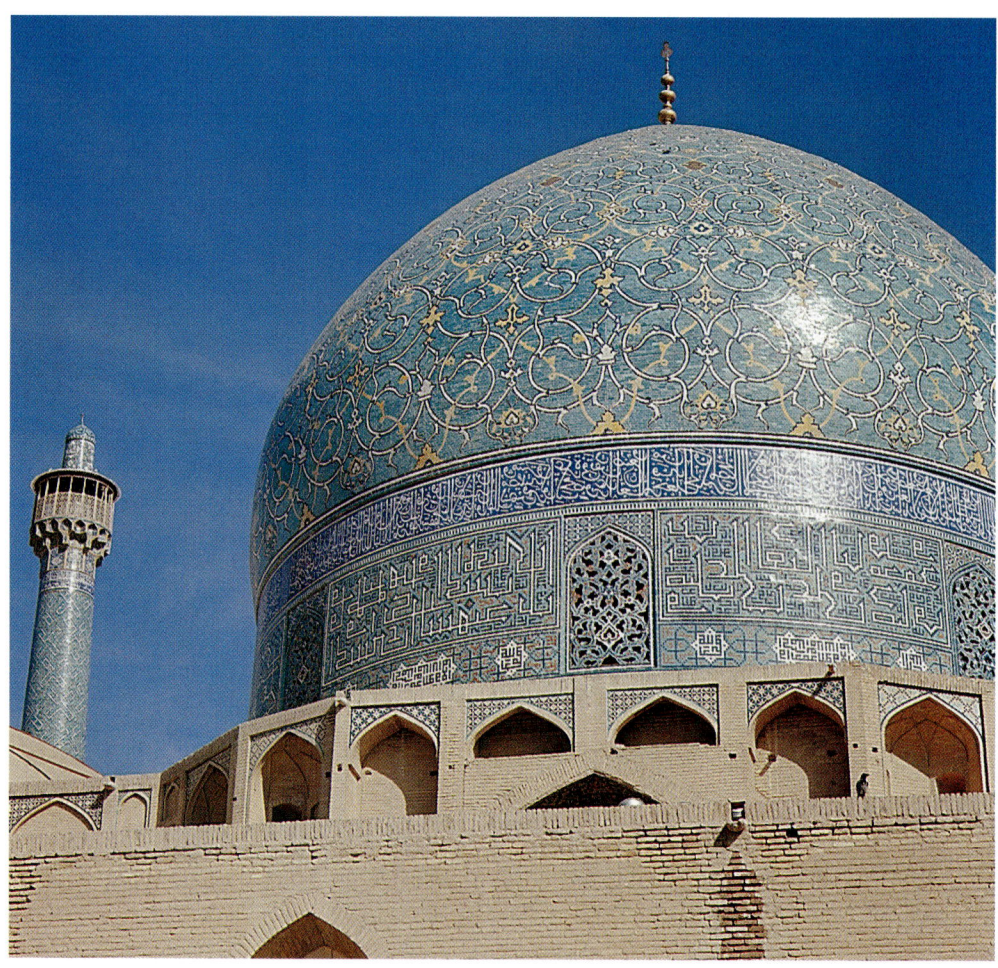

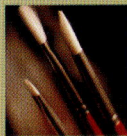

Islamic Tilework

From the Dome of the Rock (FIGS. 13-1 and 13-2), the earliest major Islamic building, to the present day, mosaics or ceramic tiles have been used to decorate the walls and vaults of mosques, madrasas, palaces, and tombs. The golden age of Islamic tilework was the sixteenth and seventeenth centuries. At that time, Islamic artists used two basic techniques to enliven building interiors with brightly colored tiled walls and to sheathe their exteriors with gleaming tiles that reflected the sun's rays.

In *mosaic tilework* (FIG. 13-26), large ceramic panels of single colors are fired in the potter's kiln and then cut into smaller pieces and set in plaster in a manner similar to the laying of mosaic tesserae of stone or glass (see "Mosaics," Chapter 11, page 314).

Cuerda seca (dry cord) tilework was introduced in Umayyad Spain during the tenth century—hence its Spanish name even in Middle Eastern and Central Asian contexts. Cuerda seca tiles (for example, FIGS. 13-1 and 13-25) are polychrome and can more easily bear complex arabesque patterns as well as Arabic script. They are more economical to use because vast surfaces can be covered with large tiles much more quickly than they can with thousands of smaller mosaic tiles. Polychrome tiles, however, have drawbacks. Because all the glazes are fired at the same temperature, cuerda seca tiles are not as brilliant in color as mosaic tiles. The preparation of the multicolored tiles also requires greater care. To prevent the colors from running together during firing, the potters outline the motifs on cuerda seca tiles with a greasy pigment containing manganese that leaves a matte black line between the colors after firing.

The Shah (or Royal) Mosque in Isfahan, which dates from the early seventeenth century, is widely recognized as one of the masterpieces of Islamic tilework. Our detail (FIG. **13-25**) shows the dome and one minaret of the qibla iwan. Beautifully adjusted to the dome's shape, the design of the spiraling tendrils is at once rich and subtle, enveloping the dome without overpowering it. In contrast to the more general Islamic tendency to disguise structure, the design here enhances the dome's form without obscuring it. On parts of the dome and on the minarets, the cuerda seca tiles are curved to conform to the shape of the architecture, a technological triumph by the Iranian ceramicists.

CERAMIC CALLIGRAPHY We noted earlier the Quran's central importance to the Islamic world and how its verses appeared in the mosaics of the earliest great Islamic building, the Dome of the Rock in Jerusalem (FIG. 13-2). Excerpts from the Quran appear on the walls of numerous other Islamic structures in a variety of media. Indeed, some of the masterworks of Arabic calligraphy are found not in manuscripts but on walls. A fourteenth-century mihrab from the Madrasa Imami in Isfahan (FIG. **13-26**) exemplifies the perfect aesthetic union between the calligrapher's art and the system of abstract Islamic ornamentation known as arabesque. The mihrab, now in the Metropolitan Museum of Art in New York, resembles the tiled dome of the Shah Mosque of Isfahan (FIG. 13-25), although it is much earlier in date. The two monuments, though also of greatly different scale, manifest the same design principles.

The pointed arch that immediately enframes the mihrab niche bears an inscription from the early Quran in Kufic, the stately rectilinear script employed for the early Quran page illustrated (FIG. 13-17). The many supple cursive styles that make up the repertoire of Islamic calligraphy are derived

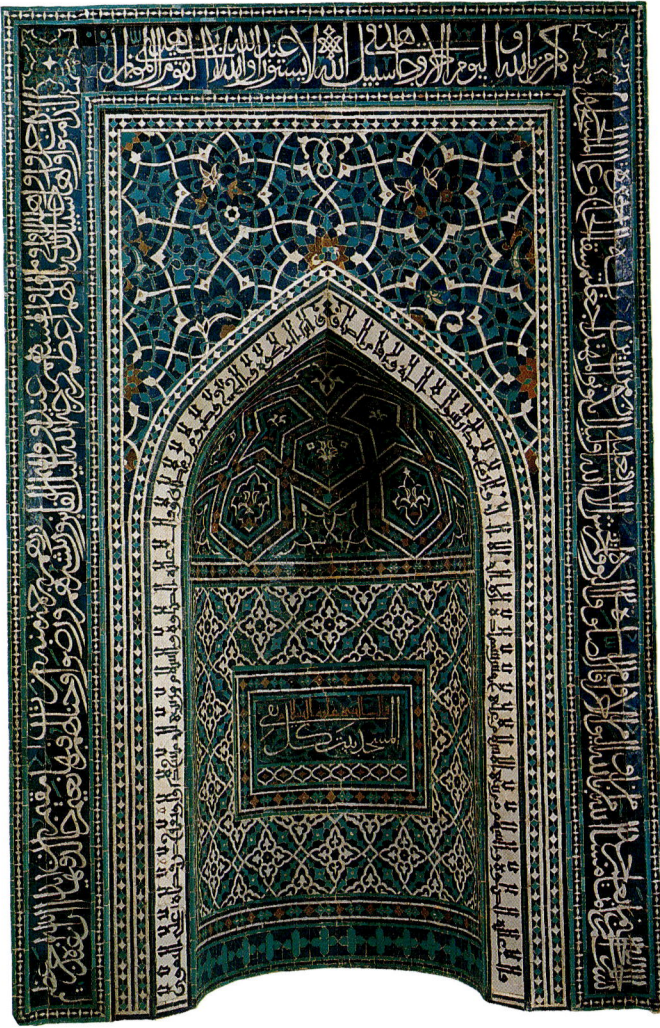

13-26 Mihrab from the Madrasa Imami, Isfahan, Iran, ca. 1354. Glazed mosaic tilework, 11′3″ × 7′6″. Metropolitan Museum of Art, New York.

from Kufic. One of these styles, known as *Muhaqqaq,* fills the mihrab's outer rectangular frame. The mosaic tile ornament on the curving surface of the niche and the *transom* (crosspiece) above the arch are composed of tighter and looser networks of geometric and abstract floral motifs. The mosaic technique is masterful. Every piece had to be sawn to fit its specific place in the mihrab—even the tile inscriptions. The framed inscription in the niche's center—proclaiming that the mosque is the domicile of the pious believer—is smoothly integrated with the subtly varied patterns. The mihrab's outermost inscription—detailing the five pillars of Islamic faith—serves as a fringelike extension, as well as a boundary, for the entire design. The calligraphic and geometric elements are so completely unified that only the practiced eye can distinguish them. The artist transformed the architectural surface into a textile surface, the three-dimensional wall into a two-dimensional hanging, weaving the calligraphy into it as another cluster of motifs within the total pattern.

PARADISE IN INDIA   Although Spain had been surrendered to the Christians at the end of the fifteenth century, in the sixteenth and seventeenth centuries Islam remained the leading religion throughout Anatolia, North Africa, the Middle East, and Central Asia, usurping other faiths in many areas. Suleyman the Magnificent, for example, presided over the Ottoman Empire from his capital at Istanbul, formerly Con-

stantinople, the seat of the Christian Byzantine Empire. In India, the Muslim Mughal dynasty held sway over a mixed population of Muslims, Hindus, and Jains (see Chapter 25). The Mughals were fabulously wealthy, and many of their cities and buildings rank among the most impressive achievements of Asian architecture.

The most famous of all the Islamic buildings of India is the fabled Taj Mahal at Agra (FIG. **13-27**). This immense mausoleum was erected by Shah Jahan (r. 1628–1658) as a memorial to his favorite wife, Mumtaz Mahal, but the ruler himself eventually was buried there as well. The central block's dome-on-cube shape is descended from that of the Samanid mausoleum at Bukhara (FIG. 13-11) and also reflects the basic form of the mausoleum of Sultan Hasan in Cairo (FIG. 13-19). But modifications and refinements have converted the earlier massive structures into an almost weightless vision of cream-colored marble. The Agra mausoleum seems to float magically above the tree-lined reflecting pools that punctuate the garden leading to it. The illusion that the marble tomb is suspended above the water is reinforced by the absence of any visible means of ascent to the upper platform. A stairway, in fact, exists, but the architect intentionally hid it from the view of anyone who approaches Mumtaz Mahal's memorial.

The Taj Mahal follows the plan of Iranian garden pavilions, except the building is placed at one end rather than in

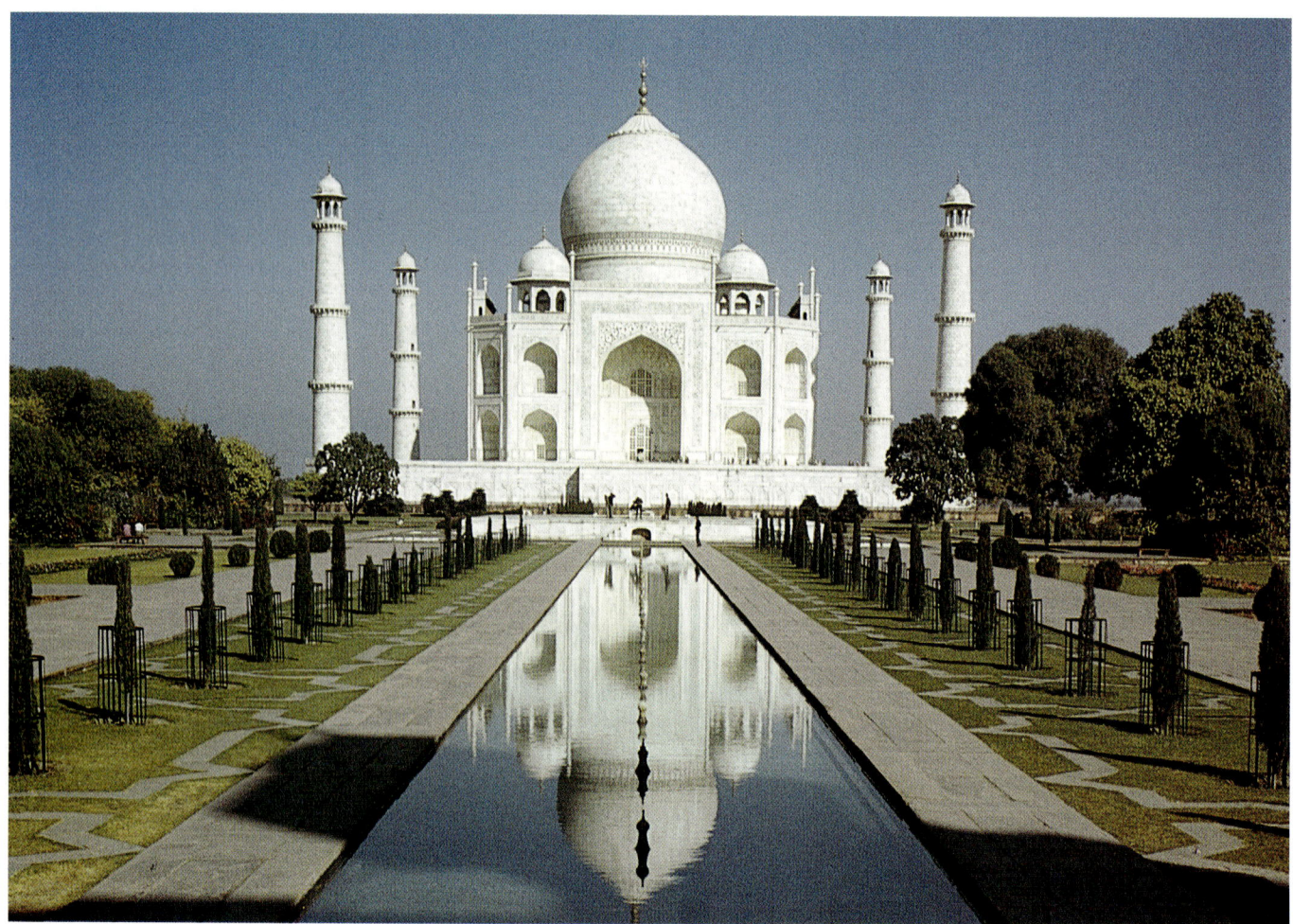

13-27   Taj Mahal, Agra, India, 1632–1647.

the center of the formal garden. The tomb is octagonal in plan with arcuated muqarnas niches on each side. The interplay of shadowy voids with gleaming marble walls that seem paper thin creates an impression of translucency. The pointed arches lead the eye in a sweeping upward movement toward the climactic balloon-shaped dome. Carefully related minarets and corner pavilions enhance, and stabilize, this soaring central theme. The architect achieved this delicate balance between verticality and horizontality by strictly applying an all-encompassing system of proportions. The Taj Mahal (without the minarets) is exactly as wide as it is tall, and the height of its dome is equal to the height of the facade. The perfect harmony and balance of dimensions were carried over into the complex as a whole. For example, the bright white mausoleum is flanked by twin red sandstone buildings (not visible in our photograph). One (at the left) is a mosque, but the other is an empty replica, constructed solely to provide compositional symmetry. Rarely has so grand a building been erected just to achieve an aesthetic effect.

Abd al-Hamid Lahori, a court historian who witnessed the construction of the Taj Mahal, compared its minarets to ladders reaching toward Heaven and the surrounding gardens to Paradise. In fact, the gateway to the gardens and the walls of the mausoleum are inscribed with carefully selected excerpts from the Quran and other Islamic texts that confirm the historian's interpretation of the tomb's symbolism. The Taj Mahal was conceived as the Throne of God perched above the gardens of Paradise on Judgment Day. The minarets hold up the canopy of that throne. In Islam, the most revered place of burial is beneath the Throne of God.

Luxury Arts

The Taj Mahal at Agra, the tile-sheathed mosques of Isfahan, Sultan Hasan's madrasa complex in Cairo, and the architecture of Sinan the Great in Edirne are enduring testaments to the brilliant artistic culture of the Mughal, Safavid, Mamluk, and Ottoman rulers of the Muslim world. But these are just some of the most conspicuous public manifestations of the greatness of later Islamic art and architecture. In the smaller-scale, and often private, realm of the luxury arts, Muslim artists also excelled. From the vast array of manuscript paintings, ceramics, textiles, and metalwork, four masterpieces may serve to suggest both the range and the quality of the inappropriately dubbed Islamic "minor arts" of the fourteenth to sixteenth centuries.

A ROYAL CARPET WITH MILLIONS OF KNOTS
The first of these artworks (FIG. **13-28**) is by far the largest, one of a pair of carpets from Ardabil in Iran. They are said to have come from the funerary mosque of Shaykh Safi al-Din (1252–1334), the founder of the Safavid line. Their origin, however, has been questioned, because the carpets are too large (the one we illustrate is almost thirty-five by eighteen feet) to fit into any of the rooms in that shrine. In any case, the carpets were made in 1540, two centuries after the mosque's erection, during the reign of Shah Tahmasp (r. 1524–1576). Tahmasp elevated carpet weaving to a national industry and set up royal factories at Isfahan, Kashan, Kirman, and Tabriz. The name of MAQSUD OF KASHAN is woven into the design of the carpet

we show. He must be the designer who supplied the master pattern to two teams of royal weavers (one for each of the two carpets). The carpet consists of roughly twenty-five million knots (some three hundred forty to the square inch; its twin has even more knots). It has been estimated that it would have taken a single weaver twenty years to complete the work.

The design consists of a central sunburst medallion, representing the inside of a dome, surrounded by sixteen pendants. Mosque lamps (appropriate motifs if the traditional attribution to the Ardabil funerary mosque is correct) are suspended from two pendants on the long axis of the carpet. The lamps are of different sizes, and some scholars have suggested that this is an optical device to make the two appear equal in size when viewed from the end of the carpet at the room's threshold (the bottom end in our illustration). The rich blue background is covered with leaves and flowers attached to a framework of delicate stems that spreads over the whole field. The entire composition presents the illusion of a heavenly dome with lamps reflected in a pool of water full of floating lotus blossoms. No human or animal figures appear, as befits a carpet intended for a mosque, although they can be found on other Islamic textiles used in secular contexts, both earlier (FIG. 13-15) and later.

MINIATURE PAINTINGS OF IRAN'S HISTORY
Shah Tahmasp was also a great patron of miniature painting. Around 1525 he commissioned an ambitious decade-long project to produce an illustrated 742-page copy of the *Shahnama (Book of Kings)*. The *Shahnama* is the Persian national epic poem by Firdawsi (940–1025). It recounts the history of Iran from the Creation until the Muslim conquest. Tahmasp's *Shahnama* contains 258 illustrations by many artists, including some of the most renowned painters of the day. It was eventually presented as a gift to Selim II, the Ottoman sultan who was the patron of Sinan's mosque at Edirne (FIGS. 13-21 to 13-23). The manuscript later entered a private collection in the West and ultimately was auctioned off as a series of individual pages, destroying its integrity—an unfortunate consequence of the esteem for Islamic art throughout the world.

The page we reproduce (FIG. **13-29**) is widely regarded as the greatest of all Persian miniature paintings. It is the work of SULTAN-MUHAMMAD and depicts Gayumars, the legendary first king of Iran, and his court. Gayumars was said to have ruled from a mountaintop when humans first learned to cook food and clothe themselves in leopard skins. In Sultan-Muhammad's representation of the story, Gayumars presides over his court (all the figures wear leopard skins) from his mountain throne. The king is surrounded by light amid a golden sky. His son and grandson are perched on multicolored rocky outcroppings to the viewer's left and right, respectively. The court encircles the ruler and his heirs. Dozens of human faces are portrayed within the rocks themselves. Many species of animals populate the lush landscape. According to the *Shahnama*, wild beasts became instantly tame in the presence of Gayumars. Sultan-Muhammad rendered the figures, animals, trees, rocks, and sky with an extraordinarily delicate touch. The sense of lightness and airiness that permeates the painting is enhanced by its placement on the page—floating, off center (our view is a detail of the full page), on a speckled background of gold leaf. The painter gave his royal patron a singular vision of Iran's fabled past.

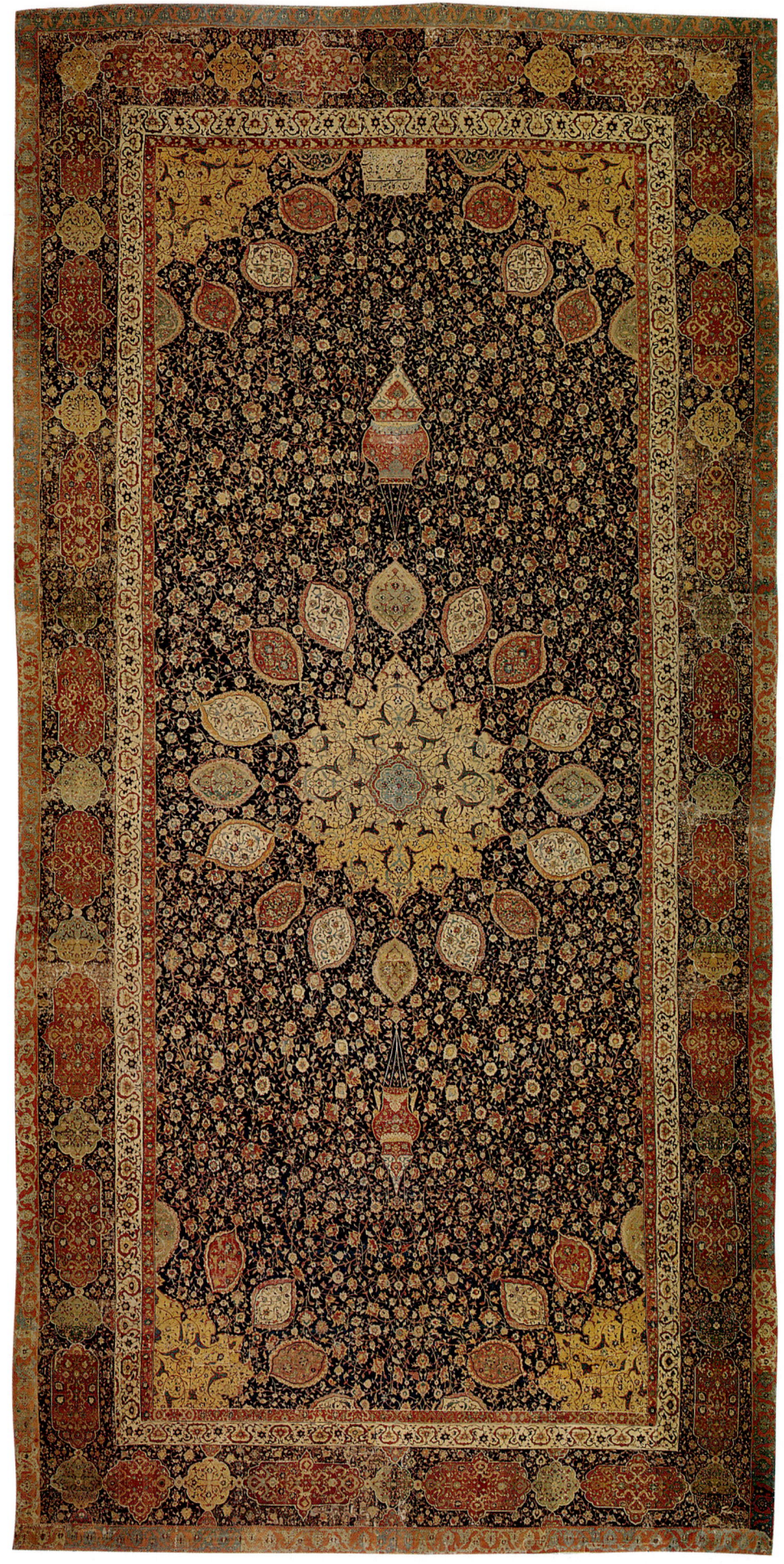

13-28 Maqsud of Kashan, carpet from the funerary mosque of Shaykh Safi al-Din(?), Ardabil, Iran, 1540. Knotted pile of wool and silk, 34′ 6″ × 17′ 7″. Victoria and Albert Museum, London.

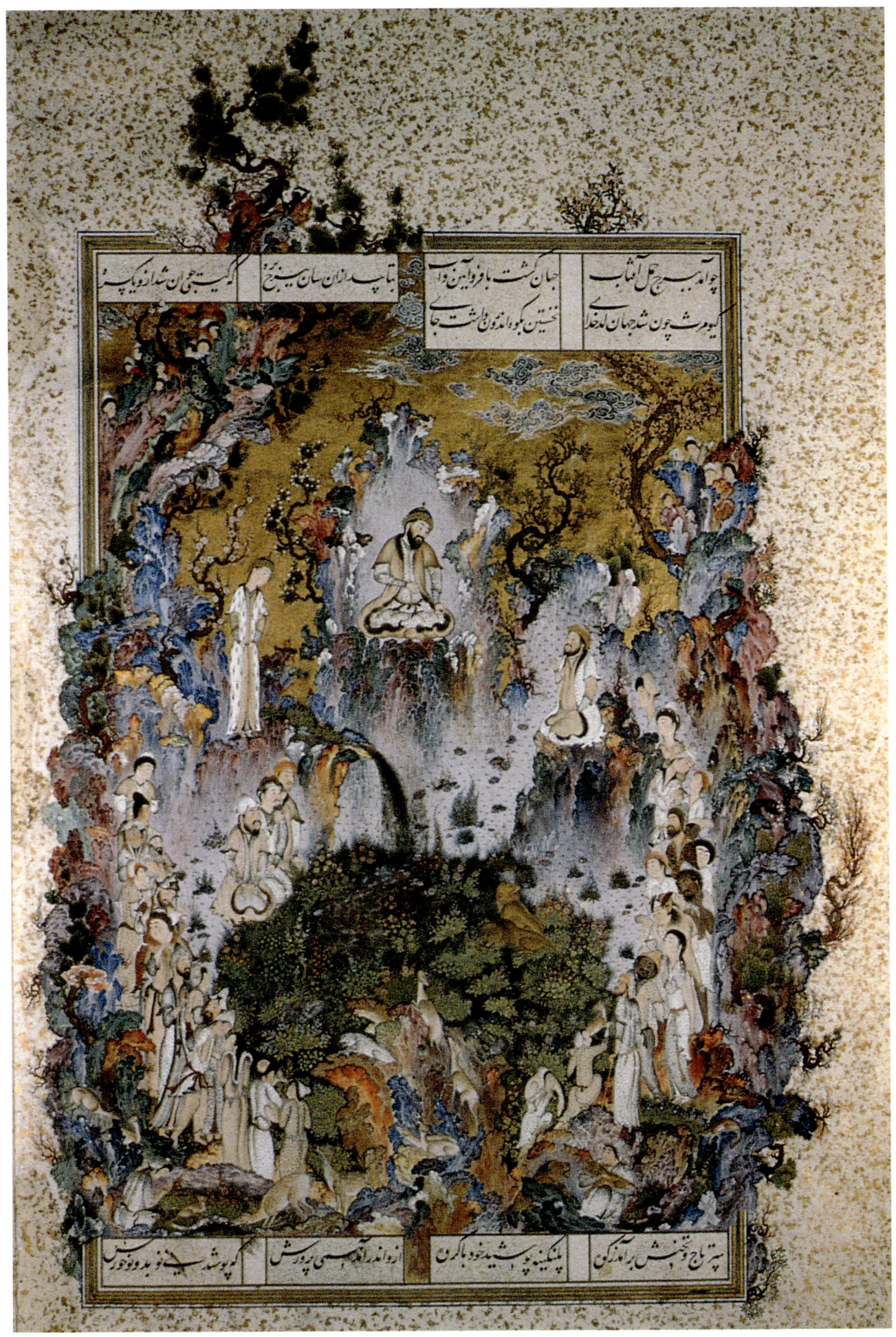

13-29 Sultan-Muhammad, the court of Gayumars, detail of folio 20 verso of the *Shahnama* of Shah Tahmasp, from Tabriz, Iran, ca. 1525–1535. Ink, watercolor, and gold on paper, full page approx. 1′ 1″ × 9″. Prince Sadruddin Aga Khan Collection, Geneva.

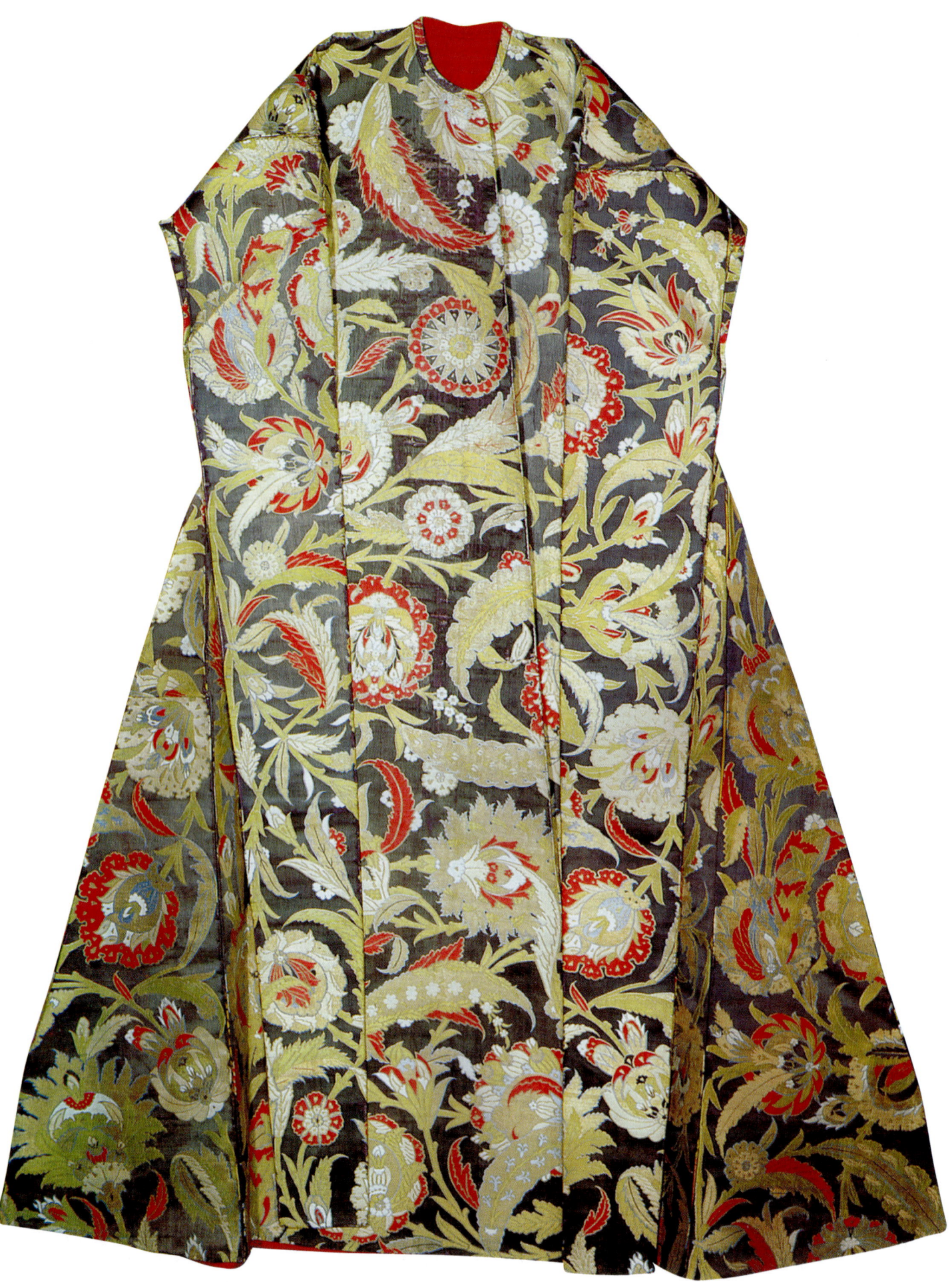

13-30 Ottoman royal ceremonial caftan, from Istanbul, Turkey, ca. 1550. Polychrome silk and gilt-metal thread, 4′ 9″ high. Topkapi Palace Museum, Istanbul.

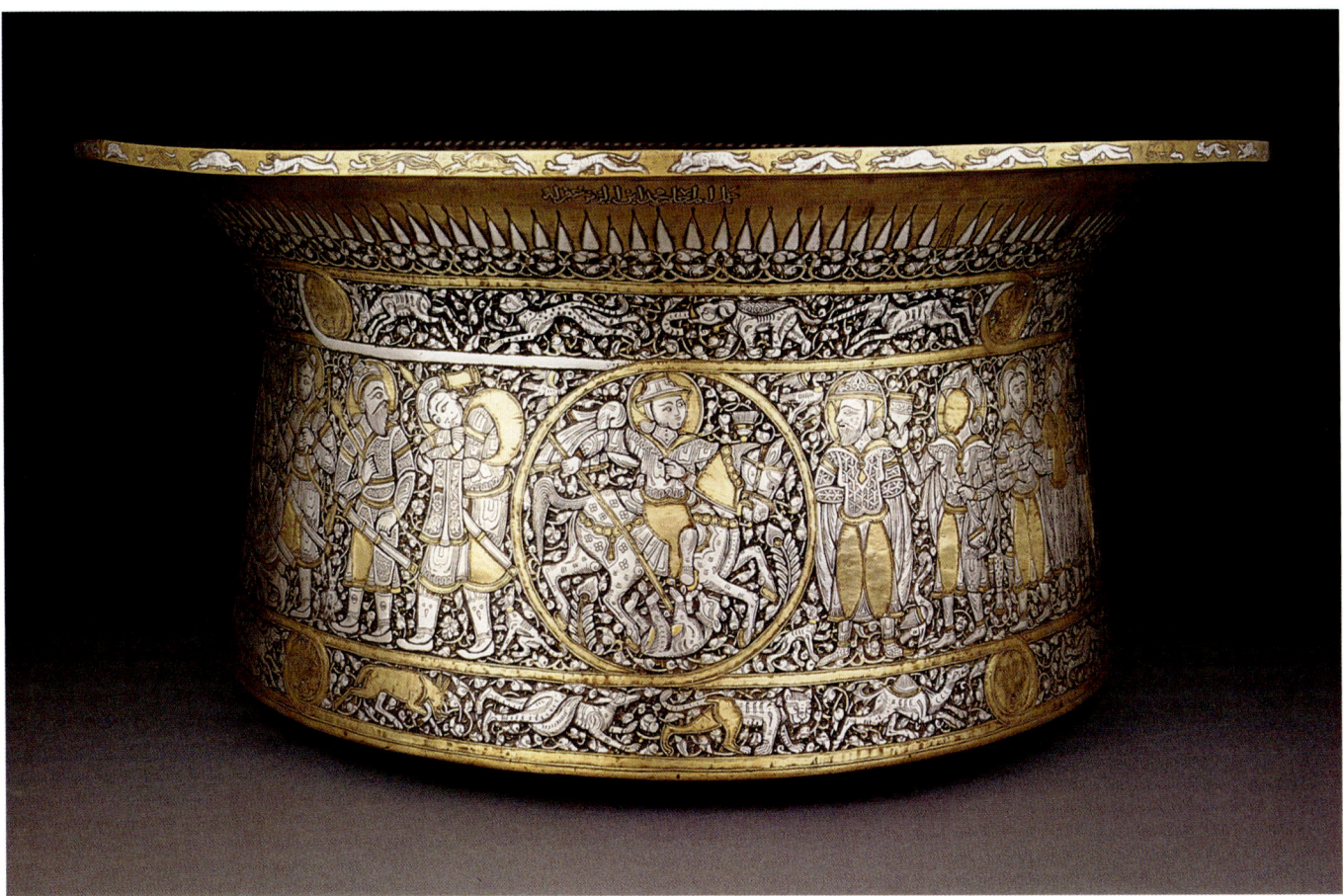

13-31 MUHAMMAD IBN AL-ZAYN, basin *(Baptistère de Saint Louis)*, from Egypt, ca. 1300. Brass inlaid with gold and silver, $8\frac{3}{4}''$ high. Louvre, Paris.

OTTOMAN POMP AND CIRCUMSTANCE When Tahmasp's *Shahnama* was presented to Selim II, the Ottoman sultan would have received the precious gift with due pomp and circumstance, perhaps wearing a ceremonial caftan like the one illustrated (FIG. **13-30**). It was woven of silk thread around 1550, perhaps for Suleyman the Magnificent's son Bayezid. More than a thousand such caftans are preserved in the Ottoman Topkapi Palace, now a museum. But this caftan was one of the most difficult to create on a loom because of its large number of colors and because of the complexity of its floral designs. This kind of distinctive Ottoman design of sinuous curved leaves and complex blossoms is known as *saz,* a Turkish term recalling an enchanted forest. The saz design is never repeated on this garment, a remarkable feat. The designer, nonetheless, made sure the pattern matched across the front opening. Court protocol dictated that Ottoman rulers stood absolutely motionless in the presence of visitors. This explains why the caftan has no fastenings to prevent it from opening. The wearer's arms protruded through slits at the shoulders. The sleeves are ankle length and served only for decoration; they were draped over the back. The rich saz arabesque of the Ottoman robe presents a telling contrast with the Byzantine sakkos of Photius (see FIG. 12-35), which is covered with Jewish and Christian narratives, saints, and Russian royalty, as well as a portrait of Photius himself.

AN ISLAMIC BASIN FOR CHRISTIAN KINGS Figures and animals do adorn one of the most impressive examples of Islamic metalwork known today, a brass basin (FIG. **13-31**) from Egypt inlaid with gold and silver and signed—six times—by the Mamluk artist MUHAMMAD IBN AL-ZAYN. The basin, used for washing hands at official ceremonies, must have been fashioned for a specific Mamluk patron. Some scholars think a court official named Salar ordered the piece as a gift for his sultan, but no inscription identifies him. The central band depicts Mamluk hunters and Mongol enemies. Running animals fill the friezes above and below. Arabesques of inlaid silver fill the background of all the bands and roundels. Figures and animals also decorate the inside and underside of the basin.

The basin has been long known as the *Baptistère de Saint Louis,* but the association with the famous French king (see "Louis IX: The Saintly King," Chapter 18, page 509) is a myth, for he died before the piece was made, The *Baptistère,* nonetheless brought to France long ago and was used in the baptismal rites of newborns of the French royal family as early as the seventeenth century. Like the Zandana silk in Toul Cathedral (FIG. 13-15), Muhammad ibn al-Zayn's basin testifies to the prestige of Islamic art in western Europe. The impact both of such imported items and of the art and architecture of Muslim Spain on European artists and builders of the later Middle Ages is examined in due course. But first this history of art through the ages steps back in time and looks at developments in the Western hemisphere and in sub-Saharan Africa.

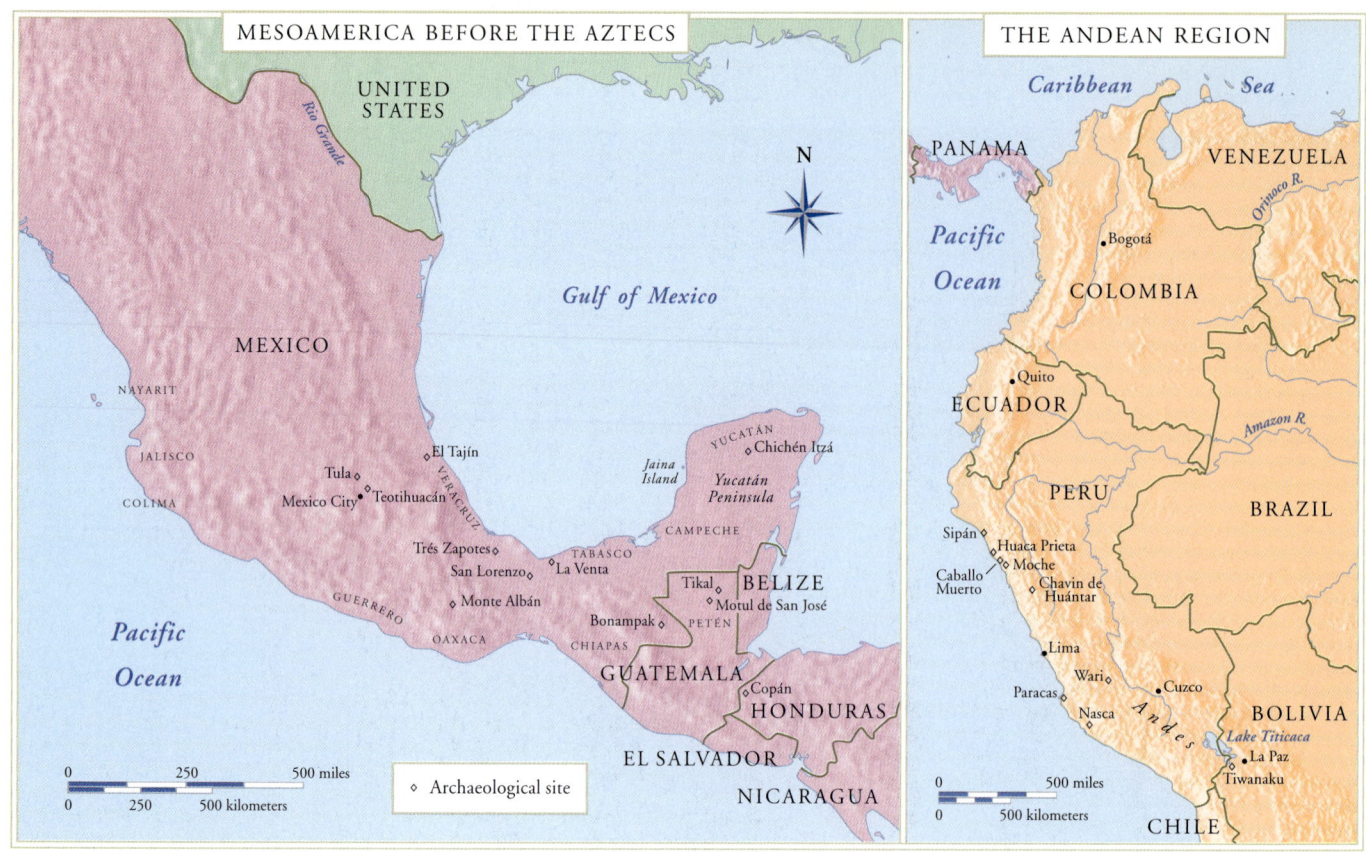

MESOAMERICA BEFORE THE AZTECS

UNITED STATES

Rio Grande

N

Gulf of Mexico

MEXICO

NAYARIT

JALISCO

COLIMA

Tula ◇
Mexico City ● ◇ Teotihuacán

El Tajín ◇

VERACRUZ

Trés Zapotes ◇
San Lorenzo ◇   ◇ La Venta

TABASCO

Jaina Island

YUCATÁN
◇ Chichén Itzá

Yucatán Peninsula

CAMPECHE

Monte Albán ◇

GUERRERO

Pacific Ocean

OAXACA

CHIAPAS

Tikal ◇   BELIZE
◇ Motul de San José
PETÉN

Bonampak ◇

GUATEMALA

◇ Copán
HONDURAS

EL SALVADOR

NICARAGUA

0 — 250 — 500 miles
0 — 250 — 500 kilometers

◇ Archaeological site

THE ANDEAN REGION

Caribbean Sea

PANAMA

VENEZUELA

Pacific Ocean

● Bogotá

COLOMBIA

Orinoco R.

● Quito

ECUADOR

Amazon R.

PERU

BRAZIL

Sipán ◇   ◇ Huaca Prieta
Caballo ◇   ◇ Moche
Muerto   ◇ Chavin de Huántar

● Lima

Wari ●   ● Cuzco

Paracas ●
Nasca ●

Andes

BOLIVIA

Lake Titicaca
● La Paz
Tiwanaku ◇

CHILE

0 — 500 miles
0 — 500 kilometers

	3000 B.C.	2000 B.C.	1000			B.C. A.D.
MESOAMERICA		PRECLASSIC (FORMATIVE)				
SOUTH AMERICA REGIONAL DEVELOPMENT PERIODS	PRECERAMIC		INITIAL PERIOD	EARLY HORIZON		EARLY INTERMEDIATE PERIOD
SOUTH AMERICA WIDESPREAD HORIZON STYLES			CABALLO MUERTO	CHAVÍN (800–200 B.C.) (SPREAD OF CULTURE 400–200 B.C.) (PARACAS 400 B.C.–A.D. 200) (NASCA 200 B.C.–A.D. 600)		

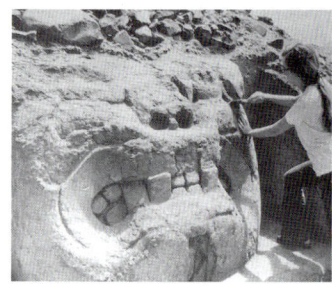

Feline head, Huaca de los Reyes
Caballo Muerto, Peru, ca. 1300 B.C

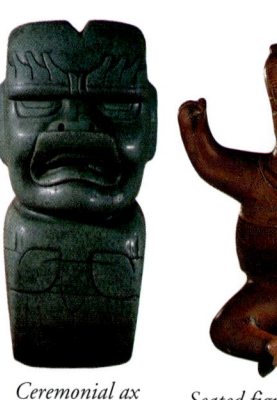

Ceremonial ax
La Venta, Mexico
900–400 B.C.

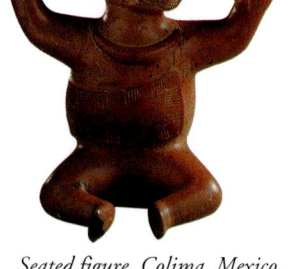

Seated figure, Colima, Mexico
ca. 200 B.C.–A.D. 250

Asian immigrants settle the Americas, 30,000–10,000 B.C.

Beginnings of plant domestication in Mesoamerica, 8000 B.C.

First monumental architecture built in Peru, of adobe and stone, ca. 3000 B.C.

Earliest Andean woven cotton textiles, ca. 2000 B.C.

Earliest Peruvian metallurgy, 2000 B.C.

First Mesoamerican ballcourt built, 1400 B.C.

Caballo Muerto, Peru, 1300 B.C.

Olmec culture spreads throughout Mesoamerica, 900–400 B.C.

Beginnings of Maya civilization, 600 B.C.

Earliest Mesoamerica writing, ca. 500 B.C.

Spread of Chavín culture, 400–200 B.C.

Paracas textiles woven, 400 B.C.–A.D. 200

Shaft-tomb cultures of West Mexico, ca. 200 B.C.–A.D. 250

Teotihuacán founded, 100 B.C.

14

FROM ALASKA TO THE ANDES

THE ARTS OF ANCIENT AMERICA

300 A.D.		900	1000	1250
CLASSIC		EARLY POST CLASSIC		
	MIDDLE HORIZON			

MOCHE (1–700)   TIWANAKU SITE (100–1000)
WARI SITE (500–800)

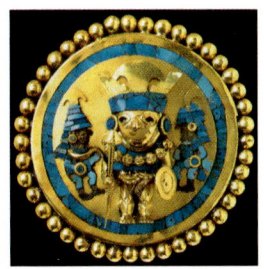

*Ear ornament
Sipán, Peru, ca. 300*

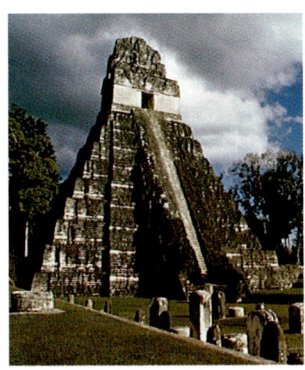

*Temple I, Tikal, Guatemala
ca. 700*

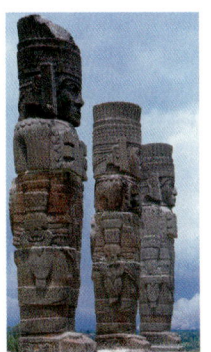

*Atlantids, Tula, Mexico
ca. 900–1180*

Moche burials at Sipán, 100–300

Nasca lines, 500

Abandonment of Teotihuacán, 700

Capture of 18-Rabbit, 738

Bonampak murals, ca. 800

Southern lowland Maya collapse, ca. 900

Ascendance of Chichén Itzá, ca. 900

Toltec domination, 1000

Tula collapses, ca. 1200

AMERICA BEFORE COLUMBUS

Among world cultures, those that flourished in Mexico, Central America, and South America before contact with European explorers were exceptional in several important ways. Some of the native peoples, such as the Maya, had a highly developed writing system and knowledge of mathematical calculation that allowed them to keep precise records and create a sophisticated calendar and a highly accurate astronomy. Although most relied on stone tools, did not use the wheel (except for toys), and had no pack animals but the llama (in South America), these peoples excelled in the engineering arts associated with the planning and construction of cities, civic and domestic buildings, roads and bridges, and irrigation and drainage systems. They mastered complex agricultural techniques using only rudimentary cultivating tools. And they produced distinctive and remarkable sculptures, paintings, and crafts. However, the sixteenth-century European invaders left most of these civilizations in ruins. Others were abandoned to the forces of nature—erosion and the encroachment of tropical forests. But despite the ruined state of many cities, archeologists have reconstructed many of them, and with art historians, reconstructed much of the art and architectural history of the Americas before the Europeans arrived.

THE PEOPLING OF THE AMERICAS The origins of the indigenous peoples of the Americas are still disputed, the debate centering primarily on the date of their arrival from Asia. Many must have crossed the now submerged land bridge called Beringia, which connected the shores of the Bering Strait between Asia and North America, sometime between 30,000 B.C. and 10,000 B.C. Some scholars also have proposed that at least some migrants reached America via boats traveling along the Pacific coast of North America. These Stone Age nomads were hunter-gatherers. They made tools only of bone, pressure-flaked stone, and wood. They had no knowledge of agriculture but possibly some of basketry. They could control fire and probably built simple shelters. For many centuries, they spread out until they occupied the two American continents. But they were always few in number. When the first Europeans arrived at the end of the fifteenth century, the total population of the Western Hemisphere may not have exceeded forty million.

Between 8000 and 2000 B.C., a number of the migrants had learned to domesticate plants like squash and maize (corn). This set the stage for the maize culture that was basic to the early peoples of the Americas. As agriculturalists, the nomads settled down in villages and learned to make clay pottery utensils and lively figurines. Metal technology, although extremely sophisticated when it existed, developed only in the Andean region of South America (eventually spreading north into modern-day Mexico) and generally met only the need for ornament, not for tools. With these skills as a base, many cultures rose and fell over long periods. Several reached a high level of social complexity and artistic achievement by the early centuries of the Christian era.

A CLASH OF CULTURES Because these civilizations abruptly collapsed with the Spanish conquests of the sixteenth century, their cultures have come to be called *pre-Columbian* in reference to Christopher Columbus's arrival in the Caribbean in 1492, even though he made only brief stops on the mainland. Others—notably Hernán Cortés in Mexico and Francisco Pizarro in Peru—completed the conquest of what people now call Latin America. In the twenty-five years following the European discovery of the "New World," the Spanish monarchs poured money into expeditions that probed the coasts of North and South America, but with little luck in finding the wealth they sought. When brief stops on the coast of Yucatán, Mexico, yielded a small but still impressive amount of gold and other precious artifacts, the Spanish governor of Cuba outfitted yet another expedition. Headed by Cortés, this contingent of Spanish explorers was the first to make contact with the great Aztec emperor Moctezuma. In two short years, with the help of guns, horses, and native allies oppressed by their Aztec overlords, Cortés managed to overthrow the vast and rich Aztec empire. His victory in 1521 opened the door to hordes of Spanish conquistadors seeking their fortunes, to missionaries eager for new converts to Christianity, and to a host of new diseases for which the native Americans had no immunity. The ensuing clash of cultures led to a century of turmoil and an enormous population decline throughout the Spanish king's new domains. Great wealth accrued to Europe, ending only with the independence of most Latin American countries in the early nineteenth century. Although the Spaniards destroyed many impressive buildings and artworks in their zeal to obliterate all traces of pagan beliefs, immediately melting down all the gold and silver objects they captured to form ingots, a surprisingly large body of magnificent artworks in many media still survives. These objects and the ruined cities where they were found serve as haunting reminders of the great civilizations that succeeded one another in the centuries before the Europeans arrived.

MESOAMERICA

GEOGRAPHY AND CLIMATE The term *Mesoamerica* names the region that comprises part of present-day Mexico, Guatemala, Belize, Honduras, and the Pacific coast of El Salvador. Mesoamerica was the homeland of several of the great civilizations that flourished before the European conquest. The principal regions of pre-Columbian Mesoamerica are the Gulf Coast region (Olmec culture); the states of Jalisco, Colima, and Nayarit, collectively known as West Mexico; the Chiapas, Yucatán, Quintana Roo, and Campeche states in Mexico and the Petén area of Guatemala (Maya culture); southwestern Mexico and the state of Oaxaca (Zapotec and Mixtec cultures); and the central plateau surrounding modern-day Mexico City (Teotihuacán, Toltec, and Aztec cultures). These cultures were often influential over extensive areas.

The Mexican highlands are a volcanic and seismic region. In highland Mexico, great reaches of arid plateau land, fertile for maize and other crops wherever water is available, lie between heavily forested mountain slopes, which at some places rise to a perpetual snow level. The moist tropical rain forests of the coastal plains yield rich crops, when the land can be cleared. In Yucatán, a subsoil of limestone furnishes abundant material both for building and carving. This limestone tableland merges with the vast Petén region of Guatemala, which separates Mexico from Honduras. Yucatán and the Petén, where dense rain forest alternates with broad stretches of grassland, host some of the most spectacular Maya ruins. The great mountain chains of Mexico and Guatemala extend into Honduras and slope sharply down to tropical coasts. Highlands and mountain valleys, with their chill and temperate climates, alternate dramatically with the humid climate of tropical rain forest and coastlines.

LANGUAGE AND CHRONOLOGY The variegated landscape of Mesoamerica may have much to do with the diversity of languages its native populations speak. Numerous languages are distributed among no fewer than fourteen linguistic families. Many of the languages spoken in the preconquest periods survive to this day. Various Mayan languages linger in Guatemala and southern Mexico. The Náhuatl of the Aztecs endures in the Mexican highlands. The Zapotec and Mixtec languages persist in Oaxaca and its environs. Diverse as the languages of these peoples were, their cultures, otherwise, had much in common. The Mesoamerican peoples shared maize cultivation, religious beliefs and rites, myths, social structures, customs, and arts. Yet each is renowned for its particular accomplishments. The Maya, for example, developed a complex writing system. The Mixtecs excelled as master craftsmen in gold and turquoise. The Aztecs were fierce warriors who in a few short years created a vast imperial state.

Archeologists, with ever increasing refinement of technique, have been uncovering, describing, and classifying Mesoamerican monuments for more than a century. Since the 1950s, when linguists made important breakthroughs in deciphering the Maya hieroglyphic script, evidence for a detailed account of Maya history and art has emerged. Many Maya rulers now can be listed by name and the dates of their reigns fixed with precision. Other writing systems, such as that of the Zapotec, who began to record dates at a very early time, are less well understood, but researchers are making rapid progress in their interpretation. The general Mesoamerican chronology is now well established and widely accepted. The standard chronology, divided into three epochs, involves some overlapping of subperiods—the Preclassic (Formative) extends from 2000 B.C. to about A.D. 300; the Classic period runs from about 300 to 900; and the Postclassic begins ca. 900 and ends with the Spanish conquest of 1521.

Preclassic (2000 B.C.–A.D. 300)

THE OLMEC "MOTHER CULTURE" The Olmec culture of the present-day states of Veracruz and Tabasco is known as the "mother culture" of Mesoamerica. Many religious, social, and artistic traditions can be traced to it. Although little is known of its origins, history, or language, the wide diffusion of Olmec institutional forms, monuments, arts, and artifacts reflects the culture's broad influence. Excavations in and around not only the principal Gulf Coast sites of Olmec culture—Tres Zapotes, San Lorenzo, and La Venta—but also in central Mexico and along the Pacific coast from the Mexican state of Guerrero to El Salvador indicate that Olmec influence was far more widespread than scholars

once supposed. The Olmec clearly were the source of the distinctive features subsequent Mesoamerican cultures shared.

Settling in the tropical lowlands of the Gulf of Mexico, the Olmec peoples cultivated a terrain of rain forest and alluvial lowland washed by numerous rivers flowing into the gulf. Here, between approximately 1500 B.C. and 400 B.C., social organization assumed the form later Mesoamerican cultures adapted and developed. The mass of the population—food-producing farmers scattered in hinterland villages—provided the sustenance and labor that maintained a hereditary caste of rulers, hierarchies of priests, functionaries, and artisans. The nonfarming population presumably lived, arranged by rank, within precincts that served ceremonial, administrative, and residential functions, and perhaps also as marketplaces. At regular intervals, the whole community convened for ritual observances at the religious-civic centers of towns such as San Lorenzo and La Venta. These centers were the formative architectural expressions of the structure and ideals of Olmec society.

COLOSSAL RULER PORTRAITS At La Venta, low clay-and-earthen platforms and stone fences enclosed two great courtyards. At the north end of the larger area was a mound almost one hundred feet high. Although now very eroded, its current fluted cone shape resembles a volcano. This early pyramid may have been built to mimic a mountain, held sacred by Mesoamerican peoples as both a life-giving source of water and a feared destructive force. (Volcanic eruptions and earthquakes still wreak havoc in this region.) The La Venta layout is an early form of the temple-pyramid and plaza complex aligned on a north-south axis that characterized later Mesoamerican ceremonial center design.

Four colossal basalt heads weighing about ten tons each and standing between six and eight feet high (FIG. 14-1) face out from the plaza. Almost as much of an achievement as the

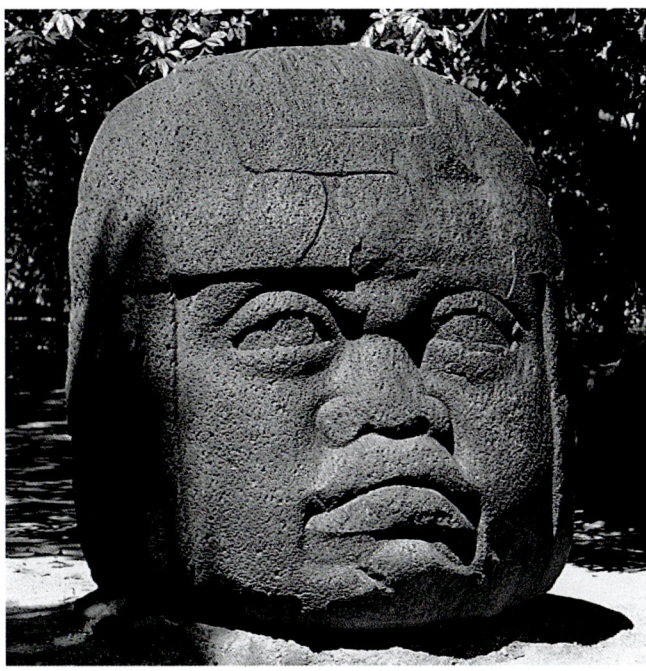

14-1   Colossal head, Olmec, La Venta, Mexico, 900–400 B.C. Basalt, 8′ high.

carving of these huge stones was their transportation across the sixty miles of swampland from the nearest known basalt source. The large heads are hallmarks of Olmec art. Several others have been found at San Lorenzo and Tres Zapotes. Although their identities are uncertain, their individualized features and distinctive headgear and ear ornaments, as well as the later Maya practice of carving monumental ruler portraits, suggest that the Olmec heads portray rulers rather than deities. The Olmec apparently mutilated their own monuments, perhaps for ritual reasons related to the end of a ruler's reign. Sometimes they reshaped sculptures for other uses, turning carved stone thrones into colossal heads, for example. But because both San Lorenzo and, later, La Venta appear to have been violently overthrown, the deliberate defacement of some monuments may represent the vandalism of particularly hostile invaders or Olmec revolutionaries.

JADE JAGUAR-HUMANS The Olmec also carved sculptures in jade, a material they acquired from unknown sources far from their homeland and that all Mesoamerican peoples highly prized. Sometimes the Olmec carved it into ax-shaped polished forms called *celts,* which they then buried as ceremonial offerings under their courtyards or platforms. The celt shape could be modified into a figural form, combining relief carving with incising. Stone-tipped drills and abrasive materials like sand were used to carve jade. Figures represented include crying babies (of unknown significance) and figures combining human and animal features and postures (FIG. **14-2**), notably those of the jaguar, the largest, most powerful, and most elusive of Mesoamerican predators. Archeologists have dubbed these jaguar-human representations "were-jaguars." Although Olmec religious beliefs and practices are little known, such human-animal representations may refer to the belief that religious practitioners known as shamans underwent dangerous transformations to wrest power from supernatural forces and harness it for the community's good.

WEST MEXICO'S RICH CERAMIC TRADITION
Far to the west of the tropical heartland of the Olmec are the Preclassic sites along Mexico's Pacific coast. The pre-Columbian peoples of the modern West Mexican states of Nayarit, Jalisco, and Colima were long thought to have existed at Mesoamerica's geographic and cultural fringes. Recent archeological discoveries, however, have revealed that although the West Mexicans did not produce large-scale stone sculpture, they did build permanent structures. These included tiered platforms and ballcourts (see "The Mesoamerican Ballgame," page 392), architectural features found in nearly all Mesoamerican cultures. Yet West Mexico is best known for its rich tradition of clay sculpture.

Distinctive tombs consisting of shafts as deep as fifty feet with chambers at their base have yielded varied offerings. These include clay sculptures, usually hollow, of humans, plants, animals, and mythological creatures. Archeologists have long neglected West Mexico. Because scientific excavations began only recently, much of what is known about tomb contents derives primarily from the artifacts grave robbers find and sell. Researchers believe, however, that most of these tombs were built and filled with elaborate offerings during the late Preclassic period.

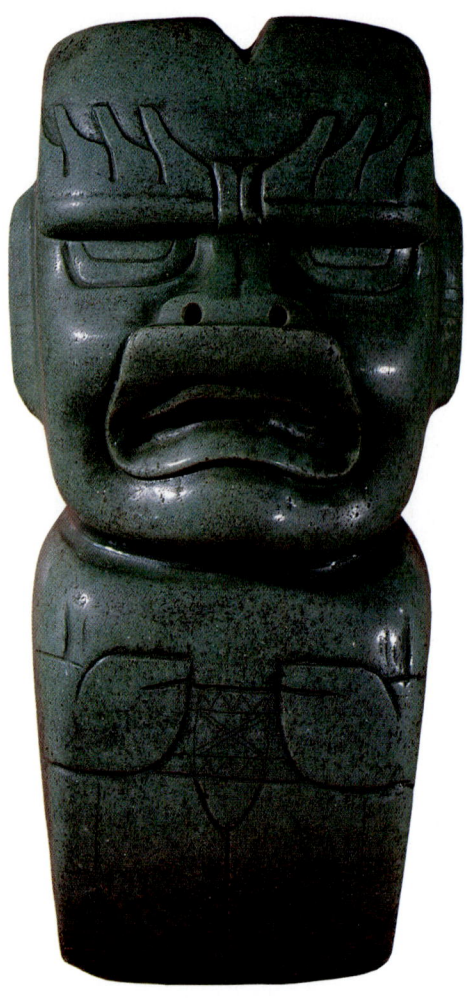

14-2   Ceremonial ax in the form of a jaguar-human, Olmec, from La Venta, Mexico, 900–400 B.C. Jadeite, 11½″ high. British Museum, London.

The large ceramic figures found in these tombs exhibit a distinct sense of volume, particularly in the swollen torsos and limbs (FIG. **14-3**). The Colima figures are consistently a highly burnished red orange, in contrast with the distinctive polychrome surfaces of the majority of other West Coast ceramics. The area also is noted for small-scale clay narrative scenes that include modeled houses and temples and numerous solid figurines shown in a variety of lively activities. Art historians have interpreted some of these sculptures as festivals, funerals, and battles. These sculptured scenes provide informal glimpses of daily life found in no other pre-Columbian Mesoamerican cultures. To some degree this viewpoint that West Mexican ceramic sculpture is anecdotal and secular rather than religious may result from scholars' limited knowledge of the region, as well as from the modern Western tendency to separate the religious from the secular. The Mesoamerican belief system does not recognize such a division. Consequently, scholars are unsure whether the figure we illustrate is a shaman with a horn on his forehead (a common indigenous symbol of special powers) or a political leader wearing a shell ornament (often a Mesoamerican emblem of rulership). He could be serving, of course, both roles.

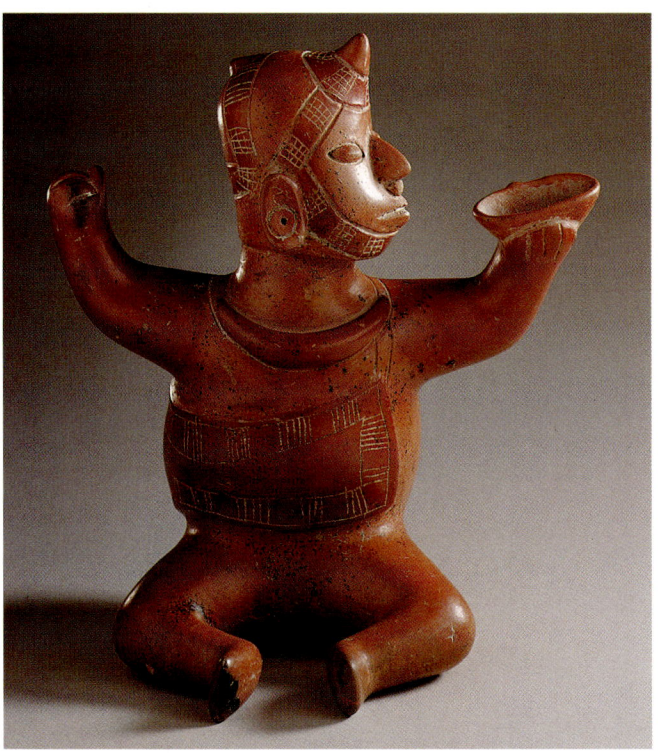

14-3 Seated figure with raised arms, from Colima, Mexico, ca. 200 B.C.–A.D. 250. Clay with orange and red slip, 1′ 1″ high. Los Angeles County Museum of Art, Los Angeles.

Classic (A.D. 300–900)

The era designated as the Classic period in Mesoamerica witnessed the rise to grandeur of several great civilizations. Although these advanced cultures originated in the late Preclassic period, they achieved their unprecedented magnificence in the Classic period.

MESOAMERICA'S FIRST METROPOLIS At Olmec La Venta, the characteristic Mesoamerican temple-pyramid-plaza layout appeared in embryonic form. At the awe-inspiring site of Teotihuacán (FIG. **14-4**), northeast of modern Mexico City, the Preclassic scheme underwent a monumental expansion into a genuine city. Teotihuacán was a large, densely populated metropolis that fulfilled a central civic, economic, and religious role for the region and indeed for much of Mesoamerica. The carefully planned area covers nine square miles, laid out in a grid pattern with the axes oriented consistently by sophisticated surveying. The city's orientation, as well as the placement of some of its key pyramids, also appear to have been related to astronomical phenomena.

At its peak, around 600, Teotihuacán may have had as many as two hundred thousand residents. It would have been at that time the sixth largest city in the world. Divided into numerous wardlike sectors, this metropolis must have had a uniquely cosmopolitan character, with Zapotec peoples located in the city's western wards and merchants from

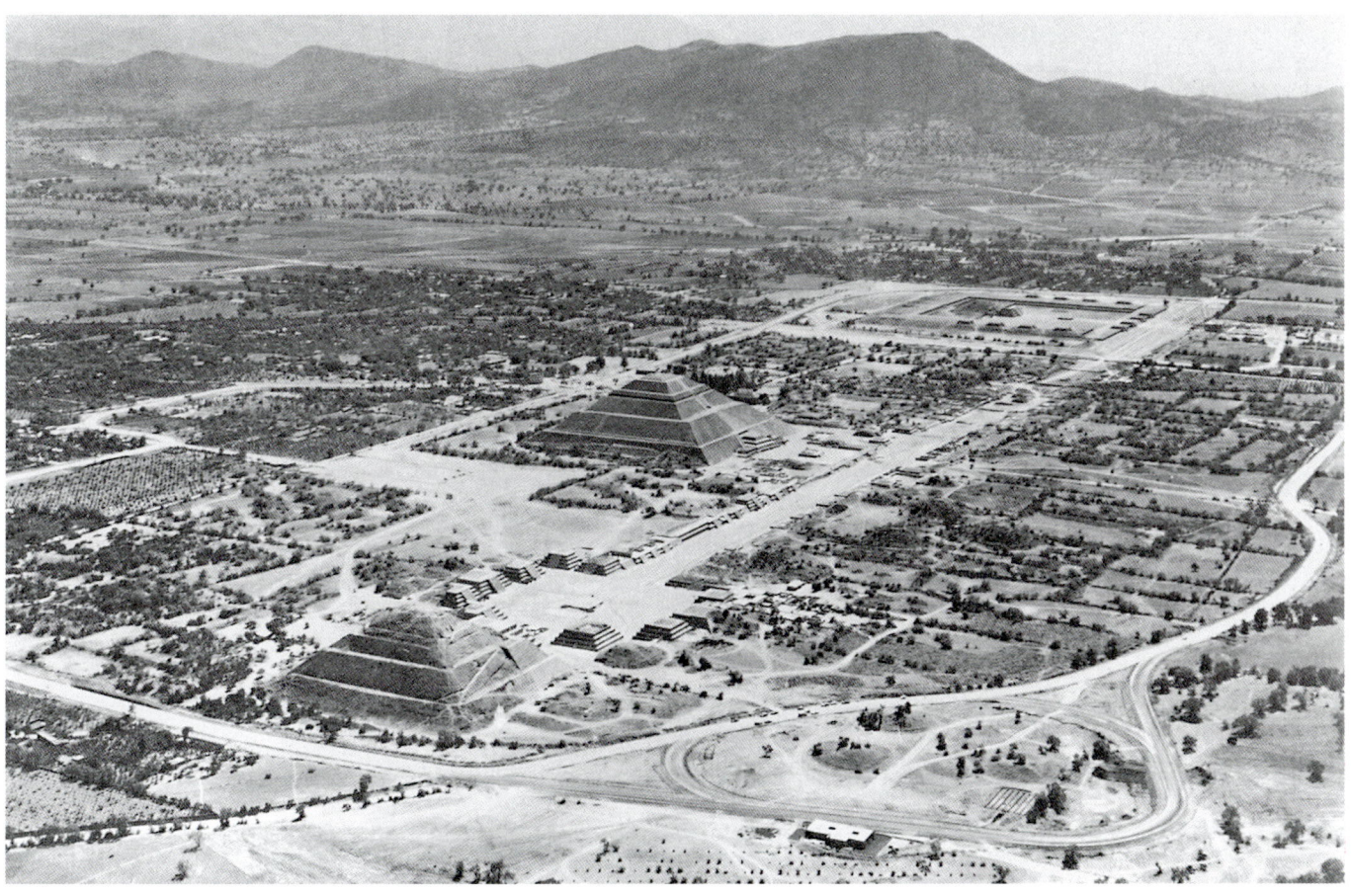

14-4 Aerial view of Teotihuacán (from the northwest), Valley of Mexico, Mexico. Pyramid of the Moon *(foreground)*, Pyramid of the Sun *(center)*, and the Citadel *(center background)*, all connected by the Avenue of the Dead; main structures ca. A.D. 50–200; site ca. 100 B.C.–A.D. 750.

Veracruz living in the eastern wards, importing their own pottery and building their houses and tombs in the style of their homelands. The city's urbanization did nothing to detract from its sacred nature. In fact, it vastly augmented Teotihuacán's importance as a religious center. The Aztecs, who visited Teotihuacán regularly and reverently long after it had been abandoned, gave it its current name, which means "the place of the gods." Because the city's inhabitants left only a handful of undeciphered hieroglyphs and linguists do not yet even know what language they spoke, the names of many major features of the site are unknown. The Avenue of the Dead and the Pyramids of the Sun and Moon are later Aztec designations that do not necessarily relate to these entities' original names.

The grid plan is quartered by a north–south and an east–west axis, each four miles in length. The rational scheme recalls Hellenistic and Roman urban planning (compare FIGS. 5-75 and 10-40). The main north–south axis, the Avenue of the Dead (FIG. 14-4), is one hundred thirty feet wide and connects the Pyramid of the Moon complex with the Citadel, which houses the well-preserved Temple of Quetzalcóatl (discussed later). It is not a continuously flat street but is broken by sets of stairs along its length, giving pedestrians a constantly changing view of the surrounding buildings and landscape. The Pyramid of the Sun, facing west on the east side of the Avenue of the Dead, is the city's centerpiece and its largest structure, rising to a height of more than two hundred feet.

The shapes of the monumental structures at Teotihuacán echo the surrounding mountains. Their imposing mass and scale surpass those of all other Mesoamerican sites. Rubble filled and faced with the local volcanic stone, the pyramids consist of stacked squared platforms diminishing in perimeter from the base to the top, much like the Stepped Pyramid of Djoser in Egyptian Saqqara (see FIG. 3-4). Ramped stairways ascend to crowning temples made of perishable materials such as wood and thatch and therefore now missing at Teotihuacán.

The Teotihuacanos built the Pyramid of the Sun over a cave, which they reshaped and filled with ceramic offerings.

The pyramid may have been constructed to honor a sacred spring within the now-dry cave. Four children were found buried at the corners of the pyramid. The later Aztec sacrificed children to bring rainfall, and Teotihuacán art abounds with references to water, so they may have shared the Aztec preoccupation with rain and agricultural fertility. The city's inhabitants rebuilt the Pyramid of the Moon (currently being excavated) at least five times in Teotihuacán's early history. It may have been positioned to mimic the shape of the mountain behind it known as Cerro Gordo, undoubtedly an important source for life-sustaining streams.

THE TEMPLE OF THE FEATHERED SERPENT
At the south end of the Avenue of the Dead is the great quadrangle of the Citadel (FIG. 14-4). It encloses a smaller pyramidal shrine, the Temple of Quetzalcóatl, the "feathered serpent." Quetzalcóatl was a major god in the Mesoamerican pantheon at the time of the Spanish conquest, hundreds of years after the fall of Teotihuacán. The later Aztecs associated him with wind, rain-bringing clouds, and life. Beneath this structure archeologists recently found a tomb looted in antiquity, perhaps that of a Teotihuacán ruler. The discovery has led them to speculate that like their contemporaries, the Maya, the Teotihuacanos also buried their elite in or under pyramids. Surrounding the tomb both beneath and around the pyramid were the remains of at least a hundred sacrificial victims. Some were adorned with necklaces made of strings of human jaws, both real and sculpted from shell, a reminder that rulership during the Classic period was not necessarily benevolent. Like most other Mesoamerican groups, the Teotihuacanos apparently felt the need to invoke and appease their gods through human sacrifice. The presence of such a large number of victims also may reflect Teotihuacán's militaristic expansion—throughout Mesoamerica, the victors often sacrificed captured warriors.

The temple's sculptured panels (FIG. **14-5**), long protected by subsequent building, are well preserved on the west facade. Massive projecting stone heads of Quetzalcóatl, which alter-

14-5 Detail of Temple of Quetzalcóatl, the Citadel, Teotihuacán, Valley of Mexico, Mexico, third century.

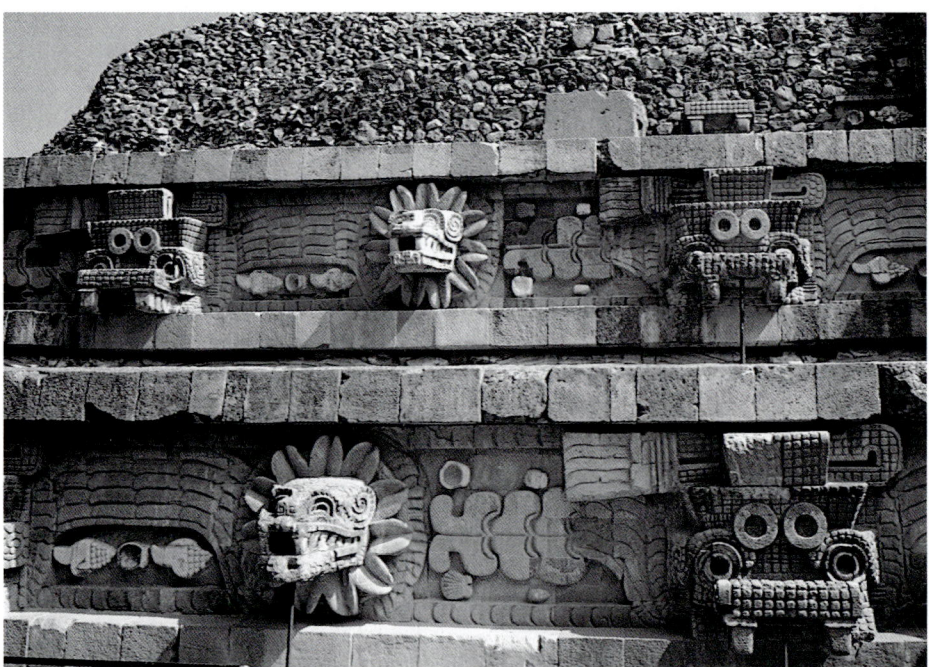

nate with heads of a long-snouted scaly creature with rings on its forehead, decorate each of the temple's six terraces. This remains the first unambiguous representation of the feathered serpent in Mesoamerica. The scaly creature's identity is unclear. Linking these alternating heads are low-relief carvings of feathered-serpent bodies and seashells. The latter reflect Teotihuacán contact with the peoples of the Mexican coasts and also symbolize water, an essential ingredient for the sustenance of an agricultural economy.

BRIGHT MURALS FOR A GREAT CITY Like those of most pre-Columbian Mesoamerican cities, Teotihucán's buildings and streets were once stuccoed over and brightly painted. In a treatment unique to Teotihuacán, however, elaborate murals covered the walls of the rooms of its elite residential compounds. These images reveal nothing about everyday life at Teotihuacán but consist largely of depictions of deities, ritual activities, and processions of priests, warriors, and even animals. Rendered as flat, repetitive motifs, the figures, although laden with elaborate costumes, are often devoid of individuality. The depiction of volume, spatial relations, or narrative interaction was not a priority.

Experimenting with a variety of surfaces, materials, and techniques over the centuries, Teotihuacán muralists finally settled on applying pigments to a smooth lime-plaster surface coated with clay. They then polished the surface to a high sheen. During one phase of Teotihuacán painting, artists limited themselves to a palette of varying tones of red (largely derived from the mineral hematite), creating subtle contrasts between figure and ground. But most Teotihuacán murals feature vivid hues arranged in flat, carefully outlined patterns.

TEOTIHUACÁN'S BOUNTY-GIVING GODDESS Once thought a man, the principal god of the city is now known to have been a woman, an earth or nature goddess, depicted here in a mural (FIG. **14-6**). Always shown frontally with her face covered by a jade mask, she is dwarfed by her large feathered headdress and reduced to a bust placed upon a stylized pyramid. She stretches her hands out to provide liquid streams filled with bounty (compare the Sumerian mural at Zimri-Lim's palace, FIG. 2-17), but the stylized human hearts that flank the frontal bird mask in her headdress reflect her dual nature. They remind viewers that the ancient Mesoamericans saw human sacrifice as essential to agricultural renewal.

The influence of Teotihuacán was all-pervasive in Mesoamerica. Colonies were established as far away as the southern borders of Maya civilization, in the highlands of Guatemala, some eight hundred miles from Teotihuacán. Political and economic interaction between Teotihuacán and the Maya in southern Mexico and Guatemala linked the two outstanding Early Classic cultures.

THE CLASSIC MAYA CITY-STATE Strong cultural influences stemming from the Olmec tradition and from Teotihuacán contributed to the development of Classic Maya culture. As with Teotihuacán, Maya civilization's foundations were laid in the Preclassic period, perhaps by 600 B.C. or even earlier. At that time, the Maya, who occupied the moist lowland areas of Belize, southern Mexico, Guatemala, and Honduras, seem to have abandoned their early somewhat egalitarian pattern of village life and adopted a hierarchical autocratic

society. This system evolved into the typical Maya city-state governed by hereditary rulers and ranked nobility. How and why this happened is still uncertain.

Stupendous building projects signaled the change. Vast complexes of terraced temple-pyramids, palaces, plazas, ballcourts, and residences of the governing elite dotted the Maya area. Unlike the Teotihuacán civilization, no one site ever achieved complete dominance as the single center of power. The new architecture, and the art embellishing it, advertised the power of the rulers, who appropriated cosmic symbolism and stressed their descent from gods to reinforce their claims to legitimate rulership. The unified institutions of religion and kingship were established so firmly, their hold on life and custom was so tenacious, and their meaning was so fixed in the symbolism and imagery of art that the rigidly conservative system of the Classic Maya lasted almost a thousand years. Maya civilization in the southern region collapsed around 900, vanishing more abruptly and unaccountably than it had appeared.

Although the causes of the beginning and end of Classic Maya civilization are obscure, researchers are gradually revealing its history, beliefs, ceremonies, conventions, and daily life patterns. Long romanticized, the Maya now enter the world history stage as believably as the peoples of other great civilizations. No longer viewed as a peaceful, benign society under theocratic rule, the Maya are now seen as flesh-and-blood peoples who glorified their rulers and oppressed the lower classes, who undertook (and broke) strategic political alliances, who waged war, and who practiced human sacrifice. This more accurate picture is the consequence of modern interdisciplinary

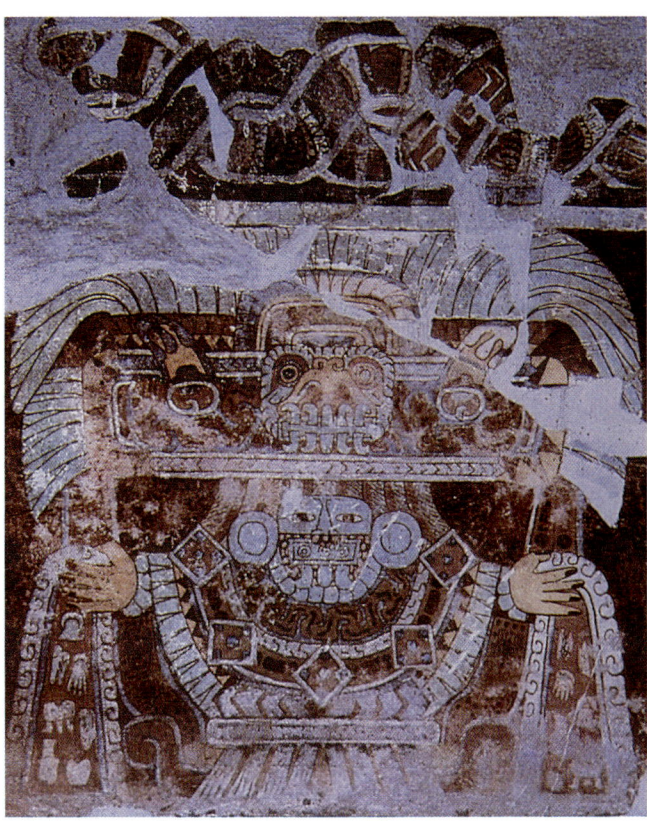

14-6 Goddess, mural painting from Tetitla apartment complex at Teotihuacán, Valley of Mexico, Mexico, 650–750. Pigments over clay and plaster.

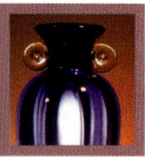

The Mesoamerican Ballgame

After witnessing the native ballgame of Mexico soon after their arrival in the sixteenth century, the Spanish conquerors took Aztec ballplayers back to Europe to demonstrate the novel sport. Their chronicles remark on the athletes' great skill, the heavy wagering that accompanied the competition, and the ball itself, made of rubber, a substance they had never seen before.

The game was played throughout Mesoamerica and into the southwestern United States, beginning at least thirty-four hundred years ago, the date of the earliest known ballcourt. The Olmec were apparently avid players. Their very name—a modern invention in the Aztec language—means "rubber people," after the latex-growing region they inhabited. Not only are ballplayers represented in Olmec art, but remnants of sunken earthen ballcourts and even rubber balls have been found at Olmec sites.

The Olmec earthen playing field evolved in other Mesoamerican cultures into a plastered masonry surface, I- or T-shaped in plan, flanked by two parallel sloping or straight walls. Sometimes the walls were wide enough to support small structures on top, as at Copán (FIG. 14-7), while at other sites temples stood at either end of the ballcourt. The largest ballcourt in Mesoamerica measures nearly five hundred feet long, while a site in rubber-rich Veracruz boasts seventeen ballcourts—at last count. Most ballcourts were adjacent to the important civic structures of Mesoamerican cities, such as palaces and temple-pyramids, as at Copán. Teotihuacán is an exception. Archeologists have not found a ballcourt there, but mural paintings at the site illustrate people playing the game with portable markers.

Researchers know surprisingly little about the rules of the ballgame itself—how many players were on the field, how goals were scored and tallied, and how competitions were arranged. Unlike a modern soccer field with its standard dimensions, Mesoamerican ballcourts vary widely in size. Some have stone rings, which a ball conceivably could have been tossed through, set high up on their walls at right angles to the ground, but many courts lack this feature. Alternatively, the ball may have been bounced against the walls and into the end zones. As in soccer, players could not touch the ball with their hands but used their heads, elbows, hips, and legs. They wore thick leather belts, and sometimes even helmets, and padded their knees and arms against the blows of the fast-moving solid rubber ball. Typically, the Maya portrayed ballplayers wearing heavy protective clothing, kneeling, and poised to deflect the ball (FIG. 14-10).

Although widely enjoyed as a competitive spectator sport, the ballgame did not serve solely for entertainment. The ball, for example, may have represented a celestial body such as the sun, its movements over the court imitating the sun's daily passage through the sky. Reliefs on the walls of ballcourts at certain sites make clear that the game sometimes culminated in human sacrifice, probably of captives taken in battle and then forced to participate in a game they were predestined to lose.

Ballplaying also had a role in Mesoamerican mythology. In the ancient Maya epic known as the *Popol Vuh (Council Book)*, first written down in Spanish in the colonial period, a legendary pair of twins is forced to play ball with the evil lords of the Underworld. The brothers lose and are sacrificed. The sons of one twin eventually travel to the Underworld, and, after a series of trials including a ballgame, outwit the lords and kill them. They revive their father, buried in the ballcourt after his earlier defeat at the hands of the Underworld gods. While the younger twins rise to the heavens to become the sun and the moon, the father becomes the god of maize, principal sustenance of all Mesoamerican peoples. The ballgame and its aftermath, then, were a metaphor for the cycle of life, death, and regeneration that permeated Mesoamerican religion.

---

scholarship. Archeologists, epigraphers (scholars who decipher writing systems), art historians, and ethnographers (those who study contemporary societies) all have contributed to a clearer understanding of ancient Maya culture.

DECODING THE MAYAN SCRIPT   Like the decipherment of Egyptian writing early in the nineteenth century, the decoding of the Mayan script has been an exciting intellectual adventure. By the end of the nineteenth century, numbers, dates, and some astronomical information could be read, but little else, leading scholars to conclude the Maya were obsessed with time and religion and uninterested in recording the mundane events of human lives. Two important breakthroughs beginning in the 1950s radically altered the understanding of both Mayan writing and the Maya worldview.

The first was the realization the Maya depicted their rulers (rather than gods or anonymous priests) in their art and noted their rulers' achievements in their texts. The second was that Mayan writing is largely phonetic; that is, the hieroglyphs are made up of signs representing sounds in the Mayan language. Fortunately, the various Mayan languages were recorded in colonial texts and dictionaries and most are still spoken today. Although perhaps only half of the ancient Mayan script can be translated accurately into spoken Mayan, today scholars can at least grasp the general meaning of many more hieroglyphs.

MAYA ASTRONOMY AND CALENDARS   The Maya possessed a highly developed knowledge of arithmetic calculation and the ability to observe and record the movements of not only the sun and moon but also numerous planets. They contrived an intricate but astonishingly accurate calendar, and although their calendric structuring of time was radically different in form from the Western calendar used today, it was just as precise and efficient. With their calendar, the Maya established the all-important genealogical lines of their rulers, which certified their claim to rule, and created the only true written history in ancient America. Although other pre-Columbian Mesoamerican societies also possessed calendars, only the Maya calendar can be translated directly into today's calendrical system.

THE CITY CENTER AS THEATRICAL STAGE

The most sacred and majestic buildings of Maya cities were raised in enclosed, centrally located precincts. The religious-civic transactions that guaranteed the order of the state and the cosmos occurred in these settings. The Maya held dramatic rituals within a sculptured and painted environment, where huge symbols and images proclaimed the nature and necessity of that order. Maya builders designed spacious plazas for vast audiences who were exposed to overwhelming propaganda. The programmers of that propaganda, the ruling families and troops of priests, nobles, and retainers, wore its symbolism in their costumes. In Maya paintings and sculptures, the Maya elite wear extravagant profusions of vividly colorful cotton tex-

tiles, feathers, jaguar skins, and jade, all emblematic of their rank and wealth. On the different levels of the painted and polished temple platforms, the ruling classes performed the offices of their rites in clouds of incense to the music of maracas, flutes, and drums. The Maya transformed the architectural complex at each city's center into a theater of religion and statecraft. In the stagelike layout of a characteristic Maya city center, its principal group, or "site core," was the religious and administrative nucleus for a population of dispersed farmers settled throughout a suburban area of many square miles.

COPÁN'S PLAZAS AND PYRAMIDS   Because Copán, on the western border of Honduras, has more hieroglyphic inscriptions and well-preserved carved monuments than any other site in the Americas, it was one of the first Maya sites excavated. It also has proved one of the richest in the trove of architectural, sculptural, and artifactual remains recovered. Archeologists are still exploring the site. Copán's heart is dominated by conspicuous plazas. In our restored view of the city center (FIG. 14-7), the Great Plaza is to the left and the smaller Middle Plaza is at the center. The latter is enclosed on three sides by the ballcourt (left side of plaza; see "The Mesoamerican Ballgame," page 392), by the towering tiered pyramid (Structure 10L-26) with its steep "Hieroglyphic Stairway," and by the so-called Acropolis, with its

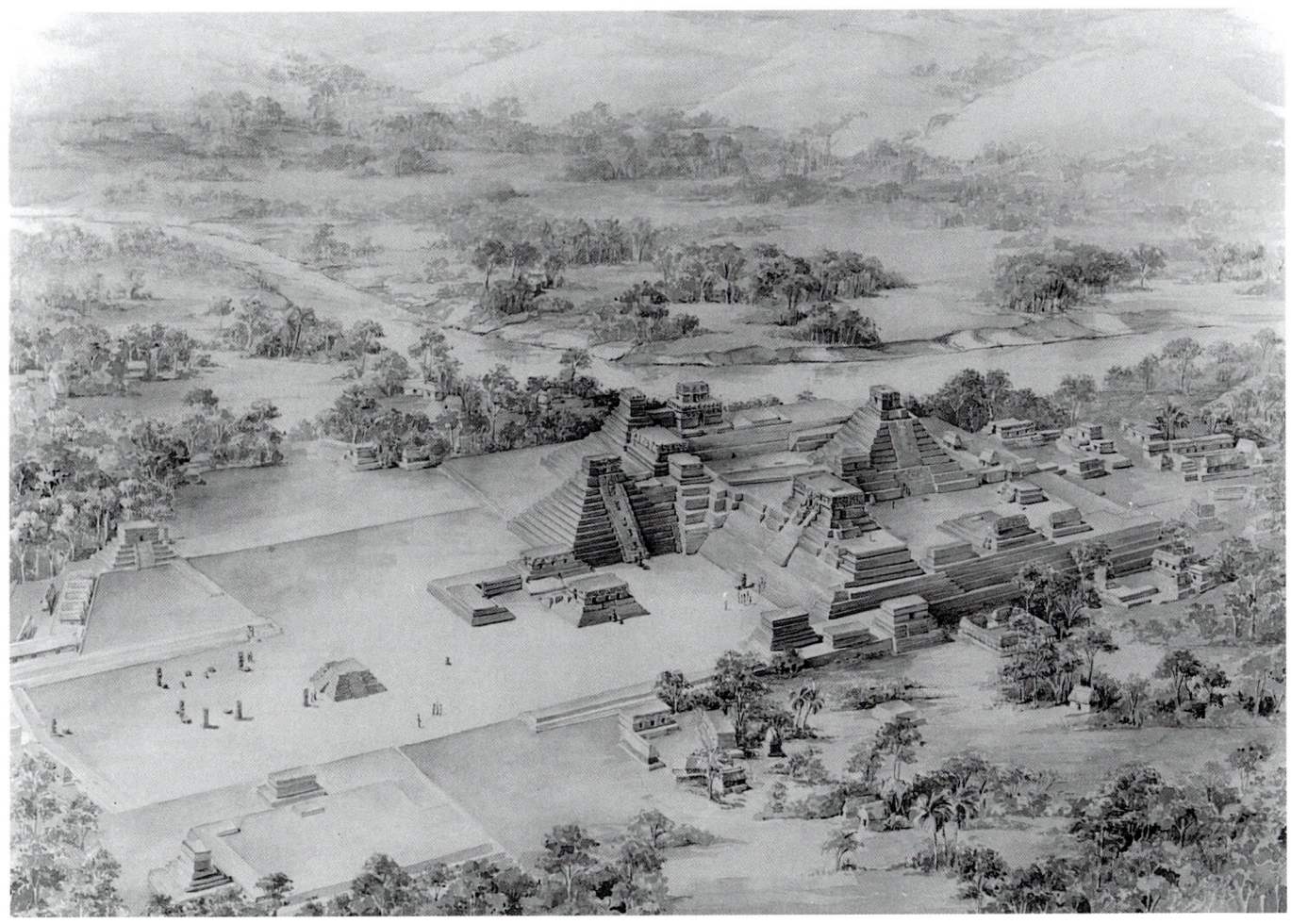

14-7   Reconstruction drawing by Tatiana Proskouriakoff of principal group of ruins at Copán, Maya, Copán Valley, Honduras. Great plaza *(left)*, Middle Plaza with Ballcourt *(two small structures at center)* and Temple of the Hieroglyphic Stairway *(center, slightly above and to right of Ballcourt)*, Acropolis *(right)*, and elite residences *(far right)*; eighth century. Peabody Museum, Harvard University.

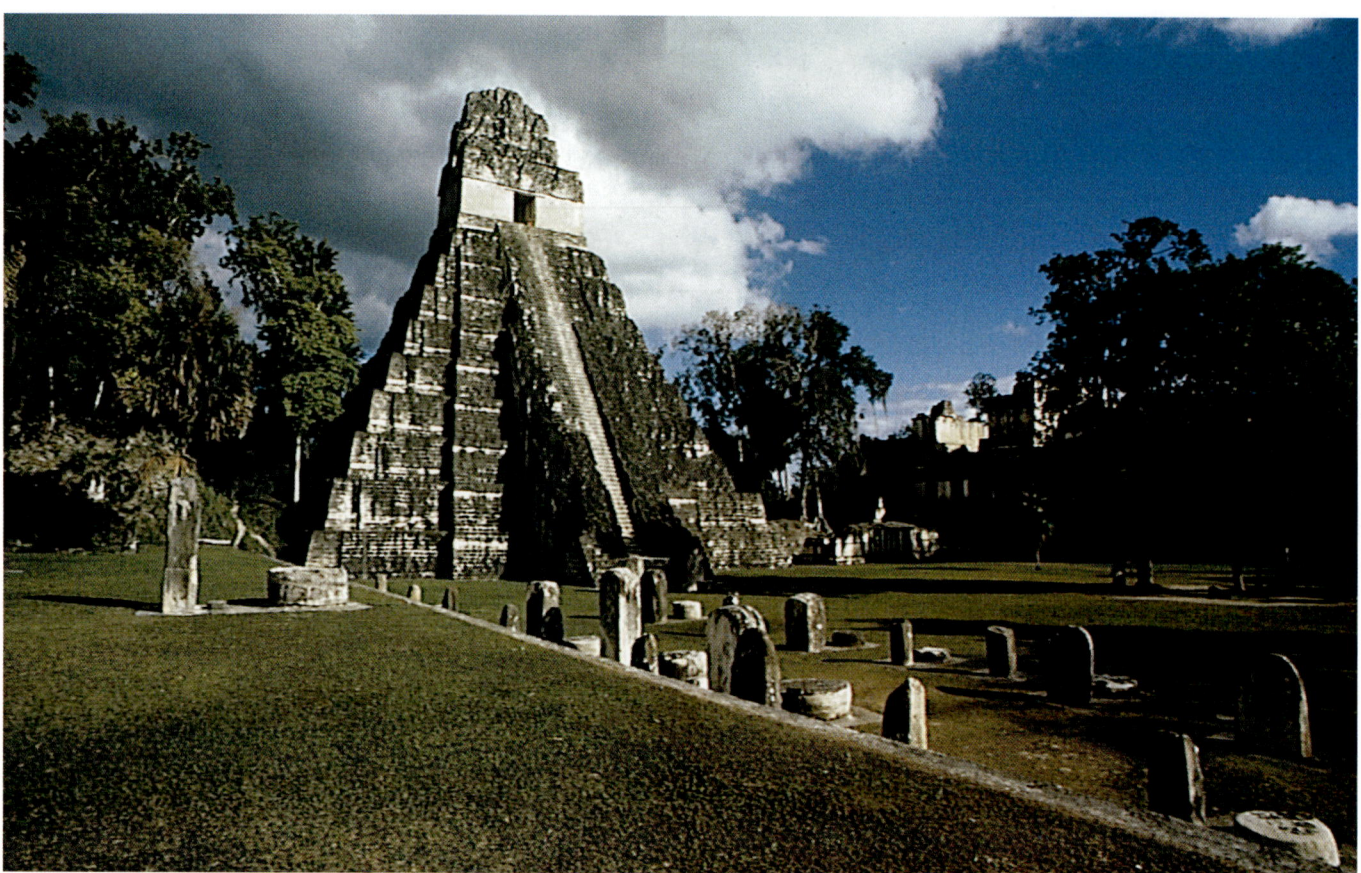

14-8   Temple I (Temple of the Giant Jaguar), Maya, Tikal, Petén, Guatemala, ca. 700.

cluster of pyramids and courtyards on a higher platform to the right of the Hieroglyphic Stairway. Beyond and below the Acropolis to the far right are elite residential buildings. In the Great Plaza the Maya set up tall, sculptured stone stelae (to the left in FIG. 14-7). Carved with the portraits of the rulers who erected them, these stelae also record their names, dates of reign, and notable achievements in glyphs on the front, sides, or back (FIG. 14-9).

A TIKAL RULER'S TEMPLE-PYRAMID TOMB
Another great Maya site of the Classic period is Tikal in Guatemala, some one hundred fifty miles north of Copán. Tikal, one of the oldest and largest of the Maya cities, rises above the thick tropical forest. The city and its suburbs originally covered some seventy-five square miles and served as the ceremonial center of a population of perhaps seventy-five thousand. The Maya did not lay out central Tikal on a grid plan like its contemporary, Teotihuacán. Instead, causeways connected irregular groupings. Modern surveys have uncovered the remains of as many as three thousand separate structures in an area of about six square miles. The site's nucleus, the Great Plaza, is studded with stelae and defined by numerous architectural complexes. The most prominent monuments are the two soaring pyramids that face each other across an open square. The taller pyramid (FIG. **14-8**), Temple I (also called the Temple of the Giant Jaguar after a motif on one of its carved wooden lintels), reaches a height of one hundred forty-four feet. It is the temple-mausoleum of a Tikal ruler, whose body was placed in a vaulted chamber under the pyramid's base. The towering structure, made up of nine sharply

inclining platforms and a narrow stairway, culminates at the summit in a three-chambered temple. The temple is surmounted by an elaborately sculpted *roof comb,* a vertical architectural projection that once bore the ruler's giant portrait modeled in stucco. This structure exhibits most concisely the pre-Columbian Mesoamerican formula for the stepped temple-pyramid and the compelling aesthetic and psychological power of Maya architecture.

MAYA PORTRAITURE The grand pyramids of Copán and Tikal are among the most imposing buildings the Maya erected. But they are only the most eye-catching monuments in cities filled with sculptures and paintings that also played a significant role in glorifying their powerful rulers. Stele D (FIG. **14-9**) in the Great Plaza at Copán (FIG. 14-7, left) represents one of the foremost of the city's rulers, 18-Rabbit (r. 695–738). In a dynastic succession of sixteen rulers, 18-Rabbit was the thirteenth. During his long reign, the city may have reached its greatest physical extent and range of political influence. On Stele D 18-Rabbit wears an elaborate headdress and ornamented kilt and sandals. He holds across his chest a double-headed serpent bar, symbol of the sky and of his absolute power. His features have the quality of a portrait likeness, although highly idealized. The Maya elite, like the Egyptian pharaohs and the rulers of some other ancient societies, tended to have themselves portrayed in a conventionalized manner and as eternally youthful. The dense, deeply carved ornamental details that frame the face and figure in florid profusion stand almost clear of the block and wrap around the sides of the stele. The high relief gives the impres-

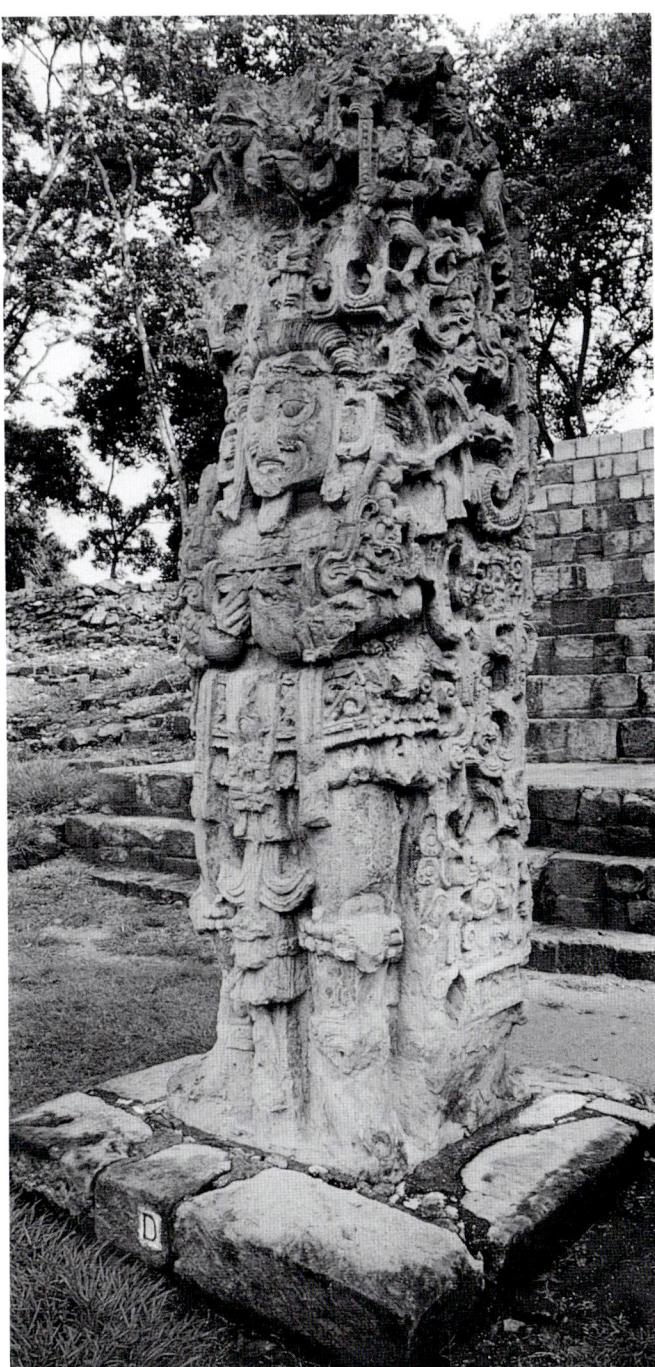

14-9 Stele D portraying the ruler 18-Rabbit, Maya, Great Plaza at Copán, Honduras, 736. Stone, 11′ 9″ high.

carefully descriptive, and even comic at times. They represent a wider range of human types and activities than is commonly depicted on Maya stelae. Ballplayers (FIG. **14-10**), women weaving, older men, dwarves, supernatural beings, and amorous couples, as well as elaborately attired rulers and warriors, comprise the figurine repertory. Many of the hollow figurines are also whistles. They were made in ceramic workshops on the mainland, often with molds, but burials on the island cemetery of Jaina, off the western coast of Yucatán, yielded hundreds of such figures, including the ballplayer we illustrate. Traces of blue remain on the figure's belt, remnants of the vivid pigments that once covered many of these figurines. The Maya used "Maya blue," a combination of a particular kind of clay and indigo, a vegetable dye, to paint both ceramics and murals. This pigment has proven virtually indestructible, unlike the other colors that largely have disappeared over time. Like the larger terracotta figures of West Mexico, these figurines were made to accompany the dead on their inevitable voyage to the Underworld. The excavations at Jaina, however, have revealed nothing more that might clarify the meaning and function of the figures. Male figurines were not found exclusively in the burials of male individuals, for example.

ROYAL RITUALS PORTRAYED ON WALLS The vivacity of the Jaina figurines and their variety of pose, costume, and occupation were reinterpreted in two dimensions at Bonampak (Mayan for "painted walls") in southeastern Mexico. Three chambers in one Bonampak structure contain mural paintings that are vivid vignettes of Maya court life.

sion of a statue in the full round, although a hieroglyphic text is carved on the flat back side of the stele. The stele was originally painted—remnants of red paint are visible on many of the other stelae at Copán. Although a powerful ruler who erected many stelae and buildings at Copán, 18-Rabbit eventually was captured and beheaded by a rival king.

EVERYDAY LIFE IN CLAY SCULPTURE The almost unlimited variety of figural attitude and gesture permitted in the modeling of clay explains the profusion of informal ceramic figurines that, like West Mexican pottery (FIG. 14-3), may illustrate aspects of everyday Maya life. Small-scale free-standing figures in the round, they are remarkably lifelike,

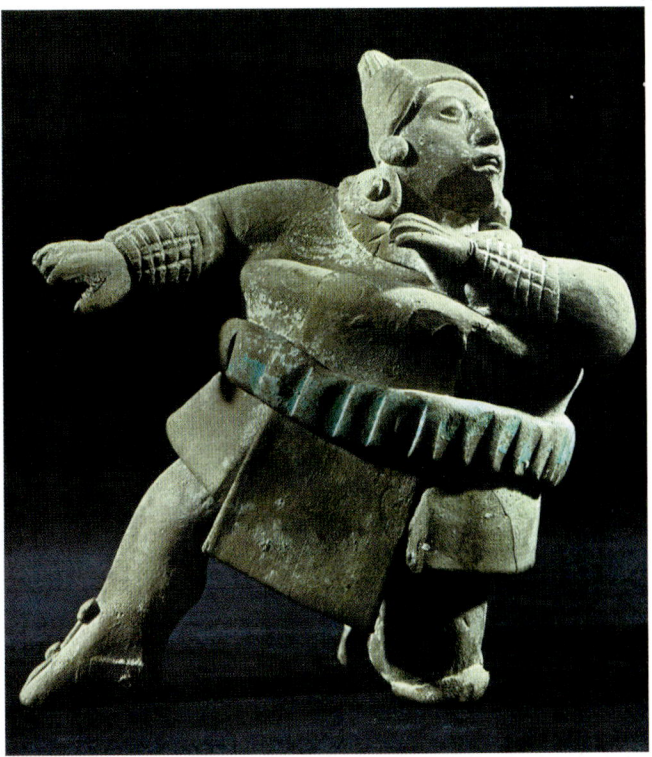

14-10 Ballplayer, Maya, from Jaina Island, Mexico, 700–900. Painted clay, $6\frac{1}{4}$″ high. National Museum of Anthropology, Mexico City.

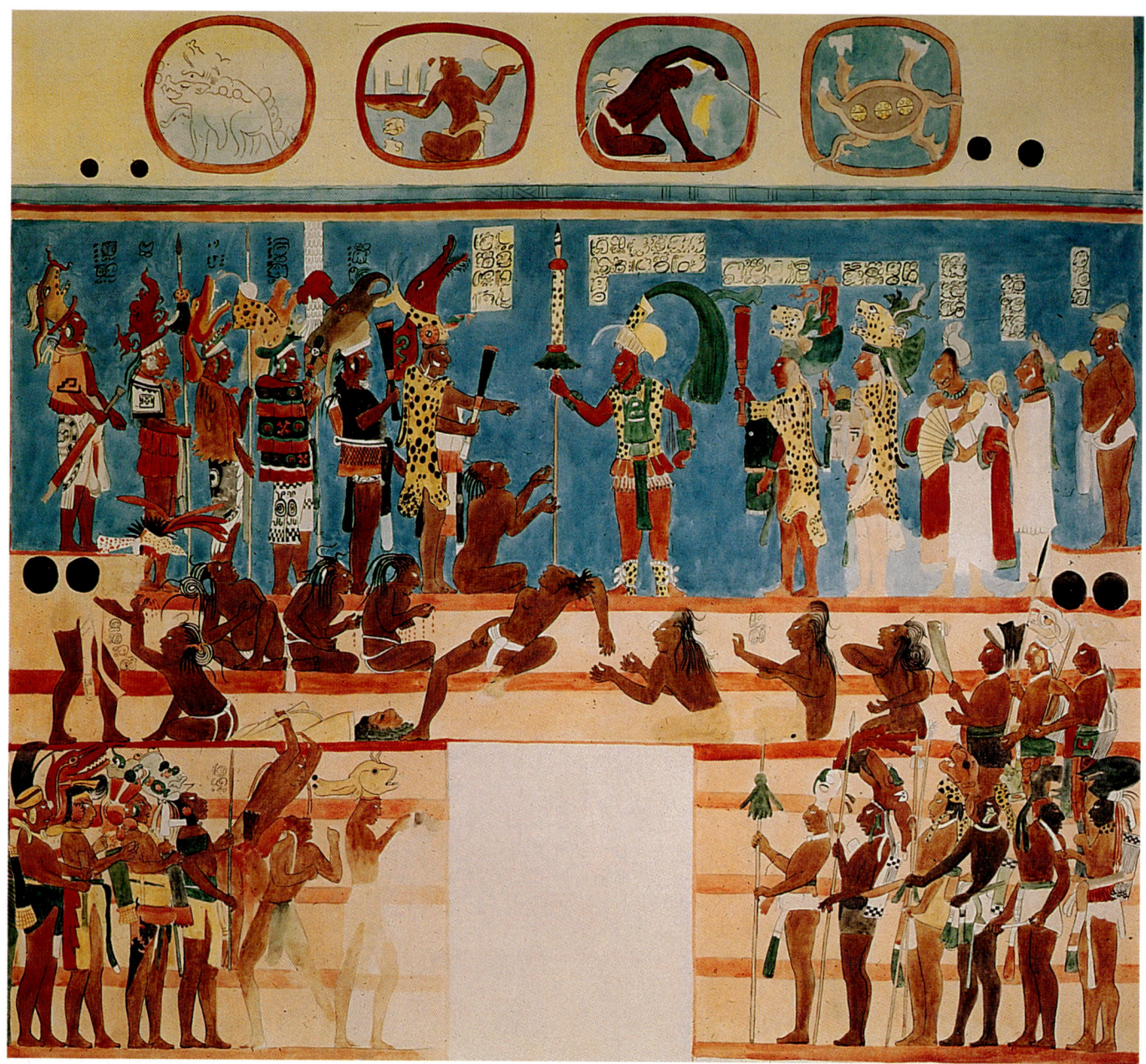

14-11   Presentation of captives to a Maya ruler, Maya, from Structure 1 at Bonampak, Mexico, late eighth century. Watercolor copy by Antonio Tejeda, housed at Peabody Museum, Harvard University, Cambridge.

The example we illustrate (FIG. **14-11**) shows warriors surrounding captives on a terraced platform. In contrast to Teotihuacán, the figures represented have naturalistic proportions and overlap, twist, turn, and gesture. The artists used fluid and calligraphic line to outline the figures, working with color to indicate both textures and volume. The Bonampak painters combined their pigments—both mineral and organic—with a mixture of water, crushed limestone, and vegetable gums and applied them to their stucco walls in a technique best described as a cross between fresco and tempera.

The Bonampak murals are filled with circumstantial detail. The information given is comprehensive, explicit, and presented with the fidelity of an eyewitness report. The royal personages are identifiable by both their physical features and their costumes, while accompanying inscriptions provide the precise day, month, and year for the events recorded. All the scenes at Bonampak relate the events and ceremonies that welcome a new royal heir (shown as a toddler in some scenes).

They include presentations, preparations for a royal fete, dancing, battle, and the taking and sacrificing of prisoners. On all occasions of state, public bloodletting was an integral part of Maya ritual. The ruler, his consort, and certain members of the nobility drew blood from their own bodies and sought union with the supernatural world. The slaughter of captives taken in war regularly accompanied this ceremony. Indeed, Mesoamerican cultures undertook warfare largely to provide victims for sacrifice. The victors forced many captives to play a fixed and fatal ballgame in courts laid out adjacent to the temples (see "The Mesoamerican Ballgame," page 392). The torture and eventual execution of prisoners served both to nourish the gods and to strike fear into enemies and the general populace.

In the scene we illustrate, depicting the presentation of prisoners to the ruler (FIG. 14-11), the painter arranged the figures in registers that may represent a pyramid's steps. On the uppermost step, against a blue background, is a file of gorgeously appareled nobles wearing animal headgear. Conspicuous among them on the right are retainers clad in jaguar pelts and jaguar headdresses. The Bonampak ruler himself, in jaguar jerkin and high-backed sandals, stands at the center, facing a crouching victim who appears to beg for mercy. Naked captives, anticipating death, crowd the middle level. One of them, already dead, sprawls at the ruler's feet. Others dumbly contemplate the blood dripping from their mutilated hands. The lower zone, cut through by a doorway into the structure housing the murals, shows clusters of attendants who are doubtless of inferior rank to the lords of the upper zone. The stiff formality of the grandees and the attendants contrasts graphically with the supple imploring attitudes and gestures of the hapless victims. The Bonampak victory was short lived. The murals were never finished, and shortly after the dates written on the walls the site seems to have been abandoned.

PAINTED VASES FOR PALACES AND TOMBS

Vivid narratives also appear on the much smaller surfaces of painted cylinder vases. A rollout view of a typical vase design (FIG. 14-12) shows a palace scene where an enthroned lord sits surrounded by courtiers and attendants. In this scene, at once regal and intimate, the participants gesture and talk. The elaborate costumes of the Copán stele and the Bonampak paintings are absent. Instead, the figures wear simple loincloths, turbans of wrapped cloth and feathers, and black body paint. The red frame that surrounds the scene suggests an architectural setting. The painter provided a glimpse of the event through the open doorways of a palace.

The horizontal band of hieroglyphs at the top describes the vessel and names the artist. Although this particular name has not been completely deciphered, the names of a handful of Maya vase painters, all male, are now known. (In pre-Columbian art, artists' signatures are almost nonexistent and even on Maya pots are very rare.) Some texts even list the vessel's contents. One pot marked with the glyph for cacao, or chocolate, still contained remnants of the prestigious drink when it was discovered. In our example, the artist may have portrayed himself among the participants. He repeats his name in one of the vertical texts, which refer to both the figures and ritual events. Some artists even recorded their parentage, clearly stating they were of noble birth and high status. Vases such as this one may have been used as drinking and food vessels for noble Maya, but their final destination was the tomb,

where they accompanied the deceased to the Underworld. They likely were commissioned by the deceased before his death or by his survivors and occasionally were sent from distant sites as funerary offerings. (The Maya intermarried with other powerful families to consolidate power between important cities, and both trade and gift exchanges were common.)

Terminal Classic and Early Postclassic (800–1250)

Throughout Mesoamerica, the Classic period ended at different times with the disintegration of the great civilizations. Teotihuacán's political and cultural empire, for example, was disrupted around 600, and its influence waned. In 700 the great city's center was destroyed by fire, possibly at the hands of invaders from the north known as the Toltecs, and within fifty years Teotihuacán was deserted. Around 900, many of the great Maya sites were abandoned to the jungle, leaving a few northern Maya cities to flourish for another century or two before they, too, became depopulated. The Classic culture of the Zapotecs, centered at Monte Albán in the state of Oaxaca, came to an end around 700, and the neighboring Mixtec peoples assumed supremacy in this area during the Postclassic period. Classic El Tajín, later heir to the Olmec in the Veracruz plain, survived the general crisis that afflicted the others but was burned sometime in the twelfth century, again by northern invaders. The war and confusion that followed the collapse of the Classic civilizations broke the great states up into small, local political entities isolated in fortified sites. The collapse encouraged even more warlike regimes and chronic aggression. The militant city-state of Chichén Itzá dominated Yucatán, while in central Mexico the Toltec and the later Aztec peoples, both ambitious migrants from the north, forged empires by force of arms.

THE ASCENDANCY OF CHICHÉN ITZÁ Yucatán, a flat, low limestone peninsula covered with scrub vegetation, lies north of the rolling and densely forested region of the Guatemalan Petén. During the Classic period, Mayan-speaking peoples sparsely inhabited this northern region. For still-debated reasons, when the southern Classic Maya sites were abandoned after 900, the northern Maya continued to build many new temples in this area. A new art style, which can be

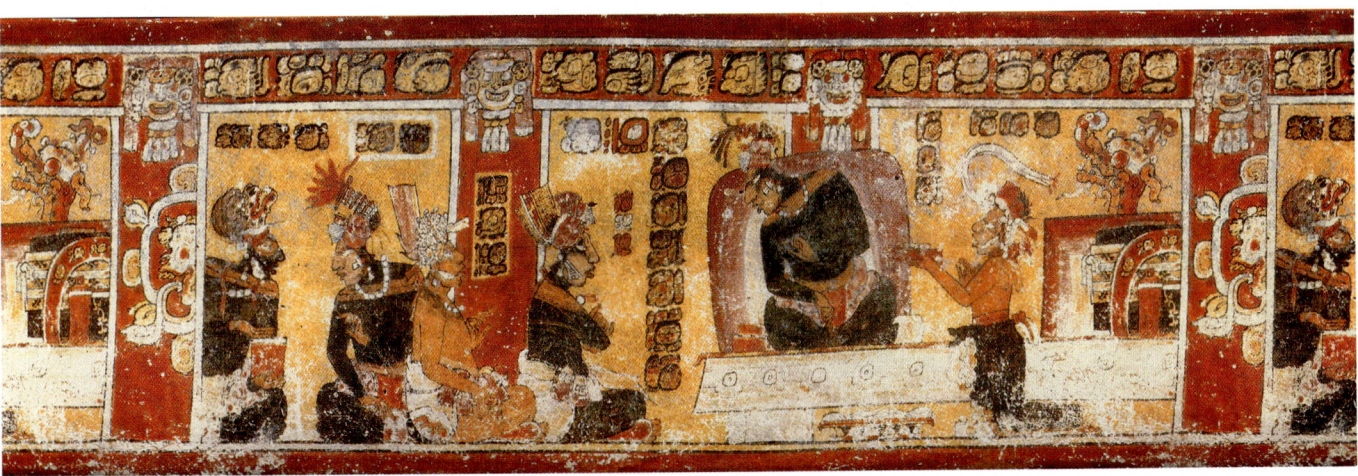

14-12 Enthroned Maya lord and courtiers, cylinder vase (rollout view), Maya, from Motul de San José region, Guatemala, 672–830. Ceramic with red, rose, orange, white, and black on cream slip, approx. 8″ high. Dumbarton Oaks Research Library and Collections, Washington.

seen in the buildings at Chichén Itzá, was contemporaneous with the political ascendancy of the Toltec at Tula, a site northwest of Mexico City. Although the two cities share striking similarities in their art and architecture—such as colonnaded structures and an emphasis on sacrificial and militaristic imagery—the nature of their relationship is still poorly understood. But the long-held notion that warriors from Tula actually invaded the Maya site has gradually been abandoned.

The Maya of Chichén Itzá left fewer written records than their cousins to the south, and the surviving texts are brief, limited to the ninth century, and written in a different style from those of Classic sites such as Tikal and Copán. Furthermore, recent hieroglyphic decipherments, as well as the site's art style, which does not focus on single figures but on groups and processions, suggest that rulership at Chichén Itzá may have been shared among nobles rather than passed from father to son.

EXPERIMENTATION IN THE NORTH The northern Maya experimented with building construction and materials to a much greater extent than the Maya farther south. Piers and columns appeared in doorways, and stone mosaics enlivened outer facades. The northern groups also invented a new type of construction, a solid core of coarse rubble faced inside and out with a veneer of square limestone plates.

The design of the structure known as the Caracol ("snail" in Spanish) at Chichén Itzá (FIG. **14-13**, foreground) suggests that the northern Maya were as inventive of architectural form as they were experimental with construction and materials. A cylindrical tower rests on a broad terrace supported, in turn, by a larger rectangular platform measuring one hundred sixty-nine feet by two hundred thirty-two feet. The tower, composed of two concentric walls, encloses a circular staircase that leads to a small chamber near the top of the structure. In plan, the building recalls the cross-section of a conch shell. Because

the conch shell was an attribute of the feathered serpent, and round temples were dedicated to him in central Mexico, this building may have been a temple to Kukulcan, the Maya name for Quetzalcóatl. Windows along the Caracol's staircase and an opening at the summit probably were used for astronomical observation, which has given the building another nickname—the Observatory. Noted astronomers, the Maya tracked celestial events closely, both for practical reasons, such as determining when to plant and the date of the next eclipse, and to foretell and attempt to manipulate the future.

THE SACRED MOUNTAIN RE-CREATED Conspicuous among the other notable structures at Chichén Itzá is the Temple of Kukulkan, which sits upon the summit platform of a great pyramid (FIG. 14-13, background). The Castillo, or "castle," as the entire monument has been long named, is of imposing size—ninety-eight feet high and one hundred eighty-two feet wide at the base—a majestic symbol of a mountain, revered as sacred throughout Mesoamerica and re-created countless times in stone. Steps on four sides of the nine-tiered pyramid converge on the temple level. Painted reliefs throughout the structure relating to the cult of Quetzalcóatl are signatures of central Mexican influence on the northern Maya of Yucatán. The Castillo is a kind of paradigm of Mesoamerican architectural form. Towering above the city's central plaza, the great stepped pyramid's quadripartite (four-part) plan echoes the four sacred directions.

TOLTEC GUARDIANS OF QUETZALCÓATL The name *Toltec*, which signifies "makers of things," generally refers to a powerful tribe of invaders from the north, whose arrival in central Mexico coincided with the great disturbances that must have contributed to the fall of the Classic civilizations. The Toltec capital at Tula flourished from about 900 to 1200. The Toltecs were great political organizers and

14-13 The Caracol *(foreground)* and the Castillo *(background)*, Chichén Itzá, Maya, Yucatán, Mexico, ca. 800–900.

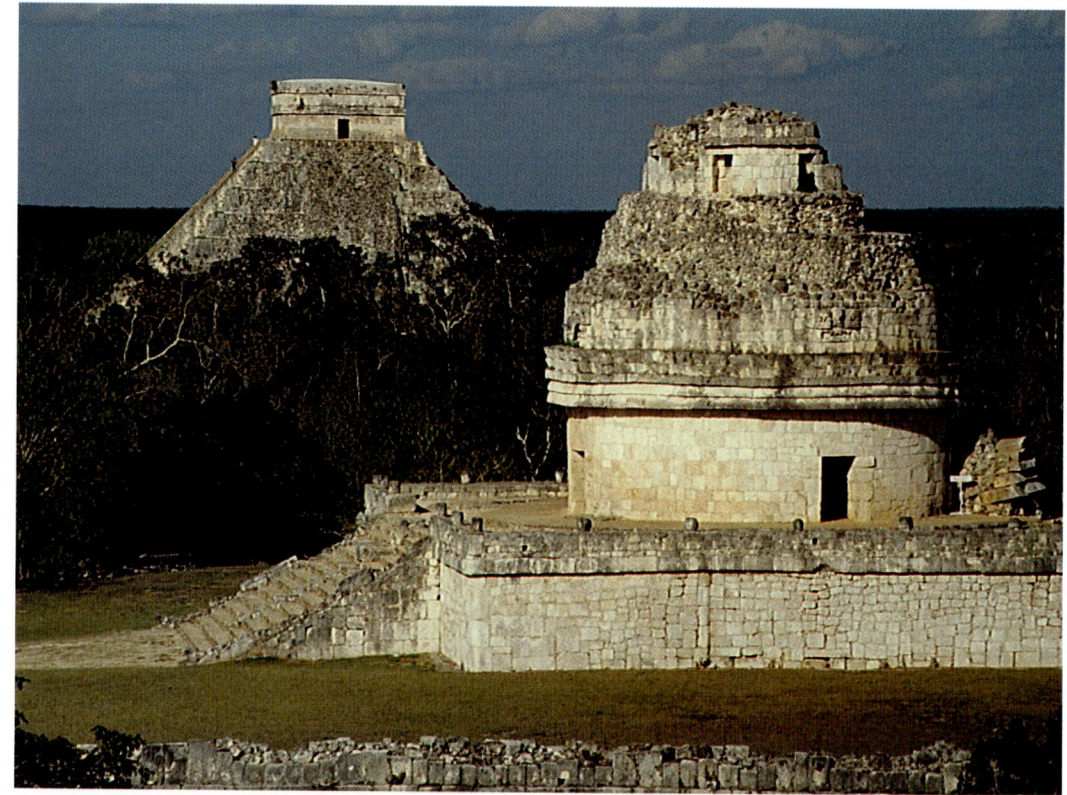

military strategists, dominating large parts of north and central Mexico. They also were respected both as master artisans and farmers, and later peoples such as the Aztec looked back on them admiringly, proud to claim descent from them.

At Tula, four colossal atlantids (male statue-columns) portraying armed warriors (FIG. **14-14**) reflect the grim, warlike regime of the Toltecs. These images of brutal authority stand eternally at attention, warding off all hostile threats. Built up of four stone drums each, the sculptures stand atop of Pyramid B, dedicated to Quetzalcóatl. They wear feathered headdresses and, as breastplates, stylized butterflies, heraldic symbols of the Toltec. In one hand they clutch a bundle of darts and in the other an *atlatl* (spear-thrower), typical weapons of highland Mexico. The figures originally supported a now-missing temple roof. Such an architectural function requires rigidity of pose, compactness, and strict simplicity of contour. The unity and regularity of architectural mass and silhouette here combine perfectly with abstraction of form.

By 1180, the last Toltec ruler abandoned Tula, followed by most of his people. Some years later, the city was catastrophically destroyed, its ceremonial buildings burned to their foundations, its walls thrown down, and the straggling remainder of its population scattered. As with the fate of the other pre-Columbian Mesoamerican civilizations, the exact reasons for the Toltecs' departure and for their city's destruction are unknown. Although the stage was set for the rise of the last great civilization of Mesoamerica, the Aztecs (see Chapter 30), they did not reach the height of their power for another three hundred years.

SOUTH AMERICA

The story of the great cultures of Andean South America is much the same as that of the pre-Columbian peoples of Mesoamerica. Native civilizations jarred against and stimulated one another, produced distinctive architecture and art, and were exterminated in violent confrontations with the Spanish conquistadors. Although long overshadowed by the better-known cultures of Mexico and Central America, those of South America are actually more ancient and in some ways surpass the accomplishments of their northern contemporaries. Andean peoples, for example, mastered metalworking much earlier, and their monumental architecture predates that of the earliest Mesoamerican culture, the Olmec, by more than a millennium.

GEOGRAPHY AND CHRONOLOGY The Central Andean region of South America lies between Ecuador and northern Chile, its western border the Pacific Ocean. It consists of three well-defined geographic zones, running north and south and roughly parallel to one another. The narrow western coastal plain is a hot desert crossed by rivers, creating habitable fertile valleys. Next, the high peaks of the great Cordillera of the Andes hem in plateaus of a temperate climate. The region's inland border, the eastern slopes of the Andes, is a hot and humid jungle.

Highly developed civilizations flourished both on the coast and in the highlands, but their origins are still obscure. As in Mesoamerica, art-producing cultures succeeded one another at irregular intervals but began at least one thousand years earlier. Andean chronology shifts between periods of independent regional development and periods known as "horizons," when a single culture appears to have dominated a broad geographic area for a relatively long period. The peoples of the earliest cultures, unidentified, lived from about 3000 B.C. to 800 B.C. The horizon art and architectural styles are represented by the cultures of Chavín (ca. 800–200 B.C.), Tiwanaku and Wari (ca. A.D. 600–1000), and, finally, the Inca (see Chapter 30), whose dominance of the Andean area was complete but brief, lasting only for the century preceding the Spanish conquest in 1532. Between the horizon periods cultural development did not lag, but it took different forms in widely separated areas. Among the many regional cultures that flourished before the Europeans arrived, the most important are those of the so-called Early Intermediate period (ca. 200 B.C.–A.D. 700), especially the Paracas and Nasca cultures of the south coast of Peru and the Moche in the north.

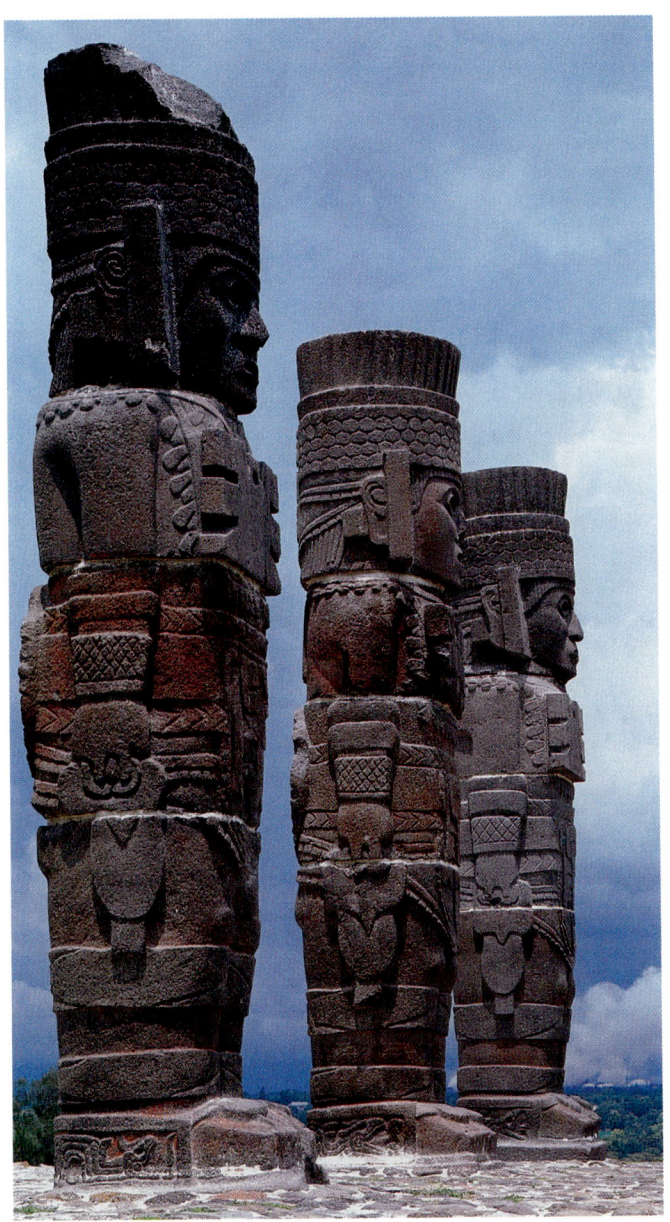

14-14 Colossal atlantids, Pyramid B, Toltec, Tula, Hidalgo, Mexico, ca. 900–1180. Stone, 16′ high.

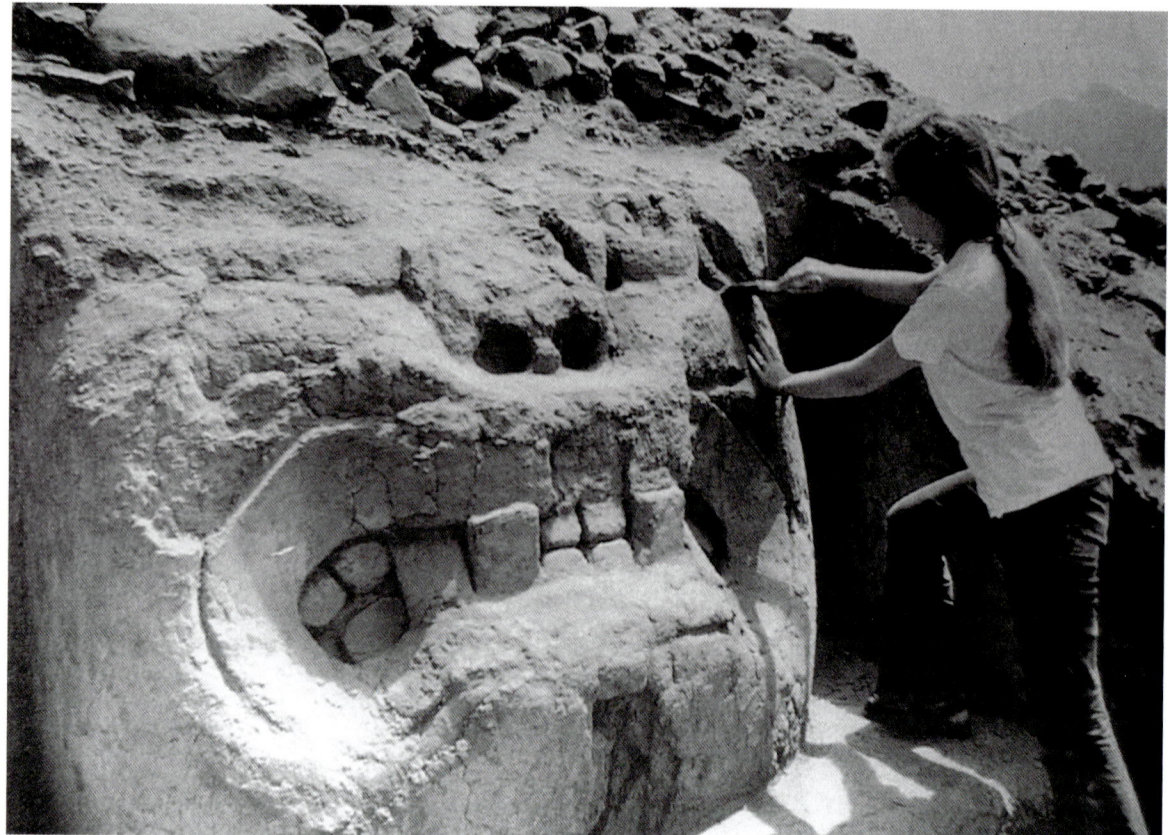

14-15   Feline head, Huaca de los Reyes mound, Caballo Muerto, Moche Valley, Peru, ca. 1300 B.C. Adobe over cobble core, probably once painted, 5′ 7″ high, 4′ 3″ wide, 2′ deep.

Early Cultures (ca. 3000–800 B.C.)

The discovery of complex ancient communities documented by radiocarbon dating is changing researchers' assessments of early South American cultures. Planned communities boasting organized labor systems and monumental architecture dot the narrow river valleys that drop from the Andes to the Pacific Ocean. In the Central Andes, these early sites began to develop around 3000 B.C., about a millenium before the invention of pottery there ca. 2000 B.C. Carved gourds, possibly imported from Ecuador, and some fragmentary twined cotton textiles survive from this early period. (*Twining* is a nonloom technique like macramé; the weaver twists two threads around each other to form the finished cloth.) They depict composite creatures, such as crabs turning into snakes, as well as doubled and then reversed images, both hallmarks of much of later Andean art.

CEREMONIAL ARCHITECTURE   The architecture of the early coastal sites typically consists of large U-shaped flat-topped platforms—some as high as a ten-story building—around sunken courtyards. Many had numerous small chambers on top. Construction materials included both uncut fieldstones and handmade *adobes* (sun-dried mud bricks) in the shape of cones, laid point to point in coarse mud plaster to form walls and platforms. Facades, ornamented with bright multicolored adobe friezes, often displayed human figures with feline or serpentine attributes or great fanged faces of massive proportions. We illustrate a large adobe feline head (FIG. **14-15**), once painted although the color disap-

peared long ago, from the Huaca de los Reyes mound at the site of Caballo Muerto in Peru. Feline and serpentine motifs reappeared throughout Andean pre-Columbian history. Undoubtedly, the early modeled images served as backdrops for large public festivals held within the open-air plazas before them. These great U-shaped complexes almost always faced toward the Andes mountains, source of the life-giving rivers these communities depended on for survival. Mountain worship, which continues in the Andean region to this day, was probably the focus of early religious practices as well.

In the highlands, archeologists also have discovered large ceremonial complexes. In place of the numerous interconnecting rooms found on top of many coastal mounds, the highland complexes have a single small chamber at the top, often with a stone-lined firepit in the center. Researchers believe these pits played a role in a highland fire ritual. Burnt offerings, often of exotic objects such as marine shells and tropical bird feathers, have been found in them.

Chavín (ca. 800–200 B.C.)

Named after the ceremonial center of Chavín de Huántar, located in the northern highlands of Peru, the Chavín culture developed and spread throughout much of the coastal region and the highlands during the first millennium B.C. From recent discoveries at other sites, archeologists have concluded that the Chavín horizon style, once thought the "mother culture" of the Andean region, was in reality the culmination of developments that began some two thousand years earlier elsewhere.

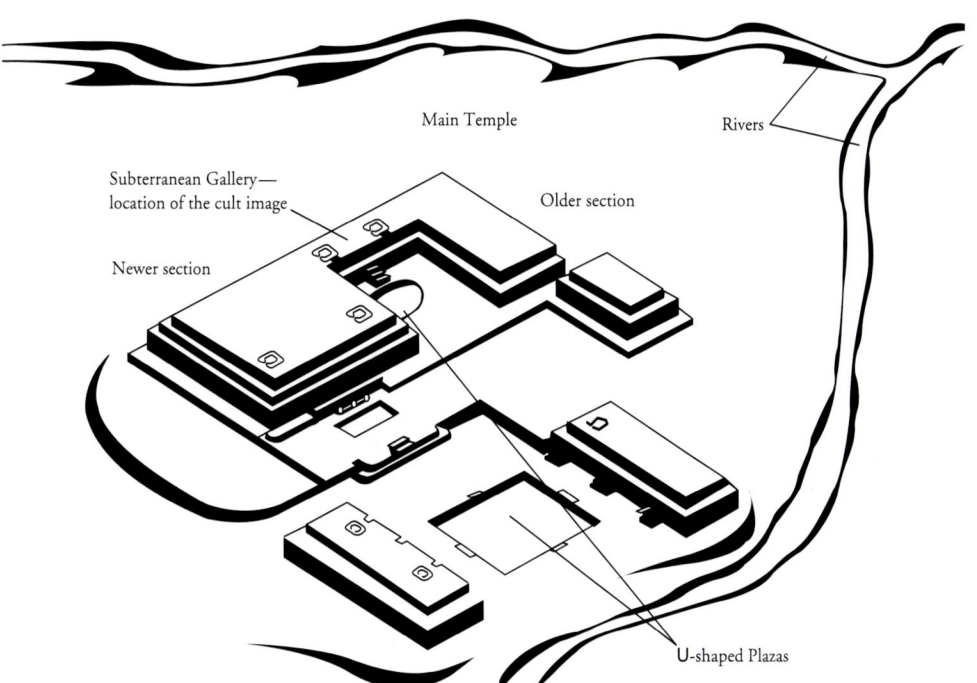

14-16 Reconstructed drawing of plan of sacred center showing temple and associated sunken courtyards, Chavín de Huántar, Peru, first millennium B.C.

Main Temple

Subterranean Gallery— location of the cult image

Older section

Newer section

Rivers

U-shaped Plazas

A SCULPTURE-FILLED TEMPLE PLATFORM

The main temple of Chavín de Huántar (FIG. **14-16**) is a U-shaped, stone-faced platform facing east toward a nearby river. Although at first glance it appears to be a solid platform with small ruined chambers on top, the temple is penetrated by a labyrinth of narrow passageways, small chambers, and stairways. The few members of Chavín society with access to these rooms must have witnessed secret and sacred ceremonies lit by torches, as no windows light the interior of the temple. The temple's builders may have attempted to re-create in stone the soaring Andean peaks that surround the valley, mountains still highly revered by Andean peoples. The temple is fronted by sunken courts, an arrangement undoubtedly adopted from earlier coastal sites. Modifications to the structure during the centuries have resulted in the asymmetrical shape seen today. The temple complex at Chavín de Huántar is famous for its extensive stone carvings. Consisting largely of low relief on panels, lintels, and columns and some rarer instances of freestanding sculpture, Chavín carving is essentially linear, hardly more than incision. An immense cult image stood in the center of the temple's oldest part. Other examples of sculpture in the round include heads of mythological creatures *tenoned* (attached by stone pegs) into the exterior walls. Although, at first glance, the subjects of Chavín stone carving appear to vary considerably, the artists most consistently emphasized composite creatures that combine feline, avian, reptilian, and human features.

A FROWNING AND SMILING GOD

The *Raimondi Stele* (FIG. **14-17**), named after its discoverer, represents the late variant of Chavín stone carving. On the lowest third of the stone is a figure called the "staff god." He appears in various versions from Colombia to northern Bolivia but seldom with the degree of elaboration found at Chavín. In this instance, the squat scowling deity, always depicted holding staffs, gazes upward. An elaborate headdress dominates the upper two-thirds of the slab. Inverting the image reveals that the headdress is composed of a series of fanged jawless faces, each emerging from the mouth of the one above it. Snakes

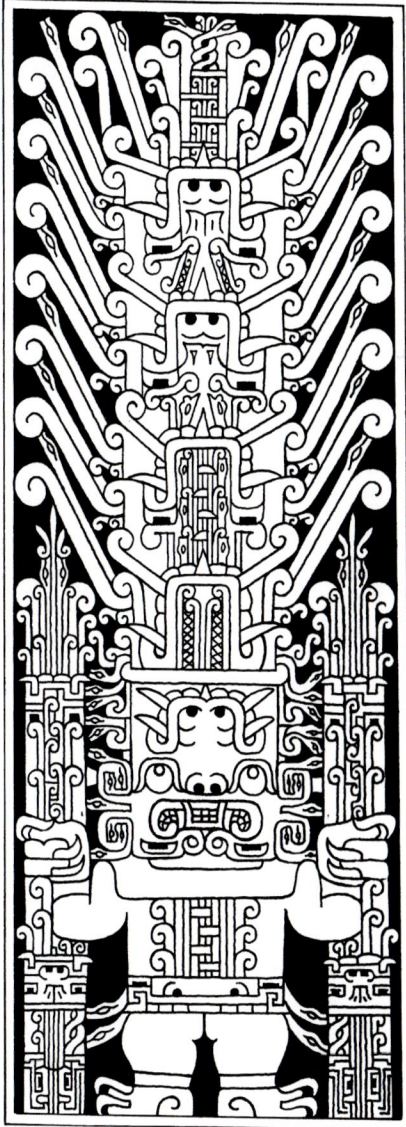

14-17 Drawing of the *Raimondi Stele,* from main temple, Chavín de Huántar, Peru, first millennium B.C. Incised green diorite, 6' high. Instituto Nacional de Cultura, Lima, Peru.

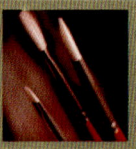

Andean Weaving

When the Inca first encountered the Spanish conquistadors, they were puzzled by the Europeans' lust for gold and silver. Finely woven cloth was infinitely more precious to the Inca than mere metal. Textiles and clothing dominated every aspect of their existence. Storing textiles in great warehouses, their leaders demanded cloth as tribute, gave it as gifts, exchanged it during diplomatic negotiations, and even burned it as a sacrificial offering. Although both men and women participated in cloth production, the Inca rulers selected women from around the empire and sequestered them for life to weave exclusively for the rulers.

Andean peoples began making textiles at least four thousand years ago. They spun into yarn the cotton grown in five different shades on the warm coast and fur sheared from highland camelids (domesticated llamas and alpacas and the wild vicuña) and then wove the yarn into cloth. Rare tropical bird feathers and small plaques of gold and silver were sometimes sewn onto cloth destined for the nobility. Andean weavers mastered nearly every textile technique known today, many executed with a simple device known as a *backstrap loom.* Such looms are still in use in the Andes. The women stretch the long *warp* (vertical) threads between two pieces of wood, one tied to a stationary object. A belt or backstrap, attached to the other piece, goes around the waist of the seated weaver, who controls the tension of the warp threads by leaning forward and back. The weaver passes the *weft* (horizontal) threads over and under the warps and pushes them tightly against each other to produce the finished cloth. In ancient textiles, the sturdy cotton often formed the warp, while the wool, which can be dyed brighter colors, served to create complex designs in the weft. *Embroidery* (see "Embroidery and Tapestry," Chapter 17, page 485), sewing threads onto a finished ground cloth to form contrasting designs, was the specialty of the Paracas culture (FIG. 14-18).

The dry deserts of coastal Peru have preserved not only numerous textiles from different periods but also hundreds of finely worked baskets containing spinning and weaving implements. These tools are invaluable sources of information about Andean textile production processes. The baskets found in documented contexts came from women's graves, attesting to both the close identity between weaving and women and the reverence for the cloth-making process.

A special problem all weavers confront is that they must visualize the entire design in advance and cannot easily change it during the weaving process. No records exist of how Andean weavers learned, retained, and passed on the elaborate patterns they wove into cloth, but Moche pottery (from a northern site discussed later) depicts weavers at work, apparently copying designs from finished models. From the earliest times, religious and political elites throughout the Andes must have tightly controlled the production of fine cloth. However, the inventiveness of individual weavers, within strict guidelines, is evident in the endless variety of colors and patterns in surviving pre-Columbian textiles.

Some motifs, such as the figures, animals, and birds embroidered on Paracas fabrics (FIG. 14-18), derived from the natural world, but most Andean textile designs are highly abstract and geometric, reflecting the right-angled relationship of warp and weft. Some of the abstract designs are actually highly stylized figures (FIG. 14-24), but many others, including those woven into fine Inca tunics during the Spanish conquest, still cannot be read with certainty. Colonial sources state only that the type and quality of clothing and accessories the Andean peoples wore reflected ethnic identity and social rank.

---

abound. They extend from the deity's belt; comprise part of the staffs; serve as whiskers and hair for the deity and the headdress creatures; and, finally, form a *guilloche* (an architectural ornament that imitates braided ribbon) at the apex of the composition. The *Raimondi Stele* clearly illustrates the Andean artistic tendency toward both multiplicity and dual readings. Upside down, the frowning god's face turns into not one but two smiling faces.

Chavín iconography spread widely throughout the Andean region through portable media such as goldwork, textiles, and ceramics. For example, more than three hundred miles from Chavín on the south coast of Peru, archeologists have discovered cotton textiles with imagery recalling Chavín sculpture. Painted staff-bearing female deities, apparently local manifestations or consorts of the highland staff god, decorate these large cloths, which may have served as wall hangings in temples. The ceramic vessels of the north coast of Peru, contemporaneous with both Huaca de los Reyes and later Chavín, are identified easily by their massive chambers, spout, surface relief, and burnished dark colors—brown, black, or grey. The motifs are much like those found on Chavín stone carvings. The stirrup spout, in which a spout emerges from a semicircular handle on top of the vessel (FIG. 14-21), became popular at this time and continued to be a commonly used North Coast form until the advent of the Spaniards.

Paracas (400 B.C.–A.D. 200)

Several coastal traditions developed during the period between about 500 B.C. and A.D. 600. Together they exemplify the great variations within Peruvian art styles. The Paracas culture, which flourished as early as the fifth century B.C., occupied a desert peninsula and a nearby river valley on the south coast of Peru.

FLYING FIGURES ON A FUNERARY MANTLE
Outstanding among the Paracas arts are the funerary textiles (FIG. **14-18**) used to wrap the bodies of the dead in multiple layers. More than a thousand examples survive. The dry desert

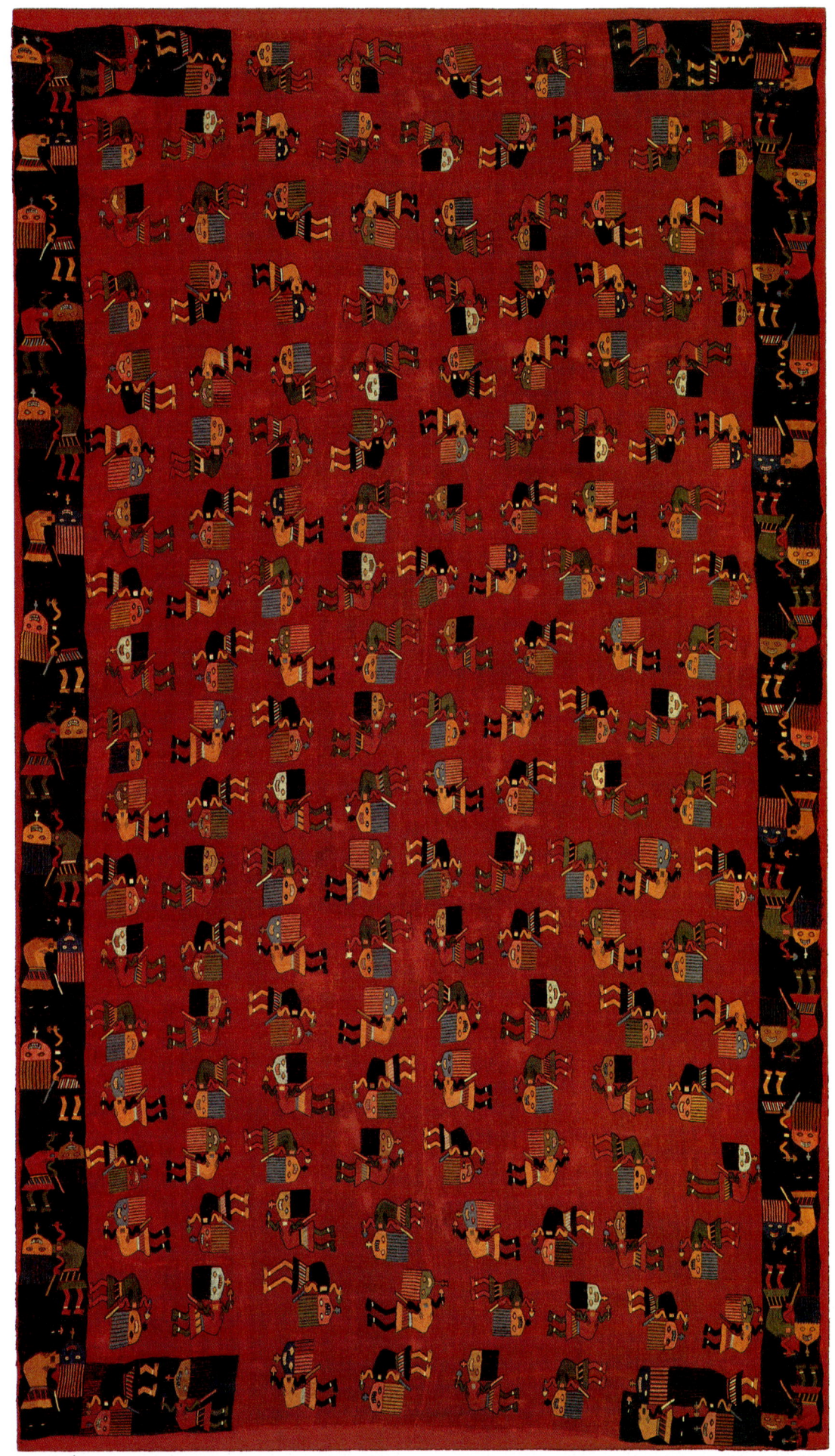

14-18 Embroidered mantle with shaman figures, Paracas, from southern coast of Peru, first century A.D. Plain weave camelid fiber with stem-stitch embroidery embroidered with camelid wool, 4′ 7⅞″ × 7′ 10⅞″. Museum of Fine Arts, Boston (William A. Paine Fund).

climate preserved the textiles, buried in shaft tombs beneath the sands. These textiles are among the enduring masterpieces of Andean art (see "Andean Weaving," page 402). Most are of woven cotton with designs embroidered onto the fabric in alpaca or vicuña wool (imported from the highlands, where these animals are herded in large numbers). The weavers used more than one hundred fifty vivid colors, the majority derived from plants. The motifs of the grave mantles have a symbolism not yet deciphered. Most distinctive is a flying figure with prominent eyes, who is repeated scores of times over the surface of the mantle we illustrate. The flying or floating beings on these cloths variously carry batons and fans (as they do here), plants, and sometimes the skulls or severed heads of enemies. Their flowing hair and the slow kicking motion of their legs suggest airy, hovering movement. Despite endless repetition of the figure, variations of detail occur throughout each textile, notably in the figures' positions and in subtle color changes. Furthermore, the mantles often had sewn borders of contrasting color, although with similar designs. Feline, bird, and serpent motifs also appear on some of the textiles, but the human figure, real or mythological, predominates. Art historians have interpreted the flying figure as a Paracas shaman dancing or flying during an ecstatic trance such as those shamans experienced in rites to cure individual illness or to insure the fertility of the community's crops.

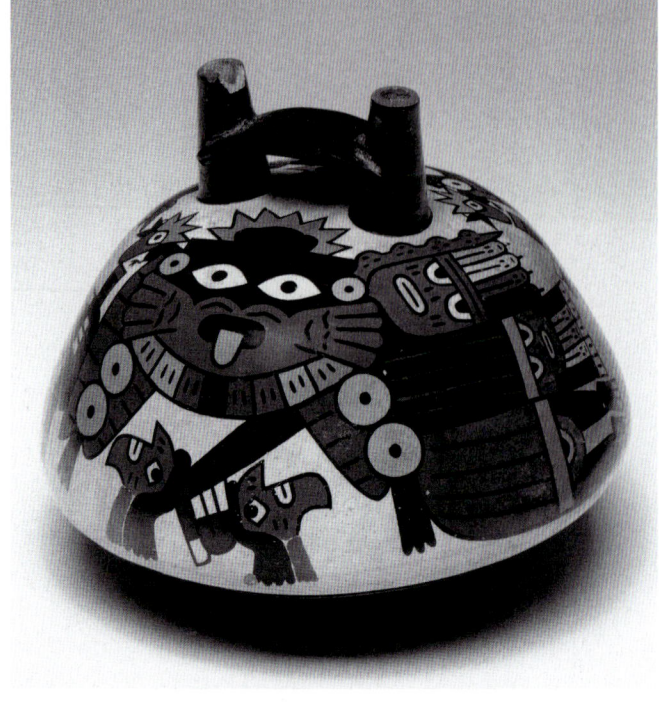

14-19   Bridge-spouted vessel depicting ceremonial figure, Nasca, from Nasca River valley, Peru, ca. 50–200. Ceramic, approx. $5\frac{1}{2}''$ high. Art Institute of Chicago, Chicago (Kate S. Buckingham Endowment).

Nasca (200 b.c. – a.d. 600)

The culture now called Nasca is named after the Nasca River valley of the south coast of Peru. The Nasca were renowned for their pottery. Thousands of their ceramic vessels survive and usually have round bottoms, double spouts connected by bridges, and smoothly burnished polychrome surfaces (FIG. **14-19**). The subjects vary greatly, with emphasis on plants, animals, and composite mythological creatures, partly human and partly animal. The painters commonly represented ritual impersonators, some of whom, like the Paracas flying figures, hold trophy heads and weapons. In the example we illustrate, two such costumed figures fly around the vessel. The painter reduced their bodies and limbs to abstract appendages and focused on the heads. The figures wear a multicolored necklace, a whiskered gold mouthpiece, circular disks hanging from the ears, and a rayed crown on the forehead. Masks or heads with streaming hair, possibly more trophy heads, flow over the impersonators' backs, increasing the sense of motion.

IMMENSE DRAWINGS ON THE NASCA PLAIN Polychrome pottery is not the sole source of Nasca's fame. Some eight hundred miles of lines, drawn in complex networks on the dry surface of the Nasca Plain in southwestern Peru, have long attracted world attention as mysterious and gigantic artworks. Nasca artists traced out about three dozen images of birds, fish, and plants on the plain. Our illustration (FIG. **14-20**) shows a hummingbird with a wingspan of more than two hundred feet. The Nasca artists also drew geometric forms, such as trapezoids, spirals, and straight lines running for miles. Uniformly, the Nasca Lines, as the im-

mense drawings are called, appear light on a dark ground. The Nasca produced the effect by scraping aside the sun-darkened desert pebbles to reveal the lighter layer of whitish clay and calcite beneath. The near-rainless environment has preserved the drawings for centuries, but modern highways and off-road vehicles have damaged many of the Nasca Lines.

Given the huge size and bewildering intricacy of the patterns, speculation continues as to the source, construction, and meaning of the Nasca Lines. Although they are best seen from the air, they are also visible from the Andean foothills and the great coastal dunes. The lines were constructed quite easily from available materials and with some rudimentary geometry. A small group of workers have made modern reproductions of them with relative ease. The lines seem to be paths laid out using simple stone-and-string methods. Some lead in traceable directions across the deserts of the Nasca River drainage, while others are punctuated by many shrine-like nodes, like the knots on a cord. The lines converge at central places usually situated close to water sources and seem to be associated with water supply and irrigation. They may have marked pilgrimage routes for those who journeyed to local or regional shrines on foot. Although astronomical functions have been proposed for the lines, this theory has not been convincingly demonstrated. Altogether, the vast arrangement of the Nasca Lines is a system—not a meaningless maze but a traversable map that plotted out the whole terrain of the Nasca material and spiritual concerns. Remarkably, until quite recently similar ritual pathways were made and used in association with shrines in highland Bolivia, demonstrating the tenacity of the Andean indigenous belief systems.

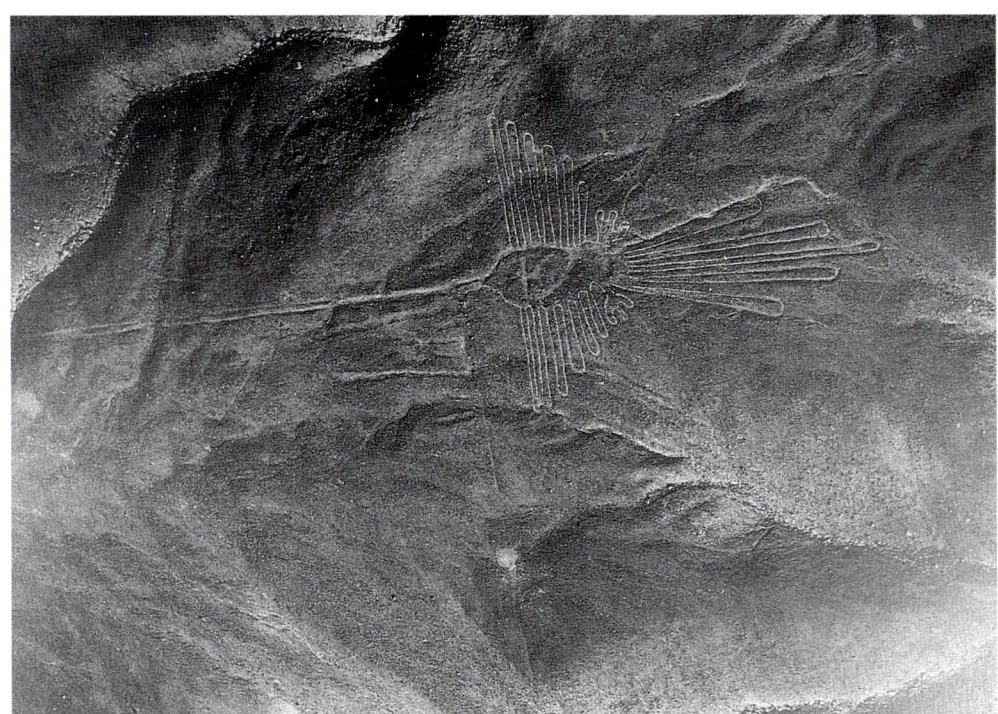

14-20 Drawing of a hummingbird on Nasca Plain, Nasca, Peru, ca. 500. Dark layer of pebbles, scraped aside to reveal lighter clay and calcite beneath; 27′ wide, 200′ wingspan, and 459′ length.

Moche (A.D. 1–700)

The Moche occupied a series of river valleys on the north coast of Peru around the same time the Nasca flourished to the south, but the Moche left behind more impressive architectural remains. Their ceremonial architecture consisted of immense pyramidal platforms that, due to the scarcity of stone, they constructed of adobe and then plastered and painted in bright colors. In the lower Moche River valley, the remains of the Temple of the Sun, which the Moche made of millions of adobe bricks, provide some idea of the scale of such construction.

MOCHE DAILY LIFE Among the most famous art objects the ancient Peruvians produced are the Moche ceramic vessels, predominantly flat-bottomed stirrup-spouted jars, generally decorated with a bichrome (two-color) slip. Although the Moche hand made early vessels without the aid of a potter's wheel, they fashioned later ones in two-piece molds. Thus, numerous near-duplicates survive. Moche potters continued to refine the stirrup spout, making it an elegant slender tube, much more slender than the Chavín prototype. This refinement may be seen in one of the famous Moche portrait bottles (FIG. **14-21**). It may depict the face of a warrior, a ruler, or even a royal retainer whose image may have been buried with many other pots to accompany his dead master. Among ancient civilizations, only the Greeks and the Maya surpassed the Moche in the information recorded on their ceramics. Moche pots illustrate architecture, metallurgy, weaving, the brewing of *chicha* (fermented maize beer), human deformities and diseases, and even sexual acts.

TREASURES OF THE LORDS OF SIPÁN Elite men, along with retinues of sacrificial victims, appear to be the occupants of several rich Moche tombs excavated near the little village of Sipán on the arid northwest coast of Peru.

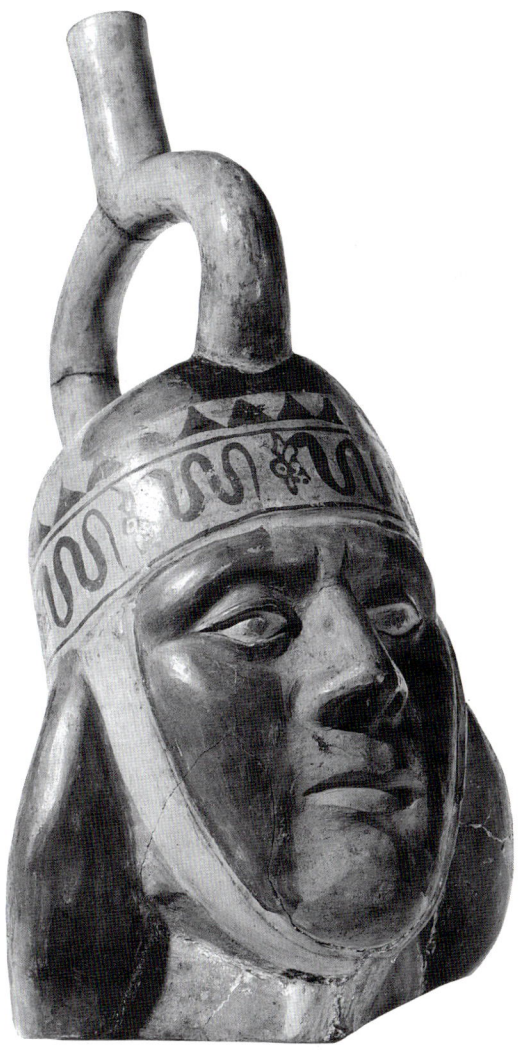

14-21 Portrait bottle, Moche, from northcoast Peru, fifth to sixth century. Painted clay, 11½″ high. American Museum of Natural History, New York.

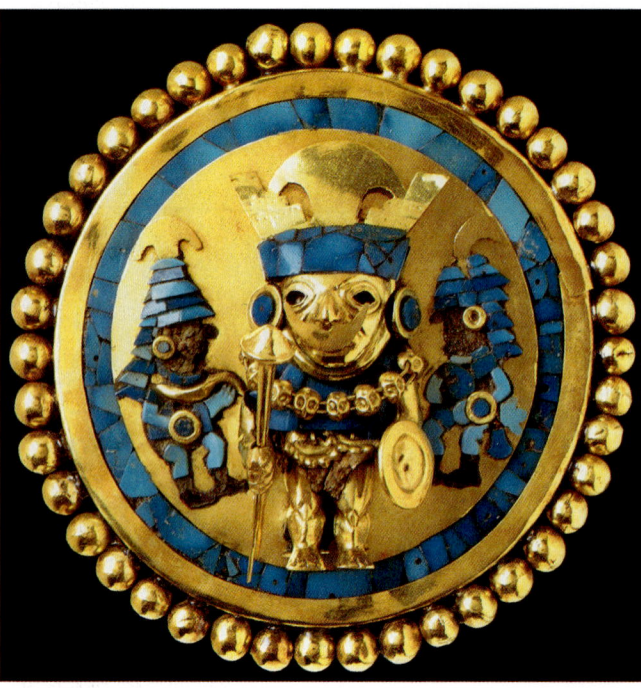

14-22   Ear ornament, from a tomb at Sipán, Moche, Peru, ca. 300. Gold and turquoise, approx. $4\frac{4}{5}$". Bruning Archeological Museum, Lambayeque.

Looted and unlooted tombs have yielded a treasure of golden artifacts and more than a thousand ceramic vessels. The tombs' discovery in the late 1980s made a great stir in the archeological world, contributing significantly to the knowledge of Moche culture. Located beneath a large adobe platform adjacent to two high but greatly eroded pyramids, the tombs had escaped the attention of village grave robbers for many years. The splendor of the funeral trappings that adorned the body of one of the dead, the so-called Lord of Sipán; the quantity and quality of the sumptuous accessories; and the bodies of the retainers buried with him indicate he was a personage of the highest rank. Indeed, he may have been one of the warrior-priests so often pictured on Moche ceramic wares and murals (and in this tomb on a golden pyramid-shaped rattle) assaulting his enemies and participating in sacrificial ceremonies.

An ear ornament of turquoise and gold found in one tomb shows a warrior-priest clad much like the dead man (FIG. **14-22**). Represented frontally, he carries a war club and shield and wears a necklace of owls' heads. The figure's bladelike crescent-shaped helmet is a replica of the large golden one buried with the warrior-priest. The ear ornament of the jewelry image is a simplified version of the piece itself. The removable nose guard and the golden chin guard also match those the deceased wore. Two retainers, with similar helmets and ear ornaments, appear in profile.

Though the Andean cultures did not develop a system of writing, they had an advanced knowledge of metallurgy long before the Mesoamericans, who must have received it via Central America as late as the tenth century. Treasure of silver and gold, of course, lured the Spanish invaders to the Americas, and the wildcat plundering of pre-Columbian tombs by grave robbers, both foreign and domestic, continues to scatter precious artifacts worldwide. The value of the Sipán find is incalculable for what it reveals about elite Moche culture.

Tiwanaku (100–1000)

The bleak highland country surrounding Lake Titicaca in southeastern Peru and southwestern Bolivia contrasts markedly with the warm valleys of the coast. Isolated in these mountains, at an altitude of twelve thousand five hundred feet, another culture developed semi-independently of the coastal cultures, beginning in the first centuries of the Christian era and ending about 1000. This culture has been named Tiwanaku, after the principal archeological site on the southern shores of the lake in Bolivia. The Tiwanaku art style then spread to the adjacent coastal area as well as to other highland areas, eventually extending from southern Peru to northern Chile.

THE GATEWAY OF THE SUN   Tiwanaku was an important ceremonial center, although today it is largely in ruins. The inhabitants constructed buildings with the region's fine stone—sandstone, andesite, and diorite—bringing much of it from great distances. Among these impressive structures is the imposing Gateway of the Sun (FIG. **14-23**), a huge monolithic block of andesite pierced by a single doorway and crowned with a sculptured lintel. Moved in ancient times from its original location within the site, the gateway now forms part of an enormous walled platform, leading nowhere. The central figure, rigidly frontal, stands on a terraced step holding a staff in each hand. From the enormous blocklike head project rays that terminate in circles and puma heads. The form recalls that of the *Raimondi Stele* (FIG. 14-17) in its frontality and in the symmetrical staffs, as well as in the geometric conventions used for human and animal representation. The "staff-god"—possibly a sky and weather deity rather than the sun deity the rayed head suggests—appears in art throughout the Tiwanaku horizon, associated, as here,

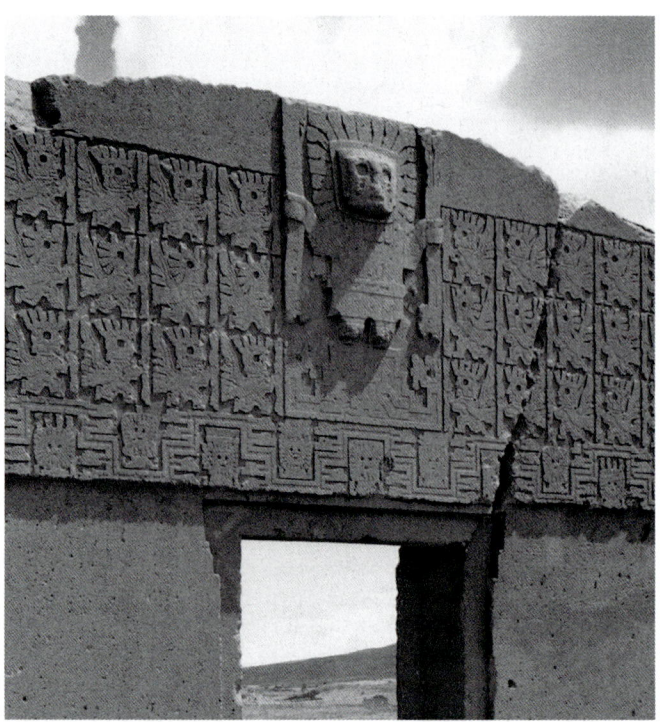

14-23   Detail of Gateway of the Sun, Tiwanaku, Bolivia, ca. 375–700.

with smaller-scale attendant figures. Carved in high relief on this lintel, the god stands out prominently against the low-relief rows of condor impersonators and winged men with weapons who run toward the center. Each of the running figures fills a square panel, giving an effect of movement, which quickens slightly the composition's otherwise static formality. A border of *frets* (an ornamental pattern of contiguous straight lines joined usually at right angles) interspersed with masklike heads forms a kind of supporting lower step. Because of the distortion of the bodily proportions, the suppression of detail, and the intricate flat relief, the Gateway imagery is difficult to decipher today. But artists once had painted the carved surface, inlaid the eyes of the figures with turquoise, poured molten gold into the recesses, and hammered sheet gold over the raised surfaces.

Wari (500–800)

The flat, abstract, and repetitive figures surrounding the central figure on the Gateway of the Sun recall woven textile designs. Indeed, the people of the Tiwanaku culture, like those of Paracas, were consummate weavers, although many fewer textiles survive from the damp highlands. However, from a contemporaneous Peruvian culture known as Wari, which dominated parts of the dry coast, many examples of weaving, especially tunics, have been recovered.

ABSTRACTION IN TAPESTRY Although Wari weavers fashioned cloth, like the earlier Paracas textiles, from both wool and cotton fibers, the resemblance between the two textile styles ends there. While Paracas motifs were embroidered onto the plain woven surface, Wari designs were woven directly into the fabric, the weft threads packed densely over the warp threads in a technique known as *tapestry* (see "Embroidery and Tapestry," Chapter 17, page 485). Some particularly fine pieces have more than two hundred weft threads per inch. Furthermore, unlike the relatively naturalistic individual figures depicted on Paracas mantles, those appearing on Wari textiles are so closely connected and so abstract as to be nearly unintelligible. Most designs, however distorted, derive from the motifs on the Gateway of the Sun at Tiwanaku. The tunic shown here, the so-called *Lima Tapestry* (FIG. **14-24**), for example, is an abstract interpretation of the Tiwanaku staff-bearing attendants. The artist expanded or compressed each figure in a different way and placed them in vertical rows pressed between narrow red bands of plain cloth. Elegant tunics such as this, worn by the elite, must have carried the message of the Tiwanaku staff god to the far reaches of the Andean region.

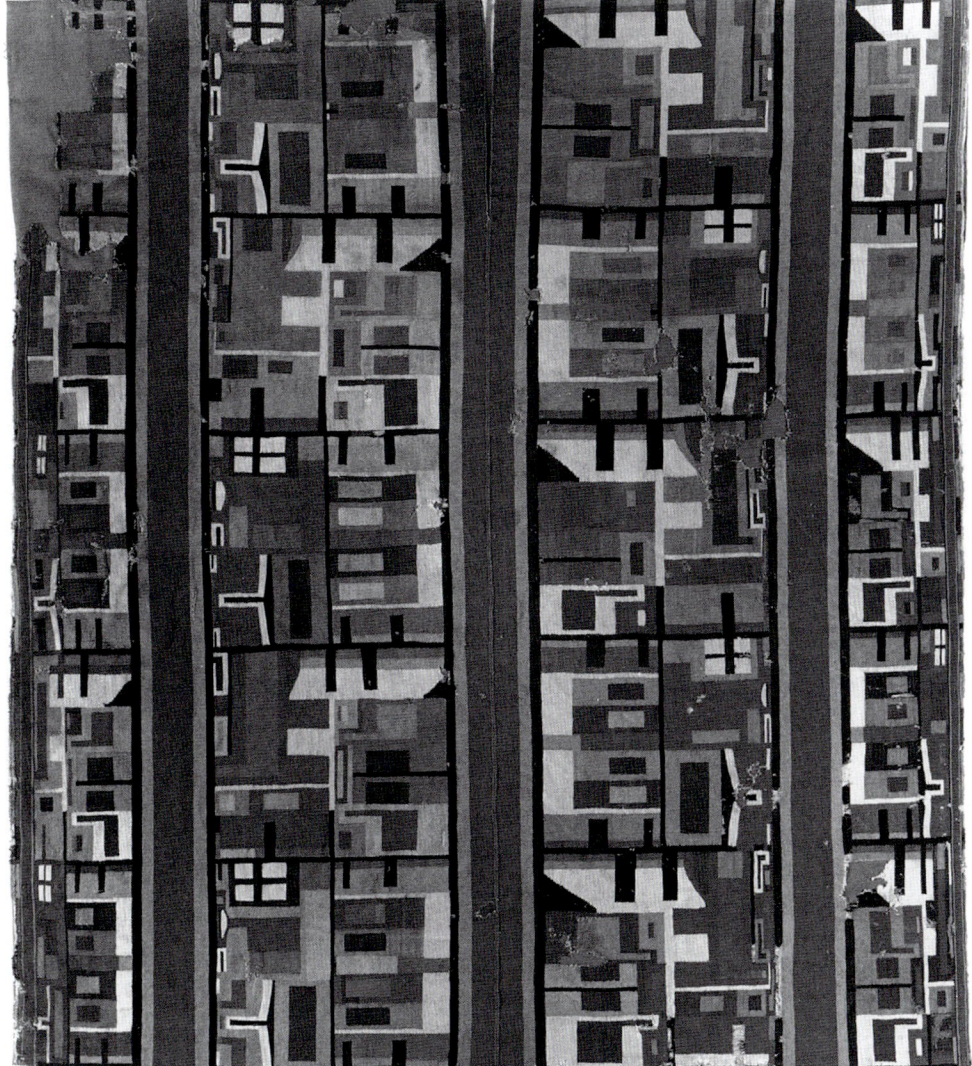

14-24 *Lima Tapestry* (tunic), Wari, from Peru, ca. 500–800. 3′ 3⅜″ × 2′ 11⅜″. National Museum of Archeology, Anthropology, and History of Peru, Lima.

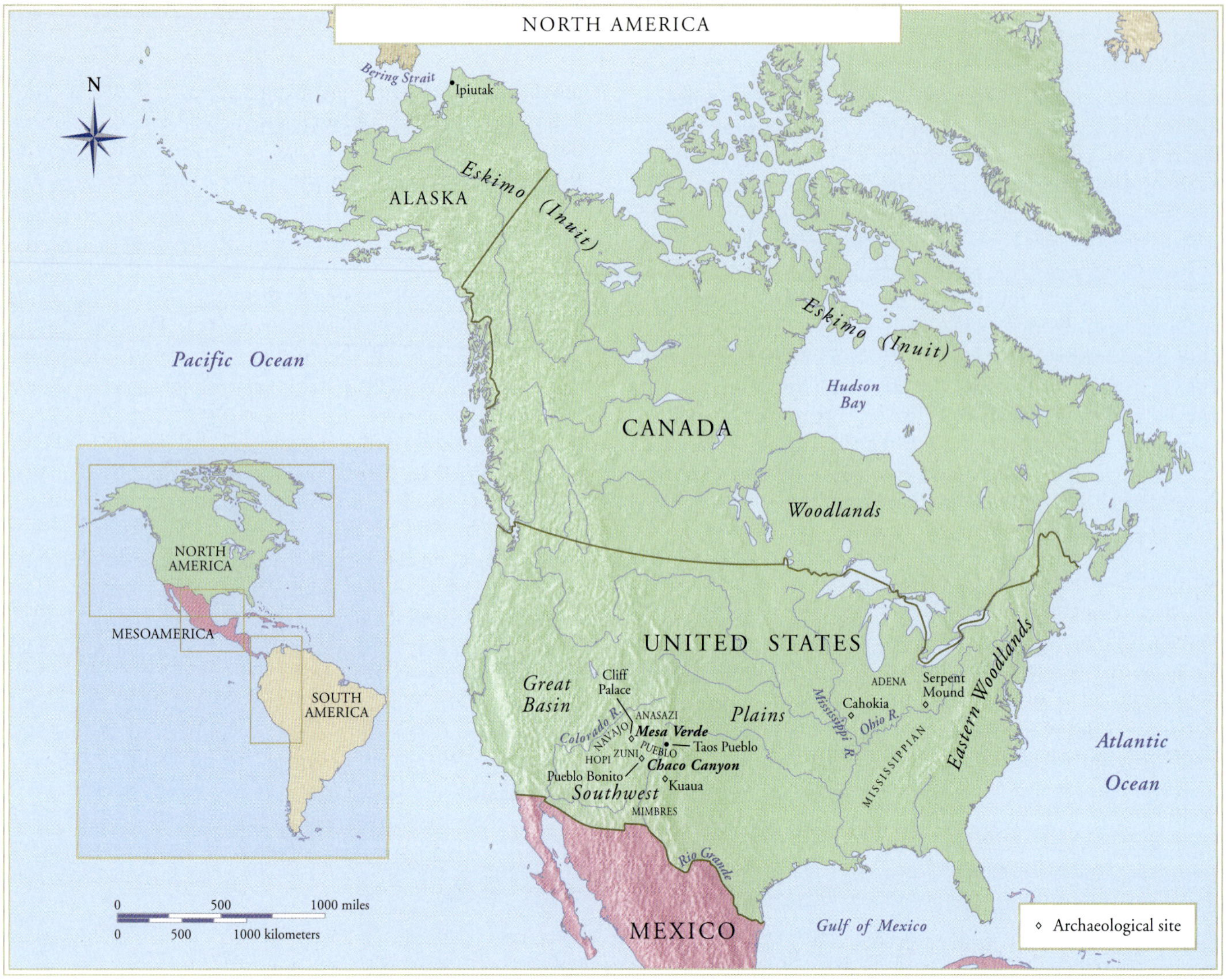

NORTH AMERICA

Bering Strait · Ipiutak

ALASKA

Eskimo (Inuit)

Eskimo (Inuit)

Pacific Ocean

NORTH AMERICA

MESOAMERICA

SOUTH AMERICA

Hudson Bay

CANADA

Woodlands

UNITED STATES

Great Basin

Cliff Palace

Plains

ADENA

Serpent Mound

Cahokia

ANASAZI

Mesa Verde

Colorado R.

NAVAJO

Taos Pueblo

HOPI ZUNI

PUEBLO

Chaco Canyon

Pueblo Bonito

Kuaua

Southwest

MIMBRES

Mississippi R.

Ohio R.

MISSISSIPPIAN

Eastern Woodlands

Atlantic Ocean

Rio Grande

MEXICO

Gulf of Mexico

◇ Archaeological site

| 0 | 500 | 1000 miles |
| 0 | 500 | 1000 kilometers |

| 1100 B.C. | A.D. 200 | 500 | 1000 | 1150 | 1500 | 1600 |

PREHISTORIC | HISTORIC

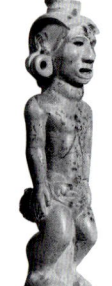

Pipe, Adena
Ohio, ca. 500 B.C.–1 A.D.

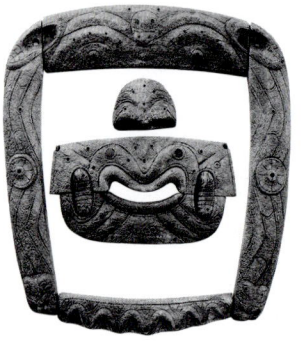

Mask, Ipiutak
Point Hope, Alaska, ca. 100

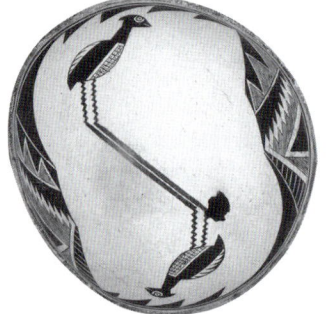

Bowl, Mimbres
New Mexico, ca. 1250

Adena culture, 1100 B.C.–A.D. 200

Earliest Eskimo/Inuit carvings in ivory, 500 B.C.

Mississippian culture dominates eastern
North America, 800–1500

Mimbres ceramic masterpieces, ca. 1000–1150

Serpent Mound, Ohio, ca. 1070

Drought forces abandonment of
Chaco Canyon, 1200

Mesa Verde abandoned, ca. 1300

Anasazi paint murals on kiva walls, ca. 1300–1500

First European colonies established,
1500–1600

NORTH AMERICA

In many parts of the United States and Canada, "prehistoric" cultures have been discovered that reach back as far as twelve thousand years ago. Most of the surviving art objects, however, come from the past two thousand years. "Historic" cultures, beginning with the earliest date of prolonged contact with Europeans, which varies from the sixteenth to the nineteenth century, have been widely and systematically recorded by anthropologists (see Chapter 30). The materials from these cultures usually reflect profound changes wrought by the impact of alien tools, materials, and values on the native peoples.

Scholars divide the vast and varied territory of North America into cultural regions based on the relative homogeneity of language and social and artistic patterns. Native lifestyles varied widely over the continent, ranging from small bands of migratory hunters to settled—at times even urban—agriculturalists. Among the peoples whose prehistoric existence is documented are the Eskimos, who hunted and fished across the Arctic from Greenland to Siberia, and the maize farmers of the American Southwest, who wrested water from their arid environment and built not only effective irrigation systems but also roads and spectacular cliff dwellings. The vast, temperate Eastern Woodlands—ranging from east-

ern Canada to Florida and from the Atlantic to the Great Plains west of the Mississippi—also were home to farmers. Some of them left behind great earthen mounds that once functioned as their elite residences or burial places.

Eskimo

A MASK OF SEVERAL FACES Eskimo sculpture, while often severely economical in the handling of form, is refined—even elegant—in the placement and precision of both geometric and representational incised designs. A carved ivory burial mask (FIG. **14-25**), datable to ca. A.D. 100, from the Ipiutak site at Point Hope in Alaska is composed of nine carefully shaped parts that are interrelated to produce several faces, both human and animal, as a visual pun. The mask is a confident, subtle composition in shallow relief, a tribute to the artist's imaginative control over the materials. For centuries, the Eskimo also carved hundreds of human and animal figurines, usually in ivory because of the scarcity of wood in most Arctic regions. These figures, as well as intricately carved hunting and fishing implements, reflect a nomadic lifestyle that required the creation of small, portable, and practical objects.

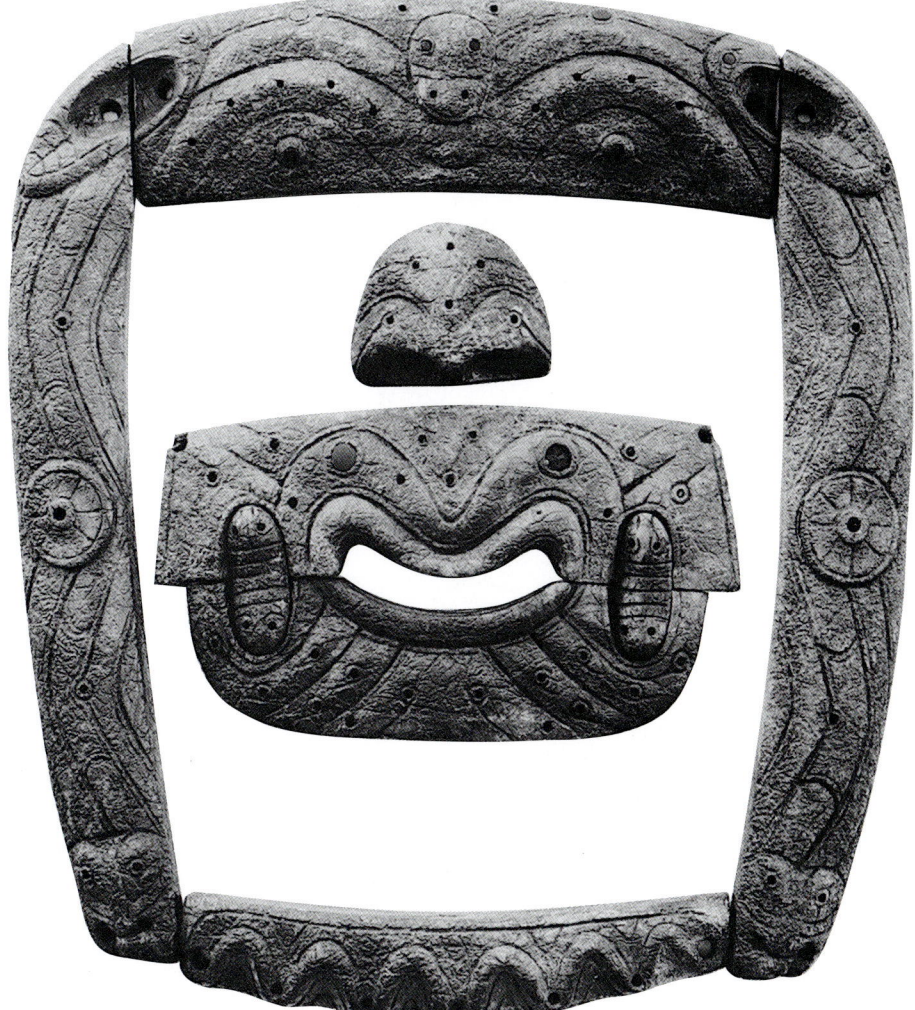

14-25 Burial mask, Ipiutak, from Point Hope, Alaska, ca. 100. Ivory, greatest width $9\frac{1}{2}''$. American Museum of Natural History, New York.

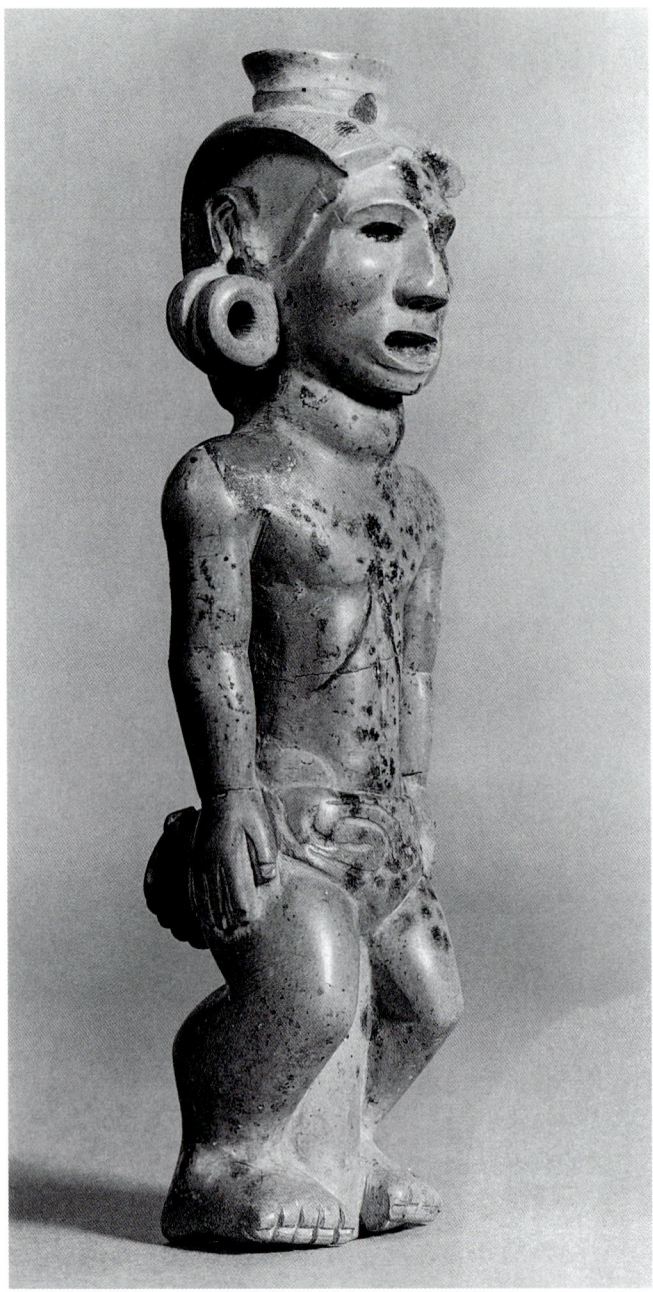

14-26 Pipe, Adena, from a mound in Ohio, ca. 500–1 B.C. Stone, 8" high. Ohio Historical Society, Columbus.

Woodlands

TWO CARVINGS A MILLENNIUM APART Early Native American artists also excelled in working stone into a variety of utilitarian and ceremonial objects. The quite realistic handling of a figural pipe bowl (FIG. **14-26**) from the Adena culture of Ohio, dated between 500 B.C. and 1 B.C., provides an interesting contrast to a much later piece from another culture. The more animated two-dimensional composition on a shell *gorget* (FIG. **14-27**), or neck pendant, is typical of the more widespread Mississippian culture. Found at a site in Tennessee, the shell gorget dates from ca. 1250 to 1300. The standing pipe figure, although simplified, has naturalistic joint articulations and musculature, a lively flexed-leg pose,

and an alert facial expression—all combining to suggest movement. The incised shell gorget depicts a running warrior wearing an elaborate headdress and carrying a mace in his left hand and a severed human head in his right. Most Adena and Mississippian objects come from burial and temple mounds and are thought to have been gifts to the dead to ensure their safe arrival and prosperity in the land of the spirits. Other art objects found in such contexts include fine mica cutouts and embossed copper cutouts of hands, bodies, snakes, birds, and other presumably symbolic forms.

CEREMONIAL MOUNDS Both *effigy mounds* (mounds built in the form of animals or birds) and complex platformed *temple mounds,* some built six thousand years ago, have been discovered at many sites in the eastern United States and the Midwest. Such elaborate earthworks exemplify the universal practice of creating visually monumental settings for ceremonial activities. The most impressive of the temple mounds is Monk's Mound at Cahokia in southern Illinois, the largest city in North America at one time (ca. 900–1200), with a population of twenty-five thousand and an area of more than six square miles. Built in stages for three centuries, Monk's Mound may have served as an elite residence, a temple, and a burial structure. Each stage was topped by wooden structures that then were destroyed in preparation for the building of a new layer. One of the finest effigy mounds is Serpent Mound (FIG. **14-28**), a twisting earthwork on a bluff overlooking a creek in Ohio. It measures nearly a quarter mile from its open jaw, which seems to clasp an oval-shaped mound in its mouth, to its tightly coiled tail. Both its date and meaning are controversial (see "Serpent Mound," page 411).

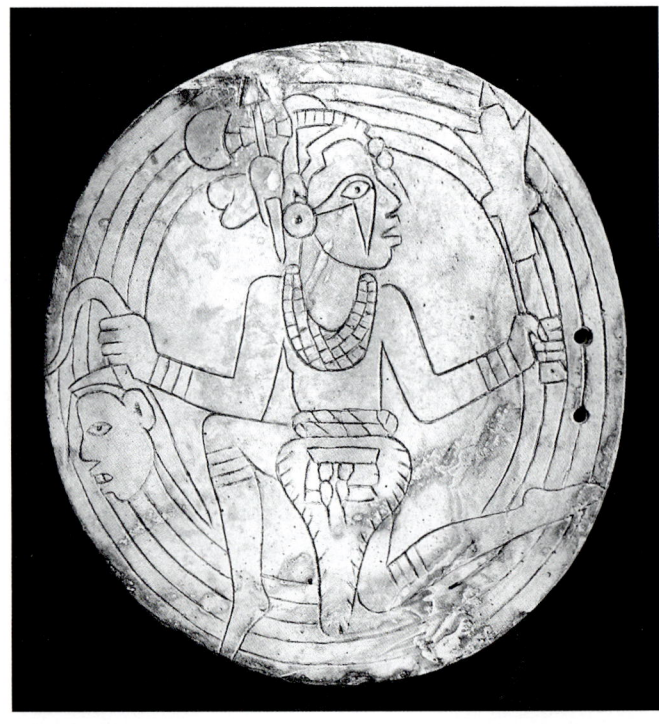

14-27 Incised shell gorget, Mississippian, from Sumner County, Tennessee, ca. 1250–1300. 4" wide. Museum of the American Indian, Smithsonian Institution, New York.

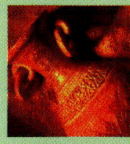

ART IN THE NEWS

Serpent Mound

Serpent Mound (FIG. 14-28) is one of the largest and best known of the Woodlands effigy mounds. Rescued from certain destruction at the hands of pot hunters and farmers a century ago (in one of the first efforts at preserving a Native American archeological site), it is today the subject of considerable controversy.

Archeologists long attributed Serpent Mound, first excavated in the 1880s, to the Adena culture, which flourished in the Ohio area for several centuries before the Christian era. New radiocarbon dates taken from the mound, however, indicate that it was built much later and thus by the people known as Mississippians. Unlike most other ancient mounds, this one contained no evidence of burials or temples. Serpents, however, were important in Mississippian iconography, appearing, for example, etched on shell gorgets similar to the one illustrated (FIG. 14-27). Snakes were strongly associated with the earth and the fertility of crops. A stone figurine found at one site, for example, depicts a woman digging her hoe into the back of a large serpentine creature whose tail turns into a vine of gourds.

But another possible meaning for the construction of Serpent Mound has been proposed recently. The new date suggested for it is 1070, not long after the brightest appearance in recorded history of Halley's Comet in 1066. Could Serpent Mound have been built in response to this important astronomical event? It even has been suggested that the serpentine form of the mound replicates the comet itself streaking across the night sky. Whatever its meaning, such a large and elaborate earthwork only could have been built by a large labor force under the firm direction of a powerful elite eager to leave its mark on the landscape forever.

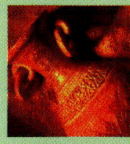

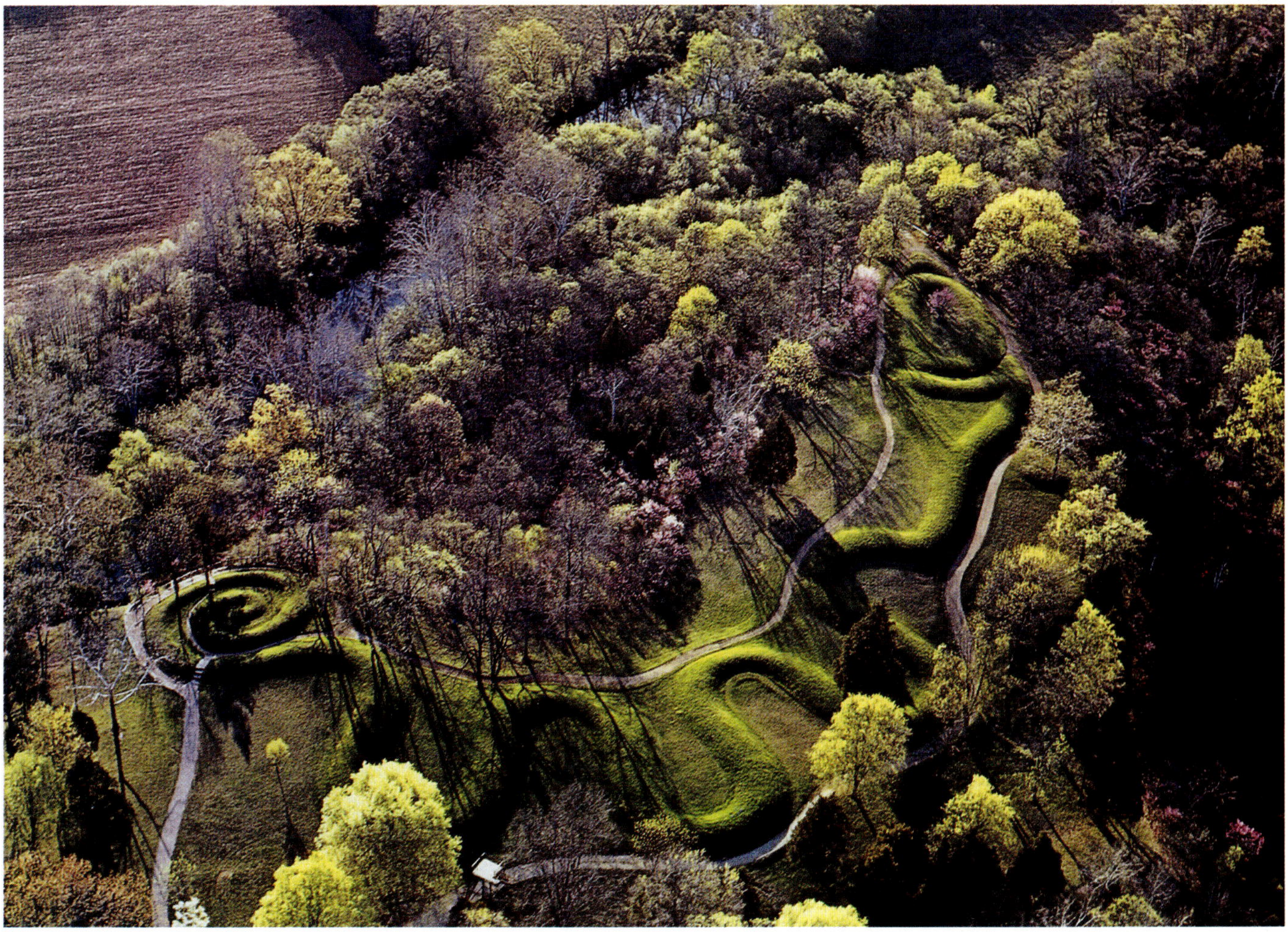

14-28 Serpent Mound, Mississippian, Ohio, late eleventh century. 1200′ long, 20′ wide, 5′ high.

Southwest

Most Native American art media span lengthy periods of time. Detailed chronological sequences of pottery styles are, in fact, the historian's major tool for dating and reconstructing the cultures of the distant past, especially in the Southwest. Many fine specimens of ceramics from the Southwest date from before the Christian era until the present, but pottery became especially fine, and its decoration most impressive, after about 1000.

MIMBRES POTTERY An animated graphic rendering of two cranes creates a dynamic tension between the black figuring and the white ground of a bowl from the Mimbres culture of southwestern New Mexico (FIG. **14-29**). The contrast between the bowl's abstract border designs and the birds creates a similar tension. Thousands of different compositions are known from Mimbres pottery. They range from lively and complex geometric patterns to often whimsical pictures of humans and animals. Almost all are imaginative creations by artists who seem to have been bent on not repeating themselves. Their designs emphasized linear rhythms balanced and controlled within a clearly defined border. Because the potter's wheel was unknown in the Americas, the artists used the coiling method to build countless sophisticated shapes of varied size, always characterized by technical excellence. Although historians have no direct knowledge about the potters' identity, the fact that pottery making was usually women's work in the Southwest during the historic period suggests that the Mimbres potters also may have been women.

Mimbres bowls have been found in burials under house floors, inverted over the head of the deceased and ritually

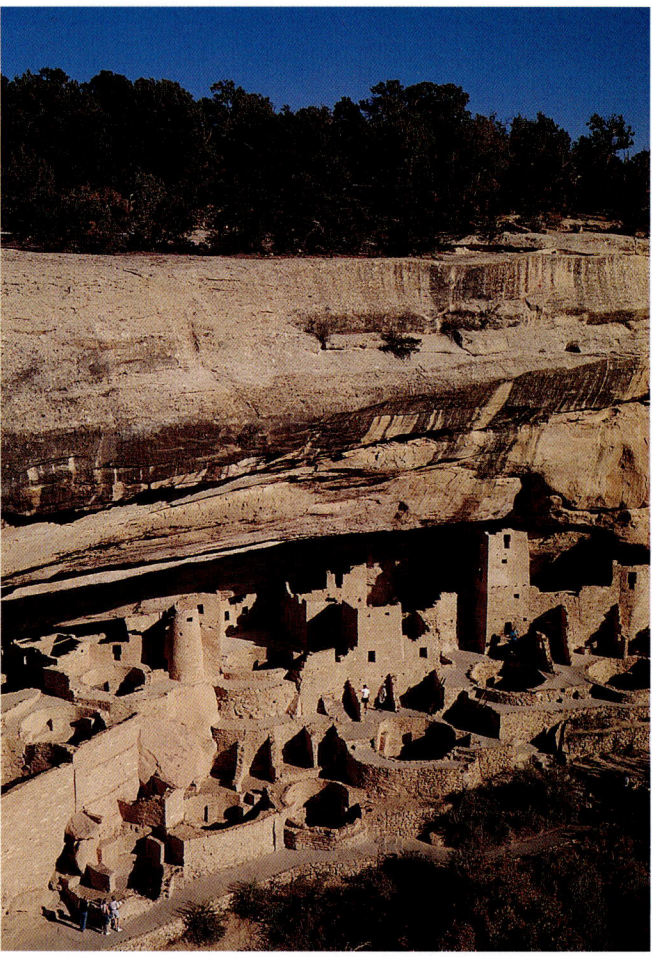

14-30 Cliff Palace, Anasazi, Mesa Verde National Park, Colorado, ca. 1150–1300.

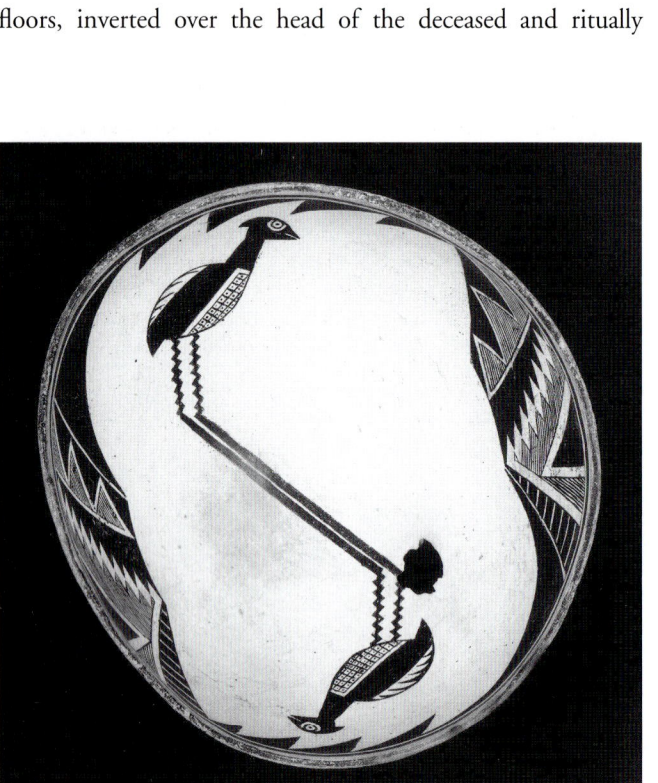

14-29 Bowl with two cranes and geometric forms, Mimbres, from New Mexico, ca. 1250. Ceramic, black-on-white, diameter approx. 1′ $\frac{1}{2}$″. Art Institute of Chicago, Chicago (Hugh L. and Mary T. Adams Fund).

"killed" by puncturing a small hole at the base, perhaps to allow the spirits of the deceased to join their ancestors in the sky (viewed as a dome by contemporary Southwestern peoples).

ANASAZI PUEBLOS In the later centuries of the prehistoric era, the Anasazi (Navajo for "enemy ancestors"), northern neighbors of the Mimbres, constructed architectural complexes that reflect masterful building skills and impressive talents of spatial organization. Many ruined *pueblos* (Spanish for "towns") are scattered throughout the Southwest. In Chaco Canyon, New Mexico, a great semicircle of eight hundred rooms reaching to five stepped-back stories was constructed, the largest of several such sites in and around the canyon. Sometime in the late twelfth century, a drought occurred and the Anasazi largely abandoned their open canyon-floor dwelling sites to move farther north to the steep-sided canyons and lusher environment of Mesa Verde in southwestern Colorado. Cliff Palace (FIG. **14-30**) is wedged into a sheltered ledge above a valley floor. It contains about two hundred rectangular rooms (mostly communal dwellings) of carefully laid stone and timber, once plastered inside and out with adobe. The location for Cliff Palace was not accidental—the Anasazi designed it to take advantage of the sun's movements to heat the pueblo and to shade it during the hot summer months.

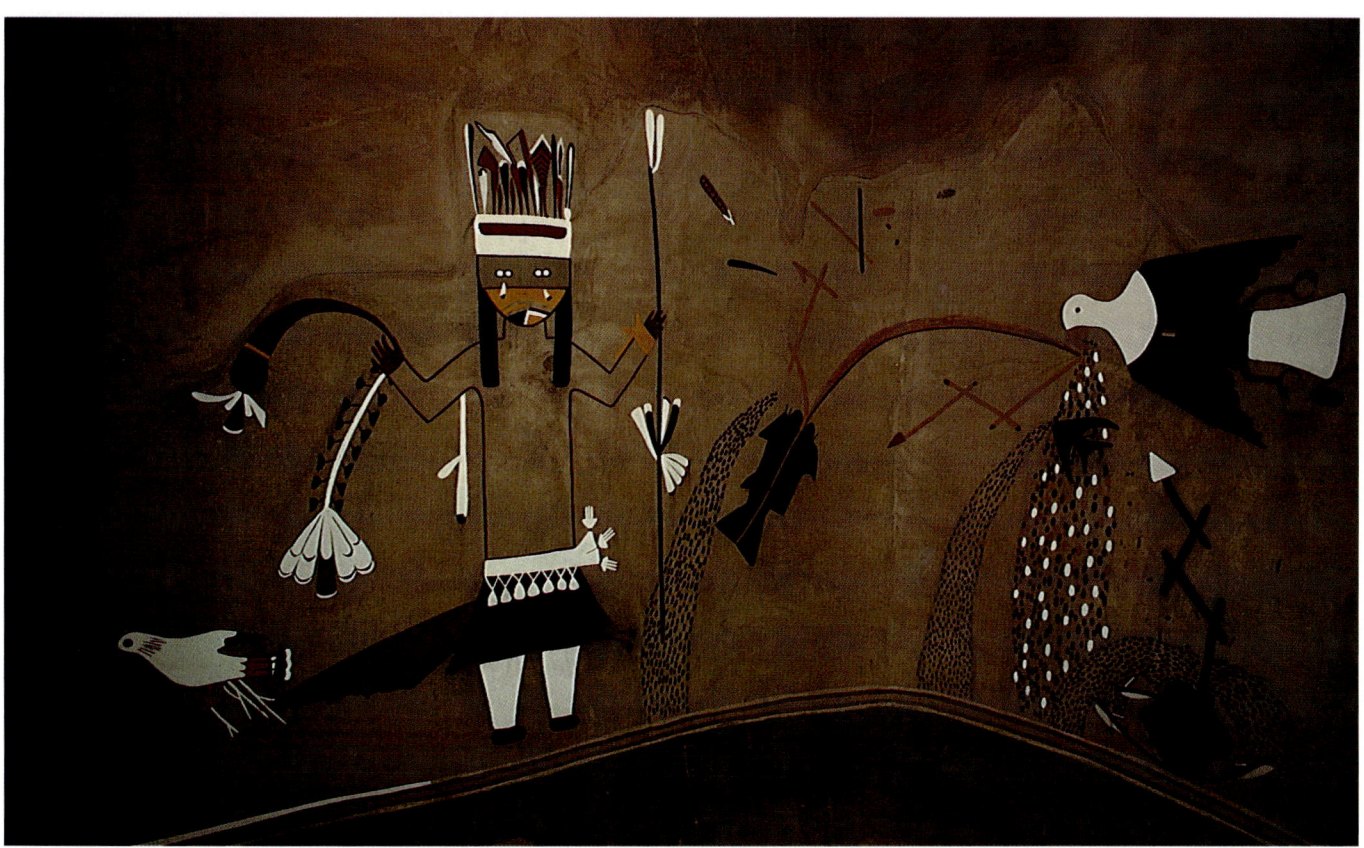

14-31 Detail of a kiva painting from Kuaua Pueblo (Coronado State Monument), Anasazi, New Mexico, late fifteenth to early sixteenth century. Museum of New Mexico, Santa Fe.

The descendants of the Anasazi built multistoried pueblos of adobe brick, with each story set back from the one beneath it to form broad roof terraces. Some, such as Taos Pueblo in Taos, New Mexico, are still at least partially occupied today.

A NEW MEXICO LIGHTNING MAN Scattered in the foreground of our Cliff Palace photograph are two dozen large circular semisubterranean structures, called *kivas,* which once were roofed over and entered with a ladder through a hole in the flat roof. These chambers were (and remain) the spiritual centers of native Southwest life, male council houses where ritual regalia are stored and private rituals and preparations for public ceremonies take place.

Between 1300 and 1500, the Anasazi decorated their kivas with elaborate mural paintings representing deities associated with agricultural fertility. According to their descendants, the present-day Hopi and Zuñi, the detail of the Kuaua Pueblo mural shown here (FIG. **14-31**) depicts a "lightning man" on the left side. Fish and eagle images (associated with rain) appear on the right side. Seeds, a lightning bolt, and a rainbow stream from the eagle's mouth. All of these figures are associated with the fertility of the earth and the life-giving properties of the seasonal rains, a constant preoccupation of Southwest farmers.

The Anasazi did not disappear but gradually evolved into the various Pueblo peoples who still live in Arizona, New Mexico, Colorado, and Utah. They continue to speak their native languages, to practice deeply rooted rituals, and to make pottery in the traditional manner (see "Native American Artists," Chapter 30, page 953). Today, collectors all over the world highly prize native arts from the Southwest—whether ceramics, jewelry, weaving, or basketry.

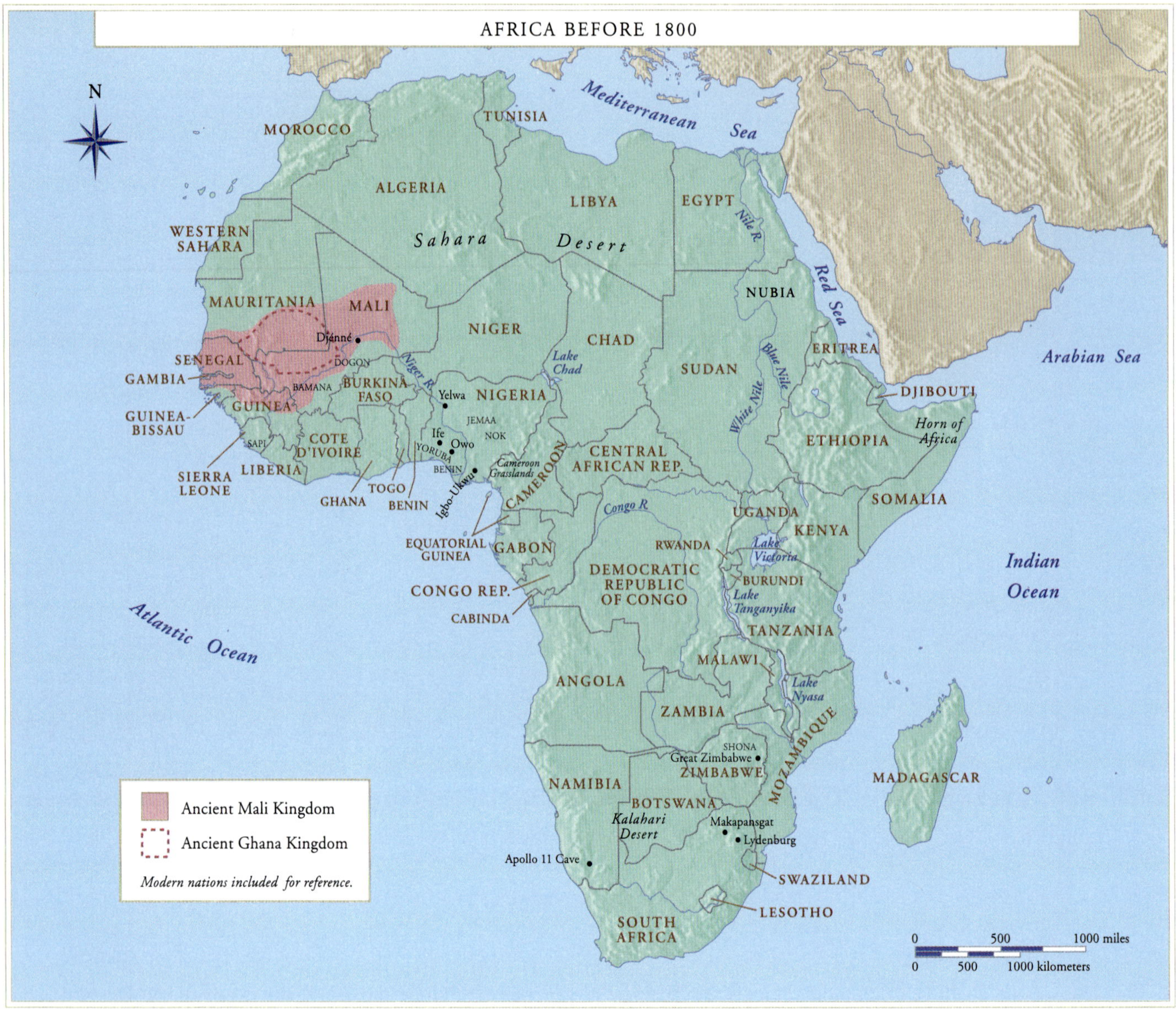

AFRICA BEFORE 1800

A map of Africa showing modern nations, with the Ancient Mali Kingdom (shaded) and Ancient Ghana Kingdom (dashed outline) highlighted. Sites labeled include Djénné, Dogon, Bamana, Yelwa, Jemaa, Nok, Ife, Owo, Yoruba, Benin, Igbo-Ukwu, Sapi, Cameroon Grasslands, Great Zimbabwe, Shona, Makapansgat, Lydenburg, and Apollo 11 Cave.

Legend:
- Ancient Mali Kingdom
- Ancient Ghana Kingdom

Modern nations included for reference.

	500 B.C.	A.D. 200	500	800	1000
NIGERIA	NOK			IGBO-UKWU	IFE
MALI AND SIERRA LEONE					DJENNE
SOUTH AFRICA AND ZIMBABWE			LYDENBURG		GREAT ZIMBABWE

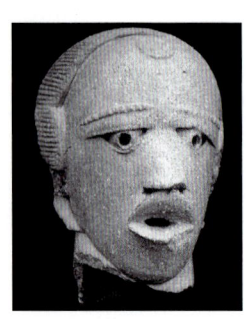

Nok head
fifth century B.C.

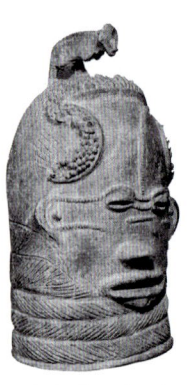

Lydenburg head
sixth–eighth century

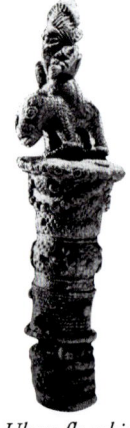

Igbo-Ukwu fly-whisk hilt
ninth–tenth century

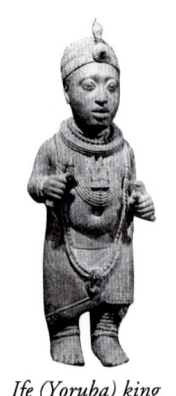

Ife (Yoruba) king
eleventh–twelfth century

First sub-Saharan ceramics, 500 B.C.–A.D. 200

Kingdom of Ghana, sixth–late eleventh century

First copper-alloy castings, 820–1000

SOUTH OF THE SAHARA

EARLY AFRICAN ART

1200		1400		1600		1800
BENIN						
		SAPI				

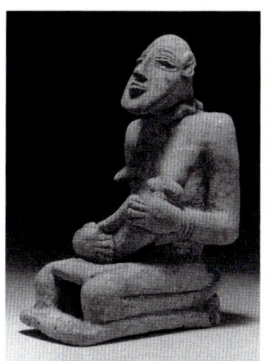

*Djenne Mother and child
eleventh–fourteenth century*

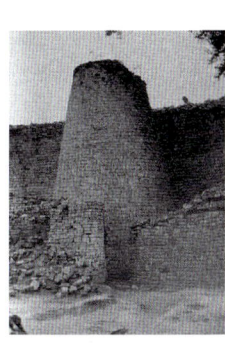

*Conical tower, Great
Zimbabwe, fifteenth century*

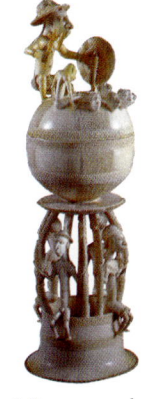

*Sapi-Portugese saltcellar
fifteenth–sixteenth century*

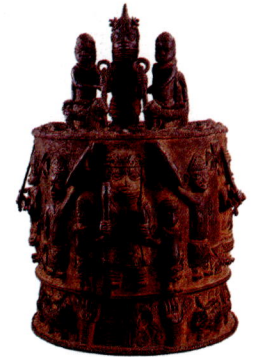

*Benin altar of the hand
seventeenth–eighteenth century*

Kingdom of Mali, early eleventh–
late fifteenth century

European contact in West and central Africa, ca. 1480–1510

THE ARTS OF AFRICA

GEOGRAPHY AND POPULATION   Vastly different topographical and ecological zones characterize Africa. Parched deserts occupy northern and southern regions, high mountains rise in the east, and lush river valleys dot the continent. Three great rivers—the Niger, the Congo (formerly called the Zaire), and the Nile, with their tributaries—support varied agricultural economies and large settled populations. Huge tracts of grassland serve agriculture or provide pasture for the animals of nomadic and semisedentary herding peoples, who reckon wealth by the size of their herds. Fishermen harvest the oceans and rivers, and some relatively small groups still prefer to hunt and gather their foods, even though they (and the herders) know about raising crops in gardens.

Hundreds of distinct ethnic, cultural, and linguistic groups, often, but inaccurately, called "tribes," long have inhabited the enormous African continent. Currently comprising the population of more than fifty-two nations, such groups historically have ranged in size from a few thousand to several million people. Groups of elders often governed smaller groups, while larger populations sometimes have joined with other ethnicities within a centralized state, as in ancient Egypt. Sometimes, as among the Yoruba, a single ethnic group has been divided for centuries into quite autonomous kingdoms.

CORE BELIEFS, ART, AND RITUAL   Within this great variety of African peoples, many share a matrix of core beliefs and practices, some dating back to ancient Egypt (see Chapter 3). This matrix includes extreme conservatism in honoring ancestrally established conventions, a profound orientation toward the spiritual in preparation for reward in the afterlife, and a tendency to elevate rulers to divine status. All of these factors have given rise to richly expressive art traditions throughout the continent. Much African sculpture demonstrates a preference for timeless stylized images, often presented without facial expression or movement. Africans also have perpetuated a love for festivals, occasions for presenting symbols of statecraft and religion through the skillful performance of costumed dancers, acrobats, musicians, and masqueraders.

THE RANGE OF AFRICAN ARTS   Over the millennia African peoples have created a vast array of visually expressive forms (see "The Role of Art in Africa and the Chronology Problem," page 417). Of numerous types, materials, and technologies, these arts range from prehistoric rock images and ceramic sculptures, made well before Christ's time, to today's cement sculptures and urban murals. Textiles, jewelry, scarification, and painting normally adorn individuals. Nations, religious organizations, and families commission architecture, often finely embellished, while artists also continue to produce pottery, furniture, and shrine objects. The larger men's or women's groups and even whole communities sponsor shrines and their architectural settings. The arts of masquerade and festival incorporate large numbers of objects essential to creating and expressing meaning in these public performances.

ART AND THE AFRICAN WORLDVIEW   Africa's visual arts encode ideas central to the ideologies and worldviews of African peoples. Although Islamic peoples in West Africa have been reading and writing Arabic since at least the twelfth century, many sub-Saharan Africans were nonliterate in the Western sense until the past few generations. Among current nonliterate groups, an art object carries a heavier burden of significance, because it replaces rather than supplements written text. Some art refers to or displays information—revealing or concealing it—while in other works the object itself is an ideological instrument, a value with no real equivalent. Art, then, helps define and create culture. It is integral to African life and thought rather than serving only as adornment.

All the hundreds of ethnic groups in Africa, speaking as many mutually unintelligible languages, made visual arts that differ according to economy and lifestyle, the materials available to them, and the specific iconography reflecting their values. Herders emphasize the arts of personal adornment. Early hunters and gatherers made many of the *pictographs* (pictures representing words or ideas) and *petroglyphs* (pictures on rock surfaces) found scattered across the continent. Farming peoples who live in settled communities have always been the major wood and clay sculptors and metalsmiths, and it is the art of these agriculturists that is stressed here.

AFRICA'S EARLIEST ART   Thousands of petroglyphs and pictographs found in hundreds of sites across the continent constitute the earliest known African art. Some painted animals from the Apollo 11 Cave in Namibia (see FIG. 1-2) date to perhaps as long ago as twenty-five thousand years, earlier than all but the oldest Paleolithic art of Europe (see Chapter 1). Since humankind apparently originated in Africa, the world's earliest art may yet be discovered there as well. The greatest concentrations of rock art are in now-dry desert regions—the Sahara to the north, the Horn in the east, and the Kalahari to the south—as well as in caves and on rock outcroppings in Namibia and South Africa. Probably because rock artists were more often herders or hunter-gatherers than farmers, these are precisely *not* the areas where most African sculpture is found. Accurately naturalistic renderings on rock surfaces show animals and humans in many different positions and activities, singly or in groups and stationary or in motion. Most of these works date to within the past four to five thousand years or slightly older and provide a rich record of the environment and of human and animal activities.

Although both precise dating and full understanding of meanings are problematic for much rock art, a considerable literature exists that describes, analyzes, and interprets the varied human and animal activities shown, as well as the evidently symbolic, more abstract patterns. Overall meanings probably coincide with those of the later arts (mostly sculpture) of agricultural areas—references to ideas and rituals about the origin, survival, and continuity of human populations.

NIGERIA

Nok Art (500 B.C.–A.D. 200)

TERRACOTTA SCULPTURES   Outside Egypt and neighboring ancient Nubia, the earliest African sculpture in the round has been found at several Nigerian archeological

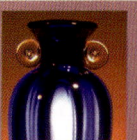

The Role of Art in Africa and the Chronology Problem

It is clear most African peoples make no distinction between "fine" and "applied" art or crafts, as is commonly the case in Europe. Until recently, too, most African peoples had not isolated visual arts into a distinct conceptual category, as suggested by the absence of a word in most African languages that translates accurately into the English word *art*. This realization connects with other issues regarding these arts, such as the importance of contexts to their understanding, the variable viewpoints of commentators, and distinctions between local African interpretations and those of outsiders. And because the arts of sub-Saharan Africa (south of the Sahara Desert) are usually unlabeled, unsigned, and undated, a central problem in organizing the vast array of African artworks is the absence of a secure chronology.

Some African cultures have left written documents that help date their artworks, even when their methods of measuring time differ from those used today. Other cultures, such as the Benin kingdom, preserve complex oral records of past events historians can check against the accounts of early travelers who visited the kingdom and recorded their observations (see "The King's Compound in Benin," Chapter 32, page 987). Where such documentation is fragmentary or unavailable, art historians sometimes try to establish chronology from an object's style, determining what sorts of changes occurred over time to forms of a similar type.

Interpretive techniques such as contextual analyses and scientific techniques such as radiocarbon dating and thermoluminescence may supplement these other kinds of dating. Archeologists use contextual analyses to help date archeological excavations. *Radiocarbon dating* refers to measuring the decay rate of carbon isotopes in organic matter to provide dates for organic materials such as wood, fiber, and ivory. *Thermoluminescence* is a method of dating amounts of radiation found within the clay of ceramic or sculptural forms, as well as in the clay cores from metal castings. Although a comprehensive history of African art remains to be written, important historical information is available for many genres and regions.

---

sites collectively designated the Nok culture. Named after one of the places where such terracotta sculptures were first discovered, Nok sites date between 500 B.C. and A.D. 200. Since their discovery in 1928 and after the 1940s, many dozens of Nok-style human and animal heads and figures have been found during tin mining operations, as well as in archeological excavations.

A representative fifth-century B.C. Nok terracotta head from a site named Jemaa (FIG. **15-1**) depicts a very expressive face with large pupils and parted lips, as if issuing a sound. The sculptor may have pierced the eyes, mouth, and ear holes to a hollow center to help equalize the clay's heating during the firing process. The swept-back hairstyle with deeply carved grooves and the raised eyebrows, along with the deeply cut triangular eyes, show that the sculptor carved some details of the head while modeling the whole. A proposed earlier artistic tradition of wood carving that has not survived archeologically may explain the lack of any known art tradition leading to the Nok culture's highly sophisticated terracotta sculptures. Perhaps a more centrally organized courtly tradition caused a shift from wood sculpture to the more permanent terracotta medium.

Recently, numerous Nok-style pieces have left Nigeria through an illegal market economy. These works lack source information and the geologic strata data from proper archeological excavation that might shed more light on Nok development (see "Archeology, Art History and the Art Market," Chapter 4, page 81, for a similar case in prehistoric Greece). At a site called Yelwa, northwest of Nok, dated to around the eighth century, a post-Nok style of terracotta sculpture has been found that extends the Nok style's influences into the late first millenium. Some scholars have noticed stylistic affinities between Nok terracottas and the arts of Ife, Benin, and the more recent pre- and post-colonial sculptures of the Yoruba. Researchers do not yet agree on the function of these objects, but a ritual context is more likely than a simply decorative one.

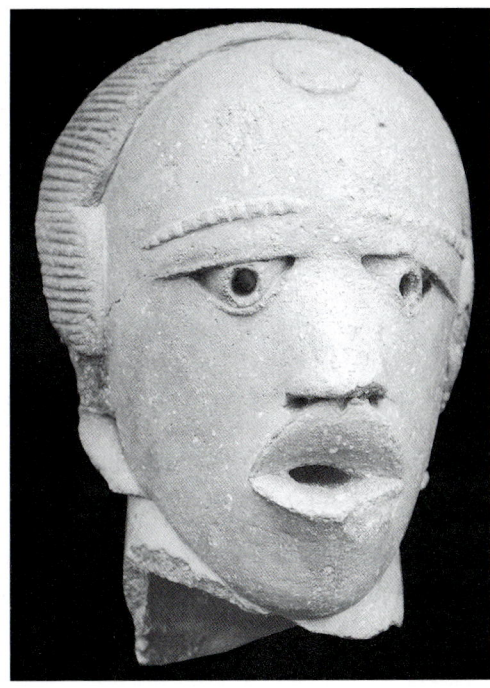

15-1 Nok head, from Jemaa, Nigeria, fifth century B.C. Terracotta, 9 $\frac{13}{16}$″ high. National Museum, Lagos.

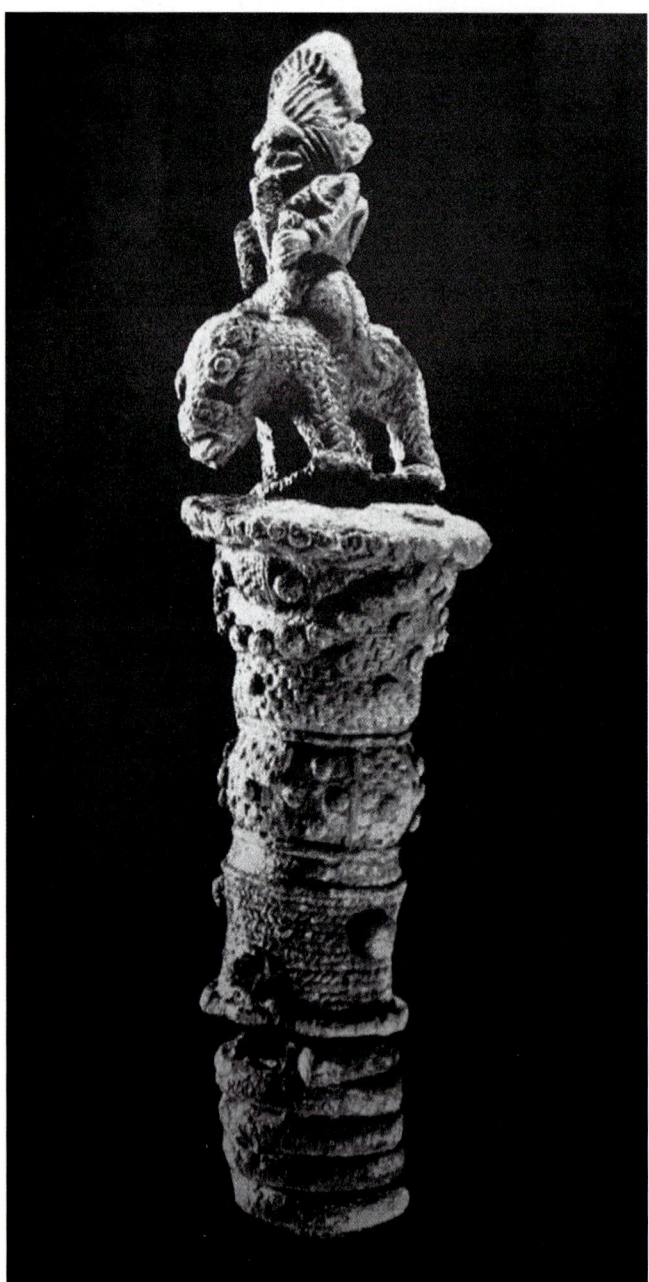

15-2   Equestrian figure on fly-whisk hilt, from Igbo-Ukwu, Nigeria, ninth to tenth century. Copper-alloy bronze, figure $6\frac{3}{16}''$ high. National Museum, Lagos.

Igbo-Ukwu Art (Ninth–Tenth Centuries)

EARLY BRONZE-CASTING   By the ninth century, a West African bronze-casting tradition of great sophistication had developed, as dozens of refined and varied objects excavated near Igbo-Ukwu in southeastern Nigeria indicate. Cast in an extremely intricate style, the copper, bronze, and iron artifacts included basins, bowls, altar stands, staffs, swords, scabbards, knives, and pendants. In the burial of a ruler at a site called Igbo-Richard, the grave goods consisted of numerous prestige objects—copper anklets, armlets, roundels, raised spiral ornaments, a strap, and a fan handle. The tomb also contained such objects as three elephant tusks, a human skull, a beaded armlet, a crown, and a bronze leopard's skull supported on a copper rod. These are the earliest metal castings known from regions south of the Sahara.

A lost-wax cast bronze equestrian figure fly-whisk hilt from Igbo-Ukwu (FIG. **15-2**) has two distinct parts. This casting method is similar to that used almost fifteen hundred years before in the ancient Mediterranean and in the Near East (see "Hollow-Casting Life-Size Bronze Statues," Chapter 5, page 124). The sculpture's upper section comprises a figure seated on a small horselike animal, and the lower section consists of an elaborately embellished flared handle with beaded and threadlike patterns adorning its surface. This figure is the earliest archeologically documented example of an equestrian figure in sub-Saharan African sculpture. The facial stripes on the human figure probably represent status-oriented marks of leadership.

Ife Art (Eleventh–Fifteenth Centuries)

By the eleventh and twelfth centuries, a very naturalistic style had appeared at Ife in western Nigeria, which long has been considered the cradle of Yoruba culture and civilization, for the Yoruba the place where the gods created the universe. Ife origin stories also account for a line of divine Yoruba rulers extending from the mythical past to the twentieth century.

IMAGES OF DIVINE KINGS   An early work, cast in a zinc-brass alloy (FIG. **15-3**), undoubtedly represents a ruler.

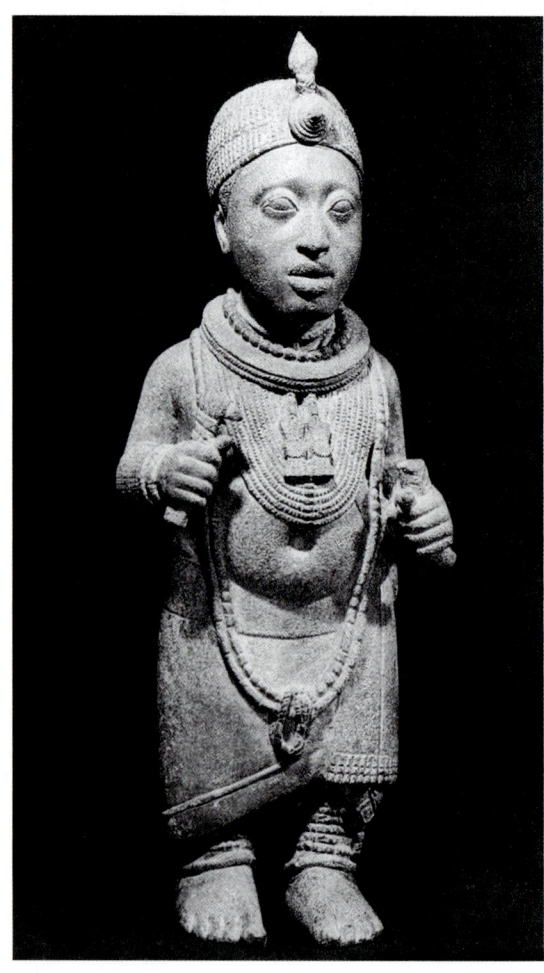

15-3   King, from Ife, Nigeria, eleventh to twelfth century. Zinc brass, $1'\,6\frac{1}{2}''$ high. Ife Museum, Ife.

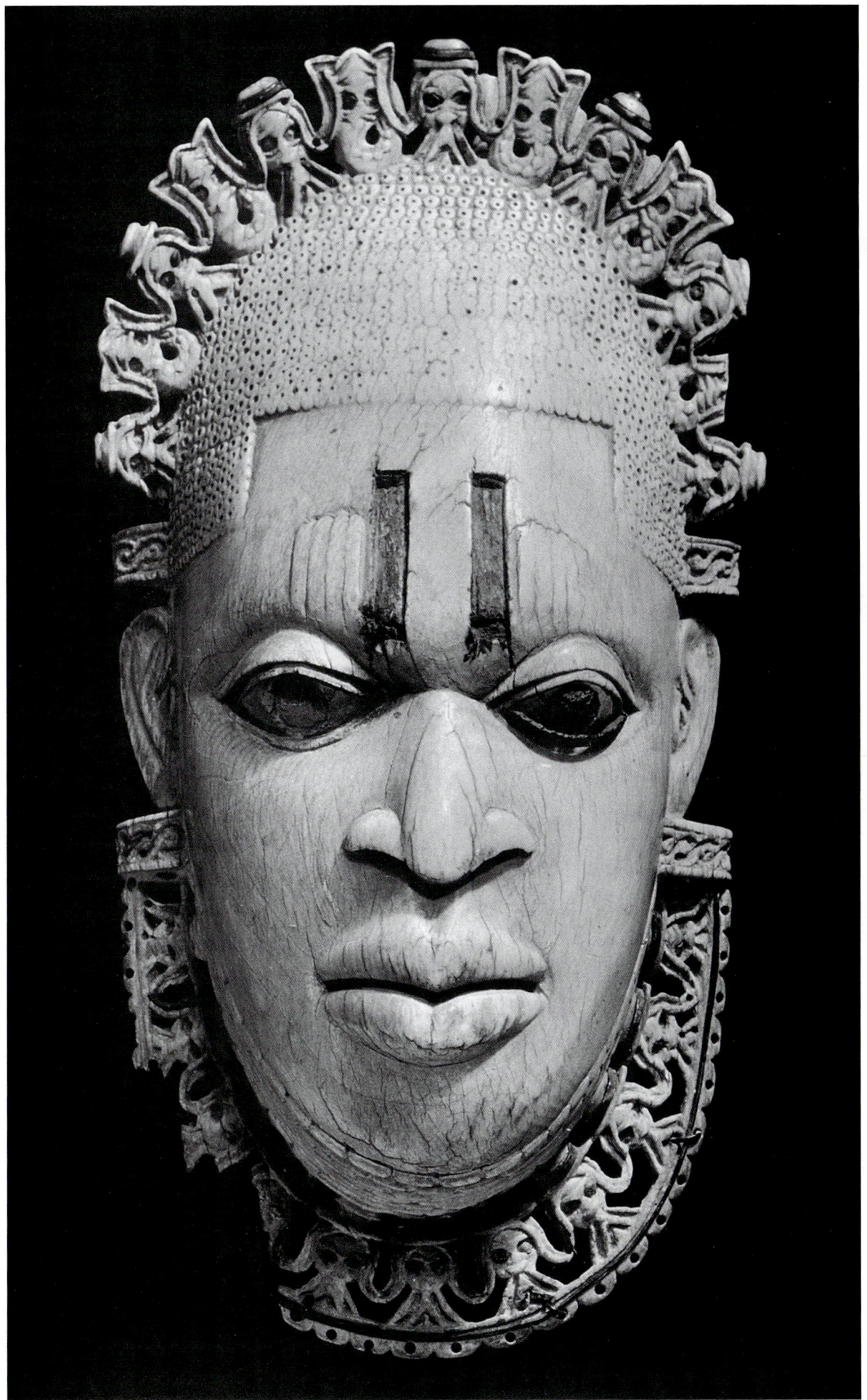

15-4   Ivory belt mask of a Queen Mother, from Benin, Nigeria, mid-sixteenth century. Ivory and iron, 9 $\frac{3}{8}$″ high. Metropolitan Museum of Art, New York (Michael C. Rockefeller Memorial Collection, gift of Nelson A. Rockefeller).

This figure, unlike most later African wood sculpture, shows fleshlike modeling, a kind of idealized naturalism in the torso and head that approaches generalized portraiture. Its proportions are less lifelike, however, than they are ideological. For modern Yoruba, the head is the locus of wisdom, destiny, and the essence of being. Such ideas probably developed some eight hundred years ago but they remain an important part of modern Yoruba culture. The casting is fine, and it accurately records precise details of the heavily beaded costume, crown, and jewelry worn by both ancient and contemporary kings in Ife and other Yoruba city-states. Ife was the source of dozens of accomplished, detailed, and sometimes realistic sculptures of heads, full figures, and animals, principally in terracotta or copper alloys. These and related works from the Yoruba kingdom of Owo, southeast of Ife, undoubtedly served in rituals supporting divine kingship.

Benin Art (Thirteenth–Eighteenth Centuries)

The Benin kingdom was established in the thirteenth century. Though the kingdom no longer exists, Benin City is today the capital of Edo State in Nigeria. By observing current rituals and regalia and talking with elderly specialists who understand the significance of these cultural features, researchers continue to learn about Benin royal art. Numerous historical and ritual ties existed between the divine kings of Ife and those of Benin, and these groups also established mutually beneficial contacts with Portuguese traders in the 1470s. Benin artists have produced many complex, finely cast copper-alloy sculptures, as well as pieces in ivory, wood, ceramic, and wrought-iron. Royalty commissioned (and sometimes still do) cast-metal works and ivory carvings from guilds of highly trained professionals. The hereditary *oba,* or divine king, and his court still use these items, also dispensing them as royal favors to title holders and other chiefs.

THE QUEEN MOTHER   In the sixteenth century, the Portuguese served in a military capacity in the army of Benin's Oba Esigie (r. ca. 1504–1550) and helped expand the Benin kingdom. Esigie's mother, Idia, helped him in warfare, and in return he created the title of Iy'oba (Queen Mother) for her and built her a separate palace and court. A mid-sixteenth-century ivory belt mask (FIG. **15-4**), used either to secure a wrapping of clothing or worn as a hip mask, probably represents Idia. The mask also contains symbolic references to Benin's trade and diplomatic relationships with the Portuguese and to the Iy'oba's link to Olokun, god of the sea. Interspersed in the front row of her hairstyle, frontally placed Portuguese heads each wear long hair and a mustache, beard, and helmet. The Benin culture probably associated the Portuguese, with their large ships, powerful weapons, and wealth in metals, with Olokun. Mudfish, which have barbels like catfish, symbolically represented Olokun and, along with other animals prevalent in Benin ritual practices, often served as sacrificial offerings.

A ROYAL ALTAR OF THE HAND   Termed an *ikegobo,* a Benin brass casting (FIG. **15-5**), most likely dating from the seventeenth or eighteenth century, comes from an oba's ancestral altar. This work features symmetrical hierarchical compositions centered on the dominant divine king, seen on both the cylinder's top and side. The composition is similar to that of the Benin royal plaque discussed in the Introduction (see FIG. Intro-16). Both use a hierarchy of scale, or the enlarging of elements considered most important. The two images of the Benin king, centrally placed both in the composition on top and directly below on the side, show him as the largest figure. The individuals depicted in the top figure group, cast nearly as freestanding figures, include the king, attendants, and leopards. The lower two sculptural zones, cast in varied levels of low to high relief, emphasize the king's importance by both his size and his positioning, flanked by and centered among his smaller attendants. The casting technique used—the lost-wax method—is still practiced in Benin today and was used elsewhere by cultures in what is now Nigeria some seven hundred years earlier.

At such personal altars, high-ranking officials, including the king, made sacrifices to their own powers of accomplishment—symbolized by the arm and hand. The altar involves power, both in the ritual's anticipated outcome and in the shrine's iconography. The inclusion of leopards on the top and around the base, along with elephant heads and crocodiles (not visible here), symbolizes this power. These animals, common in Benin arts, are also kings in their respective realms. The tame leopards flanking the king on top refer to his dominance over even this king of the wilds and thus indicate his superhuman capacities.

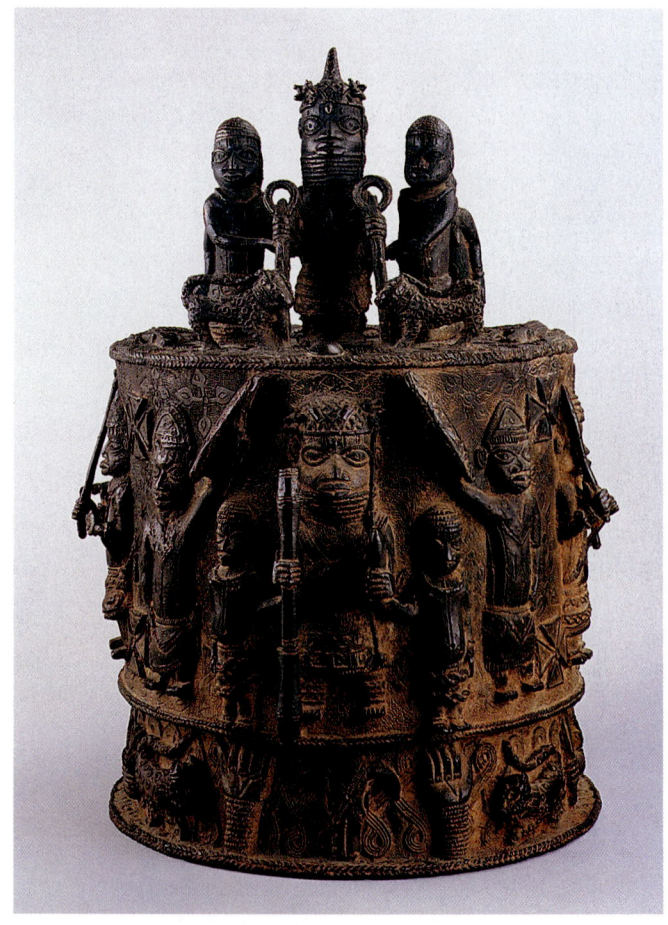

15-5   Altar of the hand, from Benin, Nigeria, seventeenth to eighteenth century(?). Bronze, 1′ 5½″ high. British Museum, London.

MALI

Djenne Art (Eleventh–Fifteenth Centuries)

Numerous ceramic (and some copper-alloy) images also have been recovered from tombs at Djenne and other sites in the inland delta of the Niger River, northwest of Nigeria in the modern nation of Mali. The dates of these sculptures fall between 1000 and 1468, roughly contemporary to the preserved artworks from the Yoruba kingdoms of Ife and Owo. This period also overlaps with two of West Africa's most important medieval empires, ancient Ghana (approximately sixth through late eleventh centuries) and Mali (early thirteenth through late fifteenth centuries). The modern nation-states took their names from these empires.

GENDER ROLES IN LIFE AND ART A terracotta statuette of a mother and child from Djenne in the inland delta (FIG. **15-6**) probably attests to gender-specific ideal roles assigned to women and men within ancient Malian societies. Women's roles involved nurturing and domestic activities, while men performed the duties of warrior/hunter and protector. Grave offerings and most likely shrine figures, such fired clay images as this include humans and animals, many in naturalistic poses and others in stiffer, more formal postures. Unfortunately, the vast majority of these terracotta figures have come to light from uncontrolled digging. Therefore, much pertinent contextual information about

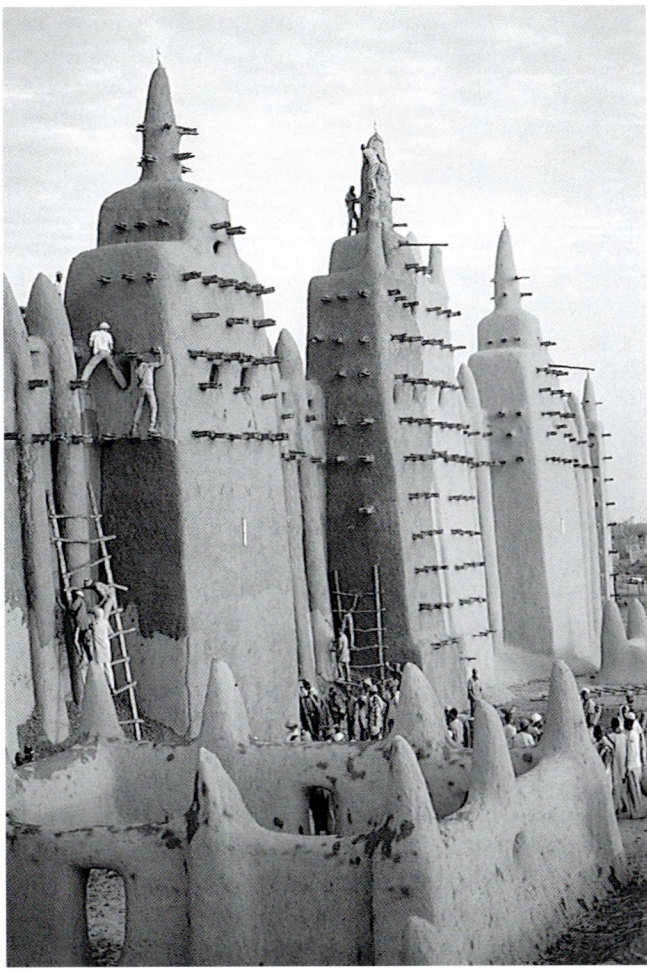

15-7 Eastern facade of Friday Mosque, Djenne, Mali, thirteenth century, rebuilt in 1906–1907.

them has been lost. Their poses, forms, and pairings suggest meanings still found in shrine art forms today among the Dogon and Bamana peoples of Mali (including the gender-specific roles mentioned and ancestral mother/father), who may have historical ties to the earlier Djenne culture (see Chapter 32).

MONUMENTAL ARCHITECTURE Over the past millennium, at least, African peoples have developed countless impressive architectural styles and building types. These range from Ethiopia's twelfth-century stone-cut churches and Mali's adobe-brick mosques from the same period and later to many sculptural and finely painted secular and sacred adobe structures still built across the West African savanna. They also include the impressive palace structures with tall carved posts and lofty thatched roofs of Cameroon kingdoms. Few early buildings survive south of the Sahara, however, because unfired adobe was so often the building material of choice. Unless well maintained, such structures deteriorate rapidly in heavy rains.

ISLAM IN MALI An exceptional surviving monumental structure is the Friday Mosque at Djenne (FIG. **15-7**), first built in the thirteenth century and still in active use. The present structure, reconstructed in 1906–1907, supposedly in the style of the first of two earlier mosques (dating to the thirteenth century) constructed on the site, boasts a strongly vertical emphasis. Three symmetrically balanced adobe towers and tall,

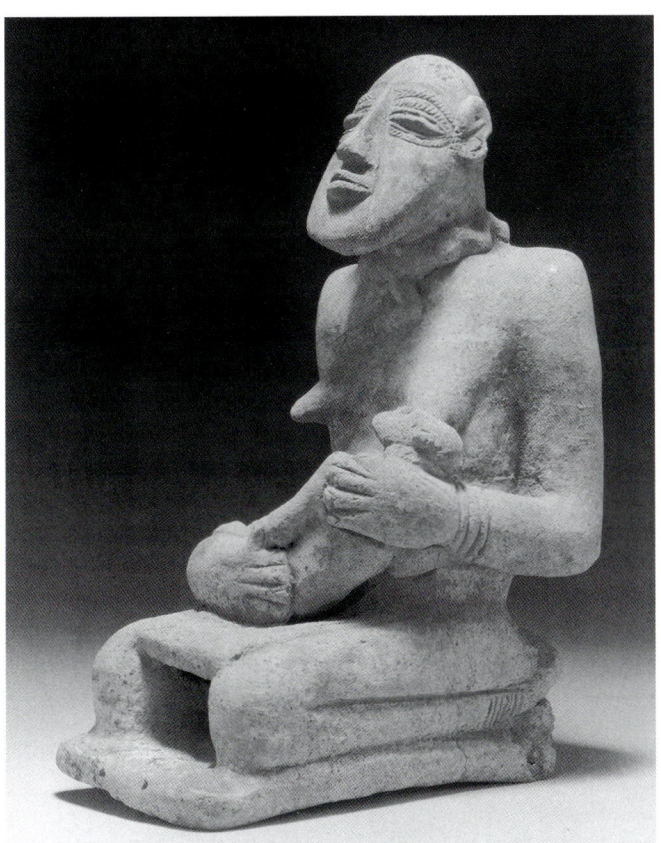

15-6 Mother and child, from Djenne, Mali, eleventh to fourteenth century. Terracotta, 11″ high. University of Iowa Museum of Art, Iowa City (Stanley Collection).

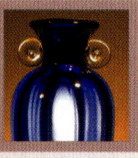

Sapi-Portuguese Ivories
A Hybrid Art Form[1]

Initial contact between Portuguese explorers and traders and West and central African groups occurred in the second half of the fifteenth century. In the first century and a half after contact, ivories became an important African export art destined for elite households and collections in Europe. Three African ethnic groups in three different regions—the Sapi of Sierra Leone, the Bini of Nigeria, and the Kongo of the lower Congo River in the Democratic Republic of the Congo (formerly Zaire)—exported ivory objects. (For information on ivory carving technique, see "Ivory Carving in Antiquity and the Early Middle Ages," Chapter 11, page 322.)

Based on information culled from archival documents, iconographic elements, and stylistic traits, researchers have concluded sculptors made the Sapi-Portuguese ivories from about 1490 to 1530. Nearly one hundred finely crafted objects have survived, including saltcellars, *pyxides* (small boxes used in church ceremonies), spoons, forks, dagger or knife handles, and hunting horns, or *oliphants*. With lids and bases carved with human and animal images in low to high relief, the saltcellars (FIG. 15-9) and pyxides were generally quite elaborate vessels. Some of the figures depicted, although African in countenance, derive their postures or compositional layouts from Christian themes, such as the Virgin and Child, the Crucifixion, or Christ's descent from the cross.

Jewish subjects of Christian significance (for example, Daniel in the lion's den and the Three Hebrews in the fiery furnace; see "Jewish Subjects in Christian Art," Chapter 11, page 305) also appear. African themes depicted include a warrior with shield riding an elephant, an executioner and his victims (FIG. 15-9), a seated man with a pipe, and a man seated on a tripod chair. Secondary male and female figures (most representing Africans) and a host of African animals, such as crocodiles, serpents, and dogs, play prominent roles.

The iconography of most of the known hunting horns features European narrative hunting scenes in low relief. In addition, the carvers commonly presented the coats of arms of ruling families on these horns, as well as Christian religious mottos such as "Hail Mary full of grace" and "Hope in God." Other European motifs include fantastic animals such as unicorns, harpies, and griffins. Many of the high-relief images found on the saltcellars are European in origin, whereas images of rulers and warriors appear African in origin and character. In contrast, most of the narrative imagery carved on the hunting horns seems derived from compositions found on European tapestries and in illustrated books.

[1] E. Bassini and W. Fagg, *Africa and the Renaissance: Art in Ivory* (New York: Center for African Art, 1988).

slender engaged columns combine to create majestic rhythms across the mosque's eastern front. This facade also features protruding beams that are partly structural and practical and partly decorative. The beams serve as perches for workers (visible in FIG. 15–7) undertaking the essential recoating of sacred clay on the exterior that occurs during an annual festival. Although this mosque is larger and grander in scale than the area's civic and domestic architecture, many of its stately features duplicate those elsewhere in these urban environments. In bygone centuries, the great Sudanic empires, such as ancient Ghana and Mali, now known best in oral traditions and from archeological excavations, embraced this architectural style.

SIERRA LEONE

Sapi Art (Fifteenth–Sixteenth Centuries)

During the fifteenth and sixteenth centuries, the Sapi people in Sierra Leone, on the Atlantic coast of West Africa, created stone figures *(nomoli)* that may have served as objects of worship in ancestral memorial shrines. The Sapi were likely ancestors of some of the modern peoples of Guinea and Sierra Leone, whose sculpture still displays stylistic affinities with the earlier group's art.

A SAPI WARRIOR Carved of serpentine, one example (FIG. **15-8**), probably representing a warrior, is notable for its

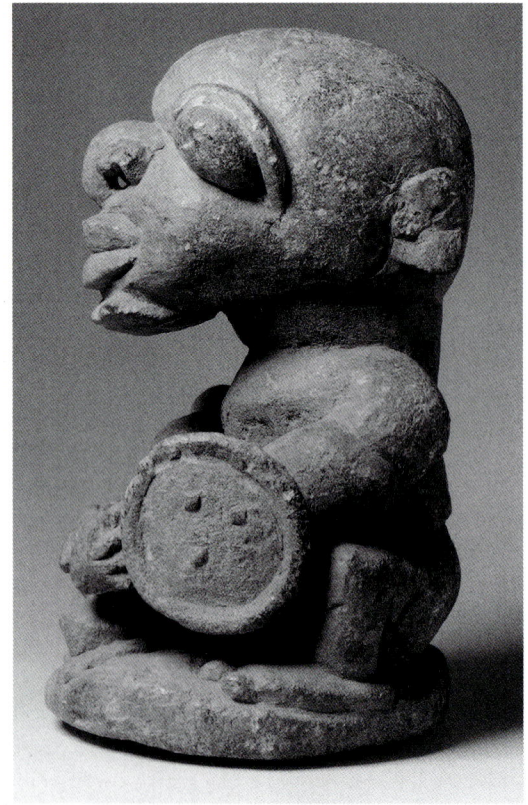

15-8 Sapi warrior, from Sierra Leone, fifteenth century. Serpentine, 7½″ high. Historisches Museum, Bern.

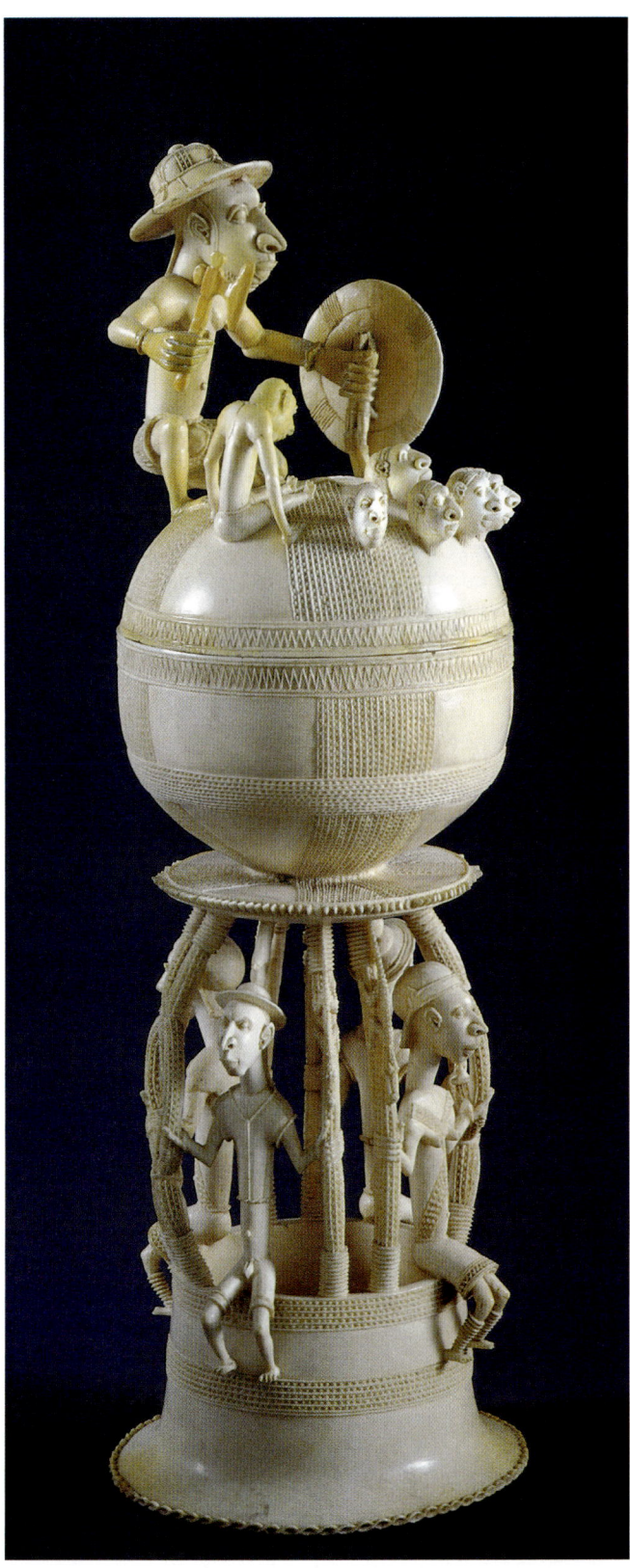

15-9 MASTER OF THE SYMBOLIC EXECUTION, saltcellar, Sapi-Portuguese, from Sierra Leone, fifteenth to sixteenth century. Ivory, $1' 4\frac{7}{8}''$ high. Museo Nazionale Preistorico e Etnografico Luigi Pigorini, Rome.

SAPI ART FOR EUROPEAN PATRONS During the late fifteenth and early sixteenth centuries, Sapi artists also created numerous skillfully crafted ivory objects for export to the wealthy classes of Europe. These items included delicate spoons and forks, *oliphants* (hunting horns), and elaborate saltcellars (containers for salt and spices). Most of these objects have been preserved in royal collections, where scholars study them today as unique hybrid objects of both African and European culture from a period of early contact and trade between the two peoples (see "Sapi-Portuguese Ivories: A Hybrid Art Form," page 422).

One saltcellar (FIG. **15-9**), standing just more than sixteen inches high, depicts an extraordinary execution scene. A kneeling figure with a shield in one hand holds an axe in the other hand over another sitting figure about to lose his head. On the ground before the executioner, six severed heads (five visible here) grimly testify to the executioner's power. A double zigzag line marks the division of the globular container's lid from the vessel below. This entire form rests on a circular platform held up by slender rods adorned with crocodile images. Two male and two female figures sit between these rods. The men wear European-style pants, and the women wear skirts, but the women have elaborate raised scarification patterns on their upper chests. The details and proportions of the heads and the scarification patterns on the female figures recall stylistic traits found on Sapi memorial figures from the same period.

Scholars have identified at least three artists' workshops active during the period from about 1500 to 1540, and they attribute about twenty-two saltcellars, or fragments thereof, to several artists in one of these workshops. The creator of this masterpiece is known as MASTER OF THE SYMBOLIC EXECUTION.

SOUTH AFRICA

Examining three art forms from two artistic traditions in southern Africa—specifically, in South Africa and Zimbabwe—enables comparison with the West African traditions just detailed. As noted previously, South African caves and rock outcroppings contain numerous examples of early rock art, but additional art forms also developed in South Africa and other southern African areas.

Lydenburg Art (Sixth–Eighth Centuries)

SOUTH AFRICA'S OLDEST SCULPTURES A terracotta head from Lydenburg (FIG. **15-10**) is one of seven recovered from that site and dated from the sixth to the eighth centuries, making it among the oldest sculptures so far discovered in southern Africa. The head (reconstructed from fragments) has a humanlike form, although its jarlike shape differs markedly from the sculptural form of the earlier Nok-style head from Jemaa (FIG. 15-1). Here, the artist created the eyes, ears, nose, and mouth by placing thin clay fillets over the head shape. The same method produced the raised scarification marks on the forehead and between the eyes and the ears. Incised marks define the neck's horizontal bands and some parts of the hair on the side and back of the head. Small clay points placed in a curving row along the front hairline create a raised coiffure effect. A small animal-like shape sits atop the head, although it is impossible to identify its species. Perhaps these heads originally served a ritual or commemorative function.

disproportionately large head with bulbous eyes, nose, and lips. The figure wears a circular war shield on his left arm and holds a smaller figure (its head missing) standing before him. The size differential and placement of these two figures imply a power relationship of superior (warrior/chief) versus inferior (vanquished or victim).

ZIMBABWE

Great Zimbabwe Art (Eleventh–Fifteenth Centuries)

RUINS OF A LOST EMPIRE   Perhaps the most famous southern African architecture is a complex of stone ruins at a major political center called Great Zimbabwe. At a site first occupied in the eleventh century, the still-standing walled enclosures date from about the late thirteenth century to the middle of the fifteenth century, when the Great Zimbabwe empire had a wide trade network. Finds of trade beads and pottery from Persia, the Near East, and China, along with copper and gold objects, show this was a prosperous trade center well before Europeans began their coastal voyaging in the late fifteenth century. Most archeologists and historians agree that the rulers at Great Zimbabwe and other nearby royal towns were ancestors of Zimbabwe's present Shona-speaking peoples.

Based on ethnographic information gathered from Portuguese accounts of the sixteenth to the early nineteenth centuries and from more recent studies of Shona customs, many scholars have tried to interpret the meanings of the buildings and artifacts found at Great Zimbabwe. Most agree the complex was a royal residence with special areas for the king (the royal hill complex), his wives and nobles, including an open

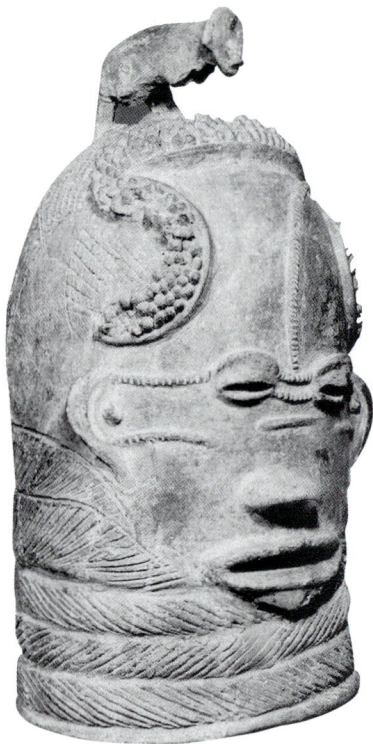

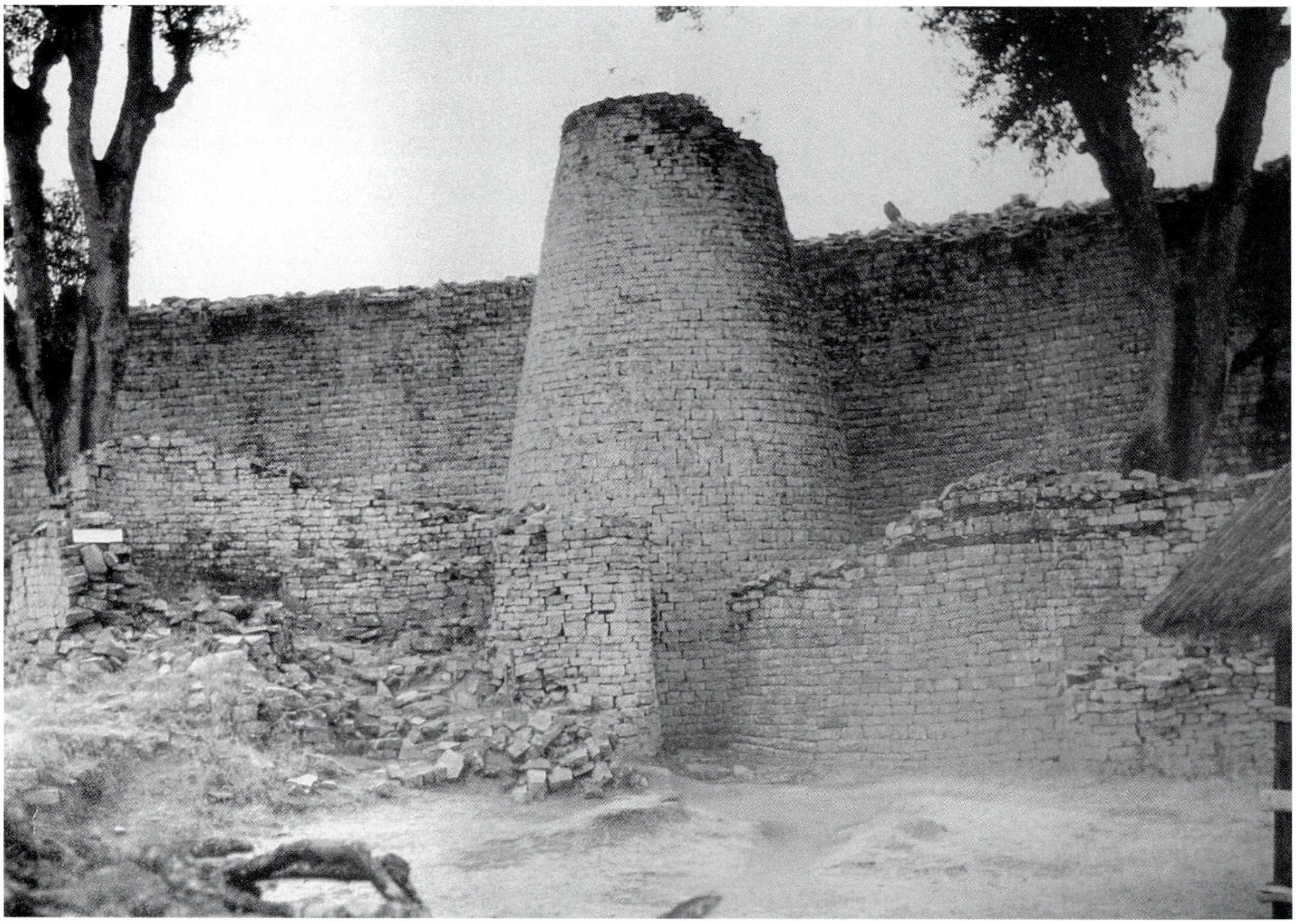

15-10   Head, from Lydenburg, South Africa, sixth to eighth century. Terracotta, 1′ 2 15/16″ high. South African Museum, Cape Town.

15-11   Conical tower, Great Zimbabwe, Zimbabwe, fifteenth century.

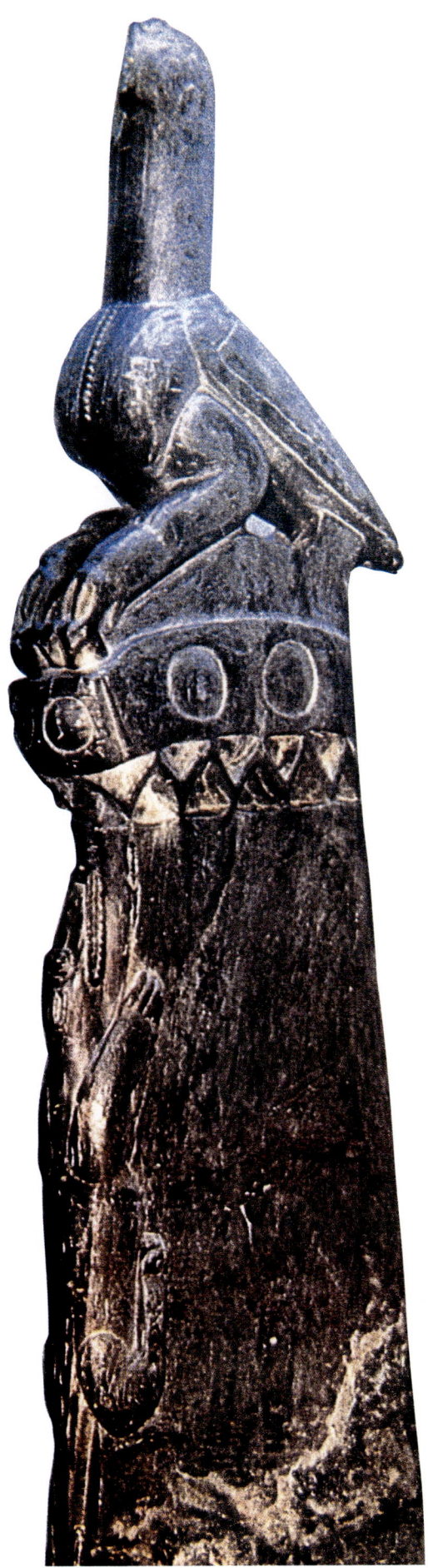

court for ceremonial gatherings. At the zenith of the empire's power, as many as eighteen thousand people may have lived in the area surrounding Great Zimbabwe, with most of the commoners living outside the enclosed structures reserved for royalty. Although actual habitations are gone, the remaining enclosures are unusual for their size and the excellence of their stonework. Some perimeter walls reach thirty feet high. One of these, known as the Great Enclosure, houses one large and several small conical stone towerlike structures (FIG. **15-11**). Scholars often have interpreted these symbolically as masculine (large) and feminine (small) forms, but their precise significance is unknown.

SOAPSTONE SCULPTURES OF BIRDS Explorations at Great Zimbabwe have yielded eight soapstone monoliths. Seven came from the royal hill complex and probably were set up as part of ritual shrines to the ancestors. The eighth soapstone bird monolith (FIG. **15-12**), found in an area now considered the ruler's first wife's ancestral shrine, stands several feet tall. Scholars have interpreted the seated bird on top as symbolizing the first wife's ancestors. (Ancestral spirits among the Shona take the form of birds, especially eagles, and are thought to communicate between the sky and the earth.) The crocodile on the front of the monolith may represent the wife's elder male ancestors, while the circles beneath the bird are called the "eyes of the crocodile" in Shona belief and represent, symbolically, elder female ancestors. The double- and single-chevron motifs represent young male and young female ancestors, respectively. The bird may represent some form of bird of prey, such as an eagle, although this and other bird sculptures from the site have feet with five humanlike toes, rather than an eagle's three-toed talons. The eagle and the crocodile may have symbolized previous rulers who would have acted as messengers between the living and the dead, as well as between the sky and the earth.

The art forms discussed in this chapter, usually made of durable materials such as fired terracotta, ivory, and cast metal (bronze or one of several copper alloys) have survived for many centuries. The complexity of many of these art forms suggests use in elite contexts such as kingship and courtly traditions. As noted, similarities with continuing and related historical traditions, such as those of the Ife-Yoruba and early Benin or contemporary Benin practices, have provided some insight into the possible meanings of these prehistoric and early historic art forms. The basis for understanding many of the art forms of later African art in sub-Saharan Africa (see Chapter 32) is firsthand study of African art traditions, which are more varied in terms of royal and nonroyal groups. The art forms also include a wider range of artistic materials and techniques, including wood carving, weaving, accumulative sculpture, and oil painting.

15-12 Bird with crocodile image on top of stone monolith, from Great Zimbabwe, Zimbabwe, fifteenth century. Soapstone, bird image 1′ 2½″ high. Great Zimbabwe Site Museum, Great Zimbabwe.

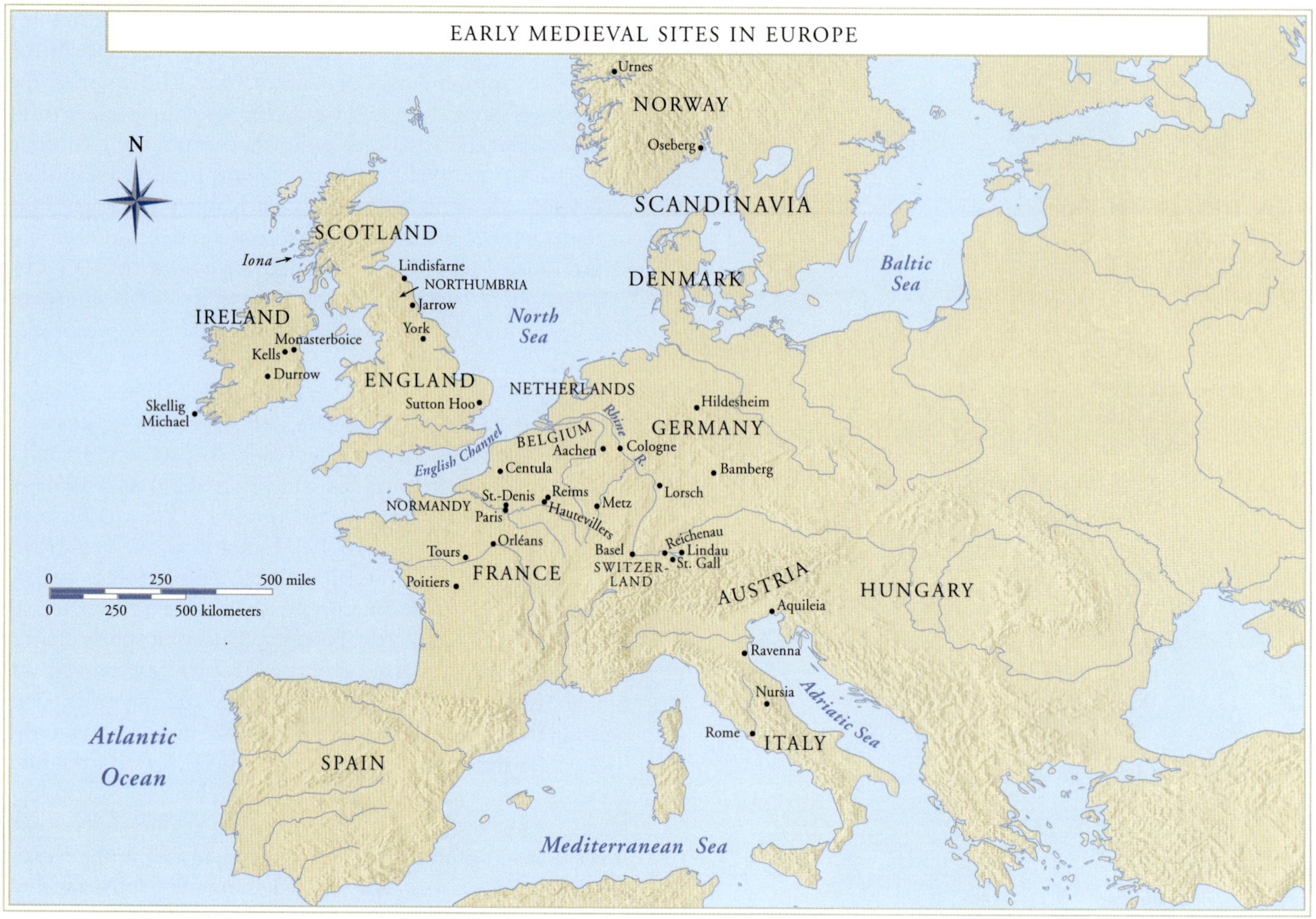

EARLY MEDIEVAL SITES IN EUROPE

Map showing Early Medieval sites in Europe including: Urnes, Oseberg (NORWAY); SCANDINAVIA; DENMARK; Baltic Sea; Iona, Lindisfarne, NORTHUMBRIA, Jarrow, York (SCOTLAND/ENGLAND); IRELAND, Monasterboice, Kells, Durrow, Skellig Michael; England, Sutton Hoo; North Sea; NETHERLANDS; Hildesheim, GERMANY, Cologne, Aachen, Bamberg, Lorsch (Rhine); BELGIUM, Centula; St.-Denis, Reims, Metz, Hautevillers, Paris, Orléans, Tours, Poitiers, NORMANDY, FRANCE; Basel, Reichenau, Lindau, St. Gall, SWITZERLAND; AUSTRIA, HUNGARY; Aquileia, Ravenna, Nursia, Rome, ITALY; Adriatic Sea; Atlantic Ocean; SPAIN; Mediterranean Sea

	476	768
FRANCE AND GERMANY	MEROVINGIAN	CAROLINGIAN
NORTHERN EUROPE	HIBERNO-SAXON PERIOD IN THE BRITISH ISLES, VIKING PERIOD IN SCANDINAVIA	

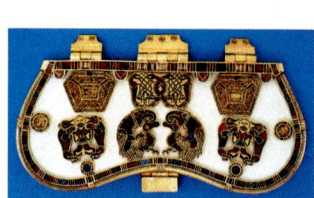

*Sutton Hoo purse cover
ca. 625*

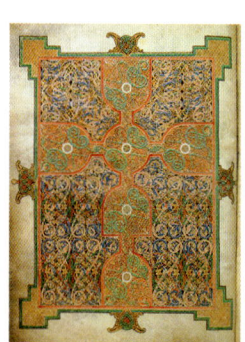

*Lindisfarne Gospels
ca. 698–721*

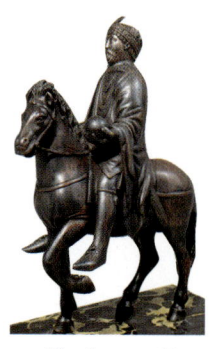

*Charlemagne(?)
early ninth century*

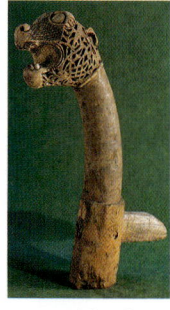

*Animal-head post
Oseberg ship
ca. 825*

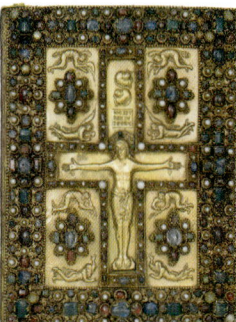

Lindau Gospels, ca. 870

End of Western Roman Empire, 476

Anglo-Saxons take over Roman Britain, ca. 480

Franks in Gaul (Merovingian dynasty), 482–768

Saint Benedict establishes Benedictine Rule for monasteries, 529

Muslims defeat Visigoths in Spain, 711

Charles Martel defeats Muslims at Poitiers, 732

Charlemagne, r. 768–814, crowned emperor in Rome, 800

Viking raids begin in Britain, 793

Louis the Pious, r. 814–840

Charles the Bald, r. 840–875

Cluniac order founded, 910

EUROPE AFTER THE FALL OF ROME

EARLY MEDIEVAL ART IN THE WEST

936		1000	1024	1050
OTTONIAN				

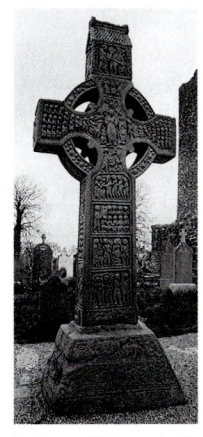

High Cross of Muiredach, 923

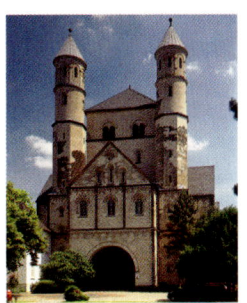

*Saint Pantaleon
Cologne, 966–980*

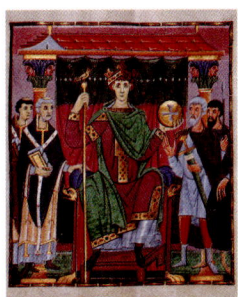

*Gospel Book of Otto III
997–1000*

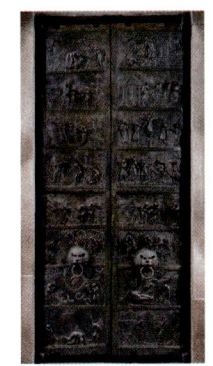

*Bronze doors, Saint Michael's
Hildesheim, 1015*

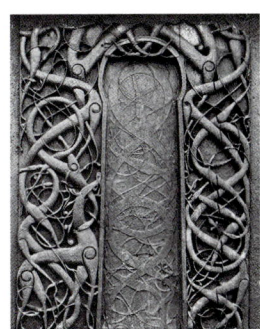

*Stave church, Urnes
ca. 1050–1070*

Otto I, r. 936–973, crowned emperor in Rome, 962

Otto II, r. 973–983; marries Byzantine princess Theophanu, 972

Otto III, r. 983–1002

Hugh Capet, king of France, r. 987–996

Bernward, bishop of Hildesheim, 993–1022

Henry II, r. 1002–1024, last Ottonian emperor

Edward the Confessor, Anglo-Saxon king of England, r. 1042–1066

MEDIEVAL EUROPE

THE ERA "IN BETWEEN"   Historians once referred to the thousand years (roughly 400 to 1400) between the dying Roman Empire's adoption of Christianity as its official religion and the rebirth (Renaissance) of interest in classical antiquity as the Dark Ages. For centuries people thought this long "interval"—between the ancient and what then was perceived as the beginning of the modern European world—was rough and uncivilized, barbarous in manners, superstitious in religion, and crude and primitive artistically. They viewed these centuries—the "Middle Ages"—as simply a blank between (in the middle of) two great civilizations.

As already shown, this judgment is far off the mark with respect to the Byzantine Empire, whose rulers always considered themselves heirs of the Roman Empire and whose artists not only created works of the highest quality but also frequently looked to the Greco-Roman tradition for inspiration. The equally negative assessment of the Middle Ages in western Europe also has been discredited. No longer do art historians consider this period a dark age devoid of invention, an era when—by classical and Renaissance standards—artists created only unsophisticated and inferior works. Historians and art historians now see these centuries with different eyes, perceiving their innovation and greatness. But the powerful force of tradition dictates that scholars continue to use the unfortunately negative term *Middle Ages* and its corresponding adjective *medieval.*

THE MEDIEVAL FUSION   Art historians date the early Middle Ages from about 500 to 1000—half a millennium of important artistic production. Early medieval civilization in western Europe represents a fusion of Christianity, the Greco-Roman heritage, and the vibrant yet very different culture of the Celtic-Germanic "barbarians," as the Greeks and Romans called the peoples who lived beyond the classical world's frontiers. Some of these so-called barbarians had, in fact, risen to prominent positions within the Roman army and government during the later Roman Empire. Others established their own areas of rule in western Europe, sometimes with Rome's approval, sometimes in opposition to imperial authority. In time these non-Romans merged with the citizens of the former Roman provinces and slowly developed political and social institutions that continued into modern times. Over the centuries a new order gradually replaced what had been the Roman Empire, resulting eventually in the foundation of today's European nations.

This period of momentous, if slow, change was characterized by countless struggles for power, not only among competing armies but also between secular and sacred authorities. The conflict between church and state is one of the distinguishing features of medieval European history and sets the West sharply apart from the Byzantine and Islamic worlds. In the West the Christian Church not only possessed extensive properties but also early on assumed major governmental responsibilities. Frequently, secular and ecclesiastical authorities found themselves in open opposition. Toward the end of the early medieval period, both sides resolved these conflicts to a large extent by recognizing the other's claim to authority in different spheres, but the tension between the two reverberates even today.

THE ART OF THE WARRIOR LORDS

As Rome's power waned in late antiquity, competition for political authority and armed conflicts became commonplace among "barbarian" groups—Huns, Vandals, Franks, Goths, and others. Once one group established itself in Italy or in one of Rome's European provinces, another often pressed in behind and compelled it to move on. The Visigoths, for example, who at one time controlled part of Italy and formed a kingdom in what is today southern France, were forced southward into Spain under pressure from the Franks, who had crossed the lower Rhine River and established themselves firmly in France, Switzerland, the Netherlands, and parts of Germany. The Ostrogoths moved from Pannonia (at the junction of modern Hungary, Austria, and the former Yugoslavia) to Italy. Under Theodoric, they established their kingdom there, only to have it fall less than a century later to the Lombards, the last of the early Germanic powers to occupy land within the limits of the old Roman Empire (see Chapter 12). In the North, Anglo-Saxons controlled what had been Roman Britain. Celts inhabited Ireland, never colonized by the Romans. In Scandinavia the great seafaring Vikings held sway.

ART AND STATUS   Art historians do not know the full range of art and architecture these "barbarian" peoples produced. What has survived is not truly representative and consists almost exclusively of small "status symbols"—weapons and items of personal adornment such as bracelets, pendants, and belt buckles archeologists have discovered in lavish furnished graves. Scholars long ignored these "minor arts" because of their small scale, seeming utilitarian nature, and abstract ornament, and because the people who made them rejected the classical idea that the representation of organic nature should be the focus of artistic endeavor. These early medieval objects gradually have been reevaluated during the past century and are now recognized as highly sophisticated masterpieces, both technically and stylistically. Produced by artists of the highest caliber, these treasures enhanced the prestige of those who owned them and testified to the stature of those who were buried with them. In the great early (possibly seventh-century) Anglo-Saxon epic *Beowulf,* the hero is cremated and his ashes placed in a huge tumulus overlooking the sea. As an everlasting tribute to Beowulf's greatness, his people "buried rings and brooches in the barrow, all those adornments that brave men had brought out from the hoard after Beowulf died. They bequeathed the gleaming gold, treasure of men, to the earth."[1]

A FRANKISH LORD'S COSTLY PIN   Most characteristic, perhaps, of the prestige adornments was the *fibula,* a decorative pin the Romans (and the Etruscans before them) favored (see FIG. 9-1). Produced in quantity by almost all the Celtic-Germanic groups, it usually was used to fasten garments. Fibulae are made of bronze, silver, or gold and often are decorated profusely, sometimes with inlaid precious or semiprecious stones. The fibula we illustrate (FIG. **16-1**) was found in France and dates to the sixth or seventh century. It once must have been the proud possession of a wealthy Frankish lord. The pin resembles, in its general form, the roughly contemporary but plain fibulae used to fasten the outer garments of some of the attendants flanking the Byzantine emperor Jus-

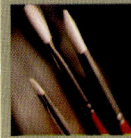

Cloisonné

One of the preferred methods of decoration in early medieval art was *cloisonné*, the richest of the luxury arts favored by the kings and warrior lords who often were called "treasure givers" in medieval poetry. This technique was employed in a masterly fashion by the artist or artists responsible for the Sutton Hoo purse cover (FIG. 16-2). First, small metal strips or *cloisons* (French for "partitions"), usually of gold, are soldered edge-up to a metal background. A glass paste (subsequently fired to give it the look of sparkling jewels) or semiprecious stones, such as garnets, or pieces of colored glass are placed in the compartments thus formed. The edges of the cloisons remain visible on the surface and are an important part of the design. The technique is a cross between mosaic (see "Mosaics," Chapter 11, page 314) and stained glass (see "Stained-Glass Windows," Chapter 18, page 500) but was employed only on a miniature scale.

---

tinian in the apse mosaic of San Vitale in Ravenna (see FIG. 12-10). (Note how much more elaborate is the emperor's clasp. In Rome, New Rome, and early medieval Europe alike, these fibulae were emblems of office and of prestige.)

The Frankish fibula's entire surface is covered with decorative patterns adjusted carefully to the basic shape of the object they adorn. They thus describe and amplify its form and structure, becoming an organic part of the object itself. Often zoomorphic elements were so successfully integrated into this type of highly disciplined, abstract decorative design that they became almost unrecognizable. One must examine a fibula carefully to discover that it contains a zoomorphic form. In our example (FIG. 16-1), a fish may be discerned just below the center of the fibula.

A KING'S FINAL VOYAGE   The *Beowulf* saga also recounts the funeral of the warrior lord Scyld, who was laid to rest in a ship set adrift in the North Sea overflowing with arms and armor and costly adornments:

> They laid their dear lord, the giver of rings, deep within the ship by the mast in majesty; many treasures and adornments from far and wide were gathered there. I have never heard of a ship equipped more handsomely with weapons and war-gear, swords and corselets; on his breast lay countless treasures that were to travel far with him into the waves' domain."[2]

In 1939, a treasure-laden ship was discovered in a burial mound at Sutton Hoo in Suffolk, England. Although unique, it epitomizes the early medieval tradition of burying great lords with rich furnishings, as recorded in *Beowulf*. Among the many precious finds were a gold belt buckle, ten silver bowls, a silver plate with the imperial stamp of the Byzantine emperor Anastasius I (r. 491–518), and forty gold coins (to pay the forty oarsmen who would row the deceased across the sea on his final voyage). Also placed in the ship were two silver spoons inscribed "Saulos" and "Paulos," Saint Paul's names in Greek before and after his baptism. They may allude to a conversion to Christianity. Historians have associated the site with the East Anglian king Raedwald, who was baptized a Christian before his death in 625 but who never fully abandoned pagan polytheism.

Most extraordinary of all the Sutton Hoo finds is a purse cover (FIG. **16-2**) decorated with cloisonné-enamel plaques (see "Cloisonné," above). Four symmetrically arranged groups of figures are in the lower row. The end groups consist of a man standing between two beasts. He faces front, and they appear in profile. This heraldic type of grouping has a venerable heritage in the ancient world (see FIG. 2-10). The two center groups represent eagles attacking ducks. The animal figures are cunningly adjusted to each other. For example, the convex beaks of the eagles fit against the concave beaks of the ducks. The two figures fit together so

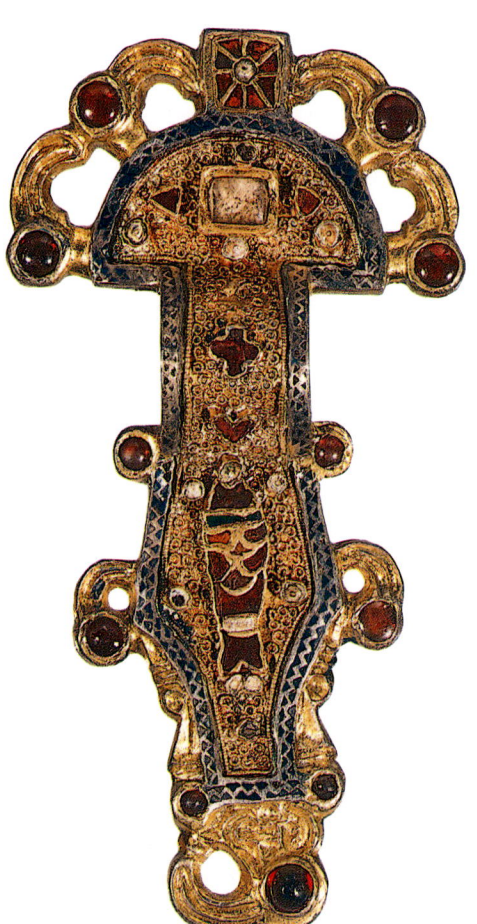

16-1   Frankish looped fibula, sixth to seventh century. Silver gilt worked in filigree, with inlays of garnets and other stones, 4″ long. Musée des Antiquités Nationales, Saint-Germain-en-Laye.

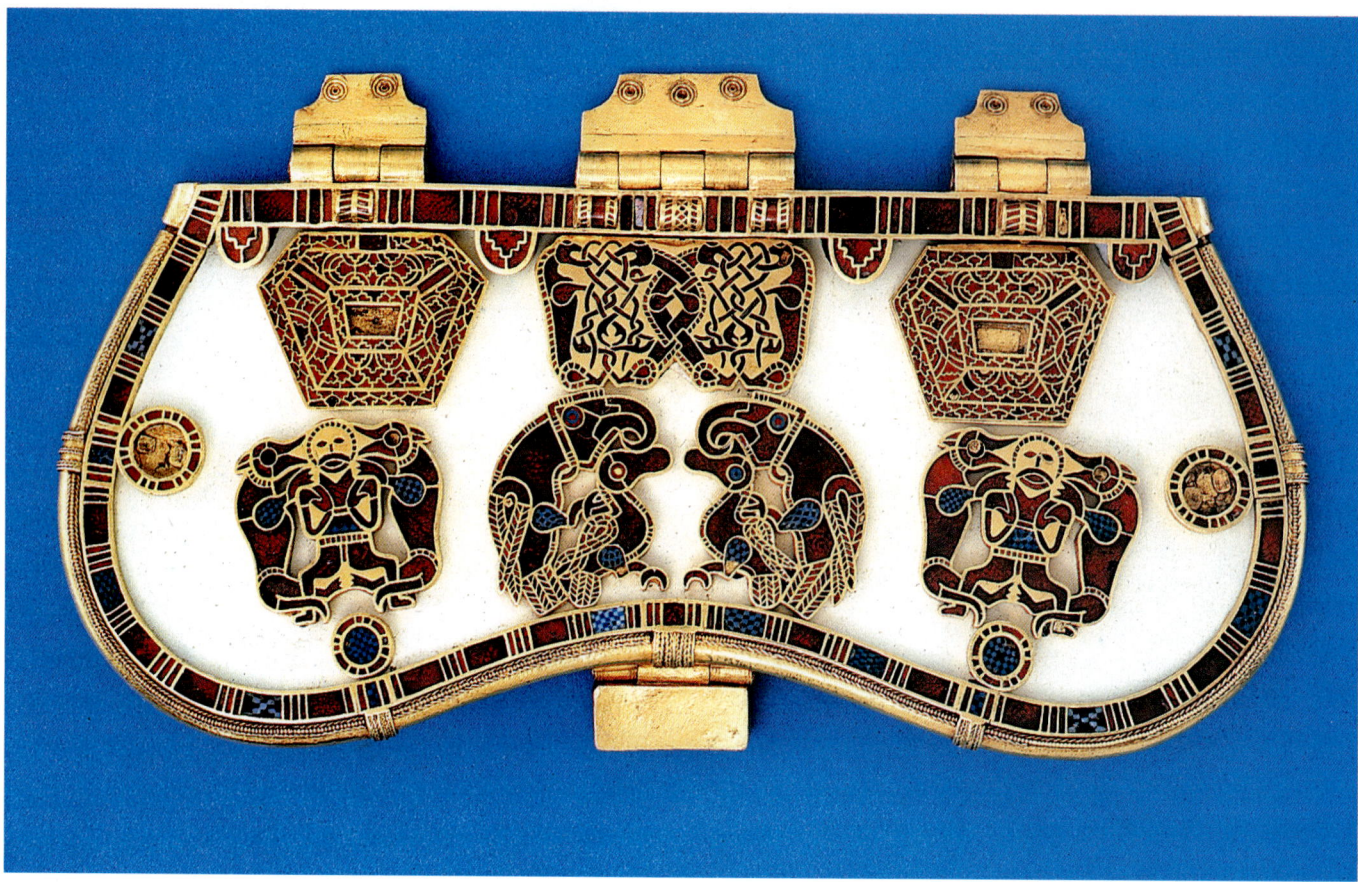

16-2   Purse cover, from the Sutton Hoo ship burial in Suffolk, England, ca. 625. Gold, glass, and enamel cloisonné with garnets and emeralds, $7\frac{1}{2}''$ long. British Museum, London.

snugly that they seem at first to be a single dense abstract design. This is true also of the man-animals motif. Above these figures are three geometric designs. The outer ones are clear and linear in style. In the central design, an interlace pattern, the interlacements turn into writhing animal figures. Elaborate interlace patterns are characteristic of many times and places, notably in the art of the Islamic world (Chapter 13). But the combination of interlace with animal figures was uncommon outside the realm of the early medieval warlords. In fact, metalcraft with a vocabulary of interlace patterns and other motifs beautifully integrated with the animal form was, without doubt, *the* art of the early Middle Ages in the West. Interest in it was so great that the colorful effects of jewelry designs were imitated in the painted decorations of manuscripts, in stone sculpture, in the masonry of churches, and in sculpture in wood, an especially important medium of Viking art.

THE PIRATES OF THE NORTH   In 793 the pagan traders and pirates known as Vikings (named after the *viks*— coves or "trading places"—of the Norwegian shoreline) set sail from Scandinavia and landed in the British Isles. They destroyed the Christian monastic community on Lindisfarne Island off the Northumbrian (northeastern) coast of England (see later discussion). Shortly after, these *Norsemen* (North men) attacked the monastery at Jarrow in England as well as that on Iona Island, off the west coast of Scotland. From this time until the mid-eleventh century, the Vikings were the terror of western Europe. From their great ships they seasonally

harried and plundered the coasts, harbors, and river settlements of the West. Their fast, seaworthy longboats took them on wide-ranging voyages, from Ireland eastward to Russia and westward to Iceland and Greenland and even, briefly, to Newfoundland in North America, long before Columbus arrived in the "New World."

The Vikings were not intent merely on a hit-and-run strategy of destruction but on colonizing the lands they occupied by conquest. Their exceptional talent for organization and administration, as well as for war, enabled them to take and govern large territories in Ireland, England, and France, as well as in the Baltic regions and Russia. For a while, in the early eleventh century, the whole of England was part of a Danish empire. When Vikings settled in northern France in the early tenth century, their territory came to be called Normandy— home of the Norsemen who became *Normans.* (Later, a Norman duke, William the Conqueror, sailed across the English Channel and invaded and became the master of Anglo-Saxon England; see FIG. 17-40.)

TWO WOMEN BURIED IN A VIKING SHIP The art of the Viking sea rovers was early associated with ships—with wood and the carving of it. Striking examples of Viking wood carving were found in a royal ship buried near Oseberg, Norway. The ship, which was covered by a mound like the earlier Anglo-Saxon royal burial at Sutton Hoo, was more than seventy feet long. It once must have carried many precious objects, but robbers removed them long before its modern discovery. When the vessel was found, it contained

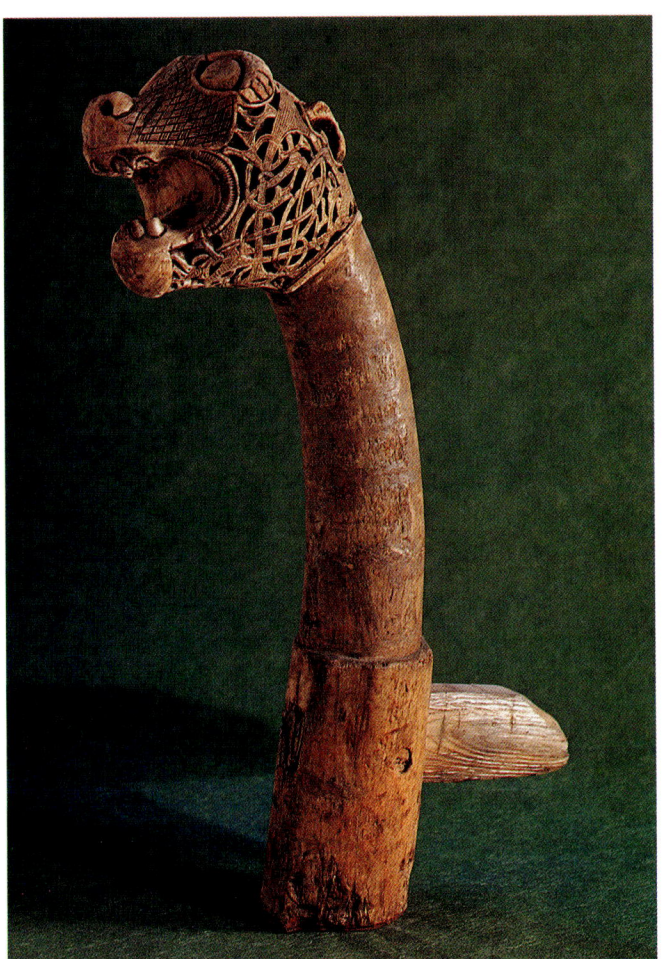

16-3   Animal-head post, from the Oseberg, Norway, ship burial, ca. 825. Wood, approx. 5″ high. Vikingskipshuset Museum, Oslo.

strous animal forms intertwine with flexible plant stalks and tendrils in spiraling rhythm. The effect of natural growth is astonishing. Yet, the elaboration of the forms is so intricate and refined that the animal-interlace art of design seems to have reached its limits of inventiveness. The Urnes style was the culmination of three centuries (the eighth to the eleventh) of Viking art. During the whole period, the art of the Norsemen interacted closely with Hiberno-Saxon art.

HIBERNO-SAXON ART

THE CONVERSION OF THE BRITISH ISLES In 432 Saint Patrick established a church in Ireland and began the Christianization of the Celts on that remote island that had never known Roman rule. The newly converted Celts, although nominally subject to the popes of Rome, quickly developed a form of monastic organization that differed from the Church of Rome in its liturgical practices and even in its calendar of holidays. The relative independence of the Irish churches was due in part to the isolation of its monasteries, which often were situated in inaccessible and inhospitable places such as Skellig Michael. There, on a craggy hillside overlooking the sea, sixth-century Irish monks and their successors lived in bare beehive-shaped stone cells far from the rest of the world's temptations and distractions.

Before long, Irish monks, filled with missionary zeal, set up monastic establishments in Britain and Scotland. In 563 Saint Columba founded an important monastery on the Scottish

little more than the remains of two women, but the size of the burial and the lavishly carved wooden ornament of the sleek ship attest to the importance of those laid to rest there.

We illustrate a wooden animal-head post (FIG. **16-3**) from the Oseberg ship that, like the other animal forms in the carved bands that follow the prow's gracefully curving lines, expresses the dynamic energy of the nothern sea rovers. This head combines in one composition the image of a roaring beast with protruding eyes and flaring nostrils and the deftly carved, controlled, and contained pattern of tightly interwoven animals that writhe, gripping and snapping, in serpentine fashion. The Oseberg animal head is a powerfully expressive example of the union of two fundamental motifs of the art of the warrior lords on the former Roman Empire's northern frontiers—the animal form and the interlace pattern.

MONSTERS WRITHING ON A CHURCH By the eleventh century, much of Scandinavia had become Christian, but the Viking artistic traditions persisted. Nowhere is this more evident than in the decoration of the portal (FIG. **16-4**) of the stave church (*staves* are wedge-shaped timbers placed vertically) at Urnes in Norway. The portal is almost all that is preserved of a mid-eleventh-century wooden church whose staves were incorporated in the walls of a twelfth-century church. The doorjambs and the connecting lintel are masterpieces of the wood-carver's art. Gracefully elongated mon-

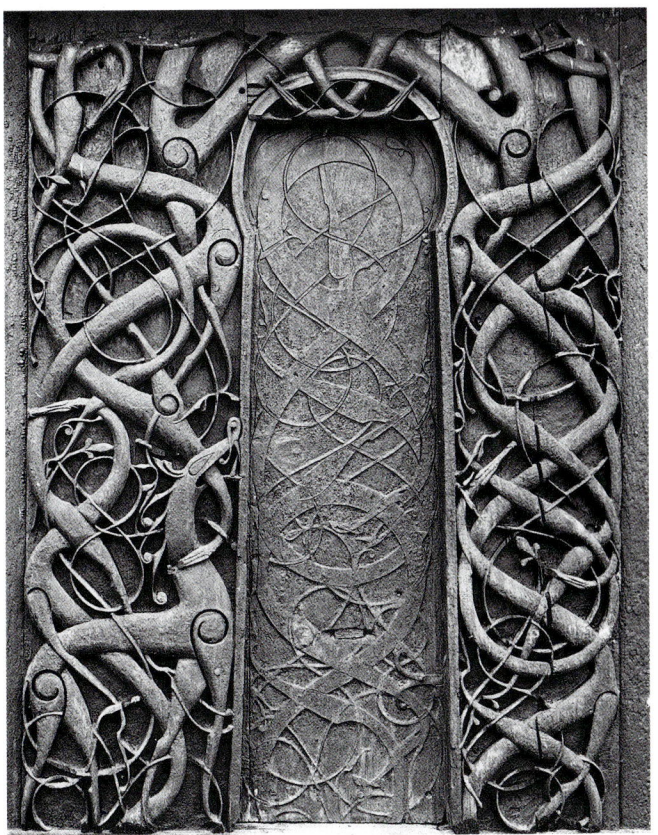

16-4   Wood-carved portal of the stave church at Urnes, Norway, ca. 1050–1070.

island of Iona, where he successfully converted the native Picts to Christianity. The monastery at Lindisfarne off the northern coast of Britain was established by Iona monks in 635. From these and other later foundations, which became great centers of learning for both Scotland and England, Irish and Anglo-Saxon missionaries journeyed through Europe, establishing great monasteries in Italy, Switzerland, Germany, and France.

HIBERNO-SAXON BOOKS A style art historians designate as *Hiberno-Saxon* (Hibernia was the ancient name of Ireland), or sometimes as *Insular* to denote the Irish-English islands where it was produced, flourished within the monasteries of the British Isles. Its most distinctive products were the illuminated manuscripts of the Christian Church (see "Medieval Books," page 434). Liturgical books became an important vehicle of miniature art and a principal medium for the exchange of stylistic ideas between the northern and the Mediterranean worlds. In an age of general illiteracy, books were scarce. For those who could read, books were jealously guarded treasures, most of them housed in the libraries and *scriptoria* (writing studios) of monasteries or major churches. The illuminated books described here survived the depredations of the ninth-century Viking invaders. They are the most important extant monuments of the brilliant culture that flourished in Ireland and Northumbria during the seventh and eighth centuries.

Among the earliest Hiberno-Saxon illuminated manuscripts is the *Book of Durrow,* a Gospel book probably written and decorated in the monastic scriptorium at Iona. (In the late Middle Ages it was housed in Durrow, Ireland—hence its modern nickname.) The Durrow Gospels already display one of the most characteristic features of Insular book illumination: full pages devoted neither to text nor to illustration but to pure embellishment. Interspersed between the Durrow text pages are so-called *carpet pages,* resembling textiles, made up of decorative panels of abstract and zoomorphic forms. The *Book of Durrow* also contains pages where the initial letters of an important passage of sacred text are enormously enlarged and transformed into elaborate decorative patterns. Examples of Hiberno-Saxon carpet pages (FIG. **16-6**) and initial pages (FIG. **16-7**) will be examined later. It is important to note at the outset that this type of manuscript decoration had no precedent in classical art.

A CHECKERBOARD-CLOAKED EVANGELIST In the *Book of Durrow* each of the four Gospel books has a carpet page facing a page dedicated to the symbol of the Evangelist who wrote that Gospel, framed by an elaborate interlace border. The symbol of Saint Matthew (FIG. **16-5**) is a man (more commonly represented later as winged), but the only human parts the artist, a seventh-century monk, chose to render are a schematic frontal head and two profile feet. The rest of the "body" is enveloped by a checkerboard cloak of yellow, red, and green squares filled with intricate abstract designs and outlined in dark brown or black. The man lacks arms and more resembles a warrior lord's cloisonné-enameled belt buckle, brooch, or purse ornament than a human figure. The Durrow artist was interested in ornamental pattern, not in reproducing physical reality. The *Book of Durrow* weds the ab-

straction of the native arts of personal adornment with classical and Early Christian pictorial imagery. The vehicle for the transmission of those Mediterranean forms was the illustrated book itself, brought to the North by Christian missionaries and deposited and reverently copied in the northern monastic scriptoria.

CARPETS AND CROSSES An excellent example of the marriage between Christian imagery and the animal-interlace style of the North is the cross-inscribed carpet page (FIG. **16-6**) of the *Lindisfarne Gospels.* The book, produced in the Northumbrian monastery on Lindisfarne Island, contains several ornamental pages and exemplifies Hiberno-Saxon art at its best. According to a later *colophon* (an inscription, usually on the last page, providing information regarding a book's manufacture), Eadfrith, Bishop of Lindisfarne between 698 and his death in 721, wrote the *Lindisfarne Gospels* "for God and Saint Cuthbert." Cuthbert's relics (see "Pilgrimages and the Cult of Relics," Chapter 17, page 457) recently had been deposited in the Lindisfarne church.

The Lindisfarne ornamental page's patterning and detail are much more intricate and compact than the *Book of Durrow*'s. Serpentine interlacements of fantastic animals devour each other, curling over and returning on their writhing, elastic shapes. The rhythm of expanding and contracting forms produces a most vivid effect of motion and change. But it is

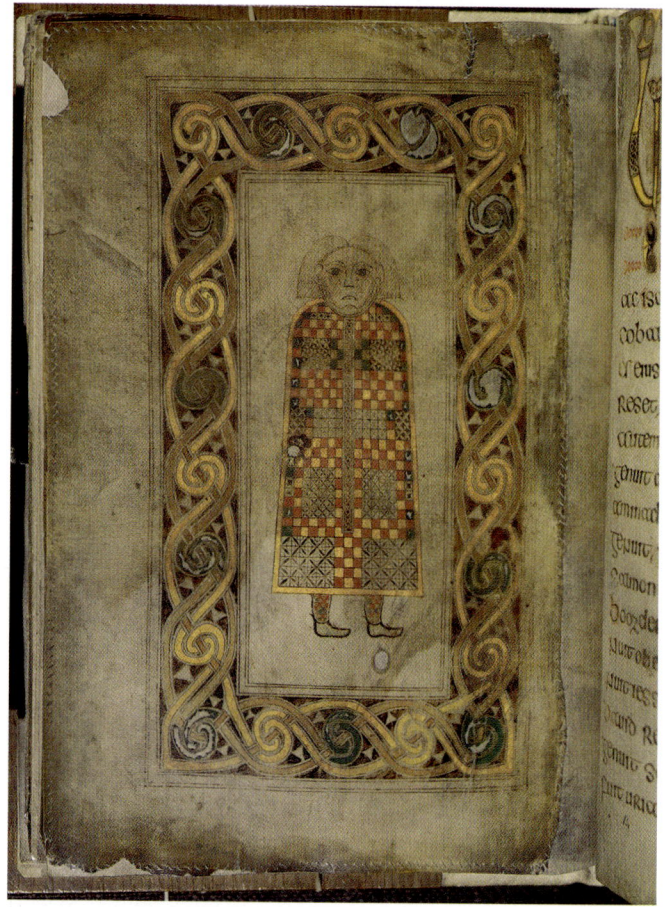

16-5 Man (symbol of Saint Matthew), folio 21 verso of the *Book of Durrow,* probably from Iona, Scotland, ca. 660–680. Ink and tempera on parchment, $9\frac{5}{8}'' \times 6\frac{1}{8}''$. Trinity College Library, Dublin.

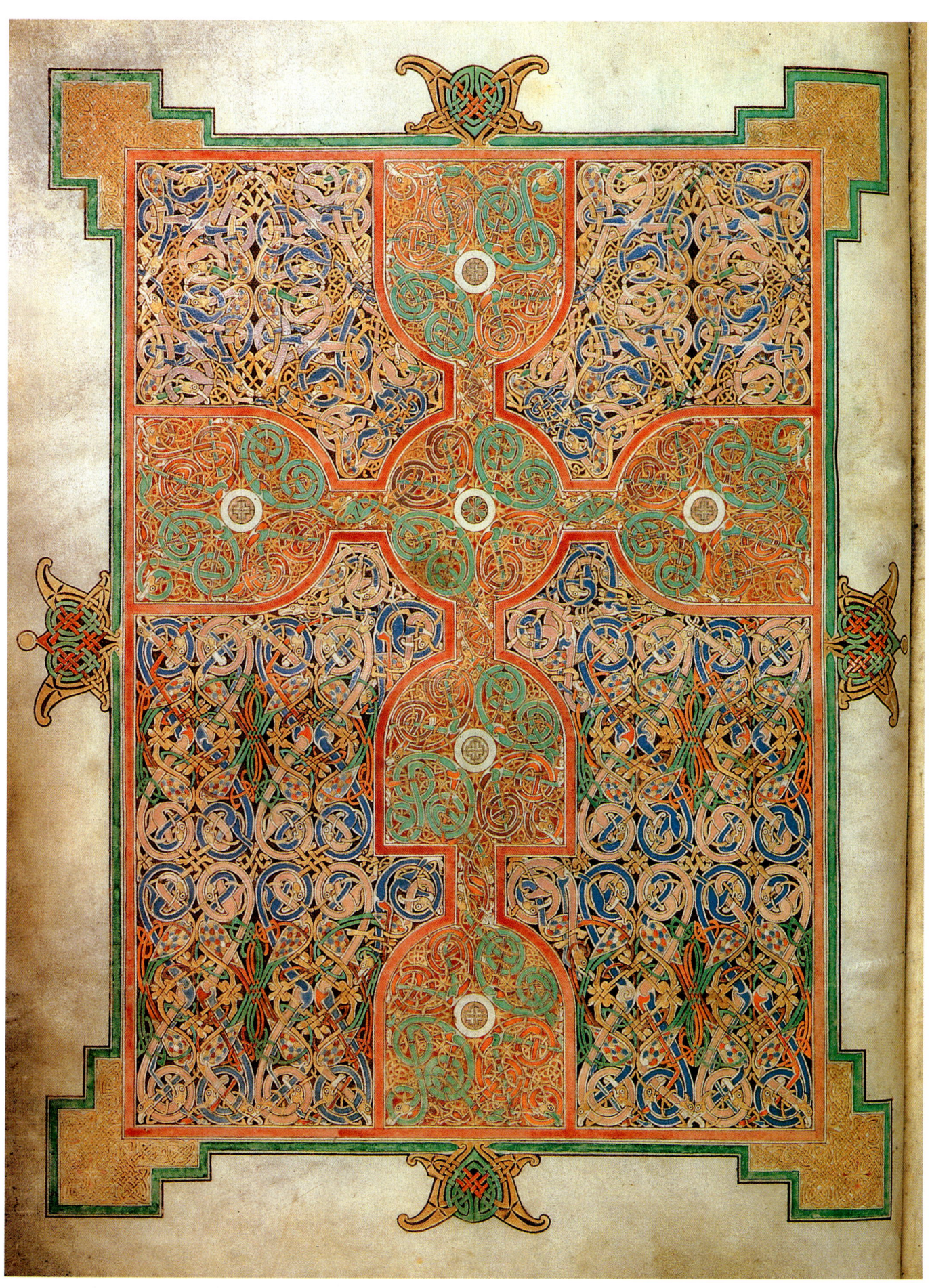

16-6 Cross and carpet page, folio 26 verso of the *Lindisfarne Gospels,* from Northumbria, England, ca. 698–721. Tempera on vellum, 1′ 1½″ × 9¼″. British Library, London.

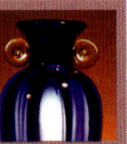

Medieval Books

The central role books played in the medieval Christian Church led to the development of a large number of specialized types for priests, monks and nuns, and laypersons.

The primary sacred text came to be called the Bible ("the Book"), consisting of the Old Testament of the Jews, originally written in Hebrew, and the Christian New Testament, written in Greek. In the late fourth century, Saint Jerome produced the canonical Latin, or *Vulgate* (vulgar, or common tongue), version of the Bible, which incorporates forty-six Old and twenty-seven New Testament books. Before the invention of the printing press in the fifteenth century, all books were written by hand ("manuscripts," from the Latin *manu scriptus*). Bibles were extremely difficult to produce, and few early medieval monasteries possessed a complete Bible. Instead, several biblical books often were gathered and published in discrete volumes.

The *Pentateuch* contains the first five books of the Old Testament, beginning with the Creation of Adam and Eve (Genesis). The *Gospels* ("good news") are the New Testament works of the Four Evangelists (Saints Matthew, Mark, Luke, and John) and tell the story of the life of Christ (see "The Life of Jesus in Art," Chapter 11, pages 308–309). Medieval Gospel books often contained *canon tables*, a concordance, or matching, of the corresponding passages of the four Gospels as compiled by Eusebius of Caesarea in the fourth century. *Psalters* contained the one hundred fifty psalms of King David, written in Hebrew and translated into both Greek and Latin.

Other types of books also were frequently employed in the Christian liturgy. The *lectionary* contains passages from the Gospels reordered to appear in the sequence they were read during the celebration of Mass throughout the liturgical year. *Breviaries* include the texts required for the daily recitations of monks. *Sacramentaries* were used by priests and incorporate the prayers they recited during Mass. *Benedictionals* contain bishops' blessings.

In the later Middle Ages religious books were developed for the private devotions of the laity, patterned after monks' readers. The most popular were *Books of Hours,* so called because they contain the prayers to be read at specified times of the day.

Many other types of books were written and copied in the Middle Ages—theological treatises, secular texts on history and science, and even some classics of Greco-Roman literature—but these were less frequently illustrated than the various sacred texts.

---

held in check by the design's regularity and by the dominating motif of the inscribed cross. The cross stabilizes the rhythms of the serpentines and, perhaps by contrast with its heavy immobility, seems to heighten the effect of motion. The illuminator placed the motifs in detailed symmetries, with inversions, reversals, and repetitions that must be studied closely to appreciate not so much their variety as their mazelike complexity. The zoomorphic forms intermingle with clusters and knots of line, and the whole design vibrates with the energy that also permeates Viking art (FIGS. 16-3 and 16-4). The color is rich yet cool. The entire spectrum is embraced, but in hues of low intensity. The painter so adroitly adjusted shape and color that a smooth and perfectly even surface was achieved. The page is the product of a master familiar with long-established conventions, yet neither the discipline nor the convention stiffens the supple lines that tirelessly and endlessly thread and convolute their way through the design.

ILLUMINATING THE WORD The greatest achievement of Hiberno-Saxon art in the eyes of almost all modern observers is the *Book of Kells* (FIG. **16-7**), the most elaborately decorated of the Insular Gospel books. Medieval commentators shared this high opinion, and one wrote in the *Annals of Ulster* for the year 1003 that this "great Gospel [is] the chief relic of the western world." The *Book of Kells* (named after the monastery in southern Ireland that owned it) was written and decorated either at Iona or a closely related Irish monastery. Fortunately, it survived the Viking raids of the early ninth century. The manuscript probably was created for display on a church altar. From an early date it was housed in an elaborate metalwork box, befitting a greatly revered "relic." The *Book of Kells* boasts an unprecedented number of full-page illumina-

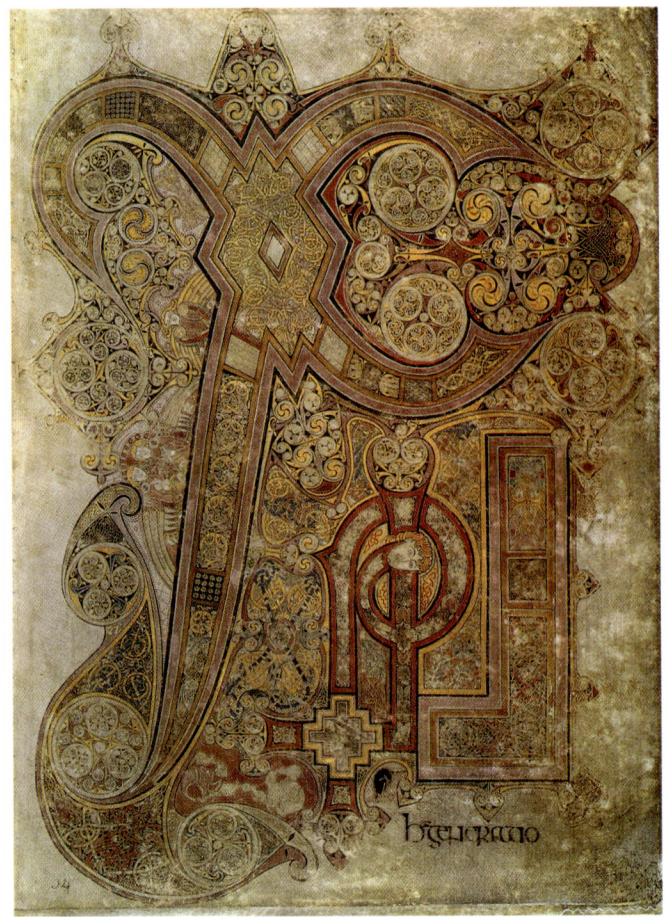

16-7 Chi-rho-iota page, folio 34 recto of the *Book of Kells,* probably from Iona, Scotland, late eighth or early ninth century. Tempera on vellum, $1' 1'' \times 9\frac{1}{2}''$. Trinity College Library, Dublin.

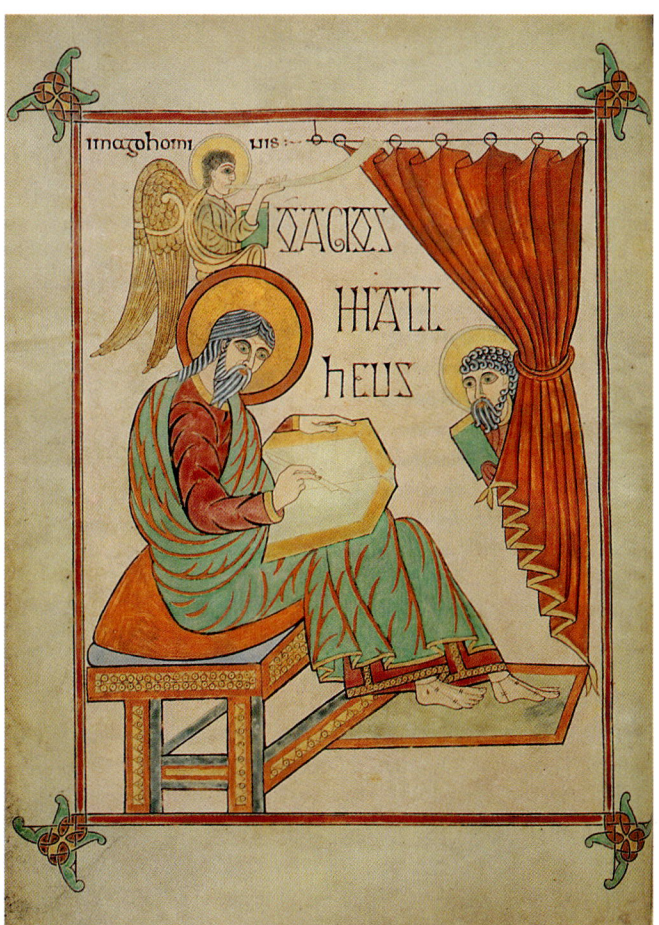

16-8   Saint Matthew, folio 25 verso of the *Lindisfarne Gospels,* from Northumbria, England, ca. 698–721. Tempera on vellum, 1′ 1½″ × 9¼″. British Library, London.

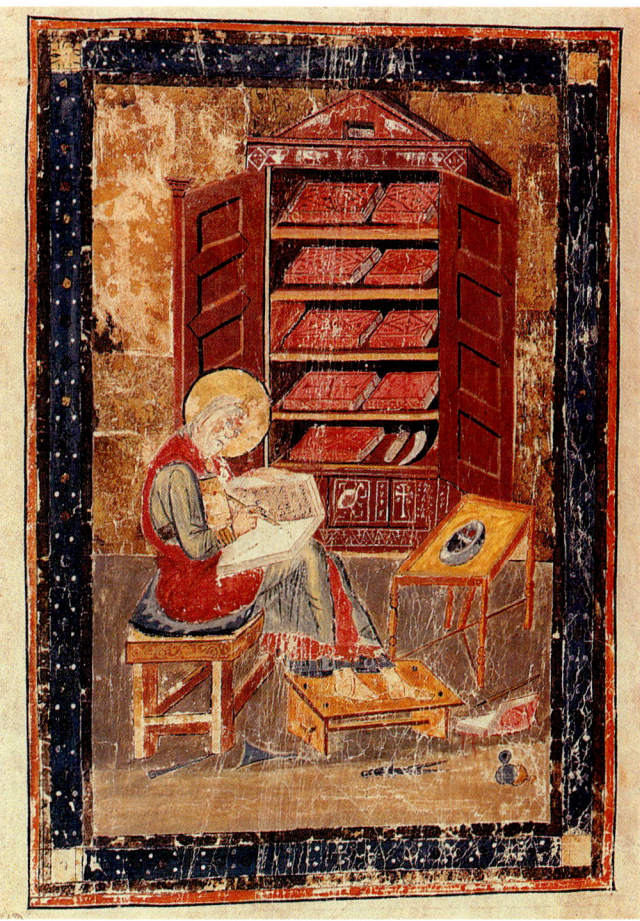

16-9   The scribe Ezra, folio 5 recto of the *Codex Amiatinus,* from Jarrow, England, ca. 689–716. Tempera on vellum, 1′ 8″ × 1′ 1½″. Biblioteca Medicea-Laurenziana, Florence.

tions, including carpet pages, evangelist symbols, portrayals of the Virgin Mary and of Christ, New Testament narrative scenes, canon tables, and several instances of monumentalized and embellished words from the Bible.

The page we reproduce (FIG. 16-7) opens the account of the nativity of Jesus in the Gospel of Saint Matthew. The initial letters of Christ in Greek (XPI, *chi-rho-iota*) occupy nearly the entire page, although two words—*autem* (abbreviated simply as *h*) and *generatio* ("Now this is how the birth of Christ came about")—appear at the lower right. The illuminator transformed the holy words into extraordinarily intricate abstract designs that recall Celtic and Anglo-Saxon metalwork. Close observation reveals that the cloisonné-like interlace is not purely abstract pattern. The letter *rho,* for example, ends in a male head, and animals are at its base to the left of *h generatio.* Half-figures look out at viewers to the left of *chi;* another head is at the very top of that letter; and so forth.

When the priest Giraldus Cambrensis visited Ireland in 1185, he described a manuscript he saw that, if not the *Book of Kells* itself, must have been very much like it:

Fine craftsmanship is all about you, but you might not notice it. Look more keenly at it and you . . . will make out intricacies, so delicate and subtle, so exact and compact, so full of knots and links, with colors so fresh and vivid, that you might say that all this was the work of an angel, and not of a man. For my part, the oftener I see the book, the more carefully I study it, the more I am lost in ever fresh amazement, and I see more and more wonders in the book.[3]

SOUTHERN MOTIFS IN THE NORTH   The three Hiberno-Saxon books examined here display the illuminators' pure joy in working on small, infinitely complex, and painstaking projects. The same may be said of the precious objects fashioned by Hiberno-Saxon goldsmiths and jewelers. Even when the illuminators depicted human figures, as in the Matthew symbol of the *Book of Durrow* (FIG. 16-5), the artists' models were generally the abstract designs of buckles and pins, not the world about them or imported works in the classical tradition. But exceptions exist. In some Insular manuscripts it is clear the northern artists copied imported Mediterranean books. This is evident at once when the author portrait of Saint Matthew from the *Lindisfarne Gospels* (FIG. 16-8) is compared with the contemporary full-page portrayal of the scribe Ezra from the *Codex Amiatinus* (FIG. 16-9). Both were "copied" from similar books Christian missionaries brought from Italy to England—but with markedly divergent results.

The figure of Ezra and the architectural environment of the *Codex Amiatinus* are closely linked with the pictorial illusionism of late antiquity. The color, although applied here and there in flat planes, is blended smoothly to model the figure and to provide gradual transitions from light to dark. By contrast, the Hiberno-Saxon artist of the Lindisfarne Matthew apparently knew nothing of the illusionistic pictorial technique nor, for that matter, of the representation of the human figure. Although the illuminator carefully copied the pose, the Insular artist interpreted the form in terms of line exclusively, "abstracting" the classical model's unfamiliar tonal scheme into a patterned figure. The Lindisfarne Matthew resembles the pictures of kings, queens, and jacks in a modern deck of playing cards. The soft folds of drapery in the *Codex Amiatinus* Ezra became, in the Hiberno-Saxon manuscript, a series of sharp, regularly spaced, curving lines. The artist used no modeling. No variations occur in light and shade. The Lindisfarne painter converted the strange Mediterranean forms into a familiar linear idiom. The illuminator studied a tonal *picture* and made of it a linear *pattern*. The result, however, is not an inferior imitation of a southern prototype but a vivid new vision of the Evangelist, unencumbered by distracting details such as the bookcase and the scattered writing instruments on the floor present in the *Codex Amiatinus* picture.

SACRED AUTHORITY IN ART   The medieval artist did not go to nature for models but to a prototype—another image, a statue, or a picture in a book. Each copy might be one in a long line of copies, and, in some cases, art historians can trace these copies back to a lost original, inferring its former existence. The medieval practice of copying pictures is closely related to the copying of books, especially sacred books such as the Scriptures and the books used in the liturgy. The medieval scribe or illuminator (before the thirteenth century, most often a monk) could have reasoned that just as the text of a holy book must be copied faithfully if the copy also is to be holy, so must the pictures be rendered faithfully. Of course, in the process of copying, mistakes were made. Although scholars seek to purge books of these textual "corruptions," "mistakes" in the copying of pictures yield new pictorial styles or represent the merging of different styles, as in the *Codex Amiatinus* and the *Lindisfarne Gospels*.

In any event, the style of medieval images, whether in sculpture or in painting, was the result of copying from sources thought to have sacred authority, not from studying natural models. Artists could not, of course, draw Christ or the saints "from life." Thus, they learned what was true from authorities who declared the truth—the Scriptures and the fathers of the Christian Church—and painted "true" images from authoritative images. In the early Middle Ages a pictorial tradition for representing many sacred figures and biblical narratives already had been codified. To deviate from iconographical conventions and investigate "nature" on one's own was unthinkable. It would have meant questioning God's truth as revealed and interpreted.

SCULPTURE ON A GRAND SCALE   The preserved art of the early Middle Ages is, as has been noted, confined almost exclusively to small and portable works. The high crosses of the British Isles, erected between the eighth and tenth centuries, are exceptional by their mass and scale—and by the very fact of their survival. These majestic monuments, some seventeen feet in height or taller, preside over burial grounds adjoining the ruins of monasteries at sites widely distributed throughout the Irish countryside, and in some instances also in England. Freestanding and unattached to any architectural fabric, the high crosses have the imposing unity, weight, and presence of both building and statue—architecture and sculpture combined.

The *High Cross of Muiredach* at Monasterboice, Ireland (FIG. **16-10**), though a late representative of the type (dated by inscription to 923), can serve as standard for the form. The

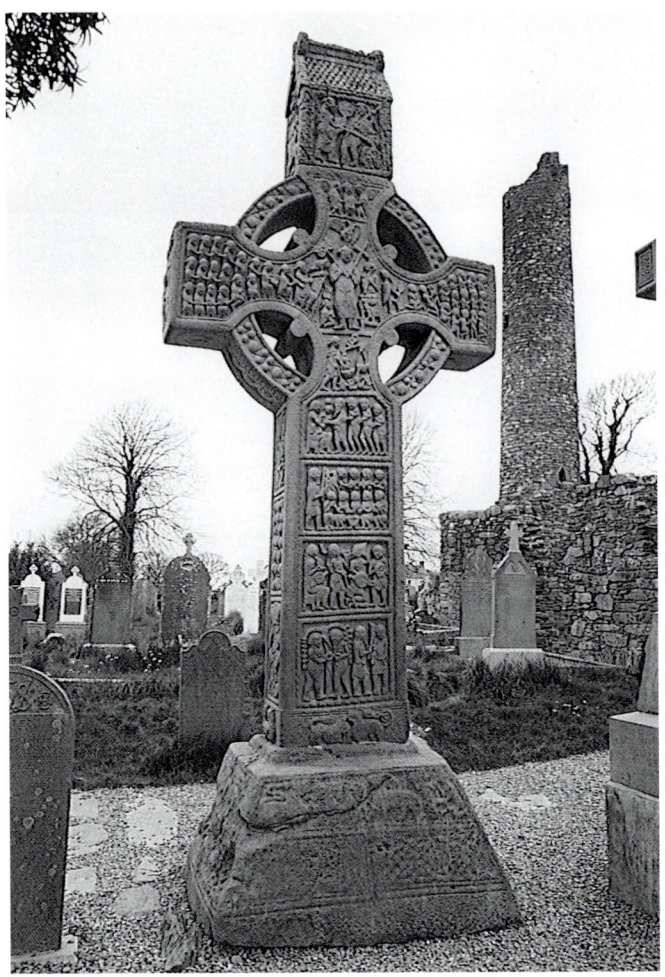

16-10   *High Cross of Muiredach,* Monasterboice, County Louth, Ireland, 923. Approx. 16′ high.

cross element crowns a four-sided stone shaft, which rises from a base with sloping sides. The concave arms of the cross are looped by four arcs that form a circle. The arms expand into squared terminals (compare FIG. 16-6). The circle intersecting the cross identifies the type as Celtic. The early high crosses bear abstract designs, especially the familiar interlace pattern. But the later ones have figured panels, with scenes from the life of Christ or, occasionally, events from the life of some Celtic saint. In addition, fantastic animals sometimes are portrayed. At the center of the Muiredach cross's transom, the risen Christ stands as judge of the world, the hope of the neighboring dead. Below him the souls of the dead are being weighed. Later, the sculptors of twelfth-century church portals (see FIG. 17-25) took up this theme with extraordinary force.

CAROLINGIAN ART

ROME RISES AGAIN   On Christmas day of the year 800, Pope Leo III crowned Charles the Great (Charlemagne), King of the Franks since 768, as emperor of Rome (r. 800–814). In time Charlemagne came to be seen as the first Holy (that is, Christian) Roman Emperor, a title his successors in the West did not formally adopt until the twelfth century. The setting for Charlemagne's coronation, fittingly, was Saint Peter's basilica in Rome (see FIG. 11-7), built by Constantine, the first Roman emperor to embrace Christianity. Born in 742, when northern Europe was still in chaos, Charlemagne consolidated the Frankish kingdom his father and grandfather bequeathed him and defeated the Lombards in Italy. He thus united Europe and laid claim to reviving the ancient Roman Empire's glory. He gave his name (Carolus Magnus in Latin) to an entire era, the *Carolingian* period.

Charlemagne's official seal bore the words *renovatio imperii Romani* (renewal of the Roman Empire). The "Carolingian Renaissance" was a remarkable historical phenomenon, an energetic, brilliant emulation of Early Christian Rome's art, culture, and political ideals. Charlemagne's (Holy) Roman Empire, waxing and waning for a thousand years and with many hiatuses, existed in central Europe until Napoleon destroyed it in 1806.

IMPERIAL IMAGERY REVIVED When Charlemagne returned home from his coronation in Rome, he ordered the transfer of an equestrian statue of the Ostrogothic king Theodoric from Ravenna to the Carolingian palace complex at Aachen. That portrait is lost, as is the grand gilded bronze statue of the Byzantine emperor Justinian that once crowned a column in Constantinople (see "The Emperors of 'New Rome,'" Chapter 12, page 327). But in the early Middle Ages both statues stood as reminders of ancient Rome's glory and of the pretensions and aspirations of the medieval successors of the pagan Roman emperors. The portrait of Theodoric may have been the inspiration for an early ninth-century bronze statuette of a Carolingian emperor on horseback (FIG. **16-11**). Charlemagne greatly admired Theodoric, the first Germanic ruler of Rome. Many have identified the small bronze figure as Charlemagne himself, although others think it portrays his grandson, Charles the Bald.

The ultimate model for the statuette was the equestrian portrait of Marcus Aurelius (see FIG. 10-59) in Rome. In the Middle Ages, it mistakenly was thought to represent Constantine, the first Christian emperor, another revered predecessor of Charlemagne and his Carolingian successors. The medieval sculptor portrayed the ninth-century emperor, like Marcus Aurelius, as overly large so that he, not the horse, is the center of attention. But unlike the Roman emperor, the Carolingian monarch sits rigidly upright. Quiet dignity replaces the torsion of Marcus Aurelius's body and the bold gesture of his right arm. Charlemagne (or Charles the Bald) is on parade, wearing imperial robes rather than a general's cloak, although his sheathed sword is visible. On his head is the imperial crown, and in his outstretched left hand he holds a globe, symbol of world dominion. The portrait proclaimed the *renovatio* of the Roman Empire's power and trappings and set the tone for much of Carolingian art.

The Art of the Book

CHARLEMAGNE'S BOOKS Charlemagne was a sincere admirer of learning, the arts, and classical culture (see "The Revival of Learning at Charlemagne's Court," page 440). He, his successors, and the scholars under their patronage placed a very high value on books, both sacred and secular, importing many and producing far more. Today four to five times as many Carolingian books exist than Latin books from all of Roman antiquity. One of these is the famous *Coronation Gospels* (also known as the *Gospel Book of Charlemagne*). An old (and probably inaccurate) legend says the book was found on Charlemagne's knees when, in the year 1000, Otto III had the emperor's tomb opened. The text is written in handsome gold letters on purple vellum.

The major full-page illuminations show the four Gospel authors at work. The page we reproduce (FIG. 16-12) depicts Saint Matthew. Such author portraits were common in medieval books and two earlier examples in the *Lindisfarne Gospels* and the *Codex Amiatinus* (FIGS. 16-8 and 16-9) have already been discussed. The theme originated in ancient book illustrations, and similar representations of seated philosophers or poets writing or reading abound in ancient art (see FIGS. 10-72 and 11-4). The Carolingian painter's technique is of the same antiquity—deft, illusionistic brushwork that easily and accurately defines the massive drapery folds wrapped around the body beneath. Color, not line, was used to create shapes. The cross-legged chair, the lectern, and the saint's toga are familiar Roman accessories. The landscape background is classicizing and the frame is filled with the kind of acanthus leaves found in Roman temple capitals and friezes (see FIG. 10-30). The whole composition seems utterly out of place

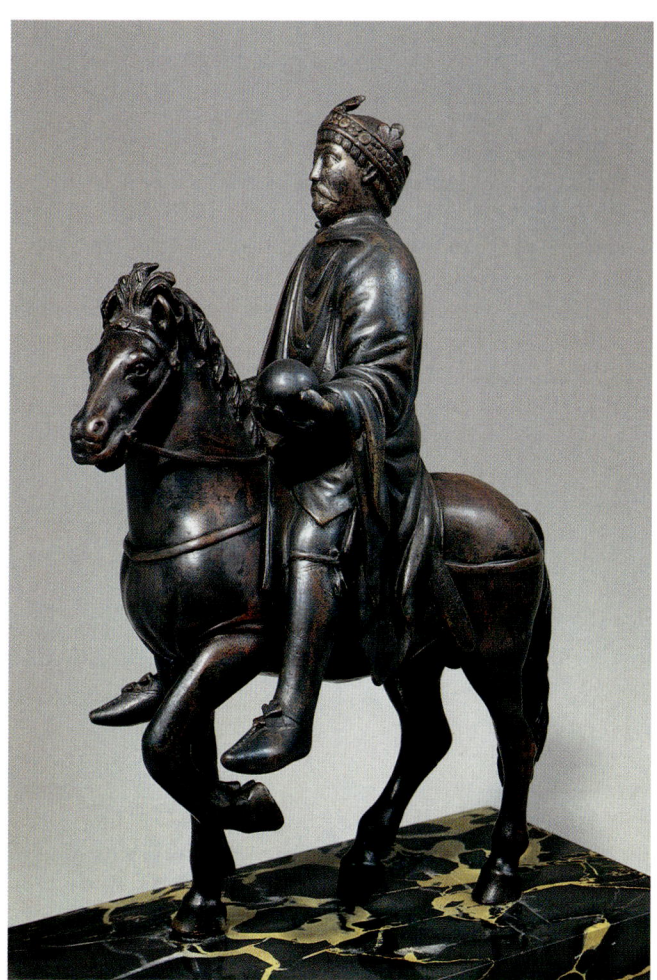

16-11 Equestrian portrait of Charlemagne(?), from Metz, Germany, early ninth century. Bronze, originally gilt, $9\frac{1}{2}$" high. Louvre, Paris.

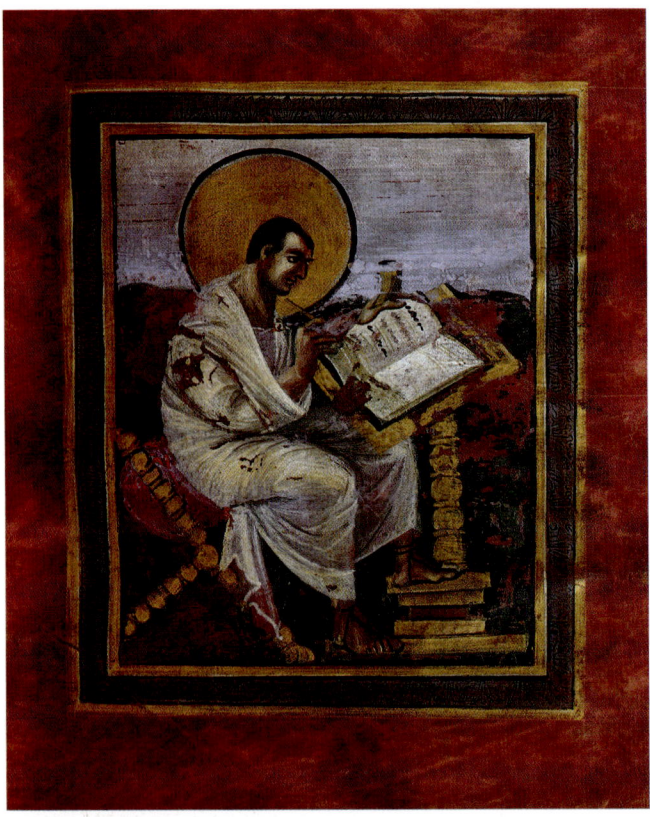

16-12   Saint Matthew, folio 15 recto of the *Coronation Gospels (Gospel Book of Charlemagne)*, from Aachen, Germany, ca. 800–810. Ink and tempera on vellum, 1′ $\frac{3}{4}$″ × 10″. Schatzkammer, Kunsthistorisches Museum, Vienna.

in the North in the ninth century. If a Frank, rather than an Italian or a Byzantine, painted the Saint Matthew and the other Evangelist portraits of the *Coronation Gospels*, the northern artist accomplished an amazing feat of approximation. Almost nothing is known in the Hiberno-Saxon or Frankish West that could have prepared the way for such a classicizing portrayal of Saint Matthew.

AN IMPASSIONED EVANGELIST   The style evident in the *Coronation Gospels* was by no means the only one that appeared suddenly in the Carolingian world. A wide variety of styles from late antique prototypes were distributed through the court schools and the monasteries. This must have been a bewildering array for the natives, who attempted to appropriate them by copying them as accurately as possible. Another Saint Matthew (FIG. **16-13**), in a gospel book made for Archbishop Ebbo of Reims, France, may be an interpretation of a prototype very similar to the one the *Coronation Gospels* master used. It resembles it in pose and in brushwork technique, but there the resemblance stops. The *Ebbo Gospels* illuminator replaced the classical calm and solidity of the *Coronation Gospels* with an energy that amounts to frenzy, and the frail saint almost leaps under its impulse. His hair stands on end, his eyes open wide, the folds of his drapery writhe and vibrate, the landscape behind him rears up alive. The painter even set the page's leaf border in motion. Matthew appears to take down in frantic haste what his inspiration (the tiny angel in the upper-right corner) dictates. The artist forsook all fi-

delity to bodily structure to concentrate on the saint's act of writing. Instead, Matthew's face, hands, inkhorn, pen, and book are the focus of the composition. This presentation contrasts strongly with the settled pose of the Saint Matthew of the *Coronation Gospels* with its even stress so that no part of the composition starts out at viewers to seize their attention.

The native power of expression is unmistakable in the *Ebbo Gospels* and became one of the important distinguishing traits of late medieval art. Just as the painter of the *Lindisfarne Gospels* Matthew (FIG. 16-8) transformed his model into something original and strong, translating the classicizing manner of a southern manuscript into his own Hiberno-Saxon idiom, so the *Ebbo Gospels* artist translated his classical prototype into a new Carolingian vernacular. This master painter brilliantly merged classical illusionism and the North's linear tradition.

ACTING OUT THE PSALMS   The Carolingians also revived narrative illustration, so richly developed in Early Christian and Byzantine art, and produced many fully illuminated books (even some large Bibles). One of the most extraordinary and enjoyable of all medieval manuscripts is the *Utrecht Psalter* (book of psalms). The text reproduces the Psalms of David in three columns of Latin capital letters emulating the script and page organization of long out-of-fashion ancient books. The artist illustrated each psalm with a pen-

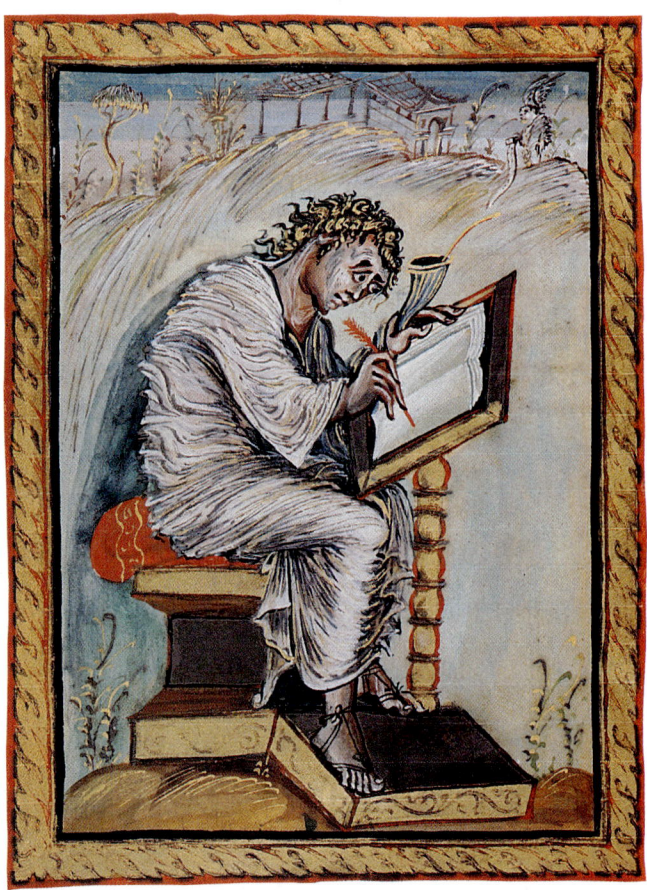

16-13   Saint Matthew, folio 18 verso of the *Ebbo Gospels (Gospel Book of Archbishop Ebbo of Reims)*, from Hautvillers (near Reims), France, ca. 816–835. Ink and tempera on vellum, 10 $\frac{1}{4}$″ × 8 $\frac{3}{4}$″. Bibliothèque Municipale, Épernay.

and-ink drawing stretching across the page's entire width. Our example (FIG. **16-14**) depicts figures acting out — literally and with a refreshing sense of humor — Psalm 43, in which the psalmist laments the plight of the oppressed Israelites. Where the text says, "Thou hast made us like sheep for slaughter," the artist drew some slain sheep fallen to the ground in front of a walled city reminiscent of cities on the Column of Trajan in Rome (see FIG. 10-42) and in Early Christian mosaics and manuscripts (see FIG. 11-19). At the left, the faithful grovel on the ground before a temple because the psalm reads "our belly cleaveth unto the earth." The artist's response to "Arise, why sleepest thou, O Lord" was to depict the Lord, flanked by six pleading angels, reclining in a canopied bed overlooking the slaughter below.

The style shows a vivid animation of much the same kind as the Saint Matthew of the *Ebbo Gospels,* and the *Utrecht Psalter* may have been produced in the same "school of Reims." As in the *Ebbo Gospels,* even the earth heaves up around the figures. The bodies are tense, shoulders hunched, heads thrust forward. The rapid, sketchy techniques used to render the figures convey the same nervous vitality as the Evangelists in the *Ebbo Gospels.* From details of the figures, their dress, and accessories, some scholars have argued that the artist followed one or more manuscripts compiled four hundred years before. If the *Utrecht Psalter* is not a copy, it certainly was designed to evoke earlier artworks and to appear "ancient." The interest in simple human emotions and actions and the variety and descriptiveness of gesture, however, are essentially medieval characteristics. Candid observation of human behavior, often in unguarded moments, lent both truth and charm to the art of the Middle Ages.

BEJEWELED BOOKS OF GOLD AND IVORY

The taste for sumptuously wrought and portable objects, shown previously in the art of the early medieval warrior lords, persisted under Charlemagne and his successors. They commissioned numerous works employing costly materials. One of the most luxurious is the psalter belonging to Charles the Bald (r. 840–877), grandson of Charlemagne and patron of the royal abbey of Saint-Denis near Paris, where the work was produced. The book's front cover (FIG. **16-15**) reveals the mastery of both metal- and ivorycraft during the Carolingian era. At the center is an ivory panel that, in shape and size if not subject, recalls late antique diptychs (see FIG. 11-22). It is set within a silver-gilt, filigreed frame inlaid with gems. The panel illustrates verses from Psalm 57:

> Oh God, in the shadow of thy wings will I make my refuge. . . . My soul is among lions; and I lie even among them that are set on fire, even the sons of men, whose teeth are spears and arrows, and their tongues a sharp sword. . . . They have prepared a net for my steps; they have digged a pit before me, into the midst thereof they are fallen themselves.

As in the earlier *Utrecht Psalter,* which, in fact, it directly copies, the narrative composition closely follows the text. Beginning at the top, the panel shows the psalmist in the Lord's lap, flanked by lions. On the next level are men armed to the teeth, and at the bottom, men are digging the pit and falling into it. The style of the carved figures — note the quick, nervous movements and exaggerated gestures — is also derived from the *Utrecht Psalter* illustrations. The cover of the *Psalter of Charles the Bald* is a model of the faithful reproduction of a prototype and exhibits the dependence of much medieval

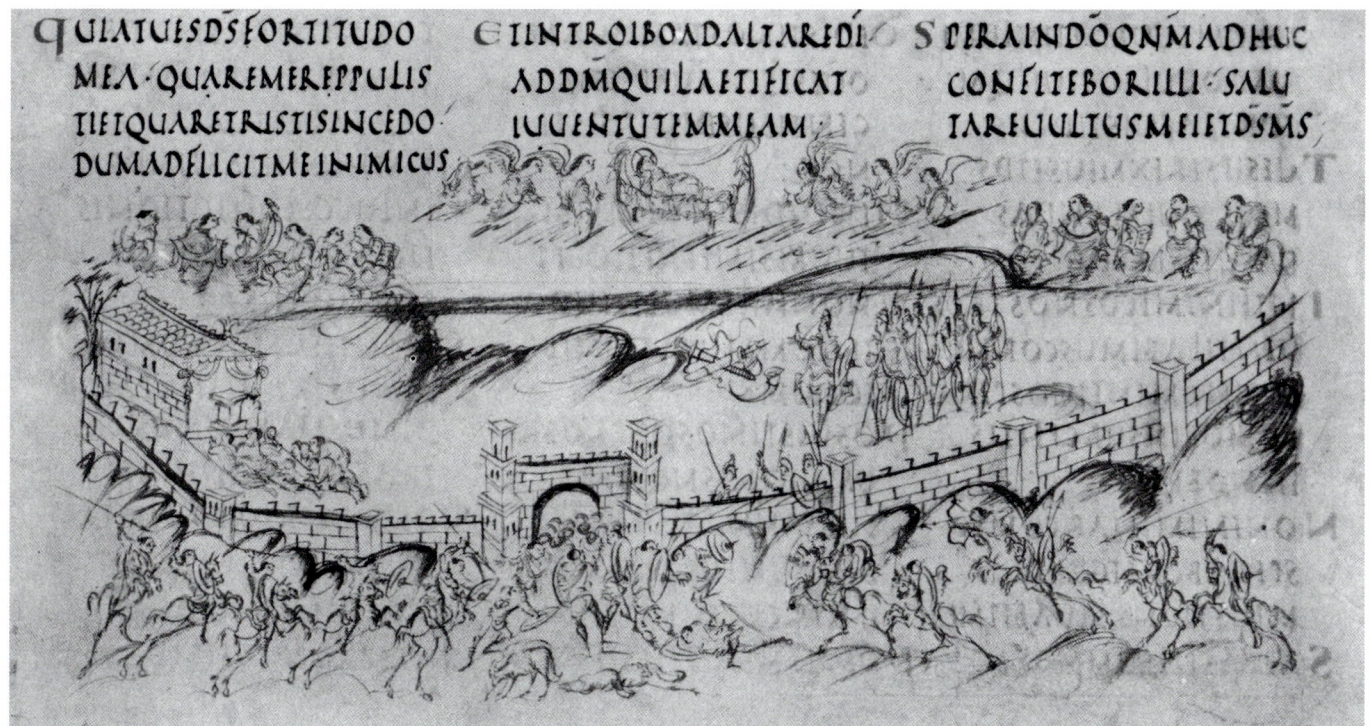

16-14   Psalm 43, detail of folio 25 recto of the *Utrecht Psalter,* from Hautvillers (near Reims), France, ca. 820–835. Ink on vellum, full page, 1′ 1″ × 9$\frac{7}{8}$″. University Library, Utrecht.

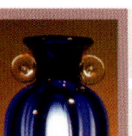

The Revival of Learning at Charlemagne's Court

To make his empire as splendid as Rome's, Charlemagne invited to his court at Aachen the best minds and the finest artisans of western Europe and the Byzantine East. Among them were Theodulf of Orléans, Paulinus of Aquileia, and Alcuin, master of the cathedral school at York, the center of Northumbrian learning. Alcuin brought Anglo-Saxon scholarship into the Carolingian setting, a major stimulus of its cultural reawakening.

Charlemagne himself, according to Einhard, his biographer, could read and speak Latin fluently, in addition to Frankish, his native tongue. He also could understand Greek, and he studied rhetoric and mathematics with the learned men he gathered around him. But he never learned to write properly—that was a task best left to professional scribes. In

fact, one of Charlemagne's dearest projects was the recovery of the true text of the Bible, which, through centuries of miscopying by ignorant scribes, had become quite corrupt. Various scholars undertook the great project at the emperor's behest, but Alcuin of York's revision of the Bible, prepared at the new monastery at Tours, became the most widely used.

Charlemagne's scribes also were responsible for the development of a new, more compact, and more easily written and legible version of Latin script called *Caroline minuscle.* The letters on this page are descended from the alphabet Carolingian scribes perfected. Later generations also owe to Charlemagne's patronage the restoration and copying of important classical texts. The earliest known manuscripts of many Greek and Roman authors are Carolingian in date.

sculpture, small or large scale, on pictorial sources. In general, manuscript illumination provided the prototypes for medieval ivory- and metalwork.

More monumental in its conception is the golden cover of the *Lindau Gospels* (FIG. **16-16**), also fashioned in one of the workshops of Charles the Bald's court. Surrounded by pearls

and jewels (raised on golden claw feet so that they can catch and reflect the light even more brilliantly and protect the delicate metal relief from denting), a youthful Christ in the Early Christian tradition is shown nailed to the cross. The statuesque open-eyed figure, rendered in *repoussé* (hammered or pressed relief), brings to mind the beardless unsuffering

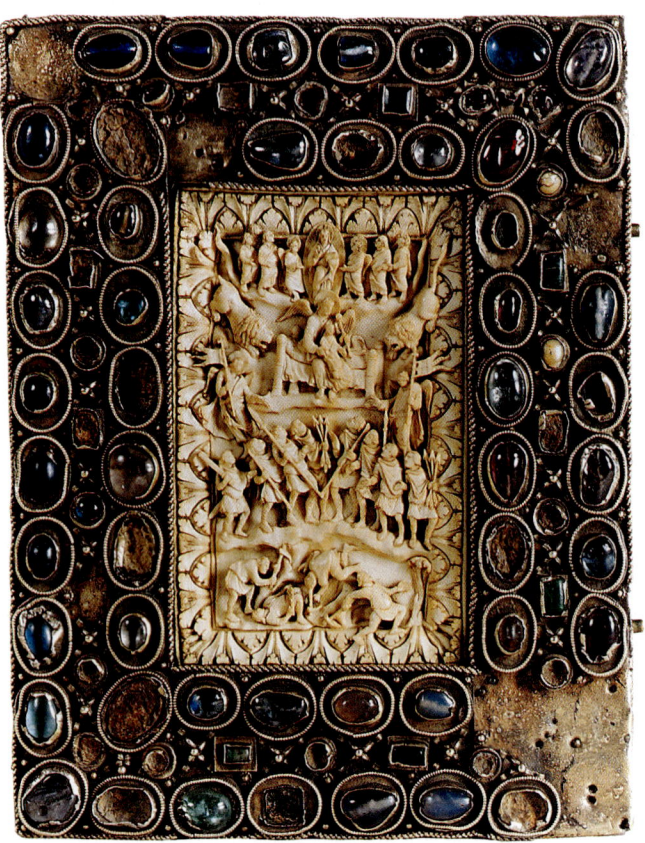

16-15 Psalm 57, front cover of the *Psalter of Charles the Bald,* from Saint-Denis, France, ca. 865. Ivory panel set in silver-gilt frame with filigree work and precious stones; panel $5\frac{1}{2}'' \times 5\frac{1}{4}''$, entire cover $9\frac{1}{2}'' \times 7\frac{3}{4}''$. Bibliothèque Nationale, Paris.

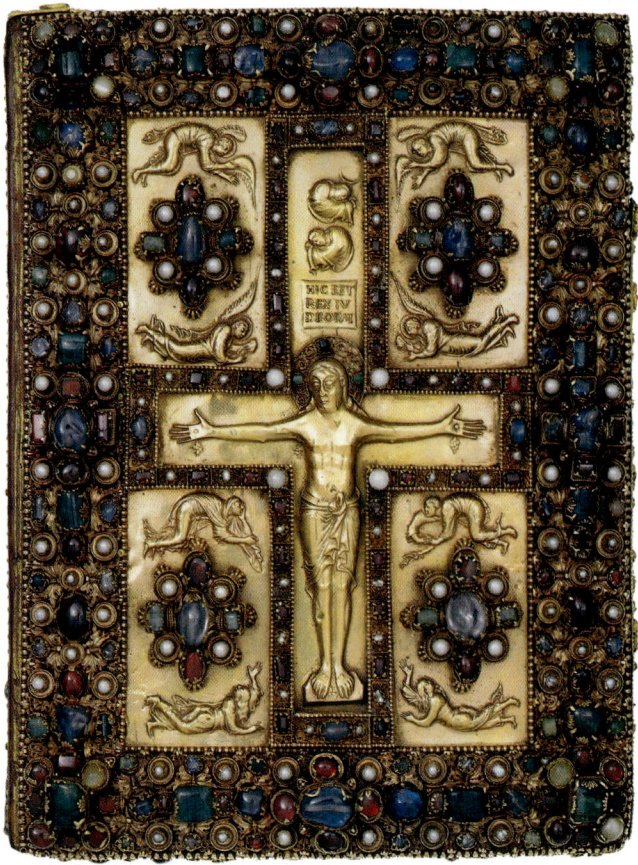

16-16 Crucifixion, front cover of the *Lindau Gospels,* ca. 870. Gold, precious stones, and pearls, $1' 1\frac{3}{8}'' \times 10\frac{3}{8}''$. Pierpont Morgan Library, New York.

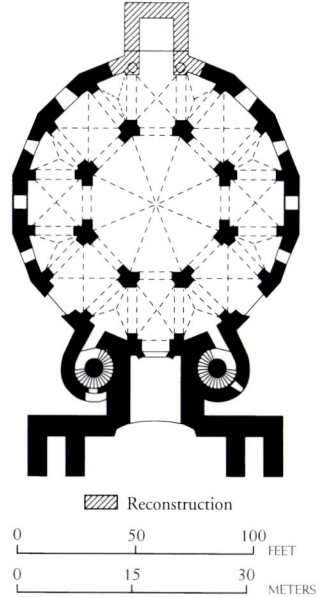

Reconstruction

0 ——— 50 ——— 100 FEET
0 ——— 15 ——— 30 METERS

16-17 ODO OF METZ, restored plan of the Palatine Chapel of Charlemagne, Aachen, Germany, 792–805.

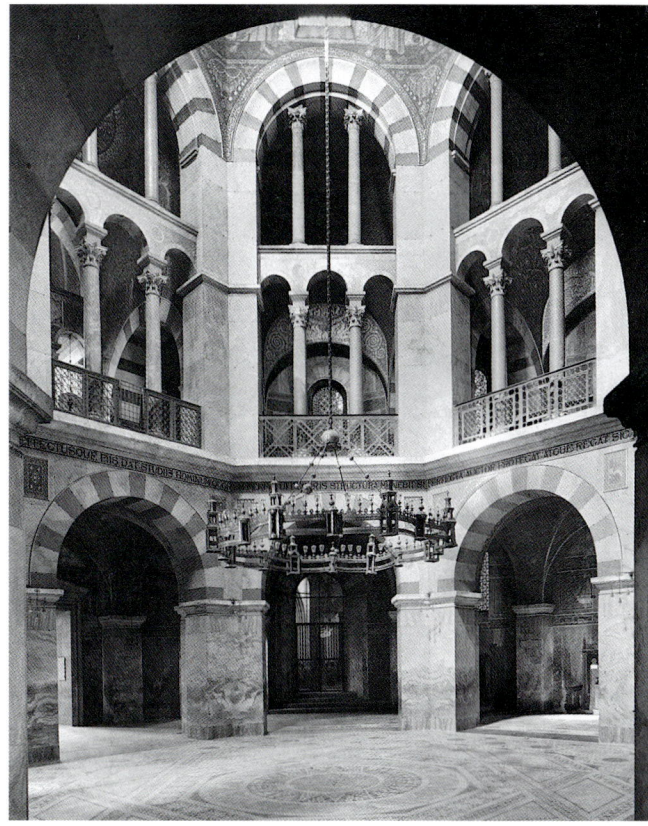

16-18 ODO OF METZ, interior of the Palatine Chapel of Charlemagne, Aachen, Germany, 792–805.

Christ of the fifth-century ivory casket from Italy in the British Museum (see FIG. 11-21). By contrast, the four angels and the personifications of the Moon and the Sun above and the crouching figures of the Virgin Mary and Saint John (and two other figures of uncertain identity) in the quadrants below display the vivacity and nervous energy of the *Utrecht Psalter* figures. This single eclectic work displays the classical and native stylistic poles of Carolingian art side by side. But at the core the translated figural style of the south prevails, in keeping with the tastes and aspirations of the Frankish emperors who brought about the "Carolingian Renaissance."

Architecture

In his eagerness to reestablish the imperial past, Charlemagne also encouraged the revival of Roman building techniques. In architecture, as in sculpture and painting, innovations made in the reinterpretation of earlier Roman Christian sources became fundamental to the subsequent development of northern European architecture. For his models, Charlemagne went to Rome and Ravenna. One was the former heart of the Roman Empire, which he wanted to revive. The other was the long-term western outpost of Byzantine might and splendor, which he wanted to emulate in his own capital at Aachen, a site chosen because of its renowned hot springs.

AACHEN: THE RAVENNA OF THE NORTH
Charlemagne often visited Ravenna, and, as already noted, he once brought an equestrian statue of Theodoric from there to display in his palace complex at Aachen, where it served as a model for Carolingian equestrian portraits (FIG. 16-11). Charlemagne also imported *porphyry* (purple marble) columns from Ravenna to adorn his Palatine Chapel, and historians long have thought he chose one of Ravenna's churches as the model for the new structure. The Aachen chapel's plan (FIG. **16-17**) resembles San Vitale's (see FIG. 12-7), and a direct relationship very likely exists between the two, although the de-

sign and construction of Charlemagne's chapel was entrusted to a Frankish builder, ODO OF METZ. (Odo was the first architect north of the Alps whose name is known.)

A comparison between the northern building, the first vaulted structure of the Middle Ages in the West, and its southern counterpart is instructive. The Aachen plan is simpler. San Vitale's apselike extensions reaching from the central octagon into the ambulatory were omitted, so the two main units stand in greater independence of each other. This solution may lack the subtle sophistication of the Byzantine building, but the Palatine Chapel gains geometric clarity. A view of the interior of the Palatine Chapel (FIG. **16-18**) shows that the "floating" quality of San Vitale (see FIG. 12-8) was converted into blunt massiveness and stiffened into solid geometric form.

Odo's conversion of a complex and subtle Byzantine prototype into a building that expresses robust strength and clear structural articulation foreshadowed the architecture of the eleventh and twelfth centuries and the style called Romanesque (see Chapter 17). So, too, did his treatment of the Palatine Chapel's exterior, where two cylindrical towers with spiral staircases flank the entrance portal. This was a first step toward the great dual-tower facades of churches in the West from the tenth century to the present. Above the portal, Charlemagne could appear in a large framing arch and be seen by those gathered in the atrium in front of the chapel (only part of the atrium is included in our plan). Directly behind that second-story arch was Charlemagne's marble throne. From there he could peer down at the altar in the apse. This was in every sense a royal chapel. Charlemagne's son, Louis the Pious (r. 814–840), was crowned there when he succeeded his father as emperor.

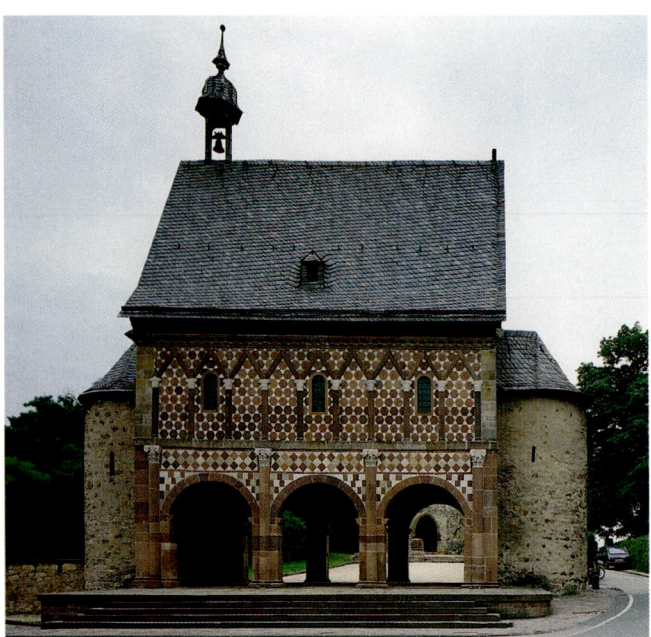

16-19 *Torhalle* (gatehouse), Lorsch, Germany, ninth century.

A MONASTIC TRIUMPHAL GATEWAY The Carolingian evocation of the Roman past is illustrated by a remarkable survival from the ninth century, the *Torhalle* (FIG. **16-19**), or gatehouse, of the Lorsch Monastery in Germany. The gate is difficult to date because it is unique. Long thought to be from Charlemagne's time, it recently has been placed later in the century. Built as a freestanding structure in the atrium of the monastic church, the Lorsch *Torhalle* is a distant relative of the Arch of Constantine (see FIG. 10-76). But it follows more closely the design of Roman city gates, with its second-story windows and flanking towers (which also recall the arrangement of the Palatine Chapel's facade at Aachen). Also inspired by Roman architecture are the fairly close copies of Composite capitals and the framing of the arcuated passageways by engaged columns. The decorative treatment of the flat wall surfaces with colored inlays of cream and pink stone imitated Roman *opus reticulatum,* a method of facing concrete walls with lozenge-shaped bricks or stones to achieve a netlike ornamental surface pattern. However, the columns support a decorative *stringcourse* (raised horizontal *molding,* or band) instead of a full entablature, and the second level was treated in a manner without parallel in classical

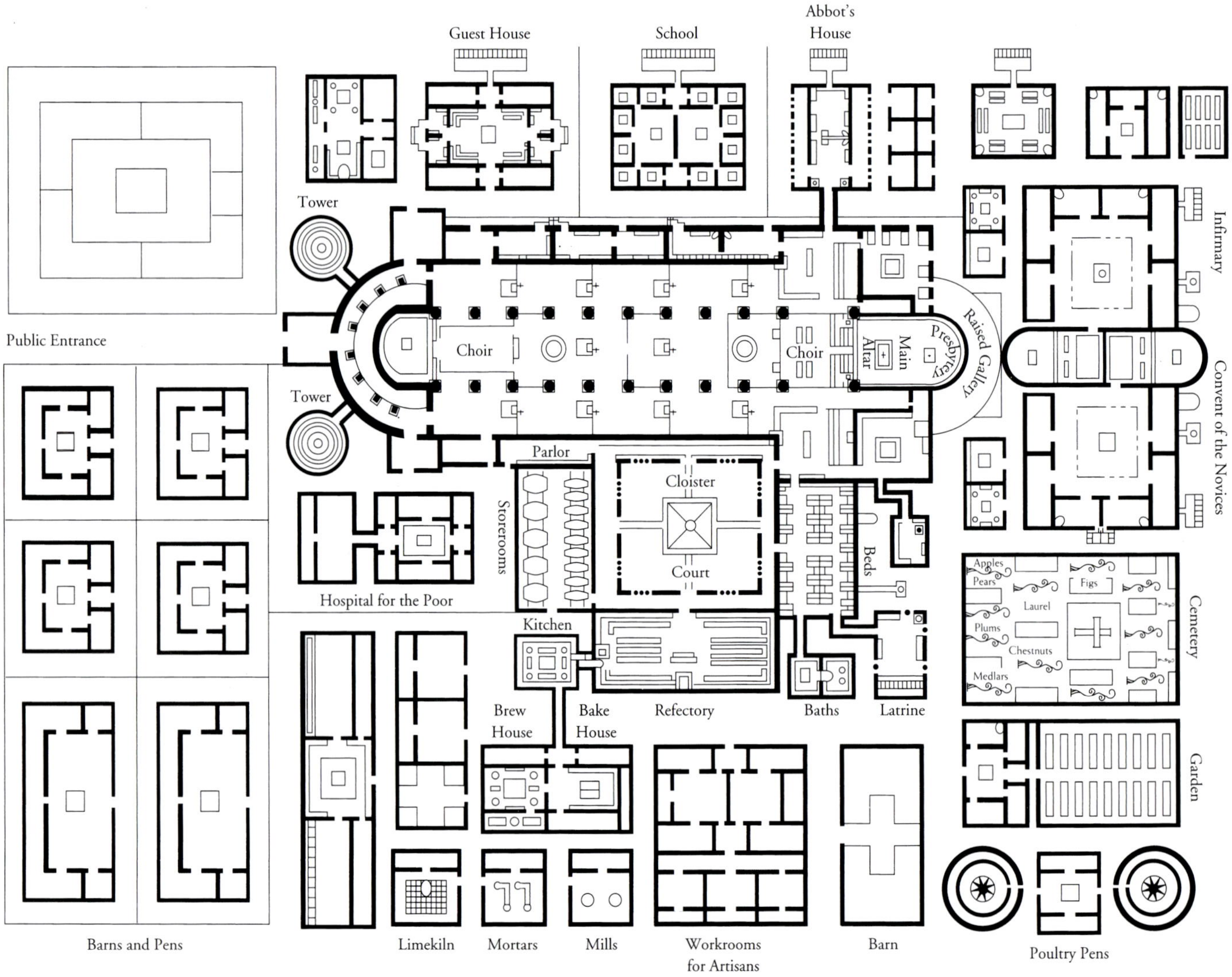

16-20 Schematic plan for a monastery at Saint Gall, Switzerland, ca. 819. (Redrawn after a ninth-century manuscript; original in red ink on parchment, 2' 4" × 3' 8⅛". Stiftsbibliothek, Saint Gall.)

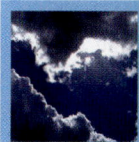

Medieval Monasteries and Benedictine Rule

Monastic foundations appeared in the West beginning in Early Christian times. The monks who established monasteries also made the rules that governed them. The most significant of these monks was Benedict of Nursia (Saint Benedict), who founded the Benedictine Order in 529. By the ninth century, the "Rule" Benedict gave *(Regula Sancti Benedicti)* had become standard for all Western monastic establishments, in part because Charlemagne had encouraged its adoption throughout the Frankish territories.

Saint Benedict believed that the corruption of the clergy that accompanied the Christian Church's increasing worldliness was rooted in the lack of firm organization and regulation. Neglect of the commandments of God and of the Church was due, as he saw it, to idleness and venality, which in turn tempted the clergy to loose living. The cure for this was communal association in an *abbey* under the absolute rule of an *abbot* the monks elected (or an *abbess* the nuns chose), who would see to it that each hour of the day was spent in useful work and in sacred reading. The emphasis was on work and study and not on meditation and austerity. This is of great historical significance. Since antiquity, manual labor had been considered disgraceful, the business of the lowborn or of slaves. Benedict raised it to the dignity of religion. The core idea of what many people today call the "work ethic" found early expression here as an essential feature of the spiritual life. By thus exalting the virtue of manual labor, Benedict not only rescued it from its age-old association with slavery, but also recognized it as the way to self-sufficiency for the entire religious community.

While some of Saint Benedict's followers emphasized spiritual "work" over manual labor, others, most notably the Cistercians (see "Saint Bernard of Clairvaux on Cloister Sculpture," Chapter 17, page 470), put his teachings about the value of physical work into practice. These monks reached into their surroundings and helped reduce the vast areas of daunting wilderness of early medieval Europe. They cleared dense forest teeming with wolves, bear, and wild boar; drained swamps; cultivated wastelands; and built roads, bridges, and dams, as well as monastic churches and their associated living and service quarters. An ideal monastery (FIG. 16-20) provided all the facilities necessary for the conduct of daily life— a mill, bakery, infirmary, vegetable garden, and even a brewery—so that the monks felt no need to wander outside its protective walls.

Such religious communities were centrally important to the revival of learning. The clergy, who were also often scribes and scholars, had a monopoly on the skills of reading and writing in an age of almost universal illiteracy. The monastic libraries and scriptoria, where books were read, copied, illuminated, and bound with ornamented covers, became centers of study. These were almost the sole repositories of what remained of the literary culture of the Greco-Roman world and early Christianity. The Benedictine Rule's requirements of manual labor and sacred reading were expanded to include writing and copying books, studying music for chanting the day's offices, and—of great significance—teaching. The monasteries were the schools of the early Middle Ages, as well as self-sufficient communities and production centers.

---

architecture. Pseudo-Ionic pilasters carry a zigzag of ornamental moldings, and the opus reticulatum was converted into a decorative pattern of hexagons and triangles that form star shapes. Finally, the steeply pitched timber roof that shelters a chapel dedicated to Saint Michael unmistakably stamps this gatehouse as a northern building. Still, the source of inspiration is clear, and if the final product no longer closely resembles the original, it is due to the fact it is not a copy but a free and fanciful interpretation of its model.

THE IDEAL MONASTERY The Carolingian monastery at Lorsch is not preserved, but scholars have learned much about the design of monastic communities at this time, thanks to a fascinating contemporary document, the ideal plan (FIG. **16-20**) for a monastery at Saint Gall in Switzerland. About 819, a schematic plan for a Benedictine community (see "Medieval Monasteries and Benedictine Rule," above) was drawn for Haito, the abbot of Reichenau and bishop of Basel, and sent to the abbot of Saint Gall. The plan provided a coherent arrangement of all the buildings of a monastic community and was intended as a guide in the rebuilding of the Saint Gall monastery. The design's fundamental purpose was to sep-

arate the monks from the laity, who also inhabited the community. Variations of the scheme may be seen in later monasteries all across western Europe.

Near the center, dominating everything, was the church with its *cloister,* a colonnaded courtyard (compare FIG. 17-24) not unlike the Early Christian atrium but situated to the side of the church rather than in front of its main portal. Reserved for the monks alone, the cloister provided the peace and quiet necessary for contemplation and was regarded as a kind of earthly paradise removed from the world at large. Around the cloister were grouped the most essential buildings: dormitory, refectory, kitchen, and storage rooms. Other structures, including an infirmary, school, guest house, bakery, brewery, and workshops, were grouped around this central core of church and cloister.

Haito invited the abbot of Saint Gall to adapt the plan as he saw fit, and the Saint Gall builders did not, in fact, follow the Reichenau model exactly. Nonetheless, if the abbot had wished, Haito's plan *could* have served as a practical guide for the Saint Gall masons because it was laid out on a *module* (standard unit) of two and one-half feet. Parts or multiples of this module were used consistently throughout the plan. For example, the nave's width, indicated on the plan as forty feet, was equal to sixteen modules; the length of each monk's bed to two and one-half modules; and the width of paths in the vegetable garden to one and a quarter modules. This systematic building up of the plan from a prescribed module reflects the medieval mind's eagerness to explain the Christian faith in terms of an orderly, rationalistic philosophy built on carefully distinguished propositions and well-planned arguments. It also parallels the Carolingian invention of that most convenient device, the division of books into chapters and subchapters.

THE BASILICAN CHURCH TRANSFORMED   The models that carried the greatest authority for Charlemagne and his builders were those from the Christian phase of the late Roman Empire. The widespread adoption of the Early Christian basilica, at Saint Gall and elsewhere, rather than the domed central plan of Byzantine churches, was crucial to the subsequent development of Western church architecture. Unfortunately, no Carolingian basilica has survived in anything approaching its original form. Nevertheless, it is possible to reconstruct the appearance of some of them with fair accuracy. Several of these structures appear to have followed their Early Christian models quite closely. But in other instances Carolingian builders subjected the basilica plan to some very significant modifications, converting it into a much more complex form. The monastery church at Saint Gall (FIG. 16-20), for example, was essentially a three-aisled basilica, but it had features not found in any Early Christian church. Most obvious is the addition of a second apse on the west end of the building, perhaps to accommodate additional altars and relics (see "Pilgrimages and the Cult of Relics," Chapter 17, page 457). Whatever its purpose, this feature remained a characteristic regional element of German churches until the eleventh century.

Not quite as evident but much more important to the subsequent development of church architecture in the North was the presence of a transept at Saint Gall, a very rare feature, but one that characterized the two greatest Early Christian basilicas in Rome, Saint Peter's (see FIG. 11-7) and Saint Paul's. The Saint Gall transept is as wide as the nave on the plan and was probably the same height. Early Christian builders had not been concerned with proportional relationships. They assembled the various portions of their buildings only in accordance with the dictates of liturgical needs. On the Saint Gall plan, however, the various parts of the building are related to one another by a geometric scheme that ties them together into a tight and cohesive unit. Equalizing the widths of nave and transept automatically makes the area where they cross (the *crossing*) a square. Most Carolingian churches shared this feature. But Haito's planner also used the crossing square as the unit of measurement for the remainder of the church plan. The transept arms are equal to one crossing square, the distance between transept and apse is one crossing square, and the nave is four and one-half crossing squares long. The fact the aisles are half as wide as the nave integrates all parts of the church in a rational, lucid, and extremely orderly plan.

THE MULTIPLICATION OF TOWERS   Old drawings of the now-destroyed church of Saint-Riquier at Centula

in northeastern France provide a good idea of what major Carolingian basilicas looked like. A monastery church like that of Saint Gall, Saint-Riquier was built toward the very end of the eighth century. It predated the Saint Gall plan by approximately twenty years. Our drawing (FIG. **16-21**) shows a feature not indicated on the plan for Saint Gall—multiple towers. The Saint Gall plan shows only two towers, both cylindrical and on the west side of the church, as at the Palatine Chapel at Aachen (FIG. 16-17), but they stand apart from the church facade. If a tower existed above the crossing, the silhouette of Saint Gall would have shown three towers rising above the nave. Saint-Riquier had six towers (not all are shown in the illustration) built directly onto or rising from the building proper. As large, vertical, cylindrical masses, these towers rose above the horizontal roofline, balancing one another in two groups of three at each end of the basilican nave. Round stair towers on the basilica's west end provided access to the upper stories of the so-called *westwork* (entrance structure) and to the big spired tower that balanced the spired tower above the eastern crossing. On the second floor, the towered westwork contained a complete chapel flanked by aisles—a small upper church available for parish services. The

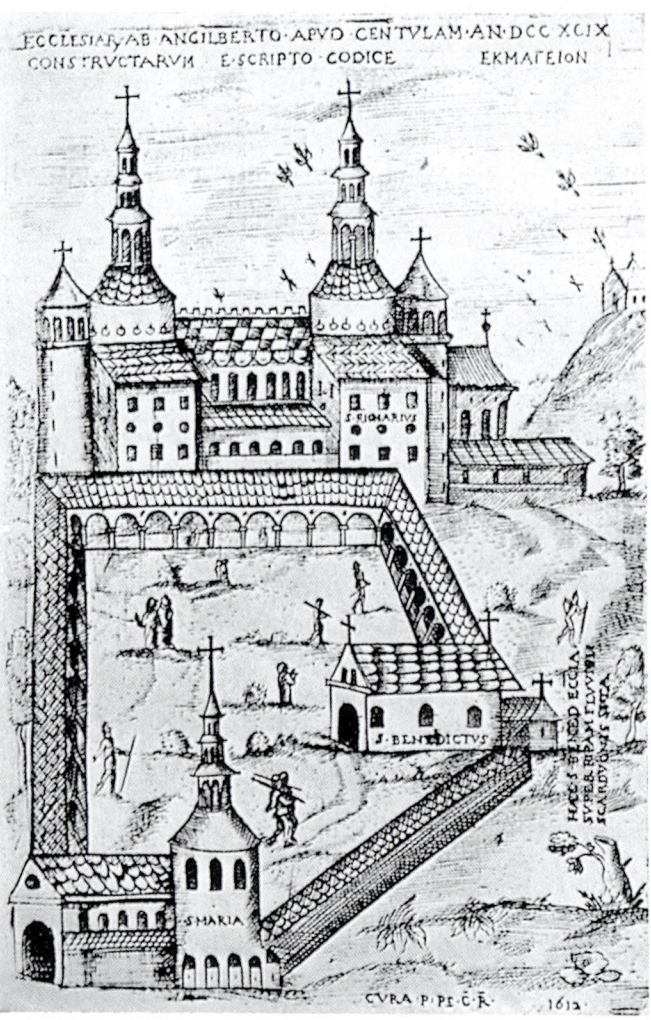

16-21   Drawing of the monastery church of Saint-Riquier, Centula, France, ca. 800. (Engraving made in 1612 after a now-destroyed eleventh-century miniature.)

building's main floor was reserved for the clergy's use. As at Aachen, a gallery opened onto the main nave, and from it, on occasion, the emperor and his entourage could watch and participate in the service below. The Saint-Riquier design, particularly the silhouette with its multiple towers, was highly influential, especially in Germany.

OTTONIAN ART

IN THE AFTERMATH OF CHARLEMAGNE Charlemagne was buried in the Palatine Chapel at Aachen. His empire survived him by less than thirty years. When his son Louis the Pious died in 840, the Carolingian Empire was divided among Louis's sons, Charles the Bald, Lothair, and Louis the German. After bloody conflicts among the brothers, a treaty was signed in 843 partitioning the Frankish lands into western, central, and eastern areas, very roughly foreshadowing the later nations of France and Germany and a third realm corresponding to a long strip of land stretching from the Netherlands and Belgium to Rome. Intensified Viking incursions in the West helped bring about the collapse of the Carolingians and the suspension of their great cultural effort. The empire's breakup into weak kingdoms, ineffectual against the invasions, brought a time of darkness and confusion to Europe. The Viking scourge in the West was complemented by the invasions of the Magyars in the East and by the plundering and piracy of the Saracen (Muslim) corsairs in the Mediterranean.

Only in the mid-tenth century did the eastern part of the former empire consolidate under the rule of a new Saxon line of German emperors called, after the names of the three most illustrious family members, the *Ottonians*. The first Otto (r. 936–973) was crowned emperor in Rome by the pope in 962, assuming the title Charlemagne's weak successors held during most of the previous century. The three Ottos made headway against the invaders from the East, remained free from Viking depredations, and not only preserved but also enriched the Carolingian period's culture and tradition. The Christian Church, which had become corrupt and disorganized, recovered in the tenth century under the influence of a great monastic reform encouraged and sanctioned by the Ottonians, who also cemented ties with Italy and the papacy. When the last of the Ottonian line, Henry II, died in the early eleventh century, the pagan marauders had become Christianized and settled, and the monastic reforms had been highly successful. Several signs pointed to a cultural renewal destined soon to produce greater monuments than had been known in the West since ancient Rome.

Architecture

TOWERING OTTONIAN SPIRES Ottonian architects followed the course of their Carolingian predecessors. In fact, the westwork of the Benedictine abbey church of Saint Pantaleon (FIG. **16-22**) at Cologne, Germany, gives an idea of the former facades of Saint-Riquier and other Carolingian churches. Begun in 966 and consecrated in 980, Saint Pantaleon was the burial site of Archbishop Bruno, brother of Otto I. It is distinguished by its towering westwork, where

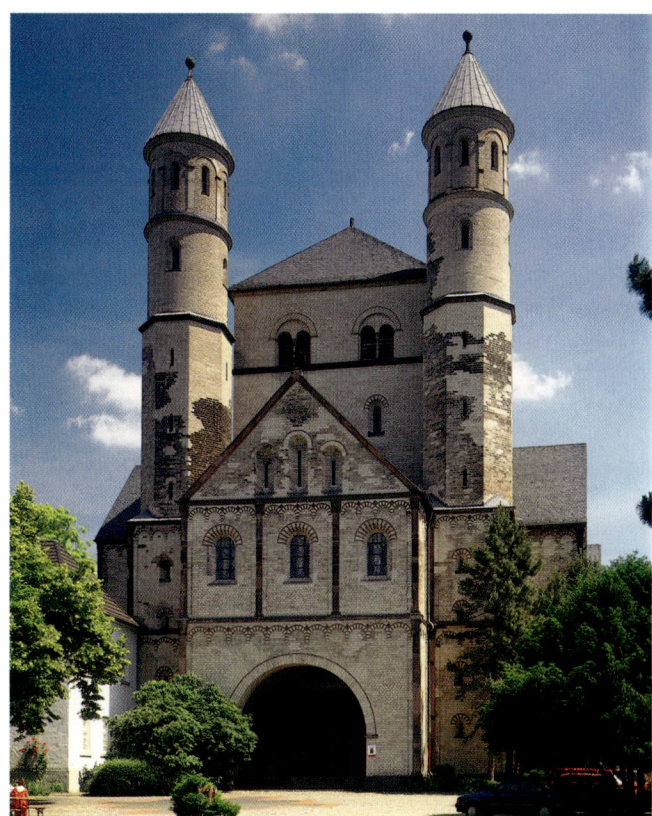

16-22 Abbey church of Saint Pantaleon, Cologne, Germany, 966–980.

two tall cylindrical spires capped by cones rise from polygonal bases and frame a less-lofty, broad, quadrilateral crossing tower. The centerpiece is a three-story entrance facade with a large arcuated portal below three rounded windows framed by pilasters, all crowned by a pediment-like upper story pierced by another set of three smaller windows. The arrangement recalls that of the Lorsch *Torhalle* (FIG. 16-19) and echoes, more distantly, the series of superimposesd arches of varying size of the Roman Pont-du-Gard (see FIG. 10-31). The pattern is repeated, in variant form, on the ends of the transept arms (not shown). The framing of the various design elements by stringcourses and pilasters creates a linear geometric grid that complements the interplay of cylinders, cubes, polygons, and pyramids of the westwork as a whole.

AN OTTONIAN BISHOP IN ROME One of the great patrons of Ottonian art and architecture was Bishop Bernward of Hildesheim, Germany. He was the tutor of Otto III (r. 983–1002) and builder of the abbey church of Saint Michael's at Hildesheim. Bernward, who made Hildesheim a center of learning, not only was skilled in affairs of state but also was an eager scholar, a lover of the arts, and, according to Thangmar of Heidelberg, his biographer, an expert craftsman and bronze caster. In 1001, he traveled to Rome as the guest of Otto III. During this stay, Bernward studied at first hand the monuments of the empire the Carolingian and Ottonian emperors had been seeking to revive.

Bernward's Saint Michael's and its sculptured decoration in precious bronze are widely acknowledged as Ottonian

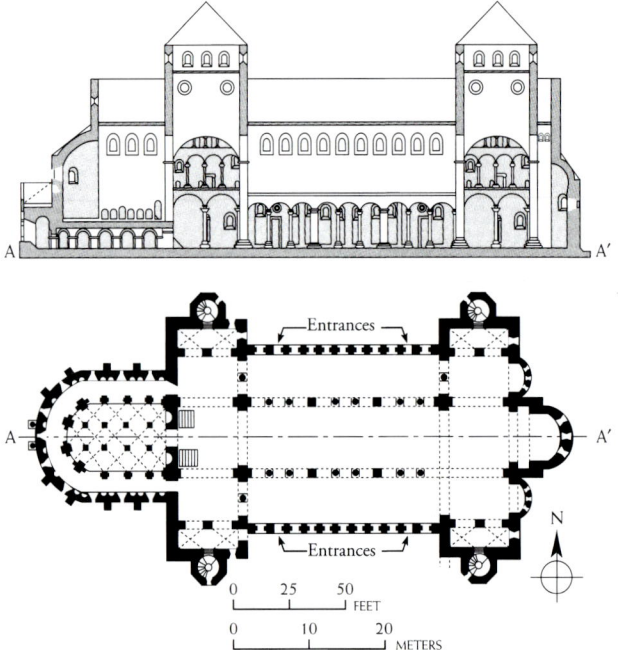

16-23 Longitudinal section *(top)* and plan *(bottom)* of the abbey church of Saint Michael's, Hildesheim, Germany, 1001–1031.

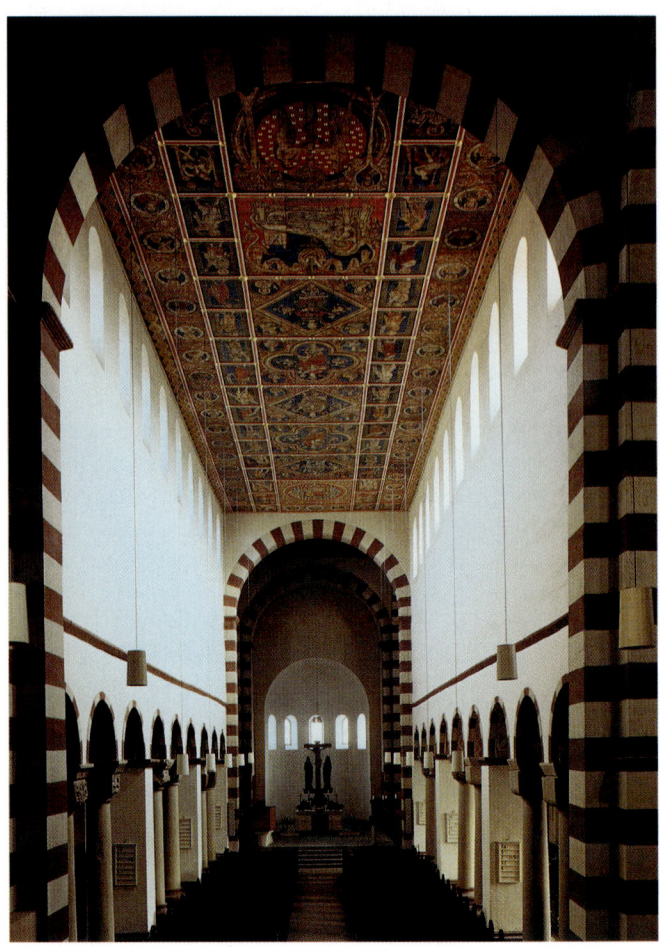

16-24 Restored nave of Saint Michael's, Hildesheim, Germany, 1001–1031.

masterpieces. Constructed between 1001 and 1031, the church has a double-transept plan, tower groupings, and a westwork similar to Saint Pantaleon's, as well as massive walls pierced only occasionally by arcuated windows. The plan and section of Saint Michael's (FIG. **16-23**) clearly show how the two transepts create eastern and western centers of gravity. The nave merely seems to be a hall that connects them. Lateral entrances leading into the aisles from the north and south additionally make for an almost complete loss of the traditional basilican orientation toward the east. Some ancient Roman basilicas, such as the Basilica Ulpia in Trajan's Forum (see FIG. 10-41), also had two apses and were entered from the side, and Bernward probably was familiar with this variant basilican plan.

At Hildesheim, as in the plan of the monastery at Saint Gall (FIG. 16-20), the builders adopted a modular approach. The crossing squares, for example, were used as the basis for the nave's dimensions—three crossing squares long and one square wide. This fact was emphasized visually by the placement of heavy piers at the corners of each square. These piers alternate with pairs of columns as wall supports to form what is called an *alternate-support system*. It became a standard element of many Romanesque churches in northern Europe.

A view of Saint Michael's interior (FIG. **16-24**) shows the rhythm of the alternating light and heavy wall supports. It shows, as well, that this rhythm is not reflected in the upper nave walls—that, in fact, it was not carried farther than the actual supports, unlike later basilicas. Although the nave's proportions had changed from those of earlier churches (it is much taller in relation to its width than a Roman basilica), it retained the continuous and unbroken appearance of its Early Christian predecessors.

Sculpture

BIBLICAL STORIES ON COLOSSAL DOORS In 1001, when Bishop Bernward was in Rome visiting the young Otto III, he resided in Otto's palace on the Aventine hill in the neighborhood of Santa Sabina (see FIG. 11-8), an Early Christian church renowned for its carved wooden doors. Those doors, decorated with episodes from both the Old and New Testaments, may have inspired the remarkable bronze doors the bishop had cast for his new church in Germany. The colossal doors (FIG. **16-25**) for Saint Michael's, dated by inscription to 1015, are more than sixteen feet tall. Each was cast in a single piece with the figural sculpture, a technological tour-de-force of lost-wax casting (see "Hollow-Casting Life-Size Bronze Statues," Chapter 5, page 124). Carolingian sculpture, like most sculpture since late antiquity, consisted primarily of small-scale art executed in ivory and precious metals, so the sixteen individual panels of the Hildesheim doors may be compared to the covers of earlier Carolingian and Ottonian books (FIGS. 16-15 and 16-16). But Bernward's doors are more public than any book cover, although they were situated at the entrance to the church from the cloister, where only the monks could pass through them. The prominent placement of narrative reliefs on the Saint Michael's portal anticipated the reinstatement of large-scale sculpture in the Romanesque period (see "The Romanesque Portal," Chapter 17, page 471).

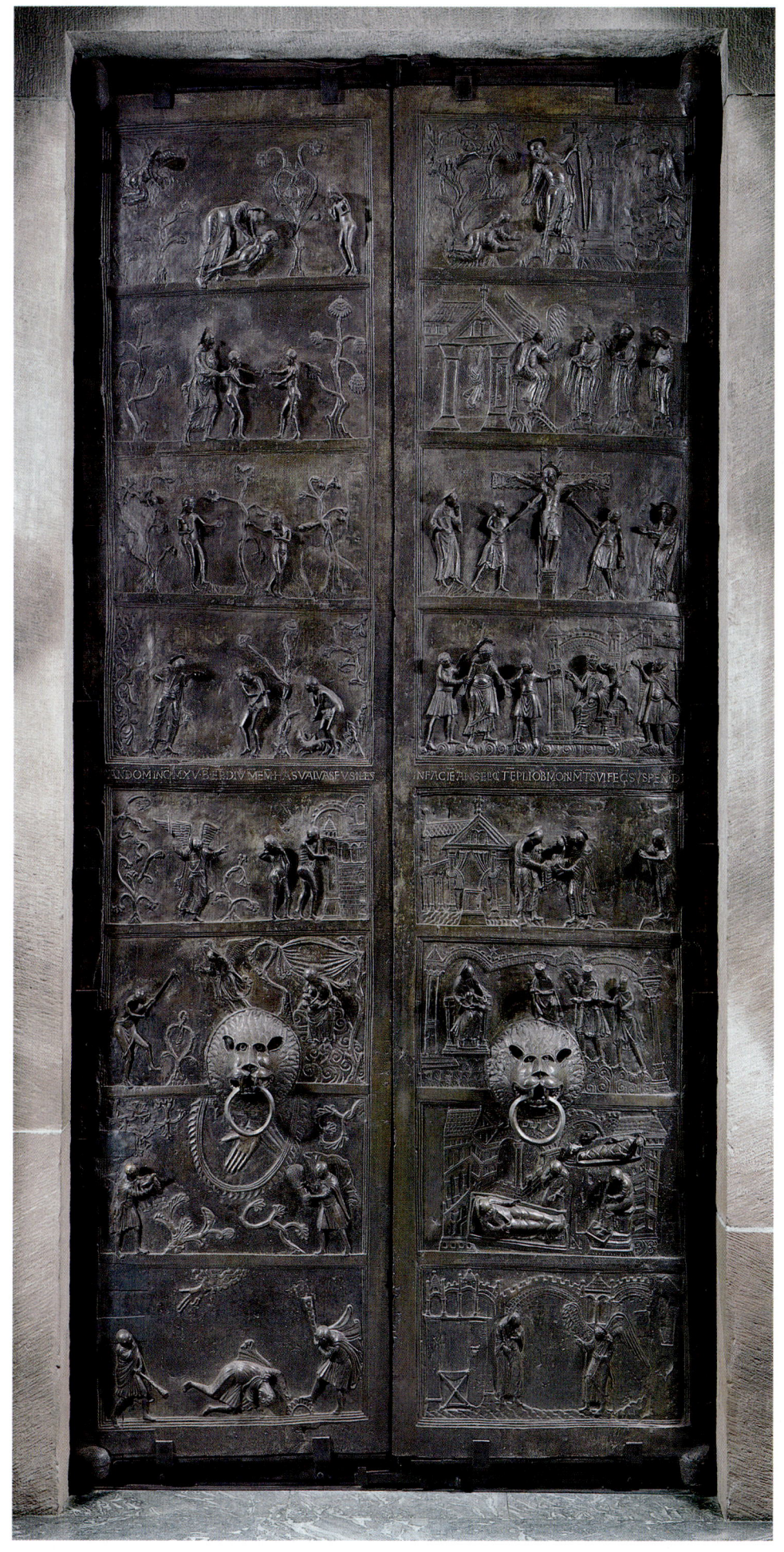

16-25 Doors with relief panels (Genesis, left door; life of Christ, right door), commissioned by Bishop Bernward for Saint Michael's, Hildesheim, Germany, 1015. Bronze, 16′ 6″ high. Saint Michael's, Hildesheim.

The left-door panels illustrate highlights from the biblical Book of Genesis, beginning with the creation of Adam (at the top) and ending with the murder of Adam and Eve's son Abel by his brother Cain (at the bottom). The right door recounts the life of Christ (reading from the bottom up), starting with the Annunciation and terminating with the appearance to Mary Magdalene of Christ after the Resurrection. Together, the doors tell the story of Original Sin and ultimate redemption, showing the expulsion from the Garden of Eden and the path back to Paradise through the Christian Church. As in Early Christian times, the Old Testament was interpreted as prefiguring the New Testament (see "Jewish Subjects in Christian Art," Chapter 11, page 305). The panel depicting the Fall of Adam and Eve, for example, is juxtaposed with the Crucifixion on the other door. Eve nursing the infant Cain is opposite Mary with the Christ Child in her lap.

The composition of many of the scenes on the doors derives from Carolingian manuscript illumination, and the style of the figures has an expressive strength that brings to mind the illustrations in the *Utrecht Psalter* (FIG. 16-14). For example, in the fourth panel from the top on the left door, God, portrayed as a man, accuses Adam and Eve after their fall from grace. As he lays on them the curse of mortality, the primal condemnation, he jabs his finger at them with the force of his whole body. The force is concentrated in the gesture, which becomes the psychic focus of the whole composition. The frightened pair crouch, not only to hide their shame but also to escape the lightning bolt of divine wrath. Each passes the blame—Adam pointing backward to Eve and Eve pointing downward to the deceitful serpent. The starkly flat setting throws the gestures and attitudes of rage, accusation, guilt, and fear into relief. The story was presented with simplicity, but with great emotional impact. The artist had a flair for anecdotal detail. Adam and Eve both struggle to point with one arm while attempting to shield their bodies from sight with the other. With an instinct for expressive pose and gesture, the sculptor brilliantly communicated their newfound embarrassment at their nakedness and their unconvincing denials of wrongdoing.

AN OTTONIAN TRIUMPHAL COLUMN The great doors of Saint Michael's were not the only large-scale masterpieces of bronze-casting Bernward commissioned. Within the church stood a bronze spiral column (FIG. **16-26**) that is preserved intact, save for its later capital and missing surmounting cross. It probably was begun sometime after the doors were set in place and completed before the bishop's death in 1022. The seven spiral bands of relief tell the story of Jesus' life in twenty-four scenes, beginning with his baptism and concluding with his entry into Jerusalem. These are the missing episodes from the story told on the church's doors.

The narrative reads from bottom to top, exactly as on the Column of Trajan in Rome (see FIG. 10-42). That ancient monument was unmistakably the model for the Hildesheim column, even though the Ottonian narrative unfolds from right to left instead of from left to right. Once again, a monument in Rome provided the inspiration for the Ottonian artists working under Bernward's direction. Both the doors and the column of Saint Michael's lend credence to the Ottonian emperors' claim to be the heirs to Charlemagne's *renovatio imperii Romani.*

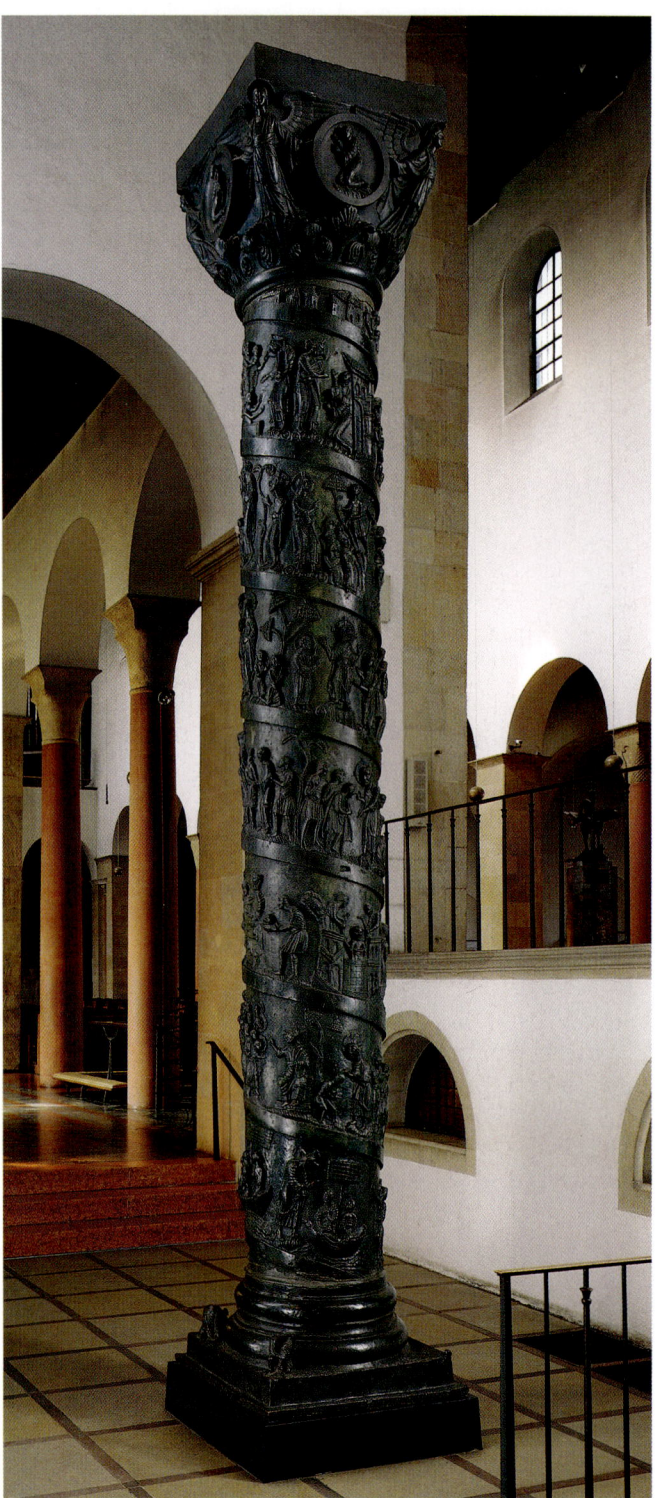

16-26   Column with reliefs illustrating the life of Christ, commissioned by Bishop Bernward for Saint Michael's, Hildesheim, Germany, ca. 1015–1022. Bronze, 12' 6" tall. Saint Michael's, Hildesheim.

SUFFERING ON A MONUMENTAL SCALE Nowhere was the revival of interest in monumental sculpture more evident than in the *Crucifix* (FIG. **16-27**) Archbishop Gero commissioned and presented to Cologne Cathedral in 970. Carved in oak and then painted and gilded, the six-foot-tall image of Christ nailed to the cross is both statue and *reliquary* (a shrine for sacred relics). A com-

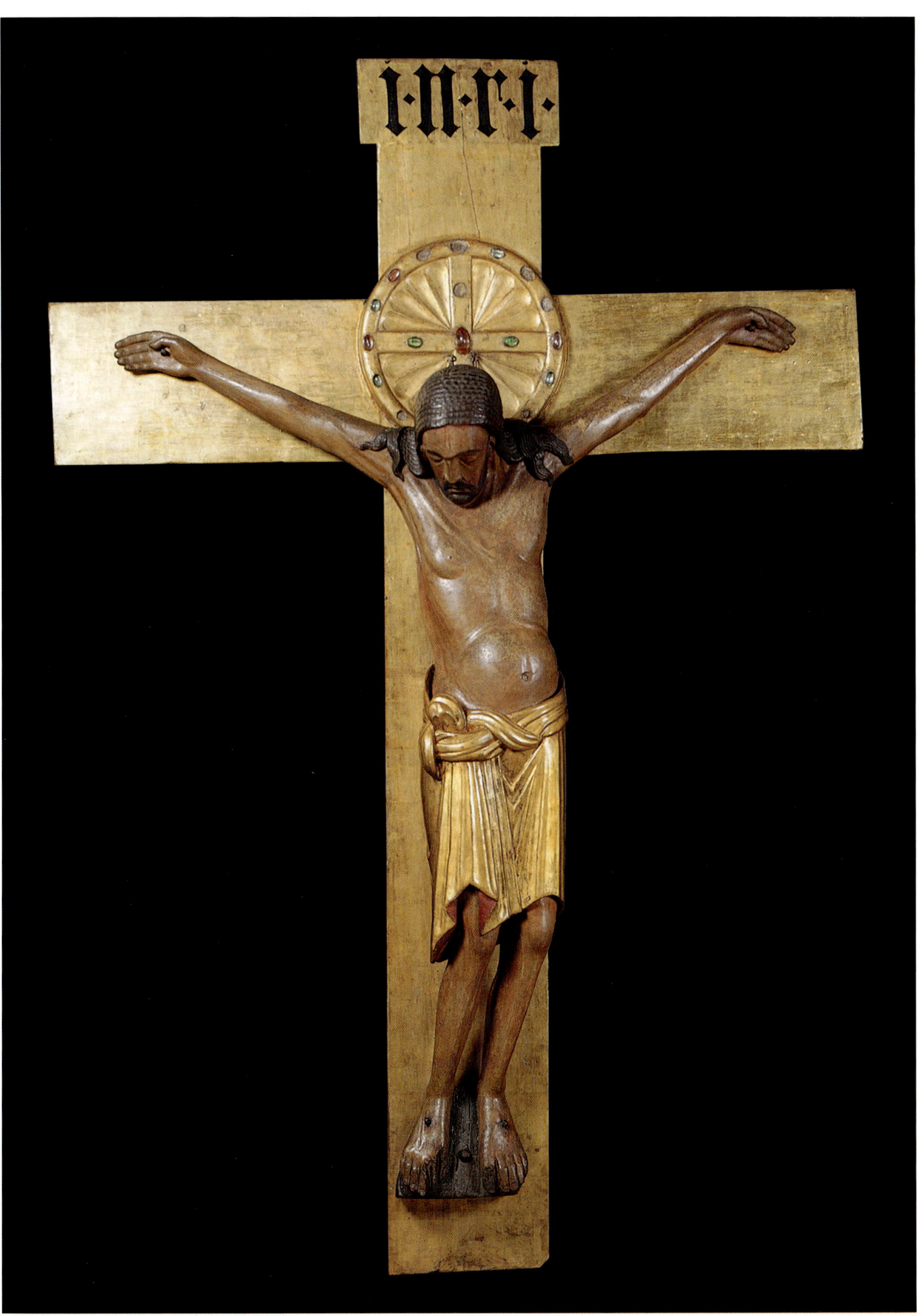

16-27 Crucifix commissioned by Archbishop Gero for Cologne Cathedral, Germany, ca. 970. Painted wood, height of figure 6′ 2″. Cathedral, Cologne.

16-28 Annunciation to the Shepherds, folio in the *Lectionary of Henry II,* from Reichenau, Germany, 1002–1014. Tempera on vellum, approx. 1′ 5″ × 1′ 1″. Bayerische Staatsbibliothek, Munich.

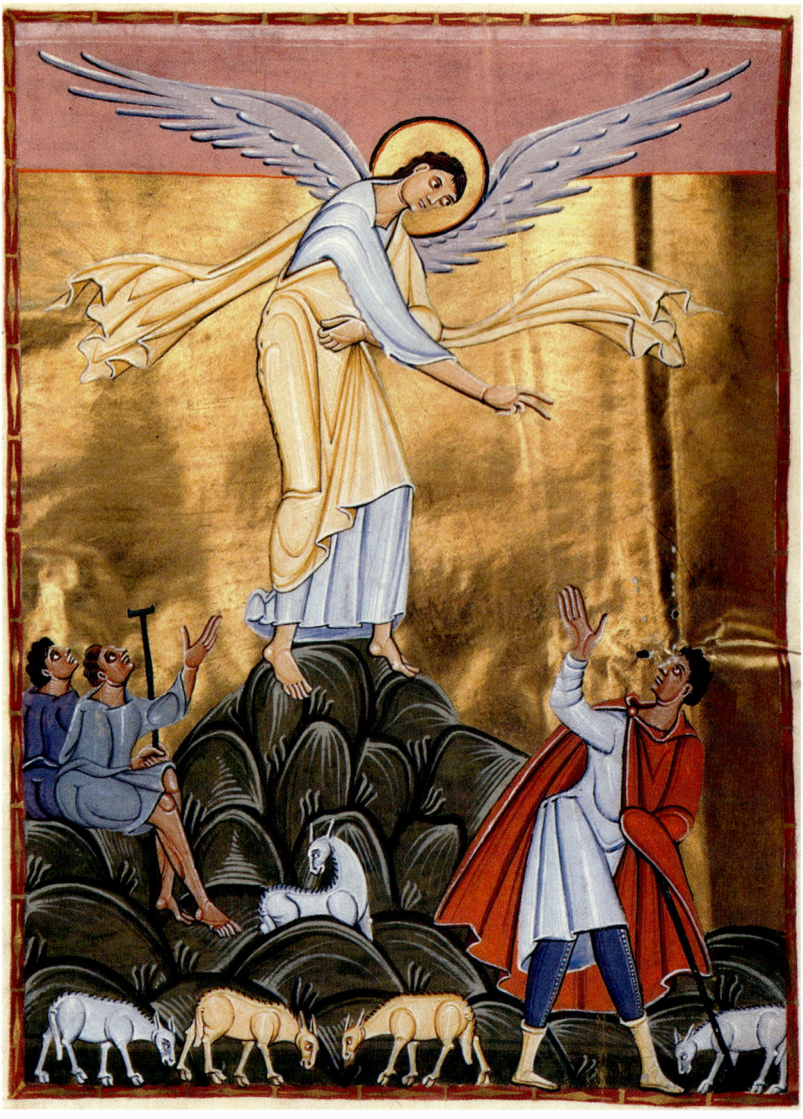

partment in the back of the head held the Host. This was a dramatically different conception of the crucified Savior than that on the cover of the *Lindau Gospels* (FIG. 16-16), which revived the Early Christian image of the youthful Christ triumphant over death. The bearded Christ of the Gero Crucifix is more akin to Byzantine representations of the suffering Jesus (see FIG. 12-20), but the Ottonian work's emotional power is greater still. The sculptor depicted Christ as an all-too-human martyr. Blood streaks down his forehead from the (missing) crown of thorns. His eyelids are closed, and his face is contorted in pain. Christ's body sags under its own weight. The muscles are stretched to the limit—those of his right shoulder and chest seem almost to rip apart. The halo behind Christ's head may foretell his subsequent Resurrection, but all the worshiper senses is his pain. Gero's Crucifix is the most powerful characterization of intense agony of the early Middle Ages.

The Art of the Book

A ROYAL LECTIONARY   Ottonian artists carried on the Carolingian tradition of producing sumptuous books for the clergy and royalty alike. One of the finest is the *Lectionary of Henry II,* the cousin of Otto III who succeeded him as em-

peror (r. 1002–1024). The book was his gift to Bamberg Cathedral. We reproduce the full-page illumination of the Annunciation of Christ's birth to the shepherds (FIG. **16-28**). The angel has just alighted on a hill, his wings still beating, and the wind of his landing agitates his draperies. Although the angel is a far cry from the dynamic marble *Nike of Samothrace* (see FIG. 5-82) of Hellenistic times, the framed panel still incorporates much that was at the heart of the classical tradition, including the rocky landscape setting with grazing animals, common also in Early Christian art (see FIG. 11-15). The golden background betrays, however, knowledge of Byzantine book illumination and mosaic decoration. (Otto II, r. 973–983, had taken as his bride the Byzantine princess Theophanu, who ruled as regent from 983 to 991, while Otto III was still a minor.) The angel looms immense above the startled and terrified shepherds, filling the golden sky, and bends on them a fierce and menacing glance as he extends his hand in the gesture of authority and instruction. Emphasized more than the message itself are the power and majesty of God's authority. The artist portrayed it here with the same emotional impact as the electric force of God's violent pointing in the Hildesheim doors.

The draperies, rendered in a hard, firm line, and the planes, partitioned in sharp, often heavily modeled shapes

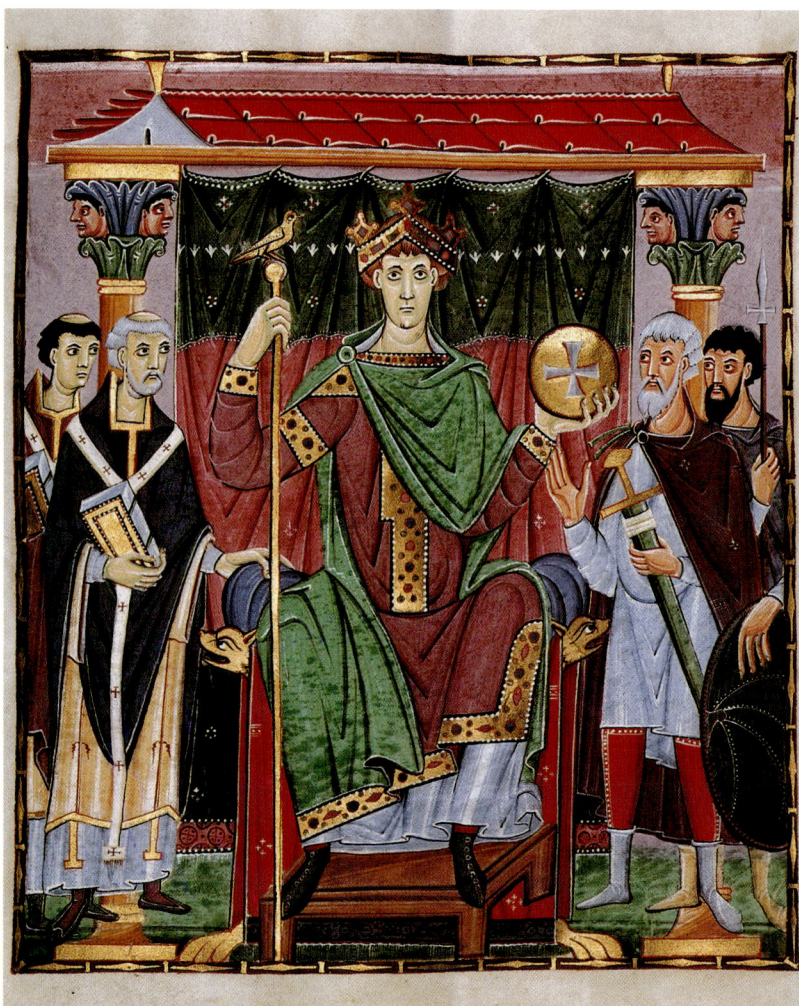

16-29 Otto III enthroned, folio 24 recto of the *Gospel Book of Otto III,* from Trier, Germany, 997–1000. Tempera on vellum, 1′ 1″ × 9 3/8″. Bayerische Staatsbibliothek, Munich.

epitomize the painter's sureness of touch. But the Ottonian figures have lost the old realism, inherited from late antiquity, of the Carolingian *Coronation Gospels* (FIG. 16-12) and move with an abrupt hinged jerkiness that is not "according to nature" but nevertheless possesses a sharp and descriptive expressiveness.

THE IMPERIAL IDEAL IN EUROPE   A picture from the *Gospel Book of Otto III,* representing the emperor himself (FIG. **16-29**), sums up much of what went before and points to what was to come. Of the three Ottos, Otto III dreamed the most of a revived Christian Roman Empire; indeed, it was his life's obsession. His mother was a Byzantine princess, and he was keenly aware of his descent from both Eastern and Western imperial lines. He moved his court, with its Byzantine ceremonial, to Rome and there set up theatrically the symbols and trappings of Roman imperialism. Otto's romantic dream of imperial unity for Europe never materialized. He died prematurely, at age twenty-one, and, at his own request, was buried beside Charlemagne at Aachen.

The illuminator represented the emperor enthroned, holding the scepter and cross-inscribed orb that represent his universal authority, conforming to a Christian imperial iconographic tradition that went back to Constantine (see FIG. 10-82). He is flanked by the clergy and the barons (the Christian Church and the state), both aligned in his support.

On the facing page (not illustrated), classicizing female personifications of Slavinia, Germany, Gaul, and Rome—the provinces of the Ottonian Empire—bring tribute to the young emperor. Stylistically remote from Byzantine art, the picture still has a clear political resemblance to the Justinianic mosaic in San Vitale (see FIG. 12-10).

The vestigial ideal of a Christian Roman Empire—awakened in the Frankish Charlemagne and preserved for a while by his Ottonian successors—gave partial unity to western Europe in the ninth, tenth, and early eleventh centuries. To this extent, ancient Rome lived on to the millennium, culminating in the frustrated ambition of Otto III. But native princes in England, France, Spain, Italy, and eastern Europe aspired to a sovereignty outside the imperial Carolingian and Ottonian domination. Staking their claims, they vied in the medieval power contests that led eventually to the formation of the modern states of Europe. The Romanesque period that followed, in fact, denied the imperial spirit that had prevailed for centuries—but not the notion of Western Christendom. A new age was about to begin, and Rome—an august memory—ceased to be the deciding influence. Europe found unity, rather, in a common religious heritage and a missionary zeal. By the year 1000, even remote Iceland had adopted Christianity. The next task for the kings and church leaders of Europe was to take up the banner of Christ and attempt to wrest control of the Holy Land from the Muslims.

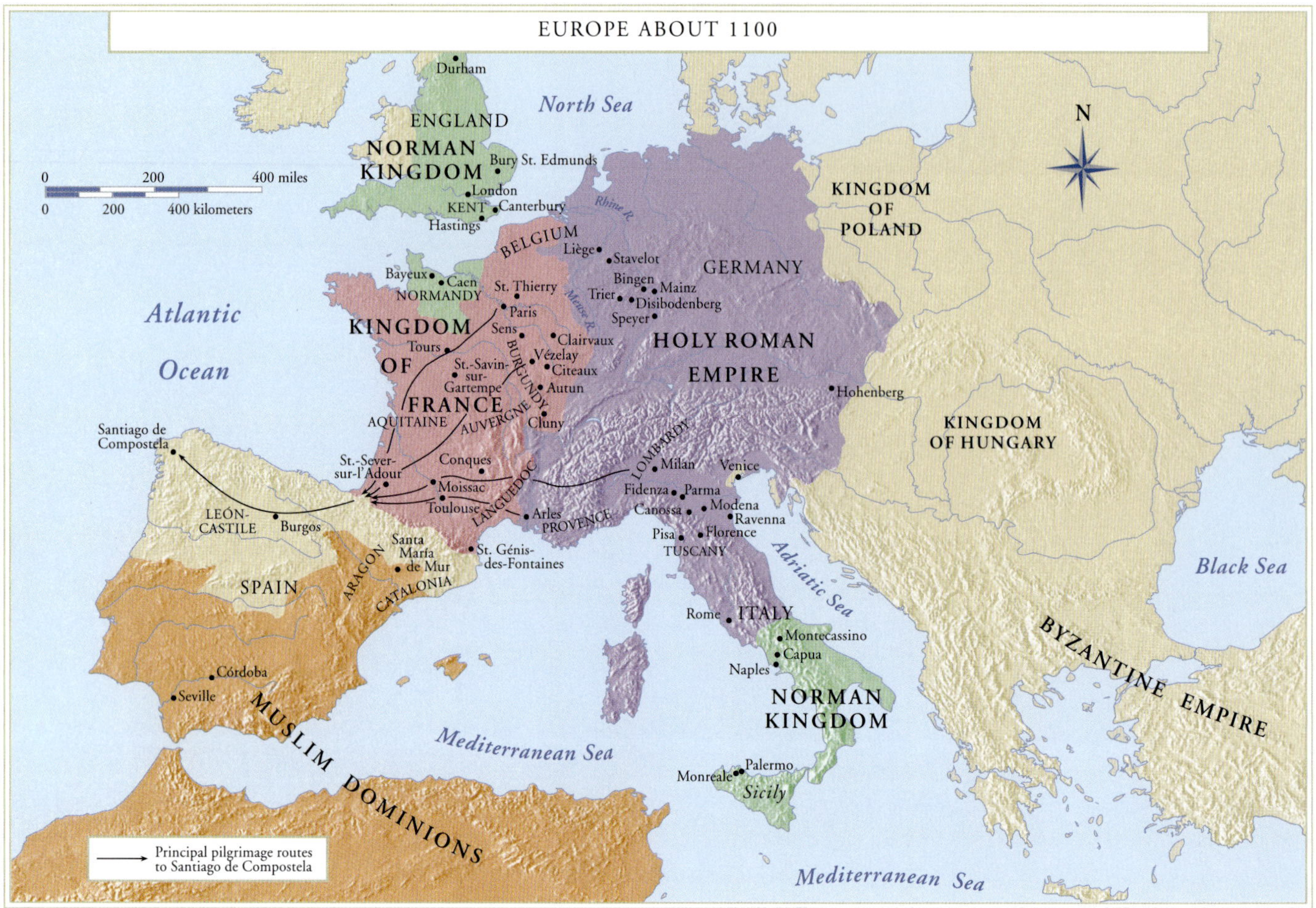

EUROPE ABOUT 1100

North Sea

Durham

ENGLAND
NORMAN KINGDOM

0 — 200 — 400 miles
0 — 200 — 400 kilometers

Bury St. Edmunds
London
KENT • Canterbury
Hastings

Atlantic Ocean

BELGIUM
Liège • Stavelot
Bingen • Mainz
St. Thierry • Trier • Disibodenberg
Speyer

Bayeux • Caen
NORMANDY
Paris
Sens
Clairvaux
Tours
Vézelay
St.-Savin-sur-Gartempe • Citeaux
Autun
Cluny

KINGDOM OF FRANCE

AQUITAINE
AUVERGNE

GERMANY

HOLY ROMAN EMPIRE

Rhine R.
Meuse R.

KINGDOM OF POLAND

Hohenberg

KINGDOM OF HUNGARY

Santiago de Compostela

St.-Sever-sur-l'Adour
Conques
Moissac
Toulouse
LANGUEDOC
Arles
PROVENCE

BURGUNDY

LOMBARDY
Milan • Venice
Fidenza • Parma
Canossa • Modena
Ravenna
Pisa • Florence
TUSCANY

LEÓN-CASTILE
Burgos

ARAGON
Santa María de Mur
CATALONIA
St. Génis-des-Fontaines

SPAIN

Adriatic Sea

Black Sea

BYZANTINE EMPIRE

Rome • **ITALY**
Montecassino
Capua
Naples

NORMAN KINGDOM

Córdoba
Seville

MUSLIM DOMINIONS

Monreale • Palermo
Sicily

Mediterranean Sea

Mediterranean Sea

N

→ Principal pilgrimage routes to Santiago de Compostela

1050	1075	1100

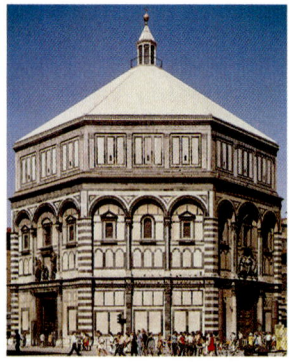

*Baptistery
Florence, dedicated 1059*

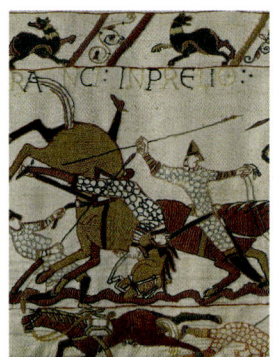

*Bayeux Tapestry
ca. 1070–1080*

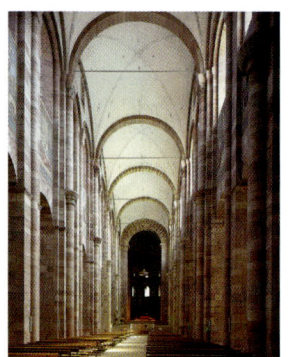

*Speyer Cathedral
Vaults, ca. 1082–1106*

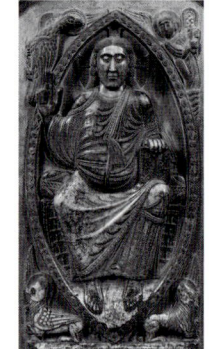

*Bernardus Gelduinus
Christ in Majesty
Saint-Sernin, Toulouse
ca. 1096*

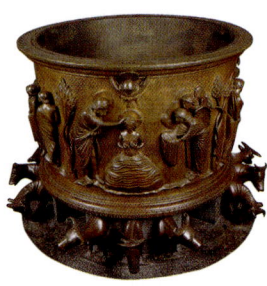

*Rainer of Huy
Baptismal font
Liège, 1107–1118*

Hugh of Semur, 1024–1109

Countess Matilda of Canossa, 1046–1115

Norman conquest of southern Italy and Sicily, 1060–1101

Norman conquest of England (Battle of Hastings), 1066

Final separation of Latin (Roman) Church from the Byzantine (Greek Orthodox) Church, 1051–1054

Pope Gregory VII (1073–1085) asserts spiritual supremacy of papacy over kings and emperors, 1077

Saint Bernard of Clairvaux, ca. 1090–1153

Pope Urban II preaches the First Crusade, 1095

Hildegard of Bingen, 1098–1179

Cistercian Order founded, 1098

Crusaders capture Jerusalem, 1099

17

THE AGE OF PILGRIMS AND CRUSADERS

ROMANESQUE ART

1150   1200

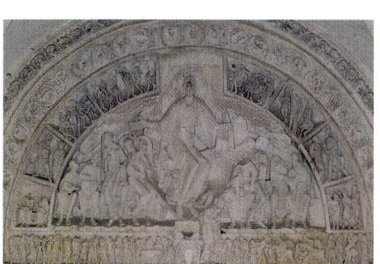

La Madeleine
Vézelay, 1120–1132

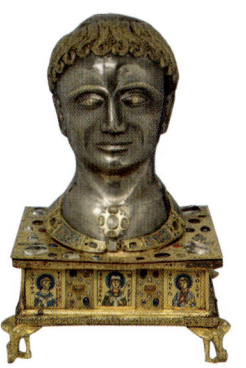

Reliquary of Saint Alexander
Stavelot, 1145

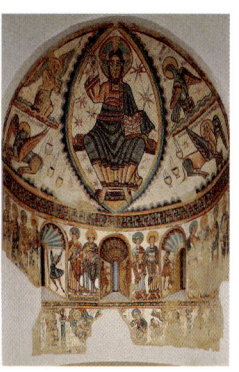

Santa María de Mur
mid-twelfth century

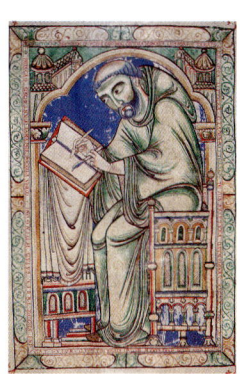

Eadwine Psalter
ca. 1160–1170

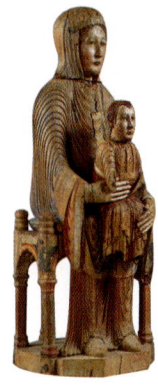

Morgan Madonna
ca. 1150–1200

Foundation of the Knights Templar, 1118

Eleanor of Aquitaine, 1122–1204

King Louis VII of France, r. 1137–1180

Gervase of Canterbury, 1141–1210

Quran translated into Latin, 1143

Second Crusade, 1147

Frederick Barbarossa, Holy
Roman Emperor, r. 1152–1190

King Henry II Plantagenet
of England, r. 1154–1189

King Philip Augustus of
France, r. 1180–1223

King Richard the Lionheart
of England, r. 1189–1199

Third Crusade, 1190

ROMANESQUE EUROPE

The Romanesque era is the first since Archaic and Classical Greece to take its name from an artistic style rather than from politics or geography. Unlike Carolingian and Ottonian art, named for emperors, or Hiberno-Saxon art, a regional term, Romanesque is a title art historians invented to describe an artistic phenomenon. *Romanesque* means "Romanlike" and first was applied in the early nineteenth century to describe European architecture of the late eleventh and the twelfth centuries. Scholars noted that certain architectural elements of this period, principally barrel and groin vaults based on the round arch, resembled those of ancient Roman architecture. Thus, the word distinguished Romanesque buildings from earlier medieval timber-roofed structures, as well as from later Gothic churches with vaults resting on pointed arches. Researchers in other fields quickly borrowed the term. Today "Romanesque" broadly designates the history and culture of western Europe between about 1050 and 1200.

FEUDALISM AND THE RISE OF TOWNS   The political, social, and economic system that governed early medieval society in much of Europe is called *feudalism*. The northern warrior lords of the early Middle Ages eventually settled down and established themselves as landholding barons. The barons, or *liege lords,* granted tenure of some of their land to *vassals.* The vassals swore allegiance to their liege and rendered him military service in return for the land and the promise of protection. Vassals could, in turn, allot parts of their *fief* to others and become lesser lords with vassals beholden to them. Peasants sustained all by their work. They tilled the soil to gain a place to live and food to eat. Some accumulated enough wealth to buy their freedom. Most remained subservient to their lords, tied to the land.

The feudal system reflected the agricultural basis of early medieval society. The focus of life was the *manor,* or estate, of the individual feudal lord. But in the Romanesque period, a sharp increase in trade, fostered in part by traveling pilgrims and Crusaders (discussed later), encouraged the growth of towns and cities. The independence the towns so proudly cherished depended on their charters. *Charters* were public documents feudal lords granted, enumerating the communities' rights, privileges, immunities, and exemptions beyond the feudal obligations they owed the lords. A community could win independence by purchasing outright a charter. Many of the new Romanesque towns rose on the sites of ancient Roman colonies, which were restored to busy urban life after centuries of relative stagnation. Often located on navigable rivers, the towns were naturally the nuclei of networks of maritime and overland commerce. Merchants, traders, moneylenders, artisans, and free peasants populated them.

ARCHITECTURE

THE "WHITE ROBE OF THE CHURCH"   The new Romanesque towns were also centers of ecclesiastical influence. Their bishops and archbishops built towers, gates, and walls, as well as churches. The immense building enterprise that raised thousands of churches in western Europe in the eleventh and twelfth centuries was not, however, due solely to the revival of urban life. It also reflected the widely felt relief and thanksgiving that the conclusion of the first Christian millennium in the year 1000 did not bring an end to the world, as many had feared. In the Romanesque age, the construction of churches became almost an obsession. Raoul Glaber (ca. 985–ca. 1046), a monk who witnessed the coming of the new millennium, noted the beginning of it:

> [After the] year of the millennium, which is now about three years past, there occurred, throughout the world, especially in Italy and Gaul, a rebuilding of church basilicas. Notwithstanding, the greater number were already well established and not in the least in need, nevertheless each Christian people strove against the others to erect nobler ones. It was as if the whole earth, having cast off the old by shaking itself were clothing itself everywhere in the white robe of the church.[1]

Great building efforts were provoked not only by the needs of growing cities, the pilgrimages, and the Crusades but also by the fact invading armies had destroyed many churches (notably in Italy and France). Architects of the time seemed to see their fundamental challenge in terms of providing a building that would have space for the circulation of its congregations and visitors and that would be solid, fireproof, well lighted, and acoustically suitable. These requirements, of course, are the necessities of any great civic or religious architecture. But, in this case, fireproofing must have been foremost in the builders' minds. Wooden-roofed churches were especially susceptible to fire, whether caused by nature or by humans (see "The Burning of Canterbury Cathedral," page 455). In the ninth and tenth centuries, these churches had burned fiercely and totally when marauders from the north, east, and south set them aflame.

The new churches had to be covered with cut stone, because the technology of concrete construction had been lost long before. The structural problems that arose from this need for a solid masonry were to help determine the "look" of Romanesque architecture throughout most of Europe. Nonetheless, regional differences abound, and some Romanesque churches, especially in Italy, retained the wooden roofs of their Early Christian predecessors long after stone vaulting had become commonplace elsewhere. Whatever their differences, all the buildings manifested a new widely shared method of architectural thinking, a new logic of design and construction. To a certain extent, Romanesque architecture can be compared to the Romance languages of Europe, which vary regionally but have a common core in Latin, the language of the Romans.

Southern France

One of the first regions to have a distinctive Romanesque architecture was southern France, the heart of ancient Gaul. This is not surprising, for of all the Roman Empire's European provinces, Gaul was the most profoundly Romanized. Visitors to the area today can go to almost any town and view both Roman remains (see FIGS. 10-30 and 10-31) and Romanesque buildings. In fact, the modern name of the French region that is the core of what once was Roman Gaul is *Provence* ("the [Roman] Province").

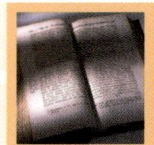

The Burning of Canterbury Cathedral

The perils of wooden construction are well documented by the chroniclers of medieval ecclesiastical history. In some cases, churches burned over and over again in the course of a single century and repeatedly had to be extensively repaired or completely rebuilt. In September 1174, for example, Canterbury Cathedral, which had been dedicated only forty-four years earlier, burned to the ground because its builders had not used the stone vaults employed at Durham (FIG. 17-12) and elsewhere in England and France. A vivid eyewitness account is preserved in the *Chronica* of Gervase of Canterbury (1141–1210), who entered the monastery at Canterbury in 1163 and wrote a history of the archbishopric from 1100 to 1199:

> During an extraordinarily violent south wind, a fire broke out before the gate of the church, and outside the walls of the monastery, by which three cottages were half destroyed. From thence, while the citizens were assembling and subduing the fire, cinders and sparks carried aloft by the high wind, were deposited upon the church, and being driven by the fury of the wind between the joints of the lead, remained there amongst the half rotten planks, and shortly glowing with increased heat, set fire to the rotten rafters; from these the fire was communicated to the larger beams and their braces, no one yet perceiving or helping. For the well-painted ceiling below, and the sheet-lead covering above, concealed between them the fire that had arisen within. . . . But beams and braces burning, the flames arose to the slopes of the roof; and the sheets of lead yielded to the increasing heat and began to melt. Thus the raging wind, finding a freer entrance, increased the fury of the fire. . . . And now that the fire had loosened the beams from the pegs that bound them together, the half-burnt timbers fell into the choir below upon the seats of the monks; the seats, consisting of a great mass of woodwork, caught fire, and thus the mischief grew worse and worse. And it was marvellous, though sad, to behold how that glorious choir itself fed and assisted the fire that was destroying it. For the flames multiplied by this mass of timber, and extending upwards full fifteen cubits [about twenty-five feet], scorched and burnt the walls, and more especially injured the columns of the church. . . . In this manner the house of God, hitherto delightful as a paradise of pleasures, was now made a despicable heap of ashes, reduced to a dreary wilderness.[1]

After the fire, the Canterbury monks summoned a master builder from Sens, a French city seventy-five miles southeast of Paris, to supervise the construction of their new church. Gervase reports that the first task WILLIAM OF SENS tackled was "the procuring of stone from beyond the sea."

[1]Quoted in Elizabeth G. Holt, *A Documentary History of Art* (New York: Doubleday Anchor Books, 1957), 1: 52–54.

A NEW CHURCH FOR FRENCH PILGRIMS

Around 1070, the counts of Toulouse, principal sponsors of the Crusades, began construction of a great new church in honor of the city's first bishop, Saint Saturninus (Saint Sernin in French), who was martyred in the middle of the third century. Toulouse was an important stop on the pilgrimage road through southwestern France to Santiago de Compostela in northwestern Spain. The grand scale of Saint-Sernin at Toulouse (FIGS. **17-1** to **17-3**) reflects the popularity of pilgrimages and of the cult of relics, which brought big crowds even to relatively isolated places (see "Pilgrimages and the Cult of Relics," page 457). Large congregations were common at the shrines along the great pilgrimage routes, and Saint-Sernin was designed to accommodate them. The twelfth-century exterior of the church is still largely intact, although the two towers of the western facade were never completed and the prominent crossing tower is largely Gothic and later. A complex interplay of rectangular, polygonal, and rounded forms enlivens the basic basilica-with-transept plan. The composition recalls but goes beyond earlier Carolingian and Ottonian experiments in the arrangement of geometric volumes on church exteriors (see FIGS. 16-21 and 16-22).

Saint-Sernin's plan (FIG. 17-2) closely resembles those of the churches of Saint James at Santiago de Compostela and Saint Martin at Tours and exemplifies what has come to be called the "pilgrimage type." At Toulouse one clearly can see how the builders provided additional space for curious pilgrims, worshipers, and liturgical processions alike. They increased the length of the nave, doubled the side aisles, extended the aisles around the eastern end to make an ambulatory, and attached a series of *radiating chapels* (for the display of relics) opening directly onto the ambulatory and the transept. In addition, upper galleries, or *tribunes,* over the inner aisle and opening onto the nave (FIG. 17-3), accommodated overflow crowds on special occasions.

The Saint-Sernin design is also extremely regular and geometrically precise. The crossing square, flanked by massive piers and marked off by heavy arches, served as the module for the entire church. Each nave bay, for example, measures exactly one-half of a crossing square, and each aisle bay measures exactly one-quarter. The architect employed similar simple ratios throughout the building. The first suggestion of such a planning scheme in medieval Europe was the Saint Gall monastery plan (see FIG. 16-20), almost three centuries earlier. The Toulouse solution was a crisply rational and highly refined realization of the germ of an idea first seen in Carolingian architecture. This approach to design became increasingly common in the Romanesque period.

FIGHTING FIRE WITH STONE VAULTS

The builders of Saint-Sernin also sought to protect the great church from the ravages of fire. To this end, they placed a semicircular stone barrel vault below the timber-roofed loft. The long cut-stone nave vault at Saint-Sernin (FIG. 17-3) put

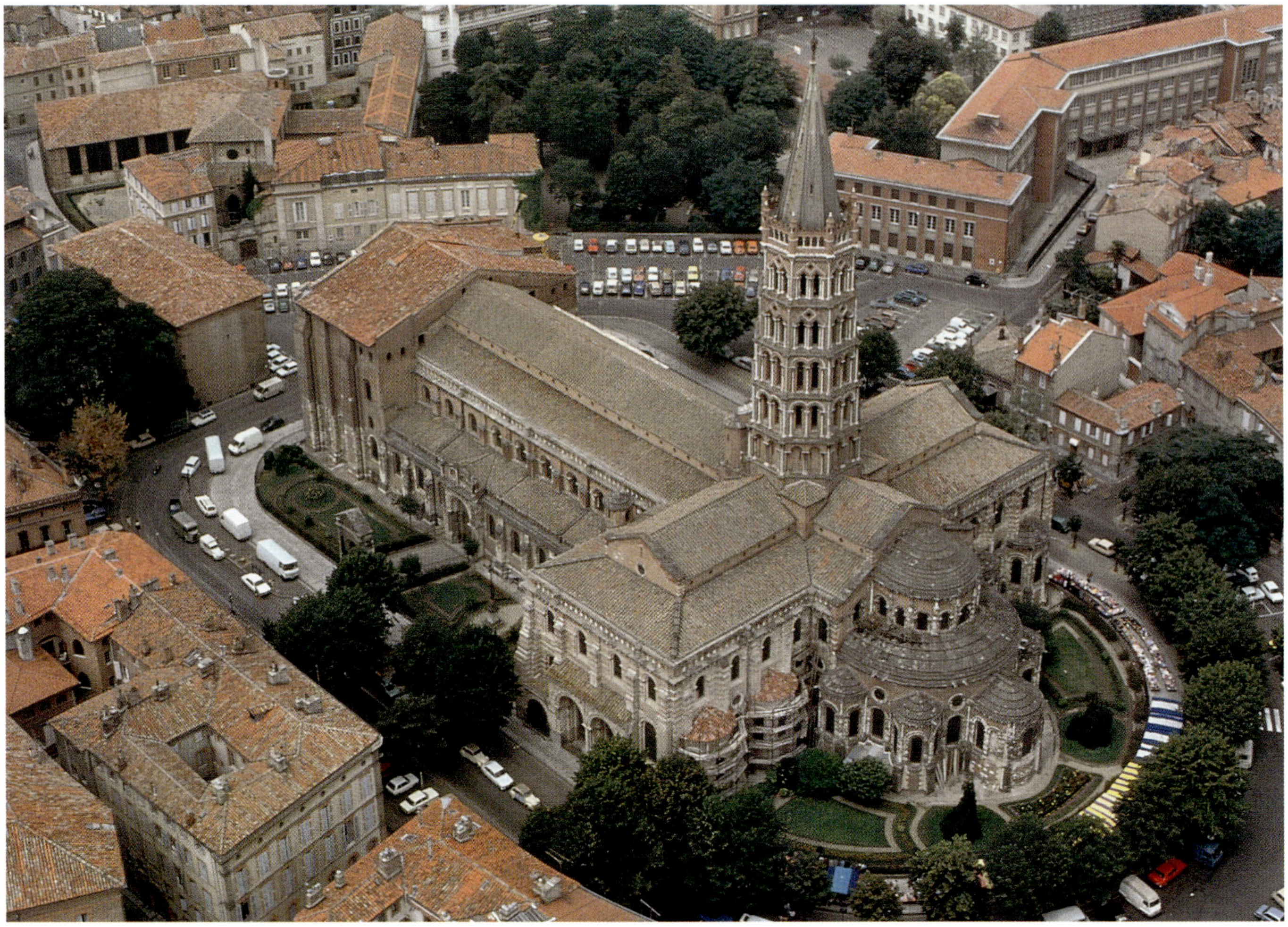

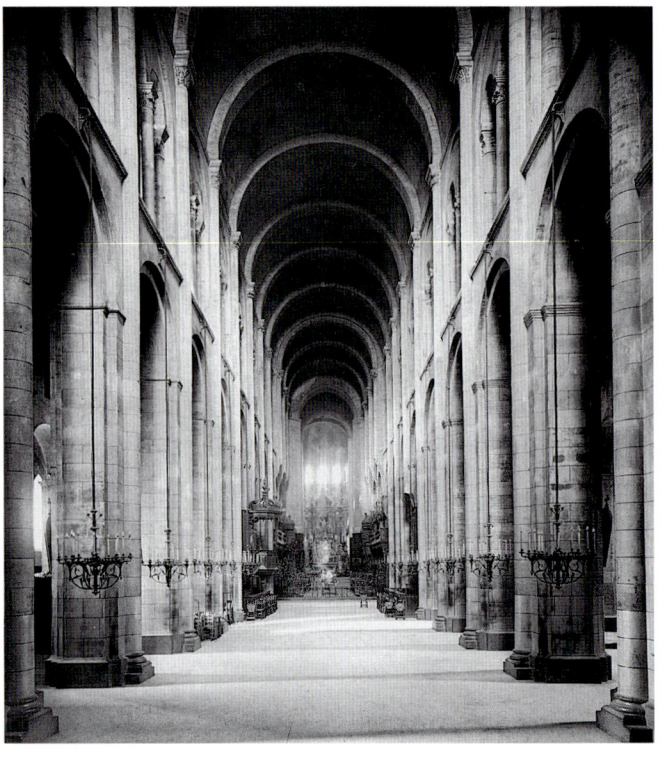

17-1   Aerial view (from the southeast) of Saint-Sernin, Toulouse, France, ca. 1070–1120.

constant pressure along the supporting masonry's entire length. In most churches where the nave is flanked by side aisles, the nave ceiling rests on arcades and the vaults over the aisles transfer the main thrust to the thick outer walls. In larger churches like Saint-Sernin, the second-story tribunes and their vaults (groin vaults at Toulouse) are an integral part of the structure, buttressing the higher vaulting over the nave.

The builders of Saint-Sernin were concerned with more than just buttressing their fireproof nave vault. They also

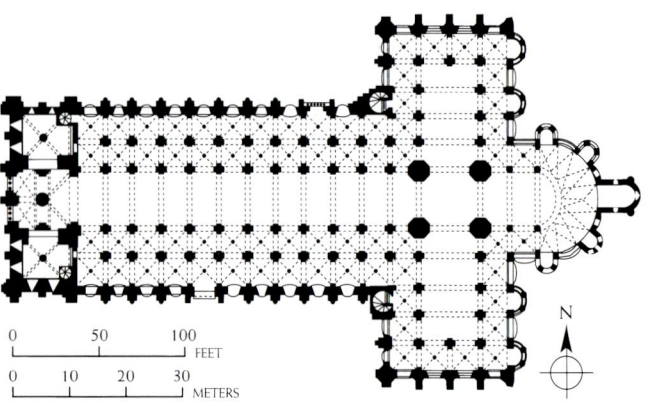

17-2   Plan of Saint-Sernin, Toulouse, France, ca. 1070–1120 (after Kenneth John Conant).

17-3   Interior of Saint-Sernin, Toulouse, France, ca. 1070–1120.

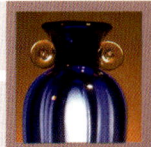

Pilgrimages and the Cult of Relics

The cult of relics was not new in the Romanesque era. For centuries Christians had traveled to sacred shrines housing the body parts of, or objects associated with, the holy family or the saints. The faithful believed such relics—bones, clothing, instruments of martyrdom, and the like—had the power to heal body and soul. As related earlier, for example, in the seventh century the relics of Saint Apollinaris were deposited in a sixth-century church at Ravenna, and, as a result, the church was rededicated and named Sant'Apollinare Nuovo (see FIG. 11-16). But the veneration of relics reached a high point in the eleventh and twelfth centuries.

In Romanesque times, pilgrimage was the most conspicuous feature of public devotion, proclaiming the pilgrim's faith in the veneration of saints and hope for their special favor. The major shrines—Saint Peter's and Saint Paul's in Rome and the Church of the Holy Sepulcher in Jerusalem—drew pilgrims from all over Europe. The visitors braved, for salvation's sake, bad roads and hostile wildernesses infested with robbers who preyed on innocent travelers. The journeys could take more than a year to complete—when they were successful. People often undertook pilgrimage as an act of repentance or as a last resort in their search for a cure for some physical disability. Hardship and austerity were means for increasing pilgrims' chances for the remission of sin or of disease. The distance and peril of the pilgrimage were measures of pilgrims' sincerity of repentance or of the reward they sought.

For those with less time or money than required for a pilgrimage to Rome or Jerusalem, holy destinations could be found closer to home. In France, for example, the church at Vézelay housed the bones of Mary Magdalene. Saint Foy's remains were enshrined at Conques, Lazarus's at Autun, Saint Martin's at Tours, and Saint Saturninus's at Toulouse. Each of these great shrines was also an important way station en route to the most venerated shrine in the West, Santiago de Compostela in northwestern Spain, where the tomb of the apostle Saint James had been discovered in the ninth century.

Hordes of pilgrims paying homage to saints placed a great burden on the churches that stored their relics, but they also provided significant revenues, making possible the erection of ever grander and more luxuriously appointed structures. The popularity of pilgrimages led to changes in church design, necessitating longer and wider naves and aisles, transepts and ambulatories with additional chapels, and second-story galleries (FIGS. 17-2 and 17-3). Pilgrim traffic also established the routes that later became the major avenues of European commerce and communication.

---

carefully coordinated the vault's design with that of the nave arcade below and with the modular plan of the building as a whole. Our view of the interior (FIG. 17-3) shows that the geometric floor plan (FIG. 17-2) is fully reflected in the nave walls, where the piers marking the corners of the bays are embellished with engaged half-columns. Architectural historians refer to piers with columns or pilasters attached to their rectangular cores as *compound piers*. At Saint-Sernin the engaged columns rise from the bottom of the compound piers to the vault's *springing* (the lowest stone of an arch) and continue across the nave as *transverse arches*.

Ever since Early Christian times, basilican interiors had been framed by long flat walls between arcades and clerestories that enclosed a single horizontal unbroken volume of space (compare FIGS. 11-8 and 16-24). In Saint-Sernin the nave's appearance is radically different. It seems to be composed of numerous identical vertical volumes of space placed one behind the other, marching down the building's length in orderly procession. This segmentation of Saint-Sernin's interior space corresponds to and renders visually the plan's geometric organization. It also is reflected in the building's exterior walls (FIG. 17-1), where buttresses frame each bay. The result is a structure with all of its parts integrated to a degree unknown in earlier Christian architecture. The new scheme, with repeated units decorated and separated by moldings, had a long future in later church architecture in the West.

AN EARTHLY DWELLING PLACE FOR ANGELS

Even grander than Saint-Sernin was the church Abbot Hugh of Semur built in Cluny at the end of the eleventh century. In 909 William, Duke of Aquitaine, had donated land near Roman Cluniacum to a community of reform-minded Benedictine monks under Berno of Baume's leadership. Since William had waived his feudal rights to the land, the abbot of Cluny was subject only to the pope in Rome, a unique privilege. Berno founded a new order at Cluny in strict adherence to the rules of Saint Benedict (see "Medieval Monasteries and Benedictine Rule," Chapter 16, page 443). Under Berno's successors, the Cluniac monks became famous for their scholarship, music, and art. Their influence and wealth grew rapidly, and they built a series of ever more elaborate monastic churches at Cluny.

The church Hugh of Semur commissioned was the third on the site. Begun in 1088, it is called Cluny III by art historians. The building is, unfortunately, largely destroyed today. During the French Revolution it ceased to function as a church. In the nineteenth century it was dismantled so that its building stones could be reused. At the time of its erection, Cluny III was the largest church in Europe, and its contemporaries considered it a place worthy for angels to dwell if they lived on earth. The church had an innovative and influential design, with five aisles, a barrel-vaulted nave, and radiating chapels, as at Saint-Sernin, but with a three-story nave elevation (arcade-tribune-clerestory) and slightly pointed nave vaults. With a nave more than five

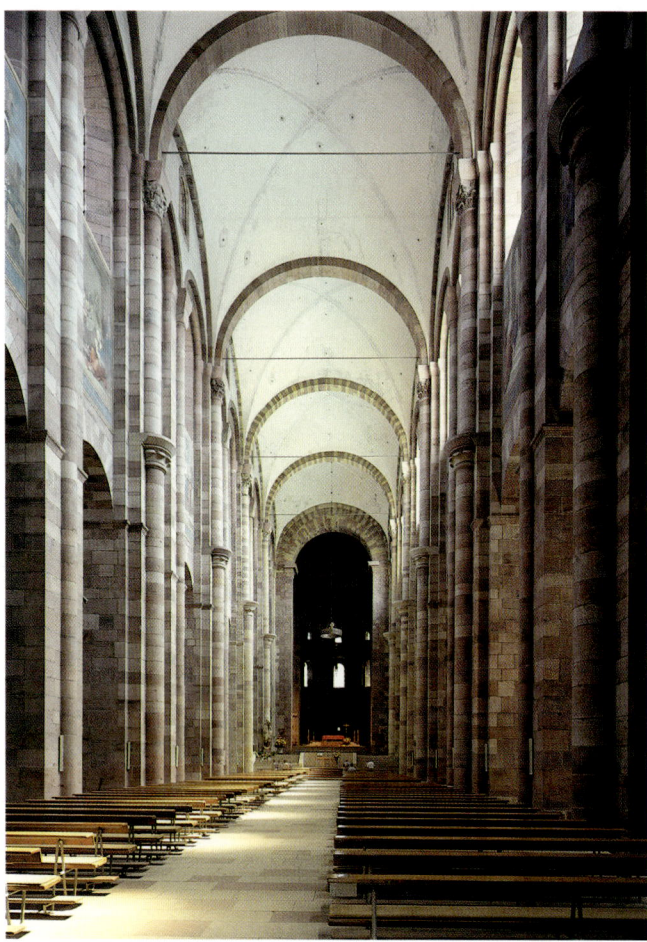

17-4   Interior of Speyer Cathedral, Speyer, Germany, begun 1030; nave vaults, ca. 1082–1106.

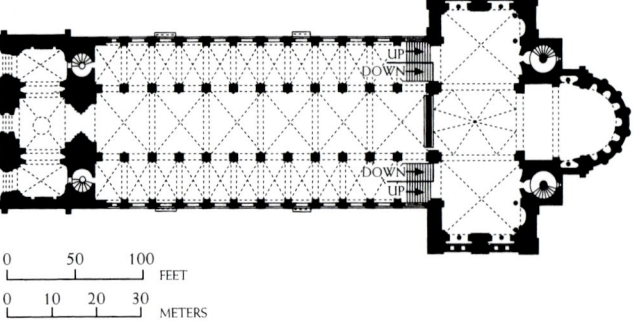

17-5   Plan of Speyer Cathedral, Speyer, Germany, begun 1030.

great Roman vaults were made possible by the use of concrete, which could be poured into forms, where it solidified into a homogeneous mass. But, as noted earlier, the technique of mixing concrete did not survive into the Middle Ages. And the technical problems of building groin vaults of cut stone and heavy rubble, which had very little cohesive quality, limited their use to the covering of small areas, such as the individual bays of Saint-Sernin's aisles and galleries. But during the eleventh century, masons, using ashlar blocks joined by mortar, developed a groin vault of monumental dimensions.

A DARING GERMAN EXPERIMENT   Speyer Cathedral (FIGS. **17-4** and **17-5**) in the German Rhineland is an early example of groin vaults used over a nave. The church was begun in 1030 and was the burial place of the Holy Roman Emperors until the beginning of the twelfth century. Like all cathedrals, Speyer was also the seat (*cathedra* in Latin) of the powerful local bishop. In its earliest form, Speyer Cathedral was a timber-roofed structure. When the emperor Henry IV rebuilt it between 1082 and 1106, his masons covered the nave with groin vaults, which made possible the insertion of a small clerestory window above each pair of tribune arches. Scholars disagree about where the first comprehensive use of groin vaulting occurred in Romanesque times, and nationalistic concerns sometimes color the debate. We will not argue here for the precedence of any one region. But no one doubts that the large groin vaults covering the nave of Speyer Cathedral (FIG. 17-4) represent one of the most daring and successful vaulting enterprises of the time. The nave is forty-five feet wide, and the crowns of the vaults are one hundred seven feet high.

Although the cathedral's plan (FIG. 17-5) has some irregularities and was not worked out as neatly and precisely as Saint-Sernin's plan, the builders' intention to employ a modular scheme is quite clear. They used the crossing, covered by an octagonal dome, as the module for the arrangement of the building's east end. Because the nave bays are not square, the use of the crossing as a measurement unit is not as obvious. In fact, every third wall support in the nave marks off an area the size of the crossing. The aisles are half the width of the nave, and each groin-vaulted nave bay corresponds to two aisle bays.

Also in contrast to Saint-Sernin, Speyer Cathedral's nave exhibits an alternate-support system, as in the Ottonian church of Saint Michael's at Hildesheim (see FIG. 16-24). At Speyer, however, the alternation continues all the way up into the vaults (FIG. 17-4), with the nave's more richly molded compound piers marking the corners of the groin vaults. The resultant bay arrangement, with a large unit in the nave

hundred feet long and more than one hundred feet high (both dimensions are about fifty percent greater than at Saint-Sernin), it epitomized the grandiose scale of the new stone-vaulted Romanesque churches.

Germany and Lombardy

A PROBLEM SOLVED: GROIN VAULTS   The barrel-vaulted naves of Cluny III and Saint-Sernin covered vast spaces and were relatively fireproof. But the barrel vaults failed in one critical requirement—lighting. Due to the great outward thrust the continuous semicircular vaults exerted, a clerestory was difficult to construct. (The designers of Saint-Sernin did not even attempt to introduce a clerestory, although their counterparts at Cluny III succeeded.) A more complex and efficient type of vaulting was needed. Structurally, the central problem of Romanesque architecture was the need to develop a masonry vault system that admitted light.

Among the numerous experimental solutions ingenious Romanesque builders devised to alleviate the problem of inadequate lighting, the groin vault turned out to be the most efficient and flexible. The groin vault had been used widely by Roman builders, who saw that its concentration of thrusts at four supporting points permitted clerestory windows (see "The Roman Architectural Revolution: Concrete Construction," Chapter 10, page 249, and FIGS. 10-68 and 10-79). The

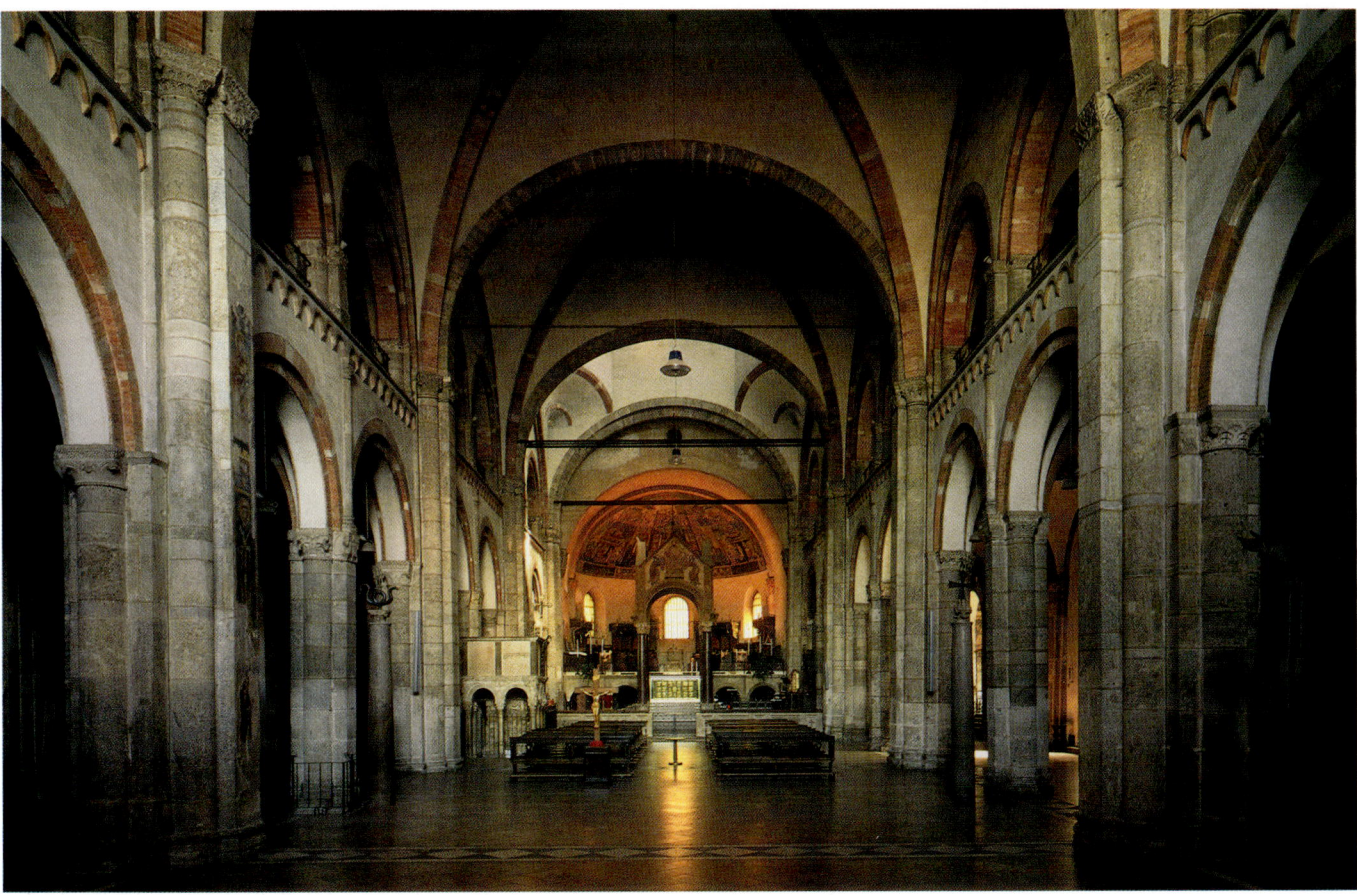

17-6 Interior of Sant'Ambrogio, Milan, Italy, late eleventh to early twelfth century.

flanked by two small units in each aisle, became almost standard in northern Romanesque architecture. Speyer's interior shows the same striving for height and the same compartmentalized effect seen in Saint-Sernin. By virtue of the alternate-support system, the Speyer nave's rhythm is a little more complex. Because each compartment is individually vaulted, the effect of a sequence of vertical spatial blocks is even more convincing.

INNOVATIVE RIB VAULTING IN LOMBARDY

Ever since Charlemagne crushed the Lombards in 773, German kings held sway over Lombardy, and the Rhineland and northern Italy cross-fertilized each other artistically. No agreement exists as to which source of artistic influence was dominant in the Romanesque age, the northern or the southern. The question, no doubt, will remain the subject of controversy until the construction date of Sant'Ambrogio in Milan (FIGS. **17-6** to **17-8**) can be established unequivocally. The church, erected in honor of Saint Ambrose, Milan's first bishop (d. 397), is the central monument of Lombard Romanesque architecture.

Whether or not it was a prototype for Speyer Cathedral, Sant'Ambrogio remains a remarkable building. It has an atrium in the Early Christian tradition (one of the last to be built), a two-story narthex pierced by arches on both levels, two bell towers (*campaniles*) joined to the building, and, over the nave's east end, an octagonal tower that recalls the crossing towers of German churches. Of the facade bell towers, the shorter one dates back to the tenth century, while the taller north campanile is a twelfth-century addition.

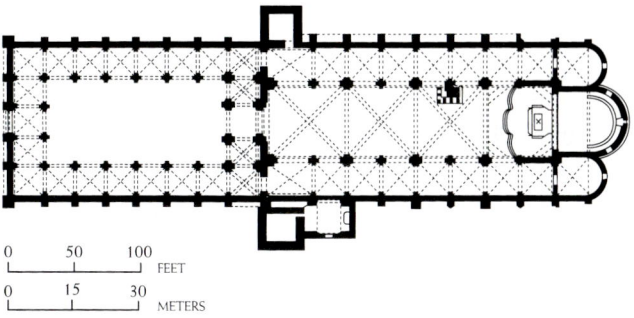

17-7 Plan of Sant'Ambrogio, Milan, Italy, late eleventh to early twelfth century.

In plan (FIG. 17-7), Sant'Ambrogio is three aisled and without a transept. The modular scheme was applied with greater consistency and precision than at Speyer. Each bay consists of a full square in the nave flanked by two small squares in each aisle, all covered with groin vaults. The main vaults are slightly domical, rising higher than the transverse arches (FIG. 17-6). An octagonal dome covers the last bay, its windows providing the major light source (the building lacks a clerestory) for the otherwise rather dark interior. The emphatic alternate-support system perfectly reflects the plan's geometric regularity. The lightest pier moldings are interrupted at the gallery level, and the heavier ones rise to support the main vaults. At Sant'Ambrogio, the compound piers even continue into the ponderous vaults, which have supporting

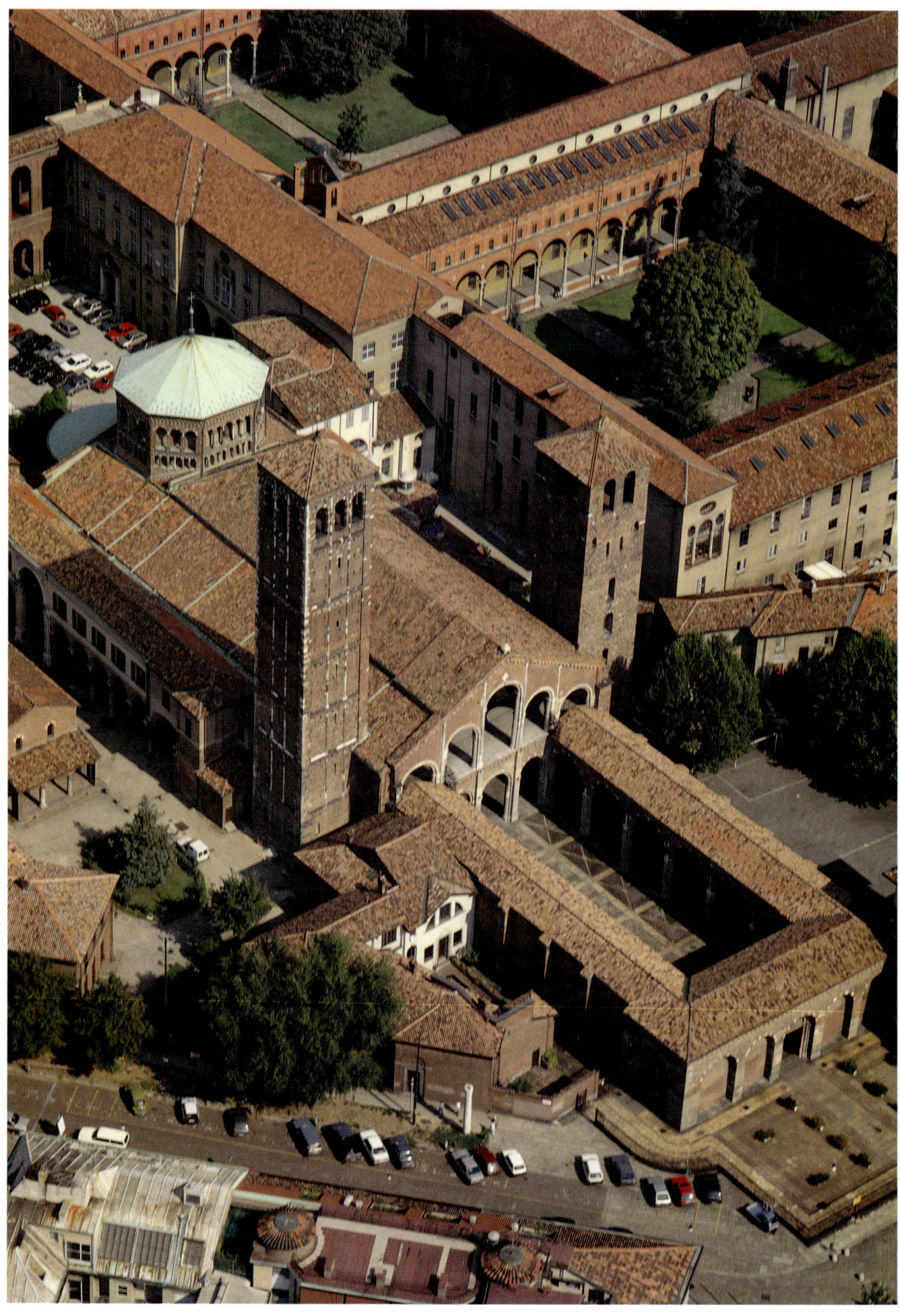

17-8 Aerial view of Sant'Ambrogio, Milan, Italy, late eleventh to early twelfth century.

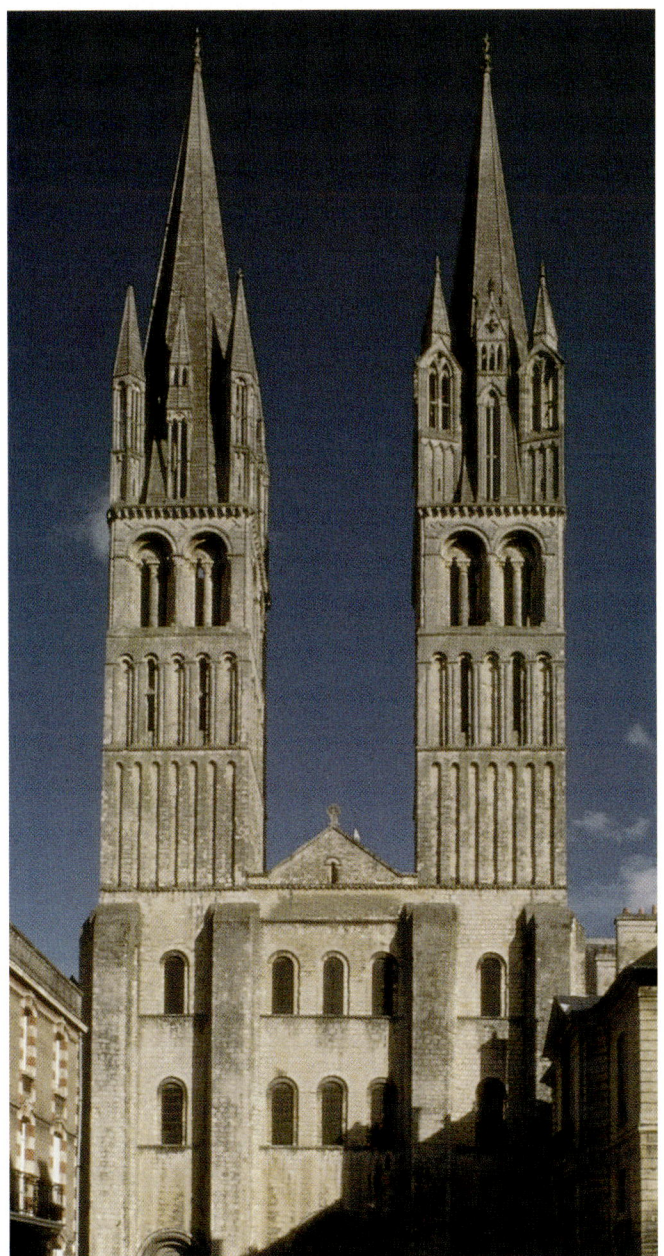

17-9 West facade of Saint-Étienne, Caen, France, begun 1067.

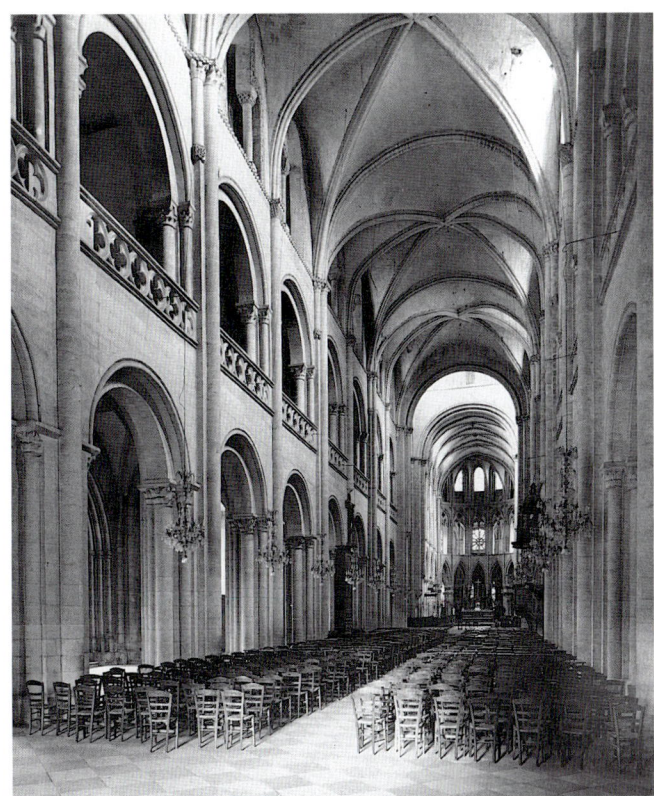

17-10 Interior of Saint-Étienne, Caen, France, vaulted ca. 1115–1120.

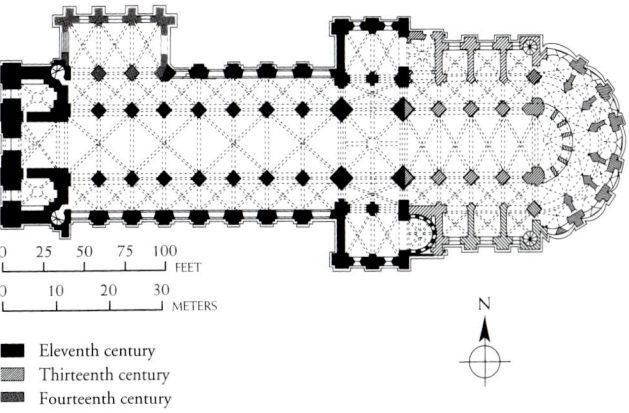

■ Eleventh century
▨ Thirteenth century
▨ Fourteenth century

17-11 Plan of Saint-Étienne, Caen, France.

arches, or *ribs,* along their groins. This is one of the first instances of rib vaulting, a salient characteristic of mature Romanesque and of later Gothic architecture (see "The Gothic Rib Vault," Chapter 18, page 494).

As noted earlier, regional differences characterize Romanesque architecture. This can be seen clearly by comparing the proportions of Sant'Ambrogio with those of both Speyer Cathedral and Saint-Sernin at Toulouse. The Milanese building does not aspire to the soaring height of the northern churches. Save for the later of the two towers (FIG. 17-8), Sant'Ambrogio's proportions are low and broad and remain close to those of Early Christian basilicas. Italian architects, with their firm roots in the venerable Early Christian style, never accepted the verticality found in northern architecture, not even during the Gothic period.

Normandy and England

After their conversion to Christianity in the early tenth century, the Vikings settled on the northern coast of France in present-day Normandy (see Chapter 16). Almost at once, they proved themselves not only aggressive warriors but also skilled administrators and builders, active in Sicily (see FIG. 12-24) as well as in northern Europe. With astounding rapidity, they absorbed the lessons to be learned from Ottonian architecture and went on to develop a distinctive Romanesque architectural style that became the major source of French Gothic architecture.

A CHURCH FOR ENGLAND'S CONQUEROR Most critics consider the abbey church of Saint-Étienne (Saint Stephen; FIGS. **17-9** to **17-11**) at Caen the masterpiece of Norman Romanesque architecture. It was begun by William of Normandy (William the Conqueror; see page 484) in 1067 and must have advanced rapidly, as he was buried there in 1087. Saint-Étienne's west facade (FIG. 17-9) is a striking design rooted in the tradition of Carolingian and Ottonian westworks, but it displays the increased rationalism of Romanesque architecture. Four large buttresses divide the facade into three bays that correspond to the nave and aisles. Above the buttresses, the towers also display a triple division and a progressively greater piercing of their walls from lower to upper stages. (The culminating spires are a Gothic addition.) The tripartite division is employed throughout the facade, both vertically and horizontally, organizing it into a close-knit, well-integrated design that reflects the careful and methodical planning of the entire structure.

The original design of Saint-Étienne called for a wooden roof, as originally at Speyer Cathedral. But from the beginning, the French church's nave walls (FIG. 17-10) were built with an alternating rhythm of compound piers with simple engaged half-columns and piers with half-columns attached to pilasters. The decision to employ an alternate-support system must have been motivated by aesthetic rather than structural concerns. When groin vaults were introduced around 1115, the varied nave piers proved an ideal match. The alternating compound piers soar all the way to the vaults' springing. Their branching ribs divide the large square-vault compartments into six sections, making a *sexpartite vault* (FIG. 17-11). These vaults rise high enough to provide room for an efficient clerestory. The resulting three-story elevation, with its large arched openings, provides more light to the interior. It also makes the nave appear even taller than it actually is. As in the Milanese church of Sant'Ambrogio (FIG. 17-8), the

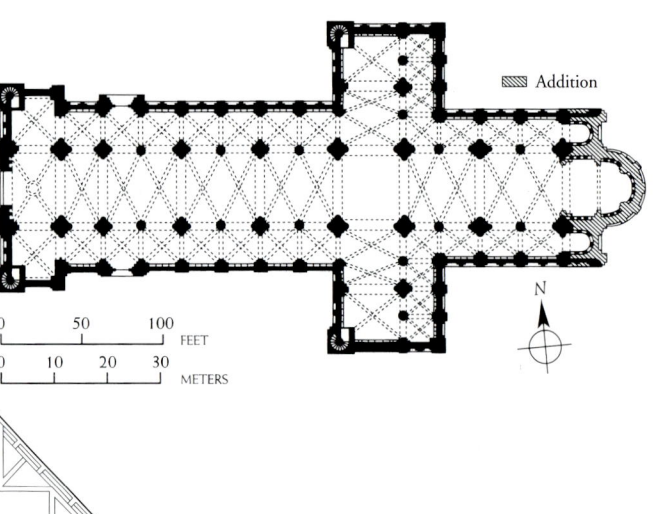

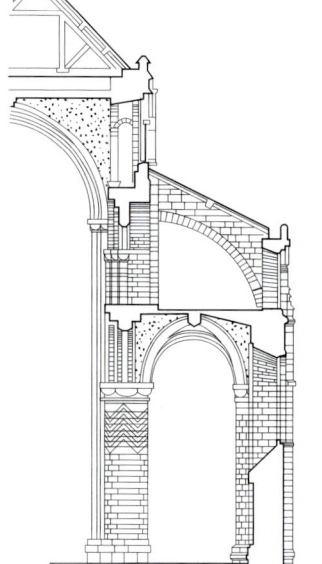

17-13 Plan *(top)* and transverse section *(bottom)* of Durham Cathedral, England (after Kenneth John Conant).

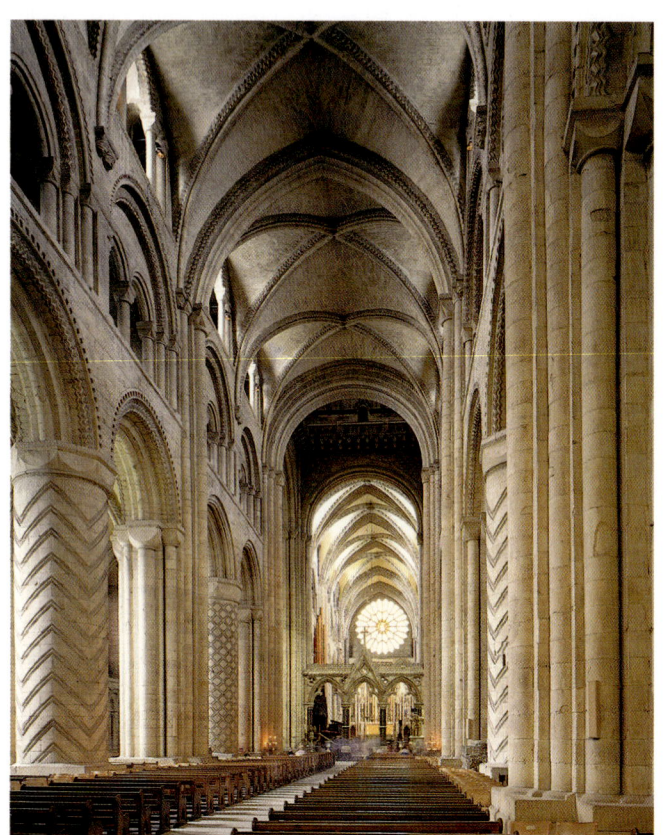

17-12 Interior of Durham Cathedral, England, begun ca. 1093.

Norman building has rib vaults. The diagonal and transverse ribs compose a structural skeleton that partially supports the still fairly massive paneling between them. But despite the heavy masonry, the large windows and reduced interior wall surface give Saint-Étienne's nave a light and airy quality that is unusual in the Romanesque period.

ROMANESQUE ON THE SCOTTISH BORDER

William of Normandy's conquest of Anglo-Saxon England in 1066 began a new epoch in English history. In architecture, it signaled the importation of French Romanesque building and design methods. Durham Cathedral (FIGS. **17-12** and **17-13**) sits majestically on a cliff overlooking the Wear River in northern England. It was begun around 1093, in the generation following the Norman conquest, and is the centerpiece of a monastery, cathedral, and fortified-castle complex on the Scottish frontier. The church's vaulted interior (FIG. 17-12), which predates that of the remodeled Saint-Étienne at Caen, retains its original severe Romanesque appearance. Ambitious in scale, its four-hundred-foot length compares favorably with that of Speyer, the great imperial cathedral. But unlike Speyer and Saint-Étienne, this building was conceived from the very beginning as a vaulted structure. Consequently, the pattern of the ribs of the nave's groin vaults is reflected in the design of the arcade below. Each seven-part nave vault covers two bays. Large simple pillars ornamented with abstract designs (diamond, chevron, and cable patterns, all originally painted) alternate with compound piers that carry the transverse arches of the vaults. The pier-vault relationship scarcely could be more visible or the building's structural rationale better expressed.

The Durham nave's bold surface patterning is a reminder that the raising of imposing stone edifices such as the Romanesque churches of England and Normandy required more than just the talents of master designers. A corps of expert masons had to transform rough stone blocks into the precise shapes necessary for their specific place in the church's fabric. Although thousands of simple quadrangular ashlar blocks make up the great walls of these buildings, much more complex shapes also needed to be produced in large numbers. To cover the nave and aisles, the stonecutters had to carve blocks with concave faces to conform to the vault's curve. Also required were blocks with projecting moldings for the ribs, blocks with convex surfaces for the pillars or with multiple profiles for the compound piers, and so forth. It was an immense undertaking, and it is no wonder that medieval building campaigns often lasted for decades.

Durham Cathedral's plan (FIG. 17-13, top) is typically English with its long, slender proportions. It does not employ the modular scheme with the same care and logic seen at Caen. But in other ways this English church is even more innovative than the French church. It is the earliest example known of a ribbed groin vault placed over a three-story nave. And in the nave's western parts, completed before 1130, rib vaults were combined with slightly pointed arches, bringing together for the first time two of the key elements that determined the structural evolution of Gothic architecture. Also of great significance is the way the nave vaults are buttressed. Our longitudinal section (FIG. 17-13, bottom) reveals that simple *quadrant arches* (arches whose curve extends for one quarter of a circle's circumference) were used in place of groin vaults in the tribune. The structural descendants of the Durham quadrant arches are the flying buttresses that epitomize the mature Gothic solution to church construction (see "The Gothic Cathedral," Chapter 18, page 498).

Tuscany

South of the Lombard region, Italy retained its ancient traditions and, for the most part, produced Romanesque architecture that was structurally less experimental than that of Lombardy. The buildings of Tuscany, along with those of Rome itself, adhered closely to the traditions of the Early Christian basilica. They underscore that diversity is the rule, not the exception, in Romanesque Europe.

A CATHEDRAL WITH UNSTABLE TOWER   The cathedral complex at Pisa (FIG. **17-14**) dramatically testifies to the prosperity that busy maritime city enjoyed. The cathedral, its freestanding bell tower, and the baptistery, where infants and converts were initiated into the Christian community, present a rare opportunity to study a coherent group of three Romanesque buildings. Save for the upper portion of the baptistery, with its remodeled Gothic exterior, the three structures are stylistically homogeneous.

Construction of Pisa Cathedral began first—in 1063, the same year work began on Saint Mark's in Venice (see FIGS.

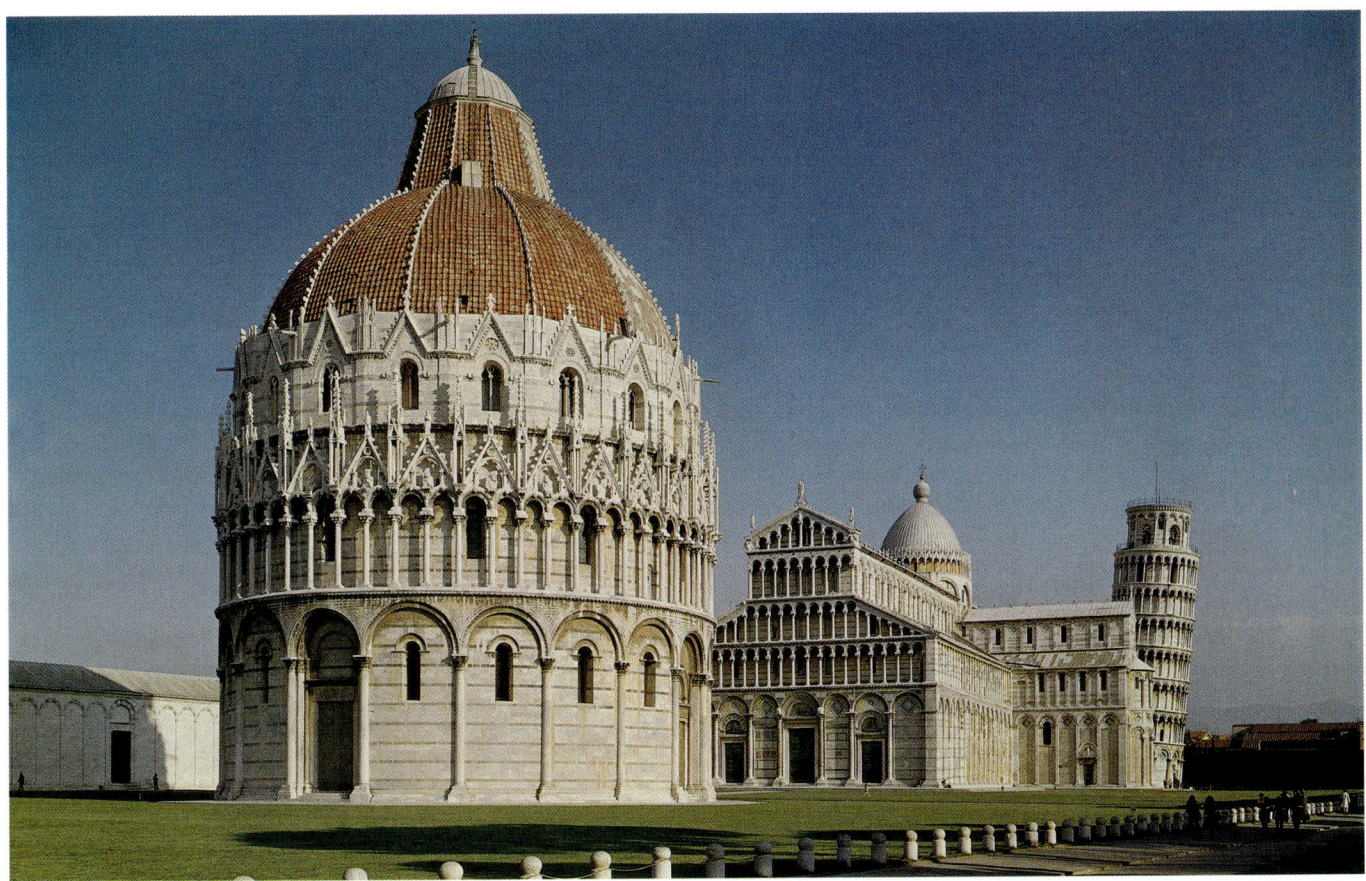

17-14 Cathedral complex, Pisa, Italy; cathedral begun 1063; baptistery begun 1153; campanile begun 1174.

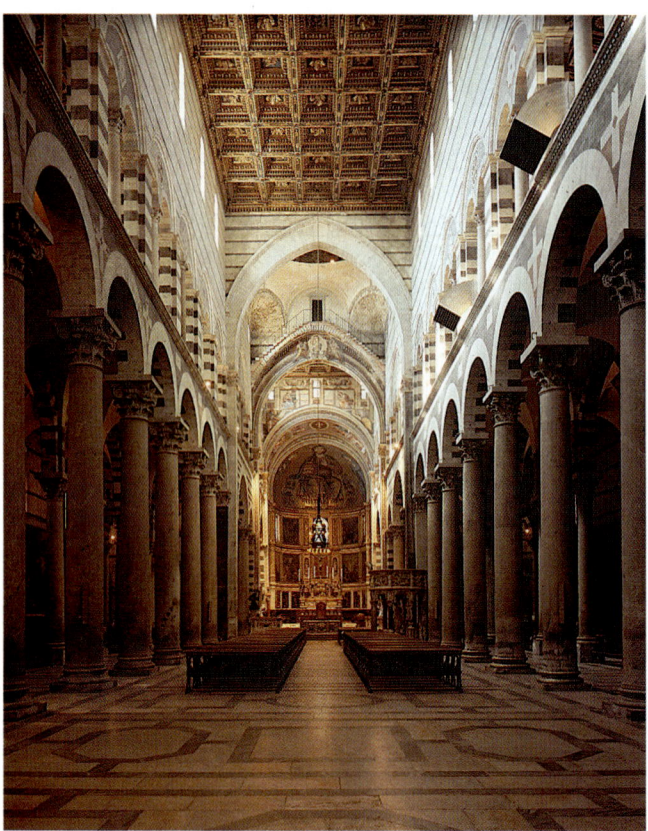

17-15   Interior of Pisa Cathedral, Pisa, Italy, begun 1063.

12-21 and 12-22), another maritime power. The Pisan project was funded by the spoils of a naval victory over the Muslims off Palermo in Sicily in 1062. The cathedral is large, five aisled, and one of the most impressive and majestic of all Romanesque churches. The Pisans, according to a document of the time, wanted their bishop's church not only to be a monument to the glory of God but also one that would bring credit to the city. At first glance, Pisa Cathedral resembles an Early Christian basilica. But the broadly projecting transept, the crossing dome, and the facade's multiple arcade galleries soon distinguish it as Romanesque. So too does the rich marble *incrustation* (wall decoration consisting of bright panels of different colors, as in the Pantheon's interior, FIG. 10-50).

The interior (FIG. **17-15**) also at first suggests the basilica, with its timber rather than vaulted ceiling (originally the rafters were exposed, as in Early Christian basilicas) and nave arcade of reused Roman columns in unbroken procession. Above the colonnade is a continuous horizontal molding, on which the gallery arcades rest. The gallery, of course, is not a basilican feature, but it is a familiar trait of churches north of the Alps. It is ultimately of Byzantine origin. Other divergences from the basilica form include the relatively great verticality of the interior and, at the crossing, the markedly unclassical pointed arch. The pointed arch probably was inspired by Islamic architecture. The striped walls of alternating dark green and cream-colored marble provide a luxurious polychromy that became a hallmark of Tuscan Romanesque and Gothic buildings.

The cathedral's campanile, detached in the standard Italian fashion, is the famous Leaning Tower of Pisa (FIG. 17-14). The tilted vertical axis is the result of a settling foundation. It began to "lean" even while under construction and now in-

clines some twenty-one perilous feet out of plumb at the top. Round, like the bell towers of Sant'Apollinare in Classe and other Ravenna churches, it is much more elaborate. Its stages are marked by graceful arcaded galleries that repeat the cathedral's facade motif and effectively relate the tower to its mother building.

A ROMANESQUE BAPTISTERY IN FLORENCE

Florence is always associated with the Renaissance of the fifteenth and sixteenth centuries, but it was already an important independent city-state in the Romanesque period. The gem of Florentine Romanesque architecture is the Baptistery of San Giovanni (Saint John; FIG. **17-16**). Dedicated to the city's patron saint by Pope Nicholas II in 1059, it was constructed during the succeeding century. Like Pisa's baptistery (FIG. 17-14), which it predates, Florence's baptistery faces that city's great cathedral. These freestanding Italian baptisteries are unusual and reflect the great significance the Florentines and Pisans attached to baptisms. On the day of a newborn child's annointment, the citizenry gathered in the baptistery to welcome a new member into their community. The Tuscan baptisteries therefore were important civic, as well as religious, structures. Some of the most renowned artists of the late Middle Ages and the Renaissance were employed to provide the Florentine and Pisan baptisteries with pulpits (see FIG. 19-2), bronze doors (see FIGS. 21-1, 21-2 , and 21-4), and mosaics.

The simple and serene classicism of San Giovanni's design places it in a direct line of descent from ancient Roman architecture—from the Pantheon (see FIG. 10-48) and imperial mausoleums such as Diocletian's (see FIG. 10-75) to the Early Christian Santa Costanza (see FIG. 11-9), the Byzantine San Vitale (see FIG. 12-6), and other central-plan structures, pagan

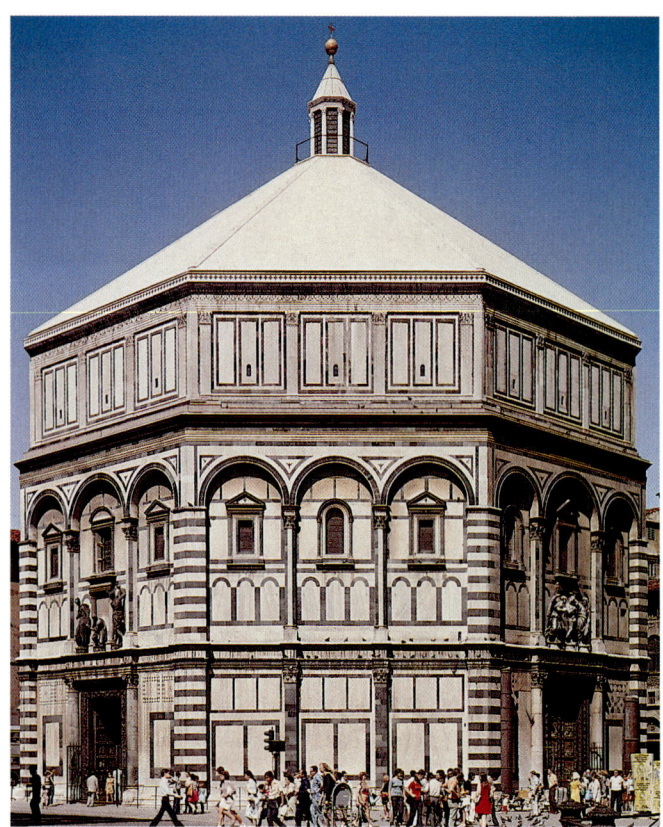

17-16   Baptistery of San Giovanni, Florence, Italy, dedicated 1059.

or Christian, including Charlemagne's Palatine Chapel at Aachen (FIG. 16-18). A distinctive Tuscan Romanesque feature is the marble incrustation that patterns the walls. These simple oblong and arcuated shapes not only outline the paneled surfaces but also assert the building's structural lines and its elevation levels. The corner piers accentuating the octagon's apexes are boldly striped in the Pisan fashion (FIG. 17-15).

In plan, San Giovanni is a domed octagon, enwrapped on the exterior by a graceful arcade, three arches to a bay. It has three entrances, one each on the north, south, and east sides. On the west side an oblong sanctuary replaces the original semicircular apse. The domical vault is some ninety feet in diameter, its construction a feat remarkable for its time.

OLD AND NEW IN A FLORENTINE BASILICA

Contemporaneous with the baptistery and stylistically affiliated with it is another Florentine building, the Benedictine abbey church of San Miniato al Monte (FIG. **17-17**). It sits, as its name implies, on a hillside overlooking the Arno River and the heart of Florence. The body of the church was completed by 1090, the gable-crowned facade during the twelfth and early thirteenth centuries. Even more than Pisa Cathedral, the structure recalls the Early Christian basilica in plan and elevation, although its elaborate geometric incrustation makes for a rich ornamental effect foreign to the earlier buildings. Though at first glance the lowest level much resembles the patterning of Florence's baptistery, the arcades and panels do not reflect the building's structure. The facade's upper levels, of much later date than the lowest level, are filled capriciously with geometrical shapes that have a purely ornamental function.

San Miniato has a quite Romanesque interior (FIG. **17-18**), despite its strong ties with the design of Early Christian basilicas. Although the church is timber roofed, as are most Tuscan Romanesque churches, the nave is divided into three equal

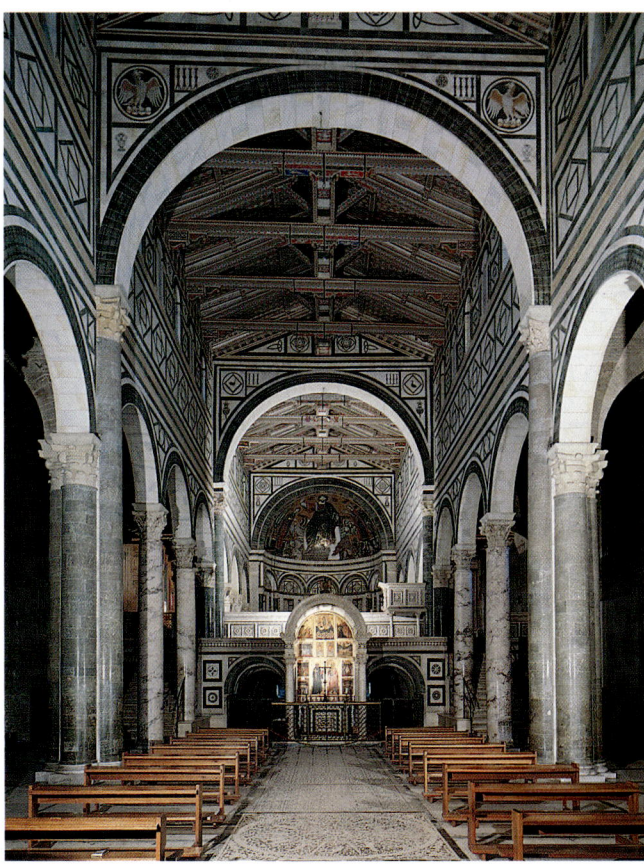

17-18   Interior of San Miniato al Monte, Florence, Italy, 1062 and twelfth century.

compartments by *diaphragm arches*. The arches rise from compound piers and brace the rather high, thin walls. They also provide firebreaks beneath the wooden roof and compartmentalize the basilican interior in the manner so popular with most Romanesque builders. The compound piers alternate with pairs of simple columns with Roman-revival Composite capitals.

SCULPTURE

Architectural Sculpture

MONUMENTAL STONE SCULPTURE REVIVED Stone sculpture, with some notable exceptions, such as the great crosses of the British Isles (see FIG. 16-10), almost had disappeared from the art of western Europe during the early Middle Ages. The revival of the technique is one of the hallmarks of the Romanesque age—and one of the reasons the period is aptly named. The inspiration for monumental stone sculpture no doubt came, at least in part, from the abundant remains of ancient stone statues and reliefs throughout Rome's northwestern provinces. As one would expect, the individual motifs and compositions Romanesque sculptors employed often originated in Carolingian and Ottonian ivory carving, metalwork, and manuscript illumination. But ancient sculptures throughout France, Italy, Germany, and Spain provided a powerful spur to the imaginations of patrons and artists alike.

The reemergence of monumental stone sculpture in western Europe coincided with the introduction of stone vaulting in Romanesque churches. But it is important to remember

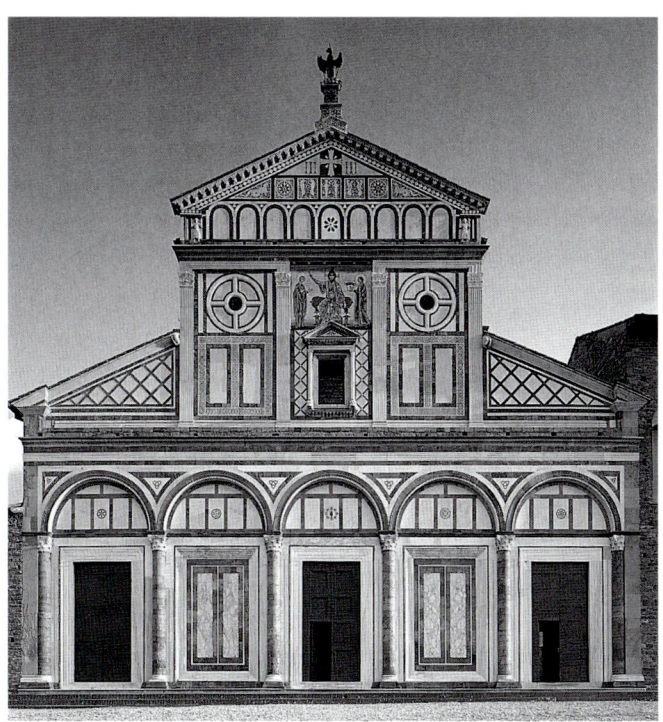

17-17   West facade of San Miniato al Monte, Florence, Italy, 1062 and twelfth century.

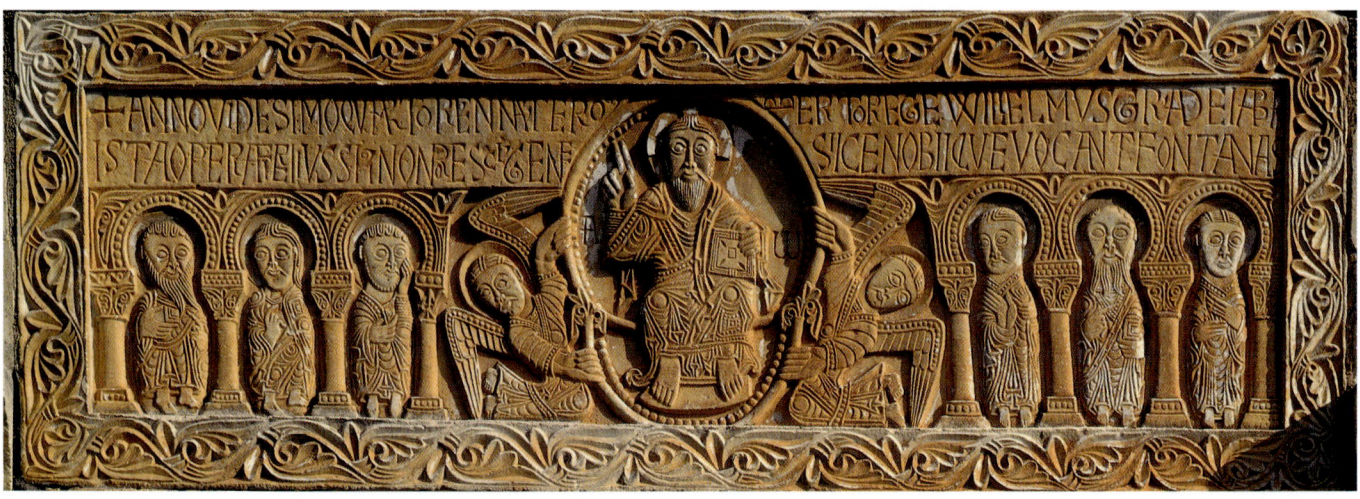

17-19   Christ in Majesty *(Maiestas Domini)* with apostles, lintel over doorway, Saint-Génis-des-Fontaines, France, 1019–1020. Marble, approx. 2′ × 7′.

that stone-walled churches and monumental westworks had been built for centuries, even if the structures bore timber ceilings and roofs. The addition of stone vaults to basilican churches is not in itself an explanation for the resurgence of stonecarving in the Romanesque period. The answer lies, rather, in the changing role of many churches in Western Christendom. In the early Middle Ages, most churches served small monastic communities, and the worshipers were primarily or exclusively clergy. These buildings were not devoid of decoration, but it took the form of *interior* mosaics or frescoes. With the rise of cities and towns in the Romanesque period, churches, especially those on the major pilgrimage routes, increasingly served the lay public. To reach this new, largely illiterate audience and to draw a wider population into their places of worship, church officials decided to display Christian symbols and stories on the *exteriors* of their buildings. Stone was the most suitable durable medium for such exterior decorative programs.

Even though the Romanesque church grew out of the Roman basilican type, the towering west facades and broad transepts of Romanesque churches had no parallels in ancient basilicas or temples. Romanesque sculptors may have derived ideas and compositional patterns from surviving Roman sculptures, but they had to develop their own attitudes toward the placement of sculpture on their churches.

CHRIST IN MAJESTY OVER A PORTAL   A very early, securely datable, example of Romanesque architectural sculpture is the carved lintel (FIG. **17-19**) over the doorway to the church of Saint-Génis-des-Fontaines, in the extreme south of France near the Spanish border. Dated 1019–1020 by inscription, the lintel depicts Christ enthroned in a lobed *mandorla* ("glory") supported by angels and flanked by apostles. To the left and right of Christ are inscribed the first and last letters of the Greek alphabet, a reference to his role as Last Judge: "I am the Alpha and the Omega, the First and the Last, the Beginning and the End" (Rev. 21:6). The Saint-Génis lintel is the earliest of many reliefs on Romanesque church facades depicting or alluding to Judgment Day and the separation of those who will be saved (the Christian faithful who frequent the churches) from those who will be damned.

The six apostles on the Saint-Génis lintel stand in an arcade of horseshoe arches of the type familiar in Is-

lamic Spain (see FIG. 13-12). The general framework, however, is typical of Roman sarcophagi (see FIG. 10-62), and a late antique or Early Christian sarcophagus in France may have been one of the relief's prototypes. But if the models were ancient, the sculptor translated those sources into a new, distinctively Romanesque idiom. The result is what one might expect of an artisan unfamiliar with the classical figural style who was asked to revive the forgotten art of monumental stone relief sculpture.

A SHRINE FOR SAINT SATURNINUS   Also precisely dated is a group of seven marble slabs, representing angels, apostles, and Christ, made for the great pilgrimage church of Saint-Sernin at Toulouse (see FIGS. 17-1 to 17-3). An inscription on a marble altar, part of the group, states that the reliefs date to the year 1096 and that the artist was a certain BERNARDUS GELDUINUS. Today the plaques are affixed to the ambulatory wall. Their original location is uncertain. Some scholars have suggested that they once formed part of a shrine dedicated to Saint Saturninus that stood in the crypt of the grand structure. Others believe the reliefs once decorated a choir screen or an exterior portal.

The sculptured figures are twice the height of those at Saint-Génis but still well under life-size. We illustrate the centerpiece of the group, the figure of Christ in Majesty (FIG. **17-20**). Christ sits in a mandorla, his right hand raised in blessing, his left hand resting on an open book inscribed with the words *Pax vobis* ("peace be unto you"). The signs of the Four Evangelists occupy the slab's corners. Above are the eagle of Saint John and the angel of Saint Matthew. Below are the ox of Saint Luke and the lion of Saint Mark. Art historians debate the sources of Gelduinus's style, but one easily can imagine such a composition used for a Carolingian or Ottonian work in metal or ivory, perhaps a book cover. The polished marble has the gloss of both materials, and the sharply incised lines and the ornamentation of Christ's aureole are characteristic of pre-Romanesque metalwork.

GENESIS ON AN ITALIAN CHURCH   Some fifteen years later, around 1110, another sculptor carved one of the first fully developed narrative reliefs in Romanesque art. The facade of Modena Cathedral in northern Italy has a frieze that extends on two levels across three of its bays. It represents scenes from Genesis set against an architectural backdrop. As at Saint-Génis-des-Fontaines (FIG. 17-19), the framing device is derived from late Roman and Early Christian sarcophagi. The segment shown (FIG. **17-21**) illustrates the creation and temptation of Adam and Eve (Gen. 2, 3:1–8), the theme employed almost exactly a century earlier on Bishop Bernward's bronze doors to Saint Michael's at Hildesheim (see FIG. 16-25). At Modena, as at Hildesheim, the faithful enter the house of the Lord with a reminder of Original Sin and the suggestion that the only path to salvation is through the Christian Church.

On the Modena frieze, Christ is at the far left, framed by a mandorla held up by angels—a variation on both the motifs and the themes of the lintel at Saint-Génis-des-Fontaines and the reliefs of Saint-Sernin. The creation of Adam, then Eve, and the serpent's temptation of Eve are to the right. Although the figures appear in an architectural frame, as at Saint-Génis, they break through the arcade's constriction to make for a more continuous narrative. Like the Toulouse Christ, they are not linear patterns but high reliefs. Some parts at Modena are almost entirely in the round. The frieze is the work of a master craftsman whose name, WILIGELMO, is given in an inscription on another relief on the facade. There he boasts, "Among sculptors, your work shines forth, Wiligelmo." The inscription is also an indication of the pride of Wiligelmo's patrons in obtaining the services of such an accomplished sculptor for their city's cathedral.

THE SECOND COMING AT MOISSAC At Modena, the frieze recounts the beginning of the human race. Some twenty-five years later, a portal at Moissac in southwestern France announces its end. The abbey of Saint-Pierre at Moissac joined the Cluniac order in 1047 and was an important stop along the pilgrimage route to the tomb of Saint James at Santiago de Compostela. The monks, enriched by the gifts of pilgrims and noble benefactors, adorned their church and its cloister with one of the most extensive series of sculptures of the Romanesque age.

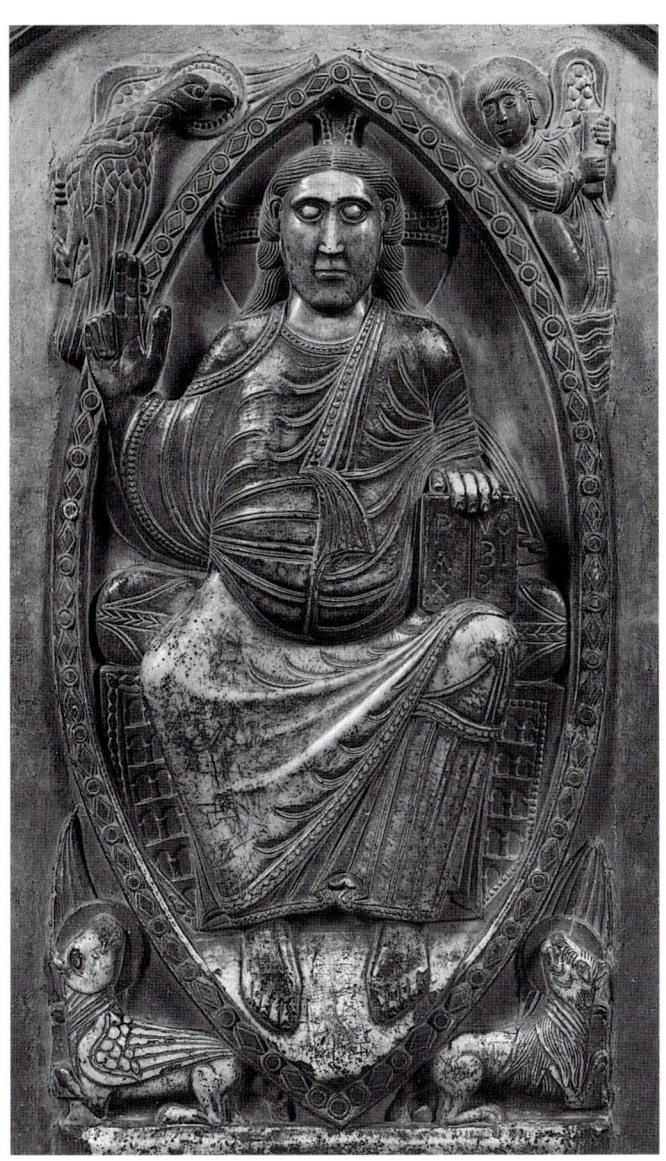

17-20 BERNARDUS GELDUINUS, Christ in Majesty, relief in the ambulatory of Saint-Sernin, Toulouse, France, ca. 1096. Marble, 4′ 2″ high.

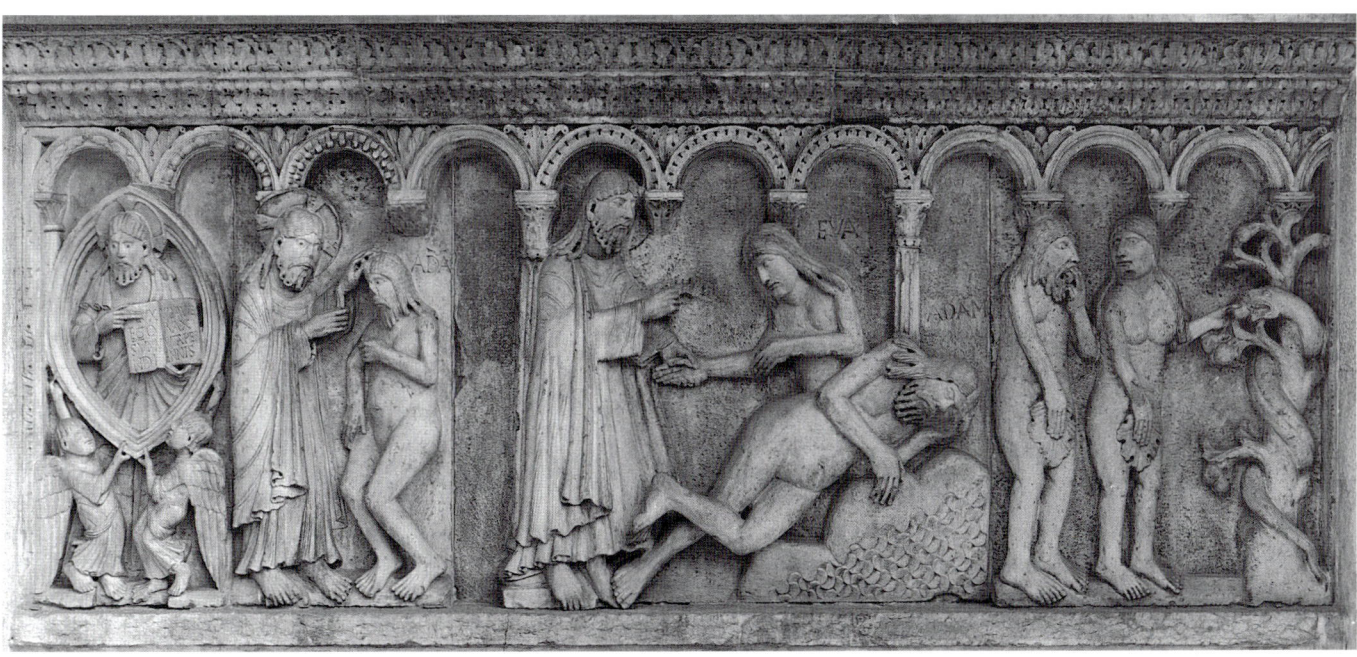

17-21 WILIGELMO, creation and temptation of Adam and Eve, frieze on the west facade, Modena Cathedral, Modena, Italy, ca. 1110. Marble, approx. 3′ high.

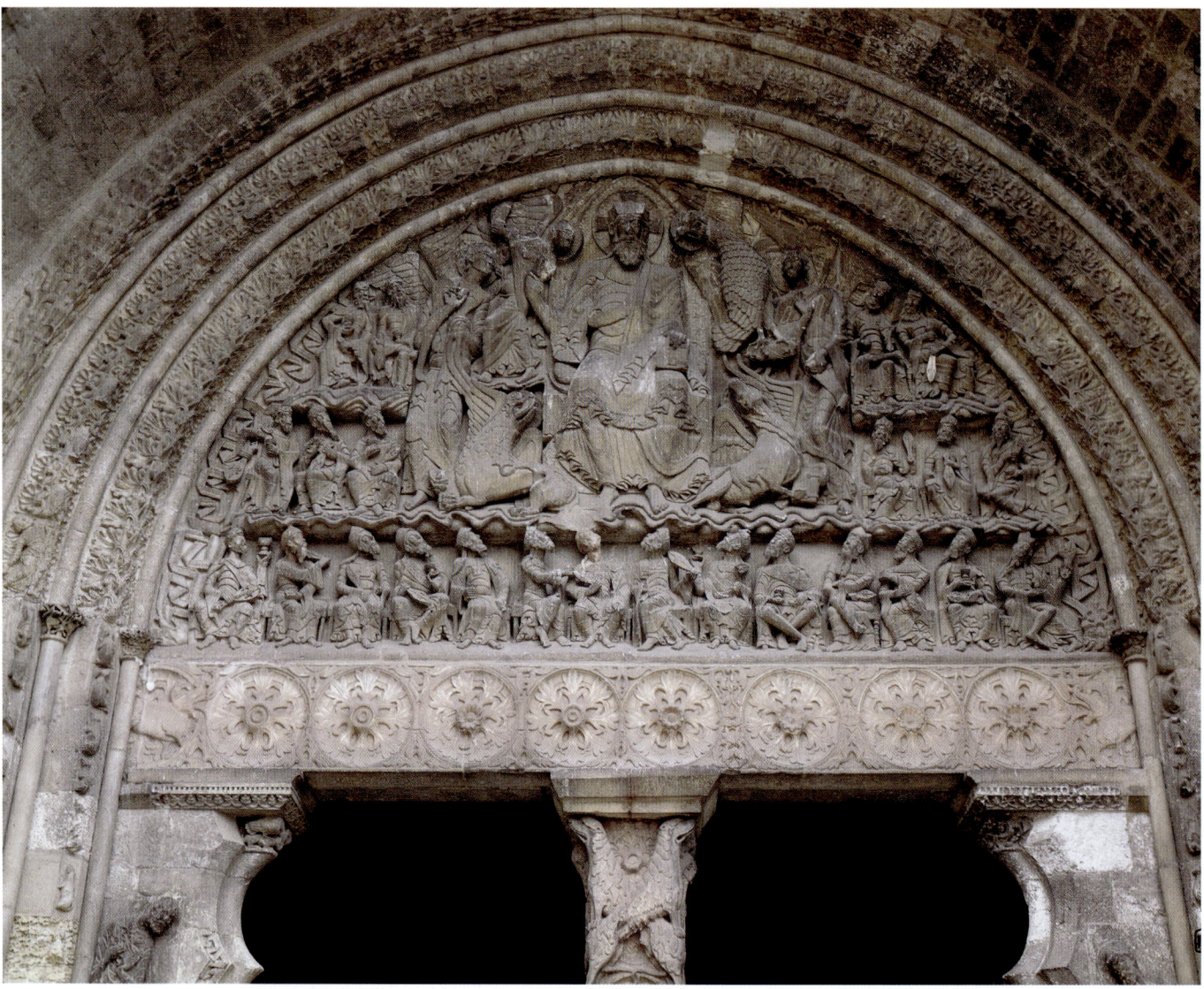

17-22   Christ in Majesty with angels and the Twenty-Four Elders, tympanum of the south portal of Saint-Pierre, Moissac, France, ca. 1115–1135. Marble, approx. 16′ 6″ wide at base.

The vast tympanum that crowns the south portal (see "The Romanesque Portal," page 471) of Saint-Pierre (FIG. **17-22**) depicts the Second Coming of Christ as King and Judge of the world in its last days, a theme already alluded to at Saint-Génis-des-Fontaines (FIG. 17-19). As befits his majesty, the enthroned Christ is at the center, reflecting a compositional rule followed since Early Christian times. The signs of the Four Evangelists flank him. On his right side are the angel and lion, and on his left side are the eagle and ox. To one side of each pair of signs is an attendant angel holding scrolls to record human deeds for judgment. The figures of crowned musicians, which complete the design, are the Twenty-Four Elders who accompany Christ as the kings of this world and make music in his praise. Each turns to face him, much as would the courtiers of a Romanesque monarch in attendance on their lord. Two courses of wavy lines symbolizing the clouds of Heaven divide the Elders into three tiers.

As many variations exist within the general style of Romanesque sculpture as within Romanesque architecture, and the figures of the Moissac tympanum contrast sharply with those of the reliefs previously examined. The extremely elongated bodies of the recording angels, the cross-legged dancing pose of Saint Matthew's angel, and the jerky, hinged movement of the Elders' heads are characteristic of the nameless Moissac master's style of representing the human figure. The zigzag and dovetail lines of the draperies, the bandlike folds of the torsos, the bending back of the hands against the body, and the wide cheekbones are also common features of this distinctive style.

A PROPHET AND LIONS ON A TRUMEAU   Below the Moissac tympanum are a richly decorated trumeau and elaborate door jambs with scalloped contours (FIG. 17-22), the latter another Romanesque borrowing from Islamic architecture (see FIG. 13-13). On the trumeau's right face is a prophet (FIG. **17-23**) identified by some as Jeremiah, by others as Isaiah. Whoever the prophet is, he displays the scroll where his prophetic vision is written. His position below the apparition of Christ as the apocalyptic Judge is yet another instance of the pairing of Old and New Testament themes. This is in keeping with an iconographic tradition established in Early Christian times (see "Jewish Subjects in Christian Art," Chapter 11, page 305).

The prophet's figure is very tall and thin, in the manner of the tympanum angels, and, like Matthew's angel, he executes folds ultimately derive from manuscript illumination and here play gracefully around the elegant figure. The long, serpentine locks of hair and beard frame an arresting image of the dreaming mystic. The prophet seems entranced by his vision of what is to come, the light of ordinary day unseen by his wide eyes. His expression is slightly melancholy—at once pensive and wistful. For people of the Middle Ages, two alternative callings were available. One calling was to *vita activa* (the active life). The other was to *vita contemplativa* (the religious life of contemplation), the pursuit of the vision of God. The sculptor of the Moissac prophet captured the very image of the vita contemplativa, a most appropriate theme for a monastic church.

Six roaring interlaced lions fill the trumeau's outer face (FIGS. 17-22 and 17-23). The animal world was never far from the medieval artist's instinct and imagination and was certainly not far from the medieval mind in general. Kings and barons often were associated with animals thought to be the most fiercely courageous—for example, Richard the Lionheart, Henry the Lion, and Henry the Bear. Lions were the church's ideal protectors. In the Middle Ages, people believed lions slept with their eyes open. But the idea of placing fearsome images at the gateways to important places had a very ancient origin. The lions and composite monsters that guarded the palaces of Assyrian and Mycenaean kings (see FIGS. 2-18, 2-21, and 4-20), the watchful sphinx in front of Khafre's pyramid (see FIG. 3-11), and the panthers and leopards in Greek temple pediments (see FIG. 5-15) and Etruscan tombs (see FIG. 9-8) are the ancestors of the interlaced lions at Moissac.

THE CLOISTER IN MONASTIC LIFE Before the great sculptures were put in place on Moissac's south portal, facing the town square and the public at large, the church's cloister (FIG. **17-24**) was decorated for the monks alone to see. *Cloister* (from the Latin word *claustrum,* an enclosed place) connotes being shut away from the world. Architecturally, the medieval church cloister expresses the seclusion of the spiritual life, the vita contemplativa. It provided the monks (and nuns) with a foretaste of Paradise. They walked in the cloister in contemplation, reading their devotions, praying and meditating in an atmosphere of calm serenity, each withdrawn into the private world where the soul communes only with God. The physical silence of the cloister is one with the silence that the more austere monastic communities required of their members. The monastery cloisters of the twelfth century are monuments to the vitality, popularity, and influence of monasticism at its peak.

At Moissac a timber-roofed walkway supported by piers and columns surrounds the cloister *garth* (garden) on four sides. Moissac's is the earliest surviving cloister with an extensive sculpture program. It consists of large figural reliefs on the piers and historiated (ornamented with figures) capitals on the columns. The pier reliefs portray the Twelve Apostles and the first Cluniac abbot of Moissac, Durandus (1047–1072), who was buried in the cloister. The seventy-six capitals alternately crown single and paired column shafts. They are variously decorated, some with abstract patterns, many with biblical scenes or the lives of saints, others with fantastic monsters of all sorts—basilisks, griffins, lizards, gargoyles, and more. Such sculptures were controversial at the time. Saint Bernard of Clairvaux, for example, complained that this kind of imagery

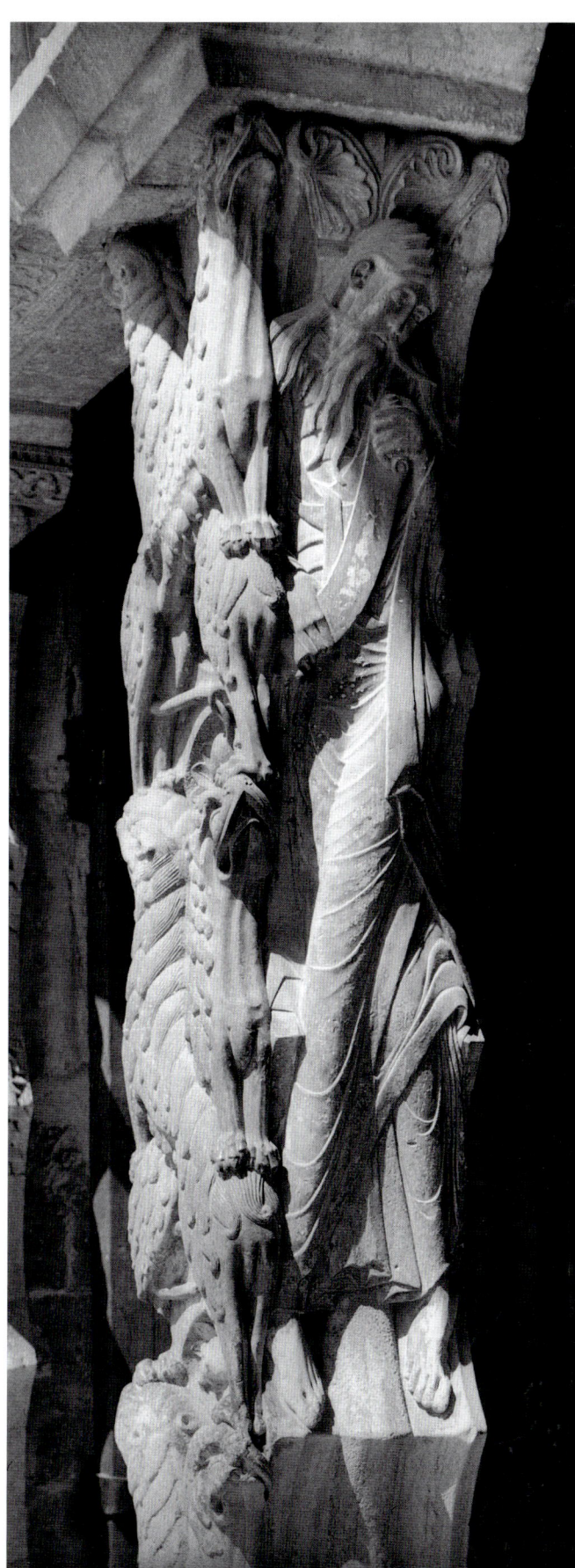

17-23 Lions and Old Testament prophet (Jeremiah or Isaiah?), from the trumeau of the south portal of Saint-Pierre, Moissac, France, ca. 1115–1130. Marble, approx. life-size.

a cross-legged step. The body's animation reveals the passionate nature of the soul within. The flowing lines of the drapery

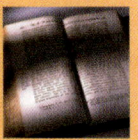

Saint Bernard of Clairvaux on Cloister Sculpture

The most influential theologian of the Romanesque era was Saint Bernard of Clairvaux (ca. 1090–1153). A Cistercian monk and abbot of the monastery he founded at Clairvaux in northern Burgundy, he embodied not only the reforming spirit of the Cistercian order but also the new religious fervor awakening in the West.

The Cistercians (so called from the Latin name for Cîteaux, France, their place of origin) were Benedictine monks who split from the older Benedictine monasticism of Cluny, which they felt had become rich and worldly. They returned to the strict observance of the Rule of Saint Benedict (see "Medieval Monasteries and Benedictine Rule," Chapter 16, page 443), changing the color of their habits from Cluniac Benedictine black to unbleached white. These so-called White Monks emphasized productive manual labor, and their systematic farming techniques stimulated the agricultural transformation of Europe. Under Bernard's leadership, they expanded rapidly. When he died in 1153, the Cistercian order had three hundred fifty abbeys. By the end of the twelfth century, five hundred thirty had been established.

Saint Bernard's impassioned eloquence made him a European celebrity and drew him into Europe's stormy politics. He intervened in high ecclesiastical and secular matters, defended and sheltered embattled popes, counseled kings, denounced heretics, and preached Crusades against the Muslims—all in defense of papal Christianity and spiritual values.

Saint Bernard's opposition to the profusion of sculpture in the Romanesque churches of his day was legendary. An excerpt from a letter he wrote in 1127 to William, abbot of Saint-Thierry, contains a tirade against the rich outfitting of churches in general and the sculptural adornment of monastic cloisters in particular:

> I say naught of the vast height of your churches, their immoderate length, their superfluous breadth, the costly polishings, the curious carvings and paintings which attract the worshipper's gaze and hinder his attention. . . . Let this pass, however: say that this is done for God's honour. . . . But in the cloister, under the eyes of the Brethren who read there, what profit is there in those ridiculous monsters, in that marvellous and deformed comeliness, that comely deformity? To what purpose are those unclean apes, those fierce lions, those monstrous centaurs, those half-men, those striped tigers, those fighting knights, those hunters winding their horns? Many bodies are there seen under one head, or again, many heads to a single body. Here is a four-footed beast with a serpent's tail; there, a fish with a beast's head. Here again the forepart of a horse trails half a goat behind it, or a horned beast bears the hinder quarters of a horse. In short, so many and so marvellous are [the sculpted figures] that we are more tempted to read in the marble than in our books, and to spend the whole day in wondering at these things rather than in meditating the law of God. For God's sake, if men are not ashamed of these follies, why at least do they not shrink from the expense?[1]

[1]Quoted in Elizabeth G. Holt, *A Documentary History of Art* (New York: Doubleday Anchor Books, 1957), 1: 19, 21.

17-24   Cloister of Saint-Pierre, Moissac, France, ca. 1100–1115. Marble, piers approx. 6′ high.

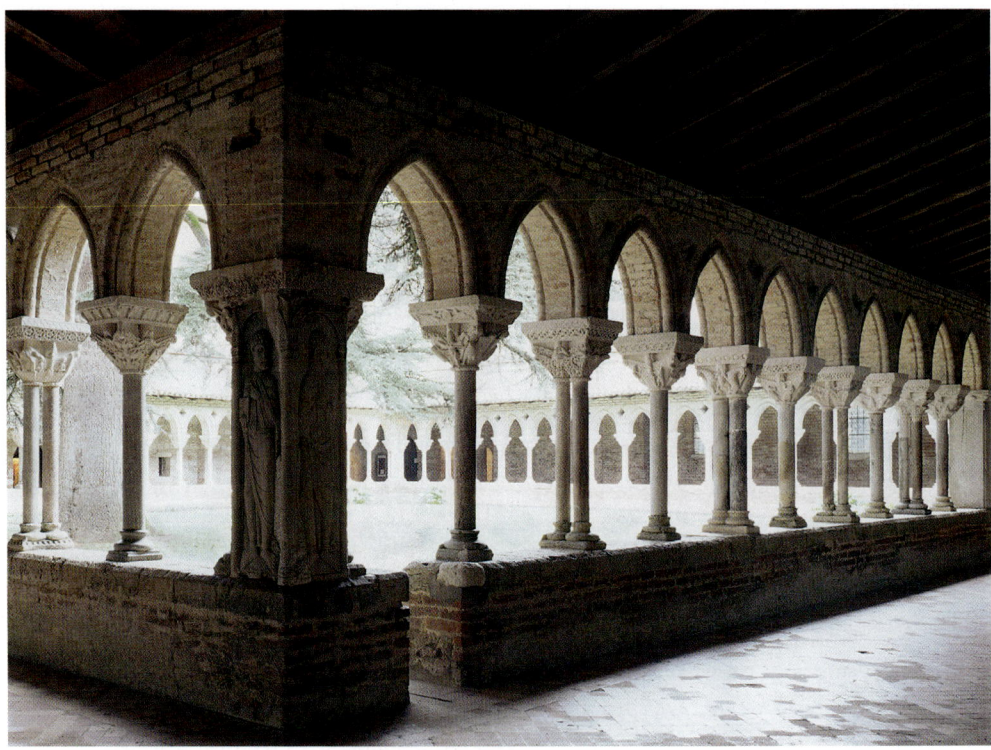

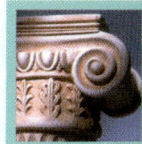

The Romanesque Portal

One of the most significant and distinctive features of Romanesque art is the revival of monumental sculpture in stone. Because of the Second Commandment's prohibition of graven images, large-scale carved Old and New Testament figures (and later saints) were almost unknown in Christian art before the Romanesque period. But in the late eleventh and early twelfth centuries, rich ensembles of figural reliefs began to appear again, although freestanding statuary, still associated with pagan idol worship, remained very rare.

Although sculpture in a variety of materials adorned different areas of Romanesque churches, it was most often found in the grand stone portals through which the faithful had to pass. Theologians undoubtedly dictated the subjects of the Romanesque portals. Church authorities felt it was just as important to have the right subjects carved in the correct places as to have the right arguments correctly arranged in a theological treatise. Sculpture had been employed in church doorways before. For example, carved wooden doors greeted Early Christian worshipers as they entered Santa Sabina in Rome. And Ottonian bronze doors decorated with Old and New Testament scenes marked the entrance to Saint Michael's at Hildesheim (FIG. 16-25). But these were exceptions. And in the Romanesque era (and during the Gothic period that followed), sculpture usually appeared in the area *around,* rather than *on,* the doors.

Our diagram shows the parts of church portals that Romanesque sculptors regularly decorated with figural reliefs:

- *Tympanum* (FIGS. 17-22, 17-25, and 17-26), the prominent semicircular *lunette* above the doorway proper, comparable in importance to the triangular pediment of a Greco-Roman temple

[Diagram of Romanesque portal labeled: Voussoirs, Archivolts, Voussoirs, Tympanum, Lintel, Jambs, Trumeau, Jambs]

- *Voussoirs* (FIG. 17-26), the wedge-shaped blocks that together form the *archivolts* of the arch framing the tympanum
- *Lintel* (FIG. 17-19), the horizontal beam above the doorway
- *Trumeau* (FIG. 17-23), the center post supporting the lintel in the middle of the doorway
- *Jambs* (FIG. 17-27), the side posts of the doorway

distracted the monks from their devotions (see "Saint Bernard of Clairvaux on Cloister Sculpture," page 470).

JUDGMENT DAY AT AUTUN The relatives of the monsters of the Moissac capitals appear as the demons of Hell in the tympanum of the Burgundian cathedral of Saint-Lazare (Saint Lazarus) at Autun (FIG. **17-25**). The Cluniac bishop Étienne de Bage had the cathedral built, and it was consecrated in 1132. At Moissac (FIG. 17-22), the faithful saw the apparition of the Divine Judge before he summoned humankind to Judgment. At Autun, the Judgment is in progress, announced by four trumpet-blowing angels.

In the tympanum's center, far larger than any other figure, is Christ, enthroned in a mandorla angels support, dispassionately presiding over the separation of the Blessed from the Damned. At the left, an obliging angel boosts one of the Blessed into the heavenly city. Below, the souls of the dead line up to await their fate. Two of the men at the left end of the lintel carry bags emblazoned with a cross and a shell.

These are the symbols of pilgrims to Jerusalem and Santiago de Compostela. Those who had made the difficult journey would be judged favorably. To their right, three small figures beg an angel to intercede on their behalf. The angel responds by pointing to the Judge above. On the right side are those who will be condemned to Hell (see FIG. Intro-6). One poor soul is plucked from the earth by giant hands. Directly above, in the tympanum, is one of the most unforgettable renditions of the weighing of souls in the history of art (compare the much earlier representation of this theme in Egypt, FIG. 3-39). Angels and devils contest at the scales, each trying to manipulate the balance for or against a soul. Hideous demons guffaw and roar. Their gaunt, lined bodies, with legs ending in sharp claws, writhe and bend like long, loathsome insects. A devil, leaning from the dragon mouth of Hell, drags souls in, while, above him, a howling demon crams souls headfirst into a furnace. The resources of the Romanesque imagination, heated by a fearful faith, provided an appalling scene.

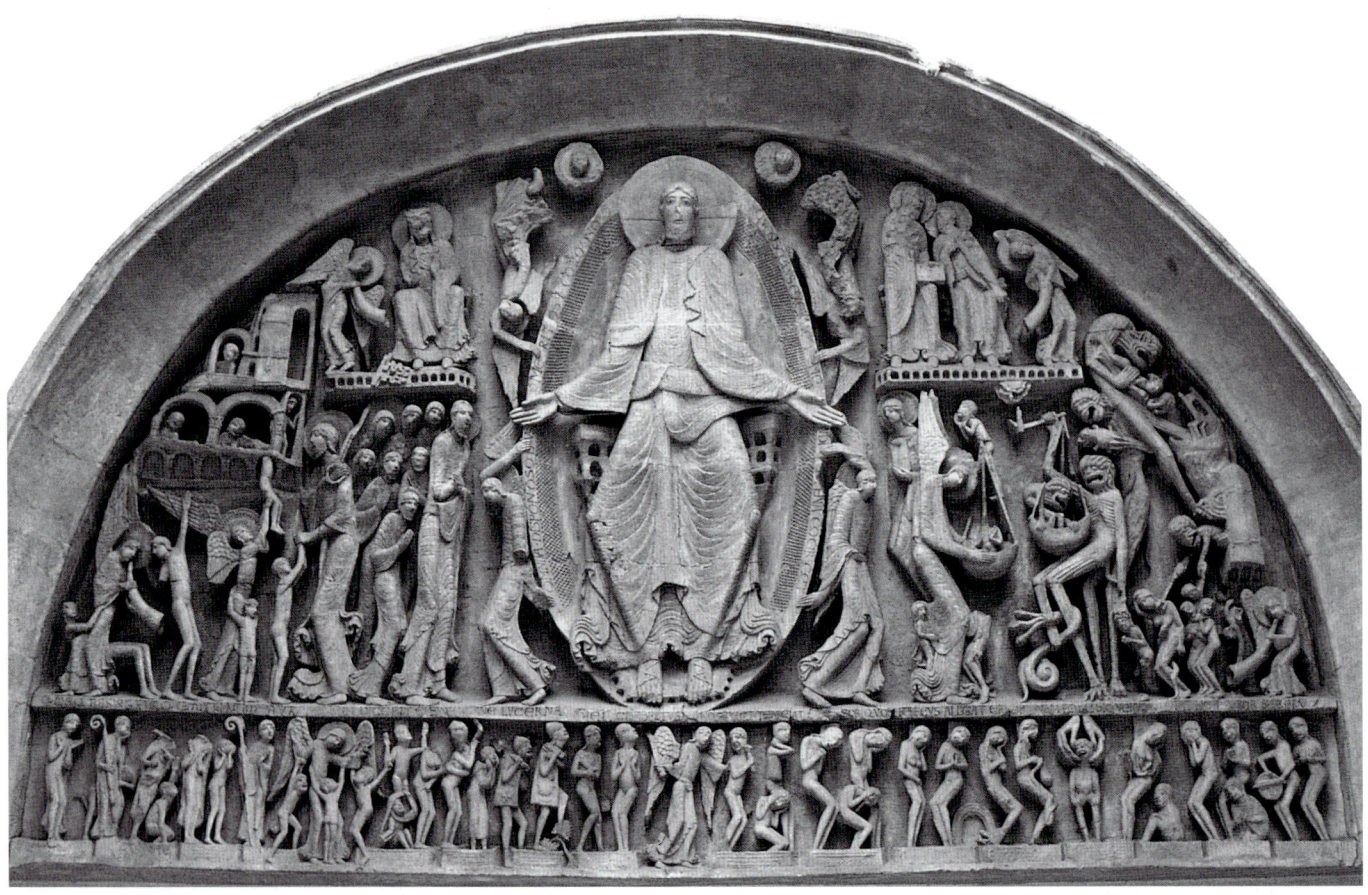

17-25 Gislebertus, *Last Judgment* (plaster cast), west tympanum of Saint-Lazare, Autun, France, ca. 1120–1135. Marble, approx. 21′ wide at base.

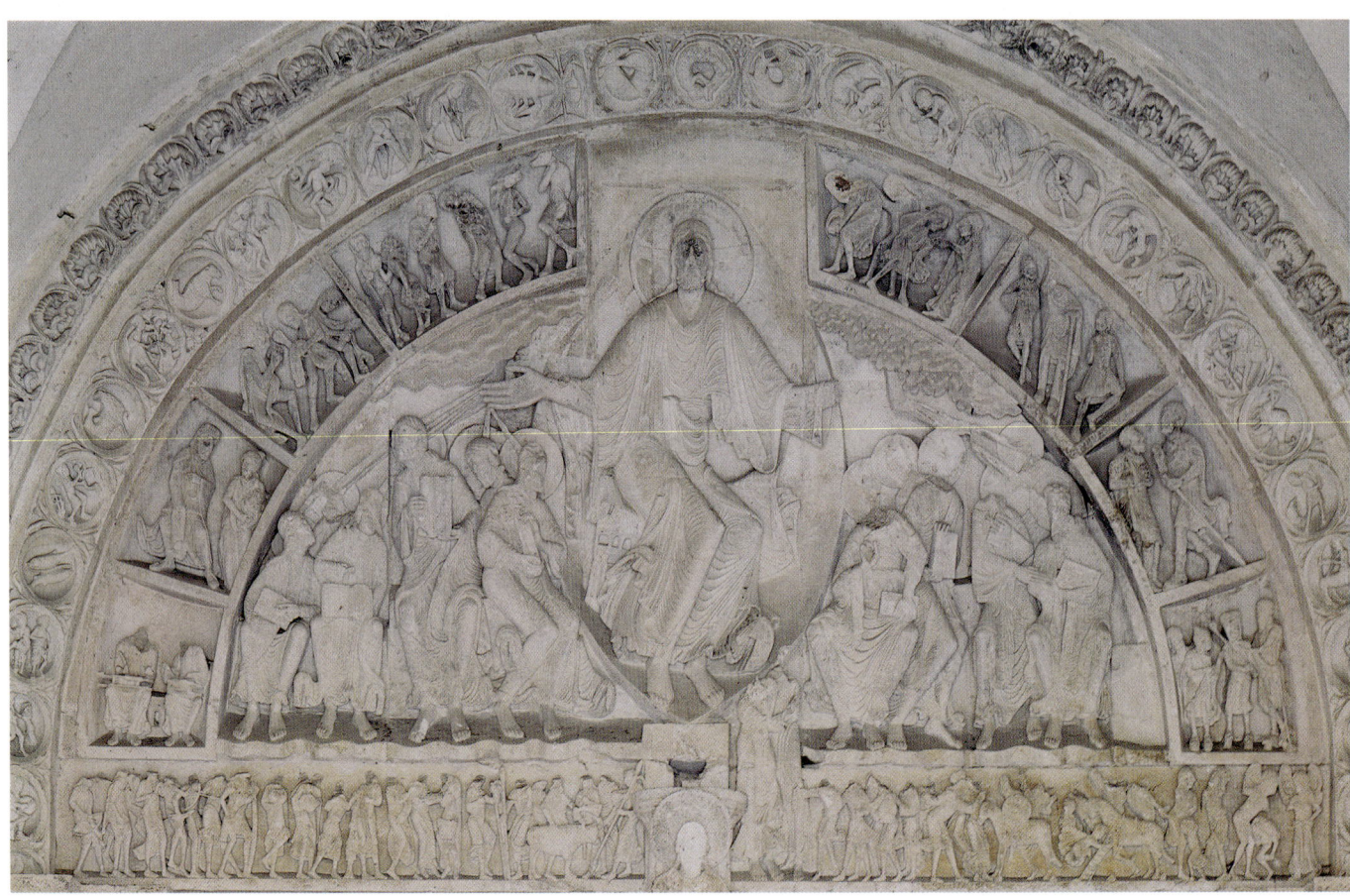

17-26 *Ascension of Christ and Mission of the Apostles*, tympanum of the center portal of the narthex of La Madeleine, Vézelay, France, 1120–1132.

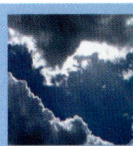

The Crusades

Between 1095, when Pope Urban II called for an assault on the Holy Land at the Council of Clermont, and 1190, Christians launched three great Crusades from France. The *Crusades* ("taking of the Cross") were mass armed pilgrimages, whose stated purpose was to wrest the Christian shrines of the Holy Land from Muslim control. Crusaders and pilgrims were bound by similar vows. They hoped not only to atone for sins and win salvation but also to glorify God and extend the Christian Church's power. The joint action of the papacy and the barons—mostly French—in this type of holy war strengthened papal authority over the long run and created an image of Christian solidarity.

The joining of religious and secular forces in the Crusades was symbolically embodied in the Christian warrior, the fighting priest, or the priestly fighter. From the early medieval warrior evolved the Christian knight, who fought for the honor of God rather than in defense of his chieftain. The first and most typical of the crusading knights were the Knights Templar. After the Christian conquest of Jerusalem in 1099, they stationed themselves next to the Dome of the Rock (see FIG. 13-1) near the site of Solomon's Temple, the source of their name. Their mission was to protect pilgrims visiting the recovered Christian shrines. Formally founded in 1118, the Knights Templar order was blessed by Saint Bernard, who gave them a rule of organization based on that of his own Cis-

tercians. Saint Bernard justified their militancy by declaring that "the knight of Christ" is "glorified in slaying the infidel . . . because thereby Christ is glorified" and the Christian knight then wins salvation. Saint Bernard saw the Crusades as part of the general reform of the Church and as the defense of the supremacy of Christendom. He himself preached the Second Crusade in 1147.

The Crusaders achieved little in the East. They established a few unstable kingdoms and princely states in Syria and the Holy Land, which the Muslims later overthrew and assimilated. But in western Europe, the Crusades' impact was much greater. They increased the power and prestige of the towns. Many communities purchased their charters from the barons when the barons needed to finance their campaigns. A middle class of merchants and artisans arose to rival the power of the feudal lords and the great monasteries. Italian maritime towns such as Pisa thrived on the commercial opportunities presented by the transportation of Crusaders overseas. The Crusades also widened the provincial West's cultural perspectives, bringing into view more civilized peoples and more exotic and opulent ways of life than anything the medieval West had yet known. And the direct exposure to the art and architecture of Byzantium and Islam had a profound impact on the character of Romanesque buildings, sculptures, reliquaries, mural paintings, and illuminated manuscripts.

One can appreciate the terror the Autun tympanum must have inspired in the believers who passed beneath it as they entered the cathedral. Even those who could not read could, in the words of Saint Bernard of Clairvaux, "read in the marble." For the literate, the Autun clergy composed explicit written warnings to reinforce the pictorial message, and had the words engraved in Latin on the tympanum. For example, beneath the weighing of souls, the inscription reads "May this terror terrify those whom earthly error binds, for the horror of these images here in this manner truly depicts what will be."[2] A second prominent inscription, directly beneath the feet of Christ, names GISLEBERTUS as the sculptor. It has been suggested that Gislebertus placed his signature on the tympanum not to advertise his own fame but as a kind of request to spectators to admire his good work and to pray for his salvation on Judgment Day. But pride in individual accomplishment was also a factor in the increasing number of artists' signatures in Romanesque times, as witnessed by Wiligelmo's boast at Modena.

VÉZELAY AND THE CRUSADES Another large tympanum (FIG. **17-26**), this one at the church of La Madeleine (Mary Magdalene) at Vézelay, not far from Autun, depicts the Ascension of Christ and the Mission of the Apostles. As related in Acts 1:4–9, Christ foretold that the Twelve Apostles would receive the power of the Holy Spirit and become

the witnesses of the truth of the Gospels throughout the world. The light rays emanating from Christ's hands represent the instilling of the Holy Spirit in the apostles (Acts 2:1–42) at the Pentecost (the seventh Sunday after Easter). The apostles, holding the Gospel books, receive their spiritual assignment, to preach the Gospel to all nations.

The world's heathen, the objects of the apostles' mission, appear on the lintel below and in eight compartments around the tympanum. The portrayals of the yet-to-be-converted constitute a medieval anthropological encyclopedia. Present are the legendary giant-eared Panotii of India, Pygmies (who require ladders to mount horses), and a host of other races, some characterized by a dog's head, others by a pig's snout, and still others by flaming hair. The assembly of agitated figures also includes hunchbacks, mutes, blind men, and lame men. Humanity, still suffering, awaits the salvation to come. The whole world is electrified by the promise of the ascended Christ, whose great figure, seeming to whirl in a vortex of spiritual energy, looms above human misery and deformity. Again, as at Autun, as worshipers enter the church, the tympanum emphatically establishes the greatness of God and the littleness of human beings.

Stylistically, the Vézelay tympanum figures are similar to those of the Moissac and Autun tympanums. Abrupt and jerky movement (strongly exaggerated at Vézelay), rapid play of line, windblown drapery hems, elongation, angularity, and

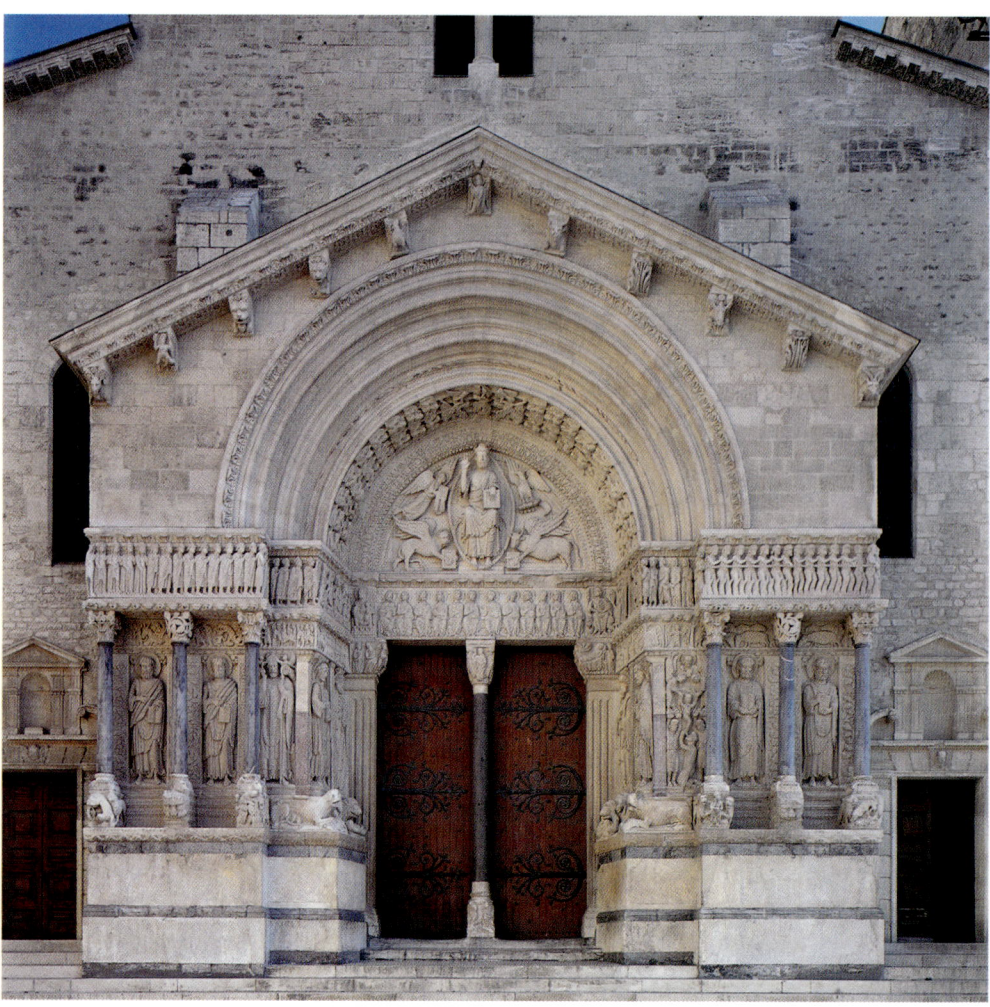

agitated poses, gestures, and silhouettes characterize this French Romanesque style. The Vézelay Christ figure is a splendid essay in calligraphic theme and variation. The drapery lines shoot out in rays, break into quick zigzag rhythms, and spin into whorls, wonderfully conveying the spiritual light and energy that flow from Christ over and into the animated apostles.

The Mission of the Apostles theme was an ideal choice for this tympanum. Vézelay is more closely associated with the Crusades (see "The Crusades," page 473) than any other church in Europe. Pope Urban II had intended to preach the launching of the First Crusade at Vézelay in 1095, twenty to thirty years before the tympanum was carved. In 1147, Saint Bernard of Clairvaux called for the Second Crusade at Vézelay, and King Louis VII of France took up the cross there. In 1190, it was from Vézelay that King Richard the Lionheart of England and King Philip Augustus of France set out on the Third Crusade. The spirit of the Crusades determined in part the iconography of the Vézelay tympanum. The Crusades were a kind of "second mission of the apostles" to convert the infidel.

ROMANESQUE PORTALS AND ROMAN ARCHES
In Provence, rich in the remains of Roman art and architecture, some Romanesque facades seem to have been inspired by Roman triumphal arches. This is the case at the mid-twelfth-century church of Saint-Trophîme at Arles, ancient Arelate, an important Roman colony Julius Caesar founded. Saint

Trophimus was an early bishop in Roman Gaul. For the church's western entrance (FIG. **17-27**), a projecting portal resembling a Roman arch was "attached" to the building's otherwise simple facade. The frieze above the freestanding columns recalls the sculptured fronts of late antique sarcophagi, which are also plentiful in the area. The figures in high relief between the columns emulate classical statuary.

The subject matter is, however, strictly Christian and thematically related to other Romanesque portals already examined here. The tympanum shows Christ surrounded by the signs of the Four Evangelists. On the lintel, directly below him, the Twelve Apostles appear at the center of a continuous frieze depicting the Last Judgment. The outermost parts of the frieze represent the Saved (on Christ's right) and the Damned in the flames of Hell (on his left). Below, in the jambs and the front bays of the portals, stand grave figures of saints draped in classical garb. The sculptor gave pride of place to Saint Trophimus, the third figure from the left. Across the doorway is a depiction of the stoning of Saint Stephen, whose relics were housed at Arles. It is the only narrative relief on the facade's lower part.

The quiet stances of the saints of Saint-Trophîme contrast with the spinning, twisting, and dancing figures seen at Moissac, Autun, and Vézelay. The Arles draperies, modeled on ancient stone sculpture rather than medieval manuscripts and metalwork, are also less agitated and show nothing of the dexterous linear play of the earlier portals. But the statuesque treatment of the figures on the Arles jambs has parallels in French Gothic art.

ing biblical figures in stone was not immediately emulated. But the idea of placing freestanding statues in niches would be taken up again in Italy by Early Renaissance sculptors (see FIGS. 21-6 and 21-8).

Metalwork and Wood Sculpture

BRONZEWORKING IN BELGIUM Another Romanesque sculptor whose name is known is RAINER OF HUY, a bronzeworker from the Meuse River valley in Belgium, an area renowned for its metalwork. In 1118 he masterfully cast in a single piece the baptismal font (FIG. **17-29**) for Notre-Dame-des-Fonts in Liège (today it is in Saint-Barthélémy). The bronze basin rests on the foreparts of twelve oxen, a reference to the "molten sea . . . on twelve oxen" cast in bronze for King Solomon's temple (1 Kings 7:23–25). The Old Testament story was thought to prefigure Christ's baptism (the twelve oxen were equated with the Twelve Apostles), which is the central scene on Rainer's font.

The style is classicizing. The figures are softly rounded, with idealized bodies and faces and heavy clinging drapery. One figure (at the left in our photo) even turns his back to observers. The three-quarter view from the rear was a popular motif in classical art. Some of Rainer's figures, including even Christ, are naked. In Romanesque art, the classical spirit lived on both north and south of the Alps.

Rainer of Huy joins the Italian Benedetto Antelami; Bernardus Gelduinus, who carved the Saint-Sernin sculptures (FIG. 17-20); Wiligelmo, sculptor of the Modena frieze (FIG. 17-21); and Gislebertus of Autun (FIG. 17-25) in the small but growing company of Romanesque artists who signed their works or whose names were recorded. In the twelfth century, artists, illuminators as well as sculptors, increasingly began to identify themselves. (The works of the manuscript painters Stephanus Garsia, FIG. 17-35; Master Hugo, FIG. 17-38; and Eadwine the

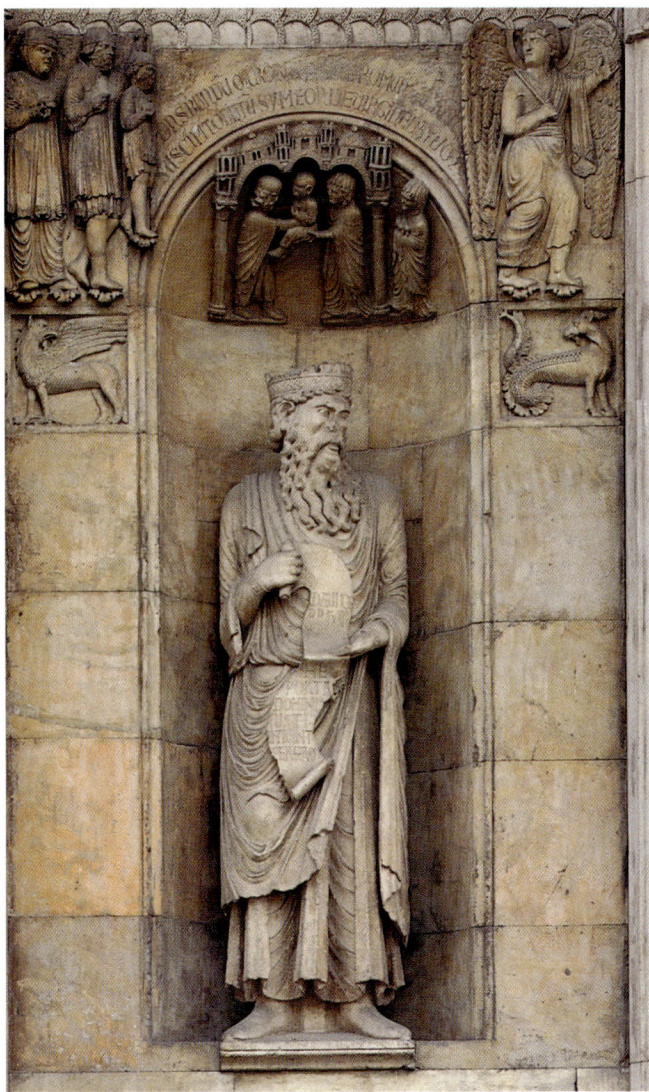

17-28 BENEDETTO ANTELAMI, King David, statue in a niche on the west facade of Fidenza Cathedral, Fidenza, Italy, ca. 1180–1190. Marble, approx. life-size.

In fact, in the north of France, near Paris, sculptors already had begun to adorn church portals with jamb figures that approximated freestanding statuary (see FIGS. 18-5 and 18-6).

THE REVIVAL OF STATUARY IN ITALY The reawakening of interest in stone sculpture in the round also may be seen in northern Italy, where the sculptor BENEDETTO ANTELAMI was active in the last quarter of the twelfth century. Several reliefs by his hand exist, including Parma Cathedral's pulpit and the portals of that city's baptistery. But his most unusual works are the monumental marble statues of two Old Testament figures he carved for Fidenza Cathedral's west facade. Antelami's King David (FIG. **17-28**) seems confined within his niche. His elbows are kept close to his body, and his stance is stiff, lacking any hint of the contrapposto that is classical statuary's hallmark. Yet the sculptor's conception of this prophet is undeniably rooted in Greco-Roman art. One need only compare the Fidenza David with the prophet on the Moissac trumeau (FIG. 17-23), who also displays an unfurled scroll, to see how much the Italian sculptor freed his figure from its architectural setting. Antelami's classical approach to portray-

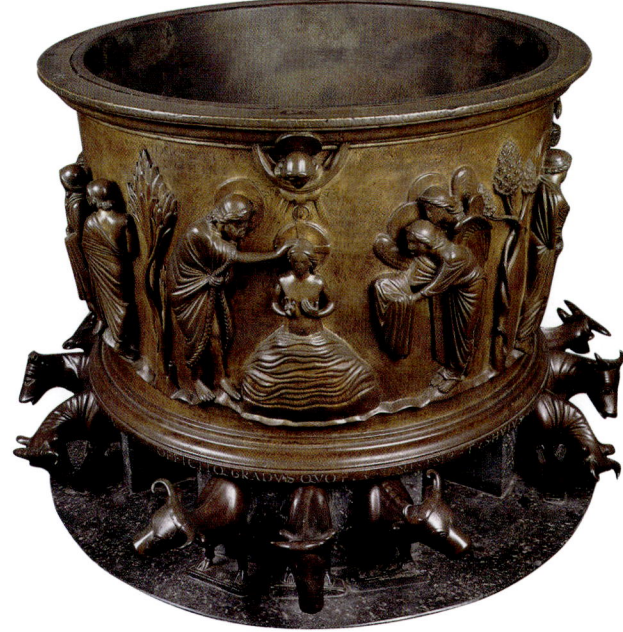

17-29 RAINER OF HUY, Baptism of Christ, baptismal font from Notre-Dame-des-Fonts, Liège, Belgium, 1107–1118. Bronze, 2′ 1″ high. Saint-Barthélémy, Liège.

Scribe, FIG. 17-39 will be introduced soon.) Although most medieval artists remained anonymous, the contrast of the Romanesque period with the early Middle Ages is striking.

THE THRONE OF WISDOM Despite the widespread use of stone relief sculptures to adorn Romanesque church portals, resistance to the creation of statues in the round—in any material—continued. The avoidance of anything that might be construed as an idol was still the rule, in keeping with the Second Commandment. Two centuries after Archbishop Gero commissioned a monumental wooden image of the crucified Christ for Cologne Cathedral (see FIG. 16-27), freestanding statues of Christ, the Virgin Mary, and the saints were still quite rare. The veneration of relics, however, brought with it a demand for small-scale images of the holy family and saints for placing on the chapel altars of the churches along the pilgrimage roads. Reliquaries in the form of saints (or parts of saints), tabletop crucifixes, and small wooden devotional images began to be produced in great numbers.

One of the most popular types, a specialty of France's Auvergne workshops, was a wooden statuette depicting the Virgin Mary with the Christ Child in her lap. The *Morgan Madonna* (FIG. **17-30**), so named because it once belonged to the financier and prolific collector J. Pierpont Morgan, is an excellent example. The type—known as the Throne of Wisdom, *sedes sapientiae*—is a western European freestanding version of the Byzantine Theotokos theme popular in icons and mosaics (see FIGS. 12-15 and 12-16). Christ, God incarnate, holds a Bible in his left hand and raises his right arm in blessing (both hands are broken off). He is the embodiment of the divine wisdom contained in the Holy Scriptures. His mother, seated on a wooden chair, is in turn the Throne of Wisdom because her lap is the Christ Child's throne. As in Byzantine art, familiar to many Romanesque painters and sculptors, both Mother and Child sit rigidly upright and are strictly frontal emotionless figures. But the intimate scale, the gesture of benediction, the once-bright coloring of the garments, and the soft modeling of the Virgin's face make the group seem much less remote than its counterparts in Byzantium.

A SAINTED POPE'S SILVER RELIQUARY Far more costly, but also created for private devotional purposes, is the reliquary of Saint Alexander (FIG. **17-31**), made in 1145 for Abbot Wibald of Stavelot in Belgium to house the hallowed pope's relics. The idealized head, which resembles portraits of youthful Roman emperors such as Augustus (see FIG. Intro-10) and Constantine (see FIG. 10-78), is almost life-size and was fashioned in beaten (repoussé) silver with bronze gilding for the hair. The saint wears a collar of jewels and enamel plaques around his neck. Enamels and gems also adorn the box on which the head is mounted. The reliquary rests on four bronze dragons—mythical animals of the kind that populated Romanesque cloister capitals. Not surprisingly, Saint Bernard of Clairvaux was as critical of church furnishings such as the Alexander reliquary as he was of Romanesque sculpture:

> [Men's] eyes are feasted with relics cased in gold, and their pursestrings are loosed. They are shown a most comely image of some saint, whom they think all the more saintly that he is the more

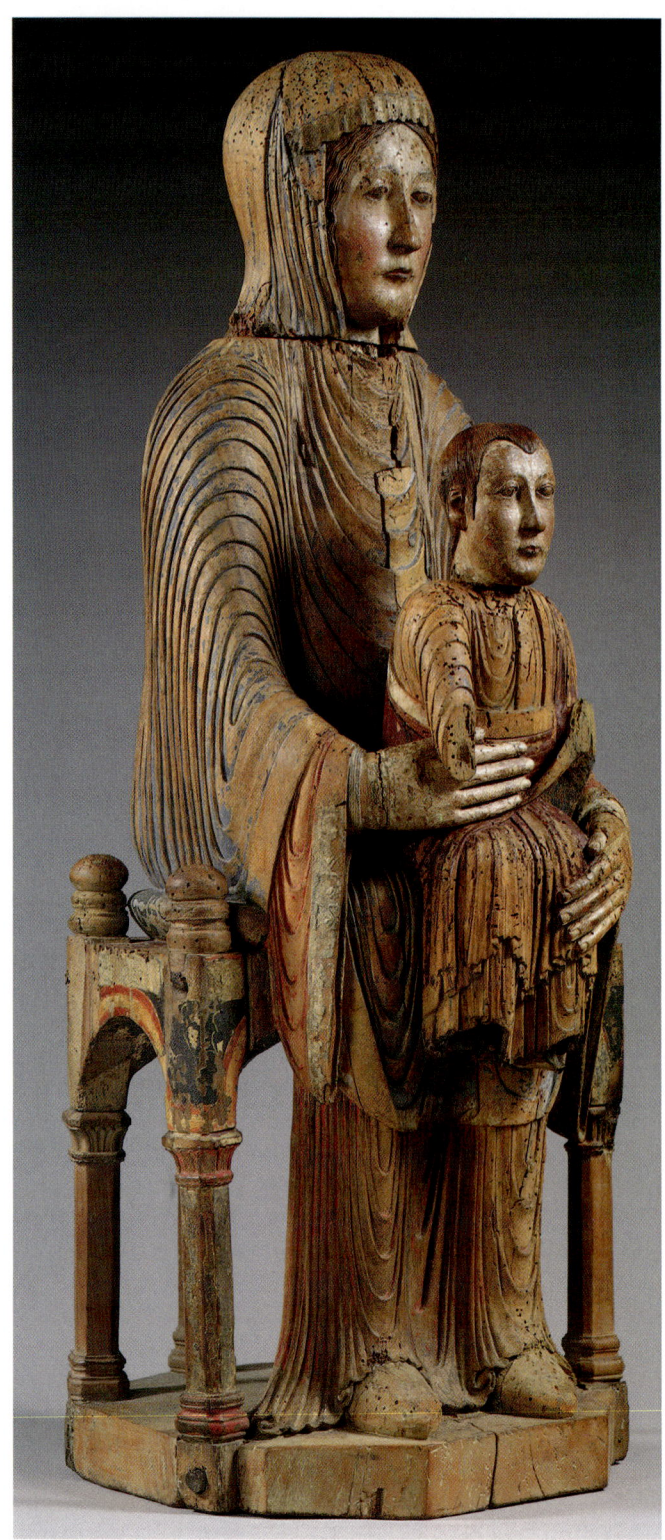

17-30 Virgin and Child *(Morgan Madonna)*, from Auvergne, France, second half of twelfth century. Painted wood, 2′ 7″ high. Metropolitan Museum of Art, New York (gift of J. Pierpont Morgan, 1916).

gaudily painted. Men run to kiss him, and are invited to give; there is more admiration for his comeliness than veneration for his sanctity. . . . O vanity of vanities, yet no more vain than insane! The church . . . clothes her stones in gold and leaves her sons naked; the rich man's eye is fed at the expense of the indigent. The curious find delight here, yet the needy find no relief.[3]

The central plaque on the front of the Stavelot reliquary depicts Pope Alexander. Saints Eventius and Theodolus flank

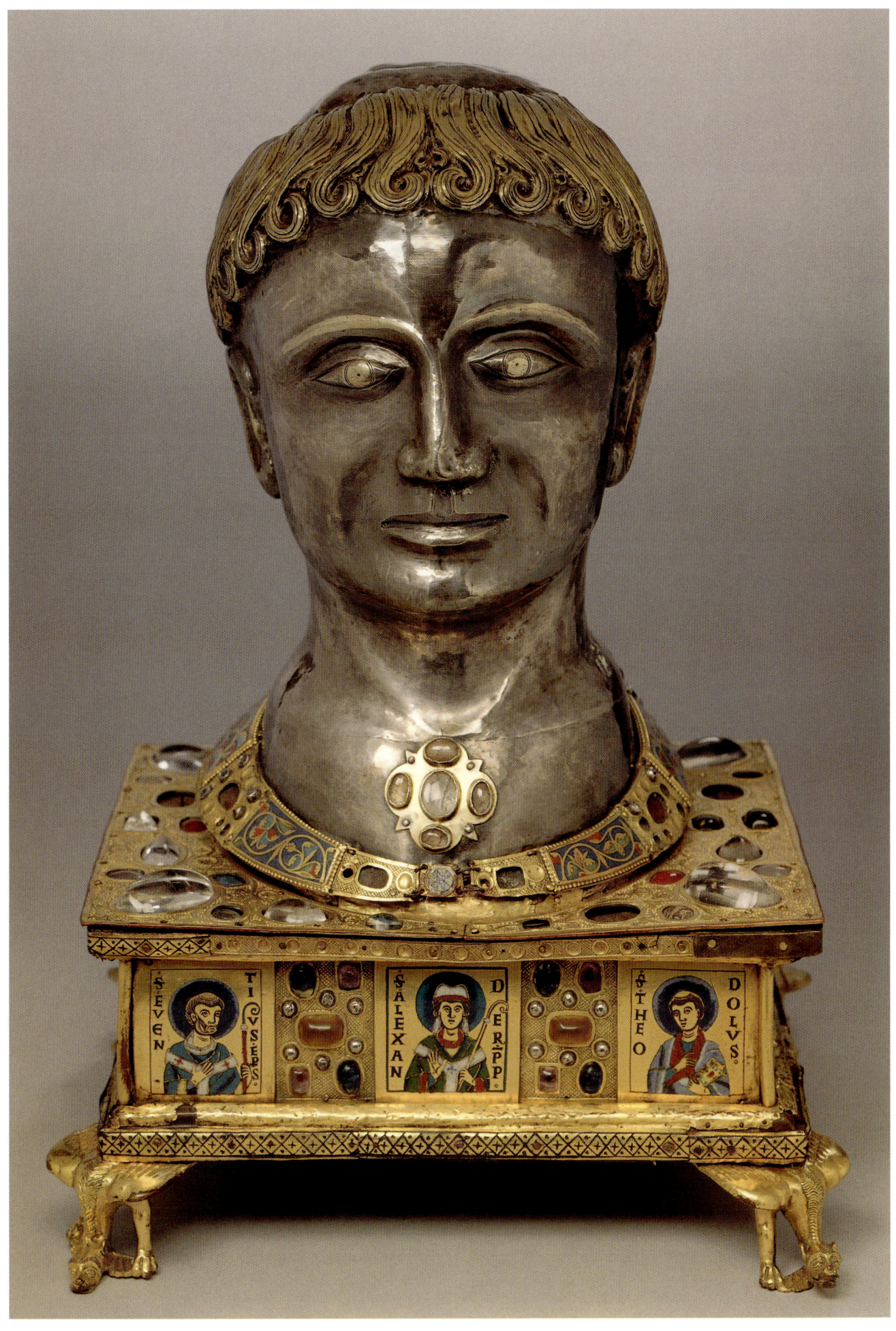

17-31 Head reliquary of Saint Alexander, from Stavelot Abbey, Belgium, 1145. Silver repoussé (partly gilt), gilt bronze, gems, pearls, and enamel, approx. 1′ 5½″ high. Musées Royaux, Brussels.

him. The nine plaques on the other three sides represent female allegorical figures—Wisdom, Piety, and Humility among them. Although a local artist produced these enamels in the Meuse River region, the models were surely Byzantine (compare FIG. 12-25). Saint Alexander's reliquary underscores the multiple sources of Romanesque art, as well as its stylistic diversity. Not since antiquity had people journeyed as extensively as they did in the Romanesque period, and artists regularly saw works of wide geographic origin. Abbot Wibald himself epitomizes the well-traveled twelfth-century clergyman. He was abbot of Montecassino in southern Italy, took part in the Second Crusade, and was sent by Frederick Barbarossa (Holy Roman Emperor, r. 1152–1190) to Constantinople to arrange Frederick's wedding to the niece of the Byzantine emperor Manuel Comnenus.

PAINTING

Unlike the practices of placing vaults over naves and aisles, and decorating building facades with monumental stone reliefs, the art of painting did not need to be "revived" in the Romanesque period. Illuminated manuscripts had been produced in large numbers in the early Middle Ages, and even the Roman tradition of mural painting had never died, especially in Italy. But the quantity of preserved frescoes and illustrated books from the Romanesque era is unprecedented. As with architecture and sculpture, Romanesque painting exhibits considerable regional and stylistic diversity. We discuss here a representative sample of Romanesque paintings from several regions in different media and formats.

Mural Painting

PAINTING IN CHRISTIAN SPAIN   In the eighth century, Muslim armies from North Africa defeated the Visigoths and occupied almost all of the Iberian Peninsula (Spain and Portugal), bringing with them both the Islamic faith and Islamic art (see Chapter 13). But in northern Spain, the Muslim conquerors never completely controlled many areas, and Christianity and Christian art still flourished. In fact, Catalonia in northeastern Spain has more Romanesque mural paintings today than anywhere else.

One of the most impressive is the fresco (FIG. **17-32**) that once filled the apse of Santa María de Mur, a monastery church not far from Lérida. (The fresco was detached from the church, and the apse has been reconstructed in the Museum of Fine Arts in Boston.) The formality, symmetry, and placement of the figures is Byzantine—compare the sixth-century apse of Saint Catherine's at Mount Sinai in Egypt (see FIG. 12-13) and the late-twelfth-century apse of the basilica at Monreale (see FIG. 12-24). But the Spanish artist rejected Byzantine mosaic in favor of direct painting on plaster-coated walls. And the iconographic scheme in the semidome of the apse is more closely tied to those of the Romanesque church portals of France (FIGS. 17-22 and 17-27).

In the Santa María de Mur fresco, Christ in a star-strewn mandorla is flanked by the signs of the Four Evangelists—the Apocalypse theme that so fascinated the Romanesque imagination. Seven lamps, or candlesticks, between Christ and the Evangelist signs symbolize the seven Christian communities

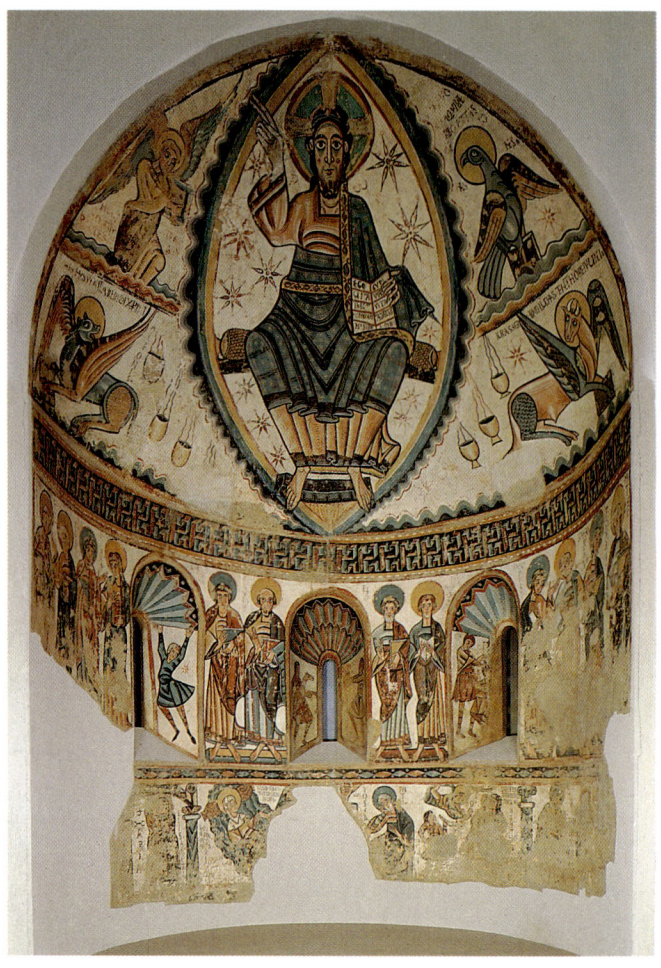

17-32   Christ in Majesty, apse fresco from Santa María de Mur, near Lérida, Spain, mid-twelfth century. 22′ × 24′. Museum of Fine Arts, Boston.

where Saint John addressed his revelation (the Apocalypse) at the beginning of his book (Rev. 1:4, 12, 20). Below stand apostles, paired off in formal frontality, much like the saints on the facade of Saint-Trophîme at Arles (FIG. 17-27), as well as in the apse at Monreale (see FIG. 12-24). The principal figures are rendered—as at Moissac (FIG. 17-22) and elsewhere in Romanesque art—with partitioning of the drapery into volumes, here and there made tubular by local shading. The painter stiffened the irregular shapes of actual cloth into geometric patterns. The effect overall is one of simple, strong, and even blunt directness of statement, reinforced by harsh, bright color, appropriate for a powerful icon.

ITALIAN MURALS AND BYZANTINE MODELS The tradition of decorating church apses with imposing images of Christ and saints is a venerable one, going back to Early Christian art. So, too, is the idea of illustrating episodes from the Old and New Testaments above the nave arcade of basilican churches, as at Santa Maria Maggiore (see FIG. 11-13) and Sant'Apollinare Nuovo (see FIG. 11-17). An extensive series of framed scenes from Christ's life—in fresco rather than mosaic—appears along both sides of the nave of Sant'Angelo in Formis, near Capua in southern Italy. (Frescoes also adorn the apse, where Christ sits on a jeweled throne with the dove of the Holy Spirit above him and the symbols of the Four Evangelists at his side.)

Abbot Desiderius (later Pope Victor III) of Montecassino, the great monastery Saint Benedict founded in the sixth cen-

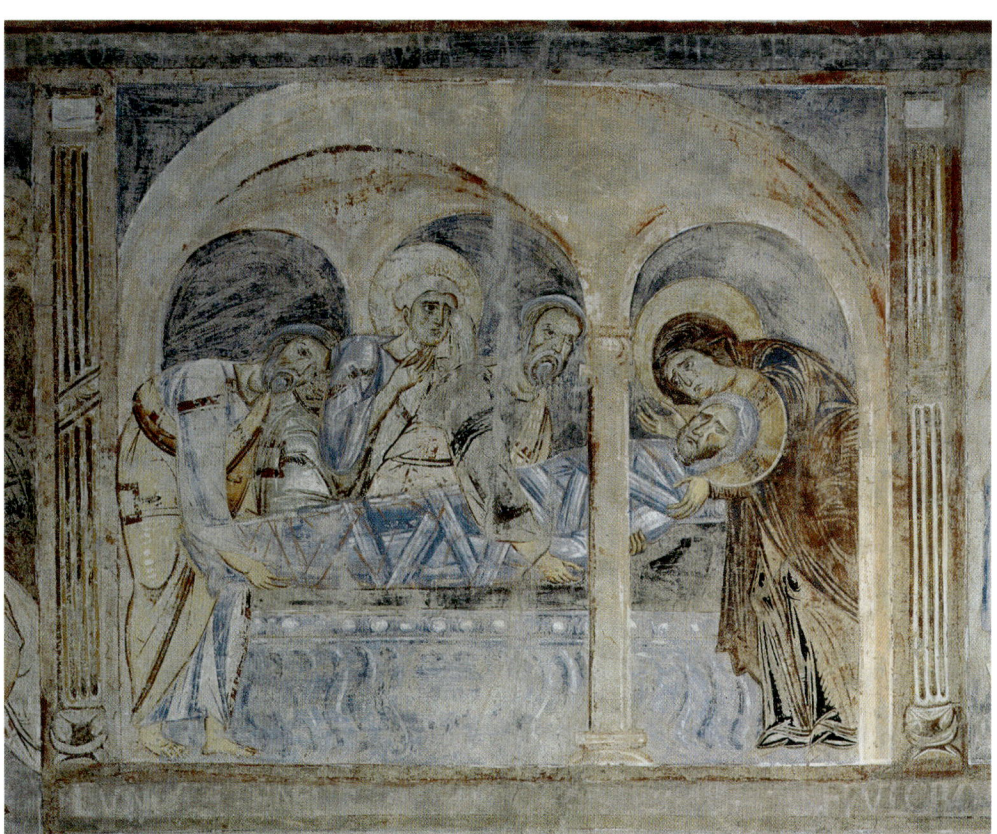

17-33 Entombment of Christ, fresco above the nave arcade, Sant'Angelo in Formis, near Capua, Italy, ca. 1085.

tury, began Sant'Angelo in Formis in 1072. The nave frescoes date to around 1085. Our detail (FIG. 17-33) shows the panel illustrating the entombment of Christ, with Mary cradling the head of her dead son as Joseph of Arimathea and Nicodemus lower him into his coffin. The weeping Saint John the Evangelist (with nimbus) watches. The fully modeled figures, the three-dimensional architectural setting, and the natural blue sky provide a sharp contrast with the Catalonian mural. But a comparison with the painted lamentation scene in Saint Pantaleimon in Macedonia (see FIG. 12-27) underscores that the Italian painter used Byzantine artworks as models. For the church at Montecassino, Desiderius imported artisans from Constantinople and instructed them to train his monks in mosaic and other arts. Sant'Angelo in Formis displays the work of these Italian pupils of Desiderius's Greek masters.

THE OLD TESTAMENT ON A BARREL VAULT
The Santa María de Mur and Sant'Angelo in Formis frescoes easily could be moved to an Early Christian basilica, where they would find ready homes in the apse and nave. But the murals of the Benedictine abbey church of Saint-Savin-sur-Gartempe were inconceivable before the mastering of stone vaulting in the Romanesque period. A continuous barrel vault supported by columns painted to appear like grained marble covers the nave (FIG. 17-34) of the French church. The structure lacks both tribune gallery and clerestory, but the absence of a direct light source did not deter the monks from commissioning paintings (not true frescoes) to decorate the ceiling's entire surface. Since the side aisles rise to the nave vault's level, more light than usual reaches the nave from the aisle windows.

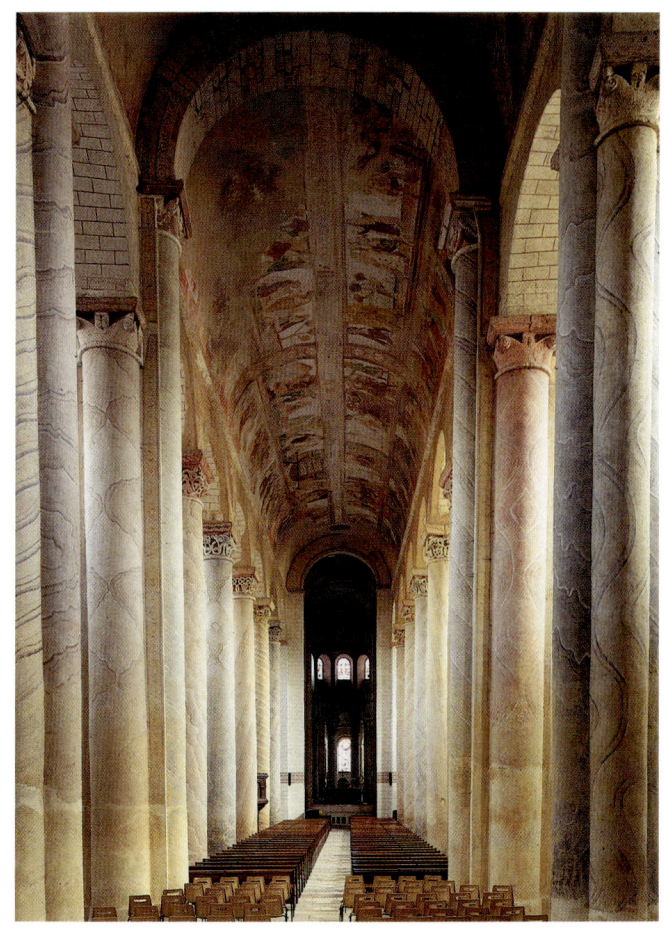

17-34 Nave of the abbey church, Saint-Savin-sur-Gartempe, France. Painted barrel vault, ca. 1100.

The subjects were all drawn from the Pentateuch, the opening five books of the Old Testament, in contrast to the New Testament themes of Sant'Angelo in Formis. They also bear little resemblance stylistically to the Byzantine-inspired murals of the Capuan and Catalonian churches. The elongated, agitated cross-legged figures of the Saint-Savin paintings are northern both in spirit and in form. They have stylistic affinities both to the reliefs of southern French portals and to some of the illuminated manuscripts discussed next.

Manuscript Illumination

THE APOCALYPSE ON TWO PAINTED FOLIOS
The apocalyptic vision of the Second Coming of Christ, recorded in the Book of Revelation and carved on the great tympanum at Moissac (FIG. 17-22), is also the subject of a double-page illumination of the third quarter of the eleventh century. The *Apocalypse of Saint-Sever* (FIG. **17-35**) contains the commentaries on the Apocalypse written by Beatus of Liébana, an eighth-century Spanish monk. The theme of the Second Coming was of such interest that numerous manuscripts of Beatus's commentary were copied and illustrated in the Romanesque era. With the exception of this book, all were produced in Spain. The monastery at Saint-Sever-sur-

l'Adour, in southwestern France near Moissac and Toulouse, is about sixty-five miles from the Spanish border. It does not seem to have had its own scriptorium. STEPHANUS GARSIA, the painter of the great vision of the Second Coming in the *Apocalypse of Saint-Sever*, therefore must have been employed especially for this manuscript.

Stephanus's two-folio painting is significant not only as a masterpiece of the illuminator's art but also as a pictorial relative of the Moissac tympanum. Such manuscript pages probably served as prototypes for the Moissac sculptor. The characters in the drama are essentially the same. Only the composition is different. In both cases, the artist strictly followed the New Testament account of the vision of Saint John (Rev. 4:6–8, 5:8–9). Christ, enthroned in a sapphire aura, appears amid the signs of the Four Evangelists, whose bodies are full of eyes and who are borne aloft by numerous wings. The crowned and music-making Twenty-Four Elders offer their golden cups of incense and their stringed viols. Flights of angels frame the great circle of the apparition. The color is intense and vivid. The agile figures were fluently drawn. The artist depicted the seated figures in a kind of bird's-eye perspective. Their bodies overlap, and some of them are seen from behind. Within a context of visionary abstraction, these deft touches of realism are noteworthy, but the characteristic patternings of Romanesque figural art still contain them.

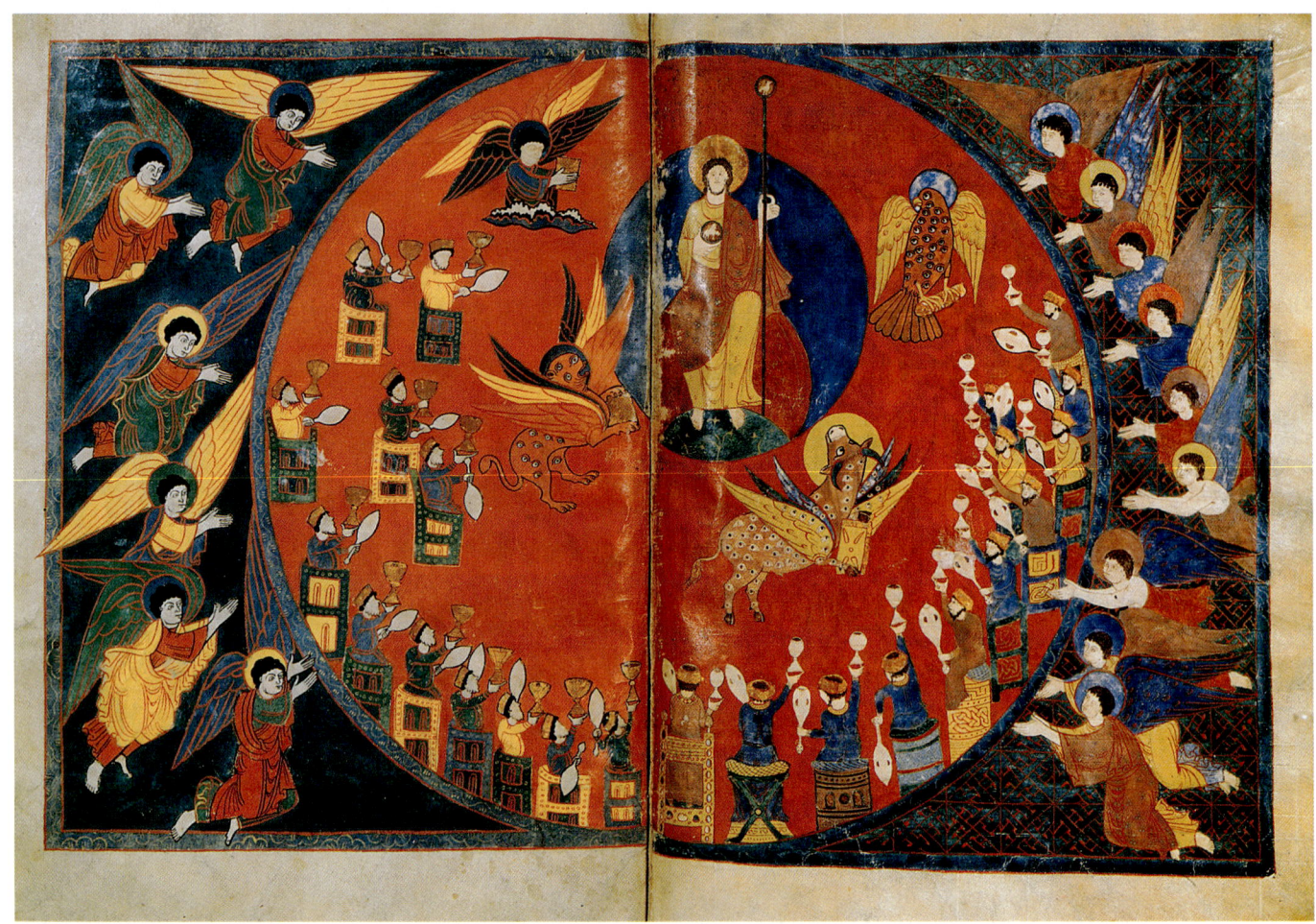

17-35   STEPHANUS GARSIA, enthroned Christ with signs of the Four Evangelists and the Twenty-Four Elders, folios 121 verso and 122 recto of the *Apocalypse of Saint-Sever*, from Saint-Sever-sur-l'Adour, France, ca. 1050–1070. Ink and tempera on vellum, approx. 1' 2$\frac{1}{2}$" × 1' 10". Bibliothèque Nationale, Paris.

nying text. Hildegard immediately sets down what has been revealed to her on a wax tablet resting on her left knee. Nearby, the monk Volmar, Hildegard's confessor, copies into a book all she has written. Here, in a singularly dramatic context, is a picture of the essential nature of ancient and medieval book manufacture—individual scribes copying and recopying texts by hand. In the early Middle Ages and during the Romanesque era, these scribes were almost exclusively monks and nuns working in the sheltered scriptoria of isolated religious communities.

A KNIGHT BATTLES DRAGONS One of the major Romanesque scriptoria was at the abbey of Cîteaux, France, home of the Cistercian order. Just before Saint Bernard joined the monastery in 1112, the monks completed work on an illuminated copy of Saint Gregory's *Moralia in Job*. It is a splendid example of Cistercian illumination before Bernard's passionate opposition to figural art led in 1134 to a ban on elaborate paintings in manuscripts. After 1134, not only were full-page illustrations prohibited but also even initial letters had to be nonfigurative and of a single color.

The historiated initial we reproduce (FIG. **17-37**) clearly would have been in violation of Saint Bernard's ban if it had not been painted before his prohibitions took effect. A knight (thought by some to be Saint George in contemporary garb), his squire, and two roaring dragons form an intricate letter *R,* the initial letter of the salutation *Reverentissimo*. This page is the

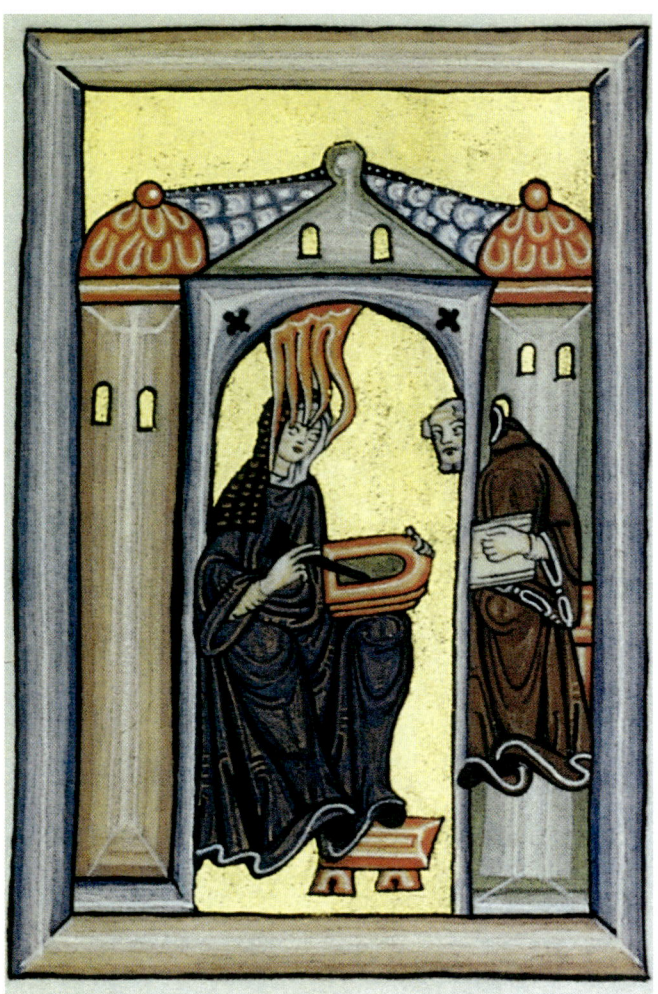

17-36 The vision of Hildegard of Bingen, detail of a facsimile of a lost folio in the *Scivias* by Hildegard of Bingen, from Trier or Bingen, Germany, ca. 1050–1079. Formerly in Hessische Landesbibliothek, Wiesbaden.

THE DIVINE VISIONS OF A GERMAN NUN
An unusual portrait of a visionary, rather than a vision, was the opening page of the *Scivias (Know the Ways [Scite vias] of God)* of Hildegard of Bingen. Hildegard was a German nun and eventually the abbess of the convent at Disibodenberg in the Rhineland (see "Romanesque Countesses, Queens, and Nuns," page 482). The manuscript, lost in 1945, is known today only through a facsimile. The original probably was written and illuminated at the monastery of Saint Matthias at Trier between 1150 and Hildegard's death in 1179, but it is possible the book was produced at Bingen under Hildegard's supervision. The *Scivias* contains a record of Hildegard's vision in the year 1141 of the divine order of the cosmos and of humankind's place in it. The vision came to her as a fiery light from the open vault of heaven that poured into her brain.

On one page of the Trier manuscript (FIG. **17-36**), Hildegard sits within the monastery walls, with her feet resting on a footstool, in much the same way the Evangelists of the *Coronation* and *Ebbo Gospels* (see FIGS. 16-12 and 16-13) were portrayed. This Romanesque page is a link in a chain of author portraits that goes back to classical antiquity. The painter showed Hildegard experiencing her divine vision by depicting five long tongues of fire emanating from above and entering her brain, just as she describes the experience in the accompa-

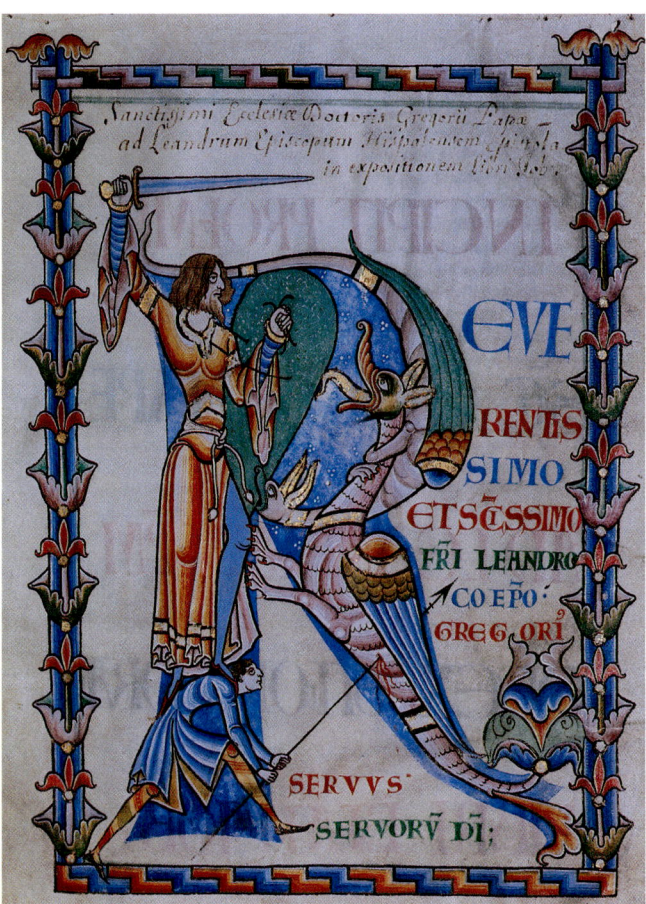

17-37 Initial *R* with knight fighting a dragon, from the *Moralia in Job,* from Cîteaux, France, ca. 1115–1125. Ink and tempera on vellum, 1′ 1¾″ × 9¼″. Bibliothèque Municipale, Dijon.

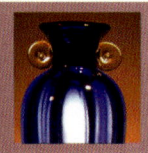

Romanesque Countesses, Queens, and Nuns

Romanesque Europe was still a man's world, but women could and did have power and influence. Countess Matilda of Canossa (1046–1115), who ruled Tuscany after 1069, was sole heiress of vast holdings in northern Italy. She was a key figure in the political struggle between the popes and the German emperors who controlled Lombardy. With unflagging resolution she defended Pope Gregory's reforms and at her death willed most of her lands to the papacy.

More famous and more powerful was Eleanor of Aquitaine (1122–1204), wife of Henry II of England. She married Henry after her marriage to Louis VII, king of France, was annulled. She was queen of France for fifteen years and queen of England for thirty-five years. During that time she bore three daughters and five sons. Two became kings—Richard I (Lionheart) and John. She prompted her sons to rebel against their father, so Henry imprisoned her. Released at Henry's death, she lived on as dowager queen, managing England's government and King John's holdings in France.

Of quite different stamp was Hildegard of Bingen (1098–1179), the most prominent nun of the twelfth century and one of the greatest religious figures of the Middle Ages. Hildegard was born into an aristocratic family that owned large estates in the German Rhineland. At a very early age she began to have visions. When she was eight, her parents placed her in the Benedictine *double monastery* (for monks *and* nuns) at Disibodenberg. She became a nun at fifteen. In 1141, God instructed Hildegard in a vision to disclose her visions to the world. Before then she had revealed them only to close confidants at the monastery. One of these was the monk Volmar, and Hildegard chose to dictate her visions to him (FIG. 17-36) for posterity. No less a figure than Saint Bernard of Clairvaux certified in 1147 that her visions were authentic. Archbishop Heinrich of Mainz joined him in endorsing Hildegard. In 1148, the Cistercian pope Eugenius III formally authorized Hildegard "in the name of Christ and Saint Peter to publish all that she had learned from the Holy Spirit." At this time Hildegard became the abbess of a new convent built for her near Bingen. As reports of Hildegard's visions spread, kings, popes, barons, and prelates sought her counsel. All of them were attracted by her spiritual insight into the truth of the mysteries of the Christian faith.

In addition to her visionary works—the most important is the *Scivias* (FIG. 17-36)—Hildegard also wrote two scientific treatises. *Physica* is a study of the natural world, and *Causae et curae (Causes and Cures)* is a medical encyclopedia. Hildegard also composed the music and wrote the lyrics of seventy-seven songs published under the title *Symphonia*, and still performed today.

Hildegard was the most famous of all Romanesque nuns, but she was by no means the only learned woman of her age. A younger contemporary, the abbess Herrad (d. 1195) of Hohenberg, Austria, was also the author of an important medieval encyclopedia. Herrad's *Hortus deliciarum (Garden of Delights)* is a history of the world intended for instructing the nuns under her supervision, but it was more widely published.

---

opening of Gregory's letter to "the very reverent" Leandro, Bishop of Seville. The knight is a slender regal figure who raises his shield and sword against the dragons while the squire, crouching beneath him, runs a lance through one of the monsters. One can gauge Saint Bernard's reaction to this kind of illumination from his tirade against the monstrous creatures and "fighting knights" of contemporary cloister capitals (see "Saint Bernard of Clairvaux on Cloister Sculpture," page 470).

Ornamented initials go back to the Hiberno-Saxon period (see FIG. 16-7), but here the artist translated the theme into Romanesque terms. This page may be a reliable picture of a medieval baron's costume. The typically Romanesque banding of the torso and partitioning of the folds (especially the servant's skirts) are evident, but the master painter deftly avoided stiffness and angularity. The partitioning actually accentuates the knight's verticality and elegance and the thrusting action of his servant. The flowing sleeves add a spirited flourish to the swordsman's gesture. The knight, handsomely garbed, cavalierly wears no armor and aims a single stroke with proud disdain.

MOSES IN AN ENGLISH BIBLE An illumination of exceedingly refined execution is the frontispiece (FIG. **17-38**) to the Book of Deuteronomy from the *Bury Bible*. The page exemplifies the sumptuous illustration common to the large Bibles produced in wealthy Romanesque abbeys not subject to the Cistercian ban. Such costly books were not only used by the monks in their studies and devotions but also lent prestige to monasteries that could afford them (see "Medieval Books," Chapter 16, page 434). MASTER HUGO, also a sculptor and metalworker, produced this volume at the Bury Saint Edmunds abbey in England around 1135. Hugo seems not to have been a monk but a secular artist, like Stephanus Garsia (FIG. 17-35), whom the abbey hired. Hugo and Stephanus were two of a growing number of professional artists and artisans who depended for their livelihood on commissions from well-endowed monasteries. They resided in the towns and traveled frequently to find work. These artists were still the exception, however, and the typical Romanesque scribes and illuminators continued to be monks and nuns working anonymously in the service of God. The Benedictine Rule, for example, specified that "craftsmen in the monastery . . . should pursue their crafts with all humility after the abbot has given permission."

Our page of the *Bury Bible* (FIG. 17-38) shows two scenes from Deuteronomy enframed by symmetrical leaf motifs in softly glowing harmonized colors. The upper register depicts

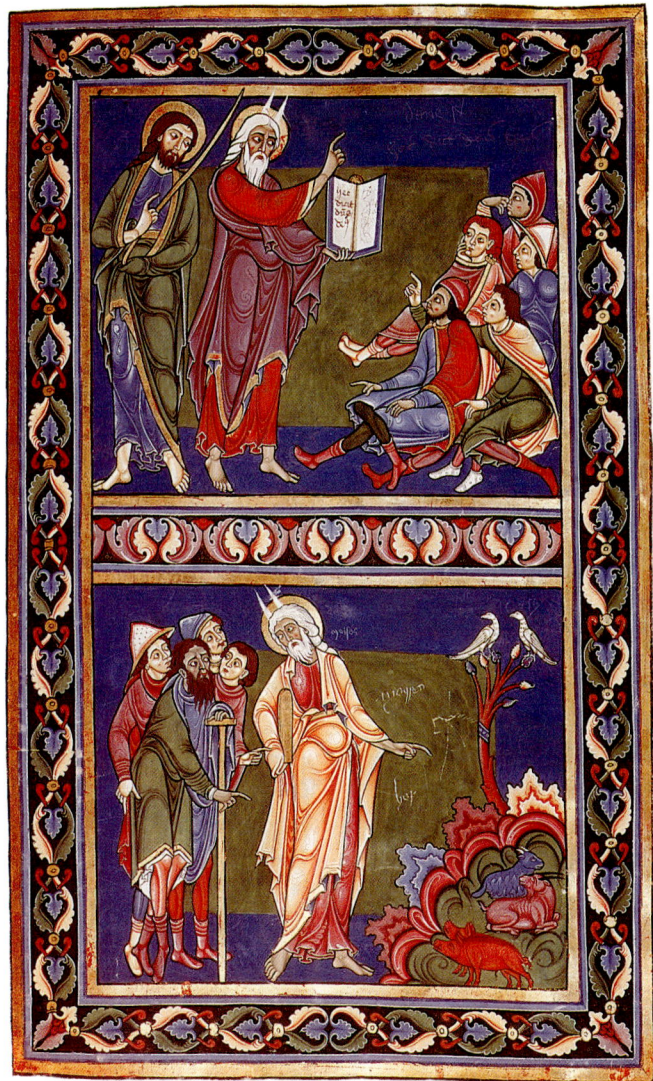

17-38 MASTER HUGO, *Moses expounding the Law*, folio 94 recto of the *Bury Bible*, from Bury Saint Edmunds, England, ca. 1135. Ink and tempera on vellum, approx. 1′ 8″ × 1′ 2″. Corpus Christi College, Cambridge.

Moses and Aaron proclaiming the law to the Israelites. Master Hugo represented Moses with horns, consistent with Saint Jerome's translation of the Hebrew word that also means "rays" (compare Michelangelo's similar conception of the Hebrew prophet, FIG. 22-10). The lower panel portrays Moses pointing out the clean and unclean beasts. The gestures are slow and gentle and have quiet dignity. The figures of Moses and Aaron seem to glide. This presentation is quite different from the abrupt emphasis and spastic movement seen in earlier Romanesque paintings. Here, as the patterning softens, the movements of the figures appear more integrated and smooth. Yet the patterning remains in the multiple divisions of the draped limbs, the lightly shaded volumes connected with sinuous lines and ladderlike folds. Hugo still thought of the drapery and body as somehow the same. The frame has a quite definite limiting function, and the painter carefully fit the figures within it.

THE "PRINCE OF SCRIBES" The last page of the *Eadwine Psalter* (FIG. **17-39**) presents a rare picture of a Romanesque artist at work. The book is the masterpiece of an English monk known as EADWINE THE SCRIBE. It contains

one hundred sixty-six illustrations, and many are variations of those in the Carolingian *Utrecht Psalter* (see FIG. 16-14). The "portrait" of Eadwine—it is probably a generic type and not a specific likeness—also has models in the past. It is in the long tradition of author portraits in ancient and medieval manuscripts (see FIGS. 16-8, 16-9, 16-12, 16-13, and 17-36), although the true author of the *Eadwine Psalter* is King David. The image of Eadwine is noteworthy because it represents a living man, a priestly scribe, not one of the Four Evangelists or another sacred person. Carolingian and Ottonian manuscripts included portraits of living men (FIG. 16-29), but those portraits were of reigning emperors, whose right to appear in sacred books was God given, just as Justinian and Theodora and their court had the right to be depicted in San Vitale's sanctuary (see FIGS. 12-10 and 12-11). Here, the inclusion of the scribe's own portrait sanctified his work. Eadwine exaggerated his importance by likening his image to that of an Evangelist writing his gospel and by including an inscription within the inner frame that identifies him and proclaims that he is a "prince among scribes." He declares that, due to the excellence of his work, his fame will endure forever and that he can offer his book as an acceptable gift to God. Eadwine, like other Romanesque sculptors and painters who signed their works, may have been concerned for his fame, but these artists, whether monks or laity, were not yet aware of the concepts of fine art and fine artist. To them, their work existed not for its own sake but for God's.

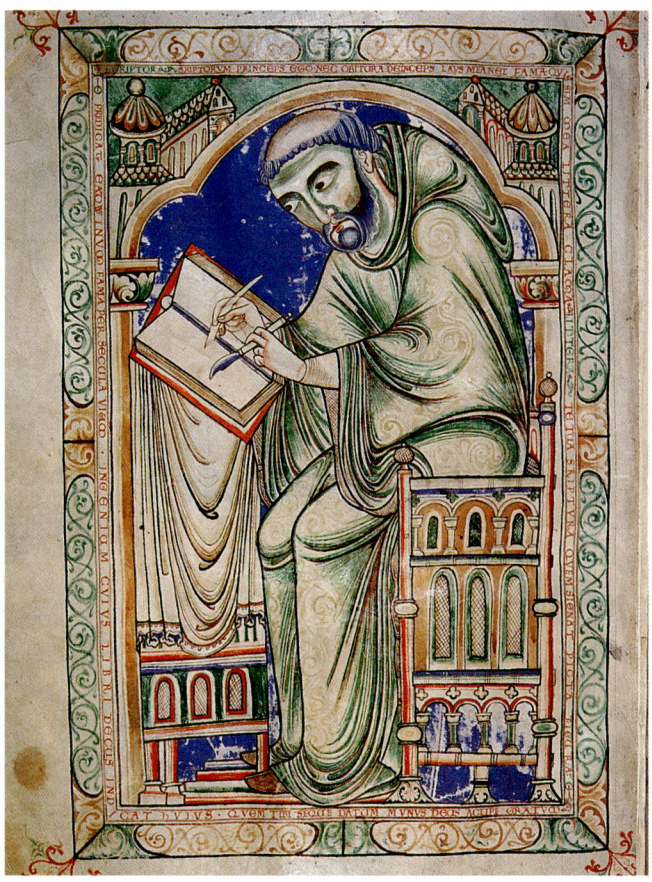

17-39 EADWINE THE SCRIBE(?), *Eadwine the scribe at work*, folio 283 verso of the *Eadwine Psalter*, ca. 1160–1170. Ink and tempera on vellum. Trinity College, Cambridge.

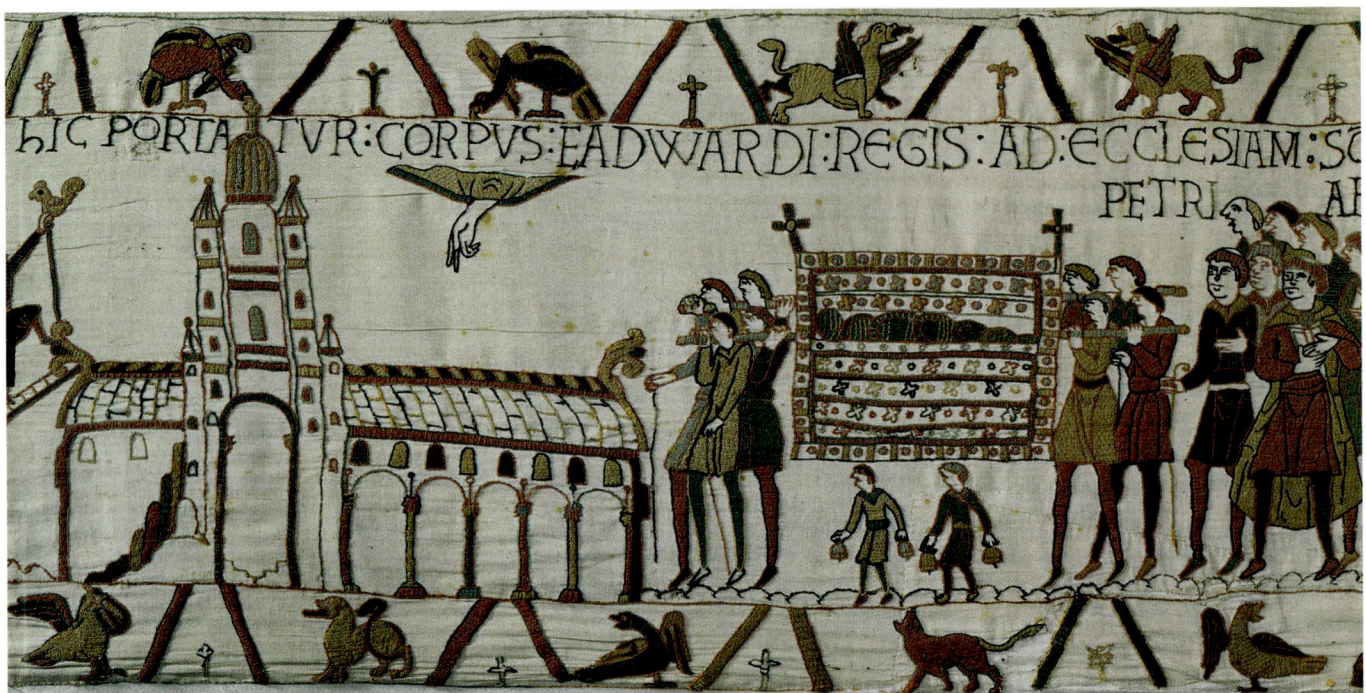

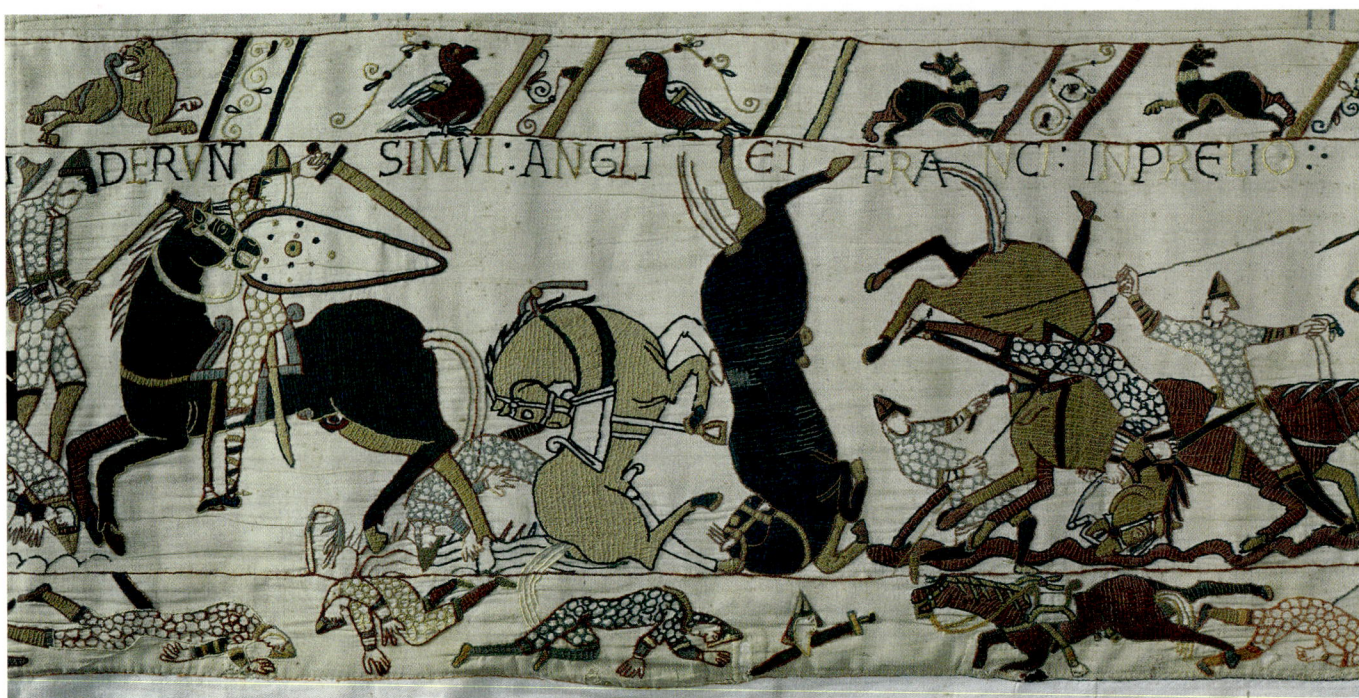

17-40   Funeral procession to Westminster Abbey *(top)* and the Battle of Hastings *(bottom)*, details of the *Bayeux Tapestry,* from Bayeux Cathedral, Bayeux, France, ca. 1070–1080. Embroidered wool on linen, 1′ 8″ high (entire length of fabric 229′ 8″). Centre Guillaume le Conquérant, Bayeux.

The Eadwine portrait's style is related to that of the *Bury Bible,* but, although the patterning is still firm (notably in the cowl and the thigh), the drapery falls more softly and follows the movements of the body beneath it. Here, the arbitrariness of many Romanesque painted and sculpted garments yielded slightly, but clearly, to the requirements of more naturalistic representation. The Romanesque artist's instinct for decorating the surface remained, as is apparent in the gown's whorls and spirals. But, significantly, these were painted in very

lightly so that they would not conflict with the functional lines that contain them.

THE CONQUEST OF ENGLAND   This account of Romanesque painting concludes with a work that is *not* a painting. Nor is the so-called *Bayeux Tapestry* (FIG. **17-40**) a woven tapestry. It is, instead, an embroidered fabric made of wool sewn on linen (see "Embroidery and Tapestry," page 485). But the *Bayeux Tapestry* is closely related to Romanesque

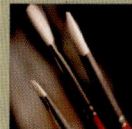

Embroidery and Tapestry

The most famous embroidery of the Middle Ages is, ironically, known as the *Bayeux Tapestry* (FIG. 17-40). Embroidery and tapestry are related, but different, means of decorating textiles. *Tapestry* designs are woven on a loom as part of the fabric. *Embroidery* patterns are sewn with threads.

The needleworkers who fashioned the *Bayeux Tapestry* were either Norman or English women. They employed eight colors of dyed wool—two varieties of blue, three shades of green, yellow, buff, and terracotta red—and two kinds of stitches. In *stem stitching*, short overlapping strands of thread form jagged lines. *Laid-and-couched work* creates solid blocks of color. In the latter technique, the needleworker first lays down a series of parallel and then a series of cross stitches. Finally, the stitcher tacks down the cross-hatched threads using couching (knotting). On the *Bayeux Tapestry*, the natural linen color was left exposed for the background, human flesh, building walls, and other "colorless" design elements. Stem stitches define the contours of figures and buildings and delineate interior details, such as facial features, body armor, and roof tiles. Laid-and-couched work was employed for clothing, animal bodies, and other solid areas.

manuscript illumination. Its borders are populated by the kinds of real and imaginary animals found in contemporaneous books, and its pictures are often accompanied by an explanatory Latin text sewn in thread.

Some twenty inches high and about two hundred thirty feet long, the *Bayeux Tapestry* is a continuous, friezelike, pictorial narrative of a crucial moment in England's history and of the events that led up to it. The Norman defeat of the Anglo-Saxons at Hastings in 1066 brought England under the control of the Normans, uniting all of England and much of France under one rule. The dukes of Normandy became the kings of England. Commissioned by Bishop Odo, the half brother of the conquering Duke William, the embroidery may have been sewn by women at the Norman court. Many art historians, however, believe it was the work of English stitchers in Kent, where Odo was earl after the Norman conquest. Odo donated the work to Bayeux Cathedral (hence its nickname), but it is uncertain whether it was originally intended for display in the church's nave, where the theme would have been a curious choice.

The circumstances leading to the Norman invasion of England are well documented. In 1066, Edward the Confessor, the Anglo-Saxon king of England, died. The Normans believed Edward had recognized William of Normandy as his rightful heir. But the crown went to Harold, earl of Wessex, the king's Anglo-Saxon brother-in-law, who had sworn an oath of allegiance to William. The betrayed Normans, descendants of the seafaring Vikings, boarded their ships, crossed the English Channel, and crushed Harold's forces.

We illustrate two episodes of the epic tale as represented in the *Bayeux Tapestry*. The first detail (FIG. 17-40, top) depicts King Edward's funeral procession. The hand of God points the way to the church where he was buried—Westminster Abbey, consecrated on December 28, 1065, just a few days before Edward's death. The church was one of the first Romanesque buildings erected in England, and the embroiderers took pains to record its main features, including the imposing crossing tower and the long nave with tribune gallery. Here William was crowned king of England on Christmas Day, 1066. (The coronation of every English monarch since then also has occurred in Westminster Abbey.)

The second detail (FIG. 17-40, bottom) shows the Battle of Hastings in progress. The Norman cavalry cuts down the English defenders. The lower border is filled with the dead and wounded, although the upper register continues the animal motifs of the rest of the embroidery. The Romanesque artist co-opted some of the characteristic motifs of Greco-Roman battle scenes. Note, for example, the horses with twisted necks and contorted bodies (compare FIG. 5-69). But the artists translated the figures into the Romanesque manner. Linear patterning and flat color replaced three-dimensional volume and modeling in light and dark hues.

The *Bayeux Tapestry* is unique in Romanesque art in that it depicts an event in full detail at a time shortly after it occurred, recalling the historical narratives of ancient Roman art. The Norman embroidery often has been likened to the scroll-like frieze of the Column of Trajan (see FIG. 10-42). Like the account on the Column of Trajan, the story told on the *Bayeux Tapestry* is the conqueror's version of history, a proclamation of national pride. And as on Trajan's Column, the narrative is not confined to battlefield successes; it is a complete chronicle of events. Included are the preparations for war, with scenes depicting the felling and splitting of trees for ship construction; the loading of equipment onto the vessels; the cooking and serving of meals; and so forth. In this respect, the *Bayeux Tapestry* is the most *Roman*-esque of all Romanesque artworks.

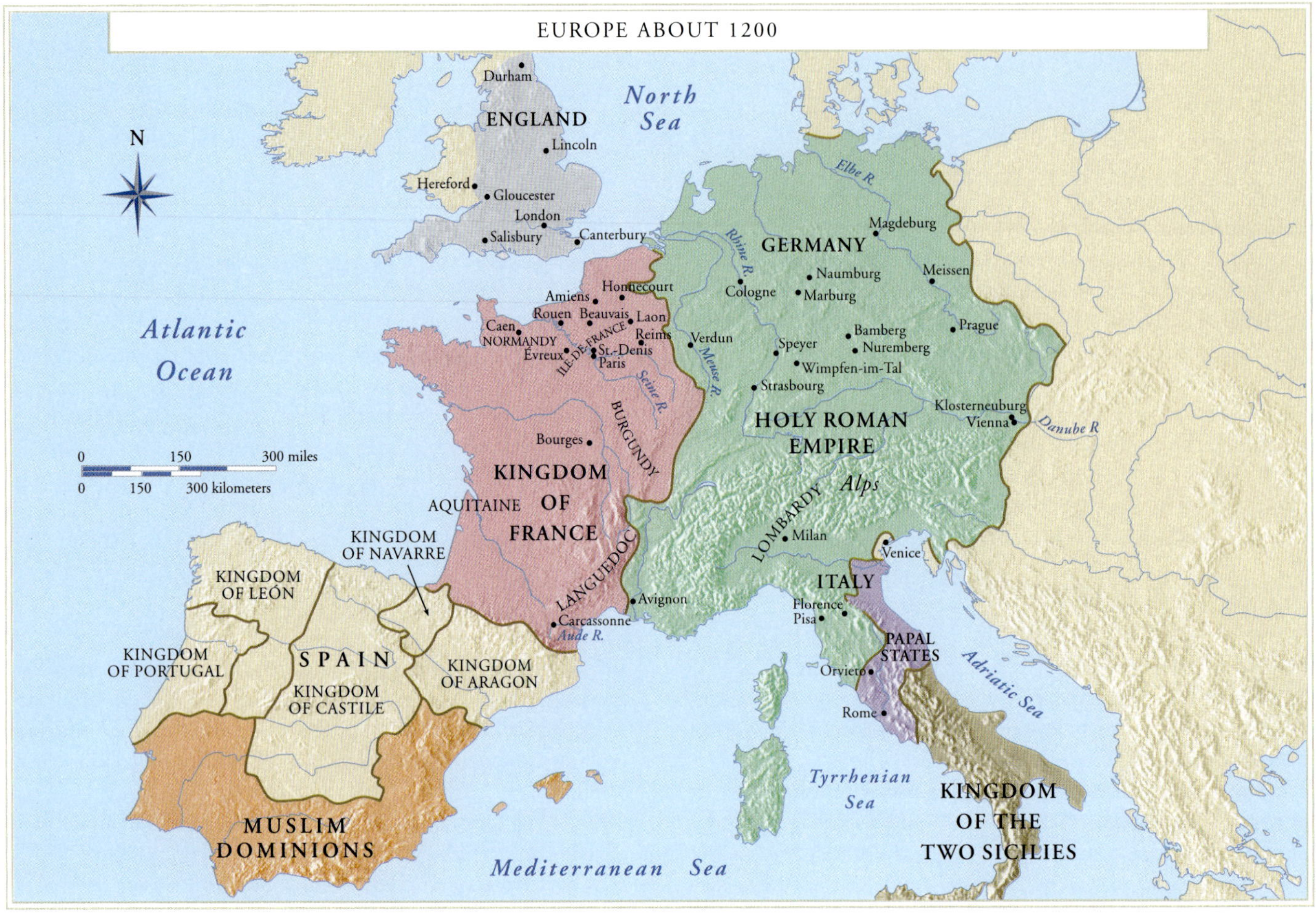

EUROPE ABOUT 1200

North Sea

ENGLAND
Durham
Lincoln
Hereford • Gloucester
London
Salisbury • Canterbury

Atlantic Ocean

N

NORMANDY
Caen
Évreux
Rouen Beauvais
Amiens Honnecourt
ILE-DE-FRANCE
St-Denis
Paris
Laon
Reims
Verdun

GERMANY
Magdeburg
Cologne
Naumburg
Marburg
Meissen
Bamberg
Speyer
Nuremberg
Prague
Wimpfen-im-Tal
Strasbourg

Elbe R.
Rhine R.
Meuse R.
Seine R.

HOLY ROMAN EMPIRE
Klosterneuburg
Vienna
Danube R.

0   150   300 miles
0   150   300 kilometers

KINGDOM OF FRANCE
Bourges
BURGUNDY
AQUITAINE
KINGDOM OF NAVARRE
LANGUEDOC
Carcassonne
Aude R.
Avignon

Alps
LOMBARDY
Milan
Venice
ITALY
Florence
Pisa
Orvieto
PAPAL STATES
Rome
Adriatic Sea

KINGDOM OF LEÓN
KINGDOM OF PORTUGAL
SPAIN
KINGDOM OF CASTILE
KINGDOM OF ARAGON
MUSLIM DOMINIONS

Tyrrhenian Sea
KINGDOM OF THE TWO SICILIES

Mediterranean Sea

1140	1194	1220
EARLY GOTHIC	HIGH GOTHIC	

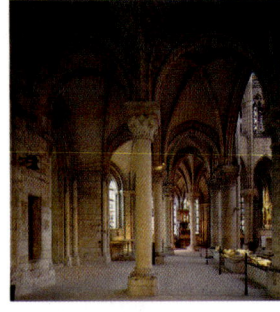
Abbey church Saint-Denis, 1140–1144

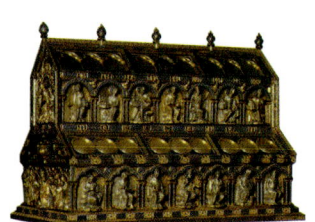
Nicholas of Verdun Shrine of the Three Kings Cologne Cathedral, begun ca. 1190

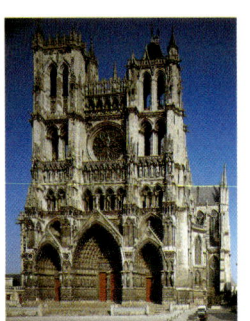
Amiens Cathedral begun ca. 1220

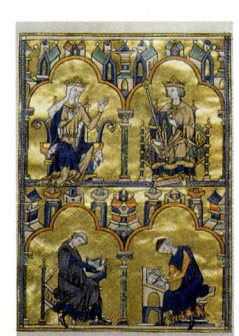
Moralized Bible of Blanche of Castile, 1226–1234

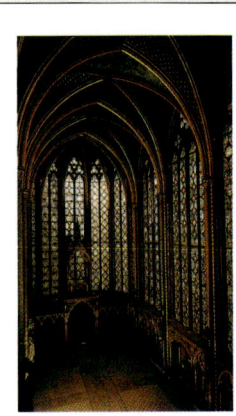
Sainte-Chapelle Paris, 1243–1248

Peter Abelard, 1079–1142

Suger, Abbot of Saint-Denis, 1122–1151

King Louis VII of France, r. 1137–1180

Second Crusade, 1147–1149

Frederick Barbarossa, Holy Roman Emperor, r. 1152–1190

Crétien de Troyes, fl. ca. 1160–1190

King Philip Augustus of France, r. 1180–1223

Saint Francis of Assisi, 1182–1226

University of Paris founded, ca. 1200

Capture of Constantinople by Latins (Fourth Crusade), 1204

King John of England signs Magna Carta, 1215

Frederick II, Holy Roman Emperor, r. 1220–1250

Romance of the Rose, Part I, ca. 1225–1235

Saint Thomas Aquinas, 1225–1274

King Louis IX (Saint Louis) of France, r. 1226–1270

Blanche of Castile, regent of France, 1226–1234

☐ **18** ☐

THE AGE OF THE
GREAT CATHEDRALS
GOTHIC ART

1250	1300		1500

LATE GOTHIC

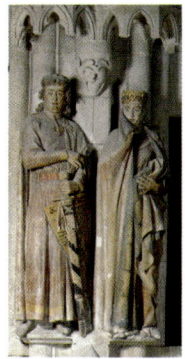

Ekkehard and Uta
Naumburg Cathedral
ca. 1249–1255

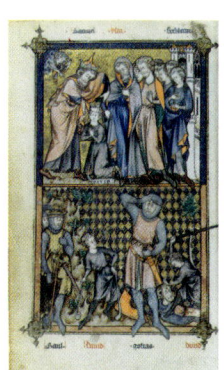

Master Honoré
Breviary of Philippe
le Bel, 1296

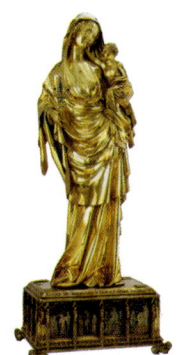

Virgin of Jeanne
d'Evreux, 1339

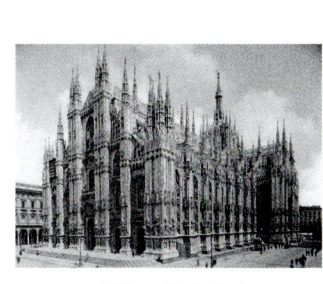

Milan Cathedral
begun 1386

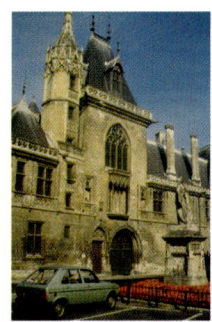

House of Jacques Coeur
Bourges, 1443–1451

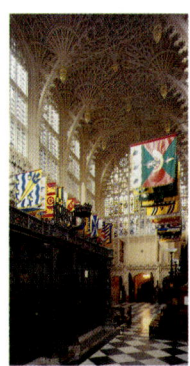

Chapel of Henry VII
London, 1503–1519

Treaty of Paris between Louis IX and Henry III of England, 1259

Byzantines retake Constantinople, 1261

Dante Alighieri, 1265–1321

Marco Polo in China, 1271–1292

Romance of the Rose, Part II, ca. 1275–1280

King Philippe le Bel of France, r. 1285–1314

Pope Boniface VIII canonizes Louis IX, 1297

King Edward II of England, r. 1307–1327

King Charles IV of France, r. 1322–1328

Hundred Years' War between France and England, 1337–1453

Geoffrey Chaucer, ca. 1343–1400

Black Death first sweeps over Europe, 1347–1350

Great Schism, 1378–1417

Fall of Constantinople to the Ottoman Turks, 1453

King Henry VII of England, r. 1471–1509

GOTHIC EUROPE

GOTHS AND "GOTHIC"   In the mid-sixteenth century, Giorgio Vasari, the "father of art history" (see "Giorgio Vasari on Raphael," Chapter 22, page 654), used "Gothic" as a term of ridicule to describe late medieval art and architecture. For him, Gothic art was "monstrous and barbarous," invented by the Goths.[1] Vasari and other admirers of Greco-Roman art believed those uncouth warriors were responsible not only for Rome's downfall but also for the destruction of the classical style in art and architecture. In the thirteenth and fourteenth centuries, however, when the Gothic style was the rage in most of Europe, especially north of the Alps, contemporary commentators considered Gothic buildings *opus modernum* (modern work) or *opus francigenum* (French work). They recognized that the great cathedrals towering over their towns displayed an exciting and new building and decoration style —and that the style originated in France. People regarded their new cathedrals not as distortions of the classical style but as images of the City of God, the Heavenly Jerusalem, which they were privileged to build on earth.

The Gothic style first appeared in northern France around 1140. In southern France (see FIG. 17-27) and elsewhere in Europe the Romanesque style still flourished. But by the thirteenth century, the opus modernum of the region around Paris had spread throughout western Europe, and in the next century further still. The Cathedral of Saint Vitus in Prague (Czech Republic), for example, begun in 1344, closely emulated French Gothic architecture.

Although it became an internationally acclaimed style, Gothic art was, nonetheless, a regional phenomenon. To the east and south of Europe, the Islamic and Byzantine styles still held sway. And many regional variants existed within European Gothic, just as distinct regional styles characterized the Romanesque period. Gothic began and ended at different dates in different places. When the banker Jacques Coeur built his home in Bourges (FIG. 18-30) in the Gothic style in the mid-fifteenth century, classicism already reigned supreme in Italy. While the Gothic church of Saint-Maclou (FIG. 18-28) was under construction in Rouen in the early years of the sixteenth century, Michelangelo was painting the ceiling of the Sistine Chapel in Rome.

TURMOIL AND CHANGE   The Gothic period was a time of not only great prosperity but also turmoil in Europe. In 1337, the Hundred Years' War began, shattering the peace between France and England. In the fourteenth century, a great plague, the Black Death, swept over western Europe and killed at least a quarter of its people. From 1378 to 1417, opposing popes resided in Rome and in Avignon in southern France during the political-religious crisis known as the Great Schism (see Chapter 19).

Above all, the Gothic age was a time of profound change in European society. The centers of both intellectual and religious life shifted definitively from monasteries to cities. In these urban areas, prosperous merchants made their homes, universities run by professional guilds of scholars formed, minstrels sang of chivalrous knights and beautiful maidens at

18-1   Ambulatory and radiating chapels, abbey church, Saint-Denis, France, 1140–1144.

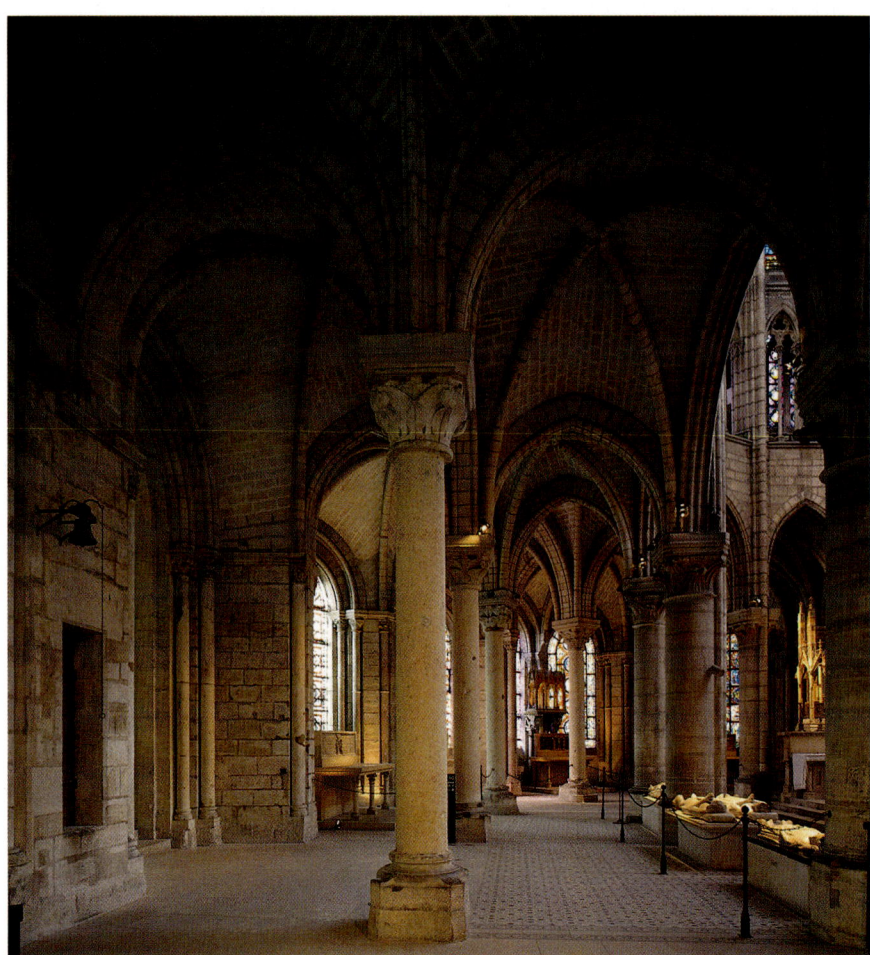

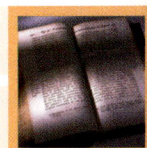

Abbot Suger and the Rebuilding of Saint-Denis

Abbot Suger of Saint-Denis (1081–1151) rose from humble parentage to become the right-hand man of both Louis VI (r. 1108–1137) and Louis VII (r. 1137–1180). When the latter, accompanied by his queen, Eleanor of Aquitaine, left to join the Second Crusade (1147–1149), Suger served as regent of France. From his youth, Suger wrote, he had dreamed of the possibility of embellishing the church in which French monarchs had been buried since the ninth century. In 1122, he became abbot of Saint-Denis and within fifteen years began rebuilding the monastery founded in the Merovingian age. In Suger's time, the French kings' power, except for scattered holdings, extended over an area not much larger than the Île-de-France, the region centered on Paris. But the kings had pretensions to rule all of France. Suger aimed to increase both the prestige of his abbey and of the monarchy by rebuilding France's royal church in grand fashion.

Suger wrote three detailed treatises about his activities as abbot of Saint-Denis. He recorded that he summoned masons and artists from many regions to help design and construct his new church. And in one important passage he described the special qualities of the new choir (FIGS. 18-1 to 18-3) dedicated in 1144:

> [I]t was cunningly provided that—through the upper columns and central arches which were to be placed upon the lower ones built in the crypt—the central nave of the old [Carolingian church] should be equalized, by means of geometrical and arithmetical instruments, with the central nave of the new addition; and, likewise, that the dimensions of the old side-aisles should be equalized with the dimensions of the new side-aisles, except for that elegant and praiseworthy extension in [the form of] a circular string of chapels, by virtue of

which the whole [church] would shine with the wonderful and uninterrupted light of most sacred windows, pervading the interior beauty.[1]

The abbot's brief discussion of the new choir's design is key to the understanding of Early Gothic architecture. But he wrote at much greater length about his church's glorious golden and gem-studded furnishings. Here, for example, is Suger's description of the *altar frontal* (hanging in front of the altar) in the choir:

> Into this panel, which stands in front of [Saint Denis's] most sacred body, we have put . . . about forty-two marks of gold [and] a multifarious wealth of precious gems, hyacinths, rubies, sapphires, emeralds and topazes, and also an array of different large pearls.[2]

The costly furnishings and the light-filled space caused Suger to "delight in the beauty of the house of God" and "called [him] away from external cares." The new church made him feel as if he was "dwelling . . . in some strange region of the universe which neither exists entirely in the slime of the earth nor entirely in the purity of Heaven." In Suger's eyes, then, his splendid new church, permeated with *lux nova* (new light) and outfitted with gold and precious gems, was a waystation on the road to Paradise, which "transported [him] from this inferior to that higher world."[3]

[1] Erwin Panofsky, trans., *Abbot Suger on the Abbey Church of Saint-Denis and Its Art Treasures,* 2nd ed. (Princeton, N.J.: Princeton University Press, 1979), 101.

[2] Ibid., 55.

[3] Ibid., 65.

royal "courts of love," and bishops erected great new cathedrals reaching to the sky. Although the papacy was at the height of its power and knights throughout Europe still gathered to wage Crusades against the Muslims, modern Europe's independent secular nations were beginning to take shape. Foremost among them was France.

FRENCH GOTHIC

Architecture and Architectural Decoration

THE BIRTH OF GOTHIC ARCHITECTURE   On June 11, 1144, King Louis VII of France, Queen Eleanor of Aquitaine, royal court members, and a host of distinguished clergy, including five archbishops, converged on the Benedictine abbey church of Saint-Denis for the dedication of its new choir (FIG. **18-1**). Saint Dionysius (Denis in French) was the apostle who brought Christianity to Gaul and who died a

martyr's death there in the third century. The church, just a few miles north of Paris, housed the saint's tomb and those of the French kings, as well as the crimson military banner said to have belonged to Charlemagne. The Carolingian basilica was France's royal church, the very symbol of the monarchy (just as Speyer Cathedral, FIGS. 17-4 and 17-5, was the burial place of the German rulers of the Holy Roman Empire). But the old building had been in disrepair and had become too small to accommodate the growing number of pilgrims. Its abbot, Suger, also had believed it was of insufficient grandeur to serve as the official church of the French kings (see "Abbot Suger and the Rebuilding of Saint-Denis," above). Thus, Suger began to rebuild the church in 1135 by erecting a new west facade with sculptured portals. In 1140, work began on the east end. Suger died before he could remodel the nave but he attended the 1144 choir dedication.

Because the French considered the old church a relic in its own right, the new choir had to conform to the dimensions of the crypt below it. Nevertheless, the elevation and plan

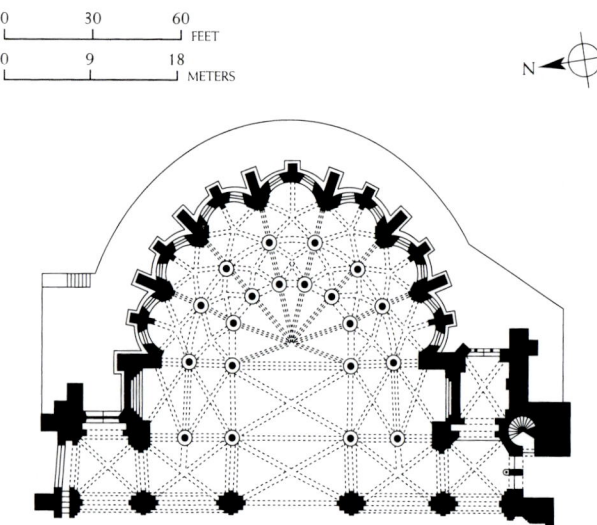

18-2 Plan of the choir, abbey church, Saint-Denis, France, 1140–1144 (after Sumner Crosby).

(FIG. **18-2**) of Suger's choir represented a sharp break from past practice. The choir of 1140–1144 is the birthplace of Gothic architecture. Innovative rib vaults resting on pointed arches (see "The Gothic Rib Vault," page 494) cover the ambulatory and chapels (FIG. **18-3**). These pioneering, exceptionally light, vaults spring from slender columns in the ambulatory and from the thin masonry walls framing the chapels. Because of the vaults' lightness, the walls between the chapels were eliminated and the outer walls opened up and filled with stained-glass windows (see "Stained-Glass Windows," page 500). Suger and his contemporaries marveled at the "wonderful and uninterrupted light" that poured in through the "most sacred windows." The abbot called the colored light *lux nova*, "new light." The polychrome rays coming through the windows shine on the walls and columns, almost dissolving them. Both the new type of vaulting and the use of stained glass became hallmarks of the French Gothic style in architecture.

ROYAL PORTALS FILLED WITH SCULPTURE
Saint-Denis is the key monument of Early Gothic art and architecture. Gothic sculpture, as well as architecture and stained glass, made its first appearance at Saint-Denis. Little of the sculpture of the abbey church's west facade survived the French Revolution, although much of the structure is intact. The west facade consists of a double-tower westwork as at Saint-Étienne at Caen (see FIG. 17-9) and has massive walls in the Romanesque tradition. A restored large central *rose window* (a circular stained-glass window) punctuates the facade's upper story, a new feature that became standard in French Gothic architecture. For the three portals, Suger imported sculptors to carry on the rich heritage of Romanesque Burgundy. But at Saint-Denis, statues of Old Testament kings, queens, and prophets attached to columns screened the jambs of all three doorways.

This innovative treatment of the portals of Suger's church appeared immediately afterward at the Cathedral of Notre Dame ("Our Lady," that is, the Virgin Mary) at Chartres, also in the Île-de-France. Work on the west facade, the "Royal Portal" (FIGS. **18-4** and **18-5**), began around 1145. (The Royal Portal is so named because of the statue columns of

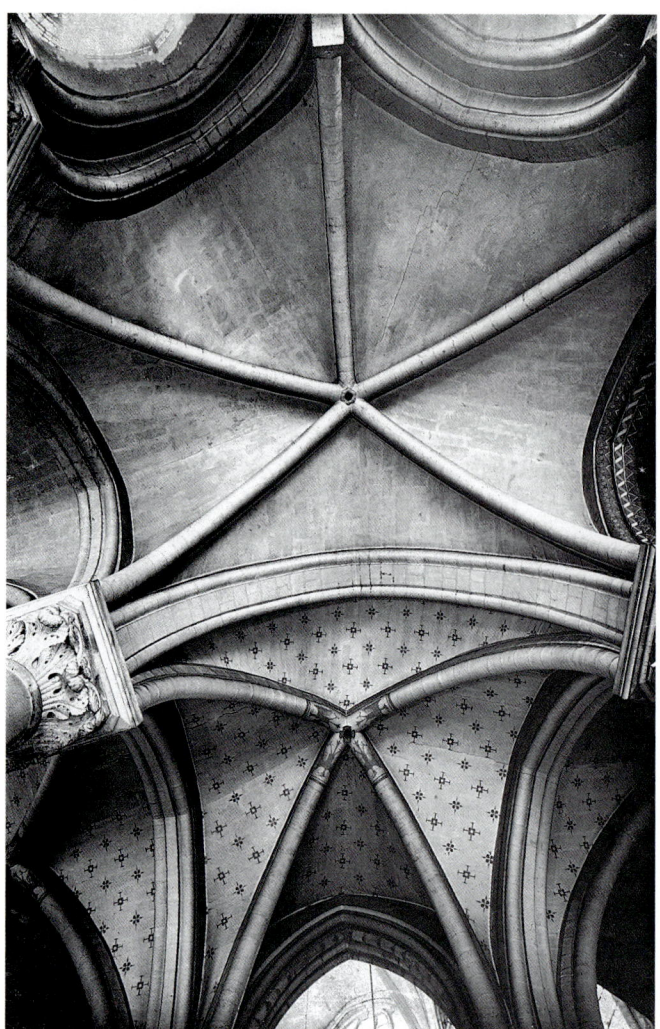

18-3 Vaults of the ambulatory and radiating chapels of the choir, abbey church, Saint-Denis, France, 1140–1144.

kings and queens flanking its three doorways.) The lower parts of the massive west towers at Chartres and the portals between them are all that survived of a cathedral begun in 1134 and destroyed by fire in 1194 before it had been completed. Reconstruction of the cathedral began immediately, but in the High Gothic style (discussed later). The west portals, however, constitute the most complete and impressive surviving ensemble of Early Gothic sculpture. Thierry of Chartres, chancellor of the School of Chartres from 1141 until his death ten years later, may have conceived the complex iconographical program. The right-portal archivolts, for example, depict the seven female Liberal Arts and their male champions. The figures represent the core of medieval learning and symbolize human knowledge, which Thierry and others believed led to true faith.

The sculptures of the west facade (FIG. 18-5) proclaim the majesty and power of Christ. To unite the three doorways iconographically and visually, the sculptors carved episodes from Christ's life on the capitals, which form a kind of frieze linking one entrance to the next. In the right-portal tympanum, Christ appears in the lap of his Virgin Mother, while scenes of his birth and early life fill the lintel below. The tympanum's theme and composition recall Byzantine representations of the Theotokos (see FIGS. 12-15 and 12-16), as well as the Romanesque Throne of Wisdom (see FIG. 17-30). But

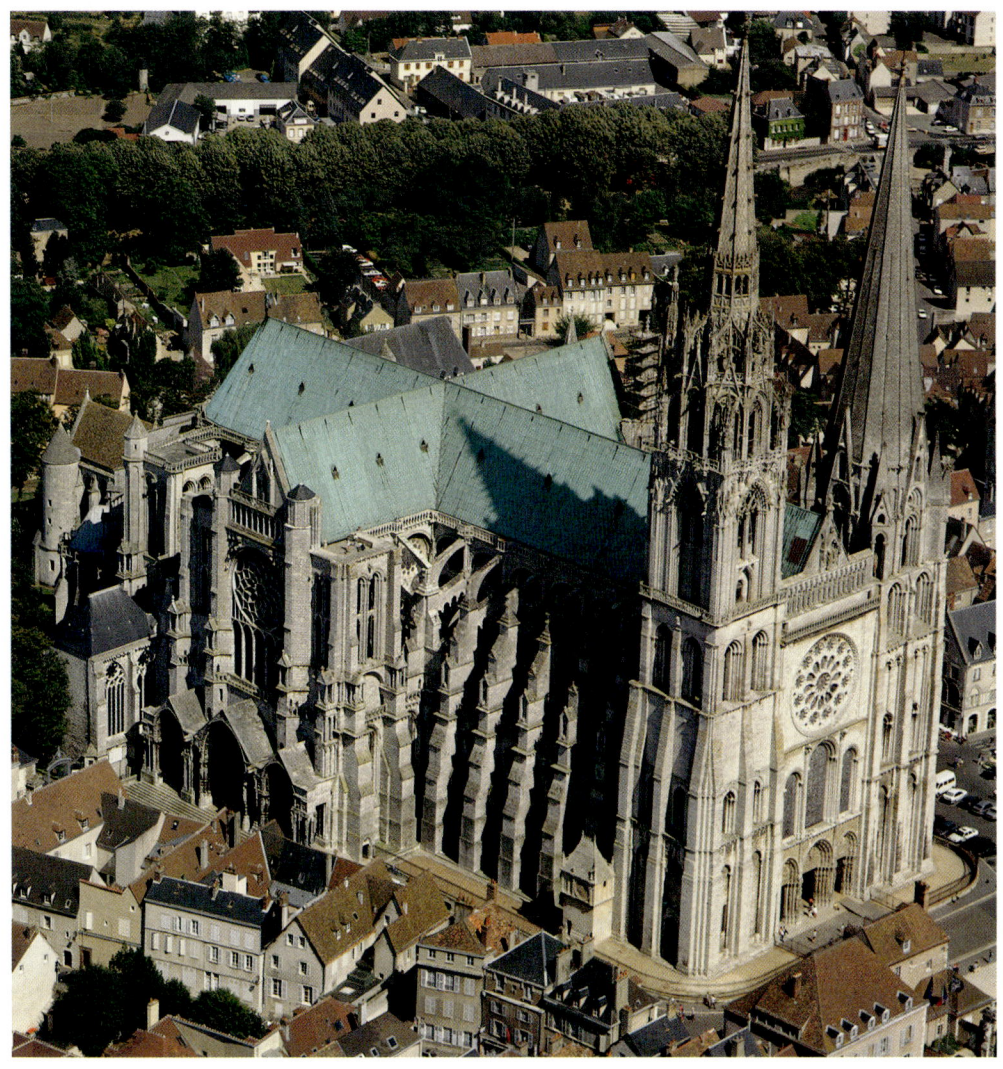

18-4 Aerial view from the northwest of Chartres Cathedral, Chartres, France, begun 1134; rebuilt after 1194.

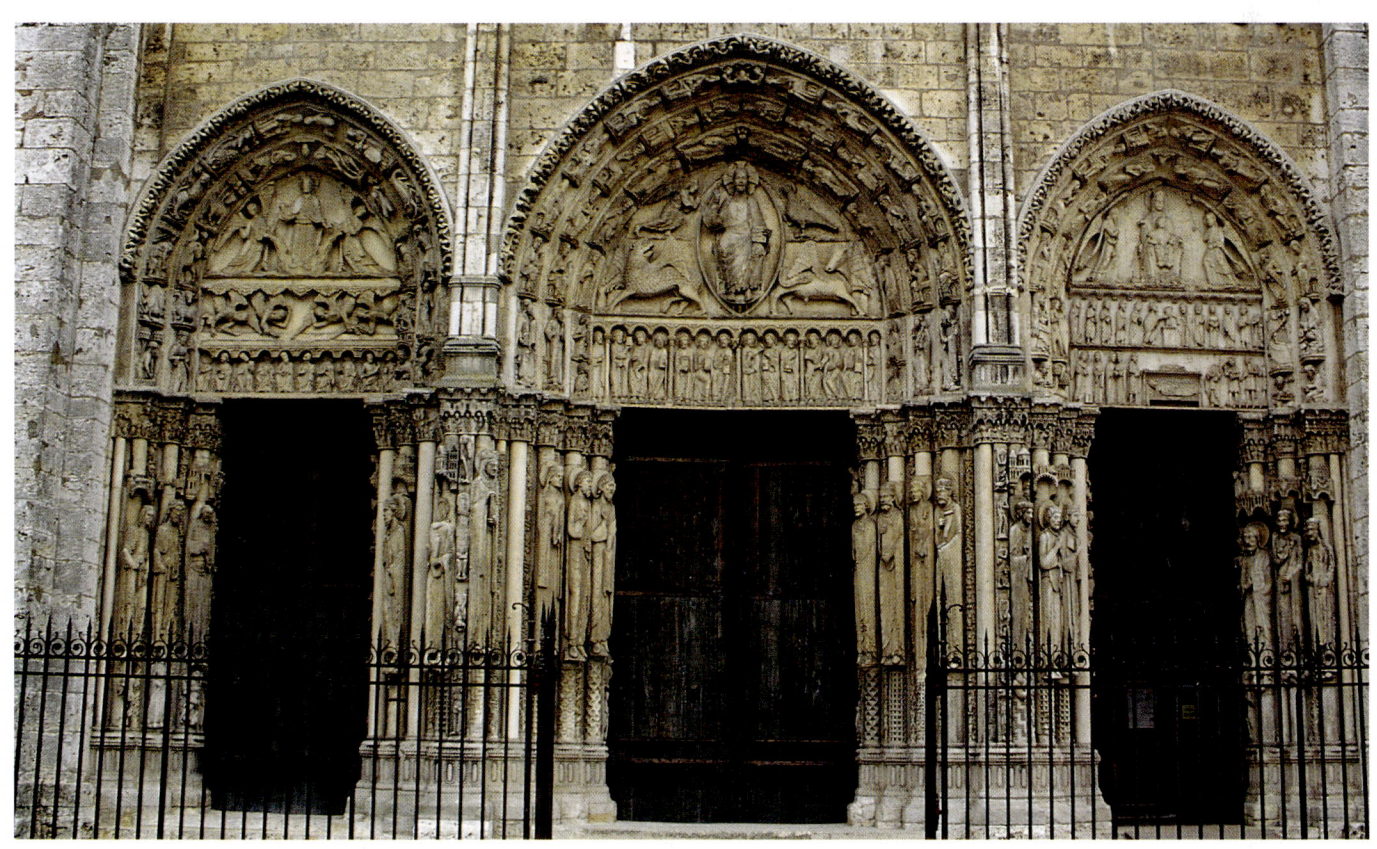

18-5 Royal Portal, west facade, Chartres Cathedral, Chartres, France, ca. 1145–1155.

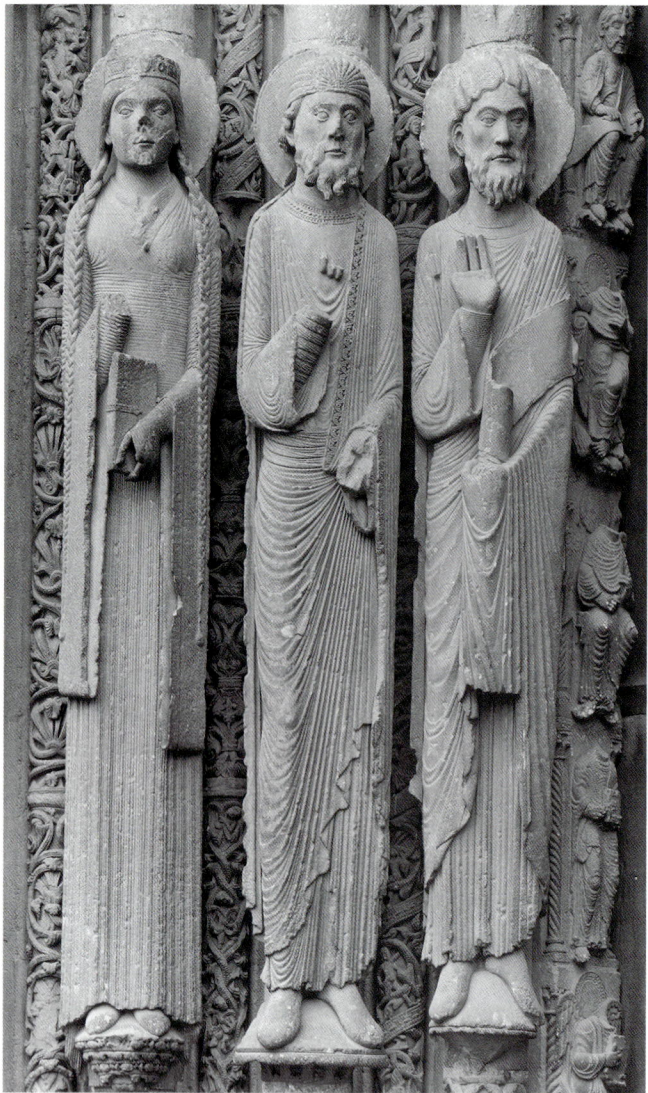

18-6 Old Testament queen and two kings, jamb statues, central doorway of Royal Portal, Chartres Cathedral, Chartres, France, ca. 1145–1155.

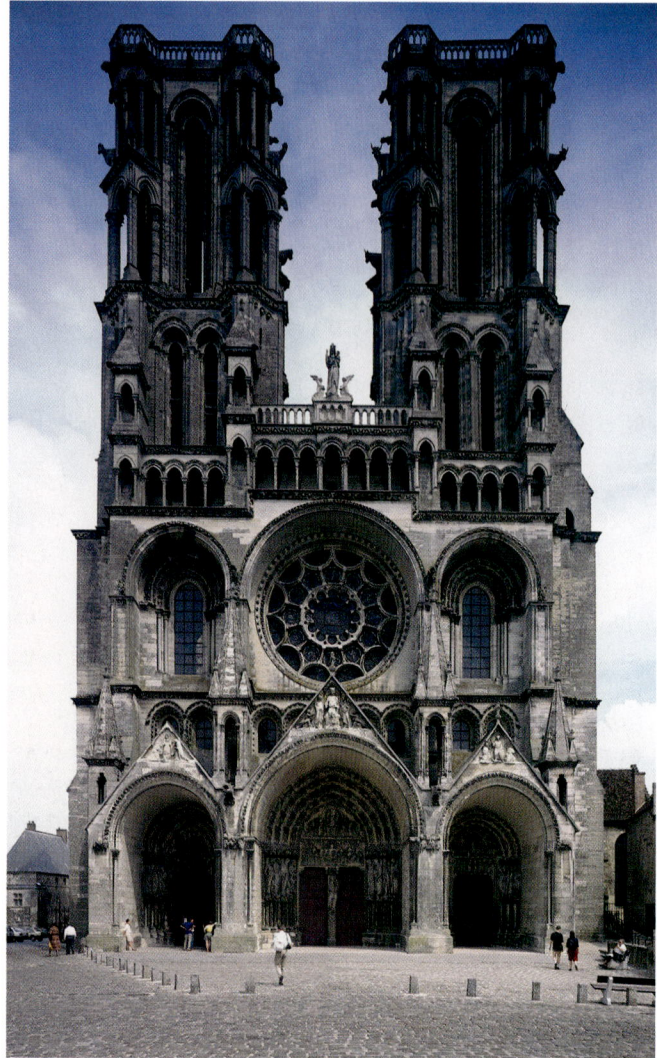

18-7 West facade of Laon Cathedral, Laon, France, begun ca. 1190.

Mary's prominence on the Chartres facade has no parallel in the decoration of Romanesque church portals. At Chartres the designers gave her a central role in the sculptural program, a position she maintained throughout the Gothic period. The cult of the Virgin Mary reached a high point in the Gothic age. As the Mother of Christ, she stood compassionately between the Last Judge and the horrors of Hell, interceding for all her faithful. Worshipers in the later twelfth and thirteenth centuries sang hymns to her, put her image everywhere, and dedicated great cathedrals to her. Soldiers carried the Virgin's image into battle on banners, and her name joined Saint Denis's as part of the French king's battle cry. Mary became the spiritual lady of chivalry, and the Christian knight dedicated his life to her. The severity of Romanesque themes stressing the Last Judgment yielded to the gentleness of Gothic art, where Mary is the kindly Queen of Heaven.

Christ's Ascension into Heaven appears in the tympanum of the left portal. All around, in the archivolts, are the signs of the zodiac and scenes representing the various labors of the months of the year. They are symbols of the cosmic and earthly worlds. The Second Coming is the central tympanum's subject. The signs of the Four Evangelists, the Twenty-

Four Elders of the Apocalypse, and the Twelve Apostles appear around Christ or on the lintel. The Second Coming—in essence, the Last Judgment theme—was still of central importance, as it was in Romanesque portals. But at Early Gothic Chartres the theme became a symbol of salvation rather than damnation.

THE EARLY GOTHIC STATUE-COLUMN   Statues of Old Testament kings and queens (FIG. **18-6**) decorate the jambs flanking each doorway of the Royal Portal. They are the royal ancestors of Christ and, both figuratively and literally, support the New Testament figures above the doorways. They wear twelfth-century clothes, and medieval observers also regarded them as images of the kings and queens of France, symbols of secular as well as of biblical authority. (This was the motivation for vandalizing the comparable figures at Saint-Denis during the French Revolution.)

Seen from a distance, the statue-columns appear to be little more than vertical decorative accents within the larger designs of the portals and facade (FIG. 18-5). The figures stand rigidly upright with their elbows held close against their hips. The linear folds of their garments—the Romanesque style's heritage, along with the elongated proportions—generally echo the vertical lines of the columns behind them. (In this respect,

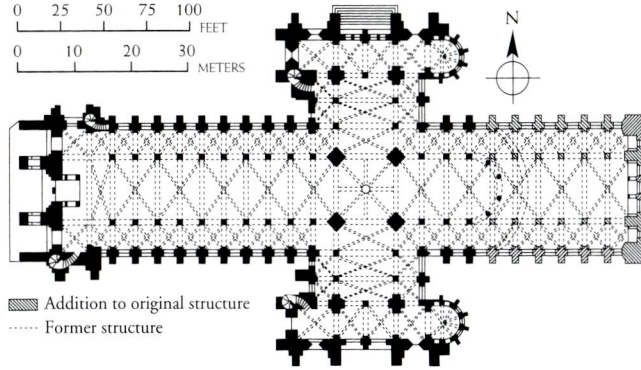

18-8 Plan of Laon Cathedral, Laon, France, ca. 1160–1205; choir extended after 1210 (after Ernst Gall).

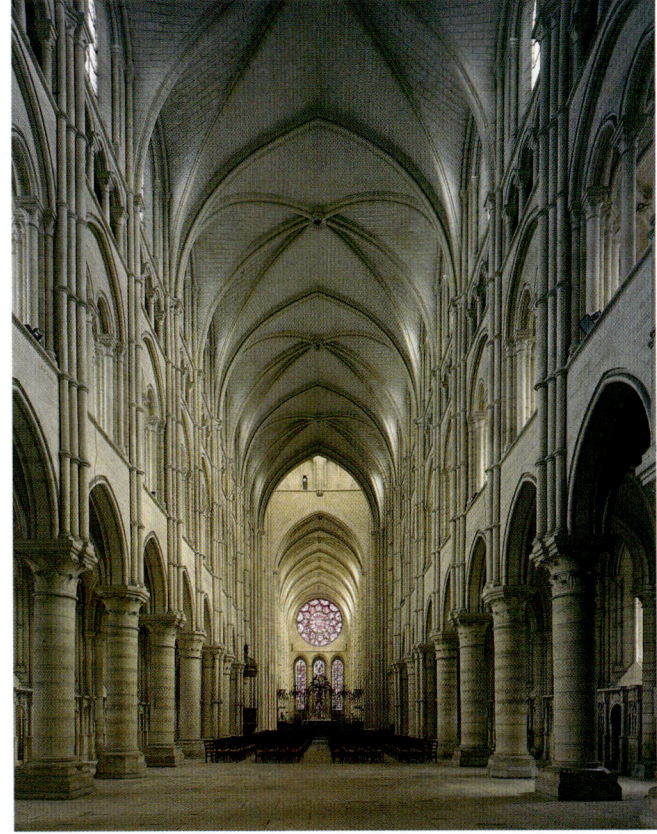

18-9 Nave of Laon Cathedral (view facing east), Laon, France, begun ca. 1190.

Gothic jamb statues differ significantly from classical caryatids; see FIG. 5-52. The Gothic figures are *attached* to columns. The classical statues *replaced* the columns.) And yet, within and despite this architectural straitjacket, the statues display the first signs of a new naturalism. They stand out from the plane of the wall. The sculptors conceived and treated the statues as three-dimensional volumes, so the figures "move" into the space of observers. The new naturalism is noticeable particularly in the statues' heads, where kindly human faces replace the masklike features of most Romanesque figures. At Chartres, a personalization of appearance began that was transformed first into idealized portraits of the perfect Christian and finally, by 1400, into the portraiture of specific individuals. The Royal Portal statues' heads announced an era of artistic concern with personality and individuality.

ROMANESQUE AND GOTHIC AT LAON As noted, Suger completed only the new choir and narthex of Saint-Denis in the twelfth century. Laon Cathedral (FIGS. **18-7** to

18-9), however, provides a fairly complete view of Early Gothic church architecture of the second half of the century. Begun about 1160 and finished shortly after 1200, this building retained many Romanesque features but combined them with the Gothic rib vault resting on pointed arches.

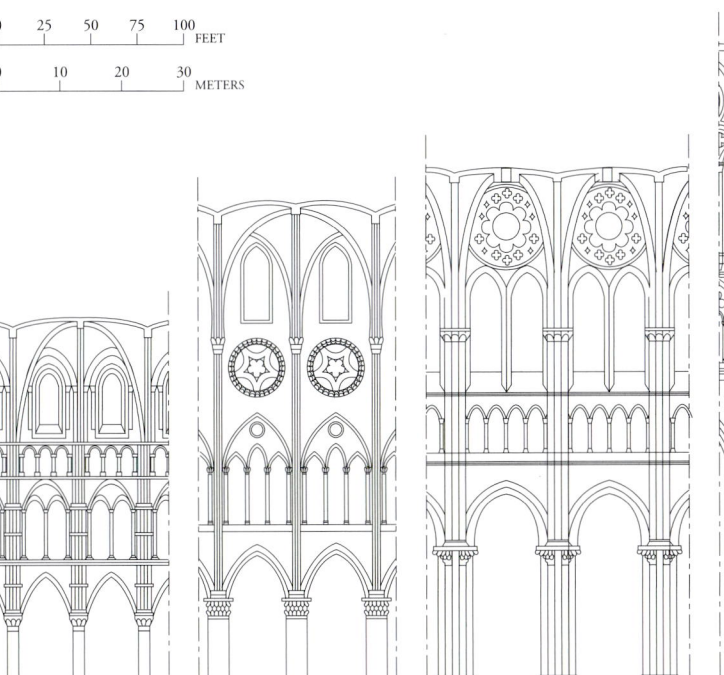

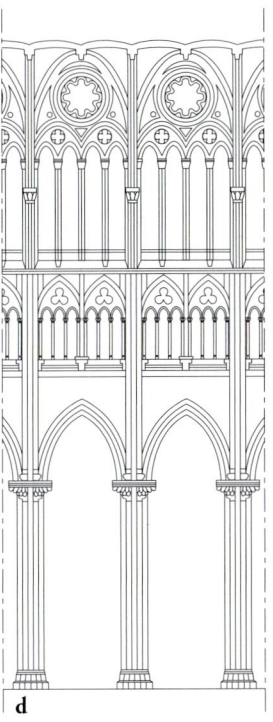

18-10 Nave elevations of four French Gothic cathedrals at the same scale (after Louis Grodecki): *(a)* Laon, *(b)* Paris, *(c)* Chartres, *(d)* Amiens.

a   b   c   d

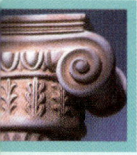

The Gothic Rib Vault

The ancestors of the Gothic rib vault are the Romanesque vaults found at Caen (see FIG. 17-10), Durham (see FIG. 17-12), and elsewhere. The rib vault's distinguishing feature is its crossed, or diagonal, arches under its groins, as seen in the Saint-Denis choir (FIG. 18-3; compare FIG. 18-20). These arches form the *armature,* or skeletal framework for constructing the vault. Gothic vaults generally have more thinly vaulted webs, or *severies,* between the arches than Romanesque vaults have. But the chief difference between Romanesque and Gothic rib vaults is the pointed arch, an integral part of the Gothic skeletal armature. Pointed arches were first widely used in Sasanian architecture (see FIG. 2-28), and Islamic builders later adopted them. French Romanesque architects (for example, at Cluny III; see Chapter 17, page 457) borrowed the form from Muslim Spain and passed it to their Gothic successors. Pointed arches allowed Gothic builders to make the crowns of all the vault's arches approximately the same level, regardless of the space to be vaulted. The Romanesque architects could not achieve this with their semicircular arches.

Our diagrams illustrate this key difference. In diagram *a,* the rectangle *ABCD* is an oblong nave bay to be vaulted. *AC* and *DB* are the diagonal ribs; *AB* and *DC,* the transverse arches; and *AD* and *BC,* the nave arcade's arches. If the architect uses semicircular arches (*AFB, BJC,* and *DHC*),

their radii and, therefore, their heights (*EF, IJ,* and *GH*), will be different, because the height of a semicircular arch is determined by its width. The result will be a vault (diagram *b*) with higher transverse arches (*DHC*) than the arcade's arches (*CJB*). The vault's crown (*F*) will be still higher. If the archi-tect uses pointed arches, the points (and hence the ribs) can have the same heights (*IK* and *GL* in diagram *a*). The result will be a Gothic rib vault (diagram *c*), where the points of the arches (*L* and K) are at the same level as the vault's crown (*F*).

A major advantage of the Gothic vault is its flexibility, which permits the vaulting of compartments of varying shapes, as may be seen in the Saint-Denis choir plan (FIG. 18-2). Pointed arches also channel the weight of the vaults more directly downward than do semicircular arches. The vaults, therefore, require less buttressing to hold them in place, in turn permitting the opening up of the walls beneath the arches with large windows. Because pointed arches also lead the eye upward, they make the vaults appear taller than they actually are. In our diagrams, the crown (*F*) of both the Romanesque (diagram *b*) and Gothic (diagram *c*) vaults is the same height from the pavement, but the Gothic vault seems taller. Both the physical and visual properties of rib vaults with pointed arches aided Gothic architects in their quest for soaring height in church interiors.

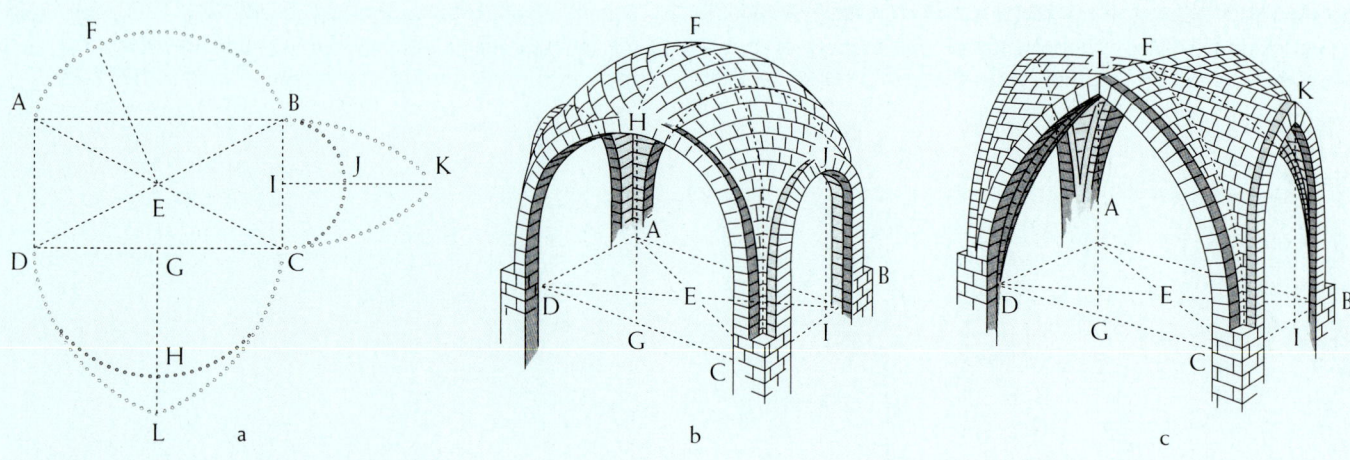

Among the plan's Romanesque features are the nave bays with their large six-part rib vaults, flanked by two small groin-vaulted squares in each aisle (FIG. 18-8). The vaulting system (except for the pointed arches), as well as the vaulted gallery above the aisles, derived from Norman Romanesque churches such as Saint-Étienne at Caen (see FIG. 17-10), which enjoyed great prestige in northern France throughout the twelfth century. A new feature found in the Laon interior, however, is

the *triforium,* the band of arcades below the clerestory (FIG. 18-9) occupying the space corresponding to the exterior strip of wall that the sloping timber roof above the galleries covers. The triforium has no practical function. Its introduction expressed a growing desire to break up and eliminate all continuous wall surfaces. The insertion of the triforium into the Romanesque three-story nave-wall elevation produced the characteristic four-story Early Gothic interior elevation (FIG. 18-9):

nave arcade, vaulted gallery, triforium, and clerestory with single *lancets* (tall, narrow windows ending in pointed arches). FIG. **18-10** compares the Laon nave elevation with those of later Gothic cathedrals.

The Laon architect also employed the alternate-support system of Caen and other Romanesque churches, but more subtly. The nave arcade does not reflect the alternation (although the builders added colonnettes to a few of the columns as work progressed). Rather, the distinction begins above the nave piers, where bundles of three and five shafts alternate in framing the aisle bays. The Laon architect moved away from the compartmentalized effect of Romanesque interiors, which tends to make visitors pause as they advance from unit to unit. Gothic builders aimed, even if rather timidly at Laon, to create a unified interior space that sweeps uninterruptedly from west to east. The level crowns of the successive nave vaults, made possible by pointed arches, enhance this longitudinal continuity (FIG. 18-9).

Laon Cathedral's west facade (FIG. 18-7) signals an even more pronounced departure from the Romanesque style still lingering at Saint-Denis and the Chartres Royal Portal. Typically Gothic are the huge central rose window, the deep porches in front of the doorways, and the open structure of the towers. (The statues of oxen on the towers refer to the local legend that oxen miraculously appeared to haul stones for an earlier church on the site.) A comparison of the facades of Laon Cathedral and Saint-Étienne at Caen (see FIG. 17-9) reveals a much deeper penetration of the wall mass in the later building. At Laon, as in Gothic architecture generally, the operating principle was to reduce sheer mass and replace it with intricately framed voids.

A NEW CATHEDRAL RISES IN PARIS About 1130, Louis VI moved his official residence to Paris, spurring much commercial activity and a great building boom. Paris soon became the leading city of France, indeed of all northern Europe (see "Paris: The Intellectual Capital of Gothic Europe," page 496), making a new cathedral a necessity. Notre-Dame of Paris (FIG. **18-11**) occupies a picturesque site on an island in the Seine River called the Île-de-la-Cité. The Gothic church replaced a large five-aisled Merovingian basilica and has a complicated building history. The choir and transept were completed by 1182; the nave, by ca. 1225; and the facade not until ca. 1250–1260. Sexpartite vaults covered the

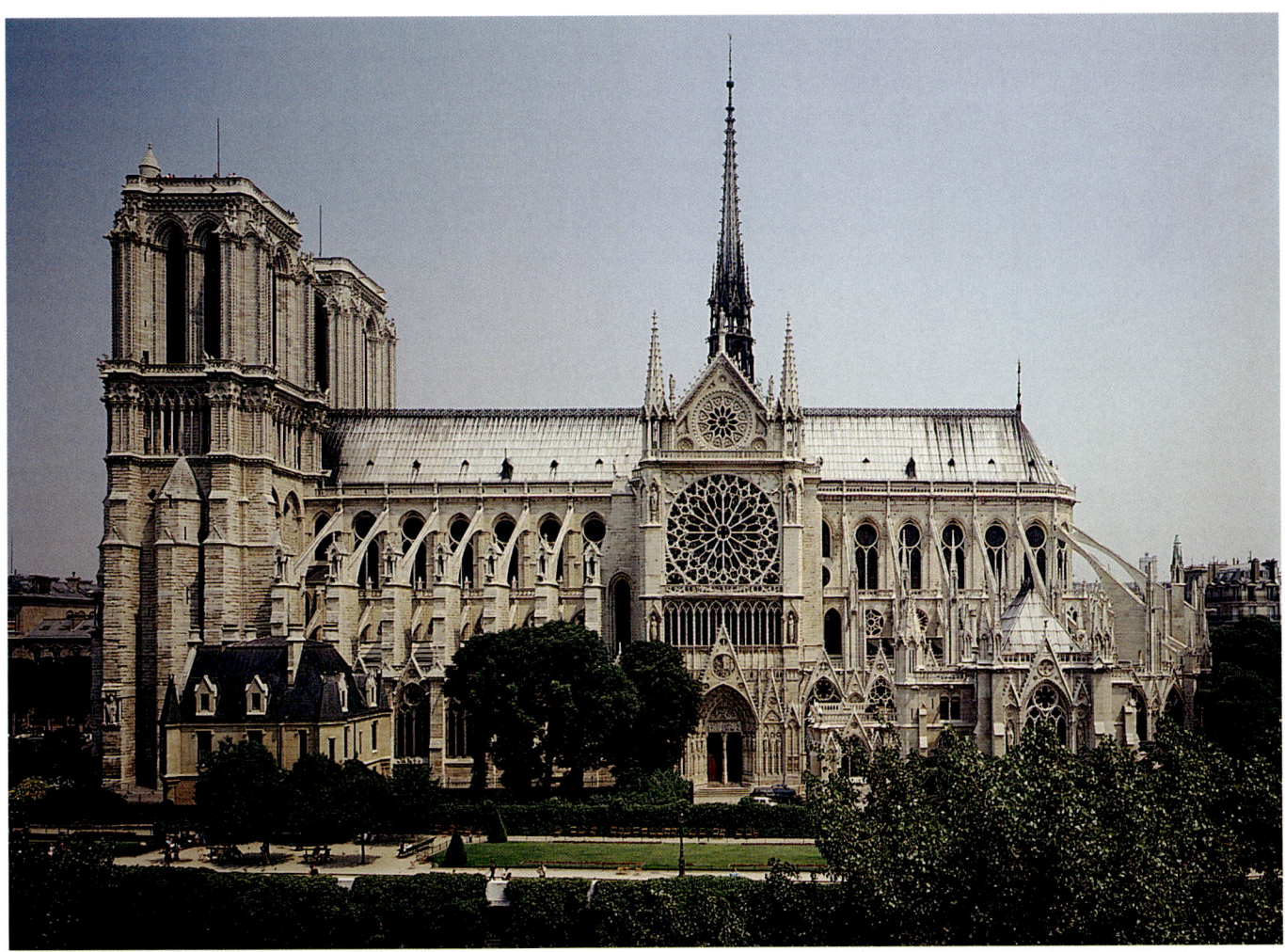

18-11 Notre-Dame (view from the south), Paris, France, begun 1163; nave and flying buttresses, ca. 1180–1200; remodeled after 1225.

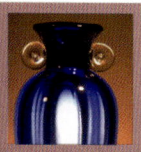

Paris
The Intellectual Capital of Gothic Europe

A few years before the formal consecration of the altar of Notre-Dame in Paris (FIG. 18-11), Philip II (Philip Augustus, r. 1180–1223) succeeded to the throne. Philip brought the barons under his control and expanded the royal domains to include Normandy in the north and most of Languedoc in the south, laying the foundations for the modern nation of France. Renowned as "the maker of Paris," he gave the city its walls, paved its streets, and built the palace of the Louvre (now one of the world's great museums) to house the royal family. Although Rome remained the religious center of western Christendom, Paris became its intellectual capital. The University of Paris attracted the best minds from all over Europe. Virtually every thinker of note in the Gothic world at some point studied or taught at Paris.

Even in the Romanesque period, Paris was a learning center. Its Cathedral School professors were known as Schoolmen and the philosophy they developed as Scholasticism. The greatest of the early Schoolmen was Peter Abelard (1079–1142), a champion of logical reasoning. Abelard and his contemporaries had been introduced to the writings of the Greek philosopher Aristotle through the Arabic scholars of Islamic Spain. Abelard applied Aristotle's system of rational inquiry to the interpretation of religious belief. Until the twelfth century, truth had been considered the exclusive property of divine revelation as given in the Holy Scriptures. But the Schoolmen, using Aristotle's method, sought to demonstrate that reason alone could lead to certain truths. Their goal was to prove the central articles of Christian faith by argument (*disputatio*). In Scholastic argument, a possibility is stated, an authoritative view is cited in objection, the positions are reconciled, and, finally, a reply is given to each of the rejected original arguments.

One of Abelard's greatest critics was Saint Bernard of Clairvaux (see "Saint Bernard of Clairvaux on Cloister Sculpture," Chapter 17, page 470), who believed Scholasticism was equivalent to questioning Christian dogma. Although Bernard succeeded in 1140 in having the Church officially condemn Abelard's doctrines, the Schoolmen's philosophy developed systematically until it became the dominant Western philosophy of the late Middle Ages. By the thirteenth century, the Schoolmen of Paris already had organized as a professional guild of master scholars, separate from the numerous Church schools the bishop of Paris oversaw. The Parisian guild's structure served as the model for many other European universities.

The greatest exponent of Abelard's Scholasticism was Thomas Aquinas (1225–1274), an Italian monk who became a saint. Aquinas settled in Paris in 1244. There, the German theologian Albertus Magnus instructed him in Aristotelean philosophy. Aquinas went on to become an influential teacher at the University of Paris. His most famous work, the *Summa Theologica* (left unfinished at his death), is a model of the Scholastic approach to knowledge. Aquinas divided his treatise into books, the books into questions, the questions into articles, each article into objections with contradictions and responses, and, finally, answers to the objections. He set forth five ways to prove the existence of God by rational argument. Aquinas's work remains the foundation of contemporary Catholic teaching.

The earliest manifestations of the Gothic spirit in art and architecture—the sculpted portals and vaulted choir of Suger's Saint-Denis (FIG. 18-1)—are contemporary with the first stages of Scholastic philosophy. Both also originated in Paris and its environs. Many art historians have noted the parallels between them, how the logical thrust and counterthrust of Gothic construction, the geometric relationships of building parts, and the systematic organization of the iconographical programs of Gothic church portals coincide with Scholastic principles and methods. Although no documents exist linking the scholars, builders, and sculptors, Gothic art and architecture shared with Scholasticism an insistence on systematic design and procedure. They both sought stable, coherent, consistent, and structurally intelligible solutions.

---

nave, as at Laon. The original elevation (the builders modified the design as work progressed) had four stories, but the scheme (FIG. 18-10*b*) differed from Laon's (FIG. 18-10*a*). In place of the triforium over the gallery, stained glass *oculi* (singular *oculus,* a small round window) opened up the wall below the clerestory lancets. As a result, of the four stories, two were filled by windows, further reducing the masonry area. (This four-story nave elevation can be seen in only one bay in FIG. 18-11, immediately to the right of the south transept, and partially hidden by it.)

THE FINAL GOTHIC INGREDIENT To hold the much thinner—and taller (compare FIGS. 18-10*a* and 18-10*b*)—walls of Notre-Dame in place, the unknown architect introduced *flying buttresses,* exterior arches that spring from the lower roofs over the aisles and ambulatory (FIG. 18-11) and counter the outward thrust of the nave vaults. Flying buttresses seem to have been employed as early as 1150 in a few smaller churches, but at Notre-Dame in Paris they circle a great urban cathedral. The internal quadrant arches the roofs at Durham conceal (see FIG. 17-13), also employed at Laon, perform a similar function and may be regarded as precedents for exposed Gothic flying buttresses. The combination of precisely positioned flying buttresses and rib vaults with pointed arches was the ideal solution to the problem of constructing towering naves with huge windows filled with stained glass. The flying buttresses, like slender extended fingers holding up the walls, also are important elements contributing to the distinctive "look" of Gothic cathedrals (see "The Gothic Cathedral," page 498).

CHARTRES AFTER THE GREAT FIRE The fire of 1194 was not the first to destroy parts of Chartres Cathedral, but it was especially devastating. Churches burned frequently in the Middle Ages (see "The Burning of Canterbury Cathedral," Chapter 17, page 455), and church officials often had to raise money suddenly for new building campaigns. In contrast to monastic churches, which usually were small and completed fairly quickly, the building histories of urban cathedrals often extended over decades and sometimes over centuries. Their financing depended largely on collections and public contributions (not always voluntary), and a lack of funds often interrupted building programs. Unforeseen events, such as wars, famines, or plagues, or friction between the town and the cathedral authorities would stop construction, which then might not resume for years. At Reims (FIG. 18-23), the clergy offered *indulgences* (pardons for sins committed) to those who helped underwrite the enormous cost of erecting the cathedral. The rebuilding of Chartres Cathedral after 1194 took a relatively short twenty-seven years, but at one point the townspeople revolted against the prospect of a heavier tax burden. They stormed the bishop's residence and drove him into exile for four years.

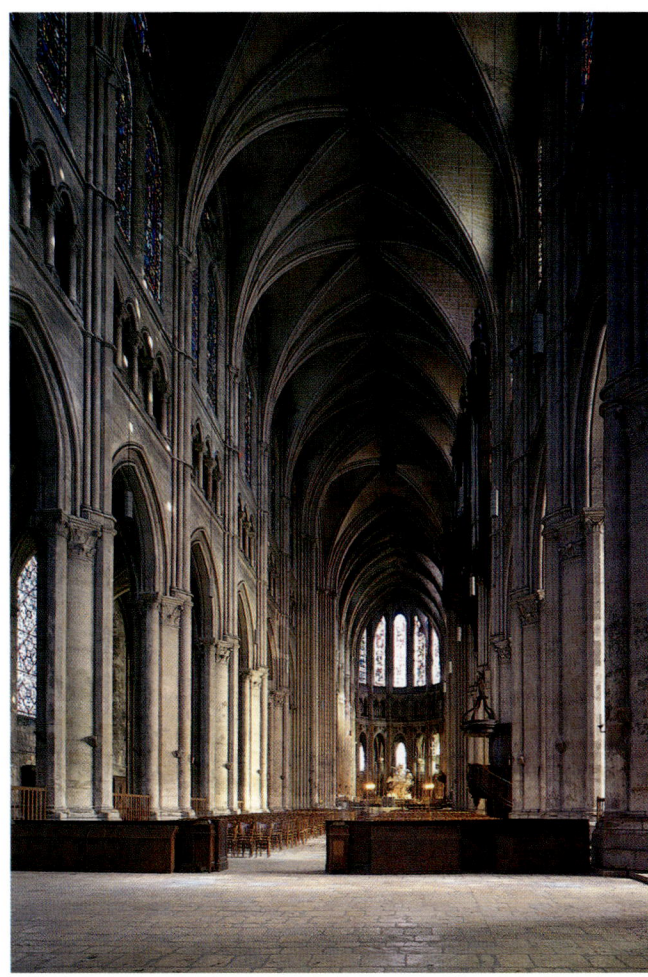

18-13 Nave of Chartres Cathedral (view facing east), Chartres, France, begun 1194.

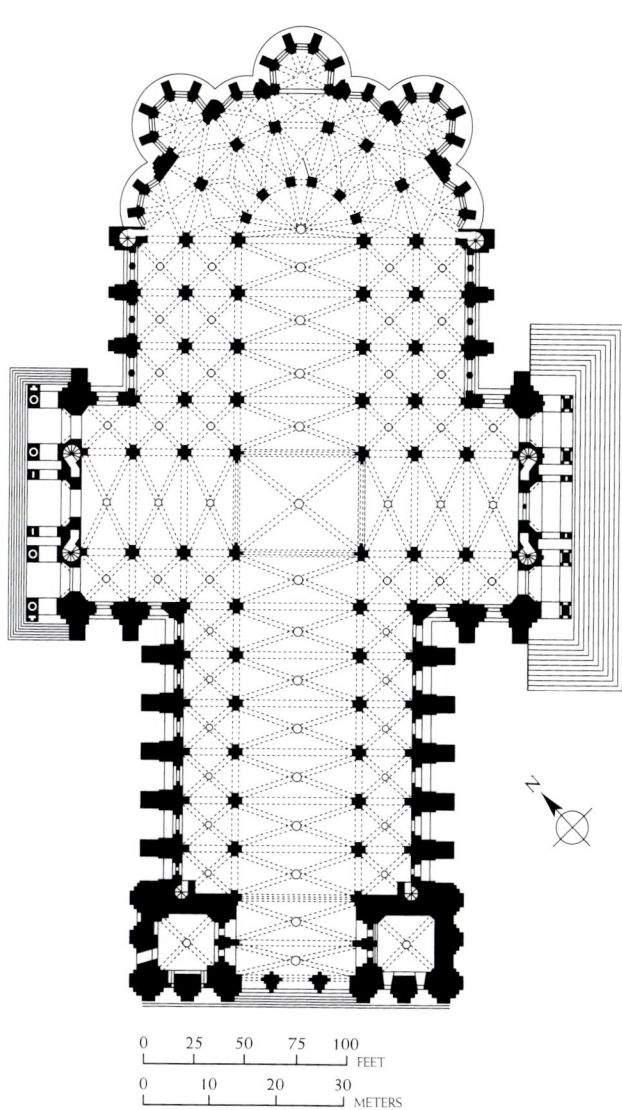

0 25 50 75 100
└─┴──┴──┴──┴──┘ FEET
0   10   20   30
└──┴────┴────┴─┘ METERS

18-12 Plan of Chartres Cathedral, Chartres, France, as rebuilt after 1194 (after Paul Frankl).

Architectural historians usually consider the new Chartres Cathedral the first High Gothic building—the first to have been planned from the beginning with flying buttresses. The mid-twelfth-century facade left standing to the west (FIGS. 18-4 and 18-5) and the masonry of the crypt to the east determined the new structure's overall dimensions. The crypt housed the most precious relic of Chartres—the mantle of the Virgin, which miraculously survived the fire. For piety and economy, the builders used the crypt for the new structure's foundation. The earlier forms did not limit the plan (FIG. 18-12), however, which reveals a new kind of organization. Rectangular nave bays replaced the square bays with six-part vaults and the alternate-support system, still present in Early Gothic churches such as Laon Cathedral (FIG. 18-8). The new system, where a rectangular unit in the nave, defined by its own vault, was flanked by a single square in each aisle rather than two, as before, became the High Gothic norm. A change in vault design and the abandonment of the alternate-support system usually accompanied this new bay arrangement. The High Gothic vault, which covered a relatively smaller area and therefore was braced more easily than its Early Gothic predecessor, had only four parts. The visual effect of these changes was to unify the interior (FIG. 18-13). The High Gothic architect aligned identical units so that viewers saw them in too rapid a sequence to perceive them as individual volumes of space. The nave became a vast, continuous hall.

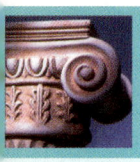

The Gothic Cathedral

The great cathedrals erected throughout Europe in the later twelfth and thirteenth centuries are the enduring symbols of the Gothic age. These towering structures are eloquent testimonies to the extraordinary skill of the architects, engineers, carpenters, masons, sculptors, glassworkers, and metalsmiths who constructed and decorated the buildings.

Most of the architectural components of Gothic cathedrals appeared in earlier structures, but the way Gothic architects combined these elements made these buildings unique expressions of medieval faith. The key ingredients of the Gothic "recipe" were rib vaults with pointed arches, flying buttresses, and huge colored-glass windows (see "Stained-Glass Windows," page 500). Our "exploded" view of a typical Gothic cathedral illustrates how these and other important Gothic architectural devices worked together.

THE VOCABULARY OF GOTHIC ARCHITECTURE

1. *Flying buttresses:* Masonry struts that transfer the thrust of the nave vaults across the roofs of the side aisles and ambulatory to a tall pier rising above the church's exterior wall. Compare the cross-section of Bourges Cathedral (see FIG. Intro-19).

2. *Pinnacle:* A sharply pointed ornament capping the piers or flying buttresses; also used on cathedral facades

3. *Vaulting web (Severy):* The masonry blocks that fill the area between the ribs of a groin vault

4. *Diagonal rib:* In plan, one of the ribs that form the X of a groin vault. In the diagrams of rib vaults on page 494, the diagonal ribs are the lines *AC* and *DB*.

5. *Transverse rib:* A rib that crosses the nave or aisle at a ninety-degree angle (lines *AB* and *DC* in the diagrams on page 494)

6. *Springing:* The lowest stone of an arch; in Gothic vaulting, the lowest stone of a diagonal or transverse rib

7. *Clerestory:* The windows below the vaults that form the nave elevation's uppermost level. By using flying buttresses and rib vaults on pointed arches, Gothic architects could build huge clerestory win-

dows and fill them with stained glass held in place by ornamental stonework called *tracery*.

8. *Triforium:* The intermediate story in a standard High Gothic three-story nave elevation consisting of arcades, usually blind (FIGS. 18-9 and 18-13) but occasionally filled with stained glass (see FIG. Intro-2)

9. *Nave arcade:* The series of arches supported by piers separating the nave from the side aisles

10. *Compound pier with shafts (responds):* Also called the *cluster pier,* a pier with a group, or cluster, of attached shafts, or *responds,* extending to the springing of the vaults

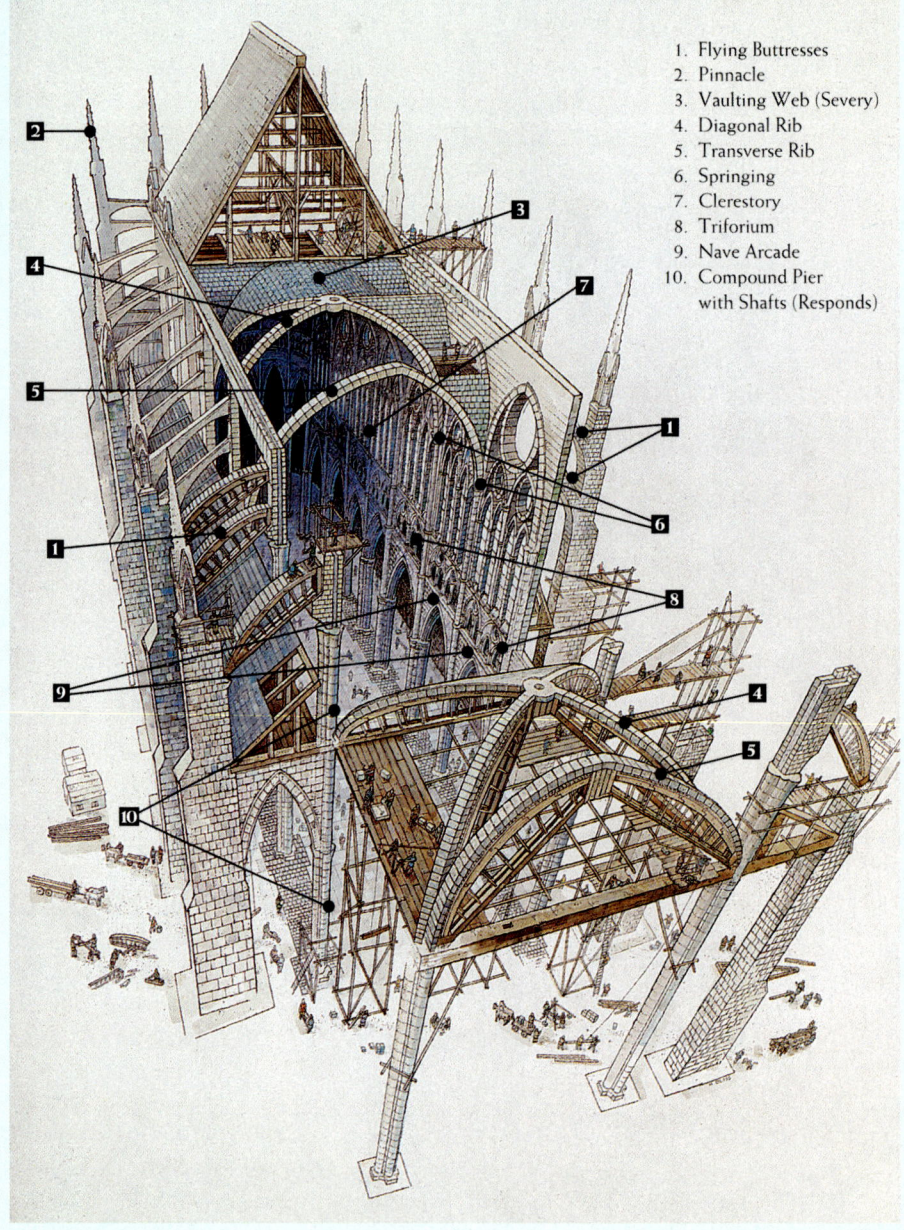

1. Flying Buttresses
2. Pinnacle
3. Vaulting Web (Severy)
4. Diagonal Rib
5. Transverse Rib
6. Springing
7. Clerestory
8. Triforium
9. Nave Arcade
10. Compound Pier with Shafts (Responds)

A new nave-wall elevation, which admitted more light to the nave through greatly enlarged clerestory windows, enhanced the organic, "flowing" quality of the High Gothic interior. Flying buttresses made it possible to eliminate the tribune gallery above the aisle, which had partially braced Romanesque and Early Gothic naves (compare FIG. 18-10*c* with FIGS. 18-10*a* and 18-10*b*). The High Gothic tripartite nave elevation, consisting of arcade, triforium, and clerestory, emphasized the large clerestory windows. Those at Chartres are almost as high as the main arcade and consist of double lancets crowned by a single oculus. The strategic placement of flying buttresses permitted the construction of nave walls whose voids dominated so that heavy masonry played a minor role.

Despite the vastly increased size of the clerestory windows, the Chartres nave is relatively dark (FIG. 18-13). The explanation for this seeming contradiction is that light-muffling colored glass fills the windows. These windows were not meant to illuminate the interior with bright sunlight but to trans-

form natural light into Suger's mystical *lux nova* (see "Stained-Glass Windows," page 500). Chartres retains almost the full complement of its original stained glass, which, although it has a dimming effect, transforms the interior's character in dramatic fashion. Gothic churches that have lost their original stained-glass windows give a false impression of what their architects intended.

THE VIRGIN'S BEAUTIFUL WINDOW   One Chartres window that survived the fire of 1194 and that the builders subsequently reused in the High Gothic cathedral is the tall single lancet the French call *Notre Dame de la Belle Verrière* (Our Lady of the Beautiful Window, FIG. **18-14**). The central section, depicting the Virgin Mary enthroned with the Christ Child in her lap, dates to ca. 1170 and has a red background. The framing angels seen against a blue ground were added when the window was reinstalled in the thirteenth-century choir. The artist represented Mary as the beautiful, young, rather worldly, Queen of Heaven, haloed, crowned,

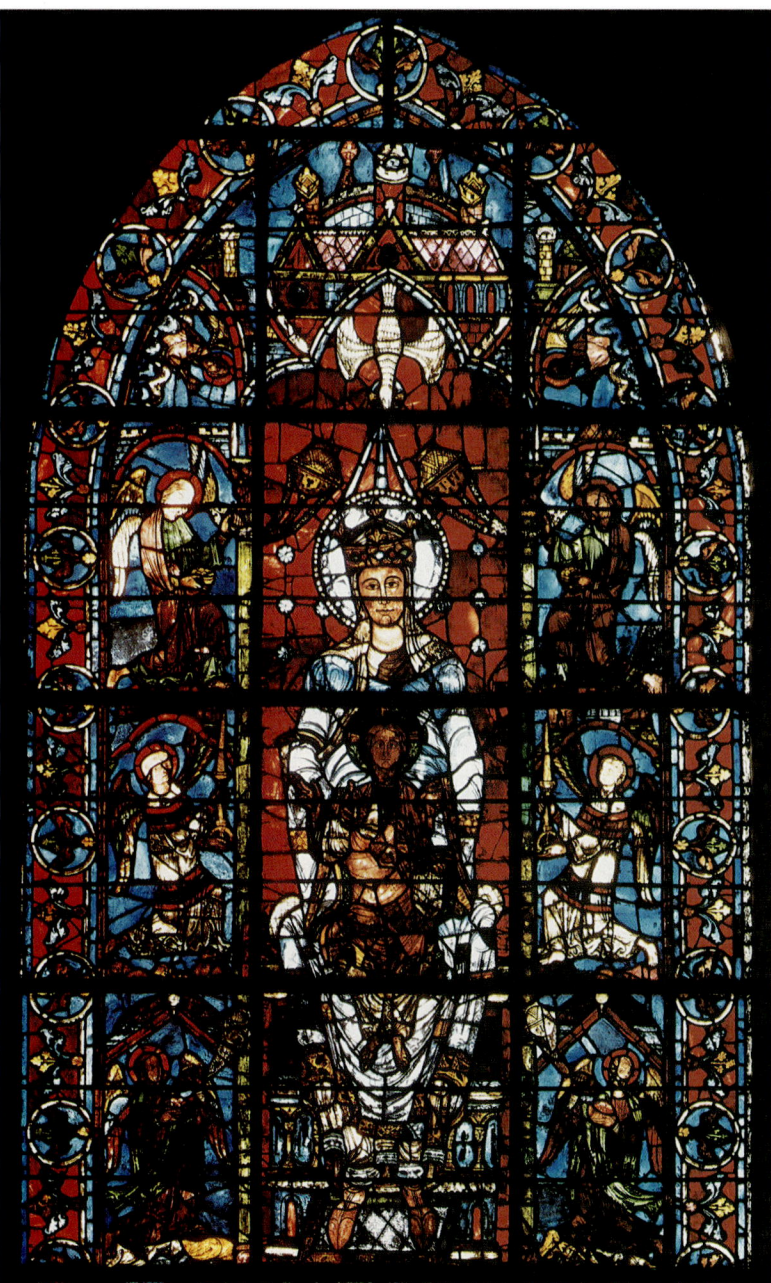

18-14 Virgin and Child and angels *(Notre Dame de la Belle Verrière)*, window in the choir of Chartres Cathedral, Chartres, France, ca. 1170, with thirteenth-century side panels. Stained glass, 16′ × 7′ 8″.

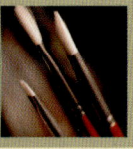

MATERIALS AND TECHNIQUES

Stained-Glass Windows

Stained glass is almost synonymous with Gothic architecture. No other age produced windows of such rich color and beauty. The art of making colored glass is, however, very old. Egyptian artists excelled at fashioning colorful glass vessels and other objects for both home and tomb. Archeologists also have uncovered thousands of colored-glass artifacts at hundreds of sites throughout the classical world.

But if the technology of manufacturing colored glass was ancient, how artists used stained glass in the Gothic period was new. Stained-glass windows were not just installed to introduce color and religious iconography into church interiors. That could have been—and was much earlier—done with both mural paintings and mosaics, often with magnificent effect. But stained-glass windows differ from those earlier techniques in one all-important respect. They do not conceal walls; they replace them. And they transmit rather than reflect light, filtering and transforming the natural sunlight as it enters the building. Abbot Suger called this colored light *lux nova* (see "Abbot Suger and the Rebuilding of Saint-Denis," page 489). Hugh of Saint-Victor (1096–1142), a prominent Parisian theologian who died while Suger's Saint-Denis was under construction, also commented on the special mystical quality of stained-glass windows. "Stained-glass windows," he wrote, "are the Holy Scriptures . . . and since their brilliance lets the splendor of the True Light pass into the church, they enlighten those inside."[1]

As early as the fourth century, architects used colored glass for church windows. Perfection of the technique came gradually. The stained-glass windows in the Saint-Denis choir (FIG. 18-1) show already a high degree of skill. According to Suger, they were "painted by the exquisite hands of many masters from different regions," proving that the art was known widely at that time.[2]

The manufacture of stained-glass windows was labor intensive and costly. First, the master designer drew the exact composition of the planned window on a wooden panel, indicating all the linear details and noting the colors for each section.

Glassblowers provided flat sheets of glass of different colors to *glaziers* (glassworkers), who cut the windowpanes to the required size and shape with special iron shears. Glaziers produced an even greater range of colors by *flashing* (fusing one layer of colored glass to another). Purple, for example, resulted from the fusing of red and blue (compare the color triangle, FIG. Intro-11). Next, painters added details such as faces, hands, hair, and clothing in enamel by tracing the master design on the wood panel through the colored glass. Then they heated the painted glass to fuse the enamel to the surface. The glaziers then *leaded* the various fragments of glass; that is, they joined them by strips of lead called *cames*. The leading not only held the (usually quite small) pieces together but also separated the colors to heighten the design's effect as a whole. The distinctive character of Gothic stained-glass windows is largely the result of this combination of fine linear details with broad flat expanses of color framed by black lead. Finally, the glassworkers strengthened the completed window with an armature of iron bands, which in the twelfth century formed a grid over the whole design (FIG. 18-14). In the thirteenth century, the bands followed the outlines of the medallions and of the surrounding areas (FIGS. 18-15 and 18-26).

The form of the stone window frames into which the glass was set also evolved throughout the Gothic era. Early rose windows, such as the one on Chartres Cathedral's west facade (FIG. 18-4), have stained glass held in place by *plate tracery*. The glass fills only the "punched holes" in the heavy ornamental stonework. *Bar tracery* (FIG. 18-15), a later development, is much more slender. The stained-glass windows fill almost the entire opening, and the stonework is unobtrusive, more like delicate leading than masonry wall.

[1]Hugh of Saint-Victor, *Seculum de mysteriis ecclesiae,* Sermo II.

[2]Erwin Panofsky, trans., *Abbot Suger on the Abbey Church of Saint-Denis and Its Art Treasures,* 2nd ed. (Princeton, N.J.: Princeton University Press, 1979), 73.

and accompanied by the Holy Spirit dove. The frontal composition is traditional. Comparing this Virgin and Child with the Theotokos and Child of Hagia Sophia (see FIG. 12-16) highlights not only the Byzantine image's greater severity and aloofness but also the sharp difference between the light-reflecting mosaic medium and Gothic light-transmitting stained glass. Byzantine and Gothic architects used light to transform the material world into the spiritual, but in opposite ways. In Gothic architecture, light was transmitted through a kind of diffracting screen of stone-set glass. In Byzantine architecture, light was reflected from myriad glass tesserae set into the thick masonry wall.

A QUEEN'S GIFT TO CHARTRES Chartres's thirteenth-century Gothic windows are even more spectacular than the *Belle Verrière* because they were designed from the outset to fill entire walls, thanks to the introduction of flying buttresses. The immense rose window (approximately forty-three feet in diameter) and tall lancets of Chartres Cathedral's north transept (FIGS. 18-4 and **18-15**) were the gift of the Queen of France, Blanche of Castile, around 1220. (The royal motifs of yellow castles on a red ground and yellow *fleurs-de-lis*—three-petaled iris flowers—on a blue ground fill the small lancets in the rose window's lower spandrels.) The enthroned Virgin and Child is again the central motif (Chartres,

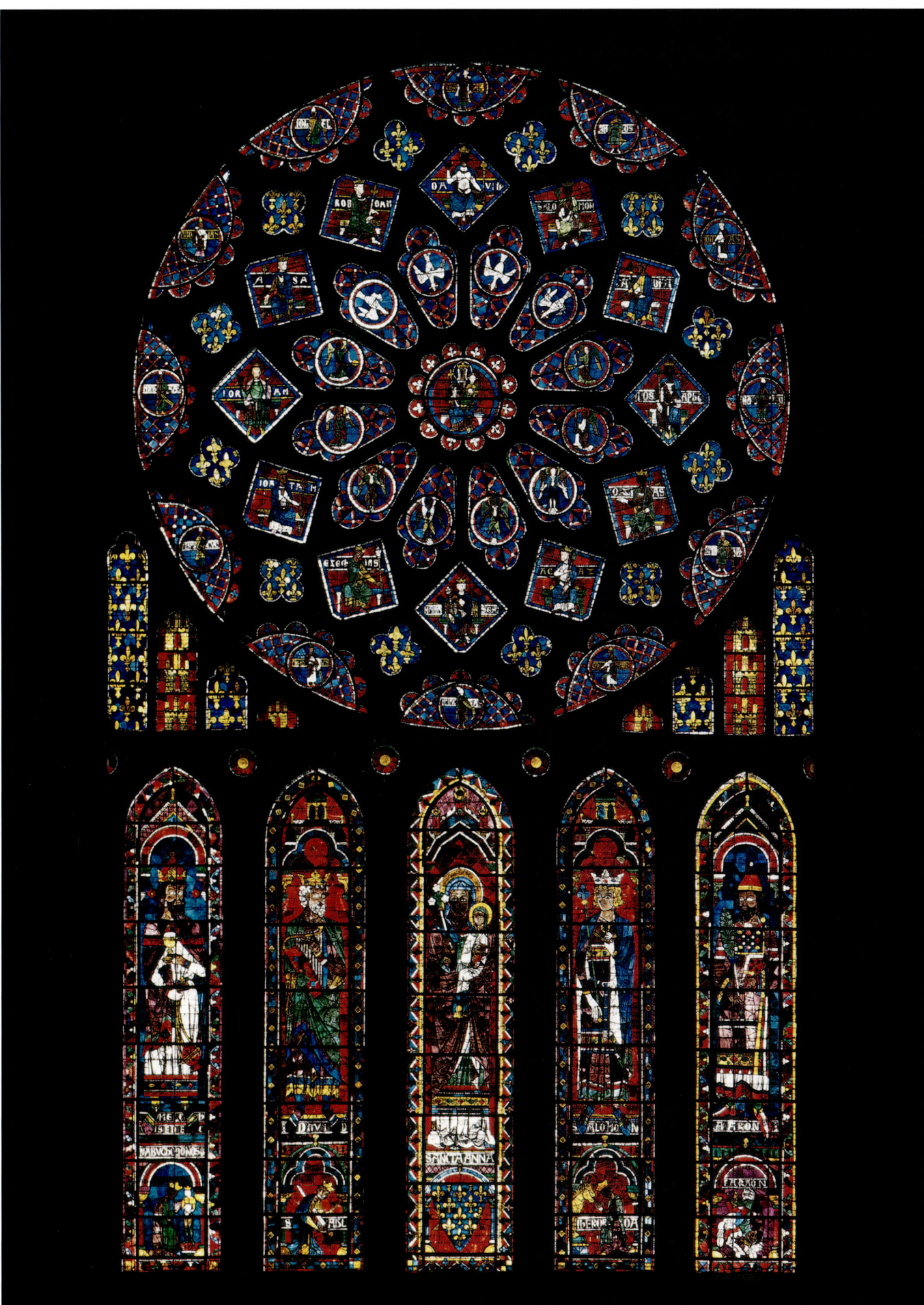

18-15 Rose window and lancets, north transept, Chartres Cathedral, Chartres, France, ca. 1220. Stained glass, rose window approx. 43′ in diameter.

as noted, was dedicated to the Virgin and housed her tunic), but the scale is much reduced. Mary appears in the roundel at the center of the rose, which resembles a gem-studded book cover or cloisonné brooch. Below, in the lancets, are Saint Anne and four Old Testament prophets, supporting the New Testament figures above, as on the Royal Portal. Many Gothic stained-glass windows also present narrative scenes, and their iconographical programs are sometimes as complex as those of the sculpted church portals.

The rose and lancets change in hue and intensity with the hours, turning solid architecture into a floating vision of the celestial heavens. Almost the entire mass of wall opens up into stained glass, which is held in place by an intricate stone armature of stone *bar tracery* that almost has the strength of steel. Here, the Gothic passion for light led to a most daring and successful attempt to subtract all superfluous material bulk just short of destabilizing the structure in order to transform hard substance into insubstantial, luminous color. That this vast, complex fabric of stone-set glass has maintained its structural integrity for almost eight hundred years attests to the Gothic builders' engineering genius.

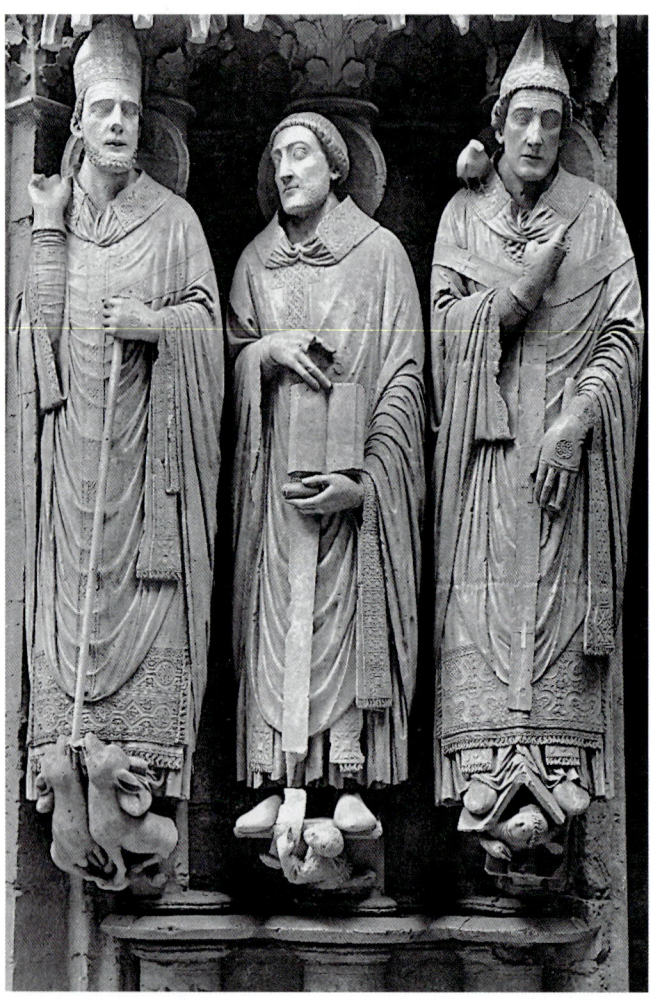

18-16 Saints Martin, Jerome, and Gregory, jamb statues, Porch of the Confessors (right doorway), south transept, Chartres Cathedral, Chartres, France, ca. 1220–1230.

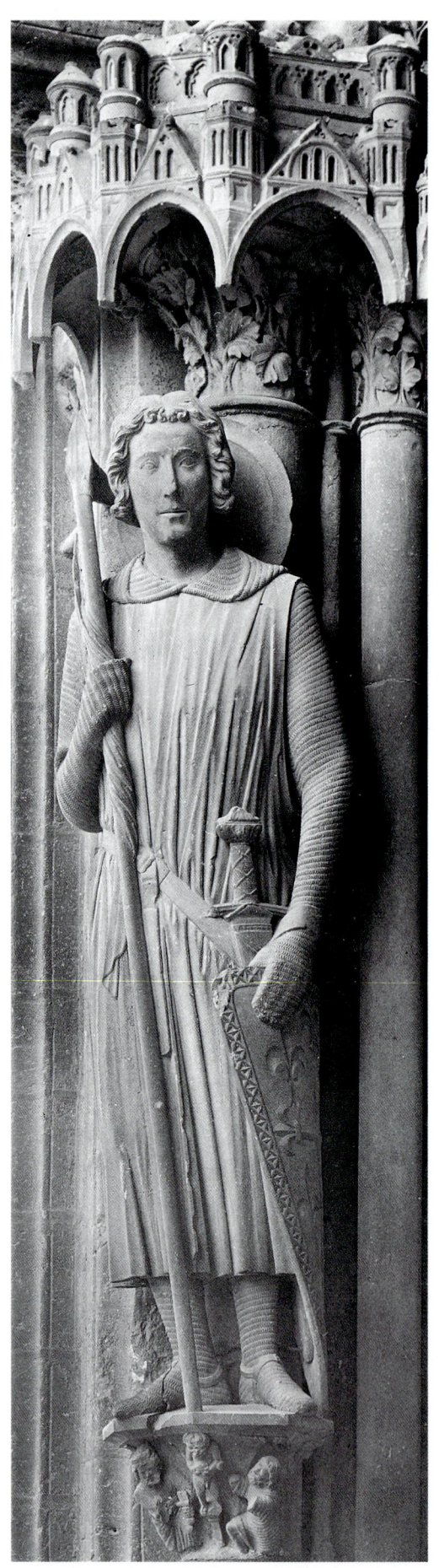

18-17 Saint Theodore, jamb statue, Porch of the Martyrs (left doorway), south transept, Chartres Cathedral, Chartres, France, ca. 1230.

ANOTHER "CLASSICAL REVOLUTION" The sculptures adorning the portals of the two new Chartres transepts erected after the 1194 fire are also prime examples of the new High Gothic spirit. As at Laon (FIG. 18-7) and Paris (FIG. 18-11), the transept portals project more forcefully from the church than do the Early Gothic portals of its west facade (compare FIGS. 18-4 and 18-5). Similarly, the statues of saints on the portal jambs are more independent from the architectural framework. Three figures from the Porch of the Confessors in the south transept (FIG. **18-16**) reveal the great changes Gothic sculpture underwent since the Royal Portal statues of the mid-twelfth century. These changes recall in many ways the revolutionary developments in ancient Greek sculpture during the transition from the Archaic to the Classical style (see Chapter 5). The Chartres transept statues we illustrate date from 1220 to 1230 and represent Saints Martin, Jerome, and Gregory. Although they are still attached to columns, the architectural setting does not determine their poses as much as it did on the west portals (FIG. 18-6). The saints communicate quietly with one another, like waiting dignitaries. They turn slightly toward and away from each other, breaking the rigid vertical lines that, on the Royal Portal, fix the figures immovably. The drapery folds are not stiff and shallow vertical accents, as on the west facade. The fabric falls and laps over the bodies in soft, if still regular, folds.

The treatment of the faces is even more remarkable. The sculptor gave the figures individualized features and distinctive personalities and clothed them in the period's liturgical costumes. Saint Martin is a tall, intense priest with gaunt features (compare the spiritually moved but not particularized face of the Moissac prophet in FIG. 17-23). Saint Jerome appears as a kindly, practical administrator-scholar, holding his copy of the Scriptures. At the right, the introspective Saint Gregory seems lost in thought as he listens to the Holy Ghost dove on his shoulder. Thus, the sculptor did not contrast the three men simply in terms of their poses, gestures, and attributes but, most particularly and emphatically, as persons. Personality, revealed in human faces, makes the real difference.

The south-transept figure of Saint Theodore (FIG. **18-17**), the martyred warrior on the Porch of the Martyrs, presents an even sharper contrast with Early Gothic jamb statues. The sculptor portrayed Theodore as the ideal Christian knight and clothed him in the cloak and chain-mail armor of Gothic Crusaders. The handsome long-haired youth holds his spear firmly in his right hand and rests his left hand on his shield. He turns his head to the left and swings out his hip to the right. The body's resulting torsion and pronounced sway call to mind Classical Greek statuary, especially the contrapposto stance of Polykleitos's *Spear Bearer* (see FIG. 5-38). It is not inappropriate to speak of the changes that occurred in thirteenth-century Gothic sculpture as a second "Classical revolution."

THE QUEST FOR HEIGHT AT AMIENS Chartres Cathedral was one of the most influential buildings in the history of architecture. Its builders set a pattern that many other Gothic architects followed, even if they refined the details. Construction of Amiens Cathedral (FIGS. **18-18** to **18-21**) began in 1220, while work was still in progress at Chartres. The architects were ROBERT DE LUZARCHES, THOMAS DE CORMONT, and RENAUD DE CORMONT. The builders finished the nave by 1236 and the radiating

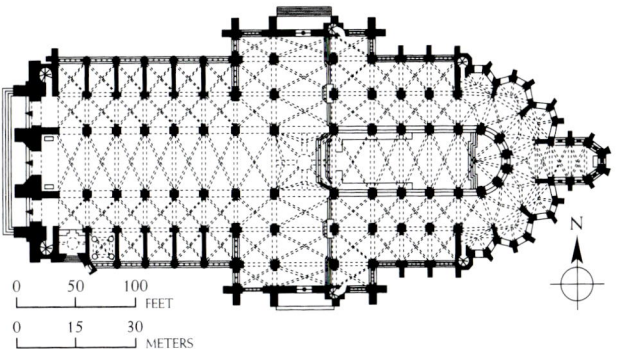

18-18 ROBERT DE LUZARCHES, THOMAS DE CORMONT, and RENAUD DE CORMONT, plan of Amiens Cathedral, Amiens, France, 1220–1288 (after Paul Frankl).

chapels by 1247, but work on the choir continued until almost 1270. The Amiens plan (FIG. 18-18) and elevation (FIGS. 18-10*d* and 18-19) derived from the High Gothic formula established at Chartres. But Amiens Cathedral's proportions are even more elegant, and the number and complexity of the lancet windows in both its clerestory and triforium are even greater. The whole design reflects the builders' confident use of the complete High Gothic structural vocabulary: the rectangular-bay system, the four-part rib vault, and a buttressing system that permitted almost complete dissolution of heavy masses and thick weight-bearing walls. At

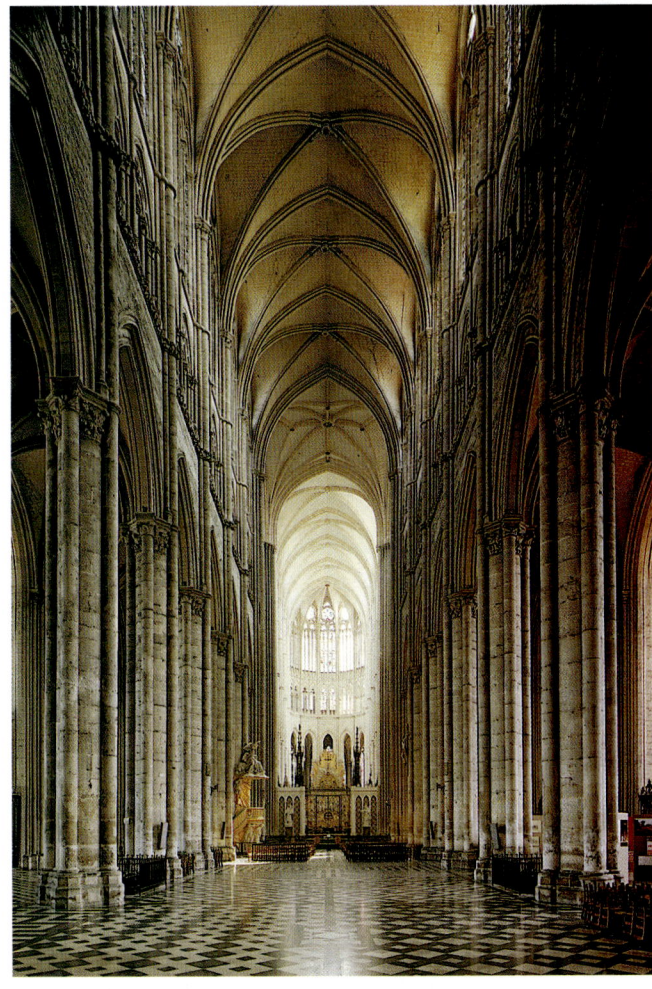

18-19 ROBERT DE LUZARCHES, THOMAS DE CORMONT, and RENAUD DE CORMONT, nave of Amiens Cathedral (view facing east), France, begun 1220.

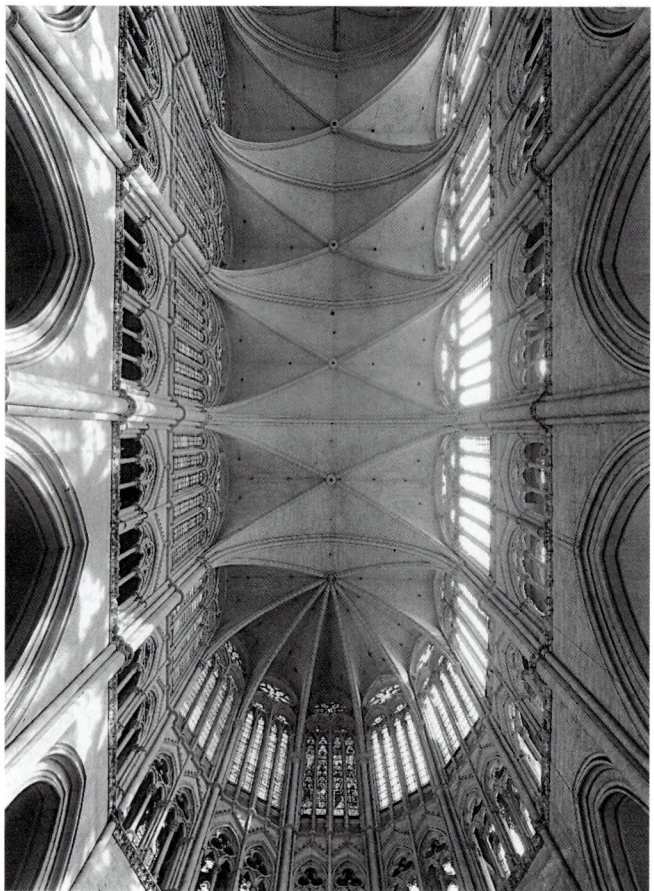

18-20   ROBERT DE LUZARCHES, THOMAS DE CORMONT, and RENAUD DE CORMONT, choir vaults of Amiens Cathedral, Amiens, France, begun 1220.

Amiens, the concept of a self-sustaining skeletal architecture reached full maturity. What remained as walls was stretched like a skin between the piers and seems to serve no purpose other than to provide a weather screen for the interior (FIG. 18-20).

Amiens Cathedral is one of the most impressive examples of the French Gothic obsession with constructing ever taller cathedrals. With their new skeletal frames of stone, French builders attempted goals almost beyond limit, pushing with ever more slender supports to new heights. The nave vaults at Laon rise to a height of about eighty feet; at Paris, to one hundred seven feet; and at Chartres, to one hundred eighteen feet. Those at Amiens are one hundred forty-four feet above the floor. The tense, strong lines of the Amiens vault ribs converge to the colonnettes and speed down the shell-like walls to the compound piers. Almost every part of the superstructure has its corresponding element below. The only exception is the *wall rib* (at the junction of the vault and the wall). The overall effect is of effortless strength, of a buoyant lightness one normally does not associate with stone architecture. Viewed directly from below, the choir vaults (FIG. 18-20) seem like a canopy, tentlike and suspended from bundled masts. The light flooding in from the clerestory makes the vaults seem even more insubstantial. The effect recalls another great building, one utterly different from Amiens but where light also plays a defining role: Hagia Sophia in Constantinople (see FIG. 12-5). Once again, not only did the architects reduce the building's physical mass by structural ingenuity and daring, but also light dematerializes further what remains. If Hagia Sophia is the

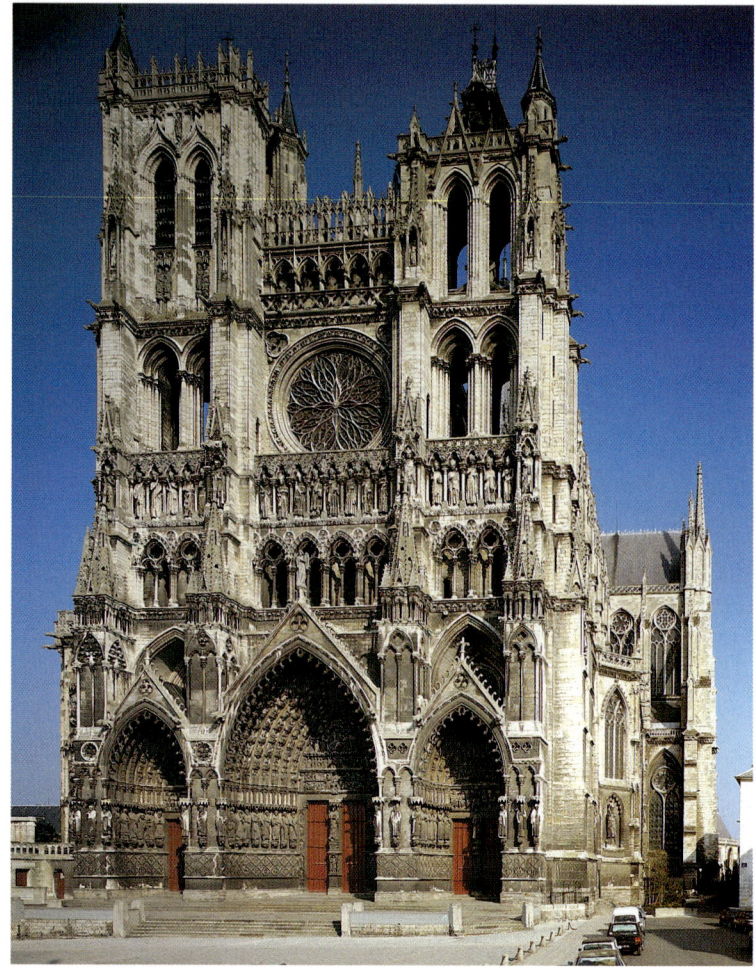

18-21   ROBERT DE LUZARCHES, THOMAS DE CORMONT, and RENAUD DE CORMONT, west facade of Amiens Cathedral, Amiens, France, begun 1220.

perfect expression of Byzantine spirituality in architecture, Amiens, with its soaring vaults and giant windows admitting divine colored light, is its Gothic counterpart.

Work began on the Amiens west facade (FIG. 18-21) at the same time as the nave (1220). Its lower parts seem to reflect the influence of Laon Cathedral (FIG. 18-7) in the spacing of the funnel-like and gable-covered portals. But the Amiens designer punctured the facade's upper parts to an even greater degree than did the Laon architect. The deep piercing of walls and towers at Amiens seems to have left few continuous surfaces for decoration, but the ones that remained were covered with a network of colonnettes, arches, pinnacles, rosettes, and other decorative stonework that visually screens and nearly dissolves the structure's solid core. Sculpture also extends to the areas above the portals, especially the band of statues (the so-called "kings' gallery") running the full width of the facade directly below the rose window (with fifteenth-century tracery). The uneven towers were later additions. The shorter one dates from the fourteenth century, the taller one from the fifteenth century.

CHRIST, THE BEAUTIFUL GOD The most prominent statue on the Amiens facade is of Christ (the *Beau Dieu*, or Beautiful God) on the central doorway's trumeau (FIG. **18-22**). The sculptor fully modeled Christ's figure, enveloping his body with massive drapery folds cascading from his waist. The statue stands freely and is as independent of its architectural setting as any Gothic facade statue ever was. Nonetheless, the sculptor still placed an architectural canopy over the figure's head. It is in the latest Gothic style, mimicking the east end of a thirteenth-century cathedral with a series of radiating chapels pierced by elegant lancet windows. Above the canopy is the great central tympanum with the representation of Christ as Last Judge (FIG. 18-21). But the *Beau Dieu* is a handsome, kindly figure who does not strike terror into sinners. Instead he blesses those who enter the church and tramples a lion and a dragon symbolizing the evil forces in the world. This image of Christ gives humankind hope in salvation. The *Beau Dieu* epitomizes the bearded, benevolent image of Christ that replaced the youthful Early Christian Christ (see FIG. 11-6) and the stern Byzantine Pantocrator (see FIG. 12-24) as the preferred representation of the Savior in later European art. The figure's quiet grace and grandeur also sharply contrast with the emotional intensity of the twisting Romanesque prophet carved in relief on the Moissac trumeau (see FIG. 17-23).

GLASS REPLACES STONE AT REIMS Construction of Reims Cathedral (FIG. 18-23) began only a few years after work commenced at Amiens. The Reims designers carried the High Gothic style of the Amiens west facade still further, both architecturally and sculpturally. The two facades, although similar, display some significant differences. The kings' gallery of statues at Reims is *above* the great rose window, and the figures stand in taller and more ornate frames. In fact, the architect "stretched" every detail of the facade. The openings in the towers and those to the left and right of the rose window are taller, narrower, and more intricately decorated, and they more closely resemble the elegant lancets of the clerestory within. A pointed arch also frames the rose window itself, and the pinnacles over the portals are taller and more elaborate than those at Amiens. Most striking, however,

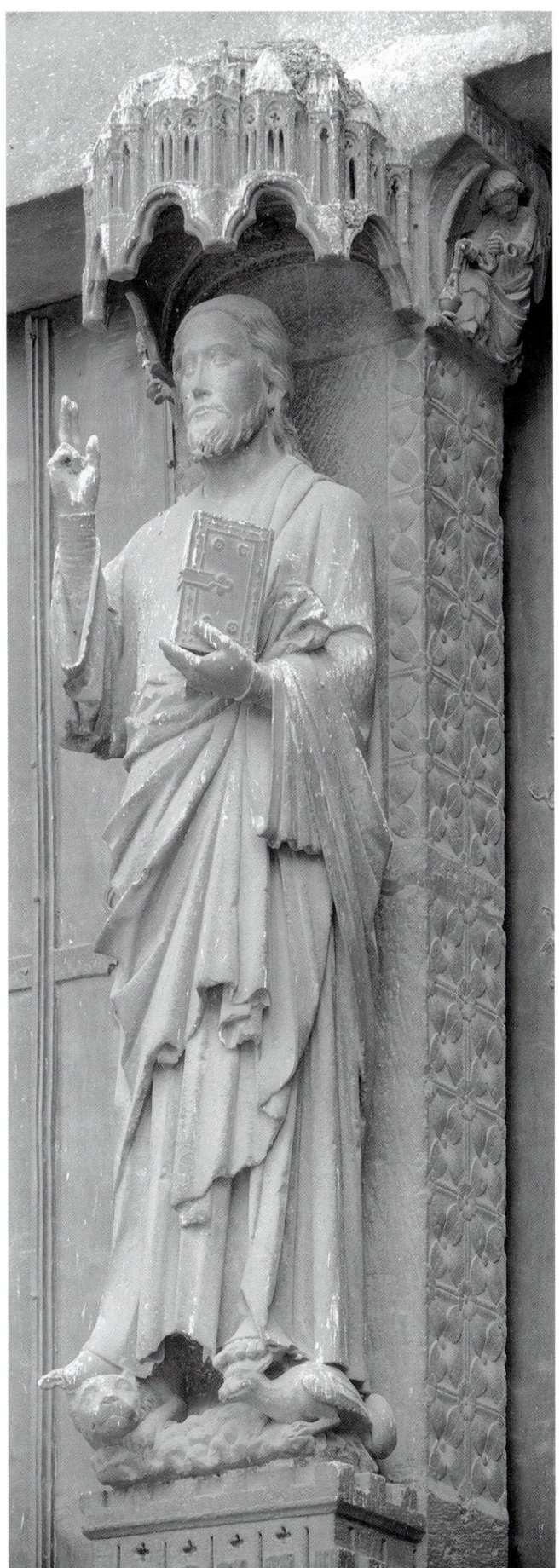

18-22 Christ *(Beau Dieu)*, trumeau statue of central doorway, west facade, Amiens Cathedral, Amiens, France, ca. 1220–1235.

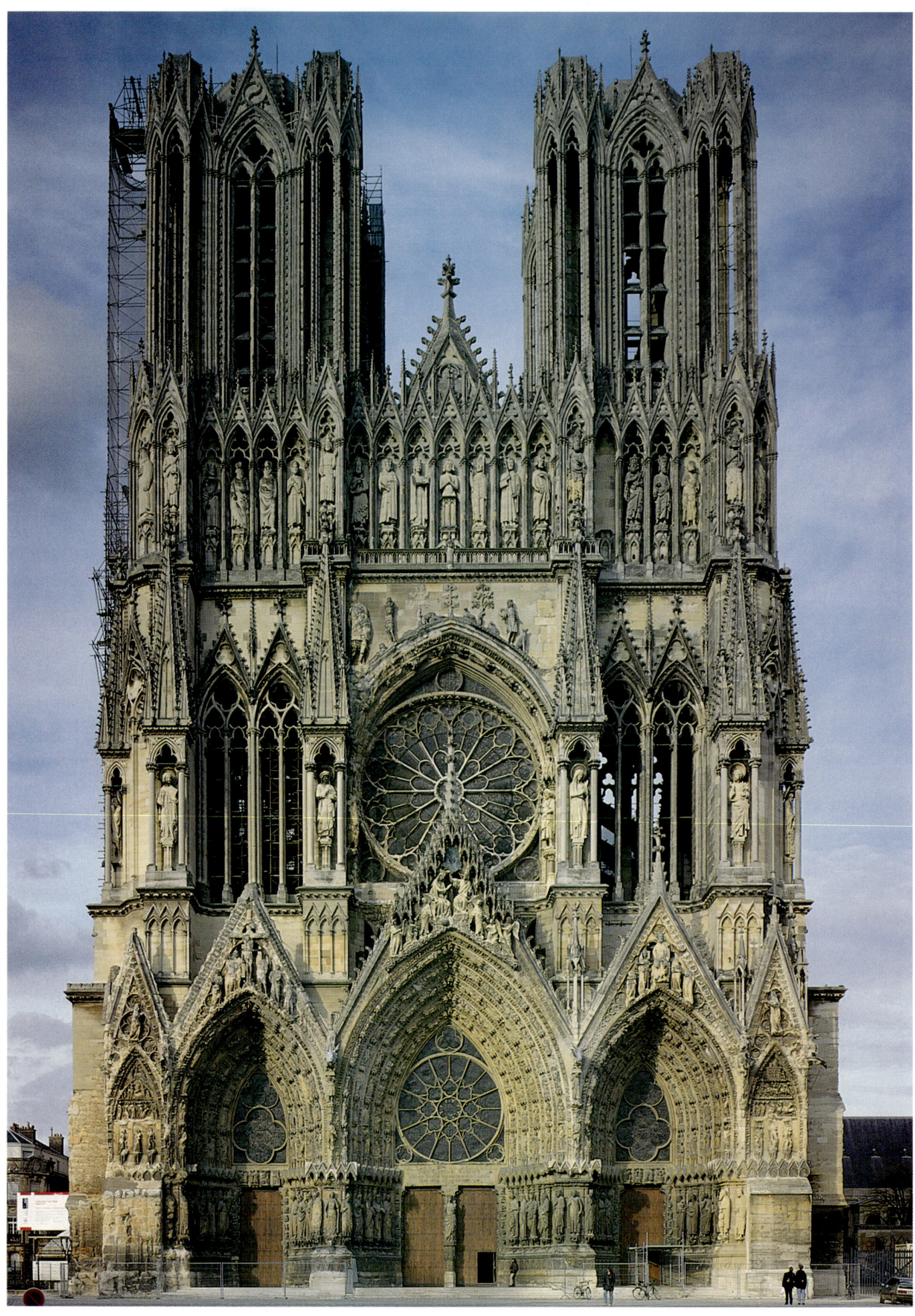

18-23 West facade of Reims Cathedral, Reims, France, ca. 1225–1290.

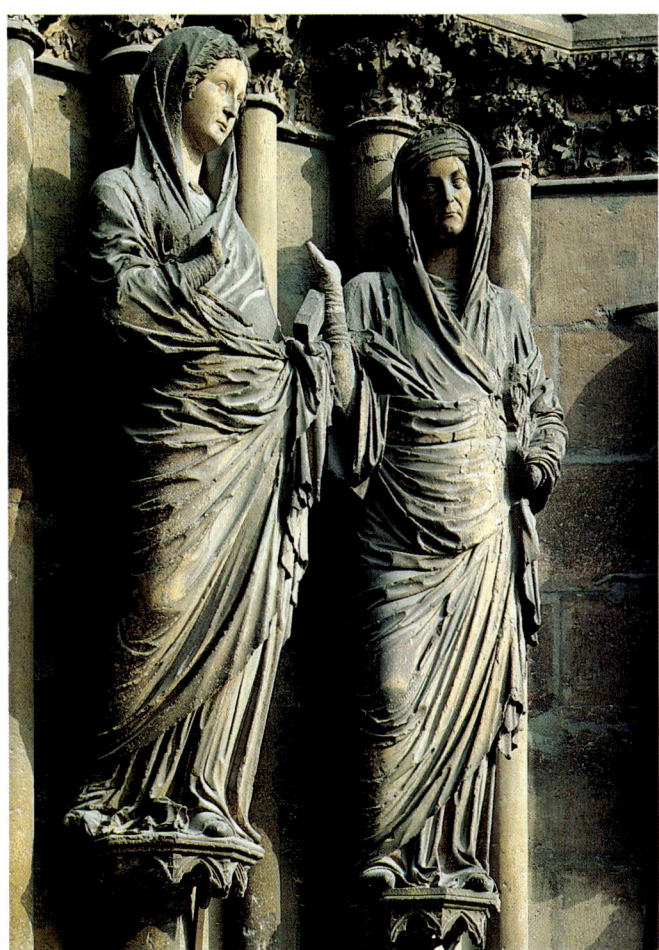

18-24 Visitation, jamb statues of central doorway, west facade, Reims Cathedral, Reims, France, ca. 1230.

is the architect's treatment of the tympanums over the doorways, replacing the stone relief sculpture of earlier facades with stained-glass windows. The contrast with Romanesque heavy masonry construction (see FIG. 17-9) is extreme. But the rapid transformation of the Gothic facade since the twelfth-century designs of Saint-Denis and Chartres (FIG. 18-4) and even Laon (FIG. 18-7) is no less noteworthy.

STATUES BEGIN TO CONVERSE   At Reims the fully ripened Gothic style also can be seen in sculpture. At first glance, the jamb statues of the west portals of Reims Cathedral (FIG. **18-24**) appear to be completely detached from their architectural background. The designer shrank the supporting columns into insignificance so that they in no way restrict the free and easy movements of the full-bodied figures. (Compare the Reims statue-columns with those of the Royal Portal of Chartres, FIG. 18-6, where the background columns occupy a volume equal to the figures' volume.) The two Reims jamb statues we illustrate portray Saint Elizabeth visiting the Virgin Mary before the birth of Jesus. They are two of a series of statues celebrating Mary's life and are further testimony to the Virgin's central role in Gothic iconography.

The sculptor of the Visitation group reveals a classicizing bent startlingly unlike anything seen since Roman times. The artist probably studied actual classical statuary in France. Although art historians have been unable to pinpoint specific models, the heads of both women look like ancient Roman

portraits. The youthful Mary, for example, resembles the women of the Antonine dynasty, especially Faustina the Younger, Marcus Aurelius's wife. Whatever the sculptor's source, the statues are astonishing approximations of the classical naturalistic style. The Reims master even incorporated the Greek contrapposto posture, going far beyond the stance of the Chartres Saint Theodore (FIG. 18-17). At Reims, the swaying of the hips is much more pronounced. The right legs bend, and the knees press through the rippling folds of the garments. The sculptor also set the figures' arms in motion. Not only do Mary and Elizabeth turn their faces toward each other, but they converse through gestures. In the Reims Visitation group, the formerly isolated Gothic jamb statue became part of a narrative group.

A RADIANT ROYAL CHAPEL   If the stained-glass windows inserted into the portal tympanums of Reims Cathedral exemplify the wall-dissolving High Gothic architectural style, Sainte-Chapelle in Paris (FIG. **18-25**) shows this principle applied to a whole building. Louis IX built

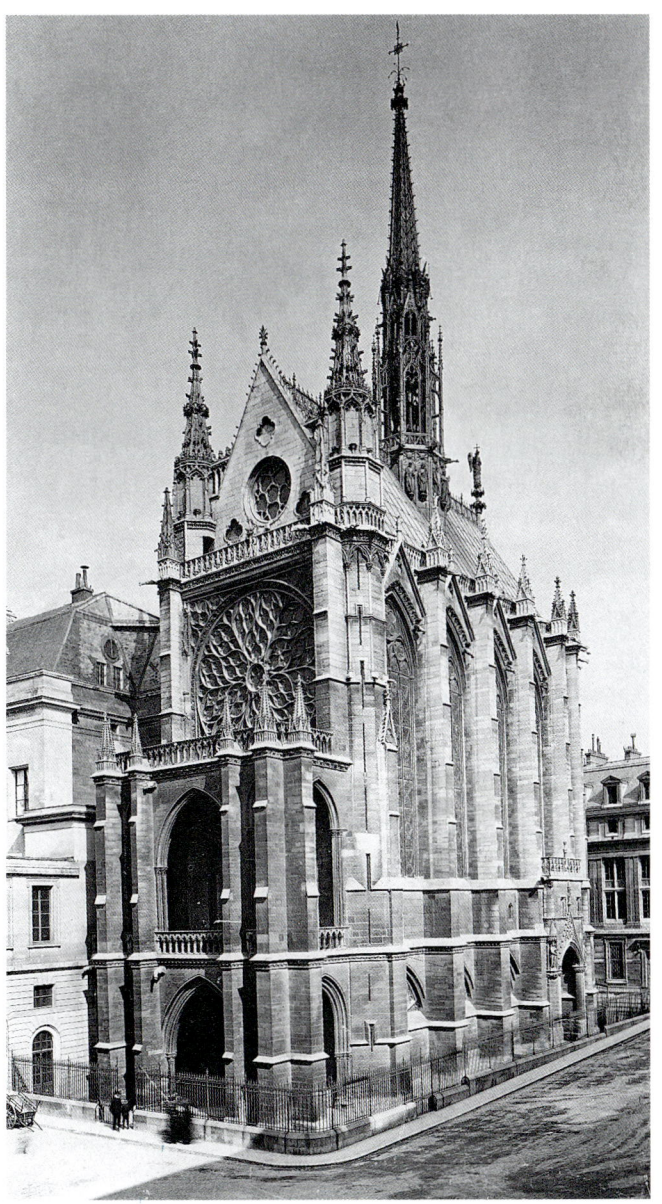

18-25 Sainte-Chapelle, Paris, France, 1243–1248.

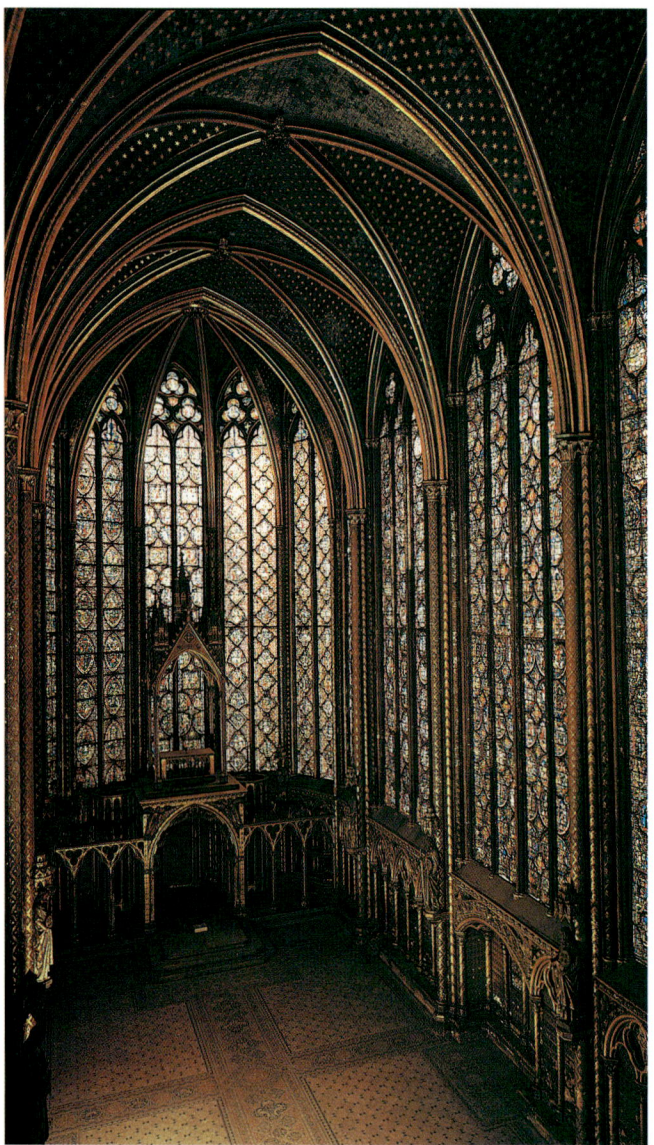

18-26   Interior of the upper chapel, Sainte-Chapelle, Paris, France, 1243–1248.

mous windows (FIG. 18-26) filter the light and fill the interior with an unearthly rose-violet atmosphere. Approximately forty-nine feet high and fifteen feet wide, they were the largest designed up to their time.

THE VIRGIN AS QUEEN   The "court style" of Saint Louis was not confined to architecture. Indeed, the elegance and delicacy displayed in Sainte-Chapelle's design permeated the pictorial arts as well. By the early fourteenth century, a mannered elegance that marks Late Gothic art in general had replaced the monumental and solemn sculptural style of the High Gothic portals. Perhaps the best example of the late French court style in sculpture is the statue nicknamed the *Virgin of Paris* (FIG. **18-27**) because of its location in the Parisian Cathedral of Notre-Dame. The sculptor portrayed Mary as a very worldly queen, decked out in royal garments and wearing a heavy gem-encrusted crown. The Christ Child is equally richly attired and is very much the infant prince in the arms of his young mother. The tender, anecdotal characterization of mother and son represents a further humanization of the portrayal of religious figures in Gothic sculpture.

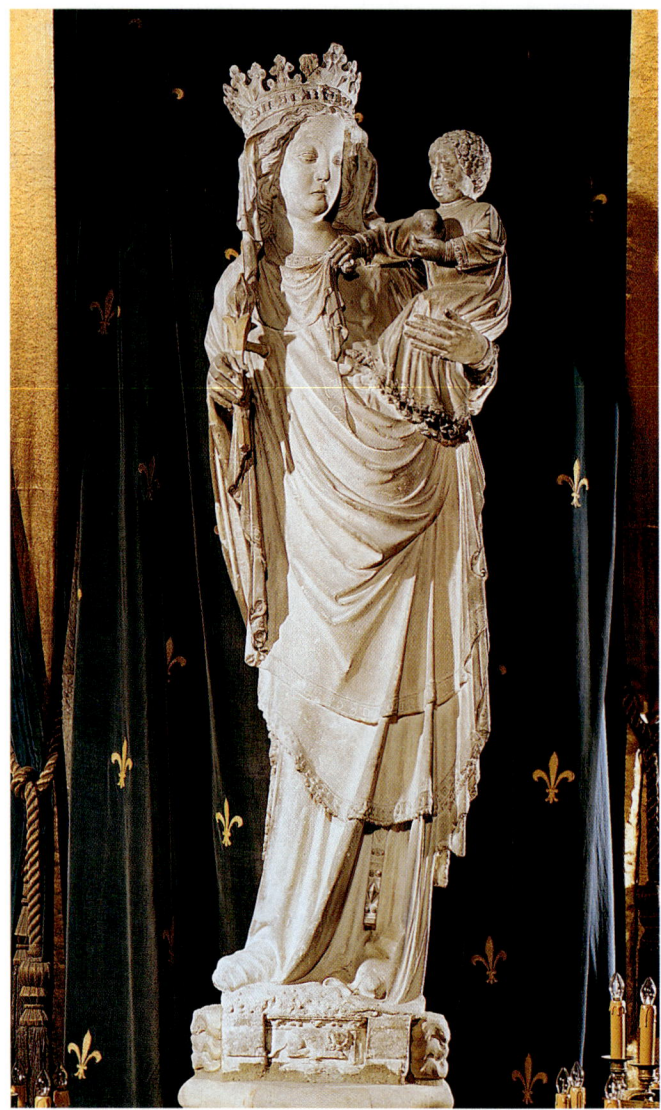

Sainte-Chapelle, joined to the royal palace, as a repository for the crown of thorns and other relics of Christ's Passion he had purchased in 1239 from his cousin Baldwin II, the Latin emperor of Constantinople. The building's resemblance to an intricately carved reliquary is intentional (compare FIG. 18-55). The structure is a prime example of the so-called *Rayonnant* (radiant) style of the High Gothic age, which dominated the second half of the century. It was associated with the royal Parisian court of Saint Louis (see "Louis IX: The Saintly King," page 509). In Sainte-Chapelle, the dissolution of walls and the reduction of the bulk of the supports were carried to the point that some six thousand four hundred fifty square feet of stained glass make up more than three-quarters of the structure (FIG. **18-26**). The supporting elements were reduced so much that they are hardly more than large *mullions,* or vertical bars. The emphasis is on the extreme slenderness of the architectural forms and on linearity in general. Although the chapel was heavily restored during the nineteenth century (after damage from the French Revolution), it has retained most of its original thirteenth-century stained glass. Sainte-Chapelle's enor-

18-27   Virgin and Child *(Virgin of Paris)*, Notre-Dame, Paris, France, early fourteenth century.

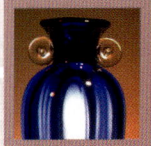

Louis IX
The Saintly King

The royal patron behind the Parisian "court style" of Gothic art and architecture was King Louis IX (1215–1270; r. 1226–1270), grandson of Philip Augustus. Louis inherited the throne when he was only twelve years old, so until he reached adulthood six years later, his mother, Blanche of Castile, granddaughter of Eleanor of Aquitaine (see "Romanesque Countesses, Queens, and Nuns," Chapter 17, page 482), served as France's regent.

The French regarded Louis as the ideal king, and in 1297, twenty-seven years after his death, Pope Boniface VIII declared him a saint. In his own time, Louis was revered for his piety, justice, truthfulness, and charity. His alms giving and his donations to religious foundations were extravagant. He especially favored the *mendicant* (begging) orders, the Dominicans and Franciscans (see "Mendicant Orders and Confraternities," Chapter 19, page 537). He admired their poverty, piety, and self-sacrificing disregard of material things.

Louis launched two unsuccessful Crusades, the Seventh (1248–1254, when, in her son's absence, Blanche was again

French regent) and the Eighth (1270). He died in Tunisia during the latter. As a crusading knight who lost his life in the service of the Church, Louis personified the chivalric virtues of courage, loyalty, and self-sacrifice. Saint Louis united in his person the best qualities of the Christian knight, the benevolent monarch, and the holy man. He became the model of medieval Christian kingship.

Louis's political accomplishments were also noteworthy. He subdued the unruly French barons, so between 1243 and 1314 no one seriously challenged the crown. He negotiated a treaty with Henry III, king of France's traditional enemy, England. Such was his reputation for integrity and just dealing that he served as arbiter in at least a dozen international disputes. So successful was he as peacekeeper that despite civil wars through most of the thirteenth century, international peace prevailed. Under Saint Louis, medieval France was at its most prosperous, and its art and architecture were admired and imitated throughout Europe.

The playful interaction of an adult and an infant in the *Virgin of Paris* may be compared with the similarly composed statuary group of Hermes and the infant Dionysos (see FIG. 5-62) by the Greek sculptor Praxiteles. Indeed, the exaggerated swaying S curve of the Virgin's body superficially resembles the shallow S curve Praxiteles introduced in the fourth century B.C. But unlike its Late Classical predecessor, the Late Gothic S curve was not organic (derived from within figures), nor was it a rational, if pleasing, organization of human anatomical parts. Rather, the Gothic curve was an artificial form imposed on figures, a decorative device that produced the desired effect of elegance but that had nothing to do with figure structure. In fact, in our example, the body is quite lost behind the heavy drapery, which, deeply cut and hollowed, almost denies the figure a solid existence. The ornamental line the sculptor created with the flexible fabric is analogous to the complex, restless tracery of the Late Gothic style in architecture, which dominated northern Europe in the fourteenth and fifteenth centuries.

A FLAMBOYANT CHURCH IN NORMANDY

The change from Rayonnant architecture to the Late Gothic, or *Flamboyant,* style (named for the flamelike appearance of its pointed bar tracery), occurred in the fourteenth century. The style reached its florid maturity nearly a century later. This period was a difficult one for the French monarchy. Long wars against England and the duchy of Burgundy sapped its economic and cultural strength, and building projects in the royal domain either ceased or never began. Archi-

tects accepted the new style most enthusiastically in regions outside the Île-de-France.

Normandy is particularly rich in Flamboyant architecture, and the church of Saint-Maclou (FIG. **18-28**) in Rouen, its capital, is a masterpiece of the Flamboyant style. The church is tiny (only about seventy-five feet high and one hundred eighty feet long) compared to the great Gothic cathedrals. Its facade presents a sharp contrast with the High Gothic style of the thirteenth century (compare FIGS. 18-21 and 18-23). The five portals (two of them blind) bend outward in an arc. Ornate gables crown the doorways, pierced through and filled with wiry, "flickering" Flamboyant tracery made up of curves and countercurves that form brittle decorative webs and mask the building's structure. The transparency of the pinnacles over the doorways permits visitors to see the central rose window and the flying buttresses, even though they are set well back from the facade. The overlapping of all features, pierced as they are, confuses the structural lines and produces a bewildering complexity of views that is the hallmark of the Flamboyant style.

A DOUBLY FORTIFIED TOWN

The Gothic age was truly "the age of the great cathedrals," but people, of course, also needed and built secular structures such as town halls, palaces, and private residences. In an age of frequent warfare, the feudal barons often constructed fortified castles in places enemies could not easily access. Sometimes thick defensive wall circuits or *ramparts* enclosed entire towns. In time, however, purely defensive wars became obsolete due to the invention of artillery and improvements in siege craft. The fortress

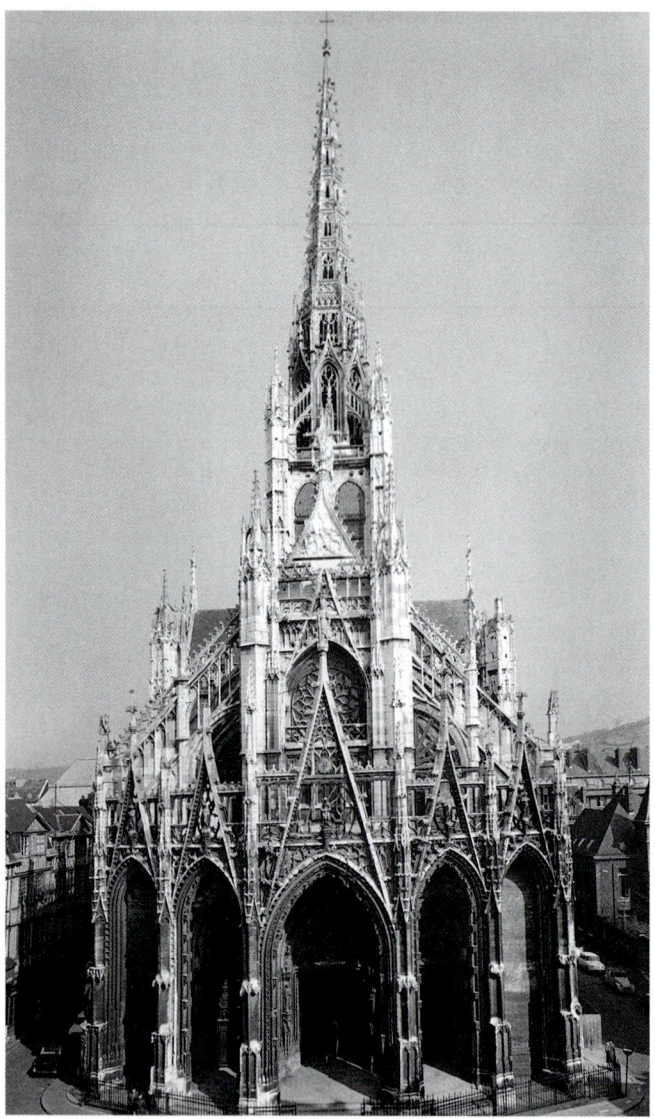

18-28   West facade of Saint-Maclou, Rouen, France, ca. 1500–1514.

era gradually passed, and throughout Europe once-mighty ramparts fell into ruin.

One of the most famous Gothic fortified towns is Carcassonne (FIG. **18-29**) in Languedoc in southern France. It was the regional center of resistance to the northern forces of royal France. Built on a hill bounded by the Aude River, Carcassonne had been fortified since Roman times. It had Visigothic walls dating from the sixth century, but in the twelfth century masons reinforced them with bastions and towers. The double ring of walls discouraged any attacking force. *Crenellations* (notches) in the *battlements* (low screen walls) protected guards patrolling the stone ring surrounding the town. Carcassonne might be made to surrender but could not easily be taken by storm.

Within the town's double walls was a fortified castle (FIG. 18-29, left) with a massive attached *keep,* a secure tower that could serve as a place of last refuge. Balancing that center of secular power was the bishop's seat, the Cathedral of Saint-Nazaire (FIG. 18-29, right). The small church, built between 1269 and 1329, may have been the work of an architect brought in from northern France. In any case, Saint-Nazaire's builders were certainly familiar with the latest developments in architecture in the Île-de-France. Today, Carcassonne provides a rare glimpse of what was once a familiar sight in Gothic France: a tightly contained complex of castle, cathedral, and town within towered walls.

A PROSPEROUS MERCHANT'S HOME   In the late Middle Ages, a new class of wealthy merchants rose to prominence throughout Europe. Although their fortunes may not have equaled those of the hereditary royalty, their power and influence were still enormous. One such figure was the French trader and financier Jacques Coeur (1395–1456), whose astonishing career illustrates how wealth and power could be won and lost by enterprising private citizens. Coeur had banking houses in every city of France and many abroad.

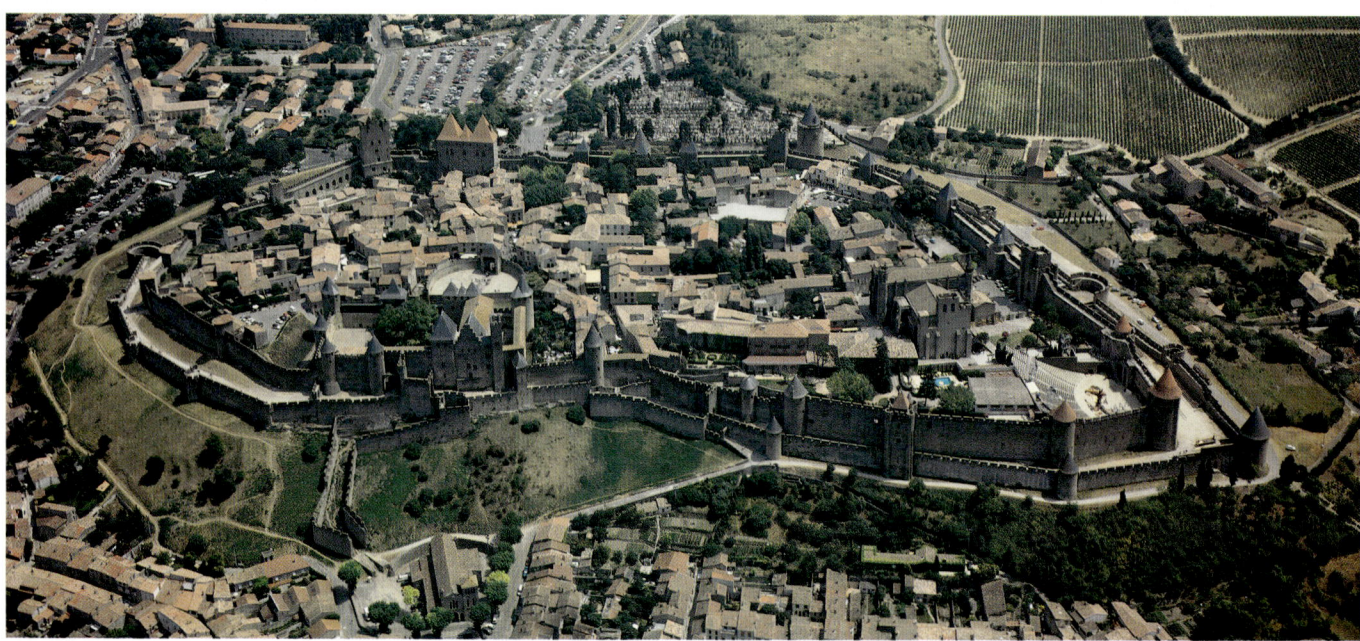

18-29   Aerial view of the fortified town of Carcassonne, France. Bastions and towers, twelfth–thirteenth centuries, restored by EUGÈNE VIOLLET-LE-DUC in the nineteenth century.

The broad facade's focus is a tall central section with a very steep pyramidal roof, a spire-capped tower with Flamboyant tracery, a large pointed-arch stained-glass window, and two doorways (one for pedestrians and the larger one for horses and carriages). The elegant canopied niche beneath the great window once housed a royal equestrian statue. A comparable statue of Coeur on horseback dominated the facade opening onto the interior courtyard. An unusual feature of the external facade is the pair of false windows with life-size relief sculptures of a male and a female servant looking down upon passersby in the street. Jacques Coeur's house is not only a splendid example of Late Gothic architecture but also a monumental symbol of the period's new secular spirit—an expression of the triumph of city culture, of capital accumulation, and of the desire for worldly convenience and proud display.

Book Illumination and Luxury Arts

Paris's claim as the intellectual center of Gothic Europe (see "Paris: The Intellectual Capital of Gothic Europe," page 496) did not rest solely on the stature of its university faculty and on the reputation of its architects, masons, sculptors, and stained-glass makers. The city was also a renowned center for the production of fine books. The famous Florentine poet Dante Alighieri (1265–1321), in fact, referred to Paris in his *Divine Comedy* of ca. 1310–1320 as the city famed for the art of illumination.[2] Indeed, the Gothic period is when book manufacture shifted from monks and nuns toiling for God's glory in scriptoria shut off from the world to urban workshops. Owned and staffed by laypersons who sold their products to the royal family, scholars, and prosperous merchants, these for-profit secular businesses, concentrated in Paris, were the forerunners of modern publishing houses.

THE ART OF GEOMETRY One of the most intriguing Parisian manuscripts preserved today was not, however, produced for sale. It is the personal sketchbook compiled by VILLARD DE HONNECOURT, an early thirteenth-century master mason. Its pages contain details of buildings, plans of choirs with radiating chapels, church towers, lifting devices, a sawmill, stained-glass windows, and other subjects of obvious interest to architects and masons. But also sprinkled liberally throughout the pages are drawings depicting religious and worldly figures, as well as animals, some realistic and others purely fantastic.

On the page we illustrate (FIG. **18-31**), Villard demonstrated the value of the *ars de geometria* (art of geometry) to artists. He showed that both natural forms and buildings are based on simple geometric shapes such as the square, circle, and triangle. Even where he claimed to have drawn his animals from nature, he composed his figures around a skeleton not of bones but of abstract geometric forms. Geometry was, in Villard's words, "strong help in drawing figures."

But geometry played a symbolic as well as a practical role in Gothic art and architecture. Gothic artists, architects, and theologians alike thought the triangle, for example, embodied the idea of the Trinity of God the Father, Christ, and the

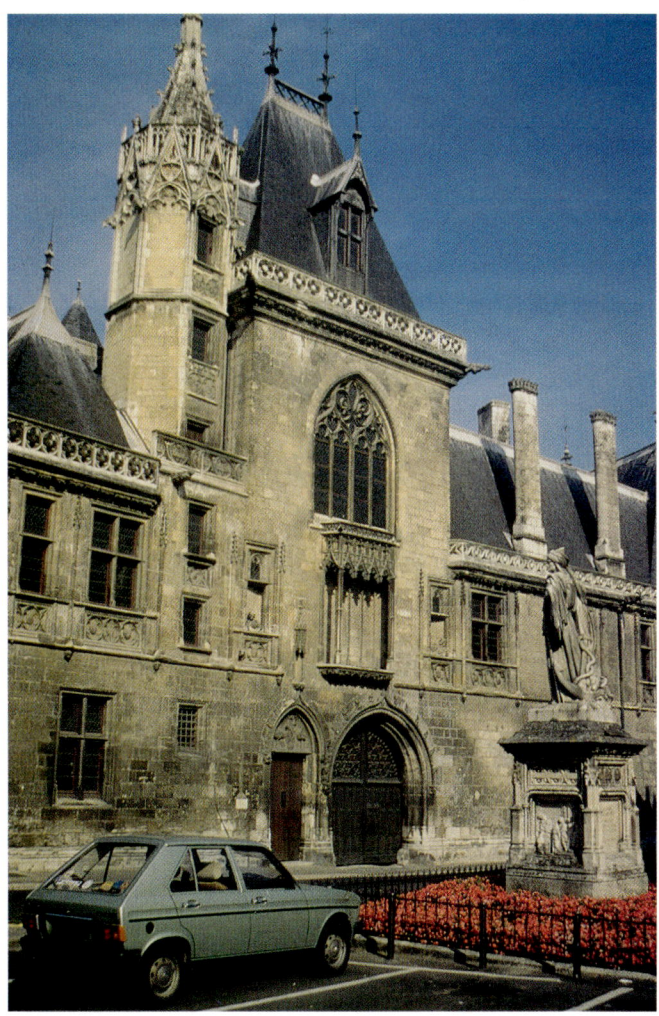

18-30 House of Jacques Coeur, Bourges, France, 1443–1451.

He employed more than three hundred agents and competed with the great trading republics of Italy. His merchant ships filled the Mediterranean. With the papacy's permission, he traded widely with the Muslims of Egypt and the Middle East and gained concessions there that benefited French commerce for centuries. He was financial adviser to King Charles VII of France and a friend of Pope Nicholas V. The animosity of hundreds of his highborn debtors and competitors eventually led to Coeur's downfall. His enemies framed him on an absurd charge of having poisoned Agnes Sorel, the king's mistress, and he was imprisoned. His vast wealth and property were confiscated and distributed among the king's people. Coeur escaped from prison and made his way to Rome, where the pope warmly received him. He died of fever while leading a fleet of papal war galleys in the eastern Mediterranean.

Jacques Coeur's great town house (FIG. **18-30**), built between 1443 and 1451 in his native city of Bourges, still stands. It is the best preserved example of Late Gothic domestic architecture. The house's plan is irregular, with the units arranged around an open courtyard. The service areas (maintenance shops and storage, servants' quarters, baths) occupy the ground level. The upper stories house the great hall and auxiliary rooms used for offices and family living rooms.

18-31 VILLARD DE HONNECOURT, figures based on geometric shapes, folio 18 verso of a sketchbook, from Paris, ca. 1220–1235. Ink on vellum, $9\frac{1}{4}'' \times 6''$. Bibliothèque Nationale, Paris.

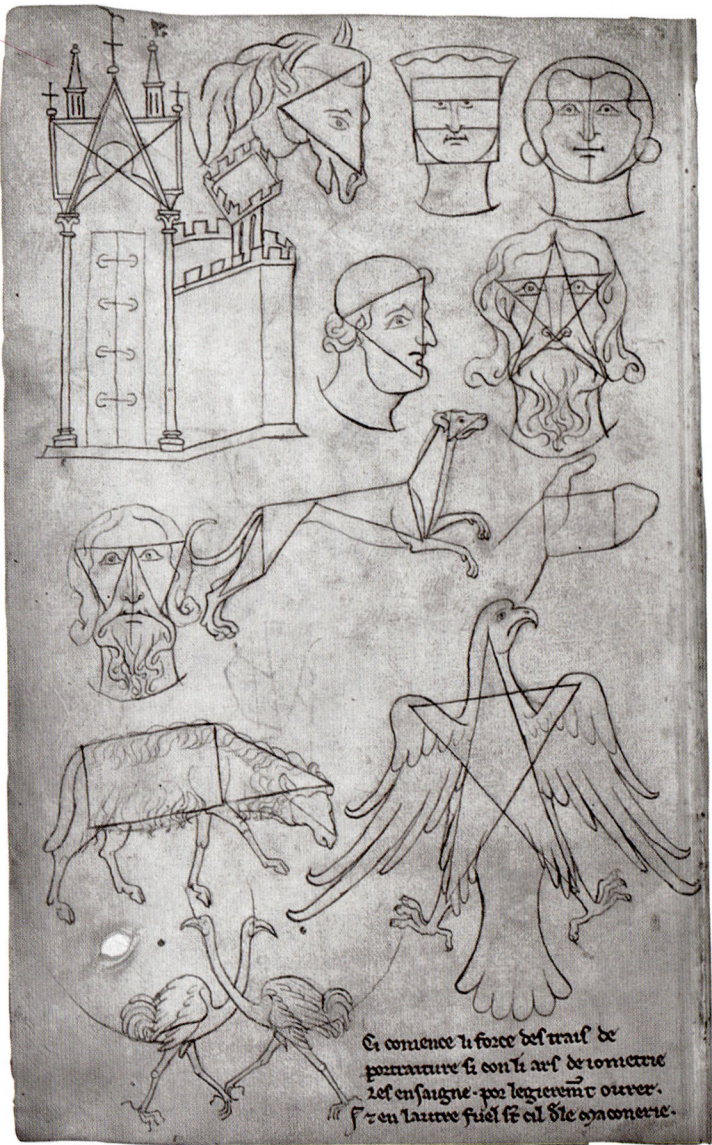

Holy Spirit. The circle, which has neither a beginning nor an end, symbolized the eternity of the one God. When Gothic architects based their designs on the art of geometry, building their forms out of abstract shapes laden with symbolic meaning, they believed they were working according to the divinely established laws of nature.

GOD AS ARCHITECT OF THE WORLD   A vivid illustration of this concept appears as the frontispiece (FIG. **18-32**) of a moralized Bible produced in Paris during the 1220s. *Moralized Bibles* are heavily illustrated, each page pairing Old and New Testament episodes with illustrations explaining their moral significance. The page we show does not conform to this formula because it is the introduction to all that follows. God appears as the architect of the world, shaping the universe with the aid of a compass. Within the perfect circle already created are the spherical sun and moon and the unformed matter that will become the earth once God applies the same geometric principles to it. In contrast to the biblical account of Creation, where God made the world by sheer force of will and a simple "Let there be . . ." command, the Gothic artist portrayed God as an industrious architect, creating the universe with some of the same tools mortal builders used.

A BIBLE FIT FOR A QUEEN   Not surprisingly, most of the finest Gothic books known today belonged to the French monarchy. Saint Louis in particular was an avid collector of both secular and religious books. The library he and his royal predecessors and successors formed was vast and eventually formed the core of France's national library, the Bibliothèque Nationale. One of the books the royal family commissioned is a moralized Bible now in the collection of New York's Pierpont Morgan Library. Louis's mother, Blanche of Castile, ordered the Bible during her regency (1226–1234) for her teenage son. The dedication page (FIG. **18-33**) has a costly gold background and depicts Blanche and Louis enthroned beneath triple-lobed arches and miniature cityscapes. The latter can be compared to the architectural canopies above the heads of contemporaneous French portal statues (FIG. 18-22). Below, in similar architectural frames, are a monk and a scribe. The older clergyman dictates a sacred text to his young apprentice. The scribe already has divided his page into two columns of four roundels each, a format often used for the paired illustrations of moralized Bibles. The inspirations for such designs were probably the roundels of Gothic stained-glass windows (compare the borders of the *Belle Verrière* window at Chartres, FIG. 18-14, and the windows of Louis's own, later, Sainte-Chapelle, FIG. 18-26).

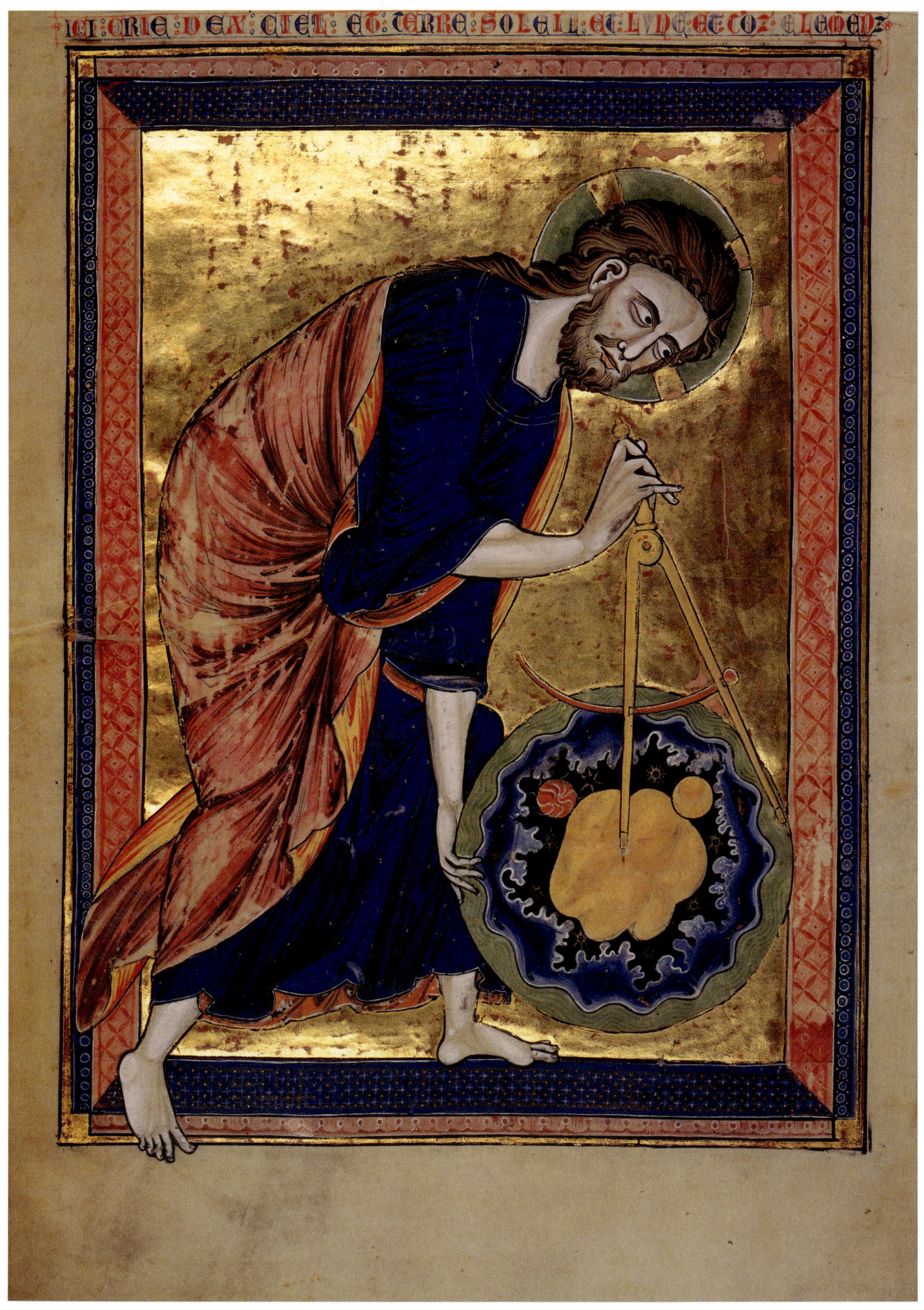

18-32 God as architect of the world, folio 1 verso of a moralized Bible, from Paris, ca. 1220–1230. Ink, tempera, and gold leaf on vellum, 1′ 1½″ × 8¼″. Österreichische Nationalbibliothek, Vienna.

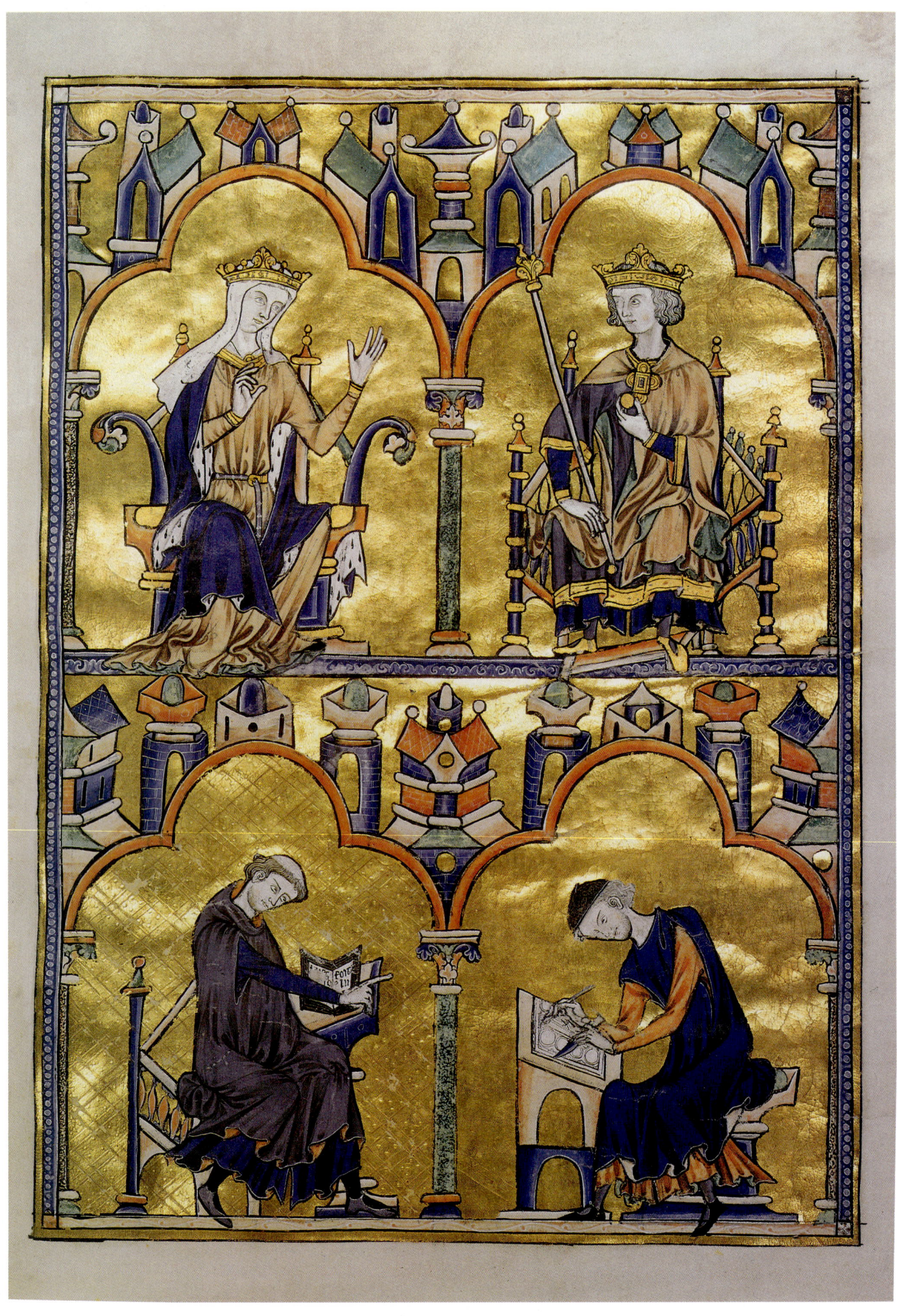

18-33 Blanche of Castile, Louis IX, and two monks, dedication page (folio 8 recto) of a moralized Bible, from Paris, France, 1226–1234. Ink, tempera, and gold leaf on vellum, 1′ 3″ × 10½″. Pierpont Morgan Library, New York.

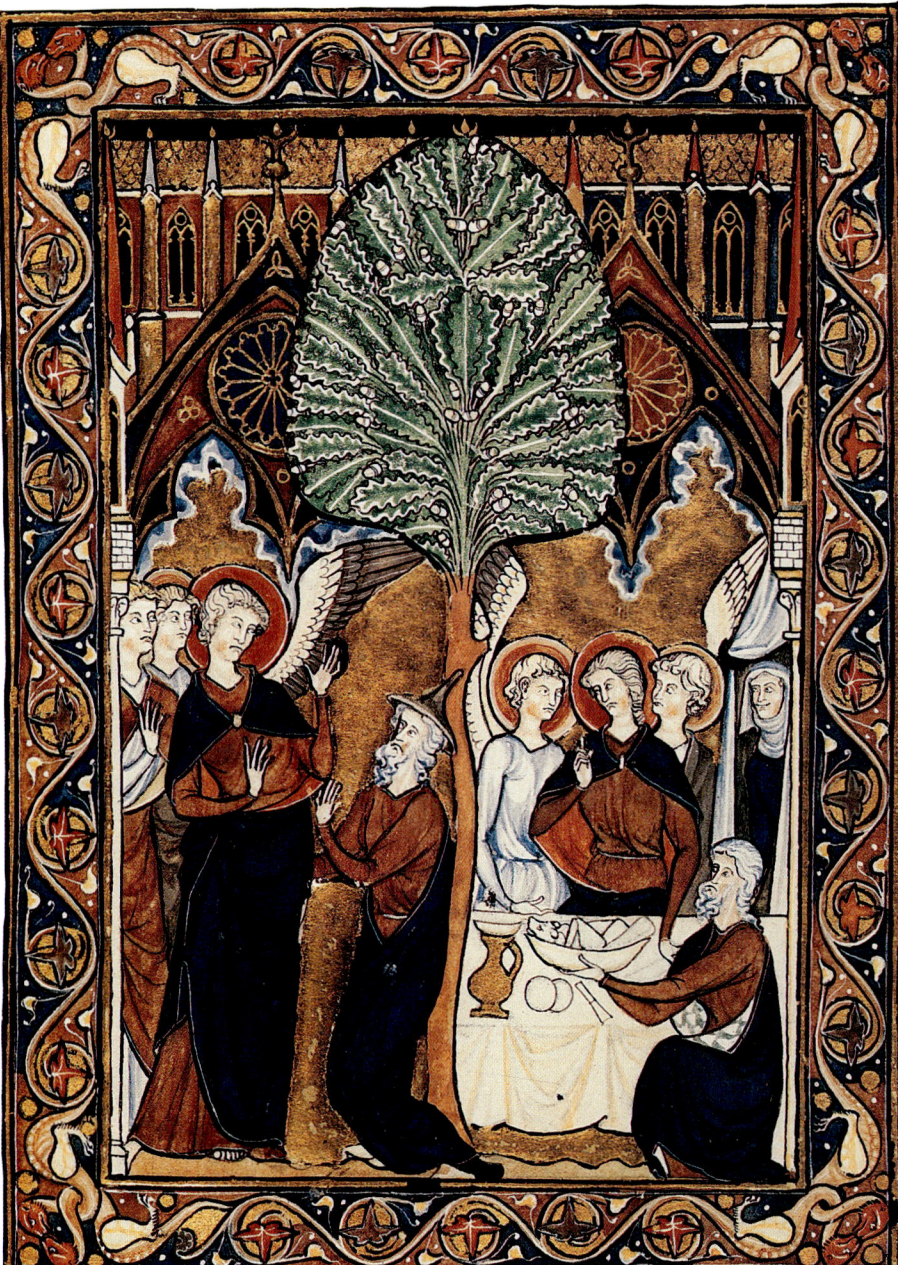

18-34 Abraham and the three angels, folio 7 verso of the *Psalter of Saint Louis,* from Paris, France, 1253–1270. Ink, tempera, and gold leaf on vellum, 5″ × 3½″. Bibliothèque Nationale, Paris.

The picture of Gothic book production on the dedication page of Blanche of Castile's moralized Bible is a very abbreviated one. The manufacturing process used in the workshops of thirteenth-century Paris involved many steps and numerous specialized artists, scribes, and assistants of varying skill levels. The Benedictine abbot Johannes Trithemius (1462–1516) described the way books were made in late medieval Europe in his treatise *In Praise of Scribes:*

> If you do not know how to write, you still can assist the scribes in various ways. One of you can correct what another has written. Another can add the rubrics [headings] to the corrected text. A third can add initials and signs of division. Still another can arrange the leaves and attach the binding. Another of you can prepare the covers, the leather, the buckles and clasps. All sorts of assistance can be offered the scribe to help him pursue his work without interruption. He needs many things which can be prepared by others: parchment cut, flattened and ruled for script, ready ink and pens. You will always find something with which to help the scribe.[3]

The preparation of the illuminated pages also involved several hands. Some artists, for example, specialized in painting borders or initials. Only the workshop head or one of the most advanced assistants would paint the main figural scenes. Given this division of labor and the assembly-line nature of Gothic book production, it is astonishing how uniform the style is on a single page, as well as from page to page, in most illuminated manuscripts.

STAINED GLASS AND A ROYAL PSALTER   The golden background of Blanche's Bible is unusual and has no parallel in Gothic windows. But the radiance of stained glass probably inspired the glowing color of other thirteenth-century Parisian illuminated manuscripts. In some cases, masters in the same urban workshop produced both glass and books. Many art historians believe that the *Psalter of Saint Louis* (FIG. **18-34**) is one of several books produced in Paris for Saint Louis by artists associated with those who made the

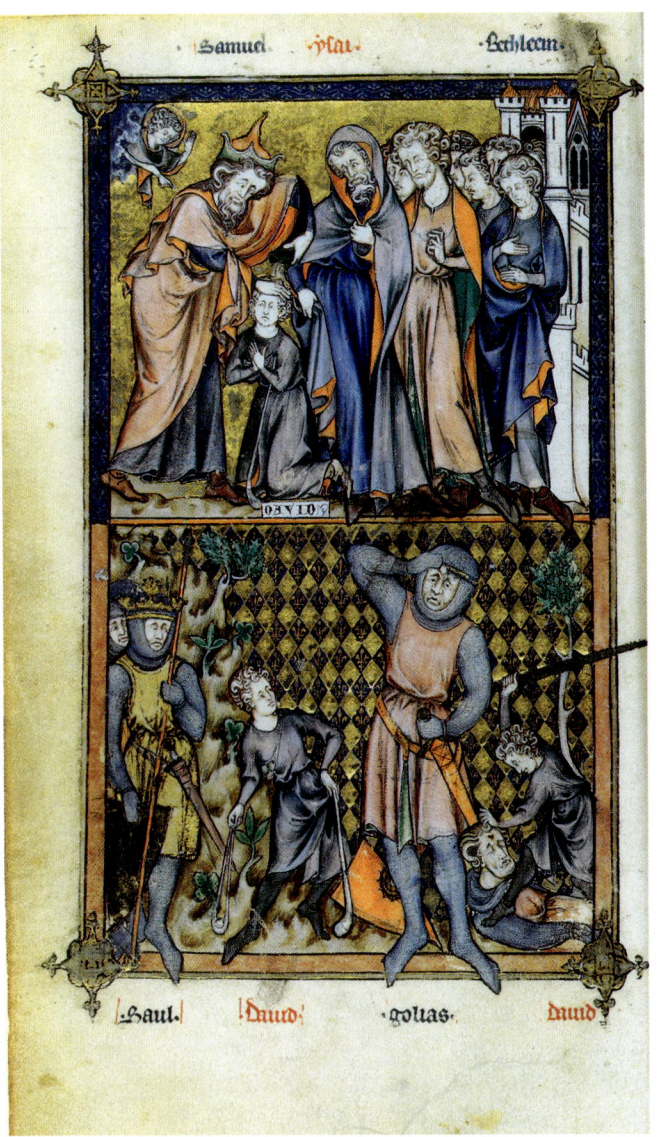

18-35   MASTER HONORÉ, David anointed by Samuel and battle of David and Goliath, folio 7 verso of the *Breviary of Philippe le Bel,* from Paris, France, 1296. Ink and tempera on vellum, $7\frac{7}{8}'' \times 4\frac{7}{8}''$. Bibliothèque Nationale, Paris.

Sarah peers at them from a tent. The figures' delicate features and the linear wavy strands of their hair have parallels in Blanche of Castile's moralized Bible, as well as in Parisian stained glass. The elegant proportions, facial expressions, theatrical gestures, and swaying poses are characteristic of the Parisian court style admired throughout Europe. A later example of this mannered style in sculpture, complete with the exaggerated contrapposto of the angel in the left foreground, is the *Virgin of Paris* (FIG. 18-27), already discussed.

A FRENCH KING'S PRAYER BOOK   As in the Romanesque period, some Gothic manuscript illuminators signed their work. The names of others appear in royal accounts of payments made and similar official documents. One of the artists who produced books for the French court was MASTER HONORÉ, whose Parisian workshop was on the street known today as rue Boutebrie. Honoré illuminated a *breviary* (a book of selected prayers and psalms) for Philippe le Bel (Philip the Fair, r. 1285–1314) in 1296. The page we illustrate (FIG. **18-35**) features two Old Testament scenes involving David. In the upper panel, Samuel anoints the youthful David. Below, while King Saul looks on, David prepares to hurl his slingshot at his most famous opponent, the giant Goliath (who already touches the wound on his forehead!). And then, in a classic example of continuous narration, David slays Goliath with his sword.

Master Honoré's linear treatment of hair, his figures' delicate hands and gestures, and their elegant swaying postures are typical of Parisian painting of the time. But this painter was much more interested than most of his colleagues in giving his figures sculptural volume and showing the play of light on their bodies. Honoré, however, was not concerned with locating his figures in space. The Goliath panel in the *Breviary of Philippe le Bel* has a textilelike decorative background, and the feet of Honoré's figures frequently overlap the border. Compared to his contemporaries, Master Honoré pioneered naturalism in figure painting. But he still approached the art of book illumination as a decorator of two-dimensional pages. He did not embrace the classical notion that a painting should be an illusionistic window into a three-dimensional world.

JEAN PUCELLE AND ITALY   David and Saul also are the subjects of a miniature painting at the top left of an elaborately decorated text page in the *Belleville Breviary* (FIG. **18-36**). JEAN PUCELLE of Paris illuminated it around 1325. He went far beyond Honoré and other French artists by placing his fully modeled figures in three-dimensional architectural settings rendered in convincing perspective. For example, Pucelle painted Saul as a weighty figure seated on a throne seen in a three-quarter view, and he meticulously depicted the receding coffers of the barrel vault over the young David's head. Such "stage sets" already had become commonplace in Italian painting, and Pucelle seems to have visited Italy and studied Duccio's work in Siena (see Chapter 19). Pucelle's (or one of his assistant's) renditions of plants, a bird, butterflies, a dragonfly, a fish, a snail, and a monkey also reveal a keen interest in and close observation of the natural world. Nonetheless, in the *Belleville Breviary* the text still dominates the figures, and the artist (and his patron) delighted in ornamental flourishes, fancy initial letters, and abstract pattern. In that respect, comparisons to monu-

stained glass for his Sainte-Chapelle. Certainly, the painted architectural setting in Saint Louis's psalter reflects the pierced screenlike lightness and transparency of royal buildings such as Sainte-Chapelle. The painted figures also express the same aristocratic elegance as the Rayonnant "court style" of architecture royal Paris favored. The intense colors, especially the blues, emulate glass. The borders resemble glass partitioned by leading. And the gables, pierced by rose windows with bar tracery, are standard Rayonnant architectural features.

The page from the *Psalter of Saint Louis* shown here (FIG. 18-34) represents Abraham and the three angels. Christians believed the Old Testament story prefigured the Christian Trinity (see "Jewish Subjects in Christian Art," Chapter 11, page 305), and the subject was also popular in Byzantine art (see FIGS. 12-8 and 12-34). The Gothic artist included two episodes on the same page, separated by the tree of Mamre mentioned in the Bible. At the left, Abraham greets the three angels. In the other scene, he entertains them while his wife

gifts to the churches they frequented. The Virgin Mary was a favored subject, reflecting her new prominence in the iconography of Gothic portal sculpture.

Perhaps the finest of these costly statuettes is the large (more than two feet tall) silver-gilt figurine known as the *Virgin of Jeanne d'Evreux* (FIG. **18-37**). The queen, wife of Charles IV (r. 1322–1328), donated the image of the Virgin and Child to the royal abbey church of Saint-Denis in 1339. Mary stands on a rectangular base decorated with enamel scenes of Christ's Passion. (Some art historians think the enamels are Jean Pucelle's work.) But no hint of grief appears in the beautiful young Mary's face. The Christ Child, also without a care in the world, playfully reaches for his mother. The elegant proportions of the two figures, Mary's swaying posture, the heavy drapery folds, and the intimate human characterization of the

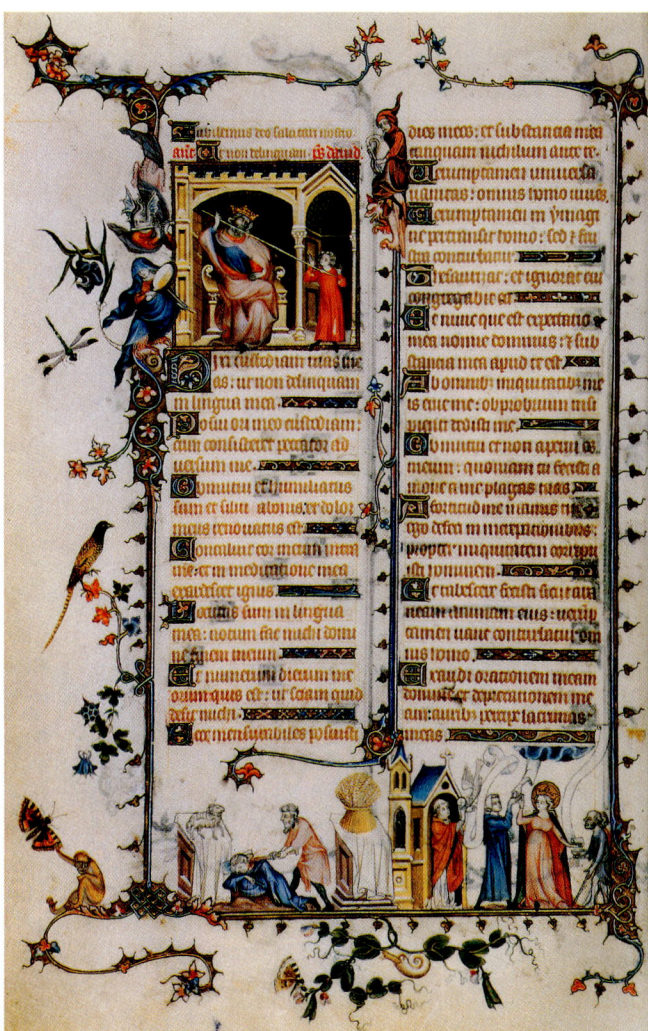

18-36 JEAN PUCELLE, David before Saul, folio 24 verso of the *Belleville Breviary*, from Paris, France, ca. 1325. Ink and tempera on vellum, $9\frac{1}{2}'' \times 6\frac{3}{4}''$. Bibliothèque Nationale, Paris.

mental panel paintings are inappropriate. Pucelle's breviary remains firmly in the tradition of book illumination.

The *Belleville Breviary* is of special interest because Pucelle's and some of his assistants' names appear at the end of the book, in a memorandum recording the payment they received for their work. Inscriptions in other Gothic illuminated books regularly state the production costs—the prices paid for materials, especially gold, and for the execution of initials, figures, flowery script, and other embellishments. By this time, illuminators were professional guild members, and their personal reputation, like modern "brand names," guaranteed the quality of their work. Though the cost of materials was still the major factor determining a book's price, individual skill and reputation increasingly decided the value of the illuminator's services. The centuries-old monopoly of the Christian Church in bookmaking had ended.

A VIRGIN AND CHILD FOR SAINT-DENIS
The royal family also patronized goldsmiths, silversmiths, and other artists specializing in the production of luxury works in metal and enamel for churches, palaces, and private homes. Especially popular among the wealthy were statuettes of sacred figures purchased either for their private devotion or as

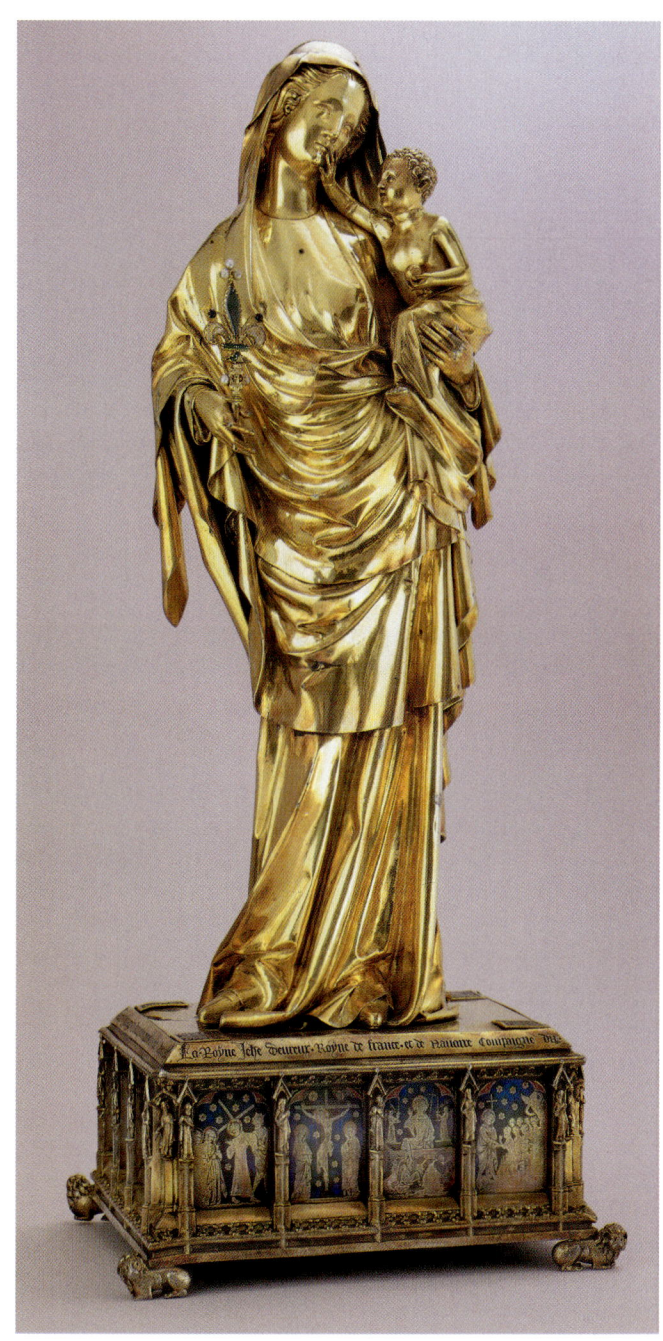

18-37 *Virgin of Jeanne d'Evreux,* from the abbey church of Saint-Denis, France, 1339. Silver gilt and enamel, $2' 3\frac{1}{2}''$ high. Louvre, Paris.

holy figures are also features of the roughly contemporary *Virgin of Paris* (FIG. 18-27). The monumental-stone sculptor and the royal silversmith working at small scale approached the representation of the Virgin and Child in a similar fashion.

In the *Virgin of Jeanne d'Evreux,* as in the *Virgin of Paris,* Mary appears not only as the Mother of Christ but as the Queen of Heaven. The Saint-Denis Mary also originally had a crown on her head, and the scepter she holds is in the form of the *fleur-de-lis,* the French monarchy's floral emblem. The statuette also served as a reliquary. The Virgin's scepter contained hairs believed to come from Mary's head.

THE CASTLE OF LOVE   Gothic artists produced luxurious objects for secular, as well as religious, contexts. Sometimes they decorated these costly pieces with stories of courtly love inspired by the romantic literature of the day, such as the famous story of Lancelot and Queen Guinevere, wife of King Arthur of Camelot. The French poet Chrétien de Troyes recorded their famous affair in the late twelfth century.

One of the most interesting objects of this type is a woman's jewelry box adorned with ivory relief panels, now in the Walters Art Gallery in Baltimore. The theme of the panel illustrated here (FIG. **18-38**) is related to the *Romance of the Rose* by Guillaume de Lorris, written ca. 1225–1235 and completed by Jean de Meung between 1275 and 1280. At the left the sculptor carved the allegory of the siege of the Castle of Love. Gothic knights attempt to capture love's fortress by shooting flowers from their bows and hurling baskets of roses over the walls from catapults. Among the castle's defenders is Cupid, who aims his arrow at one of the knights while a comrade scales the walls on a ladder. The scene in the lid's two central sections shows two knights jousting on horseback, ac-

companied by the sound of blaring trumpets. Several maidens look down on the contest from a balcony and cheer the knights on. A youth in the crowd holds a hunting falcon. The sport was a favorite pastime of the leisure class in the late Middle Ages. At the right, the victorious knight receives his prize (a bouquet of roses) from a chastely dressed maiden on horseback. The scenes on the casket's sides include the famous medieval allegory of female virtue, the legend of the *unicorn,* a white horse with a single ivory horn. Only a virgin could attract the rare animal, and any woman who could do so thereby also demonstrated her moral purity. Religious themes may have monopolized artistic production for churches in the Gothic age, but secular themes figured prominently in private contexts. Unfortunately, very few examples of the latter survive. The Baltimore casket is one of the best.

GOTHIC OUTSIDE OF FRANCE

In 1269, the prior (deputy abbot) of the church of Saint Peter at Wimpfen-im-Tal in the German Rhineland hired "a very experienced architect who had recently come from the city of Paris" to rebuild his monastery church.[4] The architect reconstructed the church *opere francigeno* (in the French manner)—that is, in the Gothic style of the Île-de-France. The spread of the Parisian Gothic style had begun even earlier, but in the second half of the thirteenth century the new style became dominant throughout western Europe. European architecture did not, however, turn Gothic all at once nor in a uniform way. Almost everywhere, patrons and builders modified the "court style" of the Île-de-France according to local preferences. Be-

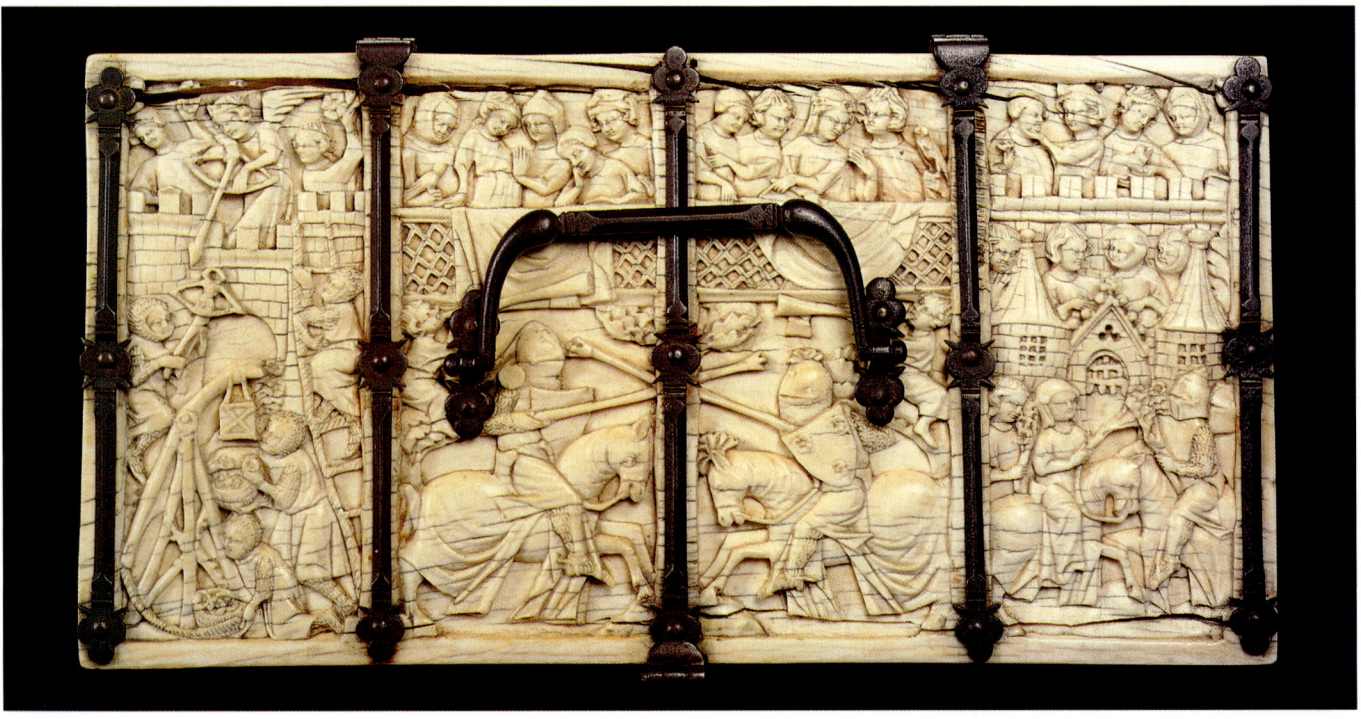

18-38   The Castle of Love and knights jousting, lid of a jewelry casket, from Paris, France, ca. 1330–1350. Ivory and iron, $4\frac{1}{2}$″ × $9\frac{3}{4}$″. Walters Art Gallery, Baltimore.

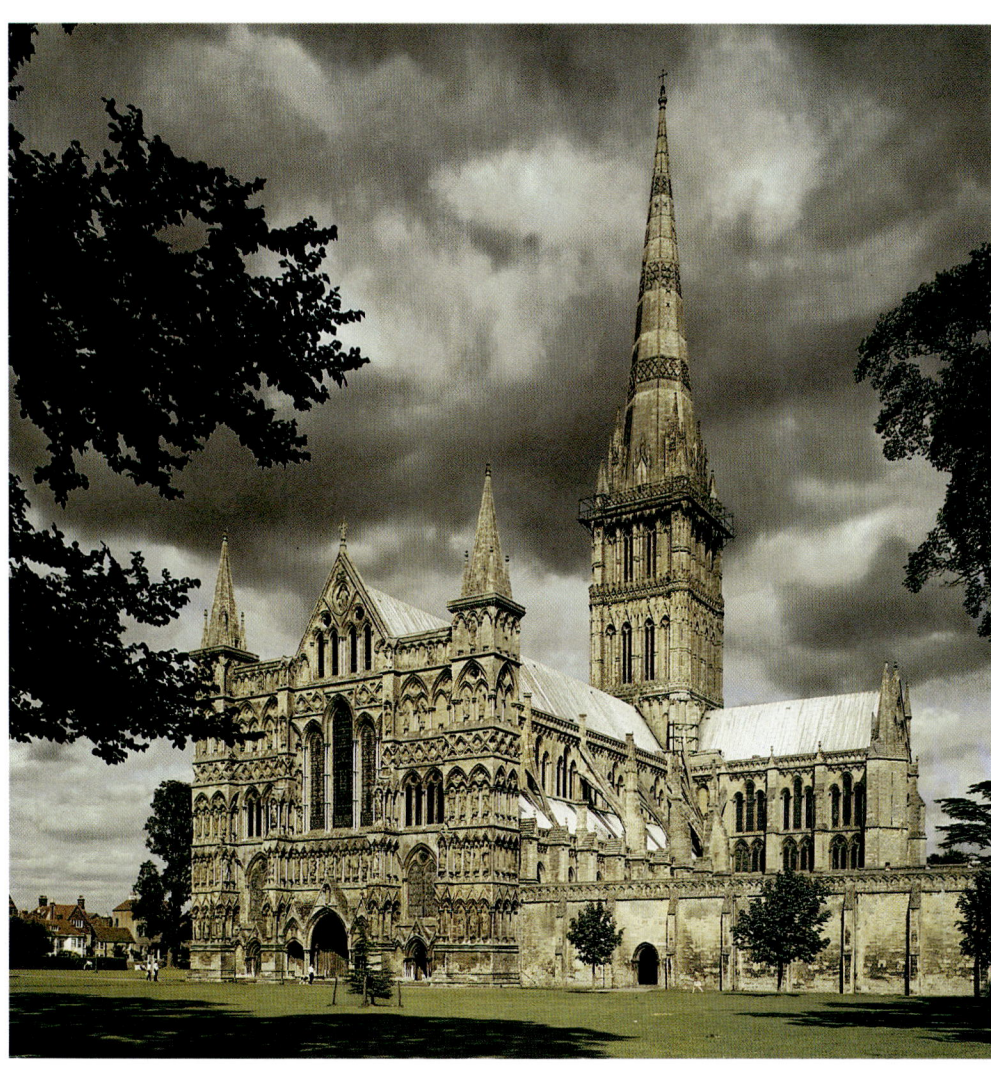

18-39 Salisbury Cathedral (view from the southwest), Salisbury, England, 1220–1258; west facade completed 1265; spire ca. 1320–1330.

cause the old Romanesque traditions lingered on in many places, each area, marrying its local Romanesque design to the new style, developed its own brand of Gothic architecture.

England

HORIZONTALITY AND COLOR AT SALISBURY
Salisbury Cathedral (FIG. **18-39**) embodies the essential characteristics of English Gothic architecture. Begun in 1220, the same year work started on Amiens Cathedral (FIGS. 18-18 to 18-21), Salisbury Cathedral was mostly completed in about forty years. The two cathedrals are, therefore, almost exactly contemporary, and the differences between them are very instructive. Although Salisbury's facade has lancet windows and blind arcades with pointed arches and statuary, it presents a striking contrast to French designs (compare Amiens, FIG. 18-21, and Reims, FIG. 18-23). The English facade is a wide and squat screen in front of the nave. Not only is the soaring height of the French facades absent, but also the English facade is wider than the building behind it. Its design does not correspond to the three-part division of the interior (nave and two aisles). Also different is the emphasis on the great crossing tower (added ca. 1320–1330), which dominates the silhouette. Salisbury's height is modest compared with that of

Amiens and Reims. And because height is not a decisive factor in the English building, the architect used the flying buttress sparingly and as a rigid prop, rather than as an integral part of the vaulting system within the church. In short, the English builders adopted some of the superficial motifs of French Gothic architecture but did not embrace its structural logic or emphasis on height.

Equally distinctive is the long rectilinear plan (FIG. **18-40**), with its double transept and flat eastern end. The latter

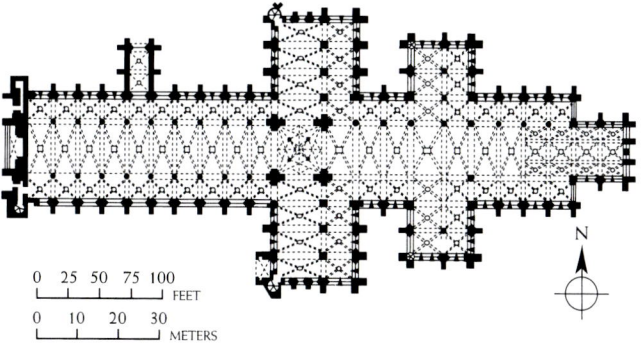

18-40 Plan of Salisbury Cathedral, Salisbury, England, 1220–1258.

18-41   Nave of Salisbury Cathedral (view facing east), Salisbury, England, 1220–1258.

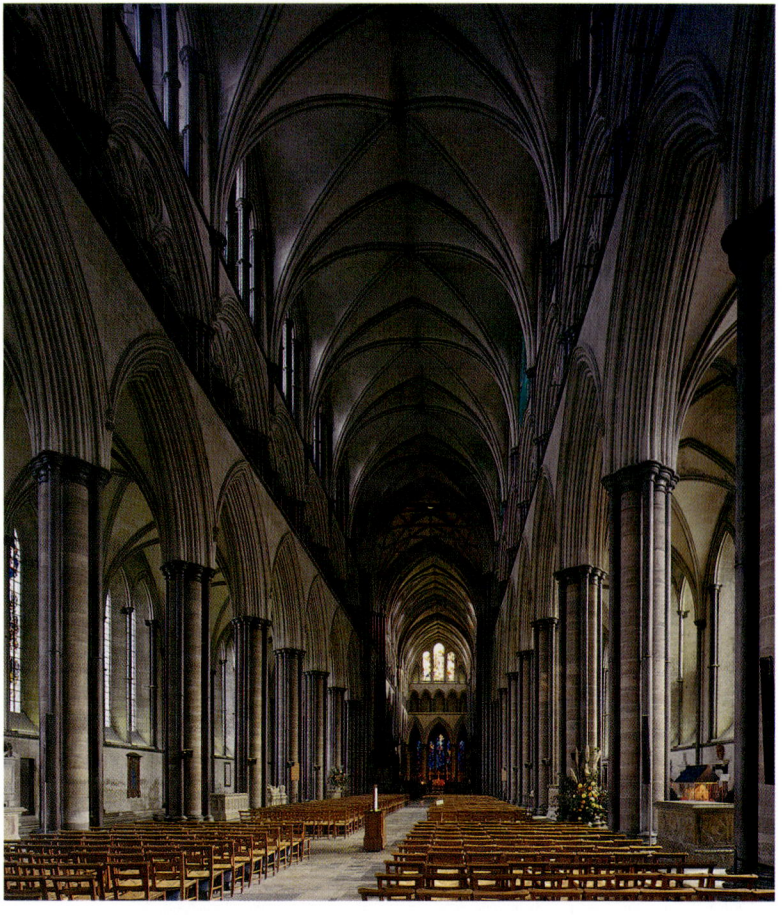

feature was characteristic of Cistercian churches and had been favored in England since Romanesque times. The interior (FIG. **18-41**), although Gothic in its three-story elevation, pointed arches, four-part rib vaults, and compound piers, conspicuously departs from the French Gothic style. The pier colonnettes stop at the springing of the nave arches and do not connect with the vault ribs (compare FIGS. 18-19 and 18-20). Instead, the vault ribs rise from corbels in the triforium, producing a strong horizontal emphasis. The rich color contrast between the light stone of the walls and vaults and the dark Purbeck marble used for the triforium moldings and corbels, compound pier responds, and other details underscores this horizontality. Once again, however, the French Gothic style's impact is clearly visible in the decorative details, especially the tracery of the triforium. Nonetheless, visitors to Salisbury could not mistake the English cathedral for a French one.

FROM DECORATED TO PERPENDICULAR   Early on, English architecture found its native language in the elaboration of architectural pattern for its own sake (compare the decorative patterning of the Romanesque piers of Durham Cathedral, FIG. 17-12). Structural logic, expressed in the building fabric, was secondary. The pier, wall, and vault elements, still relatively simple at Salisbury, became increasingly complex and decorative in the fourteenth century. Architectural historians usually call the English Gothic architectural style of that period the Decorated Style. The choir of Gloucester Cathedral (FIG. **18-42**), remodeled about a century after Salisbury, illustrates the transition from the Deco-

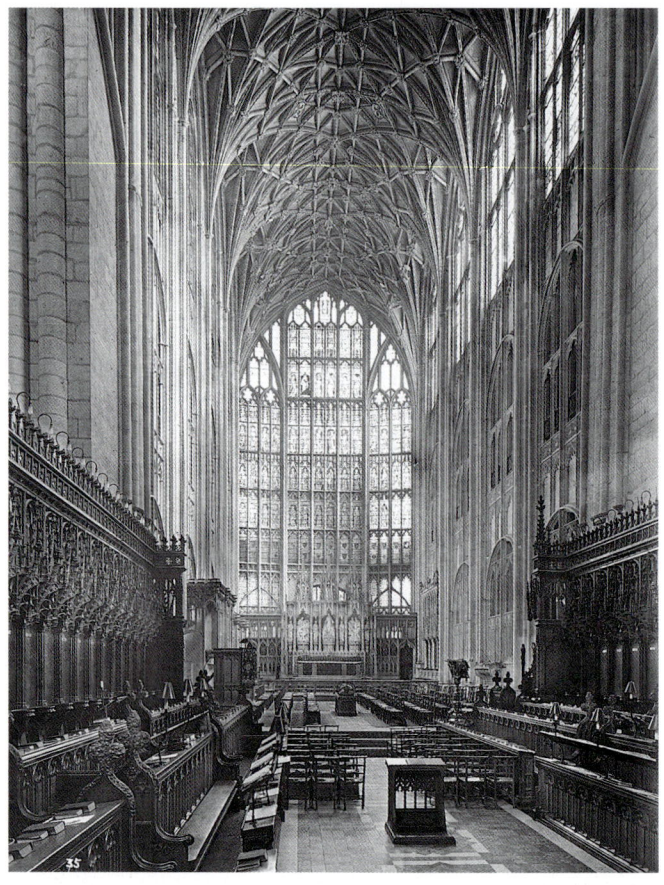

18-42   Choir of Gloucester Cathedral (view facing east), Gloucester, England, 1332–1357.

rated to the last English Gothic style, the Perpendicular Style. The newer style took its name from the pronounced verticality of its decorative details, in contrast to the horizontal emphasis of Salisbury and early English Gothic.

A single enormous window divided into tiers of small windows of like shape and proportion fills the characteristically flat east end of Gloucester Cathedral. At the top, two slender lancets flank a wider central section that also ends in a pointed arch. The design has much in common with the screen facade of Salisbury, but the proportions are different. Vertical, as opposed to horizontal, lines dominate. In the choir wall, the architect also erased Salisbury's strong horizontal accents, as the vertical wall elements lift directly from the floor to the vaulting, unifying the walls with the vaults in the French manner. The vault ribs, which designers had begun to multiply soon after Salisbury, are at Gloucester a dense thicket of entirely ornamental strands that serve no structural purpose. The choir, in fact, is not covered by rib vaults at all but by a continuous Romanesque barrel vault with applied Gothic ornament. In the Gloucester choir the taste for decorative surfaces triumphed over structural "honesty."

"FAN VAULTS" IN A KING'S CHAPEL The decorative and structure-disguising qualities of the Perpendicular Style became even more pronounced in its late phases. A primary example is the early sixteenth-century ceiling of the Chapel of Henry VII (FIG. **18-43**) adjoining Westminster Abbey in London. In this chapel, the earlier linear play of ribs became a kind of architectural embroidery, pulled into

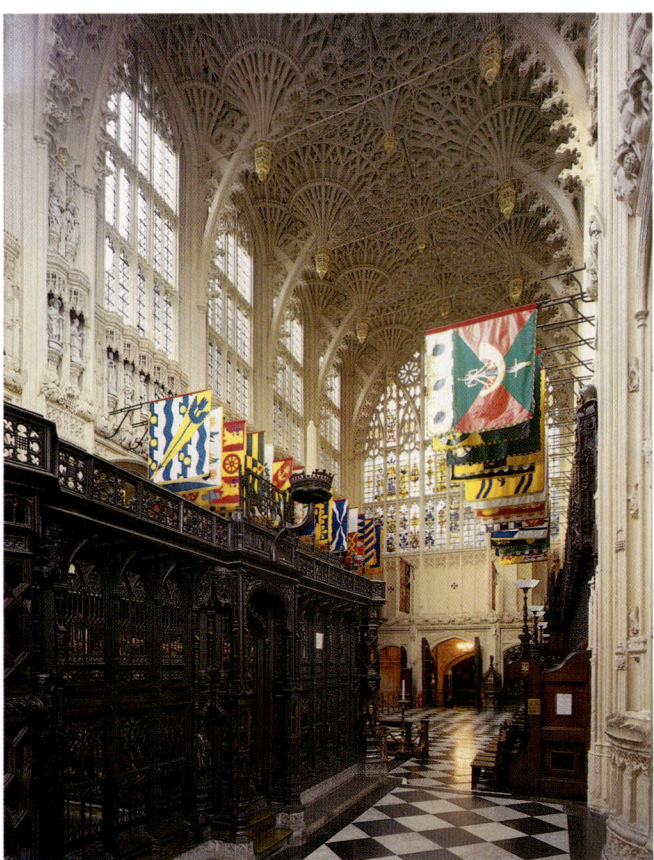

18-43 Chapel of Henry VII, Westminster Abbey, London, England, 1503–1519.

uniquely English "fan vault" shapes with large hanging *pendants* resembling stalactites. The vault looks like something organic that hardened in the process of melting. Intricate tracery recalling lace overwhelms the cones hanging from the ceiling. The chapel represents the dissolution of structural Gothic into decorative fancy. The architect released the Gothic style's original lines from their function and multiplied them into uninhibited architectural virtuosity and theatrics. The Perpendicular Style in this structure well expresses the precious, even dainty, lifestyle codified in the dying etiquette of chivalry at the end of the Middle Ages. A contemporaneous phenomenon in France was the Flamboyant Style seen in churches such as Saint-Maclou at Rouen (FIG. 18-28).

ROYALTY ENTOMBED IN CHURCHES Behind the wooden screen in Henry VII's chapel is the king's tomb in the form of a large stone coffin with sculptured portraits of Henry and his queen, Elizabeth of York, lying on their backs. This type of tomb is a familiar feature of the churches of Late Gothic England—indeed, of Late Gothic Europe. Though not strictly part of the architectural fabric, as are tombs set into niches in the church walls, freestanding tombs with recumbent images of the deceased are permanent and immovable units of church furniture. They preserve both the remains and the memory of the person entombed and testify to the deceased's piety as well as prominence.

Services for the dead were a vital part of the Christian liturgy. The Christian hope for salvation in the hereafter prompted the dying faithful to request masses sung, sometimes in perpetuity, for the eternal repose of their souls. Toward that end, the highborn and wealthy endowed whole chapels for the chanting of masses *(chantries)*, as well as made rich bequests of treasure and property to the Church. Many also required that their tombs be placed as near as possible to the choir or at some other important location in the church, if not in a chapel especially designed and endowed to house it, such as Henry's chapel at Westminster Abbey. Freestanding tombs, accessible to church visitors, had a moral as well as a sepulchral and memorial purpose. The silent image of the deceased, cold and still, was a solemn reminder of human mortality, all the more effective because the remains of the person depicted were housed directly below the portrait. A tomb of an illustrious person could bring distinction, pilgrims, and patronage to the church in which it was placed. Canterbury Cathedral, for example, became one of the most revered shrines in Europe because the martyred saint Thomas à Becket (d. 1170) was buried in its crypt.

A very elaborate example of a freestanding tomb is that of Edward II (r. 1307–1327), installed in Gloucester Cathedral several years after the king's murder in 1327 (FIG. **18-44**). Edward's successor, his son Edward III, paid for the memorial to his father, who reposes in regal robes with his crown on his head. The sculptor portrayed the dead king as an idealized Christlike figure (compare FIG. 18-22). On each side of Edward's head is an attentive angel tenderly touching his hair. At his feet is a guardian lion, emblem also of the king's strength and valor. An intricate Perpendicular Gothic canopy encases the coffin, forming a kind of miniature chapel protecting the deceased. It is a fine example of the English manner with its forest of delicate alabaster and Purbeck marble gables, buttresses, and pinnacles. A distinctive feature is the use

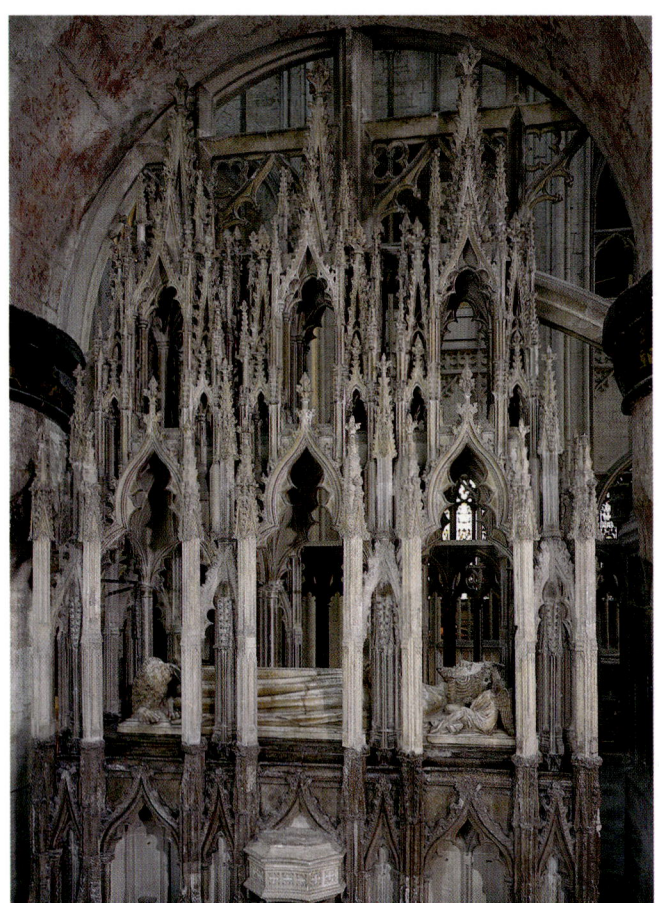

18-44 Tomb of Edward II, Gloucester Cathedral, Gloucester, England, ca. 1330–1335.

of *ogee arches* (arches made up of two double-curved lines meeting at a point), a characteristic Late Gothic form. Art historians often have compared tombs like Edward's to reliquaries. Indeed, the shrinelike frame and the church setting transform the deceased into a kind of saintly relic worthy of veneration.

A GOTHIC VIEW OF THE WORLD We conclude our survey of Gothic England with a monument of a very different kind—a large vellum map of the world (FIG. **18-45**) displayed in Hereford Cathedral. This *mappamundi* ("cloth of the world" in Latin) is probably the work of RICHARD DE BELLO, a priest attached to Lincoln Cathedral from 1264 to 1283. It is the finest thirteenth-century example of the art of mapmaking, which had its roots in antiquity, especially in the imperially commissioned geographic surveys of the then-known world. In fact, at the bottom left of the Hereford map is a picture of the Roman emperor Augustus handing a document to three surveyors and instructing them to "Go into the whole world and report back to the Senate on each continent."

The orientation of the Hereford map and of many other medieval maps is unlike that of most modern maps. North is at the left and east at the top. The explanation is that Christians believed that on Judgment Day Christ would rise in the east, like the sun. At the gabled top of the Hereford map, Christ appears as the enthroned Last Judge of humankind. An angel leads the Saved to Paradise on the left (Christ's right), while grotesque demons pull the Damned into the mouth of Hell. This iconographical theme recalls the tympanum of the

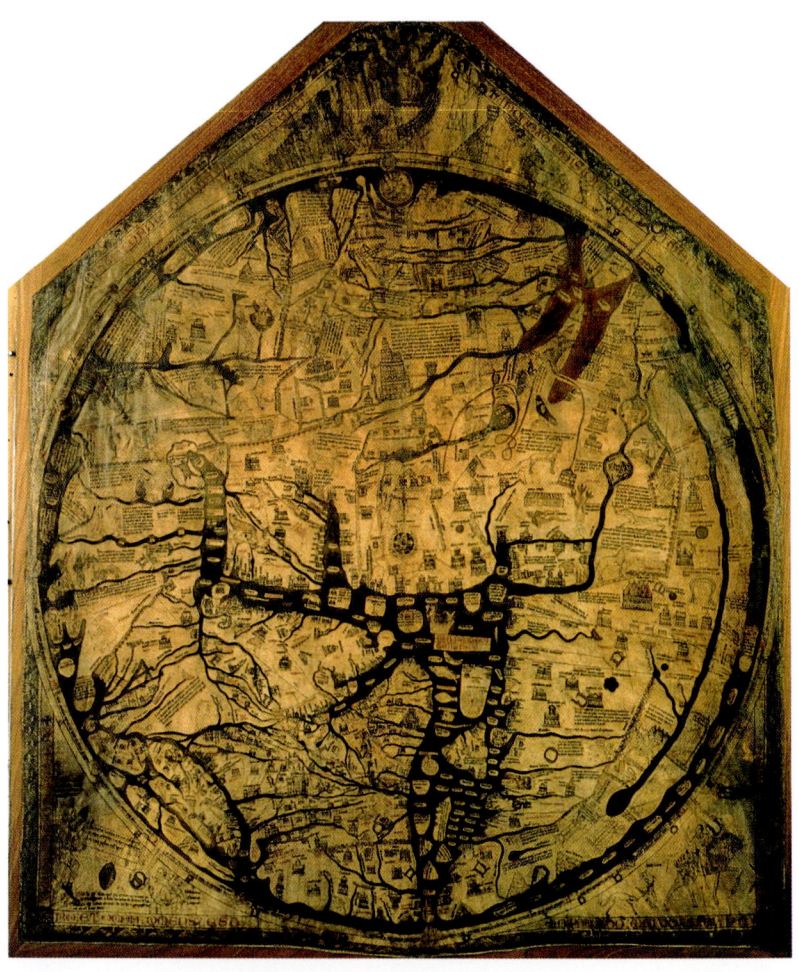

18-45 RICHARD DE BELLO(?), *Mappamundi* (world map) of Henry III, ca. 1277–1289. Tempera on vellum, approx. 5′ 2″ × 4′ 4″. Hereford Cathedral, Hereford, England.

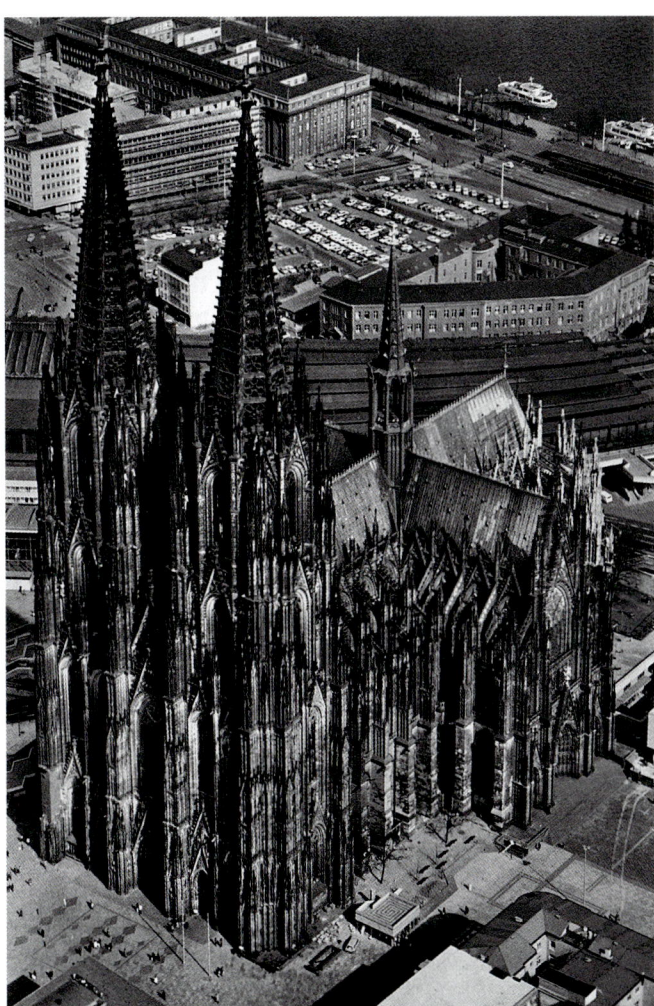

18-46 GERHARD OF COLOGNE, Cologne Cathedral (aerial view from the southwest), Cologne, Germany, begun 1248; nave, facade, and towers completed 1880.

Romanesque church of Saint-Lazare at Autun (see FIG. 17-25). A distinctive Gothic element is the presence of the Virgin Mary below Christ, interceding with her son on behalf of those who prayed to her.

At the world's exact center is Jerusalem, not because medieval mapmakers believed the earth was a flat disk with Jerusalem at its center but because of the central importance of the holy city in medieval thought. Jerusalem appears as a circular walled city accompanied by a picture of Christ on the cross. As was the norm, the Hereford artist characterized most of the world's famous places by their chief buildings. Crete's major feature, for example, is a circular maze, the legendary labyrinth of the Minoan palace at Knossos (see FIGS. 4-3 and 4-4). Babylon's Tower of Babel (see "Babylon: City of Wonders," Chapter 2, page 37) is a multistory fortress with crenellated battlements of the kind found at Carcassonne (FIG. 18-29). Alexandria's lighthouse, one of the Seven Wonders of the ancient world, stands at the Nile River's mouth in Egypt. In some places, the mapmaker provided pictures of the monstrous races that were said to inhabit the far corners of the earth, just as the sculptor of the Vézelay tympanum (see FIG. 17-26) did in the previous century. The Gothic artist also answered the question of what a traveler would find beyond the oceans that bounded the continents—*MORS* (death).

Germany

THE SOARING VAULTS OF COLOGNE The architecture of Germany remained conservatively Romanesque well into the thirteenth century. In many German churches, the only Gothic feature was the rib vault, buttressed solely by the heavy masonry of the walls. By mid-century, though, the French Gothic style began to make a profound impact. An outstanding example is Cologne Cathedral (FIGS. **18-46** and **18-47**). Begun in 1248 under the direction of GERHARD OF COLOGNE, the cathedral was not completed until more than six hundred years later, making it one of the longest building projects on record. Work halted entirely from the mid-sixteenth to the mid-nineteenth century, when the fourteenth-century design for the facade was unexpectedly found. Gothic Revival architects then completed the building according to the Gothic plans, adding the nave, towers, and facade to the east end that had stood alone for several centuries. The Gothic/Gothic Revival structure is the largest cathedral in northern Europe and boasts a giant (four hundred seventy-two feet long) nave with two aisles on each side.

The one hundred fifty-foot-high fourteenth-century choir (FIG. 18-47) is a skillful variation of the Amiens Cathedral choir (FIGS. 18-19 and 18-20) design, with double lancets in the triforium and tall, slender single windows in the clerestory above and choir arcade below. Completed four decades after Gerhard's death, but according to his plans, the choir expresses the Gothic quest for height even more emphatically than many French Gothic buildings. Despite the cathedral's seeming lack of

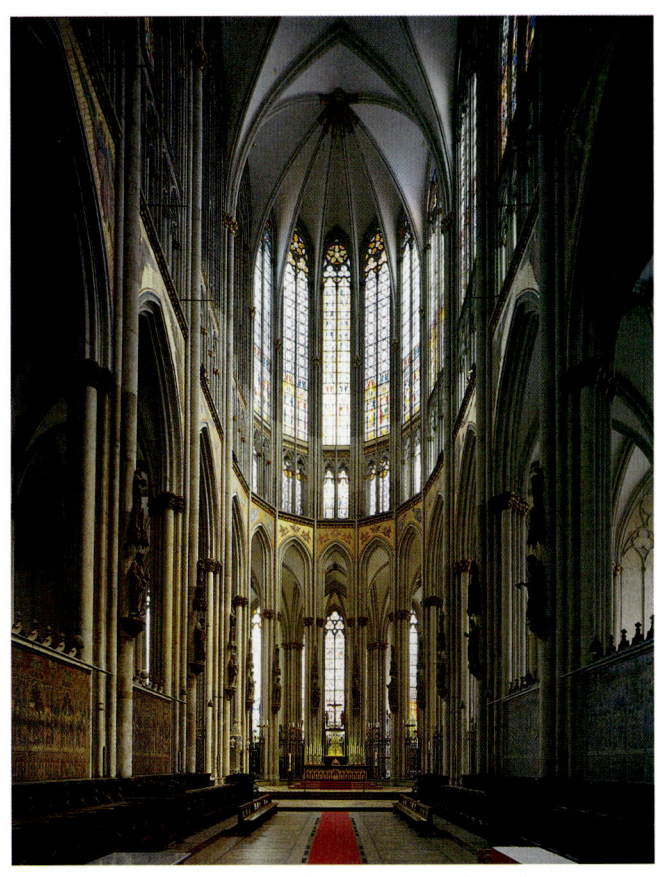

18-47 GERHARD OF COLOGNE, Choir of Cologne Cathedral (view facing east), Cologne, Germany, completed 1322.

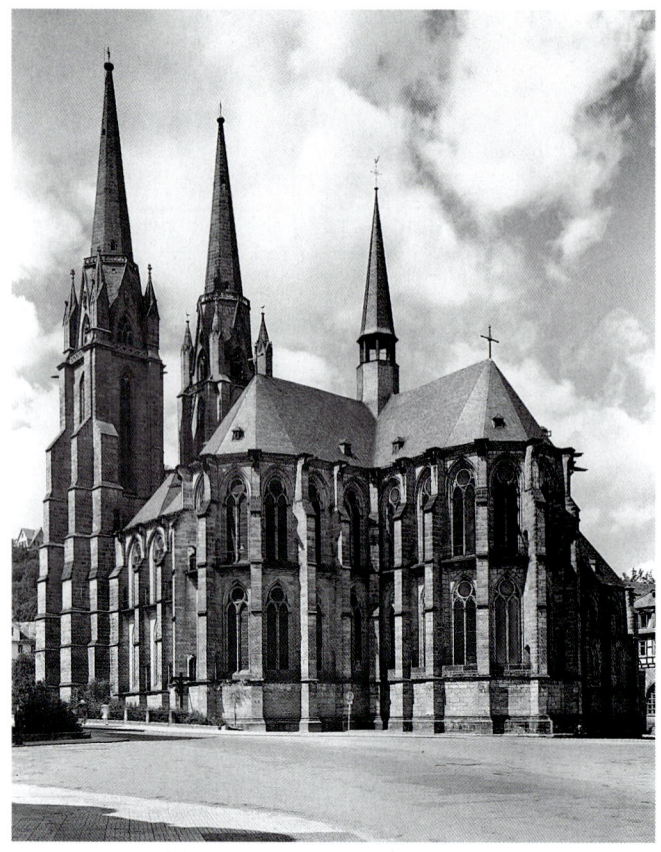

18-48   Saint Elizabeth (view from the southeast), Marburg, Germany, 1235-1283.

the standard for their counterparts abroad. In the German Rhineland, then still ruled by the successors of the Carolingian and Ottonian emperors, work began in 1176 on a new cathedral for Strasbourg, today a French city. The apse, choir, and transepts were in place by around 1240. Stylistically, these sections of the new church are Romanesque. But the reliefs of the two south-transept portals are fully Gothic and reveal the impact of contemporary French sculpture, especially that of Reims.

We illustrate the left tympanum, where the theme is the death of the Virgin Mary (FIG. **18-50**). A comparison of the Strasbourg Mary on her deathbed with the Mary of the Reims Visitation group (FIG. 18-24) suggests that the German master had studied the recently installed French jamb statues. The Twelve Apostles gather around the Virgin, forming an arc of mourners well suited to the semicircular frame. At the center Christ receives his mother's soul (the doll-like figure he holds in his left hand). Mary Magdalene, wringing her hands in grief, crouches beside the deathbed. The sorrowing figures express emotion in varying degrees of intensity, from serene resignation to gesturing agitation. The sculptor organized the group by dramatic pose and gesture but also by the rippling flow of deeply incised drapery that passes among them like a rhythmic electric pulse. The sculptor's objective was to imbue the sacred figures with human emotions and to stir emo-tional responses in observers. In Gothic France, as already noted, art became increasingly humanized and natural.

substance, the structure's stability was proven effectively during World War II, when the city of Cologne suffered from extremely heavy aerial bombardments. The church survived the war by virtue of its Gothic skeletal design. Once the first few bomb blasts had blown out all of its windows, subsequent explosions had no adverse effects, and the skeleton remained intact and structurally sound.

A LIGHT-FILLED HALL CHURCH   A different type of design, also probably of French origin but developed especially in Germany, is the *Hallenkirche,* or hall church. The term applies to buildings with aisles the same height as the nave. Hall churches, consequently, have no gallery, triforium, or clerestory. An early example of this type is the church of Saint Elizabeth at Marburg (FIGS. **18-48** and **18-49**), built between 1235 and 1283. It incorporates French-inspired rib vaults with pointed arches and tall lancet windows. The facade has two spire-capped towers in the French manner but no tracery arcades or portal sculpture. Because the aisles provide much of the bracing for the nave vaults, the German building's exterior is without the dramatic parade of flying buttresses that typically circles French Gothic churches. But the interior, lighted by double rows of tall windows in the aisle walls, is more unified and free flowing, less narrow and divided, and more brightly illuminated than the interiors of French and English Gothic churches.

HIGH DRAMA IN A GERMAN TYMPANUM
Like French Gothic architects, French sculptors also often set

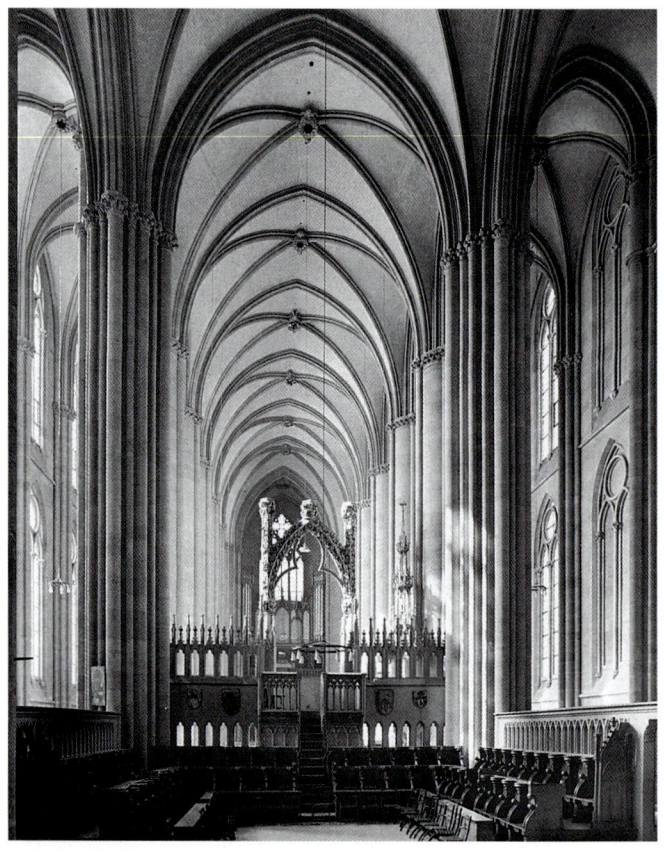

18-49   Interior of Saint Elizabeth (view facing west), Marburg, Germany, 1235–1283.

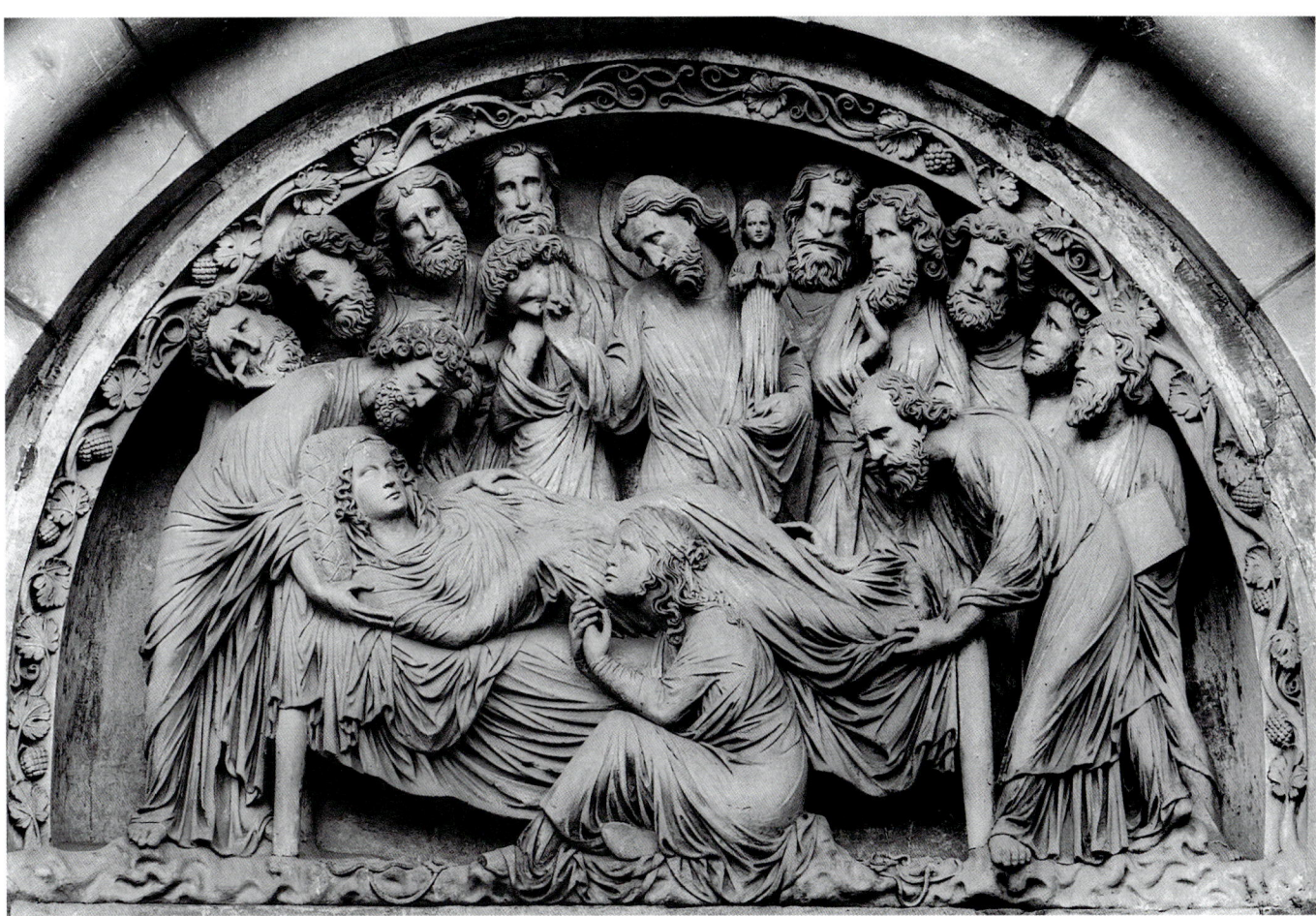

18-50 Death of the Virgin, tympanum of left doorway, south transept, Strasbourg Cathedral, Strasbourg, France, ca. 1230.

In Gothic Germany artists carried this humanizing trend even further by emphasizing passionate drama. Heightened emotionalism (or *expressionism*) proved an important ingredient of German art in succeeding centuries and even in the modern era.

"PORTRAITS" OF LONG-DEAD DONORS   The Strasbourg style, with its feverish emotionalism, was particularly appropriate for narrating dramatic events in relief. The sculptor entrusted with the decoration of the west choir of Naumburg Cathedral faced a very different challenge. The task was to carve statues of the twelve benefactors of the original eleventh-century church on the occasion of a new fundraising campaign. The Strasbourg portal's vivid gestures and agitated faces contrast with the Naumburg statues' quiet solemnity. Two of the figures stand out from the group because of their exceptional quality. They represent the margrave (German military governor) Ekkehard II of Meissen and his wife Uta (FIG. **18-51**). The statues are attached to columns and stand beneath architectural canopies, following the pattern of French Gothic portal statuary. Their location indoors accounts for the preservation of much of the original paint. Ekkehard and Uta give an idea of how the facade and transept sculptures of the French cathedrals once looked.

The period costumes and the individualized features and personalities of the margrave and his wife give the impression they sat for their own portraits, although the subjects lived well before

the sculptor's time. Ekkehard, the intense and somewhat stout knight, contrasts with the beautiful and aloof Uta. With a wonderfully graceful gesture, she draws the collar of her gown partly across her face while she gathers up a soft fold of drapery with a jeweled, delicate hand. The sculptor understood that the drapery and the body it enfolds are distinct. The artist subtly revealed the shape of Uta's right arm beneath her cloak and rendered the fall of drapery folds with an accuracy that indicates the use of a model. The two statues are arresting images of real people, even if they bear the names of aristocrats the artist never met. By the mid-thirteenth century, life-size images not only of sacred but also of secular personages had found their way into churches.

EQUESTRIAN STATUARY REVIVED   Somewhat earlier in date than the Naumburg "portraits" is the equestrian statue known as the *Bamberg Rider* (FIG. **18-52**). For centuries this statue has been mounted against a pier in Bamberg Cathedral beneath an architectural canopy that frames the rider's body but not his horse. Scholars debate whether or not the statue was made for this location or moved there, perhaps from the church's exterior. A similar equestrian statue of the same period stood in the market square of Magdeburg, Germany. Both statues revive the imagery of ancient Rome (see FIG. 10-59) and of the Carolingian Empire (see FIG. 16-11).

Like Ekkehard and Uta, the *Bamberg Rider* seems to be a true portrait. Some believe it represents a German emperor, perhaps Frederick II (r. 1220–1250), who was a benefactor of

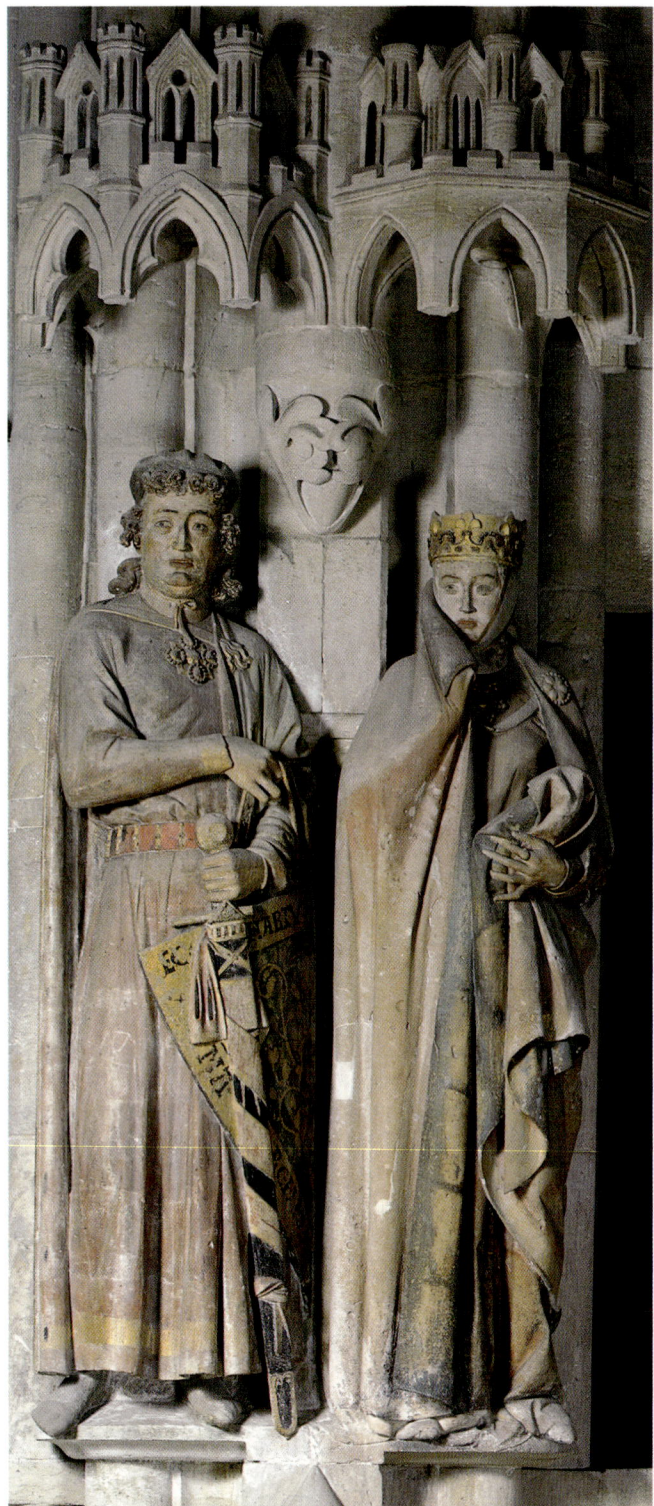

18-51 Ekkehard and Uta, statues in the west choir, Naumburg Cathedral, Naumburg, Germany, ca. 1249–1255. Painted limestone, approx. 6′ 2″ high.

Bamberg Cathedral. The many other identifications include Saint George and one of the three magi, but a historical personality is most likely the subject. The presence of a Holy Roman Emperor in the cathedral would have underscored the unity of church and state in thirteenth-century Germany. The artist carefully described the rider's costume, the high saddle, and the horse's trappings. The proportions of horse and rider are correct, although the sculptor did not quite understand the animal's anatomy, so its shape is rather stiffly schematic.

The rider turns toward the observer, as if presiding at a review of troops. The stirring and turning of this figure seem to reflect the same impatience with subordination to architecture found in the Reims portal statues (FIG. 18-24).

GRIEVING FOR AN EMACIATED CHRIST The confident thirteenth-century figures at Naumburg and Bamberg stand in marked contrast to a haunting fourteenth-century German image of the Virgin Mary holding the dead Christ in her lap (FIG. **18-53**). The widespread troubles of the fourteenth century—war, plague, famine, and social strife—brought on an ever more acute awareness of suffering. This found its way readily into religious art. The Dance of Death, Christ as the Man of Sorrow, and the Seven Sorrows of the Virgin Mary became favorite themes. A fevered and fearful piety sought comfort and reassurance in the reflection that Christ and the Virgin Mother shared humanity's woes. To represent this, artists emphasized the traits of human suffering in powerful, expressive exaggeration. In the illustrated carved and painted wood group (called a *Pietà*, "pity" or "compassion" in Italian), the sculptor portrayed Christ as a stunted, distorted human wreck, stiffened in death and covered with streams of blood gushing from a huge wound. The Virgin Mother, who cradles him like a child in her lap, is the very image of maternal anguish, her oversized face twisted in an expression of unbearable grief.

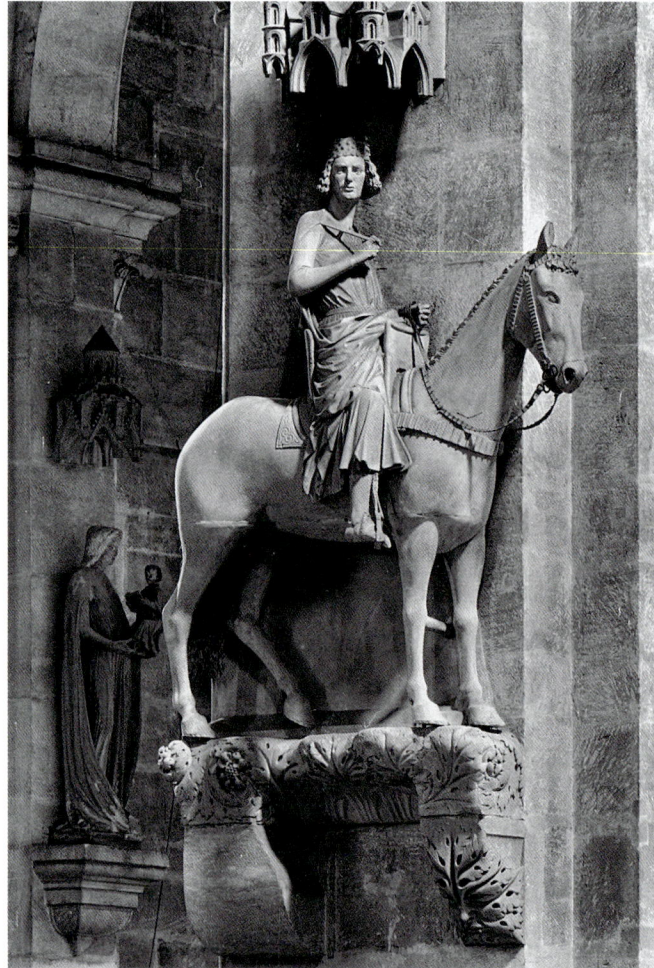

18-52 Equestrian portrait *(Bamberg Rider)*, statue in the east choir, Bamberg Cathedral, Germany, ca. 1235–1240. Sandstone, 7′ 9″ high.

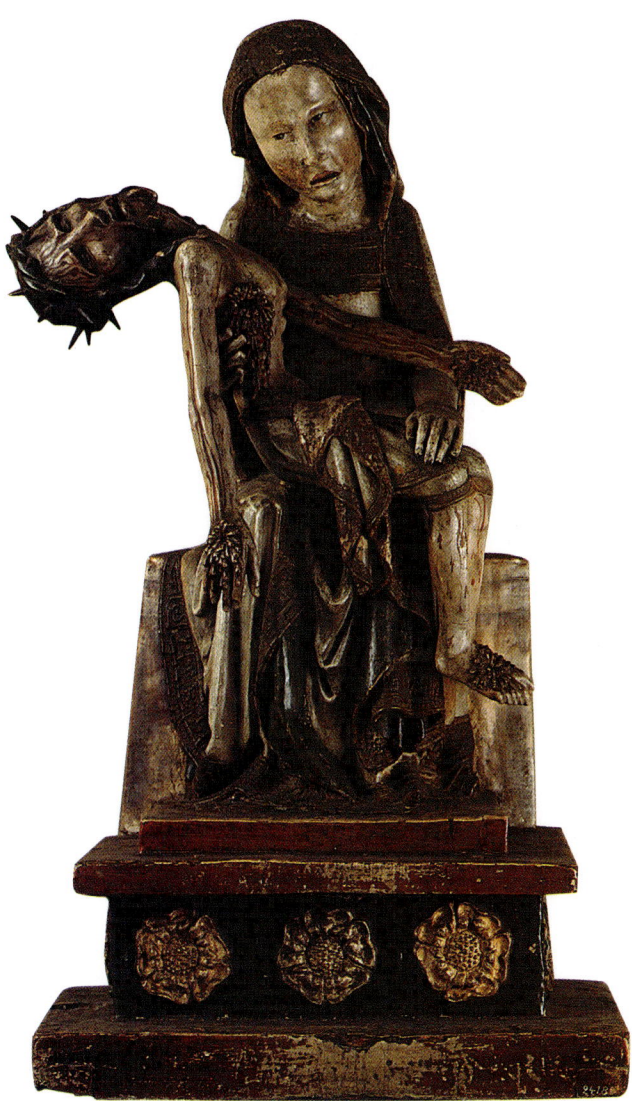

18-53 Virgin with the Dead Christ *(Röttgen Pietà)*, from the Rhineland, Germany, ca. 1300–1325. Painted wood, 2′ 10½″ high. Rheinisches Landemuseum, Bonn.

This statue expresses nothing of the serenity of Romanesque and earlier Gothic depictions of Mary (see FIGS. 17-30 and 18-5, right tympanum). Nor does the *Röttgen Pietà* (named after a collector) have anything in common with the aloof, iconic images of the Theotokos with the infant Jesus in her lap common in Byzantine art (see FIGS. 12-15 and 12-16). Here the artist forcibly confronts the devout with an appalling icon of agony, death, and sorrow that humanizes, to the point of heresy, the sacred personages. The work calls out to the horrified believer, "What is your suffering compared to this?"

The humanizing of religious themes and religious images accelerated steadily from the twelfth century. By the fourteenth century, art addressed the private person (often in a private place) in a direct appeal to the emotions. The expression of feeling accompanied the representation of the human body's motion. As the figures of the church portals began to "move" on their columns, then within their niches, and then became freestanding, their details became more outwardly related to the human audience as expressions of recognizable human emotions.

GOLD AND ENAMEL FOR THE CHURCH

When Abbot Suger wanted to install a magnificent crucifix in the new Gothic choir of Saint-Denis, he selected artists from Germany's Meuse River valley for the job. The Mosan region long had been famous for the quality of its metalworkers and enamelers (see FIGS. 17-29 and 17-31) so Suger's choice is not surprising. The Saint-Denis crucifix is lost, but Suger described it in one of his treatises on the building and adorning of the royal abbey church. The cross stood on a sumptuous base decorated with sixty-eight enamel scenes pairing Old and New Testament episodes. Costly furnishings such as this crucifix were key ingredients in Suger's plan to make his new church an earthly introduction to the splendors of Paradise (see "Abbot Suger and the Rebuilding of Saint-Denis," page 489).

The leading Mosan artist of the late twelfth and early thirteenth centuries was NICHOLAS OF VERDUN. In 1181 he completed work on a gilded-copper and enamel *ambo* (a pulpit for biblical readings) for the Benedictine abbey church at Klosterneuburg, near Vienna in Austria. After a fire damaged the pulpit in 1330, the church hired artists to convert the pulpit into an altarpiece. The pulpit's sides became the wings of a triptych. The fourteenth-century artists also added six scenes to Nicholas's original forty-five.

We illustrate the *Klosterneuburg Altar* in its final form (FIG. **18-54**), with its fifty-one enamels set into trefoil-arched niches framed by explanatory inscriptions. The central row of enamels depicts New Testament episodes, beginning with the Annunciation, and bears the label *sub gracia,* or the world "under grace," that is, after the coming of Christ. The upper and lower registers contain Old Testament scenes labeled, respectively, *ante legem,* "before the law" Moses received on Mount Sinai, and *sub lege,* "under the law" of the Ten Commandments. In this scheme, prophetic Old Testament events appear above and below the New Testament episodes they prefigure. This organization was unlikely to have been Nicholas's invention. Provost Wernher of Klosterneuburg or another church official probably formulated the iconographical program, consistent with a long tradition going back to the earliest Christian art (see "Jewish Subjects in Christian Art," Chapter 11, page 305).

On the *Klosterneuburg Altar,* the angel's Annunciation to Mary of the coming birth of Jesus, for example, is framed above and below by enamels of angels announcing the births of Isaac and Samson. In the central section of the triptych the Old Testament counterpart of Christ's Crucifixion is Abraham's sacrifice of Isaac, a parallelism already established in Early Christian times in both art (see FIG. 11-5) and literature. Nicholas of Verdun's gold figures stand out vividly from the blue enamel background. The biblical actors make lively gestures and wear garments that are almost overwhelmed by the complex linear patterns of their folds.

ENSHRINING THE MAGI'S RELICS Sculptured versions of the Klosterneuburg figures appear on the *Shrine of the Three Kings* (FIG. **18-55**) in Cologne Cathedral. Nicholas of Verdun probably began work on the huge (more than six feet long and almost as tall) reliquary in 1190. Philip von Heinsberg, archbishop of Cologne from 1167 to 1191, commissioned the shrine to contain relics of the three magi. The Holy Roman Emperor Frederick Barbarossa acquired them in the conquest of

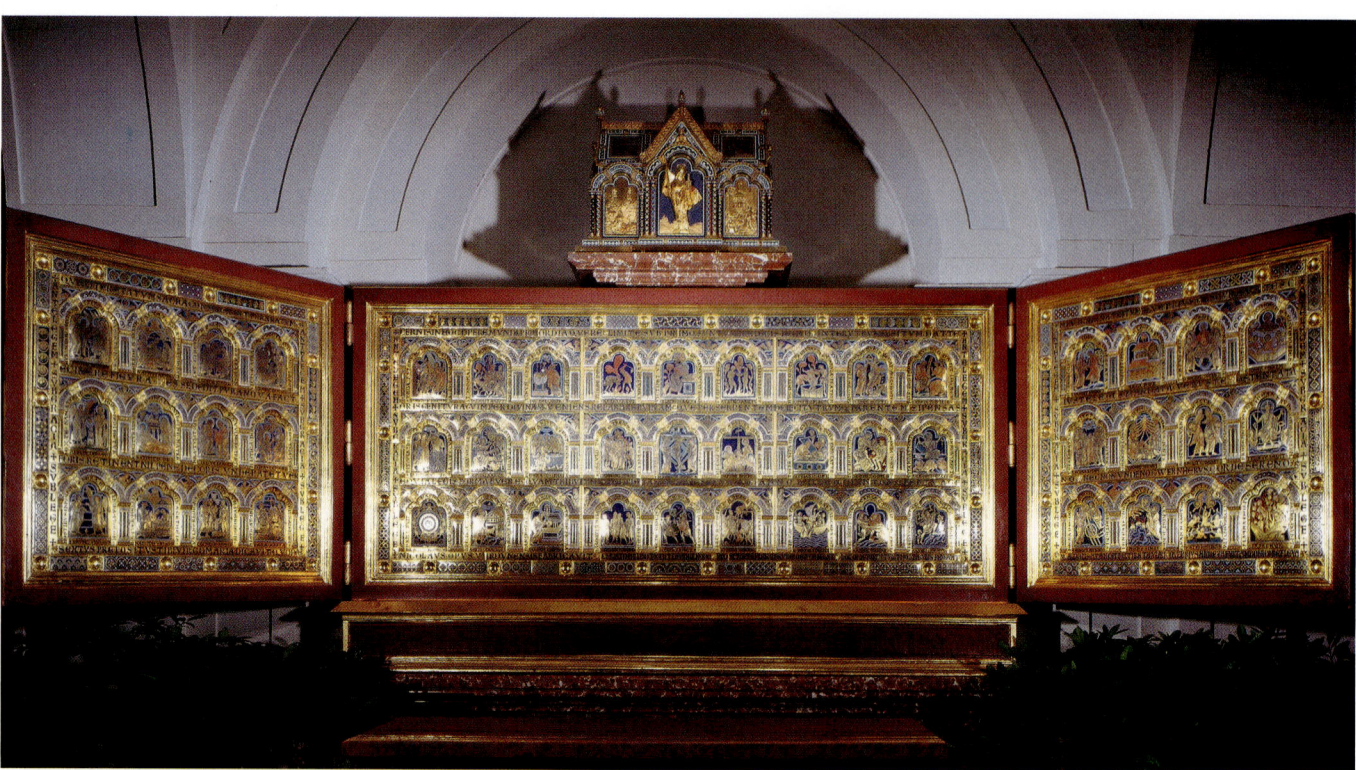

18-54   NICHOLAS OF VERDUN, the *Klosterneuburg Altar,* from the abbey church at Klosterneuburg, Austria, 1181. Gilded copper and enamel, 3′ 6¾″ high. Stiftsmuseum, Klosterneuburg.

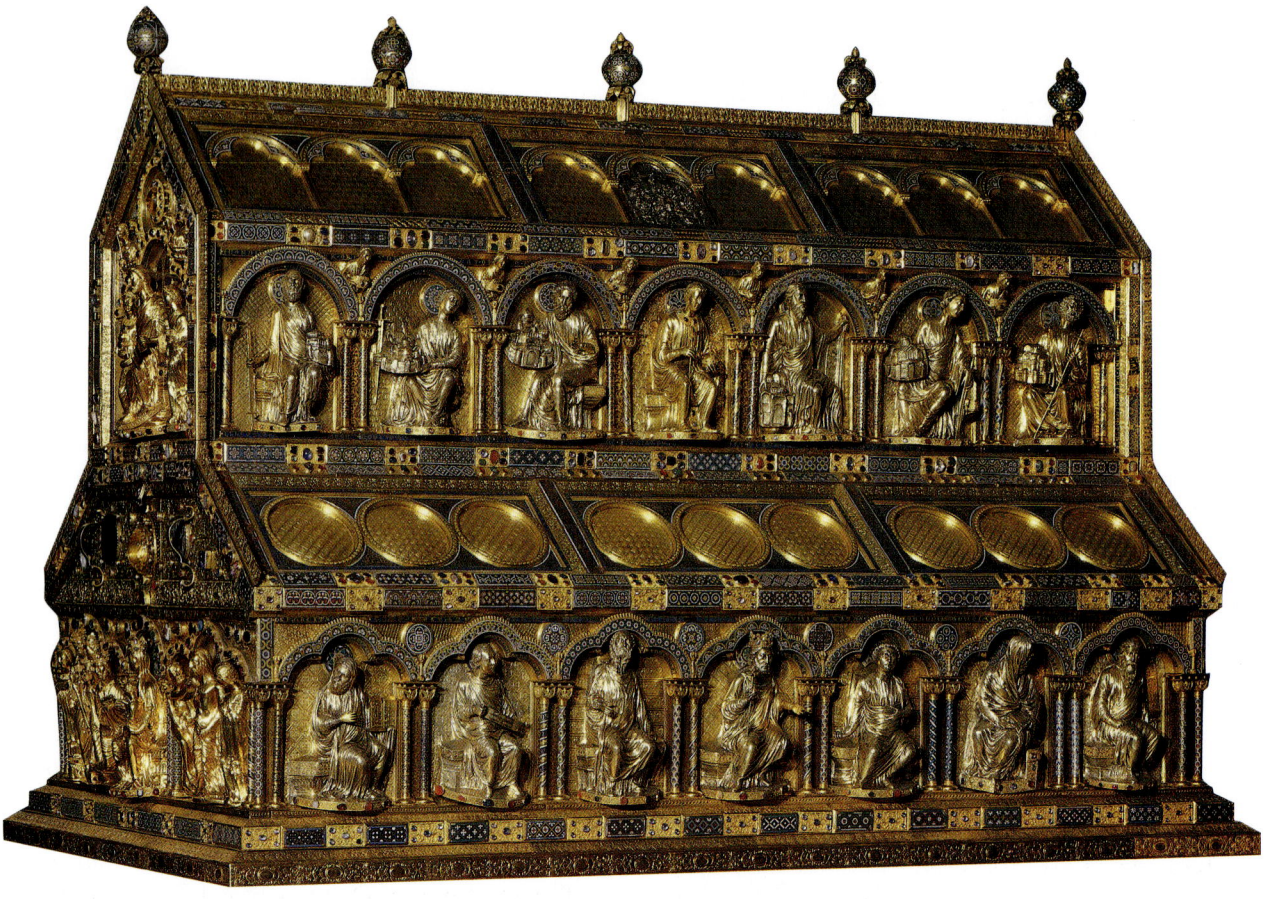

18-55   NICHOLAS OF VERDUN, *Shrine of the Three Kings,* from Cologne Cathedral, Cologne, Germany, begun ca. 1190. Silver, bronze, enamel, and gemstones, 5′ 8″ × 6′ × 3′ 8″. Cathedral Treasury, Cologne.

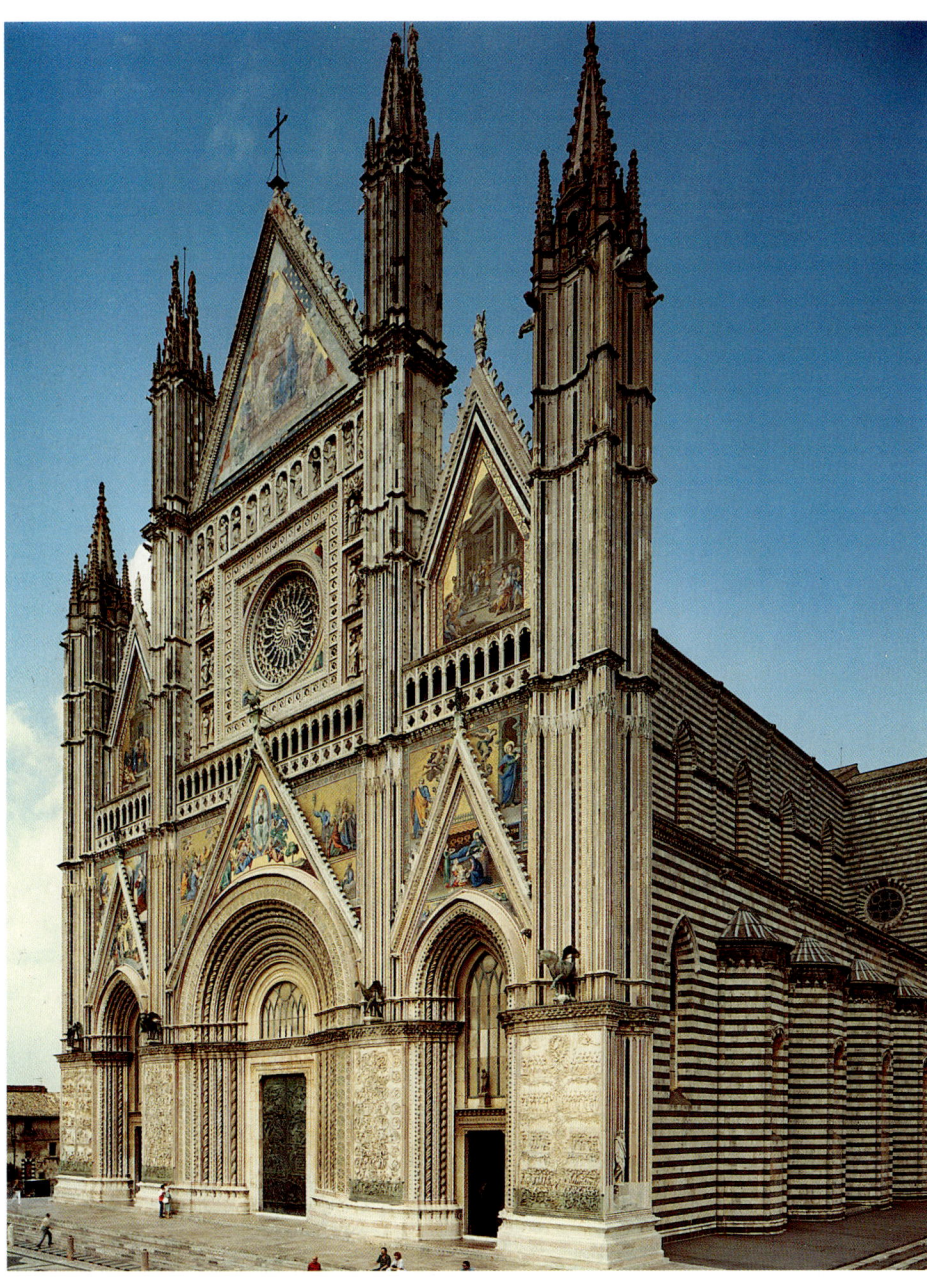

18-56 LORENZO MAITANI, west facade of Orvieto Cathedral, Orvieto, Italy, begun 1310.

Milan in 1164 and donated them to the German cathedral. Possession of the magi's relics gave the Cologne archbishops the right to crown German kings. Nicholas's reliquary, made of silver and bronze with ornamentation in enamel and gemstones, is one of the most luxurious ever fashioned, especially considering its size. The shape resembles that of a basilican church. Repoussé figures of the Virgin Mary, the three magi, Old Testament prophets, and New Testament apostles in arcuated frames are variations of those on the Klosterneuburg pulpit. The deep channels and tight bunches of the drapery folds are hallmarks of Nicholas's style. A similar figural style appeared a half century later in Strasbourg Cathedral's *Death of the Virgin* tympanum (FIG. 18-50).

Nicholas of Verdun's *Klosterneuburg Altar* and his *Shrine of the Three Kings,* together with Suger's treatises on the furnishings of Saint-Denis, are welcome reminders of how magnificently outfitted medieval church interiors were. The so-called "minor arts" played a defining role in creating a special otherworldly atmosphere for Christian ritual. These Gothic examples continued

a tradition that dates back to the Roman emperor Constantine and the first imperial patronage of Christianity (see "Constantine's Gifts to the Churches of Rome," Chapter 11, page 311).

Italy

GOTHIC AND NON-GOTHIC AT ORVIETO Nowhere is the regional diversity of Gothic architecture more evident than in Italy. In the Romanesque period, as already discussed, Italian architects stood apart from developments north of the Alps. Many Italian Romanesque churches more closely resemble Early Christian basilicas than contemporary buildings in France, Germany, or England. Similarly, few Italian architects accepted the northern Gothic style. Some architectural historians even have questioned whether it is proper to speak of late medieval Italian buildings as Gothic structures.

The west facade of Orvieto Cathedral (FIG. **18-56**) is typical of late medieval architecture in Italy. Designed in the early fourteenth century by LORENZO MAITANI, an architect from

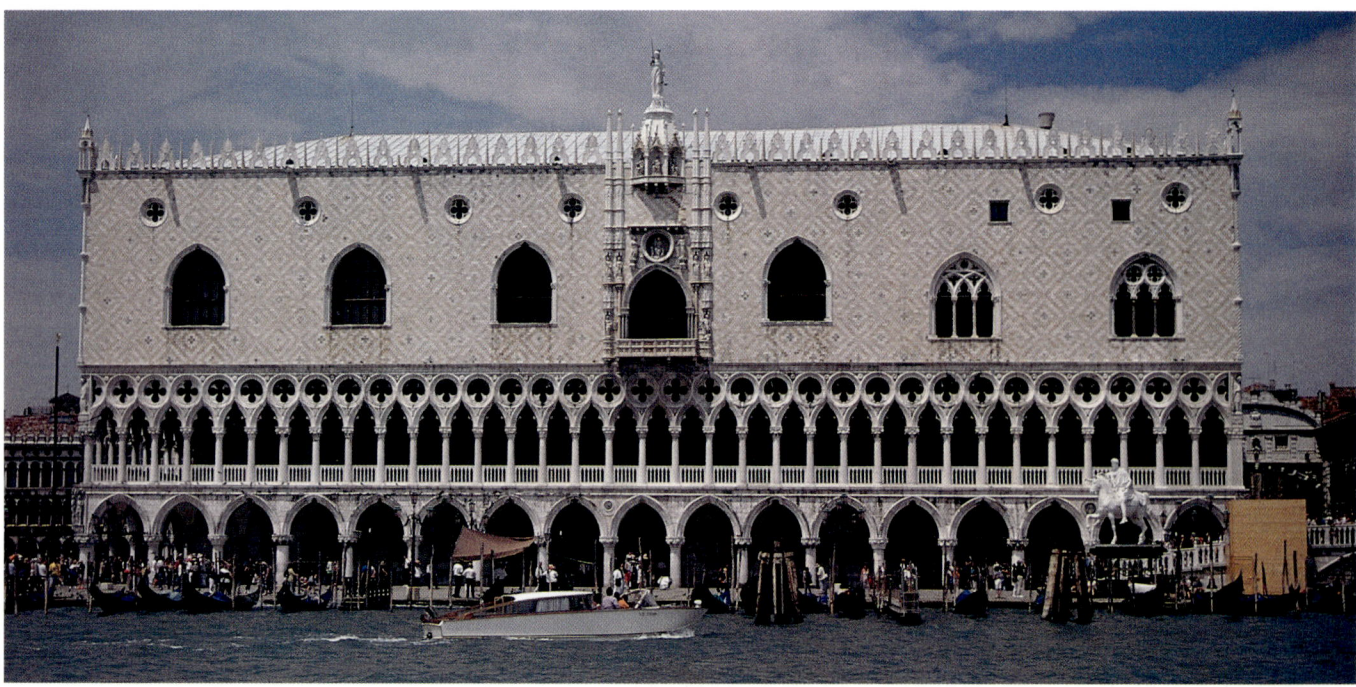

18-57   Doge's Palace, Venice, Italy, begun ca. 1340–1345; expanded and remodeled, 1424–1438.

nearby Siena, the Orvieto facade imitates some elements of the French Gothic architectural vocabulary. French influence is especially noticeable in the pointed gables over the three doorways, in the rose window in the upper zone framed by statues in niches, and in the four large pinnacles that divide the facade into three bays. The outer pinnacles serve as miniature substitutes for the big northern European west-front towers. Maitani's facade is, however, merely a Gothic overlay masking a marble-revetted structure in the Tuscan Early Christian–inspired Romanesque tradition, as our three-quarter view of the cathedral reveals. The Orvieto facade resembles a great altar screen, its single plane covered with carefully placed carved and painted ornament. In principle, Orvieto belongs with Florence's San Miniato al Monte (see FIG. 17-17) or Pisa Cathedral (see FIG. 17-14), rather than with Amiens (FIG. 18-21) or Reims (FIG. 18-23) Cathedrals. Inside, Orvieto Cathedral has a timber-roofed nave with a two-story elevation (columnar arcade and clerestory). Both the triumphal arch framing the apse and the nave arcade's arches are round as opposed to pointed.

THE EARLY CHRISTIAN TRADITION   Timber beams rather than lofty stone vaults also cover the nave and aisles of the church of Santa Croce (Holy Cross) in Florence (see FIG. Intro-3), begun in 1295. Although Santa Croce's one hundred twenty-four-foot-high nave is taller than those of Laon (FIG. 18-9) and Chartres (FIG. 18-13) Cathedrals in France, the Florentine church's interior closely resembles an Italian Early Christian basilica. The only immediately recognizable Gothic feature is the pointed arches of the nave arcade and side aisles.

The city churches of Italy, as elsewhere in Gothic Europe, were just as much monuments of civic pride as they were sites of religious ritual. To undertake the construction of great

buildings, a city had to be rich with thriving commerce. The profusion of large churches during the period attests to the prosperity of those who built and maintained them, as well as to the general revival of Italy's economy in the thirteenth and fourteenth centuries (see Chapter 19).

A GOTHIC PALACE ON A LAGOON   One of the wealthiest cities of late medieval Italy—and of Europe—was Venice, renowned for its streets of water. Situated on a lagoon on the northeastern coast of Italy, Venice was secure from land attack and could rely on a powerful navy for protection against invasion from the sea. Internally, Venice was a tight corporation of ruling families who, for centuries, provided stable rule and fostered economic growth. The Venetian republic's seat of government was the Doge's (Duke's) Palace (FIG. **18-57**). Begun around 1340–1345 and significantly remodeled after 1424, it was the most ornate public building in medieval Italy. In a stately march, the first level's short and heavy columns support rather severe pointed arches that look strong enough to carry the weight of the upper structure. Their rhythm is doubled in the upper arcades, where more-slender columns carry ogee arches, which terminate in flame-like tips between medallions pierced with quatrefoils. Each story is taller than the one beneath it, the topmost as high as the two lower arcades combined. Yet the building does not look top-heavy. This is due in part to the complete absence of articulation in the top story and in part to the walls' delicate patterning, in cream- and rose-colored marbles, which somehow makes them appear paper thin. The Doge's Palace is the monumental representative of a delightful and charming variant of Late Gothic architecture. Colorful, decorative, light and airy in appearance, and not overloaded, the Venetian Gothic is ideally suited to Venice, which floats between water and air.

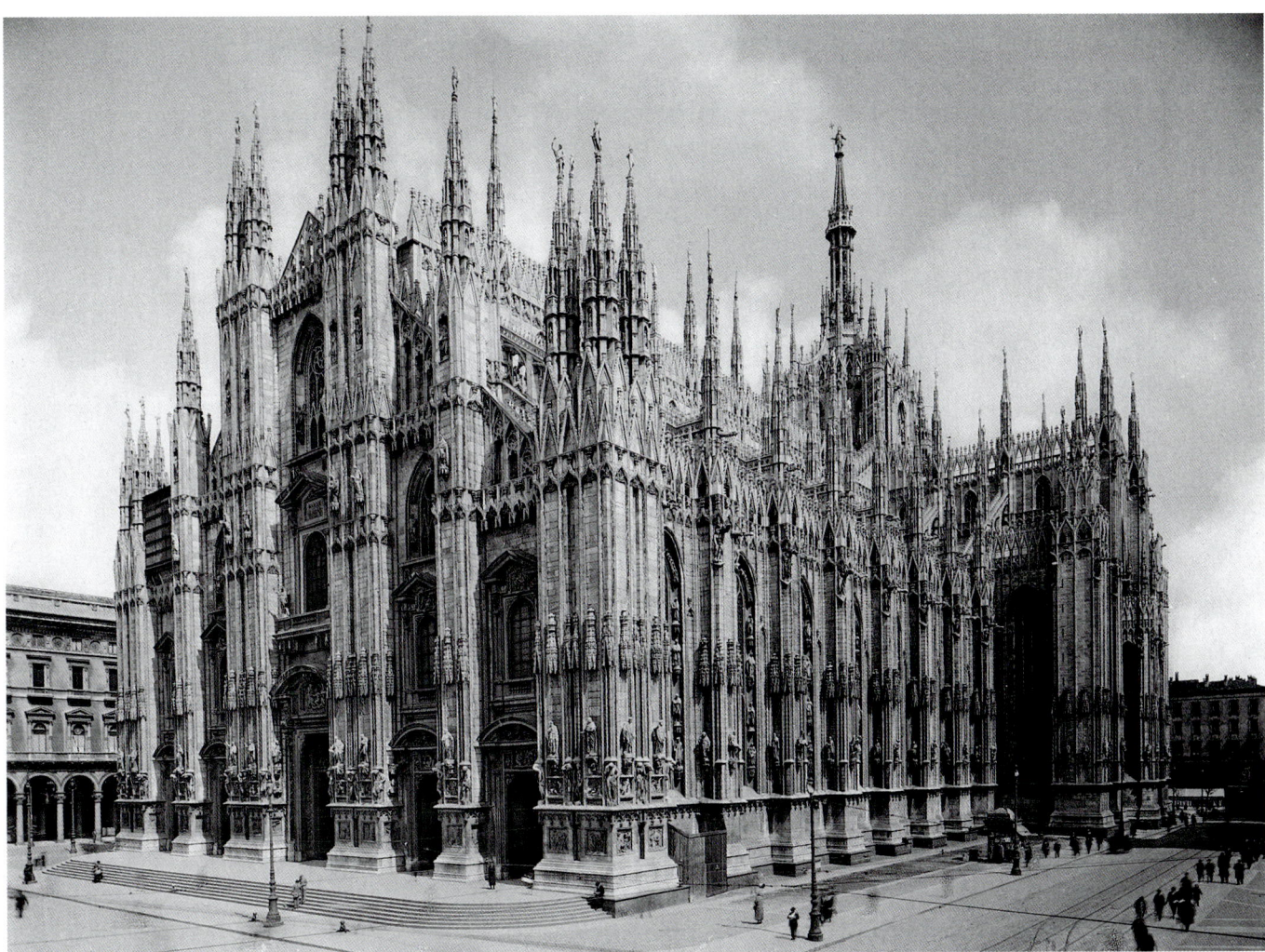

18-58 Milan Cathedral (view from the southwest), Milan, Italy, begun 1386.

MILAN'S ECLECTIC CATHEDRAL Since Roman-esque times, northern European influences had been felt more strongly in Lombardy than in the rest of Italy. When Milan's citizens decided to build their own cathedral (FIG. 18-58) in 1386, they invited experts not only from Italy but also from France, Germany, and England. These masters argued among themselves and with the city council, and no single architect ever played a dominant role. The result of this attempt at "architecture by committee" was, not surprisingly, a compromise. The building's proportions, particularly the nave's, became Italian (that is, wide in relation to

height), and the surface decorations and details remained Gothic. Clearly derived from France are the cathedral's multitude of pinnacles and the elaborate tracery on the facade, flank, and transept. But even before the building was half finished, the new classical style of the Italian Renaissance had been well launched (see Chapter 21), and the Gothic design had become outdated. Thus, Milan Cathedral's elaborate facade represents a confused mixture of Late Gothic and classicizing Renaissance elements. With its pediment-capped rectilinear portals amid Gothic pinnacles, the cathedral stands as a symbol of the waning of the Gothic style.

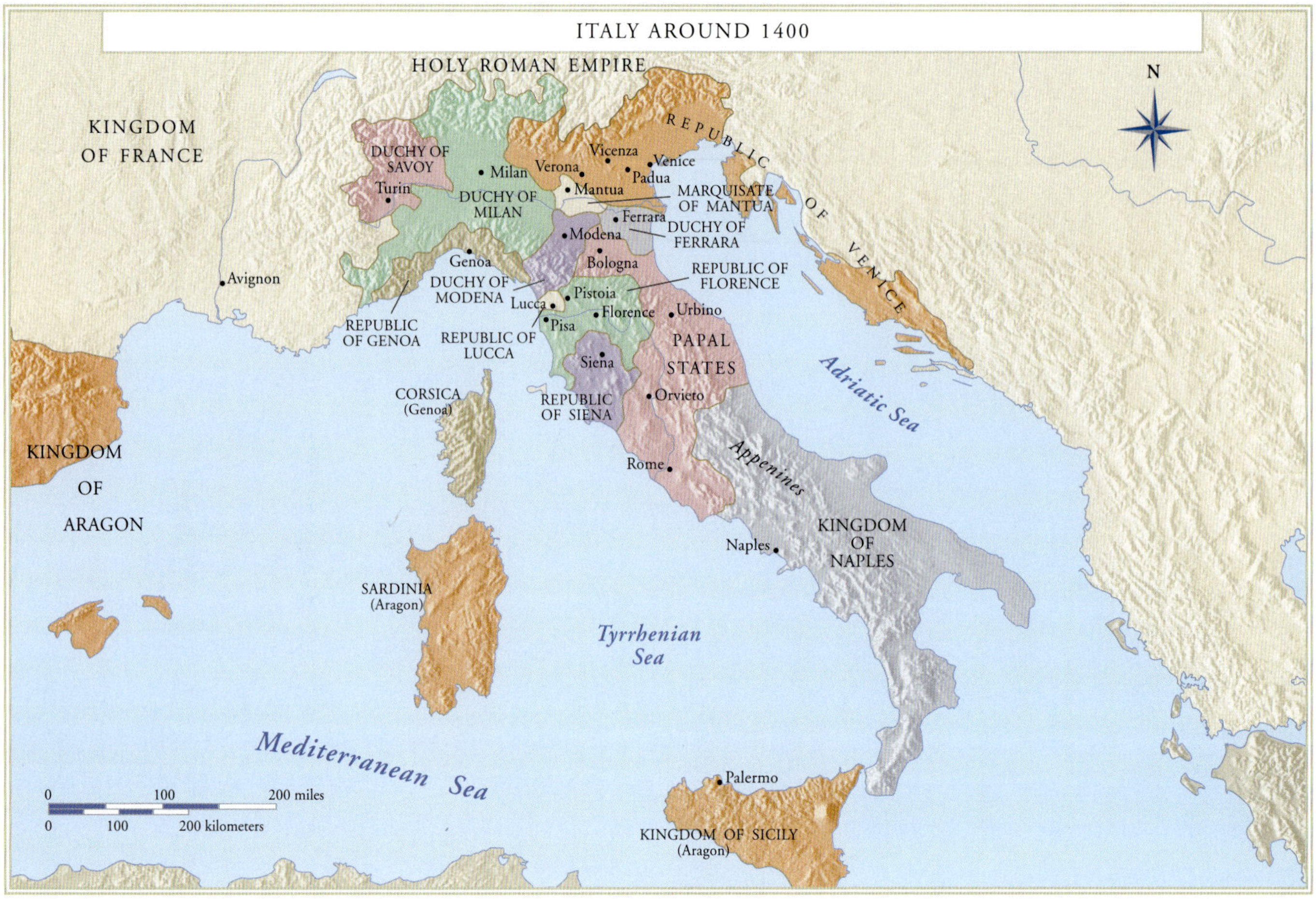

ITALY AROUND 1400

KINGDOM OF FRANCE

HOLY ROMAN EMPIRE

DUCHY OF SAVOY

Turin
• Milan

DUCHY OF MILAN

Verona
Vicenza
Padua
Venice
Mantua

MARQUISATE OF MANTUA

REPUBLIC OF VENICE

Avignon •

Genoa

DUCHY OF MODENA

• Modena

Ferrara
DUCHY OF FERRARA

Bologna

REPUBLIC OF GENOA

REPUBLIC OF LUCCA

Lucca
Pistoia
• Pisa

REPUBLIC OF FLORENCE

• Florence
• Urbino

CORSICA (Genoa)

Siena

PAPAL STATES

REPUBLIC OF SIENA

• Orvieto

Adriatic Sea

Appenines

KINGDOM OF ARAGON

Rome •

KINGDOM OF NAPLES

Naples •

SARDINIA (Aragon)

Tyrrhenian Sea

Mediterranean Sea

0   100   200 miles
0 100 200 kilometers

• Palermo

KINGDOM OF SICILY (Aragon)

N

1200	1225	1250	1300

FREDERICK II (HOLY ROMAN EMPEROR)

TRIUMPH OF THE PAPACY
FALL OF HOHENSTAUFEN HOLY ROMAN EMPERORS

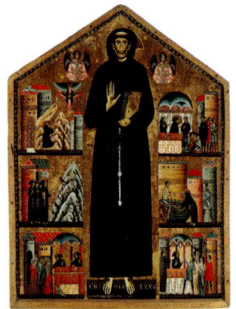

Bonaventura Berlinghieri
Saint Francis Altarpiece, 1235

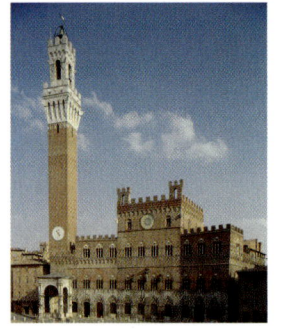

Palazzo Pubblico
Siena, 1288–1309

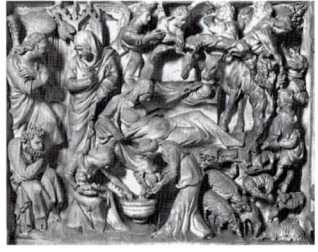

Giovanni Pisano
The Annunciation
and the Nativity, 1297–1301

Saint Dominic, ca. 1170–1221

Franciscan Order founded, 1209

Saint Francis of Assisi,
ca. 1181–1226

Dominican Order founded, 1215

Saint Thomas Aquinas, ca. 1225–1274
(Scholasticism)

Dante, 1265–1321, The Divine Comedy

FROM GOTHIC TO RENAISSANCE

THE FOURTEENTH CENTURY IN ITALY

1305	1338	1378	1400
AVIGNON PAPACY	HUNDRED YEARS' WAR BETWEEN FRANCE AND ENGLAND	GREAT SCHISM IN THE CHRISTIAN CHURCH	

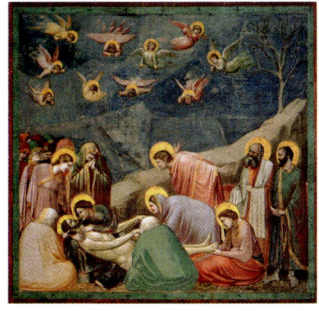

Giotto
Lamentation, 1305

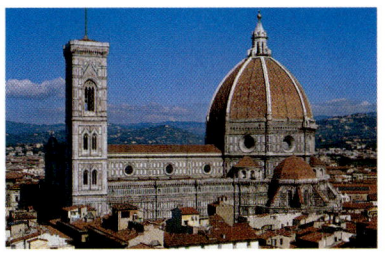

*Florence Cathedral
begun 1296
Campanile designed 1334*

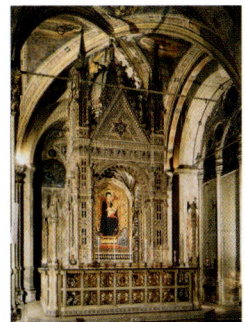

Andrea Orcagna
Tabernacle, 1350–1360

Francesco Petrarch, 1304–1374, humanist poet

Papacy moved to Avignon, 1305

Giovanni Boccaccio, 1313–1375, humanist scholar and novelist

Saint Catherine of Siena, 1347–1380

Black Death, 1348–mid 1350s

Beginning of Great Schism, 1378

Election of Clement VII (Avignon), 1378

Election of Urban VI (Rome), 1378

THE CITY-STATES: POLITICS AND ECONOMICS

In the fourteenth century, Italy did not exist as a single unified entity. Rather, it consisted of numerous city-states, each functioning independently. This fragmentation, due in part to the difficult terrain (especially the Apennines, the mountain range that traverses the country's length), precluded easy travel and communication, thereby discouraging unification. Further, these Italian city-states forcibly resisted the efforts of the German emperors and the popes to bring them under imperial or papal control. From these struggles grew a confidence and self-sufficiency that led many city-states to claim independence from kings, nobles, and papacy alike.

REPUBLICS, DUCHIES, AND KINGDOMS   Each city-state consisted of a geographic region, varying in size, dominated by a major city. For example, among the twelve city-states in the fourteenth century were the Duchy of Milan, the Republic of Venice, and the Kingdom of Naples. Most of the city-states, such as Venice, Florence, Lucca, and Siena, were republics. Other major cities—Genoa, Bologna, and Perugia—followed this governmental model at various intervals during the century as well. These republics were constitutional oligarchies—governed by executive bodies, advisory councils, and special commissions. Only a restricted group of citizens with political rights could serve on these governing boards, and because the number of these enfranchised citizens was very limited, the same individuals tended to rotate through the various legislative councils and decision-making bodies. Other powerful city-states included the Papal States, the Kingdom of Naples, and the Duchies of Milan, Modena, Ferrara, and Savoy. As their names indicate, these city-states were politically distinct from the republics.

EXPANDING TRADE AND COMMERCE   By the beginning of the fourteenth century, Italy had established a thriving international trade and held a commanding position in the Mediterranean world. The uniqueness and independence of each city-state were underscored by their separate economies. Italy's port cities—Genoa, Pisa, and Venice—controlled the ever busier and more extended avenues of maritime commerce that connected the West with the lands of Islam, with Byzantium and Russia, and overland with China. Milan dominated the arms industry, while Florence assured its centrality to banking operations by making its gold florin the standard coin of exchange everywhere. Florence's economic prosperity was further enhanced by its control of the textile industry. Florence had a large share of the wool trade with England and the Netherlands and Florentine merchants exported fine finished cloth all over Europe.

The structured organization of economic activity extended to the many trades and professions. Guilds (associations of master craftspeople, apprentices, and tradespeople), which had emerged during the twelfth century, became prominent. These associations not only protected members' common economic interests against external pressures, such as taxation, but also provided them with the means to regulate their internal operations (for example, work quality and membership training). Although members' personal security and welfare were the guilds' primary concerns, these organizations dominated city governments as well.

DISRUPTION AND CHANGE

THE BLACK DEATH   Despite the relative stability and prosperity established throughout the Italian peninsula, the eruption of the Black Death (bubonic plague) in the late 1340s threw this delicate balance into chaos. Historians generally agree that the Black Death originated in China and was introduced to Europe through Sicily by Genoese merchants returning from the Middle East. From there, it spread throughout southern Italy and up through France and Germany, extending to Scandinavia, Eastern Europe, and Russia. The most devastating natural disaster in European history, the Black Death eliminated between twenty-five percent and fifty percent of Europe's population in about five years. Italy was particularly hard hit. In large cities, where people lived in relatively close proximity, the death tolls climbed as high as fifty or sixty percent of the population. This disease's virulence may have been aided by widespread malnutrition at midcentury, the result of famine caused by disastrous weather conditions in the 1340s.

This plague wreaked havoc on all aspects of society. Ties among family members, neighbors, and communities were ripped asunder. One Sienese observer noted: "Father abandoned child, wife husband, one brother another, for the plague seemed to strike through breath and sight. And so they died. And no one could be found to bury the dead, for money or friendship."[1] People responded to the terror and hysteria in different ways. In *The Decameron,* Giovanni Boccaccio described the devil-may-care attitude adopted by some Italians, who lived "unrestrainedly." Others sought ways to earn God's forgiveness, since they saw the plague as divine punishment. Groups of flagellants, people who flogged themselves and one another with whips of hard knotted leather (sometimes with small iron spikes), roamed from town to town seeking forgiveness through their penance.

The Black Death had a significant effect on art. It stimulated religious bequests and encouraged the commissioning of devotional images. The focus on sickness and death also led to a burgeoning in hospital construction.

The Black Death's consequences were staggering. Because the disease indiscriminately afflicted various members of families and classes, the social disruption left in its wake was acute. Further, the significantly diminished population resulted in a severe labor shortage, exacerbating tension between landed nobility and peasants. Economic turmoil soon followed.

THE GREAT SCHISM   Disruptions in the religious realm also contributed to the societal upheaval. In 1305, the College of Cardinals (the collective body of all cardinals) elected a French pope, Clement V, who settled in Avignon. Subsequent French popes remained in Avignon, despite their announced intentions to return to Rome. Understandably, this did not sit well with Italians, who saw Rome as the rightful capital of the universal church. The conflict between the French and Italians resulted in the election in 1378 of two popes—Clement VII, who resided in Avignon, and Urban VI (r. 1378–1389), who remained in Rome. Thus began what became known as the Great Schism. After forty years, a council convened by the Holy

Roman Emperor Sigismund managed to resolve this crisis in the church by electing a new Roman pope, Martin V (r. 1417–1431), who was acceptable to all.

LETTERS AND LEARNING

DEVELOPING A VERNACULAR LITERATURE

Concurrent with these momentous shifts in the economic, social, and religious realms was the development of a vernacular (everyday) literature, which dramatically affected Italy's intellectual and cultural life. Latin remained the official language of church liturgy and state documents. However, the creation of an Italian vernacular literature (based on the Tuscan dialect common in Florence) expanded the audience for philosophical and intellectual concepts because of its greater accessibility. Dante (1265–1321; the author of *The Divine Comedy*), the poet and scholar Francesco Petrarch (1304–1374), and Giovanni Boccaccio (1313–1375; as noted, the author of *Decameron*) were among those most responsible for establishing this vernacular literature.

HUMANISM: REVIVING CLASSICAL VALUES

Petrarch may be said to have first put forth the values of versatile individualism and humanism. His articulation of these ideas generated interest in humanism during the fourteenth century. However, not until the fifteenth and sixteenth centuries did humanism become a central component of much of Italian art. Humanism was more a code of civil conduct, a theory of education, and a scholarly discipline than a philosophical system. As the word *humanism* suggests, the chief concerns of its proponents were human values and interests as distinct from—but not opposed to—religion's otherworldly values. The study of the Latin classics, for their practical as well as aesthetic value, led to what might be called civil ethics. These guided the conduct of life in a self-governing republic; the ancient Roman ideal and model were always in view. The humanist enthusiasm for antiquity, as Cicero's elegant Latin and the Augustan age represented, involved a conscious emulation of what proponents thought were the Roman civic virtues. These included self-sacrificing service to the state, participation in government, defense of state institutions (especially the administration of justice), and stoic indifference to personal misfortune in the performance of duty. To resurrect the spirit of classical* antiquity, humanists culled through a trove of ancient manuscripts, which they hunted eagerly, edited, and soon reproduced in books made by the new process of mechanical printing. With the help of a new interest in and knowledge of Greek, the humanists of the late fourteenth and fifteenth centuries recovered a large part of the Greek as well as the Roman literature and philosophy that had been lost, left unnoticed, or cast aside in the Middle Ages. The humanists' greatest literary contribution was, perhaps, the translation of these works. But they also wrote commentaries on them, which they used as models for their own historical, rhetorical, poetic, and philosophical writings. What

*Note: In *Art through the Ages* the adjective "Classical," with uppercase *C*, refers specifically to the Classical period of ancient Greece, 480–323 B.C. Lowercase "classical" refers to Greco-Roman antiquity in general, that is, the period treated in Chapters 5, 6, and 10.

the humanists perceived with great excitement in classical writing was a philosophy for living in this world, a philosophy primarily of human focus that derived not from an authoritative and traditional religious dogma but from reason.

Ideally, humanists sought no material reward for services rendered. The sole reward for heroes of civic virtue was fame, just as the reward for leaders of the holy life was sainthood. For the educated, the lives of heroes and heroines of the past became as edifying as the lives of the saints. Petrarch wrote a book on illustrious men, and his colleague Boccaccio complemented it with biographies of famous women—from Eve to his contemporary, Joanna, queen of Naples. Both Petrarch and Boccaccio were famous in their own day as poets, scholars, and men of letters—their achievements equivalent in honor to those of the heroes of civic virtue. In 1341, Petrarch was crowned in Rome with the laurel wreath, the ancient symbol of victory and merit. The humanist cult of fame emphasized the importance of creative individuals and their role in contributing to the renown of the city-state and of all Italy.

Yet humanism, with its revival of interest in antiquity's secular culture, was only part of the general humanizing tendency in life and art that began in the fourteenth century and became dominant in subsequent centuries. Italy, crowded with classical monuments and memorials, was the natural setting for receiving humanistic values recovered from antiquity's omnipresent influence. Dante, the supreme poet of the age, presented in the *Inferno* a whole theater of human sin and suffering. With passionate intensity, he characterized the throngs of actors in sharp, realistic detail. Significantly, he took as his guide through the infernal regions not a Christian saint but Vergil, the great Roman classical poet, who was the personification of the highest attainment of human reason. Petrarch, the careful and critical scholar of classical literature, was also the poet of an ardent personal love, freed from the conventions of the courtly kind the troubadours sang. His verses to his loved one, Laura, are intimate, emotionally complex, and psychologically insightful; they immensely influenced European literature in later centuries. Boccaccio, likewise a humanist scholar, gave in his *Decameron* a vivid narrative of the human scene in all varieties of incident, mood, and characterization, a lasting source of inspiration and material for later novelists and playwrights.

THE BIRTH OF A NEW ARTISTIC CULTURE

This litany of changes—political, social, economic, religious, and cultural—demonstrates that fourteenth-century Italy was in a period of transition. The artistic production of that century also can be seen as occupying a watershed position in the history of Italian art. This assessment is evident in the terminology used to describe late-thirteenth- and fourteenth-century Italian art. Although some scholars refer to this art as Late Gothic, connecting it with the medieval culture that preceded it, other scholars describe it as "Proto-Renaissance." The latter acknowledge the inception of a new artistic culture—the Renaissance (from the French word *renaissance* and the Italian word *rinascità,* both meaning "rebirth")—that flourished in the fifteenth and sixteenth centuries in Italy. Both of these characterizations have merit. Medieval conventions dominated late-thirteenth- and fourteenth-century art and architecture, but artists more assertively attempted to break away from these conventions.

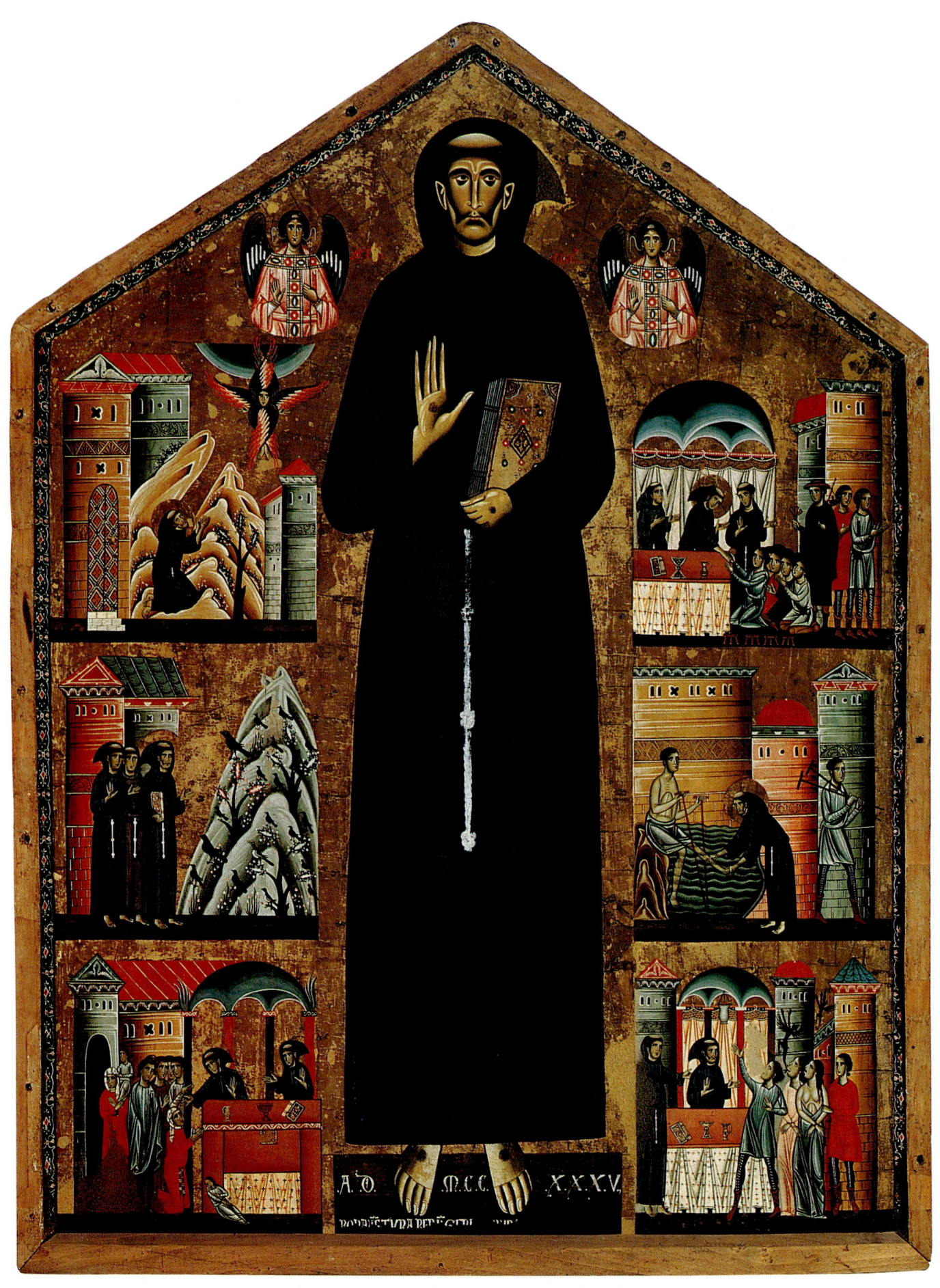

19-1 Bonaventura Berlinghieri, panel from the *Saint Francis Altarpiece,* San Francesco, Pescia, Italy, 1235. Tempera on wood, approx. 5′ × 3′ 6″.

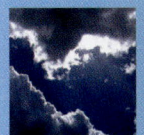

RELIGION AND MYTHOLOGY

Mendicant Orders and Confraternities

The pope's absence from Italy during much of the four-teenth century (the Avignon papacy) contributed to an in-crease in prominence of monastic orders and confraternities. Orders such as the Augustinians, Carmelites, and Servites be-came very active, ensuring a constant religious presence in the daily life of Italians. Of the monastic orders, the largest and most influential were the *mendicants* (begging friars)—the Franciscans, founded by Francis of Assisi (FIG. 19-1), and the Dominicans, founded by the Spaniard Dominic de Guzman (ca. 1170–1221). These mendicants renounced all worldly goods and committed themselves to spreading God's word, performing good deeds, and ministering to the sick and dy-ing. The Dominicans, in particular, contributed significantly to establishing urban educational institutions. The Francis-cans and Dominicans became very popular among Italian citi-zens because of their devotion to their faith and the more per-sonal relationship with God they encouraged.

Although both mendicant orders were working for the same purpose—the glory of God—a degree of rivalry still existed between the two. The Franciscans established their church, Santa Croce (see FIG. Intro-3), on Florence's eastern side, while the Dominicans built their church, Santa Maria Novella (FIGS. 19-14, 21-36, and 21-37), on the city's other side.

Confraternities, organizations comprised of laypeople who dedicated themselves to strict religious observance, also grew in popularity during the fourteenth and fifteenth centuries. The mission of confraternities included tending the sick, burying the dead, singing hymns, and performing other good works.

The mendicant orders and confraternities continued to play an important role in Italian religious life throughout the sixteenth century. They reinforced their presence by commis-sioning numerous artworks and monastic churches.

THE MOVEMENT AWAY FROM MEDIEVALISM IN ART

ECHOES OF BYZANTINE ART   The fundamentally medieval nature of much of Italian art of this period is evident in a panel of the *Saint Francis Altarpiece* (FIG. **19-1**) by BONAVENTURA BERLINGHIERI (active ca. 1235–1244). Throughout the Middle Ages, the Byzantine style dominated Italian painting. This Italo-Byzantine style, or *maniera greca* (Greek style), surfaced in Berlinghieri's altarpiece. Painted in tempera on wood panel, Saint Francis wears the belted clerical garb of the order he founded. He holds a large book and dis-plays the *stigmata*—marks like Christ's wounds—that ap-peared on his hands and feet. The saint is flanked by two an-gels, whose presentation—the frontality of their poses, prominent halos, and lack of modeling—indicates that Berlinghieri borrowed from Byzantine models. The painter enhanced this connection to earlier art forms with gold leaf (gold beaten into tissue-paper-thin sheets that then can be ap-plied to surfaces), which emphasizes the image's flatness and spiritual nature. Other scenes from Francis's life strongly sug-gest that their source is Byzantine illuminated manuscripts (compare FIG. 12-14). The central scene on the saint's right depicts Saint Francis preaching to the birds. The saint and his two attendants are aligned carefully against a shallow tower and wall, from Early Christian times a stylized symbol of a town or city. In front of the saint is another stage-scenery im-age of nested birds and twinkling plants. The composition's strict formality (relieved somewhat by the lively stippling—applied small dots or paint flecks—of the plants), the shallow space, and the linear flatness in the rendering of the forms are all familiar traits of a long and venerated tradition, soon sud-denly and dramatically replaced.

Berlinghieri's depiction of Saint Francis sheds light on more than aspects of style—it also highlights the increasingly prominent role of religious orders in Italy (see "Mendicant Orders and Confraternities," above). The Franciscan order, named after its founder, Saint Francis of Assisi (ca. 1181–1226), worked diligently to impress on the public the saint's valuable example and to demonstrate its commitment to teaching and to alleviating suffering. Berlinghieri's altar-piece, commissioned for the church of San Francesco (Saint Francis) in Pescia, was created nine years after the saint's death and is the earliest known signed and dated representation of Saint Francis. Appropriately, this image focuses on the aspects of the saint's life the Franciscans wanted to promote. Saint Francis believed he could get closer to God by rejecting worldly goods, and to achieve this he stripped himself bare in a public square and committed himself to a strict life of fast-ing, prayer, and meditation. The appearance of stigmata on his hands and feet (visible in Berlinghieri's painting) was per-ceived as God's blessing and led some followers to see Francis as a second Christ. The coarse habit he wears, tied at the waist with a rope, became the garb of the Franciscans.

THE INFLUENCE OF CLASSICAL ART   Interest in the art of classical antiquity was not unheard of during the medieval period. For example, the Visitation group statues on the west facade of Reims Cathedral (see FIG. 18-24) show an unmistakable interest in Roman sculpture, even though the facial modeling reveals their Gothic origin. However, the thirteenth-century sculpture of NICOLA PISANO (active ca. 1258–1278), contemporary with the Reims statues, exhibits an interest in classical forms unlike that found in the works of his predecessors. This interest was perhaps due in part to the influence of the humanistic culture of Sicily under its king,

Artists' Names in Renaissance Italy

In contemporary societies, people have become accustomed to a standardized method of identifying individuals. Given names are coupled with family names, although the order of the two (or more) names sometimes varies. This practice is due in large part to the prevalence of bureaucracy (for example, birth certificates, driver's licenses, and wills) and the predominance of written documents.

However, such regularity in names was not the norm in Italy during the fourteenth and fifteenth centuries. Often, individuals adopted their hometowns as one of their names. For example, sculptor Nicola Pisano (FIGS. 19-2 and 19-3) was from Pisa, Giulio Romano (see FIG. 22-48) was from Rome, and painter Domenico Veneziano was from Venice. Leonardo da Vinci (see FIGS. 22-1 to 22-5) hailed from the small town of Vinci, while Andrea del Castagno (see FIG. 21-39) was from Castagno. This information was particularly valuable when meeting someone for the first time, especially once mobility

and travel increased in the fourteenth century. Such artists are often referred to by their given names, such as *Leonardo.*

Nicknames were also common. While Masaccio (see FIGS. 21-11, 21-12, and 21-13) was "Big Thomas," his fellow artist, Masolino, was "Small Thomas." Guido di Pietro is better known today as Fra Angelico (the Angelic Friar; FIG. 21-38), and Cenni di Pepo (FIG. 19-6) is remembered as Cimabue, meaning "bull's head." Artists sometimes derived their names from their renowned works. Jacopo della Quercia was familiar to early-fifteenth-century Italians as Jacopo del Fonte (Jacopo of the Fountain) for his impressive Fonte Gaia (Gay Fountain) in the public square in front of the Palazzo Pubblico in Siena.

Not only were names not standardized, but they were also impermanent and could be changed at will. This flexibility has resulted in significant challenges for historians, who often must deal with archival documents and records.

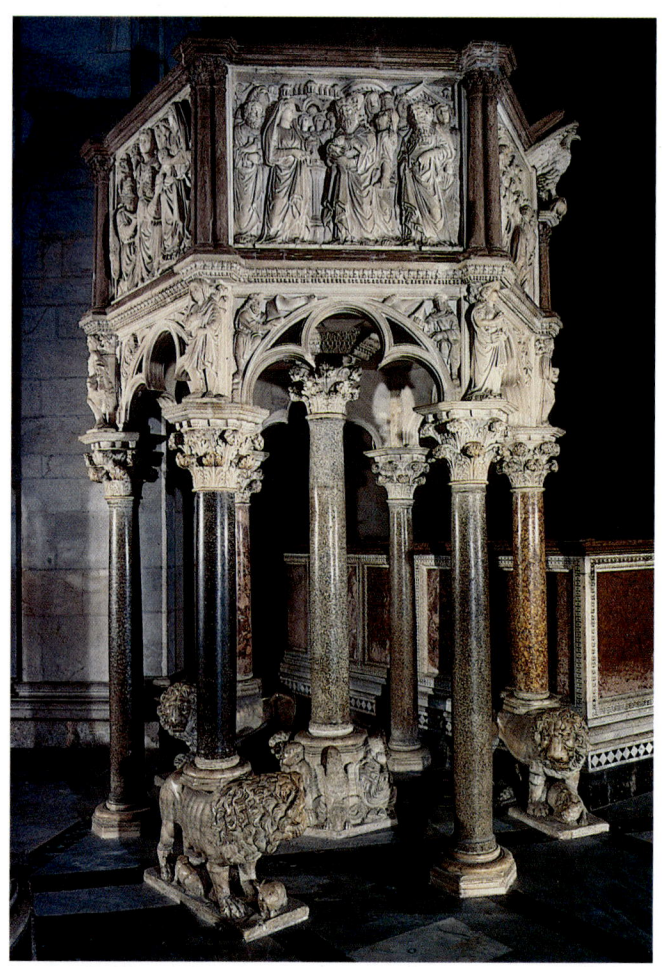

19-2 NICOLA PISANO, pulpit of Pisa Cathedral baptistery, Pisa, Italy, 1259–1260. Marble, approx. 15' high.

Holy Roman Emperor Frederick II. The king was known in his own time as "the wonder of the world" for his many intellectual gifts and other talents. Frederick's nostalgia for Rome's past grandeur fostered a revival of Roman sculpture and decoration in Sicily and southern Italy before the mid-thirteenth century. Because Nicola Pisano (see "Artists' Names in Renaissance Italy," above) may have received his early training in this environment, he may have been influenced by Roman artworks. After Frederick's death in 1250, Nicola Pisano traveled northward and eventually settled in Pisa, which was then at the height of its political and economic power. Although Florence soon emerged as the center of artistic innovation in Tuscany, artists continued to recognize Pisa as a locale for lucrative commissions (see "Art to Order: Commissions and Patronage," page 539).

Nicola Pisano's sculpture, unlike the French sculpture of the period, was not part of the extensive decoration of great portals. He carved marble reliefs and ornament for large pulpits, completing the first in 1260 for the baptistery of Pisa Cathedral (FIG. **19-2**). Some elements of the pulpit's design carried on medieval traditions (for example, the lions supporting some of the columns and the trilobed arches), but Nicola Pisano incorporated classical elements into this medieval type of structure. The large, bushy capitals are a Gothic variation of the Corinthian capital; the arches are round rather than pointed (ogival); and the large rectangular relief panels, if their proportions were altered slightly, could have come from the sides of Roman sarcophagi. The densely packed large-scale figures of the individual panels also seem to derive from the compositions found on Roman sarcophagi. In one of these panels, *The Annunciation and the Nativity* (FIG. **19-3**), the Virgin reclines in the fashion seen in Byzantine ivories,

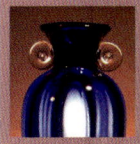

ART AND SOCIETY

Art to Order
Commissions and Patronage

Because of today's international open art market, the general public tends to see art as the creative expression of an individual—the artist. However, artists did not always enjoy this level of freedom. Historically, artists rarely undertook major artworks without a patron's concrete commission.

The patron could be a civic group, religious entity, or private individual. Guilds, although primarily economic commercial organizations, contributed to their city's religious and artistic life by subsidizing the building and decoration of numerous churches and hospitals. For example, the Arte della Lana (wool manufacturers' guild) oversaw the start of the Florence Cathedral (FIGS. 19-12 and 19-13) in 1296, and the Arte di Calimala (wool merchants' guild) supervised the completion of its dome (see FIG. 21-14).

Religious groups, such as the monastic orders, were also major art patrons. Certainly, the papacy had long been an important patron, and artists vied for the pope's prestigious commissions. The papacy's patronage became even more visible during the sixteenth and seventeenth centuries, and today the Vatican Museums hold one of the world's most spectacular art collections.

Wealthy families and individuals commissioned artworks for a wide variety of reasons. Besides the aesthetic pleasure these patrons derived from art, the images often also served as testaments to the patron's wealth, status, power, and knowledge. Art was commissioned for propagandistic, philanthropic, or commemorative purposes as well.

Because artworks during this period were the product of what was, in effect, a service contract, viewers must consider the patrons' needs or wishes when looking at commissioned art and architecture. From the few extant contracts, it appears artists normally were asked to submit drawings or models to their patrons for approval. Patrons expected artists to adhere to the approved designs fairly closely. Surviving contracts do not have the detail one might expect from a legal document. These contracts usually stipulate certain conditions, such as the insistence on the artist's own hand in the work's production, the pigment quality and amount of gold or other precious items to be used, completion date, payment terms, and penalties for failure to meet the contract's terms. Although it is clear patrons could have been very specific about the details of projects and often made many decisions about the works, those expectations are often absent from the written contracts. Regardless, the patron's role looms large in any discussion of art created before the seventeenth century, when an open art market developed.

---

mosaics, and paintings (for information on the Annunciation and the Nativity, see "The Life of Jesus in Art," Chapter 11, pages 308–309 or xxx–xxxi in Volume II). But the face types, beards, coiffures, and draperies, as well as the bulk and weight of the figures, were inspired by relief stronger than anything created in several centuries.

A SON'S SCULPTURAL RESPONSE Nicola Pisano's classicizing manner was countered by his son GIOVANNI PISANO (ca. 1250–1320). Giovanni's version of *The Annunciation and the Nativity* (FIG. **19-4**), from the pulpit in Sant'Andrea at Pistoia, was finished some forty years after the one by his father in the Pisa baptistery. It offers a striking contrast to

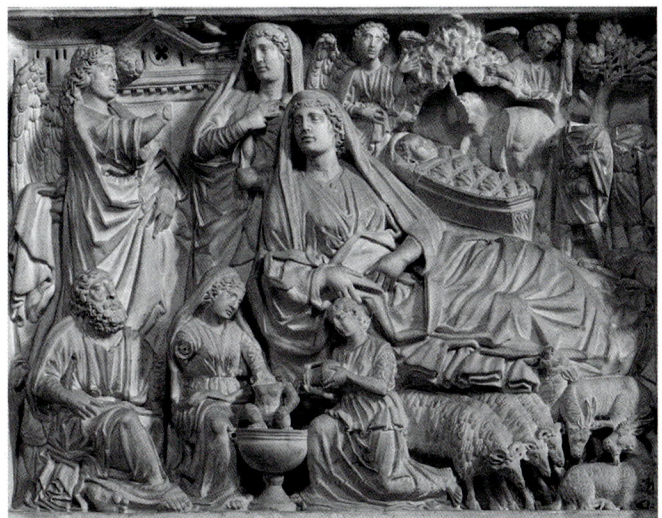

19-3 NICOLA PISANO, *The Annunciation and the Nativity*, detail of Pisa baptistery pulpit, Pisa, Italy, 1259–1260. Marble relief, approx. 2′ 10″ × 3′ 9″.

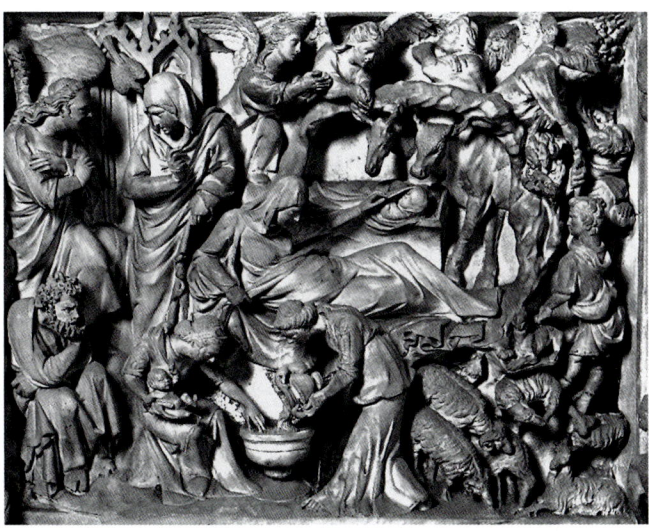

19-4 GIOVANNI PISANO, *The Annunciation and the Nativity*, detail of the pulpit of Sant'Andrea, Pistoia, Italy, 1297–1301. Marble relief, approx. 2′ 10″ × 3′ 4″.

Nicola Pisano's thick carving and placid, almost stolid, presentation of the theme. Giovanni Pisano arranged the figures loosely and dynamically. An excited animation twists and bends them, and their motion is emphasized by spaces that open deeply between them, through which they hurry while gesticulating. In the Annunciation episode, which is combined with the Nativity (as in the older version), the Virgin shrinks from the angel's sudden apparition in a posture of alarm touched with humility. The same spasm of apprehension contracts her supple body as she reclines in the Nativity scene. The drama's principals share in a peculiar nervous agitation, as if they all suddenly are moved by spiritual passion. Only the shepherds and the sheep, appropriately, do not yet share in the miraculous event. The swiftly turning, sinuous draperies; the slender figures they enfold; and the scene's general emotionalism are features not found in Nicola Pisano's interpretation. Thus, the father and son's works show, successively, two novel trends of great significance for subsequent art—a new contract with classical antiquity and a burgeoning naturalism.

SCULPTURAL FORM IN PAINTING   The art of PIETRO CAVALLINI (active ca. 1273–1308) represented one style of the Roman school of painting. A great interest in the sculptural rendering of form characterized the style, as evidenced in a detail from Cavallini's badly damaged fresco, *Last Judgment* (FIG. **19-5**), in the church of Santa Cecilia in Trastevere in Rome. Cavallini, perhaps under the influence of Roman paintings now lost, abandoned Byzantine stylized dignity and replaced it with a long-lost impression of solidity and strength in *Seated Apostles*.

A FINAL SUMMARY OF BYZANTINE STYLE
Like Cavallini, CENNI DI PEPO, better known as CIMABUE (ca. 1240–1302; see "Artists' Names in Renaissance Italy," page 538), moved beyond the limits of the Italo-Byzantine style. Inspired by the same impulse toward naturalism as Giovanni Pisano and also influenced, no doubt, by Gothic sculpture, Cimabue challenged the conventions that dominated earlier art. The formality evident in Cimabue's *Madonna Enthroned with Angels and Prophets* (FIG. **19-6**) is appropriate to the dignity of the theme represented. The artist modeled his large image on Byzantine examples (see FIG. 12-15), revealed in the painting's careful structure and symmetry. However, Cimabue constructed a deeper space for the Madonna and the surrounding figures to inhabit. He used the gold embellishments common to Byzantine art to enhance the folds and three-dimensionality of the drapery. Despite such progressive touches as the throne's solid appearance, this vast altarpiece is a final summary of centuries of Byzantine art before its utter transformation.

A MATERIAL IMAGE OF A HEAVENLY BEING
A naturalistic approach based on observation was the major contribution of GIOTTO DI BONDONE (ca. 1266–1337), who made a much more radical break with the past. Scholars still debate the sources of Giotto's style, although one source must have been the style of the Roman school of painting Cavallini represented. Another formative influence on Giotto may have been the work of the man presumed to be his teacher, Cimabue. The art of the French Gothic sculptors (perhaps seen by Giotto himself but certainly familiar to him from the sculpture of Giovanni Pisano, who had spent time in Paris) and ancient Roman art, both sculpture and painting, must have contributed to Giotto's artistic education. Some believe that new developments in contemporaneous Byzantine art further influenced him.

Yet no synthesis of these varied influences could have produced the significant shift in artistic approach that has led some scholars to describe Giotto as the father of Western pictorial art. Renowned in his own day, his reputation has never

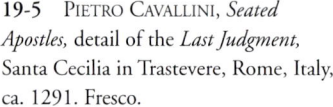

19-5   PIETRO CAVALLINI, *Seated Apostles*, detail of the *Last Judgment*, Santa Cecilia in Trastevere, Rome, Italy, ca. 1291. Fresco.

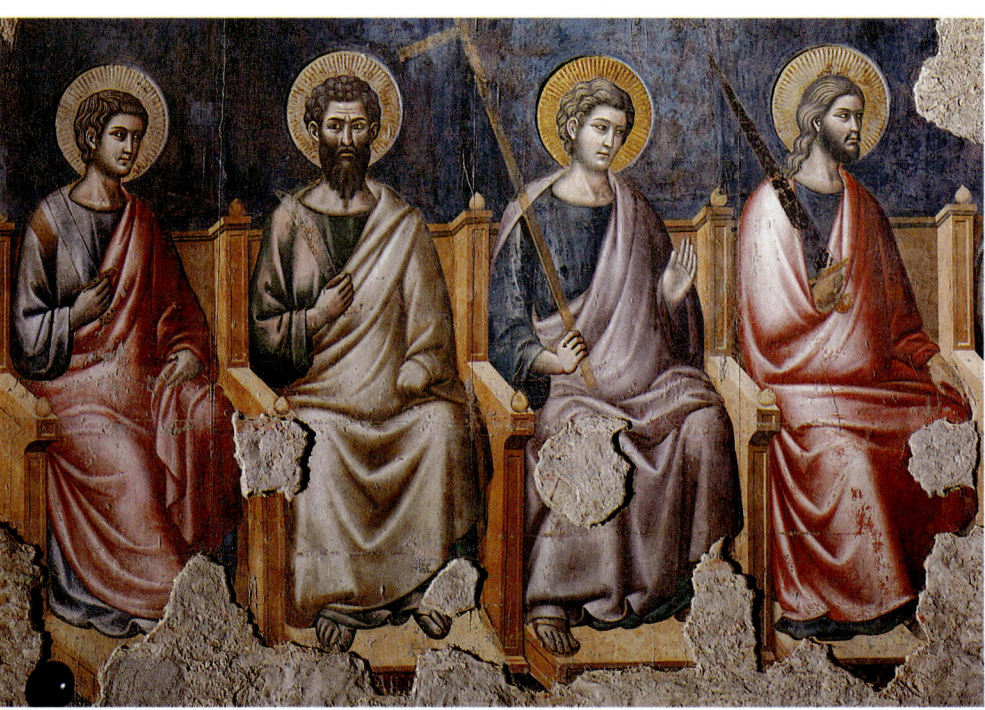

In nearly the same great scale as the Madonna Cimabue painted, Giotto depicted her (FIG. **19-7**) in a work that offers an opportunity to appreciate his perhaps most telling contribution to representational art—sculptural solidity and weight. The Madonna, enthroned with angels, rests within her Gothic throne with the unshakable stability of an ancient marble goddess. Giotto replaced Cimabue's slender Virgin, fragile beneath the thin ripplings of her drapery, with a sturdy, queenly mother, bodily of this world, even to the swelling of her bosom. Her body is not lost; it is asserted. The new art aimed, before all else, to construct a figure that has substance, dimensionality, and bulk. Works painted in the new style portray figures, like those in sculpture, that project into the light and give the illusion they could throw shadows. In Giotto's *Madonna Enthroned,* the throne is deep enough to contain the monumental figure and breaks away from the flat ground to project and enclose her.

VISUALIZING THE BODY AND THE SOUL

Projecting an illusion of solid bodies moving through space on a flat surface presents a double challenge. Constructing the illusion of a body also requires constructing the illusion of a

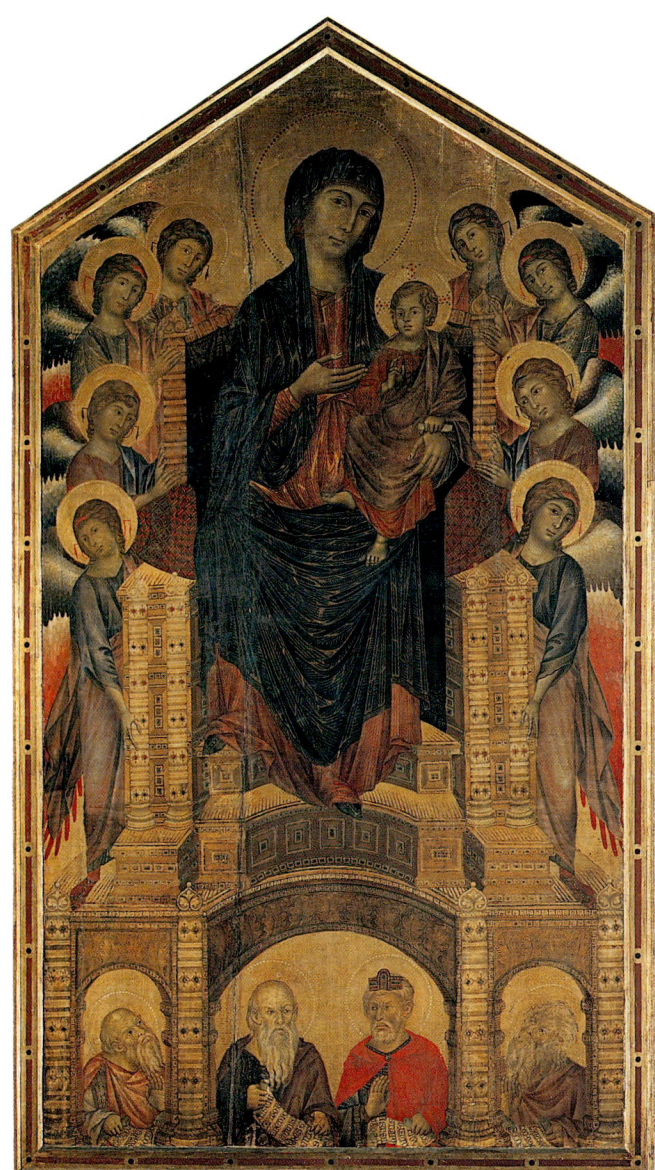

19-6 CIMABUE, *Madonna Enthroned with Angels and Prophets,* ca. 1280–1290. Tempera on wood, 12′ 7″ × 7′ 4″. Galleria degli Uffizi, Florence.

faltered. Regardless of the other influences on his artistic style, his true teacher was nature—the world of visible things.

Giotto's revolution in painting did not consist only of displacing the Byzantine style, establishing painting as a major art form for the next six centuries, and restoring the naturalistic approach invented by the ancients and largely abandoned in the Middle Ages. He also inaugurated a method of pictorial expression based on observation and initiated an age that might be called "early scientific." By stressing the preeminence of sight for gaining knowledge of the world, Giotto and his successors laid the path empirical science followed. They recognized that the visual world must be observed before it can be analyzed and understood. Praised in his own and later times for his fidelity to nature, Giotto was more than a mere imitator of it. He revealed nature while observing it and divining its visible order. In fact, he showed his generation a new way of seeing. With Giotto, Western artists turned resolutely toward the visible world as their source of knowledge of nature.

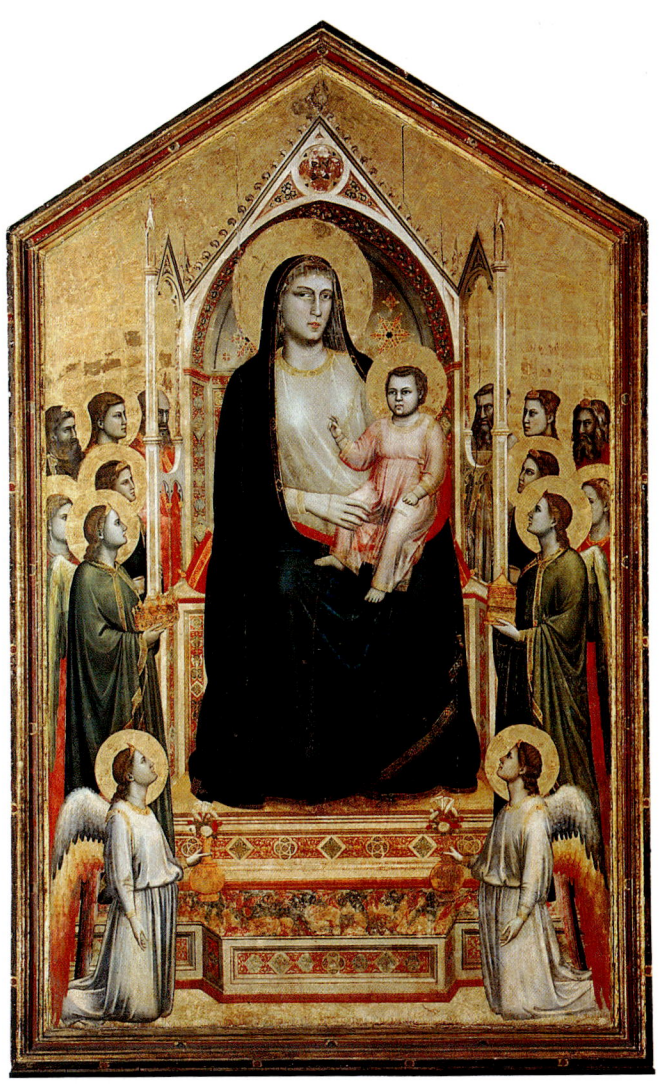

19-7 GIOTTO DI BONDONE, *Madonna Enthroned,* ca. 1310. Tempera on wood, 10′ 8″ × 6′ 8″. Galleria degli Uffizi, Florence.

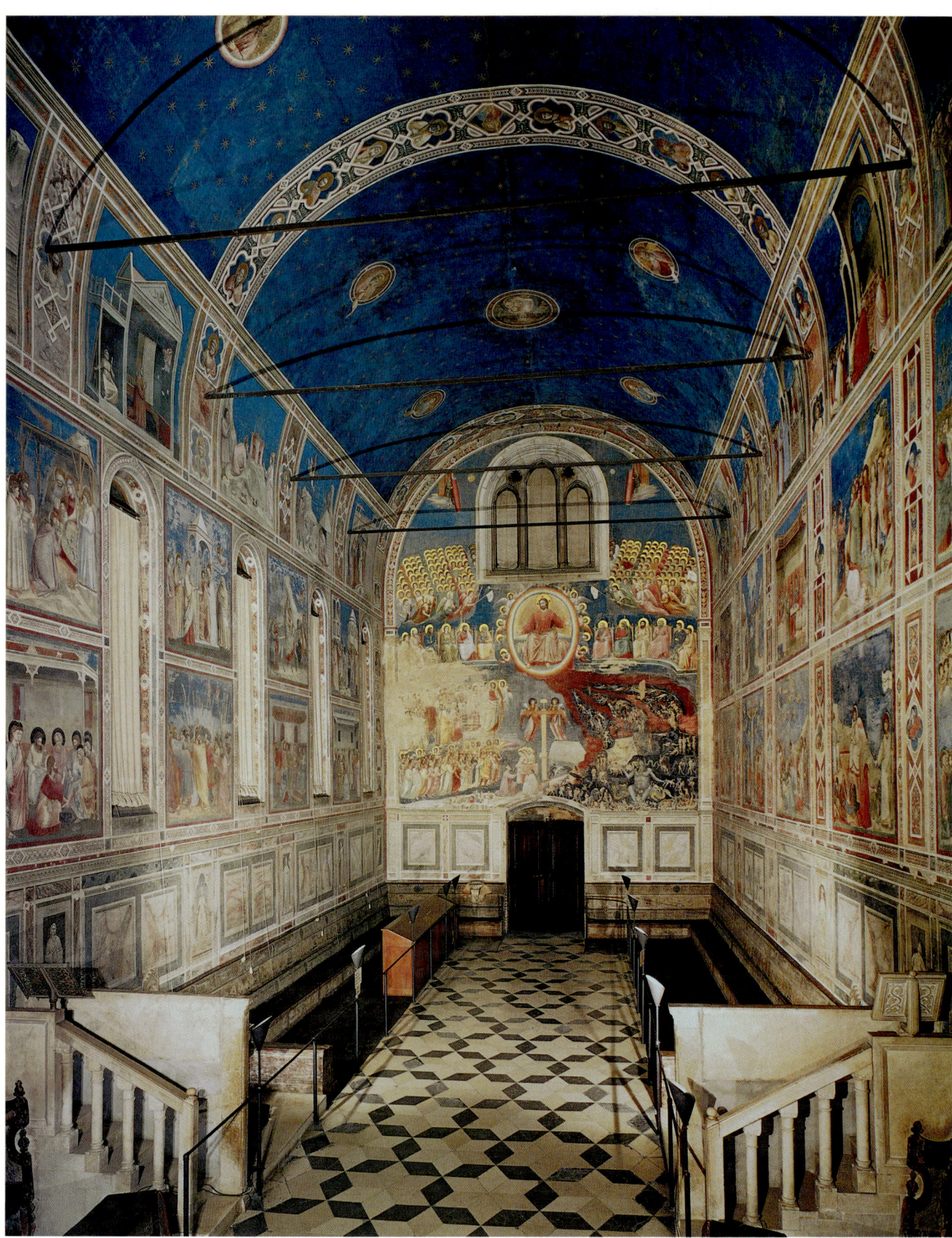

19-8 Interior of the Arena Chapel (Cappella Scrovegni), Padua, Italy, 1305–1306.

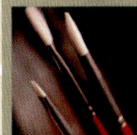

Fresco Painting

Fresco has a long history, particularly in the Mediterranean region, where the Minoans used it in Crete (see FIGS. 4-6 to 4-10) as early as 1650 B.C. Fresco (Italian for "fresh") is a mural-painting technique that involves applying permanent limeproof pigments, diluted in water, on freshly laid lime plaster. Because the pigments are absorbed into the wall's surface as the plaster dries, fresco is one of the most permanent painting techniques. The stable conditions of frescoes such as those in the Arena Chapel (FIGS. 19-8, 19-9, and 19-10) and in the Sistine Chapel (see FIGS. 22-12, 22-13, and 22-14), now hundreds of years old, testify to the longevity of this painting method. The colors have remained vivid (although dirt and soot have necessitated cleaning) because of the chemically inert pigments the artists used. In addition to this *buon fresco* ("true" fresco) technique, artists used *fresco secco* (dry fresco). Fresco secco involves painting on dried lime plaster. Although the finished product visually approximates buon fresco, the pigments are not absorbed into the wall and simply adhere to the surface, so fresco secco does not have buon fresco's longevity. Compare, for example, the current condition of Michelangelo's buon fresco Sistine Ceiling (see FIG. 22-13) with Leonardo da Vinci's *Last Supper* (see FIG. 22-3), executed largely in fresco secco (with experimental techniques and pigments).

The buon fresco process is time consuming and demanding and requires several layers of plaster. Although buon fresco methods vary, generally, the painting is built from a rough layer of lime plaster called the *trullisatio* (scratch coat), followed by the *arriccio* (brown coat), the *arenato* (sand coat), and, finally, the *intonaco* (painting coat). A cartoon (a full-sized preparatory drawing) of the composition is usually transferred to the wall after the arenato layer. Then, the intonaco is laid smoothly over the drawing in sections (called *giornate,* Italian for "days") only as large as the artist expects to complete in that session. The artist must paint fairly quickly because once the plaster is dry, it will no longer absorb the pigment. Any areas of the intonaco that remain unpainted after a session must be cut away so that fresh plaster can be applied for the next giornata.

In areas of high humidity, such as Venice, fresco was less appropriate because of the obstacle the moisture presented to the drying process. Over the centuries, fresco became less popular, although it did experience a revival in the 1930s with the Mexican muralists. Many of the older frescoes have been transferred from their original walls by lifting off the intonaco layer of plaster and readhering the images to other supports.

---

space sufficiently ample to contain that body. In Giotto's fresco cycles (he was primarily a muralist), he constantly strove to reconcile these two aspects of illusionistic painting. His frescoes (paintings on wet plaster; see "Fresco Painting," above) in the Arena Chapel (Cappella Scrovegni) at Padua (FIG. **19-8**) show his art at its finest. The Arena Chapel, which takes its name from an ancient Roman amphitheater nearby, was built for Enrico Scrovegni, a wealthy Paduan merchant, on a site adjacent to his now razed palace. This building, intended for the Scrovegni family's private use, was consecrated in 1305, and its design is so perfectly suited to its interior decoration that some scholars have suggested that Giotto himself may have been its architect.

The rectangular barrel-vaulted hall has six narrow windows in its south wall only, which left the entire north wall an unbroken and well-illuminated surface for painting. The entire building seems to have been designed to provide Giotto with as much flat surface as possible for presenting one of the most impressive and complete pictorial cycles of Christian Redemption ever rendered. With thirty-eight framed pictures, arranged on three levels, the artist related the most poignant incidents from the lives of the Virgin and her parents Joachim and Anna *(top level)*, the life and mission of Christ *(middle level)*, and his Passion, Crucifixion, and Resurrection *(bottom level)*. These three pictorial levels rest on a coloristically neutral base. Imitation marble veneer (reminiscent of ancient Roman wall decoration [see FIG. 10-14], which Giotto may have

seen) alternates with the Virtues and Vices painted in *grisaille* (monochrome grays, often used for modeling in paintings) to resemble sculpture. The climactic event of the cycle of human salvation, the Last Judgment, covers most of the west wall above the chapel's entrance.

The hall's vaulted ceiling is blue—an azure sky symbolic of Heaven; it is dotted with golden stars and medallions bearing images of Christ, Mary, and various prophets. Giotto painted the same blue in the backgrounds of the narrative panels on the walls below (some now faded or flaked). The color thereby functions as a unifying agent for the entire decorative scheme and renders the scene more realistic. For visitors to this remarkable chapel, the decorative ensemble's formal and coloristic unity become memorable standards for measuring other decorative schemes.

The individual panels are framed with decorative borders, which, with their delicate tracery, offer a striking contrast to the sparse simplicity of the images they surround. Subtly scaled to the chapel's space (only about one-half life-size), Giotto's stately and slow-moving actors present their dramas convincingly and with great restraint. *Lamentation* (FIG. **19-9**) provides a good example of his style's essentials. In the presence of angels darting about in hysterical grief, a congregation mourns over the dead body of the Savior just before its entombment. Mary cradles her son's body, while Mary Magdalene looks solemnly at the wounds in Christ's feet and Saint John the Evangelist throws his arms back dramatically. Giotto

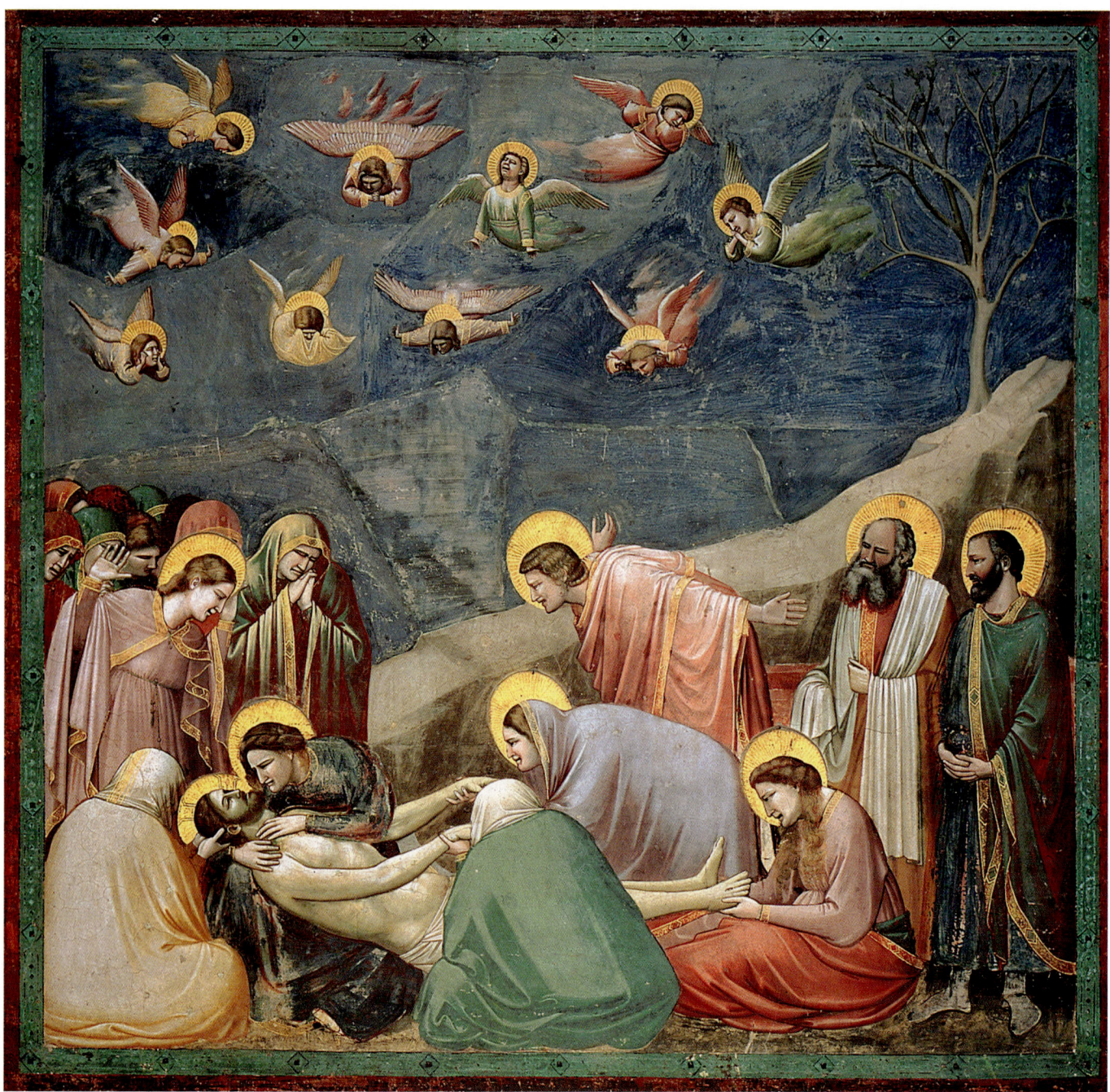

19-9 GIOTTO DI BONDONE, *Lamentation,* Arena Chapel, Padua, Italy, ca. 1305. Fresco, 6' 6$\frac{3}{4}$" × 6' $\frac{3}{4}$".

arranged a shallow stage for the figures, bounded by a thick diagonal rock incline that defines a horizontal ledge in the foreground. Though rather narrow, the ledge provides firm visual support for the figures, while the steep slope indicates the picture's dramatic focal point at the lower left. The rocky landscape also links this scene with the adjoining one. Giotto connected the framed scenes throughout the fresco cycle with such formal elements. The figures are sculpturesque, simple, and weighty, but this mass did not preclude motion and emotion. Postures and gestures that might have been only rhetorical and mechanical here convincingly express a broad spectrum of grief. They range from Mary's almost fierce despair to the passionate outbursts of Mary Magdalene and John to the philosophical resignation of the two disciples at the right and the mute sorrow of the two hooded mourners in the fore-

ground (compare FIG. 12-27). Giotto constructed a kind of stage that served as a model for artists who depicted human dramas in many subsequent paintings. His style was far removed from the isolated episodes and figures seen in art until the late thirteenth century. In *Lamentation,* a single event provokes a single intense response. This integration of formality with emotional composition was rarely attempted, let alone achieved, in art before Giotto.

The formal design of the *Lamentation* fresco, the way the figures are grouped within the constructed space, is worth close study. Each group has its own definition, and each contributes to the rhythmic order of the composition. The strong diagonal of the rocky ledge, with its single dead tree (the tree of knowledge of good and evil, which withered at the Fall of Adam), concentrates the viewer's attention on the group

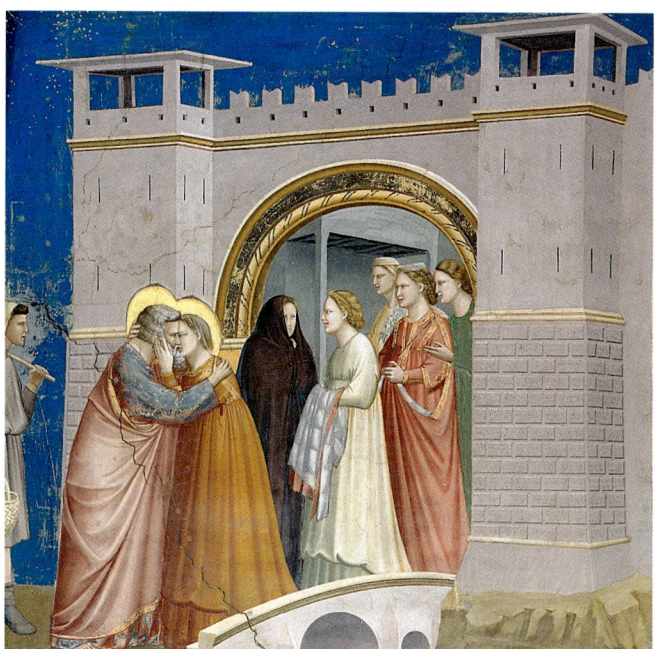

19-10   GIOTTO DI BONDONE, *The Meeting of Joachim and Anna,* Arena Chapel, Padua, Italy, ca. 1305. Fresco, 6′ 6 $\frac{3}{4}$″ × 6′ $\frac{3}{4}$″.

called the "mystery" plays. The drama of the Mass was extended into one- and two-act tableaus and scenes and then into simple narratives offered at church portals and in city squares. (Eventually, confraternities also presented more elaborate religious dramas called *sacre rappresentazioni*—sacred representations.) The great increase in popular sermons to huge city audiences prompted a public taste for narrative, recited as dramatically as possible. The arts of illusionistic painting, of drama, and of sermon rhetoric with all their theatrical flourishes were developing simultaneously and were mutually influential. Giotto's art masterfully—perhaps uniquely—synthesized dramatic narrative, holy lesson, and truth to human experience in a visual idiom of his own invention, accessible to all.

THE MASTER'S LEGACY   Giotto's frescoes served as textbooks for generations of Renaissance painters from Masaccio to Michelangelo and beyond. Another of Giotto's panels in the Arena Chapel, *The Meeting of Joachim and Anna* (FIG. **19-10**), portrays Anna greeting Joachim to inform him that she has been chosen to bear the Virgin Mary. The composition is simple and compact. The figures are carefully related to the single architectural element (the Golden Gate), where the Virgin's parents meet in triumph in the presence of splendidly dressed ladies. The latter mock the cloaked servant who refused to believe the elderly Anna (Saint Anne) would ever bear a child. The story, related in the Apocrypha (biblical writings considered canonical—orthodox—by Catholics but not by Protestants), is managed with Giotto's usual restraint, clarity, and dramatic compactness.

Influenced by Giotto, TADDEO GADDI (ca. 1300–1366), his foster son and assistant for many years, produced a similar image. In Gaddi's version of the same subject (FIG. **19-11**) in the Baroncelli Chapel in Florence's church of Santa Croce, the image (particularly the architecture) is more complex than Giotto's, and the shepherd and the court ladies are more

around the head of Christ, whose positioning is dynamically off center. All movement beyond this group is contained, or arrested, by the massive bulk of the seated mourner in the painting's left corner. The seated mourner to the right establishes a relation with the center group, who, by their gazes and gestures, draw the viewer's attention back to Christ's head. Figures seen from the back, which are frequent in Giotto's compositions, represent an innovation in the development away from the formal Italo-Byzantine style. These figures emphasize the foreground, aiding the visual placement of the intermediate figures farther back in space. This device, the very contradiction of the old frontality, in effect puts viewers behind the "observer" figures, who, facing the action as spectators, reinforce the sense of stagecraft as a model for painting.

Giotto's new devices for depicting spatial depth and bodily mass could not, of course, have been possible without his management of light and shade. He shaded his figures to indicate both the direction of the light that illuminates them and the shadows (the diminished light), giving the figures volume. In *Lamentation,* light falls upon the upper surfaces of the figures (especially the two central bending figures) and passes down to dark in their draperies, separating the volumes one from the other and pushing one to the fore, the other to the rear. The graded continuum of light and shade, directed by an even neutral light from a single steady source—not shown in the picture—was the first step toward the development of *chiaroscuro* (the use of dramatic contrasts of dark and light to produce modeling).

The stagelike settings made possible by Giotto's innovations in *perspective* (the depiction of three dimensional objects in space on a two-dimensional surface) and lighting suited perfectly the dramatic narrative the Franciscans emphasized then as a principal method for educating the faithful in their religion. In the humanizing age, the old stylized presentations of the holy mysteries had evolved into what were

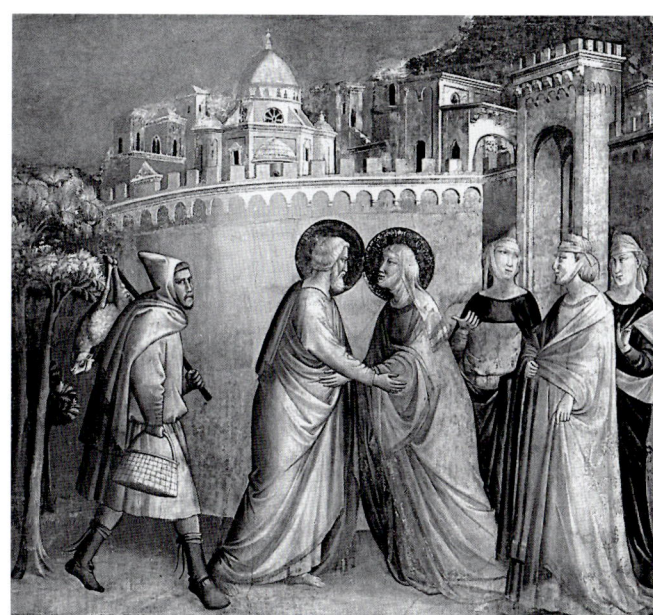

19-11   TADDEO GADDI, *Meeting of Joachim and Anna,* Baroncelli Chapel, Santa Croce, Florence, Italy, 1338. Fresco.

obtrusive. Yet, Gaddi made an important contribution to the investigation of pictorial light. In *Joachim and Anna* he took great pains to depict light falling not only on the figures but also on the architecture. A light-and-shade continuum determines the city wall's volume and curve into the background. Light strikes sharply on the facing planes of the arched gateway and the city's clustered buildings. From the light's low angle, viewers might even speculate as to the time of day represented, morning or evening.

The Republic of Florence

Among fourteenth-century Italian city-states, the Republics of Florence and Siena were notable for their strong commitment to art. Both Florence and Siena (the major cities of these two republics) were urban centers of bankers and merchants with widespread international contacts. Chroniclers and historians recognized early on the importance of these two cities for the development of art; discussions comparing their artistic contributions extend back into the fourteenth century.

THE "MOST BEAUTIFUL" TUSCAN CHURCH The Republic of Florence was a dominant city-state during the fourteenth century. This belief was reinforced by statements such as one by the early historian Giovanni Villani (ca. 1270–1348) that Florence was "the daughter and the creature of Rome," suggesting a preeminence inherited from the Roman Empire. Florentines prided themselves on what they perceived as economic and cultural superiority. They translated this pride into landmark buildings such as Florence Cathedral (FIG. **19-12**). Recognized as the center for the most important religious observances in Florence, the cathedral was begun in

1296 by Arnolfo di Cambio. Intended as the "most beautiful and honorable church in Tuscany," this structure reveals the competitiveness Florentines felt with cities such as Siena and Pisa. Cathedral authorities planned for the church to hold the city's entire population, and although it only holds about thirty thousand (Florence's population at the time was slightly less than one hundred thousand), it seemed so large that even the noted architect Leon Battista Alberti commented that it seemed to cover "all of Tuscany with its shade." Like the facade of San Miniato al Monte (see FIG. 17-17), the architects ornamented the building's surfaces, in the old Tuscan fashion, with marble-encrusted geometric designs. This matched it to the eleventh-century Romanesque Baptistery of San Giovanni nearby (see FIG. 17-16). The vast gulf that separates this Italian church from its northern European counterparts is strikingly evident when the former is compared with a full-blown German representative of the High Gothic style, such as Cologne Cathedral (see FIG. 18-46).

Cologne Cathedral's emphatic stress on the vertical produces an awe-inspiring upward rush of almost unmatched vigor and intensity. The building has the character of an organic growth shooting heavenward, its toothed upper portions engaging the sky. The pierced, translucent stone tracery of the spires merges with the atmosphere.

Florence Cathedral clings to the ground and has no aspirations to flight. All emphasis is on the design's horizontal elements, and the building rests firmly and massively on the ground. Simple geometric volumes are defined clearly and show no tendency to merge either into each other or into the sky. The dome, though it may seem to be rising because of its ogival section, has a crisp, closed silhouette that sets it off emphatically against the sky behind it. But because this dome is the monument with which architectural historians usually in-

19-12 Arnolfo di Cambio and others, Florence Cathedral (view from the south), Florence, Italy, begun 1296.

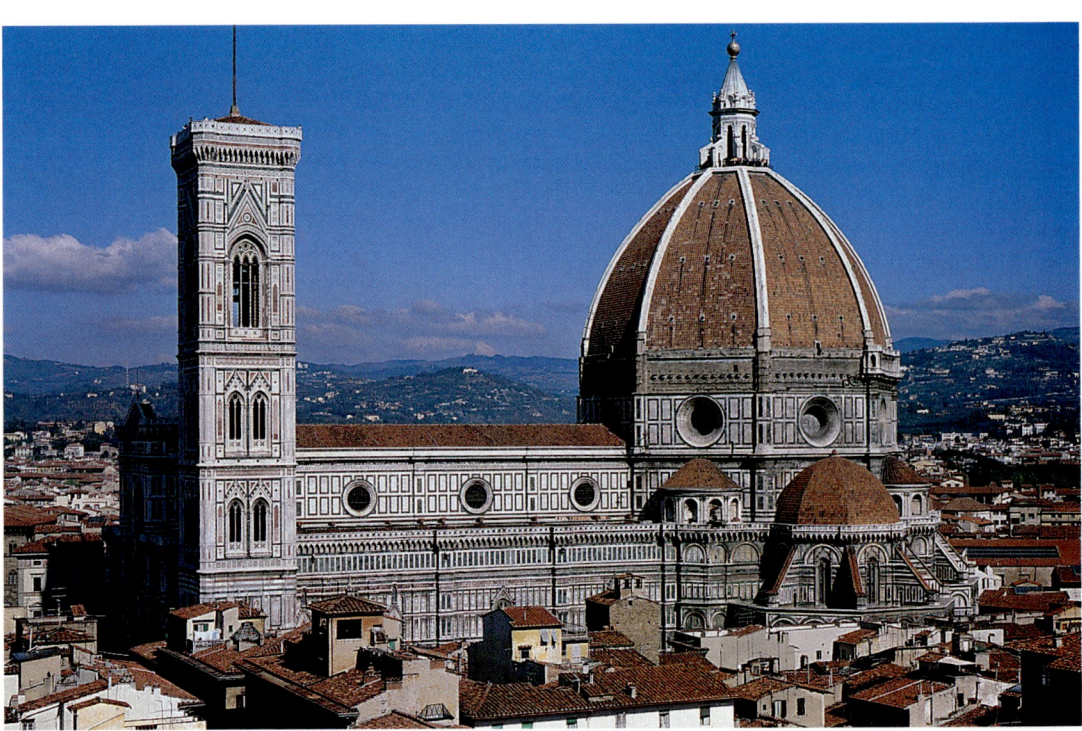

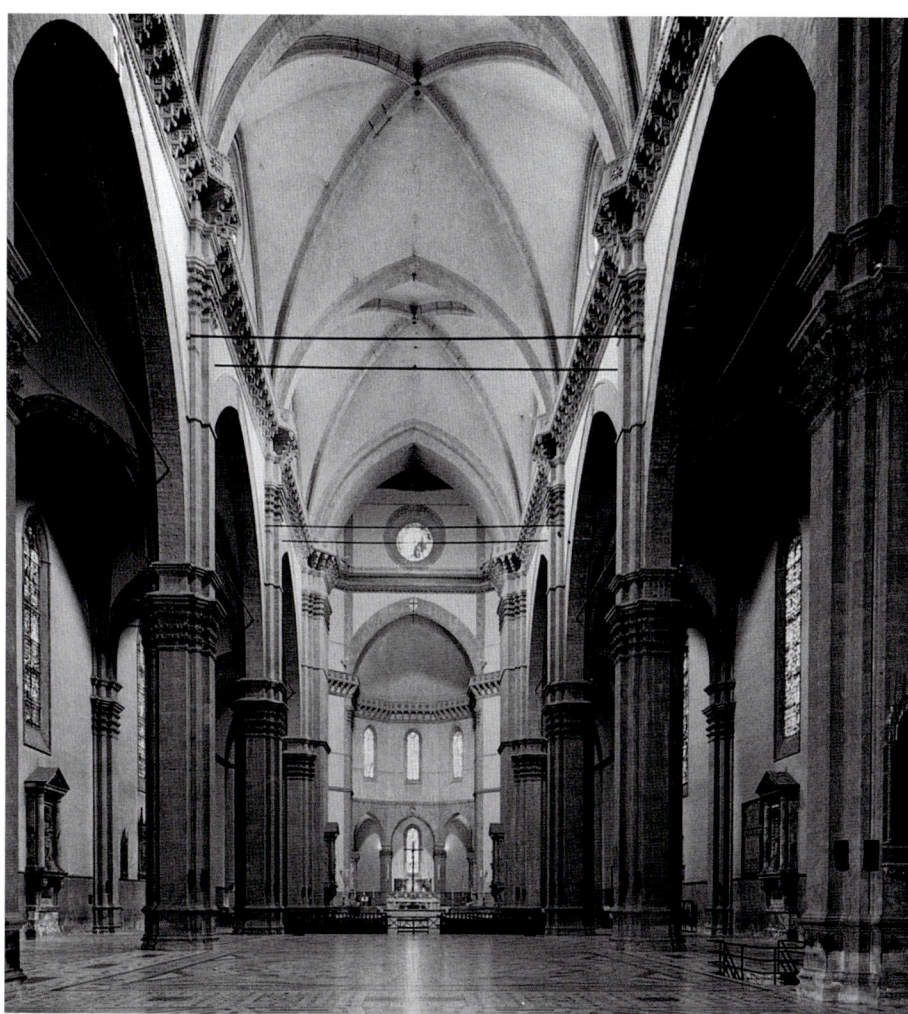

19-13   Nave of Florence Cathedral (view facing east), Florence, Italy, begun 1296.

troduce the Renaissance (it was built by Filippo Brunelleschi between 1420 and 1436), the following comparison of the campanile with the Cologne towers may be somewhat more appropriate in this discussion of fourteenth-century Italian art and architecture.

A TOWER OF BUILDING BLOCKS   Designed by the painter Giotto di Bondone in 1334 (and completed with some minor modifications after his death), the Florence campanile (FIG. 19-12) stands apart from the cathedral in the Italian tradition. In fact, it could stand anywhere else in Florence without looking out of place; it is essentially self-sufficient. The same hardly can be said of the Cologne towers (see FIG. 18-46). They are essential elements of the building behind them, and it would be unthinkable to detach one of them and place it somewhere else. No individual element in the Cologne grouping seems capable of an independent existence. One form merges into the next in an unending series of rising movements that pulls the eye upward and never permits it to rest until it reaches the sky. This structure's beauty is formless rather than formal—a beauty that speaks to the heart rather than to the intellect.

The Italian tower is entirely different. Neatly subdivided into cubic sections, Giotto's tower is the sum of its clearly distinguished parts. Not only could this tower be removed from

the building without adverse effects, but also each of the component parts—cleanly separated from each other by continuous moldings—seems capable of existing independently as an object of considerable aesthetic appeal. This compartmentalization is reminiscent of the Romanesque style, but it also forecasts the ideals of Renaissance architecture. Artists hoped to express structure in the clear, logical relationships of the component parts and to produce self-sufficient works that could exist in complete independence. Compared to Cologne's north towers, Giotto's campanile has a cool and rational quality that appeals more to the intellect than to the emotions.

In Florence Cathedral's plan, the nave almost appears to have been added to the crossing complex as an afterthought. In fact, the nave was built first, mostly according to Arnolfo's original plans (except for the vaulting), and the crossing was redesigned midway through the fourteenth century to increase the cathedral's interior space. In its present form, the area beneath the dome is the design's focal point, and the nave leads to it. To visitors from the north, the nave seems as strange as the plan; neither has a northern European counterpart. The Florence nave bays (FIG. 19-13) are twice as deep as those of Amiens (see FIG. 18-19), and the wide arcades permit the shallow aisles to become part of the central nave. The result is an interior of unmatched spaciousness. The accent

19-14   Nave of Santa Maria Novella, Florence, Italy, ca. 1246–1470.

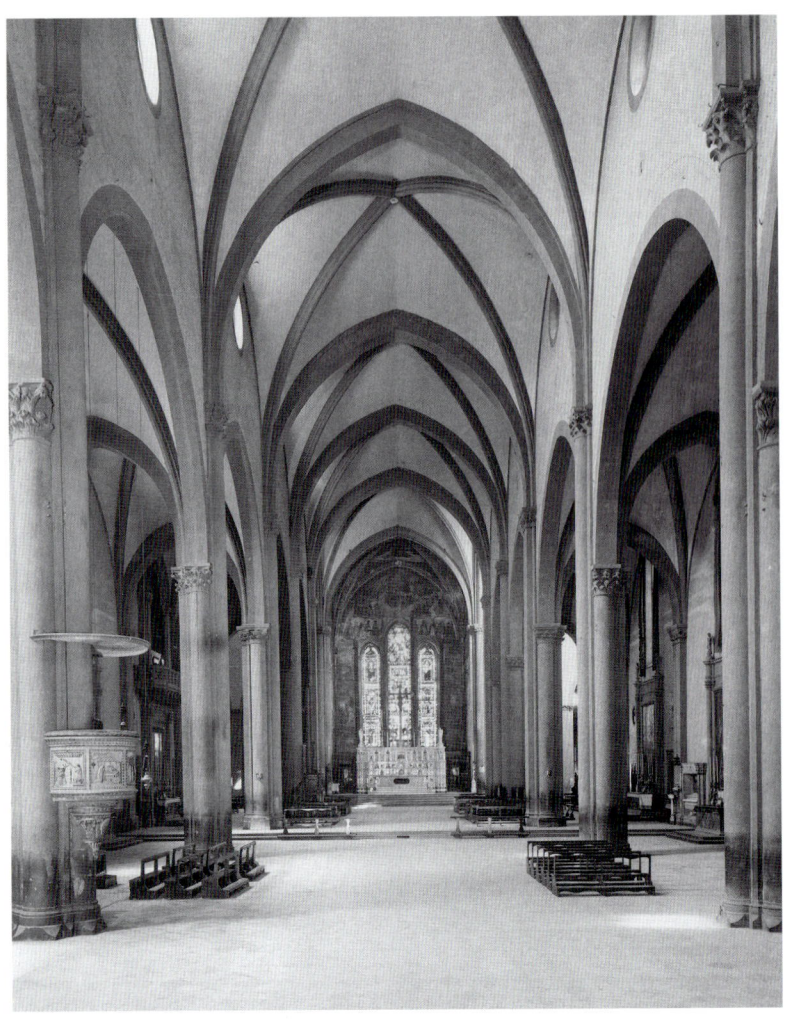

here, as on the exterior, is on the horizontal elements. The substantial capitals of the piers prevent them from soaring into the vaults and emphasize their function as supports.

The facade of Florence Cathedral was not completed until the nineteenth century and then in a form much altered from its original design. In fact, until the seventeenth century, Italian builders exhibited little concern for the facades of their churches, and dozens remain unfinished to this day. One reason for this may be that the facades were not conceived as integral parts of the structures but as screens that could be added to the church exterior at any time.

ACCOMMODATING THE FAITHFUL   The increased importance of the mendicant orders during the fourteenth century led to the construction of large churches by the Franciscans (Santa Croce; FIG. Intro-3) and the Dominicans (see "Mendicant Orders and Confraternities," page 537) in Florence. The Florentine government and contributions from private citizens subsidized the commissioning of the Dominicans' Santa Maria Novella (FIG. 19-14) around 1246. The large congregations these orders attracted necessitated the expansive scale of this church. Marble striping along the ogival arches and small *oculi* (round openings) punctuate the nave. Originally, a screen *(tramezzo)* placed across the nave separated the friars from the lay audience; the Mass was performed on sepa-

rate altars on each side of the screen. Church officials removed this screen in the mid-sixteenth century to encourage greater lay participation in the Mass. A powerful Florentine family, the Rucellai, commissioned the facade for Santa Maria Novella from architect Leon Battista Alberti in the mid-fifteenth century.

A MEMORIAL TO THE BLACK DEATH   The tabernacle of the Virgin Mary in Florence's Or San Michele (FIG. 19-15) is the work of two "Giotteschi" (followers of Giotto), ANDREA DI CIONE, known as ORCAGNA (active 1343–1368) and BERNARDO DADDI (ca. 1290–1348). Orcagna produced the work's architecture and sculpture, and Bernardo Daddi painted the panel of the Madonna, which the tabernacle enshrines. Or San Michele was originally a grain market, a *loggia* (open-sided arcade) into the street; it was transformed into a church, confraternity building, and center for the city's guilds. After the plague in 1348, upper stories were added to house a granary. Or San Michele also functioned as a guild church, and each guild was assigned a niche on the building's exterior for a commissioned statue of its patron saint. Donations prompted by the plague funded the construction of Orcagna's tabernacle, which donors no doubt perceived as a kind of memorial to both the dead and the survivors. Individuals made bequests to a supposed miraculous portrait of the Virgin, which later burned and was replaced with the image by Bernardo Daddi. The

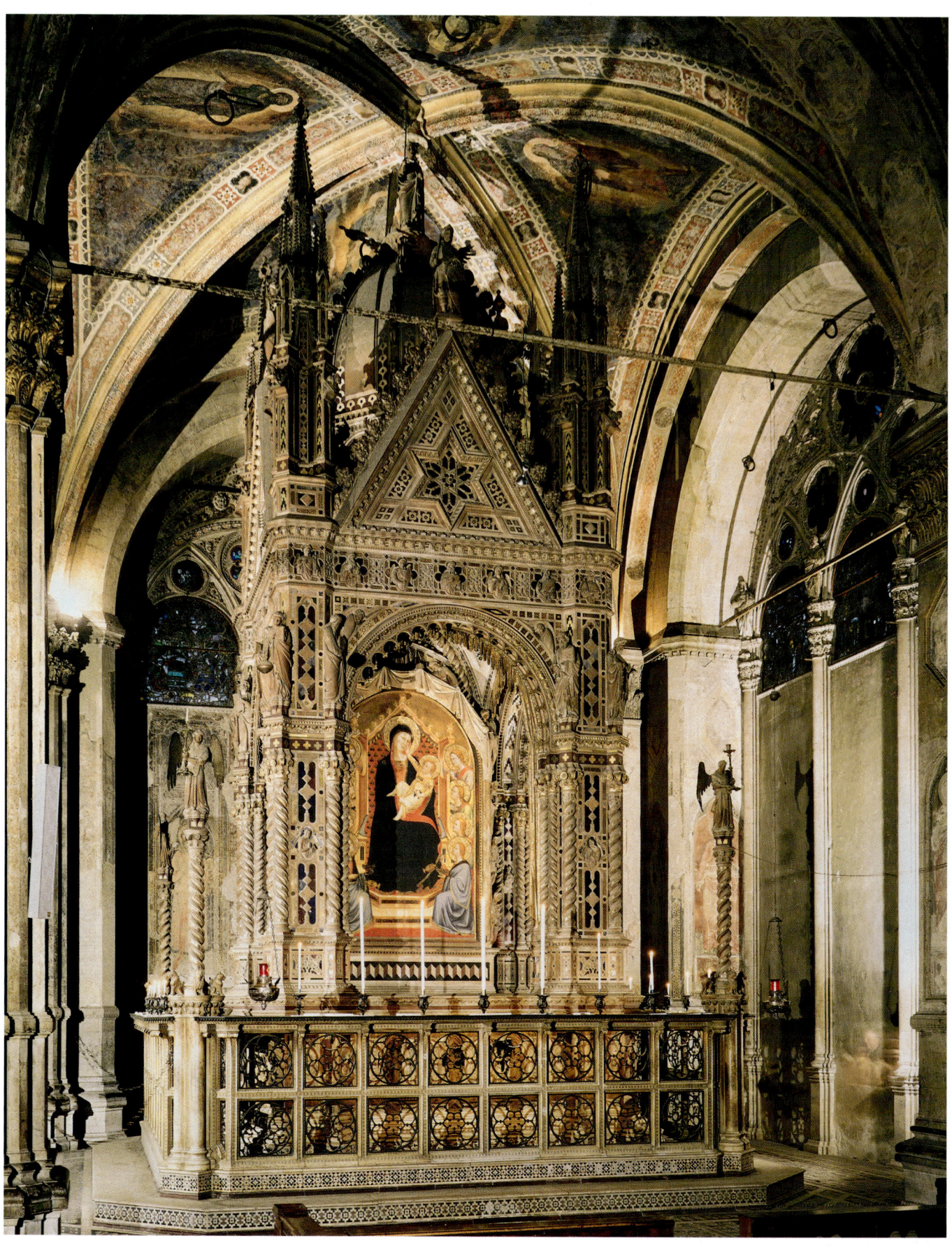

19-15 ANDREA ORCAGNA, tabernacle, Or San Michele, Florence, Italy, begun 1349. Mosaic, gold, marble, lapis lazuli. BERNARDO DADDI, *Madonna and Child with Saints,* painted panel insert, 1346–1347.

entire tabernacle, started in 1349, took ten years to complete, costing the vast sum of eighty-seven thousand gold florins.

Orcagna, an artistic virtuoso, was an architect, sculptor, and painter; he was familiar with the styles and practice of all the arts in post-Giotto Florence. The architectural enframement of the tabernacle recalls the polygonal piers and the slender spiral colonettes of the Florence Cathedral and campanile (FIG. 19-12), as well as the triangular pediment, fenestration, and pinnacles of a typical Italian Gothic facade (FIG. 18-56). The planar surfaces sparkle with gold, lapis lazuli, mosaic, and finely cut marble, all inlaid in geometric patterns called *Cosmato work* (from *Cosmati,* the name given to craftsmen who worked in marble and mosaic in the twelfth to fourteenth centuries, many belonging to a family of that name). The effect is that of a gem-encrusted, scintillating shrine or reliquary, more the work of a jeweler than an architect.

The lavish ornamentation and costly materials recall the medieval association of precious material with holy things and themes, in this case with the original miracle-working image of the Virgin, which the new *Madonna and Child* replaced. Bernardo Daddi interpreted this most popular of Gothic subjects in a light, delicate, and charming manner appropriate to the humanizing of religion and to the emotional requirements of private devotion. Flanked by angels, two of whom swing censers filled with incense, the enthroned Virgin sits within a round arch with sculptured curtains. The Christ Child playfully touches his mother's face. The composition is conventional but softened by sentiment. The architectural enframement provides an illusionistic stage for the image, composing an ensemble of architecture, painting, and sculpture to serve Marian devotion (devotion to the Virgin Mary). This tabernacle attests to the versatility of Florentine artists after Giotto as they followed the various paths his original inspiration suggested.

The Republic of Siena

A MAJESTIC PAINTING OF MARY   Siena, like Florence, was a commanding presence in fourteenth-century Italy. Particularly proud of their victory over the Florentines at the battle of Monteperti in 1260, the Sienese worshiped the Virgin Mary, whom they believed had sponsored their victory. Sienese devotion to the Virgin was paramount in the religious life of the city, whose citizens could boast of Siena's dedication to the Queen of Heaven as more ancient and venerable than that of all others. It is important that loyalty to the secular republican city-state was linked with devotion to its favorite saint. The Virgin became not only protector of every citizen but also of the city itself.

The works of DUCCIO DI BUONINSEGNA (active ca. 1278–1318) represent Sienese art in its supreme achievement. His immense altarpiece, the *Maestà,* was designed to replace a much smaller painting of the Virgin Mary. Duccio's inscription of his name at the base of the Virgin's throne in the *Maestà* is part of a prayer for himself and for the city of Siena, its cathedral, and its churches.

The *Maestà,* painted in tempera front and back and composed of many panels, was commissioned for the high altar of the Cathedral of Siena in 1308 and completed by Duccio and his assistants in 1311. As originally executed, it consisted of a seven-foot-high central panel (FIG. **19-16**), surmounted by seven pinnacles above, and a *predella,* or raised shelf, of panels at the base, altogether some thirteen feet high. Unfortunately, the work no longer can be seen in its entirety. It was dismantled in subsequent centuries, and many of its panels are now scattered as single masterpieces among the world's museums.

The main panel of the front side represents the Virgin enthroned in majesty (maestà) as Queen of Heaven amid cho-

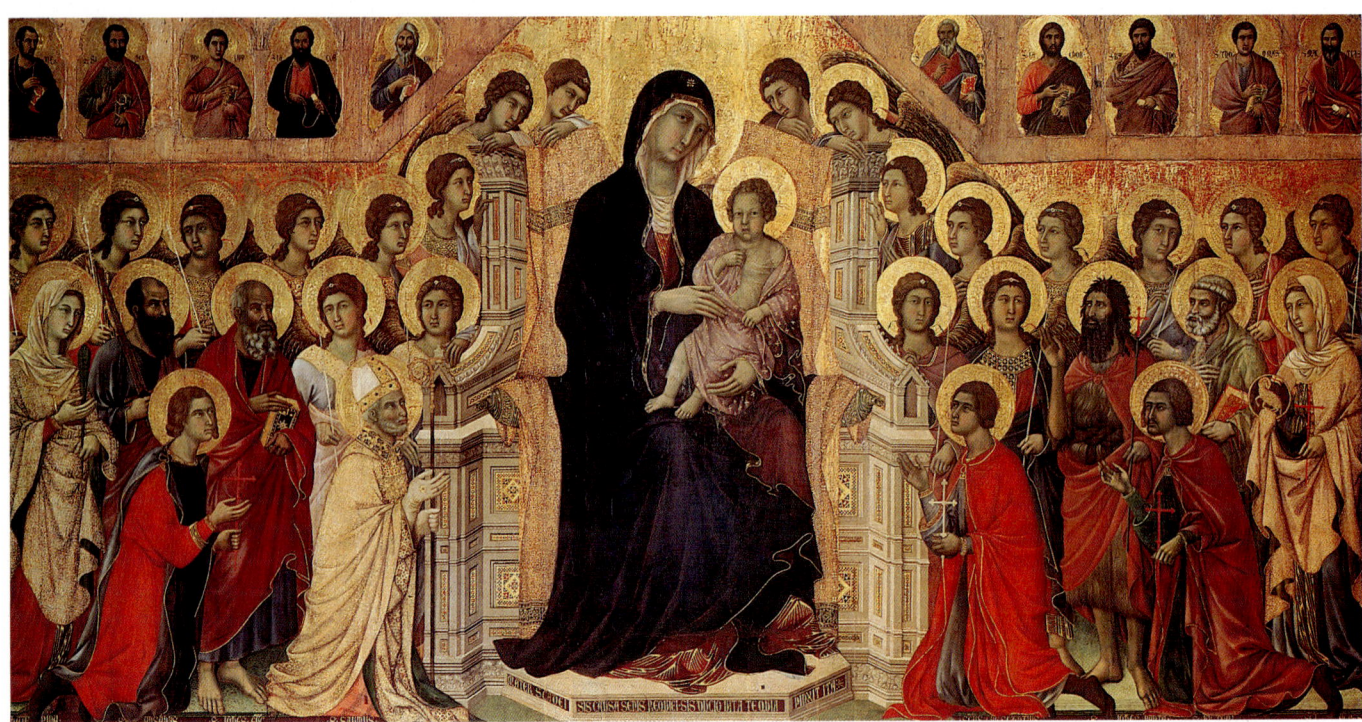

19-16   DUCCIO DI BUONINSEGNA, *Virgin and Child Enthroned with Saints,* principal panel of the *Maestà* altarpiece, from the Siena Cathedral, Siena, Italy, 1308–1311. Tempera on wood, panel 7′ × 13′. Museo dell'Opera del Duomo, Siena.

ruses of angels and saints. Duccio derived the composition's formality and symmetry, along with the figures and facial types of the principal angels and saints, from Byzantine tradition. But the artist relaxed the strict frontality and rigidity of the figures in the typical Byzantine icon and iconostasis, or apse mosaic; they turn to each other in quiet conversation. Further, Duccio individualized the faces of the four saints kneeling in the foreground who perform their ceremonial gestures without stiffness. Similarly, Duccio softened the usual Byzantine hard body outlines and drapery patterning. The drapery, particularly that of the female saints at both ends of the panel, falls and curves loosely. This is a feature familiar in northern Gothic works (see FIG. 18-37) and is a mark of the artistic dialogue that occurred between Italy and the north in the fourteenth century.

These changes are part of a new naturalism that only slowly made itself apparent in details. This is an altarpiece, and the artist respected the age-old requirement that as such it would occupy the very center of the sanctuary as the focus of worship. He knew it should be an object holy in itself—a work of splendor to the eyes, precious in its message and its materials. As such, its function naturally limited experimentation with depicting narrative action and producing illusionistic effects, such as Giotto's, by modeling forms and adjusting their placement in pictorial space.

Instead, the Queen of Heaven panel is a miracle of color composition and texture manipulation, unfortunately not apparent in a photo. Close inspection of the original reveals what the Sienese artists learned from new media and systems of ornament. In the thirteenth and fourteenth centuries, Italy was the distribution center for the great silk trade from China and the Middle East (see "Silk and the Silk Road," Chapter 7, page 194). After processing in city-states such as Lucca and Florence, merchants exported the silk throughout Europe to satisfy an immense market for sumptuous dress. (Dante, Petrarch, and many of the humanists decried the appetite for luxury in costume, which to them represented a decline in civic and moral virtue.) People throughout Europe (Duccio and other artists among them) prized fabrics from China, Persia, Byzantium, and the Islamic realms. In the *Maestà* panel, Duccio created the glistening and shimmering effects of textiles, adapting the motifs and design stratagems of exotic materials.

If on the front panel of the *Maestà* Duccio showed himself as the great master of the formal altarpiece, the small accompanying panels, front and back, reveal his powers as a narrative painter. In the numerous panels on the back, he illustrated the later life of Christ—his ministry (on the predella), his Passion (on the main panel), and his Resurrection and appearances to the disciples (on the pinnacles). In the small narrative pictures, Duccio relaxed the formalism appropriate to the iconic, symbolic representation of the maestà and revealed his ability not only as a narrator but also as an experimenter with new pictorial ideas. In a synoptic sequence on one of the small panels, *Betrayal of Jesus* (FIG. **19-17**), the

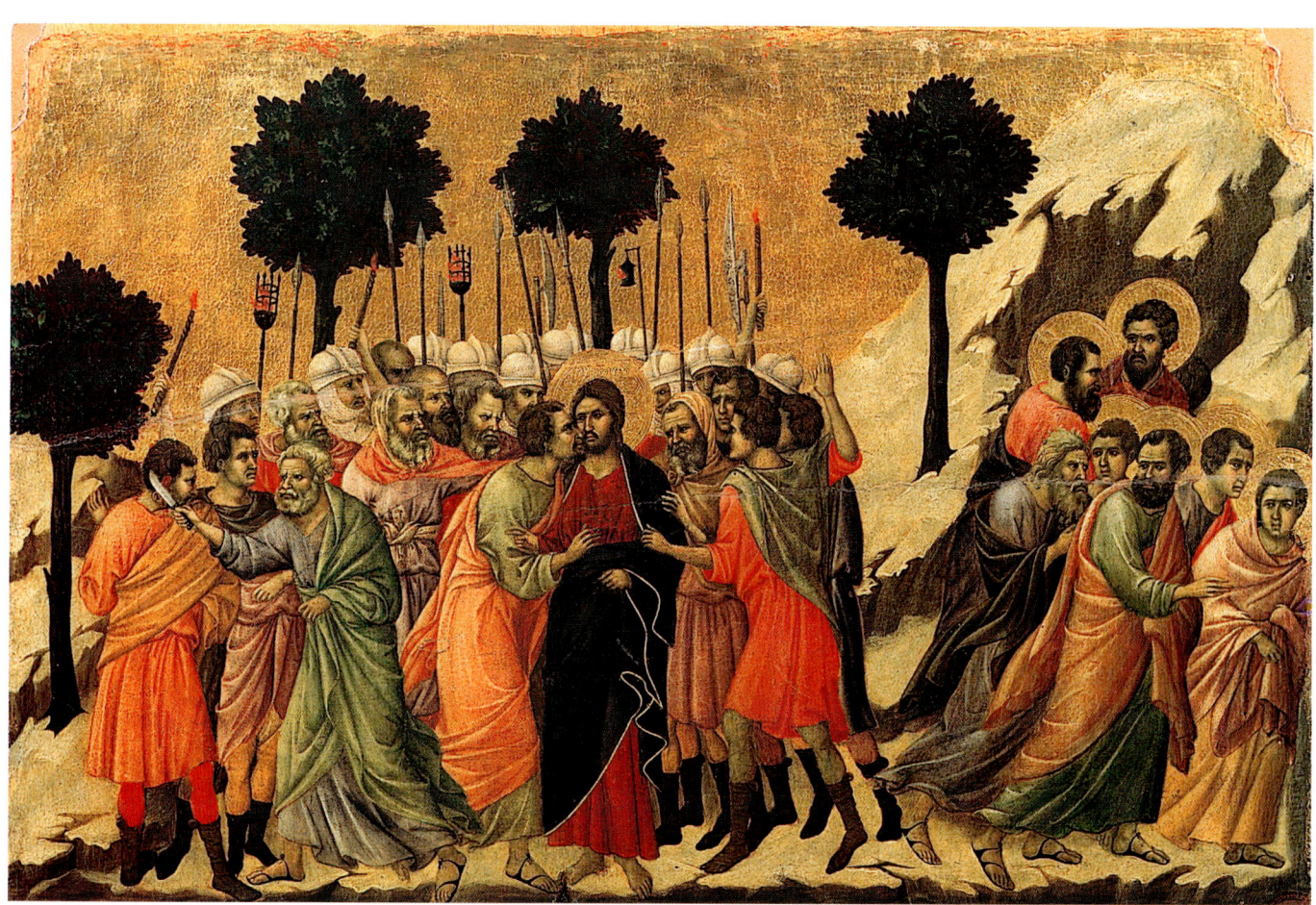

19-17 DUCCIO DI BUONINSEGNA, *Betrayal of Jesus*, detail from the back of the *Maestà* altarpiece, from the Siena Cathedral, Siena, Italy, 1309–1311. Tempera on wood, detail approx. 1′ 10$\frac{1}{2}$″ × 3′ 4″. Museo dell'Opera del Duomo, Siena.

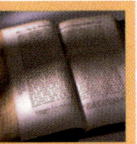

WRITTEN SOURCES

A Majestic Altarpiece
Duccio's Maestà

Agnolo di Tura del Grasso provided one of the most complete records of the completion and installation of the *Maestà* in the Cathedral of Siena. Scholars consider his account reliable, as he was the keeper of the record books of Siena's chief financial magistracy. He described the pomp and ceremony that accompanied the transport of the altarpiece to the cathedral:

> This [*Maestà*] was painted by master Duccio di Niccolò, painter of Siena, who was in his time the most skillful painter one could find in these lands. The panel was painted outside the Porta a Stalloreggi in the Borgo a Laterino, in the house of the Muciatti. The Sienese took the panel to the Cathedral at noontime on the ninth of June [1311], with great devotions and processions, with the bishop of Siena, Ruggero da Casole, with all of the clergy of the Cathedral, and with all the monks and nuns of Siena, and the Nove [that is, the Council of the Nine Lords], with the city officials, the Podestà and the Captain, and all the citizens with coats of arms and those with more distinguished coats of arms, with lighted lamps in hand. And thus, the women and children went through Siena with much devotion and around the Campo in procession, ringing all the bells for joy, and this entire day the shops stayed closed for devotions, and throughout Siena they gave many alms to the poor people, with many speeches and prayers to God and to his mother, Madonna ever Virgin Mary, who helps, preserves and increases in peace the good state of the city of Siena and its territory, as advocate and protectress of that city, and who defends the city from all danger and all evil. And so, this panel was placed in the Cathedral on the high altar. The panel is painted on the back with the Old Testament [sic], with the Passion of Jesus Christ, and on the front is the Virgin Mary with her son in her arms and many saints at the side. Everything is ornamented with fine gold; it cost three thousand gold florins.[1]

[1] James H. Stubblebine, *Duccio di Buoninsegna and His School* (Princeton, N.J.: Princeton University Press, 1979), 1:33–34.

artist represented several episodes of the event—the betrayal of Jesus by Judas's false kiss, the disciples fleeing in terror, and Peter cutting off the ear of the high priest's servant. Although the background, with its golden sky and rock formations, remains traditional, the style of the figures before it has changed quite radically. The bodies are not the flat frontal shapes of earlier Byzantine art. Duccio imbued them with mass, modeled them with a range from light to dark, and arranged their draperies around them convincingly. Even more novel and striking is how the figures seem to react to the central event. Through posture, gesture, and even facial expression, they display a variety of emotions. Duccio extended himself to differentiate among the anger of Peter, the malice of Judas (echoed in the faces of the throng about Jesus), and the apprehension and timidity of the fleeing disciples. These figures are actors in a religious drama that, in a lively performance, the artist interpreted in terms of thoroughly human actions and reactions. In this and similar narrative panels, Duccio took another decisive step toward the humanization of religious subject matter. The greatness of the *Maestà* did not have to wait for modern acclaim. A Sienese chronicler noted that nothing like it had been done anywhere else in Italy (see "A Majestic Altarpiece: Duccio's *Maestà*," above).

CREATING AN "INTERNATIONAL STYLE" Duccio's successors in the Sienese school displayed even greater originality and assurance than Duccio. SIMONE MARTINI (ca. 1285–1344) was a pupil of Duccio and a close friend of Petrarch, who praised him highly for his portrait of "Laura" (the woman to whom Petrarch dedicated his sonnets). Martini worked for the French kings in Naples and Sicily and, in his last years, produced paintings for the papal court at Avignon, where he came in contact with northern painters. By adapting the insubstantial but luxuriant patterns of the French Gothic manner to Sienese art and, in turn, by acquainting northern painters with the Sienese style, Martini was instrumental in forming the so-called International Style. This new style swept Europe during the late fourteenth and early fifteenth centuries. It appealed to the aristocratic taste for brilliant colors, lavish costumes, intricate ornamentation, and themes involving splendid processions so knights and their ladies—complete with entourages, horses, and greyhounds—could glitter to advantage.

Martini's own style did not quite reach the full exuberance of the developed International Style, but his famous *Annunciation* altarpiece (FIG. **19-18**) provides a counterpoint to Giotto's style. Elegant shapes and radiant color; flowing, fluttering line; and weightless figures in a spaceless setting characterize the *Annunciation*. The complex etiquette of the European chivalric courts dictated the presentation. The angel Gabriel has just alighted, the breeze of his passage lifting his mantle, his iridescent wings still beating. The gold of his sumptuous gown heraldically represents the celestial realm whence he bears his message. The Virgin, putting down her book of devotions, shrinks demurely from Gabriel's reverent genuflection, an appropriate gesture in the presence of royalty. She draws about her the deep blue, golden-hemmed mantle, the heraldic colors she wears as Queen of Heaven. Despite the Virgin's modesty and diffidence and the tremendous import of the angel's message, the scene subordinates

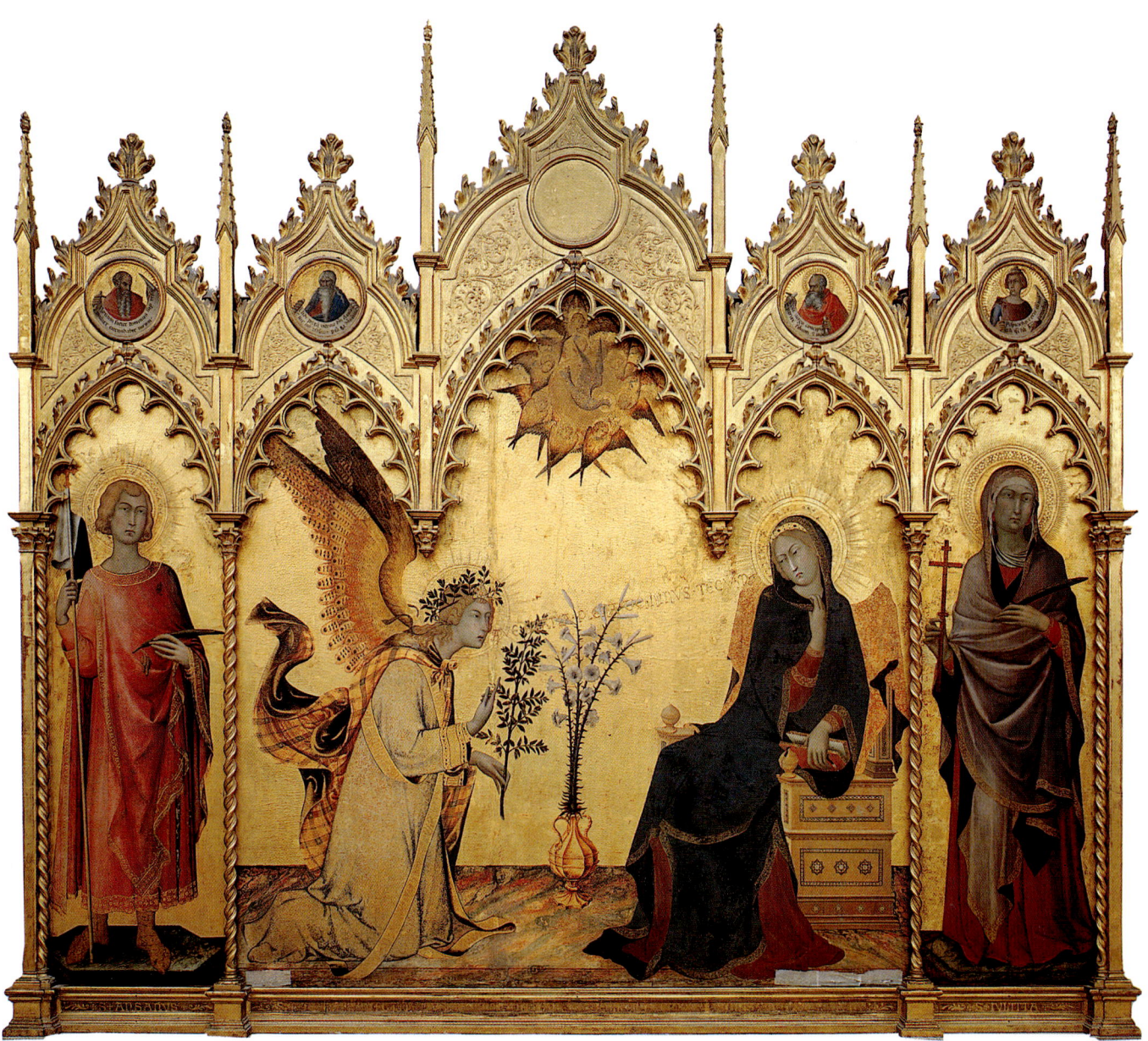

19-18   SIMONE MARTINI and LIPPO MEMMI(?), *Annunciation,* 1333 (frame reconstructed in the nineteenth century). Tempera and gold leaf on wood, approx. 10′ 1″ × 8′ 8¾″. Galleria degli Uffizi, Florence.

drama to court ritual and structural experimentation to surface splendor. The intricate tracery of the richly tooled Late Gothic frame enhances the painted splendor. Of French inspiration, it replaced the more sober, clean-cut shapes traditional in Italy, and its appearance here is eloquent testimony to the two-way flow of transalpine influences that fashioned the International Style.

Simone Martini and his student and assistant, LIPPO MEMMI, signed the altarpiece and dated it (1333). Lippo's contribution to the *Annunciation* is still a matter of debate, but historians now generally agree he painted the two lateral saints, Saint Ansanus and Saint Margaret(?). Lippo drew these figures, which are reminiscent of the jamb statues of Gothic church portals, with greater solidity and without the linear elegance of Martini's central pair. Given

the medieval and Renaissance workshop practices, it is often next to impossible to distinguish the master's hand from those of assistants, especially if the master corrected or redid part of the latter's work (see "Mastering a Craft: Artistic Training in Renaissance Italy," page 554). This uncertainty is exacerbated by the fact that *Annunciation's* current architectural enframements are dated almost a century later than the central panel.

SEEKING CONVINCING SPATIAL ILLUSION

The Lorenzetti brothers, also Duccio's students, shared in the general experiments in pictorial realism that characterized the fourteenth century, especially in their seeking of convincing spatial illusions. Going well beyond his master, PIETRO LORENZETTI (active 1320–1348) achieved remarkable success

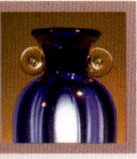

Mastering a Craft
Artistic Training in the Renaissance

In fourteenth- through sixteenth-century Italy, training to become a professional artist (earning membership in the appropriate guild) was a laborious and lengthy process. Because Italians perceived art as a trade, they expected artists to be trained as they would in any other profession. Accordingly, aspiring artists started their training at an early age, anywhere from seven to fifteen years old. Their fathers would negotiate arrangements with specific master artists, whereby each youth lived with a master for a specified number of years, usually between five and six years. During that time, they served as apprentices to the masters in the workshop, learning the trade. This living arrangement served as a major obstacle for aspiring female artists. Certainly, it was considered inappropriate for young girls to live in a master's household.

The skills apprentices learned varied with the type of studio they joined. Those apprenticed to painters learned to grind pigments, draw, prepare wood panels for painting, gild, and lay plaster for fresco. Sculptors in training learned to manipulate different materials (for example, wood, stone, terracotta, wax, bronze, or stucco), although many sculpture workshops specialized in only one or two of these materials. For stone carving, apprentices learned their craft by blocking out the master's designed sculpture.

The guilds supervised this rigorous training. Not only did they want to ensure their professional reputations by admitting only the most talented members, but they also wanted to control the number of artists (to limit undue competition). Toward this end they frequently tried to regulate the number of apprentices working under a single master. Surely the quality of the apprentices a master trained reflected the master's competence. When encouraging a prospective apprentice to join his studio, the Paduan painter Francesco Squarcione boasted he could teach "the true art of perspective and everything necessary to the art of painting. . . . I made a man of Andrea Mantegna [see FIGS. 21-47, 21-48, 21-49, and 21-50] who stayed with me and I will also do the same to you."[1]

As their skills developed, apprentices took on more-difficult tasks. After completing their apprenticeships, artists entered the appropriate guilds. For example, painters, who ground pigments, joined the guild of apothecaries; sculptors were members of the guild of stoneworkers; and goldsmiths entered the silk guild, because gold often was stretched into threads wound around silk for weaving. Such memberships served as certification of the artists' competence. Once "certified," artists often affiliated themselves with established workshops, as assistants to master artists. This was largely for practical reasons. New artists could not expect to receive many commissions, and the cost of establishing their own workshops was high. In any case, this arrangement was not permanent, and workshops were not necessarily static enterprises. Although well-established and respected studios existed, workshops could be organized around individual masters (with no set studio locations) or organized for a specific project, especially an extensive decoration program.

Generally, assistants were charged with gilding frames and backgrounds, completing decorative work, and, occasionally, rendering architectural settings. Artists regarded figures, especially those central to the represented subject, as the most important and difficult parts of a painting, and the master retained responsibility for such figures. Assistants were allowed to paint some of the less important or marginal figures, but only under the master's close supervision.

Eventually, of course, artists hoped to attract patrons and establish themselves as masters. As the anonymity of medieval art moved toward artists' emancipation during the fifteenth and sixteenth centuries, artists rose in rank from artisan to artist-scientist. The value of their individual skills—and their reputations—became increasingly important to their patrons and clients. This apprentice system—the passing of knowledge from one generation to the next—accounts for the sense of continuity people experience when reviewing Italian Renaissance art.

[1] Giuseppe Fiocco, *Mantegna: La Cappella Ovetari nella Chiesa degli Eremitani* (Milan: A. Pizzi, 1974), 7.

---

in a large panel, *The Birth of the Virgin* (FIG. **19-19**). Like Duccio's *Maestà* and Simone Martini's *Annunciation,* the panel was painted for the Siena Cathedral as part of a program honoring the Virgin Mary, heavenly Queen of the Republic. Pietro Lorenzetti painted the wooden architectural members that divide the panel into three compartments as though they extend back into the painted space, as if viewers were looking through the wooden frame (apparently added later) into a boxlike stage, where the event takes place. That one of the vertical members cuts across one of the figures,

blocking part of it from view, strengthens the illusion. In subsequent centuries, artists exploited this use of architectural elements to enhance pictorial illusion. A long, successful history of such visual illusions produced by unifying both real and simulated architecture with painted figures evolved from these experiments.

Pietro Lorenzetti did not make just a structural advance here; his very subject represents a marked step in the advance of worldly realism. Saint Anne, reclining wearily as the midwives wash the child and the women bring gifts, is the

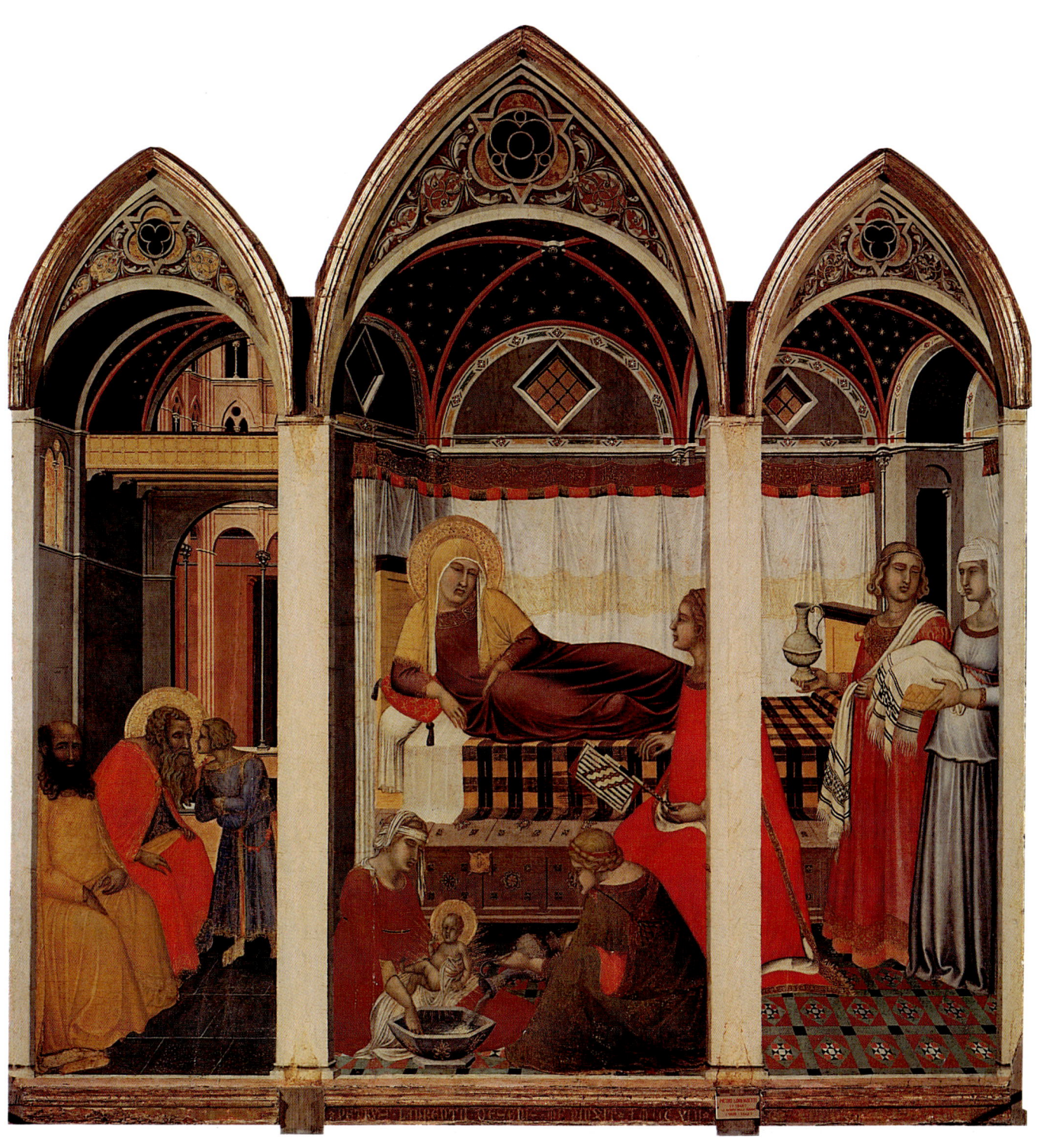

19-19 PIETRO LORENZETTI, *The Birth of the Virgin,* from Altar of Saint Savinus, Siena Cathedral, Siena, Italy, 1342. Tempera on wood, approx. 6′ 1″ × 5′ 11″. Museo dell'Opera del Duomo, Siena.

center of an episode that occurs in an upper-class Italian house of the period. A number of carefully observed domestic details and the scene at the left, where Joachim eagerly awaits the news of the delivery, place the event in an actual household, as if viewers had moved the panels of the walls back and peered inside. Pietro Lorenzetti joined structural innovation in illusionistic space with the new curiosity that led to careful inspection and recording of what lay directly before artists' eyes in the everyday world.

A BASTION OF STRENGTH AND POWER The Sinese were concerned about matters of both church and state. The city-state was a proud commercial and political rival of Florence. The secular center of the community, the town hall, was almost as much the object of civic pride as the cathedral. A building such as the Palazzo Pubblico of Siena (FIG. **19-20**) must have earned the admiration of Siena's citizens as well as of visiting strangers, inspiring in them respect for the city's power and success. More symmetrical in its design than most buildings of its type and period, it abuts a lofty tower, which (along with Giotto's campanile in Florence) is one of the finest in Italy. This tall structure served as lookout over the city and the countryside around it and as a bell tower for ringing signals of all sorts to the populace. The city, a self-contained political unit, had to defend itself against neighboring cities and often against kings and emperors. In addition, it had to be secure against internal upheavals common in the history of the Italian city-republics. Feuds between rich and powerful families, class struggle, even uprisings of the whole populace against the city governors were constant threats. The Italian town hall's heavy walls and battlements eloquently express how the city governors frequently needed to defend themselves against their own citizens. The high tower, out of reach of most missiles, includes machicolated galleries (galleries with holes in its floors to allow stones or hot liquids to be dumped on enemies below). These were built out on corbels around the top of the structures to provide openings for a vertical (downward) defense of the tower's base.

VISUALIZING GOOD AND BAD GOVERNMENTS Pietro Lorenzetti's brother AMBROGIO LORENZETTI (active 1319–1348) elaborated the Sinese advances in illusionistic representation in spectacular fashion in a vast fresco program in the Palazzo Pubblico. Ambrogio Lorenzetti produced three frescoes: *Allegory of Good Government, Bad Government and the Effects of Bad Government in the City*, and *Effects of Good Government in the City and in the Country*. The turbulent politics of the Italian cities—the violent party struggles, the overthrow and reinstatement of governments—certainly would have called for solemn reminders of fair and just administration. And the city hall was just the place for paintings such as Ambrogio Lorenzetti's.

In *Effects of Good Government in the City and in the Country*, the artist depicted the urban and rural effects of good government. *Peaceful City* (FIG. **19-21**) is a panoramic view of Siena, with its clustering palaces, markets, towers, churches, streets, and walls. The city's traffic moves peacefully, the guilds' members ply their trades and crafts, and a cluster of radiant maidens, hand in hand, perform a graceful circling dance. The artist fondly observed the life of his city, and its architecture gave him an opportunity to apply Sinese artists' rapidly growing knowledge of perspective. Passing through the city gate to the countryside beyond its walls, Ambrogio Lorenzetti's *Peaceful Country* (FIG. **19-22**) presents a bird's-eye view of the undulating Tuscan countryside—its villas, castles, plowed farmlands, and peasants going about their seasonal occupations. An allegorical figure of Security hovers above the landscape, unfurling a scroll that promises safety to all who live under the rule of the law. In this sweeping view of an actual countryside, *Peaceful Country* represented one of the first appearances of landscape in Western art since antiquity. The difference here is that the artist particularized the landscape—as well as the city view—by careful observation and endowed the painting with the character of a portrait of a specific place and environment. By combining some of Giotto's analytical powers with Duccio's narrative talent, Ambrogio Lorenzetti achieved more spectacular results than those of either of his two great predecessors.

The Black Death may have ended the careers of both Lorenzettis. They disappear from historical records in 1348, the year that brought so much horror to defenseless Europe. It is an irony of history that as Western societies drew both themselves and the world into ever-clearer visual focus, they realized even more clearly that material things are perishable. The ideas that gained momentum in the fourteenth century—humanism, direct observation, greater concern with the solidity of forms, and the interest in illusion—became prominent in the following centuries, during a period known as the Renaissance.

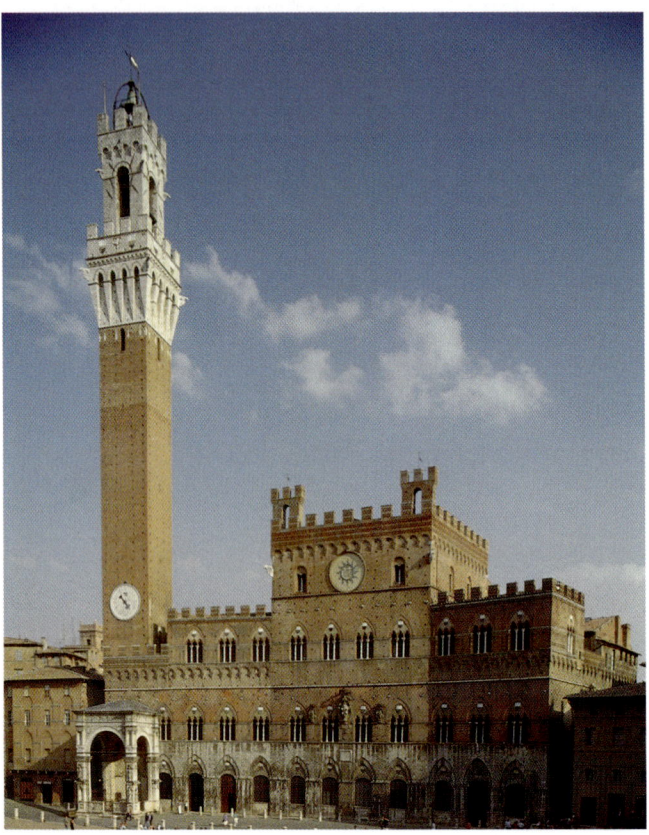

19-20 Palazzo Pubblico, Siena, Italy, 1288–1309.

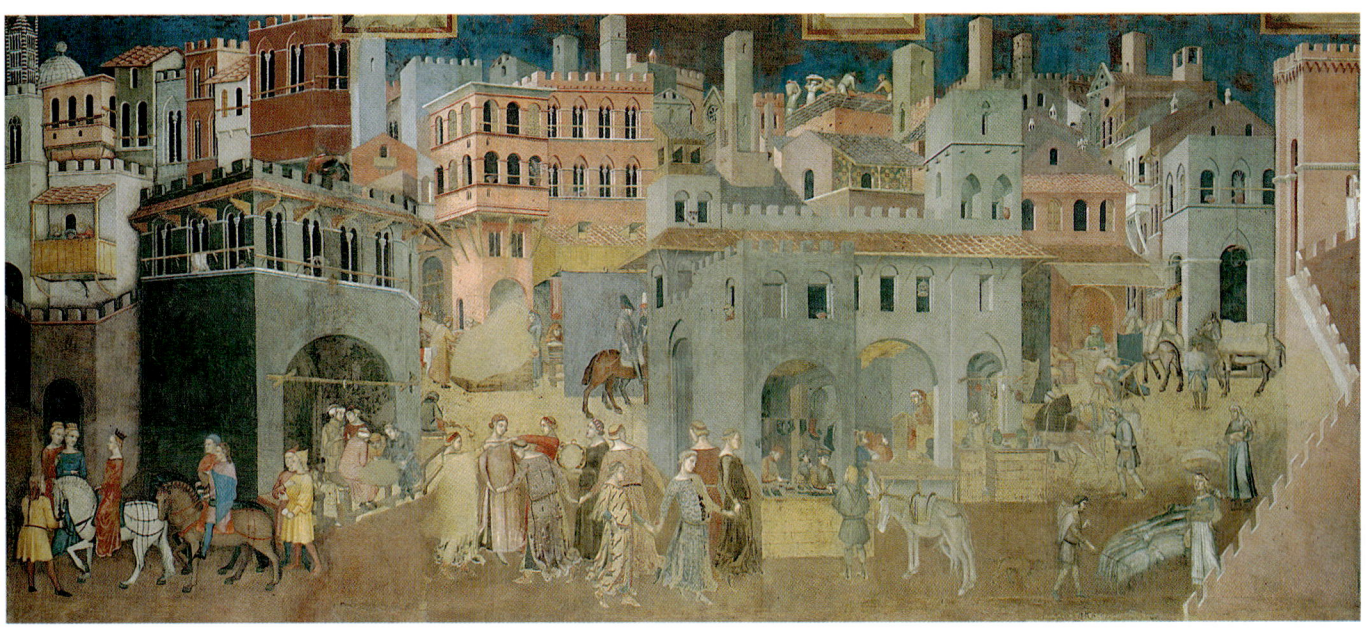

19-21   AMBROGIO LORENZETTI, *Peaceful City,* detail from the fresco *Effects of Good Government in the City and in the Country,* Sala della Pace, Palazzo Pubblico, Siena, Italy, 1338–1339.

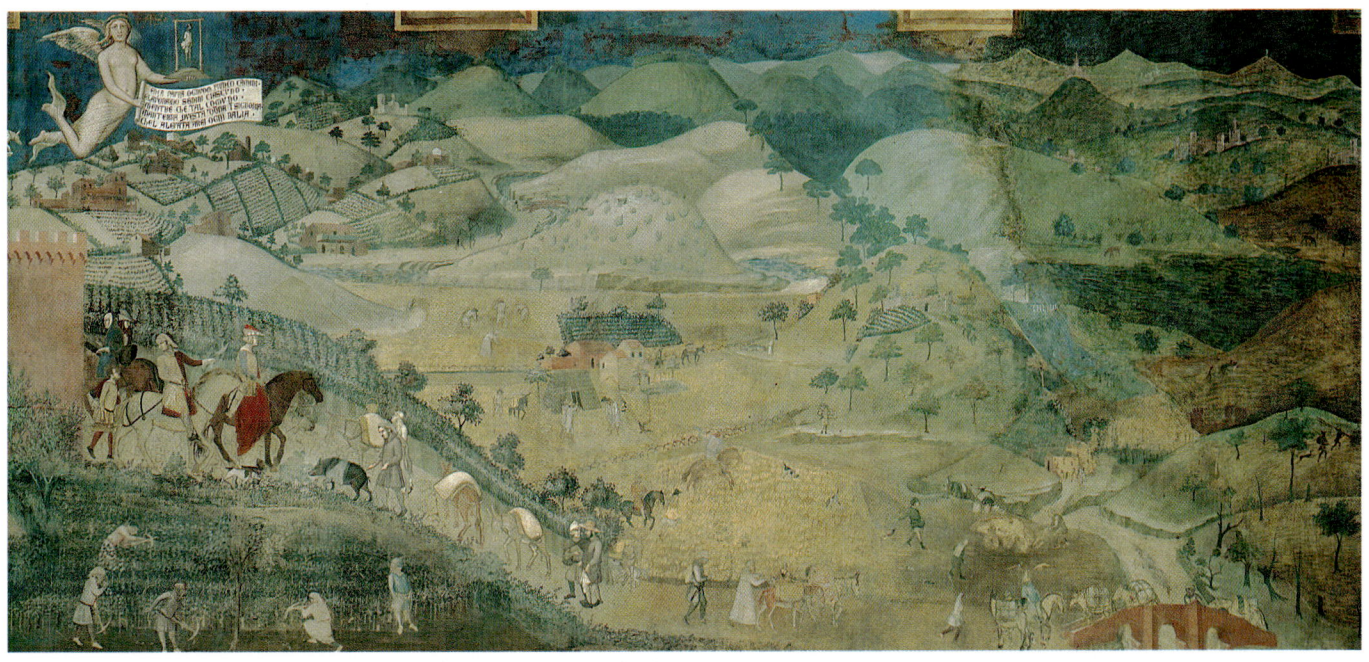

19-22   AMBROGIO LORENZETTI, *Peaceful Country,* detail from the fresco *Effects of Good Government in the City and in the Country,* Sala della Pace, Palazzo Pubblico, Siena, Italy, 1338–1339.

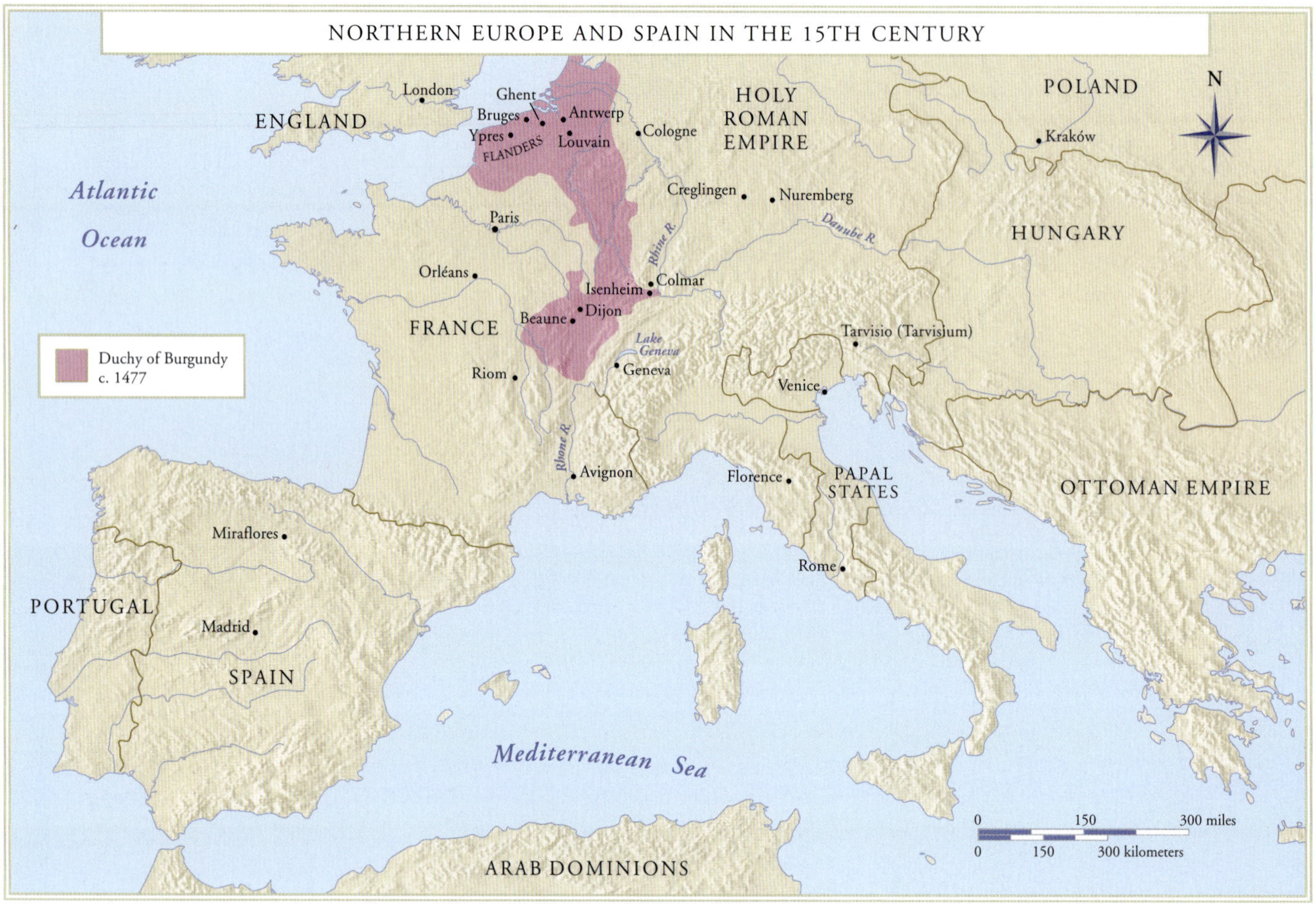

NORTHERN EUROPE AND SPAIN IN THE 15TH CENTURY

POLAND

N

ENGLAND

HOLY
ROMAN
EMPIRE

London
Ghent
Bruges
Antwerp
Ypres
Louvain
FLANDERS
Cologne

Kraków

Atlantic

Ocean

Creglingen
Nuremberg

Paris

Danube R.

Rhine R.

HUNGARY

Orléans

Isenheim
Colmar

Duchy of Burgundy
c. 1477

FRANCE
Beaune
Dijon

Tarvisio (Tarvisium)

Riom

Lake
Geneva
Geneva

Rhone R.

Venice

Avignon

Florence

PAPAL
STATES

OTTOMAN EMPIRE

Miraflores

Rome

PORTUGAL

Madrid

SPAIN

Mediterranean Sea

0   150   300 miles
0   150   300 kilometers

ARAB DOMINIONS

1375		1425
PHILIP THE BOLD (BURGUNDY)	JOHN THE FEARLESS	PHILIP THE GOOD

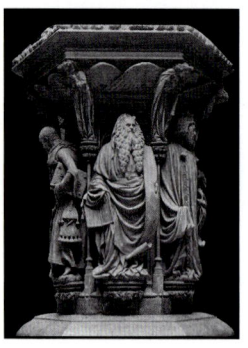

Claus Sluter
Well of Moses
1395–1406

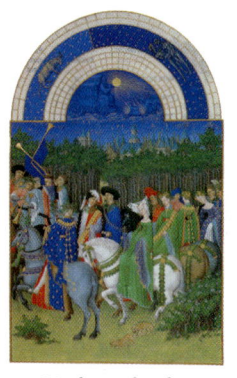

Limbourg brothers
May, from Très Riches Heures
1413–1416

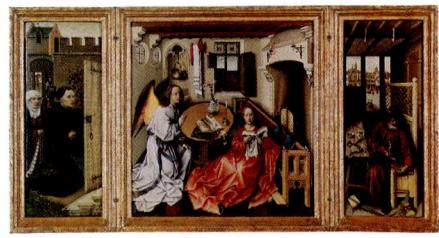

Master of Flémalle
Mérode Altarpiece
ca. 1425–1428

Hundred Years' War begins, 1337

The papacy in Avignon, 1305–1378

The Great Schism in the Church, 1378–1417

The Netherlands under the dukes of Burgundy, 1384–1477

OF PIETY, PASSION, AND POLITICS

FIFTEENTH-CENTURY ART IN NORTHERN

EUROPE AND SPAIN

1467	1477	1500

CHARLES THE BOLD

FERDINAND (ARAGON) AND ISABELLA (CASTILE), CATHOLIC RULERS OF SPAIN

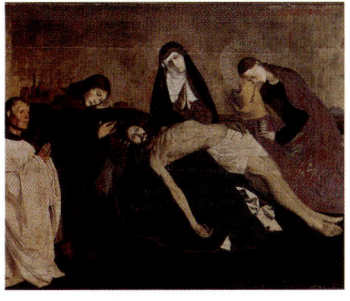

The Avignon Pietà
ca. 1455

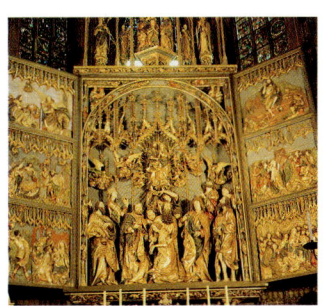

Veit Stoss
The Death and Assumption of the Virgin Mary
1477–1489

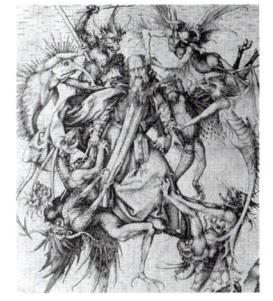

Martin Schongauer
Saint Anthony Tormented by Demons
ca. 1480–1490

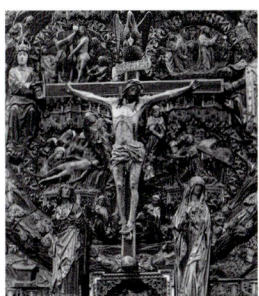

Gil de Siloé
Christ Crucified
1496–1499

Hundred Years' War ends, 1453

Burgundy and Burgundian Netherlands pass to Holy
Roman Empire Maximilian I, Hapsburg emperor, 1486

Moorish kingdom of Granada falls to Spain, 1492

Columbus arrives in West Indies, 1492

French invade Italy, 1494

POLITICAL, ECONOMIC, AND RELIGIOUS DEVELOPMENTS IN THE FIFTEENTH CENTURY

In the Late Gothic world, western Europe beyond the Alps experienced the calamities of war, plague, and the social upheavals and dislocations that accompanied dying feudalism. The Black Death that ravaged Italy in 1348 also decimated much of the rest of Europe. The Hundred Years' War (1337–1453) contributed to the instability across the European continent. Primarily a protracted series of conflicts between France and England, the Hundred Years' War also involved Flanders. Technically, Flanders was a principality or county in the Netherlands, a country that consisted of what today is Belgium, the Netherlands (more commonly called Holland), Luxembourg, and part of northern France. However, during the fifteenth century, "Flanders" also referred more generally to a broader territory. During the Hundred Years' War, urban revolts erupted in this larger Flanders, England's chief market for raw wool. France's intervention in the Flemish problem threatened England's revenues, thereby intensifying the antagonism between France and England that underlay the long-simmering war.

CONSOLIDATING POLITICAL POWER   Politically, the widespread European movement toward centralized government, begun in the twelfth century, continued apace. Structured bureaucracies, royal courts, and parliamentary assemblies were becoming the norm, creating conflicts with the lingering cumbersome arrangements of feudal governance. During the latter part of the fifteenth century, several kings successfully consolidated their authority over their respective countries, accounting for the label "new monarchies" used to describe the governmental systems in France, England, and Spain. Of course, European monarchies had existed for centuries, but these "new monarchs" exerted and expanded their authority in a more systematic and comprehensive way. For example, they suppressed the nobility, controlled the Christian Church, and insisted on the unwavering loyalty of their subjects.

EMERGING CAPITALISM   Despite the age's calamities, a new economic system also evolved—the early stage of European capitalism. Responding to the financial requirements of trade, new credit and exchange systems created an economic network of enterprising European cities. The trade in money accompanied the trade in commodities, and the former financed industry. Both were in the hands of trading companies with central offices and international branches; the Medici of Florence (see Chapter 21, pages 590, 609–15) were a notable example of such a trading firm. The origin of the French word for *stock market* demonstrates the importance of Flanders to Europe's economic development. *Bourse* came from the name of the van der Beurse family, whose Bruges (now a Belgian city) residence was a center of economic activity. The first international commercial stock exchange, established in Antwerp in 1460, became pivotal for Europe's integrated economic activity. The thriving commerce, industry, and finance contributed to the evolution of cities, as did the migration of a significant portion of the rural population to urban centers.

DIVISIVENESS IN THE CHURCH   Crisis in the religious realm exacerbated the period's political instability. The conflicts between those supporting the Avignon papacy in France and those agitating for the pope's return to Rome led to the Great Schism (see Chapter 19, pages 534–35). Because most fourteenth-century popes were French, establishing the papal residence in Avignon was not unexpected. The Italian insistence on the pope's presence in Rome also was foreseeable. This split in the Christian Church—the Great Schism—lasted from 1378 until 1417, when both sides agreed to the selection of Martin V as pope in Rome.

FRENCH MANUSCRIPT ILLUMINATION

For centuries, stained glass (see FIGS. 18-14 and 18-15) and the illuminated manuscript page (see FIGS. 18-34 and 18-35) had prevailed as the characteristic painted surfaces in northern Europe, especially in France. Northern Gothic architects had eliminated solid walls and left few continuous blank surfaces that invited painted decorations (see FIG. 18-26), unlike designers in Italy, where the climate and architecture favored mural painting in fresco (see FIG. 19-8). Northern artists had extensive experience at working not only in miniature but also with rich jewel-like colors that, especially in stained glass, have a profound luminosity, with light seemingly irradiating the forms. Manuscript illustration, working deep color into exquisitely tiny and intricate shapes and patterns, particularly showcased this color mastery. In addition, illuminations had begun to take on the character of independent paintings, expanding in size until they occupied pages completely.

TURNING THE PAGE TO A NEW ERA   The work of Jean Pucelle in the early fourteenth century, discussed in Chapter 18, represented the first step toward illumination's size expansion within texts. A page from the *Belleville Breviary* (see FIG. 18-36) shows how the illustrator took command of the entire page. The borders, extended to invade the margins, include not only decorative tendrils and a profusion of spiky ivy and floral ornaments but also a myriad of insects, small animals, and grotesques. In addition, three narrative scenes encroach on the text columns, demonstrating that manuscript illustrators were feeling less constrained by the text, both physically on the page and figuratively in the relationship between the text and image.

AN OPULENT PRAYER BOOK   In the early fifteenth century, the three LIMBOURG BROTHERS—POL (PAUL?), HENNEQUIN (JEAN? JAN?), and HERMAN—carried the size expansion of illustrations in manuscripts even further. These artists produced a gorgeously illustrated Book of Hours for Jean, the duke of Berry (1340–1416) and brother of King Charles V of France. The duke was an avid art patron and focused much of his collecting energy on manuscripts, jewels, and rare artifacts. An inventory of the duke's libraries revealed that he owned more than three hundred manuscripts, including the *Belleville Breviary* (see FIG. 18-36) and the *Hours of Jeanne d'Évreux*. The Limbourg brothers worked on the manuscript, *Les Très Riches Heures du Duc de Berry (The Very Sumptuous Hours of the Duke of Berry),* until their deaths in 1416. A Book of Hours, like a breviary, was a prayer book used for reciting prayers.

The centerpiece of a Book of Hours (see "Medieval Books," Chapter 16, page 434) was the "Office [prayer] of the Blessed Virgin," which contained liturgical passages to be read privately at seven set times during the day, from matins (dawn prayers) to compline (the last of the seven prayers recited daily). An illustrated calendar containing local religious feast days usually preceded the "Office of the Blessed Virgin." Penitential psalms, devotional prayers, litanies to the saints, and other prayers, including those of the dead and of the Holy Cross, followed the centerpiece. Such books became favorite possessions of the northern aristocracy during the fourteenth and fifteenth centuries. As prayer books, they replaced the traditional psalters, which had been the only liturgical books in private hands until the mid-thirteenth century.

The calendar pictures of *Les Très Riches Heures* are perhaps the most famous in the history of manuscript illumination. They represent the twelve months in terms of the associated seasonal tasks, alternating the occupations of nobility and peasantry. Above each picture is a lunette depicting the chariot of the sun as it makes its yearly round through the twelve months and zodiac signs. Representative is the colorful calendar picture for May (FIG. **20-1**). A cavalcade of patrician ladies and gentlemen, preceded by trumpeters, rides out to celebrate the first day of May, a spring festival that courts throughout Europe observed. Clad in springtime green and garlanded with fresh leaves, the riders sparkle with ornate finery. Behind them is a woodland and the chateau of Riom in south central France. Such great country estates, most belonging to the duke of Berry, loom in the backgrounds of most of the calendar pictures. The artists represented these estates so faithfully that those surviving can be easily recognized. The rich costume detail also speaks to the artists' careful observation and depiction of their subjects. The picture's spirit is lighthearted, chivalric, and pleasure loving. The entire book, as seen in *May*, reflects the illustrators' interest in precise detail and rich color.

Although all three Limbourg brothers worked on *Les Très Riches Heures,* art historians have never been able to ascertain which brother painted which images. Given the common practice of collaboration on artistic projects at this time, this determination of specific authorship is not very important. From what scholars know, all three brothers died in the same year, 1416, before completing this Book of Hours, and another court illustrator finished the manuscript about seventy years later. Despite this uncertainty regarding the authorship of specific pages, *Les Très Riches Heures* as a whole realized the emancipation of illustration from text. Further, the Limbourg brothers expanded the conventional range of subject matter to include genre subjects, and they gave these everyday scenes a prominent place, even in a religious book. This combination reflected the increasing integration of religious and secular concerns in both art and life at the time.

FIFTEENTH-CENTURY FLEMISH ART

The Burgundian Netherlands

EXPANDING BURGUNDIAN TERRITORIES The duke of Berry's grandnephew, Philip the Good (1396–1467), ruled a region known as the Duchy of Burgundy—hence his title, the duke of Burgundy. Burgundy was the fertile east-central region of France still known for its wines. In the late fourteenth century, one of Philip the Good's predecessors, Philip the Bold (1342–1404), had married the daughter of the count of Flanders, thereby acquiring counties in the Netherlands. With them came the rich industrial, commercial, and banking cities that together were pivotal for the economic development of northern and western Europe. The reigning duke of Burgundy wielded power over not just the county of Flanders proper but over the broader Flanders as well. Although the duke's official capital and court were at Dijon in Burgundy, the source of Burgundian wealth and power was at Bruges, the city that made Burgundy a dangerous rival of royal France.

Bruges derived its wealth from the wool trade and from banking. Until late in the fifteenth century, an arm of the North Sea, now silted up, reached inland to Bruges. There, ships brought raw wool from England and Spain and carried away fine woolen cloth that became famous throughout Europe. The wool brought bankers, among them representatives of the House of Medici, and Bruges became the financial clearinghouse for all of northern Europe. In its streets, merchants from Italy and the Near East rubbed shoulders with traders from Russia and Spain. Despite the flourishing economies of its sister cities—Ghent, Louvain, and Ypres—Bruges so dominated Flanders that the duke of Burgundy eventually chose to make the city his capital and moved his court there from Dijon in the early fifteenth century.

Due to the expanded territory and the prosperity of the "Burgundian Netherlands," the dukes of Burgundy were probably the most powerful rulers in northern Europe during the first three quarters of the fifteenth century. Although cousins of the French kings, they usually supported England (which they relied on for the raw materials used in their wool industry) during the Hundred Years' War and, at times, controlled much of northern France, including Paris. At the height of their power, the reigning duke's lands stretched from the Rhône River to the North Sea. Only the rash policies of the last of their line, Charles the Bold (1433–1477), and his death at the battle of Nancy in 1477 brought to an end the Burgundian dream of forming a strong middle kingdom between France and the Holy Roman Empire. After Charles's death, France reabsorbed the southern Burgundian lands, and the Netherlands passed to the Holy Roman Empire by virtue of the dynastic marriage of Charles's daughter, Mary of Burgundy, to Maximilian of Hapsburg.

SUBSIDIZING A MONASTERY Though all of the period's dukes of Burgundy felt a commitment to the arts, Philip the Bold, who ruled from 1364 to 1404, was among the greatest art patrons in northern Europe. His interests centered on illuminated manuscripts, arras tapestries (from Arras, a town in northeastern France famous for its fabric), and rich furnishings for his numerous castles and town houses, located throughout the duchy. He also maintained an entire workshop of sculptors. Philip's largest artistic enterprise was the building of the Chartreuse (Carthusian monastery) de Champmol, near Dijon. Founded in the late eleventh century by Saint Bruno, the Carthusian order consisted of monks who devoted their lives to solitary living and prayer. Saint Bruno established the order at Chartreuse, near Grenoble in

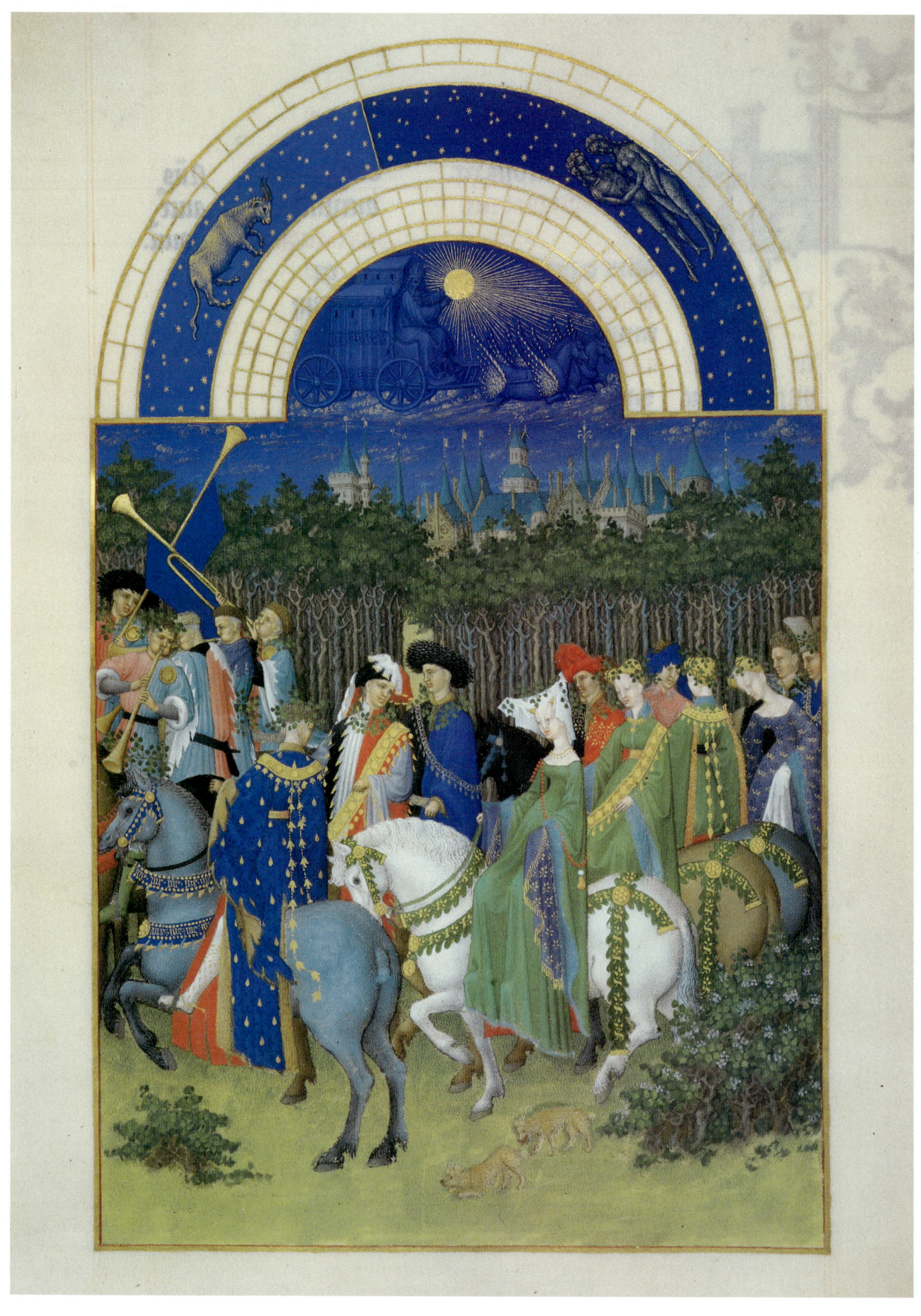

20-1 LIMBOURG BROTHERS (POL, HENNEQUIN, HERMAN), *May,* from *Les Très Riches Heures du Duc de Berry,* 1413–1416. Illumination, approx. $8\frac{1}{2}'' \times 5\frac{1}{2}''$. Musée Condé, Chantilly.

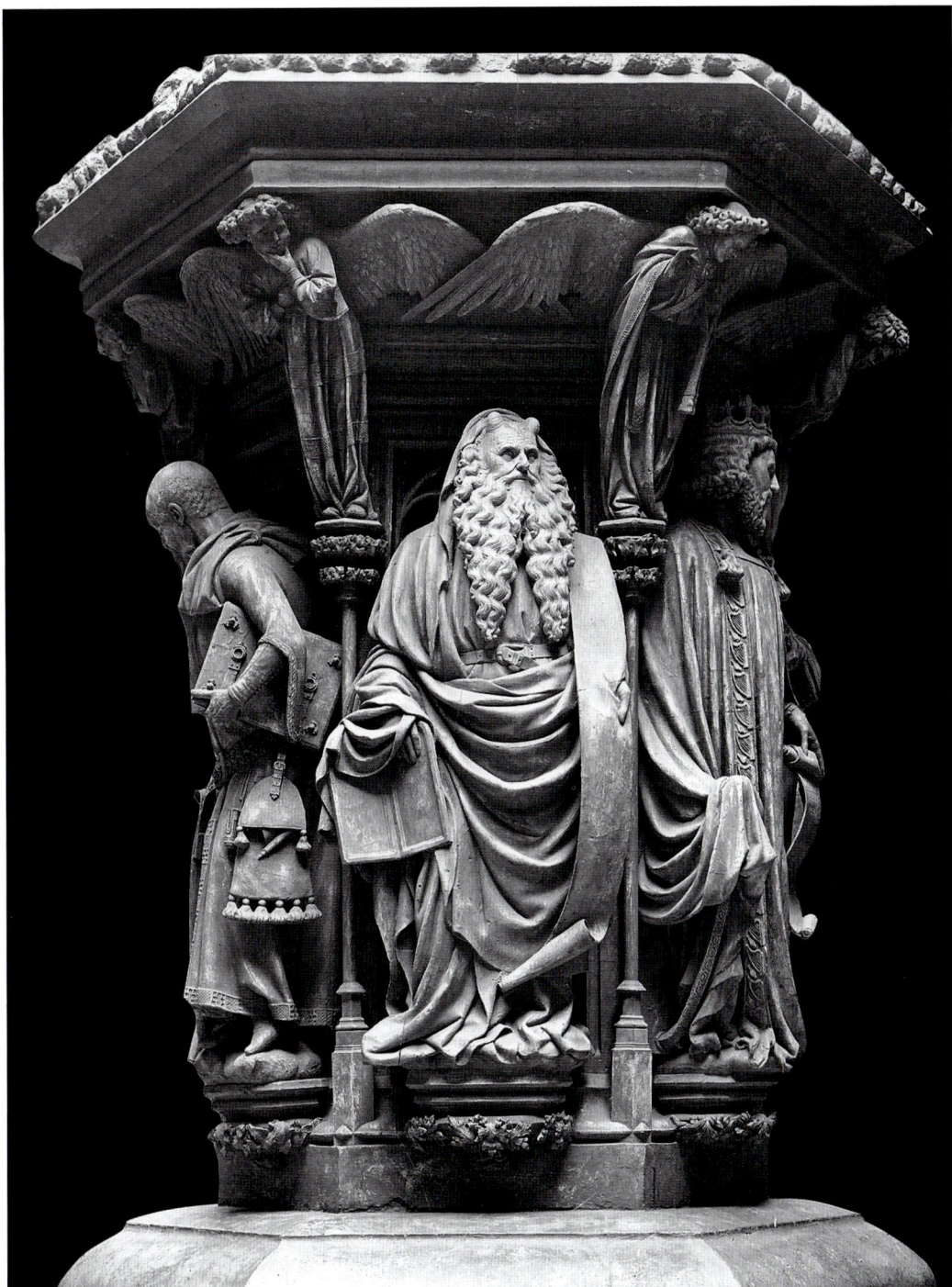

20-2 CLAUS SLUTER, *Well of Moses,* Chartreuse de Champmol, Dijon, France, 1395–1406. Stone, figures approx. 6′ high.

southeastern France; hence, the term *chartreuse* ("charter house" in English) refers to a Carthusian monastery. Because Carthusian monasteries did not generate revenues, Philip the Bold's endowment at Champmol was significant. Intended as a tomb repository for the important members of the Valois House of Burgundy, the Chartreuse's magnificent endowment attracted artists from all parts of northern Europe.

A SYMBOLIC FOUNTAIN OF LIFE Philip the Bold placed sculptor CLAUS SLUTER (active ca. 1380–1406) in charge of his sculpture workshop. For the cloister of the Chartreuse de Champmol, Sluter designed a large sculptural fountain located in a well. The well served as a water source for the monastery. It seems probable, however, that the fountain did not actually spout water, because the

Carthusian commitment to silence and prayer would have precluded anything that produced sound. Although the sculptor died before completing the entire fountain, he did finish *Well of Moses* (FIG. **20-2**). Moses, David, and four other prophets (Daniel, Isaiah, Jeremiah, and Zachariah) surround a base that once supported a Crucifixion group. Despite the nonfunctioning nature of this fountain, it had immense symbolic significance. The entire structure served as a symbolic fountain of life, with the blood of Christ (on the cross above) flowing down over the Old Testament prophets, washing away their sins and spilling into the well below. The *Well of Moses* thus represented the promise of everlasting life.

The six figures recall the jamb statues of the Gothic portals, but they far surpass even the most realistic of those (see

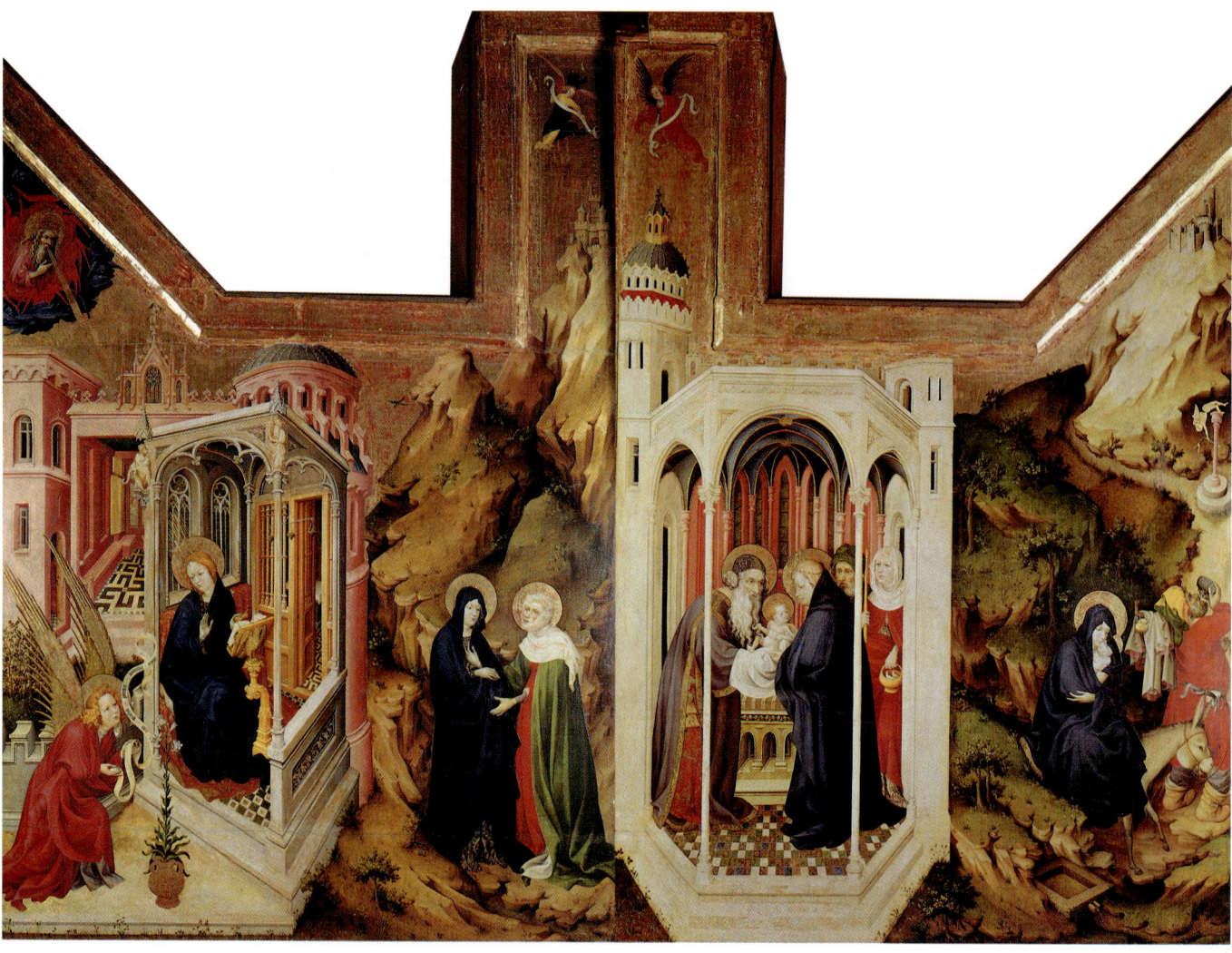

20-3   MELCHIOR BROEDERLAM, outer wings of the *Retable de Champmol. Annunciation and Visitation (left)* and *Presentation and Flight into Egypt (right),* from Chapel of the Chartreuse de Champmol, Dijon, France, installed 1399. Panels, each 5′ 5$\frac{3}{4}$″ × 4′ 1$\frac{1}{4}$″. Musée de la Ville, Dijon.

FIGS. 18-16 and 18-24). Sluter's intense observation of natural appearance provided him with the information necessary to render the figures in minute detail. Heavy draperies with voluminous folds, characteristic of Sluter's style, swath the life-size figures. The artist succeeded in making their difficult, complex surfaces seem remarkably naturalistic. He enhanced this effect by skillfully differentiating textures, from coarse drapery to smooth flesh and silky hair, and by the paint, which still adheres in places. This fascination with the specific and tangible in the visible world became one of the chief characteristics of fifteenth-century Flemish painting. Yet despite the realism of Sluter's figures, they do not evidence much physical movement or weight shift.

PANELS THAT PREFACE THE PASSION   Philip the Bold also commissioned a major altarpiece for the main altar in the chapel of the Chartreuse. A collaborative project, this altarpiece consisted of a large sculptured shrine carved by Jacques de Baerze and a pair of exterior panels (FIG. **20-3**) painted by MELCHIOR BROEDERLAM (active ca. 1387–1409). The artist depicted *Annunciation and Visitation* on the left panel and *Presentation and Flight into Egypt* on the right

panel (see "The Life of Jesus in Art," Chapter 11, pages 308–309 or xxx–xxxi in Volume II). Dealing with Christ's birth and infancy, these scenes introduce the Passion scenes (from Christ's last days on earth) de Baerze presented in the interior sculpture. The exterior panels are an unusual amalgamation of different styles, locales, and religious symbolism. The two paintings include both landscape and interior scenes, and the architecture of the structures varies from Romanesque to Gothic. Scholars have suggested that the juxtaposition of different architectural styles in the left panel is symbolic. The *rotunda* (round building, usually with a dome) refers to the Old Testament, while the Gothic porch relates to the New Testament. Stylistically, Broederlam's representation of parts of the landscape and architecture reveals an attempt to render three-dimensionality on the two-dimensional surface. Yet his staid treatment of the figures, their halos, and the flat gold background recall medieval pictorial conventions. Despite this interplay of various styles and diverse imagery, the altarpiece was a precursor of many of the artistic developments (such as the illusionistic depiction of three-dimensional objects and the representation of landscape) that preoccupied European artists throughout the fifteenth century.

The Artist's Profession in Flanders

THE ART OF BUILDING A CAREER As in Italy, guilds controlled the Flemish artist's profession. To pursue a craft, individuals had to belong to the guild controlling that craft. Painters, for example, sought admission to the Guild of Saint Luke, which included the saddlers, glassworkers, and mirrorworkers as well. The path to eventual membership in the guild began, for men, at an early age, when the father apprenticed his son in boyhood to a master, with whom the young aspiring painter lived. The master taught the fundamentals of his craft—how to make implements; how to prepare panels with gesso (plaster mixed with a binding material); and how to mix colors, oils, and varnishes. Once the youth mastered these procedures and learned to work in the master's traditional manner, he usually spent several years working as a journeyman in various cities, observing and absorbing ideas from other masters. He then was eligible to become a master and applied for admission to the guild. Through the guild, he obtained commissions. The guild also inspected his paintings to ensure he used quality materials and to evaluate workmanship and then secured him adequate payment for his labor. As a result of this quality control, Flemish artists soon gained a favorable reputation for their solid artisanship.

FLEMISH FEMALE ARTISTS Scholars know much less about the training of women artists than they do about that of men. Certainly, far fewer women participated in the art professions, although the membership records of the art guilds of Flemish cities such as Bruges list a substantial number of women in the fifteenth century and later.

Flemish women interested in pursuing art as a career most often received tutoring from fathers and husbands who were professionals and whom the women assisted in all the craft's technical procedures. Social and moral constraints would have forbidden women's apprenticeship in the homes of male masters and would have stringently limited their freedom of movement. Moreover, from the sixteenth century, when academic training courses supplemented and then replaced guild training, until the twentieth century, women would not as a rule expect or be permitted instruction in figure painting, insofar as it involved dissection of cadavers and study of the nude male model. Despite the lack of concrete information, it is clear women did not have access to the training and experience many male artists enjoyed. Yet Flemish women artists, such as Lavinia Teerlinc of Bruges, did manage to establish themselves. These artists ably negotiated the difficult path to acceptance as professionals, overcoming significant obstacles. Indeed, so successful was Teerlinc in pursuing an artistic career that she eventually was invited to England to paint miniatures for the courts of Henry VIII and his successors. There, she was a formidable rival of some of her male contemporaries and received greater compensation for her work than they did for theirs.

Public Devotional Imagery: Altarpieces

PIETY AND POLITICS Despite the resolution of the Great Schism in 1417 and the restoration of the papal seat in Rome, religion continued to play an extremely important role in Flemish lives. Accordingly, the religious orientation of art produced during the preceding Gothic period continued unabated. This commitment to religion and art pervaded all levels of Flemish society from authoritative ruler to lowly subject. Philip the Bold demonstrated his commitment to the Christian Church through commissions, generous charitable donations, and support for religious orders, such as the Carthusians (for example, the Chartreuse de Champmol commission). From his pinnacle of power, however, Philip the Bold's interest in the Church extended beyond his concern for his own salvation and setting a pious example for his subjects; he also sought to increase his power.

Using the Church to expand his authority was logical because the conflicts that precipitated the Great Schism were largely political rather than doctrinal in nature and focused on issues of power and control. Fifteenth-century sovereigns were well aware of this and recognized the value of the Church as an ally. Thus, secular leaders across Europe eagerly entered the fray between the pope in Avignon and the pope in Rome. Philip the Bold threw his support behind Clement VII in Avignon, confident that he could control that pope more easily than a pope hundreds of miles away in Rome. English support for Urban VI in Rome furthered Philip's resolve to see the Avignon papacy dominate.

This heightened politicization of the Church impacted the clergy as well. Because the duke of Burgundy determined upper-level Church appointments (for example, bishops, abbots, and deans of chapters), the political motivation that drove the duke infiltrated the clergy, many of whom owed their positions (and therefore their loyalty) to the duke. Clerical involvement in the political situation led to increased neglect of clerical functions, to immoral behavior, and to pursuit of material gain. The populace counteracted what it perceived as a decline in clerical spirituality with an upsurge in devotional practices. Pilgrimages and processions escalated, as did the worship of the Virgin Mary.

Thus, the reasons for the predominance of religious imagery in the art of fifteenth-century Flanders were numerous. Large-scale public altarpieces were among the most visible manifestations of piety. These altarpieces served a variety of functions, among them providing a backdrop for the Mass celebration, teaching church doctrine, and visually encouraging piety. A wide range of Flemish society—pious individuals, high officials, and organizations (religious orders and lay confraternities)—commissioned these devotional objects, which helped ensure the donor's eventual salvation and promoted greater devotion among the faithful. Guilds commonly commissioned art; through guilds, the middle class became more involved in art patronage.

SETTING THE STAGE FOR SALVATION These public altarpieces most often took the form of *polyptychs* (hinged multipaneled paintings) or carved relief panels. The hinges allowed users to close the polyptych's side wings over the central panel(s). Artists decorated both the exterior and interior of the altarpieces. This multi-imaged format provided artists the opportunity to construct narratives through a sequence of images, somewhat like manuscript illustration. Although scholars do not have concrete information about the specific circumstances when these altarpieces were opened or closed, evidence

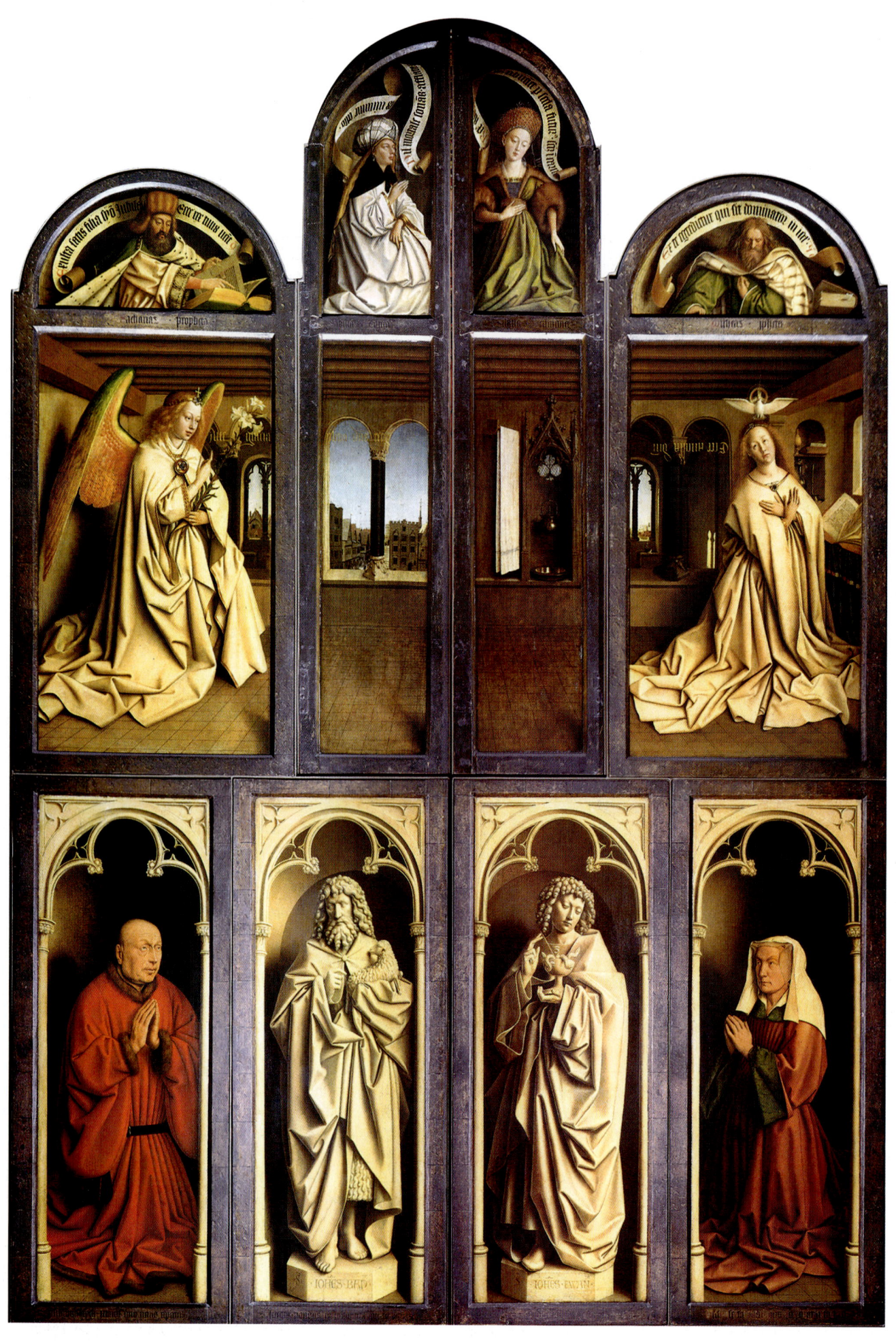

20-4 Jan van Eyck, *Ghent Altarpiece* (closed), Saint Bavo Cathedral, Ghent, Belgium, completed 1432. Oil on wood, height 11′ 5 3/4″.

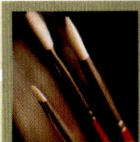

Painters, Pigments, and Panels

The generic word *paint* or *pigment* encompasses a wide range of substances artists have used over the years. Fresco aside (see "Fresco Painting," Chapter 19, page 543), during the fourteenth century, egg tempera was the material of choice for most painters, both in Italy and northern Europe. Tempera consists of egg combined with a wet paste of ground pigment. In his influential guidebook *Il Libro dell'Arte* (*The Craftsman's Handbook*), Cennino Cennini, a contemporaneous painter, mentioned that artists mixed only the egg yolk with the ground pigment, but analysis of paintings from this period has revealed that some artists chose to use the whole egg. Images painted with tempera have a velvety sheen to them and exhibit a lightness of artistic touch because thick application of the pigment mixture results in premature cracking and flaking.

Scholars have discovered that artists used oil paints as far back as the eighth century, but not until the early fifteenth century did painting with this material become widespread. Flemish artists were among the first to employ oils extensively (often mixing them with tempera), and Italian painters quickly followed suit. The discovery of better drying components in the early fifteenth century enhanced the setting capabilities of oils. Rather than apply these oils in the light flecked brushstrokes that tempera encouraged, artists laid the oils down in transparent glazes over opaque or semiopaque underlayers. In this manner, painters could build up deep tones through repeated glazing. Unlike tempera, whose surface dries quickly due to water evaporation, oils dry more uniformly and slowly, providing the artist time to rework areas. This flexibility must have been particularly appealing to artists who worked very deliberately, such as Leonardo da Vinci (Chapter 22, pages 636–42). Leonardo also preferred oil paint because its gradual drying process and consistency permitted him to blend the pigments, thereby creating the impressive *sfumato* (smoky effect) that contributed to his fame.

Both tempera and oils can be applied to different surfaces. Through the early sixteenth century, wooden panels served as the foundation for most paintings. Italians painted on poplar, while northern artists used oak, lime, beech, chestnut, cherry, pine, and silver fir. Availability of these timbers determined the wood choice. Linen canvas became increasingly popular in the late sixteenth century. Although evidence suggests that artists did not intend permanency for their early images on canvas, the material proved particularly useful in areas such as Venice where high humidity made fresco unfeasible and warped wood panels. Further, until canvas paintings were stretched on wooden stretcher bars before framing or affixed to a surface, they were more portable than wood panels.

---

suggests that they remained closed on regular days and were opened on Sundays and feast days. This schedule would have allowed viewers to see both the interior and exterior—differing imagery at various times according to the liturgical calendar.

SEEKING SALVATION AND REDEMPTION   The *Ghent Altarpiece* in the Cathedral of Saint Bavo in Ghent (FIG. **20-4**) is one of the largest and most admired Flemish altarpieces of the fifteenth century. Jodocus Vyd (Joos Vijd), burgomaster (chief magistrate) of Ghent, and his wife Isabel (Elizabeth) Borluut commissioned this *triptych* (three-paneled painting) from JAN VAN EYCK (ca. 1390–1441). Completed in 1432, the *Ghent Altarpiece* functioned as the liturgical centerpiece of the endowment established in the chapel Vyd and Borluut built in the local church dedicated to Saint John the Baptist (now Saint Bavo Cathedral).

Two of the exterior panels of the *Ghent Altarpiece* depict the donors, appropriately, at the bottom. The husband and wife, painted in illusionistically rendered niches, kneel with their hands clasped in prayer. They gaze piously at illusionistic stone sculptures of Ghent's patron saints, Saint John the Baptist and Saint John the Evangelist (who was probably also Vyd's patron saint). An Annunciation scene appears on the upper register, with a careful representation of a Flemish town outside the center panel's painted window. In the uppermost arched panels, van Eyck depicted images of the Old Testament prophets Zachariah and Micah, along with sibyls, classical mythological prophetesses whose writings the Christian Church interpreted as prophesies of Christ.

When opened, the altarpiece (FIG. **20-5**) reveals a sumptuous, superbly colored painting of the medieval conception of humanity's Redemption. In the upper register, God the Father—wearing the pope's triple tiara, with a worldly crown at his feet, and resplendent in a deep-scarlet mantle—presides in majesty. To God's right, van Eyck placed the Virgin, represented as the Queen of Heaven, with a crown of twelve stars upon her head. Saint John the Baptist sits to God's left. To either side is a choir of angels and on the right an angel playing an organ. Adam and Eve appear in the far panels. The inscriptions in the arches above Mary and Saint John extol the Virgin's virtue and purity and Saint John's greatness as the forerunner of Christ. The particularly significant inscription above the Lord's head translates: "This is God, all-powerful in his divine majesty; of all the best, by the gentleness of his goodness; the most liberal giver, because of his infinite generosity." The step behind the crown at the Lord's feet bears the inscription: "On his head, life without death. On his brow, youth without age. On his right, joy without sadness. On his left, security without fear." The entire altarpiece amplifies the central theme of salvation—though humans,

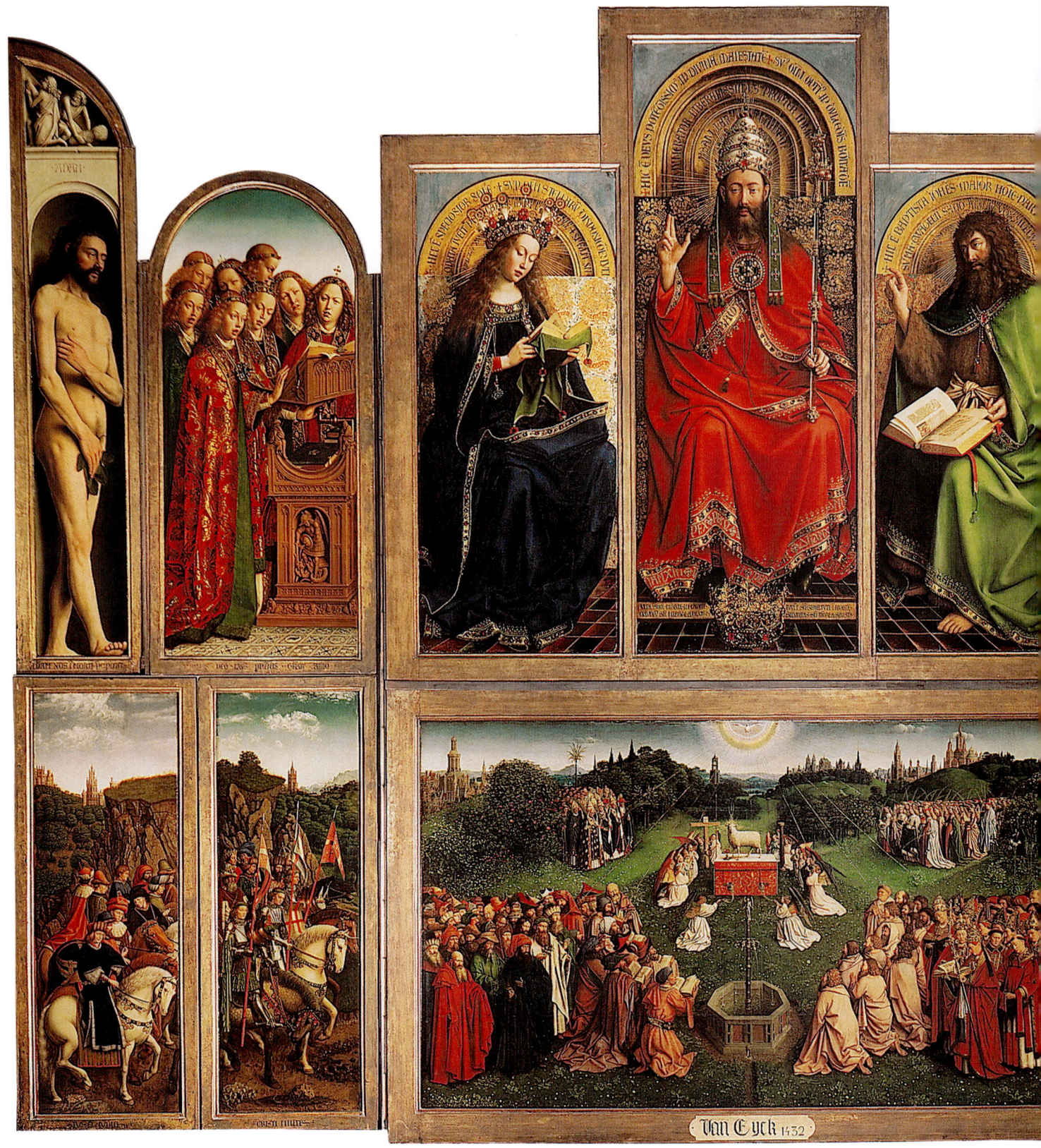

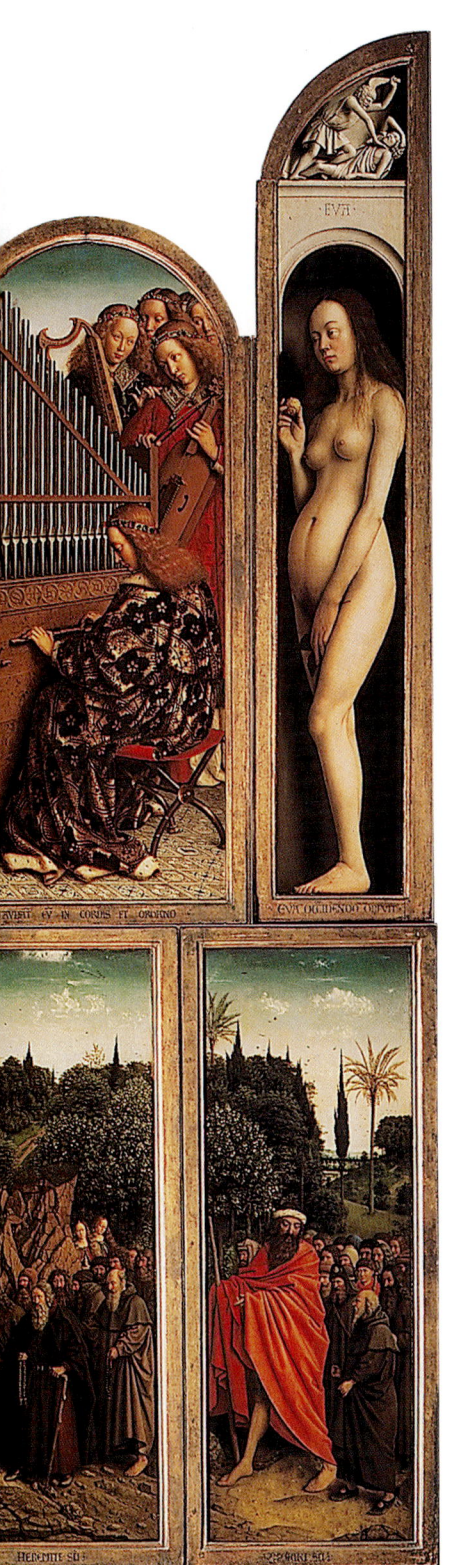

20-5 JAN VAN EYCK, *Ghent Altarpiece* (open), Saint Bavo Cathedral, Ghent, Belgium, completed 1432. Oil on wood, approx. 11′ 6″ × 15′ 1″.

symbolized by Adam and Eve, are sinful, they will be saved because God, in his infinite love, will sacrifice his own son for this purpose.

The lower register panels extend the symbolism of the upper. In the central panel, the community of saints comes from the four corners of the earth through an opulent, flower-spangled landscape. They proceed toward the altar of the Lamb and toward the octagonal fountain of life. The Lamb symbolizes the sacrificed Son of God, whose heart bleeds into a chalice, while into the fountain spills the "pure river of water of life, clear as crystal, proceeding out of the throne of God and of the Lamb" (Rev. 22:1). On the right, the Twelve Apostles and a group of martyrs in red robes advance; on the left appear prophets. In the right background come the Virgin martyrs, and in the left background the holy confessors approach. On the lower wings, other approaching groups symbolize the four cardinal virtues: the hermits, Temperance; the pilgrims, Prudence; the knights, Fortitude; and the judges, Justice. The altarpiece celebrates the whole Christian cycle from the Fall to the Redemption, presenting the Church triumphant in heavenly Jerusalem.

Van Eyck rendered the entire altarpiece in a shimmering splendor of color that defies reproduction. No small detail escaped van Eyck, trained as a miniaturist. With pristine specificity, he revealed the beauty of the most insignificant object as if it were a work of piety as much as a work of art. He depicted the soft texture of hair, the glitter of gold in the heavy brocades, the luster of pearls, and the flashing of gems, all with loving fidelity to appearance.

THE DEVELOPING USE OF OIL PAINTS Oil paints facilitated the exactitude found in the work of van Eyck and others. Although traditional scholarship credited Jan van Eyck with the invention of oil painting, recent evidence has revealed that oil paints were known for some time and that Melchior Broederlam was using oils in the 1390s. Flemish painters built up their pictures by superimposing translucent paint layers, called *glazes,* on a layer of underpainting, which in turn had been built up from a carefully planned drawing made on a white-grounded panel. With the rediscovered medium, painters created richer colors than previously had been possible. Thus, a deep, intense tonality; the illusion of glowing light; and hard enamel-like surfaces characterized fifteenth-century Flemish painting. These traits differed significantly from the high-keyed color, sharp light, and rather matte surfaces of tempera (see "Painters, Pigments, and Panels," page 567).

The brilliant and versatile oil medium suited perfectly the formal intentions of the Flemish painters, who aimed for sharply focused, hard-edged, and sparkling clarity of detail in their representation of thousands of objects ranging in scale from large to almost invisible.

The apprentice training system throughout the continent ensured the transmission of information about surfaces and pigments from generation to generation, thereby guaranteeing the painting tradition's continued viability.

THE DRAMA OF CHRIST'S DEATH Like the art of van Eyck, that of ROGIER VAN DER WEYDEN (ca. 1400–1464) had a great impact on northern painting during the fifteenth century. In particular, Rogier (as scholars refer to

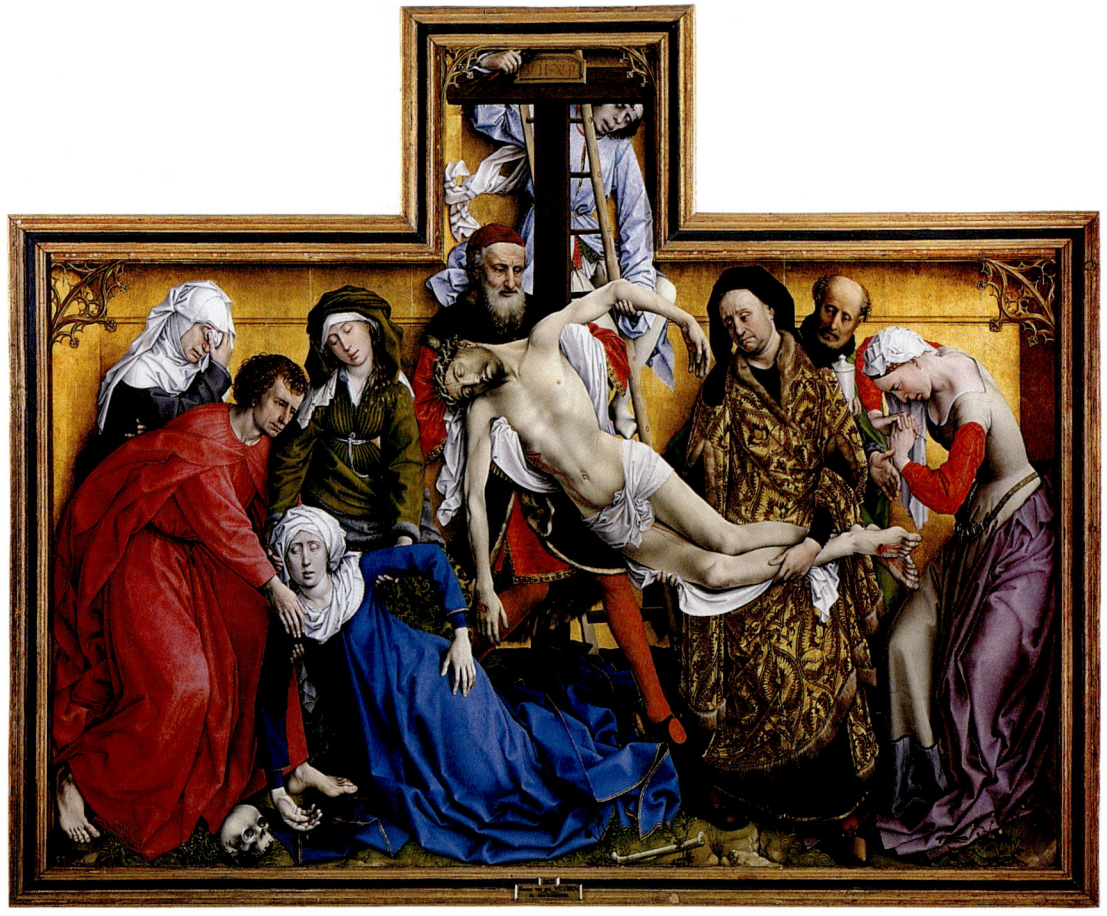

20-6 ROGIER VAN DER WEYDEN, *Deposition,*
from Notre-Dame hors-les-murs, Louvain,
Belgium, ca. 1435. Oil on wood, approx.
7′ 3″ × 8′ 7″. Museo del Prado, Madrid.

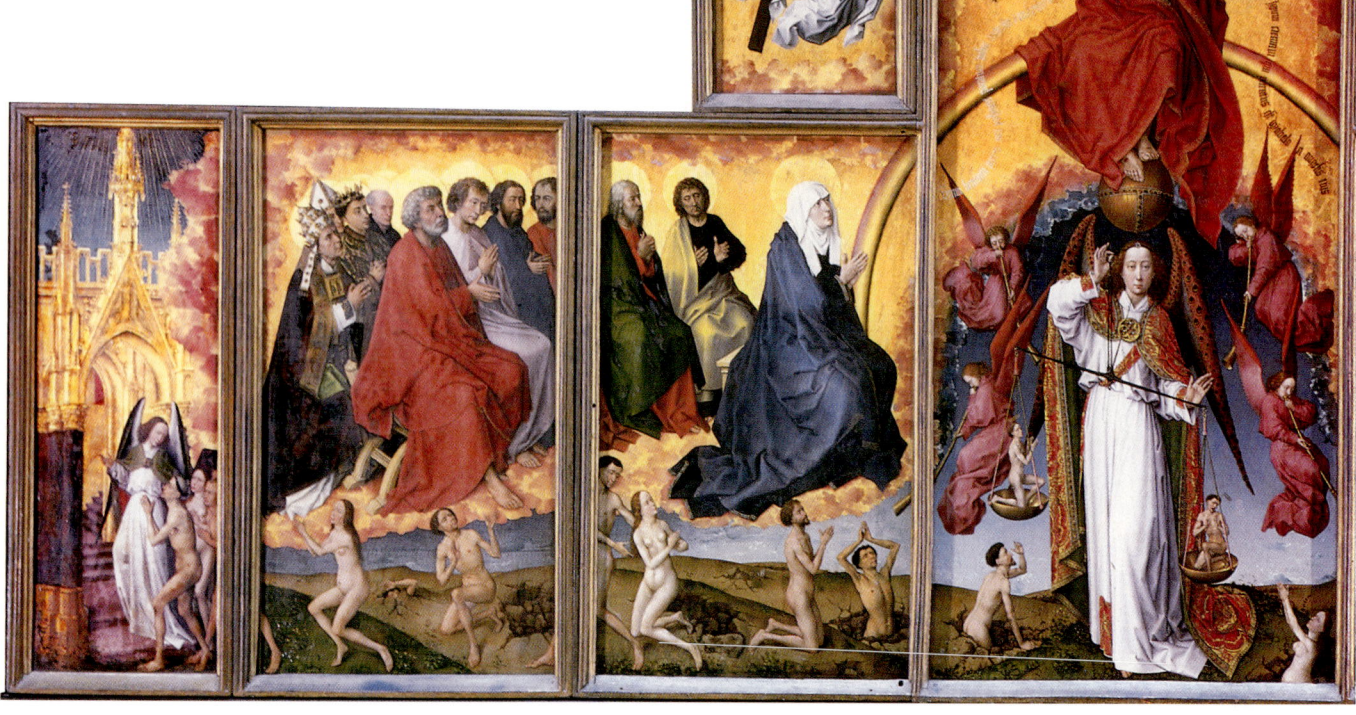

him) created fluid and dynamic compositions stressing human action and drama. He concentrated on themes such as the Crucifixion and the Pietà, moving observers emotionally by relating the sufferings of Christ.

Deposition (FIG. **20-6**) was the center panel of a triptych the Archers' Guild of Louvain commissioned for the church of Notre Dame hors-les-murs in Louvain. Rogier acknowledged the patrons of this large painting by incorporating the crossbow (the guild's symbol) into the decorative spandrels in the corners.

This altarpiece nicely sums up Rogier's early style and content. Instead of creating a deep landscape setting, as Jan van Eyck might have, he compressed the figures and action onto a shallow stage to concentrate the observer's attention. Here, Rogier imitated the large sculptured shrines so popular in the fifteenth century, especially in Germany, and the device admirably serves his purpose of expressing maximum action within a limited space. The painting, with the artist's crisp drawing and precise modeling of forms, resembles a stratified relief carving. A series of lateral undulating movements gives the group a unity, a formal cohesion that Rogier strengthened by psychological means—by the desolating anguish common to all the figures. The similar poses of Christ and the Virgin Mary further unify *Deposition*. Few painters have equaled Rogier in the rendering of passionate sorrow as it vibrates through a figure or distorts a tear-stained face. His depiction of the agony of loss is among the most authentic in religious art. The emotional impact on viewers is immediate and direct.

SAVING LIVES AND SOULS IN A HOSPITAL

Rogier further demonstrated his immense talent at orchestrating emotional visualizations in complex compositions in the *Last Judgment Altarpiece* (FIG. **20-7**). Nicholas Rolin, whom Philip the Good had appointed chancellor of the Burgundian territories, commissioned this polyptych. Created for the Hôtel-Dieu (hospital) in Beaune (also founded by Rolin), this image served an important function in the treatment of hospital patients. The public often attributed the horrific medical maladies affecting people of all walks of life to God's displeasure and perceived such afflictions as divine punishment. Thus, the general populace embraced praying to patron saints as a viable treatment component. On the altarpiece's exterior (not illustrated), Rogier depicted Saints Anthony and Sebastian, both considered plague saints—saints whose legends made them appropriate intercessors for warding off or curing the plague. This work served many purposes. It demonstrated Nicholas Rolin's devotion and generosity, aided in patient therapy, and warned of the potential fate of people's souls should they turn away from the Christian Church.

Rogier visualized this warning on the altarpiece's interior (FIG. 20-7), where he depicted the Last Judgment, a reminder of larger issues beyond earthly life and death—everlasting life or consignment to Hell. A radiant Christ appears in the center panel, above the archangel Michael, who holds the scales to weigh souls. The panels on both sides include numerous saints above the dead, while on the ends viewers witness the Saved ushered into Heaven on the left and the Damned

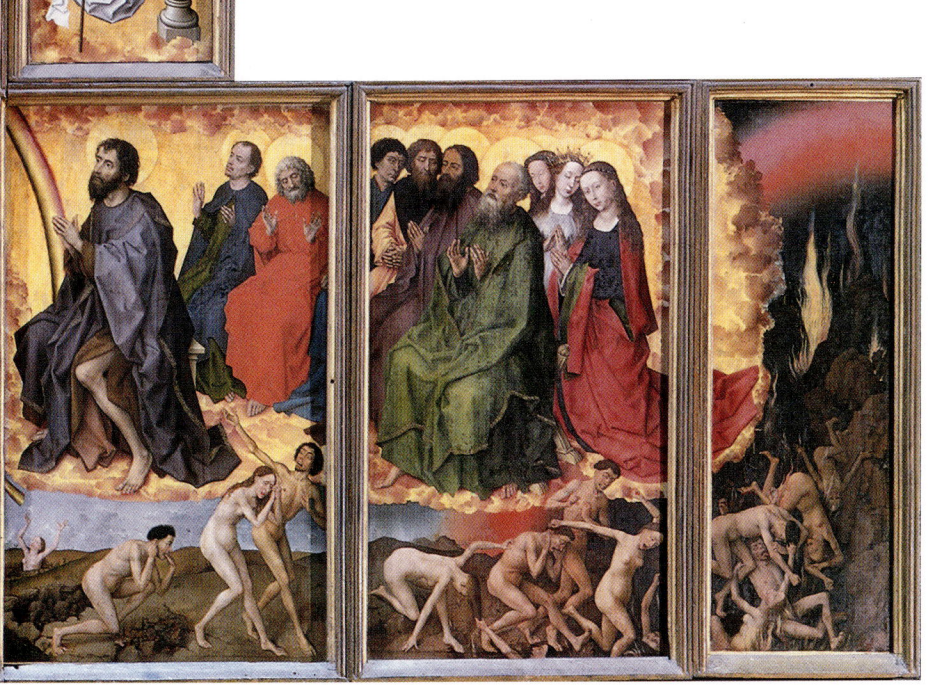

20-7 ROGIER VAN DER WEYDEN, *Last Judgment Altarpiece* (open), Hôtel-Dieu, Beaune, France, ca. 1444–1448. Panel, 7' 4⅝" × 17' 11". Musée de l'Hôtel-Dieu, Beaune.

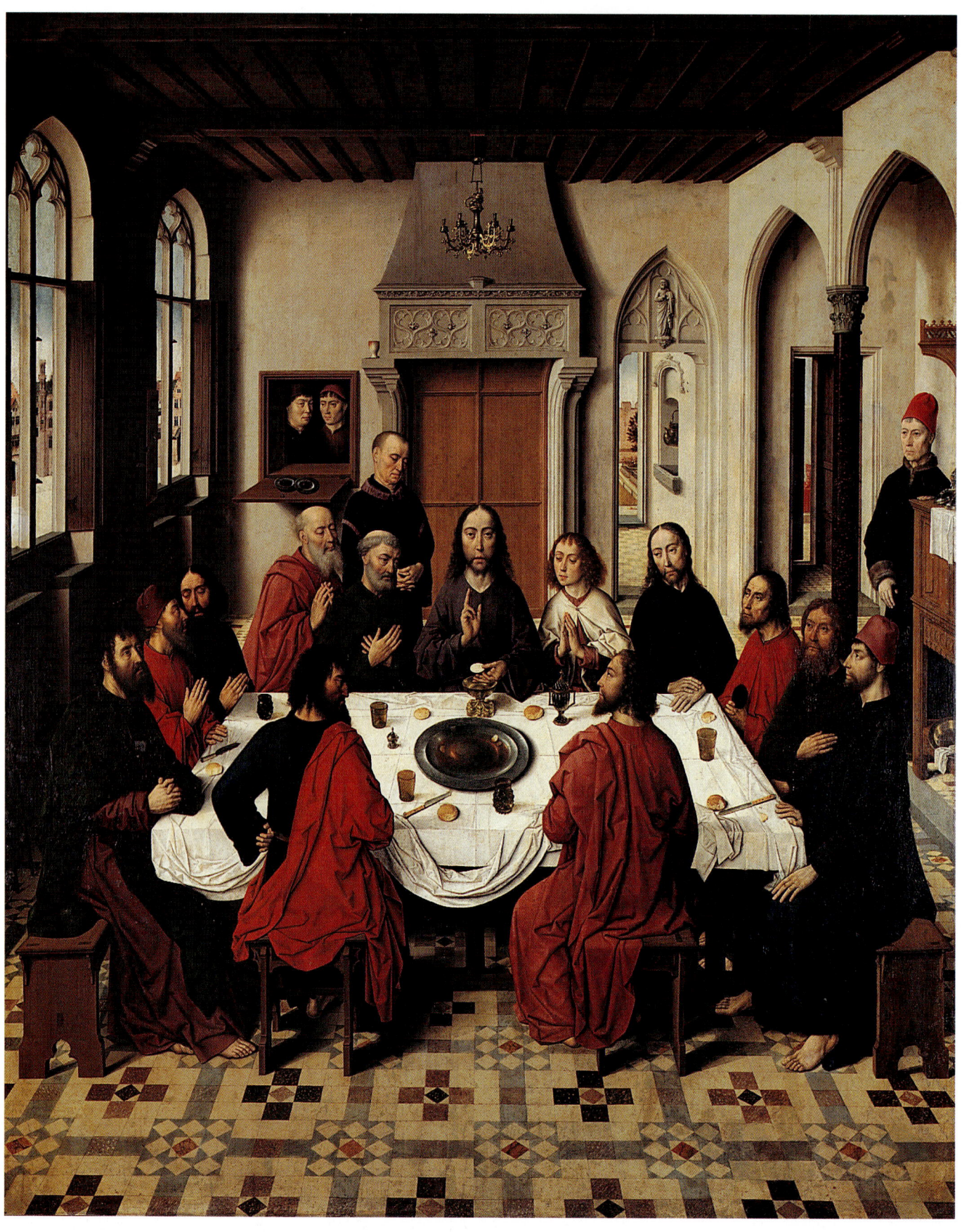

20-8 Dirk Bouts, *Last Supper* (central panel of the *Altarpiece of the Holy Sacrament*), Saint Peter's, Louvain, Belgium, 1464–1468. Oil on wood, approx. 6′ × 5′.

thrown into the fires of Hell on the right. Because this altarpiece is largely horizontal, relying solely on the common convention of distinguishing the spiritual from the mundane by placing the figures in a vertical hierarchy would not have been very effective. Therefore, Rogier used both hierarchy and scale to emphasize the relative importance of the figures. Christ appears as the largest and highest figure in the altarpiece, while the naked souls are miniscule.

A NEW PERSPECTIVE ON THE LAST SUPPER

Although Rogier may have known about the Italian science of linear perspective, he apparently chose not to use it in his paintings. Recent studies tend to give precedence in this field to Petrus Christus (see FIG. 20-14), from whom DIRK BOUTS (ca. 1415–1475) may have acquired his knowledge. In 1464, the Louvain Confraternity of the Holy Sacrament commissioned Bouts's *Altarpiece of the Holy Sacrament*. For a long time, scholars have believed the central panel of this altarpiece, *Last Supper* (FIG. **20-8**), was the first northern painting to demonstrate the use of a single vanishing point for constructing an interior. All of the depicted room's orthogonals lead to a single vanishing point in the center of the mantelpiece above Christ's head. This painting is not only the most successful fifteenth-century northern representation of an interior, but it was also the first northern one whose artist adjusted the figures' scale to correspond to the space they occupy. However, Bouts confined the perspective unity to single units of space only. The small side room has its own vanishing point, and neither it nor the vanishing point of the main room falls on the horizon of the landscape seen through the windows. Bouts's tentative manner of solving his spatial problems suggests he arrived at his solution independently and that the Italian science of perspective had not yet reached the north, except perhaps in small fragments. Regardless, Bouts's works clearly show that, by midcentury, northern artists had become involved with the same scientific formal problems that concerned Italian artists during most of the fifteenth century.

Scholars also have noted that Bouts's *Last Supper* was the first Flemish panel painting depicting this event. In this central panel, Bouts did not focus on the biblical narrative itself but instead presented Christ in the role of a priest performing a ritual from the liturgy of the Christian Church—the consecration of the Eucharistic wafer. This contrasts strongly with other Last Supper depictions, which often focused on Judas's betrayal or on Christ's comforting of John. Bouts also added to this image's complexity by including four servants (two in the window and two standing), all dressed in Flemish attire. These servants are most likely portraits of the confraternity's members responsible for commissioning the altarpiece.

FROM FLANDERS TO FLORENCE

Flemish altarpieces surfaced in countries outside of Flanders. One large-scale triptych the patron installed in a family chapel in Florence was the *Portinari Altarpiece* (FIG. **20-9**). The artist, HUGO VAN DER GOES (ca. 1440–1482), was dean of the painters' guild of Ghent from 1468 to 1475 and an extremely popular painter.

Hugo painted the triptych for Tommaso Portinari, an Italian shipowner and Medici agent who appears on the wings of the altarpiece with his family and their patron saints. The central panel is titled *Adoration of the Shepherds*. On this large surface, Hugo displayed a scene of solemn grandeur, muting the high drama of the joyous occasion. The Virgin, Joseph, and the angels seem to brood on the suffering to come rather than to meditate on the Nativity miracle. Mary kneels, somber and monumental, on a tilted ground that has the expressive function of centering the main actors. From the right rear enter three shepherds, represented with powerful realism in attitudes

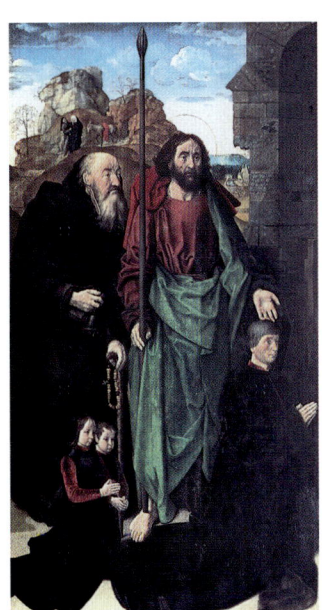
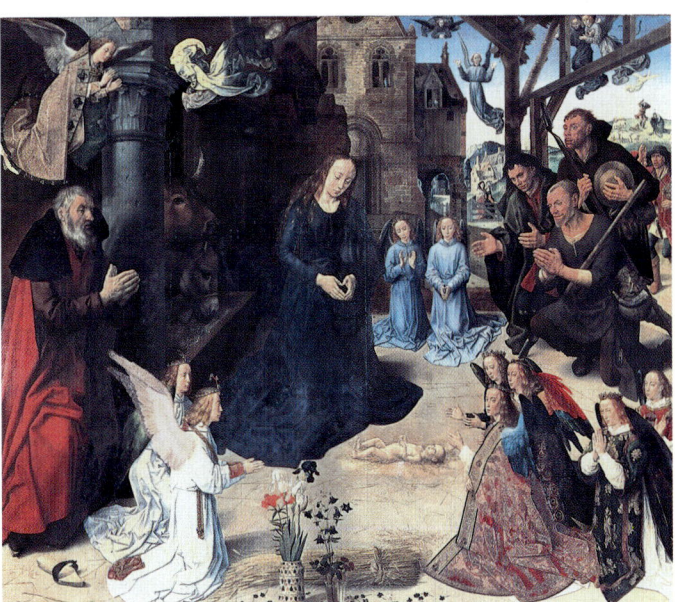
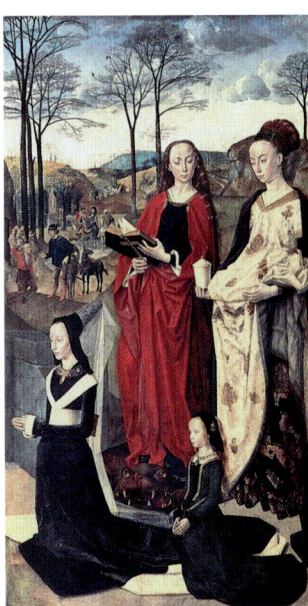

20-9 HUGO VAN DER GOES, *Portinari Altarpiece* (open), from Sant'Egidio, Florence, Italy, ca. 1476. Tempera and oil on wood, 8′ 3½″ × 10′ (center panel), 8′ 3½″ × 4′ 7½″ (each wing). Galleria degli Uffizi, Florence.

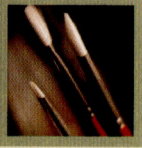

Edges and Borders
Framing Paintings

Until recent decades, when painters began to complete their works by simply affixing canvas to wooden stretcher bars, artists considered the frame an integral part of the painting. Most fifteenth- and sixteenth-century paintings included elaborate frames that artists helped design and construct. Frames were frequently polychromed (painted) or gilded, adding to the expense. Surviving contracts reveal that as much as half of an altarpiece's cost derived from the frame. For small works, artists sometimes affixed the frames to the panels before painting, creating an insistent visual presence as they worked. Occasionally, a single piece of wood served as both panel and frame, and the artist carved the painting surface from the wood, leaving the edges as a frame.

Larger images with elaborate frames, such as altarpieces, required the services of a woodcarver or stonemason. The painter worked closely with the individual constructing the frame to ensure its appropriateness for the image(s) produced. Indeed, in

some of their altarpieces, Giovanni Bellini (FIG. 22-31) and Andrea Mantegna (Chapter 21, pages 627–30) duplicated the carved pilasters of their architectural frames in their paintings, thereby enhancing the illusion of space. This interest in illusion occasionally extended to the frames. For example, the inscription that seems chiseled into the frame of Jan van Eyck's *Man in a Red Turban* (FIG. 20-15) is actually painted.

Unfortunately, over time, many frames were removed from paintings. For instance, most scholars believe individuals concerned with conserving the *Ghent Altarpiece* (FIG. 20-4) removed its elaborately carved frame and dismantled the altarpiece in 1566 to protect it from Protestant iconoclasts. As ill luck would have it, when the panels were reinstalled in 1587, no one could find the frame, which probably was destroyed. Sadly, the absence of many of the original frames deprives viewers today of the complete artistic vision of painters and, sometimes, of their hired woodcarvers.

---

of wonder, piety, and gaping curiosity. Their lined plebeian faces, work-worn hands, and uncouth dress and manner seem immediately familiar. The symbolic architecture and a continuous wintry northern landscape unify the three panels. Symbols surface throughout the altarpiece. Iris and columbine flowers symbolize the Sorrows of the Virgin; the fifteen angels represent the Fifteen Joys of Mary; a sheaf of wheat stands for Bethlehem (the "house of bread" in Hebrew), a reference to the Eucharist; and the harp of David, emblazoned over the building's portal in the middle distance (just to the right of the Virgin's head), signifies the ancestry of Christ.

To stress the meaning and significance of the depicted event, Hugo revived medieval pictorial devices. Small scenes shown in the background of the altarpiece represent (from left to right) the Flight into Egypt, the Annunciation to the Shepherds, and the Arrival of the Magi. Hugo's variation in the scale of his figures to differentiate them by their importance to the central event also reflects older traditions. Still, he put a vigorous, penetrating realism to work in a new direction, characterizing human beings according to their social level while showing their common humanity.

After Portinari placed his altarpiece in the family chapel in the Florentine church of Sant'Egidio, it created a considerable stir among Italian artists. Although the painting as a whole may have seemed unstructured to them, Hugo's masterful technique and what they thought of as incredible realism for representing drapery, flowers, animals, and, above all, human character and emotion made a deep impression on them. At

least one Florentine artist, Domenico Ghirlandaio, paid tribute to the northern master by using Hugo's most striking motif, the adoring shepherds, in one of his own Nativity paintings.

A CREATOR OF SUMPTUOUS ALTARPIECES The artistic community in Flanders held Hugo's contemporary, HANS MEMLING (ca. 1430–1494), in high esteem as well. Memling specialized in images of the Madonna; the many that survive are slight, pretty, and young princesses, each holding a doll-like infant Christ. A good example of his work is the *Saint John Altarpiece*, the central panel of which is *Virgin with Saints and Angels* FIG. **20-10**). The composition is balanced and serene; the color, sparkling and luminous; and the execution, of the highest technical quality. (Memling's paintings are among the best preserved from the fifteenth century.) The prevailing sense of isolation and the frail, spiritual human types contrast not only with Hugo's monumental and somber forms but also with van Eyck's robust ones. The patrons of this altarpiece—two brothers and two sisters of the Hospital of Saint John order in Bruges—appear on the exterior side panels (not illustrated). In the central panel, two angels, one playing a musical instrument and the other holding a book, flank the Virgin. To the sides of Mary's throne stand Saint John the Baptist on the left and Saint John the Evangelist on the right, and in the foreground are Saints Catherine and Barbara. The altarpiece exudes opulence due to the rich colors,

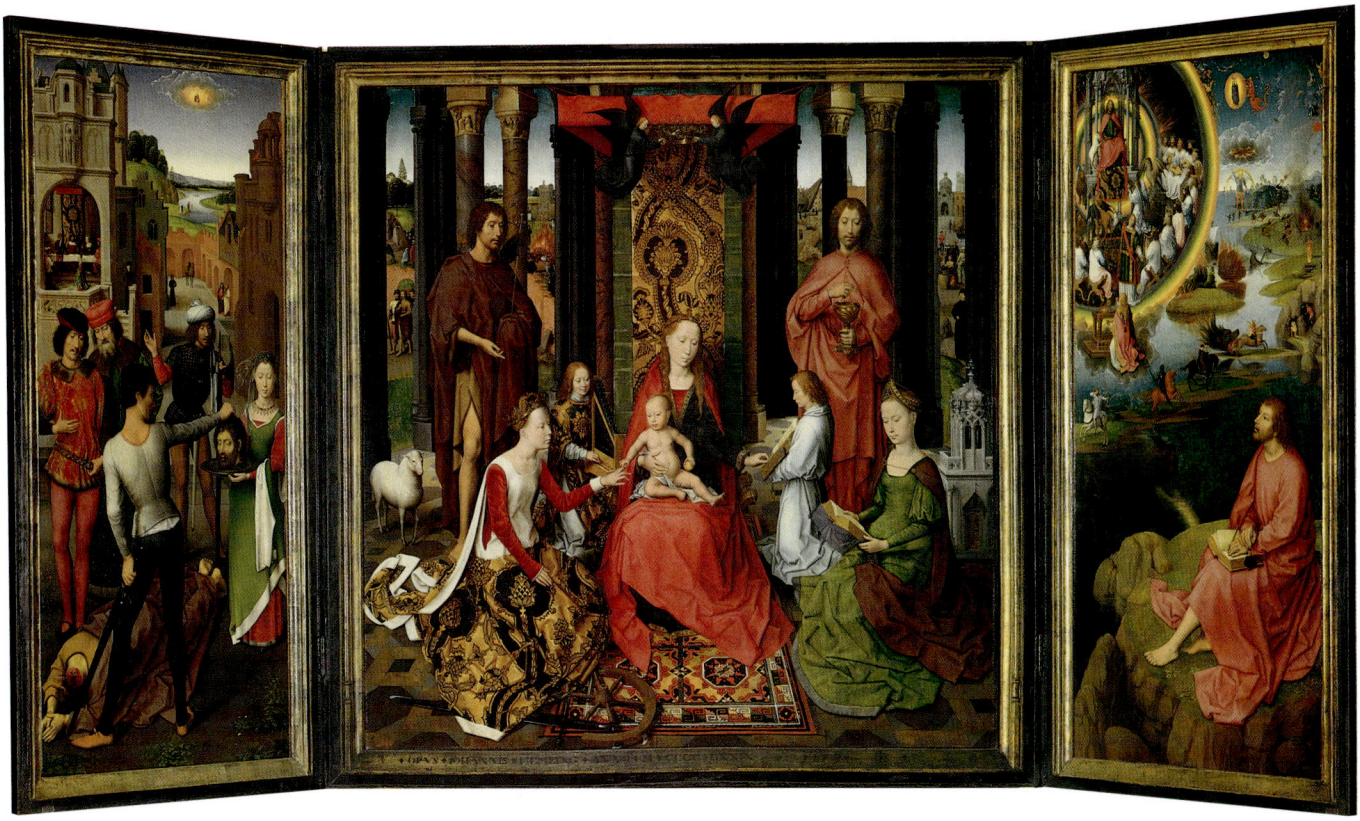

20-10   HANS MEMLING, *Altarpiece of the Virgin with Saints and Angels* (or *Saint John Altarpiece*), Hospitaal Sint Jan, Bruges, Belgium, 1479. Oil on wood, approx. 5′ 7 3/4″ × 5′ 7 3/4″ (center panel), 5′ 7 3/4″ × 2′ 7 1/8″ (each wing).

carefully depicted tapestries and brocades, and the serenity of the figures. Works such as this earned Memling the following tribute after his death: "Johannes Memlinc [Memling] was the most accomplished and excellent painter in the entire Christian world." [1]

Private Devotional Imagery

IN THE PRIVACY OF THE HOME The Flemish did not limit their demonstrations of piety to the public realm. Individuals commissioned artworks for private devotional use in the home as well. Dissatisfaction with the clergy accounted, in part, for this commitment to private prayer. In addition, popular reform movements advocated personal devotion. So strong was the impetus for private devotional imagery that it seems, based on extant Flemish religious paintings, that lay patrons outnumbered clerical patrons by a ratio of two to one.

One of the more prominent features of these images commissioned for private use is the intersection of religious and secular concerns. Although the idea, for example, of depicting a biblical scene as transpiring in a Flemish house may seem inconsistent or even sacrilegious, religion was such an integral part of Flemish life that separating the sacred from the secular became virtually impossible. As Johan Huizinga, renowned modern historian on the fifteenth century, describes it:

All life was saturated with religion to such an extent that the people were in constant danger of losing sight of the distinction between things spiritual and things temporal. If, on the one hand, all details of ordinary life may be raised to a sacred level, on the other hand, all that is holy sinks to the commonplace, by the fact of being blended with everyday life . . . the demarcation of the spheres of religious thought and that of worldly concerns was nearly obliterated.[2]

Further, the presentation in religious art of familiar settings and objects no doubt strengthened the direct bond the patron or viewers felt with biblical figures.

THE SYMBOLIC AND THE SECULAR The *Mérode Altarpiece* (FIG. **20-11**) is a good example of a triptych commissioned for private use. Scholars continue to debate the identity of the artist, generally referred to as the "MASTER OF FLÉMALLE." Although many have claimed the artist is Robert Campin (ca. 1378–1444), the leading painter of the city of Tournai, others disagree. Similar in format to large-scale Flemish public altarpieces, the *Mérode Altarpiece* is considerably smaller (the central panel is roughly two feet square), which allowed the owners to close the wings and move the painting when necessary. The popular Annunciation theme (as prophesied in Isa. 7:14) occupies the triptych's central panel. The archangel Gabriel approaches Mary, who sits reading. The artist depicted a well-kept middle-class Flemish home as the site of the event. The carefully rendered architectural scene in the background of the right wing testifies to location.

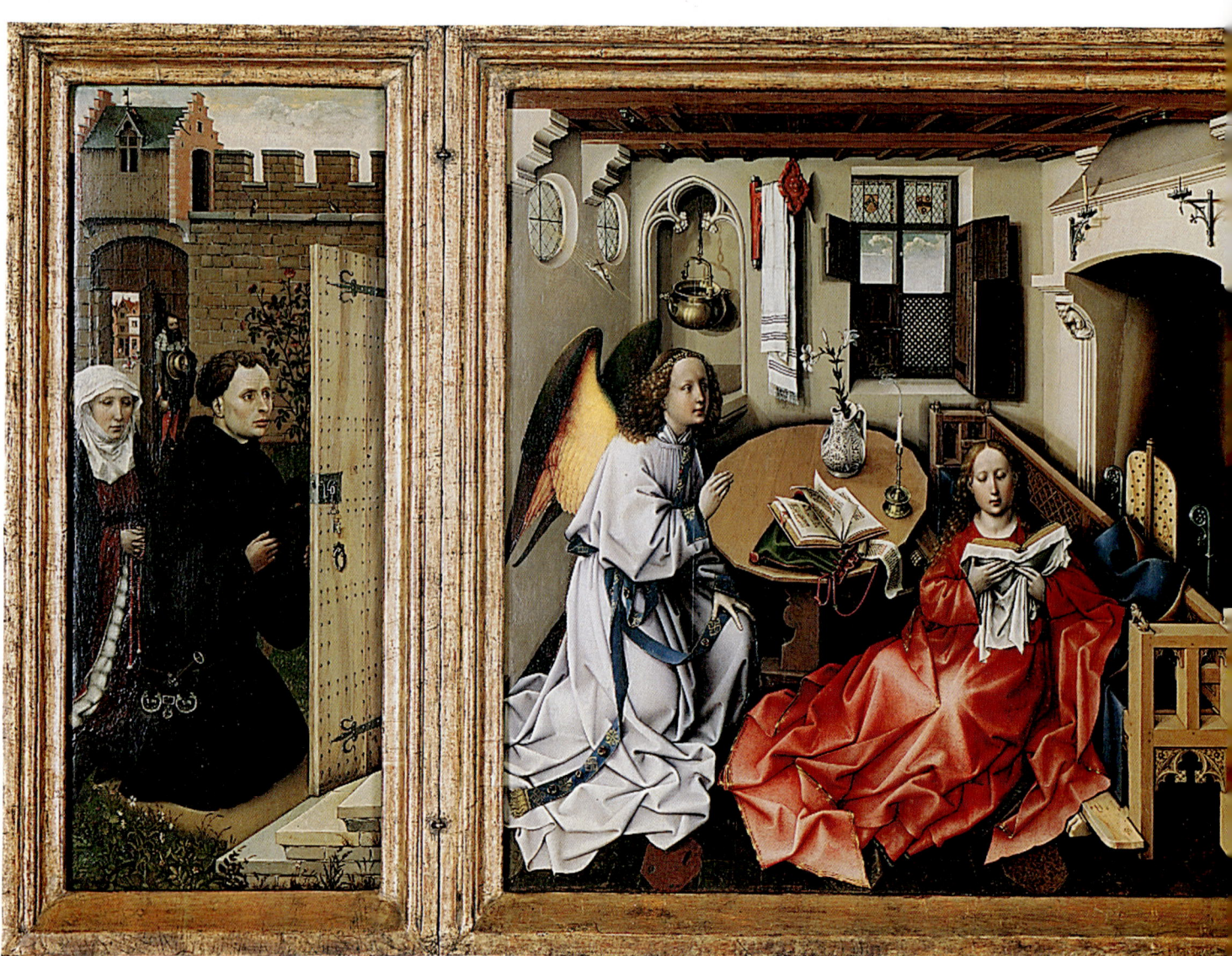

20-11 MASTER OF FLÉMALLE (Robert Campin?), *Mérode Altarpiece* (open), *The Annunciation* (center panel), ca. 1425–1428. Oil on wood, center panel approx. 2′ 1″ × 2′ 1″. Metropolitan Museum of Art, New York (The Cloisters Collection, 1956).

The Master of Flémalle included accessories, furniture, and utensils to reinforce the setting's identification. However, the objects represented are not merely decorative. They also function as religious symbols, thereby reminding viewers of the event's miraculous nature. The book, extinguished candle, lilies, copper basin (in the corner niche), towels, fire screen, and bench symbolize, in different ways, the Virgin's purity and her divine mission. In the right panel, Joseph has made a mousetrap, symbolic of the theological tradition that Christ is bait set in the trap of the world to catch the Devil. The painter completely inventoried a carpenter's shop. The ax, saw, and rod in the foreground are not only tools of the carpenter's trade but also are mentioned in Isaiah 10:15. In the left panel, the altarpiece's donor, Peter Inghelbrecht (Engelbrecht), and his wife kneel and seem to be permitted to witness this momentous event through an open door. The Inghelbrechts, a devout, middle-class couple, appear in a closed garden, symbolic of Mary's purity, and the flowers depicted—strawberries, violets, and plantains—all relate to Mary's virtues, especially humility.

The careful conceptualization of this entire altarpiece is further suggested by the fact the Annunciation theme also refers to the patron's name—Engelbrecht ("angel bringer")—and the workshop scene in the right panel also refers to his wife's name, Schrinmechers ("shrine maker").

FOR BETTER, FOR WORSE The intersection of the secular and the religious in Flemish painting also surfaces in Jan van Eyck's double portrait *Giovanni Arnolfini and His Bride* (FIG. **20-12**). Van Eyck depicted the Lucca financier (who had established himself in Bruges as an agent of the Medici family) and his betrothed in a Flemish bedchamber that is simultaneously mundane and charged with the spiritual. As in the *Mérode Altarpiece*, almost every object portrayed conveys the event's sanctity, specifically, the holiness of matrimony. Arnolfini and his bride, Giovanna Cenami, hand in hand, take the marriage vows. The cast-aside clogs indicate this event is taking place on holy ground. The little dog symbolizes fidelity (the common canine name Fido originated from the Latin *fido,* "to trust"). Behind the pair,

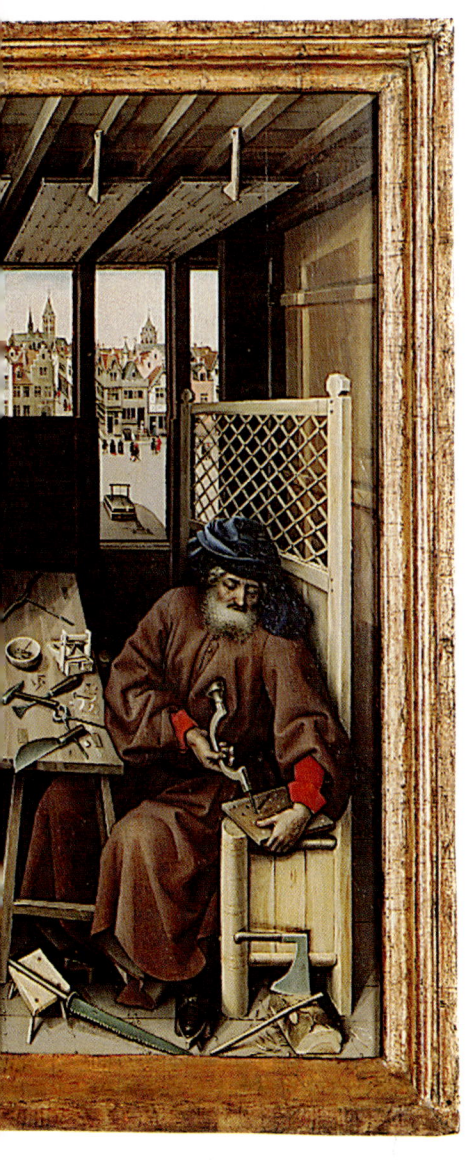

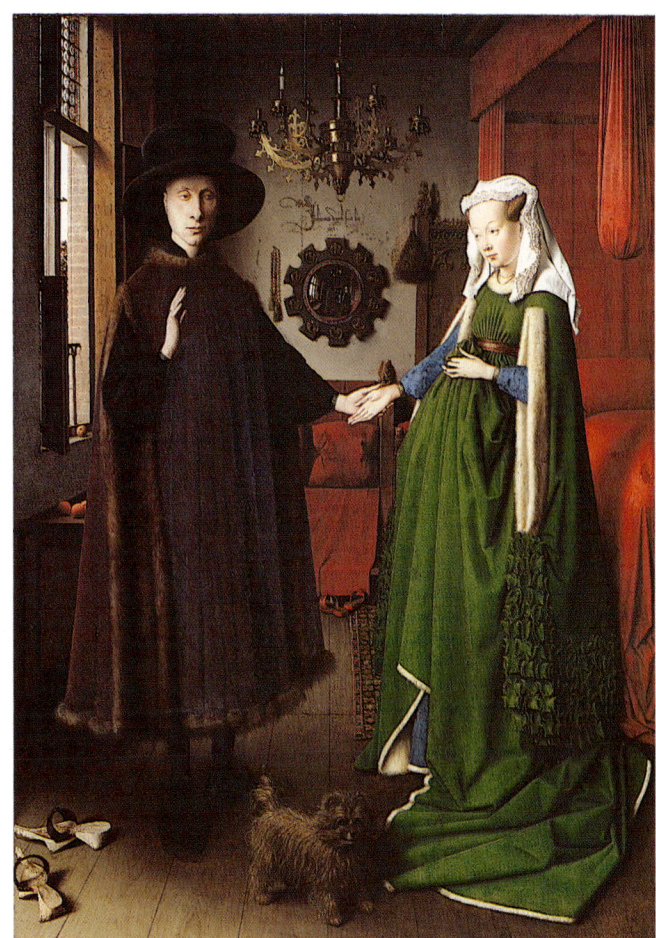

20-12 JAN VAN EYCK, *Giovanni Arnolfini and His Bride,* 1434. Oil on wood, approx. 2′ 8″ × 1′ 11½″. National Gallery, London.

20-13 JAN VAN EYCK, detail of *Giovanni Arnolfini and His Bride,* 1434.

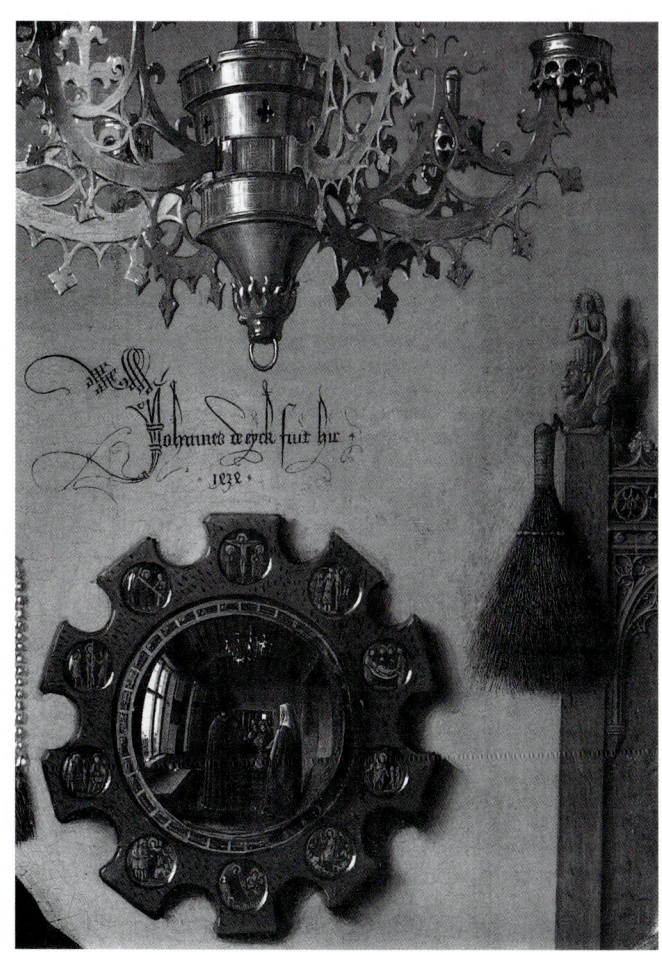

the curtains of the marriage bed have been opened. The bedpost's *finial* (crowning ornament) is a tiny statue of Saint Margaret, patron saint of childbirth. From the finial hangs a whisk broom, symbolic of domestic care. The oranges on the chest below the window may refer to fertility, and the all-seeing eye of God seems to be referred to twice. It is symbolized once by the single candle burning in the left rear holder of the ornate chandelier and again by the mirror, where viewers see the entire room reflected (FIG. **20-13**). The small medallions set into the mirror's frame show tiny scenes from the Passion of Christ and represent God's ever-present promise of salvation for the figures reflected on the mirror's convex surface.

Flemish viewers would have been familiar with many of the objects included in *Giovanni Arnolfini and His Bride* because of traditional Flemish customs. Husbands traditionally presented brides with clogs, and the solitary lit candle in the chandelier was also part of Flemish marriage practices. Van Eyck's placement of the two figures suggests conventional gender roles—the woman stands near the bed and well into the

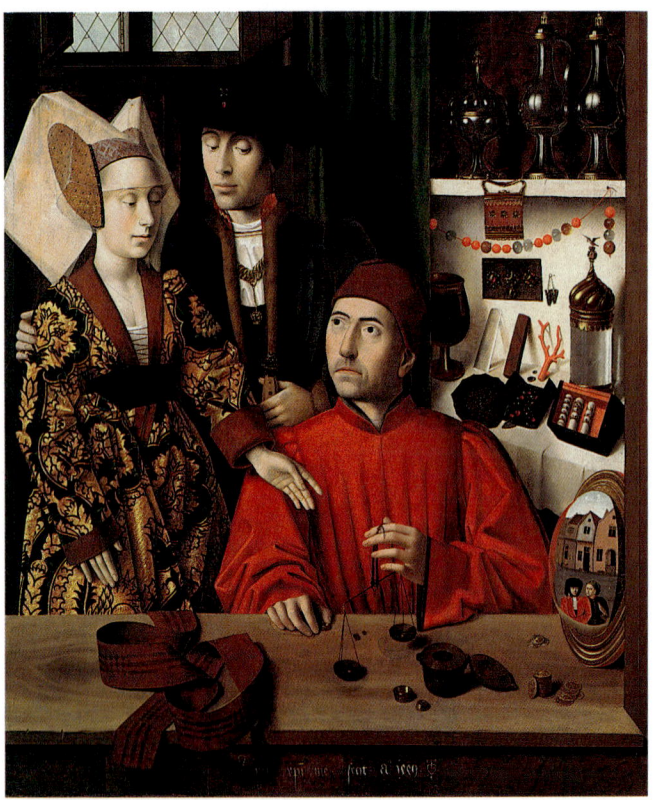

20-14   Petrus Christus, *A Goldsmith in His Shop, Possibly Saint Eligius,* 1449. Oil on wood, approx. 3′ 3″ × 2′ 10″. Metropolitan Museum of Art, New York (the Robert Lehman Collection, 1975).

room, while the man stands near the open window, symbolic of the outside world.

Van Eyck enhanced the documentary nature of this painting by exquisitely painting each object. He carefully distinguished textures and depicted the light from the window on the left reflecting off various surfaces. The artist augmented the scene's credibility by including the convex mirror (FIG. 20-13), because viewers can see not only the principals, Arnolfini and his wife, but also two persons who look into the room through the door. One of these must be the artist himself, as the florid inscription above the mirror, "Johannes de Eyck fuit hic," announces he was present. The picture's purpose, then, seems to have been to record and sanctify this marriage. Although this has been the traditional interpretation of this image, some scholars recently have taken issue with this reading, suggesting that Arnolfini is conferring legal privileges on his wife to conduct business in his absence. Despite the lingering questions about the precise purpose of *Giovanni Arnolfini and His Bride,* the painting provides viewers today with great insight into both van Eyck's remarkable skill and Flemish life in the fifteenth century.

A GOLDEN MOMENT   Like van Eyck's double portrait, *A Goldsmith in His Shop, Possibly Saint Eligius* (FIG. **20-14**) by Petrus Christus (ca. 1410–1472) involves a couple and the holy sacrament of matrimony. Scholars know little of Christus's life, except that he may have been van Eyck's student and that he settled and worked in Bruges. As with many Flemish artworks, uncertainties remain about why Christus produced

this painting and the scene depicted. Although the couple's presence suggests a marriage portrait, most scholars believe the goldsmiths' guild in Bruges commissioned this painting. Saint Eligius was the patron saint of gold- and silversmiths, blacksmiths, and metalworkers, all of whom shared a chapel in a building adjacent to their meetinghouse. This painting thus seems to fit into the tradition of vocational paintings produced for installation in guild chapels.

In *A Goldsmith in His Shop, Possibly Saint Eligius,* a goldsmith sits in his stall, showing an elegantly attired couple a selection of rings. The bride's betrothal girdle lies on the table, and the woman reaches for the ring the goldsmith weighs. The carefully depicted objects on the right side of the painting refer to the goldsmith's trade. The raw materials—precious stones, beads, crystal, coral, and seed pearls—are scattered among finished products, including rings, buckles, and brooches. Christus also meticulously painted the convex mirror in the foreground, which extends the painting's space into that of viewers, creating a greater sense of involvement.

A Goldsmith in His Shop, like the Arnolfini wedding portrait, incorporates both secular and religious elements. While focusing on an economic transaction and the goldsmith's profession, it calls attention to the sacrament of marriage and includes items such as a crystal container for Eucharistic wafers. Further, the artist's presentation of the goldsmith holding the scales easily could be read as a reference to the Last Judgment.

Portraiture

MEETING THE VIEWER'S GAZE   Despite the overwhelming incorporation of religion into Flemish everyday lives, the increasing prosperity produced by the economy's mercantilist orientation led some individuals to commission nonreligious landscapes and portraits. Two Flemish works shown so far, the *Ghent Altarpiece* (FIG. 20-4) and the *Mérode Altarpiece* (FIG. 20-11), include painted portraits of their donors. These paintings marked a significant revival of portraiture, a genre that had languished since antiquity. Jan van Eyck's *Man in a Red Turban* (FIG. **20-15**) is a completely secular portrait without the layer of religious interpretation common to Flemish painting. In this work (possibly a self-portrait), the image of a living individual apparently required no religious purpose for being—only a personal one. These private portraits began to multiply as both artists and patrons became interested in the reality (both physical and psychological) they revealed. As human beings confronted themselves in painted portraits, they objectified themselves as people. In this confrontation, the otherworldly anonymity of the Middle Ages faded away. The man van Eyck portrayed looks directly at viewers or, perhaps, at himself in a mirror. So far as studies show, this was the first Western painted portrait in a thousand years to do so. The level composed gaze, directed from a true three-quarter head pose, must have impressed observers deeply. The painter created the illusion that from whatever angle a viewer observes the face, the eyes return that gaze. Van Eyck, with his considerable observational skill and controlled painting style, injected a heightened sense of specificity to this portrait by including veins in the bloodshot left eye, the beard stubble, and the weathered and aged skin.

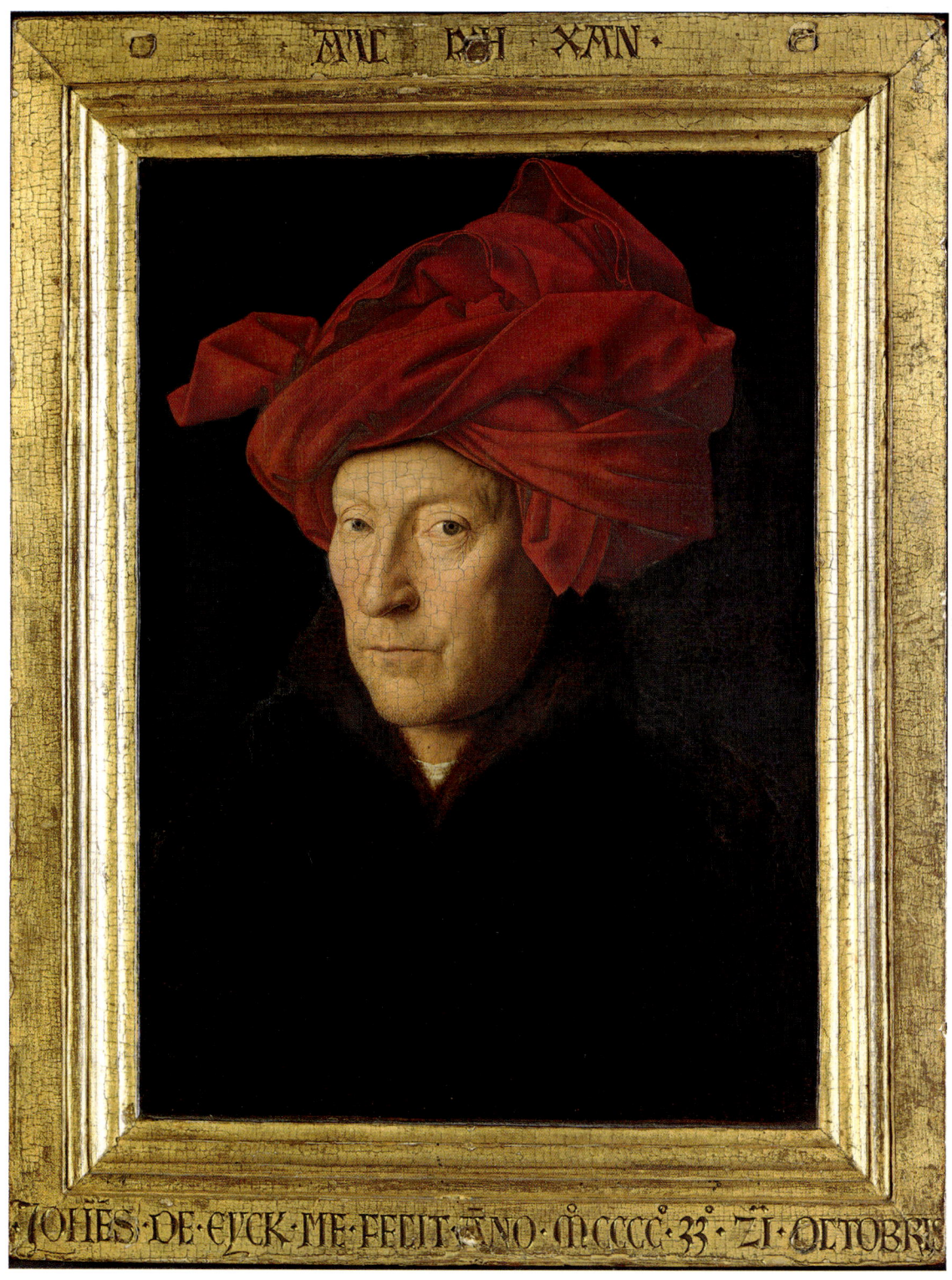

20-15   JAN VAN EYCK, *Man in a Red Turban*, 1433. Oil on wood, approx. $10\frac{1}{4}'' \times 7\frac{1}{2}''$. National Gallery, London.

Although a definitive identification of the sitter has yet to be made, the possibility *Man in a Red Turban* is a self-portrait seems reinforced by the frame's inscriptions (see "Edges and Borders: Framing Paintings," page 574). Across the top, van Eyck wrote "As I can" in Flemish using Greek letters, and across the bottom in Latin appears the statement "Jan van Eyck made me" and the date.

Admired artists, such as van Eyck, established portraiture among their principal tasks. Great patrons embraced the opportunity to have their likenesses painted for various reasons. They wanted to memorialize themselves in their dynastic lines; to establish their identities, ranks, and stations by images far more concrete than heraldic coats of arms; or to represent themselves at state occasions when they could not attend. They even used such paintings when arranging marriages. Royalty, nobility, and the very rich would send painters to "take" the likeness of a prospective bride or groom. Evidence reveals that when young King Charles VI of France sought a bride, a painter journeyed to three different royal courts to make portraits of the candidates for the king to use in making his choice.

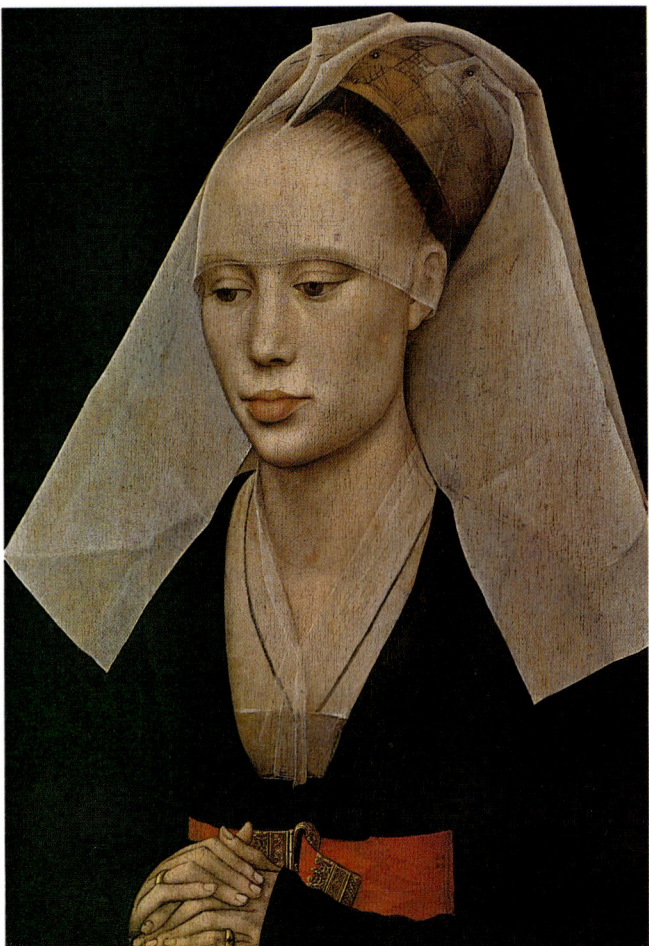

20-16   ROGIER VAN DER WEYDEN, *Portrait of a Lady,* ca. 1460. Oil on panel, 1′ 1$\frac{3}{8}$″ × 10$\frac{1}{16}$″. National Gallery, Washington (Andrew W. Mellon Collection).

CAPTURING CLASS AND CHARACTER The commission details for Rogier van der Weyden's portrait of an unknown young lady (FIG. **20-16**) remain unclear. Her dress and bearing imply noble rank. The artist provided viewers with a portrait that not only presented a faithful likeness of her somewhat plain features but also revealed her individual character. Her lowered eyes, tightly locked thin fingers, and fragile physique bespeak an introverted and devout personality. Rogier's honesty and directness, typical in the Flemish artist's approach, reveal much, despite the woman's reserved demeanor. This style contrasted with the formal Italian approach (see FIG. 21-30), derived from the profiles common to coins and medallions, which was sterner and conveyed little of the sitter's personality. Rogier was perhaps chief among the Flemish in his penetrating readings of his subjects, and, as a great pictorial composer, he made beautiful use here of flat, sharply pointed angular shapes that so powerfully suggest the rigidity of this subject's personality. Unlike Jan van Eyck, Rogier placed little emphasis on minute description of surface detail. Instead, he defined large, simple planes and volumes, achieving an almost "abstract" effect, in the modern sense, of dignity and elegance.

An Enigmatic Flemish Painter

LOVE AND MARRIAGE OR SEX AND SIN? Although certain themes in and genres of painting emerged so frequently during the fifteenth century in Flanders as to qualify as conventions, this country also produced one of the most fascinating and puzzling painters in history, HIERONYMUS BOSCH (ca. 1450–1516). Interpretations of Bosch differ widely. Was he a satirist, an irreligious mocker, or a pornographer? Was he a heretic or an orthodox fanatic like Girolamo Savonarola, his Italian contemporary? Was he obsessed by guilt and the universal reign of sin and death?

Bosch's most famous work, the so-called *Garden of Earthly Delights* (FIG. **20-17**), is also his most enigmatic, and no interpretation of it is universally accepted. This large-scale work takes the familiar form of a triptych. More than seven feet high, the painting extends to more than twelve feet wide when opened. This triptych format seems to indicate a religious function for this work, but documentation reveals that *Garden of Earthly Delights* resided in the palace of Henry III of Nassau, regent of the Netherlands, seven years after its completion. This suggests a secular commission for private use. Scholars have proposed that such a commission, in conjunction with the central themes of marriage, sex, and procreation, points to a wedding commemoration, which, as seen in *Giovanni Arnolfini and His Bride* and in *A Goldsmith in His Shop, Possibly Saint Eligius,* was not uncommon. Any similarities between these paintings end there, however. While van Eyck and Christus grounded their depictions of betrothed couples in contemporary Flemish life and custom, Bosch's image portrays a visionary world of fantasy and intrigue.

In the left panel, God presents Eve to Adam in a landscape, presumably the Garden of Eden. Bosch complicated his straightforward presentation of this event by placing it in a wildly imaginative setting that includes an odd pink fountain-like structure in a body of water and an array of fanciful and unusual animals, which may hint at an interpretation involving alchemy—the medieval study of seemingly magical changes, especially chemical changes. The right panel, in contrast, bombards viewers with the horrors of Hell. Beastly creatures devour people, while others are impaled or strung on musical instruments, as if on a medieval rack. A gambler is nailed to his own table. A spidery monster embraces a girl while toads bite her. A sea of inky darkness envelops the entire range of horror. Observers must search through the hideous enclosure of Bosch's Hell to take in its fascinating though repulsive details.

Sandwiched between Paradise and Hell is the huge central panel, with nude people blithely cavorting in a landscape dotted with bizarre creatures and unidentifiable objects. The prevalence of fruit and birds (fertility symbols) throughout the scene suggests procreation, and, indeed, many of the figures are paired off as couples. The orgiastic overtones of *Garden of Earthly Delights,* in conjunction with the terrifying image of Hell, have led some scholars to interpret this triptych, like other Last Judgment images, as a warning to viewers of the fate awaiting the sinful, decadent, and immoral.

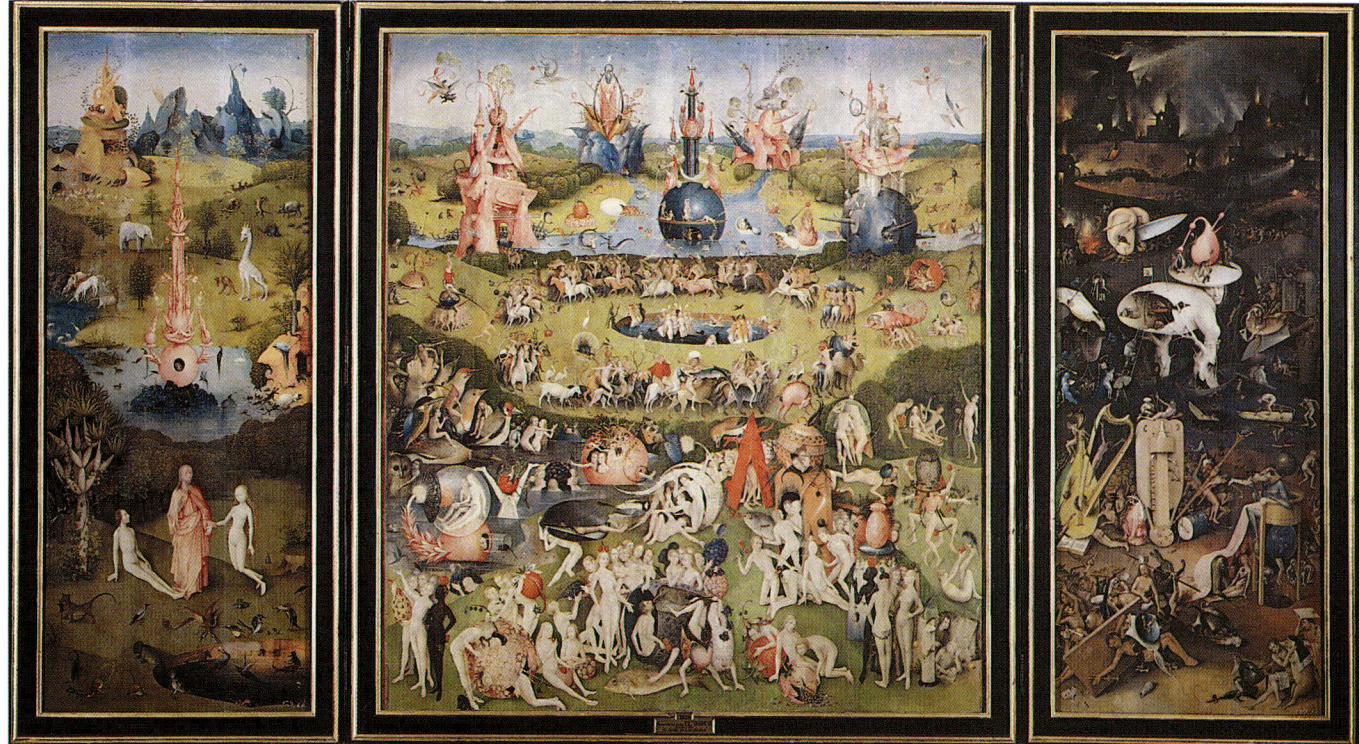

20-17 HIERONYMUS BOSCH, *Garden of Earthly Delights. Creation of Eve* (left wing), *Garden of Earthly Delights* (central panel), *Hell* (right wing), 1505–1510. Oil on wood, center panel 7′ 2⅝″ × 6′ 4¾″. Museo del Prado, Madrid.

FIFTEENTH-CENTURY FRENCH ART

In France, the Hundred Years' War decimated economic enterprise and prevented stability. The anarchy of war and the weakness of the kings gave rise to a group of duchies, each with significant power. The strongest of these, as mentioned earlier, was the Duchy of Burgundy. Despite this instability, French artists joined the retinues of the wealthiest nobility, the dukes of Berry, Bourbon, and Nemours and sometimes the royal court, where they could continue to develop their art.

PORTRAYING THE PIOUS Images for private devotional use were popular in France, as in Flanders. Among the French artists whose paintings were in demand was JEAN FOUQUET (ca. 1420–1481), who worked for King Charles VII (the patron and client of Jacques Coeur, FIG. 18-30) and for the duke of Nemours. Fouquet painted the portrait of Étienne Chevalier with his patron saint, Saint Stephen (FIG. **20-18**), in a format commonly referred to as a donor portrait because an individual commissioned (or "gave") the portrait as evidence of devotion. The kneeling donor with his standing saint recalls Flemish art, as do the three-quarter stances and the sharp, clear focus of the portraits. Despite lowly origins, Chevalier elevated himself in French society, and in 1452 King Charles VII named him treasurer of France. In *Étienne Chevalier and Saint Stephen,* the donor appears appropriately devout. The artist depicted the saint holding the stone of his martyrdom (death by stoning) atop a volume of the Scriptures, ensuring viewer identification. Fouquet rendered the entire image in meticulous detail and included a highly ornamented architectural setting.

The parallels between this French portrait and Flemish painting also include the format; this panel was originally half of a diptych. The panels were separated some time ago, and each now resides in a different museum—one in Berlin, the other in Antwerp. The second panel, not illustrated here, depicts the Virgin Mary and Christ Child. As with the *Mérode Altarpiece,* the juxtaposition of these two panels allowed the patron to bear witness to the sacred.

A PROVENÇAL PIETÀ A French artist produced the *Avignon Pietà* (FIG. **20-19**) in Provence, in the extreme south of France. Traditional scholarship has identified ENGUERRAND QUARTON (CHARONTON; ca. 1410–1466) as the artist. The *Avignon Pietà* resided, at one time, in the Chartreuse du Val de Bénédiction (the church of the Carthusians) in Villeneuve; the Carthusians supported the Avignon pope during the Great Schism. This documented placement of *Pietà* in this church thus contributes to the attribution of this work to Enguerrand Quarton, who produced other major works there. Despite this connection, much skepticism remains about the attribution.

Rogier van der Weyden's *Deposition* (FIG. 20-6) might come to mind quickly when viewing *Pietà*. Here, however, the artist chose a much more subdued, almost monochromatic, color scheme, and, unlike Rogier's placement of the figures in a box-like setting, this scene occurs in an ill-defined landscape with buildings in the far distance. The donor (whose identity remains unknown), a familiar presence in fifteenth-century depictions of sacred events, kneels at the left. His is a strikingly characteristic portrait, the face gnarled, oaken, and ascetic. The luminous gold background the artist silhouetted the figures against and incised the halos into recalls Byzantine art.

20-18 JEAN FOUQUET, *Étienne Chevalier and Saint Stephen* (from a diptych now divided), ca. 1450. Oil on wood, 3′ ½″ × 2′ 9½″. Gemäldegalerie, Staatliche Museen, Berlin.

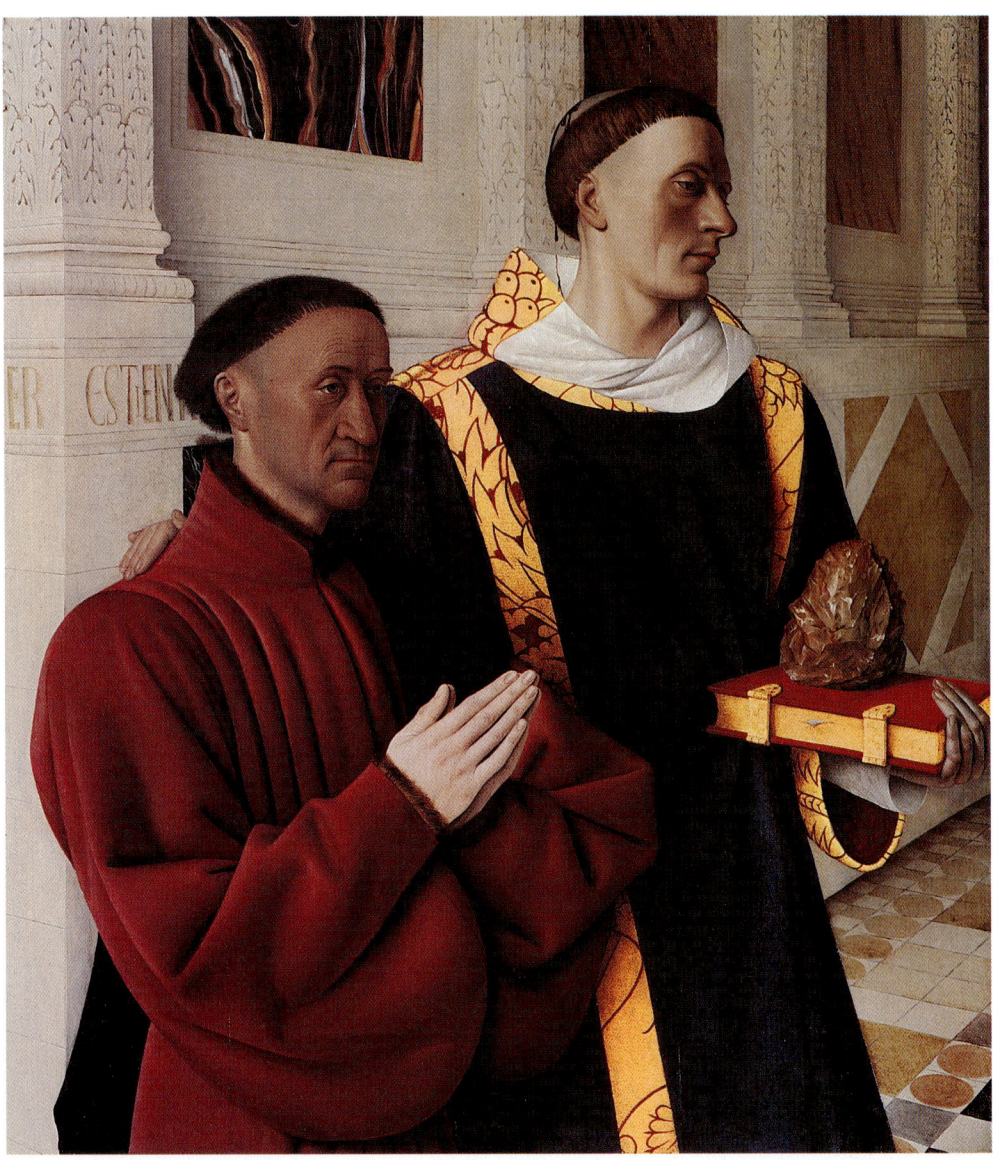

20-19 The *Avignon Pietà,* attributed to ENGUERRAND QUARTON (CHARONTON), ca. 1455. Oil on wood, approx. 5′ 4″ × 7′ 2″. Louvre, Paris.

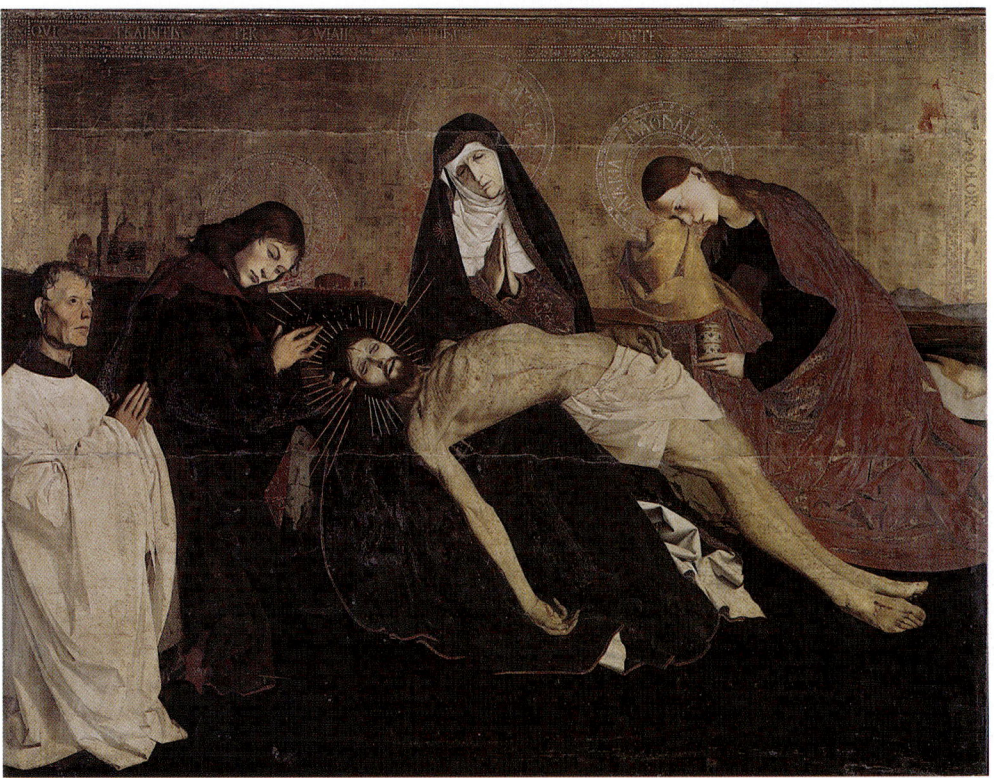

FIFTEENTH-CENTURY GERMAN ART

While the exclusive authority of the "new monarchies" in France, England, and Spain fostered cohesive and widespread developments in the arts of those countries, the lack of a strong centralized power in the Holy Roman Empire (whose core was Germany) led to provincial artistic styles that the strict guild structure perpetuated. Because the Holy Roman Empire did not participate in the long, drawn-out saga of the Hundred Years' War, its economy was stable and prosperous. Thus, in the absence of a dominant court culture to commission artworks and due to the flourishing of the middle class, wealthy merchants and clergy became the primary German patrons during the fifteenth century.

The geographic proximity of the Holy Roman Empire to Flanders (particularly the Duchy of Burgundy) nurtured artistic dialogue between artists of the two countries. A comparison of two German paintings of the Madonna, one earlier in the century (ca. 1430) and the other later (1473), will demonstrate the degree to which Flemish painting influenced German artists.

German Piety

A ROSE AMONG THORNS Most of the early years of STEPHAN LOCHNER (ca. 1400–1451) remain a mystery. Scholars have documented his artistic activity in Cologne in 1440, and by 1447 he had accrued sufficient respect to be named city councilor, representing the painters' guild.

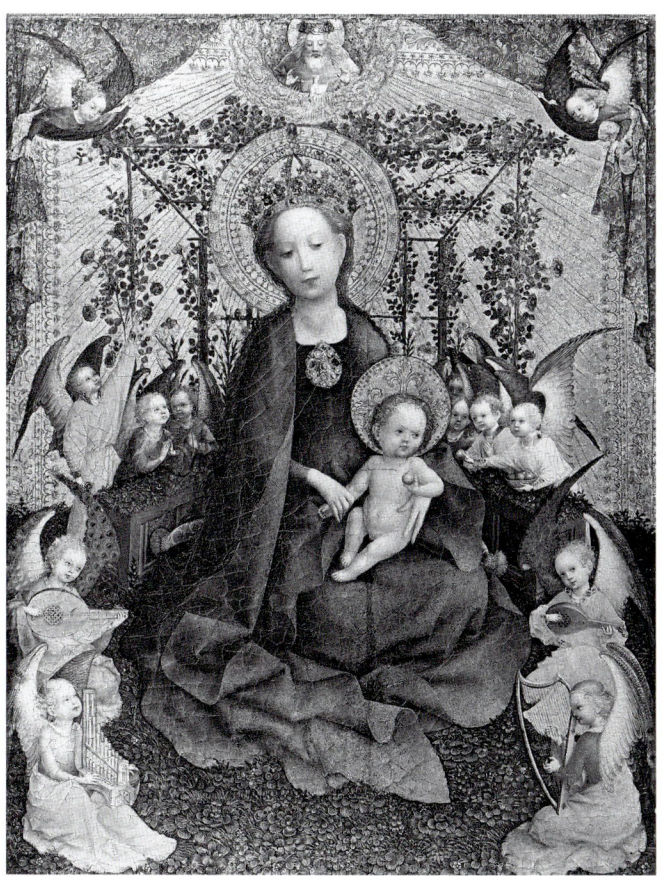

20-20 STEPHAN LOCHNER, *Madonna in the Rose Garden*, ca. 1430–1435. Tempera on wood, approx. 1′ 8″ × 1′ 4″. Wallraf-Richartz Museum, Cologne.

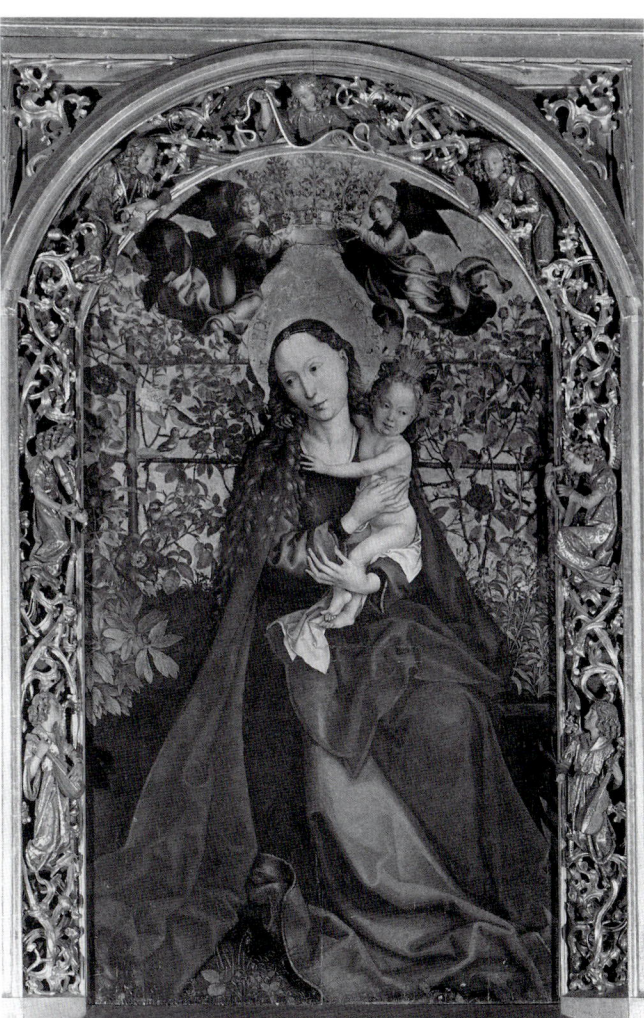

20-21 MARTIN SCHONGAUER, *Madonna and Child in a Rose Arbor*, church of Saint Martin, Colmar, France, 1473. Oil on wood, 6′ 6$\frac{3}{4}$″ × 3′ 9$\frac{1}{4}$″.

Lochner's painting from the 1430s, *Madonna in the Rose Garden* (FIG. **20-20**), presents an extremely popular theme in the Rhineland. The artist depicted the Virgin Mary and Christ Child in a rose arbor, a traditional reference to Mary's holiness ("a rose among thorns") and a symbol of her purity. Lochner presented this subject using stylized conventions. He established a symmetrical and very structured composition, and the exquisite gold background again recalls Byzantine and medieval artworks. His use of established conventions can be attributed, in part, to the new patronage. Wealthy laypeople who desired such images for private devotional purposes or as status symbols relied on a familiar, recognizable iconography and presentation.

A FLEMISH-INFLUENCED PAINTING By the latter part of the century, Flemish artistic ideas had spread throughout Europe, including the Holy Roman Empire. *Madonna and Child in a Rose Arbor* (FIG. **20-21**) by MARTIN SCHONGAUER (ca. 1430–1491) reflects this influence. Although he moved frequently during his career, Schongauer spent a substantial amount of time in Colmar (originally part of western Germany), where he produced this painting for the church of Saint Martin in 1473. The artist represented the same theme as did Lochner, but his figures have a greater physical substance. The work of Dirk Bouts and Rogier van der Weyden surely inspired this treatment of the figures.

20-22 KONRAD WITZ, *Miraculous Draught of Fish,* from the *Altarpiece of Saint Peter,* from Chapel of Notre-Dame des Maccabées in the Cathedral of Saint Peter, Geneva, Switzerland, 1444. Oil on wood, approx. 4′ 3″ × 5′ 1″. Musée d'art et d'histoire, Geneva.

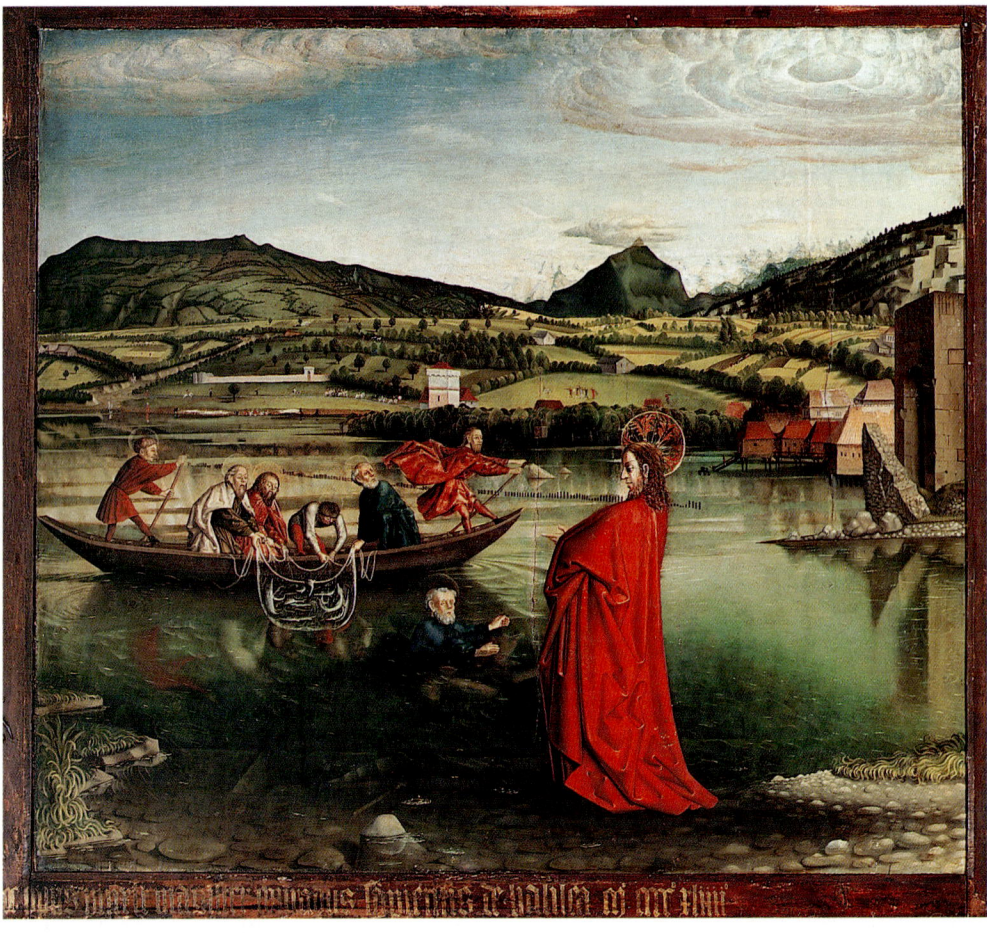

FISHING IN LAKE GENEVA As in Flanders, large-scale altarpieces were familiar sights in the Holy Roman Empire. Among the most notable of these is the *Altarpiece of Saint Peter* painted in 1444 for the chapel of Notre-Dame des Maccabées in the Cathedral of Saint Peter in Geneva. On one exterior wing of this triptych appears *Miraculous Draught of Fish* (FIG. **20-22**) by the Swiss painter KONRAD WITZ (ca. 1400–1446). The other exterior wing (not illustrated) depicts the release of Saint Peter from prison. The central panel has been lost, leaving viewers without a major component of this altarpiece. On the interior wings, Witz painted scenes of the Adoration of the Magi and of Saint Peter's presentation of the donor (Bishop François de Mies) to the Virgin and Child. *Miraculous Draught of Fish* is particularly significant because of the landscape's prominence. Witz showed precocious skill in the study of water effects—the sky glaze on the slowly moving lake surface, the mirrored reflections of the figures in the boat, and the transparency of the shallow water in the foreground. He observed and depicted the landscape so carefully that art historians have determined the exact location shown. Witz presented a view of the shores of Lake Geneva, with the town of Geneva on the right and Le Môle Mountain in the distance behind Christ's head. This painting is one of the first fifteenth-century works depicting a specific site.

WITNESSING THE VIRGIN'S ASSUMPTION The works of German artists who specialized in carving large wooden retables (altarpieces) reveal most forcefully the power of the Late Gothic style. The sculptor VEIT STOSS (1447–

1533) carved a great altarpiece (FIG. **20-23**) for the church of Saint Mary in Kraków, Poland. In the central boxlike shrine, huge figures (some are nine feet high) represent the Virgin's death and Assumption, and on the wings Stoss portrayed scenes from the lives of Christ and Mary. The altar expresses the intense piety of Gothic culture in its late phase, when artists used every figural and ornamental design resource from the vocabulary of Gothic art to heighten the emotion and to glorify the sacred event's appearance. In *The Death and Assumption of the Virgin*, the disciples of Christ congregate around the Virgin, who sinks down in death. One of them supports her, while another, just above her, wrings his hands in grief. Stoss posed others in attitudes of woe and psychic shock, striving for minute realism in every detail. Moreover, he engulfed the figures in restless, twisting, and curving swaths of drapery whose broken and writhing lines unite the whole tableau in a vision of agitated emotion. The artist's massing of sharp, broken, and pierced forms that dart flame-like through the composition—at once unifying and animating it—recalls the design principles of Late Gothic architecture (see FIG. 18-28). Indeed, in the Kraków altarpiece, Stoss merged sculpture and architecture, enhancing their union with paint and gilding.

AN ORNATE SPIRITUAL VISION TILMAN RIEMEN-SCHNEIDER (ca. 1460–1531) depicted the Virgin's Assumption in the center panel of the *Creglingen Altarpiece* (FIG. **20-24**), created for a parish church in Creglingen. He also incorporated intricate Gothic forms, especially in the altarpiece's elaborate canopy. By employing an endless and rest-

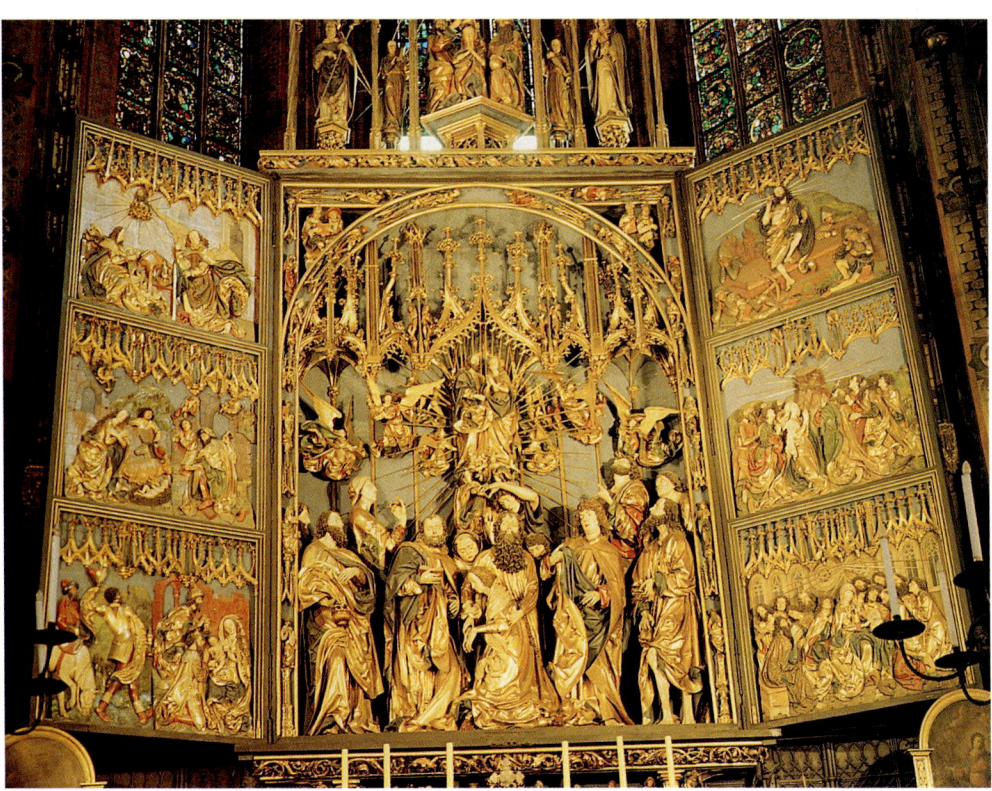

20-23 VEIT STOSS, *The Death and Assumption of the Virgin* (wings open), altar of the Virgin Mary, church of Saint Mary, Kraków, Poland, 1477–1489. Painted and gilded wood, 43′ × 35′.

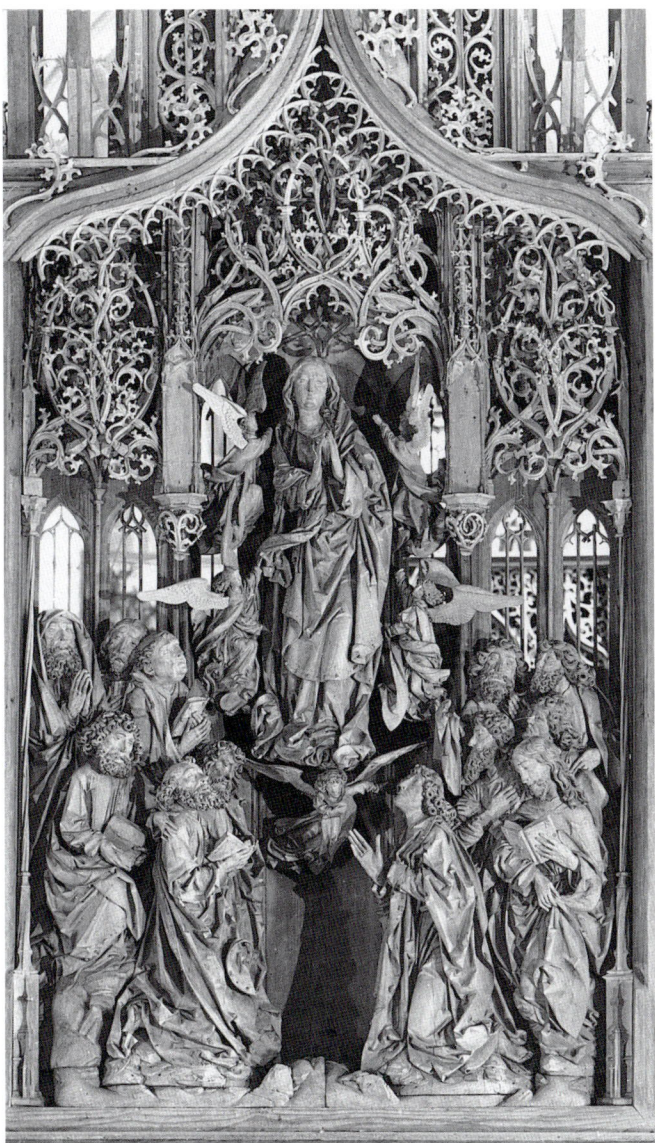

20-24 TILMAN RIEMENSCHNEIDER, *The Assumption of the Virgin*, center panel of the *Creglingen Altarpiece*, parish church, Creglingen, Germany, ca. 1495–1499. Carved lindenwood, 6′ 1″ wide.

less line that runs through the draperies of the figures in *The Assumption of the Virgin*, Riemenschneider succeeded in setting the whole design into fluid motion, and no individual element functions without the rest. The draperies float and flow around bodies lost within them, serving not as descriptions but as design elements that tie the figures to one another and to the framework. A look of psychic strain, a facial expression common to Riemenschneider's figures and consonant with the emerging age of disruption, heightens the spirituality of the figures, immaterial and weightless as they appear.

Graphic Art

GOING AGAINST THE GRAIN A new age blossomed in the fifteenth century with a sudden technological advance that shaped human experience—the German invention of the *letterpress,* printing with movable type. Printing had been known in China centuries before but had never developed, as it did in fifteenth-century Europe, into a revolution in written communication and in information generation and management. Printing provided new and challenging media for artists, and the earliest form was the *woodblock* or *woodcut print* (see "Graphic Changes: The Development of Printmaking," page 586). Using a gouging instrument, artists remove sections of wood blocks, sawing along the grain. They ink the ridges that carry the designs, and the hollows remain dry of ink and do not print. Artists produced woodblock prints well before the development of movable-type printing. But when the popularity of books (and accompanying illustrations) necessitated production on a grand

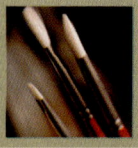

MATERIALS AND TECHNIQUES

Graphic Changes
The Development of Printmaking

The popularity of prints over the centuries attests to the medium's enduring appeal. Generally speaking, a print is an artwork on paper, usually produced in multiple impressions. The set of prints an artist creates from a single print surface is often referred to as an *edition*. The printmaking process involves the transfer of ink from a printing surface to paper, which can be accomplished in several ways. During the fifteenth and sixteenth centuries, artists most commonly used the *relief* and *intaglio* methods of printmaking.

Artists produce relief prints by carving into a surface, usually wood. The oldest and simplest of the printing methods, relief printing requires artists to conceptualize their images negatively; that is, they remove the surface areas around the images. Thus, when the printmaker inks the surface, the carved-out areas remain clean, and a positive image results when the artist presses the printing block against paper. Because artists produce *woodcuts* through a subtractive process (*removing* parts of the material), it is difficult to create very thin, fluid, and closely spaced lines. As a result, woodcut prints tend to exhibit stark contrasts and sharp edges (see FIGS. Intro-9, 23-3, and 23-4).

In contrast to the production of relief prints, the intaglio method involves a positive process; the artist incises or scratches an image on a metal plate, often copper. The image can be created on the plate manually (*engraving* or *drypoint*) using a tool (*burin* or *stylus;* see FIGS. 20-26, 21-26, 23-6, 23-7, and 23-9) or chemically (*etching*). In the latter process, an acid bath eats into the exposed parts of the plate where the artist has drawn through an acid-resistant coating. When the artist inks the surface of the intaglio plate and wipes it clean, the ink is forced into the incisions. Then the artist runs the plate and paper through a roller press, and the paper absorbs the remaining ink, creating the print. Because the artist "draws" the image onto the plate, intaglio prints possess a character different from that of relief prints. Engravings, drypoints, and etchings generally present a wider variety of linear effects. They also often reveal to a greater extent evidence of the artist's touch, the result of the hand's changing pressure and shifting directions.

The paper and inks artists use also affect the finished look of the printed image. During the fifteenth and sixteenth centuries, European printmakers had papers produced from cotton and linen rags that papermakers mashed with water into a pulp. The papermakers then applied a thin layer of this pulp to a wire screen and allowed it to dry to create the paper. As contact with the Far East increased, printmakers made greater use of what was called Japan paper (of mulberry fibers) and China paper. Artists, then as now, could select from a wide variety of inks. The type and proportion of the ink ingredients affect the consistency, color, and oiliness of inks, which various papers absorb differently.

The portability of prints—paper is lightweight, and, until recently, the size of presses precluded large prints—has appealed to artists over the years. Further, the opportunity to produce many impressions from the same print surface is an attractive option. Relatively speaking, prints can be sold at cheaper prices than paintings or sculptures, significantly expanding the buying audience. Recently, scholars have attempted to ascertain the production processes, market value, and audience for prints during the fifteenth and sixteenth centuries. The limited amount of extant documentation, however, has hindered these efforts. Regardless, the number and quality of existing prints, both from northern Europe and Italy, attest to the print medium's importance during the Renaissance.

---

scale, artists met the challenge of bringing the woodcut picture onto the same page as the letterpress.

The illustrations (more than six hundred fifty of them!) for the so-called *Nuremberg Chronicle,* a history of the world produced in the shop of the Nuremberg artist MICHEL WOLGEMUT (1434–1519) document this achievement. The page illustrated (FIG. 20-25) represents Tarvisium, a town in the extreme northeast of Italy (modern Tarvisio), as it was in the "fourth age of the world" (the Latin inscription at top). The blunt, simple lines of the woodcut technique give a detailed perspective of Tarvisium, its harbor and shipping, its walls and towers, its churches and municipal buildings, and the baronial castle on the hill. Despite the numerous architectural structures, historians cannot determine whether this illustration represents the artist's accurate depiction of the city or his fanciful imagination. Artists often reprinted the same image as illustrations of different cities; hence, this depiction of Tarvisium was likely fairly general. Regardless, the work is a monument to a new craft, which expanded in concert with the art of the printed book.

DRAWING ON METAL   The woodcut medium hardly had matured when the technique of *engraving* (inscribing on a hard surface) metal, begun in the 1430s and well developed by 1450, proved much more flexible (see "Graphic Changes: The Development of Printmaking," above). Predictably, in the second half of the century, engraving began to replace the woodcut process, both for making book illustrations and for widely popular single prints. Metal engraving produces an *intaglio* (incised) surface for printing, the incised lines (hollows) of the design, rather than the ridges, taking the ink. It is the reverse of the woodcut technique, which produces *rilievo* (relief).

Martin Schongauer was the most skilled and subtle northern master of metal engraving. His *Saint Anthony Tormented by Demons* (FIG. 20-26) shows both the medium's versatility and the artist's mastery of it. The stoic saint is caught in a revolving thornbush of spiky demons, who claw and tear at him furiously. With unsurpassed skill and subtlety, Schongauer created marvelous distinctions of tonal values and textures—from smooth skin to rough cloth, from the furry and feathery to the hairy and scaly. The method of describing forms with

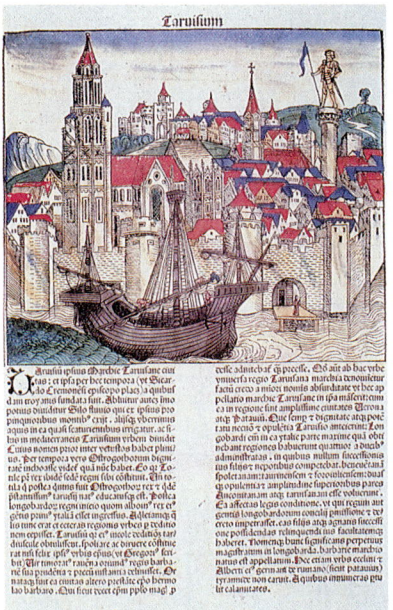

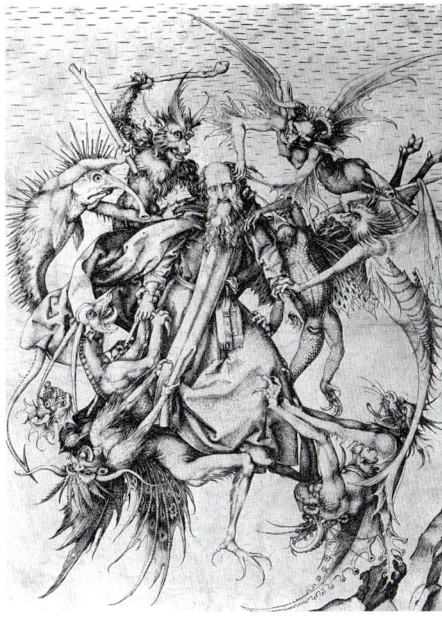

20-25 (Left) MICHEL WOLGEMUT AND SHOP, "Tarvisium," page from the so-called *Nuremberg Chronicle,* 1493. Printed by Anton Koberger.

20-26 (Right) MARTIN SCHONGAUER, *Saint Anthony Tormented by Demons,* ca. 1480–1490. Engraving, approx. 1′ 1″ × 11″. Metropolitan Museum of Art, New York (Rogers Fund, 1920).

hatching that follows them, probably developed by Schongauer, became standard among German graphic artists. The Italians preferred parallel hatching (compare Antonio Pollaiuolo's engraving, FIG. 21-26) and rarely adopted the other method, which, in keeping with the general northern approach to art, tends to describe the surfaces of things rather than their underlying structures.

FIFTEENTH-CENTURY SPANISH ART

Spain's ascent to power in Europe began in the mid-fifteenth century with the marriage of Isabella of Castile (1451–1504) and Ferdinand of Aragon (1452–1516) in 1469. A dynastic union of two rulers, Ferdinand and Isabella worked to strengthen royal control of the Spanish government. Eventually, their descendants became the most powerful monarchs in Europe.

A RETABLE OF MEDIEVAL SPIRITUALITY The ultimate masterpiece of Late Gothic art in Spain is a large, resplendent retable (detail, FIG. **20-27**), the work of the sculptor GIL DE SILOÉ (active 1485–1501). The sculptor's origins remain a mystery, but the inscriptions of his name in documents suggest he might have come from Antwerp or from Orléans in France. His style incorporates mingled Flemish and north German influence, but the uniqueness of his vision is evident. Erected over the high altar of the Cartuja (Carthusian monastery) of Miraflores, near Burgos, the retable incorporates iconography that celebrates the mystery of the Eucharist, the Lord's Supper. Its circular compartments symbolize the holy wafer of the Communion. A great halo of angels encircles the crucified Christ, the retable's centerpiece. God the Father and the personified Holy Spirit support the arms of the cross. Mary and John stand at its foot. Above it perches the pelican, symbol of self-sacrifice. In Gil de Siloé's depiction of the body of the crucified Christ, rising out of the profusion of ministering angels, he rendered a realistic image of supreme anguish. The head expresses the pain, sorrow, and resignation of the Redeemer, who by his atonement for the sins of humanity, conquers Death. This work, created at the end of the fifteenth century, consummately embodies medieval spirituality.

The northern and Spanish art in the fifteenth century was the product of political, religious, social, and economic changes. The scope and focus of the art the Burgundian dukes and the Flemish merchant/bankers commissioned reveals their strength and wealth. This situation did not last long. Charles the Bold, who had assumed the title of duke of Burgundy in 1467, died in 1477, bringing to an end the dominance of the Burgundian Netherlands. France and the Holy Roman Empire divided the Burgundian territories. Eventually, through a series of fortuitous marriages, untimely deaths, and political shifts, Charles I, the grandson of Ferdinand and Isabella of Spain, united the three major dynastic lines— Hapsburg, Burgundian, and Spanish. This made him the most powerful ruler of the sixteenth century.

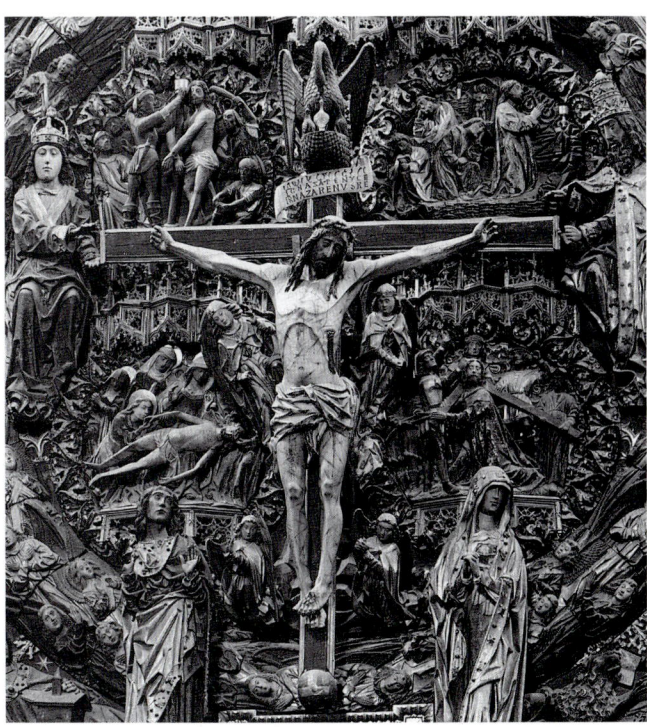

20-27 GIL DE SILOÉ, *Christ Crucified,* center detail of painted and gilded wooden altarpiece, Carthusian monastery, Miraflores, Spain, 1496–1499.

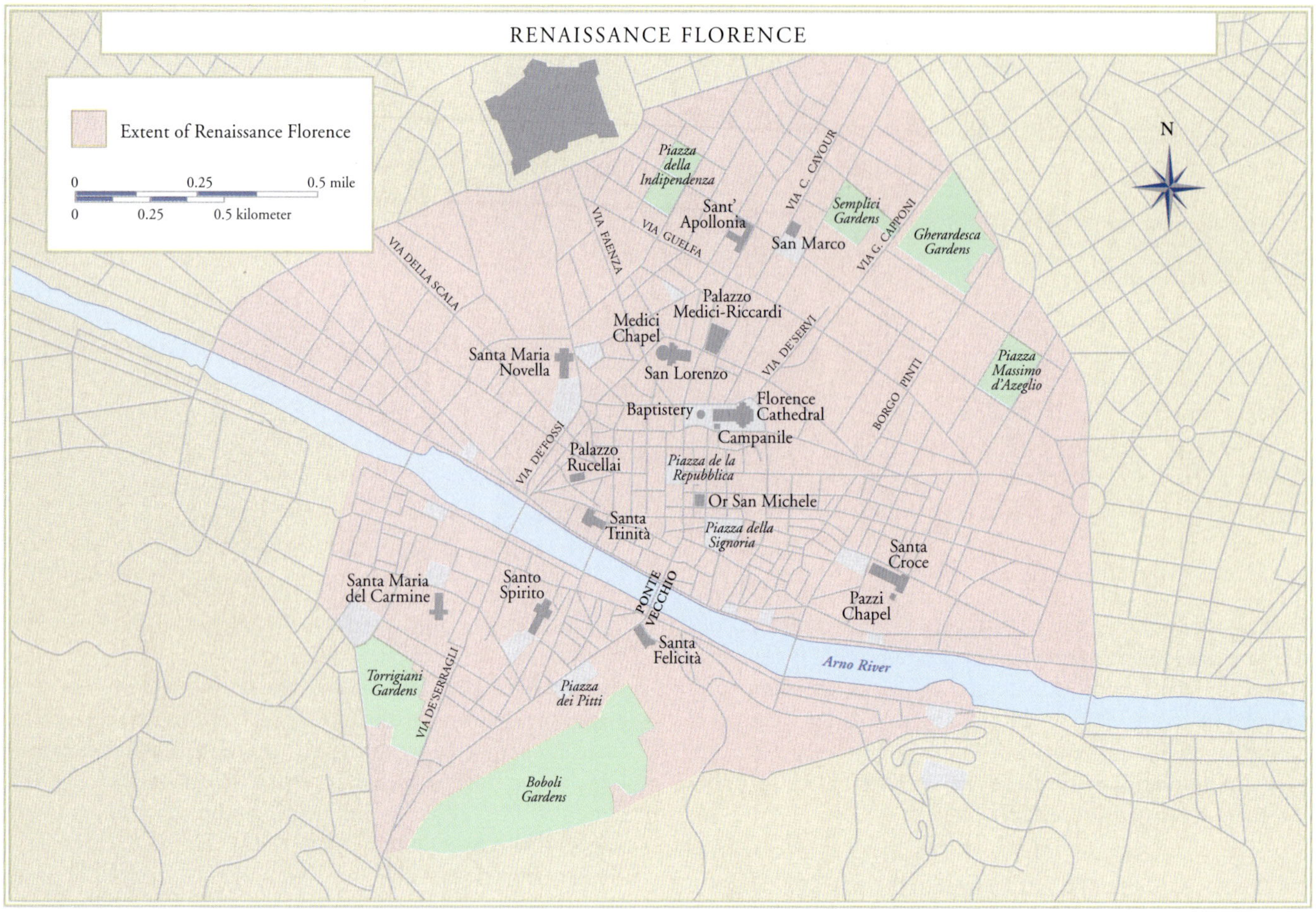

RENAISSANCE FLORENCE

Extent of Renaissance Florence

0   0.25   0.5 mile
0   0.25   0.5 kilometer

N

Piazza della Indipendenza

VIA FAENZA

VIA GUELFA

VIA C. CAVOUR

Sant' Apollonia

Semplici Gardens

VIA G. CAPPONI

San Marco

Gherardesca Gardens

VIA DELLA SCALA

Palazzo Medici-Riccardi

Medici Chapel

VIA DE'SERVI

Santa Maria Novella

San Lorenzo

BORGO PINTI

Piazza Massimo d'Azeglio

Baptistery

Florence Cathedral

VIA DE'FOSSI

Campanile

Palazzo Rucellai

Piazza de la Repubblica

Or San Michele

Santa Trinità

Piazza della Signoria

Santa Croce

Santa Maria del Carmine

Santo Spirito

PONTE VECCHIO

Pazzi Chapel

Santa Felicità

Arno River

Torrigiani Gardens

VIA DE' SERRAGLI

Piazza dei Pitti

Boboli Gardens

1420	1425	1430

EARLY RENAISSANCE

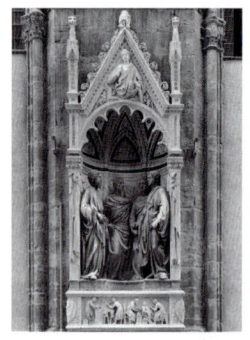

Nanni di Banco, Quattro Santi Coronati, Florence, ca. 1408

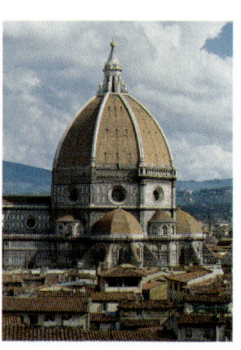

Filippo Brunelleschi Florence Cathedral Dome ca. 1420–1436

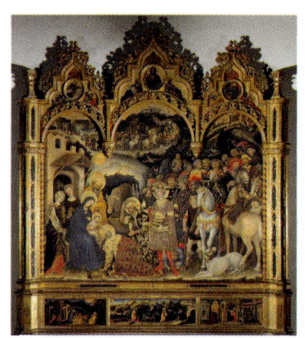

Gentile da Fabriano Adoraton of the Magi Santa Trinità, Florence, 1423

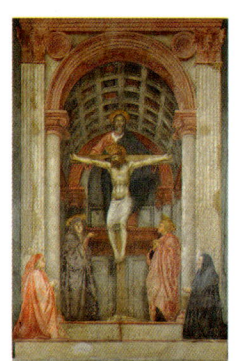

Masaccio, Holy Trinity Santa Maria Novella Florence, ca. 1428

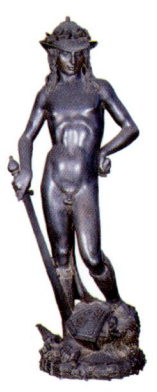

Donatello, David ca. 1428–1432

Giangaleazzo Visconti dies; Milanese armies withdraw from Tuscany, 1402

Battle of San Romano, 1432

King Ladislaus of Naples dies, 1414

End of Great Schism in Catholic Church, 1417

21

HUMANISM AND THE ALLURE OF ANTIQUITY

FIFTEENTH-CENTURY ITALIAN ART

| 1440 | 1470 | 1475 | 1480 | 1500 |

EARLY RENAISSANCE

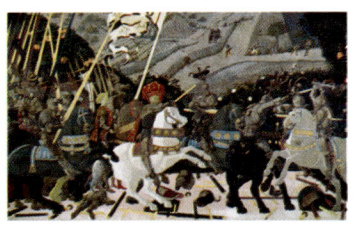

Uccello, Battle of San Romano
Florence, ca. 1455

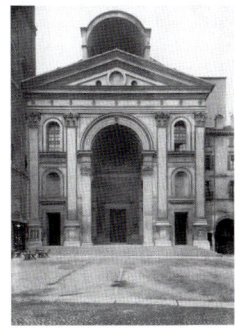

Leon Battista Alberti
Sant'Andrea, Mantua, ca. 1470

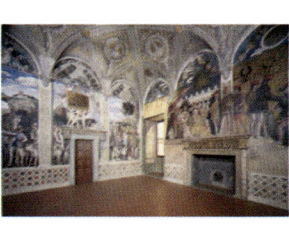

Andrea Mantegna
Camera degli Sposi
Palazzo Ducale, Mantua, 1474

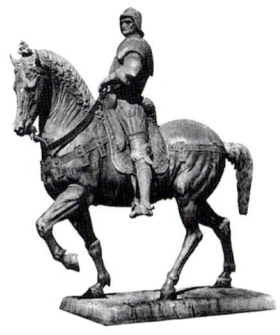

Andrea del Verrocchio
Bartolommeo Colleoni
ca. 1483–1488

Marsilio Ficino, Neo-Platonic philosopher, 1433–1499

Invention of movable metal type by Johann Gutenberg, ca. 1445

Lorenzo de' Medici, 1449–1492

Conquest of Constantinople by Turks, 1453

Medici expelled from Florence, 1494

Girolamo Savonarola assumes
power, 1496; is burned at stake, 1498

France captures Milan, 1499

THE "REBIRTH" OF ITALIAN CULTURE

The fifteenth century in Italy witnessed the flourishing of a significantly new and expanded artistic culture. For this reason, art historians and others often refer to this century as the Early Renaissance (from the French *renaissance* and the Italian *rinascità*, both meaning "rebirth"). Despite the public's enduring fascination with Italian Renaissance art of the fifteenth and sixteenth centuries, this "rebirth" had its roots in the fourteenth century. Thus, many of the developments discussed in Chapter 19 matured into what is generally referred to as the Renaissance. The designation "proto-Renaissance" for describing the fourteenth century indicates its importance in laying down the foundation for subsequent centuries.

Several factors contributed to the rise of Renaissance culture, among them the spread of humanism, political and economic fluctuations throughout Italy, and a fortunate abundance of artistic talent.

THE SPREAD OF HUMANISM The humanism Petrarch and Boccaccio popularized during the fourteenth century had greater impact as the fifteenth century progressed. Increasingly, Italians embraced the tenets underlying humanism—emphasis on education and on expanding knowledge (especially of classical antiquity), the exploration of individual potential and a desire to excel, and a commitment to civic responsibility and moral duty.

For humanists, the quest for knowledge began with the legacy of the Greeks and Romans—the writings of Plato, Socrates, Aristotle, Ovid, and others. The development of a vernacular (everyday) literature based on the Tuscan dialect expanded the audience for humanist writings. Further, the invention of movable metal type by the German Johann Gutenberg around 1445 facilitated the printing and far-reaching distribution of books. Italians enthusiastically embraced this new printing process; by 1464 Subiaco (near Rome) boasted a press, and by 1469 Venice had established one as well. Among the first books printed in Italy using this new press was Dante's vernacular classic, *The Divine Comedy*. The production of Dante's *Divine Comedy* editions in Foligno (1472), Mantua (1472), Venice (1472), Naples (1477 and 1478–1479), and Milan (1478) testifies to the widespread popularity during the fifteenth century of Dante's tale of Heaven, Purgatory, and Hell. The humanists did not restrict their learning to antique writings, however. They avidly acquired information in a wide range of fields, including science (such as botany, geology, geography, and optics), medicine, and engineering. Leonardo da Vinci's phenomenal expertise in many fields—from art and architecture to geology, aerodynamics, hydraulics, botany, and military science, among many others—explains his uncontested designation as a "Renaissance" man.

ENCOURAGING INDIVIDUAL ACHIEVEMENT Humanism also fostered a belief in individual potential and encouraged individual achievement. Whereas people in medieval society had relinquished any attempt to change the course of their lives, attributing events to divine will, those in Renaissance Italy adopted a more secular stance. Humanists not only encouraged individual improvement but also rewarded excellence with fame and honor. Achieving and excelling through hard work became moral imperatives.

GOOD CITIZENS Despite the emphasis on individualism, humanism also had a civic dimension. Citizen participation in the social, political, and economic life of their communities was obligatory. The intersection of art with humanist doctrines during the Renaissance can be seen in the popularity of subjects selected from classical history or mythology, in the increased concern with developing perspectival systems and depicting anatomy accurately, in the revival of portraiture and other self-aggrandizing forms of patronage, and in citizens' extensive participation in civic and religious art commissions.

OF WEALTH AND POWER Constant fluctuations in Italy's political and economic spheres contributed to these developments in Renaissance art as well. The shifting power relations among the numerous city-states fostered the rise of princely courts and control of cities by despots. *Condottieri* (military leaders) with large numbers of mercenary troops at their disposal played a major role in the ongoing struggle for power. Princely courts, such as those in Urbino and Mantua, emerged as cultural and artistic centers (see "Dukes, Despots, Fame, and Fortune: The Princely Courts," page 591). Certainly, high-level patronage required significant accumulated wealth, so, during the fifteenth century, individuals and families who had managed to prosper economically came to the fore. Among the best known was the Medici family, which acquired its vast fortune from banking. Not only did this money allow the Medici to wield great power, but it also permitted them to commission art and architecture on a scale rarely seen, then or since. Such lavish patrons of art and learning were the Medici that, to this day, the term "Medici" is widely used to refer to a generous patron of the fine arts.

The Medici, along with many other art patrons, princes, popes, and despots, expressed more than a passing interest in humanism. The association of humanism with education and culture appealed to accomplished individuals of high status.

The historical context that gave rise to this "rebirth" and the importance of patronage account for the character of Renaissance art. In addition, the sheer serendipity of the abundance of exceedingly talented artists also must be considered. Renaissance Italy experienced major shifts in artistic models. In part, these shifts were due to a unique artistic environment where skilled artists, through industriousness and dialogue with others, forever changed the direction and perception of art.

FLORENCE

Sculpture and Civic Pride in the Early Renaissance

The history of the Early Renaissance in art begins with a competition in 1401 for a design for the east doors of the Florence baptistery (see FIG. 17-16). Artists and public alike considered this commission particularly prestigious because of the intended placement of the doors on the baptistery's east side, facing the cathedral entrance. Even at this early date, many of the traits that characterized Renaissance art were evident.

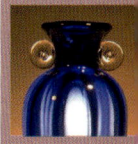

Dukes, Despots, Fame, and Fortune
The Princely Courts

The absence of a single authoritative ruler in Italy and the fragmented nature of the independent city-states provided a fertile breeding ground for the ambitions of the power hungry. Fifteenth-century Italian society witnessed the expansion of princely courts throughout the peninsula. A prince was, in essence, the lord of a territory, and, despite this generic title, he could have been a duke, marquis, cardinal, pope, tyrant, or papal vicar. In the fifteenth century, major princely courts emerged in Milan, Naples, Ferrara, Savoy, Mantua, and papal Rome. Rather than denoting a specific organizational structure or physical entity, the term "princely court" referred to a power relationship between the prince and the territory's inhabitants based on imperial models. Each prince worked tirelessly not just to preserve but also to extend his control and authority, seeking to establish a societal framework of people who looked to him for jobs, favors, protection, prestige, and leadership. The importance of these princely courts derived from their role as centers of power and culture.

The efficient functioning of a princely court required a sophisticated administrative structure. Each prince employed an extensive household staff, ranging from counts, nobles, cooks, waiters, stewards, footmen, stable hands, and ladies-in-waiting to dog handlers, leopard keepers, pages, and runners (who did menial fetching chores). The duke of Milan had more than forty chamberlains to attend to his personal needs alone. Each prince also needed an elaborate bureaucracy to oversee political, economic, and military operations and ensure his continued control. These officials included secretaries, lawyers, captains, ambassadors, and condottieri. Burgeoning international diplomacy and trade made each prince the center of an active and privileged sphere. Their domain extended to the realm of culture, for they saw themselves as more than political, military, and economic leaders. The princes felt responsible for the vitality of cultural life in their territories, and art was a major component for developing a cultured populace. Visual imagery also appealed to them as effective propaganda for reinforcing their control. As undoubtedly the wealthiest individuals in their regions, princes possessed the means to commission numerous artworks and buildings. Thus, art functioned in several capacities—as evidence of princely sophistication and culture, as a form of prestige or commemoration, as public education and propaganda, as a demonstration of wealth, and as a source of visual pleasure.

Princes often researched in advance the reputations and styles of the artists and architects they commissioned. Such assurances of excellence were necessary, because the quality of the work reflected not just on the artist but on the patron as well. Yet despite the importance of individual style, princes sought artists who also were willing, at times, to subordinate their personal styles to work collaboratively on large-scale projects.

Princes bestowed on selected individuals the title of "court artist." Serving as a court artist had its benefits, among them a guaranteed salary (not always forthcoming), living quarters in the palace, and, on occasion, status as a member of the prince's inner circle, perhaps even a knighthood. For artists struggling to elevate their profession from the ranks of craftspeople, working for a prince presented a marvelous opportunity—until the sixteenth century, they were in the same class as small shopkeepers and petty merchants. Indeed, at court dinners, artists most often were seated with other members of the salaried household: tailors, cobblers, barbers, and upholsterers. Thus, the possibility of advancement was a powerful and constant incentive.

Princes demanded a great deal from court artists. Not only did artists create the frescoes, portraits, and sculptures that have become their legacies, but they also designed tapestries, seat covers, costumes, masks, and decorations for various court festivities. Because princes constantly entertained, received ambassadors and dignitaries, and had to maintain a high profile to reinforce their authority, lavish social functions were the norm. Artists often created gifts for visiting nobles and potentates. Recipients judged such gifts on both the quality of the work and the quality of the materials. By using expensive materials—gold leaf, silver leaf, lapis lazuli, silk, and velvet brocade—princes could impress others with their wealth and good taste.

The experiences of court artists varied widely; some princes treated them as mere servants, others as trusted colleagues. At one end of the spectrum was Perino del Vaga, whose life at the papal court biographer Giorgio Vasari described: "[he had] to draw day and night and to meet the demands of the Palace, and, among other things, to make the designs of embroideries, of engravings for banner-makers, and of innumerable ornaments required by the caprice of Farnese and other Cardinals and noblemen. In short, . . . being always surrounded by sculptors, masters in stucco, wood-carvers, seamsters, embroiderers, painters, gilders, and other suchlike craftsmen, he had never an hour of repose."[1] In contrast was Leonardo da Vinci's treatment at the hands of his last patron, King Francis I of France, in whose arms the great artist is said to have died.

For princes who harbored dreams of expanding their control and who wanted to craft suitable legacies, art was indispensable. Hence, the history of Renaissance art cannot be fully understood without serious consideration of courtly culture.

---

[1] Giorgio Vasari, *Lives of the Painters, Sculptors and Architects,* trans. Gaston du C. de Vere (New York: Alfred A. Knopf, 1996), 2: 184.

These include the development of a new pictorial illusionism, patronage as both a civic imperative and personal promotion, and the esteem increasingly accorded artists.

Andrea Pisano (ca. 1270–1348), unrelated to the thirteenth-century Italian sculptors Nicola (see FIGS. 19-2 and 19-3) and Giovanni (see FIG. 19-4), had designed the south doors of the same structure between 1330 and 1335. In 1401, the Arte di Calimala (wool merchants' guild) sponsored the competition for the second set of doors, requiring each entrant to submit a relief panel depicting the sacrifice of Isaac. This biblical event centers on God's order to Abraham that he sacrifice his son Isaac as a demonstration of Abraham's devotion to God. Just as Abraham is about to comply, an angel intervenes and stops him from plunging the knife into his son's throat.

The selection of this theme may not have been random. In the late 1390s, the despot Giangaleazzo Visconti of Milan began a military campaign to take over the Italian peninsula. By 1401, when the directors of the cathedral's artworks initiated this competition, Visconti's troops had virtually surrounded Florence, and its independence was in serious jeopardy. Despite dwindling water and food supplies, Florentine officials exhorted the public to defend the city's freedom. For example, the humanist chancellor, Coluccio Salutati, whose Latin style of writing was widely influential, urged his fellow citizens to adopt the republican ideal of civil and political liberty associated with ancient Rome and to identify themselves with its spirit. To be Florentine was to be Roman; freedom was the distinguishing virtue of both. Florentine faith and sacrifice were rewarded in 1402, when Visconti died suddenly, ending the invasion threat. The sacrifice of Isaac, with its theme of sacrificing for a higher cause, paralleled the message city officials had conveyed to inhabitants. It is certainly plausible the Arte di Calimala, asserting both its preeminence among Florentine guilds and its civic duty, selected the subject with this in mind.

Those supervising this project selected as semifinalists seven artists from among the many who entered the widely advertised competition for the commission. Only the panels of the two finalists, LORENZO GHIBERTI (1378–1455) and FILIPPO BRUNELLESCHI (1377–1446), have survived. In 1402, the selection committee awarded the commission to Ghiberti. Both artists used the same French Gothic quatrefoil frames Andrea Pisano had used for the baptistery's south doors and depicted the same moment of the narrative—the angel's halting of the action. Examining these two panels provides some stylistic indications of the direction Early Renaissance art was to take during the fifteenth century.

A FATHER'S EMOTIONAL SACRIFICE Brunelleschi's panel (FIG. **21-1**) shows a sturdy and vigorous interpretation of the theme, with something of the emotional agitation Giovanni Pisano (see FIG. 19-4) favored. Abraham seems suddenly to have summoned the dreadful courage needed to kill his son at God's command—he lunges forward, draperies flying, exposing Isaac's throat to the knife. Matching Abraham's energy, the saving angel darts in from the left, grabbing Abraham's arm to stop the killing. Brunelleschi's figures demonstrate his ability to observe carefully and represent faithfully all of the elements in the biblical narrative.

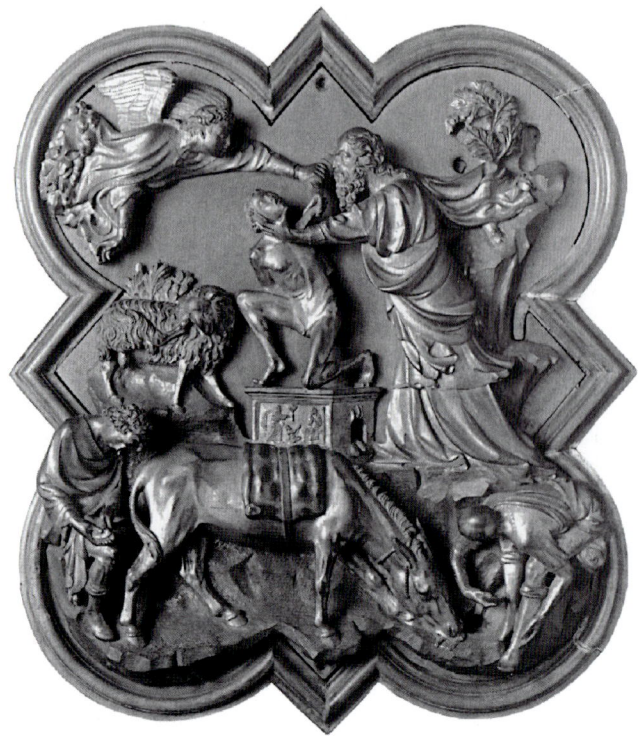

21-1 FILIPPO BRUNELLESCHI, *Sacrifice of Isaac,* competition panel for east doors, baptistery of Florence Cathedral, Florence, Italy, 1401–1402. Gilded bronze relief, 1′ 9″ × 1′ 5″. Museo Nazionale del Bargello, Florence.

A SACRIFICE IN RELIEF Where Brunelleschi imbued his image with dramatic emotion, Ghiberti emphasized grace and smoothness. In Ghiberti's panel (FIG. **21-2**), Abraham appears in the familiar Gothic S-curve pose and seems to contemplate the act he is about to perform, even as he draws his arm back to strike. The figure of Isaac, beautifully posed and rendered, recalls Greco-Roman statuary and could be regarded as the first truly classicizing nude since antiquity. (Compare, for example, the torsion of Isaac's body and the dramatic turn of his head with those of the Hellenistic statue of a Gaul thrusting a sword into his own chest, FIG. 5-80.) Unlike his medieval predecessors, Ghiberti revealed a genuine appreciation of the nude male form and a deep interest in how the muscular system and skeletal structure move the human body. Even the altar on which Isaac kneels displays Ghiberti's emulation of antique models. It is decorated with acanthus scrolls of a type that commonly adorned Roman temple friezes in Italy and throughout the former Roman Empire (see, for example, FIG. 10-30). These classical references reflect humanism's increasing influence.

Ghiberti's training included both painting and goldsmithery. His careful treatment of the gilded bronze surfaces, with their sharply and accurately incised detail, proves his skill as a goldsmith. As a painter, he was interested in spatial illusion. The rocky landscape seems to emerge from the blank panel toward viewers, as does the strongly foreshortened angel. Brunelleschi's image, in contrast, emphasizes the planar orientation of the surface.

That Ghiberti cast his panel in only two pieces (thereby reducing the amount of bronze needed) no doubt impressed the selection committee. Ghiberti's construction method differed from that of Brunelleschi, who built his from several cast

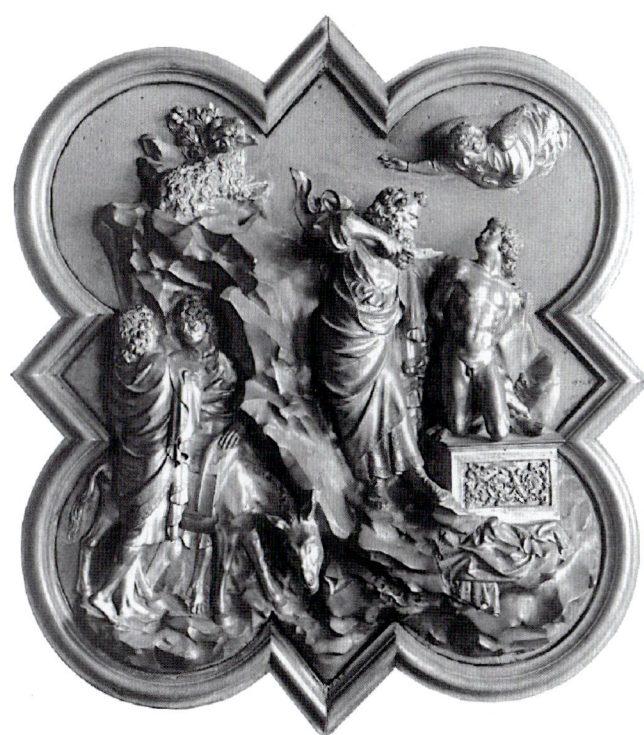

21-2   LORENZO GHIBERTI, *Sacrifice of Isaac,* competition panel for east doors, baptistery, Florence Cathedral, Florence, Italy, 1401–1402. Gilded bronze relief, 1′ 9″ × 1′ 5″. Museo Nazionale del Bargello, Florence.

pieces. Thus not only would Ghiberti's doors, as proposed, be lighter and more impervious to the elements, but they also represented a significant cost savings.

Ghiberti's submission clearly had much to recommend it, both stylistically and technically. Although Ghiberti's image was perhaps less overtly emotional than Brunelleschi's, it was more cohesive and presented a more convincing spatial illusion. Ghiberti further developed these pictorial effects, sometimes thought alien to sculpture, in his later work.

Understandably, the decision to award the commission to Ghiberti crushed Brunelleschi. Antonio Manetti, Brunelleschi's biographer, later claimed that Ghiberti's victory was due to the artist's collusion with the jury. Ghiberti's description of his award reflects the fame and glory increasingly accorded to individual achievement during the Early Renaissance:

> To me was conceded the palm of the victory by all the experts and by all . . . who had competed with me. To me the honor was conceded universally and with no exception. To all it seemed that I had at that time surpassed the others without exception, as was recognized by a great council and an investigation of learned men . . . highly skilled from the painters and sculptors of gold, silver, and marble. There were thirty-four judges. . . . The testimonial of the victory was given in my favor by all. . . . It was granted to me and determined that I should make the bronze door for this church.[1]

Ghiberti completed the twenty-eight door panels depicting scenes from the New Testament in 1424. Church officials eventually decided to move the doors to the baptistery's north side, where they remain today.

A FEAST IN PERSPECTIVE   Like Ghiberti, DONA-TELLO (ca. 1386–1466) was another sculptor who carried forward most dramatically the search for innovative forms ca-

pable of expressing the new ideas of the Early Renaissance. Donatello shared the humanist enthusiasm for Roman virtue and form. His greatness lies in an extraordinary versatility and a depth that led him through a spectrum of themes fundamental to human experience and through stylistic variations that express these themes with unprecedented profundity and force. Donatello understood the different aesthetic conventions artists routinely invoked at the time to distinguish their depictions of the real from the ideal and the earthly from the spiritual. His expansive knowledge and skill allowed him to portray this sweeping range with great facility. Further, as an astute observer of human life, Donatello could, with ease, depict figures of diverse ages, ranks, and human conditions, such as childhood, the idealized human nude, practical men of the world, military despots, holy men, derelict prelates, and ascetic old age. Few artists could match this range. That Donatello advanced both naturalistic illusion and classical idealism in sculpture remains a remarkable achievement.

This illusionism, like that Ghiberti pursued in his *Sacrifice of Isaac* panel, is evident in Donatello's bronze relief, *Feast of Herod* (FIG. **21-3**), on the baptismal font in the Siena baptistery. Salome (to the right) still dances (no doubt because she was closely modeled on a series of dancing-maenad reliefs very popular in Roman times), even though she already has delivered the severed head of John the Baptist, which the kneeling executioner offers to King Herod. The other figures recoil in horror into two groups. At the right, one man covers his face with his hand; at the left, Herod and two terrified children shrink back in dismay. The psychic explosion drives the human elements apart, leaving a gap across which the emotional electricity crackles. This masterful stagecraft obscures another drama Donatello was playing out on the stage itself. The *Feast* marked the advent of rationalized perspective space, long prepared for in the proto-Renaissance of fourteenth-century Italy and recognized by Donatello and his generation as a way

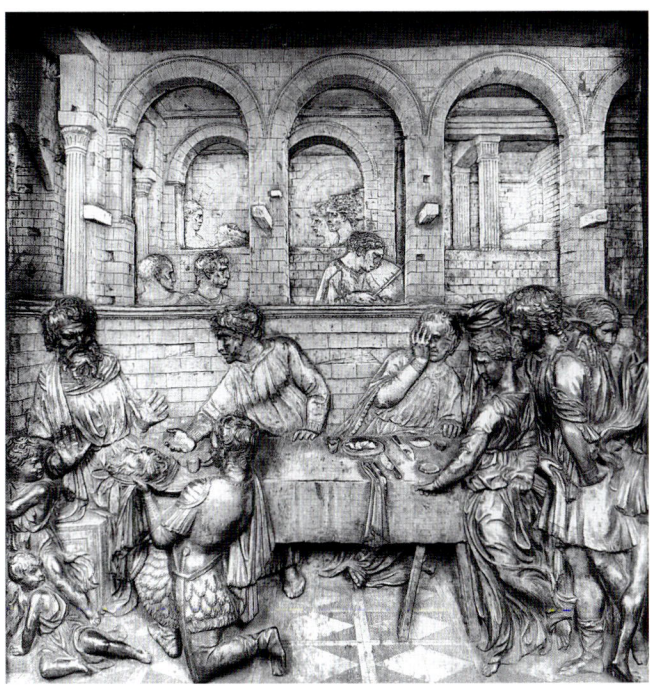

21-3   DONATELLO, *Feast of Herod,* from the baptismal font of Siena Cathedral, Siena, Italy, ca. 1425. Gilded bronze relief, approx. 1′ 11″ × 1′ 11″.

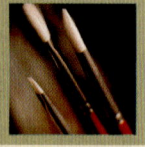

MATERIALS AND TECHNIQUES

Depicting Objects in Space
Perspectival Systems in the Early Renaissance

Scholars long have noted the Renaissance fascination with perspective. In essence, portraying perspective involves constructing a convincing illusion of space in two-dimensional imagery while unifying all objects within a single spatial system. Renaissance artists were not the first to focus on depicting illusionistic space; both the Greeks and the Romans were well versed in perspectival rendering. However, the perspectival systems developed during the Renaissance contrasted sharply with the portrayal of space during the preceding medieval period. Those artists, because of the spiritual orientation of much of their art, largely had abandoned any concern for the illusionistic presentation of objects. Renaissance perspectival systems included both linear perspective and atmospheric perspective.

Developed by Brunelleschi, *linear perspective* allows artists to determine mathematically the relative size of rendered objects to correlate them with the visual recession into space. The artist first must identify a horizontal line that marks, in the image, the horizon in the distance (hence the term *horizon line*). The artist then selects a *vanishing point* on that horizon line (often located at the exact center of the line). By drawing *orthogonals* (diagonal lines) from the edges of the pic-

ture to the vanishing point, the artist creates a structural grid that organizes the image and determines the size of objects within the image's illusionistic space. Under this system of linear perspective, artists often foreshorten a figure as the body recedes back into an illusionistic space, as seen in Andrea Mantegna's *Dead Christ* (see FIG. 21-50). Among the works that provide clear examples of linear perspective are Masaccio's *Holy Trinity* (FIG. 21-13), Leonardo da Vinci's *Last Supper* (see FIG. 22-3), and Raphael's *School of Athens* (see FIG. 22-17).

Rather than rely on a structured mathematical system (as does linear perspective), *atmospheric perspective* involves optical phenomena. Artists using atmospheric (sometimes called *aerial*) perspective exploit the principle that the farther back the object is in space, the blurrier, less detailed, and bluer it appears. Further, color saturation and value contrast diminish as the image recedes into the distance. Leonardo da Vinci used atmospheric perspective to great effect, as seen in works such as *Virgin of the Rocks* (see FIG. 22-1) and *Mona Lisa* (see FIG. 22-4).

These two methods of creating the illusion of space in pictures are not exclusive, and Renaissance artists often used both to heighten the sensation of three-dimensional space.

---

to intensify the action's optical reality and the characterization of the actors. Donatello, using pictorial perspective, opened the space of the action well into the distance, showing two arched courtyards and groups of attendants in the background. This penetration of the panel surface by spatial illusion replaced the flat grounds and backdrop areas of the medieval past. Ancient Roman illusionism (compare FIG. 10-16) had returned.

KEEPING PERSPECTIVE Fourteenth-century Italian artists, such as Duccio and the Lorenzetti brothers, had used several devices to indicate distance, but with the invention of "true" linear perspective (a discovery generally attributed to Brunelleschi), Early Renaissance artists acquired a way to make the illusion of distance mathematical and certain (see "Depicting Objects in Space: Perspectival Systems in the Early Renaissance," above). In effect, they thought of the picture plane as a transparent window through which the observers look to see the constructed pictorial world. This discovery was enormously important, for it made possible what has been called the "rationalization of sight." It brought all of our random and infinitely various visual sensations under a simple rule people could express mathematically.

Indeed, the Renaissance artists' *rediscovery* of perspective (principles already known to the ancient Greeks and Romans) reflects the emergence of science itself, which is, put simply, the mathematical ordering of our observations of the physical world. Renaissance artists were often mathematicians, and one modern mathematician asserts that artists did the most creative work in mathematics in the fifteenth century. The ob-

server's position of looking "through" a picture into the painted "world" is precisely that of scientific observers fixing their gazes on the carefully placed or located datum of their research. Of course, Early Renaissance artists were not primarily scientists; they simply found perspective a wonderful way to order and clarify their compositions.

Nonetheless, art viewers cannot doubt that perspective, with its new mathematical certitude, conferred a kind of aesthetic legitimacy on painting by making the picture *measurable* and exact. According to Plato, measure is the basis of beauty. The art of Greece certainly visualized this dictum. In the Renaissance, when humanists rediscovered Plato and eagerly read his works, artists once again exalted the principle of measure as the foundation of the beautiful in the fine arts. The projection of measurable objects on flat surfaces influenced the character of Renaissance paintings and made possible scale drawings, maps, charts, graphs, and diagrams—means of exact representation that made modern science and technology possible. Mathematical truth and formal beauty conjoined in the minds of Renaissance artists.

ADMIRING THE "GATES OF PARADISE" Many artists recognized the significance of Donatello's presentation of illusionistic space. Ghiberti, who demonstrated his interest in perspective in his *Sacrifice of Isaac*, embraced Donatello's innovations. Ghiberti's enthusiasm for a unified system for representing space is particularly evident in his famous east doors (FIG. 21-4) church officials commissioned in 1425 for the baptistery of Florence Cathedral. Michelangelo later declared these as "so beautiful that they would do well for the

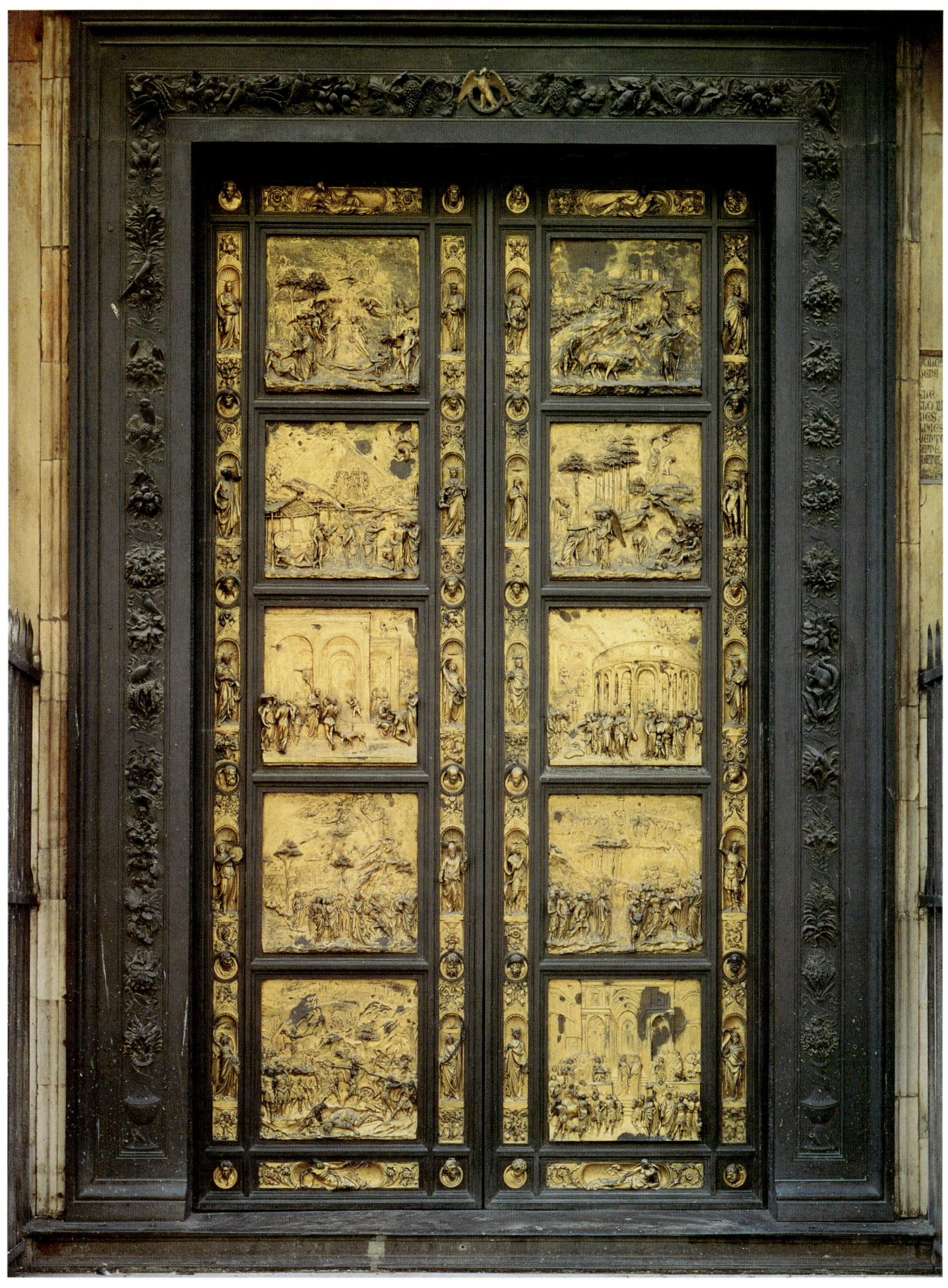

21-4 LORENZO GHIBERTI, east doors ("Gates of Paradise"), baptistery, Florence Cathedral, Florence, Italy, 1425–1452. Gilded bronze relief, approx. 17′ high.

gates of Paradise."[2] Three sets of doors provide access to the baptistery (see FIG. 17-16). Andrea Pisano created the first set, on the south side, between 1330 and 1335. Ghiberti's first pair of doors (1403–1424), the result of the competition, was moved to the north doorway so that Ghiberti's second pair of doors (1425–1452) could be placed in the east doorway. In contrast to the south and north doors, Ghiberti abandoned the quatrefoil pattern in these "Gates of Paradise" and reduced the number of panels from twenty eight to ten (probably due to time constraints). Each of the panels contains a relief set in plain moldings and depicts a scene from the Old Testament. The complete gilding of the reliefs creates an effect of great splendor and elegance.

The individual panels of Ghiberti's east doors, such as *Isaac and His Sons* (FIG. **21-5**), clearly recall painting techniques in their depiction of space as well as in their treatment of the narrative. Some exemplify more fully than painting many of the principles architect and theorist Leon Battista Alberti formulated in his 1435 treatise *On Painting*. In his relief, Ghiberti created the illusion of space partly by pictorial perspective and partly by sculptural means. He represented buildings according to a painter's one-point perspective construction, but the figures (in the bottom section of the relief, which actually projects slightly toward viewers) appear almost in the full round, some of their heads standing completely free. As the eyes progress upward, the relief increasingly flattens, concluding with the architecture in the background, which Ghiberti depicted in barely raised lines. In this manner, the artist created a sort of "sculptor's aerial perspective" with forms appearing less distinct the deeper they are in space. Ghiberti described the east doors as follows:

> I strove to imitate nature as closely as I could, and with all the perspective I could produce [to have] excellent compositions rich with many figures. In some scenes I placed about a hundred figures, in some less, and in some more. I executed that work with the greatest diligence and the greatest love. There were ten stories, all [sunk] in frames because the eye from a distance measures and interprets the scenes in such a way that they appear round. The scenes are in the lowest relief and the figures are seen in the planes; those that are near appear large, those in the distance small, as they do in reality. . . . Executed with the greatest study and perseverance, of all my work it is the most remarkable I have done and it was finished with skill, correct proportions, and understanding.[3]

Thus, like Donatello, Ghiberti harmonized an echo of the ancient and medieval past with the new science—he enhanced "proportions" and "skill" with "understanding." In these panels, Ghiberti achieved a greater sense of depth than had been possible in a relief. His principal figures, however, do not occupy the architectural space he created for them; rather, the artist arranged them along a parallel plane in front of the grandiose architecture. (According to Leon Battista Alberti, in his *De re aedificatoria*—*On the Art of Building*—the architecture's grandeur reflects the dignity of the events shown in the foreground.) Ghiberti's figure style mixes a Gothic patterning of rhythmic line, classical poses and motifs, and a new realism in characterization, movement, and surface detail. The medieval narrative method of presenting several episodes within a single frame persisted. In *Isaac and His Sons* (FIG.

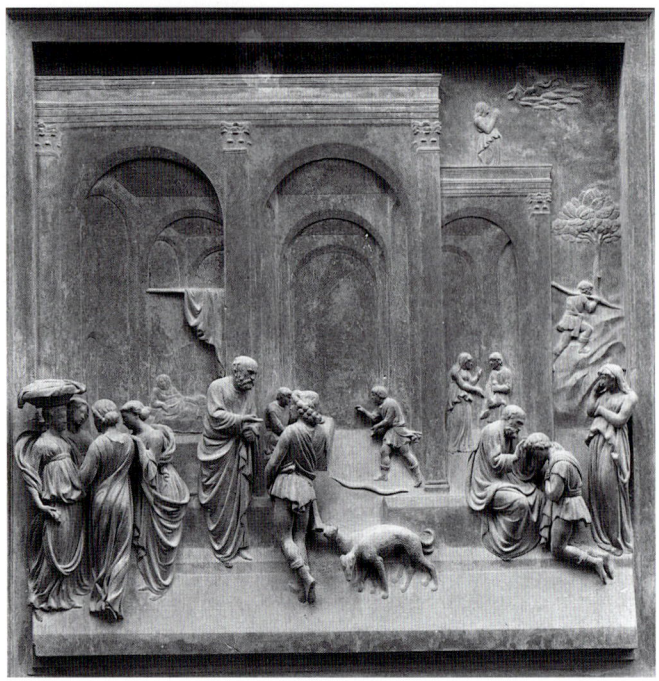

21-5   Lorenzo Ghiberti, *Isaac and His Sons* (detail of FIG. 21-4), east doors, baptistery, Florence Cathedral, Florence, Italy, 1425–1452. Gilded bronze relief, approx. 2′ 7½″ × 2′ 7½″.

21-5), the group of women in the left foreground attends the birth of Esau and Jacob in the left background; Isaac sends Esau and his hunting dogs on his mission in the central foreground; and, in the right foreground, Isaac blesses the kneeling Jacob as Rebecca looks on (Gen. 25–27). Yet viewers experience little confusion because of Ghiberti's careful and subtle placement of each scene. The figures, in varying degrees of projection, gracefully twist and turn, appearing to occupy and move through a convincing stage space, which Ghiberti deepened by showing some figures from behind. The classicism derives from the artist's close study of ancient art. His biography says he admired and collected classical sculpture, bronzes, and coins. Their influence is seen throughout the panel, particularly in the figure of Rebecca, which Ghiberti based on a popular Greco-Roman statuary type. The beginning of the practice of collecting classical art in the fifteenth century had much to do with the appearance of classicism in Renaissance humanistic art.

FILLING THE NICHES WITH STATUES   Ghiberti was just one of numerous artists who acknowledged Donatello's prodigious talent. Donatello's enviable skill at creating visually credible and engaging relief sculptures extended to sculpture in the round. His artistry impressed those in a position to commission art, a fact demonstrated by his participation, along with other esteemed sculptors, such as Ghiberti, in another major civic art program of the early 1400s—the decoration of Or San Michele.

Or San Michele was the early-fourteenth-century building that at various times housed a granary, the headquarters of the guilds, a church, and Orcagna's tabernacle (see FIG. 19-15). After construction of Or San Michele, city officials assigned

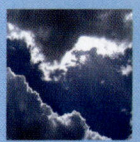

RELIGION AND MYTHOLOGY

From San Francisco to São Paulo
The Path to Sainthood

Saints are a ubiquitous element in modern society, surfacing in the names of geographic locations and churches, as well as appearing in artworks. Why is this, and what purpose do saints serve? What is the history of saints, and how does one achieve sainthood?

The word *saint* derives from the Latin word *sanctus,* meaning "made holy to God," or *sacred.* Thus, saints are people who have demonstrated a dedication to God's service. The first saints were martyrs—individuals who had suffered and died for Christianity—selected by public acclaim. The faithful called on these martyrs to intercede on their behalf. By the end of the fourth century A.D., the group of saints expanded to include confessors, individuals who merited honor for the Christian devotion they demonstrated while alive.

A more formal process of canonization emerged in the twelfth century (although the procedures in use today were established in 1634). The Roman Catholic Church derived the term *canonization* from the idea of a canon, or list, of approved saints. Canonization is a lengthy and involved process. Normally several years must pass before the Church will consider a deceased Catholic for sainthood. After a panel of theologians and cardinals of the Congregation for the Causes of Saints thoroughly evaluates the candidate's life, the pope proclaims an approved candidate "venerable" (worthy of reverence). Evidence of the performance of a miracle earns the candidate beatification (from the word *beatus,* meaning "blessed"). After proof of another miracle, the pope canonizes the candidate as a saint.

Despite the concept of a canon, no such thing as an authoritative register of all saints exists. Different groups have compiled various lists. For example, the Roman Martyrology, which is not comprehensive, contains more than forty-five hundred names. Indeed, during John Paul II's papacy alone (1978–), close to three hundred people have been canonized.

The inspiration saints provided and their teaching ability made them popular in art, especially in eras when religion dominated the lives of the populace. This was not idolatry, because viewers did not worship the images. The images simply encouraged and facilitated personal devotion. The pious called on saints to intercede on behalf of sinners (themselves or others).

The faithful admired each saint for certain traits or qualities, often having to do with the particulars of the saint's life or death. For example, the devout remembered Saint Theresa (see FIG. 24-9) for her transverberation (the piercing of her heart by the arrow of Divine Love), while they associated Saint Bartholomew (see FIGS. 22-25 and 24-28) with the manner of his martyrdom (he was flayed alive). Art viewers recognized saints by their attributes. For example, artists usually depicted Saint Sebastian—a Roman guard the emperor Diocletian ordered shot by archers for refusing to deny Christ—bound to a post or tree, his body pierced by numerous arrows. Other saints and their attributes follow:

Saint	Depicted
Francis of Assisi (see FIG. 19-1)	In a long robe tied at waist with rope; with stigmata
George (see FIG. 21-6), patron saint of soldiers and armorers	As a young knight in armor, with red cross on shield
Peter (see FIG. 23-5)	With keys signifying the power to "bind and loose" (Matt. 16:19)
Jerome (see FIG. 23-21)	As either a scholar at his desk or a hermit in the wilderness
Stephen (see FIGS. 20-18 and 23-27)	With a stone, referring to his death by stoning
Augustine (see FIG. 23-27), patron saint of theologians and scholars	In a mitre (tall pointed hat) and bishop's vestments

each of the niches on the building's exterior to a specific guild for decoration with a sculpture of its patron saint (see "From San Francisco to São Paulo: The Path to Sainthood," above). Most of the niches languished empty. By 1406, guilds had placed statues in only five of the fourteen niches. Between 1406 and 1423, however, guilds filled the nine vacant niches with statues by Donatello, Ghiberti, and Nanni di Banco. How might historians account for this flurry of activity? First, city officials issued a dictum in 1406 requiring the guilds to comply with the original plan and fill their assigned niches. Second, Florence was once again under siege, this time by King Ladislaus (r. 1399–1414) of Naples. Ladislaus had marched north, had occupied Rome and the Papal States by 1409, and then had threatened to overrun Florence. As they had previously, Florentine officials urged citizens to stand firm and defend their city-state from tyranny. As had happened with Visconti a few years earlier, Ladislaus, on the verge of military success in 1414, fortuitously died, and Florence found itself spared yet again. The guilds no doubt viewed this threat as an opportunity to perform their civic duty by rallying their fellow Florentines while also promoting their own importance and position in Florentine society. The early-fifteenth-century niche sculptures thus served various purposes, and their public placement provided an ideal vehicle for presenting political, artistic, and economic messages to a wide audience. Examining a few of these Or San Michele sculptures demonstrates the stylistic and historical significance of all these works.

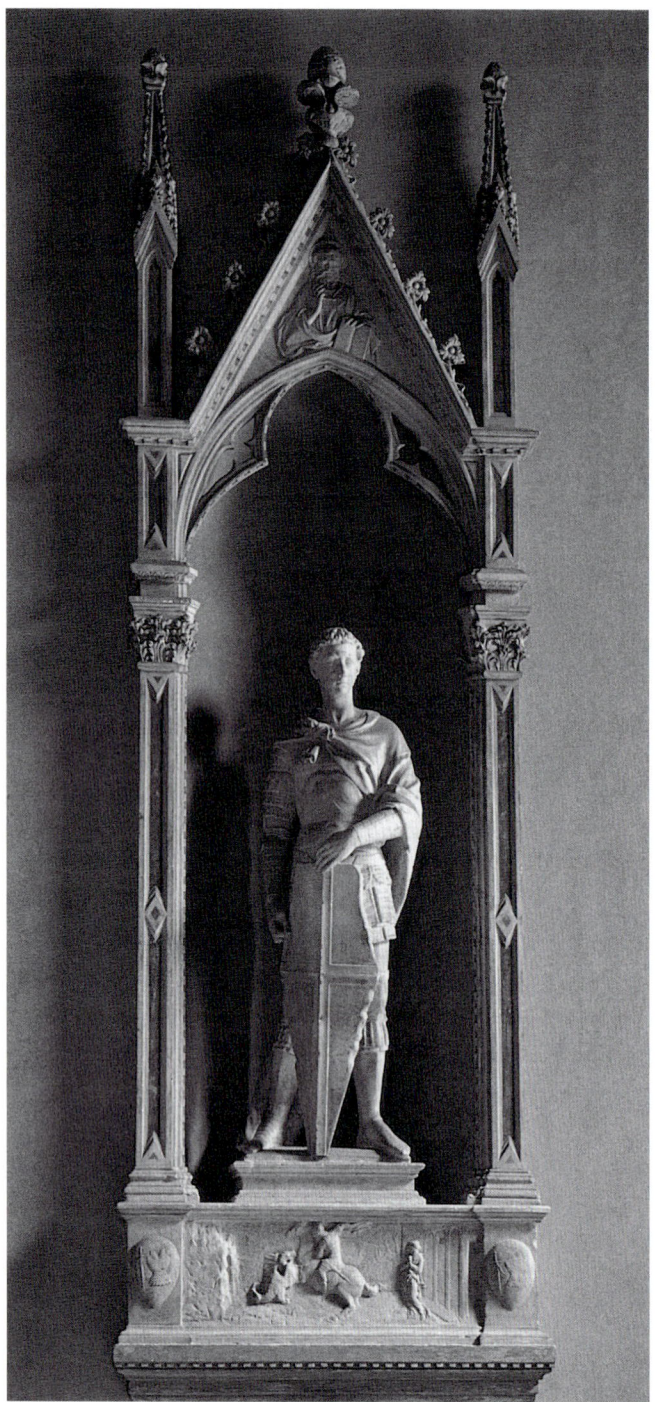

21-6 DONATELLO, *Saint George,* from Or San Michele, Florence, Italy, ca. 1415–1417. Marble (replaced in niche by a bronze copy), approx. 6′ 10″ high. Museo Nazionale del Bargello, Florence.

A KNIGHT IN MARBLE ARMOR

In *Saint George* (FIG. **21-6**), one of the three sculptures Donatello created for Or San Michele, the artist provided an image of the proud idealism of youth. The armored soldier-saint, patron of the guild of armorers and swordmakers (which commissioned Donatello to carve the statue in 1415), stands with bold firmness—legs set apart, feet strongly planted, the torso slightly twisting so that the left shoulder and arm advance with a subtle gesture of haughty and challenging readiness. The figure once wore a metal helmet and in his right hand brandished a

metal sword that projected outward from the niche into the street below. The accessories publicly identified both the figure and the guild, and the sword's positioning reinforced a greater physical connection between the warrior-saint and viewers than is evident today. Saint George's head is erect and turned slightly to his left. Beneath the furrowed brows, the dragon slayer's noble features are intent and concentrated. In its regal poise and tense anticipation, the figure contrasts sharply with the facade statues of medieval churches, which, consistent with the spiritual values of the Middle Ages, seem removed from the world and unaware of their surroundings. With *Saint George,* Donatello reasserted the prominence of individual personality that characterized the Early Renaissance in Italy.

Some art historians place *Saint George* within the chivalric traditions of the Late Gothic period; depictions of warrior-knights and knight-saints (such as Saint George and Saint Martin) were common in late medieval art. However, others argue that Donatello's *Saint George,* in addition to serving the needs of the armorers' guild, also conveyed a message of optimism in a time of military threat. When Donatello began his work on *Saint George* (this sculpture has been dated as early as 1410), Florence was in danger; Saint George, appropriately, looks ready but apprehensive. After completing the niche sculpture (and after Ladislaus's miraculous death in 1414), Donatello carved the relief sculpture at the base of the niche—a fitting relief that depicts a victorious George slaying the dragon.

FOUR MARTYRED SCULPTORS   As had *Saint George,* other niche sculptures for Or San Michele promoted the themes of sacrifice and heroism. For example, the Florentine guild of sculptors, architects, and masons chose NANNI DI BANCO (ca. 1380–1421) to create four life-size marble statues of the guild's martyred patron saints. These four Christian sculptors had defied an order from the Roman emperor Diocletian to make a statue of a pagan deity. In response, the emperor ordered them put to death. Because they placed their faith above all else, these saints were perfect role models for the fifteenth-century Florentines whom city leaders exhorted to stand fast in the face of the invasion threat by Ladislaus.

Nanni's group, *Quattro Santi Coronati* (Four Crowned Saints; FIG. **21-7**), also represented an early attempt to solve the Renaissance problem of integrating figures and space on a monumental scale. The artist's positioning of the figures, which stand in a niche that is *in* but confers some separation *from* the architecture, furthered the gradual emergence of sculpture from its architectural setting. This process began with such works as the thirteenth-century statues of the west front of Reims Cathedral (see FIG. 18-24). The niche's spatial recess permitted a new and dramatic possibility for the interrelationship of the figures. By placing them in a semicircle within their deep niche and relating them to one another by their postures and gestures, as well as by the arrangement of draperies, Nanni arrived at a unified spatial composition. Further, a remarkable psychological unity connects these unyielding figures, whose bearing expresses the discipline and integrity necessary to face adversity. While the figure on the right speaks, pointing to his right, the two men opposite listen and the one next to him looks out into space, pondering

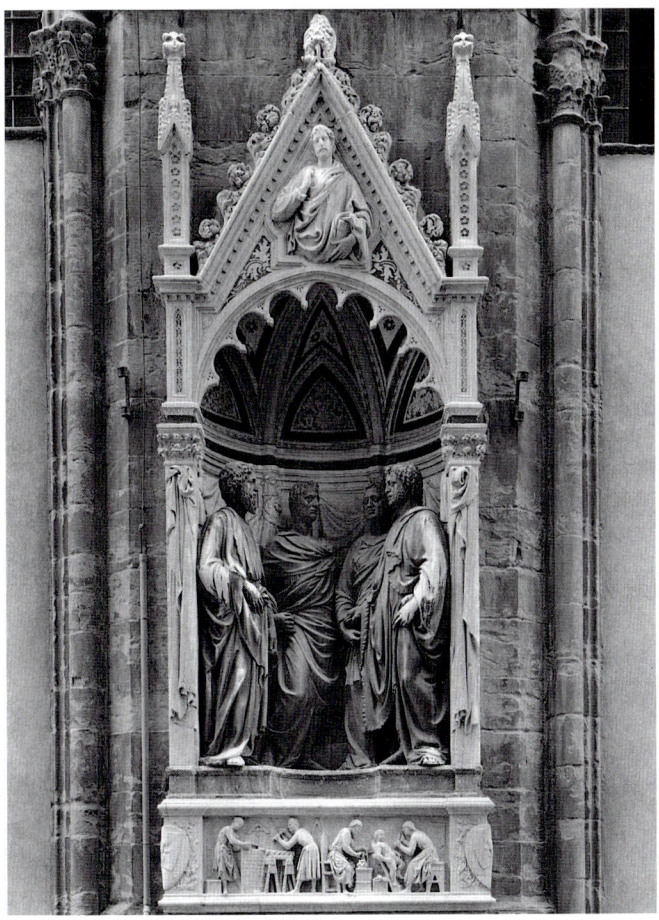

21-7 NANNI DI BANCO, *Quattro Santi Coronati,* Or San Michele, Florence, Italy, ca. 1408–1414. Marble, figures approx. life-size.

the meaning of the words. Later Renaissance artists, particularly Leonardo, exploited such reinforcement of a figural group's formal unity with psychological cross-references.

In *Quattro Santi Coronati,* Nanni also displayed a deep respect for and close study of Roman portrait statues. The emotional intensity of the faces of the two inner saints owed much to the extraordinarily moving portrayals in stone of Roman emperors of the third century A.D. (see FIG. 10-69), and the bearded heads of the outer saints reveal a familiarity with second-century A.D. imperial portraiture (see FIG. 10-60). Early Renaissance artists, like Donatello and Nanni di Banco, sought to portray individual personalities and characteristics. Roman models served as inspiration, but Renaissance artists did not simply copy them. Duplication was not the goal of Nanni and his contemporaries. Rather, they strove to interpret or offer commentary on their classical models in the manner of the humanist scholars dealing with classical texts.

SUGGESTING MOTION IN STONE Donatello's incorporation of Greek Classical principles surfaced in *Saint Mark* (FIG. **21-8**), commissioned for Or San Michele by the guild of linen drapers and completed in 1413. In this sculpture, Donatello took a fundamental step toward depicting motion in the human figure by recognizing the principle of weight shift. Earlier chapters established the importance of weight shift in the ancient world, when Greek sculptors, as

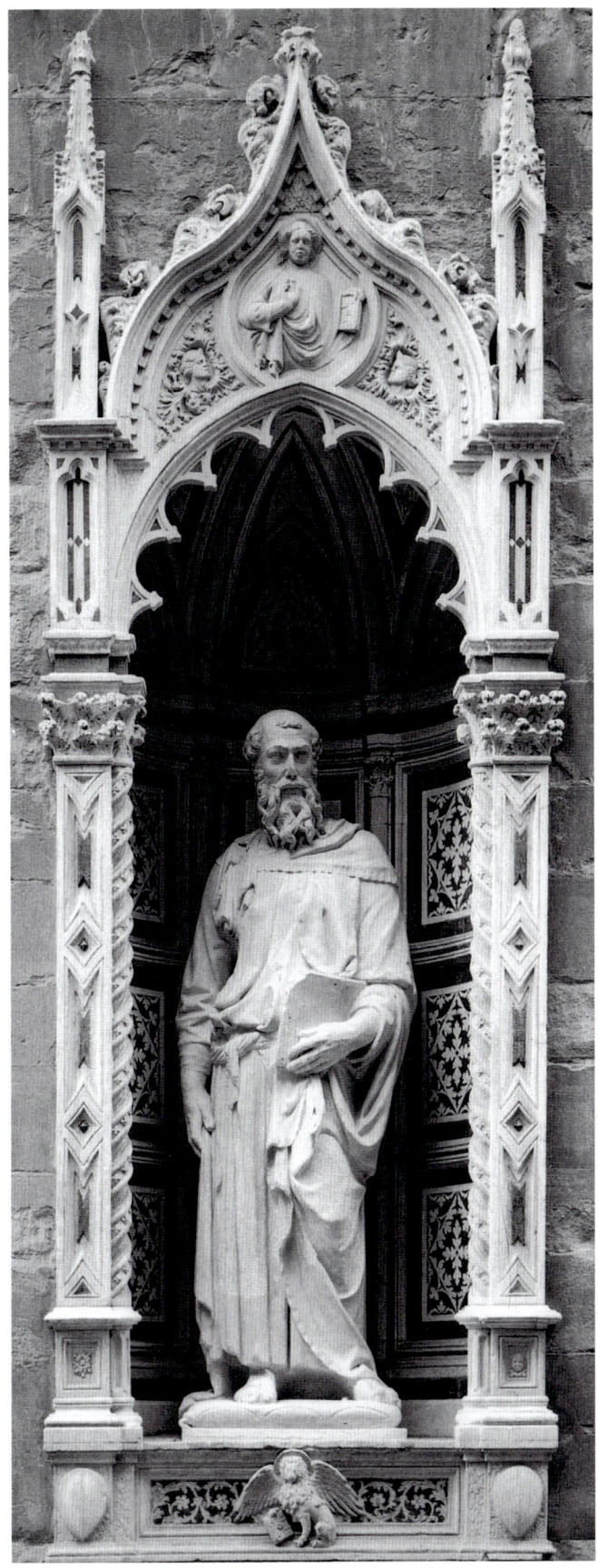

21-8 DONATELLO, *Saint Mark,* Or San Michele, Florence, Italy, 1411–1413. Marble, approx. 7′ 9″ high.

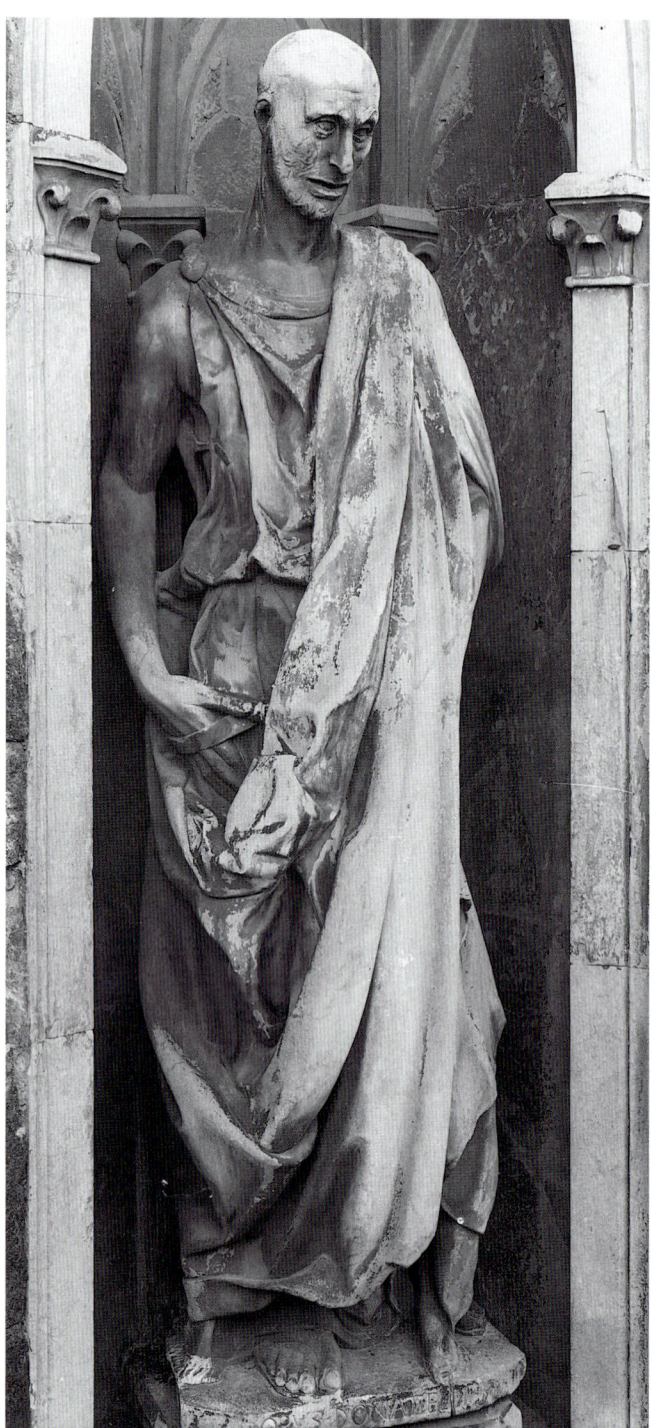

21-9 DONATELLO, prophet figure (Zuccone), from the campanile of Florence Cathedral, Florence, Italy, 1423–1425. Marble, approx. 6′ 5″ high. Museo dell'Opera del Duomo, Florence.

of support so that viewers sense the figure as a draped nude, not simply as an integrated column with arbitrarily incised drapery. This separates Donatello's *Saint Mark* from all medieval portal statuary. It was the first Renaissance figure whose voluminous drapery (the pride of the Florentine guild that paid for the statue) did not conceal but accentuated the movement of the arms, legs, shoulders, and hips. This development further contributed to the sculptured figure's independence from its architectural setting. Saint Mark's stirring limbs, the shifting weight, and the mobile drapery suggest impending movement out of the niche.

POWERFUL BELL TOWER FIGURES Between 1416 and 1435, Donatello carved five statues for niches on the *campanile* (bell tower) adjacent to Florence Cathedral—a project that, like the figures for Or San Michele, had originated in the preceding century. Unlike the Or San Michele figures, however, which were installed only slightly above eye level, the officials in charge of cathedral projects chose to place the campanile sculptures in niches at least thirty feet above the ground. At that distance, delicate descriptive details (hair, garments, and features) cannot be recognized readily. The campanile figures thus required massive garment folds that could be read from afar and a much broader, summary treatment of facial and anatomical features, all of which Donatello used to great effect. In addition, he took into account the elevated position of his figures and, with subtly calculated distortions, created images that are at once realistic and dramatic when seen from below.

The most striking of the five figures is a prophet generally known by the nickname Zuccone, or "pumpkin-head" (FIG. 21-9). This figure shows Donatello's power of characterization at its most original. The artist represented all of his prophets with a harsh, direct realism reminiscent of some ancient Roman portraits (compare FIGS. 10-6, 10-35, and 10-69). Their faces are bony, lined, and taut; Donatello carefully individualized each of them. The Zuccone is also bald, a departure from the conventional representation of the prophets but in keeping with many Roman portrait heads. Donatello's prophet wears an awkwardly draped and crumpled mantle with deeply undercut folds—a far cry from the majestic prophets of medieval portals. The head discloses a fierce personality; the deep-set eyes glare under furrowed brows, the nostrils flare, and the broad mouth is agape, as if the prophet were in the very presence of disasters that would prompt dire warnings.

Painting, Perspective, and Patronage

AN INTERNATIONAL STYLE ALTARPIECE The International Style (see FIG. 19-18), the dominant style in painting around 1400 that persisted well into the fifteenth century, developed side by side with the new styles. GENTILE DA FABRIANO (ca. 1370–1427) produced what may be the masterpiece of the International Style, his *Adoration of the Magi* (FIG. 21-10), an altarpiece in the sacristy of the church of Santa Trinità in Florence. Gentile's patron was Palla Strozzi, the wealthiest Florentine of his day, and the altarpiece, with its elaborate gilded Gothic frame, is testimony to Strozzi's lavish tastes. So, too, is the painting itself, with its gorgeous surface and sumptuously costumed kings, courtiers, captains,

shown in works such as the *Kritios Boy* (see FIG. 5-33) and the *Doryphoros* (see FIG. 5-38), grasped the essential principle that the human body is not rigid. It is a flexible structure that moves by continuously shifting its weight from one supporting leg to the other with its main masses moving in consonance. Donatello reintroduced this concept (known as *contrapposto*).

As the saint's body "moves," its drapery "moves" with it, hanging and folding naturally from and around bodily points

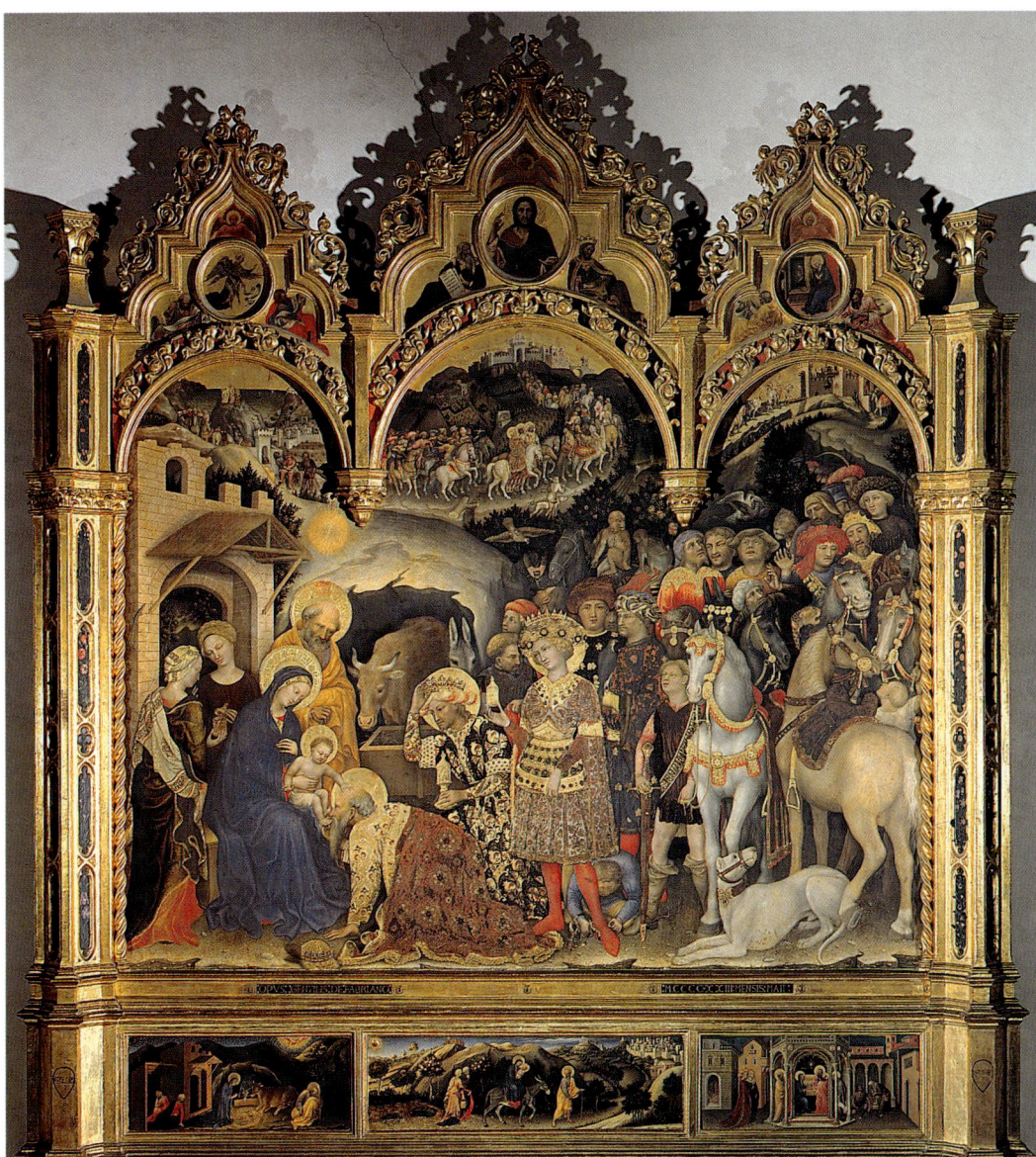

21-10 GENTILE DA FABRIANO, *Adoration of the Magi*, altarpiece from Santa Trinità, Florence, Italy, 1423. Tempera on wood, approx. 9′ 11″ × 9′ 3″. Galleria degli Uffizi, Florence.

and retainers accompanied by a menagerie of exotic and ornamental animals. Gentile portrayed all of these elements in a rainbow of color with extensive use of gold. The painting presents all the pomp and ceremony of chivalric etiquette in a scene that sanctifies the aristocracy in the presence of the Madonna and Child. Although the style is fundamentally Late Gothic, Gentile inserted striking bits of radical naturalism. Viewers encounter animals depicted from a variety of angles and foreshortened convincingly, as are tilted human heads and bodies (such as the man removing the spurs from the standing magus in the center foreground). On the right side of the predella (the ledge at the base of an altarpiece), Gentile placed the Presentation scene in a "modern" architectural setting. And on the left side of the predella, he painted what may have been the very first nighttime Nativity with the central light source—the radiant Christ Child—introduced into the picture itself. Although predominantly conservative, Gentile demonstrated he was not oblivious to contemporary experimental trends and that he could blend naturalistic and inventive elements skillfully and subtly into a traditional composition without sacrificing Late Gothic coloristic splendor.

MOMENTOUS CHANGES IN PICTORIAL STYLE

An artist much less compromising was TOMMASO GUIDI, known as MASACCIO (1401–1428). Indeed, scholars often identify Masaccio as the leading innovator in early fifteenth-century painting. Although his presumed teacher, Masolino da Panicale, had worked in the International Style, Masaccio moved suddenly, within the short span of six years, into wide-open and unexplored territory (see "Imitation and Emulation: Artistic Values in the Renaissance," page 602). Most art historians recognize no other painter in history to have contributed so much to the development of a new style in so short a time as Masaccio, whose creative career was cut short by his death at age twenty-seven. Masaccio was the artistic descendant of Giotto, whose calm monumental style he revolutionized with a whole new repertoire of representational devices that generations of Renaissance painters later studied and developed. Masaccio also knew and understood the innovations of his great contemporaries, Donatello and Brunelleschi, and he introduced new possibilities for both form and content.

The frescoes Masaccio painted in the Brancacci Chapel of Santa Maria del Carmine in Florence provide excellent

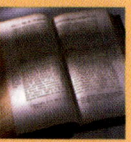

Imitation and Emulation
Artistic Values in the Renaissance

The natural human tendency is to interpret historical material from one's own vantage point and to generalize (for example, "Eastern religious beliefs" or "Third World economies"), especially when it comes to cultural or societal values. Doing so, however, results in the distortion of cultural practices and denies groups, countries, and societies their unique historical identities. Therefore, when studying material from other times and places, everyone must remain vigilant to avoid imposing their own learned and subjective values.

Among the concepts Renaissance artists most valued were *imitation* and *emulation*. The familiar premium that current Western society seems to place on originality is actually a fairly recent phenomenon. Although many Renaissance artists did develop unique, recognizable styles, convention, both in terms of subject matter and representational practices, predominated. In a review of Italian Renaissance art, certain themes, conceits, and artistic formats surface with great regularity, and the traditional training practices reveal the importance of imitation and emulation to aspiring Renaissance artists.

Imitation was the starting point in a young artist's training (see "Mastering a Craft: Artistic Training in the Renaissance," Chapter 19, page 554). Renaissance Italians believed that the best way to learn was to copy the works of masters. Accordingly, much of an apprentice's training consisted of copying exemplary artworks. Leonardo filled his sketchbooks with drawings of well-known sculptures and frescoes, while Michelangelo spent hours visiting churches around Florence and Rome and sketching the artworks he found there.

Emulation was the next step; emulation involved modeling one's art after another artist. While imitation still provided the foundation for this practice, an artist used features of another's art only as a springboard for improvements or innovations. Thus, developing artists went beyond previous artists and attempted to prove their own competence and skill by improving on established and recognized masters. Comparison and a degree of competition were integral to emulation. To evaluate the "improved" artwork, viewers had to know the original "model."

Ultimately, through this process of imitation and emulation, Renaissance artists believed that developing artists would arrive at their own unique style. Cennino Cennini (ca. 1370–1440) explained the value of this training procedure in a book he published in 1400, *Il Libro dell'Arte* (*The Craftman's Handbook*), that served as a practical guide to making art:

> Having first practiced drawing for a while as I have taught you above, that is, on a little panel, take pains and pleasure in constantly copying the best things which you can find done by the hand of great masters. And if you are in a place where many good masters have been, so much the better for you. But I give you this advice: take care to select the best one every time, and the one who has the greatest reputation. And, as you go on from day to day, it will be against nature if you do not get some grasp of his style and of his spirit. For if you undertake to copy after one master today and after another one tomorrow, you will not acquire the style of either one or the other, and you will inevitably, through enthusiasm become capricious, because each style will be distracting your mind. You will try to work in this man's way today, and in the other's tomorrow, and so you will not get either of them right. If you follow the course of one man through constant practice, your intelligence would have to be crude indeed for you not to get some nourishment from it. Then you will find, if nature has granted you any imagination at all, that you will eventually acquire a style individual to yourself, and it cannot help being good; because your hand and your mind, being always accustomed to gather flowers, would ill know how to pluck thorns.[1]

[1] Cennino Cennini, *The Craftman's Handbook (Il Libro dell'Arte)*, trans. D. V. Thompson Jr. (New York: Dover Publications, 1960), 14–15.

examples of his innovations. In *Tribute Money* (FIG. **21-11**), painted shortly before his death, Masaccio depicted a seldomly represented narrative from the Gospel of Matthew (17:24–27). As the tax collector confronts Christ at the entrance to the Roman town of Capernaum, Christ directs Saint Peter to the shore of Lake Galilee. There, as foreseen by Christ, Peter finds the half drachma tribute in the mouth of a fish and returns to pay the tax. Art historians have debated the reason for the selection of this particular biblical story. Most scholars believe that Felice Brancacci, owner of the family chapel in the early fifteenth century, commissioned the fresco. Why such an obscure narrative appealed to Brancacci or

Masaccio is unclear. Some scholars have suggested that *Tribute Money*, in which Christ condones taxation, served as a commentary on the *catasto* (state income tax) whose implementation Florentines were considering at the time. However, Brancacci's considerable wealth makes it unlikely he would have supported the *catasto*. Moreover, this fresco's placement in a private family chapel meant the public had only limited access. Therefore, because this fresco lacked the general audience enjoyed by, for example, the Or San Michele niche sculptures, it seems ill-suited for public statements.

Masaccio presented this narrative in three episodes within the fresco. In the center, Christ, surrounded by his disciples,

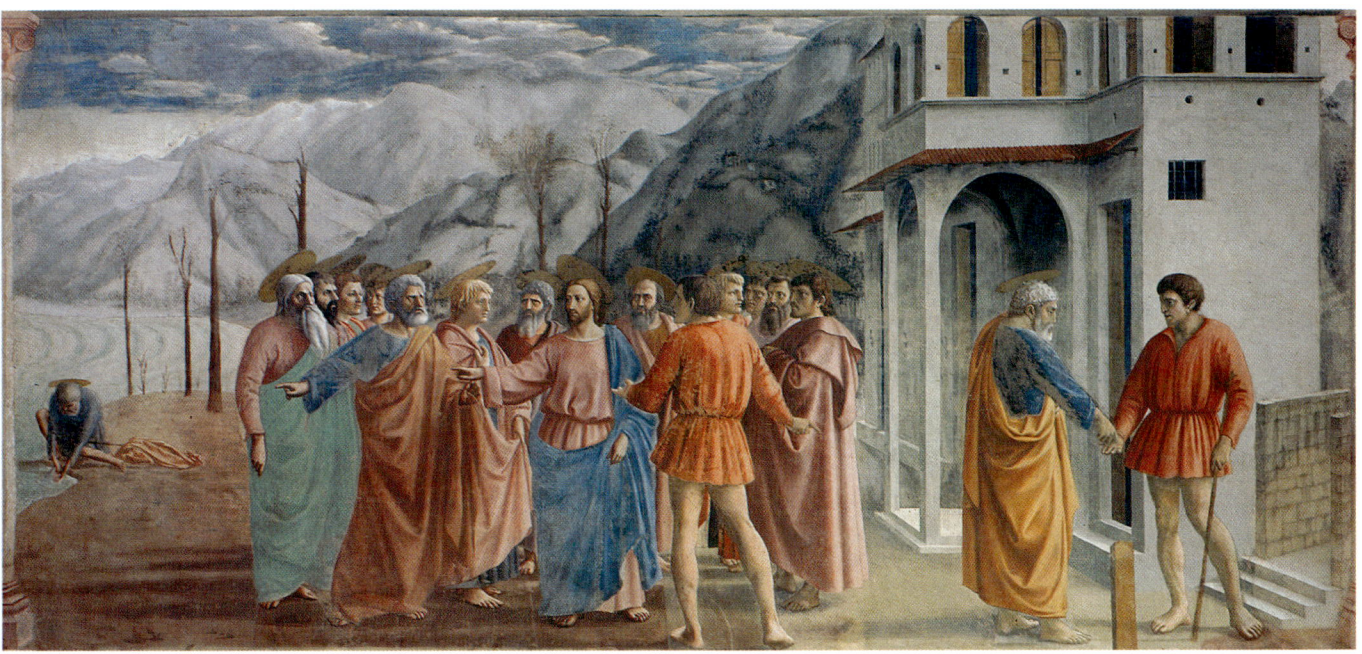

21-11 MASACCIO, *Tribute Money*, Brancacci Chapel, Santa Maria del Carmine, Florence, Italy, ca. 1427. Fresco, 8′ 1″ × 19′ 7″.

tells Saint Peter to retrieve the coin from the fish, while the tax collector stands in the foreground, his back to spectators and hand extended, awaiting payment. At the left, in the middle distance, Saint Peter extracts the coin from the fish's mouth, and, at the right, he thrusts the coin into the tax collector's hand. Masaccio's figures recall Giotto's in their simple grandeur, but they convey a greater psychological and physical credibility. Masaccio realized the bulk of the figures not through generalized modeling with a flat neutral light lacking an identifiable source but by a light coming from a specific source outside the picture. The light strikes the figures at an angle, illuminating the parts of the solids that obstruct its path and leaving the rest in deep shadow. This chiaroscuro gives the illusion of deep sculptural relief. Between the extremes of light and dark, the light appears as a constantly active but fluctuating force highlighting the scene in varying degrees, almost a tangible substance independent of the figures. In Giotto's frescoes, light is merely the modeling of a mass. In Masaccio's, light has its own nature, and the masses are visible only because of its direction and intensity. Viewers can imagine the light as playing over forms—revealing some and concealing others, as the artist directs it.

The individual figures in *Tribute Money* are solemn and weighty, but they also express bodily structure and movement, as do Donatello's statues. Masaccio's representations adeptly suggest bones, muscles, and the pressures and tensions of joints. Each figure conveys a maximum of contained energy. The figure of Christ and the two appearances of the tax collector make viewers understand what the Renaissance biographer Giorgio Vasari meant when he said: ". . . the works made before his [Masaccio's] day can be said to be painted, while his are living, real, and natural."[4]

Masaccio's arrangement of the figures is equally inventive. They do not appear as a stiff screen in the front planes. Instead, the artist grouped them in circular depth around Christ, and he placed the whole group in a spacious landscape, rather than in the confined stage space of earlier frescoes. The group itself generates the foreground space that the architecture on the right amplifies. Masaccio depicted this architecture in one-point perspective, locating the vanishing point, where all the orthogonals converge, to coincide with Christ's head. Aerial perspective, the diminishing of light and the blurring of outlines as the distance increases, unites the foreground with the background. Although ancient Roman painters used aerial perspective, medieval artists had abandoned it. Thus it virtually disappeared from art until Masaccio and his contemporaries rediscovered it, apparently independently. They came to realize that light and air interposed between viewers and what they see are parts of the visual experience called "distance."

A PICTURE OF SINNERS' ANGUISH In an awkwardly narrow space at the entrance to the Brancacci Chapel, Masaccio painted the *Expulsion of Adam and Eve from Eden* (FIG. **21-12**), another fresco displaying the representational innovations of *Tribute Money*. For example, the sharply slanted light from an outside source creates deep relief, with lights placed alongside darks, and acts as a strong unifying agent. Masaccio also presented the figures moving with structural accuracy and with substantial bodily weight. Further, the hazy, atmospheric background specifies no locale but suggests a space around and beyond the figures. Adam's feet, clearly in contact with the ground, mark the human presence on earth, and the cry issuing from Eve's mouth voices her anguish. The angel does not force them physically from Eden. Rather, they stumble on blindly, driven by the angel's will and their own despair. The composition is starkly simple, its message incomparably eloquent.

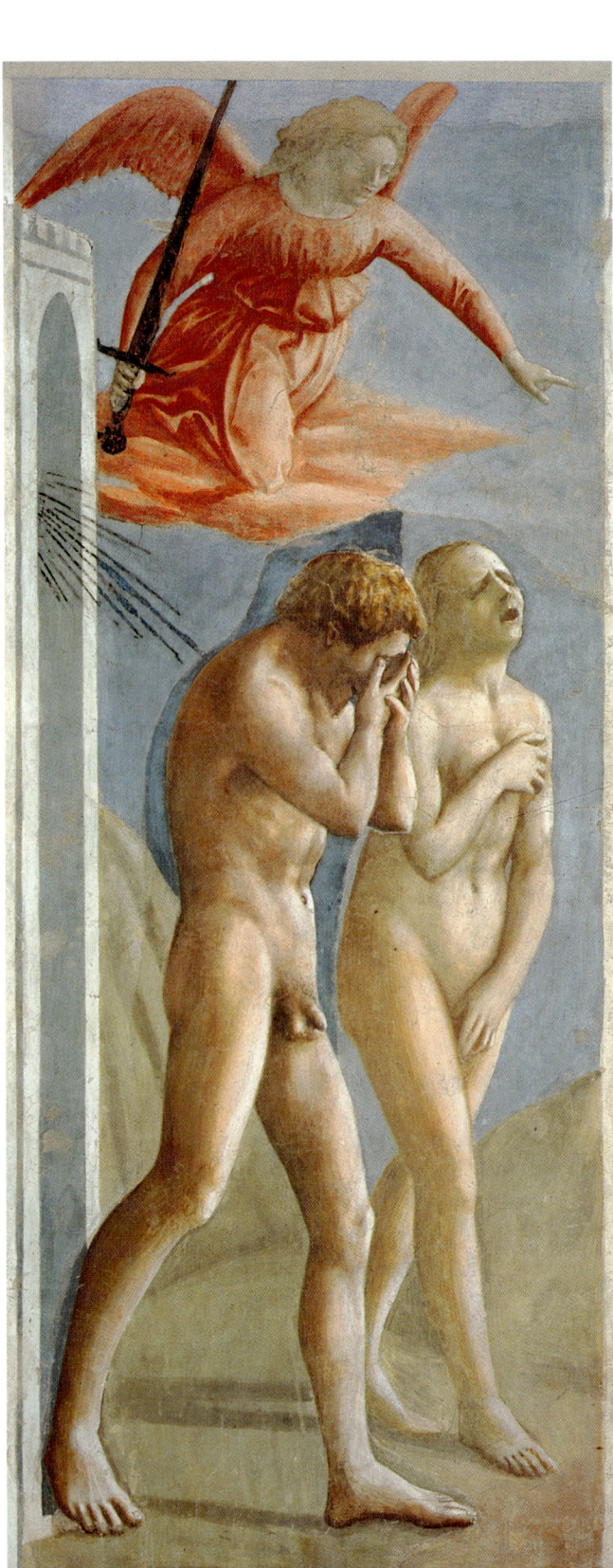

21-12   MASACCIO, *Expulsion of Adam and Eve from Eden,* Brancacci Chapel, Santa Maria del Carmine, Florence, Italy, ca. 1425. Fresco, 7′ × 2′ 11″.

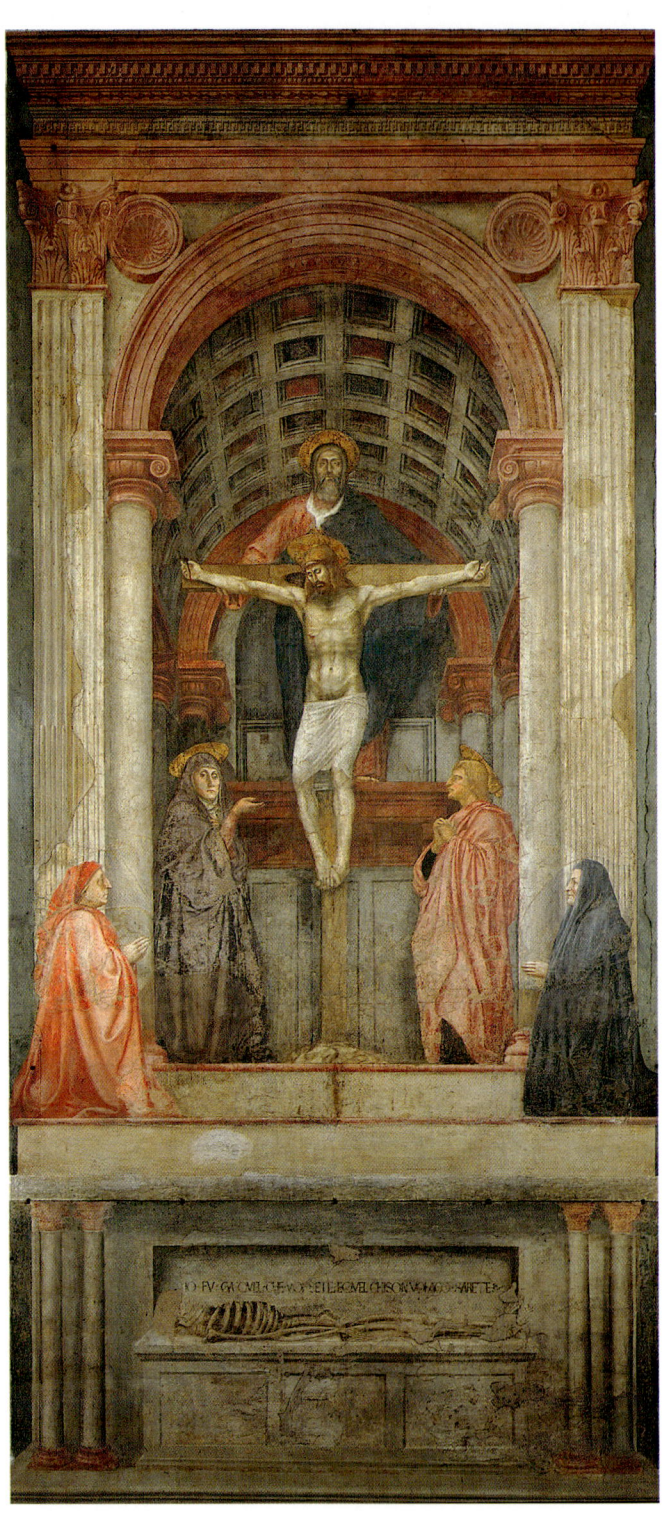

21-13   MASACCIO, *Holy Trinity,* Santa Maria Novella, Florence, Italy, ca. 1428. Fresco, 21′ × 10′ 5″.

A CONVINCING VISION OF THE TRINITY Masaccio's *Holy Trinity* fresco (FIG. **21-13**) in Santa Maria Novella, whose dating is still disputed, embodies two principal Renaissance interests. One is realism based on observation and the other is the application of mathematics to pictorial organization in the new science of perspective. The artist painted the composition on two levels of unequal height. Above, in a coffered barrel-vaulted chapel reminiscent of a Roman triumphal arch, the Virgin Mary and Saint John appear on either side of the crucified Christ. God the Father emerges from behind Christ, supporting the arms of the cross. The Dove of the Holy Spirit hovers between God's head and Christ's head. Masaccio also included portraits of the donors of the painting, Lorenzo Lenzi and his wife, who kneel just in front of the pilasters that enframe the chapel. Below the altar—a masonry insert in the depicted composition—the artist painted a tomb containing a skeleton. An inscription in Italian painted above the skeleton reminds spectators that "I was once what you are, and what I am you will become."

Although the subject matter of *Holy Trinity* may not be dramatically innovative, the illusionism of Masaccio's depiction is breathtaking. He provided viewers with a brilliant demonstration of the principles of Brunelleschi's perspective. Indeed, this work is so much in the Brunelleschian manner that some historians have suggested that Brunelleschi may have directed Masaccio. Masaccio placed the vanishing point at the foot of the cross. With this point at eye level, spectators look up at the Trinity and down at the tomb. About five feet above the floor level, the vanishing point pulls the two views together, creating the illusion of an actual structure that transects the wall's vertical plane. While the tomb projects, the chapel recedes visually behind the wall and appears as an extension of the spectators' space. This adjustment of the pictured space to the position of viewers was a first step in the development of illusionistic painting, which fascinated many artists of the Renaissance and the later Baroque period. Masaccio was so exact in his metrical proportions that it is possible to actually calculate the dimensions of the chapel (for example, the span of the painted vault is seven feet; the depth of the chapel, nine feet). Thus, he achieved not only a successful illusion but also a rational measured coherence that, by maintaining the mathematical proportions of the surface design, is responsible for the unity and harmony of this monumental composition.

Despite Masaccio's commitment to pictorial illusionism, the *Holy Trinity* fresco in the Florentine church of Santa Maria Novella still instructs the faithful through its images. In an ascending pyramid of figures, viewers move from the despair of death to the hope of resurrection and eternal life.

Early-Fifteenth-Century Architecture

ENAMORED BY ROMAN ARCHITECTURE Filippo Brunelleschi's ability to codify a system of linear perspective derived in part from his skill as an architect. Although his biographer, Manetti, reported that Brunelleschi turned to architecture out of disappointment over the loss of the baptis-

tery commission, he continued to work as a sculptor for several years and received commissions for sculpture as late as 1416. It is true, however, that as the fifteenth century progressed, Brunelleschi's interest turned increasingly toward architecture. Several trips to Rome (the first in 1402, probably with his friend Donatello), where he was captivated by the Roman ruins, heightened his fascination with architecture. It may well be in connection with his close study of Roman monuments and his effort to make an accurate record of what he saw that Brunelleschi developed his revolutionary system of geometric linear perspective that fifteenth-century artists so eagerly adopted. It made him the first acknowledged Renaissance architect.

A CROWNING ACHIEVEMENT Brunelleschi's broad knowledge of Roman construction principles, combined with an analytical and inventive mind, permitted him to solve an engineering problem that no other fifteenth-century architect could have solved. The challenge was the design and construction of a dome for the huge crossing of the unfinished Florence Cathedral (FIGS. **21-14** and 19-12). The problem was staggering; the space to be spanned (one hundred forty feet) was much too wide to permit construction with the aid of traditional wooden centering. Nor was it possible (because of the crossing plan) to support the dome with buttressed walls. Brunelleschi seems to have begun work on the problem about

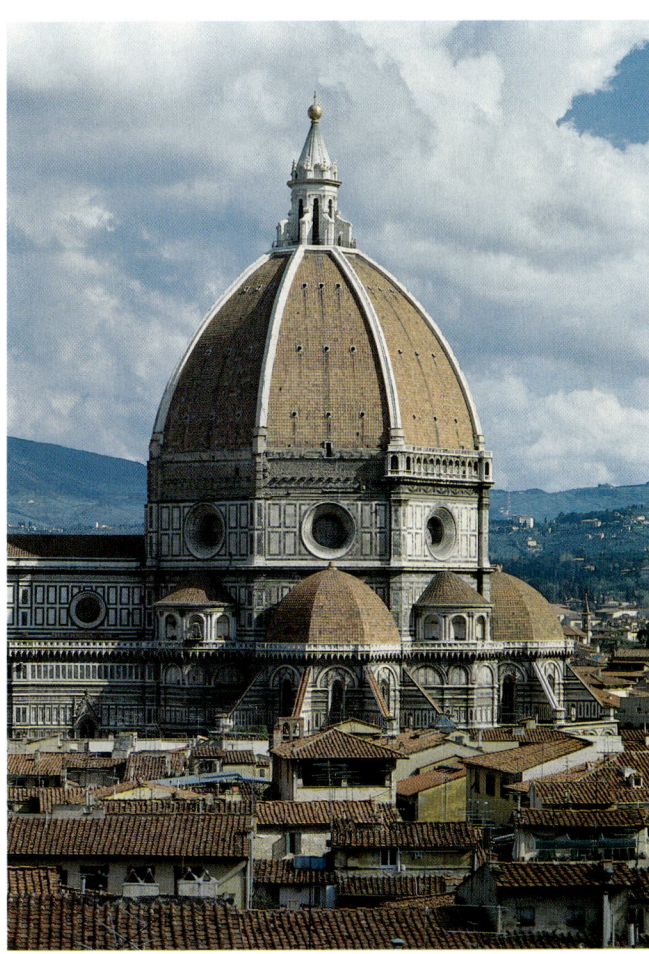

21-14 FILIPPO BRUNELLESCHI, dome of Florence Cathedral (view from the south), Florence, Italy, 1420–1436.

1417. In 1420, officials overseeing cathedral projects awarded Brunelleschi and Ghiberti a joint commission. The latter, however, soon retired from the project and left the field to his associate.

With exceptional ingenuity, Brunelleschi not only discarded traditional building methods and devised new ones, but he also invented much of the machinery necessary for the job. Although he might have preferred the hemispheric shape of Roman domes, Brunelleschi raised the center of his dome and designed it around an ogival (pointed arch) section, which is inherently more stable because it reduces the outward thrust around the dome's base. To minimize the structure's weight, he designed a relatively thin double shell (the first in history) around a skeleton of twenty-four ribs. The eight most important are visible on the exterior. Finally, in almost paradoxical fashion, Brunelleschi anchored the structure at the top with a heavy lantern, built after his death but from his design.

Despite Brunelleschi's knowledge of and admiration for Roman building techniques and even though the Florence Cathedral dome was his most outstanding engineering achievement, he arrived at the solution to this most critical structural problem through what were essentially Gothic building principles. Thus, the dome, which also had to harmonize in formal terms with the century-old building, does not really express Brunelleschi's architectural style. That is more apparent in subsequent designs when his ideas had matured.

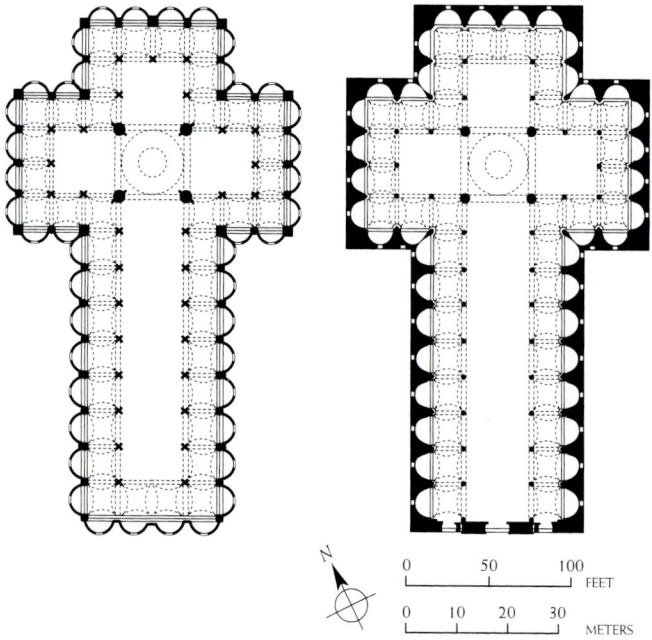

21-16 FILIPPO BRUNELLESCHI, early plan of Santo Spirito *(left)* and plan as constructed *(right)*, Florence, Italy.

APPLYING ROMAN MATHEMATICAL LOGIC

San Lorenzo and Santo Spirito, the two basilican churches Brunelleschi built in Florence, echo the clarity and classically inspired rationality that characterized much of his architecture. Of the two, the later Santo Spirito (FIGS. **21-15** and **21-16**), begun around 1436 and completed, with some changes, after Brunelleschi's death, shows the architect's mature style. Brunelleschi laid out this cruciform building in either multiples or segments of the dome-covered crossing square. The aisles, subdivided into small squares covered by shallow saucer-shaped vaults, run all the way around the flat-roofed central space. They have the visual effect of compressing the longitudinal design into a centralized one, because the various aspects of the interior resemble one another, no matter where observers stand. Originally, this centralization effect would have been even stronger; Brunelleschi had planned to extend the aisles across the front of the nave as well, as shown on the plan (FIG. 21-16, left). Because of the design's modular basis, adherence to it would have demanded four entrances in the facade, instead of the traditional and symbolic three, a feature hotly debated during Brunelleschi's lifetime and changed after his death. The appearance of the exterior walls also was modified later (compare the two plans in FIG. 21-16), when the recesses between the projecting semicircular chapels were filled in to convert the original highly sculptured wall surface into a flat one.

The major features of the interior (FIG. 21-15), however, are much as Brunelleschi designed them. He based the scale of each architectural element on a unit that served as the building block for the dimensions of every aspect of Santo Spirito. This unit, repeated throughout the interior, creates a rhythmic harmony. For example, the nave is twice as high as it is wide; the arcade and clerestory are of equal height, which means the arcade's height equals the nave's width; and so on. Crisp joinings delineate these basic facts about the building

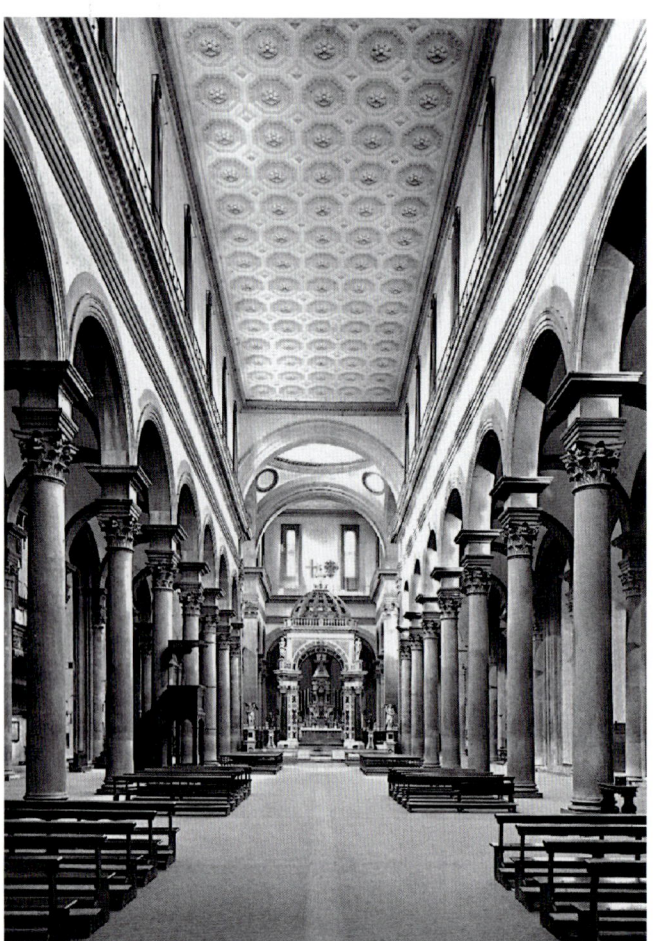

21-15 FILIPPO BRUNELLESCHI, interior of Santo Spirito (view facing east), Florence, Italy, begun ca. 1436.

does not reflect Brunelleschi's original design. The narthex, admirable as it is, seems to have been added as an afterthought, perhaps by the sculptor-architect GIULIANO DA MAIANO (1432–1490). Historians have suggested that the local chapter of Franciscan monks who held meetings in the chapel needed the expansion. Behind the narthex stands one of the first independent Renaissance buildings conceived basically as a central-plan structure. Although the plan (FIG. 21-18) is rectangular, rather than square or round, the architect placed all emphasis on the central dome-covered space. The short barrel-vault sections that brace the dome on two sides appear to be incidental appendages. The interior trim (FIG. 21-19) is done in gray stone, the so-called *pietra serena* ("serene stone"), which stands out against the white stuccoed walls and crisply defines the modular relationships of plan and elevation. As in his design for Santo Spirito, Brunelleschi used a basic unit that allowed him to construct a balanced, harmonious, and regularly proportioned space. Medallions with glazed terracotta reliefs representing the Four Evangelists in the dome's pendentives and the Twelve Apostles on the pilaster-framed wall panels provide the tranquil interior with striking color accents.

A PALACE FIT FOR A MEDICI   It seems curious that Brunelleschi, the most renowned architect of his time, did not participate in the upsurge of palace building Florence experienced in the 1430s and 1440s. This proliferation of palazzos testified to the Florentine economy's stability and to the affluence and confidence of the city's leading citizens. Brunelleschi, however, confined his efforts in this field to work on the Palazzo di Parte Guelfa (headquarters of Florence's ruling "party") and to a rejected model for a new palace that Cosimo de' Medici intended to build.

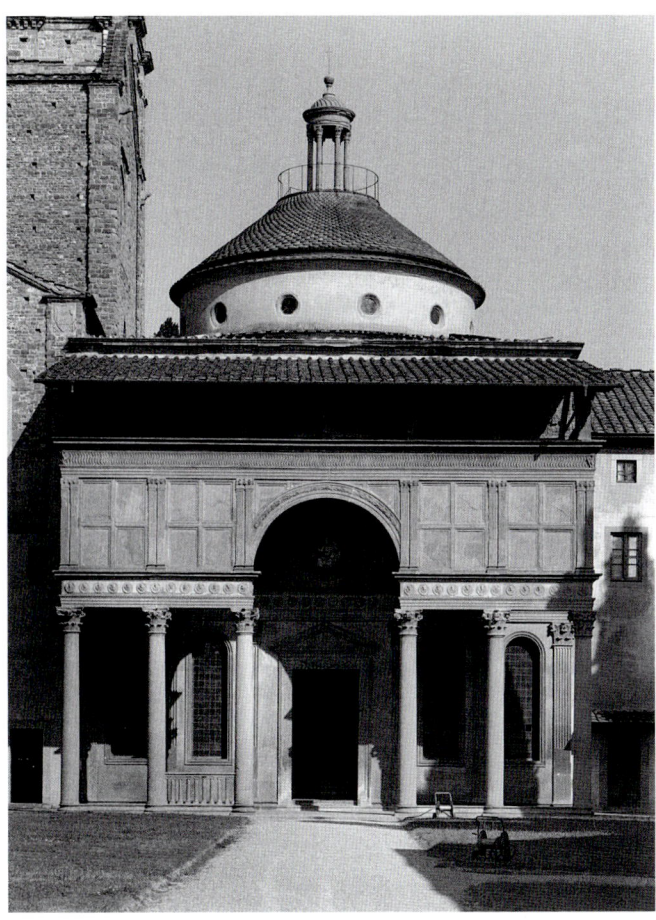

21-17 FILIPPO BRUNELLESCHI, west facade of the Pazzi Chapel, Santa Croce, Florence, Italy, begun ca. 1440.

for observers so that they can read them like mathematical equations. The austerity of the decor enhances the restful and tranquil atmosphere. Brunelleschi left no space for expansive wall frescoes that only would interrupt the clarity of his architectural scheme. The design's calculated logic echoes those of classical buildings such as Roman basilicas. Further, the rationality of Santo Spirito contrasts sharply with the soaring drama and spirituality of the vaults and nave arcades of Gothic churches. It even deviates from those in Italy, such as the Florence Cathedral nave (see FIG. 19-13), whose verticality is restrained in comparison to their northern counterparts. Santo Spirito fully expressed the new Renaissance spirit that placed its faith in reason rather than in the emotions.

A FAMILY GIFT WITH A CENTRAL DOME
Brunelleschi's apparent effort to impart a centralized effect to the interior of Santo Spirito suggests he was intrigued by the compact and self-contained qualities of earlier central-plan buildings, such as the Roman Pantheon (see FIG. 10-50). The chapel (FIGS. **21-17** to **21-19**) that was the Pazzi family's gift to the church of Santa Croce in Florence presented Brunelleschi with the opportunity to explore this interest in a structure much better suited to such a design than a basilican church. Brunelleschi began to design the Pazzi Chapel around 1440. It was not completed until the 1460s, long after his death (see "Honoring God and Family: Family Chapel Endowments," page 609). The exterior (FIG. 21-17) probably

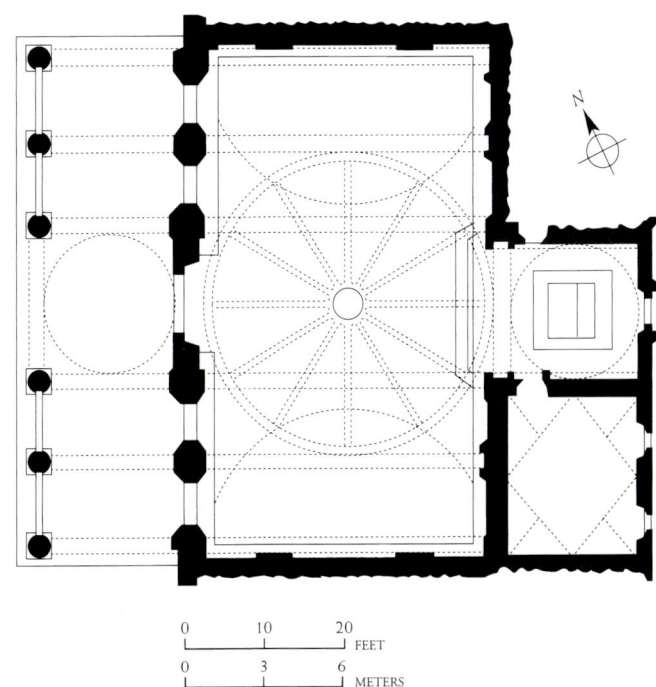

21-18 FILIPPO BRUNELLESCHI, plan of the Pazzi Chapel, Santa Croce, Florence, Italy.

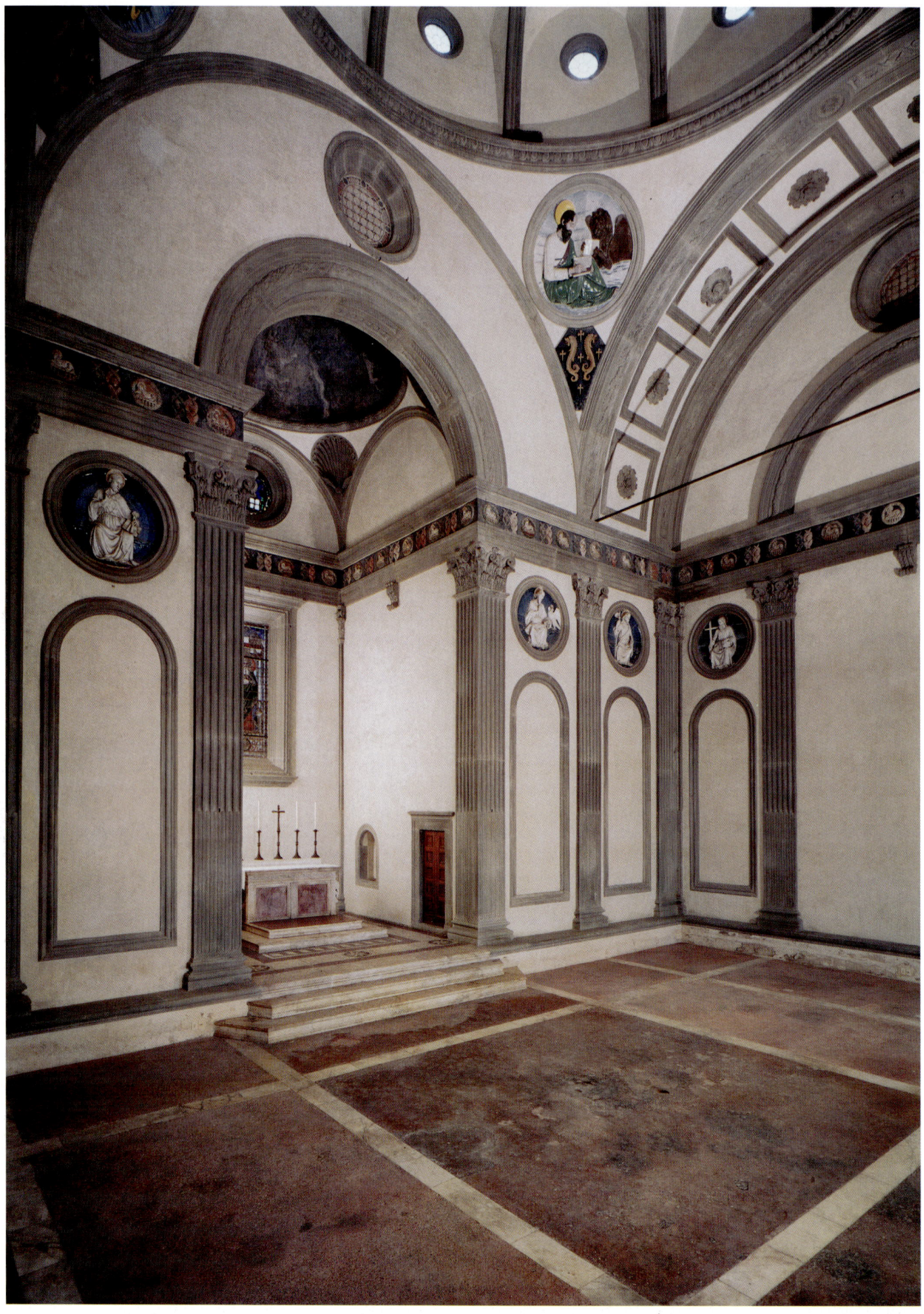

21-19 Filippo Brunelleschi, interior of the Pazzi Chapel (view facing northeast), Santa Croce, Florence, Italy, begun ca. 1440.

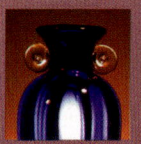

Honoring God and Family
Family Chapel Endowments

During the fourteenth through sixteenth centuries in Italy, wealthy families regularly endowed chapels in or adjacent to major churches. These family chapels usually were located on either side of the choir near the altar at the church's east end. Particularly wealthy families endowed chapels in the form of separate buildings constructed adjacent to churches. For example, the Medici chapel (Old Sacristy) abuts San Lorenzo in Florence. Powerful banking families, such as the Baroncelli, Bardi, and Peruzzi, each sponsored chapels in the Florentine church of Santa Croce. The Pazzi commissioned a chapel (FIGS. 21-17, 21-18, and 21-19) adjacent to Santa Croce, and the Brancacci family sponsored the decorative program (FIGS. 21-11 and 21-12) of their chapel in Santa Maria del Carmine.

These families sponsored such chapels as expressions of piety and devotion. The chapels also served as burial sites for important family members and as spaces for liturgical celebrations and commemorative services. Chapel owners sponsored Masses for the dead, praying to the Virgin Mary and the saints for intercession on behalf of their deceased loved ones. Changes in Christian doctrine prompted these concerted efforts to improve individuals' chances for eternal salvation. Un-

til the thirteenth century, Christians believed that after death souls went either to Heaven or Hell. After that time, the concept of Purgatory—a way station between Heaven and Hell where souls could atone for sins before Judgment Day—increasingly won favor. Pope Innocent III recognized the existence of such a place in 1215 at the Fourth Lateran Council (a major church council that dealt with redefining church doctrine). Because Purgatory represented an opportunity for the faithful to improve their chances of eventually gaining admittance to Heaven, they eagerly embraced this opportunity. They extended this idea to improving their chances while alive, so charitable work, good deeds, and devotional practices proliferated. Family chapels provided the space necessary for the performance of devotional rituals. Most chapels included altars, as well as chalices, vestments, candlesticks, and other objects used in the Mass. Most patrons also commissioned decorations, such as painted altarpieces, frescoes on the walls, and sculptural objects.

Thus, families endowed these chapels to ensure the well-being of the souls of individual family members and ancestors. The gifts also honored the families themselves and burnished their images in the larger community.

Early in the fifteenth century, Giovanni de' Medici (ca. 1360–1429) had established the family fortune. Cosimo (1389–1464) expanded his family's financial control, which led to considerable political power as well. This consolidation of power in a city that prided itself on its republicanism did not go unchallenged. In the early 1430s, a power struggle with other wealthy families led to the Medici's expulsion from Florence. In 1434, the Medici returned, and Cosimo resumed his position as de facto ruler of Florence. However, aware of the importance of public perception, he attempted to maintain a lower profile and continued to wield his power from behind the scenes. In all probability, this attitude accounted for his rejection of Brunelleschi's design for the Medici residence. Cosimo evidently found Brunelleschi's project too imposing and ostentatious to be politically wise. Cosimo eventually awarded the commission to MICHELOZZO DI BARTOLOMMEO (1396–1472), a young architect who had been Donatello's collaborator in several sculptural enterprises. Although Cosimo chose Michelozzo instead of Brunelleschi, Brunelleschi's architectural style in fact deeply influenced the young architect. To a limited extent, the Palazzo Medici-Riccardi (FIG. **21-20**) reflects Brunelleschian principles.

Later bought by the Riccardi family, who almost doubled the facade's length in the eighteenth century, the palace, both in its original and extended form, is a simple, massive structure. Heavy rustication on the ground floor accentuates its strength. Michelozzo divided the building block into stories of decreasing height by long, unbroken stringcourses (horizontal bands), which give it coherence. Dressed stone on the upper levels, which smoothens the surface with each successive story, modifies the severity of the ground floor. The building thus appears progressively lighter as the eye moves upward. The extremely heavy cornice, which Michelozzo related not to the top story but to the building as a whole, dramatically reverses this effect. Like the ancient Roman cornices that served as Michelozzo's models (compare, for example, FIGS. 10-30, 10-37, and 10-45), the Palazzo Medici-Riccardi cornice is a very effective lid for the structure, clearly and emphatically defining its proportions. Michelozzo also may have been inspired by the many extant examples of Roman rusticated masonry, and Roman precedents even exist for the juxtaposition of rusticated and dressed stone masonry on the same facade (see FIG. 10-32). However, nothing in the ancient world precisely compares to Michelozzo's design. The Palazzo Medici-Riccardi is an excellent example of the simultaneous

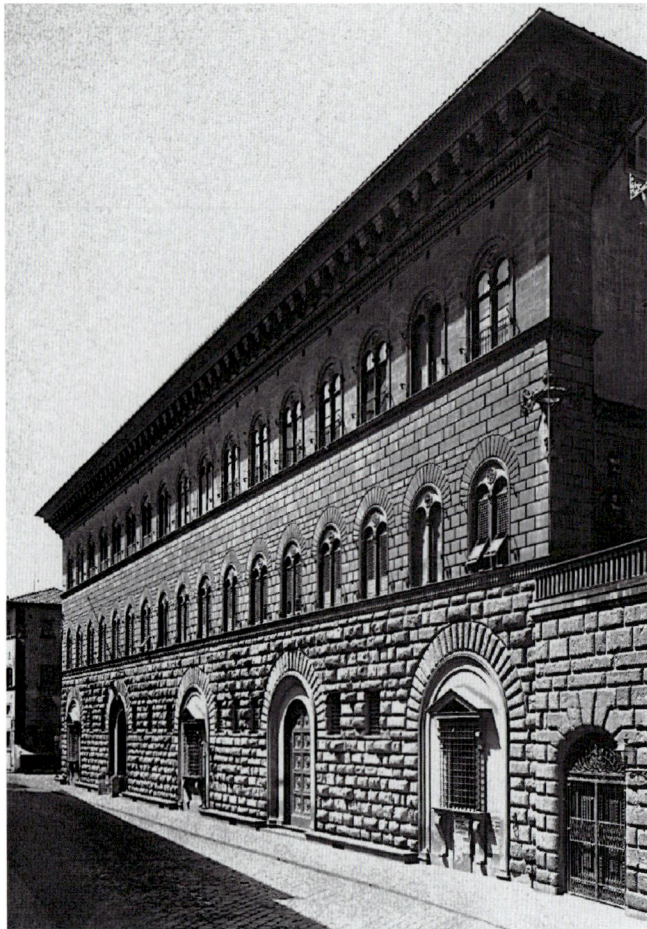

21-20 MICHELOZZO DI BARTOLOMMEO, facade of the Palazzo Medici-Riccardi, Florence, Italy, begun 1444.

respect for and independence from the antique that characterize the Early Renaissance in Italy.

The Palazzo Medici-Riccardi is built around an open colonnaded court (FIG. **21-21**) that clearly shows Michelozzo's debt to Brunelleschi. The round-arched colonnade, although more massive in its proportions, closely resembles other buildings by Brunelleschi. Ultimately, this internal court surrounded by an arcade was the first of its kind and influenced a long line of descendants in Renaissance domestic architecture.

THE MAGNIFICENT MEDICI The references to classical architecture in the Palazzo Medici-Riccardi's design were entirely appropriate for its patrons. The Medici were avid humanists. Cosimo began the first public library since the ancient world, and historians estimate that in some thirty years he and his descendants expended the equivalent of almost $20 million for manuscripts and books. Beyond their enthusiastic collecting of classical and Renaissance literature, the Medici were voracious art collectors. Scarcely a great architect, painter, sculptor, philosopher, or humanist scholar escaped the Medici's notice.

Cosimo was the very model of the cultivated humanist. His grandson Lorenzo (1449–1492), called "the Magnificent," achieved an even greater reputation for generosity than his grandfather, as his name suggests. A talented poet himself, Lorenzo gathered about him a galaxy of artists and gifted men in all fields, extending the library Cosimo had begun and revitalizing his academy for instructing artists. He also established what some have called the Platonic Academy of Philosophy

21-21 MICHELOZZO DI BARTOLOMMEO, interior court of the Palazzo Medici-Riccardi, Florence, Italy, begun 1444.

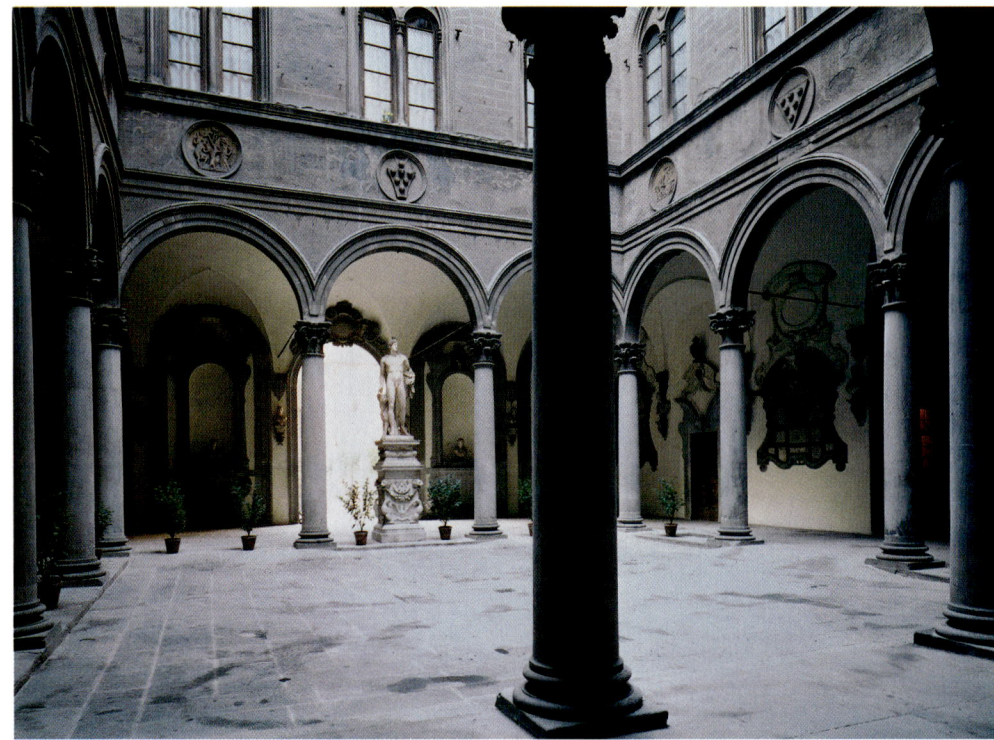

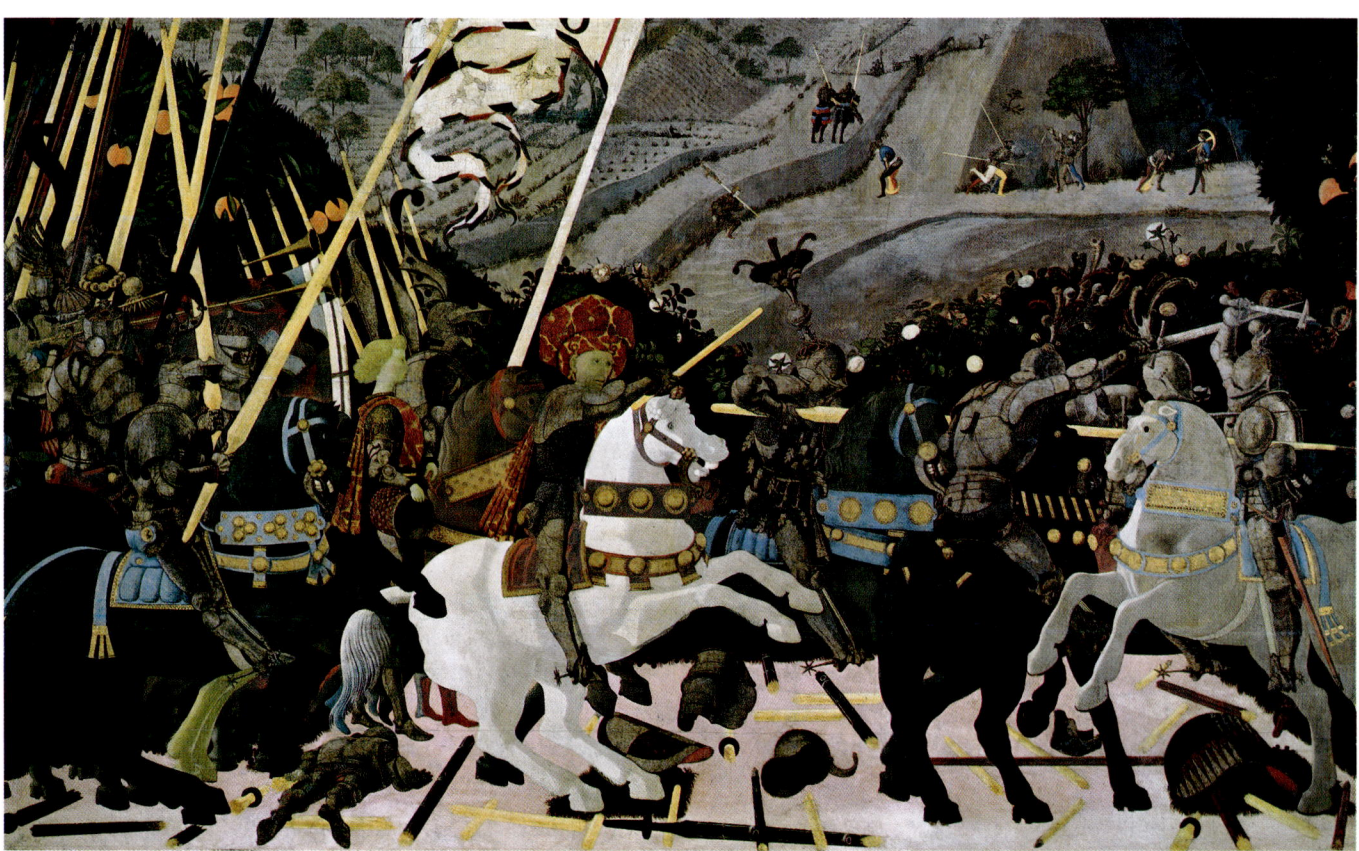

21-22 PAOLO UCCELLO, *Battle of San Romano*, ca. 1455. Tempera on wood, approx. 6′ × 10′ 5″. National Gallery, London.

(most likely an informal reading group), and lavished funds (often the city's own) on splendid buildings, festivals, and pageants. A review here of some of the hundreds of artworks the Medici commissioned reveals the family's interest in humanist ideas and its concern about its public image.

SIMULTANEOUSLY CHAOTIC AND ORDERED PAOLO UCCELLO (1397–1475), a Florentine painter trained in the International Style, received a commission from Lorenzo de' Medici to produce a series of panel paintings. Uccello painted *Battle of San Romano* (FIG. **21-22**), one of three wood panels (all with the same title), to decorate Lorenzo the Magnificent's bedchamber. The scenes commemorate the Florentine victory over the Sienese in 1432. In the panel illustrated, Niccolò da Tolentino, a friend and supporter of Cosimo, leads the charge against the Sienese. Lorenzo may have selected this particular image to commemorate Tolentino, whose subsequent death perhaps was due to his friendship with the Medici. Although the painting focuses on Tolentino's military exploits, it also acknowledges the Medici. The reference appears in symbolic form. The bright orange fruit (appropriately placed) behind the unbroken and sturdy lances on the left were known as *mela medica* (medicinal apples). Given that the name Medici means "doctor," this fruit was a fitting symbol (one of many) of the family.

Uccello's obsession with perspective undoubtedly appealed to Lorenzo. The development of perspectival systems intrigued the humanists, because perspective represented the rationalization of vision. As staunch humanists, the Medici pursued all facets of expanding knowledge. In *Battle of San Romano,* Uccello created a composition that recalls the processional splendor of Gentile's *Adoration of the Magi* (FIG. 21-10). But in contrast with the surface decoration of Gentile's International Style, Uccello constructed his world of immobilized solid forms. He foreshortened broken spears, lances, and a fallen soldier and carefully placed them along the converging orthogonals of the perspective to create a base plane like a checkerboard, on which he then placed the larger volumes in measured intervals. This diligently created space recedes to a landscape that resembles the low cultivated hillsides between Florence and Lucca. The rendering of three-dimensional form, used by other painters for representational or expressive purposes, became for Uccello a preoccupation. For him, it had a magic of its own, which he exploited to satisfy his inventive and original imagination.

A CLASSICALLY INSPIRED DAVID The Medici worked tirelessly to acquire art from the most esteemed artists, and they identified Donatello as among those worthy of receiving their coveted commissions. The bronze statue

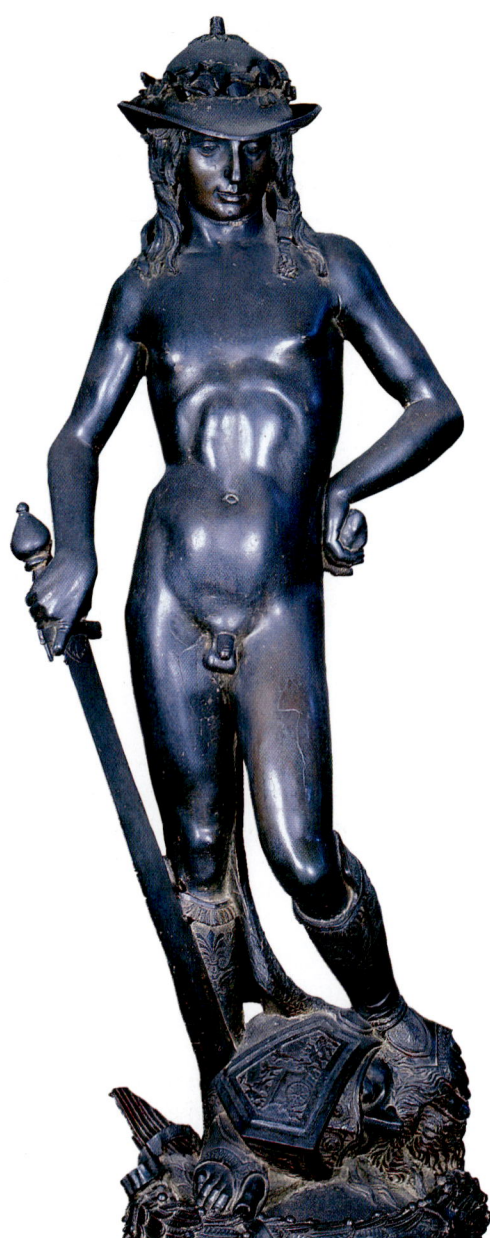

21-23 DONATELLO, *David*, ca. 1428–1432. Bronze, 5′ 2¼″ high. Museo Nazionale del Bargello, Florence.

David (FIG. **21-23**), created between about 1428 and 1432 by Donatello for the Palazzo Medici courtyard, was the first freestanding nude statue since ancient times. The nude, as such, proscribed in the Christian Middle Ages as both indecent and idolatrous, had been shown only rarely—and then only in biblical or moralizing contexts, such as the story of Adam and Eve or descriptions of sinners in Hell. Donatello reinvented the classical nude, even though his subject is not a pagan god, hero, or athlete but the biblical David, the young slayer of Goliath and the symbol of the independent Florentine republic. David possesses both the relaxed classical contrapposto stance and the proportions and sensuous beauty of Greek Praxitelean gods (see FIG. 5-62), qualities absent from medieval figures. The invoking of classical poses and formats appealed to the humanist Medici.

The Medici were aware of Donatello's earlier *David*, a sculpture located in the Palazzo della Signoria, the center of political activity in Florence. The artist had produced it during the threat of invasion by King Ladislaus, and it became a symbol of Florentine strength and independence. Their selection of the same subject suggests that the Medici identified themselves with Florence or, at the very least, saw themselves as responsible for Florence's prosperity and freedom.

CELEBRATING THE MEDICI AND FLORENCE

Another David sculpture produced by one of the most important sculptors during the second half of the century, ANDREA DEL VERROCCHIO (1435–1488), reaffirms this identification of the Medici with Florence. A painter as well as a sculptor, with something of Donatello's versatility and depth, Verrocchio directed a flourishing *bottega* (studio-shop) in Florence that attracted many students, among them Leonardo da Vinci. Verrocchio, like Donatello, also had a broad repertoire. His *David* (FIG. **21-24**) contrasts strongly in its narrative realism with the quiet, aesthetic classicism of Donatello's *David*. Verrocchio's *David*—made for Lorenzo de' Medici to exhibit in the Palazzo Medici—is a sturdy, wiry young apprentice

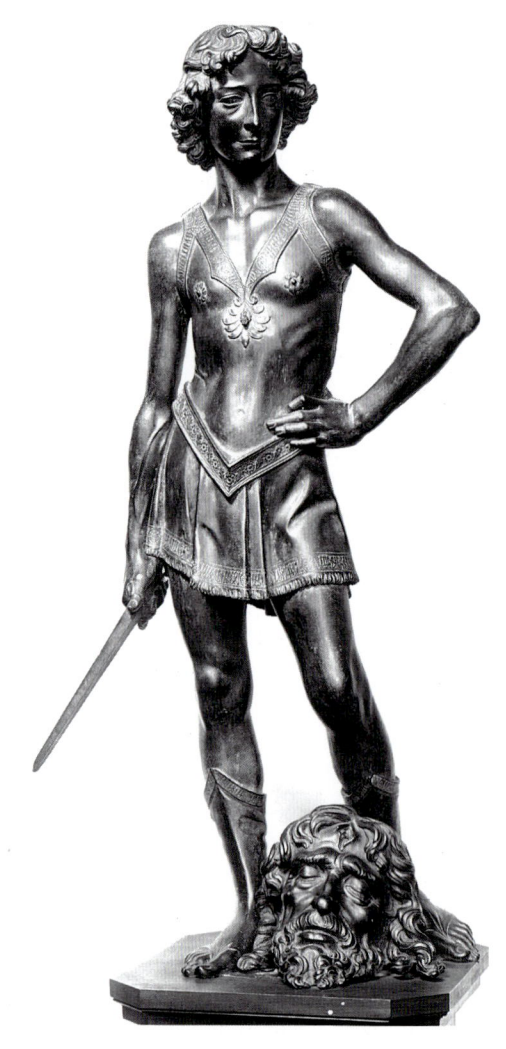

21-24 ANDREA DEL VERROCCHIO, *David*, ca. 1465–1470. Bronze, approx. 4′ 1½″ high. Museo Nazionale del Bargello, Florence.

Donatello's *David, Hercules and Antaeus* exhibits the stress and strain of the human figure in violent action. This sculpture departs dramatically from the convention of frontality that had dominated statuary art during the Middle Ages and the Early Renaissance. Not quite eighteen inches high, *Hercules and Antaeus* embodies the ferocity and vitality of elemental physical conflict. The group illustrates the Greek myth of a wrestling match between Antaeus (Antaios), a giant and son of Earth, and Hercules (Herakles). As seen earlier, Euphronios represented this story on an ancient Greek vase (see FIG. 5-21). Each time Hercules threw him down, Antaeus sprang up again, his strength renewed by contact with the earth. Finally, Hercules held him aloft, so that he could not touch the earth, and strangled him around the waist. Pollaiuolo strove to convey the final excruciating moments of the struggle—the straining and cracking of sinews, the clenched teeth of Hercules, and the kicking and screaming of Antaeus. The figures intertwine and interlock as they fight, and the flickering reflections of light on the dark gouged bronze surface contribute to the effect of agitated movement and a fluid play of planes. The subject matter, derived from Greek mythology, and the emphasis on human anatomy reveal the Medici preference for humanist-affiliated imagery. Even more specifically, Hercules had been represented on Florence's state seal since the end of the thirteenth century. As with commissions such as the two *David* sculptures, the Medici clearly embraced every opportunity to associate themselves with the glory of the Florentine republic, surely claiming much of the credit for it.

A GRAPHIC IMAGE OF BATTLING NUDES Although not commissioned by the Medici, Pollaiuolo's *Battle of the Ten Nudes* (FIG. **21-26**) further demonstrates the artist's sustained interest in the realistic presentation of human figures in action. Earlier artists, such as Donatello and Masaccio, had dealt effectively with the problem of rendering human anatomy, but they usually depicted their figures at rest or in restrained motion. As is evident in his *Hercules and Antaeus,* Pollaiuolo took delight in showing violent action and found his opportunity in subjects dealing with combat. He conceived the body as a powerful machine and liked to display its mechanisms—knotted muscles and taut sinews activate the skeleton as ropes pull levers. To show this to best effect, Pollaiuolo developed a figure so lean and muscular that it appears *écorché* (as if without skin), with strongly accentuated delineations at the wrists, elbows, shoulders, and knees. His *Battle of the Ten Nudes* engraving shows this figure type in a variety of poses and from numerous viewpoints. The composition has no specific mythological or historical subject. Rather, it was an excuse for Pollaiuolo to demonstrate his prowess in rendering the nude male figure. In this, he was a kindred spirit of late-sixth-century Greek vase painters, such as Euthymides (see FIG. 5-22), who had experimented with foreshortening for the first time in history. If Pollaiuolo's figures, even though they hack and slash at each other without mercy, seem somewhat stiff and frozen, it is because Pollaiuolo shows *all* the muscle groups at maximum tension. Not until several decades later did an even greater anatomist, Leonardo, observe that only part of the body's muscle groups are involved in any one action, while the others are relaxed.

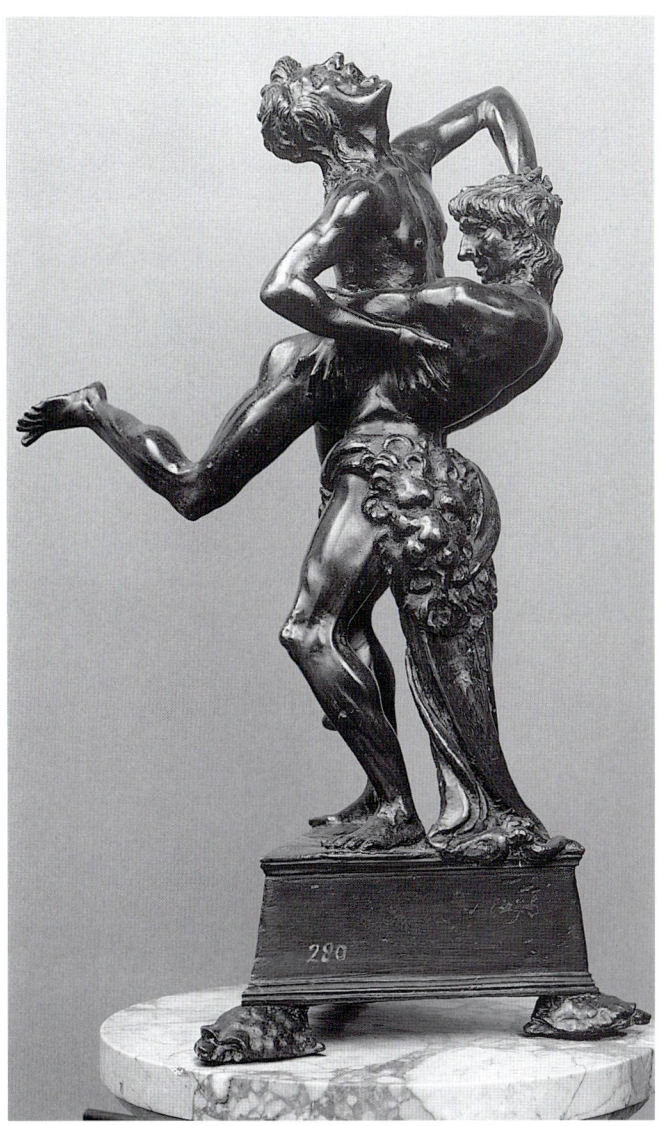

21-25 ANTONIO POLLAIUOLO, *Hercules and Antaeus,* ca. 1475. Bronze, approx. 18″ high with base. Museo Nazionale del Bargello, Florence.

clad in a leathern doublet who stands with a jaunty pride. As in Donatello's version, Goliath's head lies at David's feet. He poses like any sportsman who has just won a game or like a hunter with his kill. The easy balance of the weight and the lithe, still thinly adolescent musculature, with prominent veins, show how closely Verrocchio read the biblical text and how clearly he knew the psychology of brash and confident young men.

Lorenzo and Giuliano de' Medici eventually sold Verrocchio's bronze *David* to the Florentine *signoria* (a governing body) for placement in the Palazzo della Signoria. After the Medici were expelled from Florence, city officials appropriated Donatello's *David* for civic use and moved it to the Palazzo as well.

A MYTHIC WRESTLING MATCH Closely related in stylistic intent to Verrocchio's work is that of ANTONIO POLLAIUOLO (ca. 1431–1498). Pollaiuolo, who is also important as a painter and engraver, received a Medici commission in the 1470s to produce a small-scale sculpture, *Hercules and Antaeus* (FIG. **21-25**). In contrast to the placid presentation of

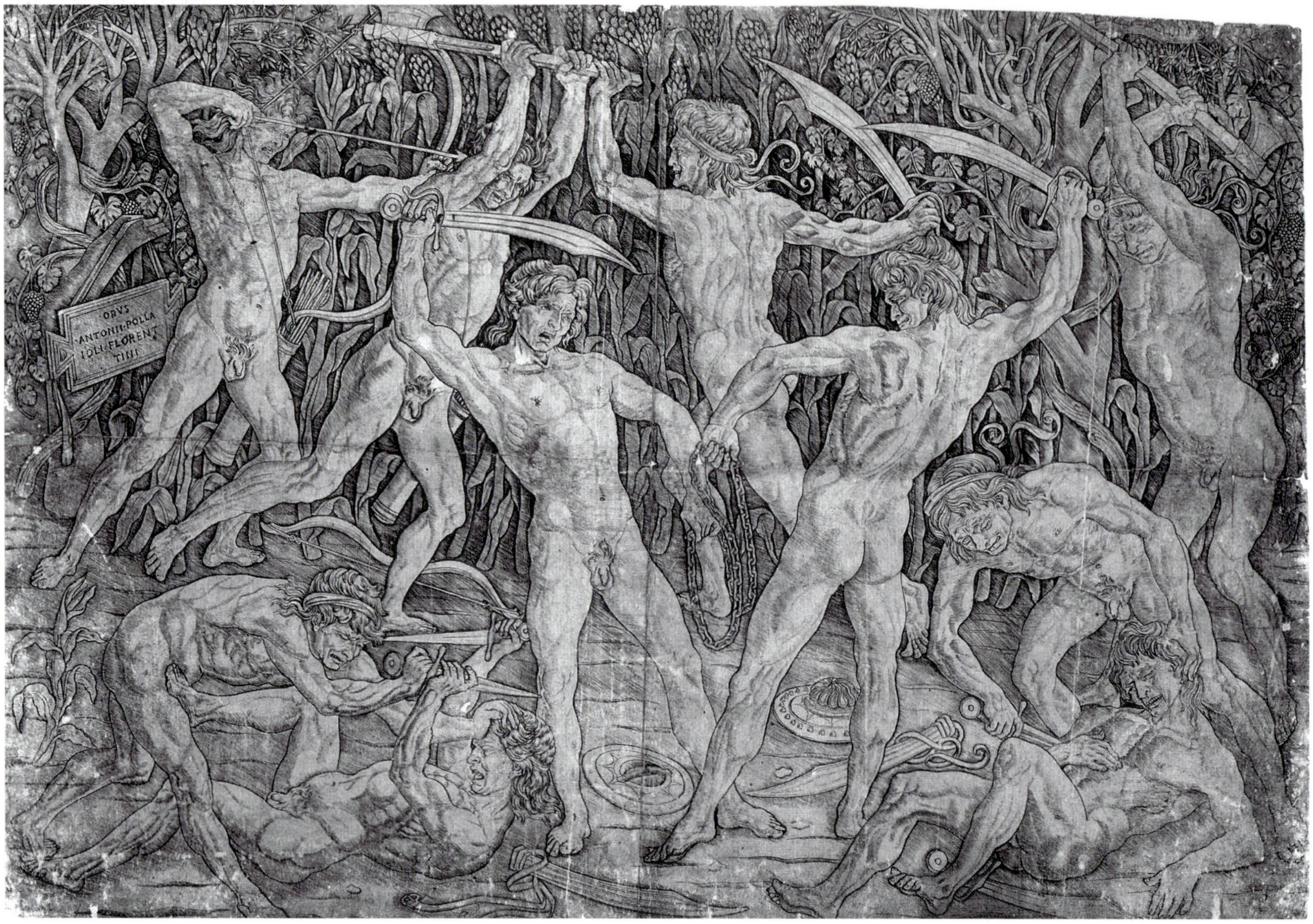

21-26 Antonio Pollaiuolo, *Battle of the Ten Nudes,* ca. 1465. Engraving, approx. 1′ 3″ × 1′ 11″. Metropolitan Museum of Art, New York (bequest of Joseph Pulitzer, 1917).

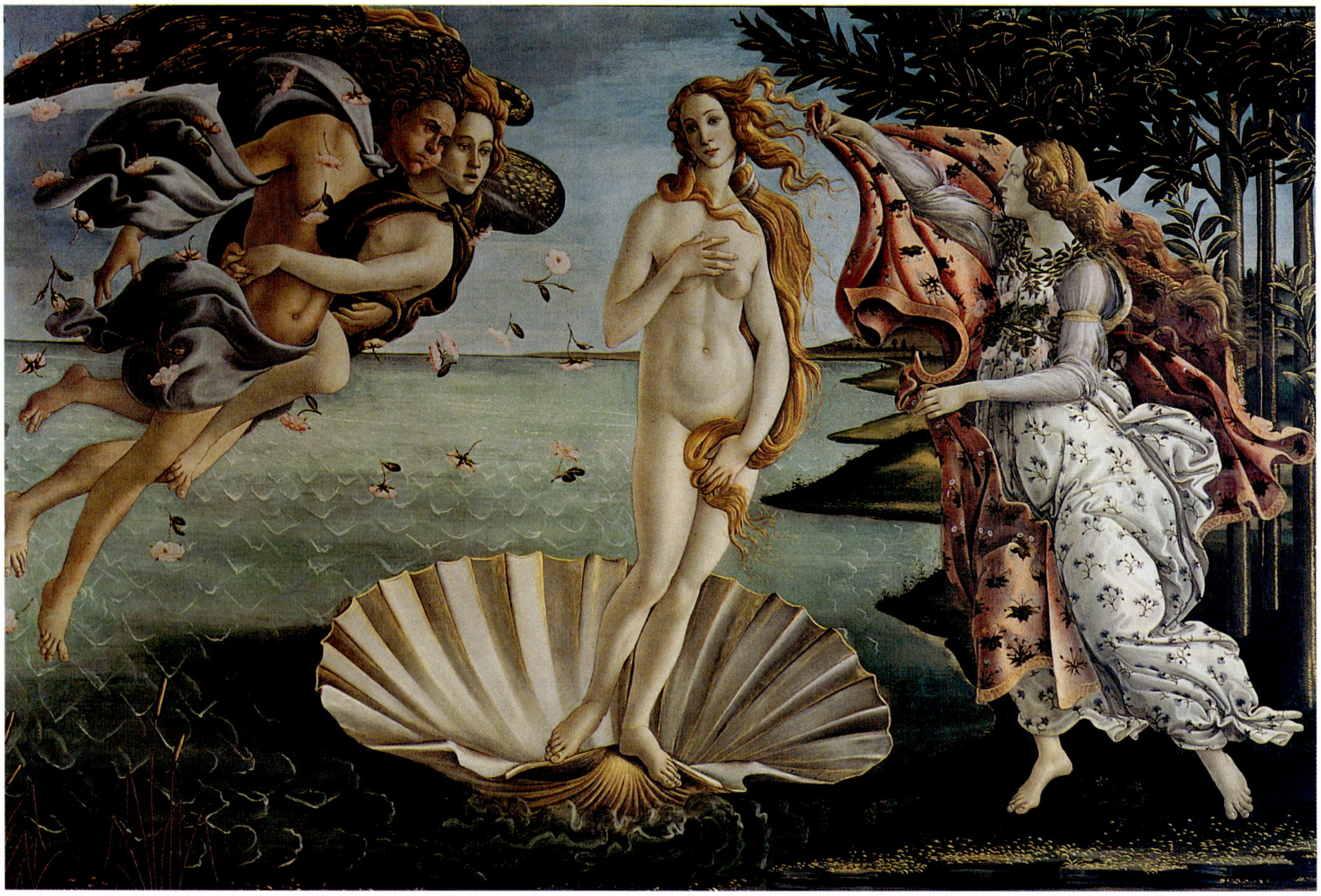

21-27 Sandro Botticelli, *Birth of Venus,* ca. 1482. Tempera on canvas, approx. 5′ 8″ × 9′ 1″. Galleria degli Uffizi, Florence.

As an engraving, Pollaiuolo's *Battle of the Ten Nudes* is a new medium, as discussed earlier, that northern European artists probably developed around the middle of the fifteenth century. But whereas German graphic artists, such as Martin Schongauer (see FIG. 20-26), described their forms with hatching that follows the forms, Italian engravers, such as Pollaiuolo, preferred parallel hatching. The former method was in keeping with the general northern approach to art, which tended to describe surfaces of forms, rather than their underlying structures, while the latter was better suited for the anatomical studies that preoccupied Pollaiuolo and his Italian contemporaries.

VISUAL POETRY SANDRO BOTTICELLI (1444–1510) remains among the best known of the artists who produced works for the Medici. One of the works he painted in tempera on canvas for the Medici was his famous *Birth of Venus* (FIG. **21-27**). A poem on that theme by Angelo Poliziano, one of the leading humanists of the day, inspired Botticelli to create this lyrical image. Zephyrus (the west wind) blows Venus, born of the sea foam and carried on a cockle shell, to her sacred island, Cyprus. There, the nymph Pomona runs to meet her with a brocaded mantle. The lightness and bodilessness of the winds move all the figures without effort. Draperies undulate easily in the gentle gusts, perfumed by rose petals that fall on the whitecaps. Botticelli's nude presentation of the Venus figure was in itself an innovation. As mentioned earlier, the nude, especially the female nude, had been proscribed during the Middle Ages. Its appearance on such a scale and the artist's use of an ancient Venus statue of the Venus *pudica* (modest Venus) type—a Hellenistic variant of Praxiteles' famous *Aphrodite of Knidos* (see FIG. 5-60)—as a model could have drawn the charge of paganism and infidelity. But in the more accommodating Renaissance culture and under the protection of the powerful Medici, the depiction went unchallenged.

Botticelli's style is clearly distinct from the earnest search many other artists pursued to comprehend humanity and the natural world through a rational and empirical order. Indeed, Botticelli's elegant and beautiful style seems to have ignored all of the scientific knowledge experimental art had gained (for example, in the areas of perspective and anatomy). His style paralleled the allegorical pageants staged in Florence as chivalric tournaments but structured around allusions to classical mythology; the same trend is evident in the poetry of the 1470s and 1480s. Artists and poets at this time did not directly imitate classical antiquity but used the myths, with delicate perception of their charm, in a way still tinged with medieval romance. Ultimately, Botticelli created a style of visual poetry, parallel to the Petrarchan love poetry Lorenzo de' Medici wrote. His paintings possess a lyricism and courtliness that appealed to cultured patrons such as the Medici.

As evidenced by these Medici commissions, the Florentine family did not restrict their collecting to any specific style or artist. Their acquisitions, as already noted, often incorporated elements associated with humanism, from mythological subject matter to concerns with anatomy and perspective. Collectively, the art of the Medici also makes a statement about the patrons themselves. Careful businessmen that they were, the Medici were not sentimental about their endowment of art

and scholarship. Cosimo acknowledged that his good works were not only for the honor of God but also to construct his own legacy. This is not to suggest that the Medici were solely self-serving—throughout the century, Medici family members demonstrated a sustained and sincere love of learning.

THE RISE OF PORTRAITURE

Portraiture in Florence

With humanism's increased emphasis on individual achievement and recognition, portraiture enjoyed a revival in the fifteenth century. Commemorative portraits of the deceased were common, and patrons also commissioned portraits of themselves. The profile pose was customary in Florence until about 1470, when three-quarter and full-face portraits began to replace it. Bust-length portraits based on Roman precedents also became prominent.

A PSYCHOLOGICAL PROFILE In about the last decade of the fifteenth century, Sandro Botticelli painted the nearly full-face *Portrait of a Youth* (FIG. **21-28**). Painters of northern Europe (see FIGS. 20-15 and 20-16) popularized three-quarter and full-face views earlier in the century. The Italian painters adopted these views believing that such poses

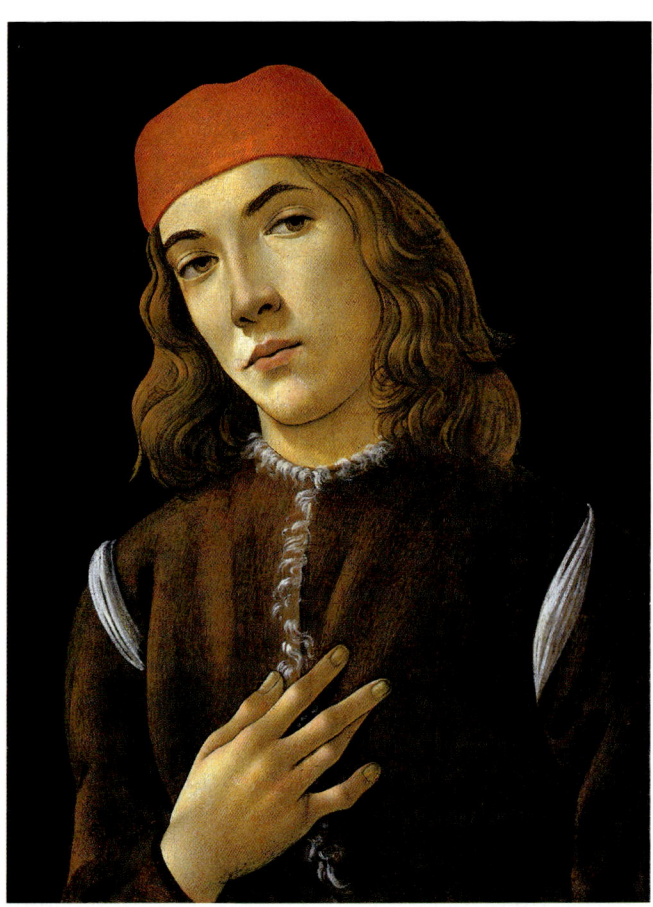

21-28 SANDRO BOTTICELLI, *Portrait of a Youth,* early 1480s. Tempera on panel, 1′ 4″ × 1′. National Gallery of Art, Washington (Andrew W. Mellon Collection).

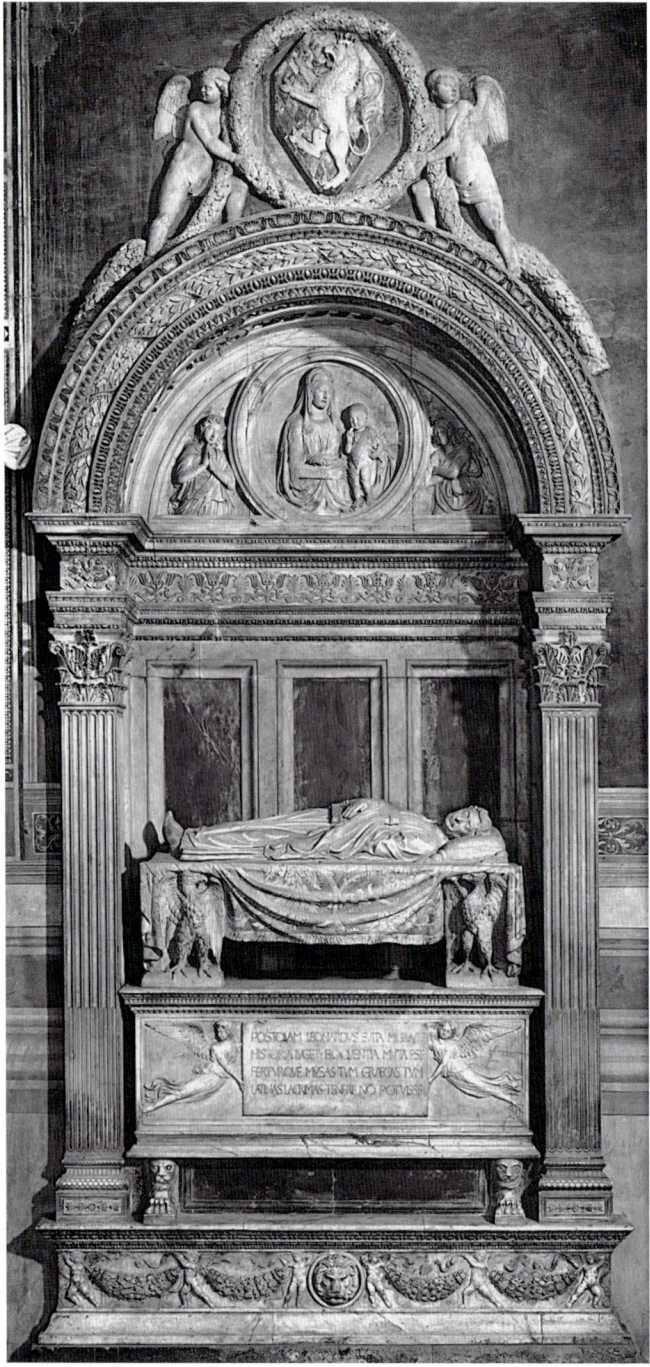

21-29 BERNARDO ROSSELLINO, tomb of Leonardo Bruni, Santa Croce, Florence, Italy, ca. 1445–1450. Marble, approx. 20′ high to top of arch.

form. Botticelli infinitely refined this method, and art historians recognize him as one of the great masters of line.

A TRIBUTE TO A HUMANIST SCHOLAR   The tomb of Leonardo Bruni (1370–1444) in Santa Croce in Florence (FIG. **21-29**) beautifully expressed the prevailing dedication to the values of classical antiquity. Its sculptor, BERNARDO ROSSELLINO (1409–1464), like the man whose tomb he built, was at one time a resident of Arezzo, a city southeast of Florence. Rossellino aimed at nothing less than the immortalization of his fellow citizen. Wall tombs have a history that reaches back into the Middle Ages, but Rossellino's version was new and definitive—the expression of an age deliberately turning away from the medieval past.

Bruni was one of the most distinguished men of Italy and served as chancellor of Florence from 1427 until his death in 1444. When he died, people from far and wide mourned his passing. As a scholar in Greek and Latin, diplomat, and apostolic secretary to four popes, Bruni's career summed up the humanist ideal. The Florentines particularly praised him for his *History of Florence*. In his honor, citizens revived the funeral oration practice and the ancient custom of crowning the deceased with laurel. The historic event of the crowning of

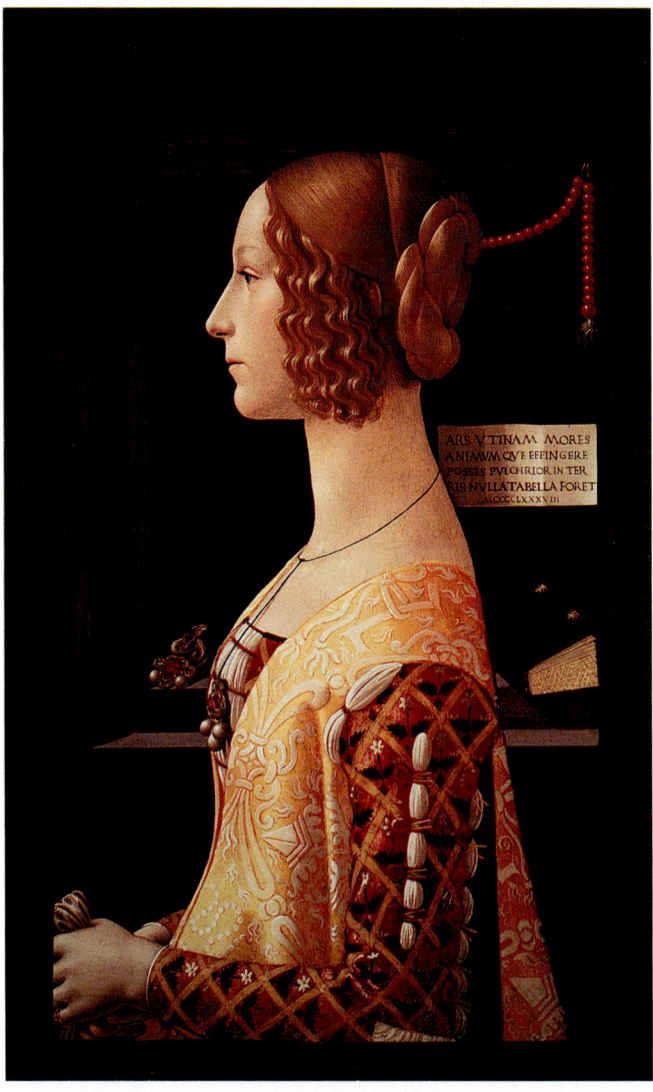

21-30 DOMENICO GHIRLANDAIO, *Giovanna Tornabuoni*(?), 1488. Oil and tempera on wood, approx. 2′ 6″ × 1′ 8″. Collection, Madrid, Spain.

increased the information available to viewers about the subject's appearance. Further, these poses permitted greater exploration of the subject's character, although Italian artists continued to favor an impersonal formality that concealed the private psychological person. An apparent exception, Botticelli's young man is highly expressive psychologically. The delicacy of the pose, the head's graceful tilt, the sidelong glance, and the elegant hand gesture compose an equivocal expression half musing and half insinuating. Botticelli merged feminine and masculine traits to make an image of rarefied beauty.

Botticelli was the pupil of Fra Filippo Lippi (FIG. 21-40), who must have taught him the method of "drawing" firm, pure outline with light shading within the contours. The effect is apparent in the portrait's explicit and sharply elegant the dead humanist may have given Rossellino his theme so that the tomb was a kind of memorialization of the laureate scene.

The deceased lies on the *catafalque* (a supporting framework) in a long gown, the *History of Florence* on his breast, with imperial Roman eagles holding up his couch drapery at the ends. Winged *genii* (guardian spirits) at the summit of the arch above the catafalque hold a great *escutcheon* (an emblem bearing a coat of arms). On the side of the sarcophagus, other genii support a Latin inscription that describes the Muses' grief at the scholar's passing. Rossellino carved Roman funeral garlands on the narrow platform at the base of the niche. The only unmistakably Christian reference is a Madonna and Child with angels in the tympanum. The artist revealed his intimate familiarity with ancient Italian art by selecting motifs that have specific sources in Etruscan and Roman funerary monuments. Rossellino would not have had to travel far to study examples of sculptured marble figures on the lids of their sarcophagi (for example, FIG. 10-62), and the conceit of having the deceased hold a book (or a scroll) attesting to his achievements in life also came directly from antiquity (see FIG. 9-14). Winged Victories displaying engraved epitaphs, putti (cherubic little boys) bearing garlands, and eagles (who carry the deceased to a heavenly afterlife) were also staples on Roman sarcophagi—which, like Bruni's, usually were set into niches in walls. A humanist and pagan classicism controls the design's mood in an evocation of the ancient Greco-Roman world.

AN ELEGANT AND CULTURED WOMAN

Women were also portrait subjects. DOMENICO GHIRLANDAIO (1449–1494) produced a portrait of an aristocratic young woman (FIG. **21-30**), probably Giovanna Tornabuoni, a member of the powerful Albizzi family and wife of Lorenzo Tornabuoni. Although artists did not often employ the profile pose to convey a character reading, this portrait reveals the proud bearing of a sensitive and beautiful young woman. It tells viewers much about the advanced state of culture in Florence, the value and careful cultivation of beauty in life and art, the breeding of courtly manners, and the great wealth behind it all. The painting also shows the powerful attraction classical literature held for Italian humanists; in the background an epitaph (Giovanna Tornabuoni died in childbirth in 1488) quotes the ancient Roman poet Martial.

SUMMARIZING PICTORIAL DEVELOPMENTS

Although Domenico Ghirlandaio did not develop a very innovative style, his art provides viewers with significant insight into artistic developments, summarizing as it does the state of Florentine art toward the end of the fifteenth century. His works expressed his times to perfection, and, because of this, he enjoyed great popularity among his contemporaries. Ghirlandaio's paintings also reveal a deep love for Florence, with its spectacles and pageantry, its material wealth and luxury. Giovanni Tornabuoni, one of the wealthiest Florentines of his day, commissioned Ghirlandaio's most representative pictures, a cycle of frescoes depicting scenes from the lives of the Virgin and Saint John the Baptist, for the choir of Santa Maria Novella. In the illustrated painting, *Birth of the Virgin* (FIG. **21-31**), Mary's mother, Saint Anne, reclines in a palace room embellished with fine *intarsia* (wood inlay) and sculpture, while midwives prepare the infant's bath. From the left comes a grave procession of women led by a young Tornabuoni family member, probably Ludovica, Giovanni's daughter. This splendidly dressed beauty holds as prominent

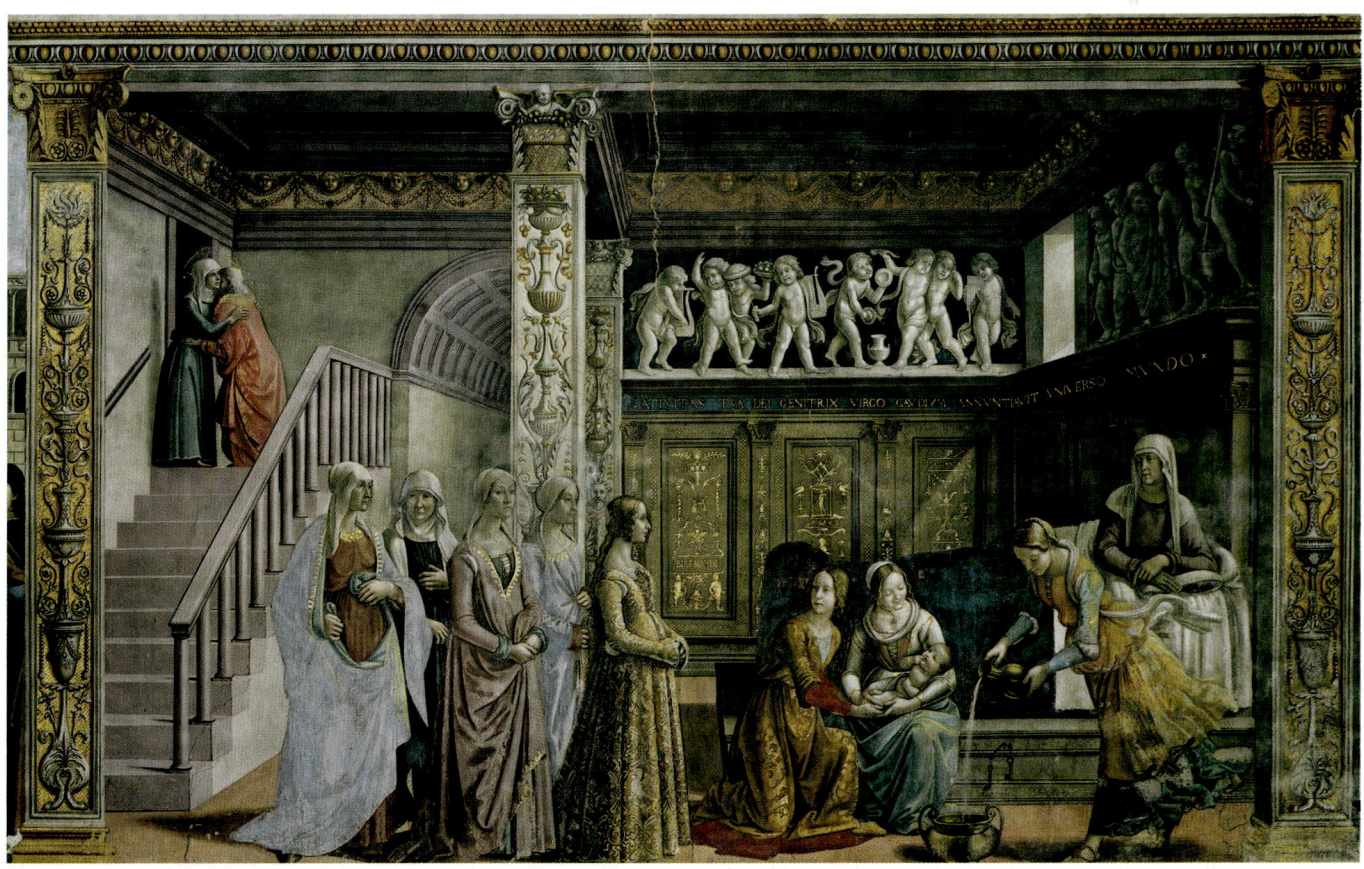

21-31 DOMENICO GHIRLANDAIO, *Birth of the Virgin,* Cappella Maggiore, Santa Maria Novella, Florence, Italy, 1485–1490. Fresco.

21-32 Donatello, *Gattamelata* (equestrian statue of Erasmo da Narni), Piazza del Santo, Padua, Italy, ca. 1445–1450. Bronze, approx. 11′ × 13′.

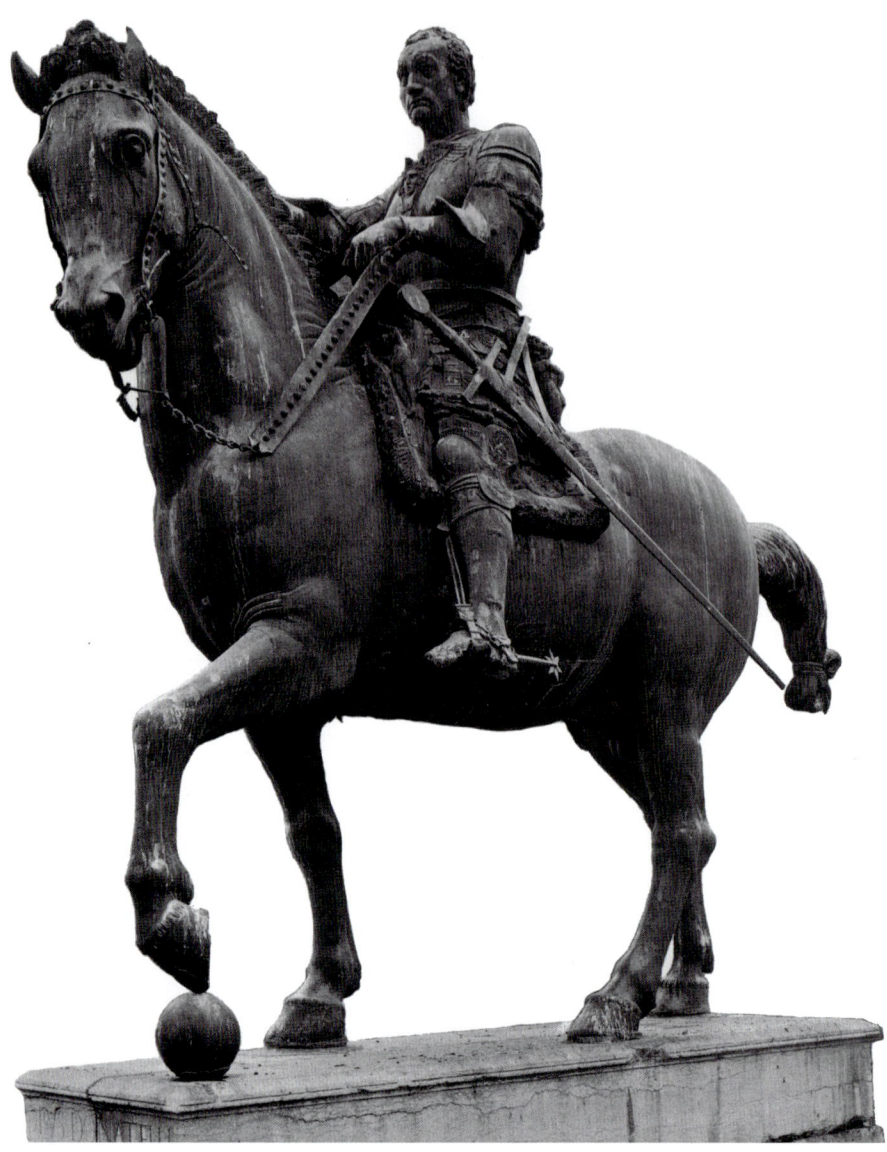

a place in the composition (close to the central axis) as she must have held in Florentine society. Her appearance in the painting (a different female member of the house appears in each fresco) is conspicuous evidence of the secularization of sacred themes—commonplace in art by this time. Artists depicted living persons of high rank not only as present at biblical dramas but also, as here, often stealing the show from the saints. The display of patrician elegance tempers the biblical narrative and subordinates the tableau's devotional nature.

Ghirlandaio's composition epitomizes the achievements of Early Renaissance painting: clear spatial representation; statuesque, firmly constructed figures; and rational order and logical relations among these figures and objects. If anything of earlier traits remains here, it is the arrangement of the figures, which still cling somewhat rigidly to layers parallel to the picture plane.

Portraiture outside of Florence

A CAT ON A HORSE   In 1443, Donatello left Florence for northern Italy to accept a rewarding commission from the Republic of Venice to create a commemorative monument in honor of the recently deceased Venetian condottiere Erasmo da Narni, nicknamed Gattamelata ("honeyed cat," a wordplay on his mother's name, Melania Gattelli). City officials asked Donatello to portray Gattamelata on horseback in a statue (FIG. **21-32**) to be erected in the square of Sant'Antonio in Padua. Although equestrian statues occasionally had been set up in Italy in the late Middle Ages, Donatello's *Gattamelata* is the first to rival the grandeur of the mounted portraits of antiquity, such as that of Marcus Aurelius (see FIG. 10-59), which the artist must have seen in Rome. Donatello's contemporaries, one of whom described Gattamelata as sitting "there with great magnificence like a triumphant Caesar," [5] recognized this reference to antiquity. The figure stands high on a lofty elliptical base, set apart from its surroundings, and almost celebrates sculpture's liberation from architecture. Massive and majestic, the great horse bears the armored general easily, for, unlike the sculptor of Marcus Aurelius, Donatello did not represent the Venetian commander as superhuman and more than life-size. The officer dominates his mighty steed by force of character rather than sheer size. Together, man and horse combine to convey an overwhelming image of irresistible strength and unlimited power—an impression Donatello reinforced visually by plac-

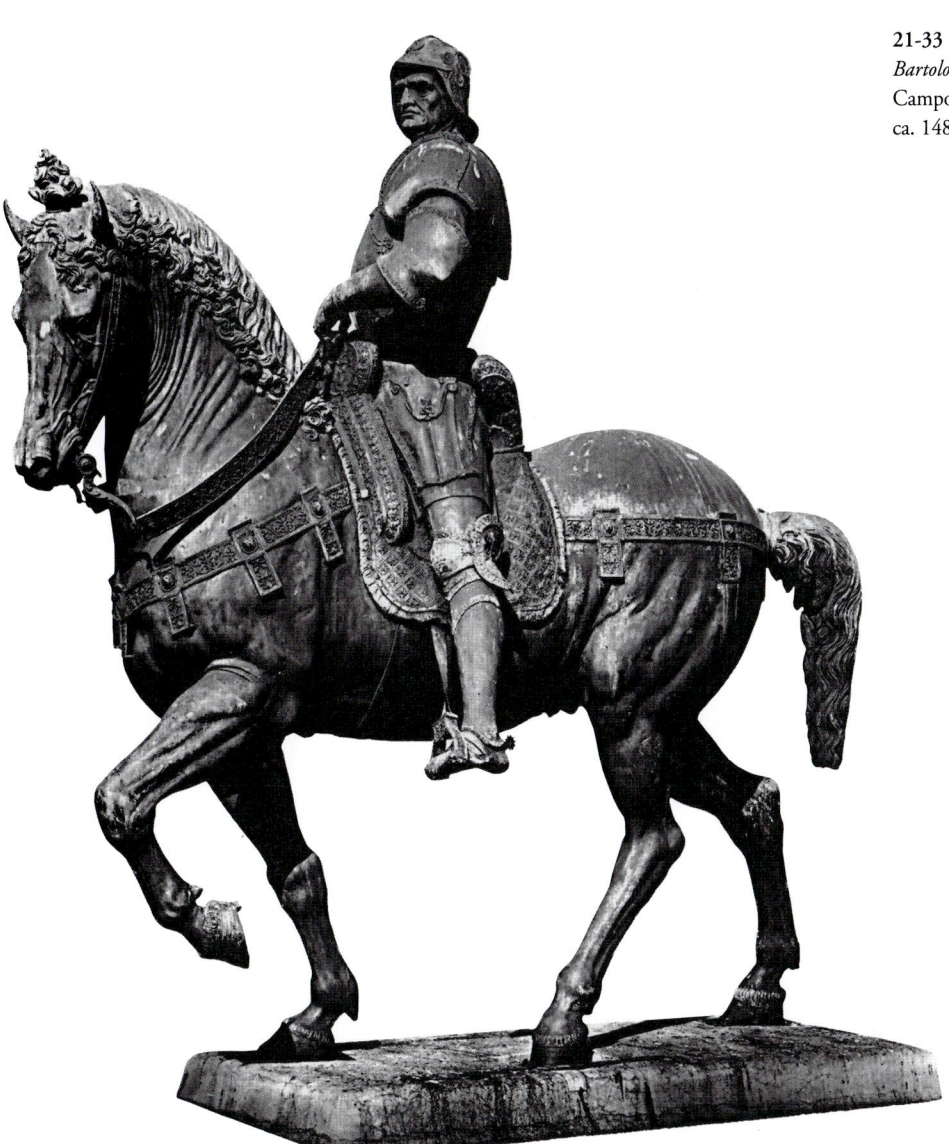

21-33 ANDREA DEL VERROCCHIO, *Bartolommeo Colleoni* (equestrian statue), Campo dei Santi Giovanni e Paolo, Venice, Italy, ca. 1483–1488. Bronze, approx. 13′ high.

ing the left forehoof of the horse on an orb, reviving a venerable ancient symbol for hegemony over the earth. The Italian rider, his face set in a mask of dauntless resolution and unshakable will, is the very portrait of the male Renaissance individualist. Such a man—intelligent, courageous, ambitious, and frequently of humble origin—could, by his own resourcefulness and on his own merits, rise to a commanding position in the world.

A DOMINATING MILITARY LEADER Verrocchio's equestrian statue of another condottiere of Venice, Bartolommeo Colleoni (FIG. **21-33**), provides a counterpoint to *Gattamelata*. Eager to garner the fame of *Gattamelata* by emulating Donatello's sculpture, Colleoni provided for the statue in his will. Both artists executed the statues after the death of their subjects, so neither Donatello nor Verrocchio knew personally the individual he portrayed. The result is a fascinating difference of interpretation (like that between the two *Davids,* FIGS. 21-23 and 21-24) as to the demeanor of a professional captain of armies. Verrocchio placed the statue of the bold equestrian general on a pedestal even higher than that Donatello used for *Gattamelata* so that viewers could see the dominating, aggressive figure above the rooftops from all ma-

jor approaches to the piazza (the Campo dei Santi Giovanni e Paolo). Silhouetted against the sky, *Bartolommeo Colleoni* with its fierce authority is unmistakable. In contrast with the near repose of *Gattamelata,* the *Colleoni* horse moves in a prancing stride, arching and curving its powerful neck, while the commander seems suddenly to shift his whole weight to the stirrups and, in a fit of impassioned emotion, to rise from the saddle with a violent twist of his body. The artist depicted the figures with an exaggerated tautness—the animal's bulging muscles and the man's fiercely erect and rigid body together convey brute strength. In *Gattamelata,* Donatello created a portrait of grim sagacity; Verrocchio's *Bartolommeo Colleoni* is a portrait of savage and merciless might. Machiavelli wrote in his famous political treatise of 1513, *The Prince,* that the successful ruler must combine the traits of the lion and the fox. It seems that Donatello's *Gattamelata* is a little like the latter and that Verrocchio's *Bartolommeo Colleoni* is much like the former.

LOOKING UP TO THE POPE Individuals in positions of religious authority also welcomed the opportunity to commission portraits. Pope Sixtus IV commissioned a series of frescoes for the Vatican Library in Rome from MELOZZO

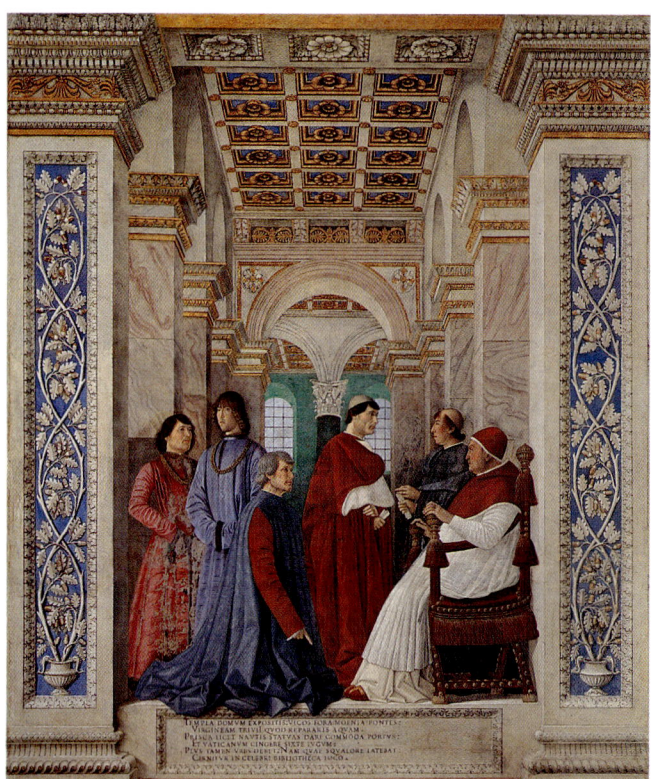

21-34 Melozzo da Forlì, *Pope Sixtus IV, His Nephews, and the Librarian Platina*, 1480–1481. Fresco originally in the Vatican Library, Rome, Italy, transferred to canvas, 13′ 1″ × 10′ 4″. Pinacoteca Vaticana, Rome.

DA FORLÌ (1438–1494). In one of these frescoes (FIG. **21-34**), the artist depicted the seated pope receiving his nephews (including the future Pope Julius II in the center, wearing red cardinal's robes) and his librarian, Platina, who kneels before him. Melozzo's debt to Masaccio appears in his weighty and solemn figures, as well as in his interest in employing perspective to unify the painted space of his fresco with that of the surrounding room. Because the fresco has been removed from the wall and transferred to the picture gallery of the Vatican Museums, viewers no longer can study Melozzo's integration of pictorial and actual space in its original location. Nevertheless, it is clear the painting once occupied a position high on the wall, because spectators look up at the pope and his entourage from below. In the foreground, Platina points downward toward a Latin inscription he wrote praising the achievements of Sixtus IV. A steady rhythm of piers rendered in precise linear perspective leads the eye farther into the background.

FURTHER DEVELOPMENTS IN ARCHITECTURE

LEON BATTISTA ALBERTI (1404–1472) entered the profession of architecture rather late in life, but, nevertheless, he made a remarkable contribution to architectural design. He was the first to study seriously the treatise of Vitruvius *(De architectura)*, and his knowledge of it, combined with his own archeological investigations, made him the first Renaissance architect to understand Roman architecture in depth. Alberti's most important and influential theoretical work, *De re aedificatoria* (written about 1450, published 1485), al-

though inspired by Vitruvius, contains much original material. Alberti advocated a system of ideal proportions and argued that the central plan was the ideal form for a Christian church. He also considered incongruous the combination of column and arch (which had persisted from Roman times, FIG. 10-51, to Brunelleschi in the fifteenth century). By arguing that the arch is a wall opening that should be supported only by a section of wall (a pier), not by an independent sculptural element (a column), Alberti (with a few exceptions) disposed of the medieval arcade used for centuries. The early impact of Alberti's ideas already was seen in the architectural backdrop of Ghiberti's *Isaac and His Sons* (FIG. 21-5) on the Florence baptistery's "Gates of Paradise."

BUILDING ON CLASSICAL ARCHITECTURE
Alberti's own architectural style represents a scholarly application of classical elements to contemporary buildings. His Palazzo Rucellai in Florence (FIG. **21-35**) probably dates from the mid-1450s. Alberti organized the facade, built over three medieval houses, in a much more severe fashion than the Palazzo Medici-Riccardi facade (FIG. 21-20), another classically inspired building. Flat pilasters, which support full entablatures, define each story of the Palazzo Rucellai. A classical cornice crowns the palace. The rustication of the wall surfaces between the smooth pilasters is subdued and uniform. Alberti created the sense that the structure becomes lighter in weight toward its top by adapting the ancient Roman manner of using different capitals for each story. He chose Tuscan (the Etruscan variant of the Greek

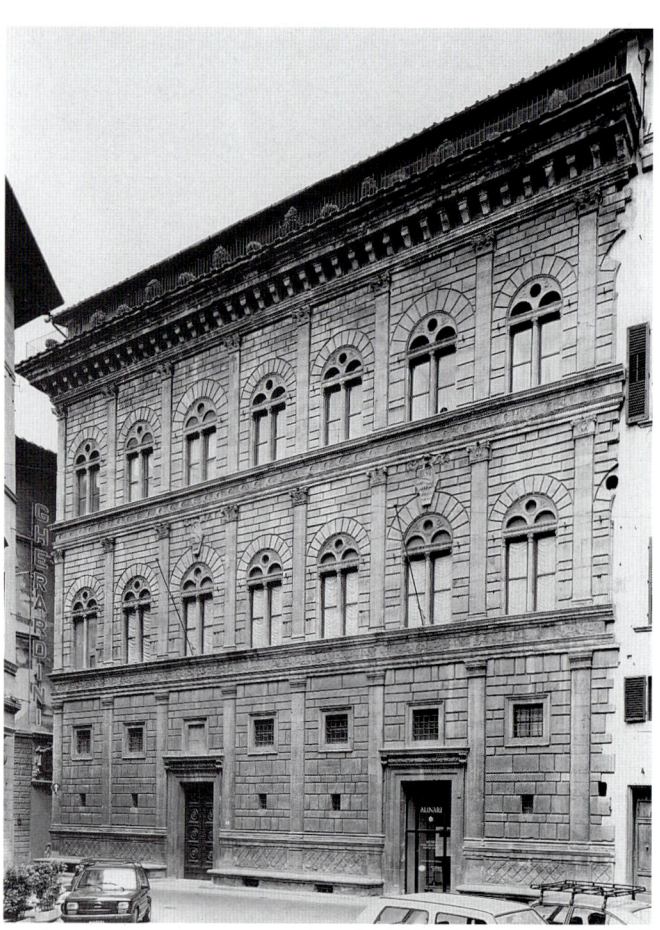

21-35 LEON BATTISTA ALBERTI, Palazzo Rucellai, Florence, Italy, ca. 1452–1470.

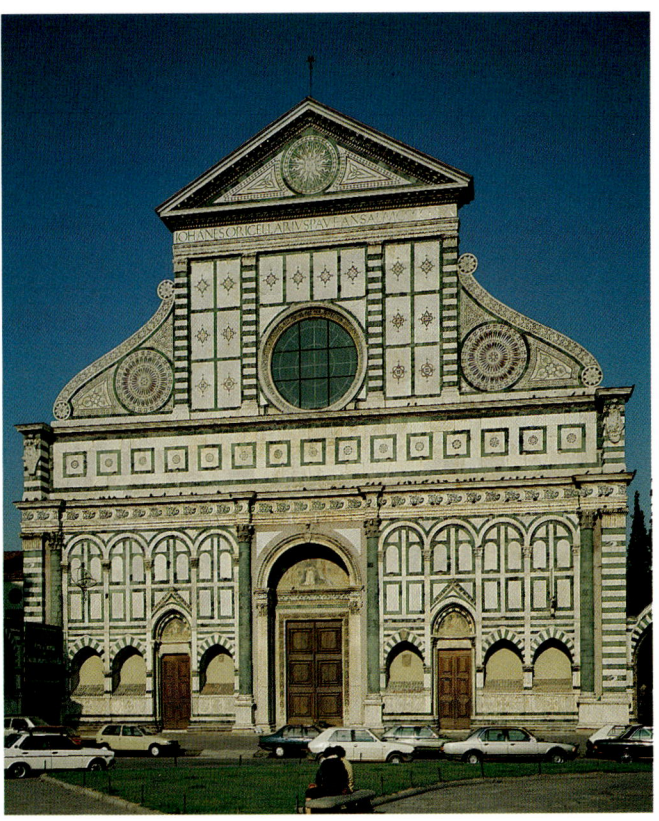

21-36 LEON BATTISTA ALBERTI, west facade of Santa Maria Novella, Florence, Italy, ca. 1458–1470.

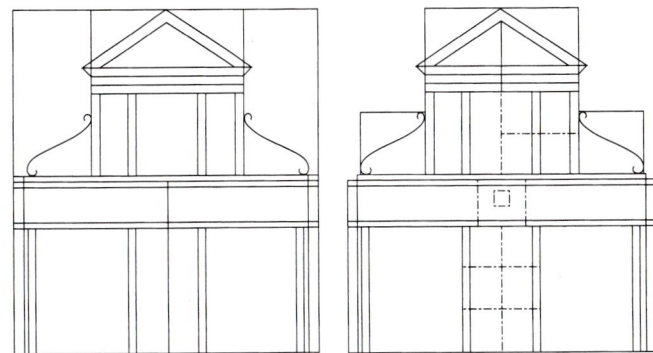

21-37 LEON BATTISTA ALBERTI, diagrams of west facade, Santa Maria Novella, Florence, Italy.

ment tip) equals its width so that the entire facade can be inscribed in a square (FIG. 21-37, left). Throughout the facade, Alberti defined areas and related them to one another in terms of proportions that can be expressed in simple numerical ratios (1:1, 1:2, 1:3, 2:3, and so on). For example, the upper structure can be encased in a square one-fourth the size of the main square (for other squares, see the right diagram). The cornice of the entablature that separates the two levels halves the major square so that the lower portion of the building is a rectangle twice as wide as it is high. Further, the areas the columns on the lower level outline are squares with sides about one-third the main unit's width. In his treatise, Alberti wrote at length to promote the necessity of such harmonic relationships for designing beautiful buildings.

Alberti shared this conviction with Brunelleschi, and this fundamental dependence on classically derived mathematics distinguished their architectural work from that of their medieval predecessors. They believed in the eternal and universal validity of numerical ratios as the source of beauty. In this respect, Alberti and Brunelleschi revived the true spirit of the High Classical age of ancient Greece, as epitomized by the sculptor Polykleitos and the architect Iktinos, who produced canons of proportions for the perfect statue and the perfect temple. But it was not only a desire to emulate Vitruvius and the Classical masters that motivated Alberti to turn to mathematics in his quest for beauty. His contemporary, the Florentine humanist Giannozzo Manetti, had argued that Christianity itself possessed the order and logic of mathematics by insisting—in his 1452 treatise, *On the Dignity and Excellence of Man*—that Christian religious truths were as self-evident as mathematical axioms.

The Santa Maria Novella facade was an ingenious solution to a difficult design problem. On one hand, it adequately expressed the organization of the structure attached to it. On the other hand, it subjected preexisting and quintessentially medieval features, such as the large round window on the second level, to a rigid geometrical order that instilled a quality of classical calm and reason. This facade also introduced a feature of great historical consequence—the scrolls that simultaneously unite the broad lower and narrow upper level and screen the sloping roofs over the aisles. With variations, such spirals appeared in literally hundreds of church facades throughout the Renaissance and Baroque periods.

Doric order) for the ground floor, Composite (the Roman combination of Ionic volutes with the acanthus leaves of the Corinthian) for the second story, and Corinthian for the third floor. Alberti modeled his facade on the most imposing Roman ruin of all, the Colosseum (see FIG. 10-34), but he was no slavish copyist. On the Colosseum's facade the capitals employed are, from the bottom up, Tuscan, Ionic, and Corinthian. Moreover, Alberti adapted the Colosseum's varied surface to a flat facade, which does not allow the deep penetration of the building's mass that is so effective in the Roman structure. By converting his ancient model's *engaged columns* (half-round columns attached to a wall) into shallow pilasters that barely project from the wall, Alberti created a large-meshed linear net. Stretched tightly across the front of his building, it not only unifies the three levels but also emphasizes the wall's flat two-dimensional qualities.

OF RATIOS AND RATIONALITY The Rucellai family also commissioned from Alberti the design for the facade of the thirteenth-century Gothic church of Santa Maria Novella in Florence (FIGS. **21-36** and **21-37**). Here, Alberti took his cue (just as Brunelleschi did occasionally) from a pre-Gothic medieval design—that of San Miniato al Monte (see FIG. 17-17). Following this Romanesque model, he designed a small, pseudoclassical, pediment-capped temple front for the facade's upper part and supported it with a broad base of pilaster-enframed arcades that incorporate the six tombs and three doorways of the extant Gothic building. But in the organization of these elements, Alberti took a long step beyond the Romanesque planners. The height of Santa Maria Novella (to the pedi-

21-38 FRA ANGELICO, *Annunciation,* San Marco, Florence, Italy, ca. 1440–1445. Fresco, 7′ 1″ × 10′ 6″.

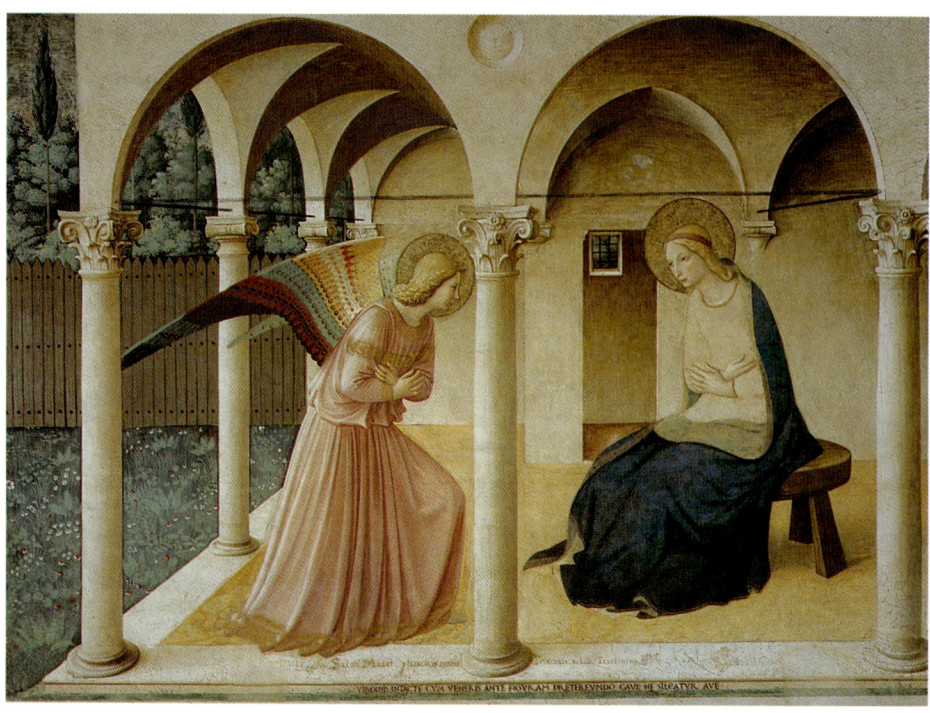

IMAGES OF PIETY AND DEVOTION

A VISUAL CALL TO PRAYER As is evident by the plethora of religious imagery produced during the fifteenth century, humanism and religion were not mutually exclusive. Yet for many artists, humanist concerns were not a primary consideration. FRA ANGELICO (ca. 1400–1455) was among those; as a friar at San Domenico at Fiesole, a village overlooking Florence, his art focused on serving the Roman Catholic Church. In the late 1430s, the abbots of the Dominican monastery of San Marco in Florence asked Fra Angelico to produce a series of frescoes for the monastery. The Dominicans of San Marco had dedicated themselves to lives of prayer and work, and the religious compound was mostly spare and austere to encourage the monks to immerse themselves in their devotional lives. Fra Angelico's frescoes illustrated a thirteenth-century text, *De modo orandi* (*The Way of Prayer*), which describes the nine ways of prayer Saint Dominic, the order's founder, used.

Among the works he completed was *Annunciation* (FIG. **21-38**), which appears at the top of the stairs leading to the friars' cells. Appropriately, Fra Angelico presented the scene of the Virgin Mary and the Archangel Gabriel with simplicity and serenity. The two figures appear in a plain loggia, and the artist painted all the fresco elements with a pristine clarity. As an admonition to heed the devotional function of the images, Fra Angelico included a small inscription at the base of the image that reads, "As you venerate, while passing before it, this figure of the intact Virgin, beware lest you omit to say a Hail Mary." Like most of Fra Angelico's paintings, *Annunciation*'s naive and tender charm still has an almost universal appeal and fully reflects the artist's simple and humble character.

DINING IN THE PRESENCE OF CHRIST ANDREA DEL CASTAGNO (ca. 1421–1457), like Fra Angelico, accepted a commission to produce a series of frescoes for a religious establishment. His *Last Supper* (FIG. **21-39**), painted in the refectory (dining hall) of Sant'Apollonia in Florence, a convent for Benedictine nuns, manifests both a commitment to the biblical narrative and an interest in perspective. The lavishly painted space Christ and his twelve disciples occupy suggests Castagno's absorption with creating the illusion of three-dimensional space. However, on scrutiny, inconsistencies are apparent, such as the fact Renaissance perspectival systems make it impossible to see both the ceiling and the roof, as Castagno depicted. Further, the two side walls do not appear parallel.

The artist chose a conventional compositional format, with the figures seated at a horizontally placed table. Castagno derived the apparent self-absorption of most of the disciples and the malevolent features of Judas (who sits alone on the outside of the table) from the Gospel of Saint John, rather than the more familiar version of the Last Supper recounted in the Gospel of Saint Luke. The prevalent exploration of perspective clearly influenced Castagno's depiction of the Last Supper, which no doubt was a powerful presence for the nuns during their daily meals.

A HUMANIZED MADONNA AND CHILD A younger contemporary of Fra Angelico, FRA FILIPPO LIPPI (ca. 1406–1469), was also a friar—but there all resemblance ends. From reports, Fra Filippo seems to have been an amiable man unsuited for monastic life. He indulged in misdemeanors ranging from forgery and embezzlement to the abduction of a pretty nun, Lucretia, who became his mistress and the mother of his son, the painter Filippino Lippi (1457–1504). Only the Medici's intervention on his behalf at the papal court preserved Fra Filippo from severe punishment and total disgrace. An orphan, Fra Filippo spent his youth in a monastery adjacent to the church of Santa Maria del Carmine, and, when about eighteen, he must have met Masaccio there and witnessed the Brancacci Chapel's decoration. Fra Filippo's early work survives only in

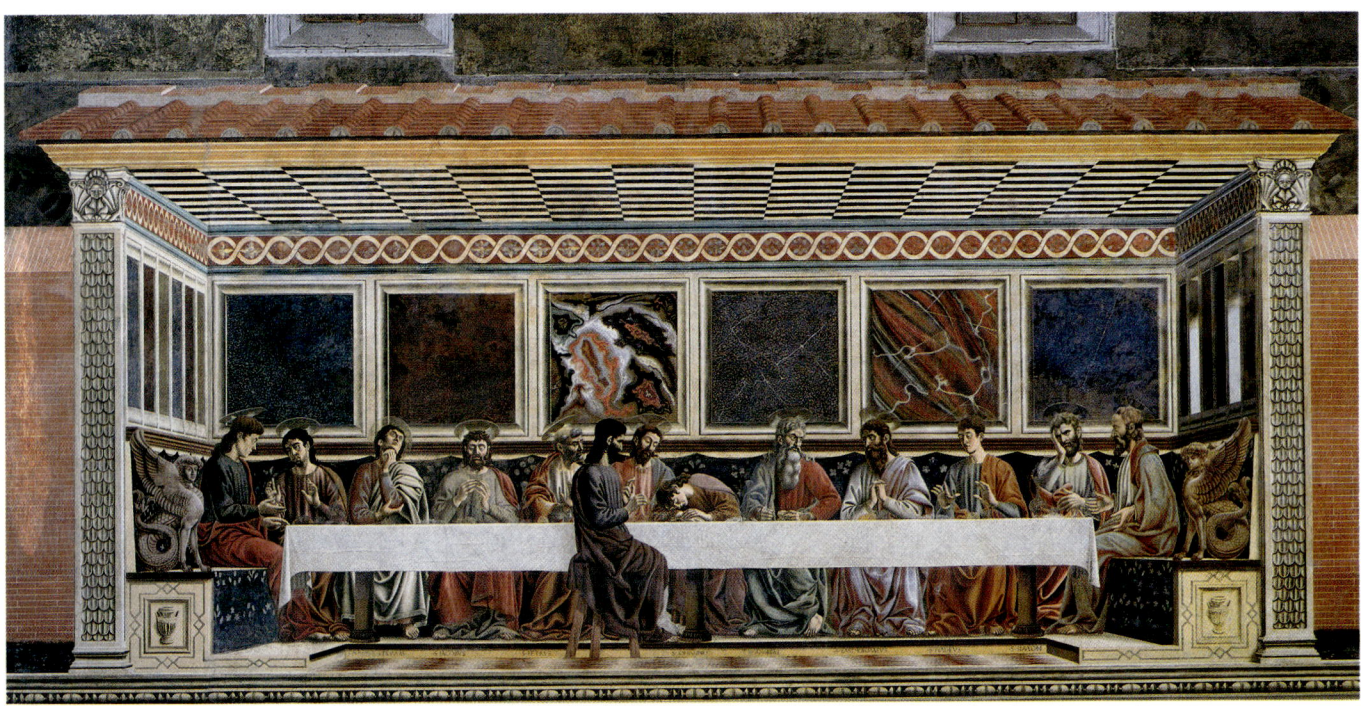

21-39 ANDREA DEL CASTAGNO, *Last Supper,* the Refectory, monastery of Sant'Apollonia, Florence, Italy, 1447. Fresco, approx. 15′ × 32′.

fragments, but these show he tried to work with Masaccio's massive forms. Later, probably under the influence of Ghiberti's and Donatello's relief sculptures, he developed a linear style that emphasized the contours of his figures and permitted him to suggest movement through flying and swirling draperies.

A painting from Fra Filippo's later years, *Madonna and Child with Angels* (FIG. **21-40**), shows his skill in manipulating line. A wonderfully fluid line unifies the composition and contributes to the precise and smooth delineation of forms. Few artists have surpassed Fra Filippo's skill in using line. He interpreted his subject here in a surprisingly worldly manner. The Madonna, a beautiful young mother, is not at all spiritual or fragile, and neither is the Christ Child, whom two angels hold up. One of the angels turns with the mischievous, puckish grin of a boy refusing to behave for the pious occasion. Significantly, all figures reflect the use of live models (that for the Madonna even may have been Lucretia). Fra Filippo plainly relished the charm of youth and beauty as he found it in this world. He preferred the real in landscape also, and the background, seen through the window, incorporates, despite some exaggerations, recognizable features of the Arno River valley. Compared with the earlier Madonnas by Giotto (see FIG. 19-7) and Duccio (see FIG. 19-16), this work shows how far artists had carried the humanization of the theme. Whatever the ideals of spiritual perfection may have meant to artists in past centuries, Renaissance artists realized such ideals in terms of the sensuous beauty of this world.

RELIEF SCULPTURE FOR THE MASSES During the latter half of the fifteenth century, increasing demand for devotional images for private chapels and shrines (rather than for large public churches) contributed to a growing seculariza-

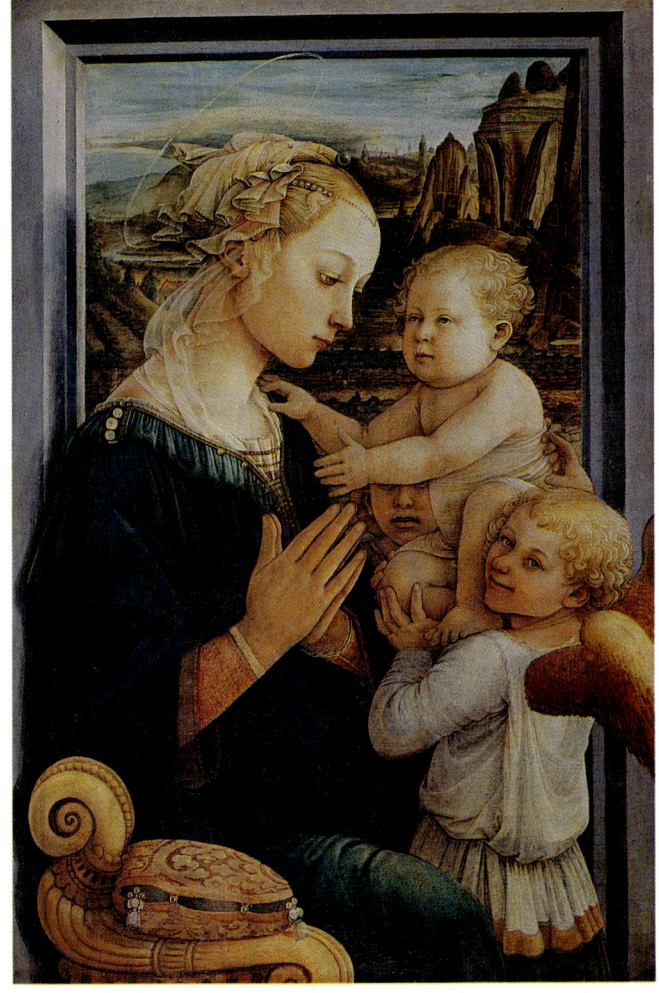

21-40 FRA FILIPPO LIPPI, *Madonna and Child with Angels,* ca. 1455. Tempera on wood, approx. 3′ × 2′ 1″. Galleria degli Uffizi, Florence.

21-41 LUCA DELLA ROBBIA, *Madonna and Child,* Or San Michele, Florence, Italy, ca. 1455–1460. Terracotta with polychrome glaze, diameter approx. 6'.

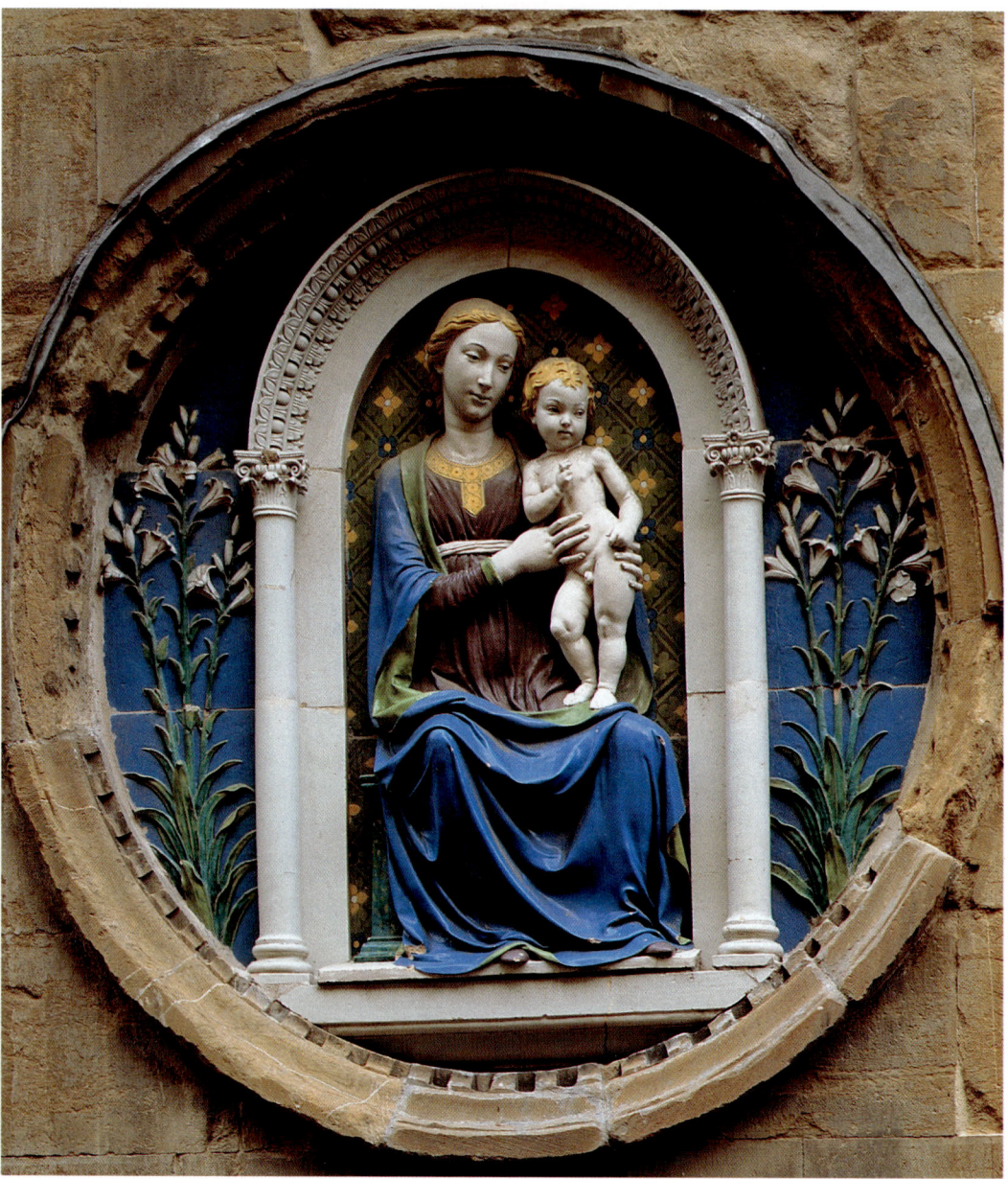

tion of traditional religious subject matter. LUCA DELLA ROBBIA (1400–1482) discovered a way to multiply Madonna images so that persons of modest means could buy them. His discovery (around 1430), involving the application of vitrified (heat fused) potters' glazes to sculpture, led to his production, in quantity, of glazed terracotta reliefs. He is best known for these works. Inexpensive, durable, and decorative, they became extremely popular and provided the basis for a flourishing family business. Luca's nephew Andrea della Robbia (1435–1525) and Andrea's sons, Giovanni della Robbia (1469–1529) and Girolamo della Robbia (1488–1566), carried on this tradition well into the sixteenth century. By then the product had become purely commercial; people still refer to it as "della Robbia ware."

An example of Luca's specialty is the *Madonna and Child* set into a wall of Or San Michele (FIG. **21-41**). The figures appear within a *tondo* (a circular painting or relief sculpture), a format that became popular with both sculptors and painters in the later part of the century. For example, Rossellino used it for the Madonna and Child of Leonardo

Bruni's tomb (FIG. 21-29), and Brunelleschi incorporated it into his design of the Pazzi Chapel's interior (FIG. 21-19), where most of the roundels are the work of Luca della Robbia himself. In his tondo for Or San Michele, Luca's introduction of high-key color into sculpture added a certain worldly gaiety to the Madonna and Child theme, and his customary light blue ground (and here the green and white of lilies and the white architecture) suggests in this work the festive Easter season and the freshness of May, the Virgin's month. Of course, the somber majesty of the old Byzantine style long since had disappeared. The young mothers who prayed before images such as this new form easily could identify with the Madonna and doubtless did. The distance between the observed and observers had vanished.

DECORATING THE NEW SISTINE CHAPEL Of course, the production of religious art extended beyond Florence. The pope's presence in Rome ensured an active artistic scene there as well. Between 1481 and 1483, Pope Sixtus

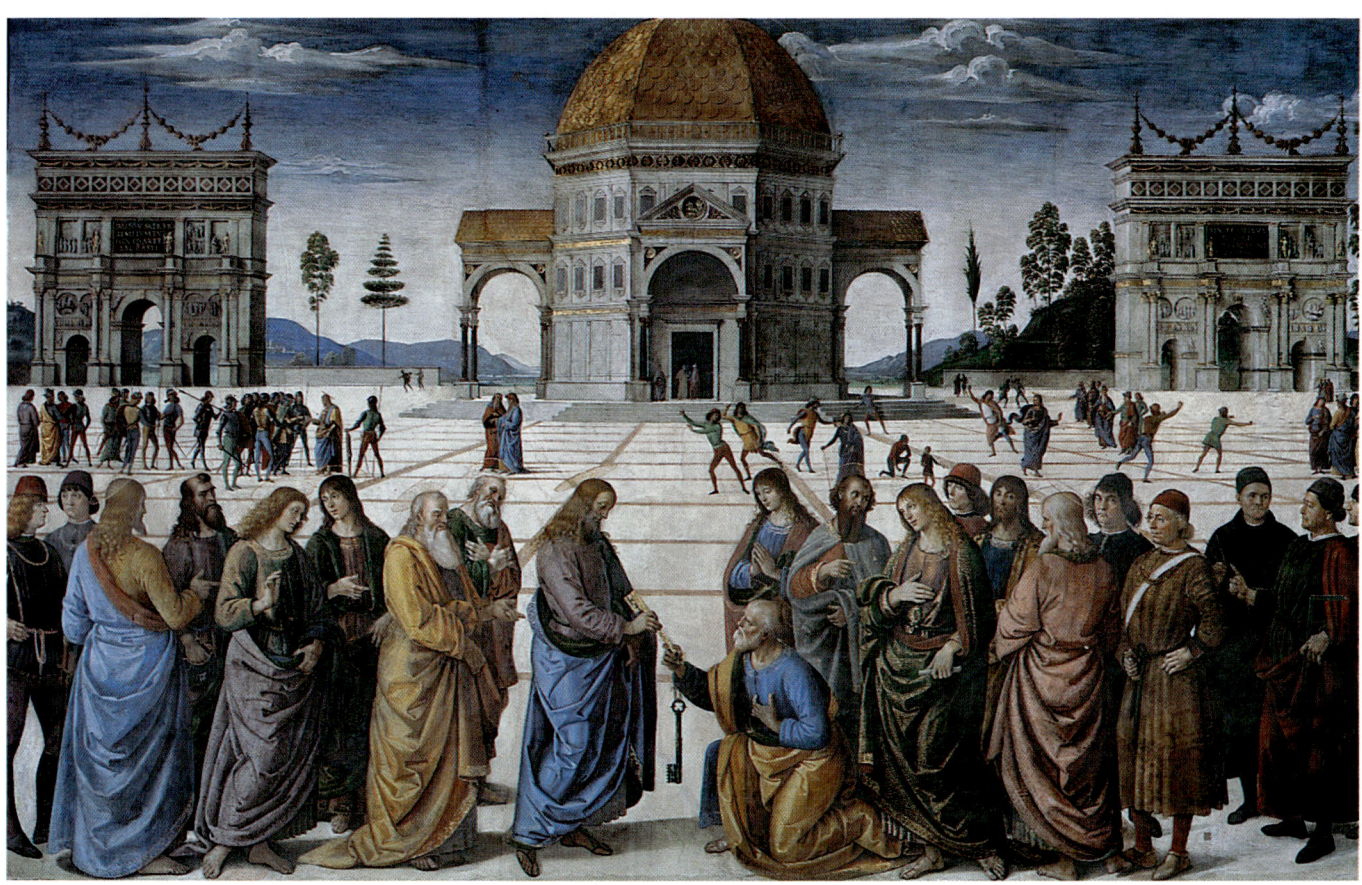

21-42   PERUGINO, *Christ Delivering the Keys of the Kingdom to Saint Peter,* Sistine Chapel, Vatican, Rome, Italy, 1481–1483. Fresco, 11′ 5½″ × 18′ 8½″.

IV summoned a group of artists, including Botticelli, Ghirlandaio, and Luca Signorelli, to Rome to decorate with frescoes the walls of the newly completed Sistine Chapel. PIETRO VANNUCCI, known as PERUGINO (ca. 1450–1523), was among this group and painted *Christ Delivering the Keys of the Kingdom to Saint Peter* (FIG. **21-42**). The papacy had, from the beginning, based its claim to infallible and total authority over the Roman Catholic Church on this biblical event. In Perugino's version, Christ hands the keys to Saint Peter, standing at the center of the Twelve Apostles and portraits of Renaissance contemporaries, who occupy the apron of a great stage space that extends into the distance to a point of convergence in the doorway of a central-plan temple. (Perugino used parallel and converging lines in the pavement to mark off the intervening space.) Figures in the middle distance complement the near group, emphasizing its density and order by their scattered arrangement. At the corners of the great piazza, duplicate triumphal arches serve as the base angles of a distant compositional triangle whose apex is in the central building. Perugino modeled the arches very closely on the Arch of Constantine in Rome, FIG. 10-76. Although an anachronism in a painting depicting a scene from Christ's life, the arches remind viewers of the close ties between Constantine and Saint Peter and of the great basilica the first Christian emperor built over Saint Peter's tomb in Rome. Christ and Peter flank the triangle's central axis, which runs through the temple's doorway, the perspective's vanishing point. Thus, the composition interlocks both two-dimensional and three-dimensional space, and the placement of central actors emphasizes the axial center. This spatial science allowed the artist to organize the action systematically. Perugino, in this single picture, incorporated the learning of generations.

THE PRINCELY COURTS

Mantua

Although virtually all the artworks discussed thus far in this chapter were Florentine, art production flourished throughout Italy in the fifteenth century. In particular, the princely courts that rulers established in cities such as Naples, Urbino, Milan, Ferrara, and Mantua deserve much credit for nurturing the arts. These princely courts consisted of the prince (lord of a territory), his consort and children, courtiers, household staff, and administrators (see "Dukes, Despots, Fame, and Fortune: The Princely Courts," page 591). The considerable wealth these princes possessed, coupled with their desire for recognition, fame, and power, resulted in major art commissions.

Marquis Ludovico Gonzaga (1412–1478) ruled one of these princely courts, the marquisate of Mantua in northern Italy. A famed condottieri, Gonzaga established his reputation as a fierce military leader while general of the Milanese armies. A visit to Mantua by Pope Pius II in 1459 stimulated the Marquis's determination to transform Mantua into a spectacular city. After the pope's departure, Gonzaga set about building a city that would be the envy of all of Italy.

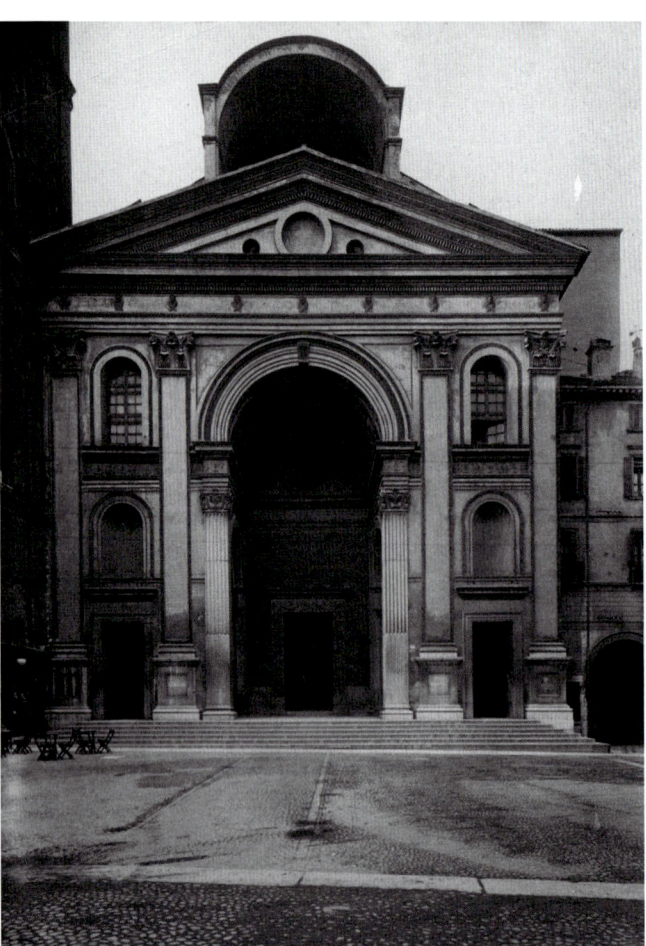

21-43   Leon Battista Alberti, west facade of Sant'Andrea, Mantua, Italy, designed ca. 1470.

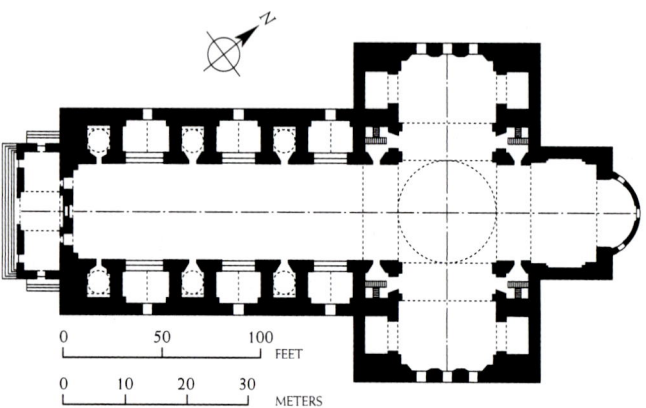

21-44   Leon Battista Alberti, plan of Sant'Andrea, Mantua, Italy, designed ca. 1470.

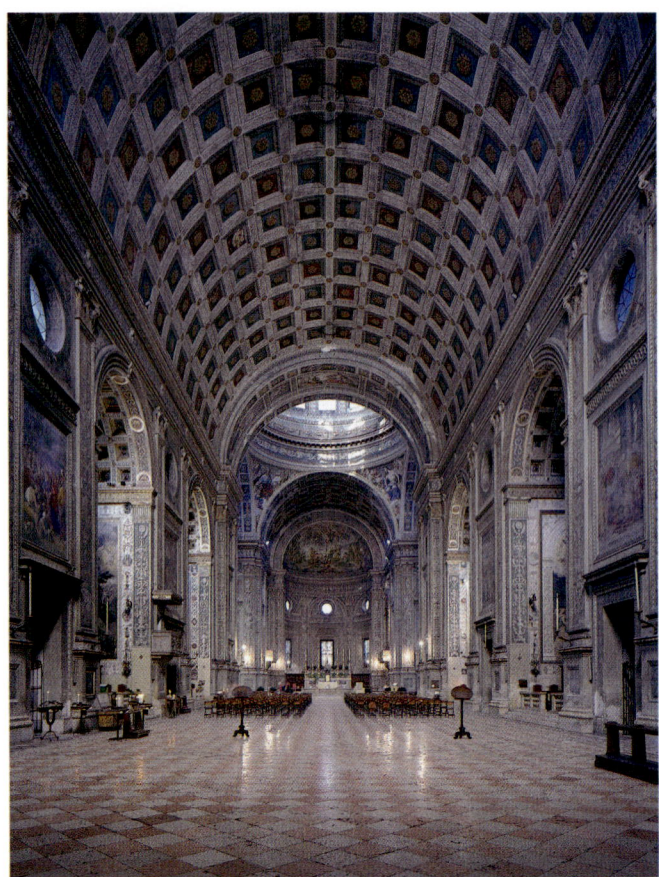

21-45   Leon Battista Alberti, interior of Sant'Andrea, Mantua, Italy, designed ca. 1470.

AN EXPANSIVE MANTUAN CHURCH One of the major projects Gonzaga instituted was the redesigning of the church of Sant'Andrea in Mantua (FIGS. **21-43** to **21-45**) to replace an eleventh-century church. Gonzaga turned to Alberti for this important commission. In the ingeniously planned facade, which illustrates the culmination of Alberti's experiments, the architect locked together two complete Roman architectural motifs—the temple front and the triumphal arch. The combination was already a feature of classical architecture. Many Roman triumphal arches incorporated

a pediment over the arcuated passageway and engaged columns, including the Augustan arch at Rimini (FIG. **21-46**), illustrated here for comparison. Alberti's concern for proportion led him to equalize the facade's vertical and horizontal dimensions, which left it considerably lower than the church behind it. Because of the primary importance of visual appeal, many Renaissance architects made this concession not only to the demands of a purely visual proportionality in the facade but also to the facade's relation to the small square in front of it, even at the expense of continuity with the body of the building. Yet, structural correspondences to the building do exist in the Sant'Andrea facade. The facade pilasters are the same height as those on the nave's interior walls, and the central barrel vault over the main exterior entrance, with smaller barrel vaults branching off at right angles, introduces (in proportional arrangement but on a smaller scale) the interior system. The facade pilasters, as part of the wall, run uninterrupted through three stories in an early application of the "colossal" or "giant" order that became a favorite motif of Michelangelo.

The tremendous vaults in the interior of Sant'Andrea (FIG. 21-45) suggest that Alberti may have been inspired by the ruined Basilica Nova of Constantine in Rome (see FIG. 10-79)—erroneously thought in the Middle Ages and Renaissance to be a Roman temple. He abandoned the medieval columned arcade Brunelleschi used in Santo Spirito (FIG. 21-15). Thick walls alternating with vaulted chapels and interrupted by a massive dome over the crossing support the huge barrel vault. Because Filippo Juvara added the present dome in the eighteenth century, the effect may be somewhat different than Alberti planned. Regardless, the vault calls to mind the vast interior spaces and dense enclosing masses of Roman architecture. In his treatise, Alberti criticized the traditional basilican plan (with continuous aisles flanking the central nave) as impractical because the colonnades conceal the ceremonies from the faithful in the aisles. For this reason, he designed a single huge hall with independent chapels branching off at right angles (FIG. 21-44). This break with a Christian building tradition that had endured for a thousand years was extremely influential in later Renaissance and Baroque church planning.

A PALATIAL ROOM OF PAINTED SPLENDOR

Like other princes, Ludovico Gonzaga believed that an impressive palace was an important visualization of his authority. One of the most spectacular rooms in Palazzo Ducale was decorated by ANDREA MANTEGNA (ca. 1431–1506) of Padua, near Venice. In the so-called Camera degli Sposi (Room of the Newlyweds; FIG. 21-47), originally the Camera Picta (Painted Room), Mantegna performed a triumphant feat of pictorial illusionism, producing the first completely consistent illusionistic decoration of an entire room. Using actual architectural elements, Mantegna painted away the room's walls in a manner that foretold later Baroque decoration. It recalls the efforts of Italian painters more than fifteen centuries earlier at Pompeii and elsewhere to integrate mural painting and actual architecture in frescoes of the so-called Second Style of Roman painting (see FIGS. 10-15 and 10-16).

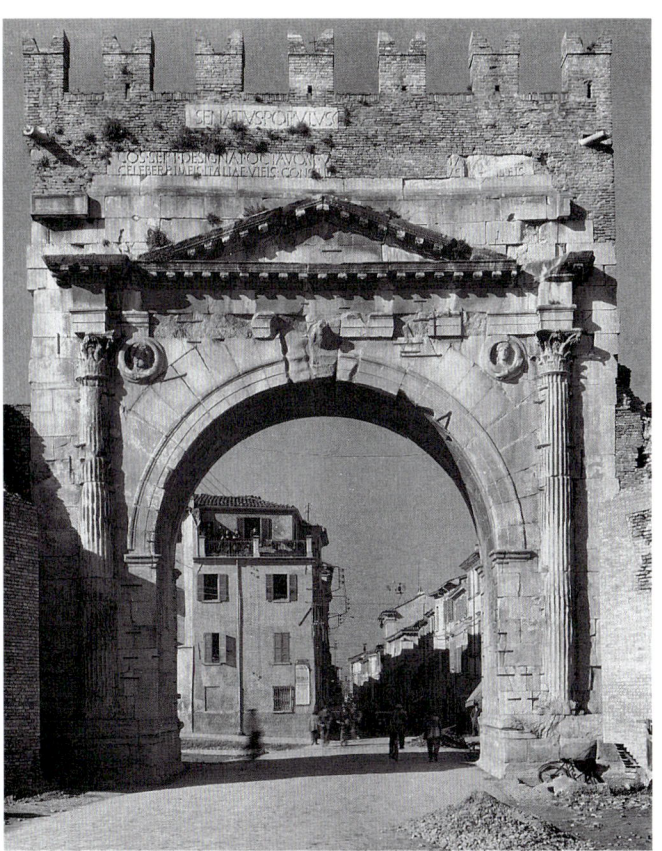

21-46   Arch of Augustus, Rimini, Italy, 27 B.C.

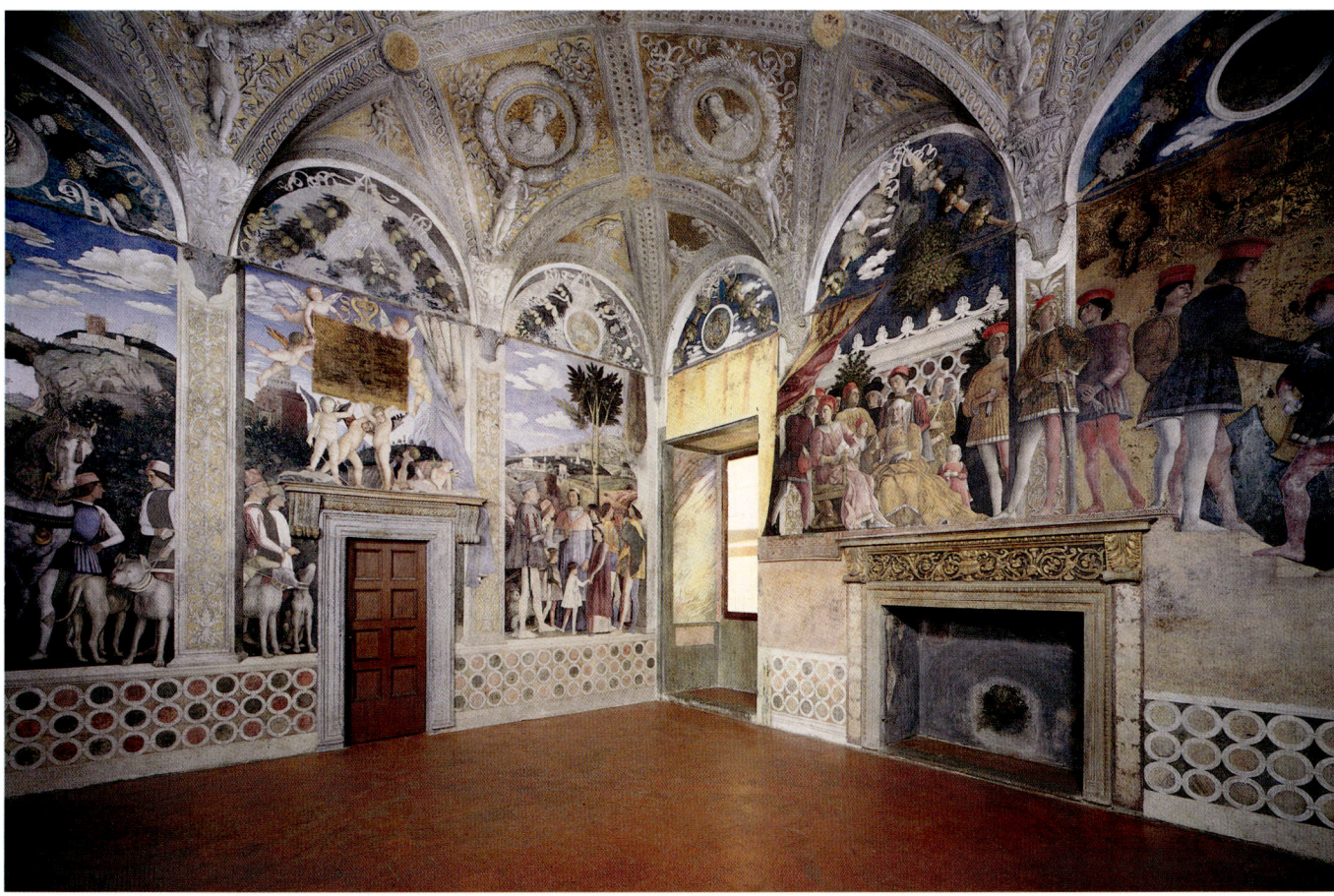

21-47   ANDREA MANTEGNA, interior of the Camera degli Sposi, Palazzo Ducale, Mantua, Italy, 1474. Fresco.

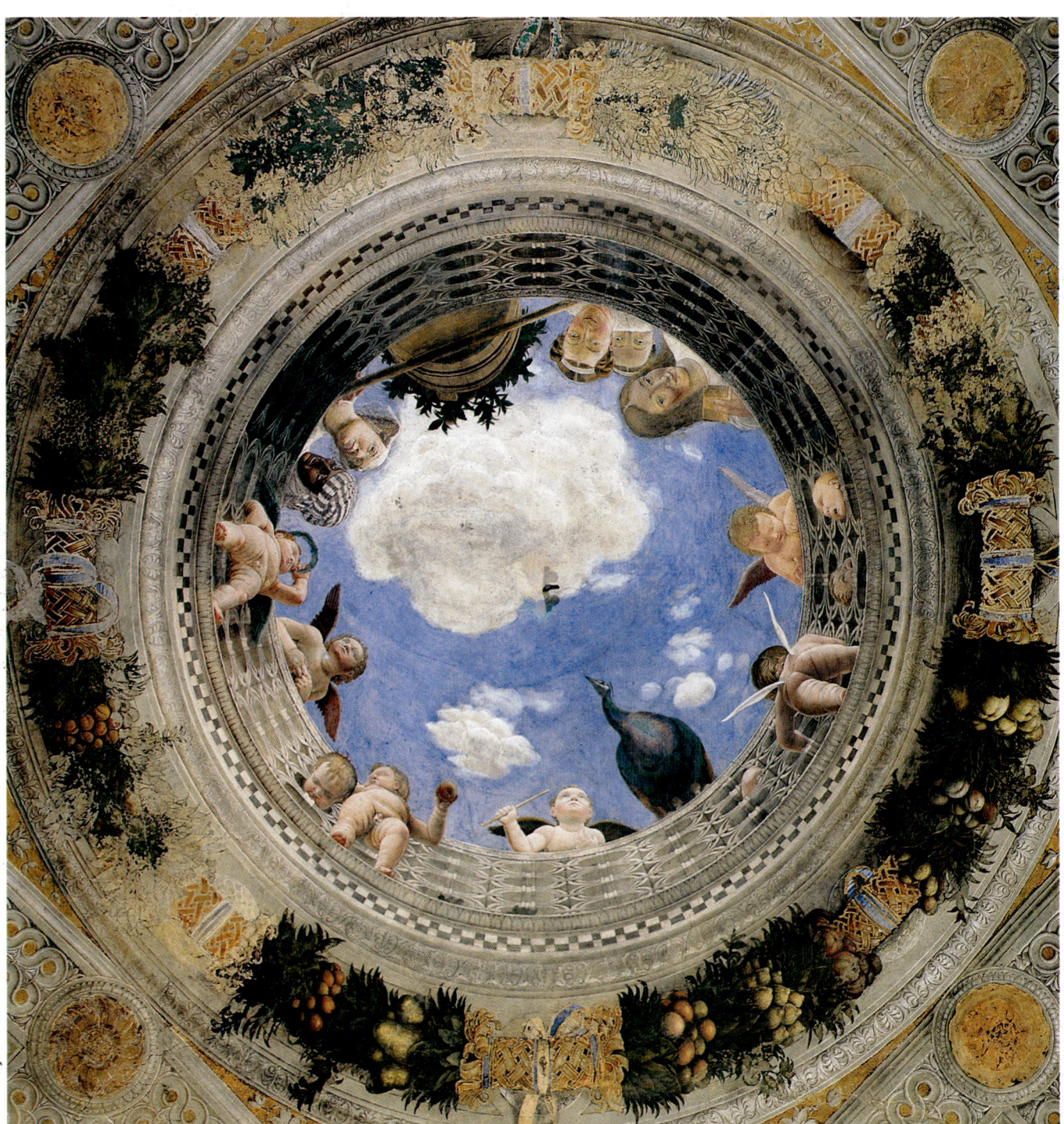

21-48 Andrea Mantegna, ceiling of the Camera degli Sposi, Palazzo Ducale, Mantua, Italy, 1474. Fresco, 8′ 9″ in diameter.

Mantegna's *trompe l'oeil* (literally, "deceives the eye") design, however, went far beyond anything preserved from ancient Italy. The Renaissance painter's daring experimentalism led him to complete the room's decoration with the first *di sotto in sù* (from below upwards) perspective of a ceiling (FIG. **21-48**). Baroque ceiling decorators later broadly developed this technique. Inside the Room of the Newlyweds, viewers become the viewed as figures look down into the room. The oculus is itself an "eye" looking down. Cupids (the sons of Venus), strongly foreshortened, set the amorous mood as the painted spectators (who are not identified) smile down on the scene. The peacock is an attribute of Juno, Jupiter's bride, who oversees lawful marriages. This

tour de force of illusionism climaxes almost a century of experiment in perspective.

A SAINT VIEWED FROM BELOW While the Gonzaga frescoes showcase Mantegna's mature style, his earlier frescoes in the Ovetari Chapel in the Church of the Eremitani (largely destroyed in World War II) in Padua reveal Mantegna's early interest in illusionism and highlight the breadth of his literary, archeological, and pictorial learning. *Saint James Led to Martyrdom* (FIG. **21-49**) depicts the condemned saint stopping, even on the way to his own death, to bless a man who has rushed from the crowd and kneels before him (while a Roman soldier restrains others from coming forward). Yet narrative does not seem to have been Mantegna's primary concern in this fresco. The painter strove for historical authenticity, much like the antiquarian scholars of the University of Padua. He excerpted the motifs that appear on the barrel-vaulted triumphal arch from the classical ornamental vocabulary. Antique attire served as the model for the soldiers' costumes.

Perspective also occupied Mantegna's attention. Indeed, he seemed to set up for himself difficult problems in perspective for the joy of solving them. Here, observers view the scene from a very low point, almost as if looking up out of a basement window at the vast arch looming above. The lines of the building to the right plunge down dramatically. Several significant deviations from true perspective are apparent, however, and establish that Mantegna did not view the scientific organization of pictorial space as an end in itself. Using artistic license, he ignored the third vanishing point (seen from below, the buildings should converge toward the top). Disregarding perspectival facts, he preferred to work toward a unified, cohesive composition whose pictorial elements relate to the picture frame. Mantegna partly compensated for the lack of perspectival logic by inserting strong diagonals in the right foreground (the banner staff, for example).

EXAMINING CHRIST'S WOUNDS One of Mantegna's later paintings, *Dead Christ* (FIG. **21-50**), is a work of overwhelming power, despite the somewhat awkward insertion (probably by a student) of the two mourning figures on the left. What seems to be a strikingly realistic study in foreshortening, however, the artist modified by reducing the size of the figure's feet, which, as he must have known, would

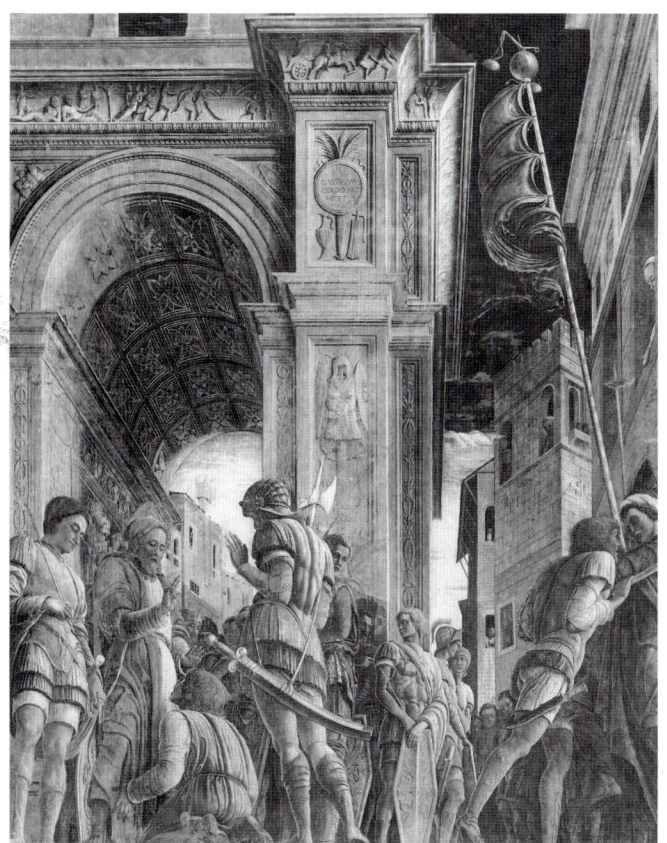

21-49 ANDREA MANTEGNA, *Saint James Led to Martyrdom,* Ovetari Chapel, Church of the Eremitani (largely destroyed, 1944), Padua, Italy, ca. 1455. Fresco, 10′ 9″ wide.

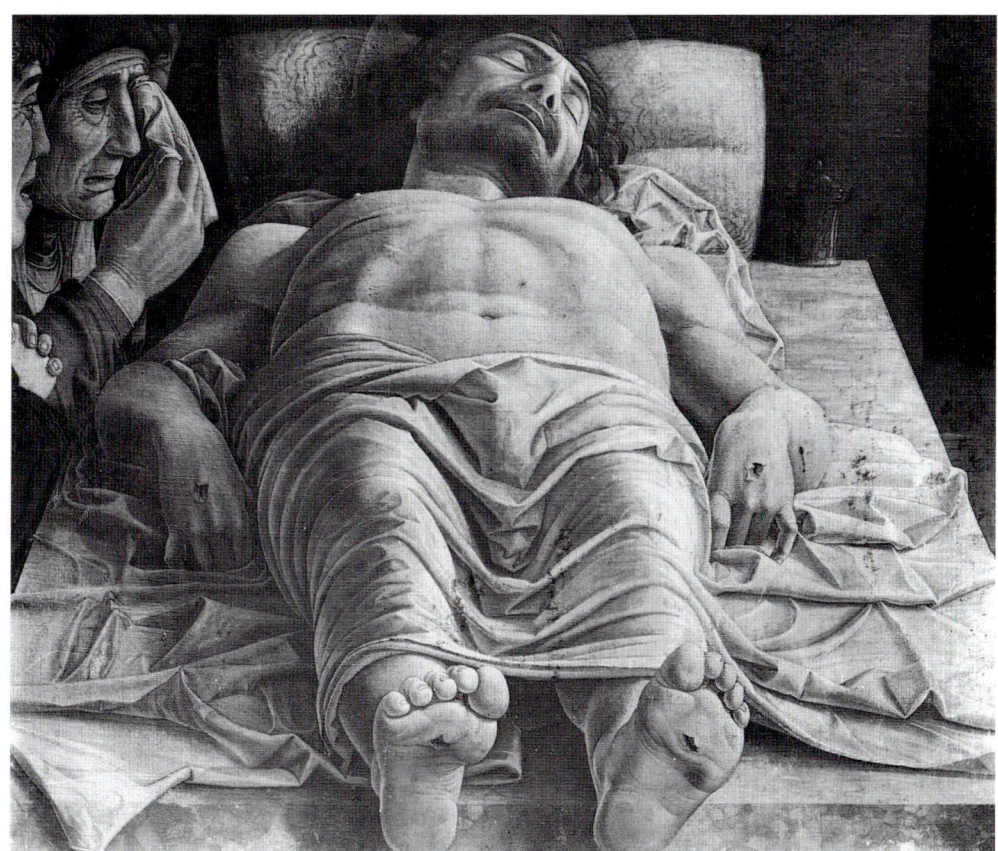

21-50 ANDREA MANTEGNA, *Dead Christ,* ca. 1501. Tempera on canvas, 2′ 2¾″ × 2′ 7⅞″. Pinacoteca di Brera, Milan.

cover much of the body if properly represented. Thus, tempering naturalism with artistic license, Mantegna presented both a harrowing study of a strongly foreshortened cadaver and an intensely poignant depiction of a biblical tragedy. The painter's harsh, sharp line seems to cut the surface as if it were metal and conveys, by its grinding edge, the theme's corrosive emotion. Remarkably, all the science of the fifteenth century here serves the purpose of devotion.

Artists in northern Italy, not only in Mantua but in Ferrara and Venice as well, attempted to follow in Mantegna's footsteps. His influence went even further, however, for he was also a great engraver (the line in the *Dead Christ* certainly suggests engraving). His prints found their way across the Alps to Germany, where they influenced Albrecht Dürer (see FIGS. 23-4 to 23-9), a leading figure in sixteenth-century art.

Urbino

Urbino, southeast of Florence across the Appenines, was another princely court; the patronage of Federico da Montefeltro (1422–1482) accounted for its status as a center of Renaissance art and culture. In fact, the humanist Paolo Cortese described Federico as one of the two greatest artistic patrons of the fifteenth century (the other was Cosimo de' Medici). Federico, like Ludovico Gonzaga, was a well-known condottieri. So renowned was Federico for his military skills that he was in demand by popes and kings across Europe, and soldiers came from across the continent to study with this military expert. One of the artists who received several commissions from Federico was PIERO DELLA FRANCESCA (ca. 1420–1492). His art projected a mind cultivated by mathematics. Piero believed that the highest beauty resides in forms that have the clarity and purity of geometric figures. Toward the end of his long career, Piero, a skilled geometrician, wrote the first theoretical treatise

on systematic perspective, after having practiced the art with supreme mastery for almost a lifetime. His association with the architect Alberti at Ferrara and at Rimini around 1450–1451 probably turned his attention fully to perspective (a science in which Alberti was an influential pioneer) and helped to determine his later, characteristically architectonic, compositions. This approach appealed to Federico, a patron fascinated by architectural space and its depiction. Observers can say fairly that Piero established his compositions almost entirely by his sense of the exact and lucid structures defined by mathematics. Within this context, however, he handled light and color with considerable sophistication, and color became the matrix of his three-dimensional forms, lending them a new density as well as fusing them with the surrounding space.

A LEGENDARY FRESCO STYLE   Before this survey considers the work Piero produced for Federico in Urbino, Piero's earlier art merits examination. One of his most important works is the fresco cycle in the apse of the church of San Francesco in Arezzo, southeast of Florence on the Arno. Painted between 1452 and 1456, the cycle represents ten episodes from the legend of the True Cross (the cross on which Christ died) and is based on a thirteenth-century popularization of the Scriptures, the *Golden Legend* by Jacobus de Voragine. In the climactic scene of Piero's Arezzo cycle, the *Finding of the True Cross and Proving of the True Cross* (FIG. **21-51**), Saint Helena, mother of Constantine, accompanied by her retinue, oversees the unearthing of the buried crosses (at left) and witnesses {at right} how the True Cross miraculously restores a dead man (the nude figure) to life. The architectural background organizes and controls the grouping of the figures; its medallions, arches, and rectangular panels are the two-dimensional counterparts of the ovoid, cylindrical, and cubic forms placed in front of it. The careful delineation of architecture suggests an architect's vision, certainly that of a man entirely

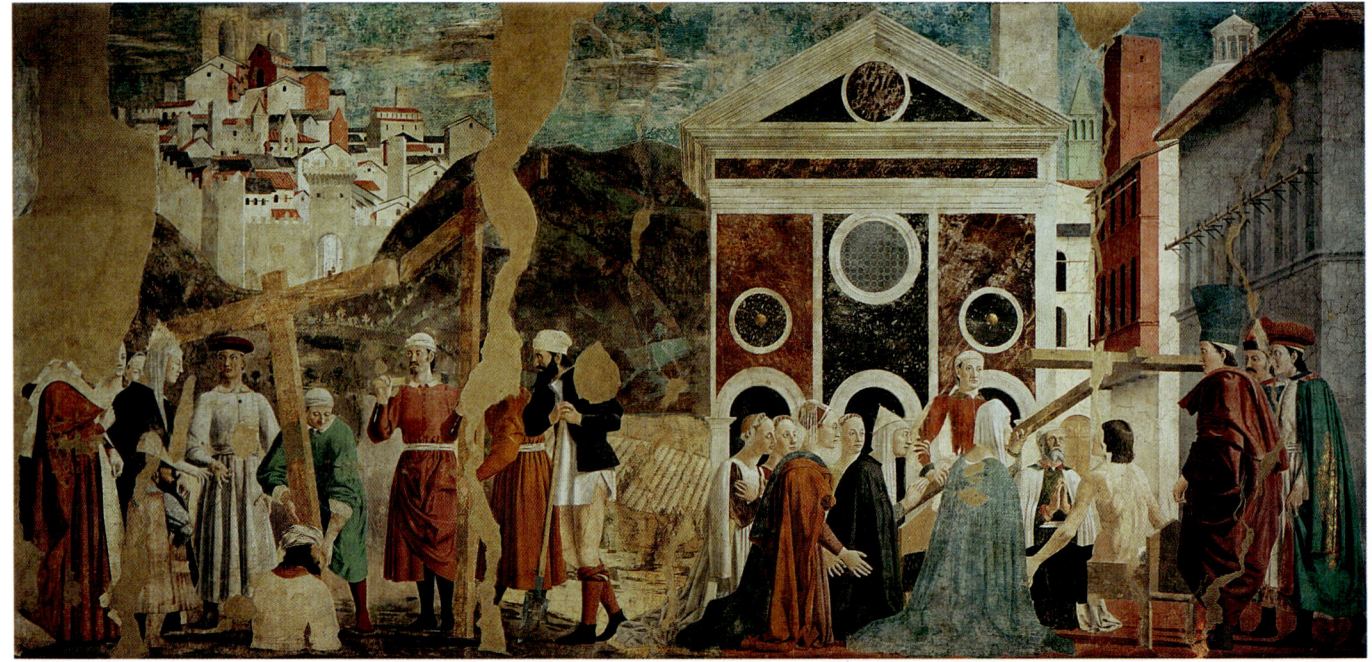

21-51 PIERO DELLA FRANCESCA, *Finding of the True Cross and Proving of the True Cross*, San Francesco, Arezzo, Italy, ca. 1455. Fresco, 11′ 8⅜″ × 6′ 4″.

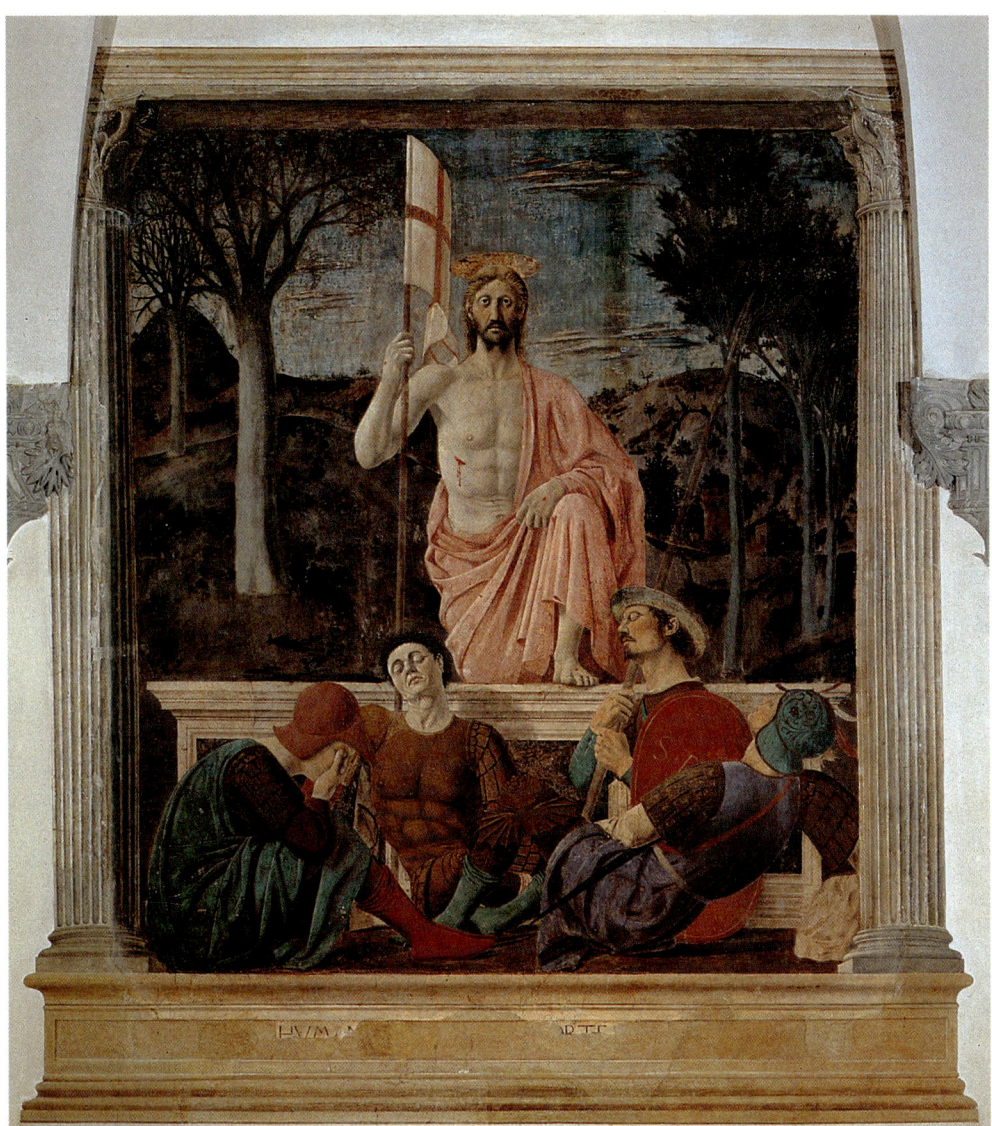

21-52 PIERO DELLA FRANCESCA, *Resurrection,* Palazzo Comunale, Borgo San Sepolcro, Italy, ca. 1463. Fresco, 7' 5" × 6' 6½".

familiar with compass and straightedge. As the architectonic nature of the abstract shapes controls the grouping, so, too, does it impart a mood of solemn stillness to the figures.

Piero's work shows, in addition, an unflagging interest in the properties of light and color. In his effort to make the clearest possible distinction between forms, he flooded his pictures with light, imparting a silver-blue tonality. To avoid heavy shadows, he illuminated the dark sides of his forms with reflected light. By moving the darkest tones of his modeling toward the centers of his volumes, he separated them from their backgrounds. With this technique, Piero's paintings lack some of Masaccio's relief-like qualities but gain in spatial clarity, as each shape forms an independent unit surrounded by an atmospheric envelope and movable to any desired position, like a figure on a chessboard.

RESURRECTING MASACCIO'S COMPOSITION In the *Resurrection* fresco in the chapel of the town hall of Borgo San Sepolcro (FIG. **21-52**), Piero's birthplace in southern Tuscany, the artist used the compositional device—the figure triangle—Masaccio had used so successfully in *Holy Trinity* (FIG. 21-13) and that enjoyed great favor with later Re-

naissance artists. To stabilize the composition, Piero arranged his figures in a group that can be circumscribed by a triangle centrally placed in the painting. The risen Christ, standing with columnar strength in the attitude of eternal triumph at the edge of the tomb, occupies the upper portion of the triangular arrangement, which rests on the broad base of the sleeping soldiers in the foreground. This triangular massing of volumes around a picture's central axis gives a painting great compositional stability and is one of the keys to the symmetry and self-sufficiency Renaissance artists strove for in their work. Here, Piero involved spectators in his triangular composition by depicting the sleeping soldier at the lower right with his back to viewers so that the figure occupies the same position relative to Christ as that of spectators. His head and those of the two seated figures closest to Christ also are seen from below; viewers look up at them, and then their gazes linger on the triumphant resurrected Christ at the very center. Piero's sophisticated handling of color draws attention to Christ, too. The bright flesh, white banner, and pink mantle contrast sharply with the dark tones used for the sleeping soldiers in the foreground. Thus, both Piero's composition and palette focus viewers' attention immediately on the radiant haloed Christ.

21-53 PIERO DELLA FRANCESCA, *Enthroned Madonna and Saints Adored by Federico da Montefeltro (Brera Altarpiece)*, ca. 1472–1474. Oil on panel, 8′ 2″ × 5′ 7″. Pinacoteca di Brera, Milan.

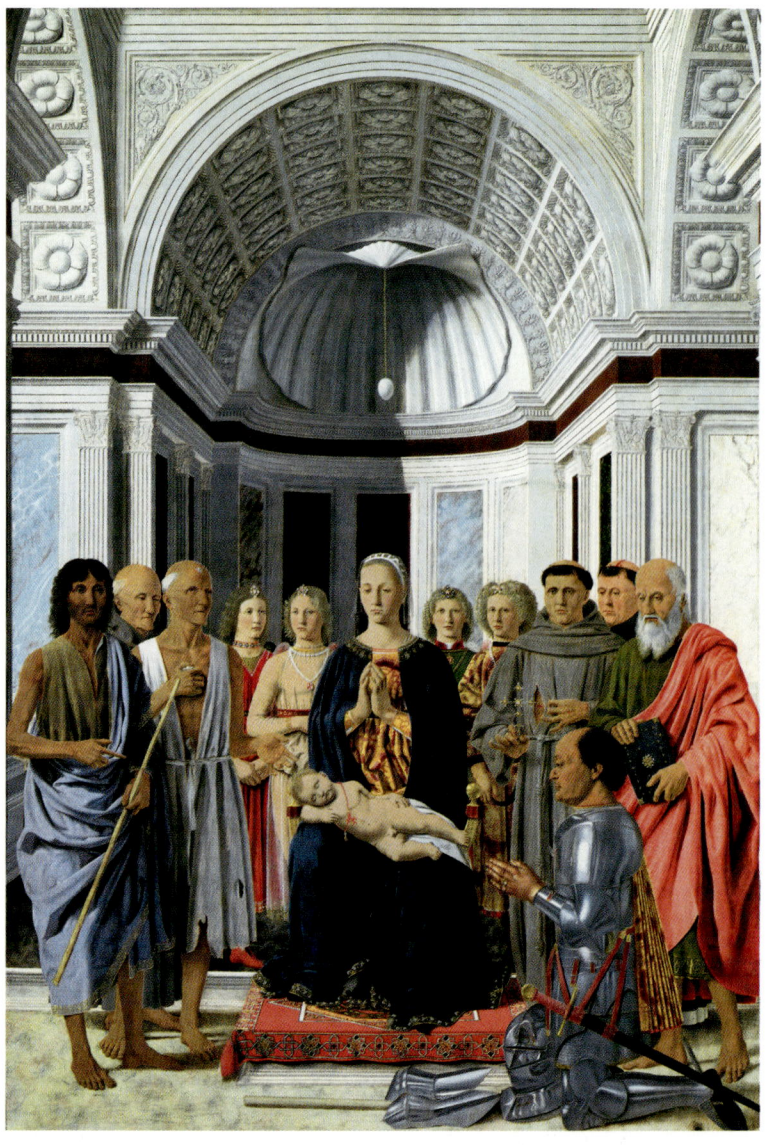

AN ARMORED PATRON AND THE MADONNA

Piero deployed all of his skills for the paintings Federico da Montefeltro commissioned. One of those works is *Enthroned Madonna and Saints Adored by Federico da Montefeltro*, also called the *Brera Altarpiece* (FIG. **21-53**). The clarity of Piero's earlier works is in full view here, as Federico, clad in armor, kneels piously at the Virgin's feet. Directly behind him stands Saint John the Evangelist, his patron saint. Where viewers would expect his wife, Battista Sforza, to appear (on the lower left, as a mirror image to Federico), no figure is present. Battista had died in 1472, shortly before Federico commissioned this painting. Thus, her absence clearly announces his loss. Piero further called attention to it by depicting Saint John the Baptist, Battista's patron saint, at the far left. The ostrich egg that hangs suspended from a shell over the Virgin's head was a common presence over altars dedicated to Mary. The figures appear in an illusionistically painted coffered barrel vault, which may have reflected the actual architecture of the painting's intended location, the church of San Bernadino degli Zoccolanti near Urbino. If such were the case, it would have enhanced the illusion, and viewers would be compelled to believe in Federico's presence before the Virgin, Christ Child, and saints. That Piero depicted Federico in profile was undoubtedly a concession to the patron. The right side of Federico's face had been badly injured in a tournament, and the resulting deformity made him reluctant to show that side of his face. The number of works (including other portraits) Piero executed for Federico reflects his success in accommodating his patron's wishes.

TURMOIL AT THE END OF THE CENTURY

A decade after Botticelli painted *Birth of Venus,* Florence underwent a political, cultural, and religious upheaval. Florentine artists and their fellow citizens responded then not only to humanist ideas but also to the incursion of French armies and especially to the preaching of the Dominican monk Girolamo Savonarola, the reforming priest-dictator who denounced the paganism of the Medici and their artists, philosophers, and poets. Savonarola exhorted the people of Florence to repent their sins, and, when Lorenzo de' Medici died in 1492 and the Medici fled, he prophesied the downfall of the city and of Italy and assumed absolute control of the state. Together with a large number of citizens, Savonarola believed that the Medici's political, social, and religious power had corrupted Florence and had invited the scourge of foreign invasion. Savonarola denounced humanism and encouraged

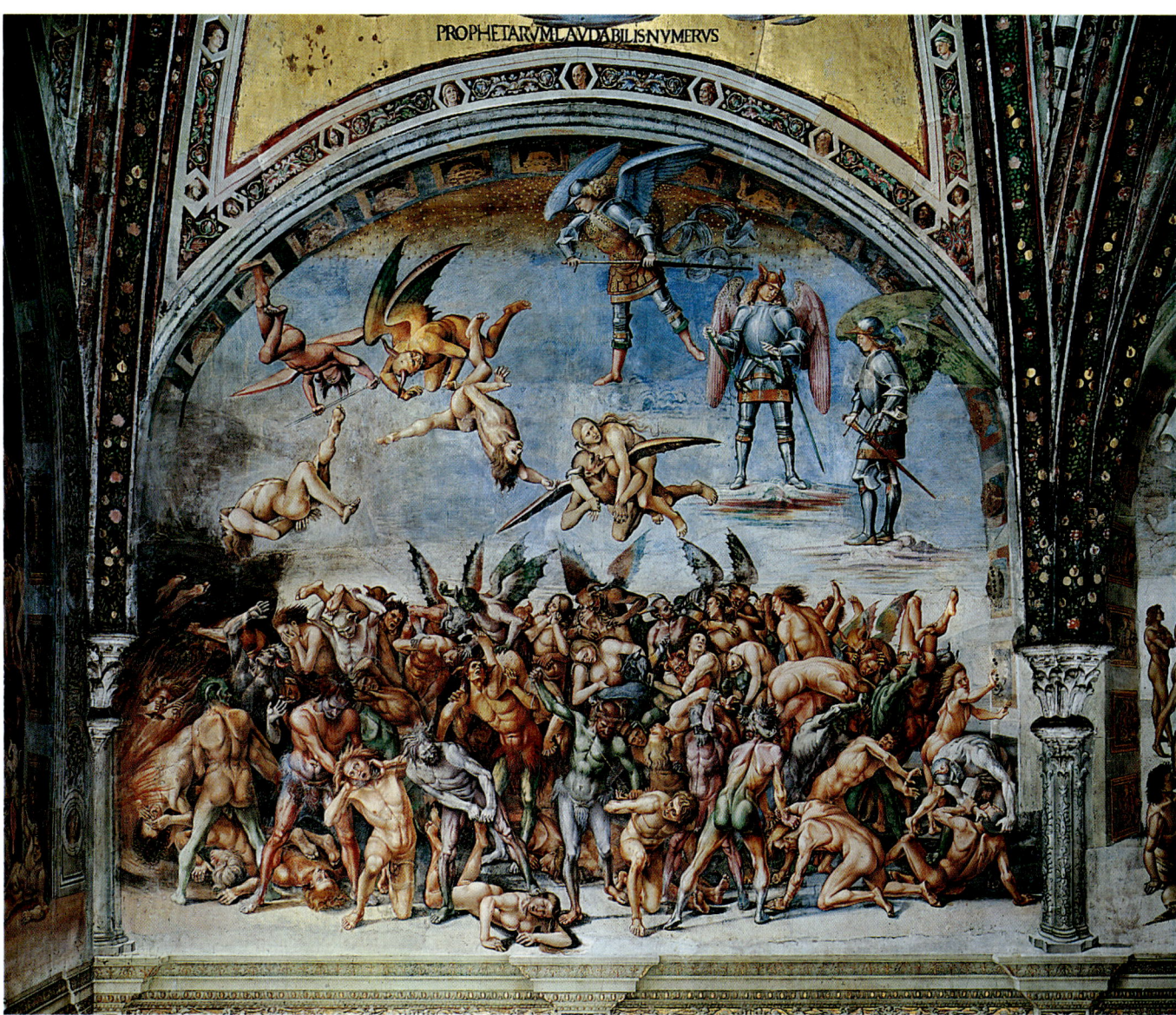

21-54 LUCA SIGNORELLI, *Damned Cast into Hell,* San Brizio Chapel, Orvieto Cathedral, Orvieto, Italy, 1499–1504. Fresco, approx. 23′ wide.

"bonfires of the vanities" for citizens to burn their classical texts, scientific treatises, and philosophical publications. Modern scholars still debate the significance of Savonarola's brief span of power. Apologists for the undoubtedly sincere monk deny that his actions played a role in the decline of Florentine culture at the end of the fifteenth century. But he did condemn humanism as heretical nonsense, and his banishing of the Medici, Tornabuoni, and other wealthy families from Florence deprived local artists of some of their major patrons. Certainly, the puritanical spirit that moved Savonarola must have dampened considerably the neopagan enthusiasm of the Florentine Early Renaissance.

A HORRIFYING VISION OF THE DAMNED
Outside Florence, the fiery passion of the sermons of Savonarola found its pictorial equal in the work of the Umbrian painter LUCA SIGNORELLI (ca. 1445–1523). The artist further developed Antonio Pollaiuolo's interest in the depiction of muscular bodies in violent action in a wide variety of poses and foreshortenings. In the San Brizio Chapel in Orvieto Cathedral, Signorelli's painted scenes depicting the end of the world include *Damned Cast into Hell* (FIG. **21-54**). Few

figure compositions of the fifteenth century have the same awesome psychic impact. Saint Michael and the hosts of Heaven hurl the Damned into Hell, where, in a dense writhing mass, demons vigorously torture them. The horrible consequences of a sinful life had not been so graphically depicted since Gislebertus carved his vision of the Last Judgment in the west tympanum of Saint-Lazare at Autun (see FIGS. 17-25 and Intro-6) around 1130. The figures—nude, lean, and muscular—assume every conceivable posture of anguish. Signorelli's skill at foreshortening the human figure was one with his mastery of its action, and, although each figure is clearly a study from a model, he fit his theme to the figures in an entirely convincing manner. Terror and rage pass like storms through the wrenched and twisted bodies. The fiends, their hair flaming and their bodies the color of putrefying flesh, lunge at their victims in ferocious frenzy.

Doubtless, Signorelli influenced Michelangelo, who made the human nude his sole and sufficient expressive motif in the next century. The many artistic experiments and directions pursued by artists of the fifteenth century served as the foundation for the work of High Renaissance masters, such as Leonardo, Michelangelo, Raphael, and Titian, among many others.

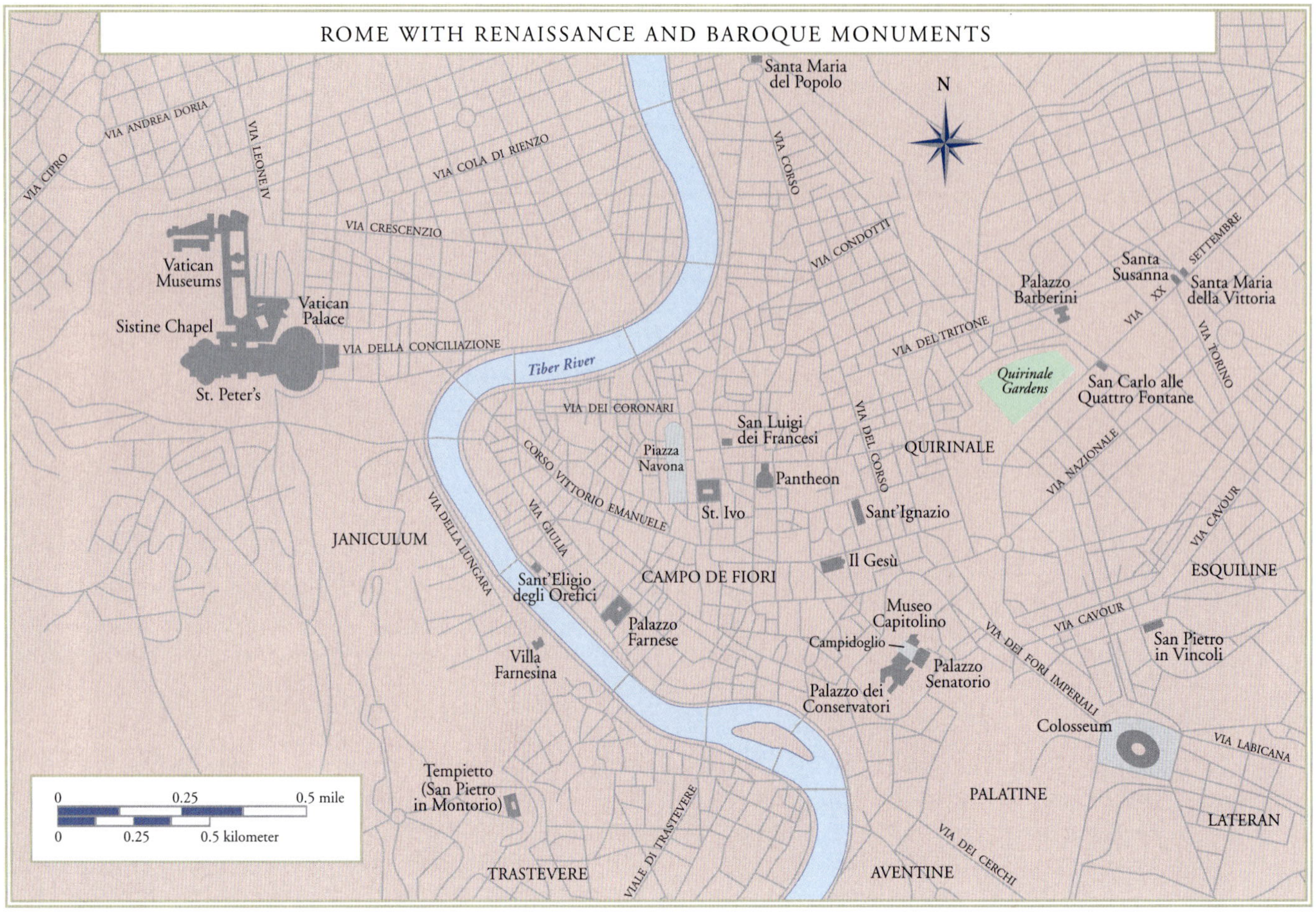

ROME WITH RENAISSANCE AND BAROQUE MONUMENTS

Santa Maria del Popolo

N

VIA ANDREA DORIA
VIA CIPRO
VIA LEONE IV
VIA COLA DI RIENZO
VIA CRESCENZIO
VIA CORSO
VIA CONDOTTI

Vatican Museums
Sistine Chapel
Vatican Palace
VIA DELLA CONCILIAZIONE
St. Peter's

Tiber River

VIA DEI CORONARI

Palazzo Barberini
Santa Susanna
Santa Maria della Vittoria
VIA XX SETTEMBRE
VIA TORINO
VIA DEL TRITONE

Quirinale Gardens
San Carlo alle Quattro Fontane

QUIRINALE

Piazza Navona
San Luigi dei Francesi
Pantheon
Sant'Ignazio
VIA DEL CORSO

VIA NAZIONALE

CORSO VITTORIO EMANUELE
St. Ivo

JANICULUM
VIA DELLA LUNGARA
VIA GIULIA

CAMPO DE FIORI
Il Gesù

VIA CAVOUR
VIA DEI FORI IMPERIALI

ESQUILINE

Sant'Eligio degli Orefici
Palazzo Farnese
Villa Farnesina

Museo Capitolino
Campidoglio
Palazzo Senatorio
Palazzo dei Conservatori

San Pietro in Vincoli

Colosseum
VIA LABICANA

Tempietto (San Pietro in Montorio)

PALATINE

LATERAN

TRASTEVERE
VIALE DI TRASTEVERE
VIA DEI CERCHI
AVENTINE

0   0.25   0.5 mile
0   0.25   0.5 kilometer

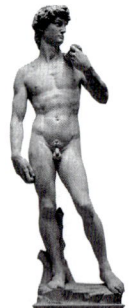

Michelangelo, David 1501–1504

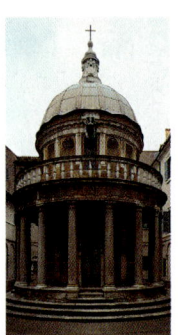

Bramante, Tempietto San Pietro in Montorio Rome, ca. 1502

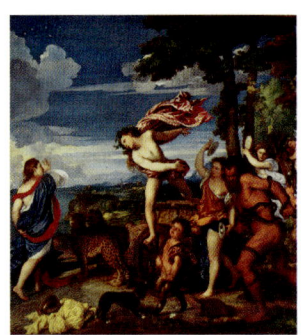

Titian, Meeting of Bacchus and Ariadne, 1522–1523

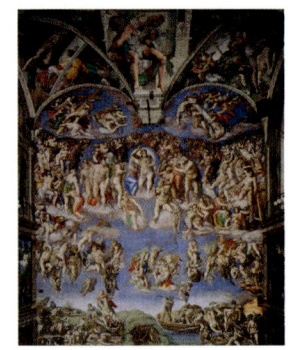

Michelangelo Last Judgment Sistine Chapel, 1534–1541

Niccolò Machiavelli (1469–1527), *The Prince*, 1532

Baldassare Castiglione (1478–1529), *The Courtier*, 1528

Pope Alexander VI (Borgia), r. 1492–1503

Pope Julius II (della Rovere), r. 1503–1513

Pope Leo X (Medici), r. 1513–1521

Protestant Reformation begins, 1517

Pope Clement VII (Medici), r. 1523–1534

Society of Jesus (the Jesuit Order) established, 1540

22

BEAUTY, SCIENCE, AND SPIRIT IN ITALIAN ART

THE HIGH RENAISSANCE AND MANNERISM

1550	1575	1600

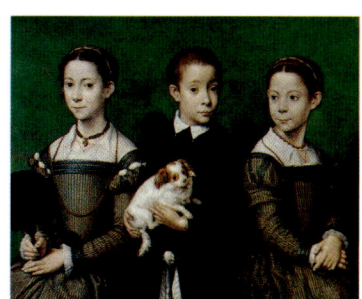

Sofonisba Anguissola
Portrait of the Artist's Sisters
and Brother, ca. 1555

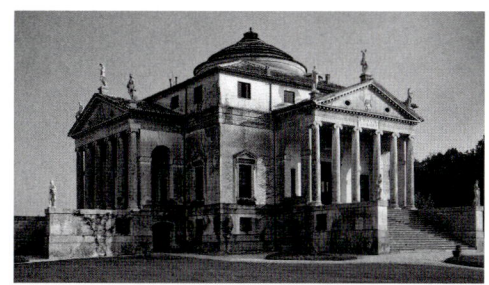

Andrea Palladio, Villa Rotonda
ca. 1566–1570

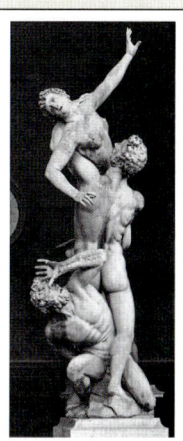

Giovanni da Bologna, Abduction of the
Sabine Women, completed 1583

Giorgio Vasari (1511–1574), *Lives of the Most Eminent Painters, Sculptors and Architects*, 1550

Council of Trent, 1545–1563

Pope Pius IV (Medici), r. 1559–1565

Pope Gregory XIII (Buoncompagni), r. 1572–1585

Pope Sixtus V (Peretti), r. 1585–1590

UPHEAVAL IN THE CHURCH

Sixteenth-century Italy witnessed major upheaval and change, particularly in the realm of religion. Widespread dissatisfaction with the leadership and policies of the Roman Catholic Church led to the Protestant Reformation, which historians often date as formally beginning in 1517. Led by clerics such as Martin Luther (1483–1546) and John Calvin (1509–1564) in the Holy Roman Empire, reformers directly challenged papal authority, especially regarding secular issues. Disgruntled Catholics voiced concerns about the sale of indulgences (pardons for sins, reducing the time a soul spent in Purgatory), nepotism (the appointment of relatives to important positions), and high Church officials pursuing personal wealth. This reform movement resulted in the establishment of Protestantism, with sects such as Lutheranism and Calvinism. Central to Protestantism was a belief in personal faith rather than adherence to decreed Church practices and doctrines. Because the Protestants believed the only true religious relationship was the personal relationship between individuals and God, they were, in essence, eliminating the need for Church intercession central to Catholicism.

The Catholic Church, in response, mounted a full-fledged campaign to counteract the migration of its members to Protestantism. This response, the Counter-Reformation, consisted of numerous initiatives. The Council of Trent, which met intermittently from 1545 through 1563, was a major component of this effort. Composed of cardinals, archbishops, bishops, abbots, and theologians, the Council of Trent dealt with issues of Church doctrine, including many the Protestants contested.

Another important facet of the Counter-Reformation was the activity of the Society of Jesus, known as the Jesuits. Ignatius of Loyola (1491–1556), a Spanish nobleman who dedicated his life to the service of God, founded the Jesuit order. He attracted a group of followers, and in 1540 the pope formally recognized this group as a religious order. The Jesuits were the papacy's invaluable allies in its quest to reassert the Catholic Church's supremacy. Particularly successful in the field of education, the order established numerous schools. Its commitment to education remains evident today in the many Jesuit colleges around the world. In addition, its members were effective missionaries and carried the message of Catholicism to the Americas, Asia, and Africa. The predominance of Catholicism in Latin America, the Philippines, and areas of Africa testifies to the Jesuit influence.

The Catholic Church's determination to win back adherents also led it to institute somewhat more extreme measures, such as the founding of the Holy Office of the Inquisition. The Inquisition was a Church court established specifically to deal with heretics. Zealous in its attempt to eradicate heresy, this court prosecuted non-Catholics, sometimes subjecting them to imprisonment or death.

The turmoil in the Church that led to both the Protestant Reformation and the Catholic Counter-Reformation provided the context for the prominence of papal art commissions during this period. Popes long had been aware of the power of visual imagery to construct and reinforce ideological claims, and sixteenth-century popes exploited this capability (see "The Role of Religious Art in Counter-Reformation Italy," page 637). Many of the major commissions came from the Church, and many of the popes initiated grandiose art programs.

THE HIGH RENAISSANCE

The Lasting Influence of Sixteenth-Century Artists

The fifteenth-century artistic developments in Italy (for example, the interest in perspectival systems and in depicting anatomy) matured during the sixteenth century, accounting for the designations "Early Renaissance" for the fifteenth century and "High Renaissance" for the sixteenth century. Although no singular style characterizes the High Renaissance, the art of those most closely associated with this period—Leonardo da Vinci, Raphael, Michelangelo, and Titian—exhibits an astounding mastery, both technical and aesthetic. High Renaissance artists created works of such authority that generations of later artists relied on these artworks for instruction.

These exemplary artistic creations further elevated the prestige of artists. Artists could claim divine inspiration, thereby raising visual art to a status formerly only given to poetry. Thus, painters, sculptors, and architects came into their own, successfully claiming for their work a high position among the fine arts. In a sense, sixteenth-century masters created a new profession with its own rights of expression and its own venerable character.

The Transition from Early Renaissance to High Renaissance

FROM A(NATOMY) TO Z(OOLOGY) The immense intellect, talent, and foresight of Leonardo da Vinci (1452–1519) allowed him to map the routes art and science were to take in the future. The scope and depth of his interests were without precedent—so great as to frustrate any hopes he might have had of realizing all his feverishly inventive imagination could conceive.

Although the discussion here focuses on Leonardo as an artist, exploring his art in conjunction with his other interests considerably enhances an understanding of his artistic production. Leonardo revealed his unquenchable curiosity in his voluminous notes, liberally interspersed with sketches dealing with botany, geology, geography, cartography, zoology, military engineering, animal lore, anatomy, and aspects of physical science, including hydraulics and mechanics. These studies informed his art. For example, Leonardo's in-depth exploration of optics provided him with an understanding of perspective, light, and color that he used in his painting. His scientific drawings are themselves artworks.

Leonardo's great ambition in his painting, as well as in his scientific endeavors, was to discover the laws underlying the processes and flux of nature. With this end in mind, he also studied the human body and contributed immeasurably to knowledge of physiology and psychology. Leonardo believed that reality in an absolute sense is inaccessible and that humans can know it only through its changing images. He considered the eyes the most vital organs and sight the most essential function, as, through these, individuals could grasp the images of reality most directly and profoundly. In his notes, he stated repeatedly that all his scientific investigations made him a better painter.

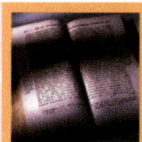

The Role of Religious Art in Counter-Reformation Italy

Both Catholics and Protestants took seriously the role of devotional imagery in religious life. However, their views differed dramatically. While Catholics deemed art as valuable for cultivating piety, Protestants believed such visual imagery could produce idolatry and could distract the faithful from their goal—developing a personal relationship with God (see Chapter 23, "Martin Luther on Religious Art," page 692). As part of the Counter-Reformation effort, Pope Paul III convened the Council of Trent in 1545 and directed them to review controversial Church doctrines. Among the council's conclusions was the following edict on the invocation (plea or call for help) of saints, the veneration of saints' relics, and the role of sacred images, published in *Canons and Decrees of the Council of Trent*:

> The holy council commands all bishops and others who hold the office of teaching and have charge of the *cura animarum* [literally, "cure of souls"—the responsibility of laboring for the salvation of souls], that in accordance with the usage of the Catholic and Apostolic Church, received from the primitive times of the Christian religion, and with the unanimous teaching of the holy Fathers and the decrees of sacred councils, they above all instruct the faithful diligently in matters relating to intercession and invocation of the saints, the veneration of relics, and the legitimate use of images. . . . Moreover, that the images of Christ, of the Virgin Mother of God, and of the other saints are to be placed and retained especially in the churches, and that due honor and veneration is to be given them; . . . because the honor which is shown them is referred to the prototypes which they represent, so that by means of the images which we kiss and before which we uncover the head and prostrate ourselves, we adore Christ and venerate the saints whose likeness they bear. That is what was defined by the decrees of the councils, especially of the Second Council of Nicaea, against the opponents of images.

Moreover, let the bishops diligently teach that by means of the stories of the mysteries of our redemption portrayed in paintings and other representations the people are instructed and confirmed in the articles of faith, which ought to be borne in mind and constantly reflected upon; also that great profit is derived from all holy images, not only because the people are thereby reminded of the benefits and gifts bestowed on them by Christ, but also because through the saints the miracles of God and salutary examples are set before the eyes of the faithful, so that they may give God thanks for those things, may fashion their own life and conduct in imitation of the saints and be moved to adore and love God and cultivate piety. . . .

And if at times it happens, when this is beneficial to the illiterate, that the stories and narratives of the Holy Scriptures are portrayed and exhibited, the people should be instructed that not for that reason is the divinity represented in picture as if it can be seen with bodily eyes or expressed in colors or figures. Furthermore, in the invocation of the saints, the veneration of relics, and the sacred use of images, all superstition shall be removed, all filthy quest for gain eliminated, and all lasciviousness avoided, so that images shall not be painted and adorned with a seductive charm, or the celebration of saints and the visitation of relics be perverted by the people into boisterous festivities and drunkenness, as if the festivals in honor of the saints are to be celebrated with revelry and with no sense of decency. . . .

That these things may be the more faithfully observed, the holy council decrees that no one is permitted to erect or cause to be erected in any place or church, howsoever exempt, any unusual image unless it has been approved by the bishop; . . .[1]

[1] Robert Klein and Henri Zerner, *Italian Art 1500–1600: Sources and Documents* (Evanston, Ill.: Northwestern University Press, 1966), 120–21.

Born in the small town of Vinci, near Florence, Leonardo trained in the studio of Andrea del Verrocchio, but he left Florence around 1481, offering his services to Ludovico Sforza, duke of Milan, who accepted them. The political situation in Florence was uncertain, and Leonardo may have felt the artistic scene in Milan would be less competitive. He devoted most of a letter to the duke of Milan to advertising his competence and his qualifications as a military engineer, mentioning only at the end his abilities as a painter and sculptor:

> And in short, according to the variety of cases, I can contrive various and endless means of offence and defence. . . . In time of peace I believe I can give perfect satisfaction and to the equal of any other in architecture and the composition of buildings, public and private; and in guiding water from one place to another. . . . I can carry out sculpture in marble, bronze, or clay, and also I can do in painting whatever may be done, as well as any other, be he whom he may.[1]

This letter illustrates the fifteenth-century artist's relation to patrons, as well as Leonardo's breadth of competence. That he should select military engineering and design to interest a patron is an index of the period's instability. By this time, especially in northern Europe, weaponry had been developed to the point that the siege cannon threatened the feudal castles of those resisting wealthy and aggressive new monarchs. By the turn of the century, when aspiring kingdoms of Europe targeted Italy for acquisition, Italians of all walks of life—not only soldiers and architects but artists and humanists as well—expressed their concern with the problem of designing a fortification system that might withstand the terrible new weapon.

PAINTING THE SOUL'S INTENTION During his first sojourn in Milan, Leonardo painted *Virgin of the Rocks*

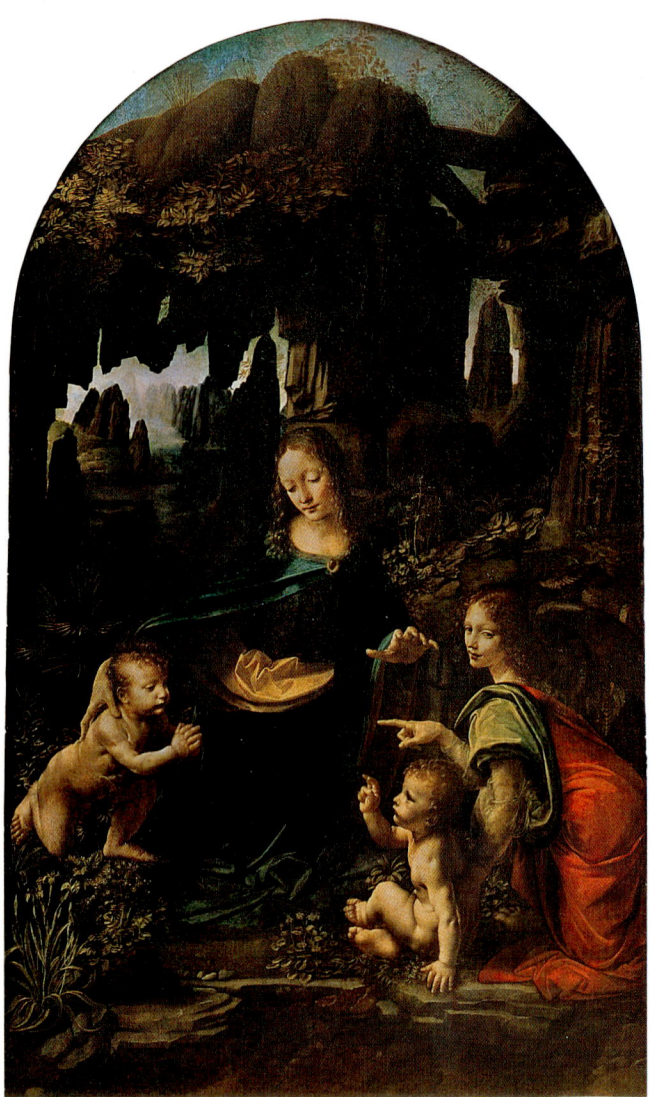

22-1 LEONARDO DA VINCI, *Virgin of the Rocks,* ca. 1485. Oil on wood (transferred to canvas), approx. 6′ 3″ × 3′ 7″. Louvre, Paris.

(FIG. **22-1**) as the central panel of an altarpiece for the chapel of the Confraternity of the Immaculate Conception (see "Mendicant Orders and Confraternities," Chapter 19, page 537) in San Francesco Grande. The painting incorporates Masaccio's great discovery of chiaroscuro, the subtle play of light and dark. Modeling with light and shadow and expressing emotional states were, for Leonardo, the heart of painting:

> A good painter has two chief objects to paint—man and the intention of his soul. The former is easy, the latter hard, for it must be expressed by gestures and the movement of the limbs. . . . A painting will only be wonderful for the beholder by making that which is not so appear raised and detached from the wall.[2]

Leonardo presented the figures in *Virgin of the Rocks* in a pyramidal grouping and, more notably, as sharing the same environment. This groundbreaking achievement—the unified representation of objects in an atmospheric setting—was a manifestation of his scientific curiosity about the invisible substance surrounding things. The Madonna, Christ Child, infant John the Baptist, and angel emerge through nuances of light and shade from the half-light of the cavernous visionary landscape. Light simultaneously veils and reveals the

forms, immersing them in a layer of atmosphere between them and viewers' eyes. Leonardo's effective use of atmospheric perspective is on full view here. The ambiguity of light and shade (familiar in dusk's optical haziness) serves the psychological ambiguity of perception. The group depicted, wrapped in subtle light and shade, eludes precise definition and interpretation. The figures pray, point, and bless, and these acts and gestures, although their meanings are not certain, visually unite the individuals portrayed. The angel points to the infant John and, through his outward glance, involves spectators in the tableau. John prays to the Christ Child and is blessed in return. The Virgin herself completes the series of interlocking gestures, her left hand reaching toward the Christ Child and her right hand resting protectively on John's shoulder. The melting mood of tenderness, enhanced by the caressing light, suffuses the entire composition. What the eye sees is fugitive, as are the states of the soul, or, in Leonardo's term, its "intentions."

A MAJESTIC PRELIMINARY DRAWING Leonardo's style fully emerges in a cartoon (a full-size preliminary drawing; see "*Disegno:* Drawing on Design Fundamentals," page 639), *Virgin and Child with Saint Anne and the Infant Saint John* (FIG. **22-2**). Here, the glowing light falls gently on the majestic forms, on a scene of tranquil grandeur and balance. Leonardo ordered every part of his cartoon with an

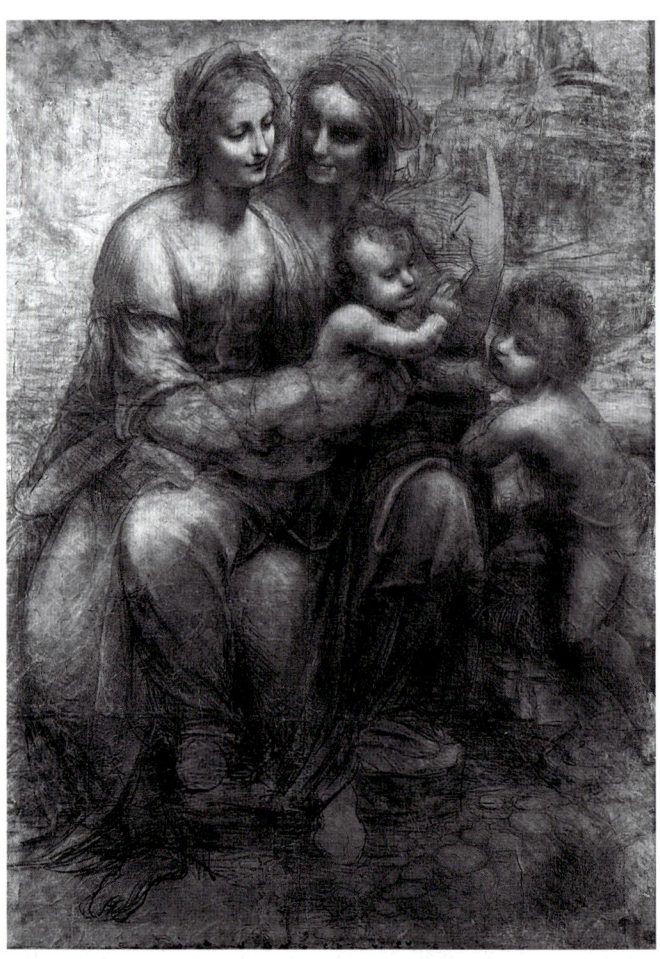

22-2 LEONARDO DA VINCI, cartoon for *Virgin and Child with Saint Anne and the Infant Saint John,* ca. 1505–1507. Charcoal heightened with white on brown paper, approx. 4′ 6″ × 3′ 3″. National Gallery, London.

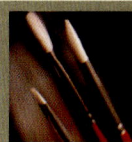

Disegno
Drawing on Design Fundamentals

In the sixteenth century in Italy, drawing (or *disegno*) assumed a position of greater prominence than ever before in artistic production. Until the late fifteenth century, the lack of availability and expense of drawing surfaces limited the production of preparatory sketches. Most artists drew on parchment (prepared from the skins of calves, sheep, and goats) or on vellum (made from the skins of young animals and therefore very expensive). Because of the cost of these materials, drawings in the fourteenth and fifteenth centuries tended to be extremely detailed and meticulously executed. Artists often drew using *silverpoint* (a stylus made of silver) because of the fine line it produced and the sharp point it maintained. The introduction of less-expensive paper made of fibrous pulp, from the developing printing industry, allowed artists to experiment more and to draw with greater freedom. As a result, sketches abounded. Artists executed these drawings in pen and ink, chalk, charcoal, brush, and graphite or lead.

The importance of drawing, however, extended beyond the mechanical or technical possibilities drawing afforded artists. The term *disegno* also referred to design, an integral component of good art. Design was the foundation of art, while drawing was the fundamental element of design, linking the two. A statement by the artist Federico Zuccaro that drawing is the external physical manifestation *(disegno esterno)* of an internal intellectual idea or design *(disegno interno)* confirms this connection.

The design dimension of art production became increasingly important as artists cultivated their own styles. The early stages of artistic training largely focused on imitation and emulation (see "Imitation and Emulation: Artistic Values in the Renaissance," Chapter 21, page 602), but, to achieve widespread recognition, artists were expected to move beyond this dependence on previous models and develop their own styles. Although the artistic community and public at large acknowledged technical skill, the artwork's conceptualization—its theoretical and formal development—was paramount. *Disegno*, or *design* in this case, represented an artist's conceptualization and intention. In the period's literature, the terms writers and critics often invoked to praise esteemed artists included *invenzione* (invention), *ingegno* (ingenuity), *fantasia* (imagination), and *capriccio* (originality).

---

intellectual pictorial logic that results in an appealing visual unity. The figures are robust and monumental, the stately grace of their movements reminiscent of the Phidian statues of goddesses in the Parthenon's pediments (FIG. 5-47). However, Leonardo and his contemporaries never saw those particular sculptures, because their acquaintance with classical art was limited to Etruscan and Roman monuments and Roman copies of Greek masterpieces unearthed in Italy.

DRAMA IN AN AUSTERE SETTING For the refectory of the church of Santa Maria delle Grazie in Milan, Leonardo painted *Last Supper* (FIG. **22-3**). Despite its ruined state (in part from the painter's unfortunate experiments with his materials) and although it often has been restored ineptly (see "Restoring the Glory of Renaissance Frescoes," page 652), the painting is both formally and emotionally his most impressive work. Christ and his twelve disciples are seated at a long table set parallel to the picture plane in a simple, spacious room. Leonardo amplified the painting's highly dramatic action by placing the group in an austere setting. Christ, with outstretched hands, has just said, "One of you is about to betray me" (Matt. 26:21). A wave of intense excitement passes through the group as each disciple asks himself and, in some cases, his neighbor, "Is it I?" (Matt. 26:22). Leonardo visualized a sophisticated conjunction of the dramatic "One of you is about to betray me" with the initiation of the ancient liturgical ceremony of the Eucharist, when Christ, blessing bread and wine, said, "This is my body, which is given for you. Do this for a commemoration of me. . . . This is the chalice, the new testament in my blood, which shall be shed for you" (Luke 22:19–20). The artist's careful conceptualization of the composition imbued this dramatic moment with force and lucidity.

In the center, Christ appears isolated from the disciples and in perfect repose, the still eye of the swirling emotion around him. The central window at the back, whose curved pediment arches above his head, frames his figure. The pediment is the only curve in the architectural framework, and it serves here, along with the diffused light, as a halo. Christ's head is the focal point of all converging perspective lines in the composition. Thus, the still, psychological focus and cause of the action is also the perspectival focus, as well as the center of the two-dimensional surface. One could say the two-dimensional, the three-dimensional, and the psychodimensional focuses are the same. Leonardo presented the agitated disciples in four groups of three, united among and within themselves by the figures' gestures and postures. The artist sacrificed traditional iconography to pictorial and dramatic consistency by placing Judas on the same side of the table as Jesus and the other disciples. His face in shadow, Judas clutches a money bag in his right hand and reaches his left forward to fulfill the Master's declaration: "But yet behold, the hand of him that betrayeth me is with me on the table" (Luke 22:21). The two disciples at the table ends are more quiet than the others, as if to bracket the energy of the composition, which is more intense closer to Christ, whose calm both halts and intensifies it.

The disciples register a broad range of emotional responses, including fear, doubt, protestation, rage, and love. Leonardo's numerous preparatory studies suggest he thought of each figure as carrying a particular charge and type of emotion. Like a skilled stage director (perhaps the first, in the modern sense), he read the gospel story carefully and scrupulously cast his

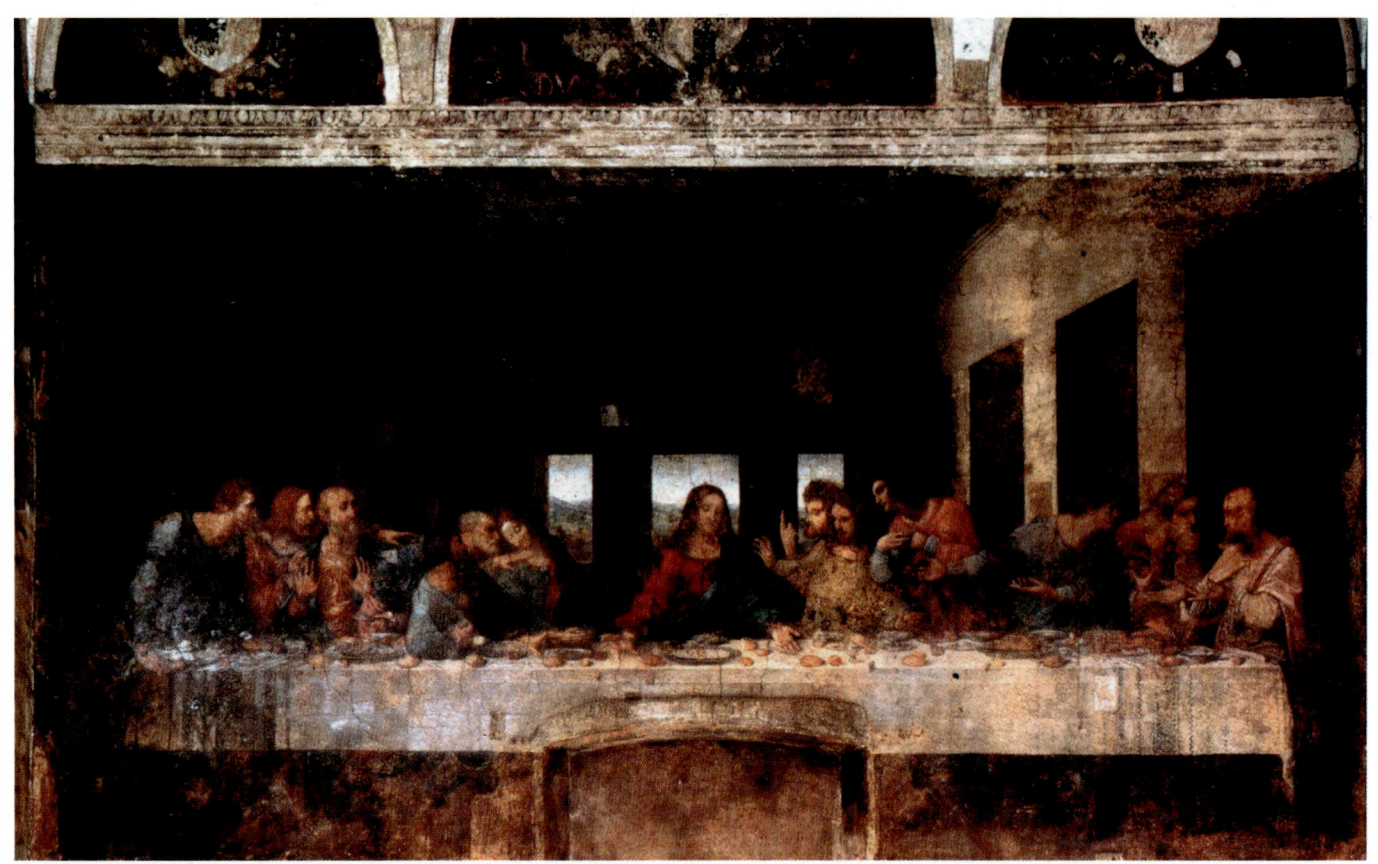

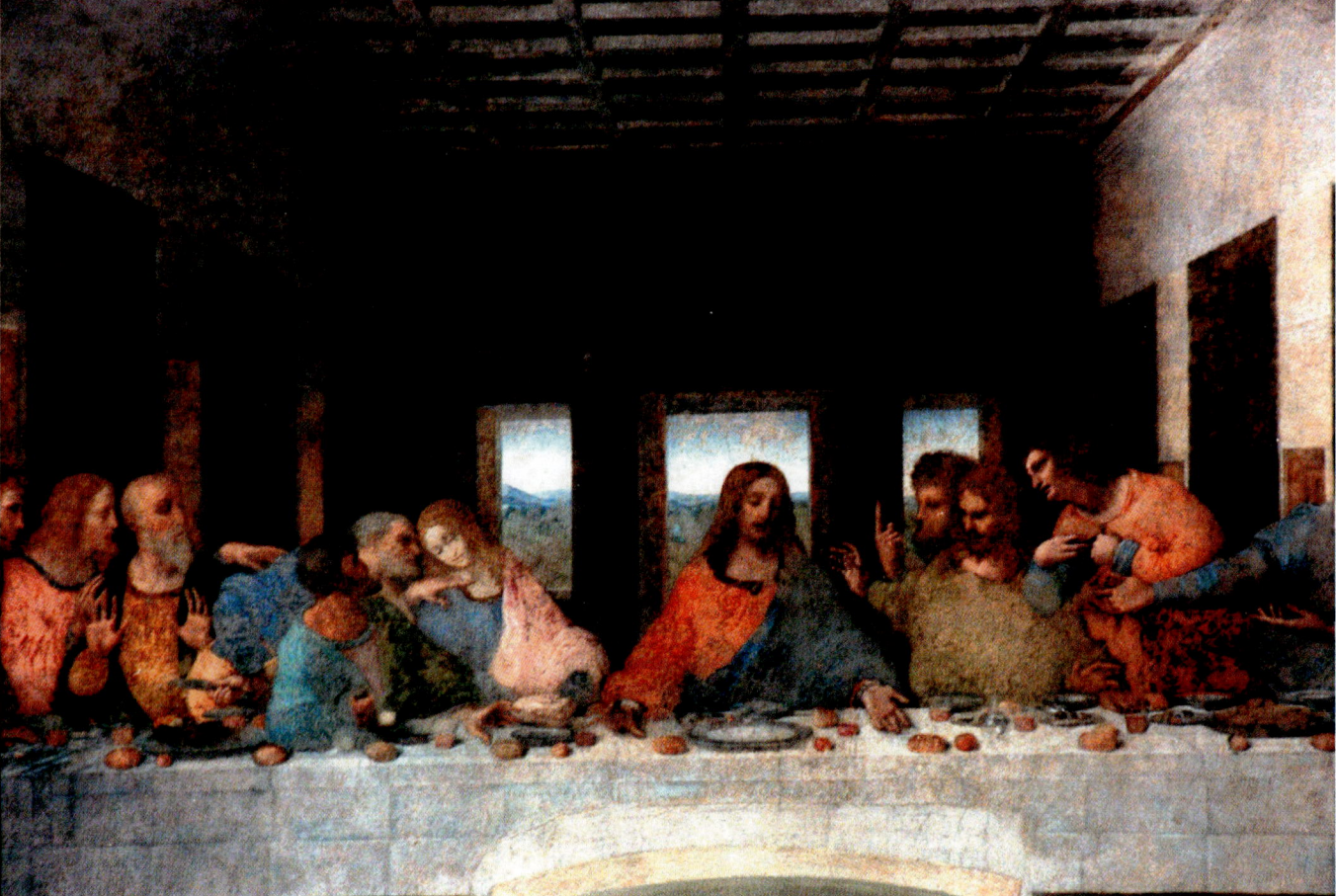

22-3 LEONARDO DA VINCI, *Last Supper* (*top,* uncleaned; *bottom,* cleaned), ca. 1495–1498. Fresco (oil and tempera on plaster), 29′ 10″ × 13′ 9″. Refectory, Santa Maria delle Grazie, Milan.

actors as the New Testament described their roles. Leonardo initiated this rhetoric of classical art that directed the compositions of generations of painters until the nineteenth century. The silence of Christ is one such powerful communication device. Indeed, art historian Heinrich Wölfflin saw that this classical element occurs precisely here, for in the silence following Christ's words, "the original impulse to the emotional excitement continues to echo, and the action is at once momentary, eternal and complete."[3] *Last Supper* and Leonardo's career leading up to it were at once a synthesis of fifteenth-century artistic developments and a first statement of the Italian High Renaissance style during the early sixteenth century.

A SMILE FOR THE AGES Leonardo's *Mona Lisa* (FIG. **22-4**) is probably the world's most famous portrait. The sitter's identity is still the subject of scholarly debate, but Renaissance biographer Giorgio Vasari asserted she is Lisa di Antonio Maria Gherardini, the wife of Francesco del Giocondo, a wealthy Florentine—hence, "Mona (an Italian contraction of *ma donna*, "my lady") Lisa." Vasari also claimed Leonardo took three years to complete the portrait after he returned to Florence from Milan. This was one of Leonardo's favorite pictures—one he could not bear to part with and that he still possessed when he died. Originally, the artist represented

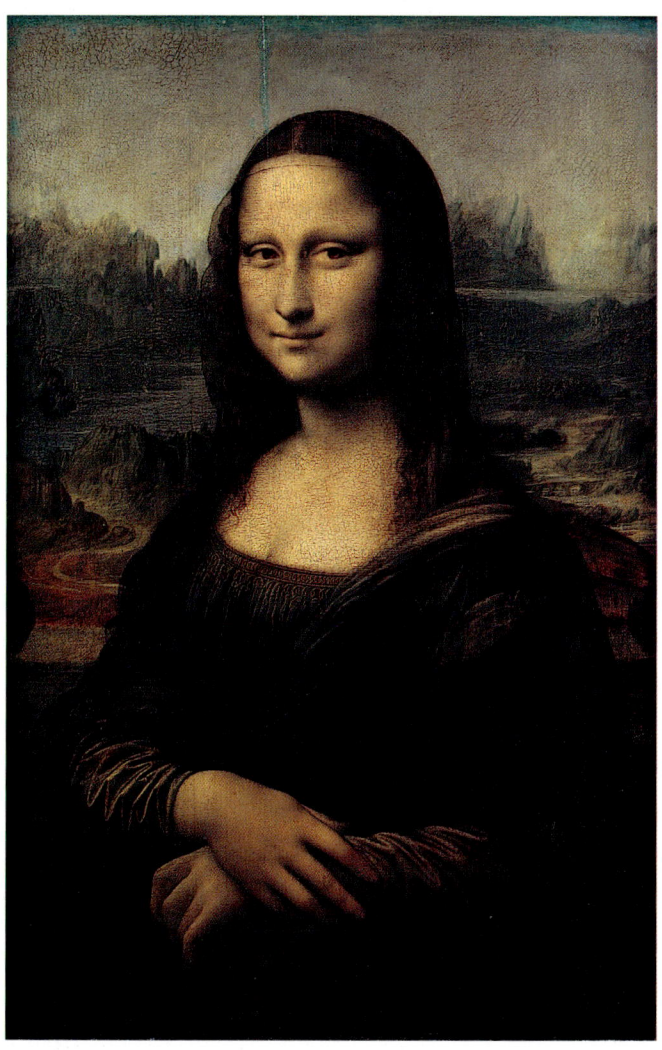

22-4 LEONARDO DA VINCI, *Mona Lisa*, ca. 1503–1505. Oil on wood, approx. 2′ 6″ × 1′ 9″. Louvre, Paris.

Mona Lisa in a loggia with columns. When the painting was trimmed (not by Leonardo), these columns were eliminated (the remains of the column bases may still be seen to the left and right of Mona Lisa's shoulders). She appears in half-length view, her hands quietly folded and her gaze directed at observers. The ambiguity of the famous "smile" is really the consequence of Leonardo's fascination and skill with chiaroscuro and atmospheric perspective, which he revealed in his *Virgin of the Rocks* (FIG. 22-1) and *Virgin and Child with Saint Anne and the Infant Saint John* (FIG. 22-2) groups. Here, they serve to disguise rather than reveal a human psyche. The artist subtly adjusted the light and blurred the precise planes—Leonardo's famous smoky *sfumato* (the misty haziness)—rendering the facial expression hard to determine.

The lingering appeal of *Mona Lisa* derives in large part from Leonardo's decision to set his subject against the backdrop of a mysterious uninhabited landscape. This landscape, with roads and bridges that seem to lead nowhere, is reminiscent of his *Virgin of the Rocks*. It also recalls Fra Filippo Lippi's "portrait," *Madonna and Child with Angels* (FIG. 21-40), with figures seated in front of a window viewers look through into a distant landscape.

THE BIRTH OF SCIENTIFIC ILLUSTRATION Leonardo completed very few paintings; his perfectionism, relentless experimentation, and far-ranging curiosity diffused his efforts. However, the drawings in his notebooks preserved an extensive record of his ideas. His interests focused increasingly on science in his later years, and he embraced knowledge of all facets of the natural world. His investigations in anatomy yielded drawings of great precision and beauty of execution. *Embryo in the Womb* (FIG. **22-5**), although it does not meet twenty-first-century standards for accuracy (for example, Leonardo regularized the uterus's shape to a sphere, and his characterization of the lining is incorrect), was an astounding achievement in its day. Analytical anatomical studies such as this epitomized the scientific spirit of the Renaissance, establishing that era as a prelude to the modern world and setting it in sharp contrast to the preceding Middle Ages. Although Leonardo may not have been the first scientist of the modern world (at least not in the modern sense of "scientist"), he certainly originated a method of scientific illustration, especially cutaway and exploded views. Art historian Erwin Panofsky stressed the importance of this: "Anatomy as a science (and this applies to all the other observational or descriptive disciplines) was simply not possible without a method of preserving observations in graphic records, complete and accurate in three dimensions."[4]

Leonardo was well known in his time as both architect and sculptor, although no actual buildings or surviving sculptures can be definitively attributed to him. From his many drawings of central-plan buildings, it appears he shared the interest of other Renaissance architects in this building type. As for sculpture, Leonardo left numerous drawings of monumental equestrian statues, and one resulted in a full-scale model for a monument to the Sforza (the duke of Milan's wealthy and influential family). The French used it as a target and shot it to pieces when they occupied Milan in 1499. Leonardo left Milan outraged at this treatment of his work and served for a while as a military engineer for Cesare Borgia, who, with the support of his father, Pope Alexander VI, tried to conquer the

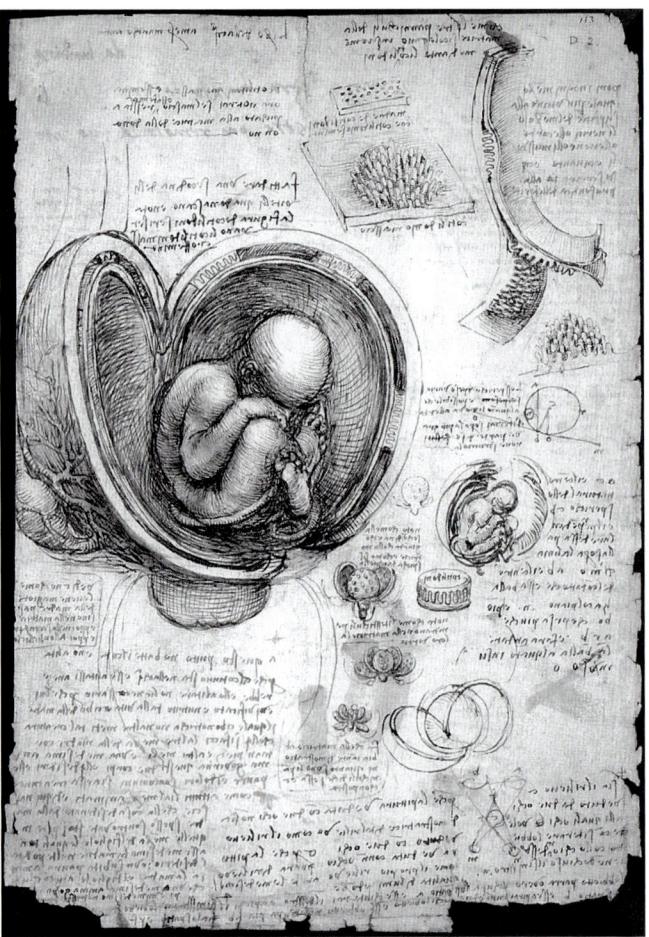

22-5 LEONARDO DA VINCI, *Embryo in the Womb,* ca. 1510. Pen and ink on paper. Royal Library, Windsor Castle.

cities of the Romagna region in north-central Italy and create a Borgia duchy. At a later date, Leonardo returned to Milan in the service of the French. At the invitation of King Francis I, he then went to France, where he died at the château of Cloux in 1519.

Julius II: A Warrior-Pope's Quest for Authority

Another individual whose interests and activities affected the course of the High Renaissance was Pope Julius II (Giuliano della Rovere, r. 1503–1513). An immensely ambitious man, Julius II's quest for authority extended beyond his responsibility as the spiritual leader of Christendom. His enthusiasm for engaging in battle, which earned him a designation as the "warrior-pope," reflected his desire for recognition as a temporal, as well as spiritual, leader. In addition, his selection of the name Julius, after Julius Caesar, reinforces the perception that the Roman Empire served as his governmental model.

Julius II's papacy is also notable for his contributions to the arts. He was an avid art patron and understood well the propagandistic value of visual imagery. After his election as pope, he immediately commissioned artworks that would present an authoritative image of his rule and reinforce the Catholic Church's primacy. Among the many projects he commissioned were a new design for Saint Peter's basilica, the construction of his tomb, the painting of the Sistine Chapel ceil-

ing, and the decoration of the papal apartments. These large-scale projects clearly required considerable financial resources. Many Church members perceived the increasing sale of indulgences as a revenue-generating mechanism to fund papal art, architecture, and lavish lifestyles. This perception, accurate or not, prompted disgruntlement among the faithful. Thus, Julius II's support for the arts, despite its exceptional artistic legacy, also contributed to the rise of the Reformation.

RE-CREATING THE ROME OF THE CAESARS   One of the most important artistic projects Julius II initiated was his plan to replace the Constantinian basilica, Old Saint Peter's (see FIG. 11-7 or page xxxiii in Volume II), with a new structure. The earlier building had fallen into considerable disrepair and, in any event, did not suit this ambitious pope's taste for the colossal. Julius wanted to gain control over the whole of Italy and to make the Rome of the popes reminiscent of (if not more splendid than) the Rome of the caesars. As the symbolic seat of the papacy, Saint Peter's represented the history of the Church. Given this importance, Julius II carefully chose the architect DONATO D'ANGELO BRAMANTE (1444–1514) for this commission. Born in Urbino and trained as a painter (perhaps by Piero della Francesca), Bramante went to Milan in 1481 and, like Leonardo, stayed there until the French arrived in 1499. In Milan, he abandoned painting to become one of his generation's most renowned architects. Under the influence of Filippo Brunelleschi, Leon Battista Alberti, and perhaps Leonardo, all of whom strongly favored the art and architecture of classical antiquity, Bramante developed the High Renaissance form of the central-plan church.

Bramante originally designed the new Saint Peter's (FIG. **22-6**) to consist of a cross with arms of equal length, each terminated by an apse. Julius II intended the new building to serve as a martyry to mark Saint Peter's grave and also hoped to have his own tomb in it. A large dome would have covered

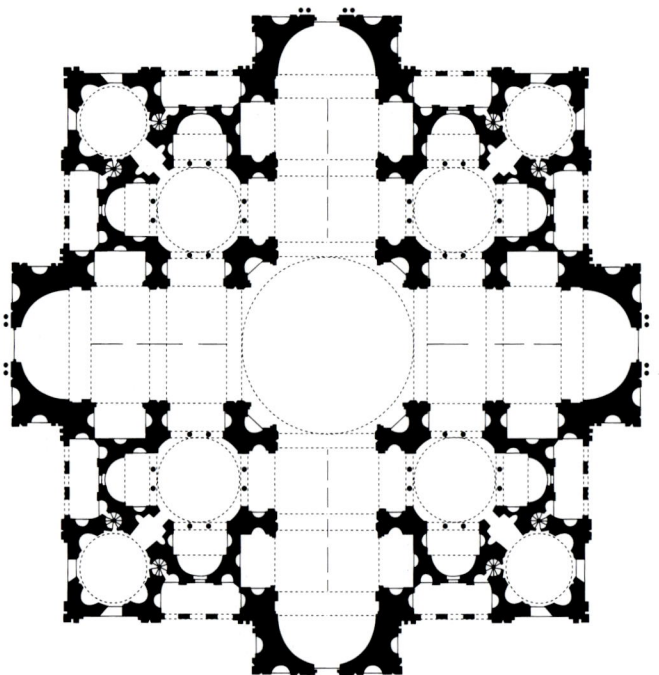

22-6 DONATO D'ANGELO BRAMANTE, plan for the new Saint Peter's, the Vatican, Rome, Italy, 1505.

the crossing, and smaller domes over subsidiary chapels would have covered the diagonal axes of the roughly square plan. Bramante's ambitious plan called for a boldly sculptural treatment of the walls and piers under the dome. His design for the interior space was complex in the extreme, with the intricate symmetries of a crystal. It is possible to detect in the plan some nine interlocking crosses, five of them supporting domes. The scale was titanic; according to sources, Bramante boasted he would place the Pantheon's dome (see FIG. 10-48) over the Basilica Nova (Basilica of Constantine; FIG. 10-79).

A commemorative medal by CHRISTOFORO FOPPA CARADOSSO (FIG. **22-7**) shows how Bramante's scheme would have attempted to do just that. The dome is hemispherical, like the Pantheon's, but, otherwise, the exterior, with two towers and a medley of domes and porticoes, breaks the massive unity, resulting in a design scaled down to human proportions in the Early Renaissance manner. In light of Julius II's interest in the Roman Empire, using the Pantheon as a model was entirely appropriate. The commemoration of Bramante's design for the new Saint Peter's on a medal is in itself significant. Such medals proliferated in the fifteenth century, reviving the ancient Roman practice of placing images of important imperial building projects on the reverses of Roman coins. Renaissance humanists prized these coins and avidly collected them; the Medici family's collection still forms the core of the coin cabinet of Florence's Archeological Museum.

During Bramante's lifetime, the actual construction of the new Saint Peter's basilica did not advance beyond the building of the crossing piers and the lower choir walls. After his death, the work passed from one architect to another and finally to Michelangelo (FIGS. 22-28 and 22-29), whom Pope Paul III appointed in 1546 to complete the building. Not until the seventeenth century, however, did the Church oversee the completion of Saint Peter's.

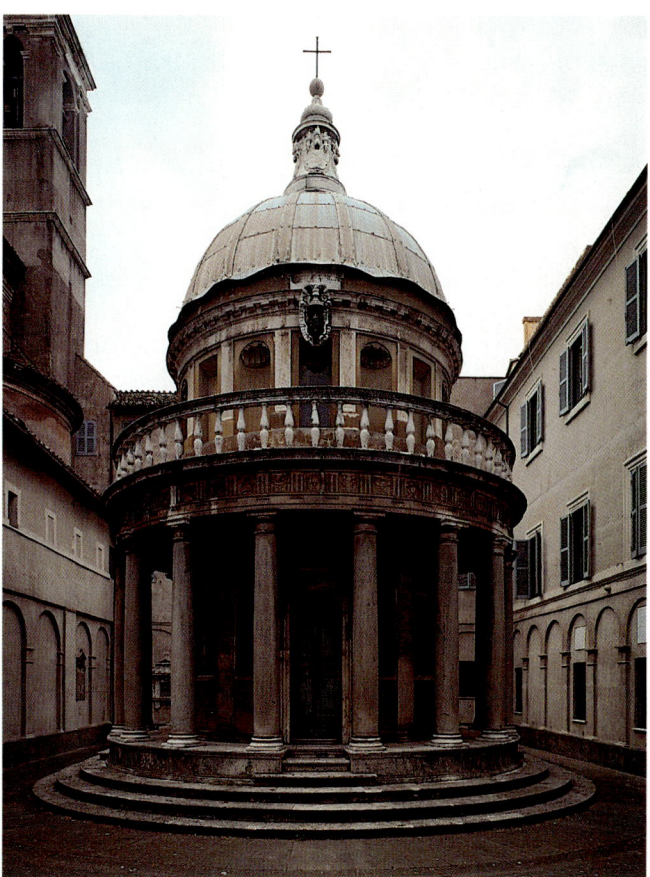

22-8   DONATO D'ANGELO BRAMANTE, Tempietto, San Pietro in Montorio, Rome, Italy, 1502(?).

REVIVING "BEAUTIFUL ARCHITECTURE" Julius II's selection of Bramante for this important commission reflected his confidence in the architect's ability to find a suitable architectural vocabulary to convey his vision of a temporal humanist authority. This vocabulary, based on Greek and Roman models, emerged in an earlier building by Bramante, often considered the perfect prototype of classical domed architecture for the Renaissance and subsequent periods. This building—the Tempietto (FIG. **22-8**)—received its name because, to contemporaries, it had the look of a small pagan temple from antiquity. "Little Temple" is, in fact, a perfectly appropriate nickname for the structure, because the round temples of Roman Italy Bramante would have known in Rome and in its environs (see FIG. 10-2) directly inspired its lower story.

King Ferdinand and Queen Isabella of Spain commissioned the Tempietto to mark the conjectural location of Saint Peter's crucifixion. Available information suggests the patrons asked Bramante to undertake the project in 1502, but some scholars have disputed that traditional dating of the building. In any case, evidence reveals that Bramante began construction of the Tempietto during the first decade of the sixteenth century.

The architect relied on the composition of volumes and masses and on a sculptural handling of solids and voids to set apart this building, all but devoid of ornament, from structures built in the preceding century. Standing inside the cloister alongside the church of San Pietro in Montorio, Rome, the Tempietto resembles a sculptured reliquary and would have looked even more like one inside the circular colonnaded courtyard Bramante planned for it but never executed. If one

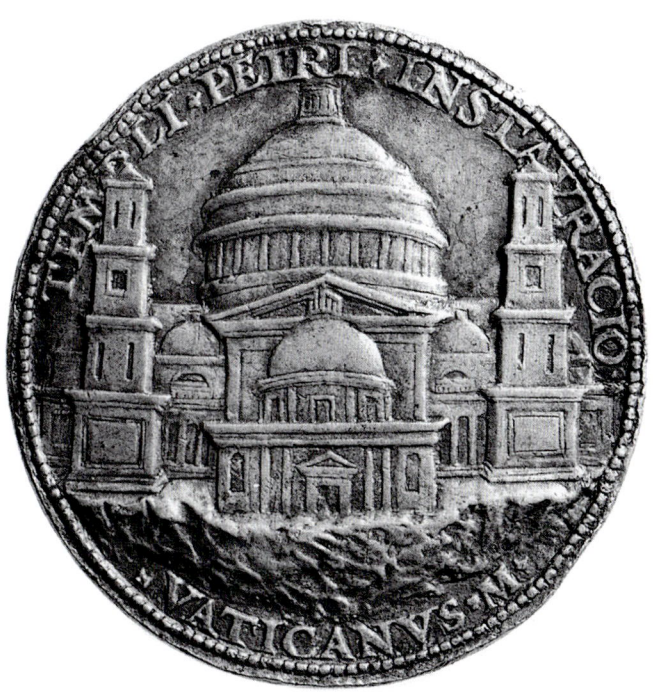

22-7   CHRISTOFORO FOPPA CARADOSSO, medal showing Bramante's design for the new Saint Peter's, 1506. British Museum, London.

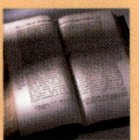

The Merits of Painting versus Sculpture
The Views of Leonardo and Michelangelo

Leonardo da Vinci and Michelangelo each produced work in a variety of artistic media, earning enviable reputations not just as painters and sculptors but as architects and draughtsmen as well. However, despite their remarkable talents, their attitudes on artistic issues diverged dramatically. In particular, Leonardo, with his intellectual and analytical mind, preferred painting to sculpture, which he denigrated as manual labor. In contrast, Michelangelo, who worked in a more intuitive manner, saw himself primarily as a sculptor. Two excerpts from their writings reveal their positions on the relative merits and drawbacks of the two mediums.

Leonardo da Vinci wrote the following in "Comparison of Painting and Sculpture" from his so-called *Treatise on Painting:*

> Painting is a matter of greater mental analysis, of greater skill, and more marvelous than sculpture, since necessity compels the mind of the painter to transform itself into the very mind of nature, to become an interpreter between nature and art. Painting justifies by reference to nature the reasons of the pictures which follow its laws: in what ways the images of objects before the eye come together in the pupil of the eye; which, among objects equal in size, looks larger to the eye; which, among equal colors will look more or less dark or more or less bright; which, among things at the same depth, looks more or less low; which, among those objects placed at equal height, will look more or less high, and why, among objects placed at various distances, one will appear less clear than the other.
>
> This art comprises and includes within itself all visible things such as colors and their diminution which the poverty of sculpture cannot include. Painting represents transparent objects but the sculptor will show you the shapes of natural objects without artifice. The painter will show you things at different distances with variation of color due to the air lying between the objects and the eye; he shows you mists through which visual images penetrate with difficulty; he shows you rain which discloses within it clouds with mountains and valleys; he shows the dust which discloses within it and beyond it the combatants who stirred it up; he shows streams of greater or lesser density; he shows fish playing between the surface of the water and its bottom; he shows the polished pebbles of various colors lying on the washed sand at the bottom of rivers, surrounded by green plants; he shows the stars at various heights above us, and thus he achieves innumerable effects which sculpture cannot attain.
>
> The sculptor says that bas-relief is a kind of painting. This may be accepted in part, insofar as design is concerned, because it shares in perspective. But with regard to shadows and lights, it is false.[1]

Michelangelo wrote these excerpts in a letter to Benedetto Varchi in 1549:

> I believe that painting is considered excellent in proportion as it approaches the effect of relief, while relief is considered bad in proportion as it approaches the effect of painting.
>
> I used to consider that sculpture was the lantern of painting and that between the two things there was the same difference as that between the sun and the moon. But . . . I now consider that painting and sculpture are one and the same thing . . . .
>
> Suffice that, since one and the other (that is to say, both painting and sculpture) proceed from the same faculty, it would be an easy matter to establish harmony between them and to let such disputes alone, for they occupy more time than the execution of the figures themselves. As to that man [Leonardo] who wrote saying that painting was more noble than sculpture, if he had known as much about the other subjects on which he has written, why, my serving-maid would have written better![2]

[1] Robert Klein and Henri Zerner, *Italian Art 1500–1600: Sources and Documents* (Evanston, Ill.: Northwestern University Press, 1966), 7–8.

[2] Michelangelo to Benedetto Varchi, ca. 1547; ibid., 13–14.

of the main differences between the Early and High Renaissance styles of architecture was the former's emphasis on detailing flat wall surfaces versus the latter's sculptural handling of architectural masses, then the Tempietto certainly broke new ground and stood at the beginning of a new High Renaissance era.

At first glance, the structure may seem severely rational with its sober circular stylobate and the cool Tuscan style of the colonnade, neither giving any indication of the placement of an interior altar or of the entrance. However, Bramante achieved a truly wonderful balance and harmony in the relationship of the parts (dome, drum, and base) to one another and to the whole. The balustrade echoes, in shorter beats, the colonnade's rhythm and averts a too-rapid visual ascent to the drum. The drum's pilasters repeat the ascending motif and lead the eye past the cornice to the dome's exposed ribs. The play of light and shade around the columns and balustrade and across the deep-set rectangular windows alternating with shallow shell-capped niches in the cella walls and drum enhances observers' experiences of the building as an interrelated sculptural mass. Although the Tempietto, superficially at least, may resemble a Greek *tholos* (a circular shrine; FIG. 5-71) and although antique models provided the inspiration for all of its details, the combination of parts and details was new and original (classical tholoi, for instance, had neither drum nor balustrade). Conceived as a tall domed cylinder projecting from the lower wider cylinder of its colonnade, this small building incorporates all the qualities of a sculptured monument.

Renaissance architects understood the significance of the Tempietto. The architect Andrea Palladio, an artistic descendant of Bramante, included it in his survey of ancient temples because Bramante was "the first to bring back to light the good and beautiful architecture that from antiquity to that time had been hidden."[5] Round in plan and elevated on a base that isolates it from its surroundings, the Tempietto conforms to Alberti's and Palladio's strictest demands for an ideal church, demonstrating "the Unity, infinite Essence, the Uniformity, and the Justice of God."[6]

A DOMINANT CREATOR OF TITANIC FORMS

The artist who Julius II deemed best able to convey his message was MICHELANGELO BUONARROTI (1475–1564), who received some of the most coveted commissions from the pope. Although he was an architect, a sculptor, a painter, a poet, and an engineer, Michelangelo thought of himself first as a sculptor, regarding that calling as superior to that of a painter because the sculptor shares in something like the divine power to "make man" (see "The Merits of Painting versus Sculpture: The Views of Leonardo and Michelangelo," page 644). Conceptually paralleling Plato's ideas, Michelangelo believed that the image the artist's hand produces must come from the idea in the artist's mind. The idea, then, is the reality that the artist's genius has to bring forth. But artists are not the creators of the ideas they conceive. Rather, they find their ideas in the natural world, reflecting the absolute idea, which, for the artist, is beauty. In this way, the strongly Platonic strain of the Renaissance theory of imitating nature makes it a revelation of the high truths hidden within nature. The theory that guided Michelangelo's hand, although never complete or entirely consistent, appears in his poetry. Two excerpts follow:

> To people of good judgment, every beauty
> seen here resembles, more than anything else does,
> that merciful fountain from which we all derive; . . .[7]

> My eyes, desirous of beautiful things,
> and my soul, likewise, of its salvation,
> have no other means to rise
> to heaven but to gaze at all such things.[8]

One of Michelangelo's best-known observations about sculpture is that the artist must proceed by finding the idea—the image locked in the stone, as it were—so, by removing the excess stone, the sculptor extricates the idea, like Pygmalion bringing forth the living form (see FIG. Intro-17). The artist, Michelangelo felt, works through many years at this unceasing process of revelation and "arrives late at novel and lofty things."[9]

Michelangelo did indeed arrive "at novel and lofty things," for he broke sharply from the lessons of his predecessors and contemporaries in one important respect. He mistrusted the application of mathematical methods as guarantees of beauty in proportion. Measure and proportion, he believed, should be "kept in the eyes." Biographer Vasari quotes Michelangelo as declaring that "it was necessary to have the compasses in the eyes and not in the hand, because the hands work and the eye judges."[10] Thus, Michelangelo set aside the ancient Roman architect Vitruvius, Alberti, Leonardo, and others who tirelessly sought the perfect measure and asserted that the artist's inspired judgment could identify other pleasing proportions. In addition, Michelangelo argued that the artist must not be bound, except by the demands made by realizing the idea. This insistence on the artist's own authority was typical of Michelangelo and anticipated the modern concept of the right to a self-expression of talent limited only by the artist's own judgment. The artistic license to aspire far beyond the "rules" was, in part, a manifestation of the pursuit of fame and success humanism fostered. In this context, Michelangelo created works in architecture, sculpture, and painting that departed from High Renaissance regularity. He put in its stead a style of vast, expressive strength conveyed through complex, eccentric, and often titanic forms that loom before viewers in

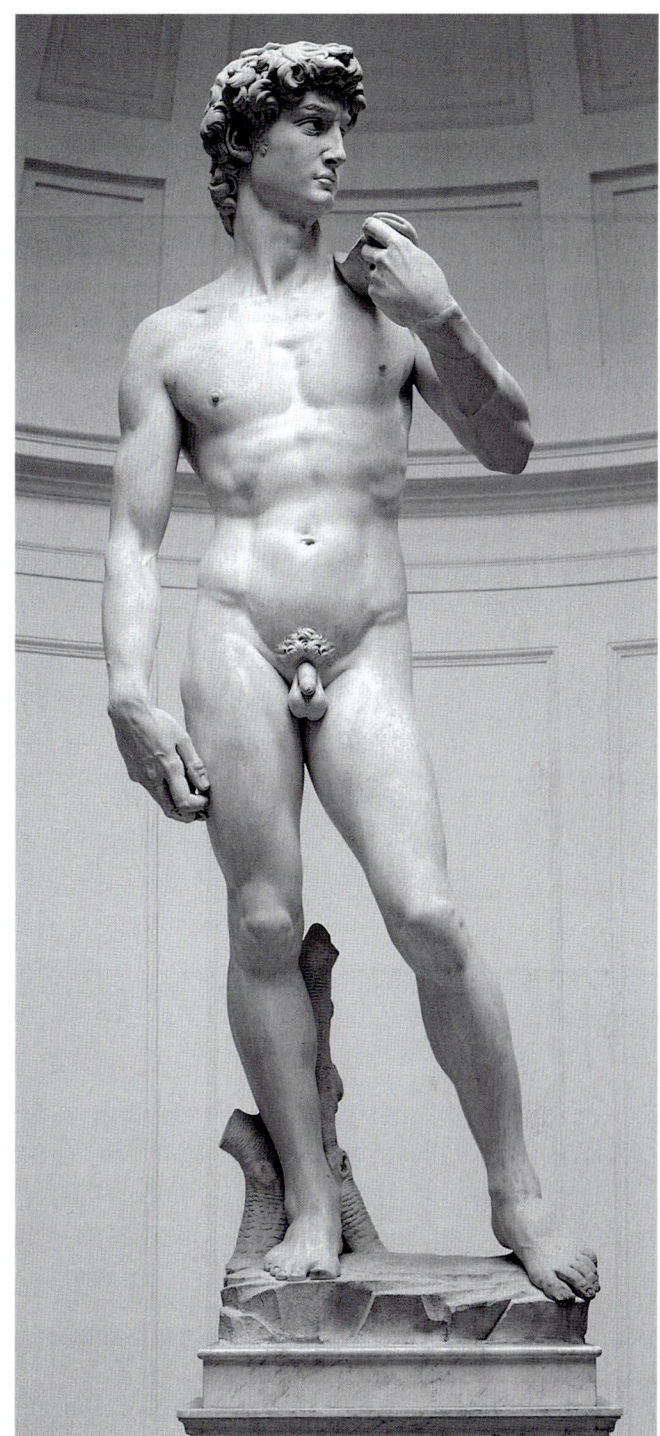

22-9 MICHELANGELO BUONARROTI, *David*, 1501–1504. Marble, 14′ 3″ high. Galleria dell'Accademia, Florence.

tragic grandeur. Michelangelo's self-imposed isolation, creative furies, proud independence, and daring innovations led Italians to speak of the dominating quality of the man and his works in one word—*terribilità,* the sublime shadowed by the awesome and the fearful.

SUBDUING A GIANT In 1501, the city of Florence asked Michelangelo to work a great block of marble, called "The Giant," left over from an earlier aborted commission. From this stone, Michelangelo crafted *David* (FIG. **22-9**), the defiant hero of the Florentine republic and, in so doing, assured his reputation then and now as an extraordinary talent. This early work reveals Michelangelo's fascination with the

22-10 MICHELANGELO BUONARROTI, *Moses,* San Pietro in Vincoli, Rome, Italy, ca. 1513–1515. Marble, approx. 8′ 4″ high.

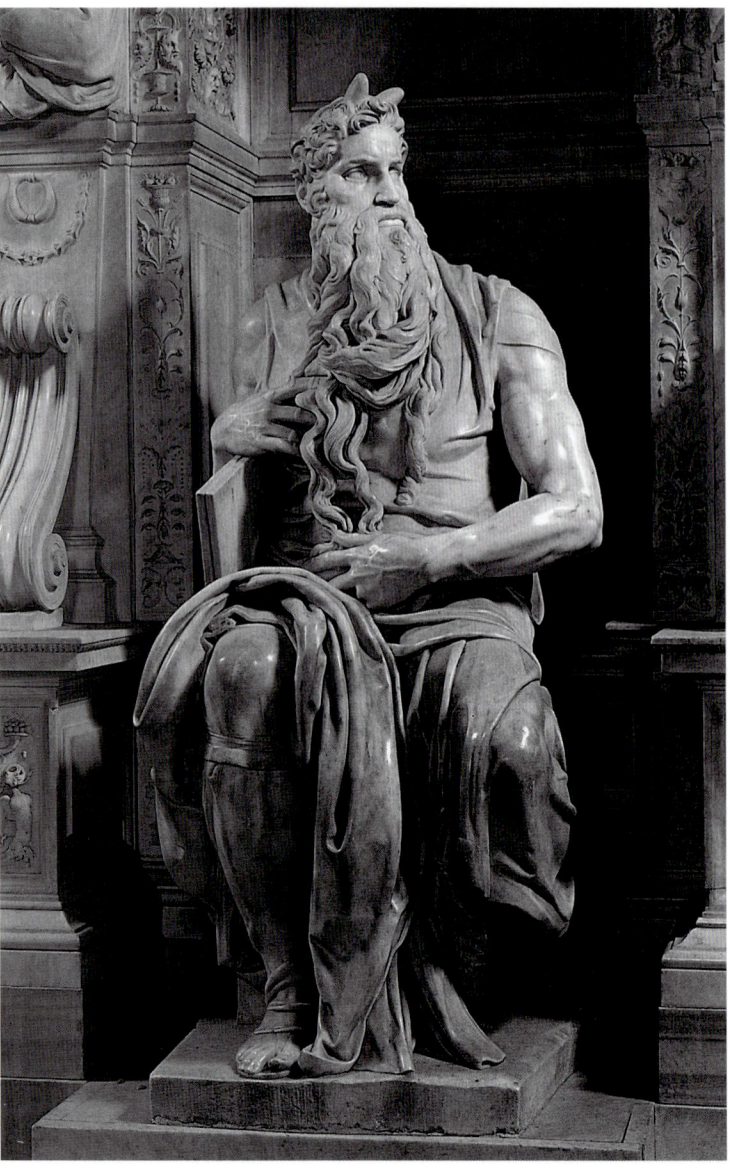

human form, and *David's* formal references to classical antiquity surely appealed to Julius II, who associated himself with the humanists and with Roman emperors. Thus, this sculpture and the fame that accrued to Michelangelo on its completion called the artist to the pope's attention, leading to major papal commissions.

For *David,* Michelangelo took up the theme Donatello (see FIG. 21-23) and Andrea del Verrocchio (see FIG. 21-24) had used successfully, but Michelangelo's resolution was highly original. The artist chose to represent David not after the victory, with Goliath's head at his feet, but turning his head to his left, sternly watchful of the approaching foe. His whole muscular body, as well as his face, is tense with gathering power. *David* exhibits the characteristic representation of energy in reserve that imbues Michelangelo's later figures with the tension of a coiled spring. The young hero's anatomy plays an important part in this prelude to action. His rugged torso, sturdy limbs, and large hands and feet, alerting viewers to the strength to come, do not consist simply of inert muscle groups, nor did the sculptor idealize them by simplification into broad masses. They serve, by their active play, to enhance

the whole mood and posture of tense expectation. Each swelling vein and tightening sinew amplifies the psychological energy of the monumental David's pose.

Michelangelo doubtless had the classical nude in mind. He, like many of his colleagues, greatly admired Greco-Roman statues, his knowledge limited mostly to Roman sculptures and Roman copies of Greek art. In particular, classical sculptors' skillful and precise rendering of heroic physique impressed Michelangelo. In his *David,* Michelangelo, without strictly imitating the antique style, captured the tension of Lysippan athletes (see FIG. 5-65) and the psychological insight and emotionalism of Hellenistic statuary (see FIGS. 5-80 and 5-81). This David differs from those of Donatello and Verrocchio in much the same way later Hellenistic statues departed from their Classical predecessors. Michelangelo abandoned the self-contained compositions of the fifteenth-century David statues by giving David's head the abrupt turn toward his gigantic adversary. Michelangelo's *David* is compositionally and emotionally connected to an unseen presence beyond the statue; this, too, is evident in Hellenistic sculpture (see FIG. 5-86). As early as the *David,* then, Michelangelo invested his efforts in presenting towering pent-up emotion rather than calm ideal beauty. He transferred his own doubts, frustrations, and passions into the great figures he created or planned. He was the spiritual heir not of Polykleitos and Phidias but of the masters of the Laocoön group (see FIG. 5-89).

IN MEMORY OF A WARRIOR-POPE The first project Julius II commissioned from Michelangelo in 1505 was the pontiff's own tomb. The original design called for a free-standing two-story structure with some twenty-eight statues. This colossal monument would have given Michelangelo the latitude to sculpt numerous human figures while providing the pope with a grandiose memorial (which Julius II intended to locate in Saint Peter's). Shortly after Michelangelo began work on this project, the pope, for unknown reasons, interrupted the commission, possibly because funds had to be diverted to Bramante's rebuilding of Saint Peter's. After Julius II's death in 1513, Michelangelo reduced the project's scale step-by-step until, in 1542, a final contract specified a simple wall tomb with fewer than one-third of the originally planned figures. Michelangelo completed the tomb in 1545 and saw it placed in San Pietro in Vincoli, Rome, where Julius II had served as a cardinal before his accession to the papacy. Given Julius's ambitions, it is safe to say that had he seen the final design of his tomb, or known where it was eventually located, he would have been bitterly disappointed.

The spirit of the tomb may be summed up in the figure *Moses* (FIG. **22-10**), which Michelangelo completed during one of his sporadic resumptions of the work in 1513. Meant to be seen from below, and balanced with seven other massive forms related in spirit to it, the *Moses* now, in its comparatively paltry setting, does not have its originally intended impact. Michelangelo depicted the Old Testament prophet seated, the Tablets of the Law under one arm and his hands gathering his voluminous beard. The horns that appear on Moses's head were a sculptural convention in Christian art and helped Renaissance viewers identify Moses (see FIG. 17-38). Here, again, Michelangelo used the turned head, which concentrates the expression of awful wrath that stirs in the mighty frame and eyes. The muscles bulge, the veins swell, and the great legs seem to begin slowly to move. If this titan ever rose to his feet, one writer said, the world would fly apart. To find such pent-up energy—both emotional and physical—in a seated statue, historians must turn once again to Hellenistic statuary (see FIG. 5-86).

STRUGGLING FOR FREEDOM OF EXPRESSION Originally, Michelangelo intended for some twenty sculptures of slaves, in various attitudes of revolt and exhaustion, to appear on the tomb. One such figure is *Bound Slave* (FIG. **22-11**). (Another such figure is FIG. Intro-17.) Considerable scholarly uncertainty about this sculpture (and three other "slave" figures) exists. Although conventional scholarship connected these statues with the Julius tomb, some art historians now doubt this. A lively debate also continues about the subject of these figures; many scholars reject their identification as "slaves" or "captives." Despite these unanswered questions, the "slaves," like *David* and *Moses,* represent definitive statements. Michelangelo made each body a different total expression of the idea of oppression, so these sculpted human figures do not so much represent a concept, as in medieval

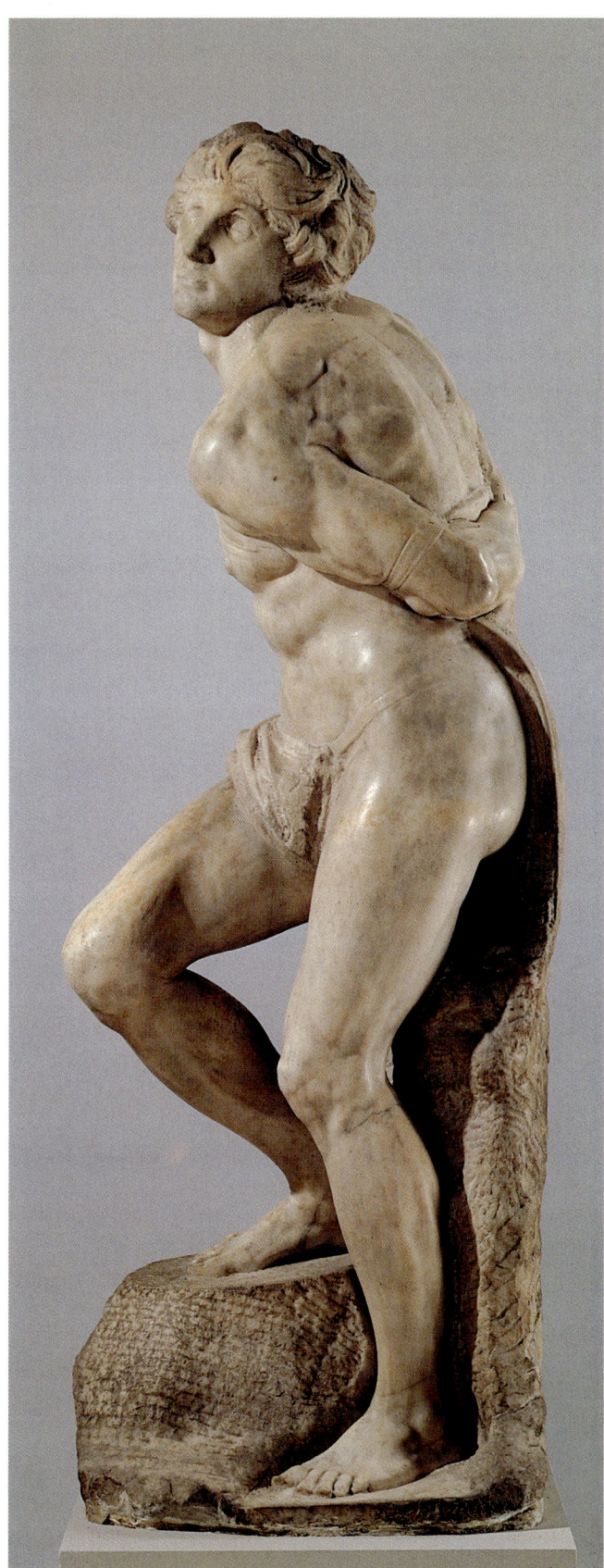

22-11 MICHELANGELO BUONARROTI, *Bound Slave,* 1513–1516. Marble, approx. 6′ 10½″ high. Louvre, Paris.

allegory, but are concrete realizations of intense feelings. Indeed, Michelangelo communicated his powerful imagination in every plane and hollow of the stone. In *Bound Slave,* the defiant figure's violent contrapposto is the image of frantic but impotent struggle. As noted earlier, many Hellenistic artists shared Michelangelo's vision of the human form. (Compare, for example, the spiral composition of his *Bound Slave* with that of the suicidal Gallic chieftain, FIG. 5-80.) The influence of the Laocoön group (see FIG. 5-89), discovered in Rome in 1506, is especially clear in the struggling *Bound Slave*. Michelangelo based his whole art on his conviction that whatever can be said greatly through sculpture and painting must be said through the human figure.

THE SISTINE CEILING: A GRAND DRAMA

Julius II's artistic program continued unabated, despite the obstacles he encountered. With the suspension of the tomb project, Julius II gave the bitter and reluctant Michelangelo the commission to paint the ceiling of the Sistine Chapel (FIGS. **22-12** and **22-13**) in 1508. The artist, insisting that painting was not his profession (a protest that rings hollow after the fact, but Michelangelo's major works until then had been in sculpture, and painting was of secondary interest to him), assented in the hope the tomb project could be revived. Michelangelo faced enormous difficulties in painting the Sistine ceiling. He had to address his relative inexperience in the fresco technique; the ceiling's dimensions (some five thousand eight hundred square feet); its height above the pavement (almost seventy feet); and the complicated perspective problems the vault's height and curve presented. Yet, in less than four

years, Michelangelo produced an unprecedented work—a monumental fresco incorporating the patron's agenda, Church doctrine, and the artist's interests. Depicting the most august and solemn themes of all, the Creation, Fall, and Redemption of humanity (most likely selected by Julius II with input from Michelangelo and a theological adviser), Michelangelo spread a colossal decorative scheme across the vast surface. He succeeded in weaving together more than three hundred figures in an ultimate grand drama of the human race.

A long sequence of narrative panels describing the Creation, as recorded in the biblical book Genesis, runs along the crown of the vault, from *God's Separation of Light and Darkness* (above the altar) to *Drunkenness of Noah* (nearest the entrance to the chapel). The Hebrew prophets and pagan sibyls who foretold the coming of Christ appear seated in large thrones on both sides of the central row of scenes from Genesis, where the vault curves down. In the four corner pendentives, Michelangelo placed four Old Testament scenes with David, Judith, Haman, and Moses and the Brazen Serpent. Scores of lesser figures also appear. The ancestors of Christ fill the triangular compartments above the windows, nude youths punctuate the corners of the central panels, and small pairs of putti in grisaille support the painted cornice surrounding the entire central corridor. The conception of the whole design no doubt contributed to the perception of Julius II as a spiritual leader, temporal power, and cultured man. For example, in

22-12   Interior of the Sistine Chapel (view facing east), Vatican City, Rome, Italy, built 1473. Copyright © Nippon Television Network Corporation, Tokyo.

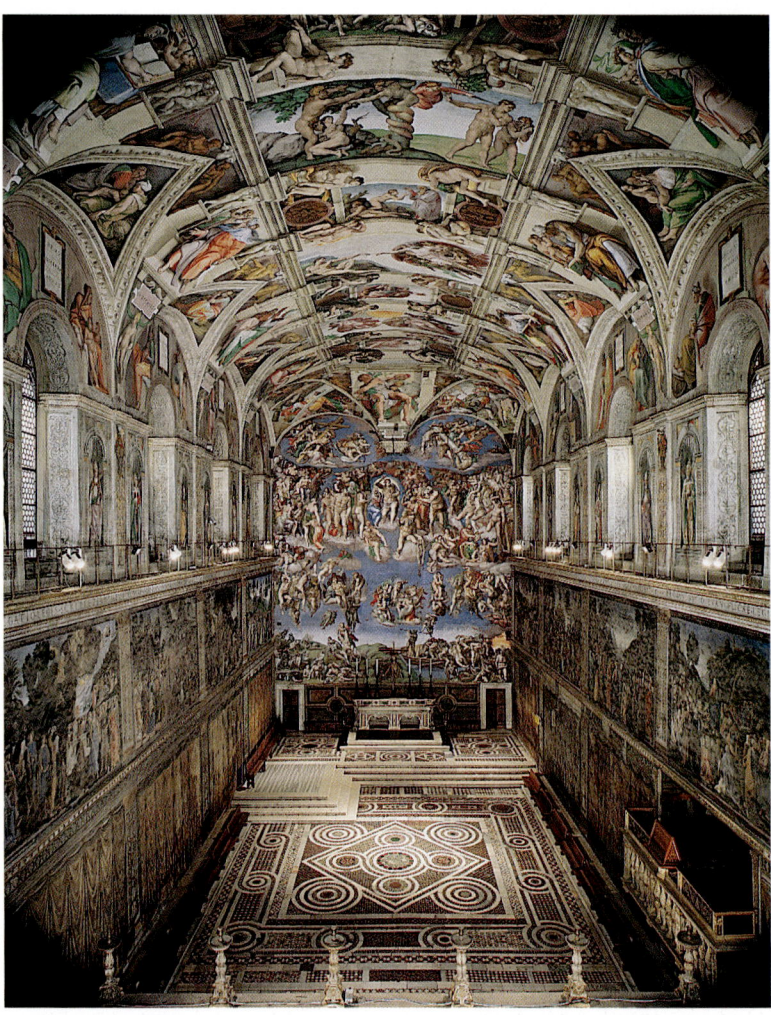

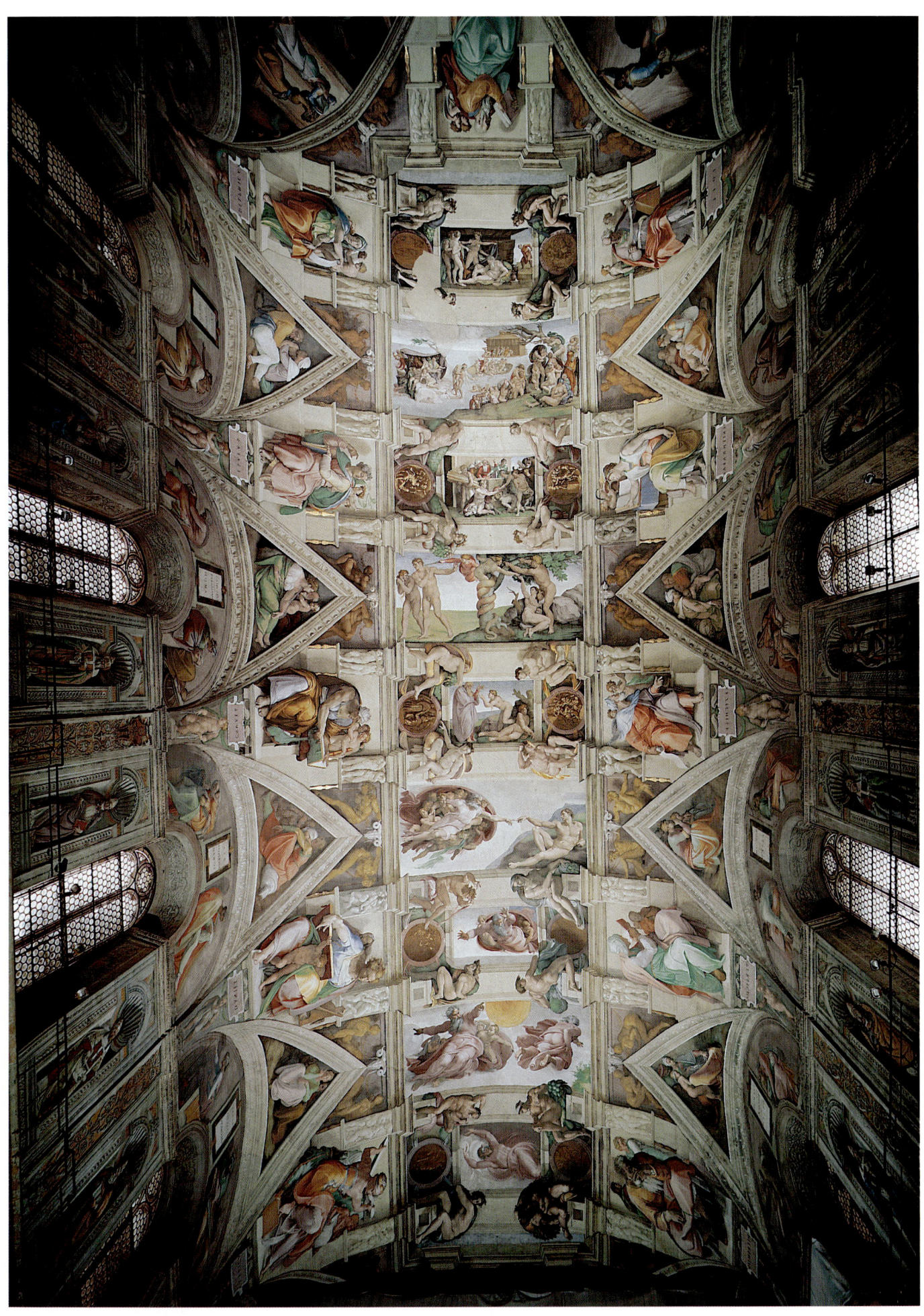

22-13 MICHELANGELO BUONARROTI, ceiling of the Sistine Chapel, Vatican City, Rome, Italy, 1508–1512. Fresco, approx. 128′ × 45′.

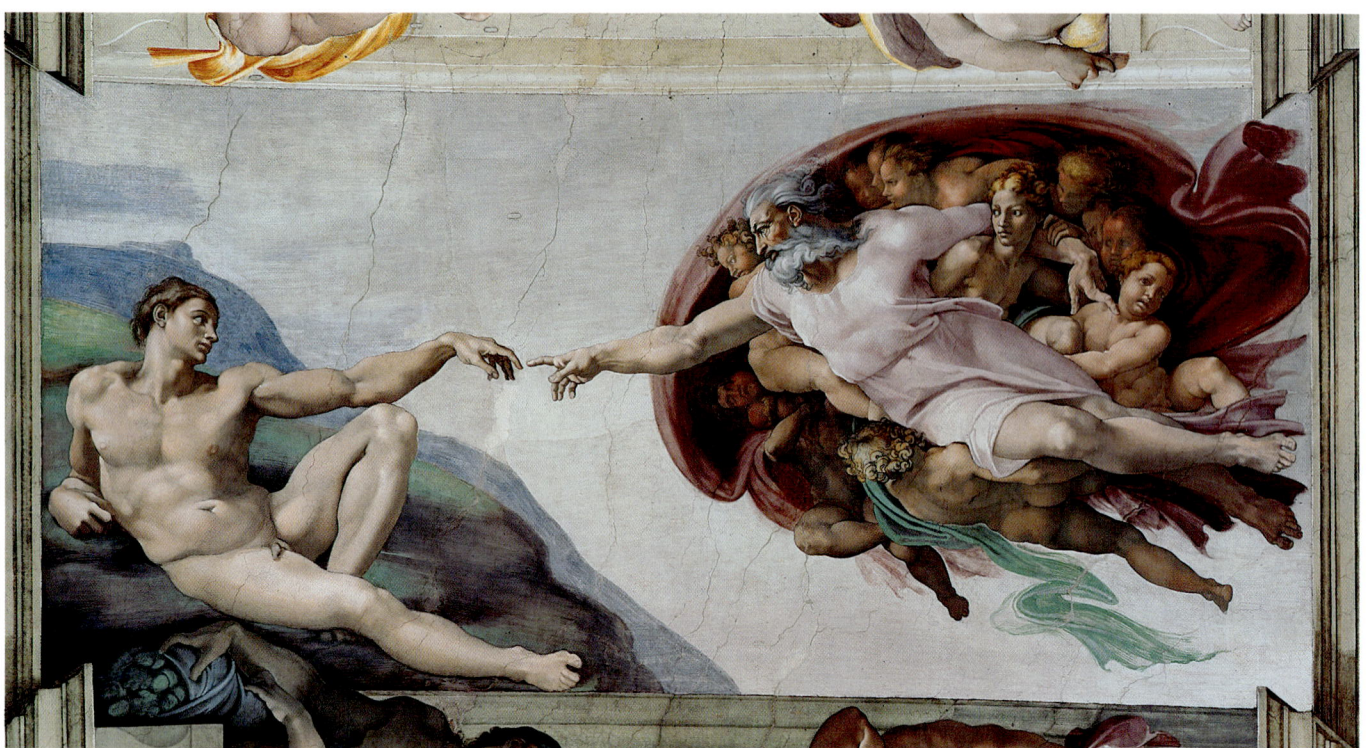

22-14 MICHELANGELO BUONARROTI, *Creation of Adam* (detail), ceiling of the Sistine Chapel, Vatican City, Rome, Italy, 1511–1512. Fresco, approx. 18′ 8″ × 9′ 2″.

the pendentives, the representation of David and Judith, Old Testament heroes who triumphed over oppressors, may allude to the pope's military exploits against invaders. Moses and Esther in the other two pendentives refer to Julius's position as a divinely ordained ruler. The conception of the entire design was astounding in itself and the articulation of it in its thousand details was a superhuman achievement.

Unlike Andrea Mantegna's decoration of the Camera degli Sposi in Mantua (see FIG. 21-48), the strongly marked unifying architectural framework in the Sistine Chapel does not construct "picture windows" enframing illusions just above. Rather, viewers focus on figure after figure, each sharply outlined against the neutral tone of the architectural setting or the plain background of the panels. Here, as in his sculpture, Michelangelo relentlessly concentrated his expressive purpose on the human figure. To him, the body was beautiful not only in its natural form but also in its spiritual and philosophical significance. The body was simply the manifestation of the soul or of a state of mind and character. Michelangelo represented the body in its most simple, elemental aspect — in the nude or simply draped, with no background and no ornamental embellishment. He always painted with a sculptor's eye for how light and shadow communicate volume and surface. It is no coincidence that many of the figures seem to be tinted reliefs or full-rounded statues.

VISUALIZING A TENET OF CHRISTIANITY
One of the ceiling's central panels is *Creation of Adam* (FIG. **22-14**). Michelangelo did not paint the traditional representation but a bold, entirely humanistic interpretation of the momentous event. God and Adam confront each other in a primordial unformed landscape where Adam is still a material part, heavy as earth. The Lord transcends the earth, wrapped in a billowing cloud of drapery and borne up by his powers.

Life leaps to Adam like a spark from the extended and mighty hand of God. The communication between gods and heroes, so familiar in classical myth, is here concrete; made of the

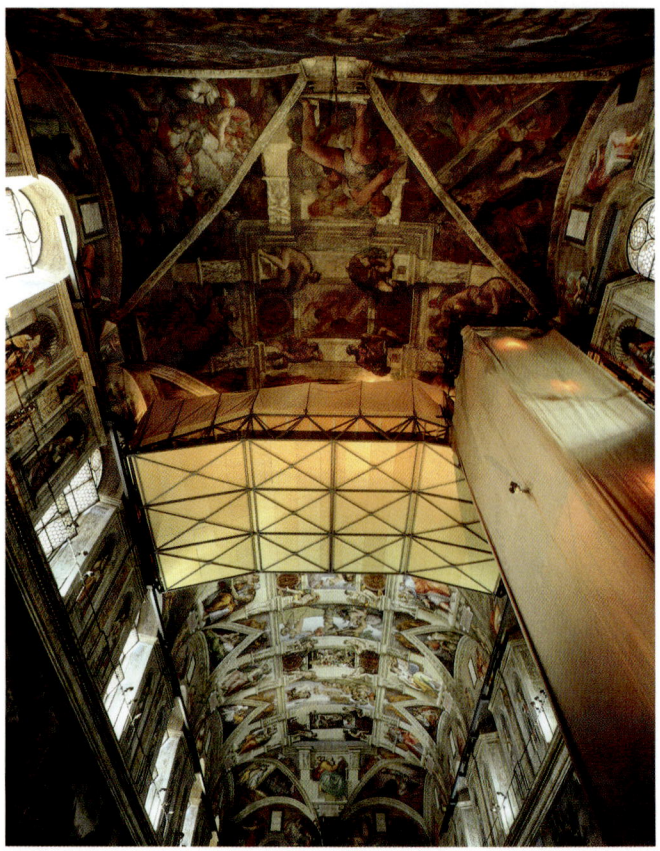

22-15 Cleaning of ceiling of Sistine Chapel, Vatican City, Rome, Italy, 1977–1989.

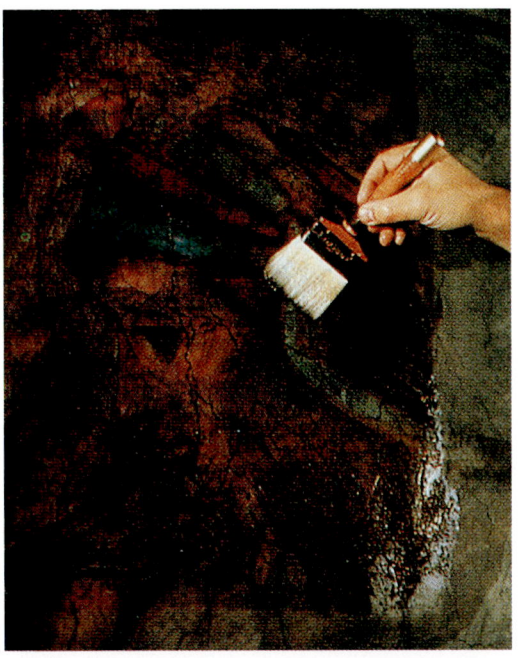
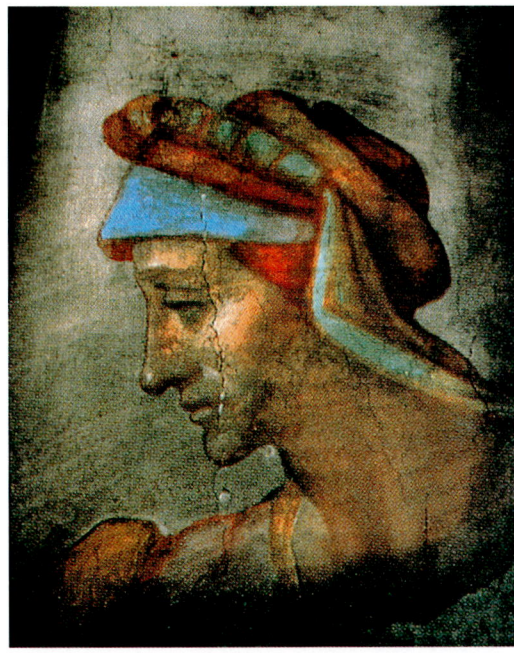
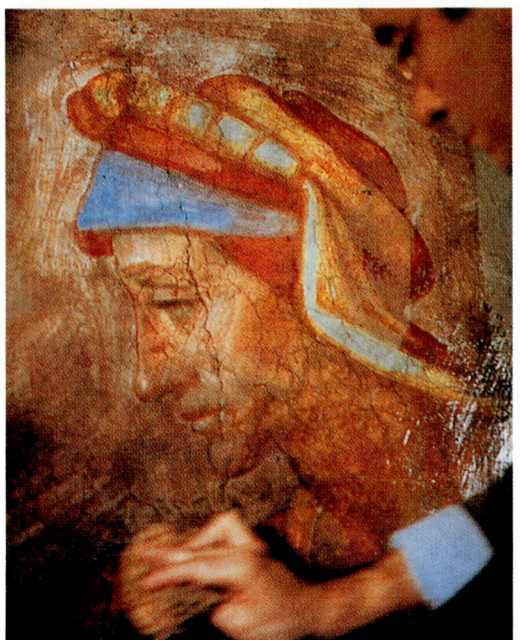
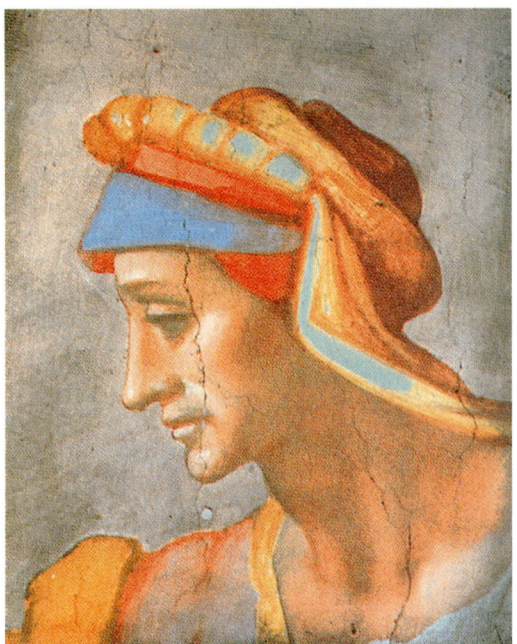

22-16 Detail of the Azor-Sadoch lunette's left side over one of the Sistine Chapel windows at various stages of the restoration process, Vatican City, Rome, Italy, 1977–1989. Copyright © Nippon Television Network Corporation, Tokyo.

same substance, both are gigantic. This blunt depiction of the Lord as ruler of Heaven in the Olympian pagan sense indicates how easily High Renaissance thought joined pagan and Christian traditions. Yet the classical trappings do not obscure the essential Christian message.

Beneath the Lord's sheltering left arm is a female figure, apprehensively curious but as yet uncreated. Scholars traditionally believed her to represent Eve but recently have suggested she may be the Virgin Mary (with the Christ Child at her knee). If the new identification is correct, it suggests Michelangelo incorporated into his fresco one of the essential tenets of Christian faith. This is the belief Adam's original sin eventually led to the sacrifice of Christ, which in turn made possible the redemption of all humankind. As God reaches out to Adam, viewers' eyes move from right to left, but Adam's extended left arm returns them back to the right, through the Lord's right arm, shoulders, and left arm to his left forefinger, which points to the Christ Child's face. The fo-

cal point of this right-to-left-to-right movement—the fingertips of Adam and the Lord—is dramatically off-center. Michelangelo replaced the straight architectural axes found in Leonardo's compositions with curves and diagonals. For example, the bodies of the two great figures are complementary—the concave body of Adam fitting the convex body and billowing "cloak" of God. Thus, motion directs not only the figures but also the whole composition. The reclining positions of the figures, the heavy musculature, and the twisting poses are all intrinsic parts of Michelangelo's style.

Visitors to the Sistine Chapel will encounter a cleaned ceiling (FIGS. 22-13 and 22-15), revealing much brighter colors (see "Restoring the Glory of Renaissance Frescoes," page 652). Controversy accompanied the execution of this restoration, and the vivid colors (FIG. 22-16) take many viewers aback. That reaction, however, probably derives from recent familiarity with the formerly soot- and grime-covered ceiling.

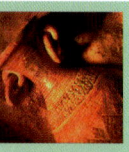

Restoring the Glory of Renaissance Frescoes

The year 1989 marked the completion of the cleaning and restoration of the Sistine Chapel ceiling—after twelve years of painstaking work. Restorers removed centuries of accumulated grime, overpainting, and protective glue, uncovering much of the artist's original craft in form, color, style, and procedure. Our before-and-after details of one of the lunettes over the windows (FIG. 22-16) depict four stages of the restoration process. In these semicircular spaces, Michelangelo painted figures representing the ancestors of Christ (Matt. 1:1–17). After computer assessment of the damage (including use of infrared and ultraviolet lights), the restorers worked carefully and slowly to clean the fresco of soot, dirt, dissolved salts, and various types of gums and varnishes made of animal glues. Over the centuries, restorers had used such varnishes to brighten the darkening fresco; unfortunately, over time the varnishes deteriorated, making the painting even darker. For the latest cleaning effort, the restorer first wet a small section of the fresco with distilled, deionized water. The application of a cleaning solution made of bicarbonates of sodium and ammonium and supplemented with an antibacterial, antifungal agent followed. Adding carboxymethylcellulose and water to this solution created a gel that clung to the ceiling fresco. After three minutes, restorers removed the gel. Our details (of the Azor-Sadoch lunette) reveal the startling product of the restorers' procedure, as the original work emerged from the dark film of time and faulty repairs.

These figures, once thought purposefully dark, now show brilliant colors of high intensity, brushed on with an astonishing freedom and verve. The fresh, luminous hues, boldly joined in unexpected harmonies, seem uncharacteristically dissonant to some experts and have aroused brisk controversy. Some believe the restorers removed Michelangelo's work along with the accumulated layers and that the apparently strident coloration cannot possibly be his. Others insist the restoration effort has revealed to modern eyes the artist's real intentions and effects—that in the Sistine Chapel Michelangelo already had paved the way for the Mannerist reaction to the High Renaissance examined later in this chapter. In any event, due to the restoration, scholars are now restudying and reassessing Michelangelo's pictorial art and its influence.

The restoration also has shed light on Michelangelo's manner of painting, because restorers constructed a bridgelike scaffolding (FIG. 22-15) similar to that the artist designed and used. Despite the persistence of stories that Michelangelo painted the ceiling lying on his back, those are merely myths. In his journals, Michelangelo complained bitterly of the pain and suffering from working on an overhead fresco while standing. One sonnet by the artist included a litany of complaints, among others: "In front my skin grows loose and long; behind, By bending it becomes more taut and strait; Crosswise I strain me like a Syrian bow."[1]

On completion of this monumental cleaning project, restorers turned their attention to Michelangelo's *Last Judgment* (FIG. 22-25) behind the altar in the Sistine Chapel. They completed their restoration of that large fresco in 1994.

The recent treatment of Leonardo's *Last Supper* (FIG. 22-3) in the refectory of Santa Maria delle Grazie in Milan presented restorers with an even greater challenge. Leonardo had mixed oil and tempera, applying much of it *a secco* (to dried, rather than wet, plaster). Thus, the wall did not absorb the pigment as in the *buon fresco* technique, and the paint quickly began to flake. The humidity of Milan further accelerated the deterioration. Over the centuries, the fresco has been subjected to frequent alterations. Napoleonic troops attacked the fresco; at other times, it was cleaned with a variety of materials. Consequently, current restorers confronted a monumental task. Their efforts, like those of the Sistine Chapel restorers, were painstaking and slow, involving extensive scholarly, chemical, and computer analysis. They recently finished their work, which took more than two decades, and they unveiled the cleaned fresco to the public in May 1999.

Like other restorations, this one was not without controversy. Dr. Pinin Brambilla Barcilon, who oversaw the cleaning project, declared: "What we have brought to light are Leonardo's original and brilliant colors. Nothing has been removed from the original painting, and nothing has been added."[2] Yet Dr. James Beck, a professor of art history at Columbia University, charges the painting is now "18–20 percent Leonardo and 80 percent by the restorer."[3] Viewers will have to judge the results for themselves. But to minimize future deterioration, viewing time is limited, and visitors are ushered through areas outfitted with special filtration systems and dust-absorbing carpets before entering the refectory.

The controversies have not put a damper on other restoration projects. Restorers have undertaken the cleaning of the frescoes in the Stanza della Segnatura in the Vatican Apartments in Rome, and the Vatican has scheduled the frescoes by Perugino and other artists in the Sistine Chapel for restoration.

[1] Robert Goldwater and Marco Treves, eds., *Artists on Art,* 3rd ed. (New York: Pantheon Books, 1958), 59.

[2] Piero Valsecchi, "It's Art, but Is It Leonardo's?" Milan Associated Press Wire, 28 May 1999.

[3] Ibid.

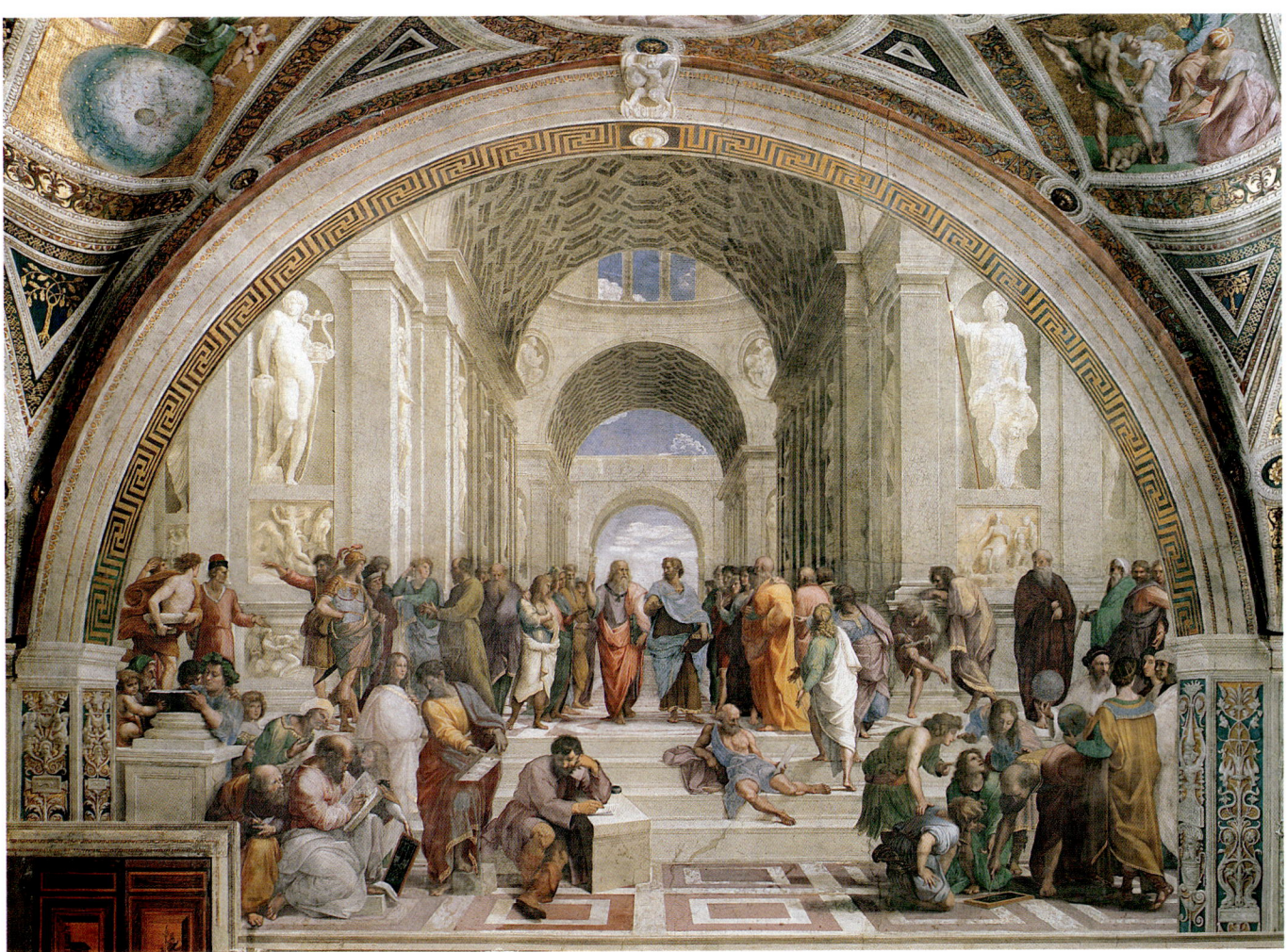

22-17 RAPHAEL, Philosophy *(School of Athens)*, Stanza della Segnatura, Vatican Palace, Rome, Italy, 1509–1511. Fresco, approx. 19′ × 27′.

A CONGREGATION OF CLASSICAL THINKERS
While Michelangelo was hard at work on the Sistine Chapel ceiling, Pope Julius II turned his attention to the papal apartments. In 1508, the pope called RAFFAELLO SANZIO, known as RAPHAEL (1483–1520), to the papal court in Rome, perhaps on the recommendation of Raphael's fellow townsman, Bramante. Born in a small town in Umbria near Urbino, Raphael probably learned the rudiments of his art from his father, Giovanni Sanzio, a provincial painter connected with the ducal court of Federico da Montefeltro.

Once in Rome, in competition with older artists such as Perugino and Luca Signorelli, Raphael received one of the largest commissions of the time—the decoration of the papal apartments in the Vatican. Of the suite's several rooms *(stanze)*, Raphael painted the Stanza della Segnatura (Room of the Signature—the papal library) and the Stanza d'Eliodoro (Room of Heliodorus). His pupils completed the others, following his sketches. On the four walls of the Stanza della Segnatura, under the headings of Theology (called *Disputà*), Law *(Justice)*, Poetry *(Parnassus)*, and Philosophy *(School of Athens)*, Raphael presented images that symbolize and sum up Western learning as Renaissance society understood it. The frescoes refer to the four branches of human knowledge and wisdom while pointing out the virtues and the learning appropriate to

a pope. Given Julius II's desire for recognition as both a spiritual and temporal leader, it is appropriate that the Theology and the Philosophy frescoes face each other. The two images present a balanced picture of the pope—as a cultured, knowledgeable individual, on the one hand, and as a wise, divinely ordained religious authority, on the other hand.

On one wall in Raphael's Philosophy mural, the so-called *School of Athens* (FIG. **22-17**), the setting is not a "school" but a congregation of the great philosophers and scientists of the ancient world. Raphael depicted these luminaries—rediscovered by Renaissance thinkers—conversing and explaining their various theories and ideas. In a vast hall covered by massive vaults that recall Roman architecture (and approximate the appearance of the new Saint Peter's in 1509, when the painting was executed), colossal statues of Apollo and Athena, patron gods of the arts and of wisdom, oversee the interactions. Plato and Aristotle serve as the central figures around whom Raphael carefully arranged the others. Plato holds his book *Timaeus* and points to Heaven, the source of his inspiration, while Aristotle carries his book *Nichomachean Ethics* and gestures toward the earth, from which his observations of reality sprang. Appropriately, ancient philosophers, men concerned with the ultimate mysteries that transcend this world, stand on Plato's side. On Aristotle's side are the philosophers

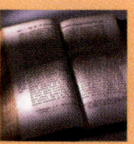

WRITTEN SOURCES

Giorgio Vasari on Raphael

Although Giorgio Vasari (1511–1574) established himself as a painter and architect, people today usually associate him with his landmark book, *Lives of the Most Eminent Painters, Sculptors and Architects,* first published in 1550. Scholars long have considered this book a major information source about Italian art and artists, although many of the details have proven inaccurate. Regardless, Vasari's *Lives* remains a tour de force — an ambitious comprehensive book dedicated to recording the biographies of artists. The following excerpt reveals Vasari's admiration for Raphael. It also demonstrates the importance of the concepts of imitation and emulation (see "Imitation and Emulation: Artistic Values in the Renaissance," Chapter 21, page 602) to the development of artistic style.

> He [Raphael] then, after having imitated in his boyhood the manner of his master, Pietro Perugino, which he made much better in draughtsmanship, coloring, and invention, believed that he had done enough; but he recognized, when he had reached a riper age, that he was still too far from the truth. For, after seeing the works of Leonardo da Vinci, who had no peer in the expressions of heads both of men and of women, and surpassed all other painters in giving grace and movement to his figures, he was left marveling and amazed; and in a word, the manner of Leonardo pleasing him more than any other that he had ever seen, he set himself to study it, and abandoning little by little, although with great difficulty, the manner of Pietro, he sought to the best of his power and knowledge to imitate that of Leonardo. . . . In time he [Raphael] found himself very much hindered and impeded by the manner that he had adopted from Pietro. . . . His being unable to forget it was the reason that he had great difficulty in learning the beauties of the nude and the methods of difficult foreshortenings from the cartoon that Michelangelo Buonarroti made for the Council Hall in Florence. . . . He then devoted himself to studying the nude and to comparing the muscles of anatomical subjects and of flayed human bodies with those of the living, which, being covered with skin, are not clearly defined, as they are when the skin has been removed; and going on to observe in what way they acquire the softness of flesh in the proper places, and how certain graceful flexures are produced by twisting the body from one view to another, and also the effect of inflating, lowering, or raising either a limb or the whole person, and likewise the concatenation [linkage] of the bones, nerves, and veins, he became excellent in all the points that are looked for in a painter of eminence. . . . To this, as Raffaello was well aware, may be added the enriching [of] those scenes with a bizarre variety of perspectives, buildings, and landscapes, the method of clothing figures gracefully, the making them fade away sometimes in the shadows, and sometimes come forward into the light, the imparting of life and beauty to the heads of women, children, young men and old, and the giving them movement and boldness, according to necessity. He considered, also, how important is the furious flight of horses in battles, fierceness in soldiers, the knowledge how to depict all the sorts of animals, and above all the power to give such resemblance to portraits that they seem to be alive, and that it is known whom they represent; with an endless number of other things, such as the adornment of draperies, footwear, helmets, armor, women's head-dresses, hair, beards, vases, trees, grottoes, rocks, fires, skies turbid or serene, clouds, rain, lightning, clear weather, night, the light of the moon, the splendor of the sun, and innumerable other things, which are called for every moment by the requirements of the art of painting. . . . Raffaello . . . devoted himself, therefore, not to imitating the manner of that master, but to the attainment of a catholic [all-inclusive] excellence in the other fields of art that have been described. . . . I have thought fit, almost at the close of this Life, to make this discourse, in order to show with what labor, study, and diligence this honored artist always pursued his art. . . .[1]

[1] Robert Klein and Henri Zerner, *Italian Art 1500–1600: Sources and Documents* (Evanston, Ill.: Northwestern University Press, 1966), 85–88.

and scientists concerned with nature and human affairs. At the lower left, Pythagoras writes as a servant holds up the harmonic scale. In the foreground, Heraclitus (probably a portrait of Michelangelo) broods alone. Diogenes sprawls on the steps. At the right, students surround Euclid, who demonstrates a theorem. This group is especially interesting; Euclid may be a portrait of the aged Bramante. At the extreme right, just to the right of the astronomers Zoroaster and Ptolemy, both holding globes, Raphael included his own portrait.

The groups appear to move easily and clearly, with eloquent poses and gestures that symbolize their doctrines and present an engaging variety of figural positions. Their self-assurance and natural dignity convey the very nature of calm reason, that balance and measure the great Renaissance minds so admired as the heart of philosophy.

Significantly, in this work, Raphael placed himself among the mathematicians and scientists, and certainly the evolution of pictorial science came to its perfection in *School of Athens.* Raphael created a vast perspectival space, within which human figures move naturally, without effort — each according to his own intention, as Leonardo might have said. The pictorial stage setting, so long in preparation, is completely realized here and this development contributed to the convincing presentation of human dramas in subsequent art. Raphael's projection of this stagelike space onto a two-dimensional surface was the consequence of the union of mathematics with pictorial science, here mastered completely.

The artist's psychological insight matured along with his mastery of the problems of physical representation. All characters in Raphael's *School of Athens,* like those in Leonardo's *Last*

Supper (FIG. 22-3), communicate moods that reflect their beliefs, and the artist's placement of each figure tied these moods together. Raphael carefully considered his design devices for relating individuals and groups to one another and to the whole. These compositional elements demand close study. From the center, where Plato and Aristotle stand, silhouetted against the sky within the framing arch in the distance, Raphael arranged the groups of figures in an elliptical movement. It seems to swing forward, looping around two foreground groups on both sides and then back again to the center. Moving through the wide opening in the foreground along the floor's perspectival pattern, the viewer's eye penetrates the assembly of philosophers and continues, by way of the reclining Diogenes, up to the here-reconciled leaders of the two great opposing camps of Renaissance philosophy. The perspectival vanishing point falls on Plato's left hand, drawing viewers' attention to *Timaeus*. In the Stanza della Segnatura, Raphael reconciled and harmonized not only the Platonists and Aristotelians but also paganism and Christianity, surely a major factor in his appeal to Julius II.

Pope Julius II was clearly a formidable force, and his selection of artists and art projects reveals his interests and agenda. Likewise, these projects—Saint Peter's, the Sistine ceiling, his tomb, and the papal apartments—provide insights into the unique contributions and skills of the artists and architects involved, individuals such as Bramante, Michelangelo, and Raphael.

Synthesizing the Period's Excellence

EPITOMIZING HIGH RENAISSANCE IDEALS
Raphael's artistic development recapitulated the fifteenth-century sequence of artistic tendencies. Although strongly influenced by Leonardo and Michelangelo, Raphael developed an individual style that, in itself, clearly depicts the ideals of High Renaissance art. His powerful originality prevailed while he learned from everyone; he assimilated what he best could use and rendered into form the classical instinct of his age. Among Raphael's early works was *Marriage of the Virgin* (FIG. **22-18**), which he painted for the Chapel of Saint Joseph in the church of San Francesco in Città di Castello, southeast of Florence. The subject is a fitting one. According to the *Golden Legend* (a thirteenth-century collection of stories about the saints' lives), Joseph competed with other suitors for Mary's hand. The high priest was to give the Virgin to whichever suitor presented to him a rod that had miraculously bloomed. Raphael depicted Joseph with his flowering rod and about to place Mary's wedding ring on her extended hand. Other virgins congregate at the left, and the unsuccessful suitors stand on the right. One of them breaks his rod in half over his knee in frustration, giving Raphael an opportunity to demonstrate his mastery of foreshortening and of the perspective system he learned from Perugino (see FIG. 21-42), his teacher. The temple in the background is Raphael's version of a centrally planned building. The painting is almost exactly contemporary to Bramante's Tempietto (FIG. 22-8), but Raphael employed Brunelleschian arcades rather than Bramante's more "modern" classicizing post-and-lintel system.

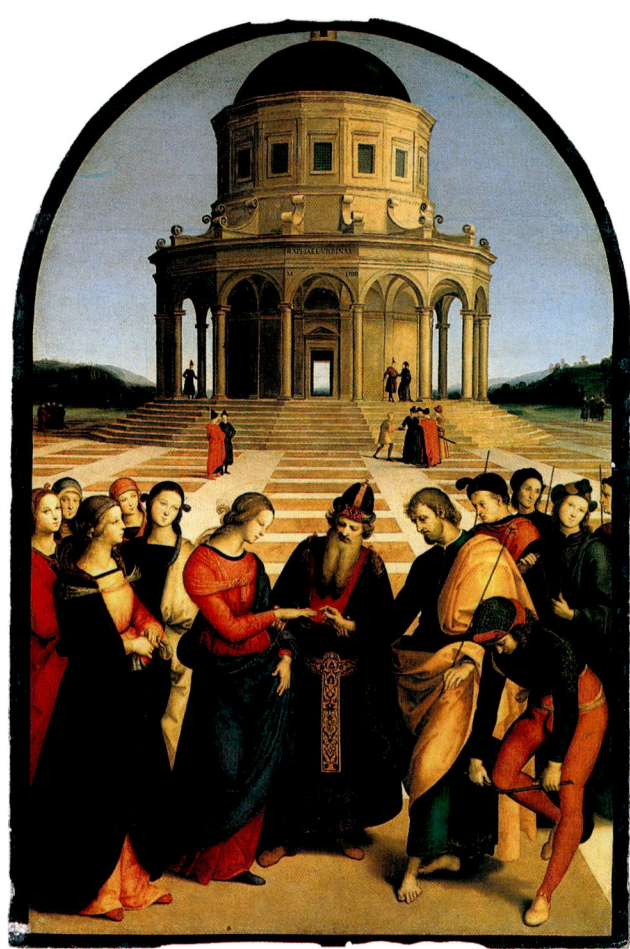

22-18 RAPHAEL, *Marriage of the Virgin,* from the Chapel of Saint Joseph in San Francesco in Città di Castello, near Florence, Italy, 1504. Oil on wood, 5′ 7″ × 3′ 10½″. Pinacoteca di Brera, Milan.

Raphael spent the four years from 1504 to 1508 in Florence. There, he discovered that the painting style he had learned so painstakingly from Perugino already was, like Brunelleschi's architectural style, outmoded. An artistic battle had developed between the two archrivals, Leonardo and Michelangelo. Crowds flocked to Santissima Annunziata to see Leonardo's recently unveiled cartoon of the Virgin, Christ Child, Saint Anne, and Saint John (probably an earlier version of *Virgin and Child with Saint Anne and the Infant Saint John,* FIG. 22-2). Michelangelo responded with the *Doni Madonna* (not illustrated). Around this time, Florentine officials commissioned both artists to decorate the council hall in the Palazzo Vecchio with frescoes memorializing Florentine victories of the past. Although neither artist completed his fresco and only some small preparatory sketches and small copies survive, this project must have had a considerable effect on artists in Florence, especially on one as gifted as Raphael (see "Giorgio Vasari on Raphael," page 654).

CHRISTIAN DEVOTION AND PAGAN BEAUTY
Under Leonardo's influence, Raphael began to modify the Madonna compositions he had learned in Umbria. In the

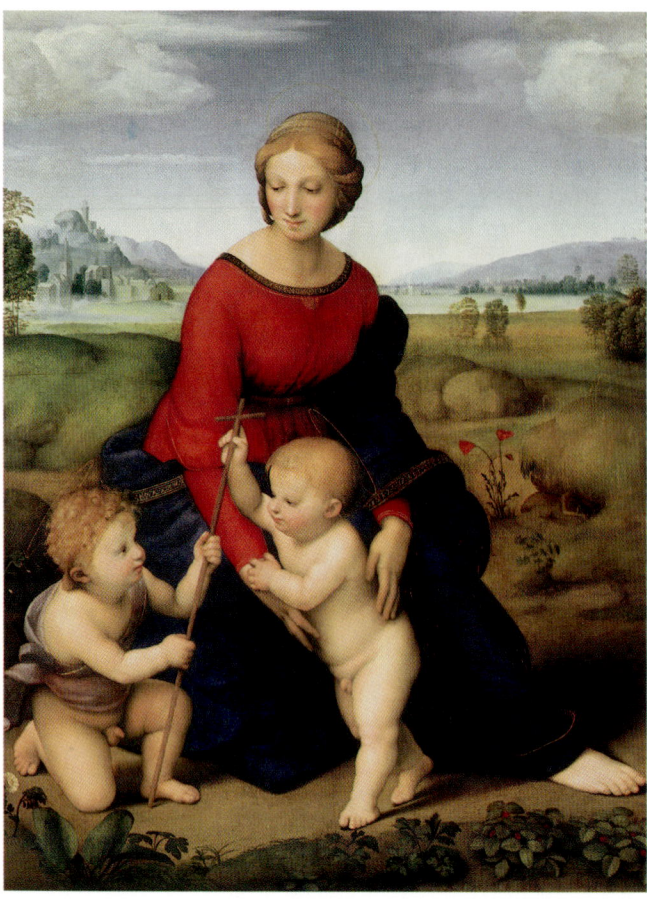

22-19   RAPHAEL, *Madonna of the Meadows,* 1505. Oil on panel, 3′ 8½″ × 2′ 10¼″. Kunsthistorisches Museum, Vienna.

noisseur. Raphael moved in the highest circles of the papal court, the star of a brilliant society. He was young, handsome, wealthy, and adulated, not only by his followers but also by Rome and all of Italy. Genial, even tempered, generous, and high minded, Raphael's personality contrasted strikingly with that of the aloof, mysterious Leonardo or the tormented and obstinate Michelangelo. The pope was not Raphael's only patron. His friend, Agostino Chigi, an immensely wealthy banker who managed the papal state's financial affairs, commissioned Raphael to decorate his palace on the Tiber with scenes from classical mythology. Outstanding among the frescoes Raphael painted in the small but splendid Villa Farnesina is *Galatea* (FIG. **22-20**), which Raphael based on *Metamorphoses* by the ancient Roman poet Ovid.

In Raphael's fresco, Galatea flees from her uncouth lover, the Cyclops Polyphemus, on a shell drawn by leaping dolphins. Sea creatures and playful cupids surround her. The painting erupts in unrestrained pagan joy and exuberance, an exultant song in praise of human beauty and zestful love. Compositionally, Raphael enhanced the image's liveliness by placing the sturdy figures around Galatea in bounding and dashing movements that always return to her as the energetic center. The cupids, skillfully foreshortened, repeat the circling motion. Raphael conceived his figures sculpturally, and Galatea's body—supple, strong, and vigorously in motion—contrasts with Botticelli's delicate, hovering, almost dematerialized Venus (see FIG. 21-27) while suggesting the spiraling compositions of Hellenistic statuary (see FIG. 5-80). Pagan myth presented in monumental form, in vivacious movement, and in a spirit of passionate delight resurrects the classical world's naturalistic art and poetry. Raphael revived the gods and heroes and the world they populated, not to venerate them but to transform them into art.

Madonna of the Meadows (FIG. **22-19**) of 1506, Raphael used the pyramidal composition of Leonardo's *Virgin of the Rocks* (FIG. 22-1). Further, Raphael may have based his modeling of faces and figures in subtle chiaroscuro on an earlier version of the theme in Leonardo's cartoon for *Virgin and Child with Saint Anne and the Infant Saint John* (FIG. 22-2). Yet, Raphael placed the large, substantial figures in a Peruginesque landscape, with the older artist's typical feathery trees in the middle ground. Although Raphael experimented with Leonardo's dusky modeling, he tended to return to Perugino's lighter tonalities. Raphael preferred clarity to obscurity, not fascinated, as Leonardo was, with mystery. His great series of Madonnas, of which this is an early example, unifies Christian devotion and pagan beauty. No artist ever has rivaled Raphael in his definitive rendering of this sublime theme of grace and dignity, of sweetness and lofty idealism.

OVID'S MYTH IN MONUMENTAL FORM   Pope Leo X (Giovanni de' Medici, r. 1513–1521), the son of Lorenzo de' Medici, succeeded Julius II as Raphael's patron. Leo was a worldly, pleasure-loving prince who spent huge sums on the arts; as a true Medici, he was a sympathetic con-

COUNTING ON CHARACTER AND GENTILITY   Raphael also excelled at portraiture. His subjects were the illustrious scholars and courtiers who surrounded Pope Leo X, among them his close friend Count Baldassare Castiglione (1478–1529), the author of a handbook on High Renaissance criteria for genteel behavior. In *Book of the Courtier,* Castiglione enumerated the perfect courtier's attributes—impeccable character, noble birth, military achievement, classical education, and knowledge of the arts. Castiglione then described a way of life based on cultivated rationality in imitation of the ancients. In Raphael's portrait of him (FIG. **22-21**), Castiglione, splendidly yet soberly garbed, looks directly at viewers with a philosopher's grave and benign expression, clear eyed and thoughtful. The figure is in half-length and three-quarter view, a pose made popular by *Mona Lisa* (FIG. 22-4). Both portraits exhibit the increasing attention High Renaissance artists paid to the subject's personality and psychic state. The muted and low-keyed tones befit the temper and mood of this reflective middle-aged man—the background is entirely neutral, without the usual landscape or architecture. The head and the hands wonderfully reveal the man, who himself had written so eloquently in *Courtier* of enlightenment from the love of beauty. Such love animated Raphael, Castiglione, and other artists of their age, and Michelangelo's poetry suggests he shared in this widely held belief.

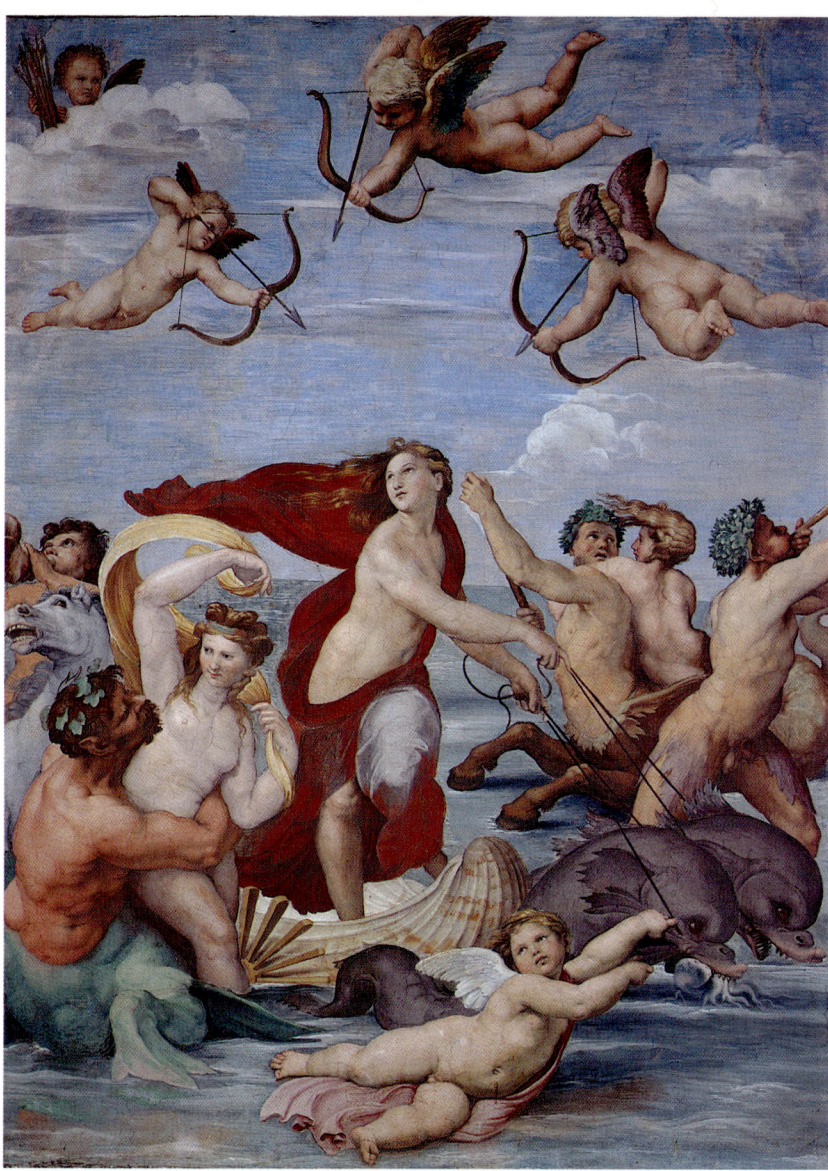

22-20 RAPHAEL, *Galatea,* Sala di Galatea, Villa Farnesina, Rome, Italy, 1513. Fresco, 9′ 8″ × 7′ 5″.

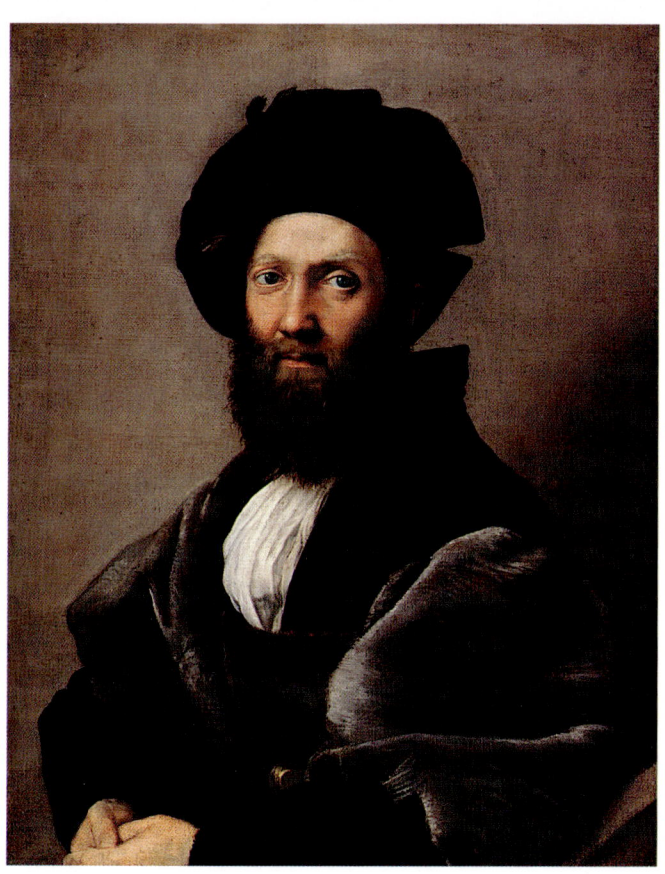

22-21 RAPHAEL, *Baldassare Castiglione,* ca. 1514. Oil on wood transferred to canvas, approx. 2′ 6¼″ × 2′ 2½″. Louvre, Paris.

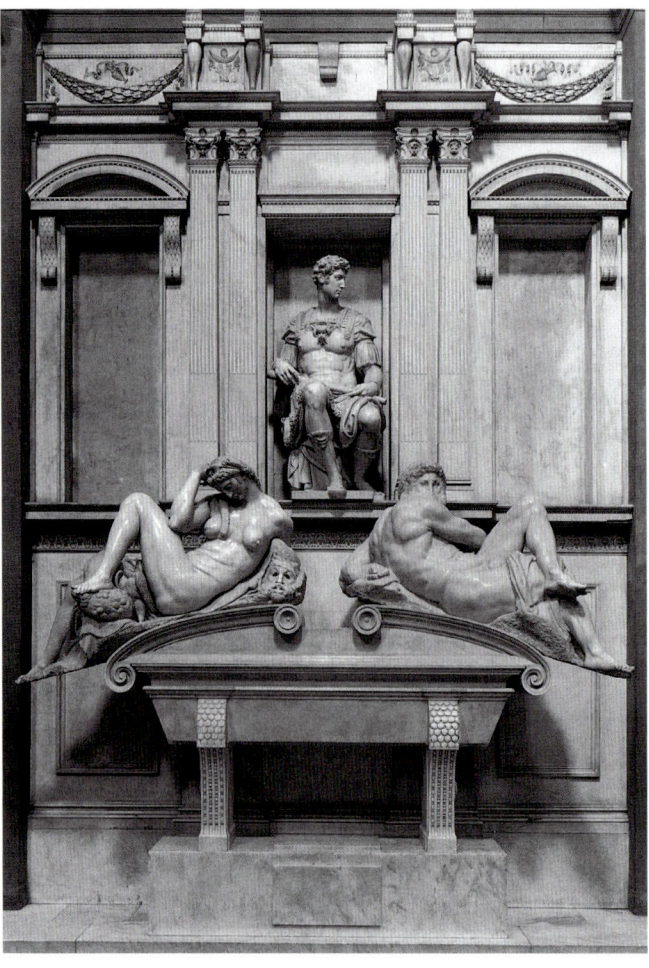

22-22 MICHELANGELO BUONARROTI, tomb of Giuliano de' Medici, New Sacristy (Medici Chapel), San Lorenzo, Florence, Italy, 1519–1534. Marble, central figure approx. 5′ 11″ high.

Michelangelo in the Service of the Medici

Following the death of Julius II, Michelangelo, like Raphael, went into the service of the Medici popes, Leo X and his successor Clement VII (Giulio de' Medici, r. 1523–1534). These Medici chose not to perpetuate their predecessor's fame by letting Michelangelo complete Julius's tomb; instead, they (Pope Leo X and the then cardinal Giulio de' Medici) commissioned him in 1519 to build a funerary chapel, the New Sacristy, in San Lorenzo in Florence.

TWO DUKES FACING OFF   At opposite sides of the New Sacristy stand Michelangelo's sculpted tombs of Giuliano, duke of Nemours (south of Paris), and Lorenzo, duke of Urbino, son and grandson of Lorenzo the Magnificent. Giuliano's tomb (FIG. **22-22**) is compositionally the twin of Lorenzo's. Michelangelo finished neither tomb. Scholars believe he intended to place pairs of recumbent river gods at the bottom of the sarcophagi, balancing the pairs of figures that rest on the sloping sides. However, despite this contention, the composition of the tombs has been a long-standing puzzle. How were they to look ultimately? What do they signify? Unfortunately, scholars possess insufficient evidence to answer these questions.

Traditional art historical scholarship suggested that the arrangement Michelangelo planned, but never completed, can be interpreted as the soul's ascent through the levels of the Neoplatonic universe. Neoplatonism, a school of thought based on Plato's idealistic, spiritualistic philosophy, experienced a renewed popularity in the sixteenth-century humanist community. The tomb's lowest level, represented by the river gods, would have signified the underworld of brute matter, the source of evil. The two statues on the sarcophagi would symbolize the realm of time—the specifically human world of the cycles of dawn, day, evening, and night. Humanity's state in this world of time was considered one of pain and anxiety, of frustration and exhaustion. At left, the female figure of Night and, at right, the male figure of Day appear to be chained into never-relaxing tensions. Both exhibit that anguished twisting of the body's masses in contrary directions, known as *figura serpentinata*, seen in the artist's *Bound Slave* (FIG. 22-11) and in his Sistine Chapel paintings. This contortion is a staple of Michelangelo's figural art. Day, with a body the thickness of a great tree and the anatomy of Hercules (or of a reclining Greco-Roman river god that may have inspired Michelangelo's statue), strains his huge limbs against each other, his unfinished visage rising menacingly above his shoulder. Night, the symbol of rest, twists as if in troubled sleep, her posture wrenched and feverish. The artist surrounded her with an owl, poppies, and a hideous mask symbolic of nightmares. Recent scholarship challenges this interpretation. These scholars argue that the personifications of night and day allude to the life cycle and the passage of time leading ultimately to death, rather than to humanity's pain.

On their respective tombs, sculptures of Lorenzo and Giuliano appear in niches at the apex of the structures. Transcending worldly existence, they represent the two ideal human types—the contemplative man (Lorenzo) and the active man (Giuliano). Together, they symbolize the two ways human beings might achieve union with God—through meditation or the active life fashioned after that of Christ. Michelangelo declined to make portraits of the actual dukes; who, he asked, would care what they looked like in a thousand years? The artist did not know the dukes personally and throughout his career demonstrated less interest in facial features and expressions than in the overall human form. The rather generic visages of the two Medici captains of the Church attest to this. The contemplation of what lies beyond the corrosion of time counted more. Giuliano, the active man (FIG. 22-22), his features quite generalized, sits clad in the armor of a Roman emperor and holding a commander's baton, his head turned alertly as if in council (he looks toward the statue of the Virgin at one end of the chapel). Across the room, Lorenzo, the contemplative man, sits wrapped in thought, his face in deep shadow. Like their predecessors, the sixteenth-century Medici made sure they enlisted the services of the best artists for constructing their legacy.

The Papacy of Pope Paul III

A PALACE FIT FOR A POPE   Pope Paul III (Alessandro Farnese, r. 1534–1549) maintained the lavish lifestyle previous popes enjoyed. However, in the wake of the Reformation, he also initiated the Counter-Reformation, establishing the Council of Trent and the Inquisition, as well as formally recognizing the Jesuit order. Paul III also continued the papal tradition of extensive art patronage. An early major project he commissioned when he was still Cardinal Farnese was the

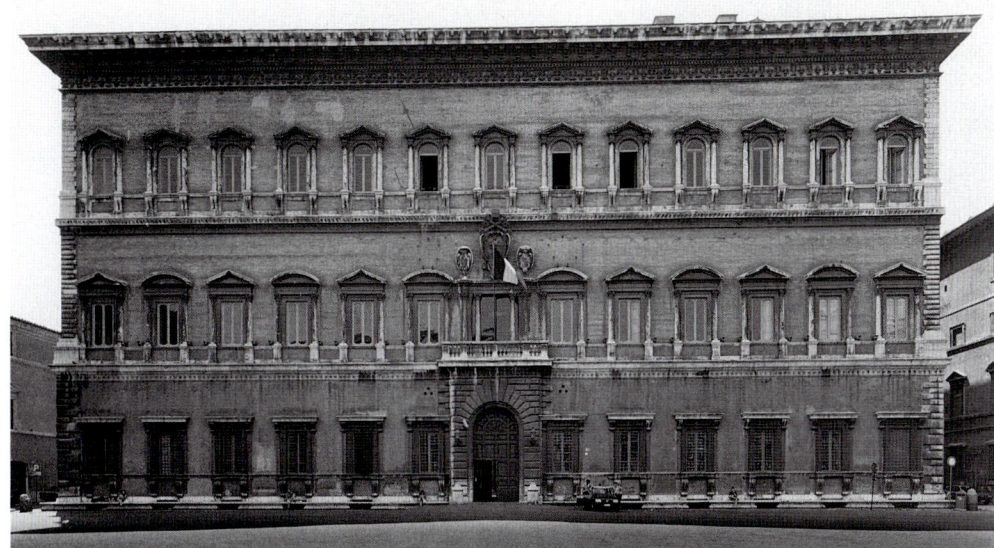

construction of the Palazzo Farnese in Rome (FIG. **22-23**). To design the palazzo, the pope selected ANTONIO DA SANGALLO THE YOUNGER (1483–1546), who established himself as the favorite architect of Pope Paul III and therefore received many commissions that might have gone to Michelangelo. Antonio, the youngest of a family of architects, went to Rome around 1503 and became Bramante's draftsman and assistant. He is the perfect example of the professional architect; indeed, his family constituted an architectural firm, often planning and drafting for other architects. Antonio built fortifications for almost the entire papal state and received more commissions for military than for civilian architecture. Although he may not have invented it, Antonio certainly laid the foundation for the modern method of bastioned fortifications.

The Palazzo Farnese set the standard for the High Renaissance palazzo and fully expresses the classical order, regularity, simplicity, and dignity of the High Renaissance. The broad majestic front of the Palazzo Farnese asserts to the public the exalted station of a great family. This impressive facade encapsulates the aristocratic epoch that followed the stifling of the nascent, middle-class democracy of European cities (especially the Italian cities) by powerful kings heading centralized states. It is thus significant that Paul chose to enlarge greatly the original, rather modest, palace to its present form after his accession to the papacy in 1534, reflecting his ambitions both for his family and for the papacy. At Antonio's death in 1546, Michelangelo assumed control of the building's completion.

Facing a spacious paved square, the facade is the very essence of princely dignity in architecture. The *quoins* (rusticated building corners) and cornice frame firmly anchor the rectangle of the smooth front, while lines of windows (the central row with alternating triangular and segmental pediments, in Bramante's fashion) mark a majestic beat across it. The window casements are not flush with the wall, as in the Palazzo Medici-Riccardi (see FIG. 21-20), but project from its surface, so instead of being a flat, thin plane, the facade is a spatially active three-dimensional mass. Antonio designed each casement as a complete architectural unit, with a *socle* (a projecting undermember), engaged columns, and a pediment. The variations in his treatment of these units prevent the

symmetrical scheme from appearing rigid or monotonous. The rusticated doorway and second-story balcony, surmounted by the Farnese coat of arms, emphasize the central axis and bring the design's horizontal and vertical forces into harmony. This centralizing feature, absent from the palaces of Michelozzo di Bartolommeo (see FIG. 21-20) and Alberti (FIG. 21-35), is the external opening of a central corridor axis that runs through the entire building and continues in the garden beyond. Around this axis, Antonio arranged the rooms with strict regularity. The interior courtyard (FIG. **22-24**) displays

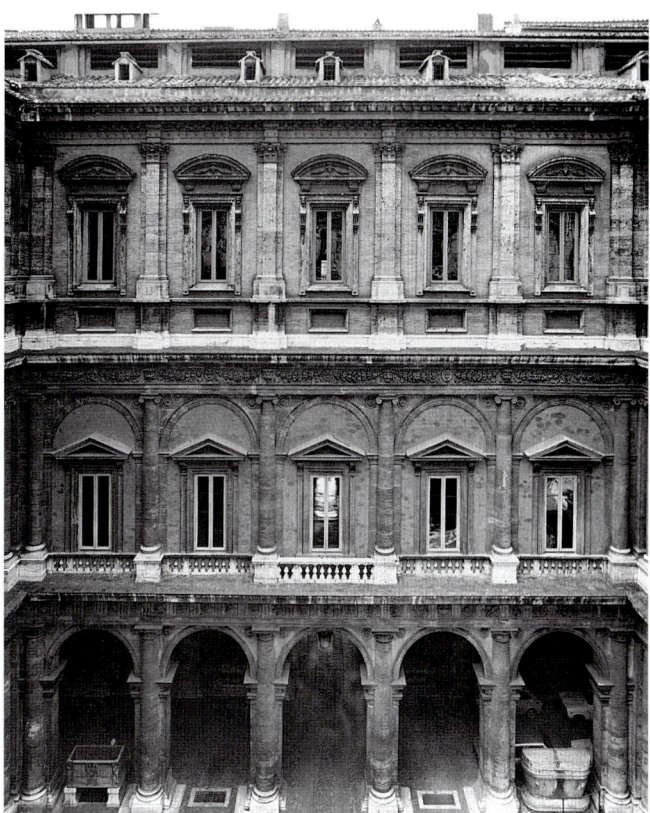

22-24 ANTONIO DA SANGALLO THE YOUNGER, courtyard of the Palazzo Farnese, Rome, Italy, ca. 1530–1546. Third story and attic by MICHELANGELO BUONARROTI, 1548.

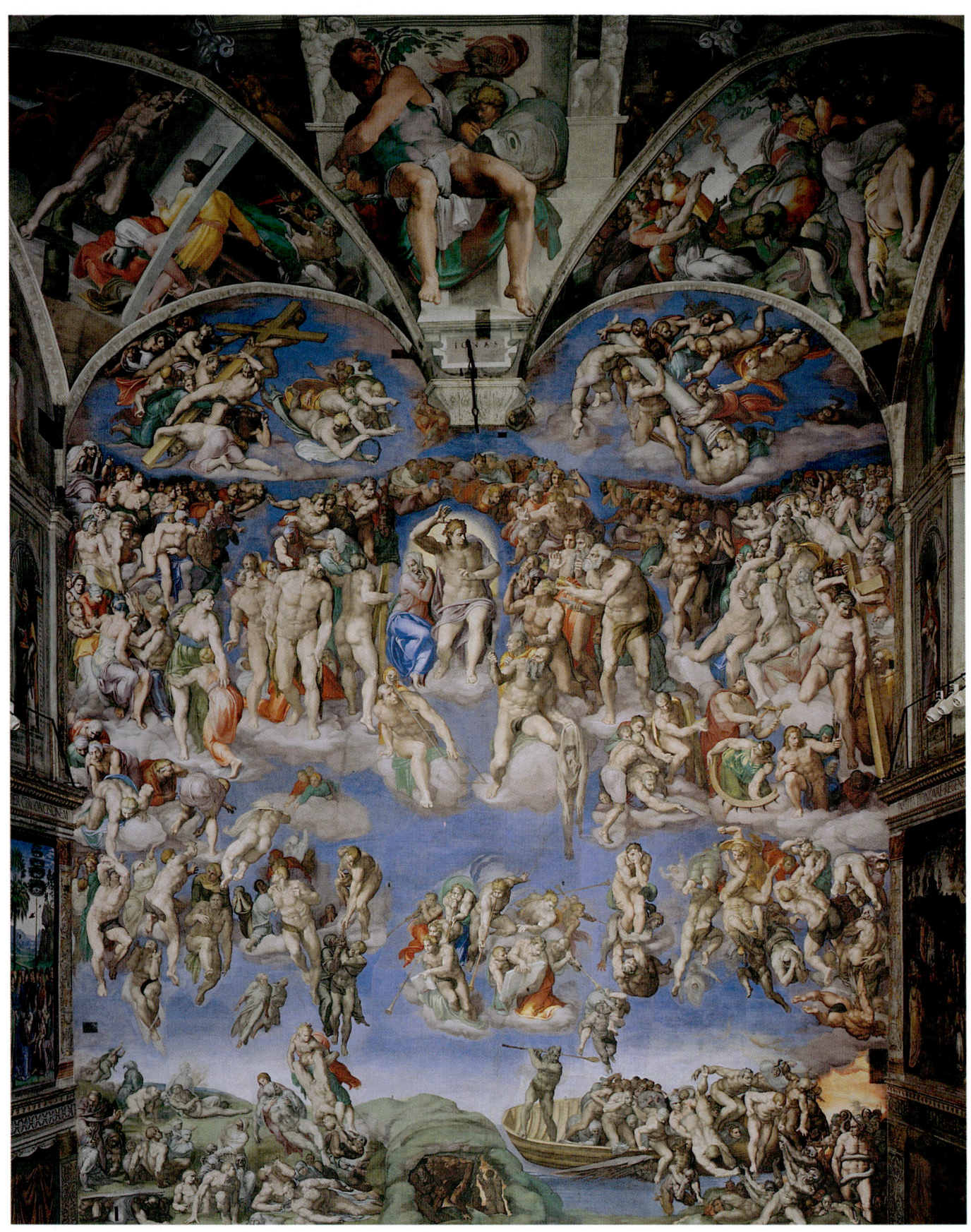

22-25 MICHELANGELO BUONARROTI, *Last Judgment,* fresco on the altar wall of the Sistine Chapel, Vatican City, Rome, Italy, 1534–1541. Copyright © Nippon Television Network Corporation, Tokyo.

stately column-enframed arches on the first two levels, as in the Roman Colosseum (see FIG. 10-34). On the third level, Michelangelo incorporated his sophisticated variation on that theme (based in part on the Colosseum's fourth-story Corinthian pilasters), with overlapping pilasters replacing the weighty columns of Antonio's design.

A MIGHTY CHRIST ON JUDGMENT DAY Once Cardinal Farnese ascended to the papacy, he extended numerous commissions to artists in the hope of restoring prominence to the Catholic Church. Thus, these projects can be viewed as an integral part of the Counter-Reformation effort. Among Paul III's first papal commissions was a large fresco for the Sistine Chapel. Michelangelo agreed to paint the large-scale *Last Judgment* fresco (FIG. **22-25**; like the Sistine ceiling, newly cleaned and restored—see "Restoring the Glory of Renaissance Frescoes," page 652) on the chapel's altar wall. Here, Michelangelo depicted Christ as the stern Judge of the world—a giant whose mighty right arm is lifted in a gesture of damnation so broad and universal as to suggest he will destroy all creation, Heaven and earth alike. The choirs of Heaven surrounding him pulse with anxiety and awe. Trumpeting angels, the ascending figures of the just, and the downward-hurtling figures of the Damned crowd into the spaces below. On the left, the dead awake and assume flesh; on the right, demons, whose gargoyle masks and burning eyes revive the demons of Romanesque tympana (see FIG. 17-25), torment the Damned.

Michelangelo's terrifying vision of the fate that awaits sinners goes far beyond even Signorelli's gruesome images (see FIG. 21-54). Martyrs who suffered especially agonizing deaths crouch below the Judge. One of them, Saint Bartholomew, who was skinned alive, holds the flaying knife and the skin, its face a grotesque self-portrait of Michelangelo. The figures are huge and violently twisted, with small heads and contorted features. Yet while this immense fresco impresses on viewers Christ's wrath on Judgment Day, it also holds out hope. A group of saved souls—the elect—crowd around Christ, and on the far right appears a figure with a cross, most likely the Good Thief (crucified with Christ) or a saint martyred by crucifixion, such as Saint Andrew.

CAPITALIZING ON ROMAN HISTORY Driven by his restive genius, Michelangelo was rarely content to grapple with only a single commission. While he was executing the *Last Judgment* fresco, he received another flattering and challenging commission from Pope Paul III. In 1537, he undertook the reorganization of the Capitoline Hill (the Campidoglio) in Rome (FIG. **22-26**). The pope wished to transform the ancient hill, which once had been the site of the Roman Empire's spiritual capitol, the greatest temple to Jupiter in the Roman world, into a symbol of the power of the new Rome of the popes. Michelangelo confronted an immense challenge. He had to incorporate into his design two existing buildings—the medieval Palazzo dei Senatori (Palace of the Senators) on the east and the fifteenth-century Palazzo dei Conservatori (Palace of the Conservators) on the south. These buildings formed an eighty-degree angle. Such preconditions might have defeated a lesser architect, but Michelangelo converted what seemed a limitation into the most impressive design for a civic unit formulated during the entire Renaissance.

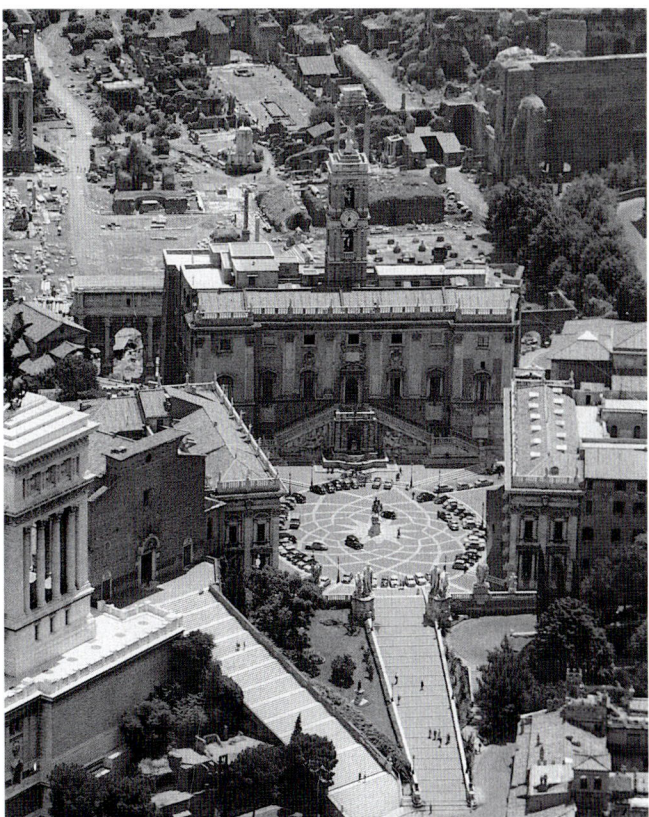

22-26 MICHELANGELO BUONARROTI, aerial view of Capitoline Hill (Campidoglio), Rome, Italy, designed ca. 1537.

He carried his obsession with human form over to architecture and reasoned that buildings should follow the human body's form. This meant organizing their units symmetrically around a central and unique axis, as the arms relate to the body or the eyes to the nose. "For it is an established fact," he once wrote, "that the members of architecture resemble the members of man. Whoever neither has been nor is a master at figures, and especially at anatomy, cannot really understand architecture."[11] It must have been with such arguments that he convinced his sponsors of the need to balance the Palazzo dei Conservatori, whose facade he was to redesign, with a similar unit on the square's north side. To achieve balance and symmetry in design, Michelangelo placed the new building (the Museo Capitolino, originally planned only as a portico with single rows of offices above and behind it) so that it stood at the same angle to the Palazzo dei Senatori as the Palazzo dei Conservatori. This yielded a trapezoidal, rather than a rectangular, plan for the piazza. Michelangelo subsequently adjusted all other design elements to this unorthodox but basic feature.

The ancient statue of Marcus Aurelius (see FIG. 10-59), the only equestrian statue of a Roman emperor to survive the Middle Ages, became the focal point for the whole design. The pope ordered it moved to the Capitoline Hill against the advice of Michelangelo, who might have preferred to carve his own centerpiece. The symbolic significance of the famous monument must have appealed to Paul III. Although the fifteenth-century humanists had rediscovered the statue's true identity (by comparison with Roman coins), the medieval identification of the portrait as Constantine the Great, the first Christian emperor, still lingered and was an integral part of its fabled history. In the sixteenth century, the image of Marcus Aurelius on horseback carried a double significance. It was the ultimate symbol of the pagan Roman Empire over which Christianity had triumphed, but Italians also associated it with Constantine, Saint Peter, and the establishment of the papacy. In short, this equestrian portrait of an omnipotent yet benevolent Roman emperor encapsulated the city's whole history from antiquity to the early Christian Church to the sixteenth-century papacy. It was the ideal centerpiece for the new civic center of Renaissance Rome and beautifully served the needs of a humanist pope during the Counter-Reformation.

To connect this central monument with the surrounding buildings, Michelangelo provided it with an oval base and placed it centrally in an oval pavement design. Michelangelo's choice of the oval is noteworthy, as other Renaissance architects considered it an unstable geometric figure and therefore shunned it. Given the piazza's trapezoidal shape, however, Michelangelo deemed the oval (which combines centralizing and axial qualities) best suited to relate the design's various elements to one another. Later artists during the Baroque period adopted the oval as their favorite geometric figure.

Facing the piazza, the two lateral palazzi, the Palazzo dei Conservatori and Museo Capitolino (FIG. **22-27**), have identical two-story facades. Michelangelo introduced viewers again to the giant order, the tall pilasters first seen in more reserved fashion in Alberti's Sant'Andrea in Mantua (see FIG. 21-43). Michelangelo used the giant order with much greater authority. The huge pilasters not only tie the two stories together but also provide a sturdy skeleton that actually functions as the structure's main support. Michelangelo all but eliminated walls. At ground level, he interposed columns to soften the transition from the massive bulk of the pilaster-faced piers to the deep voids between them. These columns carry straight lintels, in the manner Alberti earlier advocated, but Michelangelo used them with even greater logic and con-

sistency than Alberti did. For the third building on the piazza, the three-storied Palazzo dei Senatori (FIG. 22-26), the architect added a double flight of steps to the entrance. He also embellished the facade, employing the same design elements as the other two palazzi but in a less sculptural fashion. The axial building, with its greater height, thus became a distinctive and commanding accent for the ensemble, providing variety within the design without disrupting its unity.

Michelangelo might have made the piazza a roomlike enclosure, as Alberti, in his treatise, had advised for all piazzas. But the architect chose to leave one side open. He merely suggested a fourth wall with a balustrade and a thin screen of Classical statuary that effectively defines the piazza's limits without obstructing a panoramic view across the city's roofs toward the Vatican. The symbolism of this axis must have pleased the pope just as much as the piazza's dynamic design, and the sweeping vista also must have pleased Baroque planners later.

A SCULPTOR'S FINISHING TOUCH   The last project Michelangelo undertook in 1546 for Pope Paul III was the supervision of the building of the new Saint Peter's. With the Church facing challenges to its supremacy, Paul III surely felt a sense of urgency about the completion of this project. Michelangelo's work on Saint Peter's, after efforts by a succession of architects following Bramante's death, apparently became a long-term show of dedication, thankless and without pay.

Among Michelangelo's difficulties was his struggle to preserve and carry through Bramante's original plan (FIG. 22-6), which he praised (although he did modify it). Michelangelo recognized the strength of the initial design (as he had with Antonio's project for the Palazzo Farnese, FIGS. 22-23 and 22-24) and chose to retain it as the basis for his design. With Bramante's plan for Saint Peter's, Michelangelo reduced the central component from a number of interlocking crosses to a

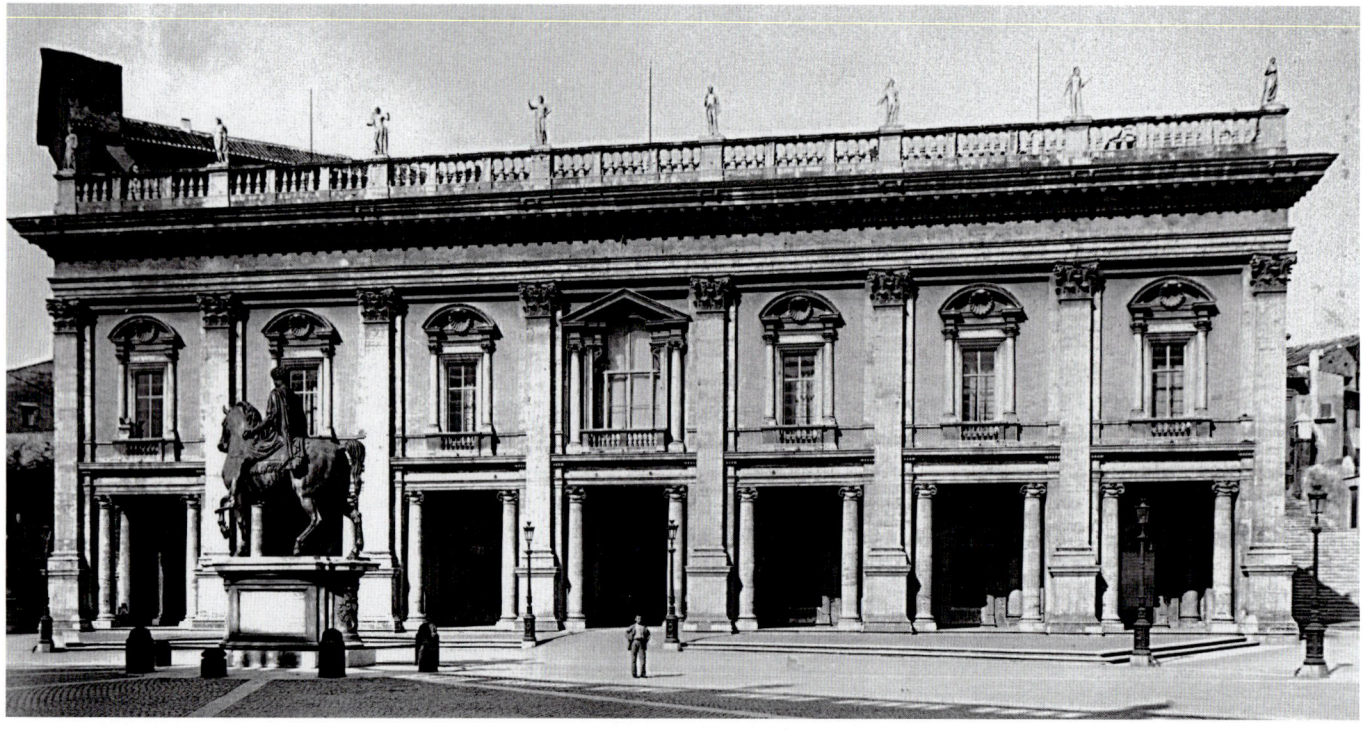

22-27   MICHELANGELO BUONARROTI, Museo Capitolino, Capitoline Hill, Rome, Italy, designed ca. 1537.

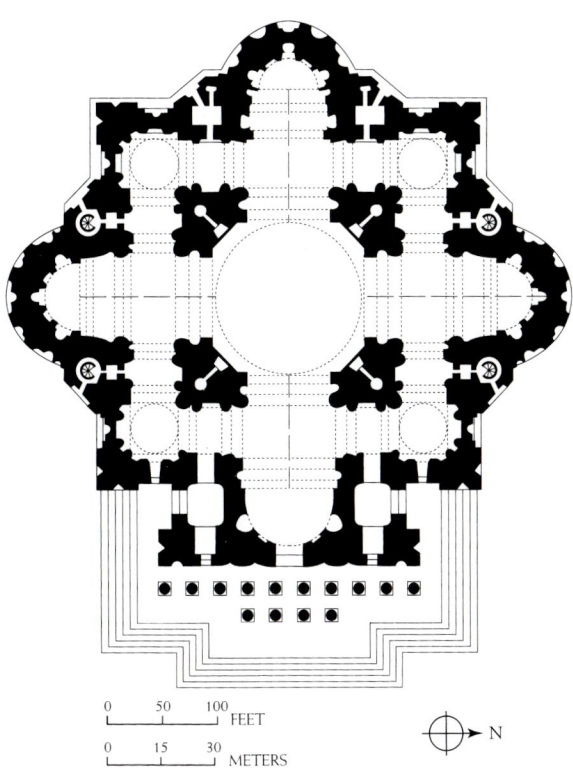

22-28 MICHELANGELO BUONARROTI, plan for Saint Peter's, Vatican City, Rome, Italy, 1546.

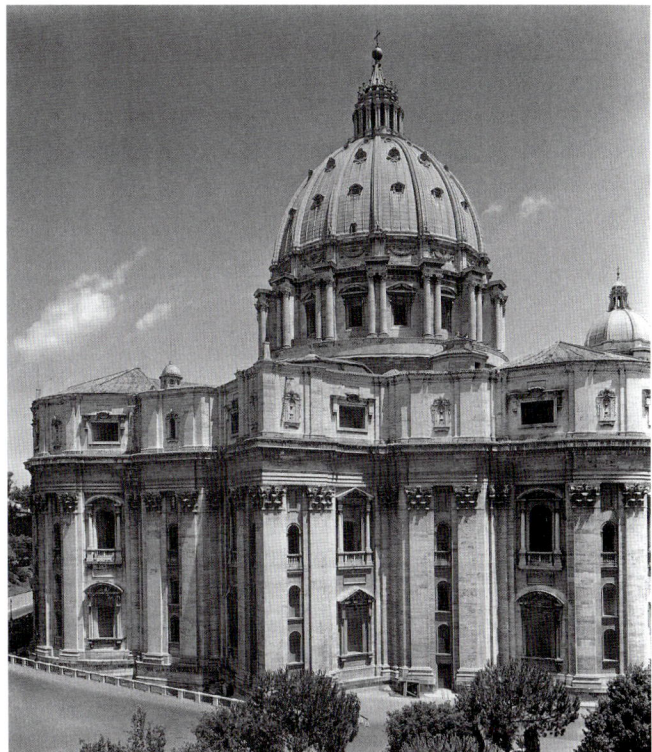

22-29 MICHELANGELO BUONARROTI, Saint Peter's (view from the northwest), Vatican City, Rome, Italy, 1546–1564. Dome completed by GIACOMO DELLA PORTA, 1590.

compact domed Greek cross inscribed in a square and fronted with a double-columned portico (FIG. **22-28**). Without destroying the centralizing features of Bramante's plan, Michelangelo, with a few strokes of the pen, converted its snowflake complexity into massive, cohesive unity.

Michelangelo's treatment of the building's exterior further reveals his interest in creating a unified and cohesive design. Because of later changes to the front of the church, the west (apse) end (FIG. **22-29**) offers the best view of his style and intention. The colossal order again served him nobly, as the giant pilasters seem to march around the undulating wall surfaces, confining the movement without interrupting it. The architectural sculpturing here extends up from the ground

through the attic stories and into the drum and the dome, unifying the whole building from base to summit. Baroque architects later learned much from this kind of integral design, which Michelangelo based on his conviction that architecture is one with the human form's organic beauty. The domed west end—as majestic as it is today and as influential as it has been on architecture throughout the centuries—is not quite as Michelangelo intended it. Originally, Michelangelo had planned a dome with an ogival section (raised silhouette), like that of Florence Cathedral (see FIG. 21-14). But in his final version he decided on a hemispheric (semicircular silhouette) dome (FIG. **22-30**) to temper the verticality of the design of the lower stories and to establish a balance between

22-30 MICHELANGELO BUONARROTI, drawing of south elevation of Saint Peter's, Vatican City, Rome, Italy, 1546–1564 (engraving by Étienne Dupérac, ca. 1569) Metropolitan Museum of Art, New York (Harris Brisbane Dick Fund, 1941).

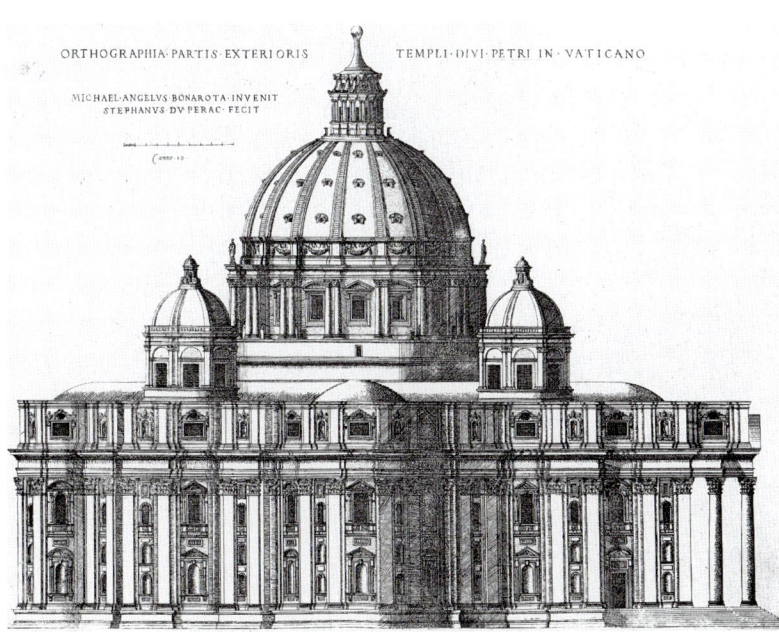

dynamic and static elements. However, when GIACOMO DELLA PORTA (ca. 1537–1602) executed the dome after Michelangelo's death, he restored the earlier high design, ignoring Michelangelo's later version. Giacomo's reasons were probably the same ones that had impelled Brunelleschi to use an ogival section for his Florentine dome—greater stability and ease of construction. The result is that the dome seems to rise from its base, rather than rest firmly on it—an effect Michelangelo might not have approved. Nevertheless, Saint Peter's dome is probably the most impressive and beautiful in the world and has served as a model for generations of architects to this day.

Michelangelo's art began in the style of the fifteenth century, developed into the epitome of High Renaissance art, and, at the end, moved toward Mannerism and the Baroque. The longevity of his career has yet to be matched by more than a handful of artists. He was eighty-nine when he died in 1564, still hard at work on both the Capitoline Hill and Saint Peter's. Few artists, then or since, could escape his influence, and variations of his style provided the foundation of art production for centuries.

Early-Sixteenth-Century Venetian Art

Venice long had been a major Mediterranean coastal port and served as the gateway to the Orient. Reaching the height of its commercial and political power during the fifteenth century, Venice saw its fortunes decline in the sixteenth century. Even so, Venice and the Papal States were the only Italian sovereignties to retain their independence during the century of strife; either France or Spain dominated all others. Although the discoveries in the New World and the economic shift from Italy to Hapsburg Germany and the Netherlands were largely responsible for the decline of Venice, even more immediate and pressing events drained its wealth and power. After their conquest of Constantinople, the Turks began to vie with Venice for control of the eastern Mediterranean and evolved into a constant threat to Venice. Early in the century, the European powers of the League of Cambrai also attacked Venice. Formed and led by Pope Julius II, who coveted Venetian holdings on Italy's mainland, the League included Spain, France, and the Holy Roman Empire, in addition to the Papal States. Despite these challenges, Venice developed a flourishing, independent, and influential school of artists.

THE ROLE OF COLOR IN VENETIAN ART The effect of Venice's soft-colored light particularly interested artists in the maritime republic. Venetian artist GIOVANNI BELLINI (ca. 1430–1516) played an important role in developing the evocative use of color and contributed significantly to creating what is known as the Venetian style. Trained in the International Style (see Chapter 19, pages 552–553) by his father, Jacopo, a student of Gentile da Fabriano, Bellini worked in the family shop and did not develop his own style until after his father's death in 1470. His early independent works show the dominant influence of his brother-in-law Andrea Mantegna. But in the late 1470s, he came into contact with the work of the Sicilian-born painter Antonello da Messina (ca. 1430–1479), which impressed him. Antonello received his early training in Naples, where he must have come in close contact with Flemish painting and mastered using mixed oil (see Chapter 20, page 569). This more flexible

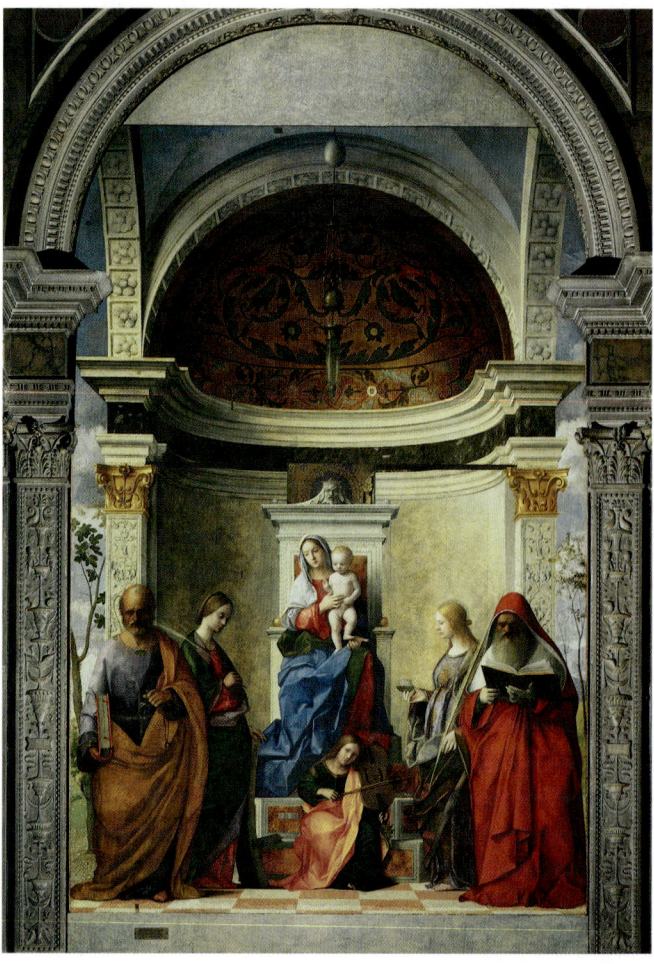

22-31 GIOVANNI BELLINI, *San Zaccaria Altarpiece,* San Zaccaria, Venice, Italy, 1505. Oil on wood transferred to canvas, approx. 16′ 5″ × 7′ 9″.

medium is wider in coloristic range than either tempera or fresco (see Chapter 19, "Fresco Painting," page 543). Antonello arrived in Venice in 1475 and during his two-year stay introduced his Venetian colleagues to the possibilities the new oil technique offered. As a direct result of Bellini's contact with him, Bellini abandoned Mantegna's harsh linear style and developed a sensuous coloristic manner that was to characterize Venetian painting in the late-fifteenth and sixteenth centuries.

Bellini earned great recognition for his many Madonnas, which he painted both in half-length (with or without accompanying saints) on small devotional panels and full-length on large, monumental altarpieces of the *sacra conversazione* (holy conversation) type. In the sacra conversazione, which gained great popularity as a theme for religious paintings from the middle of the fifteenth century on, a unified space joins saints from different epochs who seem to converse either with each other or with the audience. (Raphael employed much the same conceit in his *School of Athens,* FIG. 22-17, where he gathered Greek philosophers of different eras.) Bellini carried on the tradition in one of his large altarpieces, the *San Zaccaria Altarpiece* (FIG. **22-31**).

In the *San Zaccaria Altarpiece,* Bellini refined many of the compositional elements of his earlier altarpieces. As was conventional, the Virgin Mary sits enthroned, holding the Christ Child, with saints flanking her. Here, attributes aid the identification of all the saints but Saint Lucy—Saint Peter with his key and book, Saint Catherine with the palm of martyrdom and the broken wheel, and Saint Jerome with a book (representing his translation of the Bible into Latin). At the foot of the throne sits an angel playing a viol. Bellini placed the group in a carefully painted shrine. The refinement of his style emerged in his use of color and light. The painting radiates a feeling of serenity and spiritual calm. Viewers derive this sense less from the figures (no interaction occurs among them) than from the harmonious and balanced presentation of color and light. Bellini's method of painting here became softer and more luminous than his earlier works. Line is not the chief agent of form; indeed, outlines dissolve in light and shadow. The impact of this work is due largely to glowing color—a soft radiance that envelops the forms with an atmospheric haze and enhances their majestic serenity.

A LUSHLY COLORED MYTHOLOGICAL PICNIC
The *San Zaccaria Altarpiece* is the mature work of an inquisitive artist whose paintings spanned the development of three artistic generations in Florence. At the very end of Bellini's long life, he was still willing and able to make changes in his style and approach to keep abreast of his times—thus, he began to deal with pagan subjects.

In painting *The Feast of the Gods* (FIG. **22-32**), Bellini actually drew from the work of one of his own students, Giorgione da Castelfranco (FIGS. 22-33 and 22-34), who developed his master's landscape backgrounds into poetic Arcadian reveries. Derived from Arcadia, an ancient district of the central Peloponnesus (peninsula in southern Greece), *Arcadian* referred, by the Renaissance, to an idyllic place of rural, rustic peace and simplicity. After Giorgione's premature death, Bellini embraced his student's interests and, in *The Feast of the Gods,* developed a new kind of mythological painting. The duke of Ferrara, Alfonso d'Este, commissioned this work for a room in the Palazzo Ducale. Although Bellini drew some of the figures from the standard repertoire of Greco-Roman art—most notably, the nymph carrying a vase on her head

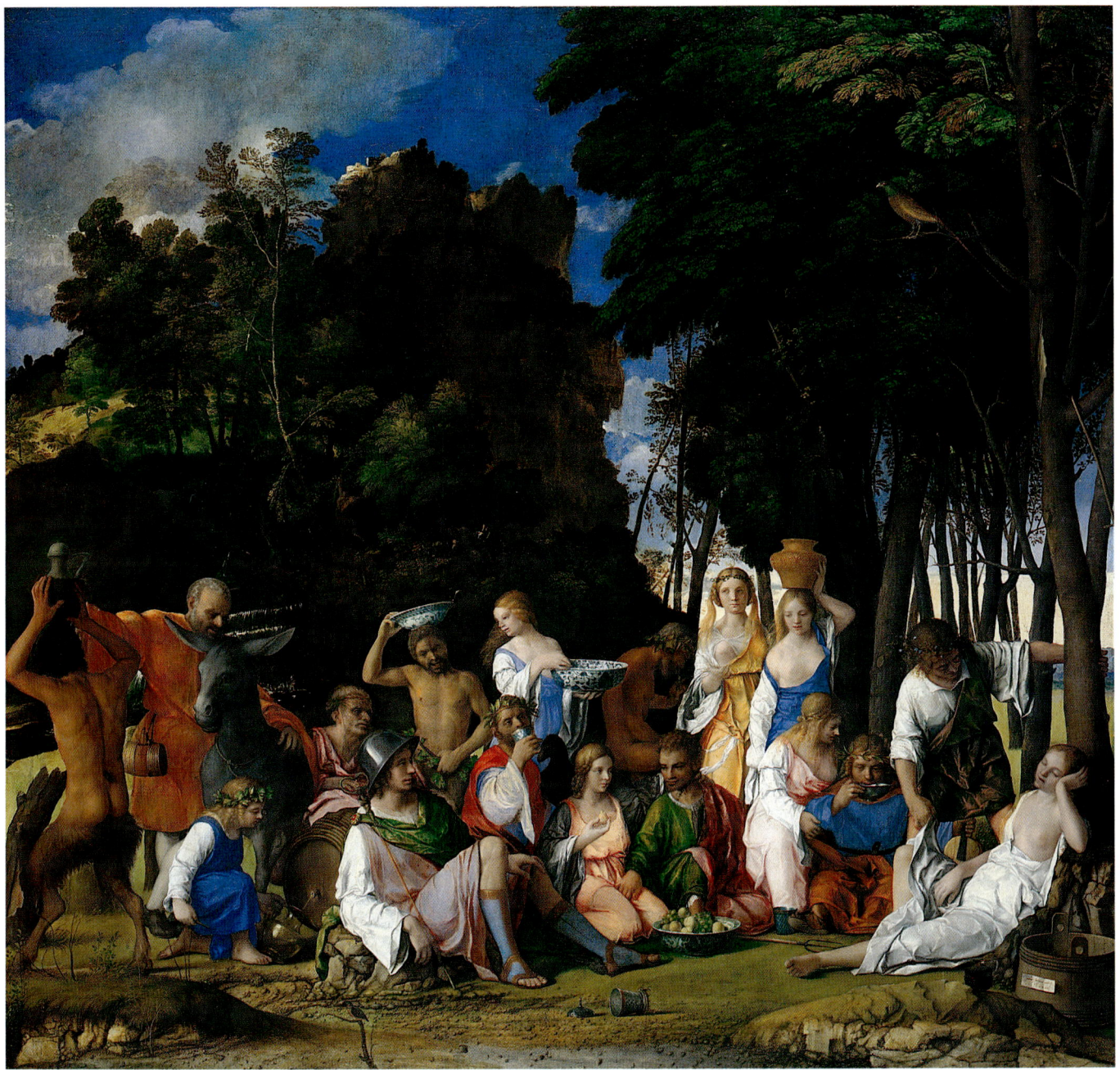

22-32 GIOVANNI BELLINI and TITIAN, *The Feast of the Gods,* 1529. Oil on canvas, approx. 5′ 7″ × 6′ 2″. National Gallery of Art, Washington (Widener Collection).

and the sleeping nymph in the lower right corner—the Olympian gods appear as peasants enjoying a heavenly picnic in a shady northern glade. Bellini's source was Ovid's *Fasti*, which describes a banquet of the gods. The artist spread the figures across the foreground. Satyrs attend the gods, nymphs bring jugs of wine, a child draws from a keg, couples engage in love play, and the sleeping nymph with exposed breast receives amorous attention. The mellow light of a long afternoon glows softly around the gathering, caressing the surfaces of colorful draperies, smooth flesh, and polished metal. Here, Bellini communicated the delight the Venetian school took in the beauty of texture revealed by the full resources of gently and subtly harmonized color. Behind the warm, lush tones of the figures, a background of cool green tree-filled glades extends into the distance; at the right, a screen of trees creates a verdant shelter. (Scholars believe that the background was modified by Titian, discussed shortly.) The atmosphere is idyllic, a lush countryside providing a setting for the never-ending pleasure of the immortal gods.

Thus, with Bellini, Venetian art became the great complement of the schools of Florence and Rome. The Venetians' instrument was color; that of the Florentines and Romans was sculpturesque form. Scholars often distill the contrast between these two approaches down to *colorito* (colored or painted) versus *disegno* (drawing and design—see *"Disegno:* Drawing on Design Fundamentals," page 639). While most central Italian artists emphasized careful design preparation based on preliminary drawing, Venetian artists focused on color and the process of paint application. These two schools have run parallel—sometimes touching and intersecting—through the history of Western art from the Renaissance to the present. In addition, their themes, in general, differed. Venetian artists painted the poetry of the senses and delighted in nature's beauty and the pleasures of humanity. Artists in Florence and Rome gravitated toward more esoteric, intellectual themes—the epic of humanity, the masculine virtues, the grandeur of the ideal, and the lofty conceptions of religion involving the heroic and sublime. Much of the history of later Western art involved a dialogue between these two traditions.

Describing Venetian art as "poetic" is particularly appropriate, given the development of *poesia,* or painting meant to operate in a manner similar to poetry. Both classical and Renaissance poetry inspired Venetian artists, and their paintings focused on the lyrical and sensual. Thus, in many Venetian artworks, discerning concrete narratives or subjects (in the traditional sense) is virtually impossible.

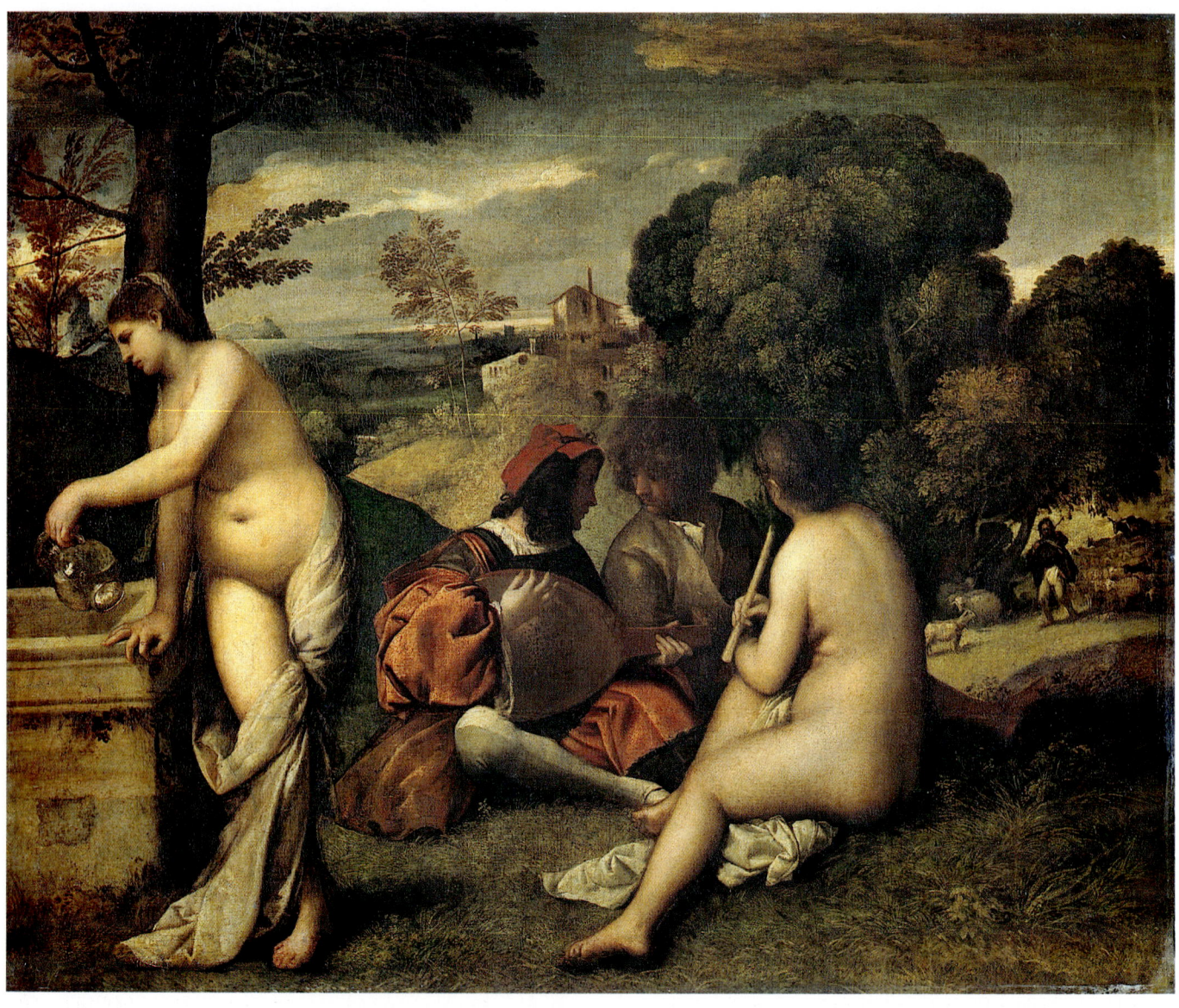

22-33 Giorgione da Castelfranco (and/or Titian?), *Pastoral Symphony,* ca. 1508. Oil on canvas, approx. 3′ 7″ × 4′ 6″. Louvre, Paris.

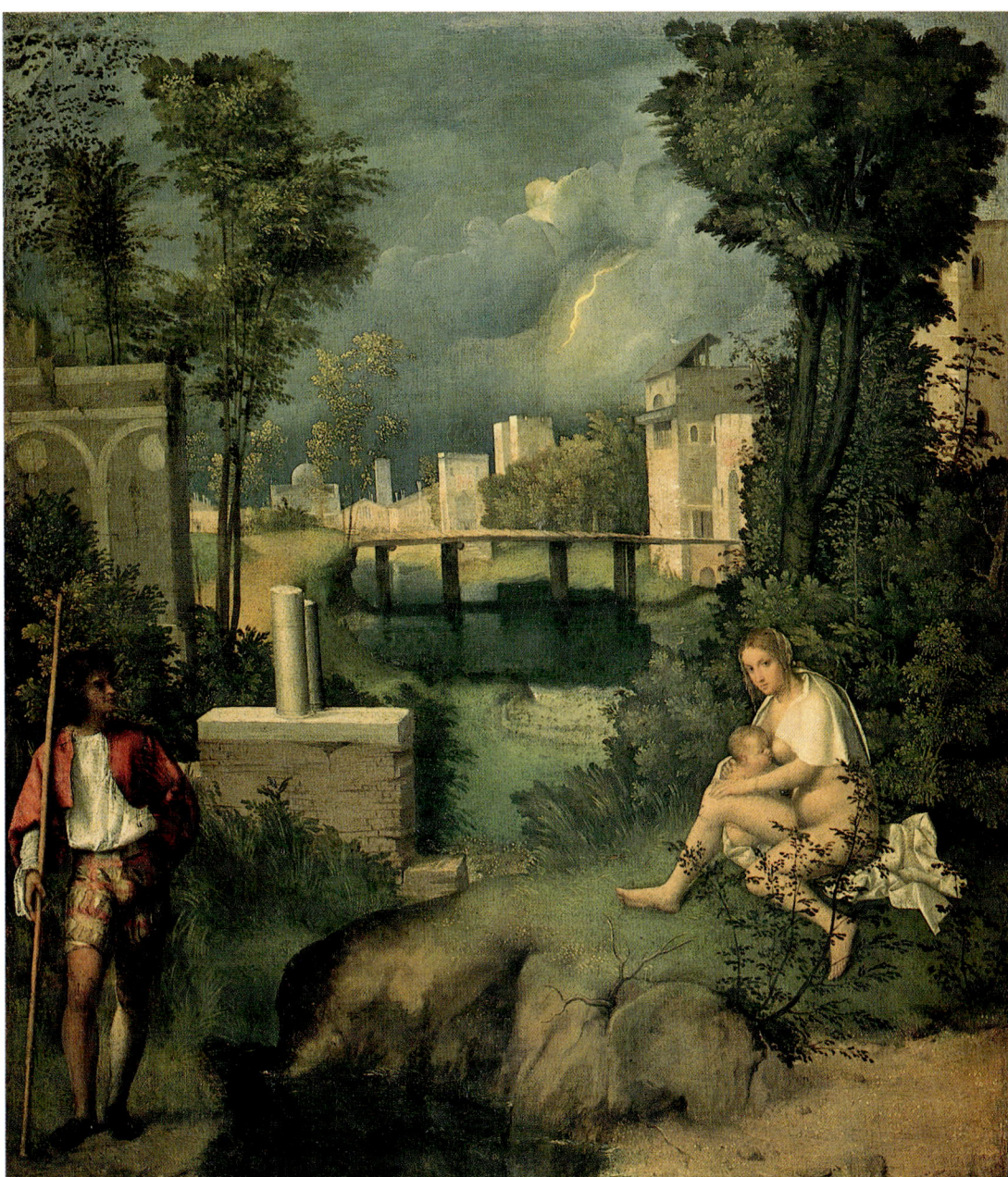

22-34 GIORGIONE DA CASTELFRANCO, *The Tempest,* ca. 1510. Oil on canvas, 2′ 7″ × 2′ 4$\frac{3}{4}$″. Galleria dell'Accademia, Venice.

POETRY IN MOTION   A Venetian artist who deserves much of the credit for developing this poetic manner of painting was GIORGIONE DA CASTELFRANCO (ca. 1477–1510). Giorgione's so-called *Pastoral Symphony* (FIG. **22-33**; some believe it an early work by his student Titian, discussed next) exemplifies poesia and surely inspired the late Arcadian scenes by Bellini, his teacher. Out of dense shadow emerge the soft forms of figures and landscape. The theme is as enigmatic as the light. Two nude females, accompanied by two clothed young men, occupy the rich, abundant landscape through which a shepherd passes. In the distance, a villa crowns a hill. The artist so eloquently evoked the pastoral mood that viewers do not find the uncertainty about the picture's precise meaning distressing; the mood is enough. The shepherd symbolizes the poet; the pipes and the lute symbolize his poetry. The two women accompanying the young men may be thought of as their invisible inspiration, their muses. One turns to lift water from the sacred well of poetic inspiration. The voluptuous bodies of the women, softly modulated by

the smoky shadow, became the standard in Venetian art. The fullness of their figures contributes to their effect as poetic personifications of nature's abundance.

As a pastoral poet in the pictorial medium and one of the greatest masters in the handling of light and color, Giorgione praised the beauty of nature, music, women, and pleasure. Vasari reported that Giorgione was an accomplished lutist and singer, and adjectives from poetry and music seem best suited for describing his painting's pastoral air and muted chords. He cast a mood of tranquil reverie and dreaminess over the entire scene, evoking the landscape of a lost but never forgotten paradise. Lingering memories of Arcadia and its happy occupants have an enduring appeal. Among the Italians, the Venetians were foremost in expressing a love of nature and in realizing its potential for painters, although they never represented it uninhabited.

STORMY WEATHER   Another Giorgione painting, *The Tempest* (FIG. **22-34**), manifests this same interest in the

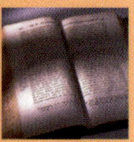

WRITTEN SOURCES

Negotiating a Contract
Titian and the Battle of Cadore

The predominance of the patronage system (see "Art to Order: Commissions and Patronage," Chapter 19, page 539) during the Renaissance compelled artists to work diligently at cultivating patrons. The following letter, from Titian to the doge of Venice, was the culmination of a protracted negotiation between the artist and the Council of the Ten (an administrative council) in 1515 (or early 1516). Due to this letter, those involved settled on a final agreement, and Titian completed the painting, *Battle of Cadore,* in 1538. A fire in the Great Council Hall subsequently destroyed the painting.

> Having understood, Your Highness, that you have decided to let those canvases in the Great Council Hall be painted, and since I, Titian, servant of Your Highness, should like to display such a canvas painted in this fashion from my hand, and have actually started on one two years ago, and it is not the most difficult and laborious to do for this Hall, I bind myself by my own will to finish it as it ought to be, at my own expense; nor do I want any other payment before the completion of the work, except only for ten ducats' worth of paints, and three ounces of that blue which is kept in the Salt Office; and I want one of the two young men that will help me to be paid for me as an advance on my account, which only amounts to 4 ducats a month, while I bind myself to pay another out of my pocket, and to take charge of any other expenditure that will be required by the painting; Your Highness would make the Salt Office promise me that when the work was completed, they would pay me half of that which was once promised to Perugino, who was supposed to paint this canvas, which would come to 400 ducats, since he would not do it for 800, and that in time I should get the office of broker of the Association of German Merchants, as was decided in the Most Illustrious Council of November 28, 1514.[1]

[1] Titian to the doge of Venice, ca. December 1515–January 1516, *Italian Art 1500–1600: Sources and Documents,* by Robert Klein and Henri Zerner (Evanston, Ill.: Northwestern University Press, 1966), 47.

poetic qualities of natural landscape humans inhabit. Dominating the scene is a lush landscape, threatened by stormy skies and lightning in the middle background. Pushed off to both sides are the human figures—a young woman nursing a baby in the right foreground and a man carrying a halberd (a combination spear and battle-ax) on the left. Much scholarly debate has centered on this painting's subject, fueled by the fact that X rays of the canvas revealed a nude female originally stood where Giorgione subsequently placed the man. This flexibility in subject has led many to believe no definitive narrative exists, appropriate for a Venetian poetic rendering. Other scholars have suggested mythological narratives or historical events. Despite this uncertainty, the painting's enigmatic quality lends it an intriguing air.

A SUPREME MASTER OF COLOR Giorgione's Arcadianism passed not only to his much older yet constantly inquisitive master, Bellini, but also to TIZIANO VECELLI, whose name has been anglicized into TITIAN (ca. 1490–1576). Titian was the most extraordinary and prolific of the great Venetian painters, a supreme colorist who cultivated numerous patrons (see "Negotiating a Contract: Titian and the Battle of Cadore," above). An important change occurring in Titian's time was the almost universal adoption of canvas, with its rough-textured surface, in place of wood panels for paintings. Titian's works established oil color on canvas as the typical medium of pictorial tradition thereafter. According to a contemporary of Titian, Palma il Giovane:

> Titian [employed] a great mass of colors, which served . . . as a base for the compositions. . . . I too have seen some of these, formed with bold strokes made with brushes laden with colors, sometimes of a pure red earth, which he used, so to speak, for a middle tone, and at other times of white lead; and with the same brush tinted with red, black and yellow he formed a highlight; and observing these principles he made the promise of an exceptional figure appear in four brushstrokes. . . . Having constructed these precious foundations he used to turn his pictures to the wall and leave them there without looking at them, sometimes for several months. When he wanted to apply his brush again he would examine them with the utmost rigor . . . to see if he could find any faults. . . . In this way, working on the figures and revising them, he brought them to the most perfect symmetry that the beauty of art and nature can reveal. . . . [T]hus he gradually covered those quintessential forms with living flesh, bringing them by many stages to a state in which they lacked only the breath of life. He never painted a figure all at once and . . . in the last stages he painted more with his fingers than his brushes.[12]

A GLORIOUS IMAGE OF THE VIRGIN Titian's remarkable coloristic sense and his ability to convey light through color emerges in a major altarpiece, *Assumption of the Virgin* (FIG. **22-35**), painted for the main altar of Santa Maria Gloriosa dei Frari in Venice. Commissioned by the prior of this Franciscan basilica, the monumental altarpiece (close to twenty-three feet high) appropriately depicts the glorious ascent of the Virgin's body to Heaven. Visually, the painting is a stunning tour de force. Golden clouds so luminous they seem to glow, radiating light into the church interior, envelop the

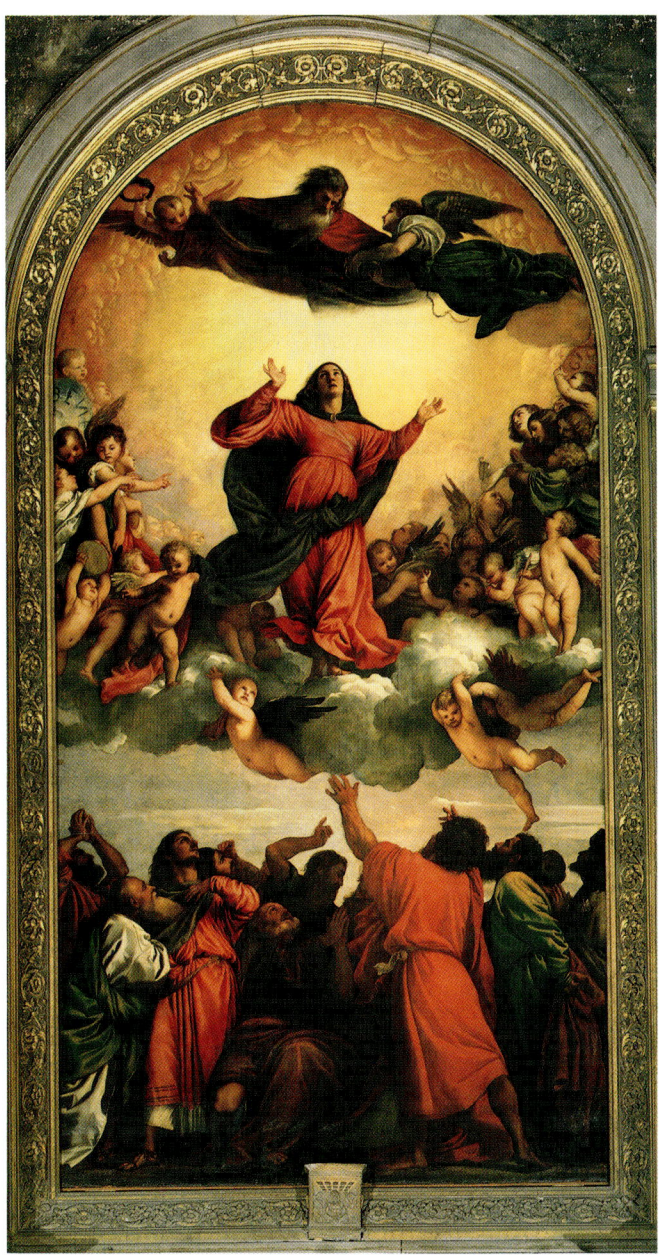

22-35 TITIAN, *Assumption of the Virgin,* Santa Maria Gloriosa dei Frari, Venice, Italy, ca. 1516–1518. Oil on wood, 22′ 6″ × 11′ 10″.

Virgin. God the Father appears above, awaiting her with open arms. Below, apostles gesticulate wildly as they witness this momentous event. Titian painted this large-scale altarpiece with exceptional clarity. Through vibrant color, he infused the image with a drama and intensity that assured his lofty reputation, then and now.

A DAZZLING DISPLAY OF COLOR Trained by both Bellini and Giorgione, Titian learned so well from them that even today scholars cannot agree about the degree of his participation in their later works. However, it is clear Titian completed several of Bellini's and Giorgione's unfinished paintings. On Giovanni Bellini's death in 1516, the republic of Venice appointed Titian as its official painter. Shortly

thereafter, Bishop Jacopo Pesaro commissioned Titian to paint *Madonna of the Pesaro Family* (FIG. **22-36**), which the patron presented to the church of the Frari. This work furthered Titian's reputation and established his personal style. Pesaro, bishop of Paphos in Cyprus and commander of the papal fleet, had led a successful expedition in 1502 against the Turks during the Venetian-Turkish war and commissioned this painting in gratitude. In a stately sunlit setting, the Madonna receives the commander, who kneels dutifully at the foot of her throne. A soldier (Saint George?) behind the commander carries a banner with the escutcheons (shields with coats of arms) of the Borgia (Pope Alexander VI) and of Pesaro. Behind him is a turbaned Turk, a prisoner of war of the Christian forces. Saint Peter appears on the steps of the throne, and Saint Francis introduces other Pesaro family members (all male — Italian depictions of donors in this era typically excluded women and children), who kneel solemnly in the right foreground.

The massing of monumental figures, singly and in groups, within a weighty and majestic architecture characterized, as already seen, the High Renaissance. But Titian did not compose a horizontal and symmetrical arrangement, as Leonardo did in *Last Supper* (FIG. 22-3) and Raphael in *School of Athens* (FIG. 22-17). Rather, he placed the figures on a steep diagonal, positioning the Madonna, the composition's focus, well off the central axis. Titian drew viewers' attention to her with the perspective lines, the inclination of the figures, and the directional lines of gaze and gesture. The banner inclining toward the left beautifully brings the design into equilibrium, balancing the rightward and upward tendencies of its main direction.

This kind of composition is more dynamic than those in the High Renaissance shown thus far and presaged a new kind of pictorial design — built on movement rather than rest. In his rendering of the rich surface textures, Titian gave a dazzling display of color in all its nuances. He entwined the human — especially the Venetian — scene with the heavenly, depicting the Madonna and saints honoring the achievements of a specific man in this particular world. A quite worldly transaction takes place (albeit beneath a heavenly cloud bearing angels) between a queen and her court and loyal servants. Titian constructed this tableau in terms of Renaissance protocol and courtly splendor.

BACCHANALIAN REVELRY In 1511, Alfonso d'Este, duke of Ferrara, asked Titian to produce a painting for his Camerino d'Alabastro (small room of alabaster). The patron had requested one bacchanalian scene each from Titian, Bellini, Raphael, and Fra Bartolommeo. Both Raphael and Fra Bartolommeo died before fulfilling the commission, and Bellini only painted one scene (FIG. 22-32), leaving Titian to produce three. One of these three paintings is *Meeting of Bacchus and Ariadne* (FIG. **22-37**). Bacchus, accompanied by a boisterous and noisy group, arrives to save Ariadne, whom Theseus has abandoned on the island of Naxos. In this scene, Titian revealed his debt to classical art; he derived one of the figures, entwined with snakes, in Bacchus's band of revelers from the ancient sculpture Laocoön (see FIG. 5-89). Titian's rich and luminous colors add greatly to the sensuous appeal of this painting, making it perfect for Alfonso's "pleasure chamber."

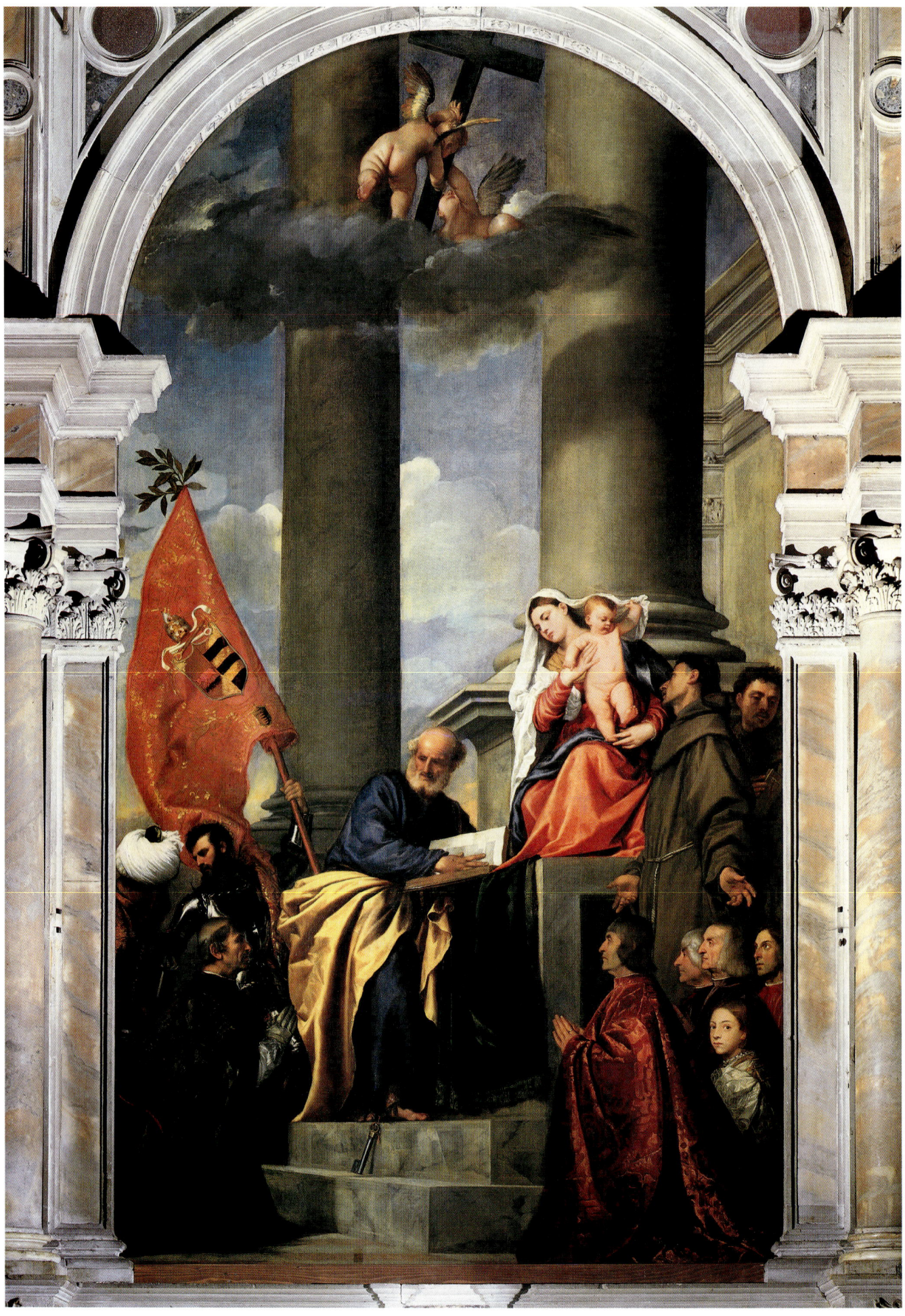

22-36 TITIAN, *Madonna of the Pesaro Family,* Santa Maria dei Frari, Venice, Italy, 1519–1526. Oil on canvas, approx. 16′ × 9′.

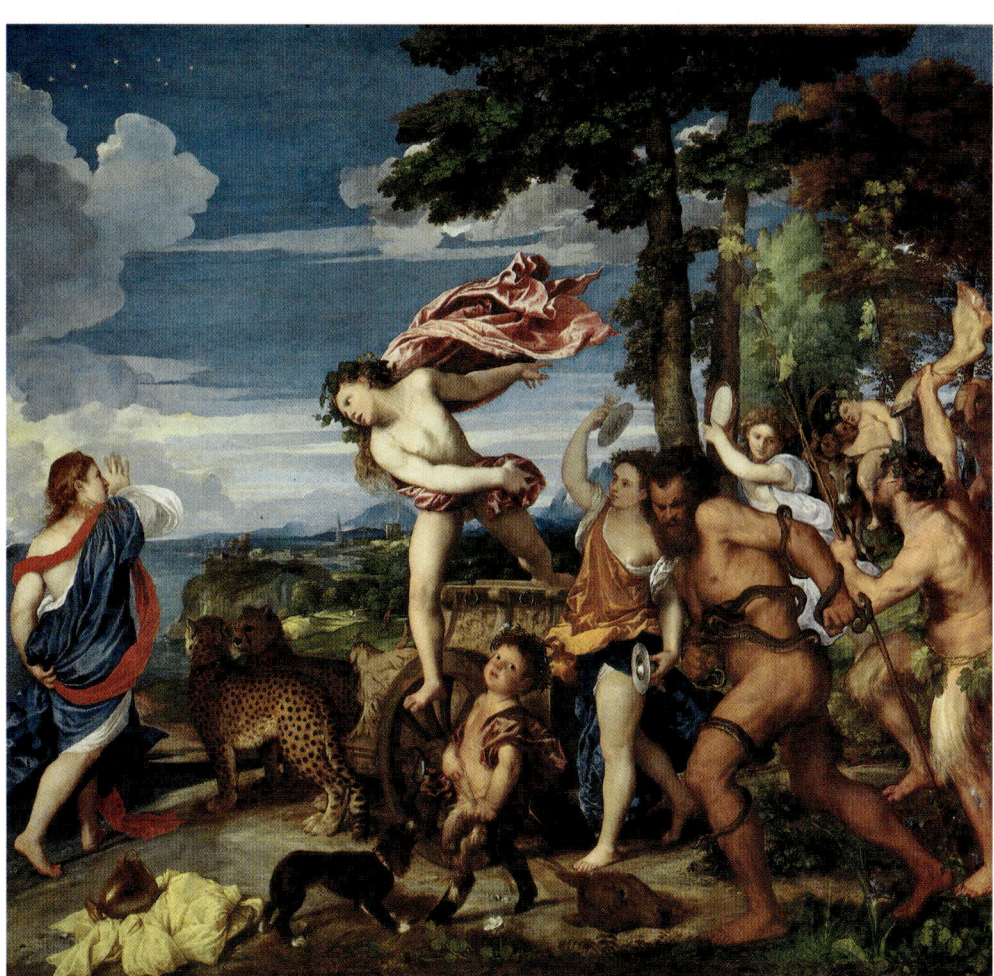

22-37 TITIAN, *Meeting of Bacchus and Ariadne,* 1522–1523. Oil on canvas, 5′ 9″ × 6′ 3″. National Gallery, London.

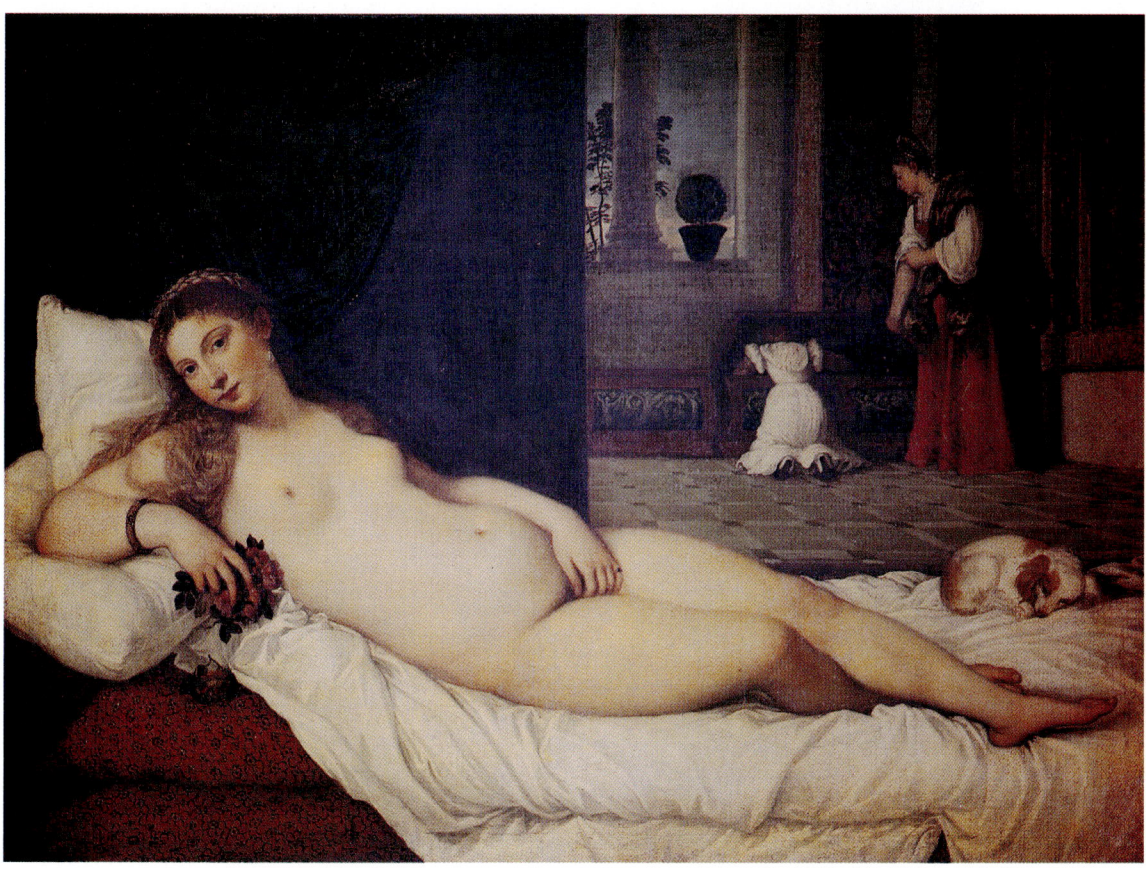

22-38 TITIAN, *Venus of Urbino,* 1538. Oil on canvas, approx. 4′ × 5′ 6″. Galleria degli Uffizi, Florence.

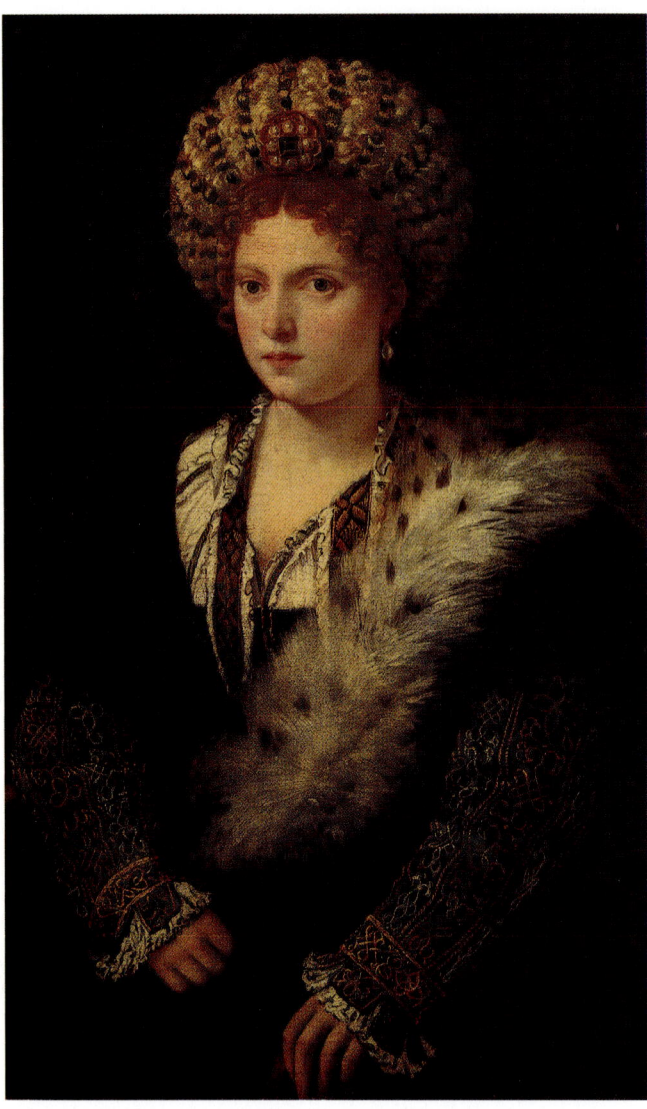

22-39   TITIAN, *Isabella d'Este*, 1534–1536. Oil on canvas, 3′ 4$\frac{1}{8}$″ × 2′ 1$\frac{3}{16}$″. Kunsthistorisches Museum, Vienna.

A VENETIAN VENUS In 1538, at the height of his powers, Titian painted the so-called *Venus of Urbino* (FIG. **22-38**) for Guidobaldo II, duke of Urbino. The title (given to the painting later) elevates what probably merely represents a courtesan in her bedchamber to the status of classical mythology, Indeed, no evidence suggests the duke intended the commission as anything more than a female nude for his private enjoyment. Whether the subject is divine or mortal, Titian based his version on an earlier (and pioneering) painting of Venus (not illustrated) by Giorgione. Here, Titian established the compositional elements and the standard for reclining female nude paintings, regardless of the many variations that ensued. This "Venus" reclines on the gentle slope of her luxurious pillowed couch, the linear play of the draperies contrasting with her body's sleek continuous volume. At her feet is a *pendant* (balancing) figure—in this case, a slumbering lap dog. Behind her, a simple drape both places her figure emphatically in the foreground and indicates a vista into the background at the right half of the picture. Two servants bend over a chest, apparently searching for garments (Renaissance households stored clothing in carved wooden chests called *cassoni*) to clothe

"Venus." Beyond them, a smaller vista opens into a landscape. Titian masterfully constructed the view backward into space and the division of the space into progressively smaller units. With his facility, he used all of the resources of pictorial representation to create original and exquisite effects of the sort that inspired generations of painters in Italy and the north.

As in other Venetian paintings, color plays a prominent role in *Venus of Urbino*. The red tones of the matron's skirt and the muted reds of the tapestries against the neutral whites of the matron's sleeves and of the kneeling girl's gown echo the deep Venetian reds set off against the pale neutral whites of the linen and the warm ivory gold of the flesh. Viewers must study the picture carefully to realize the subtlety of color planning. For instance, the two deep reds (in the foreground cushions and in the background skirt) function so importantly in the composition as a gauge of distance and as indicators of an implied diagonal opposed to the real one of the reclining figure. Here, Titian used color not simply for tinting preexisting forms but also to organize his placement of forms.

PRESENTING A POWERFUL PATRONESS Titian was also a highly esteemed portraitist and in great demand. Of his well more than fifty portraits surviving, one example, *Isabella d'Este* (FIG. **22-39**), suffices to illustrate his style (see "The Feminine Mystique: Women Patrons during the Renaissance," page 673). Isabella d'Este (1474–1539) was among the most powerful of women during the Renaissance. Daughter of the duke of Ferrara, she married Francesco Gonzaga, marquis of Mantua, and was instrumental in developing the Mantuan court into an important center of art and learning. Titian's portraits, as well as those of many of the Venetian and subsequent schools, generally make much of the artist's psychological reading of the body's most expressive parts—the head and the hands. Thus, Titian sharply highlighted Isabella's face, while her black dress fades into the background's undefined darkness. The unseen light source also illuminates Isabella's hands, and the artist painted her sleeves with incredible detail to further draw viewers' attention to her hands. This portrait reveals not only Titian's skill but the patron's wish as well. Painted when Isabella was sixty years of age, it depicts her in her twenties at her request. Titian used an earlier portrait of her as his guide, and Isabella appears not just young but also perfectly poised and self-assured.

Other Sixteenth-Century Italian Artists

ANTICIPATING BAROQUE DEVICES IN PARMA The towering achievements of Raphael and Michelangelo in Rome tend to obscure everything else created during their time. Nevertheless, aside from the flourishing Venetian school, excellent artists were active in other parts of Italy during the first part of the sixteenth century. ANTONIO ALLEGRI DA CORREGGIO (ca. 1489–1534) of Parma is almost impossible to classify. A solitary genius, Correggio pulled together many stylistic trends, including those of Leonardo, Raphael, and the Venetians. Yet he developed a unique personal style, which, if it must be labeled, might best be called "proto-Baroque." Historically, his most enduring contribution was his development of illusionistic ceiling perspectives to a point his Baroque emulators seldom surpassed. At Mantua, Man-

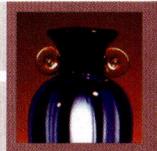

The Feminine Mystique
Women Patrons during the Renaissance

The dearth of acknowledged women artists in the Renaissance reflects the obstacles they faced. In particular, for centuries, training practices mandating residence at a master's house (see "Mastering a Craft: Artistic Training in the Renaissance," Chapter 19, page 554) precluded women from acquiring the necessary experience. In addition, social proscriptions, such as those preventing women from drawing from nude models, further hampered an aspiring female artist's advancement through the accepted avenues of artistic training.

However, despite the obstacles Renaissance women encountered as artists, they did have a significant impact on the arts in the realm of patronage. Scholars only recently have begun to explore systematically the role of women as patrons. As a result, current knowledge is sketchy at best but suggests women played a much more extensive role than previously acknowledged. Among the problems researchers face in their quest to clarify women's participation as patrons is that women often wielded their influence and decision-making power behind the scenes. Many of these women acquired their positions through marriage; their power was thus indirect and provisional, based on their husbands' wealth and status. Thus, documentation of the networks women patrons operated within and of the processes they used to exert power in a male-dominated society is less substantive than that available for male patrons.

One of the most important Renaissance patrons, male or female, was Isabella d'Este (1474–1539), marchioness of Mantua (FIG. 22-39). Brought up in the cultured princely court of Ferrara (southwest of Venice), Isabella married Francesco Gonzaga (1484–1519), marquis of Mantua, at age seventeen in 1490. Isabella's marriage gave her access to the position and wealth necessary to pursue her interest in becoming a major art patron. An avid collector, she enlisted the aid of agents who scoured Italy for appealing objects. Isabella did not limit her collection to painting and sculpture but included ceramics, glassware, gems, cameos, medals, classical texts, musical manuscripts, and musical instruments.

Isabella was undoubtedly a proud and ambitious woman well aware of how art could boost her fame and reputation. Accordingly, she commissioned several portraits of herself from the most esteemed artists of her day—Leonardo da Vinci, Andrea Mantegna, and Titian. The detail and complexity of many of her contracts with artists reveal her insistence on control over the artworks.

Another Renaissance woman who was a significant art patron was Caterina Sforza (1462–15??), daughter of Galeazzo Maria Sforza (heir to the Duchy of Milan) who married Girolamo Riario in 1484. The death of her husband, lord of Imola and count of Forlì, in 1488 gave Sforza access to power denied most women.

Lucrezia Tornabuoni (married to Piero di Cosimo de' Medici) was one of many Medici, both men and women, who earned reputations as unparalleled art patrons. Further archival investigation of women's roles in Renaissance Italy undoubtedly will produce more evidence of how women established themselves as patrons and artists and the extent they contributed to the flourishing of Renaissance art.

---

tegna created the illusion of a hole in the ceiling of the Camera degli Sposi (see FIG. 21-48). Some fifty years later, Correggio painted away the entire dome of the Parma Cathedral in *Assumption of the Virgin* (FIG. 22-40). Opening up the cupola, the artist showed his audience a view of the sky, with concentric rings of clouds where hundreds of soaring figures perform a wildly pirouetting dance in celebration of the Virgin's Assumption. Versions of these angelic creatures became permanent tenants of numerous Baroque churches in later centuries. Correggio was also an influential painter of religious panels, anticipating in them many other Baroque compositional devices. Correggio's contemporaries expressed little appreciation for his art. Later, during the seventeenth century, Baroque painters recognized him as a kindred spirit.

MANNERISM

Mannerism is a stylistic label that encompasses certain tendencies in later Renaissance art. The term derives from the Italian word *maniera* (manner) and initially referred to art produced "in the manner of" another artist (often Michelangelo). Over the years, scholars have refined their ideas about Mannerism, attempting to define this style's parameters. Chronologically, it is difficult to identify specific dates for Mannerism—it overlapped considerably with High Renaissance art, emerging in the 1520s.

Among the features most closely associated with Mannerism is *artifice*—an emphasis on staged, contrived imagery. Mannerist art evinces elegance and beauty, but not those derived directly from nature. Rather than relying on direct observation for their sources, Mannerists tended to look to earlier art, especially High Renaissance and Roman sculpture, as their models. Further, Mannerists displayed a preference for imbalanced compositions and unusual complexities, both visual and conceptual. Ambiguous space, departures from expected conventions, and unique presentations of traditional themes also surfaced frequently in Mannerist art and architecture. Where High Renaissance artists strove for balance, Mannerists sought instability. Mannerists replaced the calm equilibrium of the High Renaissance with a restlessness that led to distortions, exaggerations, and affected posturings on the one hand, and sinuous grace on the other hand. These artists, to the limits of their ingenuity and skill, abstracted forms they idealized further, so the typical Mannerist picture or statue

22-40 ANTONIO ALLEGRI DA CORREGGIO, *Assumption of the Virgin,* dome fresco of Parma Cathedral, Parma, Italy, 1526–1530.

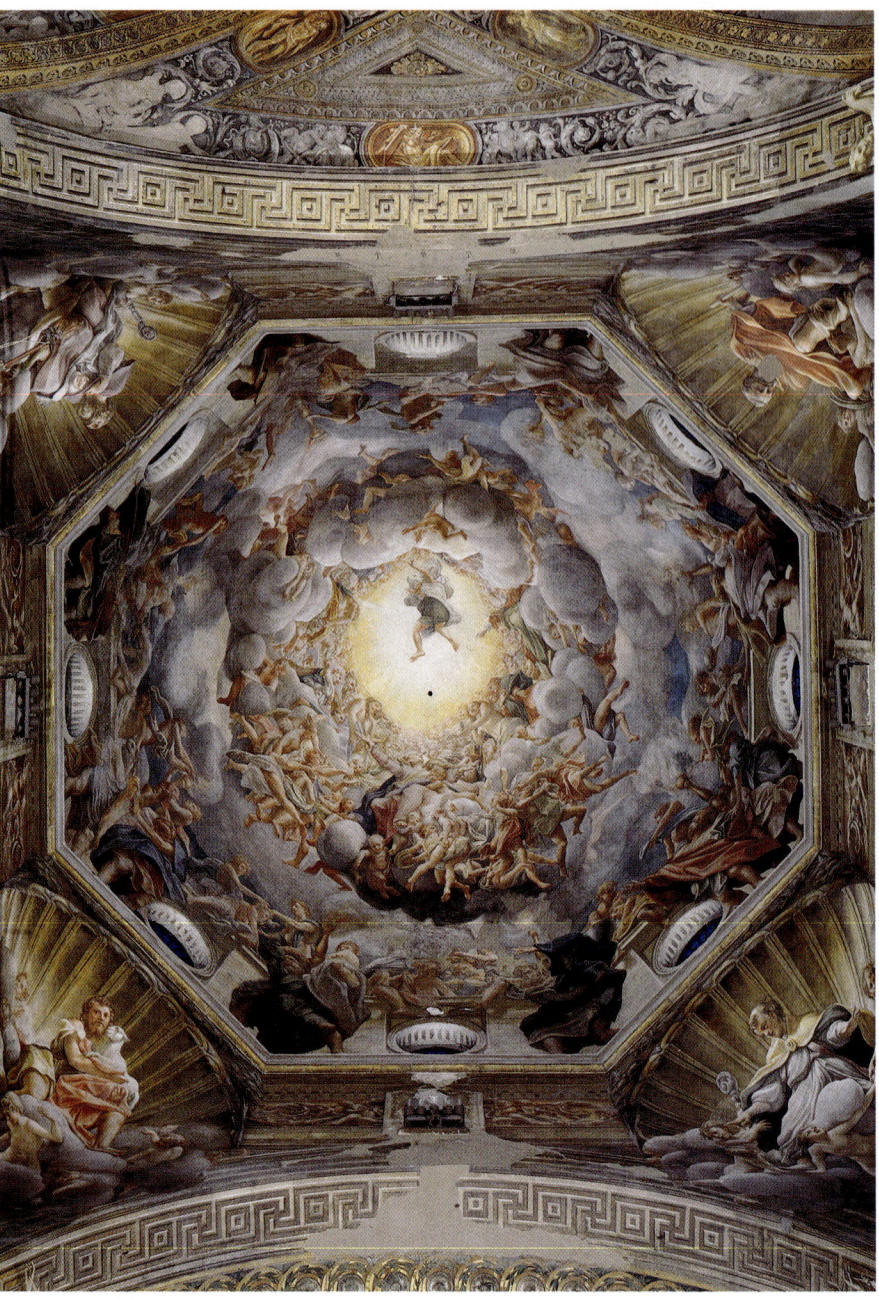

looks like an original essay in human form somewhat removed from nature. Mannerism is almost exclusively an art of the human figure. Mannerism's requirement of "invention" led its practitioners to a self-conscious stylization involving complexity, caprice, fantasy (the "conceit"), elegance, perfectionism, and polish.

Mannerist Painting

DEPARTING FROM RENAISSANCE IDEALS *Descent from the Cross* (FIG. **22-41**) by JACOPO DA PONTORMO (1494–1557) exhibits almost all of the stylistic features characteristic of Mannerism's early phase in painting. The figures crowd the composition, pushing into the front plane and almost completely blotting out the setting. Pontormo disposed the figural masses around the frame of the picture, leaving a void in the center, where High Renaissance artists had concentrated their masses. The composition has no clearly defined focal point, and the figures seem randomly placed around the painting's edges. The ambiguous representation of space typifies the Mannerist style. The space seems too shallow to contain the action within it. For example, Pontormo did not provide any space for the body belonging to the head, seen in a three-quarter rear view, that appears immediately above Christ's head.

The artist enhanced the painting's ambiguity with the curiously anxious glances the figures cast in all directions. Athletic bending and twisting characterize many of the figures, with distortions (a torso cannot bend at the point the foreground figure's does), elastic elongation of the limbs, and heads rendered as uniformly small and oval. Clashing colors add to the seeming dissonance of the image. The painting represented a departure from the balanced, harmonious structured compositions of the earlier Renaissance.

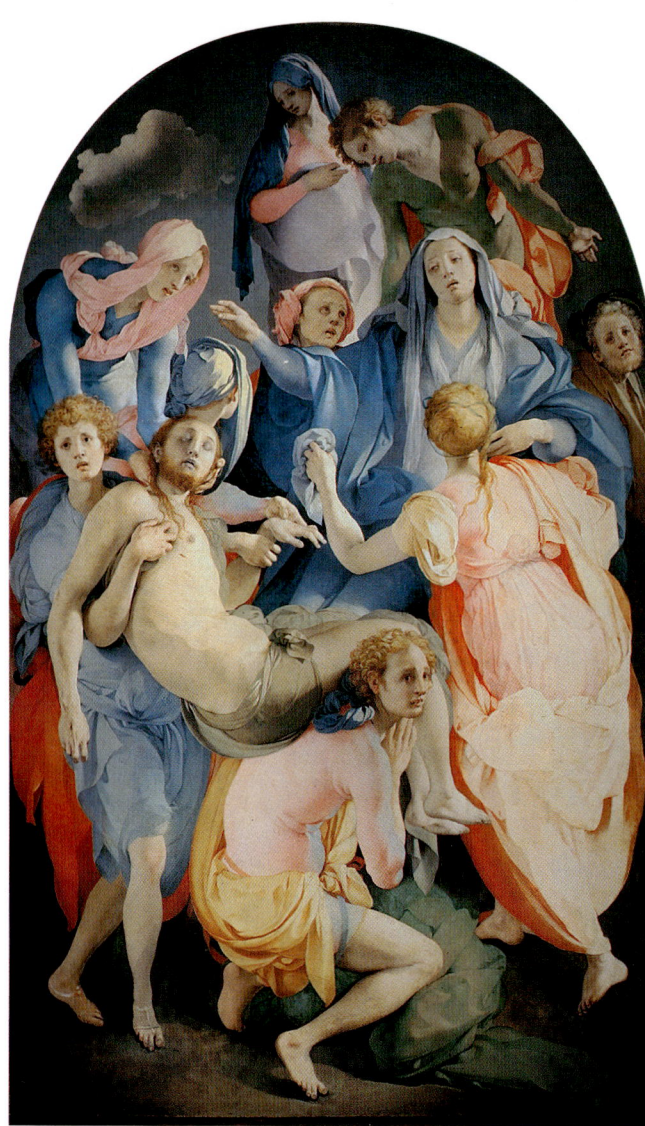

22-41 JACOPO DA PONTORMO, *Descent from the Cross,* Capponi Chapel, Santa Felicità, Florence, Italy, 1525–1528. Oil on wood, approx. 10′ 3″ × 6′ 6″.

MANNERISM'S ELEGANCE AND GRACE Correggio's pupil, GIROLAMO FRANCESCO MARIA MAZZOLA, known as PARMIGIANINO (1503–1540), achieved in his best-known work, *Madonna with the Long Neck* (FIG. **22-42**), the elegance that was a principal aim of Mannerism. He smoothly combined the influences of Correggio and Raphael in a picture of exquisite grace and precious sweetness. The Madonna's small oval head; her long, slender neck; the unbelievable attenuation and delicacy of her hand; and the sinuous, swaying elongation of her frame are all marks of the aristocratic, gorgeously artificial taste of a later phase of Mannerism. Parmigianino amplified this artificiality by expanding the Madonna's form as viewed from head to toe. On the left stands a bevy of angelic creatures, melting with emotions as soft and smooth as their limbs (the composition's left side is quite in Correggio's manner). On the right, the artist included a line of columns without capitals—an enigmatic setting for an enigmatic figure with a scroll, whose distance from the foreground is immeasurable and ambiguous.

AN ALLEGORICAL LOVE SCENE   *Venus,   Cupid, Folly, and Time,* also called *The Exposure of Luxury* (FIG. **22-43**), by AGNOLO DI COSIMO, called BRONZINO (1503–1572), also manifests all the points made thus far about Manneristic composition. A pupil of Pontormo, Bronzino was a Florentine and painter to Cosimo I, first grand duke of Tuscany. In this painting, he demonstrated the Mannerist's fondness for extremely learned and intricate allegories that often had lascivious undertones, a shift from the simple and monumental statements and forms of the High Renaissance. Bronzino depicted Cupid fondling his mother Venus, while Folly prepares to shower them with rose petals. Time, who appears in the upper right-hand corner, draws back the curtain to reveal the playful incest in progress. Other figures in the painting represent Envy and Inconstancy. The masks, a favorite device of the Mannerists, symbolize deceit. The picture seems to suggest that love—accompanied by envy and plagued by inconstancy—is foolish and that lovers will discover its folly in time. But, as in many Mannerist paintings, the meaning here is ambiguous, and interpretations of this image vary. Compositionally, Bronzino placed the figures around the front plane,

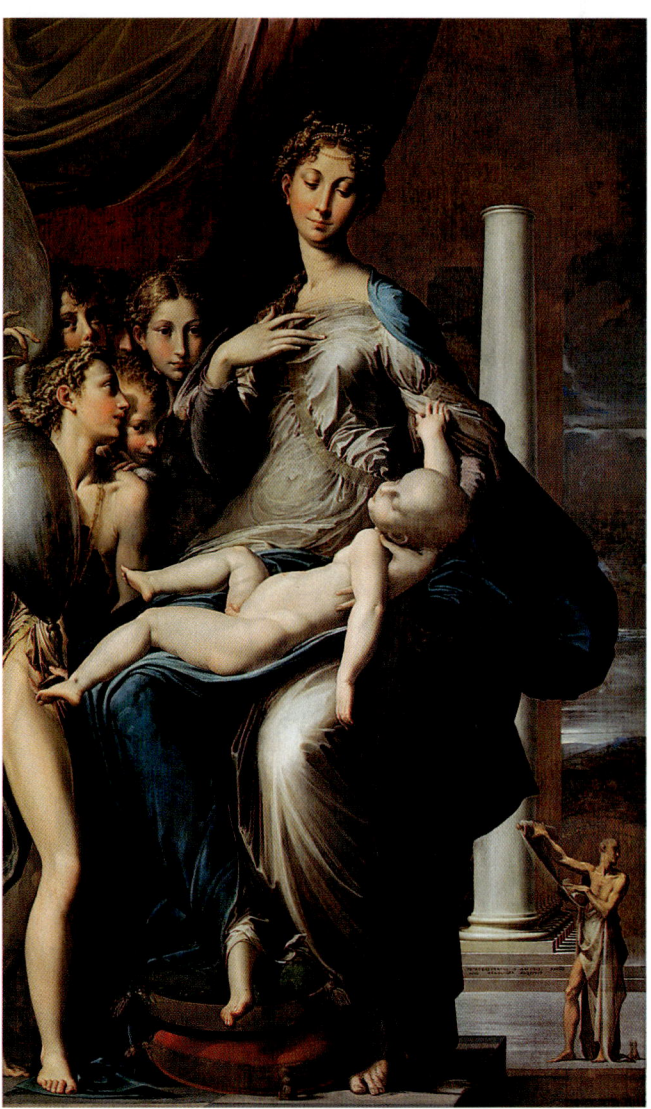

22-42 PARMIGIANINO, *Madonna with the Long Neck,* ca. 1535. Oil on wood, approx. 7′ 1″ × 4′ 4″. Galleria degli Uffizi, Florence.

22-43 Bronzino, *Venus, Cupid, Folly, and Time (The Exposure of Luxury)*, ca. 1546. Oil on wood, approx. 5′ 1″ × 4′ 8¾″. National Gallery, London.

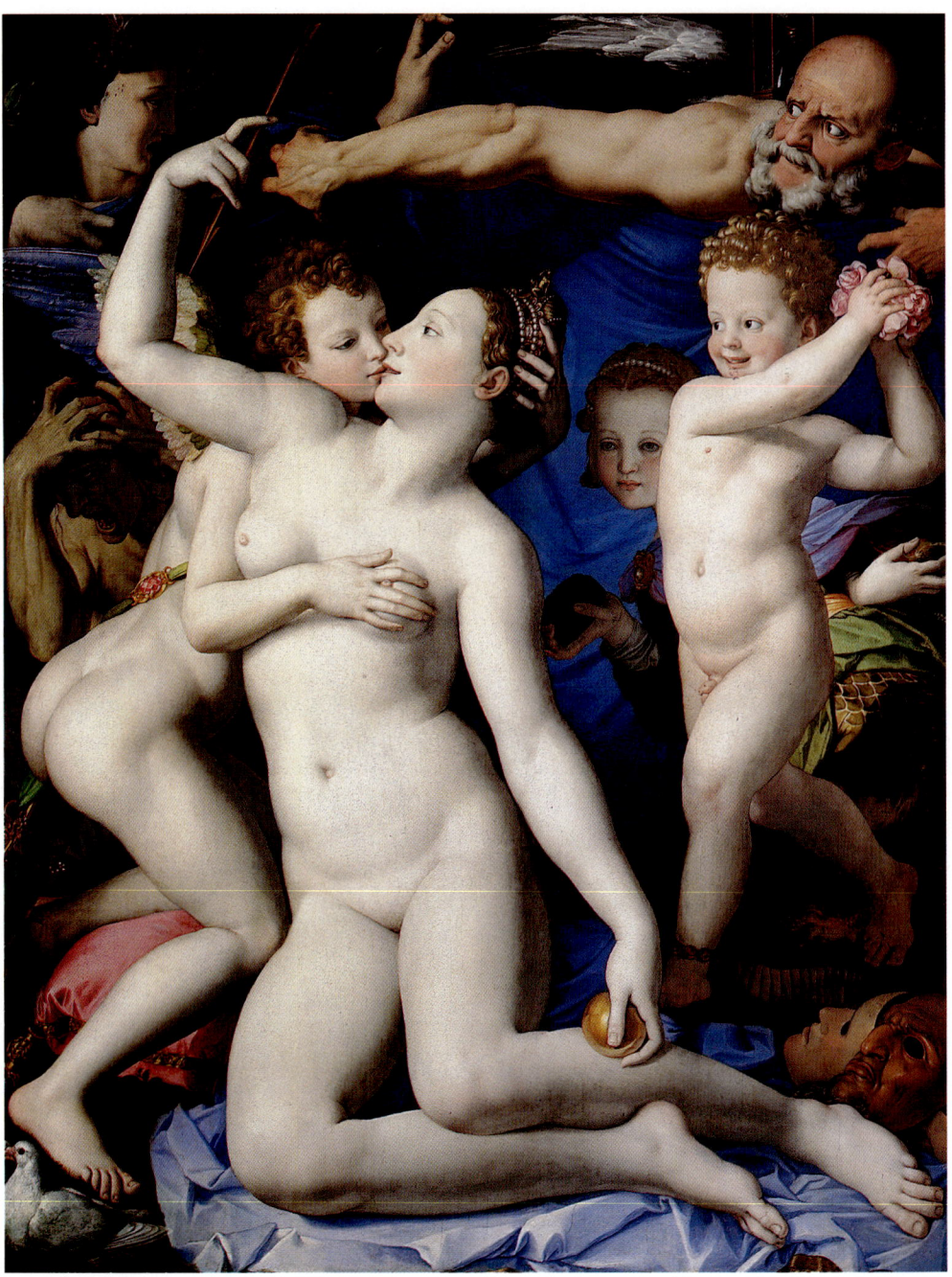

and they almost entirely block the space. The contours are strong and sculptural, the surfaces of enamel smoothness. Of special interest are the heads, hands, and feet, for the Mannerists considered the extremities the carriers of grace and the clever depiction of them evidence of artistic skill.

A MANNERED PORTRAIT Mannerist painters most often achieved the sophisticated elegance they sought in portraiture. Bronzino's *Portrait of a Young Man* (FIG. **22-44**) exemplifies Mannerist portraiture. The subject is a proud youth—a man of books and intellectual society, rather than a lowly laborer or a merchant. His cool demeanor seems carefully affected, a calculated attitude of nonchalance toward the observing world. This staid and reserved formality is a standard component of the Mannerist's portraits. It asserts the rank and station but not the personality of the subject. In

this portrait, the haughty poise, the graceful long-fingered hands, the book, the furniture's carved faces, and the severe architecture all suggest the traits and environment of the high-bred, disdainful patrician. The somber Spanish black of the young man's doublet and cap (this is the century of Spanish etiquette) and the room's slightly acid olive green walls make for a deeply restrained color scheme. Bronzino created a muted background for the subject's sharply defined, asymmetrical Mannerist silhouette that contradicts his impassive pose.

PORTRAYING FAMILIAL INTIMACY The aloof formality of Bronzino's portrait is much relaxed in the portraiture of Sofonisba Anguissola (1527–1625). A northern Italian from Cremona, Anguissola used the strong contours, muted tonality, and smooth finish familiar in Mannerist portraits. But she introduced, in a group portrait of irresistible

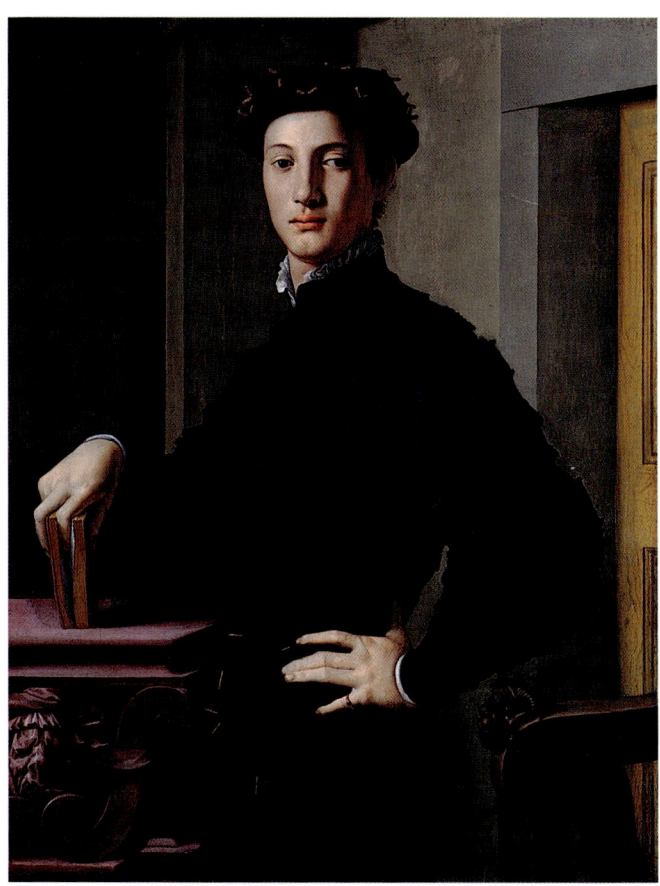

22-44 BRONZINO, *Portrait of a Young Man,* ca. 1530s. Oil on wood, approx. 3′ 1½″ × 2′ 5½″. Metropolitan Museum of Art, New York (H. O. Havemeyer Collection, bequest of Mrs. H. O. Havemeyer, 1929).

charm (FIG. **22-45**), an informal intimacy of her own. Like many of her other works done before she moved to Spain in 1559, this is a portrait of family members. Against a neutral ground, she placed her two sisters and brother in an affectionate pose meant not for official display but for private showing, much as they might be posed in a modern photo-studio portrait. The sisters, wearing matching striped gowns, flank their brother, who caresses a lap dog. The older sister (at the left) summons the dignity required for the occasion, while the boy looks quizzically at the portraitist with an expression of naive curiosity and the other girl diverts her attention toward something or someone to the painter's left.

Anguissola's use of natural poses and expressions; her sympathetic, personal presentation; and her graceful treatment of the forms did not escape the attention of her famous contemporaries. Vasari praised her art as wonderfully lifelike, declaring that Anguissola

> laboured at the difficulties of design with greater study and better grace than any other woman of our time, and she has not only succeeded in drawing, colouring, and copying from nature, and in making excellent copies of works by other hands but has also executed by herself alone some very choice and beautiful works of painting.[13]

Moreover, her "invention" inspired great praise. Although that word does not now have quite the meaning it had then, Anguissola did introduce the intimate, anecdotal, and realistic touches of *genre* painting (the painting of scenes from ordinary life) into formal portraiture. *Portrait of the Artist's Sisters and Brothers* could have been simply a good-natured portrayal of any happy middle-class family members; the figures do not

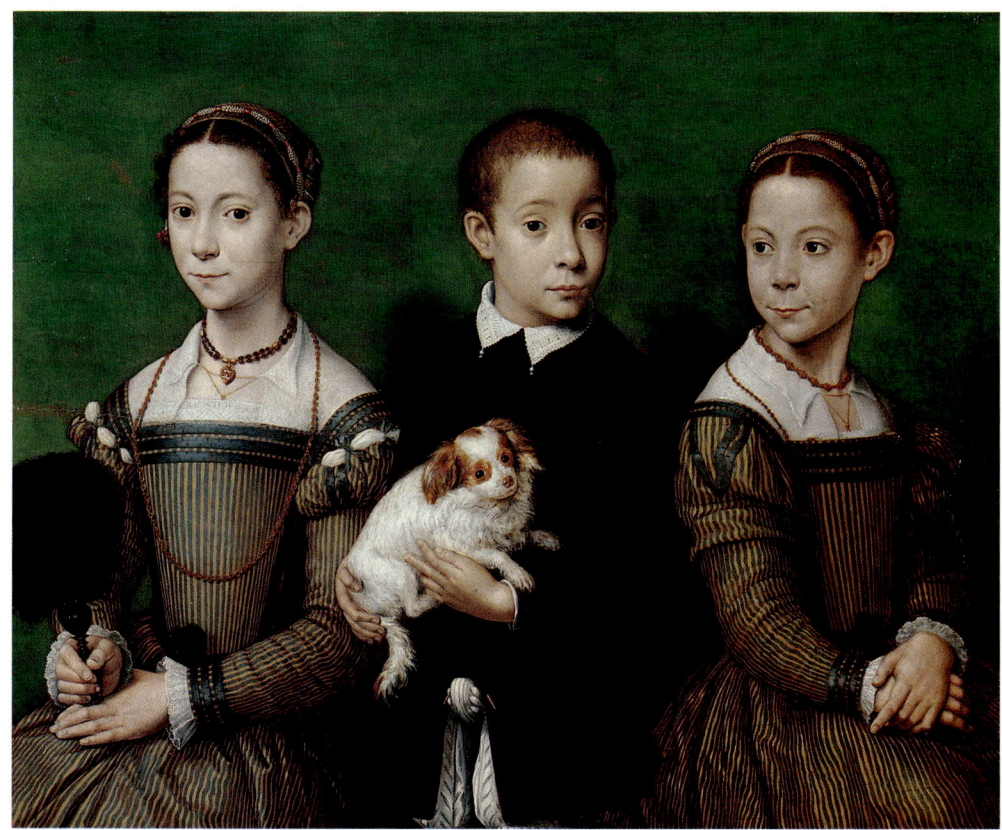

22-45 SOFONISBA ANGUISSOLA, *Portrait of the Artist's Sisters and Brother,* ca. 1555. Methuen Collection, Corsham Court, Wiltshire.

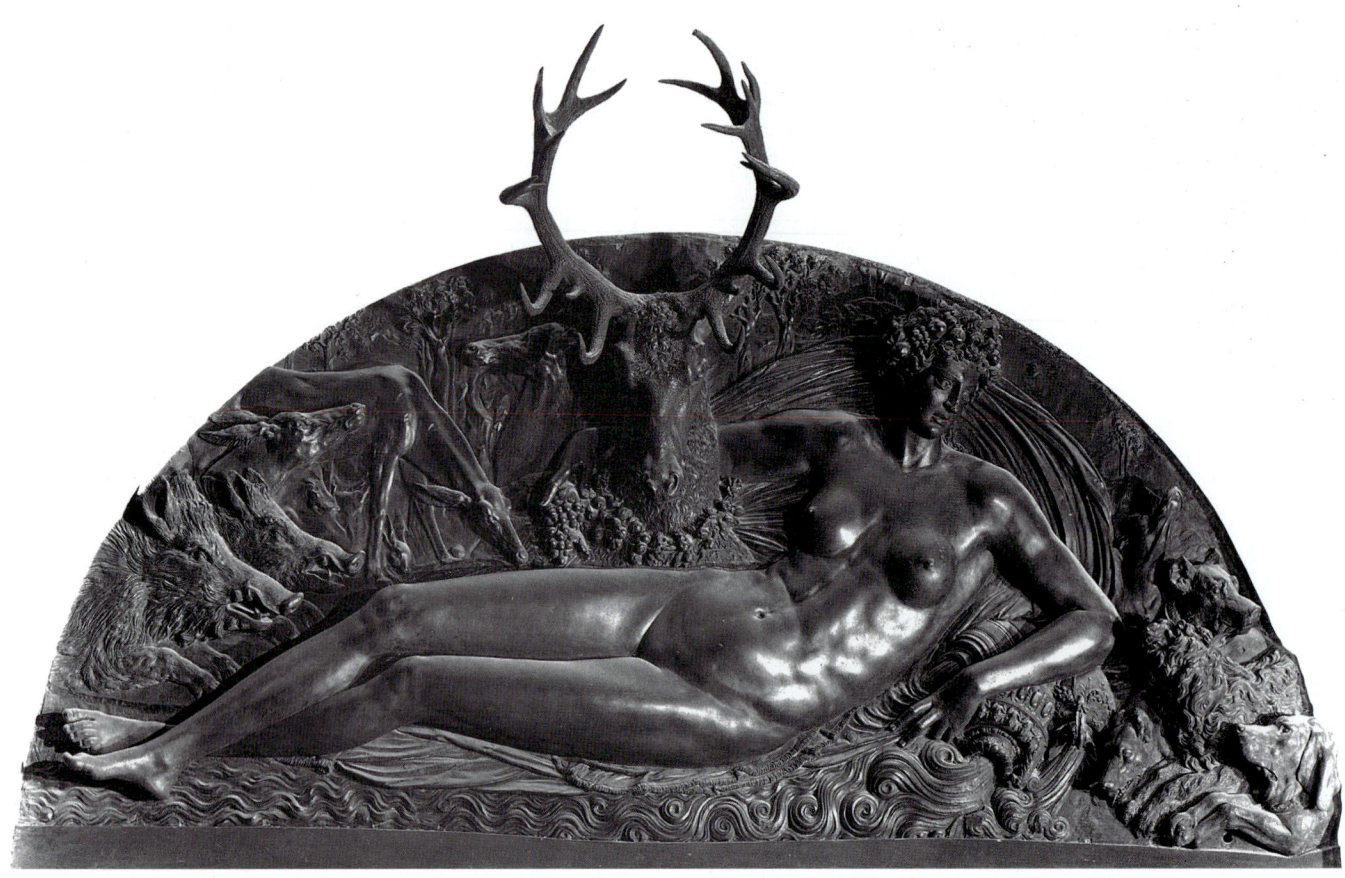

22-46   Benvenuto Cellini, *Genius of Fontainebleau,* 1543–1544. Bronze, more than life-size. Louvre, Paris.

flaunt names, titles, and elegance of dress to gain public respect. Anguissola lived a long life and enjoyed a successful career. She knew and learned from the aged Michelangelo, was court painter to Phillip II of Spain, and, at the end of her life, gave advice on art to a young admirer of her work, Anthony Van Dyck, the great Flemish master.

Mannerist Sculpture

A BRONZE GODDESS OF THE HUNT Mannerism extended beyond pictorial media; artists translated its principles into sculpture and architecture as well. BENVENUTO CELLINI (1500–1571) was among those who made their mark as Mannerist sculptors. To judge by his fascinating *Autobiography,* Cellini had an impressive proficiency as an artist, statesman, soldier, lover, and many other roles. He was, first of all, a goldsmith. Michelangelo's influence led Cellini to attempt larger works, and, in the service of Francis I, he cast in bronze *Genius of Fontainebleau* (FIG. **22-46**), which sums up Italian and French Mannerism. The female Genius, or spirit, is a composite of both Diana, the Greco-Roman goddess of the hunt, here embracing her animal the deer, and a classical personification of a spring leaning on an urn that spews forth water (compare FIG. 11-19). Her figure suggests the reclining figures in the Medici Chapel tombs (FIG. 22-22) and the female nudes, both Venuses and courtesans, that only recently had become popular subjects for Renaissance paintings (FIG. 22-38), but Cellini exaggerated their characteristics as the Mannerist's design sense dictated. The head is remarkably

small, the torso stretched out, and the limbs elongated. The contrapposto is more apparent than real, for the upper body does not compensate appropriately for the position shift of the lower body.

SPIRALING FIGURES Italian influence, working its way into France, drew a brilliant, young French sculptor, JEAN DE BOULOGNE, to Italy, where he practiced his art under the equivalent Italian name of GIOVANNI DA BOLOGNA (1529–1608). Giovanni's work provided the stylistic link between Michelangelo's sculptures and those of the Baroque master Gianlorenzo Bernini (see FIGS. 24-5 through 24-9). Giovanni's *Abduction of the Sabine Women* (FIG. **22-47**) wonderfully exemplifies Mannerism's principles of figure composition while revealing an impulse to break out of the Mannerist formulas of representation.

Drawn from early Rome's legendary history, the title—relating how the Romans abducted wives for themselves from their neighbors, the Sabines—was given to the group only after it was raised. Giovanni probably intended to present only an interesting figure composition involving an old man, a young man, and a woman, all nude in the tradition of ancient statues portraying mythological figures. This sculpture reveals the artist's knowledge of earlier art. Giovanni would have known Antonio Pollaiuolo's fifteenth-century work *Hercules and Antaeus* (see FIG. 21-25), whose Greek hero lifts his opponent off the ground. But here, unlike Giovanni's predecessor, he turned directly to classical sculpture for inspiration. *Abduction of the Sabine Women* includes references to the Laocoön

To fully appreciate the sculpture, visitors must walk around it, since the work changes radically according to the viewing point. One contributing factor to the shifting imagery is the prominence of open spaces that pass through the masses (for example, the space between an arm and a body), which have as great an effect as the solids. This sculpture was the first large-scale group since classical antiquity designed to be seen from multiple viewpoints, in striking contrast to Pollaiuolo's group, which the artist intended to be seen from the angle shown in our illustration. Giovanni's figures do not break out of this spiral vortex but remain as if contained within a cylinder. That they remain "enclosed" prevents historians from calling them Baroque. Yet the Michelangelesque potential for action and the athletic flexibility of the figures are there. Artists of the following Baroque period released their sculptured figures into full action.

Mannerist Architecture

A MANNERIST MANTUAN MANSION   Mannerism in painting and sculpture has been studied fairly extensively since the early decades of the twentieth century, but only in the 1930s did scholars discover that the term also described much of sixteenth-century architecture. The body of Mannerist architecture they have compiled since then, however, is far from homogeneous. The fact Michelangelo used classical architectural elements in a highly personal and unorthodox manner does not necessarily make him a Mannerist architect. In his designs for Saint Peter's, he certainly strove for the effects of mass, balance, order, and stability that were the very hallmarks of High Renaissance design. Unorthodox use of classical elements, however, was the precise goal of GIULIO RO-MANO (ca. 1492–1546) when he designed the Palazzo del Tè in Mantua (FIG. **22-48**) and, with it, formulated almost the entire architectural vocabulary of Mannerism.

Giulio Romano became Raphael's chief assistant in decorating the Vatican stanze. After Raphael's premature death in 1520, Giulio became his master's artistic executor, completing Raphael's unfinished frescoes and panel paintings. In 1524, Giulio went to Mantua, where he found a patron in Duke Federigo Gonzaga, for whom he built and decorated the Palazzo del Tè between 1525 and 1535.

Gonzaga intended the Palazzo del Tè to serve as both suburban summer palace and stud farm for his famous stables. Originally planned as a relatively modest country villa, Giulio's building so pleased the duke that he soon commissioned the architect to enlarge the structure. In a second building campaign, Giulio expanded the villa to a palatial scale by adding three wings, which he placed around a square central court. This once-paved court, which functions both as a passage and as the design's focal point, has a near-urban character. Its surrounding buildings form a self-enclosed unit with a large stable-flanked garden attached to it on the east side.

Giulio exhibited his Mannerist style in the facades that face the palace's interior courtyard (FIG. 22-48), where the divergences from architectural convention are so pronounced they constitute an enormous parody of Bramante's classical style. In a building laden with structural surprises and contradictions, the design of these facades is the most unconventional of all. The keystones (central voussoirs), for example, either

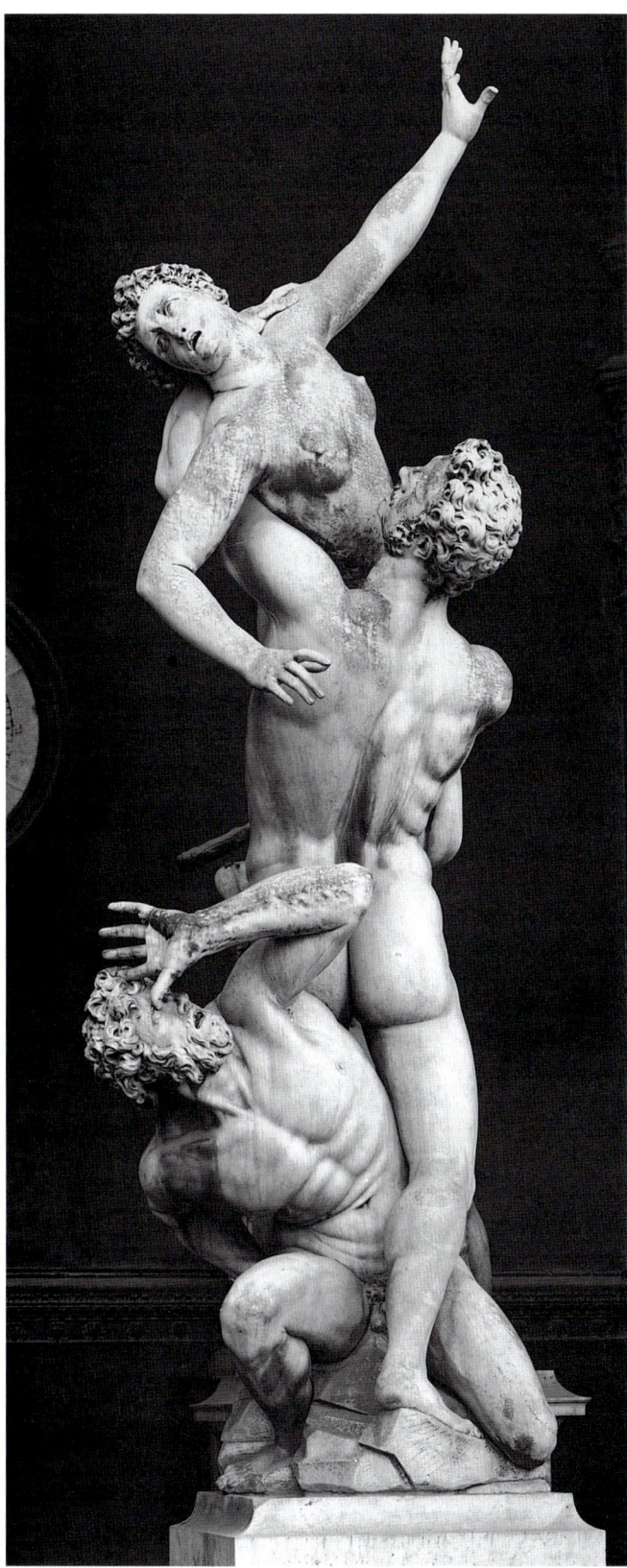

22-47   GIOVANNI DA BOLOGNA, *Abduction of the Sabine Women,* Loggia dei Lanzi, Piazza della Signoria, Florence, Italy, completed 1583. Marble, approx. 13′ 6″ high.

(see FIG. 5-89)—once in the crouching old man and again in the woman's flung up arm gesture. The three bodies interlock on a vertical axis, creating a spiral movement as viewers' eyes ascend the sculpture.

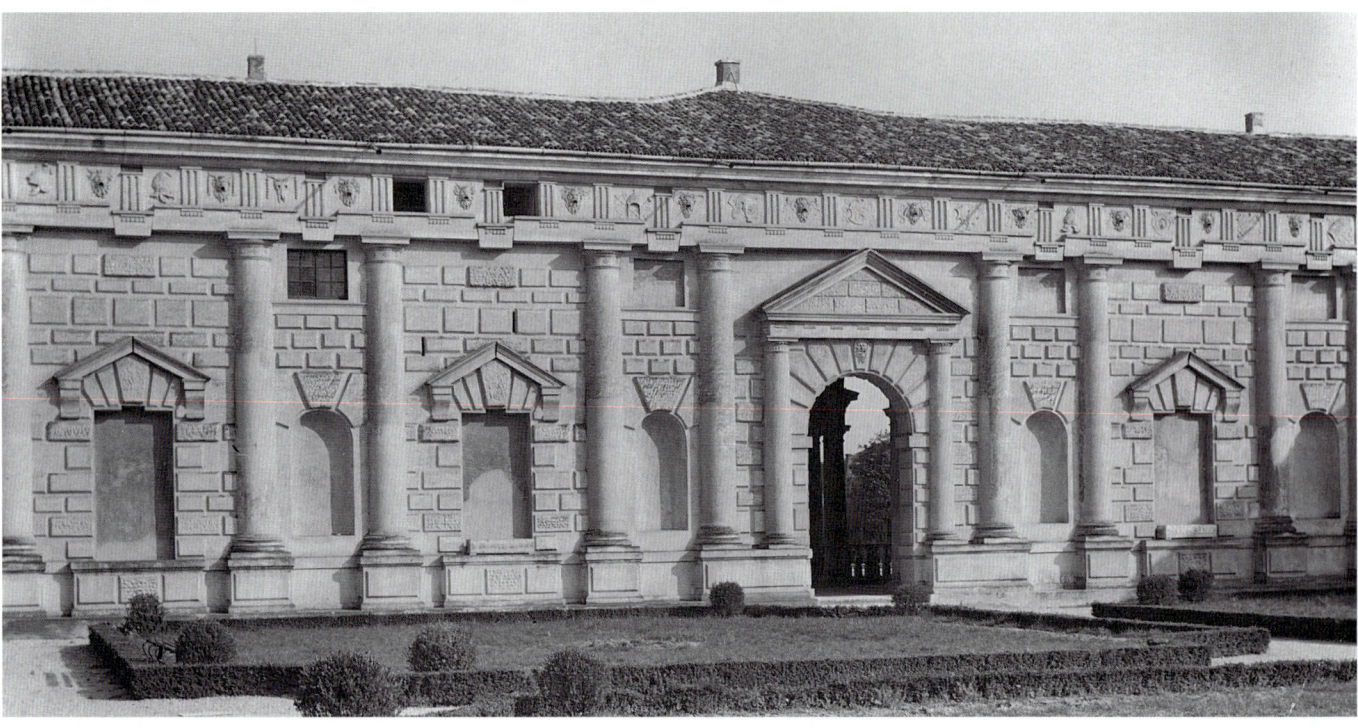

22-48   Giulio Romano, interior courtyard facade of the Palazzo del Tè, Mantua, Italy, 1525–1535.

have not fully settled or seem to be slipping from the arches—and, more eccentric still, Giulio even placed voussoirs in the pediments over the rectangular niches, where no arches exist. The massive Tuscan columns that flank these niches carry incongruously narrow architraves. That these architraves break midway between the columns stresses their apparent structural insufficiency, and they seem unable to support the weight of the triglyphs above, which threaten to crash down on the head of anyone foolish enough to stand below them. To be sure, appreciating Giulio's joke requires a highly sophisticated audience, and recognizing some quite subtle departures from the norm presupposes a thorough familiarity with the established rules of classical architecture. It speaks well for the duke's sophistication that he accepted Giulio's form of architectural humor.

In short, in his design for the Palazzo del Tè, Giulio Romano deliberately flouted most of the classical rules of order, stability, and symmetry, and he made every effort to startle and shock beholders. This desire to create ambiguities and tensions is as typical of Mannerist architecture as it is of Mannerist painting, and many of the devices Giulio invented for the Palazzo del Tè became standard features in the formal repertoire of later Mannerist buildings.

LATER SIXTEENTH-CENTURY ARCHITECTURE

Acceptance of Mannerism's style in architecture was by no means universal, neither on the part of architects nor patrons. Indeed, later sixteenth-century designs more in keeping with the High Renaissance ideals proved to have a greater impact on seventeenth-century architecture in Italy than the more adventurous, yet eccentric, works by Giulio Romano and the other Mannerists.

SETTING THE STAGE FOR THE BAROQUE Probably the most influential building of the second half of the sixteenth century was the mother church of the Jesuit order, founded in 1534, in the pontificate of Paul III. As a major participant in the Counter-Reformation, the Jesuit order needed a church appropriate to its new prominence. Because Michelangelo was late in providing the plans for this church, called Il Gesù, or Church of Jesus (FIGS. **22-49** and **22-50**), the Jesuits turned to Giacomo da Vignola (1507–1573), who designed the ground plan, and Giacomo della Porta (ca. 1533–1602), who was responsible for the facade. These two architects designed and built Il Gesù between 1568 and 1584. Chronologically and stylistically, the building belongs to the late Renaissance, but its enormous influence on later churches marks it as one of the significant monuments for the development of Baroque church architecture. Its facade (FIG. 22-49) was an important model and point of departure for the facades of Roman Baroque churches for two centuries, and many churches throughout the Catholic countries, especially in Latin America, echoed its basic scheme. The facade's design was not entirely original. The union of the lower and upper stories, effected by scroll buttresses, harks back to Alberti's Santa Maria Novella in Florence (see FIG. 21-36). Its classical pediment is familiar in Alberti's work, as well as in the work of the Venetian architect Andrea Palladio, which is examined later. And its paired pilasters appear in Michelangelo's design for Saint Peter's (FIG. 22-30). Giacomo della Porta skillfully synthesized these already existing motifs. In his facade design, he unified the two stories, the horizontal march of the pilasters and columns builds to a dramatic climax at the central bay, and the facade's bays snugly fit the nave-chapel system behind them. The later dramatic Baroque facades of Rome were architectural variations on this basic theme.

The plan of Il Gesù (FIG. 22-50) reveals a monumental expansion of Alberti's scheme for Sant'Andrea in Mantua (see

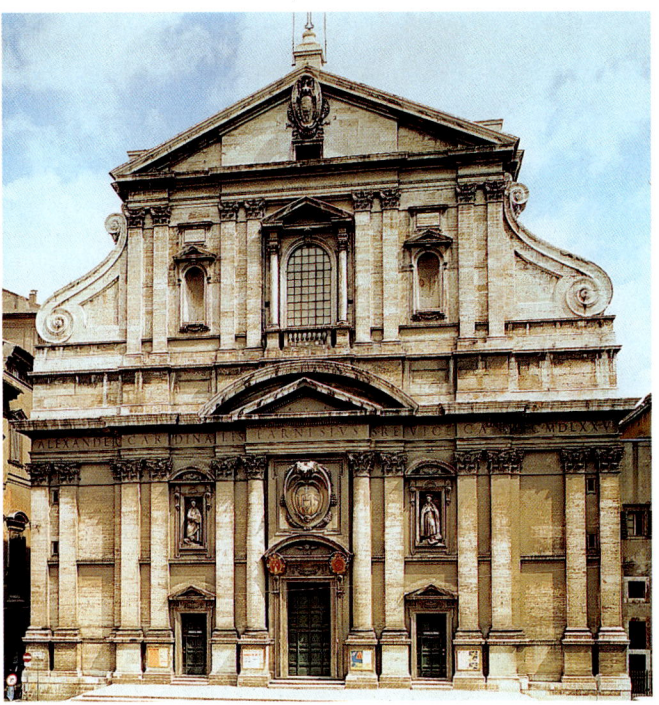

22-49 GIACOMO DELLA PORTA, facade of Il Gesù, Rome, Italy, ca. 1575–1584.

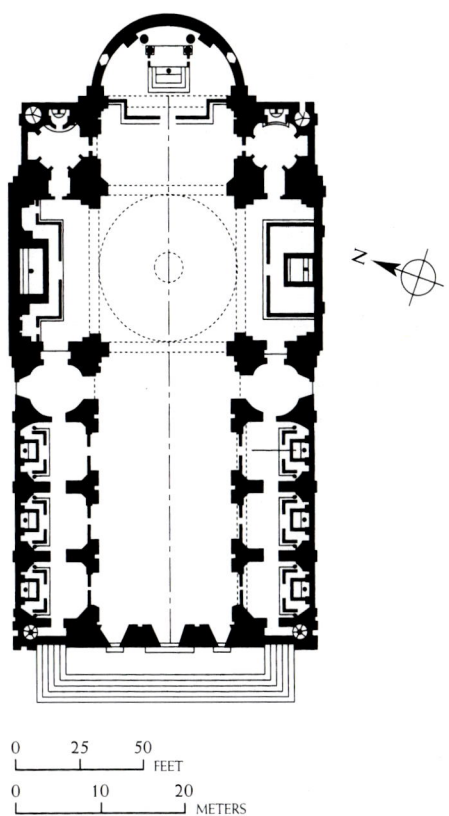

0   25   50 FEET
0   10   20 METERS

22-50 GIACOMO DA VIGNOLA, plan of Il Gesù, Rome, Italy, 1568.

FIG. 21-44). Here, the nave takes over the main volume of space, making the structure a great hall with side chapels. A dome emphasizes the approach to the altar. The wide acceptance of the Gesù plan in the Catholic world, even until modern times, speaks to its ritual efficacy. The opening of the church building into a single great hall provides an almost theatrical setting for large promenades and processions (that seemed to combine social with priestly functions). Above all, the space is adequate to accommodate the great crowds that gathered to hear the eloquent preaching of the Jesuits.

LATER SIXTEENTH-CENTURY VENETIAN ART AND ARCHITECTURE

MANNERIST DRAMA AND DYNAMISM Venetian painting of the later sixteenth century built on established Venetian ideas. JACOPO ROBUSTI, known as TINTORETTO (1518–1594), claimed to be a student of Titian and aspired to combine Titian's color with Michelangelo's drawing. Art historians often refer to Tintoretto as the outstanding Venetian representative of Mannerism. He adopted many Mannerist pictorial devices, but his dramatic power, depth of spiritual vision, and glowing Venetian color schemes seem to depart from the Mannerism's mold.

Tintoretto's art is always extremely dramatic. In his *Miracle of the Slave* (FIG. **22-51**), Saint Mark hurtles downward to assist a Christian slave, who is about to be martyred for his faith, and shatters the torture instruments. The executioner holds up these instruments to the startled judge as the throng around the central action stares. Here, Tintoretto accelerated Titian's dynamism and constructed the composition using contrary motions; for any figure leaning in one direction, another figure counters it. At the extreme left, two men, a woman, and a child wind in counterpoint directions about a

column, resembling the Mannerist twisting of Giovanni da Bologna's *Abduction of the Sabine Women* (FIG. 22-47). The main group curves deeply back into space, but Tintoretto's most dynamic touch appears in the central trio of the slave, the executioner, and the inverted Saint Mark. The two earthly figures sweep together in a great upward serpentine curve, their motion checked by the plunging figure of Saint Mark moving in the opposite direction.

The entire composition is a kind of counterpoint of motion characteristic of Mannerism. However, the picture frame firmly contains the motion, and the figures' robustness, their solid structure and firm movement, the clearly composed space, and the coherent action have little to do with Mannerist presentation. The depiction of the miraculous event, which the artist dramatized forcefully and with conviction, conveys neither hesitation nor ambiguity. Tintoretto's skillful theatricality and sweeping power of execution set him apart from the Mannerists and made him a forerunner of the Baroque, the age of theater and opera. And the tonality—the deep golds, reds, and blues—is purely Venetian.

A GLOWING LAST SUPPER Toward the end of Tintoretto's life, his art became spiritual, even visionary, as solid forms melted away into swirling clouds of dark shot through with fitful light. In Tintoretto's *Last Supper* (FIG. **22-52**), painted for the interior of Andrea Palladio's church of San Giorgio Maggiore (FIG. 22-59), the actors take part in a ghostly drama. They are as insubstantial as the shadows cast by the faint glow of their halos and the flame of a single lamp that seems to breed ghostly spirits. Only the incandescent glow around the head of Jesus identifies him as he administers the Sacrament to his disciples.

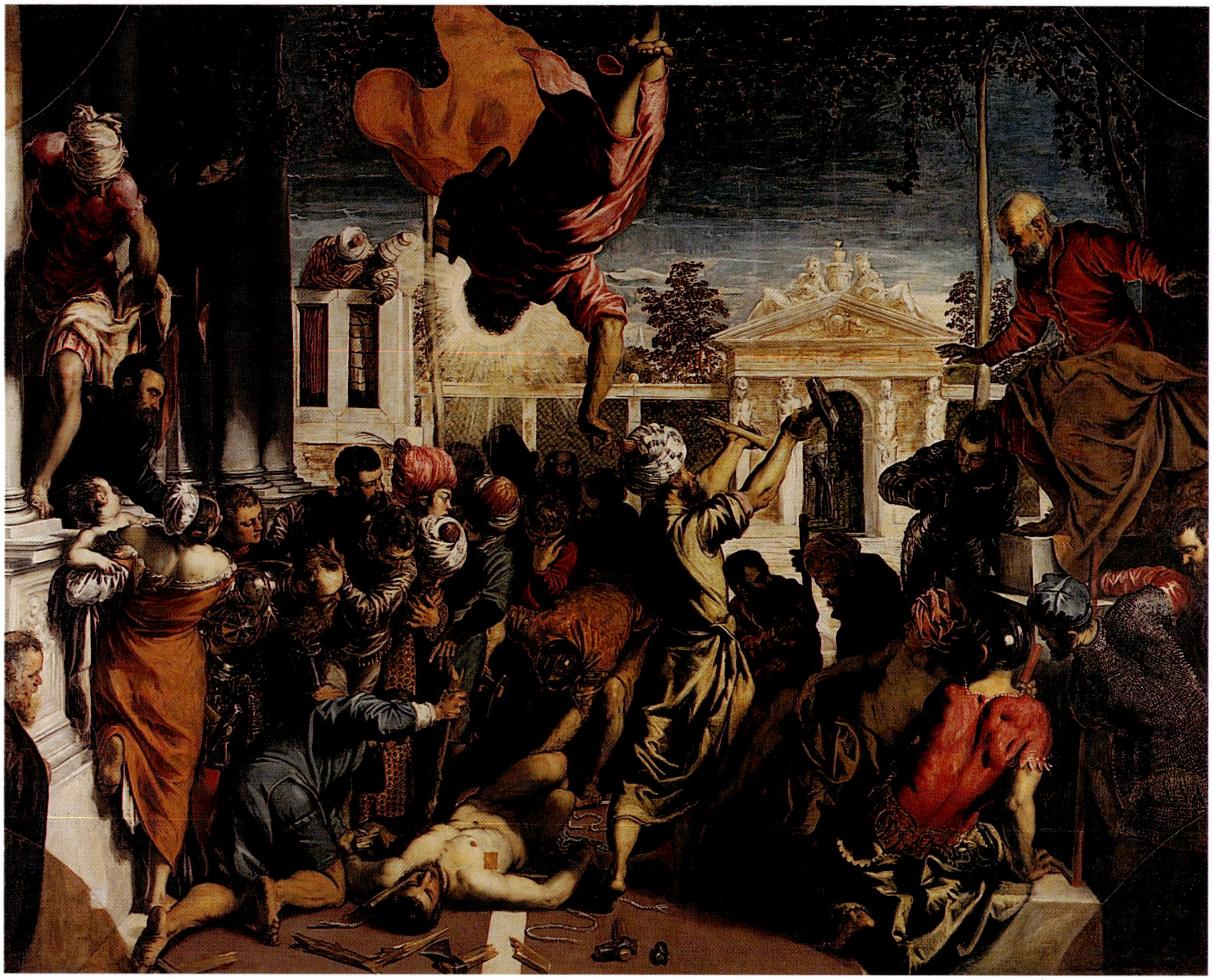

22-51   Tintoretto, *Miracle of the Slave*, 1548. Oil on canvas, approx. 14′ × 18′. Galleria dell'Accademia, Venice.

The contrast with Leonardo's *Last Supper* (FIG. 22-3) is both extreme and instructive. Leonardo's composition, balanced and symmetrical, parallels the picture plane in a geometrically organized and closed space. The figure of Christ is the tranquil center of the drama and the perspectival focus. In Tintoretto's painting, Christ is above and beyond the converging perspective lines that race diagonally away from the picture surface, creating disturbing effects of limitless depth and motion. Viewers locate Tintoretto's Christ via the light flaring, beaconlike, out of darkness. Leonardo placed his Christ by geometric and perspectival centralization. The contrast of the two represents the direction Renaissance painting took in the sixteenth century, as it moved away from architectonic clarity of space and neutral lighting toward the dynamic perspectives and dramatic chiaroscuro of the coming Baroque.

A PROBLEMATIC PAINTING OF CHRIST   Among the great Venetian masters was PAOLO CAGLIARI of Verona, called PAOLO VERONESE (1528–1588). Where Tintoretto gloried in monumental drama and deep perspectives, Veronese specialized in splendid pageantry painted in superb color and set within majestic classical architecture. Like Tintoretto, Veronese painted on a huge scale, with canvases often as large

as twenty feet by thirty feet or more. His usual subjects, painted for the refectories of wealthy monasteries, afforded him an opportunity to display magnificent companies at table.

Christ in the House of Levi (FIG. 22-53), originally called *Last Supper,* is a good example. Here, in a great open loggia framed by three monumental arches (the architectural style closely resembles the upper arcades of Jacopo Sansovino's State Library; FIG. 22-55), Christ sits at the center of the splendidly garbed elite of Venice. In the foreground, with a courtly gesture, the very image of gracious grandeur, the chief steward welcomes guests. Robed lords, their colorful retainers, clowns, dogs, and dwarfs crowd into the spacious loggia.

Painted during the Counter-Reformation, this depiction prompted criticism from the Catholic Church. The Holy Office of the Inquisition accused Veronese of impiety for painting such creatures so close to the Lord, and it ordered him to make changes at his own expense. Reluctant to do so, he simply changed the painting's title, converting the subject to a less solemn one. As Andrea Palladio (whose work is discussed later) looked to the example of classically inspired High Renaissance architecture, so Veronese returned to High

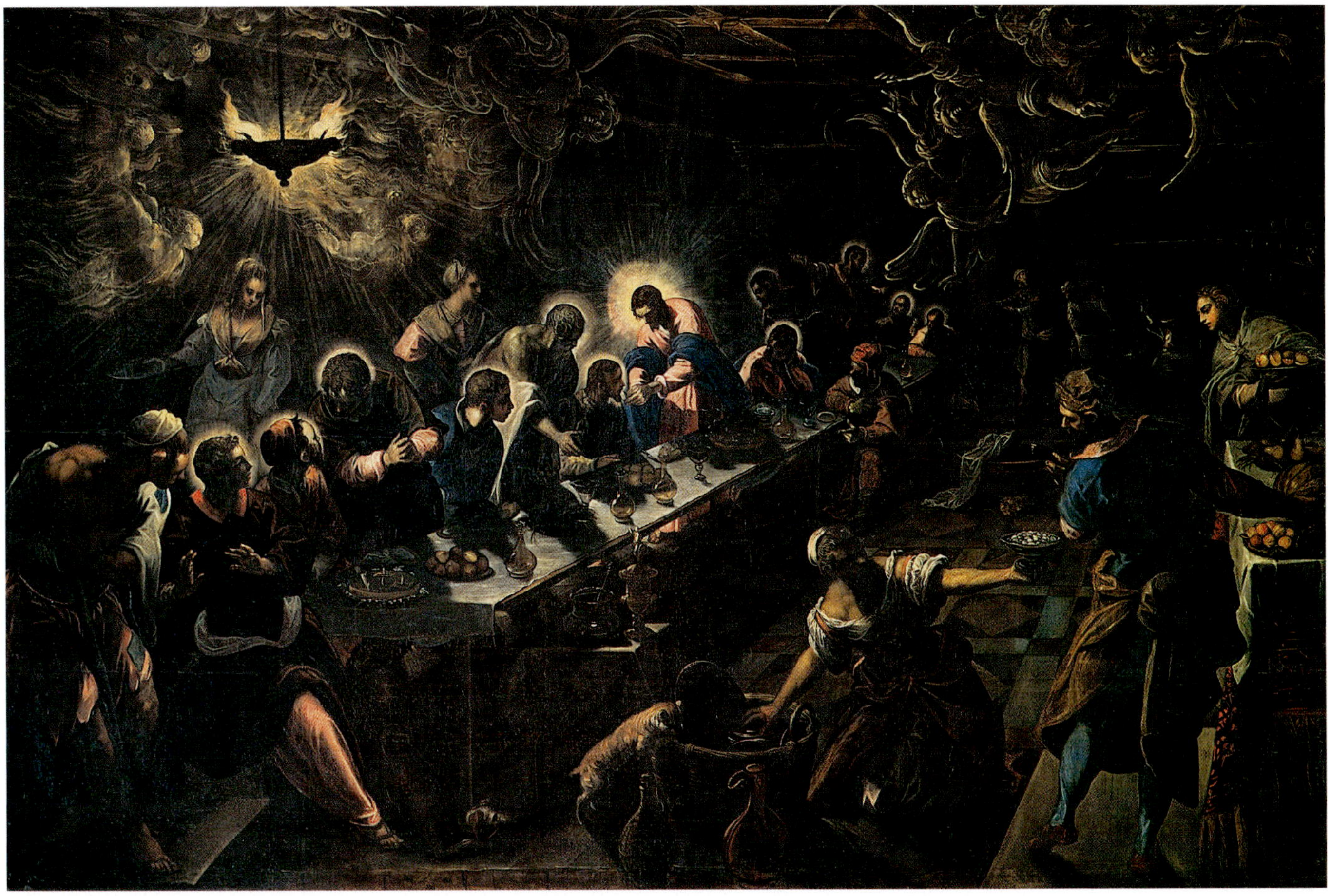

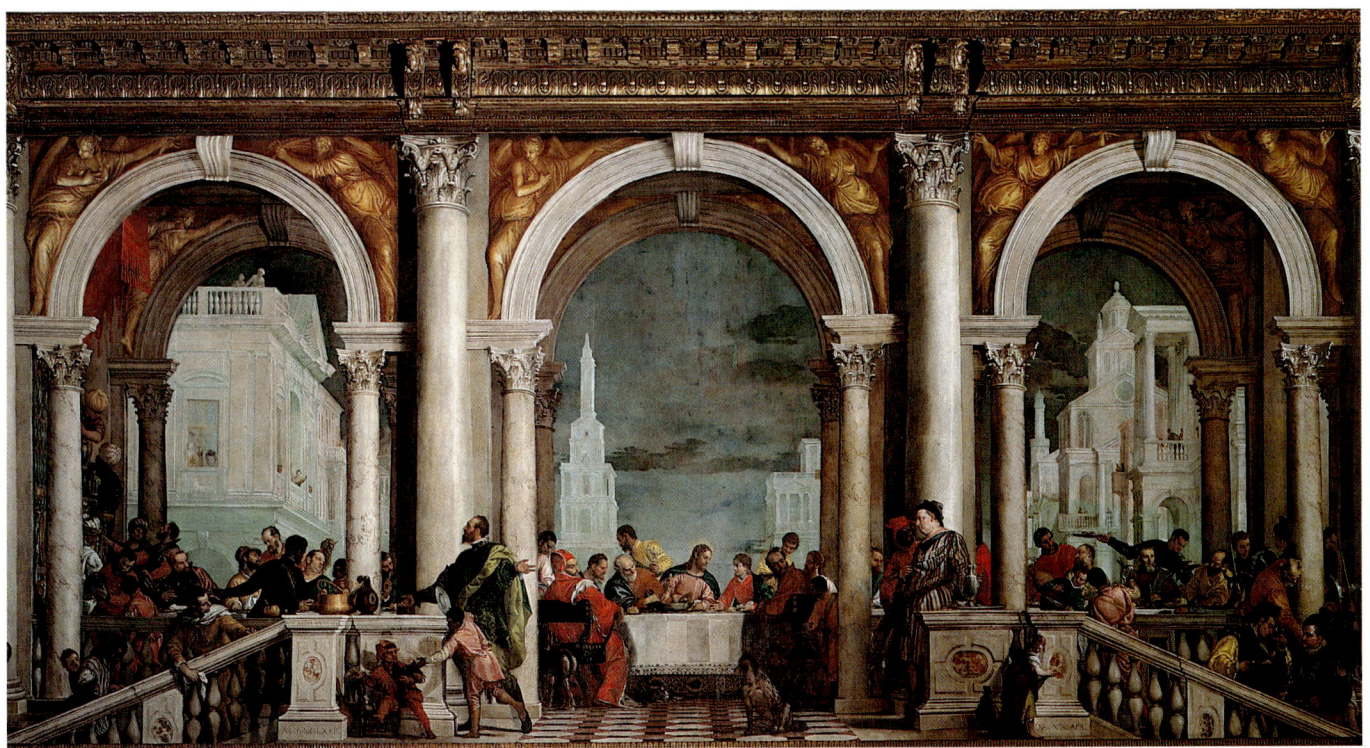

22-52 TINTORETTO, *Last Supper,* Chancel, San Giorgio Maggiore, Venice, Italy, 1594. Oil on canvas, 12′ × 18′ 8″.

22-53 PAOLO VERONESE, *Christ in the House of Levi,* 1573. Oil on canvas, approx. 18′ 6″ × 42′ 6″. Galleria dell'Accademia, Venice.

22-54 Paolo Veronese, *Triumph of Venice,* ceiling of the Hall of the Grand Council, Palazzo Ducale, Venice, Italy, ca. 1585. Oil on canvas, approx. 29′ 8″ × 19′.

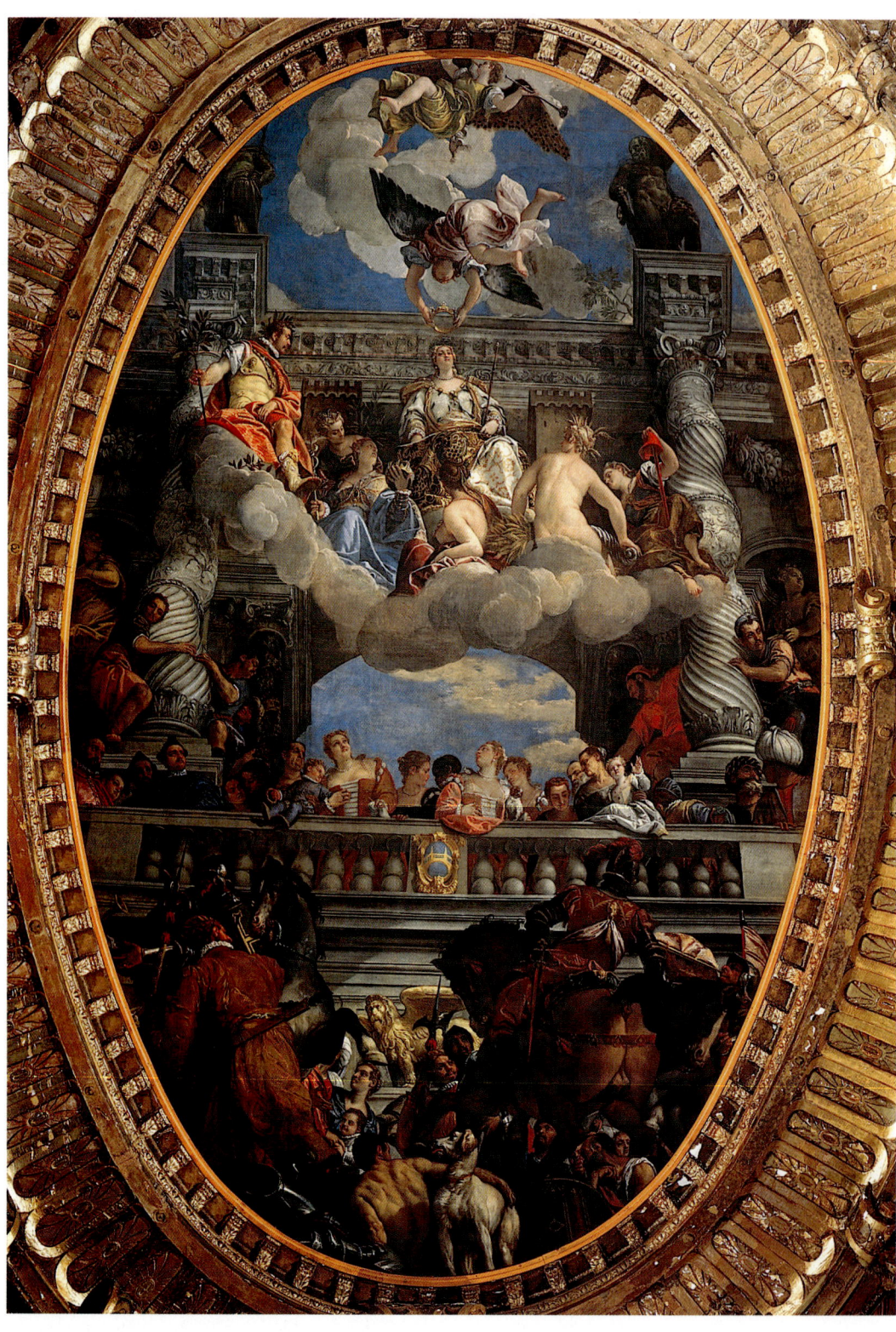

Renaissance composition, its symmetrical balance, and its ordered architectonics. His shimmering color is drawn from the whole spectrum, although he avoided solid colors for half shades (light blues, sea greens, lemon yellows, roses, and violets), creating veritable flower beds of tone.

A PICTORIAL GLORIFICATION OF VENICE
The Venetian Republic employed both Tintoretto and Veronese to decorate the grand chambers and council rooms of the Doge's Palace (see FIG. 18-57). A great and popular decorator, Veronese revealed himself a master of imposing illusionistic ceiling compositions, such as *Triumph of Venice* (FIG.

22-54). Here, within an oval frame, he presented Venice, crowned by Fame, enthroned between two great twisted columns in a balustraded loggia, garlanded with clouds, and attended by figures symbolic of its glories. This work represents one of the very first modern pictorial glorifications of a state—a subject that became very popular during the Baroque period that immediately followed. Veronese's perspective is not, like Mantegna's or Correggio's, projected directly up from below. Rather, it is a projection of the scene at a forty-five-degree angle to spectators, a technique many later Baroque decorators used, particularly the Venetian Giambattista Tiepolo in the eighteenth century.

MONEY AND MANUSCRIPTS The Florentine JACOPO TATTI, called JACOPO SANSOVINO (1486–1570), introduced Venice to the High Renaissance style of architecture. Originally trained as a sculptor under Andrea Sansovino (ca. 1467–1529), whose name he adopted, Jacopo went to Rome in 1518, where, under the influence of Bramante's circle, he turned increasingly toward architecture. When he arrived in Venice as a refugee from the sack of Rome in 1527, he quickly established himself as that city's leading and most admired architect. His buildings frequently inspired the architectural settings of the most prominent Venetian painters, including Titian and Veronese.

Sansovino's largest and most rewarding public commissions were the Mint (la Zecca) and the adjoining State Library (FIG. **22-55**) in the heart of the island city. The Mint, begun in 1535, faces the Canale San Marco with a stern and forbidding three-story facade. Its heavy rustication imbues it with an intended air of strength and impregnability. A boldly projecting, bracket-supported cornice reminiscent of the machicolated galleries of medieval castles emphasizes this fortresslike look.

Begun a year after the Mint, the neighboring State Library of San Marco, which Andrea Palladio referred to as "perhaps the most sumptuous and the most beautiful Edifice that has been erected since the time of the Ancients,"[14] exudes a very different spirit. With twenty-one bays (only sixteen were completed during Sansovino's lifetime), the library faces the Gothic Doge's Palace (see FIG. 18-57) across the Piazzetta, a

lateral extension of Venice's central Piazza San Marco. The relatively plain ground-story arcade has Tuscan-style columns attached to the arch-supporting piers in the manner of the Roman Colosseum (see FIG. 10-34). A Doric frieze of metopes and triglyphs caps it—none "slide" out of place as in the frieze of the contemporary Palazzo del Tè in Mantua (FIG. 22-48). The lower story sturdily supports the higher, lighter, and much more decorative Ionic second story, which housed the reading room with its treasure of manuscripts, keeping them safe from not-uncommon flooding. On this second level, Sansovino softened the ground story's stern system by flanking the piers with Ionic colonnettes paired in depth, rather than in the plane of the facade. Two-thirds the height of the main columns, they rise to support the springing of arches, whose spans are two-thirds those of the lower arcade, accentuating the verticality of the second story. The main columns carry an entablature with a richly decorated frieze of putti, in strongly projecting relief, supporting garlands. The oval windows of an attic story punctuate this favorite decorative motif of the ancient Romans, seen earlier in Bernardo Rossellino's tomb of Leonardo Bruni (see FIG. 21-29). Perhaps the building's most striking feature is its roofline, where Sansovino replaced the traditional straight cornice with a balustrade (reminiscent of the one on Bramante's Tempietto, FIG. 22-8) interrupted by statue-bearing pedestals. The spacing of the latter corresponds to that of the orders below so that the sculptures are the sky-piercing finials of the building's vertical design elements. Sansovino's deft application of sculpture

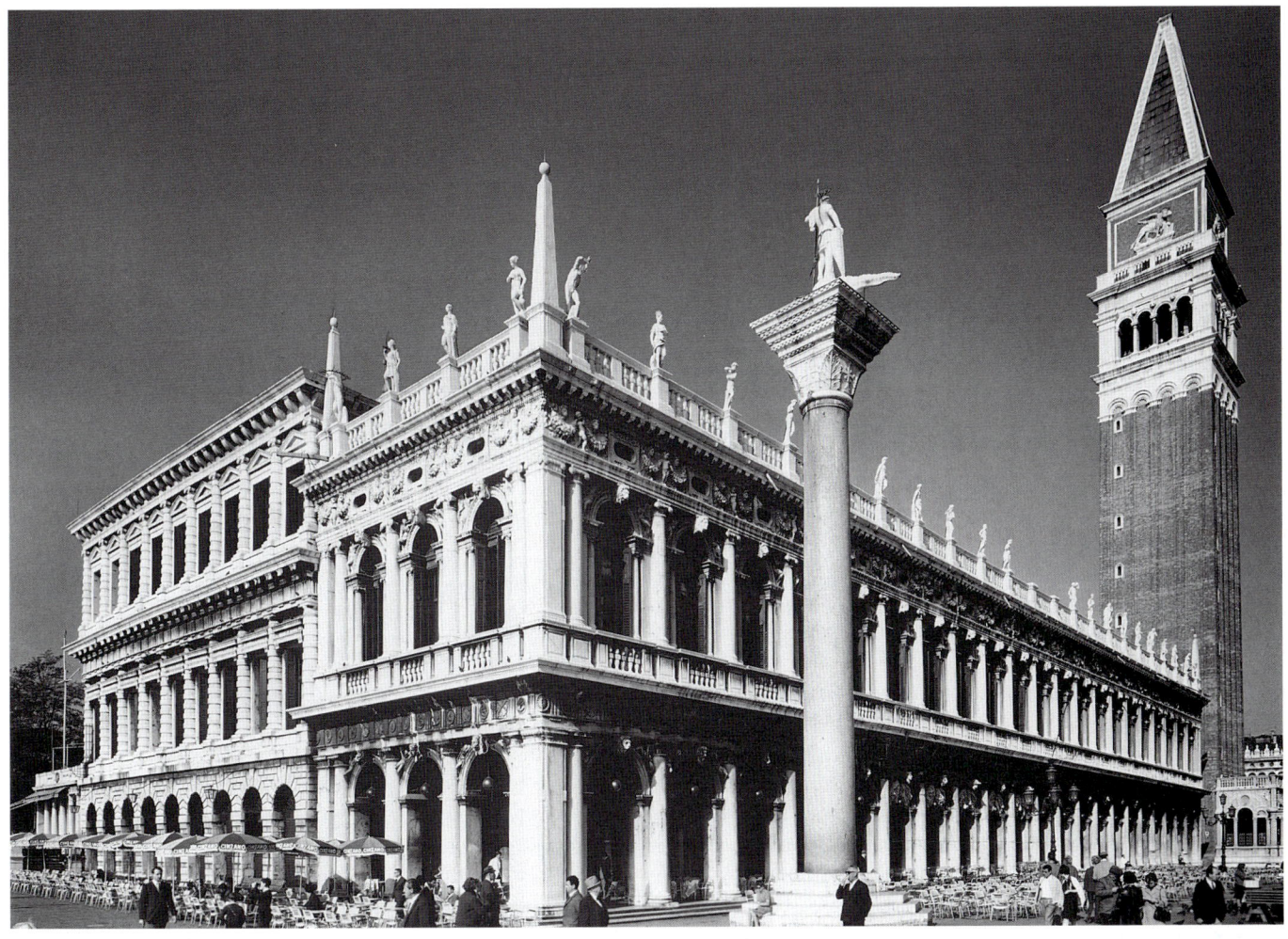

22-55 JACOPO SANSOVINO, the Mint (la Zecca), 1535–1545 *(left)* and the State Library *(right)*, begun 1536, Piazza San Marco, Venice.

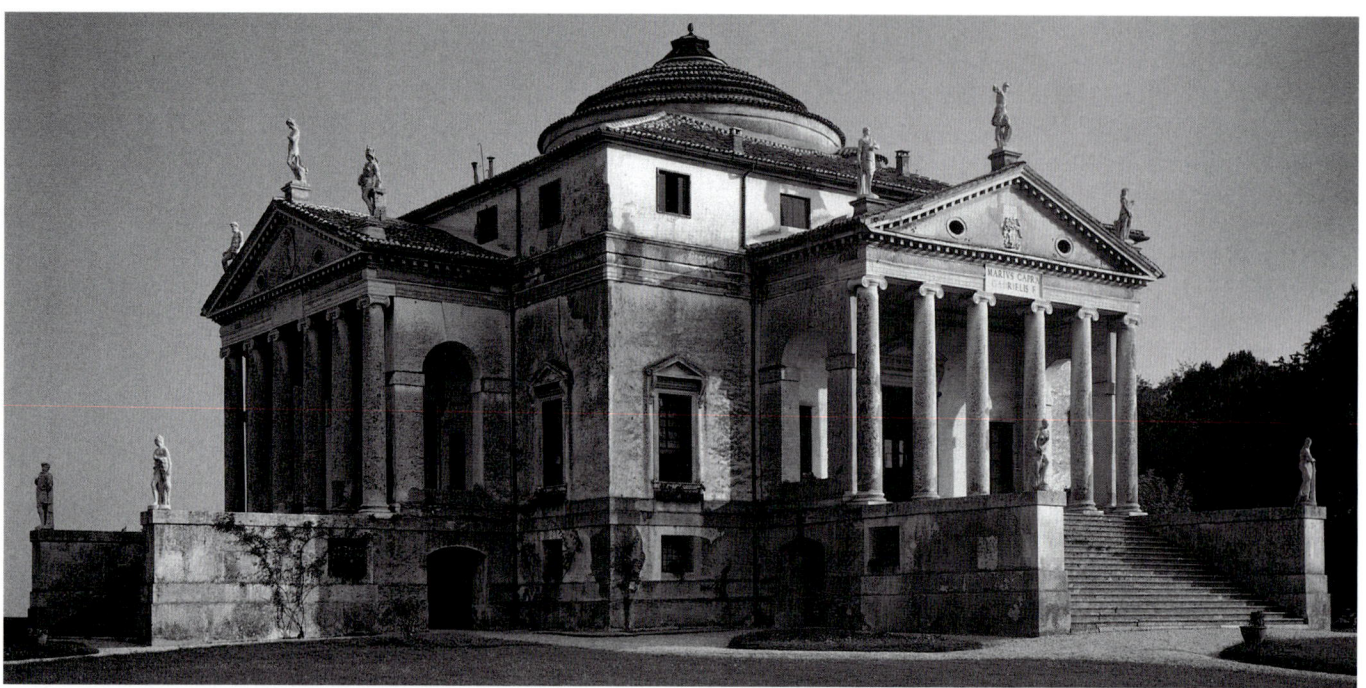

22-56 ANDREA PALLADIO, Villa Rotonda (formerly Villa Capra), near Vicenza, Italy, ca. 1566–1570.

to the building's massive framework (with no visible walls) relieves the design's potential severity and gives its aspect an extraordinary sculptural richness.

One feature rarely mentioned is how subtly the library echoes the design of the lower two stories of the decorative Doge's Palace (see FIG. 18-57) opposite it. Although Sansovino used a vastly different architectural vocabulary, he managed admirably to adjust his building to the older one. Correspondences include the almost identical spacing of the lower arcades, the rich and ornamental treatment of the second stories (including their balustrades), and the dissolution of the rooflines (with decorative battlements in the palace and a statue-surmounted balustrade in the library). It is almost as if Sansovino set out to translate the Gothic architecture of the Doge's Palace into a "modern" Renaissance idiom. If so, he was eminently successful; the two buildings, although of different spiritual and stylistic worlds, mesh to make the Piazzetta one of the most elegantly framed urban units in Europe.

AN ARCHITECT INSPIRED BY THE ANCIENTS
After Jacopo Sansovino's death, ANDREA PALLADIO (1508–1580) succeeded him as chief architect of the Venetian Republic. Beginning as a stonemason and decorative sculptor, at age thirty Palladio turned to architecture, the ancient literature on architecture, engineering, topography, and military science. Unlike the universal scholar Alberti, Palladio became more of a specialist. He made several trips to Rome to study the ancient buildings firsthand. He illustrated Daniele Barbaro's edition of *De architectura* by Vitruvius (1556), and he wrote his own treatise on architecture, *I quattro libri dell'architettura (The Four Books of Architecture)*, originally published in 1570, which had a wide-ranging influence on succeeding generations of architects throughout Europe. Palladio's influence outside Italy, most significantly in England and in colonial America, was stronger and more lasting than that of any other architect.

Palladio accrued his significant reputation from his many designs for villas, built on the Venetian mainland. Nineteen still

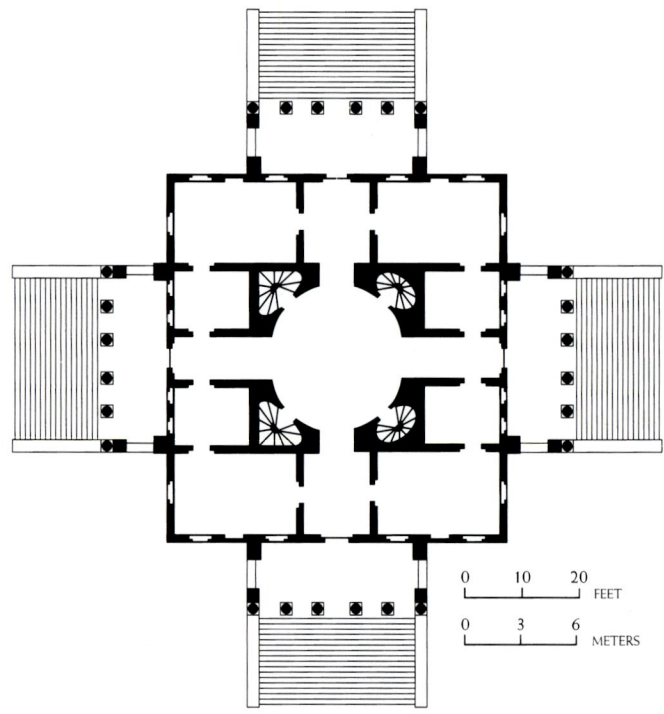

22-57 ANDREA PALLADIO, plan of the Villa Rotonda (formerly Villa Capra), near Vicenza, Italy, ca. 1566–1570.

stand, and they especially influenced later architects. The same Arcadian spirit that prompted the ancient Romans to build villas in the countryside, and that the Venetian painter Giorgione expressed so eloquently in his art, motivated a similar villa-building boom in the sixteenth century. One can imagine that Venice, with its very limited space, must have been more congested than any ancient city. But a longing for the countryside was not the only motive; declining fortunes prompted the Venetians to develop their mainland possessions with new land investment and reclamation projects. Citizens who could afford it were encouraged to set themselves up as aristocratic farmers and to develop swamps into productive agricultural land. Wealthy families could look on their villas as providential investments. The villas were thus aristocratic farms (like the much later American plantations, which Palladio's architecture influenced) surrounded by service outbuildings Palladio generally arranged in long, low wings branching out from the main building and enclosing a large rectangular court area.

Although it is the most famous, Villa Rotonda (FIG. **22-56**), near Vicenza, is not really typical of Palladio's villa style. He did not construct it for an aspiring gentleman farmer but for a retired monsignor who wanted a villa for social events. Palladio planned and designed Villa Rotonda, located on a hilltop, as a kind of belvedere (a residence on a hill), without the usual wings of secondary buildings. Its central plan (FIG. **22-57**), with four identical facades and projecting porches, is, therefore, both sensible and functional. Each of the porches can be used as a platform for enjoying a different view of the surrounding landscape. In this design, the central dome-covered rotunda logically functions as a kind of circular platform for visitors to turn in any direction for the preferred view. The result is a building with functional parts systematically related to one another in terms of calculated mathematical relationships. Villa Rotonda embodies all the qualities of self-sufficiency and formal completeness most Renaissance architects sought. The works of Alberti and Bramante and the remains of classical architecture Palladio studied in Rome influenced the young architect in his formative years. Each facade of his Villa Rotonda resembles a Roman temple. In placing a traditional temple porch in front of a dome-covered interior, Palladio doubtless had the Pantheon (FIG. 10-48) in his mind as a model. By 1550, however, he had developed his personal style, which mixed elements of Mannerism with the clarity and lack of ambiguity that characterized classicism at its most "correct."

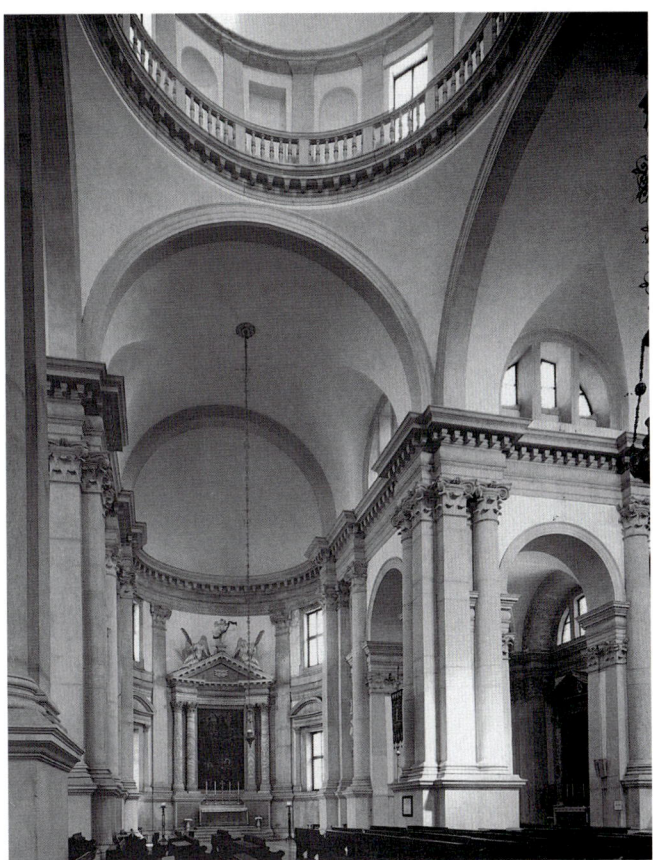

22-59 ANDREA PALLADIO, interior of San Giorgio Maggiore (view facing east), Venice, Italy, 1565.

SHADOW AND SURFACE, SEA AND SKY One of the most dramatically placed buildings in Venice is San Giorgio Maggiore (FIGS. **22-58** and **22-59**), directly across a broad canal from the Piazza San Marco. Dissatisfied with earlier solutions to the problem of integrating a high central nave and lower aisles into a unified facade design, Palladio solved it by superimposing a tall, narrow classical porch on a low broad one (FIG. 22-58). This solution reflects the building's interior arrangement (FIG. 22-59) and in that sense is coolly logical, but the intersection of two temple facades is irrational and ambiguous in Mannerist fashion. Palladio's design also introduced the illusion of three-dimensional depth, an effect the strong projection of the central columns and the shadows they cast intensify. The play of shadow across the building's surfaces, its reflection in the water, and its gleaming white against sea and sky create a remarkably colorful effect, prefiguring the Baroque. The interior of the church (FIG. 22-59) lacks the facade's ambiguity and exhibits strong roots in High Renaissance architectural style. Light floods the interior and crisply defines the contours of the rich wall decorations (pedestals, bases, shafts, capitals, and entablatures), all beautifully and "correctly" profiled—the exemplar of what classical architectural theory meant by "rational" organization.

The sixteenth century in Italy witnessed the triumph of architecture, sculpture, and painting. They achieved the status of fine arts, and High Renaissance artists, whose works have inspired generations of artists since, established an enduring tradition. The development of Mannerism, which contrasted with the rationality pervading much of High Renaissance art and architecture, paved the way for the Baroque's complexity in seventeenth-century Italy.

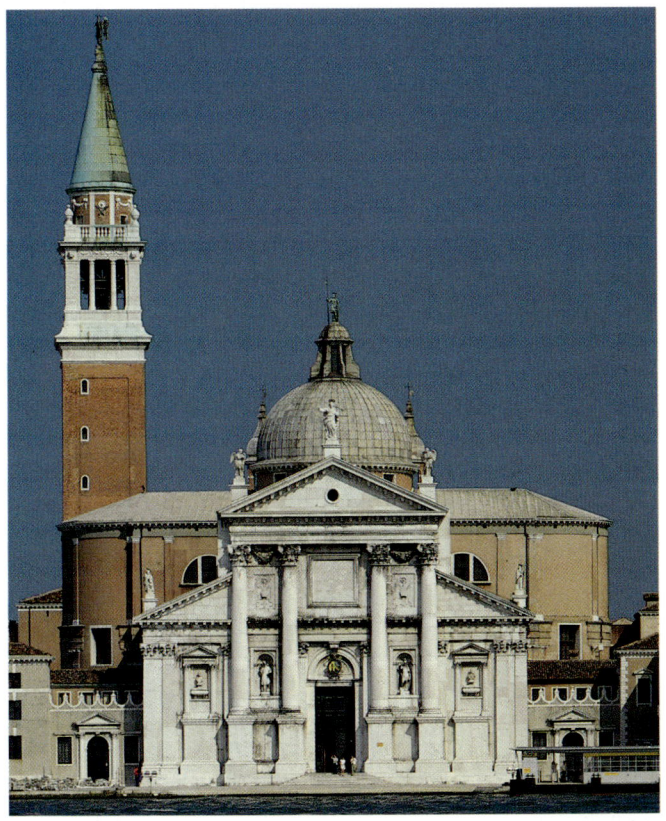

22-58 ANDREA PALLADIO, west facade of San Giorgio Maggiore, Venice, Italy.

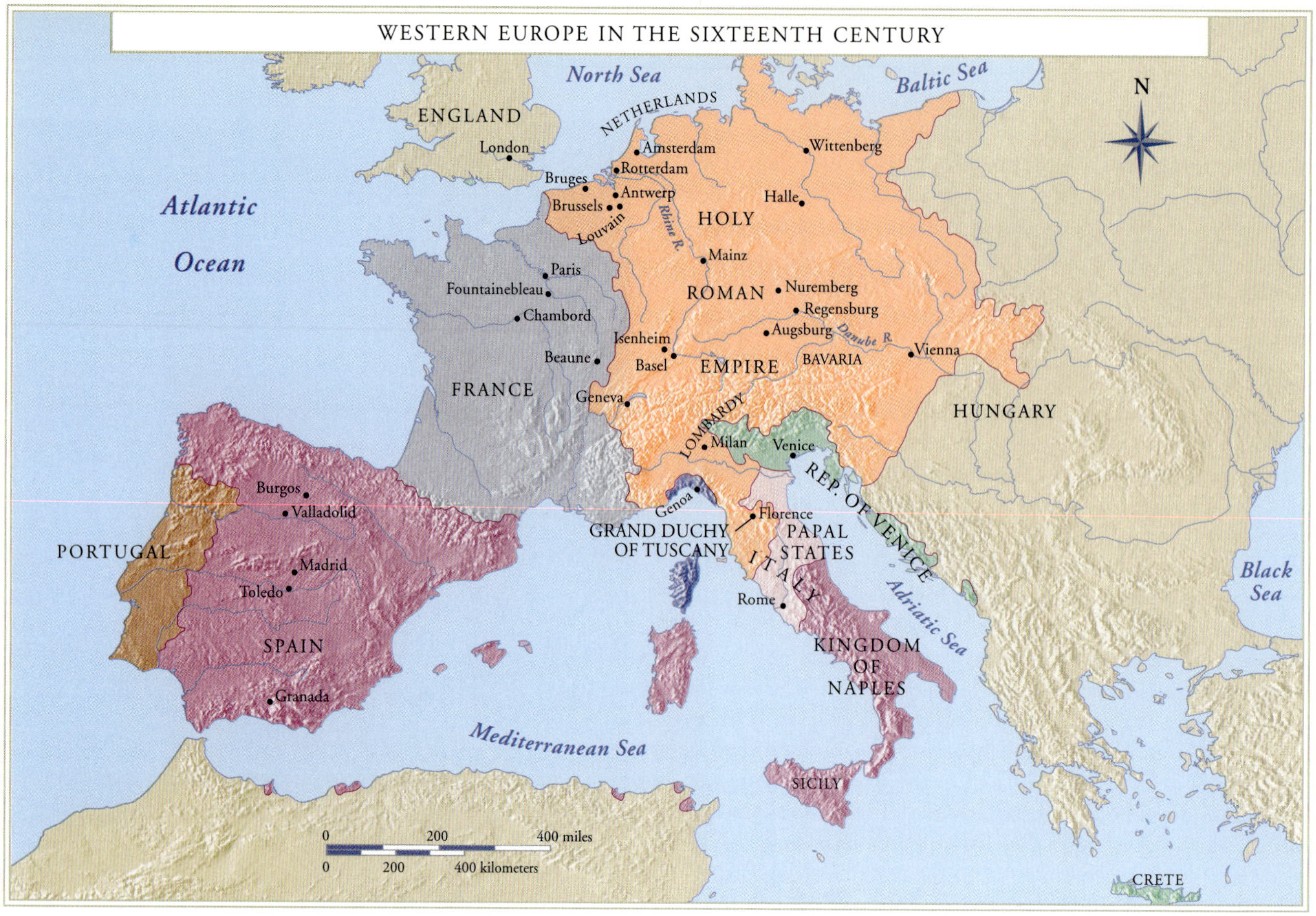

WESTERN EUROPE IN THE SIXTEENTH CENTURY

North Sea

ENGLAND
London
NETHERLANDS
Amsterdam
Rotterdam
Bruges
Antwerp
Brussels
Louvain

Baltic Sea

Wittenberg

Atlantic Ocean

Paris
Fountainebleau
Chambord
FRANCE
Isenheim
Beaune
Basel
Geneva

HOLY
Halle
ROMAN
Mainz
Nuremberg
Regensburg
Augsburg
EMPIRE
BAVARIA
Vienna
HUNGARY

LOMBARDY
Milan
Venice
REP. OF VENICE

Rhine R.
Danube R.

N

PORTUGAL
Burgos
Valladolid
Madrid
Toledo
SPAIN
Granada

Genoa
GRAND DUCHY OF TUSCANY
Florence
PAPAL STATES
ITALY
Rome
KINGDOM OF NAPLES

Adriatic Sea

Black Sea

Mediterranean Sea

SICILY

CRETE

0   200   400 miles
0   200   400 kilometers

1475	1500	1525

AGE OF EUROPEAN EXPLORATION AND COLONIZATION OVERSEAS AND PROTESTANT REFORMATION AND CATHOLIC COUNTER-REFORMATION

HRE = *Holy Roman Emperor* · MAXIMILIAN I OF HAPSBURG, HRE · CHARLES V (HAPSBURG), HRE, KING OF SPAIN AND

HENRY VIII OF ENGLAND (TUDOR)

FRANCIS I OF FRANCE (VALOIS)

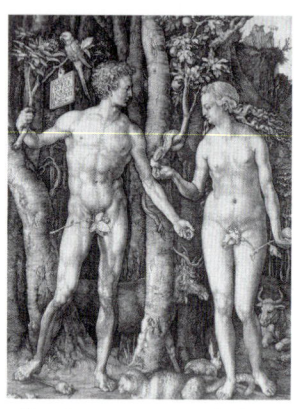

Albrecht Dürer, *The Fall of Man*
(Adam and Eve), 1504

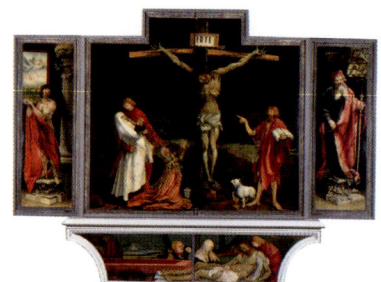

Matthias Grünewald
Isenheim Altarpiece
ca. 1510–1515

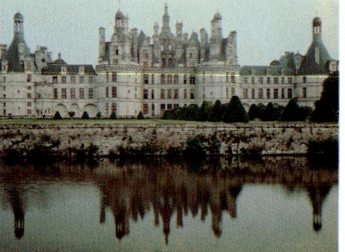

Château de Chambord
begun 1519

Erasmus of Rotterdam, 1466–1536

John Calvin, 1509–1564

Duchy of Burgundy and the Netherlands absorbed by the Holy Roman Empire and France, 1477

Sir Thomas More, 1478–1535

Beginning of Protestant Reformation, 1517

Martin Luther, 1483–1546, posts theses against Indulgences

Spanish conquest of Mexico and Peru, 1518–1536

Ulrich Zwingli, 1484–1531

House of Tudor, 1485–1603

Hapsburg-Valois Wars, 1521–1544

Spanish conquest of Muslim Granada, 1492

Hapsburg dynasty, 1493–(1918)

François Rabelais, ca. 1494–1553

Valois/Bourbon dynasty, 1498–1589/1589–(1830)

THE AGE OF REFORMATION

SIXTEENTH-CENTURY ART IN NORTHERN

EUROPE AND SPAIN

1547	1550			1575		1600
OF SPANISH AMERICA		RUDOLPH II, HAPSBURG, HRE				
PHILIP II OF SPAIN (HAPSBURG) AND OF SPANISH AMERICA						
HENRY II		FRANCIS II	CHARLES IX	HENRY III		HENRY IV OF FRANCE (BOURBON)

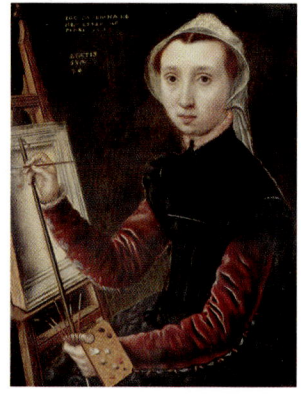

Caterina van Hemessen
Self-Portrait, 1548

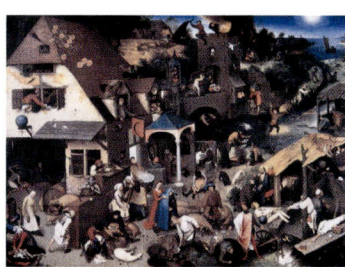

Peter Bruegel the Elder
Netherlandish Proverbs, 1559

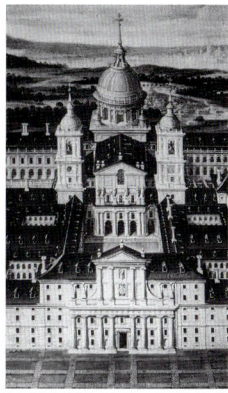

Juan de Herrera, Escorial
ca. 1563–1584

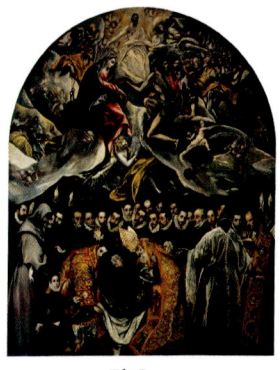

El Greco
The Burial of
Count Orgaz, 1586

Ignatius Loyola, 1491–1556, founded Jesuit Order, 1534

Spread of Calvinist Protestantism in France and Switzerland, 1530s

Henry VIII initiates Reformation in England, 1534

Council of Trent, 1545–1563

Spread of Calvinism in Scotland and the Netherlands, 1550s

Peace of Augsburg between Lutherans and Catholics, 1555

Wars of Religion in France, 1562–1598

Beginning of the revolt of the Netherlands
against Philip II of Spain, 1568

Formation of the Union of Arras, 1579

Formation of the Union of Utrecht, 1579

Netherlands House of Orange/Nassau,
1584–twenty-first century

Philip II sends the Great Armada
against Holland and England, 1588

THE PROTESTANT REFORMATION

The dissolution of the Burgundian Netherlands in 1477 led to a realignment in the European geopolitical landscape in the early sixteenth century. France and the Holy Roman Empire (at the time consisting primarily of today's Germany) expanded their territories after this breakup of Flanders. Through calculated marriages, military exploits, and ambitious territorial expansion, Spain eventually became the dominant power in Europe. Monarchs increased their authority over their subjects and cultivated a stronger sense of cultural and political unity among the populace, thereby laying the foundation for the modern state or nation. Yet a momentous crisis in the Christian Church overshadowed these power shifts. As noted earlier, concerted attempts to reform the Church led to the Reformation and the establishment of Protestantism (as distinct from Catholicism), which in turn prompted the Catholic Church's response, the Counter-Reformation. Ultimately, the Reformation split Christendom in half and produced a hundred years of civil war between Protestants and Catholics.

Replacing Church Practices with Personal Faith

The Reformation, which came to fruition in the early sixteenth century, had its roots in long-term, growing dissatisfaction with Church leadership. The deteriorating relationship between the faithful and the Church hierarchy stood as an obstacle for the millions who sought a meaningful religious experience. Particularly damaging was the perception popes concerned themselves more with temporal power and material wealth than with the salvation of the Church's members. The fact many fifteenth-century popes and cardinals came from wealthy families, such as the Medici (for example, Clement VII, or Giulio de' Medici, and Leo X, or Giovanni de' Medici) intensified this perception. Not only those at the highest levels seemed to ignore their spiritual duties. Upper-level clergy (such as archbishops, bishops, and abbots) began to accumulate numerous offices, which increased their revenues. This practice of pluralism led to negligence, because these officeholders could not be in many places at once. Due to this absenteeism, much of the responsibility for maintaining the efficient operation of the Church and for attending to the devout's needs fell on the parish priests, who often felt overburdened. Many of these priests grew to resent their superiors, who did not provide adequate support or leadership and stood as impediments to priests' advancement in the Church hierarchy.

As their relationship to the organized church hierarchy deteriorated, people sought new ways to invigorate their spiritual commitment and to ensure their eventual salvation. In the fifteenth century, as seen in Chapter 20, these attempts included embarking on pilgrimages to holy sites, joining lay confraternities and orders, and commissioning artworks as visual aids in private devotions. The Modern Devotion movement contributed to the emphasis on personal religious rituals. This movement emerged in the fourteenth century and built on the trend toward more personal devotions that the mendicant orders (see "Mendicant Orders and Confraternities," Chapter 19, page 537) developed in the thirteenth century. Its increasing prominence in the fifteenth century attested to the growing disillusionment with Church leaders. Followers of Modern Devotion, especially the lay religious order the Brothers and Sisters of the Common Life, encouraged a more direct spiritual communion with God. Although they did not advocate rejection of Church doctrines or practices, these adherents' emphasis on developing a personal relationship with God clearly diminished the primacy of Church officials.

Ninety-Five Theses and Lutheranism

By the early sixteenth century, dissatisfaction with the Church had grown so widespread that the outspoken challenge to papal authority by German theologian Martin Luther (1483–1546) was sufficient to spark the Reformation. In 1517, in Wittenberg, Luther issued his Ninety-Five Theses, which enumerated his objections to Church practices, especially the sale of indulgences. Indulgences were remittances (or reductions) of time spent in Purgatory. The increasing frequency of their sale suggested people were buying their way into Heaven.

Luther's goal was significant reform and clarification of major spiritual issues, but his ideas ultimately led to the splitting of Christendom. According to Luther, the Catholic Church's extensive ecclesiastical structure needed casting out, for it had no basis in Scripture. The Bible and nothing else could serve as the foundation for Christianity. Luther declared the pope the Antichrist (for which the pope excommunicated him), called the Church the "whore of Babylon," and denounced ordained priests, along with the sacramental systems (accepting only two sacraments, baptism and the Eucharist, the Lord's Supper) they administered, as pagan obstacles to salvation. According to Luther, Christianity needed cleansing of all the impurities of doctrine that had collected through the ages to restore its original purity.

Central to the reformers' creed was the question of salvation—how to achieve it. Rather than perceive salvation as something weak and sinful humans must constantly strive for through good deeds under a punitive God's watchful eye, Luther proposed that faithful individuals attain redemption by God's bestowal of his grace. Therefore, people could not earn salvation. Accordingly, no ecclesiastical machinery with all its miraculous rites and indulgent forgivenesses could save sinners face-to-face with God. Only absolute faith in Christ could justify sinners and ensure salvation. Justification by faith alone, with the guidance of Scripture, was the fundamental doctrine of Protestantism. Further, Luther advocated the Bible as the source of all religious truth. The Bible—the sole scriptural authority—was the word of God, not the Church's councils, law, and rituals.

Calvinism, Anabaptism, and the Anglican Church

If Scripture alone, and not the Church, was the Christian's guide to salvation, then it was imperative each Christian read and interpret the Scriptures. It soon became evident Christians could differ in their interpretations of the sacred texts, and this gave rise to serious differences among the reformers. Luther clashed with Ulrich Zwingli (1484–1531) over the meaning of the sixth chapter of John. The latter's followers called themselves Zwinglians. French scholar John Calvin (1509–1564) established the Calvinist Church, which paralleled Lutheranism in most of its major doctrines. The Calvinists' insistence on the absolute certainty of salvation contributed to their unshakable conviction they were doing God's work on earth. This belief led them to become particularly militant, filled with missionary zeal.

The Anabaptists were among the most radical of reformers. Because of their antipathy to uncontrolled authority (due to papal and clerical abuse of authority), they constructed a more democratic church structure. For example, church members selected ministers. Descendants of the Anabaptists include the Mennonites and the Amish. Thus, "Protestant," which originally referred to Luther's followers, eventually encompassed all reform movements that challenged papal authority at this time.

Once unleashed, the spirit of reform swept across Europe. Lutheranism was soon the primary religion in Denmark, Sweden, Norway, most of the Holy Roman Empire, and parts of Switzerland. Zwinglians were numerous in Switzerland and Calvinists in Geneva, France, the Netherlands, and Scotland. Sixteenth-century territorial and state politics influenced this Protestant sectarianism and the Catholic opposition. For instance, people's religious loyalty, whether Protestant or Catholic, could conflict with their loyalty to the religion of the ruler of the city, county, duchy, principality, or kingdom where they lived. By midcentury, subjects often felt compelled to either accept the religion of their sovereign or emigrate to a territory where the sovereign's religion corresponded with their own. For example, in predominantly Catholic France, some citizens embraced Protestantism, which King Francis I (r. 1515–1547) declared illegal in 1534. Consequently, the state persecuted these Protestants, the Huguenots, and drove them underground. Despite this minority status, the Huguenots' commitment to Protestantism eventually led to one of the bloodiest religious conflicts in European history when the Protestants and Catholics clashed in 1572 in a war that lasted until the end of the sixteenth century.

In England, King Henry VIII (r. 1509–1547), angered by Pope Clement VIII's refusal to annul his marriage to Catherine of Aragon, managed to force Parliament to pass the Act of Supremacy. This Act severed all ties with Rome and declared the king the "supreme head on earth of the Church of England," thereby establishing the Anglican Church.

Class distinctions also influenced religious affiliation, especially in the cities; the religion of the rich often differed from the religion of the poor. In wealthy cities such as Augsburg in the Holy Roman Empire, the merchants/bankers, publishers, printers, and artists—the city's bourgeois masters—were likely Catholic; the next lower societal levels, Lutheran; and the lowest-paid workers, Anabaptists. The German peasants, victims of a pitiless repression of the uprising they staged in 1525 demanding better economic and social conditions, saw Scripture as a liberating manifesto against feudal serfdom. Despite this view, Luther urged the Lutheran masters who quelled this revolt to "smite, slay and stab [the peasants], . . . remembering that nothing can be more poisonous, hurtful, or devilish than a rebel."[1] This incident and Luther's response

demonstrate how the Scriptures were interpreted in diverse ways and used for nonreligious ends. The Catholics also took this tone, and the story of the Reformation and Counter-Reformation tells of significant repression of dissenting voices.

In the 1540s, the Catholic Church mounted the Counter-Reformation, its campaign to counteract the popularity of Protestantism. Comprised of numerous initiatives, including the Council of Trent (convened 1545–1563 to produce needed reforms) and establishing the Jesuit order, Counter-Reformation endeavors continued well into the seventeenth century, and its effect on Italian art is discussed in Chapter 24.

Christian Humanism

Interestingly, despite the tumultuous religious conflict engulfing sixteenth-century Europe, the exchange of intellectual and artistic ideas continued to thrive. Catholic Italy and the (mostly) Lutheran Holy Roman Empire shared in a lively commerce—economic and cultural—and sixteenth-century art throughout Europe exhibited the benefits of that exchange. Humanism filtered up from Italy and spread throughout northern Europe. Northern humanists, like their southern counterparts, cultivated a knowledge of classical cultures and literature. However, they focused more on reconciling humanism with Christianity, so later scholars applied the general label "Christian humanists" to describe them.

Among the most influential Christian humanists were the Dutch-born Desiderius Erasmus (1466–1536) and the Englishman Thomas More (1478–1535). Erasmus demonstrated his interest in the intersection of Italian humanism and religion by his "philosophy of Christ," emphasizing education and scriptural knowledge. Equally well educated was Thomas More, who served King Henry VIII. Henry eventually ordered More's execution because of that humanist's opposition to England's break with the Catholic Church. In France, François Rabelais (ca. 1494–1553), a former monk who advocated rejecting stagnant religious dogmatism, disseminated the humanist spirit. The turmoil emerging during the sixteenth century lasted well into the seventeenth century and permanently affected the face of Europe. The concerted challenges to established authority and the persistent philosophical inquiry eventually led to the rise of new political systems (for example, the nation-state) and new economic systems (such as capitalism).

HOLY ROMAN EMPIRE (INCLUDING GERMANY)

Divergent Views on Religious Imagery

Largely because of Luther's presence, the Reformation initially had its greatest impact in the Holy Roman Empire. The seismic shifts occurring in all aspects of European life due to the Reformation affected the arts, particularly its patronage and the types of art commissioned. In addition to doctrinal differences, Catholics and Protestants took divergent stances on the role of visual imagery in religion. Catholics embraced church

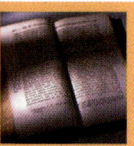

WRITTEN SOURCES

Martin Luther on Religious Art

As part of Martin Luther's quest to clarify his religious concerns and to encourage personal relationships with God, he outlined his views on religious art in his 1525 tract *Against the Heavenly Prophets in the Matter of Images and Sacraments.* He explained his attitude toward religious imagery as follows:

> I approached the task of destroying images by first tearing them out of the heart through God's Word and making them worthless and despised. . . . For when they are no longer in the heart, they can do no harm when seen with the eyes. . . . I have allowed and not forbidden the outward removal of images, so long as this takes place without rioting and uproar and is done by the proper authorities. . . .

And I say at the outset that according to the law of Moses no other images are forbidden than an image of God which one worships. A crucifix, on the other hand, or any other holy image is not forbidden. . . . However, to speak evangelically of images, I say and declare that no one is obligated to break violently images even of God, but everything is free, and one does not sin if he does not break them with violence. One is obligated, however, to destroy them with the Word of God; that is . . . with the Gospel.[1]

[1] Wolfgang Stechow, *Northern Renaissance Art 1400–1600: Sources and Documents* (Englewood Cliffs, N.J.: Prentice Hall, 1966), 129–30.

decoration as an aid to communicating with God, as seen in Italian ceiling frescoes (see FIG. 22-13; see "The Role of Religious Art in Counter-Reformation Italy," Chapter 22, page 637) and German/Polish and Spanish altarpieces (see FIGS. 20-23 and 20-27). In contrast, Protestants believed such imagery could lead to idolatry and distracted viewers from focusing on the real reason for their presence in church—to communicate directly with God (see "Martin Luther on Religious Art," above). Because of this, Protestant churches were relatively bare, and the extensive church decoration programs found especially in Italy were not as prominent in Protestant churches. This does not suggest Protestants had no use for visual images; art, especially prints (which were inexpensive and easily circulated), was a useful and effective teaching tool. The difference between Catholic and Protestant uses of art can be demonstrated by comparing two artworks, one pre-Reformation and one produced in the years after the Reformation began. Major German artists of the sixteenth century created both—Matthias Grünewald and Lucas Cranach the Elder.

VISUALIZING SICKNESS AND SALVATION MATTHIAS NEITHARDT, known conventionally as MATTHIAS GRÜNEWALD (ca. 1480–1528), worked for the archbishops of Mainz from 1511 on as court painter and decorator. He also served the archbishops as architect, hydraulic engineer, and superintendent of works. He eventually moved to northern Germany, where he settled at Halle in Saxony. Around 1510, Grünewald began work on the *Isenheim Altarpiece* (FIGS. **23-1** and **23-2**), a complex and fascinating monument.

The altarpiece, created for the monastic hospital order Saint Anthony of Isenheim, consists of a wooden shrine (carved by sculptor NIKOLAUS HAGENAUER in 1490) that includes gilded and polychromed statues of Saints Anthony Abbot, Augustine, and Jerome (FIG. 23-2). Grünewald's contribution, commissioned by the head administrator of the monastery, Guido Guersi, consists of two pairs of movable wings that open at the center. Hinged together at the sides,

one pair stands directly behind the other. Painted by Grünewald between 1510 and 1515, the exterior panels of the first pair (visible when the altarpiece is closed, FIG. 23-1) present four scenes—*Crucifixion* in the center, *Saint Sebastian* on the left and *Saint Anthony* on the right, and *Lamentation* in the predella. Opening these exterior wings, viewers encounter four additional scenes (not illustrated)—*Annunciation, Angelic Concert, Madonna and Child,* and *Resurrection.* Opening this second pair of wings reveals the interior shrine, flanked by *Meeting of Saints Anthony and Paul* and *Temptation of Saint Anthony* (FIG. 23-2).

The placement of this altarpiece in the choir of a church adjacent to the monastery hospital dictated much of the imagery. Saints associated with diseases such as the plague and with miraculous cures, such as Saint Anthony and Saint Sebastian, appear prominently both in the *Isenheim Altarpiece* and in Rogier van der Weyden's *Last Judgment Altarpiece* (see FIG. 20-7) at the Hôtel-Dieu at Beaune. Grünewald's panels, however, deal even more specifically with the themes of dire illness and miraculous healing and accordingly emphasize the suffering of the order's patron saint, Anthony. Grünewald's images served as warnings, like Rogier's *Last Judgment*, thereby encouraging increased devotion from monks and hospital patients. They also functioned therapeutically by offering some hope to the afflicted. Indeed, Saint Anthony's legend encompassed his role as both vengeful dispenser of justice (by inflicting disease) and benevolent healer. The artist enhanced the impact of this altarpiece by effectively using color. He intensified the contrasts of horror and hope by subtle tones and soft harmonies played off against shocking dissonance of color.

One of the most memorable scenes is *Temptation of Saint Anthony* (FIG. 23-2), immediately to the right of the interior sculptured shrine. It is a terrifying image of the five temptations, depicted as an assortment of ghoulish and bestial creatures in a dark landscape, attacking the saint. In the foreground Grünewald painted a grotesque image of a man, whose oozing boils, withered arm, and distended stomach all

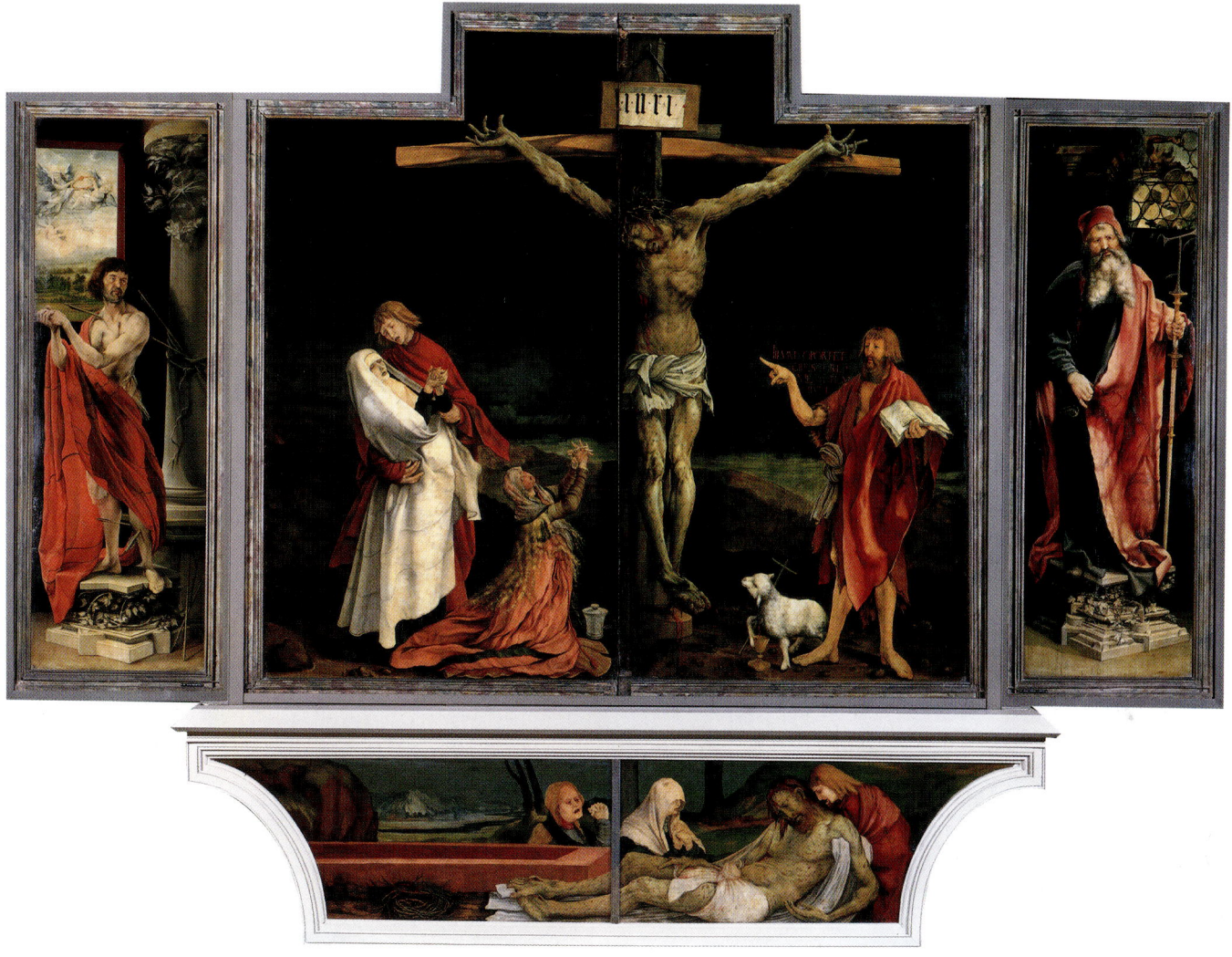

23-1 MATTHIAS GRÜNEWALD, *Isenheim Altarpiece* (closed), *Crucifixion* (center panel), from the chapel of the Hospital of Saint Anthony, Isenheim, Germany, ca. 1510–1515. Oil on panel, center panel 9′ 9½″ × 10′ 9″, each wing 8′ 2½″ × 3′ ½″, predella 2′ 5½″ × 11′ 2″. Musée d'Unterlinden, Colmar.

suggest a horrible disease. Medical experts have connected these symptoms with ergotism (a disease caused by ergot, a fungus that grows especially on rye). Although doctors did not discover the cause of this disease until about 1600, people lived in fear of its recognizable symptoms (convulsions and gangrene). The public referred to this illness as "Saint Anthony's Fire," and it was one of the major diseases treated at this hospital. The gangrene often compelled amputation, and scholars have noted that the two movable halves of the altarpiece's predella, if slid apart, make it appear as if Christ's legs have been amputated. The same observation can be made with regard to the two main exterior panels. Due to the off-center placement of the cross, opening the left panel "severs" one arm from the crucified figure.

Thus, Grünewald carefully selected and presented his altarpiece's iconography to be particularly meaningful for viewers at this hospital. In the interior shrine, the artist balanced the horrors of the disease and the punishments that awaited those who did not repent with scenes such as the *Meeting of Saints Anthony and Paul,* depicting the two saints, healthy and aged, conversing peacefully. Even the exterior panels (the closed altarpiece) convey these same concerns. The *Crucifixion* empha-

sizes Christ's pain and suffering, but the knowledge that this act redeemed humanity tempers the misery. In addition, Saint Anthony appears in the right wing as a devout follower of Christ who, like Christ and for Christ, endured intense suffering for his faith. As such, Saint Anthony's presence on the exterior reinforces the themes Grünewald intertwined throughout this entire altarpiece—themes of pain, illness, and death, as well as those of hope, comfort, and salvation.

The Protestant faith had not been formally established when Hagenauer and Grünewald produced the *Isenheim Altarpiece,* and the complexity and monumentality of the altarpiece must be viewed as Catholic in orientation. Further, Grünewald incorporated several references to Catholic doctrines, such as the lamb (symbol of the Son of God), whose wound spurts blood into a chalice in the exterior *Crucifixion* scene.

CATHOLICISM VERSUS PROTESTANTISM *Allegory of Law and Grace* (FIG. **23-3**; see "The Uses of Allegory," page 700) by LUCAS CRANACH THE ELDER (1472–1553) provides a meaningful contrast to the grandiose *Isenheim Altarpiece.* Produced in the years after the Reformation began,

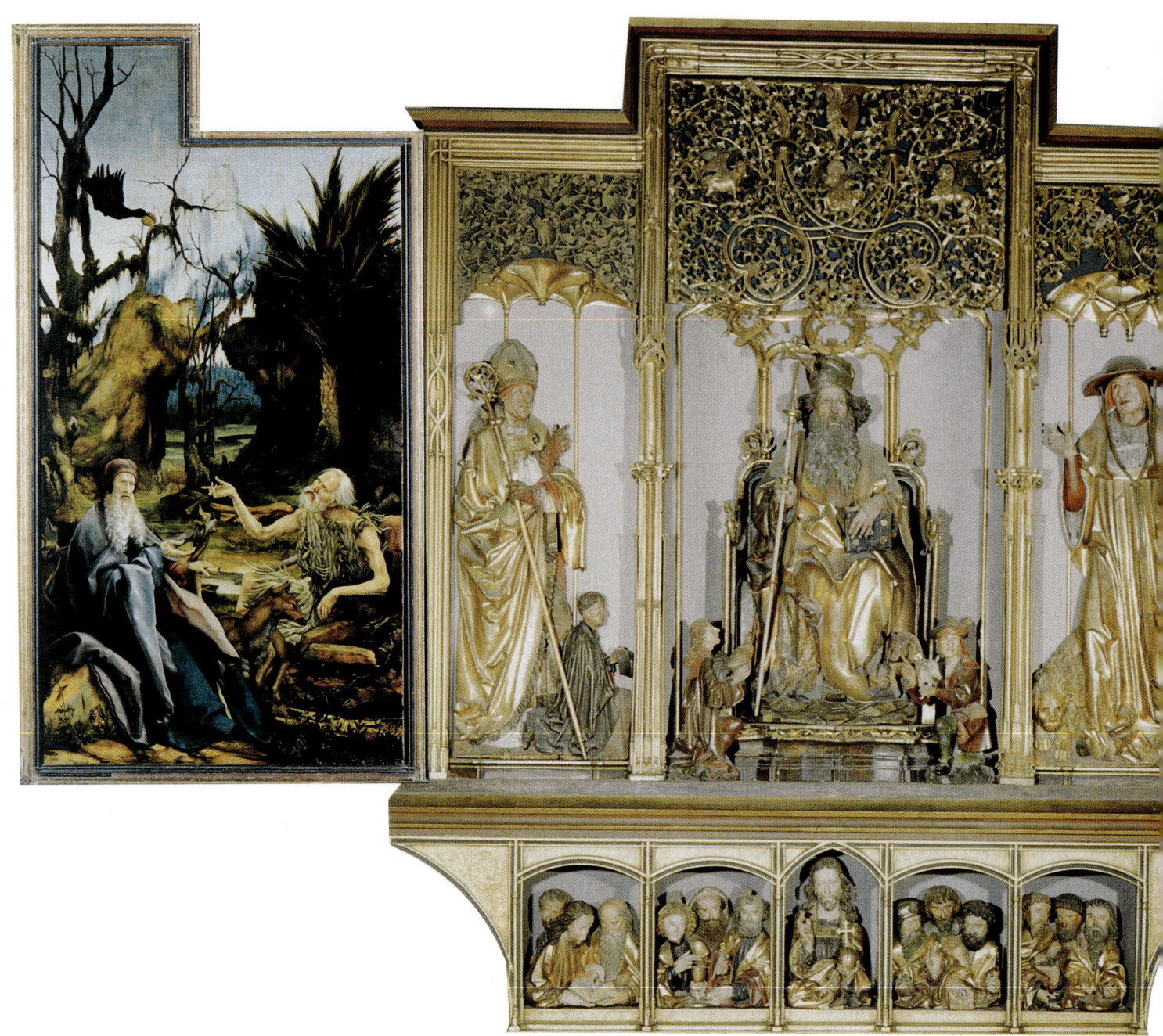

Allegory is a small woodcut print. In the early sixteenth century, northern Europe underwent a transition from handwritten manuscript (for example, illuminated manuscripts) to print media. In addition, the Protestant restrictions against visual imagery inhibited the production of large-scale altarpieces. However, Protestants viewed low-key images such as woodcut prints as useful devotional aids. Prints provided a prime opportunity for "educating the masses," because artists could print them easily, allowing the artists to sell numerous copies and to circulate them widely. In addition, woodcuts were among the least expensive of all the art forms, making them accessible to a wider audience than traditionally commissioned art, such as paintings or sculptures.

At Wittenberg, Cranach became a friend and follower of Martin Luther; indeed, his close association with Luther and the degree Luther influenced (if not guided) his imagery led scholars to refer to Cranach as the "painter of the Reformation." In *Allegory of Law and Grace,* Cranach visualized the differences between Catholicism (based on Old Testament Law, according to Luther) and Protestantism (based on a belief in God's grace) in two images separated by a centrally placed tree. On the left half, Judgment Day has arrived, as represented by Christ's appearance at the top of the scene, hovering amid a cloud halo and accompanied by angels and saints. Christ raises his left hand in the traditional gesture of damnation, and, below, a skeleton drives off a terrified person to burn for all eternity in Hell. This person tried to live a good and honorable life, but, despite his efforts, he fell short. Moses stands to the side, holding the Tablets of the Law — the commandments Catholics follow in their attempt to attain salvation. In contrast to this Catholic reliance on good works and clean living, the Protestants emphasized God's grace as the source of redemption. Accordingly, God showers the sinner in the right half of the print with grace, as streams of blood flow from the crucified Christ. On the far right, Christ emerges from the tomb and promises salvation to all who believe in him.

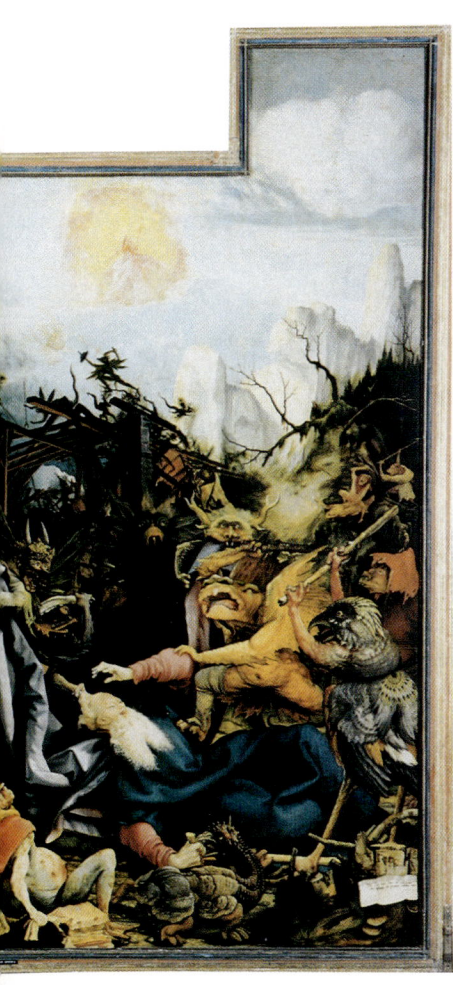

23-2 MATTHIAS GRÜNEWALD, *Isenheim Altarpiece* (open), center shrine carved by Nikolaus Hagenauer in 1490, from the chapel of the Hospital of Saint Anthony, Isenheim, Germany, ca. 1510–1515. Oil on panel, center panel 9′ 9½″ × 10′ 9″, each wing 8′ 2½″ × 3′ ½″, predella 2′ 5½″ × 11′ 2″. Musée d'Unterlinden, Colmar.

through his correspondence, and through a carefully kept, quite detailed, and eminently readable diary.

SUPPORTING THE LUTHERAN CAUSE A native of Nuremberg, one of the major cities in the Holy Roman Empire and a center of the Reformation, Dürer immersed himself in the current religious debates. Many of his works reveal his Lutheran sympathies. *Last Supper* (FIG. **23-4**) is a woodcut Dürer produced six years after Luther's issuance of his Ninety-Five Theses. Dürer's treatment of this traditional subject (see FIGS. 21-39 and 22-3) alludes to Lutheran doctrine about Communion, one of the sacraments. Rather than promote the doctrine of transubstantiation, the Catholic belief that when consecrated by the priest, the bread (Eucharist) and wine literally, miraculously, become the Body and Blood of Christ (see FIG. 24-20), Luther insisted Communion was commemorative, not a reenactment.

Dürer depicts this distinction in his *Last Supper*. The narrative moment he represented emphasizes sorrow and community; Christ has announced the betrayal, and only eleven disciples remain with Christ. The bread and wine appear prominently in the print's lower right corner, and the empty plate in the foreground refers to the commemorative, rather than literal, nature of Christ's sacrifice in the Mass. Traditional depictions often had a slaughtered lamb on the plate, conspicuously absent here.

The style of this woodcut is simple and straightforward. Compositionally, Dürer presented the figures in a conventional manner, seated behind a long horizontally placed table. Parallel lines extend throughout the entire image, with areas of crosshatching suggesting three-dimensionality. The regularity of the lines creates an evenness of value, contributing to the image's cohesiveness and directness.

EMPHASIZING THE BIBLE Dürer's support for Lutheranism surfaces in his painting *Four Apostles* (FIG. **23-5**). That he produced this work without commission and presented the two panels to the city fathers of Nuremberg in 1526 to be hung in the city hall suggests this work reflected his personal attitudes. John and Peter appear on the left panel, Mark and Paul on the right. The title, it can be argued, is something of a misnomer; Mark was an evangelist, despite conventional reference to him as an apostle. Dürer conveyed this painting's Lutheran orientation by his positioning of the figures; he relegated Saint Peter (as representative of the pope in Rome) to a secondary role by placing him behind John the Evangelist. John assumed particular prominence for Luther because of the evangelist's focus on Christ's person in his Gospel. In addition, Peter and John both read from the Bible, the single authoritative source of religious truth, according to Luther. Dürer emphasized the Bible's centrality by depicting it open to the legible passage "In the beginning was the Word, and the Word was with God, and the Word was God" (John 1:1). On the frames, Dürer included quotations from each of the Four Apostles' books in the German of Luther's translation of the New Testament. The excerpts warn against the coming of perilous times and the preaching of false prophets who will distort God's word. The individuality of each of the four men's faces, along with the detailed depiction of their attire and attributes, communicate an integrity and spirituality.

Widespread Acclaim for Exceptional Talent

The artist dominating the early sixteenth-century in the Holy Roman Empire was Grünewald's contemporary, ALBRECHT DÜRER (1471–1528). Dürer was the first artist outside Italy to become an international art celebrity. Well traveled and widely admired, he knew many of the leading humanists and artists of his time, among them Erasmus of Rotterdam and Giovanni Bellini. A man of exceptional talents and tremendous energy, Dürer achieved widespread fame in his own time and a lofty reputation ever since. Like Leonardo da Vinci, Dürer wrote theoretical treatises on a variety of subjects, such as perspective, fortification, and the ideal in human proportions. Unlike Leonardo, he both finished and published his writings. Through his prints, he exerted strong influence throughout Europe, especially in Flanders but also in Italy. Moreover, he was the first northern artist to leave a record of his life and career through several excellent self-portraits,

23-3 Lucas Cranach the Elder, *Allegory of Law and Grace,* ca. 1530. Woodcut, $10\frac{5}{8}''\times 1'\ \frac{3}{4}''$. British Museum, London.

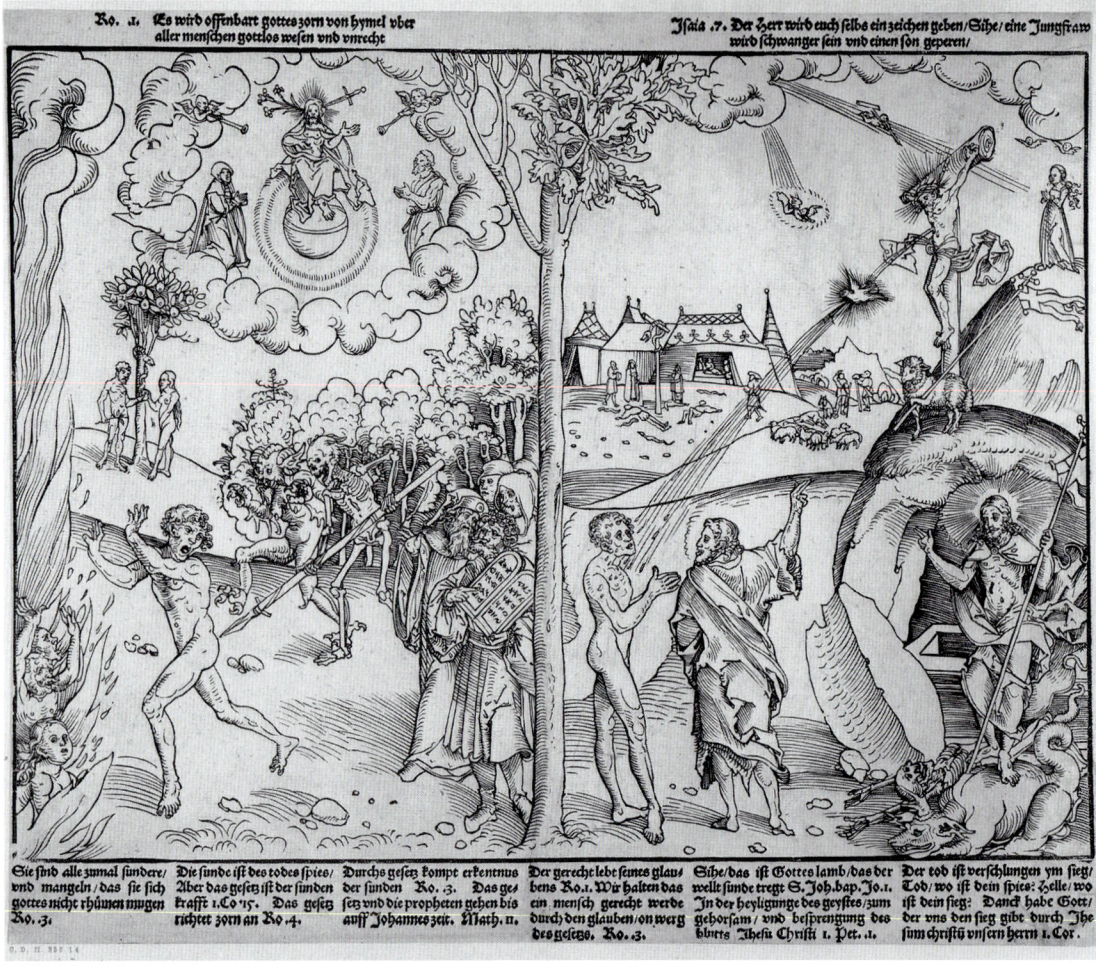

23-4 Albrecht Dürer, *Last Supper,* 1523. Woodcut, $8\frac{3}{8}''\times 11\frac{13}{16}''$. British Museum, London.

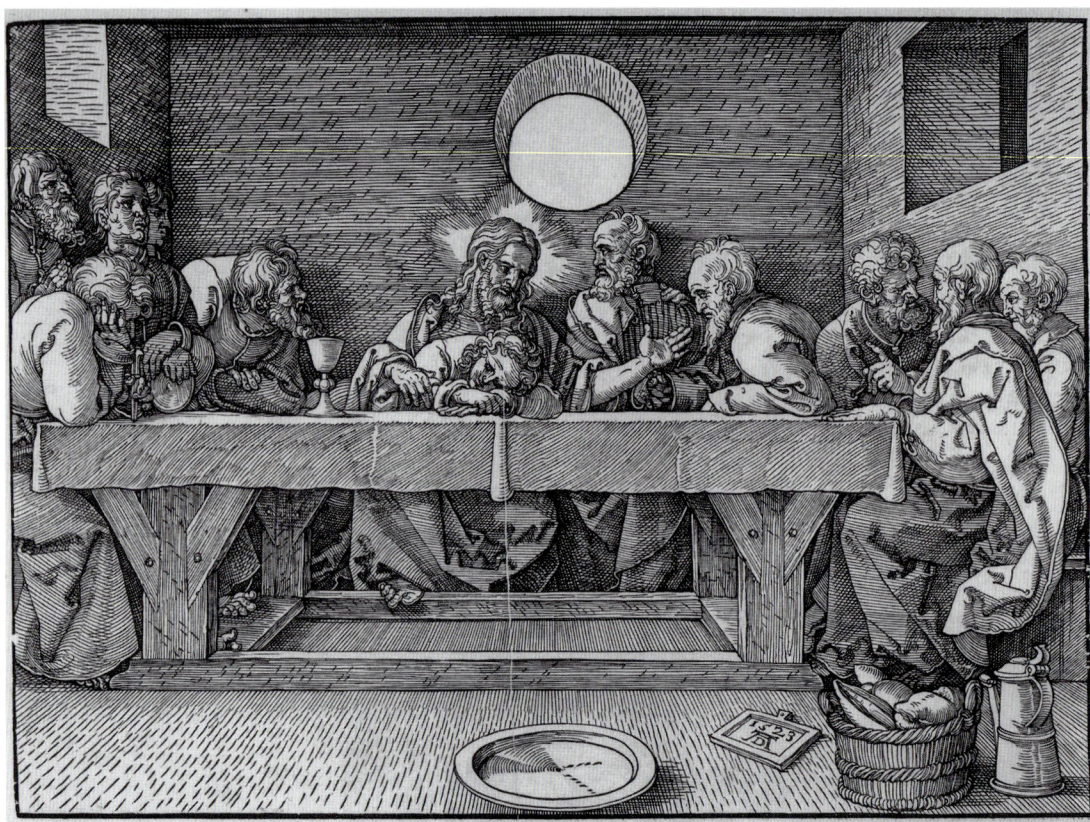

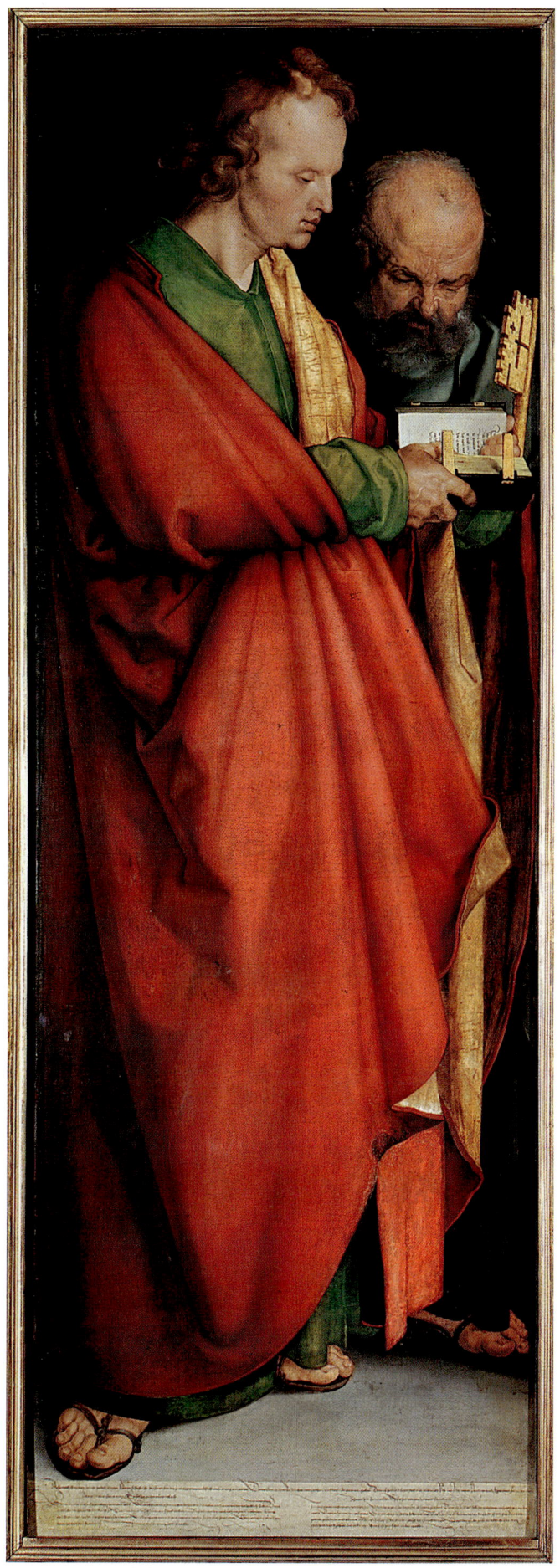
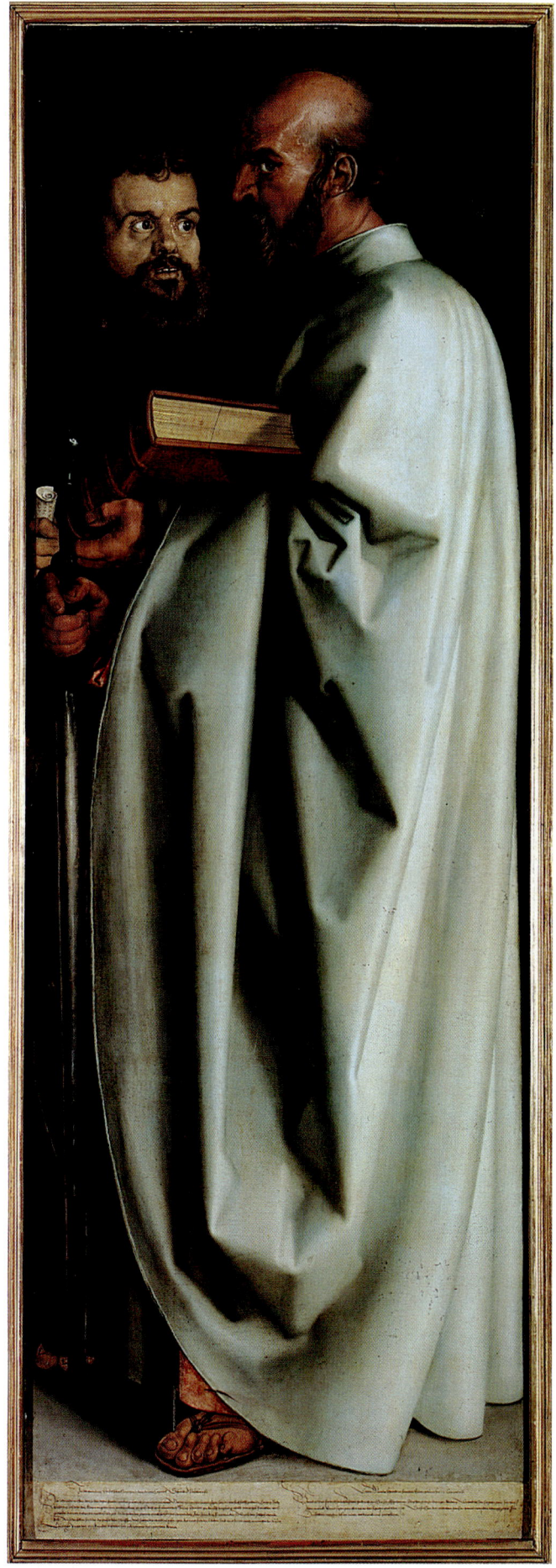

23-5 ALBRECHT DÜRER, *Four Apostles*, 1526. Oil on panel, each panel 7′ 1″ × 2′ 6″. Alte Pinakothek, Munich.

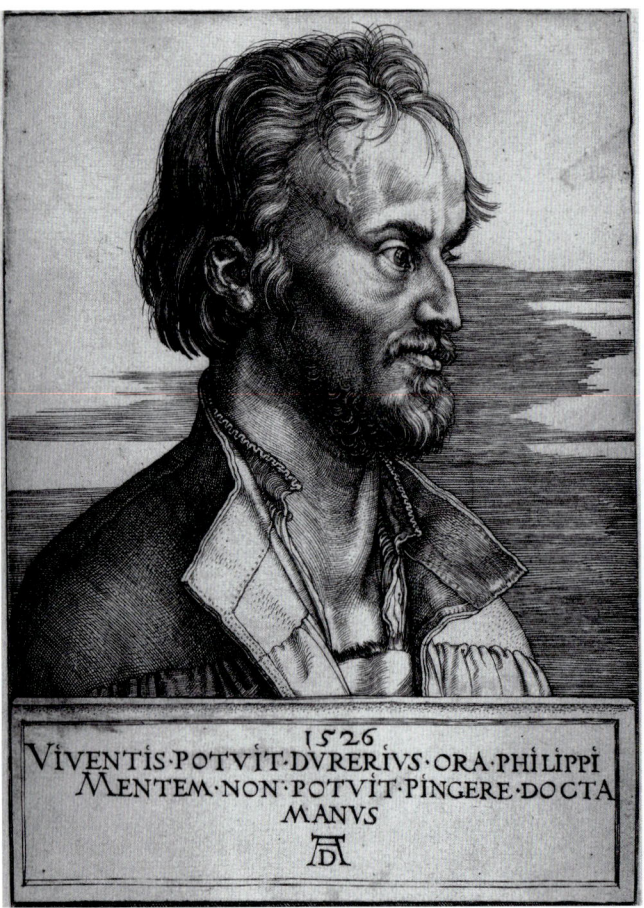

23-6 ALBRECHT DÜRER, *Philipp Melanchthon*, 1526. Engraving, $6\frac{7}{8}''$ × $5\frac{1}{16}''$. British Museum, London.

making, he developed an extraordinary proficiency in handling the burin, the engraving tool. This technical ability, combined with a feeling for the form-creating possibilities of line, enabled him to produce a body of graphic work in woodcut and engraving that seldom has been rivaled for quality and number. In addition to illustrations for books, Dürer circulated and sold prints in single sheets, which people of ordinary means could buy, expanding his audience considerably. The sale of prints also made him a wealthy man.

CLASSICAL IDEAS IN THE NORTH   Fascinated with classical ideas as transmitted through Italian Renaissance artists, Dürer was among the first northern artists to travel to Italy expressly to study Italian art and its underlying theories at their source. After his first journey in 1494–1495 (the second was in 1505–1506), he incorporated many Italian Renaissance developments into his art. Art historians have acclaimed Dürer as the first northern artist to understand fully the basic aims of the Renaissance in Italy.

An engraving, *The Fall of Man (Adam and Eve)*, FIG. **23-7**, represents the first distillation of his studies of the Vitruvian theory of human proportions, a theory based on arithmetic ratios. Clearly outlined against a northern forest's dark background, the two idealized figures of Adam and Eve stand in poses reminiscent of *Apollo Belvedere* (see FIG. Intro-7) and *Medici Venus* (not shown)—two ancient statues probably known to Dürer through graphic representations. Preceded by numerous geometric drawings, the artist's attempts to systematize sets of ideal human proportions in balanced contrapposto poses, the final print presents Dürer's 1504 concept of the "perfect" male and female figures. Yet Dürer tempered this idealization with naturalism—a commitment to observation.

Dürer demonstrated his well-honed observational skills in his rendering of the background foliage and animals. The gnarled bark of the trees and the feathery leaves authenticate the scene, as do the various creatures skulking underfoot. The animals populating the print are symbolic. The choleric cat, the melancholic elk, the sanguine rabbit, and the phlegmatic ox represent humanity's temperaments based on the "four humors," bodily fluids named by the ancient Greek physician Empedocles and a theory practiced in medieval physiology. The tension between cat and mouse in the foreground symbolizes the relation between Adam and Eve at the crucial moment in *The Fall of Man*.

Dürer agreed with Aristotle (and the new Renaissance critics) that "sight is the noblest sense of man."[2] Nature holds the beautiful, Dürer said, for the artist who has the insight to extract it. Thus, beauty lies even in humble, perhaps ugly, things, and the ideal, which bypasses or improves on nature, may not be truly beautiful in the end. Uncomposed and ordinary nature might be a reasonable object of an artist's interest, quite as much as its composed and measured aspect.

A PROTESTANT PORTRAIT OF INTELLECT Dürer also manifested his Lutheran sympathies in his portraits, which convey not only physical likeness but individual character as well. In addition to portraits of Reformation figures such as Erasmus, Dürer produced *Philipp Melanchthon* (FIG. **23-6**), an engraving of a scholar. Melanchthon (1497–1560) had arrived in Wittenberg in 1518 to teach Greek and Hebrew, but Luther's ideas captivated him, and he became a staunch supporter. Melanchthon established himself as a respected scholar, well known for reforming the German educational system. The practice of portraying such influential figures became common after Protestant leaders opposed the veneration of religious figures. Dürer depicted Melanchthon as a thoughtful, serious individual. Dürer's emphasis on Melanchthon's facial features refers to the sitter's intellect. In one of Melanchthon's eyes, a reflection of a window appears, perhaps a visualization of the notion of the eye as the window of the soul. Yet Dürer also humbly acknowledged the limitations of conventional portraiture—the inscription, in Latin, reads: "Dürer was able to depict Philipp's features as if living, but the practised hand could not portray his soul." Despite the artist's humility, he captured for perpetuity—immortalized—Philipp Melanchthon.

Through prints such as *Philipp Melanchthon*, Dürer became famous for his mastery of the graphic arts. Trained as a goldsmith by his father before he took up painting and print-

A PAINTING OF BOTANICAL ACCURACY Dürer allied himself with Leonardo's scientific studies when he painted an extremely precise watercolor study of a piece of turf; for both artists, observation yielded truth. Sight, sanctified by mystics such as Nicholas of Cusa and artists such as Jan van Eyck, became the secularized instrument of modern

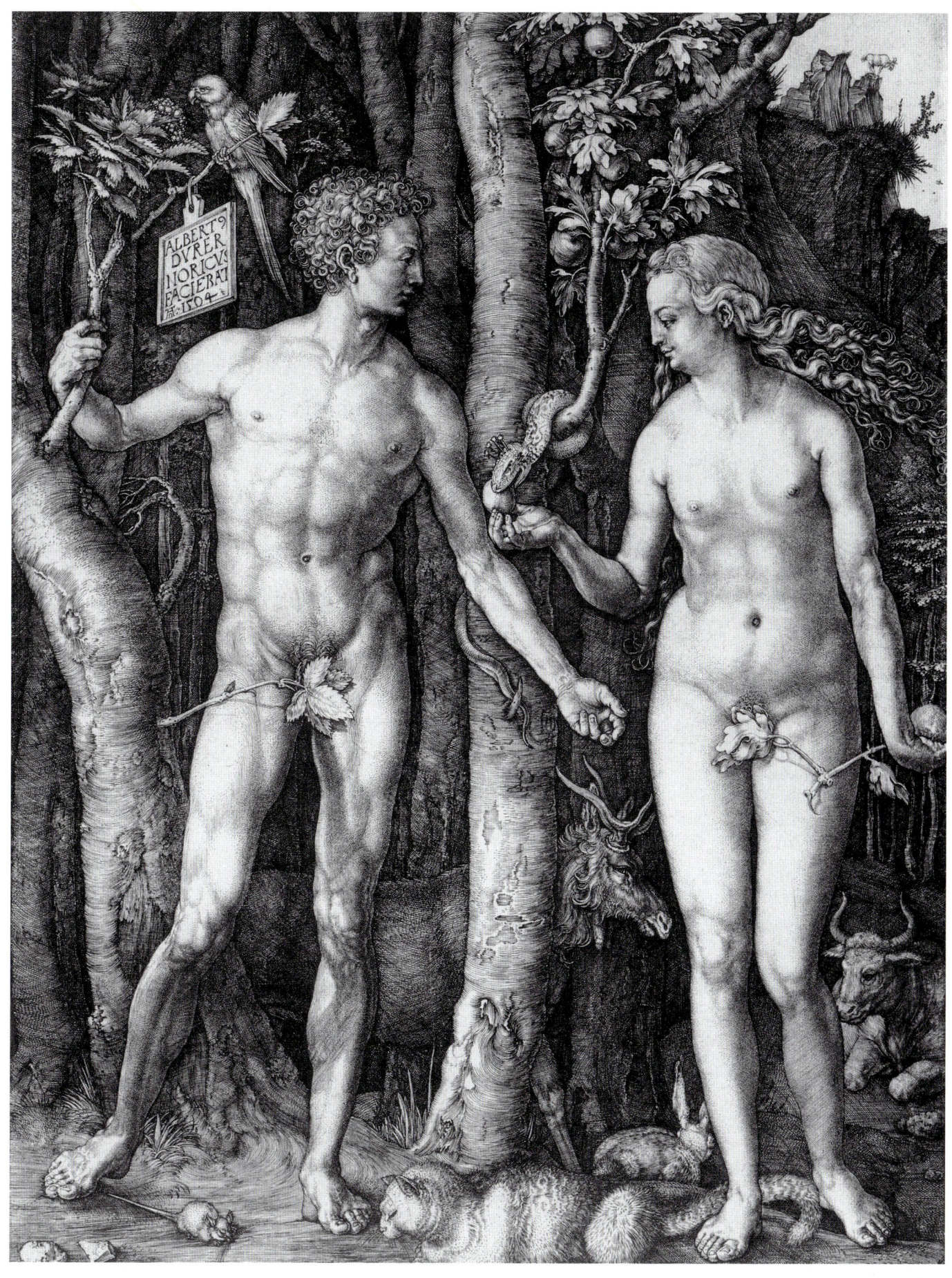

23-7 ALBRECHT DÜRER, *The Fall of Man (Adam and Eve)*, 1504. Engraving, approx. $9\frac{7}{8}'' \times 7\frac{5}{8}''$. Museum of Fine Arts, Boston (centennial gift of Landon T. Clay).

The Uses of Allegory

Western artists often employed allegory—the practice of imbuing narratives, images, or figures with symbolic meaning—to convey moral principles or philosophical ideas. For viewers to derive the deep connotations from allegorical images, the symbolic meanings of specific images had to be established as cultural convention. Among the numerous publications of Carel van Mander (1548–1606), a Netherlandish art historian and theoretician, is *Painter's Treatise* (1604), which contains a section with biographies of Netherlandish and German painters—the northern equivalent of Giorgio Vasari's *Lives of the Most Eminent Painters, Sculptors and Architects.* Van Mander outlines the functions and uses of allegory in *Handbook of Allegory,* originally published as the last section of *Painter's Treatise.* In this handbook, van Mander provides numerous examples of allegorical figures. His explication of the symbolic use of the goat and of the allegorical depiction of a common saying follow.

> The goat signifies good hearing; and some believe that she inhales and emits breath through her ears as well as through her nostrils. The goat—and this also includes the satyrs—signifies unchastity. The goat signifies the whore, who destroys the young people even as the goat gnaws off and ruins the young green sprouts. . . .
>
> In the above I have to some extent cleared the way for my young painters in order that they, without any special learning, can depict matters of significant meaning in images which all peoples with languages of their own, so far as they are at all intelligent or somewhat experienced, should be able to divine and understand; together with advice how to imagine and depict some special meaningful figures. . . . Among the common people one finds many who are amazed

when they see this kind of writing without letters, with signs or figures, in the manner of devices or verses often used by the rhetoricians. . . .

[Van Mander then takes "a common saying about the circular course of the world"—"Peace brings livelihood; livelihood, wealth; wealth, pride; pride, strife; strife, war; war, poverty; poverty, humility; humility brings peace"—and describes how a painter might render this saying allegorically through images.]

> First, peace may be represented by the cadeceus [winged staff] of Mercury or by a beehive-shaped helmet or an olive branch. Livelihood can be indicated by a coulter [plow blade], a ship's rudder, hammer, trowel, spool, and such necessary utensils, and these one could place upon the aforementioned beehive-like helmet or another peace emblem as proof that peace brings forth and supports livelihood. Above livelihood one may render wealth characterized by a purse. From the bag, or upon this purse, may rise three peacock feathers indicating pride. On the peacock feathers, loosely scattered arrows for discord or strife, with a two-headed body upon strife. A drawn bow with an arrow on the string for war. Clackdish [a dish with a moveable lid beggars often used], beggar's dish, bottle and plate for poverty that results from war. Upon poverty one may place humility, characterized by a foot stepping on a garland or a crown. This foot would then once more be followed by peace, as above; but it is unnecessary to show this again since everyone knows that it has to begin again from below, with peace as represented before.[1]

---

[1] Wolfgang Stechow, *Northern Renaissance Art 1400–1600: Sources and Documents* (Englewood Cliffs, N.J.: Prentice Hall, 1966), 71–72.

---

knowledge. The remarkable *The Great Piece of Turf* (FIG. **23-8**) is as scientifically accurate as it is poetic. Botanists can distinguish each springing plant and grass variety—dandelions, great plantain, yarrow, meadow grass, and heath rush. "[D]epart not from nature according to your fancy," Dürer said, "imagining to find aught better by yourself; . . . For verily 'art' is embedded in nature; he who can extract it, has it."[3]

ELEVATING THE ART OF ENGRAVING This lifelong interest in both idealization and naturalization surfaces in *Knight, Death, and the Devil* (FIG. **23-9**), one of three so-called Master Engravings Dürer made between 1513 and 1514. These works (the other two are *Melencolia I* and *Saint Jerome in His Study*) carry the art of engraving to the highest degree of excellence. Dürer used his burin to render differences in texture and tonal values that would be difficult to match even in the much more flexible medium of *etching* (corroding a design into metal), which artists developed later in the century. (Later in life Dürer also experimented with etching.)

Knight, Death, and the Devil depicts a mounted armored knight who rides fearlessly through a foreboding landscape. Accompanied by his faithful retriever, the knight represents a Christian knight—a soldier of God. Armed with his faith, this warrior can repel the threats of Death, who appears as a crowned decaying cadaver wreathed with snakes and shaking an hourglass as a reminder of time and mortality. The knight is equally impervious to the Devil, a pathetically hideous horned creature who follows him. The knight triumphs because he has "put on the whole armor of God that [he] may be able to stand against the wiles of the devil," as urged in Saint Paul's Epistle to the Ephesians (Eph. 6:11).

The monumental knight and his mount display the strength, movement, and proportions of the Renaissance equestrian statue. Dürer was familiar with Donatello's *Gattamelata* (see FIG. 21-32) and Verrocchio's *Bartolommeo Colleoni* (see FIG. 21-33) and had copied a number of Leonardo's sketches of horses. His highly developed feeling for the real and his meticulous rendering of it surface in the myriad details—the knight's armor and weapons, the horse's anatomy, the textures of the loathsome features of Death and the Devil, and the rock forms and rugged foliage. Dürer realized this entire range of imagery with the dense hatching of fluidly engraved lines that rivals painting's tonal range. Erasmus could rightly compliment Dürer as the "Apelles [the ancient Greek master of painting] of black lines."[4]

Dürer's use of line, whether in oil, watercolor, woodcut, or engraving, was truly exceptional. He employed line not simply to describe but to evoke as well. This ability extended beyond his impressive technical facility with the different mediums. For example, in his woodcut *The Four Horsemen* (see FIG. Intro-9), Dürer created an image of pandemonium and doom as Death, Famine, War, and Pestilence wreak havoc on society. The lines that undulate and often shift direction abruptly contribute to the scene's energy. Further, Dürer's modulation of his lines, which swell, taper, and break, along with his careful grouping of these linear elements, create impressive light and shadow effects.

Dürer's art reveals an inspired, inquisitive mind and a phenomenally gifted talent. To this day, his work serves as a model for artists, and he deserves much of the credit for expanding graphic arts' capability of conveying intellectually and emotionally complex themes.

Commenting on History and Politics

INVOKING THE PAST TO ALTER THE FUTURE
While the prominence of Reformation concerns in the Holy Roman Empire during the sixteenth century influenced the

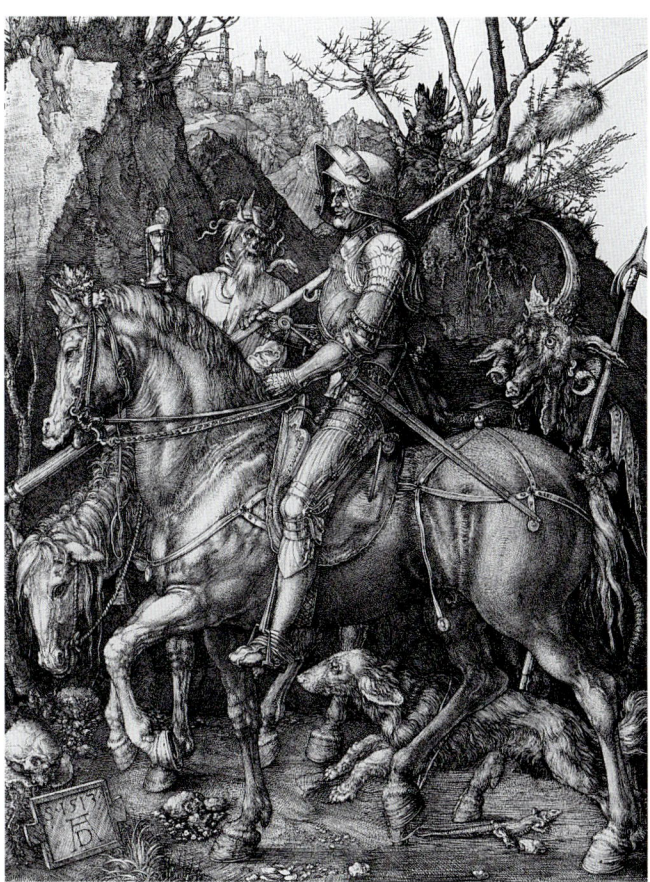

23-9 ALBRECHT DÜRER, *Knight, Death, and the Devil*, 1513. Engraving, $9\frac{5}{8}'' \times 7\frac{3}{8}''$. Metropolitan Museum of Art, New York.

period's art, artists also addressed historical and political issues. *The Battle of Issus* (FIGS. **23-10** and 5-69) by ALBRECHT ALTDORFER (ca. 1480–1538), for example, depicts the historical defeat of Darius in 333 B.C. by Alexander the Great at a town called Issus on the Pinarus River (announced in the inscription that hangs in the sky). The duke of Bavaria, Wilhelm IV, commissioned *The Battle of Issus* in 1528, concurrent with his commencement of a military campaign against the invading Turks. The parallels between the historical and contemporary conflicts were no doubt significant to the duke. Both involved societies that deemed themselves progressive engaged in battles against infidels—the Persians in 333 B.C. and the Turks in 1528. Altdorfer reinforced this connection by attiring the figures in contemporary armor and depicting them engaged in contemporary military alignments.

The scene reveals Altdorfer's love of landscape. The battle takes place in an almost cosmological setting. From a bird's eye view, the clashing armies swarm in the foreground, while in the distance craggy mountain peaks rise next to still bodies of water. Amid swirling clouds, a blazing sun descends. Despite the awesome spectacle of the topography, the artist used available historical information to produce this painting. Altdorfer derived his depiction of the landscape from maps. Specifically, he set the scene in the eastern Mediterranean with a view from Greece to the Nile in Egypt. In addition, Altdorfer may have acquired his information about this battle from an account written by Johannes Aventinus, a German scholar. In his text, Aventinus describes the bloody daylong battle and Alexander's ultimate victory. Appropriately, given Alexander's

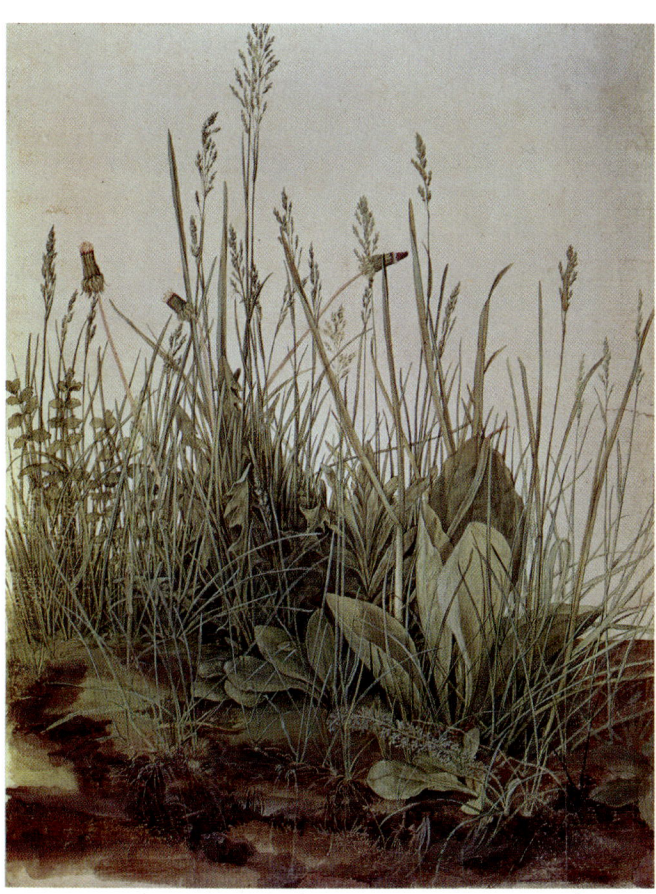

23-8 ALBRECHT DÜRER, *The Great Piece of Turf,* 1503. Watercolor, approx. $1' \, 4'' \times 1' \, \frac{1}{2}''$. Graphische Sammlung Albertina, Vienna.

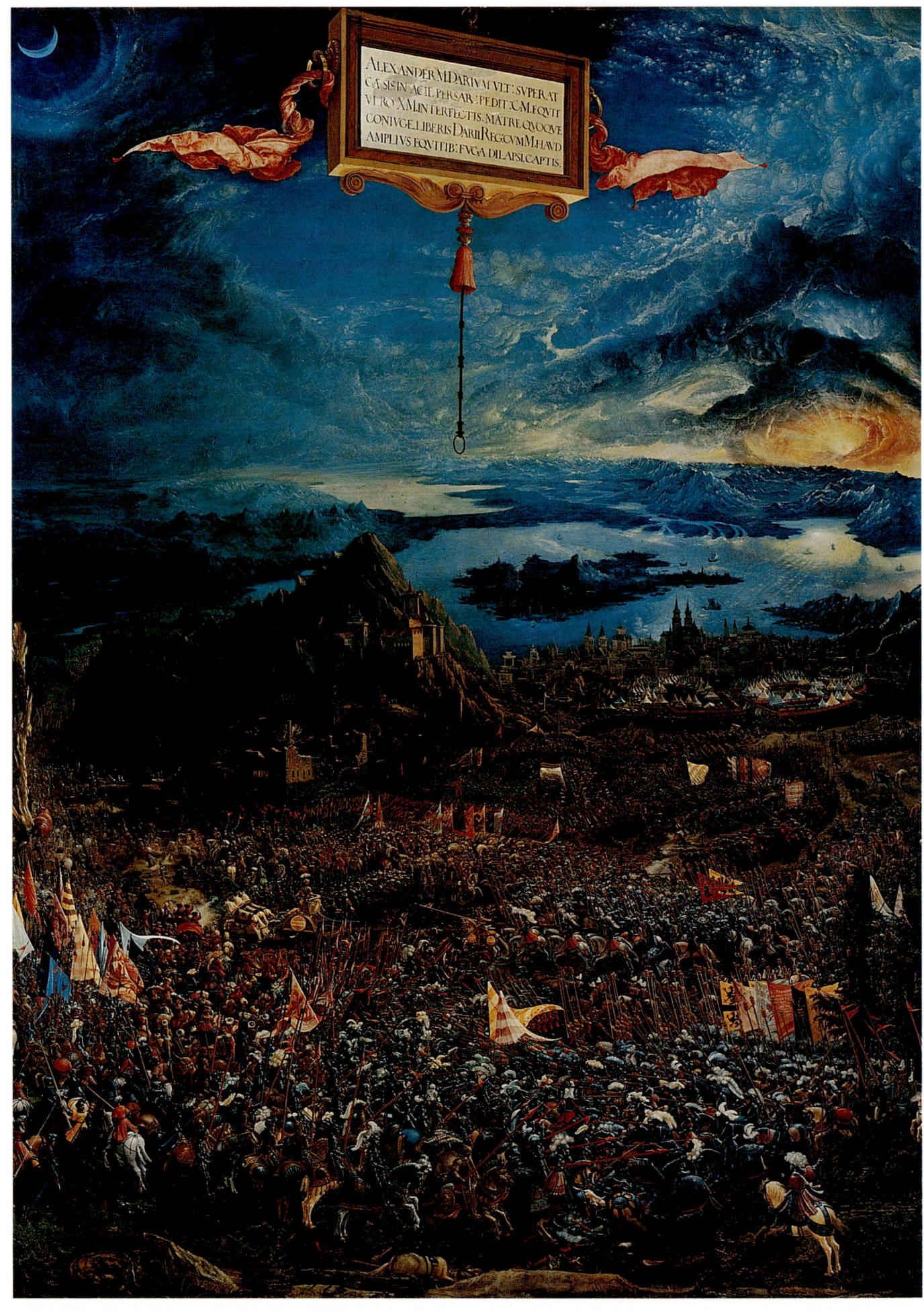

23-10 ALBRECHT ALTDORFER, *The Battle of Issus,* 1529. Oil on panel, 4′ 4¼″ × 3′ 11¼″. Alte Pinakothek, Munich.

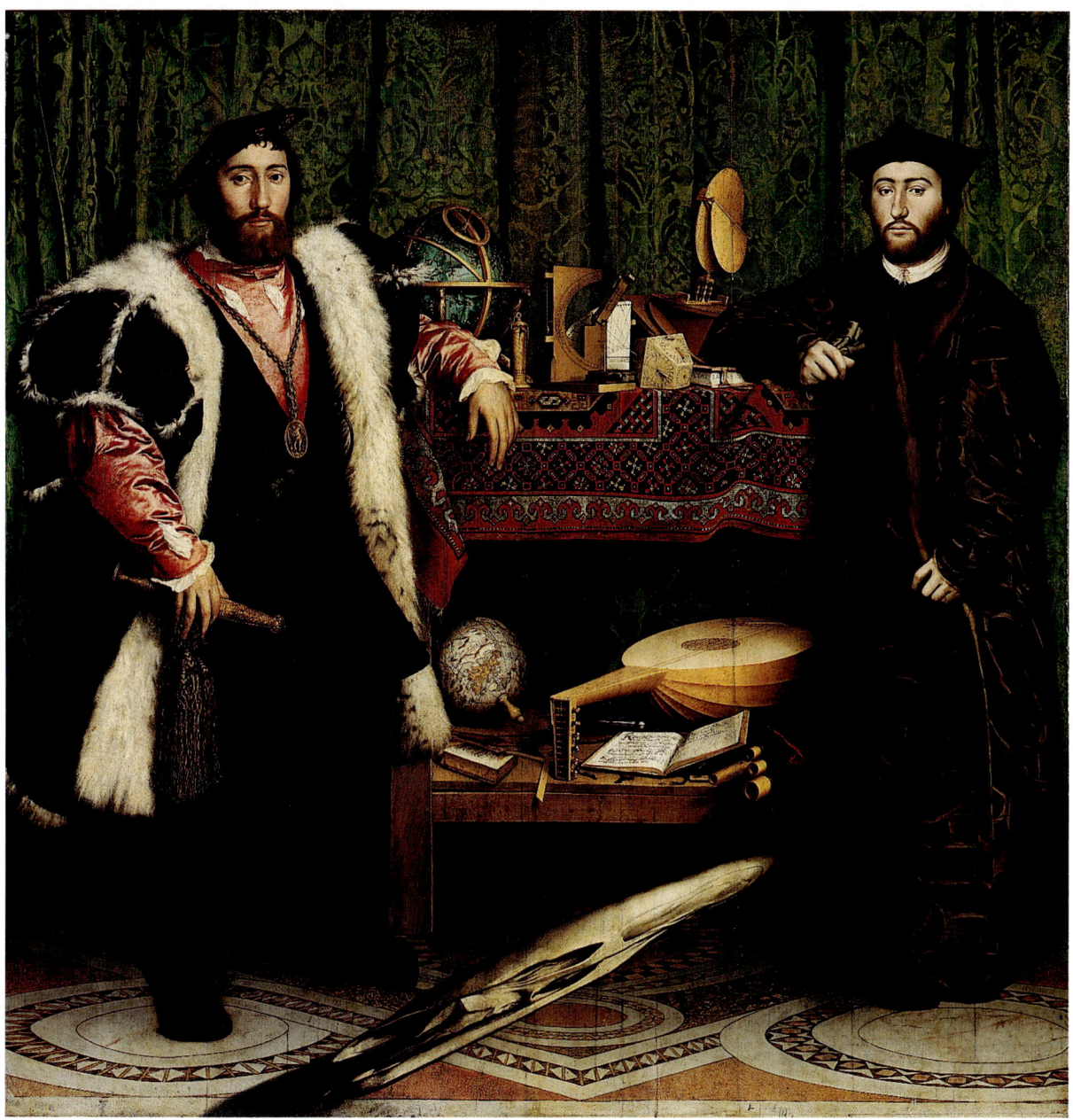

23-11 HANS HOLBEIN THE YOUNGER, *The French Ambassadors,* 1533. Oil and tempera on panel, approx. 6′ 8″ × 6′ 9½″. National Gallery, London.

designation as the "sun god," the sun sets over the victorious Greeks on the right, while a small crescent moon (a symbol of the Near East) hovers in the upper left corner over the retreating Persians.

A DIPLOMATIC SOLUTION Choosing less dramatic scenes, HANS HOLBEIN THE YOUNGER (ca. 1497–1543) excelled as a portraitist. Trained by his father, Holbein produced portraits that reflected the northern tradition of close realism that had emerged in fifteenth-century Flemish art. Yet he also incorporated Italian ideas about monumental composition, bodily structure, and sculpturesque form. The color surfaces of his paintings are as lustrous as enamel, his detail is exact and exquisitely drawn, and his contrasts of light and dark are never heavy.

Holbein began his artistic career in Basel, where he knew Erasmus of Rotterdam. Due to the immediate threat of a religious civil war in Basel, Erasmus suggested Holbein leave for England and gave him a recommendation to Thomas More, chancellor of England under Henry VIII. Holbein did move and became painter to the English court. While there, he produced a superb double portrait of the French ambassadors to England, Jean de Dinteville and Georges de Selve (FIG. **23-11**). *The French Ambassadors* exhibits Holbein's considerable talents—his strong sense of composition, his subtle linear patterning, his gift for portraiture, his marvelous sensitivity to color, and his faultlessly firm technique. This painting may have been Holbein's favorite; it is the only one signed with his full name. The two men, both ardent humanists, stand at each end of a side table covered with an oriental rug and a collection of objects reflective of their worldliness and interest in learning and the arts. These include mathematical and astronomical models and implements, a lute with a broken string, compasses, a sundial, flutes, globes, and an open hymnbook with Luther's translation of *Veni, Creator Spiritus* and of the Ten Commandments.

Of particular interest is the long gray shape that slashes diagonally across the picture plane and interrupts the stable, balanced, and serene composition. This form is an *anamorphic* image, a distorted image recognizable when viewed with a special device, such as a cylindrical mirror, or by viewing the painting at an acute angle. Viewing this painting while standing off to the right reveals this gray slash is a skull. Although scholars do not agree on this skull's meaning, at the very least, it certainly refers to death. Artists commonly incorporated skulls into paintings as reminders of mortality; indeed, Holbein depicted a skull on the metal medallion on Jean de Dinteville's hat. Holbein may have intended the skulls, in conjunction with the crucifix that appears half hidden behind the curtain in the upper left corner, to encourage viewers to ponder death and resurrection.

This painting may allude to the growing tension between secular and religious authorities; Jean de Dinteville was a titled landowner, while Georges de Selve was a bishop. The inclusion of Luther's translations next to the lute with the broken string (a symbol of discord) may also subtly refer to the religious strife. Despite scholars' uncertainty about the precise meaning of *The French Ambassadors*, it is a painting of supreme artistic achievement. Holbein rendered the still-life objects with the same meticulous care as the men themselves, as the woven design of the deep emerald curtain behind them, and as the floor tiles, constructed in faultless perspective. He surely hoped this painting's elegance and virtuosity of skill (produced shortly after Holbein arrived in England) would impress Henry VIII.

FRANCE

As *The French Ambassadors* illustrates, France in the early sixteenth century worked to secure widespread recognition as a political power. Decisive kings reorganized the country, which had been divided and harried throughout the fifteenth century. By the end of that century, France was strong enough to undertake an aggressive policy toward its neighbors. Under the rule of Francis I (r. 1515–1547), the French established a firm foothold in Milan and its environs. Francis waged a campaign (known as the Hapsburg-Valois Wars) against Charles V (the Spanish king and Holy Roman Emperor), which occupied him from 1521 to 1544. These wars erupted over disputed territories—southern France, the Netherlands, the Rhinelands, northern Spain, and Italy. Despite this distraction, Francis I also endeavored to elevate his country's cultural profile. To that end, he invited esteemed Italian artists such as Leonardo da Vinci and Andrea del Sarto to his court. Francis's attempt to glorify the state and himself meant that the religious art dominating the Middle Ages no longer prevailed, for the king and not the Christian Church held the power.

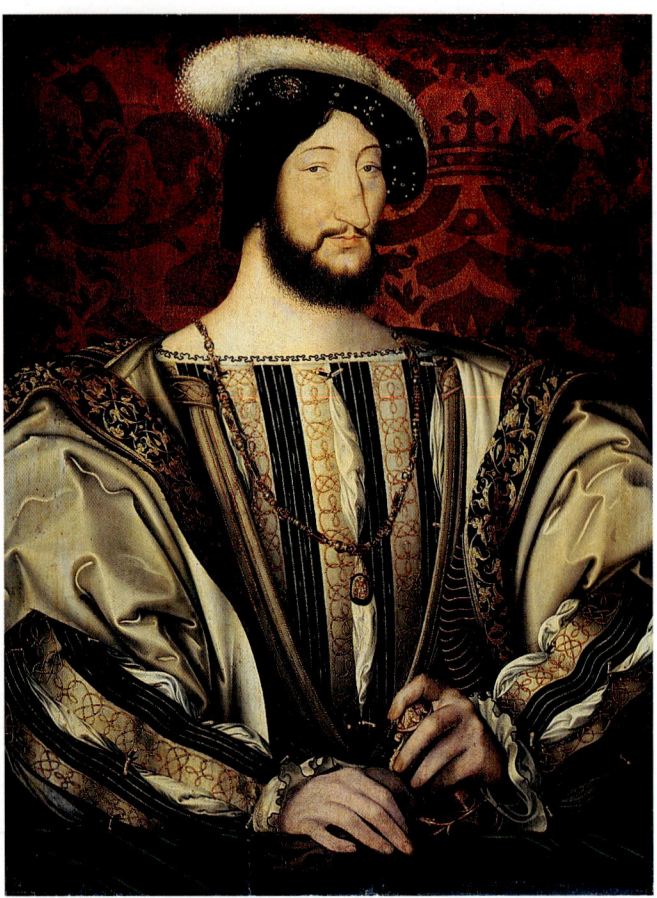

23-12 JEAN CLOUET, *Francis I*, ca. 1525–1530. Tempera and oil on panel, approx. 3′ 2″ × 2′ 5″. Louvre, Paris.

A MAGNIFICENT FRENCH MONARCH The portrait *Francis I* (FIG. **23-12**), painted by JEAN CLOUET (ca. 1485–1541), shows a worldly prince magnificently bedecked in silks and brocades, wearing a gold chain with a medallion of the Order of Saint Michael, and caressing the pommel of a dagger. Legend has it the "merry monarch" was a great lover and the hero of hundreds of "gallant" situations; appropriately, he appears suave and confident. Despite the careful detail, the portrait also exhibits an elegantly formalized quality. This characteristic is due to Clouet's suppression of modeling, resulting in a flattening of features, seen particularly in Francis's neck. The disproportion between the small size of the king's head in relation to his broad body, swathed in heavy layers of brocaded fabric, adds to the formalized nature.

A PAINTED AND PLASTERED PALACE The personal tastes of Francis and his court must have run to an art at once elegant, erotic, and unorthodox. Appropriately, Mannerism (pages 673–680) appealed to them most. Among the Italian artists who had a strong impact on French art were the Mannerists Rosso Fiorentino and Benvenuto Cellini. Rosso became the court painter of Francis I shortly after 1530. The king put ROSSO FIORENTINO (1494–1540), along with fellow Florentine FRANCESCO PRIMATICCIO (1504–1570), in charge of decorating the new royal palace at Fontainebleau. Scholars refer to the sculptors and painters who worked together on this project as the school of Fontainebleau. When Rosso and Primaticcio decorated the Gallery of King Francis I at Fontainebleau (FIG. **23-13**), they combined painting, fresco, imitation mosaic, and stucco sculpture in low and high relief. The abrupt changes in scale and texture of the figurative elements are typically Mannerist, as are the compressed space, elongated grace, and stylized poses. The formalized elegance of the paintings also appears in the stucco relief figures and caryatids, while the shift in scale between the painted and the stucco figures adds tension. The combination of painted and stucco relief decorations became extremely popular from that time on and remained a favorite ornamental technique throughout the Baroque and Rococo periods of the seventeenth and early eighteenth centuries.

CHÂTEAUX: FORTRESSES TO MANSIONS

Francis I indulged an interest in building during his reign by commissioning several large-scale châteaux, among them the Château de Chambord (FIG. **23-14**) in Chambord. Reflecting the more peaceful times, these châteaux, developed from the old countryside fortresses, served as country houses for royalty, who usually built them near forests for use as hunting lodges. Construction on Chambord began in 1519, but Francis I never saw its completion. Chambord's plan, originally drawn by a pupil of Giuliano da Sangallo, imposes Italian concepts of symmetry and balance on the irregularity of the old French fortress. A central square block with four corridors, in the shape of a cross, has a broad, central staircase that gives access to groups of rooms—ancestors of the modern suite of rooms or apartments. At each of the four corners, a round tower punctuates the square plan, and a moat surrounds the whole. From the exterior, Chambord presents a carefully contrived horizontal accent on three levels, its floors separated by continuous moldings. Windows align precisely, one exactly over another. The Italian palazzo served as the

model for this matching of horizontal and vertical features, but above the third level the structure's lines break chaotically into a jumble of high dormers, chimneys, and lanterns that recall soaring ragged Gothic silhouettes on the skyline.

REDESIGNING THE LOUVRE

Chambord essentially retains French architectural characteristics. During the reign of Francis's successor, Henry II (r. 1547–1559), however, translations of Italian architectural treatises appeared, and Italian architects themselves came to work in France. Moreover, the French turned to Italy for study and travel. Such exchanges caused a more extensive revolution in style than earlier, although certain French elements derived from the Gothic tradition persisted. This incorporation of Italian architectural ideas can be seen in the redesigning of the Louvre in Paris, originally a medieval palace and fortress. Francis I initiated this project to update and expand the royal palace but died before the work was well under way. His architect, PIERRE LESCOT (1510–1578), continued under Henry II and, with the aid of the sculptor JEAN GOUJON (ca. 1510–1565), produced the classical style later associated with sixteenth-century French architecture.

Although Chambord incorporated the formal vocabulary of the Early Renaissance, particularly from Lombardy, Lescot and his associates were familiar with the sixteenth-century Renaissance architecture of Bramante and his school. As the Square Court's west facade (FIG. **23-15**) shows, each of the Louvre's stories forms a complete order, and the cornices project enough to furnish a strong horizontal accent. The arcading on the ground story reflects the ancient Roman use of arches and produces more shadow than in the upper stories due to its recessed placement, thereby strengthening the design's visual base. On the second story, the pilasters rising from bases and the alternating curved and angular pediments supported by consoles have direct antecedents in several High

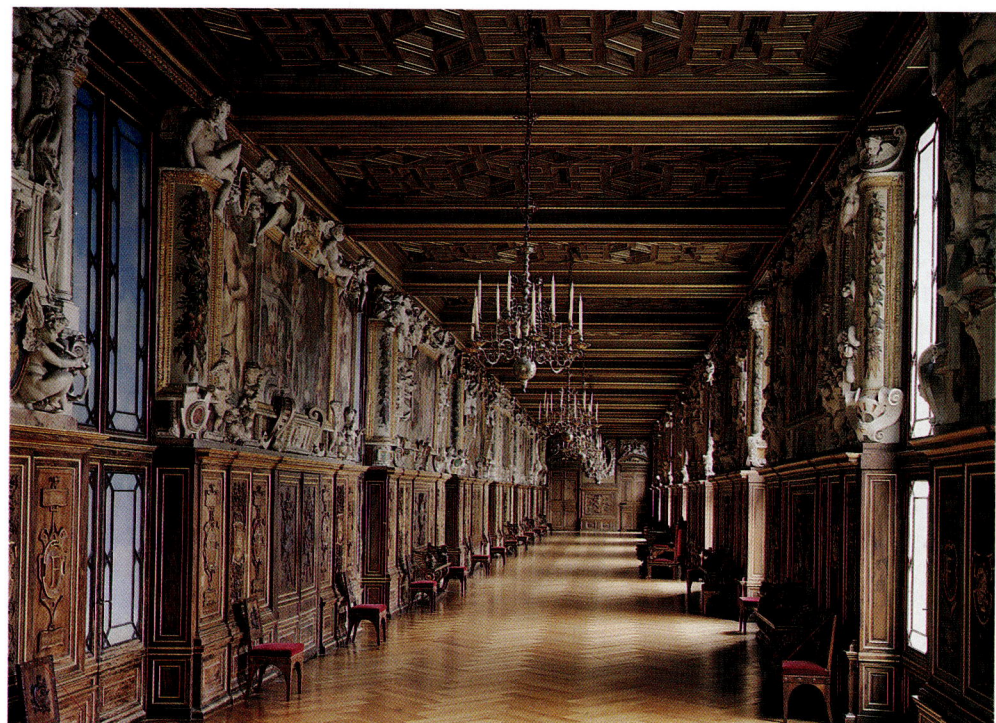

23-13 ROSSO FIORENTINO and FRANCESCO PRIMATICCIO, ensemble of architecture, sculpture, and painting, Gallery of King Francis I, Fontainebleau, France, ca. 1530–1540.

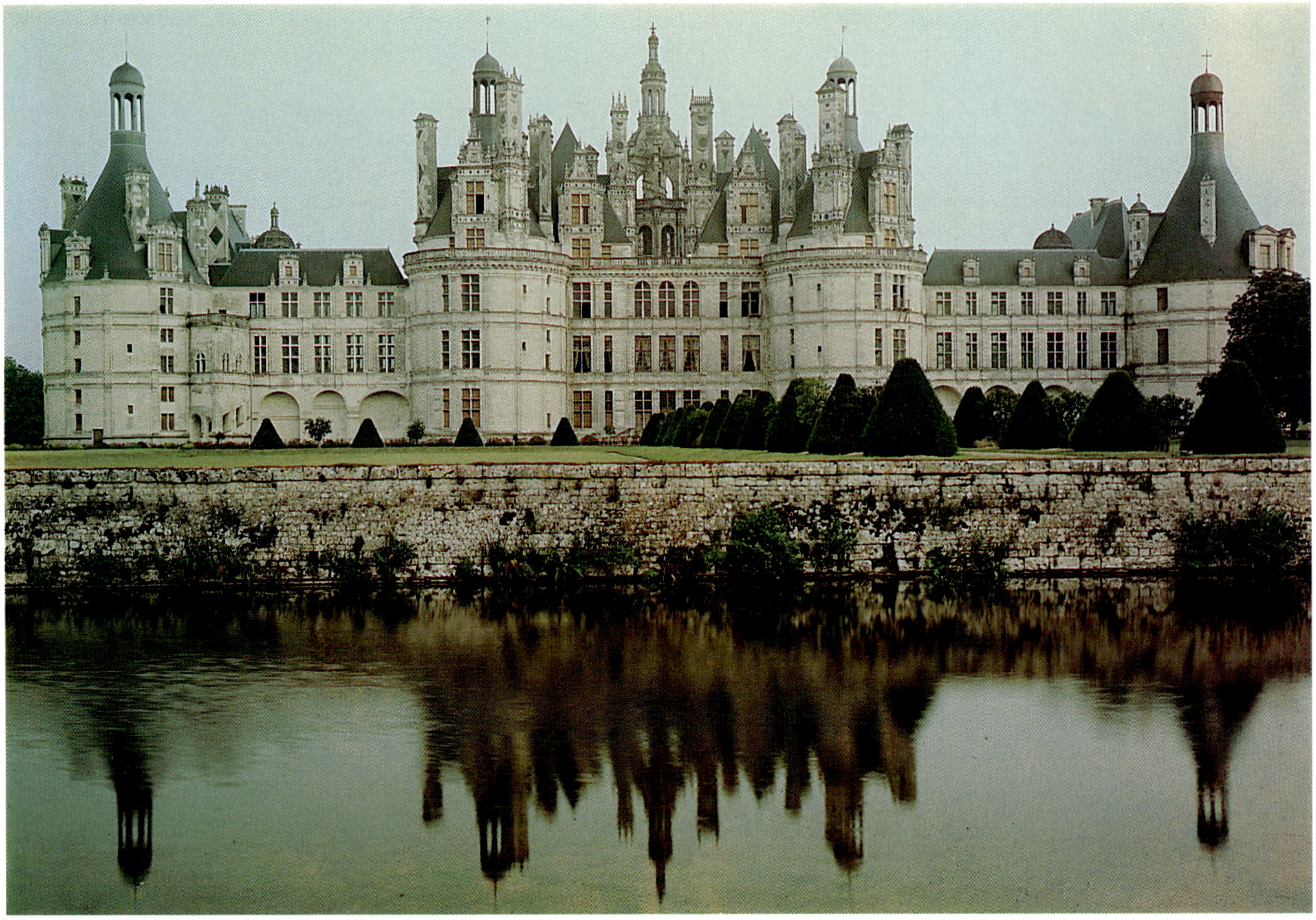

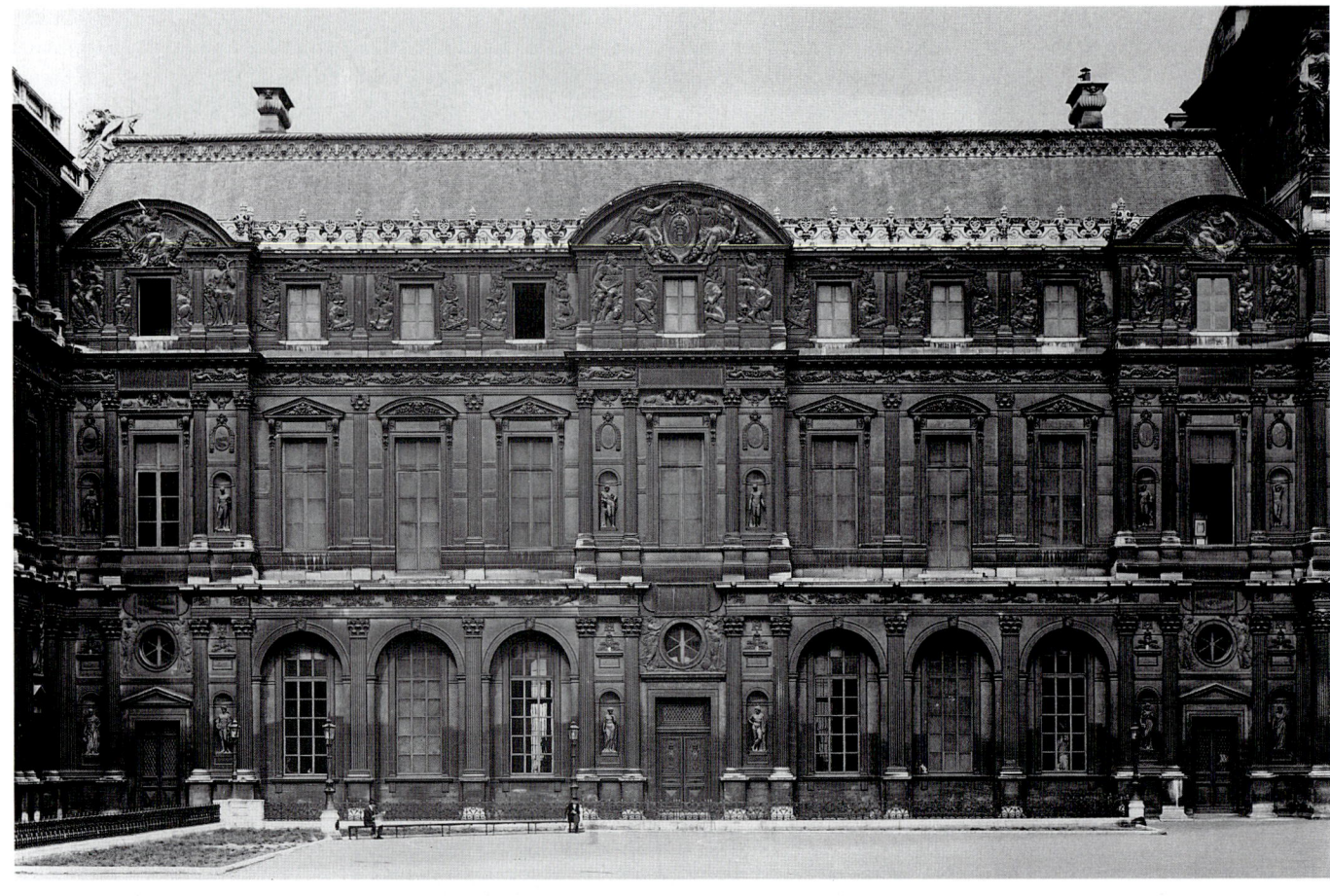

23-14 Château de Chambord, Chambord, France, begun 1519.

23-15 PIERRE LESCOT and JEAN GOUJON, west facade of the Square Court of the Louvre, Paris, France, begun 1546.

Renaissance palaces. Yet, the decreased height of the stories, the scale of the windows (proportionately much larger than in Renaissance buildings), and the steep roof suggest northern models. Especially French are the pavilions jutting from the wall. A feature the French long favored—double columns framing a niche—punctuates the pavilions. The building's vertical lines assert themselves. Openings deeply penetrate the wall, and sculptures abound. Other northern countries imitated this French classical manner—its double-columned pavilions, tall and wide windows, profuse statuary, and steep roofs—although with local variations. The modified classicism the French produced was the only classicism to serve as a model for northern architects through most of the sixteenth century. Some scholars believe the west courtyard facade of the Louvre is the best of French sixteenth-century architecture; eventually, the French purged their architecture of Italian features.

LIGHTNESS, EASE, AND GRACE The statues of the Louvre courtyard facade, now much restored, are Goujon's work. His *Nymphs* reliefs from the *Fountain of the Innocents* in Paris (FIG. **23-16**) originally decorated two facades of a fountain. Appropriately, the nymphs carry or stand next to vases of flowing water. Like the architecture of the Louvre, Goujon's nymphs recall the Italian (particularly Mannerist) canon of figural design. Certainly, their figura serpentinata poses are Mannerist. Their flowing, clinging draperies parallel the ancient "wet" drapery of Greek sculpture—the figures on the parapet of the Temple of Athena Nike (see FIG. 5-54), for example. Goujon's slender, sinuous figures perform their steps within a confined unspecified space, and they appear to make one continuous motion, an illusion produced by reversing the gestures, as they might be seen in a mirror. The style of Fontainebleau, and ultimately of Primaticcio and Cellini, guided the sculptor here, but Goujon learned the manner so

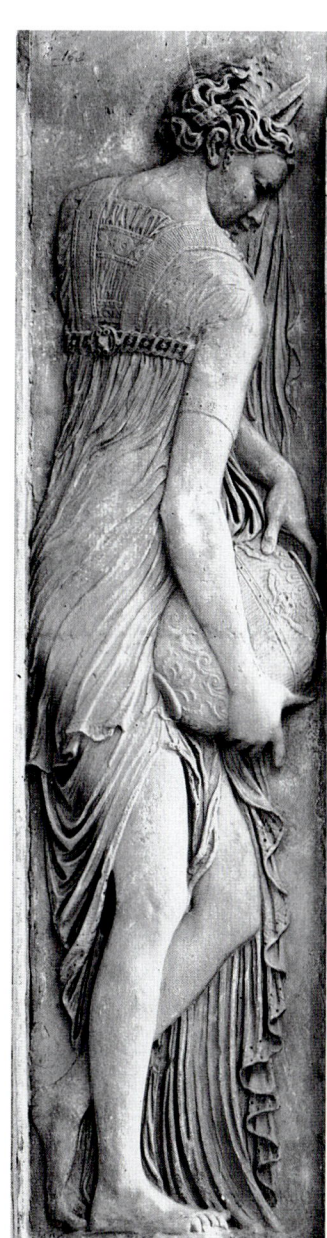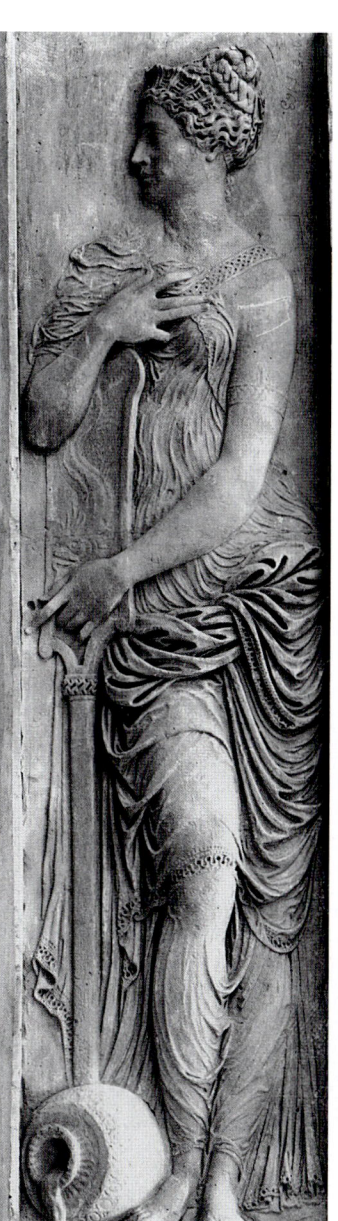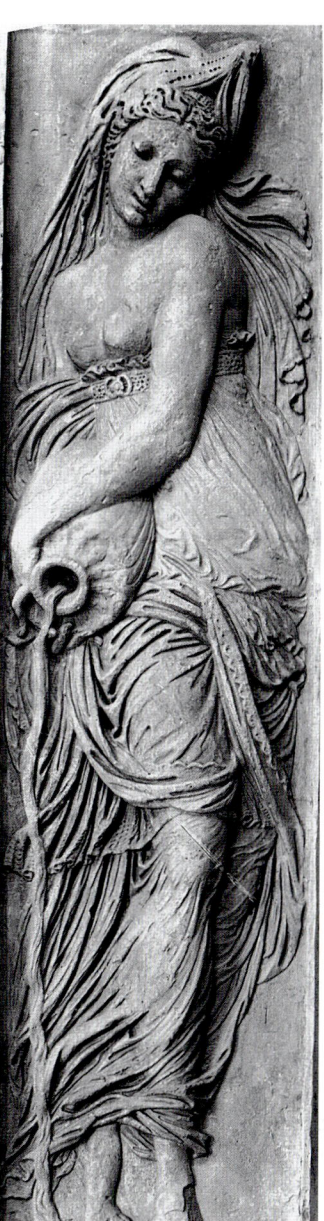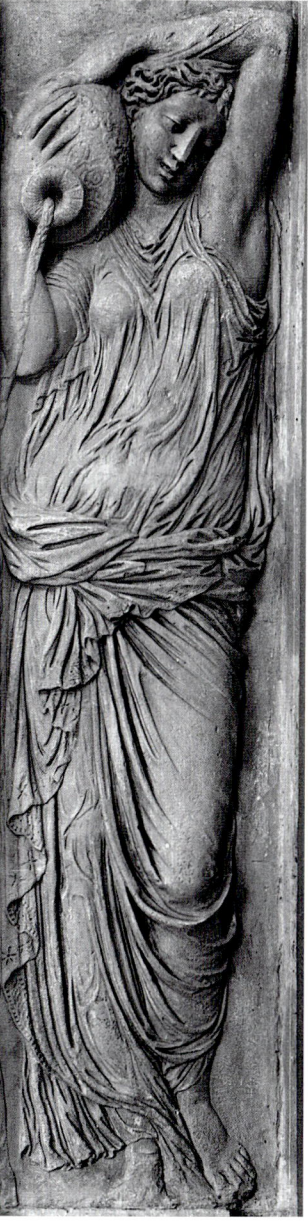

23-16 JEAN GOUJON, *Nymphs,* from the dismantled *Fountain of the Innocents,* Paris, France, 1548–1549. Marble reliefs. Each relief 6′ 4¾″ × 2′ 4¾″. Louvre, Paris.

well he created originally within it. The nymphs are truly French masterpieces, characterized by lightness, ease, and grace.

THE NETHERLANDS

With the demise of the Duchy of Burgundy in 1477 and the division of that territory between France and the Holy Roman Empire, the Netherlands at the beginning of the sixteenth century consisted of seventeen provinces (corresponding to modern Holland, Belgium, and Luxembourg). Through marriage of its rulers, the Netherlands had come under Spanish control. However, because of widespread cultural, linguistic, and religious differences, the Netherlands could hardly be considered a cohesive unit during this period. The seven northern provinces were predominantly Germanic in culture, Dutch speaking, and Calvinist, while the southern provinces were largely French and Flemish speaking, Catholic, and culturally linked to France.

Prosperous Provinces

The Netherlands was among the most commercially advanced and prosperous of European countries. Its easy access to the Atlantic Ocean and extensive network of rivers provided a setting conducive to overseas trade, and shipbuilding was one of the most profitable businesses. The geographic location of the region's commercial center changed toward the end of the fifteenth century. Partly from the silting of the Bruges estuary, traffic shifted to Antwerp, which became the hub of economic activity in the Netherlands after 1510. By midcentury, a jealous Venetian envoy had to admit that more business transactions took place in Antwerp in a few weeks than in a year in Venice. As many as five hundred ships a day passed through Antwerp's harbor, and large trading colonies from England, the Holy Roman Empire, Italy, Portugal, and Spain established themselves in the city.

The economic prosperity of the Netherlands served as a potent incentive for Philip II of Spain to strengthen his control over those provinces. He had inherited the region from his father, Charles V (r. 1519–1556), who had accumulated an expansive empire as Holy Roman Emperor. In 1566, responding to riots in the Netherlandish provinces, Philip sent ten thousand soldiers to enforce his rule. His heavy-handed tactics and repressive measures led in 1579 to further revolt, resulting in the formation of two federations. The Union of Arras, a Catholic union of southern Netherlandish provinces, remained under Spanish dominion, and the Union of Utrecht, a Protestant union of northern provinces, became the Dutch Republic.

The increasing number of Netherlandish citizens converting to Protestantism affected the arts, as evidenced by a corresponding decrease in large-scale altarpieces and religious works (although such works continued to be commissioned for Catholic churches). Much of Netherlandish art of this period provides viewers with a wonderful glimpse into the lives of various strata of society, from nobility to peasantry, capturing their activities, environment, and values.

REINTERPRETING CLASSICAL ANTIQUITY Developments in Italian Renaissance art interested many

Netherlandish artists. JAN GOSSAERT (ca. 1478–1535) associated with humanist scholars and visited Italy. There, Gossaert (who adopted the Latinized name MABUSE, after his birthplace of Maubeuge) became fascinated with classical antiquity and its mythological subjects. Giorgio Vasari, the Italian historian and Gossaert's contemporary, wrote that "Jean Gossart [sic] of Mabuse was almost the first who took from Italy into Flanders the true method of making scenes full of nude figures and poetical inventions;"[5] although it is obvious he derived much of his classicism from Dürer.

Indeed, Dürer's *The Fall of Man* (FIG. 23-7) inspired the composition and poses in Gossaert's *Neptune and Amphitrite* (FIG. **23-17**). However, unlike Dürer's exquisitely small engraving, Gossaert's painting is more than six feet tall and four feet wide. The artist executed the painting with expected Netherlandish polish, skillfully drawing and careful modeling of the figures. Gossaert depicted the sea god with his traditional attribute, the trident, and wearing a laurel wreath and an ornate conch shell, rather than Dürer's fig leaf. Amphitrite is fleshy and, like Neptune, stands in a contrapposto stance. The architecture is an unusual mix of classical elements. For example, parts of Doric and Ionic orders are combined with

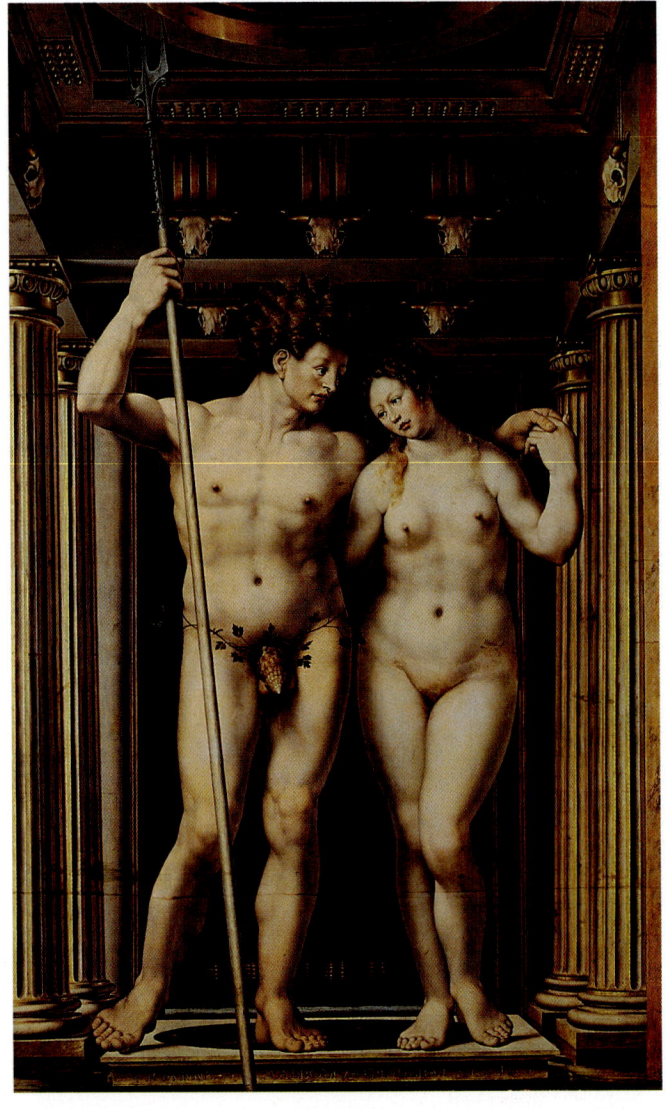

23-17 JAN GOSSAERT (MABUSE), *Neptune and Amphitrite*, ca. 1516. Oil on panel, 7′ 2″ × 4′ 1″. Gemäldegalerie, Staatliche Museen, Berlin.

egg-and-dart patterns and *bucrania* (ox skull decorations). Gossaert likely based this fanciful setting on sketches he had made of architectural structures while in Rome. He had traveled to Italy with the patron of this large-scale painting on panel, a Burgundian admiral.

BALANCING THE SECULAR AND SPIRITUAL

Antwerp's growth and prosperity, along with its wealthy merchants' propensity for collecting and purchasing art, attracted artists to the city. Among them was QUINTEN MASSYS (ca. 1466–1530), who became Antwerp's leading master after 1510. Son of a Louvain blacksmith, Massys demonstrated a willingness to explore the styles and modes of a variety of models, from van Eyck to Bosch and from van der Weyden to Dürer and Leonardo. Yet his eclecticism was subtle and discriminating, enriched by an inventiveness that gave a personal stamp to his paintings and made him a popular, as well as important, artist.

In *Money-Changer and His Wife* (FIG. **23-18**), Massys presented a professional man transacting business. He holds scales, checking the weight of coins on the table. His wife interrupts her reading of a prayer book to watch him. The artist's detailed rendering of the figures, setting, and objects suggests a fidelity to observable fact. Thus this work provides

viewers with a glimpse into the developing mercantilist activity. *Money-Changer and His Wife* also reveals Netherlandish values and mores. Although the painting highlights the financial transactions that were an increasingly prominent part of secular life in the sixteenth-century Netherlands, Massys tempered this focus on the material world with numerous references to the importance of a moral, righteous, and spiritual life. Not only does the wife hold a prayer book, but the artist also included other traditional religious symbols (for example, the carafe with water and candlestick). Two small vignettes Massys provided for viewers (not visible to the couple) refer to the balance this couple must establish between their worldly existence and their commitment to God's word. On the right, through a window, an old man talks with another man, suggesting idleness and gossip. The reflected image in the convex mirror on the counter offsets this image of sloth and foolish chatter. There, a man reads what is most likely a Bible or prayer book; behind him is a church steeple.

An inscription on the original frame (now lost) seems to have reinforced this message. According to a seventeenth-century scholar, this inscription read, "Let the balance be just and the weights equal" (Lev. 19:36), which applies both to the money changer's professional conduct and the eventual Last Judgment.

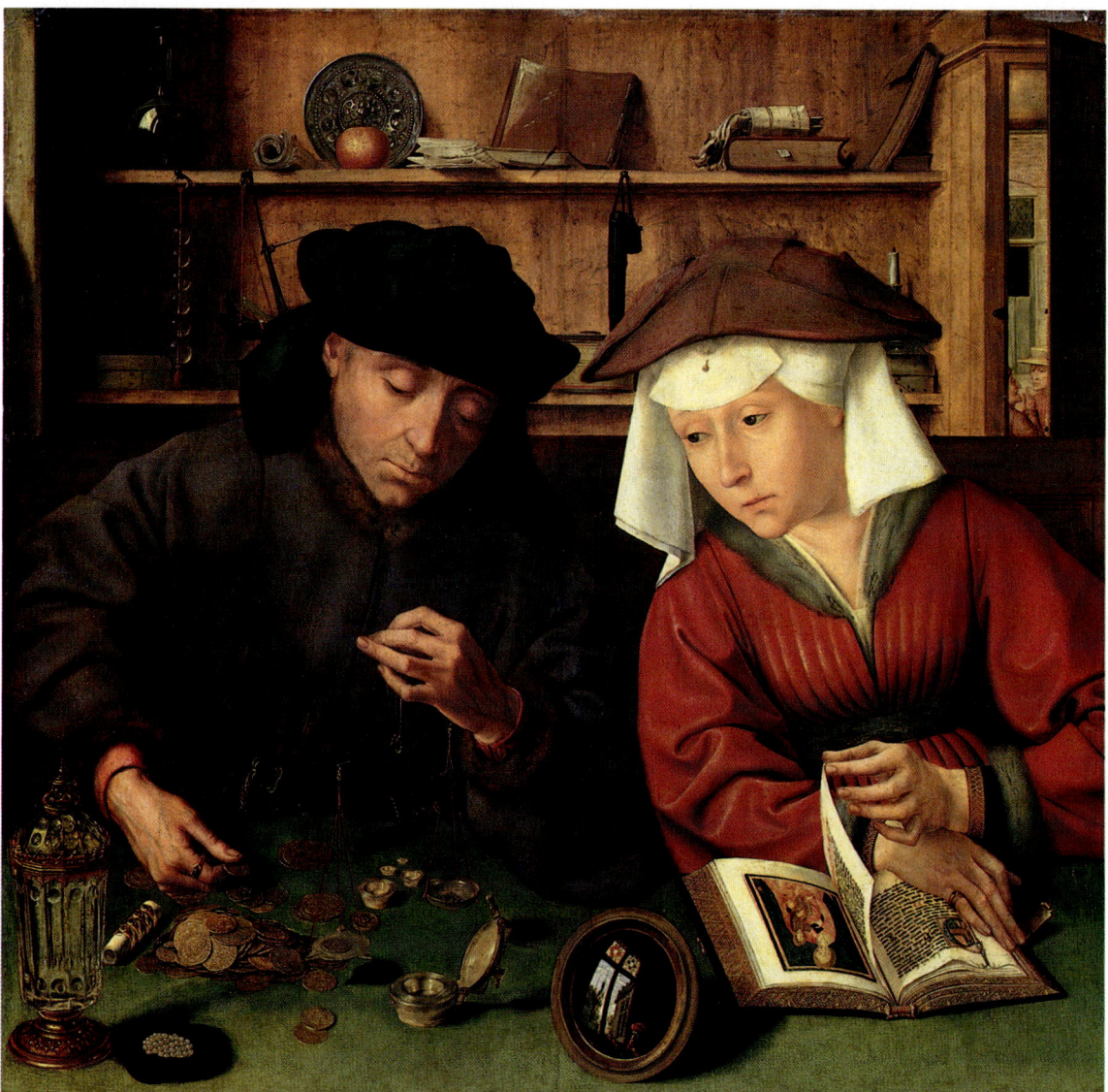

23-18
QUINTEN MASSYS, *Money-Changer and His Wife,* 1514. Oil on panel, 2′ 3¾″ × 2′ 2⅜″. Louvre, Paris.

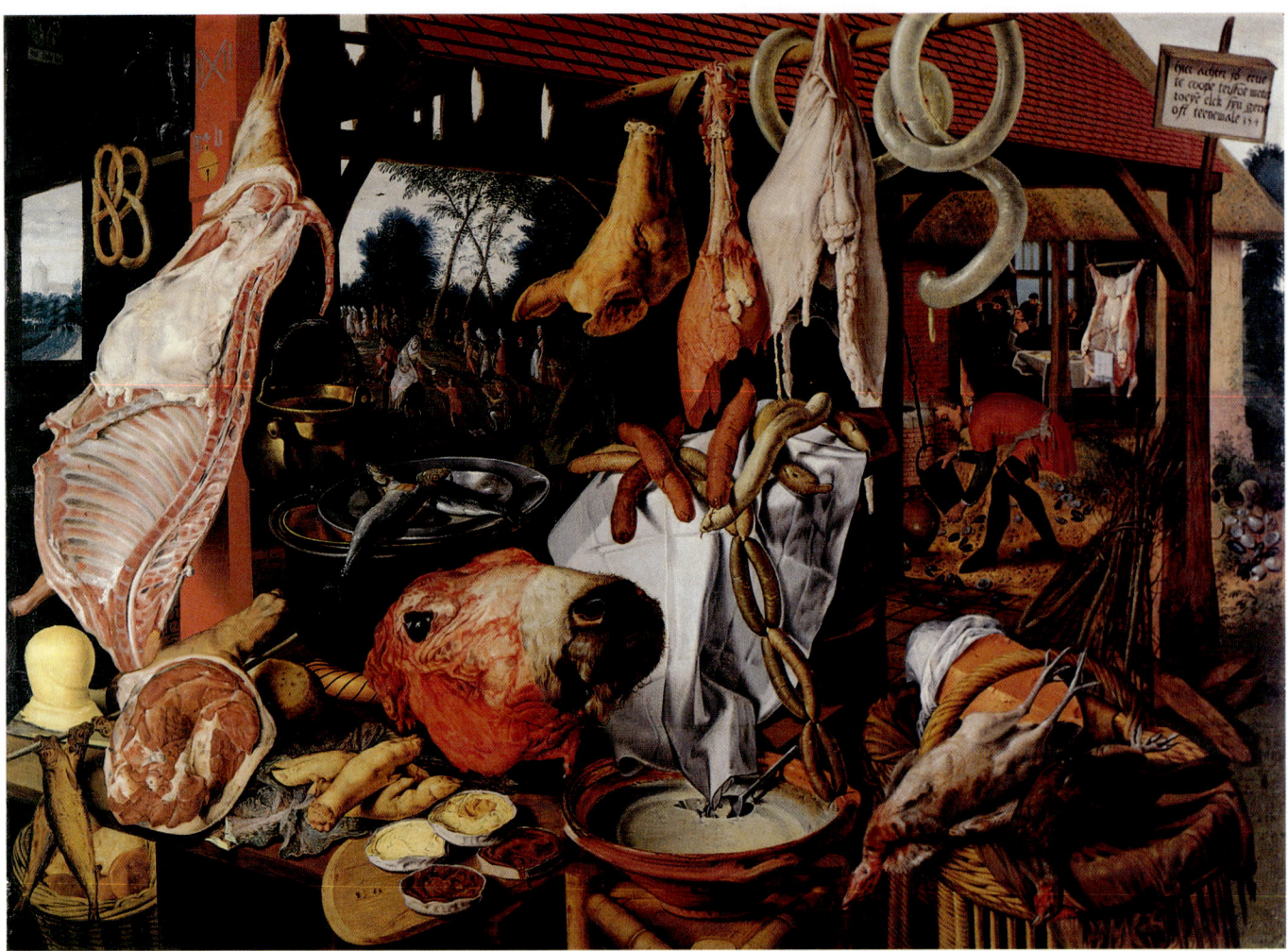

23-19   PIETER AERTSEN, *Meat Still-Life,* 1551. Oil on panel, 4′ 3/8″ × 6′ 5 3/4″. Uppsala University Art Collection, Uppsala.

MEETING SPIRITUAL OBLIGATIONS This tendency to inject reminders about spiritual well-being emerges in *Meat Still-Life* (FIG. **23-19**) by PIETER AERTSEN (ca. 1507–1575), who worked in Antwerp for more than three decades. At first glance, this painting appears to be a descriptive genre scene. Viewers encounter an array of meat products—a side of a hog, chickens, sausages, a stuffed intestine, pig's feet, meat pies, a cow's head, a hog's head, and hanging entrails. Also visible are fish, pretzels, cheese, and butter. Like Massys, Aertsen embedded strategically placed religious images as reminders to viewers. In the background of *Meat Still-Life,* Joseph leads a donkey carrying Mary and the Christ Child. The Holy Family stops to offer alms to a beggar and his son, while the people behind the Holy Family wind their way toward a church. Furthermore, the crossed fishes on the platter and the pretzels and wine in the rafters on the upper left all refer to "spiritual food" (pretzels often served as bread during Lent). Aertsen accentuated these allusions to salvation through Christ by contrasting them to their opposite—a life of gluttony, lust, and sloth. He represented this degeneracy with the oyster and mussel shells (believed by Netherlanders to possess aphrodisiacal properties) scattered on the ground on the painting's right side, along with the people seen eating and carousing nearby under the roof.

AN ACCOMPLISHED WOMAN ARTIST With the accumulation of wealth in the Netherlands, portraits increased in popularity. The self-portrait (FIG. **23-20**) by CATERINA VAN HEMESSEN (1528–1587) is purportedly the first known northern European self-portrait by a woman. Here, she confidently presented herself as an artist; she interrupts her painting to look toward viewers. She holds brushes, a palette, and a *maulstick* (a stick used to steady the hand while painting) in her left hand, and delicately applies pigment to the canvas with her right hand. Van Hemessen's father, Jan Sanders van Hemessen, a well-known painter, trained her. Caterina ensured proper identification (and credit) through the inscription in the painting: "Caterina van Hemessen painted me / 1548 / her age 20."

"A GOOD LANDSCAPE PAINTER" Landscape painting also flourished. Particularly well known for his landscapes was JOACHIM PATINIR (d. 1524). According to one scholar, the word *landscape (Landschaft)* first emerged in German literature as a characterization of an artistic genre when Dürer described Patinir as a "good landscape painter." In *Landscape with Saint Jerome* (FIG. **23-21**), Patinir subordinated the biblical scene to the exotic and detailed landscape. Saint Jerome, who removes a thorn from a lion's paw in the foreground, ap-

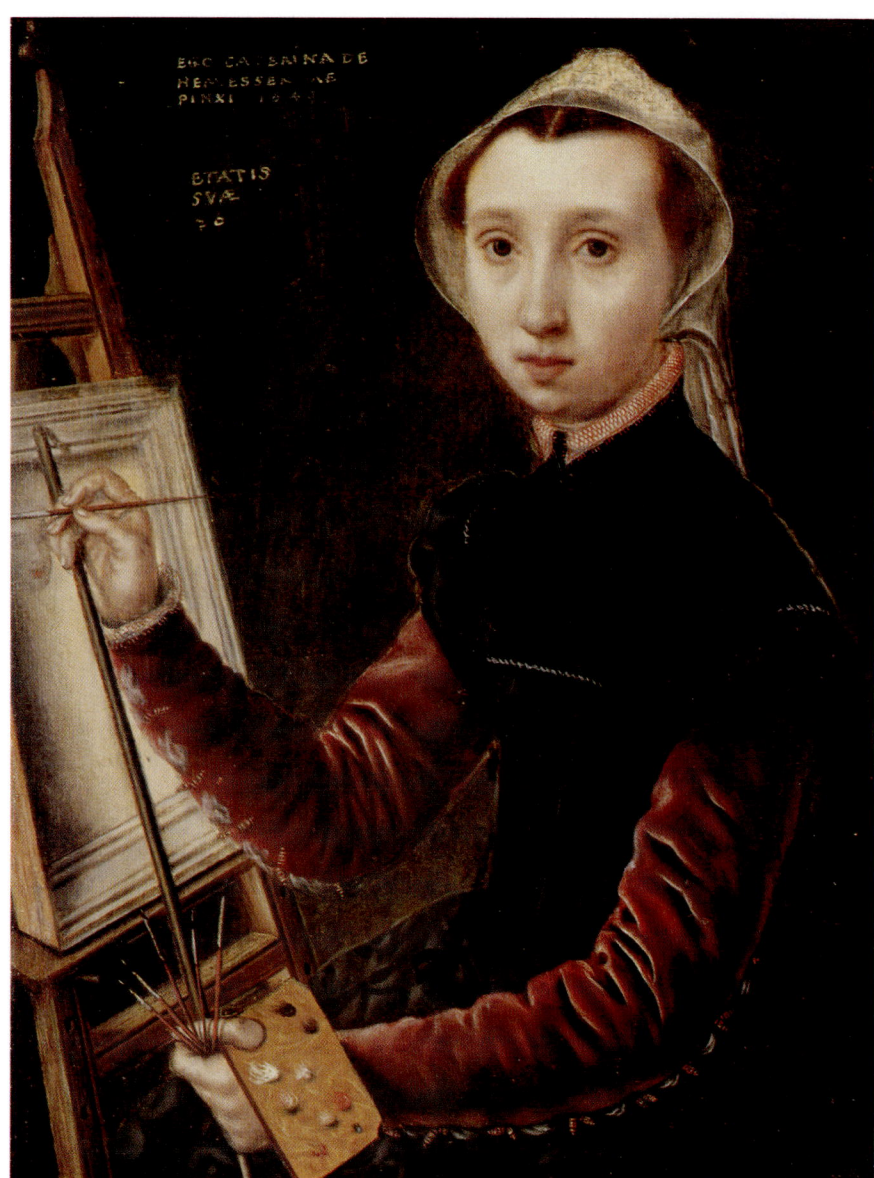

23-20 CATERINA VAN HEMESSEN, *Self-Portrait*, 1548. Panel, 1' $\frac{3}{4}$" × 9$\frac{7}{8}$". Kunstmuseum, Öffentiliche Kunstsammlung Basel.

pears dwarfed by craggy rock formations, rolling fields, and expansive bodies of water in the background. Patinir amplified the sense of distance by masterfully using color to enhance the visual effect of recession and advance.

A WINTRY NETHERLANDISH LANDSCAPE The early high-horizoned "cosmographical" landscapes of PIETER BRUEGEL THE ELDER (ca. 1528–1569) reveal both an interest in the interrelationship of human beings and nature and Patinir's influence. But in Bruegel's paintings, no matter how huge a slice of the world he shows, human activities remain the dominant theme. Like many of his contemporaries, Bruegel traveled to Italy, where he seems to have spent almost two years, going as far south as Sicily. Unlike other artists, however, Bruegel chose not to incorporate classical elements into his paintings. The impact of his Italian experiences emerges in his work most frequently in the Italian or Alpine landscape features, which he recorded in numerous drawings during his journey.

Hunters in the Snow (FIG. 23-22) is one of five surviving paintings of a series of six illustrating seasonal changes in the year. It shows human figures and landscape locked in winter cold; Bruegel's production of this painting in 1565 coincided with a particularly severe winter. The weary hunters return with their hounds, women build fires, skaters skim the frozen pond, the town and its church huddle in their mantle of snow, and beyond this typically Netherlandic winter scene lies a bit of Alpine landscape. Aside from this trace of fantasy, however, the artist rendered the landscape in an optically accurate manner. It develops smoothly from foreground to background and draws viewers diagonally into its depths. Bruegel's consummate skill in using line and shape and his subtlety in tonal harmony make this one of the great landscape paintings and an occidental counterpart of the masterworks of classical Chinese landscape.

PROVERBIAL NETHERLANDISH WISDOM Among the paintings that most comprehensively capture life

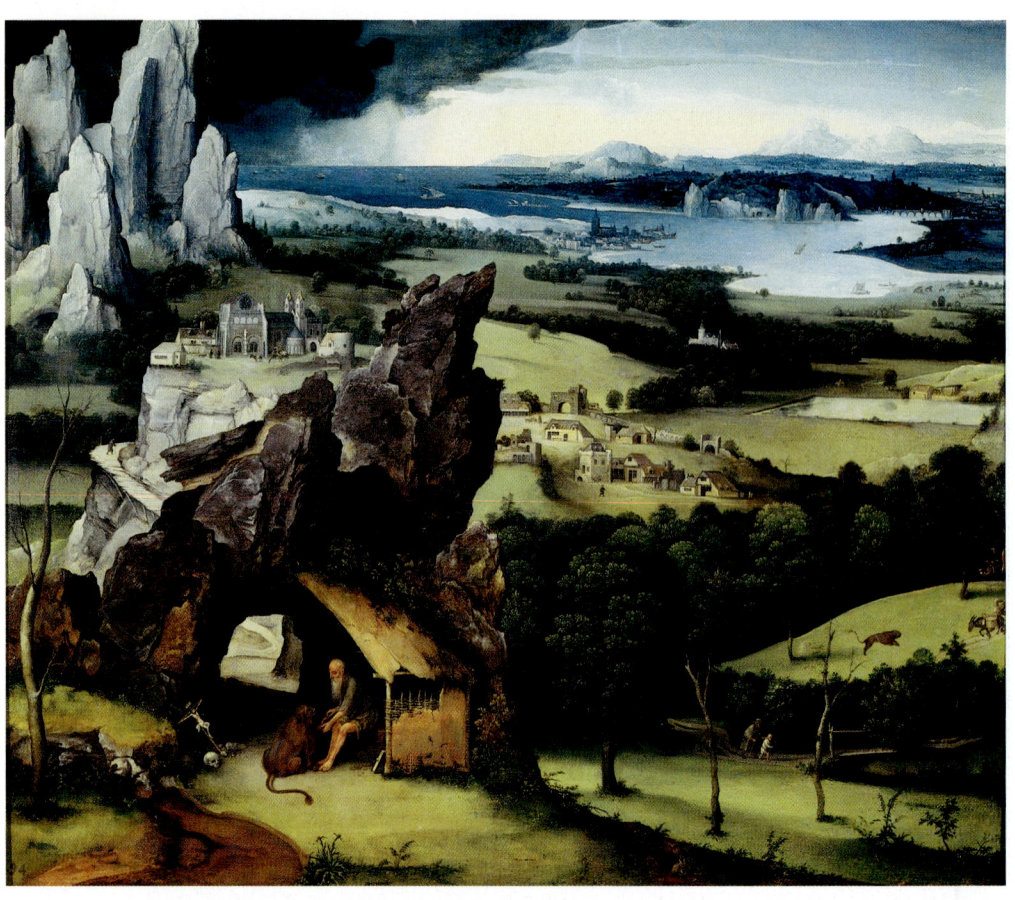

23-21 Joachim Patinir, *Landscape with Saint Jerome,* ca. 1520–1524. Oil on panel, 2′ 5⅛″ × 2′ 11⅞″. Prado, Madrid.

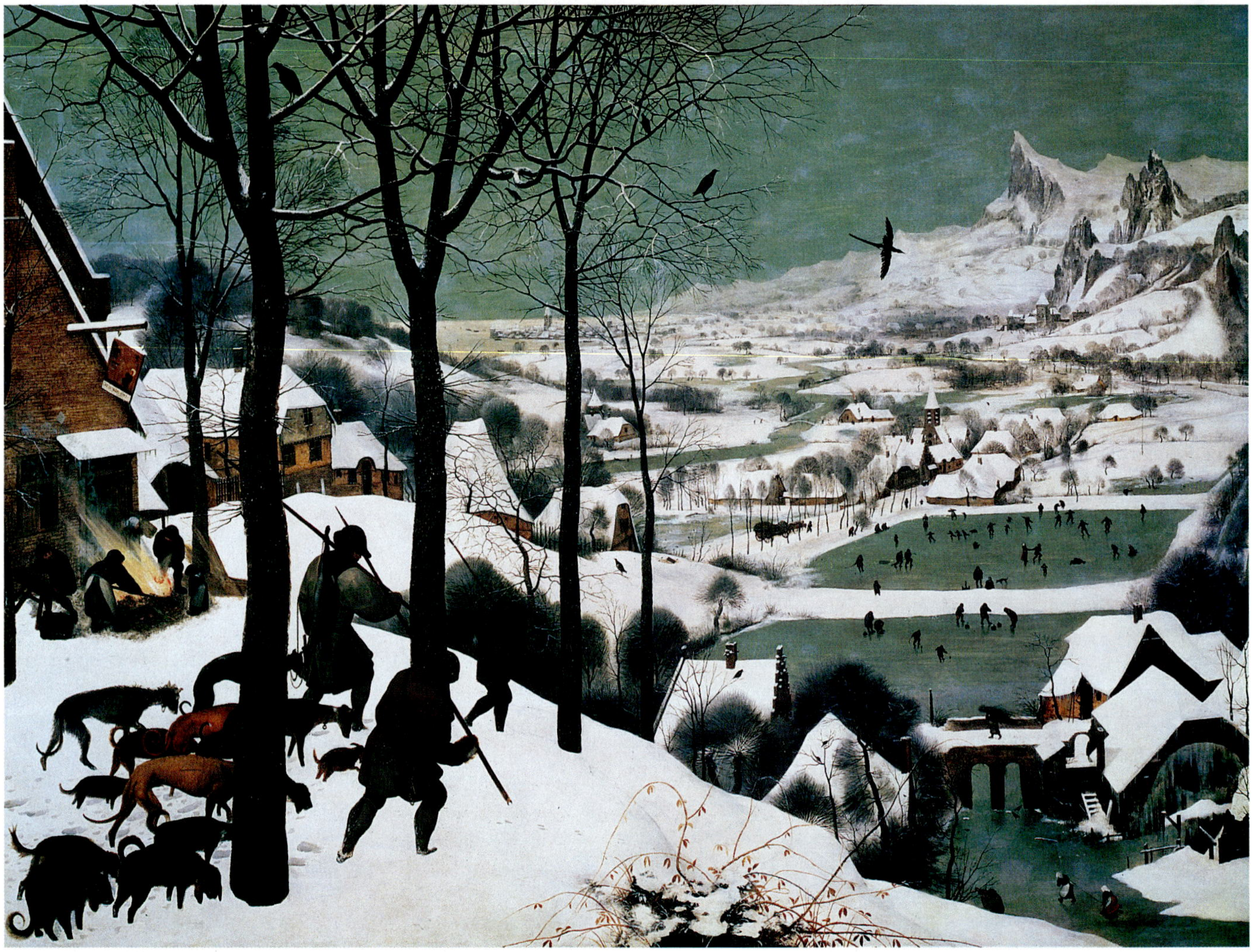

23-22 Pieter Bruegel the Elder, *Hunters in the Snow,* 1565. Oil on panel, approx. 3′ 10″ × 5′ 4″. Kunsthistorisches Museum, Vienna.

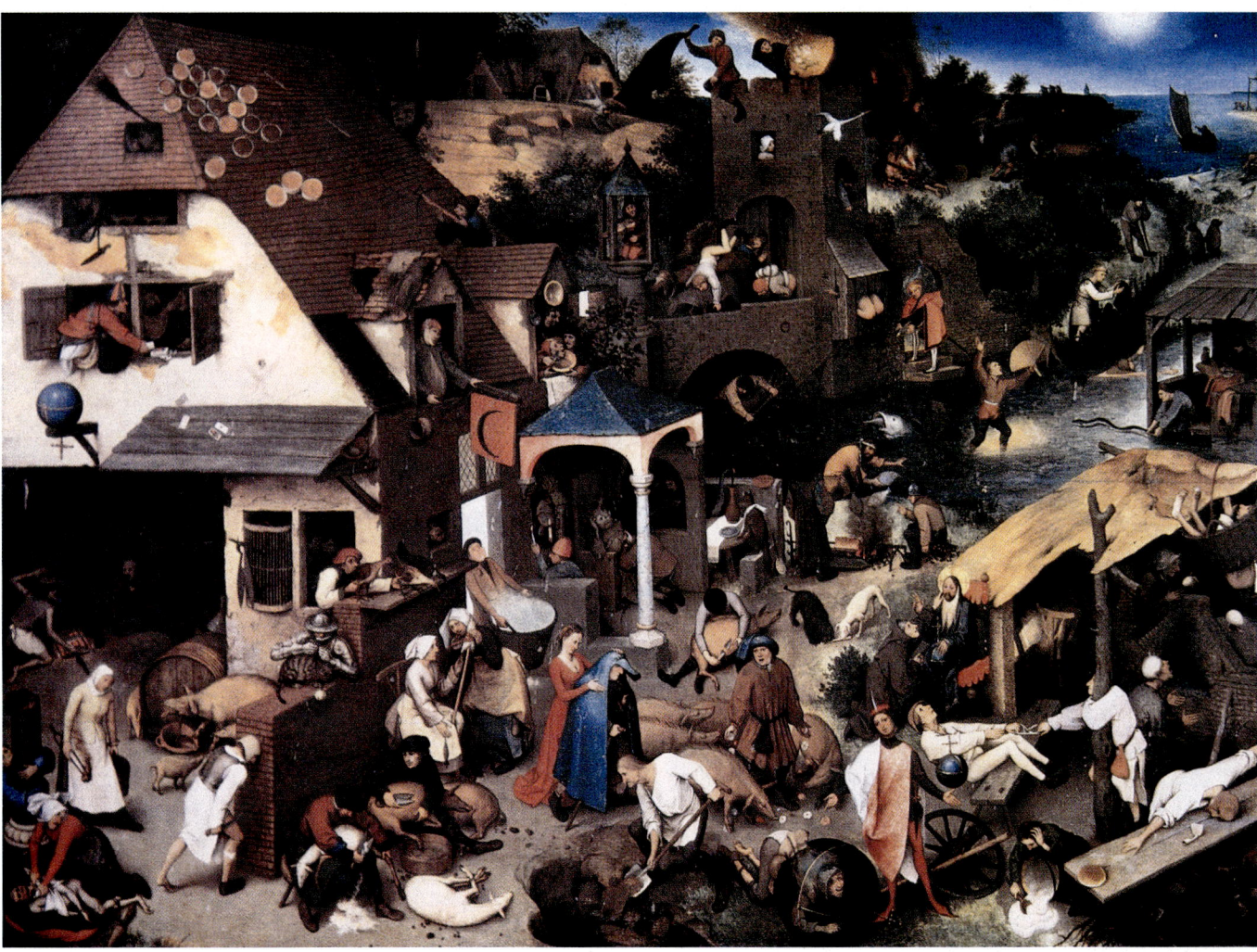

23-23 PIETER BRUEGEL THE ELDER, *Netherlandish Proverbs,* 1559. Oil on panel, 3′ 10″ × 5′ 41/8″. Gemäldegalerie, Staatliche Museen, Berlin.

in the Netherlands during the sixteenth-century is Bruegel's *Netherlandish Proverbs* (FIG. **23-23**). This work depicts a typical Netherlandish village populated by a wide range of people (nobility, peasants, and clerics). From a bird's eye view, spectators encounter a mesmerizing and mind-boggling array of activities. Beyond a mere vignette of village life, however, Bruegel illustrated more than one hundred proverbs in this one painting. It thus functions on another level and demands very close scrutiny. The proverbs depicted include, on the far left, a man in blue gnawing on a pillar ("He bites the column"—an image of hypocrisy); to his right, a man "beats his head against a wall" (an ambitious idiot); on the roof a man "shoots one arrow after the other, but hits nothing" (a short-sighted fool); and, in the far distance, the "blind lead the blind." *Netherlandish Proverbs* nicely summarizes more than just the physical facts of Netherlandish existence in the sixteenth century; it also captures the Netherlanders' morality and mentality. More generally, this artwork serves as a study of human nature.

Toward the end of his life, Bruegel's commentary on the human condition took on an increasingly bitter edge. The Netherlands, racked by religious conflict, became the seat of cruel atrocities, made even more terrible by Catholic Spain's attempts to extinguish the Reformation.

SPAIN

Spain emerged as the dominant European power at the end of the sixteenth century. Under Charles V of Hapsburg (r. 1516–1556) and his son, Philip II (r. 1556–1598), the Spanish Empire dominated a territory greater in extent than any ever known—a large part of Europe, the western Mediterranean, a strip of North Africa, and vast expanses in the New World. Spain acquired many of its New World colonies through aggressive overseas exploration. Among the most notable navigators sailing under the Spanish flag were Christopher Columbus (1451–1506), Vasco Nuñez de Balboa (ca. 1475–1517), Ferdinand Magellan (1480–1521), Hernán Cortés (1485–1547), and Francisco Pizarro (ca. 1470–1541). The Hapsburg Empire, enriched by the New World plunder, supported the most powerful military force in Europe. Spain defended and then promoted the Catholic Church's interests in its battle against the inroads of the Protestant Reformation; indeed, Philip II earned the nickname "Most Catholic King." The material and the spiritual exertions of Spain—the fanatical courage of Spanish soldiers and the ardent fervor of the great Spanish mystical saints—united. The soldiers became the terror of the Protestant and pagan worlds, while the saints served as the inspiration of the

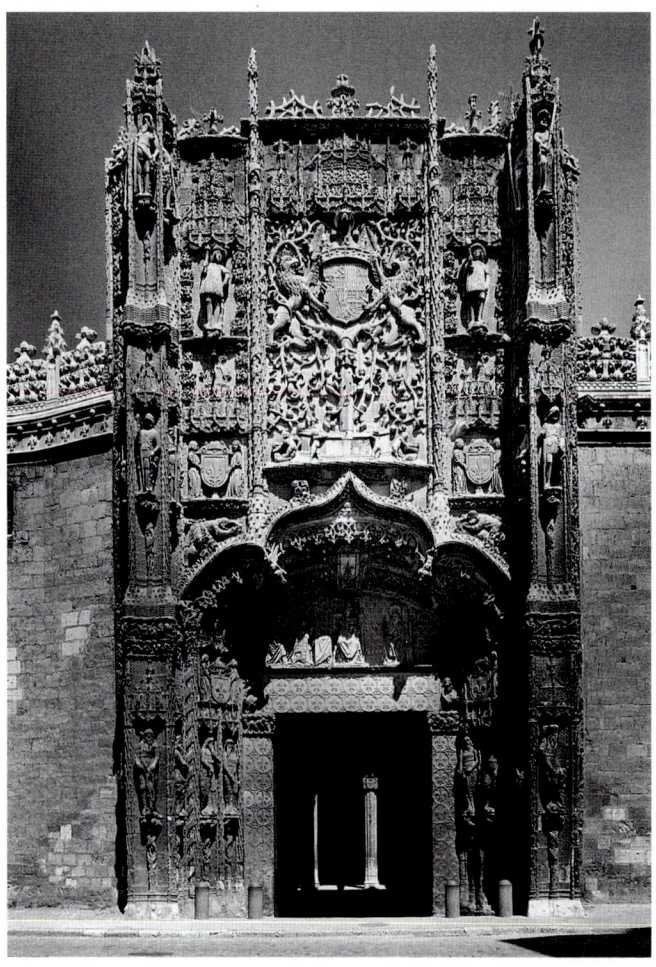
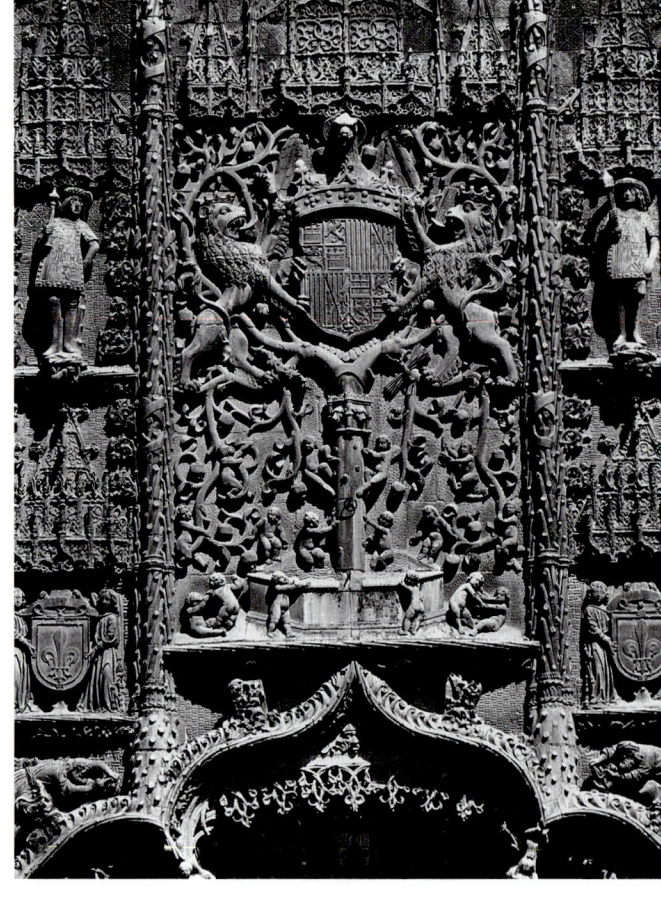

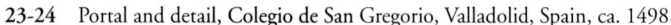

23-24   Portal and detail, Colegio de San Gregorio, Valladolid, Spain, ca. 1498.

Catholic faithful. Spain's crusading spirit, nourished by centuries of war with Islam, engaged body and soul in forming the most Catholic civilization of Europe and the Americas. In the sixteenth century, for good or for ill, Spain left the mark of Spanish power, religion, language, and culture on two hemispheres.

SILVERWORK-INSPIRED ARCHITECTURE   During the fifteenth century and well into the sixteenth, a Late Gothic style of architecture, the Plateresque, prevailed in Spain. *Plateresque* derives from the Spanish word *platero,* meaning silversmith, and relates to the style because of the delicate execution of its ornament. The Colegio de San Gregorio (Seminary of Saint Gregory; FIG. **23-24**) in the Castilian city of Valladolid handsomely exemplifies the Plateresque manner. Great carved retables, like the German altarpieces that influenced them (see FIGS. 20-23 and 20-24), appealed to church patrons and architects in Spain. They thus made them a conspicuous decorative feature of their exterior architecture, dramatizing a portal set into an otherwise blank wall. The Plateresque entrance of San Gregorio is a lofty sculptured stone screen that bears no functional relation to the architecture behind it. On the entrance level, lacelike tracery reminiscent of Moorish design hems the flamboyant ogival arches. A great screen, paneled into sculptured compartments, rises above the tracery. In the center (FIG. 23-24, detail), the

branches of a huge pomegranate tree (symbolizing Granada, the Moorish capital of Spain captured by the Hapsburgs in 1492) wreathe the coat of arms of King Ferdinand and Queen Isabella. Cupids play among the tree branches, and, flanking the central panel, niches enframe armed pages of the court, heraldic wild men (wild men symbolized aggression, and here as heralds announce the royal intentions), and armored soldiers, attesting to Spain's new proud militancy. In typical Plateresque and Late Gothic fashion, the activity of a thousand intertwined motifs unifies the whole design, which, in sum, creates an exquisitely carved panel greatly expanded in scale.

A KING'S REVIVAL OF THE CLASSICAL   Italianate classicism made its appearance in the unfinished palace of Charles V in the Alhambra in Granada (FIG. 23-25), which is the work of the painter-architect PEDRO MACHUCA (active 1520–1550). Superposed Doric and Ionic orders, which support continuous horizontal entablatures rather than arches, ring the circular central courtyard. The ornament consists only of the details of the orders themselves, which Machuca rendered with the simplicity, clarity, and authority found in the work of Bramante and his school. The lower story recalls the ring colonnade of the Tempietto (see FIG. 22-8); although here the architect reversed the curve. This pure classicism, entirely exceptional in Spain at this time, may reflect Charles V's

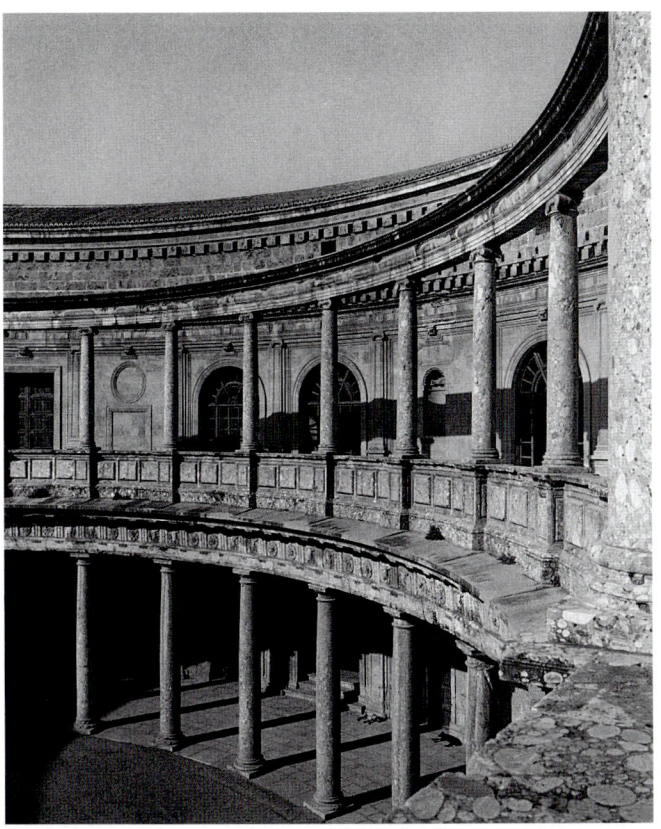

23-25   PEDRO MACHUCA, courtyard of the palace of Charles V, Alhambra, Granada, Spain, ca. 1526–1568.

personal taste acquired on one of his journeys to Italy. (The king, after all, was an enthusiastic patron of Titian.) Machuca may also have sojourned in Italy, and the courtyard may have been his attempt to incorporate elements of classical architecture.

A "DYNASTIC PANTHEON"   Charles V's successor to the Spanish throne, Philip II, appreciated the streamlined clarity of Italian-derived classicism but desired a more unique style. His tastes emerged in the expansive complex called the Escorial (FIG. 23-26), which JUAN BAUTISTA DE TOLEDO (d. 1567) and JUAN DE HERRERA (ca. 1530–1597), principally the latter, constructed for Philip II. In his will, Charles V stipulated that a "dynastic pantheon" be built to house the remains of past and future monarchs of Spain. Philip II, obedient to his father's wishes, chose a site some thirty miles northwest of Madrid in rugged terrain with barren mountains. Here, he built the Escorial, not only a royal mausoleum but also a church, a monastery, and a palace. Legend has it that the gridlike plan for the enormous complex, six hundred twenty-five feet wide and five hundred twenty feet deep, symbolized the gridiron where Saint Lawrence, patron of the Escorial, was martyred.

The whole vast structure is in keeping with Philip's austere and conscientious character, his passionate Catholic religiosity, his proud reverence for his dynasty, and his stern determination to impose his will worldwide. He insisted that the architect focus on simplicity of form, severity in the whole, nobility without arrogance, and majesty without ostentation in designing the Escorial. The result is a classicism of Doric severity, ultimately derived from Italian architecture and with

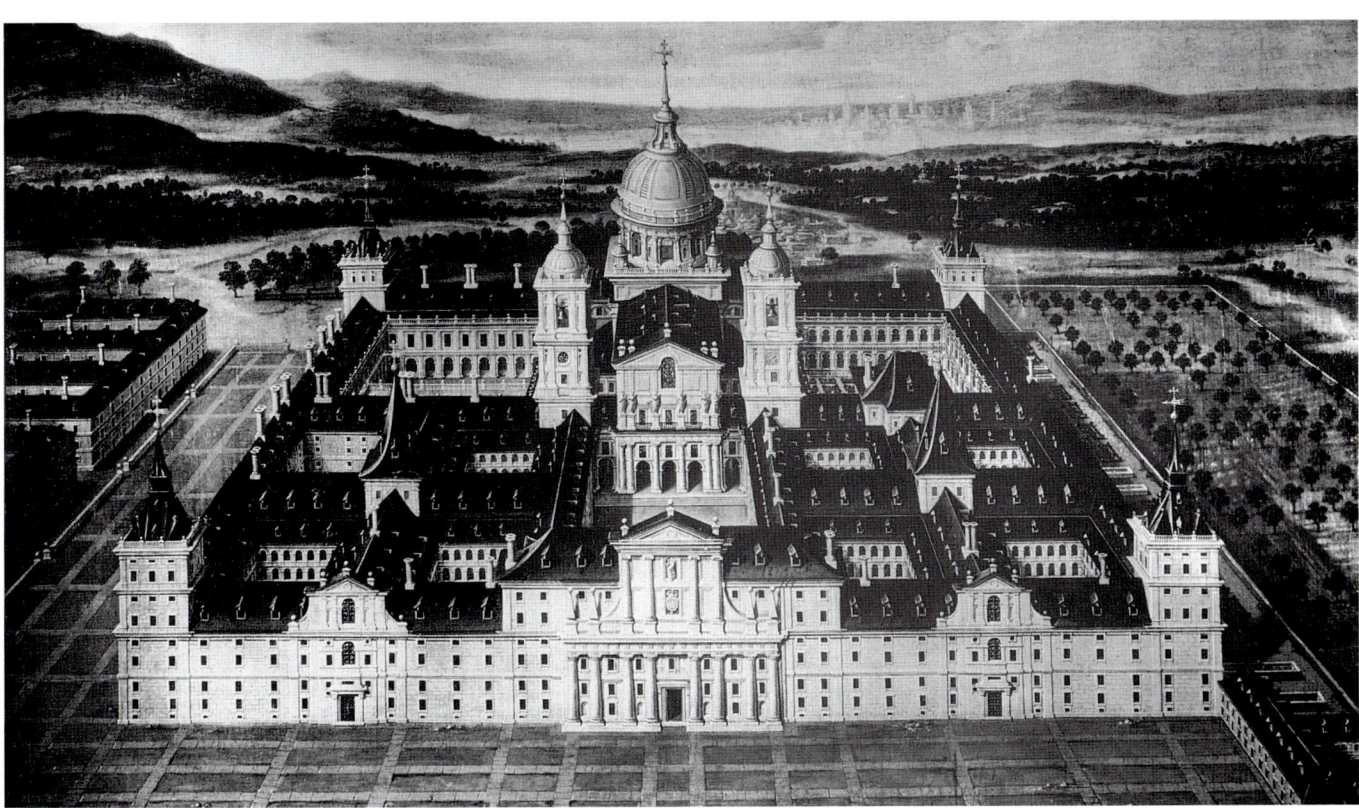

23-26   JUAN DE HERRERA, Escorial (bird's-eye view), near Madrid, Spain, ca. 1563–1584 (after an anonymous eighteenth-century painting).

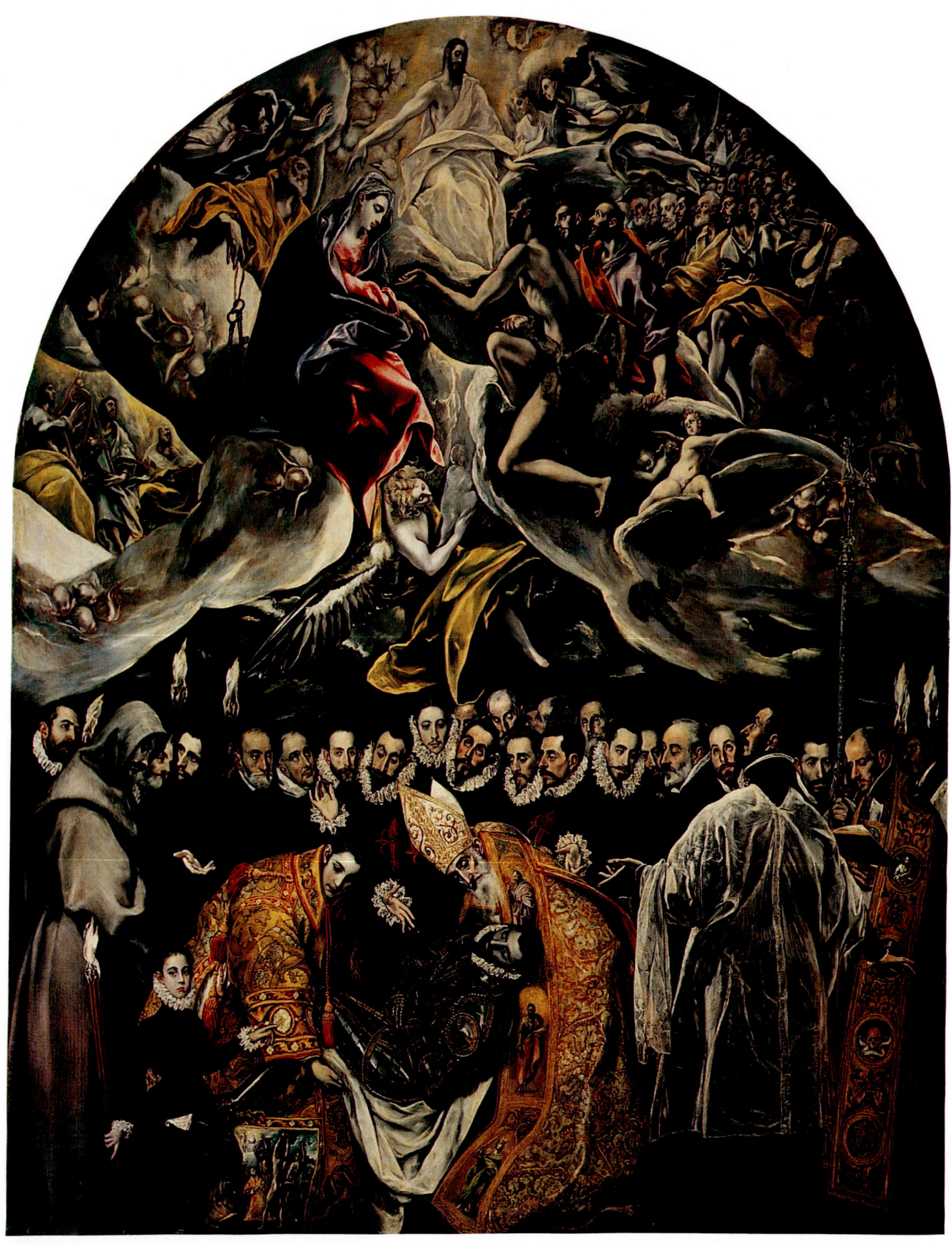

23-27 EL GRECO, *The Burial of Count Orgaz,* Santo Tomé, Toledo, Spain, 1586. Oil on canvas, approx. 16′ × 12′.

the grandeur of Saint Peter's implicit in the scheme. But it is unique in Spanish and European architecture—a matchless style, even though later structures reflect it.

Only the three entrances, with the dominant central portal framed by superposed orders and topped by a pediment in the Italian fashion, break the long sweep of the structure's severely plain walls. Massive square towers punctuate the four corners. The architect's stress on the central axis, with its subdued echoes in the two flanking portals, anticipates the three-part organization of later Baroque palace facades. The construction material for the entire complex (including the domed-cross church)—granite, a difficult stone to work—conveys a feeling of starkness and gravity. The church's massive facade and the austere geometry of the interior complex, with its blocky walls and ponderous arches produce an effect of overwhelming strength and weight.

The entire complex is a monument to the collaboration of a great king and a remarkably understanding architect. The Escorial stands as the overpowering architectural expression of Spain's spirit in its heroic epoch and of the character of Philip II, the extraordinary ruler who directed it.

A SPANISH MANNERIST DOMÉNIKOS THEOTOKÓPOULOS, called EL GRECO (ca. 1547–1614), was born on Crete but emigrated to Italy as a young man. In his youth, he absorbed the traditions of Late Byzantine frescoes and mosaics. While still young, El Greco went to Venice, where he was connected with Titian's workshop, although Tintoretto's painting seems to have made a stronger impression on him. A brief trip to Rome explains the influences of Roman and Florentine Mannerism on his work. By 1577, he had left for Spain to spend the rest of his life in Toledo.

El Greco's art is a strong personal blending of Late Byzantine and Late Italian Mannerist elements. The intense emotionalism of his paintings, which naturally appealed to the pious fervor of the Spanish, the dematerialization of form, and a great reliance on color bound him to sixteenth-century Venetian art and to Mannerism. His strong sense of movement and use of light, however, prefigured the Baroque style. El Greco's art was not strictly Spanish (although it appealed to certain sectors of that society), for it had no Spanish antecedents and little effect on later Spanish painters. Nevertheless, El Greco's hybrid style captured the fervor of Spanish Catholicism. This statement is especially true of the artist's masterpiece, *The Burial of Count Orgaz* (FIG. **23-27**), painted in 1586 for the church of Santo Tomé in Toledo. El Greco based the artwork on the legend that the count of Orgaz, who had died some three centuries before and who had been a great benefactor of Santo Tomé, was buried in the church by Saints Stephen and Augustine, who miraculously descended from heaven to lower the count's body into its sepulcher.

In the painting, the brilliant Heaven that opens above irradiates the earthly scene; El Greco carefully distinguished the terrestrial and celestial spheres. He represented the terrestrial with a firm realism, while he depicted the celestial, in his quite personal manner, with elongated undulating figures, fluttering draperies, and a visionary swirling cloud. Below, the two saints lovingly lower the count's armor-clad body, the armor and heavy draperies painted with all the rich sensuousness of the Venetian school. A solemn chorus of black-clad Spanish personages fills the background. In the carefully individualized features of these figures, El Greco demonstrated that he was also a great portraitist. These men call to mind the conquistadores, who, earlier in the century, ventured to the New World and who, two years after the completion of this picture, led the Great Armada against both Protestant England and the Netherlands.

The upward glances of some figures below and the flight of an angel above link the painting's lower and upper spheres. The action of the angel, who carries the count's soul in his arms as Saint John and the Virgin intercede for it before the throne of Christ, reinforces this connection. El Greco's deliberate change in style to distinguish between the two levels of reality gives viewers the opportunity to see the artist's early and late manners in the same work, one below the other. His relatively sumptuous and realistic presentation of the earthly sphere is still strongly rooted in Venetian art, but the abstractions and distortions El Greco used to show the immaterial nature of the Heavenly realm characterized his later style. His elongated figures existing in undefined spaces, bathed in a cool light of uncertain origin, explain El Greco's usual classification as a Mannerist, but it is difficult to apply that label to him without reservations. Although he used Mannerist formal devices, El Greco's primary concerns were emotion and expressing his religious fervor or arousing that of observers. To make the inner meaning of his paintings forceful, he developed a highly personal style so that his tapering forms, swaddled in dynamic swirls of unearthly light and color, appear as spiritual visions.

Despite the conflicts between the various European countries, it is clear extensive dialogue transpired among artists of these countries, and artistic influence and ideas traveled in many directions. The widespread religious and political conflicts continued to impact the arts well into the next century, as modern nation-states and capitalist economies solidified.

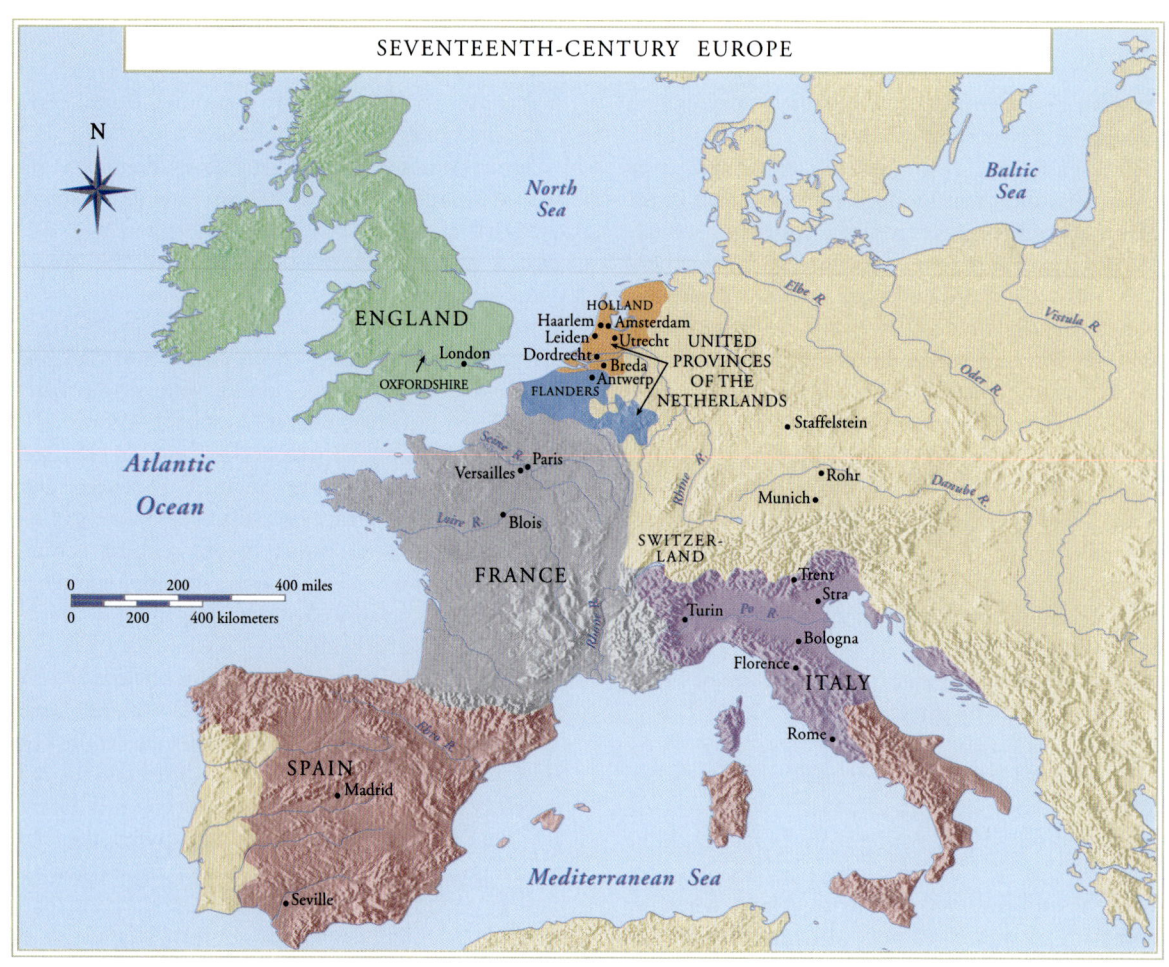

SEVENTEENTH-CENTURY EUROPE

	1600	1620	1630	1640	1650
	PHILIP III OF SPAIN	PHILIP IV OF SPAIN			
	HENRY IV OF FRANCE	LOUIS XIII OF FRANCE (DOMINATED BY CARDINAL RICHELIEU, MARIE DE MEDICI, REGENT 1610–1614)			LOUIS XIV OF
	JAMES I OF ENGLAND		CHARLES I OF ENGLAND		ENGLAND UNDER CROMWELL

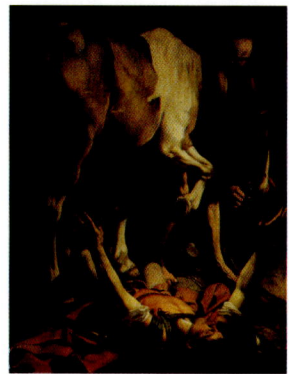

Caravaggio, Conversion of
Saint Paul, ca. 1601

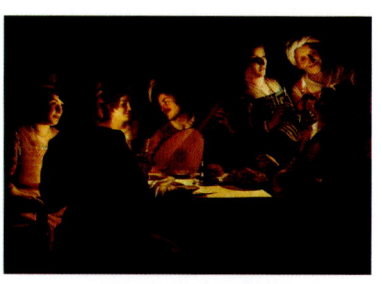

Gerritt van Honthorst
Supper Party, 1620

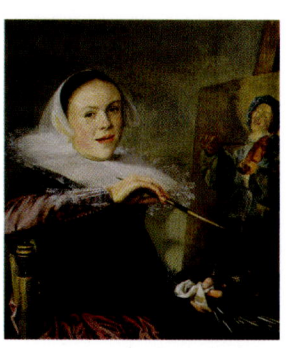

Judith Leyster
Self-Portrait, ca. 1630

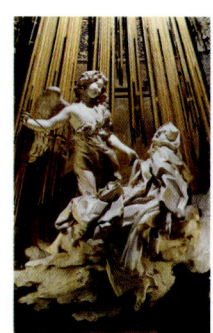

Gianlorenzo Bernini
Ecstasy of Saint Theresa
1645–1652

William Shakespeare, 1564–1616

Pope Paul V, r. 1605–1621

Galileo Galilei refines telescope, 1609

Johannes Kepler's laws of planetary motion, 1609–1619

Thirty Years' War begins, 1618

Pope Urban VIII, r. 1623–1644

Blaise Pascal, 1623–1662

William Harvey
discovers blood
circulation, 1628

René Descartes, *Discourse on Method*, 1637

Pope Innocent X, r. 1644–1655

French Royal Academy
of Painting and Sculpture
founded, 1648

United Provinces
of the Netherlands
formed, 1648

Thirty Years' War
ends, 1648

OF POPES, PEASANTS, MONARCHS, AND MERCHANTS

BAROQUE AND ROCOCO ART

1660	1670	1680	1690	1700	1710	1720	1730	1740	1750
CHARLES II OF SPAIN				PHILIP V					FERDINAND VI
FRANCE (DOMINATED BY CARDINAL MAZARIN UNTIL 1661)						LOUIS XV OF FRANCE			
CHARLES II OF ENGLAND			JAMES II	WILLIAM AND MARY	ANNE		GEORGE I OF ENGLAND	GEORGE II OF ENGLAND	

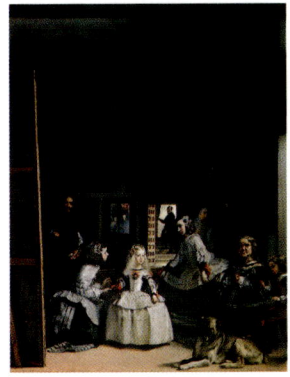

Diego Velázquez
Las Meninas, 1656

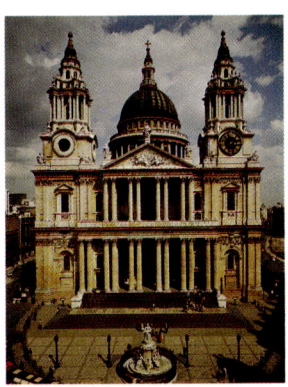

Christopher Wren
*Saint Paul's Cathredral
London, 1675–1710*

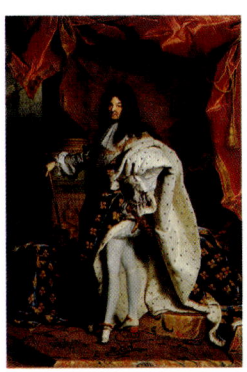

Hyacinthe Rigaud
Louis XIV, 1701

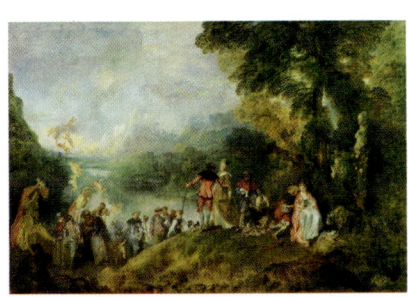

Antoine Watteau
*Return from Cythera
1717–1719*

Pope Alexander VII, r. 1655–1667

Royal Society founded in London, 1662

Sir Isaac Newton's laws of motion, gravitation, 1687

Excavation of
Pompeii
begins, 1748

THE "BAROQUE"

The cultural production of the seventeenth and early eighteenth centuries in the West is often described as "Baroque," a convenient blanket term. However, this term is problematic because the period encompasses a broad range of developments, both historical and artistic, across an expansive geographic area. Further, this term originally was used in a pejorative sense and thus had a connotation scholars long since have abandoned. (Although its origin is unclear, it may have come from the Portuguese word *barroco,* meaning an irregularly shaped pearl.) Use of the term *baroque* emerged in the late eighteenth and early nineteenth centuries, when critics disparaged the Baroque period's artistic production. This was due in large part to perceived deficiencies in comparison to the art (especially Italian Renaissance) of the period before it. Over time, this negative connotation faded, and the term is now used more generally as a period designation.

Because of the problematic associations of the term and because no commonalities can be ascribed to all of the art and cultures of this period, we have limited use of the term in this book. Wherever it is used, we have provided characteristics that anchor the term *Baroque* in particular cultures—for example, Italian Baroque as compared to Dutch Baroque.

The Shifting Geopolitical Landscape in Europe

WARRING FOR THIRTY YEARS—AND LONGER
During the seventeenth and early eighteenth centuries, numerous geopolitical shifts occurred in Europe as the fortunes of the individual countries waxed and waned. In the early years of the seventeenth century, fragile alliances, reinforced through strategic marriages, had been established. Religious conflicts, especially between Catholics and Protestants, and the political animosity between the Hapsburgs and their enemies soon eroded any stability these alliances had helped build. This volatile situation erupted into the Thirty Years' War (1618–1648), which involved Spain, France, Sweden, Denmark, the Netherlands, Germany, Austria, Poland, the Ottoman Empire, and the Holy Roman Empire. The war, which concluded with the Treaty of Westphalia in 1648, was largely responsible for the political restructuring of Europe. As a result, the Austro-Hungarian empire emerged; the United Provinces of the Netherlands (the Dutch Republic), Sweden, and France expanded their authority; and Spain and Denmark's relative power diminished. The building of nation-states was emphatically under way.

Although the Thirty Years' War was not solely responsible for the modern state system's evolution, it did contribute to the momentum of that burgeoning development. The war's causes and effects also highlight the historical and ideological issues Europe grappled with at that time. That the Thirty Years' War was symptomatic of wider disruption is revealed in one historian's claim that between 1562 and 1721 all of Europe was at peace only four years.

MOVING TOWARD SECULARIZED GOVERNMENT
One of the fundamental conflicts underlying the Thirty Years' War in particular and European turmoil in general was the ongoing friction between Catholics and Protestants. Aside from the reconfiguration of territorial boundaries, the Treaty of Westphalia in essence granted freedom of religious choice throughout Europe. This treaty thus marked the abandonment of the idea of a united Christian Europe, which the practical realities of secular political systems replaced.

Constant warfare also stimulated the movement toward the secularization of government. Military techniques had changed drastically since the medieval era. By the late sixteenth and early seventeenth centuries, warfare involved a greater use of firearms and cannons, increased flexibility and maneuverability in tactics, larger standing armies, and advanced artillery pieces that offered greater mobility during battle. The demands for expanded military forces necessitated large centralized bureaucracies to supervise military action and resources. The efficient coordination of these military operations reinforced the consolidation of power among secular authorities.

Advances in the Sciences

The growing secularization in the political realm coincided with (and certainly was linked to) the development of a new science. This new science challenged many fundamental religious tenets and emerged in astronomy, physics, biology, and mathematics. Grounded in mathematics and materialism (the belief the universe is composed of matter in motion), this momentous shift in the scientific realm laid the groundwork for the Enlightenment and its emphasis on empirical data, which is chronicled in Chapter 28.

EXPLORING THE UNIVERSE The new science rejected Aristotelian explanations of the universe, in large part because many of Aristotle's theories seemed incompatible with objective, observable fact. The great advances made in science during the late seventeenth and early eighteenth centuries relied on experimentation and tangible proof. The invention of logarithms, analytic geometry, and calculus transformed mathematics. In astronomy, Polish scientist Nicolaus Copernicus (1473–1543) argued that in contrast to traditional models of the cosmos, the Sun was the center of the universe and Earth merely a planet in orbit around it. Although this discovery occurred well before the beginning of the seventeenth century, not until his ideas were developed further by the German Johannes Kepler (1571–1630) and the Italian Galileo (1564–1642) was the notion of heliocentrism accepted throughout Europe. (Galileo provided visible proof of such astronomical conclusions with his improved tool, the telescope.)

CHEMICAL REACTIONS The study of chemical properties also advanced at a rapid pace, and discoveries in that field impacted medicine and, eventually, mechanization. For example, Englishman Robert Boyle (1627–1691) established the basis of the science of chemistry. In his book *The Sceptical Chymist,* which he published in 1661, Boyle presented an atomic explanation for matter, and he later explored the changes in atomic particles (which became known as the chemical elements). These studies led Boyle to formulate the inverse relationship between the volume and pressure of a gas (Boyle's Law) and to invent the air pump. The anatomical inquiries of Englishman William Harvey (1578–1657) resulted in his proposed anatomy of the heart, with the heart functioning like a pump and circulating blood through the entire body.

Many of the related threads of this new type of science were brought together in the work of Sir Isaac Newton (1642–1727). Although his work had an immediate impact on scientific thought after publication of his ideas (for example, the concept of force and the laws of motion and gravity), its wider implications laid the groundwork for Enlightenment thought. Thus Newtonian physics are discussed with the Enlightenment in Chapter 28. Other scientists, such as Sir Francis Bacon (1561–1626), and French philosopher René Descartes (1596–1650) were also major figures in science's advancement. Bacon was one of England's leading supporters of scientific research. Descartes explored how skepticism could be used to produce certainty. His resulting philosophy, known as Cartesianism, was based on the dual existence of matter and mind.

Although discussion of and debate about these advancements took place primarily in scientific circles, these innovative ideas did have widespread ramifications. Because this new science was based on skepticism and an insistence on demonstrable fact, it encouraged atheistic beliefs. In a historical crucible of enduring conflict between Catholics and Protestants, such beliefs seemed appallingly heretical.

The Development of a Worldwide Market

By the seventeenth century, European societies began to coordinate their long-distance trade more systematically. The allure of expanding markets, rising profits, and access to a wider range of goods all contributed to the relentless economic competition between countries during this period. Much of the foundation for worldwide mercantilism—extensive voyaging and geographic exploration, improved cartography, and advances in shipbuilding—was laid in the previous century. In fact, by the end of the sixteenth century, all of the major trade routes had been established.

COFFEE OR TEA? In the seventeenth century, however, changes in financial systems, lifestyles, and trading patterns, along with expanding colonialism, fueled the creation of a worldwide marketplace. The Dutch founded the Bank of Amsterdam in 1609, which established a uniform rate of exchange for the various currencies traded in that city. This bank eventually became the center of European transfer banking, where merchant firms held money on account, relieving traders of having to transport precious metals as payment. Trading practices became more complex. Rather than simple reciprocal trading, triangular trade (trade between three parties) allowed for a larger pool of desirable goods. Exposure to an ever-growing array of goods affected European diets and lifestyles. Coffee (from island colonies) and tea (from China) became popular beverages during the early seventeenth century. Equally explosive was the growth of sugar use. Sugar, along with tobacco and rice, were slave crops, and the slave trade expanded to accommodate the demand for these goods. Africans were enslaved and imported to European colonies and the Americas to provide the requisite labor force for producing these commodities.

Some groups (for example, the landed elite or the salaried bureaucrats) disdained trade expansion. This antipathy to trade did not impede its growth, however, and the resulting worldwide mercantile system permanently changed the face of Europe. The prosperity such trading generated affected social and political relationships, necessitating new rules of etiquette and careful diplomacy. With increased disposable income, more of the newly wealthy spent money on art (among other things), expanding the number of possible patronage sources. By 1700, the growth of a moneyed class had contributed considerably to the emergence of Rococo, a decorative style associated with the wealthy and aristocratic.

BAROQUE ART OF THE SEVENTEENTH CENTURY

Italy

Although the Catholic Church launched the Counter-Reformation—its challenge to the Protestant Reformation—during the sixteenth century, the considerable appeal of Protestantism continued to preoccupy it throughout the succeeding century. The Treaty of Westphalia in 1648 had formally recognized the principle of religious freedom, serving to validate Protestantism (predominantly in the German states). With the popes and clergy continuing to serve as major artistic patrons, as in earlier centuries, much of Italian Baroque art was aimed at propagandistically restoring Catholicism's predominance and centrality. Whereas Italian Renaissance artists often had reveled in the precise, orderly rationality of classical models, Italian Baroque artists embraced a more dynamic and complex aesthetic. During the seventeenth century, dramatic theatricality, grandiose scale, and elaborate ornateness, all used to spectacular effect, characterized Italian Baroque art and architecture. Papal Rome's importance as the cradle of Italian Baroque art production further suggests the role art played in supporting the aims of the Church. The Council of Trent, one of the Counter-Reformation initiatives, firmly resisted Protestant objection to using images in religious worship, insisting on their necessity for teaching the laity. Therefore, Italian Baroque art commissioned by the Church was not merely decorative but didactic as well.

The Catholic Church waged a lengthy campaign to reestablish its preeminence. Pope Sixtus V (r. 1585–1590) contributed significantly to this initiative. He augmented the papal treasury and intended to construct a new and more magnificent Rome. Several strong and ambitious popes—Paul V, Urban VIII, Innocent X, and Alexander VII—succeeded Sixtus V and were largely responsible for building the modern city of Rome, which bears their Baroque mark everywhere. Italian seventeenth-century art and architecture visualized the renewed energy of the Catholic Counter-Reformation and communicated it to the populace.

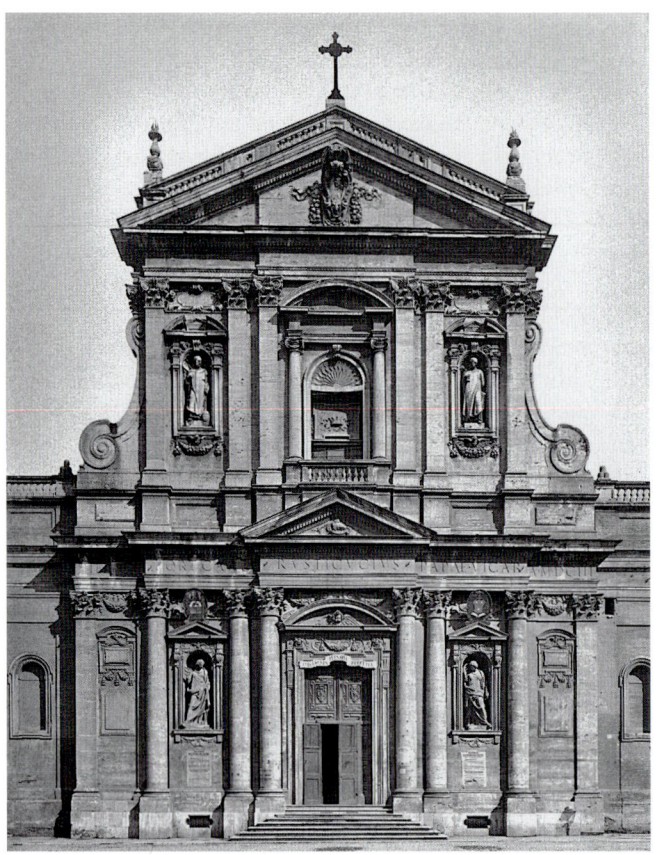

24-1 CARLO MADERNO, Santa Susanna, Rome, Italy, 1597–1603.

A VERTICAL APPEAL TO A HIGHER POWER

The facade CARLO MADERNO (1556–1629) designed at the turn of the century for the Roman church of Santa Susanna (FIG. **24-1**) stands as one of the earliest manifestations of the Baroque spirit in Italian art and architecture. In its general appearance, Maderno's facade resembles Giacomo della Porta's immensely influential design for Il Gesù (see FIG. 22-49), the seat of the Jesuit order (which played a major role in Counter-Reformation education and did expansive overseas missionary work in the New World and the Far East). But the later facade has a greater verticality, concentrating and dramatizing the major features of its model. The facade's tall central section projects forward from the horizontal lower story, and the scroll buttresses that connect the two levels are narrower and set at a sharper angle. The elimination of an arch framing the pediment over the doorway further enhances the design's vertical thrust. Strong shadows cast by Santa Susanna's vigorously projecting columns and pilasters mount dramatically toward the emphatically stressed central axis. The recessed niches, which contain statues, heighten the sculptural effect.

RESTORING SAINT PETER'S GRANDEUR

The drama inherent in Santa Susanna's facade appealed to Pope Paul V (r. 1605–1621), who commissioned Maderno in 1606 to complete Saint Peter's in Rome. As the symbolic seat of the papacy, Saint Peter's radiated enormous symbolic presence. In light of the lingering Counter-Reformation concerns, the desire of Baroque popes to conclude the extended rebuilding project and reestablish the force embodied in the mammoth structure is understandable. In many ways Maderno's facade of Saint Peter's (FIG. **24-2**) is a gigantic expansion of the elements of Santa Susanna's first level. But the compactness and verticality of the

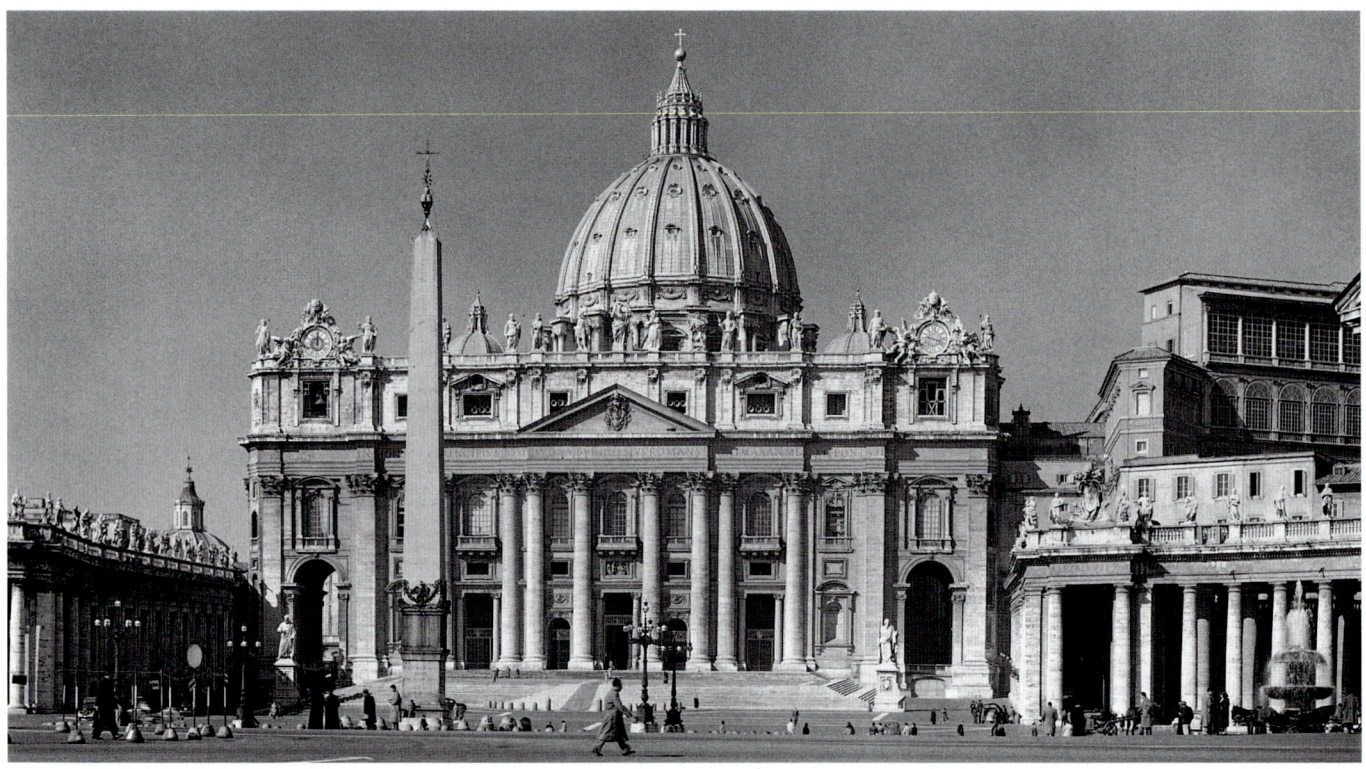

24-2 CARLO MADERNO, facade of Saint Peter's, Vatican City, Rome, Italy, 1606–1612.

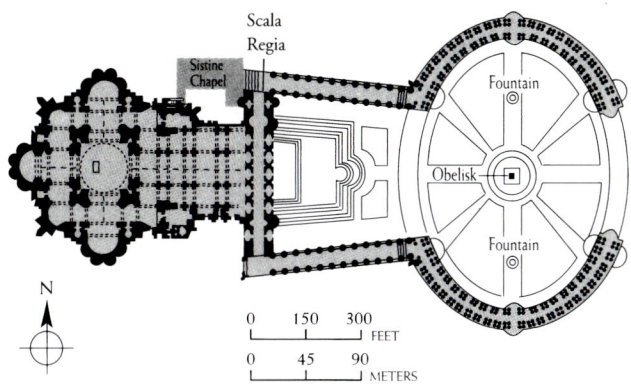

24-3   CARLO MADERNO, plan of Saint Peter's, Vatican City, Rome, Italy, with adjoining piazza designed by GIANLORENZO BERNINI.

smaller church's facade are not as prominent because Saint Peter's expansive width counterbalances them. Mitigating circumstances must be taken into consideration when assessing this design, however. The preexisting core of an incomplete building restricted Maderno, so he did not have the luxury of formulating a totally new concept for Saint Peter's. Moreover, his design for the facade was also never fully executed. The two outside bell-tower bays were not part of Maderno's original plan. Hence, had the facade been constructed according to the architect's initial design, it would have exhibited greater verticality and visual coherence.

Maderno's plan for Saint Peter's (FIG. **24-3**) also departed from the central plans designed for it during the Renaissance by Bramante (see FIG. 22-6) and, later, by Michelangelo (FIG. 22-28). Seventeenth-century clergy rejected a central plan for Saint Peter's because of its association with pagan buildings, such as the Pantheon (see FIG. 10-48). Paul V commissioned Maderno to add three nave bays to the earlier nucleus. This longitudinal plan reinforced the symbolic distinction between clergy and laity and provided a space for the processions (increasingly encouraged by the Jesuits) of ever-growing assemblies. Lengthening the nave, unfortunately, pushed the dome farther back from the facade, and the effect Michelangelo had planned—a structure pulled together and dominated by its dome—is not readily visible. When viewed at close range, the dome hardly emerges above the facade's soaring frontal plane; seen from farther back (FIG. 24-2), it appears to have no drum. Visitors must move back quite a distance from the front to see the dome and drum together and to experience the effect Michelangelo intended. Today, to truly see the structure as the sixteenth-century architect envisioned, people must view it from the back (see FIG. 22-29).

WELCOMING THE PIOUS IN ROME   The design of Saint Peter's finally was completed (except for details) by GIANLORENZO BERNINI (1598–1680). Bernini was an architect, a painter, and a sculptor—one of the most important and imaginative artists of the Italian Baroque era and its most characteristic and sustaining spirit. Bernini's largest and most

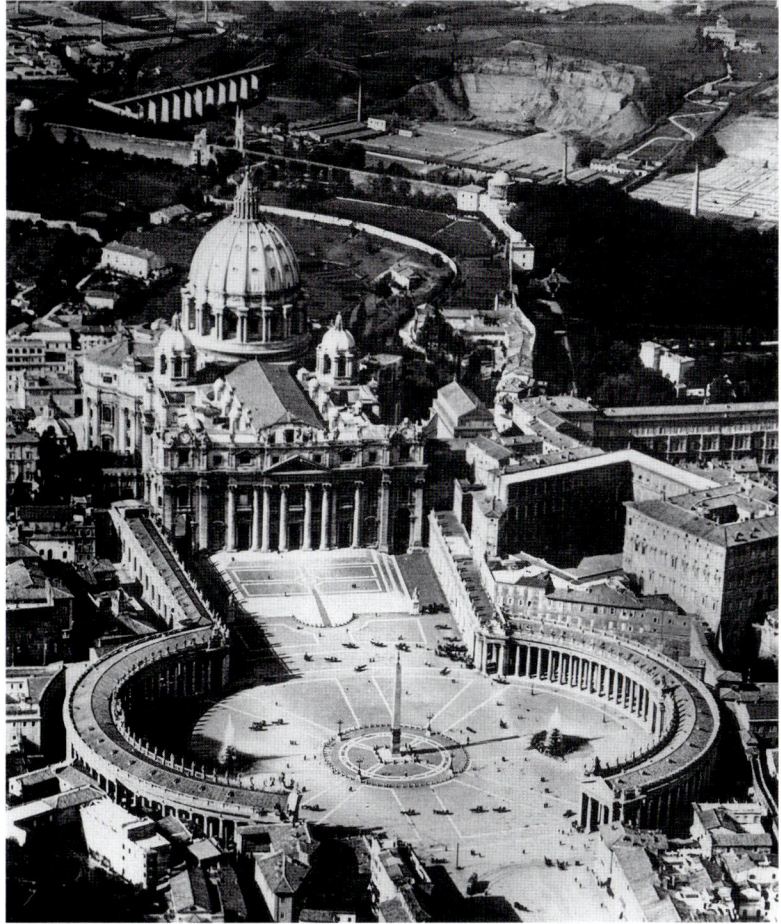

24-4   Aerial view of Saint Peter's, Vatican City, Rome, Italy, 1506–1666.

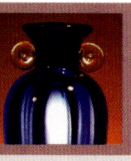

Centuries of Church History on View
Visiting Vatican City

The papacy long has been a force not only in religious matters but in the art world as well. For both of these reasons, a visit to Vatican City is a must on any trip to Italy. Vatican City is the smallest independent country in the world. It was formally established as a state in 1929 under terms of the Lateran Treaty. The complex of buildings that makes up Vatican City has more than one thousand rooms, with many open to the public.

In addition to experiencing the vast Baroque splendor of Saint Peter's (FIGS. 24-2, 24-3, 24-4, and 24-5) itself, visitors should not miss the opportunity to descend below ground (via stairs near the crossing) to view the crypts of the many popes interred there. Although Mass services are performed in Saint Peter's on occasion, opportunities to see the pope are rare. Traditionally, he makes a public appearance on Easter Sunday and, from the benediction *loggia* (the balcony) of the Saint Peter's facade, blesses the thousands who gather in the piazza.

Between the piazza and the papal apartments is the Scala Regia (FIG. 24-6) Bernini designed. Behind this staircase is the Sistine Chapel. The restoration of both the ceiling and the *Last Judgment* are complete, allowing spectators to view Michelangelo's cleaned frescoes (see FIGS. 22-13, 22-14, 22-15, 22-16, and 22-25) unimpeded by scaffolding.

The Papal Palace houses the papal apartments, government offices of the Roman Catholic Church, several chapels, and a library. The library (officially named the Biblioteca Apostolica Vaticana) contains more than one million six hundred thousand books, along with manuscripts, prints, engravings, coins, and medals, and is available for scholarly use. Most rooms in the papal apartments are open for public viewing; the Stanza della Segnatura, with Raphael's frescoes (see FIG. 22-17) is a highlight.

Vatican City is also home to an extraordinary art collection scattered throughout several Vatican Museums. In addition to paintings and sculptures, these museums house maps, tapestries, historical items, Egyptian and Etruscan artifacts, and ethnographic objects that Catholic missionaries collected.

Together, these buildings, artworks, and collections speak of a long and storied history—of art and life in the service of religion.

---

impressive single project was the design for a monumental *piazza* (plaza; 1656–1667) in front of Saint Peter's (FIGS. 24-3 and **24-4**). In much the way Michelangelo was forced to reorganize the Capitoline Hill (see FIG. 22-26), Bernini had to adjust his design to some preexisting structures on the site—an ancient obelisk the Romans brought from Egypt (which Pope Sixtus V had relocated to the piazza in 1585 as part of his vision of Christian triumph in Rome) and a fountain Maderno designed. He used these features to define the long axis of a vast oval embraced by colonnades joined to the Saint Peter's facade by two diverging wings. Four rows of huge Tuscan columns make up the two colonnades, which terminate in severely Classical temple fronts. The dramatic gesture of embrace the colonnades make as viewers enter the piazza symbolizes the welcome the Roman Catholic Church gave its members during the Counter-Reformation. Bernini himself referred to his design of the colonnade as appearing like the welcoming arms of the church.

The wings that connect the Saint Peter's facade with the oval piazza flank a trapezoidal space also reminiscent of the Campidoglio (see FIG. 22-26), but here the latter's visual effect was reversed. As seen from the piazza, the diverging wings counteract the natural perspective and tend to bring the facade closer to observers. Emphasizing the facade's height in this manner, Bernini subtly and effectively compensated for its extensive width. Thus, a Baroque transformation expanded the compact central designs of Bramante and Michelangelo into a dynamic complex of axially ordered elements that reach out and enclose spaces of vast dimension. By its sheer scale and theatricality, the complete Saint Peter's

fulfilled Catholicism's needs in the seventeenth century by presenting an awe-inspiring and authoritative vision of the Church.

A SOARING BRONZE CANOPY Long before the planning of the piazza, Bernini had been at work decorating the interior of Saint Peter's. His first commission, completed between 1624 and 1633, called for the design and erection of the gigantic bronze baldacchino (FIG. **24-5**) above the main altar under the great dome. The canopy-like structure (*baldacco* is Italian for "silk from Baghdad," such as for a cloth canopy) marks the tomb of Saint Peter. Almost one hundred feet high (the height of an average eight-story building), the baldacchino serves as a focus of the church's splendor. It at once harmonizes with the tremendous proportions of the new church and visually bridges human scale to the lofty vaults and dome above. Its four spiral columns recall those of the ancient baldacchino over the same spot in Old Saint Peter's, thereby invoking the past to reinforce the Roman Catholic Church's primacy. Partially fluted and wreathed with vines, the columns seem to deny the mass and weight of the tons of bronze resting on them. (The metal was stripped from the Pantheon's portico—ideologically appropriate, given the Church's rejection of paganism.) At the top of the columns four colossal angels stand guard at the upper corners of the canopy. Forming the canopy's apex are four serpentine brackets that elevate the orb and the cross, symbols of the Church's triumph since the time of the emperor Constantine (see FIG. 10-82, right), builder of the original Saint Peter's basilica. The baldacchino also features numerous bees, symbols of the

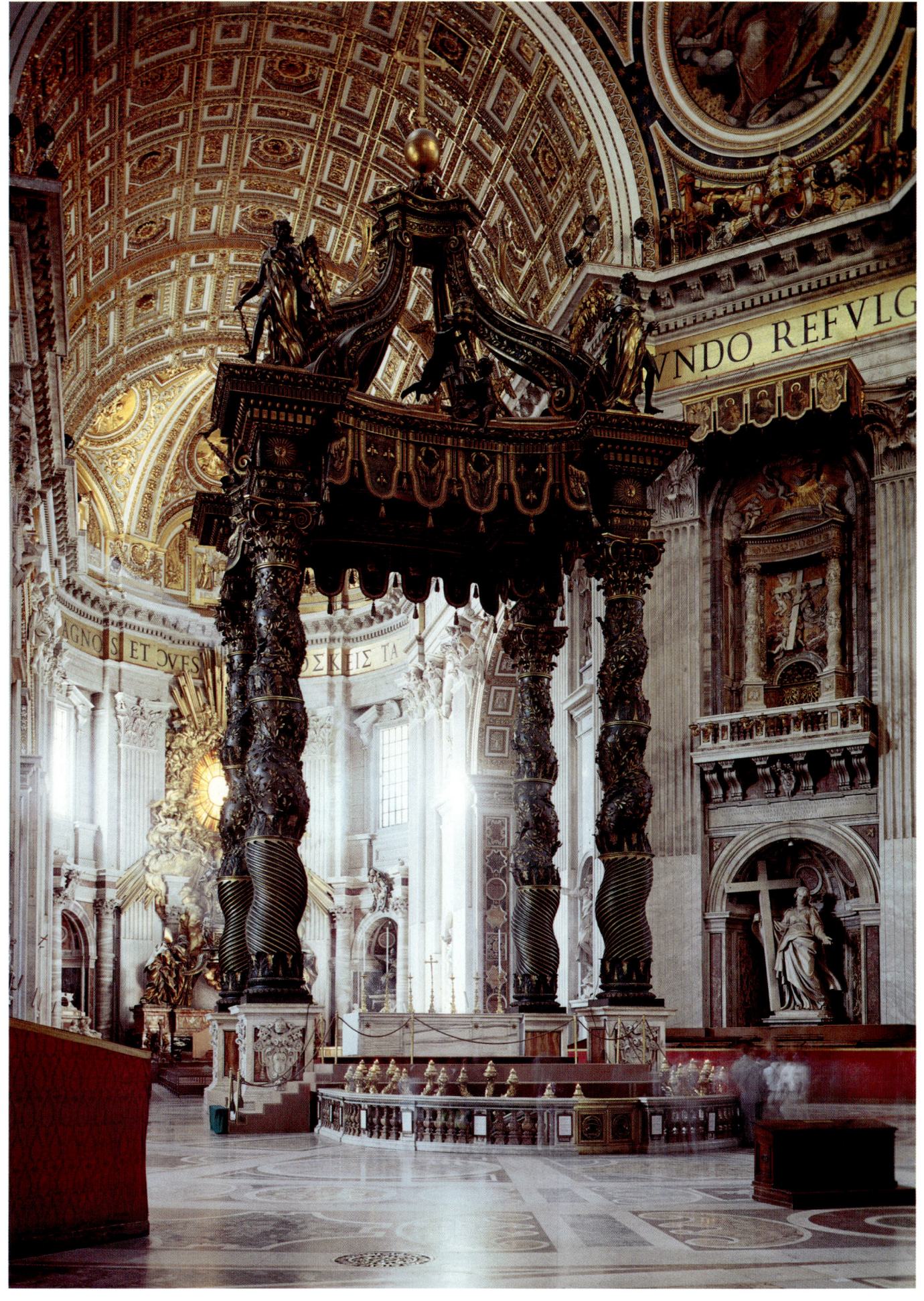

24-5 Gianlorenzo Bernini, baldacchino, Saint Peter's, Vatican City, Rome, Italy, 1624–1633. Gilded bronze, approx. 100′ high.

Barberini family. As the official patron of the work, Pope Urban VIII (Maffeo Barberini, r. 1623–1644) undoubtedly desired appropriate recognition. The structure effectively visualizes the triumph of Christianity and the papal claim to doctrinal supremacy.

The concepts of triumph and grandeur unified both the architecture and the design program of Saint Peter's during the seventeenth century (see "Centuries of Church History on View: Visiting Vatican City," page 724). Suggesting a great and solemn procession, the main axis of the complex traverses the piazza (marked but slowed by the central obelisk) and enters Maderno's nave. It comes to a temporary halt at the altar beneath the baldacchino, but it continues on toward its climactic destination at another great altar in the apse.

A STAIRWAY TO HEAVEN?   Bernini demonstrated his impressive skill at transforming space in another project he undertook in Vatican City, the Scala Regia or Royal Stairway (FIG. **24-6**). This monumental corridor of steps connects the papal apartments to the portico and narthex of Saint Peter's. Because the original passageway was irregular, dark, and dangerous to descend, Pope Alexander VII (r. 1655–1667) commissioned Bernini to replace it. The stairway, its entrance

crowned by a sculptural group of trumpeting angels and the papal arms, is covered by a barrel vault (built in two sections) carried on columns that form aisles flanking the central corridor. By gradually reducing the distance between the columns and walls as the stairway ascends, Bernini actually eliminated the aisles on the upper levels while creating an illusion of width uniformity and aisle continuity for the whole stairway. Likewise, the space between the colonnades narrows with ascent, reinforcing the natural perspective and making the stairs appear longer than they actually are. To minimize this effect, Bernini made the lighting at the top of the stairs brighter, exploiting the natural human inclination to move from darkness toward light. To make the long ascent more tolerable, he inserted an illuminated landing that provides a midway resting point. The result is a highly sophisticated design, both dynamic and dramatic, that repeats on a smaller scale, perhaps even more effectively, the processional sequence found inside Saint Peter's.

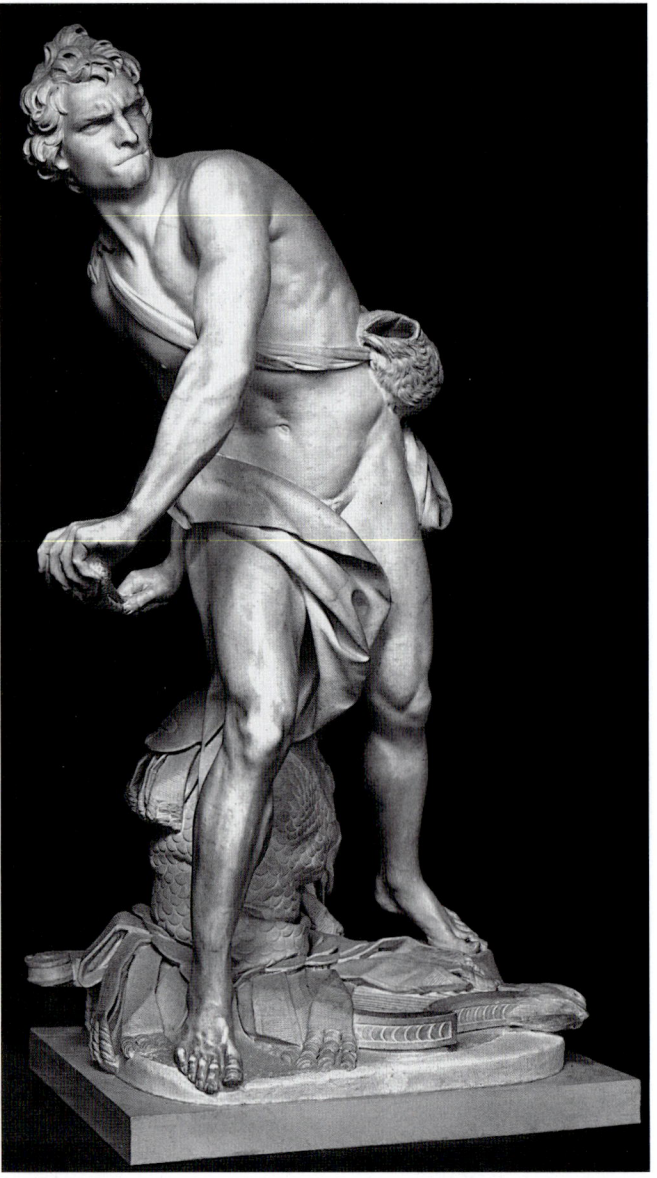

24-6   GIANLORENZO BERNINI, Scala Regia, Vatican City, Rome, Italy, 1663–1666.

24-7   GIANLORENZO BERNINI, *David,* 1623. Marble, approx. 5′ 7″ high. Galleria Borghese, Rome.

DECISIVE AND DRAMATIC ACTION Bernini devoted much of his prolific career to the adornment of Saint Peter's, where his works combine sculpture with architecture. Although Bernini was a great and influential architect, his fame rests primarily on his sculpture, which, like his architecture, energetically expresses the Italian Baroque spirit. Bernini's sculpture is expansive and dramatic, and the element of time usually plays an important role in it. A sculpture that predates his work on Saint Peter's is his *David* (FIG. **24-7**), commissioned by Cardinal Scipione Borghese. This marble statue aims at catching the figure's split-second action and differs markedly from the restful figures of David portrayed by Donatello (see FIG. 21-23), Verrocchio (see FIG. 21-24), and Michelangelo (see FIG. 22-9). Bernini's *David,* his muscular legs widely and firmly planted, is beginning the violent, pivoting motion that will launch the stone from his sling. If the action had been a moment before, his body would have been in one position; the moment after, it would have been in a completely different one. Unlike Myron, the fifth-century B.C. Greek sculptor whose Diskobolus (see FIG. 5-37) is frozen in inaction, Bernini selected the most dramatic of an implied sequence of poses, so observers have to think simultaneously of the continuum and of this tiny fraction of it. The suggested continuum imparts a dynamic quality to the statue that conveys a bursting forth of the energy seen confined in Michelangelo's figures (see FIGS. 22-9 and 22-10). Bernini's statue seems to be moving through time and through space. This is not the kind of sculpture that can be inscribed in a cylinder or confined in a niche; its indicated action demands space around it. Nor is it self-sufficient in the Renaissance sense, as its pose and attitude direct the observer's attention beyond it to its surroundings (in this case, toward an unseen Goliath). Bernini's sculptured figure moves out into and partakes of the physical space that surrounds it and observers. Further, the almost ferocious expression on David's face is a far cry from the placid visages of previous Davids and augments this sculpture's dramatic impact.

AN ECSTATIC AND RADIANT VISION Another Bernini sculpture that displays the expansive quality of Italian Baroque art and its refusal to limit itself to firmly defined spatial settings is *Ecstasy of Saint Theresa* in the Cornaro Chapel (FIG. **24-8**) of the Roman church of Santa Maria della Vittoria. For this chapel, Bernini drew on the full resources of

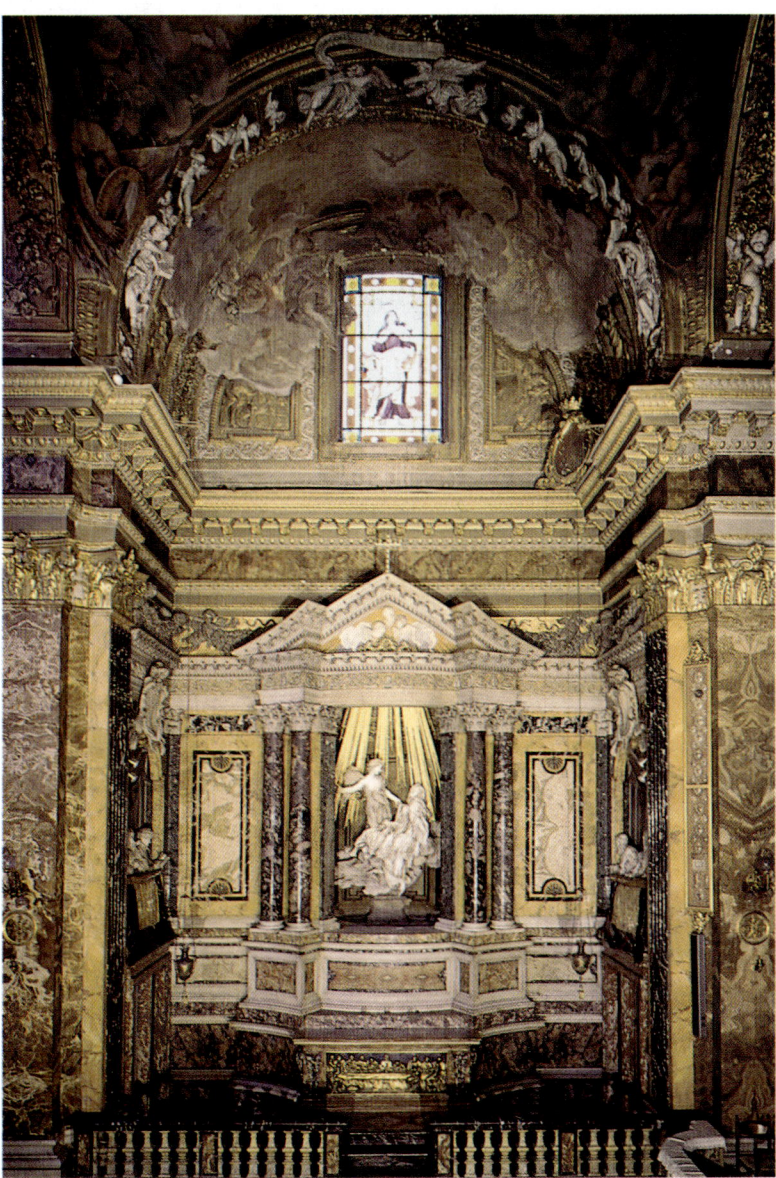

24-8 GIANLORENZO BERNINI, interior of the Cornaro Chapel, Santa Maria della Vittoria, Rome, Italy, 1645–1652.

architecture, sculpture, and painting to charge the entire area with dramatic tension. Saint Theresa was a nun of the Carmelite order and one of the great mystical saints of the Spanish Counter-Reformation. Her conversion occurred after the death of her father, when she fell into a series of trances, saw visions, and heard voices. Feeling a persistent pain, she attributed it to the fire-tipped arrow of Divine love that an angel had thrust repeatedly into her heart. In her writings, Saint Theresa described this experience as making her swoon in delightful anguish. The whole chapel became a theater for the production of this mystical drama. The niche in which it takes place appears as a shallow *proscenium* (the part of the stage in front of the curtain) crowned with a broken Baroque pediment and ornamented with polychrome marble. On either side of the chapel, relief-sculptured portraits of the Cornaro family behind draped praying desks attest to the piety of the patrons (Cardinal Federico Cornaro and his relatives) attending this heavenly drama. Bernini depicted the saint in ecstasy (FIG. **24-9**), unmistakably a mingling of spiri-

tual and physical passion, swooning back on a cloud, while the smiling angel aims his arrow. The entire sculptural group is made of white marble, and Bernini's supreme technical virtuosity is evident in the visual differentiation in texture among the clouds, rough monk's cloth, gauzy material, smooth flesh, and feathery wings. Light from a hidden window of yellow glass pours down on bronze rays that suggest the radiance of Heaven, whose painted representation covers the vault (FIG. 24-8). (Hidden lights have been installed near the top of the rays to ensure visitors to the chapel a consistent viewing experience.) The passionate drama of Bernini's sculpture correlated with the ideas disseminated by Ignatius Loyola, founder of the Jesuit order and later canonized as Saint Ignatius. In his book *Spiritual Exercises,* Ignatius argued that the re-creation of spiritual experiences for viewers would do much to increase devotion and piety. Thus, theatricality and sensory impact were useful vehicles for achieving Counter-Reformation goals. Bernini was an extremely devout Catholic, which undoubtedly contributed to his understanding of those

24-9   GIANLORENZO BERNINI, *Ecstasy of Saint Theresa,* Cornaro Chapel, Santa Maria della Vittoria, Rome, Italy, 1645–1652. Marble, height of group 11′ 6″.

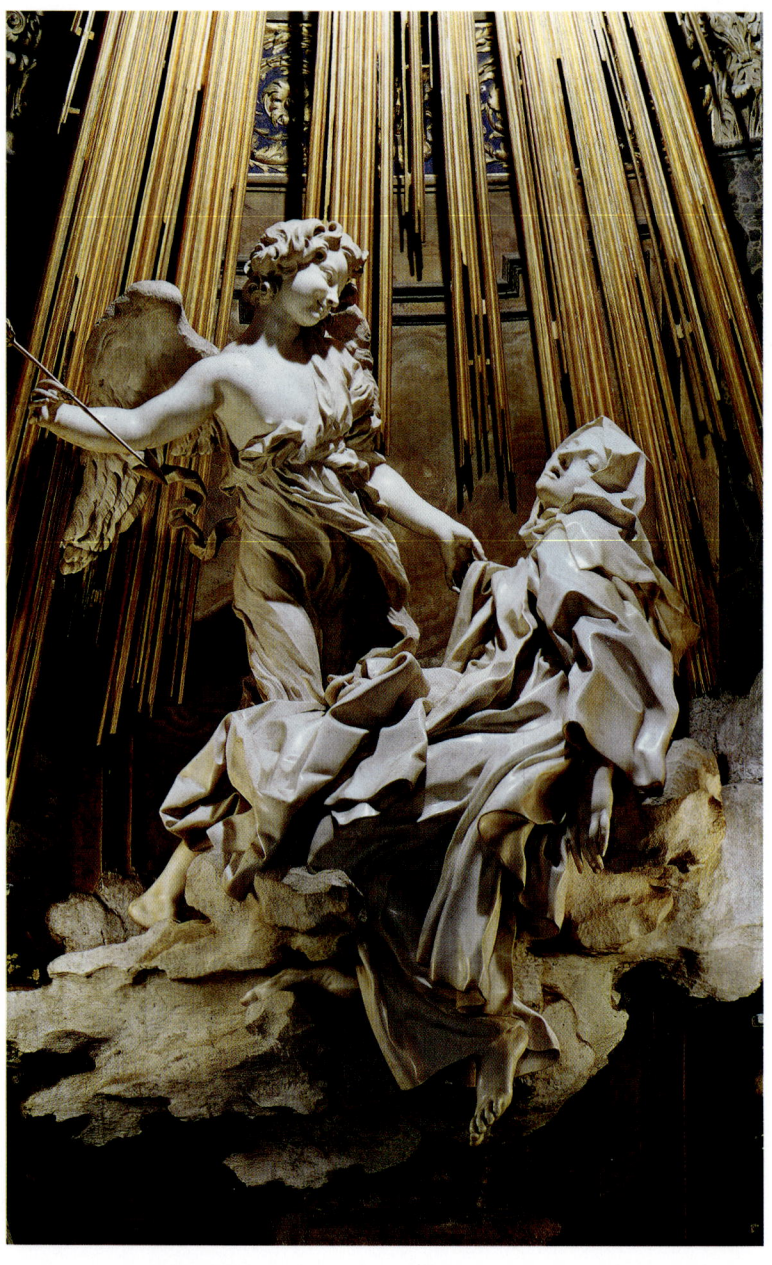

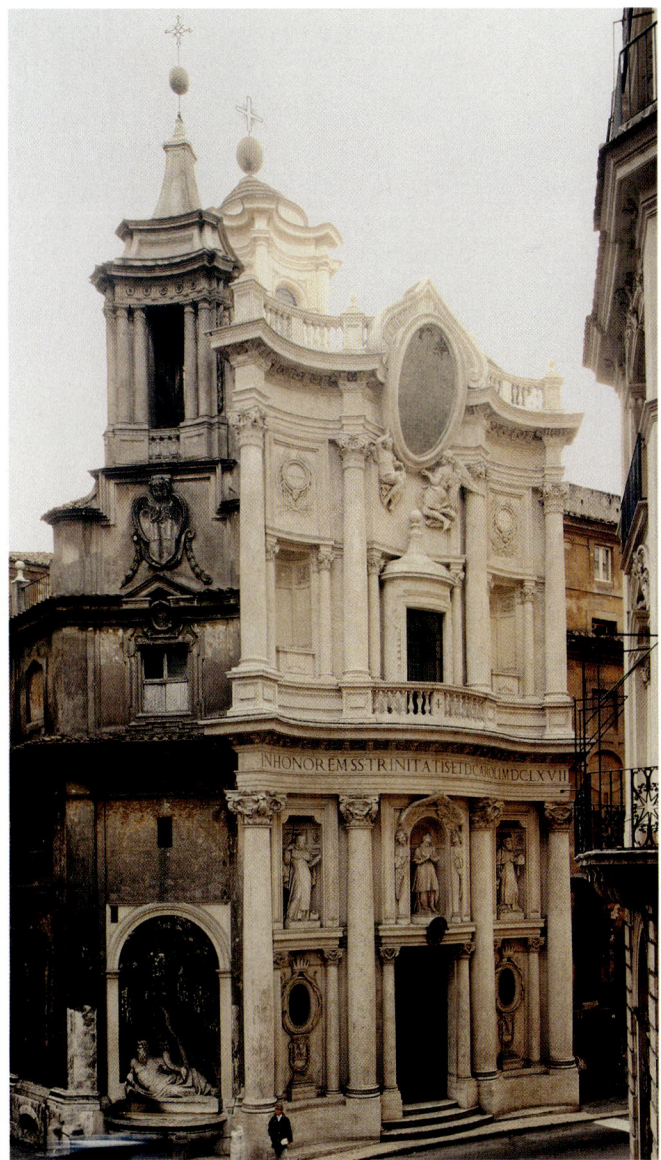

24-10 FRANCESCO BORROMINI, facade of San Carlo alle Quattro Fontane, Rome, Italy, 1665–1676.

goals. His inventiveness, technical skill, sensitivity to his patrons' needs, and energy account for his position as *the* quintessential Italian Baroque artist.

A CHURCH FACADE IN MOTION? FRANCESCO BORROMINI (1599–1667) took Italian Baroque architecture to even greater dramatic heights. A new dynamism appeared in the little church of San Carlo alle Quattro Fontane (Saint Charles of the Four Fountains; FIG. 24-10), where Borromini went well beyond any of his predecessors or contemporaries in emphasizing a building's sculptural qualities. Although Maderno incorporated sculptural elements in his designs for the facades of Santa Susanna (FIG. 24-1) and Saint Peter's (FIG. 24-2), they still develop along relatively lateral planes. Borromini set his whole facade in undulating motion, forward and back, making a counterpoint of concave and convex elements on two levels (for example, the sway of the cornices). He emphasized the three-dimensional effect with deeply recessed niches. This facade is not the traditional flat frontispiece that defines a building's outer limits. It is a pulsating, engaging component inserted between interior and exterior space, de-

signed not to separate but to provide a fluid transition between the two. This functional interrelation of the building and its environment is underlined by the curious fact it has not one but two facades. The second, a narrow bay crowned with its own small tower, turns away from the main facade and, following the curve of the street, faces an intersection. (The upper facade was completed seven years after Borromini's death, and historians cannot be sure to what degree the present design reflects his original intention.)

The interior is not only an ingenious response to an awkward site but also a provocative variation on the theme of the centrally planned church. In plan (FIG. 24-11) San Carlo looks like a hybrid of a Greek cross and an oval, with a long axis between entrance and apse. The side walls move in an undulating flow that reverses the facade's motion. Vigorously projecting columns define the space into which they protrude just as much as they do the walls attached to them. This molded interior space is capped by a deeply coffered oval dome that seems to float on the light entering through windows hidden in its base. Rich variations on the basic theme of the oval, dynamic relative to the static circle, create an interior that appears to flow from entrance to altar, unimpeded by the segmentation so characteristic of Renaissance buildings.

A COHESIVE SHELL EMBRACING THE PIOUS
The unification of interior space is carried even further in Borromini's Chapel of Saint Ivo in the courtyard of the

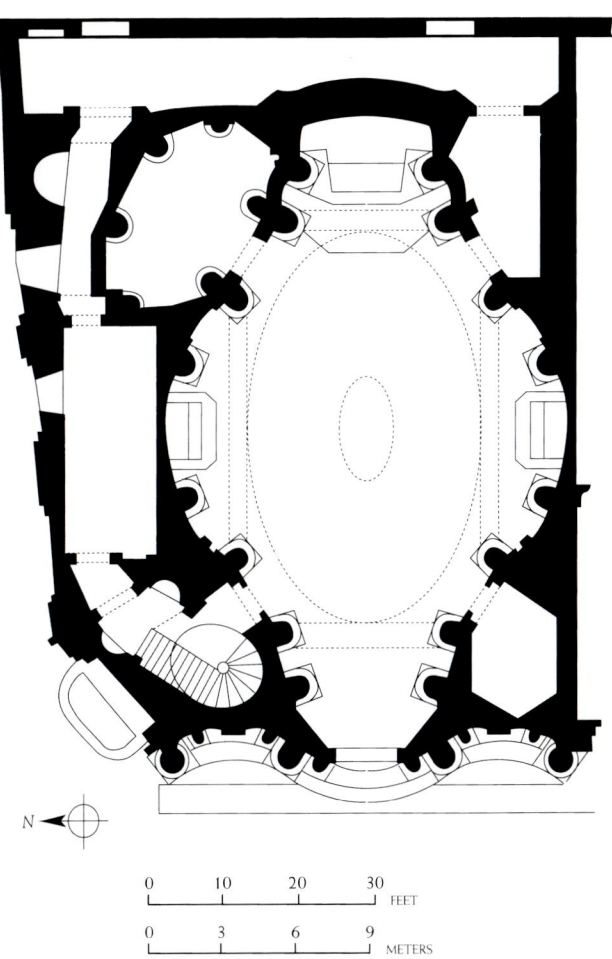

24-11 FRANCESCO BORROMINI, plan of San Carlo alle Quattro Fontane, Rome, Italy, 1638–1641.

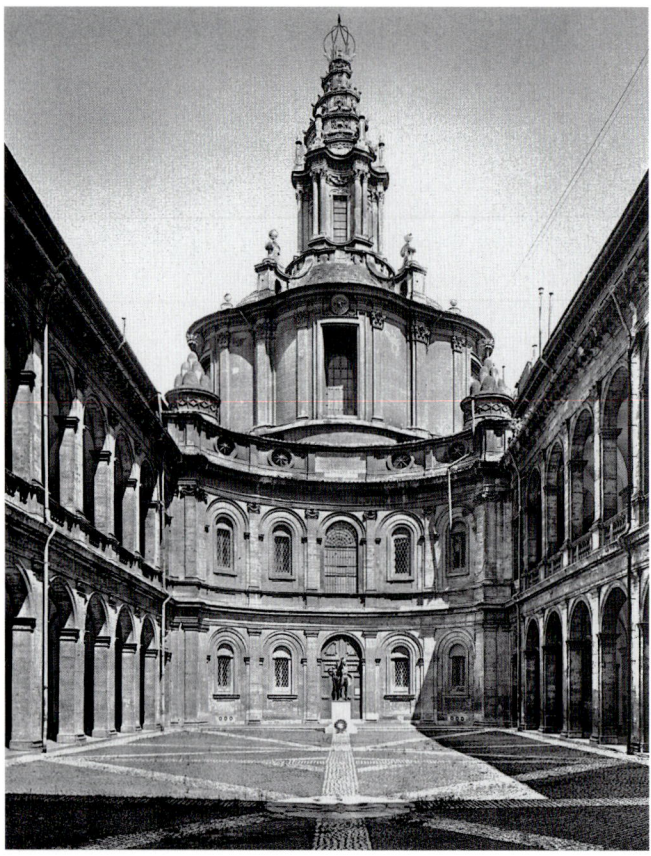

24-12 Francesco Borromini, Chapel of Saint Ivo, College of the Sapienza, Rome, Italy, begun 1642.

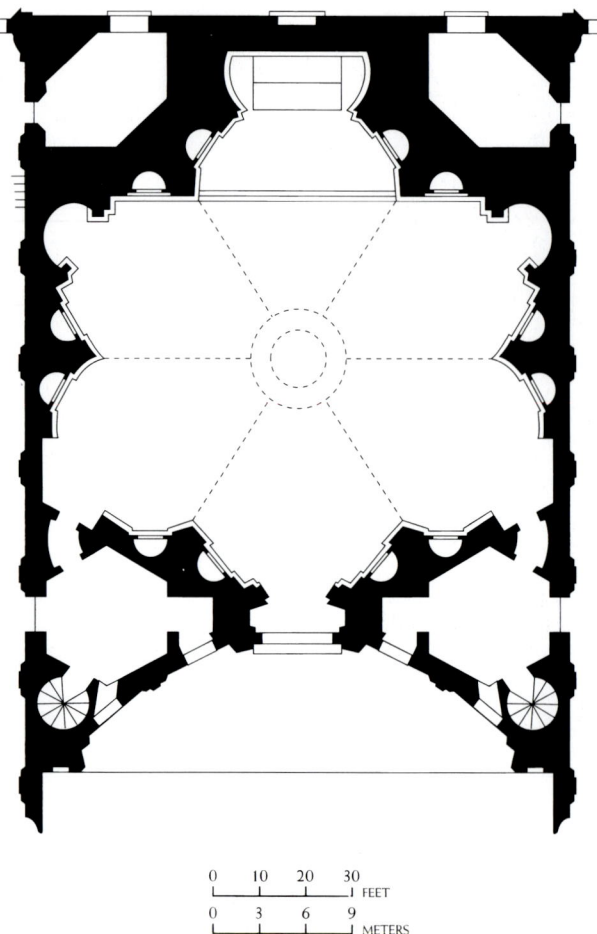

24-13 Francesco Borromini, plan of the Chapel of Saint Ivo, College of the Sapienza, Rome, Italy, begun 1642.

College of the Sapienza (Wisdom) in Rome (FIG. **24-12**). In his characteristic manner, Borromini played concave against convex forms on the upper level of this chapel's exterior. The lower stories of the court, which frame the bottom facade, were already there when Borromini began work. Above the facade's inward curve—its design adjusted to the earlier arcades of the court—rises a convex drumlike structure that supports the dome's lower parts. Powerful pilasters restrain the forces that seem to push the bulging forms outward. Buttresses above the pilasters curve upward to brace a tall, ornate lantern topped by a spiral that seems to fasten the structure, screw-like, to the sky.

The centralized plan of the Saint Ivo chapel (FIG. **24-13**) is that of a star, having rounded-off points and apses on all sides. Indentations and projections along the angled curving walls create a highly complex plan, with all the elements fully reflected in the interior elevation. From floor to lantern, the wall panels rise in a continuously tapering sweep halted only momentarily by a single horizontal cornice (FIG. **24-14**). Thus, the dome is not, as in the Renaissance, a separate unit placed on the supporting block of a building. It is an organic part that evolves out of and shares the qualities of the supporting walls, and it cannot be separated from them. This continuous complexity creates a dynamic and cohesive shell that encloses and energetically molds a scalloped fragment of universal space. Few architects have matched Borromini's ability to translate extremely complicated designs into such masterfully unified structures as Saint Ivo.

A TRIPARTITE FACADE The heir to Borromini's sculptured architectural style was GUARINO GUARINI (1624–1683), a priest, mathematician, and architect who spent the last seventeen years of his life in Turin converting that provincial Italian town into a showcase of architectural theories that later swept much of Europe. In his Palazzo Carignano (FIG. **24-15**), Guarini effectively applied Borromini's principle of undulating facades. He divided his long facade into three units, the central one curving much like the facade of San Carlo alle Quattro Fontane (FIG. 24-10) and flanked by two blocklike wings. This lateral three-part division of facades, characteristic of most Baroque palazzi, is probably based on the observation that the average person instinctively can recognize up to three objects as a unit. A greater number would require observers to count each object individually. A tripartite organization of extended surfaces thus allowed artists to introduce variety into their designs without destroying structural unity. It also permitted adding emphasis to the central axis, which Guarini did here most effectively by punching out deep cavities in the middle of his convex central block. He enhanced the variety of his design with richly textured surfaces (all executed in brick) and pilasters, which further subdivide his units into three bays each. High and low reliefs create shadows of different intensities and add to the decorative effect.

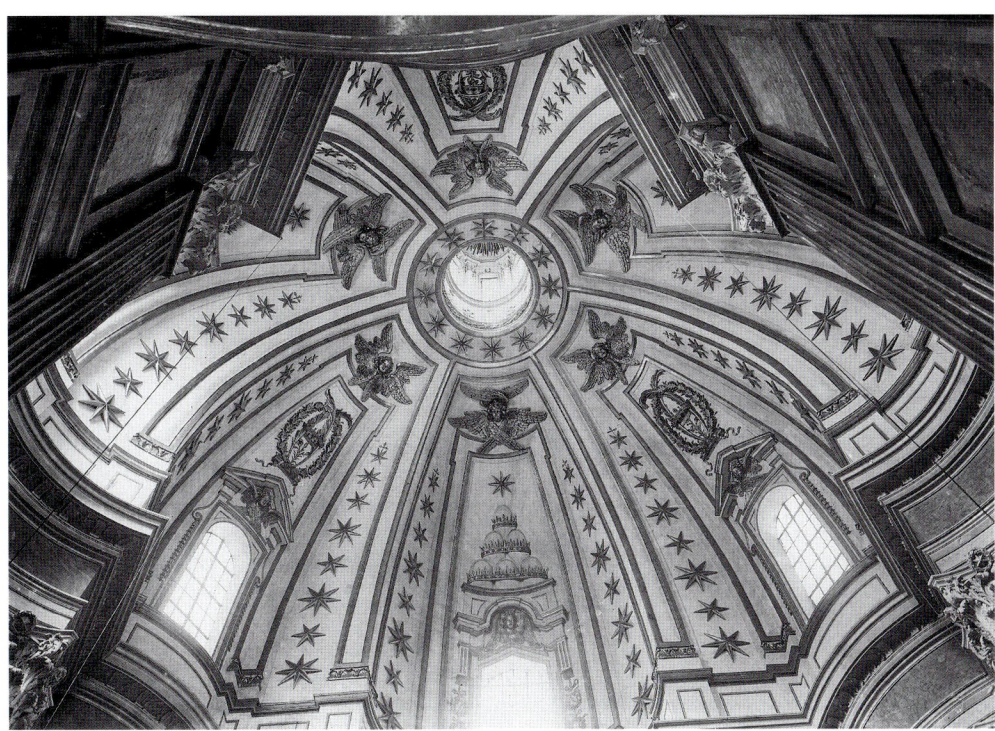

24-14   Chapel of Saint Ivo (view into dome), College of the Sapienza, Rome, Italy, begun 1642.

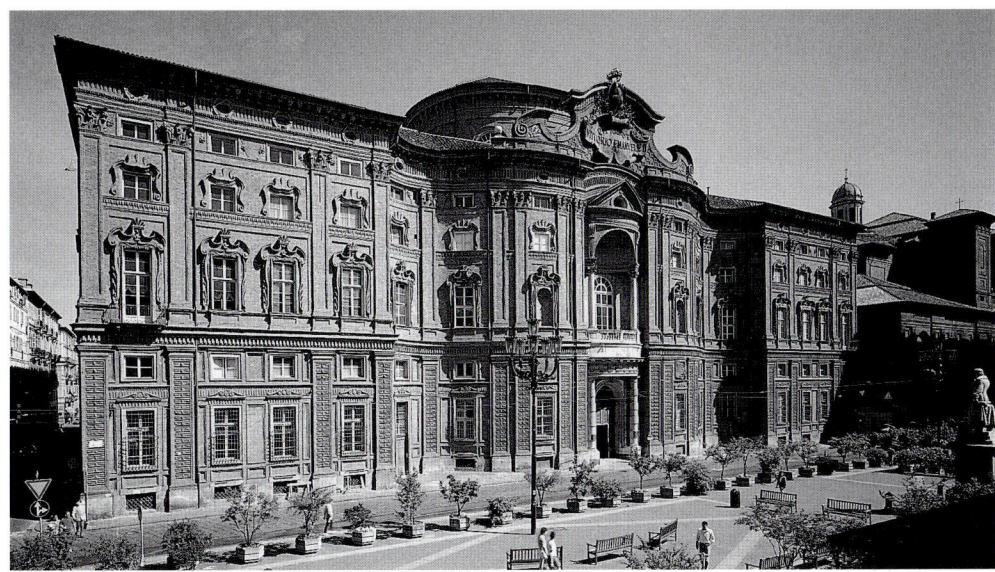

24-15   GUARINO GUARINI, Palazzo Carignano, Turin, Italy, 1679–1692.

A KALEIDOSCOPIC VISION OF HEAVEN   Guarini's mathematical talents must have guided him when he designed the extraordinarily complex dome of the Chapel of the Santissima Sindone (Holiest Shroud), a small central-plan building attached to the Turin Cathedral. A view into this dome (FIG. **24-16**) reveals a bewildering display of geometric elements appearing to move in kaleidoscopic fashion around a circular focus containing a painting of the bright Dove of the Holy Spirit. Here, the architect transformed the traditional dome into a series of segmented intersecting arches. A comparison of Guarini's dome with that of the church of Sant'Eligio degli Orefici in Rome (FIG. **24-17**), attributed both to Bramante and to Raphael

and reconstructed about 1600, indicates that a fundamental change occurred. The pristine clarity of the latter's unmodified circular shape immediately recalls the Pantheon dome (see FIG. 10-50). Guarini converted the static "dome of Heaven" of Renaissance architecture and philosophy into the dynamic Italian Baroque design that conveys a dramatic spiritual presence.

The styles of Borromini and Guarini moved across the Alps and inspired architects in Austria and southern Germany (FIG. 24-76) in the late seventeenth and early eighteenth centuries. These styles were also particularly popular in the Catholic regions of Europe and the New World (especially in Brazil).

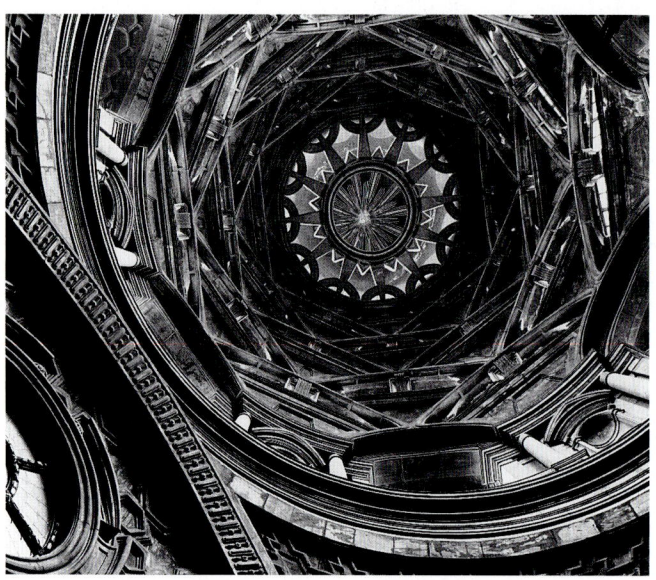

24-16   GUARINO GUARINI, Chapel of Santissima Sindone (view into dome), Turin, Italy, 1667–1694.

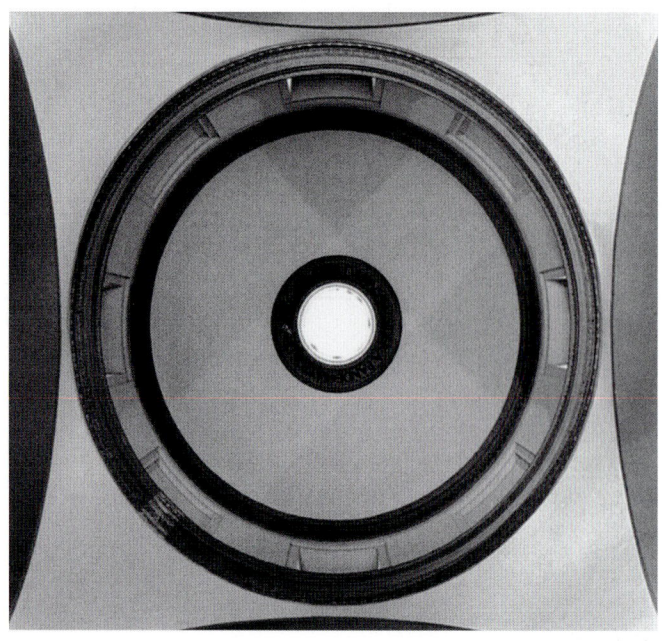

24-17   Dome of Sant'Eligio degli Orefici (view into dome), Rome, Italy, attributed to BRAMANTE and RAPHAEL, ca. 1509; reconstructed ca. 1600.

NATURALIZING RELIGIOUS ART   Although sculpture and architecture provided the most obvious vehicles for manipulating space and creating theatrical effects, painting continued to be an important art form, as it was in previous centuries. Among the most noted Italian Baroque painters were Caravaggio and Annibale Carracci, whose styles, although different, were both thoroughly in accord with the period. MICHELANGELO MERISI, known as CARAVAGGIO (1573–1610) after the northern Italian town he came from, developed a unique style that had tremendous influence throughout Europe. His outspoken disdain for the classical masters (probably more vocal than real) drew bitter criticism from many painters, one of whom denounced him as the "anti-Christ of painting." Giovanni Pietro Bellori, the most influential critic of the age and an admirer of Carracci, felt that Caravaggio's refusal to emulate the models of his distinguished predecessors threatened the whole classical tradition of Italian painting that had reached its zenith in Raphael's work. Yet despite this criticism and the problems in Caravaggio's troubled life (reconstructed from documents such as police records), many paid Caravaggio the supreme compliment of borrowing from his innovations. His influence on later artists, as much outside Italy as within, was immense. In his art, Caravaggio naturalized both religion and the classics, reducing them to human dramas played out in the harsh and dingy settings of his time and place. His unidealized figures selected from the fields and the streets were, however, effective precisely because of the Italian public's familiarity with such figures.

STARK CONTRASTS OF LIGHT AND DARK
Caravaggio painted *Conversion of Saint Paul* (FIG. **24-18**) for the Cerasi Chapel in the Roman church of Santa Maria del Popolo. It illustrates the conversion of the Pharisee Saul to Christianity, when he became the disciple Paul. The saint-to-be appears amid his conversion, flat on his back with his arms thrown up. In the background, an old hostler seems preoccupied with caring for the horse. At first inspection, little here suggests the momentous significance of the spiritual event taking place. The painting's viewers seem to be witnessing a mere stable accident, not a man overcome by a great miracle. Although Caravaggio departed from traditional depictions of such religious scenes, the eloquence and humanity with which he imbued his paintings impressed many. As a result, Caravaggio found numerous sympathetic patrons both within the Roman Catholic Church and from secular realms.

Caravaggio also employed other formal devices to compel the viewer's interest and involvement in the event. In *Conversion of Saint Paul,* he used a perspective and a chiaroscuro intended to bring viewers as close as possible to the scene's space and action, almost as if they were participating in it. The sense of inclusion is augmented by the low horizon line. Caravaggio designed *Conversion of Saint Paul* for presentation on the chapel wall, positioned at the viewers' line of sight as they stand at the chapel entrance. In addition, the sharply lit figures are meant to be seen as emerging from the dark of the background. The actual light from the chapel's windows functions as a kind of stage lighting for the production of a vision, analogous to the rays in Bernini's *Ecstasy of Saint Theresa* (FIG. 24-9). Thus, Caravaggio, like Bernini, injected the theatrical into his art.

Caravaggio's use of light is certainly dramatic. The stark contrast of light and dark was the feature of Caravaggio's style that first shocked and then fascinated his contemporaries. Caravaggio's use of dark settings enveloping their occupants, which profoundly influenced European art, has been called *tenebrism,* from the Italian word *tenebroso,* or "shadowy" manner. Although tenebrism was widespread in seventeenth-century art, it made its most emphatic appearance in the art of

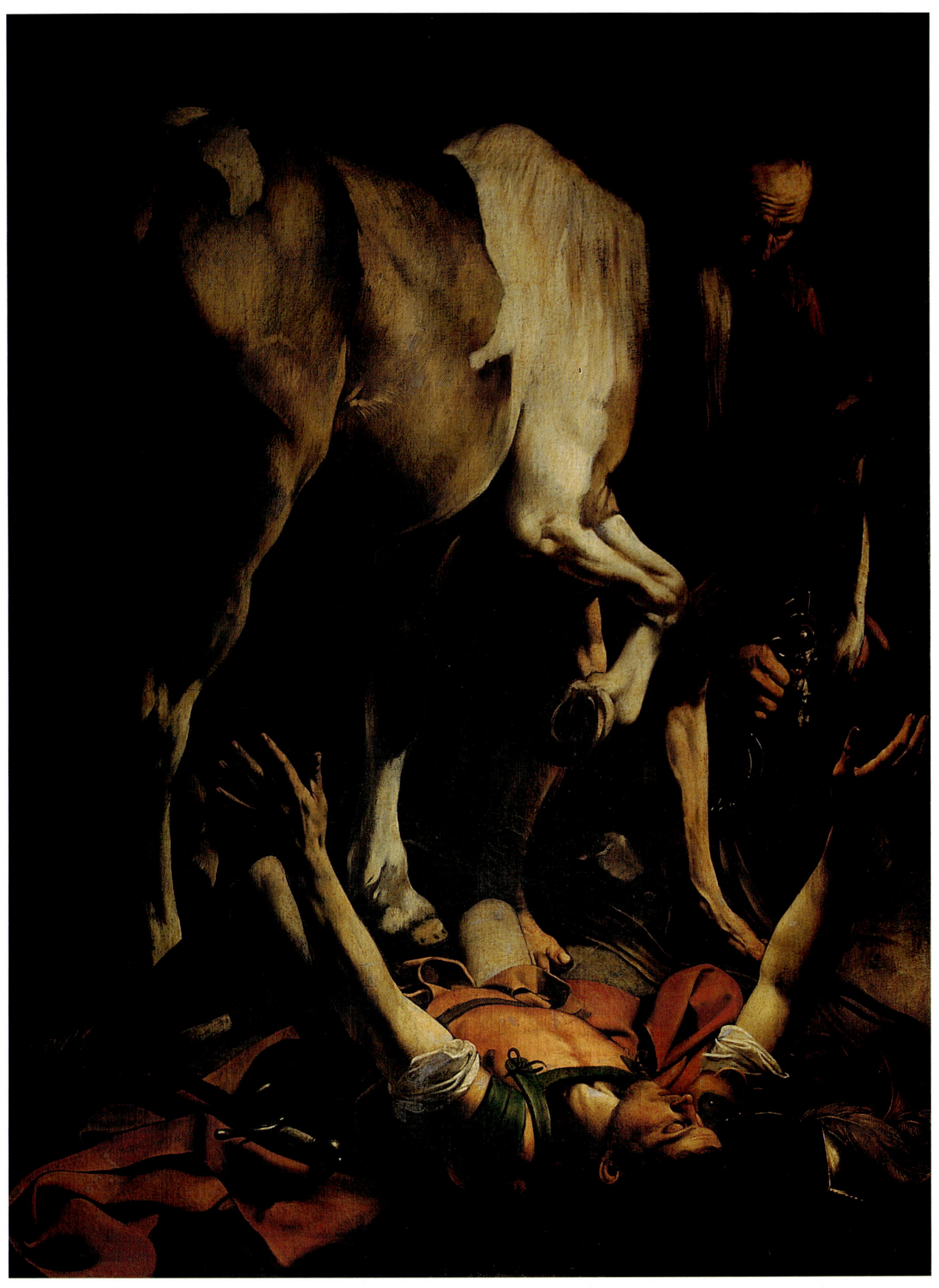

24-18 CARAVAGGIO, *Conversion of Saint Paul,* Cerasi Chapel, Santa Maria del Popolo, Rome, Italy, ca. 1601. Oil on canvas, approx. 7′ 6″ × 5′ 9″.

24-19 CARAVAGGIO, *Calling of Saint Matthew,* Contarelli Chapel, San Luigi dei Francesi, Rome, Italy, ca. 1597–1601. Oil on canvas, 11′ 1″ × 11′ 5″.

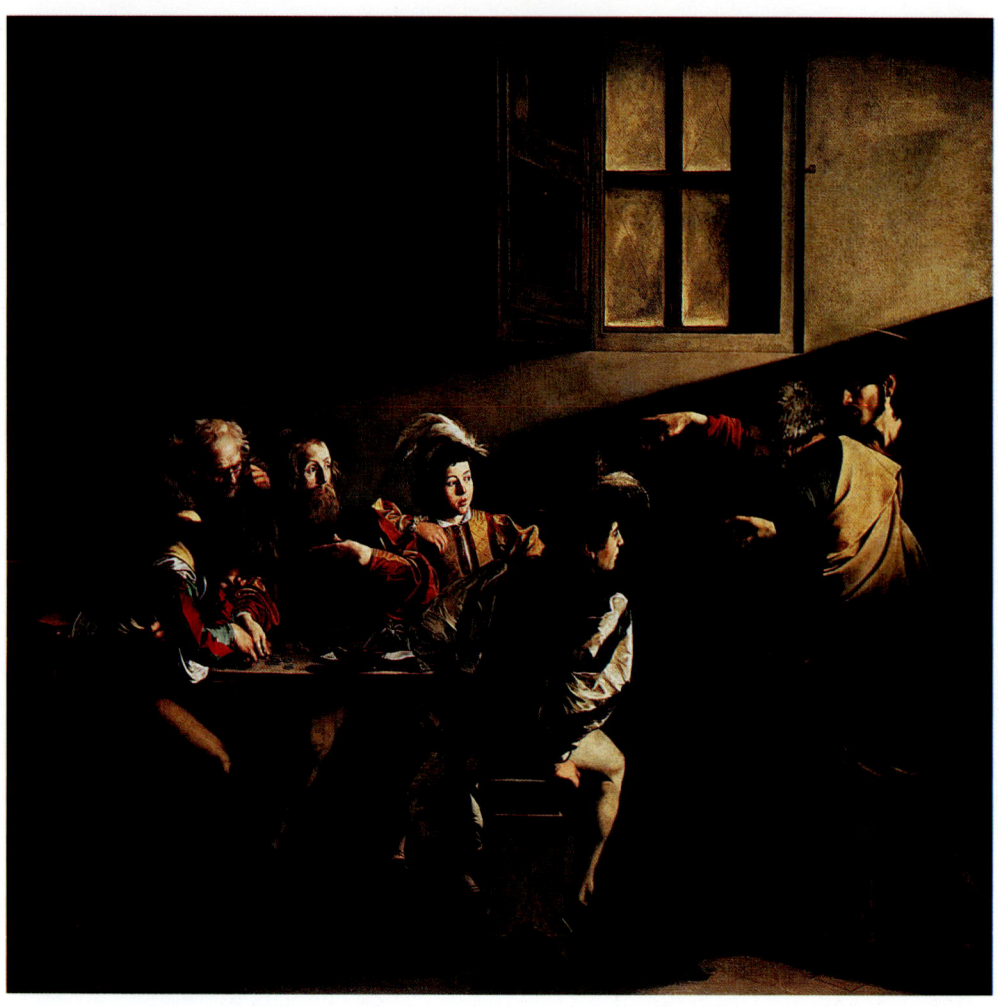

Spain and of the Netherlands. In Caravaggio's work, tenebrism also contributed mightily to the essential meaning of his pictures. In *Conversion of Saint Paul,* the dramatic spotlight shining down upon the fallen Pharisee is the light of divine revelation converting Saul to Christianity.

FROM TAX COLLECTOR TO DISCIPLE A piercing ray of light illuminating a world of darkness and bearing a spiritual message is also a central feature of one of Caravaggio's early masterpieces, *Calling of Saint Matthew* (FIG. **24-19**). It is one of two large canvases honoring Saint Matthew the artist painted for the side walls of the Contarelli Chapel in San Luigi dei Francesi in Rome. The commonplace setting is typical of Caravaggio—a bland street scene with a plain building wall serving as a backdrop. Into this mundane environment, cloaked in mysterious shadow and almost unseen, Christ, identifiable initially only by his indistinct halo, enters from the right. With a commanding gesture that recalls that of the Lord in Michelangelo's *Creation of Adam* on the Sistine Chapel ceiling (see FIG. 22-14), he summons Levi, the Roman tax collector, to a higher calling. The astonished tax collector, whose face is highlighted for viewers by the beam of light emanating from an unspecified source above Christ's head and outside the picture, points to himself in disbelief. Although Christ's extended arm is reminiscent of the Lord in *Creation of Adam,* the position of Christ's hand and wrist is similar to that of Adam. This reference is highly appropriate—theologi-

cally, Christ is the second Adam. While Adam was responsible for the Fall of Man, Christ is responsible for human redemption. The conversion of Levi (who became Matthew) brought his salvation.

VISUALIZING TRANSUBSTANTIATION In 1603, Caravaggio produced a large-scale painting, *Entombment* (FIG. **24-20**), for the Chapel of Pietro Vittrice at Santa Maria in Vallicella in Rome. This work includes all the hallmarks of Caravaggio's distinctive style: the plebian figure types (particularly visible in the scruffy, worn face of Nicodemus—a Pharisee Christ taught who holds Christ's legs in the foreground), the stark use of darks and lights, and the invitation for viewers to participate in the scene. As in *Conversion of Saint Paul,* the action takes place here in the foreground. The artist positioned the figures on a stone slab whose corner appears to extend into the viewer's space. This suggests that Christ's body will be laid directly in front of viewers.

Beyond its ability to move its audience, such a composition also had theological implications. In light of the ongoing Counter-Reformation efforts, such implications cannot be overlooked. To viewers in the chapel, it appeared as though the men were laying Christ's body onto the altar, which was in front of the painting. This served to visualize the doctrine of *transubstantiation* (the transformation of the Eucharist and wine into the Body and Blood of Christ)—a doctrine central to Catholicism but rejected by Protestants. By depicting

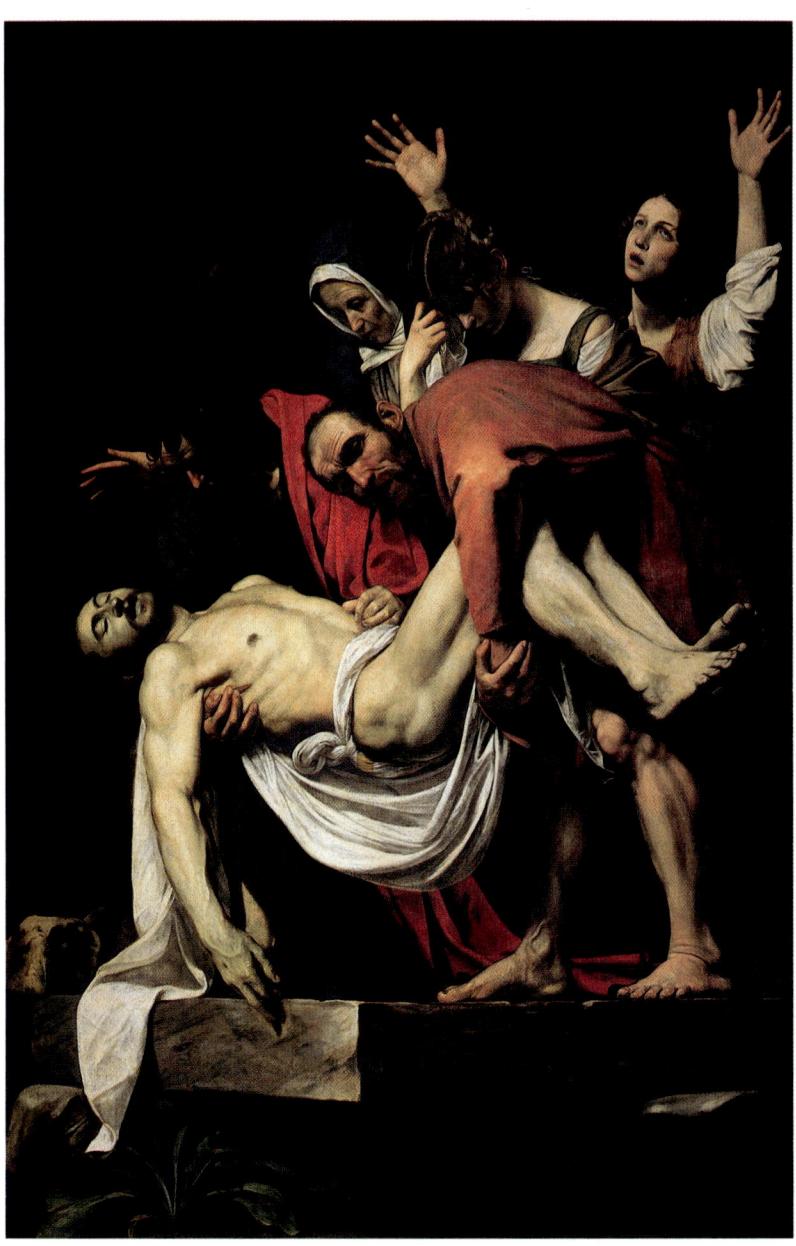

24-20 CARAVAGGIO, *Entombment,* from the chapel of Pietro Vittrice, Santa Maria in Vallicella, Rome, Italy, ca. 1603. Oil on canvas, 9′ 10$\frac{1}{8}$″ × 6′ 7$\frac{15}{16}$″. Musei Vaticani, Pinacoteca, Rome.

Christ's body as though it were physically present during the Mass, Caravaggio visually articulated an abstract theological precept. Unfortunately, viewers no longer can experience this effect.

IN THE FOOTSTEPS OF CARAVAGGIO Caravaggio's style became increasingly popular, and his combination of naturalism and drama appealed both to patrons and artists. A significant artist often discussed as a "Caravaggista" (a close follower of Caravaggio) is ARTEMISIA GENTILESCHI (ca. 1593–1653). Gentileschi was instructed by her artist father Orazio, who was himself strongly influenced by Caravaggio. Her successful career, pursued in Florence, Venice, Naples, and Rome, helped to disseminate Caravaggio's manner throughout the peninsula.

In her *Judith Slaying Holofernes* (FIG. **24-21**), Gentileschi used the tenebrism and what might be called the "dark" subject matter Caravaggio favored. Significantly, Gentileschi chose a narrative involving a heroic female, a favorite theme of hers. The story, from an Apocryphal work of the Old Testament, the Book of Judith, relates the delivery of Israel from its enemy, Holofernes. Having succumbed to Judith's charms, the Assyrian general Holofernes invited her to his tent for the night. When he fell asleep, Judith cut off his head. In this version of the scene (Gentileschi produced more than one image of Judith), Judith and her maidservant are beheading Holofernes. The event's drama cannot be evaded—blood spurts everywhere, and the strength necessary to complete the task is evident as the two women struggle with the sword. The tension and strain are palpable. The controlled highlights on the action in the foreground recall Caravaggio's work and heighten the drama here as well.

DRAWN TO THE CLASSICS In contrast to Caravaggio, ANNIBALE CARRACCI (1560–1609) not only studied but also emulated the Renaissance masters carefully. Carracci received much of his training at an academy of art in his native Bologna. Founded cooperatively by his family members, among them his cousin Ludovico Carracci (1555–1619) and brother Agostino Carracci (1557–1602), the Bolognese

24-21   ARTEMISIA GENTILESCHI, *Judith Slaying Holofernes,* ca. 1614–1620. Oil on canvas, 6' 6 $\frac{1}{3}$" × 5' 4". Galleria degli Uffizi, Florence.

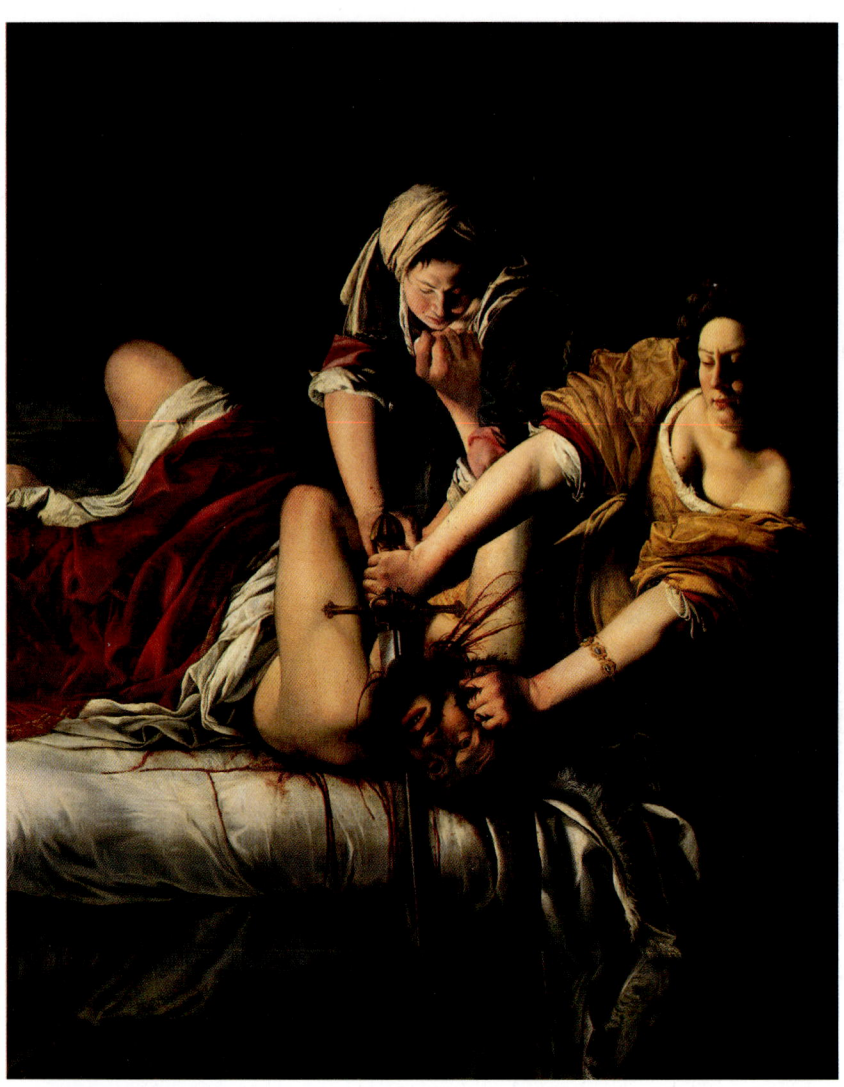

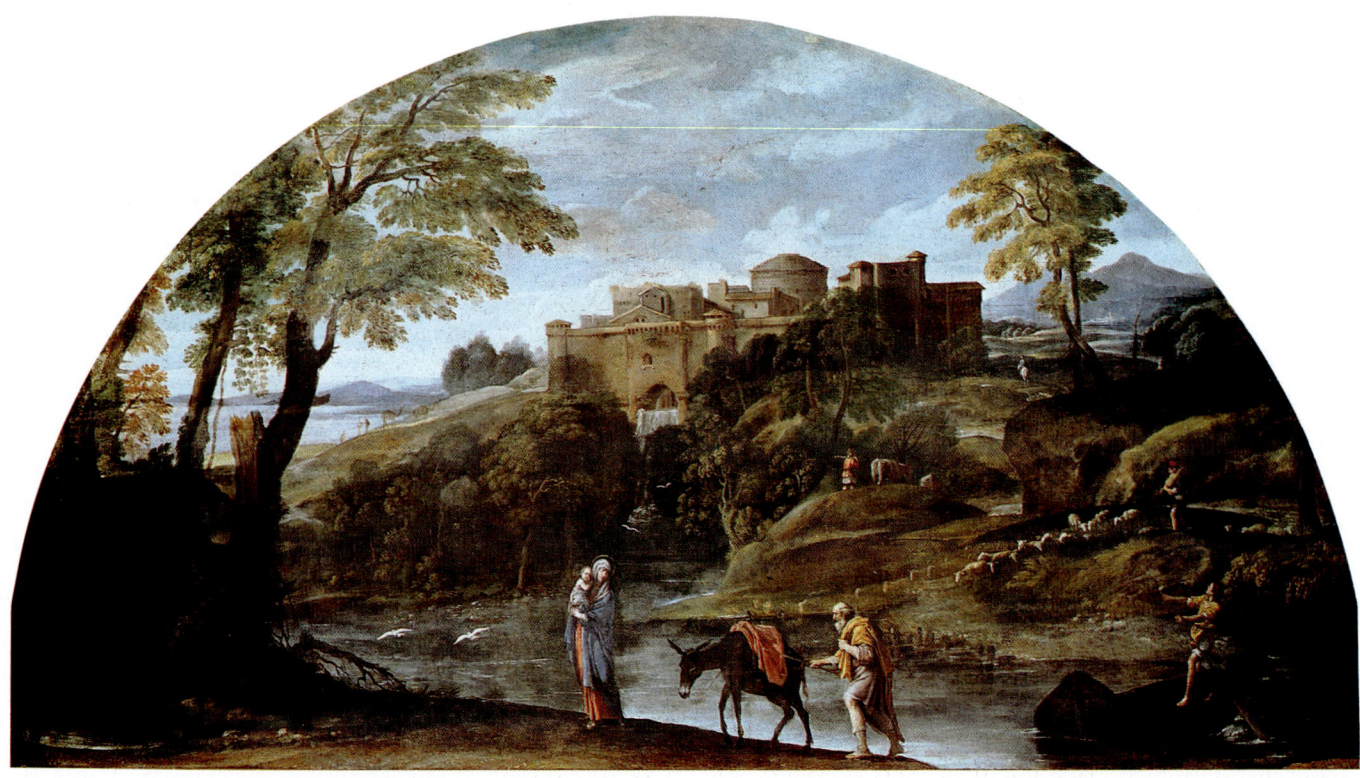

24-22   ANNIBALE CARRACCI, *Flight into Egypt,* 1603–1604. Oil on canvas, approx. 4' × 7' 6". Galleria Doria Pamphili, Rome.

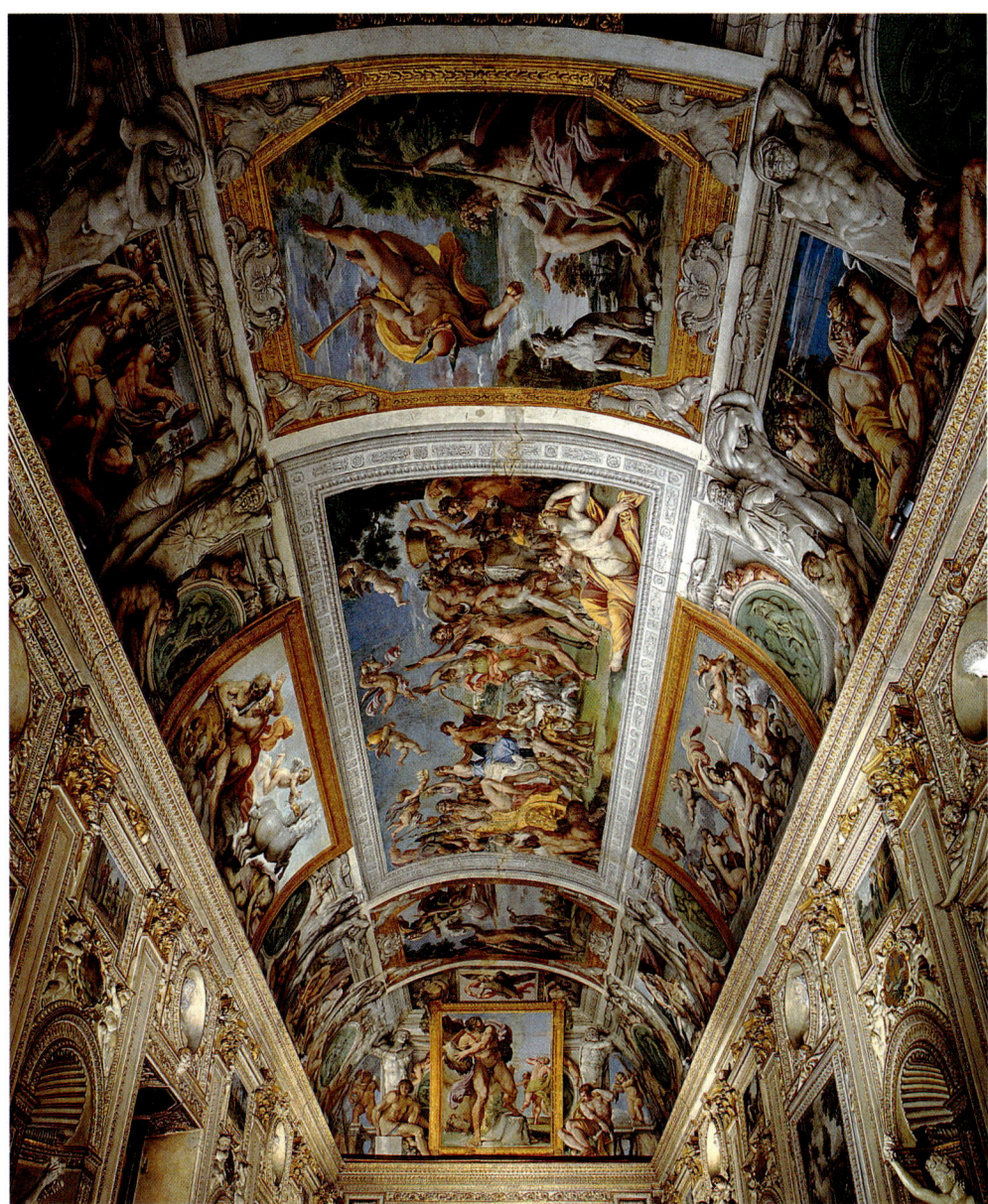

24-23 ANNIBALE CARRACCI, *Loves of the Gods,* ceiling frescoes in the gallery, Palazzo Farnese, Rome, Italy, 1597–1601.

academy was the first significant institution of its kind in the history of Western art. It was founded on the premises that art can be taught—the basis of any academic philosophy of art—and that its instruction must include the classical and Renaissance traditions in addition to studying anatomy and life drawing. Thus, in contrast to Caravaggio's more "naturalistic" style, Carracci embraced a more classically ordered style.

For example, in his *Flight into Egypt* (FIG. **24-22**), based on the biblical narrative from Matthew 2:13–14, Carracci created the "ideal" or "classical" landscape. Here he pictorially represented nature ordered by divine law and human reason. The style's roots are in the landscape backgrounds of Venetian Renaissance paintings (compare FIG. 22-33). Tranquil hills and fields, quietly gliding streams, serene skies, unruffled foliage, shepherds with their flocks—all the props of the pastoral scene and mood—expand in such paintings to fill the picture space. Carracci regularly included screens of trees in the foreground, dark against the sky's even light. In this scene, streams or terraces, carefully placed one above the

other and narrowed, zigzag through the terrain, leading the viewer's eyes back to the middle ground. There, many Venetian Renaissance landscape artists depicted architectural structures (as Carracci did in *Flight into Egypt*)—walled towns or citadels, towers, temples, monumental tombs, villas. Such constructed environments captured idealized antiquity and the idyllic life. Although the artists often took the subjects for these classically rendered scenes from religious or heroic stories, they seem to have given precedence to the pastoral landscapes over the narratives. Here, Mary, with the Christ Child, and Saint Joseph are greatly diminished in size, simply becoming part of the landscape as they wend their way slowly to Egypt after having been ferried across a stream (Matt. 2:13–14).

A CEILING FIT FOR THE GODS Among Carracci's most notable works is his decoration of the Palazzo Farnese gallery (FIG. **24-23**) in Rome. Cardinal Odoardo Farnese, a wealthy descendant of Pope Paul III, commissioned this ceiling fresco to celebrate the wedding of the cardinal's brother.

Appropriately, its iconographic program is titled *Loves of the Gods*—interpretations of the varieties of earthly and divine love in classical mythology.

Carracci arranged the scenes in a format resembling framed easel paintings on a wall, but here he painted them on the surfaces of a shallow curved vault. The Sistine Chapel ceiling (see FIG. 22-13), of course, comes to mind, although it is not an exact source. This type of simulation of easel painting for ceiling design is called *quadro riportato* (transferred framed painting). Carracci's great influence made it fashionable for more than a century. The framed pictures are flanked by polychrome seated nude youths, who turn their heads to gaze at the scenes around them, and by standing Atlas figures painted to resemble marble statues. Carracci derived these motifs from Michelangelo's Sistine Chapel ceiling. Notably, the chiaroscuro is not the same for both the pictures and the figures surrounding them. The painter modeled the figures inside the quadri in an even sculptured light. The outside figures seem to be lit from beneath, as if they were actual three-dimensional beings or statues illuminated by torches in the gallery below. This interest in illusion, already manifest in the Renaissance, continued in the grand ceiling compositions of the seventeenth century. In the crown of the vault, a long panel representing the *Triumph of Bacchus* is a quite ingenious mixture of Raphael and Titian. It reflects Carracci's adroitness in adjusting their authoritative styles to make something of his own.

A HEAVENLY SCENE BY A "DIVINE" ARTIST
Another artist trained in the Bolognese academy, GUIDO RENI (1575–1642), selected Raphael for his inspiration, as is evident in his *Aurora* (FIG. 24-24), a ceiling fresco in the Casino Rospigliosi in Rome. Aurora (Dawn) leads Apollo's chariot, while the Hours dance about it. Reni conceived *Aurora* in

quadro riportato, like the paintings in Carracci's *Loves of the Gods,* and painted a complex and convincing illusionistic frame. The fresco exhibits a suave, almost swimming, motion; soft modeling; and sure composition, without Raphael's sculpturesque strength. It is an intelligent interpretation of the master's style and of ancient classical art, for the ultimate sources of the composition were Roman reliefs (see FIG. 10-39) and coins depicting emperors in triumphal chariots accompanied by flying Victories and other personifications. Due to paintings such as *Aurora,* Reni was so much admired in his own day and well into the nineteenth century that he was known as "the divine Guido."

The impressive ceiling frescoes produced by Carracci and others inspired many artists and patrons to explore the capabilities of ceiling painting. The experience of looking up at a painting is different from simply looking at a painting hanging on a wall. The considerable height and the expansive scale of most ceiling frescoes induce a feeling of awe.

THE GLORY OF THE BARBERINI FAMILY
Patrons who wanted to burnish their public images or control their legacies found monumental ceiling frescoes perfect vehicles for such statements. In 1633, Pope Urban VIII commissioned a ceiling fresco for the Gran Salone of the Palazzo Barberini in Rome. This project was the most important decorative commission of the 1630s, and thus artists highly coveted it. Urban VIII selected PIETRO DA CORTONA (1596–1669), a fellow Tuscan who had moved to Rome in about 1612. By the 1630s, Cortona had established himself as a respected artist. The grandiose and spectacular *Triumph of the Barberini* (FIG. 24-25) overwhelms spectators with the glory of the Barberini family (and Urban VIII in particular). The iconographic program for this fresco, designed by the poet Francesco Bracci-

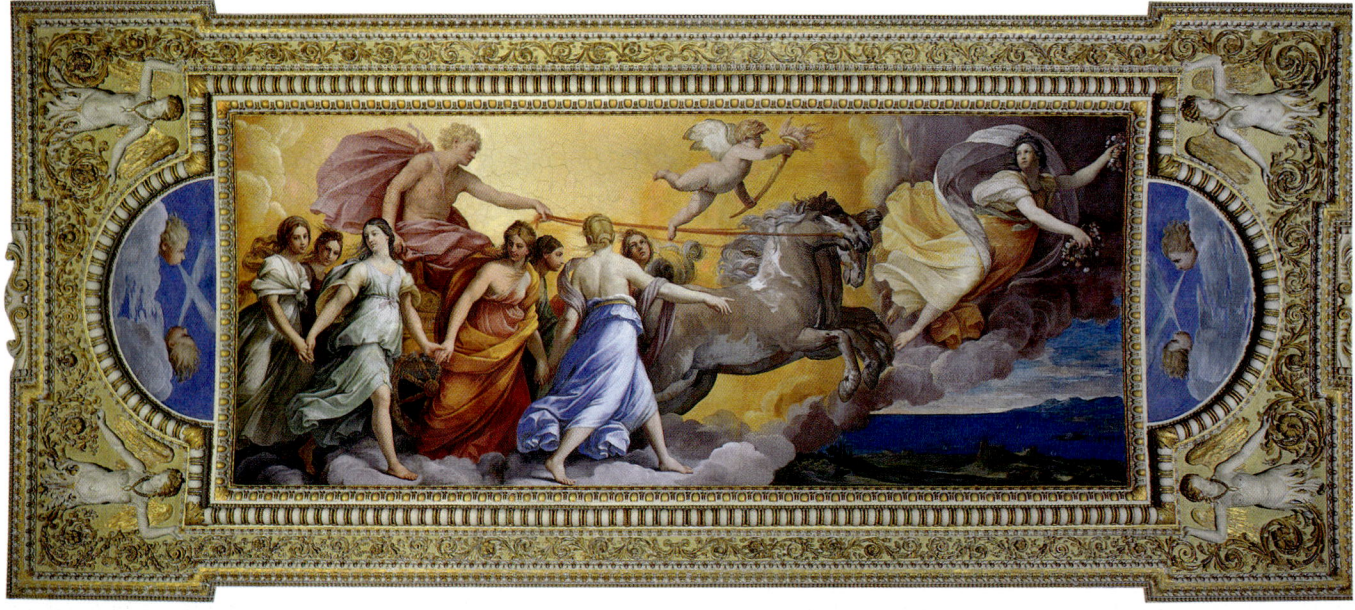

24-24 GUIDO RENI, *Aurora,* ceiling fresco in the Casino Rospigliosi, Rome, Italy, 1613–1614.

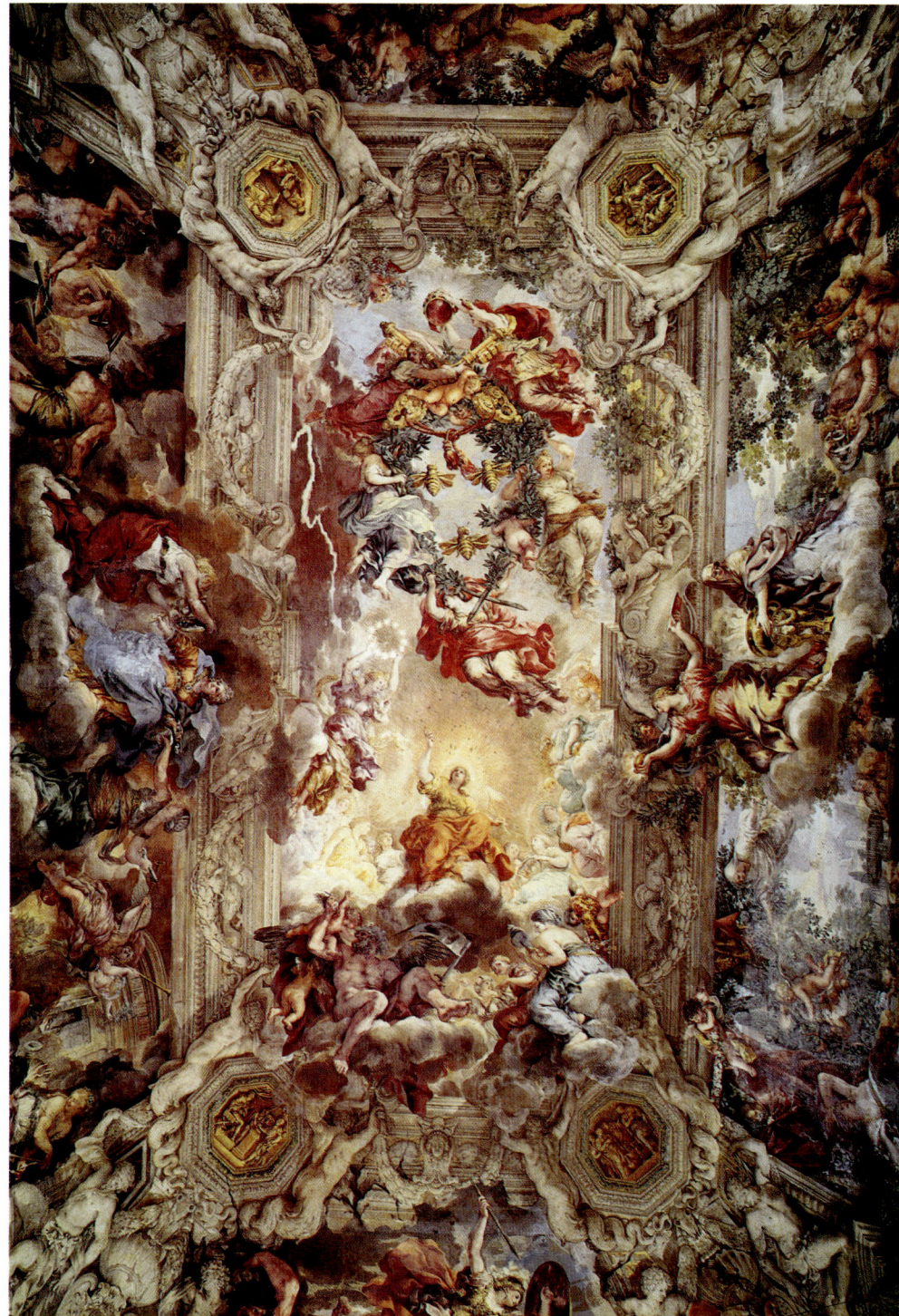

24-25 PIETRO DA CORTONA, *Triumph of the Barberini,* ceiling fresco in the Gran Salone, Palazzo Barberini, Rome, Italy, 1633–1639.

olini, centered on the accomplishments of the Barberini. Divine Providence appears in a halo of radiant light, directing Immortality, holding a crown of stars, to bestow eternal life on the Barberini family. The laurel wreath (also a symbol of immortality) reinforces the enduring Barberini legacy. It floats around the bees (the Barberini family's symbols, as already seen in Bernini's baldacchino, FIG. 24-5) and is supported by the virtues Faith, Hope, and Charity. The papal tiara and keys announcing the personal triumphs of Urban VIII are also clearly visible.

IN THE PRESENCE OF JESUS The dazzling spectacle of ceiling frescoes also proved very effective for commissions illustrating religious themes. Church authorities realized that such paintings, high above the ground, offered perfect opportunities to impress on viewers the Catholic Church's glory and power. In conjunction with the theatricality of Italian Baroque architecture and sculpture, frescoes spanning church ceilings contributed to creating transcendent spiritual environments well suited to the Church's needs in Counter-Reformation Italy.

A splendid example of the dramatic impact such ceiling frescoes could have is *Triumph in the Name of Jesus* (FIG. **24-26**), painted by GIOVANNI BATTISTA GAULLI (1639-1709). *Triumph* appears over the nave of the Church of Il Gesù in Rome (see FIGS. 22-49 and 22-50). As the mother church of the Jesuit order, Il Gesù played a prominent role in Counter-Reformation efforts. The visual effect Gaulli created is stunning. Gilded architecture opens up in the center of the ceiling to offer viewers a glimpse of Heaven. The artist represented Jesus as a barely visible monogram (IHS) in a blinding radiant light that floats heavenward. In contrast, sinners are violently thrown back down to Earth. The painter glazed the gilded architecture to suggest shadows, thereby enhancing the scene's illusionistic quality. To further heighten the illusion, Gaulli painted many of the sinners on three-dimensional stucco extensions which project outside the painting's frame.

A GLORIOUS TRIBUTE TO SAINT IGNATIUS
Another master of ceiling decoration was FRA ANDREA POZZO (1642–1709), a lay brother of the Jesuit order and a master of perspective, on which he wrote an influential treatise. Pozzo designed and executed the vast ceiling fresco *Glorifica-*

tion of Saint Ignatius (FIG. **24-27**) for the church of Sant'Ignazio in Rome. Like Il Gesù, Sant'Ignazio was prominent in Counter-Reformation Rome because of its dedication to Saint Ignatius, the founder of the Jesuit order. As Gaulli did in *Triumph in the Name of Jesus* (FIG. **24-26**), Pozzo created the illusion that Heaven is opening up above the congregation's heads. To accomplish this, the artist illusionistically continued the church's actual architecture into the vault so that the roof seems to be lifted off. As Heaven and Earth commingle, Saint Ignatius is carried to the waiting Christ in the presence of figures personifying the four corners of the world. A disk in the nave floor marks the standpoint for the whole perspectival illusion. For visitors looking up from this point, the vision is complete; they are truly in the presence of the heavenly and spiritual.

Thus, the effectiveness of Italian Baroque religious art depended on the drama and theatricality of individual images, as well as on the interaction and fusion of architecture, sculpture, and painting. Sound enhanced this experience. Churches were designed with acoustical effect in mind, and, in an Italian Baroque church filled with Baroque music, the power of both image and sound must have been immensely moving.

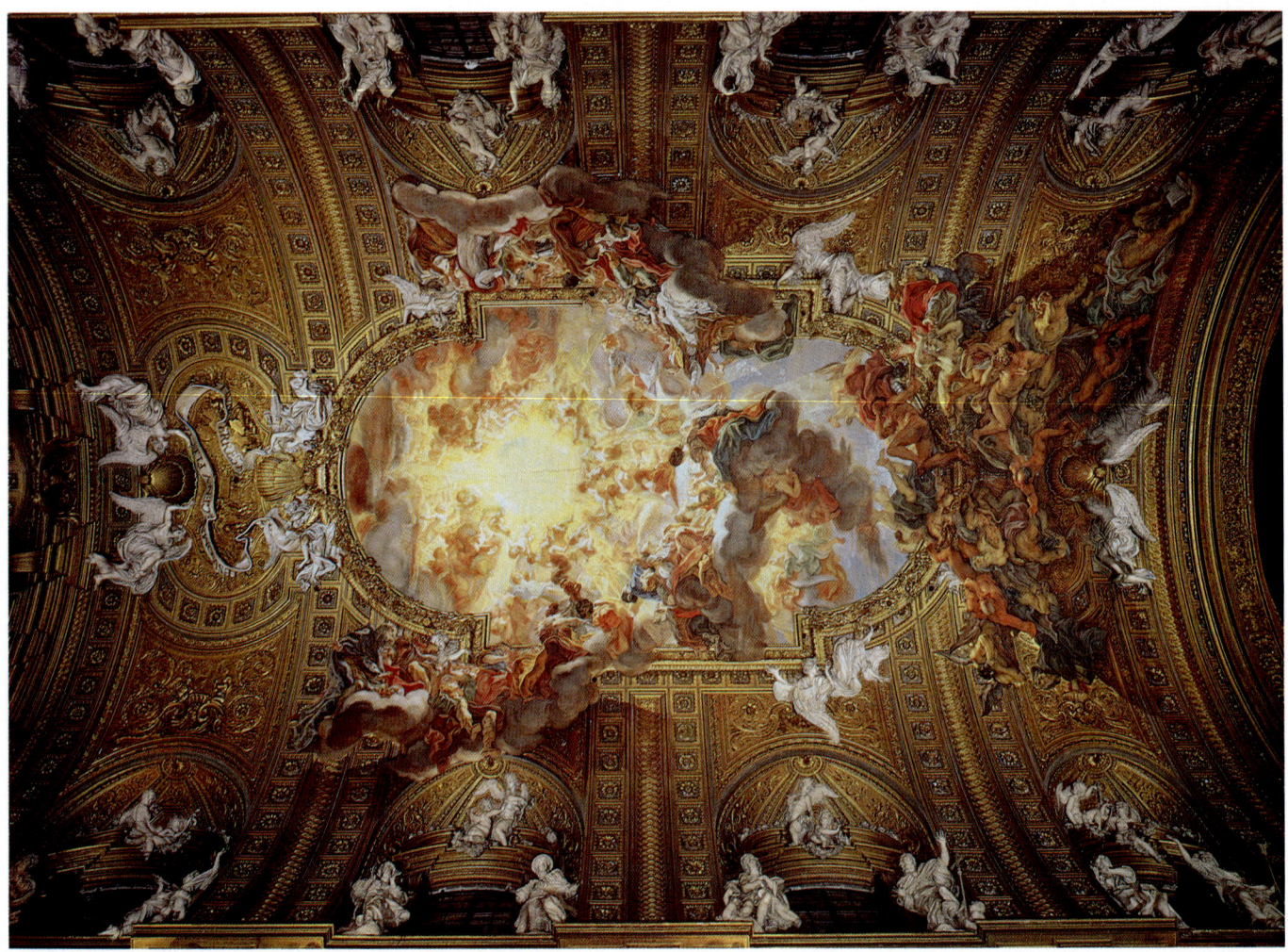

24-26 GIOVANNI BATTISTA GAULLI, *Triumph in the Name of Jesus,* ceiling fresco with stucco figures in the vault of the Church of Il Gesù, Rome, Italy, 1676–1679.

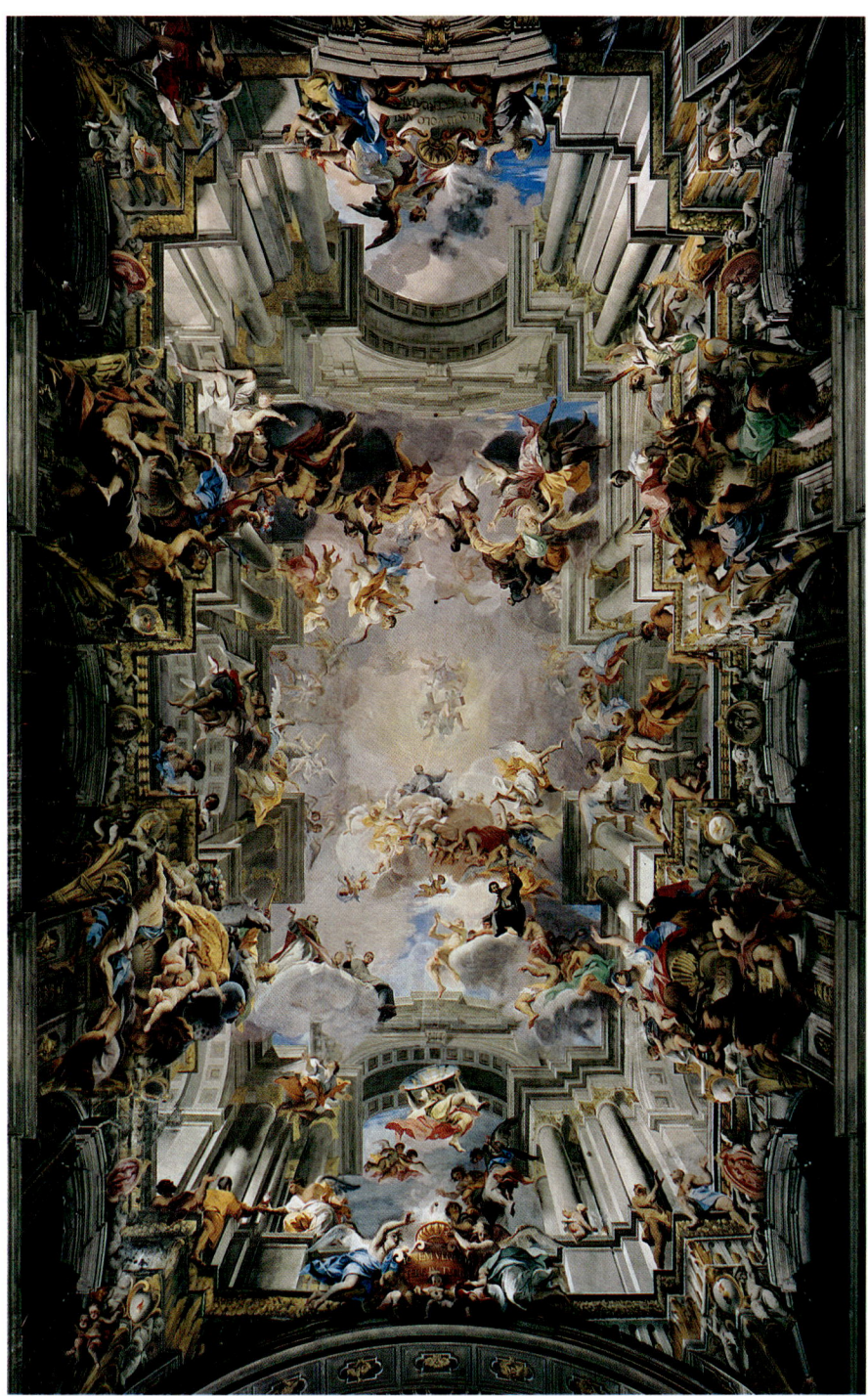

24-27 FRA ANDREA POZZO, *Glorification of Saint Ignatius,* ceiling fresco in the nave of Sant'Ignazio, Rome, Italy, 1691–1694.

Through simultaneous stimulation of both the visual and auditory senses, the faithful might well have been transported into a trancelike state that would, indeed, as England's contemporaneous poet John Milton eloquently stated in his *Paradise Lost,* "bring all Heaven before [their] eyes."

Spain

During the sixteenth century, Spain had established itself as an international power. The Hapsburg kings had built a dynastic state that encompassed Portugal, part of Italy, the Netherlands, and extensive areas of the New World. However, the animosity such dominance provoked among other European countries increased the challenges to Spanish hegemony. By the beginning of the seventeenth century, the Hapsburg empire was struggling, and although Spain mounted a very aggressive effort during the Thirty Years' War, by 1660 the imperial age of the Spanish Hapsburgs was over.

In part, the Spanish empire's demise was due to its reluctance to explore the possibility of mercantile expansion. During the height of Spanish power, the Hapsburgs had access to virtually unlimited amounts of capital, a growing population, rising consumer demand, and a far-flung overseas empire. Yet their failure to capitalize on trading opportunities allowed other countries, particularly England and the Netherlands, to develop expansive and profitable economic systems.

Thus, the dawn of the Baroque period in Spain found the country's leaders struggling to maintain control of their dwindling empire. Realizing as they did the value of visual imagery in communicating to a wide audience, Philip III (r. 1598–1621) and his son Philip IV (r. 1621–1665) were avid art patrons.

Because Spain was predominantly Catholic, it also encountered the same Counter-Reformation issues confronting Italy. As in Italy, Spanish Baroque artists sought ways to move viewers and to encourage greater devotion and piety. Particularly appealing in this regard were scenes of death and martyrdom, which provided artists with opportunities both to depict and to instill in viewers extreme feelings. Spain prided itself on its saints (for example, Saint Theresa of Avila, FIG. 24-9, and Saint Ignatius Loyola, FIG. 24-27, were both Spanish born), and martyrdom scenes surfaced frequently in Spanish Baroque art.

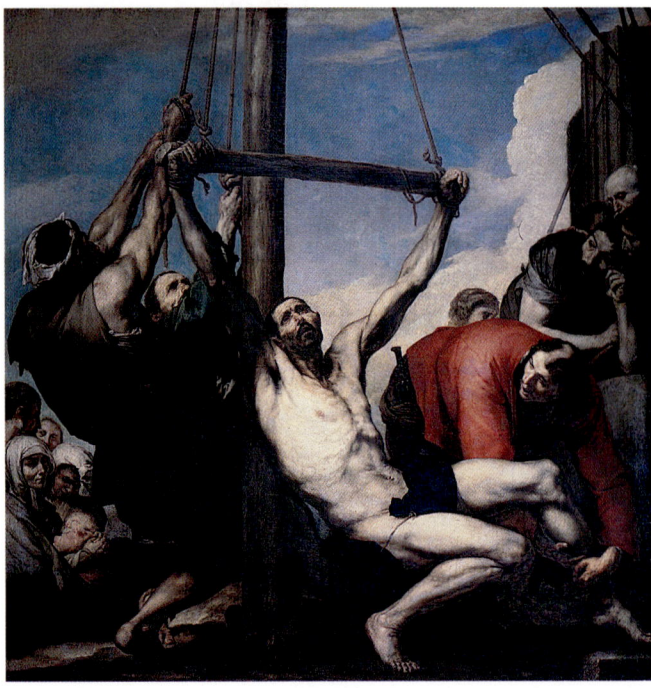

24-28   JOSÉ DE RIBERA, *Martyrdom of Saint Bartholomew*, ca. 1639. Oil on canvas, approx. 7′ 8″ × 7′ 8″. Museo del Prado, Madrid.

THE FLAYING OF A SAINT   JOSÉ (JUSEPE) DE RIBERA (ca. 1588–1652) emigrated to Naples as a young man and settled there. For that reason, he sometimes was called by his Italian nickname, Lo Spagnoletto, "the little Spaniard." Influenced by Caravaggio, Ribera imbued his work with both a naturalism and compelling drama, which lend shock value to his often brutal themes. These themes express at once the harsh times of the Counter-Reformation and a Spanish taste for the representation of courageous resistance to pain. Ribera's *Martyrdom of Saint Bartholomew* (FIG. **24-28**) is grim and dark in subject and form. Executioners are hoisting into position Saint Bartholomew, who is about to suffer the torture of being skinned alive. The saint's rough, heavy body and swarthy, plebeian features express a kinship between him and his tormentors, who are similar to the type of figures found in Caravaggio's paintings. Here, Ribera scorned idealization of any kind. In an age of merciless religious fanaticism, torture to save stubborn souls was a common and public spectacle.

A MARTYR AT PEACE   FRANCISCO DE ZURBARÁN (1598–1664) also knew Caravaggio's work through copies and works of Caravaggisti. In *Saint Serapion* (FIG. 24-29), Zurbarán used Caravaggio's presentational strategies; the figure emerges from a dark background and fills the foreground. The bright light shining on the figure calls attention to the tragic death of Saint Serapion and increases the image's dramatic impact. Saint Serapion, who participated in the Third Crusade of 1196, was martyred while preaching the Gospel to Muslims. According to one account of his martyrdom, the monk was tied to a tree, tortured, and decapitated. In Zurbarán's painting, two tree branches are barely visible in the background, and a small note next to the saint identifies him for viewers. The coarse features of the Spanish monk (who was born in England) label him as common, no doubt evoking empathy from a wide audience. In this work, as in many others, Zurbarán conveyed the fierce devotion of Catholic Spain.

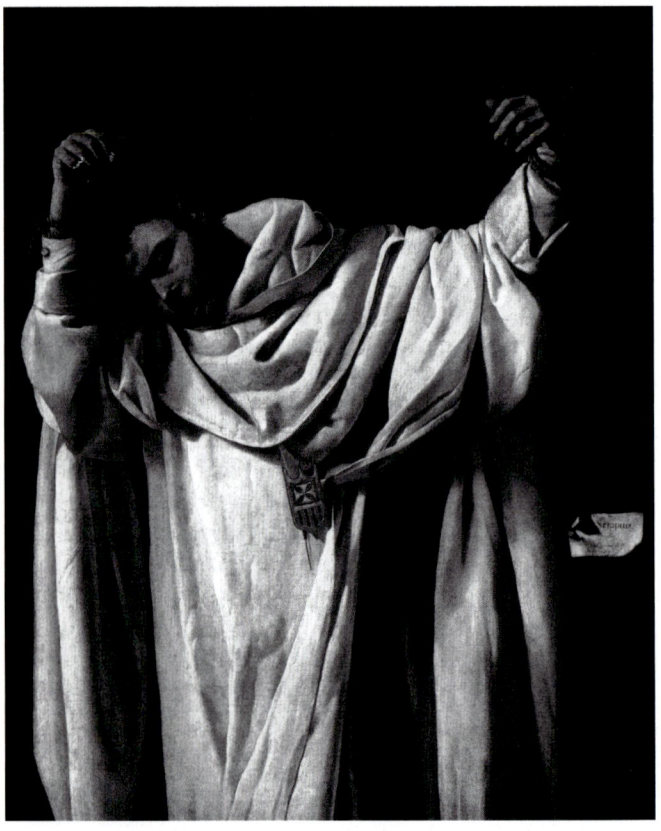

24-29   FRANCISCO DE ZURBARÁN, *Saint Serapion*, 1628. Oil on canvas, 3′ 11½″ × 3′ 4¾″. Wadsworth Atheneum, Hartford (The Ella Gallup Sumner and Mary Catlin Sumner Collection Fund).

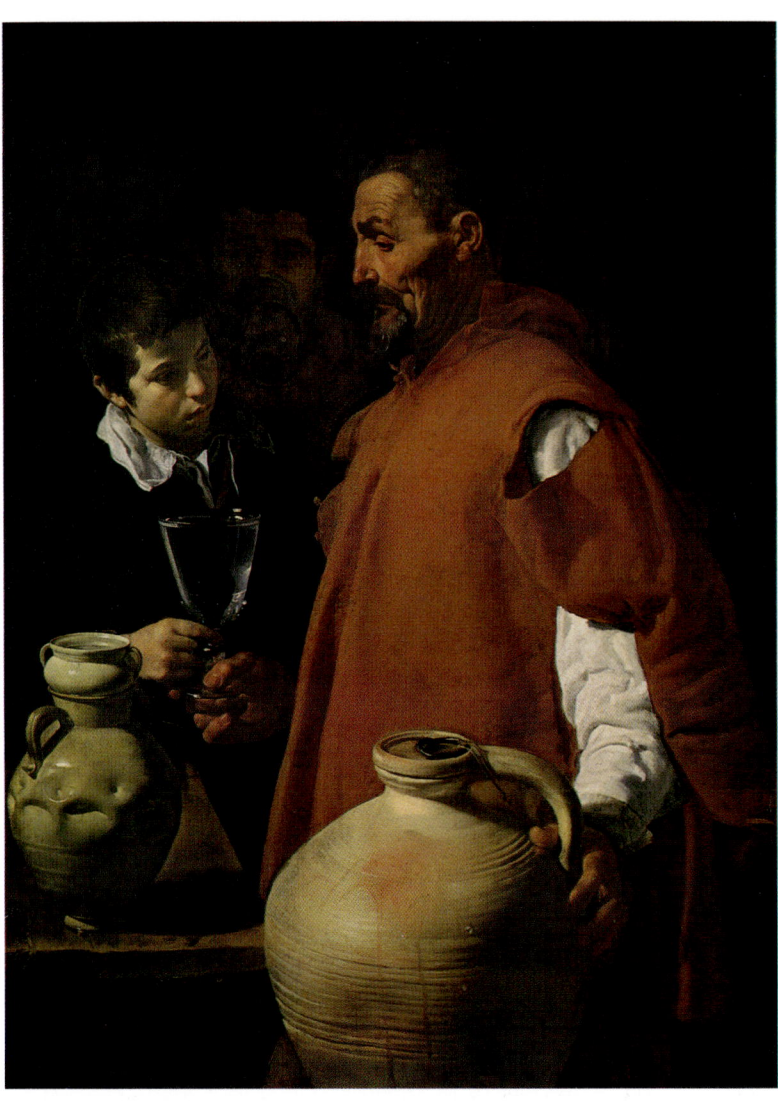

24-30 DIEGO VELÁZQUEZ, *Water Carrier of Seville*, ca. 1619. Oil on canvas, 3′ 5½″ × 2′ 7½″. Wellington Museum, London.

AN INFLUENTIAL COURT PAINTER   The artist often extolled as the greatest Spanish painter of the age is DIEGO VELÁZQUEZ (1599–1660). Velázquez, like many other Spanish artists, produced religious pictures, but he is justifiably renowned for the work he painted for his major patron, King Philip IV. Trained in Seville, Velázquez was quite young when he came to the attention of Philip IV. The king was struck by the immense talent of Velázquez and named him to the position of court painter. With the exception of two extended trips to Italy and a few excursions, Velázquez remained in Madrid for the rest of his life. His close relationship with Philip IV and his high office as marshal of the palace gave him prestige and a rare opportunity to fulfill the promise of his genius with a variety of artistic assignments.

Velázquez's skill is evident in an early work, *Water Carrier of Seville* (FIG. **24-30**), which he painted when he was only about twenty. The artist's command of his craft is impressive. He rendered the figures with clarity and dignity, and his careful depiction of the water jugs in the foreground, complete with droplets of water, adds to the scene's credibility. The contrast of darks and lights, along with the plebeian nature of the figures, reveal the influence of Car-avaggio, whose work Velázquez had studied. The artist presented this *genre scene* (one from everyday life) with such care and conviction that it seems to convey a deeper significance.

CELEBRATING A SPANISH VICTORY   As official court painter, Velázquez produced many works for Philip IV. In 1635, he painted *Surrender of Breda* (FIG. **24-31**) to commemorate the Spanish victory over the Dutch in 1625. Among the most troublesome situations for Spain was the conflict in the Netherlands. Determined to escape from Spanish control, the northern Netherlands succeeded in breaking away from the Spanish empire in the late sixteenth century. Skirmishes continued to flare up along the border between the northern (Dutch) and southern (Spanish) Netherlands, and in 1625 Philip IV sent General Ambrogio di Spínola to Breda to reclaim the town for Spain. Velázquez depicted the victorious Spanish troops, organized and well armed, on the right side of the painting. In sharp contrast, the defeated Dutch on the left appear bedraggled and disorganized. In the center foreground, the mayor of Breda, Justinus of Nassau, hands the city's keys to the Spanish general. The painting glorifies not only the strength of the Spanish

24-31   Diego Velázquez,
Surrender of Breda, 1634–1635.
Oil on canvas, 10′ 1″ × 12′ $\frac{1}{2}$″.
Museo del Prado, Madrid.

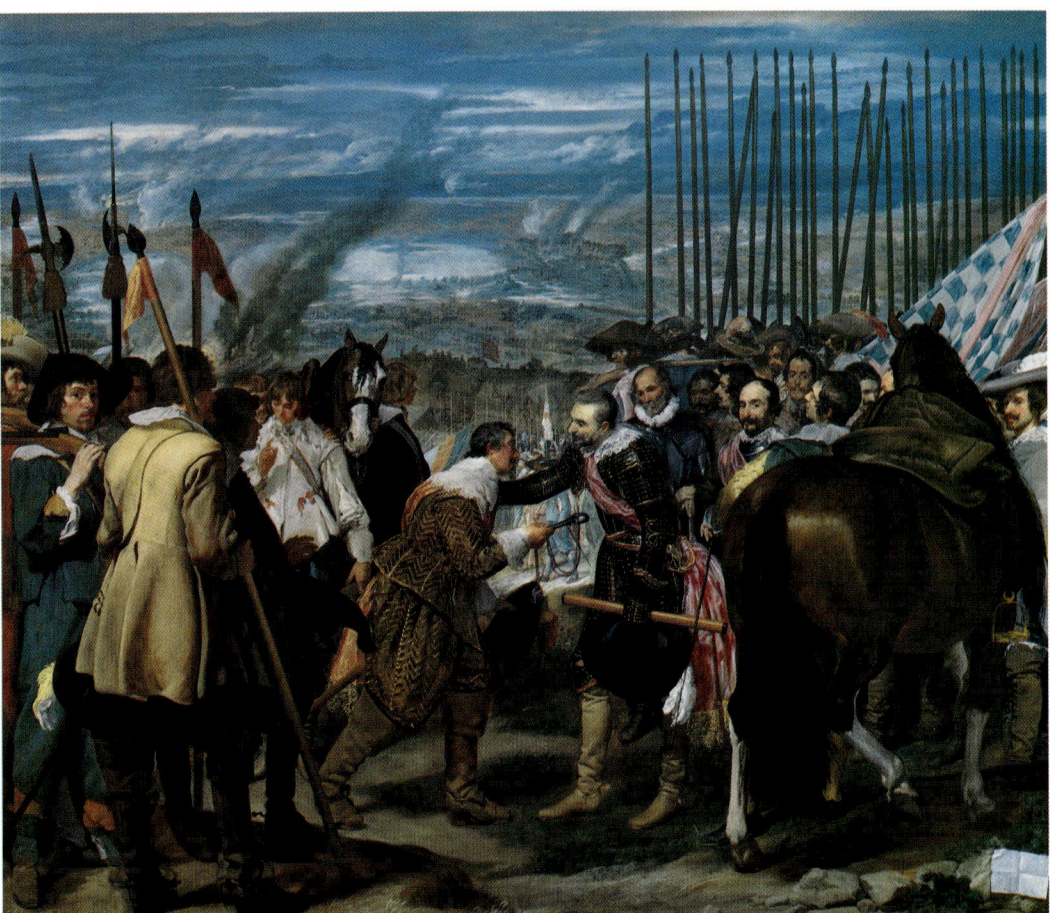

military but the benevolence of Spínola as well. Velázquez portrayed the general magnanimously patting Justinus on the shoulder—a kindly gesture, especially given the circumstances.

THE REIGN IN SPAIN   Propagandistic images such as *Surrender of Breda* were useful to Philip IV in his attempt to bolster his dwindling power. Also effective were portraits of the monarch, and Velázquez painted dozens. *King Philip IV of Spain* (FIG. **24-32**) is also known as the *Fraga Philip,* because it was painted in the town of Fraga in Aragon. Such a designation differentiates the many royal portraits from one another. Philip IV appears as a military leader, arrayed in red and silver campaign dress. Because the king was not a commanding presence and because he had inherited the large Hapsburg jaw (the result of dynastic inbreeding), Velázquez had to find creative ways to "ennoble" the monarch. He succeeded by focusing attention on the dazzling military regalia while not idealizing Philip's appearance.

OF ART AND ROYAL LIFE   After an extended visit to Rome from 1648 to 1651, Velázquez returned to Spain and painted his greatest masterpiece, *Las Meninas* (*The Maids of Honor;* FIG. **24-33**). In it, Velázquez showed his mastery of both form and content. The painter represented himself in his studio standing before a large canvas, on which he may be painting this very picture or, perhaps, the portraits of King Philip IV and Queen Mariana, whose reflections appear in the mirror on the far wall. The young *Infanta* (princess)

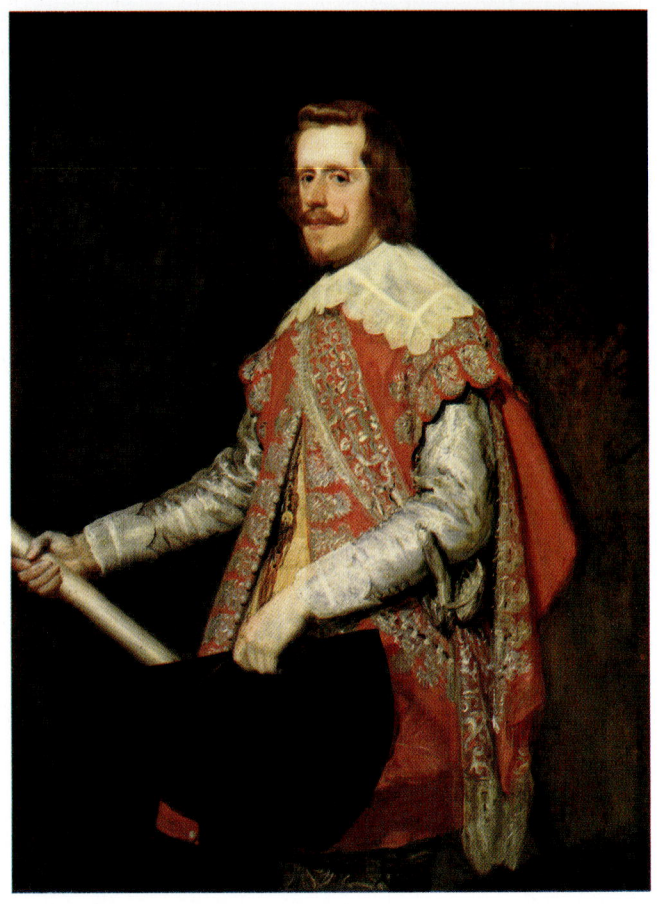

24-32   Diego Velázquez, *King Philip IV of Spain (Fraga Philip),* 1644.
Oil on canvas, 4′ 3$\frac{1}{8}$″ × 3′ 3$\frac{1}{8}$″. The Frick Collection, New York.

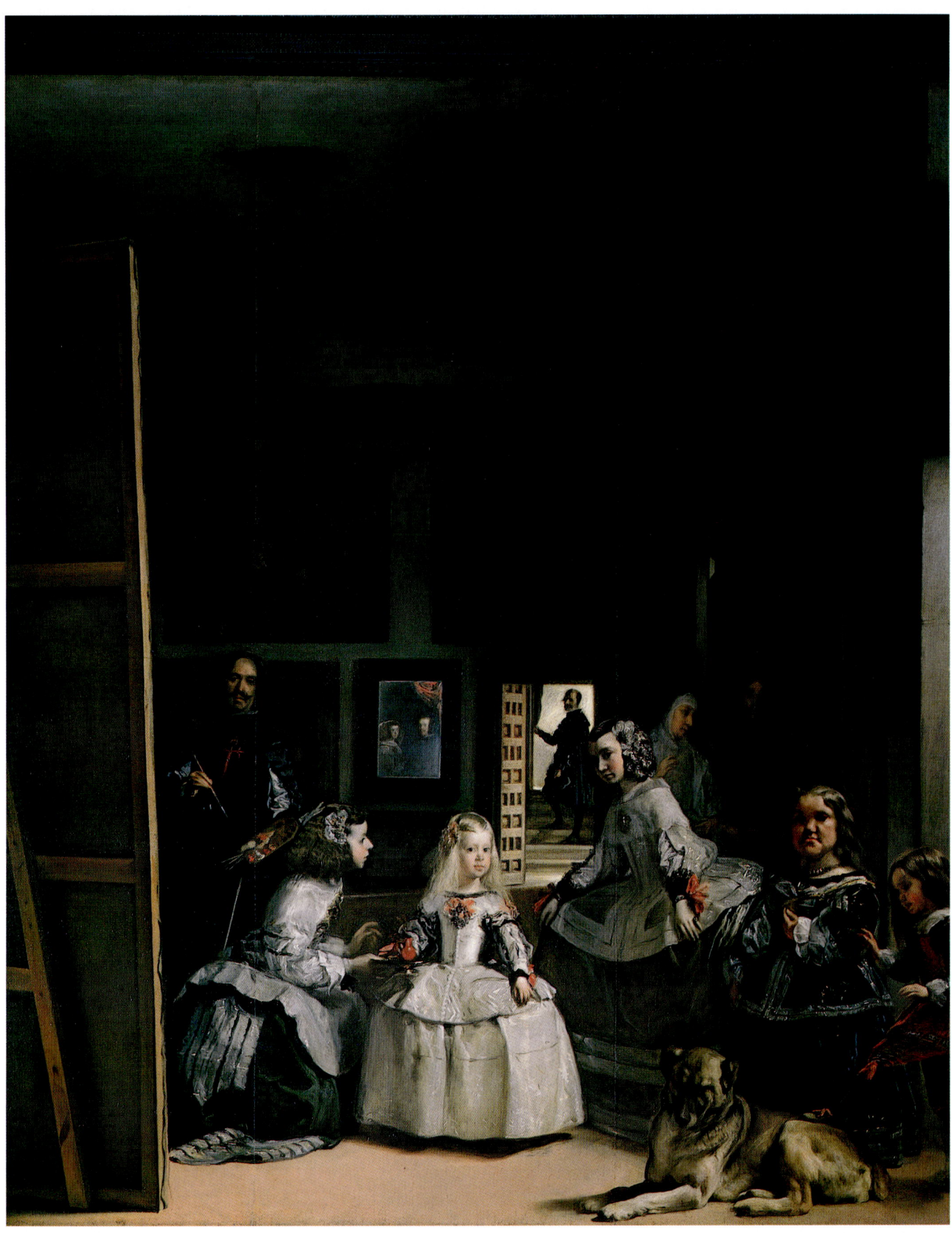

24-33 Diego Velázquez, *Las Meninas,* 1656. Oil on canvas, approx. 10′ 5″ × 9′. Museo del Prado, Madrid.

Margarita appears in the foreground with her two maids-in-waiting, her favorite dwarfs, and a large dog. In the middle ground are a woman in widow's attire and a male escort; in the background, a gentleman is framed in a brightly lit open doorway. The personages present have been identified, though we need not name them here. Noteworthy is how Velázquez extended the pictorial depth of his composition in both directions. The open doorway and its ascending staircase lead the eye beyond the artist's studio, and the mirror device and the outward glances of several of the figures incorporate the viewers' space into the picture as well. (Compare how the mirror in Jan van Eyck's *Giovanni Arnolfini and His Bride,* FIG. 20-12, also incorporates the area in front of the canvas into the picture, although less obviously and without a comparable extension of space beyond the room's rear wall.)

On the wall above the doorway and mirror in *Las Meninas,* two faintly recognizable pictures have been identified as copies of paintings by Peter Paul Rubens that represent the immortal gods as the source of art. Thus, a duality of theme exists in the Velázquez painting. It is both an informal family group portrait, seemingly casually arranged and naturalistic, and it is a genre painting—"A Visit to the Artist's Studio" would be an equally apt title. The room represented in the painting was in the palace of the Alcázar in Madrid. After the death of Prince Baltasar Carlos in 1646, Phillip IV ordered part of the prince's chambers converted into a studio for Velázquez.

As first painter to the king and as chief steward of the palace, Velázquez was conscious not only of the importance of his court office but also of the honor and dignity belonging to his profession as a painter. In this painting, he appears to have brought the roles together, asserting their equivalent value. Several pictures from the seventeenth century show painters with their royal patrons, for painters of the time continually sought to elevate their profession among the arts and to achieve by it appropriate rank and respect. Throughout his career, Velázquez hoped to be ennobled by royal appointment to membership in the ancient and illustrious Order of Santiago. Because he lacked some of the required patents of nobility, he gained entrance only with difficulty at the very end of his life, and then only through the pope's dispensation. In the painting, he wears the order's red cross on his doublet, painted there, legend says, by the king himself. The truth is that the artist painted it. In Velázquez's mind, *Las Meninas* might have embodied the idea of the great king visiting his studio, as Alexander the Great visited the studio of the painter Apelles in ancient times. The figures in the painting all acknowledge the royal presence. Placed among them in equal dignity is Velázquez, face-to-face with his sovereign. The location of the completed painting reinforced this act of looking—of seeing and being seen. *Las Meninas* hung in the personal office of Philip IV in another part of the palace. Thus, although occasional visitors admitted to the king's private quarters may have seen this painting, it was viewed primarily by Philip IV. And each time he did so, standing before the large canvas, he again participated in the work as the subject of Velázquez's painting in *Las Meninas* and as the object of the figures' gazes. The art of painting, in the person of the painter, was elevated here to the highest status. Velázquez sought ennoblement not for himself alone but for his art.

The interpretation that Velázquez, in the painting, is in the process of portraying the king and queen on the canvas before him, is standard and visually logical. Even further, Velázquez's optical report of the event, authentic in every detail, also pictorially summarizes the various kinds of images in their different levels and degrees of reality. He portrayed the realities of canvas image, of mirror image, of optical image, and of the two imaged paintings. This work—with its cunning contrasts of mirrored spaces, "real" spaces, picture spaces, and pictures within pictures—itself appears to have been taken from a large mirror reflecting the whole scene. This would mean the artist did not paint the princess and her suite as the main subjects of *Las Meninas* but himself in the process of painting them. In the Baroque period, when artists took Leonardo's dictum that "the mirror is our master" very seriously, it is not surprising to find mirrors and primitive camera-like devices used to achieve optimum visual fidelity in paintings. *Las Meninas* is a pictorial summary and a commentary on the essential mystery of the visual world, as well as on the ambiguity that results when different states or levels interact or are juxtaposed.

How did Velázquez achieve these results? Instead of putting lights abruptly beside darks, as Caravaggio had done, Velázquez allowed a great number of intermediate values of gray to come between the two extremes. His matching of tonal gradations approached effects the photography age later discovered. Velázquez did not think of figures as first drawn, next modeled into sculptural effects, and then colored. He thought of light and tone as the whole substance of painting—the solid forms only suggested, never really constructed. Observing this reduction of the solid world to purely optical sensations in a floating, fugitive skein of color tones, viewers could say the old sculpturesque form had disappeared here. The extreme thinness of Velázquez's paint and the light, almost accidental, touches of thick pigment here and there destroyed all visible structure. If viewers examine his canvas closely, everything dissolves to a random flow of paint.

Flanders

In the sixteenth century, the Netherlands had come under the crown of Hapsburg Spain when the emperor Charles V retired, leaving the Spanish throne and its Netherlandish provinces to his only son, Philip II. Philip's repressive measures against the Protestants led the northern provinces to break away from Spain and to set up the Dutch Republic. The southern provinces remained under Spanish control, and they retained Catholicism as their official religion. The political distinction between modern Holland and Belgium more or less reflects this original separation, which, in the Baroque period signalized not only religious but also artistic differences. The Baroque art of Flanders (the Spanish Netherlands) retained close connections to the Baroque art of Spain, while the Dutch schools of painting developed their own subjects and styles. This was consistent with their reformed religion and the new political, social, and economic structure of the middle-class Dutch Republic.

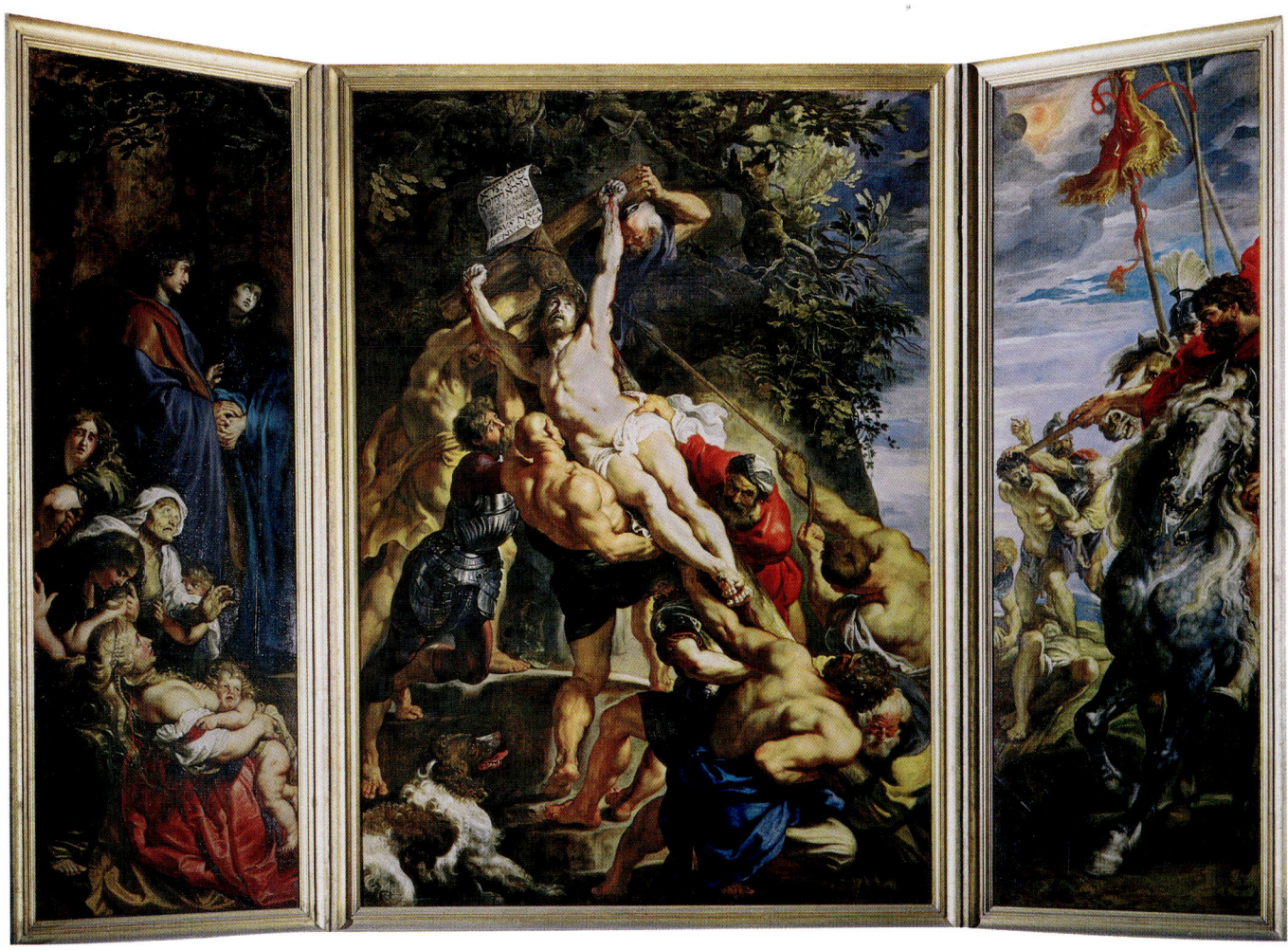

24-34 PETER PAUL RUBENS, *Elevation of the Cross,* Antwerp Cathedral, Antwerp, Belgium, 1610. Oil on panel, 15′ 2″ × 11′ 2″.

A PAN-EUROPEAN SYNTHESIS The renowned Flemish master PETER PAUL RUBENS (1577–1640) drew together the main contributions of the masters of the Renaissance (Michelangelo and Titian) and of the Italian Baroque (Carracci and Caravaggio) to synthesize in his own style the first truly pan-European manner. Rubens's art, even though it is the consequence of his wide study of many masters, is no weak eclecticism but an original and powerful synthesis. Ultimately, the influence of Rubens was international.

Among the most learned individuals of his time, Rubens possessed an aristocratic education, courtier's manner, diplomacy, and tact. All of this, along with his classical learning and language facility, made him the associate of princes and scholars. He became court painter to the dukes of Mantua (descended from Mantegna's patrons); friend of the king of Spain and his adviser on art collecting; painter to Charles I of England and Marie de' Medici, queen of France; and permanent court painter to the Spanish governors of Flanders. Rubens also won the confidence of his royal patrons in matters of state, and these patrons often entrusted him with diplomatic missions of the highest importance. In the practice of his art, scores of associates and apprentices assisted Rubens, turning out numerous paintings for an international clientele. In addition, he functioned as an art dealer, buying and selling contemporary artworks and classical antiquities. His many enterprises made him a rich man, with a magnificent town

house and a chateau in the countryside. Wealth and honors, however, did not spoil his amiable, sober, and self-disciplined character. Rubens was, like Raphael, a successful and renowned artist, a consort of kings, a shrewd man of the world, and a learned philosopher.

Rubens became a master in 1598 and went to Italy two years later, where he remained until 1608. During these years, he formulated the foundations of his style. Shortly after his return from Italy, he painted the *Elevation of the Cross* (FIG. **24-34**) for Antwerp Cathedral. This triptych reveals the result of his long study of Italian art, especially the works of Michelangelo, Tintoretto, and Caravaggio. The scene brings together tremendous straining forces and counterforces as heavily muscled men strain to lift the cross. Here, the artist had the opportunity to show foreshortened anatomy and the contortions of violent action reminiscent of the twisted figures Michelangelo sculpted and painted. Rubens placed the body of Christ on the cross as a diagonal that cuts dynamically across the picture while inclining back into it. The whole composition seethes with a power that comes from genuine exertion, from elastic human sinew taut with effort. The tension is emotional as well as physical, as reflected not only in Christ's face but also in the features of his followers in the triptych's wings. Strong modeling in dark and light, which heightens the drama, marks Rubens's work at this stage of his career; it gradually gave way to a much subtler coloristic style.

24-35 Peter Paul Rubens, drawing of Laocoön, ca. 1600-1608. Black-and-white chalk drawing with bistre wash, approx. 1′ 7″ × 1′ 7″. Ambrosiana, Milan.

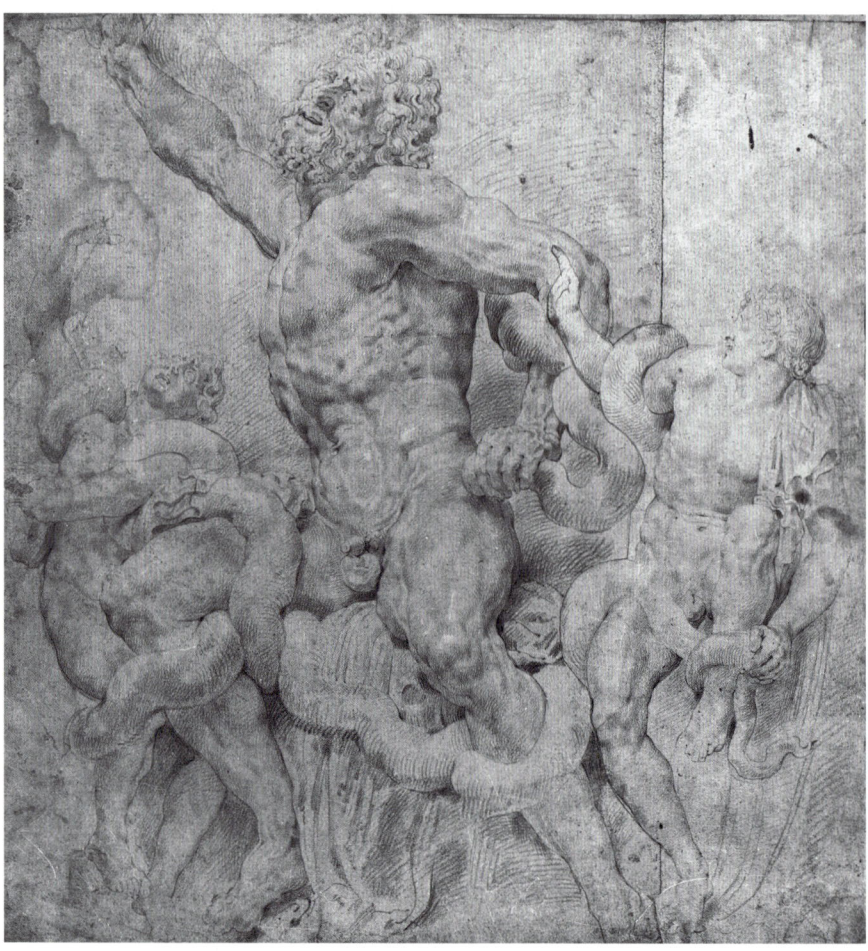

DRAWING ON THE MASTERS Rubens retained the vigor and passion of his early style throughout his career, although he modified the vitality of his work into less strained and more subtle forms, depending on the theme. One theme that remained a focus of Rubens's art was the human body, draped or undraped, male or female, and freely acting or free to act in an environment of physical forces and other interacting bodies. This interest, combined with his voracious intellect, led Rubens to copy the works of classical antiquity and of the Italian masters. These sources surfaced in Rubens's drawing of Laocoön (FIG. **24-35**), the classical sculpture discovered in 1506. Rubens apparently produced this drawing (one of a large group of drawings) sometime between 1606 and 1608, when he was in Rome. The ancient marble sculpture (FIG. 5-89) depicts the Trojan priest Laocoön and his two sons as they struggle mightily to free themselves from the death grip of sea serpents. Rubens's predominantly black chalk drawing demonstrates the artist's careful study of classical representations of the human form. In a Latin treatise he wrote titled *De imitatione statuarum (On the Imitation of Statues)*, Rubens stated: "I am convinced that in order to achieve the highest perfection one needs a full understanding of the [ancient] statues, nay a complete absorption in them. . . ."[1]

THE POWER AND MAJESTY OF ROYALTY
Rubens's interaction with royalty and aristocrats provided him with an understanding of the ostentation and spectacle of Baroque (particularly Italian) art that were appealing to those of wealth and privilege. Rubens, the born courtier, reveled in the pomp and majesty of royalty. Likewise, those in power embraced the lavish spectacle that served the Catholic Church so well in Italy. The magnificence and splendor of such Baroque imagery reinforced their authority and right to rule. Marie de' Medici, a member of the famous Florentine house, commissioned Rubens to paint a series memorializing and glorifying her career and that of her late husband, the first of the Bourbon kings of France, Henry IV. Between 1622 and 1626, Rubens, working with amazing creative energy, produced twenty-one huge historical-allegorical pictures designed to hang in the queen's new palace, the Luxembourg, in Paris.

Perhaps the most vivacious of the series is the *Arrival of Marie de' Medici at Marseilles* (FIG. **24-36**); the others are similar in mood and style. In the painting, Marie has just arrived in France after the sea voyage from Italy. As she disembarks, surrounded by her ladies-in-waiting, an allegorical personification of France, draped in a cloak decorated with the fleur-de-lis (FIG. 24-66), welcomes her. The sea and sky rejoice at her safe arrival—Neptune and the *Nereids* (daughters of the sea god Nereus) salute her, and a winged, trumpeting Fame swoops overhead. Conspicuous in the galley's opulently carved stern-castle, under the Medici coat of arms, stands the

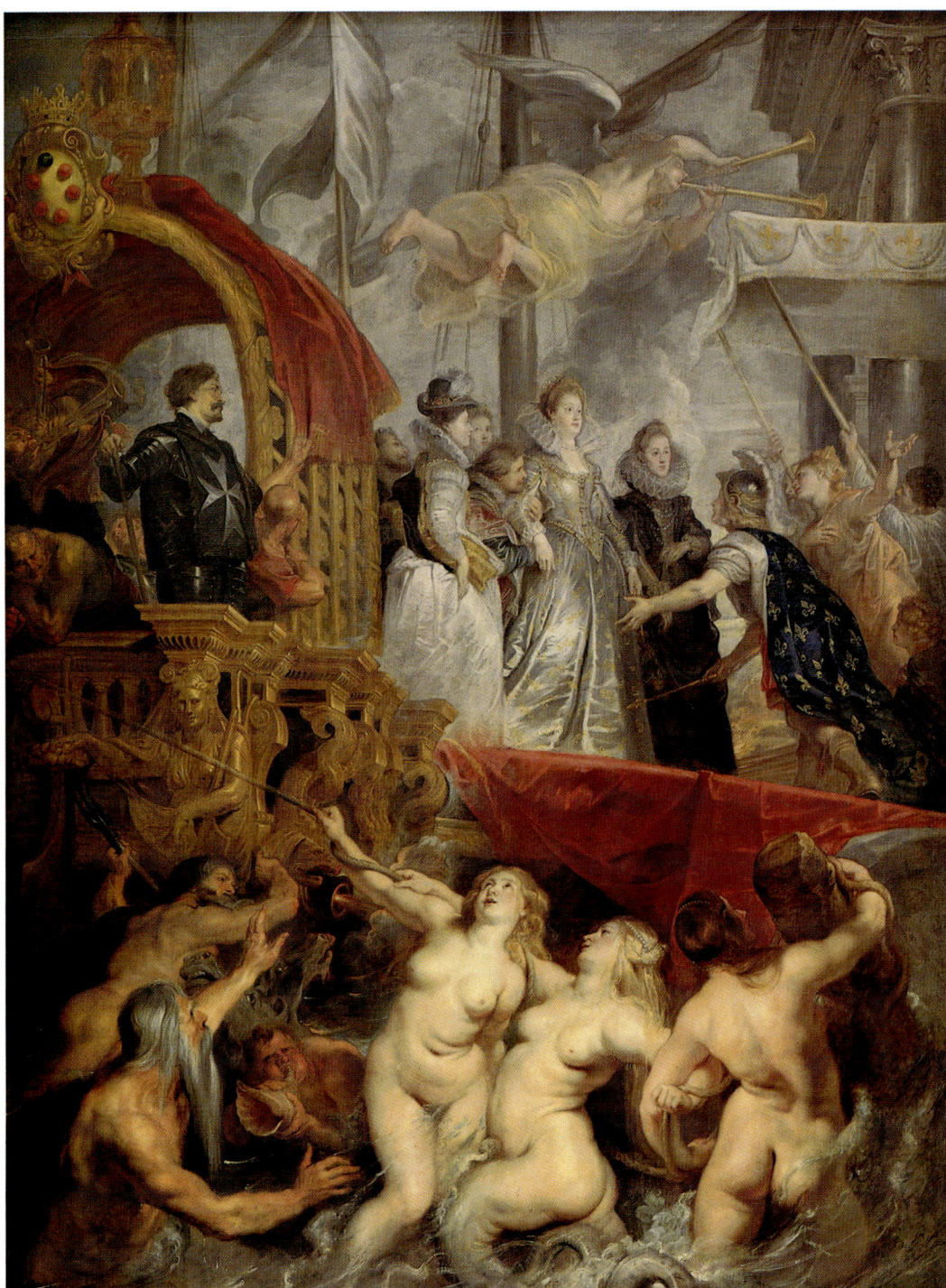

24-36 PETER PAUL RUBENS, *Arrival of Marie de' Medici at Marseilles,* 1622–1625. Oil on canvas, approx. 5′ 1″ × 3′ 9½″. Louvre, Paris.

imperious commander of the vessel. In black and silver, his figure makes a sharp accent amid the swirling tonality of ivory, gold, and red. He wears the cross of a Knight of Malta, which may identify this as a ship belonging to that order (similar to Velázquez's Order of Santiago). The only immobile figure in the composition, he could be director of and witness to the lavish welcome. The artist enriched his surfaces here with a decorative splendor that pulls the whole composition together. The audacious vigor that customarily enlivens Rubens's figures, beginning with the monumental twisting sea creatures, vibrates through the entire design.

PROTESTING WAR   Rubens also derived great insight into European politics from his diplomatic missions, and he never ceased to promote peace. Throughout most of his career, war was constant. When commissioned in 1638 to produce a painting for Ferdinando II, the Grand Duke of Tuscany, Rubens took the opportunity to express allegorically his attitude toward war. Appropriately, Rubens finished his

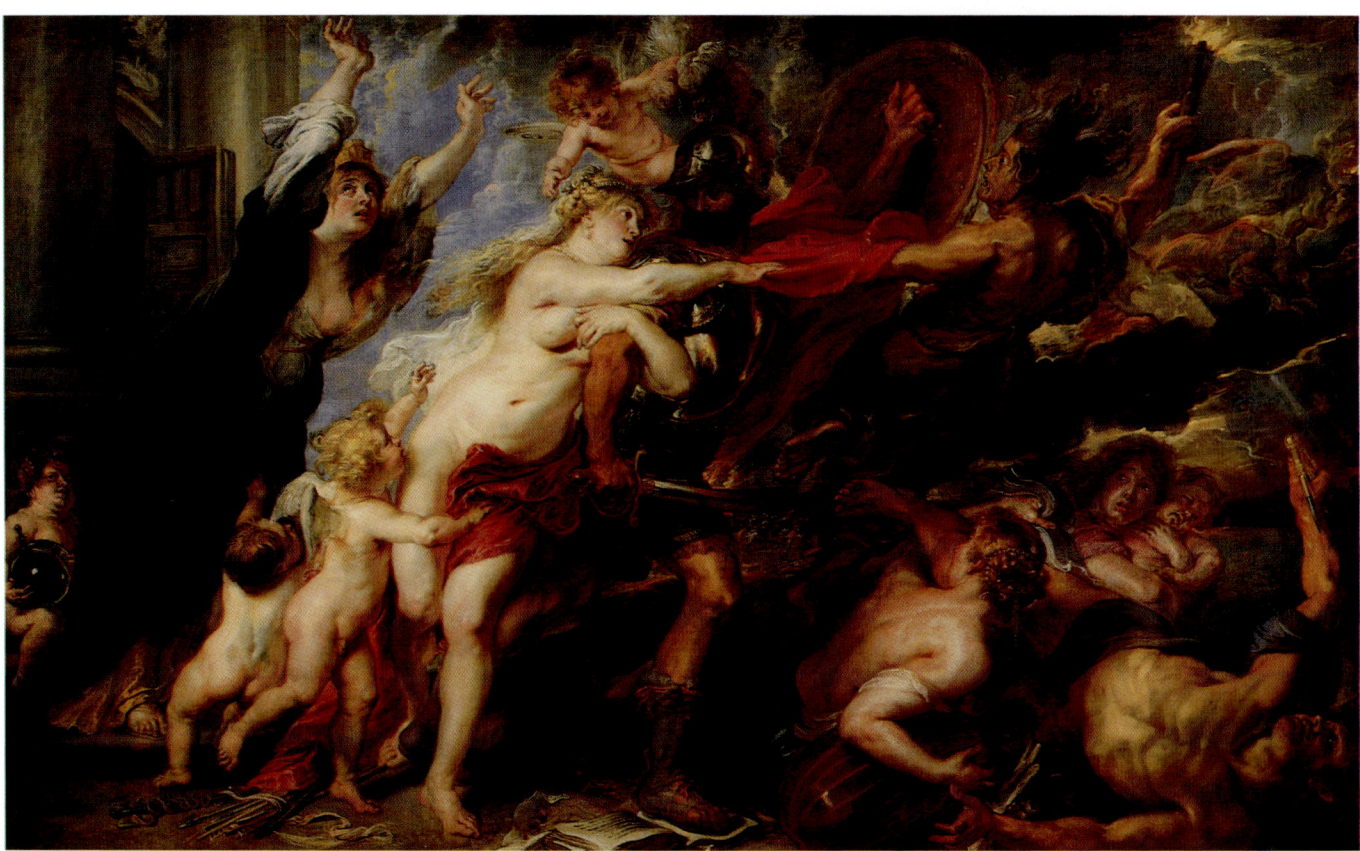

24-37   Peter Paul Rubens, *Allegory of the Outbreak of War*, 1638. Oil on canvas, 6′ 9″ × 11′ 3$\frac{7}{8}$″. Pitti Gallery, Florence.

artistic diatribe, *Allegory of the Outbreak of War* (FIG. **24-37**), during the Thirty Years' War. The fluid articulation of human forms and the energy that emanates from the chaotic scene are reminiscent of Rubens's other paintings. The artist's own description of the painting, written in a letter, provides the clearest explication of *Allegory*'s content and of his opinions on military conflict:

> The principal figure is Mars, who has left the temple of Janus open (which according to Roman custom remained closed in time of peace) and struts with his shield and his bloodstained sword, threatening all peoples with disaster; he pays little attention to Venus, his lady, who, surrounded by her little love-gods, tries in vain to hold him back with caresses and embraces. On the opposite side, Mars is pulled forward by the Fury Alecto with a torch in her hand. There are also monsters signifying plague and famine, the inseparable companions of war. Thrown to the ground is a woman with a broken lute, as a symbol that harmony cannot exist beside the discord of war; likewise a mother with a child in her arms indicates that fertility, procreation, and tenderness are opposed by war, which breaks into and destroys everything. There is furthermore an architect fallen backwards, with his tools in his hands, to express the idea that what is built in peace for the benefit and ornament of cities is laid in ruin and razed by the forces of arms . . . you will also find on the ground, beneath the feet of Mars, a book and a drawing on paper, to indicate that he tramples on literature and other refinements. . . . The sorrowing woman . . . clothed in black with a torn veil, and deprived of all her jewels and ornaments is unhappy Europe, which for so many years has suffered pillage, degradation, and misery affecting all of us so deeply that it is useless to say more about them.[2]

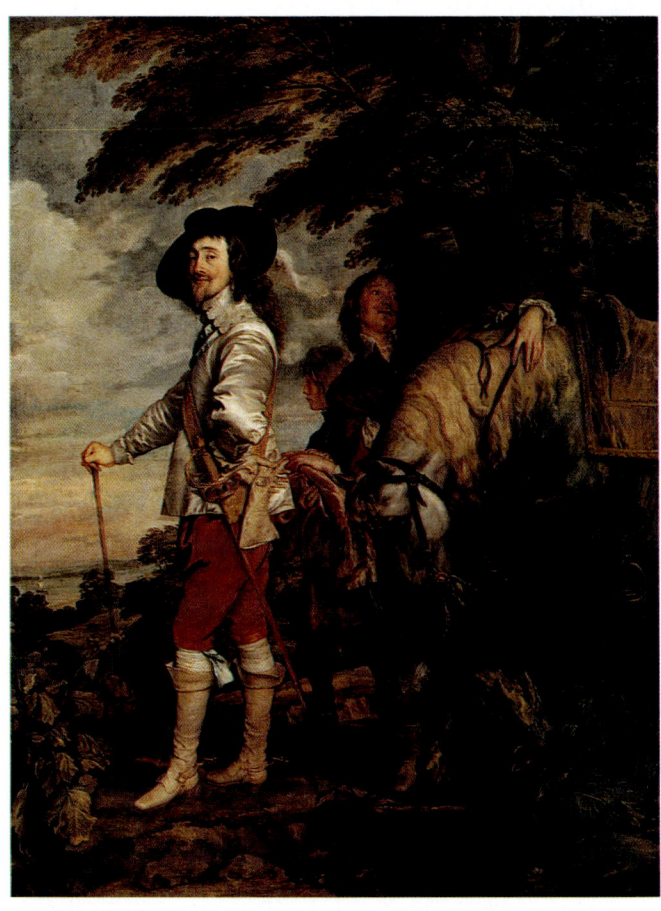

24-38   Anthony Van Dyck, *Charles I Dismounted*, ca. 1635. Oil on canvas, approx. 9′ × 7′. Louvre, Paris.

ELEGANT PORTRAITS OF ENGLAND'S KING

Most of Rubens's successors in Flanders were at one time his assistants. The most famous of these was ANTHONY VAN DYCK (1599–1641). Early on, the younger man, unwilling to be overshadowed by the master's undisputed stature, left his native Antwerp for Genoa and then London, where he became court portraitist to Charles I. Although Van Dyck created dramatic compositions of high quality, his specialty became the portrait. He developed a courtly manner of great elegance that was influential internationally. In one of his finest works, *Charles I Dismounted* (FIG. **24-38**), the ill-fated Stuart king stands in a landscape with the river Thames in the background. An equerry and a page attend Charles I. Although the king impersonates a nobleman out for a casual ride in his park, no one can mistake the regal poise and the air of absolute authority his Parliament resented and was soon to rise against. Here, King Charles turns his back on his attendants as he surveys his domain. The king's placement makes the composition exceedingly artful. He stands off center but balances the picture with a single keen glance at observers. Van Dyck even managed to portray Charles I in a position to look down on observers. In reality, the monarch's short stature forced him to exert his power in ways other than physical. Van Dyck's elegant style resounded in English portrait painting well into the nineteenth century.

The Dutch Republic

PROSPERITY IN THE PROVINCES The Dutch succeeded in securing their independence from the Spanish in the late sixteenth century. Not until 1648, however, after years of continual border skirmishes with the Spanish (as depicted in Velázquez's *Surrender of Breda,* FIG. 24-31) were the northern Netherlands officially recognized as the United Provinces of the Netherlands (the Dutch Republic). Despite attempts by the House of Orange to establish a monarchy, the republicans prevailed.

The ascendance of the Dutch Republic during the seventeenth century was largely due to its economic prosperity; Amsterdam had the highest per capita income in Europe. That city emerged as the financial center of Europe, having founded the Bank of Amsterdam in 1609. The Dutch economy benefited enormously from the country's expertise on the open seas, which facilitated establishing far-flung colonies. By 1650, Dutch trade routes extended beyond Europe proper and included North America, South America, the west coast of Africa, China, Japan, Southeast Asia, and much of the Pacific.

Due to this prosperity and in the absence of an absolute ruler, political power increasingly passed into the hands of an urban patrician class of merchants and manufacturers, especially in cities such as Amsterdam, Haarlem, and Delft. That these bustling cities were all located in Holland (the largest of the seven United Provinces) perhaps explains why the name "Holland" is used informally to refer to the entire country.

THE PROTESTANT OBJECTION TO ART Religious differences were a major consideration during the northern Netherlands' insistent quest for independence during the sixteenth and early seventeenth centuries. While Spain and the southern Netherlands were Catholic, the northern Netherlands were predominantly Protestant. The prevailing Calvinism demanded a puritanical rejection of art in churches, and thus artists produced relatively little religious art in the Dutch Republic at this time (especially in comparison to that created in areas dominated by Catholicism in the wake of the Counter-Reformation). Despite the Calvinist beliefs of much of the population, however, the Dutch were truly tolerant people, and artists (often Catholics) created the occasional religious image.

A MOVING RELIGIOUS SCENE HENDRICK TER BRUGGHEN (1588–1629), for example, painted *Calling of Saint Matthew* (FIG. **24-39**) in 1621, after returning from a trip to Italy. As a Catholic, ter Brugghen perhaps felt great affinity with artists such as Caravaggio, who painted the same

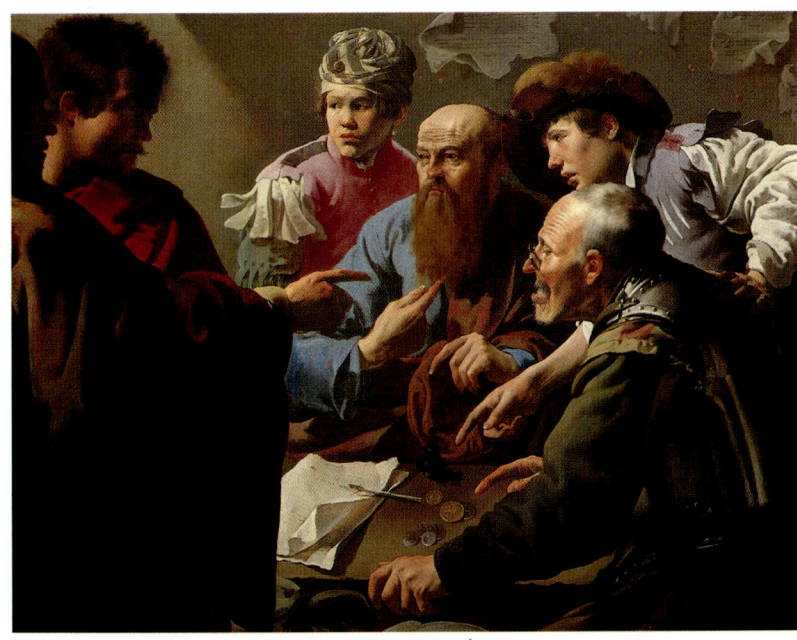

24-39 HENDRICK TER BRUGGHEN, *Calling of Saint Matthew,* 1621. Oil on canvas, 3′ 4″ × 4′ 6″. Centraal Museum, Utrecht (acquired with the aid of the Rembrandt Society).

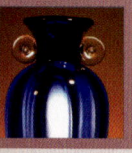

The Butcher, the Baker, the Candlestick Maker
Dutch Patronage and Art Collecting

Art collecting often has been perceived as the purview of the wealthy, and, indeed, the money necessary to commission major artworks from esteemed artists can be considerable. During the seventeenth century in the Dutch Republic, however, the widespread prosperity enjoyed by a large proportion of Dutch society significantly expanded the range of art patronage. As a result, one of the distinguishing hallmarks of Dutch art production during the Baroque period was how it catered to the tastes of a middle-class audience.

The term "middle class" is used broadly here. An aristocracy and a patriciate—an upper class of large-ship owners, rich businesspeople, high-ranking officers, and directors of large companies—still existed. These groups continued to be major patrons of the arts. With the expansion of the Dutch economy, traders, craftspeople, low-ranking officers, bureaucrats, and soldiers—the middle and lower-middle class—also became art patrons.

While steeped in the morality and propriety central to the Calvinist ethic, members of the Dutch middle class sought ways to subtly announce their success and newly acquired status. House furnishings, paintings, tapestries, and porcelain were among the items collected and displayed in the home. The Dutch disdain for excessive ostentation, attributable to Calvinism, led these collectors to favor small, low-key works—portraits, still lifes, genre scenes, and landscapes. This contrasted with the Italian Baroque penchant for large-scale, dazzling ceiling frescoes and opulent room decoration.

This new middle-class clientele, in conjunction with the developing open market (see "Mercantile Prosperity: Developing an Open Art Market," page 761), influenced the direction of Dutch Baroque art. Not only did these patrons affect the type of art produced, but they also were responsible for establishing the current mechanisms and institutions for buying and selling art.

---

scene (FIG. 24-19). The moment of the narrative depicted, the astonishment of Levi (the tax collector), and the naturalistic presentation of the figures all echo Caravaggio's work. However, ter Brugghen dispensed with the stark contrasts of dark and light and instead presented viewers with a more colorful palette of soft tints. Further, the figures are crammed into a small but well-lit space, creating a claustrophobic effect that differs from Caravaggio's careful rendering of the dark street scene.

DIFFERENT PATRONS, DIFFERENT SUBJECTS Given the absence of an authoritative ruler and the Calvinist

concern for the potential misuse of religious art, commissions from royalty or from the Christian Church, prominent in the art of other countries, were uncommon in the United Provinces. With the new prosperity, an expanding class of merchant patrons emerged, and this shift led to an emphasis on different pictorial content. Dutch Baroque art centered on genre scenes, landscapes, portraits, and still lifes, all of which appealed to the prosperous middle class (see "The Butcher, the Baker, the Candlestick Maker: Dutch Patronage and Art Collecting," above). "Middle class" often is used as a conveniently broad term to describe this developing group of patrons. However, it is important to note that despite the absence of royalty,

24-40 GERRIT VAN HONTHORST, *Supper Party,* 1620. Oil on canvas, approx. 7′ × 4′ 8″. Galleria degli Uffizi, Florence.

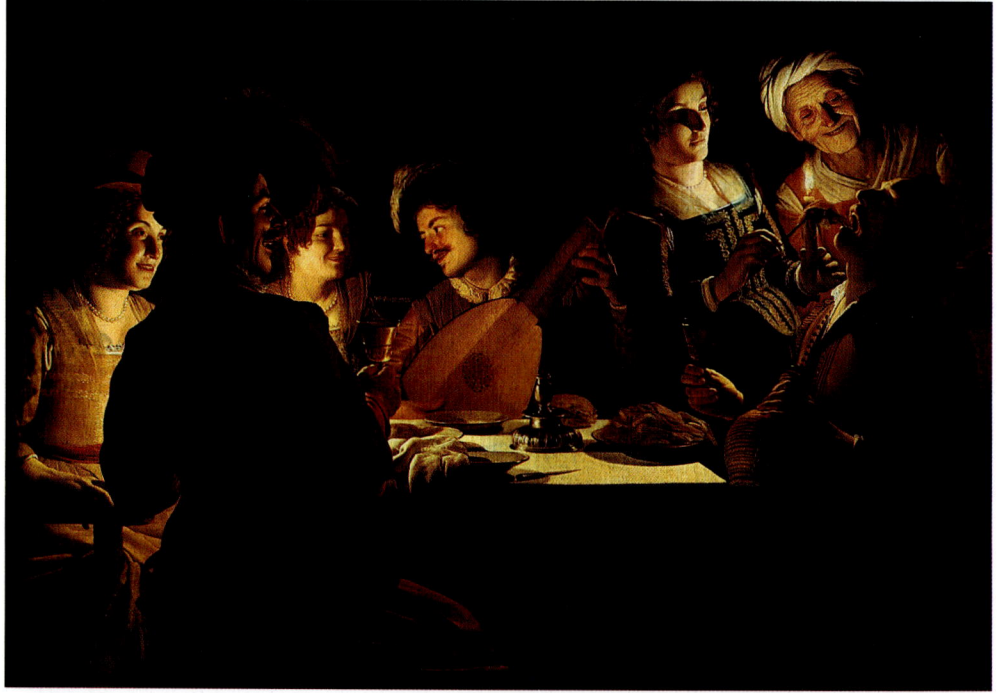

Dutch society was not totally egalitarian. The *patriciate* (leading merchants and large manufacturers) and the upper middle class (prosperous merchants, traders, and academics) were far more likely to collect art than were the middle and lower-middle classes (skilled craftspeople, workers, and servants). Regardless, art flourished in this mercantilist culture. The seventeenth century is referred to not only as the "Golden Age" of the Dutch Republic but as the "Golden Age" of Dutch art as well.

DEPICTING EVERYDAY LIFE IN HOLLAND

Typical of Dutch genre scenes is *Supper Party* (FIG. **24-40**), by GERRIT VAN HONTHORST (1590–1656) of Utrecht. In this painting, van Honthorst presented an informal gathering of unidealized human figures. While a musician serenades the group, his companions delight in watching a young woman feeding a piece of chicken to a man whose hands are both occupied—one holds a jug and the other a glass. Van Honthorst spent several years in Italy, and while there he carefully studied Caravaggio's work. The Italian artist's influence is evident in the mundane tavern setting and the nocturnal lighting. Fascinated by nocturnal effects, van Honthorst frequently placed a hidden light source in his pictures and used it as a pretext to work with dramatic and violently contrasted dark/light effects. Lighthearted genre scenes such as this were popular and widely produced in the Baroque period. Often, Dutch genre scenes could be read moralistically. For example, the *Supper Party* can be interpreted as a warning against the sins of gluttony (represented by the man on the right) and lust (the woman feeding the glutton is, in all likelihood, a prostitute with her aged procuress at her side). Or perhaps the painting represents the loose companions of the Prodigal Son (Luke 15:13)—panderers and prostitutes drinking, singing, strumming, and laughing. Strict Dutch Calvinists no doubt approved of such interpretations.

FACE-TO-FACE Dutch Baroque artists also were justifiably esteemed for their skills in portraiture, another genre, or type, of art. FRANS HALS (ca. 1581–1666) was the leading painter in Haarlem and made portraits his specialty. Portrait artists traditionally had relied heavily on convention—for example, specific poses, settings, attire, and accoutrements—to convey a sense of the sitter. Because the subject was usually someone of status or note, such as a pope, king, or wealthy individual, the artist's goal was to produce an image appropriate to the subject's station in life. With the increasing numbers of Dutch middle-class patrons, the tasks for Dutch portraitists became more challenging. Not only were the traditional conventions inappropriate and thus unusable, but also the Calvinists shunned ostentation, instead wearing uniform, subdued, and dark clothing with little variation or decoration. Despite these difficulties, or perhaps because of them, Hals produced lively portraits that seem far more relaxed than the more formulaic traditional portraiture. Not only did Hals inject an engaging spontaneity into his images, but he captured the personalities of his sitters as well. His manner of execution intensified the casualness, immediacy, and intimacy in his paintings. The touch of Hals's brush was as light and fleeting as the moment when he captured the pose, so the figure, the highlights on clothing, and the facial expression all seem instantaneously created.

Hals also excelled at group portraits, which multiplied the challenges of depicting a single sitter. *Archers of Saint Hadrian* (FIG. **24-41**) is one such painting. The Archers of Saint Hadrian were one of many Dutch civic militia groups

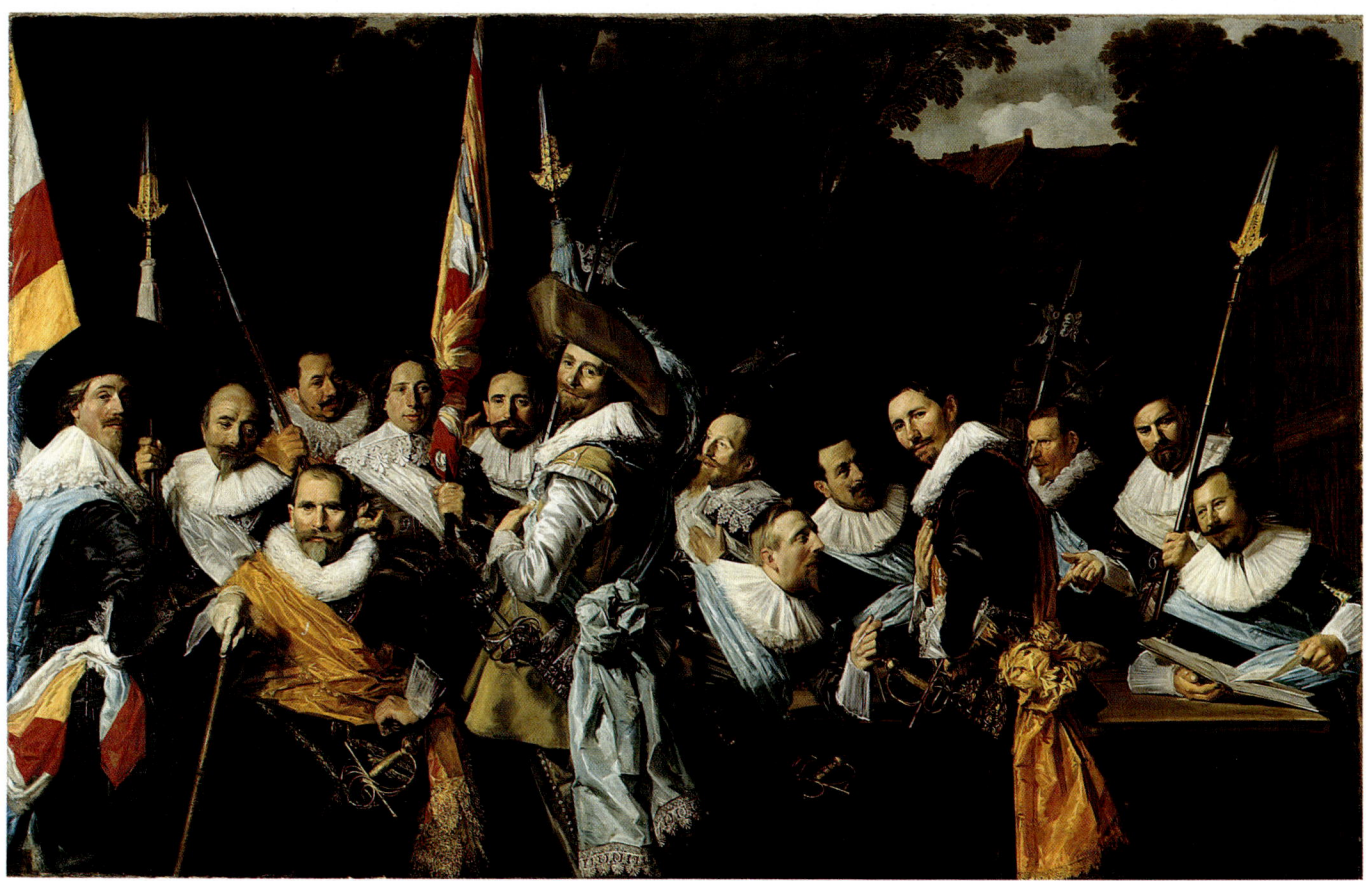

24-41 FRANS HALS, *Archers of Saint Hadrian*, ca. 1633. Oil on canvas, approx. 6' 9" × 11'. Frans Halsmuseum, Haarlem.

who claimed credit for liberating the Dutch Republic from Spain. Like other companies, the Archers met on its saint's feast day in dress uniform for a grand banquet. The celebrations sometimes lasted an entire week, prompting an ordinance limiting them to "three, or at the most four days." These events called for a group portrait, and such commissions gave Hals the opportunity to attack the problem of adequately representing each group member while retaining action and variety in the composition. Earlier group portraits in the Netherlands were rather ordered and regimented images. Hals sought to enliven the images, and the results can be seen in *Archers*. Here, each man is both a troop member and an individual with a distinct personality. Some engage viewers directly, while others look away or at a companion; where one is stern, another is animated. Each is equally visible and clearly recognizable. The uniformity of attire—black military dress, white ruffs, and sashes—does not seem to have deterred Hals from injecting a spontaneity into the work. Indeed, he used those elements to create a lively rhythm that extends throughout the composition and energizes the portrait. The impromptu effect—the preservation of every detail and fleeting facial expression—is, of course, due to careful planning. Yet Hals's vivacious brush appears to have moved instinctively, directed by a plan in his mind but not traceable in any preparatory scheme on the canvas.

PRIM AND PROPER DUTCH WOMEN   Hals captured the character of straightlaced, devout Calvinist women in *The Women Regents of the Old Men's Home at Haarlem* (FIG. **24-42**). Unlike the looser, seemingly informal character of his other group portraits, *Women Regents* communicates a stern, puritanical, and composed sensibility. The women look out from the painting (only two meet the viewer's gaze) with expressions that range from dour disinterest to kindly concern. The sombre and virtually monochromatic palette, punctuated only by the white accents of the clothing, contributes to the painting's restraint. Although this portrait may lack the vitality and spontaneity of other portraits by Hals, his unerring ability to capture both the details of the individual sitters and their general cultural characteristics is truly impressive.

A SURGICAL LESSON   Rembrandt van Rijn (1606–1669), Hals's younger contemporary, was widely recognized as the leading Dutch painter of his time. Rembrandt's move from his native Leiden to Amsterdam around 1631 provided him with a more extensive clientele, contributing to a flourishing career. In his portraits, for which he became particularly prominent, Rembrandt delved deeply into the psyche and personality of his sitters. In *Anatomy Lesson of Dr. Tulp* (FIG. **24-43**), he deviated even further from the traditional staid group portrait than had Hals. Despite Hals's de-

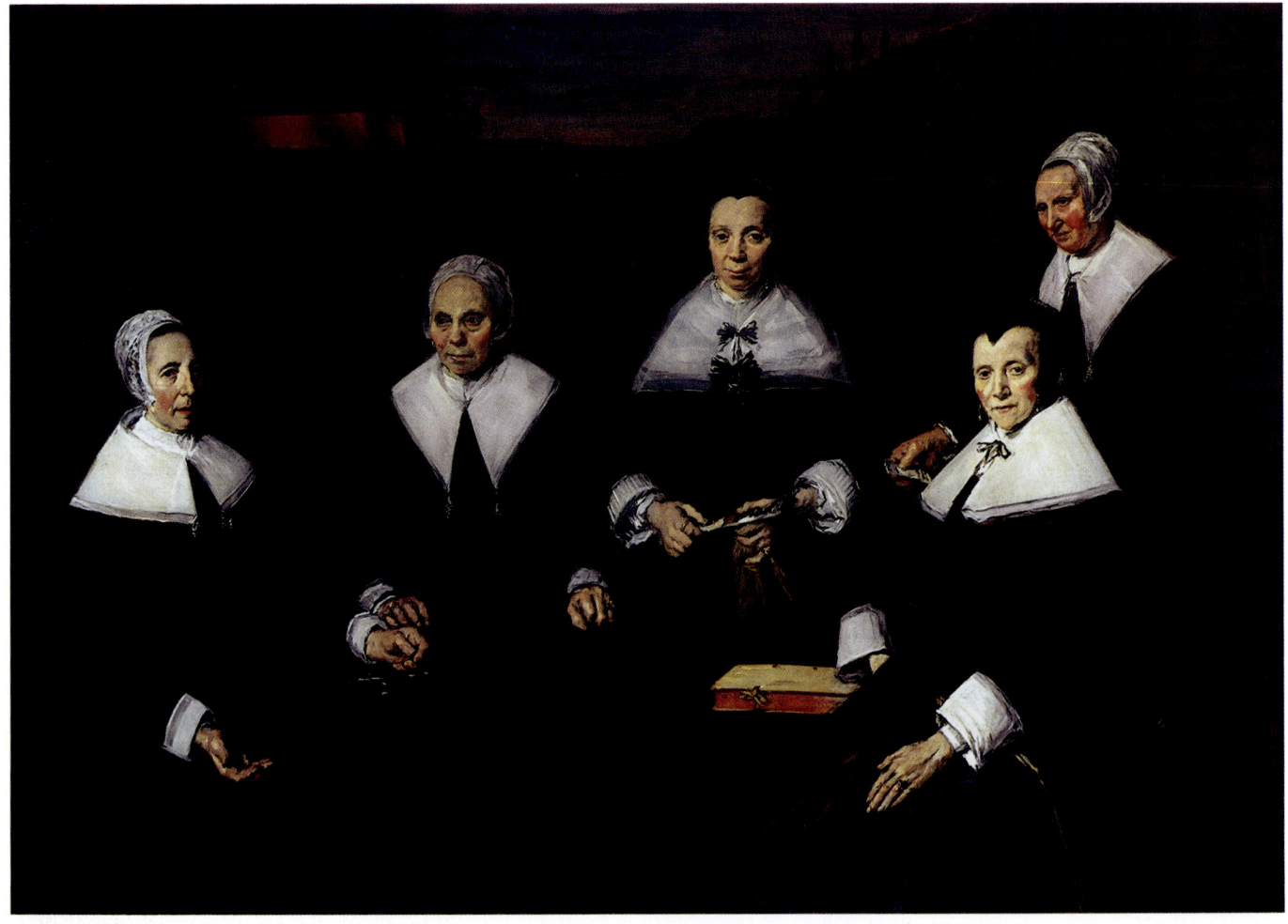

24-42   Frans Hals, *The Women Regents of the Old Men's Home at Haarlem,* 1664. Oil on canvas, 5′ 7″ × 8′ 2″. Frans Halsmuseum, Haarlem.

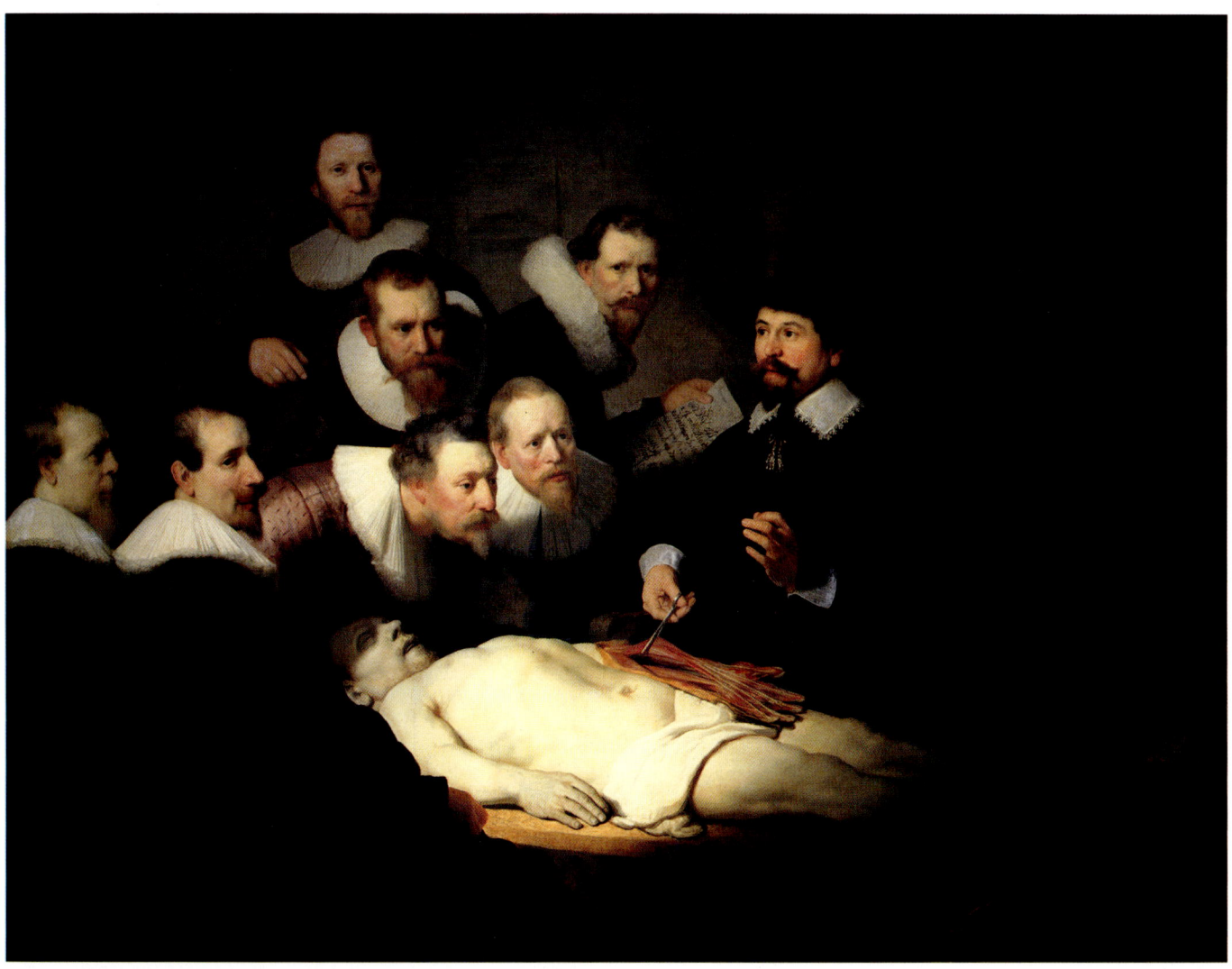

24-43 REMBRANDT VAN RIJN, *Anatomy Lesson of Dr. Tulp*, 1632. Oil on canvas, 5′ 3¾″ × 7′ 1¼″. Mauritshuis, The Hague.

termination to enliven his portraits, he still evenly placed his subjects across the canvas. In contrast, Rembrandt chose to portray the members of the surgeon's guild (who commissioned this group portrait) clustered together on the painting's left side. In the foreground appears the corpse that Dr. Tulp, a noted physician, is in the act of dissecting. Rembrandt diagonally placed and foreshortened the corpse, activating the space by disrupting the strict horizontal, planar orientation found in traditional portraiture. He depicted each of the "students" specifically, and although they wear virtually identical attire, their varying poses and facial expressions suggest unique individuals. In light of the fact Rembrandt produced this painting when he was twenty-six and just beginning his career, his innovative approach to group portraiture is all the more remarkable.

A MILITIA GROUP READYING FOR PARADE

Rembrandt amplified the complexity and energy of the group portrait in his famous painting of 1642, *The Company of Captain Frans Banning Cocq* (FIG. **24-44**), better known as *Night Watch*. This more commonly used title is, however, a misnomer—*Night Watch* is not a nocturnal scene. Rembrandt used light in a masterful way, and dramatic lighting certainly enhances this scene. However, the painting's darkness (which led to the commonly used title) is due more to the varnish the artist used, which has darkened considerably over time, than to the subject depicted.

This painting was one of many civic-guard group portraits produced during this period. From the limited information available about the commission, it appears Rembrandt was asked to paint the two officers, Captain Frans Banning Cocq and his lieutenant Willem van Ruytenburch, along with sixteen members of this militia group (each contributing to Rembrandt's fee). This work was one of six paintings commissioned from different artists around 1640 for the assembly and banquet hall of the new Kloveniersdoelen (Musketeers' Hall) in Amsterdam. Some scholars have suggested that the occasion for these commissions was the visit of Queen Marie de' Medici to the Dutch city in 1638.

Rembrandt captured the excitement and frenetic activity as the men prepared for the parade. Comparing *The Company of Captain Frans Banning Cocq* to Hals's portrait of the *Archers of Saint Hadrian* (FIG. 24-41), another militia group, reveals Rembrandt's inventiveness in enlivening what was, by then, becoming a conventional portrait format. Rather than present assembled men, the artist chose to portray the company

24-44 REMBRANDT VAN RIJN, *The Company of Captain Frans Banning Cocq (Night Watch)*, 1642. Oil on canvas (cropped from original size), 11′ 11″ × 14′ 4″. Rijksmuseum, Amsterdam.

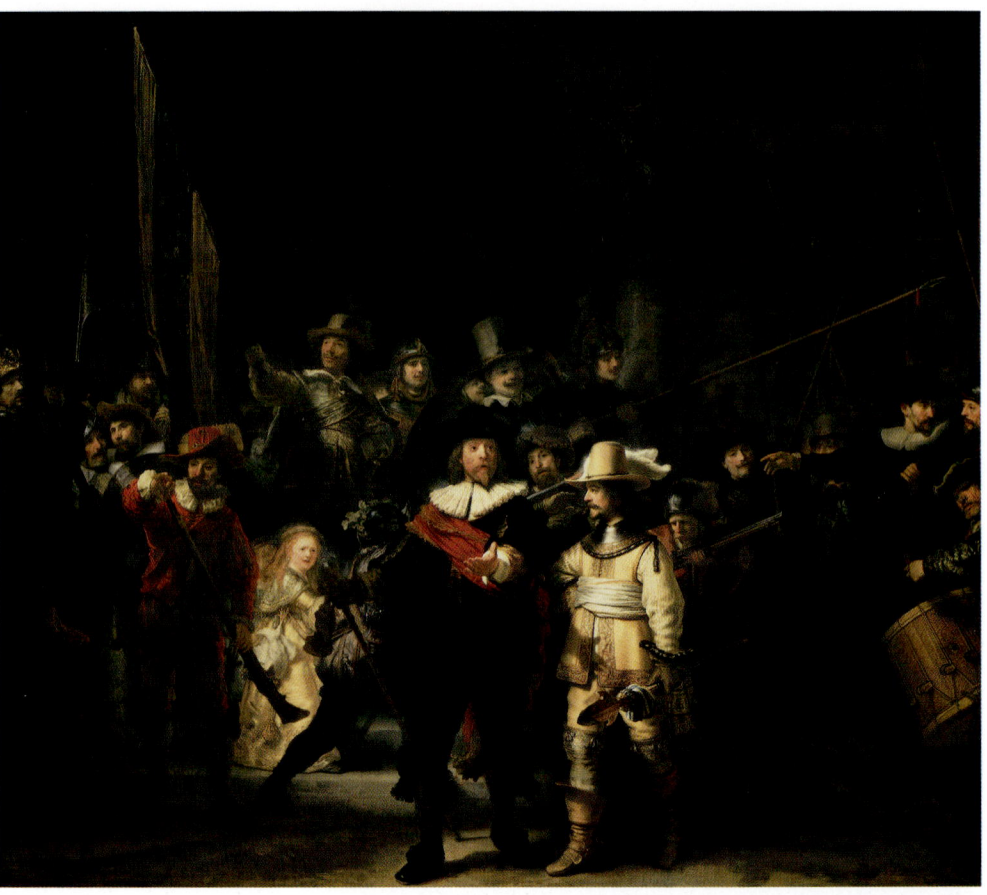

scurrying about in the act of organizing themselves, thereby animating the image considerably. Despite the prominence of the woman just to the left of center, scholars have yet to ascertain definitively her identity.

The large canvas was placed in the designated hall in 1642. Unfortunately, when the painting was subsequently moved in 1715 to the Amsterdam town hall, it was cropped on all sides, leaving viewers today with an incomplete record of the artist's final resolution to the challenge of portraying this group.

CELEBRATING THE HUMILITY OF JESUS Rembrandt's interest in probing the states of the human soul was not limited to portraiture. The Calvinist injunctions against religious art did not prevent him from making a series of religious paintings and prints. These images, however, are not the opulent, overwhelming art of Baroque Italy. Rather, his art is that of a committed Christian who desired to interpret biblical narratives in human (as opposed to lofty theological) terms. The spiritual stillness of Rembrandt's religious paintings is that of inward-turning contemplation, far from the choirs and trumpets and the heavenly tumult of Bernini or Pozzo. Rembrandt gave viewers not the celestial triumph of the Christian Church but the humanity and humility of Jesus. His psychological insight and his profound sympathy for human affliction produced, at the very end of his life, one of the most moving pictures in all religious art, *Return of the Prodigal Son* (FIG. 24-45). Tenderly embraced by his forgiving father, the son crouches before him in weeping contrition, while three figures, immersed in varying degrees in the soft shadows, note the les-

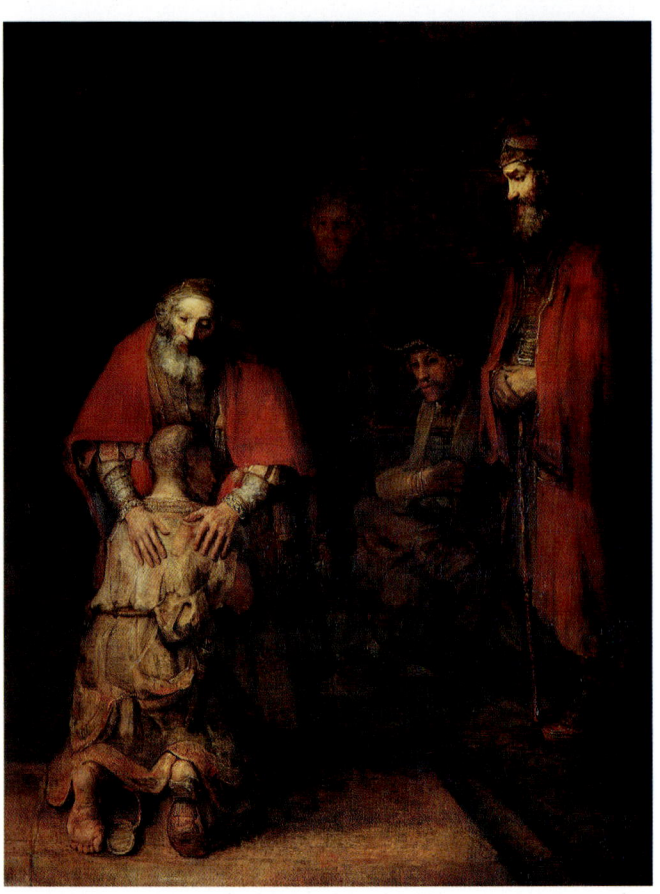

24-45   REMBRANDT VAN RIJN, *Return of the Prodigal Son,* ca. 1665. Oil on canvas, approx. 8′ 8″ × 6′ 9″. Hermitage Museum, Saint Petersburg.

son of mercy. The light, everywhere mingled with shadow, directs the viewer's attention by illuminating the father and son and largely veiling the witnesses. Its focus is the beautiful, spiritual face of the old man; secondarily, it touches the contrasting stern face of the foremost witness. *Return* demonstrates the degree to which Rembrandt developed a personal style completely in tune with the simple eloquence of the biblical passage.

LIGHTING THE WAY   From the few paintings by Rembrandt discussed thus far, it should be clear the artist's use of light is among the hallmarks of his style. Rembrandt's pictorial method involved refining light and shade into finer and finer nuances until they blended with one another. Earlier painters' use of abrupt lights and darks gave way, in the work of artists such as Rembrandt and Velázquez, to gradation. Although these later artists may have sacrificed some of the dramatic effects of sharp chiaroscuro, a greater fidelity to actual appearances offset those sacrifices. This technique is closer to reality because the eyes perceive light and dark not as static but as always subtly changing.

Generally speaking, Renaissance artists represented forms and faces in a flat, neutral modeling light (even Leonardo's shading is of a standard kind). They represented the idea of light, rather than the actual look of it. Artists such as Rembrandt discovered degrees of light and dark, degrees of differences in pose, in the movements of facial features, and in psychic states. They arrived at these differences optically, not conceptually or in terms of some ideal. Rembrandt found that by manipulating the direction, intensity, distance, and surface texture of light and shadow, he could render the most subtle nuances of character and mood, of persons, or of whole scenes. He discovered for the modern world that variation of light and shade, subtly modulated, could be read as emotional differences. In the visible world, light, dark, and the wide spectrum of values between the two are charged with meanings and feelings that sometimes are independent of the shapes and figures they modify. The theater and the photographic arts have used these discoveries to great dramatic effect.

Rembrandt carried over the spiritual quality of his religious works into his later portraits by the same means—what could be called the "psychology of light." Light and dark are not in conflict in his portraits—they are reconciled, merging softly and subtly to produce the visual equivalent of quietness. Their prevailing mood is that of tranquil meditation, of philosophical resignation, of musing recollection—indeed, a whole cluster of emotional tones heard only in silence.

AN ILLUMINATING SELF-PORTRAIT   In a late-Rembrandt self-portrait (FIG. **24-46**), the light that shines from the upper left of the painting bathes the subject's face in soft light, leaving the lower part of his body in shadow. The artist depicted himself here with dignity and strength, and the portrait can be seen as a summary of the many stylistic and professional concerns that occupied him throughout his career. Not only is Rembrandt's distinctive use of light evident, but also the assertive brushwork suggests a confidence and self-assurance. He presented himself as a working artist holding his brushes, palette, and maulstick. He is clothed in

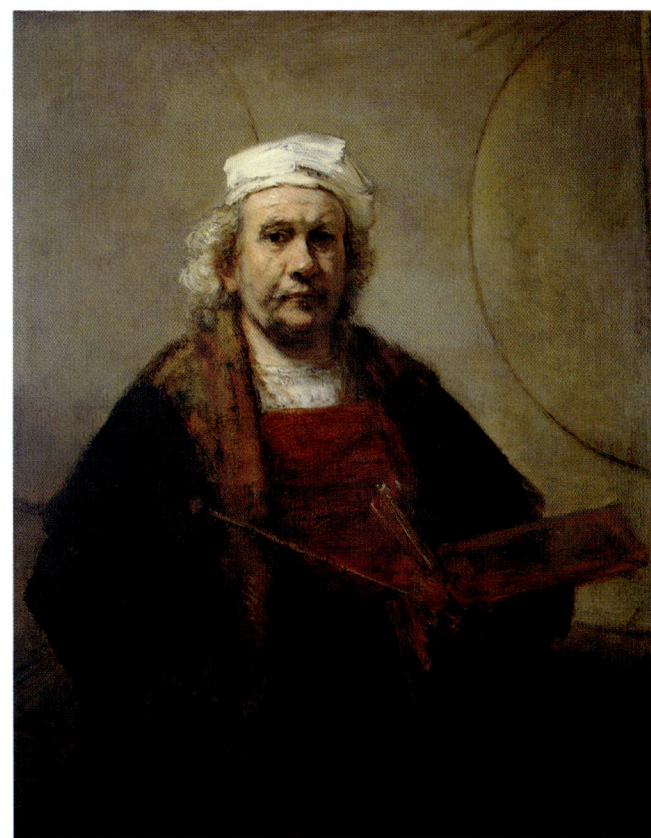

24-46   REMBRANDT VAN RIJN, *Self-Portrait*, ca. 1659–1660. Oil on canvas, approx. 3′ 8¾″ × 3′ 1″. The Iveagh Bequest, Kenwood House, London.

studio garb—a smock and painter's turban. The circles on the wall behind him (the subject of much scholarly debate) may allude to a legendary sign of artistic virtuosity—an ability to draw a perfect circle freehand. Ultimately, Rembrandt's abiding interest in revealing the human soul emerged here in his careful focus of the viewer's attention on his expressive visage. His controlled use of light and nonspecific setting contribute to this focus. Further, X rays of the painting have revealed that Rembrandt originally depicted himself in the act of painting. His final resolution, with the viewer's attention drawn to his face, produced a portrait not just of the artist but of the man as well.

COMPASSION MEMORABLY ETCHED   Rembrandt's virtuosity also extended to the graphic media—in particular, to etching. Many artists rapidly took up etching when it was perfected early in the seventeenth century. They found it far more manageable than engraving, and it allowed greater freedom in drawing the design. For etching, a copper plate is covered with a layer of wax or varnish. The artist incises the design into this surface with an etching needle or any pointed tool, exposing the metal below but not cutting into its surface. The plate is then immersed in acid, which etches, or eats away, the exposed parts of the metal, acting the same as the burin in engraving. The medium's softness gives etchers greater carving freedom than woodcutters and engravers have working directly in their more resistant media of wood and

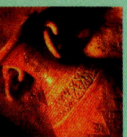

ART IN THE NEWS

Separating the Real from the Fake
The Rembrandt Research Project

Rembrandt had an active workshop and shared stylistic traits and technical methods with numerous colleagues and pupils. As a result, authenticating Rembrandt's paintings has been difficult (as is the case with many other artists). In 1968, a team of Dutch scholars organized as the Rembrandt Research Project (RRP) and set about the task of assessing the paintings attributed to Rembrandt in museums and private collections throughout the world. Their ultimate goal is the compilation of a definitive *catalogue raisonné* (a comprehensive catalog of an artist's works). RRP has relied extensively on new scientific techniques, such as X-ray, microscopic, and chemical analysis of paint samples and *dendrochronology* (the dating of wood). Of course, stylistic analysis remains an important component in assessing authorship.

The results of their investigation, which still continues, have raised vehement debate, controversy, and consternation among art historians, museum curators, collectors, and deal-

ers. Currently, the Rembrandt Research Project has published three volumes (of a projected five-volume collection) of *A Corpus of Rembrandt Paintings*. These three volumes cover Rembrandt's work from 1625 to 1642 and include not just evaluations of the numerous paintings attributed to the artist during these years but also introductory essays on Rembrandt's style, patrons, and workshop practices. Of the paintings they have examined thus far, the RRP scholars have concluded that one hundred forty-six of the paintings attributed to Rembrandt are indeed by his hand, twelve paintings are questionable, and one hundred twenty-two works previously accepted as Rembrandt's should not be attributed to him. None of this subtracts, of course, from the aesthetic value of Rembrandt's art, which certainly is inestimable. Nor does it in any way diminish his stature in the history of art. It does remind people once again that the "facts" of art history always are open to review and their interpretations open to revision.

metal. Thus, prior to the invention of the lithograph in the nineteenth century, etching was the most facile of the graphic arts and offered the greatest subtlety of line and tone.

If Rembrandt had never painted, he still would be renowned, as he principally was in his lifetime, for his prints. Prints were a major source of income for him, and he often reworked the plates so that they could be used to produce a

new issue or edition. *Christ with the Sick around Him, Receiving the Children (Hundred Guilder Print;* FIG. **24-47**) is one of Rembrandt's most celebrated etchings. Indeed, the title by which the print is best known, *Hundred Guilder Print*, refers to the high price this work brought during Rembrandt's lifetime. Like his other religious works, this print is suffused with a deep and abiding piety. Christ appears in the center

24-47 REMBRANDT VAN RIJN, *Christ with the Sick around Him, Receiving the Children (Hundred Guilder Print)*, ca. 1649. Etching, approx. $11'' \times 1' 3\frac{1}{4}''$. Pierpont Morgan Library, New York.

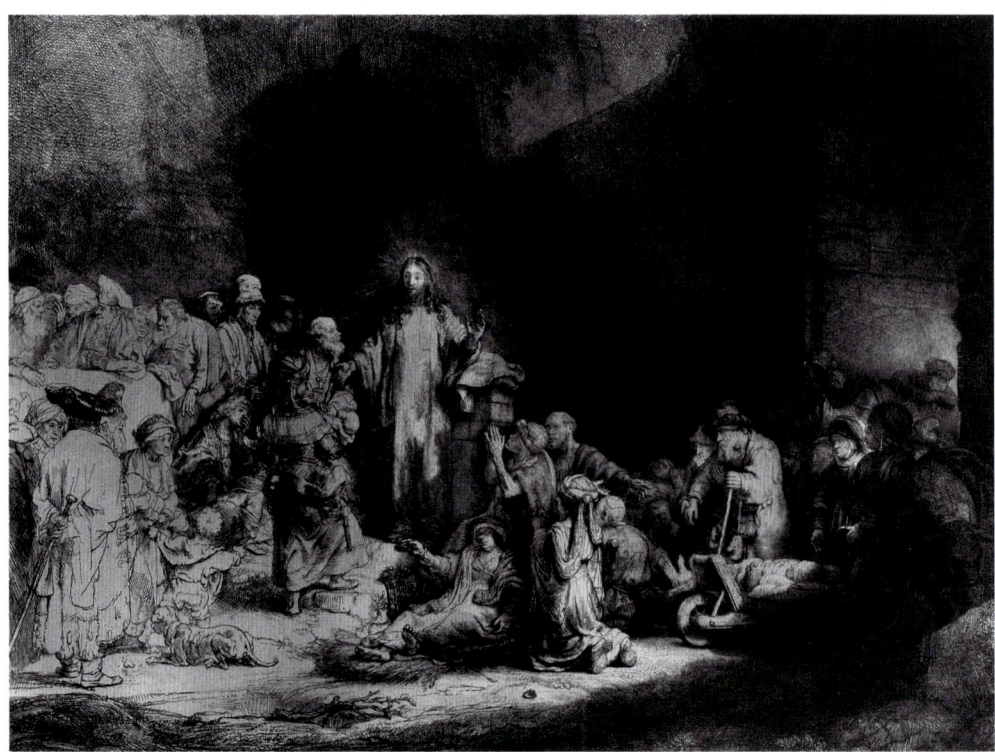

preaching compassionately to the blind, the lame, and the young. On the left, a group of Jews heatedly discuss issues among themselves. Like Rembrandt's *Return of the Prodigal Son* (FIG. 24-45), this image is about Christian humility and mercy.

Rembrandt's genius is undisputed. He is revered as an artist of great versatility, as a master of light and shadow, and as the unique interpreter of the Protestant conception of Scripture. Due to the esteem in which Rembrandt's art is held, his work and style have been the focus of many forgers. To counteract this, a group of scholars has launched the Rembrandt Research Project, whose goal is to provide definitive identification of the hundreds of works currently attributed to Rembrandt (see "Separating the Real from the Fake: The Rembrandt Research Project," page 758).

AT EASE IN FRONT OF AN EASEL JUDITH LEYSTER (1609–1660) developed a thriving career as a portraitist, like Hals, with whom she studied for a time. Her *Self-Portrait* (FIG. **24-48**) suggests the strong training she received; it is detailed, precise and accurate but also imbued with a spontaneity found in the works of Hals. In this painting, Leyster depicted herself as an artist, seated in front of a painting on an easel. The palette in her left hand and brush in her right make it clear the painting is her creation. She thus allowed viewers to evaluate her skill, which both the fiddler on the canvas and

the image of herself demonstrate as considerable. Her self-assurance is reflected in her quick smile and her relaxed pose as she stops her work to meet the viewer's gaze. Leyster produced a wide range of paintings, including genre scenes, still lifes, and floral pieces.

RECLAIMING THE LAND FROM THE SEA In addition to portraiture, the Dutch avidly collected landscapes, interior scenes, and still lifes. Each of these painting genres dealt directly with the daily lives of the urban mercantile public, accounting for their appeal. Landscape scenes abound in Dutch Baroque art. The Dutch had a unique relationship to the terrain, one that differed from other European countries due to topography and politics. After gaining independence from Spain, the Dutch undertook an extensive land reclamation project that lasted almost a century. Dikes and drainage systems cropped up across the landscape. Because of the effort expended on these endeavors, the Dutch developed a very direct relationship to the land. Further, the reclamation impacted Dutch social and economic life. The marshy and swampy nature of much of the land made it less desirable for large-scale exploitation, so the extensive feudal landowning system that existed elsewhere in Europe was never developed in the provinces. Most Dutch families owned and worked their own farms, cultivating a feeling of closeness to the Dutch terrain.

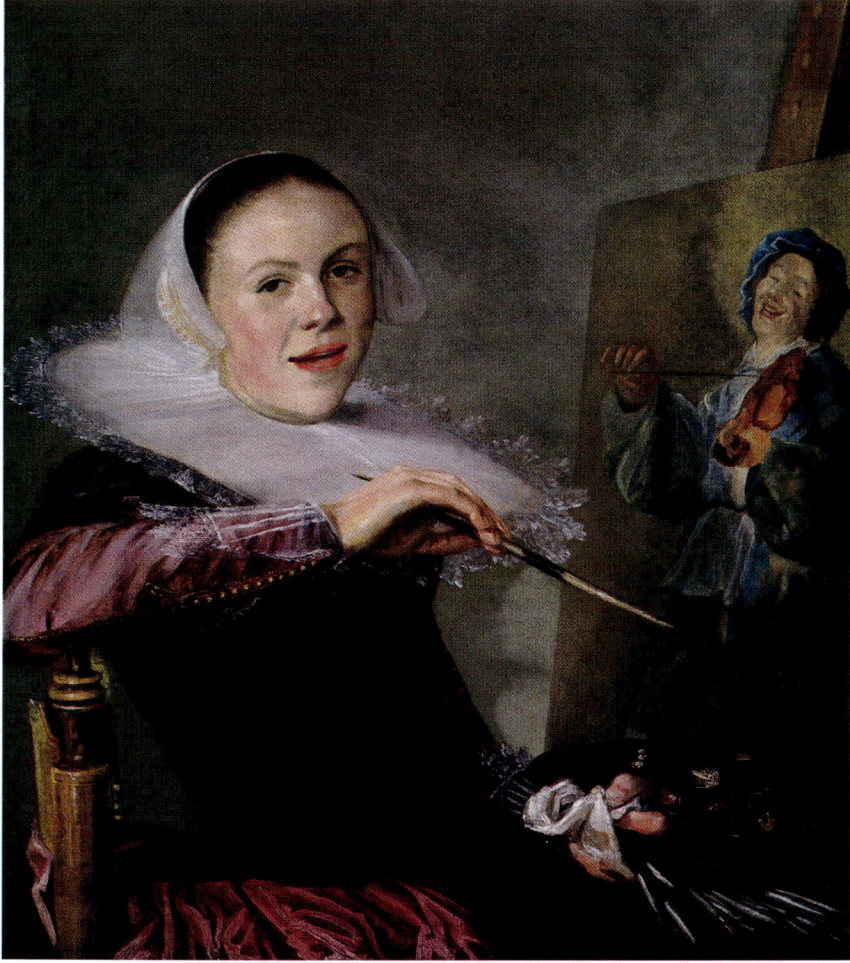

24-48 JUDITH LEYSTER, *Self-Portrait*, ca. 1630. Oil on canvas, 2' 5$\frac{3}{8}$" × 2' 1$\frac{5}{8}$". National Gallery of Art, Washington (gift of Mr. and Mrs. Robert Woods Bliss).

24-49 AELBERT CUYP, *A Distant View of Dordrecht, with a Milkmaid and Four Cows, and Other Figures (The "Large Dort")*, late 1640s. Oil on canvas, approx. 5′ 1″ × 6′ 4$\frac{7}{8}$″. National Gallery, London.

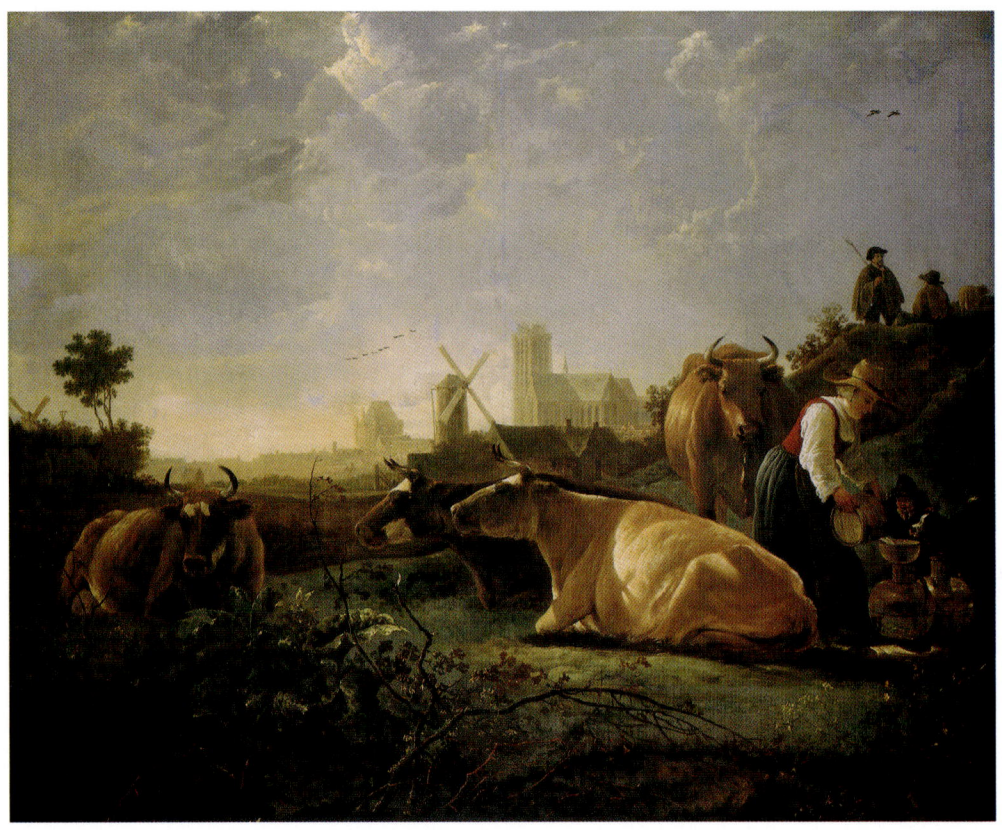

24-50 JACOB VAN RUISDAEL, *View of Haarlem from the Dunes at Overveen*, ca. 1670. Oil on canvas, approx. 1′ 10″ × 2′ 1″. Mauritshuis, The Hague.

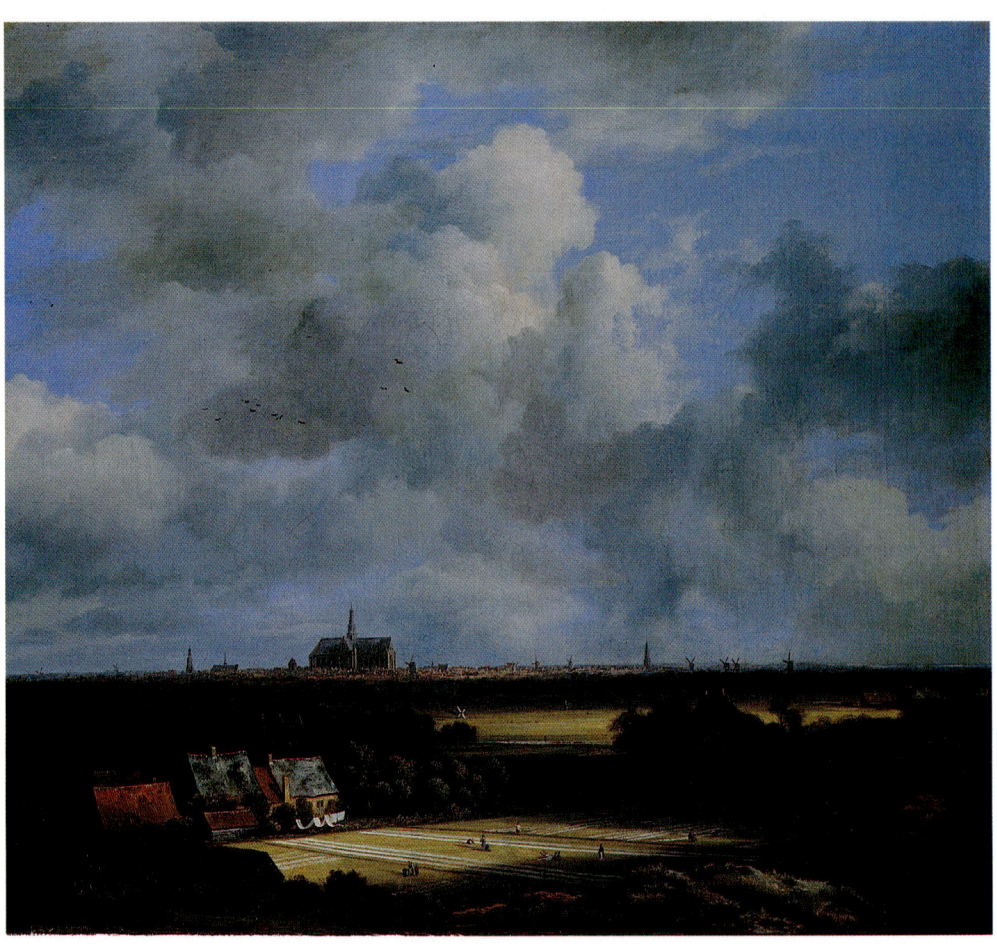

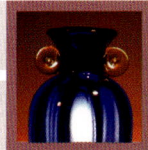

Mercantile Prosperity
Developing an Open Art Market

With the expansion of the Dutch art market (see "The Butcher, the Baker, the Candlestick Maker: Dutch Patronage and Art Collecting," page 752), commissions, the mainstay of art production in Italy and Spain, became less prevalent (except for portraiture) in the United Provinces. Dutch artists produced paintings for an anonymous market, hoping to appeal to a wide audience. To ensure success, artists adapted to the changed conditions of art production and sales. They marketed their paintings in many ways, selling their works directly to buyers who visited their studios and through art dealers, exhibitions, fairs, auctions, and even lotteries. Because of the uncertainty of these sales mechanisms (as opposed to the certainty of an ironclad contract for a commission), artists became more responsive to market demands. Specialization became common among Dutch artists of the seventeenth century. For example, painters would limit their practice to painting portraits, still lifes, or landscapes—the most popular genres among middle-class patrons. Exact prices

for Dutch paintings sold then are difficult to ascertain. Given the wide range of patrons, the prices no doubt ranged from very cheap to extravagantly expensive. Documented information about prices paid for artwork suggests that by 1700, genre scenes were the most expensive, on average, followed by history painting, religious scenes, landscapes, still lifes, and portraits. Another reason for the uncertainty about prices is that transactions often were conducted without cash. Artists frequently used their paintings to pay off loans or debts. Tavern debts, in particular, could be settled with paintings, which may explain why many art dealers (such as Jan Vermeer and his father before him) were also innkeepers. This connection between art dealing and other businesses eventually solidified, and innkeepers, for example, often would have art exhibitions in their taverns hoping to make a sale.

The institutions of the current open art market—dealers, galleries, auctions, estate sales—thus owe their establishment to the "Golden Age" of Dutch art.

A LANDSCAPE OF DORDRECHT A Dutch artist who established his reputation producing landscape paintings was AELBERT CUYP (ca. 1620–1691). His works were the products of careful observation and a deep respect for and understanding of the Dutch landscape. *A Distant View of Dordrecht, with a Milkmaid and Four Cows, and Other Figures* (FIG. **24-49**), often referred to as *The "Large Dort,"* is a good example of Cuyp's substantial skills. The title indicates that the location was important to the artist. Unlike the idealized classical landscapes that populate many Italian Renaissance paintings, this landscape is specified. In fact, the church in the background can be identified as the Grote Kerk in Dordrecht. The dairy cows, shepherds, and milkmaid in the foreground refer to a cornerstone of Dutch agriculture—the demand for dairy products such as butter and cheese, which increased with the development of urban centers. The credibility of such paintings rests on Cuyp's pristine rendering of each detail.

THE SKY'S THE LIMIT JACOB VAN RUISDAEL (ca. 1628–1682), like Cuyp, depicted the Dutch landscape with precision and sensitivity. In *View of Haarlem from the Dunes at Overveen* (FIG. **24-50**), van Ruisdael gave observers an overarching view of this major Dutch city. The specificity of the artist's image—the Saint Bavo church in the background, the numerous windmills that refer to the land reclamation efforts, and the figures in the foreground stretching linen to be bleached (a major industry in Haarlem)—endows the work with a sense of honesty and integrity. Yet this is, above all, a landscape. Although the scene is painted in an

admirably clear and detailed manner, the inhabitants and dwellings are so miniscule that they blend into the land itself. Further, the horizon line is low, so the sky fills almost three-quarters of the picture space. And the landscape is illuminated only in patches, where the sun has broken through the clouds above. In *View of Haarlem,* as in his other landscape paintings, van Ruisdael not only captured a specific and historical view of Haarlem, but he also succeeded in imbuing the work with a quiet serenity that seems almost spiritual.

HOME IS WHERE THE HEART IS The sense of peace, familiarity, and comfort that Dutch landscape paintings seem to exude also emerged in interior scenes. These paintings provide viewers with glimpses into the lives of prosperous, responsible, and cultured citizens. The best-known and most highly regarded of the Dutch interior scene painters is JAN VERMEER (1632–1675) of Delft. Vermeer derived most of his income from his work as an innkeeper and art dealer (see "Mercantile Prosperity: Developing an Open Art Market," above), and he painted no more than thirty-five paintings that definitively can be attributed to him. Vermeer's pictures are small, luminous, and captivating. Fifteenth-century Flemish artists also had painted domestic interiors, but persons of sacred significance often occupied those scenes (see, for example, the *Mérode Altarpiece* FIG. 20-11). In contrast, Vermeer and his contemporaries composed neat, quietly opulent interiors of Dutch middle-class dwellings with men, women, and children engaging in household tasks or some little recreation. These commonplace actions reflected the values of a comfortable domesticity that had a simple beauty.

24-51   Jan Vermeer, *The Letter,* 1666. Oil on canvas, 1' 5¼" × 1' 3¼". Rijksmuseum, Amsterdam.

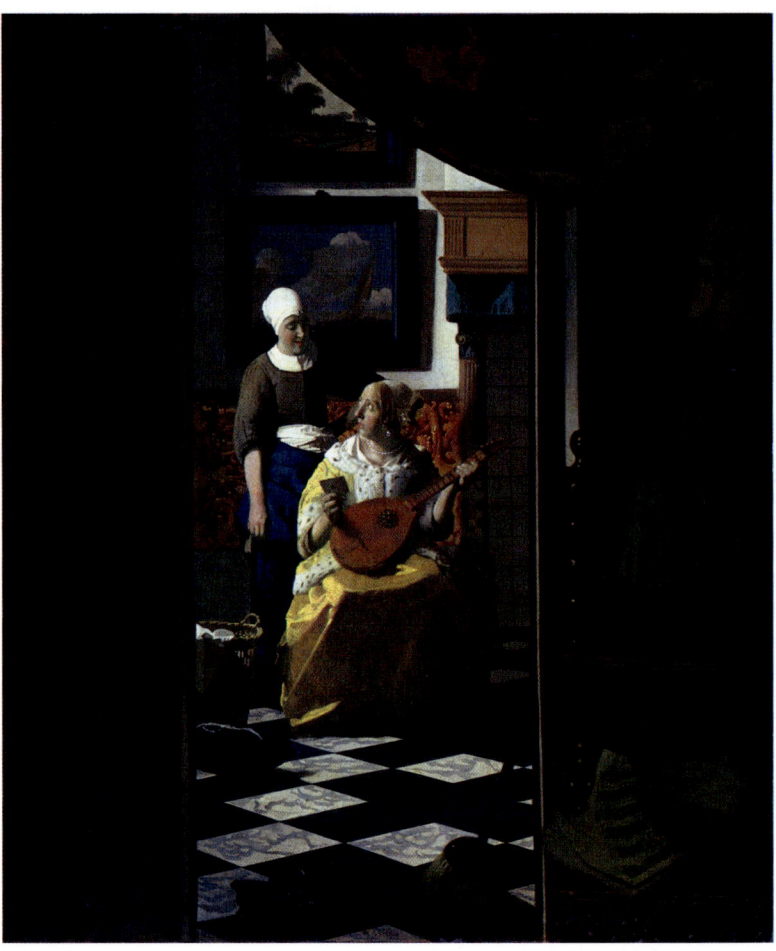

In *The Letter* (FIG. **24-51**), Vermeer ushers viewers into a room of a well-appointed Dutch house. The drawn curtain and open doorway through which they must peer reinforce the viewers' status as outsiders and affirm the scene's un-planned "normal" reality. A well-dressed woman sits framed by the doorway. Her lute playing has been interrupted by a maid, who has delivered a letter. The missive is a love letter; Vermeer included objects that would prompt this inference from a seventeenth-century Dutch audience. The lute was a traditional symbol of the music of love, and the calm seascape on the back wall served as a symbol of love requited. In the book *Love Emblems,* published in Amsterdam in 1634, the au-thor wrote: "Love may rightly be compared to the sea, consid-ering its changeableness. . . ."[3] Although the event depicted may not be historically momentous, Vermeer's care and di-rectness in recording these scenes provides viewers with im-portant insights about Dutch life and culture.

THE SCIENCE AND POETRY OF LIGHT   Vermeer was a master of pictorial light and used it with immense virtu-osity. He could render space so convincingly through his de-piction of light that in his works, the picture surface functions as an invisible glass pane the viewer looks through into the constructed illusion. Historians know Vermeer used as tools both mirrors and the *camera obscura,* an ancestor of the mod-ern camera based on passing light through a tiny pinhole or lens to project an image on a screen or the wall of a room. (In

later versions, the image was projected on a ground-glass wall of a box whose opposite wall contained the pinhole or lens.) This does not mean that Vermeer merely copied the image. Instead, these aids helped him obtain results he reworked compositionally, placing his figures and the furniture of a room in a beautiful stability of quadrilateral shapes. This gives his designs a matchless classical serenity. This quality is en-hanced by colors so true to the optical facts and so subtly modulated that they suggest Vermeer was far ahead of his time in color science. Close examination of his paintings shows that Vermeer realized that shadows are not colorless and dark, that adjoining colors affect each other, and that light is composed of colors. Thus, he painted reflections off of surfaces in colors modified by others nearby. It has been sug-gested that Vermeer also perceived the phenomenon modern photographers call "circles of confusion," which appear on out-of-focus negatives. Vermeer could have seen them in im-ages projected by the camera obscura's primitive lenses. He approximated these effects with light dabs that, in close view, give the impression of an image slightly "out of focus." When the observer draws back a step, however, as if adjusting the lens, the color spots cohere, giving an astonishingly accurate illusion of a third dimension.

All of these technical considerations reflect the scientific spirit of the age, but they do not explain the exquisite poetry of form and surface, of color and light that could come only from a great artist's sensitivity. In Marcel Proust's *Swann's Way,*

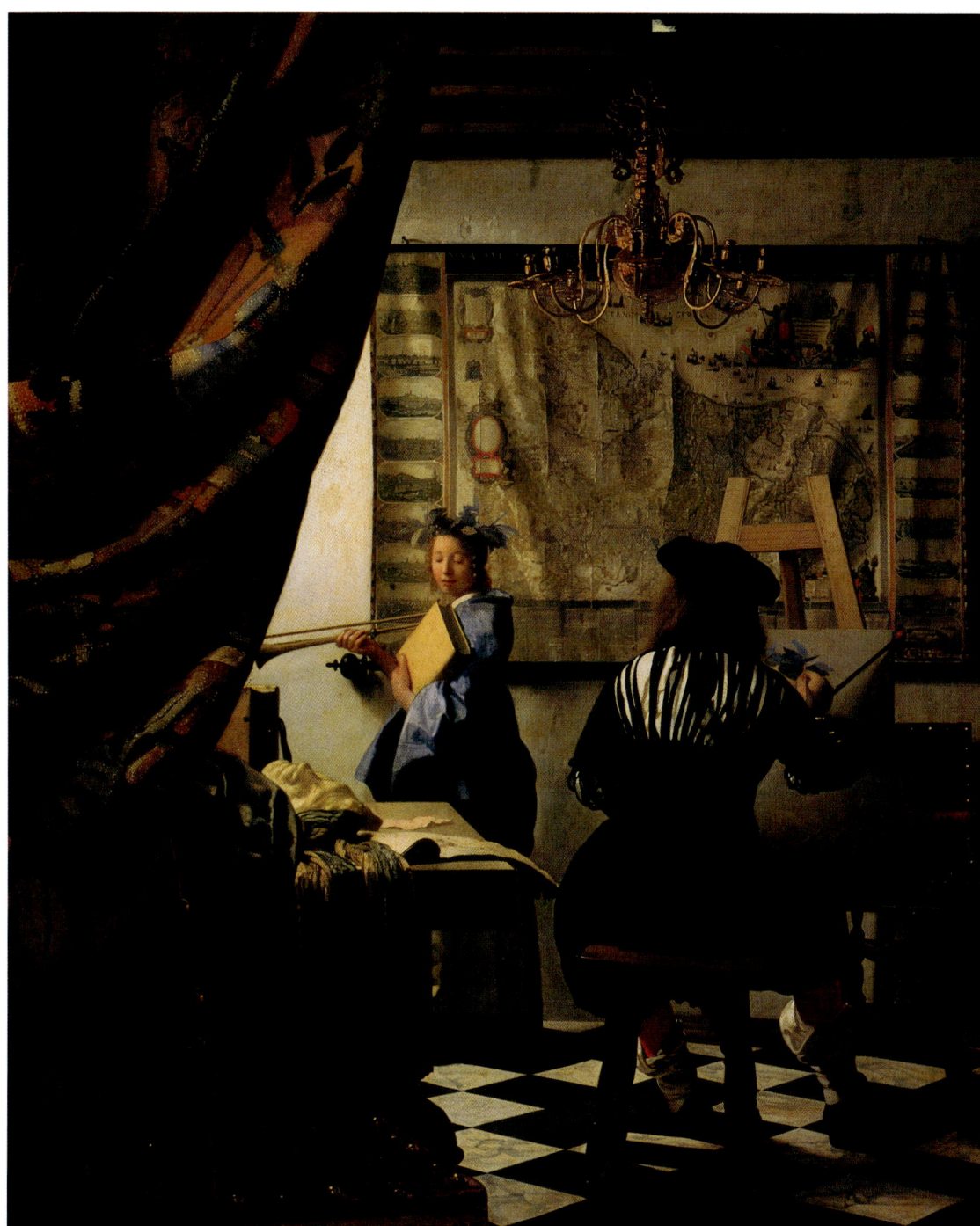

24-52 JAN VERMEER, *Allegory of the Art of Painting,* 1670–1675. Oil on canvas, 4′ 4″ × 3′ 8″. Kunsthistorisches Museum, Vienna.

the connoisseur hero, trying unsuccessfully to write a monograph on Vermeer, admits that no words could ever do justice to a single patch of sunlight on one of Vermeer's walls.

EXTOLLING THE ART PROFESSION Vermeer's stylistic precision and commitment to his profession surfaced in *Allegory of the Art of Painting* (FIG. **24-52**). The artist himself appears in the painting, with his back to the viewer and dressed in "historical" clothing (reminiscent of Burgundian attire). He is hard at work on a painting of the model who stands before him wearing a laurel wreath and holding a trumpet and book, traditional attributes of Clio, the Muse of History. The map of the provinces (an increasingly common

wall adornment in Dutch homes) on the back wall serves as yet another reference to history. As in *The Letter,* viewers are outside the space of the action, and the drawn curtain provides visual access. Some art historians have suggested that the light radiating from an unseen window on the left that illuminates both the model and the canvas being painted alludes to the light of artistic inspiration. Accordingly, this painting has been interpreted (as reflected in the title) as an allegory—a reference to painting inspired by history. This allegorical reading was affirmed when Vermeer's widow, wishing to retain this painting after the artist's death, listed it in her written claim as "the piece . . . wherein the Art of Painting is portrayed."[4]

24-53 JAN STEEN, *The Feast of Saint Nicholas,* ca. 1660–1665. Oil on canvas, 2' 8¼" × 2' 3¾". Rijksmuseum, Amsterdam.

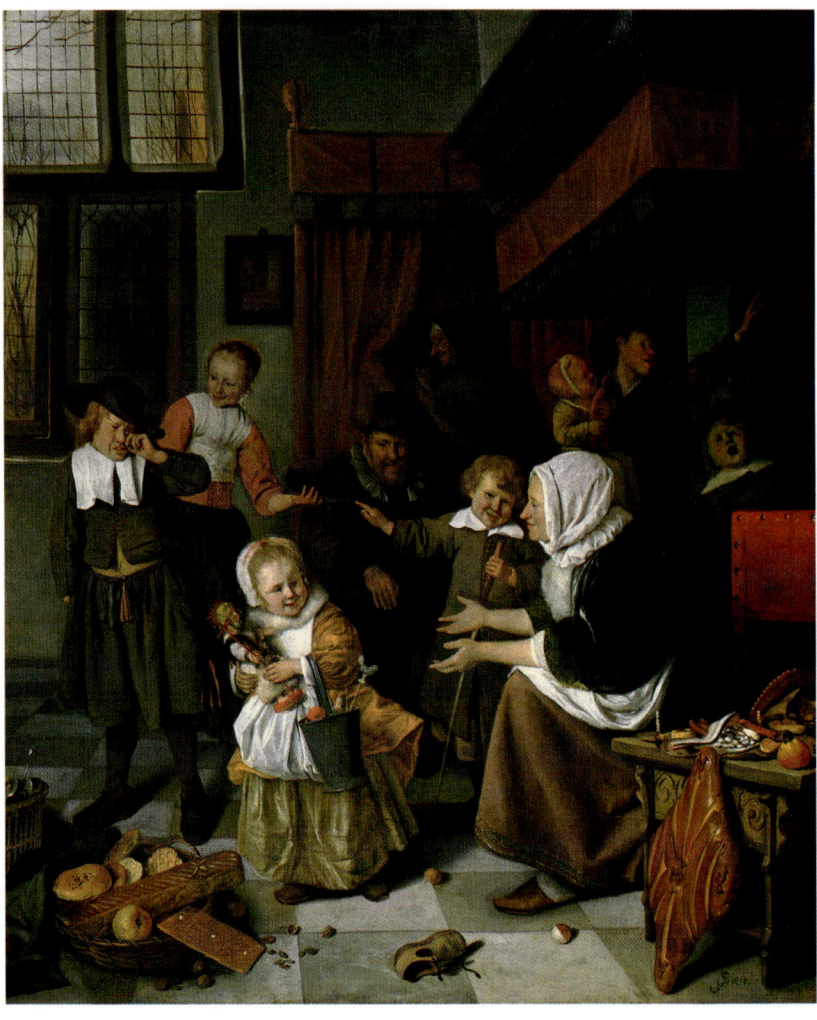

SATIRIZING DUTCH LIFE While Vermeer revealed the charm and beauty of Dutch domesticity, the work of JAN STEEN (ca. 1625–1679) provided a counterpoint. In *The Feast of Saint Nicholas* (FIG. **24-53**), rather than depicting a tidy, calm Dutch household, Steen painted a scene of chaos and disruption. Saint Nicholas has just visited this residence, and the children are in an uproar as they search their shoes for the gifts from Saint Nick. Some children are delighted—the little girl in the center clutches her gifts, clearly unwilling to share with the other children despite her mother's pleas. Others are disappointed—the boy on the left is in tears because all he has received is a birch rod. An appropriately festive atmosphere reigns, which contrasts sharply with the decorum that prevails in Vermeer's works. Like the paintings of other Dutch Baroque artists, Steen's lively scenes often take on an allegorical dimension or moralistic tone. Steen frequently used children's activities as satirical comments on foolish adult behavior. *The Feast of Saint Nicholas* can be seen as alluding to selfishness, pettiness, and jealousy.

OF BEAUTY AND DEATH The prosperous Dutch were justifiably proud of their accomplishments, and the popularity of still-life paintings—particularly images of ac-

cumulated material goods—reflected this pride. These still lifes, like Vermeer's interior scenes, are beautifully crafted images that are both scientific in their optical accuracy and poetic in their beauty and lyricism. Paintings such as *Still Life with Oysters, Rum Glass, and Silver Cup* (FIG. **24-54**) by WILLEM CLAESZ HEDA (ca. 1599–1680), reveal the pride Dutch citizens had in their material possessions, presented as if strewn across a tabletop or dresser. This pride is tempered, however, by the ever-present morality and humility central to the Calvinist faith. Thus, while appreciating and enjoying the beauty and value of the objects depicted, the artist reminded viewers of life's transience. He achieved this by including references to death. Paintings with such features are called *vanitas* paintings. In *Still Life,* references to mortality include the oysters, partially peeled fruit, broken glass, and tipped silver cup. All suggest a presence that has disappeared. Something or someone was here—and now is gone.

THE ALLURE OF PRECIOUS OBJECTS As Dutch prosperity increased, precious objects and luxury items made their way into still-life paintings. *Still Life with the Drinking Horn of Saint Sebastian's Archer's Guild* (FIG. **24-55**) by WILLEM KALF (1619–1693) reveals both the wealth Dutch

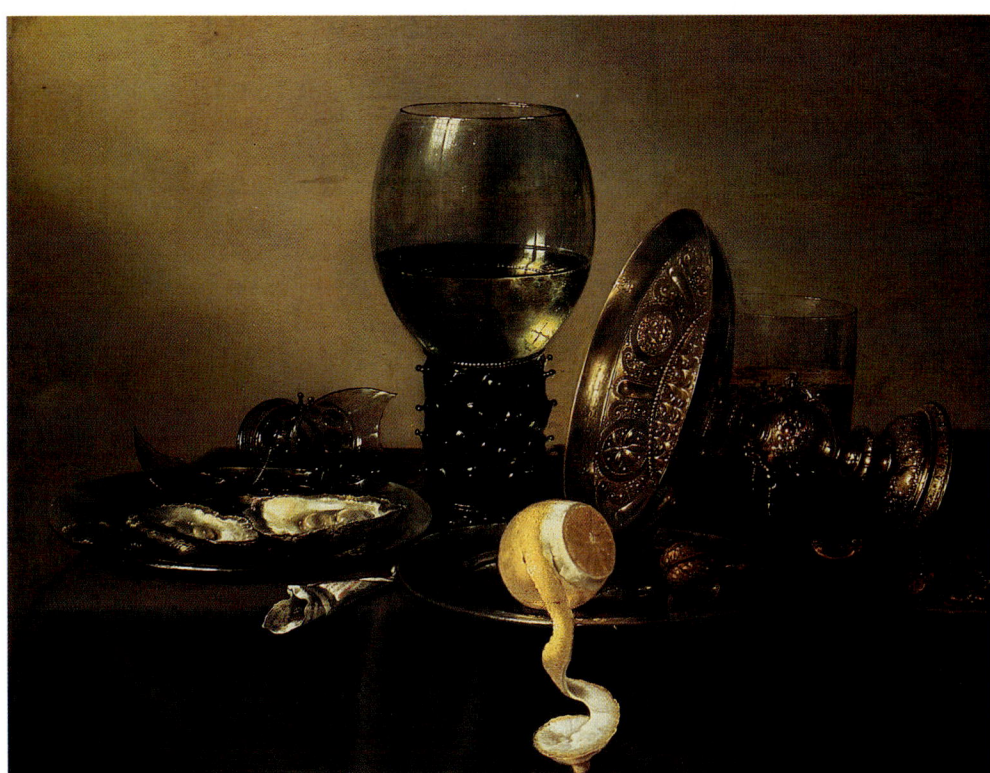

24-54 WILLEM CLAESZ HEDA, *Still Life with Oysters, Rum Glass, and Silver Cup*, Panel, 1′ 5″ × 2′ 4$\frac{7}{8}$″. Museum Boijmans-Van Beuringen, Rotterdam.

citizens had accrued and the exquisite skills—both technical and aesthetic—of Dutch Baroque artists. Kalf was enamored by highlights glinting off reflective surfaces and the lustrous sheen of fabric. His works, as is evident in this image, present an array of ornamental objects, such as the drinking horn. Kalf's inclusion of the lobster and peeled fruit suggests that these works, despite their opulence, also functioned as vanitas paintings.

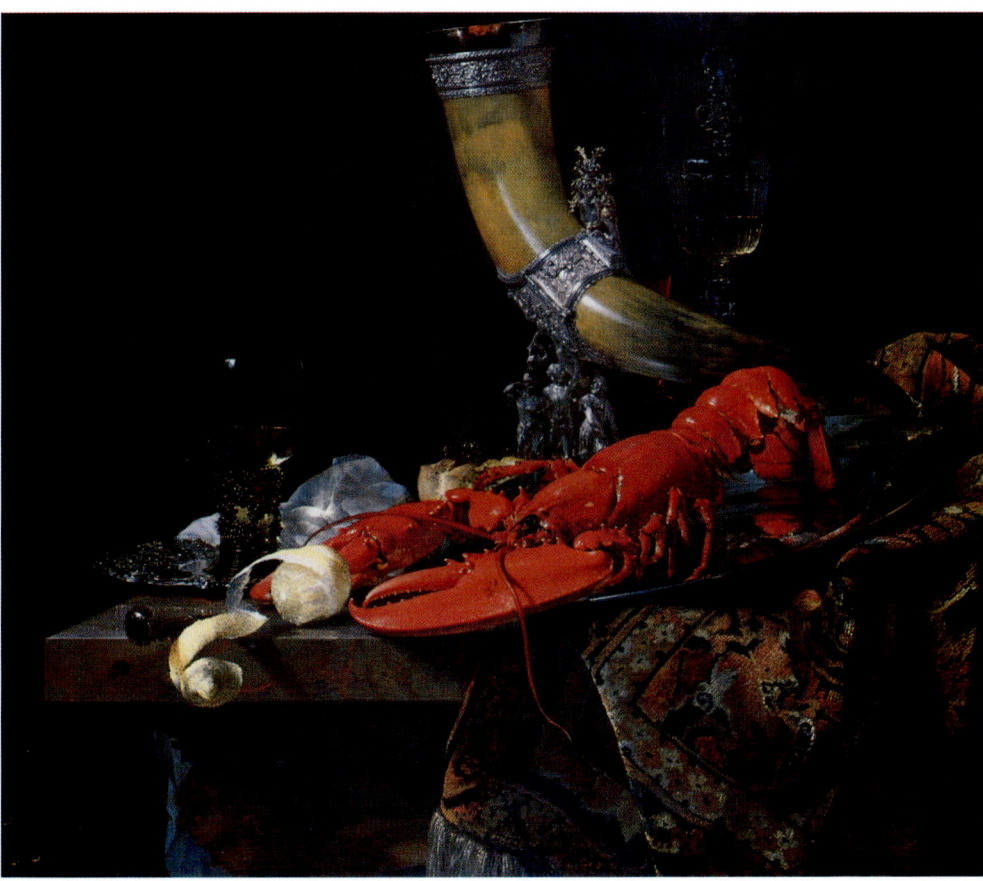

24-55 WILLEM KALF, *Still Life with the Drinking Horn of Saint Sebastian's Archer's Guild,* ca. 1653. Oil on canvas, approx. 2′ 9″ × 3′ 3$\frac{7}{8}$″. National Gallery, London.

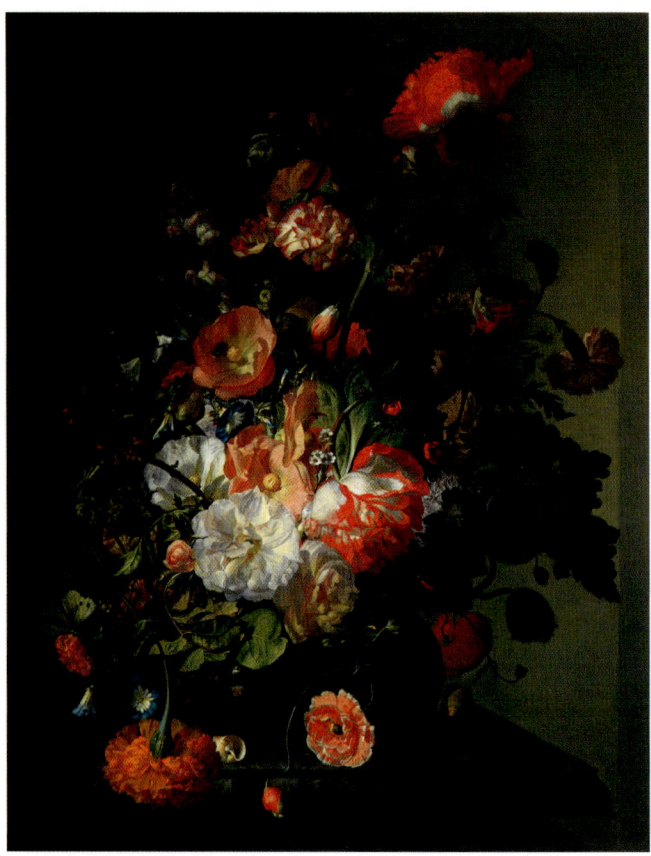

24-56 Rachel Ruysch, *Flower Still Life,* after 1700. Oil on canvas, 2′ 6″ × 2′. The Toledo Museum of Art, Toledo (purchased with funds from the Libbey Endowment, gift of Edward Drummond Libbey).

A BUDDING ARTIST Like still-life paintings, flower paintings were prominent in Dutch Baroque art. As living objects that soon die, flowers, particularly cut blossoms, appeared frequently in vanitas paintings. However, floral painting itself also flourished. Among the leading practitioners of this art was Rachel Ruysch (1663–1750). Ruysch's father was a professor of botany and anatomy, which may account for her interest in and knowledge of plants and insects. She acquired an international reputation for lush paintings such as *Flower Still Life* (FIG. **24-56**). In this image, the lavish floral arrangement is so full that many of the blossoms seem to be spilling out of the vase. Ruysch carefully constructed her paintings. Here, for example, the lower left to upper right diagonal created by her positioning of the flowers is offset by the opposing diagonal of the table edge. Ruysch became famous for her floral paintings and still lifes, and from 1708 to 1716 she served as court painter to the elector Palatine (the ruler of the Palatinate, a division of Bavaria) in Düsseldorf, Germany.

Dutch Baroque art has a unique character that sets it apart from, say, Italian Baroque, although commonalities can be uncovered. The appeal of Dutch Baroque art lies both in its beauty and its sincerity, as well as the insights it provides into Dutch life and history.

France

France's history during the Baroque period is essentially the culmination of increasing monarchical authority that had been developing for centuries. This consolidation of power was embodied in King Louis XIV (r. 1661–1715), whose ob-

sessive control determined the direction of French Baroque society and culture. The governmental investment of total authority in the absolute monarch proved France's downfall. The country's reluctance to expand economically made it unable to compete with rising powers such as the Dutch Republic. The stagnant political, economic, and social systems in France eventually led to the French Revolution in 1789.

Religious conflicts caused great tension throughout the sixteenth and seventeenth centuries. After the Reformation, Protestants in France challenged royal authority, which resulted in a sequence of religious wars between Catholics and Protestants. In 1598, King Henry IV (r. 1589–1610) issued the Edict of Nantes, which in effect decreed religious tolerance. Despite this edict, Protestants eventually were driven from the country.

REALISM, SPIRITUALISM, CLASSICISM Because of the prominence of religious issues and the value Catholics placed on the didactic capabilities of art (as in Baroque Italy), religious art did have a presence in France. Among the artists well known for their religious imagery was the painter Georges de La Tour (1593–1652). La Tour's work, particularly his use of light, suggests a familiarity with Caravaggio's art, which he may have acquired through the Dutch school of Utrecht. Although La Tour used the devices of the northern Caravaggisti, his effects are strikingly different from theirs. His *Adoration of the Shepherds* (FIG. **24-57**) makes use of the night setting favored by that school, much as van Honthorst (FIG. 24-40) portrayed it. But here, the light, its source shaded by an old man's hand, falls upon a very different company in a very different mood. A group of humble men and women, coarsely clad, gather in prayerful vigil around a luminous baby Jesus. Without the aid of the title, this might be construed as a genre piece, a narrative of some event from peasant life. Nothing in the environment, placement, poses, dress, or attributes of the figures distinguishes them as the scriptural Virgin Mary, Joseph, Christ Child, or shepherds. The artist did not portray halos, choirs of angels, stately architecture, or resplendent grandees. The light is not spiritual but material; it comes from a candle. La Tour's scientific scrutiny of the effects of material light, as it throws precise shadows on surfaces

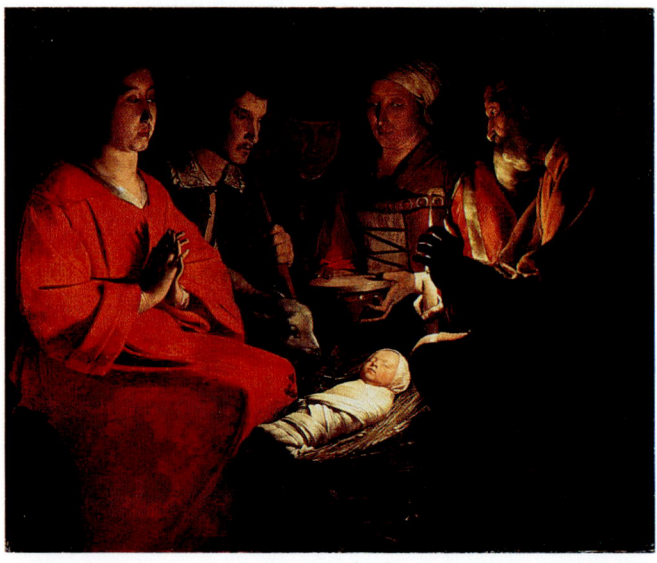

24-57 Georges de La Tour, *Adoration of the Shepherds,* 1645–1650. Oil on canvas, approx. 3′ 6″ × 4′ 6″. Louvre, Paris.

that intercept it, had, nevertheless, religious intention and consequence. The light illuminates a group of ordinary people held in a mystic trance induced by their witnessing the miracle of the Incarnation. In this timeless tableau of simple people, La Tour eliminated the dogmatic significance and traditional iconography of the Incarnation. Still, these people reverently contemplate something they regard as holy. As such, the painting is readable to the devout of any religious persuasion, whether or not they know of this central mystery of the Christian faith.

The supernatural calm that pervades this picture is characteristic of the mood of Georges de La Tour's art. He achieved this by eliminating motion and emotive gesture (only the light is dramatic), by suppressing surface detail, and by simplifying body volumes. These stylistic traits are among those associated with classical art and art based on classical principles—for example, that of Piero della Francesca (see FIGS. 21-51, 21-52, and 21-53). Several apparently contrary elements meet in the work of La Tour: classical composure, fervent spirituality, and genre realism.

THE HARDSHIP OF PEASANT LIFE   LOUIS LE NAIN (ca. 1593–1648) and his contemporary, La Tour, bear comparison with the Dutch. Subjects that in Dutch painting were opportunities for boisterous good humor the French treated with sombre stillness. *Family of Country People* (FIG. 24-58) expresses the grave dignity of a family close to the soil, one made stoic and resigned by hardship. These drab country folk surely had little reason for merriment. The peasant's lot, never easy, was miserable during the time Le Nain painted. The constant warfare (*Family* was painted during the Thirty Years' War) took its toll on France. The anguish and frustration of the peasantry, suffering from the cruel depredations of unruly armies living off the country, often broke out in violent revolts that were savagely suppressed. This family, however, is pious, docile, and calm. Because Le Nain depicted peasants with dignity and subservience, despite their harsh living conditions, some scholars have suggested he intended to please wealthy urban patrons with these paintings.

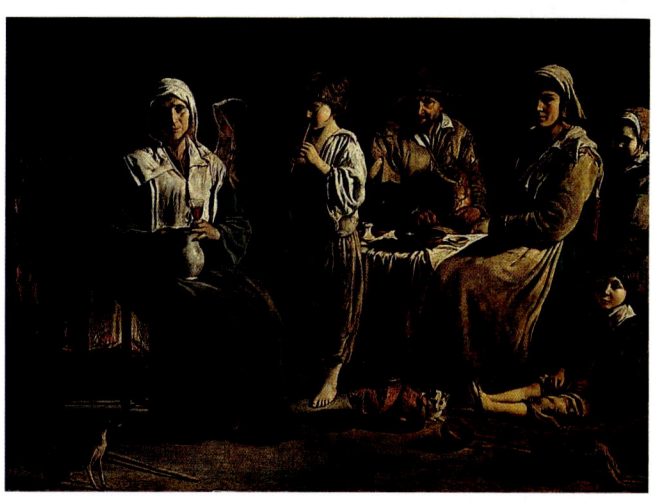

24-58   LOUIS LE NAIN, *Family of Country People,* ca. 1640. Oil on canvas, approx. 3′ 8″ × 5′ 2″. Louvre, Paris.

A STARK ETCHING OF DEATH   A record of the times appears in a series of etchings by JACQUES CALLOT (ca. 1592–1635) called *Miseries of War.* Callot confined himself almost exclusively to the art of etching and was widely influential in his time and since; Rembrandt was among those who knew and learned from his work. Callot perfected the medium and the technique of etching, developing a very hard surface for the copper plate to permit fine and precise delineation with the needle. In one small print, he would assemble as many as twelve hundred figures, which only close scrutiny can discriminate. His quick, vivid touch and faultless drawing produced panoramas sparkling with sharp details of life—and death. In the *Miseries of War* series, he observed these coolly, presenting without comment sights he himself must have seen in the wars in his own region, Lorraine.

In one etching, he depicted a mass execution by hanging (FIG. 24-59). The unfortunates in *Hanging Tree* may be war prisoners or defeated peasant rebels. The event takes place in the presence of a disciplined army, drawn up on parade with banners, muskets, and lances, their tents in the background.

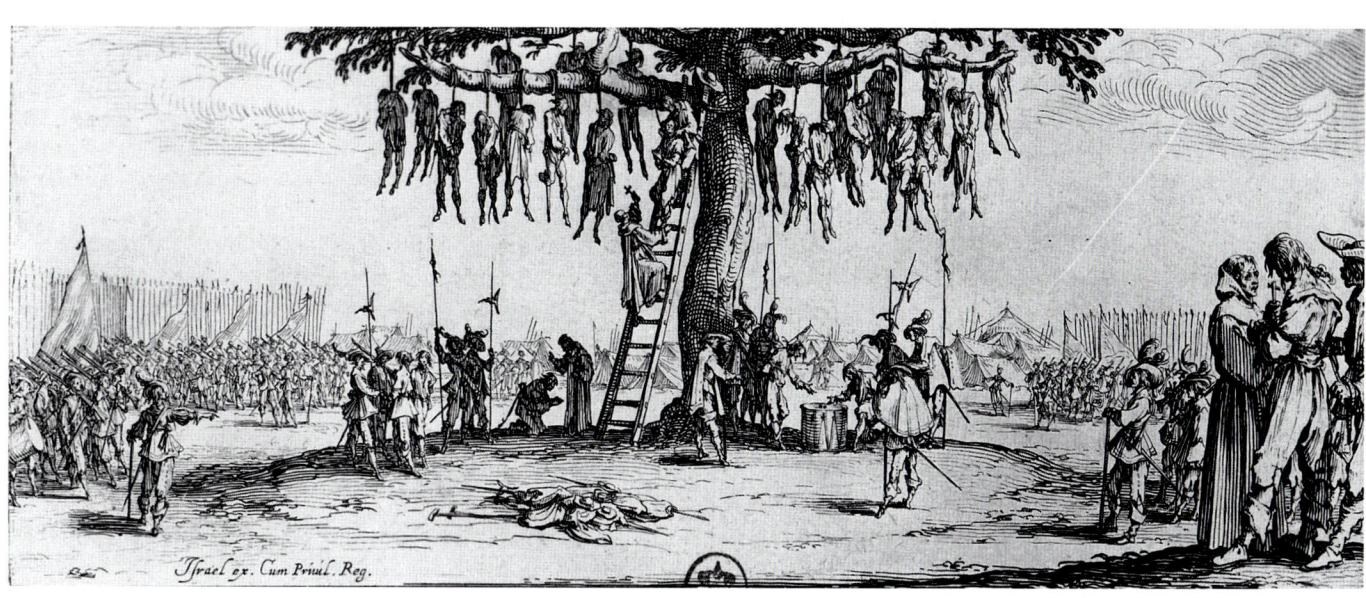

24-59   JACQUES CALLOT, *Hanging Tree,* from the *Miseries of War* series, 1621. Etching, 3¾″ × 7¼″. Bibliothèque Nationale, Paris.

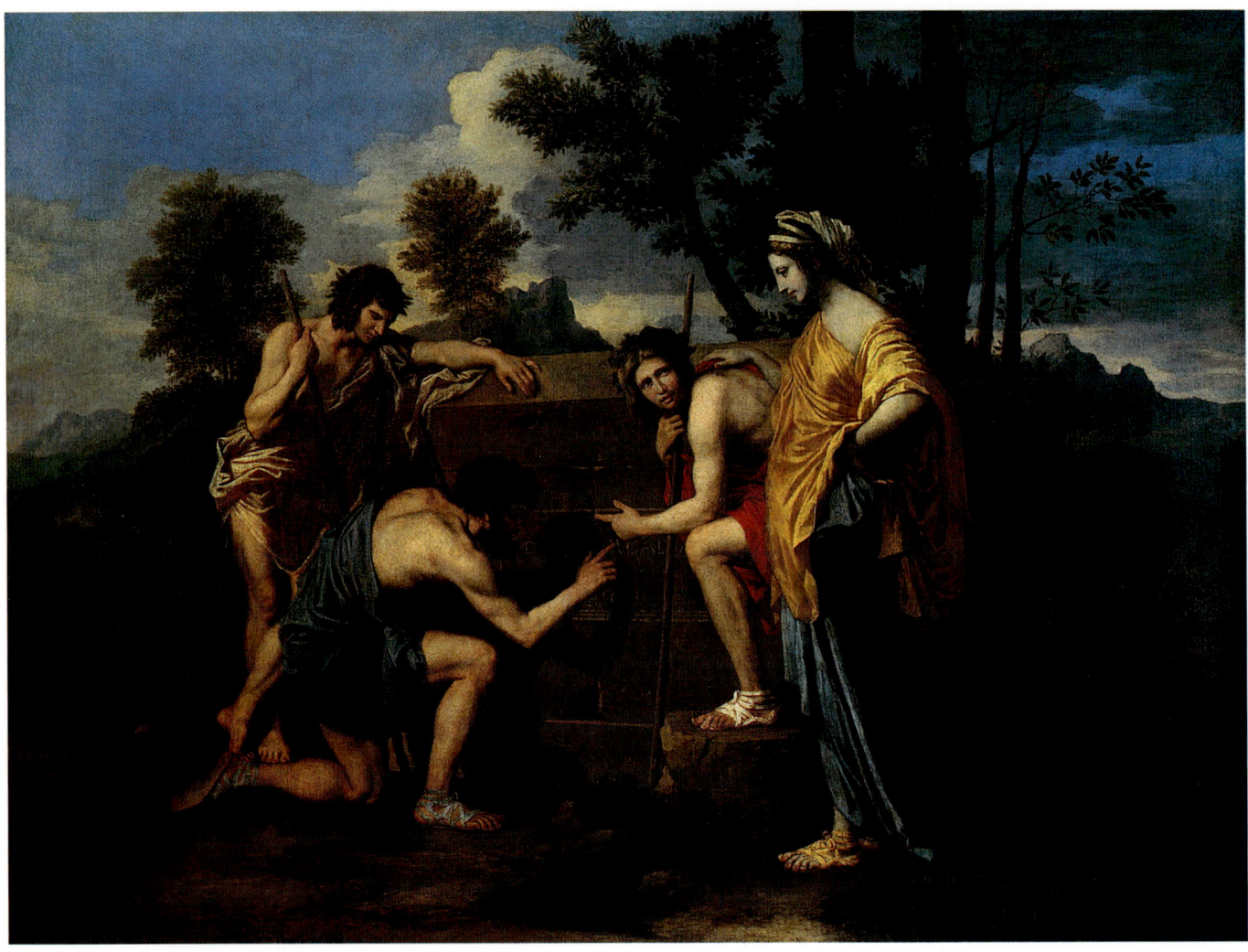

24-60   Nicolas Poussin, *Et in Arcadia Ego*, ca. 1655. Oil on canvas, approx. 2′ 10″ × 4′. Louvre, Paris.

Hanged men sway in clusters from the branches of a huge cross-shaped tree. A monk climbs a ladder, holding up a crucifix to a man while the executioner adjusts the noose around the man's neck. At the foot of the ladder, another victim kneels to receive absolution. Under the crucifix tree, men roll dice on a drumhead for the belongings of the executed. (This may be an allusion to the soldiers who cast lots for the garments of the crucified Christ.) In the right foreground, a hooded priest consoles a bound man. Callot's *Miseries of War* were among the first realistic pictorial records of the human disaster of armed conflict.

INVOKING CLASSICAL ORDER   The brisk animation of Callot's manner contrasts with the quiet composure in the art of La Tour and Le Nain, his exact contemporaries. Yet, although the art of La Tour and Le Nain exudes a calm simplicity and restraint, it remained for another contemporary, Nicolas Poussin (1594–1665), to establish classical painting as an important manifestation in French Baroque art. Poussin, born in Normandy, spent most of his life in Rome. There, inspired by its monuments and countryside, he produced his grandly severe and regular canvases modeled on the work of Titian and Raphael. He also carefully worked out a theoretical explanation of his method.

Poussin's *Et in Arcadia Ego* (*I, Too, in Arcadia*, or *Even in Arcadia, I* [am present]; FIG. 24-60) was informed by Raphael's rational order and stability and by antique statuary. Landscape, of which Poussin became increasingly fond, provides the setting for the picture. The foreground, however, is dominated by three shepherds, living in the idyllic land of Arcadia, who spell out an enigmatic inscription on a tomb as a statuesque female figure quietly places her hand on the shoulder of one of them. She may be the spirit of death, reminding these mortals, as does the inscription, that death is found even in Arcadia, supposedly a spot of Edenic bliss. The countless draped female statues surviving in Italy from Roman times supplied the models for this figure, and the youth with one foot resting on a boulder is modeled on Greco-Roman statues of Neptune, the sea god, leaning on his trident. The compact, balanced grouping of these figures; the even light; and the thoughtful, reserved, mournful mood set the tone for Poussin's art in its later, classical phase.

In notes for an intended treatise on painting, Poussin outlined the "grand manner" of classicism, of which he became the leading exponent in Rome. Artists must first of all choose great subjects: "The first requirement, fundamental to all others, is that the subject and the narrative be grandiose, such as battles, heroic actions, and religious themes."[5] Minute details should be avoided, as well as all "low" subjects, such as genre—"Those who choose base subjects find refuge in them because of the feebleness of their talents."[6] Clearly, these directives rule out a good deal of both decorative and naturalistic art.

Poussin represents a theoretical tradition in Western art that goes back to the Early Renaissance. It asserts that all good art must be the result of good judgment—a judgment based on sure knowledge. In this way, art can achieve correctness and propriety, two of the favorite categories of the classicizing artist or architect. Poussin praised the ancient Greeks, who "produced marvelous effects" with their musical "modes." He observed that "[t]he word 'mode' really means the system, or the measure and form which we use in making something. It constrains us not to pass the limits, it compels us to employ a certain evenness and moderation in all things."[7] "Evenness" and "moderation" are the very essence of French classical doctrine. In the age of Louis XIV, scholars preached this doctrine as much for literature and music as for art and architecture.

A GREEK GENERAL ABANDONED IN DEATH
Among Poussin's finest works is *Burial of Phocion* (FIG. 24-61). As was typical of Poussin, he carefully chose its subject from the literature of antiquity. His source was Plutarch's *Life of Phocion,* a biography of the distinguished Athenian general whom his compatriots unjustly put to death for treason.

Eventually, the state gave him a public funeral and memorialized him. In the foreground, Poussin represented the hero's body being taken away, his burial on Athenian soil initially forbidden. The two massive bearers and the bier are starkly isolated in a great landscape that throws them into solitary relief, eloquently expressive of the hero abandoned in death. The landscape's interlocking planes slope upward to the lighted sky at the left. Its carefully arranged terraces bear slowly moving streams, shepherds and their flocks, and, in the distance, whole assemblies of solid geometric structures (temples, towers, walls, villas, and a central grand sarcophagus). The skies are untroubled, and the light is even and form revealing. The trees are few and carefully arranged, like curtains lightly drawn back to reveal a natural setting carefully cultivated for a single human action. Unlike van Ruisdael's *View of Haarlem* (FIG. 24-50), this scene was not intended to represent a particular place and time. It was Poussin's construction of an idea of a noble landscape to frame a noble theme, much like Annibale Carracci's classical landscape (FIG. 24-22). The *Phocion* landscape is nature subordinated to a rational plan.

A LANDSCAPIST PAR EXCELLENCE
CLAUDE GEL-LÉE, called CLAUDE LORRAIN (1600–1682), modulated in a softer style the disciplined rational art of Poussin, with its sophisticated revelation of the geometry of landscape. Unlike Poussin's pictures, the figures in Claude's landscapes tell no dramatic story, point out no moral, and praise no hero.

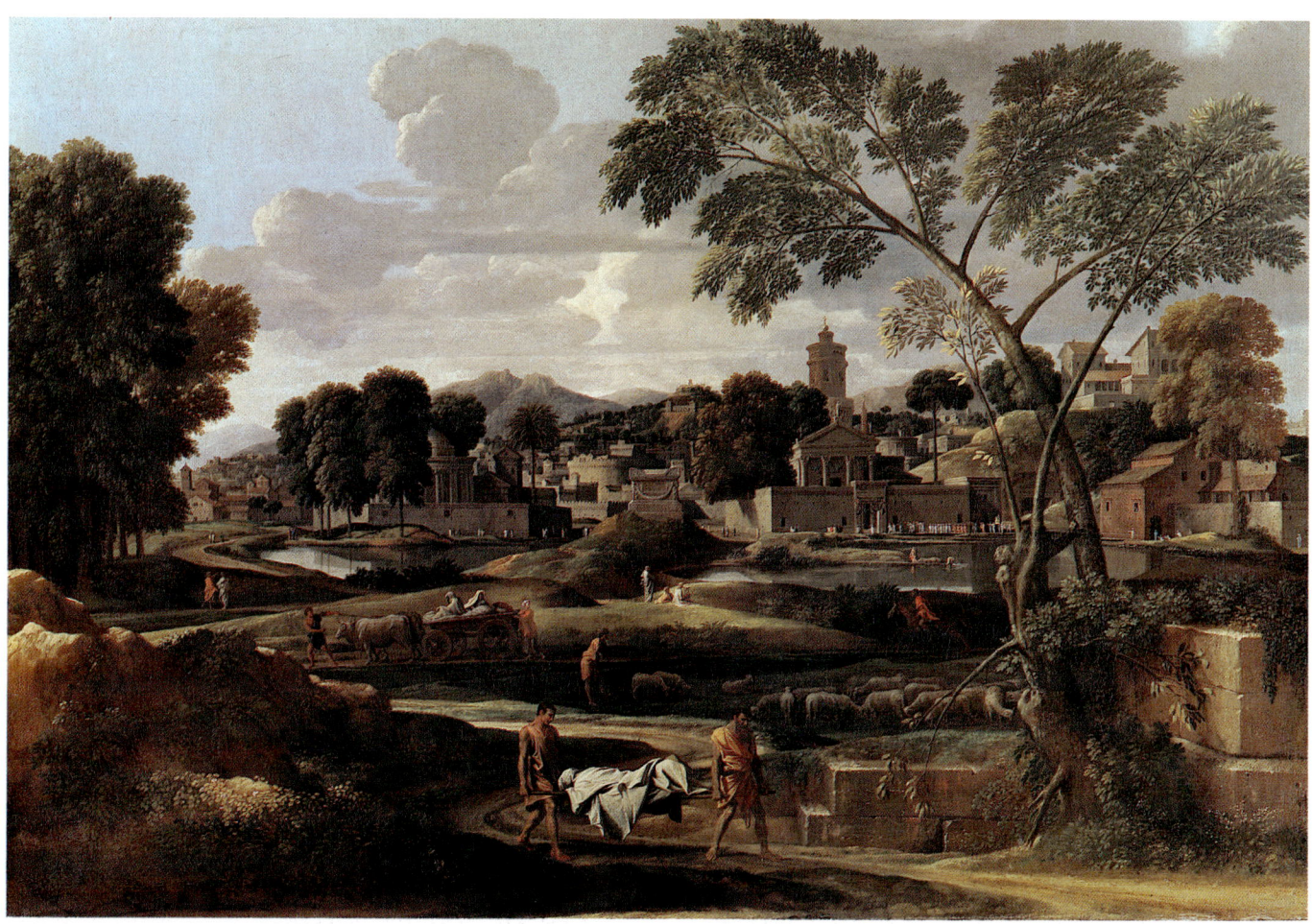

24-61 NICOLAS POUSSIN, *Burial of Phocion,* 1648. Oil on canvas, approx. 3′ 11″ × 5′ 10″. Louvre, Paris.

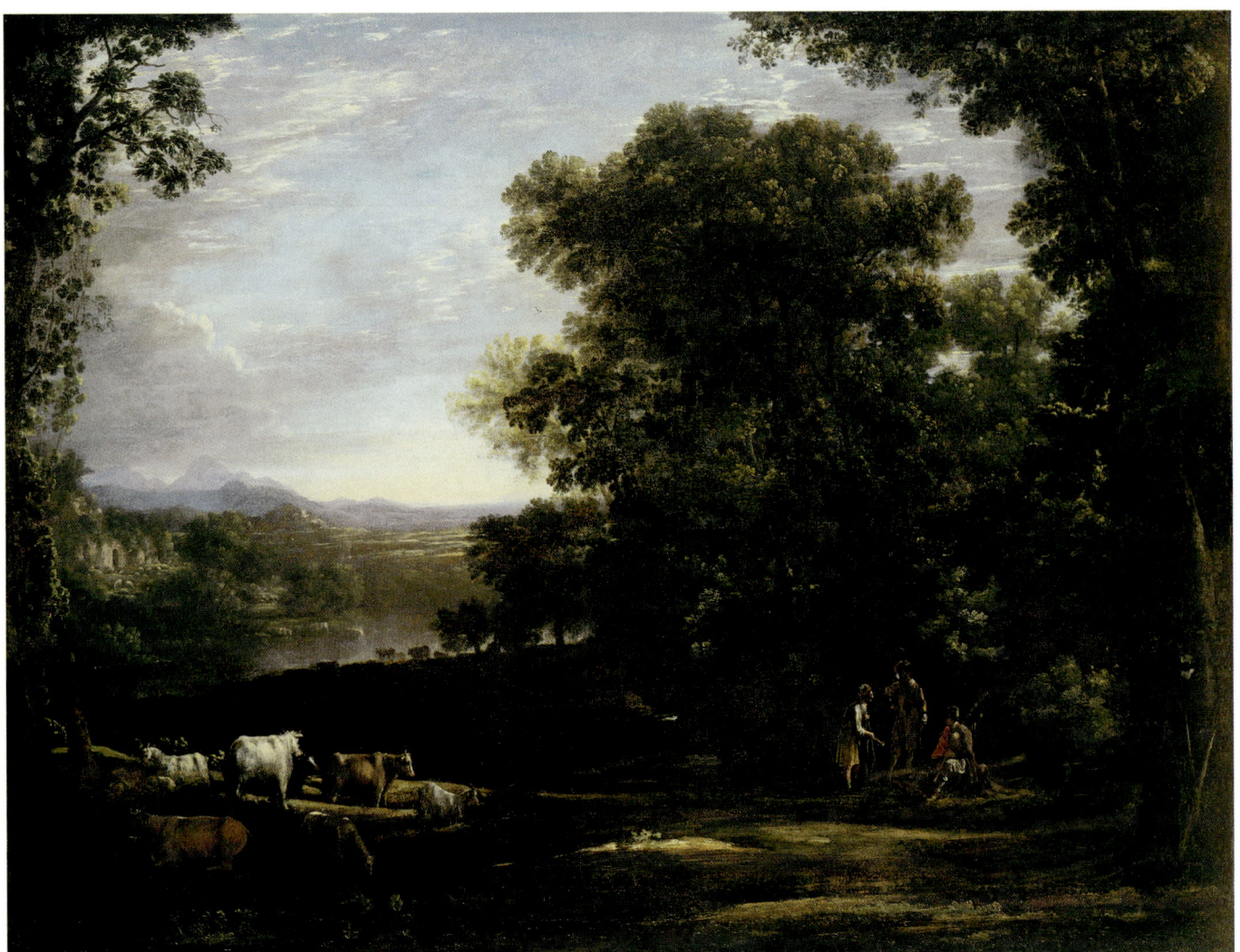

24-62 CLAUDE LORRAIN, *Landscape with Cattle and Peasants*, 1629. Oil on canvas, 3′ 6″ × 4′ 10½″. Philadelphia Museum of Art, Philadelphia (the George W. Elkins Collection).

Indeed, they often appear added as mere excuses for the radiant landscape itself. For Claude, painting involved essentially one theme—the beauty of a broad sky suffused with the golden light of dawn or sunset glowing through a hazy atmosphere and reflecting brilliantly off the rippling water.

The subject of his work often remains grounded in classical antiquity, as seen in *Landscape with Cattle and Peasants* (FIG. **24-62**). The figures in the right foreground chat in animated fashion, while in the left foreground, cattle relax contentedly and in the middle ground, cattle amble slowly away. The well-defined foreground, distinct middle ground, and dim background recede in serene orderliness, until all form dissolves in a luminous mist. Atmospheric and linear perspective reinforce each other to turn a vista into a typical Claudian vision, an ideal classical world bathed in sunlight in infinite space.

Claude's formalizing of nature with balanced groups of architectural masses, screens of trees, and sheets of water followed the great tradition of classical landscape. It began with the backgrounds of Venetian painting (see FIGS. 22-32 and 22-33) and continued in the art of Annibale Carracci (FIG. 24-22) and Poussin (FIG. 24-61). Yet, Claude, like the Dutch painters, studied the actual light and the atmospheric nuances of nature,

making a unique contribution. He recorded carefully in hundreds of sketches the look of the Roman countryside, its gentle terrain accented by stone-pines, cypresses, and poplars and by ever-present ruins of ancient aqueducts, tombs, and towers. He made these the fundamental elements of his compositions. Travelers could understand the picturesque beauties of the outskirts of Rome in Claude's landscapes.

The artist achieved his marvelous effects of light by painstakingly placing tiny value gradations, which imitated, though on a very small scale, the actual range of values of outdoor light and shade. Avoiding the problem of high-noon sunlight overhead, Claude preferred, and convincingly represented, the sun's rays as they gradually illuminated the morning sky or, with their dying glow, set the pensive mood of evening. Thus, he matched the moods of nature with those of human subjects. Claude's infusion of nature with human feeling, while recomposing it in a calm equilibrium, greatly appealed to the landscape painters of the eighteenth and early nineteenth centuries.

A GROTTO SCULPTURE FOR VERSAILLES Classicism also emerged in architecture and sculpture. FRANÇOIS GIRARDON (1628–1715) designed *Apollo Attended by the*

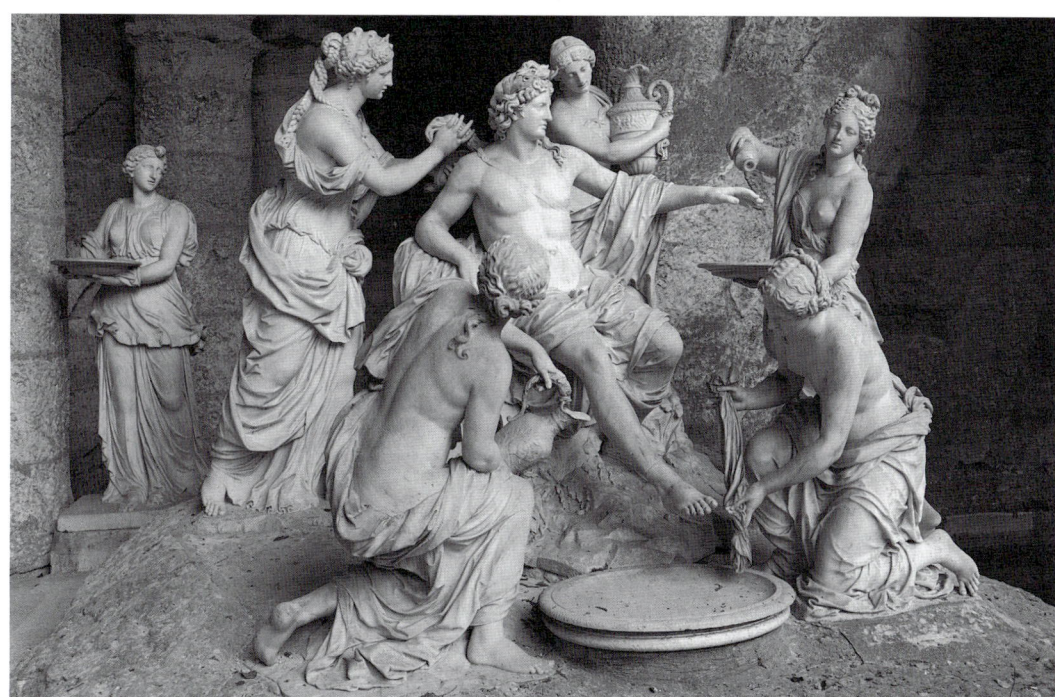

24-63 FRANÇOIS GIRARDON and THOMAS REGNAUDIN, *Apollo Attended by the Nymphs,* Grotto of Thetis, Park of Versailles, Versailles, France, ca. 1666–1672. Marble, life-size. Park of Versailles.

Nymphs (FIG. **24-63**) as a tableau group for the Grotto of Thetis in the gardens of Versailles. Both stately and graceful, the nymphs have a compelling charm as they minister to the god Apollo at the end of the day. (The three nymphs in the background are the work of THOMAS REGNAUDIN, 1622–1706.) Girardon's close study of Greco-Roman sculpture heavily conditioned his style for the figures, and Poussin's figure compositions (FIG. **24-60**) inspired their arrangement. And if this combination did not suffice, the group's rather florid reference to Louis XIV as the "god of the sun" was bound to assure its success at court. Girardon's style and symbolism were well suited to France's glorification of royal majesty.

OFFICIAL SANCTION OF CLASSICISM In contrast, departure from the principles of classicism resulted in official rejection of the work of PIERRE PUGET (1620–1694). The strained dramatic and emotional qualities in Puget's work were not at all to the court's taste. His *Milo of Crotona* (FIG. **24-64**) represents the powerful ancient hero, his hand trapped in a split stump, helpless before the attacking lion. With physical and psychic realism, Puget presented a study of immediate and excruciating agony. This approach ran counter to the official taste for heroic design dictated by King Louis XIV and Charles Le Brun, the royal painter elevated to the post of "director and general guardian of His Majesty's cabinet of paintings and drawings."[8] Although Puget was very briefly in vogue, the most original French sculptor of his time never found acceptance at the French court.

A DIGNIFIED AND ORDERED BUILDING The classical bent asserted itself early in the work of FRANÇOIS MANSART (1598–1666), as seen in the Orléans wing of the

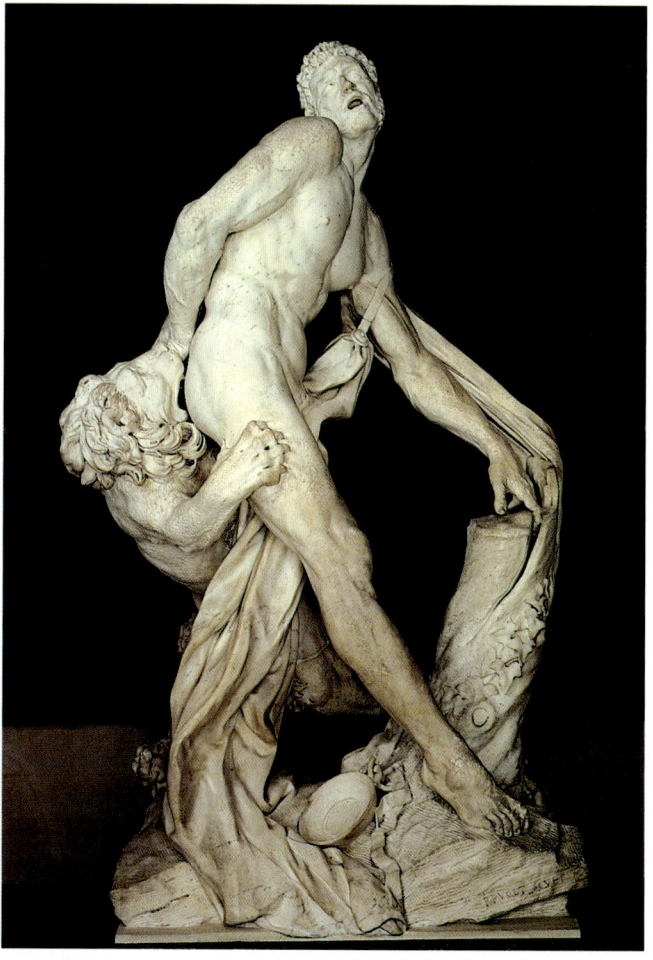

24-64 PIERRE PUGET, *Milo of Crotona,* 1671–1682. Marble, approx. 8′ 10″ high. Louvre, Paris.

24-65   FRANÇOIS MANSART, Orléans wing of the Château de Blois, Blois, France, 1635–1638.

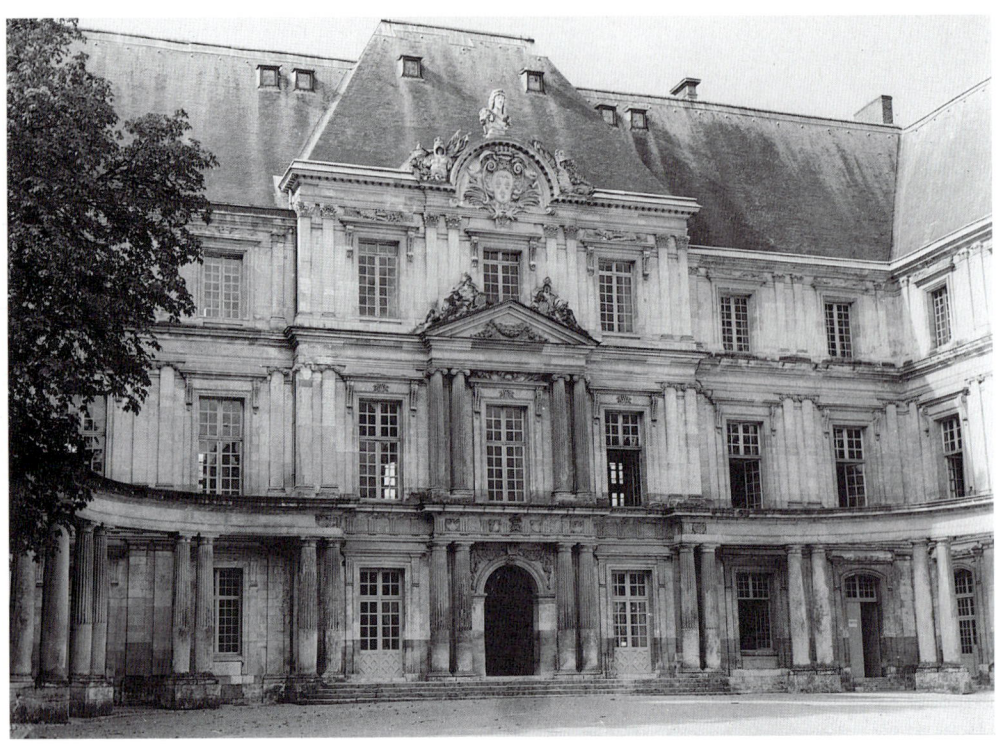

Château de Blois (FIG. **24-65**), built in Blois between 1635 and 1638. The polished dignity evident here became the hallmark of French "Classical-Baroque," contrasting with the more daring and fanciful styles of the Baroque in Italy and elsewhere. The strong rectilinear organization and a tendency to design in repeated units suggest Italian Renaissance architecture (also permeated by the classical spirit), as do the insistence on the purity of line and the sharp relief of the wall joints. Yet the emphasis on focal points—achieved with the curving colonnades, the changing planes of the walls, and the concentration of ornament around the portal—is characteristic of French Baroque architectural thinking in general.

ART IN THE SERVICE OF ABSOLUTISM The establishment of the French classical style accelerated with the foundation of the Royal Academy of Painting and Sculpture in 1648. Also, King Louis XIV and his principal adviser, Jean-Baptiste Colbert (1619–1683), were determined to organize art and architecture in the service of the state. No pains were spared to raise great symbols and monuments to the king's absolute power and to regularize taste under the academy.

Louis XIV was a master of political strategy and propaganda. He ensured subservience by anchoring his rule to the principle of the divine right of kings, which stressed a king's absolute power as God's will, rendering Louis's authority uncontestable. So convinced was he of his importance and centrality to the French kingdom that he eagerly adopted the nickname "le Roi Soleil" ("the Sun King"). Like the sun, Louis was the center of the universe. He also established a carefully crafted and nuanced relationship with the nobility.

He allowed nobles sufficient benefits to keep them pacified but simultaneously maintained rigorous control to avoid insurrection or rebellion.

Louis's desire for control extended to all realms of French life, including art. The king understood well the power of art as propaganda and the value of visual imagery for cultivating a public persona. His numerous and extravagant commissions further revealed his interest in the arts.

The portrait of Louis XIV (FIG. **24-66**) by HYACINTHE RIGAUD (1659–1743), conveys the image of an absolute monarch in control. The king, sixty-three when this work was painted, looks out at viewers with directness. The suggestion of haughtiness is perhaps due to the pose—Louis XIV stands with his left hand on his hip and with his elegant ermine-lined coronation robes thrown over his shoulder. This portrait's majesty is also derived from the composition. The king is the unmistakable focal point of the image, and the artist placed him so that he seems to look down on the viewer. Given that Louis XIV was very short in stature—only five feet, four inches, a fact that drove him to invent the red-heeled shoes he wears in the portrait—it seems the artist catered to his patron's wishes. The carefully detailed environment the king stands in also contributes to the painting's stateliness and grandiosity. So insistent was Louis XIV that the best artists serve his needs, he maintained a workshop of artists, each with a specialization—faces, fabric, architecture, landscapes, armor, or fur. Thus, many of the king's portraits were a group effort.

REDESIGNING THE LOUVRE'S EAST FACADE Once he had formally ascended to power, the first project the

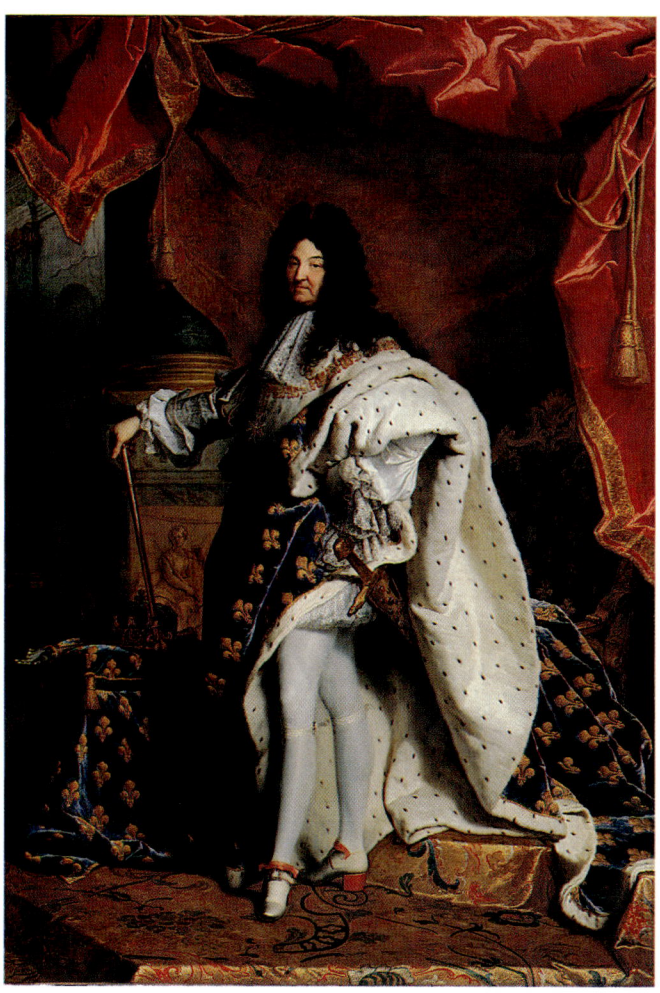

24-66 HYACINTHE RIGAUD, *Louis XIV*, 1701. Oil on canvas, approx. 9′ 2″ × 6′ 3″. Louvre, Paris.

young Louis XIV and his adviser Colbert undertook was the closing of the east side of the Louvre court, left incomplete by Lescot in the sixteenth century. Bernini, as the most renowned architect of his day, was summoned from Rome to submit plans, but he envisioned an Italian palace on a monumental scale that would have involved the demolition of all previous work. His plan rejected, Bernini returned to Rome in high indignation. Instead, the Louvre's east facade (FIG. 24-67) was a collaboration among CLAUDE PERRAULT (1613–1688), LOUIS LE VAU (1612–1670), and CHARLES LE BRUN (1619–1690). The design is a brilliant adjustment of French and Italian classical elements, culminating in a new and definitive formula. The French pavilion system was retained. The central pavilion is in the form of a classical temple front, and a giant colonnade of paired columns, resembling the columned flanks of a temple folded out like wings, is contained by the two salient pavilions at both ends. The whole is mounted on a stately basement, or podium. The designers favored an even roof line, balustraded and broken only by the central pediment, over the traditional French pyramidal roof. The emphatically horizontal sweep of this facade brushed aside all memory of Gothic verticality. Its stately proportions and monumentality were both an expression of the new official French taste and a symbol for centrally organized authority.

A HUNTING LODGE BECOMES A PALACE Work on the Louvre hardly had begun when Louis XIV decided to convert a royal hunting lodge at Versailles, a few miles outside Paris, into a great palace. A veritable army of architects, decorators, sculptors, painters, and landscape architects was assembled under the general management of former Poussin student Charles Le Brun. In their hands, the

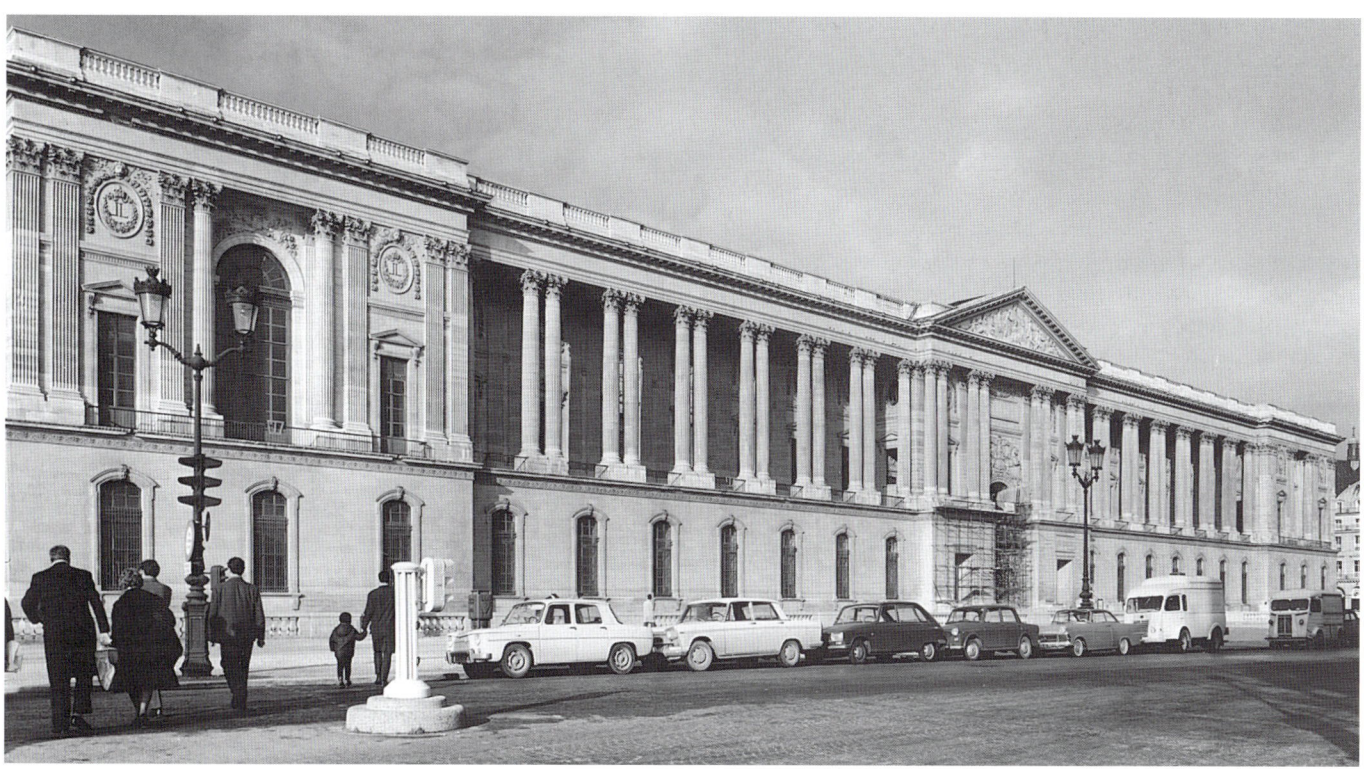

24-67 CLAUDE PERRAULT, LOUIS LE VAU, and CHARLES LE BRUN, east facade of the Louvre, Paris, France, 1667–1670.

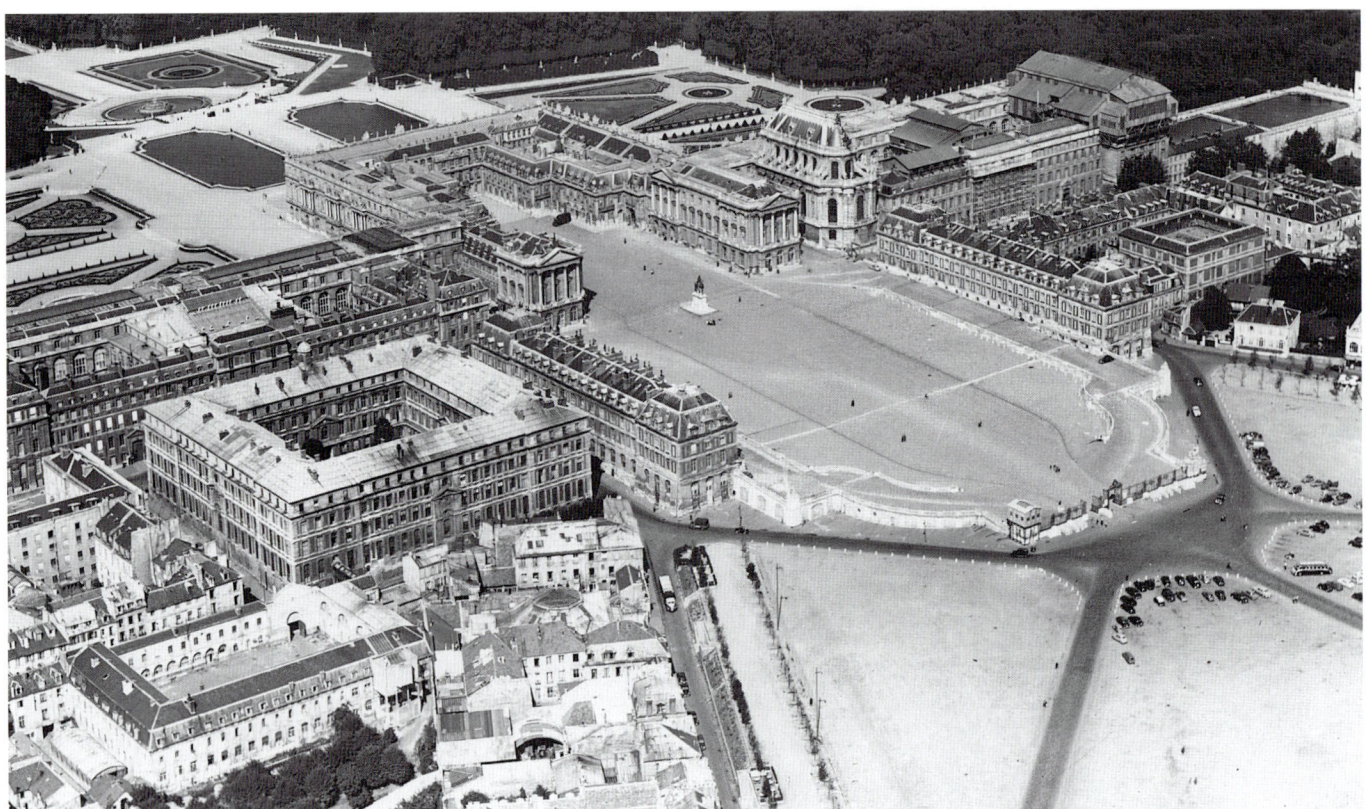

24-68 Aerial view of palace at Versailles, France, begun 1669, and a portion of the gardens and surrounding area. The white trapezoid in the lower part of the plan (FIG. 24-69) outlines the area shown here.

conversion of a simple lodge into the palace of Versailles (FIGS. **24-68** and **24-69**) became the greatest architectural project of the age—a defining statement of French Baroque style and an undeniable symbol of Louis XIV's power and ambition.

Planned on a gigantic scale, the project called not only for a large palace flanking a vast park but also for the construction of a satellite city to house court and government officials, military and guard detachments, courtiers, and servants (undoubtedly to keep them all under the king's close supervision). This town was laid out to the east of the palace along three radial avenues that converge on the palace structure itself; their axes, in a symbolic assertion of the ruler's absolute power over his domains, intersected in the king's bedroom. (As the site of the king's morning levee, this bedroom was actually an audience room, a state chamber.) The palace itself, more than a quarter of a mile long, was placed at right angles to the dominant east-west axis that runs through city and park.

Careful attention was paid to every detail of the extremely rich decoration of the palace's interior. The architects and decorators designed everything from wall paintings to doorknobs to reinforce the splendor of Versailles and to exhibit the very finest sense of artisanship. Of the literally hundreds of rooms within the palace, the most famous is the Galerie des Glaces, or Hall of Mirrors (FIG. **24-70**). This hall overlooks the park from the second floor and extends along most of the width of the central block. Although deprived of its original sumptuous furniture, which included gold and silver chairs and bejeweled trees, the Galerie des Glaces retains much of its splendor today. Its tunnel-like quality is alleviated by hundreds of mirrors, set into the wall opposite the

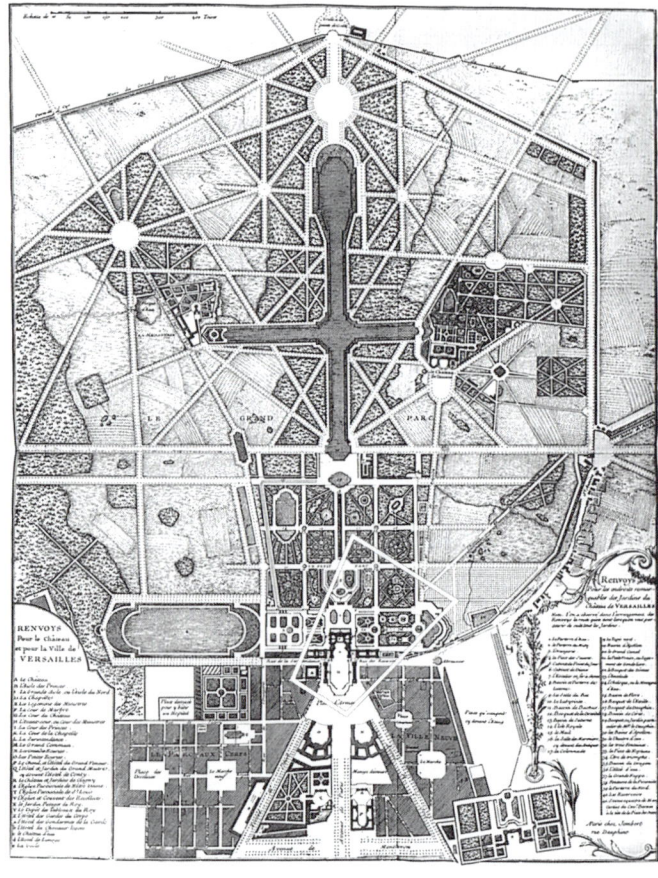

24-69 Plan of the park, palace, and town of Versailles, France, (after a seventeenth-century engraving by François Blondel). The area outlined in the white trapezoid (lower center) is shown in FIG. 24-68.

mal, dense growth and open meadows—all play against one another in unending combinations and variations. No photograph or series of photographs can reveal the design's full richness; the park unfolds itself only to people who actually walk through it. In this respect, it is a temporal artwork. Its aspects change with time and with the relative position of observers.

As a symbol of the power of absolutism, Versailles is unsurpassed. It also expresses, in the most monumental terms of its age, the rationalistic creed—based on the mathematical philosophy of Descartes—that all knowledge must be systematic and all science must be the consequence of the intellect imposed on matter. The whole stupendous design of Versailles proudly proclaims the mastery of human intelligence (and the mastery of Louis XIV) over the disorderliness of nature.

A SUBDUED ROYAL CHAPEL After Le Vau's death, JULES HARDOUIN-MANSART (1646–1708), a great-nephew of François Mansart, completed the garden facade of the Versailles palace and in 1698 received a commission to add a Royal Chapel to the complex. The chapel's interior (FIG. 24-71) is essentially a rectangular building with an apse as high as the nave, giving the fluid central space a curved

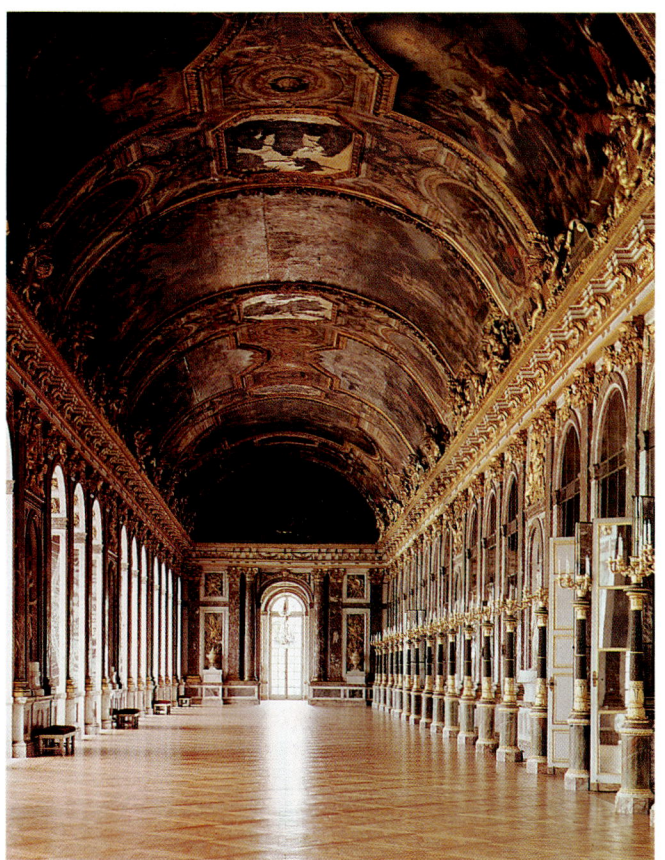

24-70 JULES HARDOUIN-MANSART and CHARLES LE BRUN, Galerie des Glaces (Hall of Mirrors), palace of Versailles, Versailles, France, ca. 1680.

windows, that illusionistically extend the room's width. The mirror, that ultimate source of illusion, was a favorite element of Baroque interior design; here, it also enhanced the dazzling extravagance of the great festivals Louis XIV was so fond of hosting.

CONTROLLING NATURE The enormous palace might appear unbearably ostentatious were it not for its extraordinary setting in the vast park that makes it almost an adjunct. The Galerie des Glaces is dwarfed by the sweeping vista (seen from its windows) down the park's tree-lined central axis and across terraces, lawns, pools, and lakes toward the horizon. The park of Versailles, designed by ANDRÉ LE NÔTRE (1613–1700), must rank among the world's greatest artworks in both size and concept. Here, an entire forest was transformed into a park. Although the geometric plan (FIG. 24-69) may appear stiff and formal, the park, in fact, offers an almost unlimited variety of vistas, as Le Nôtre used not only the multiplicity of natural forms but also the terrain's slightly rolling contours with stunning effectiveness.

The formal gardens near the palace provide a rational transition from the frozen architectural forms to the natural living ones. Here, the elegant forms of trimmed shrubs and hedges define the tightly designed geometric units. Each unit is different from its neighbor and has a focal point in the form of a sculptured group, a pavilion, a reflecting pool, or perhaps a fountain. Farther away from the palace, the design loosens as trees, in shadowy masses, screen or frame views of open countryside. Le Nôtre carefully composed all vistas for maximum effect. Dark and light, formal and infor-

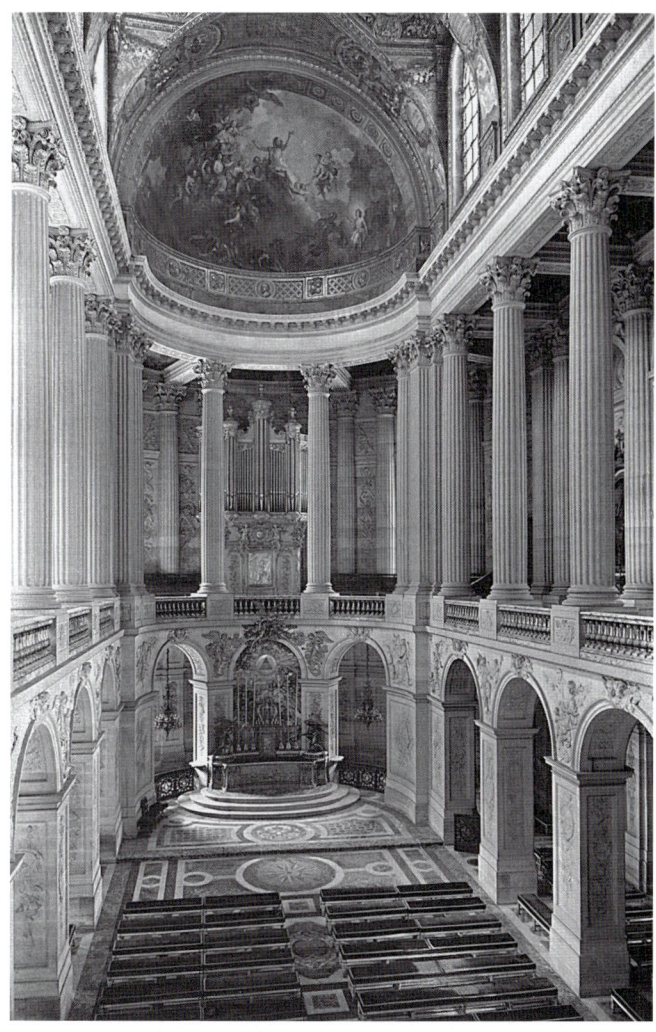

24-71 JULES HARDOUIN-MANSART, Royal Chapel, with ceiling decorations by ANTOINE COYPEL, palace of Versailles, Versailles, France, 1698–1710.

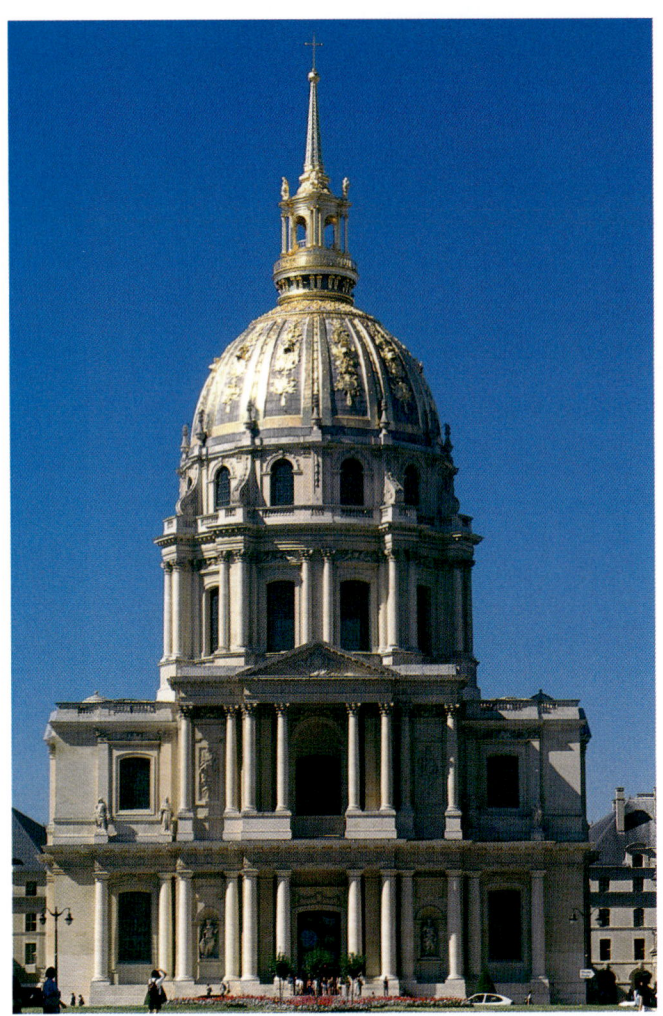

24-72 Jules Hardouin-Mansart, Église de Dôme, Church of the Invalides, Paris, France, 1676–1706.

tude, as is the way that its designer aimed for theatrical effects of light and space. The dome is built of three shells, the lowest cut off so that interior visitors look up through it to the one above, which is painted illusionistically with the *apotheosis* (deification) of Saint Louis, patron of France. This second dome, filled with light from hidden windows in the third, outermost dome, creates an impression of the open, limitless space and brightness of the heavens. Below, the building's interior is only dimly illuminated and is designed in a classicism only less severe than that of the Escorial (see FIG. 23-26).

England

The authority of the absolute monarchy that prevailed in France was not found in England. Common law and the Parliament kept royal power in check. Thus, during the seventeenth and early eighteenth centuries, England experienced the development of both limited monarchy and constitutionalism. Although religion was an important part of English life, religion was not the contentious issue it was on the continent. The religious affiliations of the English included Catholicism, Anglicanism, Protestantism, and *Puritanism* (the English version of Calvinism). In the economic realm, England was the one country (other than the Dutch Republic) to take advantage of the opportunities overseas trade offered. As an island country, England, like the Dutch Republic, possessed a powerful and large navy, as well as excellent maritime capabilities.

English Baroque art does not have the focused character of either Dutch or Italian Baroque art. The one area of cultural production England made great strides in was architecture, and much of it incorporated classical elements.

Baroque quality. But the light entering through the large clerestory windows lacks the directed dramatic effect of the Italian Baroque, instead illuminating the interior's precisely chiseled details brightly and evenly. Pier-supported arcades carry a majestic row of Corinthian columns that define the royal gallery. The royal pew occupies its rear, accessible directly from the king's apartments. The decoration is restrained, and, in fact, only the illusionistic ceiling decorations, added in 1708 to 1709 by Antoine Coypel (1661–1722), suggest the drama and complexity of Italian Baroque art.

A CHURCH FOR DISABLED SOLDIERS References to Italian Baroque architecture also surface in Hardouin-Mansart's masterwork, the Église de Dôme, Church of the Invalides in Paris (FIG. **24-72**). An intricately composed domed square of great scale, the church is attached to the veterans' hospital Louis XIV set up for the disabled soldiers of his many wars. Two firmly separated levels, the upper one pedimented, comprise the frontispiece. The grouping of the orders and of the bays they frame is not unlike that in Italian Baroque. The compact facade is low and narrow in relation to the vast drum and dome, seeming to serve simply as a base for them. The overpowering dome, conspicuous on the Parisian skyline, is itself expressive of the Italian Baroque love for dramatic magni-

KEEPING UP WITH JONES The revolution in English building was primarily the work of one man, Inigo Jones (1573–1652), architect to the kings James I and Charles I. Jones spent considerable time in Italy. He greatly admired the classical authority and restraint of Palladio's structures and studied his treatise on architecture with great care. From Palladio's villas and palaces, Jones took many motifs, and he adopted Palladio's basic design principles for his own architecture. The nature of his achievement is evident in the buildings he did for his royal patrons, among them the Banqueting House at Whitehall (FIG. **24-73**) in London. For this structure, a symmetrical block of great clarity and dignity, Jones superimposed two orders, using columns in the center and pilasters near the ends. The balustraded roof line, uninterrupted in its horizontal sweep, predated the Louvre's facade (FIG. 24-67) by more than forty years. Palladio would have recognized and approved all of the design elements, but the building as a whole is not a copy of his work. While relying on the revered Italian's architectural vocabulary and syntax, Jones retained his own independence as a designer. For two centuries his influence was almost as authoritative in English architecture as Palladio's. In a fruitful collaboration recalling the combination of Veronese paintings and Palladian architecture in northern Italian villas, Jones's interior at Whitehall is adorned with several important Rubens paintings.

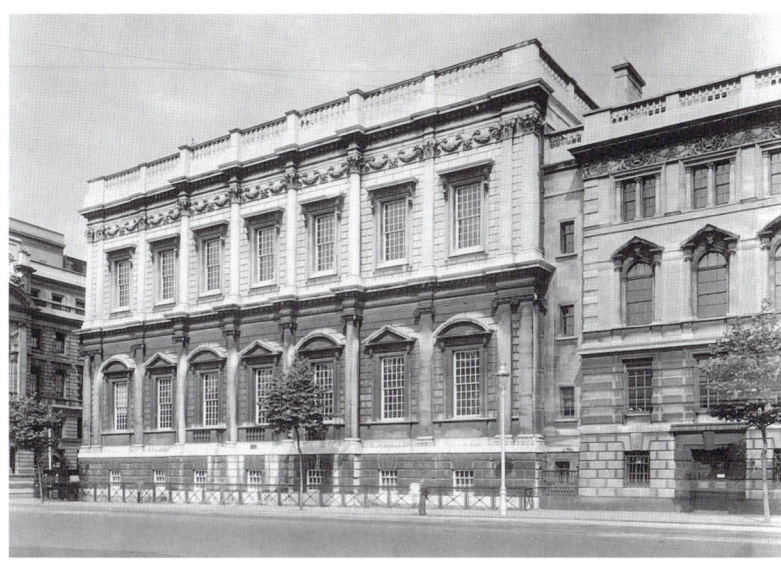

24-73 INIGO JONES, Banqueting House at Whitehall, London, England, 1619–1622.

A TOWERING ARCHITECTURAL TALENT Until almost the present, the dominant feature of the London skyline was the majestic dome of Saint Paul's Cathedral (FIG. **24-74**), the work of England's most renowned architect, CHRISTOPHER WREN (1632–1723). A mathematical genius and skilled engineer whose work won Isaac Newton's praise, Wren was appointed professor of astronomy in London at age twenty-five.

Mathematics led to architecture, and Charles II asked Wren to prepare a plan for restoring the old Gothic church of Saint Paul. Wren proposed to remodel the building based on Roman structures. Within a few months, the Great Fire of London, which destroyed the old structure and many churches in the city in 1666, gave Wren his opportunity. He built not only the new Saint Paul's but numerous other churches as well.

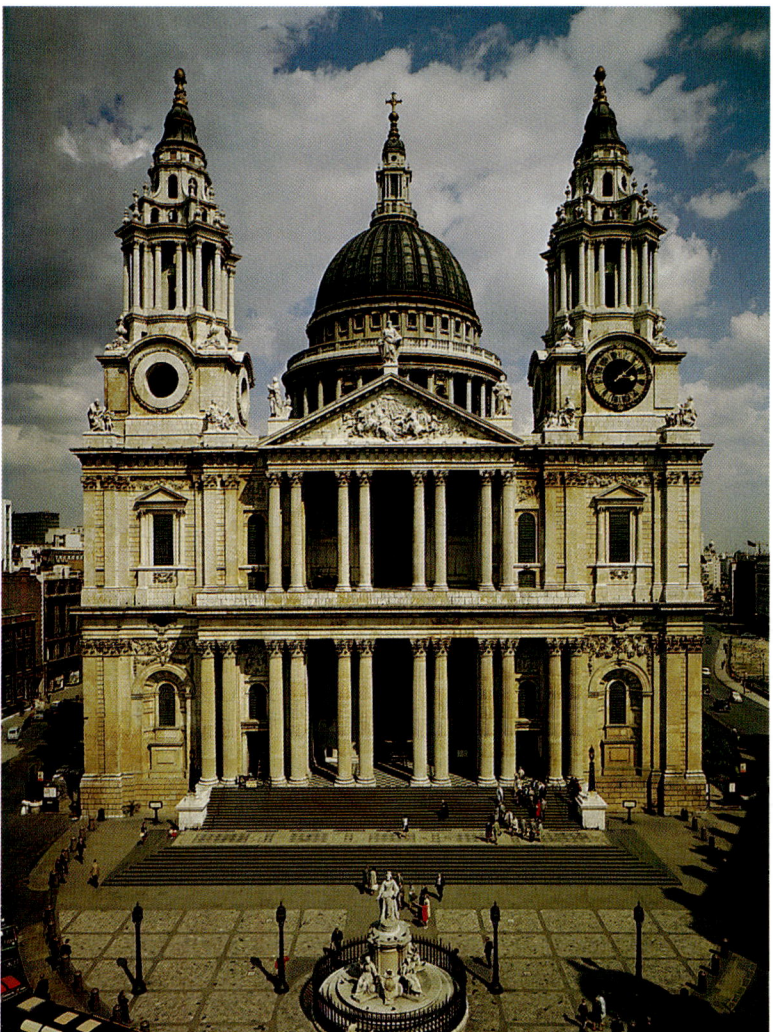

24-74 CHRISTOPHER WREN, new Saint Paul's Cathedral, London, England, 1675–1710.

Although Jones's work strongly influenced Wren, he also traveled in France, where he must have been much impressed by the splendid palaces and state buildings being created in and around Paris at the time of the competition for the Louvre design. Wren also must have closely studied prints illustrating Baroque architecture in Italy, for he harmonized Palladian, French, and Italian Baroque features in Saint Paul's.

In view of its size, the cathedral was built with remarkable speed—in a little more than thirty years—and Wren lived to see it completed. The building's form was constantly refined as it went up, and the final appearance of the towers was not determined until after 1700. In the splendid skyline composition, two foreground towers act effectively as foils to the great dome. This must have been suggested to Wren by similar schemes that Italian architects devised to solve the problem of the facade/dome relation of Saint Peter's in Rome (see FIGS. 22-29 and 24-2). Certainly, the upper levels and lanterns of the towers are Borrominesque (FIG. 24-12), the lower levels are Palladian, and the superposed paired columnar porticoes recall the Louvre facade (FIG. 24-67). Wren's skillful eclecticism brought all of these foreign features into a monumental unity.

Wren's designs for the city churches were masterpieces of careful planning and ingenuity. His task was never easy, for the churches often had to be fitted into small, irregular areas. Wren worked out a rich variety of schemes to meet awkward circumstances. When designing the church exteriors, he concentrated his attention on the towers, the one element that would set the building apart from its crowding neighbors. The skyline of London, as Wren left it, is punctuated with such towers, which served as prototypes for later buildings both in England and in colonial America.

LATE BAROQUE ART OF THE EARLY EIGHTEENTH CENTURY

Late Baroque Architecture in England

In 1705, while Saint Paul's was being completed, the British government commissioned a monumental palace in Oxfordshire, Blenheim (FIG. 24-75), for John Churchill, duke of Marlborough. The palace was a reward for Churchill's military exploits; people throughout the country acclaimed his victory over the French in 1704 at the Battle of Blenheim during the War of the Spanish Succession. Designed by JOHN VANBRUGH (1664–1726), Blenheim was one of the largest of the splendid country houses built during the period of prosperity resulting from Great Britain's expansion into the New World. At that time, a small group of architects associated with the aging Sir Christopher Wren was responsible for briefly returning Italian Baroque complexity to favor over the streamlined Palladian classicism of Inigo Jones. Vanbrugh was the best known of this group. The picturesque silhouette he created for Blenheim, with its inventive architectural detail, recalls Italian Baroque architecture. The design demonstrates his love of variety and contrast, tempered by his ability to create focus areas such as those found so frequently in seventeenth-century architecture. The tremendous forecourt, the hugely projecting pavilions, and the extended colonnades simultaneously recall Saint Peter's and Versailles (FIGS. 24-4 and 24-68). Perhaps because Vanbrugh had begun his career as a writer of witty and popular comedies and as the builder of a theater for producing them, all of his architecture tended toward

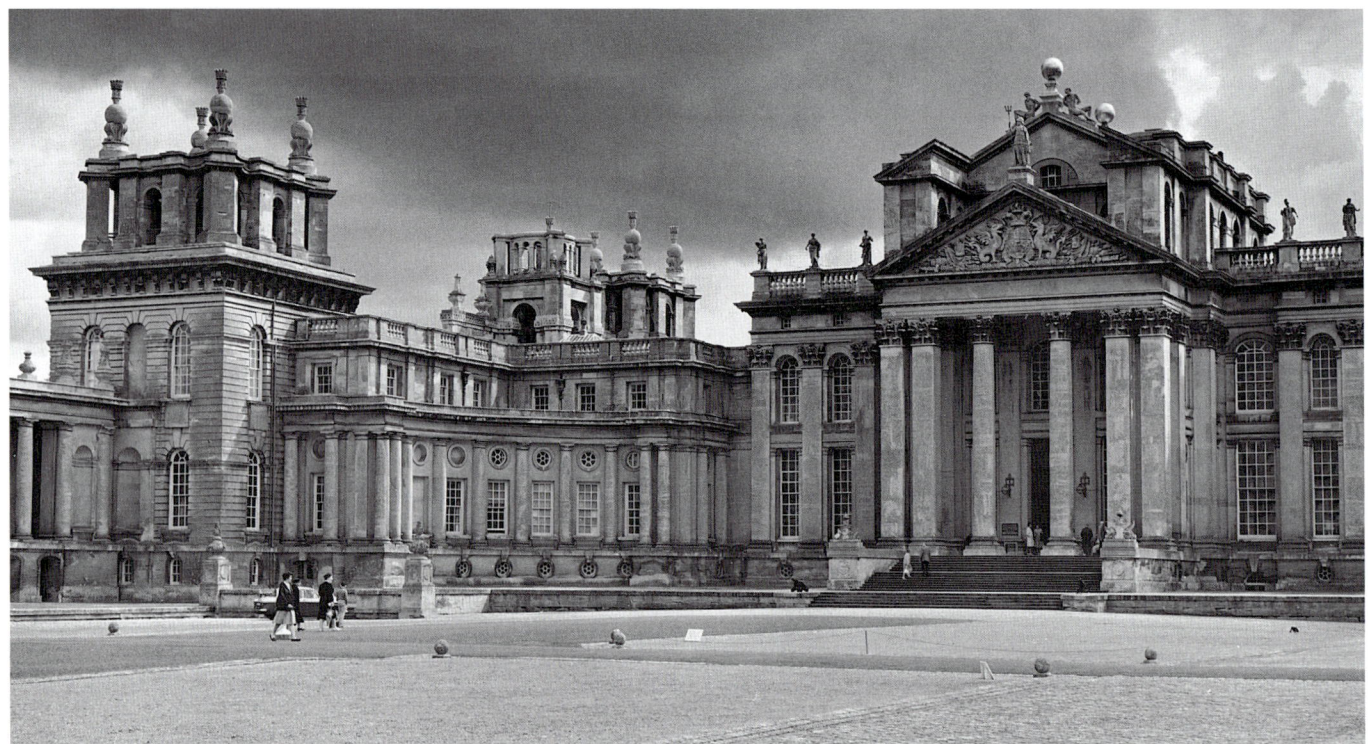

24-75 JOHN VANBRUGH, Blenheim Palace, Oxfordshire, England, 1705–1722.

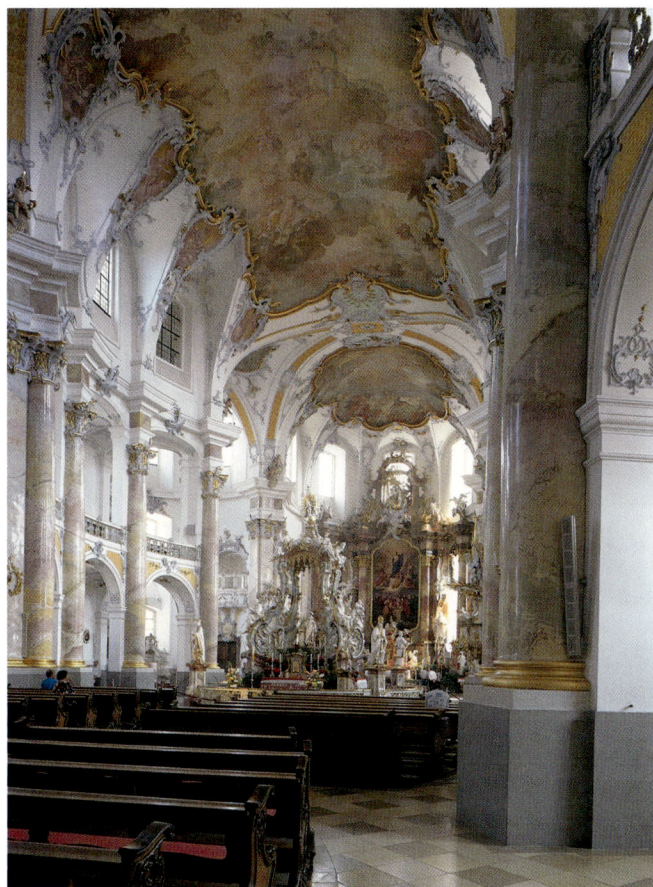

24-76 BALTHASAR NEUMANN, interior of the pilgrimage chapel of Vierzehnheiligen, near Staffelstein, Germany, 1743–1772.

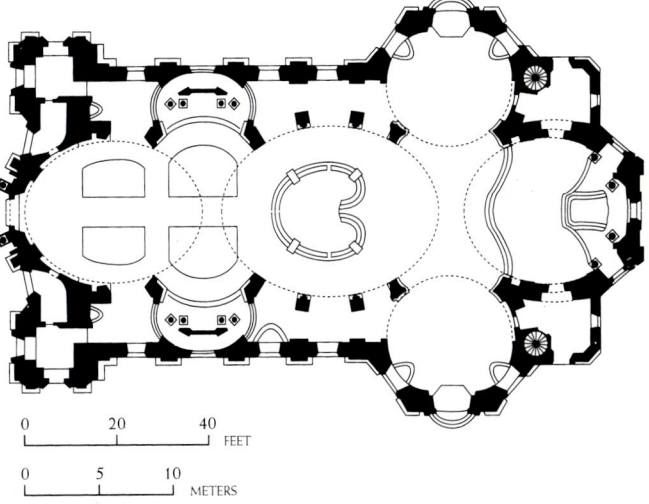

24-77 Plan of Vierzehnheiligen, near Staffelstein, Germany.

the theatrical on a mighty and extravagant scale. Like many Baroque architects, he even sacrificed convenience for dramatic effect, as in placing the Blenheim kitchen some two hundred feet from the majestic dining salon. Vanbrugh's architecture pleased his patrons in the beginning, but even before Blenheim was completed, critics were condemning what they considered its ponderous and bizarre qualities.

Late Baroque Art and Architecture in Germany and Italy

The work of Italians Borromini and Guarini strongly influenced the ecclesiastical architecture of southern Germany and Austria. One of the most splendid of the German buildings is the pilgrimage church of Vierzehnheiligen (Fourteen Saints) designed by BALTHASAR NEUMANN (1687–1753) and built near Staffelstein. Born in the German part of Bohemia, Neumann traveled in Austria and northern Italy and studied in Paris before returning home to become one of the most active architects working in his native land. Numerous large windows in the richly decorated but continuous walls of Vierzehnheiligen flood the interior with an even, bright, and cheerful light. The pilgrimage church sanctuary (FIG. **24-76**) exhibits a vivacious play of architectural fantasy that retains Italian Baroque's dynamic energy but banishes all its dramatic qualities.

Vierzehnheiligen's complexity is readable in its ground plan (FIG. **24-77**), which has been called one of the most ingenious pieces of architectural design ever conceived. The straight line seems to have been banished deliberately. The composition is made up of tangent ovals and circles, achieving a quite different interior effect within the essential outlines of the traditional Gothic church (apse, transept, nave, and western towers). Undulating space is in continuous motion, creating unlimited vistas bewildering in their variety and surprise effects. The structure's features pulse, flow, and commingle as if they were ceaselessly in the process of being molded. The design's fluency of line, the floating and hovering surfaces, the interwoven spaces, and the dematerialized masses combine to suggest a "frozen" counterpart to the intricacy of voices in a Bach fugue. The church is a brilliant ensemble of architecture, painting, sculpture, and music, dissolving the boundaries of the arts in a visionary unity.

SCULPTURE RENDERED WEIGHTLESS The desire to achieve this unity of various artistic mediums propelled architects and artists in Germany and Austria to explore further the illusionistic capabilities of each medium. EGID QUIRIN ASAM (1692–1750) created the group *Assumption of the Virgin* (FIG. **24-78**) for the space above the altar in the monastery church at Rohr, Germany. Asam designed the church in collaboration with his brother Cosmas Damian Asam (1686–1739). Influenced by the Late Baroque architecture they saw on a trip to Rome, the brothers returned to Germany with a feeling for illusionistic spectacle. In Egid Quirin Asam's *Assumption of the Virgin,* as in Bernini's *Ecstasy of Saint Theresa* (FIG. 24-9), the miraculous is made real before the viewer's eyes, a spiritual vision materially visible. The Virgin, effortlessly borne aloft by angels, soars to the glowing paradise above her, while the apostolic witnesses below gesticulate in astonishment around her vacant tomb. The figures ascending to Heaven have gilded details that set them apart from those remaining on Earth. The setting is a luxuriously ornamented theater. The scene itself is pure opera—an art perfected and very popular in

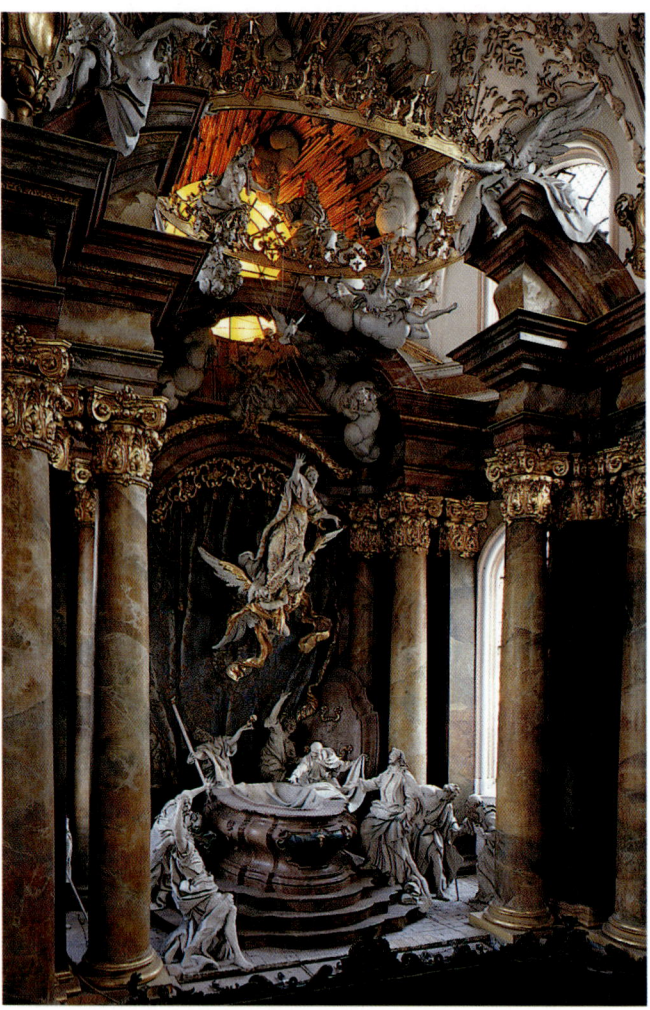

24-78 EGID QUIRIN ASAM, *Assumption of the Virgin,* monastery church at Rohr, Germany, 1723.

the eighteenth century. Here, sculpture dissolves into painting, theater, and music, its mass rendered weightless, its naturally compact composition broken up and diffused. In this instance, Asam used sculpture, paradoxically, to disguise substance and function, weight and tactility, in the interest of eye-deceiving mystical illusion.

PAINTED FESTIVALS FOR THE IMAGINATION
Illusion in painting, particularly for the ceilings of churches and palaces in Italy and France, was already a venerable tradition by the beginning of the eighteenth century. The ceilings of Late Baroque palaces sometimes became painted festivals for the imagination. The master of such works, GIAMBATTISTA TIEPOLO (1696–1770), was the last great Italian painter to have an international impact until the twentieth century. Of Venetian origin, Tiepolo worked for patrons in Austria, Germany, and Spain, as well as in Italy, leaving a strong impression wherever he went. His bright, cheerful colors and his relaxed compositions were ideally suited to Late Baroque architecture. *The Apotheosis of the Pisani Family* (FIG. **24-79**), a ceiling fresco in the Villa Pisani at Stra in northern Italy, shows airy populations fluttering through vast sunlit skies and fleecy clouds, their figures making dark accents

against the brilliant light of high noon. As *apotheosis* indicates, Pisani family members are elevated here to the rank of the gods in a heavenly scene that recalls the ceiling paintings of Correggio (see FIG. 22-40) and Pozzo (FIG. 24-27). While retaining the seventeenth-century illusionistic tendencies, Tiepolo softened the rhetoric and created pictorial schemes of great elegance and grace, unsurpassed for their sheer effectiveness as decor.

ROCOCO: THE FRENCH TASTE

The death of Louis XIV in 1715 brought many changes in French high society. The court of Versailles was at once abandoned for the pleasures of town life. Although French citizens still owed their allegiance to a monarch, the early eighteenth century saw a resurgence in aristocratic social, political, and economic power. Appropriately, some historians refer to the eighteenth century as the great age of the aristocracy. The nobility not only exercised their traditional privileges (for example, exemption from certain taxes and from forced labor on public works) but also sought to expand their power. This aristocratic resurgence extended to dominance as art patrons. The *hôtels* (town houses) of Paris soon became the centers of a new softer style called Rococo. The sparkling gaiety the new age cultivated (see "Of Knowledge, Taste, and Refinement: Salon Culture," page 782), associated with the regency that followed the death of Louis XIV and with the reign of Louis XV, found perfectly harmonious expression in this new style. Rococo appeared in France in about 1700, primarily as a style of interior design. The French Rococo exterior was most often simple, or even plain, but Rococo exuberance took over the interior. *Rococo* came from the French word *rocaille,* which literally means "pebble," but the term referred especially to the small stones and shells used to decorate grotto interiors. Such shells or shell forms were the principal motifs in Rococo ornament.

A PERMANENTLY "FESTIVE" ROOM A typical French Rococo room is the Salon de la Princesse (FIG. **24-80**) in the Hôtel de Soubise in Paris, designed by GERMAIN BOFFRAND (1667–1754). Comparing this room with the Galerie des Glaces at Versailles (FIG. 24-70) reveals (immediately) the fundamental difference. Boffrand softened the earlier style's strong architectural lines and panels into flexible, sinuous curves luxuriantly multiplied in mirror reflections. The walls melt into the vault. Irregular painted shapes, surmounted by sculpture and separated by the typical rocaille shells, replaced the hall's cornices. Painting, architecture, and sculpture combine to form a single ensemble. The profusion of curving tendrils and sprays of foliage blend with the shell forms to give an effect of freely growing nature, suggesting that the designer permanently decked the Rococo room for a festival.

Rococo was a style preeminently evident in small works. Artists exquisitely wrought furniture, utensils, and accessories of all sorts in the characteristically delicate, undulating Rococo line. French Rococo interiors were designed as lively total works of art with elegant furniture, enchanting small sculptures, ornamented mirror frames, delightful

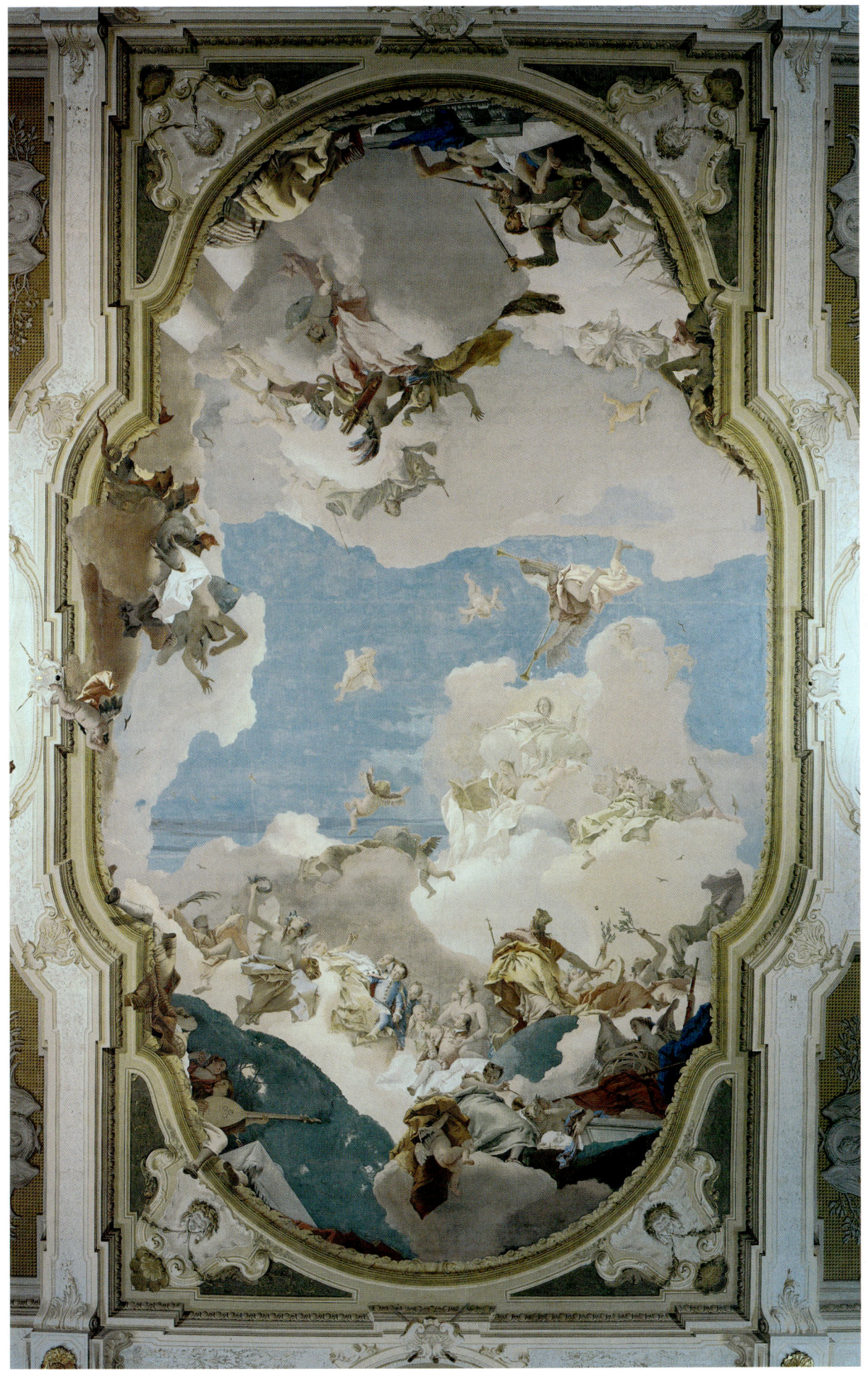

24-79 GIAMBATTISTA TIEPOLO, *The Apotheosis of the Pisani Family,* ceiling fresco in the Villa Pisani, Stra, Italy, 1761–1762.

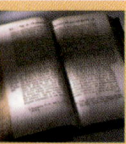

WRITTEN SOURCES

Of Knowledge, Taste, and Refinement
Salon Culture

The feminine look of the Rococo style suggests that the age was dominated by the taste and social initiative of women—and, to a large extent, it was. Women—Madame de Pompadour in France, Maria Theresa in Austria, and Elizabeth and Catherine in Russia—held some of the highest positions in Europe, and female influence was felt in numerous smaller courts. The Rococo salon was the center of early-eighteenth-century Parisian society, and Paris was the social capital of Europe. Wealthy, ambitious, and clever society hostesses competed to attract the most famous and the most accomplished people to their salons. The medium of social intercourse was conversation spiced with wit, repartee as quick and deft as a fencing match. Artifice reigned supreme, and participants considered enthusiasm or sincerity in bad taste. These salon women referred to themselves as "femmes savantes," or "learned women." Among these learned women was Julie de Lespinasse (1732–1776), one of the most articulate, urbane, and intelligent French women of the time. She held daily salons from five o'clock until nine in the evening. The *Memoirs of Marmontel* documented the liveliness of these gatherings and the remarkable nature of this hostess:

> The circle was formed of persons who were not bound together. She had taken them here and there in society, but so well assorted were they that once there they fell into harmony like the strings of an in-

strument touched by an able hand. Following out that comparison, I may say that she played the instrument with an art that came of genius; she seemed to know what tone each string would yield before she touched it; I mean to say that our minds and our natures were so well known to her that in order to bring them into play she had but to say a word. Nowhere was conversation more lively, more brilliant, or better regulated than at her house. It was a rare phenomenon indeed, the degree of tempered, equable heat which she knew so well how to maintain, sometimes by moderating it, sometimes by quickening it. The continual activity of her soul was communicated to our souls, but measurably; her imagination was the mainspring, her reason the regulator. Remark that the brains she stirred at will were neither feeble nor frivolous. . . . Her talent for casting out a thought and giving it for discussion to men of that class, her own talent in discussing it with precision, sometimes with eloquence, her talent for bringing forward new ideas and varying the topic-always with the facility and ease of a fairy . . . these talents, I say, were not those of an ordinary woman. It was not with the follies of fashion and vanity that daily, during four hours of conversation, without languor and without vacuum, she knew how to make herself interesting to a wide circle of strong minds.[1]

[1] Jean François Marmontel, *Memoirs of Marmontel,* trans. Brigit Patmore (London: G. Routledge & Sons, 1930), 270.

24-80 GERMAIN BOFFRAND, Salon de la Princesse, with painting by CHARLES-JOSEPH NATOIRE and sculpture by J. B. LEMOINE, Hôtel de Soubise, Paris, France, 1737–1740.

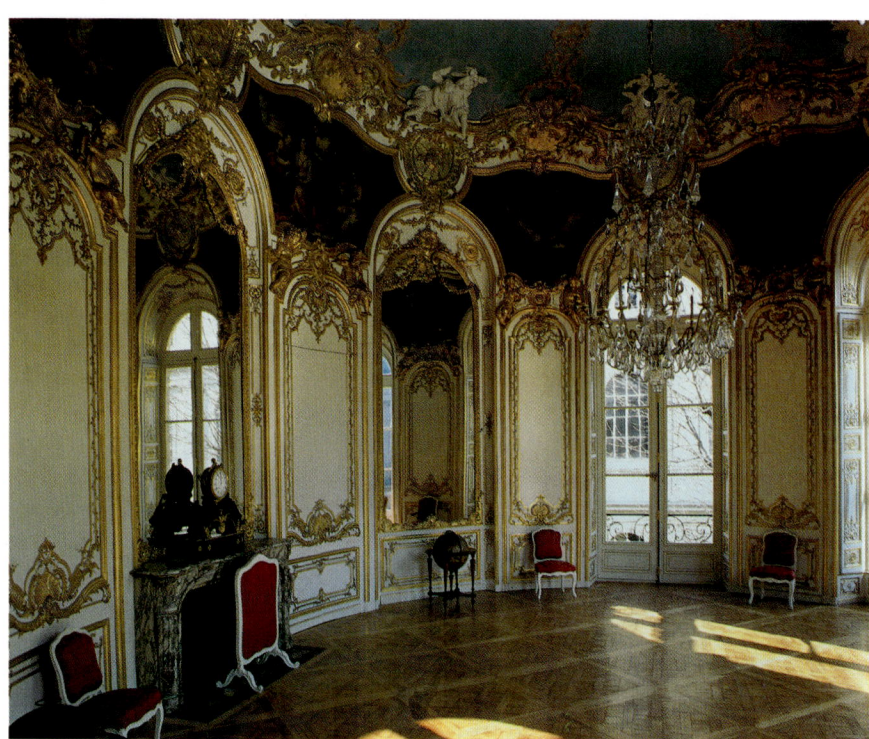

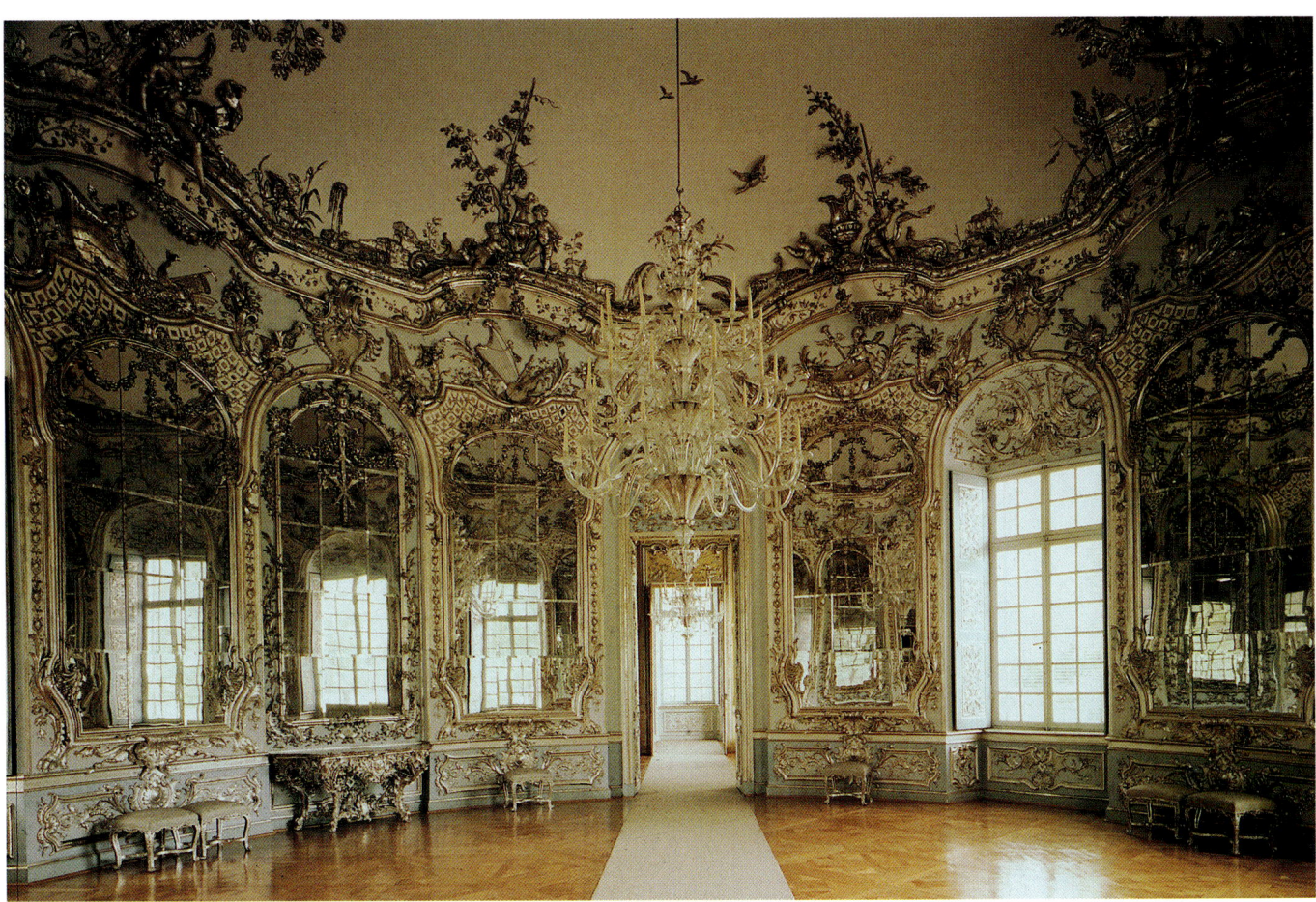

24-81   FRANÇOIS DE CUVILLIÈS, Hall of Mirrors, the Amalienburg, Nymphenburg Palace park, Munich, Germany, early eighteenth century.

ceramics and silver, a few "easel" paintings, and decorative tapestry complementing the architecture, relief sculptures, and wall paintings. As seen today, French Rococo interiors, such as the Salon de la Princesse, have lost most of the moveable "accessories" that once adorned them. Viewers can imagine, however, how such rooms—with their alternating gilded moldings, vivacious relief sculptures, and daintily colored ornament of flowers and garlands—must have harmonized with the chamber music played in them, with the elaborate costumes of satin and brocade, and with the equally elegant etiquette and sparkling wit of the people who graced them.

FRENCH ROCOCO IN A GERMAN LODGE   A brilliant example of French Rococo in Germany is the Amalienburg, a small lodge FRANÇOIS DE CUVILLIÈS (1695–1768) built in the park of the Nymphenburg Palace in Munich. Although Rococo was essentially a style of interior design, the Amalienburg beautifully harmonizes the interior and exterior elevations through the curving flow of lines and planes that cohere in a sculptural unity of great elegance. The most spectacular interior room in the lodge is the circular Hall of Mirrors (FIG. **24-81**), a silver-and-blue ensemble of architecture, stucco relief, silvered bronze mirrors, and crystal. It dazzles the eye with myriad scintillating motifs, forms, and figurations the

designer borrowed from the full Rococo ornamental repertoire. This room displays the style's zenith. Facets of silvery light, multiplied by windows and mirrors, sharply or softly delineate the endlessly proliferating shapes and contours that weave rhythmically around the upper walls and the ceiling coves. Everything seems organic, growing, and in motion, an ultimate refinement of illusion that the architect, artists, and artisans, all magically in command of their varied media, created with virtuoso flourishes.

A DELICATE DANCER   The painter scholars most associate with French Rococo is ANTOINE WATTEAU (1684–1721). The differences between the Baroque age in France and the Rococo age can be seen clearly by contrasting Rigaud's portrait of Louis XIV (FIG. 24-66) with one of Watteau's paintings, *L'Indifférent* (*The Indifferent One;* FIG. **24-82**). Rigaud portrayed pompous majesty in supreme glory, as if the French monarch were reviewing throngs of bowing courtiers at Versailles. Watteau's painting, in contrast, is not as heavy or staid and is more delicate. The artist presented a languid, gliding dancer whose mincing minuet might be seen as mimicking the monarch's solemnity if the paintings were hung together. In Rigaud's portrait, stout architecture, bannerlike curtains, flowing ermine, and fleur-de-lis exalt the king. In Watteau's painting, the dancer

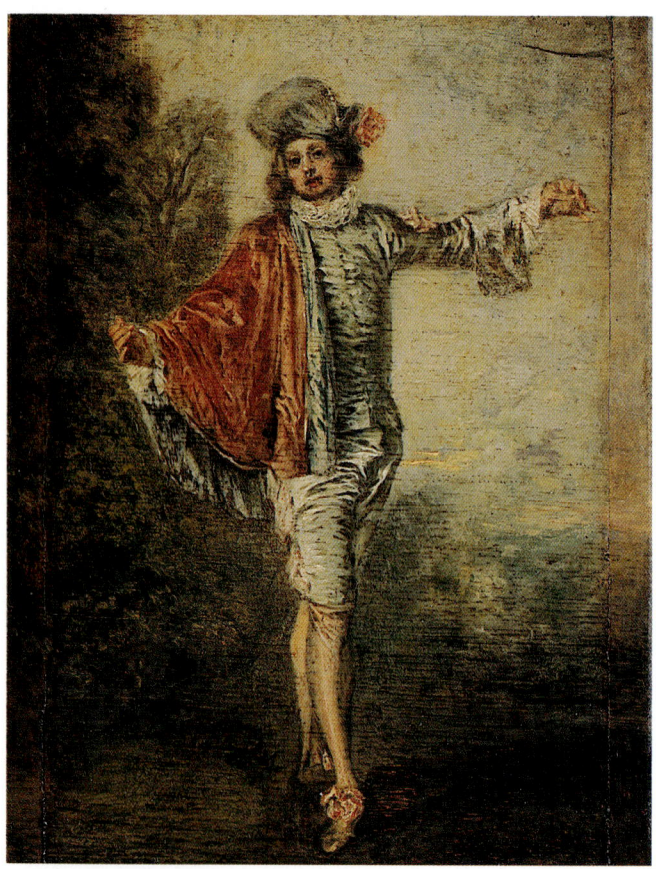

24-82   ANTOINE WATTEAU, *L'Indifférent,* ca. 1716. Oil on canvas, approx. 10″ × 7″. Louvre, Paris.

moves in a rainbow shimmer of color, emerging onto the stage of the intimate comic opera to the silken sounds of strings. The portrait of the king is very large, the "portrait" of "the indifferent one" quite small.

CELEBRATING THE GOOD LIFE   Watteau was largely responsible for creating a specific type of Rococo painting, called a *fête galante* painting. These paintings depicted the outdoor entertainment or amusements of upper-class society. *View through the Trees in the Park of Pierre Crozat (La Perspective),* FIG. **24-83**, is such a painting. Although at first glance this may seem to be a genre scene, relatively few people lived such a privileged life, so this cannot be considered "everyday life." Watteau's style in this work is emphatically Rococo—soft and feathery brushstrokes, dainty figures, and muted colors. This painting exudes a graceful elegance and delicacy.

Watteau's masterpiece (painted in two versions) is *Return from Cythera* (FIG. **24-84**), completed between 1717 and 1719 as the artist's acceptance piece for admission to the Royal Academy. Watteau was Flemish, and his style was a beautiful derivative of Rubens's style—a kind of refinement of it.

At the turn of the century, the French Royal Academy was divided rather sharply between two doctrines. One doctrine upheld the ideas of Le Brun (the major proponent of French Baroque under Louis XIV), who followed Nicolas Poussin in teaching that form was the most important element in paint-

24-83   ANTOINE WATTEAU, *View through the Trees in the Park of Pierre Crozat (La Perspective),* ca. 1715. Oil on canvas, 1′ 6⅜″ × 1′ 9¾″. Museum of Fine Arts, Boston (Maria Antoinette Evans Fund).

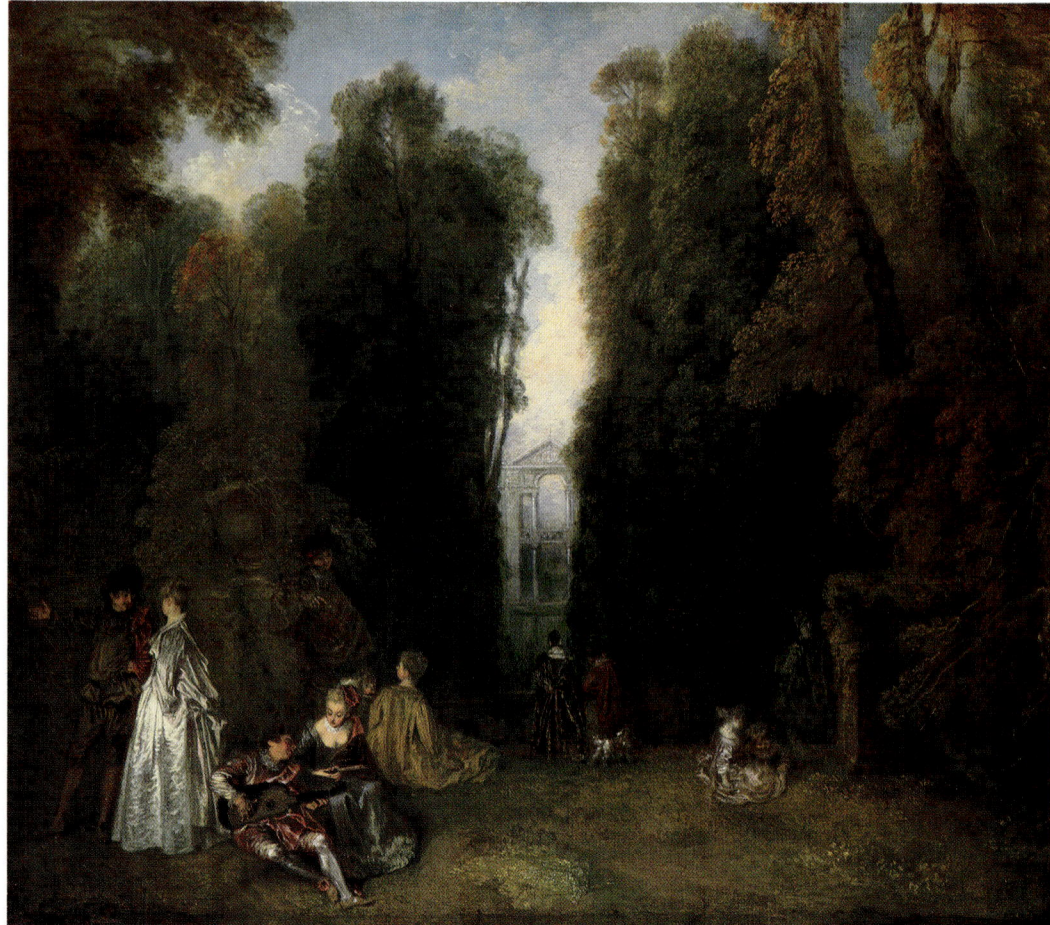

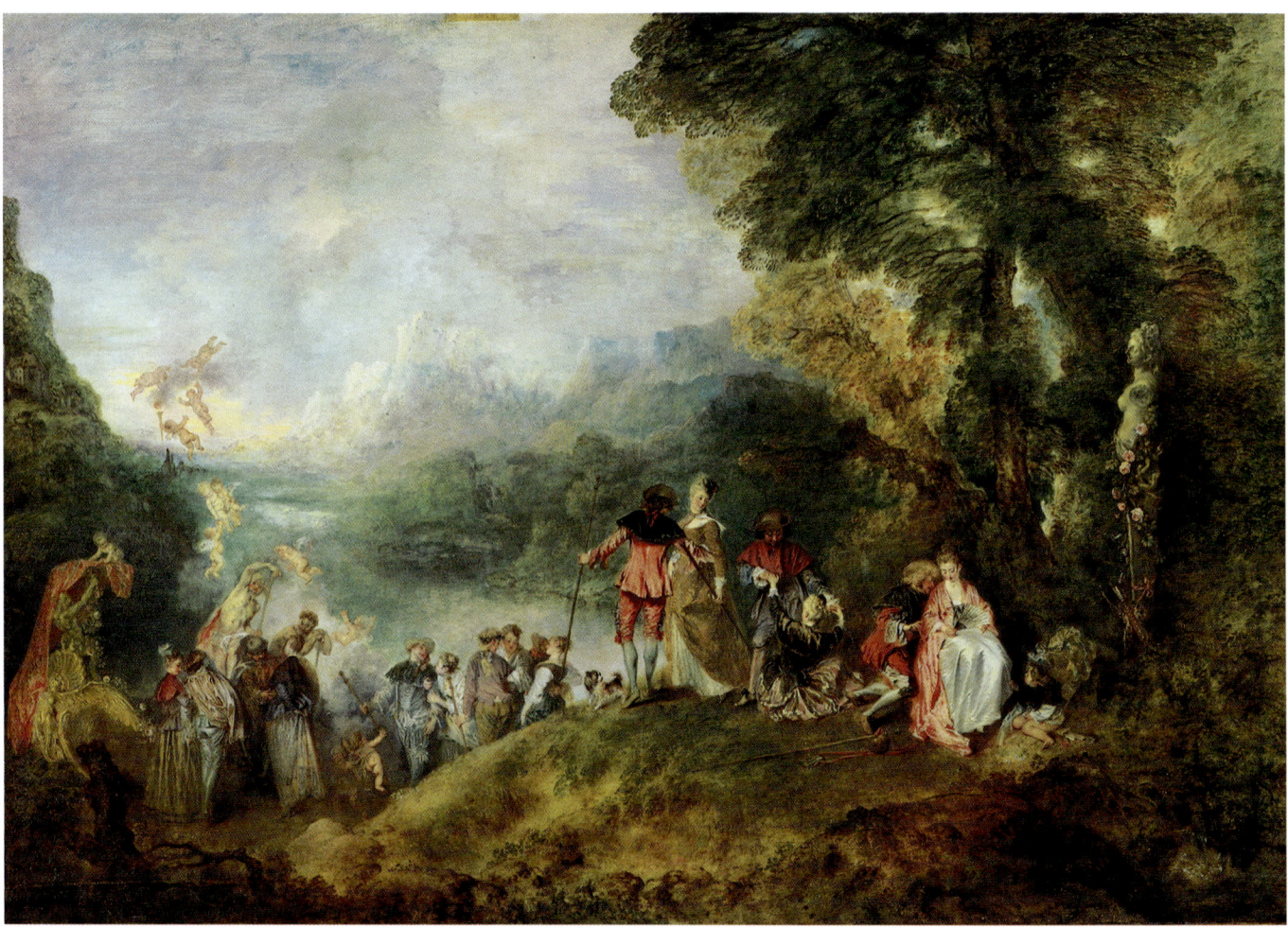

24-84   ANTOINE WATTEAU, *Return from Cythera*, 1717–1719. Oil on canvas, approx. 4′ 3″ × 6′ 4″. Louvre, Paris.

ing, while "colors in painting are as allurements for persuading the eyes," additions for effect and not really essential.[9] The other doctrine, with Rubens as its model, proclaimed the supremacy of color as natural and the coloristic style as the artist's proper guide. Depending on which side they took, academy members were called "Poussinistes" or "Rubénistes." With Watteau in their ranks, the Rubénistes carried the day, and they established the Rococo style in painting on the colorism of Rubens and the Venetians.

Watteau's *Return from Cythera* represents a group of lovers preparing to depart from the island of eternal youth and love, sacred to Aphrodite. Young and luxuriously costumed, they perform, as it were, an elegant, tender, and graceful ballet, moving from the protective shade of a woodland park, peopled with amorous cupids and voluptuous statuary, down a grassy slope to an awaiting golden barge. Watteau studied carefully the attitudes of the figures; no one has equaled his distinctive poses, which combine elegance and sweetness. He composed his generally quite small paintings from albums of superb drawings that have been preserved and are still in fine condition. These show he observed slow movement from difficult and unusual angles, obviously intending to find the smoothest, most poised, and most refined attitudes. As he sought nuances of bodily poise and movement, Watteau also strove for the most exquisite shades of color difference, defin-

ing in a single stroke the shimmer of silk at a bent knee or the iridescence that touches a glossy surface as it emerges from shadow.

Art historians have noted that the theme of love and Arcadian happiness (observed here since Giorgione and which Watteau may have seen in works by Rubens) in Watteau's pictures is slightly shadowed with wistfulness, or even melancholy. Perhaps Watteau, during his own short life, meditated on the swift passage of youth and pleasure. The haze of color, the subtly modeled shapes, the gliding motion, and the air of suave gentility were all to the taste of the Rococo artist's wealthy patronage.

A PLAYFUL ROCOCO FANTASY   Watteau's successors never quite matched his taste and subtlety. Their themes were about love, artfully and archly pursued through erotic frivolity and playful intrigue. After Watteau's early death at age thirty-seven, his follower, FRANÇOIS BOUCHER (1703–1770), painter for Madame de Pompadour (the influential mistress of Louis XV), rose to the dominant position in French painting. Although he was an excellent portraitist, Boucher's fame rested primarily on his graceful allegories, with Arcadian shepherds, nymphs, and goddesses cavorting in shady glens engulfed in pink and sky blue light. *Cupid a Captive* (FIG. **24-85**) presents viewers with a rosy pyramid of infant and female

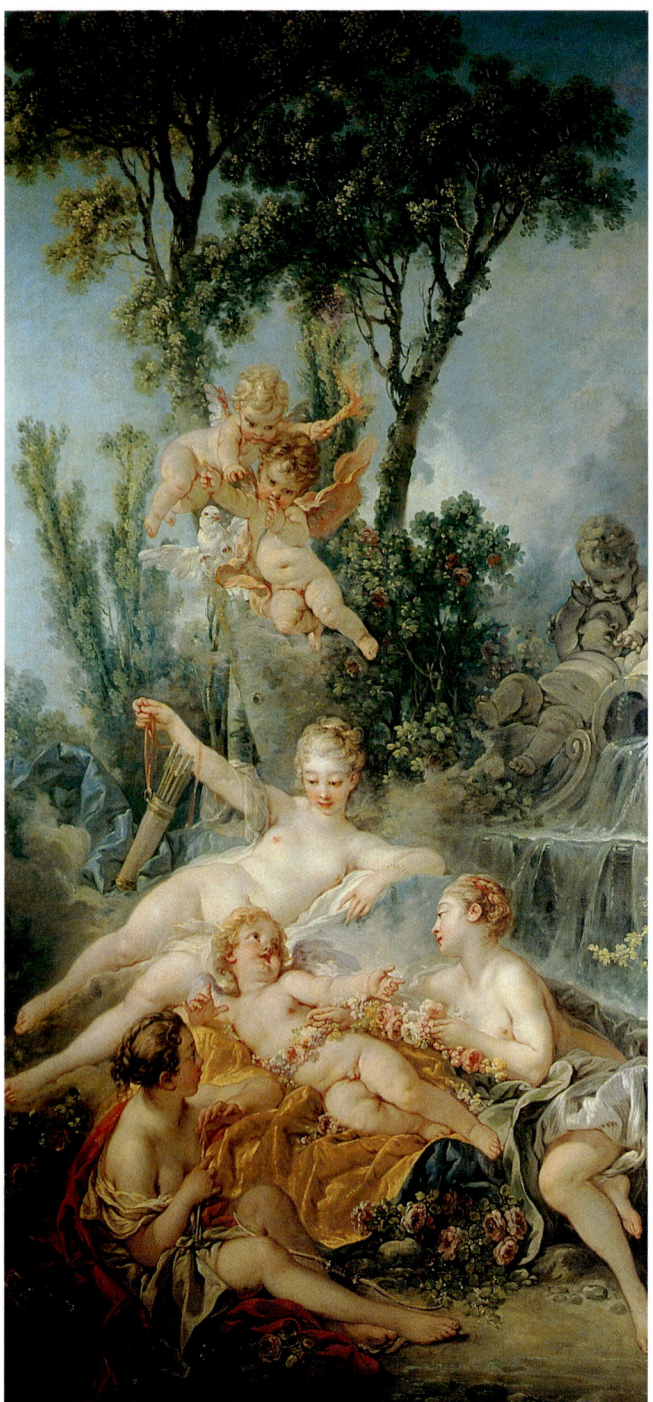

24-85 FRANÇOIS BOUCHER, *Cupid a Captive,* 1754. Oil on canvas, approx. 5′ 6″ × 2′ 10″. The Wallace Collection, London.

AN INTRIGUING FLIRTATION JEAN-HONORÉ FRAGONARD (1732–1806), Boucher's student, was a first-rate colorist whose decorative skill almost surpassed his master's. An example of his manner can stand as characteristic not only of him but also of the later Rococo in general. *The Swing* (FIG. **24-86**) is a typical "intrigue" picture. A young gentleman has managed an arrangement whereby an unsuspecting old bishop swings the young man's pretty sweetheart higher and higher, while her lover (and the work's patron), in the lower left-hand corner, stretches out to admire her ardently from a strategic position on the ground. The young lady flirtatiously and boldly kicks off her shoe at the little statue of the god of discretion, who holds his finger to his lips. The landscape setting is out of Watteau—a luxuriant perfumed bower in a park that very much resembles a stage scene for the comic opera. The glowing pastel colors and soft light convey, almost by themselves, the theme's sensuality.

ECHOES OF BERNINI IN SENSUOUS ROCOCO The Rococo mood of sensual intimacy also permeated many of the small sculptures designed for the eighteenth-century salons. Artists such as CLAUDE MICHEL, called CLODION (1738–1814), specialized in small, lively sculptures that combined the sensuous Rococo fantasies with lightened echoes of Bernini's dynamic figures. Perhaps historians should expect such influence in Clodion's works. He lived and worked in Rome for some years after discovering the city's charms during his tenure as the recipient of the cherished Prix de Rome. The Royal Academy annually gave the *Prix de Rome* (Rome Prize) to the artist who produced the best history painting, subsidizing the winning artist's stay in Rome (from three to five years).

Clodion's small group, *Nymph and Satyr* (FIG. **24-87**), has an open and vivid composition suggestive of its dynamic roots. But the artist overlaid that source with the erotic playfulness of Boucher and Fragonard to energize his eager nymph and the laughing satyr into whose mouth she pours a cup of wine. Here, the Rococo style's sensual exhilaration is caught in diminutive scale and inexpensive terracotta. As with so many Rococo artifacts, and most of Clodion's best work, the artist designed this group for a tabletop.

THE DIVERSE LEGACIES OF THE BAROQUE The art produced during the seventeenth and early eighteenth centuries was truly diverse, making any comprehensive summary of the "Baroque" period impossible. Each country encountered a different set of historical challenges, and even within country boundaries a wide variety of art forms emerged. Despite this period's lack of consistency in artistic development, its legacy was lasting. Many of the hallmarks of seventeenth-century and early-eighteenth-century art, such as direct observation, emotional intensity, and facility with light and color, laid the foundation for two styles that emerged in the late eighteenth century, Neoclassicism and Romanticism. Further, the influence of artists such as Caravaggio, Bernini, Velázquez, Rubens, Rembrandt, Vermeer, and Watteau, among many others, resonates in art to the present day.

flesh set off against a cool, leafy background, with fluttering draperies both hiding and revealing the nudity of the figures. Boucher used the full range of Italian and French Baroque devices to create his masterly composition: the dynamic play of crisscrossing diagonals, curvilinear forms, and slanting recessions. But in his work he dissected powerful Baroque curves into a multiplicity of decorative arabesques, dissipating Baroque drama into sensual playfulness. Lively and lighthearted, Boucher's artful Rococo fantasies became mirrors for his patrons, the wealthy French, to behold the ornamental reflections of their cherished pastimes.

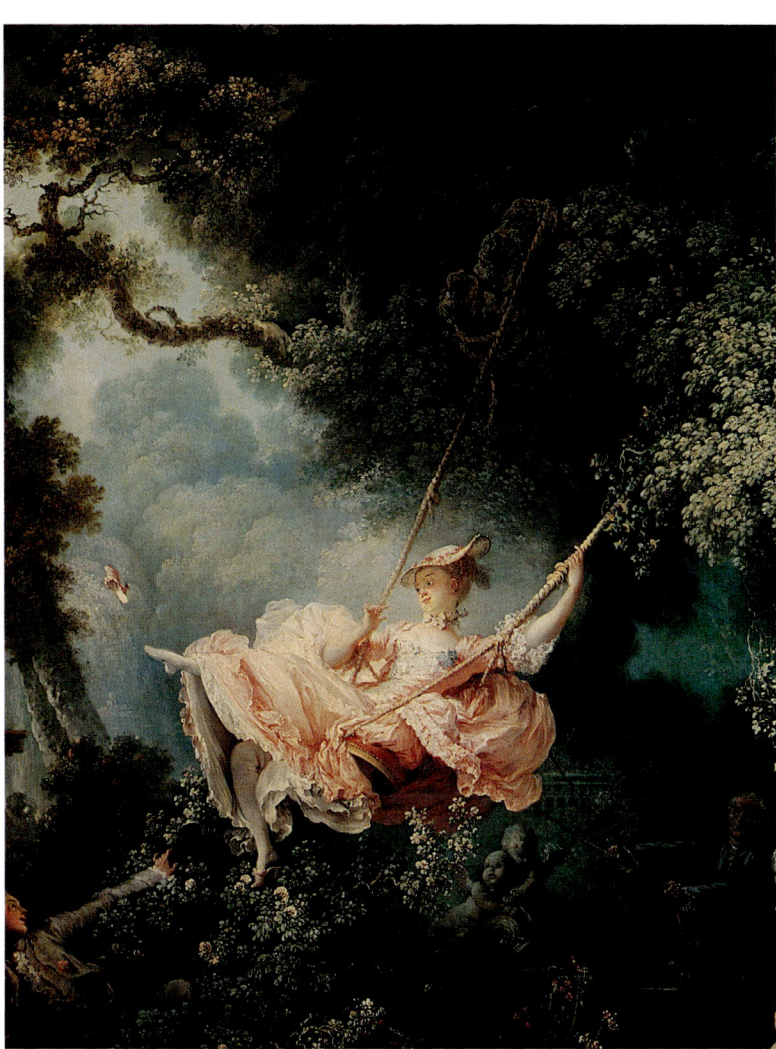

24-86 JEAN-HONORÉ FRAGONARD, *The Swing,* 1766. Oil on canvas, approx. 2′ 11″ × 2′ 8″. The Wallace Collection, London.

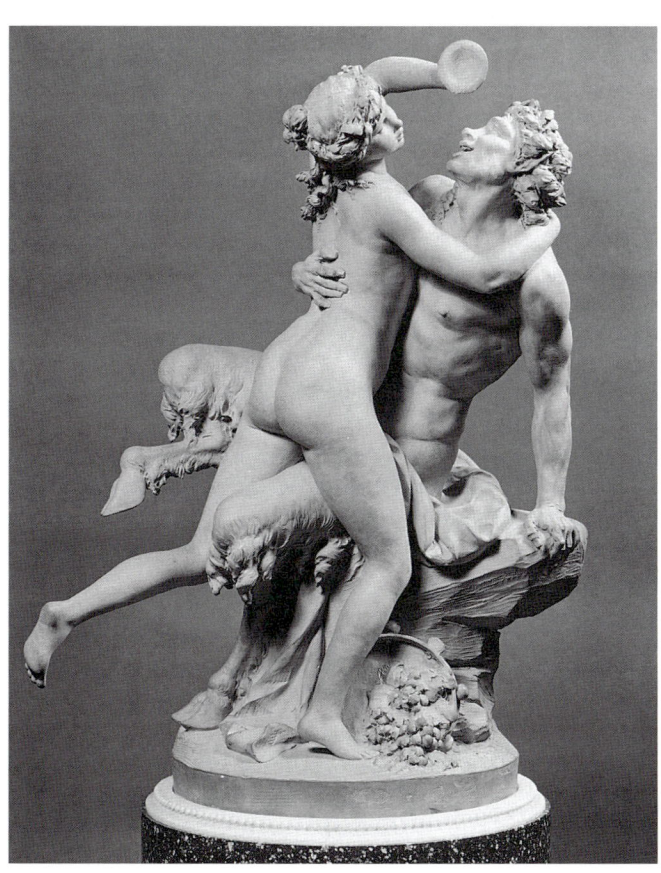

24-87 CLODION, *Nymph and Satyr,* ca. 1775. Terracotta, approx. 1′ 11″ high. Metropolitan Museum of Art, New York (bequest of Benjamin Altman, 1913).

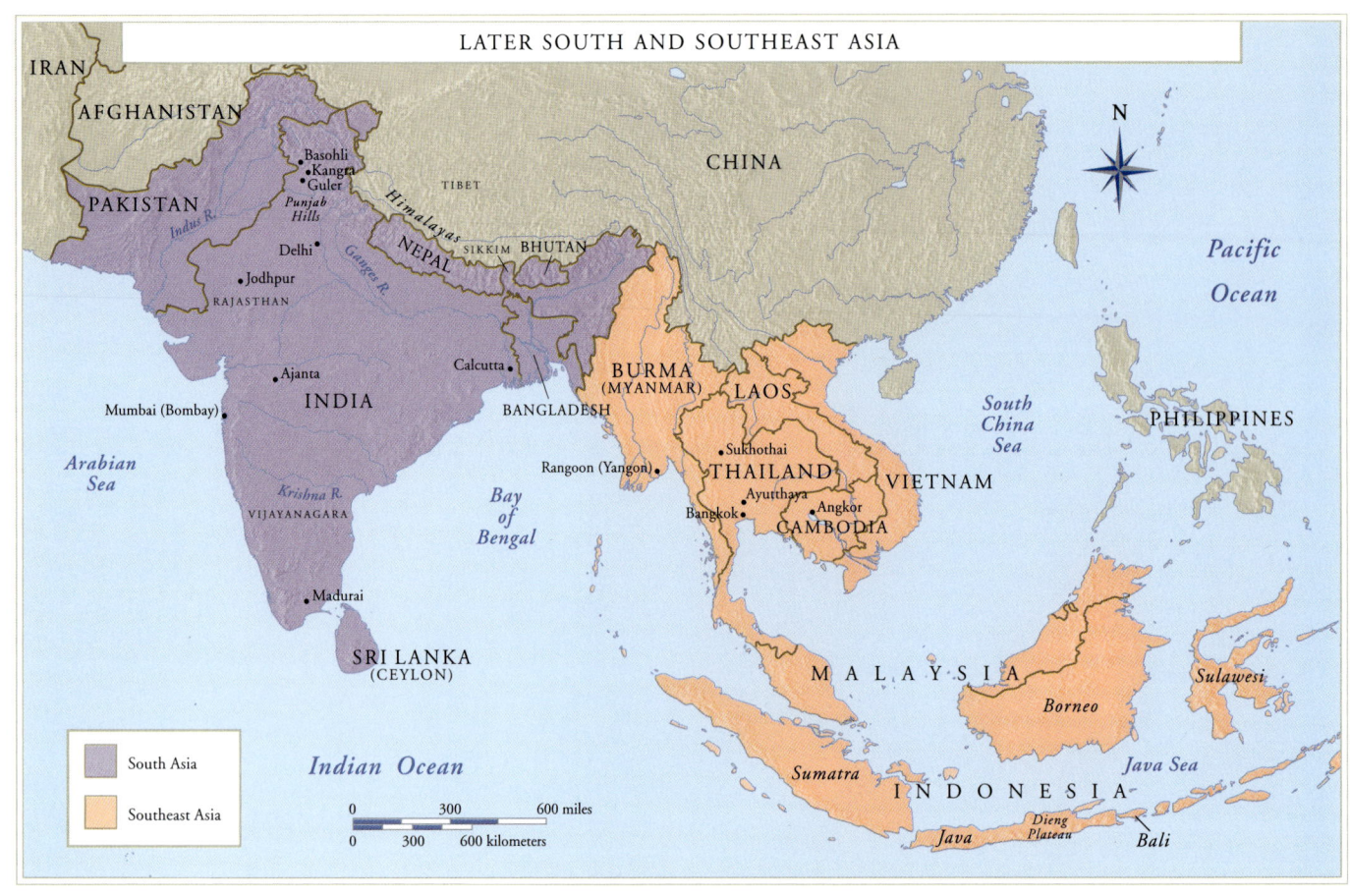

LATER SOUTH AND SOUTHEAST ASIA

	1000	1200	1250	1300	1400	1500
INDIA	LATER HINDU AND BUDDHIST DYNASTIES			VIJAYANAGARA DYNASTY		
THAILAND			SUKHOTHAI DYNASTY			
BURMA						
VIETNAM	LY DYNASTY		TRAN DYNASTY			

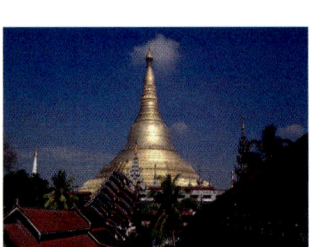

Schwedagon Pagoda, Rangoon
(Yangon), Burma (Myanmar)
fourteenth century or earlier

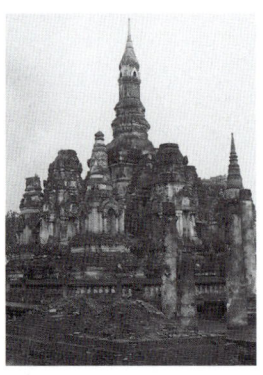

Wat Mahathat, Sukhothai
Thailand, fourteenth century

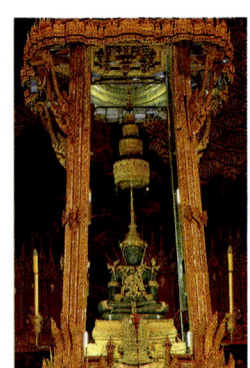

Emerald Buddha, Bangkok
Thailand, fifteenth century

Vietnamese independence from China, tenth century

Jayadeva writes *Gita Govinda* (India), twelfth century

King Ramkhamhaeng (Thailand), r. 1279–1299

Ayuthaya founded (Thailand), 1350

Ceramic trade in Southeast Asia,
fifteenth–seventeenth centuries

25

RELIGIOUS CHANGE AND COLONIAL RULE

THE LATER ART OF SOUTH AND SOUTHEAST ASIA

1500	1600	1700	1800	1900	1932	1947	1975	1982

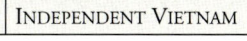

NAYAK DYNASTY

MUGHAL DYNASTY

ENGLISH RULE

INDEPENDENT INDIA

CONSTITUTIONAL THAILAND

INDEPENDENT BURMA

INDEPENDENT VIETNAM

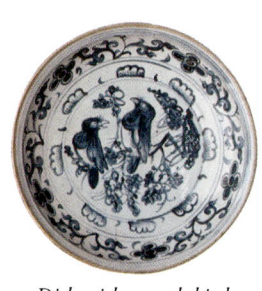

Dish with mynah birds
Vietnam, sixteenth century

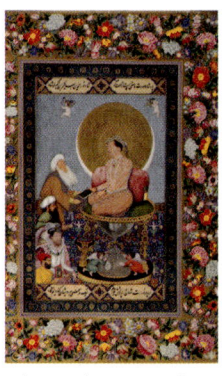

Bichitr, Jahangir Preferring
a Sufi Shaikh to Kings
ca. 1615–1618

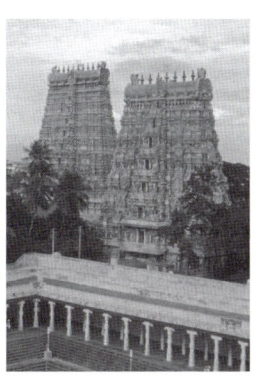

Great Temple, Madurai
India, seventeenth century

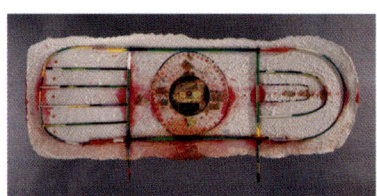

Kamol Tassananchalee
Buddha Footprint
Nang-Yai Series II, 1982

King Krishnadevaraya (India), r. 1509–1529

Emperor Akbar (India), r. 1556–1605

Battle of Talikota (India), 1564

Emperor Jahangir (India), r. 1605–1627

Emperor Shah Jahan (India), r. 1627–1658

Emerald Buddha brought to Bangkok, 1778

England formally governs India, 1858

Mararaja Jaswant Singh rules
Jodhpur (India), 1873–1895

India's independence from England, 1947

Goddess Santoshi Ma introduced
in Indian film, 1975

INDIA AND SOUTHEAST ASIA

SPIRITUALITY AND POWER Indian and Southeast Asian peoples experienced various cultural, political, and artistic changes beginning in the thirteenth century in some areas and in the fourteenth and fifteenth centuries in others. In India, Buddhism was nearing extinction in the thirteenth century, while Islam was growing, both as a religion and as a political force. Hinduism, always India's principal religion in numbers of adherents, was politically in retreat. While Hindu kings continued to rule in northern India, they did so by giving their fidelity to the Islamic rulers, although some Hindu kings resisted or revolted outright. As the Islamic kings' power increased, they pushed farther to the south, where Hindu kings maintained strong, independent kingdoms through the sixteenth and seventeenth centuries. The British, present in India from the sixteenth century on, formally took governmental control in 1858 and declared Queen Victoria empress of India in 1877. India gained its independence from Britain in 1947.

In Southeast Asia, the thirteenth and fourteenth centuries also saw major shifts in the wielding of political power and in religious affiliations. The Khmer of Angkor (see Chapter 6), after reaching the height of their power at the beginning of the thirteenth century, lost one of their outposts in northern Thailand to their Thai vassals at midcentury. The newly founded Thai kingdoms quickly replaced Angkor as the region's major power, while Theravada Buddhism (see "Buddhism and Buddhist Iconography," Chapter 6, page 164 or page xxix in Volume II) became the religion of the entire mainland except Vietnam. The Vietnamese, restricted to the northern region of today's Vietnam, gained independence in the tenth century after a thousand years of Chinese political and cultural domination. They pushed to the south, ultimately destroying the indigenous Cham culture which had dominated there for more than a millennium. A similar Burmese drive southward in Burma matched the Thai and Vietnamese expansions, all resulting in demographic changes during the second millennium that led to the cultural, political, and artistic transformation of mainland Southeast Asia. A religious shift also occurred in Indonesia. With Islam growing in importance, all but the island of Bali became predominantly Muslim by the sixteenth century.

INDIA

Painting

The early tradition of Indian painting is almost entirely lost due to the use of impermanent materials such as palm leaf and wood. Very little remains of the once extensive paintings on the wooden walls of Indian palaces and homes. But the fifth-century wall paintings in the caves at Ajanta (see FIG. 6-12) testify to the outstanding quality of ancient Indian painting. A few twelfth- and thirteenth-century manuscript pages on palm leaf in the Jain and Buddhist traditions still exist, but only Indian paintings from the fifteenth and sixteenth centuries or later have survived in any numbers.

HAND-HELD MINIATURES Indian painters often intended their works to be held in the hands. Only one or two people at a time usually would look at the illustrations created for books or to be kept in albums. Thus, such paintings are usually small, as in the Islamic world (see FIG. 13-29) and in Western medieval books (see Chapters 16 to 18). Because of their small size—about the size of a page in this book—art historians call them *miniatures*. Viewers did not place Indian paintings in frames and only very rarely hung them on walls. Instead, they kept them as books, sometimes bound or as separate sheets in albums brought out and admired on select occasions. Many shared the page with the written text they illustrated. Indian artists used a painting technique known as *gouache*, pigments ground in water, and produced their own fine paper, although until the early seventeenth century the best paper came from Persia.

Art historians have divided Indian paintings after the thirteenth century into several schools, including the Mughal, named after the Muslim Mughal dynasty (see Chapter 13) and the Rajput, named after the powerful Hindu clan that ruled in Rajasthan. The Mughal emperors commissioned the Mughal paintings from the sixteenth to eighteenth centuries. The Rajput paintings extend into the nineteenth century but otherwise overlap in date with the Mughal paintings. The various Hindu kings and their courts located in the state of Rajasthan and the Punjab Hills were the patrons of Rajput painting.

THE EMPEROR ABOVE TIME The Mughal court, especially under the three emperors Akbar (r. 1556–1605), Jahangir (r. 1605–1627), and Shah Jahan (r. 1627–1658), had no equal before or after in India in its lavish patronage of the arts (see "Mughal Kings' Attitudes toward Painting," page 792). In contrast to the anonymity of artists in the Hindu and Buddhist traditions, many Mughal artists signed their work. BICHITR (active early seventeenth century to late 1650s) painted a watercolor portrait of Jahangir seated on an hourglass throne (FIG. **25-1**). Bichitr also included his own portrait in the painting. He is the figure, almost hidden in the lower left corner, wearing a red turban. The three other figures standing with the artist are King James I of England (r. 1603–1625), a Turkish sultan, and an important Muslim holy man, Shaikh Husain, who receives a copy of the Koran from the emperor. The artist signed his name across the top of the footstool Jahangir used to step up to his throne. Thus, the ruler stepped on Bichitr's name, suggesting the painter's placement beneath the emperor's foot. Bichitr clearly knew his place in the hierarchy. The symbolism indicates Jahangir is above both the secular and sacred leaders of the day. His placement on an hourglass-shaped throne indicates he is above time as well.

The two angels kneeling at the throne's base with pens in their hands wrote on the throne, "Oh Shah [Jahangir], may the span of your life be a thousand years."[1] Angels appear in both the Judeo-Christian and Islamic artistic traditions, although the form they take in the Mughal painting follows the European style. Islam evolved out of the same cultural complex as Judaism and Christianity and shares with them many characteristics (see Chapter 13). In the painting, a flaming halo backed by an even larger combined sun and moon underscores the emperor's unique position, implying both his holiness and that he is the center of the universe and its light source. Jahangir had a special fondness for using light symbolism to indicate his relationship to the divine. His most

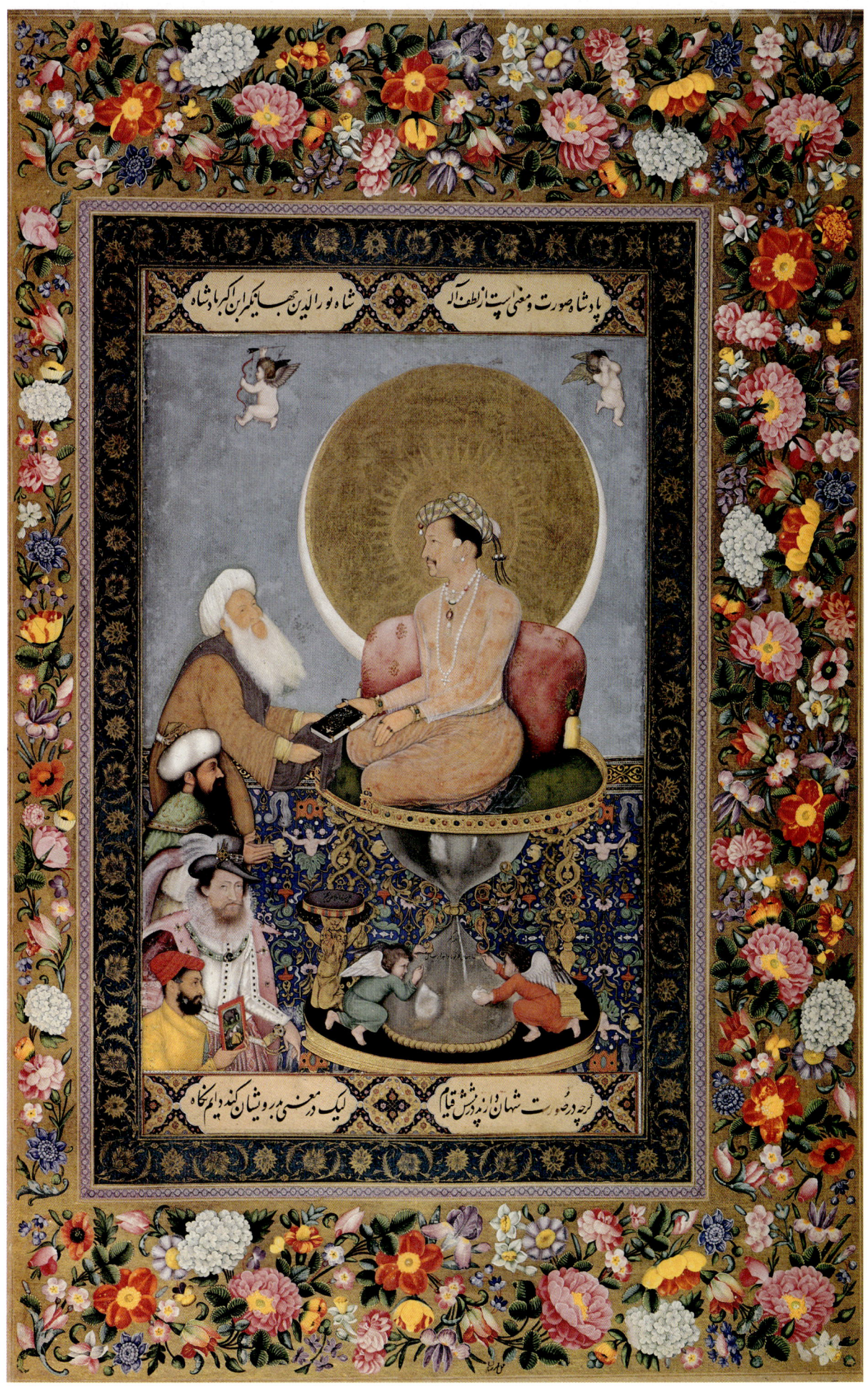

25-1 BICHITR, *Jahangir Preferring a Sufi Shaikh to Kings,* Mughal painting, India, ca. 1615–1618. Opaque watercolor on paper, 1′ 6$\frac{7}{8}$″ × 1′ 1″. Freer Gallery of Art, Washington.

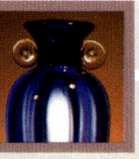

ART AND SOCIETY

Mughal Kings' Attitudes toward Painting

The emperor Akbar had a keen interest in painting. He directed his painters—a workshop of about a hundred artists—to undertake several ambitious projects. One task, an illustrated text of *Hamza-nama*—the story of Hamza, Muhammad's uncle—presented in some fourteen hundred pictures, took fifteen years to complete. Akbar felt painting could teach as well as entertain. His fascination extended to the question of how form could carry meaning, and he concluded that painting could use form to reveal the inner meaning of reality. Akbar had portraits made of his followers, feeling he could read in their faces their true psychology and the extent to which he could trust them.

For Jahangir, Akbar's son and successor, the appreciation of painting developed into full-fledged connoisseurship. He was more interested in the paintings as paintings than in what they might teach or how they could entertain. Connoisseurs are interested in the identification and categorization of artistic style, particularly the styles of individual artists. They judge artistic quality, ranking artists and works and making

the best of both a standard for judging others. Connoisseurs collect art to view and admire it. The connoisseurship of Jahangir and the Mughal court broke with traditional Indian views about art, wherein art's function was primarily to represent the gods and their world. The Mughal emperors therefore shared artistic values with the post-Renaissance West.

By the time of Jahangir's son and successor, Shah Jahan, the Mughal court had become a place for the ostentatious display of wealth. Objects made of jewels, gold, and precious stones fascinated Shah Jahan more than paintings. He also commissioned many building projects, including the famous Taj Mahal at Agra (see FIG. 13-27 for a discussion in the context of late Islamic art) which was the tomb he constructed for his wife. But he maintained the imperial painting studio his predecessors had established, which focused on pictures recording important events, especially occasions such as weddings, court ceremonies, and royal hunts. Each scene generally included dozens of individualized portraits of those present at the event.

---

frequently seen title, *Nur-un-din,* used in one inscription on the painting, translates as "Light of the Faith." Bichitr's picture elaborately states Jahangir's supremacy over every aspect of Mughal life, both secular and sacred.

The painting's title, *Jahangir Preferring a Sufi Shaikh to Kings,* comes from another inscription on the work: "Shah Nur ad-din Jahangir, . . . Although to all appearances kings stand before him,/He looks inwardly toward the dervishes [for guidance]." By giving the Koran to the Muslim holy man (a dervish), Jahangir shows him honor over the two kings depicted and gives up worldly life and control for the spiritual. The little angels above cry at the loss of the emperor's worldly life and hold a broken bow and arrows, indicating the release of political control. Of course, the emperor did not actually give up secular power, and the painting shows him *above* both worldly and spiritual leaders.

Jahangir, like the other Mughal emperors, had many portraits painted, not only of himself but also of various courtiers, friends, enemies, and even foreigners, such as King James I. Neither the emperor nor Bichitr had ever seen the king, so the painter used a portrait by an English artist, John de Critz, as his source. The Mughal patrons demanded a very realistic style in these portraits so that viewers could identify individuals by their unique features. Women at the court (particularly the emperor's wives and women in the harem), unlike men, were rarely the subject of portraits. Female dancers or musicians, depicted not as individuals but as standard types, did not have to remain hidden from men and thus do appear in paintings.

The Mughal artists learned realistic techniques from Western models, readily available at the court in European books

and engravings (frequently Flemish or German). Such items often arrived with Christian missionaries. Missionaries, traders, and diplomats also brought prints. Portuguese Jesuits brought one particularly important source, the eight-volume *Royal Polyglot Bible,* as a gift to Akbar in 1580. This massive set of books, printed in Antwerp, was illustrated with engravings by several Flemish artists. Akbar immediately set his painters to copying the engravings.

DEVI, ANIMATOR OF THE UNIVERSE   The bold areas of color, stylized figures, and flat picture plane of a work produced in Basohli, one of the seventeenth-century Hindu courts of the Punjab Hills north of Delhi, contrast markedly with the Mughal work's realism. In about 1660, the Basohli court artists produced a series of seventy or more Rajput paintings depicting the Devi or Goddess (see "Goddess Worship in India," page 793). Thirty-two of these works are known today, including *Bhadrakali within the Rising Sun* (FIG. 25-2) depicting the goddess Bhadrakali, one of the Devi's thousands of forms. A poetic stanza accompanies each painting, written in Sanskrit on the back. The poem on the reverse of the painting shown reads,

> She loves to reside
> in the mandala of the rising sun
> with a face full as the forest lotus
> dark-hued One
> with gait graceful as a young swan
> breasts high, rounded and mature
> wearing a garland of lotus blossoms

> book in hand
> clad in yellow garments
> standing upon a corpse
> She constantly visits
> the sacrificial space
> I praise Bhadrakali.[2]

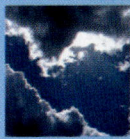

Goddess Worship in India

The three most important deities Hindus throughout India worship are Devi, or the Goddess, and the male deities Shiva and Vishnu (see "Hinduism and Hindu Iconography," Chapter 6, page 173). Like Shiva and Vishnu, the Goddess takes a variety of forms. Hindus worship her alone, as a consort or wife of male gods, and as a mother. She has both benign and horrific forms; she both creates and destroys. Alone and unmarried, Devi can be dangerous and uncontrolled. In one manifestation, she is Durga, a multiarmed goddess often accompanied by a lion, the vehicle on which she rides. Durga kills a buffalo demon threatening the balance between the gods and the demons. In another manifestation, the Goddess is Kali, the "black one," a fierce form who demands blood sacrifices (Bhadrakali in FIG. 25-2 is one form of Kali). In other forms, worshiped alone as Lakshmi, the goddess of wealth, or Sarasvati, the goddess of learning, Devi assumes the form of benevolent and benign deities. As the consort of the male gods, she is Parvati or Uma, the wife of Shiva, and

Lakshmi, the wife of Vishnu, as well as Radha, the lover of Krishna, an incarnation of Vishnu (FIG. 25-3). She also appears as a mother, frequently holding a baby or child and called simply "Ma," or mother. All of these forms (and thousands of others) are aspects of one Devi or Goddess, a deity whose female power, called *shakti*, animates the matter of the cosmos.

Modern practice permits the introduction of new goddesses even now in India. Santoshi Ma, created and introduced in a 1975 movie, is one of the most popular goddesses in India today. Hindu practice usually considers these new goddesses (and gods) as more manifestations or forms of such inclusive deities as Shiva, Vishnu, or Devi. The most important deity worshiped at the Great Temple at Madurai (FIG. 25-5) is a goddess, Minakshi Devi, or "fish-eyed goddess." Minakshi is the focus of numerous festivals throughout the year. Her marriage to Shiva at which Vishnu officiates brings more than a half million devotees to the temple for a period of ten days each year.

The painting (conforming closely to the poetic description) depicts Bhadrakali, book in hand, standing on the broken body of a male corpse at the center of the radiating sun. The dark-skinned goddess wears pink lotuses and strands of pearls around her neck. Writhing cobras twist about her neck

and arms. Basohli artists typically used iridescent green beetle-wing cases, glued onto the paper, to mimic jewels. Hindus consider the Goddess the animator of the universe, the force activating the world matter, visualized as male. Thus, the male corpse serves as the matter she will awaken to action. It also

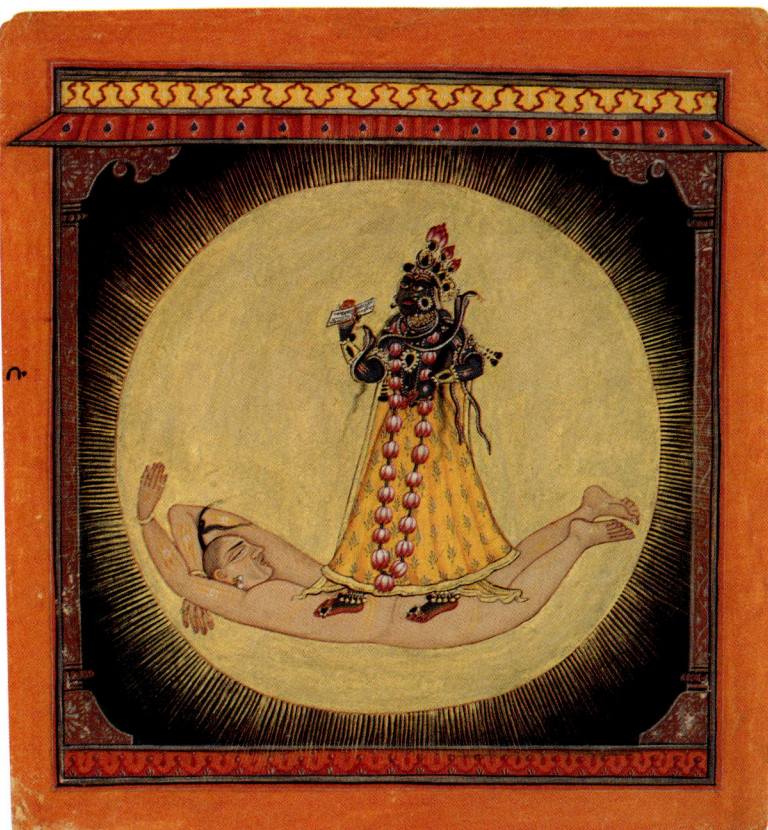

25-2 *Bhadrakali within the Rising Sun,* folio 10 from the Tantric Devi series, from Punjab Hills, Basohli, India, ca. 1660–1670. Opaque watercolor, gold, silver, and beetle-wing cases on paper, $9\frac{3}{4}'' \times 8\frac{1}{4}''$. Private collection of Dr. Alvin O. Bellak, Philadelphia.

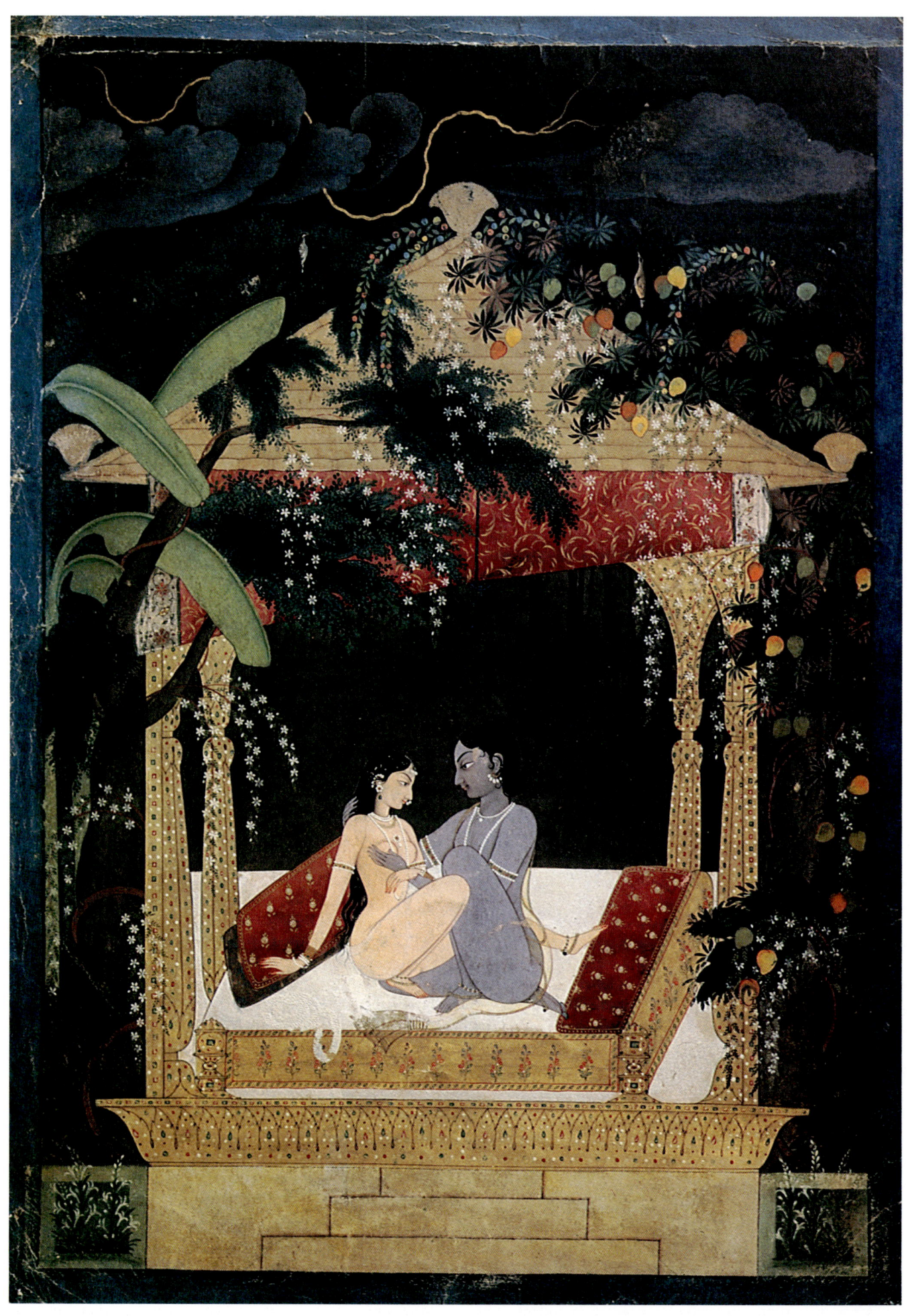

25-3 *Krishna and Radha in a Pavilion,* from Punjab Hills, Kangra(?), India, ca. 1760. Opaque watercolor on paper, $11\frac{1}{8}'' \times 7\frac{3}{4}''$. National Museum, New Delhi.

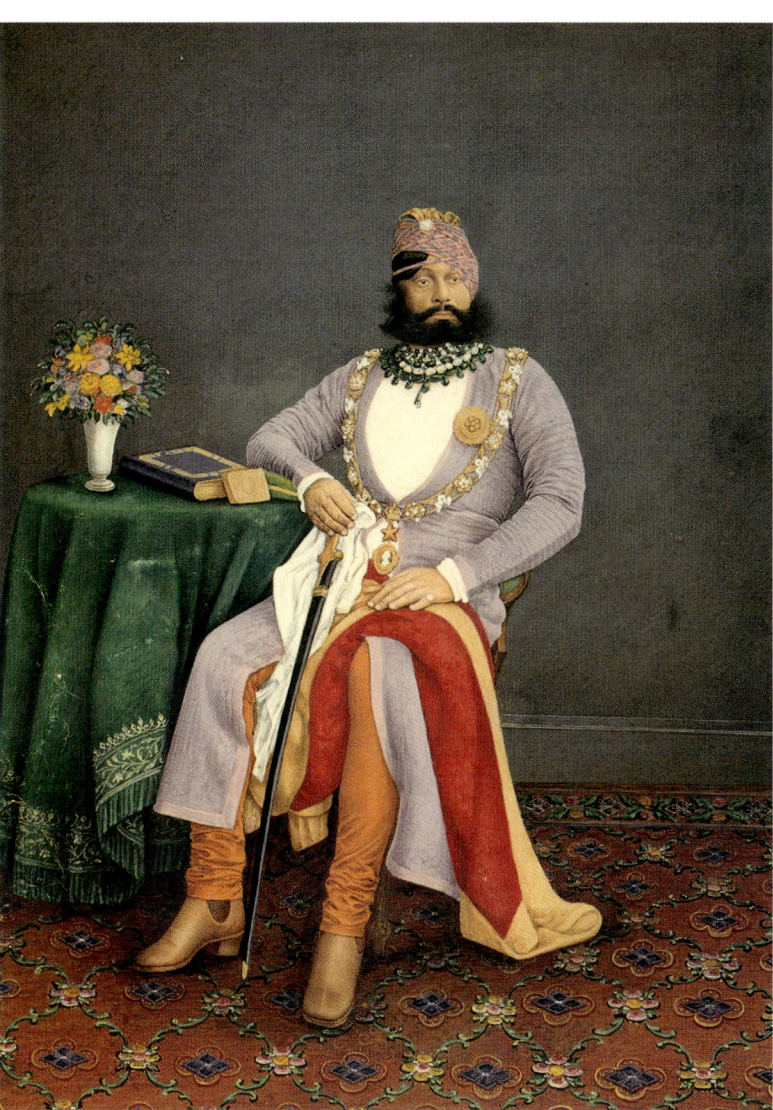

25-4 *Maharaja Jaswant Singh of Marwar,* from Jodhpur, India, ca. 1880. Opaque watercolor on paper, $1' \, 3\frac{1}{2}'' \times 11\frac{5}{8}''$. The Brooklyn Museum (gift of Mr. and Mrs. Robert L. Poster).

represents the bodily sacrifice of the worshiper, who places himself at the Goddess's mercy. Devi's positioning can be compared to Jahangir's placement as the sun's center in Bichitr's Mughal painting (FIG. 25-1), a contrast between the Hindu court's deity-centered world and the deified but human emperor as world center.

VISHNU THE LOVER One of the most popular topics for Punjab Hill paintings involved Krishna, an avatar of Vishnu, and his many amorous adventures. (As mentioned in Chapter 6, an avatar is an incarnation of the deity in a visible form while the god performs a sacred function on earth. Literally, the term translates as "descent," based on the concept that the avatar descends from the celestial Vishnu.) Krishna was a cowherd who spent an idyllic existence tending his cows, fluting, and sporting with beautiful herdswomen. His favorite lover was Radha. In *Krishna and Radha in a Pavilion* (FIG. 25-3), the couple sit naked on a bed beneath a jeweled pavilion in a lush garden. Krishna gently touches Radha's breast while looking directly into her face. Radha shyly averts her gaze. It is night, the time of illicit trysts, and the dark monsoon sky momentarily lights up with a lightning flash indicating the moment's electric passion. Lightning is one of the standard symbols used in Rajput paintings for sexual excitement.

In its realism, this picture, painted either at Kangra or Guler about a century later than the Basohli painting, relates stylistically to the Mughal tradition (FIG. 25-1). It shares with the Mughal paintings naturalistically proportioned individuals who participate in realistic settings. The artist who created *Krishna and Radha in a Pavilion* took great care to depict details accurately, as seen in the mango tree, the palm leaves, and the designs on the bed textiles. The love between Krishna and Radha is a model for the love, or *bhakti,* devotees felt for the deity. The story of Krishna and Radha's love was told in *Gita Govinda* or *Song of the Herdsman,* by Jayadeva, a twelfth-century poet. The poem inspired devotion by Krishna worshipers and was the source for hundreds of paintings.

THE RULER AS BRITISH GENTLEMAN The maharaja (a term meaning "great king") Jaswant Singh ruled Jodhpur in Rajasthan from 1873 to 1895, when the British controlled India. By this time, India's rulers and citizenry long had been involved in adapting to British or, more generally, Western culture and ideas. When the maharaja sat for his portrait (FIG. 25-4), he chose to sit alone in an ordinary chair, rather than on a throne, with his arm resting on a simple table with a bouquet and a book on it. In other words, he posed like an ordinary British gentleman in his sitting room.

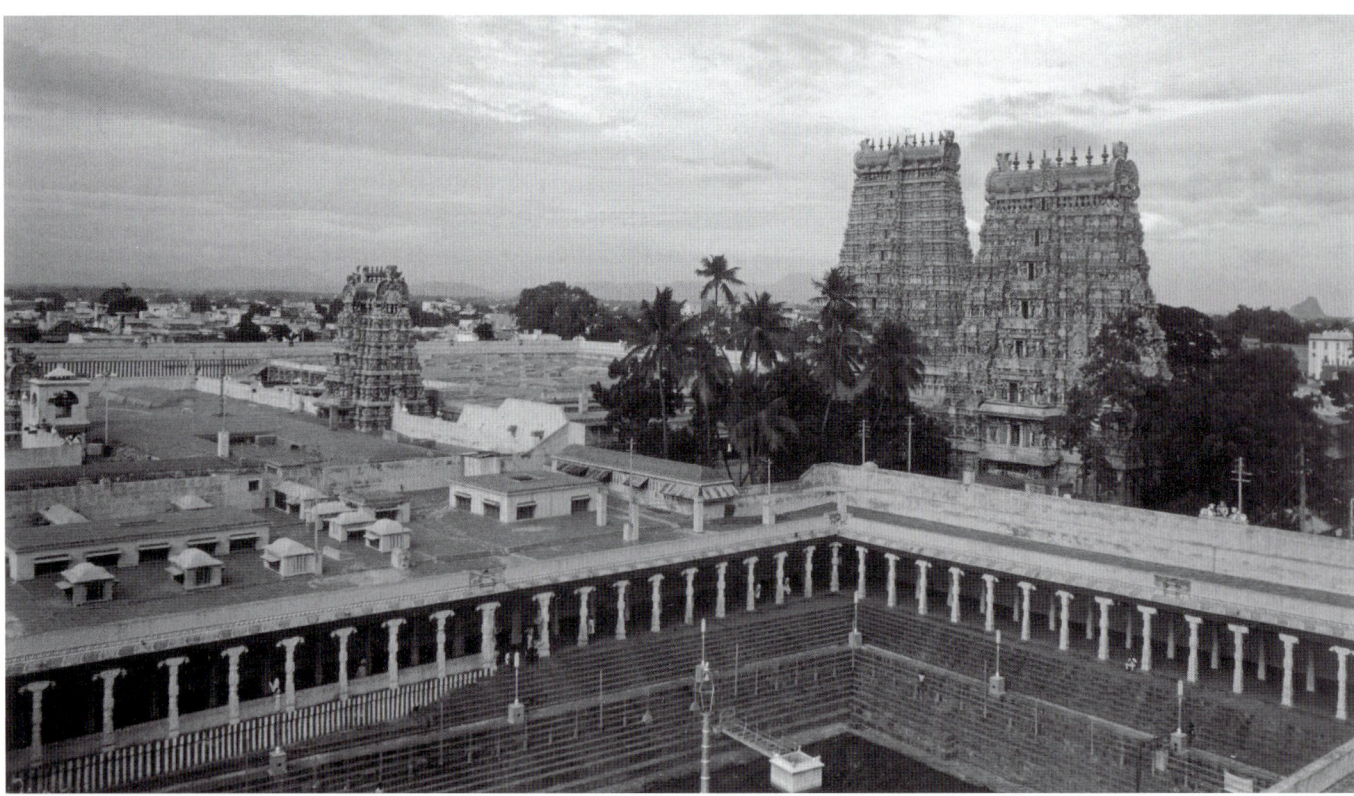

25-5 Great Temple, Madurai, India, seventeenth century.

Yet the painting leaves no question of the maharaja's regal presence and pride. His powerful chest and arms, along with the sword and his leather riding boots, indicate his abilities as a warrior and hunter. His curled beard, indicating fierceness and intended as menacing, and unflinching gaze record his confidence. Perhaps the two necklaces he wears best exemplify the combination of his two worlds. One necklace is a bib of huge emeralds and diamonds, the heritage of the wealth and splendor of his family's rule. The other, a wide gold band with a cameo, is the Order of the Star of India, a high honor his British overlords bestowed on him.

The interest in realism in Indian paintings reached a climax in works such as *Maharaja Jaswant Singh of Marwar*. The artist copied the maharaja's portrait from a photograph, thus producing a very realistic image of the ruler. Indian artists sometimes even painted directly on top of the photographs. Photography arrived in India at an early date; in 1840, just one year after its invention in Paris, the daguerreotype had been introduced in Calcutta. Indian artists readily adopted the new medium, not just to produce portraits but also to record landscapes and monuments.

Architecture

CITY-SIZED TEMPLE COMPLEXES The Nayak rulers, once vassals of the Vijayanagara kings, came to power with their former overlords' defeat and continued Hindu rule in the far south of India during the seventeenth and eighteenth centuries. Construction of some of the largest temple complexes in India occurred during this period. The builders of these huge complexes expanded them outward from the center by erecting ever larger enclosure walls, punctuated by directional *gopuras* (gateway towers). Positioned like boxes within boxes, each set of walls had taller gopuras than those of the previous wall, the towers reaching monumental size and dwarfing the actual central temples. The outer gopuras of the Great Temple at Madurai (FIG. **25-5**) stand about one hundred fifty feet tall. Also typical of late temples are large and numerous *mandapas* (pillared halls), as well as great water tanks the worshipers used for ritual bathing. Such temples were, and continue to be, almost independent cities, with thousands of pilgrims, worshipers, merchants, and priests flocking from far and near to the many yearly festivals hosted by the temples.

THAILAND

Southeast Asians practiced both Buddhism and Hinduism (see Chapter 6), but by the thirteenth century, Hinduism was dying out and Buddhism was dominating much of the mainland. Two prominent Buddhist kingdoms came to power in Thailand during the thirteenth and early fourteenth centuries. Historians date the beginning of the Sukhothai kingdom to 1292, the year King Ramkhamhaeng (r. 1279–1299) erected a four-sided stele bearing the first inscription written in the Thai language (see "King Ramkhamhaeng and the Thai Nation," page 798). (The kingdom shares its name with its major city and with the period involved.) Sukhothai's political dominance was, however, short lived. Ayuthaya, a city founded in central Thailand in 1350, quickly became the more powerful kingdom and warred sporadically with other states in Southeast Asia until the mid-eighteenth century. The art produced at Sukhothai, often of high quality and exhibiting great imagination, set a standard for Thai art to the present.

THE MONASTERY OF THE GREAT RELIC   At the center of Sukhothai stood Wat Mahathat (FIG. **25-6**), the city's most important Buddhist monastery (wats). Although largely in ruins today, Wat Mahathat's major features are clear. The central monument, a stupa, housed a relic of the Buddha (Mahathat means "Great Relic"). Although not a circular mound like earlier Indian stupas (see FIGS. 6-5 and 6-9), the Mahathat stupa had a similar function—to enshrine relics. A central lotus-bud tower and eight surrounding towers stand on the stupa's lower podium. Only a small portion of the brick structure's stucco decoration remains today. In front were halls (vihan) with walls and roof of brick, stucco, wood, and ceramic tiles. These do not survive, but the heavy stone pillars still stand. Two monumental standing Buddha images flank the stupa, each tightly enclosed in a brick building (mondop). Numerous other smaller stupas and towers, almost all reduced to their brick foundations, stand scattered in the area.

WALKING BUDDHAS   The Thai people revere the distinctive type of Buddha image that developed at Sukhothai as the city's crowning artistic achievement. The Sukhothai Buddhas are highly idiosyncratic. A flame leaps from the top of their heads, and a sharp nose projects from their rounded faces. A clinging robe reveals fluid rounded limbs and inflated bodies. Although images in stone exist, the Sukhothai artists handled bronze best, a material well suited to the forms' elasticity. The Sukhothai walking-Buddha statuary type (FIG. **25-7**) does not occur elsewhere in Buddhist art. In *Walking Buddha,* the Buddha strides forward, raising his heel off the ground, his left arm raised with the hand held in the fear-not gesture of a deity encouraging worshipers to come forward in reverence. The right arm hangs loosely, seemingly without muscles or joints, like an elephant trunk. The Sukhothai artists intended the body type to suggest a supernatural being. It expresses the Buddha's beauty and perfection.

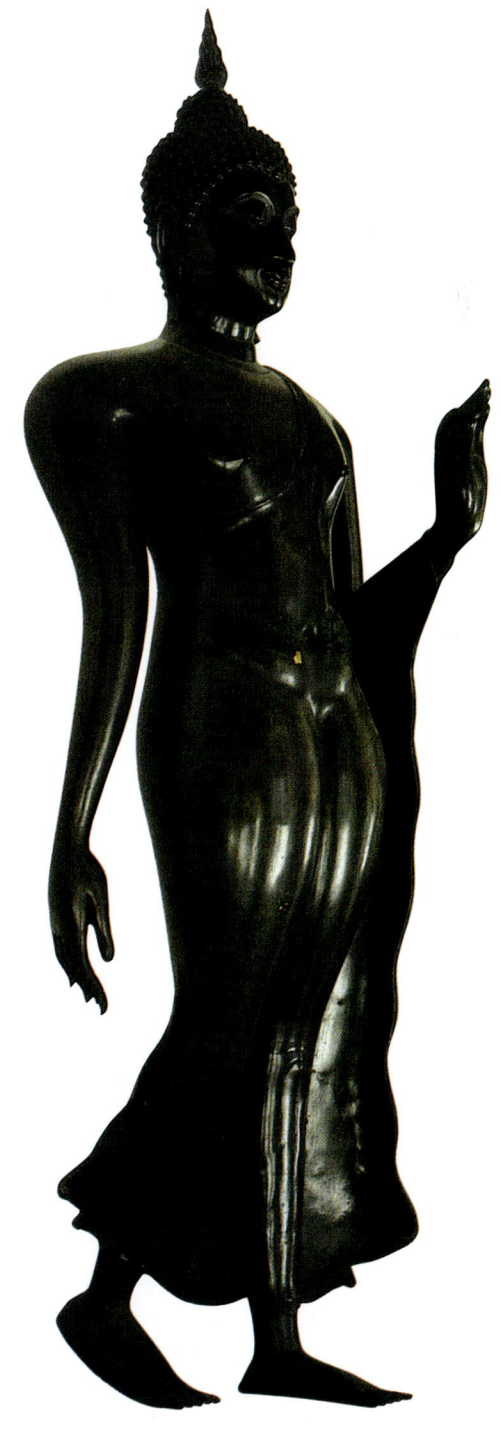

25-6 Wat Mahathat, Sukhothai, Thailand, fourteenth century.

25-7 *Walking Buddha,* from Sukhothai, Thailand, fourteenth century. Bronze, 7′ 2½″ high. Wat Bechamabopit, Bangkok.

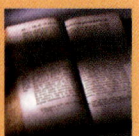

King Ramkhamhaeng and the Thai Nation

The first and most important document written in the Thai language is the so-called Inscription Number 1, dated 1292, carved into a stele found at Sukhothai in the eighteenth century and brought to Bangkok by King Mongkut. Researchers cannot identify the original location of the stele at Sukhothai, as the site was largely abandoned when Mongkut discovered it, but they do know that King Ramkhamhaeng set up the stele. The inscription constitutes Thailand's intellectual foundation and begins as follows:

> My father's name was Sri Indraditya. My mother's name was Nang Suang. My elder brother's name was Ban Muang. We were five brothers and sisters of the same womb, three boys and two girls. . . . When I grew up to nineteen years, Khun Sam Chon, Chief of Muang Chot, came to clash with Muang Tak. My father went to fight Khun Sam Chon on the left. . . . Khun Sam Chon charged in force. My father's people fled, scattered in confusion. I fled not. I rode the elephant Nakabol. I drove in before my father. . . . Khun Sam Chon fled in defeat. So my father gave me the name of Phra [an honorific title] Ram Khamhaeng, for I had thrust Khun Sam Chon's elephant.[1]

Ramkhamhaeng means "Rama the strong." After saving his father's fledgling kingdom, Ramkhamhaeng went on to thrust the kingdom of Sukhothai, centered around the city of the same name, into historical prominence. In the inscription, the king describes Sukhothai as having monasteries, many Buddha images, and a stone platform for preaching. He also mentions he had planted groves of many different kinds of trees— palm, coconut, jackfruit, mango, and tamarind. According to Ramkhamhaeng, the city drew people to its festivals, when he would light candles and set off fireworks.

In his inscription, Ramkhamhaeng also boasts, "In the lifetime of King Ram Khamhaeng, this Muang [city] Sukhothai is good. In the water there are fish, in the fields there is rice."[2] In fact, scholars regard the Sukhothai kingdom, although politically dominant for only about a century and a half, as defining a golden period in Thai history. In this time, the paternalistic nature of Thai kingship took form. The king acted like a father to his people; they regarded themselves as his children. Theravada Buddhism also became dominant in Thailand during this period, and Thai art reached levels of perfection rarely matched since.

[1] *Stone Inscriptions of Sukhothai,* trans. H. R. H. Prince Wan Waithayakon (Bangkok: The Siam Society, 1965), 9.

[2] Ibid.

BANGKOK'S *EMERALD BUDDHA*   A second distinctive Buddha image from northern Thailand is the *Emerald Buddha* (FIG. 25-8), the most famous and important statue in Thailand today. Housed in Bangkok in an *ubosoth,* or ordination hall, in the Emerald Temple on the Royal Palace grounds, the image is not only revered by the Thais, but also is the reason thousands of foreign tourists visit Bangkok each year.

The sculpture is small, only about thirty inches tall. It first appears in historical records in 1434 in northern Thailand, where Buddhist chronicles record its story. The chronicles state that the Buddha image was covered in plaster, and thus no one knew it was made of green stone. A lightning bolt caused some of the plaster to flake off, disclosing its gemlike nature. Taken by various rulers to a series of cities in northern Thailand and in Laos for more than three hundred years, the small image finally reached Bangkok in 1778 in the possession of the founder of the present Thai royal dynasty.

The *Emerald Buddha* is not carved from an actual emerald, but is probably green jade, yet its nature as a gemstone gives it unusual power. The magical gem enables the universal king, or *chakravartin,* possessing the statue to bring the rains. The historical Buddha renounced his secular destiny for that of the spiritual life. Yet, his likeness carved from the gem of a universal king allows fulfillment of the Buddha's royal destiny as well. The Buddha also can be regarded as the universal king. Thus, the combination of the sacred and the secular in the small image explains its symbolic power. The Thai king dresses the *Emerald Buddha* during the year alternately in a monk's robe and a king's robe (in FIG. 25-8 the Buddha wears

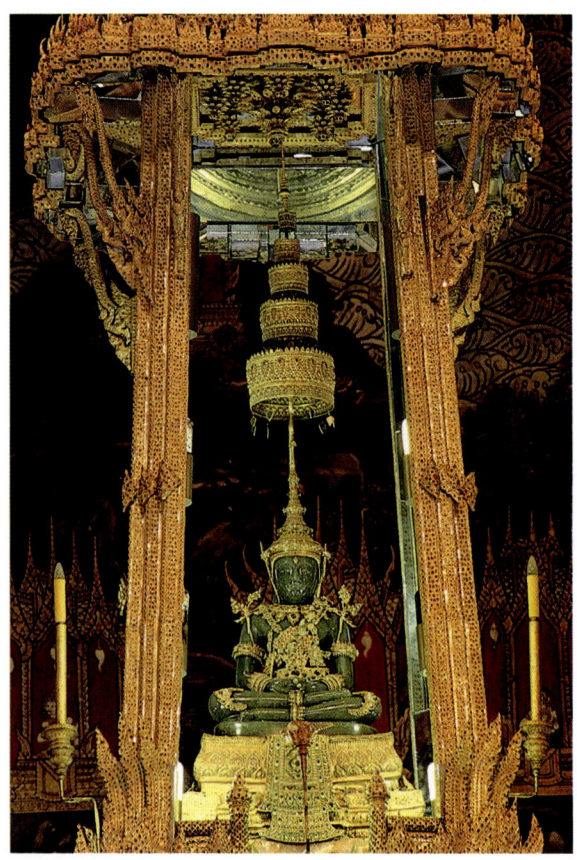

25-8   *Emerald Buddha,* ubosoth of Emerald Temple, Bangkok, Thailand, fifteenth century. Jade or jasper, 2′ 6″ high.

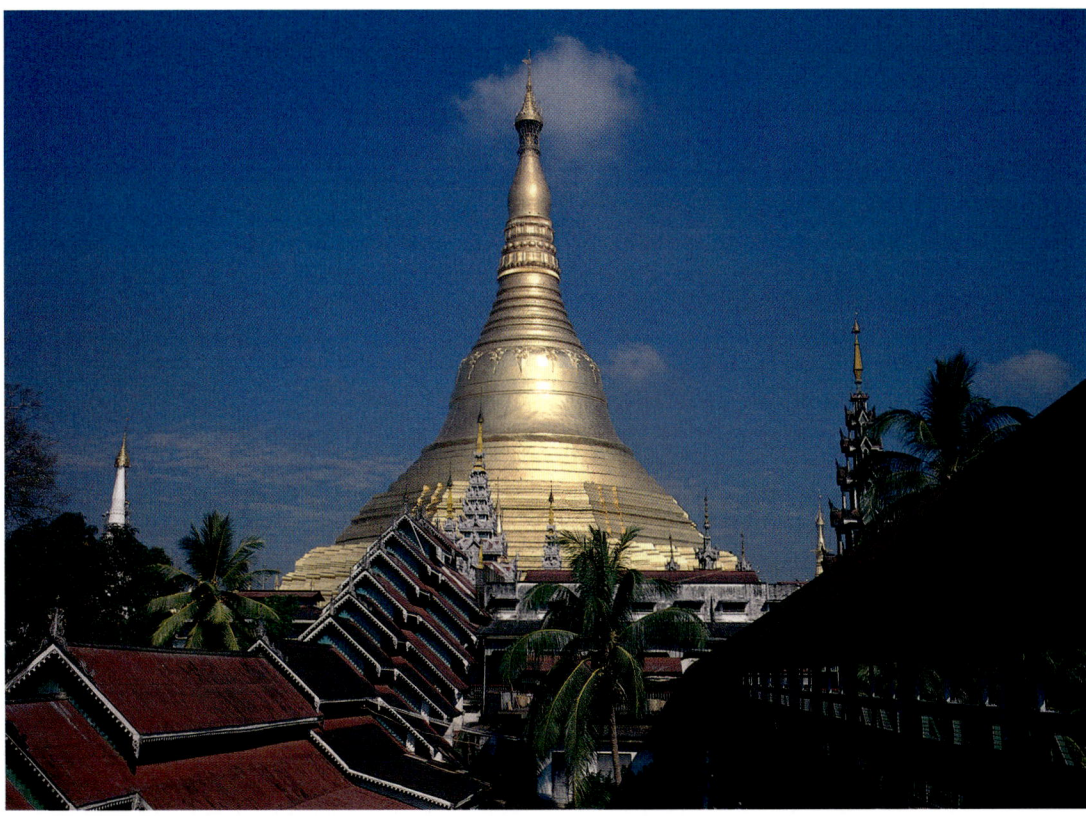

25-9 Schwedagon Pagoda, Rangoon (Yangon), Burma (Myanmar), fourteenth century or earlier (rebuilt several times). Stupa, gold, silver, and jewel encrusted, approx. 344′ high. Top of stupa, gold ball inlaid with 4,351 diamonds, one approx. 76 carats.

the royal garment), reflecting the image's dual nature and accentuating that it symbolizes both Buddha and king. The Thai king possessing the image therefore has both religious and secular authority.

BURMA

RANGOON'S GOLD-PLATED STUPA Burma, like Thailand, is overwhelmingly a Theravada Buddhist country today. Important Buddhist monasteries and monuments dot the countryside. In fact, one of the largest stupas in the world is the Shwedagon Pagoda (FIG. **25-9**) in Rangoon. (*Pagoda* reflects the European pronunciation of a local Indian word for stupa.) It houses two of the Buddha's hairs, traditionally said to have been brought to Burma by merchants who received them from the Buddha himself. The Burmese rebuilt this highly revered stupa several times. Renowned for the gold, silver, and jewels encrusting its surface, the Shwedagon Stupa stands three hundred forty-four feet high. Its upper part is covered with thirteen thousand one hundred fifty-three plates of gold, each about a foot square. At the very top is a seven-tiered umbrella crowned with a gold ball inlaid with four thousand three hundred fifty-one diamonds, one weighing seventy-six carats. This great wealth was a gift to the Buddha from the Burmese laypeople to produce merit. The stupa is at the center of an enormous complex of buildings, including wooden shrines filled with Buddha images. Shops selling all sorts of foods and gifts line the lengthy entrance stairs. Here, worshipers buy flowers, candles, and incense, gifts given to the Buddha for many centuries.

VIETNAM

VIETNAM'S MASTER CERAMICISTS Vietnam's art history is particularly complex, as it reveals both an Indian-related art and culture, broadly similar to the rest of Southeast Asia, and a unique and intense relationship with China's art and culture. Vietnamese ceramic tradition goes back to the Han period (206 B.C.–A.D. 220), when the Chinese began to govern the northern area of Vietnam. China directly controlled Vietnam for a thousand years, and early Vietnamese ceramics closely reflected Chinese wares. But during the Ly (1009–1225) and Tran (1225–1400) dynasties, when Vietnam had regained its independence, Vietnamese potters developed an array of ceramic shapes, designs, and glazes that brought their wares to the highest levels of quality and creativity. Comparing Chinese and Vietnamese ceramics of these periods reveals that the spontaneity, power, and playfulness of the Vietnamese wares contrast with the formality and perfection of the Chinese wares.

Burma, Thailand, and Vietnam all had important ceramic traditions. These included a variety of architectural ceramics, such as roof tiles for decorating their wood and brick buildings, as well as ceramic wares, such as dishes, jars, and pots. Thailand and Vietnam in particular produced great quantities of ceramic wares, especially during the fifteenth and sixteenth centuries, when they exported ceramics throughout Southeast Asia and to the Middle East (see "Ceramic Trade in Southeast Asia during the Fifteenth to Seventeenth Centuries," page 800).

In the fourteenth century, the Vietnamese began producing and exporting underglaze-cobalt-painted wares modeled on the blue-and-white ceramics first produced in China (see "Chinese Porcelain," Chapter 26, page 807). A sixteenth-century dish with two mynah birds on a flowering branch

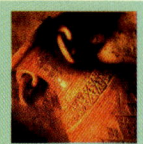

Ceramic Trade in Southeast Asia during the Fifteenth to Seventeenth Centuries

The vast majority of early Vietnamese ceramics (FIG. 25-10) have not been found in Vietnam but in Indonesia, particularly on the islands of Java and Sulawesi, and in the Philippines. The Vietnamese exported their ceramic wares to Southeast Asian island markets as early as the fourteenth century but primarily during the fifteenth through seventeenth centuries, when Vietnamese ceramics reached markets even more distant—the Middle East, Egypt, Turkey, and Persia. In the Middle East, Vietnamese ceramics entered royal collections, while in the Southeast Asian islands they served as grave goods buried with the dead, accounting for their survival today.

Chinese and European—primarily English, Dutch, and Portuguese—merchants traded the Vietnamese wares, along with ceramics from China and Thailand. According to the inventory of a Dutch ship that arrived in Java in 1669, the ship's cargo included three hundred eighty-one thousand two hundred Vietnamese ceramic bowls.

Recent finds of shipwrecks with their cargoes of ceramic wares intact, discovered in the waters along the mainland coasts and around the islands in the South China Sea, are helping to clarify the dating and interrelationships among the various ceramic traditions. Before investigation of the shipwrecks began, art historians had to rely on buried Vietnamese ceramics, which rarely could be dated. It was usually impossible to know dates of the individual pieces gathered together in the burial. Researchers thus cannot ascertain whether the buried ceramics date from different centuries or are contemporaneous.

The recent shipwreck finds have shown that many of the assumptions based on stylistic analysis of Southeast Asian ceramics were incorrect. Researchers often can date shipwrecks rather precisely, especially if any wood remains that they can analyze using radiocarbon dating techniques. The ceramics in shipwrecks, then, can be placed together at a precise moment. Wrecks have revealed groupings of ceramics that, until now, were considered separated in time. The technology of underwater archaeology is leading to new understandings of the entire Vietnamese ceramic tradition.

(FIG. **25-10**) demonstrates the painter's spontaneity and sureness. The artist suggested the foliage by squiggles and looped lines, not raising the brush frequently off the surface. This technique facilitated rapid production and, combined with the painter's control, allowed a fresh and unique design. Either lifting the brush or working more slowly would have yielded a very different result.

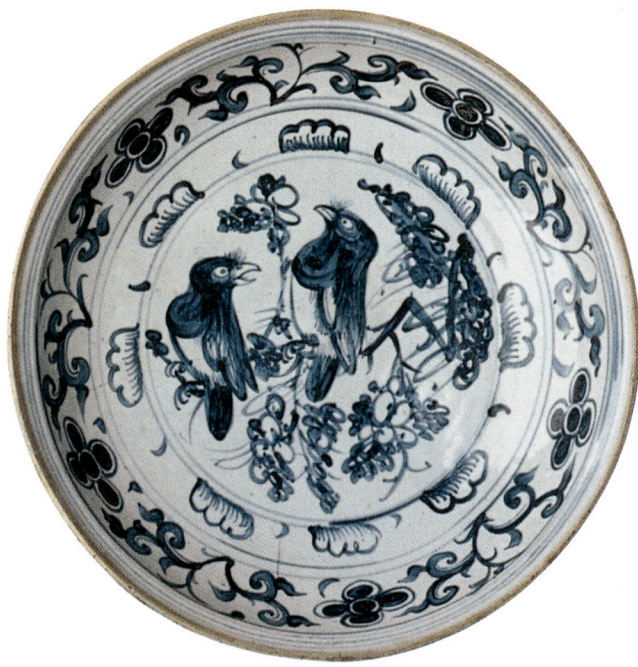

25-10   Dish with two mynah birds on flowering branch, from Vietnam, sixteenth century. Stoneware painted with underglaze-cobalt, 1' 2½" in diameter. Pacific Asia Museum, Pasadena, California.

CONTEMPORARY ART IN INDIA AND SOUTHEAST ASIA

LOCAL AND INTERNATIONAL ART   Contemporary art in India and Southeast Asian countries falls into two general categories—art made following the local traditions and art created for the international market. In India, traditional artists work at the village level, making images of deities out of inexpensive materials, such as clay, plaster, and papier-mâché, for local use. Artists in the cities use these same materials to produce sometimes elaborate religious tableaus, such as depictions of the goddess Durga killing the buffalo demon (see "Goddess Worship in India," page 793), during the annual ten-day Durga Festival in Calcutta. Participants in the festival often ornament the tableaus with thousands of colored electric lights. The most popular art form for religious imagery, however, is color lithography, brightly colored prints sold for only a few rupees each. In the Buddhist countries of Southeast Asia (Thailand, Cambodia, Burma, and Laos), artists continue to produce thousands of images of the Buddha, primarily in bronze, for worship in homes, businesses, and temples.

Artists working in the international style, however, hope their creations will be bought as art objects for decorating homes or for display in museums around the world. Indeed, many of these artists received their training in schools in Europe or the United States and, although Asian born, work outside their home countries. They face one of the fundamental quandaries of many contemporary Asian artists—how to identify themselves and situate their work between local and international, traditional and modern, and non-Western and Western cultures.

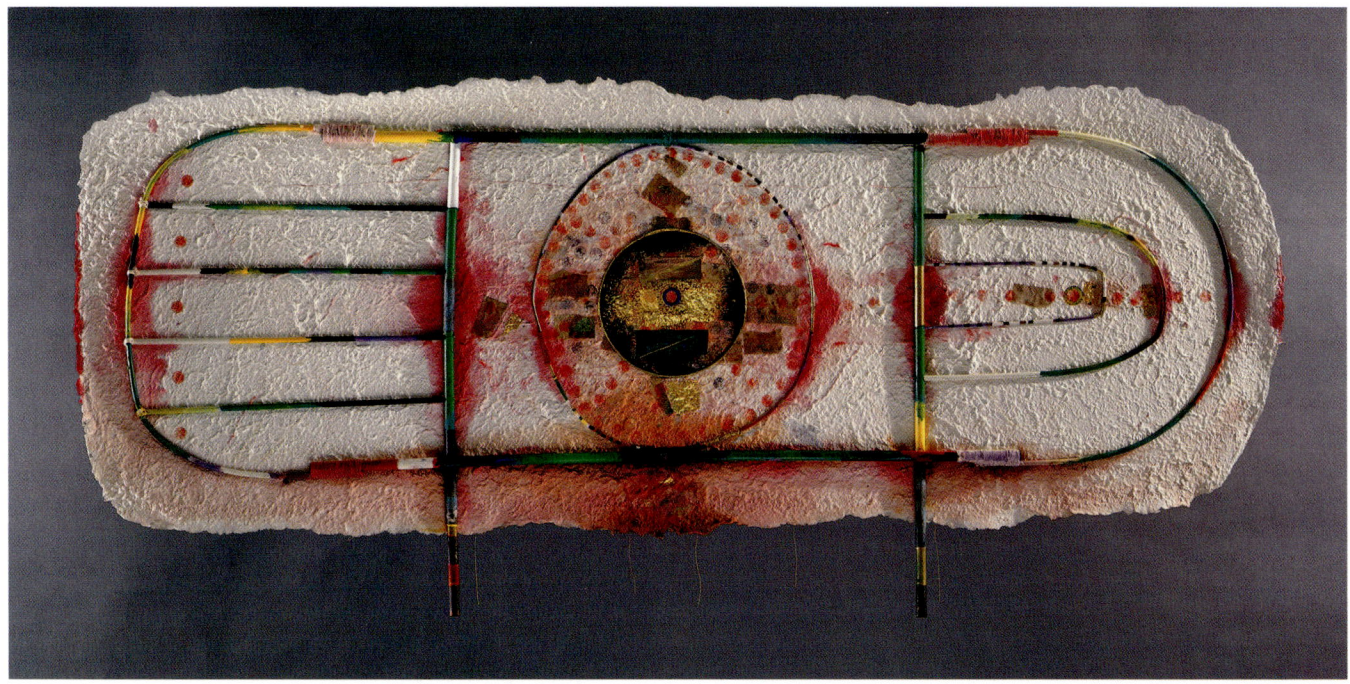

25-11 KAMOL TASSANANCHALEE, *Buddha Footprint, Nang-Yai Series II,* 1982. Handmade paper, acrylic, gold leaf, ink, thread, and wood dowels, approximately $2\frac{1}{2}' \times 5'$. The National Cultural Center of Thailand Collection, Bangkok.

THE BUDDHA'S FOOTPRINT   KAMOL TASSANAN-CHALEE is a Thai artist who has lived and worked in both Los Angeles and Bangkok since the 1970s. His 1982 work, *Buddha Footprint, Nang-Yai Series II* (FIG. **25-11**), is a mixed-media sculpture of a type he developed for two decades. *Nang-yai,* which literally translates as "large-leather," is the Thai term for shadow puppets cut from large pieces of leather and held above the heads of performers by two sticks tied to a wood frame. Kamol (Thai surnames are the second name but individuals are referred to by their first name) transformed this Thai folk art by using different materials, including handmade paper, acrylic, and ink. Here, he created a footprint of the Buddha, a common focus of Buddhist worship, suggesting

the five toes and rounded heel using the wood frame. The central circle reflects the wheel *(chakra)* that sometimes marks the Buddha's feet as a supernatural sign or lakshana. Kamol states in the catalogue of his recent retrospective exhibition, "The themes expressed in my artwork are developed from my life experience, which is a balance between two hemispheres of the globe. With the stable mind of the Thai artist, I am on my own journey, combining East and West together in my works."[3] As do many contemporary Asian artists, Kamol feels he bridges cultures, as well as places, and uses this very modern experience to create art that is both Thai and American — or, in a word, international.

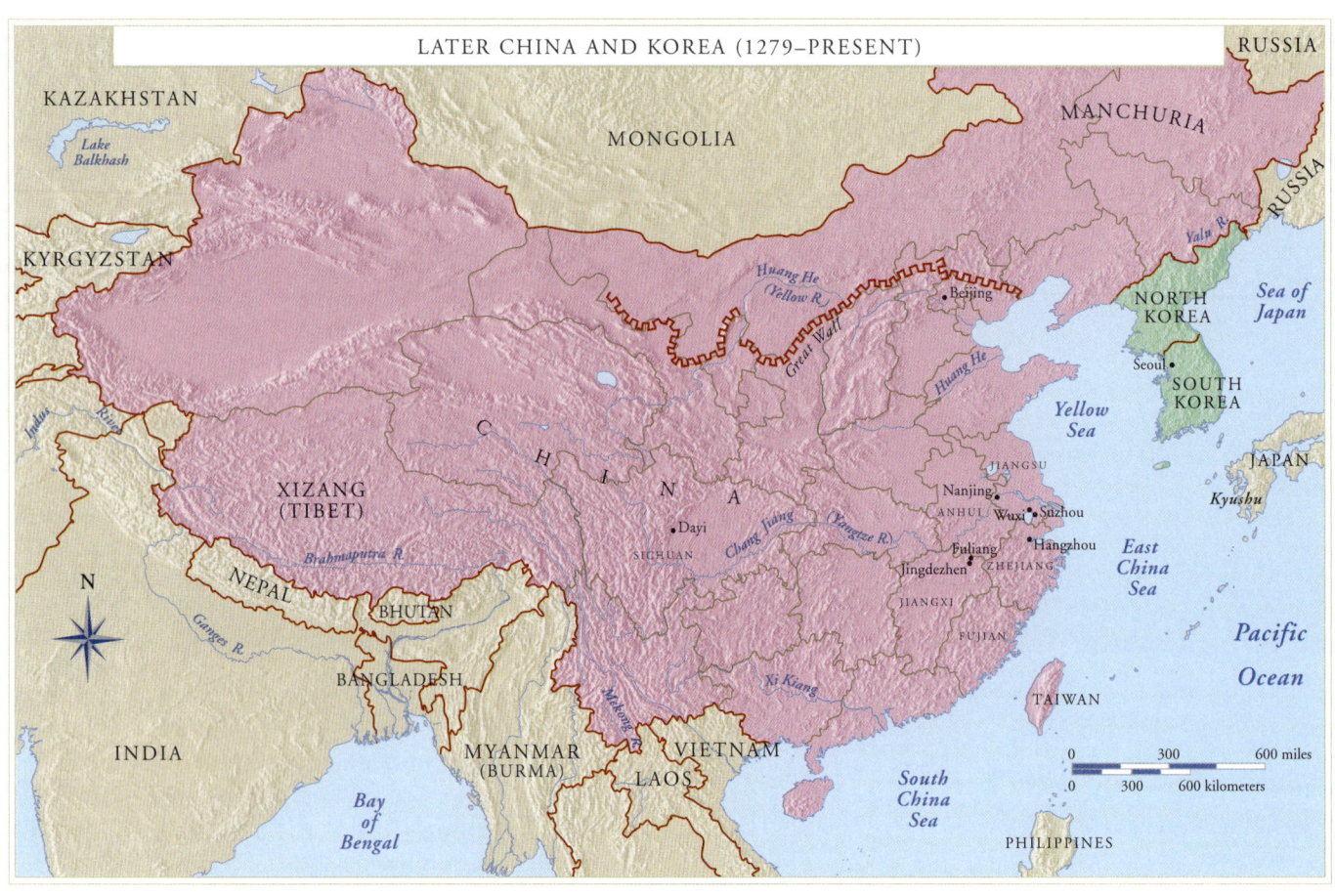

LATER CHINA AND KOREA (1279–PRESENT)

	1279	1300	1368	1392	1450	1500	1644
CHINA	YUAN DYNASTY		MING DYNASTY				QING DYNASTY
KOREA				CHOSON DYNASTY			

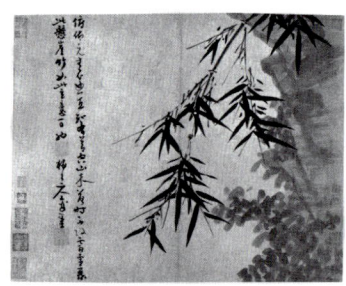

Wu Zhen
Bamboo, 1350

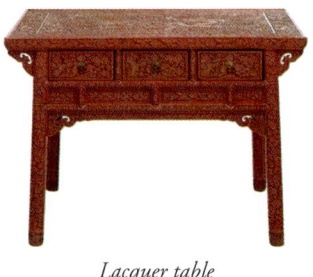

Lacquer table
ca. 1426–1435

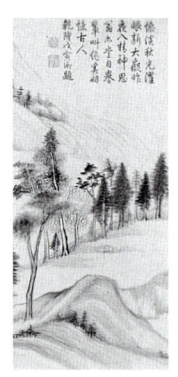

Dong Qichang, Autumn Mountains
early seventeenth century

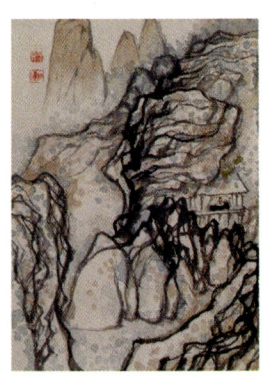

Shitao, landscape
late seventeenth century

Mongols seize power in China, 1279

Jingdezhen, China, established as ceramic center, ca. 1325

Suzhou, China, begins to flourish as cultural center, 1450

Portuguese reach China by ship, 1514

Manchus seize power
in China, 1644

26

INCURSION, RESTORATION, AND TRANSFORMATION

THE ART OF LATER CHINA AND KOREA

1700	1800	1911	1945	1949		
		REPUBLIC OF CHINA		PEOPLE'S REPUBLIC OF CHINA		
		JAPANESE RULE	POSTWAR PARTITION			

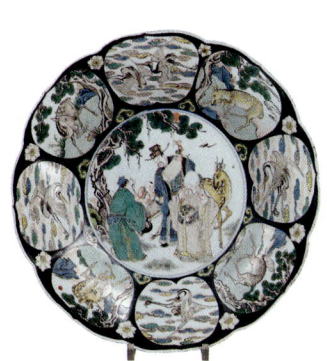

*Dish with lobed rim
ca. 1700*

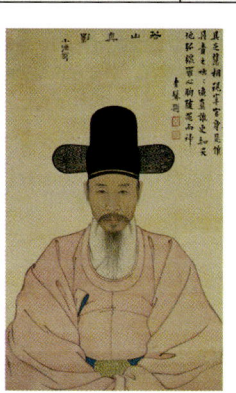

*Yi Chae-gwan, Portrait
of Kang Yi-o, early
nineteenth century*

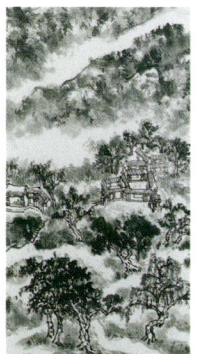

*Huang Binhong
Recluse Dwelling on
Xixia Mountian, 1954*

European trade begins to flourish, ca. 1720   Japan annexes Korea, 1910

Abdication of China's last emperor, 1912

Korea given postwar independence from Japan, 1945

Republic of Korea (South Korea) and Democratic People's Republic of Korea (North Korea) established, 1948

People's Republic of China established, 1949

Korean War between North and South Korea, 1950–1953

CHINA

Ancient Chinese culture laid the foundations for later east Asian civilization. It provided a system of writing; fundamental tenets and ideals in philosophy and religion; numerous basic technologies; standard aesthetic principles; and the formats, materials, basic forms, and subjects of art and architecture (see Chapter 7). All of these had attained a high level of development well before the end of the first millennium.

Yuan Dynasty (1279–1368)

In 1279, the Song dynasty crumbled beneath the continued onslaughts of the Mongol armies led by Genghis Khan's grandson, Kublai Khan (1215–1294), China's self-proclaimed emperor and founder of the Yuan dynasty. The Mongols, nomads from beyond China's northern borders, overwhelmed areas from central Europe to modern Iraq from roughly 1210 through the mid-fourteenth century. Yuan, the invaders' dynasty, dominated China only until 1368, yet it profoundly affected the country's culture and particularly the art of painting.

SU DONGPO AND THE LITERATI   In the late Northern Song period, new notions of value in painting had begun to shape what became a major force in Chinese art. These notions continued to gain momentum during the Yuan dynasty. The celebrated Song poet, amateur painter, and statesman Su Dongpo (1036–1101) led a theoretical attack against skillful representation and elegant compositional formulae as signs of value in painting. To Su, such characteristics merely showed the skills of professional painters and members of the court painting academy but were not true signs of elevated character. Instead, he championed less polished but more "sincere" efforts by scholar-amateurs, or *literati*. The literati were typically landed gentry whose educations earned them responsible positions in the bureaucracy or led them toward a life of reclusion and self-cultivation. Su supported their paintings as expressions of their elevated characters.

They achieved these results through learned allusions to antique styles, sometimes couched in deliberately awkward or naive forms. The scholar-amateurs painted primarily to express their moods and the philosophical ideals and religious beliefs they shared with others of their educational level and social status.

TEXTURED MOUNTAINS   Literati painting reached maturity in the Yuan dynasty, in part due to the social circumstances of some members of the literati class. Many scholar-painters chose to retreat to the provinces to avoid service under the Mongols, a group they considered barbarian usurpers, in Beijing where Kublai Khan had established his capital. Forced by their retirement to reappraise their place in the world, these artists no longer looked at a landscape as an idyllic retreat from the city. It had become a more integral part of their environment. This new intimacy is evident in *Dwelling in the Fuchun Mountains* (FIG. **26-1**) by one of the great Yuan literati painters, HUANG GONGWANG 1269–1354). Here, the painter replaced the misty atmosphere of the Southern Song landscapes (see FIG. 7-24) with massive forms richly textured with fibrous brush strokes. The rhythmic play of brush and ink renders the landscape's inner structure and momentum.

THE ART OF CALLIGRAPHY   Many literati paintings bear inscriptions (FIG. 26-6), sometimes covering a significant portion of their surfaces (see "Inscriptions on Chinese Paintings," page 805). In theory, the expressiveness of the painters' brushwork makes the literati paintings themselves close to calligraphy. This writing art depends for its effects on the controlled vitality of individual brush strokes and on the dynamic relationships of strokes within a character and among the characters themselves. Training in calligraphy was a fundamental part of the education and self-cultivation of Chinese scholars and officials.

BAMBOO AND THE GENTLEMAN   Markedly different in style from Huang Gongwang's paintings are those of

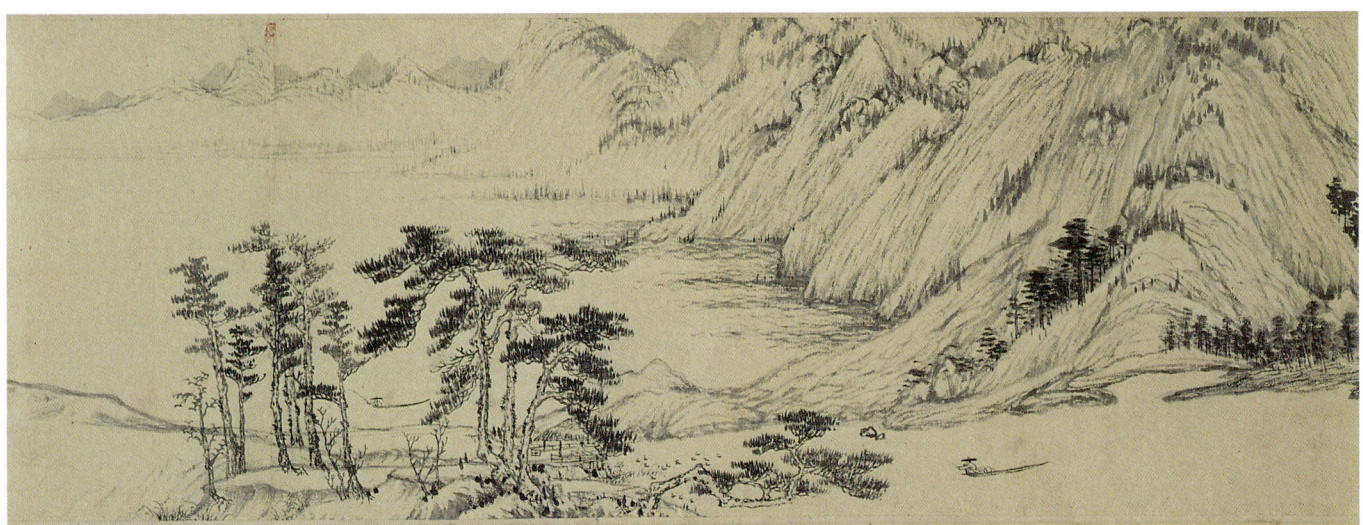

26-1 HUANG GONGWANG, *Dwelling in the Fuchun Mountains,* China, Yuan dynasty, 1347–1350. Section of a handscroll, ink on paper, 1′ 1″ high. National Palace Museum, Taipei.

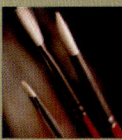

Inscriptions on Chinese Paintings

Many Chinese paintings bear *inscriptions,* texts written on the same surface as the picture, or *colophons,* written texts on attached pieces of paper or silk. Throughout Chinese history, close connections existed between writing and painting. Even the primary implements and materials for writing and drawing are the same—a round tapered brush, *india ink* (soot-based ink), and paper or silk.

Scholars sometimes refer to the calligraphic characters as *pictograms,* in the manner of early Egyptian hieroglyphics, and some basic characters indeed reveal such origins. However, the thousands of fully developed Chinese characters are best described as *logograms,* each character corresponding to one meaningful language unit. The brushing of characters in different styles—*calligraphy*—always has been a highly regarded art form in China and the rest of eastern Asia. Many stylistic variations exist. At the most formal extreme, each character is separated from the next and comprised of distinct straight and angular strokes. At the other extreme, the characters flow together as cursive abbreviations with many rounded forms. The inscriptions on the paintings by Wu Zhen (FIG. 26-2) and Dong Qichang (FIG. 26-6) show much of this range, although these examples do not include the most formal style.

A long theoretical tradition in China links pictures and texts, especially poems, metaphorically. Some ancient theorists even have said that poems were paintings without form, while paintings were poems with form—in other words, different ways to express the same observations, ideas, sentiments, and responses to nature. In a more concrete vein, famous poems frequently provided subjects for paintings, and poets composed poems inspired by paintings. Either practice might prompt inscriptions on art, some addressing painted subjects and others praising the painting's quality and the painter's character. Other inscriptions, some by the painters, simply explain the work's circumstances. Later admirers and owners of paintings often brushed on their own appreciative words.

Painters, inscribers, and even owners usually also added red seals (FIGS. 26-1, upper left, and 26-2, along the left edge) to identify themselves and their roles, using special forms of Chinese characters. With all of these textual additions, some long-admired paintings that have passed through many collections may seem too cluttered to Western eyes. However, the historical importance given to such inscriptions and ownership history has been a critical aspect of painting appreciation in China.

WU ZHEN (1280–1354), which are softer and more relaxed in manner. The Chinese at this time particularly favored paintings of bamboo (FIG. **26-2**), for which Wu is famous. The plant is a symbol of the ideal Chinese gentleman, who bends in adversity but does not break. Moreover, the pattern of bamboo leaves, like that of calligraphic script, provided

painters with an excellent opportunity to display brushwork proficiency.

THE INVENTION OF PORCELAIN   By the Yuan period, Chinese potters had extended their mastery to fully developed porcelains, a technically very demanding medium

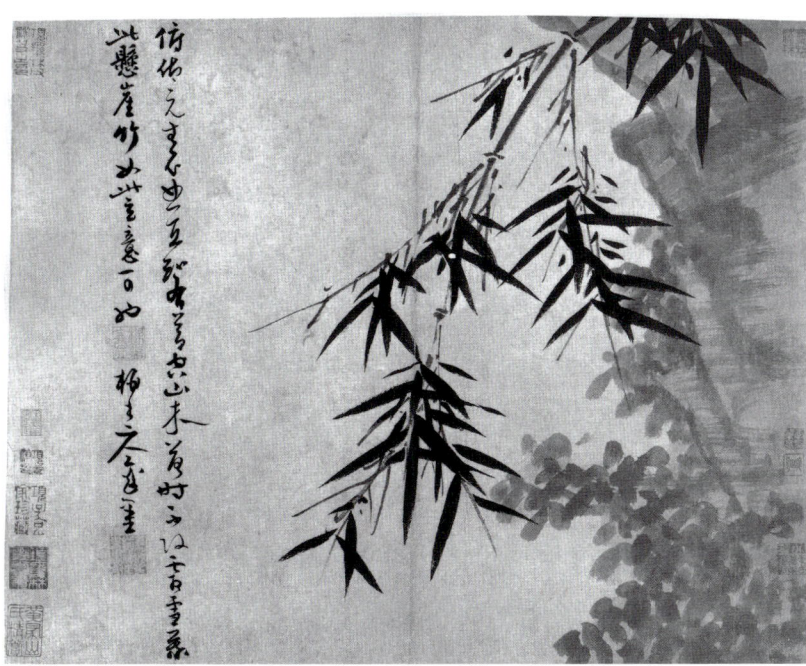

26-2   WU ZHEN, *Bamboo,* China, Yuan dynasty, 1350. Album leaf, ink on paper, 1′ 4″ × 1′ 9″. National Palace Museum, Taipei.

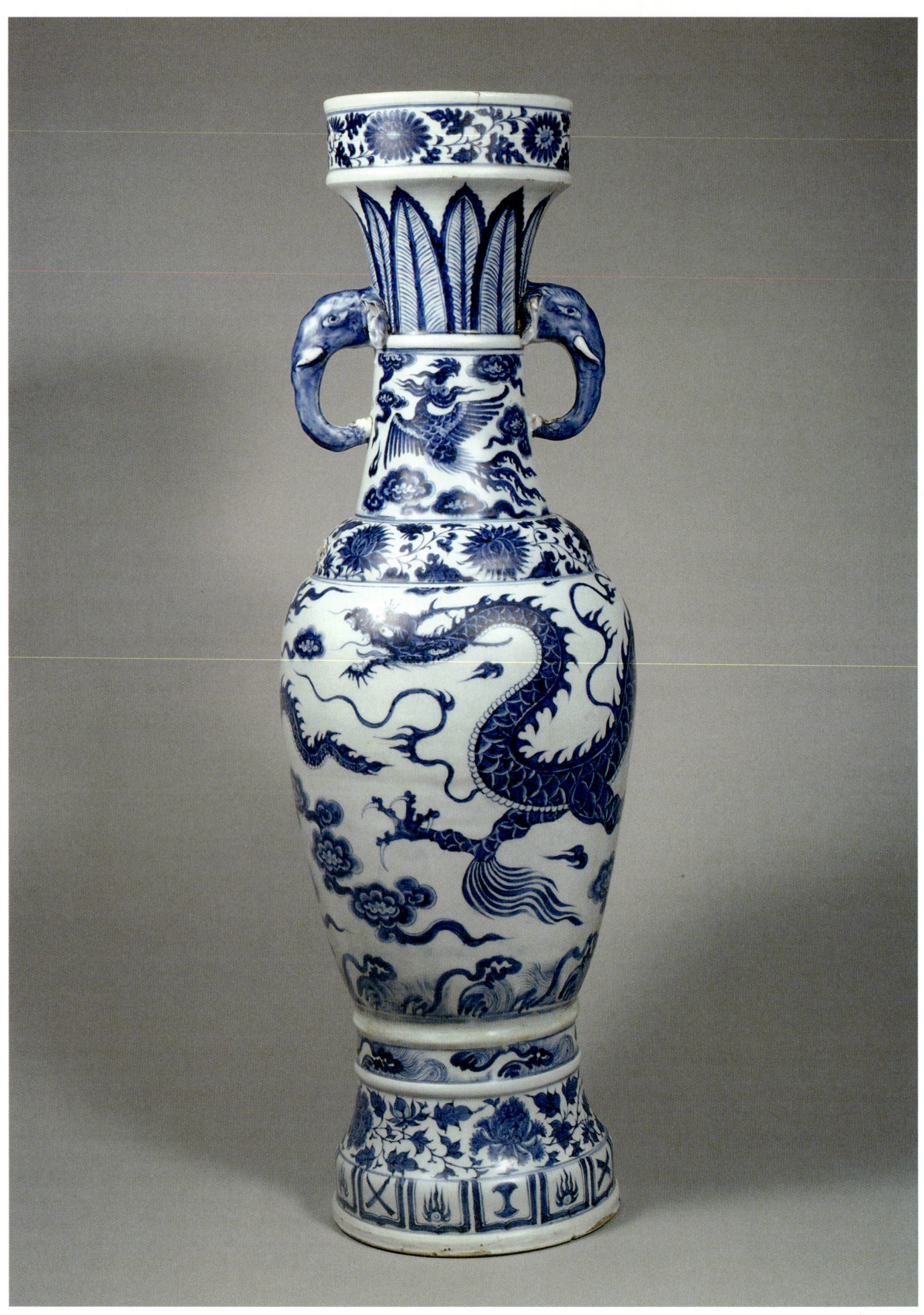

26-3 Temple vase, China, Yuan dynasty, 1351. White porcelain with cobalt blue underglaze, 2′ 1″ × 8⅛″. Percival David Foundation of Chinese Art, London.

Chinese Porcelain

Many scholars consider China's invention of porcelain (FIGS. 26-3 and 26-7) its greatest contribution to world material culture. No other Chinese objects have been so admired by the rest of the world, have inspired such imitation, or have penetrated so deeply into everyday life. Long imported by neighboring countries as luxury goods and treasures, Chinese porcelains later captured great attention in the West, where potters avidly sought the secrets of their creation. Success in replicating porcelain in the West did not occur until the early eighteenth century.

In China, primitive porcelains emerged during the Tang dynasty (618–907) and mature forms in the Yuan (1279–1368). Today, factories and individual potters worldwide produce porcelain in great quantities. Like stoneware (see "Chinese Earthenwares and Stonewares," Chapter 7, page 189), porcelain is fired at an extremely high temperature in a kiln (well over 2000 degrees Fahrenheit) until its clay body is fully fused into a dense hard substance resembling stone or glass. Liquids cannot pass into or through it. Unlike stoneware, however, porcelain is made from a fine white clay called *kaolin* mixed with ground *petuntse* (a type of feldspar). True porcelain is translucent and rings when struck.

The surfaces of most porcelains carry painted designs or pictures. The decorators work with finely ground minerals suspended in water and a binding agent (like glue). The minerals change color dramatically in the kiln. The painters apply some of the mineral colors to the clay surface before the main firing and then apply a clear glaze over them. Such *underglaze* decoration fully bonds to the piece in the kiln, but only a few colors are possible, because the raw materials must stand up to such intense heat. By far the most stable and widely used coloring agents for porcelains are cobalt compounds, which fire to an intense blue (see FIGS. 25-10 and 26-3). Much more rarely, the potters use copper compounds to produce stunning reds by carefully manipulating the kiln's temperature and oxygen content. To obtain a wider palette, ceramic decorators must paint on top of the glaze after the work has been fired (FIG. 26-7). The *overglaze* colors, or *enamels,* then fuse to the glazed surface in an additional firing at a much lower temperature. Enamels also offer glaze decorators a much brighter palette, with colors ranging from deep browns to brilliant reds and greens, but they do not have the durability of underglaze decoration.

(see "Chinese Porcelain," above). A tall temple vase from the Jingdezhen kilns (FIG. **26-3**), in a city section later named Fuliang, is one of a nearly identical pair dated by inscription to 1351. The inscription also says the vases, together with an incense burner, made up an altar set donated to a Buddhist temple as a prayer for peace, protection, and prosperity for the donor's family. The vase is one of the earliest dated examples of fine porcelain with cobalt blue underglaze decoration. It reveals the foundations for the technical brilliance of the potters and decorators at Jingdezhen, which during the Ming dynasty became the official source of porcelains for the court and government. The dramatic elephant-head handles of the Jingdezhen temple vase symbolize strength. The painted decoration consists of bands of floral motifs between broader zones containing favorable symbols. The two most important symbols are the phoenixes in the lower part of the neck and the dragons (compare FIG. 7-4) on the vessel's main body, both among clouds. These motifs may suggest the donor's high character or invoke prosperity blessings. Because of their vast power and associations with nobility and prosperity, the dragon and the phoenix also can symbolize the emperor and empress, respectively, and often appear on objects made for the imperial household. The dragon also may represent *yang,* the Chinese principle of active masculine energy, while the phoenix may represent *ying,* the principle of passive feminine energy, both permeating the universe in varying proportions.

Ming Dynasty (1368–1644)

In 1368, a popular uprising drove out the Mongol rulers, and from that date until 1644, the native Ming dynasty ruled China. During this time, court painting flourished and important regional schools emerged. The Ming court's lavish appetite for luxury goods also gave new impetus to brilliant technical achievement in the decorative arts.

THE ART OF LACQUER After the Ming rulers came to power, the court quickly established workshops to produce luxury goods under its direct supervision. Like the Yuan rulers, their Ming successors turned to the Jingdezhen kilns for fine porcelains. For objects in lacquered wood, including full-scale furniture, their patronage went to a large workshop known today as the Orchard factory. *Lacquer,* produced from the sap of the lacquer bush and often colored with mineral pigments, cures to great hardness and has a lustrous surface. Lacquer art has flourished in China from ancient times to the present. Skill in working lacquer already had reached very high technical standards by the fifteenth century. One of the

26-4   Table with drawers, China, Ming dynasty, ca. 1426–1435. Carved red lacquer on a wood core, 3′ 11″ long. Victoria and Albert Museum, London.

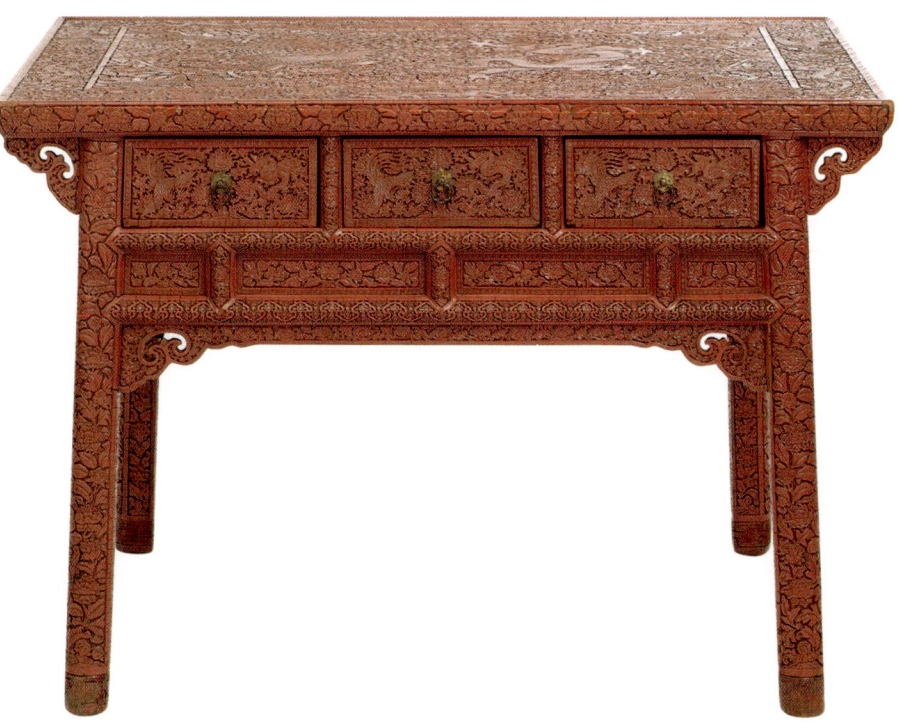

early masterpieces is a table with drawers (FIG. **26-4**) made in the Orchard factory between 1426 and 1435. The artist carved floral motifs, along with the dragon and phoenix imperial emblems, into the thick cinnabar-colored lacquer itself, which had to be built up in numerous layers. Other techniques for decorating lacquer include inlaying metals and lustrous materials, such as mother-of-pearl, and sprinkling gold powder into the still-wet lacquer. Such techniques also flourished in both Korea and Japan (see FIG. 27-10).

ZHE AND OTHER SCHOOLS   The painters at the Ming court took as their primary models the works of their Southern Song predecessors, such as those of Ma Yuan (see FIG. 7-24), but they produced their own variations. DAI JIN

(1388–1452) served at the court until his dismissal for a minor infraction, when he returned to his native city, Hangzhou. There he became extremely influential as the founder of the Zhe School of painting. As seen in *Fishermen* (FIG. **26-5**), the Zhe School painters adopted elements of the academic style developed in the Song Dynasty, especially the careful rendering of forms, sharp contrasts in ink tonalities, and a concern for atmosphere. But they handled these elements with greater looseness and freedom, replacing Ma Yuan's precise rendering of forms and fine lines with, as in this work, more rapid, expressive brush strokes. Likewise, in *Fishermen*, an asymmetrical weighting of foreground elements recalls Ma's pictorial precedents. But Dai's composition stresses a lively arrangement of forms over the careful representation

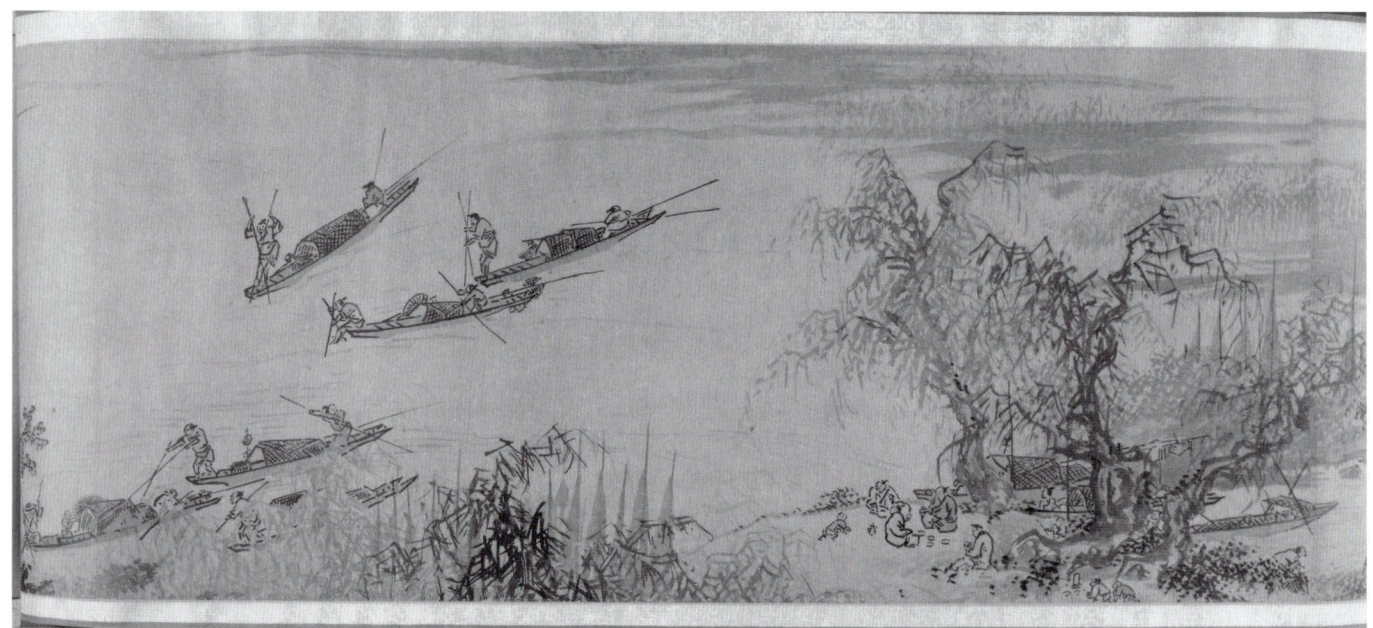

26-5   DAI JIN, *Fishermen*, China, Ming dynasty, fifteenth century. Detail of handscroll, ink and color on paper, 1′ 6$\frac{1}{8}$″ high. Freer Gallery of Art, Smithsonian Institution, Washington.

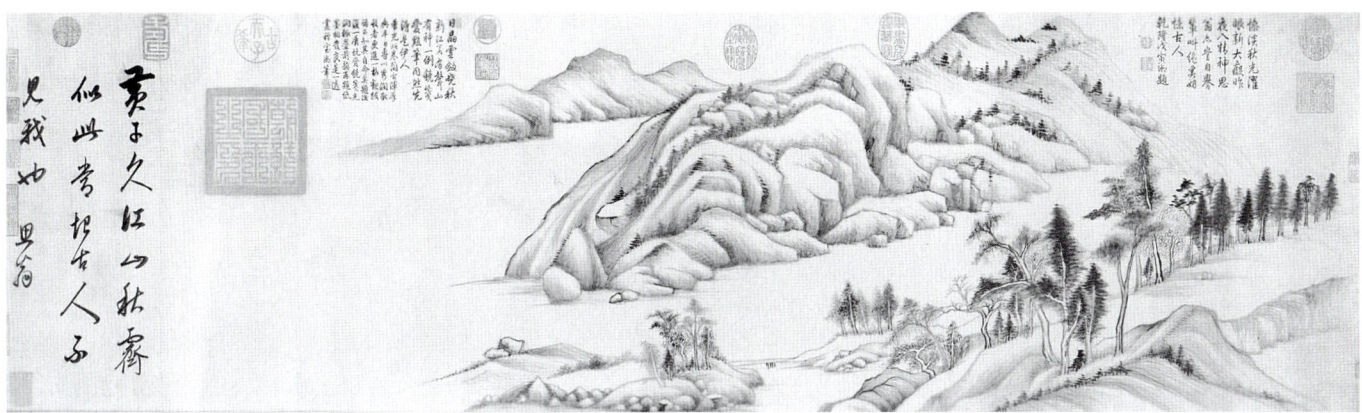

26-6 DONG QICHANG, *Autumn Mountains,* China, Ming dynasty, early seventeenth century. Handscroll, ink on paper, 1′ 3$\frac{1}{8}$″ × 4′ 5$\frac{7}{8}$″. Cleveland Museum of Art, Cleveland, Ohio (purchase from the J. H. Wade Fund).

of spatial recession for which the Southern Song painter was famous. Dai's approach here is especially congenial to his subject—a lively fleet of small fishing boats.

Other local schools of painting, such as those centered in Nanjing and in Suzhou, also assumed important roles. The Suzhou group included many highly educated amateur painters inspired by the Yuan literati painters. Professional artists, active in Suzhou and elsewhere, executed works that displayed great skill and spontaneity.

RADICAL COMPOSITIONS The influential critic, statesman, and artist DONG QICHANG (1555–1636) codified the distinction between scholar-amateur and academic-professional traditions rather artificially in writings at the end of the Ming period. Dong's glorification of the Yuan period's amateur, or literati, school reflected his own voracious study of and collecting of old paintings. His theories promoted creating an orthodoxy in painting that could be stifling, but his own works were true to his ideal of transforming old styles, rather than sterilely imitating them. In Dong's landscapes, he attempted to reveal the inner structure and momentum of nature, often radically reorganizing forms (FIG. **26-6**). He tilted and shifted ground planes, boldly arranging rocks and trees to emphasize repeated abstract shapes and textures without regard for natural scale and surface qualities. Thus, his paintings may seem arbitrarily distorted or even crude. What they lack in harmony of surface or representational accuracy, however, is more than made up in qualities of monumentality and power.

Qing Dynasty (1644–1911)

The Ming bureaucracy's internal decay permitted another group of invaders, the Manchus of Manchuria, to overrun China in the seventeenth century. Established in 1644 as the Qing dynasty, these northerners quickly adapted themselves to Chinese life. The early Qing emperors cultivated knowledge of China's arts, and the decorative arts especially flourished under their direction and patronage.

HAPPINESS, RANK, AND LONGEVITY Qing potters, especially at the imperial kilns at Jingdezhen, continued

to expand on the Yuan and Ming achievements in developing fine porcelain pieces with underglaze and overglaze decoration. A dish with a lobed rim (FIG. **26-7**) exemplifies the latter technique. All of its colors—black, green, brown, yellow, and even blue—come from applying overglaze enamels. As with many eastern Asian objects, the painter decorated this dish with positive symbols. In the center are Fu, Lu, and Shou, the three star gods of happiness, rank, and longevity. The cranes, spotted deer, and pine trees all around the rim are age-old symbols of long life.

PRIMORDIAL LINE Literati painting continued to be fashionable among conservative artists under the Manchus, but other painters experimented with extreme effects of

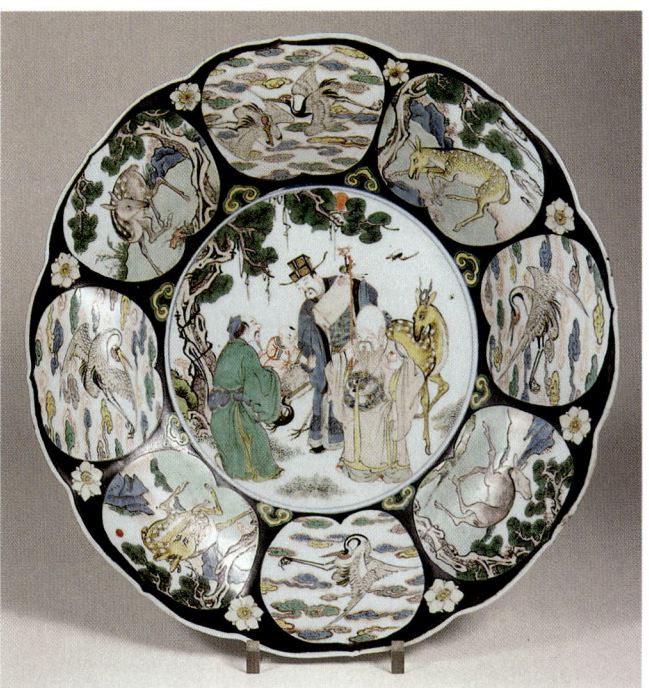

26-7 Dish with lobed rim, China, Qing dynasty, ca. 1700. White porcelain with overglaze, 2$\frac{1}{4}$″ × 1′ 2″. The Percival David Foundation of Chinese Art, London.

26-8 Shitao, landscape, China, Qing dynasty, late seventeenth century. Album leaf, ink and colors on paper, $9\frac{1}{2}'' \times 11''$. C. C. Wang Collection, New York.

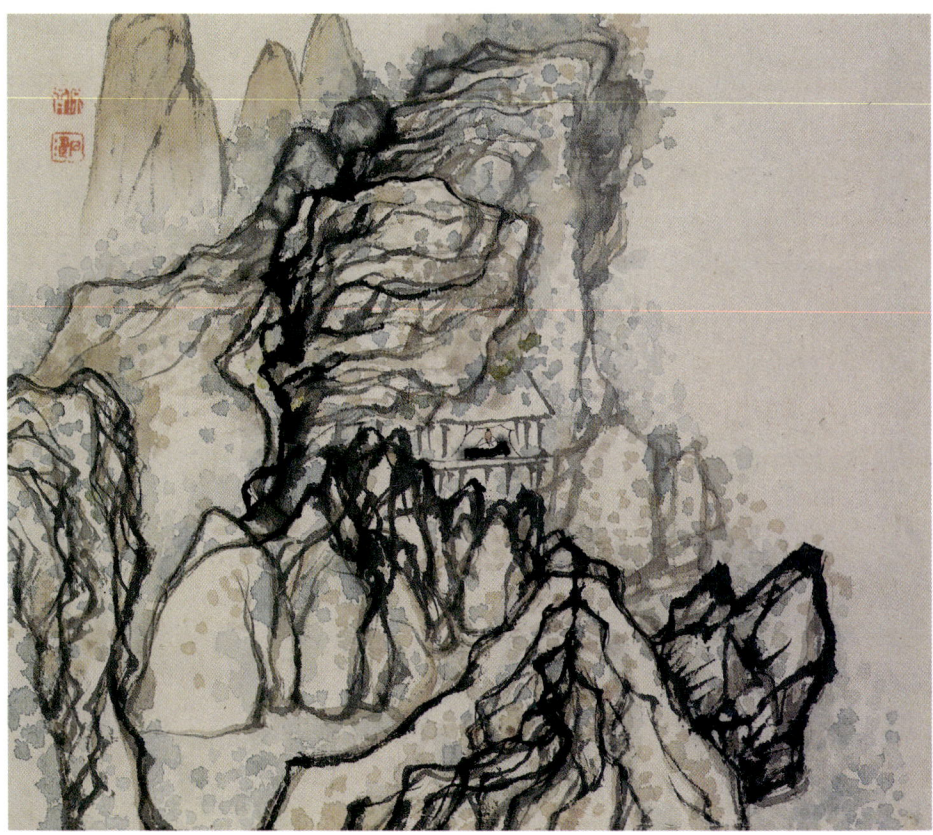

massed ink or individualized brushwork patterns. Bold and freely manipulated compositions with a new, expressive force began to appear. The most famous painter in this mode was Shitao (Dao Ji, 1642–1707), whose theoretical writings called for a return to wellsprings of creativity through use of the "single brush stroke" or "primordial line" as the root of all phenomena and representation. The figure in a hut in one of Shitao's album leaves (FIG. **26-8**) is surrounded by the surging energy of free-floating colored dots and multiple sinuous contour lines suggesting an organism's vital arteries. The artist did not so much depict the landscape's appearance as the animating, molding forces running through it—the prime focus of Chinese landscape art from the earliest times.

DECORATIVE ARTWORKS After they came to power in 1644, the Manchus commissioned decorative artworks in vast quantities. In general, they favored technical brilliance and elaborate style. Until warfare destroyed the great kilns at Fuliang (an ancient part of Jingdezhen) in the mid-nineteenth century, they flourished and produced enormous numbers of finely crafted, superbly decorated porcelains. A brief revival of Song simplicity occurred during the reign of Yong Zheng (r. 1723–1735), but a later ruler's reaction soon led to a more elaborate style. Fine embroidered and woven textiles, created for lavish court ceremonies, followed the age's general style, becoming more intricate and more delicate as time passed. As the eighteenth century waned, huge workshops, much like modern production-line factories, continued to provide masses of materials for imperial use. Specialists, instead of designer-craftspersons, worked on each manufacturing stage. By the mid-nineteenth century, this system had drained much of the vitality from the decorative arts.

Houses and Gardens

Chinese house and garden designs after the thirteenth century stem from two different philosophies, the house from the Confucianist and the garden from the Daoist (see "Daoism and Confucianism," Chapter 7, page 193). The two philosophies embrace contrasting, but not necessarily conflicting, notions of harmony. The Confucians seek harmony of the moral and social order, and the Daoists seek the harmony of humankind within, and resonant with, the forces of nature. Confucianism stresses the qualities of regularity, symmetry, balance, and finiteness. Daoism stresses irregularity, asymmetry, and the instability and incompleteness of eternal change. Confucianists thus emphasize control and definition, while Daoists emphasize yielding to the undefined, the infinite forces of nature enveloping and moving humankind as everything else, animate or inanimate.

HOUSES AND THE CONFUCIAN IDEAL Chinese houses, like Chinese temples and cities, are axial groupings of halls and courtyards within enclosures. The house plan expresses the Confucian ideal of a patriarchal society based on the patriarchal family, so residents are subordinate to the elders' commanding role and position. The religion of ancestor worship and its traditional observances sanctify this ideal. Strict rules determine the arrangements of halls, courtyards, and living quarters in Chinese houses, although the plans may differ in minor details. The orientation often depends on fengshui ("wind and water") beliefs that wind scatters the breath of life and water must stop it. Therefore, building orientation must balance the forces of wind and water. In addition, concerns regarding the influence of favorable

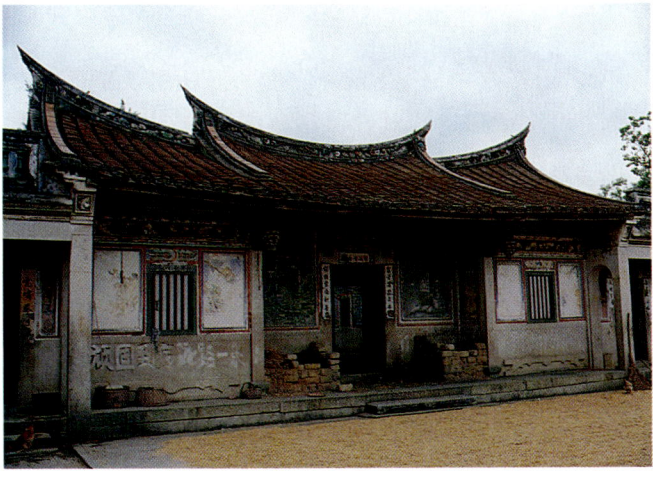

26-9   Courtyard house exterior, Fujian Province, China, primarily Qing dynasty.

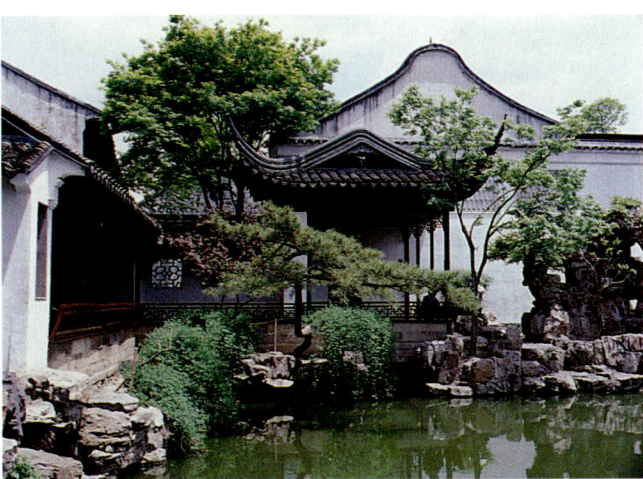

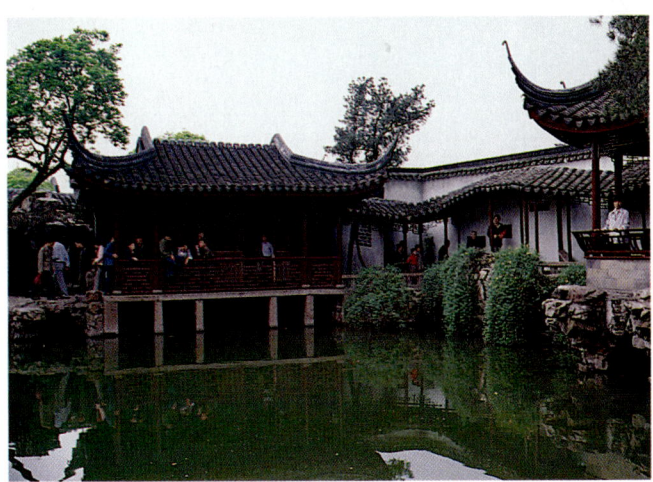

26-11   Wangshi Yuan (Garden of the Master of the Fishing Nets), veranda, pavilion, and pool, Suzhou, Jiangsu Province, China.

or unfavorable spiritual forces may decide the placement of home entrances and exits.

The facade of the Chinese house, such as one in Wuxi (FIG. **26-9**) primarily built in the Qing period, masks its private interior. It is most often modest, fronting an already narrow masonry street, and its entrance might bear an inscription invoking happiness and warding off the threat of demonic powers. The private areas, set off by walls within, may open out into verandas, as seen in a Fujian Province house (FIG. **26-10**), where the family and visitors can view another enclosure, the garden. The garden is an artfully designed fragment of nature, an aesthetic, intellectual, and spiritual resource prized in China as perhaps nowhere else.

THE REPLICATION OF NATURE   The Chinese logogram for garden provides its definition—"a place enclosed by walls, within which are buildings, waterways, rocks, trees, and flowering plants." An example is Wangshi Yuan (Garden of the Master of the Fishing Nets; FIG. **26-11**) in Suzhou. Historically, gardens served multiple, some quite practical, purposes. One important aspect of garden design has been the replication in miniature of nature's fullness in all its variety—the produc-

tion of an environment for the soul to immerse itself and find tranquillity and peace. Chinese poets never cease to sing of the restorative effect of gardens on mind and spirit. Garden design is a great art, akin to composing a poem or a landscape painting. It is not a matter of cultivating plants in rows or of laying out terraces, *parterres* (raised flower beds), and avenues in geometric fashion. Chinese gardens are rather cunningly contrived scenic arrangements of natural and artificial elements intended to reproduce the irregularities of uncultivated nature. Chinese architects often build verandas over ponds and pavilions on stilts rising above the water. A principal feature of gardens, pavilions control a variety of views. Stone bridges, paths, and causeways encourage wandering through ever-changing vistas of trees, flowers, rocks, and their reflections in the ponds. The typical design is a sequence of carefully contrived visual surprises as visitors move. A favorite garden element, fantastic rockwork, represents primitive nature and, ideally, should be "grotesque, spare, and porous," as portrayed at Liu Yuan (Lingering Garden), Guanyun Peak (Cloud-Capped Peak; FIG. **26-12**), in Suzhou. Chinese gardens are sanctuaries where people commune with nature in all its representative forms and as an ever-changing and boundless presence.

THE FORBIDDEN CITY'S THRONE ROOM   The conservatism of Confucian China, as expressed in its architecture, can be seen in the Taihe Dian (Hall of supreme

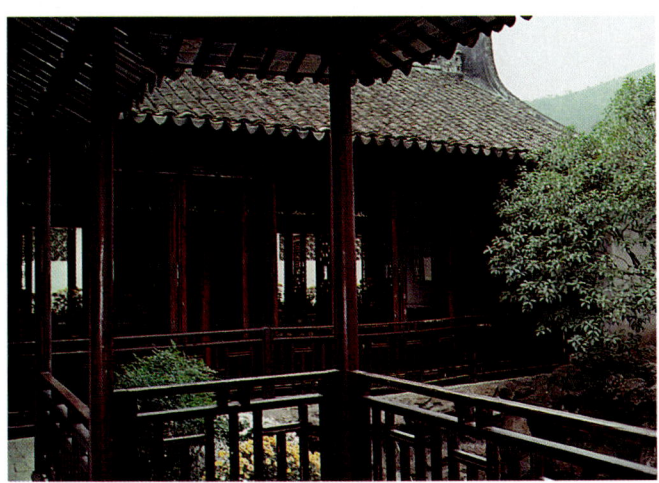

26-10   Courtyard house interior veranda, Wuxi, Jiangsu Province, China.

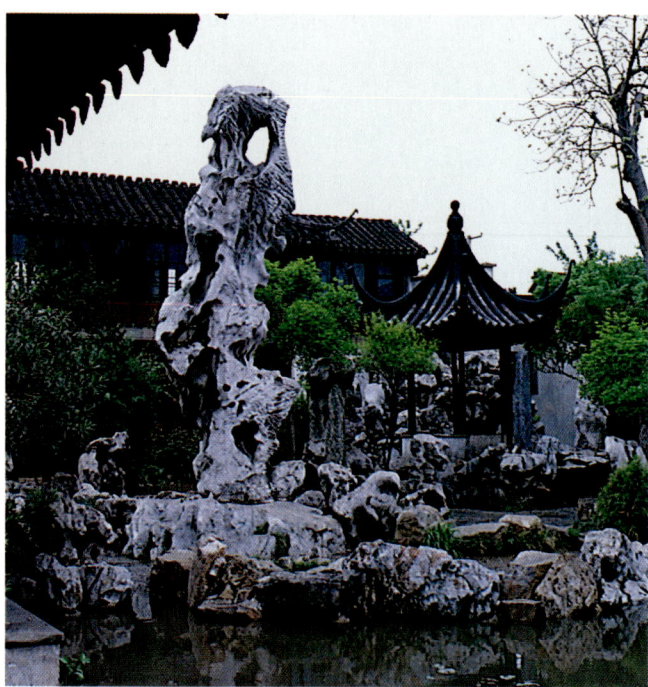

26-12 Liu Yuan (Lingering Garden), Guanyun Peak (Cloud-Capped Peak), Suzhou, Jiangsu Province, China.

26-13 Taihe Dian, Imperial Palace, Forbidden City, Beijing, China, Ming and Qing dynasties, seventeenth century and later.

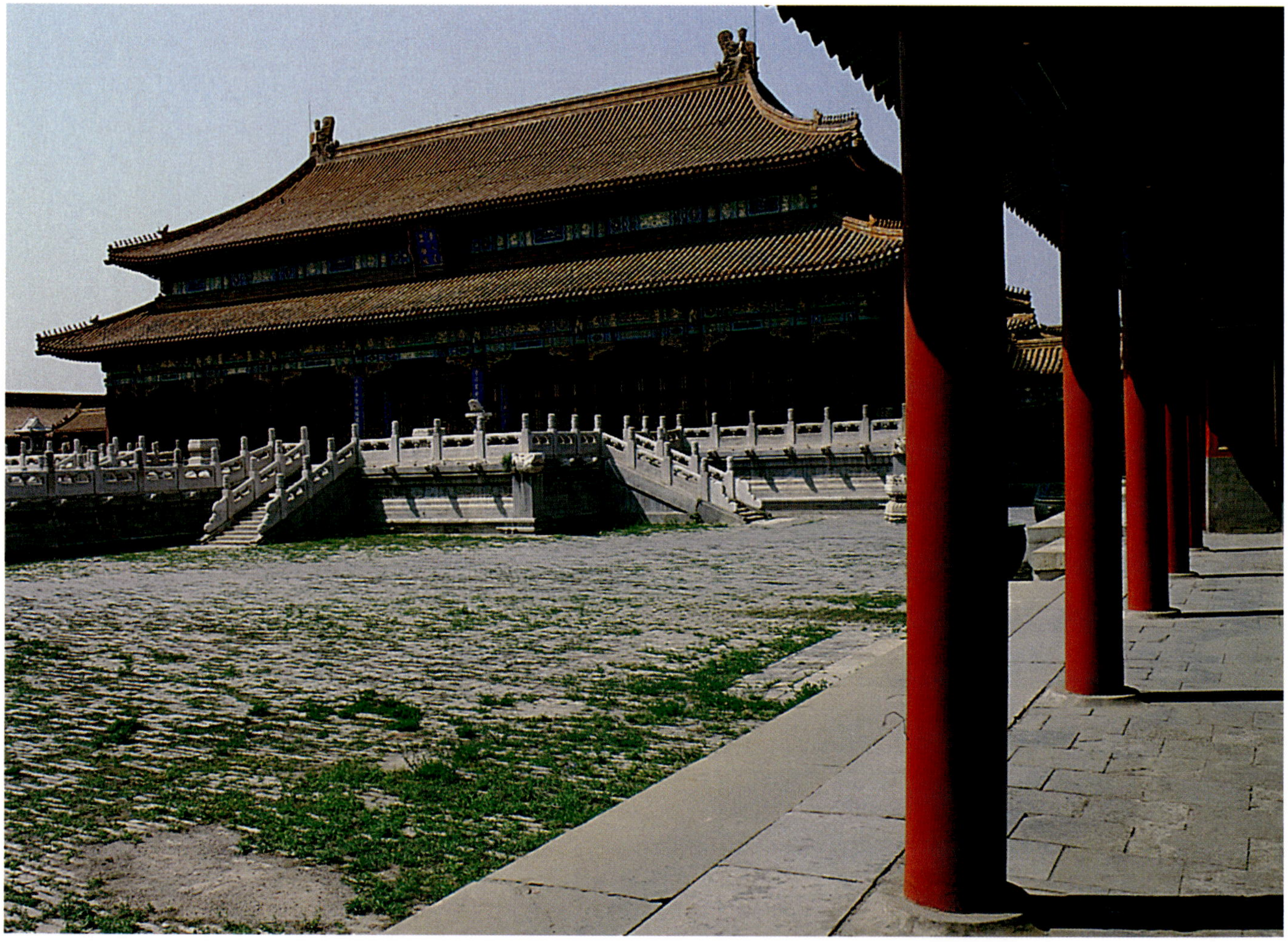

harmony; FIG. **26-13**), one of the principal monuments of the Ming and Qing dynasties. The Taihe Dian is the largest building and centerpiece of the grand, typically axial design of the "Forbidden City" in China's capital, Beijing. The former Imperial Palace compound is known as the Forbidden City because only the emperor's closest family members, attendants, and advisers could enter there. The compound itself is centered on Beijing's main north-south axis.

The great hall functioned as the emperor's throne room and audience hall. Built in 1627, rebuilt in 1697, and restored in 1765, it is a late and monumental example of the persistence of the standard Chinese architectural style. Of great scale, some two hundred feet long and one hundred feet deep, it has a weighty, majestic formality appropriate for the staging of sacred imperial ceremonies. Raised high on a terraced white marble podium, the massive wooden structure, with its overhanging eaves and upturned roof lines, dominates several smaller halls flanking it symmetrically and grouped behind it. Repeating the design of Taihe Dian, these halls with their hipped roofs and upswept eave lines align with the north-south axis running through the rectangular moat-surrounded imperial compound. The auxiliary halls, with their courtyards, provided the imperial family's private quarters, service quarters, harems, places for study, gardens, and spaces enclosed for the innumerable activities of elaborate court life. The whole immense composition is faithfully laid out according to rules for design and structure set down and followed for more than a millennium.

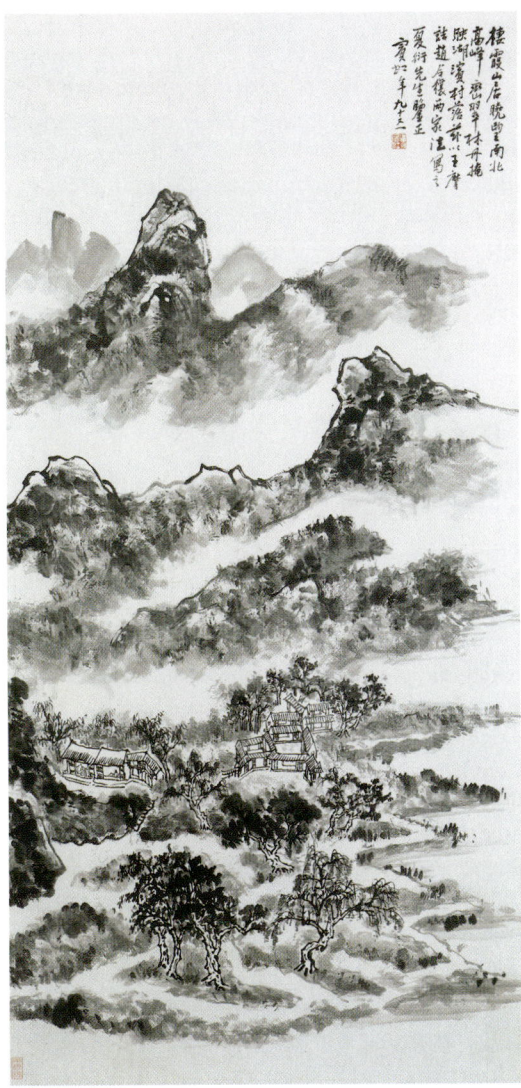

26-14 HUANG BINHONG, *Recluse Dwelling on Xixia Mountain,* 1954. Hanging scroll, ink and color on paper, 3′ 11½″ × 1′ 11½″. Metropolitan Museum of Art, New York (gift of Robert Hatfield Ellsworth, in memory of LaFerne Hatfield Ellsworth, 1986).

Modern China (1911–Present)

The overthrow of the Qing dynasty and establishment of the Republic of China in 1911 accelerated debates in China over the place of its traditional culture in a modern world. Even during the Qing dynasty's final years, both Western and east Asian painting had been taught in schools. To a great degree those debates continue today in the People's Republic of China, established in 1949.

TRADITIONALISM TODAY Some Chinese artists continue to produce works based on the old traditions. For example, HUANG BINHONG (1864–1955) found the free brush expressive and maintained the calligraphic tradition with vitality, as seen in his *Recluse Dwelling on Xixia Mountain* (FIG. **26-14**). Huang played a vital role in integrating traditional painting into a modern world. He edited the first Chinese books to reproduce paintings photographically, and he taught at newly established art schools.

MARXIST ART FOR THE PEOPLE In contrast to Huang's continuing allegiance to traditional philosophies and techniques, Marxism has sometimes inspired a social realism in art familiar to today's world that breaks drastically with traditional Chinese art. The intended purpose of such art is to serve the people in the struggle to liberate and elevate the masses. In *Rent Collection Courtyard* (FIG. **26-15,** detail), a life-size tableau located in Dayi, an anonymous team of sculptors grimly depicted the old times in a scene common enough before the revolution. Peasants, worn and bent by toil, bring their taxes (in produce) to the courtyard of their merciless, plundering landlord. The message is clear—this kind of thing must not happen again. The anonymity of the artists who depicted the event is significant in itself. Only collective action could effect the transformations the People's Republic seeks.

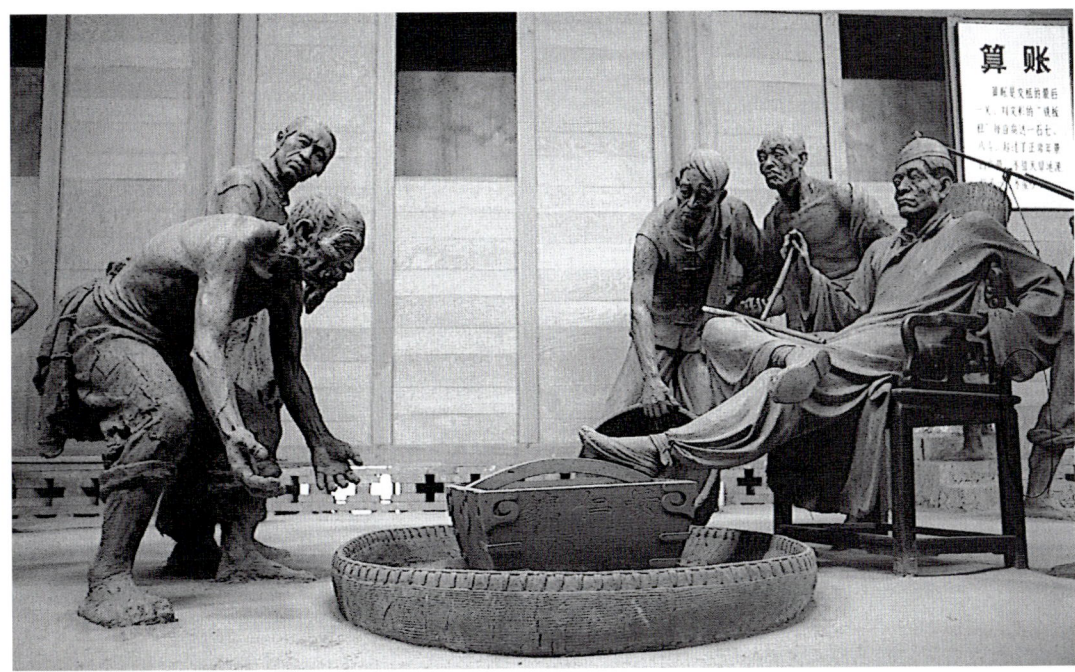

26-15 *Rent Collection Courtyard* (detail of larger tableau), Dayi, Sichuan Province, China, 1965. Clay-plaster, life-size.

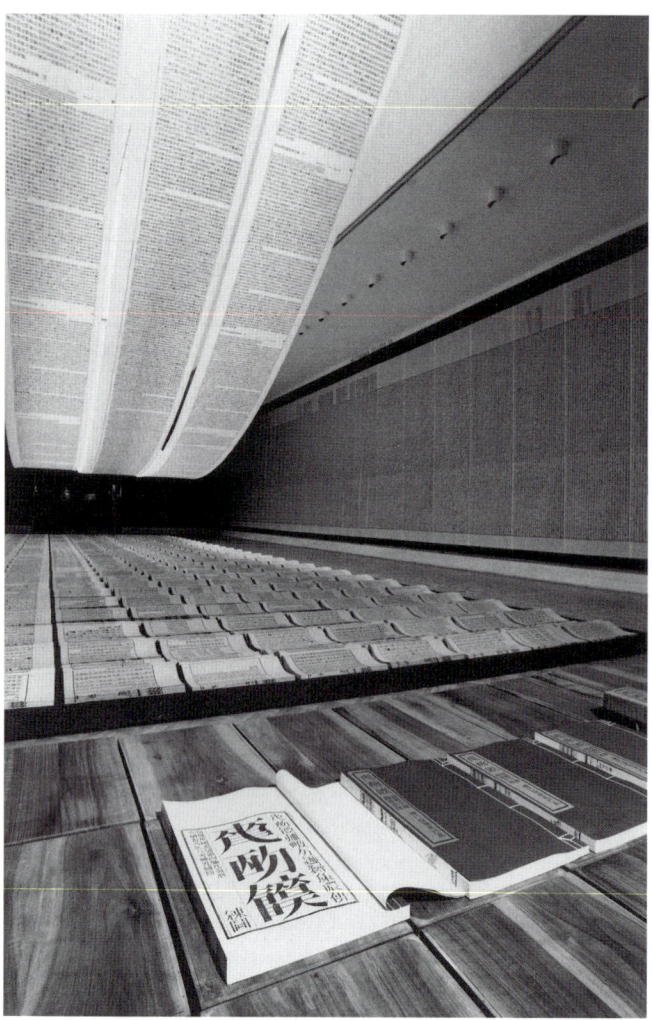

26-16   XU BING, *A Book from Heaven,* installation at Elvehjem Museum of Art, University of Wisconsin, Madison, 1987–1991. Movable-type prints and books.

A HEAVENLY BOOK   In the late 1980s and 1990s, Chinese artists in touch with their country's traditions began to make a mark on the postmodern international scene. A large installation called *A Book from Heaven* (FIG. **26-16**) by XU BING (b. 1955) provides a striking example. First exhibited in China and then in Japan, the United States, and Hong Kong, the work presents an enormous number of

wood-block-printed texts in characters that look Chinese but that the artist invented. Producing them required both an intimate knowledge of actual characters and extensive training in block carving. Xu's work points to the extreme difficulties inherent in making a place for age-old traditions in an increasingly international world dominated by American pop culture, but it also suggest the rich benefits of doing so.

KOREA

Choson Dynasty (1392–1910)

The last of the native Korean dynasties was the Choson (1392–1910), whose founder took over the Koryo state in 1392. During the Choson, the long reign of Buddhism as Korea's dominant religion ended. In its place, a strict, formalistic neo-Confucianism turned greater attention to public and worldly concerns, and the problems of daily life took control. Meanwhile, the ancient ideals of nature worship reemerged (mingled with Chinese Daoism), and artistic themes frequently came from the local flora, fauna, and landscape of the human environment. The Japanese invasion of the kingdom (1592–1598) transferred many Korean potters to Kyushu, Japan's southernmost island, where they were instrumental in inaugurating the Japanese porcelain industry. Rustic Korean-made bowls became valued accessories in the Japanese tea ceremony (see Chapter 27), and Japan naturalized them as cultural treasures.

THE GATEWAY TO SEOUL   Public building projects helped give the new Korean state an image of dignity and power. One impressive early monument, built for the new capital of Seoul, is the city's south gate, or Nandaemun (FIG. **26-17**). It combines the imposing strength of its impressive stone foundations with the sophistication of the intricately bracketed wooden superstructure. In eastern Asia, elaborate gateways, often in a processional series, were a standard element in city designs, as well as royal and sacred compounds, all usually surrounded by walls. Such gateways served as magnificent symbols of the ruler's authority or of the hallowed nature of what stood on the other side. Passage into the city

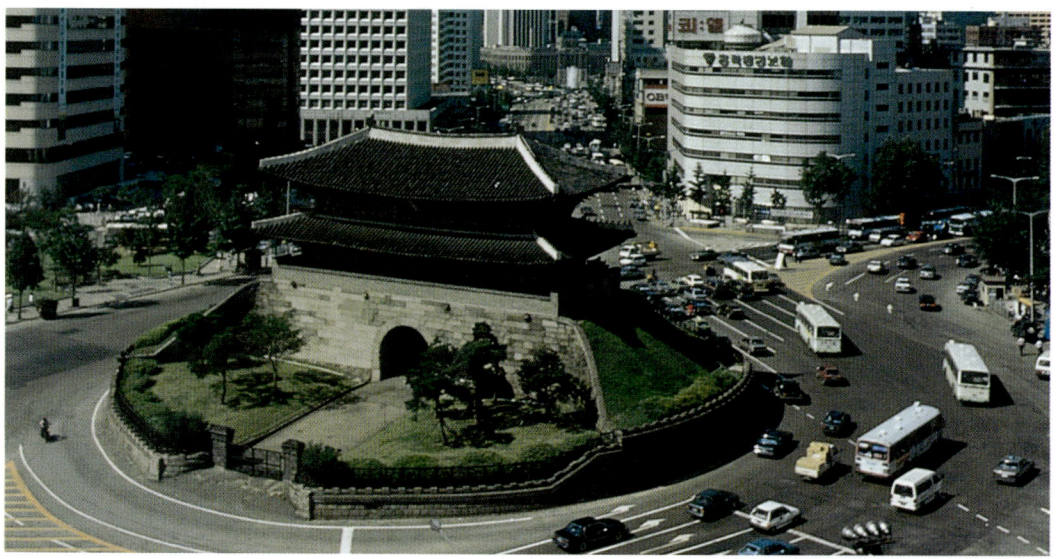

26-17   Nandaemun, Seoul, Korea, Choson dynasty, first built in 1398.

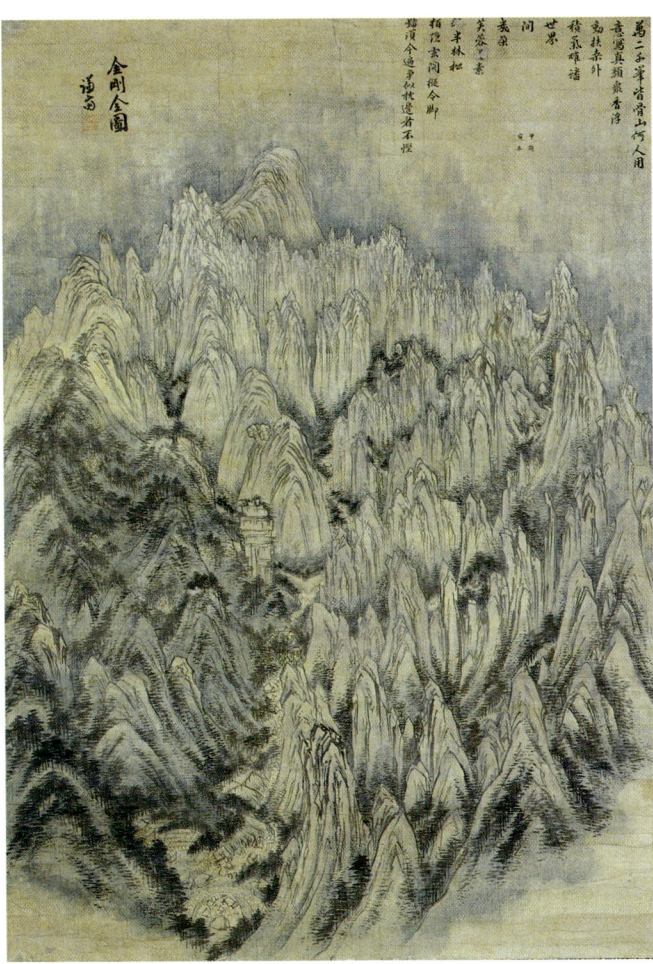

26-18 CHONG SON, *The Kumgang Mountains,* Korea, Choson dynasty, 1734. Hanging scroll, ink on paper, 4′ 3½″ × 1′ 11¼″. Hoam Art Museum, Kyunggi-Do.

through such an impressive monument reminded the populace of the Choson state's power.

THE DIAMOND MOUNTAINS Over the long course of the Choson dynasty, many varieties of painting flourished. These included scholar-amateur, or literati, painting in a particularly Korean manner, formal portraiture, and genre painting. Unlike their Chinese counterparts, Korean literati painters were not immersed in the arguments of style and meaning Dong Qichang promoted. They freely incorporated a wide variety of Chinese styles into their repertoires, especially in the first half of the Choson dynasty. In the eighteenth century, however, such painters studied Chinese literati styles more closely and produced their own brilliant, idiosyncratic fusions, as seen in the *Kumgang* (Diamond) *Mountains* (FIG. **26-18**) by CHONG SON (1676–1759). The artist transformed an actual scene into an imaginative landscape using sharper, darker versions of the fibrous brush strokes much favored by Chinese literati, such as Huang Gongwang (FIG. 26-1). Chong used these strokes to represent the bright crystalline appearance of the mountains and to emphasize their spiky forms. This gave a more intense sense of rhythmic vitality to the surface, rather than the softness and depth of Huang's picture.

A PORTRAIT WITH A SILK HAT As in China and Japan, portraiture was a very important art throughout most of Korean history. Ancestor worship and ceremonial practices honoring teachers and leaders gave portraits, serving a func-

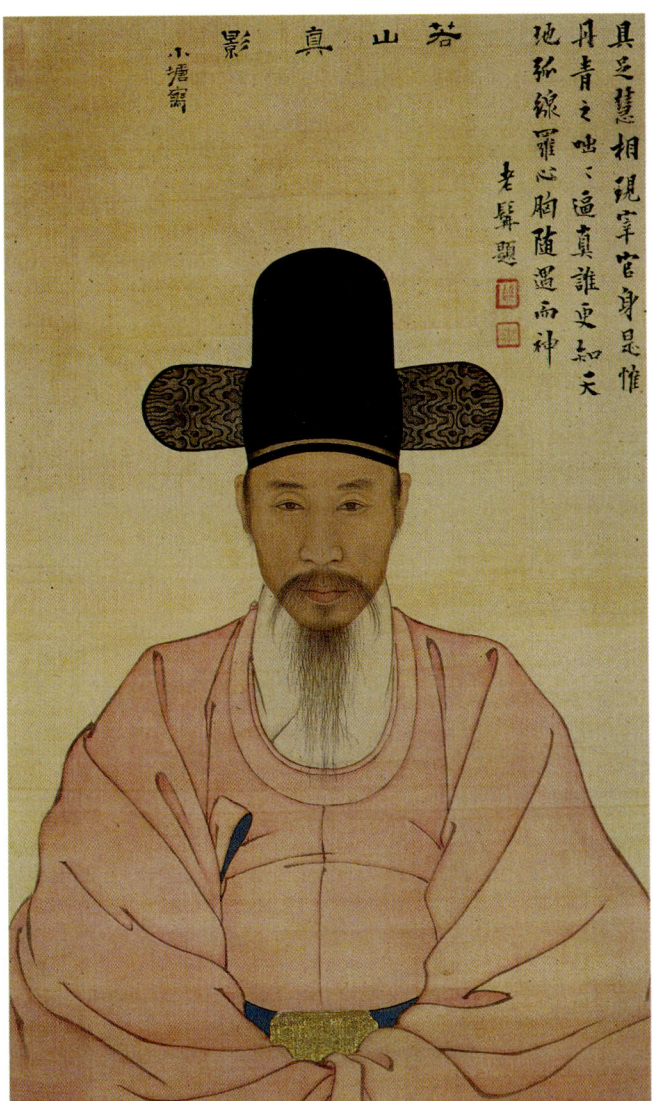

26-19 YI CHAE-GWAN, *Portrait of Kang Yi-o,* Korea, Choson dynasty, early nineteenth century. Hanging scroll, ink and colors on silk, 2′ 1″ high. National Museum of Korea, Seoul.

tion very similar to religious icons, a vital role in east Asian cultures. *Portrait of Kang Yi-o* (FIG. **26-19**), a picture of a local magistrate by YI CHAE-GWAN (1783–1837), shows the standard features of such paintings. The artist's meticulous rendering of garments and other attributes indicates the sitter's social identity in his official position. The sensitive likeness of the face records personal (and perhaps something of family) identity for posterity. In this particular picture, the winged silk hat is unmistakably that of a Korean official.

POSTSCRIPT Except for the enforced connection with China, Korea had shut off all other foreign contacts until the nineteenth century, when Japan and other nations, including the United States, forced open its doors. Japan annexed Korea in 1910, and it remained part of Japan until 1945, when the Western Allies and the Soviet Union took Korea at the end of World War II. Although divided into North and South Korea today, at least South Korea has emerged as a fully industrialized nation of great economic potential. Perhaps a united Korea will take a larger place in world affairs in the twenty-first century, and its prominence may help make a place on the international scene for particularly Korean versions of postmodern art.

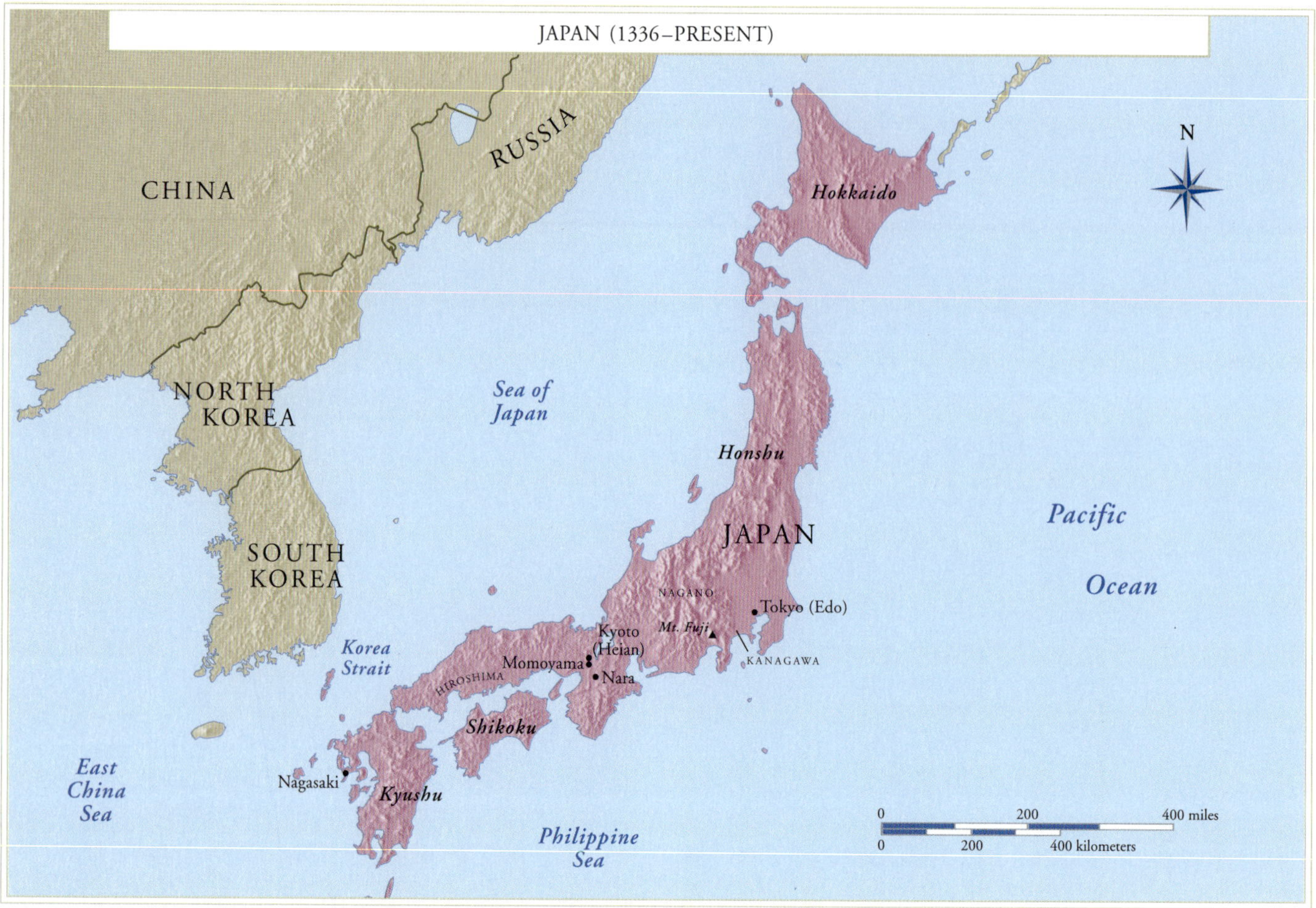

JAPAN (1336–PRESENT)

CHINA

RUSSIA

NORTH KOREA

SOUTH KOREA

Korea Strait

East China Sea

Nagasaki

Kyushu

Shikoku

HIROSHIMA

Momoyama

Kyoto (Heian)

Nara

NAGANO

Mt. Fuji

Tokyo (Edo)

KANAGAWA

Sea of Japan

Honshu

JAPAN

Hokkaido

Pacific Ocean

Philippine Sea

N

| 0 | 200 | 400 miles |
| 0 | 200 | 400 kilometers |

1334	1400		1500	1573
MUROMACHI				MOMOYAMA

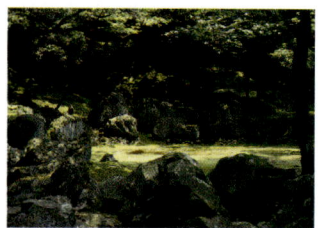

Dry cascade and pools
Saihoji, Kyoto
fourteenth century

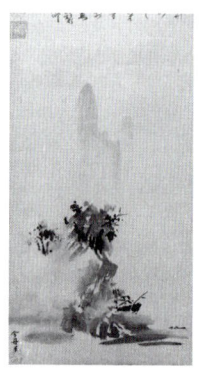

Toyo Sesshu
landscape, 1495

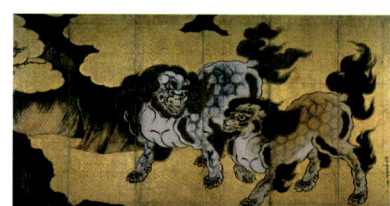

Kano Eitoku
Chinese Lions
late sixteenth century

Restoration of imperial power, 1334–1336

Ashikaga Shogunate established, 1336

Official relations established with China's Ming government, 1401

Emergence of Tosa and Kano Schools, fifteenth and sixteenth centuries

Construction of great castles/fortresses, sixteenth century

Reunification of Japan begins, ca. 1560s

Tea ceremony emerges as exercise of cultivation and refinement, sixteenth and seventeenth centuries

FROM THE SHOGUNS TO THE PRESENT

THE ART OF LATER JAPAN

1615	1700	1868	1926	1964
EDO		MEIJI AND TAISHO	SHOWA AND HEISEI	

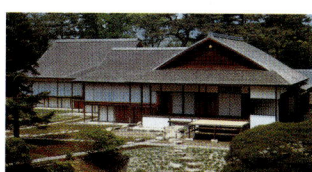

Katsura Imperial Villa
Kyoto, 1620–1663

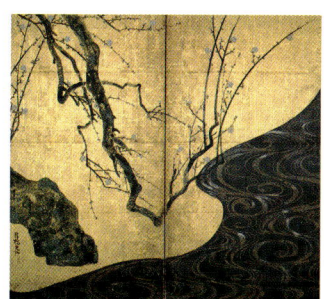

Ogata Korin
White Plum Blossoms
ca. 1710–1716

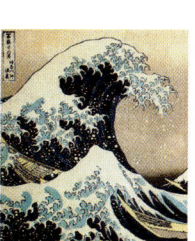

Katsushika Hokusai
The Great Wave
off Kanagawa
ca. 1826–1833

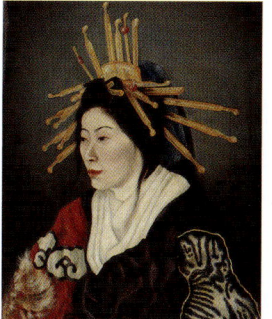

Takahashi Yuichi
Oiran (Courtesan)
Meiji period, 1872

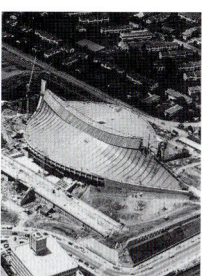

Kenzo Tange
Olympic stadiums, 1964

Tokugawa Ieyasu consolidation of power, 1615

Closing of Japan to foreigners, 1639

Rapid developments in printing industry, late seventeenth century

Social and cultural restlessness, seventeenth and eighteenth centuries

Meiji leaders promote emulation of Western culture, nineteenth century

Reaction against Westernization, nineteenth century

Arrival of American warships to force open Japan, 1853

Enthronement of Emperor Mutsuhito (Meiji), 1867

Beginning of cabinet system, 1885

Surrender of Japan to United States, 1945

American occupations end, 1952

Tokyo hosts Olympic Games, 1964

FEUDAL JAPAN

Muromachi Period (1334–1573)

SHOGUNS, SAMURAI, AND BUDDHISM In 1336, after Japan's emperor briefly restored civil authority, a warrior family once again dominated the country, as had occurred for more than a century. At that time, the Ashikaga clan seized power and formed Japan's second *shogunate,* or military government. They ruled from the Muromachi district of Kyoto. In theory, a *shogun* managed the country and maintained unity on the ruling emperor's behalf, but, in reality, the latter was little more than a figurehead, and the imperial court had very limited resources. Even the Ashikaga shoguns never gained firm control over Japan, and they ruled under a largely feudal arrangement wherein local lords had considerable power over affairs in their own domains. Under that arrangement, the shoguns' authority tended to diminish over time and essentially disappeared in the late fifteenth century. Although the Ashikaga shogunate continued in name until 1573, the great local lords vied in violent confrontations for territory and ultimately for control of the country.

During the Muromachi period, Zen (*Chan* in Chinese) Buddhism (see "Zen and Zen Art: Ideal and Realities," page 819) flourished alongside the older sects, especially Pure Land

Buddhism. Unlike the Pure Land faith, which stressed reliance on the saving grace of Amida, the Buddha of the West, Zen emphasized rigorous discipline and personal responsibility. For this reason, Zen held a special attraction for *samurai* (warriors), whose behavioral codes placed high values on loyalty, courage, and self-control. Zen, however, was not simply the religion of Zen monks and the samurai. Aristocrats, merchants, and others also studied at and supported Zen temples. Furthermore, those who embraced Zen, including samurai, also generally embraced other Buddhist teachings, especially ideas of the Pure Land sects. These sects gave much greater attention to the problems of death and salvation. Zen temples stood out not only as religious institutions but also as centers of secular culture, where people could study Chinese Song and Yuan art, literature, and learning (see Chapter 26), which the Japanese imported along with Zen Buddhism.

ZEN SPIRITUALITY AND ROCK GARDENS The Saihoji temple gardens in Kyoto bear witness to both the continuities and transitions that marked religious art in the Muromachi period. In the fourteenth century, this Pure Land temple with its extensive gardens was transformed into a Zen institution. However, Zen leaders did not attempt to erase older beliefs, and the Saihoji gardens in their totality contin-

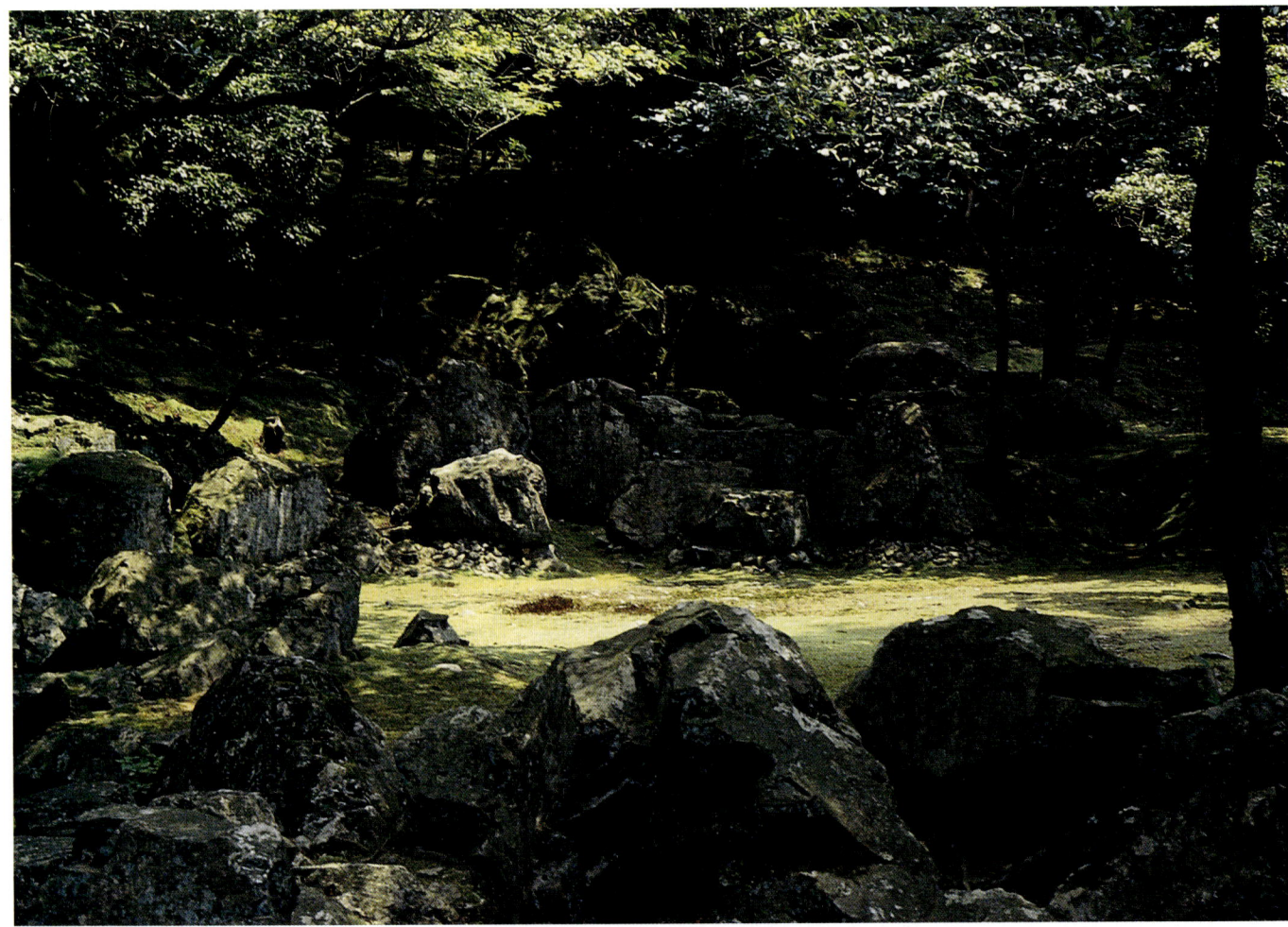

27-1   Dry cascade and pools, upper garden, Saihoji temple, Kyoto, Japan, modified in Muromachi period, fourteenth century.

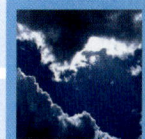

Zen and Zen Art
Ideals and Realities

Zen, as a fully developed Buddhist sect, entered Japan in the twelfth century and had its most pervasive impact on Japanese culture starting in the fourteenth century. Zen teachings assert everyone has the potential for enlightenment but worldly knowledge and mundane thought patterns suppress it. People cannot, however, according to Zen beliefs, awaken the potential for enlightenment through studying scriptures, good deeds, ceremonies and rituals, or image worship. Instead, followers must break through the boundaries of everyday perception and logic. Zen practices center on direct study with a master. Chains of master-pupil connections back through time form a monk's "Zen lineage." Some Zen schools stress meditation as a long-term practice eventually leading to enlightenment, while others stress the benefits of sudden shocks to the worldly mind, as through the posing of unanswerable questions.

In practice, Japanese Zen temples meet a variety of needs beyond those of full-time pupils. Zen teachings view mental calm, lack of fear, and spontaneity as signs of a person's advancement on the path to enlightenment. Thus, Zen training could apply to dealing with everyday life, and early Zen temples were also centers of Chinese learning in general. Some monks spent more time on such studies, including recently imported forms of philosophy and poetry, than they did on Zen. Even on the religious side, actual practices at Zen temples embraced many traditional Buddhist observances that had little to do with Zen per se, such as performing rituals before images. Local Zen temples also handled funeral rites.

Zen monks and lay followers painted pictures and produced other artworks that appear to reach toward Zen ideals through their subjects and in the feel of spontaneity in their making. However, some of the most famous painter-monks, such as Toyo Sesshu, were more devoted to art than to Zen. For most of his adult life, Sesshu did not live at a temple, as did the typical Zen monk, and he attracted many students to study painting with him. His inscription on a splashed-ink landscape (FIG. 27-2) identifies the picture as a gift to one such pupil. Other monks, although they lived and painted in temples, produced paintings of great variety, ranging from portraits to landscapes. The works that seem to be simple personal "Zen expressions" were frequently produced at the behest of temple authorities and secular patrons. Thus, the majority of Zen painter-monks worked in a largely professional capacity, and the Zen qualities of their pictures came from studying earlier paintings, as well as from institutional agreement on appropriate imagery. In fact, Kano Motonobu, who painted *Zen Patriarch Xiangyen Zhixian Sweeping with a Broom* (FIG. 27-4) at one of the great Zen temples, was a professional painter with no real Zen connection at all.

Zen ideals of spontaneity and rejection of worldliness reverberated throughout Japanese culture as the teachings spread. For example, the tea ceremony, or ritual drinking of tea, as it developed in the fifteenth and sixteenth centuries, offered a temporary respite from everyday concerns, a brief visit to a quiet retreat with a meditative atmosphere, such as the Taian teahouse (FIG. 27-6). Although the tea ritual itself was anything but spontaneous, tea aesthetics after the mid-sixteenth century placed a high value on utensils with unlabored forms and decoration. One example is the Shino water jar (FIG. 27-5), whose rough surface inspired its name, *Kogan* (literally, "ancient stream bank").

ued to evoke the beauty of Amida's Pure Land even as they served the Zen faith's more meditative needs. In this way, they perfectly echo the complementary roles of the two Buddhist sects in the Muromachi period, the former providing a promise of salvation and the latter promoting study and meditation.

Saihoji's lower gardens owe their renown today to their iridescently green mosses, whose beauty almost seems to belong to another world. In contrast, arrangements of rocks and sand on the hillsides of the upper garden, especially the dry cascade and pools (FIG. **27-1**), are treasured early examples of Muromachi dry landscape gardening. The designers stacked the rocks to suggest a swift mountain stream rushing over the stones to form pools below. In eastern Asia, people long considered wandering in the mountains and gazing at dramatic natural scenery highly beneficial to the human spirit. Such activities refreshed people after too much contact with daily affairs and helped them reach beyond mundane reality. The dry landscape, or rock garden, became very popular in Japan in the Muromachi period and afterward, especially at Zen temples. Excluding actual water and arranging stones to suggest far more expansive landscapes, as seen in Chinese paintings (see FIG. 7-19), encouraged deep mental, aesthetic, and spiritual engagement with the scene, which could be fully visualized only in the mind.

SPLASHED-INK PAINTING   Many painters produced pictures primarily in India ink during the Muromachi period. As was common in the long history of Japanese art, styles and subjects usually followed Chinese precedents closely, and painters filled their pictures with Chinese scenes and figures. Most of the ink painting masters were at least ostensibly Zen monks. The most celebrated was TOYO SESSHU (1420–1506), who spent little of his adult life in Zen temples. One of the very few painters who actually traveled to China, he learned much from contemporaneous Ming painters (see FIGS. 26-5 and 26-6). Sesshu (people who lived before 1868 are referred to by their personal names, which come second) worked in a great variety of styles, ranging from tight compositions in precise brushwork to dramatic works in the *splashed-ink style,* a technique Zen monks in eastern Asia often, but not exclusively, adopted.

The painter of a splashed-ink picture paused to visualize the image, loaded the brush with ink, and then applied primarily broad, rapid strokes, sometimes even dripping the ink on the paper. The result often hovers at the edge of legibility, without dissolving into sheer abstraction. This balance between spontaneity and a thorough knowledge of the painting tradition gave the pictures their artistic strength. In one of Sesshu's splashed-ink landscape paintings (FIG. **27-2**), viewers readily can appreciate the signs of a bravura performance with ink brush and paper, but knowledgeable viewers will also im-

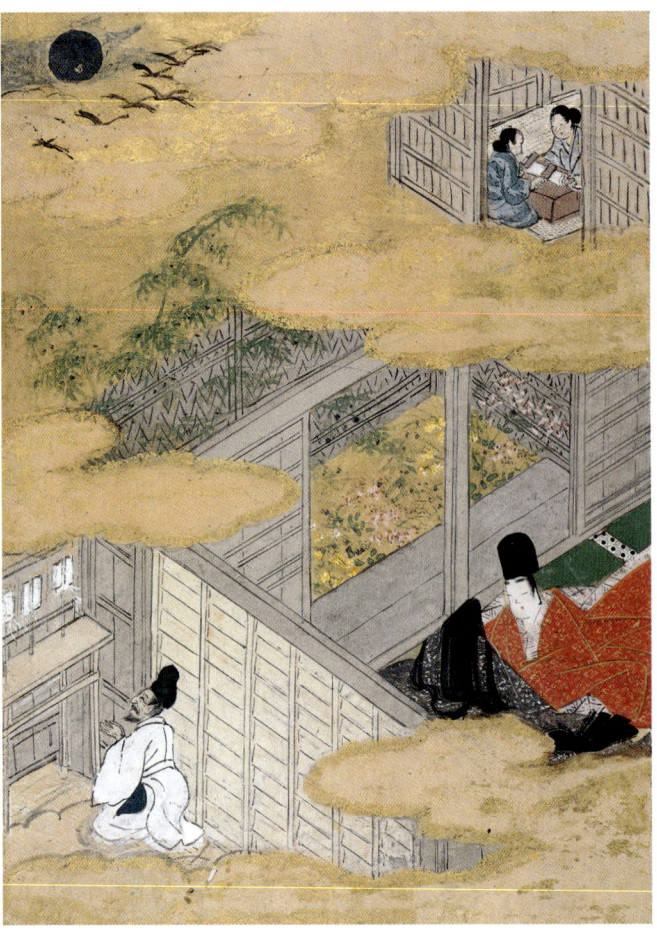

27-3 Attributed to TOSA MITSUNOBU, *Tale of Genji* ("Yugao," scene 4), Japan, Muromachi period, early sixteenth century. Album, ink and color on paper, approx. $9\frac{1}{2}'' \times 7''$. Arthur M. Sackler Museum, Harvard University, Cambridge (bequest of the Hofer Collection of the Arts of Asia).

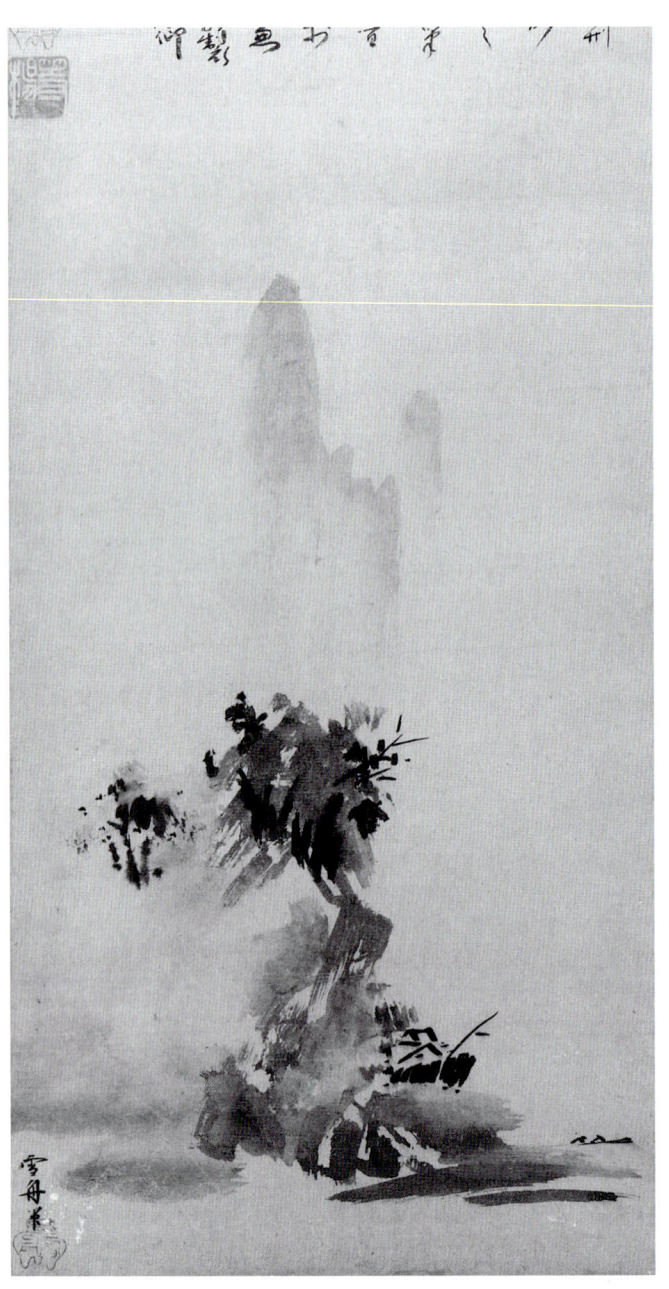

27-2 TOYO SESSHU, splashed-ink landscape, Japan, Muromachi period, 1495. Hanging scroll, ink on paper, $4' \ 10\frac{1}{4}'' \times 1' \ \frac{7}{8}''$. Tokyo National Museum, Tokyo.

mediately recognize familiar mountains, trees, and buildings. Two figures appear in a boat (to the lower right), and the two swift strokes nearby represent the pole and banner of a wine shop, a favorite destination of Chinese gentlemen boating on the river.

Ink painting was far from the only type of painting that flourished in the Muromachi period. Artists at court, in temples, and in the service of various powerful families painted portraits, icons, narrative handscrolls, folding screens, and other types of pictures in rich colors. Sesshu, for example, did not limit his work to monochrome.

THE TOSA SCHOOL   Two major painting schools emerged in Japan during the fifteenth and sixteenth centuries, the Tosa School and the Kano School. The director of the Painting Bureau (see "Japanese Artists, Workshops, and Patrons," Chapter 8, page 228) and chief painter at the imperial court in the late Muromachi period was TOSA MITSUNOBU (1434–1525). By Mitsunobu's time, the imperial court's resources had declined considerably, so his own workshop probably was not a separate official facility. Mitsunobu served the needs not only of the court but also of great temples allied to the court and the Ashikaga shoguns. Best known today for his surviving narrative handscrolls and paintings on six-panel screens, he also painted portraits, Buddhist icons, and illustrations of the *Tale of Genji,* such as the one attributed to him

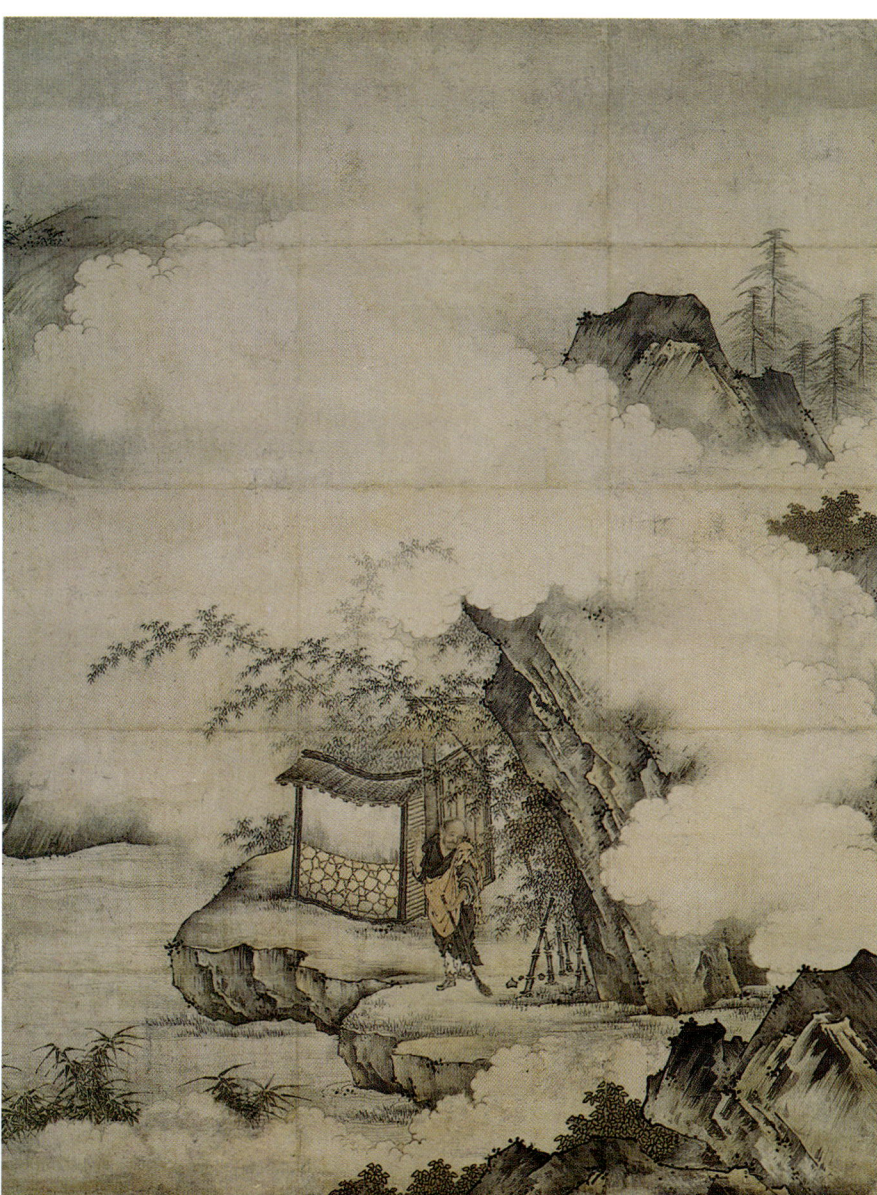

27-4   KANO MOTONOBU, *Zen Patriarch Xiangyen Zhixian Sweeping with a Broom,* Japan, Muromachi period, ca. 1513. Hanging scroll, ink and color on paper, 5′ 7$\frac{3}{8}$″ × 2′ 10$\frac{3}{4}$″. Tokyo National Museum, Tokyo.

(FIG. **27-3**). As do most examples going back to the twelfth century (see FIG. 8-11), his *Genji* illustrations show a continued emphasis on colorism and two-dimensional display of the narrative elements. However, Mitsunobu's pictures incorporate more narrative elements in elegant arrangement but do not possess the intimate moods earlier versions did.

In this image, Prince Genji and one of his many lovers sit talking in her house, which is crowded into a run-down neighborhood. The scene depicts the sounds they hear—the fulling (pounding) of cloth in the upper right and the man praying in the lower left. In the upper left, flying geese indicate autumn. By Mitsunobu's day, the task of the tale's illustrator had changed. Appreciation centered less on the narrative's rich emotional content and more on its status as a great classic of the Heian period (see Chapter 8). *Genji* paintings had become symbols of cultural sophistication intended for donation, presentation, and display.

Mitsunobu is the pivotal figure in the history of what art historians usually call the Tosa School. Several painters bearing the Tosa name, of uncertain family relationship, preceded Mitsunobu. However, starting in the early sixteenth century with Tosa's son, the Painting Bureau director inherited the position for the first time. From that time onward, a more distinct Tosa School clearly existed, but it never had the influence of its contemporary, the Kano School.

THE RISE OF THE KANO SCHOOL   KANO MOTONOBU (1476–1559) was the son of a painter in service to the eighth Ashikaga shogun and very likely the son-in-law of Tosa Mitsunobu. His training allowed him to paint in many varied styles suitable to subjects encompassing Chinese landscapes, Zen figures, *Genji* illustrations, portraits, Buddhist icons, and pictures of flowers and birds. As an independent painter in the tumultuous early sixteenth century, when the last vestiges of civil order were crumbling, he formed an efficient workshop and adapted his own broad repertoire to its needs. So successful were Motonobu and his successors that the Kano School became a virtual national academy in the seventeenth century, ending only in the late nineteenth century. Motonobu's *Zen Patriarch Xiangyen Zhixian Sweeping with a Broom* (FIG. **27-4**) depicts the monk experiencing the moment of enlightenment 5. As he swept the ground near his rustic retreat, a stone struck against a stalk of bamboo. The patriarch's Zen training was so deep that the resonant sound propelled him into an awakening. This work shows Motonobu's most precise mode of painting in ink and light color. It incorporates stylistic features of Chinese academic modes of ink painting, such as the sharp, angular rock forms Japanese painters, including Sesshu, long had adopted and adapted. Motonobu's picture of the patriarch is one of a set of sliding doors he and his assistants painted at a Zen temple. During the sixteenth century, such architectural decoration formed a growing component of the repertoires of the Kano School and later rivals.

Momoyama Period (1573–1615)

THE ROLE OF THE TEA CEREMONY To be considered legitimate rulers in eastern Asia, leaders had to display their support of and participation in refined cultural activities. The favorite exercise of cultivation and refinement in the Momoyama period was the tea ceremony (see "The Japanese Tea Ceremony," page 823). In Japan this important cultural activity eventually carried political and ideological implications. It provided a means for those relatively new to political or economic power to assert authority in the cultural realm as well. So serious did the tea ceremony's political implications become that warlords granted or refused their vassals the right to practice it. The ceremony also acquired special social significance as it gained acceptance as a major expression of aesthetic and even spiritual sophistication.

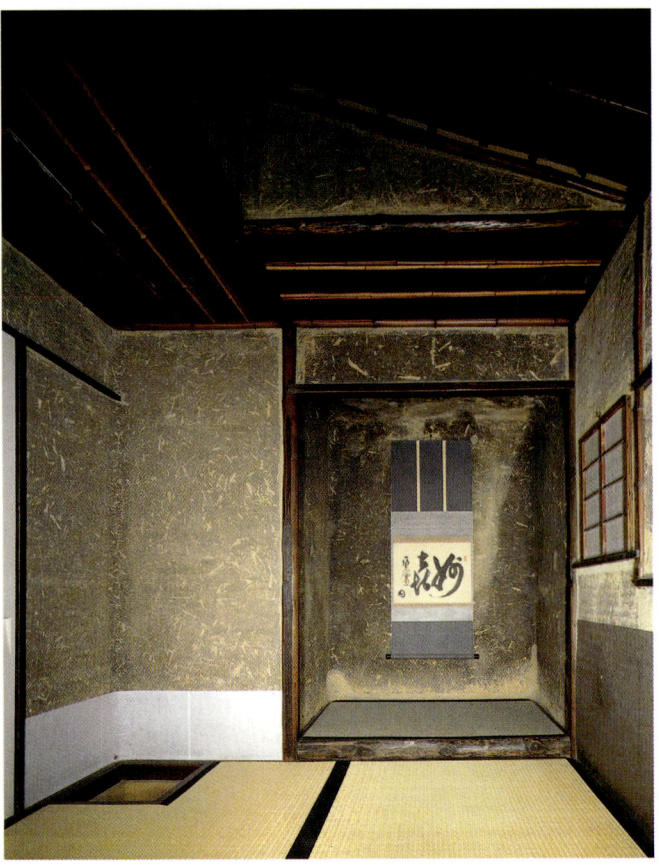

27-6   SEN NO RIKYU, Taian teahouse (interior view), Myokian Temple, Kyoto, Japan, Momoyama period, ca. 1582.

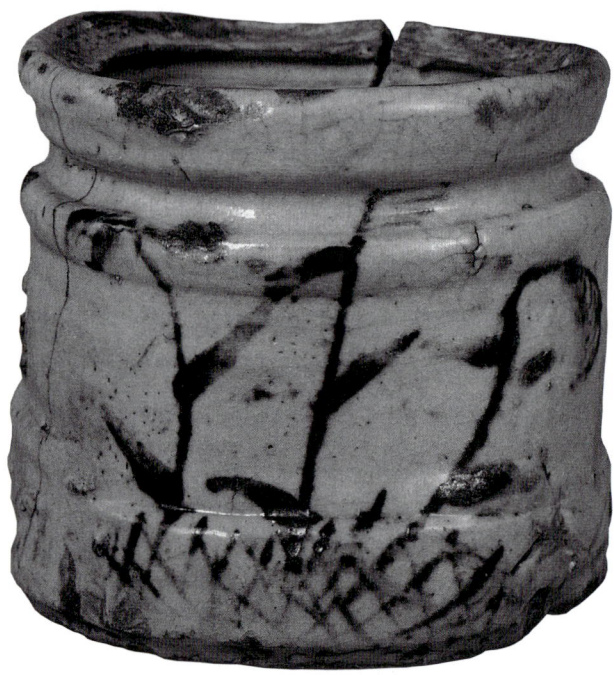

27-5   Tea-ceremony water jar, or *Kogan* ("ancient stream bank"), Japan, Momoyama period, late sixteenth century. Shino ware with underglaze design, 7″ high. Hatakeyama Memorial Museum, Tokyo.

A NEW REFINED RUSTICITY Starting around the late fifteenth century, admiration of the technical brilliance of Chinese objects slowly gave way to ever greater appreciation of the virtues of rustic Korean and Japanese wares. This new aesthetic of refined rusticity, or *wabi,* included the design of very simple tea rooms and houses that evoked the hut of a recluse in the mountains. Zen concepts also played an important role in this shift.

The Shino water jar named *Kogan* (FIG. **27-5**) shows the wabi aesthetic's influence in the tea ceremony. (The jar's name, which means "ancient stream bank," comes from the painted design on its surface, as well as from the coarse texture and rough form, both reminiscent of earth cut by water.) Shino wares, typically simple forms with rough surfaces, feature heavy glazes that fire to white, pinkish red, or gray, depending on additions of iron and firing conditions. The coarse stoneware body, simple form, and casual decoration offer the same sorts of aesthetic and interpretive challenges and opportunities as the dry landscape gardens of Zen temples (FIG. **27-1**).

TEA ROOMS AS CEREMONIAL SPACES The ultimate representation of the new wabi aesthetic in the Momoyama period was the Taian (FIG. **27-6**), a teahouse designed under the direction of the most renowned of the tea masters, SEN NO RIKYU (1522–1591), who came from a wealthy, cultivated merchant background. The interior displays two standard features of Japanese residential architecture

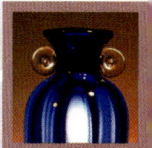

ART AND SOCIETY

The Japanese Tea Ceremony

The Japanese tea ceremony involves the ritual preparation, serving, and drinking of green tea. The fundamental practices began in China, but they developed in Japan to a much higher degree of sophistication, peaking in the Momoyama period. Simple forms of the tea ceremony started in Japan in Zen temples as a symbolic withdrawal from the ordinary world to cultivate the mind and spirit. The practices spread to other social groups, especially warriors and, by the late sixteenth century, wealthy merchants. Until the late Muromachi period, grand tea ceremonies in warrior residences served primarily as an excuse to display treasured collections of Chinese objects, such as porcelains, lacquers, and paintings.

The participants in the tea ceremony include a host and guests. The ceremony takes place in a tea room (FIG. 27-6; preferably with a garden) and involves several utensils, many of them ceramic (FIG. 27-5). The host's responsibilities included serving the guests, selecting utensils, and determining the tea room's decoration, which changed according to occasion and season. Acknowledged as having superior aesthetic sensibilities, individuals recognized as master tea ceremony practitioners (tea masters) advised patrons on the ceremony and acquired students. Tea masters even directed or influenced the design of teahouses and tea rooms within larger structures (including interiors and gardens), as well as the design of tea utensils. They often made simple bamboo implements and occasionally even ceramic vessels.

---

that developed in the late Muromachi period and only recently have begun to go out of fashion—very thick, rigid straw mats called *tatami* and an alcove called a *tokonoma*. The tatami accommodate the traditional Japanese customs of not wearing shoes indoors and of sitting on the floor. The tokonoma developed as a place to hang scrolls of painting or calligraphy and to display other prized objects.

The Taian tokonoma and the tea room as a whole have unusually dark walls, with earthen plaster covering even some of the square corner posts. The room's dimness and tiny size (about six feet square) produce a cavelike feel and force intimacy among the tea host and guests. The guests enter from the garden outside through a small sliding door that forces them to crawl inside. Such conditions emphasize a guest's passage into a ceremonial space—set apart from the ordinary world—where, in theory, all are equal. Rikyu was tea adviser to two of Japan's great reunifiers and no doubt served them in such humble settings. In contrast, the second Momoyama warlord held grand tea ceremonies in lavish surroundings and possessed a portable teahouse sheathed entirely in gold. Such were the extremes of Momoyama aesthetic choices.

MOMOYAMA PAINTING In the Momoyama period, a succession of three great warlords imposed peace on a country civil war had ravaged since the late fifteenth century. The period takes its name from the second warlord's seat of power. The great warlords and lesser lords erected huge castles with palatial residences—partly as symbols of power and partly as fortresses. The new rulers asked the Kano painters and their rivals to paint the castle walls, sliding doors, and folding screens in ink, color, and gold leaf. Gold screens had been known since Muromachi times, but Momoyama painters made them even bolder, reducing in number and often greatly enlarging the motifs against flat, shimmering fields of gold leaf.

CHINESE LIONS ON A JAPANESE SCREEN The grandson of Motonobu, KANO EITOKU (1543–1590), was the dominant painter of such murals and screens, though little of his work survives due to the eventual destruction of all the great castles he helped decorate. However, a painting of Chinese lions on a single six-panel screen (FIG. **27-7**) offers a glimpse of his work's grandeur. The colorful beasts' powerfully muscled bodies, defined and flattened by broad contour lines, stride forward within a gold field and minimal setting elements. Lions were unknown in eastern Asia except as such stylized images derived ultimately from elements of Buddhist iconography originating in southern Asia. In *Chinese Lions*, they seem more like brash emblems of power than Buddhist symbols. Because of the enormous scope of Eitoku's decoration projects, he often worked in the monumental style this painting typifies. Momoyama painting was not limited to such bold displays of isolated forms, however. It also included native and Chinese figural subjects rich in cultural, religious, and philosophical meanings.

A FOREST IN THE MIST Nor did Momoyama painters work exclusively in the colorful style exemplified by Eitoku's *Chinese Lions*. HASEGAWA TOHAKU (1539–1610), was a protégé of Rikyu with close connections to Zen temples. He became familiar with the aesthetics and techniques of Chinese Zen (Chan) painters and sometimes painted in ink monochrome using loose brushwork with brilliant success as seen in *Pine Forest* (FIG. **27-8**). His wet brush strokes—long and slow, short and quick, dark and pale—present a grove of great pines shrouded in mist. His trees emerge from and recede into the heavy atmosphere, as if the landscape hovers at the edge of formlessness. In Zen terms, the picture suggests the illusory nature of mundane reality while evoking a calm, meditative mood.

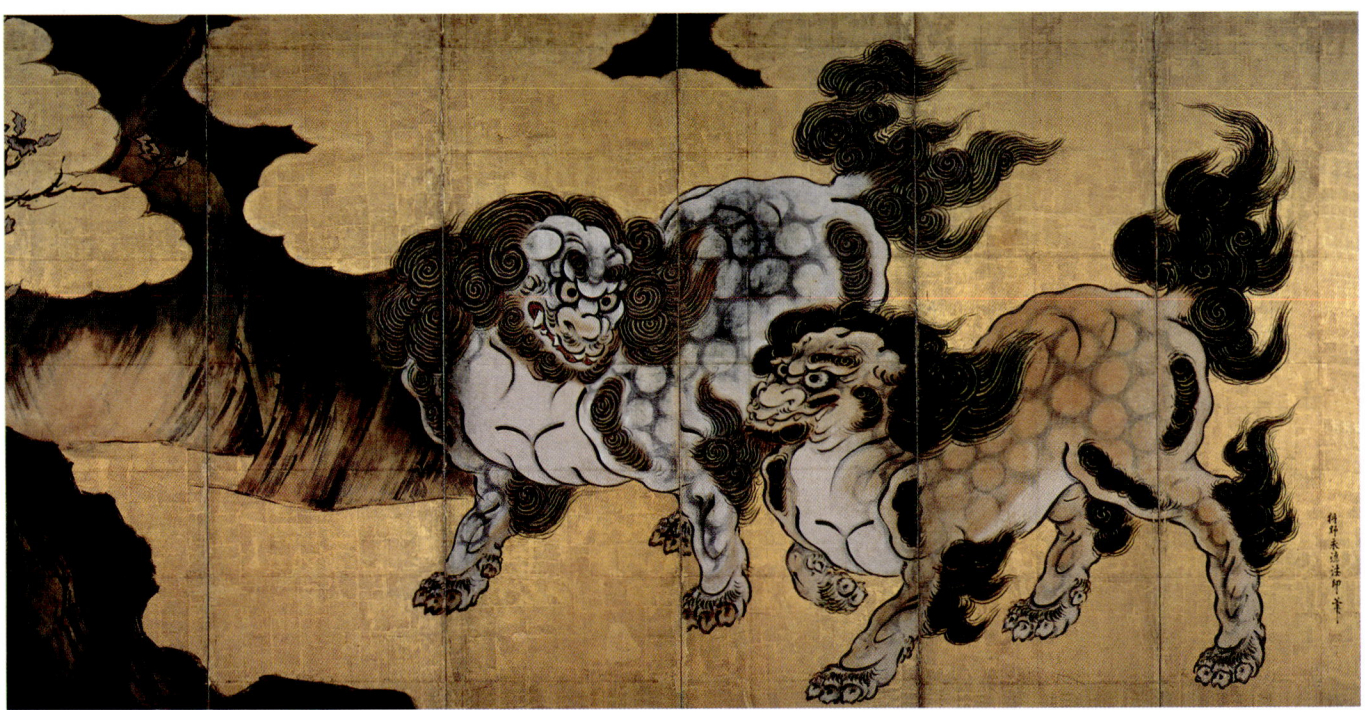

27-7   KANO EITOKU, *Chinese Lions,* Japan, Momoyama period, late sixteenth century. Six-panel screen, color, ink, and gold-leaf on paper, 7′ 4″ × 14′10″. Imperial Household Agency, Tokyo.

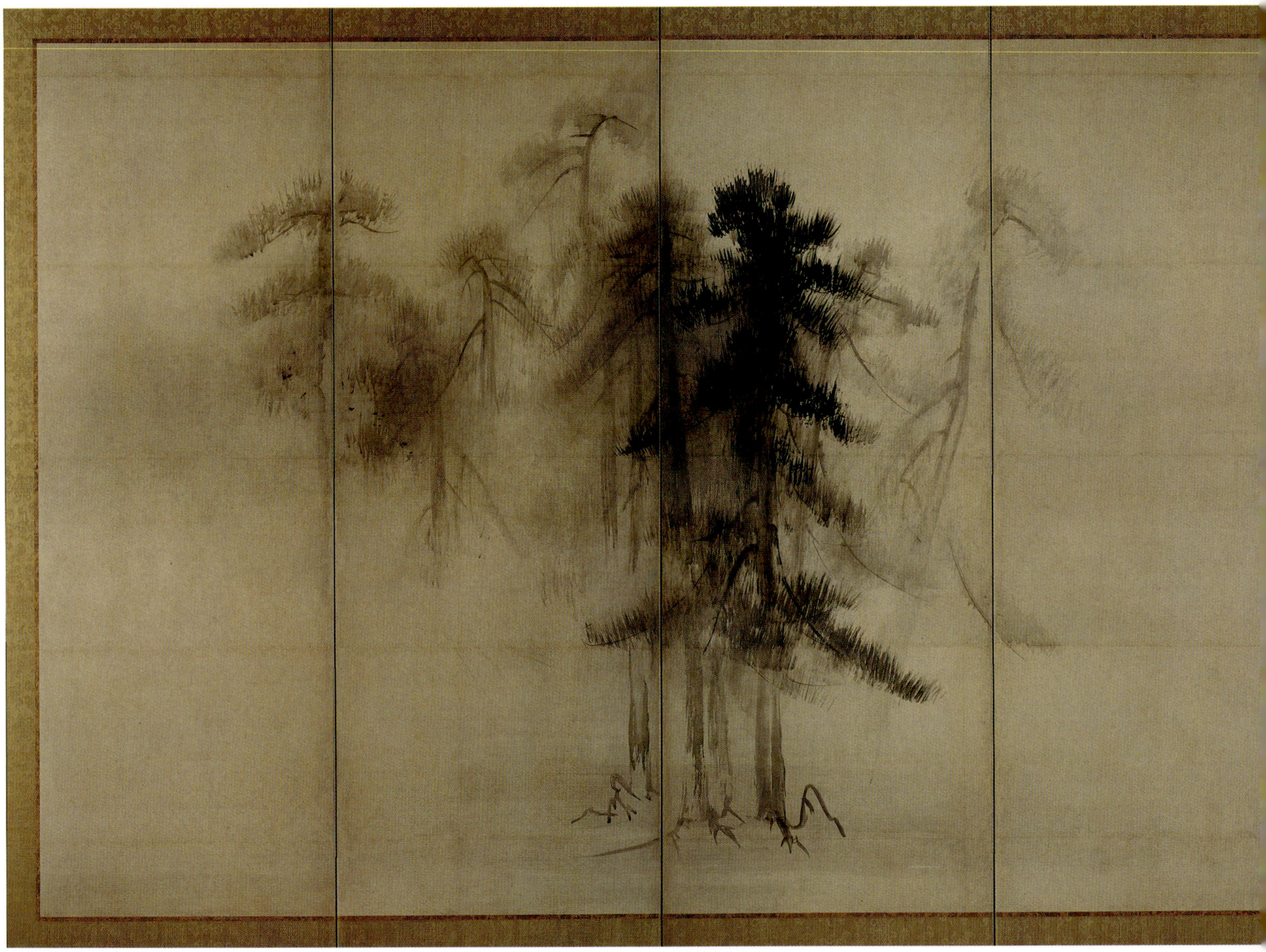

Edo Period (1615–1868)

In 1615, shogun Tokugawa Ieyasu, the final reunifier, consolidated power and established a new shogunate that lasted until 1868. He set up his seat of power in Edo (modern Tokyo), also the name for this period. The new regime instituted many policies designed to limit severely Japan's pace of social and cultural change. The Tokugawa rulers banned Christianity and expelled all Western foreigners except the Dutch, who were confined to a trading enclave far to the southwest at Nagasaki. Those in power transformed Confucian ideas of social stratification and civic responsibility into public policy, and they tried to control the social influence of urban merchants, some of whose wealth far outstripped that of most warrior leaders. However, the population's great expansion in urban centers, the spread of literacy in the cities and beyond, and a growing thirst for knowledge and diversion made for a very lively popular culture not easily susceptible to tight control.

A PRINCELY VILLA AT KYOTO   The imperial court's power remained as it had been for centuries, symbolic and ceremonial, but the court continued to wield influence in matters of taste and culture. For example, for a period of some fifty years in the seventeenth century, a princely family developed a modest country retreat into a villa that became the admired, but rarely equaled, standard for domestic Japanese architecture. Since the early twentieth century, it has inspired architects worldwide, even as ordinary living environments in Japan became increasingly Westernized in structure and decor. The Katsura Imperial Villa (FIG. **27-9**), built between 1620 and 1663, dates to the time of the tea ceremony's greatest popularity. Therefore, many of the villa's design features and tasteful subtleties derive from earlier teahouses, such as Rikyu's Taian (FIG. 27-6). However, more recent tea aesthetics had moved away from Rikyu's wabi extremes, and the Katsura Villa's designers and carpenters incorporated elements of courtly gracefulness as well.

Ornament that disguises structural forms has little place in this architecture's appeal, which relies instead on subtleties of proportion, color, and texture. A variety of textures (stone, wood, tile, and plaster) and subdued colors and tonal values enrich the villa's lines, planes, and volumes. Subtlety and finesse in the treatment of the building components were important. Artisans painstakingly rubbed and burnished all surfaces to bring out the natural beauty of their grains and textures. The rooms are not large, but parting or removing the

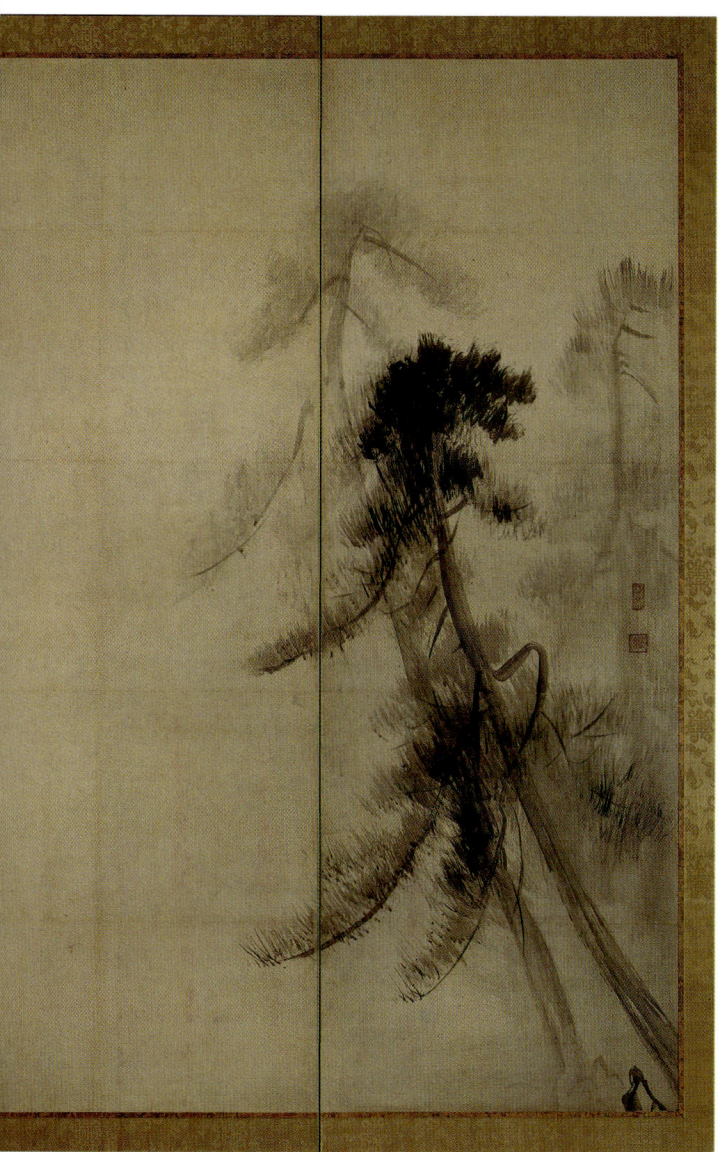

27-8   HASEGAWA TOHAKU, *Pine Forest,* Japan, Momoyama period, late sixteenth century. One of a pair of six-panel screens, ink on paper, 5′ 1⅜″ × 11′ 4″. Tokyo National Museum, Tokyo.

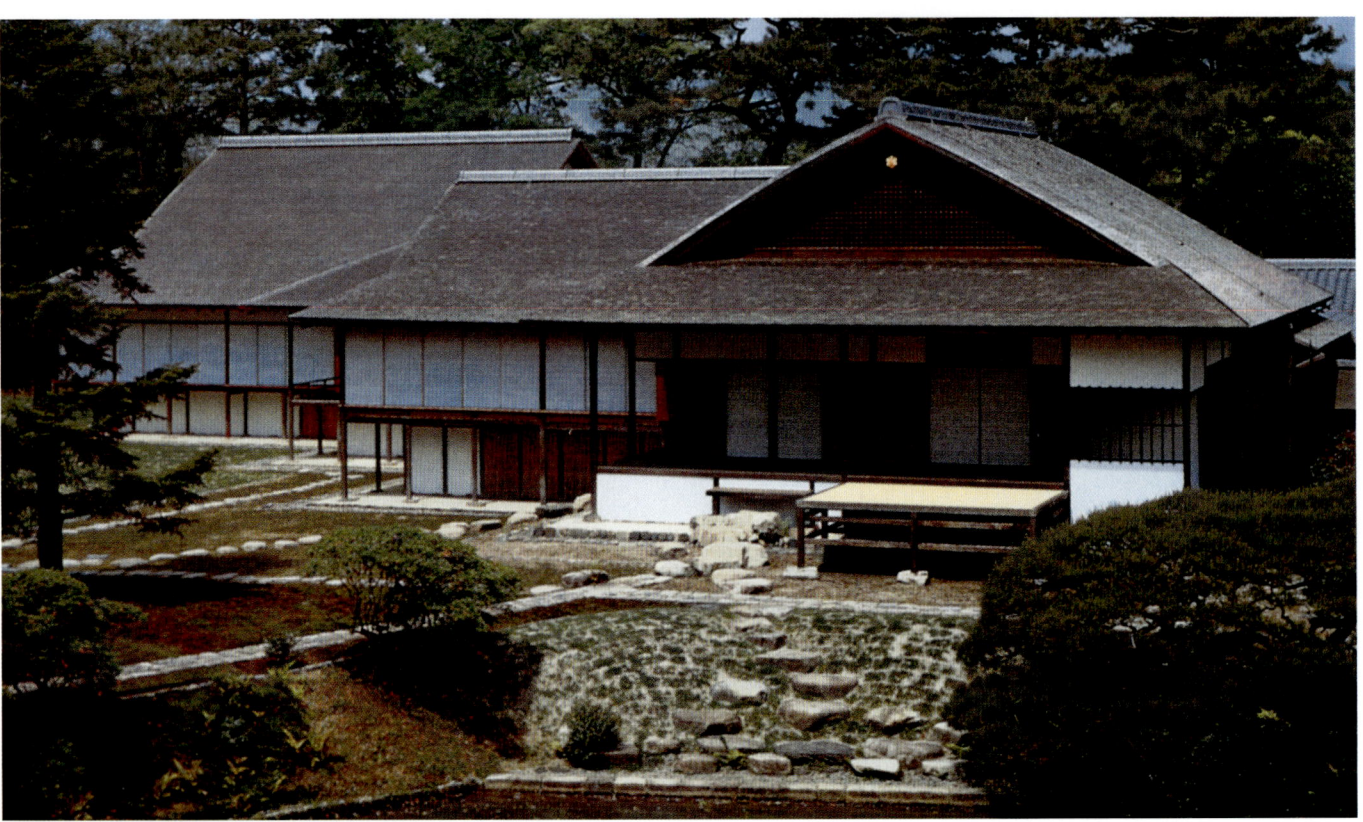

27-9   Eastern facade of Katsura Imperial Villa, Kyoto, Japan, Edo period, 1620–1663.

sliding doors between them can create broad rectangular spaces. Perhaps most important, the residents can open the doors to the outside to achieve a harmonious integration of building and garden — one of the great ideals of Japanese residential architecture.

THE RINPA SCHOOL EMERGES   In painting, the Edo period artists produced a dazzling variety. The Kano School enjoyed official governmental sponsorship, and its workshops provided paintings to the Tokugawa and their major vassals. By the mid-eighteenth century, at least, Kano masters also served as the primary painting teachers for nearly everyone aspiring to a career in the field. Nonetheless, individualist painters and other schools emerged and flourished, working in quite distinct styles.

The earliest major alternative school to emerge in the Edo period, Rinpa, was quite different in nature from the Kano and Tosa Schools. It did not have a similar continuity of lineage and training through father and son, master and pupil. Instead, Rinpa aesthetics and principles attracted over time a variety of individuals as practitioners and champions. Rinpa takes its first syllable from the last syllable in the name of its ostensible founder, Ogata Korin. However, two closely linked artists, HONAMI KOETSU (1558–1637) and Tawaraya Sotatsu (1576–1643), laid its foundations a few generations earlier.

COMBINING ANCIENT TRADITIONS   Koetsu was the heir to an important family of sword experts in the ancient capital of Kyoto and a greatly admired calligrapher. He also participated in the tea ceremony and made tea ceramics. Many scholars credit him with overseeing the design of lacquers (primarily wooden objects with lacquer decoration), perhaps with the aid of Sotatsu, the proprietor of a fan-painting shop. Schol-

ars do know that together they drew on ancient traditions of painting and craft decoration to develop a style that collapsed boundaries between the two arts. Paintings, the lacquered surfaces of writing boxes, and ceramics shared motifs and compositions. Most Rinpa motifs display an intimate knowledge of court literary and material traditions.

In typical fashion, Koetsu's *Boat Bridge* writing box (FIG. **27-10**) exhibits motifs drawn from classical poetry. The lid presents a subtle, gold-on-gold scene of small boats lined side by side in the water to support the planks of a temporary bridge. The bridge itself, a dull metal inlay, forms a band across the lid's convex surface. The raised dull linear forms on the water, boats, and bridge are a few Japanese characters from the poem, which describes the experience of crossing such a bridge as evoking reflection on life's insecurities. The box also shows the dramatic contrasts of form, texture, and color marking Rinpa aesthetics, especially the juxtaposition of the bridge's dull metal inlay and the brilliant gold surface. The gold decoration comes from careful sprinkling of actual gold dust in wet lacquer. Whatever Koetsu's contribution to the design process, specialists well versed in the demanding techniques of inlaying and sprinkling gold actually applied the lacquer decoration.

PLUM BLOSSOMS AND *TARASHIKOMI*   OGATA KORIN (1658–1716) took the principles Koetsu and Sotatsu developed into the eighteenth century. The son of an important textile merchant, Korin was primarily a painter but also designed lacquers in Koetsu's manner. One of Korin's painted masterpieces is a pair of twofold screens depicting red and white blossoming plum trees separated by a stream (FIGS. **27-11** and Intro-13). As Koetsu did with his writing box, Korin reduced the motifs to a minimum to offer a dramatic contrast

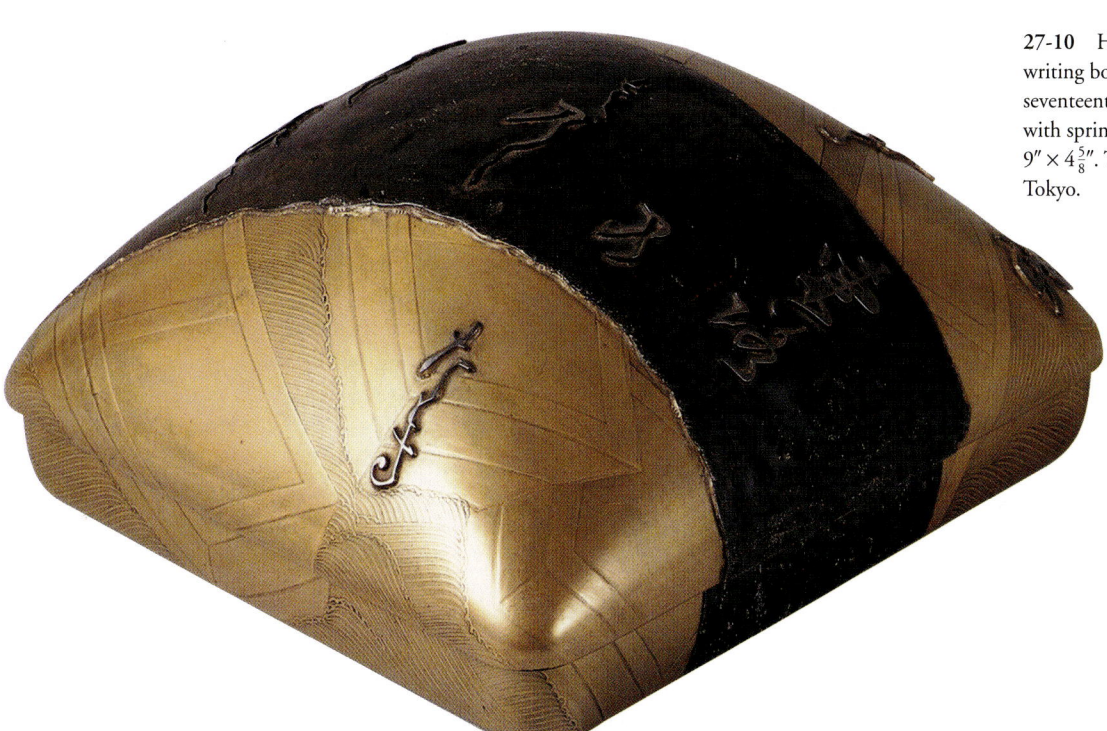

27-10 HONAMI KOETSU, *Boat Bridge,* writing box, Japan, Edo period, early seventeenth century. Lacquered wood with sprinkled gold and inlay, $9\frac{1}{2}'' \times 9'' \times 4\frac{5}{8}''$. Tokyo National Museum, Tokyo.

27-11 OGATA KORIN, *White Plum Blossoms,* Japan, Edo period, ca. 1710–1716. One of pair of twofold screens (see FIG. Intro-13), ink, color, and gold and silver leaf on paper, each screen $5'\ 1\frac{5}{8}'' \times 5'\ 7\frac{7}{8}''$. Museum of Art, Atami.

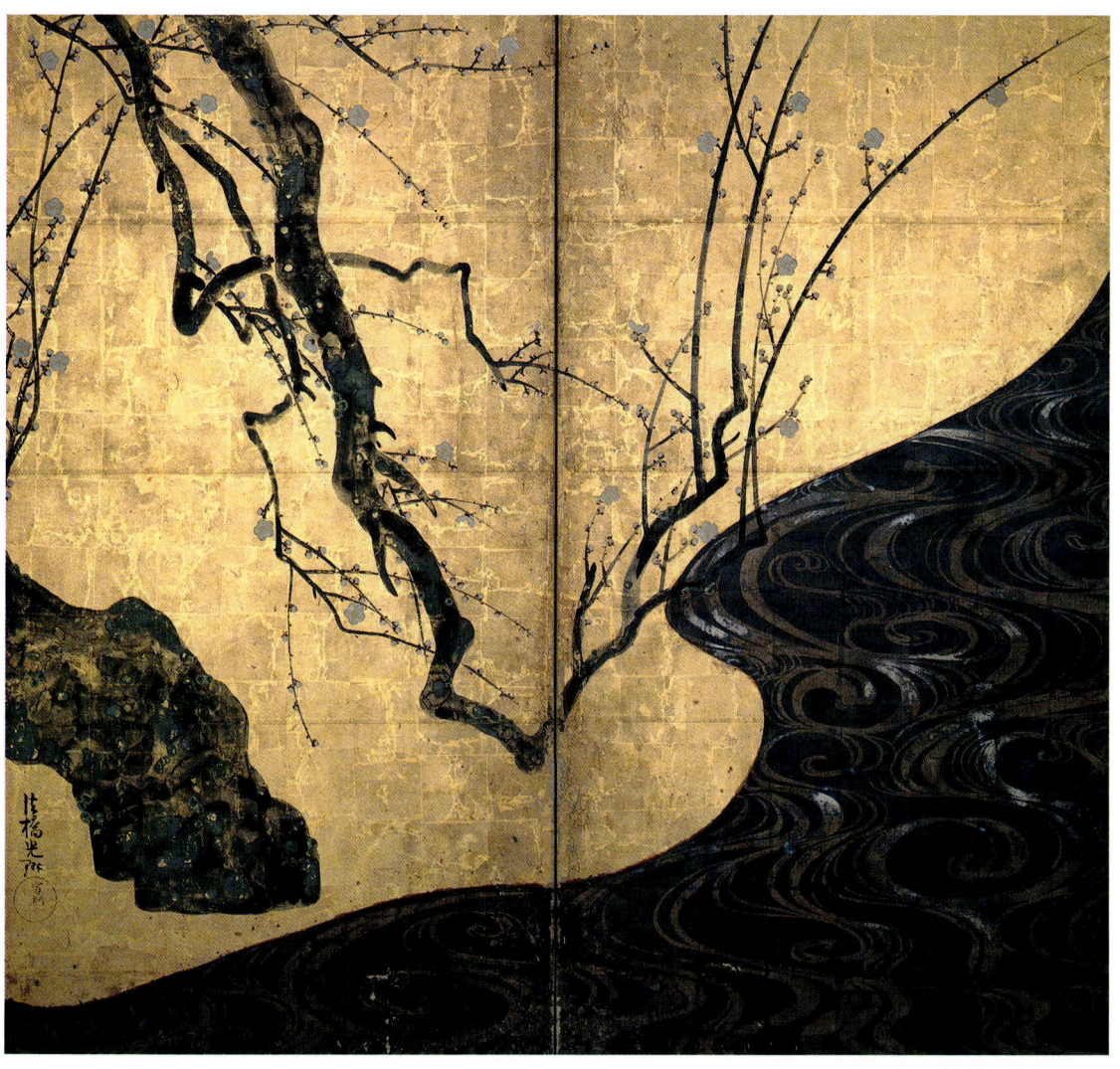

of forms and visual textures. Beneath delicate, slender branches, the gnarled, aged tree trunks exhibit flashes of bright color as they flank the stream's smooth, precise curves and muted tones. The contrast reaches even to the painting techniques. The mottling of the trees comes from a signature Rinpa technique called *tarashikomi,* the dropping of ink and pigments onto surfaces still wet with previously applied ink and pigments. In striking contrast, the pattern in the stream has the precision and elegant stylization of a textile design produced by applying pigment through the forms cut in a paper stencil.

THE LITERATI STYLE   In the seventeenth and eighteenth centuries, Japan's increasingly urban, educated population spurred a cultural and social restlessness among commoners and samurai of lesser rank that the policies of the restrictive Tokugawa could not suppress. People eagerly sought new ideas and images, directing their attention primarily to China, as had happened throughout Japanese his-

tory, but also to the West. From each direction dramatically new ideas (for the isolated Japanese) about painting emerged.

Starting in the late seventeenth century, several individual Japanese painters and their followers embraced elements of the Chinese literati style (see Chapter 26). Their inspiration came from earlier Chinese artists, such as Huang Gongwang (see FIG. 26-1), but only very indirectly. Illustrations in printed books and actual paintings of lesser quality brought limited knowledge of the literati style into Japan. However, the newly seen Chinese models supported emerging ideals of self-expression in painting by offering a worthy alternative to the Kano School's standardized repertoire.

One of the outstanding early representatives of Japanese literati painting was YOSA BUSON (1716–1783), whose *Cuckoo Flying over New Verdure* (FIG. 27-12) shows his fully mature style. He incorporated in this work basic elements of Chinese and Japanese literati style by rounding the landscape forms, by rendering their soft texture in fine fibrous brush strokes, and in his painting of dense foliage patterns. Although Buson imitated the vocabulary of brush strokes associated with the Chinese literati, his touch was bolder and more abstract, and the gentle palette of pale colors was very much his own.

NEW IDEAS FROM THE WEST   While the Japanese literati, such as Buson, catered to people of intellectual bent, a less demanding school, that of MARUYAMA OKYO (1733–1795), achieved a wide following among people attracted to naturalism combined with sheer painterly skill. Okyo looked to a variety of east Asian styles and also to the West. His sketches of animals, insects, and plants suggest an almost Western emphasis on observation, and, indeed, Western approaches to naturalistic depiction had become fairly widely known in Japan by this time. From the Dutch enclave in Nagasaki, European and Chinese books, including those with discussions and illustrations of Western pictorial art, had been filtering into Japan. In fact, groups formed to study "Dutch learning," and some painters experimented with oils and copperplate engraving techniques.

The staple of Okyo and his followers was not extreme naturalism but a blending of naturalism with elements of Kano painting and a type of Chinese painting one might call "decorative naturalism." His *Peacocks and Peonies* (FIG. 27-13) is an outstanding example of this synthesis. The rich detail in Okyo's depiction of the plumage and the brilliant colors of the bird and flowers dazzle the eyes. Meanwhile, the peacock's slight roundness, especially in its neck, and the modeling of the rocks in gradations of light and shadow grant the image substance. The combination appealed to the sensuality and materiality of urban sensibilities.

EDO'S FLOATING WORLD   The urban population's restlessness also found outlet in the more direct pursuit of sensual pleasure and entertainment. The Tokugawa tried to hold such activities in check, but largely in vain. In the brash, popular theaters and the pleasure houses of Edo's Yoshiwara brothel district, prosperous townspeople, as well as many samurai, sought entertainment and gratification. Those of lesser means could partake vicariously. Rapid developments in the printing industry led to the availability of numerous books and printed images (see "Japanese Wood-

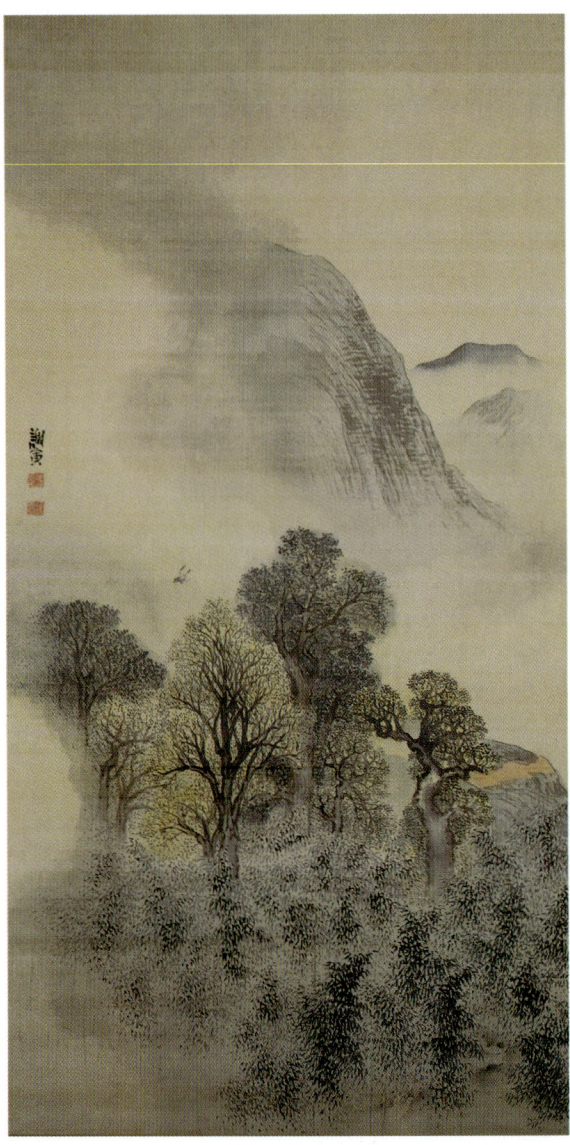

27-12   YOSA BUSON, *Cuckoo Flying over New Verdure,* Japan, Edo period, late eighteenth century. Hanging scroll, ink and color on silk, $5' \frac{1}{2}'' \times 2' 7\frac{1}{4}''$. Hiraki Ukiyoe Museum, Yokohama, Japan.

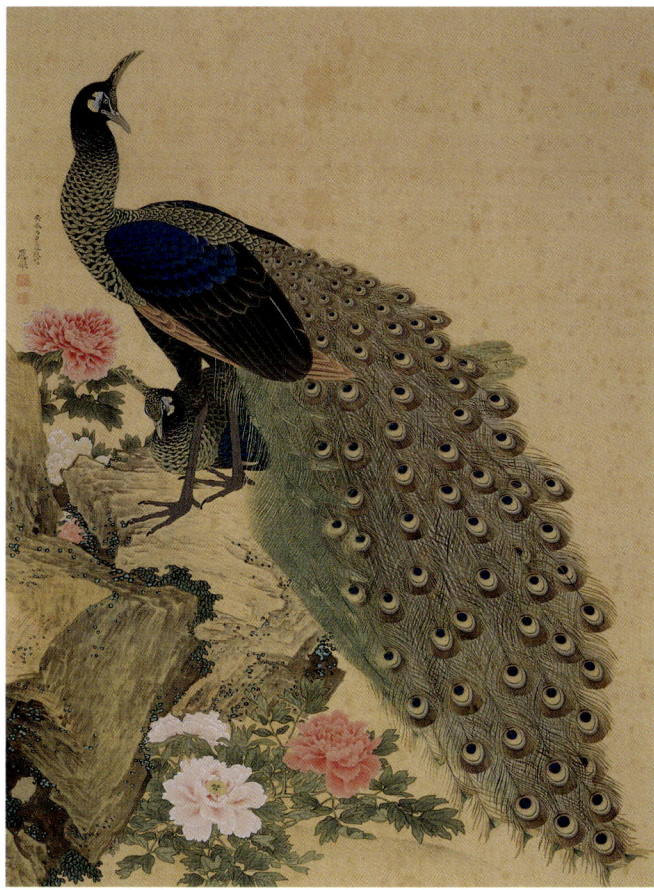

27-13 MARUYAMA OKYO, *Peacocks and Peonies,* Japan, Edo period, 1776. Hanging scroll, color on silk, 4′ 3$\frac{1}{3}$″ × 2′ 2$\frac{7}{8}$″. Imperial Household Collection, Tokyo.

Beautiful young women and the city's sensual pleasures are not the sole subjects of Harunobu's parlor series, however. The prints draw playfully on an ancient Chinese landscape theme popular in Japan for several centuries—usually titled *Eight Views of the Xiao and Xiang Rivers.* Instead of the traditional temple bell of the Chinese works, however, Harunobu depicted a modern clock. This juxtaposition of past and present has a humorous quality but also displays the cultural sophistication of the floating world's inhabitants. Not all prints engage viewers on so many levels. Many are more straightforward posterlike representations of famous courtesans and popular actors in their roles. Others depict birds and flowers, still lifes, and graphic erotica.

WESTERN PERSPECTIVE IN PRINTS Another printmaking subject that emerged in the late eighteenth century, landscapes, often incorporated Western perspective techniques. One of the most famous designers in this genre was KATSUSHIKA HOKUSAI (1760–1849), whose famous print, *The Great Wave off Kanagawa* (FIG. **27-15**), belongs to a wood-block series called *Thirty-Six Views of Mount Fuji.* In this view, the huge foreground wave dwarfs the artist's representation of a distant Fuji. This contrast and the whitecaps' ominous fingers magnify the wave's threatening aspect. The fishermen bend low to dig their oars against the rough sea and drive their long low vessels past the danger. This print, although it draws somewhat on Western techniques, also engages the Japanese pictorial tradition. Against a background with the low horizon typical of Western perspective painting, Hokusai placed the wave's more traditionally flat and powerfully graphic forms in the foreground.

block Prints," page 831), and these could convey the city's delights for a fraction of the cost of actual participation. Taking part in the emerging urban culture involved more than simple physical satisfactions and rowdy entertainments. Many who participated were highly educated in literature, music, and the other arts. The best-known products of this sophisticated counterculture are the paintings and especially prints whose main subjects come from the *ukiyo-e* (floating world) of pleasure—the Yoshiwara brothels and the popular theater.

VIEWS OF AN UKIYO-E PARLOR The urban appetite for ukiyo-e pleasures allowed many print designers to flourish, and competition among publishing houses led to ever greater refinement and experimentation. One of the most admired and emulated eighteenth-century designers, SUZUKI HARUNOBU (ca. 1725–1770), played a key role in developing some of the earliest *brocade prints,* pictures printed (not hand painted) in many colors. Harunobu gained a tremendous advantage over his fellow designers when he received commissions from members of a poetry club to design limited-edition prints of the highest quality. Harunobu brought much of what he learned from these to his design of more commercial prints. He even issued some of the private designs later under his own name for popular consumption. An outstanding example of his sophisticated work is *Evening Bell at the Clock* (FIG. **27-14**) from a series called *Eight Views of the Parlor.* Its flatness and rich color recall the traditions of court painting (FIG. **27-3**), a comparison many ukiyo-e artists openly sought.

MODERN JAPAN

The Meiji and Taisho Periods (1868–1926)

The Edo Period and samurai rule ended in 1868, when the Tokugawa shogunate toppled, in part because of its inability to handle increasing pressure from Western nations for Japan to throw open its doors to the outside world. Led by samurai from provinces far removed from Edo, the rebellion restored direct sovereignty to the imperial throne, but real power rested with the emperor's cabinet, instead of the emperor himself. As a symbol of imperial authority, however, this new period was officially called the Meiji after the emperor's chosen reign name. This became the standard still followed today. From the last years of the Edo period into the Meiji, Japanese leaders worried that Japan might suffer the colonial fate of so many other nations Westerners deemed "uncivilized." Therefore, they greatly emphasized catching up with the West in military capacity, science, and technology. They also promoted Western cultural elements as signs of Japan's status as a "civilized" nation. Japanese culture had, after all, long "upgraded" itself through similar emulation of China, as in the Nara period (see Chapter 8). To catch up with the West as quickly as possible, the government imported Western architects and artists. Many of them taught Japanese students in newly established programs and schools.

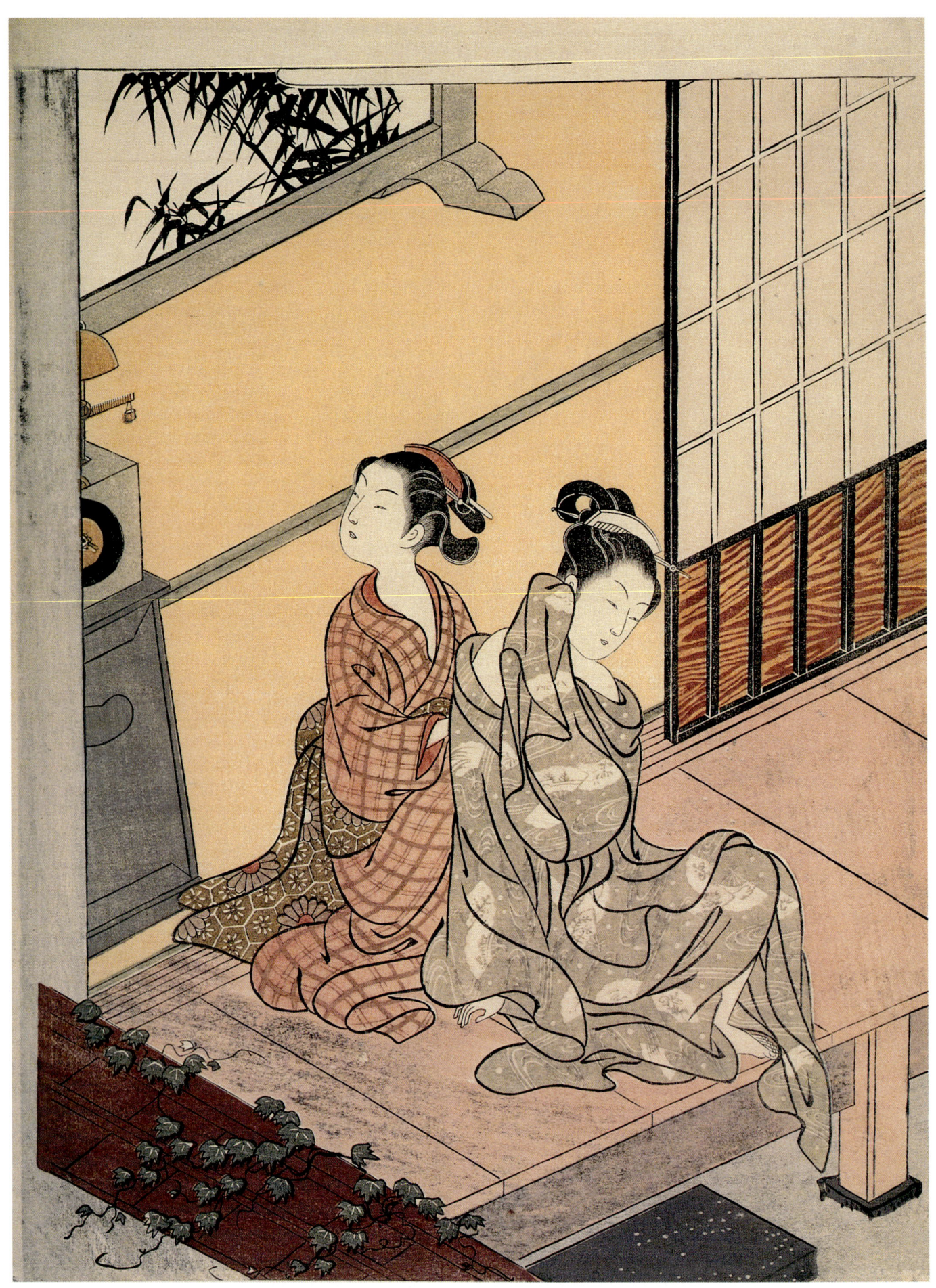

27-14 Suzuki Harunobu, *Evening Bell at the Clock*, from *Eight Views of the Parlor* series, Japan, Edo period, ca. 1765. Woodblock print, $11\frac{1}{4}'' \times 8\frac{1}{2}''$. Art Institute of Chicago, Chicago (Clarence Buckingham Collection).

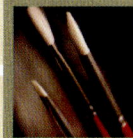

Japanese Woodblock Prints

During the Edo period, *ukiyo-e* (floating world) woodblock prints became enormously popular. Sold in small shops and on the street, an ordinary print went for the price of a bowl of noodles. People of very modest income, therefore, could collect prints in albums or paste them on their walls. A highly efficient production system made this wide distribution of Japanese graphic art possible.

The ukiyo-e artists took no direct part in the actual making of the prints that made them so famous both in their own day and today. As the designers, they sold painted originals to publishers, who in turn oversaw their printing. The publishers also played a role in creating ukiyo-e prints by commissioning specific designs or adapting them before printing. Certainly, the names of both designer and publisher appear on the final prints.

Unacknowledged in nearly all cases are the individuals who actually made the prints, the block-carvers and printers. Using skills polished since childhood, they worked with both speed and precision for relatively low wages and thus made possible the economies of ukiyo-e prints as a popular art. The master ukiyo-e printmakers seem all to have been men. Women, especially wives and daughters, often assisted painters and other artists, but few gained separate recognition. Among the exceptions, the daughter of Katsushika Hokusai (FIG. 27-15), Katsushika Oi, became well known as a painter and probably helped her father with his print designs.

That Japanese prints tended to have black outlines separating distinct color areas (FIG. 27-14) affected the printing process. A master carver pasted painted designs face down on a wooden block. Wetting and gently scraping the thin paper revealed the reversed image to guide the cutting of the block.

After the carving, only the outlines of the forms and other elements that would be black in the final print remained raised in relief. The master printer then coated the block with black ink and printed several initial outline prints. These master prints became the guides for carving the other blocks, one for each color used. On each color block, the carver left in relief only the areas to be printed in that color. Even ordinary prints sometimes required up to twenty colors and thus twenty blocks. To print a color, a printer applied the appropriate pigment to a block's raised surface, laid a sheet of paper on it, and rubbed the paper's back with a smooth flat object. Then another printer would print a different color on the same sheet of paper. Perfect alignment of the paper in each step was critical to prevent overlapping of colors, so the block-carvers included printing guides—an L-shaped ridge in one corner and a straight ridge on one side—in their blocks. The printers could cover small alignment errors with a final printing of the black outlines from the last block.

The materials used in printing varied over time but by the mid-eighteenth century had reached some level of standardization. The blocks were planks of fine-grained hardwood, usually cherry. The best paper came from the white layer beneath the bark of mulberry trees, because its long fibers helped the paper stand up to repeated rubbing on the blocks. The printers used a few mineral pigments but tended to favor rather inexpensive dyes made from plants for most colors. As a result, the colors of ukiyo-e prints were and are highly susceptible to fading, especially when exposed to strong light. In the early nineteenth century, more permanent European synthetic dyes began to enter Japan. The first, Prussian Blue, can be seen in Hokusai's *The Great Wave off Kanagawa* (FIG. 27-15).

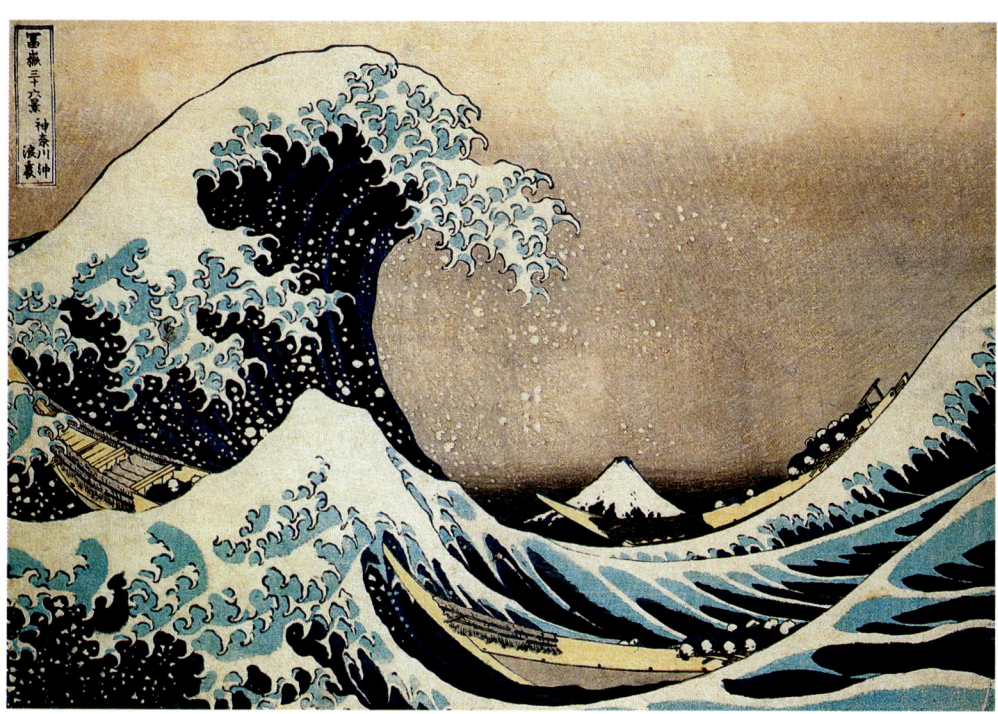

27-15 KATSUSHIKA HOKUSAI, *The Great Wave off Kanagawa*, from *Thirty-Six Views of Mount Fuji* series, Japan, Edo period, ca. 1826–1833. Woodblock print oban, ink and colors on paper, $9\frac{7}{8}''$ × 1' $2\frac{3}{4}''$. Museum of Fine Arts, Boston (Spaulding Collection).

WESTERN OIL PAINTING   Oil painting became a major genre in Japan in the late nineteenth century. Ambitious students studied with Westerners at government schools and during trips abroad. One oil painting highlighting the cultural foment of the early Meiji period is *Oiran* (literally, "Grand courtesan"; FIG. **27-16**), painted by TAKAHASHI YUICHI (1828–1894). The artist created it for a client nostalgic for vanishing elements of Japanese culture. Ukiyo-e print-makers frequently represented such grand courtesans of the pleasure quarters. In this painting, however, Takahashi (historical figures from the Meiji period onward usually are referred to by their family names, which come first) did not portray the courtesan's features in the idealizing manner of ukiyo-e artists but in the more analytical manner of Western portraiture. Yet, the painter's more abstract rendering of the garments reflects a very old practice in east Asian portraiture (see FIG. 26-19).

RESISTANCE TO WESTERNIZATION   Unbridled enthusiasm for Westernization in some quarters led to resistance and concern over a loss of distinctive Japanese identity in other quarters. Ironically, one of those most eager to preserve "Japaneseness" in the arts was an American professor of philosophy and political economy at Tokyo Imperial University, Ernest Fenollosa (1853–1908). He and a former student named Okakura Kakuzo (1862–1913) joined with others in a movement that eventually led to the founding of an arts university dedicated to Japanese arts under Okakura's direction. Their goal for Japanese painting was to make it viable in the modern age rather than preserve it as a relic, so they encouraged incorporating some Western techniques in basically Japanese-style paintings. The resulting style was called *nihonga* (Japanese painting), as opposed to *yoga* (Western painting).

Kutsugen (FIG. **27-17**), a silk scroll in the Itsukushima Shrine at Hiroshima Prefecture by YOKOYAMA TAIKAN (1868–1958) provides a good example of the former. It combines a low horizon line and subtle shading effects taken from

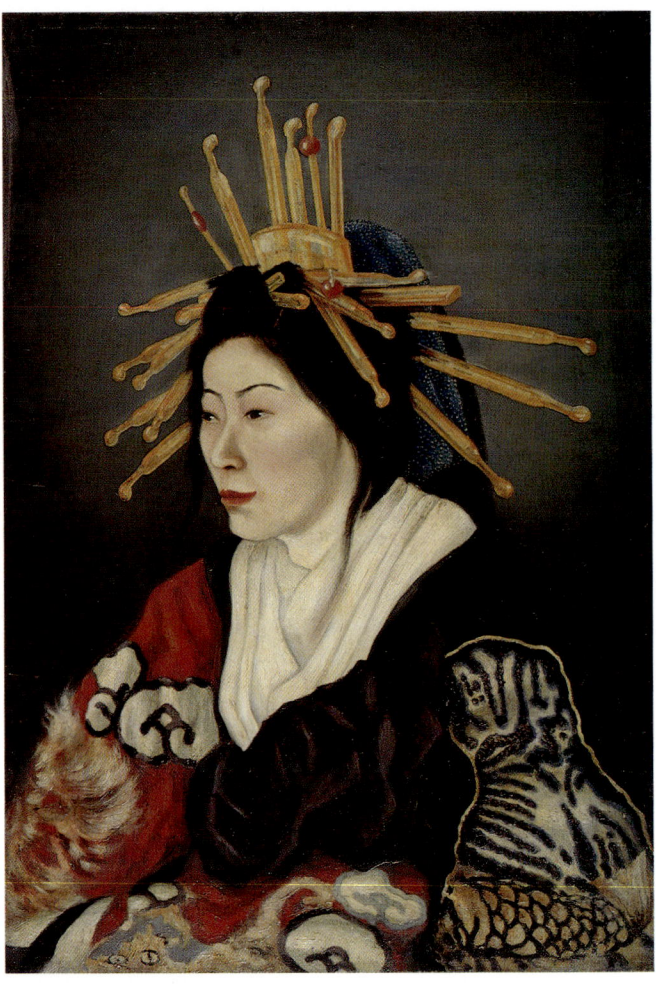

27-16   TAKAHASHI YUICHI, *Oiran* ("Grand courtesan"), Japan, Meiji period, 1872. Oil on canvas, $2' 6\frac{1}{2}'' \times 1' 9\frac{5}{8}''$. Tokyo National University of Fine Arts and Music, Tokyo.

Western painting with east Asian features, such as a composition anchored in one corner (see FIGS. 7-24 and 26-5), strong ink brushwork in its contours, washes of water-and-glue-

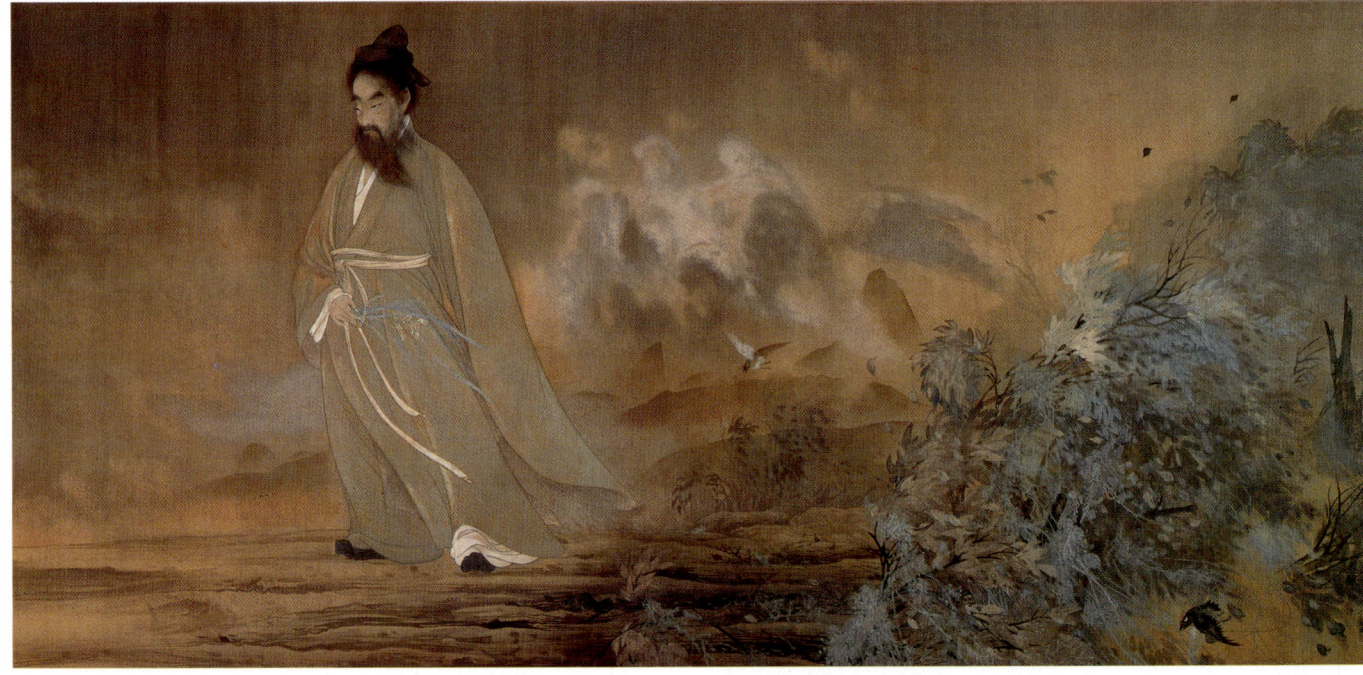

27-17   YOKOYAMA TAIKAN, *Kutsugen*, Itsukushima Shrine, Hiroshima Prefecture, Japan, Meiji period, 1898. Hanging scroll, color on silk, $4' 4'' \times 9' 6''$.

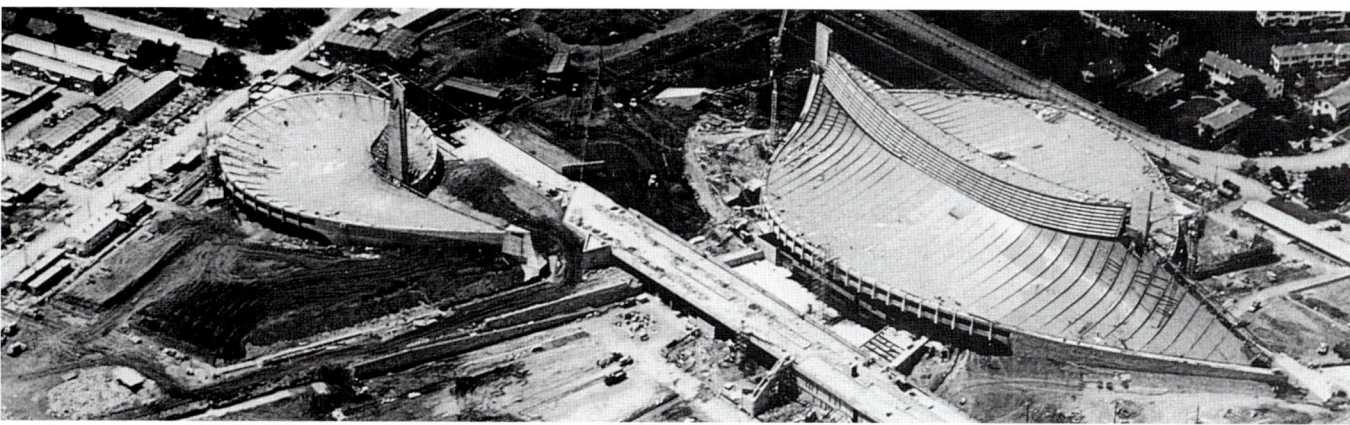

27-18   KENZO TANGE, national indoor Olympic stadiums, Tokyo, Japan, Showa period, 1963–1964.

based pigments, and applications of heavy mineral pigments. The painting's subject, a Chinese poet who fell out of the emperor's favor, may have resonated with Taikan and his associates, living in Japan when things Japanese needed defense. The poet in the picture stands resolutely against strong winds, suggesting the spirit of the early nihonga painters, who resisted powerful forces of change.

The Showa and Heisei Periods
(1926–Present)

Developments during the twentieth century brought Japan increasing prominence on the world stage in areas of economics, politics, and culture. One tragic result for Japan was the widespread devastation of World War II. During the succeeding occupation period, the United States imposed new democratic institutions on Japan, with the emperor serving as a ceremonial head of state, and Japan rebounded with remarkable speed. From the second half of that century to the present, Japan also has taken a positive and productive place in the international art world. As in earlier times in its relationship to the art and culture of China and Korea, it has internalized Western lessons and transformed them into a part of its own vital culture.

A HOME FOR THE OLYMPICS   Japanese architecture, especially public and commercial building, rapidly transformed along Western lines. In fact, architecture may be the art form providing Japanese practitioners the most substantial presence on the world scene. They have made major contributions to both modern and postmodern developments. One of the most daringly experimental architects of the post-World War II period is KENZO TANGE (b. 1913). When designing the stadiums for the 1964 Olympics (FIG. **27-18**), he employed a cable suspension system to shape steel and concrete into remarkably graceful structures. His attention to both the sculptural qualities of each building's raw concrete form and the fluidity of its spaces puts him with architects worldwide who carried on the legacy of the late style of Le Corbusier in France (see FIG. 34-40). His stadiums thus bear comparison with Joern Utzon's Sydney Opera House (see FIG. 34-42).

CONTINUING TRADITIONAL CERAMICS   The other Japanese art form of the twentieth century attracting great attention worldwide is ceramics, but not for its international fla-

vor. Like other international folk art, traditional Japanese ceramics and other so-called crafts are highly valued today. A formative figure in Japan's folk art movement, the philosopher Yanagi Soetsu (1889–1961), promoted an ideal of beauty that only could be achieved in functional objects made of natural materials by anonymous craftspeople. The potter HAMADA SHOJI (1894–1978) espoused those selfless ideals but, nevertheless, gained international fame and received official recognition in Japan as a "Bearer of Important Intangible Cultural Properties," more commonly called a "Living National Treasure." Works such as his dish with casual slip designs (FIG. **27-19**) are unsigned but easily recognized as his by connoisseurs. Such stoneware is coarser, darker, and heavier than porcelain and lacks the latter's fine decoration. To those who appreciate simpler, earthier beauty, however, this dish holds great attraction.

INNOVATION THROUGH ADAPTATION   The great strength of Japanese art always has been innovation through adaptation. Contact with the rest of eastern Asia and later the world's other areas, as well as knowledge of Japan's own past, provided artists and patrons a wealth of aesthetic and ideological options. As they integrated the new, they found cultural spaces where less radical adaptations of the old could survive. Even today, as Japan embraces a vision of its postindustrial future, very traditional artists, as well as thoroughly contemporary ones, flourish side by side as in no other industrialized nation.

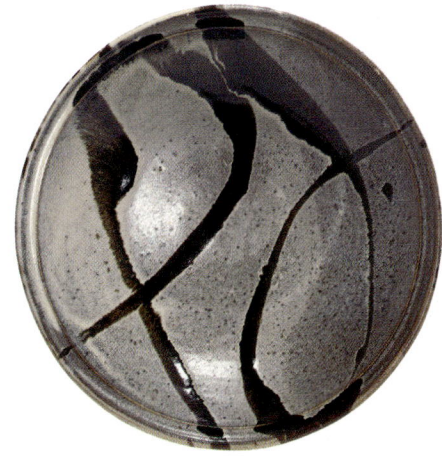

27-19   HAMADA SHOJI, large bowl, 1962. Black trails on translucent glaze, $5\frac{7}{8}''\times 1'\ 10\frac{1}{2}''$. National Museum of Modern Art, Kyoto.

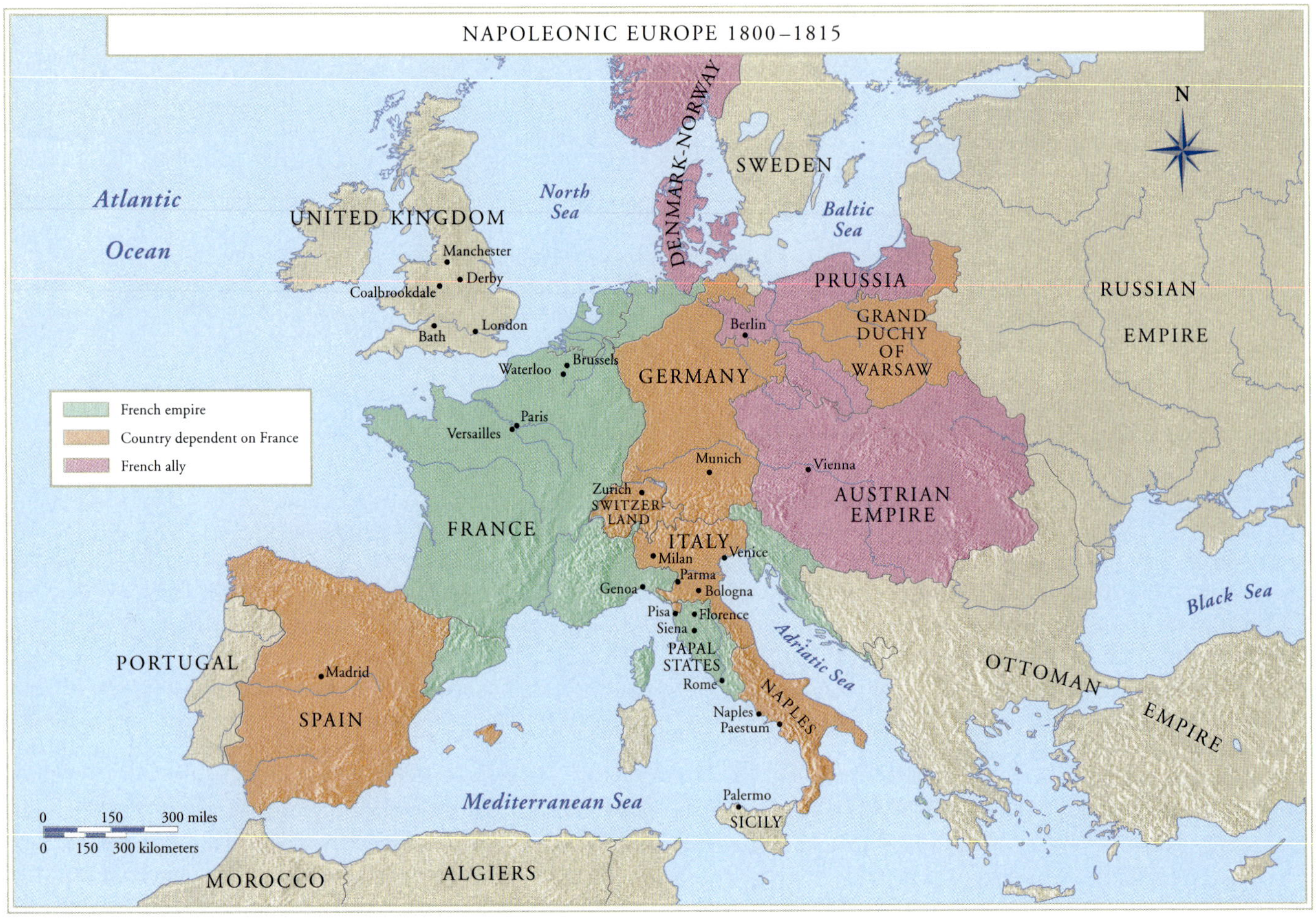

NAPOLEONIC EUROPE 1800–1815

Atlantic Ocean

North Sea

Baltic Sea

UNITED KINGDOM

- Manchester
- Derby
- Coalbrookdale
- London
- Bath
- Waterloo
- Brussels

DENMARK-NORWAY

SWEDEN

RUSSIAN EMPIRE

PRUSSIA
- Berlin

GRAND DUCHY OF WARSAW

GERMANY

FRANCE
- Paris
- Versailles

- Munich

- Vienna

AUSTRIAN EMPIRE

SWITZERLAND
- Zurich

ITALY
- Milan
- Venice
- Parma
- Genoa
- Bologna
- Pisa
- Florence
- Siena

PAPAL STATES
- Rome

NAPLES
- Naples
- Paestum

Adriatic Sea

Black Sea

OTTOMAN EMPIRE

PORTUGAL

SPAIN
- Madrid

Mediterranean Sea

- Palermo
SICILY

MOROCCO

ALGIERS

N

Legend:
- French empire
- Country dependent on France
- French ally

0   150   300 miles
0   150   300 kilometers

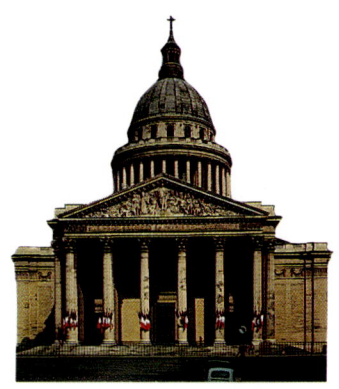

Jacques-Germain Soufflot
the Panthéon, 1755–1792

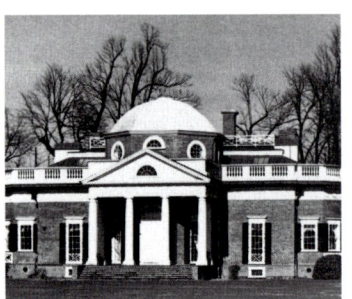

Thomas Jefferson
Monticello, 1770–1806

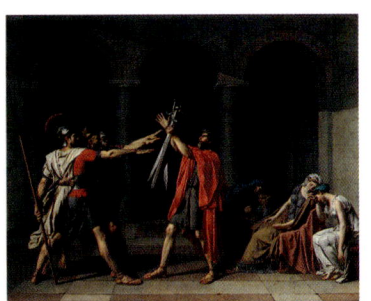

Jacques-Louis David
Oath of the Horatii, 1784

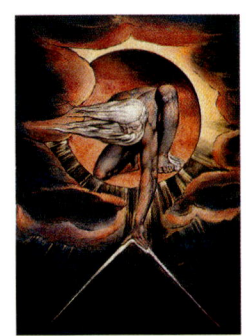

William Blake
Ancient of Days, 1794

Voltaire, 1694–1778

Jean-Jacques Rousseau, 1712–1778

Denis Diderot, 1713–1784,

Frederick II (The Great) of Prussia, r. 1740–1780

Johann Wolfgang von Goethe, 1749–1832

Encyclopédie, 1751–1780

American Revolution, 1763–1783

England's Royal Academy of Arts founded, 1766

New steam engine patented, 1769

Sir Walter Scott, 1771–1832

French Revolution, 1789–1795

28

THE ENLIGHTENMENT AND ITS LEGACY

NEOCLASSICISM THROUGH THE
MID-NINETEENTH CENTURY

1800			1820		1830		1840		1851	
GEORGE III OF ENGLAND				GEORGE IV		WILLIAM IV		VICTORIA		
FIRST REPUBLIC	NAPOLEON I (THE EMPIRE)		LOUIS XVIII		CHARLES X	LOUIS PHILIPPE			SECOND REPUBLIC	SECOND EMPIRE

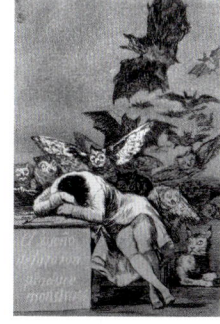

Francisco Goya
The Sleep of Reason
Produces Monsters, ca. 1798

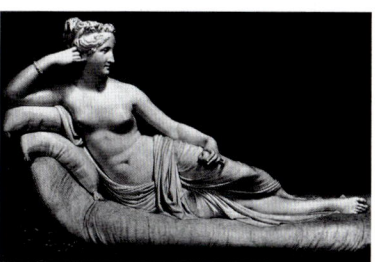

Antonio Canova
Pauline Borghese as Venus, 1808

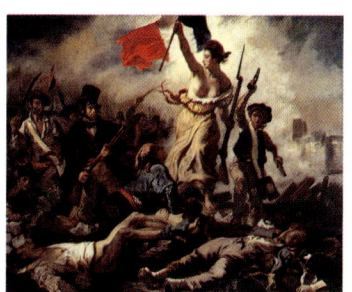

Eugène Delacroix
Liberty Leading the People, 1830

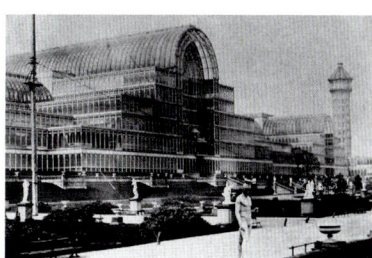

Joseph Paxton
Crystal Palace, 1850–1851

Napoleon Bonaparte, First Consul of France, 1800

Chateaubriand, *Genius of Christianity*, 1802

Napoleon crowned emperor, 1804

Napoleon abdicates, 1814

Battle of Waterloo, 1815

Restoration of the Bourbons, 1815

Revolution of 1830 in France

Constitutional monarchy in France, 1830–1848

Daguerreotype presented, 1839

Karl Marx, 1816–1883,
Communist Manifesto, 1848

Revolution of 1848 in France

THE ENLIGHTENMENT: PHILOSOPHY AND SOCIETY

During the eighteenth century, the expanding boundaries of European knowledge marked what has been called the Age of Enlightenment. The Enlightenment was in essence a new way of thinking critically about the world and about humankind, independently of religion, myth, or tradition. The new method was based on using reason to reflect on the results of physical experiments and involved the critical analysis of texts. It was grounded in empirical evidence. Enlightenment thought promoted the scientific questioning of all assertions and rejected unfounded beliefs about the nature of humankind and of the world. The enlightened mind was skeptical of doctrines and theories such as superstitions and old wives' tales that no verifiable evidence could prove. Thus the Enlightenment encouraged and stimulated the habit and application of mind known as the scientific method.

"THE DOCTRINE OF EMPIRICISM"   The Enlightenment had its roots in the seventeenth century, with the mathematical and scientific achievements of René Descartes, Blaise Pascal, Isaac Newton, and Gottfried Wilhelm von Leibnitz. England and France were the principal centers of the Enlightenment, though its dictums influenced the thinking of intellectuals throughout Europe and in the American colonies. Benjamin Franklin, Thomas Jefferson, and other American notables were educated in its principles. Of particular importance for Enlightenment thought was the work of Britons Isaac Newton (1642–1727) and John Locke (1632–1704).

In Newton's scientific studies, he insisted on empirical proof of his theories and encouraged others to avoid metaphysics and the supernatural—realms that extended beyond the natural physical world. This emphasis on both tangible data and concrete experience became a cornerstone of Enlightenment thought. In addition, Newton's experiments seemed to reveal a rationality in the physical world. Enlightenment thinkers transferred such concepts to the sociopolitical world by promoting a rationally organized society. John Locke, whose works acquired the status of Enlightenment gospel, developed these ideas further. What we know, wrote Locke, comes to us through sense perception of the material world and is imprinted on the mind as on a blank tablet. From these perceptions alone we form ideas. Our ideas are not innate or God given; it is only from experience that we can know (this is called the "doctrine of empiricism"). Locke believed human beings are born good, not cursed by original sin. The law of Nature grants them the natural rights of life, liberty, and property, as well as the right to freedom of conscience. Government is by contract, and its purpose is to protect these rights; if and when government abuses these rights, we have the further natural right of revolution. Locke's ideas empowered people to take control of their own destinies.

"THE DOCTRINE OF PROGRESS"   The work of Newton and Locke also inspired French intellectuals. New philosophies placing individuals and societies-at-large as part of physical nature were advanced by thinkers in France, who are still known by their French designation *philosophes*. They shared the conviction that the ills of humanity could be remedied by applying reason and common sense to human problems. They criticized the powers of church and state as irrational limits placed on political and intellectual freedom. They believed that, by the accumulation and propagation of knowledge, humanity could advance by degrees to a happier state than it had ever known. This conviction matured into the characteristically modern "doctrine of progress" and its corollary doctrine of the perfectibility of humankind. Previous societies, for the most part, perceived the future as inevitable—the life and death cycle and fate determined by religious beliefs. This notion of progress—the systematic and planned improvement of society—was developed first during the eighteenth century.

A COMPENDIUM OF KNOWLEDGE   Animated by their belief in human progress and perfectibility, the philosophes took the task of gathering knowledge and making it accessible to all who could read. Their program was, in effect, the democratization of knowledge. Denis Diderot's (1713–1784) brilliant, critical intelligence greatly influenced the Enlightenment's rationalistic and materialistic thinking. He became editor of the pioneering *Encyclopédie,* a compilation of articles and illustrations written by more than one hundred contributors, including all of the leading philosophes. The *Encyclopédie* was truly comprehensive (its formal title was *Systematic Dictionary of the Sciences, Arts, and Crafts*) and included all available knowledge—historical, scientific, and technical, as well as religious and moral—and political theory. The first volume was published in 1751, and the project (thirty-five volumes of text and illustrations) was completed in 1780. This notion of the accumulation and documentation of knowledge was new to Western society; such cultures had relied heavily on tradition and convention. The *Encyclopédie* was instrumental in shattering the complacency of Western thought.

Diderot's contemporary, Comte de Buffon (1707–1788), undertook a kind of encyclopedia of the natural sciences. His *Natural History,* a monumental work of forty-four volumes, was especially valuable for its zoological study and had the general effect of inspiring in the reading public an interest in the world of nature. These collections of information were consistent with the rationalistic and empiricist foundation of the Enlightenment.

REVOLUTIONARY CHANGE   The political, economic, and social consequences of this expanding knowledge were explosive. It is no coincidence that two of the major revolutions of recent centuries—the French Revolution and the Industrial Revolution in England—occurred during this period. The Enlightenment idea of a participatory and knowledgeable citizenry contributed to the revolt against the French monarchy in 1789. The immediate causes of the French Revolution were France's economic crisis and the clash between the Third Estate (bourgeoisie, peasantry, and urban and rural workers) and the First (clergy) and Second Estates (nobility). They fought over the issue of representation in the legislative body, the Estates-General, which had been convened to decide the taxation issue. However, the ensuing revolution revealed the instability of the monarchy and of the French society's traditional structure and resulted in a succession of republics and empires as France struggled to find a way to adjust to these decisive changes.

The celebration of "progress," along with technological advances, led to the Industrial Revolution. Although it is impossible to assign specific dates to the Industrial Revolution, technological innovations began to make their mark in the 1740s. By 1850, England had a manufacturing economy. This development was revolutionary because for the first time in history, societies were capable of producing a limitless supply of goods and services. England's production capability was due to the new manufacturing technology, along with advances in heating, lighting, and transportation.

These developments precipitated yet other major changes. The growth of cities and of an urban working class were two such changes. Colonialism expanded as the demand for cheap labor and raw materials increased. For example, England feuded with France over the North American continent and the subcontinent of India. This enthusiasm for growth eventually emerged in the newly established United States as well in the form of the doctrine of Manifest Destiny—the ideological justification for continued territorial expansion. As John L. O'Sullivan expounded in the earliest known use of the term in 1845: "Our manifest destiny [is] to overspread the continent allotted by Providence for the free development of our yearly multiplying millions."[1]

Thus, the Age of Enlightenment ushered in a new way of thinking and affected historical developments worldwide. Artists entered into this dialogue about the state and direction of society and played an important role in encouraging public consideration of these momentous changes. In the arts, this new way of thinking can be seen in the general label "modern" used to describe the art from the late eighteenth century on. Such a vague and generic term, covering centuries of art, renders any concrete definition of "modern art" virtually impossible. However, one defining characteristic scholars and critics traditionally have ascribed to the modern era is an awareness of history. People know their culture perpetuates or rejects previously established ideas or conventions. The concept of *modernity*—the state of being modern—involves being up to date, implying a distinction between the present and past. Recent art historical scholarship has posited an even earlier date for the inception of the modern era. Many art historians now assert that this historical consciousness was present in much earlier societies. This accounts for current use of the term "early modern" to describe Renaissance and even medieval cultures.

THE ENLIGHTENMENT: SCIENCE AND TECHNOLOGY

CHAMPION OF ENLIGHTENMENT THOUGHT François Marie Arouet, better known as Voltaire (1694–1778) became, and still is, the most representative figure—almost the personification—of the Enlightenment's spirit. Voltaire was instrumental in introducing Newton and Locke to the French intelligentsia. The sculptor JEAN-ANTOINE HOUDON (1741–1828) produced a famous marble bust of Voltaire as an old man (FIG. **28-1**). The smile Houdon recorded so strikingly reflects the grim satisfaction Voltaire must have felt at the changes of state and consciousness he brought about by his tireless critical activism. He hated, and attacked through his writings, the arbitrary despotic rule of

kings, the selfish privileges of the nobility and the church, religious intolerance, and, above all, the injustice of the *ancien regime* (the "old order"). In his numerous books and pamphlets, which the authorities regularly condemned and burned, he protested against government persecution of the freedoms of thought and religion. Voltaire believed that the human race could never be happy until the traditional obstructions to the progress of the human mind and welfare were removed. His personal and public involvement in the struggle against established political and religious authority gave authenticity to his ideas. It converted a whole generation to the conviction that fundamental changes were necessary. This conviction paved the way for a revolution in France that Voltaire never intended, and he probably never would have approved of it. He was not convinced that "all men are created equal," the credo of Jean-Jacques Rousseau, Thomas Jefferson, and the American Declaration of Independence.

Voltaire was not a scientist ("natural philosopher" as it was then called), though he dabbled in experiments. Yet he declared that enlightenment was based on experience and physics and even asserted that all philosopy could be reduced to physics.

Mathematical physics ruled all the other sciences, so in the history of the natural sciences Voltaire can be considered one

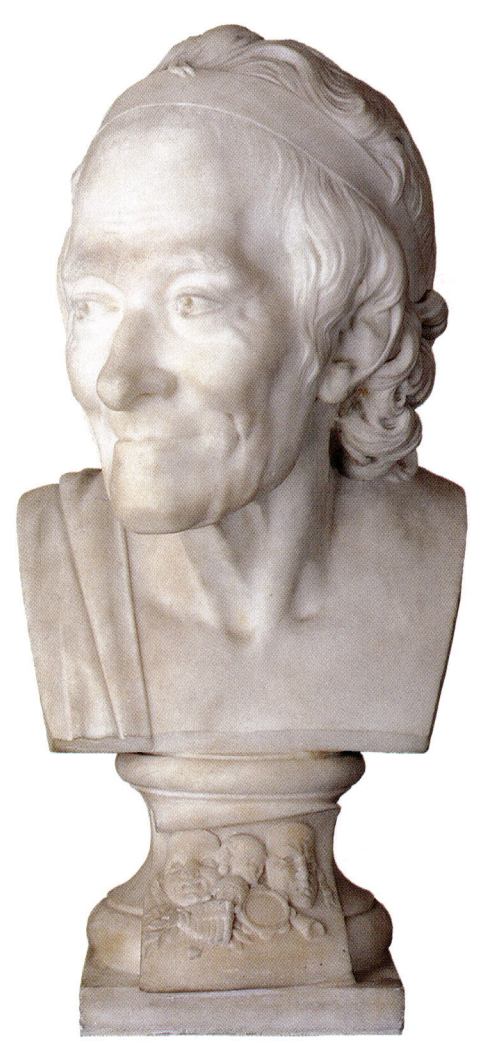

28-1 JEAN ANTOINE HOUDON, *Voltaire*, 1781. Marble, life-size. Victoria and Albert Museum, London.

of the great propagators because he lent all his prestige to their advancement.

ALL CREATURES GREAT AND SMALL   Biomechanical and chemical studies of living nature advanced that field of human knowledge. In addition to Buffon's immense collection of information on plants and animals, his contemporary, the Swedish botanist Carolus Linnaeus (1707–1778), established a system of plant classification. It is still, despite its limitations, serviceable in arranging the vast universe of biological data. Biology's number of verifiable theories was far behind Newton's physical theories. It focused on the collection, description, and classification of the data, while physical theory was at once open to demonstration and could be the guide and model for all subsequent observation.

For the sciences of life, the study of the human body—its structure, function, and disorders—naturally would be at the center of scientific interest. Since the Renaissance, artists had been concerned with learning about the body by dissecting it. Historians long have recognized the part Leonardo played in inaugurating the descriptive science of anatomy (see FIG. 22-5). As that description became more exact and complete (FIG. **28-2**), the anatomical artist's skill became a specialty, an instrument for the education and practice of physicians and surgeons. As such, it was not simply a preliminary study, a guide for a painter or sculptor constructing an image of the human body, but a tool for specialists in an entirely different discipline. In this respect it made its contribution as a technological device, an art or craft applied to a science. The technological applications of drafting and model building proved indispensable to science's development well into the computer age.

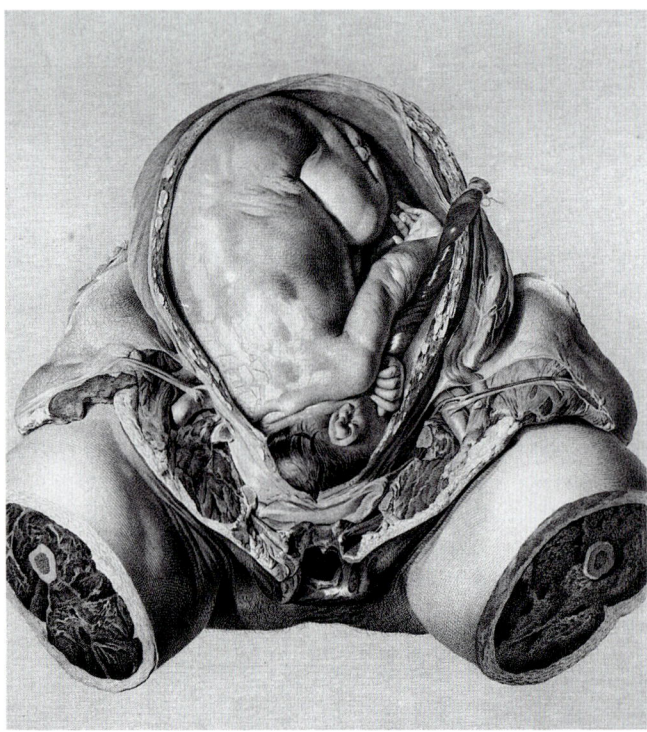

28-2   WILLIAM HUNTER, *Child in Womb, drawing from dissection of a woman who died in the ninth month of pregnancy,* from *Anatomy of the Human Gravid Uterus,* 1774.

GROWTH OF TECHNOLOGY AND INDUSTRY
Scientific investigation and technological invention opened up new possibilities for human understanding of the world and for control of its material forces. Research into the phenomena of electricity and combustion, along with the discovery of oxygen and the power of steam, had enormous consequences. Steam power as an adjunct to, or replacement for, human labor began a new era in world history. The invention of steam engines in England for industrial production and, later, their use for transportation marked the beginning of the technological and industrial revolutions, which occurred from about 1740 onward. All of Europe was destined to be transformed within a century by the harnessed power of steam, coal, oil, iron, steel, and electricity working in concert. These scientific and technological advances also affected the arts, particularly leading to the development of photography and changes in architecture.

THE WONDERS OF THE UNIVERSE   Technological advance depended on the new enthusiasm for mechanical explanations for the wonders of the universe. The fascination it had for ordinary people as well as for the learned is the subject of *A Philosopher Giving a Lecture at the Orrery (in which a lamp is put in place of the sun),* FIG. **28-3**), by the English painter JOSEPH WRIGHT OF DERBY (1734–1797). Wright specialized in the drama of candlelit and moonlit scenes. He loved subjects such as the orrery demonstration, which could be illuminated by a single light from within the picture. In the painting, a scholar uses a special technological model (called an *orrery*) to demonstrate the theory that the universe operates like a gigantic clockwork mechanism. Light from the lamp, representing the sun, pours forth from in front of the boy silhouetted in the foreground to create dramatic light and shadows that heighten the scene's drama. Awed children crowd close to the tiny metal orbs that represent the planets within the arcing bands that symbolize their orbits. An earnest listener makes notes, while the lone woman seated at the left and the two gentlemen at the right look on with rapt attention. Everyone in Wright's painting is caught up in the wonders of scientific knowledge; an ordinary lecture takes on the qualities of a grand "history painting." Wright scrupulously rendered with careful accuracy every detail of the figures, the mechanisms of the orrery, and even the books and curtain in the shadowy background. His realism appealed to the great industrialists of his day. Scientific-industrial innovators such as Josiah Wedgwood and Sir Richard Arkwright often purchased works such as *Orrery.* (Wedgwood pioneered many techniques of mass-produced pottery; Wedgwood fine china and pottery are still produced today. Arkwright's spinning frame revolutionized the textile industry.) To them, Wright's elevation of the theories and inventions of the Industrial Revolution to the plane of history painting was exciting and appropriately in tune with the future.

BRIDGING THE AGES WITH IRON   Eighteenth-century engineering, especially, foreshadowed the future, particularly its use of industrial materials. Two men first used iron in bridge design for the cast-iron bridge built in England over the Severn River, near the site at Coalbrookdale where ABRAHAM DARBY III (1750–1789) ran his family's cast-iron business. Previous bridges had been constructed of wood and

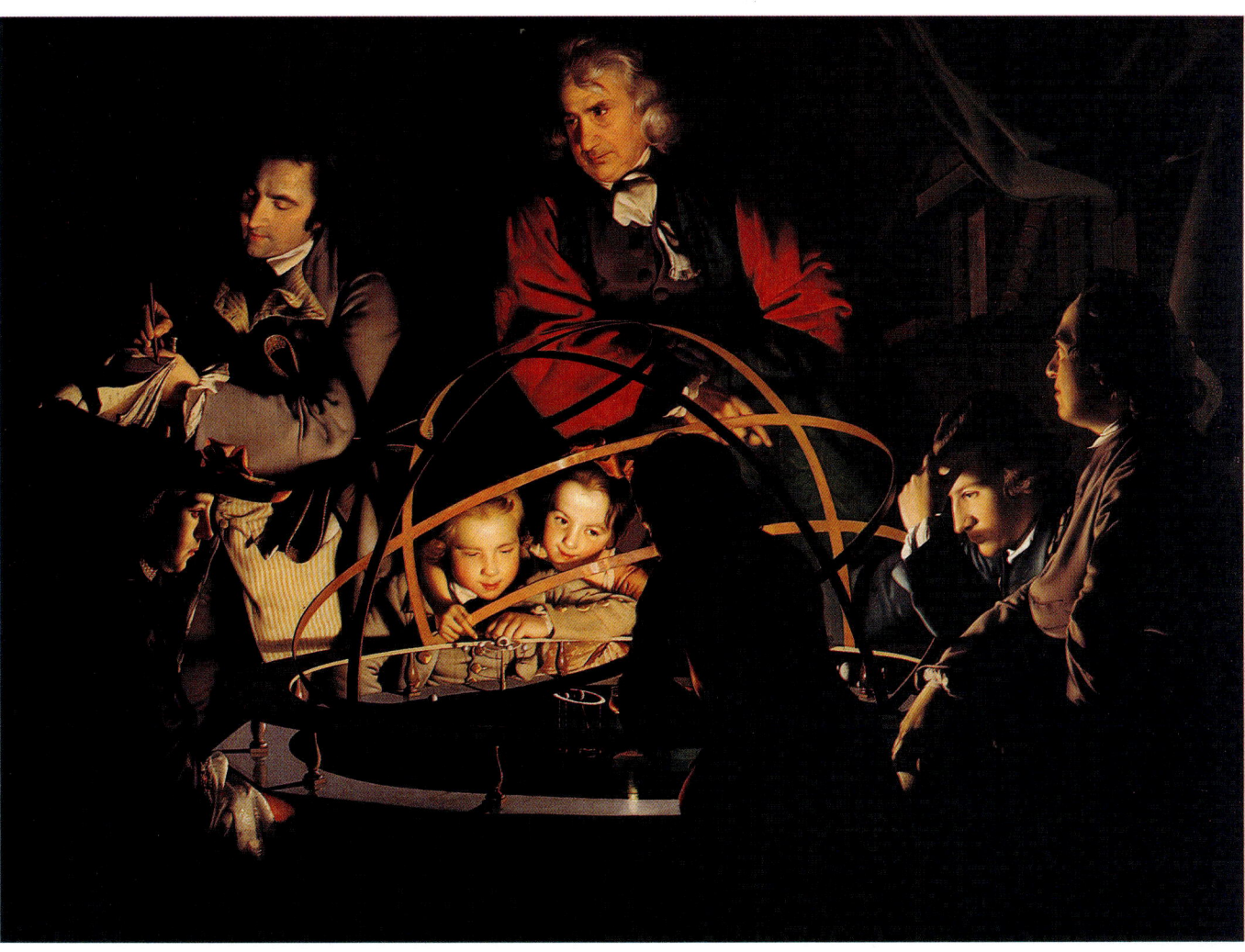

28-3 JOSEPH WRIGHT OF DERBY, *A Philosopher Giving a Lecture at the Orrery (in which a lamp is put in place of the sun)*, ca. 1763–1765. Oil on canvas, 4′ 10″ × 6′ 8″. Derby Museums and Art Gallery, Derby, Derbyshire.

spanned relatively short distances, limiting their use for high-volume industrial traffic. The Darby family had spearheaded the evolution of the iron industry in England, and they vigorously supported the investigation of new uses for the material. The fabrication of cast-iron rails and bridge elements inspired Darby to work with architect THOMAS F. PRITCHARD (1723–1777) in designing the Coalbrookdale Bridge (FIG. **28-4**). The cast-iron armature that supports the roadbed springs from stone pier to stone pier until it leaps the final one hundred feet across the Severn River gorge. The style of the graceful center arc echoes the grand arches of Roman aqueducts (see FIG. 10-31). At the same time, the exposed structure of the bridge's cast-iron parts prefigured the skeletal use of iron and steel in the nineteenth century. Such visible structural armatures became expressive factors in the design of buildings such as the Crystal Palace (FIG. 28-60) and the Eiffel Tower (see FIG. 29-57).

VOLTAIRE VERSUS ROUSSEAU: SCIENCE VERSUS THE TASTE FOR THE "NATURAL"

The name of Jean-Jacques Rousseau (1712–1778) is traditionally invoked along with that of Voltaire as representative of the French Enlightenment and as individuals instrumental in preparing the way ideologically for the French Revolution. Yet Voltaire, as has been noted, thought the salvation of humanity was in science's advancement and in society's rational improvement. In contrast, Rousseau declared that the arts, sciences, society, and civilization in general had corrupted "natural man"—people in their primitive state—and that humanity's only salvation was a return to something like "the ignorance, innocence and happiness" of its original condition. According to Rousseau, human capacity for feeling, sensibility, and emotions came prior to reason: "To exist is to feel; our feeling is undoubtedly earlier than our intelligence, and we had feelings before we had ideas." Nature alone must be the guide: "all our natural inclinations are right." Rousseau's basic point: "Man by nature is good . . . he is depraved and perverted by society." He rejected the idea of progress, insisting: "Our minds have been corrupted in proportion as the arts and sciences have improved."[2]

These and similar sentiments expressed by Rousseau shocked Voltaire, who responded to them with acid sarcasm in a letter to Rousseau that reveals their fundamentally different outlook.

I have received, Sir, your new book against the human race [*Dissertation on the Origin of Inequality*, 1755]. . . . You paint with very true

28-4 ABRAHAM DARBY III and THOMAS F. PRITCHARD, iron bridge at Coalbrookdale, England (first cast-iron bridge over the Severn River), 1776–1779. 100′ span.

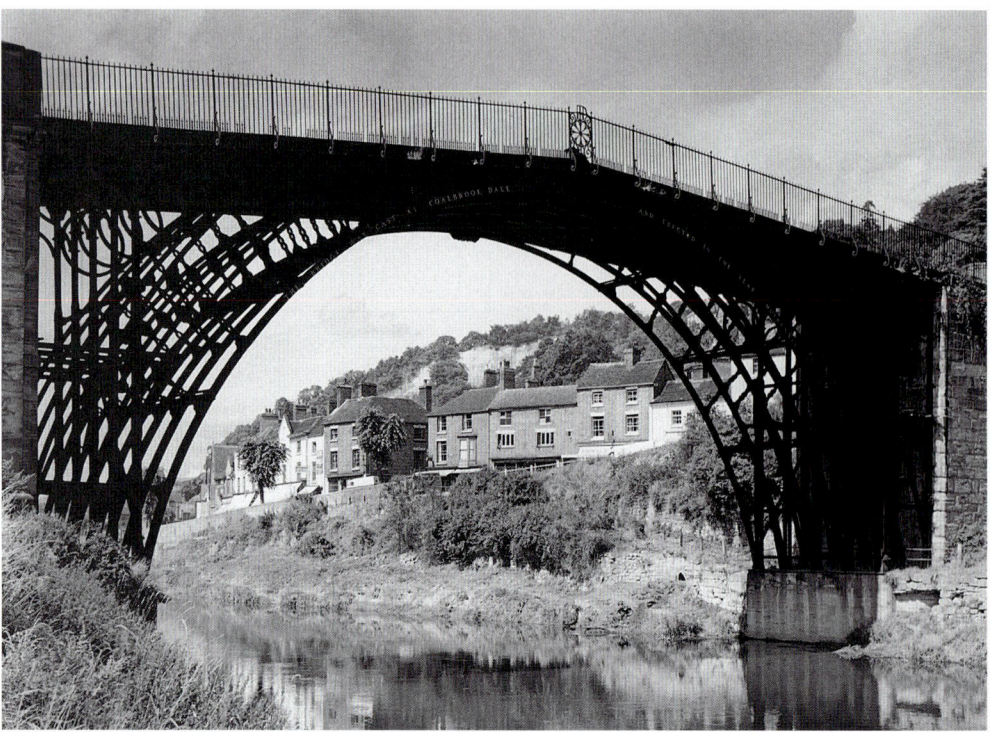

colors the horrors of human society. . . . Never has so much intelligence been used in seeking to make us stupid. One acquires the desire to walk on all fours when one reads your book. Nevertheless, since I lost this habit more than sixty years ago, I unfortunately feel that it is impossible for me to take it up again. [3]

The society Rousseau attacked and Voltaire defended in general terms was in fact the one they both knew and moved in; its center was Paris, ornamented in the Rococo style. Rousseau's views, widely read and popular, were largely responsible for the turning away from the Rococo sensibility and the formation of a taste for the "natural," as opposed to the artificial.

The "Natural" Landscape

The eighteenth-century public sought "naturalness" in artists' depictions of landscapes. Documentation of particular places became popular, in part due to growing travel opportunities and the expanding colonial imperative. Such depictions of geographic settings also served the needs of the many scientific expeditions mounted during the century and satisfied the desires of genteel tourists for mementos of their journeys. By this time, a "Grand Tour" of the major sites of Europe was considered part of every well-bred person's education (see "Grand Tour: Travel, Education, and Italy's Allure," page 842). Naturally, those on tour wished to leave with things that would help them remember their experiences and that would impress those at home with the wonders they had seen.

A PICTURESQUE VIEW OF VENICE   The English were especially eager collectors of pictorial souvenirs. Certain artists in Venice specialized in painting the most characteristic scenes, or *vedute* (views), of that city to sell to British visitors. The *veduta* paintings of ANTONIO CANALETTO (1697–1768) were eagerly acquired by English tourists, who hung them on the walls of great houses such as Chiswick (FIG. 28-22) and

Blenheim (see FIG. 24-75) as visible evidence of their visit to the city of the Grand Canal. It must have been very cheering amid a gray winter afternoon in England to look up and see a sunny, panoramic view such as that in Canaletto's *Basin of San Marco from San Giorgio Maggiore* (FIG. **28-5**), with its cloud-studded sky, calm harbor, varied water traffic, picturesque pedestrians, and well-known Venetian landmarks all painted in scrupulous perspective and minute detail.

Canaletto had trained as a scene painter with his father, but his easy mastery of detail, light, and shadow soon made him one of the most popular *"vedutisti"* in Venice. Occasionally, he painted his scenes directly from life, but usually he made drawings "on location" to take back to his studio as sources for paintings. To help make the on-site drawings true to life, he often used a *camera obscura*. The *camera obscura* (see page 762) allowed Canaletto (and other artists) to create visually convincing paintings that included variable focus of objects at different distances. His paintings give the impression of capturing every detail, with no "editing." Actually, he presented each site within Renaissance perspectival rules and exercised great selectivity about which details to include and which to omit to make a coherent and engagingly attractive picture. In addition, the mood in each of his works was constructed carefully to be positive and alluring. Everything in the world Canaletto presented is clean and tidy. The sun always shines, and every aspect of the weather is serene; the viewer never got even a hint of the dreary rainy season in Venice.

The Taste for the "Natural" in France

Rousseau, in placing feelings above reason as the most primitive—hence most "natural"—of human expressions, called for the cultivation of sincere, sympathetic, and tender emotions. This led him to exalt the peasant's simple life, with its honest and unsullied emotions, as ideal and to name it as a model for imitation. The joys and sorrows of uncorrupted "natural" people, described everywhere in novels (for example,

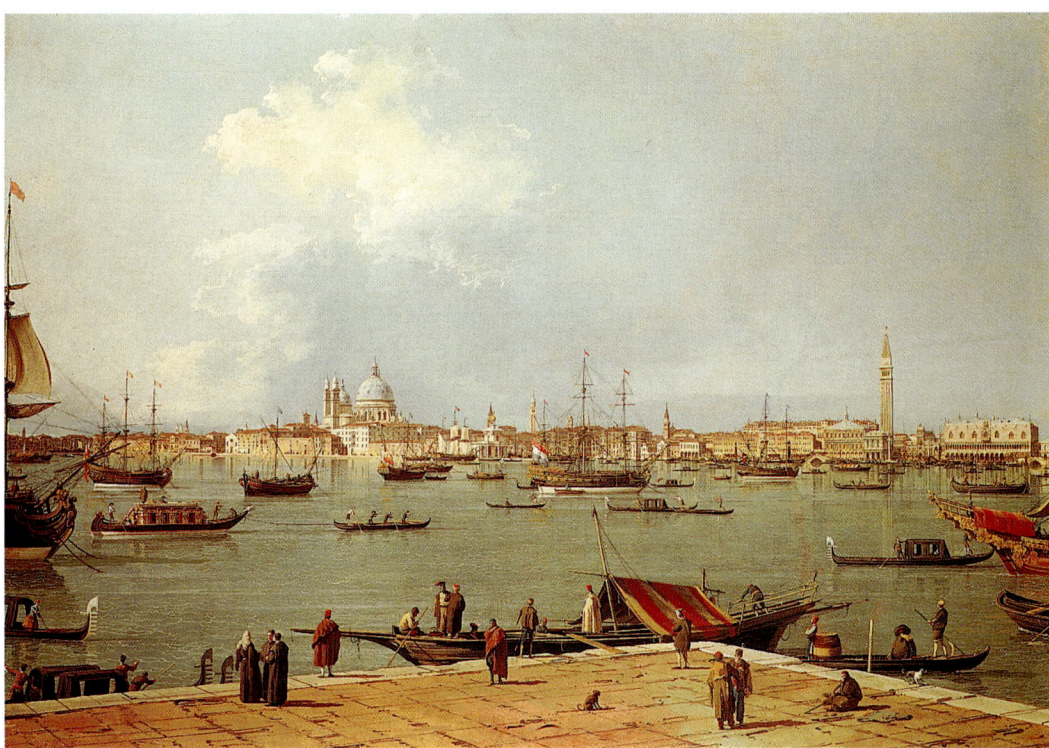

28-5 ANTONIO CANALETTO, *Basin of San Marco from San Giorgio Maggiore*, ca. 1740. Oil on canvas. The Wallace Collection, London.

Oliver Goldsmith's *The Vicar of Wakefield*, 1766, or Bernardin de Saint-Pierre's *Paul and Virginia*, 1787), soon drowned Europe in floods of tears. It became fashionable to weep, to fall to one's knees, and to languish in hopeless love. Hopelessly in love, Goethe's hero in *The Sorrows of Young Werther* (1774) kills himself under the moon.

THE SENTIMENTALITY OF RURAL ROMANCE

The sentimental narrative in art became the specialty of French artist JEAN-BAPTISTE GREUZE (1725–1805), whose most popular work, *The Village Bride* (FIG. **28-6**), sums up the genre's characteristics. The setting is an unadorned room in a rustic dwelling. In a notary's presence, the elderly father has passed his daughter's dowry to her youthful husband-to-be and blesses the pair, who gently take each other's arms. The old mother tearfully gives her daughter's arm a farewell caress, while the youngest sister melts in tears on the demure bride's shoulder. An envious older sister broods behind her father's

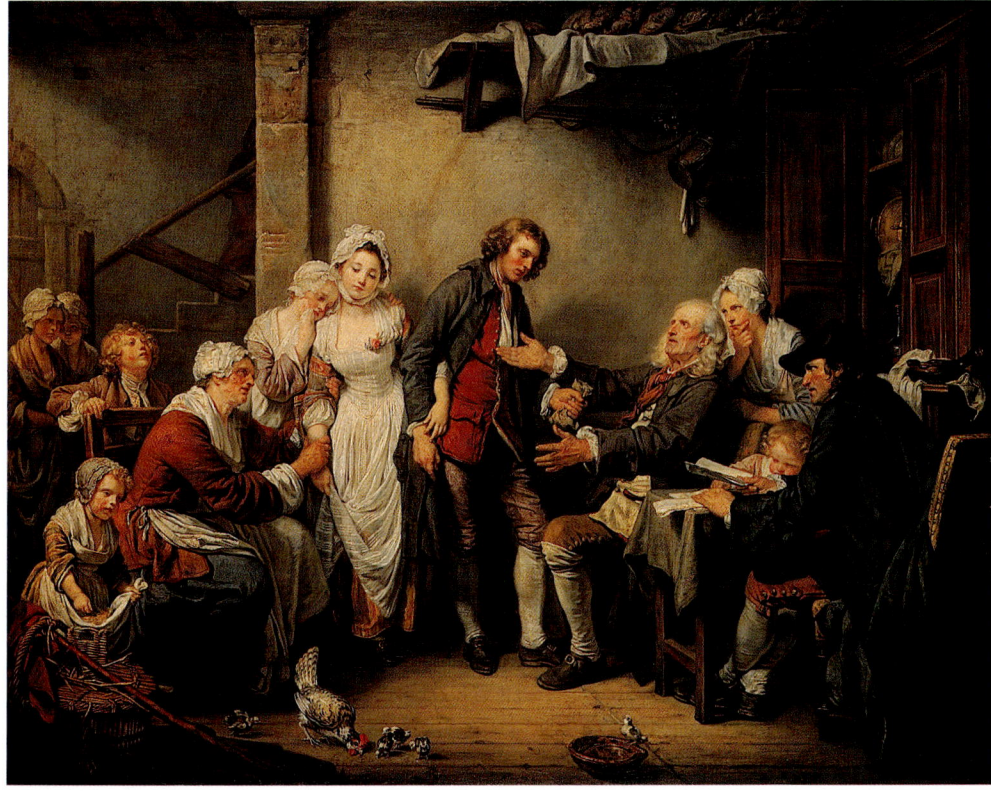

28-6 JEAN-BAPTISTE GREUZE, *The Village Bride*, 1761. Oil on canvas, 3′ × 3′ 10½″. Louvre, Paris.

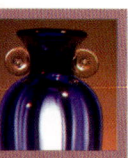

ART AND SOCIETY

Grand Tour
Travel, Education, and Italy's Allure

Although travel throughout Europe was commonplace in the eighteenth century, Italy became a particularly popular travel site. This "pilgrimage" of aristocrats, the wealthy, politicians, and diplomats from France, England, Germany, Flanders, Sweden, the United States, Russia, Poland, and Hungary came to be known as the Grand Tour. Italy's allure fueled classicism's revival, which became most formalized in Neoclassicism. In turn, Neoclassicism's prominence drove this fascination with Italy. One British observer noted: "All our religion, all our arts, almost all that sets us above savages, has come from the shores of the Mediterranean."[1]

The Grand Tour was not simply leisure travel. The education available in Italy to the inquisitive mind made such a trip an indispensable experience for anyone who wished to play an important role in society. The Enlightenment had made knowledge of ancient Rome and Greece imperative, and a steady stream of Europeans and Americans traveled to Italy in the late eighteenth and early nineteenth centuries. These tourists aimed to increase their knowledge of literature and the arts (the visual arts, architecture, theater, and music), ancient and modern history, politics and economics, and customs and folklore. Given this extensive agenda, it is not surprising that a Grand Tour could take a number of years to complete, and most travelers moved from location to location, following an established itinerary.

The British were the most avid travelers, and they established the initial "tour code," including important destinations and required itineraries. Although they established Rome early on as the primary mecca, visitors traveled as far north as Venice and as far south as Naples. Eventually, Paestum, Sicily, Florence, Genoa, Milan, Siena, Pisa, Bologna, Parma, and Palermo all appeared in guidebooks and in *veduta* paintings. Joseph Mallord William Turner (FIG. 28-51) and Joseph Wright of Derby (FIG. 28-3) were among the many British artists to undertake a Grand Tour.

Eventually, the Grand Tour's scope extended well beyond Italian borders. In large part, the archeological discoveries at Herculaneum and Pompeii were responsible for whetting people's appetites to visit Greece. The Grand Tour eventually metamorphosed into package tours, which remain popular to the present day, revealing the continuing allure of Mediterranean and classical cultures.

[1]Cesare de Seta, "Grand Tour: The Lure of Italy in the Eighteenth Century," in *Grand Tour: The Lure of Italy in the Eighteenth Century,* eds. Andrew Wilton and Ilaria Bignamini (London: Tate Gallery, 1996), 13.

---

chair. Rosy-faced healthy children play around the scene. The picture's story is simple—the happy climax of a rural romance. The picture's moral is just as clear—happiness is the reward of "natural" virtue.

The audience—as said today—loved it. They carefully analyzed each gesture and each nuance of sentiment and reacted with tumultuous enthusiasm. At the Salon (the annual academy exhibition—see "The Academies: Defining the Range of Acceptable Art," Chapter 29, page 898) of 1761, Greuze's picture received enormous attention. The great compiler of the *Encyclopédie*, Diderot, who reviewed the picture for the press, declared that it was difficult to get near it because of the throngs of admirers.

THE CHARM OF THE COMMONPLACE Adherents to the taste for the "natural" often preferred narratives that taught moral lessons, dismissing the frivolities and indecent gallantries of the Rococo. The audience of French painter JEAN-BAPTISTE-SIMÉON CHARDIN (1699–1779) was gratified to find moral values in quiet scenes of domestic life. The artist seemed to praise the simple goodness of ordinary people, especially mothers and young children, who, in spirit, occupation, and environment, lived far from corrupt society. (In the eighteenth century, *taste* also could mean the appreciation of moral as well as aesthetic qualities.) Rousseau measured human quality in terms of the degree to which it was out of reach of society's bad influence. He found it in country folk or, as here, in the urban middle class's unpretentious houses. In *Grace at Table* (FIG. **28-7**), Chardin ushers viewers into a modest room where a mother and her small daughters are about to dine. The mood of quiet attention is at one with the hushed lighting and mellow color and with the closely studied still-life accessories whose worn surfaces tell their own humble domestic history. Viewers witness a moment of social instruction, when mother and older sister supervise the younger sister in the simple, pious ritual of giving thanks to God before a meal. In his own way, Chardin was the poet of the commonplace and the master of its nuances. A gentle sentiment prevails in all of his pictures, an emotion not contrived and artificial but born of the painter's honesty, insight, and sympathy. (It is interesting that this picture was owned by King Louis XV, the royal personification of the Rococo in his life and tastes.)

PORTRAIT OF A WOMAN ARTIST *Self-Portrait* (FIG. **28-8**) by ÉLISABETH LOUISE VIGÉE-LEBRUN (1755–1842) is another variation of the "naturalistic" impulse in eighteenth-century French portraiture. In the new mode, Vigée-Lebrun looks directly at viewers and pauses in her work to return their gaze. Although her mood is lighthearted and her costume's details echo the serpentine curve beloved by Rococo artists and wealthy patrons, nothing about Vigée-Lebrun's pose or her mood speaks of Rococo frivolity. Hers is the self-confi-

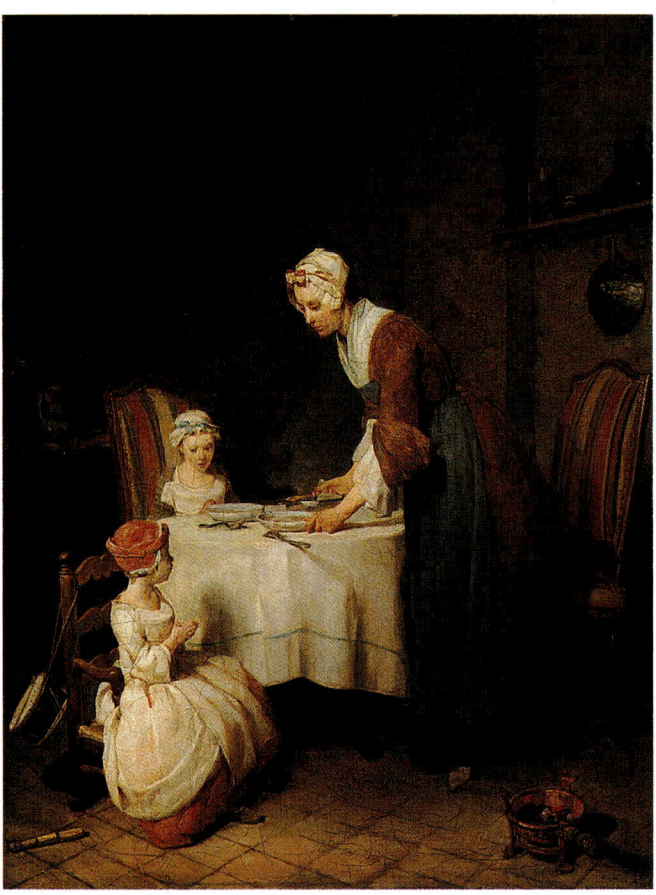

28-7 JEAN-BAPTISTE-SIMÉON CHARDIN, *Grace at Table,* 1740. Oil on canvas, 1′ 7″ × 1′ 3″. Louvre, Paris.

dent stance of a woman whose art has won her an independent role in her society. Like many of her contemporaries, Vigée-Lebrun lived a life of extraordinary personal and economic independence, working for the nobility throughout Europe. She was famous for the force and grace of her portraits, especially those of highborn ladies and royalty. She was successful during the age of the late monarchy in France and was one of few women admitted to the Academy (the established art school—see "The Academies: Defining the Range of Acceptable Art," Chapter 29, page 898). After the French Revolution, her membership in the Academy was rescinded, because women were no longer welcome in that organization. Vigée-Lebrun's continued success was indicative of her talent, her wit, and her ability to forge connections with those in power in the postrevolutionary period. For her self-portrait, Vigée-Lebrun painted herself in a close-up, intimate view at work on one of the portraits that won her renown, that of Queen Marie Antoinette. The naturalism and intimacy of her expression are similar to those in Thomas Gainsborough's portrait of Mrs. Sheridan (FIG. 28-10). Vigée-Lebrun's attitude reflects the ideals of independence and self-reliance she exhibited as a woman.

The Taste for the "Natural" in England

VISUALIZING MORALITY THROUGH SATIRE
The taste of the newly prosperous and confident middle class

in England was expressed in the art of WILLIAM HOGARTH (1697–1764), who satirized contemporary life with comic zest and with only a modicum of Rococo "indecency." With Hogarth, a truly English style of painting emerged. Traditionally, painters (such as Holbein, Rubens, and Van Dyck) were imported from the continent. Hogarth waged a lively campaign throughout his career against the English feeling of dependence on, and inferiority to, continental artists. Although Hogarth would have been the last to admit it, his own painting owed much to the work of his contemporaries across the channel in France, the Rococo artists. Yet his subject matter, frequently moral in tone, was distinctively English. It was the great age of English satirical writing, and Hogarth (who knew and admired this genre and included Henry Fielding, the author of *Tom Jones,* among his closest friends) clearly saw himself as translating satire into the visual arts.

Hogarth's favorite device was to make a series of narrative paintings and prints, in a sequence like chapters in a book or scenes in a play, that followed a character or group of characters in their encounters with some social evil. He was at his best in pictures such as the *Breakfast Scene* (FIG. 28-9) from *Marriage à la Mode.* In it, the marriage of a young viscount, arranged through one father's social aspirations and through the need for money of the other, is just beginning to founder. The moment portrayed is just past noon; husband and wife are tired after a long night spent in separate pursuits. The music and the musical instrument on the overturned chair in the foreground and the disheveled servant straightening the chairs and tables in the room at the back indicate that the wife had stayed at home for an evening of cards and music making. She stretches with a mixture of sleepiness and coquettishness, casting a glance toward her young husband, who clearly had been away from the house for a night of suspicious business. Still dressed in hat and social finery, he slumps in discouraged boredom on a chair near the fire. His hands are thrust deep into the empty money-pockets of his breeches, while his wife's small dog sniffs inquiringly at a lacy woman's cap protruding from his coat pocket. A steward, his hands full of unpaid bills, raises his eyes to Heaven in despair at the actions of his noble master and mistress. The house is palatial, but Hogarth filled it with witty clues to the dubious taste of its occupants. The mantelpiece is crowded with tiny statuettes and a classical bust, which hide everything in the architecturally framed painting on the wall behind except a winged Eros figure. Paintings of religious figures hang on the upper wall of the distant room. This demonstration of piety is countered by the curtained canvas at the end of the row that, undoubtedly, depicts an erotic subject. Appropriately, this painting is discretely hidden from the eyes of casual visitors and ladies, according to the custom of the day, but is available at the pull of a curtain cord for the gaze of the master and his male guests. In this composition, as in all his work, Hogarth proceeded as a novelist might, elaborating on his subject with carefully chosen detail, whose discovery heightens the comedy. This scene is one in a sequence of six paintings that satirize the immoralities the moneyed classes in England practiced within marriage. Hogarth designed the marriage series to be published as a set of engravings. The prints of this and his other moral narratives were so popular that unscrupulous entrepreneurs produced unauthorized versions almost as fast as the artist created his originals.

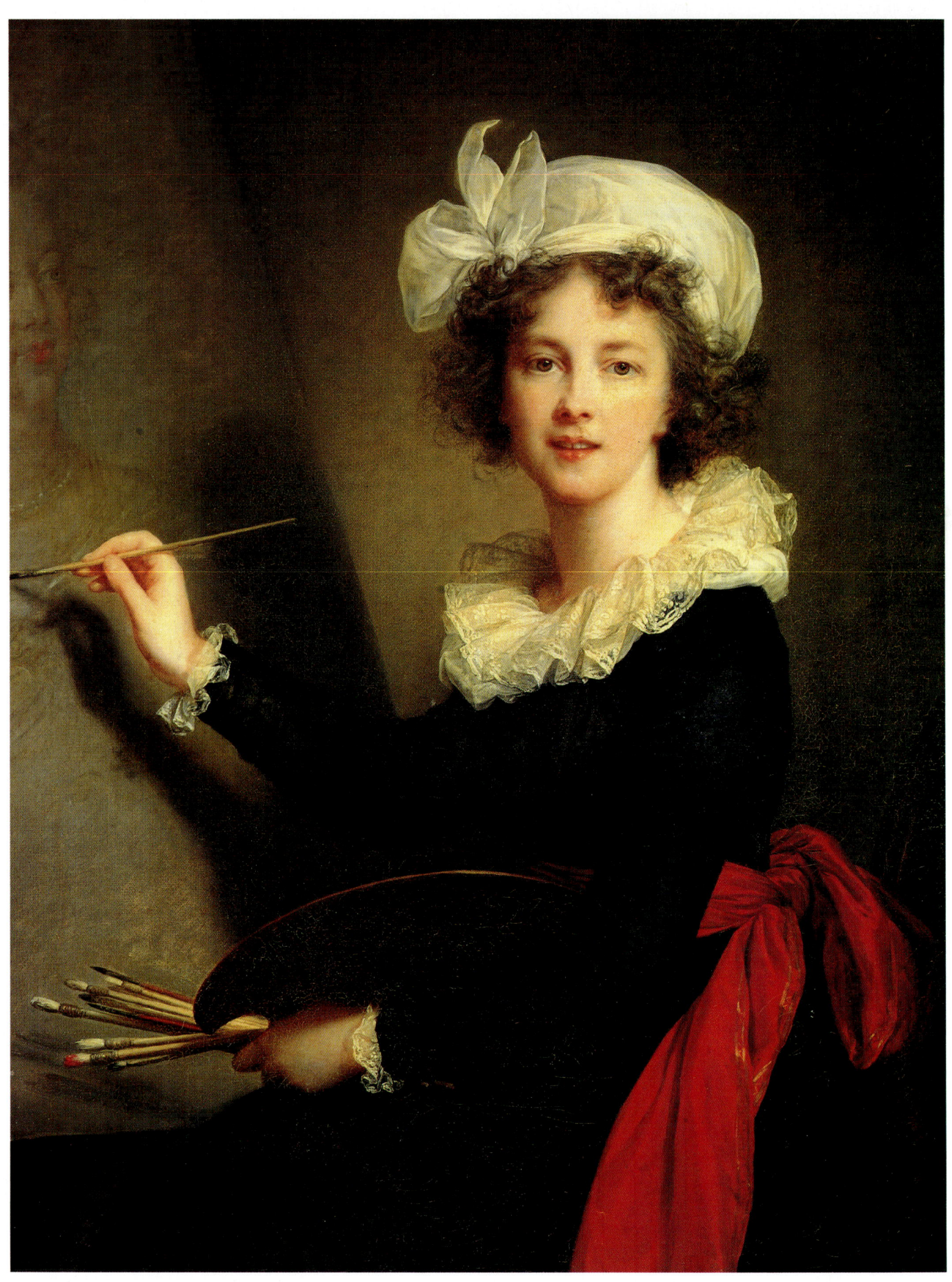

28-8 ÉLISABETH LOUISE VIGÉE-LEBRUN, *Self-Portrait,* 1790. Oil on canvas, 8′ 4″ × 6′ 9″. Galleria degli Uffizi, Florence.

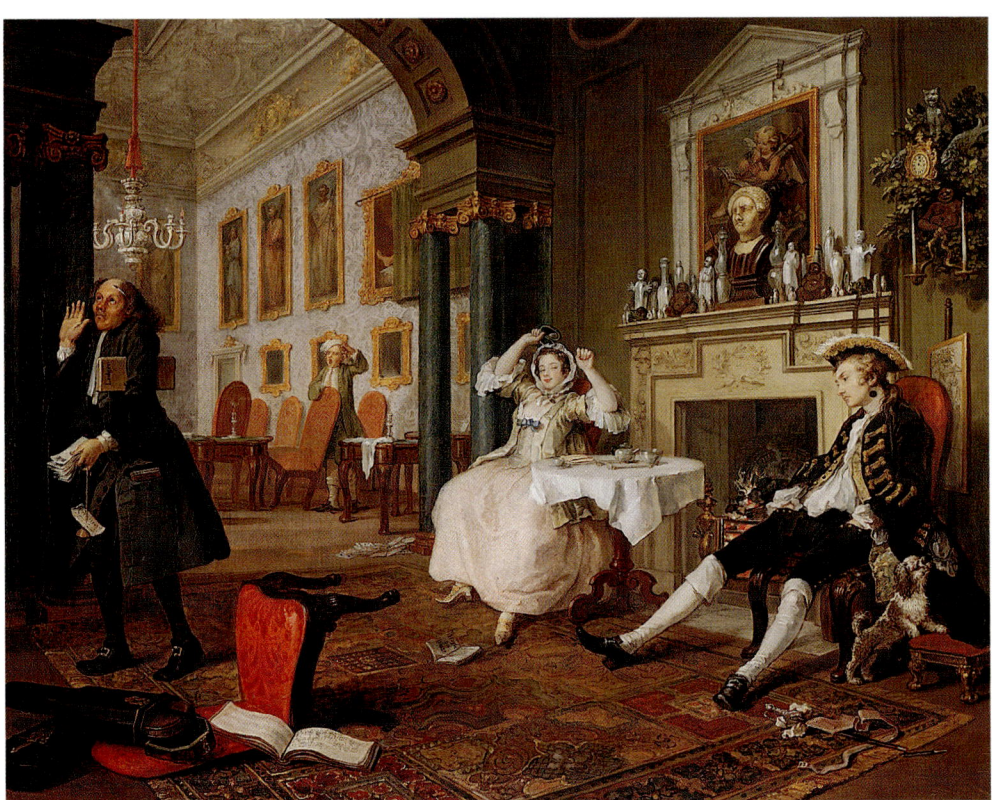

28-9 WILLIAM HOGARTH, *Breakfast Scene*, from *Marriage à la Mode*, ca. 1745. Oil on canvas, approx. 2′ 4″ × 3′. National Gallery, London.

GRAND MANNER PORTRAITURE   A contrasting blend of "naturalistic" representation and Rococo setting is found in the portrait of *Mrs. Richard Brinsley Sheridan* (FIG. **28-10**) by the British painter THOMAS GAINSBOROUGH (1727–1788). This portrait shows the lovely woman, dressed informally, seated in a rustic landscape faintly reminiscent of Watteau (see FIG. 24-84) in its soft-hued light and feathery brushwork. Gainsborough intended to match the natural landscape's unspoiled beauty with the subject's natural beauty. Her dark brown hair blows freely in the slight wind, and her clear unassisted "English" complexion and air of ingenuous sweetness contrast sharply with the pert sophistication of continental Rococo portraits. The artist originally had planned to give the picture "a more pastoral air" by adding several sheep, but he did not live long enough to paint them in. Even without this element, Gainsborough's deep interest in the landscape setting is evident. Although he won greater fame in his time for his portraits, he had begun as a landscape painter and always preferred painting scenes of nature to the depiction of human likenesses.

Such a portrait is representative of what became known as "Grand Manner portraiture," and Gainsborough was recognized as one of the leading practitioners of this genre. Although clearly depicting individualized people, Grand Manner portraiture also elevated the sitter by conveying refinement and elegance. Such grace and class were communicated through certain standardized conventions, such as the large scale of the figures relative to the canvas, the controlled poses, the landscape (often Arcadian) setting, and the low horizon line. Thus, despite the naturalism central to Gainsborough's portraits, he tempered it with a degree of artifice. This imbues the portraits with a sense of mastery and control, thereby revealing an important social function of such portraiture.

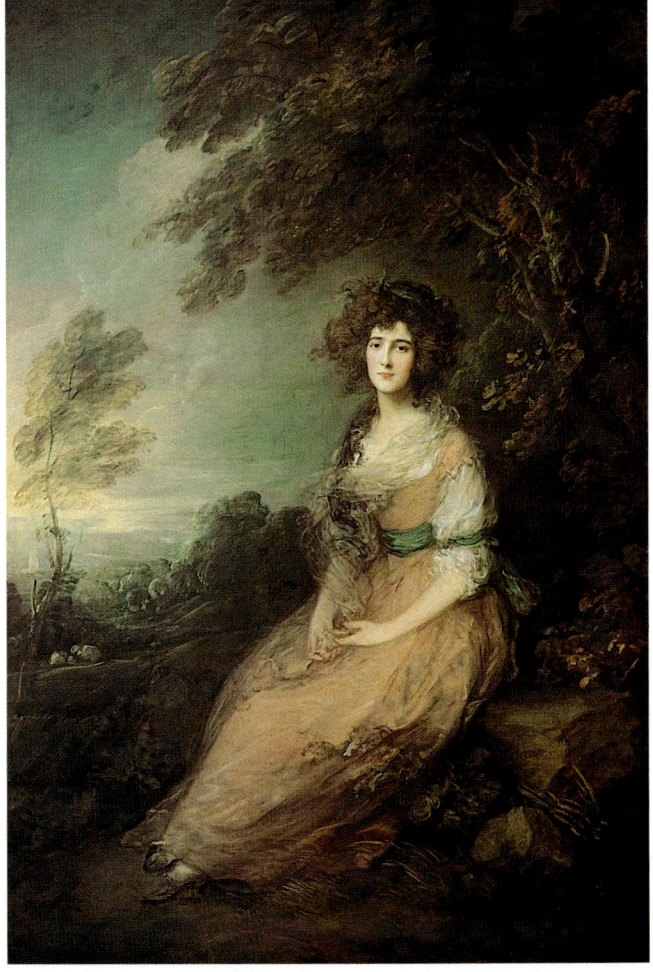

28-10   THOMAS GAINSBOROUGH, *Mrs. Richard Brinsley Sheridan*, 1787. Oil on canvas, approx. 7′ 2$\frac{5}{8}$″ × 5′ $\frac{5}{8}$″. National Gallery of Art, Washington (Andrew W. Mellon Collection).

THE VIRTUES OF HONOR AND VALOR Morality of a very different tone, yet in harmony with "naturalness," included the virtues of honor, valor, and love of country. Eighteenth-century Western societies believed that these virtues produced great people and great deeds. The concept of "nobility" especially as discussed by Rousseau referred to character, not to aristocratic birth. As the century progressed and people felt the tremors of coming revolutions, these virtues of courage and resolution, patriotism, and self-sacrifice assumed greater importance. The modern military hero, risen from humble origins, not the decadent aristocrat, brought the excitements of war into the company of the "natural" emotions.

DEFENDING THE ROCK OF GIBRALTAR: SIR JOSHUA REYNOLDS (1723–1792) specialized in portraits of contemporaries who participated in the great events of the latter part of the century. Not least among these paintings was *Lord Heathfield* (FIG. **28-11**). Reynolds was at his best with a subject such as this burly, ruddy English officer, commandant of the fortress at Gibraltar. Heathfield doggedly had defended the great rock against the Spanish and the French, so he later was honored with the title Baron Heathfield of Gibraltar. His victory is symbolized here by the huge key to the fortress, which he holds thoughtfully. He stands in front of a curtain of dark smoke rising from the battleground, flanked by one cannon that points ineffectively downward and another whose tilted barrel indicates that it lies uselessly on its back. Reynolds portrayed the features of the general's heavy, honest

face and his uniform with a sense of unidealized realism. But Lord Heathfield's posture and the setting dramatically suggest the heroic theme of battle and refer to the actual revolutions (American and French) then taking shape in deadly earnest, as the old regimes faded into the past.

The Taste for the "Natural" in the United States

THE HEROIC DEATH OF GENERAL WOLFE American artists also addressed the "death in battle of a young military hero" theme, familiar in art and literature since the ancient Greeks. Although American artist BENJAMIN WEST (1738–1820) was born in Pennsylvania, on what was then the colonial frontier, he was sent to Europe early in life to study art and then went to England, where he met with almost immediate success. He was a cofounder of the Royal Academy of Arts and succeeded Sir Joshua Reynolds as its president. He became official painter to King George III and retained that position during the strained period of the American Revolution. While in England, West became well acquainted with the work of both Gainsborough and Reynolds. In *The Death of General Wolfe* (FIG. **28-12**), West depicted the mortally wounded young English commander just after his defeat of the French in the decisive battle of Quebec in 1759, which gave Canada to Great Britain. West chose to portray a contemporary historical subject, and his characters wear contemporary costume (although the military uniforms are not completely accurate in all details). However, West blended this realism of detail with the grand tradition of history painting by arranging his figures in a complex and theatrically ordered composition. His modern hero dies among grieving officers on the field of victorious battle in a way that suggests the death of a great saint. West wanted to present this hero's death in the service of the state as a martyrdom charged with religious emotions. His innovative combination of the conventions of traditional heroic painting with a look of modern realism was so effective that it won viewers' hearts in his own day and continued to influence history painting well into the nineteenth century.

PAUL REVERE, SILVERSMITH American artist JOHN SINGLETON COPLEY (1738–1815) matured as a painter in the Massachusetts Bay Colony. Like West, Copley later emigrated to England, where he absorbed the fashionable English portrait style. But unlike Grand Manner portraiture, Copley's *Portrait of Paul Revere* (FIG. **28-13**), painted before Copley left Boston, conveys a sense of directness and faithfulness to visual fact that marked the taste for "downrightness" and plainness many visitors to America noticed during the eighteenth and nineteenth centuries. When the portrait was painted, Revere was not yet the familiar hero of the American Revolution. In the picture, he is working at his everyday profession of silversmithing. The setting is plain, the lighting clear and revealing. The subject sits in his shirtsleeves, bent over a teapot in progress; he pauses and turns his head to look observers straight in the eye. The artist treated the reflections in the tabletop's polished wood with as much care as Revere's figure, his tools, and the teapot resting on its leather graver's pillow. Copley gave special prominence to the figure's eyes by reflect-

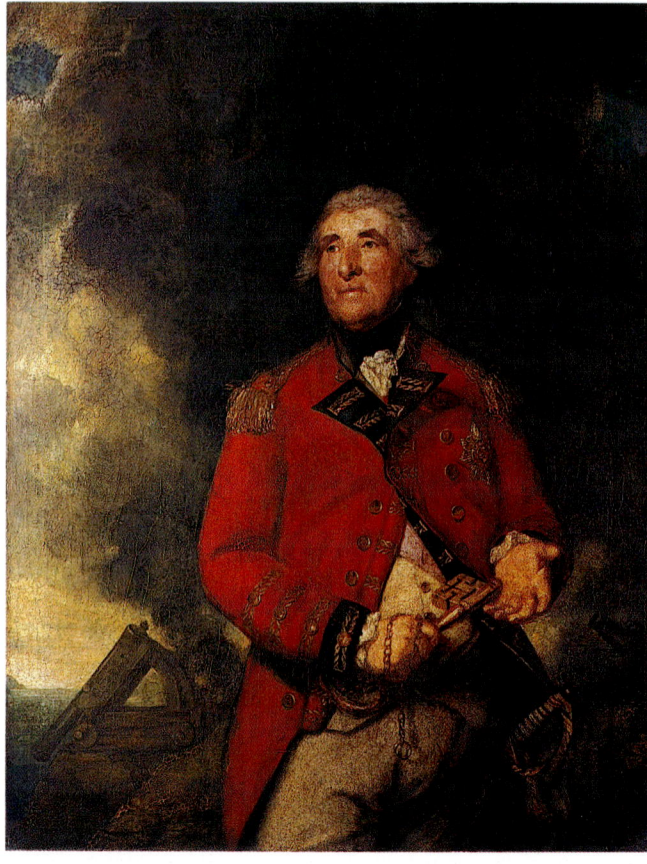

28-11 SIR JOSHUA REYNOLDS, *Lord Heathfield*, 1787. Oil on canvas, approx. 4′ 8″ × 3′ 9″. National Gallery, London.

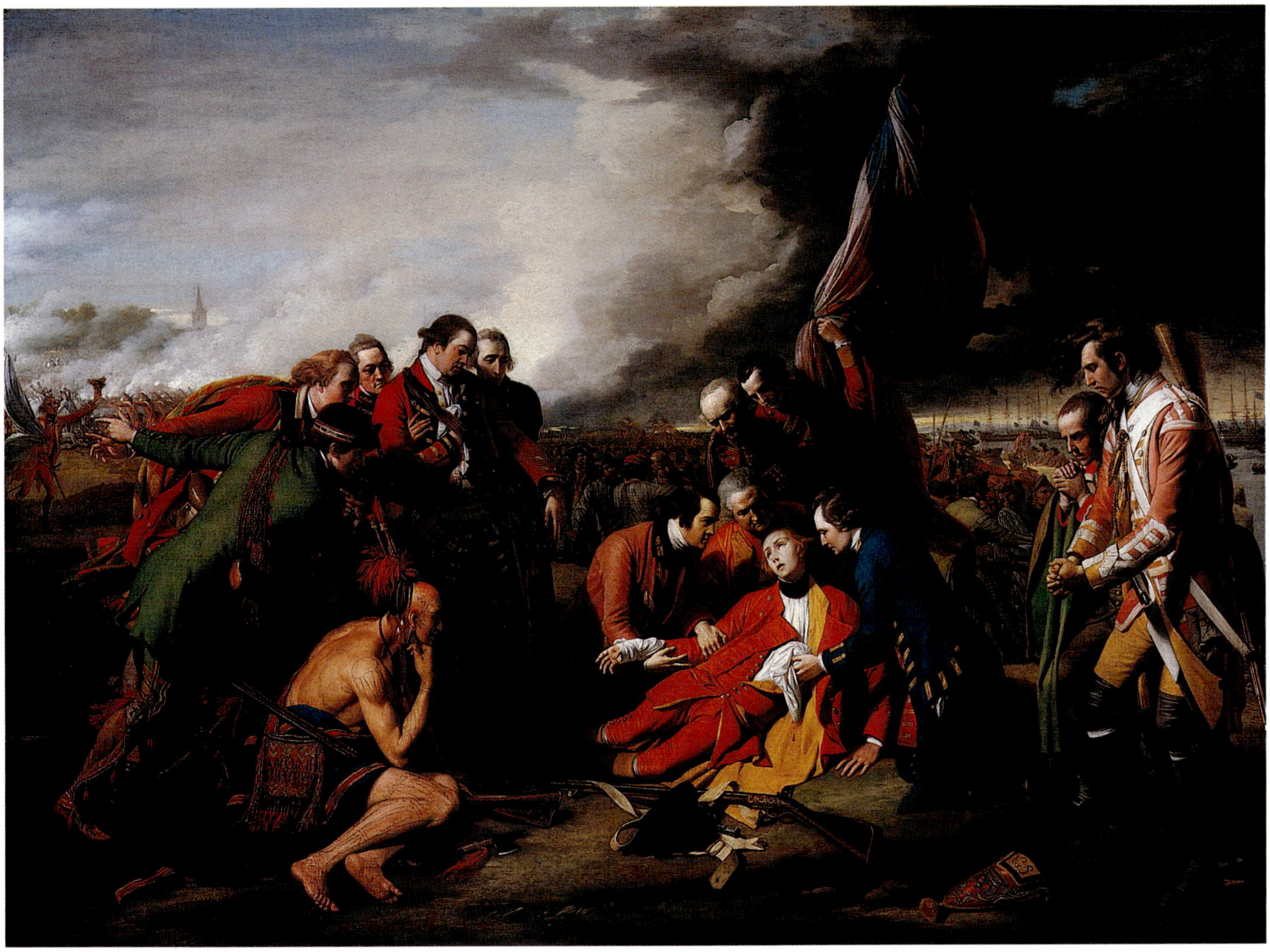

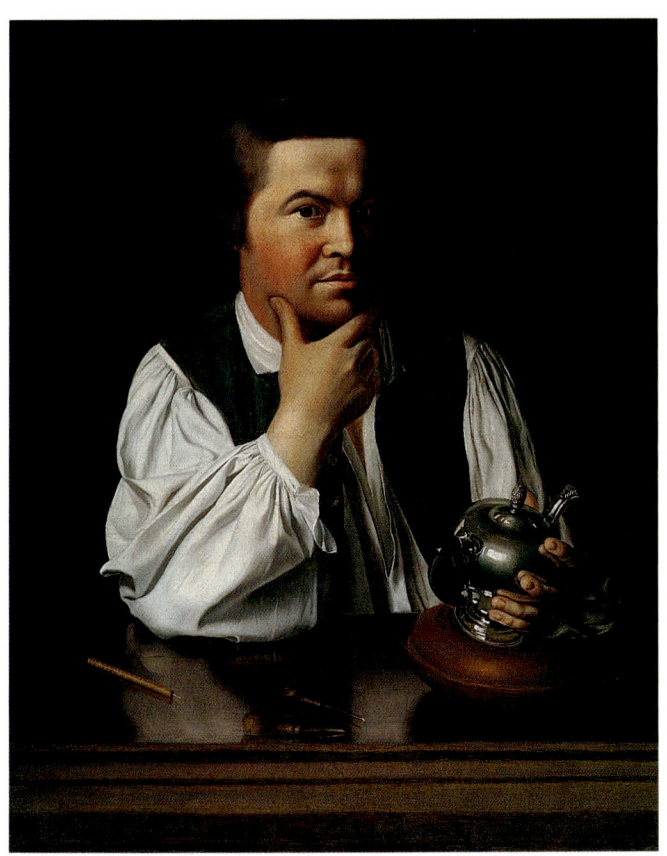

28-12 BENJAMIN WEST, *The Death of General Wolfe,* 1771. Oil on canvas, approx. 5′ × 7′ National Gallery of Canada, Ottawa (gift of the Duke of Westminster, 1918).

ing intense reddish light onto the darkened side of the face and hands. The informality and the sense of the moment link this painting to contemporaneous English and European portraits. But the spare style and the emphasis on the sitter's down-to-earth character differentiate this American work from its British and continental counterparts (FIG. 28-10).

THE REVIVAL OF INTEREST IN CLASSICISM

MODELS OF ENLIGHTENMENT   One of the defining characteristics of the late eighteenth century was a renewed interest in classical antiquity. Although the Neoclassical movement in art that encompassed painting, sculpture, and architecture is often regarded as the most prominent manifestation of this interest, fascination with Greek and Roman culture was widespread and extended to the public culture of fashion and home decor. The Enlightenment's emphasis on rationality in part fueled this classical focus. The geometric harmony of classical art and architecture seemed to embody Enlightenment ideals. In addition, classical cultures

28-13   JOHN SINGLETON COPLEY, *Portrait of Paul Revere,* ca. 1768–1770. Oil on canvas, 2′ 11$\frac{1}{8}$″ × 2′ 4″. Museum of Fine Arts, Boston (gift of Joseph W., William B., and Edward H. R. Revere).

represented the height of civilized society, and Greece and Rome served as models of enlightened political organization. These cultures, with their traditions of liberty, civic virtue, morality, and sacrifice, served as ideal models during a period of great political upheaval. Given such traditional associations, it is not coincidental that Neoclassicism was particularly appealing during the French and American Revolutions. The public appetite for classicism was whetted further by the excavations of Herculaneum (begun in 1738) and Pompeii (1748), which the volcanic eruption of Mount Vesuvius in A.D. 79 had buried (see "Rising from the Ashes: The Excavation of Herculaneum and Pompeii," page 849).

The enthusiasm for classical antiquity permeated much of the scholarship of the time. In the late eighteenth century, the ancient world increasingly became the focus of scholarly attention. A visit to Rome stimulated Edward Gibbon to begin his monumental *Decline and Fall of the Roman Empire,* which appeared between 1776 and 1788. Earlier, in 1755, Johann Joachim Winckelmann, the first modern art historian, published his *Thoughts on the Imitation of Greek Art in Painting and Sculpture,* uncompromisingly designating Greek art as the most perfect to come from human hands. Winckelmann characterized Greek sculpture as manifesting a "noble simplicity and silent greatness."[4] In his *History of Ancient Art* (1764), he described each monument and positioned it within a huge inventory of works organized by subject matter, style, and period. Before Winckelmann, art historians had focused on biography, as reflected in Giorgio Vasari's *Lives of the Most Eminent Italian Architects, Painters and Sculptors* (first published in 1550). Winckelmann thus initiated one modern method thoroughly in accord with Enlightenment ideas of or-

dering knowledge. His was clearly a system of description and classification that provided a pioneering model for the understanding of stylistic evolution. As was the norm, Winckelmann's familiarity with classical art was derived predominantly from Roman works and Roman copies of Greek art. Yet Winckelmann was instrumental in bringing to scholarly attention the distinctions between Greek and Roman art. Thus, he paved the way for more thorough study of the unique characteristics of the art and architecture of these two cultures. Winckelmann's writings also laid a theoretical and historical foundation for the enormously widespread taste for Neoclassicism that lasted well into the nineteenth century.

Setting the Stage for Neoclassicism in Art

A ROMAN EXAMPLE OF VIRTUE   In the art of Angelica Kauffmann (1741–1807), Greuze's simple figure types, homely situations, and contemporary settings in moral, "natural" pictures were transformed by a Neoclassicism that still contained echoes of the Rococo style. Born in Switzerland and trained in Italy, Kauffmann spent many of her productive years in England. A student of Sir Joshua Reynolds, and an interior decorator of many houses Robert Adam built, she was a founding member of the British Royal Academy of Arts and enjoyed a fashionable reputation. Her *Cornelia Presenting Her Children as Her Treasures,* or *Mother of the Gracchi* (FIG. **28-14**), is a kind of set piece of early Neoclassicism. Its subject is an informative *exemplum virtutis* (example or model of virtue) drawn from Greek and Roman history and literature. The

28-14 Angelica Kauffmann, *Cornelia Presenting Her Children as Her Treasures,* or *Mother of the Gracchi,* ca. 1785. Oil on canvas, 3' 4" × 4' 2". Virginia Museum of Fine Arts, Richmond (the Adolph D. and Wilkins C. Williams Fund).

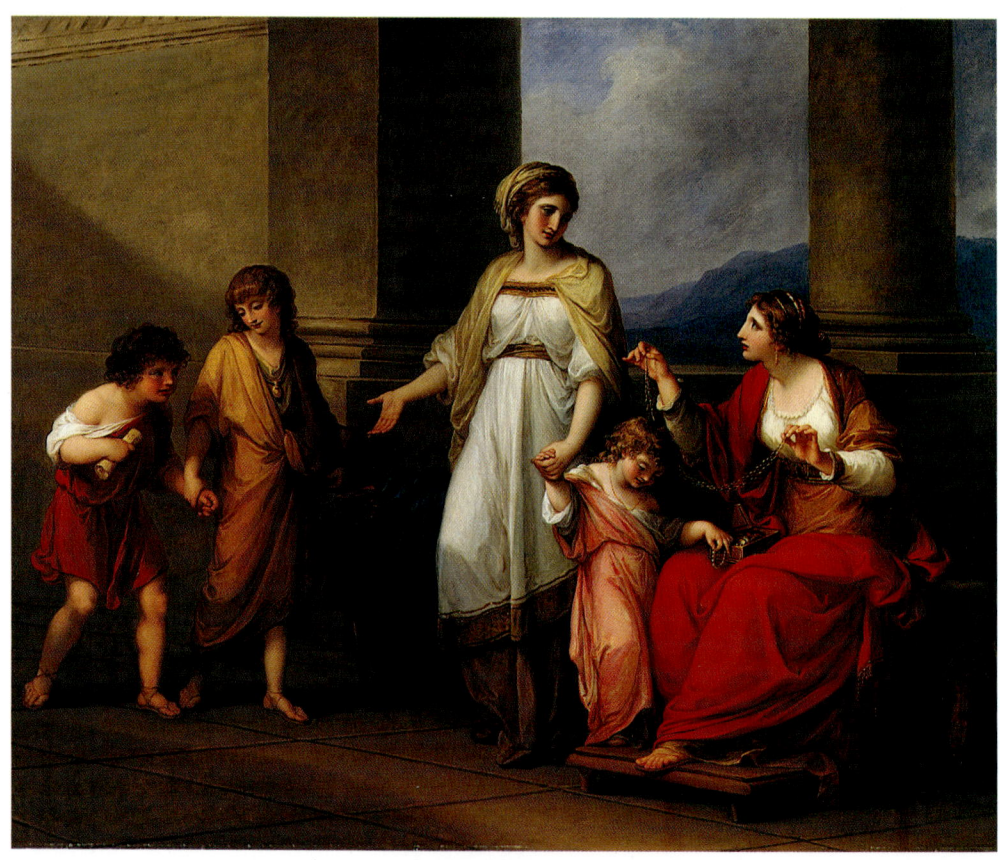

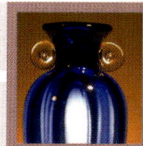

Rising from the Ashes
The Excavation of Herculaneum and Pompeii

Among the events that fueled the European fascination with classical antiquity were the excavations of two ancient cities, Herculaneum and Pompeii. The violent eruption of Mount Vesuvius in August A.D. 79 had buried both cities, located on the Bay of Naples, under volcanic ash and mud (see "An Eyewitness Account of the Eruption of Mount Vesuvius," Chapter 10, page 252). Although each of these cities had been "rediscovered" at various times during the following centuries, not until the mid-1700s did systematic excavation of both sites begin. Excavation of Pompeii, in particular, has been an extensive undertaking. That city holds the distinction as the oldest archeological site in more or less continuous excavation.

Because of how these cities were destroyed, their excavations produced unusually complete reconstructions of art and life in these Roman towns. Not only were buildings discovered, but paintings, sculptures, furniture, vases, silverware, small objects, and human skeletons were also unearthed. As a result, European imagination about and interest in ancient Rome grew tremendously.

Europeans acquired many of these uncovered objects. For example, Sir William Hamilton, British consul in Naples from 1764 to 1800, collected numerous vases and small objects, which he sold to the British Museum in 1772. The finds at Pompeii and Herculaneum, therefore, were available to a wide public.

Although the Enlightenment was largely responsible for the revival of interest in classical antiquity, these excavations were a major factor in stimulating the public's fascination with not just Rome but the entire ancient world. Soon, "Pompeian" style was all the rage, evident in the interior designs of Robert Adam (FIG. 28-25) and in the pottery designs of John Flaxman (1755–1826) and Josiah Wedgwood (1730–1795). Wedgwood established his reputation in the 1760s with his creamware inspired by ancient art. He eventually produced vases based on what were thought to be Etruscan designs and expanded his business by producing small busts of classical figures, as well as cameos and medallions adorned with copies of antique reliefs and statues. The archeological finds also affected garden and landscape designs. Fashion based on classical garb became popular, and Emma Hamilton, wife of Sir William Hamilton, often gave lavish parties dressed in floating and delicate Greek-style drapery.

Thus, despite the tragic demise of these two Roman cities ages ago, their importance has endured through the centuries, and their excavations in the eighteenth century did much to stimulate the Neoclassical taste.

---

moralizing pictures of Hogarth and Greuze already had marked a change in taste, but Kauffmann replaced the modern setting and characters of their works. She clothed her actors in ancient Roman garb and posed them in classicizing Roman attitudes within Roman interiors. The theme in this painting is the virtue of Cornelia, mother of the future political leaders Tiberius and Gaius Gracchus, who, in the second century B.C., attempted to reform the Roman Republic. Cornelia's character is revealed in this scene, which takes place after a lady visitor had shown off her fine jewelry and then haughtily requested that Cornelia show hers. Instead of rushing to get her own precious adornments, Cornelia brings her sons forward, presenting them as her jewels. The architectural setting is severely Roman, with no Rococo motif in evidence, and the composition and drawing have the simplicity and firmness of low-relief carving. Only the Rococo style's charm and grace linger—in the arrangement of the figures, in the soft lighting, and in Kauffmann's own tranquil manner.

Neoclassicism in France

PLANTING THE SEEDS OF GLORY The lingering echoes of Rococo disappeared in the work of JACQUES-LOUIS DAVID (1748–1825), the Neoclassical painter-ideologist of the French Revolution and the Napoleonic empire. David was a distant relative of Boucher and followed Boucher's style until a period of study in Rome won the younger man over to the classical art tradition. David favored the academic teachings about basing art elements on rules taken from the ancients and from the great Renaissance masters. In his individual style, David reworked the classical and academic traditions. He rebelled against the Rococo as an "artificial taste" and exalted classical art as the imitation of nature in her most beautiful and perfect form. He praised Greek art enthusiastically, although he, like Winckelmann, knew almost nothing about it firsthand: "I want to work in a pure Greek style. I feed my eyes on ancient statues, I even have the intention of imitating some of them."[5]

David concurred with the Enlightenment belief that subject matter should have a moral and should be presented so that the "marks of heroism and civic virtue offered the eyes of the people [will] electrify its soul, and plant the seeds of glory and devotion to the fatherland."[6] A milestone painting in David's career, *Oath of the Horatii* (FIG. **28-15**), depicts a story from pre-Republican Rome, the heroic phase of Roman history. The topic was not an arcane one for David's audience. This story of conflict between love and patriotism, first recounted by the ancient Roman historian Livy, had been retold in a play by Pierre Corneille performed in Paris several years earlier, making it familiar to David's viewing public. According to the story, the leaders of the warring cities of Rome and

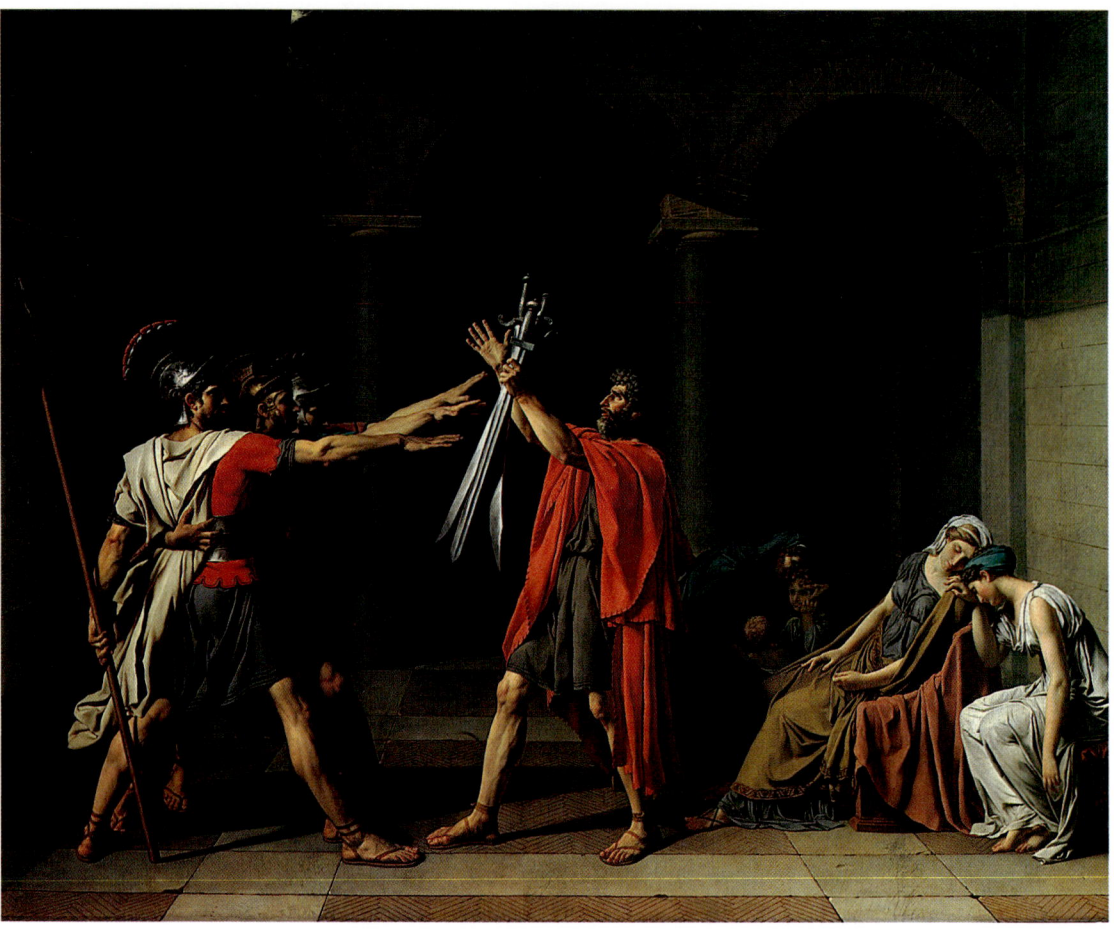

Alba decided to resolve their conflicts in a series of encounters waged by three representatives from each side. The Roman champions, the three Horatius brothers, were sent to face the three sons of the Curatius family from Alba. A sister of the Horatii, Camilla, was the bride-to-be of one of the Curatius sons, while the wife of the youngest Horatius was the sister of the Curatii.

David's painting shows the Horatii as they swear on their swords, held high by their father, to win or die for Rome, oblivious to the anguish and sorrow of their female relatives. In its form, *Oath of the Horatii* is a paragon of the Neoclassical style. Not only does the subject matter deal with a narrative of patriotism and sacrifice excerpted from Roman history, but the image is also presented with admirable force and clarity. David presented the scene in a shallow space much like a stage setting, defined by a severely simple architectural framework. The statuesque and carefully modeled figures are deployed across the space, close to the foreground, in a manner reminiscent of ancient relief sculpture. The rigid, angular, and virile forms of the men on the left effectively contrast with the soft curvilinear shapes of the distraught women on the right. This visually pits virtues the Enlightenment leaders ascribed to men (such as courage, patriotism, and unwavering loyalty to a cause) against the emotions of love, sorrow, and despair that the women in the painting express. The French viewing audience perceived such emotionalism as characteristic of the female nature. The message was clear and of a type readily identifiable to the prerevolutionary French public. The picture created a sensation when it was exhibited in Paris in 1785, and although it had been painted under royal patron-

age and was not intended as a revolutionary statement, its Neoclassical style soon became the revolution's semiofficial voice. David may have painted in the academic tradition, but he made something new of it. He created a program for arousing his audience to patriotic zeal.

ART IN THE SERVICE OF REVOLUTION   When the French Revolution broke out in 1789, David was thrust amid this momentous upheaval. He believed "the arts must . . . contribute forcefully to the education of the public,"[7] and he realized that the emphasis on patriotism and civic virtue perceived as integral to classicism would prove effective in dramatic, instructive paintings. However, rather than continuing to create artworks that focused on scenes from antiquity, David began to portray scenes from the French Revolution itself.

The Oath of the Tennis Court (FIG. **28-16**) is one such work and served not only to record an important event in the revolution but also to provide inspiration and encouragement to the revolutionary forces. David depicted the moment when delegates from the Third Estate (the middle and lower classes), rejecting the structure and voting policies of the Estates General (a representative governing body King Louis XVI convened), gathered on a nearby tennis court. Reconstituting themselves as the National Assembly, they vowed to remain as a permanent assembly until they had produced a new French constitution. David captured the moment's fervor and chaos. In contrast to the severe clarity and simplicity of his earlier Neoclassical works, this work is crowded with figures. The presiding figure is Jean-Sylvain Bailly, who became mayor

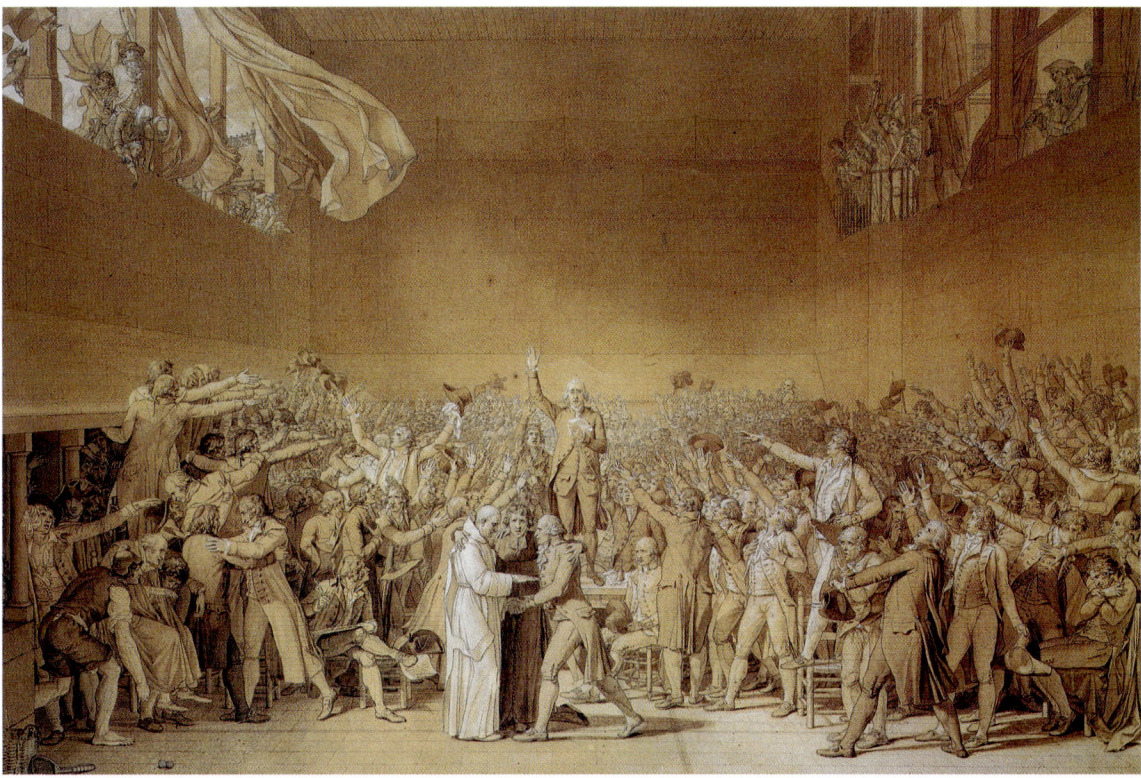

28-16 JACQUES-LOUIS DAVID, *The Oath of the Tennis Court*, 1791. Graphite, ink, sepia, heightened with white on paper, approx. 2′ 1½″ × 3′ 5⅓″. Musée national du Château de Versailles, Versailles.

of Paris. The curtain blowing in from the window on the upper left amplifies the drama and action that pervades the scene. It suggests the "fresh air" the revolution was introducing to the stagnant political structure then existing.

A radical and militant faction known as the Jacobins commissioned David to paint this subject, intending to hang the final work in the National Assembly building as a constant reminder of the ideals for which the revolutionaries were fighting. In large part because of the political situation's instability, David never finished the monumental painting (the foreground figures were to be life-sized), and viewers must be content with this preliminary drawing.

A MARTYRED REVOLUTIONARY David became increasingly involved with the revolution and threw in his lot with the Jacobins. He accepted the role of de facto minister of propaganda, organizing political pageants and ceremonies that included floats, costumes, and sculptural props. The tragic assassination of Jean-Paul Marat, a revolutionary radical, a writer, and David's personal friend, prompted David to paint another one of his French Revolution-inspired works: *The Death of Marat* (FIG. **28-17**). David depicted the martyred revolutionary after he was stabbed to death in his medicinal bath by Charlotte Corday, a member of a rival political faction. The artist ensured proper identification of this hero. The makeshift writing surface, the inscription on the writing stand, and the medicinal bath (Marat was afflicted with a painful skin disease) all provide specific references to Marat. David presented the scene with directness and clarity. The cold neutral space above Marat's figure, slumped in the tub, makes for a chilling oppressiveness. The painter vividly placed narrative details—the knife, the wound, the blood, the letter

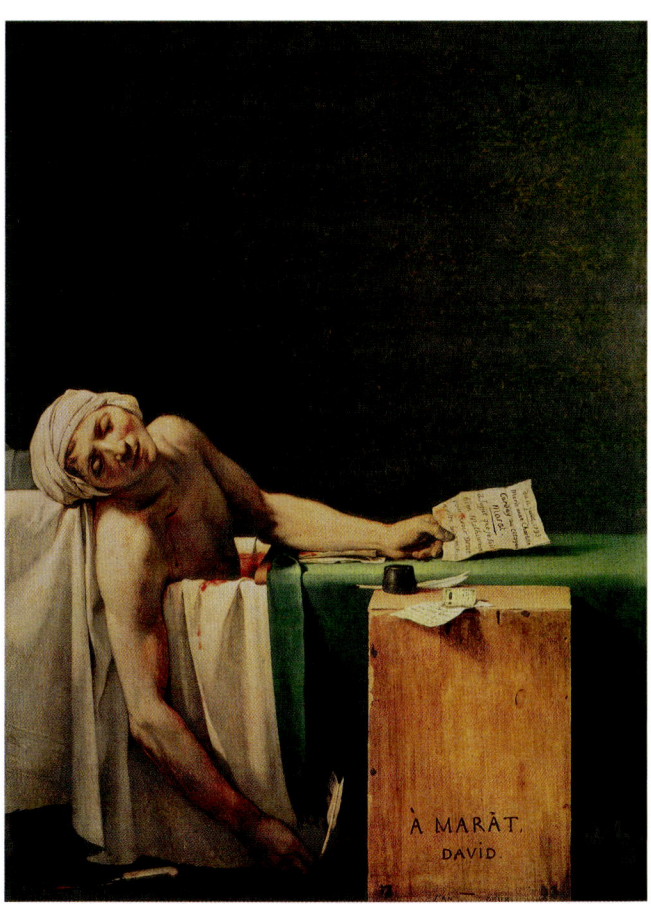

28-17 JACQUES-LOUIS DAVID, *The Death of Marat*, 1793. Oil on canvas, approx. 5′ 3″ × 4′ 1″. Musées Royaux des Beaux-Arts de Belgique, Brussels.

with which the young woman gained entrance—to sharpen the sense of pain and outrage and to confront viewers with the scene itself. Although David's depiction was based on historical events, his composition reveals his close study of Michelangelo, especially the Renaissance artist's Christ in the *Pietà* in Saint Peter's in Rome. *The Death of Marat* is convincingly real, yet it was masterfully composed to present Marat to the French people as a tragic martyr who died in the service of their state. In this way, the painting was meant to function as an "altarpiece" for the new civic "religion;" it was designed to inspire viewers with the saintly dedication of their slain leader. Rather than the grandiosity of spectacle characteristic of West's *The Death of General Wolfe* (FIG. 28-12), David's *Marat* was stripped to a severe Neoclassical spareness, yet it retains its drama and ability to move spectators.

THE EMPIRE STRIKES BACK   At the fall of the French revolutionist Robespierre (1758–1794) and his party in 1794, David barely escaped with his life. He was tried and imprisoned, and after his release in 1795 he worked hard to resurrect his career. When Napoleon Bonaparte (1769–1821)—who had ascended to power due to the revolutionary disarray—approached David and offered him the position of First Painter of the Empire, David seized the opportunity. One of the major paintings David produced for Napoleon was *The Coronation of Napoleon* (FIG. **28-18**), a large-scale work that documents the pomp and pageantry of Napoleon's coronation in December of 1804.

The Coronation of Napoleon is a monumental (twenty feet by thirty-two feet) painting that reveals the interests of both patron and artist. Napoleon was well aware of the utility of art for constructing a public image and of David's skill in producing inspiring, powerful images. To a large extent, David adhered to historical fact regarding the coronation. He was present at this momentous event and recorded his presence in the painting (he appears in one of the tribunes, or loges, constructed for spectators). The ceremony was held in Notre-Dame Cathedral, whose majestic interior David faithfully reproduced. The artist also duly recorded those in attendance. In addition to Napoleon, his wife Josephine (being crowned), and Pope Pius VII (seated behind Napoleon), others present included Joseph and Louis Bonaparte, Napoleon's ministers, the retinues of the emperor and empress, and a representative group of the clergy. It is clear, however, from preliminary studies and drawings that David made changes at Napoleon's request. For example, Napoleon insisted that the painter depict the pope with his hand raised in blessing. Further, Napoleon's mother appears prominently in the center background, yet she had refused to attend the coronation and apparently was included in the painting at the emperor's insistence.

Despite the numerous figures and the lavish pageantry involved in this event, David retained the structured composition central to the Neoclassical style. Like David's *Oath of the Horatii,* the action here was presented as if on a theater stage. In addition, as with the arrangement of the men and women in *Oath,* David conceptually divided the painting to reveal polarities. In this case, the pope, prelates, and priests repre-

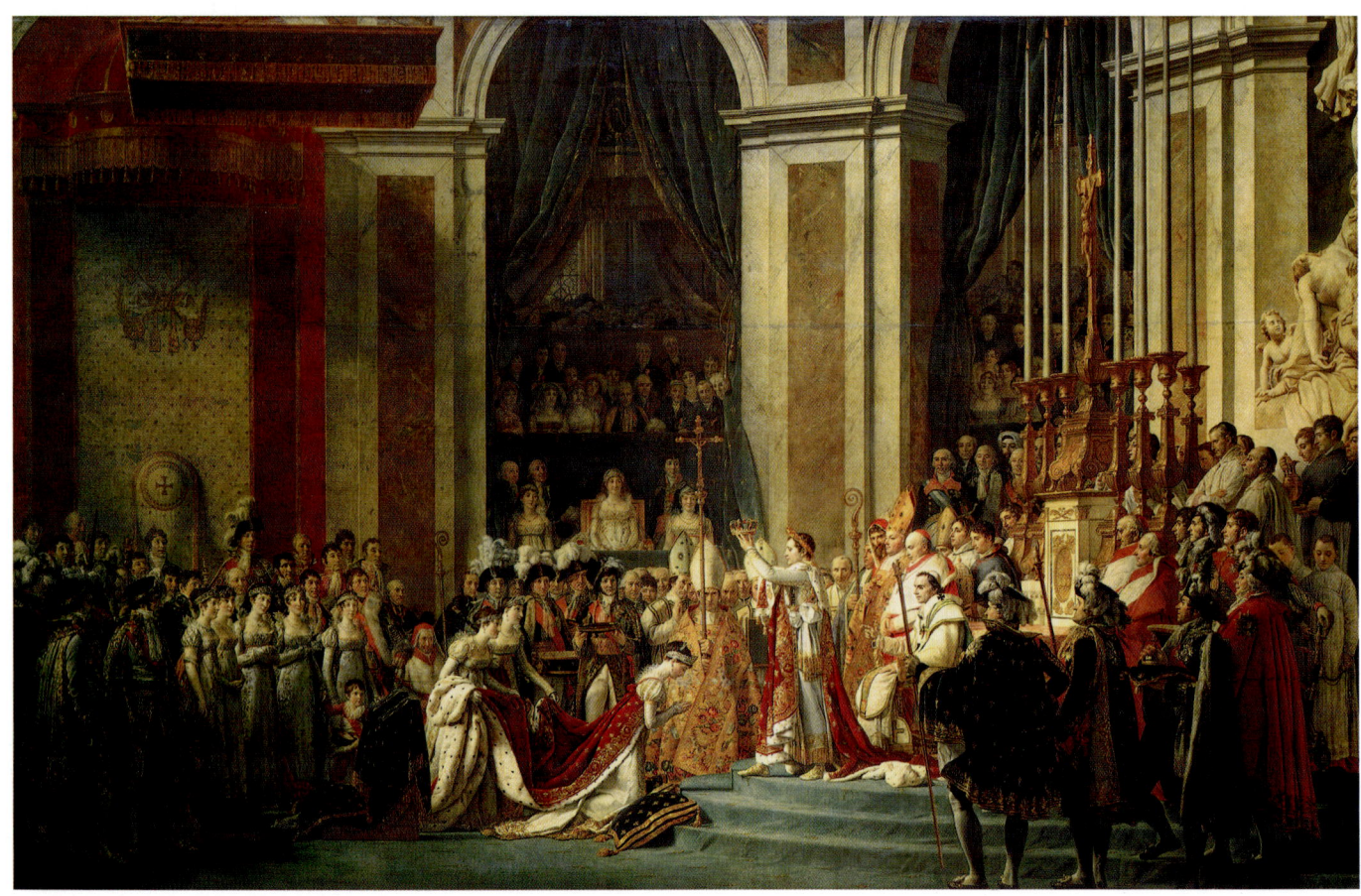

28-18   JACQUES-LOUIS DAVID, *The Coronation of Napoleon,* 1805–1808. Oil on canvas, 20′ 4½″ × 32′ 1¾″. Louvre, Paris.

senting the Catholic Church appear on the right, contrasting with members of Napoleon's imperial court on the left. The relationship between the Church and state was one of this period's most contentious issues. Napoleon's decision to crown himself, rather than allowing the pope to perform the coronation, as was traditional, revealed Napoleon's concern about the power relationship between church and state. Napoleon's insistence on emphasizing his authority is evidenced by his selection of the moment depicted; having already crowned himself, Napoleon places a crown on his wife's head. Thus, although this painting represents an important visual document in the tradition of history painting, it also represents a more complex statement about the changing politics in Napoleonic France.

It was not just David's individual skill but Neoclassicism in general that appealed to Napoleon. When Napoleon Bonaparte ascended to power, he embraced all links with the classical past as sources of symbolic authority for his short-lived imperial state. Such associations, particularly connections to the Roman Empire, served Napoleon well and were invoked in architecture and sculpture, as well as painting.

ROMAN GRANDEUR IN FRANCE Architecture provided an excellent vehicle for consolidating authority because of its public presence. Napoleon, however, was not the first to rely on classical models. Fairly early in the eighteenth century, architects began to turn away from the theatricality and ostentation of Baroque and Rococo design and embraced a more streamlined classicism. The Neoclassical portico of the Parisian church of Sainte-Geneviève (FIG. **28-19**), now the Panthéon, was designed by JACQUES-GERMAIN SOUFFLOT (1713–1780). It stands as testament to the revived interest in Greek and Roman cultures. The Roman ruins at Baalbek in Syria, especially a titanic colonnade, provided much of the inspiration for this portico. The columns, reproduced with studied archeological exactitude, are the first revelation of Roman grandeur in France. The walls are severely blank, except for a repeated garland motif near the top. The colonnaded dome, a Neoclassical version of the domes of Saint Peter's in Rome (see FIG. 22-29), the Church of the Invalides in Paris (see FIG. 24-72), and Saint Paul's in London (see FIG. 24-74), rises above a Greek-cross plan. Both the dome and vaults rest on an interior grid of splendid freestanding Corinthian columns, as if the portico's colonnade were continued within. Although the whole effect, inside and out, is Roman, the structural principles employed are essentially Gothic. Soufflot was one of the first eighteenth-century builders to suggest that Gothic engineering was highly functional structurally and could be applied to modern buildings. In his work, the curious, but not unreasonable, conjunction of Gothic and classical has a structural integration that foreshadowed nineteenth-century admiration of Gothic engineering.

A NAPOLEONIC "TEMPLE OF GLORY" La Madeleine (FIG. **28-20**) was briefly intended as a "temple of glory" for Napoleon's armies and a monument to the newly won glories of France. Begun as a church in 1807, at the height of Napoleon's power (some three years after he proclaimed himself emperor), the structure reverted again to a church after his defeat and long before its completion in 1842. Designed by PIERRE VIGNON (1763–1828), this

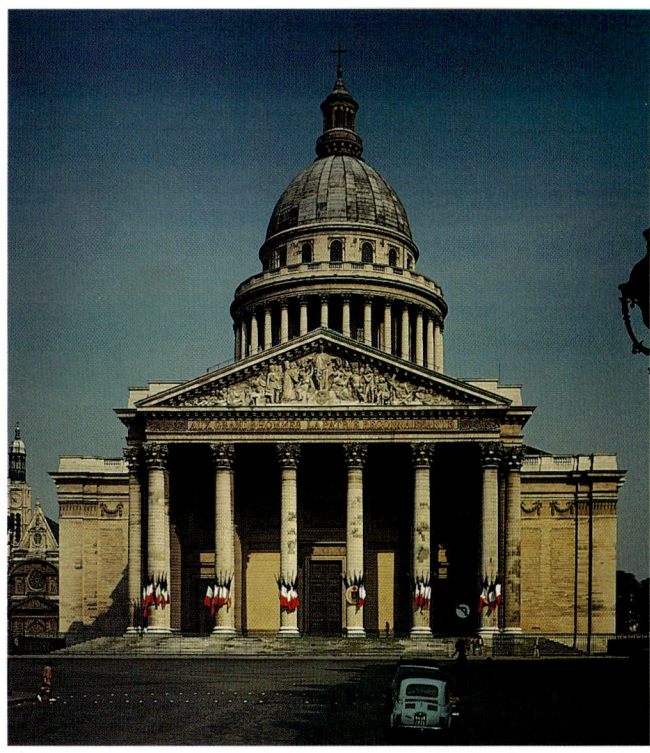

28-19   JACQUES-GERMAIN SOUFFLOT, the Panthéon (Sainte-Geneviève), Paris, France, 1755–1792.

grandiose temple includes a high podium and broad flight of stairs leading to a deep porch in the front. These architectural features, coupled with the Corinthian columns, recall Roman imperial temples (such as the Maison Carrée, FIG. 10-30, in Nîmes, France), making La Madeleine a symbolic link between the Napoleonic and Roman empires. Curiously, the building's classical shell surrounds an interior covered by a sequence of three domes, a feature found in Byzantine and Aquitanian Romanesque churches. It is as though Vignon clothed this Christian church in the costume of pagan Rome.

THE EMPEROR'S SISTER AS GODDESS Under Napoleon, classical models were prevalent in sculpture as well. The emperor's favorite sculptor was ANTONIO CANOVA (1757–1822), who somewhat reluctantly left a successful career in Italy to settle in Paris and serve the emperor. Once in France, Canova became Napoleon's admirer and made numerous portraits, all in the Neoclassical style, of the emperor and his family. Perhaps the best known of these works is the marble portrait of Napoleon's sister, *Pauline Borghese as Venus* (FIG. **28-21**). Initially, Canova had suggested depicting Borghese as Diana, goddess of the hunt. The subject of the work, however, insisted on being shown as Venus, the goddess of love. Thus she appears, reclining on a divan and gracefully holding the golden apple, a symbol of the goddess's triumph in the judgment of Paris. Although Canova clearly derived the figure from Greek art—the sensuous pose and drapery recall Greek sculpture—the work is not as idealized as might be expected. The sculptor's sharply detailed rendering of the couch and drapery suggest a commitment to naturalism as well.

The public perception of Pauline Borghese influenced the sculpture's design and presentation. Napoleon Bonaparte had

28-20 Pierre Vignon, La Madeleine, Paris, France, 1807–1842.

arranged the marriage of his sister to an heir of the noble Roman Borghese family. Once in Rome, Pauline's behavior was less than dignified, and the public gossiped extensively about her affairs. Her insistence on portrayal as the goddess of love reflected her self-perception. Due to his wife's questionable reputation, Prince Camillo Borghese, the work's official patron, kept the sculpture sequestered in the Villa Borghese. Relatively few people were allowed to see it (and then only by torchlight). Still, the sculpture increased both the artist and

subject's notoriety, although the sculpture's enduring fame was established only after Canova's death in 1822.

Neoclassicism in England

Classical antiquity's appeal extended well beyond French borders. The popularity of Greek and Roman cultures was due not only to their association with morality, rationality, and in-

28-21 Antonio Canova, *Pauline Borghese as Venus,* 1808. Marble, life-size. Galleria Borghese, Rome.

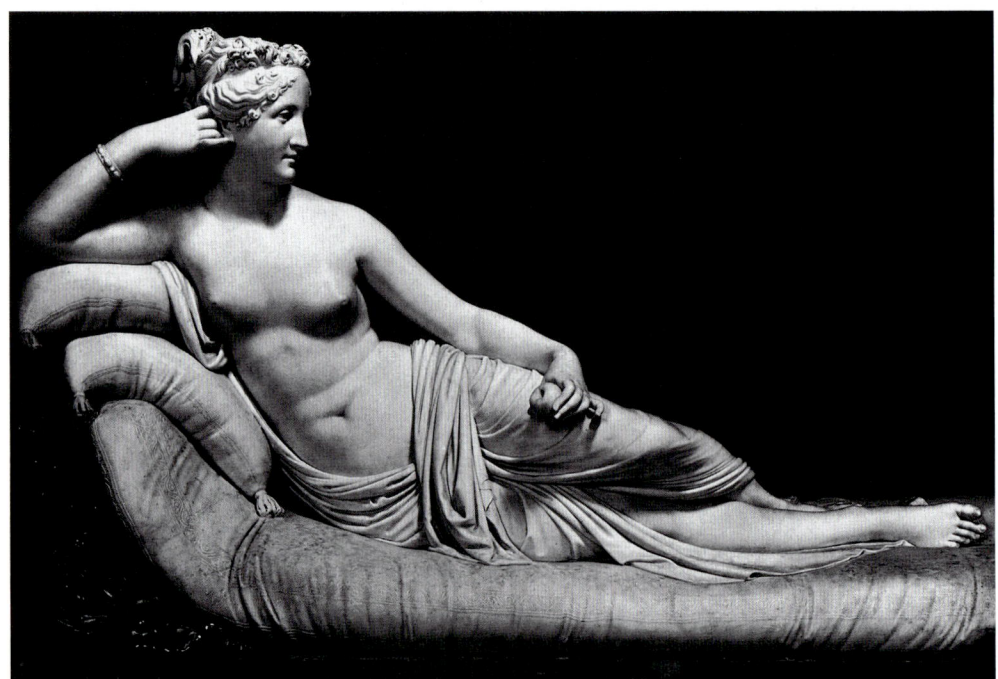

tegrity but also to their connection to political systems ranging from Athenian democracy to Roman imperial rule. Thus, in parliamentary England, as in revolutionary and imperial France, Neoclassicism was highly regarded. In England, Neoclassicism's appeal also may have been due to the Baroque style's connection with the showy rule of absolute monarchy—something to be played down in parliamentary England. In English architecture, the preference for a simple and commonsensical style led straight from the authority of the classical Roman architect Vitruvius, through Andrea Palladio's work (see FIGS. 22-56, 22-57, 22-58, and 22-59), and on to that of Inigo Jones (see FIG. 24-73). As Alexander Pope, in his *Fourth Moral Epistle* (1731), advised his friend, the statesman and architectural amateur RICHARD BOYLE, earl of Burlington (1695–1753):

> *You too proceed! make falling Arts your care,*
> *Erect new wonders, and the old repair,*
> *Jones and Palladio to themselves restore,*
> *And be whate'er Vitruvius was before.*[8]

INVOKING PALLADIO Lord Burlington took the advice and strongly restated Jones's Palladian doctrine in a new style in Chiswick House (FIG. **28-22**), which he built on London's outskirts with the help of the talented professional WILLIAM KENT (ca. 1686–1748). The way had been paved for this shift in style by, among other things, the publication of Colin Campbell's *Vitruvius Britannicus* (1715), three volumes of engravings of ancient buildings in Britain, prefaced by a denunciation of Italian Baroque and high praise for Palladio and Jones.

Chiswick House is a free variation on the theme of Palladio's Villa Rotonda (see FIG. 22-56). The exterior design provided a clear alternative to the colorful splendors of Versailles. In its simple symmetry, unadorned planes, right angles, and stiffly wrought proportions, Chiswick looks very classical and "rational." But, like so many Palladian villas in England, the effect is modified by its setting within informal gardens, where a charming irregularity of layout and freely growing uncropped foliage dominate the scene. Just as irregularity was cultivated in the landscaping surrounding English Palladian

villas, early eighteenth-century building interiors sometimes were ornamented in a style more closely related to the Rococo decoration fashionable on the continent than to the severe classical Palladian exteriors. At Chiswick, the interior design creates a luxurious Late Baroque foil to the stern symmetry of the exterior and the plan. Despite such "lapses," Palladian Classicism prevailed in English architecture until about 1760, when it began to evolve into Neoclassicism.

A RESORT TOWN OF PALLADIAN SPLENDOR
At just about this time of change, John Wood the Elder (ca. 1704–1754) and his son JOHN WOOD THE YOUNGER (1728–1782) laid out an extensive complex of buildings for the fashionable resort town of Bath in Somersetshire. The structures are grouped around simple geometrical spaces—the square, circle, and semicircle—and are called Queen's Square, the Circus, and the Royal Crescent (FIG. **28-23**), the last exclusively the work of John Wood the Younger. These early ingenious solutions to the problems of urban design were intended not for royalty but for the well-to-do members of society who came "to take the waters" at the city's hot springs. Restored and operating in the eighteenth century, the baths had been famous since Roman times and had given Bath its name. In both the Circus and the Royal Crescent, the houses are linked into rows behind a single continuous Palladian facade, which transforms the joined units into one palatial edifice. The Royal Crescent joins thirty residences in a great semiellipse, originally intended to have a matching semiellipse facing it across an intersecting roadway, so as to suggest the ancient Roman Colosseum (see FIG. 10-34). Bath, with its ancient Roman associations, prompted the younger John Wood to refer to Rome not only for the Colosseum-like plan but also for the imperial scale and majesty of the building's elevation. Especially "Roman" is the sweeping parade of colossal Ionic columns along the lofty, curving basement; the roofline, punctuated regularly with clusters of chimney pots, is traditionally English. The Bath designs, with many variations, became a standard for British urban architecture for a century. Here, they announced a new classical Roman presence in what was still a Palladian edifice.

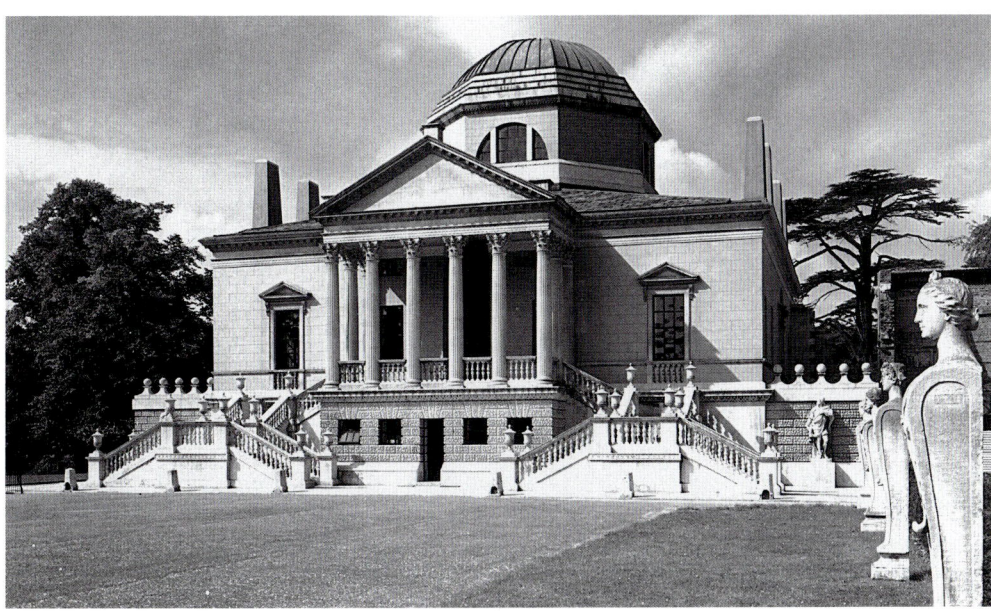

28-22 RICHARD BOYLE (earl of Burlington) and WILLIAM KENT, Chiswick House, near London, England, begun 1725. British Crown Copyright.

28-23 JOHN WOOD THE YOUNGER, the Royal Crescent, Bath, England, 1769–1775.

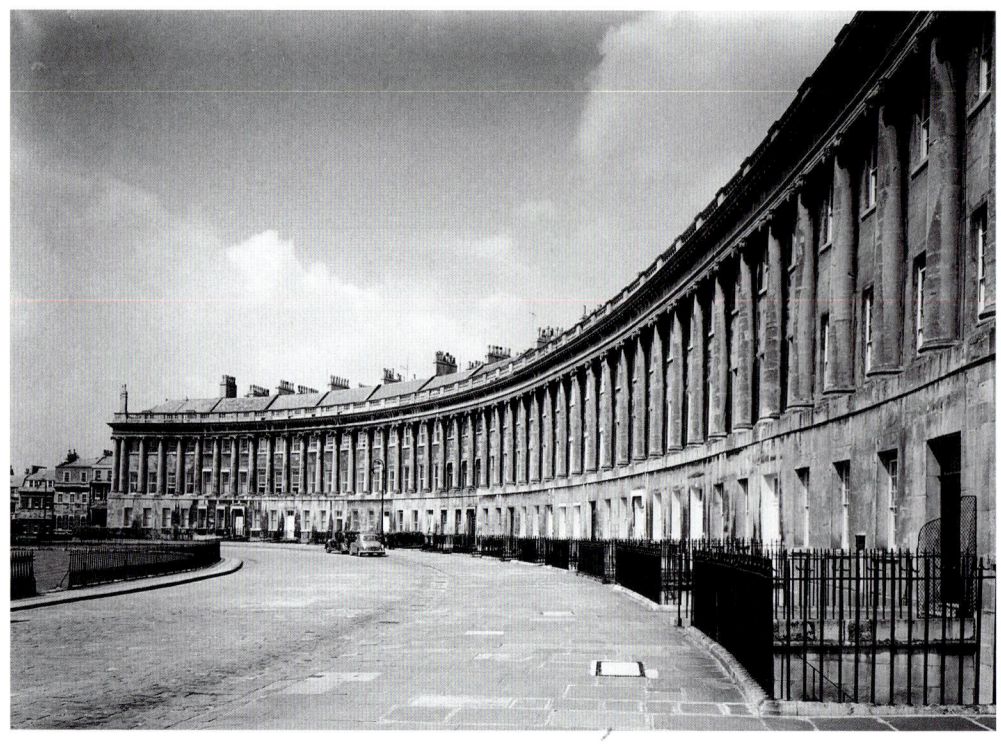

A GREEK PORTICO IN ENGLAND British painter and architect JAMES STUART (1713–1788), along with Nicholas Revett (1720–1804), also a painter and architect, introduced to Europe the splendor and originality of Greek art in the enormously influential *Antiquities of Athens,* whose first volume appeared in 1762. These volumes firmly distinguished Greek art from the "derivative" Roman style that had served as the model for classicism since the Renaissance. Stuart's design for the portico at Hagley Park (FIG. **28-24**) in Worcestershire, based on the Doric temple in Athens known as the Theseion, reflects his preference for Greek art and architecture.

NEOCLASSICISM MOVES INDOORS Eighteenth-century Neoclassical interiors also were directly inspired by new discoveries of "the glory that was Greece / And the grandeur that was Rome"[9] and summarized the conception of a noble classical world. The first great archeological event of modern times, the discovery and initial excavation of the ancient buried Roman cities of Herculaneum (see FIGS. 10-14, 10-22, and 10-24) and Pompeii (see FIGS. 10-9 to 10-13, 10-15, 10-21, and 10-23) in the 1730s and 1740s, startled and thrilled all of Europe (see "Rising from the Ashes: The Excavation of Herculaneum and Pompeii," page 849). The excavation of these cities was the veritable resurrection of the ancient world, not simply a dim vision of it inspired by a few moldering ruins. Historical reality replaced fancy with fact. The wall paintings and other artifacts of Pompeii inspired the slim, straight-lined, elegant "Pompeian" style that, after mid-century, almost entirely displaced the curvilinear Rococo.

ADAPTING POMPEIAN DECOR In England, the Pompeian manner emerged most recognizably in the work of ROBERT ADAM (1728–1792), whose interior architecture was influential throughout Europe. The Etruscan Room at Oster-

ley Park House (FIG. **28-25**) in Middlesex was begun in 1761. If compared with the Rococo salons of the Hôtel de Soubise (see FIG. 24-80) and the Amalienburg (see FIG. 24-81), this room shows how completely symmetry and rectilinearity returned. But this return was achieved with great delicacy and with none of the Louis XIV style's massive splendor. The architect took the decorative motifs (medallions, urns, vine scrolls, sphinxes, and tripods) from Roman art and, as in Roman stucco work, arranged them sparsely within broad, neutral spaces and slender margins (see FIGS. 10-18 and 10-20). Adam was an archeologist as well, and he had explored and written accounts of the ruins of Diocletian's palace at Split

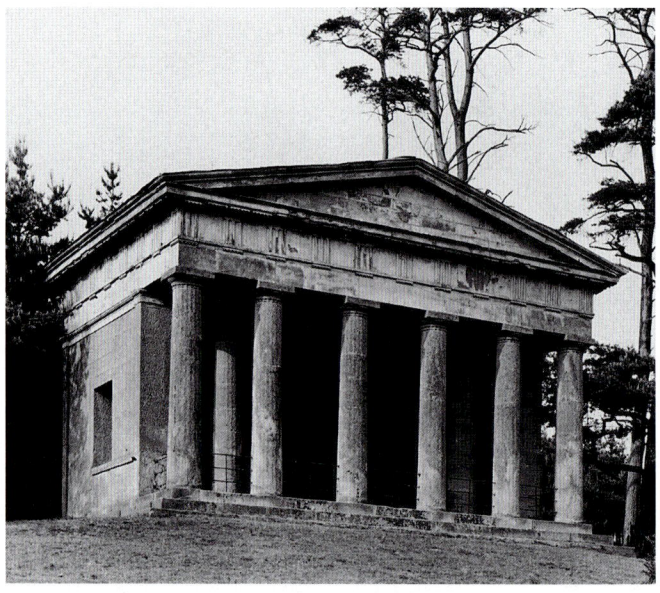

28-24 JAMES STUART, Doric portico, Hagley Park, Worcestershire, England, 1758.

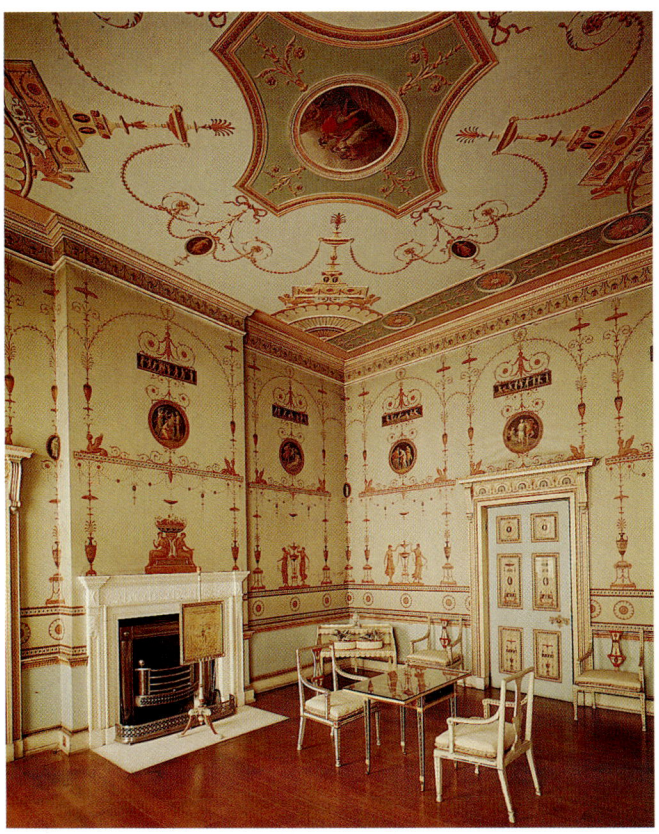

28-25   ROBERT ADAM, Etruscan Room, Osterley Park House, Middlesex, England, begun 1761. Victoria and Albert Museum, London.

(see FIG. 10-75). Kedleston House in Derbyshire, Adelphi Terrace in London, and a great many other structures he designed also show the Split palace's influence on his work.

Neoclassicism in the United States

JEFFERSONIAN IDEALISM   Neoclassicism's versatility and the appeal of the qualities with which it was connected—morality, idealism, patriotism, and civic virtue—allowed Neoclassicism to be associated with everything from revolutionary aspirations for democratic purity to imperial ambitions for unshakable authority. Thus, Napoleon invoked classical references to serve his imperial agenda. Meanwhile, in the new American republic, THOMAS JEFFERSON (1743–1826) spearheaded a movement to adopt a symbolic Neoclassicism (a style he saw as representative of U.S. democratic qualities) as the national architecture.

Scholar, economist, educational theorist, statesman, and gifted amateur architect, Jefferson was, by nature, attracted to classical architecture. He worked out his ideas in his design for his own home, Monticello (FIG. 28-26), which was begun in 1770. Jefferson admired Palladio immensely and read carefully the Italian architect's *Four Books of Architecture*. Later, while minister to France, Jefferson studied French eighteenth-century classical architecture and city planning and visited the Maison Carrée, a Roman temple at Nîmes (see FIG. 10-30). After his European trip, Jefferson completely remodeled Monticello, which he first had designed in an English Georgian style. In his remodeling, he emulated Palladio's manner, with a facade inspired by Robert Adam's work. The final version of Monticello is somewhat reminiscent of the Villa Rotonda (see

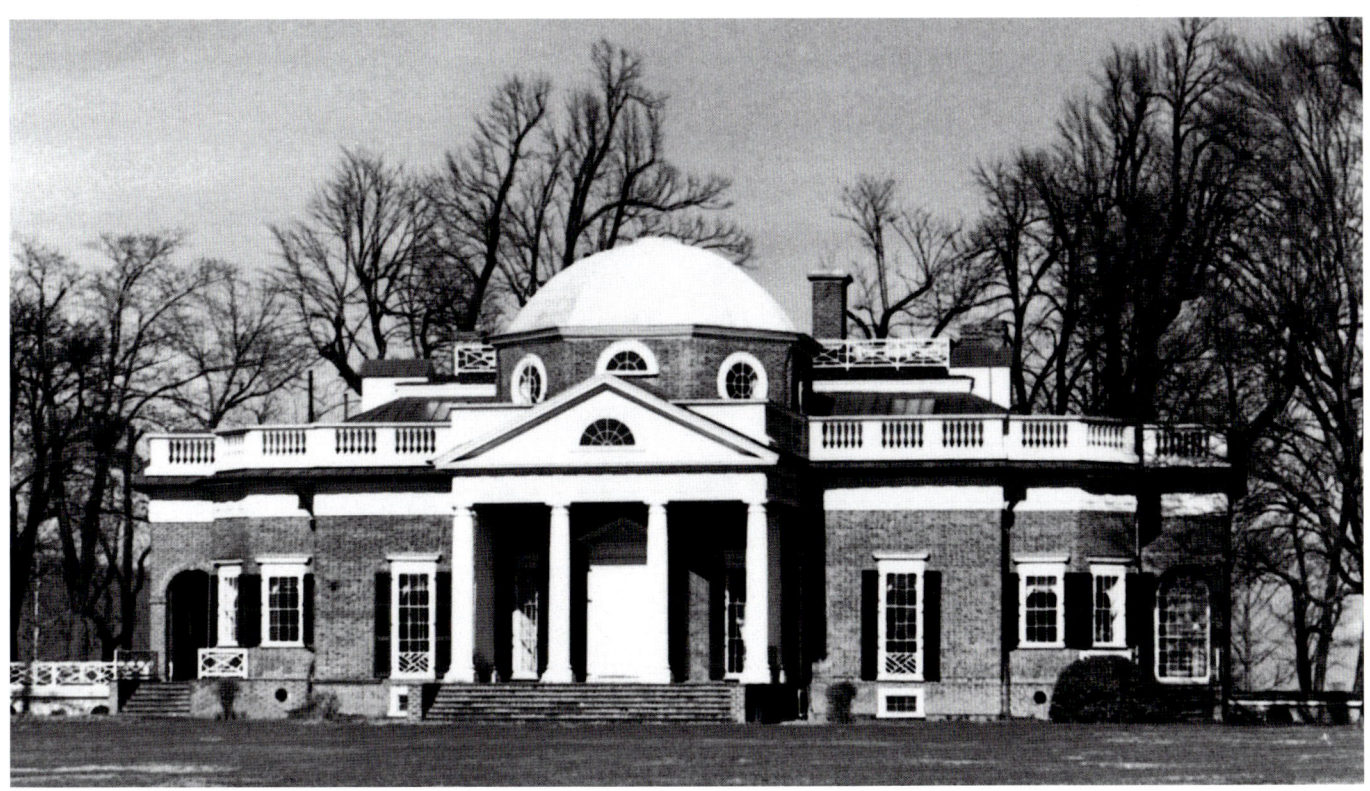

28-26   THOMAS JEFFERSON, Monticello, Charlottesville, United States, 1770–1806.

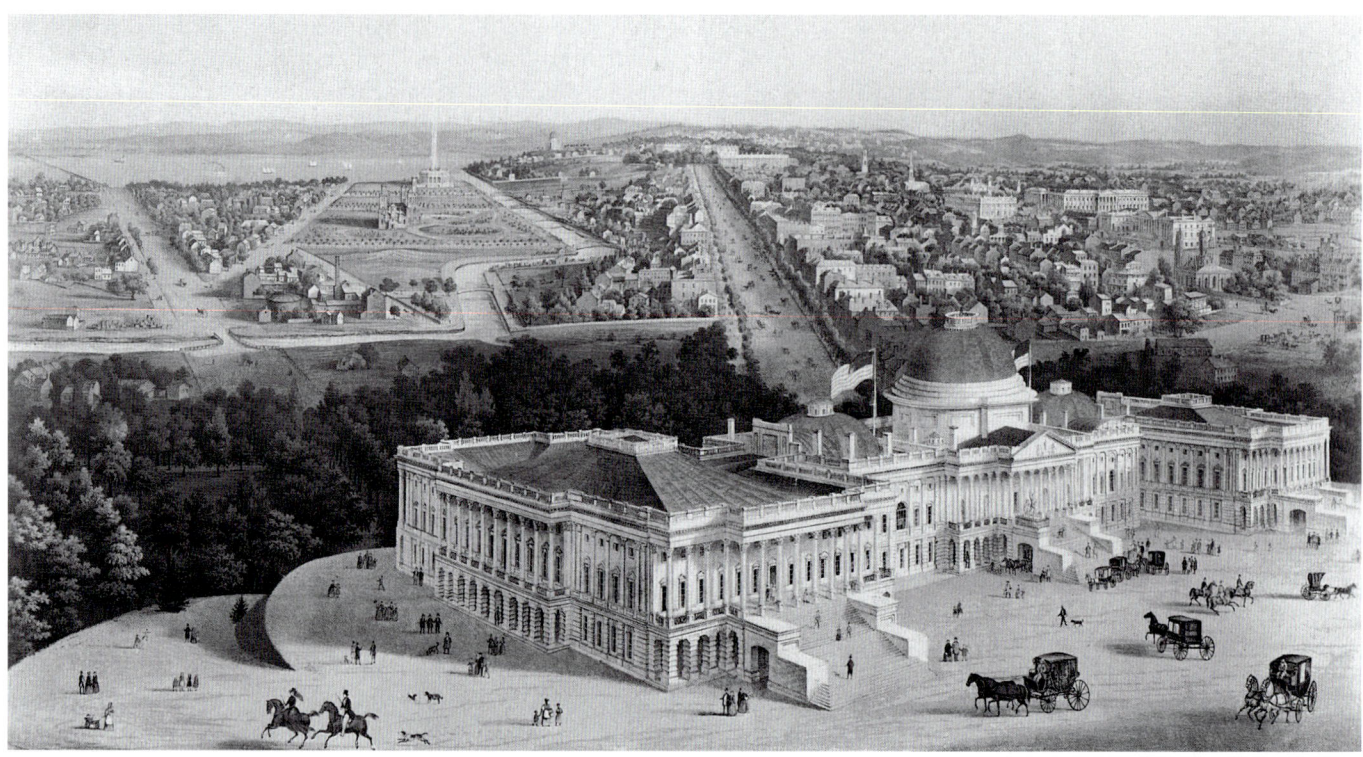

28-27   Drawing of view of Washington, 1852, showing Benjamin Latrobe's Capitol (1803–1807) and Major L'Enfant's plan (created in 1791) of the city.

FIG. 22-56) and of Chiswick House (FIG. 28-22), but its materials are the local wood and brick used in Virginia.

Turning from the private domain to public spaces, Jefferson began to carry out his dream of developing a classical style for the official architecture of the United States. Here, his Neoclassicism was an extension of the Enlightenment belief in the perfectibility of human beings and in art's power to help achieve that perfection. As secretary of state to George Washington, Jefferson supported the logically ordered city plan for Washington, D.C., created in 1791 by the French-American architect Major Pierre L'Enfant (1724–1825). The plan extended earlier ordered designs for city sections, such as Wood's designs for Bath (FIG. 28-23), to an entire community. As an architect, Jefferson also incorporated the specific look of the Maison Carrée (see FIG. 10-30) into his design for the Virginia State Capitol in Richmond. He approved William Thornton's initial Palladian design for the federal Capitol in 1793. As president, in 1803 he selected Benjamin H. Latrobe (1764–1820) to take over the design of the structure (FIG. **28-27**), with the goal of creating "a building that would serve as a visible expression of the ideals of a country dedicated to liberty." Jefferson's choice of a Roman style was influenced partly by his admiration for its beauty and partly by his associations of it with an idealized Roman republican government and, through that, with ancient Greece's democracy. Latrobe committed himself to producing a building that "when finished will be a durable and honorable monument of our infant republic, and will bear favorable comparisons with the remains of the same kind of ancient republics of Greece and Rome."[10] To that end, in the Capitol's architecture, Latrobe transformed the Roman eagle symbol into the American bald eagle, and devised a special new Corinthian order that replaced acanthus leaves with corn plants. He also designed the sculptured representation of

Liberty to abandon traditional trappings and to hold a liberty cap in one hand and rest her other hand on the Constitution.

GEORGE WASHINGTON AS GREEK GOD?   The Neoclassical style's limitations are apparent in a statue of George Washington (FIG. **28-28**), by the American sculptor Horatio Greenough (1805–1852). Here, the Neoclassical style Jefferson had championed so successfully for the new democracy's architecture (FIG. 28-27) turned out to be less suitable for commemorative portraits. Commissioned by the United States Congress to honor Washington as the country's first president, the sculptor used as a model for the head a popular bust of Washington by Houdon (a work with the same lively realism as Houdon's *Voltaire*, FIG. 28-1). For the statue's body, Greenough aimed at the monumental majesty inspired by a lost, but famous, sculpture of the Greek god Zeus by Phidias. The sheathed sword, offered hilt forward, was intended to symbolize "Washington the peacemaker," rather than "Washington the revolutionary war general." The representation of the "father of his country," deified as a half-naked pagan god, however, was, at the time, beyond the American public's taste. The statue was considered a failure in Greenough's time precisely because it manifested, more than many Neoclassical sculptures, the contradictions that sometimes develop when idealistic and realistic illusion meet. While Canova appeared to harmonize these two trends in *Pauline Borghese as Venus* (FIG. 28-21), Greenough put them in opposition. Although Greenough's statue was never thrown into the Potomac River "to hide it from the world," as one congressman suggested, it also was never placed in its intended site beneath the Capitol dome. Today, the work is more highly regarded and is displayed at the National Portrait Gallery in Washington, D.C. Although to some it

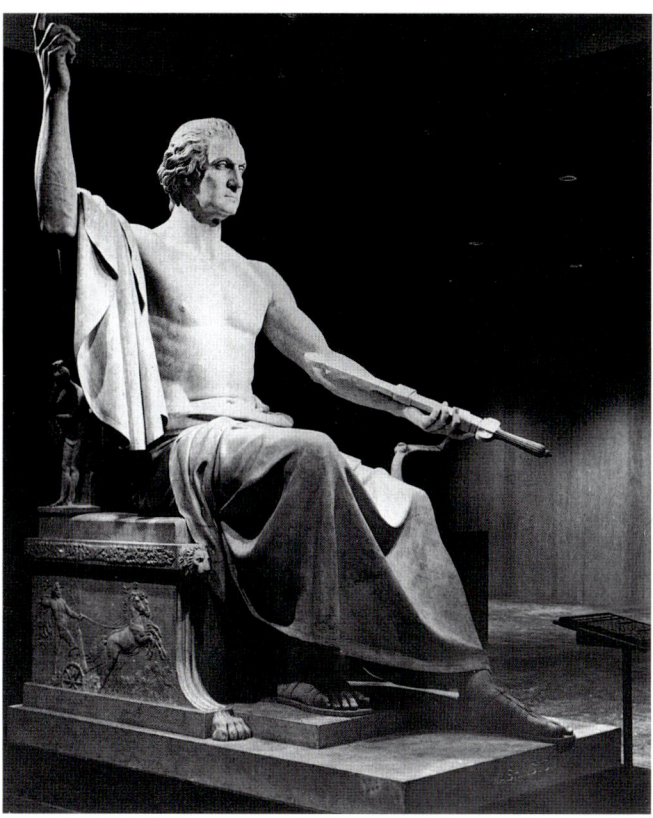

28-28 HORATIO GREENOUGH, *George Washington*, 1832–1841. Marble, approx. 11′ 4″ high. National Portrait Gallery, Smithsonian Institution, Washington.

may seem stiff, cold, or simply unconvincing, it does have an imperious majesty appropriate to its subject's national memory.

FROM NEOCLASSICISM TO ROMANTICISM

Given Jacques-Louis David's stature and prominence as an artist, along with the popularity of Neoclassicism, it is not surprising he attracted numerous students and developed an active and flourishing teaching studio. David gave practical instruction to and deeply influenced many important artists of the period, including the three discussed next. So strong was David's commitment to classicism that he encouraged all of his students to learn Latin so that they could better immerse themselves in and understand classical culture. Even further, David initially demanded that his pupils select their subjects from Plutarch, the ancient author of *Lives of the Great Greeks and Romans* and a principal source of standard Neoclassical subject matter. Due to this thorough classical foundation, David's students all produced work that, at its core, retains Neoclassical elements. Yet despite this apparent dogmatism, David was open minded and far from authoritarian in his teaching and encouraged his students to find their own visual voices.

A departure from the structured confines of Neoclassicism is evident in the work of Antoine-Jean Gros, Anne-Louis Girodet-Trioson, and Jean-Auguste-Dominique Ingres, each David's pupil. In moving beyond Neoclassicism, these artists laid the foundation for the Romantic movement, discussed in detail later. They explored the realm of the exotic and the erotic and often turned to fictional narratives for the subjects of their paintings, as Romantic artists also did.

NAPOLEON AMONG THE SICK AND DYING Like his teacher David, ANTOINE-JEAN GROS (1771–1835) was aware of the benefits that could accrue to artists favored by those in power. Following David's lead, Gros produced several paintings that contributed to the growing mythic status of Napoleon Bonaparte in the early 1800s. In *Napoleon at the Pesthouse at Jaffa* (FIG. **28-29**), which Napoleon ordered Gros to paint, the artist referred to an outbreak of the bubonic plague that erupted during the Near Eastern campaigns of 1799. This fearsome disease struck both Muslim and French forces alike, and in March of 1799 Napoleon himself visited the pesthouse at Jaffa to quell the growing panic and hysteria. Gros depicted Napoleon's staff officers covering their noses against the stench of the place, while Napoleon, amid the dead and dying, is fearless and in control. He comforts those still alive, who are clearly awed by his presence and authority. Indeed, by depicting the French leader touching the sores of a plague victim, Gros almost seemed to confer on Napoleon the miraculous power to heal by invoking the king's legendary touch (the "*touche des écouelles*"). This exaltation of the French leader was necessary to counteract the negative publicity he was subject to at the time. Apparently, two months after his visit to the pesthouse, Napoleon ordered all plague-stricken French soldiers poisoned to relieve him of having to return them to Cairo or of abandoning them to the Turks. Some of the soldiers survived, and from their accounts the damaging stories about Napoleon began to circulate. Gros's large painting was a clear attempt at damage control— to resurrect the event and rehabilitate Napoleon's compromised public image.

Gros structured his composition in a manner reminiscent of David's major paintings, with the mosque courtyard's horseshoe arches and Moorish arcades providing a backdrop for the unfolding action. In addition, Gros's placement of Muslim doctors ministering to plague-stricken Muslims on the left is contrasted with Napoleon and his soldiers on the right, bathed in radiant light. David had used this polarized compositional scheme to great effect in works such as *Oath of the Horatii* (FIG. 28-15). However, Gros's fascination with the exoticism of the Near East, as evidenced by his attention to the unique architecture, attire, and terrain, represented a departure from Neoclassicism. This, along with the artist's emphasis on death, suffering, and an emotional rendering of the scene, presaged prominent aspects of Romanticism.

A TRAGIC SUICIDE IN LOUISIANA Another of David's students, ANNE-LOUIS GIRODET-TRIOSON (1767–1824), also produced works that conjured images of exotic locales and cultures. Moving further into Romanticism's domain, his painting *The Burial of Atala* (FIG. 28-30) was based on a popular novel, *The Genius of Christianity*, by French writer Chateaubriand. The section of the novel dealing with Atala was published as an excerpt a year before the entire book's publication in 1802. Both the excerpt and the novel were enormously successful, and, as a result, Atala became almost a cult figure. In keeping with the movement

28-29 ANTOINE-JEAN GROS, *Napoleon at the Pesthouse at Jaffa*, 1804. Oil on canvas, approx. 17′ 5″ × 23′ 7″. Louvre, Paris.

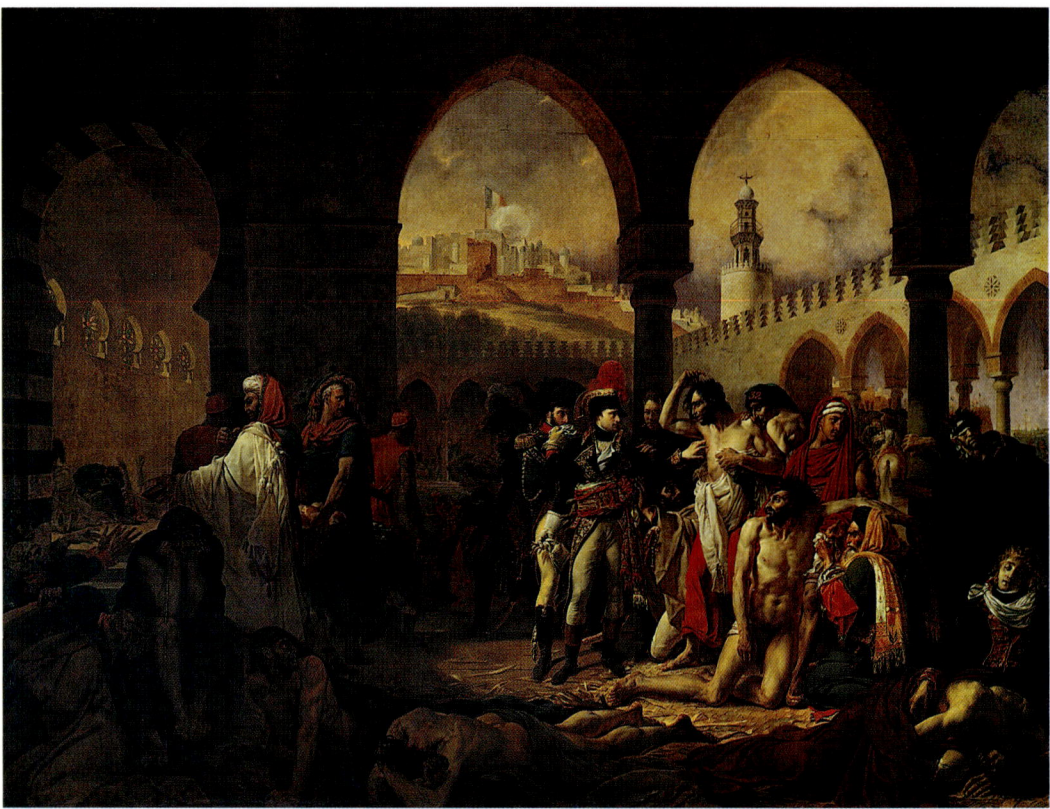

toward Romanticism, interest in *Genius of Christianity* was due in large part to the exoticism and eroticism integral to the narrative. Set in Louisiana, Chateaubriand's work focuses on two Native American youths, Atala and Chactas. The two, from different tribes, fall in love and run away together through the wilderness. The book is highly charged with erotic passion, and Atala, sworn to lifelong virginity, finally commits suicide rather than break her oath. Girodet's painting depicts this tragedy, as Atala is buried in the shadow of a cross by her grief-stricken lover, Chactas. Assisting in the burial is a cloaked priest, whose presence is appropriate given Chateaubriand's emphasis on the revival of Christianity (and the Christianization of the New World) in his novel. Like

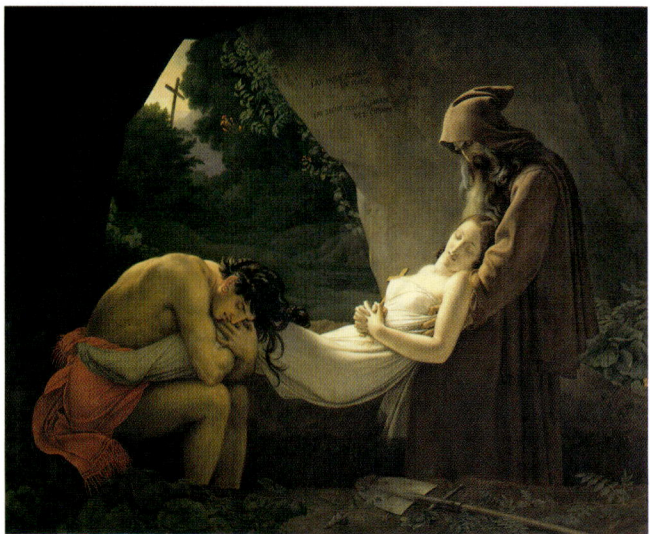

28-30 ANNE-LOUIS GIRODET-TRIOSON, *The Burial of Atala*, 1808. Oil on canvas, approx. 6′ 11″ × 8′ 9″. Louvre, Paris.

Gros's depiction of the foreign Muslim world, Girodet's representation of American Indian lovers in the Louisiana wilderness appealed to the public's fascination (whetted by the Louisiana Purchase in 1803) with what it perceived as the passion and primitivism of Native American tribal life. *The Burial of Atala* speaks here to emotions, rather than inviting philosophical meditation or revealing some grand order of nature and form. Unlike David's appeal to the feelings that manifest themselves in public action in the *Oath of the Horatii* (FIG. 28-15), the appeal here is to the viewer's private world of fantasy and emotion.

A SUMMARY OF NEOCLASSICAL PRINCIPLES
JEAN-AUGUSTE-DOMINIQUE INGRES (1780–1867) arrived at David's studio in the late 1790s after Girodet-Trioson had left to establish an independent career. Ingres's study there was to be short lived, however, as he soon broke with David on matters of style. This difference of opinion involved Ingres's adoption of what he believed to be a truer and purer Greek style than that David employed. The younger artist adopted flat and linear forms approximating those found in Greek vase painting. In many of Ingres's works, the figure is placed in the foreground, much like a piece of low-relief sculpture.

Ingres's huge composition, the *Apotheosis of Homer* (FIG. 28-31), was exhibited at the Salon of 1827. It presented in a single statement the doctrine of ideal form, of Neoclassical taste, and generations of academic painters remained loyal to that style. Enthroned before an Ionic temple, the epic poet Homer is crowned by Fame or Victory. At his feet are two statuesque women, who personify *The Iliad* and *The Odyssey*, the offspring of his imagination. Symmetrically grouped about him is a company of the "sovereign geniuses"—as Ingres called them—who expressed humanity's highest ideals in

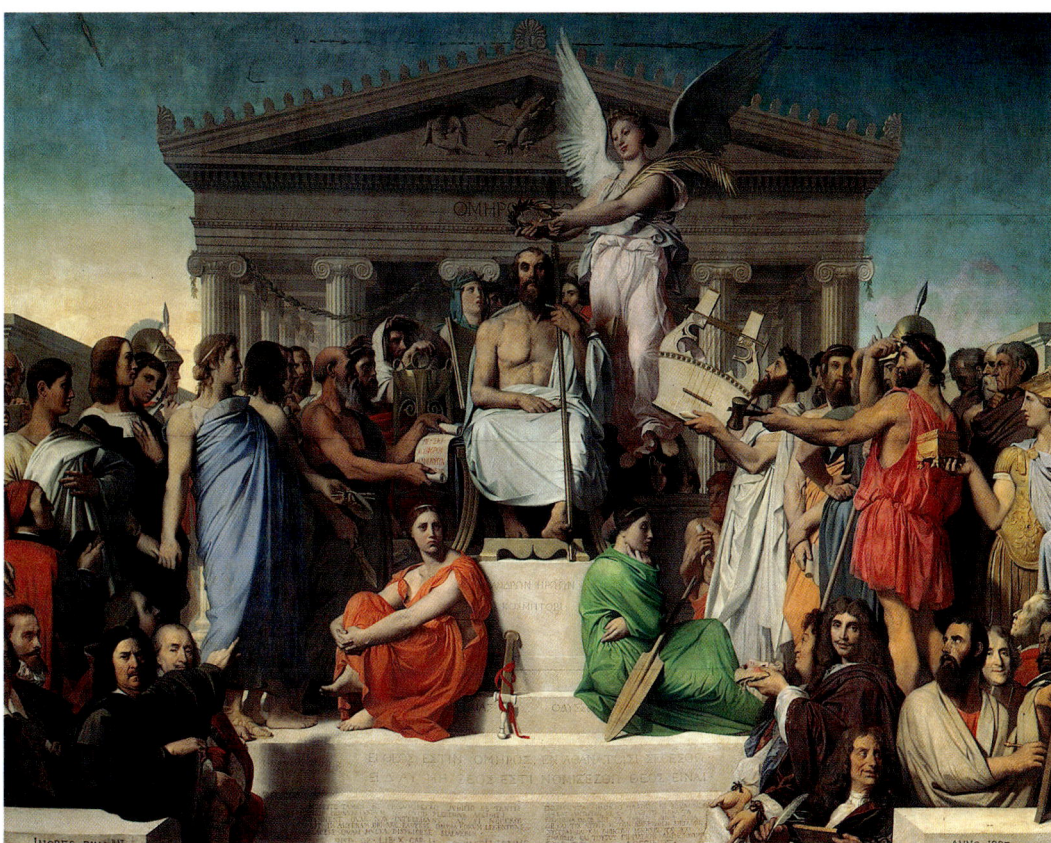

28-31 JEAN-AUGUSTE-DOMINIQUE INGRES, *Apotheosis of Homer,* 1827. Oil on canvas, approx. 12′ 8″ × 16′ 10¾″. Louvre, Paris.

philosophy, poetry, music, and art. To Homer's left are Anacreon with his lyre, Phidias with his sculptor's hammer, and Plato, Socrates, and other ancient worthies. To his far right are Horace, Virgil, Dante, and, conspicuously, Raphael, the painter Ingres most admired. Among the forward group on the painting's left side are Poussin (pointing) and Shakespeare (half concealed), and at the right are French writers Jean Baptiste Racine, Molière, Voltaire, and François de Salignac de la Mothe Fénelon. Ingres had planned a much larger and more inclusive group, but the project was never completed. For years he agonized over whom to choose for this select company of humanities' heroes.

It is obvious that Raphael's *School of Athens* (see FIG. 22-17) inspired the idea for *Apotheosis* and, to a degree, the composition. As Ingres developed as an artist, he turned more and more to Raphael, perceiving in his art the essence of classicism. Ingres disdained, in proportion, the new "modern" styles (the "romantic" and the "realistic," as they were then called) as destructive of true art. "We must ever turn to the past," he said.

> Let me hear no more of that absurd maxim: "We need the new, we must follow our century, everything changes, everything is changed." Sophistry—all of that! Does nature change, do the light and air change, have the passions of the human heart changed since the time of Homer? "We must follow our century": but suppose my century is wrong.[11]

This was the cry of the great conservative, rejecting the modern. It expressed precisely the classicist's resistance to the new school of Romantic color and passion that changed the school of ideal form, of which Ingres had become high priest and first master.

COMBINING THE IDEAL WITH THE EXOTIC
Despite Ingres's commitment to ideal form and careful compositional structure, he also produced works that, like those of Gros and Girodet, his contemporaries saw as departures from Neoclassicism. One such painting is *Grande Odalisque* (FIG. **28-32**). Ingres's subject, the reclining nude figure, is traditional enough and goes back to Giorgione and Titian (see FIG. 22-38). Further, the work shows his admiration for Raphael in his borrowing of that master's type of female head. The figure's languid pose, her proportions (small head and elongated limbs), and the generally cool color scheme also reveal his debt to such Mannerists as Parmigianino (see FIG. 22-42). However, by converting the figure to an *odalisque* (a member of a Turkish harem), the artist made a strong concession to the contemporary Romantic taste for the exotic.

This rather strange mixture of artistic allegiances—the precise adherence to classical form while incorporating Romantic themes—prompted confusion, and when *Grande Odalisque* was first shown in 1814, the painting drew acid criticism. In both form and content, critics initially saw Ingres as a kind of rebel; they did not cease their attacks until the mid-1820s, when another enemy of the official style, Eugène Delacroix, appeared. Then they suddenly perceived that Ingres's art, despite its innovations and deviations, still contained many elements that adhered to the official Neoclassicism—the taste for the ideal. Ingres soon led the academic forces in their battle against the "barbarism" of Théodore Géricault, Delacroix, and their "movement." Gradually, Ingres warmed to the role his critics had cast for him, and he came to see himself as the conservator of good and true art, a protector of its principles against its would-be "destroyers."

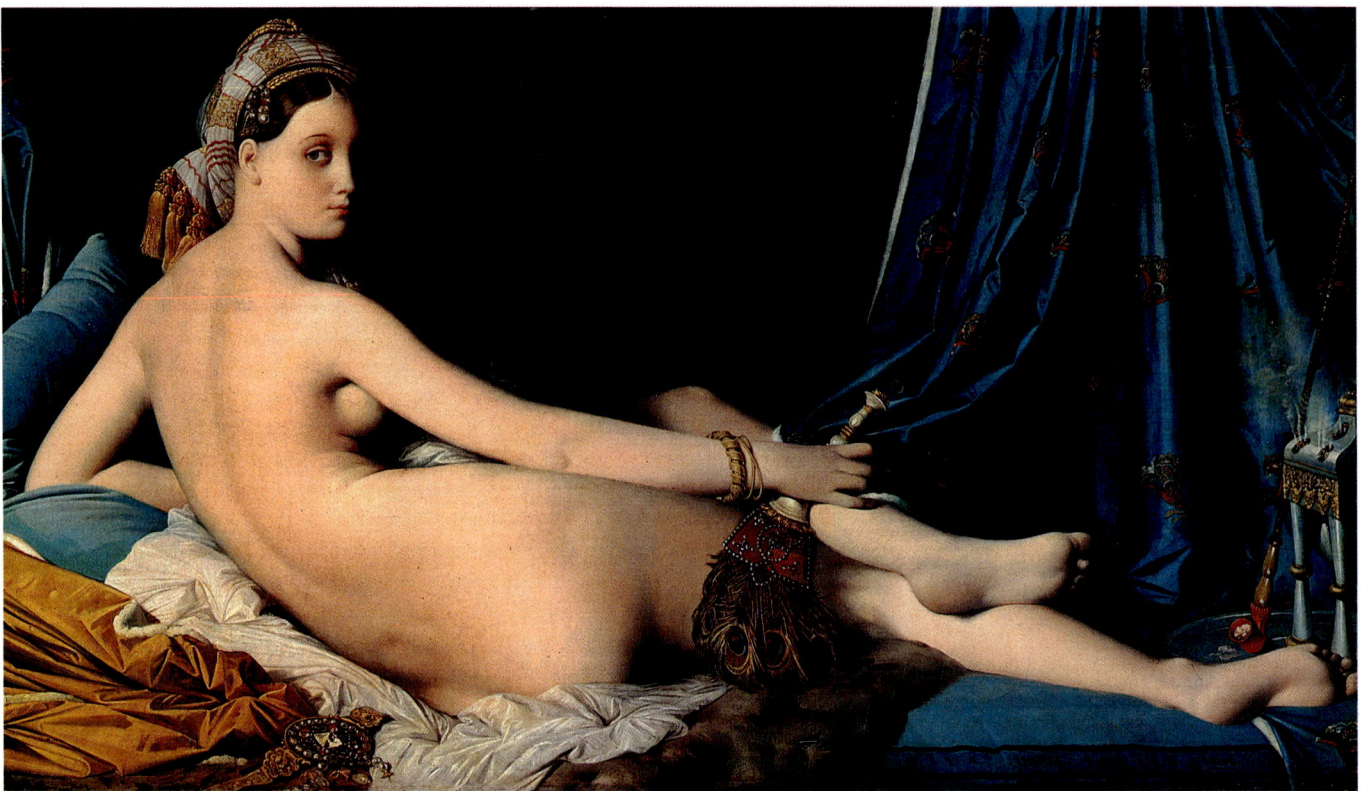

28-32   JEAN-AUGUSTE-DOMINIQUE INGRES, *Grande Odalisque,* 1814. Oil on canvas, approx. 2′ 11″ × 5′ 4″. Louvre, Paris.

DRAWN TO THE MUSIC In his many portraits, Ingres mingled the real and the ideal. He always insisted that he painted exactly what he saw, despite what one critic declared as his "genius for idealizing." Through the painted forms of Ingres's portraits, viewers sense the meticulous drawing. The value Ingres placed on the flow of the contour was a characteristic of his style throughout his career. Contour, which is simply shaded line, was everything for Ingres, and drawing was the means of creating contour. Ingres has been credited with the famous slogan that became his school's battle cry: "Drawing is the probity of art."[12] His pencil portrait of the great violin virtuoso Niccoló Paganini (FIG. **28-33**) speaks to this. Ingres was a creditable amateur violinist, passionately fond of music (he wanted to include Mozart among the immortals surrounding Homer—FIG. 28-31), and he knew Paganini personally. The portrait, executed with that marvelously crisp, clean descriptive line found in all of Ingres's portraits, painted or drawn, is entirely literal in its report of Paganini's features and demeanor. Ingres offered the musician's appearance as a kind of official likeness, enhanced by a suggestive likeness and sense of setting. Paganini, sharing a certain fragility and suppleness with his violin and bow, seems about to make his introductory bow to his audience. The portrait is formal, but it is a graceful, not stiff, formality. The musician is face-to-face with the public world, rising as always to the familiar occasion, which he knows he can command. The ideal of the great musician rises through Paganini's faithfully real likeness.

THE RISE OF ROMANTICISM

Neoclassicism's appeal and applicability were truly extensive. Yet although Neoclassicism's rationality reinforced Enlighten-

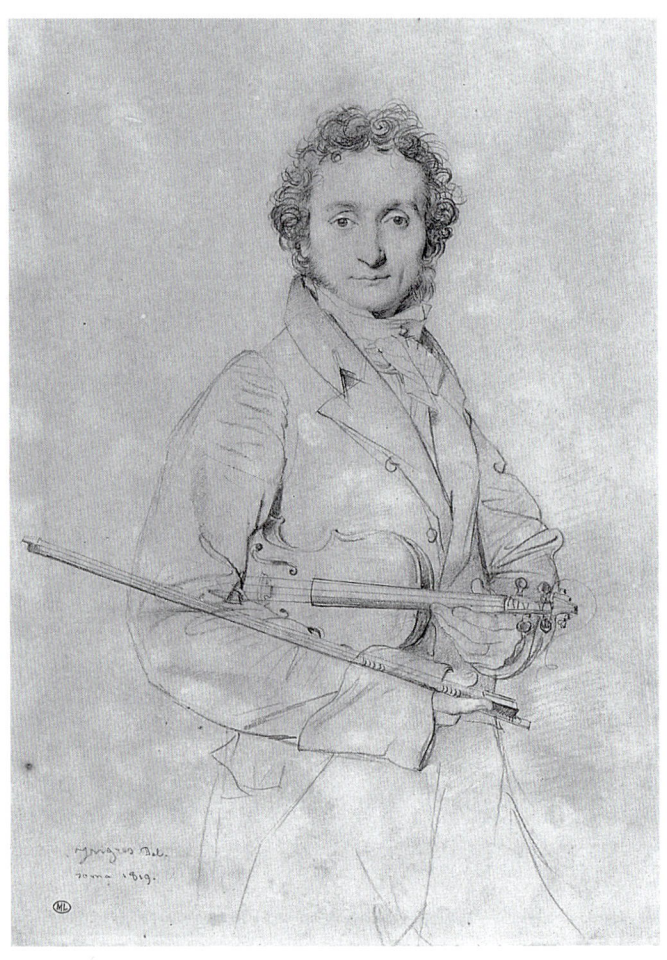

28-33   JEAN-AUGUSTE-DOMINIQUE INGRES, *Paganini,* 1819. Pencil drawing, approx. 1′ × 8½″. Louvre, Paris.

ment thought, particularly that promoted by Voltaire, Jean-Jacques Rousseau's ideas contributed to the rise of Romanticism. Rousseau's exclamation that "Man is born free, but is everywhere in chains!" summarizes a fundamental premise of Romanticism. This declaration appeared in the opening line of his *Social Contract* (1762), a book many of those involved in the late-eighteenth- and nineteenth-century revolutions carefully read and pondered. Romanticism emerged from a desire for freedom—not only political freedom, but also freedom of thought, of feeling, of action, of worship, of speech, and of taste, as well as all the other freedoms. Romantics asserted that freedom is the right and property of one and all, though for each individual the kind or degree of freedom might vary. In the opening paragraph of his *Confessions* (published posthumously 1781 to 1788), Rousseau made the following claim for each Romantic soul by making it for himself: "I am like no one in the whole world. I may be no better, at least I am different." Every individual's freedom and unique subjectivity combined was the first principle of Romanticism and key to the understanding of much that has happened and is believed in the modern world.

Those who affiliated themselves with Romanticism believed that the path to freedom was through *imagination* rather than reason and functioned through *feeling* rather than through thinking. The Romantic spirit's allure grew dramatically during the late eighteenth century. Since that time, scholars have debated the definition and the historical scope of Romanticism; to this day, the controversy has not ended. Many scholars refer to Romanticism as a phenomenon that began around 1750 and ended about 1850. The term *Romanticism* is also used more narrowly to denote a movement that rose and declined in the course of modern art, flourishing from about 1800 to 1840, between Neoclassicism and Realism. This book discusses Romanticism in general terms first to explain the nature and appeal of this mindset in the late eighteenth and early nineteenth centuries before dealing with the Romantic movement.

Though Rousseau was the prophet of Romanticism, he never knew it as such. The term *Romanticism* originated toward the end of the eighteenth century among German literary critics, who aimed to distinguish peculiarly "modern" traits from the Neoclassical traits that already had displaced Baroque and Rococo design elements.

"FEELING IS ALL!"   Romanticism was preceded by the so-called Age of Sensibility, roughly 1750 to 1780, when thinkers such as Rousseau preached the value of sincere feeling and natural human sympathy over artful reason and the cold calculations of courtly societies. The slogan of sensibility was "Trust your heart rather than your head," or, as German writer Johann Wolfgang von Goethe (1749–1832) put it, "Feeling is all!" All that was false and artificial was to be banished as the enemy of honest emotion. Thus Romanticism was based on the predominance of feeling and imagination.

The transition from Neoclassicism to Romanticism was manifested in a shift in emphasis from reason to feeling, from calculation to intuition, and from objective nature to subjective emotion. Among Romanticism's manifestations were the interest in the "Gothick" and in the sublime. The Romantic imagination discovered the Middle Ages, the Gothick world, as it was then known and spelled. (We here use the eighteenth-century spelling of *Gothick* to identify a specific sensibility within the late eighteenth and nineteenth century and to avoid confusion with the actual medieval Gothic period.) For people living in the eighteenth century, the Middle Ages were the "dark ages," a time of barbarism, superstition, dark mystery, and miracle. The Gothick imagination stretched its apparition of the Middle Ages into all the worlds of fantasy

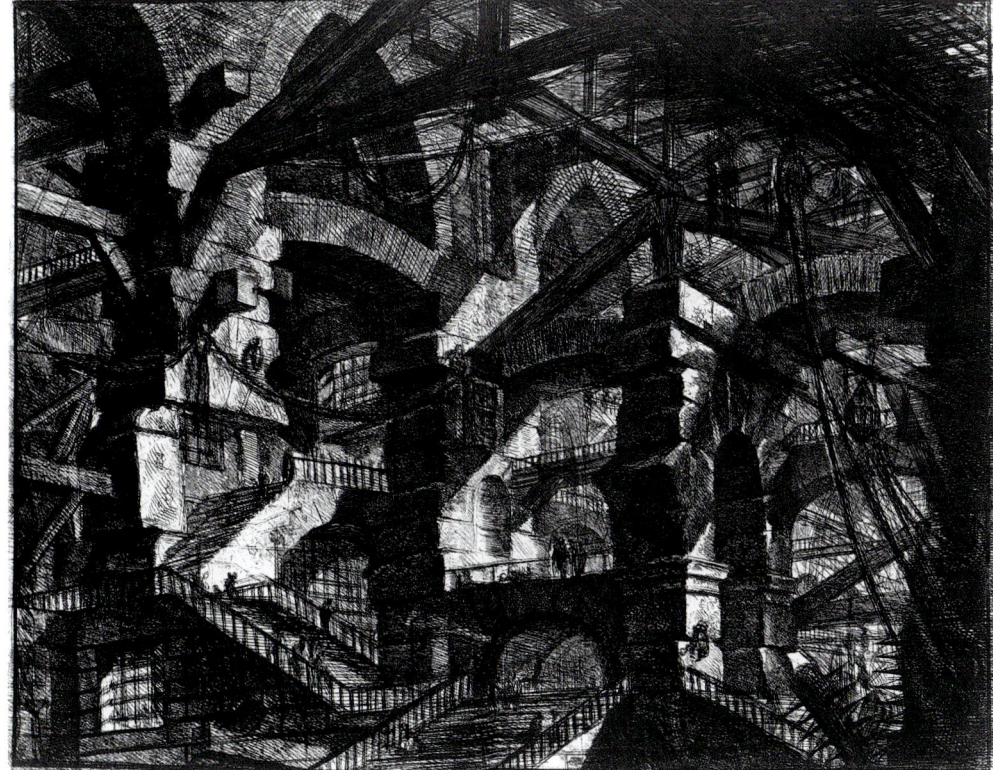

28-34   GIOVANNI BATTISTA PIRANESI, *Carceri 14,* ca. 1750. Etching, second state, approx. 1′ 4″ × 1′ 9″. Ashmolean Museum, Oxford.

open to it, including the ghoulish, the infernal, the terrible, the nightmarish, the grotesque, the sadistic, and all the remaining imagery that comes from the chamber of horrors when reason is asleep. Related to the Gothick was the period's notion of the "sublime." As articulated by Edmund Burke, the sublime inspires feelings of awe mixed with terror—the feelings people experience when they look on vast, impassable mountain peaks or great storms at sea. Accompanying this taste for the sublime was the taste for the fantastic, the occult, and the macabre—for the adventures of the soul voyaging into the dangerous reaches of consciousness.

A CLAUSTROPHOBIC DUNGEON

A work that could illustrate Burke's theory of the sublime, laced with the infernal, is an etching (FIG. **28-34**) by GIOVANNI BATTISTA PIRANESI (1720–1778). It is the second state (a working version) of one of a series of prints of imaginary dungeons, the *Carceri* (prisons). Piranesi conjured awe-inspiring visions of bafflingly complicated architectural masses, piled high and spread out through gloomy spaces. In such pictures, vistas are multiplied and broken by a seeming infinity of massive arches, vaults, piers, and stairways. Small, insectlike human figures move stealthily through them. Despite wandering, soaring perspectives, a suffocating sense of enclosure overwhelms observers; the spaces are locked in, and no exit is visible. These grim places are filled with brooding menace and hopelessness. Within this series of etchings, Piranesi often darkened subsequent editions to make them even more sinister. Our picture, *Carceri 14*, is one of these. It reminds viewers that the Rococo's gaiety and the Enlightenment's rationality coexisted with an eighteenth-century sensibility for the sublime that returned in the nineteenth century to haunt the night imaginings of many a Romantic artist and poet.

A NIGHTMARISH VISION

The concept of the nightmare is specifically addressed in *The Nightmare* (FIG. **28-35**) by HENRY FUSELI (1741–1825). Fuseli specialized in night moods of horror and in Gothick fantasies—in the demonic, in the macabre, and often in the sadistic. Swiss by birth, Fuseli settled in England and eventually became a member of the Royal Academy and an instructor there (see "The Academies: Defining the Range of Acceptable Art," Chapter 29, page 898). Largely self-taught, he contrived a distinctive manner to express the fantasies of his vivid imagination. *The Nightmare* is one of four versions of this terrifying theme. The beautiful young woman lies asleep, draped across the bed with her limp arm dangling over the side. An incubus, a demon believed in medieval times to prey, often sexually, on sleeping women, squats ominously on her body. In the background, a ghostly horse with flaming eyes bursts into the scene from beyond the curtain. Despite the temptation to see the painting's title as a pun because of this horse, the word *nightmare* is actually derived from the words *night* and *mara*. Mara was a spirit in northern mythology that was thought to torment and suffocate sleepers. As disturbing and perverse as Fuseli's art may be, he was among the first to attempt to depict the dark terrain of the human subconscious that became fertile ground for the Romantic artists to harvest.

In their images of the sublime and the terrible, artists often combined something of Baroque dynamism with natural details in their quest for grippingly moving visions. These preferences became the mainstay of Romantic art and contrasted with the more intellectual, rational Neoclassical themes and presentations. This is not to suggest that the two were mutually exclusive. As revealed in the earlier discussion of Gros, Girodet-Trioson, and Ingres, elements of Neoclassicism could be effectively integrated with Romanticism.

28-35 HENRY FUSELI, *The Nightmare,* 1781. Oil on canvas, 3′ 4″ × 4′ 2″. The Detroit Institute of the Arts (Founders Society Purchase with funds from Mr. and Mrs. Bert L. Smokler and Mr. and Mrs. Lawrence A. Fleishman).

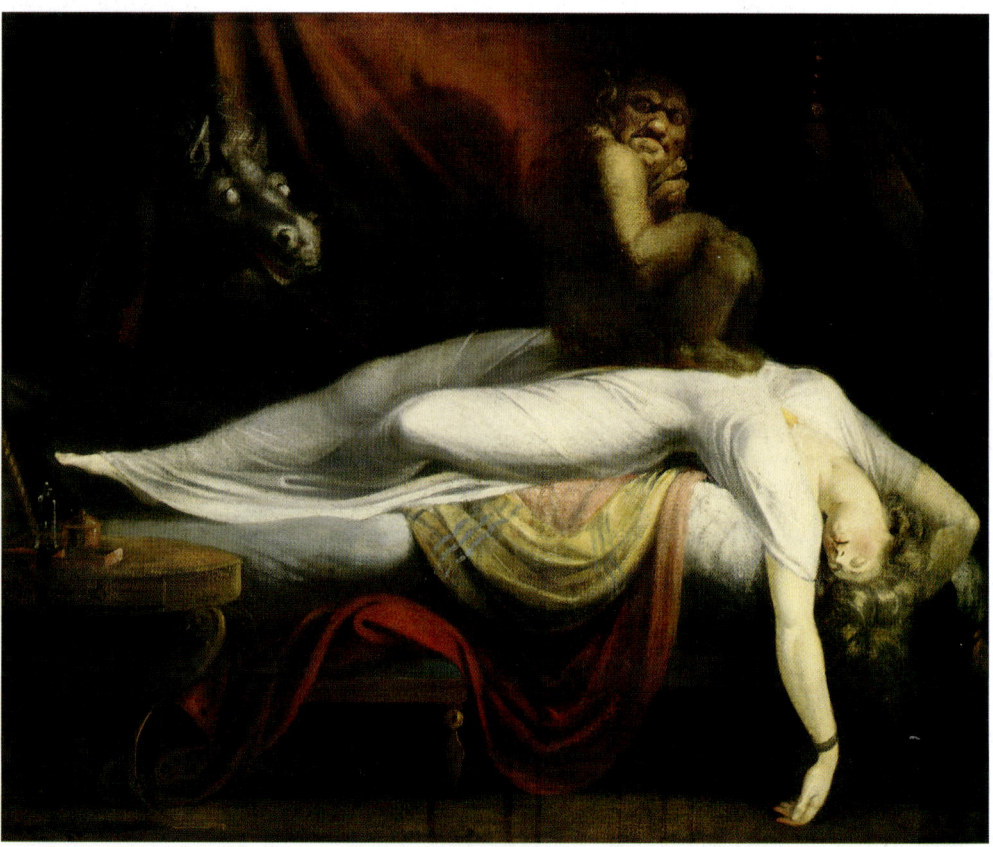

INSPIRED BY THE SPIRITS The visionary English poet, painter, and engraver WILLIAM BLAKE (1757–1827) is frequently classified as a Romantic artist. His work, however, incorporates classical references. Blake greatly admired ancient Greek art because it exemplified the mathematical and, thus, the eternal. Yet Blake did not align himself with prominent Enlightenment figures. Blake, like many other Romantic artists, also was drawn to the art of the Middle Ages—the Gothick mindset. Blake derived the compositions of many of his paintings and poems from spirits who visited him in dreams. The importance he attached to these experiences led him to believe that rationalism's search for material explanations of the world stifled human nature's spiritual side. He also believed the stringent rules of behavior imposed by orthodox religions killed the individual creative impulse. Blake's vision of the Almighty in *Ancient of Days* (FIG. **28-36**) combines his ideas and interests in a highly individual way. For Blake, this figure combined the concept of the Creator with that of wisdom as a part of God. *Ancient of Days*, printed as the frontispiece for Blake's book *Europe: A Prophecy*, was published with a quotation ("When he set a compass upon the face of the deep") from Proverbs (8:27) in the Old Testament. Most of that Bible chapter is spoken by Wisdom, identified as a female, who tells the reader how she was with the Lord through all the time of the Creation (Prov. 8:22–23, 27–30).

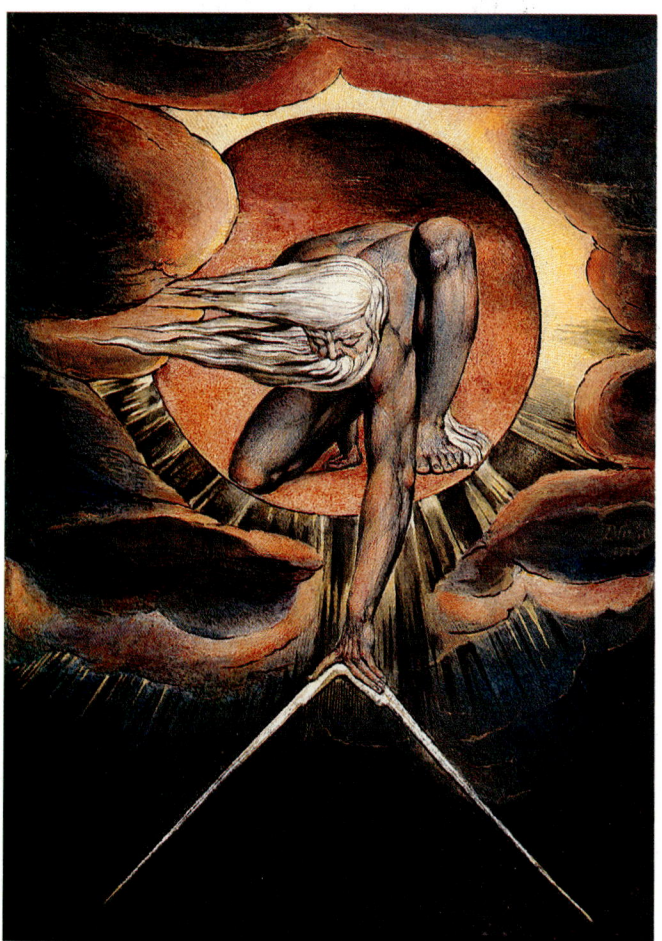

28-36 WILLIAM BLAKE, *Ancient of Days*, frontispiece of *Europe: A Prophecy*, 1794. Metal relief etching, hand colored, approx. $9\frac{1}{2}'' \times 6\frac{3}{4}''$. The Whitworth Art Gallery, The University of Manchester.

Energy fills Blake's composition. The Ancient of Days leans forward from a fiery orb, peering toward earth and unleashing power through his outstretched left arm into twin rays of light. These emerge between his spread fingers like an architect's measuring instrument. A mighty wind surges through his thick hair and beard. Only the strength of his "Michelangelesque" physique keeps him firmly planted within his heavenly perch. Here, ideal classical anatomy merges with the inner dark dreams of Gothick Romanticism, which were expressed often in the nineteenth century. With his independence and individual artistic vision, Blake was very much a man of the modern age.

Dramatic Action, Emotion, and Color

In the early nineteenth century, Romantic artists increasingly incorporated dramatic action, all the while extending their exploration of the exotic, erotic, fictional, or fantastic. One artist whose works reveal these compelling dimensions is the Spaniard FRANCISCO JOSÉ DE GOYA Y LUCIENTES (1746–1828). Goya was David's contemporary, but one scarcely could find two artists living at the same time and in adjacent countries who were so completely unlike each other. Goya, the great independent, disdained the Neoclassical and the model of classical antiquity, acknowledging only Velázquez, Rembrandt, and "nature" as his teachers.

RECONSIDERING REASON Goya did not arrive at his general dismissal of Neoclassicism without considerable thought about the Enlightenment and the Neoclassical penchant for rationality and order. This reflection emerges in works such as *The Sleep of Reason Produces Monsters* (FIG. **28-37**), an etching and aquatint from a series titled *Los Caprichos (The Caprices)*. In this print, Goya depicted himself asleep, slumped onto a table or writing stand, while threatening creatures converge on him. Seemingly poised to attack the artist are owls (symbols of folly) and bats (symbols of ignorance). Viewers might read this as a portrayal of what emerges when reason is suppressed and, therefore, as advocating Enlightenment ideals. However, it also can be interpreted as Goya's commitment to the creative process and the Romantic spirit—the unleashing of imagination, emotions, and even nightmares.

DEPICTING THE SPANISH ROYAL FAMILY The emotional art Goya produced during his long career stands as testimony not only to the allure of the Romantic vision but also to the turmoil in Spain and to the conflicts in Goya's own life. Goya's skills as a painter were recognized early on, and in 1786 he was appointed Pintor del Rey (Painter to the King). In this capacity (he was promoted to First Court Painter in 1799) Goya produced works such as *The Family of Charles IV* (FIG. **28-38**). Here King Charles IV and Queen Maria Luisa are surrounded by their children. As a court painter and artist enamored with the achievements of his predecessor Diego Velázquez, Goya appropriately used Velázquez's *Las Meninas* (see FIG. 24-33) as his inspiration for this image. As in *Las Meninas*, the royal family appears facing viewers in an interior space while the artist included himself on the left, dimly visible, in the act of painting on a large

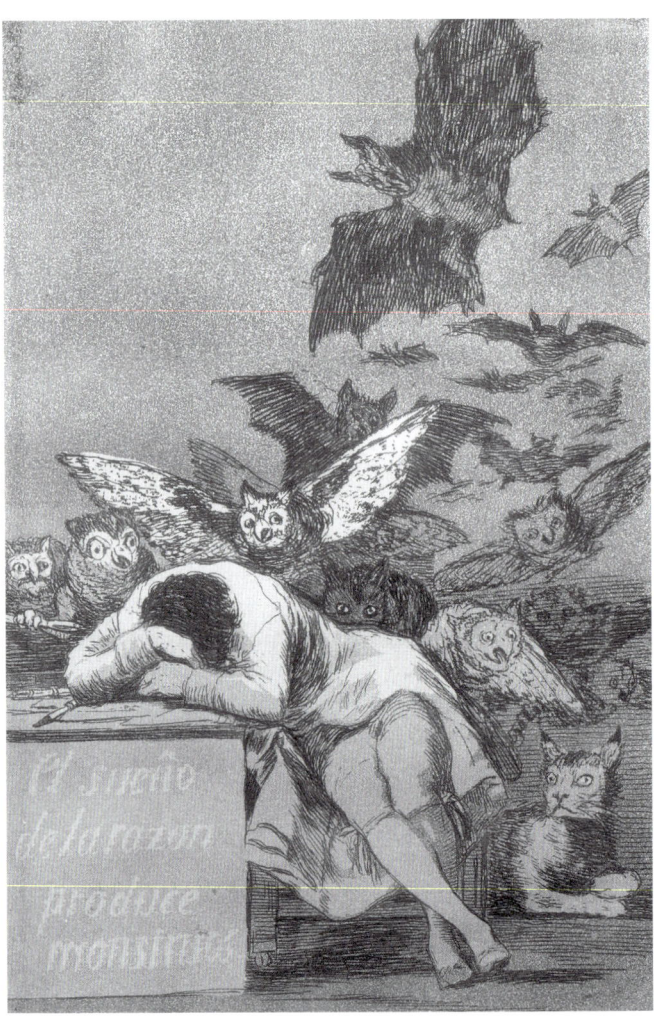

28-37 FRANCISCO GOYA, *The Sleep of Reason Produces Monsters,* from *Los Caprichos,* ca. 1798. Etching and aquatint, $8\frac{1}{2}'' \times 6''$. Metropolitan Museum of Art, New York (gift of M. Knoedler & Co., 1918).

canvas. Goya's portrait of the royal family has been subjected to intense scholarly scrutiny, resulting in a variety of interpretations. These range from naturalistic depiction to pointed commentary in a time of Spanish turmoil. It is clear his patrons authorized the painting's basic elements—the royal family members, their attire, and Goya's inclusion. Little evidence exists as to how this painting was received. Although some scholars have argued the royal family was dissatisfied with the portrait, others have suggested the painting confirmed the Spanish monarchy's continuing presence and strength and thus elicited a positive response from the patrons.

TURMOIL IN SPAIN   As dissatisfaction with the rule of Charles IV and Maria Luisa increased, the political situation grew more tenuous. The Spanish people eventually threw their support behind Ferdinand VII, son of Charles IV and Maria Luisa, in the hope he would initiate reform. To overthrow his father and mother, Ferdinand VII enlisted the aid of Napoleon Bonaparte, whose authority and military expertise in France at that time were uncontested. Napoleon had designs on the Spanish throne and thus willingly sent French troops to Spain. Not surprisingly, once Charles IV and Maria Luisa were ousted, Napoleon revealed his plan to rule Spain himself by installing his brother Joseph Bonaparte on the Spanish throne.

28-38 FRANCISCO GOYA, *The Family of Charles IV,* 1800. Oil on canvas, approx. $9' 2'' \times 11'$. Museo del Prado, Madrid.

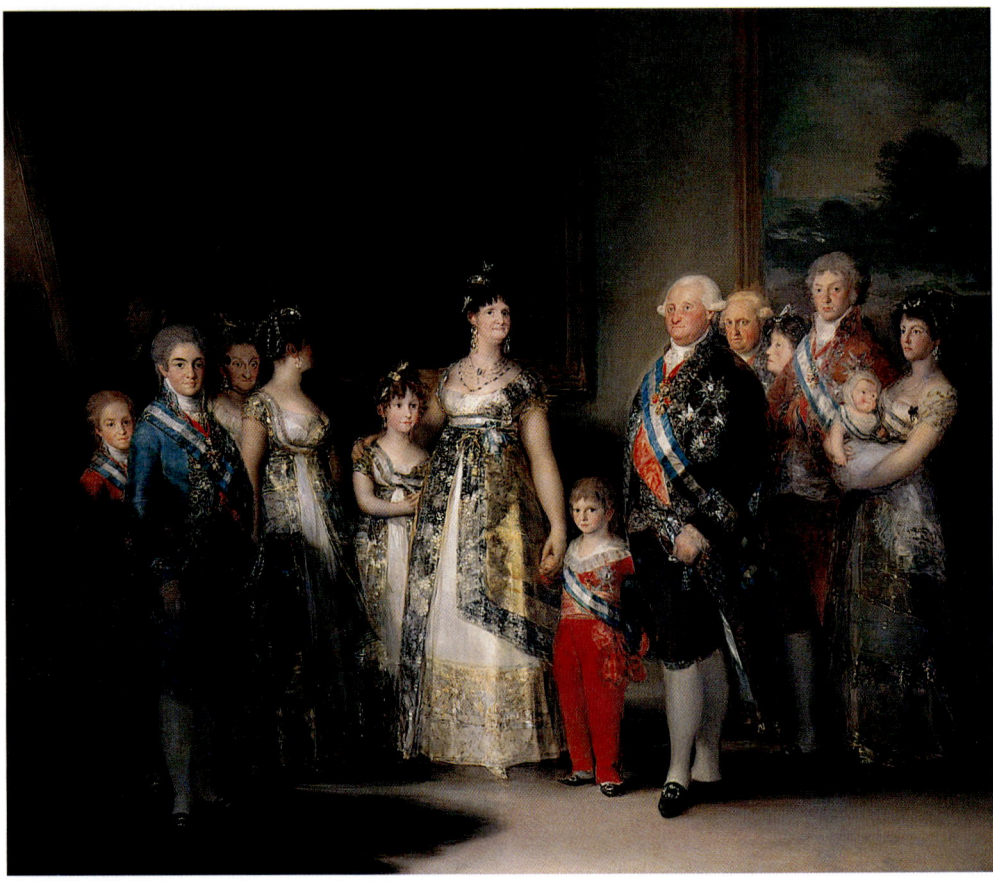

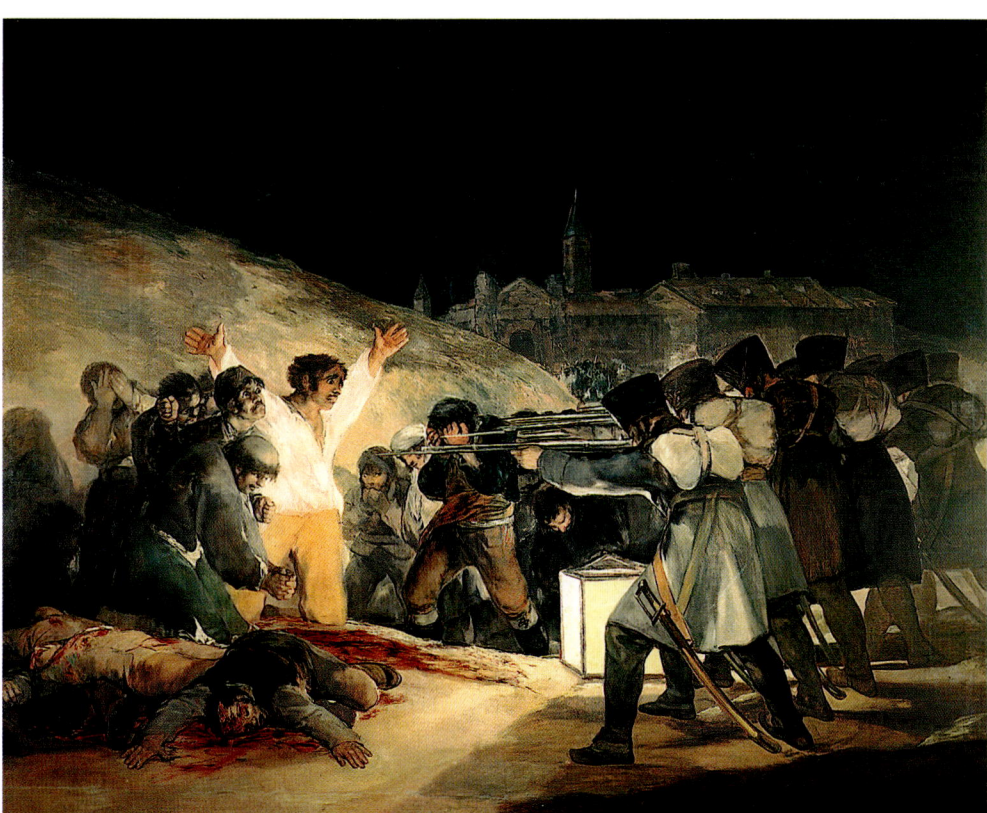

28-39 FRANCISCO GOYA, *The Third of May 1808,* 1814. Oil on canvas, approx. 8′ 8″ × 11′ 3″. Museo del Prado, Madrid.

THE MASSACRE OF MAY 3, 1808 The Spanish people, finally recognizing the French as invaders, sought a way to expel the foreign troops. On May 2, 1808, in frustration, the Spanish attacked the Napoleonic soldiers in a chaotic and violent clash. In retaliation and as a show of force, the French responded the next day by executing numerous Spanish citizens. This tragic event is the subject of Goya's most famous painting, *The Third of May 1808* (FIG. **28-39**).

In emotional fashion, Goya depicted the anonymous murderous wall of Napoleonic soldiers ruthlessly executing the unarmed and terrified Spanish peasants. The artist encouraged viewer empathy for the Spanish by portraying horrified expressions and anguish on their faces, endowing them with a humanity absent from the firing squad. Further, the peasant about to be shot throws his arms out in a cruciform gesture, providing a parallel to Christ.

Goya heightened the drama of this event through his stark use of darks and lights. In addition, Goya's choice of imagery extended the time frame and thus the tragedy's emotion. Although he captured a specific moment when one man is about to be executed, others lie dead at his feet, their blood staining the soil of Príncipe Pío hill, while many others have been herded together to be subsequently shot.

Its depiction of the resistance and patriotism of the Spanish people notwithstanding, *The Third of May 1808* was painted in 1814 for Ferdinand VII, who had been restored to the throne after the ouster of the French. Although the Spanish citizens had placed great faith in Ferdinand to install more democratic policies than were in place during the reign of his father Charles IV, Ferdinand VII increasingly emulated his father, resulting in the restoration of an authoritative monarchy.

PAINTINGS OF DARK EMOTIONS Over time, Goya became increasingly disillusioned and pessimistic; his declining health only contributed to this state of mind. Among his later works is a series of frescoes called the "Black Paintings." Goya painted these frescoes on the walls of his farmhouse in Quinta del Sordo, outside Madrid. Because Goya created these works solely on his terms and for his viewing, one could argue that they provide great insight into the artist's outlook. If so, the vision is terrifying and disturbing. *Saturn Devouring One of His Children* (FIG. **28-40**), one of the Black Paintings, depicts the raw carnage and violence of Saturn (the Greek god Kronos, see "The Gods and Goddesses of Mount Olympus," Chapter 5, page 99 or page xxviii in Volume II), wild eyed and monstrous, as he consumes one of his children. Because of the similarity of Kronos and Khronos (the Greek word for *time*), Saturn has come to be associated with time. This has led to an interpretation of Goya's painting about the artist's despair over the passage of time. Despite the image's simplicity, it conveys a wildness, boldness, and brutality that cannot help but evoke an elemental response from any viewer.

Goya's work, rooted both in a personal and a national history, presents darkly emotional images well in keeping with Romanticism. The demons that haunted Goya emerged in his art. As historian Gwyn Williams nicely sums up: "As for the grotesque, the maniacal, the occult, the witchery, they are precisely the product of the sleep of *human* reason; they are *human* nightmares. *That these monsters are human is, indeed, the point.*"[13]

DEATH AND DESPAIR ON A RAFT In France, Théodore Géricault and Eugène Delacroix were the artists most

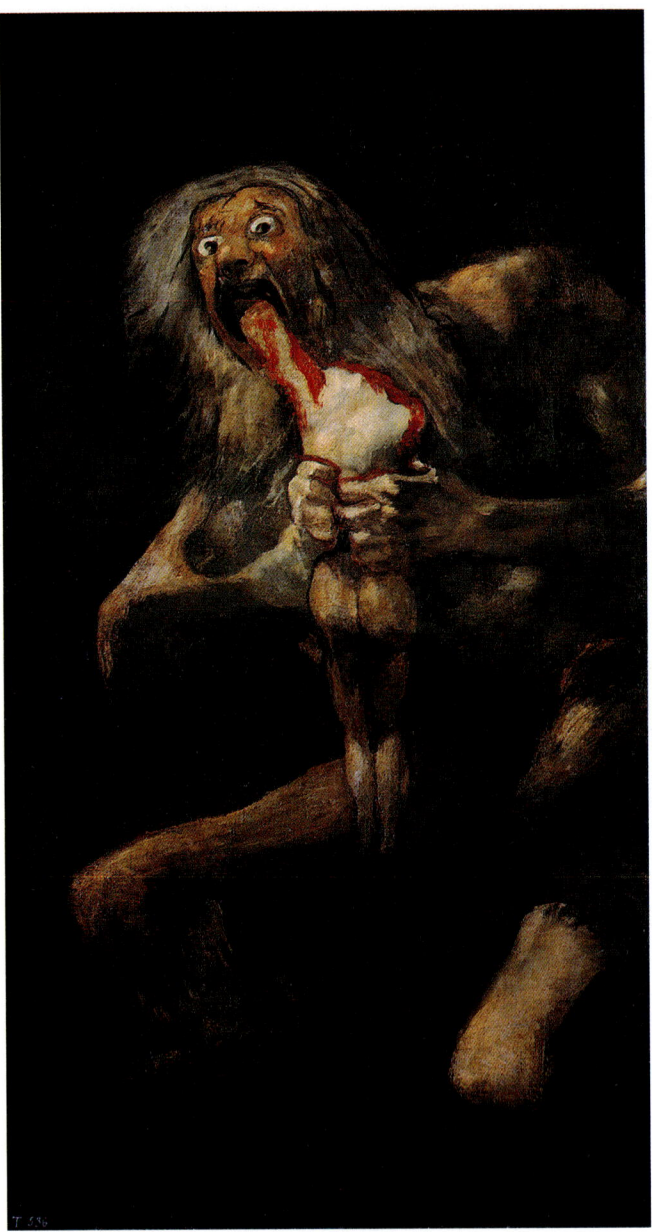

28-40 FRANCISCO GOYA, *Saturn Devouring His Children*, 1819–1823. Detail of a detached fresco on canvas, full size approx. 4′ 9″ × 2′ 8″. Museo del Prado, Madrid.

closely associated with the Romantic movement. THÉODORE GÉRICAULT (1791–1824) studied with an admirer of David, P. N. Guérin (1774–1833). Although Géricault retained an interest in the heroic and the epic and was well trained in classical drawing, he chafed at the Neoclassical style's rigidity, eventually producing works that captivate the viewer with their drama, visual complexity, and emotional force.

Géricault's most ambitious project was a large-scale (approximately sixteen feet by twenty-three feet) painting titled *Raft of the Medusa* (FIG. **28-41**). The painting's subject is a shipwreck that took place in 1816 off the African coast. The French frigate *Medusa,* carrying soldiers and settlers to the French colony of Senegal, ran aground on a reef due to the incompetence of the captain, a political appointee. Because of the limited number of lifeboats (which the captain and his officers commandeered), hundreds were left to fend for themselves on the sinking ship. As a last ditch effort to survive, 150 of those remaining built a makeshift raft from the disintegrat-

ing ship. The raft drifted for twelve days, and the number of survivors dwindled to 15. Without food or water and exposed to the elements, the raft's passengers succumbed quickly, and many of those who did not die were driven mad. The remaining people soon were forced to eat the flesh of corpses to survive. Finally, the raft was spotted and the emaciated survivors were rescued. This horrendous event became political dynamite once it became public knowledge.

In Géricault's huge painting, which took him eight months to complete, he sought to confront viewers with the tragedy's horror, chaos, and emotion while invoking the grandeur and impact of large-scale history painting. He depicted the few weak, despairing survivors as they summon what little strength they have left to flag down the passing ship far on the horizon. Géricault departed from the straightforward organization of Neoclassical compositions and instead presented a jumble of writhing bodies. The survivors and several corpses are piled onto one another in every attitude of suffering, despair, and death (recalling Gros's *Napoleon,* FIG. 28-29) and are arranged in a powerful X-shaped composition. One light-filled diagonal axis stretches from bodies at the lower left up to the black man raised on his comrades' shoulders and waving a piece of cloth toward the horizon. The cross axis descends from the storm clouds and dark wind-filled sail at the upper left to the shadowed upper torso of the body trailing in the open sea. Géricault's decision to place the raft at a diagonal so that a corner juts out toward viewers further compels their participation in this scene. Indeed, it seems as though some of the corpses are sliding off the raft into the viewing space. The subdued palette and prominent shadows lend an ominous pall to the scene.

Despite the theatricality and dramatic action that imbues this work with a Romantic spirit, Géricault did in fact go to great lengths to ensure a degree of accuracy. He visited hospitals and morgues to examine corpses, interviewed the survivors, and had a model of the raft constructed in his studio.

Géricault also took this opportunity to insert a comment on the practice of slavery. The artist was a member of an abolitionist group that sought ways to end the slave trade in the colonies. Given Géricault's antipathy to slavery, it is appropriate that he placed Jean Charles, a black soldier and one of the few survivors, at the top of the pyramidal heap of bodies.

PICTURING INSANITY Mental aberration and the irrational states of the mind hardly could have failed to interest the rebels against Enlightenment rationality. Géricault, like many of his contemporaries, examined the influence of mental states on the human face and believed, as others did, that a face accurately revealed character, especially in madness and at the instance of death. He made many studies of the inmates of hospitals and institutions for the criminally insane, and he studied the severed heads of guillotine victims. Scientific and artistic curiosity were not easily separated from the morbidity of the Romantic interest in derangement and death. Géricault's *Insane Woman (Envy),* FIG. **28-42**—her mouth tense, her eyes red rimmed with suffering—is one of several of his "portraits" of insane subjects that have a peculiar hypnotic power. These portraits present the psychic facts with astonishing authenticity, especially in contrast to earlier idealized commissioned portraiture. The more the Romantics became involved with nature, sane or mad, the more they hoped to reach the truth.

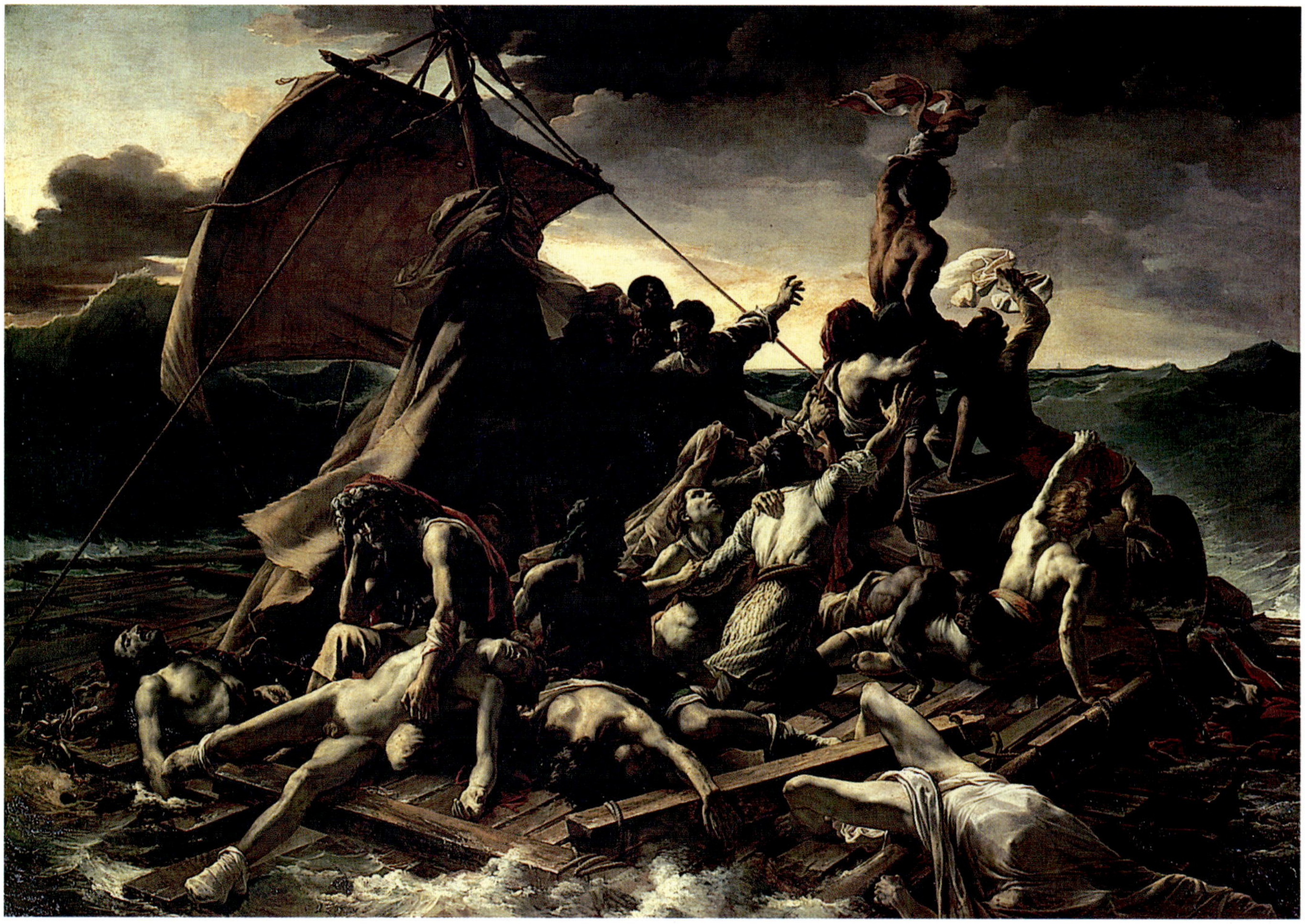

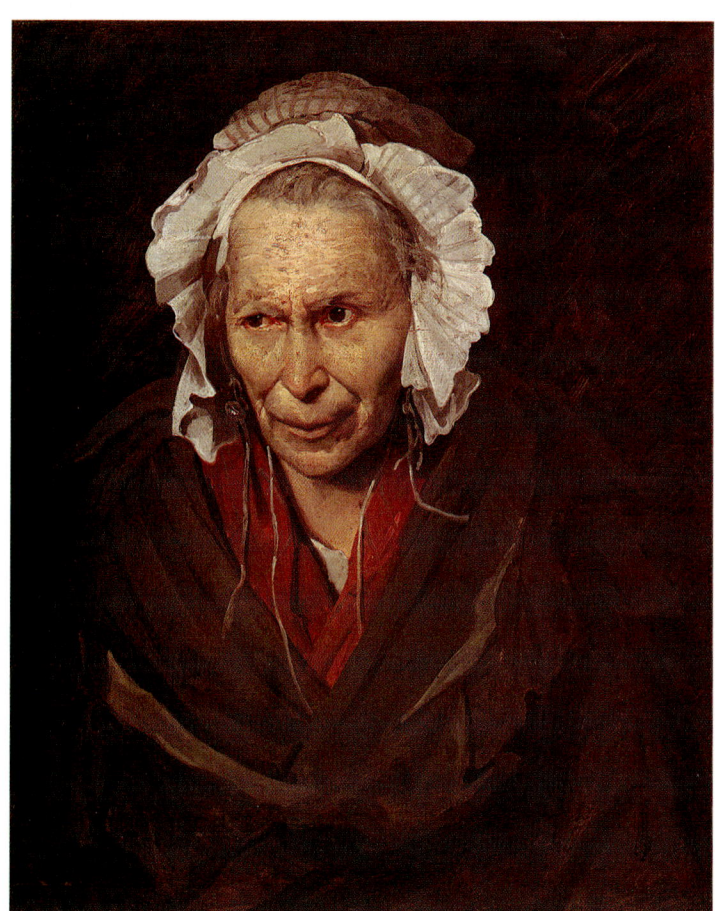

28-41   THÉODORE GÉRICAULT, *Raft of the Medusa,* 1818–1819. Oil on canvas, approx. 16′ × 23′. Louvre, Paris.

28-42   THÉODORE GÉRICAULT, *Insane Woman (Envy),* 1822–1823. Oil on canvas, approx. 2′ 4″ × 1′ 9″. Musée des Beaux-Arts, Lyon.

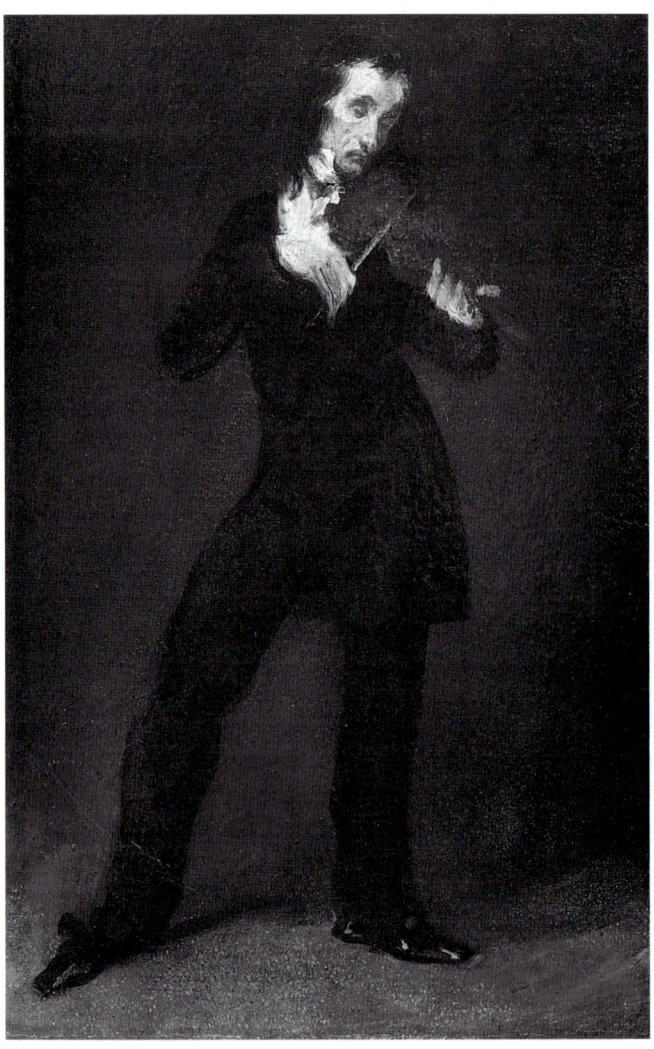

28-43 EUGÈNE DELACROIX, *Paganini,* 1831. Oil on cardboard on wood panel, 1′ 5⅝″ × 11⅞″. The Phillips Collection, Washington.

LINE VERSUS COLOR Like Géricault, Delacroix's name is consistently invoked in discussions of Romanticism. The history of nineteenth-century painting in its first sixty years often has been interpreted as a contest between two major artists—Ingres the draftsman and EUGÈNE DELACROIX (1798–1863) the colorist. Their dialogue reached back to the end of the seventeenth century in the quarrel between the Poussinistes and the Rubénistes. As discussed earlier, the Poussinistes were conservative defenders of academism who held drawing as superior to color, while the Rubénistes proclaimed color's importance over line (the line quality being more intellectual and thus more restrictive than color). Although the differences between Ingres and Delacroix were clear, it is impossible to make categorial statements about any artist. As shown, Ingres's work, though steeped in Neoclassical tradition, does incorporate elements of Romanticism. In the end, Ingres and his great rival Delacroix complemented rather than contradicted each other. Their work stands as visualizations of the great Neoclassical and Romantic dialogue.

A PORTRAIT OF MUSIC This dialogue is evident in a comparison of Ingres's pencil portrait of the great violin virtu-

oso Paganini (FIG. 28-33) with Delacroix's painted version of the same personality (FIG. **28-43**). These works disclose the difference in approach that separated the two artists. Ingres's objective formal public portrait of Paganini is a faithful likeness of the subject, historians believe, yet it is heightened into a kind of ideal image—"the Virtuoso." Delacroix's *Paganini* presents a likeness not of the virtuoso's form but of his performance. Forgetting his audience and no longer in formal confrontation with his listeners, Paganini yields himself completely to the whirlwind of his inspiration, which envelops his reedlike frame, making it vibrate in tune to his instrument's quivering strings. Delacroix tried to suggest the portrait, as it were, of Paganini's music as it plays to the musician's own ear and spirit. Ingres portrayed the outside aspect of his subject and tried to perfect the form as presented to the eye. Delacroix instead represented the inner substance—the musician transformed by his music—in an attempt to realize the truth as given to the imagination.

Critics now regard both masters as equally great. But Delacroix's celebration of the imagination, the faculty that captures the essential in life and transforms mundane experience, defined the fundamental difference between Ingres and Delacroix. Delacroix called the art of Ingres "the complete expression of an incomplete intellect," incomplete because he felt it was unleavened with imagination. In a passage from his famous *Journal,* Delacroix wrote: "Baudelaire [a well-known and influential nineteenth-century poet and art critic] . . . says that I bring back to painting the feeling . . . which delights in the terrible. He is right."[14] Delacroix, who knew and admired Géricault, greatly expanded the expressive possibilities of Romantic art by developing its themes and elaborating its forms in a direction of ever-greater emotional power.

INSPIRING FICTION AND VERSE Delacroix's works were products of his view that the artist's powers of imagination would in turn capture and inflame viewers' imagination. Literature of imaginative power served Delacroix (and many of his contemporaries) as a useful source of subject matter. The prominent Romantic critic and novelist, Théophile Gautier, recalled:

> In those days painting and poetry fraternized. The artists read the poets, and the poets visited the artists. We found Shakespeare, Dante, Goethe, Lord Byron and Walter Scott in the studio as well as in the study. There were as many splashes of color as there were blots of ink in the margins of those beautiful books which we endlessly perused. Imagination, already excited, was further fired by reading those foreign works, so rich in color, so free and powerful in fantasy.[15]

ORGIASTIC DESTRUCTION AND DEATH Delacroix's *Death of Sardanapalus* (FIG. **28-44**) is an example of pictorial grand drama. Undoubtedly, Delacroix was inspired by Lord Byron's 1821 narrative poem *Sardanapalus,* but the painting does not illustrate that text (see "The Romantic Spirit in Music and Literature," page 873). Instead, Delacroix depicted the last hour of the Assyrian king (who received news of his armies' defeat and the enemies' entry into his city) in a much more tempestuous and crowded setting than Byron described. Here, orgiastic destruction replaces the sacrificial suicide found in the poem. In the painting, the king

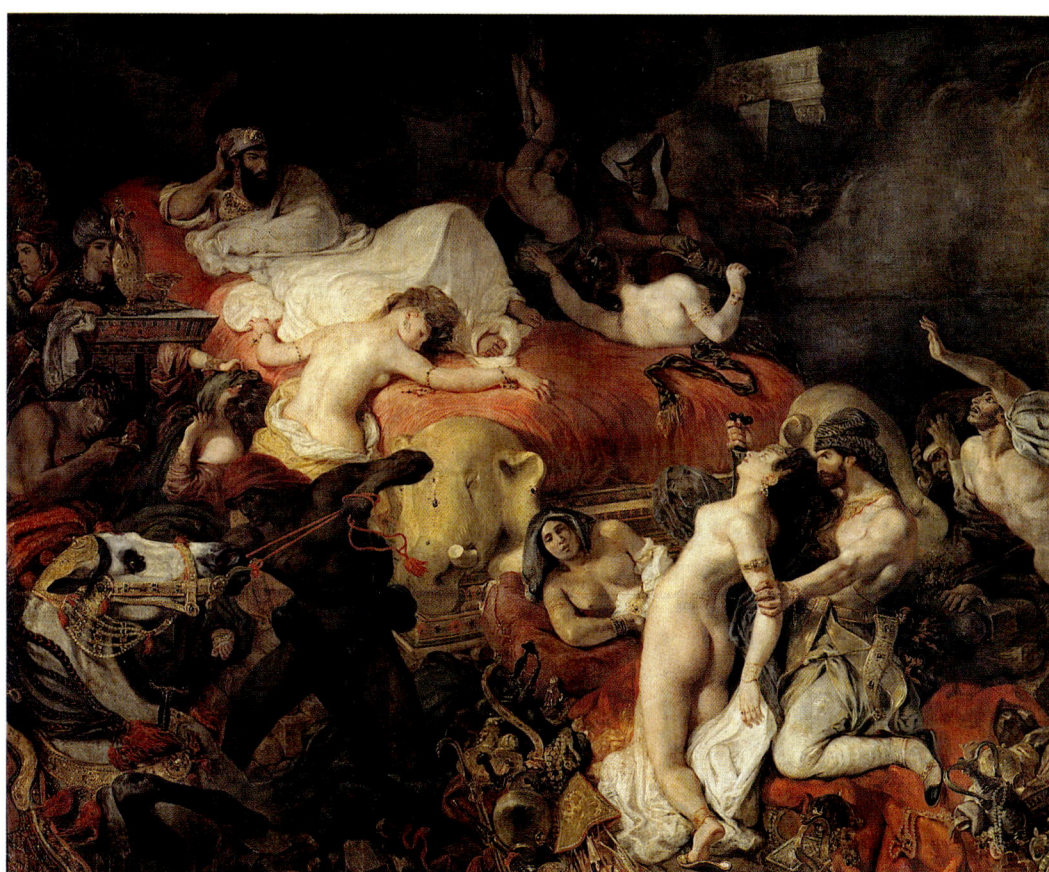

28-44 EUGÈNE DELACROIX, *Death of Sardanapalus,* 1826. Oil on canvas, approx. 12′ 1″ × 16′ 3″. Louvre, Paris.

watches gloomily from his funeral pyre, soon to be set alight, as all of his most precious possessions—his women, slaves, horses, and treasure—are destroyed in his sight. Sardanapalus's favorite concubine throws herself on the bed, determined to go up in flames with her master. The king presides like a genius of evil over the panorama of destruction. Most conspicuous are the tortured and dying bodies of the harem women. In the foreground, a muscular slave plunges his knife into the neck of one woman. This spectacle of suffering and death is heightened by the most daringly difficult and tortuous poses and by the richest intensities of hue. With its exotic and erotic overtones, *Death of Sardanapalus* taps into the fantasies of both the artist and some viewers.

LEADING THE MASSES IN UPRISING While *Death of Sardanapalus* reveals Delacroix's fertile imagination, like Géricault he also turned to current events, particularly tragic or sensational ones, for his subject matter. For example, he produced several images based on the Greek War for Independence (1821–1829). Certainly, the French perception of the Greeks locked in a brutal struggle for freedom from the cruel and exotic Ottoman Turks generated great interest. Closer to home, Delacroix captured the passion and energy of the Revolution of 1830 in his painting *Liberty Leading the People* (FIG. **28-45**). Based on the Parisian uprising against the rule of Charles X at the end of July 1830, it depicts the allegorical personification of Liberty, defiantly thrusting forth the republic's tricolor banner as she urges the masses to fight on. This struggle's urgency is reinforced by the scarlet Phrygian cap (the symbol of a freed slave in antiquity) she wears. Arrayed around her are bold Parisian types—the street boy brandishing his pistols, the menacing worker with a cutlass,

and the intellectual dandy in top hat with sawed-off musket. As in Géricault's *Raft of the Medusa,* dead bodies are strewn about. In the background, the Notre-Dame towers rise through the smoke and haze. The painter's inclusion of this recognizable Parisian landmark announces the specificity of locale and event. It also reveals Delacroix's attempt, like Géricault in *Raft,* to balance contemporary historical fact with poetic allegory (Liberty). This desire for balance is further revealed in the Salon title of this work, *The 28th of July: Liberty Leading the People.*

THE ALLURE OF MOROCCO An enormously influential event in Delacroix's life that affected his art in both subject and form was his visit to North Africa in 1832. Things he saw there shocked his imagination with fresh impressions that lasted throughout his life. He discovered, in the sun-drenched landscape and in the hardy and colorful Moroccans dressed in robes reminiscent of the Roman toga, new insights into a culture built on proud virtues. He believed it was a culture more classical than anything European Neoclassicism could conceive. "I have Romans and Greeks on my doorstep," he wrote to a friend, "it makes me laugh heartily at David's Greeks."[16] The gallantry, valor, and fierce love of liberty made the Moroccans, in Delacroix's eyes, "nature's noblemen"—unspoiled heroes uninfected by European decadence.

The Moroccan journey renewed Delacroix's Romantic conviction that beauty exists in the fierceness of nature, natural processes, and natural beings, especially animals. After Morocco, more and more of Delacroix's subjects involved combats between beasts and between beasts and men. He painted snarling tangles of lions and tigers, battles between horses, and clashes of Muslims with great cats in swirling hunting

28-45 EUGÈNE DELACROIX, *Liberty Leading the People,* 1830. Oil on canvas, approx. 8′ 6″ × 10′ 8″. Louvre, Paris.

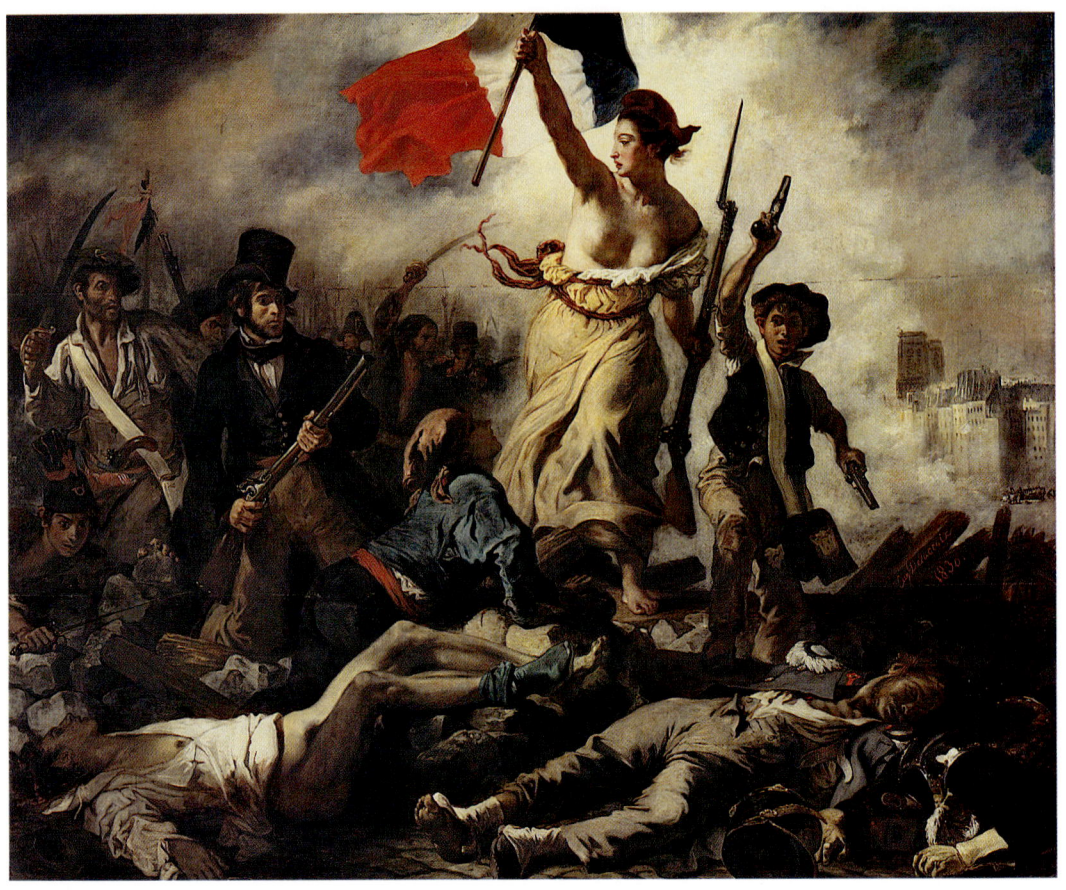

28-46 EUGÈNE DELACROIX, *Tiger Hunt,* 1854. Oil on canvas, approx. 2′ 5″ × 3′. Louvre, Paris.

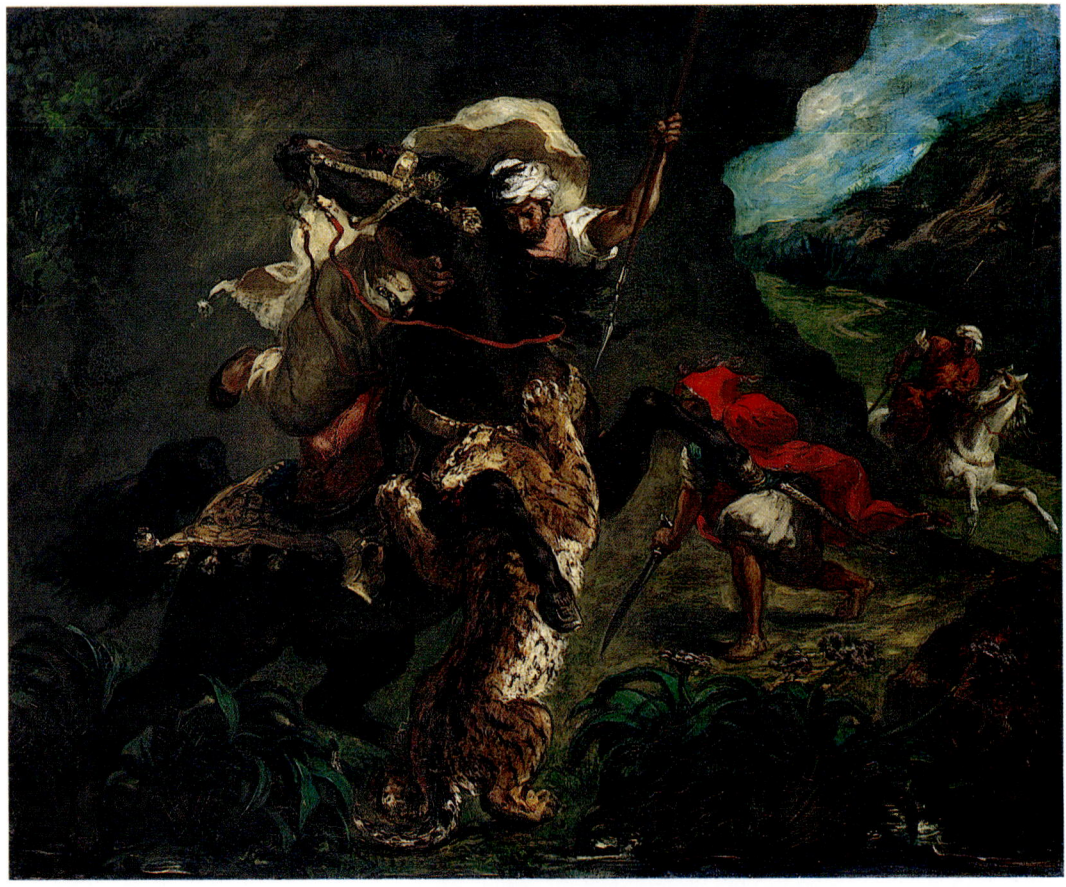

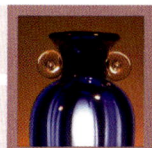

The Romantic Spirit in Music and Literature

The appeal of Romanticism, with its emphasis on freedom and feeling, extended well beyond the realm of the visual arts. In European music, literature, and poetry, the Romantic spirit was a dominant presence during the late eighteenth and early nineteenth centuries. These artistic endeavors rejected classicism's structured order in favor of the emotive and expressive. In music, the compositions of Franz Schubert (1797–1828), Franz Liszt (1811–1886), Frédéric Chopin (1810–1849), and Johannes Brahms (1833–1897) all emphasized the melodic or lyrical. These composers believed music had the power to express the unspeakable and to communicate the subtlest and most powerful human emotions.

In literature, Romantic poets such as John Keats (1795–1821), William Wordsworth (1770–1850), and Samuel Taylor Coleridge (1772–1834) published volumes of poetry that intersected with the Romantic interest in lyrical drama. *Ozymandias,* by Percy Bysshe Shelley (1792–1822), speaks of faraway, exotic locales. Lord Byron's poem of 1821, *Sardanapalus,* is set in the kingdom of Assyria in the seventh century B.C. It conjures images of eroticism and fury unleashed—images Delacroix visualized in his painting *Death of Sardanapalus* (FIG. 28-44). One of the best examples of the Romantic spirit is the engrossing novel *Frankenstein,* written in 1818 by Mary Wollstonecraft Shelley (1797–1851), who was married to Romantic poet Percy Bysshe Shelley. This fantastic tale of a monstrous creature run amok is filled with drama and remains popular to the present. As was true of many Romantic artworks, this novel not only embraces the emotional but also rejects the rationalism that underlay Enlightenment thought. Dr. Frankenstein's monster was a product of science, and this novel easily could have been interpreted as an indictment of the tenacious belief in science promoted by Enlightenment thinkers such as Voltaire. *Frankenstein* thus served as a cautionary tale of the havoc that could result from unrestrained scientific experimentation and from the arrogance of scientists like Dr. Frankenstein.

The imagination and vision that characterized Romantic paintings and sculptures were equally moving and riveting in musical or written form. The sustained energy of Romanticism is proof of the captivating nature of this movement and spirit.

---

scenes using compositions reminiscent of those of Rubens. One such work, *Tiger Hunt* (FIG. **28-46**), clearly speaks to the Romantic interest in faraway lands and exotic cultures.

DELACROIX'S COLORFUL LEGACY Delacroix's African experience also further heightened his already considerable awareness of the expressive power of color and light. What Delacroix knew about color he passed on to later painters of the nineteenth century, particularly the Impressionists. He observed that pure colors are as rare in nature as lines, that color appears only in an infinitely varied scale of different tones, shadings, and reflections, which he tried to recreate in his paintings. He recorded his observations in his *Journal,* which became a veritable body of knowledge of pre-Impressionistic color theory and was acclaimed as such by the Post-Impressionist painter Paul Signac. Delacroix anticipated the later development of Impressionist color science. But that art-science had to await the discoveries by Michel Eugène Chevreul and Hermann von Helmholtz of the laws of light decomposition and the properties of complementary colors before the problems of color perception and juxtaposition in painting could be properly formulated (see "Nineteenth-Century Color Theory," Chapter 29, page 920). Nevertheless, Delacroix's observations were significant, and he advised other artists not to fuse their brushstrokes, as the brushstrokes would appear to fuse naturally from a distance.

"PASSIONATELY IN LOVE WITH PASSION" No other painter of the time explored the domain of Romantic subject and mood as thoroughly and definitively as Delacroix. Delacroix's technique was impetuous, improvisational, and instinctive, rather than deliberate, studious, and cold. It epitomized Romantic-colorist painting, catching the impression quickly and developing it in the execution process. His contemporaries commented on how furiously Delacroix worked once he had an idea, keeping the whole painting progressing at once. The fury of his attack matched the fury of his imagination and his subjects. In the end, his friend Silvestre, in the language of Romanticism, delivered a eulogy that amounts to a definition of the Romantic artist:

> Thus died, almost with a smile on August 13, 1863, . . . Ferdinand Victor Eugène Delacroix, . . . who for forty years played upon the keyboard of human passions and whose brush—grandiose, terrible, or suave—passed from saints to warriors, from warriors to lovers, from lovers to tigers, and from tigers to flowers.[17]

The Dramatic in Sculpture

ALLEGORIZING OF FRANCE'S GLORY As one might expect, the Romantic spirit pervaded all of the media during the early nineteenth century. Many sculptors, like the period's painters, produced work that incorporated both

Neoclassical and Romantic elements. The colossal group *La Marseillaise* (FIG. **28-47**), mounted on one face of Chalgrin's Arc de Triomphe in Paris is one such sculpture. Its creator, FRANÇOIS RUDE (1784–1855), carved here an allegory of the national glories of revolutionary France by depicting the volunteers of 1792 departing to defend the nation's borders against the Revolution's foreign enemies. The Roman goddess of war, Bellona (who here personifies Liberty, as well as the revolutionary hymn, now France's national anthem), soars above patriots of all ages, exhorting them forward with her thundering battle cry. The figures recall David's classically armored (FIG. 28-15) or nude heroes, as do the rhetorical gestures of the wide-flung arms and the striding poses. Yet the densely packed, overlapping masses; the jagged contours; and violence of motion relate more closely to the compositional method of dramatic Romanticism, as found in Géricault (FIG. 28-41) and Delacroix (FIG. 28-45). La Marseillaise's allegorical figure is the spiritual sister of Delacroix's Liberty (FIG. 28-45); they share the same Phrygian cap, the badge of liberty. But, though the works are almost exactly contemporaneous, the figures in the sculpted group are represented in classical costume, while those in Delacroix's painting wear modern Parisian costumes. Both works are allegorical, but one looks to the past and the other to the present.

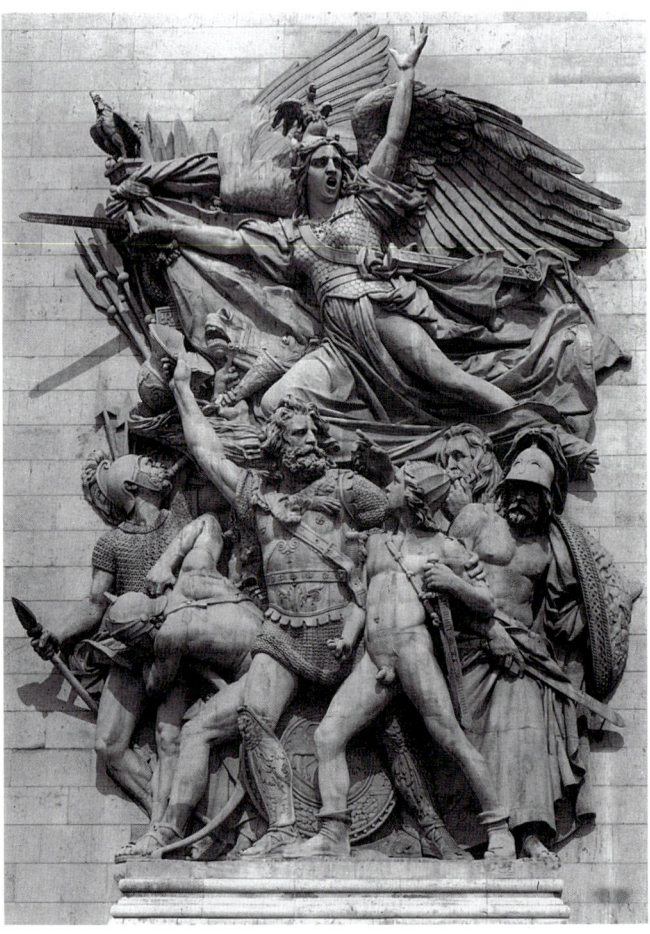

28-47 FRANÇOIS RUDE, *La Marseillaise,* Arc de Triomphe, Paris, France, 1833–1836. Approx. 42′ × 26′.

THE FEROCITY OF ANIMALS   Delacroix's fascination with brute beauty and beastial violence is echoed in *Jaguar Devouring a Hare* (FIG. **28-48**), a much smaller group in bronze by ANTOINE-LOUIS BARYE (1795–1875). Painful as the subject is, Barye's work draws viewers irresistibly by its fidelity to brute nature. The belly-crouching cat's swelling muscles, hunched shoulders, and tense spine—even the switch of the tail—tell of the sculptor's long sessions observing the animals in the Jardin des Plantes, the Parisian zoo. This work shows the influence of the vast new geographies opening before the naturalistic eyes and temper of nineteenth-century artists while demonstrating Romanticism's obsession with strong emotion and untamed nature. Nineteenth-century sensibility generally prevented humans from showing animal ferocity but enthusiastically accepted its portrayal in Romantic depictions of wild beasts.

IMAGINATION AND MOOD IN LANDSCAPE PAINTING

Landscape painting came into its own in the nineteenth century as a fully independent and respected genre. Briefly eclipsed at the century's beginning by the taste for ideal form, which favored figural composition and history, landscape painting flourished as leading painters made it their profession.

The eighteenth-century artists had regarded the pleasurable, aesthetic mood natural landscape inspired as making the landscape itself "picturesque," that is, worthy of being painted. Early on, they considered the "natural" English garden picturesque. Later, the sensitive Romantic translated landscape vistas, colored by the viewer's mood, into aesthetic form, poetry, or painting. Rather than provide simple descriptions of nature, poets and artists often used nature as allegory. In this manner, artists commented on spiritual, moral, historical, or philosophical issues. Landscape painting was a particularly effective vehicle for such commentary because it allowed artists to "naturalize" conditions, thereby making such conditions appear normal, acceptable, or inevitable.

Landscape Painting in Germany

Early in nineteenth-century northern Europe, mainly Germany, most landscape painting to some degree expressed this Romantic, pantheistic view (first extolled by Rousseau) of nature as a "being" that included the totality of existence in organic unity and harmony. In nature—"the living garment of God," as German poet and dramatist Johann Wolfgang von Goethe called it—artists found an ideal subject to express the Romantic theme of the soul unified with the natural world. As all nature was mysteriously permeated by "being," landscape artists had the task of interpreting the signs, symbols, and emblems of universal "spirit" disguised within visible material things. Artists no longer merely beheld a landscape but participated in its spirit. No longer were they painters of mere things but translators of nature's transcendent meanings, arrived at through feelings landscapes inspired.

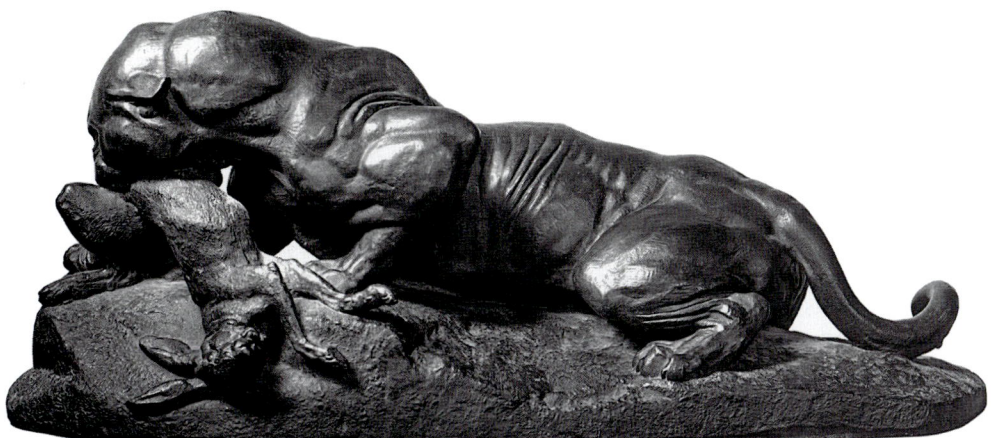

28-48   ANTOINE-LOUIS BARYE, *Jaguar Devouring a Hare,* 1850–1851. Bronze, approx. 1′ 4″ × 3′ 1″. Louvre, Paris.

THE REVERENTIAL LANDSCAPE   CASPAR DAVID FRIEDRICH (1774–1840) was among the Northern European artists who were the first to depict the Romantic transcendental landscape. For Friedrich, landscapes were temples; his paintings themselves were altarpieces. The reverential mood of his works demands from viewers the silence appropriate to sacred places filled with a divine presence. *Cloister Graveyard in the Snow* (FIG. **28-49**) is like a solemn requiem. Under a winter sky, through the leafless oaks of a snow-covered cemetery, a funeral procession bears a coffin into the ruins of a Gothic chapel. The emblems of death are everywhere—the season's desolation, leaning crosses and tombstones, the black of mourning worn by the grieving and by the skeletal trees, the destruction time wrought on the chapel. The painting is a kind of meditation on human mortality, as Friedrich himself remarked: "Why, it has often occurred to me to ask myself, do I so frequently choose death, transience, and the grave as subjects for my paintings? One must submit oneself many times

to death in order some day to attain life everlasting."[18] The artist's sharp-focused rendering of details demonstrates his keen perception of everything in the physical environment relevant to his message. Friedrich's work balances inner and outer experience. "The artist," he wrote, "should not only paint what he sees before him, but also what he sees within him."[19] Although Friedrich's works may not have the theatrical energy of the paintings of Géricault or Delacroix, they are pervaded by a resonant and deep emotion.

Landscape Painting in England

One of the most momentous developments in Western history—the Industrial Revolution—impacted the evolution of Romantic landscape painting in England. Although discussion of the Industrial Revolution invariably focuses on technological advances, factory development, and growth of ur-

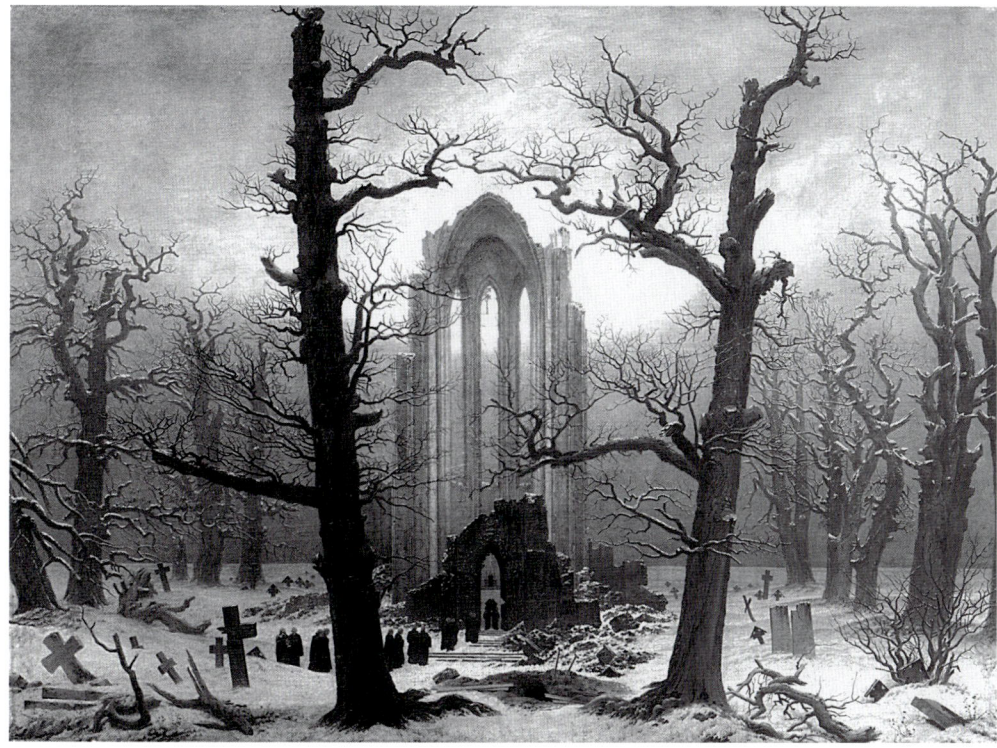

28-49   CASPAR DAVID FRIEDRICH, *Cloister Graveyard in the Snow,* 1810. Oil on canvas, approx. 3′ 11″ × 5′ 10″ (painting destroyed during World War II).

ban centers, its effect on the countryside and the land itself was no less severe. The detrimental economic impact industrialization had on the prices for agrarian products produced significant unrest in the English countryside. In particular, increasing numbers of displaced farmers could no longer afford to farm their small land plots.

NOSTALGIC IMAGES OF AGRARIAN ENGLAND

This situation is addressed in the landscape paintings of JOHN CONSTABLE (1776–1837), perhaps the best known of the English landscape artists. *The Haywain* (FIG. **28-50**) is representative of Constable's art and reveals much about his outlook. In this large painting, Constable presented a placid, picturesque scene of the countryside. A small cottage appears on the left, and in the center foreground a man leads a horse and wagon across the stream. Billowy clouds float lazily across the sky, and the scene's tranquility is augmented by the muted greens and golds and by the delicacy of Constable's brushstrokes. The artist portrayed the oneness with nature the Romantic poets sought; the relaxed figures are not observers but participants in the landscape's being. Constable made countless studies from nature for each of his canvases, which helped him produce the convincing sense of reality in his works that his contemporaries praised. In his quest for the authentic landscape, Constable studied it like a meteorologist (which he was by avocation). His special gift was for capturing the texture the atmosphere (the climate and the weather, which delicately veil what is seen) gave to landscape. He also could reveal that atmosphere as the key to representing the ceaseless process of nature, which changes constantly through the hours and through shifts of weather and season. Constable's use of tiny dabs of local color, stippled with white, created a sparkling shimmer of light and hue across the canvas's surface—the vibration itself suggestive of movement and process.

The Haywain is also significant for precisely what it does not show—the civil unrest of the agrarian working class and the outbreaks of violence and arson that resulted. Indeed, this painting has a nostalgic, wistful air to it. To a certain extent, this scene (although carefully detailed) is linked to Constable's memories of a disappearing rural pastoralism. The artist came from a family of considerable wealth; his father was a rural landowner, and many of the scenes Constable painted (*The Haywain* included) depict his family's property near East Bergholt in Suffolk, East Anglia.

The people that populate Constable's landscapes blend into the scenes and are one with nature. Rarely do viewers see workers engaged in tedious labor. This nostalgia, presented in such naturalistic terms, renders Constable's works Romantic in tone. That Constable felt a kindred spirit with the Romantic artists is revealed by his comment: ". . . painting is but another word for feeling, . . ."[20]

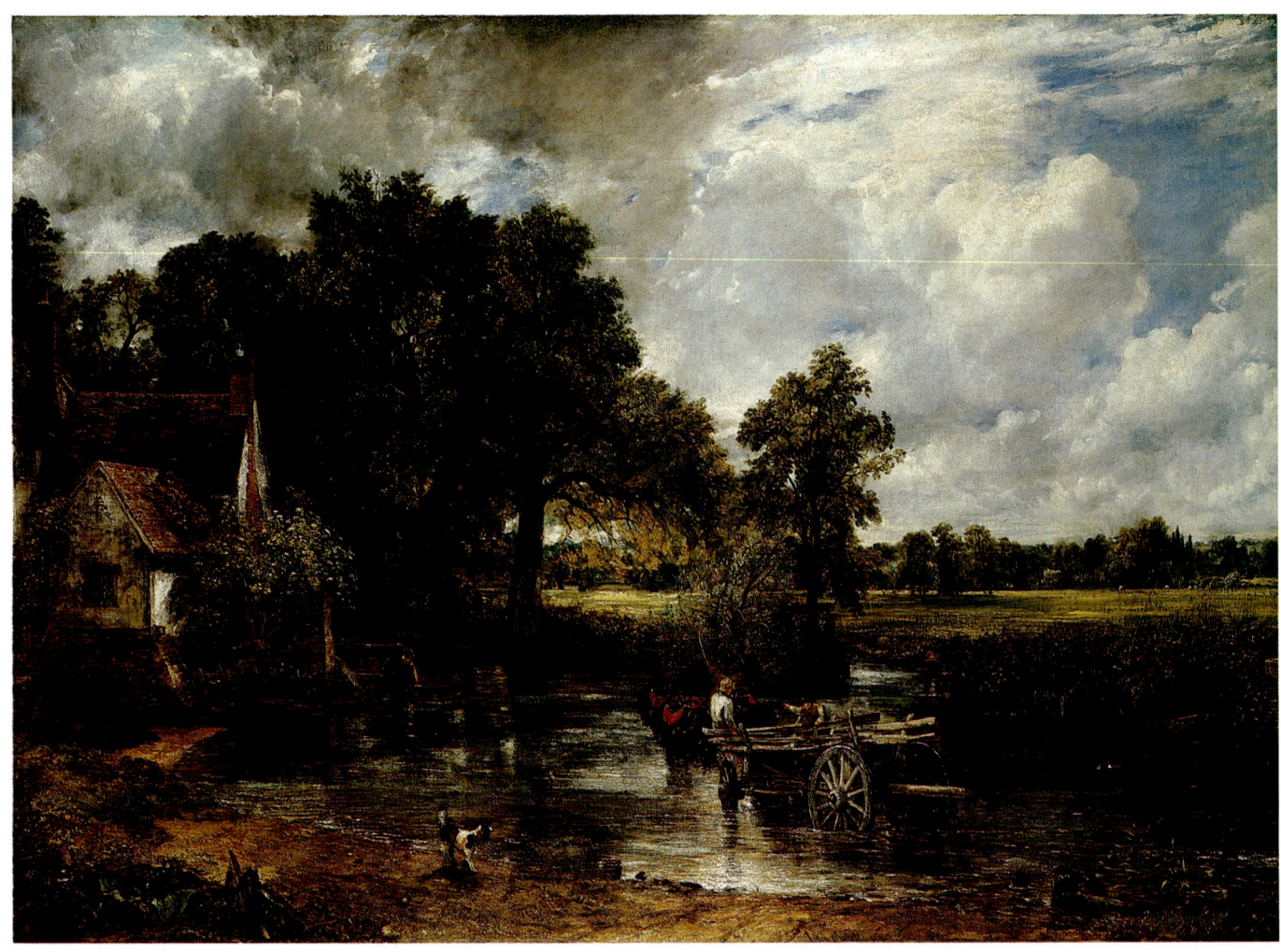

28-50 JOHN CONSTABLE, *The Haywain,* 1821. Oil on canvas, 4′ 3″ × 6′ 2″. National Gallery, London.

THE HORRORS OF THE SLAVE TRADE JOSEPH MALLORD WILLIAM TURNER (1775–1851), Constable's contemporary in the English school of landscape painting, produced work that also responded to the encroaching industrialization. However, where Constable's paintings are serene and precisely painted, Turner's are composed of turbulent swirls of frothy pigment. The passion and energy of Turner's works not only reveal the Romantic sensibility that provided the foundation for his art, but also they clearly illustrate Edmund Burke's concept of the sublime—awe mixed with terror.

Among Turner's most notable works is *The Slave Ship* (FIG. 28-51). Its subject is an incident that occurred in 1783 and was reported in a extensively read book titled *The History of the Abolition of the Slave Trade* by Thomas Clarkson. Because the book just had been reprinted in 1839, Clarkson's account probably prompted Turner's choice of subject for this 1840 painting. The incident involved the captain of a slave ship who, on realizing his insurance company would reimburse him only for slaves lost at sea but not for those who died en route, ordered the sick and dying slaves thrown overboard. Appropriately, the painting's full title is *The Slave Ship (Slavers Throwing Overboard the Dead and Dying, Typhoon Coming On)*, Turner's frenzied emotional depiction of this act matches its barbaric nature. The sun is transformed into an incandescent comet amid flying scarlet clouds. The slave ship moves into the distance, leaving in its wake a turbulent sea choked with the bodies of slaves sinking to their death. The event's particulars are almost lost in the boiling colors; however, on closer inspection, the cruelty is evident. Viewers can see the iron shackles and manacles around the wrists and ankles of the drowning slaves, denying them any chance of saving themselves.

The Slave Ship is clearly more specifically a seascape rather than a landscape painting. Yet Turner's interest in the slave trade indicates his fascination with the Industrial Revolution's effects. In his other paintings, many of them landscapes, Turner revealed a more inquisitive attitude toward industrialization than did Constable.

Turner's style, often referred to as visionary, was deeply rooted in the emotive power of pure color. The haziness of his forms and the indistinctness of his compositions imbued color and energetic brushstrokes with greater impact. Turner was a great innovator whose special invention in works such as *The Slave Ship* was to release color from any defining outlines to express both the forces of nature and the painter's emotional response to them. In works such as

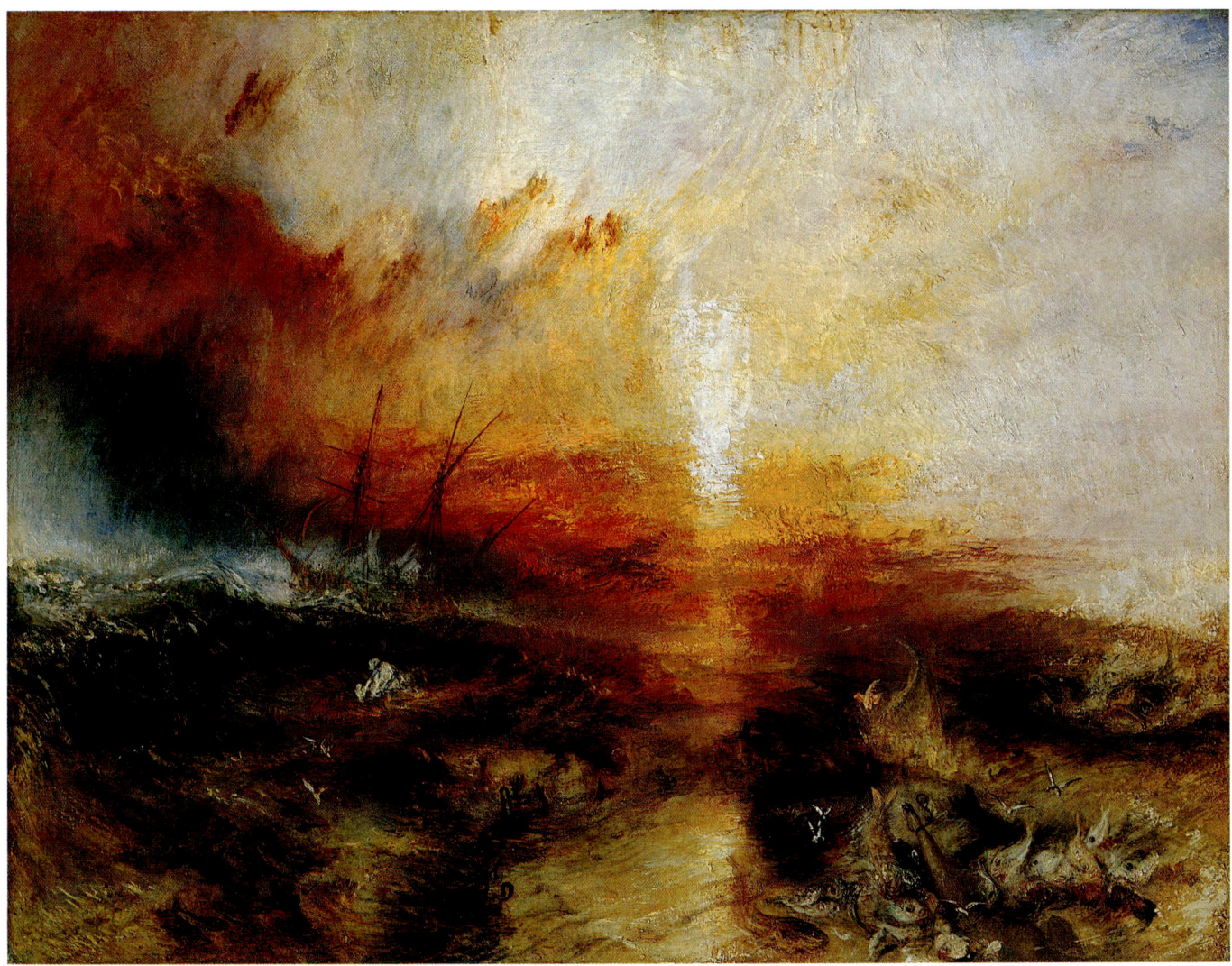

28-51 JOSEPH MALLORD WILLIAM TURNER, *The Slave Ship (Slavers Throwing Overboard the Dead and Dying, Typhoon Coming On)*, 1840. Oil on canvas, 2′ 11¹¹⁄₁₆″ × 4′ ⁵⁄₁₆″. Museum of Fine Arts, Boston (Henry Lillie Pierce Fund).

this, the reality of color is one with the reality of feeling. Turner's methods had an incalculable effect on modern art's development. His discovery of the aesthetic and emotive power of pure color and his pushing of the medium's fluidity to a point where the subject is almost manifest through the paint itself were important steps toward twentieth-century abstract art, which dispensed with shape and form altogether.

Landscape Painting in the United States

AMERICA'S FUTURE DIRECTION? In America, landscape painting was most prominently pursued by a group of artists known as the Hudson River School, because its members drew their subjects primarily from the uncultivated regions of the Hudson River valley. Many of these painters, however, depicted scenes from across the country and, thus, "Hudson River School" is actually too restrictive geographically. Like the early-nineteenth-century landscape painters in Germany and England, the Hudson River School artists not only presented Romantic panoramic landscape views but also participated in the ongoing exploration of the individual's and the country's relationship to the land. Acknowledging the unique geography and historical circumstances in each country and region, American landscape painters frequently focused on identifying qualities that rendered America unique. One American painter of English birth, THOMAS COLE (1801–1848), often referred to as the Hudson River School's leader, articulated this idea:

> Whether he [an American] beholds the Hudson mingling waters with the Atlantic—explores the central wilds of this vast continent, or stands on the margin of the distant Oregon, he is still in the midst of American scenery—it is his own land; its beauty, its magnificence, its sublimity—all are his; and how undeserving of such a birthright, if he can turn towards it an unobserving eye, an unaffected heart![21]

Another issue that surfaced frequently in Hudson River School paintings was the moral question of America's direction as a civilization. Cole presented viewers with this question in *The Oxbow (View from Mount Holyoke, Northampton, Massachusetts, after a Thunderstorm)*, FIG. **28-52**. A splendid scene opens before viewers, dominated by the lazy oxbow turning of the Connecticut River. The composition is divided, with the dark, stormy wilderness on the left and the more developed civilization on the right. The miniscule artist in the bottom center of the painting (wearing a top hat), dwarfed by the landscape's scale, turns to viewers as if to ask for their input in deciding the country's future course. In their depiction of expansive wilderness, Cole's landscapes incorporated reflections and moods so romantically appealing to the public.

WILD, WILD WEST Other Hudson River artists used the landscape genre as an allegorical vehicle to address moral and spiritual concerns. ALBERT BIERSTADT (1830–1902) traveled west in 1858 and produced many paintings depicting the Rocky Mountains, Yosemite Valley, and other sites in California. These works, such as *Among the Sierra Nevada Mountains, California* (FIG. **28-53**), present viewers with breathtaking scenery and natural beauty. This panoramic view (the painting is ten feet wide) is awe inspiring. Deer and waterfowl appear at the edge of a placid lake, while rugged and steep mountains soar skyward on the left and in the distance. A stand of trees, uncultivated and wild, frame the lake on the right. To impress on viewers the almost transcendental nature of this scene, Bierstadt depicted the sun's rays breaking through the clouds overhead, which suggests a heavenly consecration of the land. That Bierstadt focused attention on the West is not insignificant. By calling national attention to the splendor and uniqueness of the regions beyond the Rocky Mountains, Bierstadt's paintings reinforced Manifest Destiny. This popular nineteenth-century doctrine held that westward expansion across the continent was the logical destiny of the

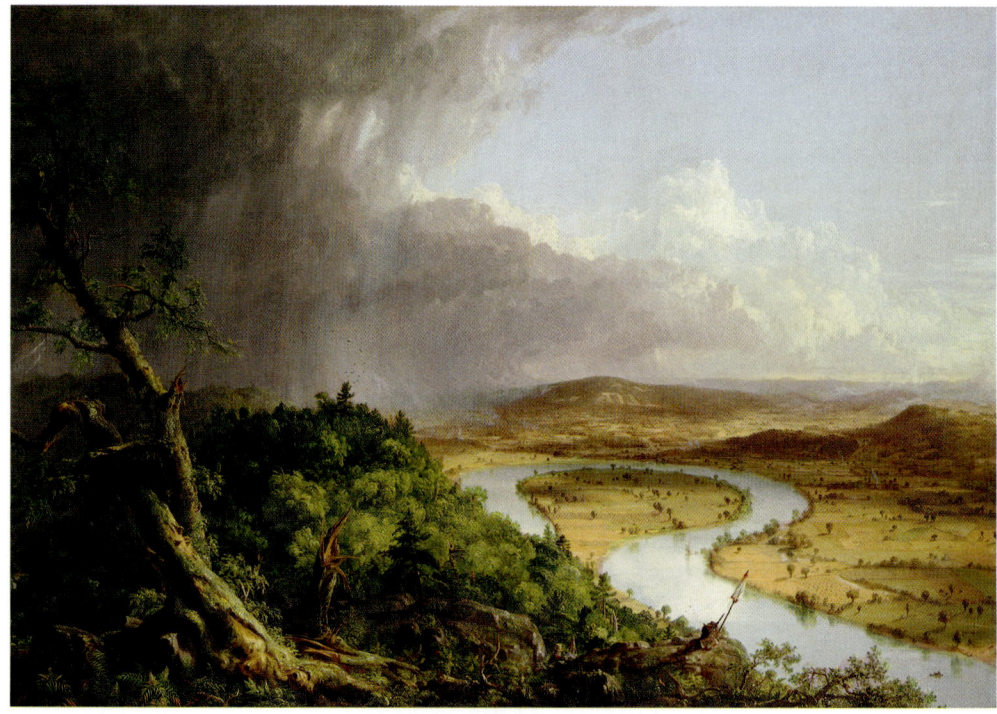

28-52 THOMAS COLE, *The Oxbow (View from Mount Holyoke, Northampton, Massachusetts, after a Thunderstorm)*, 1836. Oil on canvas, 4' 3½" × 6' 4". Metropolitan Museum of Art, New York (gift of Mrs. Russell Sage, 1908).

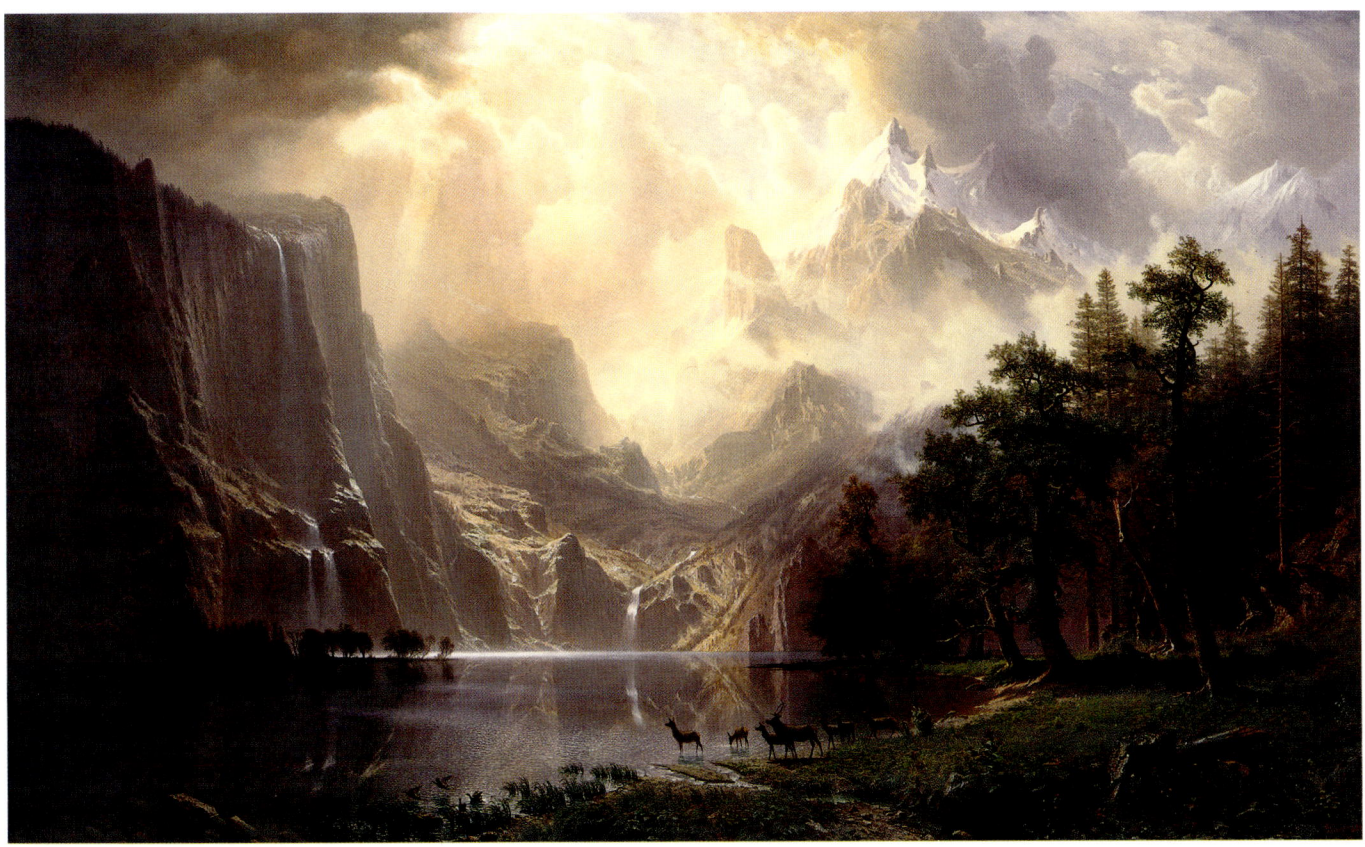

28-53   ALBERT BIERSTADT, *Among the Sierra Nevada Mountains, California,* 1868. Oil on canvas, 6′ × 10′. National Museum of American Art, Smithsonian Institution, Washington.

United States. Such artworks thereby muted growing concerns over the realities of conquest, the displacement of the Native Americans, and the exploitation of the environment. It should come as no surprise that among those most eager to purchase Bierstadt's work were mail-service magnates and railroad builders—entrepreneurs and financiers involved in westward expansion.

REAFFIRMING AMERICA'S RIGHTEOUSNESS FREDERIC EDWIN CHURCH (1826–1900) also has been associated with the Hudson River School. His interest in landscape scenes was not limited to America; during his life he traveled to South America, Mexico, Europe, the Middle East, Newfoundland, and Labrador. Church's paintings are instructive because, like the works of Cole and Bierstadt, they are firmly entrenched in the idiom of the Romantic sublime. Yet they also reveal contradictions and conflicts in the constructed mythology of American providence and character. *Twilight in the Wilderness* (FIG. **28-54**) presents an awe-inspiring panoramic view of the sun setting over the majestic landscape. Beyond Church's precise depiction of the spectacle of nature, the painting is remarkable for what it does not depict. Like John Constable, Church and the other Hudson River School painters worked in a time of great upheaval. *Twilight in the Wilderness* was created in 1860, when the Civil War was decimating the country. Yet not only does this painting not display evidence of turbulence or discord, but also it does not include even a trace of humanity. By constructing such an idealistic and comforting view, Church contributed to the national mythology of righteousness and divine providence—a

mythology that had become increasingly difficult to maintain in the face of conflict.

THE AFTERMATH OF CIVIL WAR That these American landscape paintings participated in the public discourse about philosophical, moral, and political issues is seen in the work of WINSLOW HOMER (1836–1910). Homer had firsthand knowledge of the Civil War; when it broke out in 1860, he joined the Union campaign as an artist-reporter for *Harper's Weekly.* In 1865 at the end of the Civil War, Homer painted *The Veteran in a New Field* (FIG. **28-55**). Although it is fairly simple and direct, this painting provides significant commentary on the effects and aftermath of this catastrophic national conflict. The painting depicts a man with his back to the viewer, harvesting wheat. That he is a veteran is clear not only from the painting's title but also from the uniform and canteen carelessly thrown on the ground in the lower right corner. The veteran's involvement in meaningful and productive work suggests a smooth transition from war to peace. Indeed, one could suggest that the veteran turned from harvesting men to harvesting wheat. This transition to work after the end of the Civil War and the fate of disbanded soldiers were of national concern. The *New York Weekly Tribune* commented: "Rome took her great man from the plow, and made him a dictator—we must now take our soldiers from the camp and make them farmers."[22] America's ability to effect a smooth transition was seen as evidence of its national strength. "The peaceful and harmonious disbanding of the armies in the summer of 1865," poet Walt Whitman wrote, was one of the "immortal proofs of democracy, unequall'd in

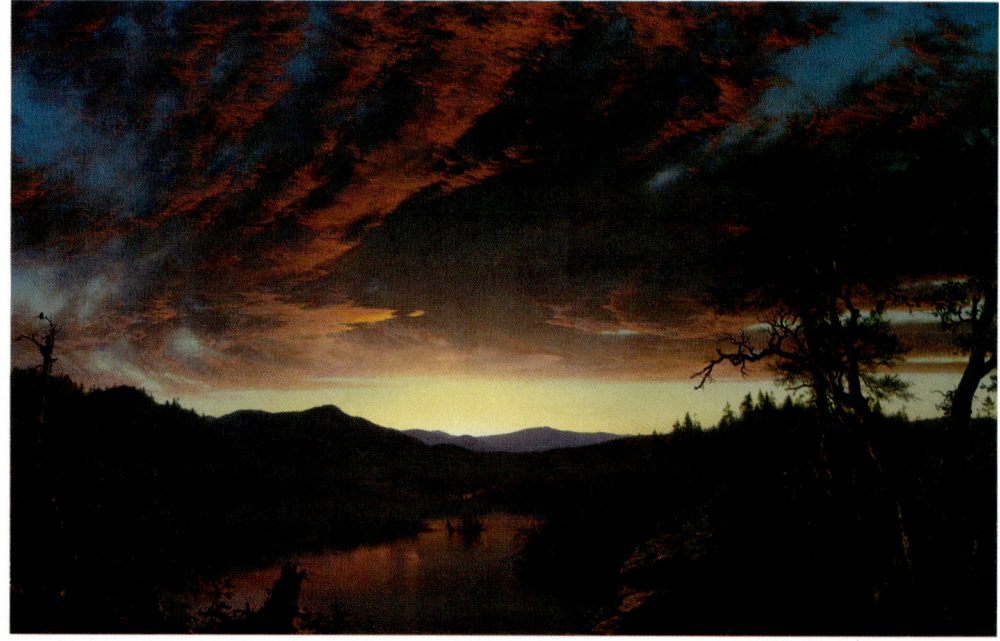

28-54   FREDERIC EDWIN CHURCH, *Twilight In the Wilderness,* 1860s. Oil on canvas, 3′ 4″ × 5′ 4″. Cleveland Museum of Art, Cleveland, Ohio (Mr. and Mrs. William H. Marlatt Fund, 1965.233).

all the history of the past."[23] Homer's painting thus reinforced the perception of the country's greatness.

The Veteran in a New Field also comments symbolically about death—both the deaths of the soldiers and of Abraham Lincoln. By the 1860s, farmers used cradled scythes to harvest wheat. However, Homer chose not to insist on this historical reality and painted a single-bladed scythe. This transforms the veteran into a symbol of Death—the Grim Reaper himself—and the painting into an elegy to the thousands of soldiers who died in the Civil War and into a lamentation on the death of the recently assassinated president. As with *Twilight in the Wilderness,* Homer's landscape painting contributed to the continuing mythmaking about national conditions and to the mediation of national discourse in difficult times.

Landscape painting was immensely popular in the late eighteenth and early nineteenth centuries, in large part be-

cause it provided viewers with breathtaking and sublime spectacles of nature. Artists also could allegorize nature, and it was rare for a landscape painting not to touch on spiritual, moral, historical, or philosophical issues. Landscape painting became the perfect vehicle for artists (and the viewing public) to "naturalize" conditions, rendering debate about contentious issues moot and eliminating any hint of conflict.

VARIOUS REVIVALIST STYLES IN ARCHITECTURE

RECONSIDERING THE PAST   As nineteenth-century scholars gathered the documentary materials of European history in extensive historiographic enterprises, each nation came to value its past as evidence of the validity of its ambitions

28-55   WINSLOW HOMER, *The Veteran in a New Field,* 1865. Oil on canvas, 2′ $\frac{1}{8}$″ × 3′ 2$\frac{1}{8}$″. Metropolitan Museum of Art, New York (bequest of Miss Adelaide Milton de Groot, 1967).

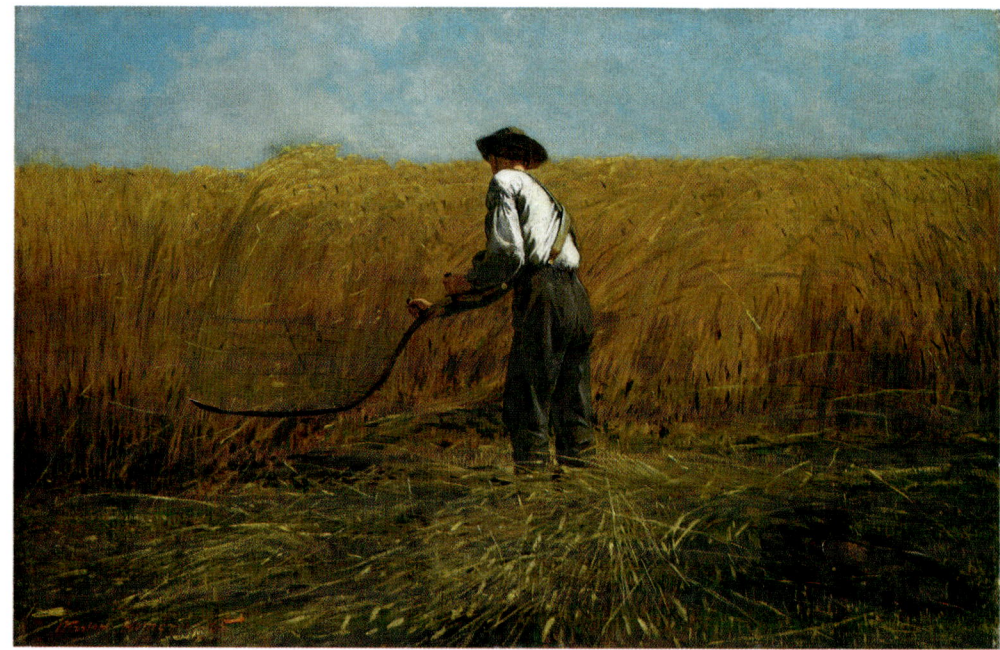

and claims to greatness. Intellectuals appreciated the art of the remote past as a product of cultural and national genius. In 1773, Goethe, praising the Gothic cathedral of Strasbourg in *Of German Architecture,* announced the theme by declaring that the German art scholar "should thank God to be able to proclaim aloud that it is German Architecture, our architecture." He also bid the observer, "approach and recognize the deepest feeling of truth and beauty of proportion emanating from a strong, vigorous German soul."[24] In 1802, the eminent French writer François René de Chateaubriand published his influential *Genius of Christianity,* which defended religion on the grounds of its beauty and mystery rather than on the grounds of truth. Gothic cathedrals, according to Chateaubriand, were translations of the sacred groves of the Druidical Gauls into stone and must be cherished as manifestations of France's holy history. In his view, the history of Christianity and of France merged in the Middle Ages.

RESTORING MEDIEVAL ARTISANSHIP   Modern nationalism thus prompted a new evaluation of the art in each country's past. In London, when the old Houses of Parliament burned in 1834, the Parliamentary Commission decreed that designs for the new building be either "Gothic or Elizabethan." CHARLES BARRY (1795–1860), with the assistance of A. W. N. PUGIN (1812–1852), submitted the winning design (FIG. **28-56**) in 1835. By this time, style had become a matter of selection from the historical past. Barry had traveled widely in Europe, Greece, Turkey, Egypt, and Palestine, studying the architecture in each place. He preferred the classical Renaissance styles, but he had designed some earlier Neo-Gothic buildings, and Pugin successfully influenced him in the direction of English Late Gothic. Pugin was one of a group of English artists and critics who saw moral purity and spiritual authenticity in the religious architecture of the Middle Ages. They glorified the careful medieval artisans who had produced it. The Industrial Revolution was flooding the market with cheaply made and ill-designed commodities. Machine work was replacing handicraft. Many, such as Pugin, believed

in the necessity of restoring the old artisanship, which had honesty and quality. The design of the Houses of Parliament, however, is not genuinely Gothic, despite its picturesque tower groupings (the Clock Tower, containing Big Ben, at one end, and the Victoria Tower at the other). The building has a formal axial plan and a kind of Palladian regularity beneath its Tudor detail. Pugin himself is reported to have said of it: "All Grecian, Sir. Tudor details on a classical body."[25]

THE IMPACT OF IMPERIALISM   Although the Neoclassical and Neo-Gothic styles were dominant in the early nineteenth century, exotic new styles of all types soon began to appear, in part due to European imperialism. Great Britain's forays throughout the world, particularly India, had exposed English culture to a broad range of non-Western artistic styles. The Royal Pavilion (FIG. **28-57**), designed by JOHN NASH (1752–1835), exhibits a wide variety of these styles. Nash was an established architect, known for Neoclassical buildings in London, when he was asked to design a royal pleasure palace in the seaside resort of Brighton for the prince regent (later King George IV). The structure's fantastic exterior is a conglomeration of Islamic domes, minarets, and screens that has been called "Indian Gothic," while sources ranging from Greece and Egypt to China influenced the interior decor. Underlying the exotic facade is a cast-iron skeleton, an early (if hidden) use of this material in noncommercial building. Nash also put this metal to fanciful use, creating life-size palm-tree columns in cast iron to support the Royal Pavilion's kitchen ceiling. The building, an appropriate enough backdrop for gala throngs pursuing pleasure by the seaside, served as the prototype for numerous playful architectural exaggerations still found in European and American resorts.

ADAPTING BAROQUE OPULENCE   The Baroque also was adapted in architecture to convey a grandeur worthy of the riches acquired during this age of expansion by those who heeded the advice of the French historian and statesman

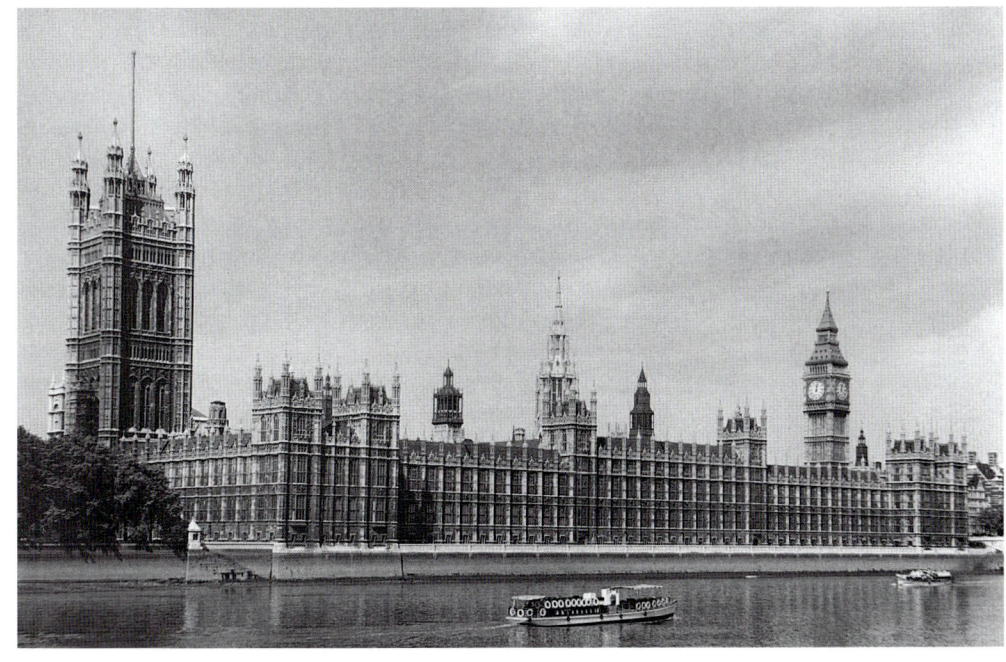

28-56   CHARLES BARRY and A. W. N. PUGIN, Houses of Parliament, London, England, designed 1835.

28-57   JOHN NASH, Royal Pavilion, Brighton, England, 1815–1818.

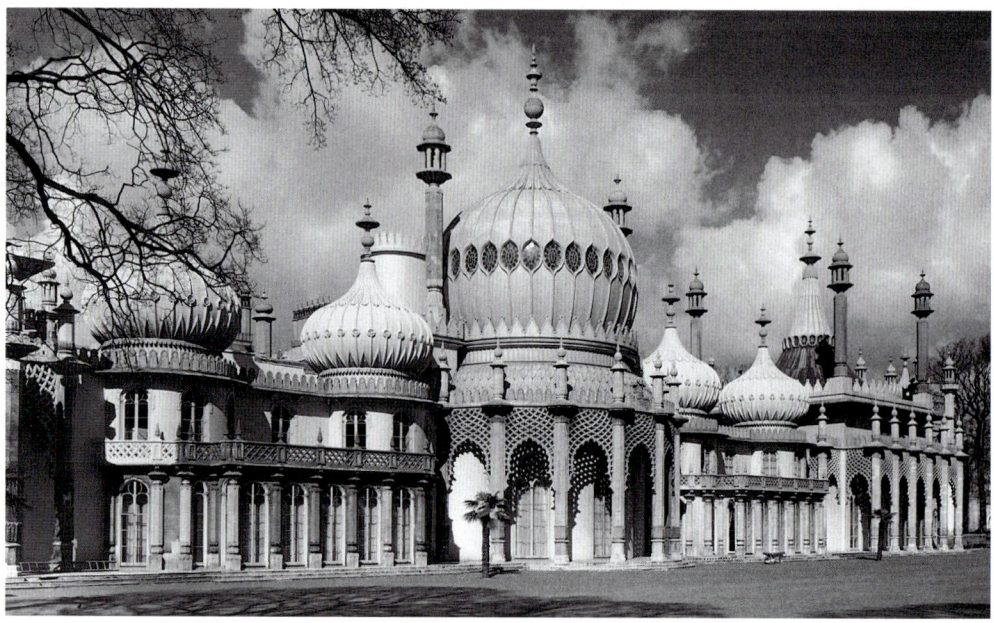

François Guizot to "get rich." The opulence reflected in the lives of these few was mirrored in the Paris Opéra (FIG. **28-58**), designed by J. L. CHARLES GARNIER (1825–1898). The Opéra parades a festive and spectacularly theatrical Neo-Baroque front that could be compared with the Louvre's facade (see FIG. 24-67), which it mimics to a degree. Garnier ingeniously planned the interior for the convenience of human traffic. Intricate arrangements of corridors, vestibules, stairways, balconies, alcoves, entrances, and exits facilitate easy passage throughout the building and provide space for entertainment and socializing at intermissions. The Baroque grandeur of the layout and of the opera house's ornamental appointments proclaims and enhances its function as a gathering place for glittering audiences in an age of conspicuous wealth. The style was so attractive to the moneyed classes who supported the arts that theaters and opera houses continued to reflect the Paris Opéra's design until World War I transformed society.

The epoch-making developments in architecture were more rational, pragmatic, and functional than the historical designs. As the years moved toward the end of the nineteenth century, architects gradually abandoned sentimental and Romantic designs from the historical past. They turned to honest expressions of a building's purpose. Since the eighteenth century, bridges had been built of cast iron (FIG. 28-4), and most other utility architecture—factories, warehouses, dockyard structures, mills, and the like—long had been built simply and without historical ornament. Iron, along with other industrial materials, permitted engineering advancements in the construction of larger, stronger, and more fire-resistant structures than before. The tensile strength of iron (and especially of steel, available after 1860) permitted architects to create new designs involving vast enclosed spaces, as in the great train sheds of railroad stations and in exposition halls.

IRONING OUT ARCHITECTURAL "DRAPERY"
The Bibliothèque Sainte-Geneviève (1843–1850), built by HENRI LABROUSTE (1801–1875), shows an interesting modification of a revived style—in this case, Renaissance—to accommodate the skeletal cast-iron elements (FIG. **28-59**). The row of arched windows in the facade recalls Renaissance buildings, and the division of its stories distinguishes its interior levels—the lower, reserved for stack space, and the upper, for the reading rooms. The latter consists essentially of two barrel-vaulted halls, roofed in terracotta and separated by a row of slender cast-iron columns on concrete pedestals. The columns, recognizably Corinthian, support the iron roof arches, which are pierced with intricate vine-scroll ornament out of the Renaissance architectural vocabulary. One scarcely could find a better example of how the peculiarities of the new structural material aesthetically transformed the forms of traditional masonry architecture. Nor could one find a better example of how reluctant the nineteenth-century architect was to surrender traditional forms, even when fully aware of new possibilities for design and construction. Architects scoffed at "engineers' architecture" for many years and continued to clothe their steel-and-concrete structures in the Romantic "drapery" of a historical style.

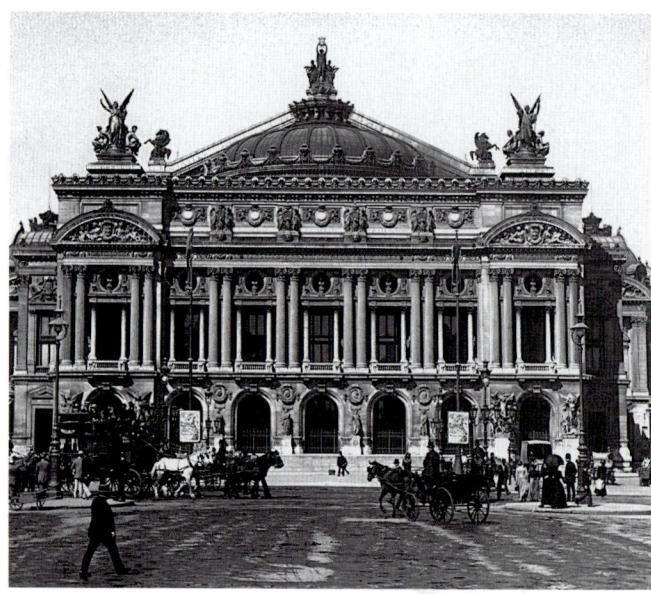

28-58   J. L. CHARLES GARNIER, the Opéra, Paris, France, 1861–1874.

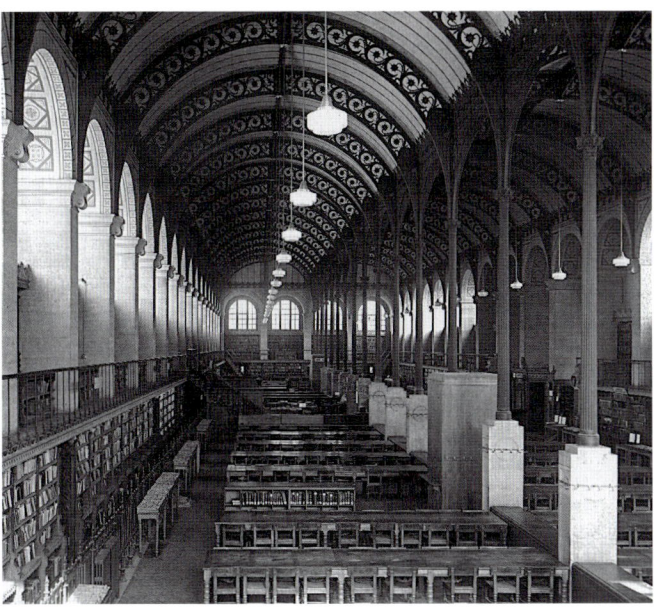

28-59 HENRI LABROUSTE, reading room of the Bibliothèque Sainte-Geneviève, Paris, France, 1843–1850.

CRYSTALLIZING CONSTRUCTION TECHNIQUES
Completely "undraped" construction first became popular in the conservatories (greenhouses) of English country estates. JOSEPH PAXTON (1801–1865) built several such structures for his patron, the duke of Devonshire. In the largest—three hundred feet long—he used an experimental system of glass-and-metal roof construction. Encouraged by this system's success, Paxton submitted a winning glass-and-iron building plan to the design competition for the hall to house the Great Exhibition of 1851, organized to gather "Works of Industry of All Nations" together in London. Paxton's exhibition building, the Crystal Palace (FIG. **28-60**), was built with prefabricated parts. This allowed the vast structure to be erected in the then-unheard-of time of six months and dismantled at the exhibition's closing to avoid permanent obstruction of the

park. The plan borrowed much from ancient Roman and Christian basilicas, with a central flat-roofed "nave" and a barrel-vaulted crossing "transept." The design provided ample interior space to contain displays of huge machines as well as to accommodate such decorative touches as large working fountains and giant trees. The public admired the building so much that when it was dismantled, it was reerected at a new location on the outskirts of London, where it remained until fire destroyed it in 1936.

THE BEGINNINGS OF PHOTOGRAPHY

THE CAMERA'S IMPACT A technological device of immense consequence for the modern experience was invented shortly before midcentury: the camera, with its attendant art of photography. Almost everyone is familiar with what the camera equips them to do—report and record optical experience at will. People have come to assume that a very close correlation exists between the photographic image and the fragment of the visual world it records. The evidence of the photograph is proof that what people think they see is really there. Americans, for example, experience the authority and credibility their culture endows on photography in the form of driver's licenses, passport photos, and security cameras.

Photography was celebrated as embodying a kind of revelation of visible things from the time Frenchman Louis J. M. Daguerre and Briton Henry Fox Talbot announced the first practical photographic processes in 1839. The medium, itself a product of science, was an enormously useful tool for recording the century's discoveries. The relative ease of the process seemed a dream come true for scientists and artists, who for centuries had grappled with less satisfying methods for capturing accurate images of their subjects. Photography also was perfectly suited to an age that saw artistic patronage continue to shift away from the elite few toward a broader base of support. The growing and increasingly powerful

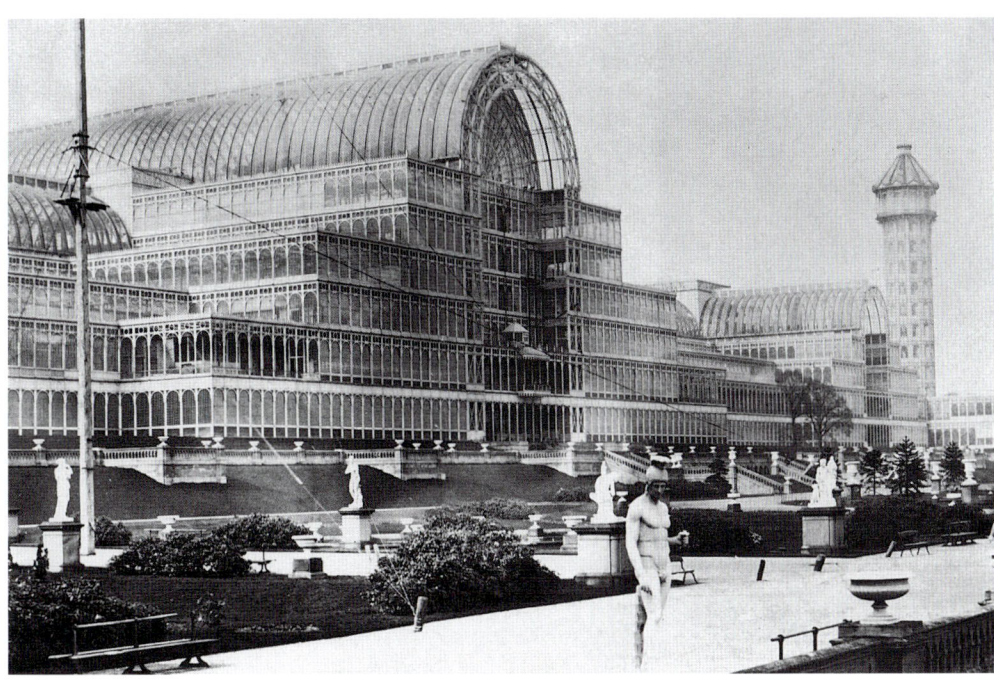

28-60 JOSEPH PAXTON, Crystal Palace, London, England, 1850–1851. Iron and glass. Victoria and Albert Museum, London.

middle class embraced both the comprehensible images of the new medium and its lower cost.

ARTISTIC RESPONSES TO PHOTOGRAPHY

For the traditional artist, photography suggested new answers to the great debate about what is real and how to represent the real in art. It also challenged the place of traditional modes of pictorial representation originating in the Renaissance. Artists as diverse as Delacroix, Ingres, the Realist Jean Désiré Gustave Courbet, and the Impressionist Edgar Degas welcomed photography as a helpful auxiliary to painting. They increasingly were intrigued by how photography translated three-dimensional objects onto a two-dimensional surface. Other artists, however, saw photography as a mechanism capable of displacing the painstaking work of skilled painters dedicated to representing the optical truth of chosen subjects. Photography's challenge to painting, both historically and technologically, seemed to some an expropriation of the realistic image, until then painting's exclusive property. But just as some painters looked to the new medium of photography for answers on how best to render an image in paint, so some photographers looked to painting for suggestions about ways to imbue the photographic image with qualities beyond simple reproduction. The collaborative efforts of Delacroix and the photographer EUGÈNE DURIEU (1800–1874) as seen in *Draped Model (back view)*, FIG. **28-61**, demonstrate the symbiotic relationship between painters and photographers. Although such a photograph provided Delacroix with a permanent image of the posed nude female model, photographers sometimes also attempted, as here, to create a mood through careful lighting and the draping of cloth.

DEVELOPING THE DAGUERREOTYPE

"Reality," "truth," "fact"—that elusive quality artists throughout time sought with painstaking effort in traditional media such as paint, crayon, and pen-and-ink—could seemingly be captured readily and with breathtaking accuracy by the new mechanical medium of photography. Artists themselves were instrumental in the development of this new technology. As early as the seventeenth century, artists such as Vermeer (see FIGS. 24-51, 24-52) had used an optical device called the camera obscura (literally, "dark room") to help them render the details of their subjects more accurately. These instruments were darkened chambers (some virtually portable closets) with optical lenses fitted into a hole in one wall that light entered through to project an inverted image of a subject onto the chamber's opposite wall. The artist could trace the main details from this image for later reworking and refinement. In 1807, the invention of the *camera lucida* (lighted room) replaced the enclosed chamber. Instead, a small prism lens, hung on a stand, projected the image of the object it had been "aimed" downward at onto a sheet of paper. Artists using either of these devices found this process long and arduous, no matter how accurate the resulting work. All yearned for a more direct way to capture a subject's image. Two very different scientific inventions that accomplished this were announced, almost simultaneously, in France and England in 1839.

The first new discovery was the *daguerreotype process,* named for LOUIS-JACQUES-MANDÉ DAGUERRE (1789–1851), one of its two inventors. The second, the calotype process, is discussed later. Daguerre had trained as an architect before becoming a theatrical set painter and designer. This background led him to open (with a friend) a popular entertainment called the Diorama. Audiences witnessed performances of "living paintings" created by changing the lighting effects on a "sandwich" composed of a painted backdrop and several layers of painted translucent front curtains. Daguerre used a camera obscura for the Diorama, but he wanted to find a more efficient and effective procedure. Through a mutual acquaintance, he was introduced to Joseph Nicéphore Nièpce, who in 1826 had successfully made a permanent picture of the cityscape outside his upper-story window by exposing, in a camera obscura, a metal plate covered with a light-sensitive coating. Although the eight-hour exposure time needed to record Nièpce's subject hampered the process, Daguerre's excitement over its possibilities led to a partnership between the two men to pursue its development. Nièpce died in 1833, but Daguerre continued to work on his own. He made two contributions to the process. He discovered latent development, bringing out the image through chemical solutions, which considerably shortened the length of time needed for exposure. Daguerre also discovered a better way to "fix" the image (again, chemically) by stopping the action of light on the photographic plate, which otherwise would continue to darken until the image could no longer be discerned.

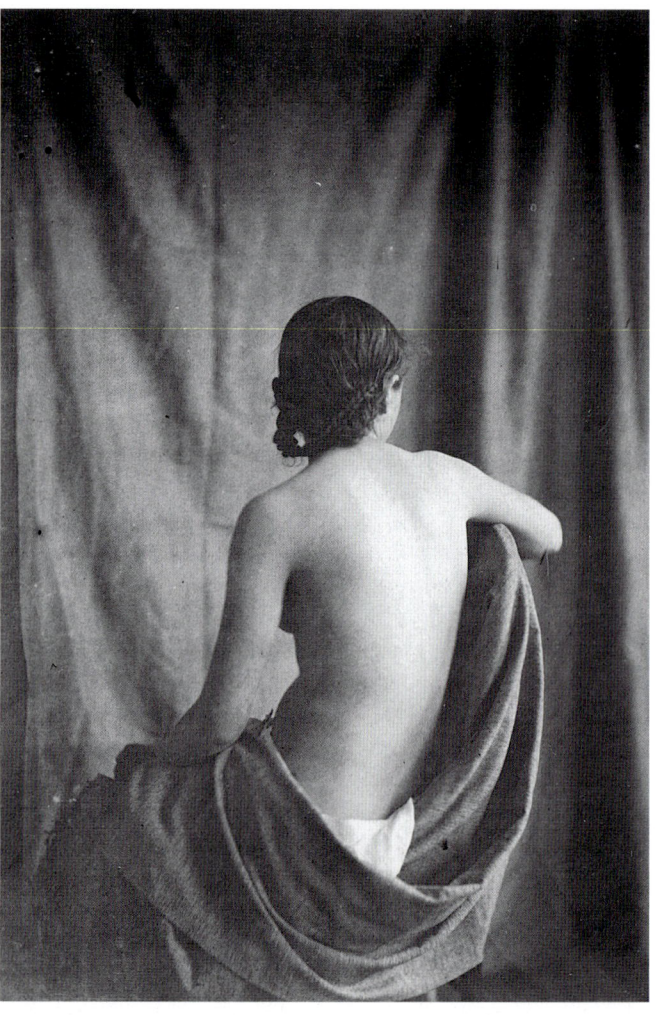

28-61 EUGÈNE DURIEU and EUGÈNE DELACROIX, *Draped Model (back view)*, ca. 1854. Albumen print, $7\frac{5}{16}'' \times 5\frac{1}{8}''$. J. Paul Getty Museum, Los Angeles.

The French government presented the new daguerreotype process at the Academy of Science in Paris on January 7, 1839, with the understanding that its details would be made available to all interested parties without charge (although the inventor received a large annuity in appreciation). Soon, people worldwide were taking pictures with the daguerreotype "camera" (a name shortened from *camera obscura*) in a process almost immediately christened *photography,* from the Greek *photos* (light) and *graphos* (writing). From the start, painters were intrigued with the possibilities of the process as a new art medium. Paul Delaroche, a leading painter of the day, wrote in an official report to the French government:

> Daguerre's process completely satisfies all the demands of art, carrying certain essential principles of art to such perfection that it must become a subject of observation and study even to the most accomplished painters. The pictures obtained by this method are as remarkable for the perfection of the details as for the richness and harmony of the general effect. Nature is reproduced in them not only with truth, but also with art.[26]

Each daguerreotype is a unique work, possessing amazing detail and finely graduated tones from black to white. Both qualities are evident in *Still Life in Studio* (FIG. **28-62**), one of the first successful plates Daguerre produced after perfecting his method. The process captured every detail—the subtle shapes, the varied textures, the diverse tones of light and shadow—in Daguerre's carefully constructed tableau. The three-dimensional forms of the sculptures, the basket, and the bits of cloth spring into high relief and are convincingly there within the image. Its composition was clearly inspired by seventeenth-century Dutch still lifes, such as those of Heda (see FIG. 24-54). Like Heda, Daguerre arranged his objects to reveal clearly their textures and shapes. Unlike a painter, however, Daguerre could not alter anything within his arrangement to effect a stronger image. However, he could suggest a symbolic meaning within his array of objects. Like the oysters and fruit in Heda's painting, Daguerre's sculptural and architectural fragments and the framed print of an embrace suggest that even art is vanitas and will not endure forever.

A PICTURE-PERFECT OPERATION In the United States, where the first daguerreotype was taken within two months of Daguerre's presentation in Paris, two particularly avid and resourceful advocates of the new medium were JOSIAH JOHNSON HAWES (1808–1901), a painter, and ALBERT SANDS SOUTHWORTH (1811–1894), a pharmacist and teacher. Together, they ran a daguerreotype studio in Boston that specialized in portraiture, then popular due to the shortened exposure time required for the process (although it was still long enough to require head braces to help subjects remain motionless while their photographs were taken).

The partners also, however, took their equipment outside the studio to record places and events of particular interest to them. One such image is *Early Operation under Ether, Massachusetts General Hospital* (FIG. **28-63**). This daguerreotype was taken from the vantage point of the gallery of a hospital operating room, putting viewers in the position of medical students looking down on a lecture-demonstration typical through the nineteenth century. An image of historic record, this early daguerreotype gives viewers a glimpse into the whole of Western medical practice. The focus of attention in *Early Operation* is the white-draped patient, who is surrounded by a circle of darkly clad doctors. The details of the figures and the room's furnishings are recorded clearly, but the slight blurring of several of the figures betrays motion during the exposure. The elevated viewpoint flattens the spatial perspective and emphasizes the relationships of the figures in ways the Impressionists, especially Degas, found intriguing.

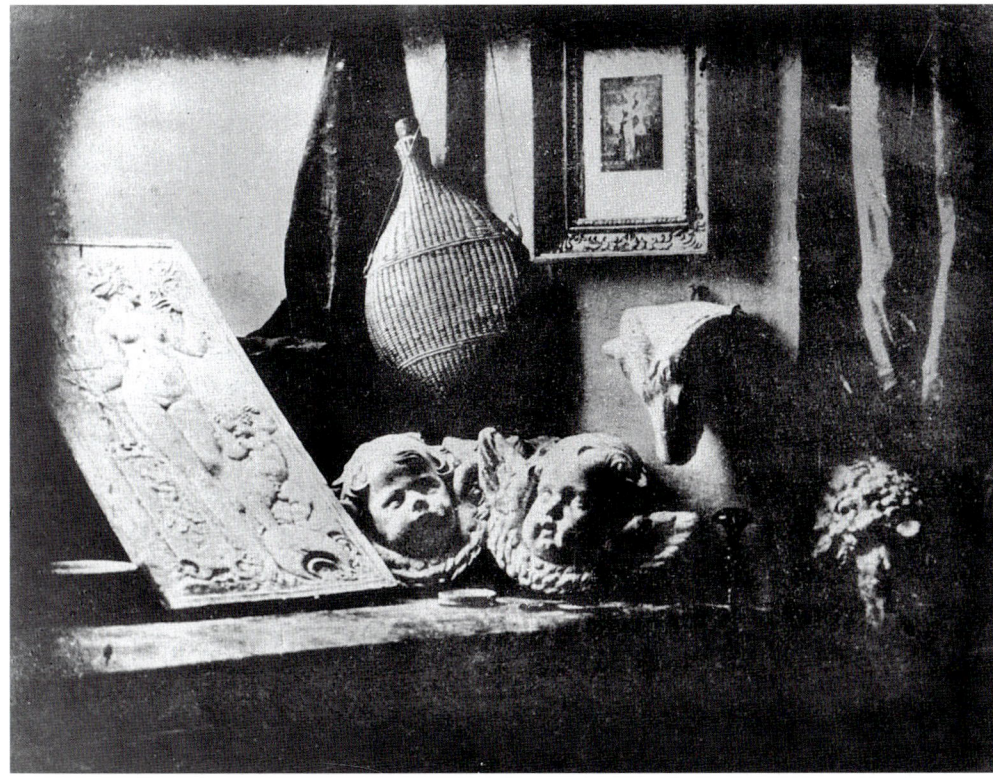

28-62 LOUIS-JACQUES-MANDÉ DAGUERRE, *Still Life in Studio,* 1837. Daguerreotype. Collection Société Française de Photographie, Paris.

28-63 Josiah Johnson Hawes and Albert Sands Southworth, *Early Operation under Ether, Massachusetts General Hospital,* ca. 1847. Daguerreotype. Massachusetts General Hospital Archives and Special Collections, Boston.

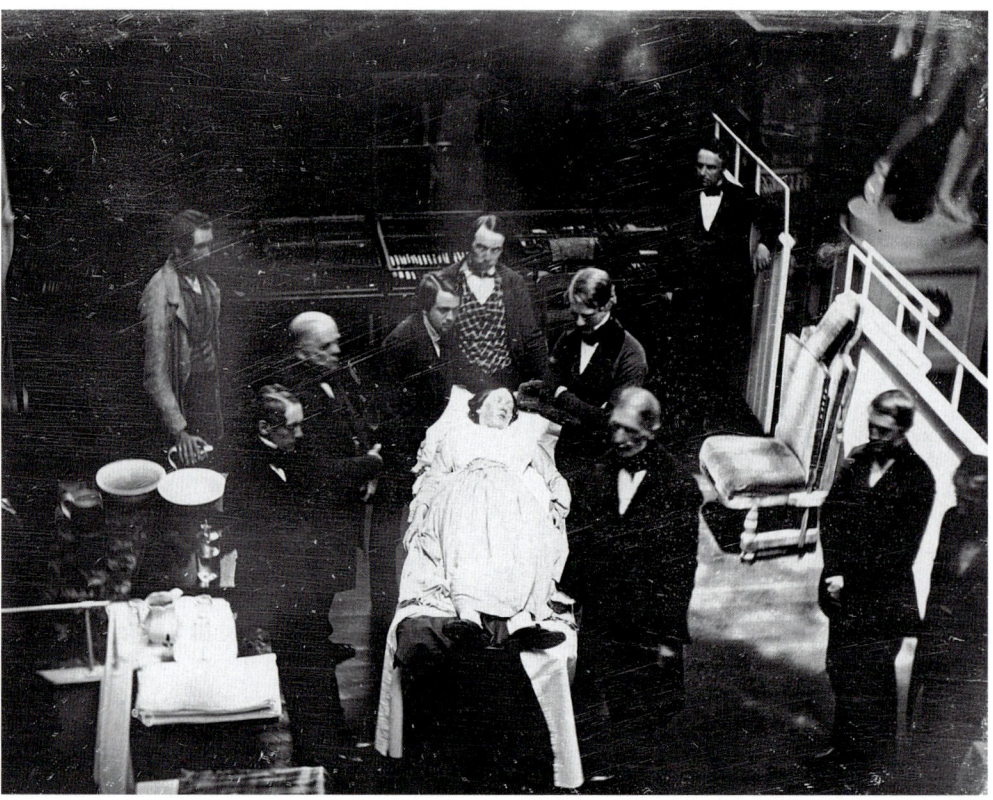

A BEAUTIFUL TYPE OF PHOTOGRAPHY The daguerreotype reigned supreme in photography until the 1850s, but the second major photographic invention was announced less than three weeks after Daguerre's method was unveiled in Paris and eventually replaced it. It was the ancestor of the modern negative-print system. On January 31, 1839, William Henry Fox Talbot (1800–1877) presented a paper on his "photogenic drawings" to the Royal Institution in London. As early as 1835, Talbot made "negative" images by placing objects on sensitized paper and exposing the arrangement to light. This created a design of light-colored silhouettes recording the places where opaque or translucent objects had blocked light from darkening the paper's emulsion. In his experiments, Talbot next exposed sensitized papers inside simple cameras and with a second sheet created "positive" images. He further improved the process with more light sensitive chemicals and a chemical development of the negative image. This technique allowed multiple prints. However, Talbot's process, which he named the *calotype* (a term he derived from the Greek term *kalos,* meaning "beautiful"), was limited by the fact its images incorporated the paper's texture. This produced a slightly blurred, grainy effect very different from the crisp detail and wide tonal range available with the daguerreotype. Aside from these drawbacks, the calotype image's widespread adoption primarily was prevented by the stiff licensing and equipment fees charged for many years after Talbot patented his new process in 1841. Due to both the look and the cost of the calotype, many photographers elected to stay with the daguerreotype until photographic technology could expand the calotype's capabilities.

CAPTURING AN ARTIST'S LIKENESS Portraiture was one of the first photography genres to use a technology that improved the calotype. Making portraits was an important economic component for most photographers, as Southworth and Hawes proved, but the greatest of the early portrait photographers was, undoubtedly, the Frenchman Gaspar-Félix Tournachon (1820–1910). Tournachon adopted the name Nadar for his professional career as novelist, journalist, enthusiastic balloonist, caricaturist, and, later, photographer. Photographic studies for his caricatures, which followed the tradition of Honoré Daumier's most satiric lithographs (see fig. 29-5), led Nadar to open a portrait studio. So talented was he at capturing the essence of his subjects that the most important people in France, including Delacroix, Daumier, Courbet, and the Impressionist Édouard Manet, flocked to his studio to have their portraits made. Nadar said he sought in his work "that instant of understanding that puts you in touch with the model—helps you sum him up, guides you to his habits, his ideas, and character and enables you to produce . . . a really convincing and sympathetic likeness, an intimate portrait."[27]

Nadar's skill in the genre can be seen in *Eugène Delacroix* (fig. **28-64**), which shows the painter at the height of his career. In this photograph, the artist appears with remarkable presence; even in half-length, his gesture and expression create a revealing mood that seems to tell viewers much about him. Perhaps Delacroix responded to Nadar's famous gift for putting his clients at ease by assuming the pose that best expressed his personality. The new photographic materials made possible the rich range of tones in Nadar's images. Glass negatives and albumen printing paper (prepared with egg white) could record finer detail and a wider range of light and shadow than Talbot's calotype process.

The new "wet-plate" technology (because this plate was exposed, developed, and fixed while wet) almost at once replaced both the daguerreotype and the calotype and became arms. Yet, with the wet plate, artists could make remarkable photographs of battlefields, the Alps, and even the traffic flow in crowded streets (see FIG. 29-22).

DOCUMENTING THE TRAGEDY OF WAR The photograph's documentary power was immediately realized. Thus began the story of the medium's influence on modern life and the immense changes it brought to communication and information management. For the historical record it was of unrivaled importance. Great events could be recorded on the spot and the views preserved for the first time. The photographs taken of the Crimean War (1856) by Roger Fenton (1819–1869) and of the American Civil War by Matthew B. Brady (1823–1896), Alexander Gardner (1821–1882), and TIMOTHY O'SULLIVAN (1840–1882) are still unsurpassed as incisive accounts of military life, unsparing in their truth to detail and poignant as expressions of human experience.

Of the Civil War photographs, the most moving are the inhumanly objective records of combat deaths. Perhaps the most reproduced of these Civil War photographs is O'Sullivan's *A Harvest of Death, Gettysburg, July 1863* (FIG. **28-65**). Although viewers might see this image as simple reportage, it also functions to impress on people the war's high price. Corpses litter the battlefield as far as the eye can see. O'Sullivan presented a scene that stretches far to the horizon. As the photograph modulates from the precise clarity of the bodies of Union soldiers in the foreground, boots stolen and pockets picked, to the almost illegible corpses in the distance, the suggestion of innumerable other dead soldiers is unavoidable. This "harvest" is far more sobering and depressing than that in Winslow Homer's Civil War image, *The Veteran in a New Field* (FIG. 28-55). Though it was years before photolithography could reproduce photographs like this in newspapers, they were publicly exhibited and made an impression that newsprint engravings never could.

Photography continued to impact significantly many aspects of art and public perceptions of "reality." The issues of reality and realism were addressed specifically in the movement that followed on the heels of Romanticism, Realism.

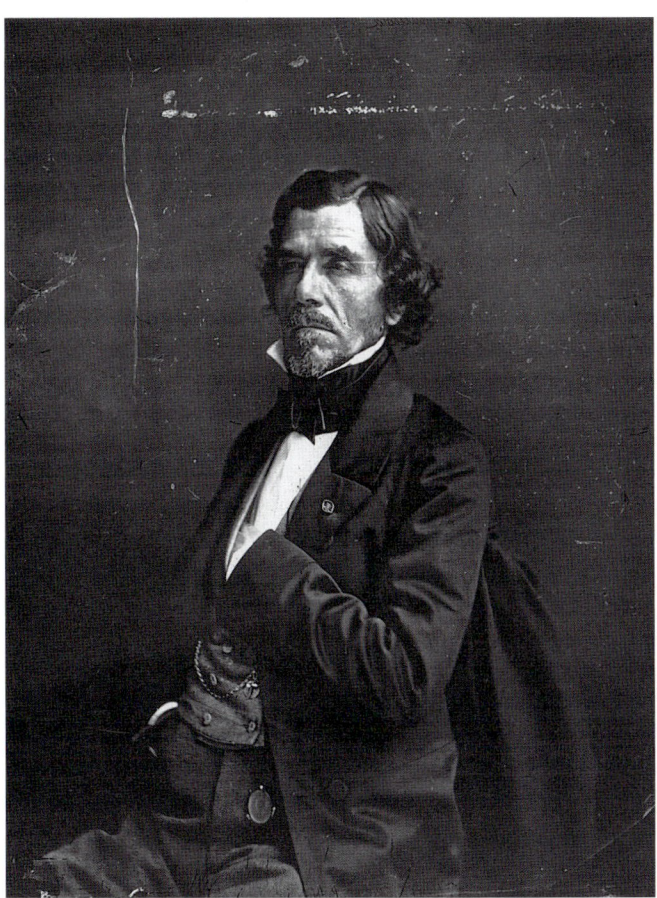

28-64 NADAR (GASPARD-FÉLIX TOURNACHON), *Eugène Delacroix,* ca. 1855. Modern print from original negative in the Bibliothèque Nationale, Paris.

the universal way of making negatives up to 1880. However, wet-plate photography had drawbacks. The plates had to be prepared and processed on the spot. To work outdoors meant taking along a portable darkroom of some sort—a wagon, tent, or box with light-tight sleeves for the photographer's

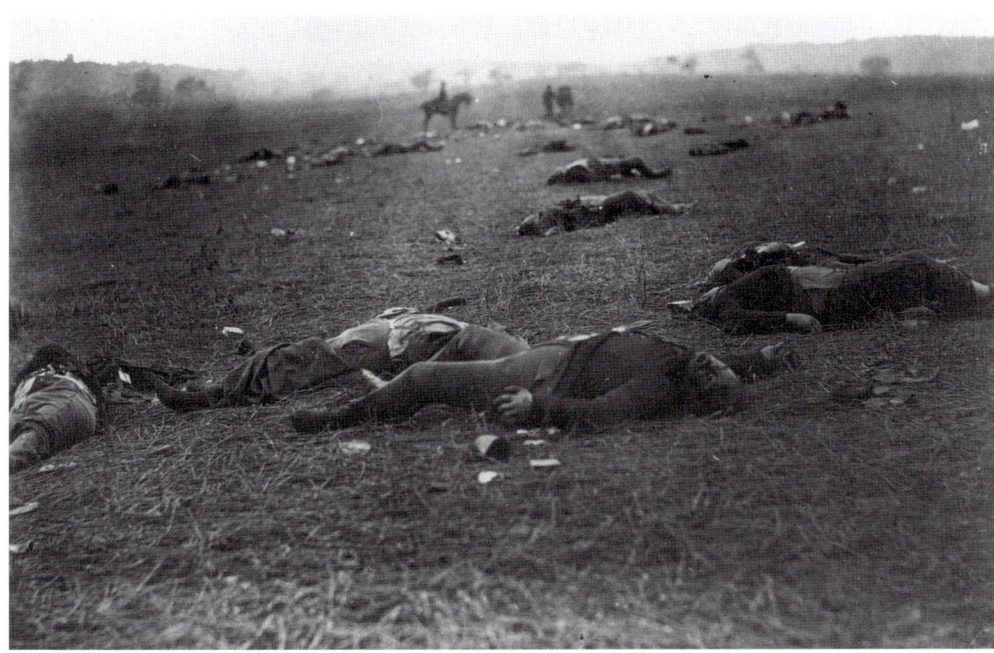

28-65 TIMOTHY O'SULLIVAN, *A Harvest of Death, Gettysburg, Pennsylvania, July 1863.* Negative by Timothy O'Sullivan. Original print by Alexander Gardner. The New York Public Library (Astor, Lenox and Tilden Foundations, Rare Books and Manuscript Division), New York.

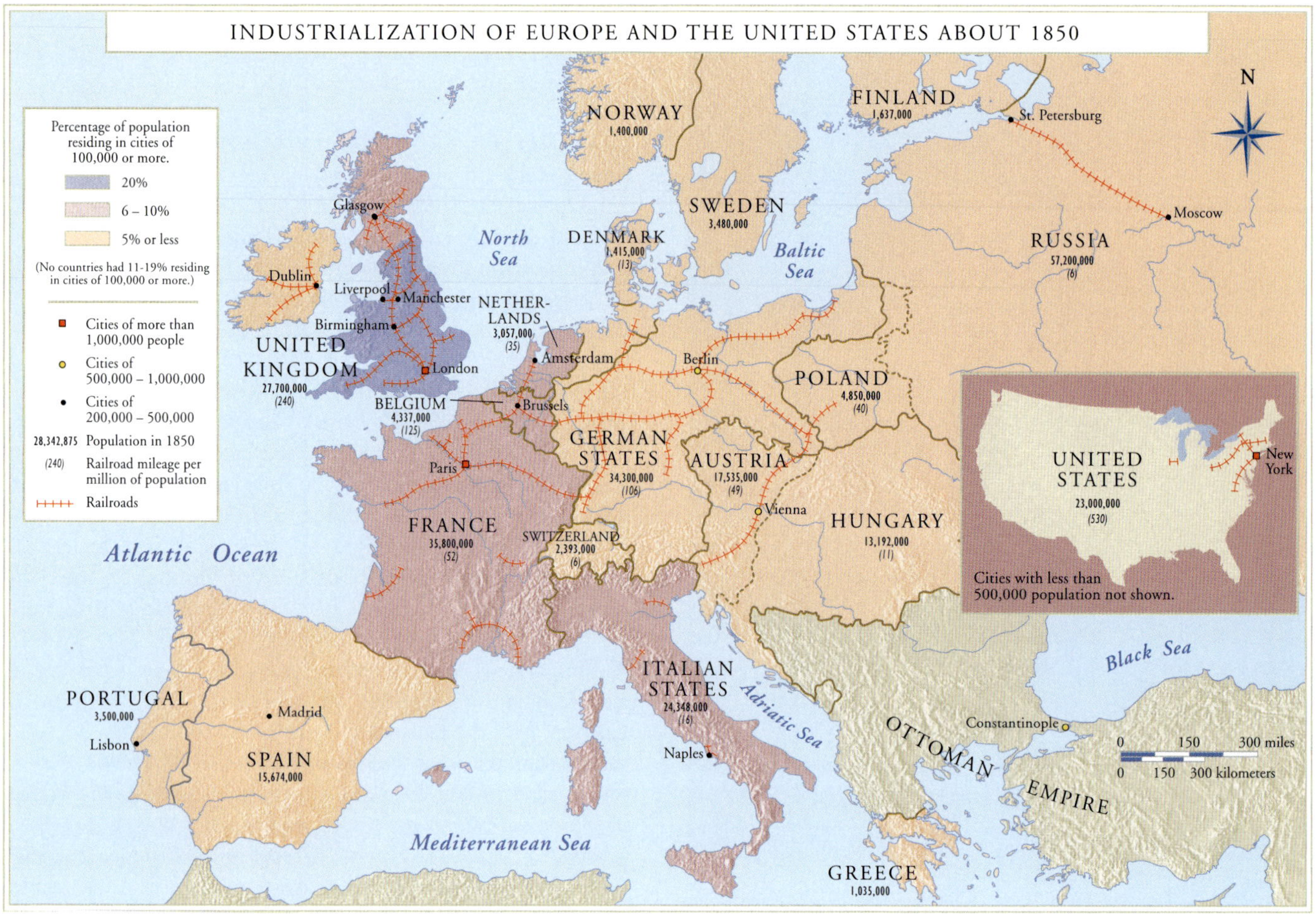

INDUSTRIALIZATION OF EUROPE AND THE UNITED STATES ABOUT 1850

Percentage of population residing in cities of 100,000 or more.

- 20%
- 6 – 10%
- 5% or less

(No countries had 11-19% residing in cities of 100,000 or more.)

- ■ Cities of more than 1,000,000 people
- ○ Cities of 500,000 – 1,000,000
- • Cities of 200,000 – 500,000

28,342,875 Population in 1850

(240) Railroad mileage per million of population

┼┼┼┼ Railroads

NORWAY 1,400,000

SWEDEN 3,480,000

FINLAND 1,637,000

St. Petersburg

Moscow

RUSSIA 57,200,000 (6)

DENMARK 1,415,000 (13)

Glasgow

UNITED KINGDOM 27,700,000 (240)

Dublin

Liverpool · Manchester

Birmingham

London

NETHER-LANDS 3,057,000 (35)

Amsterdam

Berlin

BELGIUM 4,337,000 (125)

Brussels

POLAND 4,850,000 (40)

Paris

GERMAN STATES 34,300,000 (106)

AUSTRIA 17,535,000 (49)

Vienna

FRANCE 35,800,000 (52)

SWITZERLAND 2,393,000 (6)

HUNGARY 13,192,000 (11)

North Sea

Baltic Sea

Atlantic Ocean

PORTUGAL 3,500,000

Lisbon

Madrid

SPAIN 15,674,000

ITALIAN STATES 24,348,000 (16)

Naples

Adriatic Sea

OTTOMAN EMPIRE

Constantinople

Black Sea

GREECE 1,035,000

Mediterranean Sea

UNITED STATES 23,000,000 (530)

New York

Cities with less than 500,000 population not shown.

| 0 | 150 | 300 miles |
| 0 | 150 | 300 kilometers |

| 1850 | 1860 | 1870 | 1880 |

VICTORIA   SECOND REPUBLIC

NAPOLEON III (THE SECOND EMPIRE)   THIRD REPUBLIC

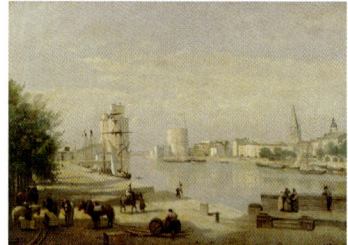

*Jean-Baptiste-Camille Corot
The Harbor of La Rochelle
(Le Port de la Rochelle), 1851*

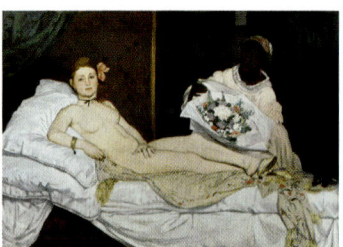

*Edouard Manet
Olympia, 1863*

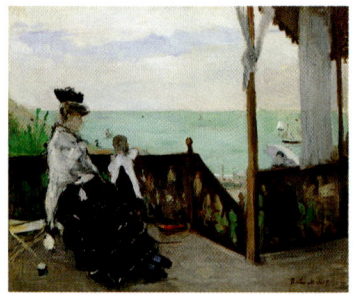

*Berthe Morisot
Villa at the Seaside, 1874*

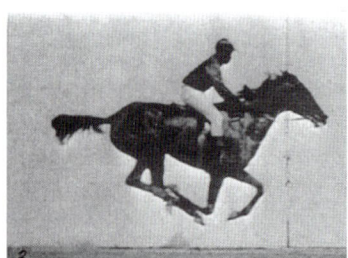

*Eadweard Muybridge
Horse Galloping, 1878*

Charles Darwin 1809–1882, *Origin of Species*, 1859

Karl Marx, 1818–1883

Fredrich Engels, 1820–1895

American Civil War 1861–1865

Paris Commune, 1870–1871

Franco-Prussian War, 1870–1871

Foundation of German Empire, 1871

Third Republic, 1871–1940

Unification of Italy, 1871

Clerk-Maxwell theory of electromagnetic radiation, 1873

THE RISE OF
MODERNISM

THE LATER NINETEENTH CENTURY

1885	1890	1895	1900	1905

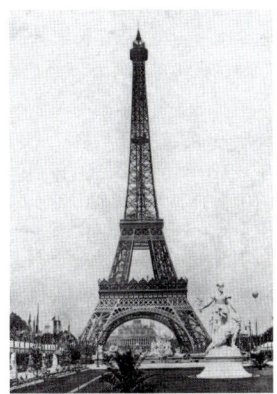

Alexandre Gustave Eiffel
Eiffel Tower, Paris, 1889

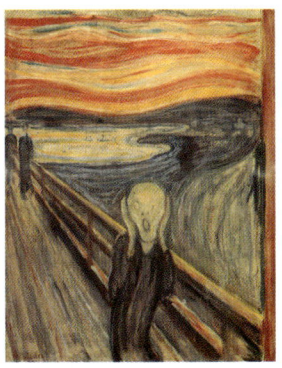

Edvard Munch
The Cry, 1893

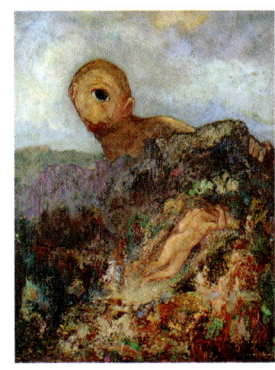

Odilon Redon
The Cyclops, 1898

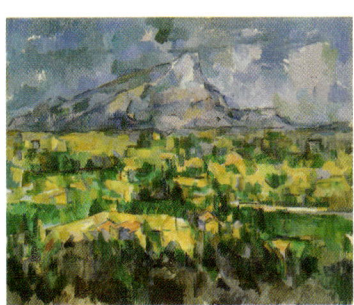

Paul Cézanne
Mont Sainte-Victoire, 1902–1904

First movie camera patented, 1891

European colonization
of African completed, 1900

INDUSTRIALIZATION, URBANIZATION, AND EXPANDING GLOBAL CONSCIOUSNESS

THE SECOND INDUSTRIAL REVOLUTION   The momentous Western developments of the early nineteenth century—industrialization, urbanization, and increased economic and political interaction worldwide—matured quickly during the latter half of the century. The Industrial Revolution in England, which had distinguished that country from others on the European continent, spread throughout Europe and to the United States. Because of this dramatic expansion, the third quarter of the nineteenth century is often referred to as the Second Industrial Revolution. While the first Industrial Revolution centered on textiles, steam, and iron, the second was associated with steel, electricity, chemicals, and oil. The discoveries in these fields provided the foundation for developments in plastics, machinery, building construction, and automobile manufacturing and paved the way for the invention of the radio, electric light, telephone, and electric streetcar.

One of the most significant consequences of industrialization was urbanization. The number and size of Western cities grew dramatically during the latter part of the nineteenth century, largely due to migration from rural regions. Rural dwellers relocated to urban centers because of expanded agricultural enterprises that squeezed the smaller property owners from the land. The widely available work opportunities in the cities, especially in the factories, were also a major factor in this migration. In addition, the improving health and living conditions in the cities contributed to their explosive growth.

REAFFIRMING A FAITH IN SCIENCE   An increasing emphasis on science was another characteristic of this period. Advances in industrial technology reinforced the Enlightenment's foundation of rationalism. The connection between science and progress seemed obvious to many, both in intellectual circles and among the general public, and, increasingly, people embraced empiricism (the search for knowledge based on observation and direct experience). Indicative of the widespread faith in science was the influence of positivism, a Western philosophical model that promoted science as the mind's highest achievement. Positivism was developed by the French philosopher Auguste Comte (1798–1857), who advocated a purely scientific, empirical approach to nature and society. Comte believed that scientific laws governed the environment and human activity and could be revealed through careful recording and analysis of observable data.

THE SURVIVAL OF THE FITTEST   The English naturalist Charles Darwin (1809–1882) and his theory of natural selection did much to increase interest in science. Although the concept of evolution had been suggested earlier, Darwin and his compatriot Alfred Russel Wallace (1823–1913), working independently, articulated the theory of natural selection, which proposed a model for the process of evolution. They based this theory on mechanistic laws, rather than attributing evolution to random chance or God's plan, and argued for a competitive system in which only the fittest survived. Darwin's ideas, as presented in *Origin of Species* (1859), sharply contrasted with the biblical narrative of Cre-

ation and thus were highly controversial. By challenging traditional Christian beliefs, Darwinism contributed to a growing secular attitude.

Other theorists and social thinkers, most notably British philosopher Herbert Spencer, applied Darwin's principles to the rapidly changing socioeconomic realm. As in the biological world, they asserted, industrialization's intense competition led to the survival of the most economically fit companies, enterprises, and countries. This logic served to justify the rampant Western racism, imperialism, nationalism, and militarism that marked the late nineteenth and early twentieth centuries. Because of the pseudoscientific basis of this Social Darwinism, those who espoused this theory perceived such conflict and struggle as inevitable.

KARL MARX AND CLASS STRUGGLE   The concept of conflict was central to the ideas of Karl Marx (1818–1883), another dominant figure of the period. Born to German-Jewish parents in Trier, Marx received a doctorate in philosophy from the University of Berlin. After moving to Paris, he met fellow German Friedrich Engels (1820–1895), who became his lifelong collaborator. Together they wrote the *Communist Manifesto* (1848), which called for the working class to overthrow the capitalist system. Like Darwin and other empiricists, Marx believed that scientific, rational law governed nature and, indeed, all human history. For Marx, economic forces based on class struggle induced historical change. Throughout history, insisted Marx, those who controlled the means of production conflicted with those whose labor was exploited to benefit the wealthy and powerful. This constant opposition—the dynamic he called "dialectical materialism"—caused change. Marxism's ultimate goal was to create a socialist state—the seizure of power by the working class and the destruction of capitalism. Marxism, which had great appeal to the oppressed as well as to many intellectuals, emphasized class conflict and was instrumental in the rise of trade unions and socialist groups.

COLONIZING THE WORLD   Many of these important developments—for example, industrialization and Social Darwinism—help to explain this period's extensive imperialism. Industrialization required a wide variety of natural resources, and Social Darwinists easily translated their intrinsic concept of social hierarchy into racial and national hierarchies. These hierarchies provided Western leaders with justification for the colonization of peoples and cultures that they deemed "less advanced." By 1900, the major economic and political powers had divided up much of the world. The French had colonized most of North Africa and Indochina, while the British occupied India, Australia, and large areas of Africa, including Nigeria, Egypt, Sudan, Rhodesia, and the Union of South Africa. The Dutch were a major presence in the Pacific, and the Germans, Portuguese, Spanish, and Italians all established themselves in various areas of Africa.

MODERNITY AND MODERNISM   The combination of the extensive technological changes and increased exposure to other cultures, coupled with the rapidity of these changes, led to an acute sense in Western cultures of the world's lack of fixity or permanence. The Darwinian ideas of evolution and Marx's emphasis on a continuing sequence of conflicts and resolutions reinforced this awareness of a constantly shifting reality. These societal changes prompted a greater consciousness of and interest in modernity—the state of being modern. This avid exploration of the conditions of modernity and of people's position relative to a historical continuum permeated the Western art world as well, resulting in the development of *modernism*. Modernist art is differentiated from modern art by its critical function. Modern art, as discussed in Chapter 28, is more or less a chronological designation, referring to art of the past few centuries. Modern artists were and are aware of the relationship between their art and that of previous eras. Modernism developed in the second half of the nineteenth century and is "modern" in that modernist artists, then and now, often seek to capture the images and sensibilities of their age. However, modernism goes beyond simply dealing with the present and involves the artist's critical examination of or reflection on the premises of art itself. *Modernism* thus implies certain concerns about art and aesthetics that are internal to art production, regardless of whether or not the artist is producing scenes from contemporary social life.

Clement Greenberg, a twentieth-century American art critic, explained: "The essence of Modernism lies . . . in the use of the characteristic methods of a discipline to criticize the discipline itself—not in order to subvert it, but to entrench it more firmly in its area of competence."[1] He explains further what he means by "criticize the discipline:" "Realistic, illusionist art had dissembled [disguised] the medium, using art to conceal art. Modernism used art to call attention to art. The limitations that constitute the medium of painting—the flat surface, the shape of the support, the properties of pigment—were treated by the Old Masters as negative factors that could be acknowledged only implicitly or indirectly. Modernist painting has come to regard these same limitations as positive factors that are to be acknowledged openly."[2] The two major modernist art movements of the later nineteenth century were Realism and Impressionism, and both were conditioned by the historical and theoretical milieu in which they incubated.

This critical, modernist stance challenged the more conservative approach of the academies, where artists received traditional training. Eventually, toward the end of the century, the aggressiveness of modernism led to the development of the avant-garde—artists whose work emphatically rejected the past and transgressed the boundaries of conventional artistic practice. The subversive dimension of the avant-garde was in sync with the anarchic, revolutionary sociopolitical tendencies in Europe at the time. The art of the Post-Impressionists, such as Vincent van Gogh, Paul Gauguin, Georges Seurat, and Paul Cézanne, was among the first labeled "avant-garde." The end of the nineteenth century, with its unique *fin-de-siècle* (end of the century) culture, paved the way for the entrenchment of modernism and the avant-garde in the twentieth century.

REALISM: THE PAINTING OF MODERN LIFE

Realism was a movement that developed in France around midcentury. GUSTAVE COURBET (1819–1877), long regarded as the leading figure of the Realist movement in nineteenth-century art, used the term "realism" when exhibiting his own works, even though he shunned labels. In and since Courbet's time, confusion about what Realism is has been widespread. Writing in 1857, Jules-Francois-Félix Husson Champfleury (1821–1889), one of the first critics to recognize and appreciate Courbet's work, declared: "I will not define *Realism*. . . . I do not know where it comes from, where it goes, what it is; . . . The name horrifies me by its pedantic ending; . . . there is enough confusion already about that famous word."[3] Confusion, or at least disagreement, about Realism still exists among historians of nineteenth- and, for that matter, twentieth-century art.

REDEFINING REALITY The work of the Realists, in essence, provides viewers with a reevaluation of "reality." Like the empiricists and positivists, Realist artists argued that only the things of one's own time, what people can see for themselves, are "real." Accordingly, Realists focused their attention on the experiences and sights of everyday contemporary life and disapproved of traditional and fictional subjects on the grounds that they were not real and visible and were not of the present world. Courbet declared in 1861:

> To be able to translate the customs, ideas, and appearances of my time as I see them—in a word, to create a living art—this has been my aim. . . . [T]he art of painting can consist only in the representation of objects visible and tangible to the painter . . . , [who must apply] his personal faculties to the ideas and the things of the period in which he lives. . . . I hold also that painting is an essentially *concrete* art, and can consist only of the representation of things both *real* and *existing*. . . . An *abstract* object, invisible or nonexistent, does not belong to the domain of painting. . . . Show me an angel, and I'll paint one.[4]

This sincerity about scrutinizing the world around them led the Realists to expand their repertoire of subject matter beyond the conventional, established themes and scenes. The Realists portrayed objects and images that until then had been deemed unworthy of depiction—the mundane and trivial, working class laborers and peasants, and so forth. Even further, the Realists depicted these scenes on a scale and with an earnestness and seriousness previously reserved for grand history painting.

THE LOWEST OF THE LOW In *The Stone Breakers* (FIG. **29-1**), Courbet presented viewers with a glimpse into the life of a rural toiler. Courbet captured on canvas in straightforward manner two males—one mature, the other very young—in the act of breaking stones, traditionally the lot of the lowest in society. Their menial labor is neither romanticized nor idealized but is shown with directness and accuracy. Courbet revealed to viewers the drudgery of this labor. His palette's dirty browns and grays convey the dreary and dismal nature of the task, while the angular positioning of the older stone breaker's limbs suggests a mechanical monotony.

This interest in the laboring poor as subject matter had special meaning for the mid-nineteenth-century French audience. In 1848, workers rebelled against the bourgeois leaders of the newly formed Second Republic and against the rest of the nation, demanding better working conditions and a redistribution of property. The army quelled the revolution in

29-1 GUSTAVE COURBET, *The Stone Breakers,* 1849. Oil on canvas, 5′ 3″ × 8′ 6″. Formerly at Gemäldegalerie, Dresden (destroyed in 1945).

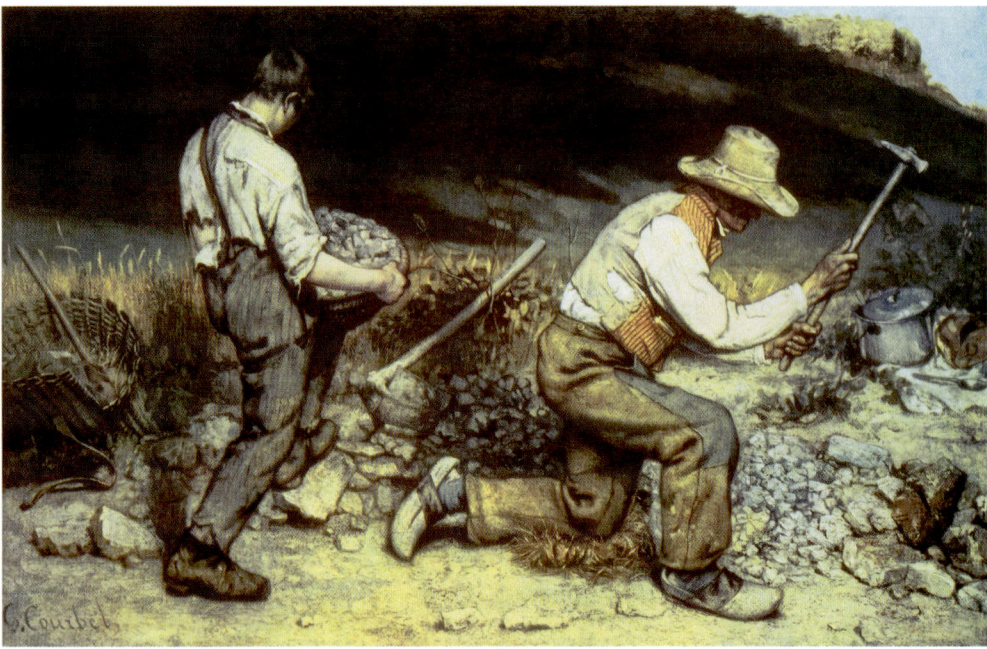

three days, but not without significant loss of life and long-lasting trauma. The Revolution of 1848 thus raised the issue of labor as a national concern and placed workers on center stage, both literally and symbolically. Courbet's depiction of stone breakers in 1849 was thus truly authentic and populist.

THE ANONYMITY OF PEASANT LIFE Also representative of Courbet's work is *Burial at Ornans* (FIG. **29-2**), which depicts a funeral in a bleak provincial landscape attended by "common, trivial" persons, the type of people Honoré de Balzac and Gustave Flaubert presented in their novels.[5] While an officious clergyman reads the Office of the Dead, those attending cluster around the excavated gravesite, their faces registering all degrees of response to the situation.

Although the painting has the monumental scale of a traditional history painting, the subject's ordinariness and the starkly antiheroic composition horrified contemporary critics. Arranged in a wavering line extending across the broad horizontal width of the canvas, the figures are portrayed in groups—the somberly clad women at the back right, a semi-circle of similarly clad men by the open grave, and assorted churchmen at the left. The observer's attention, however, is wholly on the wall of figures, seen at eye level in person, that blocks any view into deep space. The faces are portraits; some of the models were Courbet's friends. Behind and above the figures are bands of overcast sky and barren cliffs. The dark

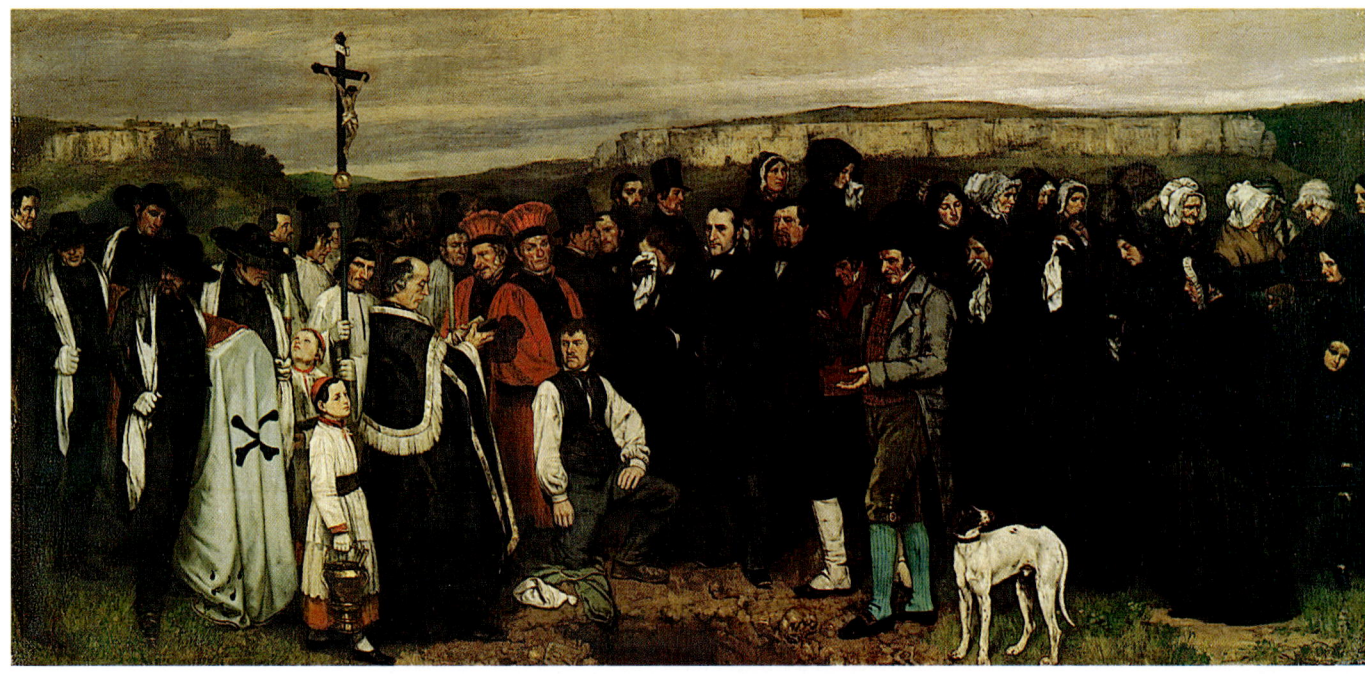

29-2 GUSTAVE COURBET, *Burial at Ornans,* 1849. Oil on canvas, approx. 10′ × 22′. Louvre, Paris.

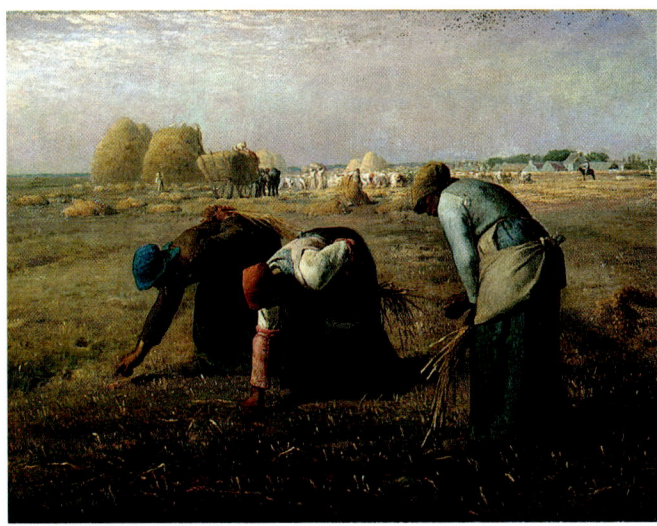

29-3 JEAN-FRANÇOIS MILLET, *The Gleaners,* 1857. Oil on canvas, approx. 2′ 9″ × 3′ 8″. Louvre, Paris.

pit of the grave opens into the viewer's space in the center foreground. Despite the unposed look of the figures, the artist controlled the composition in a masterful way by his sparing use of bright color. The heroic, the sublime, and the terrible are not found here—only the drab facts of undramatized life and death. In 1857, Champfleury wrote of *Burial at Ornans,* ". . . it represents a small-town funeral and yet reproduces the funerals of *all* small towns."[6] Unlike the superhuman or non-human actors on the grand stage of the Romantic canvas, this Realist work moves according to the ordinary rhythms of contemporaneous life.

EMPHASIZING THE PAINTED SURFACE   Viewed as the first modernist movement by many scholars and critics,

Realism also involved a reconsideration of the painter's primary goals and departed from the established priority on illusionism. Accordingly, Realists called attention to painting as a pictorial construction by their pigment application or composition manipulation. Courbet's intentionally simple and direct methods of expression in composition and technique seemed unbearably crude to many of his more traditional contemporaries, and he was called a primitive. Although his bold, somber palette was essentially traditional, Courbet often used the palette knife for quickly placing and unifying large daubs of paint, producing a roughly wrought surface. His example inspired the young artists who worked for him (and later Impressionists such as Claude Monet and Auguste Renoir), but the public accused him of carelessness and critics wrote of his "brutalities."

Because of both the style and content of Courbet's paintings, they were not well received. The jury selecting work for the Paris International Exhibition in 1855 rejected two of his paintings on the grounds that his subjects and figures were too coarsely depicted (so much so as to be plainly "socialistic") and too large. In response, Courbet set up his own exhibition outside the grounds, calling it the Pavilion of Realism. Courbet's pavilion and his utterances amounted to the new movement's manifestoes. Although he maintained he founded no school and was of no school, he did, as the name of his pavilion suggests, accept the term "realism" as descriptive of his art.

A PAINTER OF COUNTRY LIFE   Like Courbet, JEAN-FRANÇOIS MILLET (1814–1878) found his subjects in the people and occupations of the everyday world. Millet was one of a group of French painters of country life who, to be close to their rural subjects, settled near the village of Barbizon in the forest of Fontainebleau. This "Barbizon" school specialized in detailed pictures of forest and countryside. Millet,

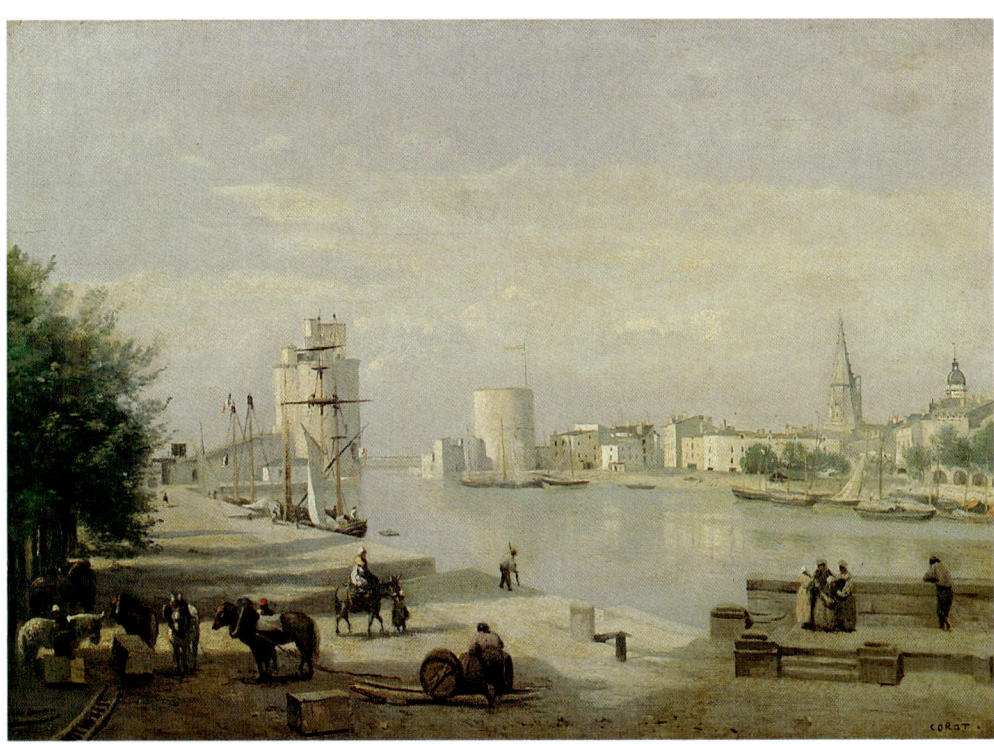

29-4 JEAN-BAPTISTE-CAMILLE COROT, *The Harbor of La Rochelle (Le Port de la Rochelle),* 1851. Oil on canvas, approx. 1′ 8″ × 2′ 4″. Yale University Art Gallery, New Haven (bequest of Stephen Carlton Clark, B.A., 1903).

perhaps their most prominent member, was of peasant stock and identified with the hard lot of the country poor. In *The Gleaners* (FIG. **29-3**), he depicted three peasant women performing the back-breaking task of gleaning the last wheat scraps. These women were members of the lowest level of peasant society, and such impoverished people were permitted to pick up the remainders left in the field after the harvest. Millet characteristically placed his monumental figures in the foreground, against a broad sky. Although the field stretches back to a rim of haystacks, cottages, trees, and distant workers and a flat horizon, viewers' attention is drawn to the gleaners quietly doing their tedious and time-consuming work.

Although Millet's works have a sentimentality absent from those of Courbet, the French public reacted to paintings such as *The Gleaners* with disdain and suspicion. In the aftermath of the Revolution of 1848, Millet's investing the poor with solemn grandeur did not meet with the approval of the prosperous classes. The middle-class mind linked it with the dangerous, newly defined working class, which was finding outspoken champions in men such as Karl Marx, Friedrich Engels, Pierre Proudhon, Honoré de Balzac, Gustave Flaubert, Émile Zola, and Charles Dickens. Socialism was a growing movement, and its views on property and its call for social justice, even economic equality, frightened the bourgeoisie. Millet's sympathetic depiction of the poor seemed to many like a political manifesto.

COROT'S PRECISE LANDSCAPES   The Realist nature of *The Gleaners* is evident on comparing it to a landscape painting, *The Harbor of La Rochelle* (FIG. **29-4**) by JEAN-BAPTISTE-CAMILLE COROT (1796–1875), another French artist closely associated with the Barbizon school. Although both paintings share a calm mood and precise composition, Corot's interest in *The Harbor of La Rochelle* is clearly on the landscape as a setting, and the people depicted—small in

scale—populate the scene like any other object, the trees, barrels, or horses. For Millet, however, the gleaners and their laborious task were central. Corot is not generally viewed as a Realist, although his commitment to the faithful rendering of scenes he encountered allies him with the Realist spirit.

LAMPOONING THE POWERS THAT BE   Because people widely recognized the power of art to serve political means, the political and social agitation accompanying the violent revolutions in France and the rest of Europe in the later eighteenth and early nineteenth centuries prompted the French people to suspect artists of subversive intention. A person could be jailed for too bold a statement in the press, in literature, in art—even in music and drama. Realist artist HONORÉ DAUMIER (1808–1879) boldly confronted authority with social criticism and political protest, and in response the authorities imprisoned the artist. Daumier—painter, sculptor, and, like Goya, one of the world's great masters of the graphic (print) medium—was a defender of the urban working classes, as Millet was a defender of the farming poor. The satirical lithographs Daumier contributed to the liberal French Republican journal *Caricature* found a wide audience. In these prints, he mercilessly lampooned the foibles and misbehavior of politicians, lawyers, doctors, and the rich bourgeoisie in general. His in-depth knowledge of the acute political and social unrest in Paris during the revolutions of 1830 and 1848 endowed his work with truthfulness and, therefore, impact.

His lithograph, *Rue Transnonain* (FIG. **29-5**), depicts an atrocity with the same shocking impact as Goya's *The Third of May, 1808* (see FIG. 28-39). The title refers to a street in Paris where an unknown sniper killed a civil guard, part of a government force trying to repress a worker demonstration. Because the fatal shot had come from a workers' housing block, the remaining guards immediately stormed the building

29-5   HONORÉ DAUMIER, *Rue Transnonain,* 1834. Lithograph, approx. 1′ × 1′ 5$\frac{1}{2}$″. Philadelphia Museum of Art, Philadelphia (bequest of Fiske and Marie Kimball).

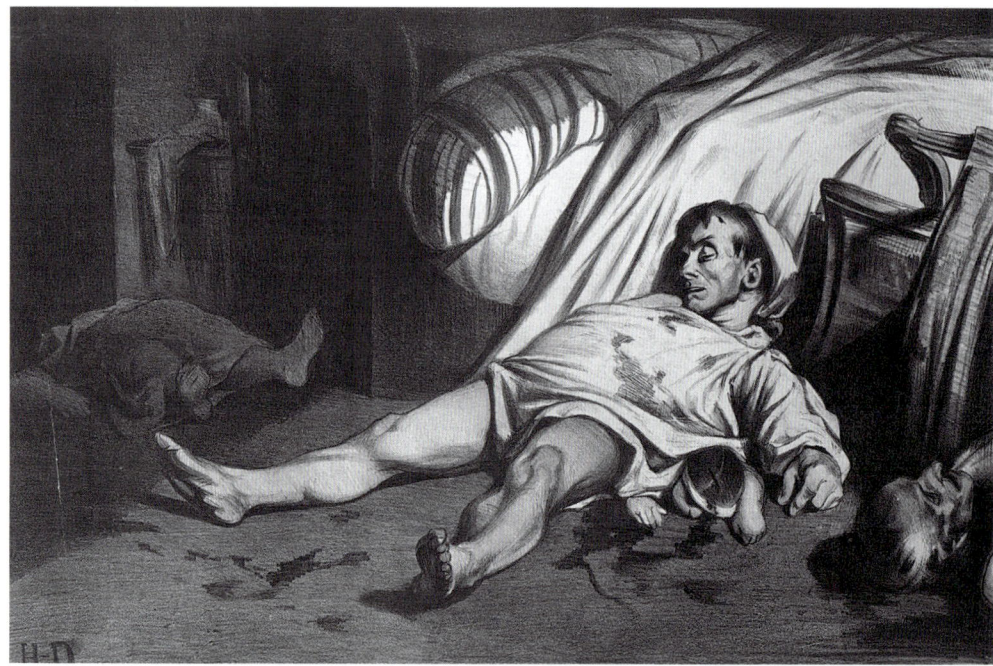

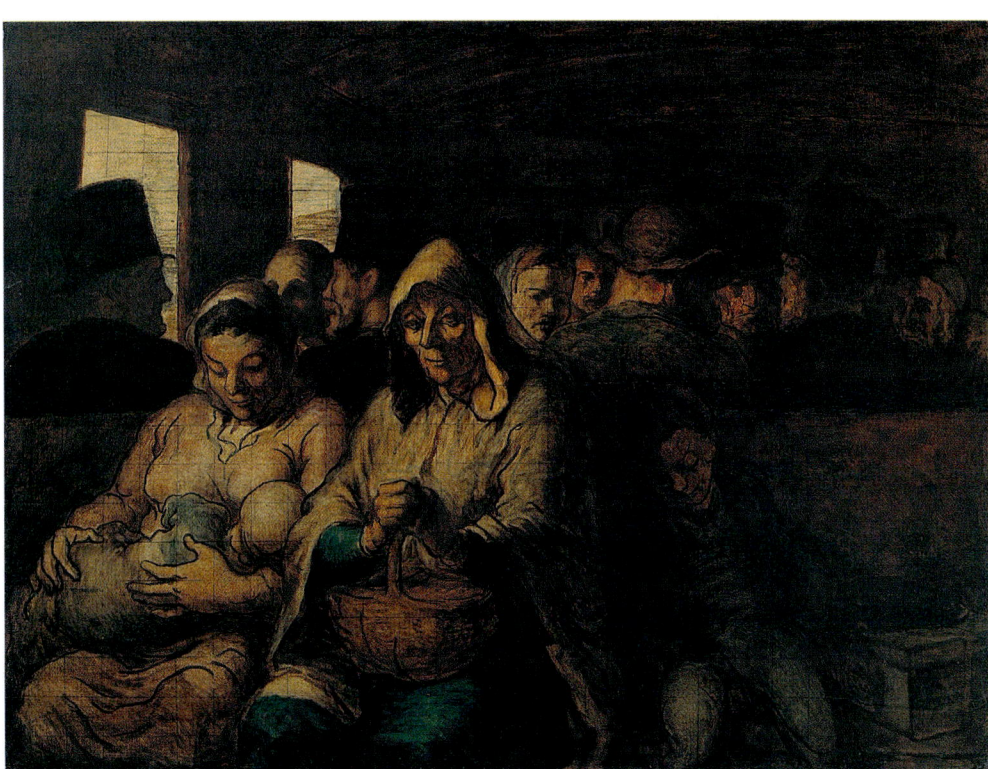

29-6 HONORÉ DAUMIER, *The Third-Class Carriage,* ca. 1862. Oil on canvas, 2' 1¾" × 2' 11½". Metropolitan Museum of Art, New York (H. O. Havemeyer Collection, bequest of Mrs. H. O. Havemeyer, 1929).

massacred all of its inhabitants. With Goya's power, Daumier created a view of the atrocity from a sharp, realistic angle of vision. He depicted not the dramatic moment of execution but the terrible, quiet aftermath. The broken, scattered forms lie amid violent disorder, as if newly found. The print's significance lies in its factualness. It is an example of the period's increasing artistic bias toward using facts as subject, and not always illusionistically. Daumier's pictorial manner is rough and spontaneous; how it carries expressive exaggeration is part of its remarkable force. Daumier's work is true to life in content, but his style is uniquely personal.

THE PLIGHT OF THE URBAN POOR Daumier brought the same convictions exhibited in his graphic work to the paintings he did, especially after 1848. His unfinished *The Third-Class Carriage* (FIG. **29-6**) provides a glimpse into the cramped and grimy railway carriage of the 1860s. The riders are poor and can afford only third-class tickets. While first- and second-class carriages had closed compartments, third-class passengers were crammed together on hard benches that filled the carriage. The disinherited masses of nineteenth-century industrialism were Daumier's indignant concern, and he made them his subject repeatedly. He showed them in the unposed attitudes and unplanned arrangements of the millions thronging the modern cities—anonymous, insignificant, dumbly patient with a lot they could not change. Daumier saw people as they ordinarily appeared, their faces vague, impersonal, and blank—unprepared for any observers. He tried to achieve the real by isolating a random collection of the unrehearsed details of human existence from the continuum of ordinary life. Daumier's vision anticipated the spontaneity and candor of scenes captured with the modern snapshot camera by the end of the century.

PROMISCUITY IN A PARISIAN PARK? Like Gustave Courbet, the commitment of ÉDOUARD MANET (1832–1883) to Realist ideas was instrumental in affecting the course of modernist painting. Manet was a pivotal figure during the nineteenth century. Not only was his work critical for the articulation of Realist principles, but his art played an important role in the development of Impressionism in the 1870s. When attempting to explain the critique of the discipline central to modernism, art historians often have looked to Manet's paintings (FIGS. 29-7, 29-8, and 29-24) as prime examples. Manet's interest in Realism and in modernist principles is evident in *Le Déjeuner sur l'herbe,* or *Luncheon on the Grass* (FIG. **29-7**).

Although historians can suggest precedents for the theme of *Le Déjeuner* (for example, the pastoral paintings of Giorgione, Titian, and Watteau), nothing about the painting's foreground figures recalls those earlier models. In fact, the foreground figures were all based on living, identifiable people. The seated nude is Victorine Meurend (Manet's favorite model at the time), and the gentlemen are his brother Eugène (with cane) and the sculptor Ferdinand Leenhof. The two men wear fashionable Parisian attire of the 1860s, and the foreground nude is not only a distressingly unidealized figure type, but she also seems disturbingly unabashed and at ease, looking directly at the viewer without shame or flirtatiousness.

This outraged the public—rather than a traditional pastoral scene, *Le Déjeuner* seemed merely to represent the promiscuous in a Parisian park. One hostile critic, no doubt voicing public opinion, said:

> A commonplace woman of the demimonde [the realm of the promiscuous woman, especially prostitutes], as naked as can be, shamelessly lolls between two dandies dressed to the teeth. These

29-7 ÉDOUARD MANET, *Le Déjeuner sur l'herbe (Luncheon on the Grass)*, 1863. Oil on canvas, approx. 7′ × 8′ 10″. Musée d'Orsay, Paris.

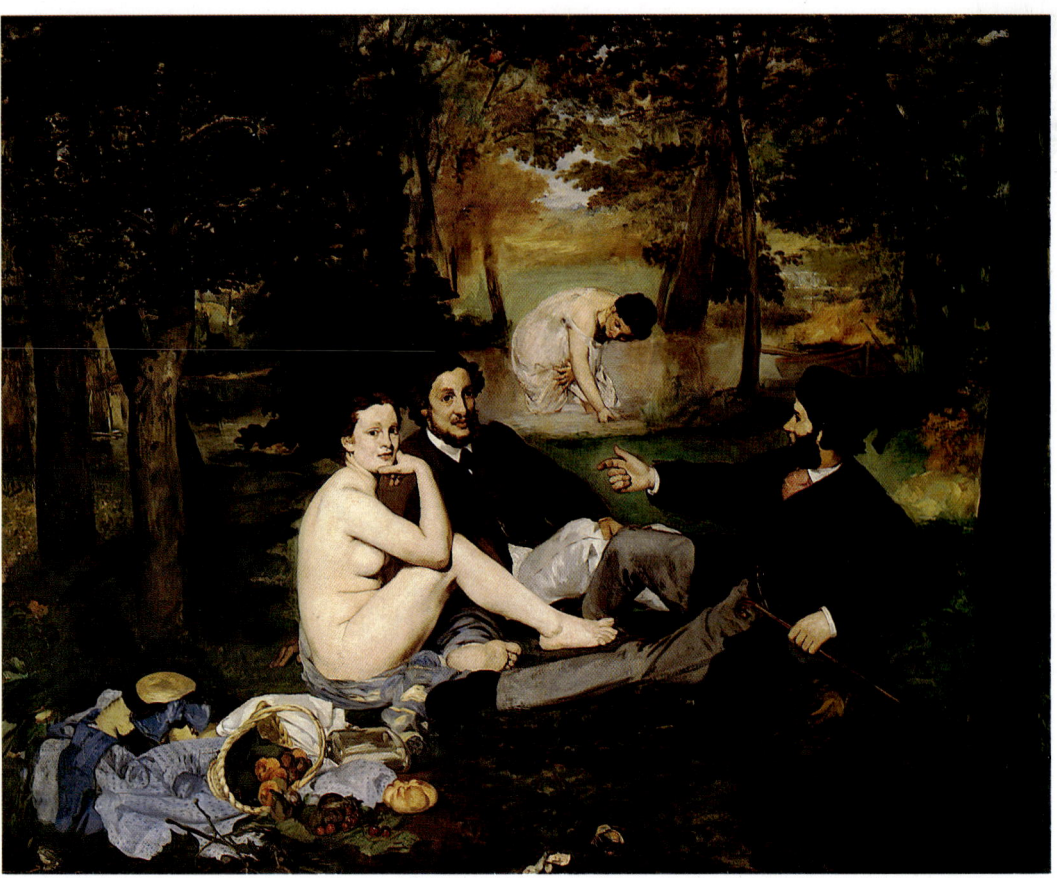

latter look like schoolboys on a holiday, perpetrating an outrage to play the man. . . . This is a young man's practical joke—a shameful, open sore.[7]

Manet's work would have been acceptable had he shown men and women as nymphs and satyrs in classical dress or undress, as did his contemporary Bouguereau (FIG. 29-9). In *Le Déjeuner,* Manet lifted the veil of allusion and bluntly confronted the public with reality.

The public and the critics disliked Manet's subject matter only slightly less than how he presented his figures. He rendered in soft focus and broadly painted the landscape, including the pool in which the second woman bathes, compared with the clear forms of the harshly lit foreground trio and the pile of discarded female attire and picnic foods at the lower left. The lighting creates strong contrasts between darks and highlighted areas. In the main figures, many values are summed up in one or two lights or darks. The effect is both to flatten the forms and to give them a hard snapping presence. Form, rather than a matter of line, is only a function of paint and light. Manet himself declared that the chief actor in the painting is the light. In true modernist fashion, Manet was using art "to call attention to art"—in other words, he was moving away from illusion and toward open acknowledgement of painting's properties, such as the flatness of the painting surface. The public, however, saw only a crude sketch without the customary "finish."

SCANDALOUS SHAMELESSNESS AND AUDACITY

Even more scandalous to the French viewing public was Manet's 1863 painting *Olympia* (FIG. **29-8**). This work depicts a young white woman reclining on a bed that extends across the foreground. Entirely nude except for a thin black ribbon tied around her neck, a bracelet on her arm, an orchid in her hair, and fashionable mule slippers on her feet, Olympia meets viewers' eyes with a look of cool indifference. Behind her appears a black woman, who presents her a bouquet of flowers.

Public and critics alike were horrified. Although images of prostitutes were not unheard of during this period, viewers were taken aback by the shamelessness of Olympia and her look that verges on defiance. The depiction of a black woman was also not new to painting, but the viewing public perceived Manet's inclusion of both a black maid and a nude prostitute as evoking moral depravity, inferiority, and animalistic sexuality. One critic described Olympia as "a courtesan with dirty hands and wrinkled feet . . . her body has the livid tint of a cadaver displayed in the morgue; her outlines are drawn in charcoal and her greenish, bloodshot eyes appear to be provoking the public, protected all the while by a hideous Negress."[8]

From this statement, it is clear viewers were responding not just to the subject matter but to Manet's artistic style as well. Manet's brushstrokes are rougher and the shifts in tonality are more abrupt than those found in traditional academic painting (see "The Academies: Defining the Range of Acceptable Art," page 898). This departure from accepted practice exacerbated the audacity of the subject matter.

ACADEMIC ART'S CONVENTIONS AND APPEAL

To better explain the public's reaction to such modernist painting, a comparison of *Olympia* to a work by a highly acclaimed French academic artist of the time, ADOLPHE-WILLIAM BOUGUEREAU (1825–1905), is instructive. In works such as *Nymphs and Satyr* (FIG. **29-9**), Bouguereau depicted

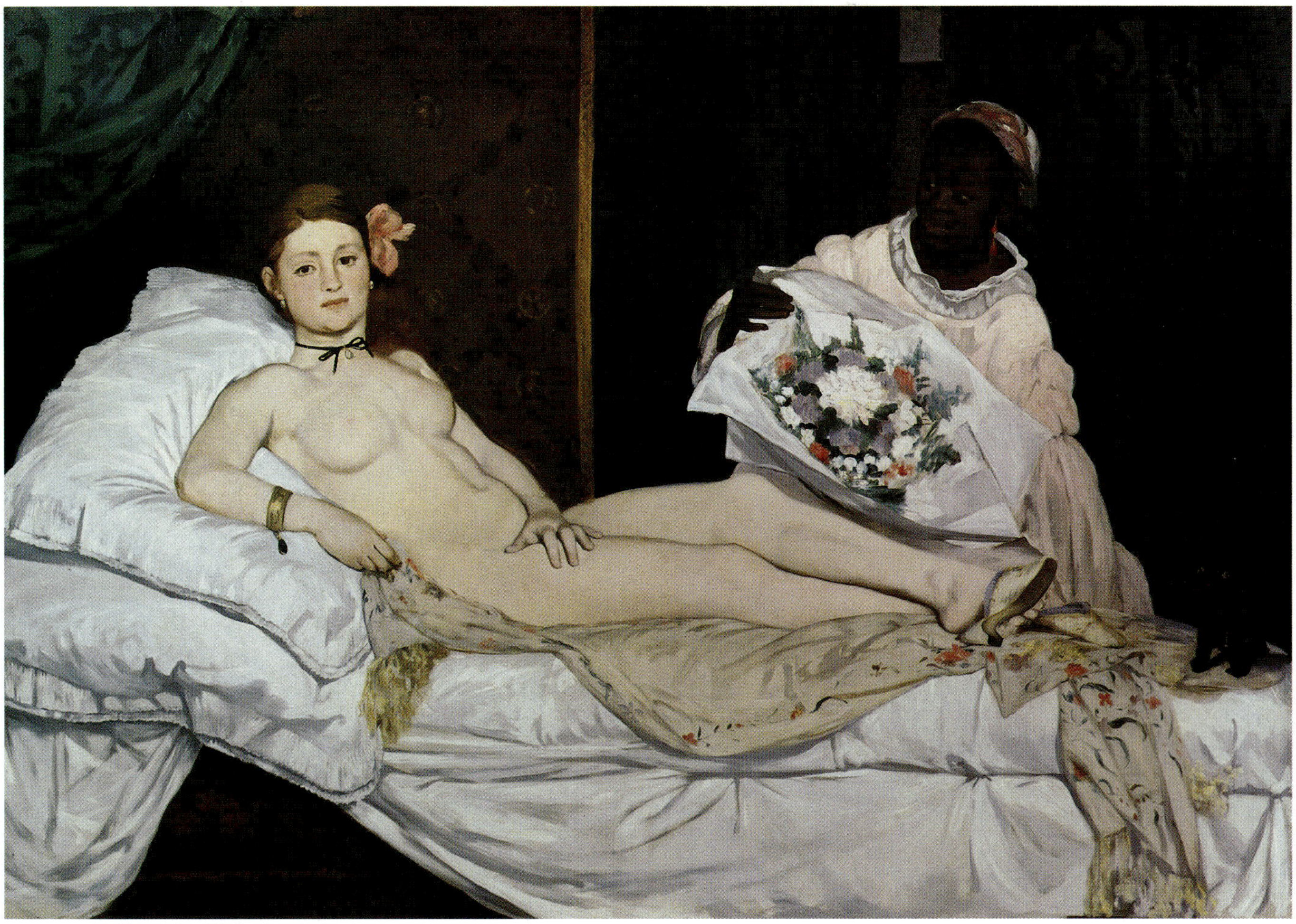

29-8 ÉDOUARD MANET, *Olympia*, 1863. Oil on canvas, 4′ 3″ × 6′ 3″. Musée d'Orsay, Paris.

classical mythological subjects with a polished illusionism. In this painting, the flirtatious and ideally beautiful nymphs strike graceful poses yet seem based as closely on nature as are the details of their leafy surroundings. They playfully pull in different directions the satyr, the mythical beast-man, with a goat's hindquarters and horns, a horse's ears and tail, and a man's upper body. Although Bouguereau arguably depicted this scene in a very naturalistic (visually realistic or illusionistic) manner, it is emphatically not Realist. His choice of a fictional theme and adherence to established painting conventions could have been seen only as staunchly traditional. Bouguereau was immensely popular during the later nineteenth century, enjoying the favor of state patronage throughout his career.

A REALIST PAINTER OF ANIMALS   Another French artist who received great acclaim during her career was MARIE-ROSALIE (ROSA) BONHEUR (1822–1899). Awarded a Légion d'honneur (Legion of Honor) in 1865, Bonheur was the most celebrated woman artist of the nineteenth century. Although Bonheur's work contains Realist elements, she is perhaps more appropriately considered a "naturalist" as described by French critic Jules Castagnary. Trained as an artist by her father, Bonheur founded her career on his belief that as a woman and an artist, she had a special role to play in creating a new and perfect society. A Realist passion for accuracy in painting drove Bonheur, but she resisted depicting the

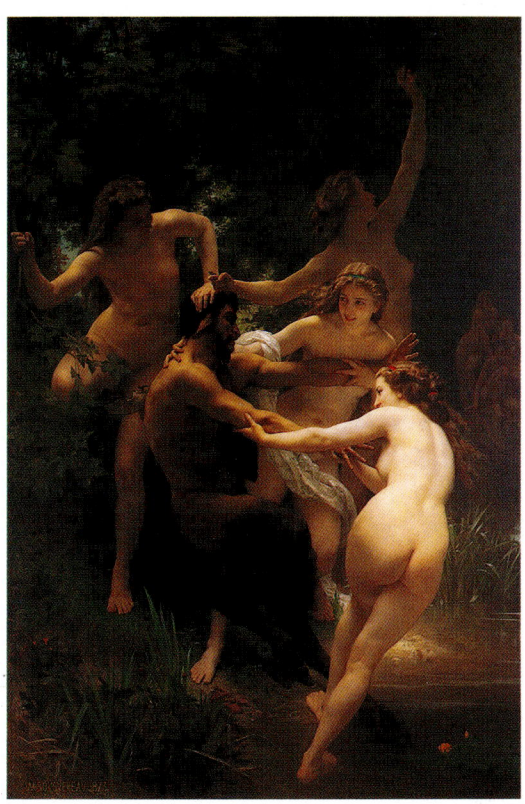

29-9 ADOLPHE-WILLIAM BOUGUEREAU, *Nymphs and Satyr,* 1873. Oil on canvas, approx. 8′ 6″ high. Sterling and Francine Clark Art Institute, Williamstown, Massachusetts.

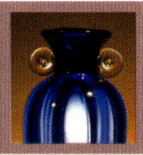

The Academies
Defining the Range of Acceptable Art

Modernist art is often discussed in contrast to academic art. What is academic art? The term is used to refer to art sanctioned by the academies, established art schools such as the Royal Academy of Painting and Sculpture in France (founded in 1648) and the Royal Academy of Arts in Britain (founded in 1768). Both of these academies provided instruction for art students and sponsored exhibitions. During the long existence of these organizations, they exerted great control over the art scene. The annual exhibitions, called "Salons" in France (not the same as the seventeenth-century social salons), were highly competitive, as was membership in these academies. Subsidized by the government, the French Royal Academy thus supported a limited range of artistic expression, focusing on traditional subjects and highly polished technique. Because of the challenges modernist art presented to established artistic conventions, the Salons and other exhibitions often rejected it. In 1863, for example, Emperor Napoleon III established the Salon des Refusés (Salon of the Rejected) to show all of the works the academy's jury had not accepted for exhibition in the regular Salon. Works such as Manet's *Le Déjeuner sur l'herbe* (FIG. 29-7) were included in the Salon des Refusés and were met with derision by much of the public.

The Impressionists reinforced the perception of these academies as bastions of conservatism. After repeated rejections, these artists decided to form their own society in 1873 and began holding their own exhibitions in Paris. This decision allowed the Impressionists much freedom, for they did not have to contend with the academies' authoritative and confining viewpoint. The Impressionist exhibitions were held at one- or two-year intervals from 1874 until 1886. Another group of artists unhappy with the Salon's conservative nature adopted this same renegade idea. In 1884, these artists formed the Sociéte des Artistes Indépendant (Society of Independent Artists) and held annual Salons des Indépendants.

social complexity and contradictions seen in the work of Courbet, Manet, and other Realists. Rather, she turned to the animal world. In her work, she combined a naturalist's knowledge of equine anatomy and motion with an honest love and admiration for the brute strength of wild and domestic animals. She went to great lengths to observe the anatomy of living horses at the great Parisian horse fair, where the animals were shown and traded, and also spent long hours studying the anatomy of carcasses in the Paris slaughterhouses. For her best-known work, *The Horse Fair* (FIG. **29-10**), she adopted a panoramic composition similar to that in Courbet's *Burial at Ornans* (FIG. 29-2), painted a few years earlier. In contrast to the still figures in *Burial,* Bonheur filled her broad canvas with the sturdy farm Percherons and their grooms seen on parade at

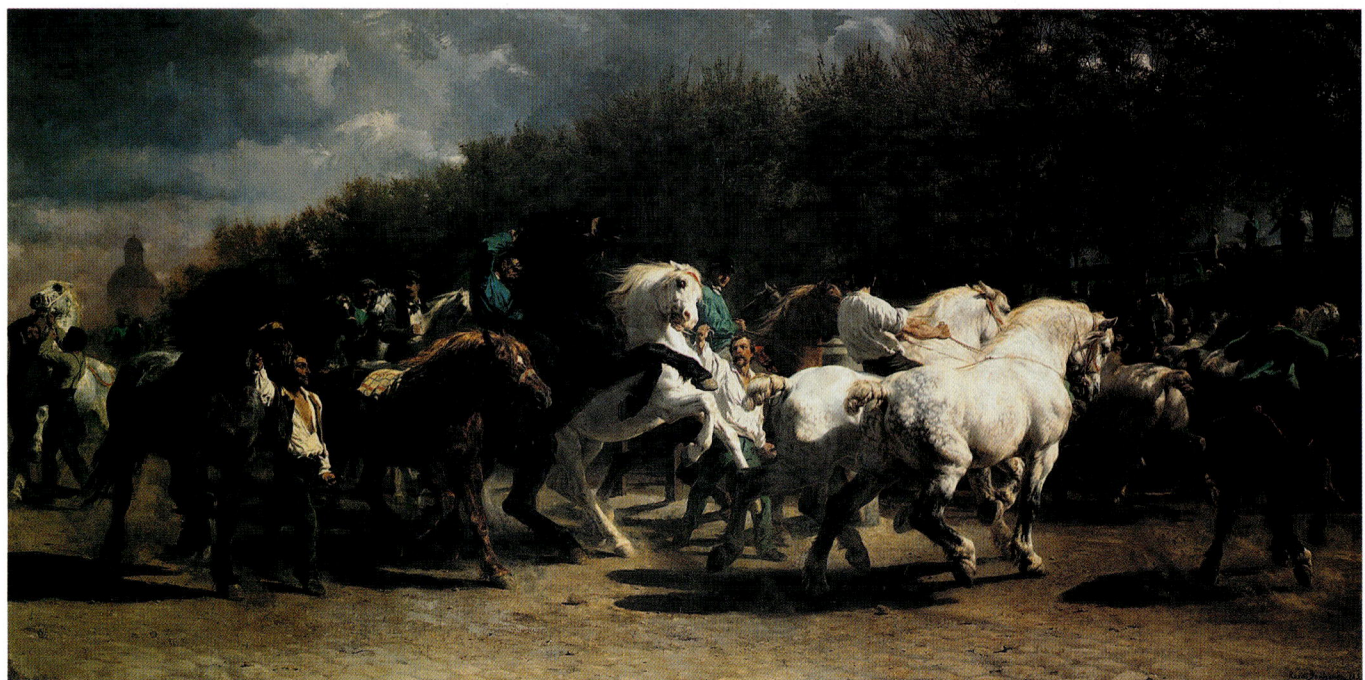

29-10 MARIE-ROSALIE (ROSA) BONHEUR, *The Horse Fair,* 1853–1855. Oil on canvas, $8' \frac{1}{4}'' \times 16' 7\frac{1}{2}''$. Metropolitan Museum of Art, New York (gift of Cornelius Vanderbilt, 1887).

the annual Parisian horse sale. Some horses, not quite broken, rear up; others plod or trot, guided on foot or ridden by their keepers. The uneven line of the march, the thunderous pounding, and the Percherons' seemingly overwhelming power clearly were based on close observation from life, even though Bonheur acknowledged some inspiration from the Classical model of the Parthenon frieze (see FIG. 5-48). The dramatic lighting, loose brushwork, and rolling sky also reveal her admiration of the style of Géricault (see FIG. 28-41). Bonheur's depiction of equine drama in *The Horse Fair* captivated viewers, who eagerly bought engraved reproductions of the work, making it one of the most well-known paintings of the century.

Despite the public's derision, the French Realists—Courbet, Millet, Daumier, Manet, and other artists—challenged the whole iconographic stock of traditional art and called public attention to what Baudelaire termed the "heroism of modern life."[9] In so doing, they not only changed the course of Western art, but they also left succeeding generations of viewers with a broader understanding of French life and culture in the later nineteenth century.

REALISM OUTSIDE FRANCE

Although French artists took the lead in promoting Realism and the notion that artists should depict the realities of modern life, this movement was not exclusively French. The Realist foundation in empiricism and positivism appealed to artists in many countries, including Germany, Russia, England, and the United States. Realism emerged in a variety of forms and places and was well established by the end of the century.

AN AMERICAN REALIST In the United States, a dedicated appetite for showing the realities of the human experience made THOMAS EAKINS (1844–1916) a master Realist portrait and genre painter. He studied both painting and medical anatomy in Philadelphia before undertaking further study under French artist Jean-Léon Gérôme (1824–1904). Eakins was resolutely a Realist; his ambition was to paint things as he saw them rather than as the public might wish them portrayed. This attitude was very much in tune with nineteenth-century American taste, combined an admiration for accurate depiction with a hunger for truth. These twin attributes are reflected in Ralph Waldo Emerson's observation that the American character delights in accurate perception and in Henry David Thoreau's insistence that the value of a fact is that it eventually flowers in a truth.

AN IMAGE NOT FOR THE SQUEAMISH The too-brutal Realism of Eakins's early masterpiece, *The Gross Clinic* (FIG. **29-11**), prompted the art jury to reject it for the Philadelphia exhibition that celebrated the American independence centennial. The work presents the renowned surgeon Dr. Samuel Gross in the operating amphitheatre of the Jefferson Medical College in Philadelphia, where the painting now hangs. That Eakins chose to depict such an event testifies to the public's increasing faith in scientific and medical progress. Dr. Gross, with bloody fingers and scalpel, lectures

about his surgery on a young man's leg. The patient suffered from osteomyelitis, a bone infection. The surgeon, acclaimed for his skill in this particular operation, is accompanied by colleagues, all of whom historians have identified, and by the patient's mother, who covers her face. Indicative of the contemporaneity of this scene is the anesthetist's presence in the background, holding the cloth over the patient's face. Anesthetics had been introduced in 1846, and their development eliminated a major obstacle to extensive surgery. The painting is, indeed, an unsparing description of a contemporaneous event, with a good deal more reality than many viewers could endure. "It is a picture," one critic said, "that even strong men find difficult to look at long, if they can look at it at all."[10] It was true to the artistic program of "scenes from modern life," as Southworth and Hawes had been in their daguerreotype of a similar setting (see FIG. 28-63). Both images recorded a particular event at a particular time.

Eakins believed that knowledge—and where relevant, scientific knowledge—was a prerequisite to his art. As a scientist (in his anatomical studies), Eakins preferred a slow, deliberate method of careful invention based on his observations of the perspective, the anatomy, and the actual details of his subject. This insistence on scientific fact corresponded to the dominance of empiricism during the latter half of the nineteenth century. Eakins's concern for anatomical correctness led him to investigate the human form and humans in motion, both with regular photographic apparatuses and with a special camera that the French *kinesiologist* (a person who studies the physiology of body movement) Étienne-Jules Marey devised. Eakins's later collaboration with Eadweard Muybridge in the photographic study of animal and human action of all types drew favorable attention in France, especially from Degas, and anticipated the motion picture.

EVERYTHING BUT THE CLATTER OF HOOFS The Realist photographer and scientist EADWEARD MUYBRIDGE (1830–1904) came to the United States from England in the 1850s and settled in San Francisco, where he established a prominent international reputation for his photographs of the western United States. (His large-plate landscape images of the Yosemite region won him a gold medal at the Vienna Exposition of 1873.) In 1872, the governor of California, Leland Stanford, sought Muybridge's assistance in settling a bet about whether, at any point in a stride, all four feet of a horse galloping at top speed are off the ground. Through his sequential photography, as seen in *Horse Galloping* (FIG. **29-12**), Muybridge proved they were. This experience was the beginning of Muybridge's photographic studies of the successive stages in human and animal motion—details too quick for the human eye to capture. These investigations culminated in 1885 at the University of Pennsylvania with a series of multiple-camera motion studies that recorded separate photographs of progressive moments in a single action. His discoveries received extensive publicity through the book *Animal Locomotion*, which Muybridge published in 1887. Muybridge's motion photographs earned him a place in the history of science, as well as art. His sequential motion studies, along with those of Eakins and Marey, influenced many other artists, including their contemporary, the painter and sculptor Edgar Degas, and twentieth-century artists such as Marcel Duchamp.

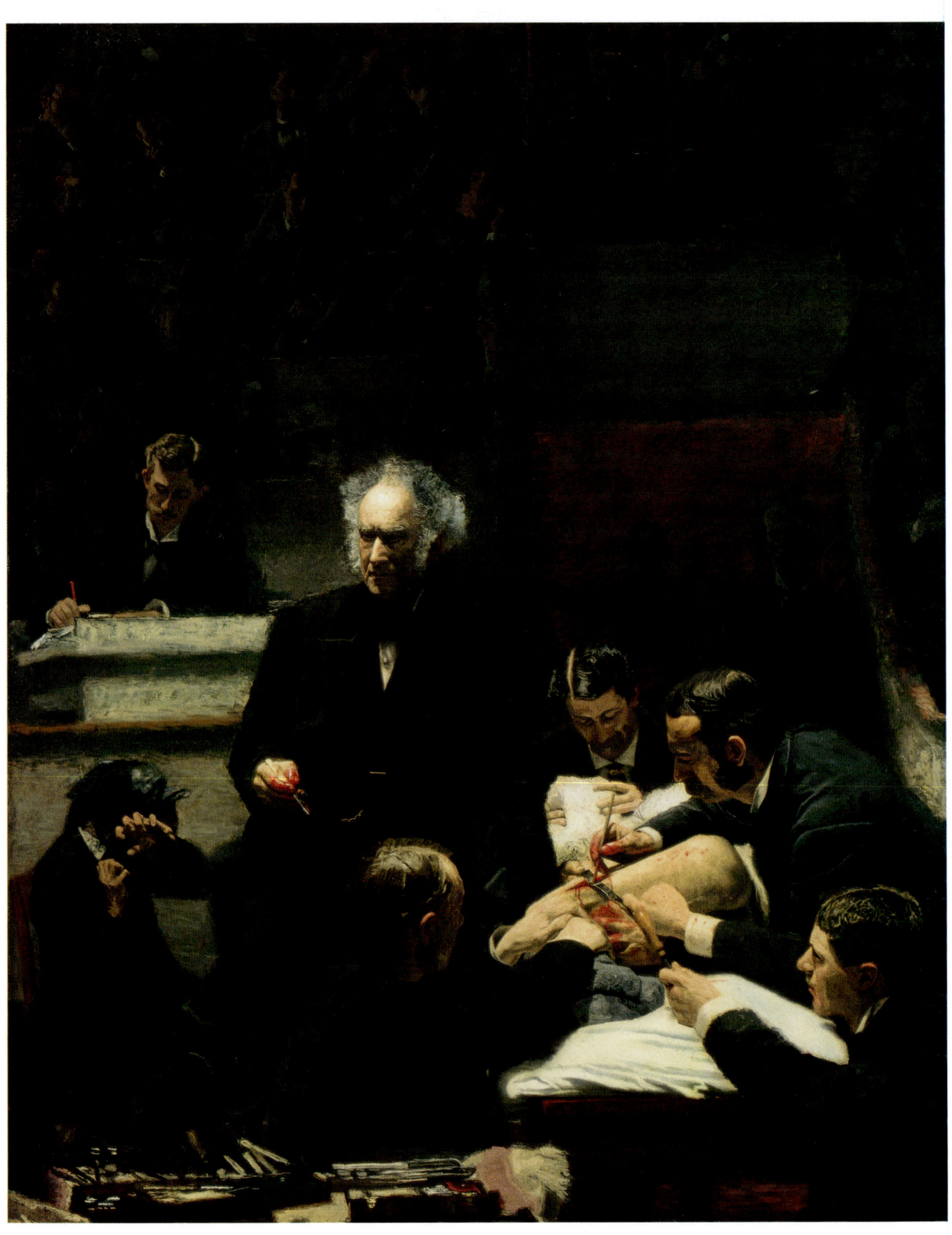

29-11 THOMAS EAKINS, *The Gross Clinic,* 1875. Oil on canvas, 8′ × 6′ 6″. Jefferson Medical College of Thomas Jefferson University, Philadelphia.

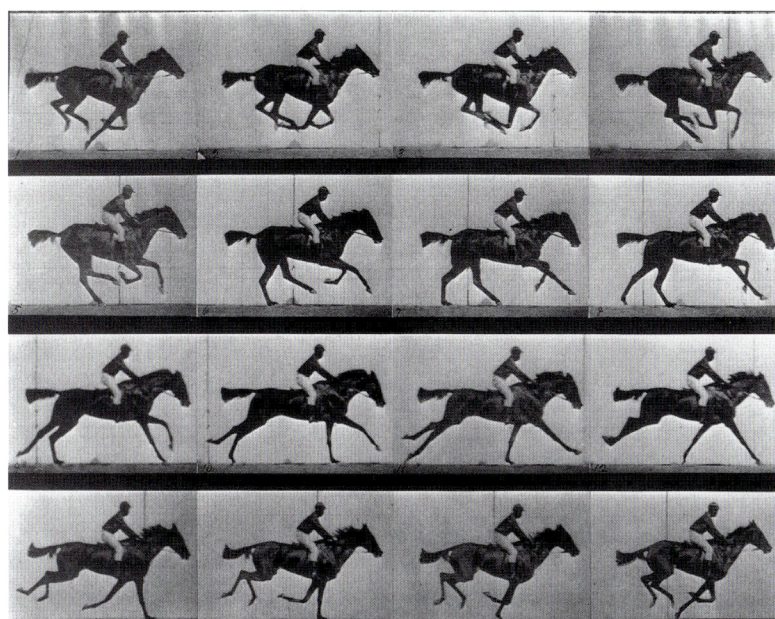

29-12 EADWEARD MUYBRIDGE, *Horse Galloping,* 1878.
Collotype print. George Eastman House, Rochester, New York.

Muybridge presented his work to scientists and general audiences with a device called the zoopraxiscope, which he invented to project his sequences of images (mounted on special glass plates) onto a screen. The result was so lifelike one viewer said it "threw upon the screen apparently the living, moving animals. Nothing was wanting but the clatter of hoofs upon the turf."[11] The illusion of motion here was created by a physical fact of human eyesight called "persistence of vision." Stated simply, it means the brain holds whatever the eye sees for a fraction of a second after the eye stops seeing it. Thus, viewers saw a rapid succession of different images merging one into the next, producing the illusion of continuous change. This illusion lies at the heart of the "realism" of all cinema.

AMERICAN REALIST PORTRAITURE The expatriate American artist JOHN SINGER SARGENT (1856–1925) was a younger contemporary of Eakins and Muybridge. In contrast to Eakins's carefully rendered details, Sargent developed a looser, more dashing Realist portrait style. Sargent studied art in Paris before settling in London, where he was renowned both as a cultivated and cosmopolitan gentleman and as a facile and fashionable portrait painter. He learned his fluent brushing of paint in thin films and his effortless achievement of quick and lively illusion from his study of Velázquez, whose masterpiece, *Las Meninas* (see FIG. 24-33), may have influenced Sargent's family portrait *The Daughters of Edward Darley Boit* (FIG. **29-13**). The four girls (the children of one of Sargent's close friends) appear in a hall and small drawing room in their Paris home. The informal, eccentric arrangement of their slight figures suggests how much at ease they are within this familiar space and with objects such as the monumental Japanese vases, the red screen, and the fringed rug, whose scale subtly emphasizes the children's diminutive stature. Sargent must have known the Boit daughters well and liked them. Relaxed and trustful, they gave the artist an opportunity to record a gradation of young innocence. He sensitively captured the naive, wondering openness of the little girl in the foreground, the grave artlessness of the ten-year-old child, and the slightly self-conscious poise of the adolescents. Sargent's casual posi-

tioning of the figures and seemingly random choice of the setting communicate a sense of spontaneity. The children seem to be attending momentarily to an adult who has asked them to interrupt their activity and "look this way." Here is a most effective embodiment of the Realist belief that the artist's business is to record the modern being in modern context.

THE DEVOTION OF ORDINARY PEOPLE Typical of the Realist painter's desire to depict the lives of ordinary people is the early work of the American artist HENRY OSSAWA TANNER (1859–1937). Tanner studied art with Eakins before moving to Paris. There he combined Eakins's belief in careful study from nature with a desire to portray with dignity the life of the ordinary people he had been raised among as the son of an African-American minister in Pennsylvania. The mood in *The Thankful Poor* (FIG. **29-14**) is one of quiet devotion not far removed from the Realism of Millet (FIG. 29-3). In Tanner's painting, the grandfather, grandchild, and main objects in the room are painted with the greatest detail, while everything else dissolves into loose strokes of color and light. Expressive lighting reinforces the painting's reverent spirit, with deep shadows intensifying the man's devout concentration and golden light pouring in the window to illuminate the quiet expression of thanksgiving on the younger face. The deep sense of sanctity expressed here in terms of everyday experience became increasingly important for Tanner. Within a few years of completing *The Thankful Poor,* he began painting biblical subjects grounded in direct study from nature and in the love of Rembrandt that had inspired him from his days as a Philadelphia art student.

Over time, Realist artists throughout Europe and America expanded and diversified their subjects to embrace all classes and levels of society, all types of people and environments. These included the urban and rural working class, the big-city inhabitants, the small-town citizens, the leisure class at its resorts, and the rustics of the provinces. Added to the social sympathies found in the works of Daumier, Courbet, and Millet were motives of an anthropological kind, reflecting interest in national and regional characteristics, in folk customs and culture, and in the quaintness of local color.

29-13 JOHN SINGER SARGENT, *The Daughters of Edward Darley Boit,* 1882. Oil on canvas, 7′ 3⅜″ × 7′ 3⅝″. Courtesy of Museum of Fine Arts, Boston (gift of Mary Louisa Boit, Florence D. Boit, Jane Hubbard Boit and Julia Overing Boit, in memory of their father, Edward Darley Boit, 19.124).

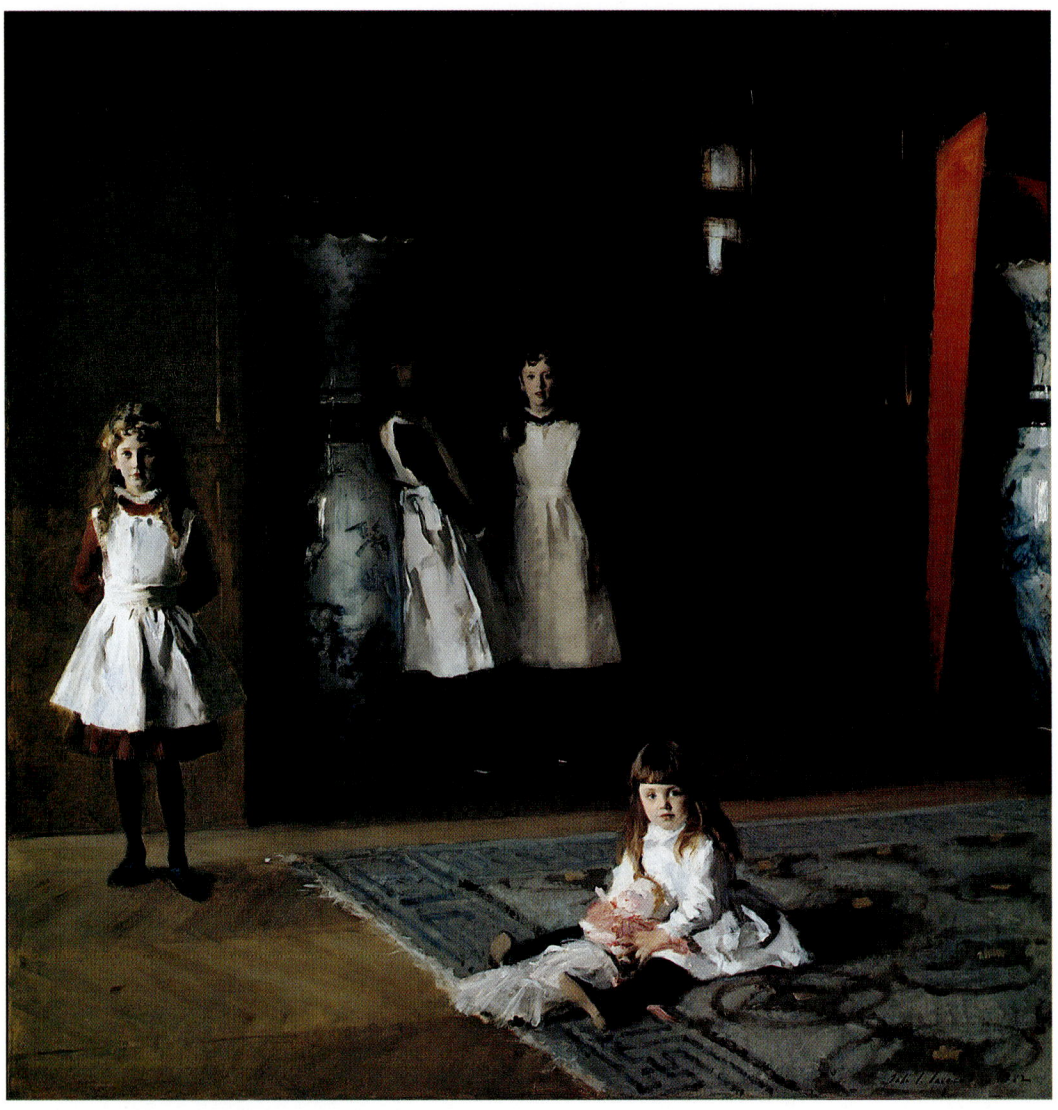

29-14 HENRY OSSAWA TANNER, *The Thankful Poor,* 1894. Oil on canvas, 3′ 8¼″ × 2′ 11½″. Collection of William H. and Camille Cosby.

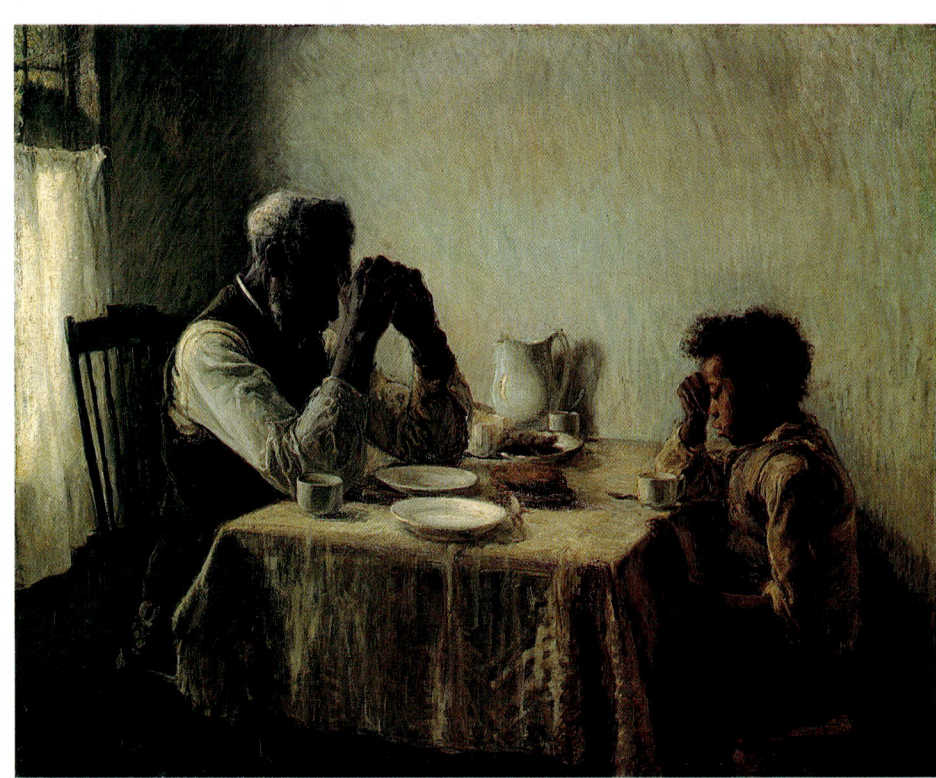

THE PRE-RAPHAELITE BROTHERHOOD

EMBRACING THE PRE-INDUSTRIAL PAST In England, JOHN EVERETT MILLAIS (1829–1896) was among a group of artists who refused to be limited to the contemporary scenes strict Realists portrayed. These artists chose instead to represent fictional, historical, and fanciful subjects but to do so using Realist techniques. So painstakingly careful was Millais in his study of visual facts closely observed from nature that Baudelaire called him "the poet of meticulous detail." Millais was a founder of the so-called Pre-Raphaelite Brotherhood. This group of artists, organized in 1848, wished to create fresh and sincere art, free from what they considered the tired and artificial manner the successors of Raphael propagated in the academies. Influenced by the influential critic, artist, and writer John Ruskin (1819–1900), Millais agreed with his distaste for the materialism and ugliness of the contemporary industrializing world and Millais also shared the Pre-Raphaelites' appreciation for the spirituality and idealism (as well as the art and artisanship) of past times, especially the Middle Ages and the Early Renaissance.

A SHAKESPEAREAN HEROINE DROWNED Millais's method is apparent in *Ophelia* (FIG. **29-15**), which he exhibited in the Universal Exposition in Paris in 1855, where Courbet set up his Pavilion of Realism. The subject, from Shakespeare's *Hamlet,* is the drowning of Ophelia, who, in her madness, is unaware of her plight:

> *Her clothes spread wide,*
> *And mermaidlike awhile they bore her up—*
> *Which time she chanted snatches of old tunes,*
> *As one incapable of her own distress.*
> (4.7.176–79)

Attempting to make the pathos of the scene visible, Millais became a faithful and feeling witness of its every detail, reconstructing it with a lyricism worthy of the original poetry. Although Millais's technique was optically realistic, orthodox nineteenth-century Realists would have complained the subject was not—that it was playacting. It may be that this conflict between what is actually seen or experienced and the realistic representation of fictitious or past events was eventually resolved in modern cinema. The kind of drama Millais depicted in *Ophelia,* which brought the fictive action of a theatrical event before viewers' eyes with optical fidelity, anticipated the dramatic motion pictures whose creators presented fictions and facts to the eye as equally real. Nineteenth-century Realists might have objected that picture dramas such as *Ophelia* were not paintings but stage productions and could only be judged as such.

A "PICTORIAL" PHOTOGRAPHIC METHOD Photography, the artificial eye, the medium created to serve the taste for visual fact, for realistic report of the world, was itself the creator of a new Realism. But it also could be manipulated by talented photographers to produce quite Romantic

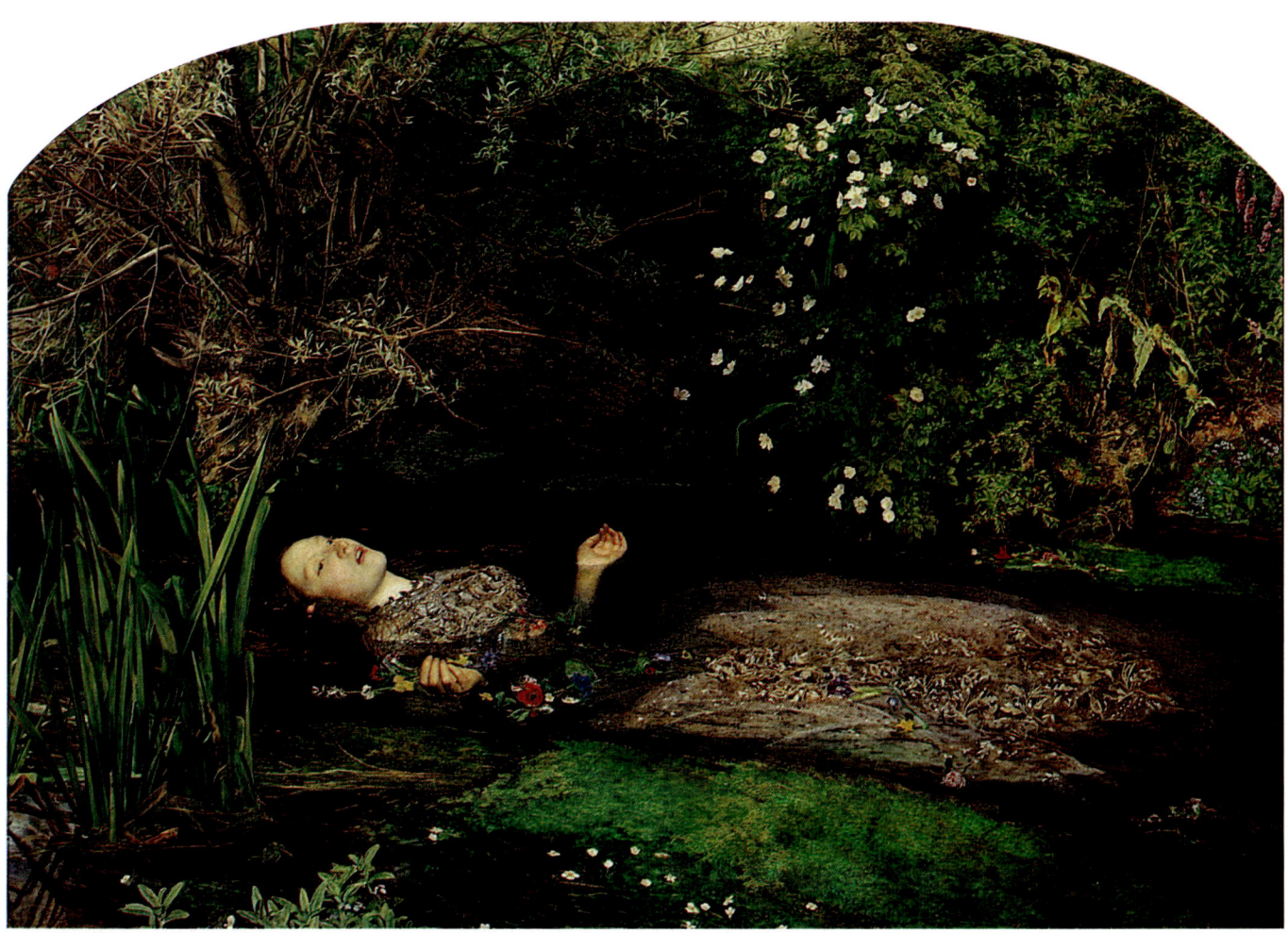

29-15 JOHN EVERETT MILLAIS, *Ophelia,* 1852. Oil on canvas, 2′ 6″ × 3′ 8″. Tate Gallery, London.

effects. After the first great breakthroughs, which bluntly showed what was before the eye, photographers imitated Romantic arrangements of nature, filtering natural appearance through sentiment—soft-focusing it, as it were. In the later century, with much public approval, photography had a Romantic-Realist school of its own. The photographers thought of it as a "pictorial" method.

One of the leading practitioners of the Pictorial style in photography was the American GERTRUDE KÄSEBIER (1852–1934). Käsebier took up photography in 1897 after raising a family and working as a portrait painter. She soon became famous for photographs with symbolic themes, such as *Blessed Art thou Among Women* (FIG. **29-16**). The title repeats the phrase the angel Gabriel used in the New Testament to announce to the Virgin Mary that she will be the mother of Jesus. In the context of Käsebier's photography, the words suggest a parallel between the biblical "Mother of God" and the modern mother in the image, who both protects and sends forth her daughter. The white setting and the mother's pale gown shimmer in soft focus behind the serious girl, who

is dressed in darker tones and captured with sharper focus. Here, as in her other works, the ideas about naturalism in photography championed by photographer Peter Henry Emerson (1856–1936) influenced Käsebier. Yet she deliberately ignored his teachings about differential focusing, combining an out-of-focus background with a sharp or almost-sharp foreground, in favor of achieving an "expressive" effect by blurring the entire image slightly. In *Blessed Art thou,* the whole scene is invested with an aura of otherworldly peace by the soft focus, the appearance of the centered figures, the vertical framing elements, and the relationship between the frontally posed girl and her gracefully bending mother. As one contemporaneous critic wrote: "The manner in which modern dress was handled, subordinated, and made to play its proper part in the composition . . . evidenced great artistic feeling."[12] *Blessed Art thou* is a superb example of Käsebier's moving ability to invest scenes from everyday life with a sense of the spiritual and the divine.

IMPRESSIONISM: CAPTURING THE FUGITIVE IMAGES OF MODERN LIFE

Impressionism, both in content and style, was an art of industrialized, urbanized Paris. As such, it furthered some of the Realists' concerns and was resolutely an art of its time. But whereas Realism focused on the present, Impressionism focused even more acutely on a single moment. Although Impressionism often is discussed as a coherent movement, it was actually a nebulous and shifting phenomenon. People have perceived the Impressionists as a group largely because they exhibited together in the 1870s and 1880s. However, participation in these shows was a constant source of contention and debate among the artists.

IMPRESSIONISM AND THE SKETCH   A hostile critic applied the label *Impressionism* in response to the painting *Impression: Sunrise* (FIG. **29-17**) by CLAUDE MONET (1840–1926). The artist exhibited this work in the first Impressionist show in 1874, and, although the critic intended the term to be derogatory, by the third Impressionist show in 1878 the artists themselves were using that label.

The term *impressionism* had been used in art before but in relation to sketches. Impressionist paintings incorporated the qualities of sketches—abbreviation, speed, and spontaneity. The Impressionist work thus was "finished" in the sense of a complete thought or the characterization of a specific moment, rather than through the polish and reworking typical of academic works. This is apparent in *Impression: Sunrise.* The brushstrokes are clearly evident; Monet made no attempt to blend the pigment to create smooth tonal gradations and an optically accurate scene. Although this painting is not a sketch, technically speaking, it has a sketchy quality. This increased concern with acknowledging the paint and the canvas surface continued the modernist direction the Realists began.

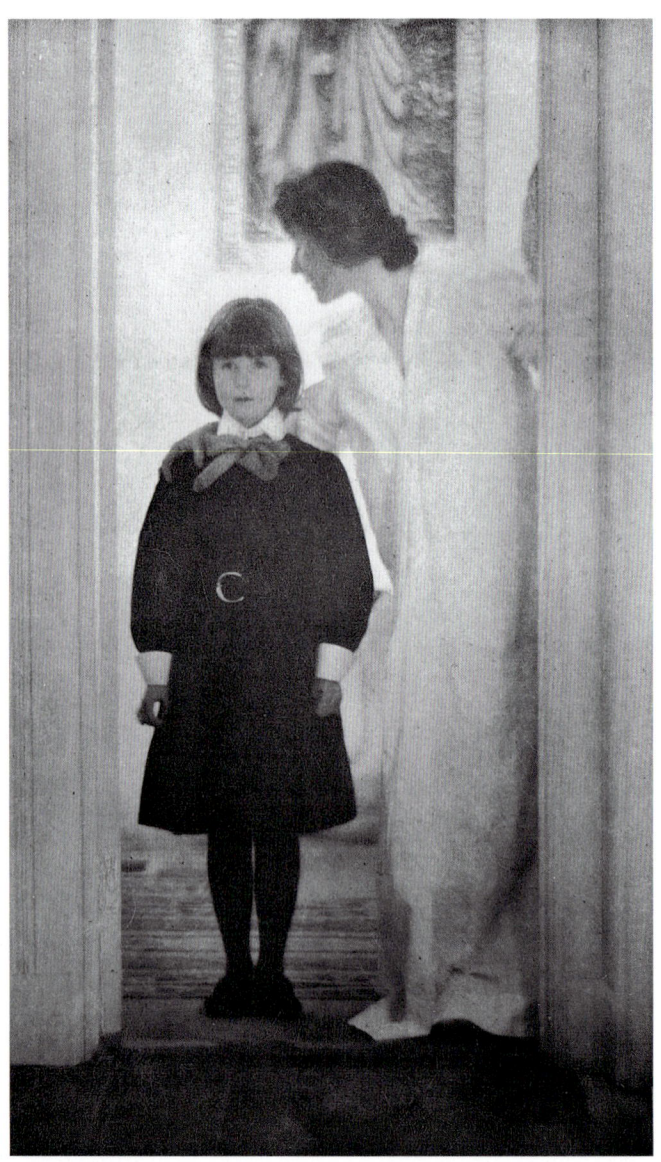

29-16   GERTRUDE KÄSEBIER, *Blessed Art thou Among Women,* 1899. Platinum print on Japanese tissue, $9\frac{3}{8}'' \times 5\frac{1}{2}''$. Museum of Modern Art, New York (gift of Mrs. Hermine M. Turner).

CAPTURING A FLEETING MOMENT   The lack of pristine clarity characteristic of most Impressionist works is also historically grounded. The extensive industrialization and urbanization that occurred in France during the latter half of the nineteenth century can be described only as a brutal and

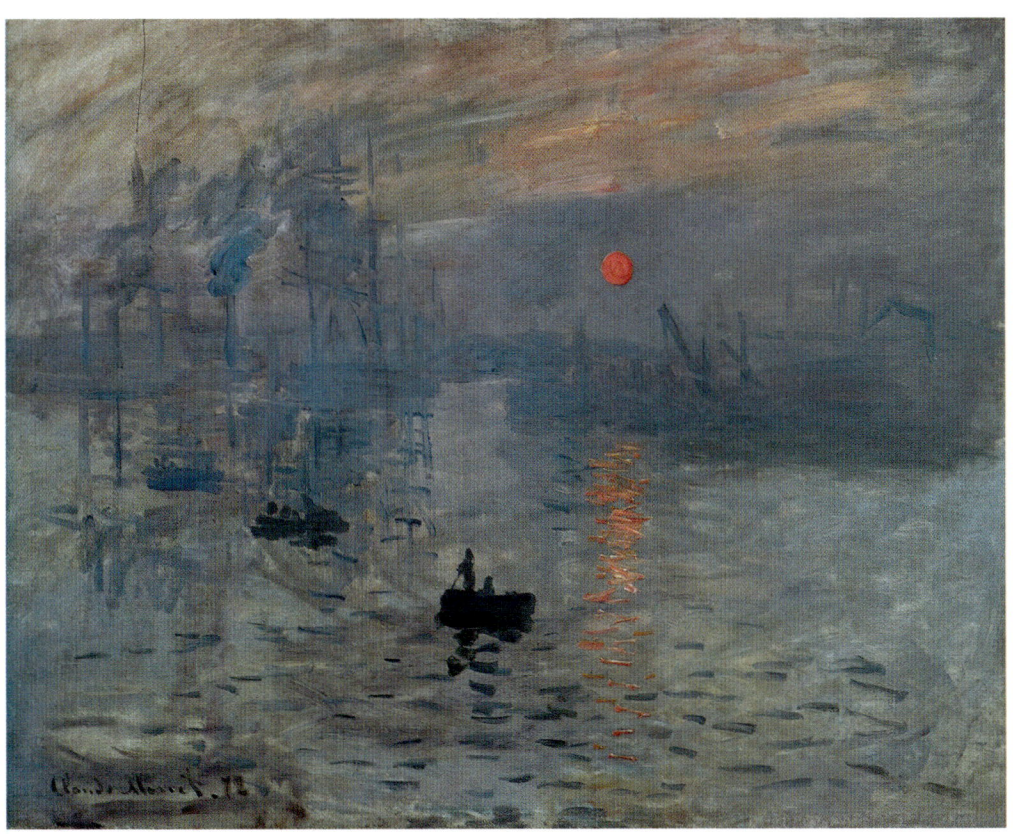

29-17   CLAUDE MONET, *Impression: Sunrise,* 1872. Oil on canvas, 1′ 7½″ × 2′ 1½″. Musée Marmottan, Paris.

chaotic transformation. The rapidity of these changes made the world seem unstable and insubstantial. As noted French poet Charles Baudelaire observed: "[M]odernity is the transitory, the fugitive, the contingent."[13] Accordingly, Impressionist works represent an attempt to capture a fleeting moment—not in the absolutely fixed, precise sense of a Realist painting but by conveying the elusiveness and impermanence of images and conditions.

THE RAILROADS AND PARISIAN LIFE   That Impressionism was firmly anchored in the industrial development of the time and in the concurrent process of urbanization is also revealed by the artists' choice of subjects. Most of the Impressionists depicted scenes in and around Paris, where industrialization and urbanization had their greatest impact. Monet's *Saint-Lazare Train Station* (FIG. **29-18**) depicts a dominant aspect of Parisian life. The expanding railway

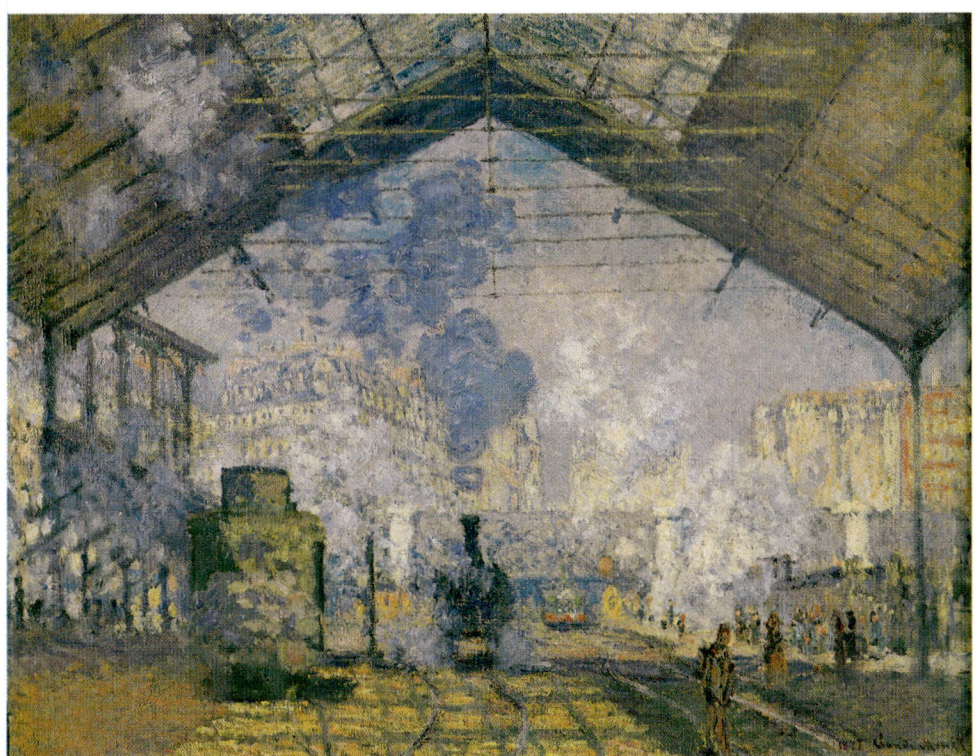

29-18   CLAUDE MONET, *Saint-Lazare Train Station,* 1877. Oil on canvas, approx. 2′ 5¾″ × 3′ 5″. Musée d'Orsay, Paris.

network had made travel more convenient, bringing throngs of people into Paris. Saint-Lazare Station was centrally located, adjacent to the Grands Boulevards, a bustling, fashionable commercial area. Monet captured the area's energy and vitality; the train, emerging from the steam and smoke it emits, comes into the station. Through the background haze, viewers can make out the tall buildings that were becoming a major component of the Parisian landscape. Monet's agitated paint application contributes to the sense of energy and conveys the atmosphere of urban life.

THE HAUSSMANIZATION OF PARIS Other Impressionists also represented facets of city life. GUSTAVE CAILLEBOTTE (1849–1893) depicted yet another scene in *Paris: A Rainy Day* (FIG. **29-19**). His setting is a junction of spacious boulevards that resulted from the redesigning of Paris begun in 1852. The city's population had reached close to one and a half million by midcentury, and to accommodate this congregation of humanity, Emperor Napoleon III ordered Paris rebuilt. The emperor named Baron Georges Haussmann, a city superintendent, to oversee the entire project; consequently, this process became known as "Haussmanization." In addition to new water and sewer systems, street lighting, and new residential and commercial buildings, a major component of the new Paris was the creation of wide, open boulevards. These great avenues, whose construction caused the demolition of thousands of ancient buildings and streets, transformed medieval Paris into the present modern city, with its superb vistas and wide uninterrupted arteries for the flow of vehicular and pedestrian traffic. Caillebotte chose to focus on these markers of the city's rapid urbanization.

The artist deliberately used an informal and asymmetrical composition. The figures seem randomly placed, with the

frame cropping them arbitrarily. Well-dressed Parisians of the leisure class share the viewers' space. Viewers and subjects all participate in the same weather, which the painter carefully indicated, not only by the umbrellas but also by the wet cobblestones, puddles, and faint reflections that blend into the monochromatic tonality of a gray day. Caillebotte did not dissolve his image into the broken color and brushwork characteristic of Impressionism. But in the apparently chance arrangement of his figures, their motion suspended in a moment already passed, Caillebotte's *Paris: A Rainy Day* is certainly an "impression," an instant long gone.

A GLIMPSE OF A PARISIAN BOULEVARD SCENE Like Caillebotte, EDGAR DEGAS (1834–1917) took to the Parisian boulevards to watch the pedestrians, to catch the chance arrangements and the shifting patterns of their motion that his picture frame would crop as they passed. His *Viscount Lepic and His Daughters* (FIG. **29-20**) summarizes what the artist had learned from photography, from his own painstaking research, and from what his generation absorbed from the Japanese print—the clear, flat pattern; the unusual viewpoint; and the informal glimpse of contemporary life. Whatever his subject, Degas saw it in terms of clear line and pattern observed from a new and unexpected angle. In *Viscount Lepic and His Daughters,* the divergent movements of the father and his small daughters, of the man entering the picture at the left, and of the horse and carriage passing across the background provide a vivid pictorial account of a moment in time at a particular position in space. In another instant, this scene in real life would have disappeared, for each of the figures would have moved in a different direction and the group would have dissolved. Here again, Degas, like Caillebotte, made clever use of the street to integrate viewers into the

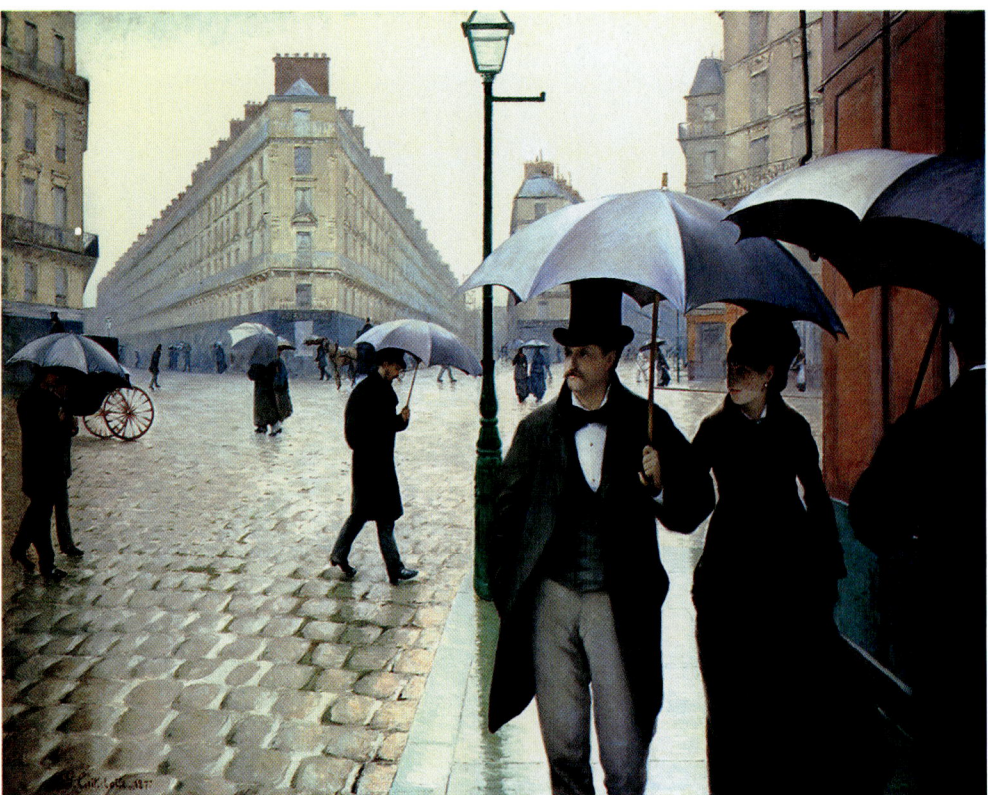

29-19 GUSTAVE CAILLEBOTTE, *Paris: A Rainy Day,* 1877. Oil on canvas, approx. 6′ 9″ × 9′ 9″. The Art Institute of Chicago, Chicago, Worcester Fund.

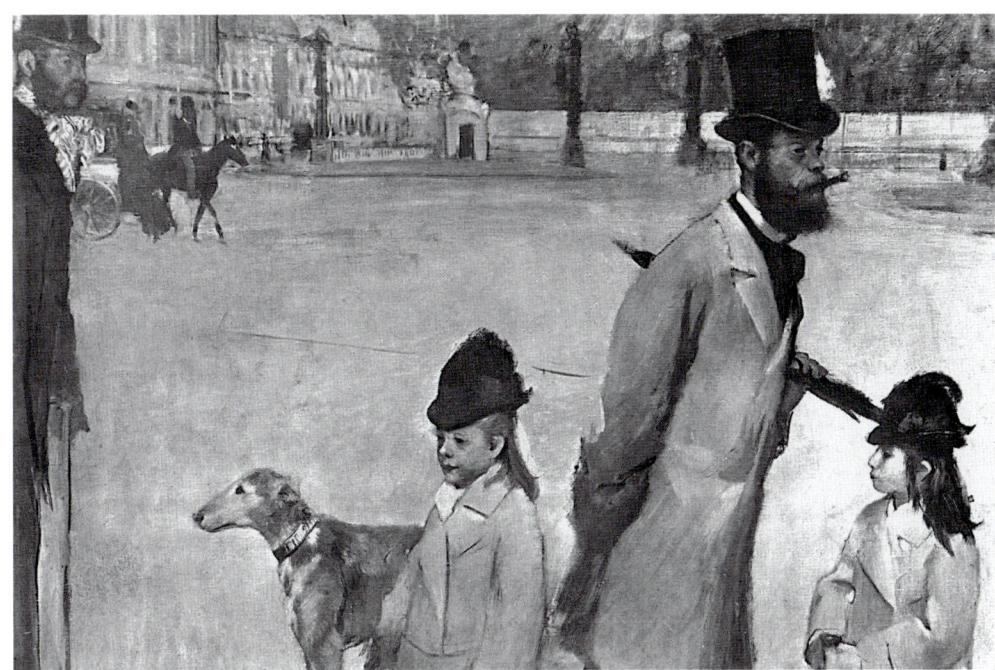

29-20 EDGAR DEGAS, *Viscount Lepic and His Daughters,* 1873. Oil on canvas, approx. 2′ 8″ × 3′ 11″. The Hermitage, Saint Petersburg.

space containing the figures. Actually, the painter seems to have taken into account the full sweep of a viewer's glance—everything one would see in a single split-second inspection.

A PANORAMA OF BUSTLING CROWDS *La Place du Théâtre Français* (FIG. **29-21**) is one of many panoramic scenes by CAMILLE PISSARRO (1830–1903) of the spacious boulevards and avenues that were the product of Haussmanization. In this painting, Pissarro recorded a panorama of blurred dark accents against a light ground that represents clearly his visual sensations of a crowded Paris square viewed from several stories above street level. Like many of the other Impressionists, Pissarro sought to capture a moment in time, but the moment in *La Place du Théâtre Français* is not so much of fugitive light effects as it is of the street life, achieved through a deliberate casualness in the figural arrangement.

Pissarro sometimes used the amazing "reality" of photography to supplement work directly from a model, like many of

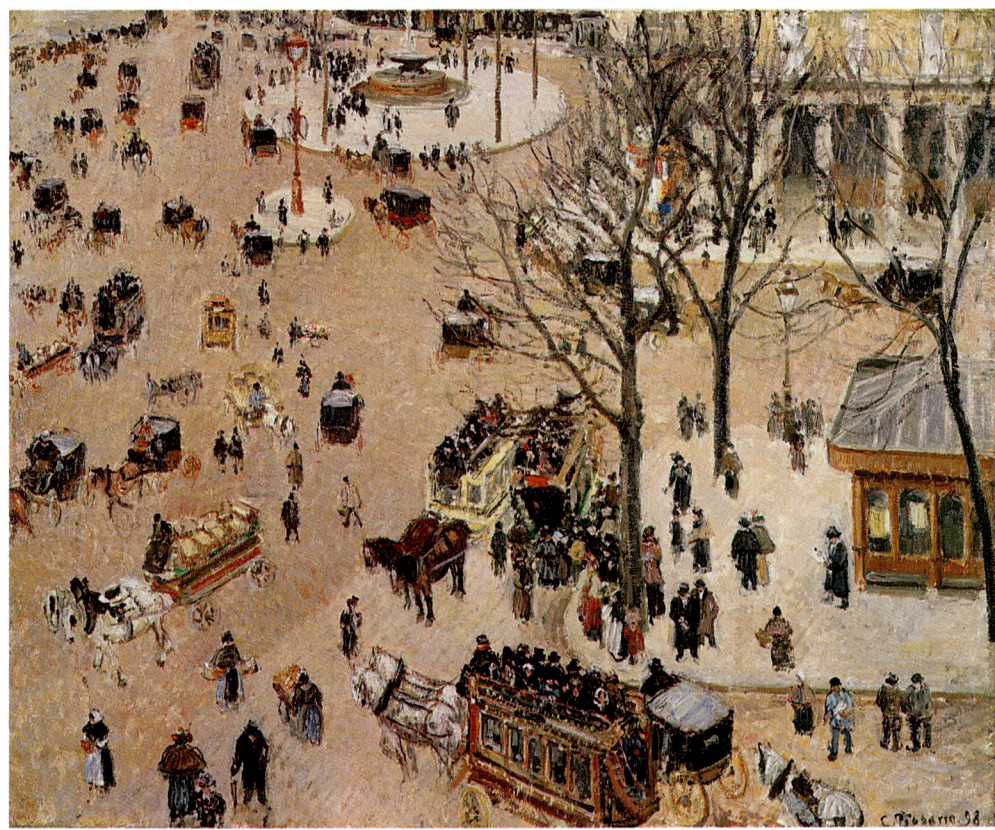

29-21 CAMILLE PISSARRO, *La Place du Théâtre Français,* 1898. Oil on canvas, 2′ 4½″ × 3′ ½″. Los Angeles County Museum of Art, Los Angeles (the Mr. and Mrs. George Gard De Sylva Collection).

29-22 HIPPOLYTE JOUVIN, *The Pont Neuf, Paris,* ca. 1860–1865. Albumen stereograph.

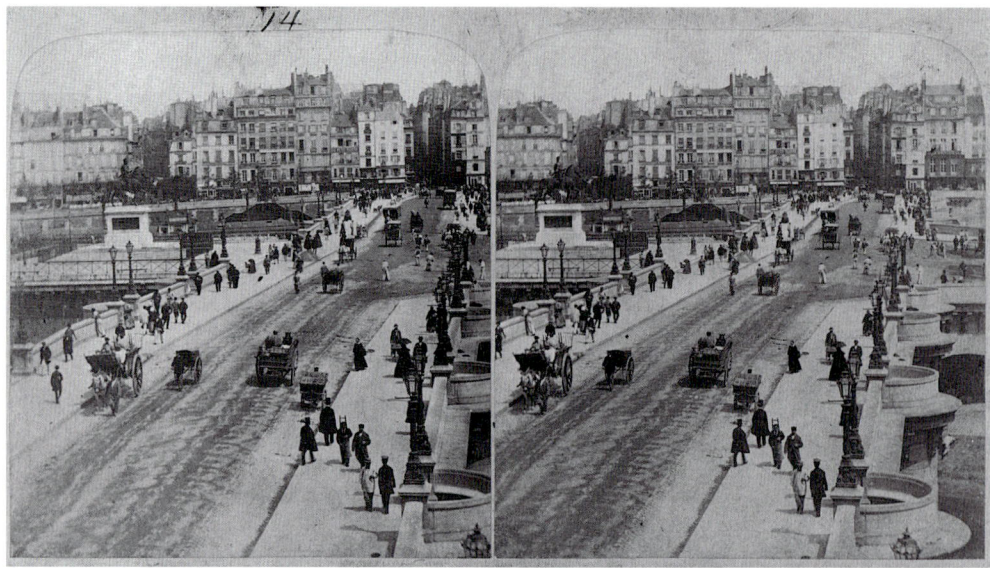

his fellow Impressionists. Although he may not have known the stereophotograph *The Pont Neuf, Paris* (FIG. **29-22**), its effect is remarkably similar to his *La Place du Théâtre.* With a special twin-lensed camera, HIPPOLYTE JOUVIN (active mid-1800s) made the stereograph, viewed with an apparatus, a stereoscope, to re-create the illusion of three dimensions. In this double image, the viewer's vantage point is from the upper story of a building along the roadway of the "New Bridge," which stretches diagonally from lower left to upper right. Hurrying pedestrians are dark silhouettes, and the scene moves from sharp focus in the foreground to soft focus in the distance. Because of the familiarity Pissarro and the other Im-

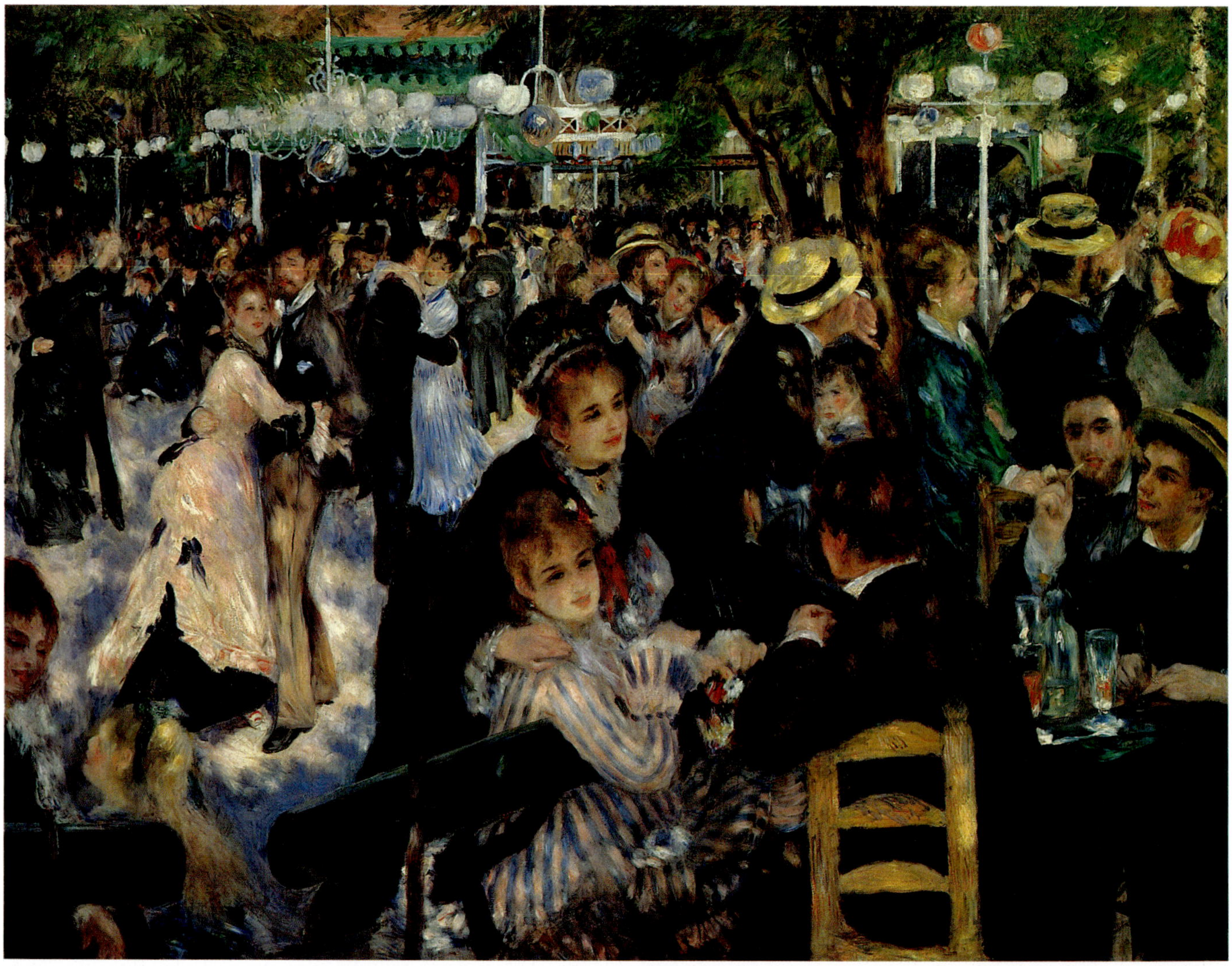

29-23   PIERRE-AUGUSTE RENOIR, *Le Moulin de la Galette,* 1876. Oil on canvas, approx. 4′ 3″ × 5′ 8″. Louvre, Paris.

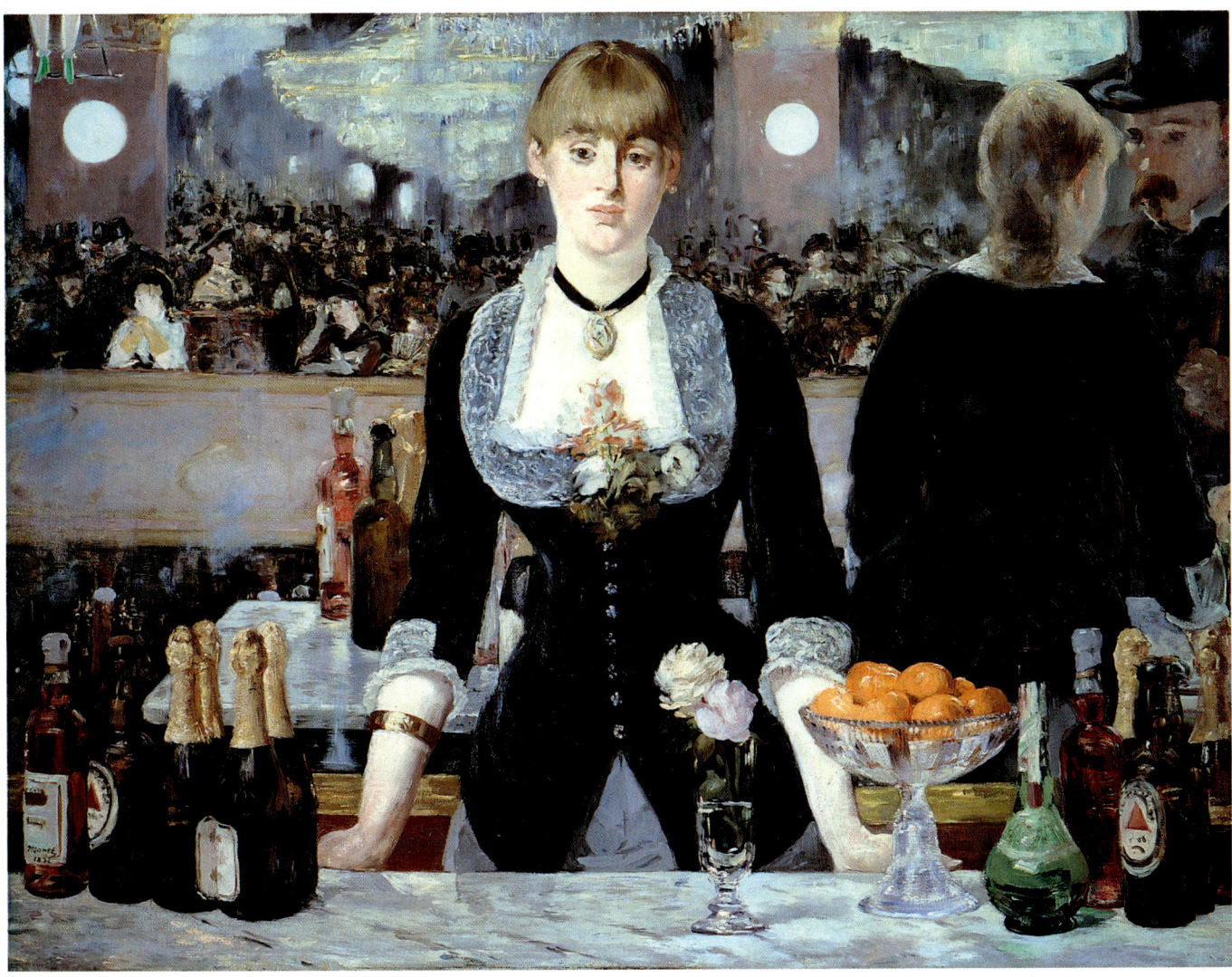

29-24   ÉDOUARD MANET, *A Bar at the Folies-Bergère,* 1882. Oil on canvas, approx. 3′ 1″ × 4′ 3″. The Courtauld Gallery, London.

pressionists had with photography, scholars have been quick to point out the visual parallels between Impressionist paintings and photographs. These parallels include, here, the arbitrary cutting off of figures at the frame's edge and the curious flattening spatial effect the high viewpoint caused.

LEISURE AND RECREATION   Another facet of the new, industrialized Paris that drew the Impressionists' attention was the leisure activities of its inhabitants. Scenes of dining, dancing, the café-concerts, the opera, the ballet, and other forms of enjoyable recreation were mainstays of Impressionism. Although seemingly unrelated to industrialization, these activities were facilitated by it. With the advent of set working hours, people's schedules became more regimented, allowing them to plan their favorite pastimes.

SOCIALIZING AT A PARISIAN DANCE HALL   *Le Moulin de la Galette* (FIG. **29-23**) by PIERRE-AUGUSTE RENOIR (1841–1919) depicts a popular Parisian dance hall. Throngs of people have gathered; some people crowd the tables and chatter, while others dance energetically. So lively is the atmosphere that viewers virtually can hear the sounds of music, laughter, and tinkling glasses. The whole scene is dappled by sunlight and shade, artfully blurred into the figures to produce just the effect of floating and fleeting light the Impres-

sionists so cultivated. Renoir's casual unposed placement of the figures and the suggested continuity of space, spreading in all directions and only accidentally limited by the frame, position viewers as participants, rather than as outsiders. Whereas classical art sought to express universal and timeless qualities, Impressionism attempted to depict just the opposite—reality's incidental, momentary, and passing aspects.

A PERPLEXING IMAGE OF A BARMAID   Édouard Manet's masterpiece, *A Bar at the Folies-Bergère* (FIG. **29-24**), was painted in 1882. The Folies-Bergère was a popular Parisian café-concert (a café with music-hall performances). Not only were these cafés fashionable gathering places for the throngs of revelers, but many of the Impressionists also frequented these establishments. In *Folies-Bergère,* viewers are confronted by a barmaid, centrally placed, who looks back but who seems disinterested or lost in thought. This woman appears divorced from the patrons as well as from viewers.

Manet blurred and roughly applied the brushstrokes, particularly those in the background, and the effects of modeling and perspective are minimal. This painting method further calls attention to the surface by forcing viewers to scrutinize the work to make sense of the scene. On such scrutiny, visual discrepancies seem to emerge. For example, what initially

29-25 EDGAR DEGAS, *Ballet Rehearsal (Adagio)*, 1876. Oil on canvas, 1′ 11″ × 2′ 9″. Glasgow Museum, Glasgow (The Burrell Collection).

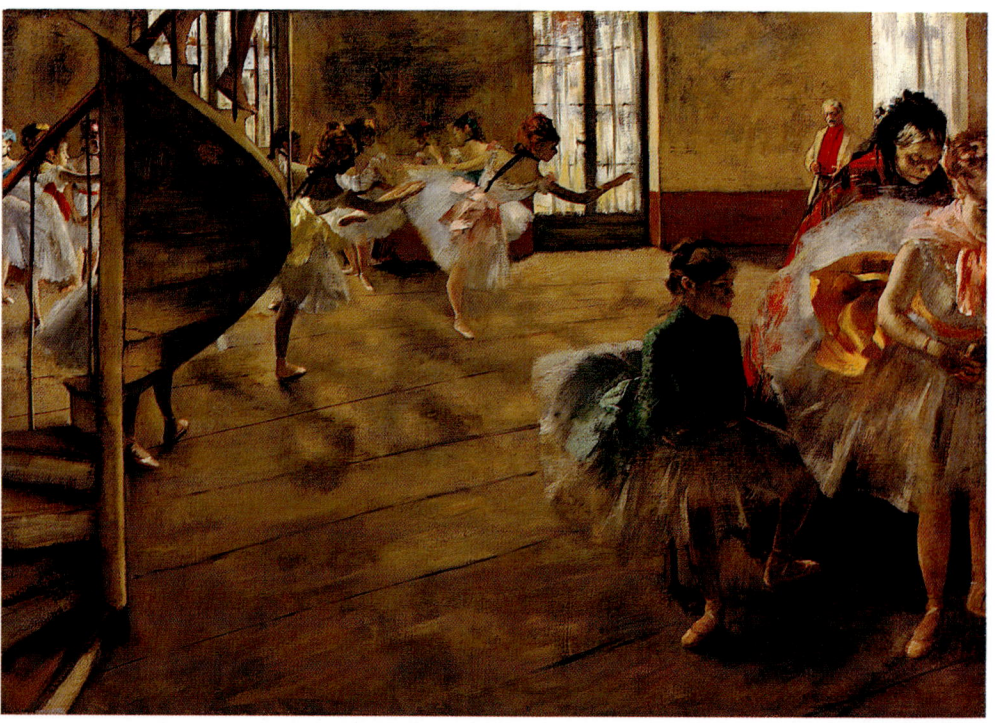

seems easily recognizable as a mirror behind the barmaid creates confusion throughout the rest of the painting. Is the woman on the right the barmaid's reflection? If so, it is impossible to reconcile the spatial relationship between the barmaid, the mirror, the bar's frontal horizontality, and the barmaid's seemingly displaced reflection. Manet's insistence on calling attention to the pictorial structure of this painting through these visual contradictions continued his Realist interest in examining the medium's basic premises. This radical break with tradition and redefinition of the function of the picture surface explains why many scholars position Manet as the first modernist artist.

OF MUSIC AND DANCE: BALLET IMAGES Impressionists also depicted more formal leisure activities. Edgar Degas's fascination with patterns of motion brought him to the Paris Opéra and its ballet school. There, his great observational power took in the formalized movements of classical ballet, one of his favorite subjects. In *Ballet Rehearsal (Adagio)*, FIG. **29-25**, Degas used several devices to bring observers into the pictorial space. The frame cuts off the spiral stair, the windows in the background, and the group of figures in the right foreground. The figures are not centered but rather, arranged in a seemingly random manner. The prominent diagonals of the wall bases and floorboards carry viewers into and along the directional lines of the dancers. Finally, as is customary in Degas's ballet pictures, a large, off-center, empty space creates the illusion of a continuous floor that connects observers with the pictured figures. By seeming to stand on the same surface with them, viewers are drawn into their space.

The often arbitrarily cutoff figures, the patterns of light splotches, and the blurriness of the images in this and other Degas works indicate the artist's interest in reproducing single moments. Further, they reveal his fascination with photogra-

phy. Degas not only studied the photography of others, but he also used the camera consistently to make preliminary studies for his works, particularly photographing figures in interiors. Other inspirational sources for paintings such as *Ballet Rehearsal* were eighteenth-century Japanese woodblock prints (see "Japonisme: The Allure of the Orient," page 912). The cunning spatial projections in Degas's paintings probably derived in part from Japanese prints, such as those by Suzuki Harunobu (see FIG. 27-14). Japanese artists used diverging lines not only to organize the flat shapes of figures but also to direct viewers' attention into the picture space. The Impressionists, acquainted with these prints as early as the 1860s, greatly admired their spatial organization, the familiar and intimate themes, and the flat unmodeled color areas and drew much instruction from them.

SAILING ALONG THE SEINE The Impressionists were drawn to painting outdoor leisure activity, and many of their prototypical works depict scenes from resort areas along the Seine River, such as Argenteuil, Bougival, and Chatou. Argenteuil was connected to Paris by the railway line that carried people to and from Saint-Lazare Station, so transportation was not an obstacle. Parisians often would take the train out to Argenteuil for a day of sailing, picnicking, and strolling along the Seine.

Claude Monet's many paintings of Argenteuil often have been seen as quintessentially Impressionist. In *Argenteuil Basin* (FIG. 29-26), sailboats float serenely on the intensely blue water. Sailing was a particularly popular recreational activity, and because the Seine was wider and deeper at Argenteuil than at other locations, it attracted those interested in boating.

Despite the rather static composition, the shimmering reflections of the boats on the water enliven the scene and impart a feeling of vibrancy. Monet enhanced this sense of

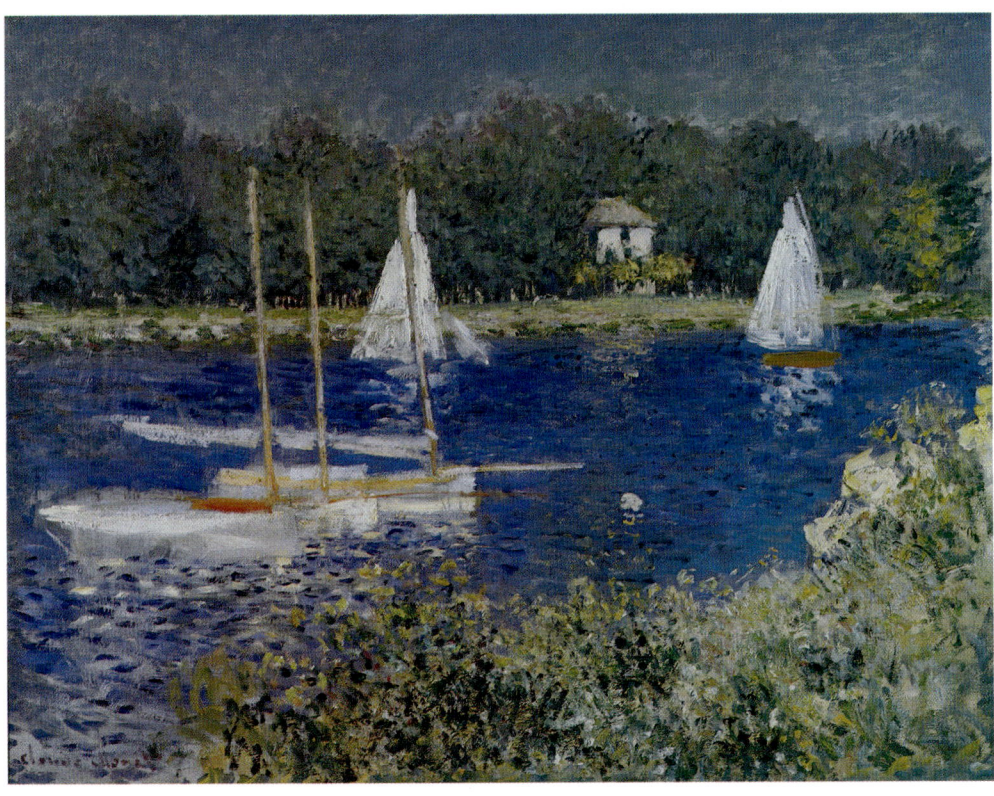

29-26 CLAUDE MONET, *Le Bassin d'Argenteuil,* ca.1875. Oil on canvas, approx. $21\frac{3}{4}''$ × $29\frac{1}{4}''$. Museum of Art, Rhode Island School of Design, Providence (gift of Mrs. Murray S. Danforth).

spontaneity with choppy brushstrokes, which suggest the breeze that plays across the surface of the water or through the trees and bushes, setting the leaves aflutter.

RELAXED LEISURE BY THE SEASIDE   BERTHE MORISOT (1841–1895) regularly exhibited with the Impres-

sionists and was well acquainted with those artists (Manet was her brother-in-law). Most of her paintings focus on domestic scenes, the one realm of Parisian life where society allowed an upper-class woman such as Morisot free access. Morisot's considerable skills are evident in *Villa at the Seaside* (FIG. **29-27**). Both the subject and style correlate well with

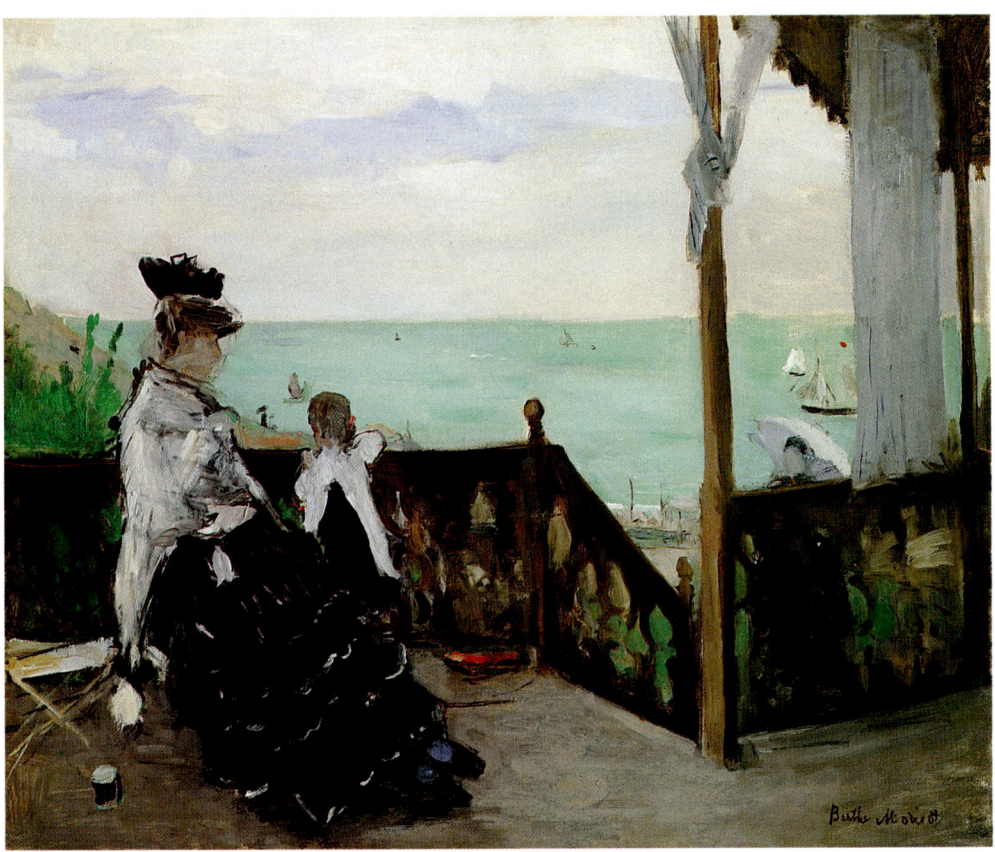

29-27 BERTHE MORISOT, *Villa at the Seaside,* 1874. Oil on canvas, approx. 1′ 8″ × 2′. Norton Simon Art Foundation, Los Angeles.

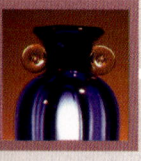

Japonisme
The Allure of the Orient

Despite Europe and America's rampant colonization during the nineteenth century, Japan avoided Western intrusion until 1853–1854, when Commodore Matthew Perry and American naval forces exacted trading and diplomatic privileges from Japan. From the increased contact, Westerners became familiar with Japanese culture. So intrigued were the French with Japanese art and culture that a specific label—"Japonisme"—was introduced to describe the Japanese aesthetic. Japonisme appealed to the fashionable segment of Parisian society, which no doubt was attracted to both the beauty and the exoticism of this foreign culture. In 1867 at the Universal Exposition in Paris, the Japanese pavilion garnered more attention than any other. Soon, Japanese kimonos, fans, lacquer cabinets, tea caddies, folding screens, tea services, and jewelry flooded Paris. Japanese-themed novels and travel books were immensely popular as well. As demand for Japanese merchandise grew in the West, the Japanese began to develop import-export businesses, and the foreign currency that flowed into Japan helped to finance much of its industrialization.

Artists in particular were drawn to Japanese art. Among those the Japanese aesthetic influenced were most of the Im-

pressionists and Post-Impressionists, especially Manet, James Abbott McNeill Whistler, Degas, Mary Cassatt, Vincent van Gogh, Paul Gauguin, and Henri de Toulouse-Lautrec. For the most part, the Japanese presentation of space in woodblock prints (see FIGS. 27-14 and 27-15), which were more readily available to the West than any other art form, intrigued these artists. Because of the simplicity of the wood-block printing process—a separate block is made for each color, and each block is printed in sequence—these prints are characterized by areas of flat color with a limited amount of modulation or gradation. This flatness interested modernist painters, who sought ways to call attention to the picture surface. The right side of Degas's *The Tub* (FIG. 29-29) has this two-dimensional quality. Degas, in fact, owned a print by Japanese artist Torii Kiyonaga (1752–1815) titled *Women's Bath* (ca. 1780) that inspired *The Tub*. The decorative quality of Japanese images also appealed to the artists associated with Art Nouveau (FIGS. 29-52, 29-53, and 29-54) and intersected nicely with two fundamental principles of the Arts and Crafts movement (FIGS. 29-50 and 29-51). These were that art should be available to the masses and that functional objects should be artistically designed, which account for that group's interest.

Impressionist concerns. The setting is the shaded veranda of a summer hotel at a fashionable seashore resort. A woman elegantly but quietly dressed sits gazing out across the railing to a sunlit beach with its umbrellas and bathing cabins. Her child, its discarded toy boat a splash of red, is attentive to the passing sails on the placid sea. The mood is of relaxed leisure. Morisot used the open brushwork and the *plein-air* (outdoor) lighting characteristic of Impressionism. Her brushwork is telegraphic in its report of her quick perceptions. Everything is suggested by swift, sketchy strokes, and nowhere did Morisot linger on contours or enclosed details. She presented the scene in a slightly filmy soft focus that conveys a feeling of airiness. The composition is also reminiscent of the work of other Impressionists; the figures fall informally into place, as someone who shared their intimate space would perceive them. Morisot was both immensely ambitious and talented, as her ability to catch the pictorial moment demonstrates. She escaped the hostile criticism directed at most of the other Impressionists; people praised her work for its sensibility, grace, and delicacy.

MONET'S STUDIES OF LIGHT AND COLOR

Monet's experiences painting outdoors sharpened his focus on the roles light and color play in capturing an instantaneous representation of atmosphere and climate. Monet, of all the Impressionists, carried the systematic investigation of light and color furthest. However, all of the artists associated with this movement recognized the importance of carefully observing

and understanding how light and color operate. Such thorough study permitted the Impressionists to present images that truly conveyed a sense of the momentary and transitory.

Scientific studies of light and the invention of chemical pigments increased artists' sensitivity to the multiplicity of colors in nature and gave them new colors for their work. After scrutinizing the effects of light and color on forms, the Impressionists concluded that *local color*—an object's actual color—usually is modified by the quality of the light in which it is seen, by reflections from other objects, and by the effects juxtaposed colors produce. Shadows do not appear gray or black, as many earlier painters thought, but seem to be composed of colors modified by reflections or other conditions. If artists use complementary colors (see Introduction, page xl in combined volumes or page xx in Volume II) side by side over large enough areas, the colors intensify each other, unlike the effect of small quantities of adjoining mixed pigments, which blend into neutral tones. Furthermore, the juxtaposition of colors on a canvas for the eye to fuse at a distance produces a more intense hue than the same colors mixed on the palette. It is not strictly true the Impressionists used only primary hues, juxtaposing them to create secondary colors (blue and yellow, for example, to create green). But they did achieve remarkably brilliant effects with their characteristically short, choppy brushstrokes, which so accurately caught the vibrating quality of light. The fact that their canvas surfaces look unintelligible at close range and their forms and objects appear only when the eye fuses the strokes at a certain distance accounts for much of the early adverse criticism leveled at their work. One such conjecture was that the Impressionists fired their paint at the canvas with pistols. Lila Cabot Perry, a student of Monet's late in his career, gave this description of Monet's approach:

> I remember his once saying to me: "When you go out to paint, try to forget what objects you have before you—a tree, a house, a field, or whatever. Merely think, here is a little square of blue, here an oblong of pink, here a streak of yellow, and paint it just as it looks to you, the exact color and shape, until it gives your own naïve impression of the scene before you." He said he wished he had been born blind and then had suddenly gained his sight so that he could have begun to paint in this way without knowing what the objects were that he saw before him.[14]

Monet's intensive study of the phenomena of light and color is especially evident in several series of paintings of the same subject. One series had some forty views of *Rouen Cathedral* (FIG. **29-28**). For each canvas in this series, Monet observed the cathedral from the same viewpoint but at differ-

ent times of the day or under various climatic conditions. With a scientific precision, he created an unparalleled record of the passing of time as seen in the movement of light over identical forms. Later critics accused Monet and his companions of destroying form and order for fleeting atmospheric effects, but Monet focused on light and color precisely to reach a greater understanding of form.

DEGAS'S PASTEL AND LINE DRAWING While color and light were major components of the Impressionist quest to capture fleeting sensations, these artists considered other formal elements as well. Degas, for example, became a superb master of line, so much so that his works often differ significantly from those of Monet and Renoir. Degas specialized in studies of figures in rapid and informal action, recording the quick impression of arrested motion, as is evident in *Ballet Rehearsal*. He often employed lines to convey this sense of movement. In *The Tub* (FIG. **29-29**), a young woman crouches in a washing tub. The artist outlined the major objects in the painting—the woman, tub, and pitchers—and covered all surfaces with linear hatch marks. Degas achieved this leaner quality with pastels, his favorite medium. Using these dry sticks of powdered pigment, Degas drew directly on the paper, as one would with a piece of chalk, thus accounting for the linear basis of this work. Further, although the applied pastel can be smudged, the colors tend to retain their autonomy, so they appear fresh and bright.

The Tub also reveals how Degas's work, like that of the other Impressionists, continues the modernist exploration of the premises of painting by acknowledging the artwork's surface. Although viewers clearly perceive the woman as a depiction of a three-dimensional form in space, the tabletop or shelf on the right of the image appears severely tilted, so much so that it seems to parallel the picture plane. The two pitchers on the table complicate this visual conflict between the table's flatness and the illusion of the bathing woman's three-dimensional volume. The limited foreshortening of the pitchers and their shared edge, in conjunction with the rest of the image, create a visual perplexity for viewers.

THE TENDERNESS OF MOTHER AND CHILD In the Salon of 1874, Degas admired a painting by a young American artist, MARY CASSATT (1844–1926), the daughter of a Philadelphia banker. "There," he remarked, "is someone who feels as I do."[15] Degas befriended and influenced Cassatt, who exhibited regularly with the Impressionists. She had trained as a painter before moving to Europe to study masterworks in France and Italy. As a woman, she could not easily frequent the cafés with her male artist friends, and she was responsible for the care of her aging parents, who had moved to Paris to join her, two facts limiting her subject choices. Because of these restrictions, Cassatt's subjects were principally women and children, whom she presented with a combination of objectivity and genuine sentiment. Works such as *The Bath* (FIG. **29-30**) show the tender relationship between a mother and child. Like Degas's *The Tub*, the visual solidity of the mother and child contrasts with the flattened patterning of the wallpaper and rug. Cassatt's style in this work owed much to the compositional devices of Degas and of Japanese prints, but the painting's design has an originality and strength all its own.

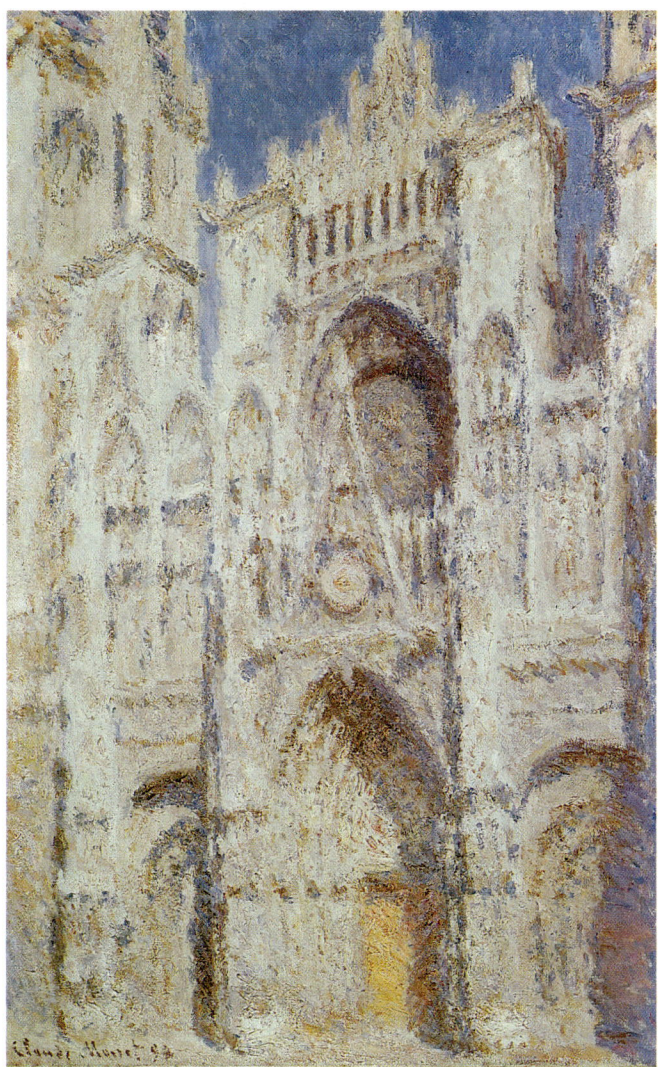

29-28 CLAUDE MONET, *Rouen Cathedral: The Portal (in Sun)*, 1894. Oil on canvas, 3' 3¼" × 2' 1⅞". Metropolitan Museum of Art, New York (Theodore M. Davis Collection, bequest of Theodore M. Davis, 1915).

29-29   EDGAR DEGAS, *The Tub*, 1886. Pastel, 1′ 11½″ × 2′ 8⅜″. Musée d'Orsay, Paris.

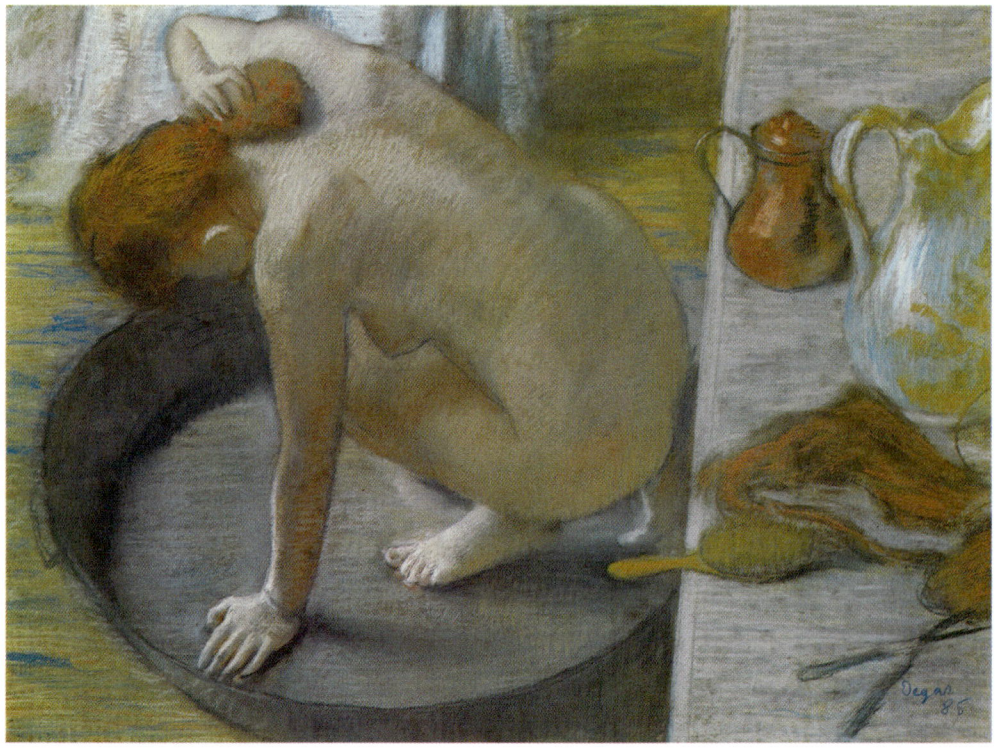

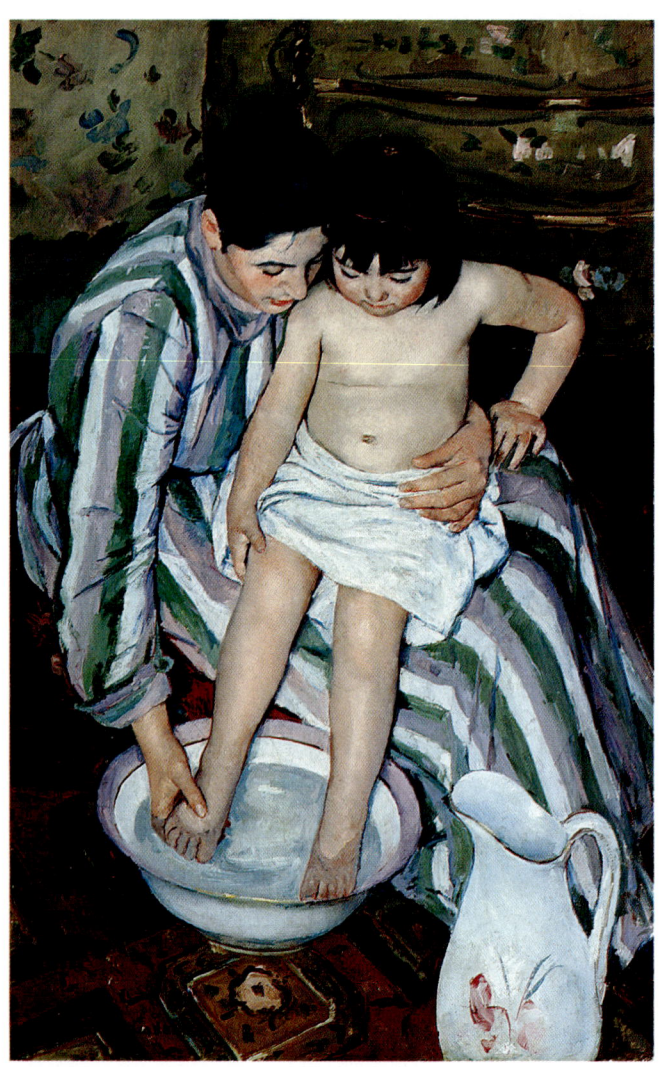

29-30   MARY CASSATT, *The Bath*, ca. 1892. Oil on canvas, 3′ 3″ × 2′ 2″. The Art Institute of Chicago, Chicago (Robert A. Walker Fund).

EXPLORING THE NIGHTLIFE OF PARIS French artist HENRI DE TOULOUSE-LAUTREC (1864–1901) was interested in capturing the sensibility of modern life and deeply admired Degas. Because of this interest and admiration, his work intersects with that of the Impressionists. However, his work has an added satirical edge to it and often borders on caricature. Toulouse-Lautrec's art was, to a degree, the expression of his life. Self-exiled by his odd stature and crippled legs from the high society his ancient aristocratic name entitled him to enter, he became a denizen of the night world of Paris, consorting with a tawdry population of entertainers, prostitutes, and other social outcasts. He reveled in the energy of cheap music halls, cafés, and bordellos. In *At the Moulin Rouge* (FIG. **29-31**), the influences of Degas, of the Japanese print, and of photography can be seen in the oblique and asymmetrical composition, the spatial diagonals, and the strong line patterns with added dissonant colors. But Toulouse-Lautrec so emphasized or exaggerated each element, although he closely studied such scenes in actual life and they were already familiar to viewers in the work of the earlier Impressionists, that the tone is new. Compare, for instance, this painting's mood with the relaxed and casual atmosphere of Renoir's *Le Moulin de la Galette* (FIG. 29-23). Toulouse-Lautrec's scene is nightlife, with its glaring artificial light, brassy music, and assortment of corrupt, cruel, and masklike faces. (He included himself in the background—the tiny man with the derby accompanying the very tall man, his cousin.) Such distortions by simplification of the figures and faces anticipated Expressionism (Chapter 33, page 1004), when artists' use of formal elements—for example, brighter colors and bolder lines than ever before—increased their images' impact on observers.

ORCHESTRATING ART JAMES ABBOTT MCNEILL WHISTLER (1834–1903) was an American expatriate artist

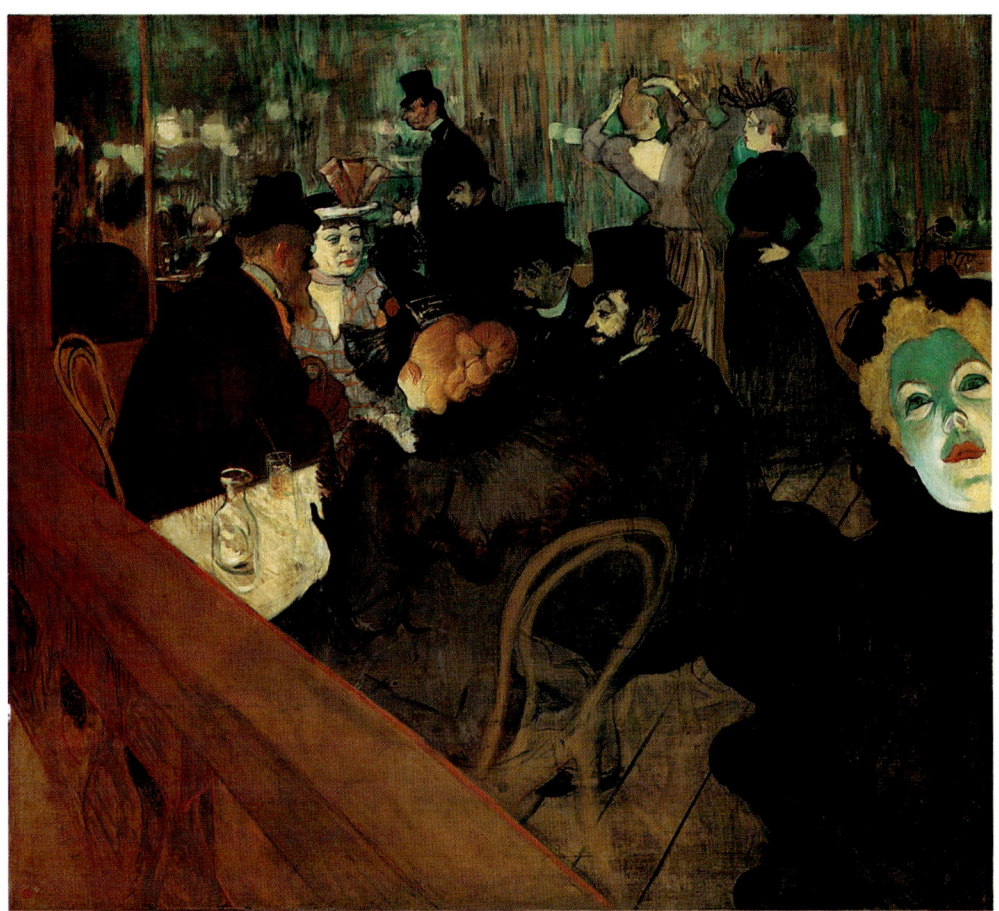

29-31 HENRI DE TOULOUSE-LAUTREC, *At the Moulin Rouge,* 1892–1895. Oil on canvas, approx. 4′ × 4′ 7″. The Art Institute of Chicago, Chicago (Helen Birch Bartlett Memorial Collection).

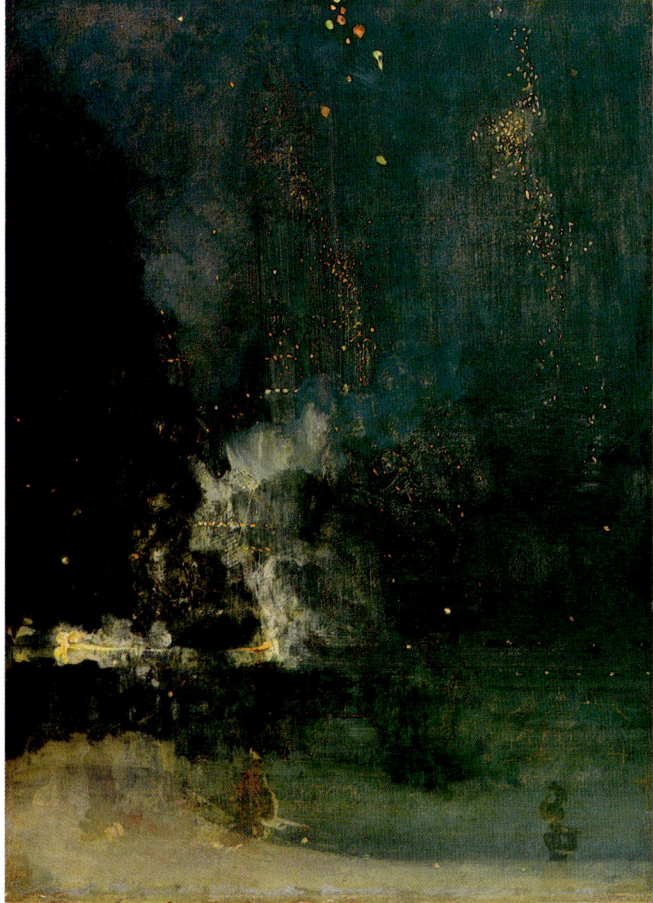

who worked on the European continent before settling finally in London. In Paris, he knew many of the Impressionists, and his art is an interesting mixture of some of their concerns and his own. Whistler shared their interests in the subject of contemporary life and the sensations color produces on the eye. To these influences he added his interest in creating harmonies paralleling those achieved in music:

> Nature contains the elements, in color and form, of all pictures, as the keyboard contains the notes of all music. But the artist is born to pick, and choose, and group with science, these elements, that the result may be beautiful—as the musician gathers his notes, and forms his chords, until he brings forth from chaos glorious harmony.[16]

To underscore his artistic intentions, Whistler began calling his paintings "arrangements" or "nocturnes." *Nocturne in Black and Gold (The Falling Rocket)*, FIG. **29-32**, is a daring painting with gold flecks and splatters that represent the exploded firework punctuating the darkness of the night sky. The artist was clearly more interested in conveying the atmospheric effects than he was in providing details of the actual scene. He emphasized creating a harmonious arrangement of shapes and colors on the rectangle of his canvas, an approach that interested many twentieth-century artists.

29-32 JAMES ABBOTT MCNEILL WHISTLER, *Nocturne in Black and Gold (The Falling Rocket),* ca. 1875. Oil on panel, 1′ 11$\frac{5}{8}$″ × 1′ 6$\frac{1}{2}$″. Detroit Institute of Arts, Detroit (gift of Dexter M. Ferry Jr.).

"FLINGING PAINT IN THE PUBLIC'S FACE"
Such works angered many viewers. The British critic John Ruskin responded to this painting by writing a scathing review accusing Whistler of "flinging a pot of paint in the public's face" with his style. In reply, Whistler sued Ruskin for libel. During the trial, Whistler was asked about the subject of *Nocturne:*

> "What is the subject of the *Nocturne in Black and Gold*?"
> "It is a night piece and represents the fireworks at Cremorne," answered Whistler.
> "Not a view of Cremorne?"
> "If it were a view of Cremorne, it would certainly bring about nothing but disappointment on the part of the beholders. It is an artistic arrangement. . . . It is as impossible for me to explain to you the beauty of that picture as it would be for a musician to explain to you the beauty of a harmony in a particular piece of music if you have no ear for music."[17]

Although Whistler won the case, his victory had sadly ironic consequences for him. The judge in the case, showing where his—and perhaps the public's—sympathies lay, awarded the artist only one farthing (less than a penny) in damages and required him to pay all of the court costs, which ruined him financially. He continued to produce etchings and portraits for two decades after his bankruptcy.

POST-IMPRESSIONISM: EXPERIMENTING WITH FORM AND COLOR

By 1886, most critics and a large segment of the public accepted the Impressionists as serious artists. Just when their images of contemporary life no longer seemed crude and unfinished, however, some of these painters and a group of younger followers came to feel Impressionists were neglecting too many of the traditional elements of picture making in their attempts to capture momentary sensations of light and color on canvas. In a conversation with the influential art dealer Ambroise Vollard in about 1883, Renoir commented: "I had wrung [I]mpressionism dry, and I finally came to the conclusion that I knew neither how to paint nor how to draw. In a word, [I]mpressionism was a blind alley, as far as I was concerned."[18] By the 1880s, four artists in particular were much more systematically examining the properties and the expressive qualities of line, pattern, form, and color: Vincent van Gogh, Paul Gauguin, Georges Seurat, and Paul Cézanne. Both van Gogh and Gauguin focused their artistic efforts on exploring the expressive capabilities of formal elements, while Seurat and Cézanne were more analytical in orientation. Because their art diverged so markedly from earlier Impressionism (although each of these painters initially based their work on Impressionist precepts and methods), these four artists and others sharing their views have become known as the Post-Impressionists. This classification also signifies their chronological position in nineteenth-century Western painting.

"THE TERRIBLE PASSIONS OF HUMANITY"
VINCENT VAN GOGH (1853–1890) explored the capabilities of colors and distorted forms to express his emotions as he confronted nature. The son of a Dutch Protestant pastor, van Gogh believed he had a religious calling and did missionary work in the slums of London and in the mining districts of Belgium. Repeated professional and personal failures brought him close to despair (see "From Pariah to Paragon: The Shifting Fortunes of Vincent van Gogh," page 917). Although the image of van Gogh as a madman persists in the public imagination, van Gogh is better described as a tormented individual who suffered from epileptic seizures. Only after he turned to painting did he find a way to communicate his

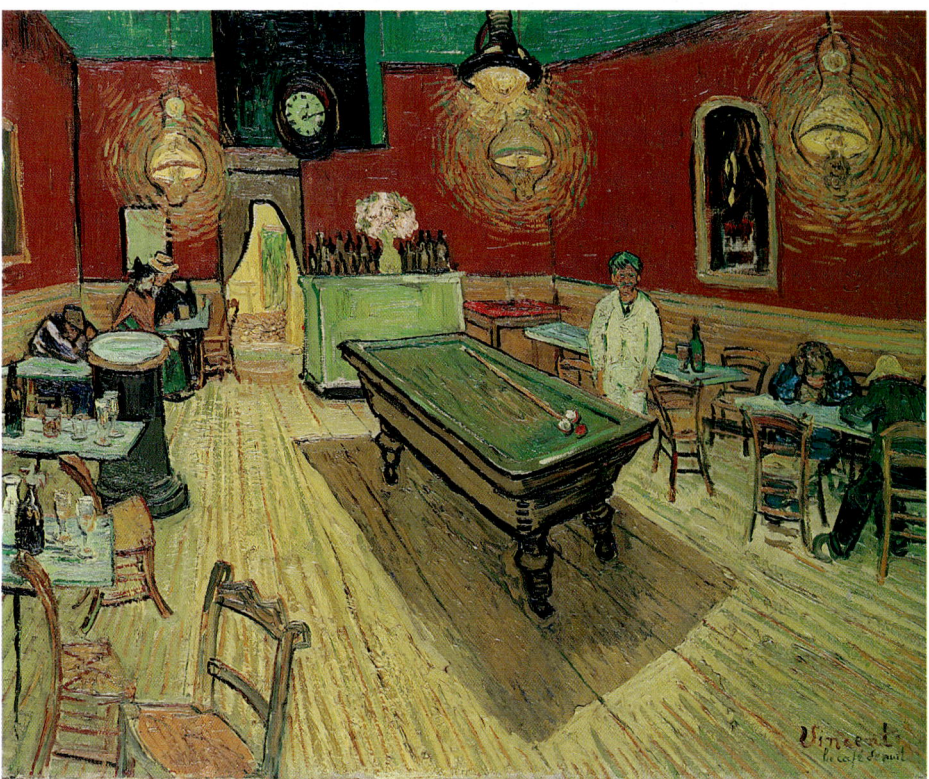

29-33 VINCENT VAN GOGH, *The Night Café,* 1888. Oil on canvas, approx. 2' 4½" × 3'. Yale University Art Gallery, New Haven (bequest of Stephen Carlton Clark, B.A., 1903).

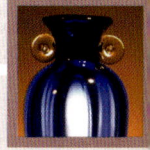

From Pariah to Paragon
The Shifting Fortunes of Vincent van Gogh

When van Gogh died of a self-inflicted gunshot wound in 1890 at age 37, he considered himself a failure as an artist. He felt himself an outcast not only from artistic circles but also from society at large. The hostile reception to his work, both from fellow artists and the general public, no doubt reinforced this perception. Throughout his brief career, he encountered great difficulty selling his work; indeed, he sold only one painting during his lifetime.

Since his death, however, his reputation and the appreciation of his art have grown dramatically, and it is no exaggeration to state that van Gogh is today one of the most revered and respected artists. This reevaluation speaks volumes about his art, yet it actually says more about the fluctuations in public taste and the ongoing assessment central to the art historical enterprise. Taste, both cultural and personal, is notoriously unpredictable, as evidenced by the constantly and frequently shifting preferences in fashion, design, architecture, and art. Art history, as a discipline, is based on the continual study of previous art. Therefore, conclusions about the work of artists are always subject to change.

Today, van Gogh's work stands as an important contribution to the development of an expressionistic art, and it has deeply influenced generations of artists. Although monetary value does not necessarily reflect artistic value, it is worth noting that in recent years, van Gogh's paintings consistently have brought the highest prices at auction. In 1987, *Sunflowers* (1888) sold for $39.9 million to a Japanese insurance company. The following year, *Irises* (1889) was purchased for $53.9 million by Alan Bond, an Australian brewing and real estate tycoon. (Bond eventually defaulted on the payment for the painting, and the J. Paul Getty Museum in Los Angeles subsequently bought the work.) In 1990, *Portrait of Dr. Gachet* (1890) was sold to Ryoei Saito, a Japanese paper manufacturing magnate, for $82.5 million, the most ever paid for an artwork.

It is sobering to think an artist who has had such a dramatic impact on the direction of art and on the general public died thinking himself a failure.

---

experiences. In one of the many revealing letters he wrote to his brother, Theo, van Gogh admitted: "In both my life and in my painting, I can very well do without God but I cannot, ill as I am, do without something which is greater than I, which is my life—the power to create."[19] For van Gogh, the power to create involved the expressive use of color. As he wrote to Theo: "Instead of trying to reproduce exactly what I have before my eyes, I use color more arbitrarily so as to express myself forcibly."[20] In another letter, he explained that the color in one of his paintings was "not locally true from the point of view of the delusive realist, but color suggesting some emotion of an ardent temperament."[21]

Van Gogh's insistence on the expressive values of color led him to develop a corresponding expressiveness in his paint application. The thickness, shape, and direction of his brush strokes created a tactile counterpart to his intense color schemes. He moved the brush vehemently back and forth or at right angles, giving a textilelike effect, or squeezed dots or streaks onto his canvas from his paint tube. This bold, almost slapdash attack enhanced the intensity of his colors.

After relocating to Arles in southern France in 1888, van Gogh painted *The Night Café* (FIG. **29-33**), an interior scene. Although the subject is apparently benign, van Gogh invested it with a charged energy. As van Gogh described it, the painting was meant to convey an oppressive atmosphere— "a place where one can ruin oneself, go mad, or commit a crime. . . ."[22] He communicated this by selecting vivid hues whose juxtaposition augmented their intensity. Van Gogh described it in a letter to Theo:

> I have tried to express the terrible passions of humanity by means of red and green. The room is blood red and dark yellow with a green billiard table in the middle; there are four citron-yellow lamps with a glow of orange and green. Everywhere there is a clash and contrast of the most disparate reds and greens in the figures of little sleeping hooligans, in the empty, dreary room, in violet and blue. The blood-red and the yellow-green of the billiard table, for instance, contrast with the soft, tender Louis XV green of the counter, on which there is a pink nosegay. The white coat of the landlord, awake in a corner of that furnace, turns citron-yellow, or pale luminous green.[23]

The proprietor rises like a specter from the edge of the billiard table, which the painter depicted in such a steeply tilted perspective that it threatens to slide out of the painting into the viewers' space. Van Gogh took an innocuous scene and imbued it with "the terrible passions of humanity."

GLIMMERS OF HOPE? Just as illustrative of van Gogh's "expressionist" method is *Starry Night* (FIG. **29-34**), which the artist painted in 1889, the year before his death. At this time, van Gogh was living at Saint-Paul-de-Mausole, an asylum in Saint-Rémy where he had committed himself. In *Starry Night,* the artist did not represent the sky in a manner that can be described as realistic. Rather, he communicated the vastness of the universe, filled with whirling and exploding stars and galaxies of stars, the earth and humanity huddling beneath it. The church nestled in the center of the village below can be seen, perhaps, as van Gogh's attempt to express or reconcile his conflicted feelings about religion. Although van Gogh's style in *Starry Night* suggests a very personal vision, this work does correspond in many ways to the view available to the painter from the window of his room in Saint-Paul-de-Mausole. The existence of cypress trees and the placement of the constellations have been confirmed as matching the view that

29-34 Vincent van Gogh, *Starry Night,* 1889. Oil on canvas, approx. 2′ 5″ × 3′ $\frac{1}{4}$″. Museum of Modern Art, New York (acquired through the Lillie P. Bliss Bequest).

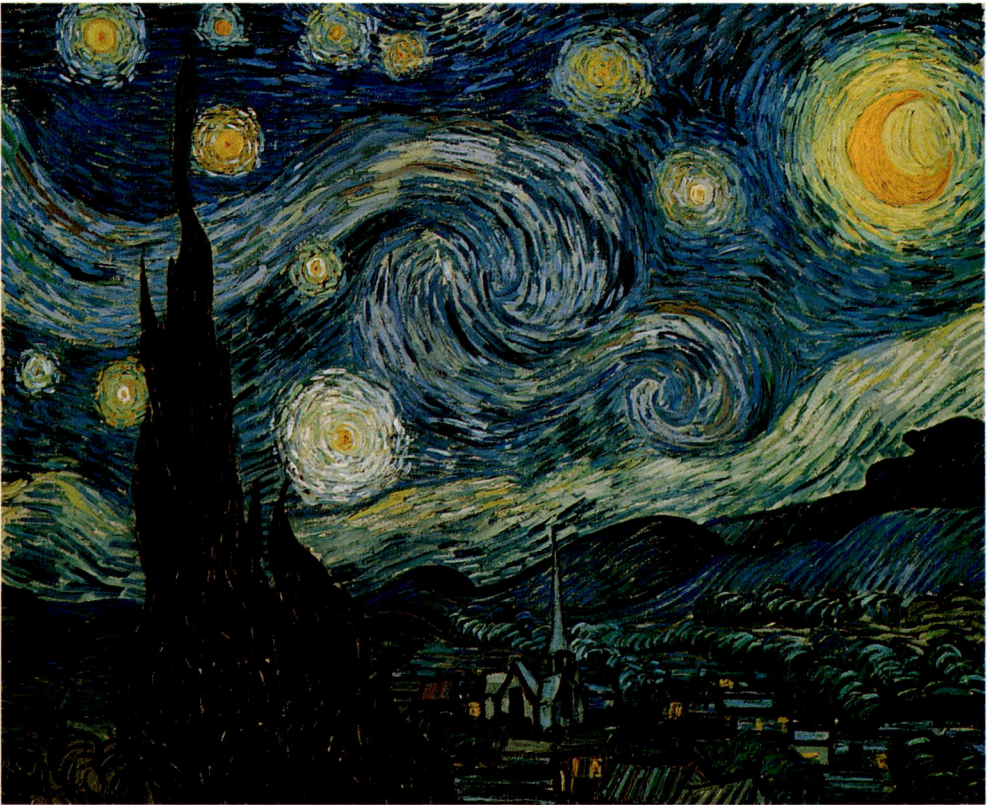

would have been visible to van Gogh during his stay in the asylum. Still, the artist took any visible objects and translated them into his unique vision. Given van Gogh's determination to use color to express himself forcibly, the dark, deep blue that pervades the entire painting cannot be overlooked. Together with the turbulent brushstrokes, the color suggests a quiet but pervasive depression. Van Gogh's written observation to his brother reveals his contemplative state of mind:

> Perhaps death is not the hardest thing in a painter's life. . . . [L]ooking at the stars always makes me dream, as simply as I dream over the black dots representing towns and villages on a map. Why, I ask myself, shouldn't the shining dots of the sky be as accessible as the black dots on the map of France? Just as we take the train to get to Tarascon or Rouen, we take death to reach a star.[24]

FROM IMPRESSIONISM TO FLAT COLOR Like van Gogh, the French painter Paul Gauguin (1848–1903) rejected objective representation in favor of subjective expression. He also broke with the Impressionistic studies of minutely contrasted hues because he believed color above all must be expressive and that the artist's power to determine the colors in a painting was a seminal element of creativity. However, while van Gogh's heavy, thick brush strokes were an important component of his expressive style, Gauguin's color areas appear flatter, often visually dissolving into abstract patches or patterns. Gauguin had painted as an amateur, but after taking lessons with Pissarro, he resigned from his prosperous brokerage business in 1883 to devote his time entirely to painting.

In 1886, Gauguin moved to Pont-Aven in Brittany, the remotest province of France. There he painted a work that decisively rejects Realism and Impressionism, *The Vision after the Sermon,* or *Jacob Wrestling with the Angel* (FIG.

29-35). Gauguin was attracted to Brittany's unspoiled culture, its ancient Celtic folkways, and the still medieval Catholic piety of its people. In his view, these were "natural" men and women, perfectly at ease in their unspoiled peasant environment. The story of Jacob's encounter with the Angel (the Lord) is told in Genesis 32:24–30. The painting shows Breton women, wearing their starched white Sunday caps and black dresses, visualizing a sermon they have just heard at church on Jacob's encounter with the Holy Spirit. They pray devoutly before the apparition, as they would have before the roadside crucifix shrines that were familiar features of the Breton countryside.

Gauguin departed from an optical realism and composed the picture elements to focus viewers' attention on the idea and intensify its message. The images are not what the Impressionist eye would have seen and replicated but what memory would have recalled and imagination would have modified. Thus the artist twisted the perspective and allotted the space to emphasize the innocent faith of the unquestioning women, while he shrank Jacob and the Angel, wrestling in a ring enclosed by a Breton stone fence, to the size of fighting cocks. The women are spectators at a contest, which, like a cockfight, is for them perfectly real.

Gauguin did not unify the picture with a horizon perspective, light and shade, or a naturalistic use of color. Instead, he abstracted the scene into a pattern. Pure unmodulated color fills flat planes and shapes bounded by firm line. Here are the white caps, black dresses, and the red field of combat. The shapes are angular, even harsh. The caps, the sharp fingers and profiles, and the hard contours suggest the austerity of peasant life and ritual. Gauguin was receptive to the influences of Japanese prints, stained glass, and cloisonné enamels (see FIG. 16-2). These contributed to his own daring experiment to transform traditional painting and Impressionism into ab-

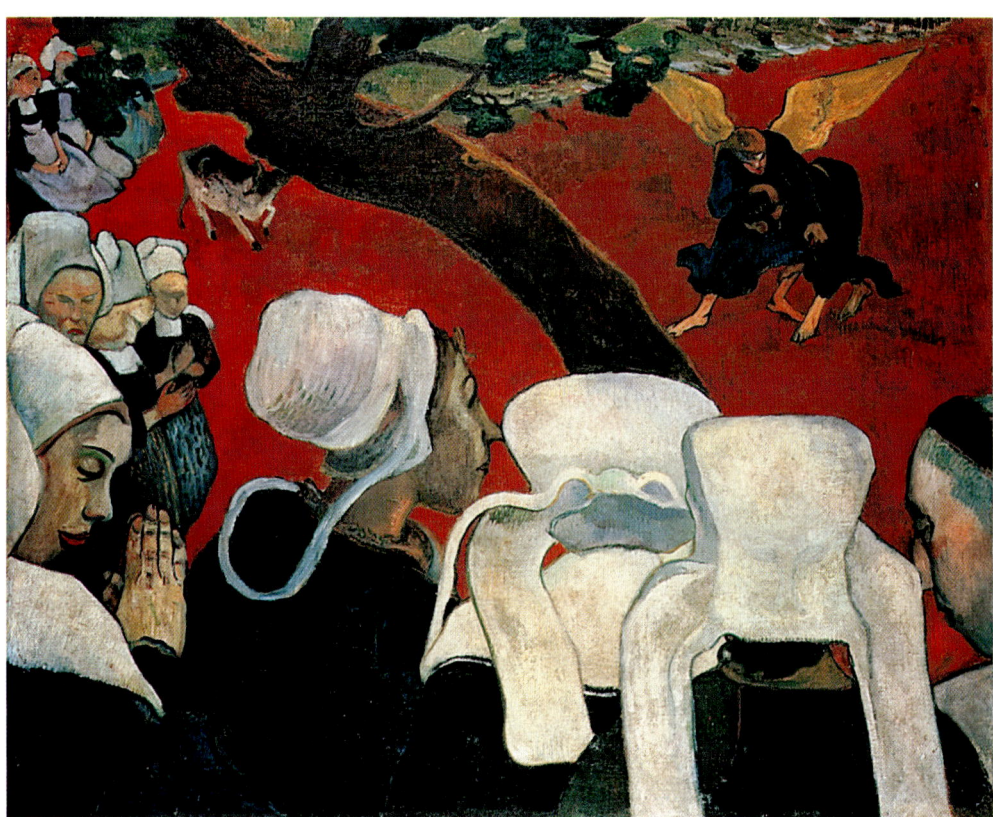

29-35 PAUL GAUGUIN, *The Vision after the Sermon* or *Jacob Wrestling with the Angel*, 1888. Oil on canvas, 2′ 4¾″ × 3′ 1½″. National Gallery of Scotland, Edinburgh.

stract, expressive patterns of line, shape, and pure color. His revolutionary method found its first authoritative expression in *The Vision After the Sermon.*

After a brief period of association with van Gogh in Arles in 1888, Gauguin, in his restless search for provocative subjects and for an economical place to live, settled in Tahiti. He spent the last years of his life in the South Pacific, where he expressed his fascination with primitive life and brilliant color in a series of striking decorative canvases. Gauguin often based the design, although indirectly, on native motifs, and the color owed its peculiar harmonies of lilac, pink, and lemon to the tropical flora of the islands.

A SUMMARY OF LIFE AND ART Despite the allure of the South Pacific, Gauguin continued to struggle with life. His health suffered, and his art was not well received. In 1897, worn down by these obstacles, Gauguin decided to take his own life, but not before painting a large canvas titled *Where Do We Come From? What Are We? Where Are We Going?* (FIG. **29-36**). From the title and based on Gauguin's state of mind, this painting can be read as a summary of his artistic methods (especially the use of flat shapes of pure unmodulated color) and his views on life.

The scene is a tropical landscape, populated with native women and children. Although any message Gauguin

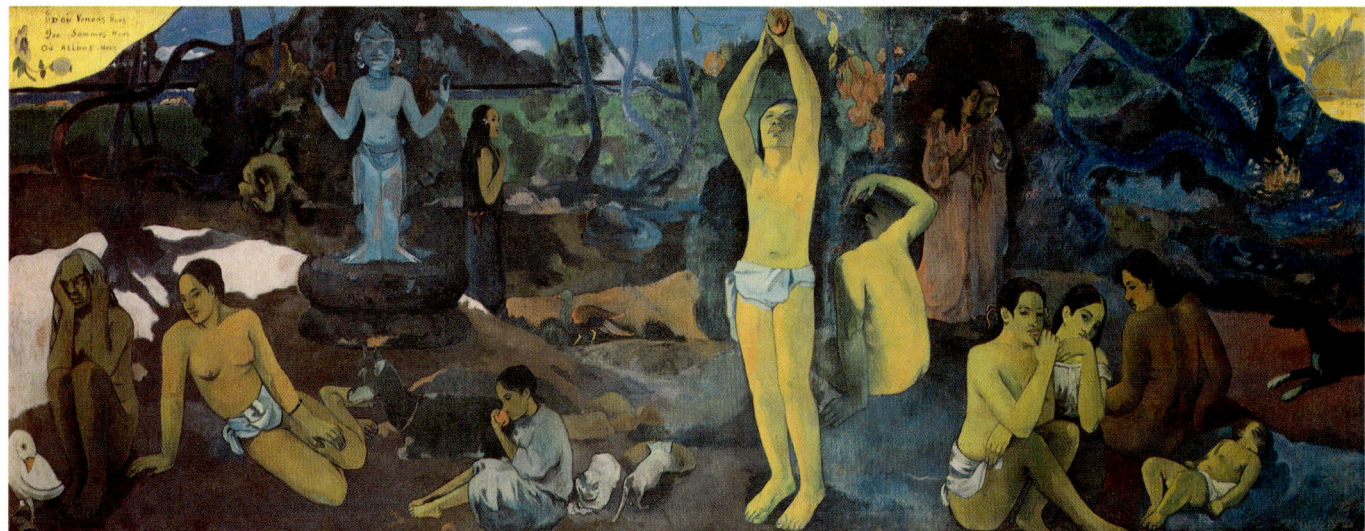

29-36 PAUL GAUGUIN, *Where Do We Come From? What Are We? Where Are We Going?*, 1897. Oil on canvas, 4′ 6¹³⁄₁₆″ × 12′ 3″. Museum of Fine Arts, Boston (Tompkins Collection).

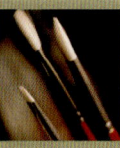

Nineteenth-Century Color Theory

With the increasing reliance on science and industry during the latter half of the nineteenth century, the interest in the science of optics is not surprising. Many physicists, chemists, and aestheticians (experts in art and artistic principles) immersed themselves in studying optical reception and the behavior of the human eye in response to light of differing wavelengths. Painter Georges Seurat was well read and very familiar with the work of these artists and scientists, and he used many of their theories to develop pointillism (FIG. 29-37).

Discussions of color often focus on hue (for example, red, yellow, and blue), but it is important to consider the other facets of color—saturation (the hue's brightness or dullness) and value (the hue's lightness or darkness). Most artists during the nineteenth century understood the primary colors as red, yellow and blue and the complementary secondary colors as those produced by mixing pairs of these primaries—green (blue plus yellow), violet (red plus blue), and orange (red plus yellow). Chemist Michel-Eugène Chevreul extended artists' understanding of color dynamics by formulating the law of simultaneous contrast of colors, based on his observations as director of dyeing at the Gobelins tapestry workshops. Chevreul asserted that juxtaposed colors affect the eye's reception of each, making the two colors as dissimilar as possible, both in hue and value. For example, placing light green next to dark green has the effect of making the light green look even lighter and the dark green darker. Chevreul further provided an explanation of *successive contrasts*—the well-known phenomenon of colored afterimages. When a person looks intently at a color (green, for example) and then shifts to a white area, the fatigued eye momentarily perceives the complementary color (orange).

Seurat was probably also familiar with the work of aesthetician Charles Blanc, who coined the term "optical mixture" to describe the visual effect of juxtaposed complementary colors.

Blanc asserted that the smaller the areas of adjoining complementary colors, the greater the tendency for the eye to "mix" the colors, so that the viewer perceives a grayish or neutral tint. Seurat used this principle frequently in his paintings.

The observations of James Clerk Maxwell also were crucial for color theory development and for Seurat's color use. Maxwell was instrumental in designing an objective method of color measurements, using algebraic color-matching equations. Maxwell's studies, it should be noted, applied to the mixing of colored lights, not the mixing of colored pigments. In other words, Maxwell's explanations dealt with how the eye sees color, not how painters should combine pigments on their palettes.

Particularly influential for Seurat was the work of physicist Ogden Rood, who published his ideas in *Modern Chromatics, with Applications to Art and Industry* in 1879. Rood expanded on the ideas of Chevreul, Blanc, and Maxwell and constructed an accurate and understandable diagram of contrasting colors. Further (and particularly significant to Seurat), Rood explored representing color gradation. He suggested that placing small dots or lines of color side by side so that, when viewed from a distance, "the blending is more or less accomplished by the eye of the beholder" is one way to achieve gradation.[1]

Although these discoveries intrigued Seurat and he purchased a copy of Rood's book, making notes from one section of it, his goal was not solely to create a scientific painting method. Seurat's work, though characterized by discipline and a systematic approach, also incorporated his concerns about the emotional tone of the images. The investigations of these color theorists, however, continued to be important and impacted the development of art in the twentieth century.

[1] John Leighton and Richard Thomson, *Seurat and the Bathers* (London: National Gallery Publications, 1997), 49.

---

intended is ambiguous at best, statements he made in a letter to his friend, Charles Morice, shed light on his philosophical conclusions.

> Where are we going? Near to death an old woman. . . . What are we? Day to day existence. . . . Where do we come from? Source. Child. Life begins. . . . Behind a tree two sinister figures, cloaked in garments of sombre colour, introduce, near the tree of knowledge, their note of anguish caused by that very knowledge in contrast to some simple beings in a virgin nature, which might be paradise as conceived by humanity, who give themselves up to the happiness of living.[25]

Gauguin's description of this work as "comparable to the Gospels"[26] indicates the expansiveness of his vision, but *Where Do We Come From?* remains a sobering, pessimistic im-

age of the life cycle's inevitability. In terms of style, this painting demonstrates Gauguin's commitment to the expressive ability of color. Although the venue is recognizable as a landscape, most of the scene, other than the figures, is composed of flat areas of unmodulated color, which convey a lushness and intensity.

Gauguin's attempt to commit suicide was unsuccessful, and he ultimately died a few years later, in 1903, in the Marquesas Islands. Members of the younger generation especially felt the influence of Gauguin's art and ideas. Parisian artist Maurice Denis (1870–1943) wrote in "The Influence of Paul Gauguin" in 1903:

> Gauguin freed us from all the hindrances imposed upon our painters' instincts by the idea of copying. . . . For instance, if we could paint in vermillion that tree which appeared to us very reddish

at a certain moment, . . . [w]hy not stress even to the point of distortion the curve of a lovely shoulder, . . . stylize the symmetry of a branch . . . ?[27]

THE SCIENCE OF COLOR   In contrast to the expressionistic nature of the work of van Gogh and Gauguin, the art of Frenchman GEORGES SEURAT (1859–1891) was resolutely intellectual. He devised a disciplined and painstaking system of painting that focused on color analysis. Seurat was less concerned with the recording of immediate color sensations than he was with their careful and systematic organization into a new kind of pictorial order. He disciplined the free and fluent play of color that characterized Impressionism into a calculated arrangement based on scientific color theory (see "Nineteenth-Century Color Theory," page 920). Seurat's system, known as *pointillism* or *divisionism,* involved carefully observing color and separating it into its component parts. The artist then applied these pure component colors to the canvas in tiny dots (points) or daubs (FIG. **29-37**). Thus, the shapes, figures, and spaces in the image only become totally comprehensible from a distance, when viewers' eyes blend the many pigment dots.

Pointillism was on view at the eighth and last Impressionist exhibition in 1886, when Seurat showed his *A Sunday on La Grande Jatte* (FIG. **29-38**). The subject of the painting is reminiscent of the Impressionist interest in recreational themes. And although Seurat was also interested in analyzing light and color (as were the Impressionists), this painting seems strangely rigid and remote, unlike the spontaneous representations of Impressionism. Seurat applied pointillism to produce a carefully composed and painted image. By using meticulously calculated values, the painter carved out a deep rectangular space. He played on repeated motifs to create both flat patterns and suggested spatial depth. Reiterating the profile of the female form, the parasol, and the cylindrical forms of the figures, Seurat placed each in space to set up a rhythmic movement in depth, as well as from side to side. The picture is filled with sunshine but not broken into transient patches

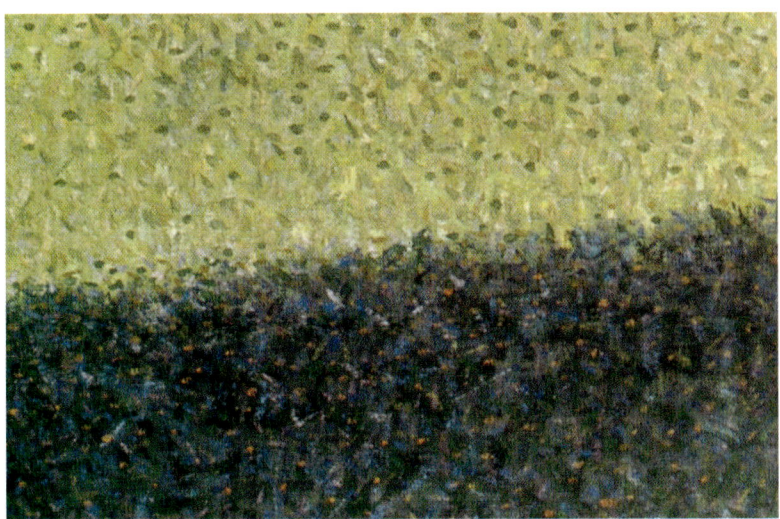

29-37   GEORGES SEURAT, detail of *Sunday on La Grande Jatte,* 1884–1886.

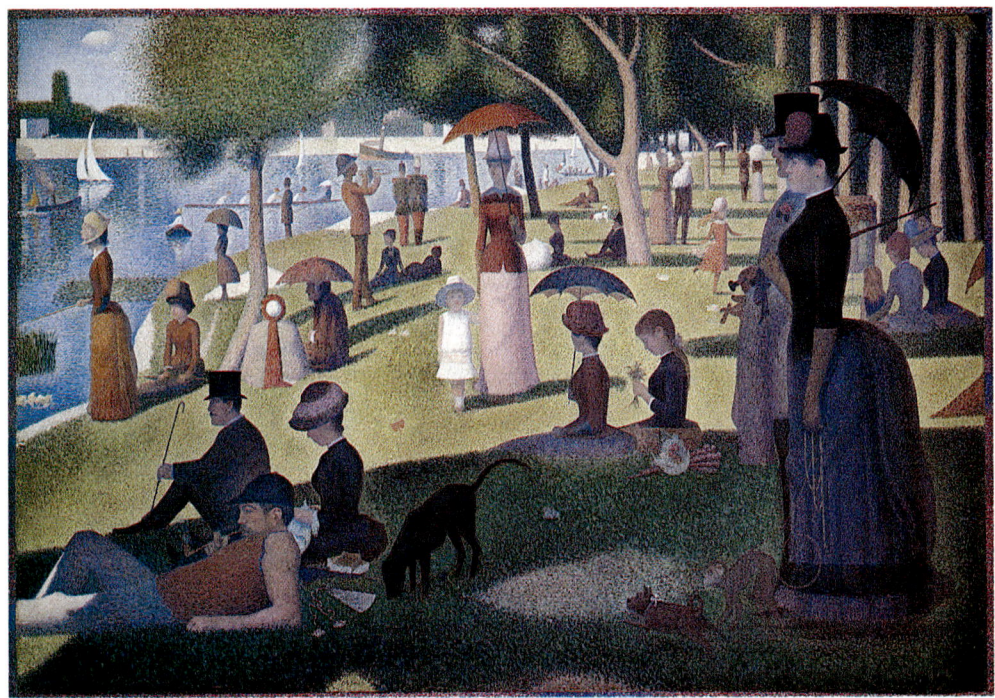

29-38   GEORGES SEURAT, *A Sunday on La Grande Jatte,* 1884–1886. Oil on canvas, approx. 6′ 9″ × 10′. The Art Institute of Chicago, Chicago (Helen Birch Bartlett Memorial Collection, 1926).

of color. Light, air, people, and landscape are fixed in an abstract design whose line, color, value, and shape cohere in a precise and tightly controlled organization.

Seurat's art is severely intellectual. He said of it, "They see poetry in what I have done. No, I apply my method, and that is all there is to it."[28] In *La Grande Jatte,* Seurat turned traditional pictorial stage space into a pattern by applying a color formula based on the belief that human optical experience of space can be only a function of color, which makes space a fairly unimportant variable. For previous artists, the reality was space with color something added, but for Seurat color was the reality and spaces and solids were merely illusion. Having found the formula of color relationships, artists no longer needed to rely on the dubious evidence of their impressions. Paul Signac, Seurat's collaborator in the design of the "neo-impressionist" method, described their discovery:

> By the elimination of all muddy mixtures, by the exclusive use of the optical mixture of pure colors, by a methodical divisionism and a strict observation of the scientific theory of colors, the neoimpressionist insures a maximum of luminosity, of color intensity, and of harmony—a result that had never yet been obtained.[29]

MAKING IMPRESSIONISM "DURABLE" Like Seurat, the French artist PAUL CÉZANNE (1839–1906) turned from Impressionism to developing a more analytical style. Although a lifelong admirer of Delacroix, Cézanne allied himself, early in his career, with the Impressionists, especially Pissarro, and at first accepted their color theories and their faith in subjects chosen from everyday life. Yet his own studies of the Old Masters in the Louvre persuaded him that Impressionism lacked form and structure. Cézanne declared he wanted to "make of Impressionism something solid and durable like the art of the museums."[30]

The basis of Cézanne's art was his unique way of studying nature in works such as *Mont Sainte-Victoire* (FIG. **29-39**). His aim was not truth in appearance, especially not photographic truth, nor was it the "truth" of Impressionism but a lasting structure behind the formless and fleeting visual information the eye absorbs. Instead of employing the Impressionists' random approach when he was face-to-face with nature, Cézanne attempted to intellectually order his presentation of the lines, planes, and colors that comprised nature. He did so by constantly and painstakingly checking his painting against the part of the actual scene—he called it the "motif"—he was studying at the moment. When Cézanne wrote of his goal of "doing Poussin over entirely from nature,"[31] he apparently meant that Poussin's effects of distance, depth, structure, and solidity must be achieved not by traditional perspective and chiaroscuro but in terms of the color patterns an optical analysis of nature provides.

With special care, Cézanne explored the properties of line, plane, and color and their interrelationships. He studied the effect of every kind of linear direction, the capacity of planes to create the sensation of depth, the intrinsic qualities of color, and the power of colors to modify the direction and depth of lines and planes. To create the illusion of three-dimensional form and space, Cézanne focused on carefully selecting colors. He understood that the visual properties—hue, saturation, and value—of different colors vary (see Introduction, page xl in combined volumes or page xx in Volume II). Cool colors tend to recede, while

29-39 PAUL CÉZANNE, *Mont Sainte-Victoire,* 1902–1904. Oil on canvas, 2′ 3½″ × 2′ 11¼″. Philadelphia Museum of Art, Philadelphia (The George W. Elkins Collection).

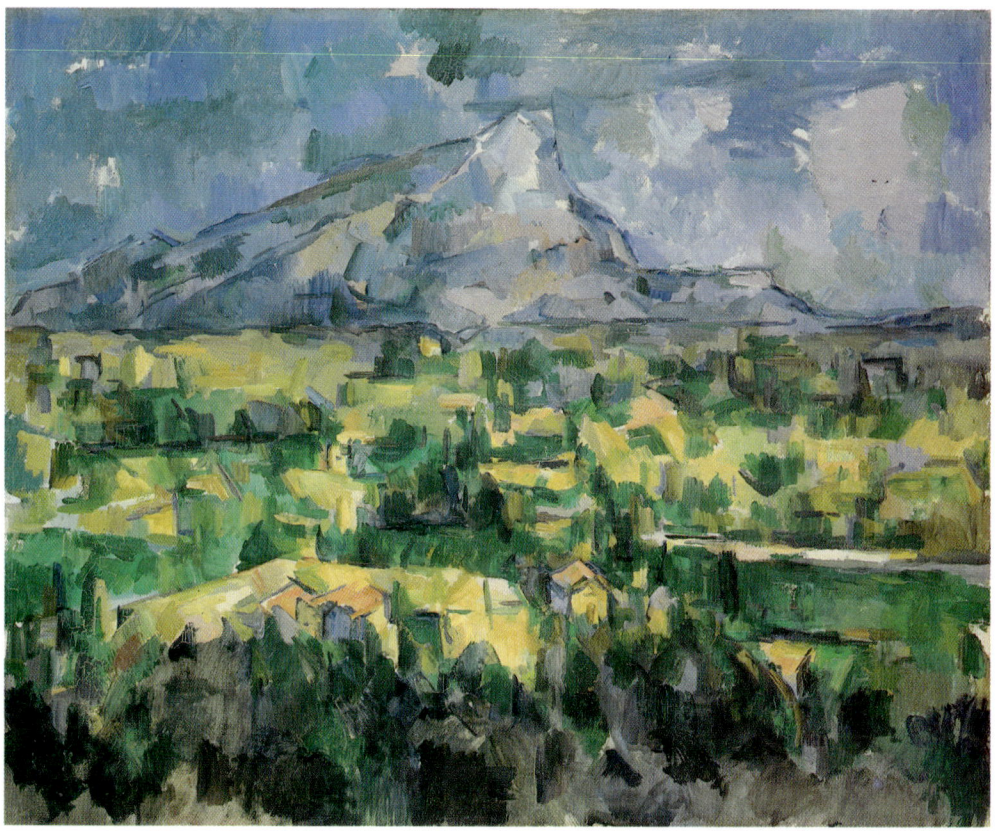

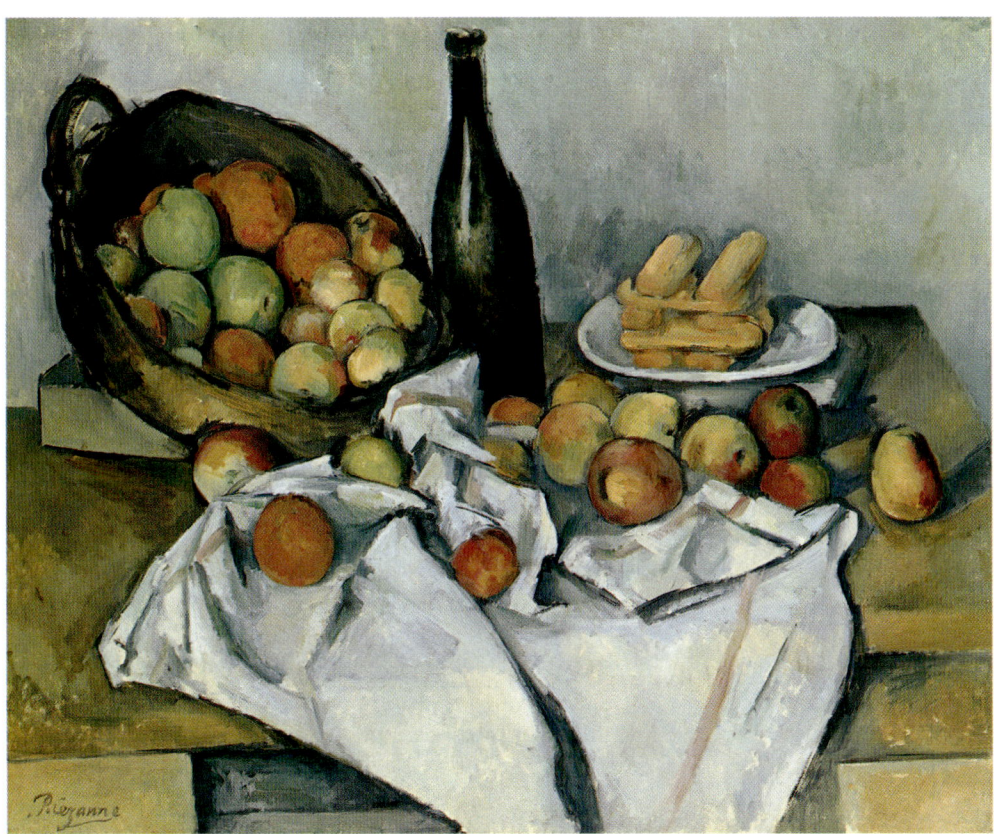

29-40 PAUL CÉZANNE, *The Basket of Apples,* ca. 1895. Oil on canvas, 2′ ⅜″ × 2′ 7″. The Art Institute of Chicago, Chicago (Helen Birch Bartlett Memorial Collection, 1926).

warm ones advance. By applying to the canvas small patches of juxtaposed colors, some advancing and some receding, Cézanne created volume and spatial depth in his works. On occasion, the artist depicted objects chiefly in one hue and achieved convincing solidity by modulating the intensity (or saturation). At other times, he juxtaposed contrasting colors—for example, green, yellow, and red—of like saturation (usually in the middle range, rather than the highest intensity) to compose specific objects, such as fruit or bowls.

Mont Sainte-Victoire is one of many views Cézanne painted of this mountain near his home in Aix-en-Provence. In it, he replaced the transitory visual effects of changing atmospheric conditions, effects that occupied Monet, with a more concentrated, lengthier analysis of the colors in large lighted spaces. The main space stretches out behind and beyond the canvas plane and includes numerous small elements, such as roads, fields, houses, and the viaduct at the far right, each seen from a slightly different viewpoint. Above this shifting, receding perspective rises the largest mass of all, the mountain, with an effect—achieved by equally stressing background and foreground contours—of being simultaneously near and far away. This portrayal approximates the actual experience a person observing such a view might have if apprehending the landscape forms piecemeal. The relative proportions of objects would vary, rather than being fixed by a strict one- or two-point perspective, such as that normally found in a photograph. Cézanne immobilized the shifting colors of Impressionism into an array of clearly defined planes that compose the objects and spaces in his scene. Describing his method in a letter to a fellow painter, he wrote:

Treat nature by the cylinder, the sphere, the cone, everything in proper perspective so that each side of an object or a plane is directed towards a central point. Lines parallel to the horizon give breadth, that is a section of nature. . . . Lines perpendicular to this horizon give depth. But nature for us men is more depth than surface, whence the need of introducing into our light vibrations, represented by reds and yellows, a sufficient amount of blue to give the impression of air.[32]

REVEALING THE UNDERLYING STRUCTURE In Cézanne's *The Basket of Apples* (FIG. **29-40**), the objects have lost something of their individual character as bottles and fruit and approach the condition of cylinders and spheres. The still life was another good vehicle for the artist's experiments, as he could arrange a limited number of selected objects to provide a well-ordered point of departure. So analytical was Cézanne in preparing, observing, and painting these still lifes (in contrast to the Impressionist emphasis on the idea of the spontaneous) that he had to abandon using real fruit and flowers because they tended to rot. In *The Basket of Apples,* he captured the solidity of each object by juxtaposing color patches. Cézanne's interest in the study of volume and solidity is evident from the disjunctures in the painting—the table edges are discontinuous, and various objects seem to be depicted from different vantage points. In his zeal to understand three-dimensionality and to convey the placement of forms relative to the space around them, Cézanne explored his still life arrangements from different viewpoints. This resulted in paintings that, while conceptually coherent, do not appear optically realistic. Cézanne created what might be called, paradoxically, an architecture of color.

In keeping with the modernist concern with the integrity of the painting surface, Cézanne's methods never allow viewers to disregard the actual two-dimensionality of the picture plane. In this manner, Cézanne achieved a remarkable feat—presenting viewers with two-dimensional and three-dimensional images simultaneously.

THE RISE OF THE AVANT-GARDE

REJECTING ARTISTIC CONVENTIONS   Each successive modernist movement of the nineteenth century—Realism, Impressionism, and Post-Impressionism—challenged artistic conventions with greater intensity. This relentless challenge gave rise to the *avant-garde*. Use of this term has expanded over the years; it now serves as a synonym for any particularly new or cutting-edge cultural manifestation. *Avant-garde*, which means "front guard," derived from nineteenth-century French military usage. The avant-garde were soldiers sent ahead of the army's main body to reconnoiter and make occasional raids on the enemy. Politicians who deemed themselves visionary and forward thinking subsequently adopted the term. It then migrated to the art world in the 1880s, where it referred to artists who were ahead of their time and who transgressed the limits of established art forms. These artists were the vanguard, or trailblazers. The avant-garde were modernists in that they rejected the classical, academic, or traditional and they adopted a critical stance toward their respective media. Yet they departed from modernism in their art's extreme transgressiveness or subversiveness. Further, the avant-garde increasingly disengaged themselves from a public audience. In zealously exploring the premises and formal qualities of painting, sculpture, or other media, avant-garde artists created an insular community whose members seemed to speak only to one another in their work. The Post-Impressionists, whose work the general public found incomprehensible, were the first artists labeled avant-garde. Avant-garde principles appealed to greater numbers of artists (such as the Fauves, Cubists, and Dada artists) as the twentieth century dawned, and the momentum it gained made the avant-garde a major force throughout much of the past century.

SYMBOLISM: FREEDOM OF IMAGINATION, EXPRESSION, AND FORM

Modernist artists, in particular the Impressionists and Post-Impressionists, concentrated on using emotion and sensation to transform perceived nature. By the end of the nineteenth century, the representation of nature became completely subjectivized, to the point that artists did not imitate nature but created free interpretations of it. Artists rejected the optical world as observed in favor of a fantasy world, of forms they conjured in their free imagination, with or without reference to things conventionally seen. Technique and ideas were individual to each of these artists. Color, line, and shape, divorced from conformity to the optical image, were used as symbols of personal emotions in response to the world. These artists who rejected the visual world were solely concerned with expressing reality in accord with their spirit and intuition. Deliberately choosing to stand outside of convention and tradition, such artists spoke like prophets, in signs and symbols.

REALITY BEYOND THE TANGIBLE WORLD   Many of the artists following this path adopted an approach to subject and form that associated them with a general European movement called Symbolism. The term had application to both art and literature, which, as critics in both fields noted, were in especially close relation at this time. Symbolists disdained the "mere fact" of Realism as trivial and asserted that fact must be transformed into a symbol of the inner experience of that fact. The task of Symbolist visual and verbal artists was not to see things but to see through them to a significance and reality far deeper than what superficial appearance gave. In this function, as the poet Arthur Rimbaud insisted, artists became beings of extraordinary insight. (One group of Symbolist painters, influenced by Gauguin, called it-

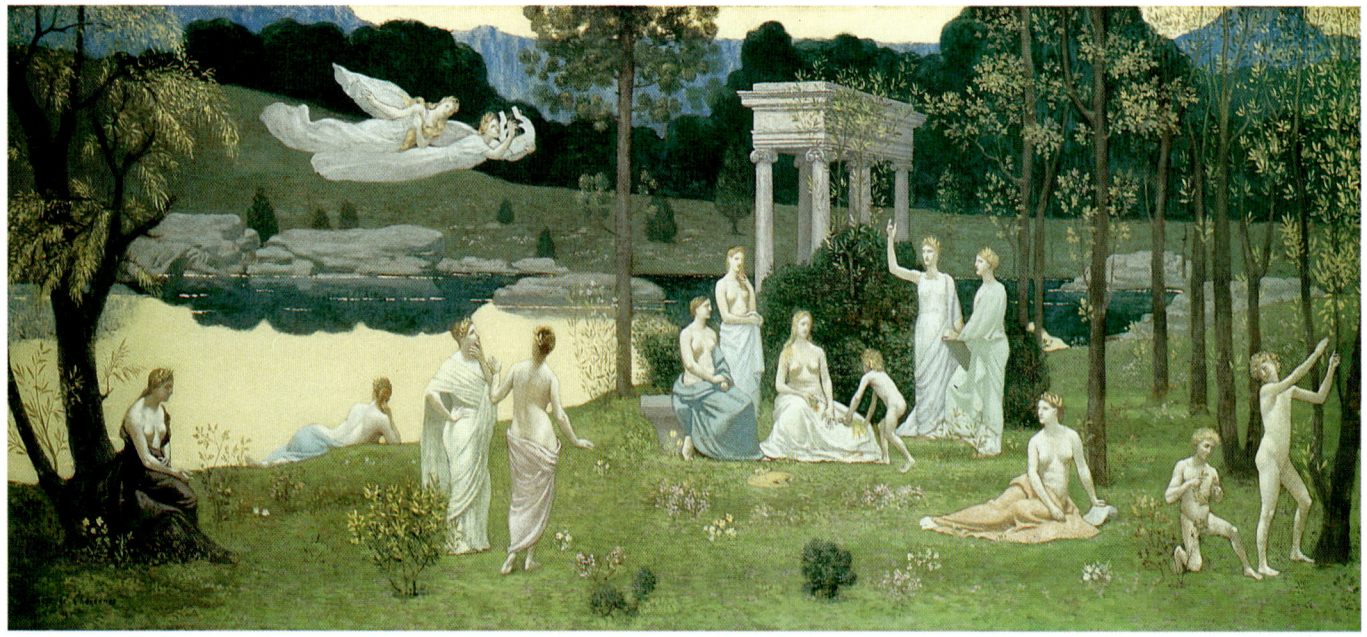

29-41   PIERRE PUVIS DE CHAVANNES, *The Sacred Grove*, 1884. Oil on canvas, 2′ 11½″ × 6′ 10″. The Art Institute of Chicago, Chicago (Potter Palmer Collection).

self Nabis, the Hebrew word for prophet.) Rimbaud, whose poems had great influence on the artistic community, went so far as to say, in his *Lettre du Voyant (Letter from a Prophet)*, that to achieve the seer's insight, artists must become deranged. In effect, they must systematically unhinge and confuse the everyday faculties of sense and reason, which served only to blur artistic vision. The artists' mystical vision must convert the objects of the commonsense world into symbols of a reality beyond that world and, ultimately, a reality from within the individual.

IMAGINATION, FANTASY, AND INNER VISION

The extreme subjectivism of the Symbolists led them to cultivate all the resources of fantasy and imagination, no matter how deeply buried or obscure. Moreover, they urged artists to stand against the vulgar materialism and conventional mores of industrial and middle-class society. Above all, by their philosophy of aestheticism, the Symbolists wished to purge literature and art of anything utilitarian, to cultivate an exquisite aesthetic sensitivity, and to make the slogan "art for art's sake" into a doctrine and a way of life.

The subjects of the Symbolists, conditioned by this reverent attitude toward art and exaggerated aesthetic sensation, became increasingly esoteric and exotic, mysterious, visionary, dreamlike, and fantastic. (Perhaps not coincidentally, contemporary with the Symbolists, Sigmund Freud, the founder of psychoanalysis, began the new century and the age of psychiatry with his *Interpretation of Dreams,* an introduction to the concept and the world of unconscious experience.)

Elements of Symbolism appeared in the works of both Gauguin and van Gogh, but their art differed from mainstream Symbolism in their insistence on showing unseen powers as linked to a physical reality, instead of attempting to depict an alternate, wholly interior, life. The writers overshadowed the artists who participated in the actual Symbolist movement, but two French artists—Gustave Moreau and Odilon Redon—had a strong influence on the movement. And several other painters, such as Puvis de Chavannes, followed the Symbolist-related path of imagination, fantasy, and inner vision in their works. Prominent figures in this latter group were the Frenchman Henri Rousseau and the Norwegian Edvard Munch. All of these artists were visionaries who anticipated the strong twentieth-century interest in creating art that expressed psychological truth.

THE "PROPHET" OF SYMBOLISM

PUVIS DE CHAVANNES (1824–1898) was a French artist who rejected Realism and Impressionism and went his own way in the nineteenth century, serenely unaffected by these movements. Although he never formally identified himself with the Symbolists, he became the "prophet" of those artists. Puvis produced an ornamental and reflective art—a dramatic rejection of Realism's noisy everyday world. In *The Sacred Grove* (FIG. **29-41**), he deployed statuesque figures in a tranquil landscape with a classical shrine. Their motion has been suspended in timeless poses, their contours are simple and sharp, and their modeling is as shallow as bas-relief. The calm and still atmosphere suggests some consecrated place, where all movements and gestures have a permanent ritual significance. The stillness and simplicity of the forms, the linear patterns their rhythmic contours create, and the suggestion of their symbolic import amount to a kind of program of anti-Realism.

The effect impressed younger painters such as Paul Gauguin and the Symbolists, who saw in Puvis the prophet of a new style that would replace Realism. Puvis had a double reputation. The Academy and the government accepted him for his classicism, and the avant-garde revered him for his vindication of imagination and his artistic independence from the world of materialism and the machine.

A DEATH-INDUCING VISION OF SPLENDOR

GUSTAVE MOREAU (1826–1898), an influential teacher, gravitated toward subjects inspired by dreaming solitude and as remote as possible from the everyday world, in keeping with Symbolist tenets. The artist presented these subjects sumptuously, and his natural love of sensuous design led him to incorporate gorgeous color, intricate line, and richly detailed shape.

Jupiter and Semele (FIG. **29-42**) is one of Moreau's rare finished works. The mortal girl Semele, one of Jupiter's loves,

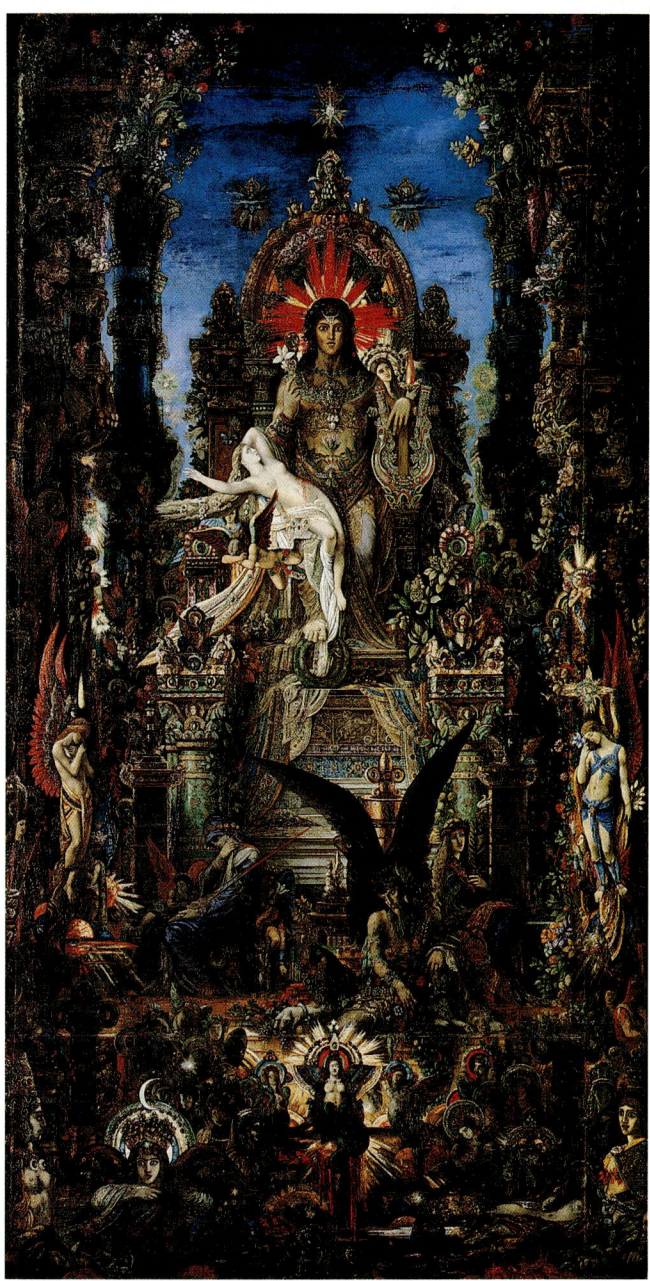

29-42 GUSTAVE MOREAU, *Jupiter and Semele,* ca. 1875. Oil on canvas, approx. 7′ × 3′ 4″. Musée Gustave Moreau, Paris.

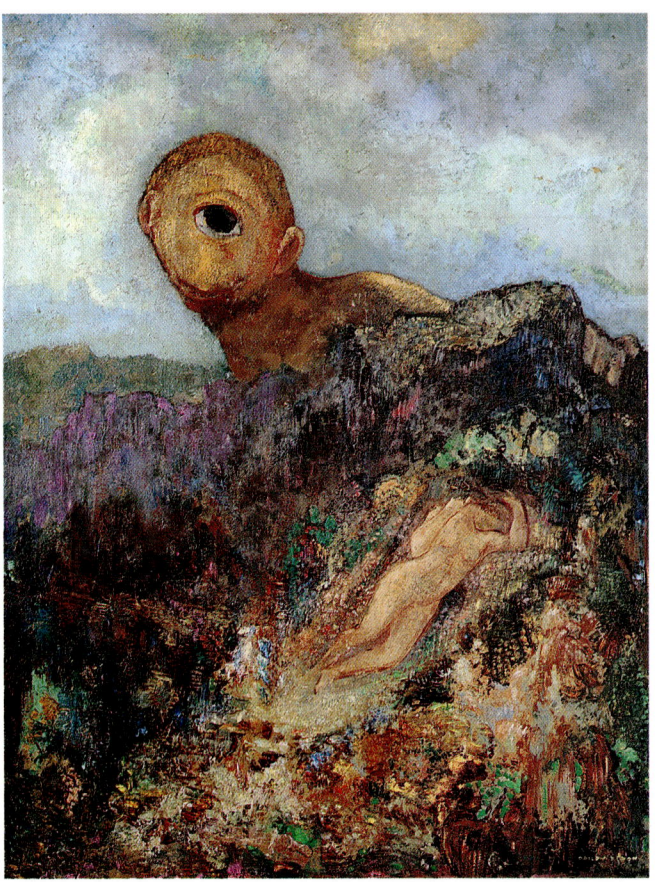

29-43   ODILON REDON, *The Cyclops,* 1898. Oil on canvas, 2′ 1″ × 1′ 8″. Kröller-Müller Museum, Otterlo, The Netherlands.

picted the royal hall of Olympus as shimmering in iridescent color, with tabernacles filled with the glowing shapes that enclose Jupiter like an encrustation of gems. In *Jupiter and Semele,* the rich color is harmonized with the exotic hues of medieval enamels, Indian miniatures, Byzantine mosaics, and the designs of exotic wares then influencing modern artists. Semele, in Jupiter's lap, is overwhelmed by the apparition of the god, who is crowned with a halo of thunderbolts. Her languorous swoon and the suspended motion of all the entranced figures show the "beautiful inertia" that Moreau said he wished to render with all "necessary richness."

HAUNTED BY "IMAGINARY THINGS"   Like Moreau, ODILON REDON (1840–1916) was a visionary. He had been aware of an intense inner world since childhood and later wrote of "imaginary things" that haunted him. Redon adapted the Impressionist palette and stippling brushstroke for a very different purpose. In *The Cyclops* (FIG. **29-43**), Redon projected a figment of the imagination as if it were visible, coloring it whimsically with a rich profusion of fresh saturated hues that harmonized with the mood he felt fitted the subject. The fetal head of the shy, simpering Polyphemus, with its huge loving eye, rises balloonlike above the sleeping Galatea. The image born of the dreaming world and the color analyzed and disassociated from the waking world come together here at the artist's will. As Redon himself observed: "My originality consists in bringing to life, in a human way, improbable beings and making them live according to the laws of probability, by putting—as far as possible—the logic of the visible at the service of the invisible."[33]

begged the god to appear to her in all his majesty, a sight so powerful that she died from it. The artist presented the theme within an operalike setting, a towering opulent architecture. (Moreau loved Wagner's music and, like that great composer, dreamed of a grand synthesis of the arts.) The painter de-

A POWERFUL WORLD OF PERSONAL FANTASY The imagination of the French artist HENRI ROUSSEAU (1844–1910) engaged a different but equally powerful world of personal fantasy. Gauguin had journeyed to the South Seas in search of primitive innocence; Rousseau was a "primitive"

29-44   HENRI ROUSSEAU, *The Sleeping Gypsy,* 1897. Oil on canvas, 4′ 3″ × 6′ 7″. Museum of Modern Art, New York (gift of Mrs. Simon Guggenheim).

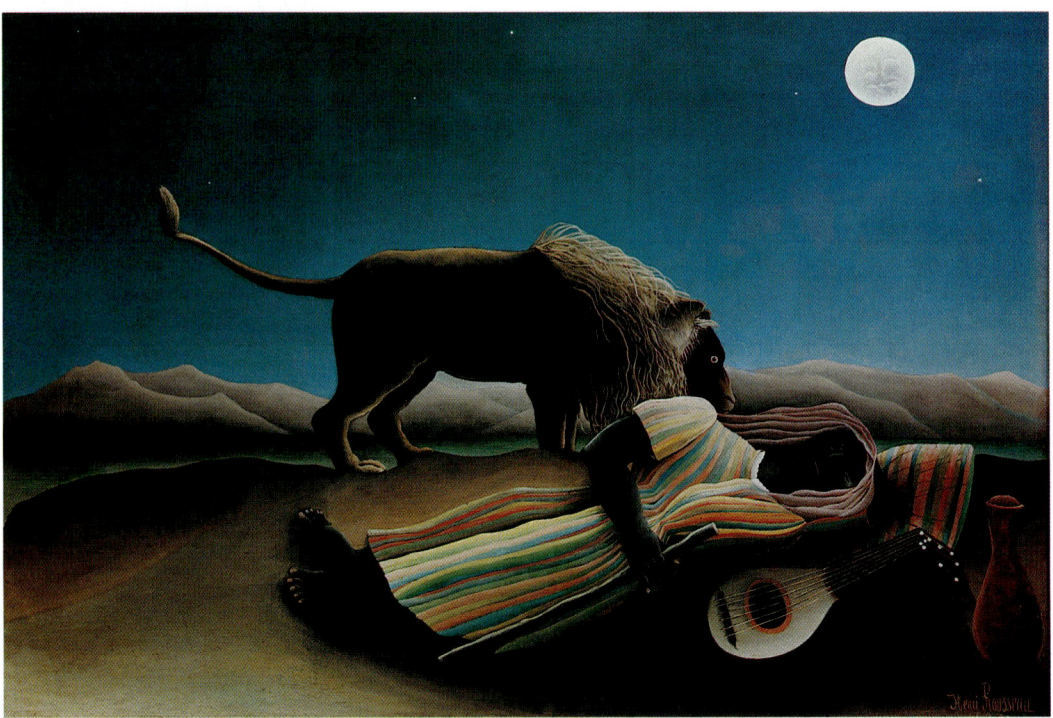

without leaving Paris—an untrained amateur painter. Rousseau produced an art of dream and fantasy in a style that had its own sophistication and made its own departure from the artistic currency of the time. He compensated for his apparent visual, conceptual, and technical naiveté with a natural talent for design and an imagination teeming with exotic images of mysterious tropical landscapes. In perhaps his best-known work, *The Sleeping Gypsy* (FIG. **29-44**), the figure identified in the title occupies a desert world, silent and secret, and dreams beneath a pale, perfectly round moon. In the foreground, a lion that resembles a stuffed, but somehow menacing, animal doll sniffs at the Gypsy. A critical encounter impends—an encounter of the type that recalls the uneasiness when a person's vulnerable subconscious self is menaced during sleep.

DESCRIBING THE "MODERN PSYCHIC LIFE"

Linked in spirit to the Symbolists was the Norwegian painter and graphic artist EDVARD MUNCH (1863–1944). Munch felt deeply the pain of human life. His belief that humans were powerless before the great natural forces of death and love and the emotions associated with them—jealousy, loneliness, fear, desire, and despair—became the theme of most of his art. Because Munch's goal was to describe the conditions of "modern psychic life," as he put it, Realist and Impressionist techniques were inappropriate, focusing as they did on the tangible world. In the spirit of Symbolism, Munch developed a style of putting color, line, and figural distortion to expressive ends.

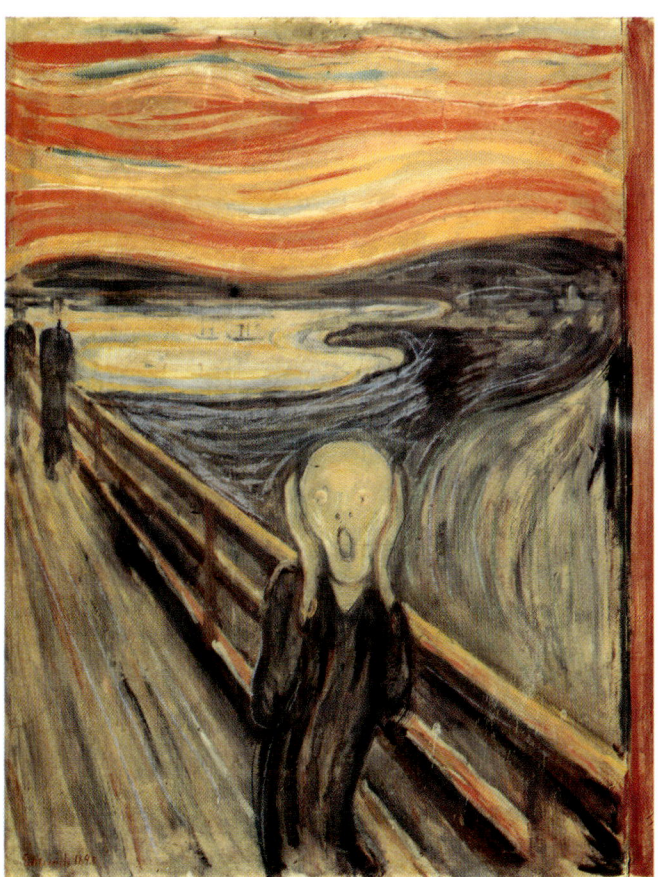

29-45 EDVARD MUNCH, *The Cry*, 1893. Oil, pastel, and casein on cardboard, 29 11¾″ × 2′ 5″. National Gallery, Oslo.

ANGUISH AND DESPAIR Munch's well-known painting, *The Cry* (FIG. **29-45**), is an example of this style. The image is grounded in the real world—a man standing on a bridge or jetty in a landscape can be clearly discerned—but it departs significantly from a visual reality. Instead, the work evokes a visceral, emotional response from viewers because of Munch's dramatic presentation. The man in the foreground, simplified to almost skeletal form, emits a primal scream. The landscape's sweeping curvilinear lines reiterate the curvilinear shape of the mouth and head, almost like an echo, as it reverberates through the landscape. The fiery red and yellow stripes that give the sky an eerie glow also contribute to this work's resonance. The emotional impulse that led Munch to produce *The Cry* is revealed in an epigraph Munch wrote to accompany the painting: "I stopped and leaned against the balustrade, almost dead with fatigue. Above the blue-black fjord hung the clouds, red as blood and tongues of fire. My friends had left me, and alone, trembling with anguish, I became aware of the vast, infinite cry of nature."[34] Appropriately, this work originally was titled *Despair*.

Gauguin's work, not only his paintings but also the woodblocks he produced from them, had influenced Munch. Munch also made prints that carried the same high emotional charge as his painted works, and both his intense images and the print medium that carried them were major sources of inspiration for the German Expressionists in the early twentieth century.

SCULPTURE IN THE LATER NINETEENTH CENTURY

The three-dimensional art of sculpture was not readily adaptable to capturing the optical sensations many painters favored in the later nineteenth century. Its very nature—its tangibility and solidity—suggests permanence. Sculpture thus served predominantly as an expression of supposedly timeless ideals, rather than of the transitory. But that did not stop sculptors during this period from pursuing many of the ideas fundamental to movements such as Realism and Impressionism.

A SCULPTURAL VISION OF HELL In his sculptures, JEAN-BAPTISTE CARPEAUX (1827–1875) combined his interest in Realism with a love of Baroque and ancient sculpture and of Michelangelo's work. Carpeaux's group *Ugolino and His Children* (FIG. **29-46**) is based on a passage from Dante's *Inferno* and shows Count Ugolino with his four sons shut up in a tower to starve to death. In Hell, Ugolino relates to Dante how, in a moment of extreme despair,

> *I bit both hands for grief. And*
> *they, thinking I did it for hunger,*
> *suddenly rose up and said, "Father"...*
> *[and offered him their own flesh as food.]*
> (33. 58–75)

The powerful forms—twisted, intertwined, and densely concentrated—suggest the self-devouring torment of frustration and despair that wracks the unfortunate Ugolino. A careful student of Michelangelo's male figures, Carpeaux also said he had the Laocoön group (see FIG. 5-89) in mind. Certainly, the storm and stress of *Ugolino and His Children* recall similar

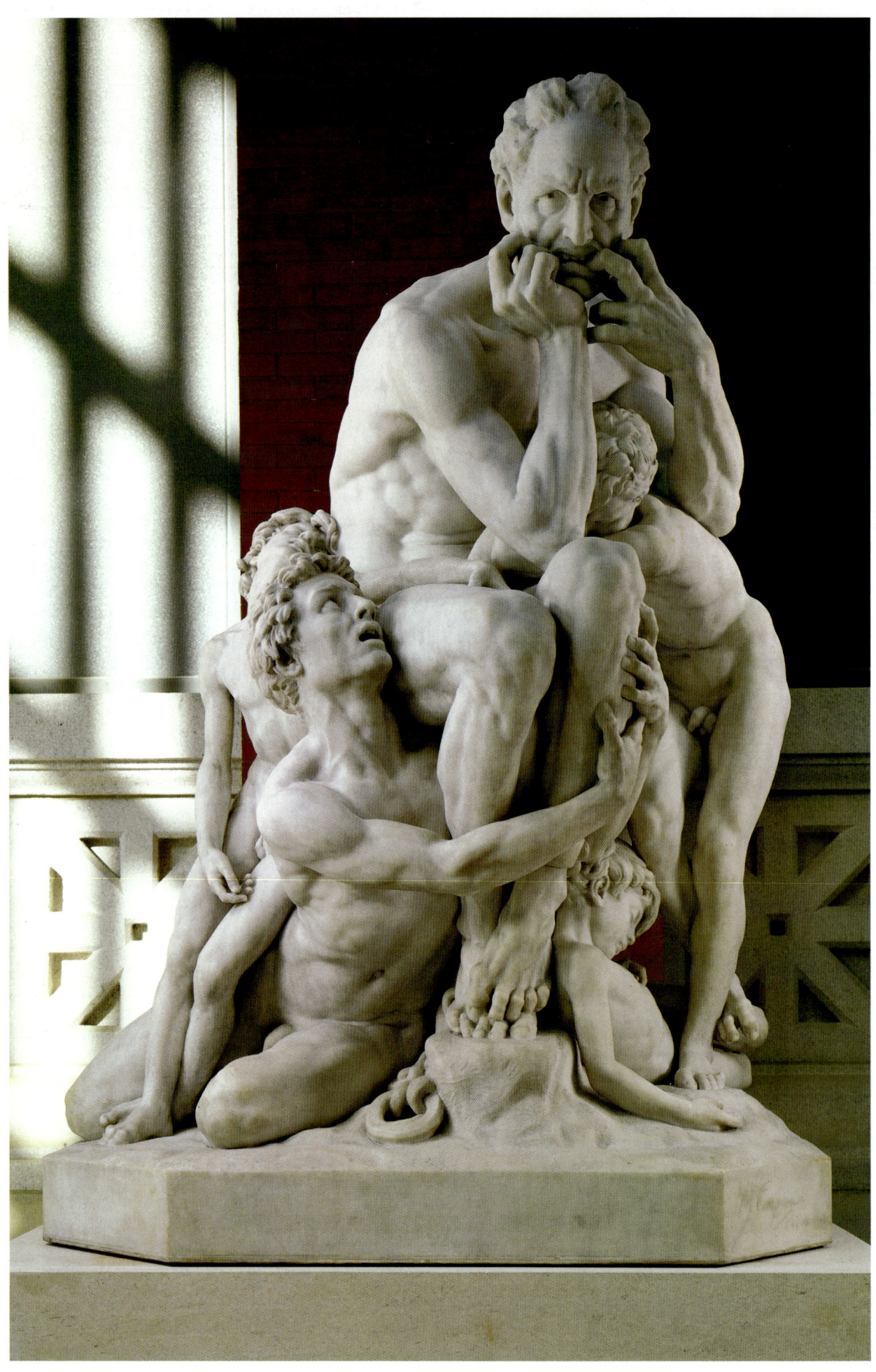

29-46 Jean-Baptiste Carpeaux, *Ugolino and His Children,* 1865–1867. Marble, 6′ 5″ high. Metropolitan Museum of Art, New York (Josephine Bay Paul and C. Michael Paul Foundation, Inc. and the Charles Ulrich and Josephine Bay Foundation, Inc., gifts, 1967).

of artistic developments such as Impressionism. Although color was not a significant factor in Rodin's work, Impressionist influence manifested itself in the artist's abiding concern for the effect of light on the three-dimensional surface. When focusing on the human form, he joined his profound knowledge of anatomy and movement with special attention to the body's exterior, saying, "The sculptor must learn to reproduce the surface, which means all that vibrates on the surface, soul, love, passion, life. . . . Sculpture is thus the art of hollows and mounds, not of smoothness, or even polished planes."[35] Primarily a modeler of pliable material rather than a carver of hard wood or stone, Rodin worked his surfaces with fingers sensitive to the subtlest variations of surface, catching the fugitive play of constantly shifting light on the body. In his studio, he often would have a model move around in front of him, while he modeled sketches with coils of clay.

In the cast bronze *Walking Man* (FIG. **29-48**), Rodin captured the sense of a body in motion. Headless and armless, the figure is caught in midstride at the moment when weight is transferred across the pelvis from the back leg to the front. As with many of his other early works, Rodin executed *Walking Man* with such careful attention to details of muscle, bone,

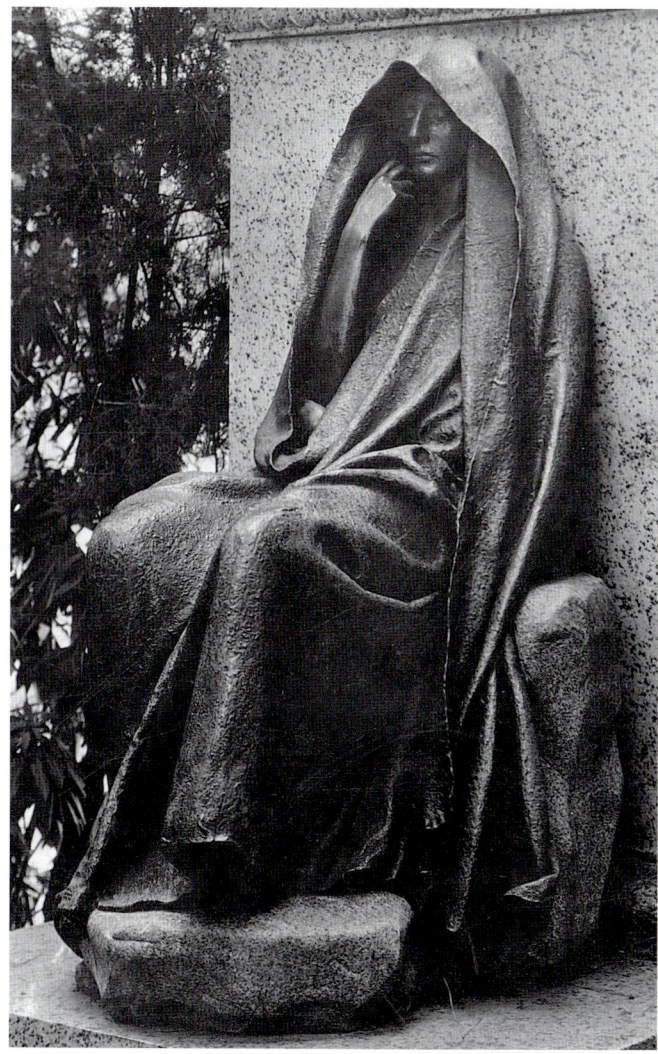

29-47 AUGUSTUS SAINT-GAUDENS, Adams Memorial, Rock Creek Cemetery, Washington 1891. Bronze, 5′ 10″ high.

characteristics of that group and other ancient "baroque" artworks, such as the battling gods and giants on the frieze of the Pergamon altar (see FIG. 5-79). Regardless of such influences, the sense of vivid reality about the anatomy of the *Ugolino* figures shows Carpeaux's interest in study from life.

A MAJESTIC PORTRAIT AUGUSTUS SAINT-GAUDENS (1848–1907), an American sculptor trained in France, used Realism effectively in a number of his portraits, where Realism was highly appropriate. However, when designing a memorial monument of Mrs. Henry Adams (FIG. **29-47**), Saint-Gaudens chose, instead, a classical mode of representation, which he modified freely. The resultant statue is that of a woman of majestic bearing sitting in mourning, her classically beautiful face partly shadowed by a sepulchral drapery that voluminously enfolds her body. The immobility of her form, set in an attitude of eternal vigilance, is only slightly stirred by a natural, yet mysterious and exquisite, gesture.

OF SURFACE AND SUBSTANCE In contrast, French artist AUGUSTE RODIN (1840–1917) was imbued with the Realist spirit, and he conceived and executed his sculptures with that sensibility. Like Muybridge and Eakins, Rodin was fascinated by the human body in motion. He was also well aware

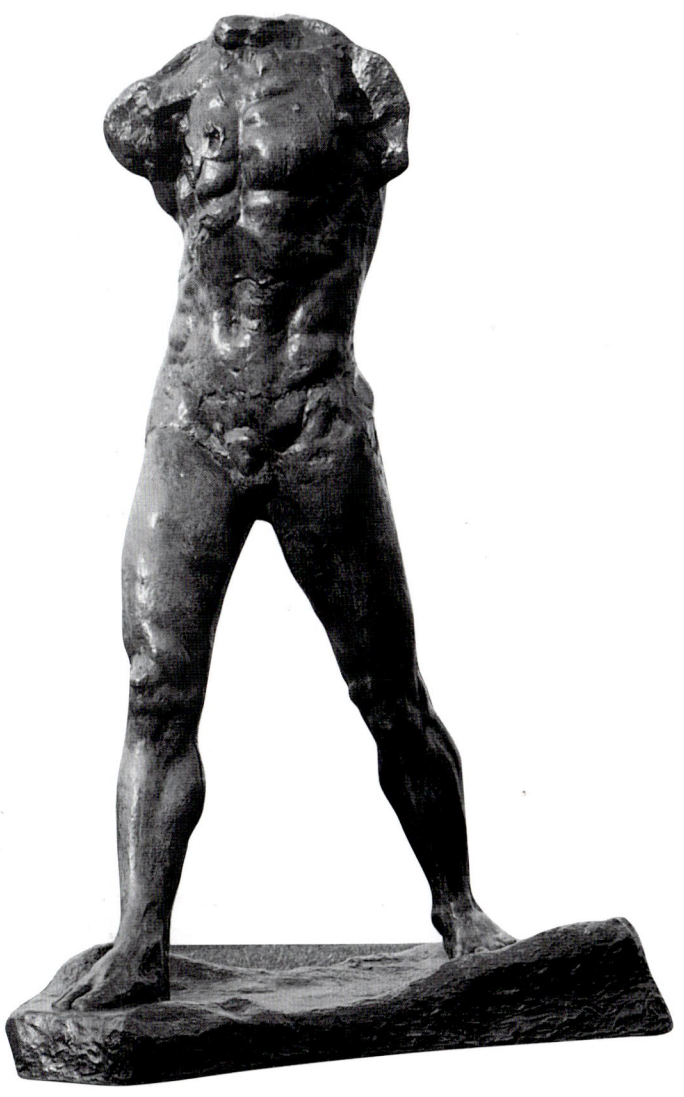

29-48 AUGUSTE RODIN, *Walking Man,* 1905, cast 1962. Bronze, 6′ 11¾″ high. Hirshhorn Museum and Sculpture Garden, Smithsonian Institution, Washington (gift of Joseph H. Hirshhorn, 1966).

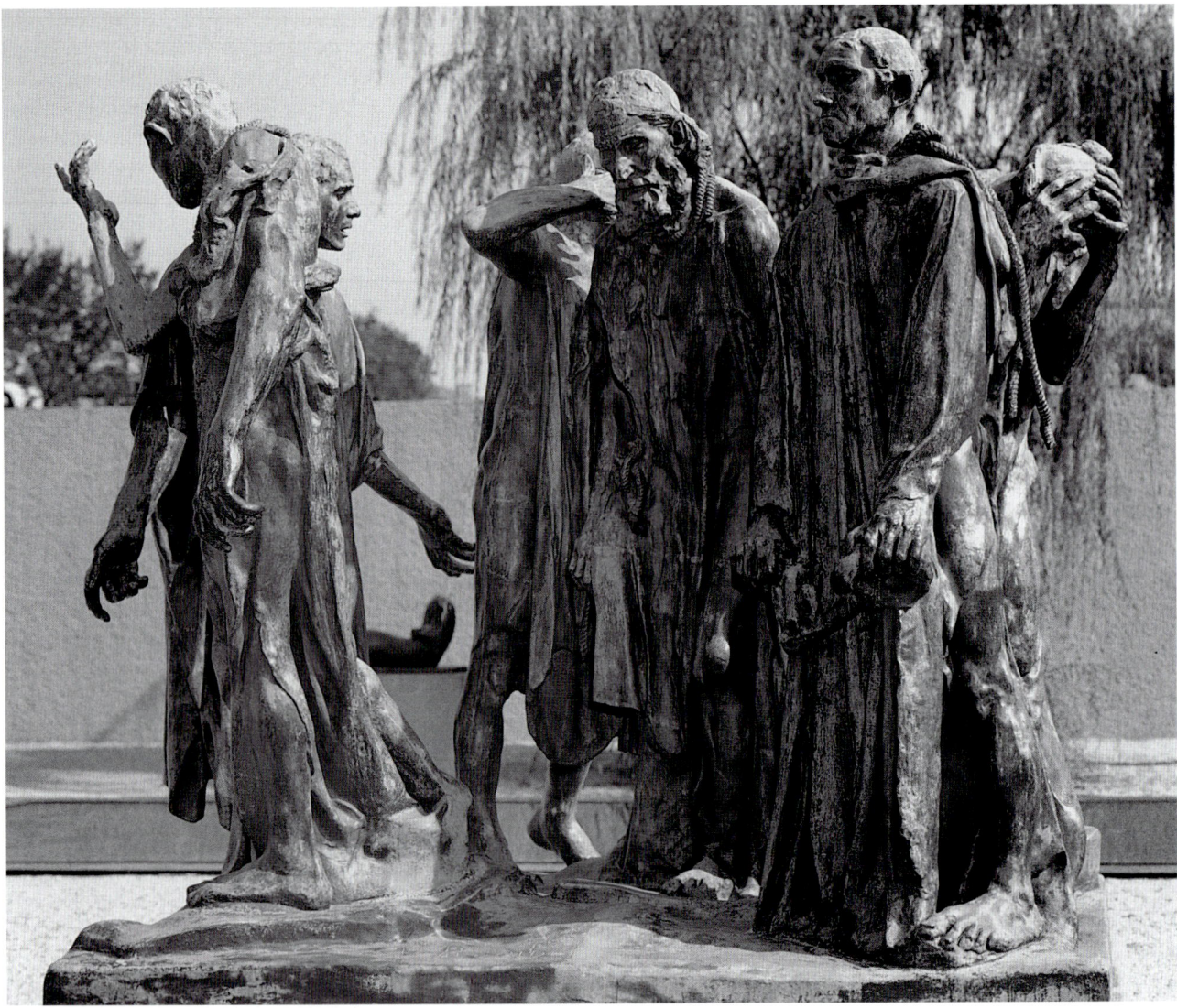

29-49   Auguste Rodin, *Burghers of Calais,* 1884–1889, cast ca. 1953–1959. Bronze, 6′ 10½″ high, 7′ 11″ long, 6′ 6″ deep. Hirshhorn Museum and Sculpture Garden, Smithsonian Institution, Washington (gift of Joseph H. Hirshhorn, 1966).

and tendon that it is filled with forceful reality, augmented by his sketchy modeling of the torso. Rodin conceived this figure as a study for his sculpture *Saint John the Baptist Preaching,* part of his process for building his conception of how the human body would express the larger theme's symbolism.

A STUDY OF DESPAIR AND DEFIANCE   Similarly, Rodin made many nude and draped studies for each of the figures in the life-size group *Burghers of Calais* (FIG. **29-49**). This cast bronze monument was commissioned to commemorate a heroic episode in the Hundred Years' War. During the English siege of Calais, France, in 1347, six of the city's leading citizens agreed to offer their lives in return for the English king's promise to lift the siege and spare the rest of the populace. Each of the bedraggled-looking figures is a convincing study of despair, resignation, or quiet defiance. Rodin achieved the psychic effects through his choreographic placement of the group members. Rather than clustering in a tightly formal composition, the burghers (middle-class citizens) seem to wander aimlessly. The roughly textured surfaces

add to the pathos of the figures and compel viewers' continued interest. Rodin designed the monument without the traditional high base in the hope that the citizens of Calais would be inspired by the sculptural representation of their ancestors standing eye-level in the city center and preparing eternally to set off on their sacrificial journey. The government commissioners found the Realism of Rodin's vision so offensive, however, that they banished the monument to a remote site and modified the work's impact by placing it high on an isolating pedestal.

Many of Rodin's projects were left unfinished or were deliberate fragments. Seeing the aesthetic and expressive virtue of these works, modern viewers and sculptors have developed a taste for how the sketch, the half-completed figure, the fragment, and the vignette lifted out of context all have the power of suggestion and understatement. Rodin's ability to capture the quality of the transitory through his highly textured surfaces while revealing larger themes and deeper, lasting sensibilities explains the impact he had on twentieth-century artists.

THE ARTS AND CRAFTS MOVEMENT

The decisive effects of industrialization were impossible to ignore, and although many artists embraced this manifestation of "modern life" or at least explored its effects, other artists decried the impact of rampant industrialism. One such response came from the Arts and Crafts movement in England. This movement, which developed during the last decades of the nineteenth century, was shaped by the ideas of art critic and writer John Ruskin (1819–1900) and WILLIAM MORRIS (1834–1896), an artist. Both of these men shared a distrust of machines and industrial capitalism, which they believed alienated workers from their own nature. Accordingly, they advocated an art "made by the people for the people as a joy for the maker and the user."[36] This condemnation of capitalism and support for manual laborers were compatible with socialism, and many artists in the Arts and Crafts movement considered themselves socialists and participated in the labor movement.

This democratic, or at least populist, attitude carried over to the art they produced as well. Members of the Arts and Crafts movement dedicated themselves to producing functional objects with high aesthetic value for a wide public. The style they advocated was based on natural, rather than artificial, forms and often consisted of repeated designs of floral or geometric patterns. For Ruskin, Morris, and others in the Arts and Crafts movement, quality artisanship and honest labor were crucial. This movement generated numerous guilds, workshops, and schools committed to the promotion of this ideal.

PATTERNS FROM FLOOR TO CEILING Morris wholeheartedly contributed to this more populist art by forming a decorating firm, Morris, Marshall, Faulkner, and Co., Fine Arts Workmen in Painting, Carving, Furniture, and Metals. This firm's services were in great demand, and they produced wallpaper, textiles, tiles, furniture, books, rugs, stained glass, and pottery. In 1867, Morris decorated the Green Dining Room (FIG. **29-50**) at London's South Kensington Museum (now the Victoria & Albert Museum), the center of public art education and home of decorative art collections. The range of room features—windows, lights, and wainscoting (paneling on the lower part of walls)—Morris decorated to create this unified, beautiful, and functional environment is overwhelming; nothing escaped Morris's eye. His design for this room also reveals the penchant of Arts and Crafts designers for intricate patterning.

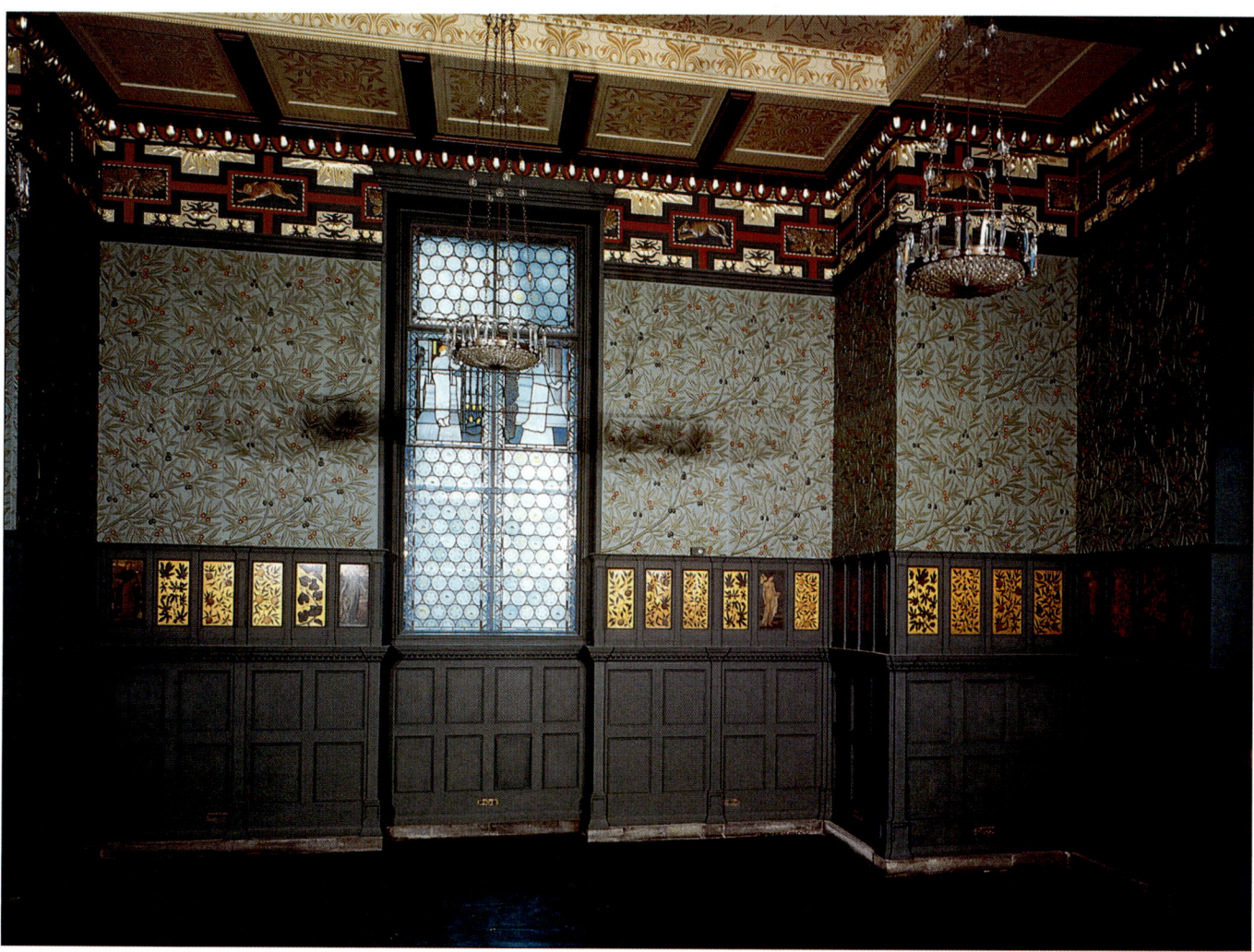

29-50 WILLIAM MORRIS, Green Dining Room, 1867. Victoria & Albert Museum, London.

29-51 CHARLES RENNIE MACKINTOSH, reconstruction (1992–1995) of Ladies' Luncheon Room, Ingram Street Tea Room, Glasgow, Scotland, 1900–1912. Glasgow Museum, Glasgow.

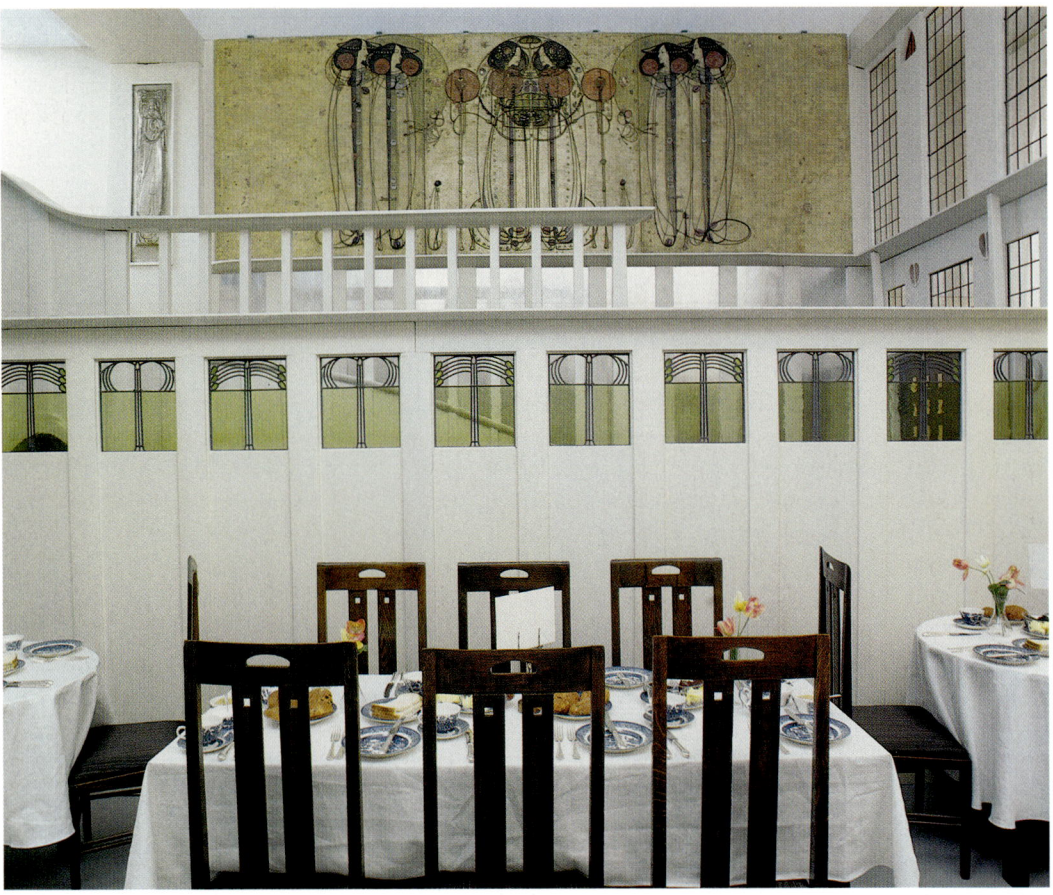

LUNCHING IN STYLE   Numerous arts and crafts societies in America, England, and Germany carried on this ideal of artisanship. In Scotland, the work of CHARLES RENNIE MACKINTOSH (1868–1929) popularized this ideal. Mackintosh designed a number of tea rooms, including the Ladies' Luncheon Room (FIG. **29-51**) located in the Ingram Street Tea Room in Glasgow. As reconstructed by Glasgow Museum in 1992–1995, the room decor is consistent with Morris's vision of a functional, exquisitely designed art. The chairs, stained-glass windows, and large panels of colored gesso with twine, glass beads, thread, mother-of-pearl, and tin leaf (made by Margaret Macdonald Mackintosh, an artist-designer and Mackintosh's wife who collaborated with him on many projects) are all pristinely geometric and rhythmical in design.

ART NOUVEAU

METALLIC PLANT LIFE   An architectural and design movement that developed out of the ideas the Arts and Crafts movement promoted was Art Nouveau. The international style of Art Nouveau took its name from a shop in Paris dealing with "L'Art Nouveau" (new art) and was known by that name in France, Belgium, Holland, England, and the United States. In other places, it had other names—Jugendstil in Austria and Germany (after the magazine *Der Jugend,* "youth"), Modernismo in Spain, and Floreale or Liberty in Italy. Proponents of this movement tried to synthesize all the arts in a determined attempt to create art based on natural forms that could be mass-produced for a large audience. The Art Nouveau style emerged at the end of the nineteenth cen-

tury and adapted the twining plant form to the needs of architecture, painting, sculpture, and all of the decorative arts. The mature Art Nouveau style was first seen in houses designed in Brussels in the 1890s by VICTOR HORTA (1861–1947). The staircase in the Van Eetvelde House (FIG. **29-52**), which Horta built in Brussels in 1895, is a good example of his Art Nouveau work. Every detail functions as part of a living whole. Furniture, drapery folds, veining in the lavish stone panelings, and the patterning of the door moldings join with real plants to provide graceful counterpoints for the twining plant theme. Metallic tendrils curl around the railings and posts, delicate metal tracery fills the glass dome, and floral and leaf motifs spread across the fabric panels of the screen (left background).

Several influences can be identified in Art Nouveau. In addition to the rich, foliated two-dimensional ornament of and artisan's respect for materials of the Arts and Crafts movement, the free, sinuous whiplash curve of Japanese print designs (see FIG. 27-14) inspired Art Nouveau artists. Art Nouveau also borrowed from the expressively patterned styles of Vincent van Gogh (FIGS. 29-33 and 29-34), Paul Gauguin (FIGS. 29-35 and 29-36), and their Post-Impressionist and Symbolist contemporaries.

THE PEACOCK'S SWEEPING CURVES   AUBREY BEARDSLEY (1872–1898) was one of a circle of English artists whose work existed at the intersection of Symbolism and Art Nouveau. For *Salomé,* an illustration for a book by Oscar Wilde, Beardsley drew *The Peacock Skirt* (FIG. **29-53**), a dazzlingly decorative composition perfectly characteristic of his

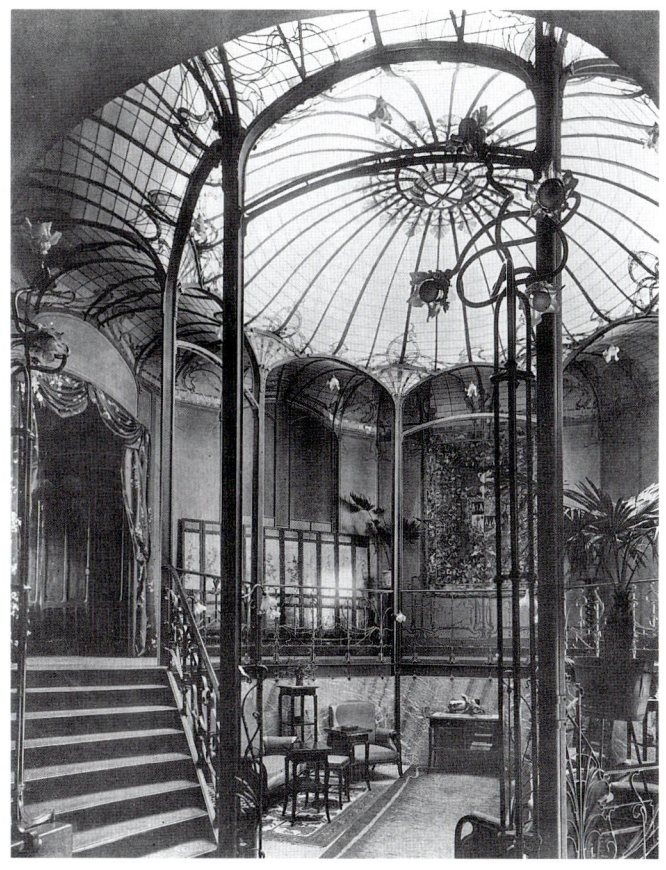

29-52 VICTOR HORTA, staircase in the Van Eetvelde House, Brussels, 1895.

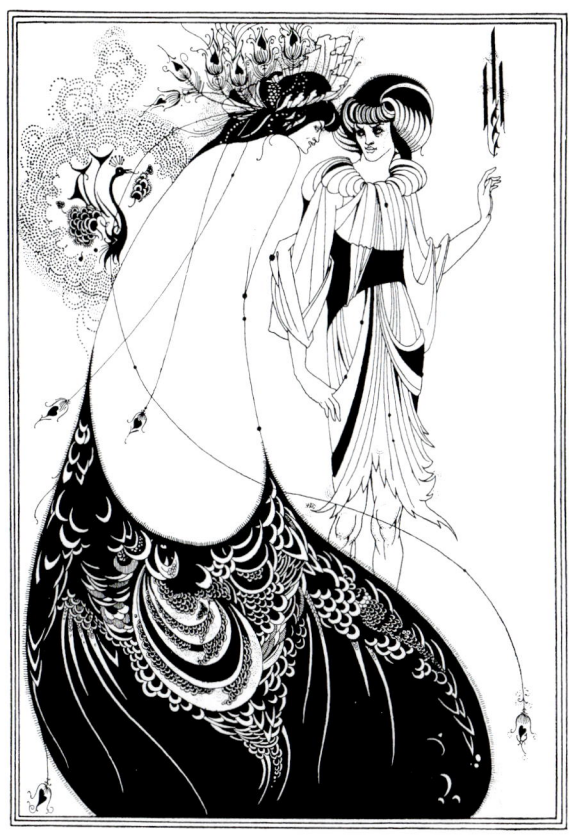

29-53 AUBREY BEARDSLEY, *The Peacock Skirt,* 1894. Pen-and-ink illustration for Oscar Wilde's *Salomé.*

29-54 ANTONIO GAUDI, Casa Milá, Barcelona, 1907.

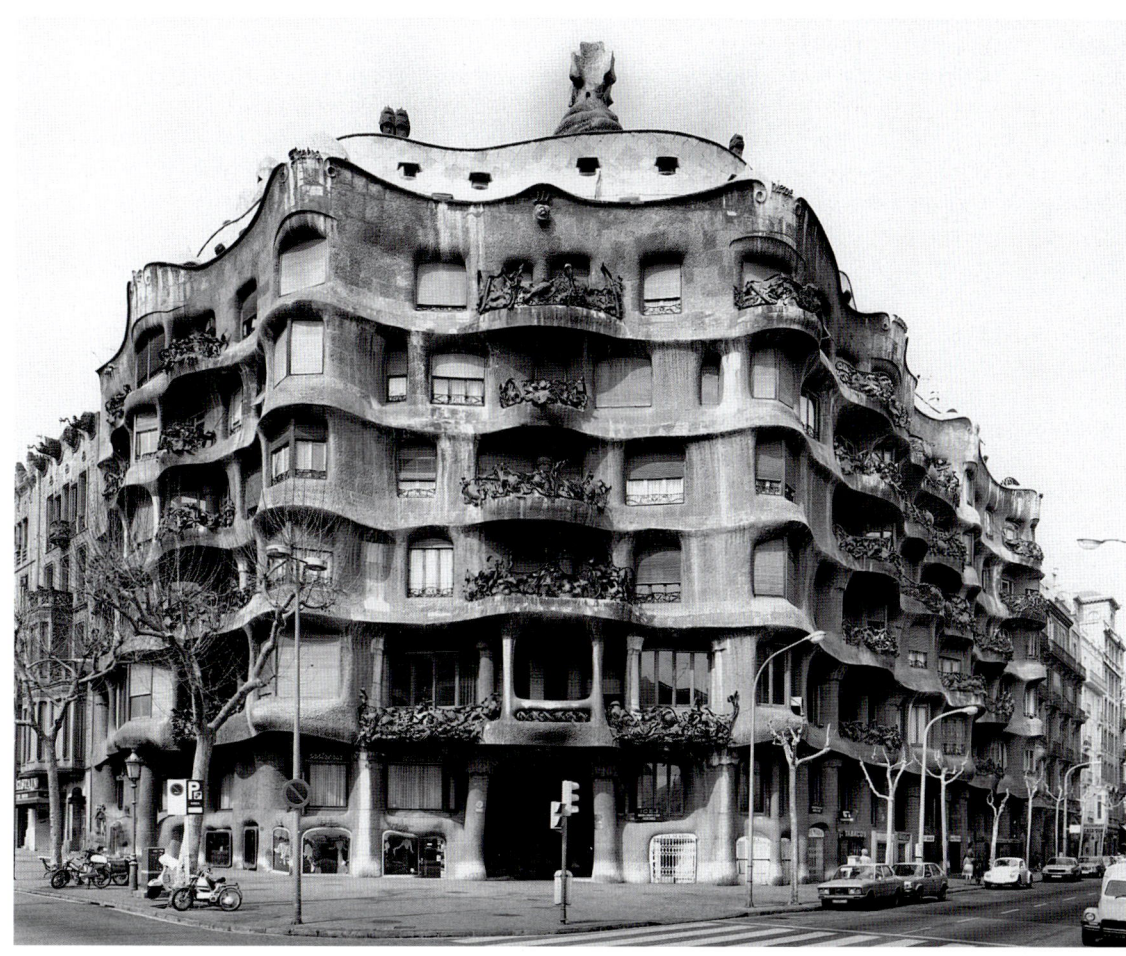

style. The Japanese print influence is obvious, although Beardsley assimilated it into his unique manner. Banishing Realism, he confined himself to lines and to patterns of black and white, eliminating all shading. His tense, elastic line encloses sweeping curvilinear shapes that lie flat on the surface—some left almost vacant, others filled with swirling complexes of mostly organic motifs. Beardsley's unfailing sense of linear rhythms and harmonies supports his mastery of calligraphic line. In his short lifetime—he died at age 26—he expressed in both his life and art the aesthete's ideal of "art for art's sake."

A BUILDING SEEMINGLY MOLDED FROM CLAY Art Nouveau achieved its most personal expression in the work of the Spanish architect ANTONIO GAUDI (1852–1926). Before becoming an architect, Gaudi had trained as an ironworker. Like many young artists of his time, he longed to create a style that was both modern and appropriate to his country. Taking inspiration from Moorish-Spanish architecture and from the simple architecture of his native Catalonia, Gaudi developed a personal aesthetic. He conceived a building as a whole and molded it almost as a sculptor might shape a figure from clay. Although work on his designs proceeded slowly under the guidance of his intuition and imagination, Gaudi was a master who invented many new structural techniques that facilitated the actual construction of his visions. His apartment house, Casa Milá (FIG. 29-54), is a wondrously free-form mass wrapped around a street corner. Lacy iron railings enliven the swelling curves of the cut-stone facade. Dormer windows peep from the undulating tiled roof, which is capped by fantastically writhing chimneys that poke energetically into the air above. The rough surfaces of the stone walls suggest naturally worn rock. The entrance portals look like eroded sea caves, but their design also may reflect the excitement that swept Spain following the 1879 discovery of Paleolithic cave paintings at Altamira. Gaudi felt that each of his buildings was symbolically a living thing, and the passionate naturalism of his Casa Milá is the spiritual kin of early-twentieth-century Expressionist painting and sculpture.

FIN-DE-SIÈCLE CULTURE

As the end of the nineteenth century neared, the momentous changes to which the Realists and Impressionists responded had become familiar and ordinary. As noted earlier, the term *fin-de-siècle,* which literally means "end of the century," is used to describe this period. This designation is not merely chronological but also refers to a certain sensibility. The cultures this term applies to experienced a significant degree of political upheaval toward the end of the nineteenth century. Moreover, prosperous wealthy middle classes dominated these societies—middle classes that aspired to the advantages the aristocracy already enjoyed. These people were determined to live "the good life," which evolved into a culture of decadence and indulgence. This fin-de-siècle culture was unrestrained and freewheeling, but the determination to enjoy life masked an anxiety prompted by the fluctuating political situation and uncertain future. The country most closely associated with fin-de-siècle culture was Austria.

THE SENSUALITY OF FIN-DE-SIÈCLE ART One Viennese artist whose works capture this period's flamboyance but temper it with unsettling undertones was GUSTAV KLIMT (1863–1918). In *The Kiss* (FIG. 29-55), Klimt depicted a couple locked in an embrace. All that is visible of the couple, however, is a segment of each person's head. The rest of the painting dissolves into shimmering, extravagant flat patterning. This patterning has clear ties to Art Nouveau and to the Arts and Crafts movement. Such a depiction also is reminiscent of the conflict between two- and three-dimensionality intrinsic to the work of Degas and other modernists. Paintings such as *The Kiss* were visual manifestations of fin-de-siècle spirit because they captured a decadence conveyed by opulent and sensuous images. Yet, such images attempted to mask, with varying degrees of success, anxiety about an uncertain and foreboding future.

REBELLING AGAINST THE ESTABLISHMENT Klimt, along with eighteen other artists, formally banded together in 1897 to promote the arts, calling themselves the Vienna Secession. This group formed in opposition to (or seceded from) the established conservative artists' society in Vienna, a society that held a virtual monopoly on art exhibitions. Because these younger, more experimental artists faced repeated rejection from these exhibitions, they decided to create their own exhibition program. In addition, they called for greater integration between art objects and the surrounding interior environment (as did the Arts and Crafts movement). Architect JOSEPH MARIA OLBRICH (1867–1918), a founding member of the Secession, designed the Vienna Secession Building (FIG. 29-56) in 1897–1898. To accommodate the unconventional needs of exhibiting members, Olbrich provided an interior of skylit flexible space with movable walls. The exterior, although formidable, incorporates the ornate and elaborate decoration that was a defining element of fin-de-siècle style. A lavish gilded laurel-leaf dome surmounts the large building. The dialogue between the geometric, staid building and the sensual, organic decorative elements reflects Olbrich's interest in invoking the solemnity and grandeur of classicism while expressing a unique and personal sensibility.

OTHER ARCHITECTURE IN THE LATER NINETEENTH CENTURY

The Beginnings of a New Style

In the later nineteenth century, new technology and the changing needs of urbanized, industrialized society affected architecture throughout the Western world. Since the eighteenth century, bridges had been built of cast iron (see FIG. 28-4), and most other industrial architecture—factories, warehouses, dockyard structures, mills, and the like—long had been built simply. Iron, along with other industrial materials, permitted engineering advancements in the construction of larger, stronger, and more fire-resistant structures. The tensile strength of iron (and especially of steel, available after 1860) permitted architects to create new designs involving vast enclosed spaces, as in the great train sheds of railroad stations and in exposition halls.

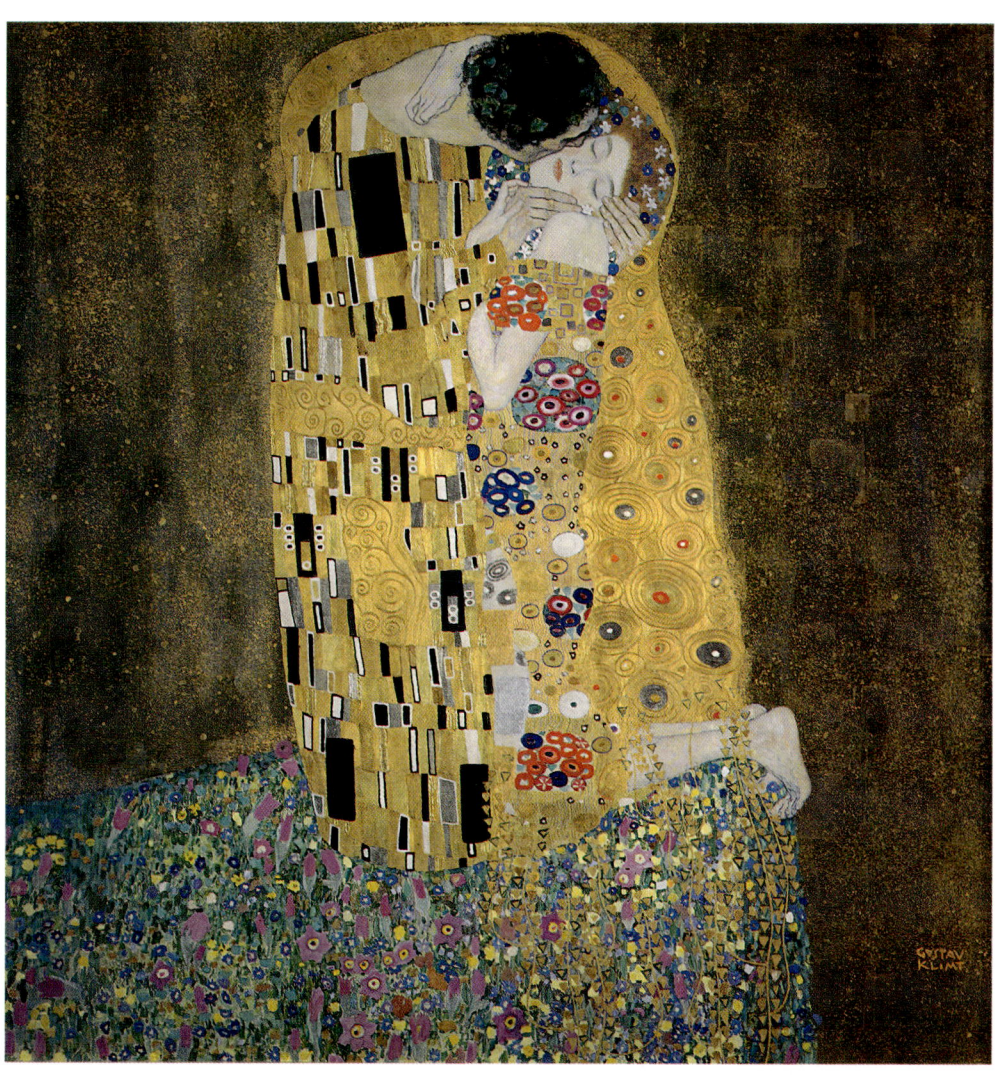

29-55 GUSTAV KLIMT, *The Kiss,* 1907–1908. Oil on canvas, approx. 5′ $10\frac{3}{4}''$ × 5′ $10\frac{3}{4}''$. Austrian Gallery, Vienna.

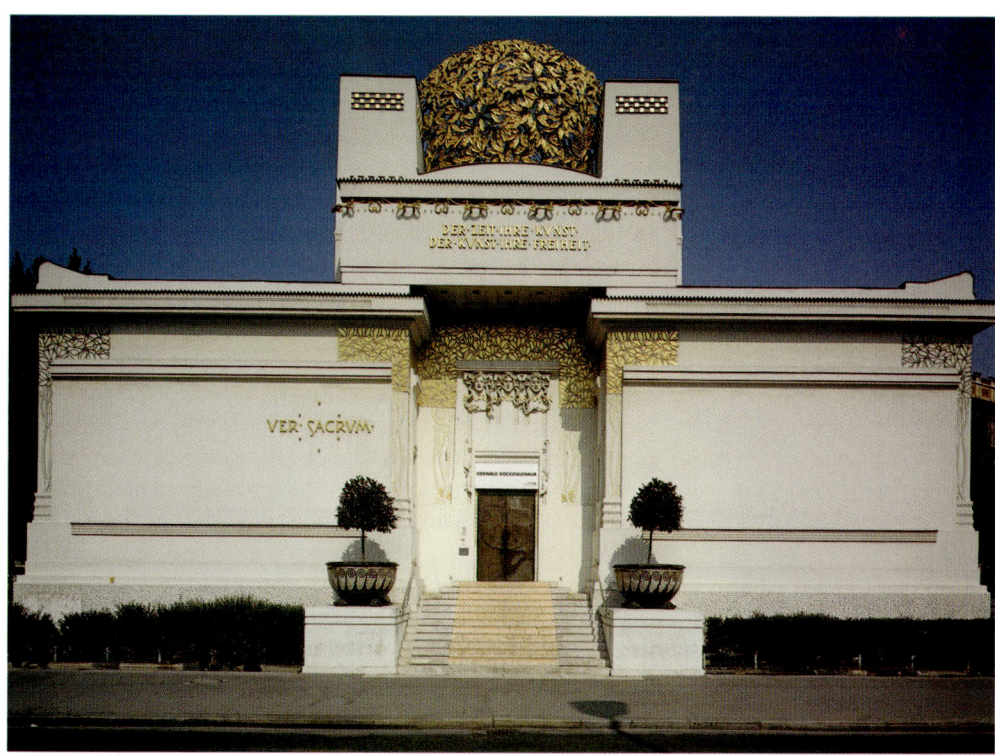

29-56 JOSEPH MARIA OLBRICH, Vienna Secession Building, Vienna, 1897–1898.

A SOARING METAL SKELETON The Realist impulse encouraged an architecture that honestly expressed a building's purpose, rather than elaborately disguising a building's function. The elegant metal skeleton structures of the French engineer-architect ALEXANDRE-GUSTAVE EIFFEL (1832–1923) can be seen as responses to this idea, and they constituted an important contribution to the development of the twentieth-century skyscraper. A native of Burgundy, Eiffel trained in Paris before beginning a distinguished career designing exhibition halls, bridges, and the interior armature for France's anniversary gift to the United States—Frédéric Auguste Bartholdi's *Statue of Liberty.* Eiffel designed his best-known work, the *Eiffel Tower* (FIG. **29-57**), for a great exhibition in Paris in 1889. Originally seen as a symbol of modern Paris and still considered a symbol of nineteenth-century civilization, the elegant metal tower thrusts its needle shaft nine hundred eighty-four feet above the city, making it at the time of its construction (and for some time to come) the world's highest structure. The tower's well-known configuration rests on four giant supports connected by gracefully arching open-frame skirts that provide a pleasing mask for the heavy horizontal girders needed to strengthen the legs. Visitors can take two elevators to the top, or they can use the internal staircase. Architectural historian Siegfried Giedion described well the effect of the tower when he wrote:

The airiness one experiences when at the top of the tower makes it the terrestrial sister of the aeroplane. . . . To a previously unknown extent, outer and inner space are interpenetrating. This effect can only be experienced in descending the spiral stairs from the top, when the soaring lines of the structure intersect with the trees, houses, churches, and the serpentine windings of the Seine. The interpenetration of continuously changing viewpoints create, in the eyes of the moving spectator, a glimpse into four-dimensional experience.[37]

This interpenetration of inner and outer space became a hallmark of twentieth-century art and architecture. At the time of their construction, however, Eiffel's metal skeleton structures and the iron skeletal frames designed by Labrouste (see FIG. 28-59) and Paxton (see FIG. 28-60) jolted some in the architectural profession into a realization that the new materials and new processes might germinate a completely new style and a radically innovative approach to architectural design.

The desire for greater speed and economy in building, as well as for a reduction in fire hazards, prompted the use of cast and wrought iron for many building programs, especially commercial ones. Designers in both England and the United States enthusiastically developed cast-iron architecture until a series of disastrous fires in the early 1870s in New York, Boston, and Chicago demonstrated that cast iron by itself was far from impervious to fire. This discovery led to encasing the metal in masonry, combining the first material's strength with the second's fire resistance.

In cities, convenience required closely grouped buildings, and increased property values forced architects literally to raise the roof. Even an attic could command high rentals if the building were provided with one of the new elevators, used for the first time in the Equitable Building in New York (1868–1871). Metal could support such tall structures, and the American skyscraper was born. With rare exceptions, however, as in Louis Sullivan's work (FIGS. 29-59 and 29-60), did designers treat successfully this innovative type of building and produce distinguished architecture.

A MASSIVE MASONRY MART Sullivan's predecessor, HENRY HOBSON RICHARDSON (1838–1886), frequently used heavy round arches and massive masonry walls. Because he was particularly fond of the Romanesque architecture of the Auvergne area in France, his work sometimes is thought of as a Romanesque revival. This designation does not do credit to the originality and quality of most of the buildings Richardson designed during the brief eighteen years of his practice. The Trinity Church in Boston and his smaller public libraries, residences, railroad stations, and courthouses in New England and elsewhere best demonstrate his vivid imagination and the solidity (the sense of enclosure and permanence) so characteristic of his style. However, his most important and influential building was the Marshall Field wholesale store (now demolished) in Chicago (FIG. **29-58**), which was begun in 1885. This vast building, occupying a city block and designed for the most practical of purposes, recalled historical styles without imitating them at all. The tripartite elevation of a Renaissance palace (see FIG. 21-20) or of the Roman aqueduct near Nîmes, France (see FIG. 10-31), may have been close to Richardson's mind. But he used no

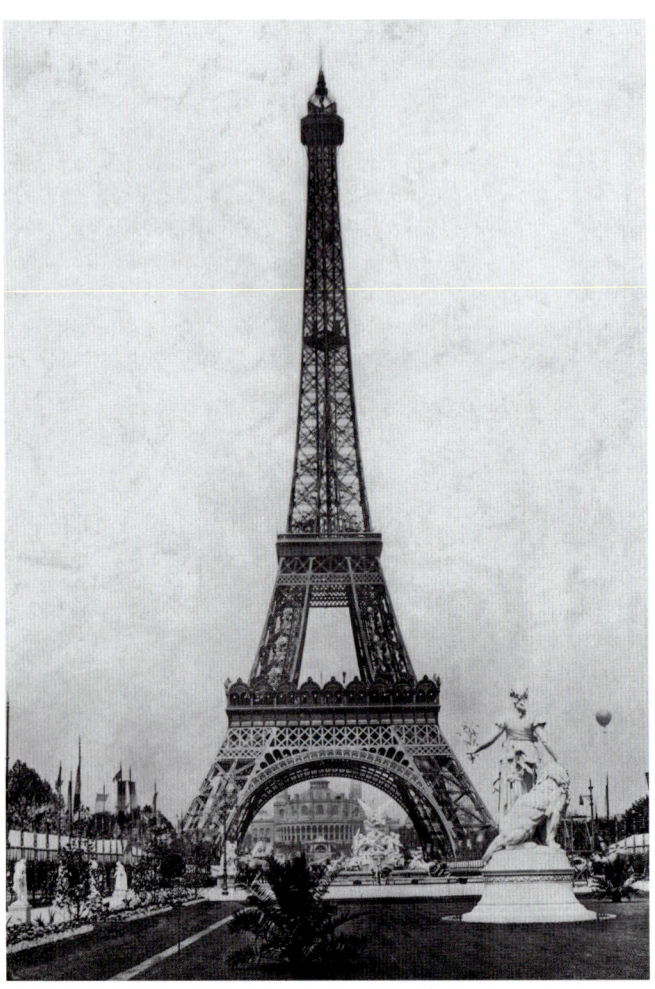

29-57 ALEXANDRE-GUSTAVE EIFFEL, Eiffel Tower, Paris, 1889 (photo: 1889–1890). Wrought iron, 984′ high.

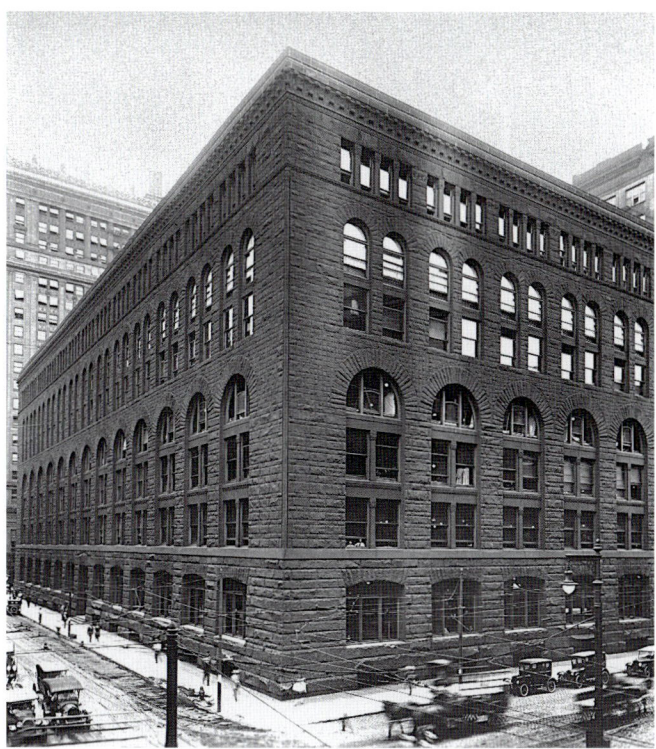

29-58 HENRY HOBSON RICHARDSON, Marshall Field wholesale store (demolished), Chicago, 1885–1887.

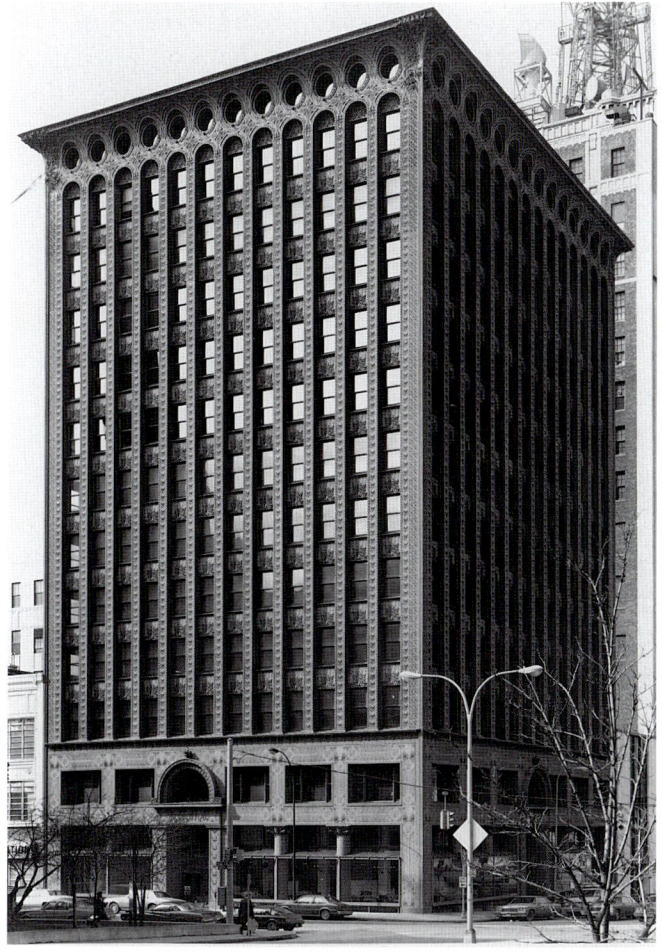

29-59 LOUIS SULLIVAN, Guaranty (Prudential) Building, Buffalo, 1894–1895.

classical ornament, made much of the massive courses of masonry, and, in the strong horizontality of the windowsills and the interrupted courses that defined the levels, stressed the long sweep of the building's lines, as well as its ponderous weight. Although the structural frame still lay behind and in conjunction with the masonry screen, the great glazed arcades opened up the walls of this large-scale building. They pointed the way to the modern total penetration of walls and the transformation of them into mere screens or curtains that serve both to echo the underlying structural grid and to protect it from the weather.

"FORM FOLLOWS FUNCTION"   LOUIS HENRY SULLI-VAN (1856–1924), who has been called the first truly modern architect, recognized Richardson's architectural innovations early in his career and worked forward from them when designing his tall buildings, especially the Guaranty (Prudential) Building in Buffalo, New York (FIG. **29-59**), built between 1894 and 1895. Here, he expressed the interior's subdivision on the exterior, as well as the skeletal (as opposed to the bearing-wall) nature of the supporting structure. Nothing more substantial than windows occupies most of the space between the terracotta-clad vertical members. In Sullivan's designs, viewers can be sure of an equivalence of interior and exterior design, not at all the case in Richardson's wholesale store or in Henri Labrouste's Library (see FIG. 28-59). Yet, Sullivan kept something of old convention; the Guaranty Building has a base and a cornice, even though the base is penetrated in such a way as to suggest the later free supports of twentieth-century architecture.

The building's form, then, began to express its function, and Sullivan's famous dictum that "form follows function," long the slogan of early-twentieth-century architects, found its illustration here. Sullivan did not mean by this slogan that a functional building is automatically beautiful, nor did he advocate a rigid and doctrinaire correspondence between exterior and interior design. Rather, he espoused a free and flexible relationship—one his pupil, Frank Lloyd Wright, later described as similar to that between the hand's bones and tissue.

TURNING A BUILDING INSIDE OUT   Sullivan took a further step in unifying exterior and interior design in his Carson, Pirie, Scott Building in Chicago, Illinois (FIG. **29-60**), built between 1899 and 1904. A department store, this building required broad, open, well-illuminated display spaces. The minimal structural steel skeleton permitted the singular achievement of this goal. The relation of spaces and solids here is so logical that nothing had to be added for structural facing, and the skeleton is clearly revealed on the exterior. The decklike stories, decoratively faced in white ceramic slabs, seem to sweep freely around the building and show several irregularities (notably the stressed bays of the corner entrance) that help the design break out of the cubical formula of Sullivan's older buildings. The architect gave over the lowest two levels of the Carson, Pirie, Scott Building to an ornament in cast iron (of his invention) made of wildly fantastic motifs that bear little resemblance to anything traditional architecture could show. Sullivan led the general search for a new style at the end of the century. He gave as much attention to finding new directions in architectural ornament as in architecture

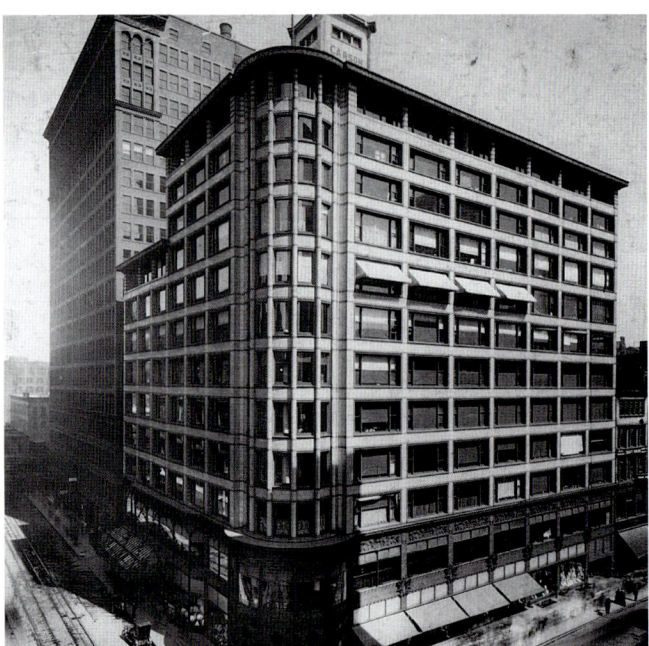

29-60 LOUIS SULLIVAN, Carson, Pirie, Scott Building, Chicago, 1899–1904.

itself. In this respect, he was an important figure in the Art Nouveau movement.

Although these new architectural models and materials were greatly important, these innovations were not immediately and widely accepted. Well into the twentieth century historical styles were still prominent in architectural design.

Especially in the nineteenth century's last decades, huge accumulations of wealth in the hands of industrialists and railway magnates permitted constructing lavishly expensive villas, mansions, and palatial town houses. Historical styles seemed appropriate to the newly rich who lived like medieval barons or Renaissance princes.

A "PALACE" IN AMERICA? RICHARD MORRIS HUNT (1827–1895) specialized in serving the building ambitions of America's new aristocracy. He brought Renaissance and Baroque form to the design of their ostentatious plans. Hunt had studied architecture in Switzerland and Paris and was happy to arbitrarily combine the historical styles to suit the tastes of his patrons. He built The Breakers (FIG. **29-61**) for Cornelius Vanderbilt II, the railroad king. It is a splendid private palace in Newport, Rhode Island, a favorite summer vacation spot for the affluent, who competed with one another in the magnitude and majesty of their mansions. Occupying a glorious promontory above the sea, with a splendid view of the incoming wave breakers, the residence resembles more a sixteenth-century Italian palazzo (with touches of French style) than a large summer cottage. The interior rooms are grand in scale and sumptuously rich in decor, each having its own variation of classical columns, painted ceilings, lavish fabrics, and sculptured trimmings. The entry hall, rising some forty-five feet above the majestic main stairway, signals the opulence of the rooms beyond. This hall and most of the main rooms offer magnificent views over the grounds and the ocean, views Hunt's positioning of the building on the property assured.

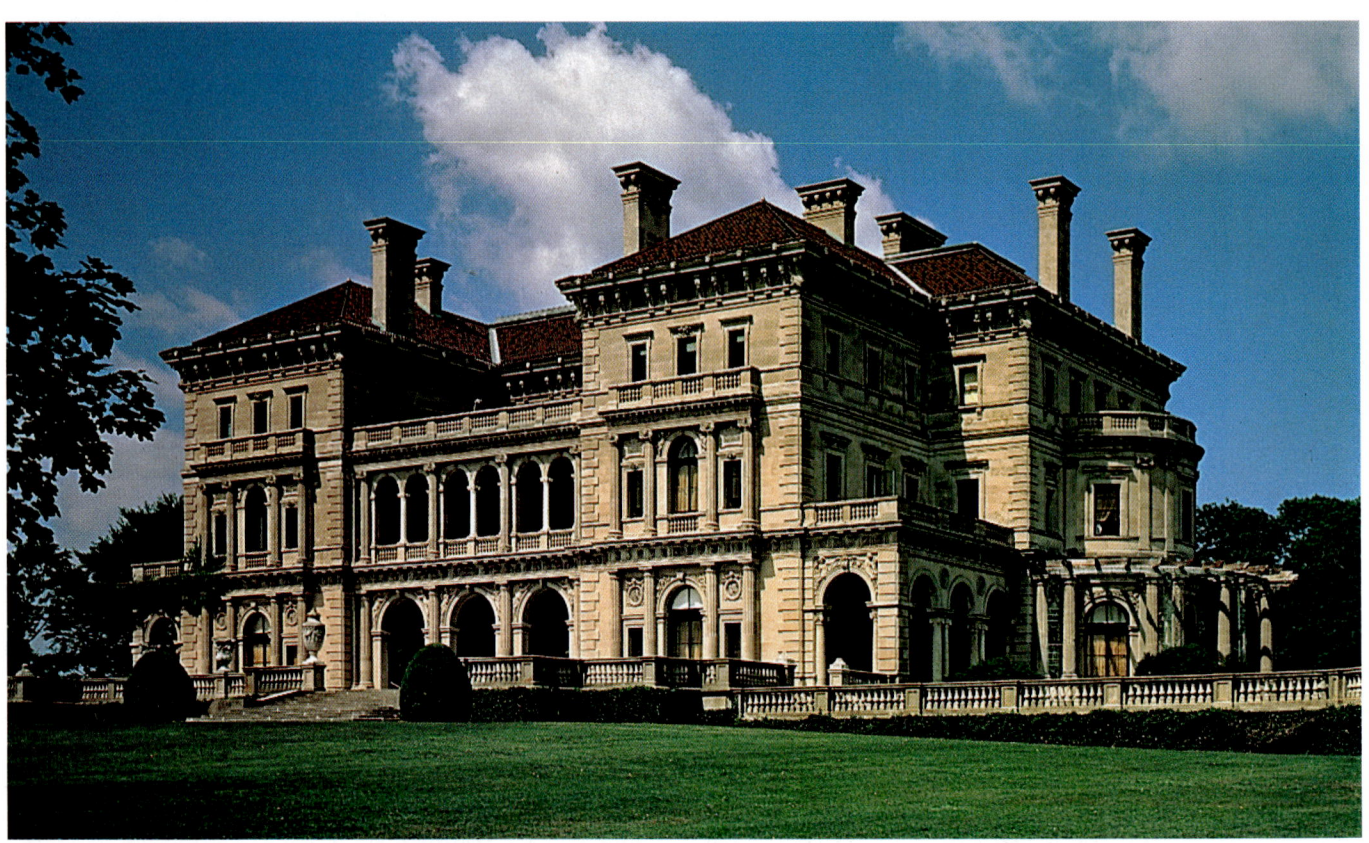

29-61 RICHARD MORRIS HUNT, The Breakers, Newport, Rhode Island, 1892.

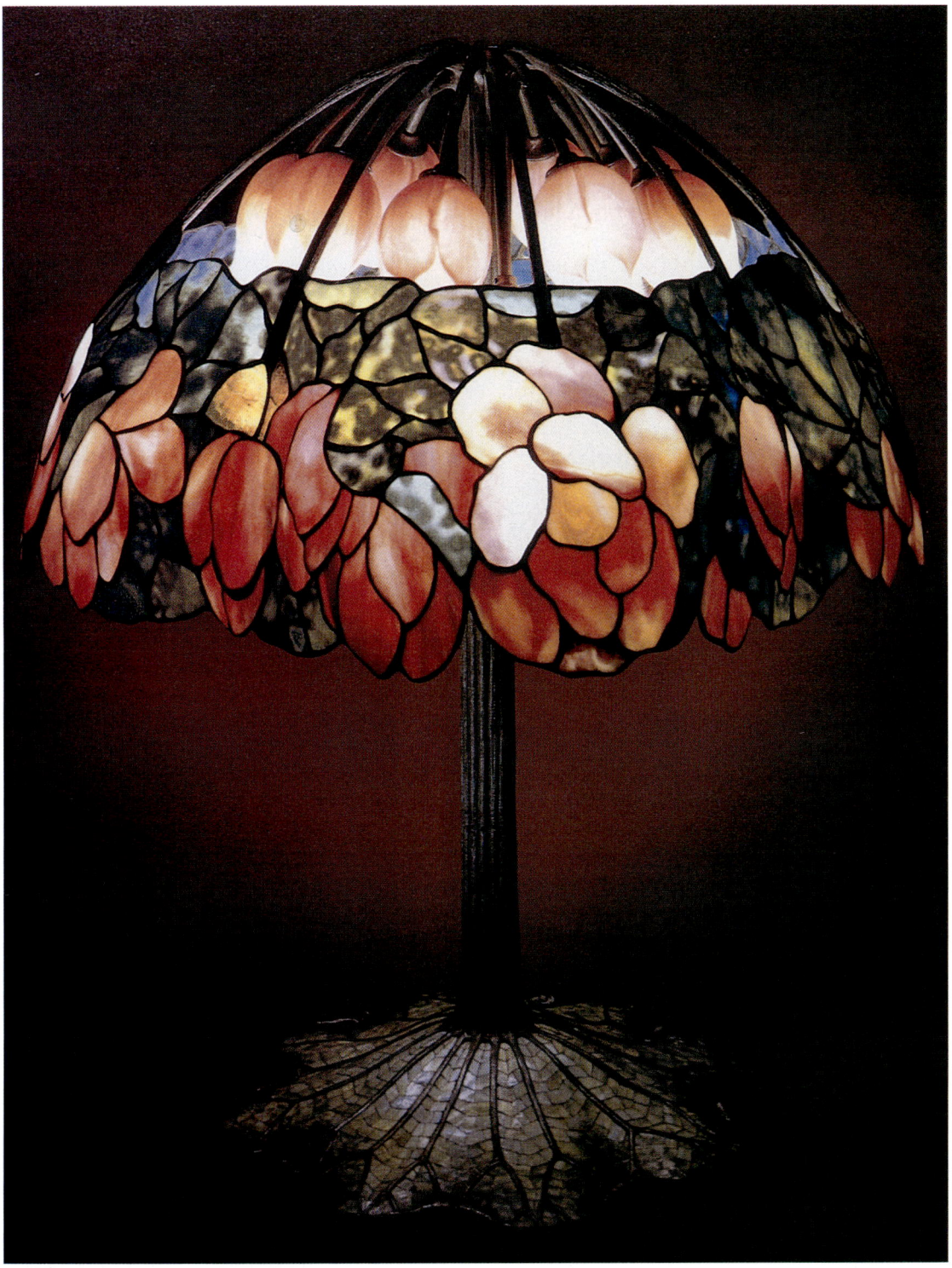

29-62   LOUIS COMFORT TIFFANY, Lotus table lamp, ca. 1905. Leaded Favrile glass, mosaic, and bronze, 2' 10½" high. Private collection.

FLORAL STAINED-GLASS LAMPS The period's extravagance and ostentation in architecture extended to the interior decor. Objects such as furniture, lights, rugs, and wallpaper with designs inspired by the sensuous opulence of Art Nouveau or fin-de-siècle art were popular. The stained-glass lamps of Louis Comfort Tiffany are one such example. His lotus table lamp (FIG. **29-62**), constructed of leaded glass, mosaic, and bronze, is based on the curvilinear floral forms of the lotus. Intended for wealthy buyers, this was the most expensive lamp ($750) Tiffany Studios produced in 1906. Because of the expense, labor, and time involved in producing this lamp, only one was made at a time. This ensured the quality artisanship so prized by the Arts and Crafts movement, whose ideas took root in America.

The grandeur and lavishness of this architectural and decorating style remained popular with the ultrarich until World War I shattered the bright period known as *la belle époque*.

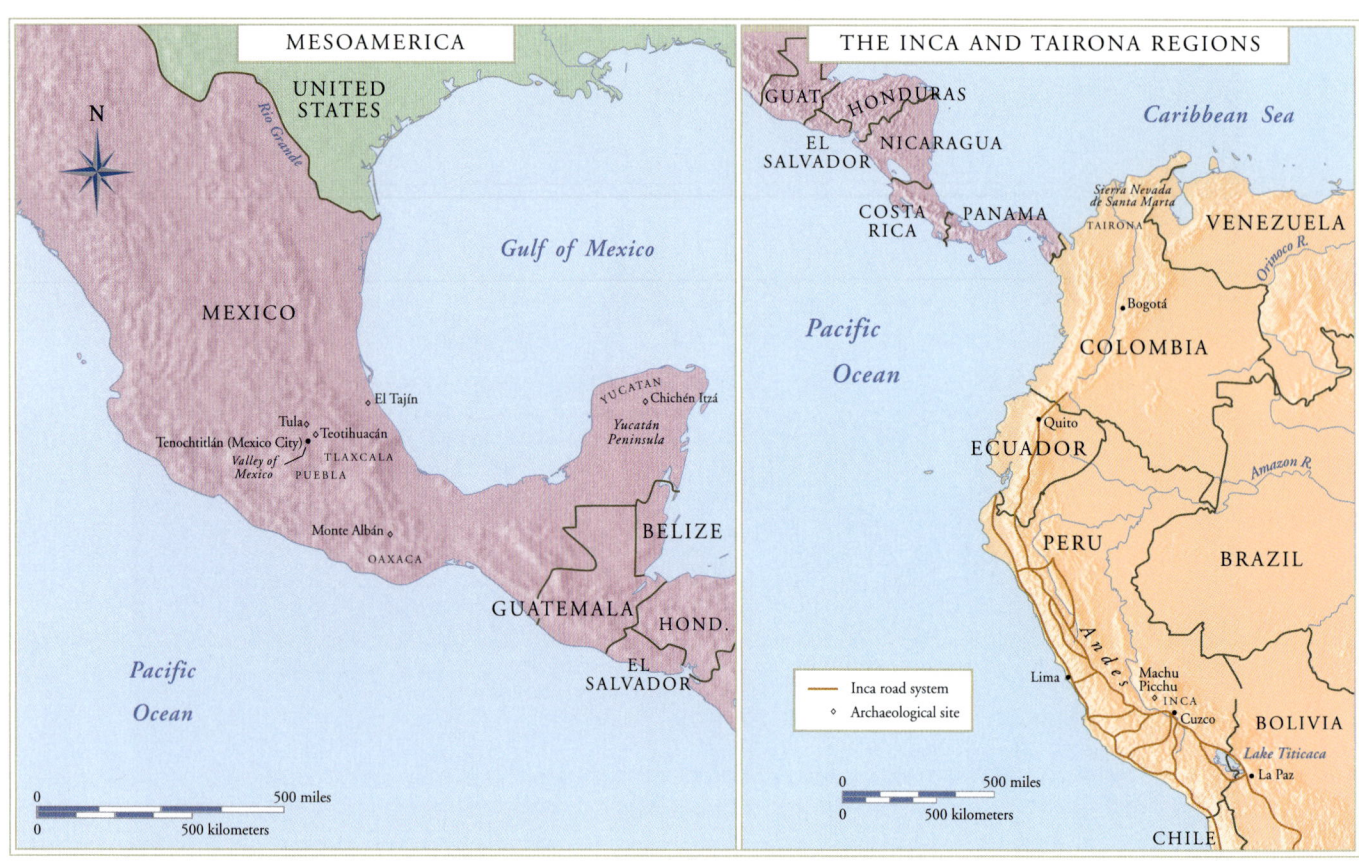

| MESOAMERICA | THE INCA AND TAIRONA REGIONS |

	800	900	1000	1100
MESOAMERICA		EARLY POSTCLASSIC		
SOUTH AMERICA			LATE INTERMEDIATE	

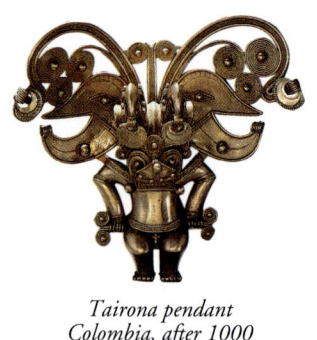

Tairona pendant
Colombia, after 1000

Inca arrive in Valley of Cuzco, 1000

Central and South American goldworking
chiefdoms flourish, 1000–early 1500s

Aztecs arrive in Valley
of Mexico, ca. 1193

30

BEFORE AND AFTER THE CONQUISTADORS

NATIVE ARTS OF THE AMERICAS AFTER 1000

1200	1300	1400	1500	1600

LATE POSTCLASSIC

LATE HORIZON

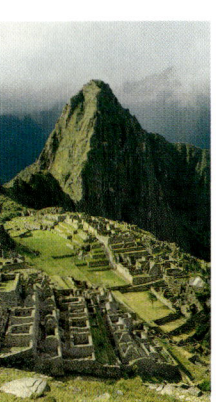

Machu Picchu
Peru, fifteenth century

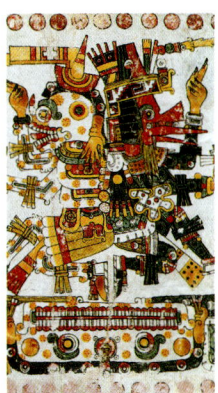

Borgia Codex
Puebla/Tlaxcala(?)
Mexico, ca. 1400–1500

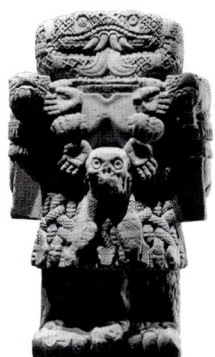

Coatlicue
Tenochtitlán, Mexico
ca. 1487–1520

Mixtecs later become accomplished Mesoamerican goldsmiths, ca. 1200

Fall of Tula and Chichén Itzá by 1200

Founding of Tenochtitlán, 1325

Surviving Mesoamerican codices painted, 1400–1500

Aztecs become an imperial power, 1427

Inca Empire begins to expand, 1438

Last rebuilding of Templo
Mayor, Tenochtitlán, 1487

Cortés arrives in Mexico, 1519

Cortés topples
Aztec Empire, 1521

Pizarro conquers
Inca Empire, 1532

MESOAMERICA

After the fall and destruction of the great central Mexican city of Teotihuacán in the eighth century and the mysterious abandonment of the southern Maya sites around 900, new cities arose to take their places. Notable were the Maya city of Chichén Itzá in Yucatán and Tula, the Toltec capital not far from modern Mexico City (see Chapter 14, pages 397–99). Their dominance was relatively short lived, however. Neither city left extensive written records; Tula seems not to have had much writing at all, although a few relief carvings there may display the names of the warriors depicted. Thus, Mesoamerican history in the early Postclassic period (ca. 900–1250) is less well documented than that of earlier groups, such as the southern Maya and the Zapotecs in Oaxaca, whose written texts carved on stone reliefs are among the earliest in Mesoamerica. For the cultures that succeeded them in the late Postclassic period (ca. 1250–1521), such as the Mixtecs and some other highland Mexican groups, however, a handful of illustrated manuscripts miraculously survived the depredations of the Spanish invasion in the sixteenth century, and their history is better known.

Postclassic Central Highland Groups

GOLD, MOSAICS, AND BOOKS The Mixtecs, who succeeded the Zapotecs at Monte Albán after 700, extended their political sway in Oaxaca by dynastic intermarriage, as well as by war. The treasures found in the tombs at Monte Albán bear witness to Mixtec wealth, and the quality of these works demonstrates the high level of Mixtec artistic achievement. Metallurgy was introduced into Mexico in Late Classic times, and the Mixtec became the skilled goldsmiths of Mesoamerica. Also renowned for their work in mosaic, they used turquoise obtained from far-off regions such as present-day New Mexico.

Seven Mixtec books survive, largely genealogical and historical in content. For Postclassic Mesoamericans, books were precious vehicles for recording not only history but also rituals, astronomical tables, calendric calculations, maps, and trade and tribute accounts. The book artists painted on long sheets of bark paper or deerskin, which they first coated with fine white lime plaster and folded into accordion-like pleats. Wooden covers protected the manuscripts, called *codices* (singular form, *codex*). The Postclassic Maya were preeminent in the art of writing and had libraries of such painted books. Their books consisted of columnar hieroglyphic texts designed to be read in zigzag fashion from left to right and top to bottom. Only four pre-Columbian Maya books survive, one discovered only thirty years ago. Bishop Diego de Landa, the sixteenth-century Spanish chronicler of the Maya of Yucatán, explains why: "We found a large number of books in these [Indian] characters and, as they contained nothing in which there were not to be seen superstition and lies of the devil, we burned them all, which they regretted to an amazing degree, and which caused them much affliction."[1]

THE JOINING OF OPPOSITES The extensively illuminated *Borgia Codex,* from somewhere in central highland Mexico (possibly the states of Puebla or Tlaxcala), is one of a different group of codices, which though slightly related to Mixtec geneological codices, treats primarily ritual subjects. The page we illustrate (FIG. **30-1**) shows the god of life, the black Quetzalcóatl (depicted here as a masked human rather than in the usual form of a feathered serpent), seated back-to-back with the god of death, the white Mictlantecuhtli. Below them is an inverted skull with a double keyboard of teeth, a symbol of the Underworld, which could be entered through the mouth of a great earth monster. Both figures hold scepters in one hand and gesticulate with the other. The image conveys the joining of opposites and the inevitable relationship of life and death, an important theme in much Mesoamerican art. Symbols of the twenty days of the two hundred sixty-day Mesoamerican ritual calendar appear in panels in the margins. The origins of this calendar, used even today in remote parts of Mexico and Central America, are lost in time. Except for the Mixtec genealogical codices, most codices painted before and immediately after the Spanish conquest deal with astronomy, calendrics, divination, and ritual and are still poorly understood.

Aztec

ANARCHY AND THE RISE OF THE AZTECS The destruction of Tula in about 1200 and the disintegration of the Toltec Empire in central Mexico made for a century of anarchy in the Valley of Mexico, the vast highland valley seven thousand feet above sea level that now contains sprawling Mexico City. Barbaric northern invaders, who must have wrought the destruction, gradually organized into small warring city-states. Nevertheless, they civilized themselves on the cultural remains and traditions of the Toltecs. Valley occupants regarded the last wave of northern invaders, when they appeared, as detestable savages.

These conquerors were the Aztecs. With astonishing rapidity, they transformed themselves within a few generations from migratory outcasts and serfs to mercenaries for local rulers and then to masters in their own right of the Valley of Mexico's petty kingdoms. In the process, they acquired, like their neighbors, the Toltec culture. They had begun to call themselves *Mexica,* and, following a legendary prophecy that they would build a city where they saw an eagle perched on a cactus with a serpent in its mouth, they settled on an island in Lake Texcoco (Lake of the Moon). Their settlement grew into the magnificent city of Tenochtitlán, which in 1519 so amazed the Spanish conqueror Hernán Cortés and his small band of adventurers.

THE AZTEC REIGN OF TERROR Recognized by those they subdued as fierce in war and cruel in peace, the Aztecs indeed seemed to glory in warfare and in military prowess. They radically changed the social and political situation in Mexico. The Aztecs believed they had a divine mission to propagate the cult of their tribal god, Huitzilopochtli, the hummingbird god of war (see "Aztec Religion," page 944). This goal meant forcing conformity on all peoples they conquered. Subservient groups not only had to submit to Aztec military power but also had to accept the cult of Huitzilopochtli and to provide victims for sacrifices to him and the many other Aztec gods. Thus, Aztec statecraft used the gods to achieve and maintain ruthless political dominion.

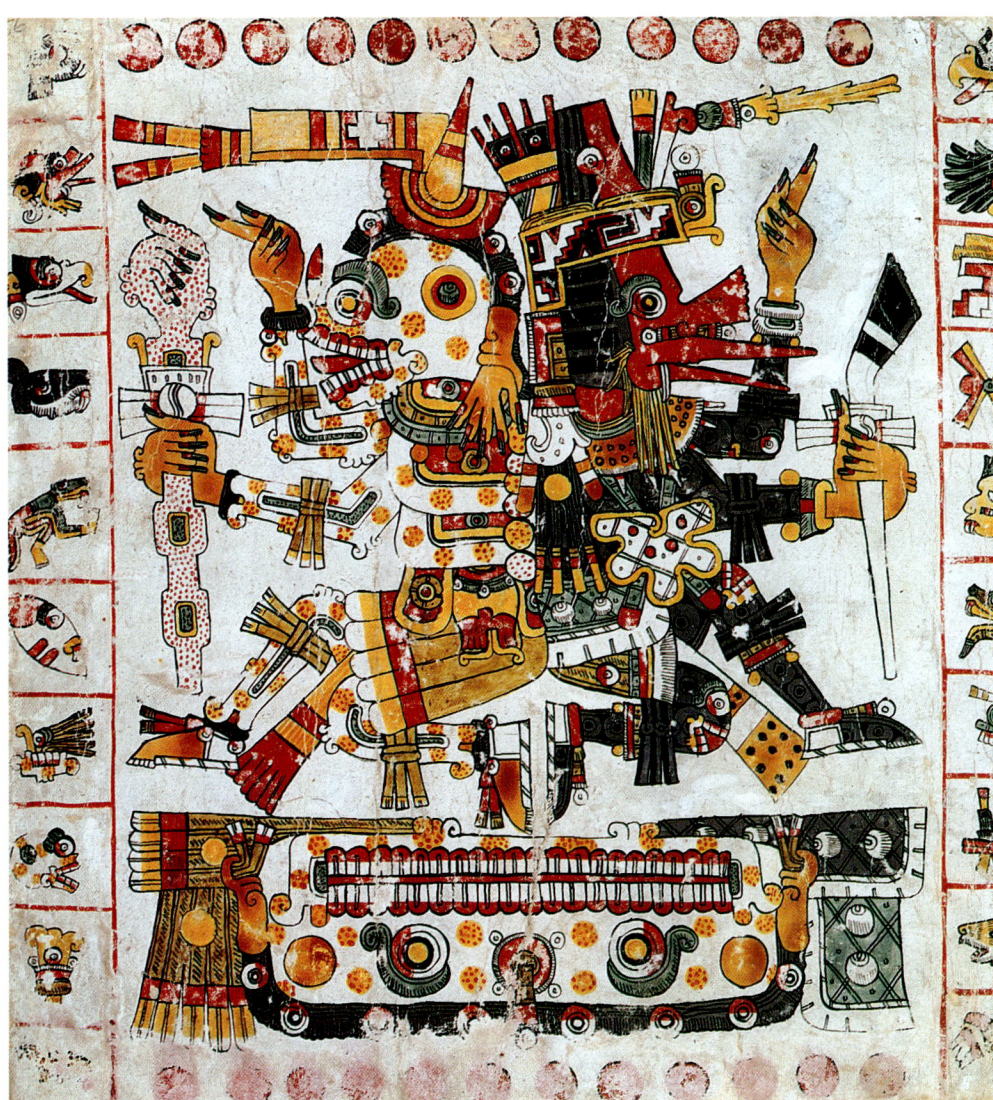

30-1 Mictlantecuhtli and Quetzalcóatl (death and life deities), illuminated page from the *Borgia Codex,* from Puebla/Tlaxcala (?), Mexico, ca. 1400–1500. Deerskin, $10\frac{2}{3}'' \times 4''$. Biblioteca Apostolica Vaticana, Rome.

Human sacrifice increased vastly in a reign of terror designed to keep the inhabitants of the Aztec Empire under control. To this end, unwilling subjects regularly had to pay tribute in the form of sacrificial victims, and the Aztecs waged special battles, called the "flowery wars," expressly to obtain captives for future sacrifice. It is no wonder that Hernán Cortés, in his conquest of the Aztec state, found ready allies among the peoples the Aztec had subjugated.

TENOCHTITLAN: CAPITAL OF AN EMPIRE
The ruins of the Aztec capital, Tenochtitlán, lie directly beneath the center of modern-day Mexico City. In the late 1970s, Mexican archeologists identified the exact location of many of the most important structures within the Aztec "sacred precinct," and extensive excavations near the cathedral in Mexico City continue. The principal building is the Templo Mayor or Great Temple (FIG. 30-2), a temple-pyramid honoring the Aztec god Huitzilopochtli and the local rain god Tlaloc. Two great staircases originally swept upward from the plaza level to the double sanctuaries at the summit. The Great Temple is a remarkable example of *superimposition,* a common trait in Mesoamerica. The excavated structure, composed of seven shells, indicates how the earlier walls nested within the later. (Today, only two of the inner structures are visible, the

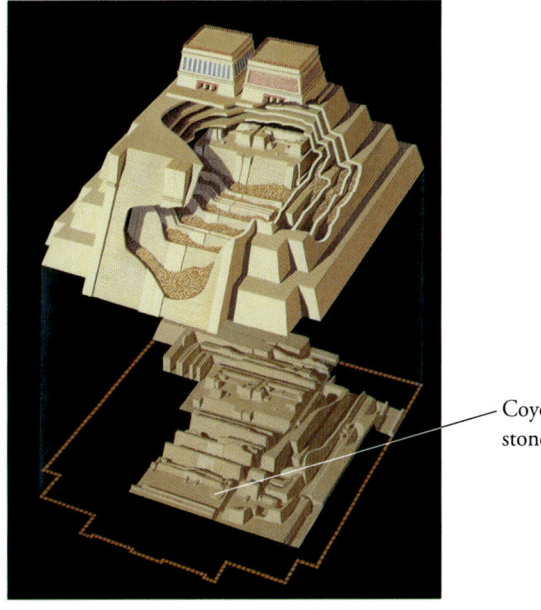

Coyolxauhqui stone (FIG. 30-3)

30-2 Reconstruction drawing with cutaway view of various rebuildings of the Great Temple, Aztec, Tenochtitlán, Mexico City, Mexico, ca. 1400–1500.

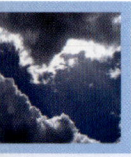

RELIGION AND MYTHOLOGY

Aztec Religion

The Aztecs saw their world as a flat disk resting on the back of a monstrous earth deity. Tenochtitlán, their capital, was at its center, with the Great Temple (FIG. 30-2) representing a sacred mountain and forming the axis passing up to the heavens and down through the Underworld. The four cardinal points each had its own god, color, tree, and calendrical symbol. The sky consisted of thirteen layers, while the Underworld had nine. The Aztec Underworld was an unpleasant place where nearly every dead person was destined to spend eternity, no matter what his or her behavior or rank during life. More agreeable afterlives awaited the souls of small children, drowned people, women who died in childbirth, and warriors.

The Aztecs often adopted the gods of conquered peoples, and their pantheon was complex and varied. When the Aztecs arrived in the Valley of Mexico, their own patron, Huitzilopochtli, a war and sun deity, joined such well-established Mesoamerican gods as Tlaloc and Quetzalcóatl, the feathered serpent who was a benevolent god of life, wind, and learning and culture, as well as the patron of priests. As the Aztecs went on to conquer much of Mesoamerica, they appropriated the gods of their subjects, such as Xipe Totec, a god of early spring and patron of goldworkers imported from the Gulf Coast and Oaxaca. Idols of the various gods made of stone, wood, and even dough (eaten at the end of rituals!) stood in their temples.

The Aztec ritual cycle was very full, given that they celebrated events in two calendars—the sacred (two hundred sixty-day) calendar and the solar (three hundred sixty days plus five unlucky and nameless days). The Spanish friars of the sixteenth century noted that the solar calendar dealt largely with agricultural matters. Almost every Aztec festival involved human sacrifice. For Tlaloc, the rain god, small children were especially desirable, because their tears brought the rains. For Xipe Totec's ceremony, the Aztecs flayed victims and then impersonators wore the skins for twenty days. This ritual symbolized the dry husk enclosing the living seed within and, more generally, the renewal of the earth's vegetation in the spring. Aztec ceremonies involved the burning of incense (made from *copal,* a resin from conifer trees), colorfully attired dancers and actors, and music provided by conch

shell trumpets, drums, rattles, rasps, bells, whistles, and, of course, the human voice.

The two Mesoamerican calendars functioned simultaneously, requiring fifty-two years for the same date to recur in both. A ritual called the New Fire Ceremony commemorated this rare event. Pots were broken and new ones made for the next period, pregnant women were hidden away, and all fires were extinguished. At midnight on a mountaintop, fire priests took out the heart of a sacrificial victim and with a fire drill renewed the flame in the exposed cavity. Bundles of sticks representing the fifty-two years that had just passed then were set ablaze, insuring that the sun would rise in the morning and that another cycle would begin.

Rituals also marked the completion of important religious structures. The dedication of the last major rebuilding of the Great Temple at Tenochtitlán in 1487, for example, reportedly involved the sacrifice of thousands of captives from recent wars in the Gulf Coast region. Varied offerings have been found within earlier layers of the temple, many representing tribute from subjugated peoples. These include blue-painted stone and ceramic vessels representing the rain deity Tlaloc, conch shells, a jaguar skeleton, flint and obsidian knives, and even Mesoamerican "antiques"—carved stone Olmec and Teotihuacán masks made hundreds of years before and probably looted by the Aztecs.

The Aztec high priest was the ruler, befitting a culture that did not separate religion and statecraft. Thousands of priests served in Aztec temples. Novices lived austerely, practicing autosacrifice by piercing their skin with cactus spines to draw blood and receiving instruction in the esoteric complexities of Aztec religion. Distinctive hairstyles, clothing, and black body paint identified the priests. Women served as priestesses, particularly in temples dedicated to various earth-mother cults. The Spanish conqueror Bernal Díaz del Castillo was shocked to witness a group of foul-smelling priests with uncut fingernails, long hair matted with blood, and ears covered in cuts, not realizing they were undergoing some sort of special penance in honor of the deities they served. Despite their unkempt appearance, these priests were the most educated of all Aztecs. They were the astronomers, diviners, teachers, cult specialists, codex painters, and scribes.

later ones destroyed at the time of the Spanish conquest.) The sacred precinct also contained the temples of other deities, a ballcourt, a skull rack for the exhibition of the heads of victims killed in sacrificial rites, and a school for the nobility's children.

Tenochtitlán was a city laid out on a grid plan in quarters and wards, reminiscent of Teotihuacán (see FIG. 14-4), which, long abandoned, had become a pilgrimage site for the Aztecs. Tenochtitlán's island location required conducting communication and transport via canals and other waterways. Many of

the Spaniards thought of Venice in Italy when they saw the city rising from the waters like a radiant vision. Crowded with buildings, plazas, and courtyards, the city also boasted a vast and ever-busy marketplace. In the words of Bernal Díaz del Castillo, a soldier who accompanied Cortés when the Spaniards first entered Tenochtitlán, "Some of the soldiers among us who had been in many parts of the world, in Constantinople, and all over Italy, and in Rome, said that so large a marketplace and so full of people, and so well regulated and arranged, they had never beheld before."[2] The city proper had a population of more than one hundred thousand people. Researchers estimate that the total population of the area of Mexico the Aztecs dominated at the time of the conquest was eleven million.

THE MOON GODDESS DISMEMBERED The Temple of Huitzilopochtli at Tenochtitlán commemorated the god's victory over his brothers and sister. The myth signifies the conquest by the sun, a role sometimes assumed by Huitzilopochtli, of the stars and the moon. Avenging the death of his mother, Coatlicue (She of the Serpent Skirt), at the hands of his half-siblings, Huitzilopochtli killed them and dismembered the body of his evil sister, the moon goddess Coyolxauhqui (She of the Bells, referring to the copper bells on her cheeks) at a hill near Tula (represented by the pyramid itself). The mythical event is depicted on a huge stone disk (FIG. **30-3**) whose discovery in 1978 set off the ongoing archeological investigations near the main plaza in Mexico City. About eleven feet in diameter, the relief had been placed at the foot of the staircase leading up to Huitzilopochtli's shrine. Carved on it is an image of the segmented, nearly naked body of Coyolxauhqui. In addition to representing human sacrifice—victims' bodies were hurled down the temple stairs to land on this stone—the broken body refers to the waxing and waning of the moon itself.

The disk is an unforgettable expression of Aztec temperament and taste. The image proclaimed the power of the Aztec gods over their enemies and the inevitable fate that must befall them when defeated. Marvelously composed, the relief has a kind of dreadful, yet formal, beauty. Within the circular space, the design's carefully balanced, richly detailed components are so adroitly placed that they seem to have a slow turning rhythm, like a revolving galaxy. The carving is confined to a single level, a smoothly even, flat surface raised

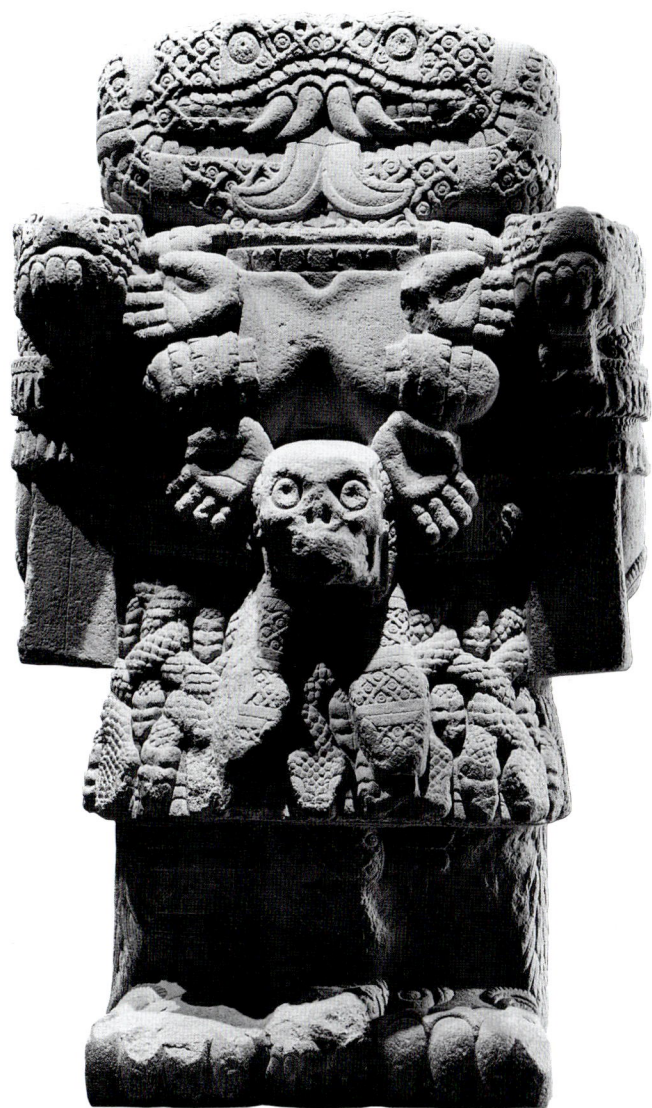

30-4 Coatlicue (She of the Serpent Skirt), Aztec, from Tenochtitlán, Mexico City, ca. 1487–1520. Andesite, approx. 8′ 6″ high. National Museum of Anthropology, Mexico City.

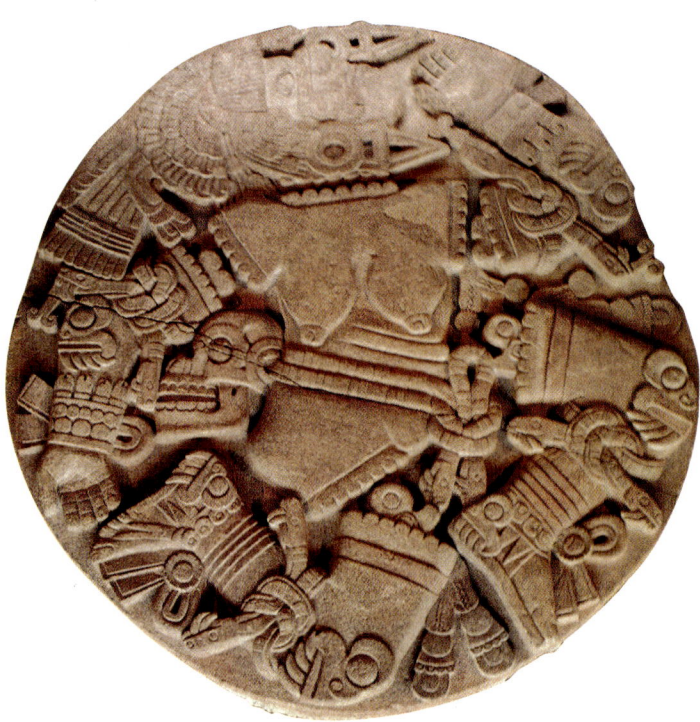

30-3 Coyolxauhqui (She of the Bells), Aztec, from the Great Temple of Tenochtitlán, Mexico City, late fifteenth century. Stone, diameter approx. 11′. Museum of the Great Temple, Mexico City.

from a flat ground. It is the sculptural equivalent of the line and flat tone, the figure and neutral ground, characteristic of Mesoamerican painting.

A COLOSSAL EARTH GODDESS In addition to relief carving, the Aztecs produced sculpture unbound to architecture, freestanding and in the round. A colossal statue of Coatlicue (FIG. **30-4**), ancient earth mother of the gods Huitzilopochtli and Coyolxauhqui, is a massive apparition of dread congealed into stone. Discovered in 1790 near Mexico City's cathedral, the sculpture's original setting is unknown. Colonial authorities, appalled by its frightening appearance, reburied it for many years. The main forms are carved in high relief, the details executed either in low relief or by incising. The overall aspect is of an enormous blocky mass, its ponderous weight looming over awed viewers.

The beheaded goddess is composed of an inventory of gruesome objects. Up from her headless neck writhe two serpents whose heads meet to form a tusked mask. Coatlicue wears a necklace of severed human hands and excised human hearts. The pendant of the necklace is a skull. Entwined snakes form her skirt. From between her legs emerges another serpent, symbolic perhaps of both menses and the male member. Like most Aztec deities, Coatlicue has both masculine and feminine traits. Her hands and feet have great claws, which she used to tear the human flesh she consumed. All of her attributes symbolize sacrificial death. Yet, in Aztec thought, this mother of the gods combined savagery and tenderness, for out of destruction arose new life, a theme seen earlier at Teotihuacán (see FIG. 14-6).

SPANIARDS CONQUER THE AZTECS Given the Aztecs' almost meteoric rise from obscurity to their role as the dominant culture of Mesoamerica, the quality of the art they sponsored is astonishing. Granted, they swiftly appropriated the best artworks and most talented artists of conquered territories, bringing both back to Tenochtitlán. Thus, craftspeople from other areas, such as the Mixtecs of Oaxaca, may have created much of the exquisite pottery, goldwork, and turquoise mosaics the Aztec elite used. Gulf Coast artists probably made the life-size terracotta sculptures of eagle warriors found at the Templo Mayor.

Although the Aztecs may have sacked what remained of Tula, dragging Toltec stone sculptures back to Tenochtitlán, their own sculptural style, developed at the height of their power in the later fifteenth century, is unsurpassed. Unfortunately, much of Aztec and Aztec-sponsored art did not survive the Spanish conquest and subsequent period of evangelization. The conquerors took Aztec gold artifacts back to Spain and melted them down, zealous friars destroyed "idols" and codices, and perishable materials such as textiles and wood largely disappeared. A handful of beautifully worked feathered objects ended up in Europe, including a magnificent headdress that once may have belonged to Moctezuma (r. 1502–1521), the last Aztec ruler before the conquest. Aztec artisans even created mosaic-like images with feathers, an art they put to service for the Catholic Church for a brief time after the Spanish conquest, creating religious pictures and decorating ecclesiastical clothing with the bright tropical bird feathers.

The Spanish conquerors found it impossible to reconcile the beauty of the great city of Tenochtitlán with its hideous cults. They admired its splendid buildings ablaze with color, its luxuriant and spacious gardens, its sparkling waterways, its teeming markets, and its grandees resplendent in exotic bird feathers. But when Moctezuma brought Cortés and his entourage into the shrine of Huitzilopochtli's temple, the newcomers started back in horror and disgust from the huge statues clotted with dried blood. Cortés was furious. Denouncing Huitzilopochtli as a devil, he proposed to put a high cross above the pyramid and a statue of the Virgin in the sanctuary to exorcise its evil.

This proposal came to symbolize the avowed purpose and the historic result of the Spanish conquest of Mesoamerica. The conquerors venerated the cross and the Virgin, triumphant, in new shrines raised on the ruins of the plundered temples of the Indian gods, and the banner of the Most Catholic King of Spain waved over new atrocities of a European kind.

SOUTH AMERICA

Inca

A VAST ANDEAN EMPIRE The Inca were a small highland group who established themselves in the Cuzco Valley of Andean South America around 1000, with the city of Cuzco as their capital. In the fifteenth century, however, they rapidly extended their power until their empire stretched from modern Quito, Ecuador, to central Chile, a distance of more than three thousand miles. Perhaps twelve million subjects inhabited the area the Inca ruled.

The Inca's story, like those of the pre-Columbian peoples of Mesoamerica, ended in extermination in violent confrontations with the Spanish conquistadors. In the Andean region, however, smallpox spreading south from Spanish-occupied Mesoamerica killed the Inca emperor and his heir before they ever laid eyes on a Spaniard, plunging the Inca empire into a civil war that only aided the Europeans in their conquest of the territory soon afterward. In 1532, Francisco Pizarro, the Spanish explorer of the Andes, ambushed the Inca ruler Atawalpa shortly after the latter had vanquished his rival half-brother and was on his way to be crowned at Cuzco. Although Atawalpa paid a ransom of enough gold and silver to fill a room, the Spaniards killed him and took control of his vast domain, only a decade after Cortés had defeated the Aztecs in Mexico.

The vast Inca empire required skillful organizational and administrative control, and the Inca had rare talent for both (see "Inca Clothing and Social Status," page 947). In this respect, they resembled the Romans (see Chapter 10, page 246). They divided their Andean empire into sections and subsections, provinces and communities, whose boundaries all converged on, or radiated from, Cuzco (meaning "navel of the world" in Quechua, the Inca language). The Inca's constructional prowess matched their organizational talent. They were skillful engineers who knitted together the fabric of their empire with networks of roads and bridges. Lacking wheeled vehicles and horses, they used their highway system to move goods and armies throughout their territories. The Inca mastered the difficult problems of Andean agriculture with expert terracing and irrigation. Metallurgists, they mined extensively, accumulating the fabled troves of gold and silver that motivated Pizarro to conquer them.

RECORD-KEEPING, ROADS, AND RUNNERS Unlike their Aztec contemporaries in Mexico, the Inca never developed a writing system. Nevertheless, they maintained strict control over their vast empire by developing a remarkably complex communication system. The only known Andean record-keeping device, the *quipu,* was not a book or tablet but was made of fibers. From a main cord hung numerous knotted strings. The color and position of each cord, as well as the kind of knot and its location, apparently recorded numbers and categories of things, whether people, llamas, or crops. Studies of quipus have demonstrated the Inca used the decimal system and were familiar with the zero concept. The Inca census taker or tax collector could easily roll up and carry the quipu.

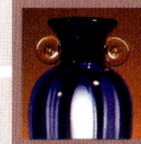

ART AND SOCIETY

Inca Clothing and Social Status

The Inca aimed at imposing not only political control but also their art style throughout their realm, subjugating local traditions to those of the empire. Control even extended to clothing, which communicated the social status of the person wearing the garment. The Inca wove bands of small squares of various repeated abstract designs into their fabrics. Scholars believe the patterns had political meaning, connoting membership in particular social groups. Such motifs completely covered the Inca ruler's tunics, perhaps to indicate his control over all such groups. Those the Inca conquered, however, had to wear their characteristic local dress at all times, a practice reflected in the distinctive and varied clothing of today's indigenous Andean peoples.

The Incas built more than fourteen thousand miles of roads, one main highway running through the highlands and another along the coast, with connecting roads linking the two regions. They established a highly efficient swift communication system of runners who carried messages in relays the length of the empire. It was said the Inca emperor in Cuzco could get fresh fish from the coast in only three days. Where the terrain was too steep for a paved flat surface, the Inca built stone steps, while their rope bridges crossed canyons high over impassable rivers. They placed small settlements along the roads no more than a day apart where travelers could rest and obtain supplies for the journey.

Like the Romans, the imperial Inca were great architects. Although they also worked with the ancient building material of adobe, the Inca were supreme masters of shaping and fitting stone. In addition, they had an almost instinctive grasp of the

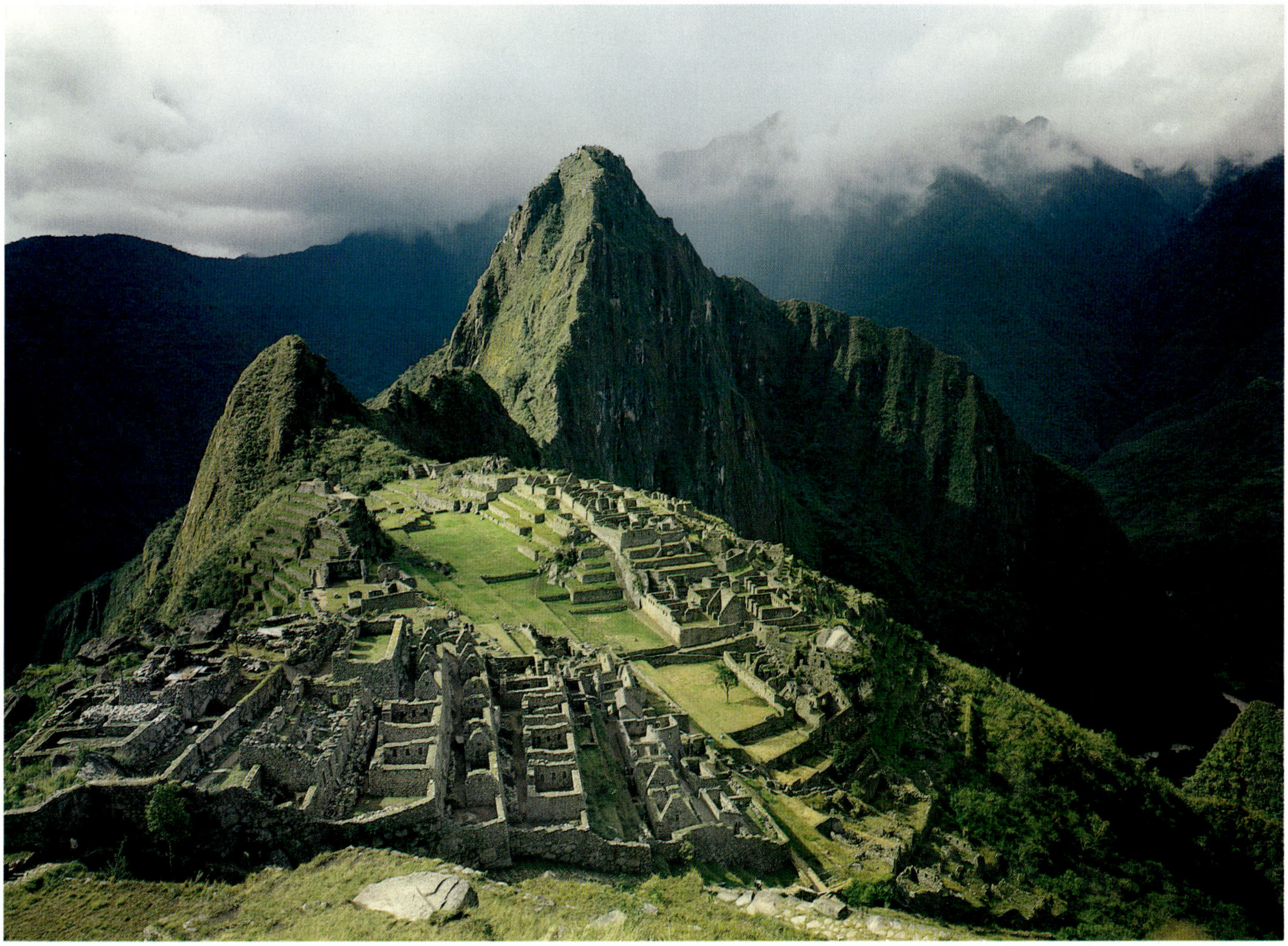

30-5   Machu Picchu (view from adjacent peak), Inca, Peru, fifteenth century.

proper relation of architecture to site. As a militant conquering people, they selected naturally fortified sites and further strengthened them by building various defensive structures.

Archeologists have found many small clay and stone architectural models the Inca may have used for planning buildings or even entire towns. Some large boulders that have carved architectural features such as plazas and stairs also survive. Researchers, however, have been unable to find any correlation between an existing structure or settlement and these supposed models. Thus, they still do not know how Inca architects planned and constructed important civic and religious monuments.

UNDISTURBED MACHU PICCHU

One of the world's most awe-inspiring sights, the Inca city of Machu Picchu (FIG. **30-5**) perches on a ridge between two jagged peaks nine thousand feet above sea level. Completely invisible from the Urubamba River valley some sixteen hundred feet below, the site remained unknown to the outside world until American explorer Hiram Bingham discovered it in 1911. In the very heart of the Andes, Machu Picchu is about fifty miles north of Cuzco and, like some of the region's other cities, was the private estate of a powerful mid-fifteenth-century Inca ruler. Though relatively small and insignificant among its neighbors (with a resident population of little more than a thousand), the city is of great archeological importance as a rare site left undisturbed since Inca times. The accommodation of its architecture to the landscape is so complete that Machu Picchu seems a natural part of the mountain ranges that surround it on all sides. The Inca even cut large stones to echo the shapes of the mountain beyond. Terraces spill down the mountainsides and are built even up to the very peak of Huayna Picchu, the great hill just beyond the city's main plaza. The Incas carefully sited buildings so that windows and doors framed spectacular views of sacred peaks and facilitated the recording of important astronomical events.

CUZCO: THE PUMA CITY

The Inca capital, Cuzco, was largely destroyed during the Spanish conquest and subsequent colonial period. Thus, most of what is known about the city has been gleaned from often-contradictory Spanish sources rather than from archeology. Some descriptions state that Cuzco's plan was in the shape of a puma, with a great shrine-fortress on a hill above the city representing its head and the southeastern convergence of two rivers forming its tail. Cuzco residents still refer to the river area as "the puma's tail." A great plaza, still the hub of the modern city, was nestled below the animal's stomach. The puma referred to Inca royal power, but feline symbolism dates back to the very beginnings of Andean art (see Chapter 14, page 400) and occurs in nearly every medium (see FIG. 14-15).

DRY-JOINED MASONRY: THE CORICANCHA

The Inca, as already noted, were masters of stone masonry. Their technique of *dry-joining* (fitting stone blocks together without mortar) ashlar construction is famous. The ashlar's joints could be beveled to show their tightness or laid in courses with per-

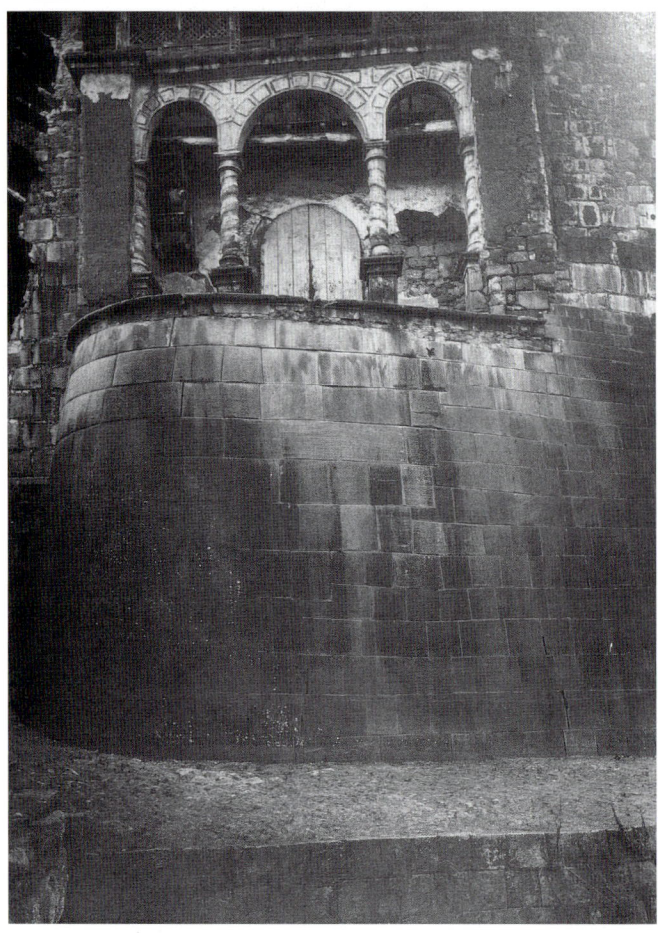

30-6 Wall of the Golden Enclosure (surmounted by the church of Santo Domingo), Inca, Cuzco, Peru, fifteenth century.

fectly joined faces so that the lines of separation were hardly visible. The Inca produced the close joints of their masonry by abrasion alone. Masons swung each stone in a sling against its neighbor until the surfaces were ground to a perfect fit. For the walls of more important buildings, such as temples or administrative palaces, the workers usually laid the stones in regular horizontal courses. For lesser structures, they set the blocks in polygonal (mostly trapezoidal) patterns. (The trapezoid was a favorite architectural figure, commonly appearing as the shape of niches, doorways, windows, and even the plans of plazas.) With Inca stonecraft, builders could fashion walls with curved surfaces, their planes as level and continuous as if they were a single form poured in concrete.

A prime example of the single-form effect is a surviving wall from the Temple of the Sun in Cuzco (FIG. **30-6**). Originally known as Coricancha (Golden Enclosure), this structure was the most magnificent of all Inca shrines. The temple was dedicated to the worship of several Inca deities, including the creator god Viracocha and the gods of the sun, moon, stars, and the elements. Sixteenth-century Spanish chroniclers wrote in awe of Coricancha's gold-and-silver splendor, its interior veneered with sheets of gold, silver, and emeralds. The remaining hewn stones, precisely fitted and polished, form a curving semiparabola (sickle shape) and were set for flexibility in earthquakes, allowing for a temporary dislocation of the courses, which then return to their original position.

During the Inca revolt against the Spaniards in the mid-1530s, the Temple of the Sun was badly burned. Later, the church of Santo Domingo, in the Spanish Colonial style, was erected on what remained of it, the curved section of wall serving as the foundation for the apse. Although parts of the original Inca building were always visible, a violent earthquake in 1950 seriously damaged the church and revealed even more of the temple, with its chambers, courtyards, and trapezoidal niches and doorways. Santo Domingo has been rebuilt, and the two contrasting structures remain standing one atop the other (FIG. 30-6). The Coricancha is of more than architectural and archeological interest. It is a symbol of the Spanish conquest of the Americas and serves as a composite monument to it—one civilization built on the ruins of another.

Intermediate Area

Between the highly developed civilizations of Mesoamerica and the Andes lies a region archeologists have dubbed the "Intermediate Area." Comprised of part of Ecuador, part of Venezuela, and all of Colombia and the modern Central American countries of Panama, Costa Rica, Nicaragua, and parts of El Salvador and Honduras, at the time of the European invasion it was by no means a unified political territory but was occupied by many small rival chiefdoms. Although the people of the Intermediate Area did not produce monumental architecture on the scale of their neighbors to the north and south and, unlike the Mesoamericans, left no written records, they, too, were consummate artisans. Potters in the Intermediate Area made some of the earliest ceramics of the Americas, and they continued to create an astonishing variety of terracotta vessels and figures until the time of the Spanish conquest. Among the other arts practiced in the Intermediate Area was stone sculpture, including not only large-scale figures but also elaborately carved *metates* (ceremonial grinding stones, possibly used as thrones). The ancient Costa Ricans excelled at carving jade as well, particularly anthropomorphic and zoomorphic celts in a style quite different from those the Olmec made centuries earlier (see Chapter 14, page 388). Throughout the area, goldworking was prized, and the first Europeans to make contact here were astonished to see the inhabitants nearly naked but covered in gold jewelry.

THE GOLD OF THE TAIRONA In Colombia, the country that occupies the northwestern corner of the South American continent, the Andes form four parallel ranges separated by deep valleys. Another individual mountain group, the lofty Sierra Nevada de Santa Marta, rises above the Caribbean to the northeast. In this area of the Sierra Nevada, the topography of high mountains and river valleys allowed for considerable isolation and the independent development of various groups. Late inhabitants of this region (from about 1000 to contact with the Spanish conquerors, in the poorly documented chronology of the area) included a group known as the Tairona, whose metalwork is among the finest of all of the pre-Columbian goldworking styles.

Goldsmiths in Peru, Ecuador, and southern Colombia produced technologically advanced and aesthetically sophisticated work in gold mostly by cutting and hammering thin gold sheets. The Tairona smiths, however, who had to obtain gold by trade, used the lost-wax process (see "Hollow-Casting Life-Size Bronze Statues," Chapter 5, page 124) in part to preserve the scarce amount of the precious metal available to them. They cast small works of the highest quality in both fabrication and design. Distant peoples sought Colombian goldwork even before the arrival of the Spanish explorers. The inhabitants of Chichén Itzá, Mexico (see Chapter 14, pages 397–98), tossed objects of Colombian manufacture into their Sacred Well at a time when Mesoamericans had just begun to work with gold themselves. The legend of El Dorado, a Colombian chief who coated himself in gold as part of his accession rites, was largely responsible for the Spanish invaders' ruthless plunder of the region.

Peruvian and Colombian metalworkers often fashioned gold and silver into pendants not meant to be worn simply as rich accessories to costume but as amulets or talismans representing spiritual beings who gave the wearer protection and status. The glow of the burnished material itself was symbolic of the light of the heavens. The Inca, and likely their northern neighbors, regarded gold as "the sweat of the sun" and silver as the "tears of the moon."

Our illustrated pendant (FIG. **30-7**), a bilaterally symmetrical design, shows a bat-faced man, arms akimbo, wearing an immense headdress made up of two birds in the round, two great beaked heads, and a series of spirals crowned by two overarching stalks. The harmony of repeated curvilinear motifs, the rhythmic play of their contours, and the precise delineation of minute detail bespeak the anonymous artist's technical control and aesthetic sensitivity. The mastery of the jeweler's craft manifested here is common to the numerous specimens of pre-Columbian metal art that survived Spanish despoliation.

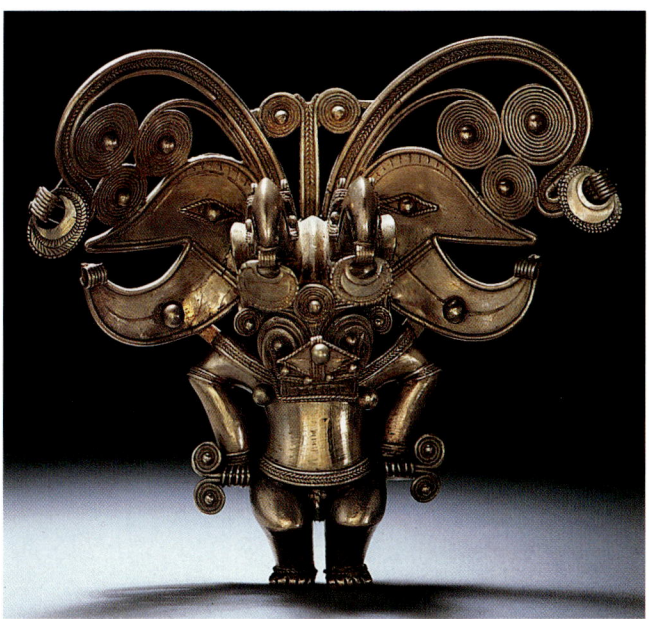

30-7 Tairona pendant in the form of a bat-faced man, Northeast Colombia, after 1000. Gold, $5\frac{1}{4}''$ high. Metropolitan Museum of Art, New York (Jan Mitchell Collection).

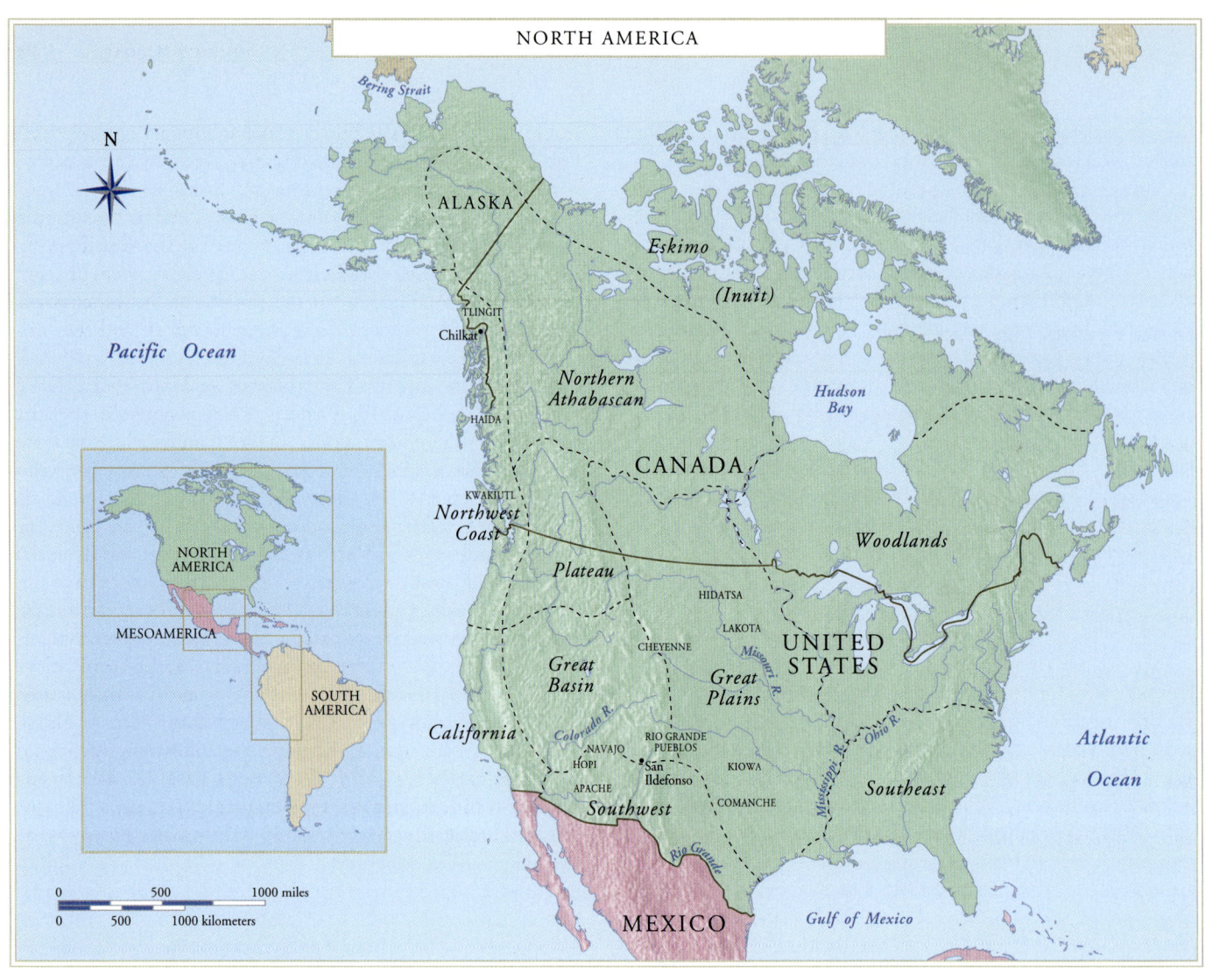

NORTH AMERICA

Bering Strait

N

ALASKA

Eskimo

(Inuit)

Pacific Ocean

TLINGIT
Chilkat

Northern
Athabascan

Hudson
Bay

HAIDA

CANADA

NORTH
AMERICA

MESOAMERICA

SOUTH
AMERICA

KWAKIUTL

Northwest
Coast

Woodlands

Plateau

HIDATSA

LAKOTA

UNITED
STATES

Great
Basin

CHEYENNE

Great
Plains

Missouri R.

California

Colorado R.

NAVAJO

RIO GRANDE
PUEBLOS

Ohio R.

Atlantic
Ocean

HOPI

San
Ildefonso

KIOWA

Mississippi R.

APACHE

Southwest

COMANCHE

Southeast

Rio Grande

MEXICO

Gulf of Mexico

0   500   1000 miles

0   500   1000 kilometers

| 1200 | 1300 | 1400 | 1500 | 1600 | 1700 |

PREHISTORIC

HISTORIC

Ancestors of Apache and Navajo arrive
from Canada, ca. 1200–1500

Contemporary Hopi and Pueblo
peoples evolve from Anasazi, 1200–1500

Columbus reaches Americas, 1492

First European colonies in North
America, late sixteenth century

Navajo learn
weaving from Hopi
and Pueblo, ca. 1600

Plains peoples utilize horses
(introduced earlier by Europeans), 1760

Metal more widely available for tools
and artworks, late eighteenth century

Europeans explore
Northwest Coast and
initiate trade, 1778

NORTH AMERICA

Southwest

By the time of the first European contact in the sixteenth century, the ancient peoples of the Southwest, such as the Anasazi who built Pueblo Bonito and Cliff Palace (see FIG. 14-30), had evolved into the "Pueblo Indians." The name for these Native Americans comes from the Spanish word *pueblo,* or urban settlement. The Pueblo Indians include linguistically diverse, but culturally similar peoples such as the Hopi of northern Arizona and the Rio Grande Pueblos of New Mexico. Living among them are the descendants of nomadic hunters who arrived in the Southwest from their homelands far away in northwestern Canada sometime between 1200 and 1500. These are the Apache and Navajo, who although culturally quite distinct from the original inhabitants of the Southwest, adopted many features of Pueblo life.

NAVAJO RITUALS AND SANDPAINTINGS

Among these borrowed elements is sand painting, which the Navajo learned from the Pueblos but transformed into an extraordinarily complex ritual art form. The temporary sandpaintings (also known as dry paintings), constructed to the accompaniment of prayers and chants, are an essential part of ceremonies for curing disease. (In the healing cere-

mony, the patient sits in the painting's center to absorb the life-giving powers of the gods and their representations.) The Navajo perform similar rites to assure success in hunting and to promote fertility in human beings and nature alike. The artists who supervise the making of these complex images are *shamans,* medicine men (rarely women) thought to have direct contact with the powers of the supernatural world, which they use to help both individuals and the community.

The natural materials used—corn pollen, charcoal, sand, and varicolored powdered stones—play a symbolic role that reflects the Native Americans' preoccupation with the forces of nature. The paintings, which depict the gods and mythological heroes whose help is sought, are destroyed in the process of the ritual, so no models exist. Still, the traditional prototypes, passed on from artist to artist, must be adhered to as closely as possible. Mistakes can render the ceremony ineffective. Navajo dry-painting style is rigid—composed of simple curves, straight lines, and serial repetition—despite the potential freedom of freehand drawing. A fine example is *Nightway: Whirling Logs* (FIG. **30-8**), a reproduction. (Anglo artist Franc J. Newcomb, who lived for many years in Navajo territory, was permitted to make watercolor reproductions of sandpaintings after gaining the confidence of a respected Navajo medicine man.) The iconography is complex but explicit as a text. The central figures are the logs whirling in the

1800	1850	1900	1950	1990

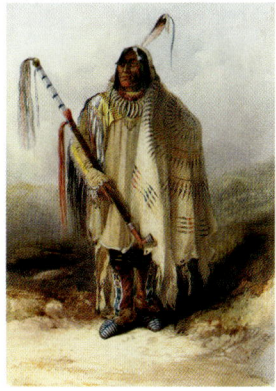

Karl Bodmer, Hidatsa Warrior Pehriska-Ruhpa, 1833

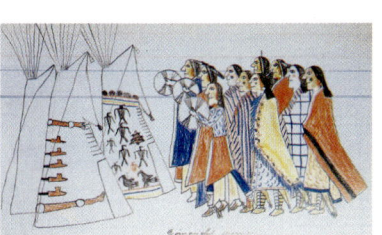

Ledger painting Kiowa, 1880

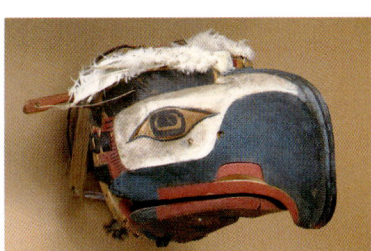

Eagle transformation mask (closed) Kwakiutl, late nineteenth century

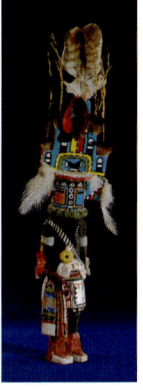

Otto Pentewa Kachina Doll Hopi, pre-1959

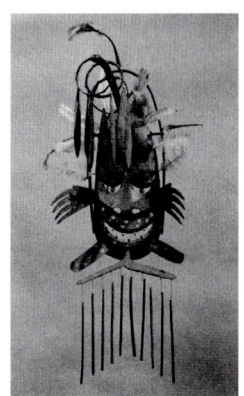

Mask, Yup'ik Eskimo Alaska, early twentieth century

European and North American artists record Plains life, 1800

U.S. government removes and resettles Native Americans, 1830s

Reservation period on Plains; many ledger books painted, beadwork flourishes, beginning 1860s

Smallpox epidemic reduces Haida population, 1862

Tourists create demand for Southwestern native crafts, 1880s

White hunters nearly wipe out buffalo on Plains, by 1890

Lakota massacre at Wounded Knee, South Dakota, 1890

María and Julian Martínez invent black-on-black pottery, ca. 1918

First exhibitions of Indian art, 1920–1940s

Native Americans receive U.S. citizenship, 1924

U.S. Government sponsors Native art programs, 1930s

Canadian Inuit form co-ops for sculpture and print sales, 1950s

Revival of Northwest Coast arts begins, 1960s

Congress authorizes National Museum of the American Indian, 1989

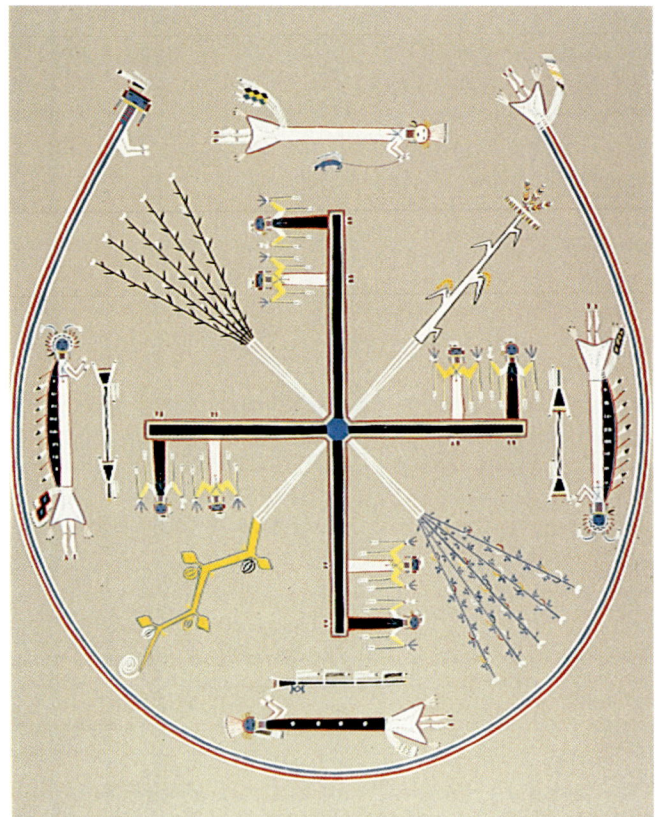

30-8 *Nightway: Whirling Logs,* reproduction of Navajo sandpainting (painted by Franc J. Newcomb), before 1933. $22\frac{5}{8}'' \times 28\frac{3}{4}''$, Wheelwright Museum of the American Indian, Santa Fe.

meeting of rivers from which grow the four holy plants—black tobacco, blue beans, yellow squash, and white corn. On each log stand two *Yei,* or Holy People. At the east (top, on this image) is Talking God, the god who talks to men, carrying his blue squirrelskin medicine bag. At the north and the south are two Humpbacks, the gods who brought seeds to men in their packs. They have mountain sheep horns and woodpecker feathers on their heads. Near them are their *gishes,* or medicine canes. At the west is the Calling God with his cane in front of him.

By the mid-seventeenth century, the Navajo also had learned how to weave from their Hopi and Pueblo neighbors, quickly adapting to new materials such as sheep's wool and synthetic dyes introduced by Spanish settlers and, later, by Anglo Americans. They rapidly transformed their simple wearing blankets into handsome rugs in response to the new market created by the arrival of the railroad and early tourists in the 1880s. The Navajo mastered an incredible variety of designs, including vivid abstract designs known as "eye dazzlers" and copies of sandpaintings (altered slightly to preserve the sacred quality of the impermanent ritual images).

HOPI KACHINAS Another art form from the Southwest, the *Kachina* doll, also has deep roots in the area. Kachinas are benevolent supernatural spirits personifying natural elements and living in mountains and water sources. Humans, too, join their world after death. Among contemporary Pueblo groups,

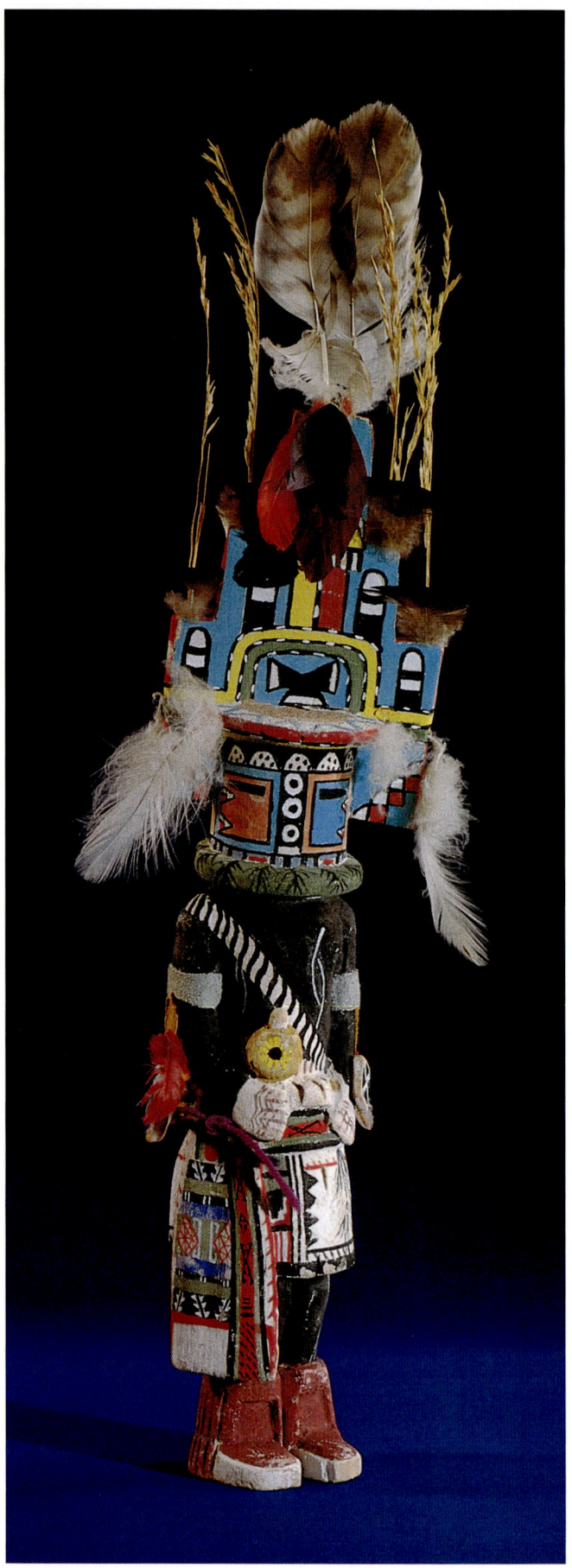

30-9 Otto Pentewa, Kachina doll (Niman or Hemis), Hopi, New Oraibi, Arizona, carved before 1959. Cottonwood root, about 1′ high. Arizona State Museum, University of Arizona, Tucson.

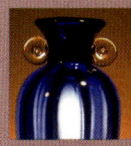

Native American Artists

Although both Native American women and men created art objects, they traditionally worked in different media or at different tasks. Among the Navajo, for example, weavers tend to be women, while among the neighboring Hopi the men weave. According to Navajo myth, long ago Spider Woman's husband built her a loom for weaving. In turn, she taught Navajo women how to spin and weave so that they might have clothing to wear. Today, young girls learn how to work the loom from their mothers, just as Spider Woman instructed their ancestors, passing along the techniques and designs from one generation to the next.

Among the Pueblos, pottery making normally has been the domain of women. But in response to heavy demand for her wares, María Martínez, of San Ildefonso Pueblo in New Mexico, coiled, slipped, and burnished her pots, while her husband Julian painted the designs. Although they worked in many styles, some based on prehistoric ceramics, around 1918 they invented the black-on-black ware that made María, and indeed the whole pueblo, famous (FIG. 30-10). The elegant shapes of the pots, as well as the traditional but abstract designs, were particularly compatible with the Art Deco style in architecture and interior design, and collectors avidly sought (and continue to seek) them. When nonnative buyers suggested she sign her pots to increase their value, María obliged, but, in the communal spirit typical of the Pueblos, she also signed her neighbors' names so that they might share in her good fortune. Though María died in 1980, her descendants continue to garner awards as outstanding potters.

Women also produced the elaborately decorated skin and, later, trade-cloth clothing of the Woodlands and Plains by using moosehair, dyed porcupine quills, and imported beads. Among the Cheyenne, quillworking was a sacred art, and young women worked at learning both proper ritual and correct techniques to obtain membership in the prestigious quillworkers' guild. Women gained the same honor and dignity from creating finely worked utilitarian objects as men did from warfare. Both women and men painted on tipis and clothing, with women creating abstract designs (FIG. 30-16) and men working in a more realistic narrative style, often celebrating their exploits in war (FIG. 30-17).

In the far north, women tended to work with soft materials such as animal skins, while men were sculptors of wood masks among the Alaskan Eskimos and of ivory pieces throughout the Arctic. The introduction of printmaking, a foreign medium with no established gender associations, to some Canadian Inuit communities in the 1950s provided the native women with a new creative outlet. Printmaking became an important source of economic independence vital to these isolated and once-impoverished settlements. Today, both Inuit women and men make prints, but men still dominate in carving stone sculpture, another new medium also produced for and sold to outsiders.

Throughout North America, indigenous artists continue to work in traditional media, such as ceramics, beadwork, and basketry, marketing their wares through museum shops, galleries, and regional competitions and art fairs. Many also obtain degrees in art and express themselves in European media such as oil painting and mixed-media sculpture (see FIG. 34-69).

---

masked dancers ritually impersonate Kachinas during yearly festivals dedicated to rain, fertility, and good hunting. To educate young girls in ritual lore, the Hopi traditionally give them Kachina dolls, miniature representations of the masked dancers. We illustrate a Hopi Kachina, carved by OTTO PENTEWA before 1959, of a rain-bringing deity (FIG. **30-9**) who wears a mask painted in geometric patterns symbolic of water and agricultural fertility. The mask is topped by a stepped shape signifying thunderclouds and, finally, by feathers to carry the Hopis' airborne prayers. The origins of the Kachina dolls have been lost in time (they even may have developed from carved saints the Spanish introduced during the colonial period). However, the cult is probably very ancient and may be represented in the scenes found in precontact kiva murals, rock art, and pottery.

PUEBLO POTTERY The Southwest also has provided some of the finest examples of North American pottery. Originally producing utilitarian forms, Southwest potters worked without the potter's wheel and instead coiled shapes that they then slipped, polished, and fired. Decorative motifs, often abstract and conventionalized, dealt largely with forces of nature—clouds, wind, and rain. The efforts of San Ildefonso Pueblo potter MARÍA MARTINEZ (ca. 1881–1980) and her husband JULIAN MARTINEZ (ca. 1879–1943) (see "Native American Artists," above) in the early decades of the twentieth century revived old techniques to produce forms of striking shape, proportion, and texture. Her black-on-black pieces (FIG. **30-10**) feature matte designs on highly polished surfaces achieved by extensive polishing and special firing in an oxygen-poor atmosphere.

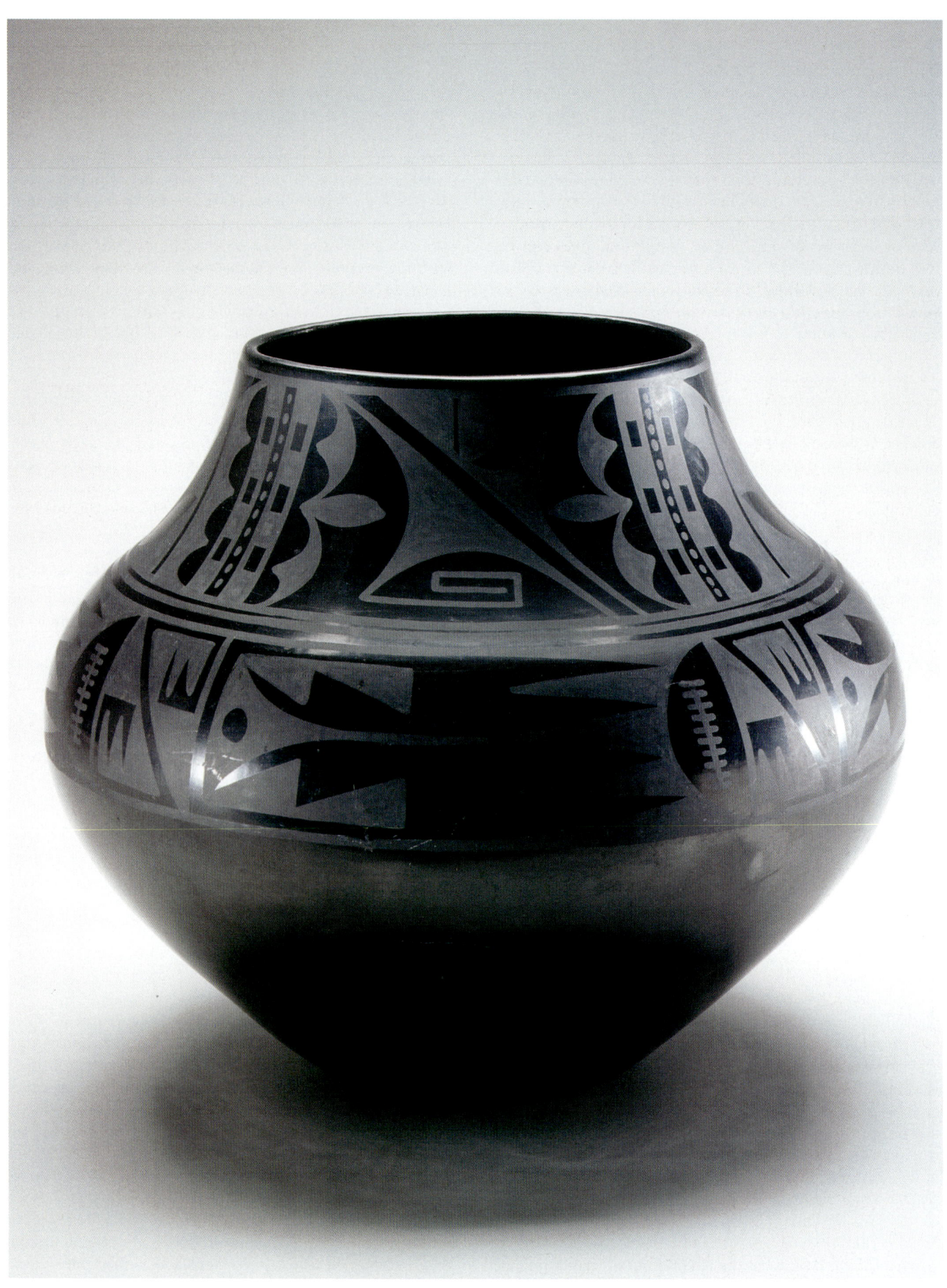

30-10 María Montoya Martínez, jar, San Ildefonso Pueblo, New Mexico, ca. 1939. Blackware, $11\frac{1}{8}''$ × 1′ 1″. The National Museum of Women in the Arts (gift of Wallace and Wilhelmina Hollachy).

Northwest Coast

The Native Americans of the coasts and islands of northern Washington state, the province of British Columbia in Canada, and southern Alaska were blessed with a rich and reliable environment. They fished, hunted sea mammals and game, gathered edible plants, and made their homes, utensils, ritual objects, and even clothing from the region's great cedar forests. Among the numerous groups who make up the Northwest Coast area are the Kwakiutl of southern British Columbia, the Haida who live on the Queen Charlotte Islands off the coast of the province, and the Tlingit of southern Alaska. In the Northwest, a class of professional artists developed, in contrast to the more typical Native American pattern of part-time artisans.

MASKS FOR TRANSFORMATION RITES Working in a highly formalized, subtle style, these Northwest Coast artists have produced a wide variety of art objects for more than five thousand years: totem poles, masks, rattles, chests, bowls, clothing, charms, and decorated houses and canoes. They carved masks for shamans to use in their healing rites and for other male participants to use in dramatic public performances during the winter ceremonial season. The animals and mythological creatures represented in masks and a host of other carvings derive from the Northwest Coast's rich oral tradition and celebrate the mythological origins and inherited privileges of high-ranking families. Meant to be seen in flickering firelight, the Kwakiutl mask we illustrate (FIG. **30-11**) was ingeniously constructed to open and close rapidly when the

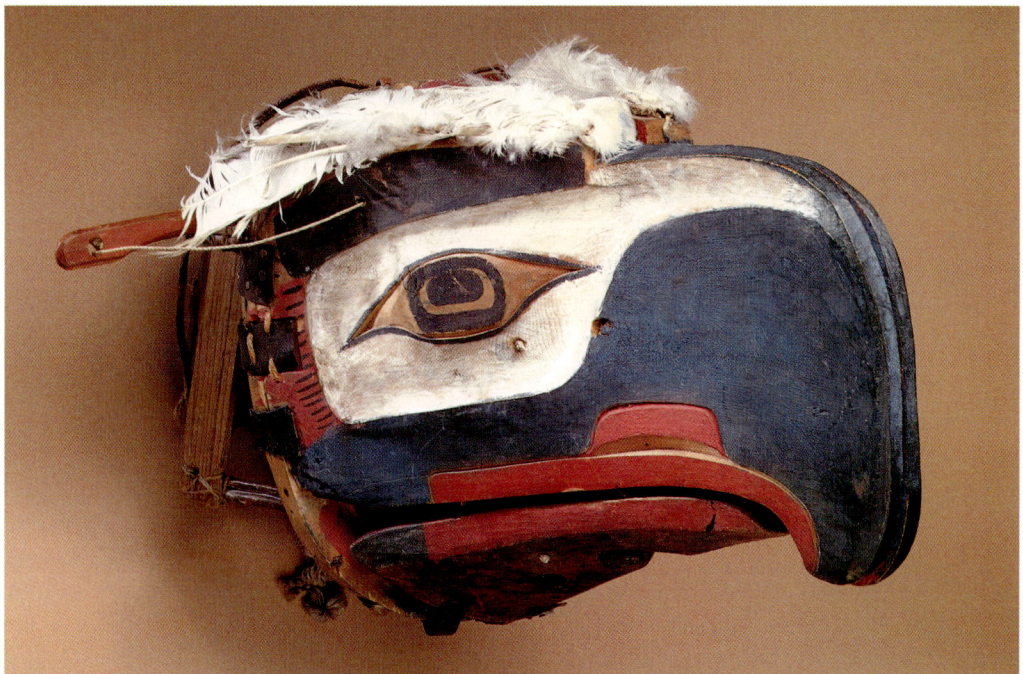

30-11 Eagle transformation mask, closed and open views, Kwakiutl, Alert Bay, late nineteenth century. Wood, feathers, and rope, approx. 1' 10" × 11". American Museum of Natural History, New York.

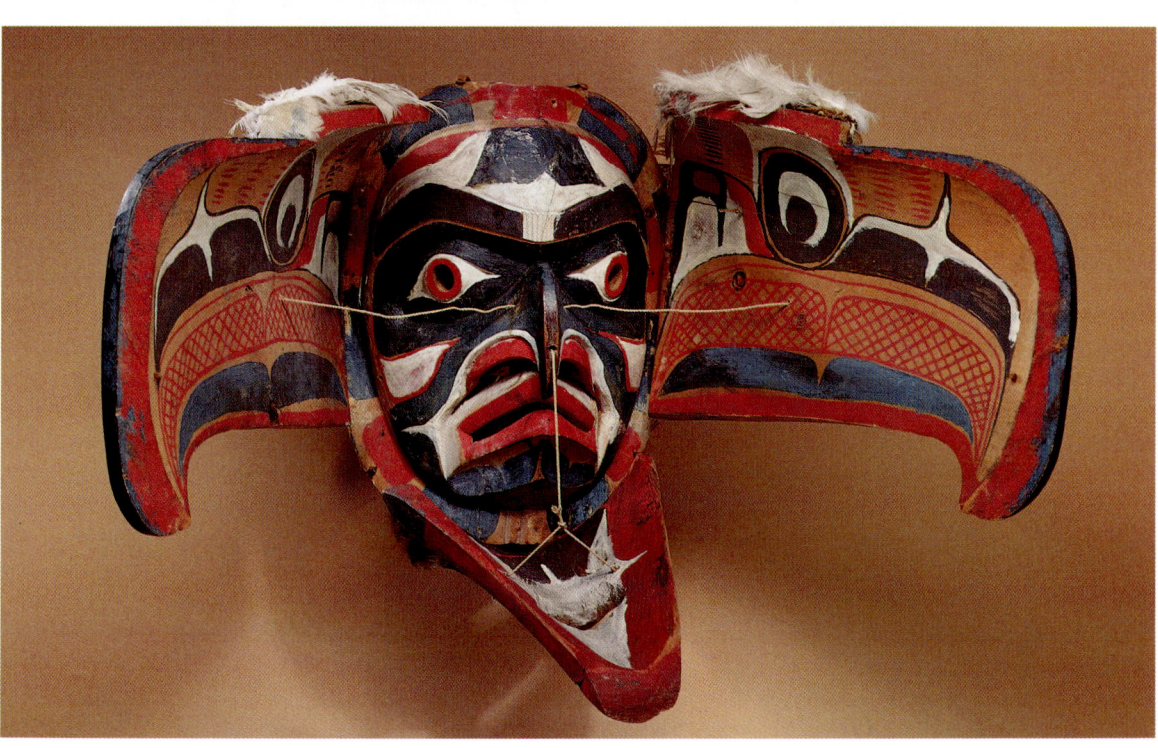

wearer manipulated hidden strings. He could thus magically transform himself from human to eagle and back again as he danced. The mask's human aspect also owes its dramatic character to the exaggeration and distortion of facial parts—such as the hooked beaklike nose and flat flaring nostrils—and to the deeply undercut curvilinear depressions, which form strong shadows. In contrast to the carved human face, but painted in the same colors, is the two-dimensional abstract image of the eagle painted on the inside of the outer mask.

AN INTIMIDATING WAR HELMET

The Kwakiutl mask (FIG. 30-11) is a refined, yet forceful, carving typical of the area's more dramatic styles. Others are more subdued, and some, such as a wooden Tlingit war helmet (FIG. **30-12**), are exceedingly naturalistic. Although the helmet mask may be an actual portrait, it also might represent a spirit being from the realm of the dead whose powers enhance the wearer's strength. In either case, the artist surely created its grimacing expression to intimidate the enemy.

CLAN HISTORY ON HAIDA POLES

Although Northwest Coast arts have a spiritual dimension, they are often more important as expressions of social status. Haida house frontal poles, displaying totemic emblems of clan groups before the clan chief's house, strikingly express this interest in prestige and family history. Our example of nineteenth-century poles (FIG. **30-13**) is from a reconstructed Haida village BILL REID (1920–1998, Haida) and his assistant DOUG KRANMER (b. 1917, Kwakiutl) completed in 1962. Each of the superimposed figures carved on these poles represents a crest, an animal, or a supernatural being who figures in the clan's origin story. Additional crests also could be obtained through marriage and trade. The right to own and display such crests was so jealously guarded that even warfare could break out over the disputed ownership of a valued crest. In the

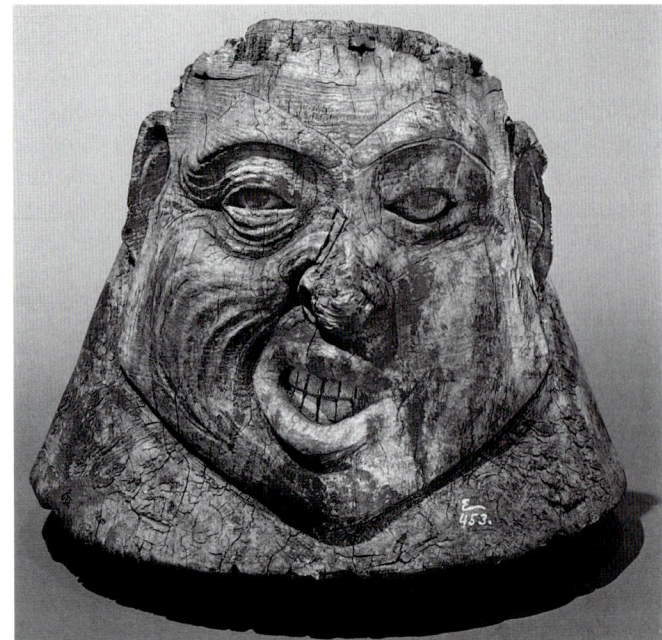

30-12 War helmet, Tlingit, collected 1888–1893. Wood, 1' high. Courtesy of Department Library Services, American Museum of Natural History, New York.

larger pole shown, the crests represented include an upside-down dogfish (a small shark) at the top, an eagle with a down-turned beak at the center, and a killer whale with a crouching human between its snout and its upturned tail flukes at the base. During the nineteenth century, the Haida erected more poles and made them larger in response to greater competitiveness and the availability of metal tools. The artists carved poles up to sixty feet tall from the trunk of single cedar trees. Because of the damp coastal climate, however, the poles decayed in a century or less, and as a result only a handful of well-preserved nineteenth-century poles exist in museum collections.

30-13 BILL REID (Haida), assisted by DOUG KRANMER (Kwakiutl), reconstruction of a nineteenth-century Haida village with frontal poles, original village on Queen Charlotte Island, completed 1962. Museum of Anthropology, University of British Columbia, Vancouver.

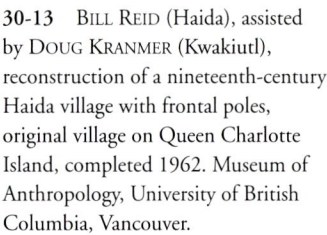

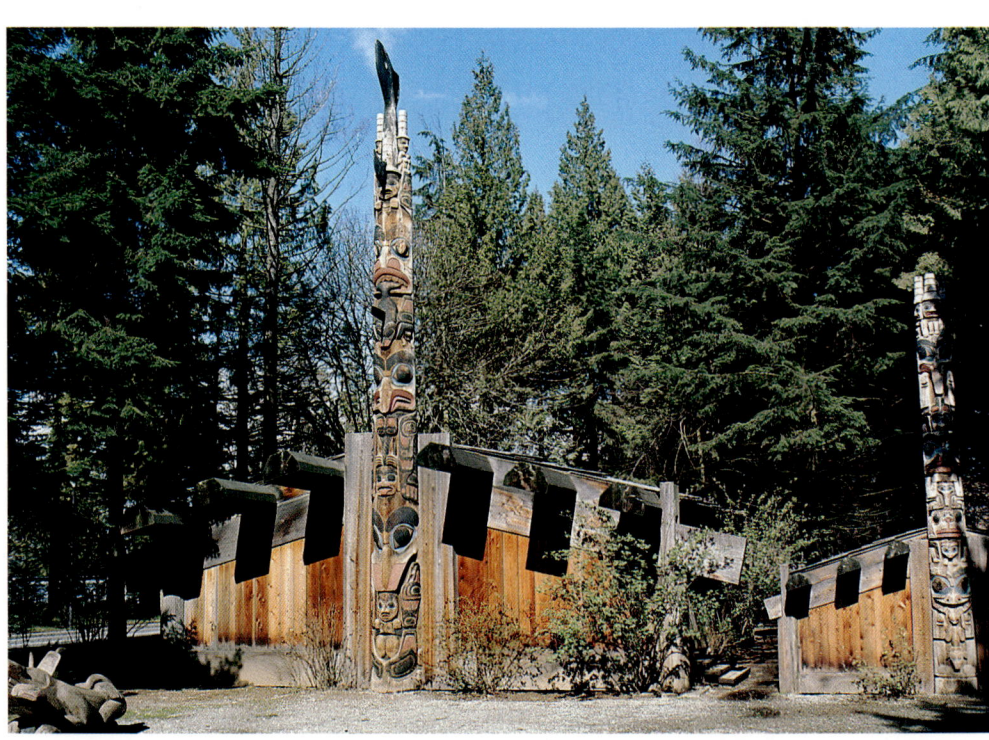

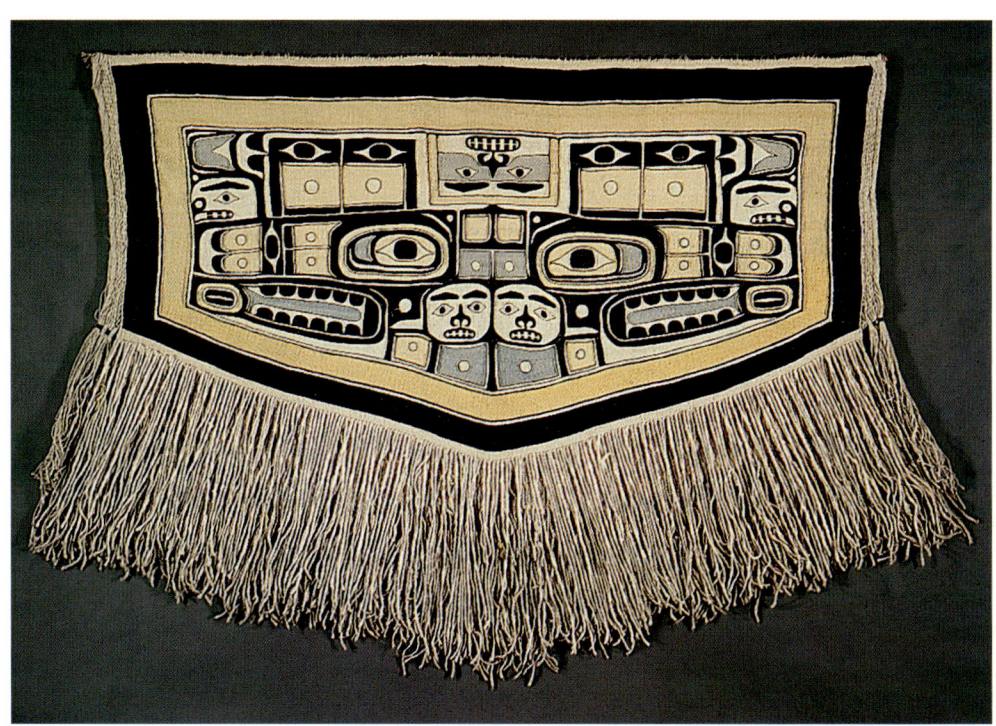

30-14 Chilkat blanket with stylized animal motifs, Tlingit, early twentieth century. Mountain goat's wool and cedar bark, 6′ × 2′ 11″. Southwest Museum, Los Angeles.

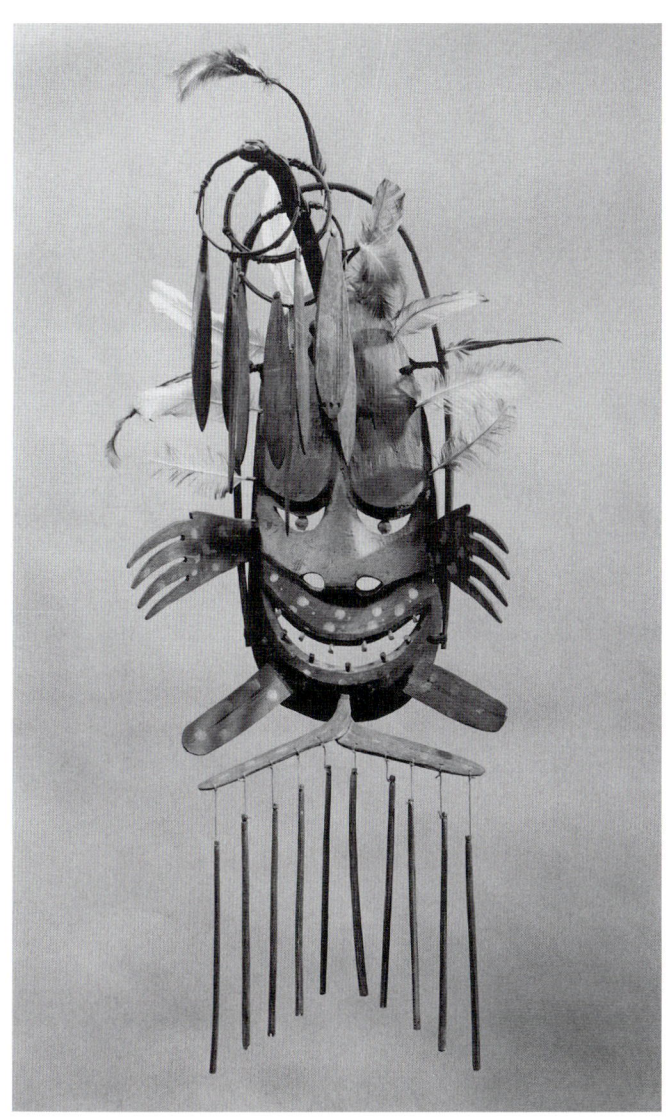

30-15 Mask, Yup'ik Eskimo, Alaska, early twentieth century. Wood and feathers, approx. 3′ 9″ high. Metropolitan Museum of Art, New York.

ALASKAN CEREMONIAL BLANKETS Another characteristic Northwest Coast art form is the Chilkat blanket (FIG. **30-14**), named for an Alaskan Tlingit village where the blankets were woven. Male designers provided the templates for these blankets in the form of wooden pattern boards for the female weavers. Woven of shredded cedar bark and mountain goat wool on an upright loom, the Tlingit blankets took at least six months to complete. Actually robes worn over the shoulders, these became widespread prestige items of ceremonial dress during the nineteenth century. They display several recurrent characteristics of the Northwest Coast style in all media: symmetry and rhythmic repetition, schematic abstraction of animal motifs (in the robe illustrated, a bear), eye designs, a regularly swelling and thinning line, and a tendency to round off corners.

Many critics and collectors hold Northwest Coast art elegant, precise, and highly accomplished technically as one of the sophisticated high points of Native American artistic accomplishment. The devastating effects of nineteenth-century epidemics, coupled with government and missionary repression of Northwest Coast ritual and social activities, threatened to wipe out the traditional arts entirely. Nevertheless, a handful of outstanding artists continued to produce fine art objects, some for the nonnative trade. The last half century has seen an impressive revival of traditional art forms, as well as the development of new ones, such as printmaking.

Eskimo

THE NORTH WIND'S MASK The nineteenth-century Yup'ik Eskimos living around the Bering Strait of Alaska also had a highly developed ceremonial life focused on pleasing game animals, particularly seal. Shamans wore highly imaginative masks with moving parts. Our example (FIG. **30-15**) represents the spirit of the north wind, its face surrounded by a hoop representing the universe, its voice re-created by the rattling appendages. The paired human hands commonly found on such masks refer to the shaman's power to attract animals for hunting. The painted white spots represent snowflakes. Surrealists in the 1920s (see Chapter 33, page 1037) much appreciated these masks due to their fanciful forms and odd juxtapositions of images and materials. (Because the Yup'ik generally made masks for single occasions and then abandoned them, it was not difficult to purchase them, so many masks ended up in museums and private collections.)

In more recent years, Canadian Eskimos, known as the Inuit, have set up cooperatives to produce and market stone carvings and prints. With these new media, artists generally depict themes from the rapidly vanishing traditional Inuit way of life.

Great Plains

After the Europeans introduced the horse to North America and colonial governments disrupted settled indigenous communities on the East Coast, a new mobile Native American culture flourished for a short time on the Great Plains. Artists of the Great Plains worked in materials and styles quite differ-

ent from those of the Northwest Coast and Eskimo. Much artistic energy went into the decoration of leather garments, pouches, and horse trappings, first with compactly sewn quill designs and later with beadwork patterns. Artists painted tipis, tipi linings, and buffalo-skin robes with geometric and stiff figural designs prior to about 1830. After that, they gradually introduced naturalistic scenes, often of war exploits, in styles adapted from those of visiting European artists.

COSTUME AS ART   Because, at least in later periods, most Plains peoples were nomadic, they focused their aesthetic attention largely on their clothing and bodies and on other portable objects, such as shields, clubs, pipes, tomahawks, and various containers. Transient but important Plains art forms sometimes can be found in the paintings and drawings of visiting American and European artists. The Swiss KARL BODMER, for example, accurately portrayed the personal decoration of Two Ravens (FIG. 30-16), a Hidatsa warrior, in a watercolor from 1833. Titled *Hidatsa Warrior Pehriska-Ruhpa (Two Ravens)*, it depicts his pipe, painted buffalo robe, bearclaw necklace, and feather decorations, all symbolic of his affiliations and military accomplishments. They may be called his biography—a composite artistic statement in several media— that neighboring Native Americans could have "read" easily.

30-16 KARL BODMER, *Hidatsa Warrior Pehriska-Ruhpa (Two Ravens)*, 1833. Watercolor, 1' 3⅞" × 11½". Joslyn Art Museum, Omaha (gift of the Enron Art Foundation).

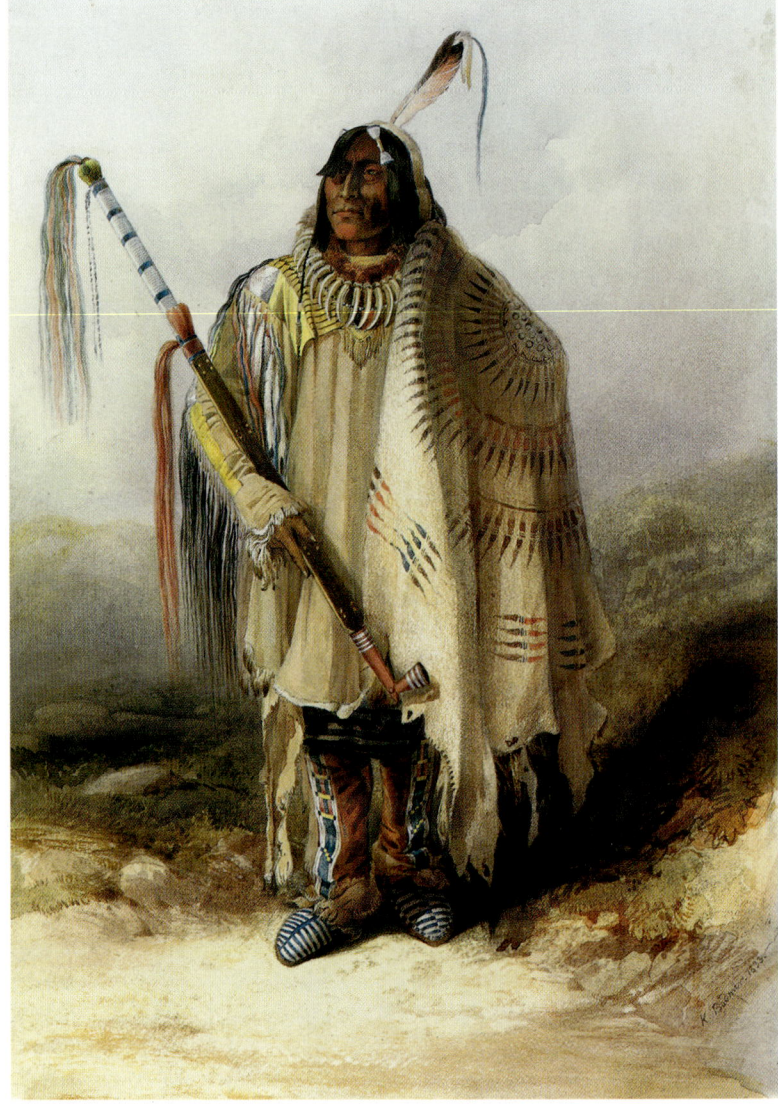

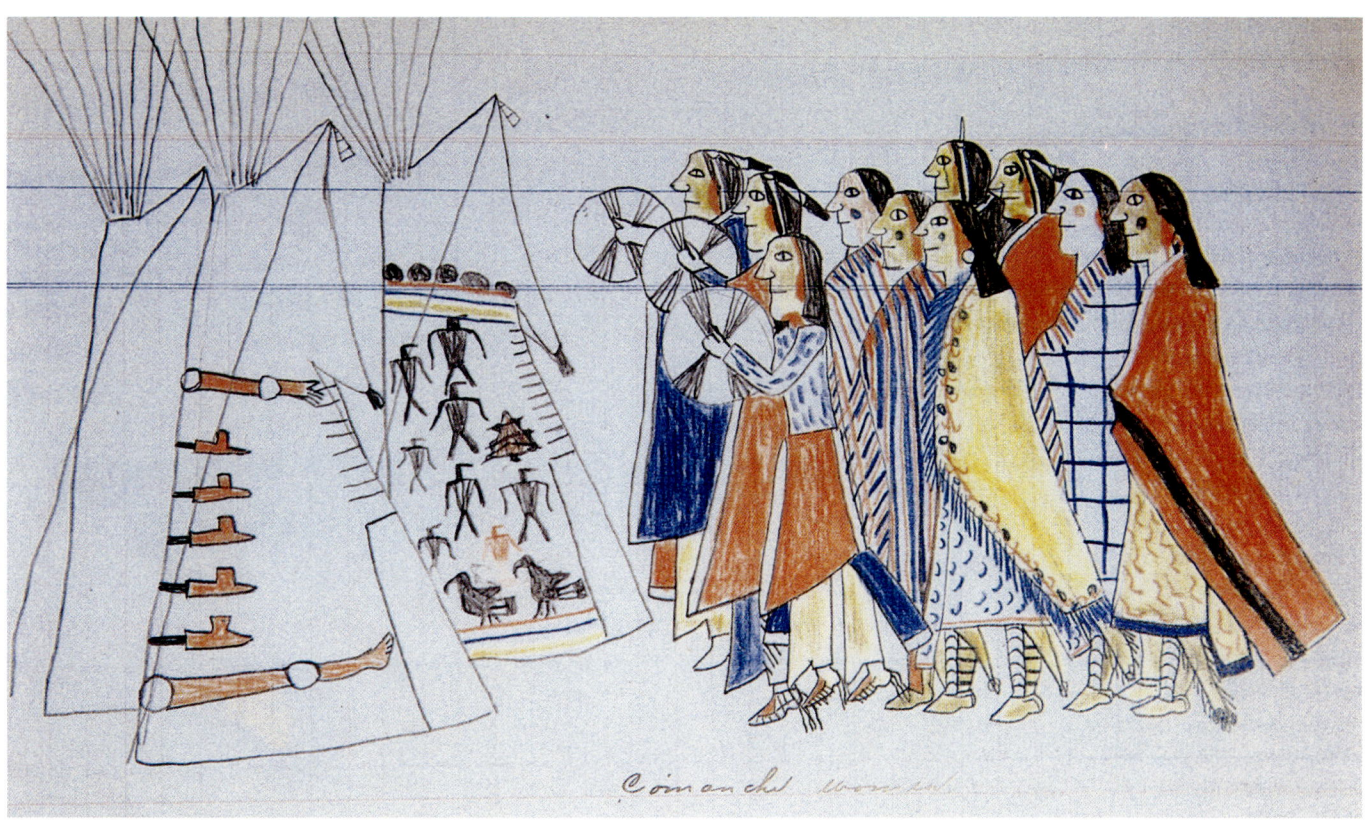

30-17 Honoring song at painted tipi, in Julian Scott Ledger, Kiowa, 1880. Pencil, ink, and colored pencil, $7\frac{1}{2}'' \times 1'$. Mr. and Mrs. Charles Diker Collection.

The concentric circle design over his left shoulder, for example, represents an abstract rendering of an eagle-feather warbonnet.

Plains peoples also made shields and shield covers that were both artworks and "power images." Shield paintings often derived from personal religious visions. The owners believed the symbolism, the pigments themselves, and added materials, such as feathers, provided them with magical protection and supernatural power.

Plains warriors battled incursions into their territory throughout the nineteenth century, but they were finally defeated by a combination of broken treaties, the rapid extinction of the buffalo, and military defeats at the hands of the U.S. Army. The pursuit of Plains natives culminated in the 1890 slaughter of Lakota participants who had gathered for a ritual known as the Ghost Dance at Wounded Knee Creek, South Dakota. Indeed, from the 1830s on, U.S. troops had forcibly removed Native Americans from their homelands and resettled them in other parts of the country. Toward the end of the century, governments confined them to reservations in both the United States and Canada.

PAINTINGS IN LEDGER BOOKS Ironically, during the reservation period some Plains arts flourished, notably beadwork for the women and painting in ledger books for the men. Traders, the army, and Indian agents had for years provided Plains peoples with pencils and new or discarded ledger books. They, in turn, used them to draw their personal exploits for themselves or for interested Anglo buyers. Sometimes warriors carried them into battle where U.S. Army opponents retook the ledgers. After confinement to reservations, Plains artists began to record not only their heroic past and vanished lifestyle but also their reactions to their new surroundings, frequently in a state far from home. These images, often poignant and sometimes humorous, are important native documents of a time of great turmoil and change. In our example (FIG. **30-17**) by an unknown Kiowa artist, a group of men and women, possibly Comanches (allies of the Kiowa), appear to dance an honoring song before three tipis, the left forward one painted with red stone pipes and dismembered legs and arms. The women (at the center and right) wear the mixture of clothing typical of the late nineteenth century among the Plains Indians—traditional high leather moccasins, dresses made from calico trade cloth, and (on the right) a red Hudson's Bay blanket with a black stripe.

Although ledger-book paintings are no longer made, beadworking has never completely died out. The ancient art of creating quilled, beaded, and painted clothing has evolved into the elaborate costumes displayed today at competitive dances called *powwows*.

Whether secular and decorative or spiritual and highly symbolic, the diverse styles and forms of Native American art testify to the ancient and continuing artistic sensibility of the peoples of North America. Their creative use of local materials and pigments constitutes an artistic reshaping of nature that, in many cases, reflects the Native Americans' reliance on and reverence toward the environment they considered it their privilege to inhabit. They demonstrate resilience by their ability to adopt new materials and new media without losing their innate creativity.

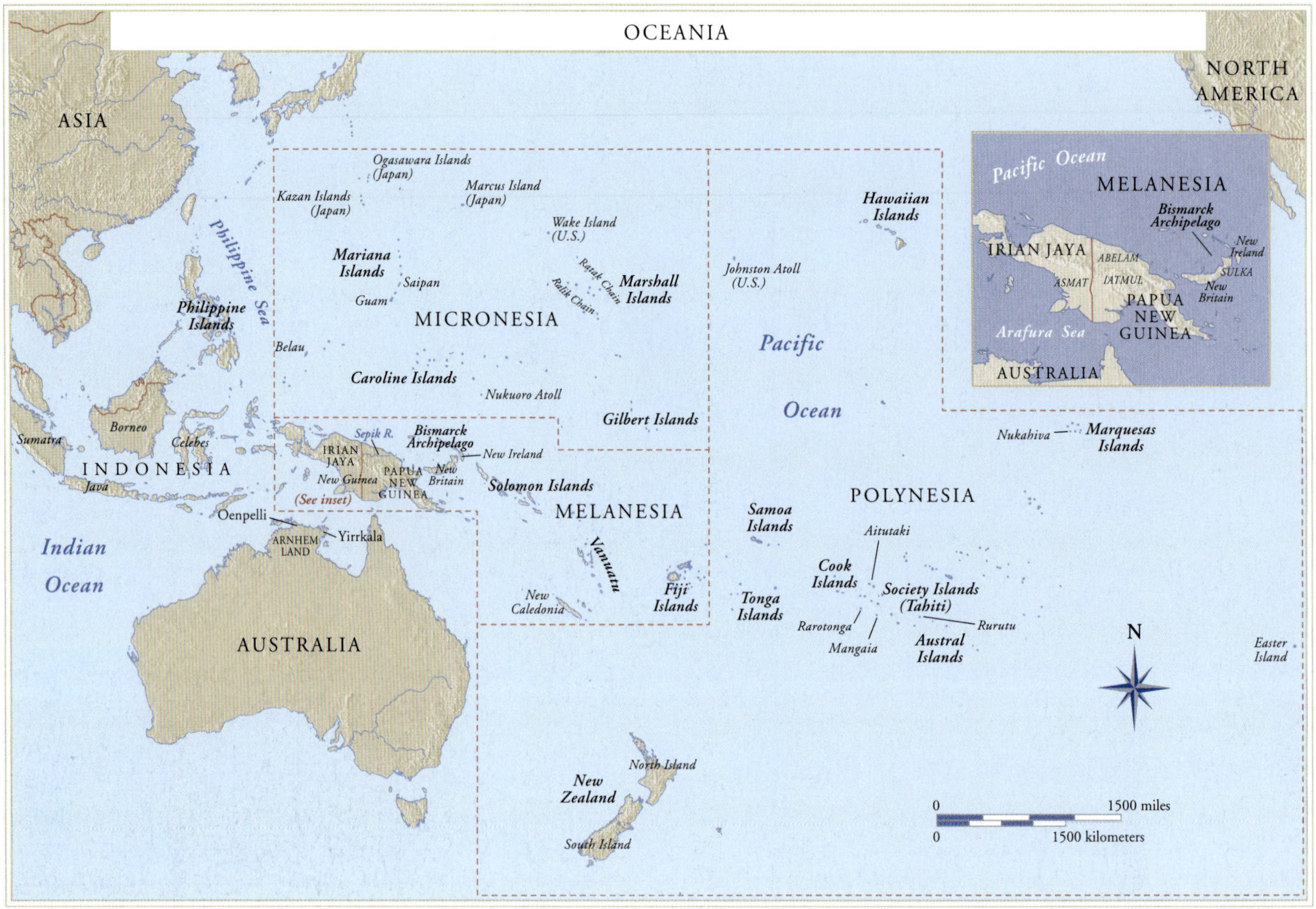

Map of Oceania

NORTH AMERICA

ASIA

Philippine Sea

Ogasawara Islands *(Japan)*

Kazan Islands *(Japan)*

Marcus Island *(Japan)*

Wake Island *(U.S.)*

Mariana Islands

Saipan

Guam

Belau

Philippine Islands

Rarak Chain

Ralik Chain

Marshall Islands

MICRONESIA

Johnston Atoll *(U.S.)*

Hawaiian Islands

Pacific

Caroline Islands

Nukuoro Atoll

Gilbert Islands

Ocean

MELANESIA

Pacific Ocean

MELANESIA

Bismarck Archipelago

New Ireland

IRIAN JAYA

ABELAM

ASMAT

IATMUL

SULKA

New Britain

PAPUA NEW GUINEA

Arafura Sea

AUSTRALIA

Sumatra

Borneo

Celebes

INDONESIA

Java

Indian Ocean

Oenpelli

ARNHEM LAND

Yirrkala

Sepik R.

IRIAN JAYA

New Guinea

Bismarck Archipelago

PAPUA NEW GUINEA

New Britain

New Ireland

(See inset)

Solomon Islands

MELANESIA

Vanuatu

New Caledonia

Fiji Islands

AUSTRALIA

Samoa Islands

Tonga Islands

Cook Islands

Aitutaki

Rarotonga

Mangaia

Society Islands (Tahiti)

Rurutu

Austral Islands

POLYNESIA

Nukahiva

Marquesas Islands

N

Easter Island

New Zealand

North Island

South Island

0 —— 1500 miles
0 —— 1500 kilometers

1800   1850   1900

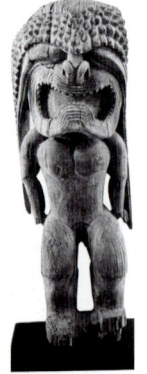

Kukailimoku, Hawaii
eighteenth–nineteenth centuries

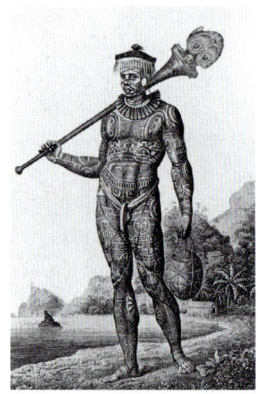

Tattooed warrior, Marquesas
nineteenth century

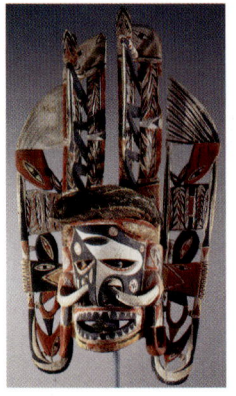

Malanggan mask
New Ireland
late nineteenth century

Captain James Cook and other European explorers (re)discover Polynesia, late eighteenth century

Christianity spreads throughout Polynesia by mid-1850s

European colonization of most of Oceania complete, 1880s–1920

ELDERS, "BIG MEN," CHIEFS, AND KINGS

THE ARTS OF OCEANIA

1950   2000

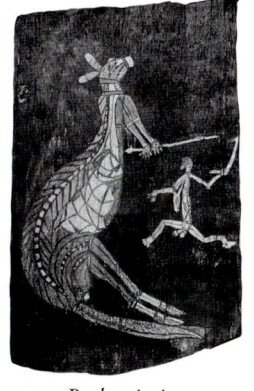

Bark painting,
Australia, ca. 1913

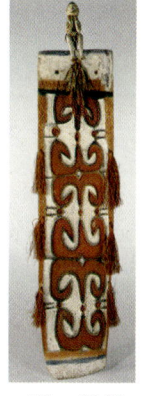

War shield
Irian Jaya, ca. 1961

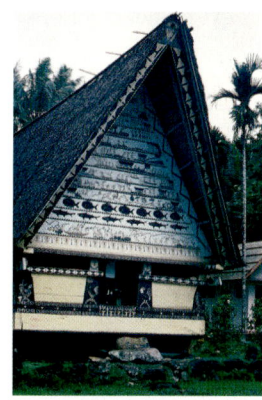

Ceremonial men's house
Belau, photographed 1992

Europeans first contact highlanders in New Guinea, 1930s

World War II, 1940–1945

Independence for most Oceanic peoples, 1960s–1970s

THE ISLANDS OF OCEANIA

The South Pacific island group known as Oceania includes four major regions: Melanesia ("islands of the blacks"), Micronesia ("small islands"), Polynesia ("many islands"), and Australia ("land to the south"). Although documentary evidence does not exist for Oceania until the arrival of seafaring Europeans in the early sixteenth century, archeologists have determined that the islands have been inhabited for tens of thousands of years. Researchers have assigned early habitation dates of forty or more thousand years ago to sites on the island continent of Australia. Sites on the island of New Guinea and on some of the nearby islands of the Bismarck Archipelago, such as New Ireland, were populated more than thirty thousand years ago. Dates for human occupation in the Melanesian islands to the east and those in Micronesia are much more recent, more on the order of two to three thousand years ago.

The last islands of Oceania humans colonized were those of Polynesia. A pottery-making culture called Lapita (after a site in New Caledonia in Melanesia) settled western Polynesia by about 1000 B.C. From there, the central and eastern Polynesian islands were occupied starting from about the time of Christ. Humans settled all the outlying islands of Polynesia, including Hawaii, New Zealand, and Easter Island, by about A.D. 800–1000. The ongoing efforts of archeologists, linguists, ethnologists, and art historians continue to shed light on the development of the early arts of Oceania. But, as in Stone Age Europe and Africa (see Chapter 1), scholars have been able to determine only a vague chronology. This chapter focuses on Oceanic art from the European discovery of the islands until the present.

MELANESIA

Melanesia includes, from west to east, New Guinea, the islands of the Bismarck Archipelago, the Solomon Islands, New Caledonia, Vanuatu, and the Fijian Islands. The art forms of Melanesia seem to suggest a variety of historical overlays of styles and symbolism. These were brought about both by a complex series of early and late migrations on New Guinea and other islands to the east and by adaptation to various ecological environments and diverse living conditions. Art styles are numerous and extremely varied. Typical Melanesian societies are more democratic than Polynesian societies and relatively unstratified. Their cults and art forms address a host of legendary ancestral and nature spirits. Masks, very rare in Polynesia, are central to many Melanesian spirit cults. Elaborate festivals displaying masks and other art forms occur with some frequency.

MIGRANTS AND ECOSYSTEMS   New Guinea consists today of parts of two countries—Irian Jaya, a province of nearby Indonesia on the island's western end, and Papua New Guinea on the eastern end. New Guinea's inhabitants together speak nearly eight hundred different languages, almost one quarter of the world's known languages. For tens of thousands of years people settled on the island and on the nearby continent of Australia when the two land masses were connected during periods ice covered them. The water levels in the oceans were several hundred feet shallower than today, allowing migrations over lands now under water. These early migrants settled throughout the twelve-hundred-mile-long New Guinea and adapted to various ecosystems. These ecosystems included highlands with permanently snow-capped mountains and a variety of tropical and subtropical forest regions, as well as low-lying tropical river systems, which emptied out into New Guinea's northern, southwestern, southeastern, and eastern lowlands. The various ecosystems afforded numerous adaptations for survival. These included intense agriculture and husbandry (involving especially the domesticated pig) in the highlands and forest regions, as well as hunting, fishing, and gathering of wild species of plants and animals in all regions of New Guinea.

LANGUAGE AND SOCIETY   The descendants of these early settlers in New Guinea speak a language group called non-Austronesian (also sometimes called Old Papuan after early black-skinned peoples living throughout the island's southeastern sections). These peoples tend to organize in egalitarian social units with political power vested in groups of elder males and in some areas elder women. The elders handle the people's affairs in a communal, more or less democratic, fashion. Within some of these groups are persons of local distinction, known as "Big Men," individuals renowned for their political, economic, and warrior attributes. Later seagoing migrants to New Guinea and the other Melanesian islands spoke Austronesian languages (also called Malayo-Polynesian languages), which are related to languages found in areas of Southeast Asia, Indonesia, Micronesia, and Polynesia. These cultures in New Guinea tend to stratify more and frequently have chiefs at the top of the social system, with various peoples under their power socially, politically, and economically.

The Asmat, Iatmul, and Abelam peoples of New Guinea all speak non-Austronesian languages and descend from the early settlers who came to the island in the remote past. Each of these peoples has an important and distinctive artistic culture that will be discussed in turn. But they represent just three of the hundreds of art styles found on New Guinea. These artistic traditions are quite different from those of the more stratified art-producing cultures of Austronesian-speakers in other parts of New Guinea, Melanesia, Micronesia, Polynesia, and Australia.

Asmat Art (West New Guinea)

Asmat culture and arts revolve around mythological ancestral beliefs associated with competition, warfare, and head-hunting. Life in the Asmat areas of southwestern New Guinea is harsh, and each community ekes out an existence by hunting and gathering the varied flora and fauna found in the mangrove swamps, rivers, and tropical forests where they live. They fill their art with symbols of ancestors, as well as animals and insects associated with head-hunting. These include the fruit-eating bat (flying fox), hornbill, heron, cockatoo, and praying mantis. The Asmat people liken the fruit the flying fox eats from the tops of trees to the trees' heads, and, symbolically, they see the bat as a headhunter. They also see the hornbill, heron, and cockatoo as efficient hunters and their eating behaviors as similar to taking heads and eating the victims. The Asmat consider the female praying mantis's practice of beheading her mate after copulation and eating him as another form of head-hunting/cannibalism they symbolize in their art.

The Asmat headhunt as a way of maintaining a balance of spirit power. When a person dies, either by natural causes, or by homicide, the Asmat attribute the loss of the person to a taking away of ancestral power. A natural death would be understood to be the result of sorcery by an enemy, death by homicide is yet another form of losing one's ancestral spirit to another. In order to restore a balance an enemy's head must be taken to avenge one's relative's death and to add to one's communal spirit power.

ANCESTOR POLES TO HONOR THE DEAD

The Asmat erect ancestor poles (FIG. **31-1**) in special commemorative ceremonies marking the death of their men, often due to head-hunting, warfare, or sorcery. The lifelike standing figures on the poles' vertical axis represent individuals who have died. Below them, on each pole, a seated, more abstracted, figure symbolizes both a praying mantis and an ancestor. A large curved flaglike sculptural element protrudes from the lower torso of each figure at the top of the poles. This pierced openwork form contains praying-mantis-like ancestor figures as well as S shapes symbolizing the spine and ancestors. After ceremonies, the Asmat discard the ancestor poles in the nearby swamp to begin a symbolic death-rebirth cycle.

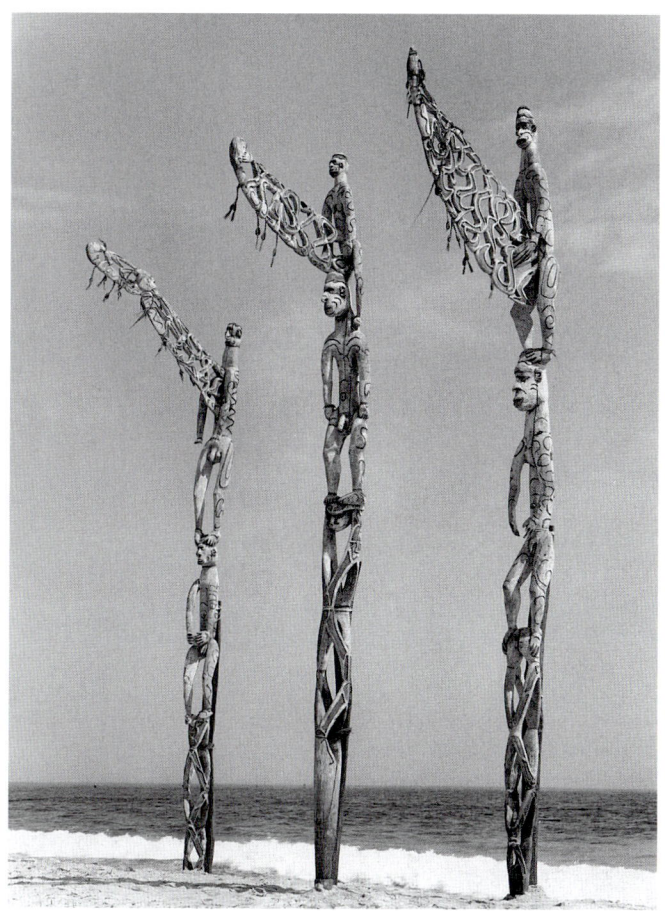

31-1   Ancestral poles, central Asmat, from Irian Jaya, 1960. Wood, paint, and sago palm leaves, 17′ 11″ high (tallest pole). Metropolitan Museum of Art, New York.

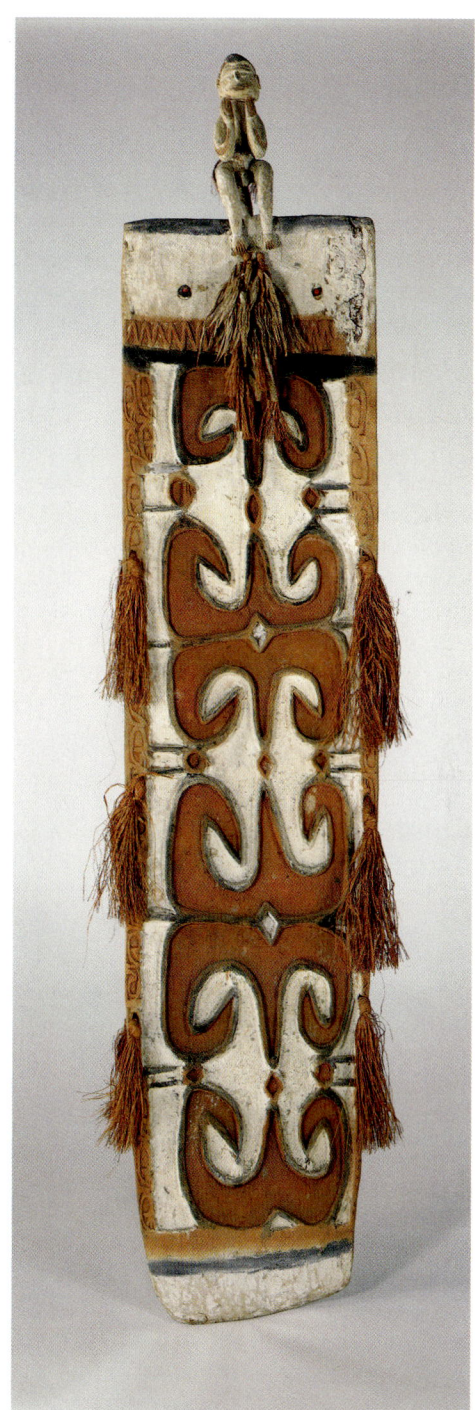

31-2   War shield, central Asmat, from Irian Jaya, collected in 1961. Wood, paint, charcoal, and sago leaf fiber, 7′ 1$\frac{12}{16}$″. Rijksmuseum voor Volkenkunde, Leiden.

WAR SHIELDS TO PROTECT THE LIVING In a culture where warfare was once common, war shields were an important defensive weapon for each man. Today, the Asmat make war shields primarily for sale; however, they are still an important part of the culture. They are kept in the men's house where initiated men sleep and congregate separately from the uninitiated boys and women, and they are placed near each man's section for ready access in time of need. The artist carved the war shield illustrated here (FIG. **31-2**) in low relief with symbols and images of ancestors and head-hunting. The Asmat believe the images have the power to help protect

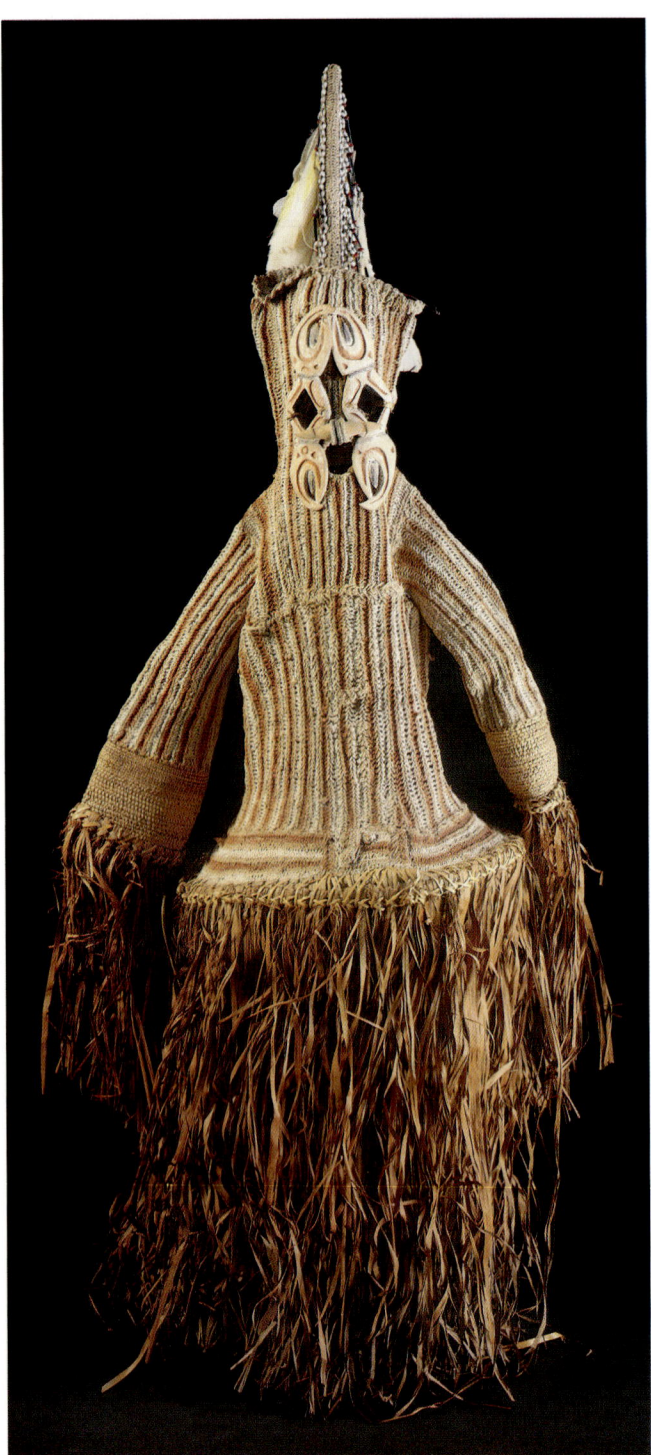

31-3 Rope mask ancestral costume (used in jipae), northwest Asmat, West New Guinea, 1953. Rope, wood, paint, sago leaf fiber, and cassowary feathers and quills, 6' 8⅞". Rijksmuseum voor Volkenkunde, Leiden.

the warrior behind the shield. The shapes on the shield sometimes look like recognizable human forms—for example, the centrally placed figure on the top. Other shapes, such as the paired, symmetrically stacked curved winglike forms down the shield's center, represent abstractions of a frontally positioned fruit-eating bat with outstretched wings. This bat form symbolically represents both the protective powers of the ancestors and head-hunting.

ANCESTRAL COSTUMES   In some areas, the Asmat perform special ancestral rites to appease the spirit of a dead

ancestor. During these rites, known as *jipae*, the Asmat wear a dramatic woven-fiber basketry costume (FIG. **31-3**). Its face and head create an otherworldly effect. The eye shapes, a pair of carved birdlike forms in profile, can be read simultaneously as the eyes of the ancestor and as hornbills. The Asmat use these masked costumes in nocturnal ceremonies to capture the dead ancestor's spirit, to remove it from the village, and to aid its journey to the west where the sun descends in the land of the dead. Afterward, they burn these masks or throw them back into the swamp in a symbolic death-rebirth cycle.

Abelam Art (East New Guinea)

INITIATION RITES IN CEREMONIAL HOUSES The Abelam people are agriculturalists living in the hilly regions north of the Sepik River. They elaborately paint the facade of their decorated men's houses (FIG. **31-4**) with representations of ancestral spirits connected to the fertility of the gardens, where yams are the primary food grown. The house itself symbolizes male and female generative and fertility notions. Entering the house requires crawling through the small doorway on the lower right, known as the womb of the house. The carved lintel about one-third up the facade represents a pair of male and female ancestors engaging in sexual intercourse. This symbolically links ancestors to human and

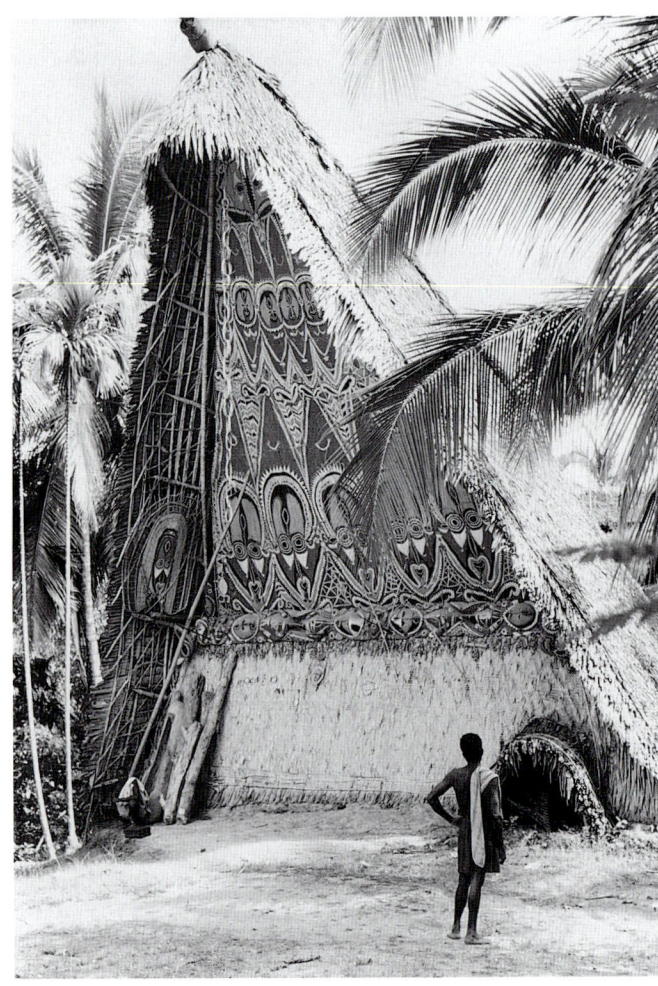

31-4 Ceremonial men's house, Abelam, Papua New Guinea, photographed in 1970.

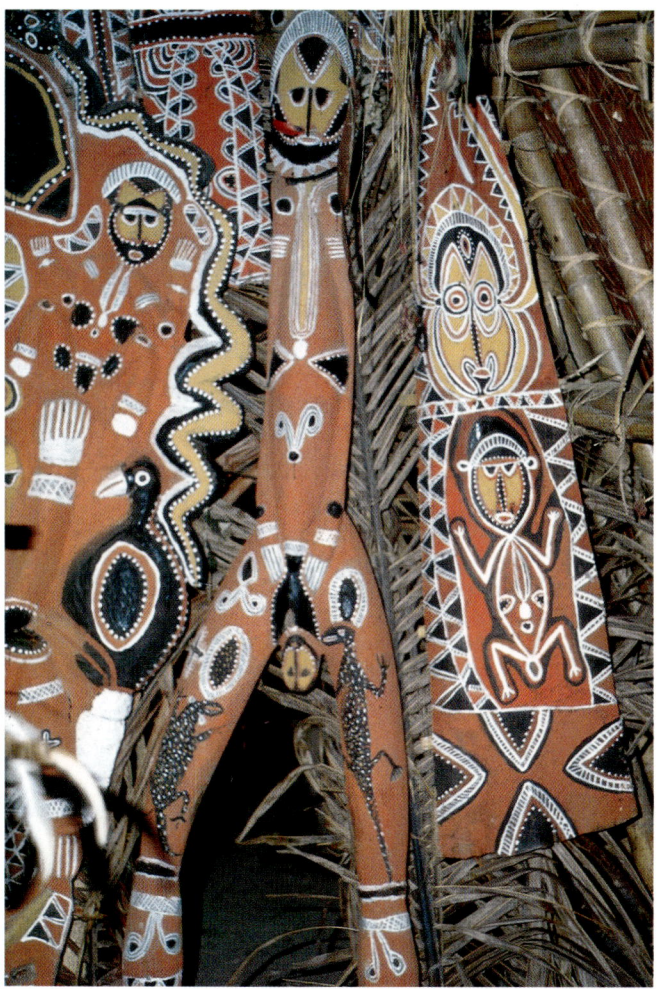

31-5 Interior initiation room doorway in a ceremonial men's house, Abelam, Papua New Guinea, photographed in the 1960s.

agricultural fertility. A monstrous female witch's face near the overhanging gable tops the painted ancestral faces organized in two rows on the facade. The protruding element on the peak of the ceremonial house is called its penis.

During initiation celebrations, young men enter the outer doorway and pass through an inner doorway under a carving of a female ancestral figure giving birth (FIG. **31-5**). The female figure straddles this interior opening. Thus, the initiates are symbolically reborn as they enter and leave the ceremonial house. Inside they undergo special instruction in all aspects of their roles as adult males in their society.

Iatmul Art (East New Guinea)

MEN'S HOUSES AND FEMALE ANCESTORS
The Iatmul live along the middle Sepik River in Papua New Guinea, and their settlements are noted for their massive saddle-shaped men's ceremonial houses. By tradition, the house illustrated (FIG. **31-6**) represents a monstrous female ancestor. Normally, the gable ends of such houses are covered and contain a protective giant female gable mask (similar in concept to the witch's face in FIG. 31-4), making the symbolism more apparent. However, when this house was reconstructed after damage during the Second World War, it was never fully completed, thereby exposing interior carvings normally hidden from view. The Iatmul placed carved images of clan an-

cestors on the five central ridge-support posts and on the twelve roof-support posts on both sides of the house. (One central post and two roof-support posts are fully visible in our photograph.) They topped each roof-support post with large faces representing mythical spirits of the clans. Below them, birds symbolizing the war spirit of the village men sit above carvings of male ancestors.

The house's interior is subdivided into three parts—a front, middle, and end—representing the three major clans who built the house. These parts are further subdivided into additional subclan areas, which also have support posts carved with images of mythical male and female ancestors. Normally taboo to women and uninitiated boys, the house serves as the place of initiation of local youths and for ceremonies linked to the Iatmul's ancestors. Beneath the house, each clan keeps large carved slit-gongs (at the lower right in FIG. 31-6) to serve as both instruments of communication (for sending drum messages within and between villages) and as the voices of ancestral spirits. The Iatmul placed carvings of female ancestors in this ceremonial house above the two ladders leading to the second level. On horizontal crossbeams (see the carving in the open gable space in FIG. 31-6), these figures symbolize female clan ancestors in a birthing position. The Iatmul house and its female ancestral figures symbolize a reenacted death and rebirth when a clan member enters and exits the house.

MASKS OF SPIRIT ANCESTORS The Iatmul keep various types of portable art in their ceremonial houses. These include ancestors' skulls overmodeled with clay in a likeness

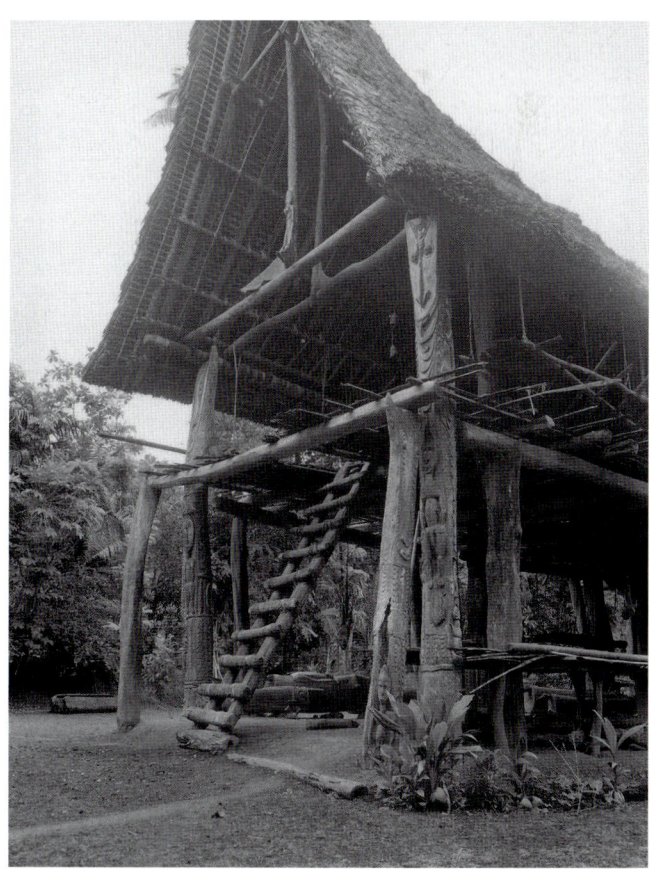

31-6 Exposed interior of ceremonial men's house, Iatmul, Papua New Guinea, photographed in 1953–1954.

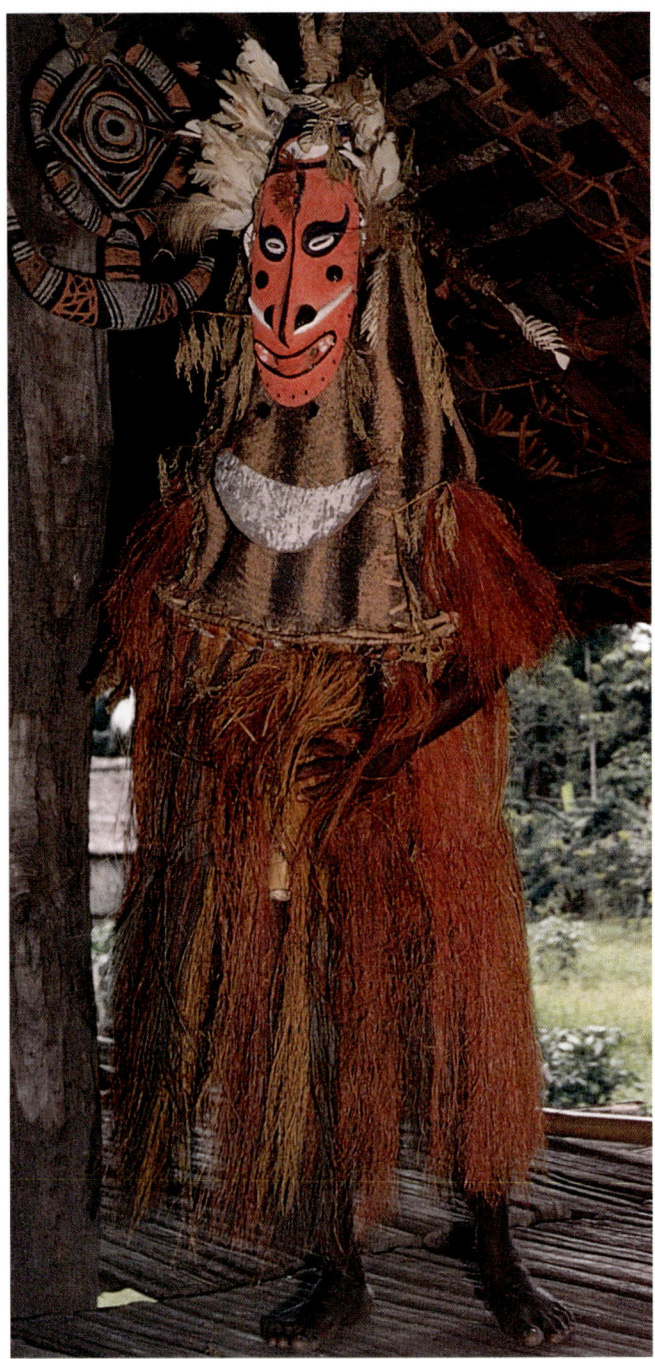

31-7   Abwan masked costume, Iatmul, Papua New Guinea, photographed in 1953–1954. Wood, paint, fibers, shell, and feathers, approx. 6' high with fiber costume.

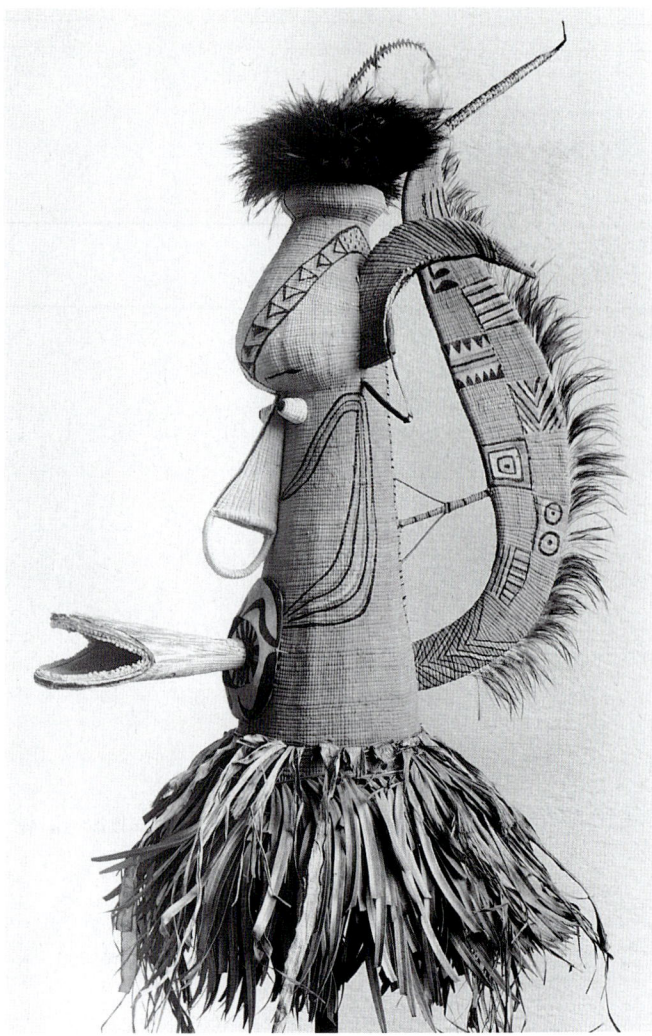

31-8   Gitvung-Susu mask, Sulka, New Britain, Papua New Guinea, 1900–1910. Fiber structure covered with pith, feathers, wood, and paint, 2' 3" high (without leaf skirt). Übersee-Museum, Bremen.

of the deceased, ceremonial chairs, sacred flutes, hooks for hanging sacred items and food, and several types of masks, including an anthropomorphic type called Abwan. In the Abwan masked costume illustrated here (FIG. **31-7**), the artist painted the spirit ancestor with elaborate clan-specific patterns on the face. The ancestor wears various decorative feathers and shell ornaments that clan members also wear during ceremonial events.

Sulka Art (East New Britain)

SERPENT-TONGUED INITIATION MASKS   The non-Austronesian-speaking Sulka people of the island of New

Britain in Papua New Guinea are known for elaborate surreal masks used in ceremonies of birth, initiation, men's house dedications, and mortuary rites. The Sulka make two basic types of masks. One type, called Hemlaut, has a large umbrella-like form on top of the mask. A second type, called Susu, appears in several distinct forms, including an anthropomorphized cone-shaped form called a Gitvung-Susu (FIG. **31-8**). The Sulka associate the Gitvung-Susu mask with the initiation of youth into adulthood. In our example, the mask's pierced nose, elongated earlobes, and blackened teeth are direct symbolic links to the operations performed on Sulka males during initiation. The extraordinary serpent form on the back of the head, which extends out from the mouth as a serpent tongue, symbolizes a supernatural snake spirit called Kot, which the Sulka greatly fear.

Malanggan Art (Northern New Ireland)

ANCESTRAL IMAGES AND MORTUARY RITES
The Austronesian-speaking peoples of the island of northern New Ireland in Papua New Guinea use elaborately carved polychrome sculptures called *malanggan* in large displays to honor the dead. The relevant rituals both commemorate ancestors and initiate youths into adulthood. In a 1930 field

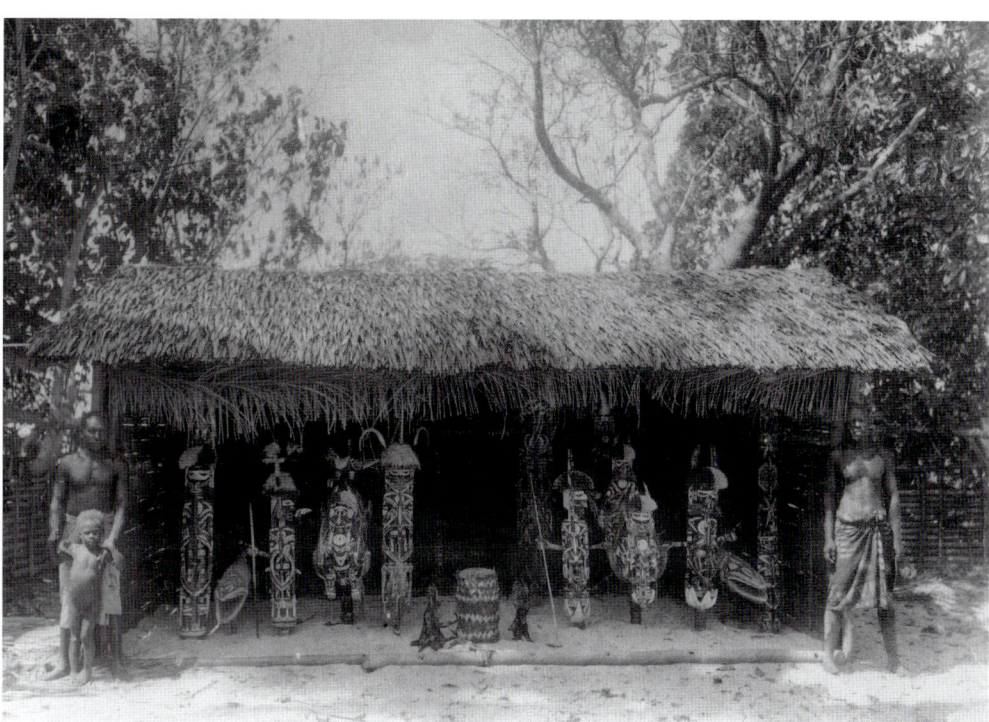

31-9 Malanggan house display, from northern New Ireland, Papua New Guinea, photographed in 1930.

photograph of a malanggan display (FIG. 31-9), all of the vertical sculptures contain representations of ancestors. Carved and painted birds, fish, and other animals, as well as plant forms, cover the surface of each ancestral image. These flora and fauna indicate the place of origin—bush (forest) or sea—of each clan ancestor represented in the display. The forms' bewildering intricacy stems from generous use of openwork and sliverlike projections and from overpainting in minute geometric patterns that further subdivide the image. The result is a splintered or fragmented and airy effect. This style is even more remarkable because the sculptors carved most of these forms from a single block of wood. After the malanggan rites conclude, the community discards the sculptures and allows them to decay. Artists carve new malanggan sculptures for each commemorative rite.

MASKS TO LIFT TABOOS The masks for malanggan rites include a dramatic taboo-lifting mask called Matua (FIG. 31-10). Made from wood, feathers, vegetal materials, and paints, the mask is a study in surreal imagery. The face is split into two asymmetrical parts by the painted subdivision of the lower face and forehead. Inside the toothy mouth, a tonguelike shape may represent the Matua eating a human liver (reenacting its cannibal-like attributes). The spirit's ears are made of large carved and painted planks set into the sides of the mask. Matching images of fish heads, bird heads with protruding tongues, and eye shapes decorate the ears' vertical axes. Above the forehead vertical and diagonal planks represent fish, snakes, and inverted sea eagle heads. The clan who made the mask associates these animal images with their clan's totemic animals.

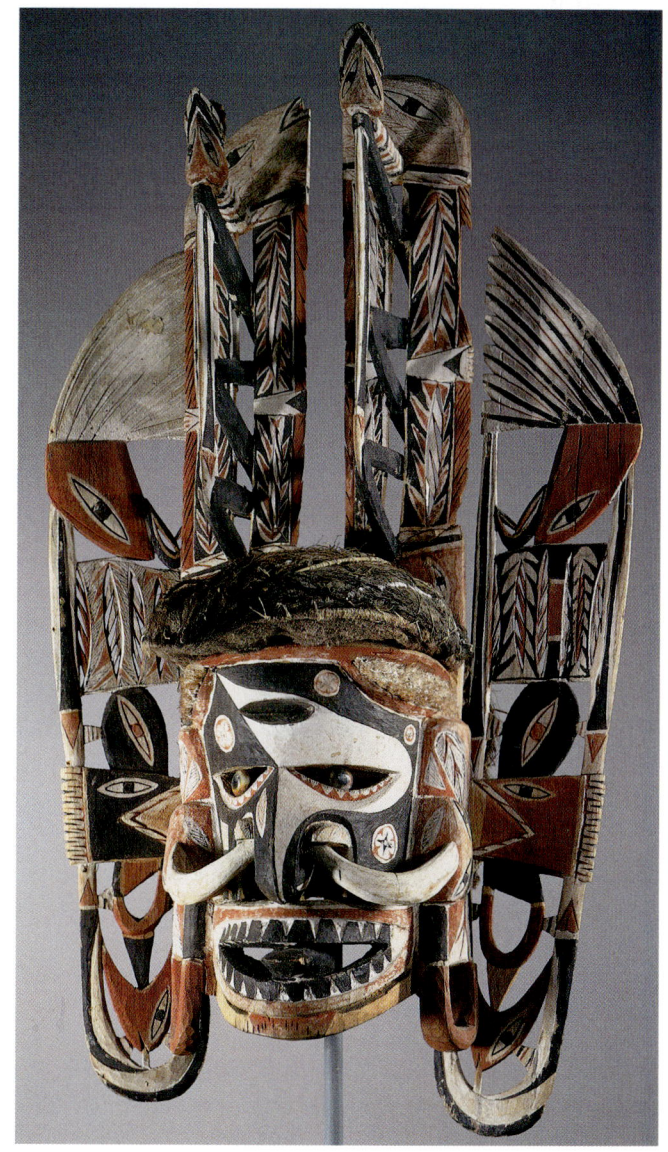

31-10 Malanggan mask for lifting taboos (Matua), from northern New Ireland, Papua New Guinea, late nineteenth century. Wood, pigment, and fiber, 2′ 1½″ high. Museum der Kulturen, Basel.

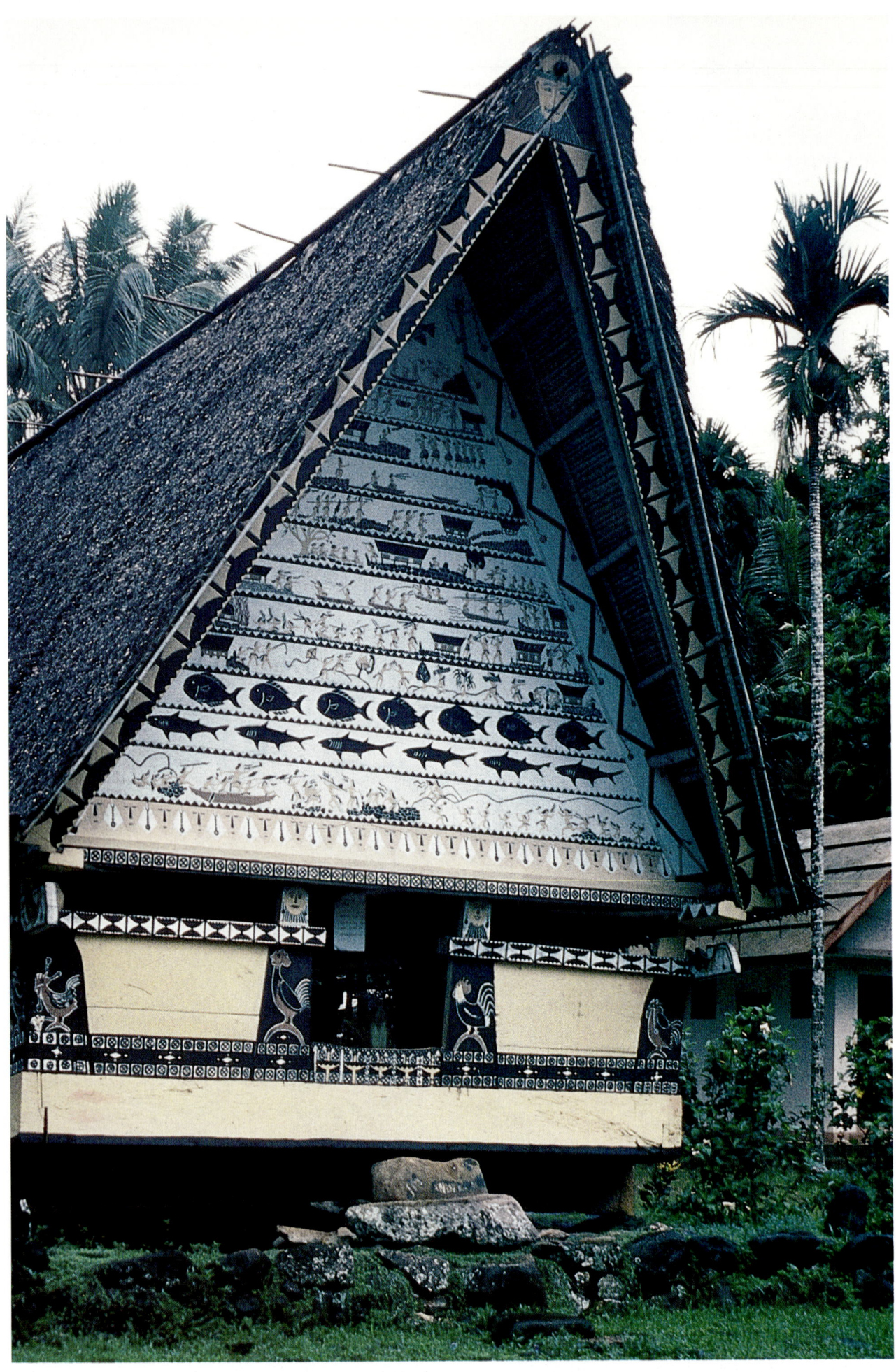

31-11 Men's ceremonial house *(bai)*, at Airai, Belau (Palau), Republic of Belau, photographed 1992.

MICRONESIA

The Austronesian-speaking cultures of Micronesia and related Polynesian outlier islands in Micronesia and Melanesia tend to stratify more than those found in non-Austronesian cultures in New Guinea and other Melanesian areas. These outliers are islands where Polynesian peoples back-migrated westward after living earlier on islands to the east. Such cultures are frequently organized around chieftainships with craft and ritual specializations, and their religions include named deities as well as honored ancestors. Virtually all Micronesian cultures center life around the sea through fishing, trading, and long-distance travel in large oceangoing vessels. For this reason, they connect much of the imagery in their arts in one way or another with the sea. Micronesian arts include carved canoes, charms, and deity images used to protect travelers at sea and for fishing and fertility magic. Micronesian artists also tend to simplify and to abstract the natural forms of animals, humans, and plants geometrically. This characteristic often differentiates Micronesian art from the arts of Melanesia, Polynesia, and Australia.

Belau Art (Caroline Islands)

CEREMONIAL HOUSE STORYBOARDS On Belau (formerly Palau) in the Caroline Islands, the islanders put much effort into creating and maintaining elaborately painted men's ceremonial clubhouses called *bai*. The recently constructed (ca. 1991) bai we illustrate (FIG. **31-11**) has a steep overhanging roof decorated with geometric patterns along the roof boards. Belau artists carved the gable in low relief and painted it with horizontal bands of narrative scenes and recognizable fish imagery, as well as various abstracted forms of the shell money used traditionally on Belau as currency. These decorated "storyboards" illustrate important historical events and myths related to the clan who built the bai. In the illustration, the rooster images on the lower facade symbolize a Belau deity, whereas the profiled "money birds" on the projecting support beams under the roof ends represent the source of shell money. The multiple frontal human faces carved and painted along the lower painted gable beams and on the vertical elements above the rooster images represent a deity called Blellek. He warns women to stay away from the ocean and the bai or he will molest them. The god serves as a social control mechanism within Belau society.

Artists also carved and painted the crossbeams on the inside of the house with similar narratives recounting clan histories and myths. The shell-like abstract patterns found on the exterior roof beams and lower sections of the house all refer to the shell-money wealth of the clan and its chief. While the Abelam and Iatmul make their ceremonial houses, discussed earlier, by elaborate tying, lashing, and weaving of different-sized posts, trees, saplings, and grasses, the Belau people make the main structure of the bai entirely of worked, fitted, joined, and pegged wooden elements, which they can take apart and put together at will.

Nukuoro Art (Caroline Islands)

COMMUNAL SPIRIT HOUSE SCULPTURE In Micronesia, as well as on Polynesian outliers, the inhabitants often carved deities as very refined abstracted human forms. Two excellent examples, representing a male and female deity pair known as Tino (FIG. **31-12**), came from Nukuoro Island in the eastern Caroline Islands in Micronesia. The pair dates to the late nineteenth century. Carvings such as these were often part of an ensemble of large and small deity figures set up on a shrine in a spirit house *(amalau)* that served as a communal religious structure for men and women. Large figures represented major deities, while smaller ones, such as those in our illustration, represented minor deities. The male figure on

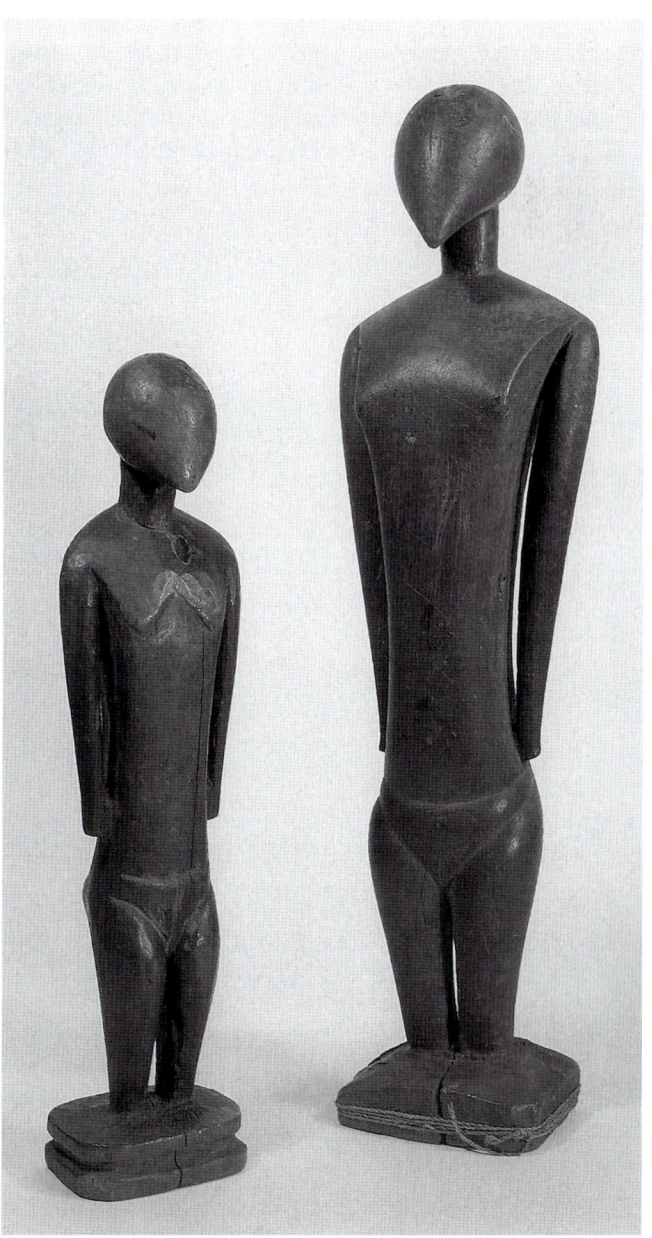

31-12 Male and female deity pair (Tino), from Nukuoro, Caroline Islands, late nineteenth century. Wood; female figure *(left)*, 1′ 2⅛″; male figure *(right)*, 2′ 6½″. Museum für Volkerkunde, Leipzig.

the right is taller than the female on the left. Both have abstracted heads with pointed chins. The artist did not indicate eyes, nose, or mouth. The result is a human head abstraction similar to later abstract works Western artists created (see Chapter 33). The male figure's chest flares out slightly to suggest a broad pectoral region, while the clearly defined pair of downward pointing triangular shapes on the female figure represent pendulant breasts. Both figures have elongated arms attached to the sides of their torsos, ending slightly above the waist. The figures' legs appear to grow out of a horizontal rectangular base with no indication of feet, knees, or toes.

The smooth, elegant abstracted human forms of the Nukuoro Island Tino contrast strongly with human forms seen in the Asmat, Abelam, Iatmul, and malanggan arts already discussed. This tendency to simplify and abstract the human form into essential geometric planes is common in the art of Micronesia and of western (Tonga) and central Polynesia (Tahiti, Rurutu, and Aitutaki). In other Polynesian areas, such as on Rarotonga, Easter Island, the Marquesas Islands, Hawaii, and New Zealand, artists favored more varied and robust expressions of human imagery. These developed into distinctly recognizable artistic traditions by the time of early contact with European explorers in the eighteenth century.

POLYNESIA

Polynesia was one of the last areas in the world humans colonized. It was not settled until about the end of the first millennium B.C. in the west and the first millennium A.D. in the east. Its inhabitants brought complex sociopolitical and religious institutions with them. Polynesian societies typically are aristocratic, with ritual specialists and chiefs heading elaborate political organizations. Polynesians often make art forms for upholding spiritual power, or *mana*. They vest this mana in the ranked nobility and believe it to exist in many objects humans make, as well as in natural forms and in places associated with religious shrines and temples or in historically significant sites. The counterpart to mana, *tapu* (the source of the English word *taboo*), creates with mana a dynamic opposition of forces dominating Polynesian social and religious concepts and practices. In Polynesia, art forms imbued with mana include those serving as examples of the power of ancestors or deities and objects that high-ranking persons of noble or high religious background own and use. People could be tapu to others, depending on their status within the hierarchy.

Polynesian artists traditionally have excelled in carving figural sculptures in wood, stone, and ivory. The artworks range in size from the gigantic fabled stone images of Easter Island

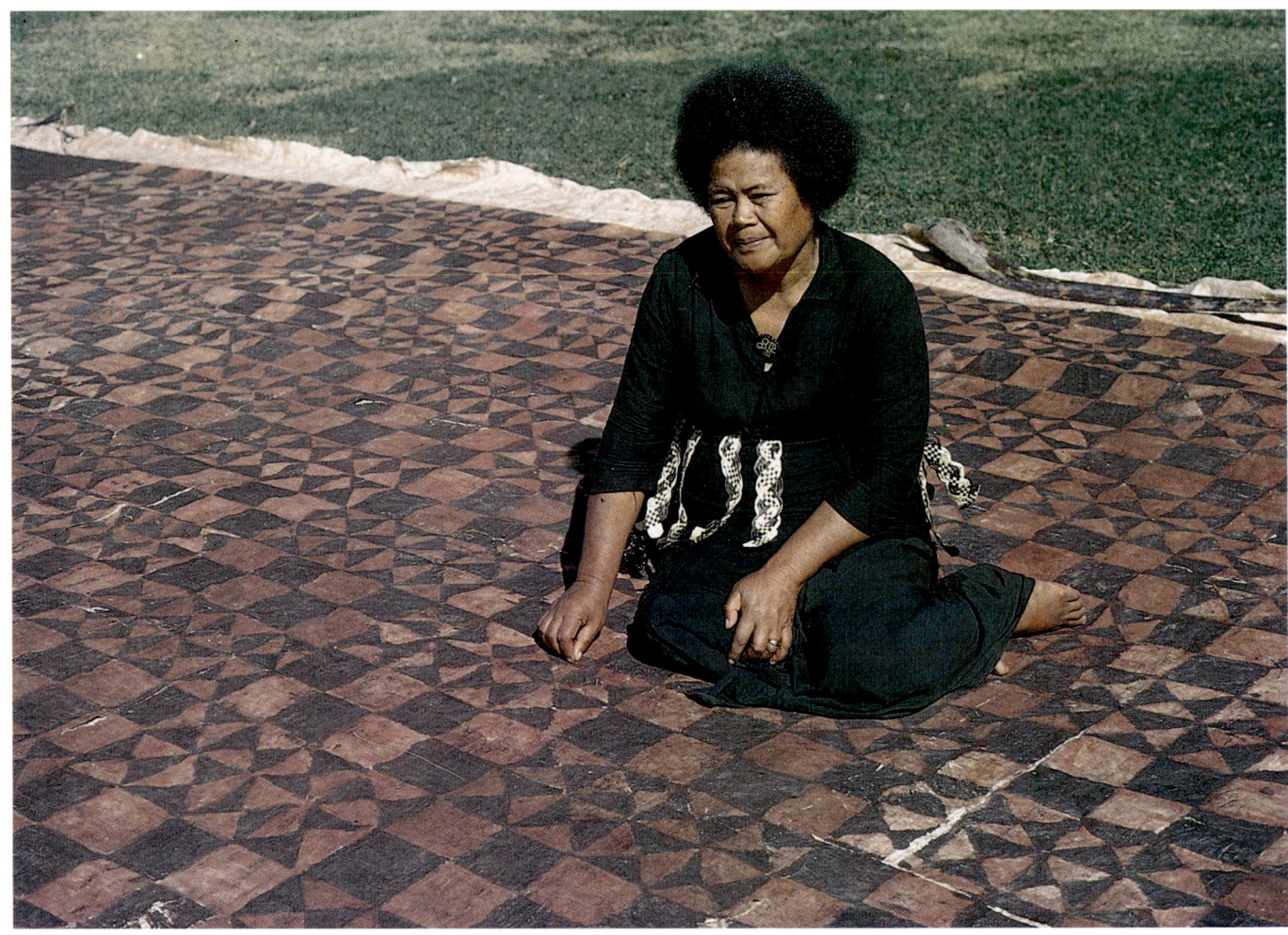

31-13   Mele Sitani, decorated barkcloth *(ngatu)* with two-bird *(manulua)* designs, Tonga, 1967.

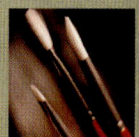

Polynesian Barkcloth

Throughout Polynesia women make decorated barkcloth using the inner bark of the paper mulberry tree (*Broussonetia papyrifera*). The finished product goes by various names in Polynesia, including *ahu* (Tahiti), *autea* (Cook Islands), *aute* (New Zealand), *kapa* (Hawaii), *hiapo* (Marquesas Islands), *siapo* (Samoa), and *masi* (Fiji). As these varied names for decorated barkcloth indicate, only the Hawaiian word *kapa* relates linguistically to *tapa*, the generally accepted term for barkcloth in Polynesia. During the nineteenth century, *tapa* became a widely used reference word for decorated barkcloth in Polynesia and still is today.

At the time of early contact between Europeans and Polynesians in the late eighteenth and early nineteenth centuries, ranking women in Tonga (western Polynesia) made decorated barkcloth. Today, women's organizations called *kautaha* make Tongan decorated barkcloth (*ngatu*). The kautaha may have the honorary patronage of ranking women. In Tonga, men plant the paper mulberry tree and harvest it in two to three years. They cut the trees into about ten-foot lengths and allow them to dry out for several days. Then the women strip off the outer bark and soak the inner bark in water to prepare it for further processing. They then place these soaked inner bark strips over a wooden anvil and repeatedly strike them with a wooden beater until they spread out and flatten. Folding and layering the strips while beating them, a felting process, results in a wider piece of ngatu than the original strips. Afterward, the beaten barkcloth dries and bleaches in the sun.

The next stage of artistic handling of the barkcloth involves first placing these thin sheets of barkcloth over semicircular-shaped boards. The women then fasten embroidered design tablets (*kupesi*) of low-relief leaf, coconut leaf midribs, and string patterns to the boards. They transfer the patterns on the design tablets to the outer barkcloth by rubbing. Then, the women fill in the lines and patterns by painting, covering the large white spaces with painted figures. The Tongans use brown, red, and black pigments derived from various types of bark, clay, fruits, and soot to create the colored patterns on ngatu. Sheets, rolls, and strips of ngatu are made for use on special occasions, such as weddings, funerals, and ceremonial presentations for ranking persons.

We illustrate a traditionally patterned ngatu (FIG. 31-13) made in 1967 for the coronation of King Tupou IV of Tonga. It clearly shows the richness of pattern, subtlety of theme, and variation of geometric forms that characterize Tongan royal barkcloths. One of the women barkcloth specialists— MELE SITANI, who made this presentation piece—kneels in the middle of an ngatu covered in triangular patterns known as *manulua*. This pattern is made from the intersection of three or four triangular points. *Manulua* means "two birds," and the design gives the illusion of two birds flying together. The motif symbolizes chiefly status derived from both parents.

---

to tiny one-inch-long ivory Marquesan earplugs. Generally full-volumed monochromatic human figures, these sculptures are often dynamic in pose. Polynesians also adeptly make decorative barkcloth, called *tapa*, which plays a crucial role in Polynesian society as clothing, bedding, and gift articles (FIG. 31-13). Barkcloth making and decorating is one of the major art forms Polynesian women create (see "Polynesian Barkcloth," above). The art of tattooing is highly developed as well. In fact, the word *tattoo* is of Polynesian origin.

Rarotongan Art (Cook Islands)

Even though Polynesians were skillful navigators, various island groups remained sufficiently isolated from one another for centuries by the vast distances they would have had to cover in open outriggers. This allowed distinct regional styles to develop within a recognizable general Polynesian style. Deity images from Rarotonga and Mangaia in the Cook Islands and from Rurutu in the Austral Islands have multiple figures attached to their bodies. These carvings probably also represented clan ancestors, revered for their protective and procreative powers. All such images refer ultimately to the creator deities the Polynesians revere for their central role in human fertility.

A STAFF GOD WRAPPED IN BARKCLOTH The central Polynesian island residents of Rarotonga used various types of carved deity figures well into the early decades of the nineteenth century, when Christians converted the islanders and destroyed their deities as part of the conversion process. These included carved wooden fishermen's gods, large naturalistic deity images, and at least three types of staff gods (also called district gods), some more than twenty feet long. An example of one of these staff gods (of the smaller type, only forty-five inches long) shows a profile figure with multiple layers of barkcloth wrapped around its center (FIG. **31-14**). The artist painted the tapa with dark zigzag patterns. The deity has an elongated-profile head with a sharp jutting jawline, lips with a slight protruding form, and an oval-shaped ear set behind a pointed oval-shaped eye. A simplified arm extends down the shaft and covers a small secondary frontal figure placed slightly beneath the jutting lower jaw. Directly beneath this second figure is a third one, seen only as a profile head above the barkcloth, with no recognizable body parts below. On the other end of the staff god, the artist carved a well-defined phallus with glans exposed. Directly behind this, a pair of figures stand back-to-back, and a third profile figure faces down the staff. The exact meanings of the primary and secondary figures are unknown and forever lost due to the abrupt conversion to Christianity and the near total destruction of Rarotongan religious imagery in the early nineteenth century. However, the procreative symbolism and multiple small figures found on this staff god suggest a generative deity creating minor deities from his own body, a trait found frequently in central Polynesian art and religion.

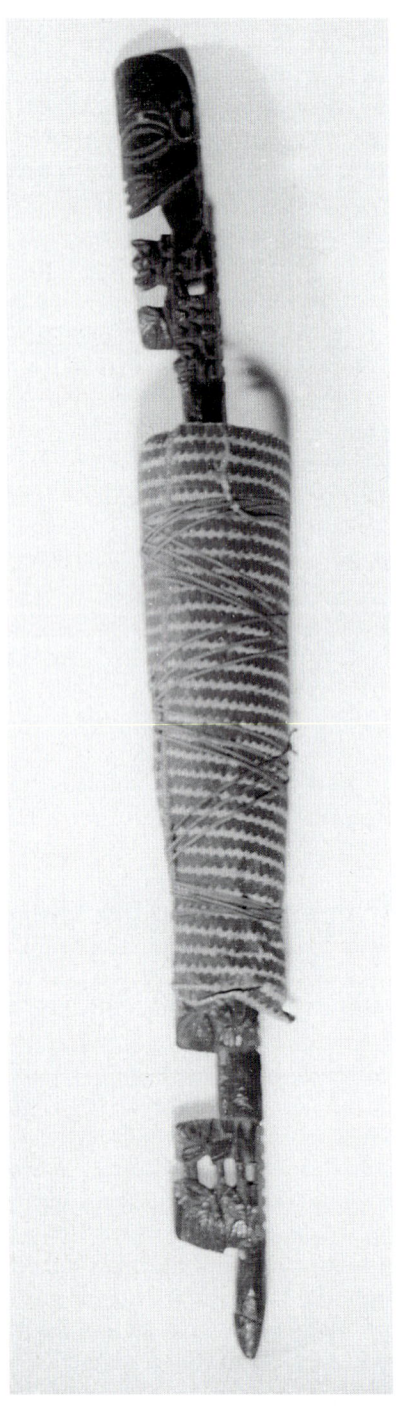

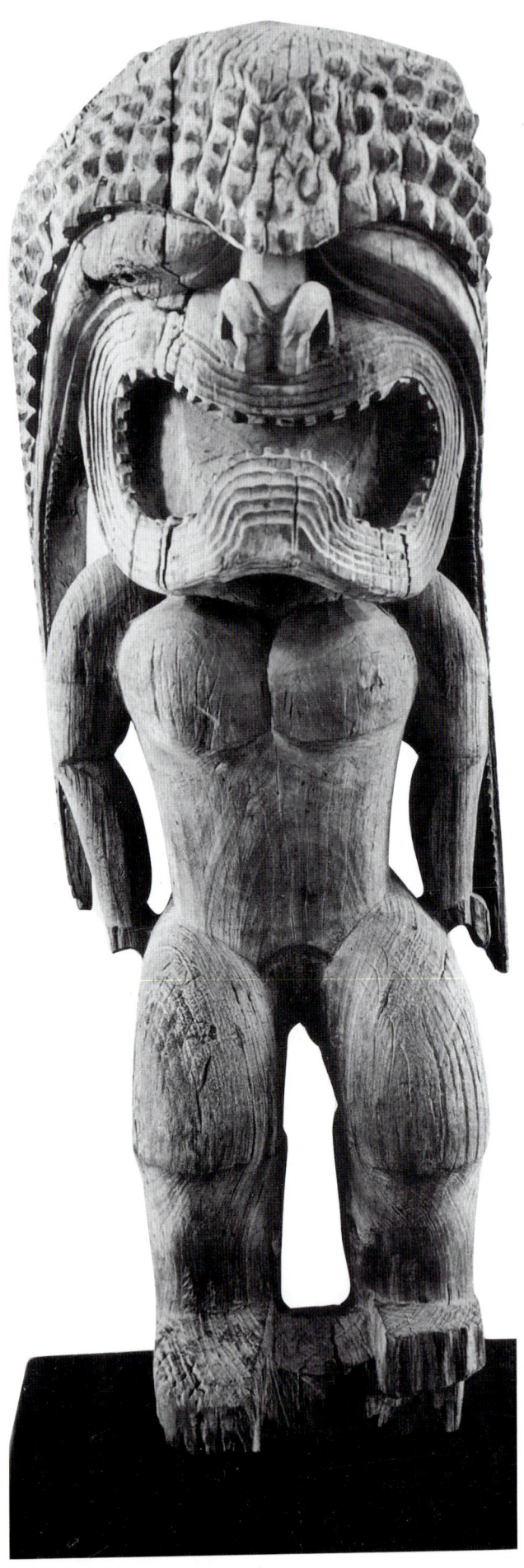

31-14   Staff god, from Raratonga, central Polynesia, nineteenth century. Wood, barkcloth, pigment, and sennit, 3′ 9″ high. Otago Museum, Dunedin.

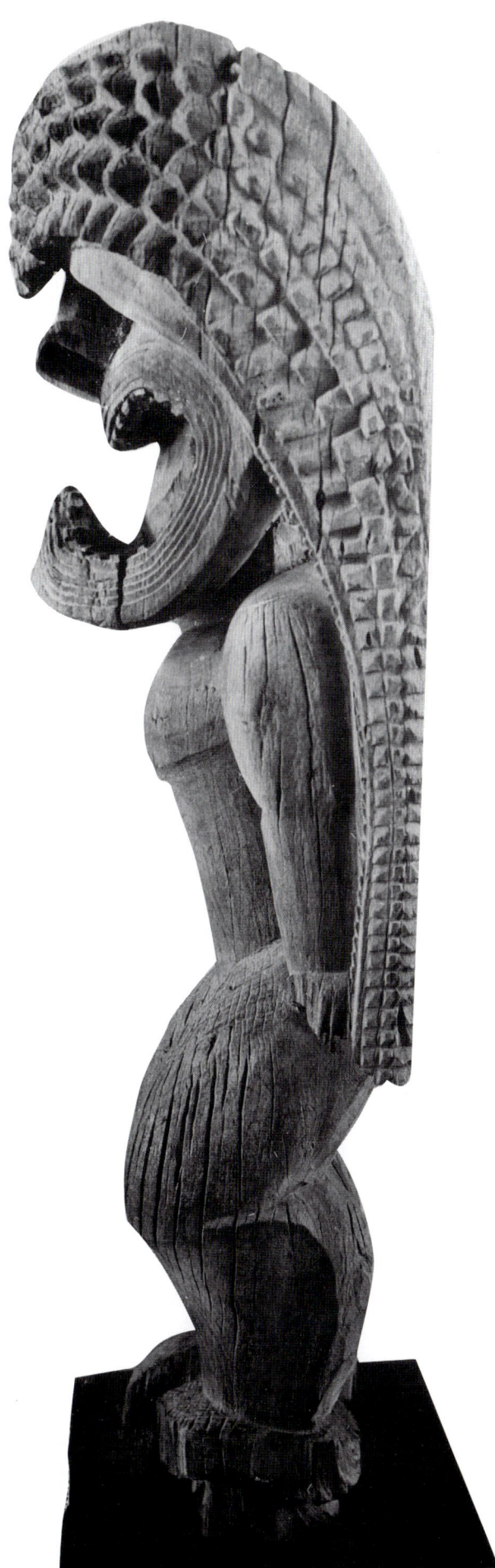

Hawaiian Art (Hawaiian Islands)

A DEFIANT WAR GOD A late-eighteenth- or early-nineteenth-century Hawaiian wooden temple image of the war god Kukailimoku (FIG. **31-15**), more than six feet tall, sharply contrasts with the refined, abstracted, and subtle procreative imagery seen on the Rarotongan staff god. This war god's head is nearly a third the size of his entire body, and his wide-open figure-eight-shaped mouth, with its rows of teeth, expresses aggression and defiance. His muscular body appears to stand slightly flexed, as if ready to act. The artist realized this Hawaiian war god's overall athleticism through the full-volumed sculptural treatment of his arms, legs, and the pectoral area of the chest. In the late eighteenth and early nineteenth centuries, the Hawaiians placed deities such as this and other similar large temple images in semicircular (and opposing) rows within an enclosed temple area *(heiau)*. They also carved smaller versions of lesser deity and ancestral images. The styles differ in the various islands of the Hawaiian chain, but the sculptured figures share a tendency toward athleticism and expressive defiance.

Marquesan Art (Marquesas Islands)

TATTOOING AND SOCIAL STATUS Polynesians developed the painful but prestigious art of tattoo more fully than many other Oceanic peoples, although tattooing also was common in Micronesia. Nobles and warriors, especially, accumulated various tattoo patterns over the years to increase their status, mana, and personal beauty.

An early-nineteenth-century engraving (FIG. **31-16**) provides an example of a Marquesan warrior from Nukahiva

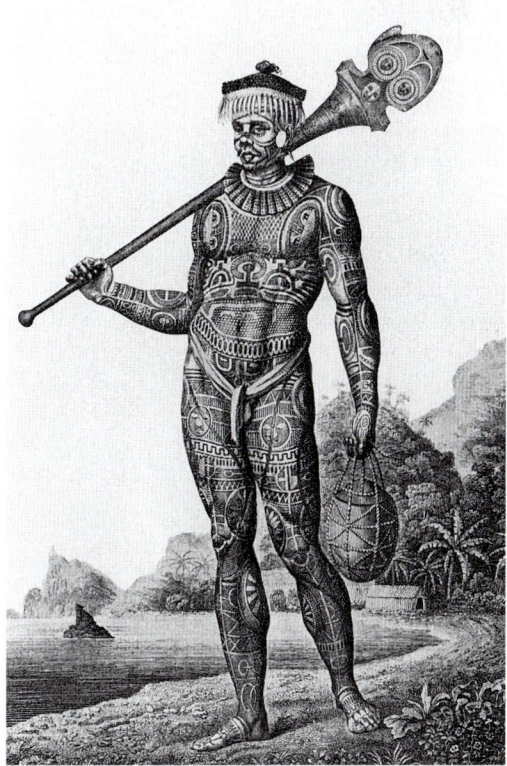

31-15 Kukailimoku (war god), temple image, from Hawaii, eighteenth–nineteenth century. Wood, 6′ 7″ high (figure only). Peabody Museum of Salem, Salem.

31-16 Tattooed warrior with war club, Nukahiva, Marquesas Islands, nineteenth century. Engraving.

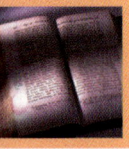

WRITTEN SOURCES

Chief Rangihaeata's Meeting House on Mana

The English artist, botanist, traveler, and writer GEORGE FRENCH ANGAS (1822–1886) spent six months in New Zealand in 1844. He painted watercolor studies of Maori architecture, canoes, settlements, weapons, and utilitarian wares, as well as clothing and modes of tattooing and self-decoration. His numerous paintings and their accompanying descriptions provide a glimpse of Maori art and culture shortly after the early European colonization and missioning of the Maori in the first half of the nineteenth century. Angas's painting (below) and description of an early-nineteenth-century Maori meeting house are especially valuable documents of Maori architecture just prior to the decline of pre-European artistic traditions.

> The houses of the New Zealanders are generally collected into villages, fortified with high wooden fences, and supported at intervals by huge carved posts, some of which bear grotesque representations of the human figure; within the enclosure, which when thus fortified, is termed "E Pa," the houses are grouped about, each family having a court-yard of their own, divided with a slight fence, and connected by stiles leading from the narrow ways that run between the various compartments. Great skill and taste are displayed in the carving and ornaments of the more important buildings, which are generally raised by some chief, either to commemorate a battle, or to shew his proficiency in the art of carving, they are otherwise always painted red with Kokowai, an ochre from Taranaki [North Island's west-central peninsula and Maori battleground], and the ridge pole, and boards that support the roof, are richly covered with spiral arabesques in red, white and black. . . . The House represented in the Plate [illustrated here] is designated by the cannibal name of 'Kai Tangata,' or eat man; it was built many years ago by Rangihaeata, the formidable warrior of the Nga-ti-toa tribe, who massacred the Europeans at Wairau Valley [northern South Island]. It stands on the small island of Mana, or Table Island, in Cook's Strait, and is one of the finest specimens of elaborately ornamented dwellings yet extant; most of the carving was executed by Rangihaeata's own hand, and the image supporting the ridge pole, is intended to represent himself.[1]

Rangihaeata's house has a carved gable face surmounted by a smaller face with a full figure standing on its head. The roof planks are unadorned until a point near where they overhang the ground. At this point their decoration includes elaborate curvilinear spiral motifs (tattoo patterns) that have six-fingered extensions at both ends. Two large figures hold up the roof boards at the ends of the porch. Both figures stick out their tongues in a gesture of aggression and defiance. Carved spiral tattoo patterns cover their shoulders and knees. Painted rafter boards line the underside of the outer porch, and carvings frame both the window and the doorway. A large lintel spans the doorway, decorated with two figures surrounded by spiral patterns. Carved support posts stand on both sides. Barely visible inside the doorway is a small humanlike figure at the bottom of a roof-support post that probably represents Rangihaeata himself.

[1] George French Angas, *New Zealanders Illustrated* (London: Thomas McLean, 1847), text accompanying Plate IV.

GEORGE FRENCH ANGAS, *Rangihaeata's House on the Island of Mana, called "Kai Tangata" (Eat Man)*, 1844. Watercolor.

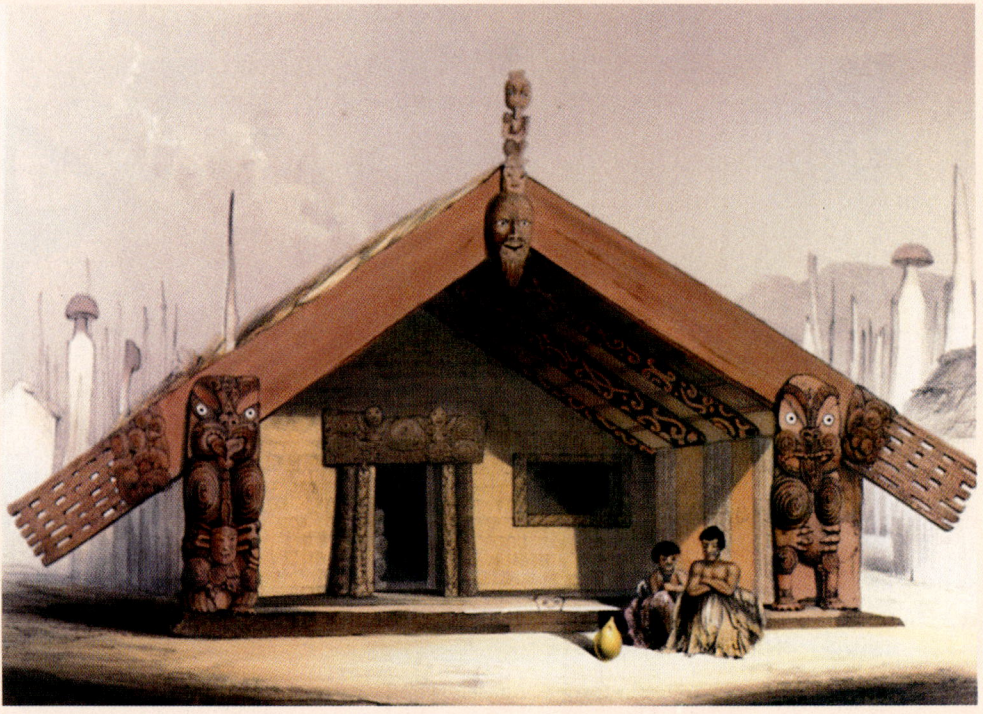

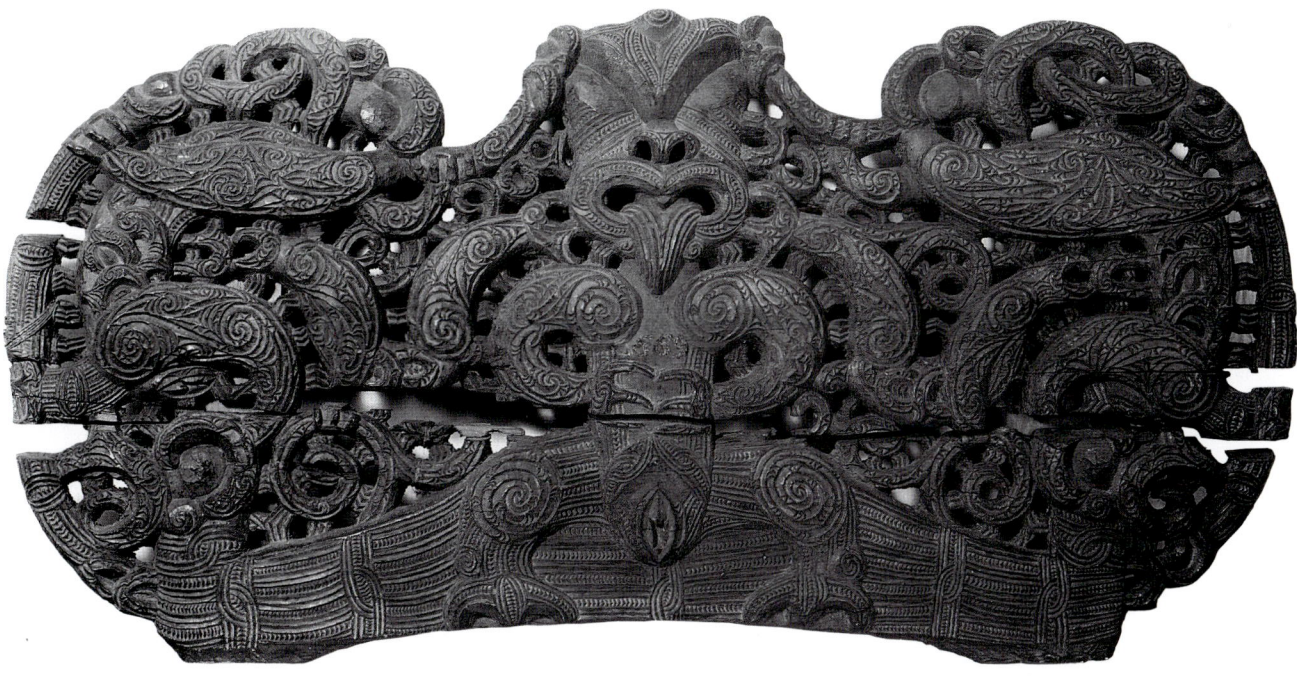

31-17   Door lintel of a meeting house, Maori, from New Zealand, nineteenth century. Wood, 1' 7" × 3' 9". Peabody Museum of Salem, Salem.

Island covered with elaborate tattoo patterns. The warrior holds a large wooden war club over his right shoulder and carries a decorated water gourd in his left hand. The various tattoo patterns marking his entire body seem to subdivide his body parts into zones on both sides of a line down the center. Some tattoos seem to accentuate joint areas, while others seem to separate muscle masses into horizontal and vertical geometric shapes. The warrior also covered his face, hands, and feet with tattoos.

Maori Art (New Zealand)

A TATTOOED EARTH GODDESS The highly distinctive arts of the Maori peoples of New Zealand merge a tendency toward decorative embellishment with an underlying human-figure style in dynamic intricate images. Major forms are bold, but minute curvilinear detailing covers and interconnects all surface areas. We illustrate a door lintel *(pare)* from a Maori meeting house (FIG. **31-17**) that is generously decorated, inside and out, with technically refined complex imagery. The central female figure probably represents an earth goddess (Papa) giving birth to the gods. Her tongue protrudes in a defiant gesture. Various carved tattoo patterns, similar to those the Maori decorated their own bodies with (see FIG. Intro-20), cover her entire form, including her face, legs, and arms. On both sides of her, profile figures representing mythological creatures called *manaia* face outward. The two manaia's faces are in profile at the top on both sides of the central goddess's head and face upward with their eyebrow, eye, nose, and open mouth clearly defined. Directly beneath their horizontally placed faces are their arms covered in tattoo patterns, each arm terminating on the outer edge in three fingers that grasp at the outer border of the pare. The Maori associate these manaia with death and destruction in the world.

This panel, with deities of life and death, symbolically represents the world's constant dynamic between creative and de-

structive forces. When entering and exiting from the Maori meeting house, community members passing beneath this lintel were symbolically transformed from one state of existence in the outside world to another within the meeting house. Figure carvings on and in the meeting house represented real and mythological ancestors and deities. The Maori sought their advice and protection for the political, war-making, and ritual deliberations occurring within the meeting house. Countless Maori prestige items and weapons display this same unique style. So, too, did the tattoos on their faces and bodies.

Meeting houses played an important role in Maori life before the Europeans arrived in the nineteenth century. A primary example is that of Chief Rangihaeata on the island of Mana, recorded by an English artist in 1844 (see "Chief Rangihaeata's Meeting House on Mana," page 974). Similar meeting houses still constructed today are among the most recent examples of a Maori cultural revival in New Zealand. These contemporary structures serve not just as meeting places but also as community centers and as symbols of Maori cultural identity.

AUSTRALIA

For the past forty thousand years, the Aboriginal peoples of Australia spread out over the entire continent and adapted to a variety of ecological conditions, ranging from those of tropical and subtropical areas in the north to desert regions in the continent's center and more temperate locales in the south. European explorers reaching the region in the late-eighteenth and early-nineteenth centuries found that the Aborigines had a special relationship with the land they lived on, developed primarily by hunting and gathering. Aboriginal origin myths emphasize a group's place of origin in terms of a specific tribal land the group had sprung from in the distant past and where they subsist in the present. Most objects the Aborigines make for ceremonial use symbolically link them with this

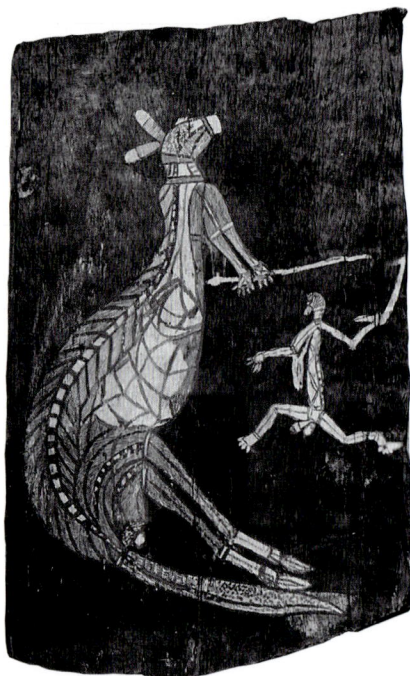

31-18 Hunter and kangaroo, from Oenpelli, Arnhem Land, Australia, collected in 1913. Pigment on bark, 4′ 3″ × 2′ 8″. National Museum of Victoria, Melbourne.

mythological place of origin. They recite creation myths in concert with songs and dances, and many art forms—body painting, carved figures, sacred objects, decorated stones, and rock and bark painting—serve as essential props in these dramatic recreations.

Aboriginal Art (Arnhem Land)

X-RAY BARK PAINTING Two bark paintings from different locations within a region of northern Australia known as Arnhem Land can serve as representative examples of Aboriginal art. The first (FIG. 31-18), a painting created before World War I, depicts a black kangaroo a hunter is about to spear. This painting comes from an area of western Arnhem Land called Oenpelli, where the Kakadu-speaking Aborigines created an X-ray style for depicting animal and human forms. In this style, the artist simultaneously depicts the subject's interior (internal organs) and exterior. The painting possesses a fluid and dynamic quality, with the X-ray-like figures clearly defined against a red ochre background. The artist also painted the small, elongated humanlike figure to the right side of the composition to appear something like an X ray. The hunter has just launched his spear from a spear-thrower and carries a dilly bag over one shoulder to transport small useful items during the hunt. The painter clearly depicted the hunter's penis and scrotum hanging beneath his outstretched legs. The kangaroo has risen to flee just before the spear strikes him on the upper chest.

Although his outer contour is clearly a naturalistic rendering of a kangaroo species, the depiction of his internal organs and bones constitutes a good example of the X-ray style. This type of bark painting probably served as a magical aid in hunting, as well as a form of visual aid to teach Aboriginal youths about hunting practices and mythology connected to the hunt.

AN ABORIGINAL ORIGIN MYTH   The second Aboriginal bark painting (FIG. 31-19), from eastern Arnhem Land at the Yirrkalla area, was painted about 1959 by the Yolngu-speaking Aboriginal artist MAWALAN MARIKA (1908–1967). Marika's painting, titled *The Djanggawul Sisters,* illustrates several incidents from the Yirrkalla Aborigines' origin myth of the same name. In contrast to the large-figure composition from Oenpelli, with its clear images of a kangaroo and hunter, Marika's composition subdivides the rectangular surface into four crowded panels. He further divided

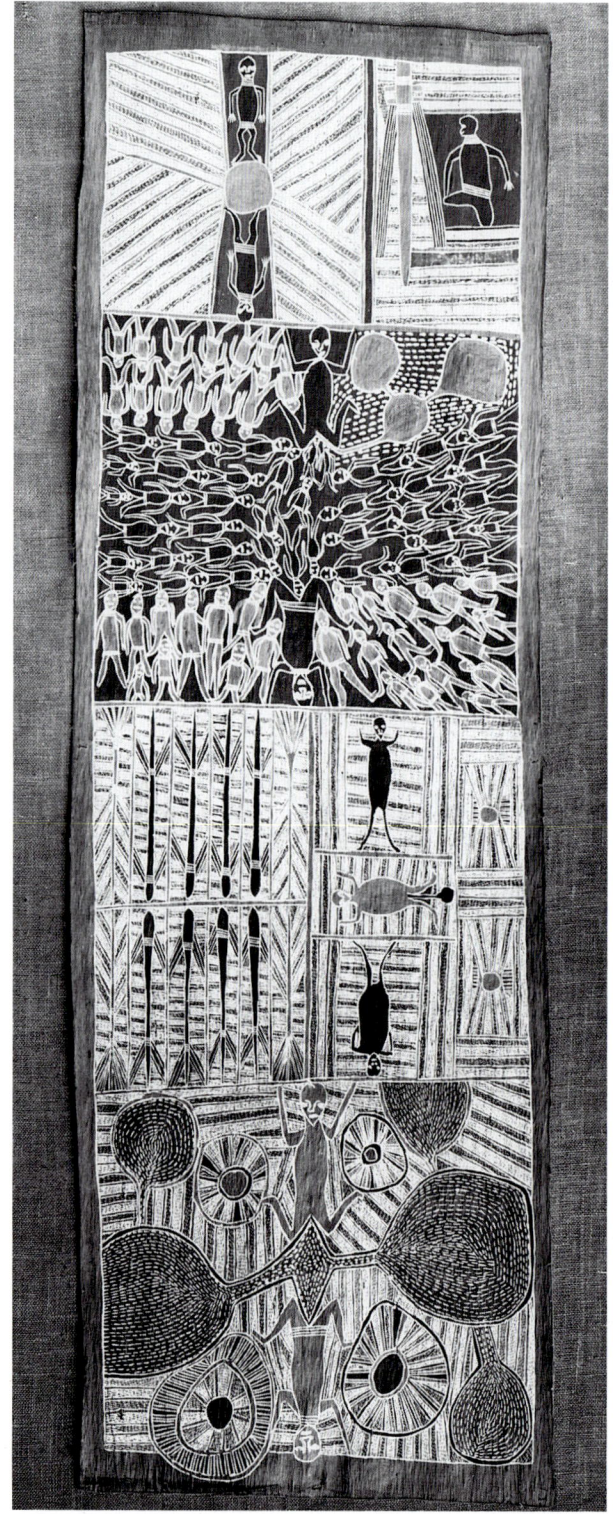

31-19 MAWALAN MARIKA, *The Djanggawul Sisters,* from Yirrkala, Arnhem Land, Australia, collected in 1959. Pigment on bark. Art Gallery of New South Wales, Sydney.

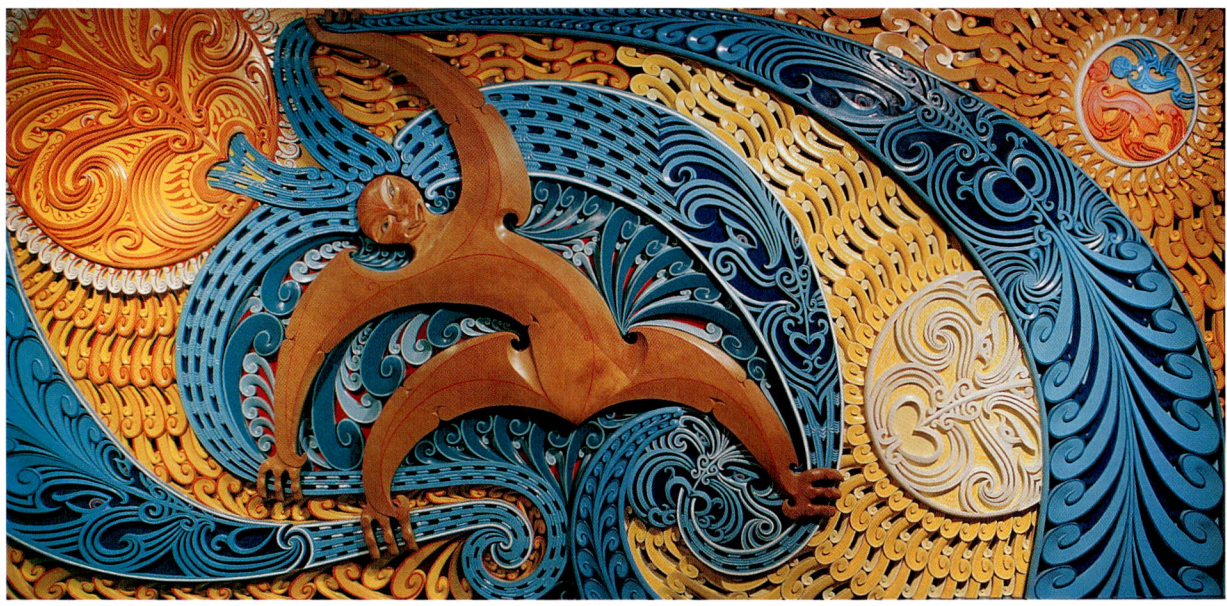

31-20   CLIFF WHITING (TE WHANAU-A-APANUI), *Tawhiri-Matea (God of the Winds),* Maori, 1984. Oil on wood and fiberboard, approx. 6′ 4⅜″ × 11′ 10¾″. Meteorological Service of New Zealand Ltd. Collection, Wellington.

two of these panels (the second from the bottom and the upper panel) into two smaller panels. Each panel illustrates a separate episode from the Djanggawul origin myth.

The bottom panel shows the two sisters in a birthing position creating male and female babies, represented by the small dash marks. The left side of the second panel from the bottom depicts eight decorated sacred sticklike clan emblems *(rangga)* the mythical originators used to create springs, waterholes, and trees. On the right are the two sisters and their brother (with the long penis). Two rectangles on the outer right edge of the panel represent the rising and setting sun. The Djanggawul sisters and brother started their journey of creation in the east, where the sun rises, and ended it in the west, where the sun sets. Along the way the mythical trio created specific places sacred to the Yirrkalla Aborigines. The third panel from the bottom shows the two sisters giving birth to these Aborigines. Here, dozens of smaller human figures depicted frontally represent the large numbers of people the Djanggawul sisters originally created. In the upper panel the sisters stand by a sacred spring (the circular form at their feet), with water flowing outward as diagonal lines radiating from the center spring. In the panel's small upper right side, Marika depicted himself sitting before his sacred rangga singing songs from the Djanggawul origin myth.

OCEANIC ART TODAY

Many of the traditional native arts of Oceania, particularly in Polynesia's central and peripheral islands, are not now practiced, for they no longer have critical roles insuring cultural continuity and survival. Yet, in several places, with the stimulus of cosmopolitan contacts in a shrinking world, these arts have been revitalized and flourish energetically. New, confident cultural awareness has led native artists to assert their inherited values with pride and to express them in a resurgence of traditional arts, such as weaving, painting, tattooing, and carving.

MAORI CULTURAL RENEWAL   One example that represents the many cases of cultural renewal in native Oceanic art is the vigorously productive school of New Zealand artists who draw on their Maori heritage for formal and iconographic inspiration. The historic Maori woodcarving craft brilliantly reemerges in what the artist CLIFF WHITING (TE WHANAU-A-APANUI) calls a "carved mural" (FIG. **31-20**). Whiting's *Tawhiri-Matea (God of the Winds)* is a masterpiece of woodcrafting designed for the very modern environment of an exhibition gallery or for embellishing a corporation wall. The artist suggested the wind turbulence with the restless curvature of the main motif and its myriad of serrated edges. The 1984 mural depicts events in the Maori creation myth. The central figure, Tawhiri-Matea, god of the winds, wrestles to control *te whanau puhi,* the children of the four winds, seen as blue spiral forms. Ra, the sun, energizes the scene from top left, complemented by Marama, the moon, in the opposite corner. The top right image refers to the primal separation of Ranginui, the Sky Father, and Papatuanuku, the Earth Mother. Spiral *koru* motifs symbolizing growth and energy flow through the composition. Blue waves and green fronds around Tawhiri suggest his brothers Tangaroa and Tane, gods of the sea and forest.

The artist is securely at home with the native tradition of form and technique, as well as with the worldwide aesthetic of modernist design. Out of the seamless fabric made by uniting both, he feels something new can develop that loses nothing of the power of the old. "Our people," Whiting declares, "must develop new forms with which they can identify. . . . We need to train the young to have, to find responsibility, within our culture, so that we can be assured of the transmission of the culture."[1] This is a call not only for renewing Maori cultural life in terms of its continuity in art but also for educating the young in the values that made that culture great, values they are asked to perpetuate. The salvation of their native identity will depend on their success in making the Maori culture once again their own.

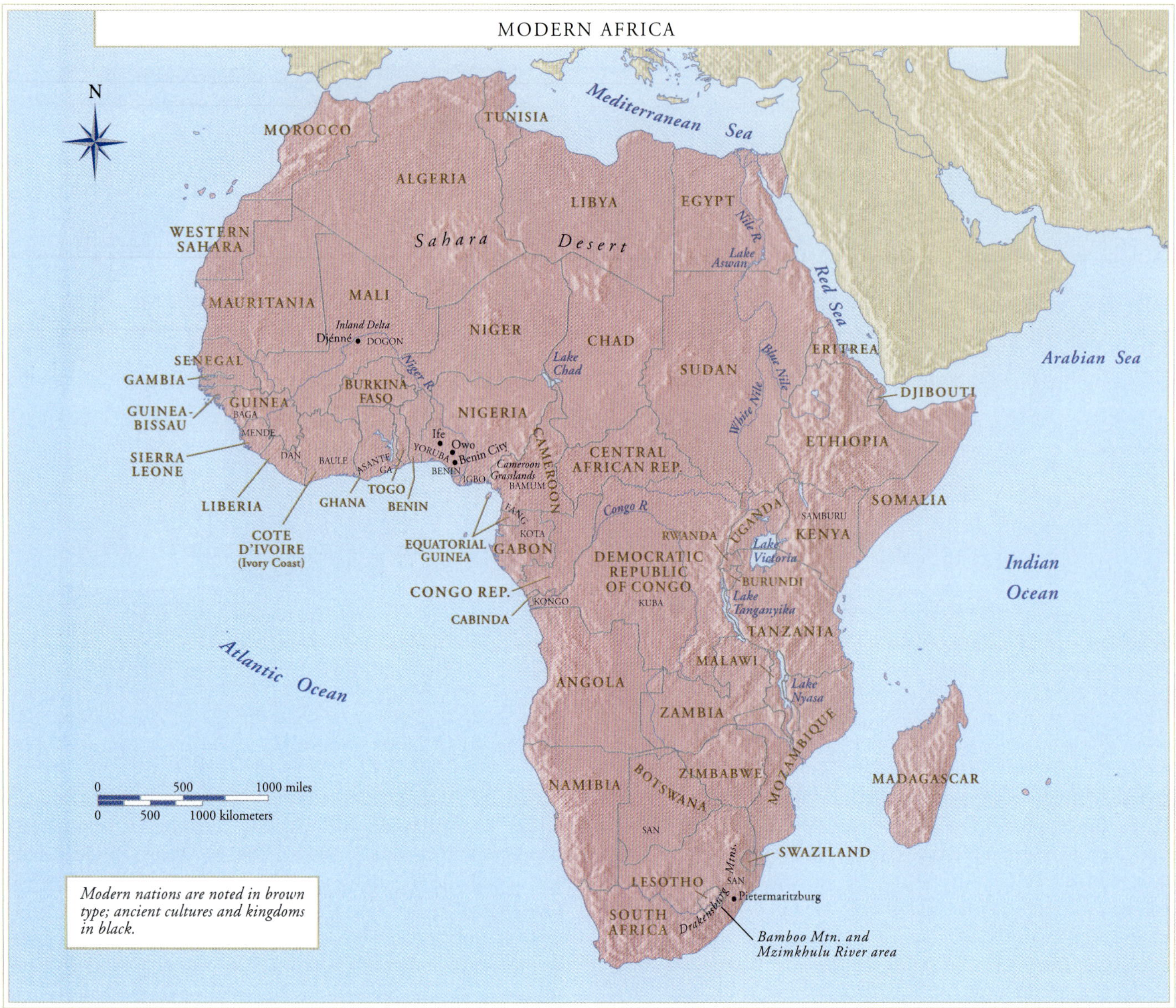

MODERN AFRICA

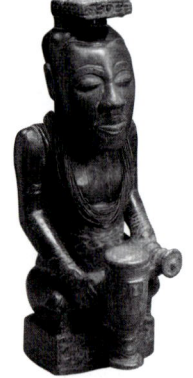

MOROCCO
TUNISIA
Mediterranean Sea
WESTERN SAHARA
ALGERIA
LIBYA
EGYPT
Sahara Desert
Nile R.
Lake Aswan
MAURITANIA
MALI
NIGER
CHAD
Red Sea
ERITREA
SENEGAL
Inland Delta
Djenné
DOGON
Niger R.
Lake Chad
SUDAN
Blue Nile
DJIBOUTI
Arabian Sea
GAMBIA
BURKINA FASO
NIGERIA
GUINEA
BAGA
GUINEA-BISSAU
MENDE
Ife
Owo
Benin City
CENTRAL AFRICAN REP.
ETHIOPIA
SIERRA LEONE
DAN
BAULE
ASANTE
GA
YORUBA
BENIN
IGBO
Cameroon Grasslands
BAMUM
White Nile
SOMALIA
LIBERIA
GHANA
TOGO
BENIN
CAMEROON
FANG
KOTA
Congo R.
SAMBURU
UGANDA
KENYA
COTE D'IVOIRE (Ivory Coast)
EQUATORIAL GUINEA
GABON
RWANDA
DEMOCRATIC REPUBLIC OF CONGO
Lake Victoria
CONGO REP.
KONGO
KUBA
BURUNDI
Lake Tanganyika
Indian Ocean
CABINDA
TANZANIA
Atlantic Ocean
ANGOLA
MALAWI
ZAMBIA
Lake Nyasa
MOZAMBIQUE
MADAGASCAR
NAMIBIA
BOTSWANA
ZIMBABWE
SAN
SWAZILAND
Mtns.
SAN
LESOTHO
Pietermaritzburg
Drakensberg
SOUTH AFRICA
Bamboo Mtn. and Mzimkhulu River area

0   500   1000 miles
0   500   1000 kilometers

Modern nations are noted in brown type; ancient cultures and kingdoms in black.

1700   1800   1850   1875   1900

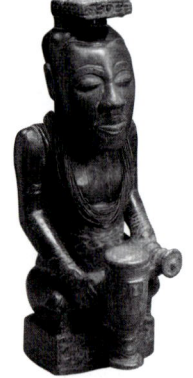

Male figure, King Kot a-Ntshey Democratic Republic of Congo eighteenth–nineteenth century

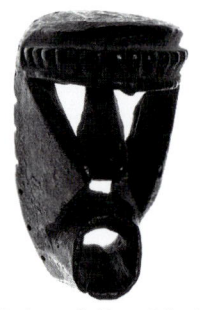

Kagle mask, Dan, Liberia nineteenth century

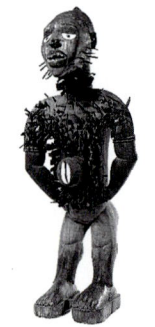

Nail figure, Kongo Democratic Republic of Congo ca. 1875–1900

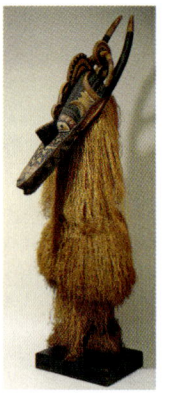

Banda mask Baga, Guinea late nineteenth century

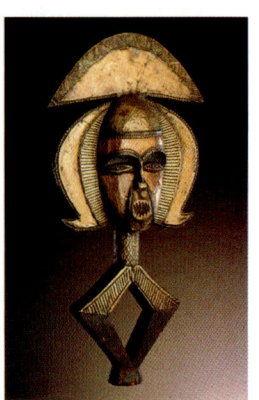

Guardian figure, Kota, Gabon nineteenth–twentieth century

Active missionizing by various Christian groups, eighteenth–nineteenth century

European countries colonize most of Africa, ca. 1885–1924

Colonial interest in African natural resources and trade, nineteenth century

British punitive expedition sacks Benin, 1897

Liberia achieves independence, 1847

European and American collectors and museums begin systematically collecting African arts, late nineteenth and early twentieth centuries

Pressure on traditional values alters African art forms and functions, 1890–present

EXPLORATION, COLONIZATION, AND INDEPENDENCE

LATER AFRICAN ART

1960   2000

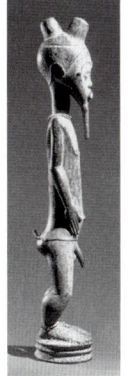

*Trance diviner
Baule, Côte d'Ivoire
nineteenth–twentieth century*

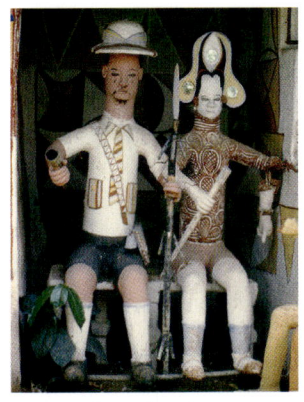

*Clay Mbari figures
Igbo, Nigeria, photographed 1966*

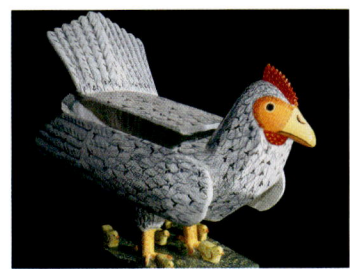

*Kane Kwei, hen-shaped coffin
Ga, Ghana, 1989*

Most African countries (besides Liberia) achieve independence
from Britain or France, beginning ca. 1960

International art market venues more common throughout
sub-Saharan Africa, late twentieth century

New tendencies develop toward realism, broader subject
range, urban settings, painting, new materials, and
greater emphasis on personal style, late twentieth century

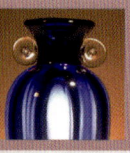

A San Rock Painting as a Historical Document

Numerous rock paintings found at southern African sites appear in shelters in mountainous areas of Zimbabwe, Botswana, South Africa, and Lesotho. In South Africa's Drakensberg Mountain region, scholars have associated many of the complex compositions containing animal and human forms with the San (formerly called Bushmen), who speak Khoisan. These compositions often depict several game animals hunted for food, as well as animals, such as the eland, considered effective in spirit and ancestor rituals. By the early to mid-nineteenth century, the increasing development of colonial settlements (farms and ranches) and Bantu-speaking settlements of agriculturists had greatly impacted the lifestyle and movement patterns of the San hunters and gatherers. In some Drakensberg Mountain regions, the San began to raid local settlements for livestock and horses as an alternate food source. Some San rock shelter paintings near the Mzimkhulu River source at Bamboo Mountain may represent pictures made after a series of stock raids over a period from about 1838 to 1848. Various South African military and police forces unsuccessfully pursued San raiders after many stock raids. Inclement weather, with frequent rains and fog, added to the difficulty of capturing a people who had lived in the region as hunters and gatherers for many years and were familiar with its terrain.

The painting illustrated here is about eight feet long. After having it photographed in situ in 1910, officials later removed it to the Natal Museum in Pietermaritzburg, South Africa. On the right side of the composition, two San riders on horses laden with meat drive a large herd of cattle and horses toward a San encampment located left of center and encircled by a linear outline. Within the encampment are various women and children. To the far left, a single figure (perhaps a diviner or rainmaker) leads a large animal toward the encampment. The similarity of this scene (a human leading an animal) to other rock paintings with mystical interpretations suggests that this may represent a spiritual leader in a trance state, calling on rain to foil the attempts of the government soldiers and police to locate and punish the San raiders. The close correspondence between the painting's imagery and the actual events of 1838–1848 adds to the certainty that this work both indirectly records government and police action and was designed to facilitate rainmaking.

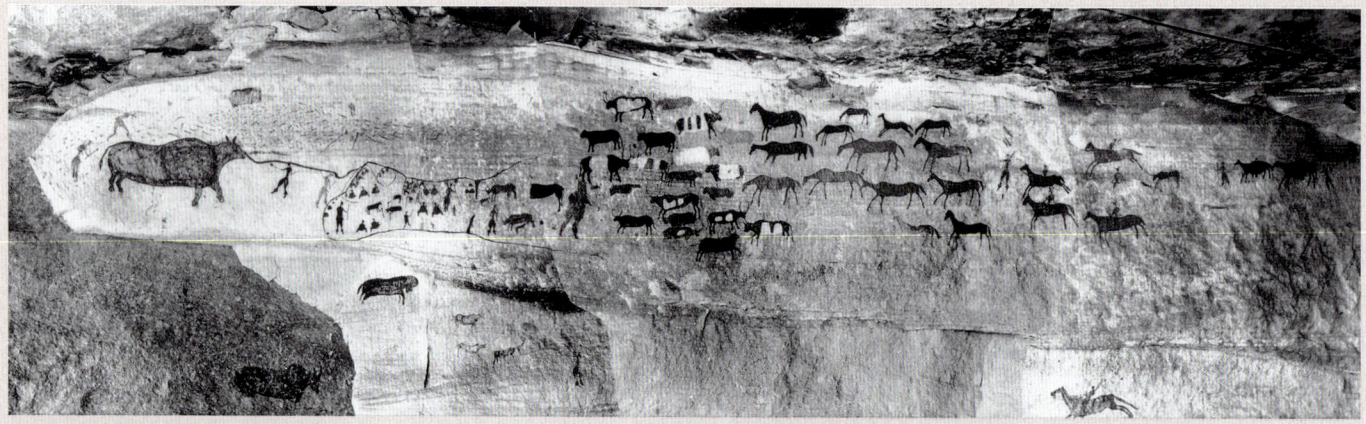

Bamboo Mountain stock raid with cattle, horses, encampment, and magical "rain animal," San, from South Africa, mid-nineteenth century, photographed in 1910. Pigments on rock, approx. 8′ long. Natal Museum, Pietermaritzburg, South Africa.

EUROPEAN CONTACT AND EARLY COLONIZATION

EXPLORERS AND MISSIONARIES The early contact period between Europeans and Africans extended from the late fifteenth century to the beginning of the nineteenth century. With few exceptions, early European explorers seldom ventured beyond the coastal sections (where they often constructed forts) and had no real access to interior regions or peoples. European wars and revolutions between the sixteenth and early nineteenth centuries lessened contact with African peoples, although the slave trade between Europe and Africa, established by the late fifteenth century, continued well into the mid-nineteenth century.

The slave trade's decline spurred greater exploration inland and various missionizing efforts. Limited zones of areas of late-fifteenth-century Portuguese contact and trade with the kingdoms of Benin (Nigeria) and the Kongo (Democratic Republic of Congo, formerly Zaire) had seen conversions and missionizing to Christianity. Islam had expanded southward through the Sahara Desert since the ninth and tenth centuries (see FIG. 15-7). By the late nineteenth century, many indigenous peoples had converted to Islam along a line that bisected the continent from west to east, including (at its southern boundary) present-day Senegal, most of Mali and Niger, northern Nigeria, most of Chad and Sudan, the eastern coast of Ethiopia (with a large Christian enclave throughout most of the country), Somalia, and Tanzania. Christian missionaries were active in the eighteenth and nineteenth centuries throughout most of the rest of the continent's southern two-thirds, moving inland from coastal settlements. These imported religions affected the local traditional reverence for spirits and ancestor worship, especially in the more elite cultures (kingdoms). They had less impact in the more egalitarian cultures dominating most areas of sub-Saharan Africa.

Many Christian missionaries (both Protestant and Catholic) sent collections of art (masks, figures, decorative arts) back to their home missions, often as evidence of "idolatry," "devil worship," or conversion to Christianity. Therefore, major religious institutions, such as the Vatican, the London Missionary Society, and the Basel (Switzerland) Mission, have important African art collections, as well as manuscript and photographic archives helpful in reconstructing a history of African art. Many artworks from the colonization period are themselves useful documents for historical reconstruction (see "A San Rock Painting as a Historical Document," page 980). In addition, questions asked about a figure or mask in an African community often elicit answers describing origin or changes over time. This information is essential to understanding the history of a people or region or specific art form.

COLONISTS AND COLLECTORS Throughout the colonization period, African art objects also trickled into European royal collections and other high-status or mercantile collections. An increasing interest in Africa's natural resources, such as exotic woods, diamonds, and precious metals, characterized the nineteenth century, and many European nations began to create colonies in Africa during this time. Between about 1885 and 1924, British, Belgian, French, German, Italian, Portuguese, and Spanish trade interests carved virtually the entire continent into European colonies with vast trade networks. Even earlier, Portugal's extensive trade with Africa had led to the creation of African art objects in Sierra Leone expressly for export to Europe (see "Sapi-Portuguese Ivories: A Hybrid Art Form," Chapter 15, page 422). The colonialism period persisted until well after World War II, with most countries in Africa attaining their independence sometime during the early 1960s.

During the late nineteenth century and the early decades of the twentieth century, many European and American museums began to collect art and artifacts from peoples all over the African continent. These collections often came from anthropological field expeditions (later also focusing on art) that sought to amass human artifacts from around the world for comparative study. Predictably, each European colonial power supported expeditions in its own colonies (although some ranged more broadly in the pursuit of collectibles). For example, some of the earliest collections of art from the Asante of

Ghana and Benin in Nigeria now reside in the British Museum, both Ghana and Nigeria being former British colonies. Similarly, German museums hold major art collections from Germany's colonies in present-day Togo, Cameroon, and Tanzania.

THE NATURE OF AFRICAN ART

Context and Meaning

Arts in Africa function in greatly varied human and physical contexts, and knowledge of these contexts is essential for understanding the artworks. Among herding peoples such as the Samburu of Kenya (FIG. **32-1**), for instance, the types of costumes, hairstyles, and jewelry worn are gender specific and age graded so that a Samburu man or woman immediately can tell other group members' ages and marital status by their everyday (as well as ceremonial) clothing and adornments. Most outside observers would not recognize the significance of the different costumes, coiffures, and jewelry.

Among other African groups, wherever dancers present *masquerades* (several maskers together), a performance is understood in one way by a performer but in an entirely different way by an uninitiated child or by a woman the masquerader chases. Further, a single dancer is usually only one unit in a larger ceremonial whole. The ceremony includes the performances, for example, of several or even dozens of different masqueraders who may reenact origin stories or invoke multiple ancestors and nature spirits, as among the Dogon of Mali (FIG. 32-15). In addition, a mask may become more powerful as it grows older, and it eventually may occupy an honored place in a shrine as a power object. Then, no longer a ceremonial mask, both its context and its meaning may have changed. A mask changes radically into a commodity when offered for sale to an art dealer. Spotlighting the same mask under Plexiglas in a museum or using it to adorn a collector's living room also transforms it substantially. Each context offers new viewpoints, a different audience, fresh opportunities for interpretation, and separate meanings.

This chapter briefly surveys African art and artists after about 1800 and explores varied contexts. It combines local information on use, function, and meaning derived from research in Africa with interpretive strategies devised for the most part by outsiders. (Those who reclassify African objects that Africans use socially, spiritually, and politically into "artworks" also are usually outsiders.) We have divided our treatment of African art into three major categories—leadership arts, spiritual arts, and masquerades—but these are only devices for classification. Some art forms operate in two or even all three categories. A Benin royal altar (FIG. 32-4), for instance, is the site of sacrifices that strengthen the king as a ruler. The altar is also an assemblage of historical and ritual "documents" or "texts" that aid in reconstructing Benin art history and ceremonial process. The altar exemplifies other vital dimensions of art, such as its active centrality in the lives of the people who commissioned and use it, its capacity for encoding values and levels of knowledge, and its varied kinds of symbolism.

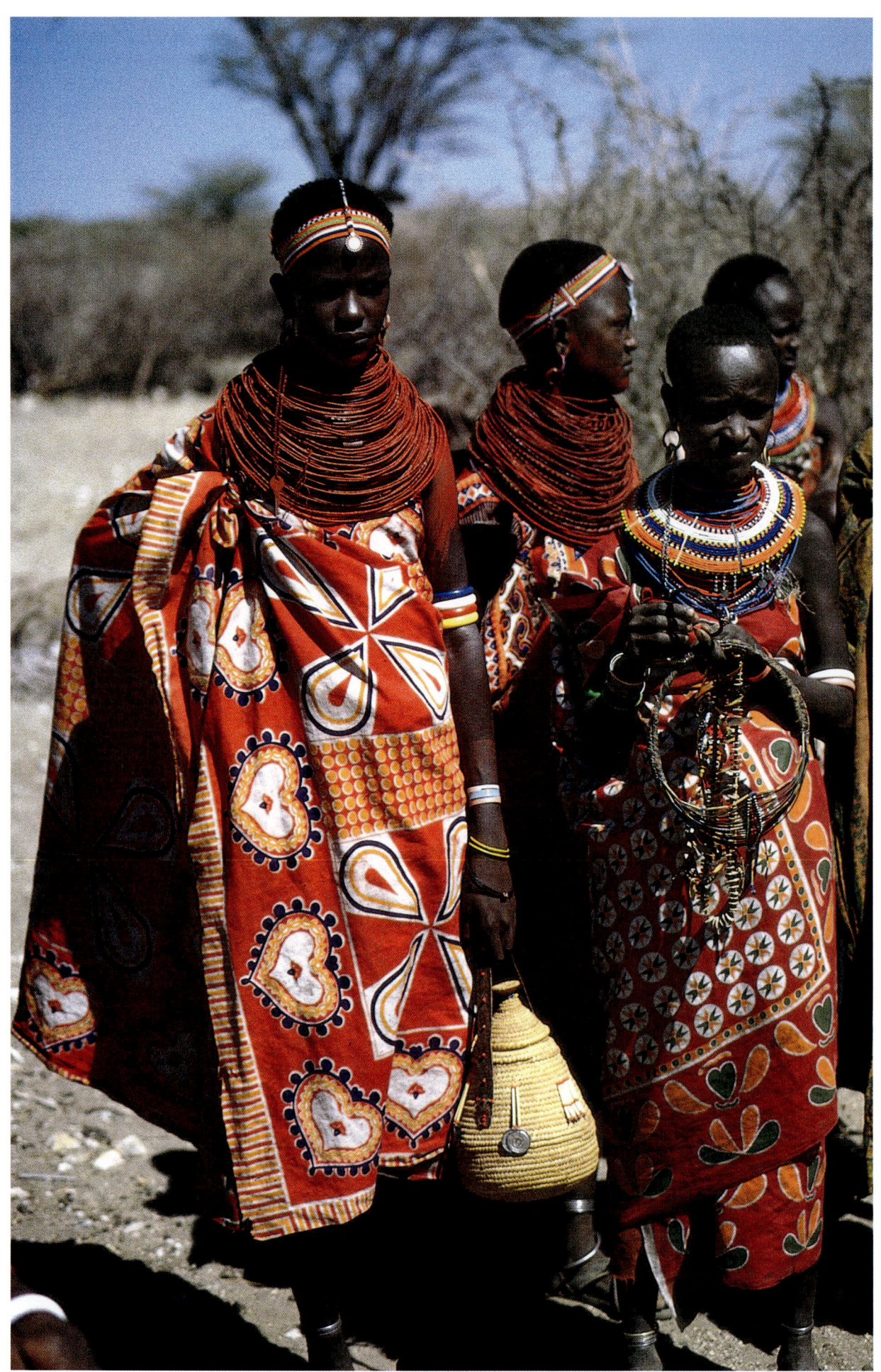

32-1 Unmarried women with printed cloth and beaded jewelry, Samburu, Kenya, photographed in 1987.

Style and Artistic Production

As shown throughout this book, art styles vary not only by individual artist but also according to time and place of manufacture. The notions of period, regional, and personal styles are also valid for Africa, even though early researchers stressed what they saw as fairly homogeneous styles developed by entire ethnic groups. Early observers also saw the art styles of groups such as the Yoruba, Dogon, Dan, Baga, or Baule as fixed over long periods. Recent scholarship documents a far greater diversity and fluidity of style. The Yoruba or Igbo, for example, have many regional styles, and it is now clear that these, as well as individual styles, changed over time.

CONVENTIONALIZATION   Degrees of conventionalization generally characterize African sculpture and painting. Most artists work from a conceptual model rather than perceptually translate observed living human or animal models. Thus each sculptural or painting genre tends to have its own formal conventions, often held in the artist's mind and normally shared by others from the region working in the same genre. Akan peoples of Ghana, for instance, have a longstanding convention of making figures with flat disc-shaped heads. Women who model commemorative ceramic sculpture for display in royal funerary rites and graveyards (FIG. **32-2**) work in this style. So, too, do Asante (an Akan group) men who carve small wooden fertility figures (known individually as *akua ba* or collectively as *akua mma;* FIG. **32-3**), often placed on shrines after a woman successfully con-

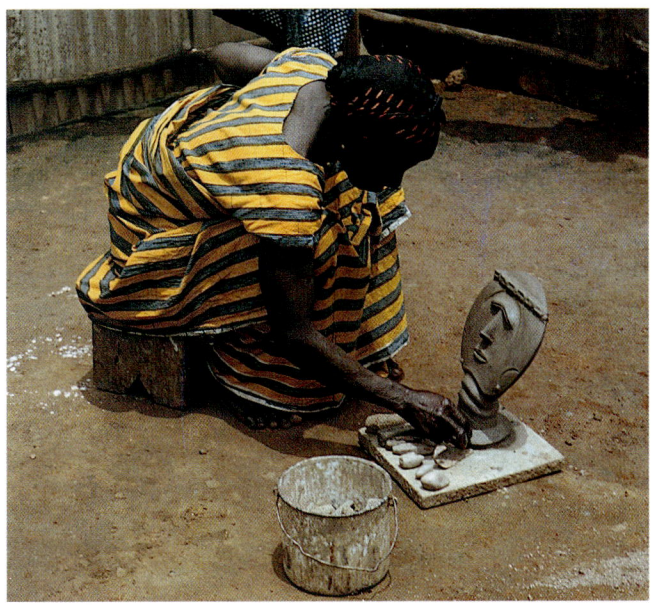

32-2   Woman sculptor finishing ceramic ancestral portrait, Akan, Ghana, photographed in 1965.

ceives a child. Each artist works from and incrementally alters these conceptual models with each new work, as the variations seen in the figures indicate. In the past few decades and in response to influences from Europe and America, however, sculptors often have significantly altered earlier conventions. This chapter later examines some of these changes.

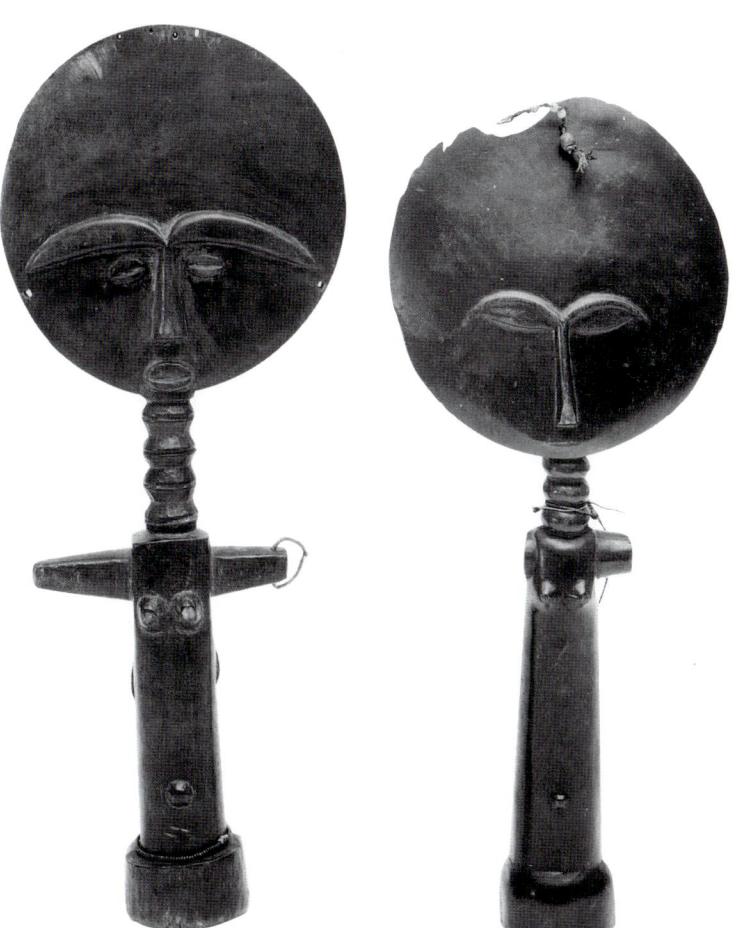

32-3   Two shrine figures *(akua mma)*, Asante, Ghana. Wood, left figure 1′ 1⅝″ high; right figure 1′ 13/16″ high. British Museum, London.

GENDER ROLES IN ART PRODUCTION   Until the past decade or two, art production in Africa has been quite rigidly gender specific. Men have been (and largely still are) ironsmiths and gold and copper-alloy casters, as well as architects, builders, and carvers. Women are wall and body painters, calabash decorators, potters, and often ceramic sculptors, although men do this in some areas. Both men and women work with beads and weave, men executing narrow strips (later sewn together) on horizontal looms and women working wider pieces of cloth on vertical looms. Much art in process, however, is collaborative. Men may build a clay wall, for example, but women will decorate it. Festivals, invoking virtually all the arts, are truly collaborative. In most regions, too, until recently Africans had not greatly emphasized artists' individuality, even when personal styles are clearly recognizable. This does not mean art is anonymous or that artists are not honored locally. Rather, Africans have tended not to exalt individual innovative artists as much as Western countries have (see "Artists in Africa: The Dan and the Benin Court," page 985).

SUBJECTS AND THEMES

Leadership Arts

The relationships between art and leaders in Africa are pervasive, complex, and multileveled. Art forms leaders invoke range from the obvious—regalia and royal altars—to the more veiled and subtle, such as masquerades conducted for social control and community shrines served by religious specialists who have considerable authority. Leadership arts often overlap, of course, with arts manifesting supernatural aspects.

Numerous formal and functional traits characterize leadership arts, but the overriding one is their contrast with objects ordinary people own or invoke. Elite arts are more durable, more iconographically complex, and more expensive than those of commoners. Wealthy and powerful chiefs, kings, and religious leaders commission art and display and otherwise use it instrumentally—to get things done. Artistically elaborated swords, ancestor heads, and altarpieces from Benin are good examples. They derive their power in part from their placement on the shrines of dynastic ancestors, creating multiple levels of meaning.

ROYAL ANCESTRAL SHRINES   A Benin shrine to the heads of divine royal ancestors (FIG. **32-4**), with its base constructed of sacred riverain clay, features cast-copper-alloy heads, each fitted with an ivory tusk carved in relief. The formerly polished heads, believed to repel evil forces, represent the enduring qualities of kingship through the durability of their material. In Benin, the king's head refers to wisdom, good judgment, and divine guidance for the kingdom (see "The King's Compound in Benin," page 987). Elephant tusk reliefs commemorate important events and personages in the kingdom's history. The bleached white color also signifies purity and the tusks themselves, the vast physical power of elephants, which, like leopards, are metaphors for the king. Other ritual arts on the altar include carved wood rattle-staffs referencing generations of dynastic ancestors in their segmented forms. Such staffs also function musically, as do the several pyramidal bells, to call ancestral spirits.

The central sculpture in the overall hierarchical composition depicts a sacred king flanked by his entourage. The living king, with animal sacrifices at such altars, purifies his own "head" by calling on the collective strength of his ancestors, represented by heads. Thus the varied objects and materials comprising this

32-4 Royal ancestral altar, Benin, Nigeria. Clay, copper alloy, wood, ivory, photographed in 1970.

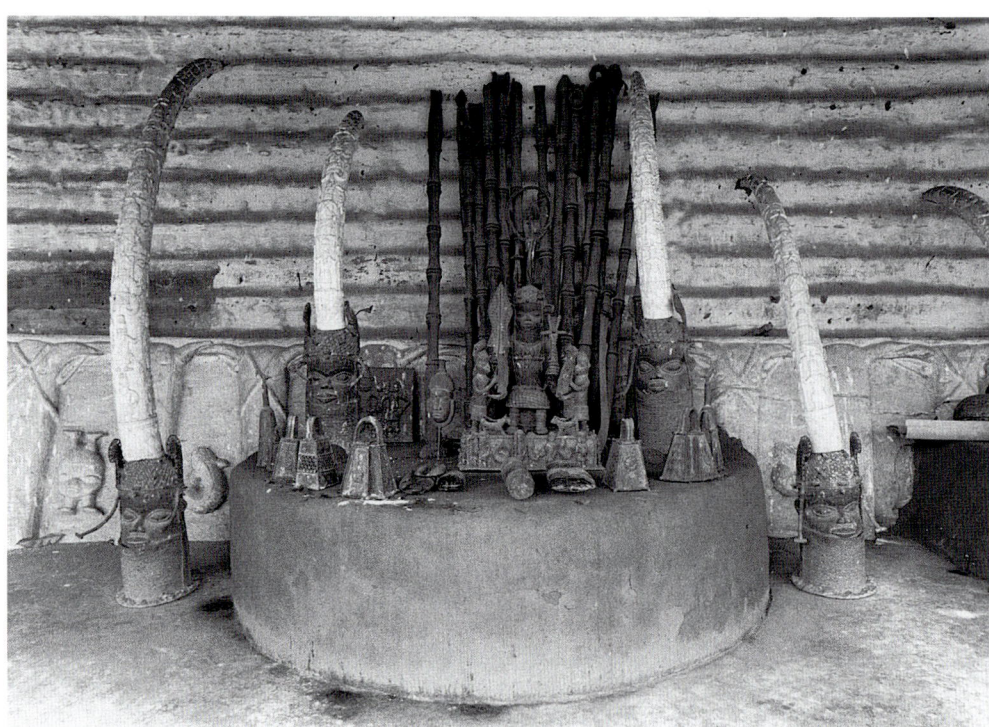

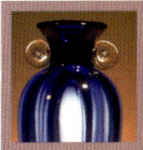

Artists in Africa
The Dan and the Benin Court

As in other times and places, the roles of artists vary significantly among African societies. The differing training and working methods, as well as various artist-patron relationships, can be illustrated effectively by comparing the position of artists in two West African societies—the stateless society of the Dan (Côte d'Ivoire, or Ivory Coast) and royal Benin (Nigeria).

Traditional artists in Dan society were frequently artist-farmers, artist-hunters, artist-blacksmiths, and so forth. In other words, they were not just artists. Most Dan wood-carvers could not support themselves solely as carvers and needed to do other tasks to provide for their wives and families. Dan artists usually apprenticed to acknowledged master carvers and learned the Dan style of making masks and figures by imitating the masters until these teachers felt the apprentices had achieved a level of competence sufficient to go off on their own. Such artists worked on commission for anyone who needed a mask, figure, or utilitarian object, such as a carved ladle. Depending on their reputation, they might carve for patrons from near their village or from far afield, including patrons from neighboring ethnic groups.

Once a patron accepted a work and paid for it, the art object took on a life of its own, gaining prestige and fame according to its ritual and ceremonial effectiveness over time. Its meaning sometimes changed from its original meaning. For instance, a female (singing) spirit mask might become known, over time, as a male (dancing or judging) spirit mask, even though the carver intended its original form and meaning as female.

Artists at the Benin royal court, by contrast, were specialists and belonged to hereditary guilds located in specific parts of the city of Benin in wards for brass casters, blacksmiths, ivory workers, wood-carvers, and so forth. Their patron was first the king (Oba) and second the titled chiefs and lesser dignitaries. Each Benin guild was subdivided into titled rankings, which further organized the types of art objects each could make or assist in making. Benin government included palace associations that managed state affairs. The highest ranking members of the royal artists' guilds belonged to the palace association entrusted with creating royal arts and perpetuating certain past learning. Some of these individuals also had the prerogative of interpreting many of the motifs incorporated in royal art objects.

Within a certain amount of time after each Benin ruler's installation as Oba, he established a shrine to his father. He then instructed the highest ranking artists of the hereditary royal ivory-carvers' guild, for instance, to provide a set of elephants' tusks covered with carved designs for incorporation into the royal ancestral altar (FIG. 32-4). The carvers used motifs passed down for generations, as well as personal inspiration, to create their designs. Carvers of lesser rank were charged with the carving of many other ivory objects, such as bracelets or armlets.

---

altar contribute both artistically and ritually to the imaging of royal power, as well as to its renewal and perpetuation. Altars of lesser chiefs and other high-ranking individuals often have similar altar furnishings, although frequently made of more perishable materials, such as wood or clay.

EMBLEMS OF ROYAL POWER Other African art forms, especially finely decorated stools and chairs, elevate leaders, contributing to their actual and figurative superiority and grandeur. Weapons, umbrellas, and other regalia—clothing, hats, staffs, fly whisks—amplify leaders, contributing to their monumentality, their commanding presence. The image of the Bamum, Cameroon, King Njoya sitting on a wooden, cloth-covered, and beaded throne outside his palace (FIG. 32-5) attests to the sumptuousness of courtly display and testifies to his power over his subjects and his enemies. Carved male and female figures stand behind him, and a row of smaller figures decorates the footrest. Various figures used as support posts on his palace facade refer to his many male and female subjects. The royal imagery incorporates varied power symbols, such as spiders and double-headed snakes, as well as servants and people who make up the king's retinue. The armed warriors on guard signify his military strength.

"AESTHETIC OVERLOAD" Seated in state, walking or riding in a festival, and supported by a costumed entourage, African chiefs and kings with rich attire and symbolic implements evoke both majesty and mystery. Rich, complex images of leaders project political and spiritual powers. These messages derive frequently from what scholars have called "intentional design redundancy" and "aesthetic overload." Such phrases refer to the conscious layering of luxurious garments, jewelry, and weapons; the proliferation of detailing and symbolic iconography; the complexity, cost, and sheer size of compositions; and a general sense of excess. The king (nyim) of the Kuba peoples of the Democratic Republic of Congo, Kot a-Mbweeky III (FIG. 32-6), epitomizes such an assemblage, which constructs him as "larger than life." Messages of wealth and power radiate from the overload of beads, shells, cloth, animal skins and teeth, and feathers used in his costume. A living collage, he embodies power and authority.

The Kuba and related peoples use the raffia palm to make textiles. On a vertical loom, the men weave a plain cloth from this palm's stripped and split leaves. Afterward, the women create elaborate geometric patterns on the cloth by embroidery (to create the pattern outlines) and cut-pile (also called plush) stitching. In the cut-pile technique, women pull

32-5 King Njoya on beaded throne, front of palace, Bamum, Cameroon, photographed in 1912.

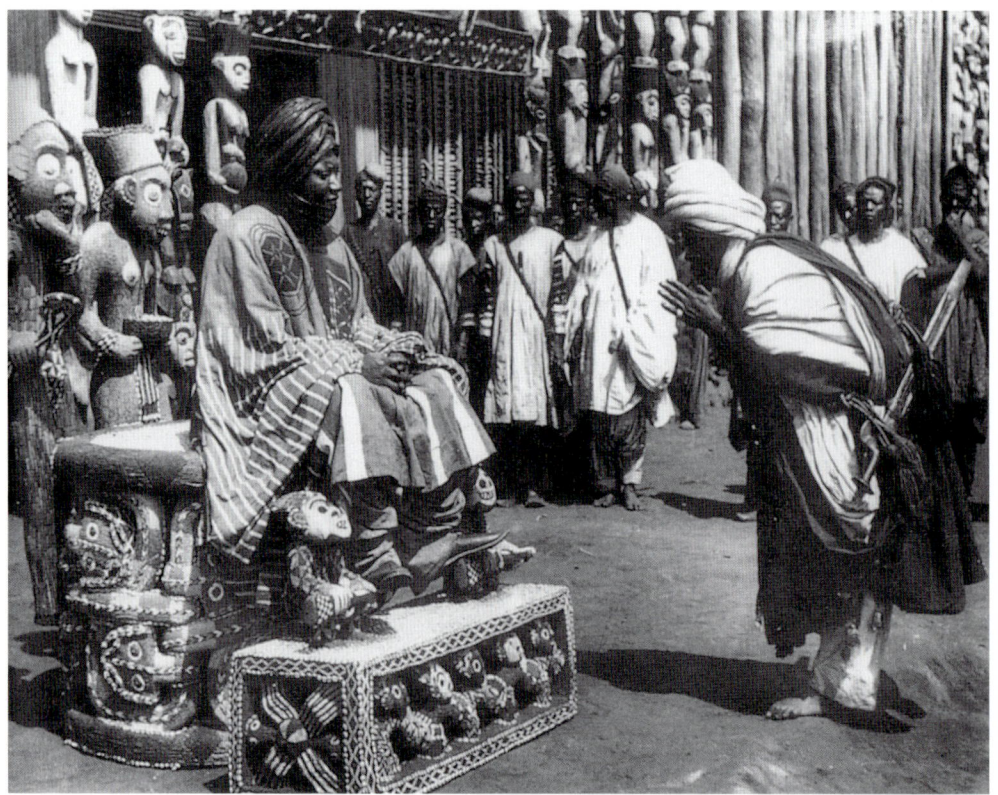

32-6 Kuba King Kot a-Mbweeky III (who has ruled from 1969 to the present) during a display for photographer and filmmaker Eliot Elisofon in early 1970. Mushenge, Democratic Republic of Congo.

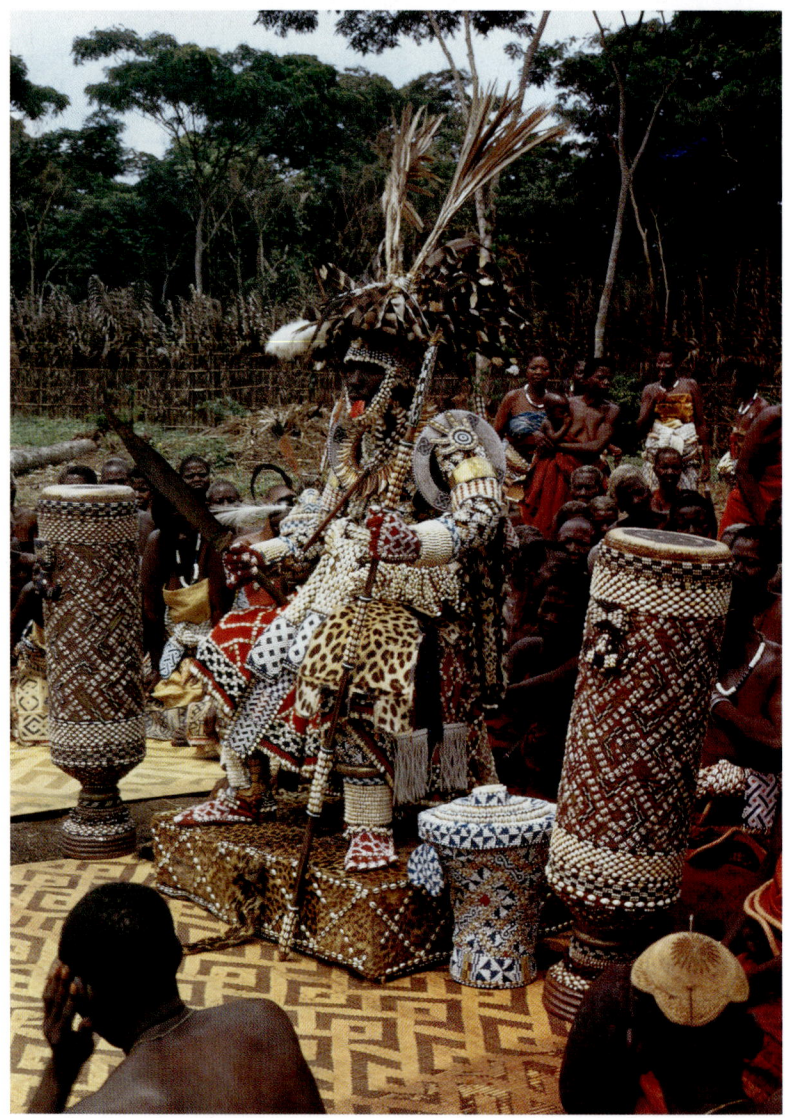

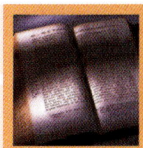

The King's Compound in Benin

In 1897, the British medical doctor H. Ling Roth partici- pated in the British Punitive Expedition that sacked Benin. In 1903, in a book whose title reflects European attitudes at the time toward African art and society in general, he recorded information on the context of Benin art and archi- tecture that remains invaluable today.[1] Roth's book, in addi- tion to providing the most complete account known for Benin City's arts between the seventeenth and late nineteenth centuries, also attests to the continuity of Benin arts and rit- ual-related beliefs from the colonial period to the present. In the first of two passages here, Roth details the placement and appearance of brass heads surmounted by ivory carvings found within the late-nineteenth-century king's personal compound. The description approximates that of the figures shown in a Benin shrine (FIG. 32-4) photographed in 1970.

> Starting with the king's compound and houses and going up the main road on the right, there is an immense wall 20 feet high and 3 or 4 feet at the base, and perhaps 2 feet wide at the top. At the back of this there is a big compound or open space, and it is entered through a doorway, the big door of which is lined with sheets of brass with stamped figures of men and leopards' heads. . . .
>
> Passing through the central door we come to the compound; in it there is a big tree and at its foot there is a deep pit. . . . On the other side of the compound facing the big wall is another wall partly roofed in, and along this is a row of brass heads, and on top of every head is a long, heavy, weather-worn finely carved ivory tusk; near

them and against the wall were the wooden rattles with which, as we were told, captives were killed by being struck on the neck; between the brass heads were brass castings of men on horseback, in armour, in chain mail, etc., and many other articles which have since become familiar to us.[2]

(See FIG. Intro-16, a bronze plaque of the Benin King, mounted on horseback.) Roth then describes the Benin king's reception hall:

> Through this compound to the right is the king's palaver or meeting house, where the king used to sit to meet strangers, etc. The first thing which strikes one here is the metal roof on which, just facing you, is an immense brass snake crawling down with its big head close to the gutter of the roof. There is a sloping roof of Muntz metal [im- ported from Europe] all round this compound, leaving the centre of the compound open to the air and skies. This place is fairly lofty, and all the rafters are of wood carved with rough figures; some of the rafters have been covered with brass sheeting on which figures have been punched. The roof is supported by over a hundred pillars made of bronze sheets riveted together, giving a very good effect. Round the sides, hundreds of people can find accommodation.[3]

[1] H. Ling Roth, *Great Benin: Its Customs, Art and Horrors* (Halifax, England: F. King & Sons, 1903).

[2] Ibid., 175.

[3] Ibid., 175–77.

a small length of raffia fiber strand (or a small bundle of them) through the plain raffia cloth and then cut it, leaving a small tuft on each side about two to three millimeters long. Scraping these tuft ends with a knife blade spreads them out, creating a velvetlike surface. Dyed in various colors, such as red, black, and yellow, these strands create varied geometric decorative fields on the natural beige of the original raffia cloth.

Across the continent, today as in the past, sculpture and regalia, shrines and altars, and masquerades (see later discus- sion) serve temporal and spiritual leaders both as active in- struments of rule or more passive emblems or commemora- tions. African leaders clearly understand the arts as valuable to both exercising and materializing power and authority.

Spiritual Arts

A high percentage of African art has a spiritual dimension. Most figures and masks are symbolic visualizations of unseen supernatural forces. Countless images and shrines have been created as aids to contacting various deities, such as gods of

nature, legendary founding ancestors, and the spirits of peo- ple who have actually lived.

PRIMORDIAL DOGON ANCESTORS A wooden couple from Dogon country in Mali (FIG. 32-7) embodies complex information in a large carving integrating a man and woman on a common base. Although scholars lack proof of this sculpture's exact place of origin, as well as information about its original context, it clearly depicts a married couple and almost certainly represents the primordial founding an- cestors of a subgroup or important family among the Dogon people. The man has a quiver and the woman a baby on their backs. Thus, the work establishes primary social roles—the man as hunter-warrior and the woman as child- bearer-nurturer. The man is also shown as dominant, typi- cally indicated by size, and protective, by his gesture. The carver rejected naturalism in favor of a rectilinear conceptu- alization some scholars view as based on philosophical sym- bolism and characterizing several Dogon styles. The sculptor depicted all body parts but simplified them, rendering them tubular and defining them geometrically to reveal complex vertical and horizontal rhythms. The woman's tubular lip plug, or *labret,* echoes the man's beard. The man's right hand

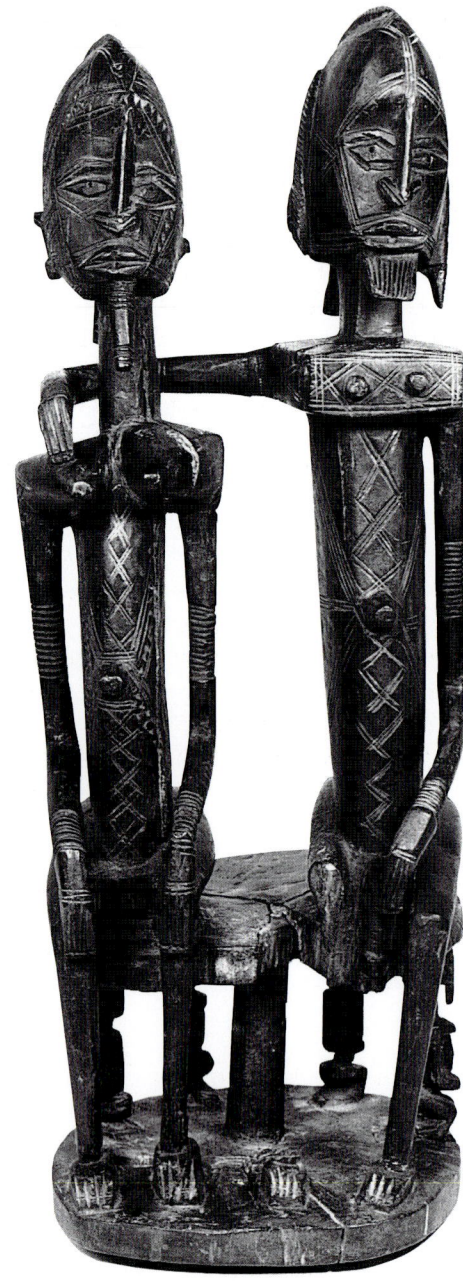

32-7 Ancestral couple(?), Dogon, Mali, circa nineteenth century, photographed in 1975. Wood, 2′ 6″ high.

rests over the top of the woman's right breast, while his left hand rests over his genitals, perhaps symbolically referring to fertility. Heads and torsos are exaggerated, probably for ideological emphasis, as is documented for several other African peoples. It is likely this carving served a symbolic and spiritual function, probably in a shrine for an entire community.

SHRINES FOR BAULE DIVINERS Most Baule figural sculptures of Cote d'Ivoire, such as the male and female seen here (FIG. **32-8**), appear in personal shrines hidden away in the interiors of their owners' houses. A trance diviner ordered these figures, probably bush spirits, as a source of inspiration and power. Offerings made on or near such figures to feed and honor the spirits thus appeased them and thereby induced them to care for, cure, or otherwise bless human petitioners. Diviners may have several such carved shrine figures,

fashioned to represent handsome people in the prime of life. Even though by local standards bush spirits are believed to be unattractive or even ugly, carvers make refined and deliberately beautiful sculptures of them, with delicate hairstyles and carefully rendered scarification.

IGBO HOUSES FOR THE GODS Among the Igbo of southeastern Nigeria, powerful nature gods sometimes demand that their human constituents build an Mbari house. These elaborate unified complexes consist of numerous unfired clay sculptures and paintings, occasionally more than a hundred in one Mbari, in a specially designed architectural setting. The Igbo build these adobe houses as sacrifices to major community deities, often Ala, goddess of the earth. In the Mbari shown (FIG. **32-9**), the thunder god Amadioha sits next to his wife. He wears modern clothing, while his wife appears with traditional body markings and coiffure. These differing modes of dress relate to the Igbo concepts of modernity and tradition, both viewed as positive aspects of one's existence. The artist enlarged and extended both figures' torsos, necks, and heads to express their aloofness, dignity, and

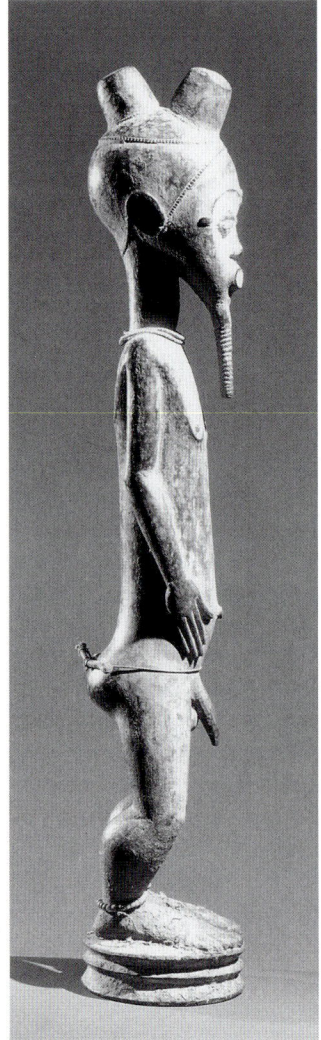
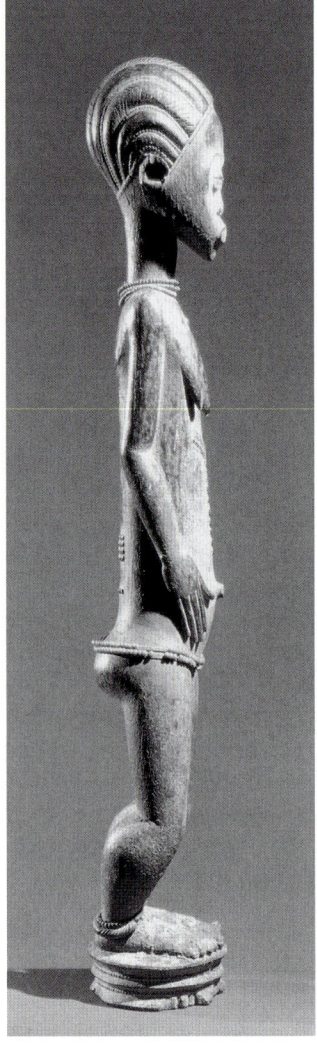

32-8 Bush spirit(?) pair for trance diviner, Baule, from Côte d'Ivoire, nineteenth and early twentieth centuries. Wood, beads, kaolin, male 1′ 9¾″ high, female 1′ 8⅝″ high. Metropolitan Museum of Art, New York (Michael C. Rockefeller Memorial Collection, gift of Nelson A. Rockefeller).

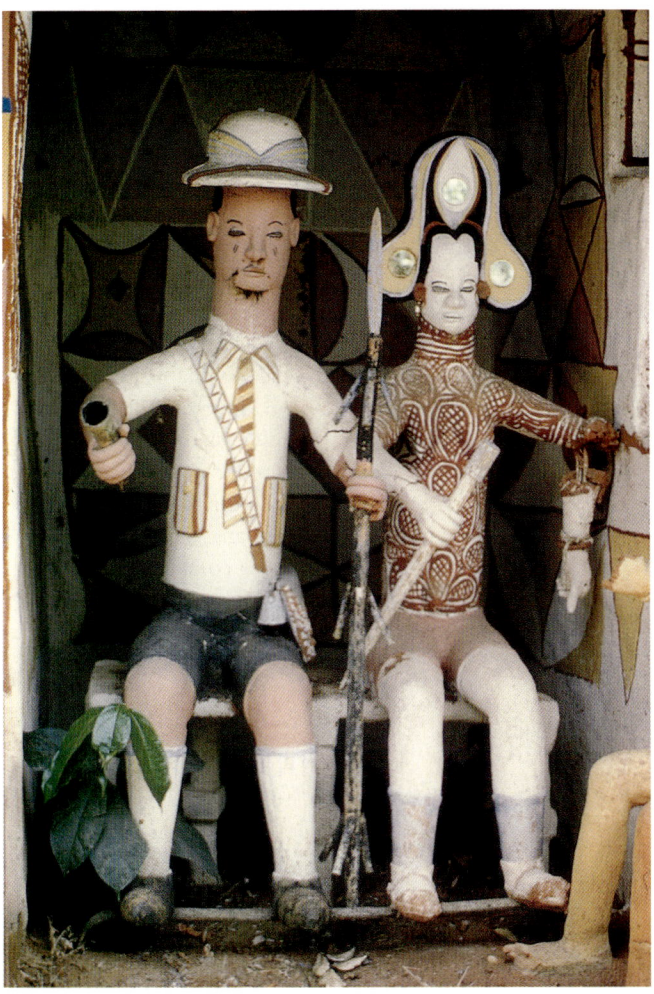

32-9 Mbari thunder god (Amadioha) in modern dress with wife, Igbo, Umugote Orishaeze, Nigeria, photographed in 1966. Clay. .

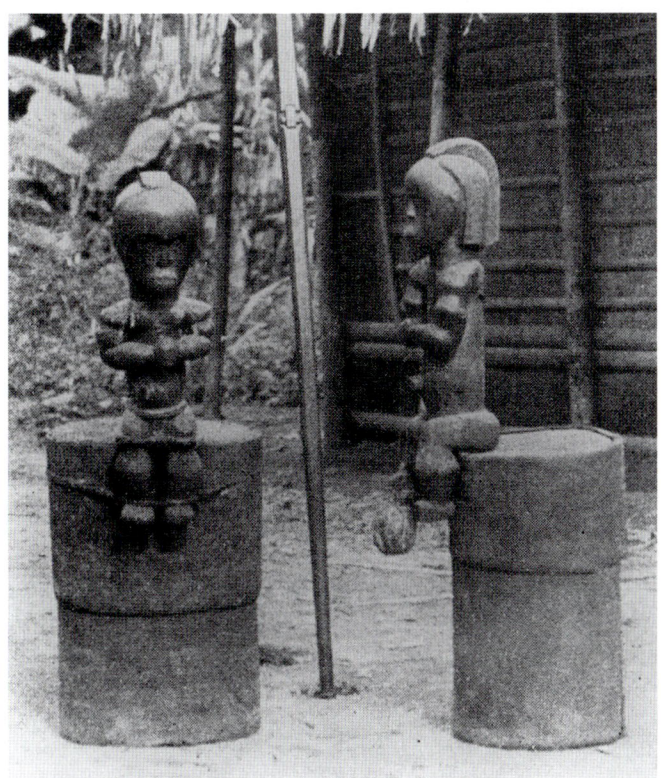

32-10 Reliquary guardian figures on bark boxes, Fang, Cameroon, photographed in 1914. Wood.

power. More informally posed figures and groups appear on the other sides of the house—beautiful, amusing, or frightening figures of animals, humans, and spirits taken from mythology, history, dreams, and everyday life.

The Mbari construction process, veiled in secrecy behind a fence, is a stylized world-renewal ritual, while the completed monument shows off that world after the Mbari is ritually opened. Ceremonies for opening the house to public view indicate that the god accepted the sacrificial offering (of the house) and, for a time at least, will be benevolent. An Mbari house never undergoes repair. Instead, the Igbo allow it to disintegrate and return to its source, the earth. Unfortunately, the Igbo today rarely make Mbari complexes for ritual purposes, and two recent ones, sponsored by the Nigerian government essentially as "museums," were constructed of cement.

RELIQUARY GUARDIANS Among the Kota (Ndassa-Wumbu) of Gabon and Fang of southern Cameroon and Gabon, reliquary figures function in a virtually identical way, although the artistic forms of both differ. Both types of figures protect objects important to the gods. Two wooden Fang reliquary figures sitting atop circular bark boxes containing ancestral relics (FIG. 32-10) are both studies in sculptural power held in check by their erect postures and contained gestures, their hands resting across the upper chest. The front and back views of a Kota reliquary guardian (Mbulu-Ngulu) figure (FIG. 32-11), more abstract in form, emphasize the head and headdress while leaving out any reference to the body except for a lozenge shape that may refer to arms held in a downward diamond-shaped gesture.

A KUBA ROYAL PORTRAIT In royal artistic traditions such as that of the Kuba of the Democratic Republic of Congo, figures commemorating living and dead kings remained at the court for ceremonial use. One of these, a male figure (ndop), represents King Kot a-Ntshey (formerly Kata Mbula; FIG. 32-12), who reigned in the first half of the eighteenth century. In this image, the king wears a simple hat, a cowrie-covered belt, and arm and leg rings. In addition, a drum carved in front of him symbolizes his skill as a musician. In contrast to the martial and power-oriented display of the living Kuba king (FIG. 32-6), this figure seems peaceful and contemplative. According to Kuba royal traditions, such figures were placed next to an ailing king near death to absorb some of his life essence. They also were kept in his wives' quarters as a symbolic surrogate during his lifetime and when he was absent from the palace.

KONGO IMAGES OF WOMEN AND MEN Ancestral and power images of the Kongo peoples of the Democratic Republic of Congo, conventionalized sculptural forms, serve a variety of purposes—commemoration, healing, divination, and social regulation. The woman and child carving we illustrate (FIG. 32-13) represents Kongo royalty. It may commemorate an ancestor or more probably a legendary founding clan mother, a genetrix. The Kongo called some of these figures "white chalk," a reference to the spiritual strength of white kaolin clay. Diviners owned them.

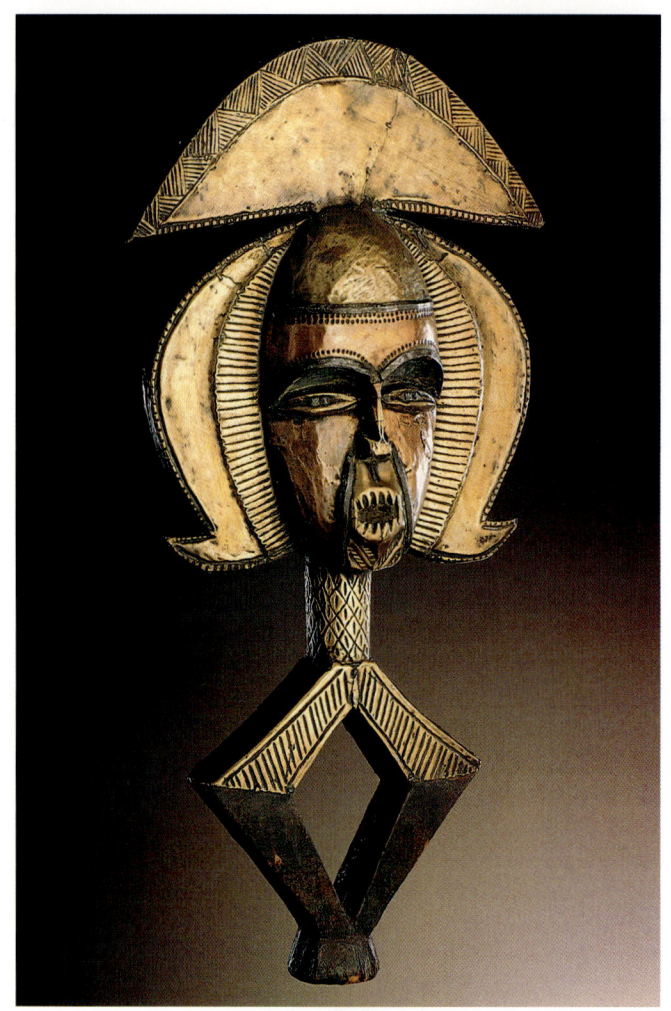

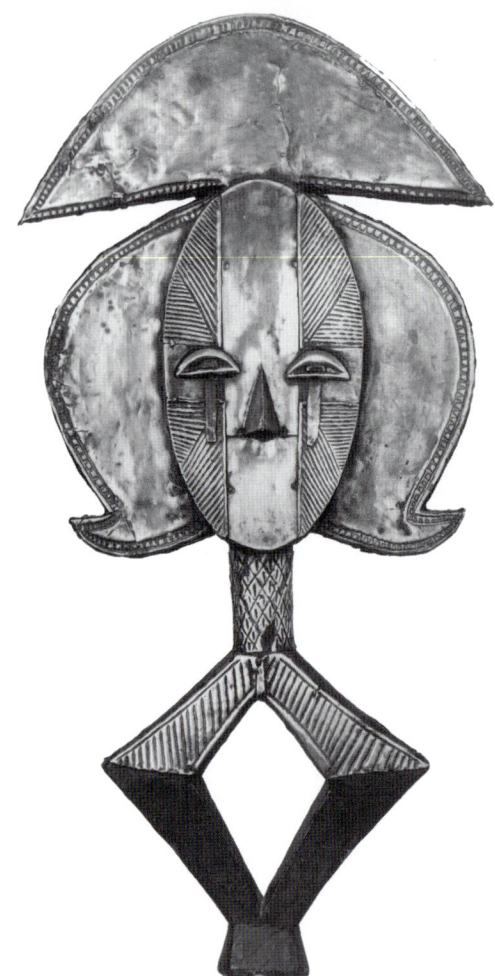

32-11 Front and back view of reliquary guardian figure (Mbulu-Ngulu), Kota (Ndassa-Wumbu), from Gabon, nineteenth and twentieth centuries. Wood, copper, iron, brass, 1′ 9 1/16″ high. Barbier-Mueller Museum, Geneva.

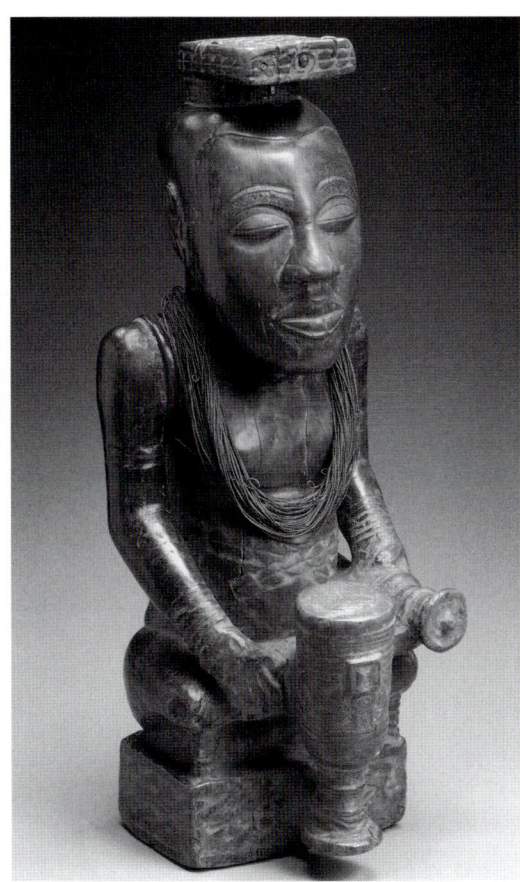

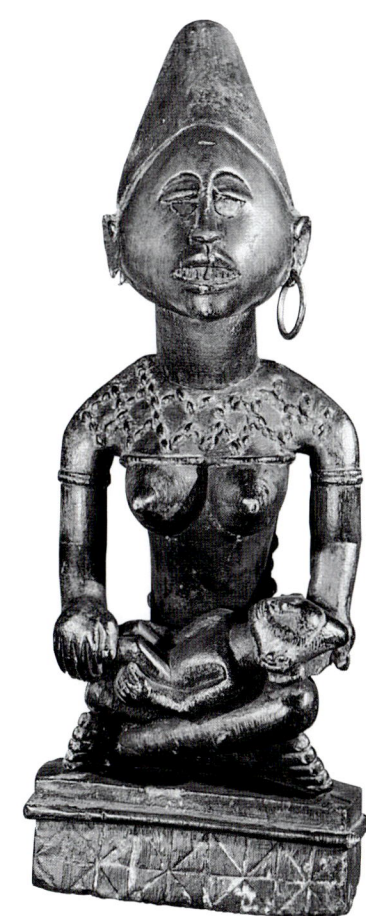

32-12 Male figure *(ndop)* representing King Kot a-Ntshey (formerly Kata Mbula), Kuba, from Democratic Republic of Congo, eighteenth and nineteenth centuries approx. 1′ 8″. Wood, beads, metal. Musée Royal de l'Afrique Centrale, Tervuren.

The large standing male carving (FIG. **32-14**), bristling with nails and blades, is a Kongo power figure *(Nkisi n'kondi)* consecrated by a trained priest using precise ritual formulas. When still in use in Africa, such images embodied spirits believed to heal and give life or sometimes capable of inflicting harm, disease, or even death. Each power figure had its own specific role, just as it wears its particular medicines—here protruding from the abdomen and featuring a cowrie shell.

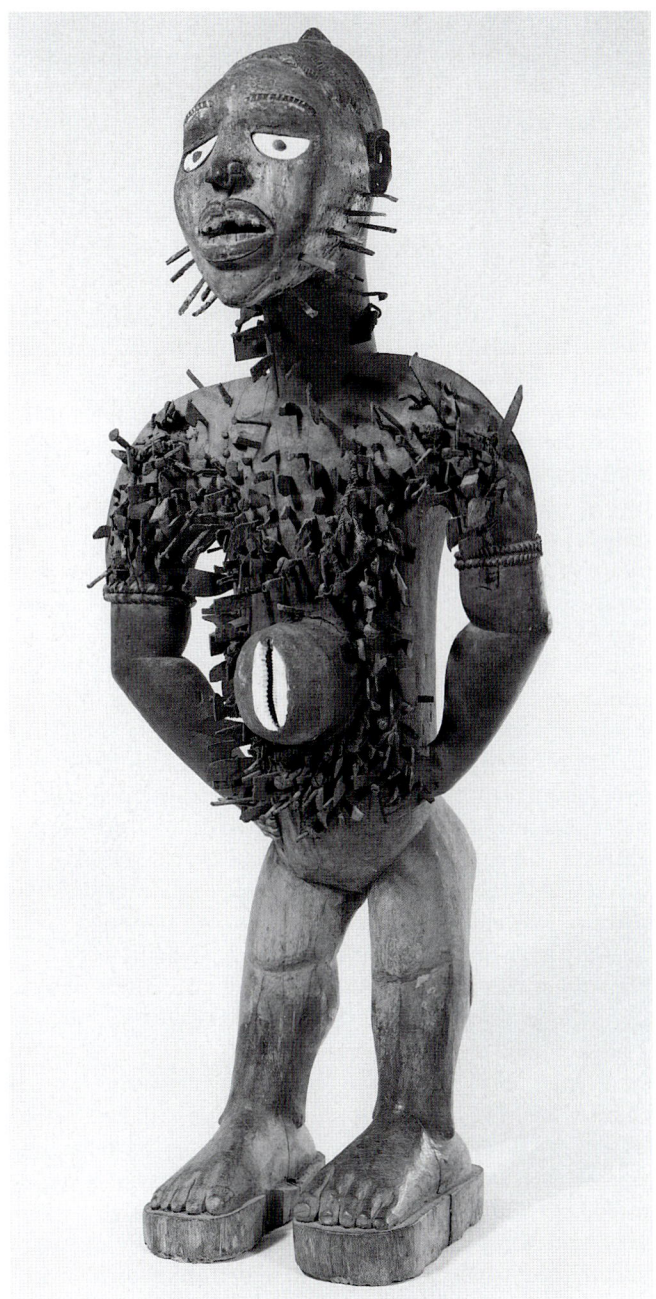

32-13 Ancestral figure, Kongo, from Democratic Republic of Congo, nineteenth and twentieth centuries. Wood and brass, 1′ 4″ high. Musée Royal de l'Afrique Centrale, Tervuren.

32-14 Nail figure (Nkisi n'kondi), Kongo, from Shiloango River area, Democratic Republic of Congo, ca. 1875–1900. Wood, nails, blades, medicinal materials with cowrie shell, 3′ 10¾″ high. Detroit Museum of Art, Detroit, Michigan (Eleanor Clay Ford Fund for African Art).

The Kongo also activated every image differently. Owners appealed to the forces lodged in this Kongo figure each time they inserted a nail or blade. People invoke other spirits by a certain chant, by rubbing them, or by applying special powders. Their roles varied enormously, from curing minor ailments to stimulating crop growth and from punishing thieves to weakening an enemy in warfare. Very large figures, such as the Kongo male, had exceptional ascribed powers. Although benevolent for their owners (entire communities, in some cases), the figures stood at the boundary between life and death, and most villagers held them in awe. Today, however, power images of this sort are more likely found in museums than in villages.

The pervasive religious arts of Africa greatly vary, from small, simple disc-headed figures aiding women in childbirth to purifying community-sponsored Mbari rituals involving the construction of a new symbolic world. People throughout Africa still invoke ancestors and different spirit powers, especially those of nature, to help them maintain productivity, good health, and a balanced social order. Although traditional religious institutions have been weakened in recent decades, they are still viable in many areas.

Masquerades

The masquerade arts are crucially important in Africa even today, but especially before the advent of colonial rule, African masking societies boasted extensive regulatory and judicial powers. These governmental functions were particularly forceful in stateless societies, such as those of the Dan or Igbo, where masks sometimes became so powerful they had their own priests and served as oracles. Societies empowered maskers to apprehend witches (usually defined as socially destructive people) and sometimes to take human life. Normally, however—especially today—masks are less threatening and more educational and entertaining. Masked dancers embody either ancestors, seen as briefly returning to the human realm, or various nature spirits called upon for their special powers.

A mask, a costume ensemble's focal point, combined with held objects, music, and dance gestures invokes a specific named spirit character. The several maskers of a masquerade perform more-or-less strongly ritualized dramas. Some masked dramas reenact creation stories, while others may parody behavior considered deviant or excessive. The maskers perform a very broad range of dramatic behaviors. Sometimes they enact animal traits, but more often their behavior symbolizes various human characteristics. African masks, in fact, vary in function or effect along a continuum from weak spirit power and strong entertainment value to those rarely, if ever seen but possessing vast executive powers backed by powerful shrines. Most function between these extremes, crystallizing varieties of human behavior—caricatured, ordinary, amusing, bizarre, serious. Such actions inform and affect audience members because they are staged and framed within the masquerade performance, normally only an occasional event.

Thus, masks and masquerades mediate between men and women, youths and elders, the initiated and uninitiated, the powers of nature and those of human agency, and even life and death. For many groups in West and central Africa, masking plays an active role in the socialization process, especially for men, who control most masking on the continent. Maskers carry boys away from their mothers to bush initiation camps, put them through ordeals and schooling, and welcome them back to society months or even years later as men.

DOGON MASQUERADES   Elaborate cyclical Dogon masquerades in Mali dramatize creation stories. According to these legends, women were the first ancestors to imitate spirit maskers and thus the first human masqueraders. Men later took masks over, forever barring women from direct involvement with masking processes. A mask, Satimbe (FIG. 32-15), who appears to represent all women, commemorates this legend. In ceremonies called Dama, held every three to six years to honor the lives of people who have died since the last

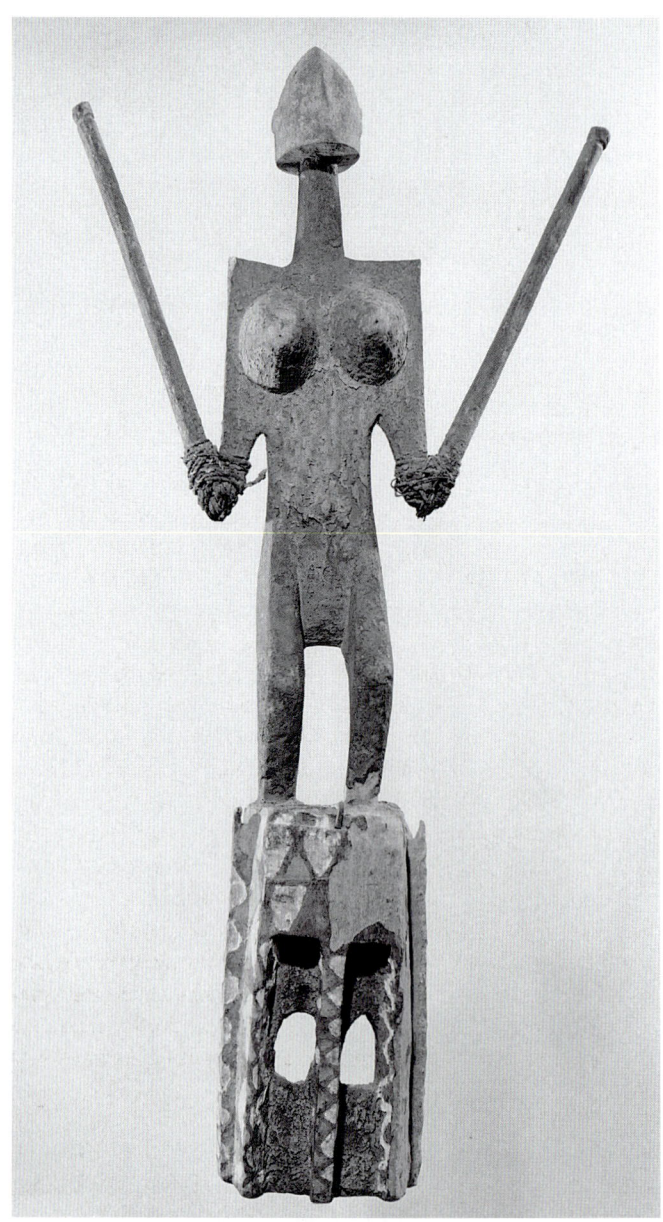

32-15   Satimbe mask, Dogon, from Mali, early twentieth century. Wood. Private collection.

full pendulous breasts, characterizes the ideal Baga woman, who bears many healthy children. Young men who aspire to hard work in the fields wear this heavy mask, thereby associating it with agricultural fertility and well-being. The male Banda mask embodies the forms of a crocodile (jaw), human (face and coiffure), antelope (horns), serpent (body patterns), and chameleon (tail) in a truly imaginative composite of the supernatural. It appears that earlier in the twentieth century, this mask served a sacred policing function, whereas today it primarily entertains.

WOMEN AS MASK DANCERS   Although men own and perform most masks, women control and dance certain masks in several adjacent cultures of Sierra Leone and Liberia, such as the Mende (see "Mende Women as Maskers," page 995). With a glistening black surface evoking ancestral spirits newly emergent from their underwater

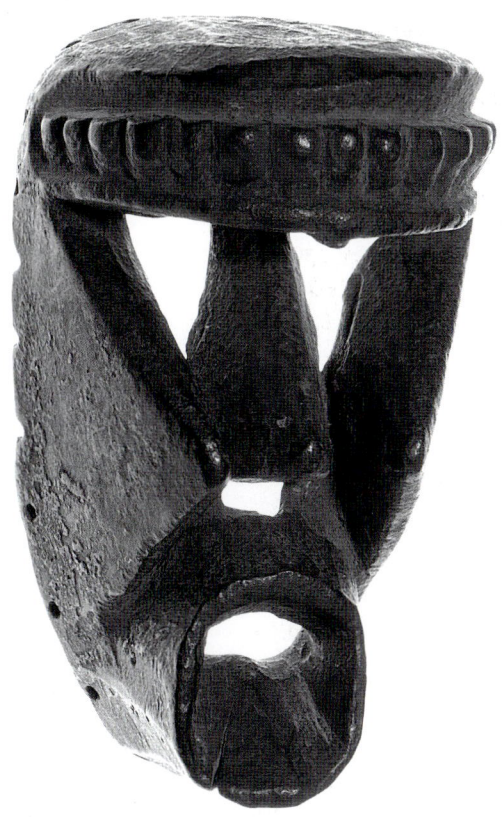

32-16   Mask (Kagle), Dan, from Liberia, nineteenth century. Wood, 9″ high. Yale University Art Gallery, New Haven, Connecticut (gift of Mr. and Mrs. James M. Osborn for the Linton Collection of African Art).

Dama, Satimbe is among the dozens of different masked spirit characters who escort dead souls away from the village, sending them off to the land of the dead. Once they are ancestors, the deceased are enjoined to benefit their living descendants and stimulate agricultural productivity. Thus the Dogon invite ancestors back into the human community periodically to be fed, praised, and shown respect by the living.

DAN SPIRIT MASKS   Among the noncentralized Dan people of Liberia, the ownership of spirits—some manifested as masks—provides major access to sociopolitical and spiritual power. The numerous mask types, all controlled and danced by men, include police, chasers, pretty singers, firemen, warriors, strangers, and animals. The same Dan artist might carve fairly naturalistic polished female masks and rougher abstracted male masks composed of thrusting and receding positive and negative shapes (FIG. **32-16**). Without field information, the exact spirit character or use of these masks cannot be known, because functions change over time. A mask could begin its "life" as a benign female entertainer yet gain spiritual energy over a few generations to become a powerful judge or oracle.

MALE AND FEMALE BAGA MASKS   Two types of masks embodying female/male complementary opposition include a female headdress, the dance of D'amba (FIG. **32-17**), and the elaborate Banda (or Kumbaruba) mask (FIG. **32-18**) from the Baga Sitemu of Guinea. The D'amba mask, with its

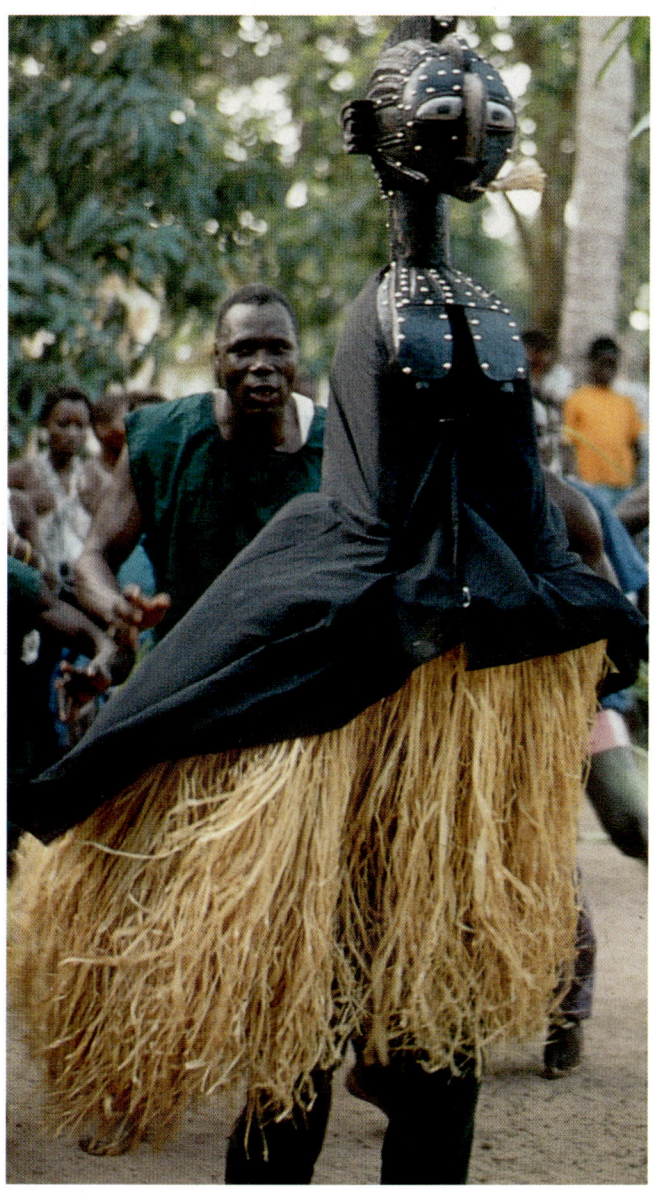

32-17   Female headdress (D'amba dance), Baga Sitemu, Guinea, photographed in 1990.

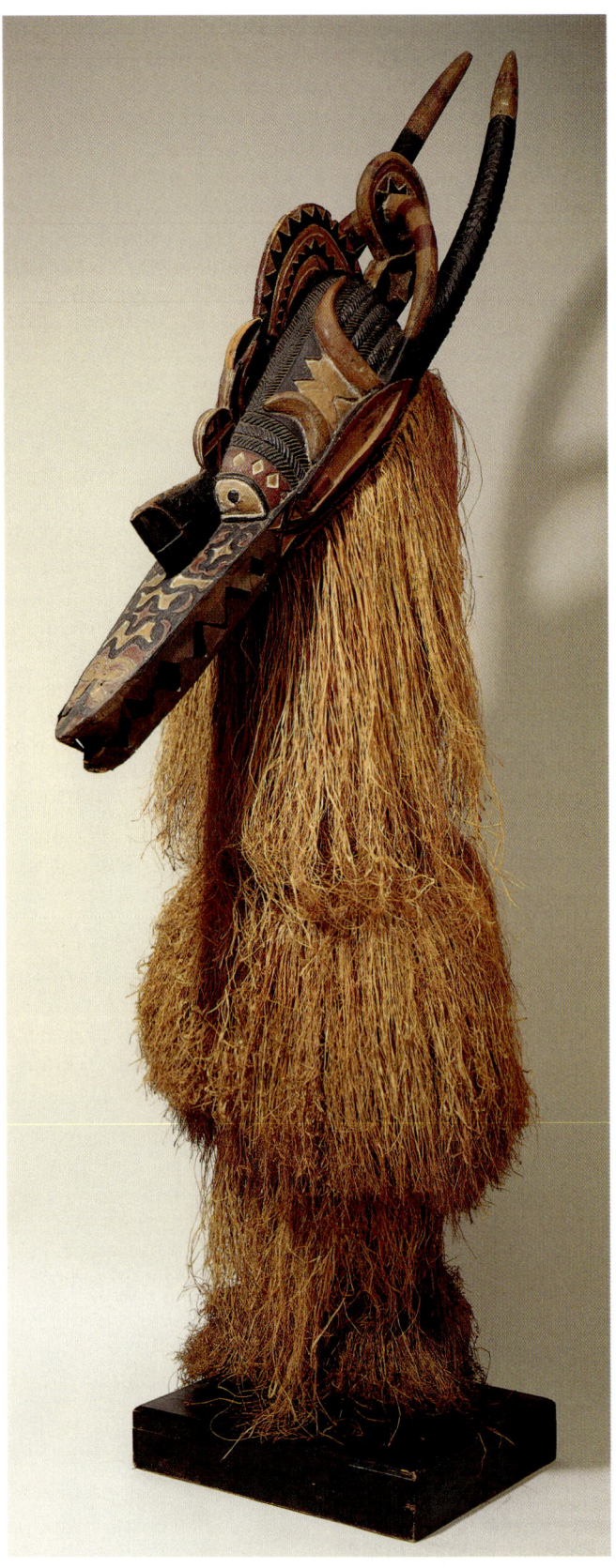

32-18 Mask (Banda/Kumbaruba), Nalu/Baga, from Guinea, late nineteenth century. Wood, metal, pigment, raffia, 5′ 2 3/16″. Bernisches Historisches Museum, Bern.

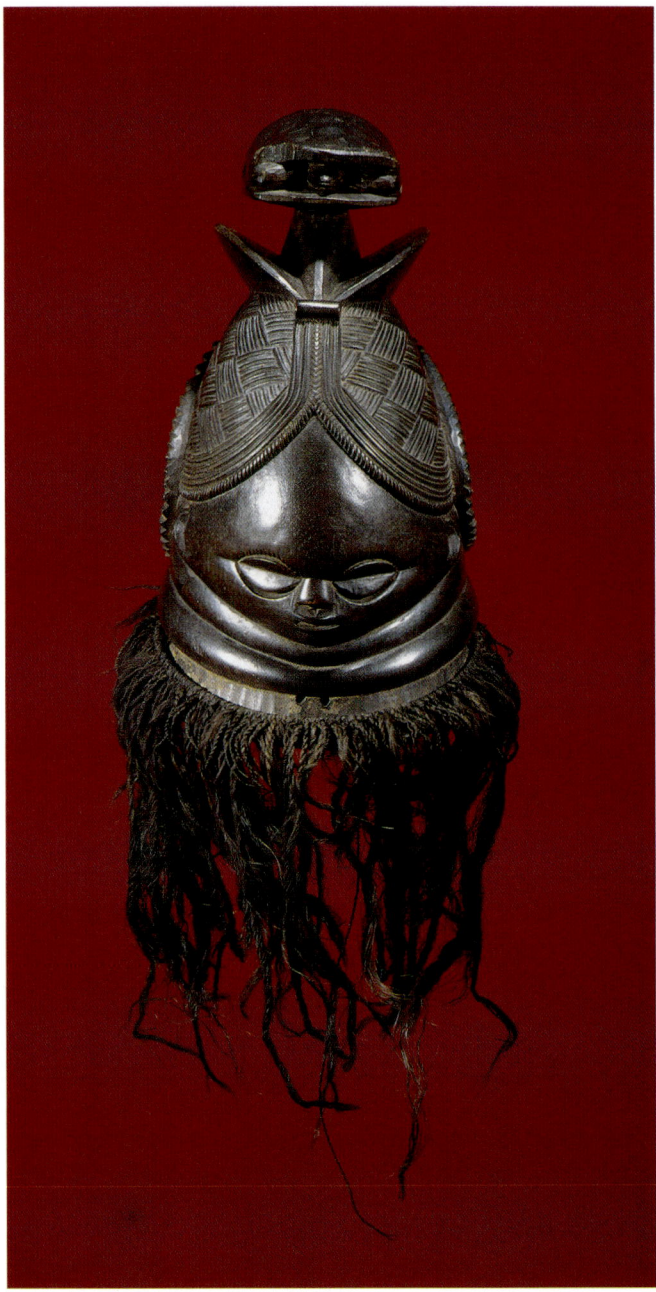

32-19 Female mask, Mende, from Sierra Leone. Wood, pigment, 1′ 2 2/4″ high. Fowler Museum of Cultural History, University of California, Los Angeles (gift of the Wellcome Trust).

homes (also symbolized by the turtle on top; FIG. **32-19**), this mask and its parts refer to ideals of female beauty, morality, and behavior. A high broad forehead signifies wisdom and success. Intricately woven or plaited hair is the essence of harmony and order found in ideal households, also symbolized by mats and textiles. A small closed mouth and downcast eyes indicate the silent, serious demeanor expected of recent initiates.

A BAULE PORTRAIT MASK Among the Baule people of Côte d'Ivoire, Gbagba masks entertain in performances symbolizing the importance of civilized aspects of village life and culture. The performers wear various animal and human masks in a hierarchy ranging from domesticated animals to bush animals to ideal humans in female and male

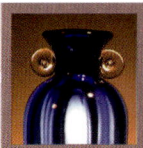

ART AND SOCIETY

Mende Women as Maskers

The Mende and neighboring peoples of Sierra Leone and Liberia are unique in Africa in that women actually wear masks (FIG. 32-19) and costumes that conceal them totally from the audience in attendance on the occasion of their performance. The Sande society of the Mende is the women's counterpart to the men's Poro society. Both societies are associated with the initiation, education, and acculturation of female and male youth, respectively, into productive adulthood. Women leaders who dance these masks serve as priestesses and judges during the three years the women's society controls the ritual calendar (alternating with the men's society in this role), thus serving the community as a whole. Women maskers, also initiators, teachers, and mentors, help girl novices with their transformations into educated and marriageable women. Masked spirits and their symbolic attributes play a major role in girls' initiations among the Mende and several neighboring peoples.

The male Poro society uses masked costumes called Gbini and Goboi in their society rites, associating these masqueraders with powerful bush spirits and the color white in the domain of male chiefly powers. The Sande society associates their Sowie masks with water spirits and the color black, which the society, in turn, connects with human skin color and the civilized world. The women wear these helmet masks on top of their heads as headdresses, with black raffia and cloth costumes to hide the wearers' identity during public performances. Elaborate coiffures, shiny black color, dainty triangular-shaped faces with slit eyes, rolls around the neck, and actual and carved versions of amulets and various emblems on the top commonly characterize Sowie masks. These symbolize the adult women's roles as wives, mothers, providers for the family, and keepers of medicines for use within the Sande society and the society at large.

Sande society patrons commission the masks from male carvers, with the carver and patron determining the type of mask needed for a particular society purpose. The Mende often keep, repair, and reuse masks for many decades, thereby preserving them as models for subsequent generations of carvers.

portrait masks (Mblo). The example illustrated here (FIG. 32-20) is a portrait mask carved about 1913 by OWIE KIMOU (d. 1948) to represent madame Moya Yanso, an individual celebrated during her youth for her great beauty and her ability as a dancer. Throughout her long life, madame Yanso (the woman pictured, beside her stepson) accompanied her mask as a nonmasked dancer, while first her husband and then later other close male relatives donned the mask that honored her youthful charms and accomplishments. When she no longer could dance with it in old age, her granddaughter accompanied the mask, until it was sold in the mid-1990s.

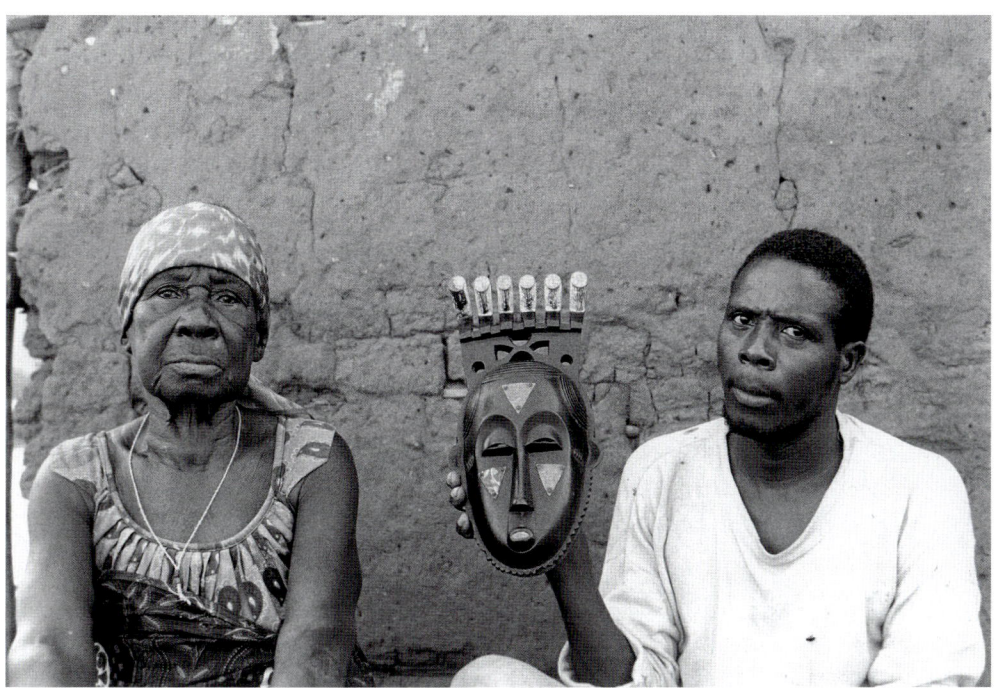

32-20 OWIE KIMOU, Gbagba portrait mask (Mblo) of Moya Yanso and stepson, Kouame Ndri, Kami village, Baule, Côte d'Ivoire, carved around 1913, photographed in 1971.

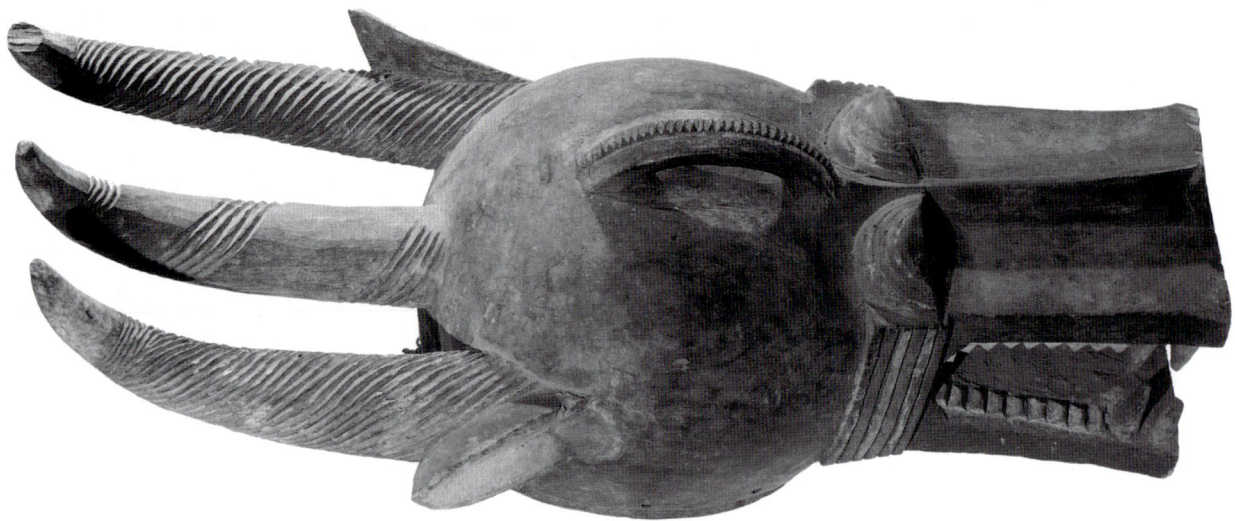

32-21 Three-horned bush-spirit mask *(bo nun amuin),* Baule, from Côte d'Ivoire, late nineteenth century. Wood and pigment, 2′ 11$\frac{7}{16}$″ long. Musée de l'Homme, Paris.

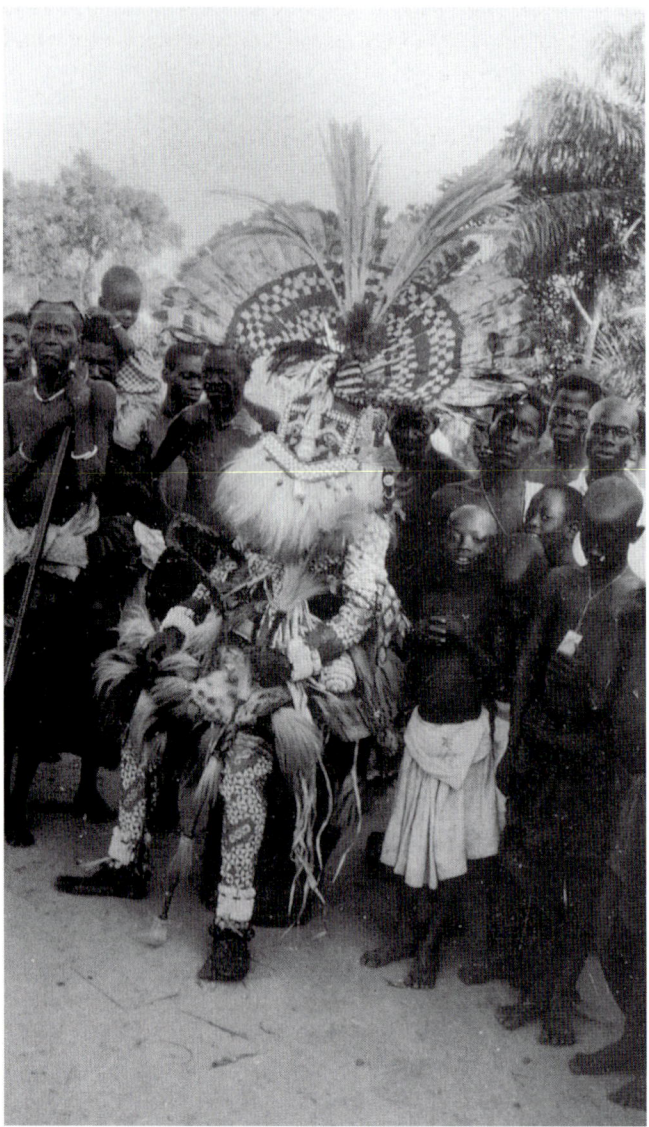

32-22 Mythical ancestor mask *(moshambwooy* at rest), Kuba, Democratic Republic of Congo, photographed in 1938.

THE POWER OF THE BUSH In direct contrast and opposition to the Mblo portrait and other Gbagba animal and human village masks, the Baule composite imaginary animal masks *(bo nun amuin,* FIG. **32-21**) represent powers of the male-oriented bush. The costume accompanying these masks consists of raffia from the bush, rather than cloth—a product of the civilized village. Such masks often feature horizontal placement of forms, with a monstrous toothy mouth, horns thrusting upward, and bulging cone-shaped eyes, all

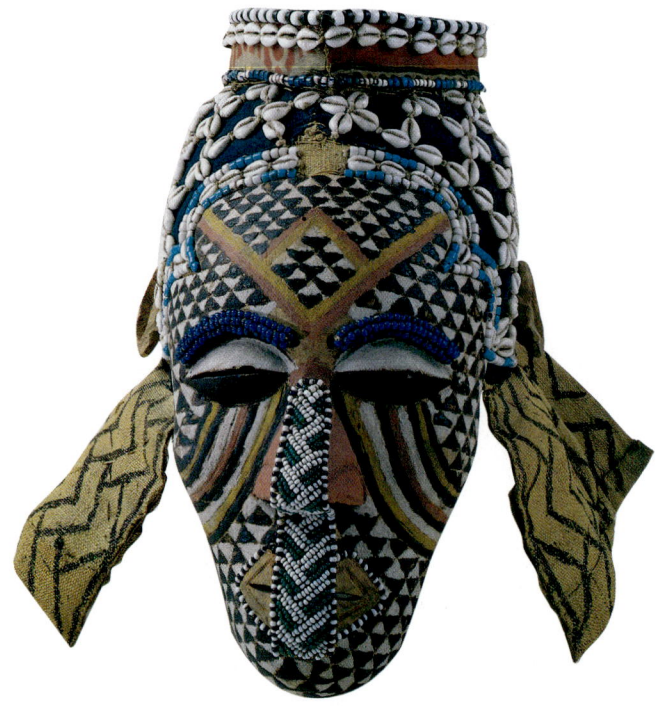

32-23 Mythical ancestor mask *(ngady amwaash),* Kuba, from Democratic Republic of Congo, collected between 1890 and 1910. Peabody Museum, Harvard University, Cambridge.

adding to the masks' otherworldly spirit power. Serving a social policing function within traditional Baule society, these masks are sacred and secret compared to the more secular performative aspects of portrait masks.

NATURE SPIRITS AND ANCESTORS   At the court of Kuba kings, three masks, known as *moshambwooy, bwoom,* and *ngady amwaash,* represent legendary ancestors. Moshambwooy (FIG. **32-22**) represents a primordial nature spirit *(ngesh)* that serves social control functions and embodies the king's supernatural and political powers. Another mask, bwoom, with its bulging forehead, is said to represent a legendary dwarf or pygmy who often vies for the attention of the beautiful female ancestor ngady amwaash (FIG. **32-23**). These three characters reenact creation stories while rehearsing various forms of archetypal behavior that instruct young men during initiation and reinforce basic Kuba societal values. The masks and their costumes, with elaborate beads, feathers, animal pelts, cowrie shells, cut-pile cloth, and ornamental trappings, echo the sumptuousness of the Kuba king himself (FIG. 32-6).

These few examples of masks and masquerades, from among the thousands performed on the continent, exemplify the exceptionally diverse and important values and meanings characterizing this art form. Since African nations gained independence, and often earlier under colonial domination, masks that once had powerful roles in social control have become at least partially secularized. Yet masking generally remains viable and socially relevant in many parts of the continent.

AFTERWORD: THE PRESENT

The past fifty to a hundred years have witnessed many changes in the forms and functions of African arts. Colonial governments, followed by those of modern independent nations,

have contributed to the erosion of leadership arts even though regalia and court ceremonial attire can still be seen in festivals that continue to be value-laden events. The encroachments of Christianity, Islam, Western education, and market economies have led to increasing secularization in all arts. Many figures and masks earlier commissioned for shrines and serious dances are now made only for purchase by outsiders, essentially as tourist arts. In cities, nontraditional murals and cement sculptures appear frequently, often making at least implicit comments about modern life. Despite the growing importance of urbanism (pre-European in some areas), however, most African people still live in rural communities. Traditional values, although under pressure, hold considerable force in villages especially, and many people adhere to spiritual beliefs that uphold the kinds of art forms discussed above. Yet art-supporting institutions are also changing, with international art market venues becoming more common throughout sub-Saharan Africa.

African art always has changed and developed in response to the continent's evolving history, both before and after the European presence in Africa. At the beginning of the twenty-first century, several tendencies are clear. African artists emphasize realism more than conventionalization and prefer a broader range of subjects, urban rather than rural settings, more painting than sculpture, brighter colors, new materials, and a greater accent on personal style.

DOGON HOUSES OF WORDS   Most of these trends can be seen in recently installed colorful posts in Dogon men's houses, called *togu na* (FIG. **32-24**). The togu na (known as a "house of words" because men's deliberations vital to community welfare take place under its sheltering roof) is considered the "head" and the most important part of the community, which the Dogon characterize with human attributes. Earlier posts, such as the central one, show schematic renderings of legendary female ancestors, similar to stylized ancestral couples (FIG. 32-7) or Satimbe mask

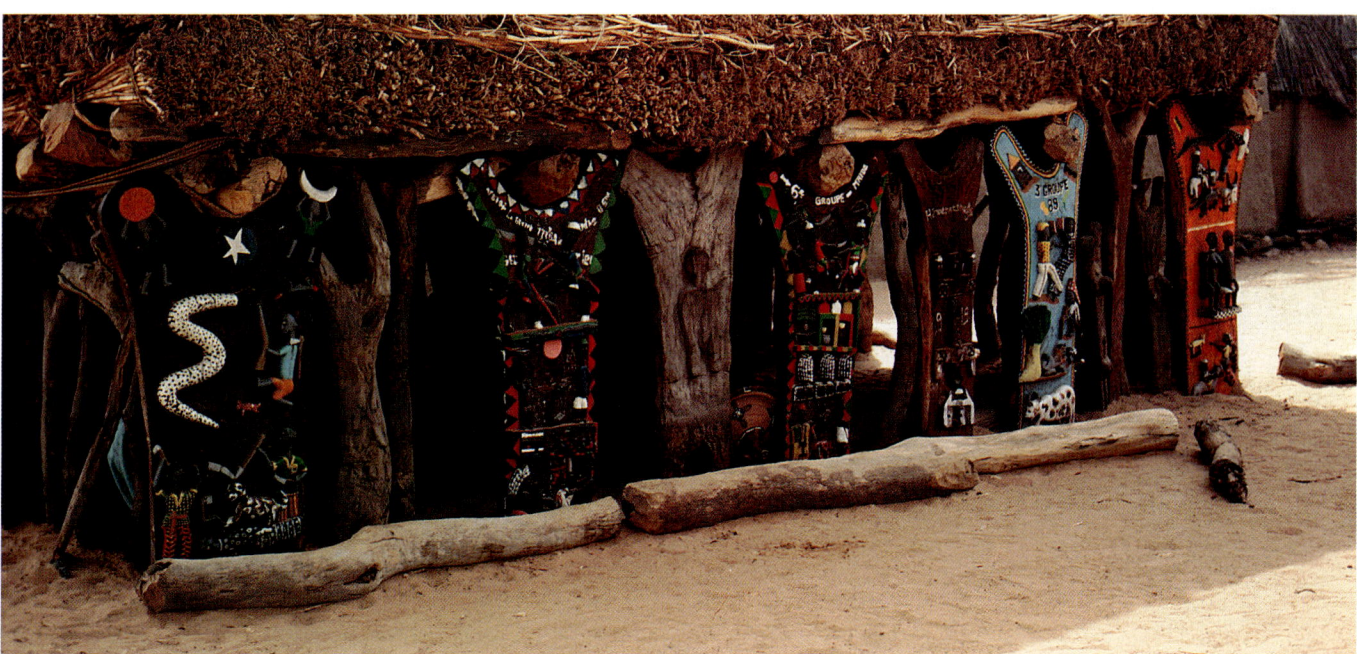

32-24   Togu na (men's "house of words"), Dogon, Mali, photographed in 1989. Wood and pigment.

figures (FIG. 32-15). Recent replacement posts feature narrative and topical scenes of varied subjects, more descriptive detail, writing, polychrome painting in enamels, and their artists' desired recognition.

GA WOODEN CASKETS Today's African artists also tend to use new forms and materials within older functional categories. Carved wooden caskets, created by KANE KWEI (1924–1991) of the Ga people, a non-Akan-speaking group in southern Ghana, exemplify this type of art. Kwei created caskets intended to reflect on the deceased's life and occupation, and he created such diverse shapes as a boat, a fish, a whale, a bird, various agricultural products (such as an onion and a cocoa pod), airplanes, a Mercedes-Benz, and a modern villa. He also created coffins in traditional Akan forms, such as an eagle, an elephant, a leopard, and a stool. The Akan use the type of coffin illustrated here (FIG. **32-25**), a hen with chicks, for senior women with large families.

A CONGOLESE INTERNATIONALIST TRIGO PIULA (b. ca. 1950), a contemporary painter of the "international school" (trained in Western artistic forms, techniques, and styles) from the Democratic Republic of Congo, creates works that fuse Western and Congolese images and objects into a pictorial blend that socially comments on present-day Congolese culture. *Ta Tele* (FIG. **32-26**) depicts a group of Congolese citizens staring transfixed at colorful pictures of consumerism displayed on fourteen television screens on a background wall. The television images include references to travel to exotic places (such as Paris with the Eiffel Tower), sports events, love, the earth seen from a satellite, and worldly goods reflecting Western consumer products. A traditional lower Kongo power figure (called *nkisi nduda*), associated with warfare and divination, stands at the composition's center as a visual mediator between the anonymous foreground viewers and the background television images. In traditional Kongo contexts (FIG. 32-14), the figure's feather headdress associates it with supernatural and magical powers from the sky above, such as lightning and storms. In Piula's rendition, the headdress probably refers to the power of airborne television images. In the stomach area, where Kongo power figures sometimes have a mirror embedded, Piula placed a television screen with a second image of the power figure, as if doubling its power. Piula depicts some of the television audience members with a small, white image of consumer-culture objects— cars, shoes, hearts (signifying love), bottles, and knives and

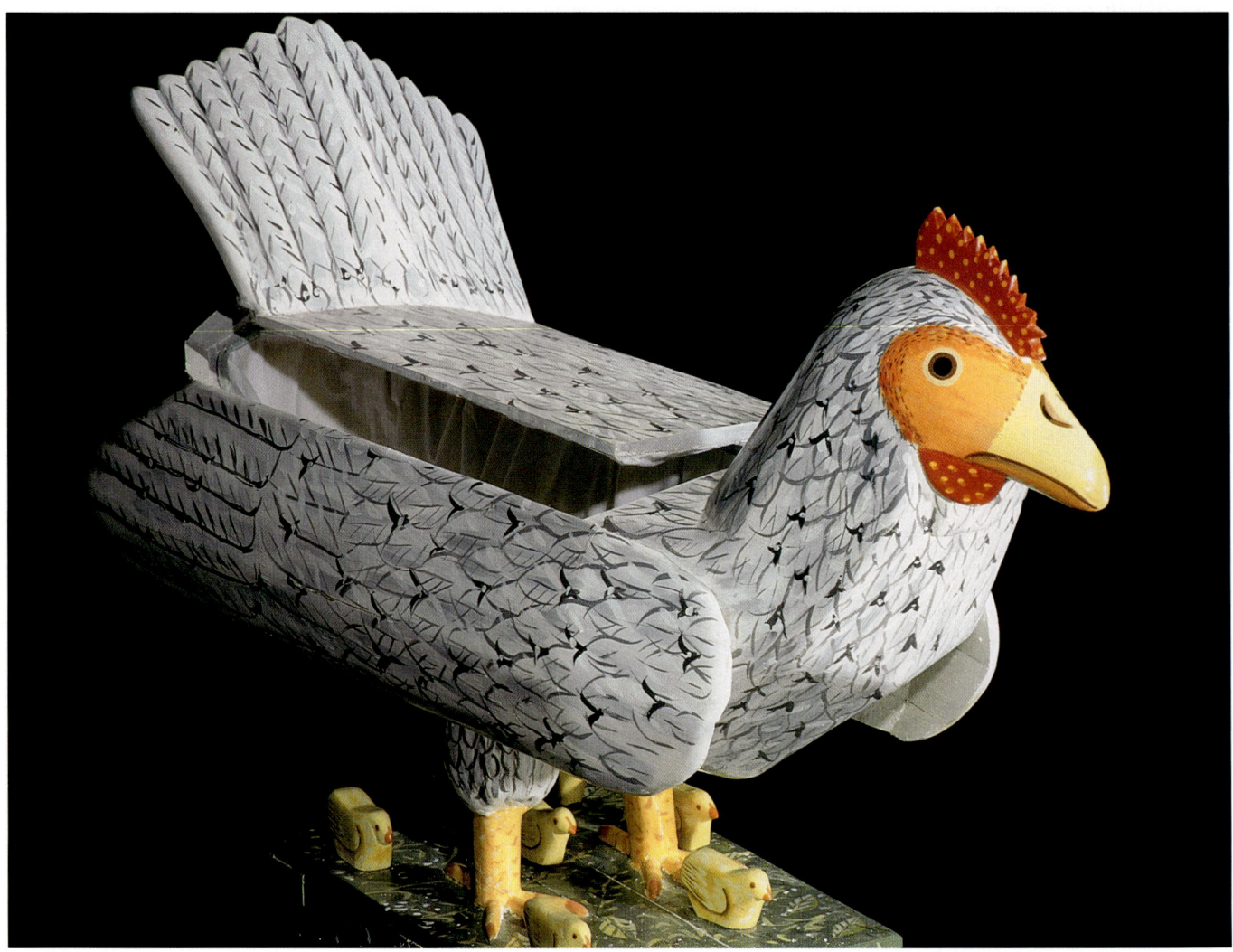

32-25 KANE KWEI, coffin in shape of hen with chicks, Ga, from Ghana, 1989. Wood, pigment, 7′ 6½″ long. Museum voor Volkenkunde, Rotterdam.

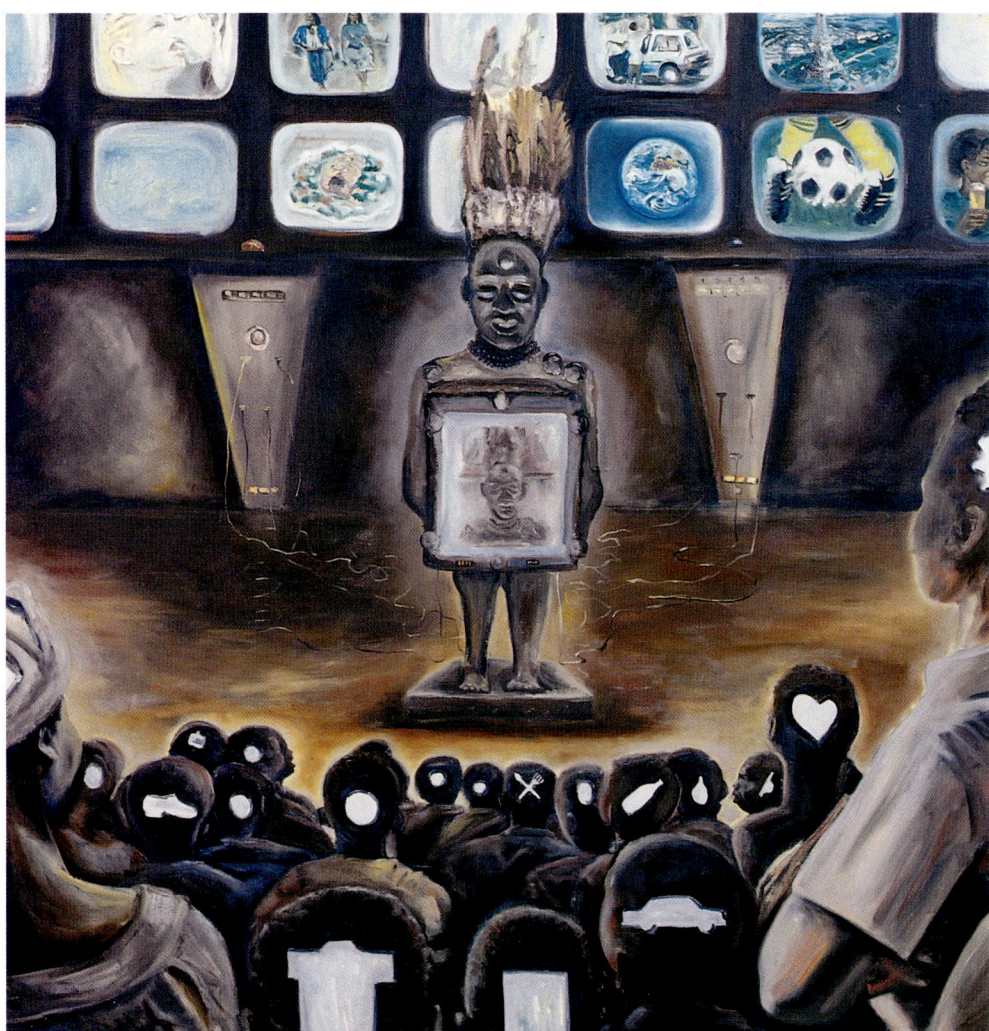

32-26 TRIGO PIULA, *Ta Tele,* from Democratic Republic of Congo, 1988. Oil on canvas, 3′ 3⅜″ × 3′ 4⅜″.

forks—on the back of their heads while others have a small circular shape there.

The meaning appears to be that the television messages have deadened contemporary Congolese peoples' minds with the need for modern commodities. The power figure stands squarely on brown earth. Two four-sided speakers, set against the back wall beneath the television screens, seem to point downward toward the earth (like tombstones?). In traditional Kongo thinking and color symbolism, the color white and earth tones are associated with spirits and the land of the dead. Perhaps Piula suggests that as with past traditional power figures, the contemporary world's new television-oriented consumerism is affecting the minds and souls of the Congolese people as if by magic or sorcery. The resulting image clearly indicts contemporary consumerism in central Africa and beyond.

Many contemporary African art forms are formally vibrant, as well as relevant to emerging social and political issues. Art in South Africa, for example, first reflected protests against apartheid and then celebrated its demise and the consequent democratically elected government. Change will continue to affect the types, forms, styles, symbolism, uses, and subjects of African arts, as it always has.

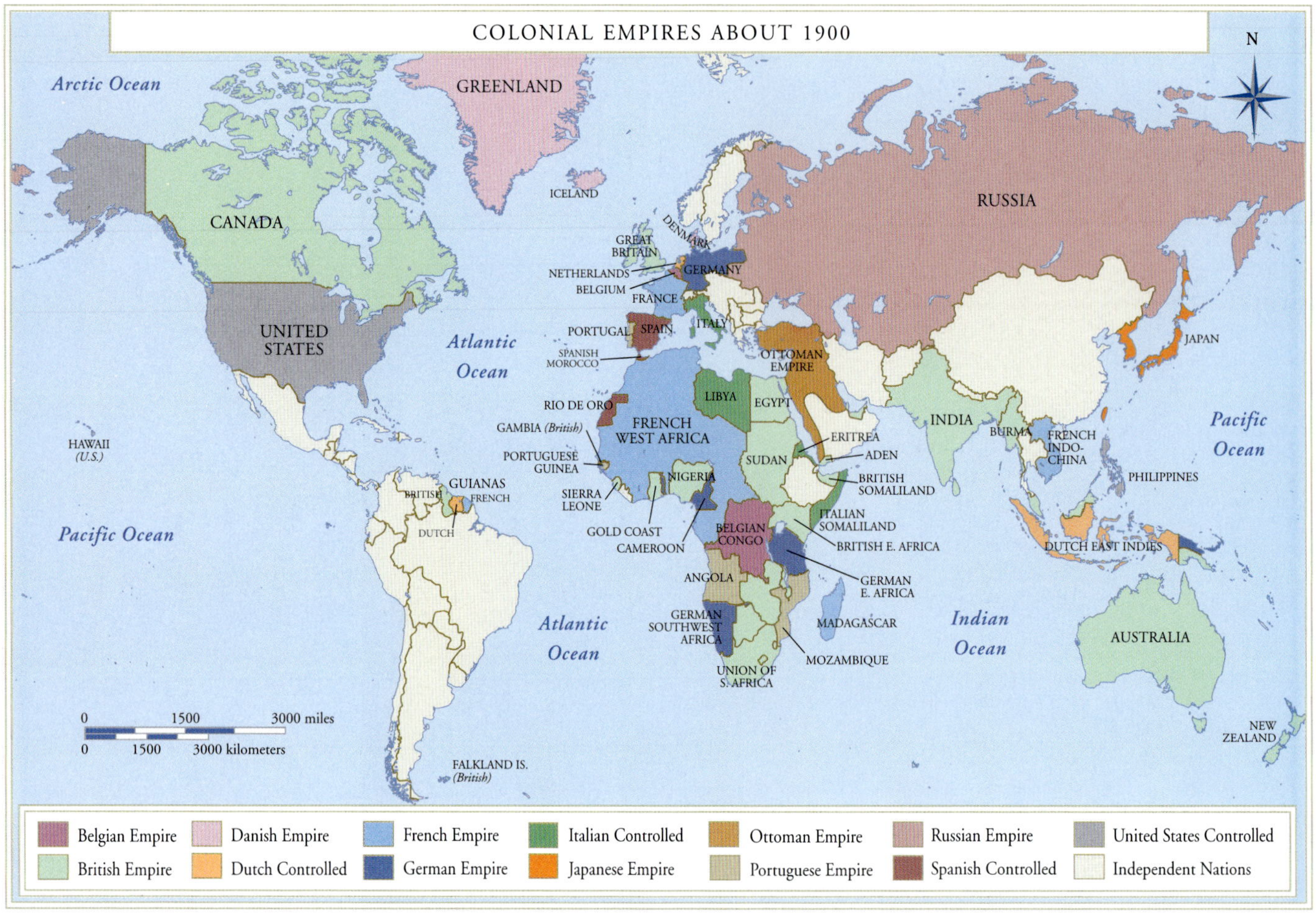

COLONIAL EMPIRES ABOUT 1900

N

Arctic Ocean

GREENLAND

ICELAND

CANADA

RUSSIA

UNITED STATES

Atlantic Ocean

GREAT BRITAIN

NETHERLANDS

BELGIUM

FRANCE

GERMANY

DENMARK

PORTUGAL   SPAIN   ITALY

SPANISH MOROCCO

JAPAN

HAWAII (U.S.)

RIO DE ORO

GAMBIA (British)

PORTUGUESE GUINEA

OTTOMAN EMPIRE

LIBYA   EGYPT

FRENCH WEST AFRICA

ERITREA

ADEN

INDIA

BURMA

FRENCH INDO-CHINA

Pacific Ocean

Pacific Ocean

GUIANAS
BRITISH
FRENCH
DUTCH

SIERRA LEONE

NIGERIA

GOLD COAST

CAMEROON

SUDAN

BRITISH SOMALILAND

ITALIAN SOMALILAND

BRITISH E. AFRICA

PHILIPPINES

DUTCH EAST INDIES

BELGIAN CONGO

ANGOLA

GERMAN SOUTHWEST AFRICA

GERMAN E. AFRICA

MADAGASCAR

MOZAMBIQUE

Indian Ocean

AUSTRALIA

Atlantic Ocean

UNION OF S. AFRICA

NEW ZEALAND

FALKLAND IS. (British)

0   1500   3000 miles
0   1500   3000 kilometers

Belgian Empire	Danish Empire	French Empire	Italian Controlled	Ottoman Empire	Russian Empire	United States Controlled
British Empire	Dutch Controlled	German Empire	Japanese Empire	Portuguese Empire	Spanish Controlled	Independent Nations

---

1900 **1915** **1925**

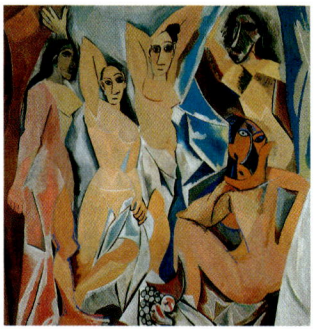

Pablo Picasso
Les Demoiselles d'Avignon, 1907

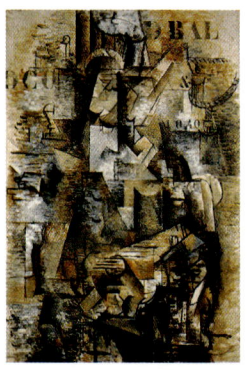

Georges Braque
The Portuguese, 1911

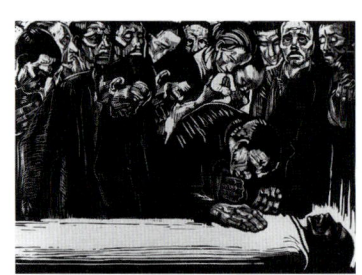

Käthe Kollwitz
Memorial to Karl Liebknecht, 1919

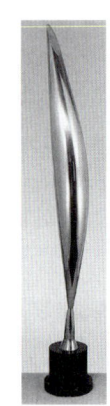

Constantin Brancusi
Bird in Space, 1928

Sigmund Freud, 1856–1939; *The Interpretation of Dreams*, 1900

Max Planck, 1858–1947; quantum theory, 1900

Die Brücke, formed 1905

Les Fauves, formed 1905

Albert Einstein, 1879–1955; theory of relativity, 1905–1915

Futurist Manifesto, 1909

Niels Bohr, 1885–1962; atomic theory, 1913

Die Blaue Reiter, formed 1911

Queen Victoria's reign ends, 1901

World War I, 1914–1918

First Transatlantic radio signal, 1901

Wright brothers' first flight, 1903

Russian Revolution, Communist regime, 1917–1921

Bauhaus founded, 1919

Treaty of Versailles, 1919–1921

Commercial television, 1920s

League of Nations, 1921–1939

U.S.S.R. officially established, 1923

Surrealist Manifesto, 1924

Mexican Revolution ends, 1924

THE TRIUMPH OF MODERNIST ART

THE EARLY TWENTIETH CENTURY

1930   1936   1940

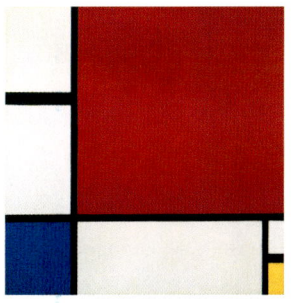

Piet Mondrian, Composition (Blue, Red, and Yellow), 1930

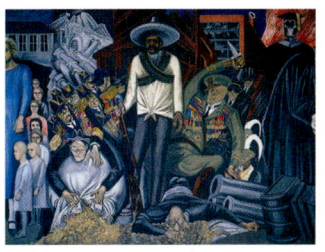

José Clemente Orozco Epic of American Civilization: Hispano-America, (panel 16) ca. 1932–1934

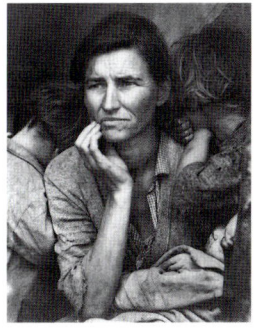

Dorothea Lange Migrant Mother, Nipomo Valley, 1935

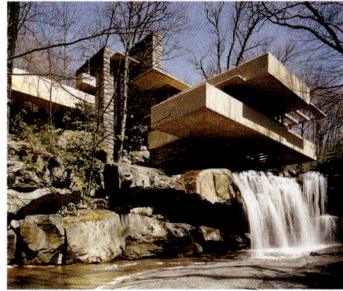

Frank Lloyd Wright Kaufmann House (Fallingwater), 1936–1939

Carl Jung, 1875–1961 (analytical psychology)

Fascism in Italy, 1920–1930s

Stock market crashes, 1929

The Great Depression, 1930s

Rise of Nazism in Germany, 1930s

Roosevelt's "New Deal" in United States, 1933–1939

Spanish Civil War, 1936–1939

Japan invades China, 1937

World War II 1939–1945

The decisive changes that marked the nineteenth century—industrialization, urbanization, and the growth of nationalism and imperialism—are chronicled in Chapter 29. These developments continued to affect countries dramatically throughout the twentieth century. The rampant industrialization matured into international industrial capitalism, which fueled the rise of consumer economies.

As in the nineteenth century, these developments presented societies with great promise, as well as significant problems. Appropriately, these changes prompted both elation and anxiety. The combination of euphoria and alienation that was the hallmark of fin-de-siècle culture in Europe (Chapter 29, page 934) carried through the next decades. Momentous historical events—World War I, the Great Depression, the rise of totalitarianism, and World War II—exacerbated this rather schizophrenic attitude.

Twentieth-Century Intellectual Developments

In the early twentieth century, societies worldwide contended with discoveries and new ways of thinking in a wide variety of fields, including science, technology, economics, and politics. These new ideas forced people to radically revise how they understood their worlds. In particular, the values and ideals that were the legacy of the Scientific Revolution (during the Age of Newton) and the Enlightenment began to yield to innovative views. Thus, intellectuals questioned eighteenth- and nineteenth-century assumptions about progress and reason with ideas challenging traditional thoughts about the physical universe, the structure of society, and human nature.

CHALLENGING NEWTONIAN PHYSICS   One of the fundamental Enlightenment beliefs was faith in science. Because it was based on empirical, or observable, fact, science provided a mechanistic conception of the universe, which reassured a populace finding traditional religions less certain. As promoted in the classic physics of Isaac Newton, the universe was a huge machine consisting of time, space, and matter. The early twentieth century witnessed an astounding burst of scientific activity challenging this model of the universe. It amounted to what has been called "the second scientific/technological revolution." Particularly noteworthy was the work of German physicist Max Planck (1858–1947), German-born Albert Einstein (1879–1955), and British physicist Ernest Rutherford (1871–1937) and Danish physicist Niels Bohr (1885–1962). With their discoveries, each of these scientists shattered the existing faith in the objective reality of matter and, in so doing, paved the way for a new model of the universe. Planck's quantum theory (1900) raised questions about the emission of atomic energy. He maintained that a heated body radiated energy discontinuously in irregular units he called "quanta." Einstein furthered these studies of thermodynamics. In his 1905 paper, *The Electrodynamics of Moving Bodies,* he outlined his theory of relativity. He argued that space and time are not absolute, as postulated in Newtonian physics. Rather, Einstein explained that time and space are relative to the observer and linked in what he called a four-dimensional space-time continuum. He also concluded that matter, rather than a solid, tangible reality, was actually an-

other form of energy. Einstein's famous equation $E = mc^2$, where E stands for energy, m for mass, and c^2 for the speed of light, provided a formula for understanding atomic energy. Rutherford's and Bohr's exploration of atomic structure between 1906 and 1913 contributed to this new perception of matter and energy. The 1896 discovery of radioactivity in uranium and later research opened the way for world-transforming electronic technology. Together, all these scientific discoveries constituted a changed view of physical nature and raised the curtain on the Atomic Age.

TECHNOLOGY: CHEMICAL AND ELECTRICAL Scientific developments were not limited to the realm of physics. Advances in chemistry, biology, biochemistry, microbiology, and medicine in the early twentieth century yielded knowledge of polymers, plastics, fertilizers, enzymes, viruses, vitamins, hormones, and antibiotics. Molecular biologists analyzed and described the structure of cells and tissues, as well as the electrical nature of the brain and nervous system. Their investigations into proteins and nucleic acids led to an understanding of the genetic structure of life.

The most conspicuous technological advances, which largely depended on the scientific discoveries, were in communication and transportation. People adapted to radios, radar, televisions, and talking cinema, as well as automobiles, airplanes—from propeller-driven to jet, electrified railway and municipal transit systems, and electrification of street lighting and home appliances.

Chemical technology became an industry as important as electrical technology. It had its greatest impact in the world of materials, in mining, metals, oil refining, textiles, pharmaceuticals, agriculture, food production and food processing. It was particularly useful in the fight against disease and famine, although at this time its long-term ecological effects were unknown.

The field of mechanical engineering experienced great advances as well. Mass production and the assembly line became indispensable to industry. Chemical and biological researchers found scientific instruments such as the electron microscope essential to their work. The requirements of calculation, vastly expanded by the new complexities of scientific research and the machine environment, demanded electronic instrumentation and control mechanisms. Cybernetic theory and early computer models were in place by midcentury.

MIND OVER MATTER   In other realms of thought—philosophy, psychology, and economic theory—significant challenges to the primacy of reason and objective reality emerged. Friedrich Nietzsche (1844–1900), a German intellectual, rejected the rational. In his existentialist publications, he argued that Western society was decadent and incapable of any real creativity precisely because of its excessive reliance on reason at the expense of emotion and passion. Nietzsche blamed Christianity for much of Western civilization's decay, and he insisted societies only could attain liberation and renewal when they acknowledged God is dead.

Also instrumental in examining the irrational mind and destabilizing the entrenched belief in the rational nature of humanity and the world was the Viennese doctor Sigmund Freud (1856–1939). He developed the fundamental principles for what became known as psychoanalysis. In his book *The Inter-*

pretation of Dreams (1900), Freud argued that the unconscious and inner drives (of which people are largely unaware) control human behavior. He used both hypnosis and dream analysis to understand behavior. Freud concluded that this control by the unconscious is due to repression, or individuals mentally burying uncomfortable experiences or memories. This repression occurs in the brain due to a struggle between three forces—the id, the ego, and the superego. While the id contains unconscious drives and desires, the ego is rational and coordinates this struggle of forces. The superego consists of the inhibitions and values that societal forces, such as parents or friends, impose. Making patients aware of repressed memories or unconscious conflicts through psychoanalysis, Freud believed, could assure patients' mental well-being.

During the twentieth century, Freud's ideas gained popularity. Another very influential psychiatrist who expanded on Freud's theories was Carl Jung (1875–1961). This Swiss doctor felt Freud's theories were too narrowly focused. Instead, Jung proposed a model connecting a person's dreams in a unique arrangement he called "the process of individuation." Therapists could understand the behavior and personality of an individual by identifying this pattern of dreams. Further, Jung asserted that the unconscious is composed of two facets, a "personal unconscious" and a "collective unconscious." The collective unconscious comprises memories and associations all humans share, such as archetypes (original models) and mental constructions. According to Jung, the collective unconscious accounts for the development of myths, religions, and philosophies.

The Rise of Industrial Capitalism

The industrialization so prominent during the nineteenth century matured quickly. By the early part of the twentieth century, boards of directors controlled large-scale firms. These were often far-flung enterprises with enormous factories. The owners and managers of such industrial giants, known as "captains of industry," wielded extraordinary economic and political power. Due to the widening gap between these captains of industry and the laborers, Marxism (Chapter 29, page 890) grew in popularity. Marxism's championing of the working classes held great appeal, so enrollment in trade unions and socialist parties increased. Although the socialists did not have unified strategies, they all agreed the capitalist profit system exploited the workers and enriched the owners, causing the deplorable living and working conditions of most workers.

As dramatic as the societal changes were in the nineteenth century, twentieth-century individuals encountered even greater uncertainty and anxiety. Not only were the conditions of their lives very different, but also they faced fundamental, indeed revolutionary, challenges in how they viewed the world, prompted by thinkers such as Einstein, Freud, and Nietzsche.

World War I and the Russian Revolution

The development of advanced industrial societies in Europe and America led to frenzied imperialist expansion. Countries controlled far-flung empires and spread their spheres of influence worldwide. By the beginning of the twentieth century, Britain, France, Germany, Belgium, Italy, Spain, and Portugal all had footholds in Africa. In Asia, Britain ruled India, the Dutch controlled Indonesia's vast archipelago, the French held power in Indochina, and the Russians ruled Central Asia and Siberia. Japan began rising as a new and formidable Pacific power that would stake its claims to empire in the 1930s. Such imperialism was capitalist and expansionist, establishing colonies as raw-material sources, as manufacturing markets, and as territorial acquisitions. Imperialism also often had the missionary dimension of bringing the "light" of Christianity and civilization to "backward peoples" and educating "inferior races." This mission, driven by Social Darwinism (Chapter 29, page 890), based its beliefs on Charles Darwin's idea of the "survival of the fittest." Social Darwinism found its major proponent in the British philosopher Herbert Spencer (1820–1903), who argued that societies and cultures conflicted and only the strongest survived.

THE GREAT WAR Although many people optimistically hoped the development of nation-states would result in peace and harmony, this was not to be. Rather than cooperation, the prevalent nationalism and rampant imperialism led to competition. Eventually, countries negotiated alliances to protect their individual interests. The conflicts between the two major blocs—the Triple Alliance (Germany, Austria-Hungary, and Italy), and the Triple Entente (Russia, France, and Great Britain)—led to World War I. In July 1914, Austria-Hungary declared war on Serbia. The "Great War" lasted until 1918 and involved virtually all of Europe. Allegiances shifted with the changing fortunes of different countries; for example, Italy betrayed the rest of the Triple Alliance by entering the war in 1915 on the side of the Allies. The initial enthusiasm of the war effort revealed the strength of nationalist sentiments.

The slaughter and devastation soon destroyed any romantic illusions soldiers held about World War I. Not only were millions of men killed in battle, but the introduction of poison gas in 1915 also added to the horror of humankind's inhumanity to itself. Although the United States tried to remain neutral, it finally felt compelled to enter the war in 1917.

The twenty-seven Allied nations finally negotiated the official end of World War I in 1919. The national interests of the individual countries complicated these deliberations. Separate peace treaties with the various participants resulted in a fragile peace. The devastation of World War I brought widespread misery, social disruption, and economic collapse. All the world viewed the ultimate effects of nationalism, imperialism, and expansionist goals.

THE DEMISE OF THE TSAR IN RUSSIA The Russian Revolution exacerbated the global chaos when it erupted in 1917. Dissatisfaction with the regime of Tsar Nicholas II had led workers to stage a general strike, and the monarchy's rule ended with the tsar's abdication in March. In late 1917 the Bolsheviks wrested control of the country from the ruling Provisional Government. The Bolsheviks, a faction of Russian Social Democrats led by V. I. Lenin (1870–1924), promoted violent revolution and were eventually renamed the Communists. Once in power, Lenin nationalized the land and turned it over to the local rural soviets (councils of workers' and soldiers' deputies). After extensive civil war, the Communists succeeded in retaining control of Russia, officially renamed the Soviet Union in 1923.

The Great Depression and World War II

The resolution of World War I was indeed tenuous; the Great Depression of the 1930s dealt a serious blow to the stability of Western countries. Largely due to the international scope of banking and industrial capitalism, the economic depression deeply affected the United States and many European countries. By 1932, 25 percent of the British workforce was unemployed, while 40 percent of German workers were without jobs. Production in the United States plummeted by 50 percent.

THE UNHEEDED LESSONS OF WORLD WAR I This economic disaster, along with the failure of postwar treaties and the League of Nations to keep the peace, provided a fertile breeding ground for dangerous forces to once again emerge. In the 1920s and 1930s, totalitarian regimes came to the fore in several European countries. Benito Mussolini (1883–1945) headed the Fascist regime in Italy, derived from a staunch nationalism. Mussolini explained: "Fascism is totalitarian, and the Fascist State, the synthesis and unity of all values, interprets, develops and gives strength to the whole life of the people."[1] Joseph Stalin (1879–1953) gained control of the Communist Party in the Soviet Union in 1929. Concurrently, Adolf Hitler (1889–1945) consolidated his power in Germany by building the National Socialist German Workers' Party (or Nazi for short) into a mass political movement.

These ruthless seizures of power and the desire to develop "total states" led to the many conflicts that evolved into World War II. This catastrophic struggle erupted in 1939 when Germany invaded Poland and in response Britain and France declared war on Germany. Eventually, this conflict earned its designation as a world war; while Germany and Italy fought most of Europe and the Soviet Union, Japan invaded China and occupied Indochina. After the Japanese bombing of Pearl Harbor in Hawaii in 1941, the United States declared war on Japan. Germany, in loose alliance with Japan, declared war on the United States. Although most of the concerns of individual countries participating in World War II were territorial and nationalistic, other agendas surfaced as well. The Nazis, propelled by Hitler's staunch anti-Semitism, were determined to build a racially exclusive Aryan state. This resolve led to the horror of the Holocaust, the killing of nearly two out of every three European Jews.

World War II drew to an end in 1945, when the Allied forces defeated Germany and the United States dropped atomic bombs on Hiroshima and Nagasaki in Japan. The shock of the war's physical, economic, and psychological devastation immediately tempered the elation people felt at the conclusion of these global hostilities.

The Evolution of Modernism and the Avant-Garde

Like other members of society, artists were deeply affected by the upheaval of the early twentieth century. At times, they responded with energy and optimism, while at other times they descended into bleak despair. Changes in the art world itself also influenced artistic developments. The challenges of Impressionism, Post-Impressionism, and the various renegade exhibitions diminished the academies' authority, although still a presence.

For artists, working within the crucible of historical turmoil, contending with shifting institutional structures within the art world, and acknowledging modernism's significance led to an incredibly fertile period for the evolution of art. In particular, the avant-garde (Chapter 29, page 924), first discussed in conjunction with the Post-Impressionists, became a major force. Like their nineteenth-century predecessors, early-twentieth-century avant-garde artists positioned themselves in the forefront by aggressively challenging traditional and often cherished notions about art and its relation to society. As the old social orders collapsed and new ones, from communism to corporate capitalism, took their places, one of the self-imposed tasks school after school of twentieth-century avant-gardes embraced was the search for new ways to communicate in a radically changed world. This does not suggest, however, that the avant-garde represented a unified group—far from it. Some avant-garde artists used their art to powerfully criticize political and social institutions. Because the term avant-garde emerged in art after its use in politics, these critiques prompted the general public to associate avant-garde artists with radical political thought and anarchism. In contrast, other avant-garde artists, in essence, withdrew from society and concentrated their attention on art as a unique activity, separate from society-at-large. These artists pursued an introspective examination of artistic principles and elements (continuing the modernist critique) which increasingly focused on formal qualities.

EXPRESSIONISM IN EARLY-TWENTIETH-CENTURY EUROPE

Aspects of all these avant-garde strains contributed to the emergence of "expressionism." The term *expressionism* has been used over the years to refer to a wide range of art. Simply put, *expressionism* refers to art that is the result of the artist's unique inner or personal vision and that often has an emotional dimension. This contrasts, for example, with art focused on visually describing the empirical world. The term first gained currency in the early twentieth century and was popularized in *Der Sturm,* an avant-garde periodical initially published in Munich. Herwarth Walden, the editor of *Der Sturm,* proclaimed: "We call the art of this century Expressionism in order to distinguish it from what is not art. We are thoroughly aware that artists of previous centuries also sought expression. Only they did not know how to formulate it."[2]

In this chapter and the next, several movements are classified as expressionist, from German Expressionism of the 1910s to Abstract Expressionism, which emerged in the United States in the 1940s. Some of this expressionist art evokes visceral emotional responses from viewers, while other such artworks rely on the artist's introspective revelations. One of the first movements to tap into this pervasive desire for expression was Fauvism. In their work, these artists explored both facets of expressionism. They combined outward expressionism in the form of a bold release of internal feelings through wild color and powerful, even brutal, brushwork and inward expressionism, awakening viewers' emotions by these very devices. Often the expressionists offended viewers and even critics, but the expressionists sought empathy—connection between the internal states of artists and viewers—not sympathy.

Fauvism

In 1905, the first signs of a specifically twentieth-century movement in painting appeared in Paris. In that year, at the third Salon d'Automne, a group of young painters under the leadership of Henri Matisse exhibited canvases so simplified in design and so shockingly bright in color that a startled critic described the artists as *fauves* (wild beasts). The Fauves were totally independent of the French Academy and the "official" Salon. The Fauve movement was driven by a desire to develop an art that had the directness and antitheoretical orientation of Impressionism but that also used intense color juxtapositions and their emotional capabilities, the legacy of artists such as van Gogh and Gauguin. The Fauves had seen the works of these two artists (shown in retrospective exhibitions in Paris in 1901 and 1903), but the Fauves went even further in liberating color from its descriptive function and using it for both expressive and structural ends. They produced portraits, landscapes, still lifes, and nudes of spontaneity and verve, with rich surface textures, lively linear patterns, and, above all, bold colors. The Fauves went beyond any earlier artist by newly intensifying color with startling contrasts of vermilion and emerald green and of cerulean blue and vivid orange held together by sweeping brush strokes and bold patterns.

The Fauve painters never officially organized, and the looseness of both personal connections and stylistic affinities caused the Fauve movement to begin to disintegrate almost as soon as it emerged. Within five years, most of the artists had departed from a strict adherence to Fauve principles and developed their own, more personal, styles. During its brief existence, however, the Fauve movement made a remarkable contribution to the direction of art by demonstrating color's structural, expressive, and aesthetic capabilities.

THE PRIMACY OF COLOR The Fauve use of color is particularly apparent in the work of HENRI MATISSE (1869–1954), who was the centrifugal force of this group. Matisse realized the primary role color could play in conveying meaning and focused his efforts on developing this notion. His *Woman With the Hat* (FIG. **33-1**) is an instructive example of this. Matisse depicted his wife, Amélie, in a rather conventional manner compositionally. However, the seemingly arbitrary colors immediately strike viewers. The entire image—the woman's face, clothes, hat, and background—consists of patches and splotches of color juxtaposed in ways that sometimes produce jarring contrasts. Matisse explained his approach: "What characterized fauvism was that we rejected imitative colors, and that with pure colors we obtained stronger reactions—more striking simultaneous reactions,

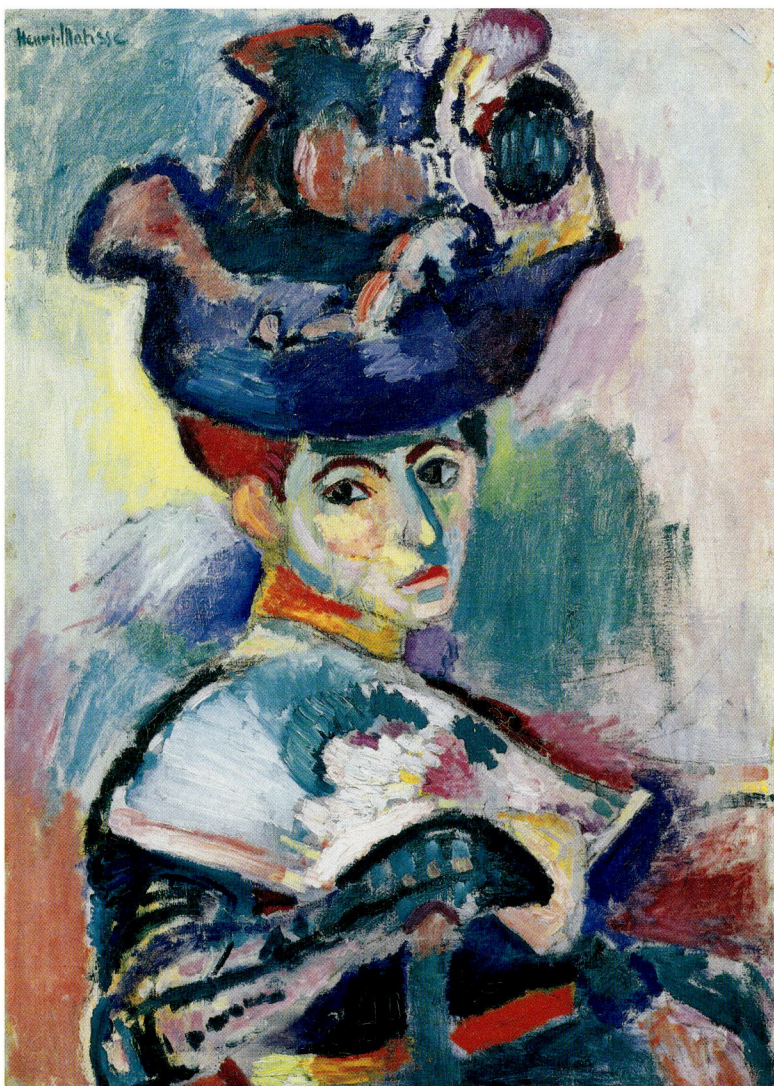

33-1 HENRI MATISSE, *Woman with the Hat,* 1905. Oil on canvas, 2′ 7$\frac{3}{4}$″ × 1′ 11$\frac{1}{2}$″. San Francisco Museum of Modern Art, San Francisco (bequest of Elise S. Haas).

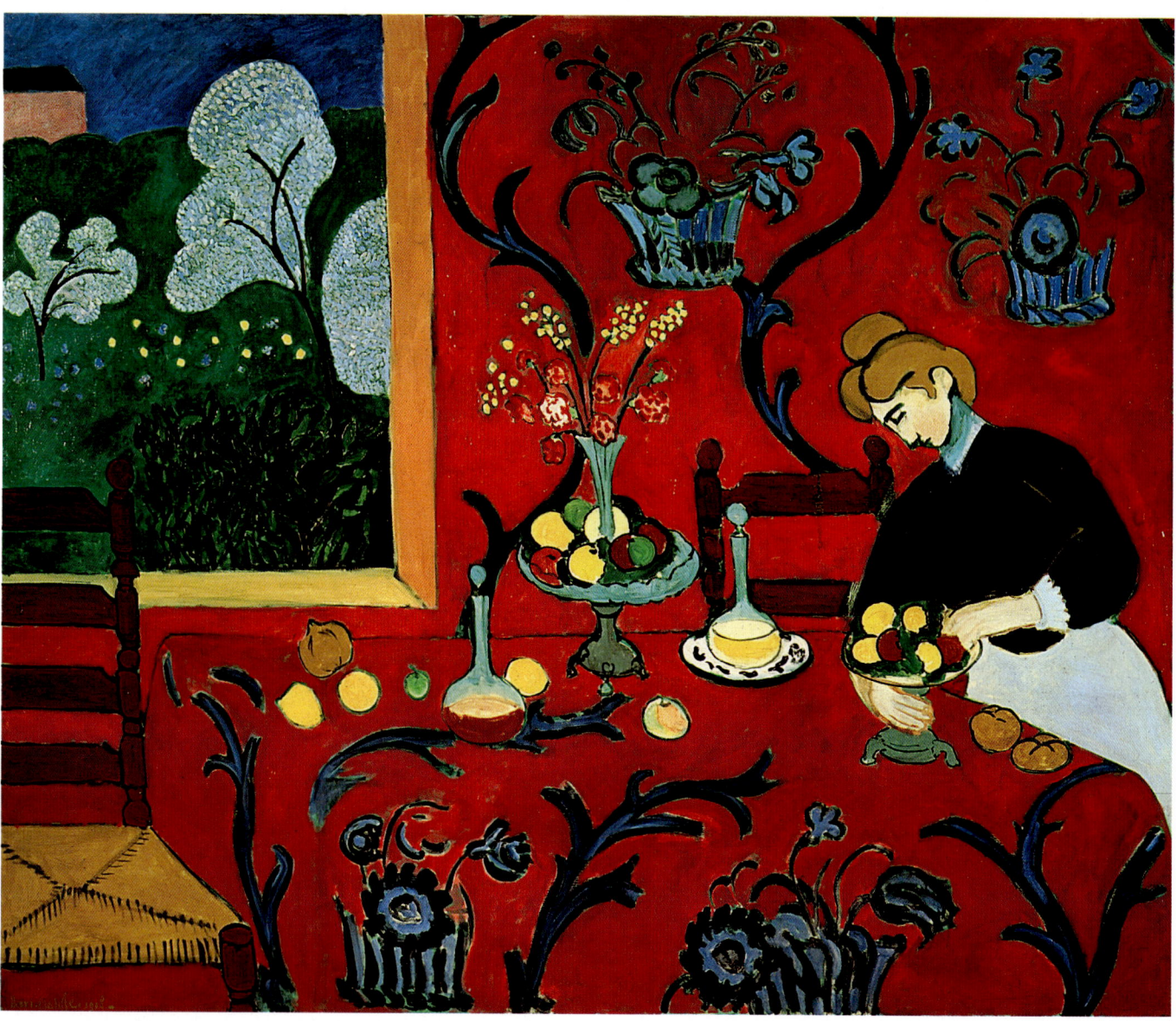

33-2   HENRI MATISSE, *Red Room (Harmony in Red)*, 1908–1909. Oil on canvas, approx. 5′ 11″ × 8′ 1″. State Hermitage Museum, Saint Petersburg.

and there was also the luminosity of our colors."[3] Matisse's reference to luminosity linked him to Cézanne, who argued that painters could not reproduce light but must represent it by color. For Matisse and the Fauves, therefore, color became the formal element most responsible for pictorial coherence and the primary conveyor of meaning.

FROM GREEN, TO BLUE, TO RED   The maturation of these color discoveries can be seen in Matisse's *Red Room (Harmony in Red)*, FIG. **33-2**. Here, viewers are confronted with the interior of a comfortable, prosperous household with a maid placing fruit and wine on the table. The artist's color selection and juxtapositions generate much of the feeling of warmth and comfort. He depicted objects in simplified and schematized fashion and flattened out the forms—for example, he eliminated the front edge of the table, making the table, with its identical patterning, as flat as the wall behind it. The colors, however, contrast richly and intensely. Matisse's process of overpainting reveals color's importance for striking the right chord in viewers. Initially, this work was

predominantly green, and then he repainted it blue. Neither color seemed appropriate to Matisse, and not until he repainted this work red did he feel he had struck the proper chord. Like van Gogh and Gauguin, Matisse expected color to provoke an emotional resonance in viewers. He declared: "Color was not given to us in order that we should imitate Nature. It was given to us so that we can express our own emotions."[4]

EXPRESSING CONTENT WITH COLOR   ANDRÉ DERAIN (1880–1954), also a Fauve group member, worked closely with Matisse. Like Matisse, Derain worked to use color to its fullest potential—for aesthetic and compositional coherence, to increase luminosity, and to elicit emotional responses from viewers. *London Bridge* (FIG. **33-3**) is typical of Derain's art. The perspective appears distorted, and color delineates space. In addition, the artist indicated light and shadow not by differences in value, but by contrasts of hue. Finally, color does not describe the local tones of objects; instead, it expresses the picture's content.

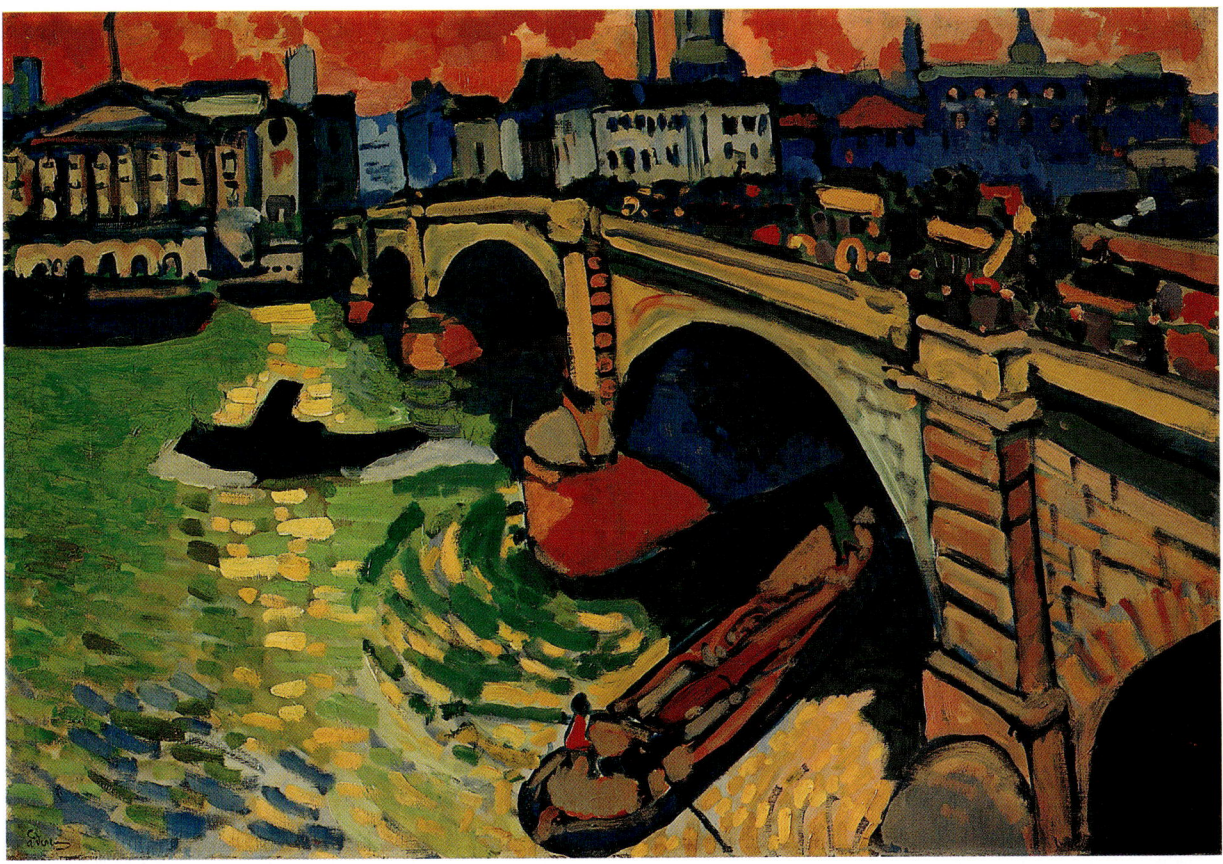

33-3 ANDRÉ DERAIN, *London Bridge,* 1906. Oil on canvas, 2′ 2″ × 3′ 3″. Museum of Modern Art, New York (gift of Mr. and Mrs. Charles Zadok).

FAUVE COLOR TO REVEAL SOCIAL TRUTHS

French artist GEORGES ROUAULT (1871–1958) was not a member of the Fauve circle, but he did study with Gustave Moreau, the teacher who had so influenced Matisse's development. And he clearly based his works on a similar interest in the evocative power of color. However, although the work of the Fauves generally did not include strong social or political content, Rouault's work is moving precisely because it reveals social truths and comments on the forces that crush the spirit. Rouault is best known for his expressive portraits of clowns, prostitutes, and actors, all appearing as universal tragic figures. Given Rouault's strong religious convictions, it is not surprising many of his works have religious overtones. Rouault's intersection with the Fauve program comes from his use of intense colors to impart a lushness and luminosity to the images, adding to their power.

The evocative power of Rouault's work is manifested in *The Old King* (FIG. **33-4**). The artist painted the single figure of the king, whose fierce visage appears in sharp profile, in rich jewel tones—deep glowing reds, emerald greens, and midnight blues. Rouault divided the color areas and outlined the figure in harsh black lines, a mainstay of his style. The parallel of this style to stained-glass windows is not coincidental. Rouault worked as a glassmaker's apprentice as a youth and remained impressed by the depth and intensity of color

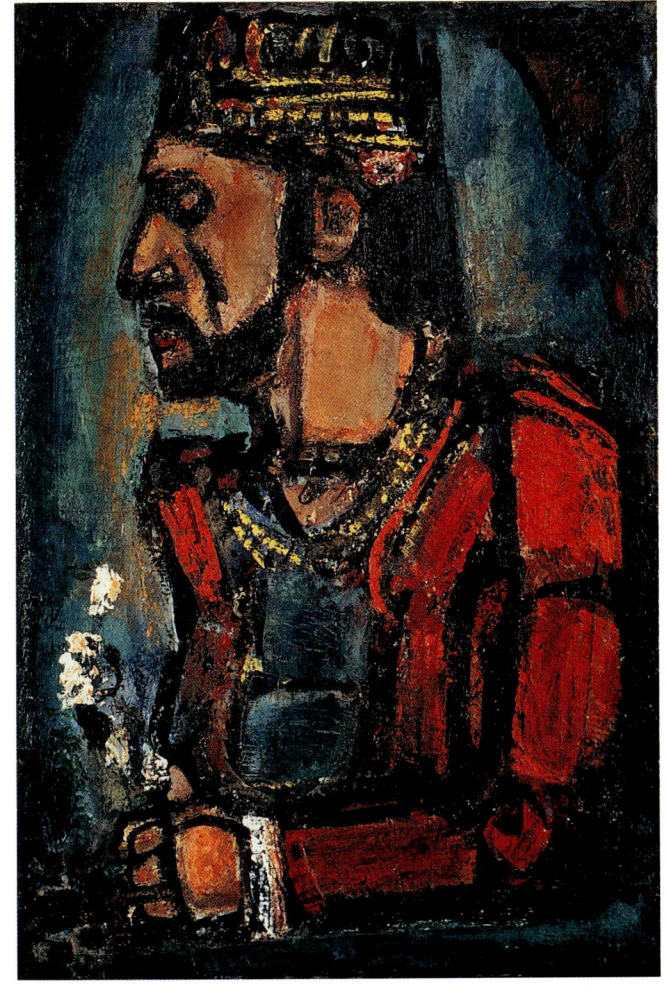

33-4 GEORGES ROUAULT, *The Old King,* 1916–1936. Oil on canvas, 2′ 6¼″ × 1′ 9¼″. Carnegie Museum of Art, Pittsburgh (Patrons Art Fund, 1940).

in glass. The king's severe aquiline features, dark complexion, and thick black hair suggest an authoritative despot in brooding reverie. The sharp and rugged simplification of the forms and harsh, hacked-out edges convey with blunt force an aspect of monarchic vengeance. Here, Rouault produced a powerful, defiant image of merciless authority, a ruler somewhat ravaged by time. Paradoxically, the king appears to clutch flowers in his fist.

German Expressionism: Die Brücke

The immediacy and boldness of the Fauve images appealed to many artists, including the German Expressionists. However, although color plays a prominent role in the work of the German Expressionists, the expressiveness of their images is due as much to the wrenching distortions of form, ragged outline, and agitated brushstrokes. This resulted in savagely powerful, emotional canvases in the years leading to World War I.

The first group of German artists to explore expressionist ideas gathered in Dresden in 1905 under the leadership of ERNST LUDWIG KIRCHNER (1880–1938). The group's members thought of themselves as paving the way for a more perfect age by bridging the old age to the new. They derived their name Die Brücke (The Bridge) from this concept. Kirchner's early studies in architecture, painting, and the graphic arts had instilled in him a deep admiration for German medieval art. Like the British artists associated with the Arts and Crafts movement, such as William Morris (see FIG. 29-50), this admiration stirred the group to model themselves on their ideas of medieval craft guilds by living together and practicing all

the arts equally. Kirchner described their lofty goals in a ringing statement:

> With faith in development and in a new generation of creators and appreciators we call together all youth. As youth, we carry the future and want to create for ourselves freedom of life and of movement against the long-established older forces. Everyone who with directness and authenticity conveys that which drives him to creation, belongs to us.[5]

These artists protested the hypocrisy and materialistic decadence of those in power. Kirchner, in particular, focused much of his attention on the detrimental effects of industrialization, such as the alienation of individuals in cities, which he felt fostered a mechanized and impersonal society. This perception was reinforced when most of the group, including Kirchner, moved to Berlin, a teeming metropolis. Further, the tensions leading to World War I exacerbated the discomfort and anxiety evidenced in the works of Die Brücke.

URBAN LIFE IN PREWAR DRESDEN   Kirchner's *Street, Dresden* (FIG. 33-5) provides viewers with a glimpse into the frenzied urban activity of a bustling German city before the First World War. Rather than the distant, panoramic urban view of the Impressionists, this street scene is jarring and dissonant. The women in the foreground loom large, approaching viewers somewhat menacingly. The steep perspective of the street, which threatens to push the women directly into the viewing space, increases their confrontational nature. Harshly rendered, the women's features make them appear zombielike and ghoulish, and the garish, clashing colors—juxtapositions of bright orange, emerald green, acrid chartreuse, and pink—add to the image's expressive impact.

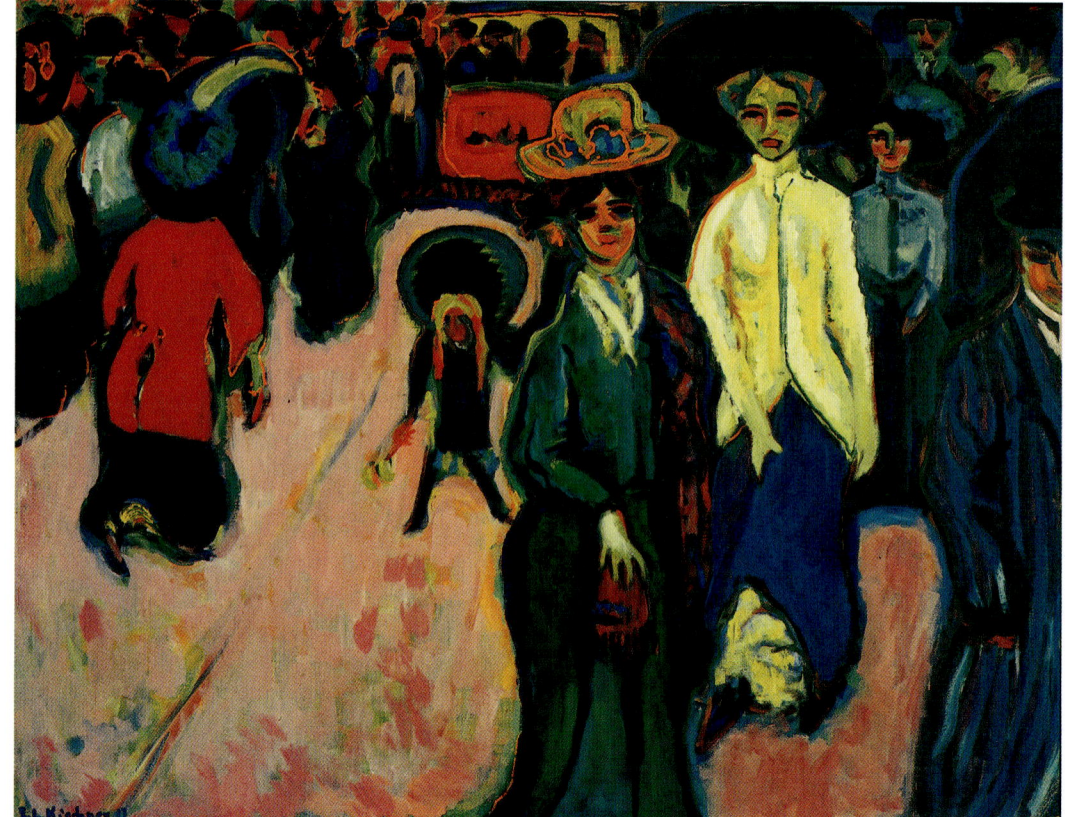

33-5   ERNST LUDWIG KIRCHNER, *Street, Dresden,* 1908 (dated 1907). Oil on canvas, 4′ 11¼″ × 6′ 6⅞″. Museum of Modern Art, New York (purchase).

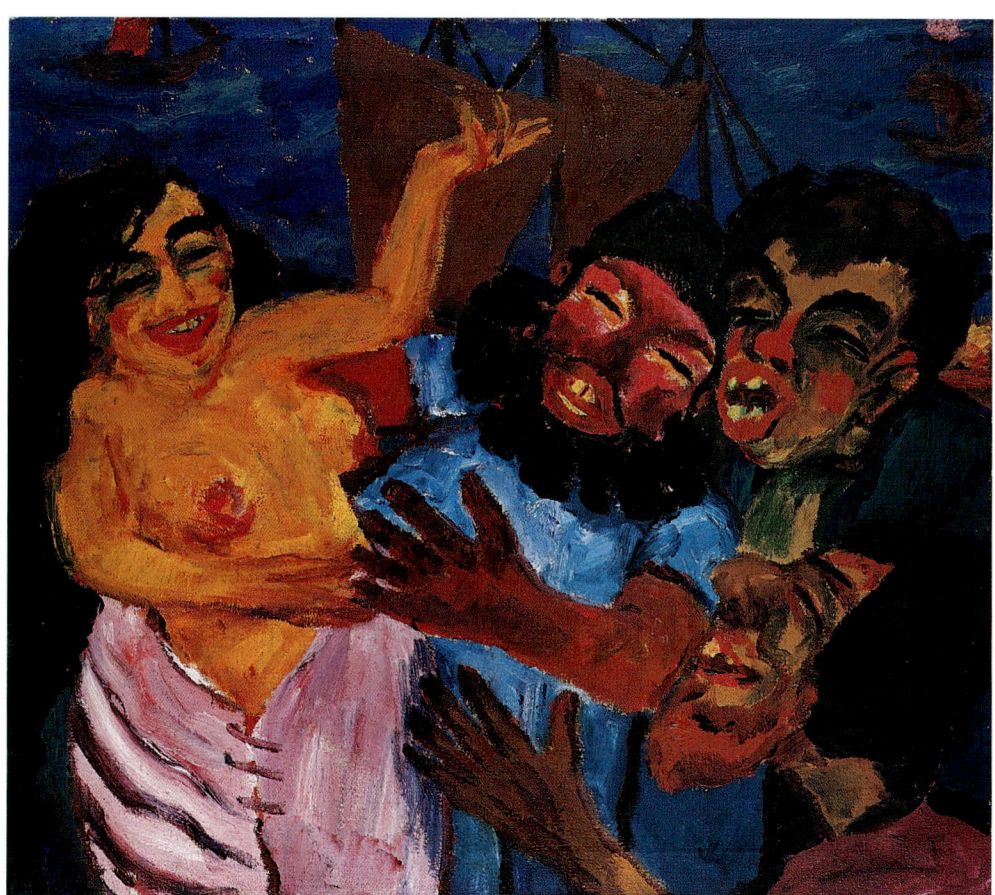

33-6 EMIL NOLDE, *Saint Mary of Egypt among Sinners,* 1912. Left panel of a triptych, oil on canvas, approx. 2'10" × 3'3". Hamburger Kunsthalle, Hamburg.

BIBLICAL LUST AND LECHERY EMIL NOLDE (1867–1956) was much older than most Die Brücke artists, but because he was pursuing similar ideas in his work, he was invited to join the group in 1906 and became an important member for a year and a half. The content of Nolde's work centered, for the most part, on religious imagery. In contrast to the quiet spirituality and restraint of traditional religious images, however, Nolde's paintings are visceral and forceful. A good example is *Saint Mary of Egypt among Sinners* (FIG. **33-6**). Mary Magdalene, before her conversion, entertains lechers whose lust magnifies their brutal ugliness. The distortions of form and color (especially the jarring juxtaposition of blue and orange) and the rawness of the brushstrokes amplify the harshness of the leering faces.

Borrowing ideas from van Gogh, Munch, the Fauves, and African and Oceanic art, Die Brücke artists created a wide range of images. The harsh colors, aggressively brushed paint, and distorted forms expressed the painters' feelings about the injustices of society and their belief in a healthful union of human beings and nature. Their use of such diverse sources reflects the expanding scope of global contact from colonialism and international capitalism. By 1913, the group dissolved, and each member continued to work independently.

German Expressionism: Der Blaue Reiter

A second major German Expressionist group, Der Blaue Reiter (The Blue Rider) formed in Munich in 1911. The two founding members, VASSILY KANDINSKY (1866–1944) and FRANZ MARC (1880–1916), whimsically selected this name because of their mutual interest in the color blue and horses.

Like Die Brücke and other expressionist artists, this group produced paintings that captured their feelings in visual form while also eliciting intense visceral responses from viewers.

BLUEPRINTS FOR ENLIGHTENMENT Born in Russia, Vassily Kandinsky, one of the driving forces of Der Blaue Reiter, moved to Munich in 1896 and soon developed a spontaneous and aggressively avant-garde expressive style. Indeed, Kandinsky was one of the first artists to explore complete abstraction, as evidenced by *Improvisation 28* (FIG. **33-7**). Kandinsky fueled his elimination of representational elements with his interest in theosophy (a religious/philosophical belief system incorporating a wide range of tenets from, among other sources, Buddhism and mysticism) and the occult, as well as with advances in the sciences. A true intellectual widely read in philosophy, religion, history, and the other arts, especially music, Kandinsky was also one of the few early modernists to read with some comprehension the new scientific theories of Einstein's era. Rutherford's exploration of atomic structure, for example, convinced Kandinsky that material objects had no real substance, thereby shattering his faith in a world of tangible things.

The painter articulated his ideas in an influential treatise, *Concerning the Spiritual in Art,* published in 1912. Artists, Kandinsky believed, must express the spirit and their innermost feelings by orchestrating color, form, line, and space. He produced numerous works like *Improvisation 28,* conveying feelings with color juxtapositions, intersecting linear elements, and implied spatial relationships. Ultimately, Kandinsky saw these abstractions as evolving blueprints for a more enlightened and liberated society emphasizing spirituality.

33-7 VASSILY KANDINSKY, *Improvisation 28* (second version), 1912. Oil on canvas, 3′ 7⅞″ × 5′ 3⅞″. Solomon R. Guggenheim Museum, New York (gift of Solomon R. Guggenheim, 1937).

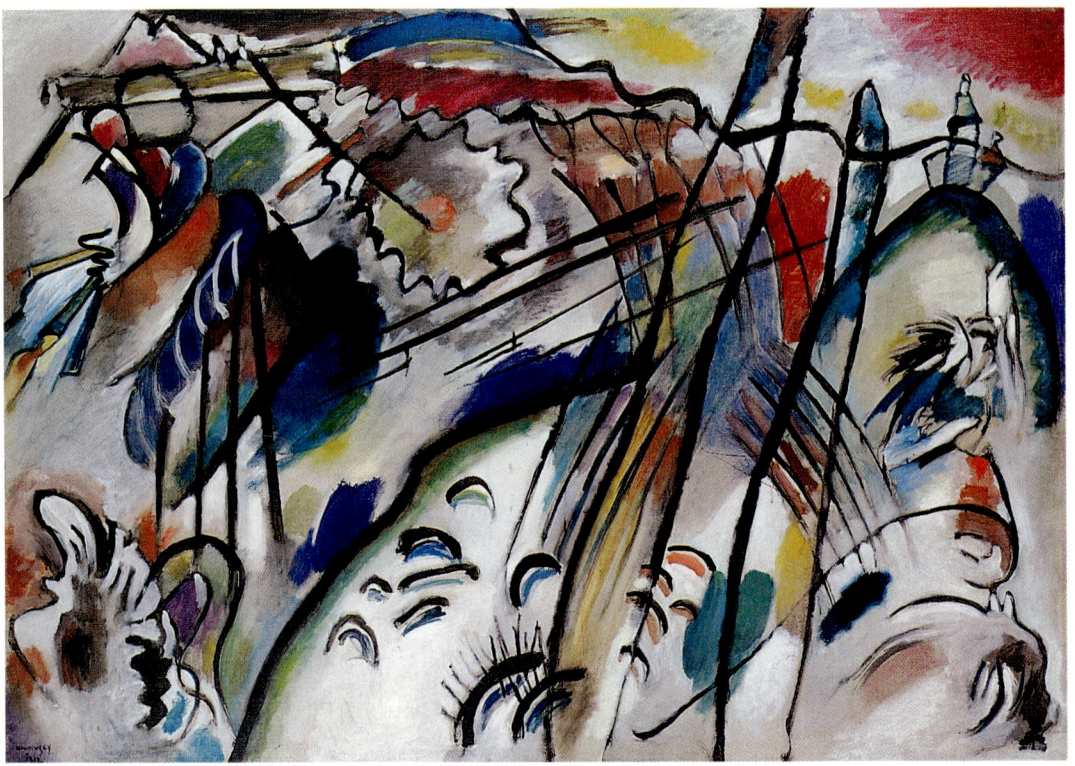

EXPRESSING AN "INNER TRUTH" As noted earlier, Kandinsky's friend and cofounder of Der Blaue Reiter was Franz Marc. Like many of the other German Expressionists, Marc grew increasingly pessimistic about the state of humanity, especially as World War I loomed on the horizon. His perception of human beings as deeply flawed led him to turn to the animal world for his subjects. Animals, he believed, were "more beautiful, more pure" than humanity and thus more appropriate as a vehicle to express an inner truth.[6] In his quest to imbue his paintings with greater emotional intensity, Marc focused on color and developed a system of colors expressing specific feelings or ideas. In a letter to a fellow Blaue Reiter, Marc explained: "Blue is the *male* principle, severe and spiritual. Yellow is the *female* principle, gentle, happy and sensual. Red is *matter,* brutal and heavy. . . ."[7] He based this correspondence between colors and emotions on his perceptions. Marc's attempts to create, in a sense, an iconography (or representational system) of color links him to other avant-garde artists struggling to find new ways to communicate.

Fate of the Animals (FIG. **33-8**) represents the culmination of Marc's color explorations. It was painted in 1913, when the tension of impending cataclysm had pervaded society and

33-8 FRANZ MARC, *Fate of the Animals,* 1913. Oil on canvas, 6′ 4¾″ × 8′ 9½″. Kunstmuseum, Basel.

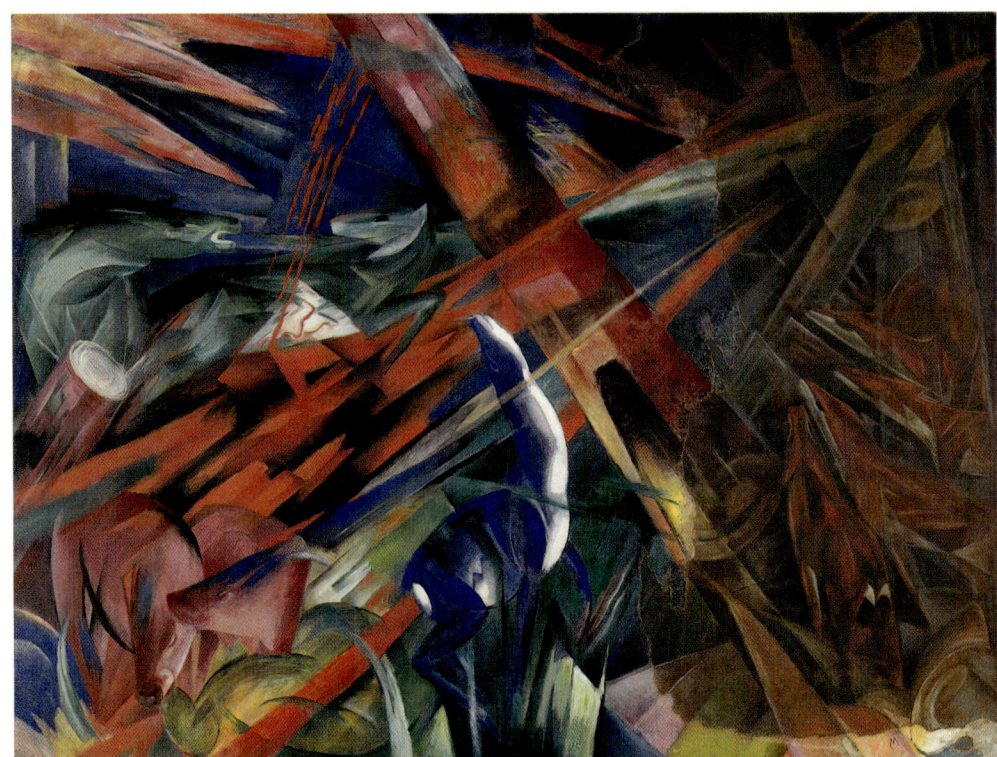

emerged in Marc's art. The animals appear trapped in a forest, some apocalyptic event destroying them. The entire scene is distorted—shattered into fragments. More significantly, the lighter and brighter colors—the passive, gentle, and cheerful ones—are absent, and the colors of severity and brutality dominate the work. Marc discovered just how well his painting portended war's anguish and tragedy when he ended up at the front the following year. His experiences in battle prompted him to write to his wife that *Fate of the Animals* "is like a premonition of this war—horrible and shattering. I can hardly conceive that I painted it."[8] His contempt for people's inhumanity and his attempt to express that through his art ended, with tragic irony, in his death in action in World War I in 1916.

EARLY EXPRESSIONIST SCULPTURE

CLASSICAL GRACE AND BEAUTY Just as painters sought maximum expressive effect through line, color, and manipulation of shape, many early-twentieth-century sculptors pursued a similar direction. They moved away from literally depicting objects and sought to imbue their works with greater emotional resonance. The French sculptor ARISTIDE MAILLOL (1861–1944) wanted his sculptures, predominantly figurative, to embody the abstractions of beauty, repose, and tranquility. His works, such as *The Mediterranean* (FIG. **33-9**), capture the essence of those ideals through a graceful simplicity of pose and gesture. The clean lines and apparent timelessness of Maillol's sculpture reveal that he deeply imbued his art with the classical spirit. In fact, it has been suggested *The Mediterranean* is a metaphor of cultural geography in how it captures the character of the Greek and Roman cultures once populating the Mediterranean region. Maillol was born in Banyuls, a Mediterranean fishing village near the Spanish border, which well may explain his sensitivity to the classical legacy.

EMBRACING ABSTRACTION

A Spanish artist whose importance in the history of art is uncontested is PABLO PICASSO (1881–1973). His extensive artistic production during his lengthy career covered a wide range of media (painting, sculpture, ceramics, prints, and drawings) and styles. He made staggering contributions to the development of abstraction and to new ways of representing the surrounding world.

Picasso was a precocious student who had mastered all aspects of late-nineteenth-century Realist technique by the time he entered the Barcelona Academy of Fine Art in the late 1890s. His prodigious talent led him to experiment with a wide range of visual expression, first in Spain and then in Paris, where he settled in 1904. Throughout his career, Picasso remained a traditional artist in making careful preparatory studies for each major work. He characterized the modern age, however, in his enduring quest for innovation, his lack of complacency, and his insistence on constantly challenging himself and those around him. Picasso revealed this modernity in his constant experimentation, in his sudden shifts from one style to another, and in his startling innovations in painting, graphic art, and sculpture, among other media. By the time he settled permanently in Paris, his work had evolved from Spanish painting's sober Realism through an Impressionistic phase (for a time, influenced by Toulouse-Lautrec's early works) to the so-called Blue Period (1901–1904). Picasso's melancholy state of mind prompted the Blue Period, when he used primarily blue colors to depict worn, pathetic, and alienated figures.

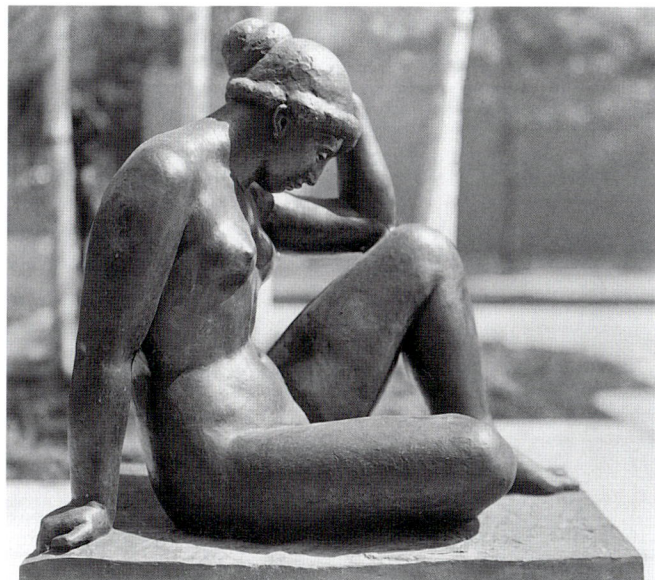

33-9 ARISTIDE MAILLOL, *The Mediterranean*, 1902–1905 (base ca. 1951–1953). Bronze, 3′ 5″ high; base, 3′ 9″ × 2′ 5″. Museum of Modern Art, New York (gift of Stephen C. Clark).

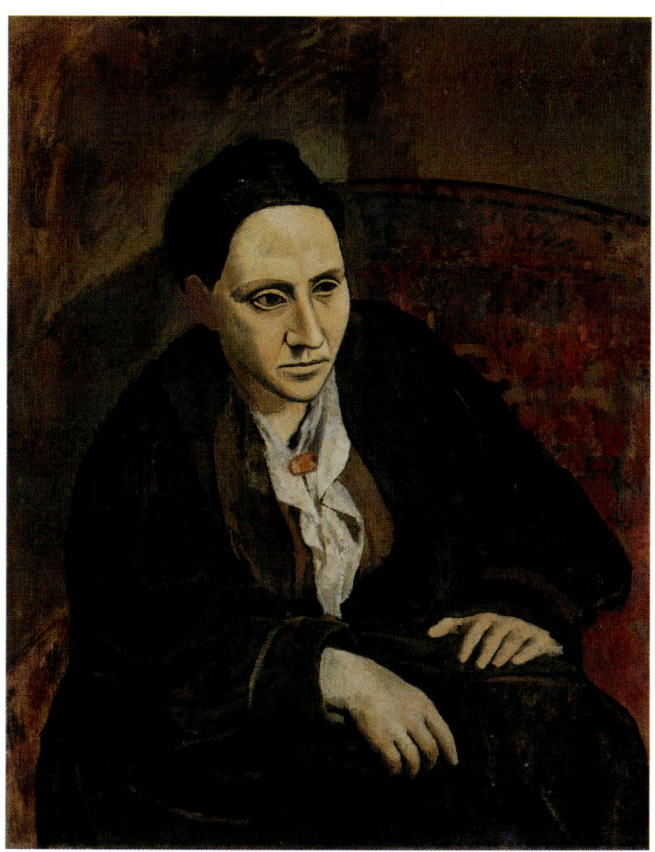

33-10 PABLO PICASSO, *Gertrude Stein*, 1906–1607. Oil on canvas, 3′3$\frac{3}{8}$″ × 2′8″. Metropolitan Museum of Art, New York (bequest of Gertrude Stein, 1947).

The Fragmentation of Forms in Space

A PLANAR PORTRAIT OF A WRITER   By 1906, Picasso was searching restlessly for new ways to depict form. He found clues in African sculpture, in ancient Iberian sculpture, and in the late paintings of Cézanne. (The expansion of colonial empires in the late nineteenth and early twentieth centuries resulted in wider exposure of European and American artists to art from Africa, India, and other faraway lo-

cales.) Inspired by these sources, Picasso returned to a portrait of Gertrude Stein (FIG. **33-10**), his friend and patron (see "Nurturing the Avant-Garde: Gertrude and Leo Stein as Art Patrons," page 1015). Picasso had started the painting earlier that year but had left it unfinished after more than eighty sittings by Stein because, the artist told her, "I can't see you any longer when I look."[9] On resuming his work on the portrait, Picasso painted Stein's head as a simplified planar form, incorporating aspects derived from his wide-ranging sources.

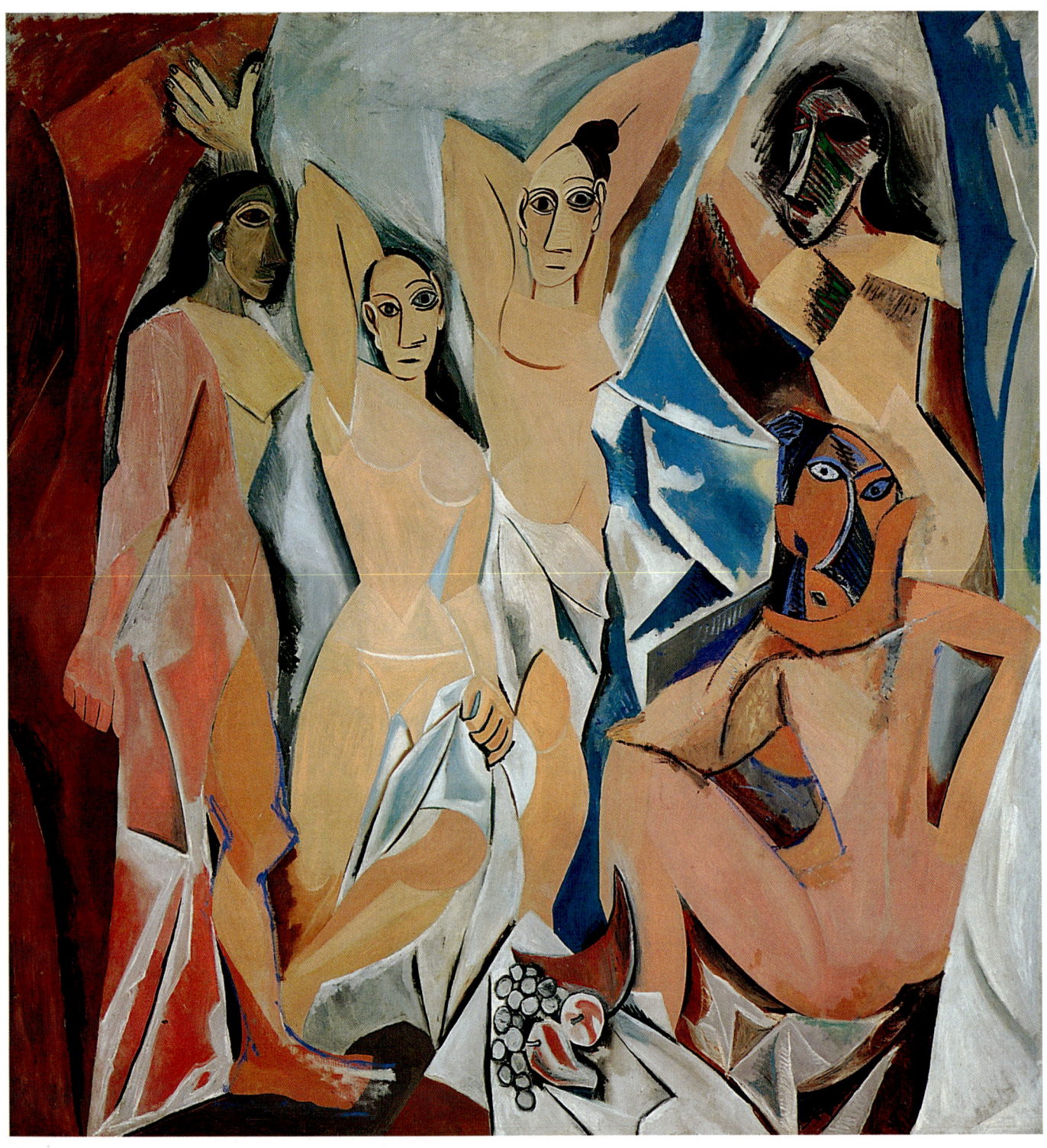

33-11   PABLO PICASSO, *Les Demoiselles d'Avignon,* June–July 1907. Oil on canvas, 8′ × 7′ 8″. Museum of Modern Art, New York (acquired through the Lillie P. Bliss Bequest).

"I PAINT FORMS AS I THINK THEM" The influence of African, Iberian, and European art also surfaces in *Les Demoiselles d'Avignon* (The young ladies of Avignon; FIG. 33-11), which opened the door to a radically new method of representing form in space. Picasso began the work as a symbolic picture to be titled *Philosophical Bordello,* portraying male clients intermingling with women in the reception room of a brothel (Avignon Street in Barcelona was located in the red-light district). By the time the artist finished, he had eliminated the male figures and simplified the room's details to a suggestion of drapery and a schematic foreground still life. Picasso had become wholly absorbed in the problem of finding a new way to represent the five female figures in their interior space. Instead of representing the figures as continuous volumes, he fractured their shapes and interwove them with the equally jagged planes that represent drapery and empty space. Indeed, the space, so entwined with the bodies, is virtually illegible. Here Picasso pushed Cézanne's treatment of form and space to a new tension. The tension between Picasso's representation of three-dimensional space and his statement of painting as a two-dimensional design lying flat on the surface of a stretched canvas is a tension between representation and abstraction.

The artist extended the radical nature of *Les Demoiselles d'Avignon* even further by inconsistently depicting the figures. The calm, ideal features of the three young women at the left were inspired by ancient Iberian sculptures, which Picasso saw during summer visits to Spain. The energetic, violently striated features of the two heads to the right emerged late in Picasso's production of the work and grew directly from his increasing fascination with the power of African sculpture. Perhaps responding to the energy of these two new heads, Picasso also revised their bodies. He broke them into more ambiguous planes suggesting a combination of views, as if the figures are seen from more than one place in space at once. The woman seated at the lower right shows these multiple views most clearly, seeming to present observers simultaneously with a three-quarter back view from the left, another from the right, and a front view of the head that suggests seeing the figure frontally as well. Gone is the traditional concept of an orderly, constructed, and unified pictorial space that mirrors the world. In its place are the rudimentary beginnings of a new representation of the world as a dynamic interplay of time and space. Clearly, *Les Demoiselles d'Avignon* represents a dramatic departure from the careful presentation of a visual reality. Explained Picasso: "I paint forms as I think them, not as I see them."[10]

For many years, Picasso showed *Les Demoiselles* only to other painters. One of the first to see it was GEORGES BRAQUE (1882–1963), a Fauve painter who was so agitated and challenged by it that he began to rethink his own painting style. Using the painting's revolutionary ideas as a point of departure, together Braque and Picasso formulated Cubism around 1908.

Cubism

Cubism represented a radical turning point in the history of art, nothing less than a dismissal of the pictorial illusionism that had, over the years, dominated Western art. The Cubists rejected naturalistic depictions, preferring compositions of shapes and forms "abstracted" from the conventionally perceived world. These artists pursued the analysis of form central to Cézanne's artistic explorations, and they adopted Cézanne's suggestion that artists use the simple forms of cylinders, spheres, and cones to represent nature in art. They dissected life's continuous optical spread into its many constituent features, which they then recomposed, by a new logic of design, into a coherent aesthetic object. For the Cubists, the art of painting had to move far beyond the description of visual reality. This rejection of accepted artistic practice illustrates both the period's aggressive avant-garde critique of pictorial convention and the public's dwindling faith in a safe, concrete Newtonian world, fears fostered by the physics of Einstein and others. Although not immune to the effects of the societal turbulence of the early twentieth century, the Cubists increasingly directed their energies into their critique of traditional aesthetics. The French writer and theorist Guillaume Apollinaire summarized well the central Cubism concepts in 1913:

> Authentic Cubism [is] the art of depicting new wholes with formal elements borrowed not from the reality of vision, but from that of conception. This tendency leads to a poetic kind of painting which stands outside the world of observation; for, even in a simple cubism, the geometrical surfaces of an object must be opened out in order to give a complete representation of it. . . . Everyone must agree that a chair, from whichever side it is viewed, never ceases to have four legs, a seat and back, and that if it is robbed of one of these elements, it is robbed of an important part.[11]

The new style received its name after Matisse described some of Braque's work to a critic, Louis Vauxcelles, as having been painted "avec des petits cubes" (with little cubes), and the critic went on in his review to speak of "cubic oddities."[12] Thus, critics, through their choice of labels, in part formed public understanding of this original and trailblazing painting method.

Analytic Cubism

Historians often refer to the first phase of Cubism, developed jointly by Picasso and Braque, as Analytic Cubism. Because Cubists could not achieve the kind of total view Apollinaire described by the traditional method of drawing or painting models from one position, these artists began to dissect the forms of their subjects. They presented that dissection for viewers to inspect across the canvas surface. In simplistic terms, Analytic Cubism involves analyzing form and investigating the visual vocabulary (that is, the pictorial elements) for conveying meaning.

A SHIFTING PORTRAIT OF A MUSICIAN Georges Braque's painting *The Portuguese* (FIG. 33-12) is a striking example of Analytic Cubism. The artist derived the subject from his memories of a Portuguese musician seen years earlier in a bar in Marseilles. In this painting, Braque concentrated his attention on dissecting the form and placing it in dynamic interaction with the space around it; he reduced color to a monochrome of brown tones. Unlike the high-keyed paintings of the Fauves and German Expressionists, the Cubists used subdued hues to focus viewers' attention on form. In *The Portuguese,* the artist carried his analysis so far that viewers must work diligently to discover clues to the

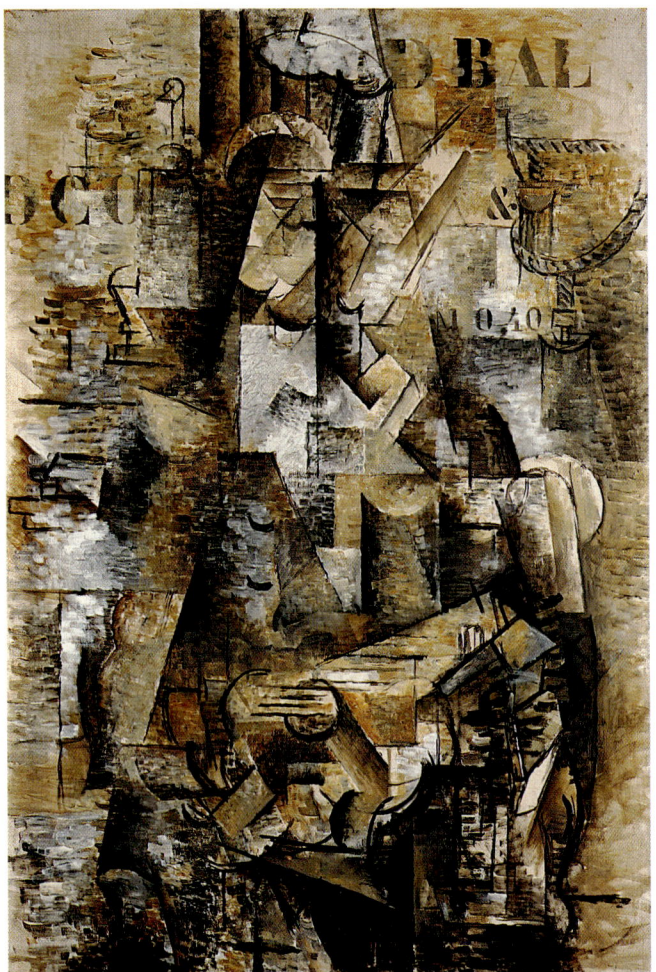

33-12 GEORGES BRAQUE, *The Portuguese,* 1911. Oil on canvas, $3'10\frac{1}{8}'' \times$ $2' 8''$. Offentliche Kunstsammlung Basel, Kunstmuseum, Basel (gift of Raoul La Roche, 1952).

subject. The construction of large intersecting planes suggests the forms of a man and a guitar. Smaller shapes interpenetrate and hover in the large planes. The way Braque treated light and shadow reveals his departure from conventional artistic practice. Light and dark passages suggest both chiaroscuro modeling and transparent planes that allow viewers to see through one level to another. As observers look, solid forms emerge only to be canceled almost immediately by a different reading of the subject.

The stenciled letters and numbers add to the painting's complexity. Letters and numbers are flat shapes. On a book's pages, they exist outside three-dimensional space, but as shapes in a Cubist painting such as *The Portuguese,* they allow the painter to play with viewers' perception of two- and three-dimensional space. The letters and numbers lie flat on the painted canvas surface, yet the image's shading and shapes seem to flow behind and underneath them, pushing the letters and numbers forward into the viewing space. Occasionally, they seem attached to the surface of some object within the painting. Picasso and Braque pioneered precisely this exploration of visual vocabulary—for example, composition, two-dimensional shape, three-dimensional form, color, and value—and its role in generating meaning. Ultimately, the constantly shifting imagery makes it impossible to arrive at any definitive or final reading of the image. Even today, examining such a painting is a disconcerting excursion into ambiguity and doubt.

KALEIDOSCOPIC COLORED SHARDS Picasso and Braque avoided bright color in their Analytic Cubist works. Artists and art historians generally have seen this suppression of color as crucial to Cubism's success. These two artists employed this strategy to unify paintings that radically disrupted viewer expectations about the representation of time and space. Their contemporary, ROBERT DELAUNAY (1885–1941), worked toward a kind of color Cubism. The French poet Guillaume Apollinaire called this art style Orphism, after Orpheus, the Greek god with magical powers of music. Apollinaire believed art, like music, was divorced from representation of the visible world. *Champs de Mars,* or *The Red Tower* (FIG. 33-13), is one of many paintings Delaunay produced between 1909 and 1912 depicting the Eiffel Tower. People in the early twentieth century still considered this tower, constructed in 1889, a marvel of modern engineering technology. The title *Champs de Mars* refers to the Parisian field in which the Eiffel Tower is located, named after the Campus Martius (Field of Mars) located outside the walls of Republican Rome.

The artist broke the monument's perceptual unity into a kaleidoscopic array of colored shards, which variously leap forward or pull back according to the relative hues and values of the broken shapes. The structure ambiguously rises and collapses. Beyond its formal links to Cubism, the fragmentation of the Eiffel Tower in *Champs de Mars* also has been interpreted in political terms as a commentary on the societal collapse in the years leading to World War I. In unedited notes, Delaunay himself described the collapsing tower imagery as "the synthesis of a period of destruction; likewise a prophe-

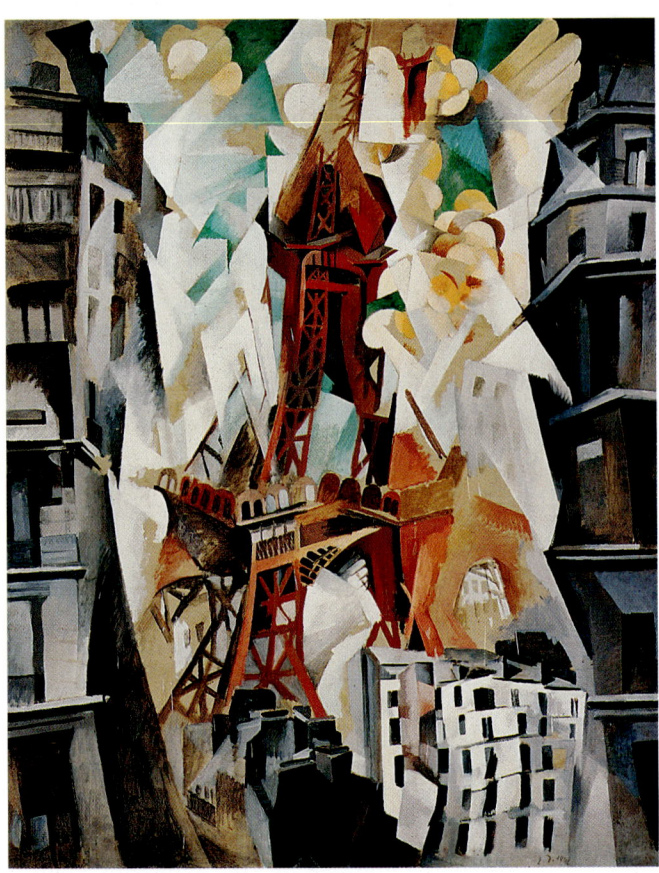

33-13 ROBERT DELAUNAY, *Champs de Mars* or *The Red Tower,* 1911. Oil on canvas, $5' 3'' \times 4' 3''$. Art Institute of Chicago, Chicago.

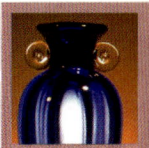

ART AND SOCIETY

Nurturing the Avant-Garde
Gertrude and Leo Stein as Art Patrons

The rebellious and antagonistic stance avant-garde artists adopted in all media understandably engendered much hostility and resistance to their art by the public. This response rather restricted the social circles within which avant-garde artists traveled. Gertrude (1874–1946) and Leo (1872–1947) Stein played a pivotal role in the history of the avant-garde in the early twentieth century because they provided, in their Paris house, a hospitable environment. Artists, writers, musicians, collectors, and critics interested in progressive art and ideas could meet there to talk and socialize. Born in Pennsylvania, brother and sister Leo and Gertrude moved to Paris in 1903, setting up a home at 27, rue de Fleurus. Gertrude's experimental writing stimulated her interest in the latest developments in the arts; conversely, the avant-garde ideas discussed at the Steins's house influenced her unique poetry, plays, and other literary forms. She is perhaps best known for *The Autobiography of Alice B. Toklas* (1933), a unique memoir written in the persona of her longtime companion.

The Steins's interest in the exciting and invigorating debates taking place in avant-garde circles led them to welcome visitors to their Saturday salons, which included lectures, thoughtful discussions, and spirited arguments. Often, these "salon" gatherings lasted until dawn. They became renowned and included not only the French but also visiting Americans, British, Swedes, Germans, Hungarians, Spaniards, Poles, and Russians. Among the hundreds who welcomed the opportunity to visit the Steins's were the artists Matisse, Picasso, Georges Braque, Cassatt, Duchamp, Alfred Stieglitz, and Arthur B. Davis; the writers Ernest Hemingway, F. Scott Fitzgerald, John dos Passos, Jean Cocteau, and Guillaume Apollinaire; art dealers Daniel Kahnweiler and Ambroise Vollard; critics Roger Fry and Clive Bell; and collectors Sergei Shchukin and Ivan Morosov.

The art decorating the walls of 27, rue de Fleurus also attracted many visitors. The Steins were avid art collectors. One of the first paintings Leo purchased was Matisse's notorious *Woman with the Hat* (FIG. 33-1), and he subsequently bought numerous important paintings by Matisse and Picasso, along with works by Gauguin, Cézanne, Renoir, and Braque. Picasso, who developed a close friendship with Gertrude, asked to paint her portrait, and the well-known painting (FIG. 33-10), which he finished in 1907 after more than one year of work and numerous sittings by Gertrude, today hangs in the Metropolitan Museum of Art. So taken by the completed portrait, Gertrude kept it by her all her life and bequeathed it to the Metropolitan only after her death in 1946.

Ultimately, Gertrude and Leo Stein played a central role in the avant-garde's development in the early twentieth century, both as collectors and as facilitators of interaction among avant-garde artists, writers, musicians, and others in the art world. Their passion for and fascination with the international art scene undeniably contributed to the history of twentieth-century art.

---

tic vision with social repercussions: war, and the base crumbles."[13] This statement encapsulates well the social and artistic climate during these years—the destruction of old world orders and of artistic practices deemed obsolete, as well as the avant-garde's prophetic nature and its determination to subvert tradition.

Ultimately, Delaunay's experiments with color dynamics strongly influenced the Futurists (discussed later) and the German Expressionists (he exhibited with Der Blaue Reiter, as well as with Cubists). These artists found in his art means for intensifying expression by suggesting violent motion through shape and color.

Synthetic Cubism

ILLUSION OR REALITY? In 1912, Cubism entered a new phase when the style no longer relied on a decipherable relation to the visible world. In this new phase, called Synthetic Cubism, artists constructed paintings and drawings from objects and shapes cut from paper or other materials to represent parts of a subject. The work marking the point of departure for this new style was Picasso's *Still Life with Chair-Caning* (FIG. **33-14**), a painting that included a piece of oil-cloth pasted on the canvas after it was imprinted with the photolithographed pattern of a cane chair seat. It is framed with a piece of rope. This work challenges viewers' understanding of "reality." The photographically replicated chair caning seems so "real" that one expects the holes to break any brush strokes laid upon it. But the chair caning, although optically suggestive of the real, is actually only an illusion or representation of an object. In contrast, the painted abstract areas do not refer to tangible objects in the real world. Yet the fact they do not imitate anything makes them more "real" than the chair caning—no pretense exists. Picasso extended the visual play by making the letter *U* escape from the space of the accompanying *J* and *O* and partially covering it with a cylindrical shape that pushes across its left side. The letters *JOU* appear in many Cubist paintings; these letters formed part of the masthead of the daily French newspapers (journals) often found among the objects represented. Picasso and Braque especially delighted in the punning references to *jouer* and *jeu*—the French words for "to play" and "game."

PAPER GLUED ON CANVAS After *Still Life with Chair-Caning*, both Picasso and Braque continued to explore the new medium of collage introduced in that work. From the French word meaning "to stick," a collage is a composi-

33-14   PABLO PICASSO, *Still Life with Chair-Caning,* 1911–1912. Oil and oilcloth on canvas on canvas, $10\frac{5}{8}$″ × 1′ $1\frac{3}{4}$″. Musée Picasso, Paris.

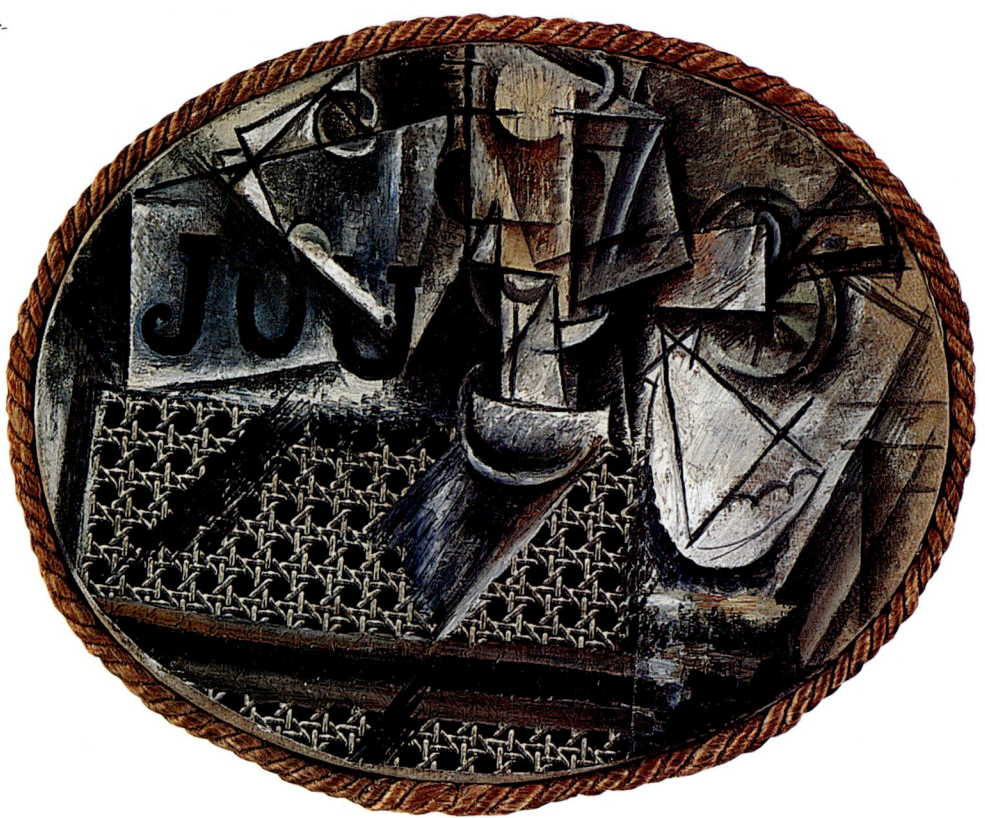

tion of bits of objects, such as newspaper or cloth, glued to a surface. Its possibilities also can be seen in Braque's *Fruit Dish and Cards* (FIG. **33-15**), done in a variant of collage called *papier collé* (stuck paper), or gluing assorted paper shapes to a drawing or painting. Here, charcoal and pencil lines and shadows provide clues to the Cubist multiple views of table, dishes, playing cards, and fruit. Roughly rectangular strips of wood-grained, gray, and black paper run vertically up the composition. They overlap each other to create a layering of unmistakably flat planes that both echo the space the lines suggest and establish the flatness of the work's surface. All shapes in the image seem to oscillate, pushing forward and dropping back in space. Shading seems to carve space into flat planes in some places and to turn planes into transparent surfaces in others. The bottom edge of the ace of clubs, for example, seems to extend forward over a strip of wood-grained paper, while its top corner appears to slip behind a filmy plane.

Viewers of *Fruit Dish and Cards* are kept aware that this is an artwork an artist created and that they must enter the visual game to decipher all levels of representation. Braque no longer analyzed the three-dimensional qualities of the physical world. Here, he constructed or synthesized objects and space alike from the materials he used. Picasso stated his views on Cubism at this point in its development: "Not only did we try to displace reality; reality was no longer in the object. . . . [In] the *papier collé* . . . [w]e didn't any longer want to fool the eye; we wanted to fool the mind. . . . If a piece of newspaper can be a bottle, that gives us something to think about in connection with both newspapers and bottles, too."[14]

Like all collage, the papier collé technique was modern in its medium—mass-produced materials never before found in "high" art—and modern in how the artist embedded the art's "message" in the imagery and in the nature of these everyday

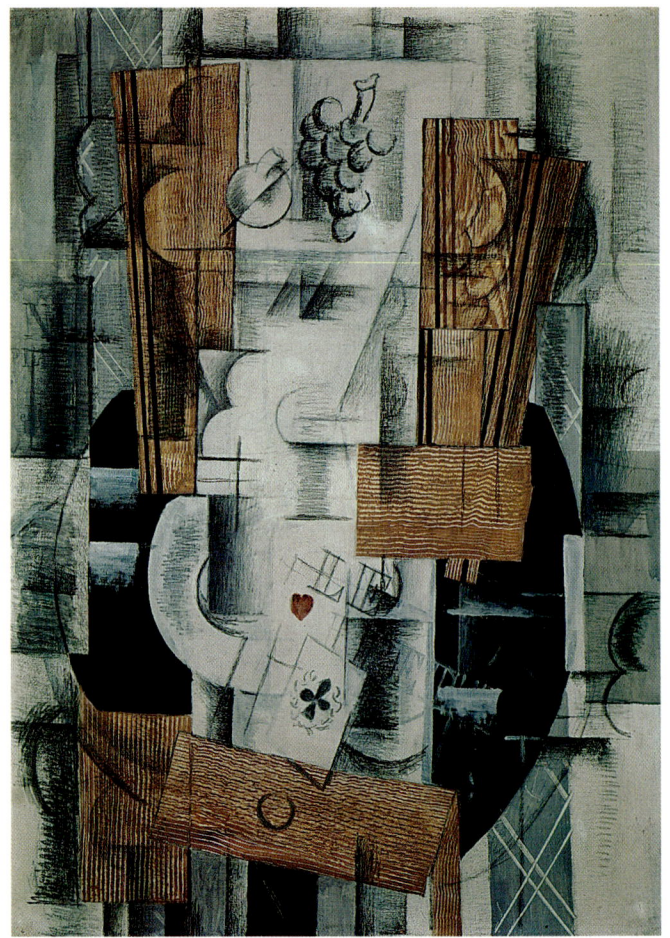

33-15   GEORGES BRAQUE, *Fruit Dish and Cards,* 1913. Oil, pencil, paper collage, and charcoal on canvas, 2′ $7\frac{7}{8}$″ × 1′ $11\frac{5}{8}$″. Musée Nationale d'Art Moderne, Centre Georges Pompidou, Paris (gift of Paul Rosenberg).

materials. Although most discussions of Cubism and collage focus on the formal innovations they represented, it is important to note that the public also viewed the revolutionary and subversive nature of Cubism in sociopolitical terms. Cubism's attacks on artistic convention and tradition were easily expanded to encompass an attack on society's complacency and status quo. Many artists and writers of the period allied themselves with various anarchist groups whose social critiques and utopian visions appealed to progressive thinkers. It was, therefore, not a far leap to see radical art, like Cubism, as having political ramifications. Indeed, many critics in the French press consistently equated Cubism with anarchism, revolution, and disdain for tradition. The impact of Cubism thus extended beyond the boundaries of the art world itself.

A WHIMSICAL MUSICAL TRIO Braque and Picasso eventually used found materials in collages to reintroduce color into their work. In the 1920s, Picasso developed a colorful variant of Synthetic Cubism into a highly personal painting style that mimicked the look of the earlier pasted works. In paintings such as *Three Musicians* (FIG. **33-16**), Picasso constructed figures from simple flat shapes that interlock and interpenetrate in a composition that whimsically combined a modernist statement of the canvas's flat plane with traditional modes of representation. The floor and walls of the room where this lively musical trio performs suggest Renaissance perspective gone slightly awry, while the table, with an unexpected still life resting on its surface, appears in reverse perspective. A jumble of flat shapes materializes into the figures

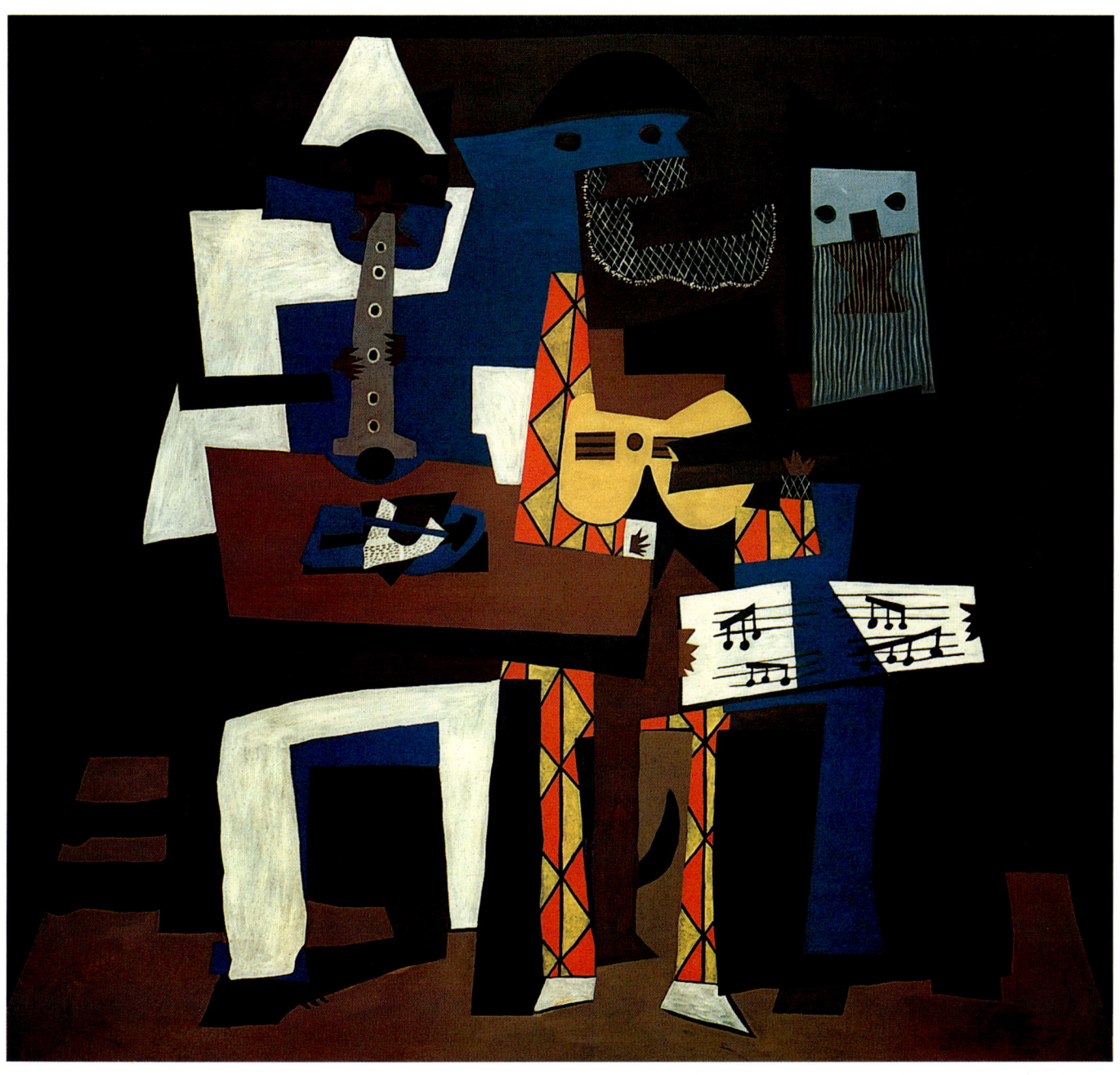

33-16 PABLO PICASSO, *Three Musicians*, Fontainebleau, summer 1921. Oil on canvas, 6′ 7″ × 7′ 3″. Museum of Modern Art, New York, (Mrs. Simon Guggenheim).

of Pierrot (the French pantomime character in white) on clarinet, Harlequin (a French clown in mask and tights) on guitar, and a mysterious masked monk as vocalist. Miraculously, the flat irregular yet rhythmic shapes give each musician a different personality and simultaneously suggest the sprightly tune they are performing. Careful inspection reveals an alert dog sprawled behind the troupe, apparently beating its tail vigorously in time to the music. By the 1920s, Picasso and Braque were going their separate ways as artists, but their Cubist contributions had dramatic and widespread impact, and each continued to produce significant artworks for many years.

Cubist Sculpture

DISSOLVING THREE-DIMENSIONAL FORM Cubism did not just open new avenues for representing form on two-dimensional surfaces; it also inspired new approaches to sculpture. Picasso explored Cubism's possibilities in sculpture throughout the years he and Braque developed the style.

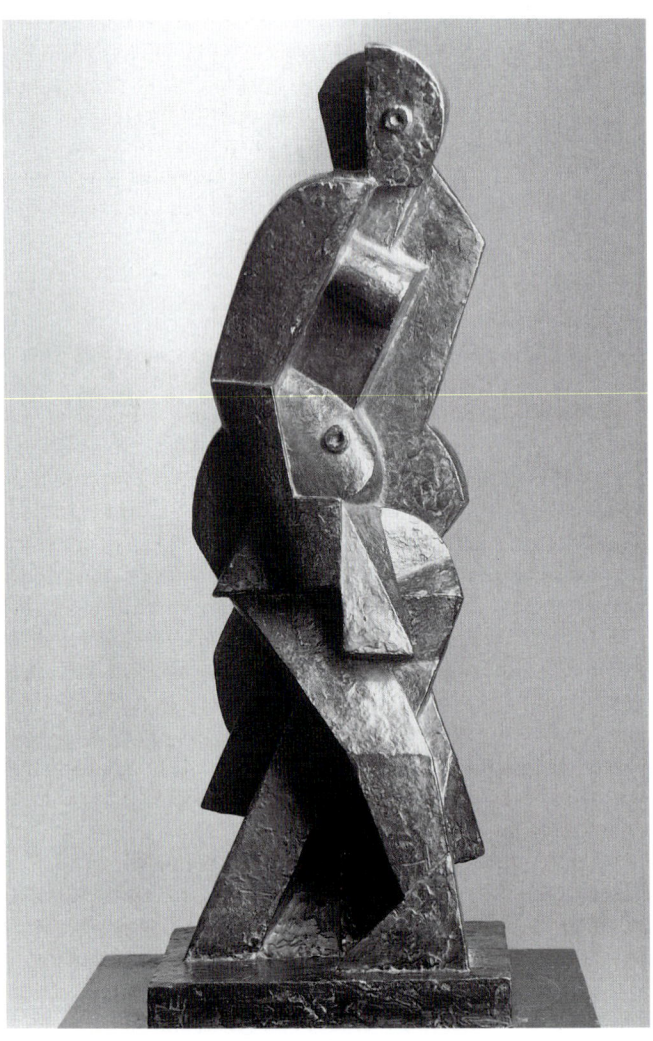

33-17 JACQUES LIPCHITZ, *Bather*, 1917. Bronze, 2′ 10¾″ × 1′1¼″ × 1′1″. Nelson-Atkins Museum of Art, Kansas City (gift of the Friends of Art). Copyright © Estate of Jacques Lipchitz/Licensed by VAGA, New York/ Marlborough Gallery, NY.

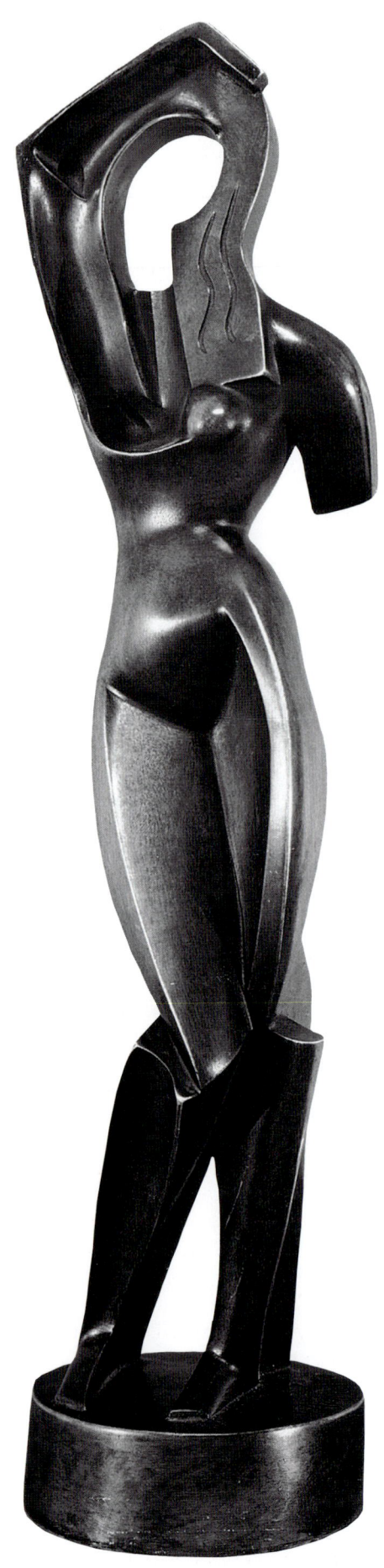

33-18 ALEKSANDR ARCHIPENKO, *Woman Combing Her Hair,* 1915. Bronze, approx. 1′1¾″ high. Museum of Modern Art, New York (bequest of Lillie P. Bliss).

the body when the hand rests on the hip, as in Verrocchio's *David* (see FIG. 21-24). But here the space penetrates the figure's continuous mass and is a defined form equal in importance to the mass of the bronze. It is not simply the negative counterpart to the volume. Archipenko's figure shows the same fluid intersecting planes seen in Cubist painting, and the relation of the planes to each other is similarly complex. Thus, in painting and sculpture, the Cubists broke through traditional limits and transformed the medium. Archipenko's figure is still somewhat representational, but sculpture (like painting) executed within the Cubist idiom tended to cast off the last vestiges of representation.

WELDED METAL SCULPTURES OF THE 1930s

A friend of Picasso, JULIO GONZÁLEZ (1876–1942) shared his interest in the artistic possibilities of new materials and new methods borrowed from both industrial technology and traditional metalworking. Born into a family of metalworkers in Barcelona, Spain, González helped Picasso construct a number of welded sculptures. This contact with Picasso, in turn, allowed González to refine his own sculptural vocabulary. Using ready-made bars, sheets, or rods of welded or wrought iron and bronze, González created dynamic sculptures with both linear elements and volumetric forms. In his *Woman Combing Her Hair* (FIG. **33-19**); (compare with Archipenko's version of the same subject), the figure is reduced to an interplay of curves, lines, and planes—virtually a complete abstraction. Although González's sculpture received limited exposure during his lifetime, it became particularly important for sculptors in subsequent decades who focused their attention on the capabilities of welded metal.

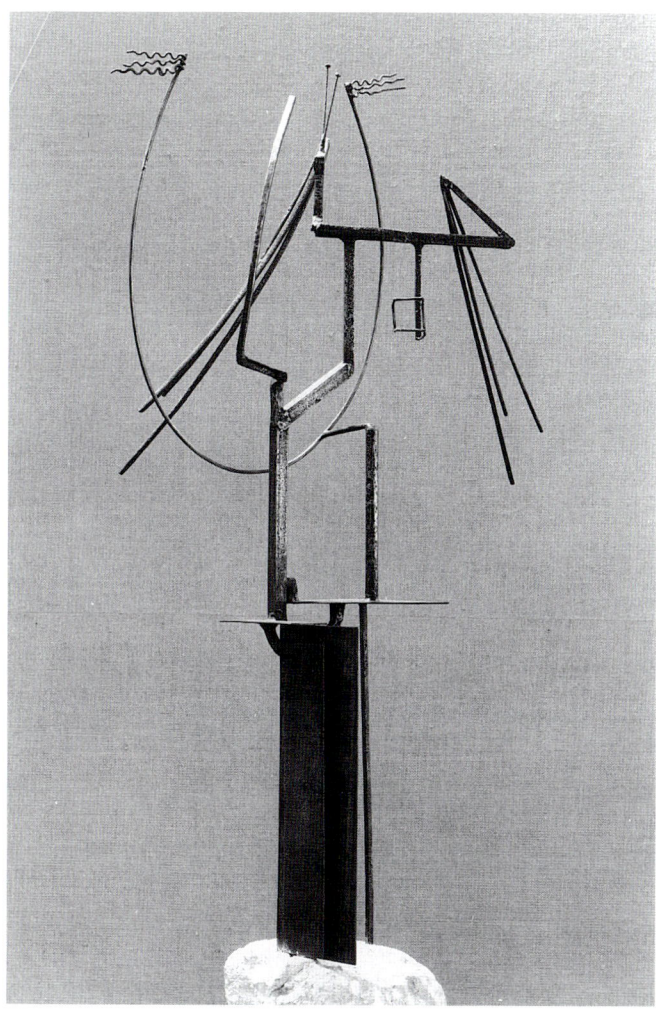

33-19 JULIO GONZÁLEZ, *Woman Combing Her Hair,* ca. 1930–1933. Iron, 4′ 9″ high. Moderna Museet, Stockholm.

One of the most successful sculptors to adapt into three dimensions the planar, fragmented dissolution of form central to Analytic Cubist painting was JACQUES LIPCHITZ (1891–1973). Born in Latvia, Lipchitz resided for many years in France and the United States. He worked out his ideas for many of his sculptures in clay before creating them in bronze or in stone. *Bather* (FIG. **33-17**) is typical of his Cubist style. Lipchitz broke the continuous form in this work into cubic volumes and planes. The interlocking and gracefully intersecting irregular facets and curves recall the paintings of Picasso and Braque and represent a parallel analysis of dynamic form in space. Lipchitz later produced less volumetric sculptures that included empty spaces outlined by metal shapes. In these sculptures, Lipchitz pursued even further the Cubist notion of spatial ambiguity and the relationship between solid forms and space.

THE INTERPLAY OF MASS AND SPACE

The Russian sculptor ALEKSANDR ARCHIPENKO (1887–1964) explored similar ideas, as seen in *Woman Combing Her Hair* (FIG. **33-18**). This statuette introduces, in place of the head, a void with a shape of its own that figures importantly in the whole design. Enclosed spaces always have existed in figurative sculpture—for example, the space between the arm and

Purism

THE MACHINE AESTHETIC Charles Edouard Jeanneret, known as Le Corbusier, is today best known as one of the most important modernist architects (see later discussion, pages 1056–57). But also a painter, he founded in 1918 a movement called Purism, which opposed Synthetic Cubism on the grounds that it was becoming merely an esoteric, decorative art out of touch with the machine age. Purists maintained that machinery's clean functional lines and the pure forms of its parts, should direct the artist's experiments in design, whether in painting, architecture, or industrially produced objects. This "machine esthetic" inspired FERNAND LÉGER (1881–1955), a French painter who had early on painted with the Cubists. He devised an effective compromise of tastes, bringing together meticulous Cubist analysis of form with the Purist's broad simplification and machinelike finish of the design components. He retained from his Cubist practice a preference for cylindrical and tube-shaped motifs, suggestive of machined parts such as pistons and cylinders.

Léger's works have the sharp precision of the machine, whose beauty and quality he was one of the first artists to discover. His contemporary, modern composer George Antheil, wrote a score for a Léger film, *Ballet Mécanique* (1924). The film contrasted inanimate objects such as functioning machines with humans in dancelike variations. Preeminently the

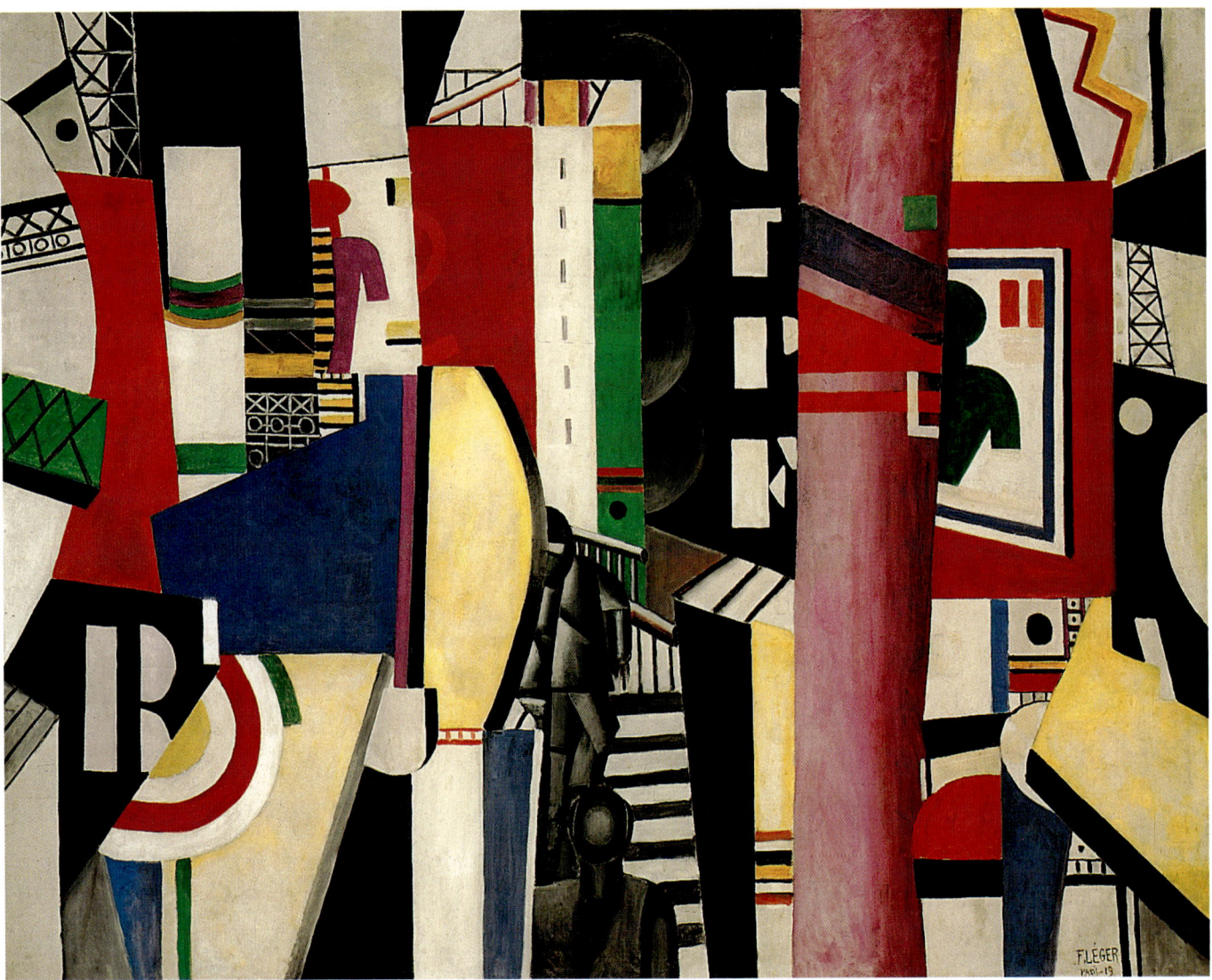

33-20   FERNAND LÉGER, *The City,* 1919. Oil on canvas, approx. 7′ 7″ × 9′ 9½″. Philadelphia Museum of Art, Philadelphia (A. E. Gallatin Collection).

painter of modern urban life, Léger incorporated into his work the massive effects of modern posters and billboard advertisements, the harsh flashing of electric lights, the noise of traffic, and the robotic movements of mechanized people. These effects appear in an early work—modulated, however, by the aesthetic of Synthetic Cubism—*The City* (FIG. **33-20**). Its monumental scale suggests that Léger, had he been given the opportunity, would have been one of the great mural painters of his age. In a definitive way, he depicted the mechanical commotion of contemporary cities then and now.

Futurism

Artists associated with another early-twentieth-century movement, Futurism, pursued many of the ideas the Cubists explored. The contributions of the Futurists, however, were not only artistic. These artists also had a well-defined sociopolitical agenda. Inaugurated and given its name by the charismatic Italian poet and playwright Filippo Tommaso Marinetti in

1909, Futurism began as a literary movement but soon encompassed the visual arts, cinema, theater, music, and architecture. Indignant over the political and cultural decline of Italy, the Futurists published numerous manifestoes in which they aggressively advocated revolution, both in society and in art. Like Die Brücke and other avant-garde artists, the Futurists aimed at ushering in a new, more enlightened era.

In their quest to launch Italian society toward a glorious future, the Futurists championed war as a means of washing away the stagnant past. Indeed, they saw war as a cleansing agent. Marinetti declared: "We wish to glorify war—sole hygiene to the world."[15] The Futurists agitated for the destruction of museums, libraries, and similar institutions, which they described as mausoleums. They also called for radical innovation in the arts. Of particular interest to the Futurists were the speed and dynamism of modern technology. Marinetti insisted that "a speeding automobile. . . is more beautiful than the Nike of Samothrace" (see FIG. 5-82, by then representative of Classicism and the glories of past civilizations).[16] Appropriately, Futurist art often focuses on motion in time and space, incorporating the Cubist discoveries from analyzing form.

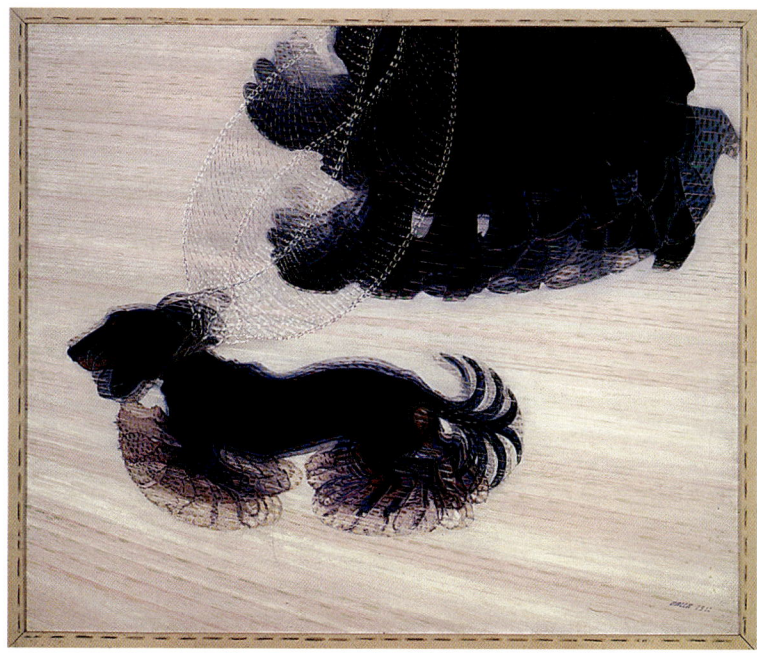

33-21 GIACOMO BALLA, *Dynamism of a Dog on a Leash,* 1912. Oil on canvas, $2'11\frac{3}{8}'' \times 3'7\frac{1}{4}''$. Albright-Knox Art Gallery, Buffalo, New York (bequest of A. Conger Goodyear, gift of George F. Goodyear, 1964).

SIMULTANEITY OF VIEWS The Futurists' interest in motion and in the Cubist dissection of form is evident in *Dynamism of a Dog on a Leash* (FIG. **33-21**) by GIACOMO BALLA (1871–1958). Here, observers focus their gazes on a passing dog and its owner, whose skirts the artist placed just within visual range. Balla achieved the effect of motion by repeating shapes, as in the dog's legs and tail and in the swinging line of the leash. Simultaneity of views, as demonstrated here, was central to the Futurist program.

CAPTURING THE SENSATION OF MOTION UMBERTO BOCCIONI (1882–1916) applied Balla's representational technique to sculpture. What we want, he claimed, is not fixed movement in space but the sensation of motion itself: "Owing to the persistence of images on the retina, objects in motion are multiplied and distorted, following one another like waves in space. Thus, a galloping horse has not four legs, it has twenty."[17] Clearly, this description applies to *Dynamism of a Dog on a Leash.* Though Boccioni in this instance was talking about painting, his observation helps explain what is perhaps the definitive work of Futurist sculpture, his *Unique Forms of Continuity in Space* (FIG. **33-22**).

This piece highlights the formal and spatial effects of motion rather than their source, the striding human figure. The "figure" is so expanded, interrupted, and broken in plane and contour that it disappears, as it were, behind the blur of its movement. Boccioni's search for sculptural means for expressing dynamic movement reached a monumental expression here. In its power and sense of vital activity, this sculpture surpasses similar efforts in painting (by Boccioni and his Futurist companions) to create images symbolic of the dynamic quality of modern life. To be convinced by it, people need only reflect on how details of an adjacent landscape appear in their peripheral vision when they are traveling at great speed on a highway or in a low-flying airplane. Although Boccioni's figure bears a curious resemblance to the ancient *Nike of Samothrace* (see FIG. 5-82), a cursory comparison reveals how far the modern work departs from the ancient one.

This Futurist representation of motion in sculpture has its limitations. The eventual development of the motion picture, based on the rapid sequential projection of fixed images,

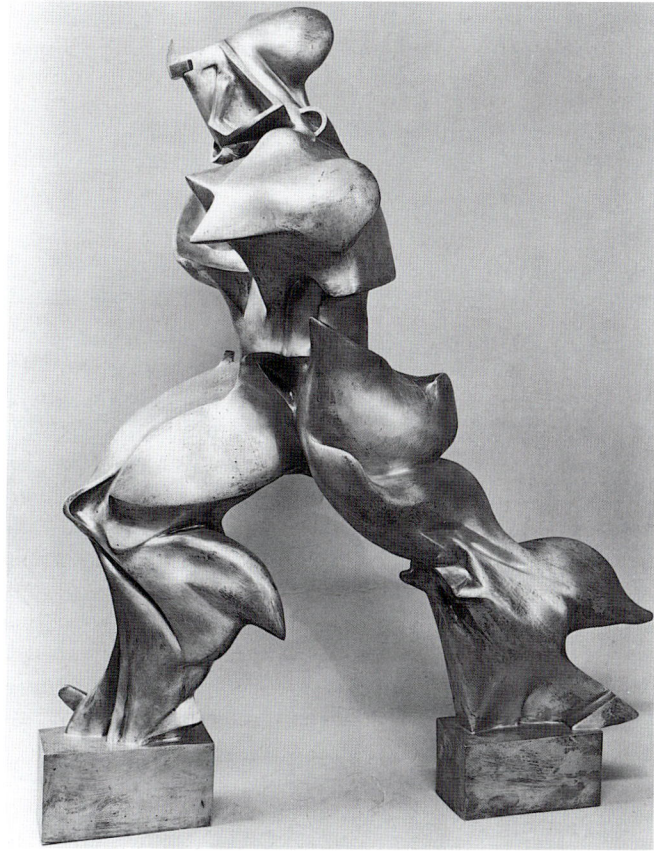

33-22 UMBERTO BOCCIONI, *Unique Forms of Continuity in Space,* 1913 (cast 1931). Bronze, $3'7\frac{7}{8}''$ high $\times 2'10\frac{7}{8}'' \times 1'3\frac{3}{4}''$. Museum of Modern Art, New York (acquired through the Lillie P. Bliss Bequest).

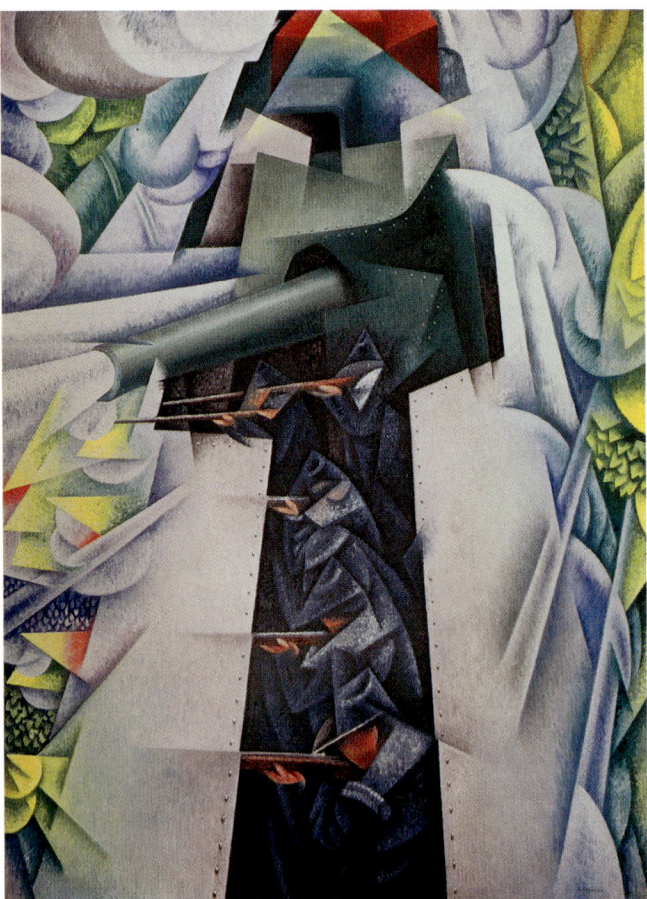

33-23   GINO SEVERINI, *Armored Train*, 1915. Oil on canvas, 3'10" × 2'10⅛". Collection of Richard S. Zeisler, New York.

produced more convincing illusions of movement. And several decades later in sculpture, Alexander Calder (FIG. 33-73) pioneered the development of kinetic sculpture—with actual moving parts. However, in the early twentieth century, Boccioni's sculpture was notable for its ability to capture the sensation of motion.

"WAR—SOLE HYGIENE TO THE WORLD" *Armored Train* (FIG. **33-23**) by GINO SEVERINI (1883–1966) nicely encapsulates the Futurist program, both artistically and politically. The artist depicted a high-tech armored train with its rivets glistening and a huge booming cannon protruding from the top. Submerged in the bowels of the train, a row of soldiers train guns at an unseen target. Severini's painting reflects the Futurist faith in the cleansing action of war. Not only are the colors predominantly light and bright, but the artist also omitted death and destruction—the tragic consequences of war—from the image. This sanitized depiction of war contrasts sharply with Francisco Goya's *Third of May 1808* (see FIG. 28-39), which also depicts a uniform row of anonymous soldiers in the act of shooting. Goya, however, graphically presented the dead and those about to be shot, and the dark tones of the work cast a dramatic and sobering pall. *Armored Train* captures the dynamism and motion central to Futurism. In Cubist fashion, Severini depicted all of the objects, from the soldiers to the smoke emanating from the cannon, broken into facets and planes, suggesting action and movement.

Once World War I broke out, the Futurist group began to disintegrate, largely because so many of them felt compelled to join the Italian Army. Some of them, including Umberto Boccioni, were killed in the war. The ideas the Futurists promoted became integral to the fascism that emerged in Italy shortly thereafter.

CHALLENGING ARTISTIC CONVENTIONS

Although the Futurists celebrated the war and the changes they hoped it would effect, the mass destruction and chaos of World War I horrified other artists. Humanity had never before witnessed such wholesale slaughter on so grand a scale over such an extended period. Millions were killed, wounded, or missing (blown to bits) in great battles. For example, in 1916, the battle of Verdun (lasting five months) left five hundred thousand casualties. On another day in 1916, the British lost sixty thousand men in the opening battle of the Somme. The new technology of armaments, bred of the age of steel, made it a "war of the guns" (as in Severini's *Armored Train*). In the face of massed artillery hurling millions of tons of high explosives and gas shells and in the sheets of fire from thousands of machine guns, attack was suicidal, and battle movement congealed into the stalemate of trench warfare, stretching from the English Channel almost to Switzerland. The mud, filth, and blood of the trenches, the pounding and shattering of incessant shell fire, and the terrible deaths and mutilations were a devastating psychological, as well as physical, experience for a generation brought up with the doctrine of progress and a belief in the fundamental values of civilization.

Dada

With the war as a backdrop, many artists contributed to an artistic and literary movement that became known as Dada. This movement emerged, in large part, in reaction to what many of these artists saw as nothing more than an insane spectacle of collective homicide. They clearly were "revolted by the butchery of the World War."[18] The international scope of Dada proves this revulsion was widespread; although Dada began independently in New York and Zurich, it also emerged in Paris, Berlin, and Cologne, among other cities. Dada was more a mind-set or attitude than a single identifiable style. As André Breton, founder of the slightly later Surrealist movement, explained: "Cubism was a school of painting, futurism a political movement: DADA is a state of mind."[19] The Dadaists believed reason and logic had been responsible for the unmitigated disaster of world war, and they concluded that the only route to salvation was through political anarchy, the irrational, and the intuitive. Thus, an element of absurdity is a cornerstone of Dada, even reflected in the movement's name. "Dada" is a term unrelated to the movement; according to an often repeated anecdote, the Dadaists chose the word at random from a French-German dictionary. Although *dada* does have meaning—it is French for a child's hobby horse—it satisfied the Dadaists' desire for something irrational and nonsensical. (It should be noted, however, that this is just one among many explanations for the name selected for this movement.)

Further, the pessimism and disgust of these artists surfaced in their disdain for convention or tradition, characterized by a concerted and sustained attempt to undermine cherished notions and assumptions about art. Because of this destructive dimension, art historians often describe Dada as a nihilistic enterprise. This nihilism, Dada's contempt for all traditional and established values, and its derisive iconoclasm can be read at random from its numerous manifestoes and declarations of intent:

> Dada knows everything. Dada spits on everything. Dada says "knowthing," Dada has no fixed ideas. Dada does not catch flies. Dada is bitterness laughing at everything that has been accomplished, sanctified. . . . Dada is never right. . . . No more painters, no more writers, no more religions, no more royalists, no more anarchists, no more socialists, no more police, no more airplanes, no more urinary passages. . . . Like everything in life, Dada is useless, everything happens in a completely idiotic way. . . . We are incapable of treating seriously any subject whatsoever, let alone this subject: ourselves. [Dadaists, describing their own movement, said] Dada was a phenomenon bursting forth in the midst of the post-war economic and moral crisis, a savior, a monster, which would lay waste to everything in its path. [It was] a systematic work of destruction and demoralization. . . . In the end it became nothing but the act of sacrilege.[20]

Although the artists' cynicism and pessimism inspired Dada, what developed was phenomenally influential and powerful. By attacking convention and logic, the Dada artists unlocked new avenues for creative invention, thereby fostering a more serious examination of the basic premises of art than had prior movements. Dada was, in its subversiveness, extraordinarily avant-garde and tremendously liberating. In addition, although horror and disgust about the war initially prompted Dada, an undercurrent of humor and whimsy—sometimes sardonic or irreverent—runs through much of the art. For example, Marcel Duchamp painted a moustache on a reproduction of Leonardo's *Mona Lisa*. The French painter Francis Picabia (1879–1953), Duchamp's collaborator in setting up Dada in New York, nailed a toy monkey to a board and labeled it *Portrait of Cézanne*.

In its emphasis on the spontaneous and intuitive, Dada paralleled the psychoanalytic views of Sigmund Freud, Carl Jung, and others. Particularly interested in the exploration of the unconscious Freud promoted, the Dada artists believed art was a powerfully practical means of self-revelation and catharsis. In addition, they were convinced the images arising out of the subconscious mind had a truth of their own independent of conventional vision. A Dada filmmaker, Hans Richter, summarized the attitude of the European Dadaists:

> Possessed, as we were, of the ability to entrust ourselves to "chance," to our conscious as well as our unconscious minds, we became a sort of public secret society. . . . We laughed at everything. . . . But laughter was only the expression of our new discoveries, not their essence and not their purpose. Pandemonium, destruction, anarchy, anti-everything of the World War? How could Dada have been anything but destructive, aggressive, insolent, on principle and with gusto?[21]

THE ANARCHY OF CHANCE CREATIONS A Dada artist whose works serve as good examples of the "chance" Richter refers to is the Zurich-based artist JEAN (HANS) ARP (1887–1966). Arp pioneered the use of chance in composing his images. Tiring of the look of some Cubist-related collages he was making, he took some sheets of paper, tore them into roughly shaped squares, haphazardly dropped them to a sheet of paper on the floor, and glued them into the resulting arrangement. The rectilinearity of the shapes guaranteed a somewhat regular design, but chance had introduced an imbalance that seemed to Arp to restore to his work a special mysterious vitality he wanted to preserve. *Collage Arranged According to the Laws of Chance* (FIG. **33-24**) is a work he created by this method. The operations of "chance" were for Dadaists a crucial part of this kind of improvisation. As Richter stated: "For us chance was the 'unconscious mind' that Freud had discovered in 1900. . . . Adoption of chance had another purpose, a secret one. This was to restore to the work of art its primeval magic power and to find a way back to the immediacy it had lost through contact with . . . classicism."[22] Further, in its renunciation of artistic control, Arp's reliance on chance when creating his compositions reinforced the anarchy and subversiveness inherent in Dada.

FREEING ART FROM CONVENTION Perhaps the most influential of all the Dadaists was Frenchman MARCEL

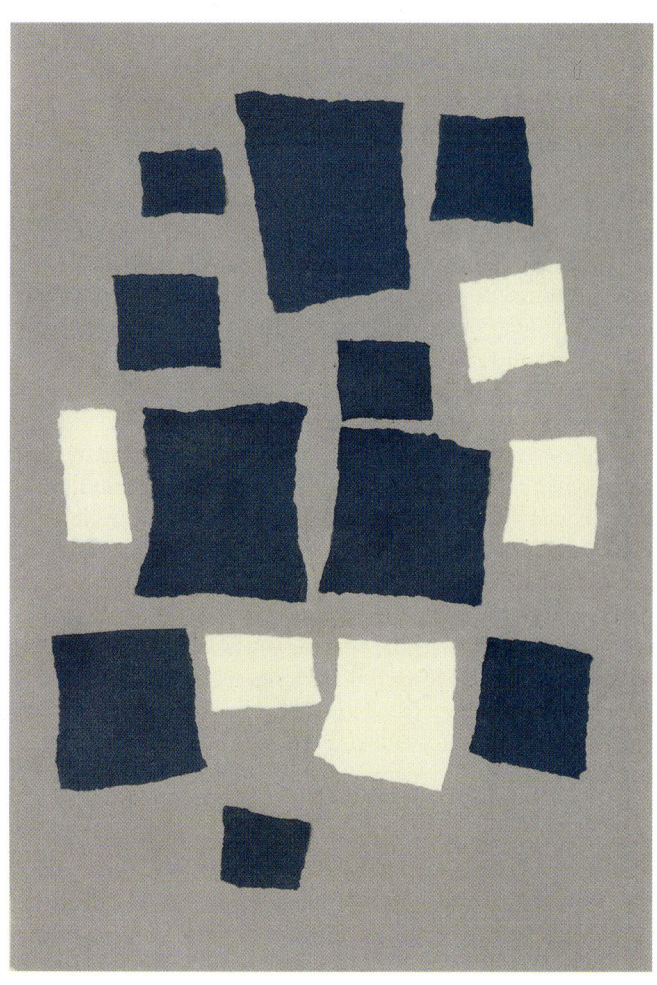

33-24 JEAN ARP, *Collage Arranged According to the Laws of Chance*, 1916–1917. Torn and pasted paper, 1' 7$\frac{1}{8}$" × 1' 1$\frac{5}{8}$". Museum of Modern Art, New York (purchase).

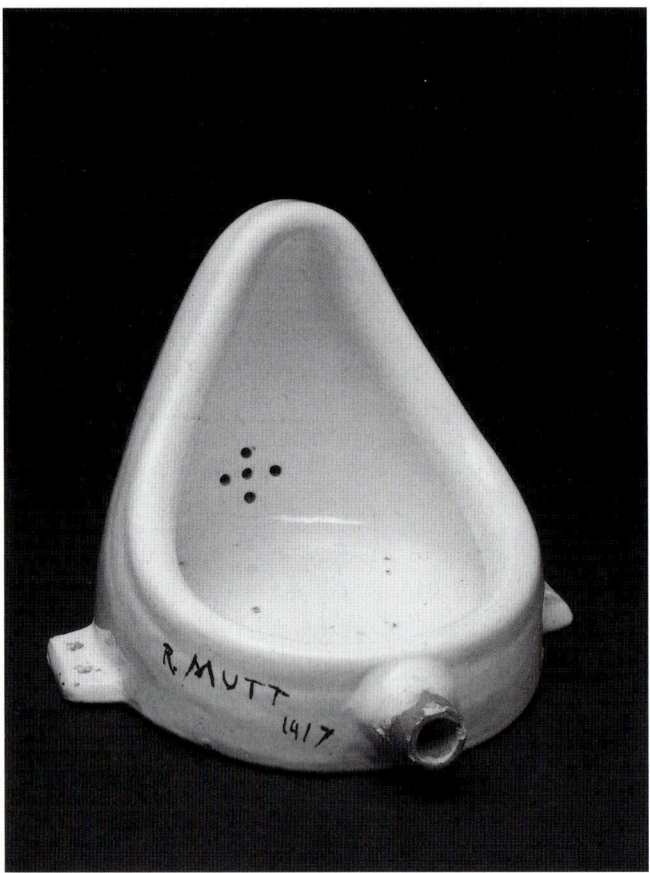

33-25   MARCEL DUCHAMP, *Fountain, (second version),* 1950. Ready-made glazed sanitary china with black paint, 12″ high. Philadelphia Museum of Art, Philadelphia (purchased with proceeds from the sale of deaccessioned works of art).

DUCHAMP (1887–1968), the central artist of New York Dada and active in Paris at the end of the Dada movement. In 1913, he exhibited his first "ready-made" sculptures, which were mass-produced common objects the artist selected and sometimes "rectified" by modifying their substance or combining them with another object. Such works, he insisted, were created free from any consideration of either good or bad taste, qualities shaped by a society he and other Dada artists found aesthetically bankrupt. Perhaps his most outrageous ready-made was *Fountain* (FIG. **33-25**), a porcelain urinal presented on its back, signed "R. Mutt," and dated. The "artist's signature" was, in fact, a witty pseudonym derived from the Mott plumbing company's name and that of the short half of the Mutt and Jeff comic-strip team. As with Duchamp's other ready-mades, he did not select this object for exhibition because of its aesthetic qualities. The "artness" of this work lies in the artist's choice of this object, which has the effect of conferring the status of art on it and forces viewers to see the object in a new light. As he wrote in a "defense" published in 1917, after the exhibition committee for an unjuried show rejected *Fountain* for display: "Whether Mr. Mutt with his own hands made the fountain or not has no importance. He chose it. He took an ordinary article of life, placed it so that its useful significance disappeared under the new title and point of view—created a new thought for that object."[23] It is hard to imagine a more aggressively avant-garde approach to art; Dada persistently presented staggering challenges to artistic conventions.

Duchamp (and the generations of artists after him profoundly influenced by his art and especially his attitude) considered life and art matters of chance and choice freed from the conventions of society and tradition. Within his approach to art and life, each act was individual and unique. Every person's choice of found objects would be different, for example, and each person's throw of the dice would be at a different instant and probably would yield a different number. This philosophy of utter freedom for artists was fundamental to the history of art in the twentieth century. Duchamp spent much of World War I in New York, inspiring a group of American artists and collectors with his radical rethinking of the role of artists and of the nature of art.

A VIEW OF "THE GREAT DADA WORLD"   Dada spread throughout much of western Europe, arriving as early as 1917 in Berlin, where it soon took on an activist political edge, partially in response to the economic, social, and political chaos in that city in the years at the end of and immediately after World War I. The Berlin Dadaists developed to a new intensity a technique used earlier in popular art postcards. Pasting parts from many pictures together into one image, the Berliners christened their version of the technique *photomontage.* The technique of creating a composition by pasting together pieces of paper had been used in private and popular arts long before the twentieth century. A few years earlier, the Cubists had named the process "collage." Unlike Cubist collage, the parts of a Dada collage were made almost entirely of "found" details, such as pieces of magazine photographs, usually combined into deliberately antilogical compositions. Collage lent itself well to the Dada desire to use chance when creating art and antiart, but not all Dada collage was as savagely aggressive as that of the Berlin photomontagists.

One of the Berlin Dadaists who perfected this photomontage technique was HANNAH HÖCH (1889–1978). Höch's photomontages were particularly incisive because they operated at the intersection of so many timely discourses. Her works not only advanced the absurd illogic of Dada by presenting viewers with chaotic, contradictory, and satiric compositions, but they also provided scathing and insightful commentary on two of the most dramatic developments during the Weimar Republic (1918–1933) in Germany—the redefinition of women's social roles and the explosive growth of mass print media. She revealed these combined themes in her powerful photomontage *Cut with the Kitchen Knife Dada through the Last Weimar Beer Belly Cultural Epoch of Germany* (FIG. **33-26**). The artist arranged an eclectic mixture of cutout photos in seemingly haphazard fashion. On closer inspection, however, viewers can see Höch carefully placed photographs of some of her fellow Dadaists among images of Marx, Lenin, and other revolutionary figures in the lower right section, aligning this movement with other revolutionary forces. She promoted Dada in prominently placed cutout lettering—"Die grosse Welt dada" ("The great Dada world"). Certainly, juxtaposing the heads of German military leaders with exotic dancers' bodies provided the wickedly humorous critique central to much of Dada. Höch also positioned herself in this topsy-turvy world she created. A photograph of her head appears in the lower right corner, juxtaposed to a map of Europe showing the progress of women's enfranchisement. Aware of the power both women and Dada had to destabilize society, Höch made forceful visual manifestations of that belief.

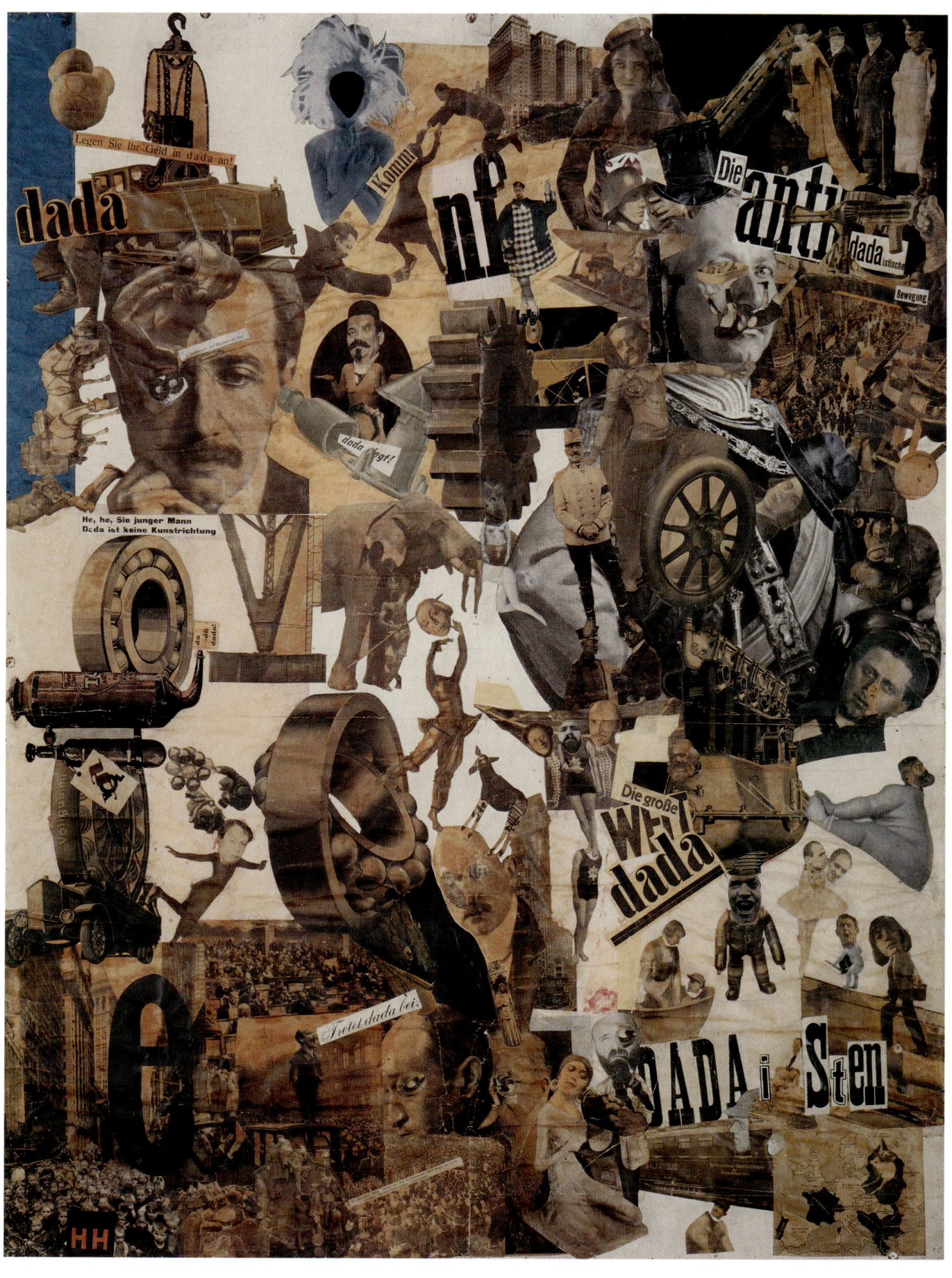

33-26 HANNAH HÖCH, *Cut with the Kitchen Knife Dada through the Last Weimar Beer Belly Cultural Epoch of Germany*, 1919–1920. Photomontage, 3′ 9″ × 2′ 11½″. Neue Nationalgalerie, Staatliche Museen, Berlin.

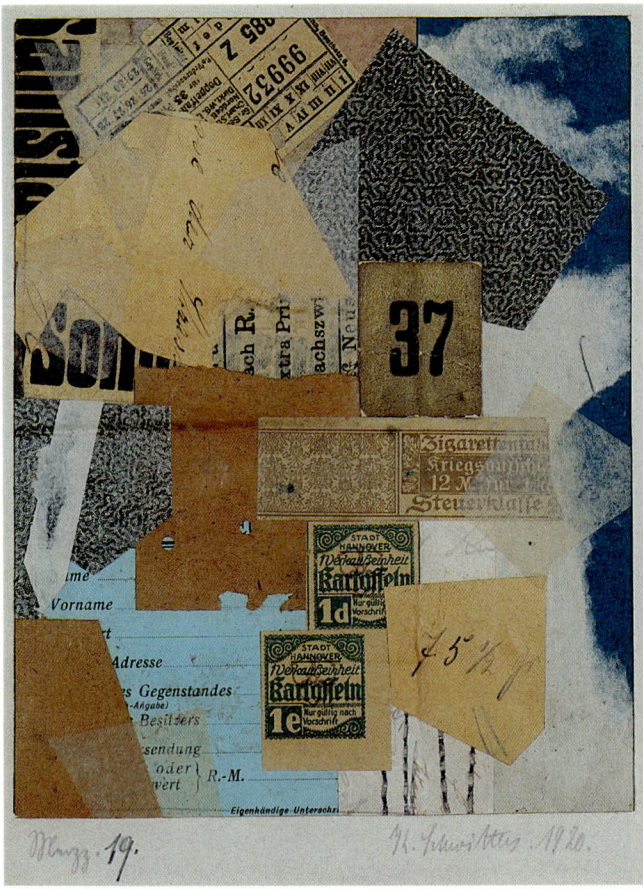

33-27   KURT SCHWITTERS, *Merz 19*, 1920. Paper collage, approx. $7\frac{1}{4}''$ × $5\frac{7}{8}''$. Yale University Art Gallery, New Haven, (gift of Collection Société Anonyme).

THE VISUAL POETRY OF RUBBISH   The Hanover Dada artist KURT SCHWITTERS (1887–1948) followed a gentler muse. Inspired by Cubist collage but working nonobjectively, Schwitters found visual poetry in the cast-off junk of modern society and scavenged in trash bins for materials, which he pasted and nailed together into designs such as *Merz 19* (FIG. 33-27). The term *merz*, which Schwitters used as a generic title for a whole series of collaged images, derived, nonsensically, from the word *kommerzbank* (commerce bank) and appeared as a word fragment in one of his collages. Although nonobjective, his compositions still resonate with the "meaning" of the fragmented found objects they contain. The recycled elements of Schwitters's collages, like Duchamp's ready-mades, acquire new meanings through their new uses and locations. Elevating objects that are, essentially, trash to the status of high art certainly fits within the parameters of the Dada program and parallels the absurd dimension of much of Dada art. Contradiction, paradox, irony, and even blasphemy are Dada's bequest. They are, in the view of Dada and its successors, the free and defiant artist's weapons in what has been called the hundred years war with the public.

TRANSATLANTIC ARTISTIC DIALOGUES

The energy and enthusiasm of artists undertaking these avant-garde experiments were not limited to Europe. A wide range of artists engaged in a lively exchange of artistic ideas and significant transatlantic travel. In the latter part of the nineteenth century, American artists such as John Singer Sargent, James Abbott McNeil Whistler and Mary Cassatt spent much of their productive careers in Europe, while many European artists ended their careers in America, especially in anticipation of and, later, in the wake of World War I.

The Armory Show and Its Legacy

CHALLENGING ARTISTIC REGIMENTATION One of the major vehicles for disseminating information about European artistic developments in the United States was the Armory Show, which occurred in early 1913. This large-scale and ambitious endeavor got its name from its location. After a year of searching for a suitable site, the exhibition's coordinators settled on the armory of the New York National Guard's 69th Regiment. Organized in large part by two artists, Walt Kuhn and Arthur B. Davies, the Armory Show (FIG. 33-28) contained more than sixteen hundred artworks both by American and European artists. Among the European artists represented were Matisse, Derain, Picasso, Braque, Duchamp, Kandinsky, Kirchner, and expressionist sculptor Wilhelm Lehmbruck and organic sculptor Constantin Brancusi, both discussed later. In addition to exposing American artists and the public to the latest in European artistic developments, this show also provided American artists with a prime showcase for their work.

AN "EXPLOSION IN A SHINGLE FACTORY" On its opening, this provocative exhibition served as a lightning rod for commentary, immediately attracting heated controversy. The *New York Times* described the show as "pathological," and other critics demanded closing the exhibition as a menace to public morality. The work the press most maligned was Marcel Duchamp's *Nude Descending a Staircase* (FIG. 33-29). The painting, a single figure in motion down a staircase in a time continuum, suggests the effect of a sequence of overlaid film stills. Although earlier discussion of Duchamp focused on his contributions to the Dada movement, *Nude Descending a Staircase* has more in common with the work of the Cubists and the Futurists. The monochromatic palette is reminiscent of Analytic Cubism, as is Duchamp's faceted presentation of the human form. The artist's interest in depicting the figure in motion reveals an affinity to the Futurists' ideas. One critic described this work as "an explosion in a shingle factory,"[24] and newspaper cartoonists had a field day lampooning the painting.

A PHOTOGRAPHER'S AVANT-GARDE GALLERY The Armory Show traveled to Chicago and Boston after it closed in New York and was a significant catalyst for discussion and serious thought about recent developments in art. Another catalyst in the period's artistic ferment was the artist ALFRED STIEGLITZ (1864–1946). Committed to promoting the avant-garde in the United States, Stieglitz established an art gallery at 291 Fifth Avenue in New York, which eventually became known simply as "291." His gallery was renowned for

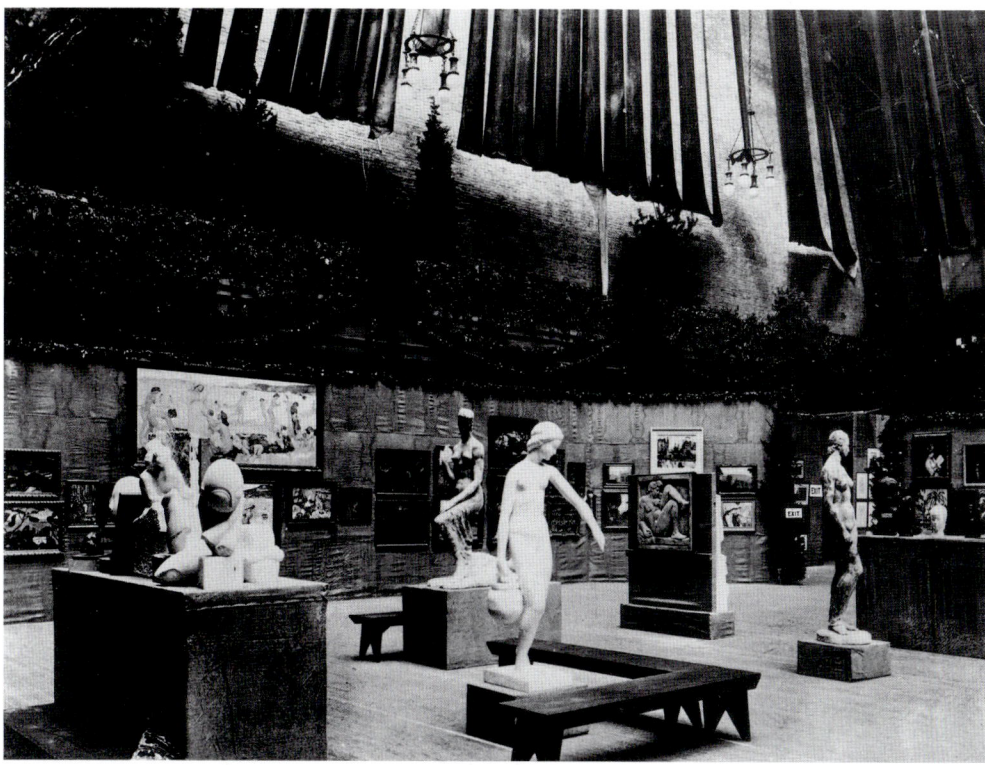

33-28 Installation photo of the Armory Show, New York National Guard's 69th Regiment, New York, 1913. Courtesy of the Museum of Modern Art, New York.

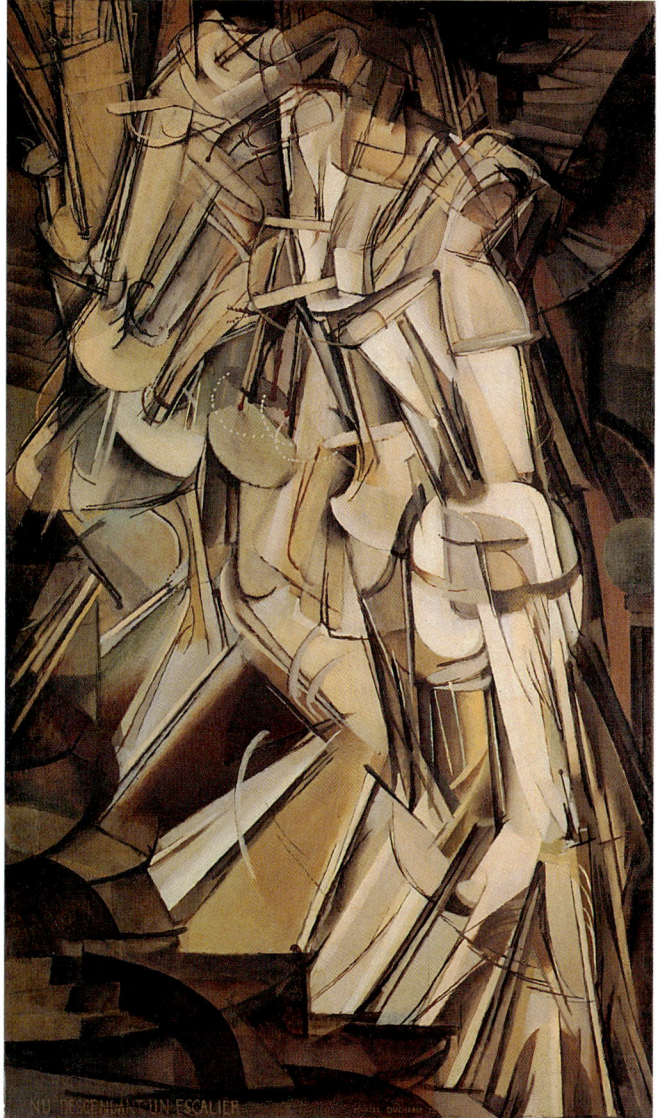

exhibiting the latest in both European and American art and, thus, like the Armory Show, played an important role in the history of early-twentieth-century art in America.

Stieglitz also channeled his artistic energies into producing photography. Taking his camera everywhere he went, he photographed whatever he saw around him, from the bustling streets of New York City to cloudscapes in upstate New York and the faces of friends and relatives. He believed in making only "straight, unmanipulated" photographs.[25] Thus, he exposed and printed them using basic photographic processes, without resorting to techniques such as double-exposure or double-printing that would add information not present in the subject when he released the shutter. Stieglitz said he wanted the photographs he made with this direct technique "to hold a moment, to record something so completely that those who see it would relive an equivalent of what has been expressed."[26]

He began a lifelong campaign to win a place for photography among the fine arts while a student of photochemistry in Germany. Returning to New York, he founded the Photo-Secession group, which mounted traveling exhibitions in the United States and sent loan collections abroad, and he also published an influential journal titled *Camera Work*. In his own works, Stieglitz specialized in photographs of his environment and saw these subjects in terms of form and of the "colors" of his black-and-white materials. He was attracted above all to arrangements of form that stirred his deepest emotions. His aesthetic approach crystallized during the making of one of his best-known works, *The Steerage* (FIG.

33-29 MARCEL DUCHAMP, *Nude Descending a Staircase, No. 2,* 1912. Oil on canvas, approx. 4' 10" × 2' 11". Philadelphia Museum of Art, Philadelphia (Louise and Walter Arensberg Collection).

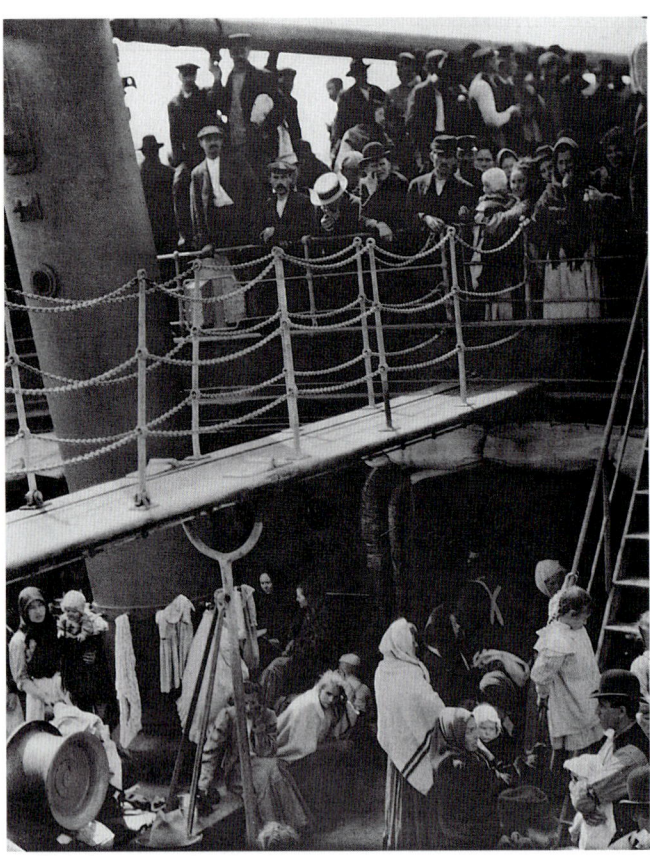

33-30 ALFRED STIEGLITZ, *The Steerage*, 1907 (print 1915). Photogravure (on tissue), 1′ $\frac{3}{8}″$ × 10 $\frac{1}{8}″$. Courtesy of Amon Carter Museum, Fort Worth.

33-30), taken during a voyage to Europe with his first wife and daughter in 1907. Traveling first class, Stieglitz rapidly grew bored with the company of the prosperous passengers in the ship's first-class section. He walked as far forward on that level as he could, when the rail around the opening onto the lower deck brought him up short. This level was reserved for "steerage" passengers the government was returning to Europe after refusing them entrance into the United States for any one of many reasons. Later, Stieglitz described what happened next:

> The scene fascinated me: A round hat; the funnel leaning left, the stairway leaning right; the white drawbridge, its railing made of chain; white suspenders crossed on the back of a man below; circular iron machinery; a mast that cut into the sky, completing a triangle. I stood spellbound. I saw shapes related to one another—a picture of shapes, and underlying it, a new vision that held me: simple people; the feeling of ship, ocean, sky; a sense of release that I was away from the mob called rich. Rembrandt came into my mind and I wondered would he have felt as I did. . . . I had only one plate holder with one unexposed plate. Could I catch what I saw and felt? I released the shutter. If I had captured what I wanted, the photograph would go far beyond any of my previous prints. It would be a picture based on related shapes and deepest human feeling—a step in my own evolution, a spontaneous discovery.[27]

The finished print fulfilled Stieglitz's vision so well that it shaped his future photographic work, and its haunting mixture of found patterns and human activity has continued to stir viewers' emotions to this day.

MOVING TOWARD ABSTRACTION Stieglitz's concern for positioning photography as an art form with the same fine art status as painting and sculpture was also pursued by EDWARD WESTON (1886–1958). In addition to "straight" photography, like that Stieglitz produced, Weston experimented with photographs that moved toward greater abstraction, paralleling developments in other media. *Nude* (FIG. **33-31**) is a good example of this photographic style. The image's simplicity and the selection of a small segment of the human body as the subject result in a lyrical photograph of dark and light areas that at first glance suggests a landscape. Further inspection reveals the fluid curves and underlying skeletal armature of the human form. This photograph, in its reductiveness, formally expresses a study of the body that verges on the abstract.

A WICKEDLY FUNNY GIFT The American artist MAN RAY (1890–1976), who worked closely with Duchamp through the 1920s, produced art with a decidedly Dada spirit. Man Ray incorporated found objects into many of his paintings, sculptures, movies, and photographs. Trained as an architectural draftsman and engineer, Man Ray earned his living as a graphic designer and portrait photographer. He brought to his personal work an interest in mass-produced objects and technology, as well as a dedication to exploring the psychological realm of human perception of the exterior world. Like Schwitters, Man Ray used chance and the dislocation of ordinary things from their everyday settings to surprise his viewers into new awareness. His displacement of found objects was particularly effective in works such as *Cadeau (Gift)* (FIG. **33-32**). For this sculpture, he equipped a laundry iron with a row of wicked-looking spikes, subverting its proper function of smoothing and pressing. The malicious humor of *Cadeau (Gift)*—seen throughout Dada and, indeed, in much of contemporary art—gives it a characteristic edge that can cut the unwary.

SYNCOPATED CUBISM Other American artists developed personal styles that intersected with movements such as Cubism. STUART DAVIS (1894–1964), for example, created what he believed was a modern American art style by combining the flat shapes of Synthetic Cubism with his sense of jazz tempos and his perception of the energy of fast-paced American culture. *Lucky Strike* (FIG. **33-33**) is one of several Tobacco still lifes Davis began in 1921. A heavy smoker, Davis was fascinated by tobacco products and their packaging. He insisted the late-nineteenth-century introduction of packaging was evidence of high civilization and, therefore, he concluded, of the progressiveness of American culture. Davis depicted the Lucky Strike package in fragmented form, reminiscent of Synthetic Cubist collages. However, although the work does incorporate flat printed elements, these are illusionistically painted, rather than glued onto the canvas surface. The discontinuities and the interlocking planes imbue *Lucky Strike* with a dynamism and rhythm not unlike American jazz or the pace of life in a lively American metropolis. This work is both resolutely American and modern.

A VOICE OF THE HARLEM RENAISSANCE Also deriving his personal style from Synthetic Cubism was African-American artist AARON DOUGLAS (1898–1979), who used the

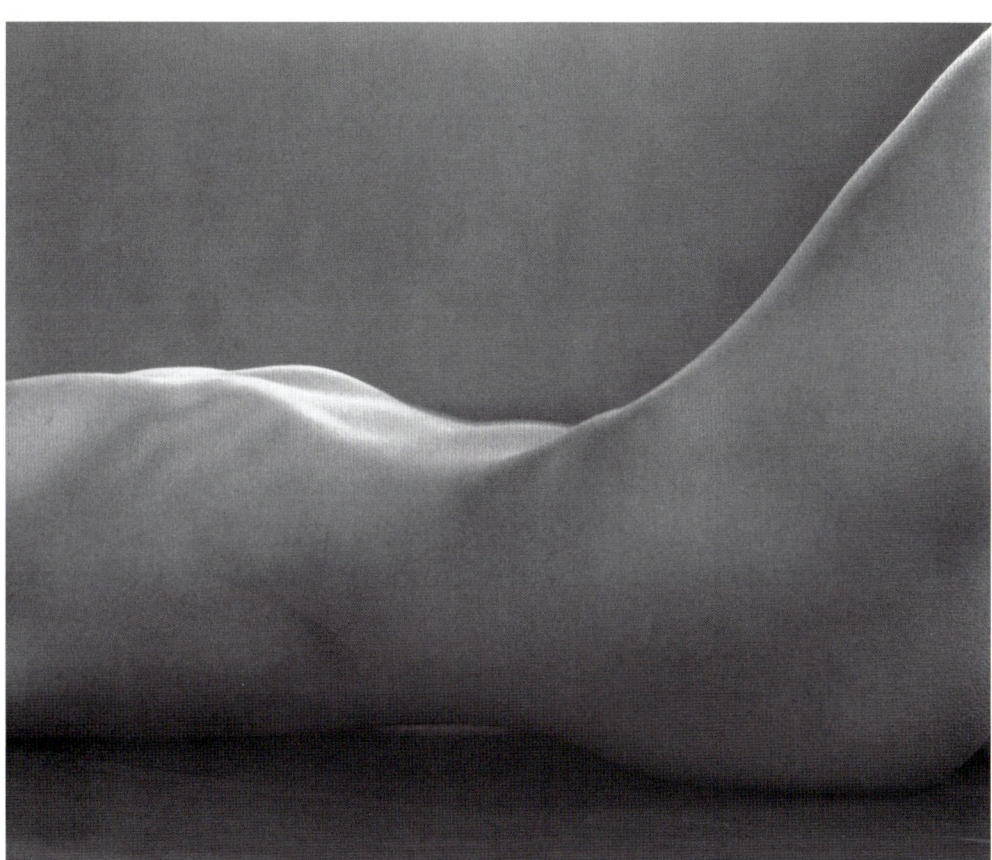

33-31 EDWARD WESTON, *Nude,*
1925. Platinum print. Collection,
Center for Creative Photography,
University of Arizona, Tucson.

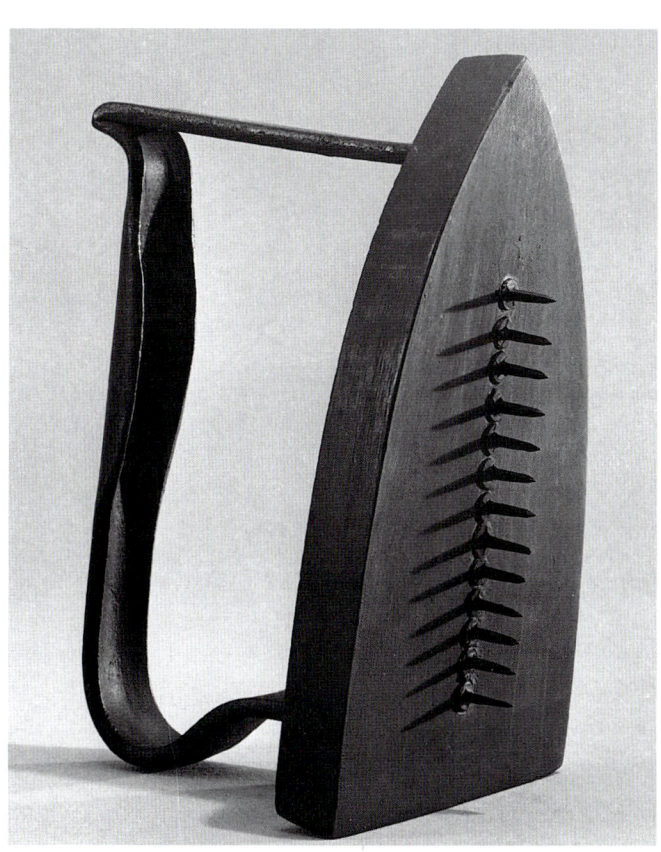

33-32 MAN RAY, *Cadeau (Gift),* ca. 1958 (replica of 1921 original).
Painted flatiron with row of 13 tacks with heads glued to the bottom, $6\frac{1}{8}''$
high, $3\frac{5}{8}''$ wide, $4\frac{1}{2}''$ deep. Museum of Modern Art, New York (James Thrall
Soby Fund).

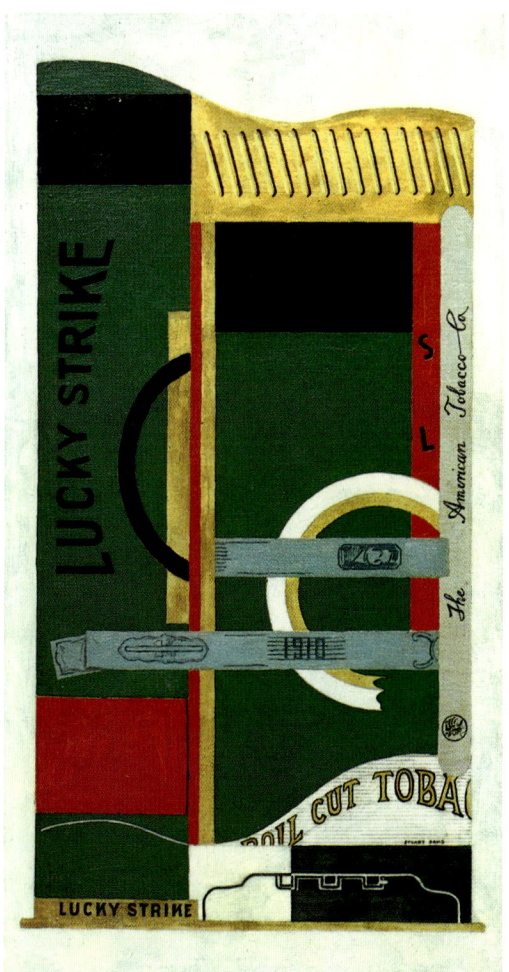

33-33 STUART DAVIS, *Lucky Strike,* 1921. Oil on canvas, $2'\ 9\frac{1}{4}'' \times 1'\ 6''$.
Museum of Modern Art, New York (gift of The American Tobacco
Company, Inc.). Copyright © Estate of Stuart Davis/Licensed by VAGA,
New York, NY.

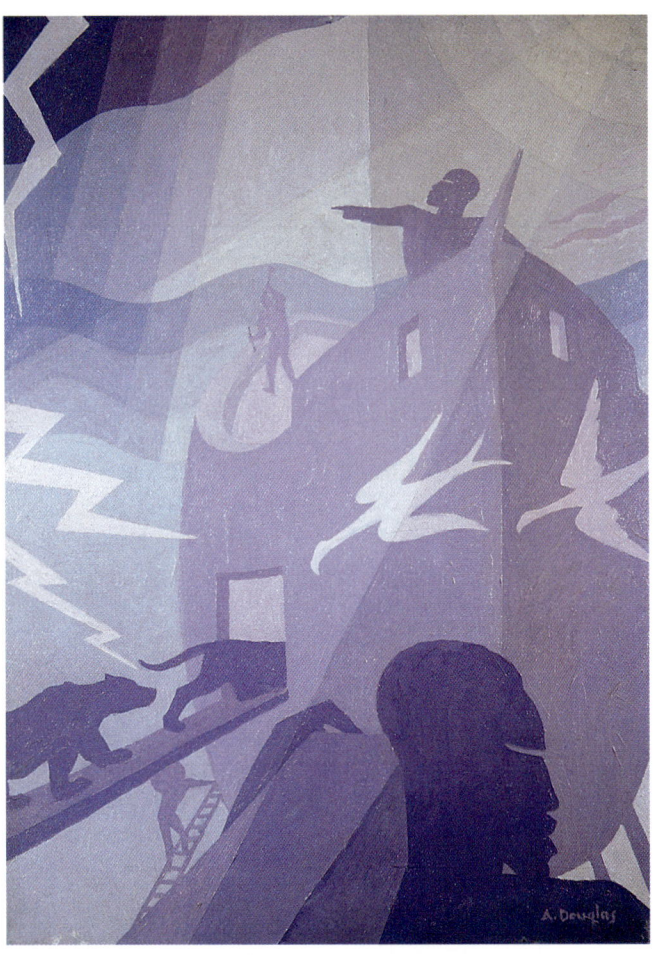

33-34 Aaron Douglas, *Noah's Ark,* ca. 1927. Oil on masonite, 4′ × 3′. Fisk University Galleries, Nashville, Tennessee.

intrigued by the latest European avant-garde art, from Cubism to Dada. However, these artists did not just absorb passively the ideas transported across the Atlantic. For many American artists, the challenge was to understand the ideas this modernist European art presented and then filter them through an American sensibility. Ultimately, many American artists set as their goal the development of a uniquely American art.

One group of such artists became known as Precisionists. This was not an organized movement, and these artists rarely exhibited together (although once the similarities in their work were revealed they were grouped together in shows), but they did share certain thematic and stylistic traits in their art. Precisionism developed in the 1920s out of a fascination with the machine's precision and importance in modern life. Although many European artists (for example, the Futurists) had demonstrated interest in burgeoning technology, Americans, generally, seemed more enamored by the prospects of a mechanized society than did Europeans. Even French artist Francis Picabia (associated with both Cubism and Dada) noted: "Since machinery is the soul of the modern world, and since the genius of machinery attains its highest expression in America, why is it not reasonable to believe that in America the art of the future will flower most brilliantly?"[28] The efforts of others in the art world also supported this observation. Alfred Stieglitz's gallery 291 was instrumental in exhibiting mechanistically oriented works, thereby championing the "age of the machine."

style to represent symbolically the historical and cultural memories of African Americans. Born in Kansas, he studied in Nebraska and Paris before settling in New York City, where he became part of the flowering of art and literature in the 1920s known as the Harlem Renaissance. Encouraged by the German artist Winold Reiss to create art that would express the cultural history of his race, Douglas incorporated motifs from African sculpture into compositions painted in a version of Synthetic Cubism that stressed transparent angular planes. *Noah's Ark* (FIG. **33-34**) was one of seven paintings based on a book of poems by James Weldon Johnson called *God's Trombones: Seven Negro Sermons in Verse.* Douglas used flat planes to evoke a sense of mystical space and miraculous happenings. In *Noah's Ark,* lightning strikes and rays of light crisscross the pairs of animals entering the ark, while men load supplies in preparation for departure across the heaving seas. The artist suggested deep space by differentiating the size of the large human head and shoulders of the worker at the bottom and the small person at work on the far deck of the ship. Yet, the composition's unmodulated color shapes create a pattern on the masonite surface that cancels any illusion of three-dimensional depth. Here, Douglas used Cubism's formal language to express a powerful religious vision.

Precisionism

It is obvious from viewing the American art in the period immediately after the Armory Show that American artists were

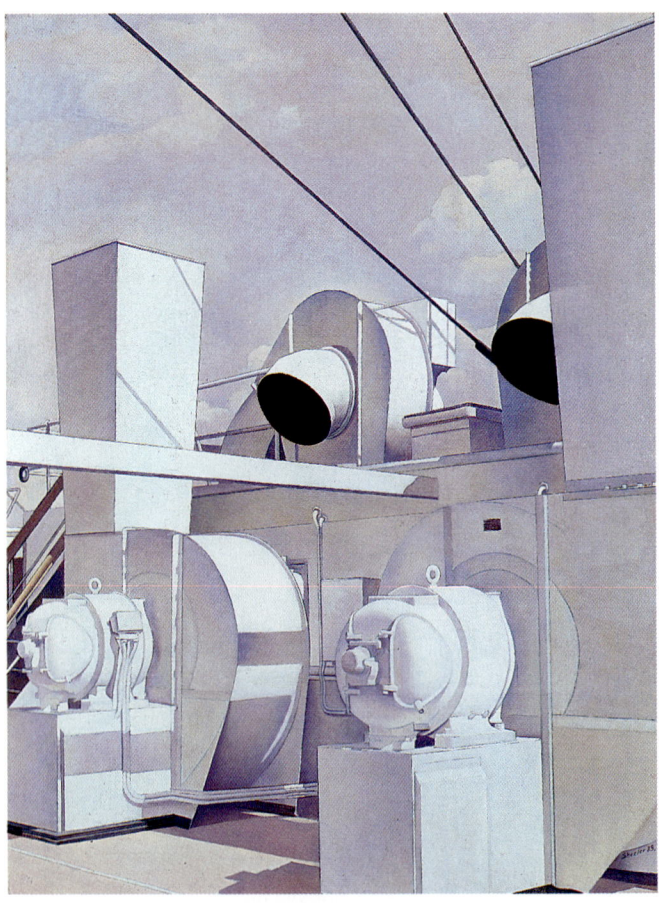

33-35 Charles Sheeler, *The Upper Deck,* 1929. Oil on canvas, 2′ 5$\frac{1}{8}$″ × 1′ 10$\frac{1}{8}$″. Courtesy of the Fogg Art Museum, Harvard University Art Museums, Cambridge, Massachusetts (Louise E. Bettens Fund).

Precisionism, however, expanded beyond the exploration of machine imagery. Many artists associated with this group gravitated toward Synthetic Cubism's flat, sharply delineated planes as an appropriate visual idiom for their imagery, adding to the clarity and precision of their work. Eventually, Precisionism was characterized by a merging of a familiar native style in American architecture and artifacts with a modernist vocabulary largely derived from Synthetic Cubism.

A TIGHTLY ORDERED GEOMETRY *Upper Deck* (FIG. **33-35**) by CHARLES SHEELER (1883–1965) is a pristinely and meticulously rendered image of a ship's ventilation system. More visually coherent than many Synthetic Cubist images, this particular painting was based on a commissioned photograph Sheeler took on board the German ocean liner S.S. *Majestic* for a publicity brochure and is thus firmly grounded in a specific visual reality. Still, a tightly ordered geometry pervades the work. *Upper Deck* was special for Sheeler; it represented his attainment of an artistic goal. "I had come to feel that a picture could have incorporated in it the structural design implied in abstraction and be presented in a wholly realistic manner."[29]

AMERICAN PYRAMIDS? More informed by Synthetic Cubism is the work of CHARLES DEMUTH (1883–1935). Demuth had spent the years 1912–1914 in Paris and thus had firsthand exposure to Cubism and other avant-garde directions in art. He incorporated the spatial discontinuities characteristic of Cubism into his work, focusing much of it on industrial sites near his native Lancaster, Pennsylvania. *My Egypt* (FIG. **33-36**) is a prime example of Precisionist painting. Demuth depicted the John W. Eshelman and Sons grain elevators, which he reduced to simple geometric forms. The grain elevators remain insistently recognizable and solid. However, the painting is disrupted by the "beams" of transparent planes and the diagonal force lines that threaten to destabilize the image and that correspond to Cubist fragmentation of space. Not only does this adaptation of Cubist vocabulary place Demuth in the more progressive ranks of American artists of the time, but it also reveals his sensitivity to the effects of the expanding technology. A writer described these effects:

> [A]ll these instruments: telephone, microscope, magnifying glass, cinematograph, lens, microphone, gramophone, automobile, kodak, aeroplane, are not merely dead objects. [These] machines become part of ourselves, interposing themselves between the world and us, filtering reality as the screen filters radium emanations. Thanks to them we have no longer a simple, clear, continuous, constant notion of an object. . . . The world for people today is like descriptive geometry, with its infinite planes of projection."[30]

Although this passage was not written about Demuth's painting, *My Egypt* provides a perfect illustration of an industrial site "filtering reality" and its "descriptive geometry, with its infinite planes of projection." The degree to which Demuth intended to extol the American industrial scene is unclear. The title, *My Egypt,* is sufficiently ambiguous in tone to accommodate differing readings. On the one hand, Demuth could have been suggesting a favorable comparison between

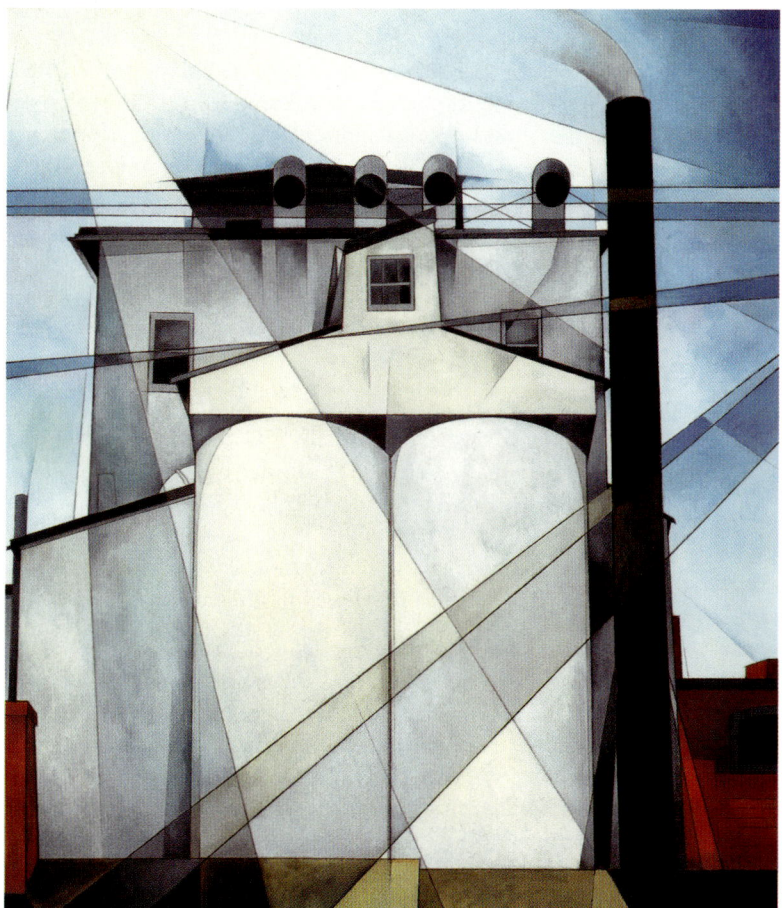

33-36 CHARLES DEMUTH, *My Egypt,* 1927. Oil on composition board, 2' 11 $\frac{3}{4}$" × 2' 6". Collection of Whitney Museum of American Art, New York (purchase, with funds from Gertrude Vanderbilt Whitney).

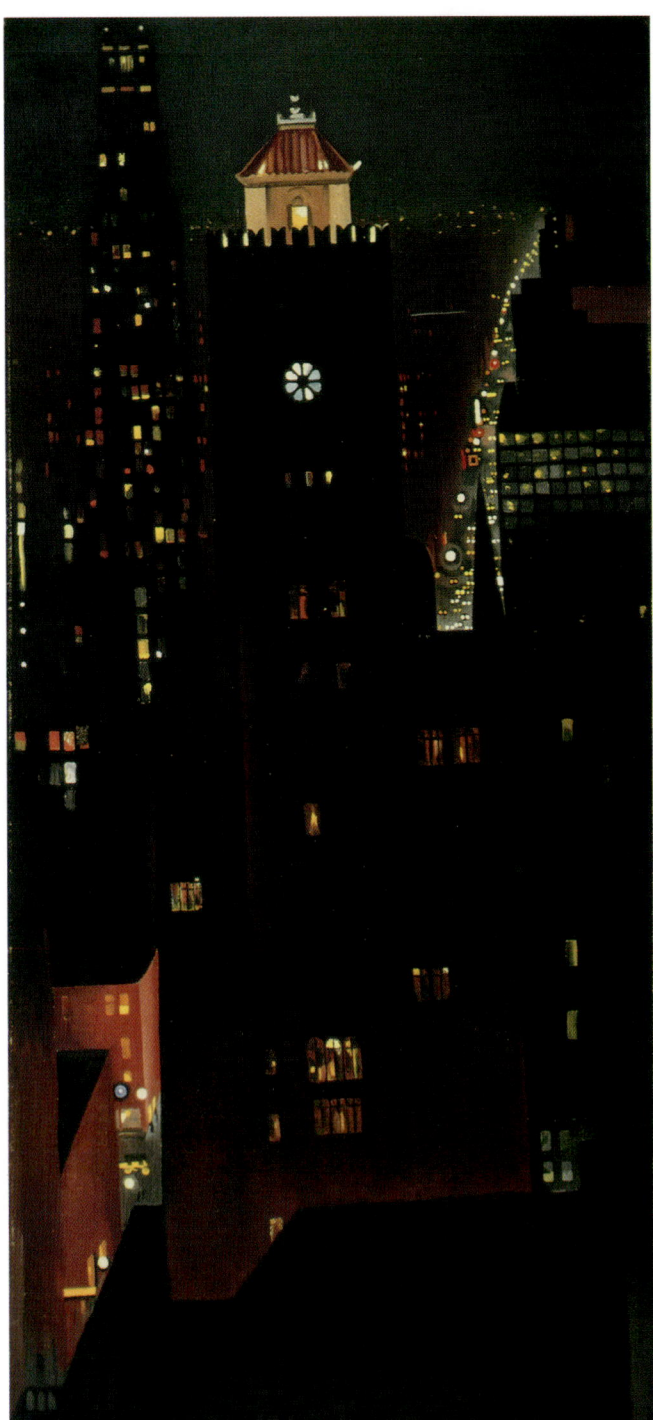

33-37 GEORGIA O'KEEFFE, *New York, Night*, 1929. Oil on canvas, 3′ 4⅛″ × 1′ 7⅛″. Sheldon Memorial Art Gallery, Lincoln, Nebraska (Nebraska Art Association, Thomas C. Woods Memorial Collection).

the Egyptian pyramids and American grain elevators as cultural icons. On the other hand, the title could be read cynically, as a negative comment on the limitations of American culture.

CAPTURING THE RHYTHM OF CITY LIFE

The work of GEORGIA O'KEEFFE (1887–1986), like that of many artists, changed stylistically throughout her career. During the 1920s, O'Keeffe was affiliated with Precisionism. She had moved from the tiny town of Canyon, Texas, to

New York City in 1918 (although she had visited on occasion previously), and what she found there both overwhelmed and excited her. "You have to live in today," she told a friend, "Today the city is something bigger, more complex than ever before in history. And nothing can be gained from running away. I couldn't even if I could."[31] While in New York, O'Keeffe met Alfred Stieglitz, who had seen and exhibited some of her earlier work, and she was drawn into the circle of painters and photographers surrounding Stieglitz and his gallery. Stieglitz became one of O'Keeffe's staunchest supporters and, eventually, her husband. The interest of Stieglitz and his circle in capturing the sensibility of the machine age intersected with O'Keeffe's fascination with the fast pace of city life, and she produced paintings during this period, such as *New York, Night* (FIG. 33-37), that depict the soaring skyscrapers dominating the city. Like other Precisionists, O'Keeffe reduced her images to flat planes, here punctuated by small rectangular windows that add rhythm and energy to the image, countering the monolithic darkness of the looming buildings.

THE PURE FORM OF GROWING PLANTS Despite O'Keeffe's affiliation with the Precisionist movement, she is probably best known for her paintings of cow skulls and of flowers. One such painting, *Jack in the Pulpit IV* (FIG. Intro-4) reveals the artist's interest in stripping her subjects to their purest forms and colors to heighten their expressive power. In this work, O'Keeffe reduced the incredible details of her subject to a symphony of basic colors, shapes, textures, and vital rhythms. Exhibiting the natural flow of curved planes and contour, O'Keeffe simplified the form almost to the limit of the flower's identity. The fluid planes unfold like undulant petals from a subtly placed axis—the white jet-like streak—in a vision of the slow, controlled motion of growing life. O'Keeffe's painting, in its graceful, quiet poetry, reveals the organic reality (Brancusi would say its "essence") of the object by strengthening its characteristic features, in striking contrast with either Kandinsky's explosions (FIG. 33-7) or Mondrian's rectilinear absolutes (FIG. 33-56). In 1946, O'Keeffe moved permanently to New Mexico and continued to paint for decades.

EUROPEAN EXPRESSIONISM IN THE WAKE OF WORLD WAR I

That American artists could focus on these modernist artistic endeavors with such commitment was due to the fact World War I was fought entirely on European soil. Thus, its effects were not as devastating as they were both on Europe's geopolitical terrain and on individual and national psyches. After the war concluded, many European artists were drawn to the expressionist idiom (as developed by the Fauves and the German Expressionists) both to express and to deal with the trauma of world war.

Neue Sachlichkeit

As shown earlier, the war severely impacted many artists, notably those associated with German Expressionism and Dada. Neue Sachlichkeit (New Objectivity) grew directly out of the war experiences of a group of German artists. All of the artists associated with Neue Sachlichkeit served, at some point, in the German army and thus had firsthand involvement with the military. Their military experiences deeply influenced their world views and informed their art. This was not an organized movement, and the label "Neue Sachlichkeit" was coined by museum director G. F. Hartlaub in 1923. The label does, however, capture their aim—to present a clear-eyed, direct, and honest image of the war and its effects. As George Grosz, one of the Neue Sachlichkeit artists, explained: "I am trying to give an absolutely realistic picture of the world. . . ."[32]

SCATHING DEPICTIONS OF THE MILITARY

GEORGE GROSZ (1893–1958) was, for a time, associated with the Dada group in Berlin, but his work, with its harsh and bitter tone, seems more appropriately linked with Neue Sachlichkeit. Grosz observed the onset of World War I with horrified fascination, but that feeling soon turned to anger and frustration. He reported:

> Of course, there was a kind of mass enthusiasm at the start. But this intoxication soon evaporated, leaving a huge vacuum. . . . And then after a few years when everything bogged down, when we were defeated, when everything went to pieces, all that remained, at least for me and most of my friends, were disgust and horror.[33]

Grosz produced numerous paintings and drawings, such as *Fit for Active Service* (FIG. **33-38**), that were caustic indictments of the military. In these works, he often depicted military officers as heartless or incompetent. This particular drawing may relate to Grosz's personal experience. On the verge of

a nervous breakdown in 1917, he was sent to a sanatorium where doctors examined him and, much to his horror, declared him "fit for service." In this biting and sarcastic drawing, an army doctor proclaims the skeleton before him "fit for service." None of the other military officers or doctors attending seem to dispute this evaluation. The spectacles perched on the skeleton's face, very similar to the gold-rimmed glasses Grosz wore, further suggests he based this on his experiences. The simplicity of the line drawing contributes to the directness and immediacy of the work, which scathingly portrays the German army.

WORLD VIOLENCE INVADES THE HOME

MAX BECKMANN (1884–1950), like Grosz, enlisted in the German army and initially rationalized the war. He believed the chaos would lead to a better society, but over time the mass destruction increasingly disillusioned him. Soon his work began to emphasize the horrors of war and of a society he saw descending into madness. His disturbing view of society is evident in *Night* (FIG. **33-39**). As best described, *Night* depicts a cramped room three intruders have forcefully invaded. The bound woman apparently was raped. Her husband appears on the left; one of the intruders hangs him, while another one twists his left arm out of its socket. An unidentified woman cowers in the background. On the far right, the third intruder prepares to flee with the child.

Although this image does not depict a war scene, the wrenching brutality and violence pervading in the home is a searing and horrifying comment on society's condition. Beckmann also injected a personal reference by using himself, his wife, and his son as the models for the three family members.

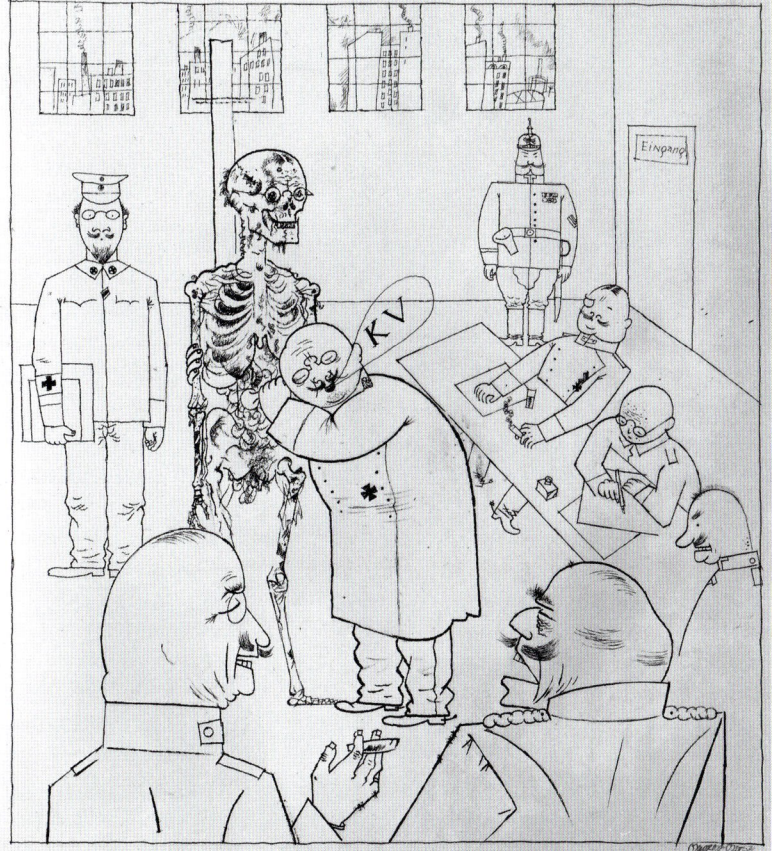

33-38 GEORGE GROSZ, *Fit for Active Service,* 1916–1917. Pen and brush and ink on paper, 1′ 8″ × 1′ 2⅜″. Museum of Modern Art, New York (A. Conger Goodyear Fund). Copyright © Estate of George Grosz/Licensed by VAGA, New York, NY.

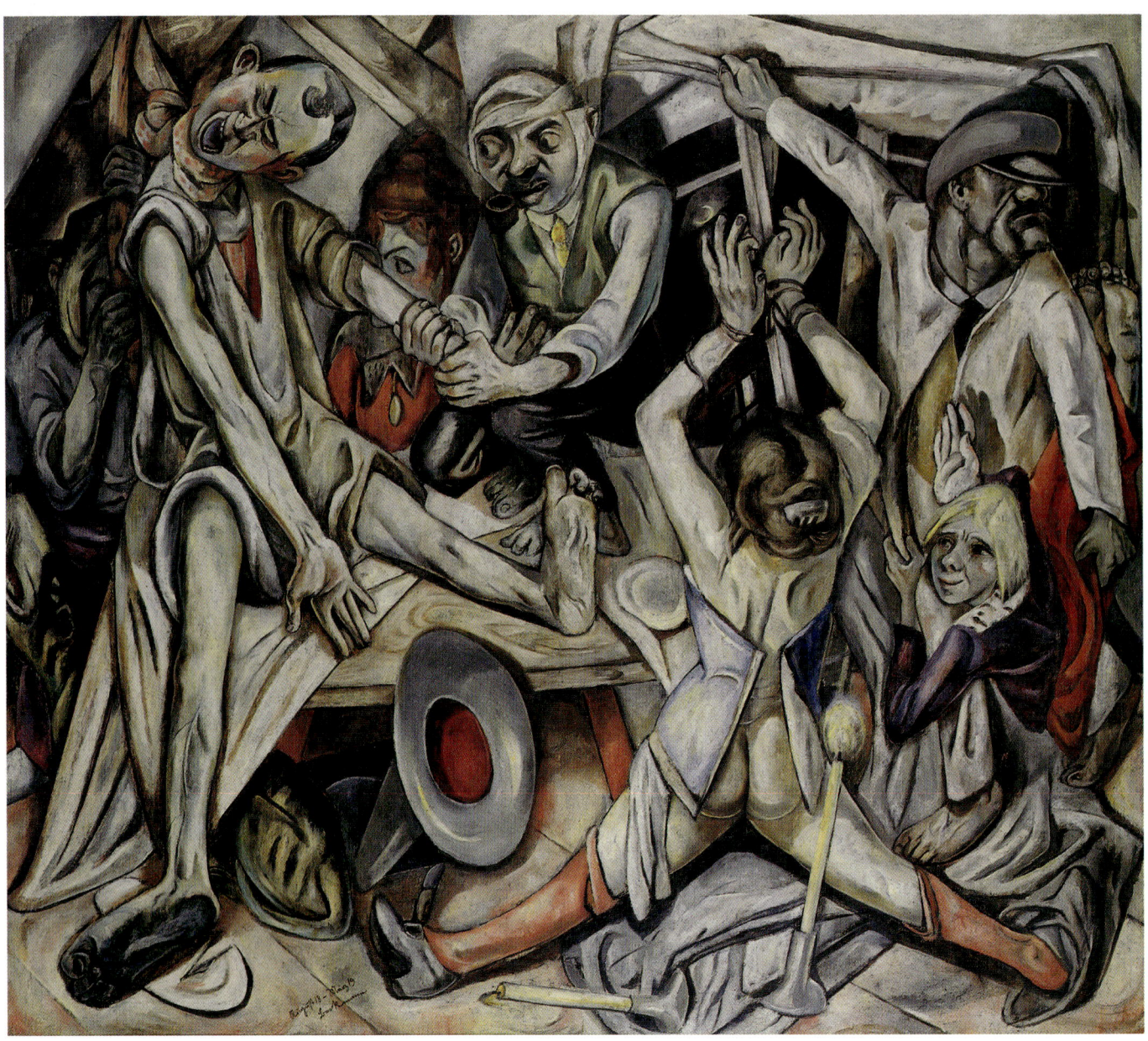

33-39 MAX BECKMANN, *Night*, 1918–1919. Oil on canvas, 4′ 4⅜″ × 5′ ¼″. Kunstsammlung Nordrhein-Westfalen, Dusseldorf.

The stilted angularity of the figures and the roughness of the paint surface contribute to the image's savageness. In addition, the artist's treatment of forms and space reflects the world's violence. Objects seem dislocated and contorted, and the space appears buckled and illogical. For example, the woman's hands are bound to the window that opens from the room's back wall, but her body appears to hang vertically, rather than lying across the plane of the intervening table. Despite the fact images such as *Night* do not directly depict war's carnage or violence, Beckmann's art is undeniably powerful and honest.

THE DEVASTATION OF WAR OTTO DIX (1891–1959) was the third artist who, along with Beckmann and Grosz, most closely was associated with Neue Sachlichkeit. Although Beckmann, for the most part, avoided specific war imagery, Dix embraced it. Having served as both a machine gunner and an aerial observer, he was well acquainted with

war's effects. Like Grosz, he initially tried to find redeeming value in the apocalyptic event. Dix explained: "The war was a horrible thing, but there was something tremendous about it, too. . . . You have to have seen human beings in this unleashed state to know what human nature is. . . . I need to experience all the depths of life for myself, that's why I go out, and that's why I volunteered."[34] This idea of experiencing the "depths of life" stemmed from Dix's interest in the philosophy of Friedrich Nietzsche, best known for his existentialist writings. In particular, Dix avidly read Nietzsche's *The Joyous Science,* deriving from it a belief in life's cyclical nature—procreation and death, building up and tearing down, and growth and decay.

As the war progressed, however, Dix's faith in the potential improvement of society dissipated, and he began to produce unflinchingly direct and provocative artworks. His *Der Krieg (The War)* (FIG. **33-40**) vividly captures the panoramic devastation war inflicts, both on the terrain and on humans. In the

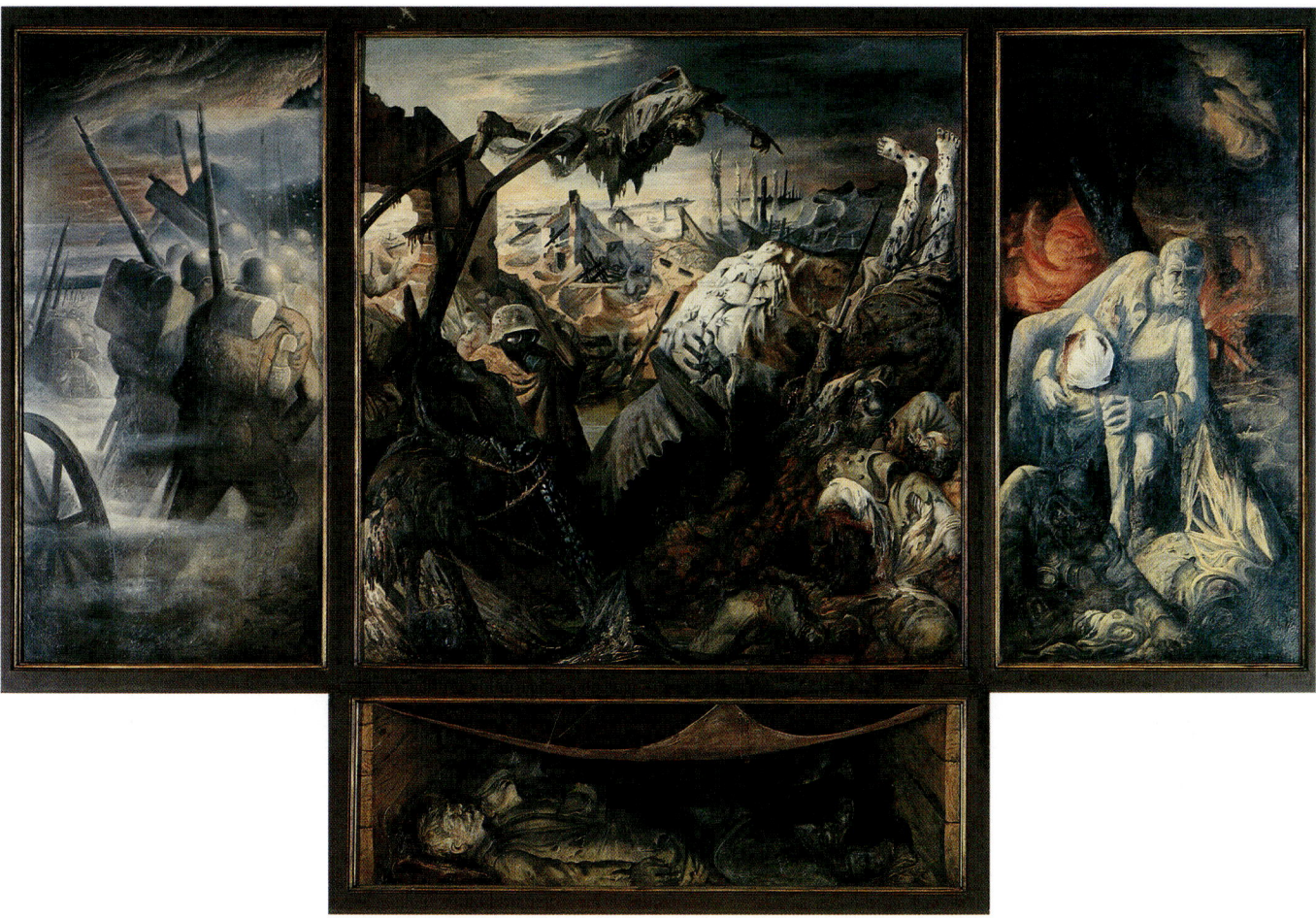

33-40 OTTO DIX, *Der Krieg (The War)*, 1929–1932. Oil and tempera on wood, 6′ 8$\frac{1}{3}$″ × 13′ 4$\frac{3}{4}$″. Staatliche Kunstsammlungen, Gemäldegalerie Neue Meister, Dresden.

left panel, armed and uniformed soldiers march off into the distance. Dix graphically displayed the horrific results in the center and right panels, where mangled bodies, many riddled with bullet holes, are scattered throughout the eerily lit apocalyptic landscape. As if to emphasize the intensely personal nature of this scene, the artist painted himself into the right panel as the ghostly but determined soldier who drags a comrade to safety. In the bottom panel, in a coffinlike bunker, lie soldiers asleep—or perhaps dead. Dix significantly chose to present this sequence of images in a triptych format, and the work recalls triptychs such as Matthias Grünewald's *Isenheim Altarpiece* (see FIG. 23-1). Christ's death and suffering there serve as reference points for Dix's dead soldiers. However, the hope of salvation extended to viewers of *Isenheim Altarpiece* through Christ's eventual Resurrection is absent from *War Triptych*. Like his fellow Neue Sachlichkeit artists, Dix felt compelled to lay bare the realities of his time, which the war's violence dominated. Even years later, Dix still maintained:

> You have to see things the way they are. You have to be able to say yes to the human manifestations that exist and will always exist. That doesn't mean saying yes to war, but to a fate that approaches you under certain conditions and in which you have to prove yourself. Abnormal situations bring out all the depravity, the bestiality of human beings. . . . I portrayed states, states that the war brought about, and the results of war, as states.[35]

Other Postwar Expressionist Art in Germany

POIGNANT PRINTS The emotional range of German Expressionism extends from passionate protest and satirical bitterness to the poignantly expressed pity for the poor in the woodblock prints of the independent artist KÄTHE KOLLWITZ (1867–1945). The graphic art of Gauguin and Munch stimulated a revival of the print medium in Germany, especially the woodcut, and the forceful block prints cut in the days of the German Reformation, such as those of Holbein, proved inspiring models. The harsh, black, and splintered lines of woodblock prints were ideal for the stark forms and blunt emphasis of message the modern expressionists prized. In her *Memorial to Karl Liebknecht* (FIG. **33-41**), Kollwitz represented the sorrowing poor gathered around the bier of the assassinated leader of the 1919 socialist revolution. When World War I concluded, Liebknecht, along with Rosa Luxemburg and other radical left-wing socialists, formed the German Communist Party. The Communists challenged the Social Democrats for control of Germany but were brutally suppressed. Kollwitz was not formally affiliated with Neue Sachlichkeit or any of the organized German Expressionist groups. However, this is a classic of expressionism, a masterful presentation of the theme of mourning for the lost leader and a strong political protest presented in a moving, eloquent visual statement.

33-41 Käthe Kollwitz, *Memorial to Karl Liebknecht,* 1919. Woodcut. Käthe Kollwitz Museum, Berlin.

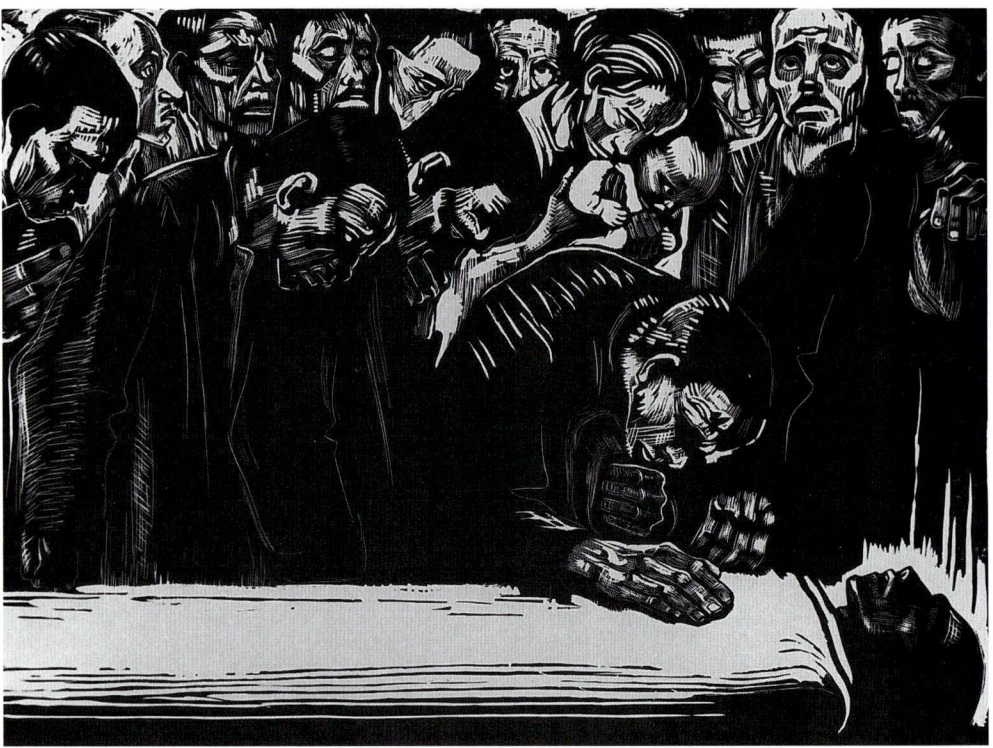

AN ELONGATED, EXPRESSIVE SCULPTURE Like Kollwitz, the war deeply affected German artist WILHELM LEHMBRUCK (1881–1919). His figurative sculpture exudes a quiet mood but still possesses a compelling emotional sensibility. Lehmbruck studied sculpture, painting, and the

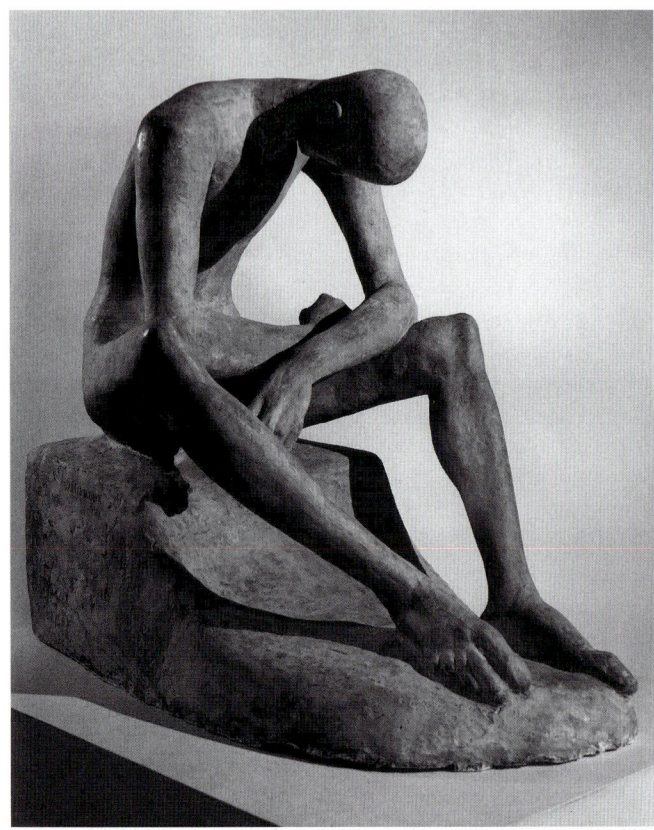

33-42 WILHELM LEHMBRUCK, *Seated Youth,* 1917. Composite tinted and plaster, 3′ 4⅝″ × 2′ 6″ × 3′ 9″. National Gallery of Art, Washington. (Andrew W. Mellon Fund).

graphic arts in Dusseldorf before moving to Paris in 1910, where he developed the style of his *Seated Youth* (FIG. **33-42**). His sculpture combines the expressive qualities he much admired in the work of two fellow sculptors—the classical idealism of Maillol (FIG. 33-9) and the psychological energies of Rodin (see FIGS. 29-48 and 29-49). In Lehmbruck's *Seated Youth,* the poignant elongation of human proportions, the slumped shoulders, and the hands that hang uselessly all impart an undertone of anguish to the rather classical figure. Lehmbruck's figure communicates by pose and gesture alone. Although its extreme proportions may recall Mannerist attenuation (such as Parmigianino's *Madonna with the Long Neck,* FIG. 22-42), its distortions announce a new freedom in interpreting the human figure. For Lehmbruck, as for Rodin, the human figure could express every human condition and emotion. The quiet, contemplative nature of this sculpture serves both as a personal expression of Lehmbruck's increasing depression and as a powerful characterization of the general sensibility in the wake of World War I. Appropriately, *Seated Youth* was originally titled *The Friend,* in reference to the artist's many friends who lost their lives in the war. After Lehmbruck's tragic suicide in 1919, officials placed this sculpture as a memorial in the soldiers' cemetery in Lehmbruck's native city of Duisburg.

A SUSPENDED, HAUNTING MEMORIAL OF WAR A work more spiritual in its expression is the *War Monument* (FIG. **33-43**) the German sculptor ERNST BARLACH (1870–1938) created for the cathedral in his hometown of Güstrow in 1927. Working often in wood, Barlach sculpted single figures usually dressed in flowing robes and portrayed in strong, simple poses that embody deep human emotions and experiences such as grief, vigilance, or self-comfort. Barlach's works combine sharp, smoothly planed forms with intense expression. The cast-bronze hovering figure of his *War Monument* is

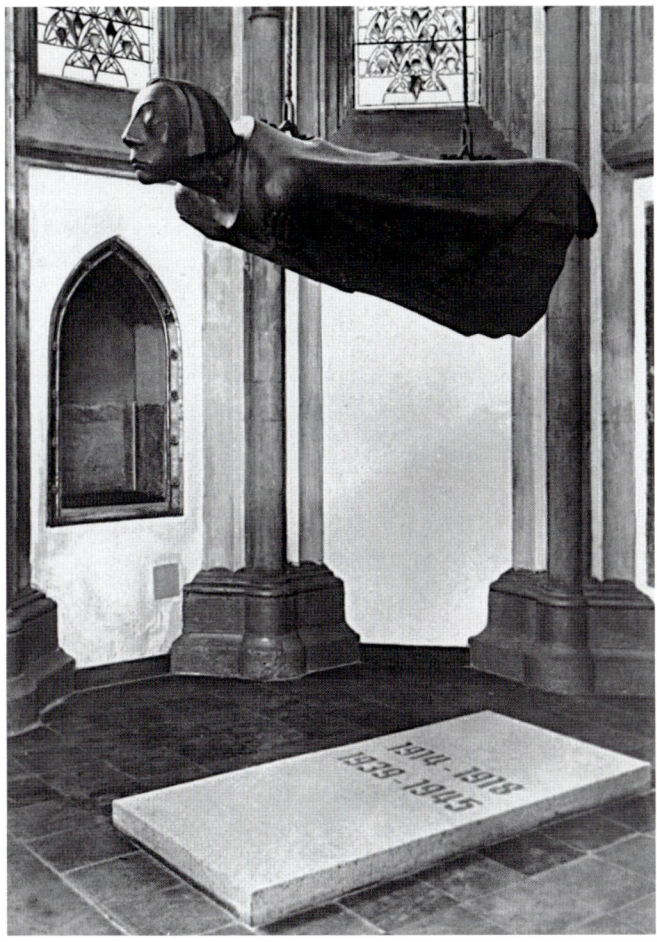

33-43 ERNST BARLACH, *War Monument,* from Güstrow Cathedral, Güstrow, Germany, 1927. Bronze. Schildergasse Antoniterkirche, Cologne.

one of the poignant memorials of World War I. Unlike traditional war memorials depicting heroic military figures, often engaged in battle, Barlach created a hauntingly symbolic figure that speaks to the experience of all caught in the conflict of war. The floating human form, suspended above a tomb inscribed with the dates 1914–1918 and the later added 1939–1945, suggests a dying soul at the moment when it is about to awaken to everlasting life—the theme of death and transfiguration. The rigid economy of surfaces concentrates attention on the simple but expressive head. The spiritual anguish the disaster of war evokes and the release from that anguish through hope of salvation rarely have been expressed as movingly as in *War Monument.* So powerful was this sculpture that the Nazis had it removed from the cathedral in 1937 and melted down for ammunition. Luckily, a friend hid another version by Barlach; a Protestant parish in Cologne purchased this surviving cast, from which a new cast was made for the Güstrow cathedral.

Surrealism and Fantasy Art

The exuberantly aggressive momentum of the Dada movement that emerged during World War I was only sustained for a short time. By 1924, with the publication in France of the *First Surrealist Manifesto,* most of the artists associated with Dada joined the Surrealist movement and its determined exploration of ways to express in art the world of

dreams and the unconscious. Given this transition, it is not surprising the Surrealists incorporated many of the Dadaists' improvisational techniques. They believed these methods important for engaging the elements of fantasy and activating the unconscious forces that lie deep within every human being. The Surrealists were determined to explore the inner world of the psyche, the realm of fantasy and the unconscious. Inspired in part by the ideas of the psychoanalysts Sigmund Freud and Carl Jung, the Surrealists especially were interested in the nature of dreams. They viewed dreams as occurring at the level connecting all human consciousness and as constituting the arena in which people could move beyond their environment's constricting forces to reengage with the deeper selves society had long suppressed. In 1924, one of the leading Surrealists thinkers, the young Parisian writer André Breton, provided a definition of Surrealism:

> Pure psychic automatism, by which one intends to express verbally, in writing, or by any other method, the real functioning of the mind. Dictation by thought, in the absence of any control exercised by reason, and beyond any esthetic or moral preoccupation. . . . Surrealism is based on the belief in the superior reality of certain forms of association heretofore neglected, in the omnipotence of dreams, in the undirected play of thought. . . . I believe in the future resolution of the states of dream and reality, in appearance so contradictory, in a sort of absolute reality, or surreality.[36]

Thus, the Surrealists' dominant motivation was to bring the aspects of outer and inner "reality" together into a single position, in much the same way life's seemingly unrelated fragments combine in the vivid world of dreams. The projection in visible form of this new conception required new techniques of pictorial construction. The Surrealists adapted some Dada devices and invented new methods such as automatic writing and various types of planned "accidents" not so much to reveal a world without meaning as to provoke reactions closely related to subconscious experience.

Surrealism developed along two lines. Some artists gravitated toward an interest in biomorphic (life forms) Surrealism with automatism—"dictation of thought without control of the mind"—predominating. Biomorphic Surrealists such as Joan Miró produced largely abstract compositions, although they sometimes suggested organisms or natural forms. Naturalistic Surrealists, in contrast, presented recognizable scenes that seem to have metamorphosed into a dream or nightmare image. The artists Salvador Dalí and René Magritte are most closely associated with this variant of Surrealism.

METAPHYSICAL PAINTING   The Italian painter GIORGIO DE CHIRICO (1888–1978) produced emphatically ambiguous works that position him as a precursor of Surrealism. De Chirico's paintings of cityscapes and shop windows were part of a movement called *pittura metafisica,* or Metaphysical Painting. Returning to Italy after study in Munich, de Chirico found hidden reality revealed through strange juxtapositions, such as those seen on late autumn afternoons in the city of Turin, when the setting sun's long shadows transformed vast open squares and silent public monuments into "the most metaphysical of Italian towns." De Chirico translated this vision into paint in works such as *Melancholy and*

33-44 GIORGIO DE CHIRICO, *Melancholy and Mystery of a Street,* 1914. Oil on canvas, 2′ 10¼″ × 2′ 4½″. Private collection.

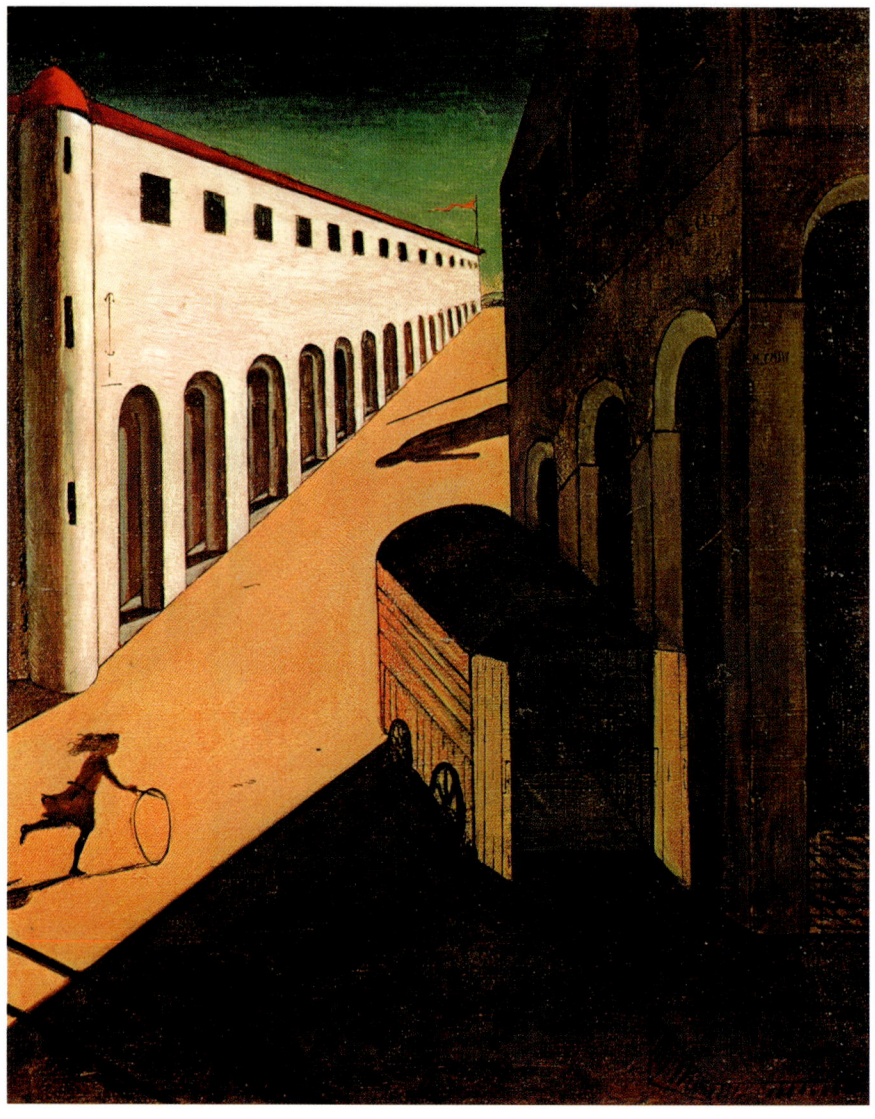

Mystery of a Street (FIG. **33-44**), where the squares and palaces of Roman and Renaissance Italy evoke a disquieting sense of foreboding. The choice of the term "metaphysical" to describe de Chirico's paintings suggests that these images transcend their physical appearances. *Melancholy and Mystery of a Street,* for all of its clarity and simplicity, takes on a rather sinister air. Only a few inexplicable and incongruous elements punctuate the scene's solitude—a small girl with her hoop in the foreground, the empty van, and the ominous shadow of a man emerging from behind the building. The sense of strangeness de Chirico could conjure with familiar objects and scenes recalls Nietzsche's "foreboding that underneath this reality in which we live and have our being, another and altogether different reality lies concealed."[37]

De Chirico's paintings were reproduced in periodicals almost as soon as he completed them, and his works quickly influenced artists outside Italy, including both the Dadaists and, later, the Surrealists. The incongruities in his work intrigued the Dadaists, while the eerie mood and visionary quality of paintings such as *Melancholy and Mystery of a Street* excited and inspired Surrealist artists who sought to portray the world of dreams.

SEEKING THE SENSE OF THE PSYCHIC Originally a Dada activist in Cologne, Germany, MAX ERNST (1891–1976) became one of the early adherents of the Surrealist circle Breton anchored. As a child living in a small community near Cologne, Ernst had found his existence fantastic and filled with marvels. In autobiographical notes, written mostly in the third person, he said of his birth: "Max Ernst had his first contact with the world of sense on the 2nd April 1891 at 9:45 A.M., when he emerged from the egg which his mother had laid in an eagle's nest and which the bird had incubated for seven years."[38] Ernst's service in the German army during World War I swept away his early success as an expressionist; in his own words:

> Max Ernst died on 1st August 1914. He returned to life on 11th November 1918, a young man who wanted to become a magician and find the central myth of his age. From time to time he consulted the eagle which had guarded the egg of his prenatal existence. The bird's advice can be detected in his work.[39]

Before joining the Surrealists, Ernst explored every means to achieve the sense of the psychic in his art. Like other Dadaists,

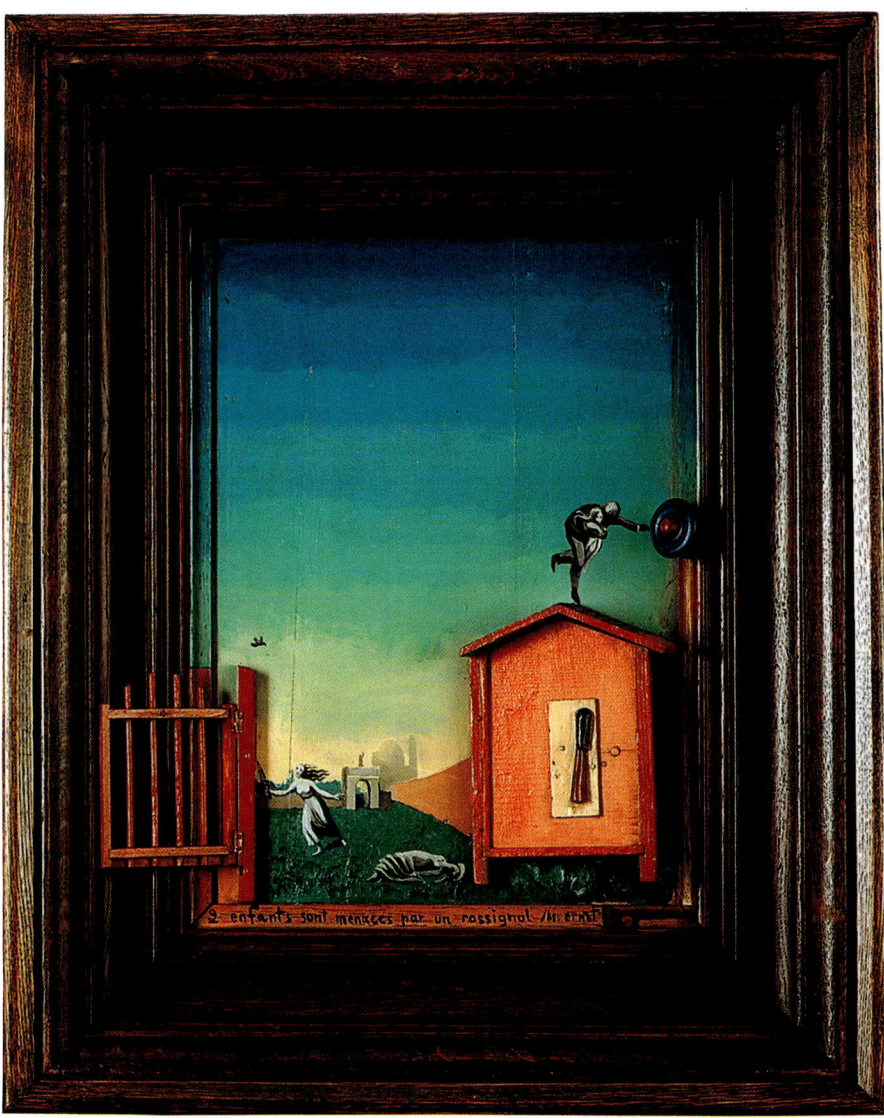

33-45 MAX ERNST, *Two Children Are Threatened by a Nightingale,* 1924. Oil on wood with wood construction, 2′ 3½″ high, 1′ 10½″ wide, 4½″ deep. Museum of Modern Art, New York (purchase).

he set out to incorporate found objects and chance into his works. Using a process called *frottage,* he created some works by combining the patterns achieved by rubbing a crayon or another medium across a sheet of paper placed over a surface with a strong and evocative textural pattern. In other works, he joined fragments of images he had cut from old books, magazines, and prints to form one hallucinatory collage.

Ernst soon began making paintings that shared the mysterious dreamlike effect of his collages. In 1920, his works brought him into contact with Breton, who instantly recognized Ernst's affinity with the Surrealist group. In 1922, Ernst moved to Paris. His *Two Children Are Threatened by a Nightingale* (FIG. **33-45**) manifests many of the creative bases of Surrealism. Here, Ernst displayed a private dream that challenged the post-Renaissance idea that a painting should resemble a window looking into a "real" scene rendered illusionistically three-dimensional through mathematical perspective. In *Two Children Are Threatened,* the artist painted the landscape, the distant city, and the tiny flying bird in conventional fashion; he followed all the established rules of aerial and linear perspective. The three sketchily rendered figures, however, clearly belong to a dream world, and the liter-

ally three-dimensional miniature gate, the odd button knob, and the strange closed building "violate" the bulky frame's space. Additional dislocation occurs in the traditional museum identification label, which Ernst displaced into a cutaway part of the frame. Handwritten, it announces the work's title (taken from a poem Ernst wrote before he painted this), adding another note of irrational mystery.

Like the title of many Surrealist works, *Two Children Are Threatened by a Nightingale* is ambiguous and uneasily relates to what spectators see. Viewers must struggle to decipher connections between the image and words. When Surrealists (and Dadaists and Metaphysical artists before them) used such titles, they intended for the seeming contradiction between title and picture to act like a "blow to the mind," knocking spectators off balance with all expectations challenged. Much of the impact of Surrealist works begins with viewers' sudden awareness of the incongruity and absurdity of what is pictured.

A DISTURBING BLUE DREAMSCAPE   Spaniard SALVADOR DALÍ (1904–1989), an established Surrealist painter, also explored his psyche and dreams in his paintings,

33-46 SALVADOR DALÍ *The Persistence of Memory*, 1931. Oil on canvas, $9\frac{1}{2}$″ × 1′ 1″. Museum of Modern Art, New York (given anonymously).

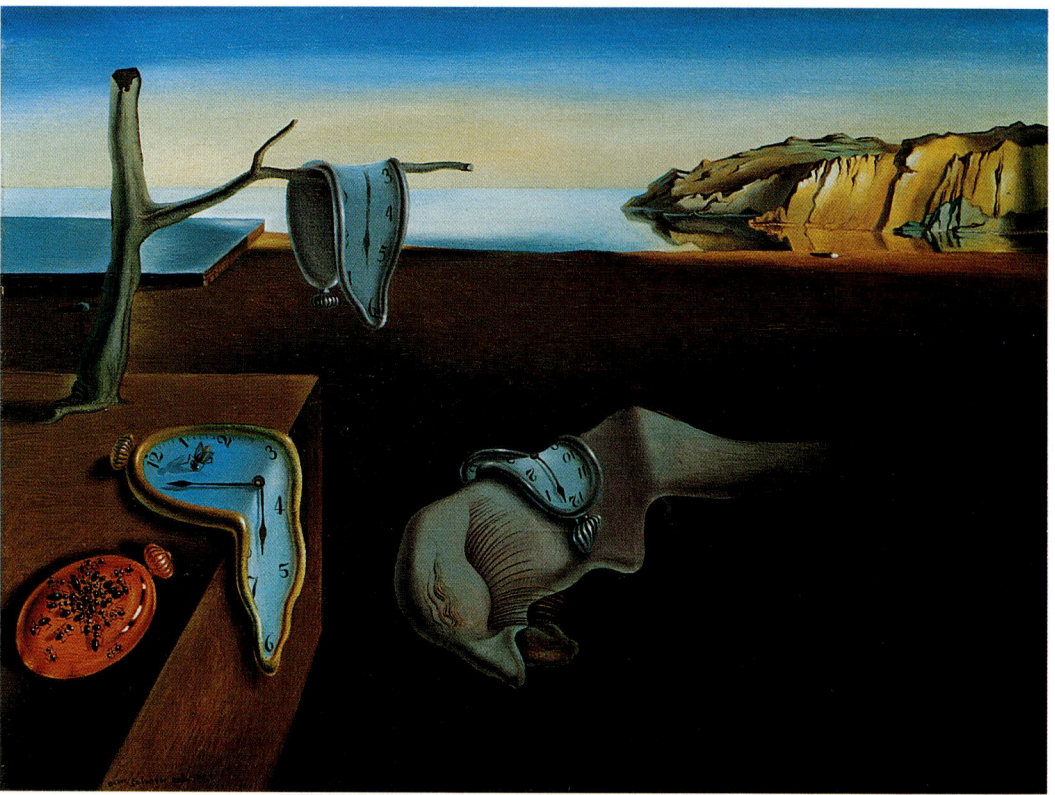

sculptures, jewelry, and designs for furniture and movies. Dalí probed a deeply erotic dimension through his work, studying the writings of Sigmund Freud and Richard von Krafft-Ebing and inventing what he called the "paranoiac-critical method" to assist his creative process. As he described it, in his painting he aimed "to materialize the images of concrete irrationality with the most imperialistic fury of precision . . . in order that the world of imagination and of concrete irrationality may be as objectively evident . . . as that of the exterior world of phenomenal reality."[40] All these aspects of Dalí's style can be seen in *The Persistence of Memory* (FIG. **33-46**). Here, he created a haunting allegory of empty space where time has ended. An eerie never-setting sun illuminates the barren landscape. An amorphous creature sleeps in the foreground; it is based on a figure in the Paradise section of Hieronymous Bosch's *Garden of Earthly Delights* (see FIG. 20-17). Dalí draped his creature with a limp pocket watch. Another watch hangs from the branch of a dead tree that springs unexpectedly from a blocky architectural form. A third watch hangs half over the edge of the rectangular form, beside a small timepiece resting dial-down on the block's surface. Ants swarm mysteriously over the small watch, while a fly walks along the face of its large neighbor, almost as if this assembly of watches were decaying organic life—soft and sticky. Dalí rendered every detail of this dreamscape with precise control, striving to make the world of his paintings as convincingly real as the most meticulously rendered landscape based on an actual scene from nature.

WORDS CONTRADICTING IMAGES The Belgian painter RENÉ MAGRITTE (1898–1967) also expressed in ex-

emplary fashion the Surrealist idea and method—the dreamlike dissociation of image and meaning. His works administer disruptive shocks because they subvert viewers' expectations based on logic and common sense. The danger of relying on rationality when viewing a Surrealist work is glaringly apparent in Magritte's *The Treachery (or Perfidy) of Images* (FIG. **33-47**). Magritte presented a meticulously rendered trompe l'oeil depiction (a very illusionistic rendering; literally, "fools the eye") of a briar pipe. The caption beneath the image, however, contradicts what seems obvious: "Ceci n'est pas une pipe" ("This is not a pipe"). The discrepancy between image and caption clearly challenges the assumptions underlying the reading of visual art. Like the other Surrealists' work, this painting wreaks havoc on viewers' reliance on the conscious and the rational.

FUZZY LOGIC The Surrealists also were enamored with sculpture, whose concrete tangibility made their art all the more disquieting. *Object (Le Déjeuner en fourrure)*, translated as "Luncheon in fur" (FIG. **33-48**), by Swiss artist MERET OPPENHEIM (1913–1985) captures the incongruity, humor, visual appeal, and, often, eroticism characterizing Surrealism. The artist presented a fur-lined teacup inspired by a conversation she had with Picasso. After admiring a bracelet Oppenheim had made from a piece of brass covered with fur, Picasso noted that anything might be covered with fur. When her tea grew cold, Oppenheim responded to Picasso's comment by ordering "un peu plus de fourrure" ("a little more fur"), and the sculpture had its genesis. *Object (Le Déjeuner en fourrure)* takes on an anthropomorphic quality, animated by the quirky combination of the fur with a functional ob-

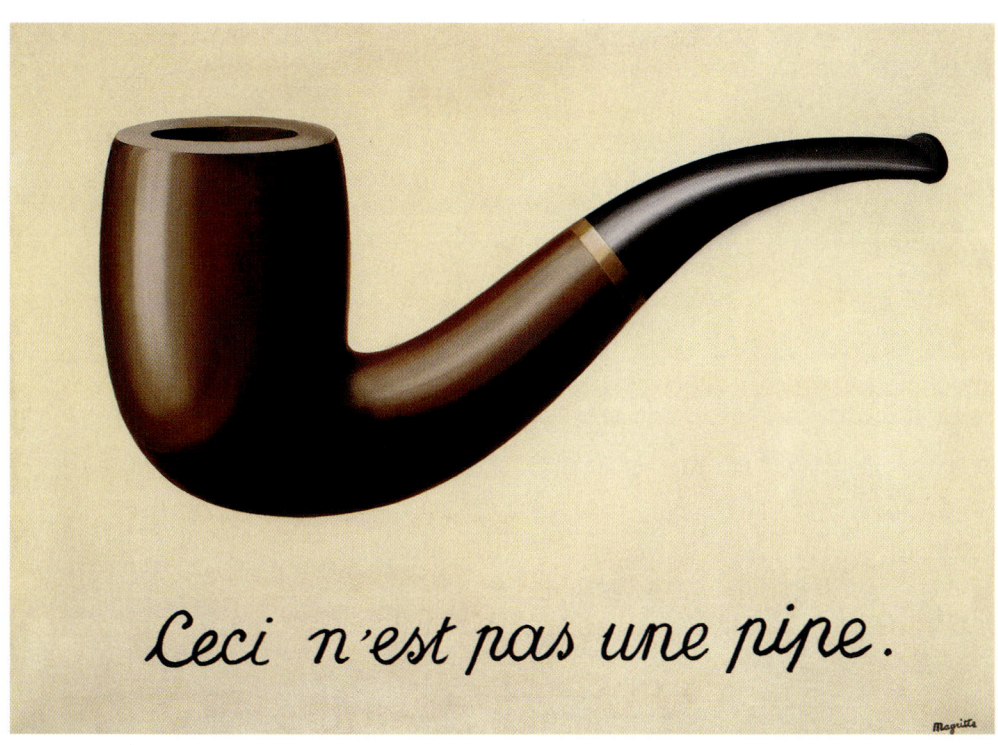

33-47 RENÉ MAGRITTE, *The Treachery (or Perfidy) of Images*, 1928–1929. Oil on canvas, 1' 11⅝" × 3' 1". Los Angeles County Museum of Art, Los Angeles (purchased with funds provided by the Mr. and Mrs. William Preston Harrison Collection).

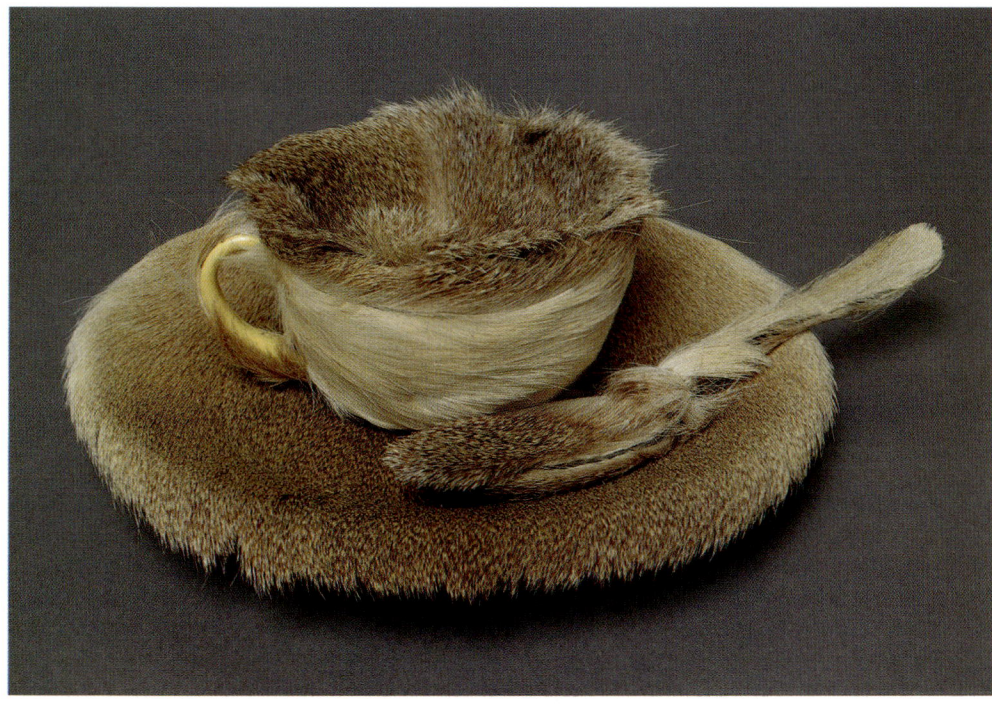

33-48 MERET OPPENHEIM, *Object (Le Déjeuner en fourrure)*, 1936. Fur-covered cup, 4⅜" in diameter; saucer, 9⅜" in diameter; spoon, 8". Museum of Modern Art, New York (purchase).

ject. Further, the sculpture captures the Surrealist flair for alchemical, seemingly magical or mystical, transformation. It incorporates a sensuality and eroticism (seen here in the seductively soft, tactile fur lining the concave form) that are also components of much of Surrealist art. That visitors to the Surrealist exhibition at the Museum of Modern Art in New York in 1937 selected *Object* as the quintessential Surrealist symbol reveals that it seemed to epitomize the Surrealist vision.

WEARING HER HEART ON HER SLEEVE The Mexican painter FRIDA KAHLO (1907–1954), who used the details of her life as powerful symbols for the psychological pain of human existence, often has been discussed as a Surrealist. The psychic and autobiographical issues she dealt with in her art account for this association. Indeed, Breton himself deemed her a natural Surrealist. Yet Kahlo consciously distanced herself from the Surrealist group, and it was left to others to impose Surrealist connections on her. Kahlo began

33-49 FRIDA KAHLO, *The Two Fridas,* 1939. Oil on canvas, 5′ 7″ × 5′ 7″. Collection of the Museo de Arte Moderno, Mexico City.

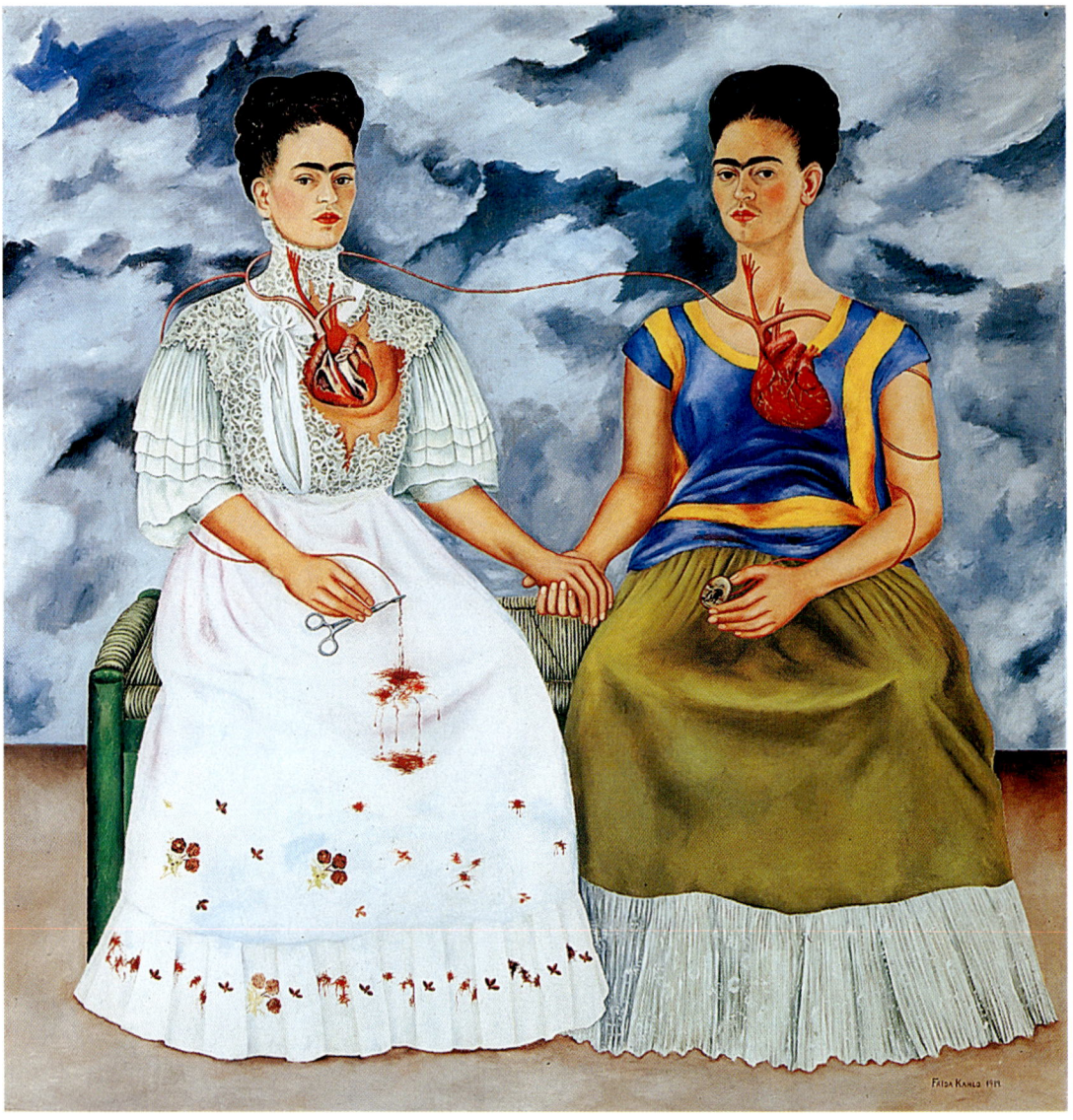

painting seriously as a young student, during convalescence from an accident that tragically left her in constant pain. Her life became a heroic and tumultuous battle for survival against illness and stormy personal relationships. *The Two Fridas* (FIG. **33-49**), one of the few large-scale canvases Kahlo ever produced, is typical of her long series of unflinching self-portraits. The twin figures sit side by side on a low bench in a barren landscape under a stormy sky. One figure wears a simple Mexican costume, while the other is dressed in what might be an elaborate wedding dress. The figures suggest different sides of the artist's personality, inextricably linked by the clasped hands and by the thin artery that stretches between them, joining their exposed hearts. The artery ends on one side in surgical forceps and on the other in a miniature portrait of her husband, the artist Diego Rivera (FIG. 33-81), as a child. Kahlo's deeply personal paintings touch sensual and psychological memories in her audience.

THE CONSCIOUS AND THE UNCONSCIOUS
Like the Dadaists, the Surrealists used many methods to free the creative process from reliance on the kind of conscious control they believed society had shaped too much. Dalí used his paranoiac-critical approach to encourage the free play of

association as he worked. Other Surrealists used automatism—the creation of art without conscious control and various types of planned "accidents" to provoke reactions closely related to subconscious experience. The Spanish artist JOAN MIRÓ (1893–1983) was a master of this approach. Although Miró resisted formal association with any movement or group, including the Surrealists, André Breton identified him as "the most Surrealist of us all."[41] From the beginning, his work contained an element of fantasy and hallucination. Introduced to using chance to create art by Surrealist poets in Paris, the young Spaniard devised a new painting method that allowed him to create works such as *Painting* (FIG. **33-50**). Miró began this painting by making a scattered collage composition with assembled fragments cut from a catalogue for machinery. The shapes in the collage became motifs the artist freely reshaped to create black silhouettes—solid or in outline, with dramatic accents of white and vermilion. They suggest, in the painting, a host of amoebic organisms or constellations in outer space floating in an immaterial background space filled with soft reds, blues, and greens.

Miró described his creative process as a switching back and forth between unconscious and conscious image making: "Rather than setting out to paint something, I begin painting

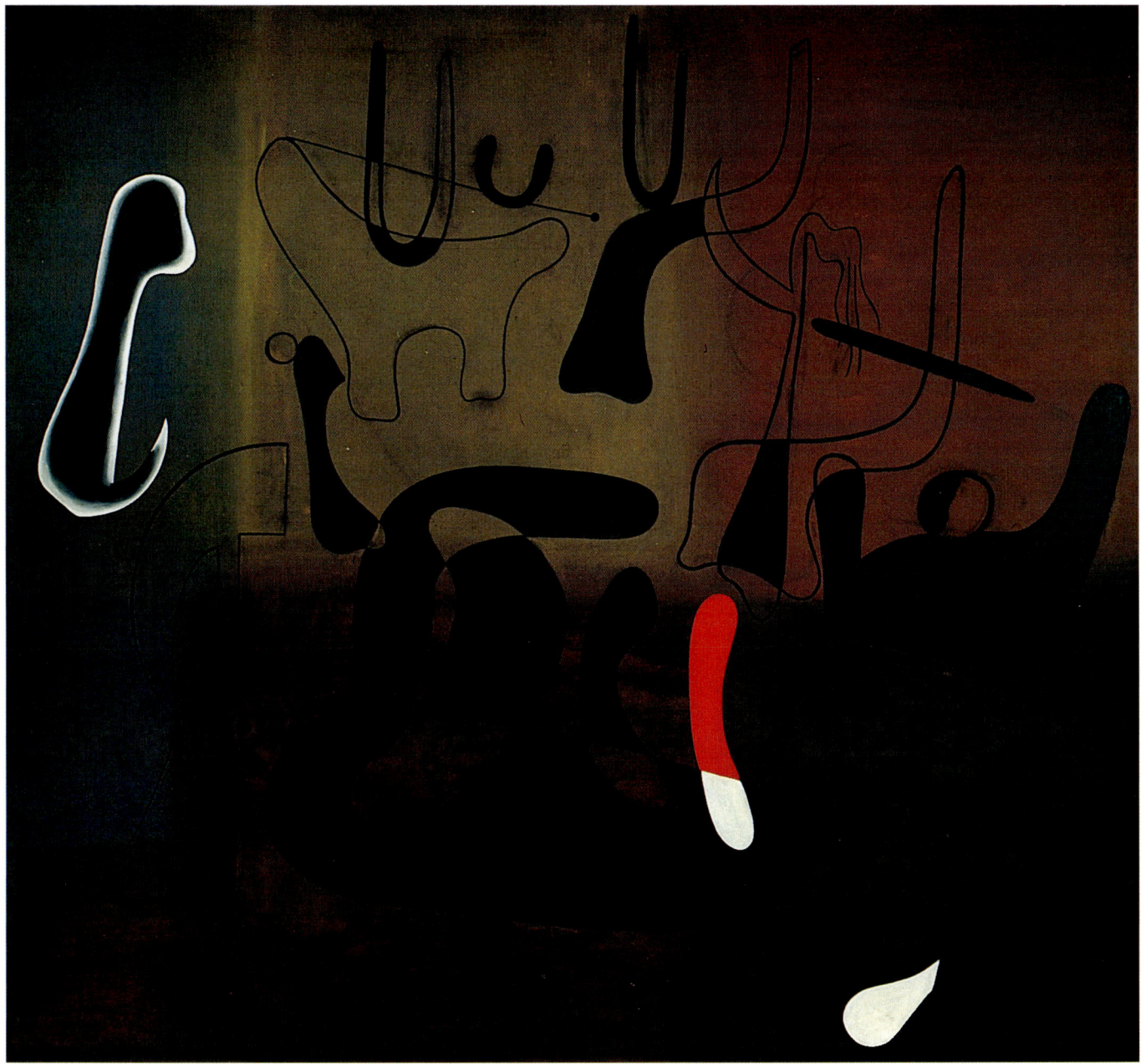

33-50 JOAN MIRÓ, *Painting*, 1933. 5′ 8″ × 6′ 5″. Museum of Modern Art, New York (Loula D. Lasker Bequest by exchange).

and as I paint the picture begins to assert itself, or suggest itself under my brush. The form becomes a sign for a woman or a bird as I work. . . . The first stage is free, unconscious. . . . The second stage is carefully calculated."[42] Even the artist could not always explain the meanings of pictures such as *Painting*. They are, in the truest sense, spontaneous and intuitive expressions of the little-understood, submerged unconscious part of life.

MECHANICAL BIRDS Perhaps the most inventive artist using fantasy images to represent the non-visible world was the Swiss-German painter PAUL KLEE (1879–1940). Like Miró, he shunned formal association with groups such as the Dadaists and Surrealists but pursued their interest in the subconscious. Klee shared the widespread modern apprehension about the rationalism driving a technological civilization that could destroy as much as construct. As do some psychologists,

he sought clues to humanity's deeper nature in primitive shapes and symbols. Like Jung, Klee seems to have accepted the existence of a collective unconscious that reveals itself in archaic signs and patterns and that is everywhere evident in the art of so-called "primitive" cultures (see "'Primitivism,' Colonialism, and Early-Twentieth-Century Western Art," page 1044). The son of a professional musician and himself an accomplished violinist, Klee thought of painting as similar to music in its expressiveness and in its ability to touch its viewers' spirit through a studied use of color, form, and line:

Art does not reproduce the visible; rather it makes visible. . . . The formal elements of graphic art are dot, line, plane and space—the last three charged with energy of various kinds. . . . Formerly we used to represent things visible on earth, things we either liked to look at or would have liked to see. Today we reveal the reality that is behind visible things. . . . By including the concepts of good and evil, a moral sphere is created. . . . Art is a simile of the Creation.[43]

"Primitivism," Colonialism, and Early-Twentieth-Century Western Art

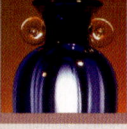

Many scholars have noted that one of the major sources for much of early-twentieth-century art is non-Western culture. Picasso, Matisse, the German Expressionists, Brancusi, Klee, the Dadaists, and the Surrealists all incorporated stylistic elements from the artifacts of Africa, Oceania, and the native peoples of the Americas.

These artists benefited from the numerous non-Western objects displayed in European and American collections and museums. During the second half of the nineteenth century, anthropological and ethnographic museums began to proliferate. In 1882, the Musée d'Ethnographie (now the Musée de l'Homme, the Museum of Man) in Paris opened its doors to the public. The Musée Permanent des Colonies (now the Musée national des Arts d'Afrique et d'Oceanie) in Paris also provided the public with a wide array of objects—weapons, tools, basketwork, headdresses—from colonial territories, as did the Musée Africain in Marseilles. In Germany, the Berlin Museum für Völkerkunde (Museum of Ethnology) housed close to ten thousand African tribal objects by 1886, when it opened for public viewing. In addition, private collecting of such material was fairly widespread—even Matisse and Picasso collected African and Oceanic artifacts. The Expositions Universelles, regularly scheduled exhibitions in France designed to celebrate industrial progress, included products from Oceania and Africa after 1851, familiarizing the public with these cultures. By the beginning of the twentieth century, significant non-Western collections were on view in museums in Liverpool, Glasgow, Edinburgh, London, Hamburg, Stuttgart, Vienna, Berlin, Munich, Leiden, Copenhagen, and Chicago.

The availability of these collections and materials was due to the rampant colonialism central to the geopolitical dynamics of the nineteenth century and much of the twentieth century. Most of the Western powers maintained colonies. For example, the Dutch, Americans, and French all kept a colonial presence in the Pacific. Britain, France, Germany, Belgium, Holland, Spain, and Portugal divided up the African continent. People often perceived these colonial cultures as "primitive," and many of the non-Western artifacts displayed in museums were referred to as "artificial curiosities" or seen as fetish objects. Indeed, the exhibition of these objects collected during expeditions to the colonies served to reinforce the "need" for a colonial presence in these countries. As previously noted, colonialism often had a missionary dimension. These objects, which often seemed to depict strange gods or creatures, reinforced the perception that these peoples were "barbarians" who needed to be "civilized" or "saved," thereby justifying colonialism worldwide.

Whether avant-garde artists were aware of the imperialistic implications of their appropriation of non-Western culture is unclear. Certainly, however, many artists reveled in the energy and freshness of non-Western images and forms. These different cultural products provided Western artists with new ways of looking at their own art. Matisse always maintained he saw African sculptures as simply "good sculptures . . . like any other."[1] Picasso, in contrast, believed these objects were "magical things," "mediators" between humans and the forces of evil.[2] Further, "primitive" art seemed to embody a directness, closeness to nature, and honesty that appealed to modernist artists determined to reject conventional models. Ultimately, non-Western art served as an important revitalizing and energizing force in Western art, and this influence continues to the present.

[1] Jean-Louis Paudrat, "From Africa," in *"Primitivism" in 20th Century Art: Affinity of the Tribal and the Modern,* ed. William Rubin (New York: Museum of Modern Art, 1984), 1:141.

[2] Ibid.

To penetrate the reality behind visible things, Klee studied nature avidly, taking special interest in analyzing processes of growth and change. He coded these studies in diagrammatic form in notebooks, and the knowledge he gained in this way became so much a part of his consciousness that it influenced the "psychic improvisation" he used to create his art.

Klee's works, such as *Twittering Machine* (FIG. **33-51**), are small and intimate in scale. A viewer must draw near to decipher the delicately rendered forms and enter this mysterious dream world. The artist joined the ancient world of nature and the modern world of machines in this picture. Four diagrammatic birds, like those in a cuckoo clock, appear forced into twittering action—in this case, by the turning of a crank-driven mechanism. It is not too far-fetched to associate birds with life and machines with the human ability to control nature. (Indeed, a 1921 drawing by Klee called *Concert on a Twig* shows these four birds with their double-curved perch clearly attached to a tree.) In *Twittering Machine,* however, Klee linked the birds permanently to the machine, creating an ironic vision of existence in the modern age. Each bird responds in such an individual way that viewers may see all of them as metaphors for themselves—beings trapped by the operation of the industrial society they either created or maintain. Some observers see an even darker meaning in *Twittering Machine.* The individual birds may represent the four temperaments of the ancient, medieval, and Renaissance periods, while their loony appearance also features avian shapes capable of luring real birds into a trap in the rectangular trough at the bottom of the image. Perhaps no other artist of the twentieth century matched Klee's subtlety as he deftly created a world of ambiguity and understatement that draws each viewer into finding a unique interpretation of the work.

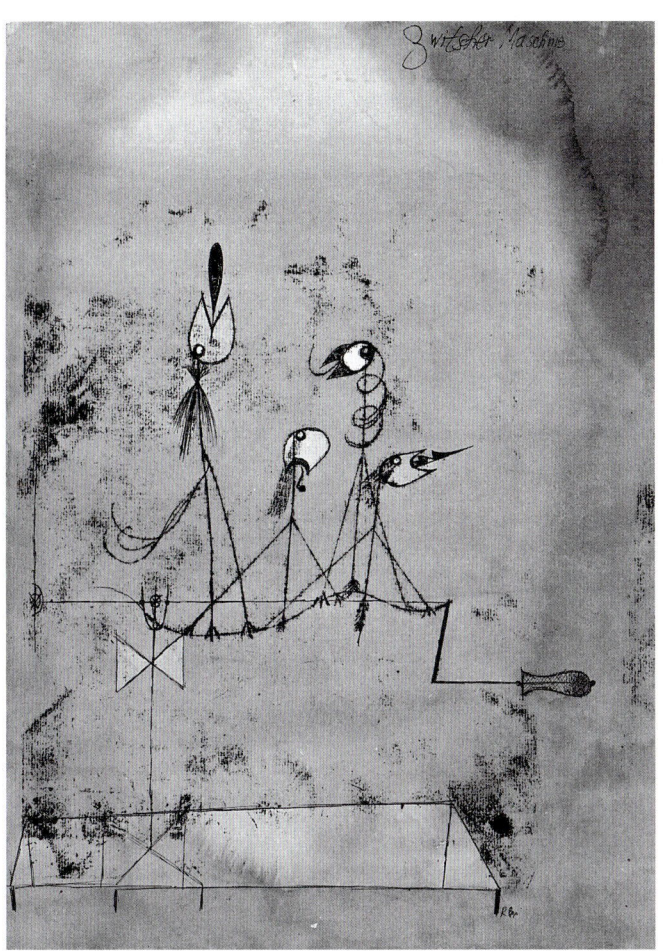

33-51 PAUL KLEE, *Twittering Machine,* 1922. Watercolor and pen and ink, on oil transfer drawing on paper, mounted on cardboard, 2′ 1″ × 1′ 7″. Museum of Modern Art, New York (purchase).

MEMORIES OF A RUSSIAN CHILDHOOD   Not formally associated with either Dada or Surrealism but sharing their philosophy of the primacy of the subconscious in artistic creation was the Russian artist MARC CHAGALL (1887–1985). He maintained a more-or-less independent stance, producing his personal world of free fantasy. He created works filled with the extremes of visionary joy and despair, achieved through both symbols and fantasy. Chagall studied and worked in Paris and Berlin and incorporated into his work elements of expressionism, Cubism, and Fauvism. However, he never forgot his early years in the small Russian village of Vitebsk, and themes from his childhood emerge repeatedly in his art as if in dreams and memories. Some, gay and fanciful, suggest the simpler pleasures of folk life; others, somber and even tragic, recall the trials and persecutions of the Jewish people. Through all of his work runs a sense of deep religious experience, an integral part of his early life. In *I and the Village* (FIG. **33-52**) Chagall portrayed an assortment of images from his memories of his homeland—peasants and their families, a woman milking a cow, and a row of houses. These variously sized images overlap with others, all depicted in Fauve colors and Cubist fragmented space. The painting, clearly a mental construct rather than a logical narrative, has a fairy-tale, lyrical quality to it. A highly individual artist,

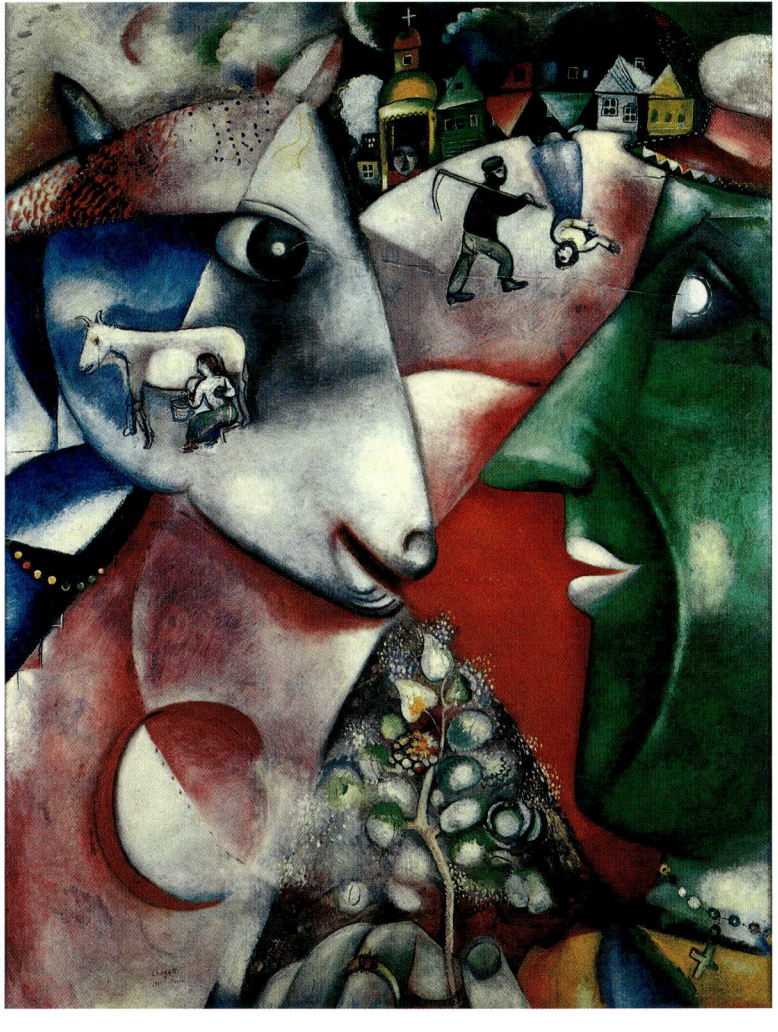

33-52 MARC CHAGALL, *I and the Village,* 1911. Oil on canvas, 6′ 3⅝″ × 4′ 11⅝″. Museum of Modern Art, New York (Mrs. Simon Guggenheim Fund).

Chagall intuitively used diverse avant-garde styles to help him transform the personal themes of his Russian childhood into symbols suggesting broader human experience.

NEW ART FOR A NEW SOCIETY— UTOPIAN IDEALS

The pessimism and cynicism of movements such as Dada are thoroughly understandable in light of the historical circumstances. However, not all artists gravitated toward alienation from society and its profound turmoil. Some avant-garde artists promoted utopian ideals, believing staunchly in art's ability to contribute to improving society and all humankind. These efforts often surfaced in the face of significant political upheaval, illustrating the link established early on between revolution in politics and revolution in art. Among the art movements espousing utopian notions were Suprematism and Constructivism in Russia, De Stijl in Holland, and the Bauhaus in Germany.

Suprematism and Constructivism

THE SUPREMACY OF PURE FEELING Although Russia was geographically far removed from Paris, the center of the international art world in the early twentieth century, Russians had a long history of cultural contact and interaction with the West. Russian artists were thus well aware of early-twentieth-century artistic developments, especially Fauvism, Cubism, and Futurism. Among the artists who pursued the

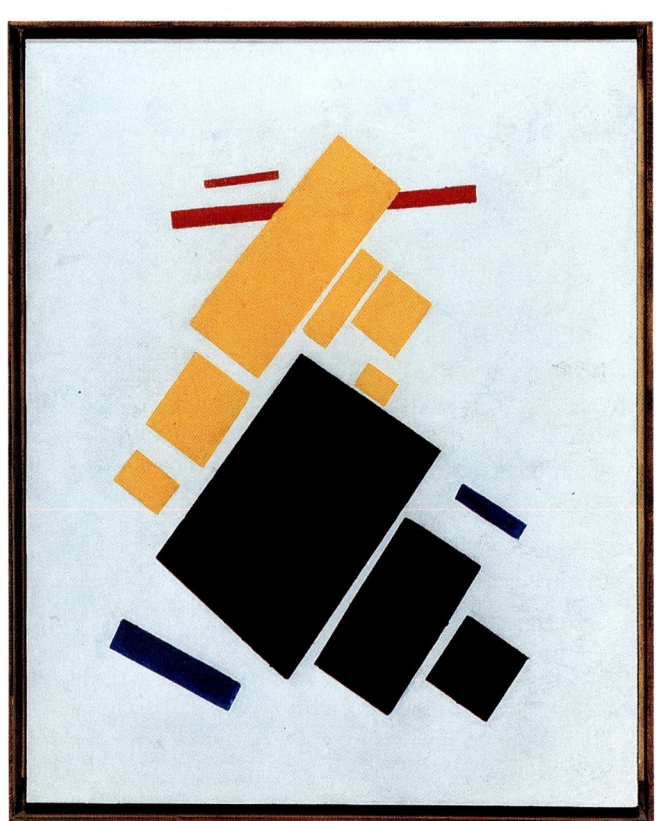

33-53 KAZIMIR MALEVICH, *Suprematist Composition: Airplane Flying,* 1915 (dated 1914). Oil on canvas, $1'10\frac{7}{8}'' \times 1'7''$. Museum of Modern Art, New York (purchase).

avant-garde direction Cubism introduced was the Russian painter KAZIMIR MALEVICH (1878–1935). Malevich developed an abstract style to convey his belief that the supreme reality in the world is pure feeling, which attaches to no object. Thus, this belief called for new, nonobjective forms in art— shapes not related to objects in the visible world. Malevich had studied painting, sculpture, and architecture and had worked his way through most of the avant-garde styles of his youth before deciding none were suited to expressing the subject he found most important—"pure feeling." He christened his new artistic approach Suprematism, explaining: "Under Suprematism I understand the supremacy of pure feeling in creative art. To the Suprematist, the visual phenomena of the objective world are, in themselves, meaningless; the significant thing is feeling, as such, quite apart from the environment in which it is called forth. . . . The Suprematist does not observe and does not touch—he feels."[44]

The basic form of Malevich's new Suprematist nonobjective art was the square. Combined with its relatives, the straight line and the rectangle, the square soon filled his paintings, such as *Suprematist Composition: Airplane Flying* (FIG. **33-53**). In this work, the brightly colored shapes float against and within a white space, and the artist placed them in dynamic relationship to one another. Malevich believed all peoples easily would understand his new art because of the universality of its symbols. It used the pure language of shape and color that everyone could respond to intuitively. Having formulated his artistic approach, Malevich welcomed the Russian Revolution, which broke out in 1917, as a political act that would wipe out past traditions and begin a new culture. He believed his art could play a major role because of its universal accessibility. In actuality, after a short period when the new regime heralded avant-garde art, the political leaders of the postrevolution Soviet Union decided the new society needed a more "practical" art. This art would teach citizens about their new government or produce goods that would improve their lives. Malevich was horrified; to him, true art was forever divorced from such practical connections with life. As he explained, "Every social idea, however great and important it may be, stems from the sensation of hunger; every art work, regardless of how small and insignificant it may seem, originates in pictorial or plastic feeling. It is high time for us to realize that the problems of art lie far apart from those of the stomach or the intellect."[45]

Disappointed and unappreciated in his own country, Malevich eventually stopped painting and turned his attention to other things, such as mathematical theory and geometry, logical fields given his interest in pure abstraction.

THE ABSOLUTE REALITY OF SPACE/TIME Like Malevich, the Russian-born sculptor NAUM GABO (1890–1977) wanted to create an innovative art to express a new reality, and, also like Malevich, Gabo believed such art would spring from sources separate from the everyday world. For Gabo, the new reality was the space/time world described by early-twentieth-century advances in science. As he wrote in *Realistic Manifesto,* published with his brother Anton Pevsner in 1920: "Space and time are the only forms on which life is built and hence art must be constructed." Later, he explained: "We are realists, bound to earthly matters. . . . The shapes we are creating are not abstract, they are absolute. They are released from any already existent thing in nature and their content lies in themselves. . . . It is impossible to comprehend the content of an absolute shape by reason alone. Our emotions are the real manifestation of this content."[46]

Gabo was associated with a group of Russian sculptors known as Constructivists. The name *Constructivism* may have come originally from the title *Construction,* which the Russian artist Vladimir Tatlin had used for some relief sculptures he made in 1913 and 1914. According to Gabo, he called himself a Constructivist partly because he built up his sculptures piece by piece in space, instead of carving or modeling them in the traditional way. This method freed the Constructivists to work with "volume of mass and volume of space" as "two different materials" for creating compositions filled with the "kinetic rhythms" humans perceive as "real time." [47]

Although Gabo experimented briefly with real motion in his work, most of his sculptures relied on the relationship of mass and space to suggest the nature of space/time. To indicate the volumes of mass and space more clearly in his sculpture, Gabo used some of the new synthetic plastic materials, including celluloid, nylon, and lucite, to create constructions whose space seems to flow through as well as around the transparent materials. In works such as *Column* (FIG. **33-54**), the sculpture's depth is visible, because the sculptor opened up the column's circular mass so that viewers can experience the volume of space it occupies. Two transparent planes extend through its diameter, crossing at right angles at the center of the implied cylindrical column shape. The opaque colored planes at the base and the inclined open ring set up counter rhythms to the crossed upright planes. They establish the sense of dynamic kinetic movement Gabo always sought to express as an essential part of reality.

"THE CULTURE OF MATERIALS" In the years immediately following the Russian Revolution, a new art movement emerged in the Soviet Union whose members devoted their talents to designing a better environment for human beings. The Russians called their movement Productivism. It developed as an offshoot of the Constructivist movement, and one of its most gifted leaders was VLADIMIR TATLIN (1885–1953). Influenced by Cubism's formal analysis, the dynamism of Futurism, and the rhythmic compositions of flat curved planes in traditional Russian icon paintings (see FIG. 12-29), Tatlin produced abstract relief constructions and models for stage sets. He experimented with every kind of material—glass, iron, sheet metal, wood, and plaster—to lay the basis for what he called the "culture of materials."

The revolution had been the signal to Tatlin and other avant-garde artists in Russia that the hated old order was ending. They were determined to play a significant role in creating a new world, one that would fully use the power of industrialization to benefit all the people. Initially, like Malevich and Gabo, Tatlin believed nonobjective art was ideal for the new society, free as such art was from any past symbolism. For a few years, all Russian avant-garde artists worked together designing public festivals and demonstrations. They presented plays and exhibitions intended to help educate the public about their new government and the possibilities for their future. The Russian Futurist-Constructivist poet Vladimir Mayakovsky proclaimed their new goal: "We do not need a dead mausoleum of art where dead works are worshiped, but a living factory of the human spirit—in the streets, in the tramways, in the factories, workshops, and workers' homes."[48]

These artists reorganized art schools such as the College of Painting, Sculpture, and Architecture in Moscow, combining them with craft schools to form new educational programs—they renamed the one in Moscow Vkhutemas (Higher Artistic-Technical Studios). Tatlin, Malevich, and Gabo's brother, Pevsner, had studios there. Gabo (a frequent visitor) described the school's activities, which were much like those of Germany's Bauhaus, discussed later:

> [It was] both a school and a free academy where not only the current teaching of special professions was carried out (. . . painting, sculpture, architecture, ceramics, metalwork, and woodwork, textile, and typography) but general discussions were held and seminars conducted amongst the students on diverse problems where the public could participate, and artists not officially on the faculty could speak and give lessons. . . . During these seminars . . . many ideological questions between opposing artists in our abstract group were thrashed out.[49]

As Gabo's statement indicates, a split was developing among avant-garde members. On one side were Malevich, Gabo, Kandinsky (who had returned to Moscow in 1914), and all the other artists who believed art was an expression of

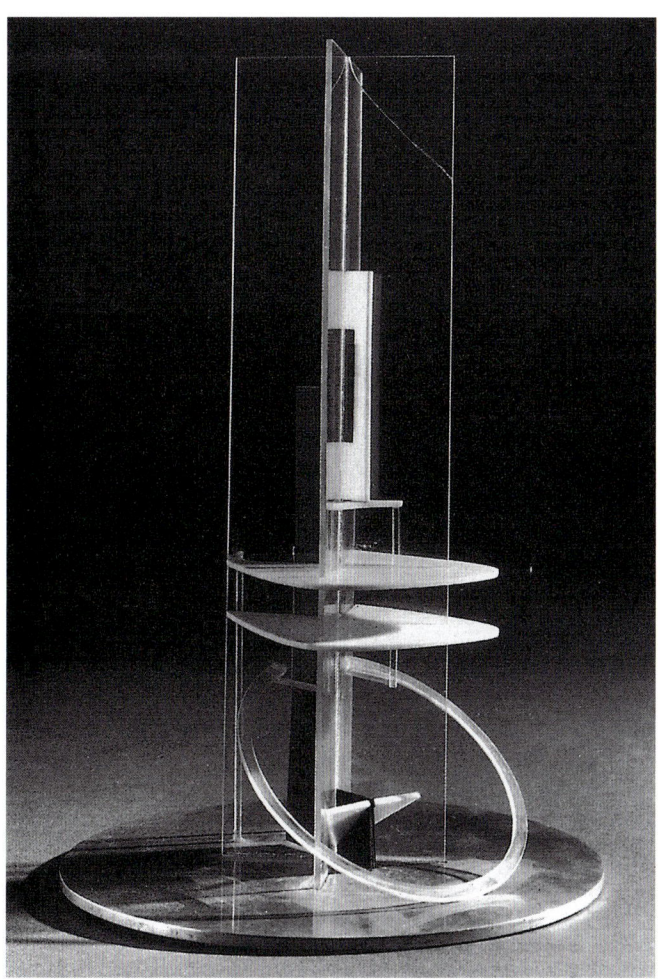

33-54 NAUM GABO, *Column,* ca. 1923 (reconstructed 1937). Perspex, wood, metal, glass, 3′ 5″ × 2′ 5″ × 2′ 5″. Solomon R. Guggenheim Museum, New York.

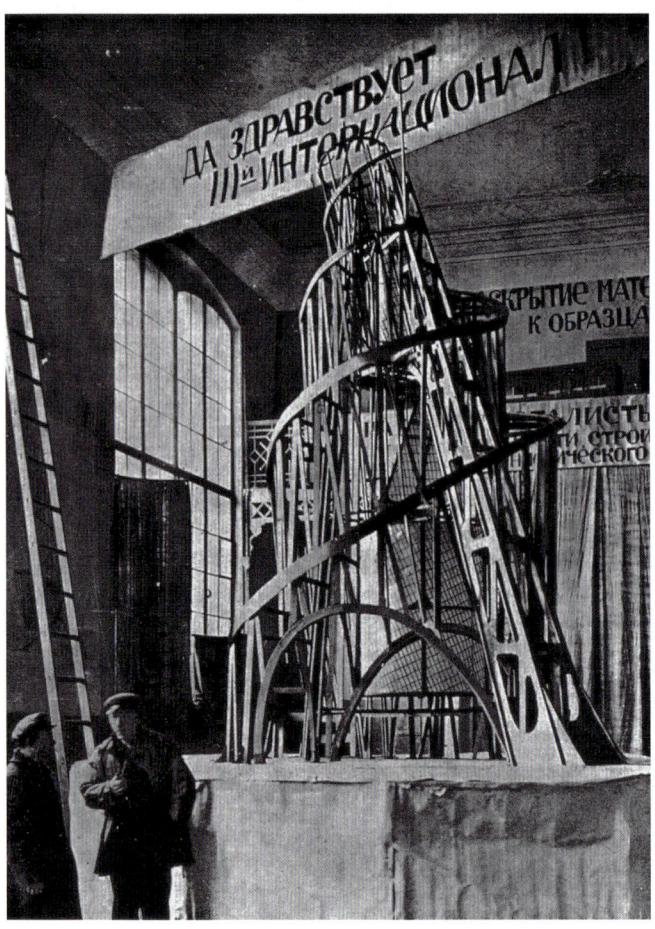

33-55 VLADIMIR TATLIN, *Monument to the Third International*, 1919–1920. Model in wood, iron, and glass. Re-created in 1968 for exhibition at the Moderna Museet, Stockholm. Copyright © Estate of Vladimir Tatlin/Licensed by VAGA, New York, NY.

humanity's spiritual nature. On the other side were the Productivists—Tatlin and other artists who felt artists must direct art toward creating useful products for the new society. The Productivists connected their position to that of a group called Proletkult (Organization for Proletarian Culture). Founded in 1906, it became free to follow its primary doctrine ("Art is a social product, conditioned by the social environment") only after the 1917 revolution. Tatlin enthusiastically abandoned abstract art for functional art by designing such products as an efficient stove and a "functional" set of worker's clothing. For a time, he even worked in a metallurgical factory near Petrograd (after 1989 once again Saint Petersburg).

Tatlin's most famous work is his design for *Monument to the Third International* (FIG. **33-55**), commissioned by the Department of Artistic Work of the People's Commissariat for Enlightenment early in 1919 to honor the Russian Revolution. His concept was for a huge glass-and-iron symbol building that would have been twice as high as the Empire State Building. Widely influential, "Tatlin's Tower," as it became known, was viewed as a model for those seeking to encourage socially committed and functional art. On its proposed site in the center of Moscow, it would have served as a propaganda and news center for the Soviet people. Within a dynamically tilted spiral cage, three geometrically shaped chambers were to rotate around a central axis, each chamber housing facilities

for a different type of governmental activity and rotating at a different speed. The one at the bottom, a huge cylindrical glass structure for lectures and meetings, was to revolve once a year. Higher up was a cone-shaped chamber intended for administrative functions and monthly rotations. At the top, a cubic information center would have revolved daily, issuing news bulletins and proclamations via the most modern means of communication. These included an open-air news screen (illuminated at night) and a special instrument designed to project words on the clouds on any overcast day. The proposed decreasing size of the chambers as visitors ascended the monument paralleled the decision-making hierarchy in the political system, with the most authoritative, smallest groups near the building's apex.

Tatlin's design thus served as a visual reinforcement of a social and political reality. Tatlin envisioned the whole complex as a dynamic communications center perfectly suited to the exhilarating pace of the new age. In addition, the design's reductive geometry demonstrates Tatlin's connection to the artistic programs of the Suprematists and the Constructivists. Due to the desperate economic situation in Russia during these years, Tatlin's ambitious design was never realized as a building. It existed only in metal-and-wood models exhibited on various official occasions before disappearing. The only records of the models are found in a few drawings, photographs, and recent reconstructions, such as the one illustrated.

De Stijl

In 1917, a group of young artists in Holland formed a new movement and began publishing a magazine, calling both movement and magazine De Stijl (The Style). The group was cofounded by the painters PIET MONDRIAN (1872–1944) and Theo van Doesburg (1883–1931). Group members promoted utopian ideals and believed in the birth of a new age in the wake of World War I. They felt it was a time of balance between individual and universal values, when the machine would assure ease of living: "There is an old and a new consciousness of the age. The old one is directed toward the individual. The new one is directed toward the universal."[50] The goal was a total integration of art and life:

> We must realize that life and art are no longer separate domains. That is why the "idea" of "art" as an illusion separate from real life must disappear. The word "art" no longer means anything to us. In its place we demand the construction of our environment in accordance with creative laws based upon a fixed principle. These laws, following those of economics, mathematics, technique, sanitation . . . are leading to a new, plastic unit.[51]

THE UNIVERSALITY OF NONOBJECTIVITY Toward this goal of integration, Piet Mondrian created a resolutely monistic style—that is, it was based on a single ideal principle. The choice of the term *De Stijl* reflected Mondrian's confidence that this style revealed the underlying eternal structure of existence. De Stijl artists reduced their artistic vocabulary to simple geometric elements. Study in Paris, just before World War I, introduced Mondrian to modes of abstraction in avant-garde art such as Cubism. However, as his attraction to contemporary theological writings grew, Mon drian sought to purge his art of every overt reference to individual objects in the external world. (He especially favored the teachings of theosophy, a tradition basing knowledge of nature and the human condition on knowledge of the divine nature or spiritual powers.) His fellow theosophist, Vassily Kandinsky (FIG. 33-7) was pursuing a similar path. Mondrian turned toward a conception of nonobjective or pictorial design—"pure plastic art"— he believed expressed universal reality. He articulated his credo with great eloquence in 1914:

> What first captivated us does not captivate us afterward (like toys). If one has loved the surface of things for a long time, later on one will look for something more. . . . The interior of things shows through the surface; thus as we look at the surface the inner image is formed in our soul. It is this inner image that should be represented. For the natural surface of things is beautiful, but the imitation of it is without life. . . . Art is higher than reality and has no direct relation to reality. Between the physical sphere and the ethereal sphere there is a frontier where our senses stop functioning. . . . The spiritual penetrates the real . . . but for our senses these are two different things. To approach the spiritual in art, one will make as little use as possible of reality, because reality is opposed to the spiritual. We find ourselves in the presence of an abstract art. Art should be above reality, otherwise it would have no value for man.[52]

Mondrian soon moved beyond Cubism because he felt "Cubism did not accept the logical consequences of its own discoveries; it was not developing towards its own goal, the expression of pure plastics."[53] Caught by the outbreak of hostilities while on a visit to Holland, Mondrian remained there during World War I, developing his theories for what he called Neoplasticism—the new "pure plastic art." He believed all great art has polar but coexistent goals, the attempt to create "universal beauty" and the desire for "aesthetic expression of oneself."[54] The first goal is objective in nature, while the second is subjective, existing within the individual's mind and heart. To create such a universal expression, an artist must communicate "a real equation of the universal and the individual."[55] To express this vision, Mondrian eventually limited his formal vocabulary to the three primary colors (red, blue, and yellow), the three primary values (black, white, and gray), and the two primary directions (horizontal and vertical). Basing his ideas on a combination of teachings, he concluded that primary colors and values are the purest colors and therefore are the perfect tools to help an artist construct a harmonious composition. Using this system, he created numerous paintings locking color planes into a grid of intersecting vertical and horizontal lines, as in *Composition in Red, Blue, and Yellow,* (FIG. **33-56**). In each of these paintings, Mondrian altered the grid patterns and the size and placement of the color planes to create an internal cohesion and harmony. This did not mean inertia; rather, Mondrian worked to maintain a dynamic tension in his paintings from the size and position of lines, shapes, and colors.

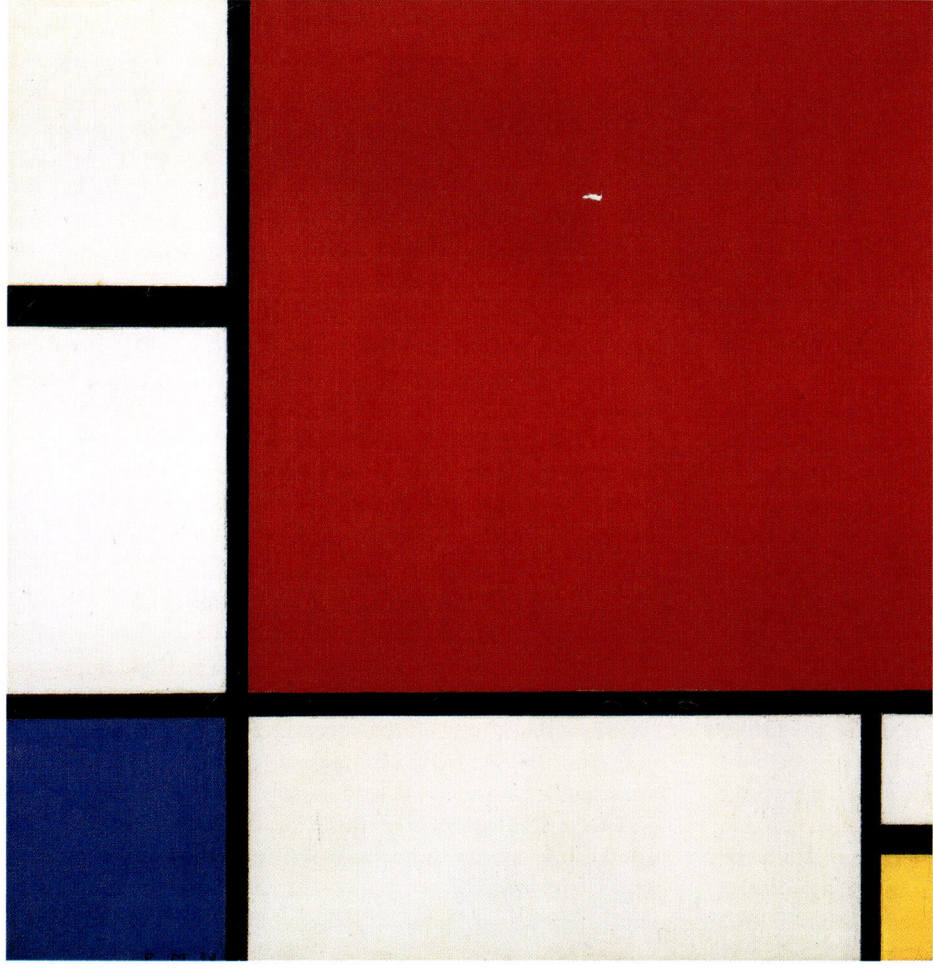

33-56 PIET MONDRIAN, *Composition in Red, Blue, and Yellow,* 1930. Oil on canvas, 2′ 4⅝″ × 1′ 9¼″. Private Collection.

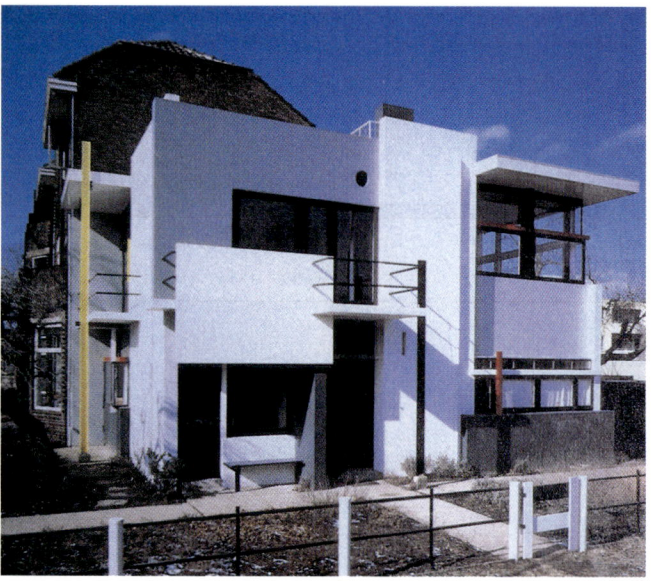

33-57   GERRIT RIETVELD, Schröder House, Utrecht, the Netherlands, 1924.

DE STIJL STYLE IN SPACE   Architects also explored many of the ideas Mondrian and De Stijl artists pursued. One of the masterpieces of De Stijl architecture is the Schröder House in Utrecht, Holland (FIG. **33-57**), built in 1924 by GERRIT THOMAS RIETVELD (1888–1964). Rietveld came to the group as a cabinetmaker and made De Stijl furnishings throughout his career. His architecture carries the same spirit into a larger integrated whole and perfectly expresses van Doesburg's definition of De Stijl architecture:

> The new architecture is anti-cubic, i.e., it does not strive to contain the different functional space cells in a single closed cube, but it throws the functional space (as well as canopy planes, balcony volumes, etc.) out from the centre of the cube, so that height, width, and depth plus time become a completely new plastic expression in open spaces. . . . The plastic architect . . . has to construct in the new field, time-space.[56]

The main living rooms of the Schröder House are on the second floor, with more private rooms on the ground floor. However, Rietveld's house has an open plan and a relationship to nature more like the houses of his contemporary, the American architect Frank Lloyd Wright (FIG. 33-67 and FIG. 33-69). Rietveld designed the entire second floor with sliding partitions that can be closed to define separate rooms or pushed back to create one open space broken into units only by the furniture arrangement. This shifting quality appears also on the outside, where railings, free-floating walls, and long rectangular windows give the effect of cubic units breaking up before viewers' eyes. Rietveld's design clearly links all the arts. Rectangular planes seem to slide across each other on the Schröder House facade like movable panels, making this structure a kind of three-dimensional projection of the rigid but carefully proportioned flat planes in Mondrian's paintings.

The Bauhaus

The De Stijl group developed not only an appealing simplified geometric style, but it also promoted the notion that art should be thoroughly incorporated into living environments. As Mondrian had insisted, "Art and life are *one;* art and life are both expressions of truth."[57] In Germany, a particular vision of "total architecture" was developed by the architect WALTER GROPIUS (1883–1969), who made this concept the foundation not only of his own work but also of the work of generations of pupils under his influence at a school called the Bauhaus. In 1919, Gropius was appointed the director of the Weimar School of Arts and Crafts in Germany, founded in 1906. Under Gropius, the school was renamed Das Staatliche Bauhaus (roughly translated as "State School of Building") and referred to as the Bauhaus.

Gropius's goal was to train artists, architects, and designers to accept and anticipate twentieth-century needs. He designed an extensive curriculum based on certain principles. First, Gropius staunchly advocated the importance of strong basic design (including principles of composition, two- and three-dimensionality, and color theory) and craftsmanship as fundamental to good art and architecture. Declared Gropius: "Architects, sculptors, painters, we must all go back to the crafts. . . . There is no essential difference between the artist and the craftsman."[58] To achieve this, both a technical instructor and a "teacher of form"—an artist—taught each department.

Second, Gropius promoted the unity of art, architecture, and design. "Architects, painters, and sculptors," he insisted, "must recognize anew the composite character of a building as an entity."[59] To encourage eliminating boundaries that traditionally separated art from architecture and art from craft, the Bauhaus offered courses in a wide range of artistic disciplines. These included weaving, pottery, bookbinding, carpentry, metalwork, stained glass, mural painting, stage design, and advertising and typology, in addition to painting, sculpture, and architecture.

Third, because Gropius wanted the Bauhaus to produce graduates who could design progressive environments that satisfied twentieth-century needs, he emphasized thorough knowledge of machine-age technologies and materials. He felt that to produce truly successful designs, the artist/architect/craftsperson had to understand industry and mass production. Ultimately, Gropius hoped for a marriage between art and industry—a synthesis of design and production.

Like the De Stijl movement, the Bauhaus was founded on utopian principles. Gropius's declaration reveals the idealism of the entire Bauhaus enterprise: "Together let us conceive and create the new building of the future, which will embrace architecture and sculpture and painting in one unity and which will rise one day toward heaven from the hands of a million workers like a crystal symbol of a new faith."[60] In its reference to a unity of workers, this statement also reveals the undercurrent of socialism present in Germany at the time.

Gropius hired some of the period's most innovative and avant-garde artists and thinkers to teach at the Bauhaus, and their influence—at the Bauhaus and long after its demise, as a group and individually—was monumental.

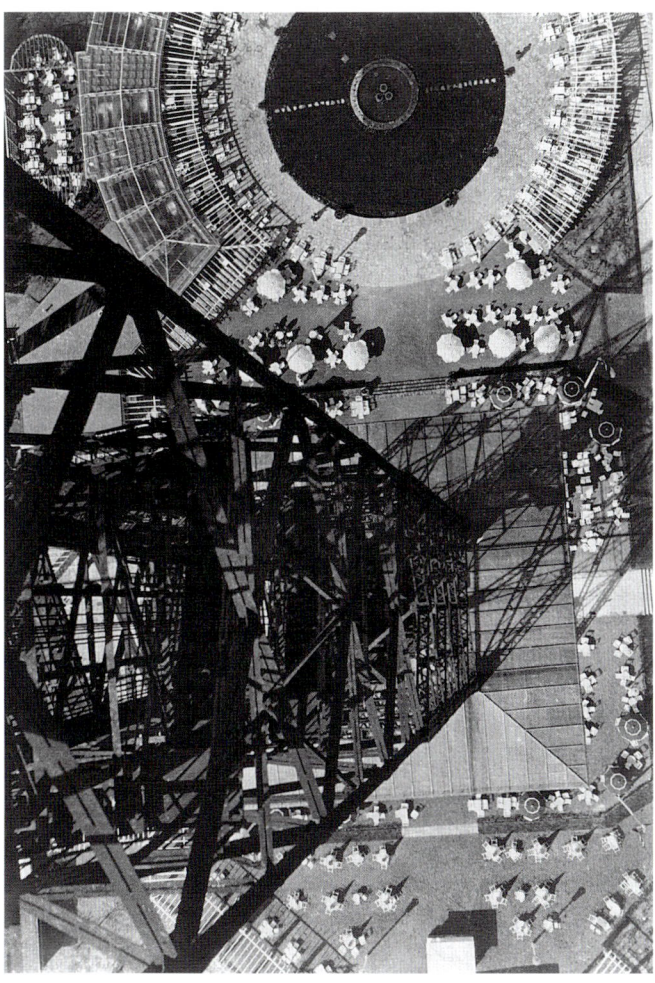

33-58 László Moholy-Nagy, *From the Radio Tower Berlin,* 1928, Gelatin silver print. The Art Institute of Chicago, Chicago.

Given this fascination with space/time relationships, it is not surprising Moholy-Nagy increasingly turned his attention to photography and film. Not only does *From the Radio Tower Berlin* (FIG. **33-58**) depict a marvel of the modern age—a radio tower—but the photo also exercises his "new vision," taken as it is from the top looking straight down. This vertical aerial viewpoint presented viewers with a new perspective on the world (an increasingly common one with the development of aerial flight) and new formal patterns and visual relationships.

THE PRIMACY OF DESIGN PRINCIPLES   Another Bauhaus teacher who left a lasting legacy is the German artist JOSEF ALBERS (1888–1976). Although he initially worked in the Bauhaus's glass and furniture workshops, his greatest contribution to the school was his revision of the basic design course required of all students. There he refined his ideas, declaring: "We learn which formal qualities are important today: harmony or balance, free or measured rhythm, geometric or arithmetic proportion, symmetry or asymmetry, central or peripheral emphasis."[62] This systematic and thorough investigation of art's formal aspects characterized his own work, as evidenced in his best-known series *Homage to the Square* (FIG. **33-59**). Although Albers executed this series between 1950 and 1976, some time after his departure from the Bauhaus and his emigration to the United States in 1933, it encapsulates the design concepts he developed while at the Bauhaus. Consisting of hundreds of paintings that were simply color variations on the same composition of concentric squares, *Homage to the Square* reflected Albers's belief that art originates in "the discrepancy between physical fact and psychic effect."[63]

Among these teachers were Vassily Kandinsky (FIG. 33-7), Paul Klee (FIG. 33-51), and the De Stijl artists Theo van Doesburg and Piet Mondrian (participating as a guest teacher; FIG. 33-56).

EXPLORING SPACE/TIME RELATIONSHIPS
One of the most important Bauhaus teachers was Hungarian-born artist LÁSZLÓ MOHOLY-NAGY (1895–1946), who embraced Gropius's notion that art should be all encompassing. Accordingly, Moholy-Nagy produced paintings, sculptures, prints, photograms, advertisements, set designs, photographs, and special effects for film. He was particularly interested in the character of the modern age and believed society was

> heading toward a kinetic, time-spatial existence; toward an awareness of the forces plus their relationships which define all life and of which we had no previous knowledge and for which we have as yet no exact terminology. . . . Space-time stands for many things: relativity of motion and its measurement, integration, simultaneous grasp of the inside and outside, revelation of the structure instead of the facade. It also stands for a new vision concerning materials, energies, tensions, and their social implications.[61]

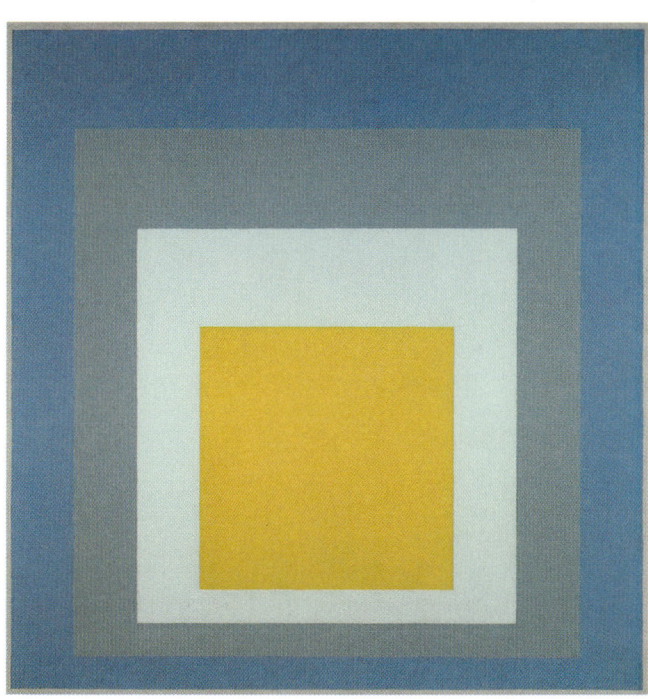

33-59 JOSEF ALBERS, *Homage to the Square: "Ascending",* 1953. Oil on composition board, $3' 7\frac{1}{2}'' \times 3' 7\frac{1}{2}''$. Collection of Whitney Museum of American Art, New York (purchase).

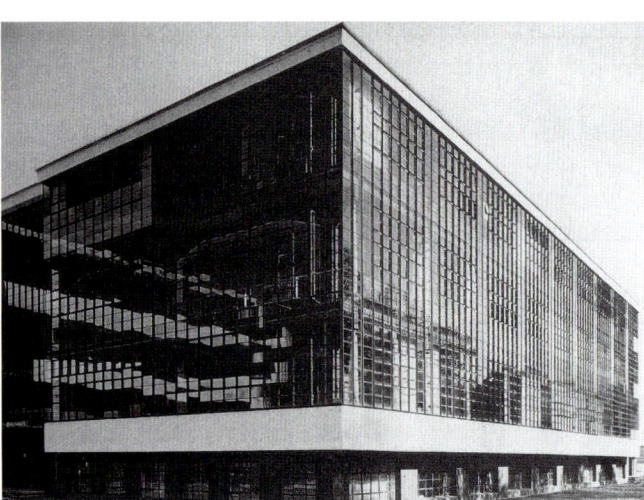

33-60 WALTER GROPIUS, Shop Block, the Bauhaus, Dessau, Germany, 1925–1926.

The building Gropius designed for the Bauhaus at Dessau visibly expressed these goals and can be seen as the Bauhaus's architectural manifesto. The building consisted of workshop and class areas, a dining room, a theater, a gymnasium, a wing with studio apartments, and an enclosed two-story bridge housing administrative offices. Of the major wings, the most dramatic was the Shop Block (FIG. **33-60**). The Nazi government tore down this building, but the Bauhaus's main buildings were later reconstructed. Three stories tall, the Shop Block housed a printing shop and dye works facility, in addition to other work areas. The builders constructed the skeleton of reinforced concrete but set these supports well back, sheathing the entire structure in glass, creating a streamlined and light effect. This design's simplicity followed Gropius's dictum that architecture should avoid "all romantic embellishment and whimsy." Further, he realized the "economy in the use of space" articulated in his list of principles in his interior layout of the Shop Block, which consisted of large areas of freeflowing undivided space. Gropius believed such a spatial organization encouraged interaction and the sharing of ideas. One student described the "wonderful community spirit" such a layout generated.

The former interior decor of this Dessau building also reveals the comprehensiveness of the Bauhaus program. Because carpentry, furniture design, and weaving were all part of the Bauhaus curriculum, Gropius gave students and teachers the task of designing furniture and light fixtures for the building.

TUBULAR STEEL BAUHAUS FURNITURE One of the memorable furniture designs that emerged from the Bauhaus was the tubular steel chair (FIG. **33-61**) crafted by the Hungarian MARCEL BREUER (1902–1981). Breuer supposedly was inspired to use tubular steel while riding his bicycle and admiring the handlebars. In keeping with Bauhaus

Because the composition in each of these paintings remains constant, the works succeed in revealing the relativity and instability of color perception. Albers varied the hue (color), saturation (brightness or dullness), and value or tone (lightness or darkness) of each square in the paintings in this series. As a result, the sizes of the squares from painting to painting appear to vary (although they remain the same), and the sensations emanating from the paintings range from clashing dissonance to delicate serenity. Albers explained his motivation for focusing on color juxtapositions: "They [the colors] are juxtaposed for various and changing visual effects. . . . Such action, reaction, interaction . . . is sought in order to make obvious how colors influence and change each other; that the same color, for instance—with different grounds or neighbors—looks different. . . . Such color deceptions prove that we see colors almost never unrelated to each other . . ."[64]

In keeping with the Bauhaus's encouragement of proficiency in a wide range of media, Albers produced versions of *Homage* in oil painting on masonite, in lithographs, in screenprints, on Aubusson (French densely patterned carpet) and other tapestries, and on large interior walls. Albers's ideas about design and color were widely disseminated, not only during his years at the Bauhaus but also during his subsequent residency in the United States.

THE BAUHAUS MOVES TO DESSAU After encountering increasing hostility from a new government elected in 1924, the Bauhaus was forced to move north to Dessau in early 1925. By this time, the Bauhaus program had matured. In a statement, Walter Gropius listed the school's goals more clearly:

- A decidedly positive attitude to the living environment of vehicles and machines.
- The organic shaping of things in accordance with their own current laws, avoiding all romantic embellishment and whimsy.
- Restriction of basic forms and colours to what is typical and universally intelligible.
- Simplicity in complexity, economy in the use of space, materials, time, and money.[65]

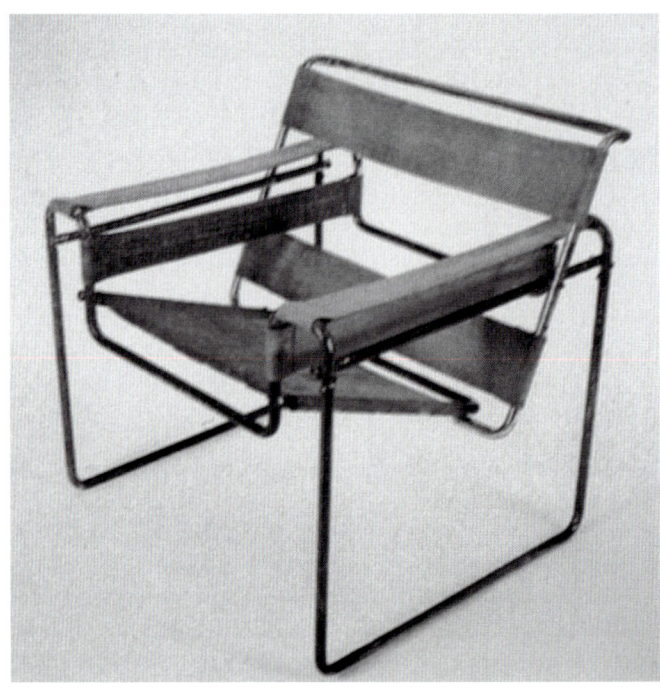

33-61 MARCEL BREUER, tubular chair, 1925.

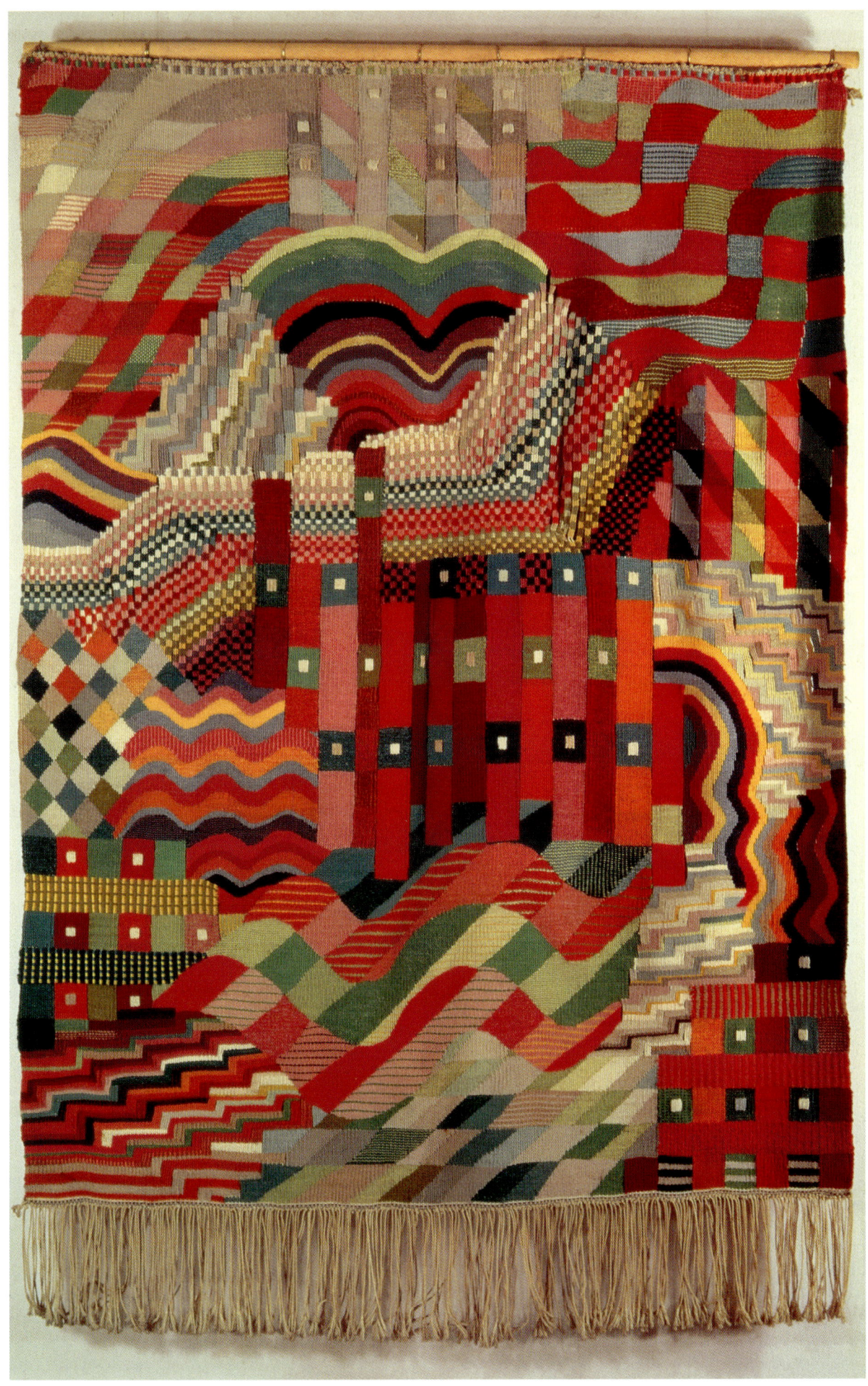

33-62 Gunta Stölzl, Gobelin tapestry, 1926–1927. Linen and cotton.

aesthetics, his chairs have a streamlined, simple geometric look to them, and the leather or cloth supports add to the furniture's comfort and functionality. These chairs also were easily mass produced and thus stand as epitomes of the Bauhaus program.

This reductive, spare geometric aesthetic served many purposes—artistic, practical, and social. Bauhaus and De Stijl artists alike championed this style. Theo van Doesburg, an important De Stijl member, promoted this simplified artistic vocabulary, in part accepted because of its association with the avant-garde and progressive thought. Such an aesthetic also evoked the machine. Appropriately, it easily could be applied to all art forms, from stage design to advertising to architecture, and therefore was perfect for mass production. Even further, this aesthetic fit in well with Gropius's directive that artists, architects, and designers restrict their visual vocabulary "to what is typical and universally intelligible," revealing the social dimension of the Bauhaus agenda in its adherence to socialist principles.

THE VITALITY OF BAUHAUS FIBER CRAFTS
The universal applicability of this aesthetic is seen in a tapestry (FIG. **33-62**) designed by GUNTA STÖLZL (1897–1983), the only woman on the Bauhaus staff. More lively than many of the other Bauhaus-produced designs, this intricate and colorful work retains the emphasis on geometric patterns and clear intersection of verticals and horizontals. Stölzl was largely responsible for the vitality of the weaving workshop at the Bauhaus, creating numerous handwoven carpets, curtains, and runners. In accordance with Bauhaus principles, she also designed weavings for machine production. In terms of establishing production links with outside businesses, her department was one of the most successful at the school.

"LESS IS MORE"   In 1928, Gropius left the Bauhaus, and architect LUDWIG MIES VAN DER ROHE (1886–1969) eventually took over the directorship, moving the school to Berlin. In his architecture and furniture, he made such a clear and elegant statement of the International Style (see FIGS. 33-64 and 33-65) that his work had enormous influence on modern architecture. Taking as his motto "less is more" and calling his architecture "skin and bones," his aesthetic was already fully formed in the model for a glass skyscraper building he conceived in 1921 (FIG. **33-63**). This model received extensive publicity when it was exhibited at the first Bauhaus exhibition in 1923. Working with glass provided Mies van der Rohe with new freedom and many expressive possibilities.

In the glass model, three irregularly shaped towers flow outward from a central court designed to hold a lobby, a porter's room, and a community center. Two cylindrical entrance shafts rise at the ends of the court, each containing elevators, stairways, and toilets. Wholly transparent, the perimeter walls reveal the regular horizontal patterning of the cantilevered floor planes and their thin vertical supporting elements. The bold use of glass sheathing and inset supports was, at the time, technically and aesthetically adventurous. A few years later, Gropius pursued it in his design for the Bauhaus building in Dessau. The weblike delicacy of the lines of the glass model, its radiance, and the illusion of movement created by reflection and by light changes seen through it pre-

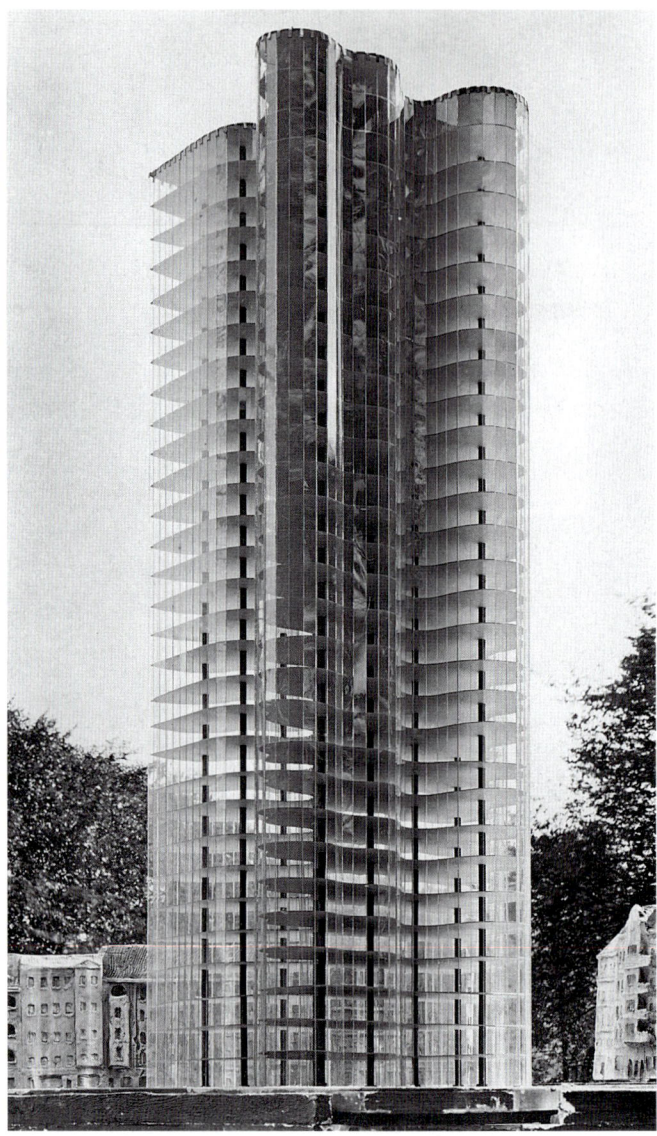

33-63   LUDWIG MIES VAN DER ROHE, model for a glass skyscraper, Berlin, Germany, 1922 (no longer extant).

figured many of the glass skyscrapers found in major cities throughout the world today.

THE DEMISE OF THE BAUHAUS   In 1933, the Nazis finally occupied the Bauhaus and closed the school for good, one of Hitler's first acts after coming to power (see "'Degenerate Art,'" page 1055). During its fourteen-year existence, the beleaguered school graduated fewer than five hundred students, yet it achieved legendary status. Its phenomenal impact extended beyond painting, sculpture, and architecture to interior design, graphic design, and advertising. Even further, the Bauhaus greatly influenced art education, and art schools everywhere structured their curricula in line with that the Bauhaus pioneered. The Bauhaus philosophy and aesthetic were disseminated widely, in large part by the numerous instructors who fled Nazi Germany, many to the United States. Walter Gropius and Marcel Breuer ended up at Harvard University, while Mies van der Rohe and László Moholy-Nagy moved to Chicago and taught there. Josef Albers moved to the United States in 1993, teaching at Black Mountain College in North Carolina and later at Yale University.

"Degenerate Art"

Estrangement between the avant-garde and the public evolved into a defining characteristic of their relationship—a distance artists often consciously cultivated because they perceived it as confirming the innovative nature of their art. Despite the avant-garde's strong commitment to its art, such constant ridicule by and hostility from the public (and the art world's more conservative segment) must have been difficult and wearying.

At times, this hostility went beyond mere derision to outright political persecution. The Bauhaus endured years of harassment by the National Socialists (Nazis) before they forced it to close its doors in 1933. But perhaps the most dramatic and moving example of the persecution avant-garde artists suffered is the infamous *Entartete Kunst* (Degenerate art) exhibition Adolf Hitler and the Nazis mounted in 1937.

Hitler aspired to become an artist himself, producing numerous drawings and paintings. These works reflected Hitler's firm belief that nineteenth-century realistic genre painting represented the zenith of Aryan art development. Accordingly, he denigrated anything that did not conform to that standard—in particular, avant-garde art. Hitler ordered confiscation of more than sixteen thousand artworks he considered "degenerate," and to publicize his condemnation of this art, he ordered his minister for public enlightenment and propaganda (and second in command) Joseph Goebbels to organize a massive exhibition of this "degenerate art." Hitler defined "degenerate art" as works that "insult German feeling, or destroy or confuse natural form, or simply reveal an absence of adequate manual and artistic skill."[1] The term "degenerate" also had other specific connotations at the time and was used to designate supposedly inferior racial, sexual, and moral types. Hitler's order to Goebbels to target twentieth-century avant-garde art for inclusion in this exhibition was intended to impress on viewers the general inferiority of these individuals. To make this point all the more dramatic, Hitler ordered the organization of another exhibition, the *Grosse Deutsche Kunstausstellung* (Great German art exhibition), which ran concurrently and presented an extensive array of Nazi-approved conservative art.

Entartete Kunst opened in Munich on July 19, 1937, and included more than 650 paintings, sculptures, prints, and books. Among the 112 artists whose works the Nazis presented for ridicule were Ernst Barlach, Max Beckmann, Marc Chagall, Otto Dix, Max Ernst, George Grosz, Vassily Kandinsky, Ernst Kirchner, Paul Klee, Wilhelm Lehmbruck, Franz Marc, László Moholy-Nagy, Piet Mondrian, Emil Nolde, and Kurt Schwitters. The photograph here shows Hitler visiting the exhibition, pausing in front of the Dada wall, where works by Schwitters, Klee, and Kandinsky were initially deliberately hung askew. No avant-garde or even modernist artist was safe from Hitler's attack; only six of the artists in the exhibition were Jewish. Indeed, despite his status

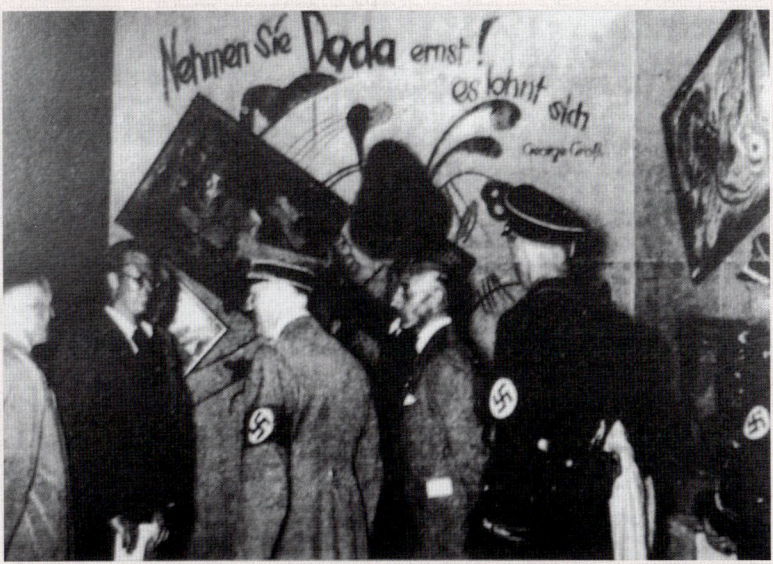

Adolf Hitler, accompanied by Nazi commission members photographer Heinrich Hoffmann, Wolfgang Willrich, Walter Hansen, and painter Adolf Ziegler, viewing the *Entartete Kunst* show on July 16, 1937. The curators deliberately hung askew these works by Kandinsky, Klee, and Schwitters (although the paintings were subsequently straightened for the duration of the exhibition).

as a charter member of the Nazi party, Emil Nolde was singled out for particularly harsh treatment. The Nazis confiscated more than one thousand of Nolde's works from German museums and included twenty-seven of them in the exhibition, more than almost any other artist.

Entartete Kunst was immensely popular; roughly twenty thousand viewers visited the show daily. By the end of its four-month run, it had attracted more than two million viewers, and nearly a million more viewed it as it traveled through Germany and Austria.

Clearly, artists needed monumental courage to defy tradition and produce avant-garde art. Commitment to the avant-garde demanded a resoluteness that extended beyond issues of aesthetics and beyond the confines of the art world. Such persecution exacted an immense toll on these artists. Kirchner, for example, responded to the stress of Nazi pressure by destroying all of his woodblocks and burning many of his works. A year later, in 1938, he committed suicide. Beckmann and his wife fled to Amsterdam on the exhibit's opening day, never to return to their homeland. Although *Entartete Kunst* was just a fragment of the tremendous destruction of life and spirit Hitler and the Nazis wrought, Hitler's insistence on suppressing and discrediting this art dramatically demonstrates art's power to affect viewers.

[1] Stephanie Barron, *"Degenerate Art": The Fate of the Avant-Garde in Nazi Germany* (Los Angeles: Los Angeles County Museum of Art, 1991), 19.

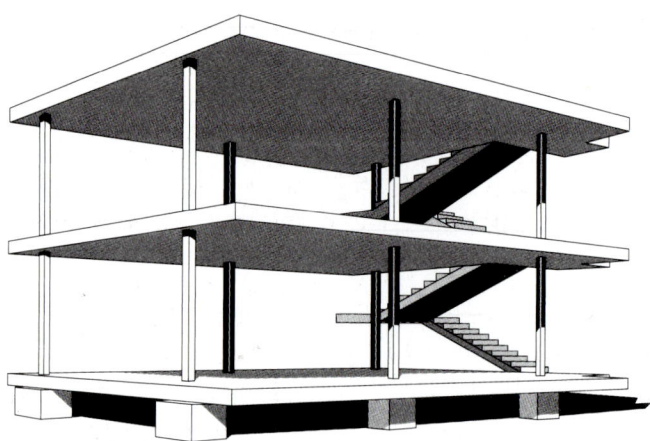

33-64   LE CORBUSIER, perspective drawing for Domino House project, Marseille, France, 1914.

The International Style

DESIGNING FUNCTIONAL LIVING SPACES
The simple streamlined aesthetic Gropius and Mies van der Rohe developed became known as the International Style (different from the Early Renaissance painting style) because of its widespread popularity. Of the architectural purists—perhaps, puritans—of this style, the first and staunchest adherent was the Swiss architect CHARLES-EDOUARD JEANNERET (1887–1965), called LE CORBUSIER. Trained in Paris and Berlin, he was also a painter (see page 1019) but was best known as an influential architect and theorist on modern architecture. As such, he applied himself to designing a "functional" living space, which he described as a "machine for living."[66]

The drawing for his Domino House project (FIG. **33-64**) shows the skeleton of his ideal dwelling. Every level can be used. Reinforced concrete slabs serve the double function of ceiling and floor, supported by thin steel columns rising freely inside the perimeter of the structure's interior spaces. The whole building is raised above ground on short blocks so that the design uses the space underneath, as well as that on the roof. Exterior walls can be suspended from the projecting edges of the concrete slabs in this model, like free-hanging curtains. Because the skeleton supports itself, architects using this plan have complete freedom to subdivide the interior, wherever desired, with light walls that bear no structural load. This drawing illustrates one of the major principles associated with the International Style—eliminating the bearing wall. New structural systems using materials such as structural steel and ferroconcrete (reinforced concrete) made this idea possible.

The scheme allows architects to provide for what Le Corbusier saw as the basic physical and psychological needs of every human being—sun, space, and vegetation combined with controlled temperature, good ventilation, and insulation against harmful and undesired noise. He also believed in basing dwelling designs on human scale, because the house is humankind's assertion within nature. The Domino House system's main principles were anticipated about half a decade earlier in the designs of the German architects Walter Gropius and Peter Behrens (with whom Le Corbusier worked early in his career). However, Le Corbusier's drawing depicts their ideas with such elegant simplicity that it has had enormous influence. It is the primary statement of the design concepts governing the structural principles used in many modern office buildings and skyscrapers.

A "PURIST" HOUSE   Le Corbusier used the basic ideas of the Domino House project in many single-family dwellings. The most elegant is the Villa Savoye (FIG. **33-65**), located at Poissy-sur-Seine near Paris. This country house sits conspicuously within its site, tending to dominate it, and has a broad view of the landscape. A cube of lightly enclosed and deeply penetrated space, the Villa Savoye has only a partially

33-65   LE CORBUSIER, Villa Savoye, Poissy-sur-Seine, France, 1929.

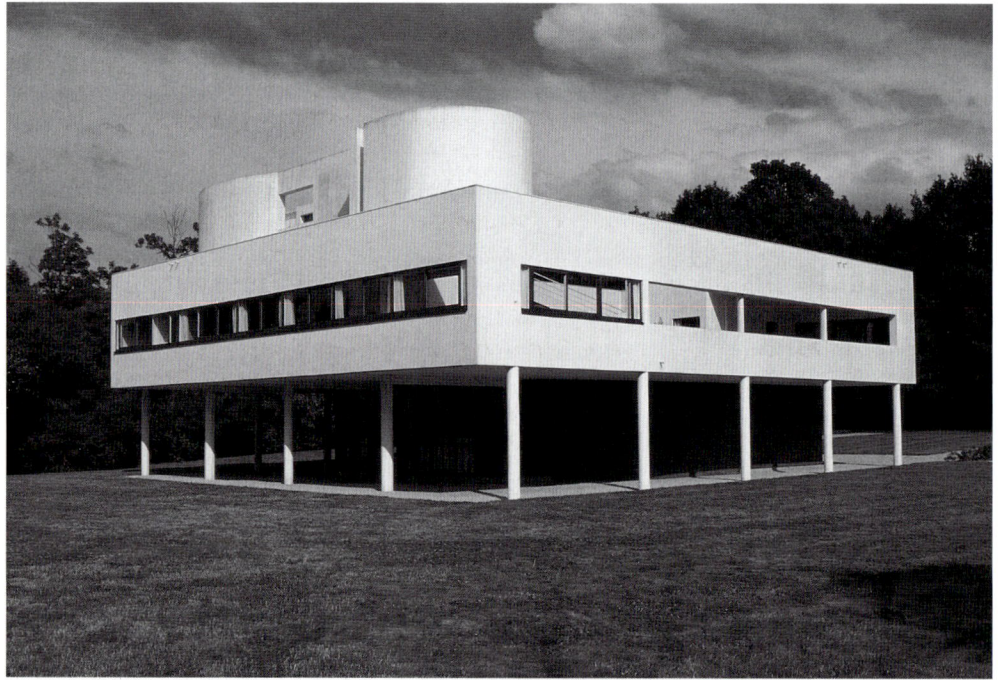

confined ground floor (containing a three-car garage, bedrooms, a bathroom, and utility rooms). Much of the house's interior is open space, with the thin columns supporting the main living floor and the roof garden area. The major living rooms in the Villa Savoye are on the second floor, wrapping around an open central court and lighted by strip windows that run along the membranelike exterior walls. From the second floor court, a ramp leads up to a flat roof-terrace and garden protected by a curving windbreak along one side. The ostensible approach to Villa Savoye does not define an entrance; the building has no traditional facade. People must walk around and through the house to comprehend its layout. Spaces and masses interpenetrate so fluently that "inside" and "outside" space intermingle. The machine-planed smoothness of the surfaces, entirely without adornment; the slender "ribbons" of continuous windows; and the buoyant lightness of the whole fabric—all combine to reverse the effect of traditional country houses (compare Andrea Palladio's Villa Rotunda, FIG. 22-56, and John Vanbrugh's Blenheim, FIG. 24-75).

Le Corbusier inverted the traditional design practice of placing light elements above and heavy ones below by refusing to enclose the ground story of the Villa Savoye with masonry walls. This openness makes the "load" of the Villa Savoye's upper stories appear to hover lightly on the slender column supports. Le Corbusier used several colors on this building's exterior—originally, a dark-green base, cream walls, and a rose-and-blue windscreen on top. They were a deliberate analogy for the colors in the contemporary machine-inspired Purist style of painting (FIG. 33-20) he actively practiced.

EFFICIENT AND HUMANE CITY PLANNING

The Villa Savoye was a marvelous house for a single family, but, like the De Stijl architects, Le Corbusier also dreamed of extending his ideas of the house as a "machine for living" to designs for efficient and humane cities. He saw great cities as spiritual workshops and he proposed to correct the deficiencies in existing cities caused by poor traffic circulation, inadequate living units, and the lack of space for recreation and exercise. Le Corbusier suggested replacing such cities with three types of new communities. Vertical cities would house workers and the business and service industries. Linear-industrial cities would run as belts along the routes between the vertical cities and would serve as centers for the people and processes involved in manufacturing. Finally, separate centers would be constructed for people involved in intensive agricultural activity. Le Corbusier's cities would provide for human cultural needs in addition to serving every person's physical, mental, and emotional comfort needs.

The Domino House project was a key part of Le Corbusier's thinking because the module design could be repeated almost indefinitely, both horizontally and vertically. Its volumes could be manipulated and interlocked to provide interior spaces of different sizes and heights. It was not site specific and could stand comfortably in any setting. Later in Le Corbusier's career, he designed a few of his vertical cities, most notably the Unité d'Habitation in Marseille (1945–1952). He also created the master plan for the entire city of Chandigarh, the capital city of the Punjab, India (1950–1957). He ended his career with a personal expressive style in his design

of the Chapel of Notre Dame du Haut at Ronchamp (see FIGS. 34-40 and 34-41).

Art Deco

In theory and practice, the new architecture (particularly that associated with the Bauhaus) rejected ornament of any kind. Pure form emerged from functional structure and required no decoration. Yet popular taste still favored ornamentation, especially in public architecture. A movement in the 1920s and 1930s sought to upgrade industrial design in competition

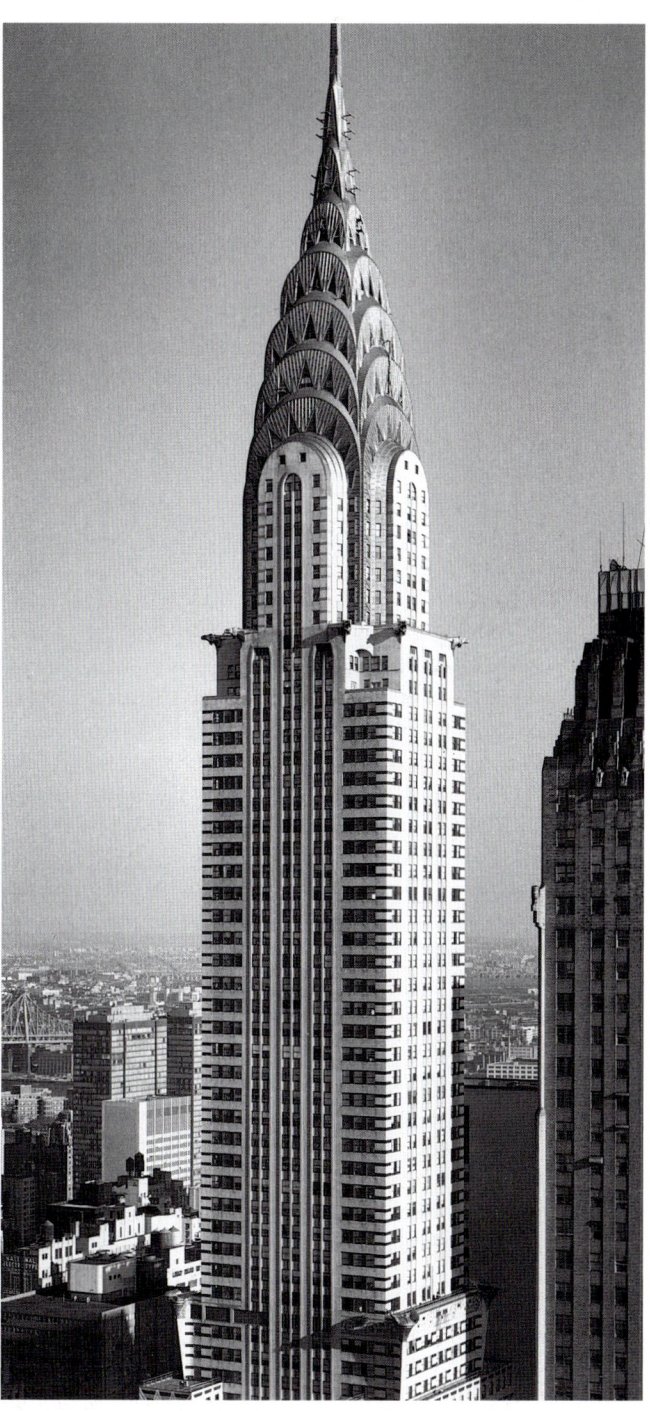

33-66 WILLIAM VAN ALEN, Chrysler Building, New York, New York, 1928–1930. Spire of stainless steel, overall height 1,048′.

with "fine art." Proponents wanted to work new materials into decorative patterns that could be either machined or handcrafted and that could, to a degree, reflect the simplifying trend in architecture. A remote descendant of Art Nouveau, this movement became known as Art Deco. (Like its predecessor, it was an event in the history of industrial design, not in the history of architecture.) Art Deco had universal application—to buildings, interiors, furniture, utensils, jewelry, fashions, illustration, and commercial products of every sort. Art Deco products have a "streamlined," elongated symmetrical aspect; simple flat shapes alternate with shallow volumes in hard patterns simulating mainline modern architecture. As a cultural phenomenon, it is associated with Jazz Age flair, flippancy, and elegance and with the gorgeous salons of the great ocean liners ferrying the carefree rich in the days of the "lost generation."

A GLITTERING SPIRE OF STAINLESS STEEL Art Deco's exemplary masterpiece is the stainless-steel spire of the Chrysler Building in New York City (FIG. **33-66**), designed by WILLIAM VAN ALEN (1882–1954). The building and spire are monuments to the fabulous twenties, when American millionaires and corporations competed with one another to raise the tallest skyscrapers in the biggest cities. Built up of diminishing fan shapes, the spire glitters triumphantly in the sky, a resplendent crown honoring the business achievements of the great auto manufacturer. As a temple of commerce, the Chrysler Building was dedicated to the principles and success of American business, before its chastening in the Great Depression.

EMPHASIZING THE ORGANIC

It was impossible for early-twentieth-century artists to ignore the increasingly intrusive expansion of mechanization and growth of technology. However, not all artists embraced these developments, as had the Futurists. In contrast, many artists attempted to overcome the predominance of mechanization in society by immersing themselves in a search for the organic and natural.

Organic Architecture

One of the most striking personalities in the development of early-twentieth-century architecture was FRANK LLOYD WRIGHT (1867–1959). Born in Wisconsin, Wright attended a few classes at the University of Wisconsin in Madison before moving to Chicago, where he eventually joined the firm headed by Louis Sullivan (see FIGS. 29-59 and 29-60). Wright set out to create "architecture of democracy."[67] Early influences were the volumetric shapes in a set of educational blocks the German educator Friedrich Froebel (from Wright's childhood) designed, the organic unity of a Japanese building Wright saw at the Columbian Exposition in Chicago in 1893, and a Jeffersonian belief in individualism and populism. Always a believer in architecture as "natural" and "organic," Wright saw it as serving free individuals who have the right to move within a "free" space, envisioned as a nonsymmetrical design interacting spatially with its natural surroundings. He

sought to develop an organic unity of planning, structure, materials, and site. Wright identified the principle of continuity as fundamental to understanding his view of organic unity: "Classic architecture was all fixation. . . . Now why not let walls, ceilings, floors become seen as component parts of each other? . . . You may see the appearance in the surface of your hand contrasted with the articulation of the bony structure itself. This ideal, profound in its architectural implications . . . I called . . . continuity.[68]

Wright manifested his vigorous originality early, and by 1900 he had arrived at a style entirely his own. In his work during the first decade of the twentieth century, his cross-axial plan and his fabric of continuous roof planes and screens defined a new domestic architecture.

A "WANDERING" HOUSE ON THE PRAIRIE Wright fully expressed these elements and concepts in Robie House (FIG. **33-67**), built between 1907 and 1909. Like other buildings in the Chicago area he designed at about the same time, this was called a "prairie house." Wright conceived the long, sweeping ground-hugging lines, unconfined by abrupt wall limits, as reaching out toward and capturing the expansiveness of the Midwest's great flatlands. Abandoning all symmetry, the architect eliminated a facade, extended the roofs far beyond the walls, and all but concealed the entrance. Wright filled the "wandering" plan of the Robie House (FIG. **33-68**) with intricately joined spaces (some large and open, others closed), grouped freely around a great central fireplace. (He believed strongly in the hearth's age-old domestic significance.) Wright designed enclosed patios, overhanging roofs, and strip windows to provide unexpected light sources and glimpses of the outdoors as people move through the interior space. These elements, together with the open ground plan, create a sense of space-in-motion inside and out. Wright matched his new and fundamental interior spatial arrangement in his exterior treatment. He set masses and voids in equilibrium; the flow of interior space determined the exterior wall placement. The exterior's sharp angular planes meet at apparently odd angles, matching the complex play of interior solids, which function not as inert containing surfaces but as elements equivalent in role to the design's spaces.

INTEGRATING INTERIOR AND EXTERIOR The Robie House is a good example of Wright's "naturalism," his adjusting of a building to its site. However, in this particular case, the confines of the city lot constrained the building-to-site relationship more than did the sites of some of Wright's more expansive suburban and country homes. The Kaufmann House, nicknamed "Fallingwater" (FIG. **33-69**) and designed as a weekend retreat at Bear Run near Pittsburgh, is a prime example of the latter. Perched on a rocky hillside over a small waterfall, this structure extends the Robie House's blocky masses in all four directions. The contrast in textures between concrete, painted metal, and natural stones in its walls enliven its shapes, as does Wright's use of full-length strip windows to create a stunning interweaving of interior and exterior space.

The implied message of Wright's new architecture was space, not mass—a space designed to fit the patron's life and enclosed and divided as required. Wright took special pains to meet his clients' requirements, often designing all the accessories of a house (including, in at least one case, gowns for his

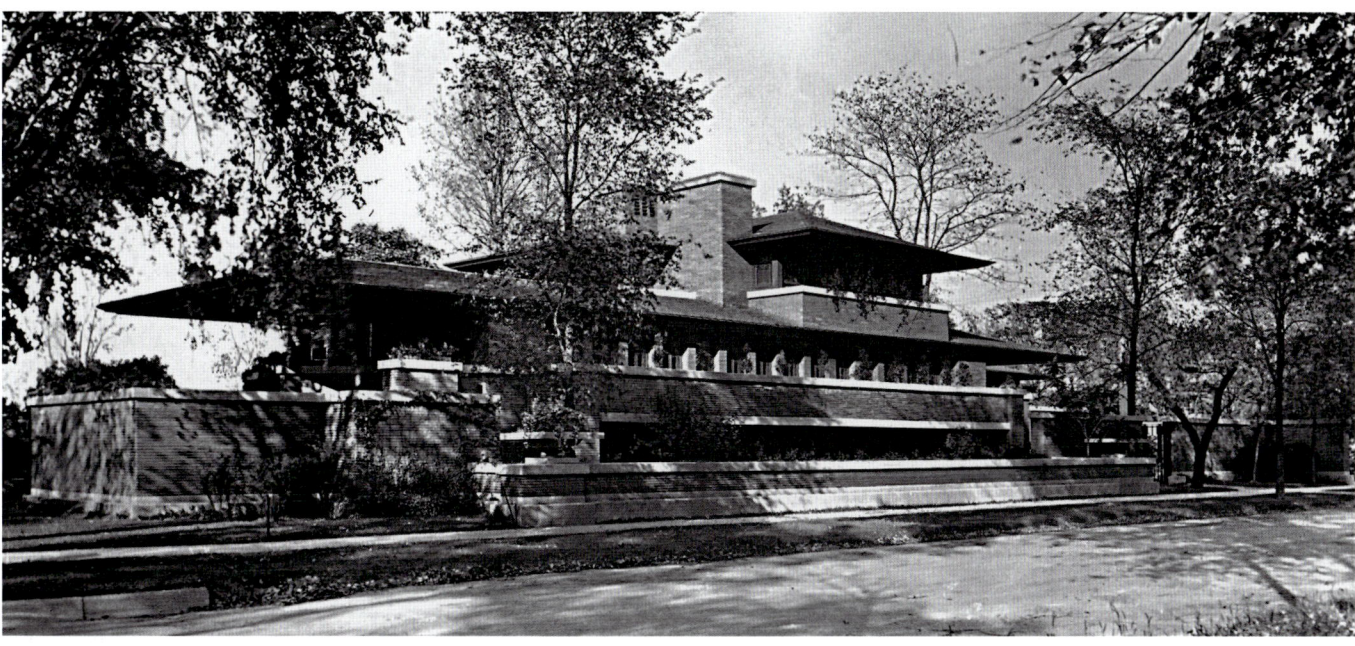

33-67 FRANK LLOYD WRIGHT, Robie House, Chicago, Illinois, 1907–1909.

1. Porch
2. Living room
3. Dining room
4. Balcony
5. Guest room
6. Kitchen
7. Servants
8. Billiard room
9. Children's playroom

10. Entrance hall
11. Boiler room
12. Laundry
13. Garage
14. Court
15. Garden
16. Lavatory or bath
17. Fireplace
18. Bedrooms

Roof

Outdoor walls (garden, terrace, balcony, etc.)

Structures above or below level

Third Level

Second Level

First Level

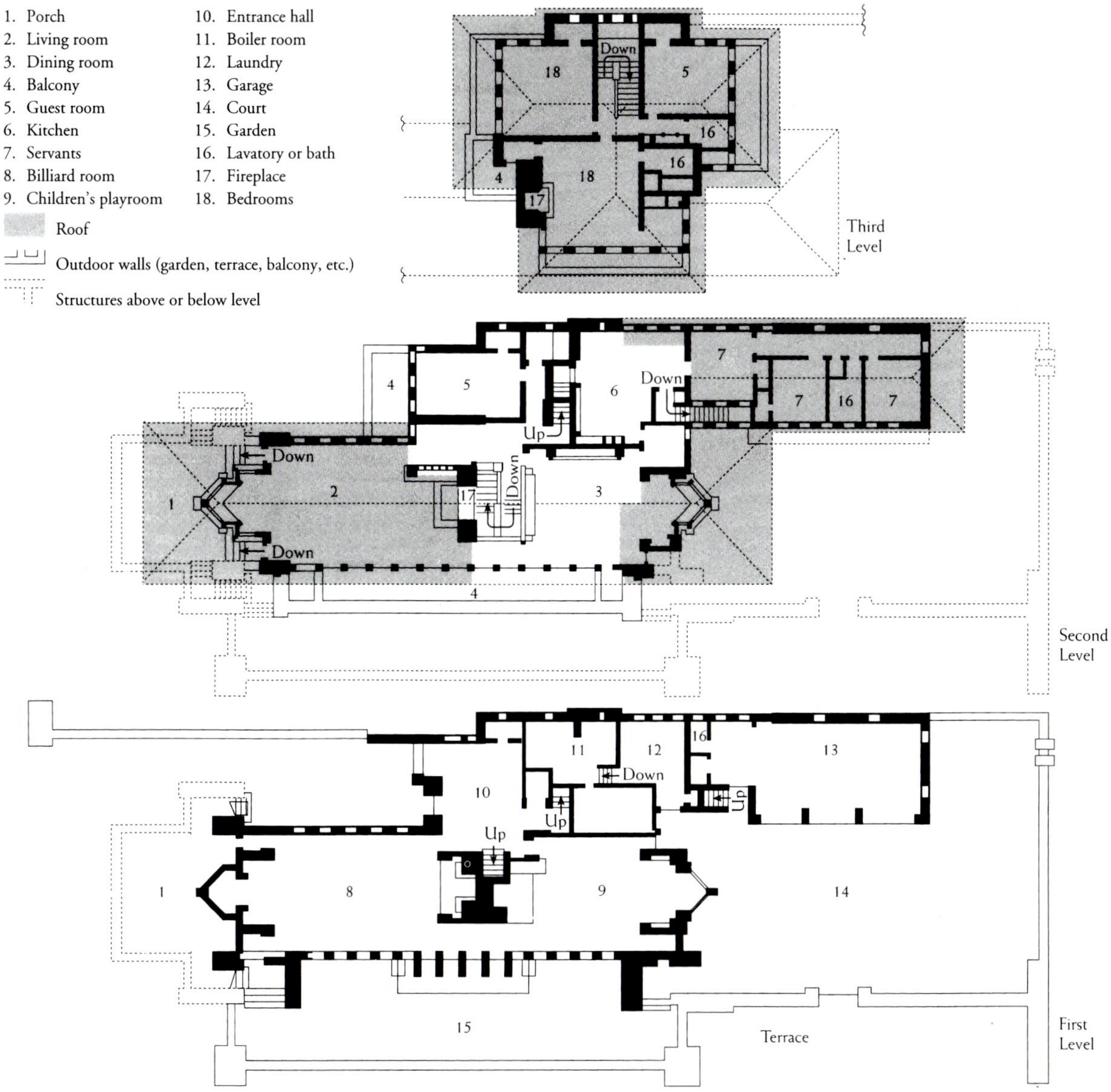

33-68 FRANK LLOYD WRIGHT, plan of the Robie House, Chicago, Illinois, 1907–1909.

33-69 FRANK LLOYD WRIGHT, Kaufmann House (Fallingwater), Bear Run, Pennsylvania, 1936–1939.

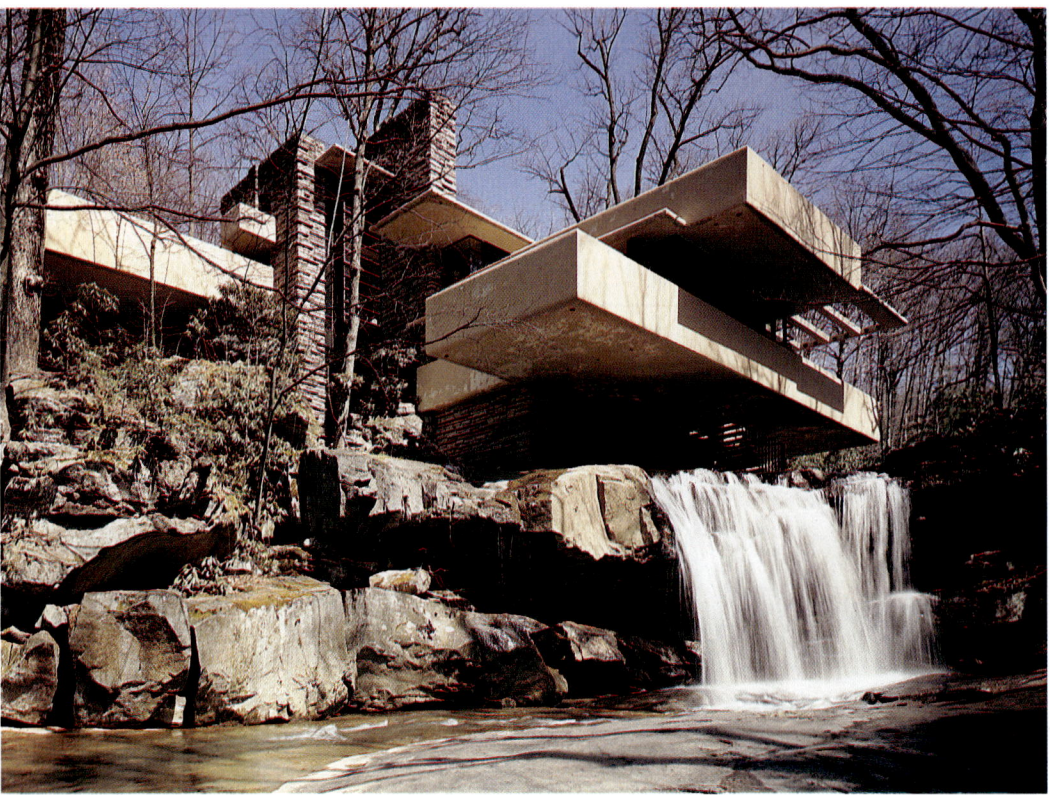

client's wife!). In the late 1930s, he acted on a cherished dream to provide good architectural design for less prosperous people by adapting the ideas of his prairie house to plans for smaller, less-expensive dwellings.

The publication of Wright's plans brought him a measure of fame in Europe, especially in Holland and Germany. The issuance in Berlin in 1910 of a portfolio of his work and an exhibition of his designs the following year stimulated younger architects to adopt some of his ideas about open plans that afforded clients freedom. Some forty years before his career ended, his work was already of revolutionary significance. The modern architect Mies van der Rohe wrote in 1940 that the "dynamic impulse from [Wright's] work invigorated a whole generation. His influence was strongly felt even when it was not actually visible."[69]

Organic Sculpture

SEEKING THE ESSENCE OF FLIGHT Romanian artist CONSTANTIN BRANCUSI (1876–1957) was one of many sculptors eager to produce works emphasizing the natural or organic. Often composed of softly curving surfaces and ovoid forms, his sculptures refer, directly or indirectly, to the cycle of life. Brancusi sought to move beyond surface appearances to capture the essence or spirit of the object depicted. He claimed: "What is real is not the external form but the essence of things. Starting from this truth it is impossible for anyone to express anything essentially real by imitating its exterior surface."[70] Brancusi's ability to design rhythmic, elegant sculptures conveying the essence of his subjects is evident in *Bird in Space* (FIG. **33-70**). Clearly not a literal depiction of a bird, the work is the final result of a long process. Brancusi started with the image of a bird at rest with its wings folded at its sides and ended with an abstract columnar form sharply ta-

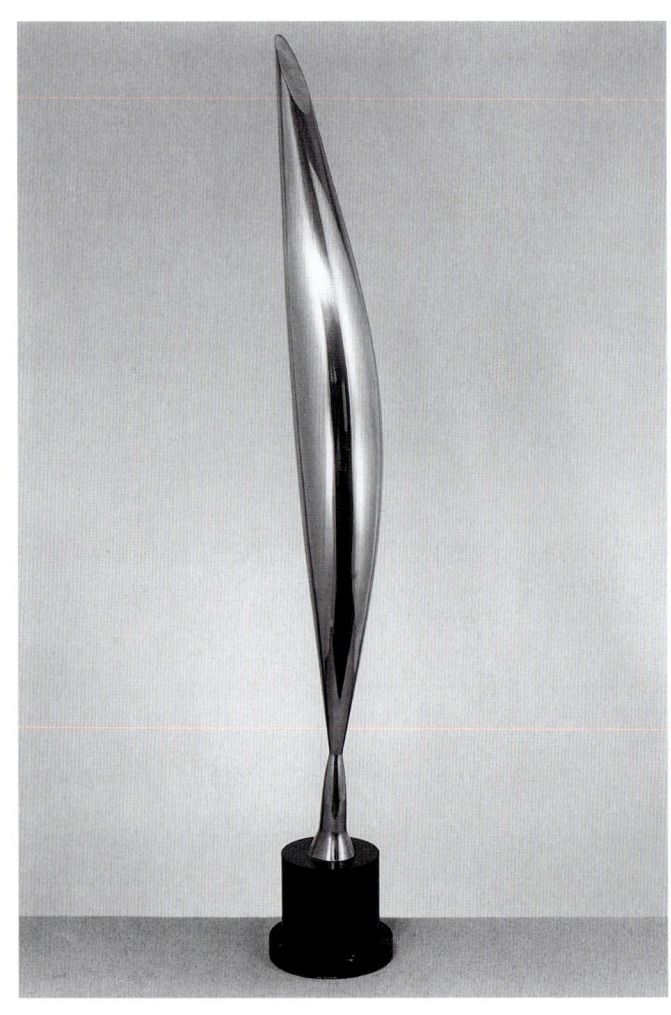

33-70 CONSTANTIN BRANCUSI, *Bird in Space,* 1928. Bronze (unique cast), 4′ 6″ × 8″ × 6″ high. Museum of Modern Art, New York (given anonymously).

pered at each end. Despite the abstraction, the sculpture retains the suggestion of a bird about to soar in free flight through the heavens. Even further, Brancusi succeeded in capturing the essence of flight. The highly reflective surface of the polished bronze does not allow the eye to linger on the sculpture itself (as do, for example, Rodin's agitated and textured surfaces, FIG. 29-48). Instead, viewers' eyes follow the gleaming reflection along the delicate curves right off the tip of the work, thereby inducing a feeling of flight. Brancusi stated: "All my life I have sought the essence of flight. Don't look for the mysteries. I give you pure joy. Look at the sculptures until you see them. Those nearest to God have seen them."[71]

Despite the seeming grandiosity of those claims, Brancusi was deeply immersed in exploring the emotional chords sculpture could strike in its viewers. Indeed, he envisioned many of his works, including this one, enlarged to monumental scale. The subtitle for this work was *Project of Bird Which, When Enlarged, Will Fill the Sky,* and the sculptor spoke of the work's ability on that scale to fill viewers with comfort and peace. Brancusi always paid special attention to the intrinsic qualities of the materials he used. He made sculptures in wood, marble, stone, and bronze. In each medium, he tried to create forms that respected and worked with the nature of the material, extracting from it its maximum expressive effect.

EVOKING ORGANIC VITALITY   BARBARA HEPWORTH (1903–1975) developed her own kind of essential sculptural form, combining pristine shape with a sense of organic vitality. She sought a sculptural idiom that would express her sense both of nature and the landscape and of the person who is in and observes nature:

The forms which have had special meaning for me since childhood have been the standing form (which is the translation of my feeling towards the human being standing in landscape); the two forms (which is the tender relationship of one living thing beside another); and the closed form, such as the oval, spherical, or pierced form (sometimes incorporating colour) which translates for me the association and meaning of gesture in the landscape. . . . In all these shapes the translation of what one feels about man and nature must be con-

veyed by the sculptor in terms of mass, inner tension, and rhythm, scale in relation to our human size, and the quality of surface which speaks through our hands and eyes.[72]

Three Forms (FIG. 33-71) was the first in a series of works Hepworth began soon after she became the mother of triplets in 1934, an experience that perhaps stimulated her to explore the relationship of size, shape, and position in space among three elements arranged on a thin base. In this piece, a small ovoid form nestles close to a larger form, a kind of inflated relative of it. A petite sphere rests on the corner of the base farthest from the other two forms. The artist gathered here the basic organic forms that had special meaning for her. Although human hands have shaped these smooth marble forms, they have a simplicity and "naturalness" to them. Like the forms in all of Hepworth's mature works, those in *Three Forms* are basic and universal, expressing a sense of eternity's timelessness.

CELEBRATING THE NATURAL CONDITION
The English sculptor HENRY MOORE (1898–1986) shared Brancusi's profound love of nature and knowledge of organic forms and materials. Moore was interested in vitalism—a philosophy that celebrated the natural condition. He maintained that every "material has its own individual qualities" and that these qualities could play a role in the creative process. "It is only when the sculptor works direct, when there is an active relationship with his material, that the material can take its part in the shaping of an idea."[73] Accordingly, the forms and lines of Moore's lead and stone sculptures tend to emphasize the material's hardness and solidity, while his fluid wood sculptures draw attention to the flow of the wood grain. One major recurring theme in Moore's work is the reclining female figure with simplified and massive forms. A tiny photograph of a Chac Mool figure from pre-Columbian Mexico originally inspired this motif. Thought perhaps to represent gods or worshipers bearing offerings, Chac Mool figures usually were carved in stone, in semireclining positions, with their heads turned abruptly to one side.

Although viewers can recognize a human figure in most of Moore's works, the artist simplified and abstracted the figure, attempting to express a universal truth beyond the physical

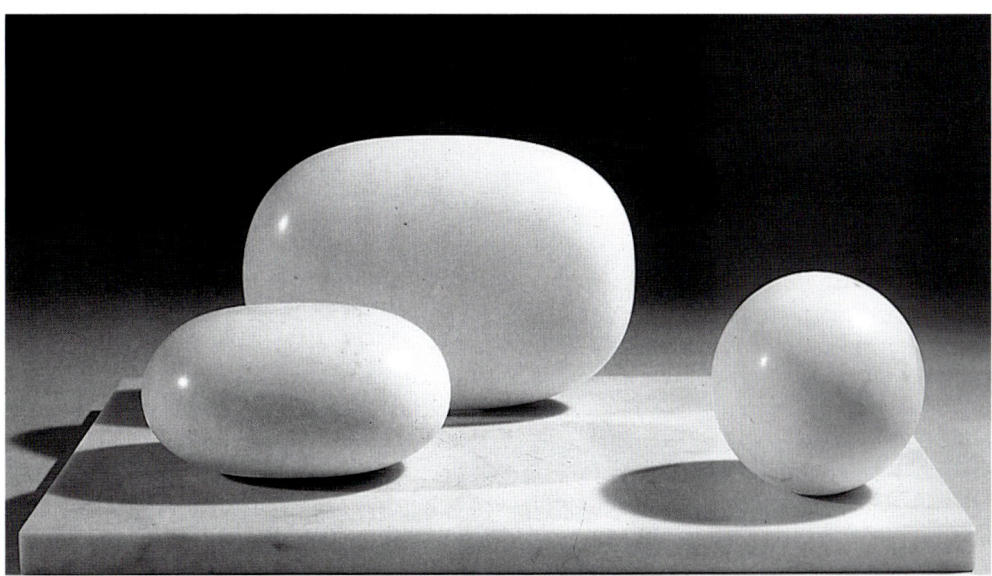

33-71 BARBARA HEPWORTH, *Three Forms,* 1935. Marble. Tate Gallery, London.

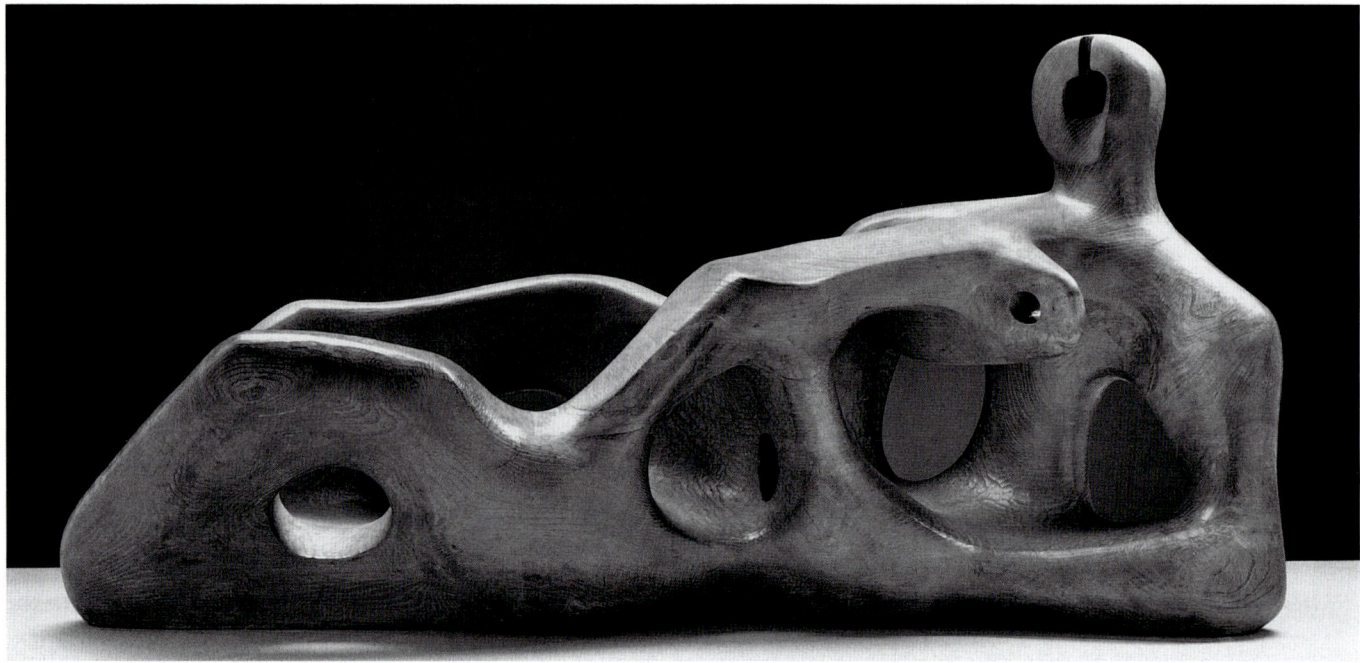

33-72 HENRY MOORE, *Reclining Figure,* 1939. Elm wood, 3′ 1″ × 6′ 7″ × 2′ 6″. Detroit Institute of Arts, Detroit (Founders Society purchase with funds from the Dexter M. Ferry, Jr. Trustee Corporation).

world. He summarized his feelings about abstract figurative form in two passages from essays written in the 1930s:

> Because a work does not aim at reproducing natural appearances, it is not, therefore, an escape from life—but may be a penetration into reality. . . . My sculpture is becoming less representational, less an outward visual copy . . . but only because I believe that in this way I can present the human psychological content of my work with greatest directness and intensity.[74]

Reclining Figure (FIG. **33-72**) is a wonderful example of Moore's handling of the human form and his responsiveness to his chosen material—elm wood. The figure's massive shapes suggest Surrealist biomorphic forms (FIG. 33-50), but Moore's recumbent woman is also a powerful earth mother whose undulant forms and hollows suggest nurturing human energy. Similarly, they evoke the contours of the Yorkshire hills where Moore was raised and the wind-polished surfaces of weathered wood and stone. The sculptor heightened the allusions to landscape and to Surrealist organic forms in his work by interplaying mass and void, based on the intriguing qualities of cavities in nature. As he explained, "The hole connects one side to the other, making it immediately more three-dimensional. . . . The mystery of the hole—the mysterious fascination of caves in hillsides and cliffs."[75] The concern with the void—the holes—recalls the sculpture of artists such as Aleksandr Archipenko (FIG. 33-18). The contours and openings of *Reclining Figure* follow the grain of the wood. Above all, the work combines the organic vocabulary central to Moore's philosophy—bone shapes, eroded rocks, and geologic formations—to communicate the human form's fluidity, dynamism, and evocative nature.

LARGE-SCALE KINETIC SCULPTURES The belief of Moholy-Nagy (FIG. 33-58) that modern experience is spa-

tial-temporal and his interest in new materials could have served as a program for the American sculptor ALEXANDER CALDER (1898–1976). Using his thorough knowledge of engineering techniques, Calder combined nonobjective organic forms and motion, to create a new kind of sculpture that expressed reality's innate dynamism. Both the artist's father and grandfather were sculptors, but Calder initially studied mechanical engineering. Fascinated all his life by motion, he explored that phenomenon and its relationship to three-dimensional form in much of his sculpture.

As a young artist in Paris in the late 1920s, Calder invented a circus full of wire-based miniature performers he activated into realistic analogues of the motion of their counterparts in life. After a visit to Mondrian's studio in the early 1930s, Calder was filled with a desire to set the brightly colored rectangular shapes in the Dutch painter's compositions into motion. (Marcel Duchamp, intrigued by Calder's early motorized and hand-cranked examples of moving abstract pieces, named them mobiles.) Calder's engineering skills soon helped him to fashion a series of balanced structures hanging from rods, wires, and colored organically shaped plates, such as *125* (FIG. **33-73**), designed much later for New York's John F. Kennedy International Airport. The sculptor carefully planned each nonmechanized mobile so that any air current would set the parts moving to create a constantly shifting dance in space. When air currents activate the sculpture, its patterns suggest clouds, leaves, or waves blown by the wind.

Mondrian's work may have provided the initial inspiration for the mobiles, but their organic shapes resemble those in Joan Miró's Surrealist paintings (FIG. 33-50) and Calder's love of nature actually generated them. Indeed, Calder's forms can be read either as geometric or organic. Geometrically, the lines suggest circuitry and rigging, while the shapes are irregular

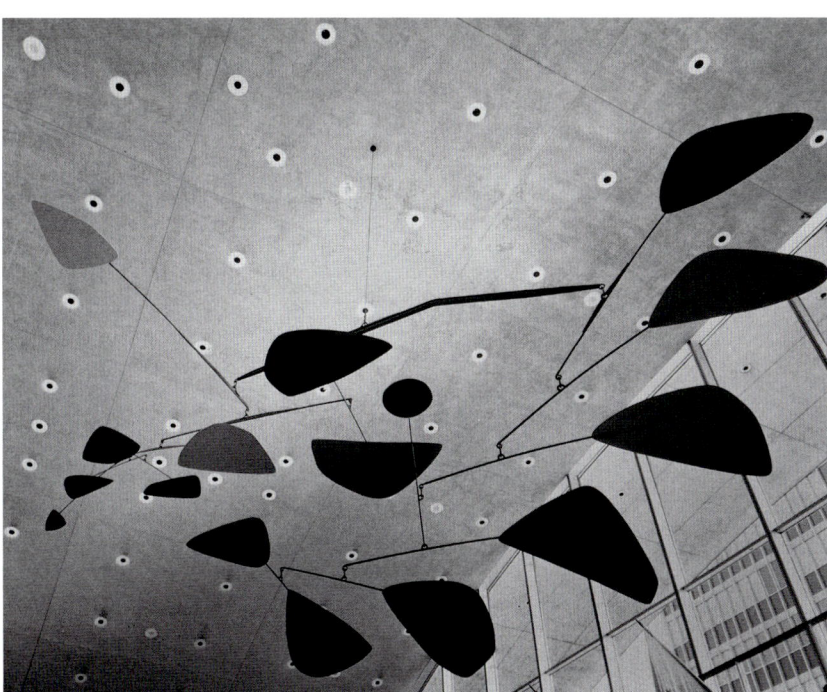

33-73 ALEXANDER CALDER, *125*, 1957. Approx. 42' long. John F. Kennedy International Airport, New York.

sections of the cone. Organically, the lines suggest nerve axons, and the shapes are cells, leaves, fins, wings, and other bioforms.

ART AS POLITICAL STATEMENT IN THE 1930S

Throughout history, art regularly has served political ends and addressed political themes and issues. With the phenomenal upheaval the Western world experienced during the first half of the twentieth century—for example, World War I, the Russian Revolution, the Spanish Civil War, and World War II—numerous artists felt compelled to speak out and use their art to make a political statement.

DEPICTING SOCIAL INJUSTICE The American painter BEN SHAHN (1898–1969) used photographs as a point of departure for semi-abstract figures he felt would express the emotions and facts of social injustice that were his main subject throughout his career. Shahn came to the United States from Lithuania in 1906 and trained as a lithographer before broadening the media in which he worked to include easel painting, photography, and murals. He focused on the lives of ordinary people and the injustices often done to them by the structure of an impersonal society. In the early 1930s, he completed a cycle of twenty-three paintings and prints inspired by the trial and execution of the two Italian anarchists Nicola Sacco and Bartolommeo Vanzetti. Accused of killing two men in a holdup in 1920 in South Braintree, Massachusetts, the Italians were convicted in a trial that many people thought resulted in a grave miscarriage of justice. Shahn felt he had found in this story a subject the equal of any in Western art history: "Suddenly I realized . . . I was living through another crucifixion."[76] Basing many of

the works in this cycle on newspaper photographs of the events, Shahn devised a style that adapted his knowledge of Synthetic Cubism and his training in commercial art to an emotionally expressive use of flat, intense color in figural compositions filled with sharp, dry, angular forms. The major work in the series was called simply *The Passion of Sacco and Vanzetti* (see FIG. Intro-5). This tall, narrow painting condenses the narrative in terms of both time and space. The two executed men lie in coffins at the bottom of the composition. Presiding over them are the three members of the commission chaired by Harvard University president A. Laurence Lowell, who declared the original trial fair and cleared the way for the executions to take place. A framed portrait of Judge Webster Thayer, who handed down the initial sentence hangs on the wall of a simplified government building. The gray pallor of the dead men, the stylized mask-faces of the mock-pious mourning commissioners, and the sanctimonious, distant judge all contribute to the mood of anguished commentary that makes this image one of Shahn's most powerful works.

Guernica and the Spanish Civil War

A MONUMENTAL OUTCRY OF HUMAN GRIEF Although previous discussion of Pablo Picasso focused on his immersion in aesthetic issues, he also maintained a political commitment throughout his life. He declared: "Painting is not made to decorate apartments. It is an instrument for offensive and defensive war against the enemy."[77] This political commitment became more acute as Picasso watched his homeland descend into civil war in the late 1930s. In January 1937, the Spanish Republican government in exile in Paris asked Picasso to produce the work for the Spanish pavilion at the Paris International Exposition that summer. Like the Mexican muralists (FIGS. 33-80 and 33-81), artists interested in disseminating political and so-

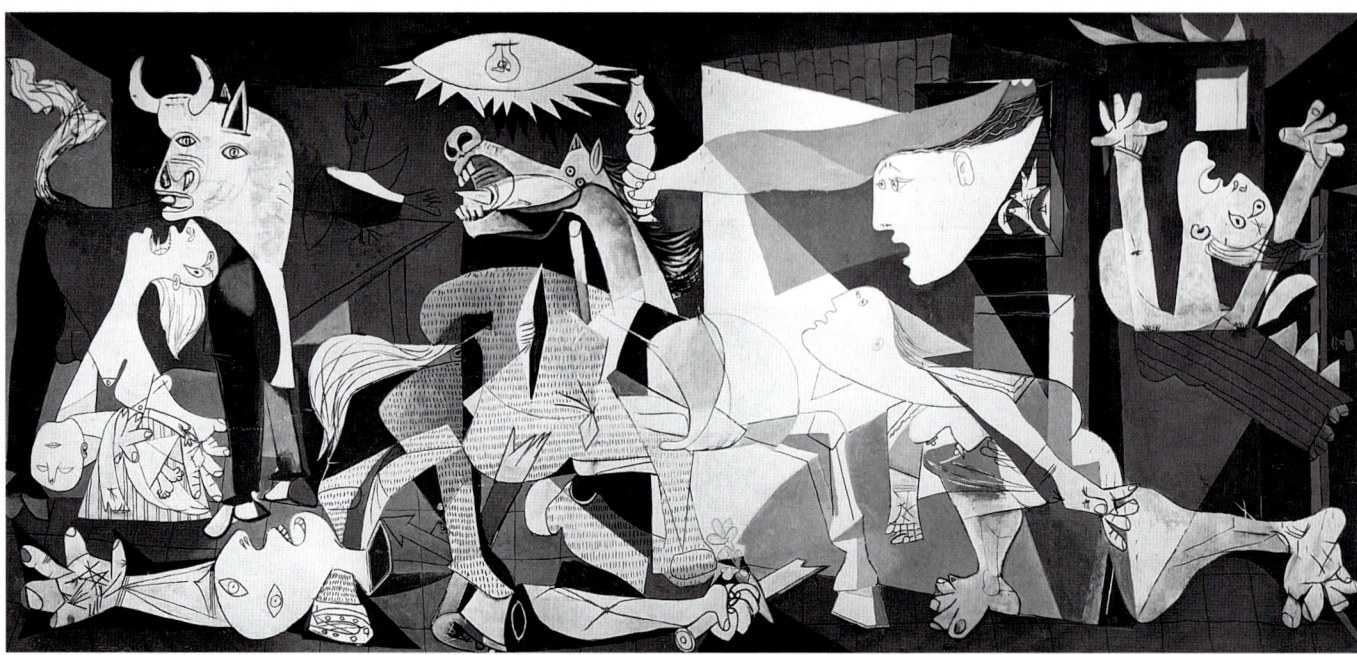

33-74   PABLO PICASSO, *Guernica,* 1937. Oil on canvas, 11′ 5½″ × 25′ 5¾″. Museo Nacional Centro de Arte Reina Sofia, Madrid.

cial messages with their art realized the importance of placing their work in public arenas. Picasso also was well aware of the immense visibility and large international audience this opportunity afforded him. He therefore accepted this invitation but was not inspired to work on the project until he received word the Basque capital, Guernica, had been almost totally destroyed in an air raid on April 26 by Nazi bombers acting on behalf of the rebel general Francisco Franco. Not only did the Germans decimate the city itself, but also, because they attacked at the busiest hour of a market day, they killed or wounded many of the seven thousand citizens. The event jolted Picasso into action; by the end of June, he completed the mural-sized canvas of *Guernica* (FIG. **33-74**).

Picasso produced this monumental painting condemning the senseless bombing without specific reference to the event—depicting no bombs nor German planes. Rather, the collection of images in *Guernica* combine to create a visceral outcry of human grief. In the center, along the lower edge of the painting, lies a slain warrior clutching a broken and useless sword. A gored horse tramples him and rears back in fright as it dies. On the left, a shrieking anguished woman cradles her dead child. On the far right, a woman on fire runs screaming from a burning building, while another woman flees mindlessly. In the upper right-hand corner, a woman, represented only by a head, emerges from the burning building, thrusting forth a light to illuminate the horror. Overlooking the destruction is a bull, which, according to the artist, represents "brutality and darkness."[78]

Picasso used aspects of his Cubist discoveries to expressive effect in *Guernica,* particularly the fragmentation of objects and the dislocation of anatomical features. This Cubist fragmentation visualizes the horror. What happened to these figures in the artist's act of painting—the dissections and contortions of the human form—parallels what happened to

them in real life. To emphasize the scene's severity and starkness, Picasso reduced his palette to black, white, and shades of gray.

Revealing his political commitment and his awareness of the power of art, Picasso refused to allow exhibition of *Guernica* in Spain while Generalissimo Franco was in power. At the artist's request, *Guernica* hung in the Museum of Modern Art (see "The Museum of Modern Art and the Avant-Garde," page 1065) in New York City after the World's Fair concluded. Not until after Franco's death (ending his right-wing dictatorship) in 1975 did Picasso allow the mural patriated to his homeland. It was moved in 1981 and hangs today in the Centro de Arte Reina Sofia in Madrid as a testament to a tragic chapter in Spanish history.

The Depression and Its Legacy

As a momentously catastrophic event in American history, the stock market crash of October 1929 and the subsequent Great Depression of the 1930s had a widespread national impact. Artists were particularly affected. The limited art market virtually disappeared, and museums curtailed both their purchases and exhibition schedules. Many artists sought financial support from the federal government, which established numerous programs to provide relief, aid recovery, and promote reform. Among the programs supporting artists were the Treasury Relief Art Project, founded in 1934 to commission art for federal buildings, and the Works Progress Administration (WPA), founded in 1935 to relieve all unemployment. Under the WPA, varied activities of the Federal Art Project paid artists, writers, and theater people a regular wage in exchange for work in their professions. Another important program was the Resettlement Administration (RA), later the Farm Securities Administration (FSA). The FSA

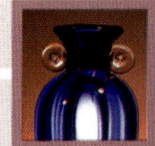

ART AND SOCIETY

The Museum of Modern Art and the Avant-Garde

The Museum of Modern Art in New York City is consistently identified as the institution most responsible for developing modernist art. Established in 1929, the Museum of Modern Art (or MoMA, as it is often called) owes its existence to a trio of remarkable women—Lillie P. Bliss, Mary Quinn Sullivan, and Abby Aldrich Rockefeller. These visionary and influential women, themselves art collectors, saw the need for a museum to collect and exhibit modernist art. Together they founded MoMA, which became (and continues to be) the most influential museum of modern art in the world. Their efforts and success are all the more extraordinary considering the skepticism and hostility greeting much of modernist art. Indeed, at the time, few American museums were inclined to show late-nineteenth- and twentieth-century art at all. Abby Aldrich Rockefeller's son Nelson (later governor of New York and involved with MoMA's administration) noted the boldness and courage required of these women: "It was the perfect combination. The three women among them had the resources, the tact, and the knowledge of contemporary art that the situation required. More to the point, they had the courage to advocate the cause of the modern movement in the face of widespread division, ignorance, and a dark suspicion that the whole business was some sort of Bolshevik plot."[1]

Over the years, MoMA has become a leader in museology and in promoting modernist art. Its ambitious exhibition schedule, trailblazing museum organization, and expansive collection place MoMA at the forefront of art institutions. In its quest to expose the public to the energy and challenge of modernist, particularly avant-garde, art, the museum developed unique and progressive exhibitions. Among the memorable exhibitions MoMA mounted were *Cubism and Abstract Art* and *Fantastic Art, Dada, Surrealism* in 1936. The museum also organized such groundbreaking exhibitions as *American Sources of Modern Art (Aztec, Maya, Inca)* in 1933 and *African Negro Art* in 1935, among the first exhibitions to deal with such artifacts in artistic rather than anthropological terms.

The organization of MoMA's administrative structure and scope of the museum's activities were also remarkable and were due, in large part, to the vision and energy of MoMA's first director, Alfred H. Barr Jr. Influenced by the Bauhaus and by art history courses he had taken emphasizing the interrelationship of all the arts, Barr insisted on establishing departments at MoMA not only for painting and sculpture but also for the other arts. He developed a library of books on modern art and a film library, which have become world-class collections, as well as an extensive publishing program. More recently, critic John Russell summarized the ambitious and landmark structure of MoMA:

> The Museum of Modern Art as it is today has certain clearly defined characteristics. It is truly international. It covers not only painting and sculpture, but photography, prints and drawings, architecture, design, the decorative arts, typography, stage design, and artists' books. It has its own publishing house, its own movie house, and its own department of film and video. It has a shop in which everyday objects of every kind may be on sale. . . . It is a palace of pleasure, but it is also an unstructured university. You don't get grades for going there, but in a mysterious, unquantifiable way, you become alert to the energies of modern art.[2]

Through exciting exhibitions and educational activities, MoMA succeeds in encouraging the public to make modernist art a regular part of their lives. While the museum pursues its founders' desire to appeal to a larger audience, it also works to establish itself within the scholarly community through publishing serious and high-quality books and catalogs.

It is the museum's art collection, however, that has drawn the most attention. By cultivating an enlightened and influential group of patrons, MoMA has developed an extensive and enviable collection of late-nineteenth- and twentieth-century art. Its collection includes such important works as Picasso's *Les Demoiselles d'Avignon* (FIG. 33-11), van Gogh's *Starry Night* (see FIG. 29-34), and Brancusi's *Bird in Space* (FIG. 33-70). Simply reading through the illustration captions in this textbook reveals how many significant artworks reside in the Museum of Modern Art.

The dominance of this institution also has made it the target of critics. Some observers believe MoMA's position as the preeminent collector of modernist art has made it an overly influential judge. They suggest that rather than simply documenting artistic developments, MoMA actively influences the direction of art through its exhibitions and acquisitions. Although the museum's influence cannot be denied, its enduring legacy will be the public access to a broad range of art it provides.

[1] Sam Hunter, *The Museum of Modern Art, New York: The History and Collection* (New York: Harry N. Abrams, 1984), 10.

[2] Ibid., 11–12.

oversaw emergency aid programs for farm families caught in the depression and provided information to the public about both the government programs and the plight of the people such programs served.

PERSONIFYING DEPRESSION SUFFERING The RA hired American photographer DOROTHEA LANGE (1895–1965) in 1936, sending her to photograph the dire situation of the rural poor the Great Depression displaced.

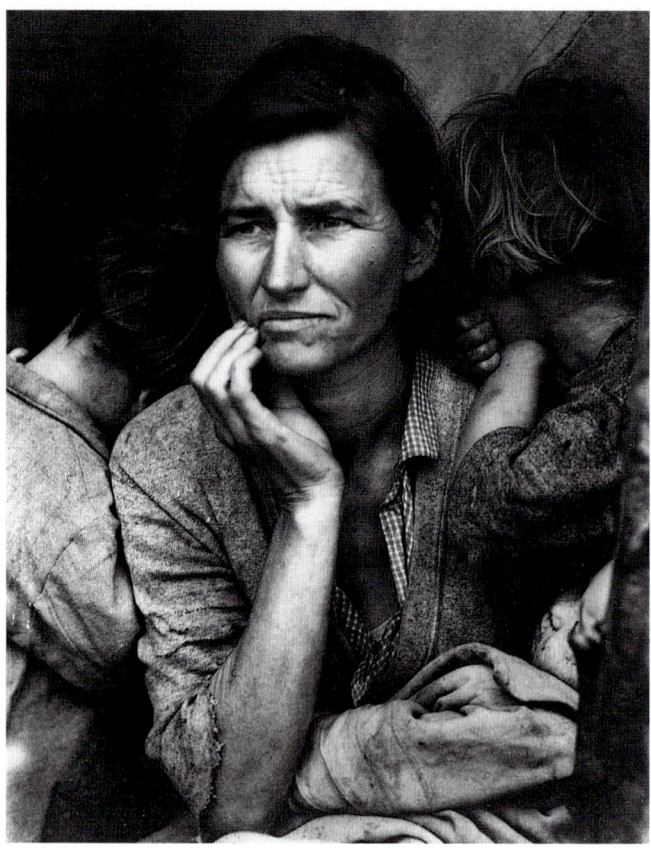

33-75   DOROTHEA LANGE, *Migrant Mother, Nipomo Valley,* 1935. Gelatin silver print. Copyright © the Dorothea Lange Collection, The Oakland Museum of California, City of Oakland (gift of Paul S. Taylor).

At the end of an assignment to document the lives of migratory pea pickers in California, Lange stopped at a camp in Nipomo and found the migrant workers there starving because the crops had frozen in the fields. Among the pictures she made on this occasion was *Migrant Mother, Nipomo Valley* (FIG. **33-75**), which, like *American Gothic* (FIG. 33-78), has achieved iconic status. Generations of viewers have been moved by the mixture of strength and worry in the raised hand and careworn face of a young mother, who holds a baby on her lap. Two older children, who cling to her trustfully while turning their faces away from the camera, flank her. Lange described how she got the picture:

> [I] saw and approached the hungry and desperate mother, as if drawn by a magnet. I do not remember how I explained my presence or my camera to her, but I remember she asked me no questions. I made five exposures, working closer and closer from the same direction. . . . There she sat in that lean-to tent with her children huddled around her, and she seemed to know that my pictures might help her, and so she helped me.[79]

Although viewers often perceive such "documentary" photography as a reflection of reality, they must acknowledge that people always read visual images through the lens of cultural conditioning. With this in mind, it seems logical the one government-commissioned photograph that has emerged as representative of the depression experiences of millions depicts a mother with her children. Such an image draws strongly on cultural values associated with familial and social stability,

constructing a reassuring depiction of noble and undeserved suffering rather than focusing the spotlight on major economic problems. The response to this photo indicates the ability of *Migrant Mother, Nipomo Valley* to strike a sympathetic chord in viewers. Within days after this image was printed in a San Francisco newspaper, people rushed food to Nipomo to feed the hungry workers.

VISIONS OF LONELINESS AND ISOLATION

EDWARD HOPPER (1882–1967) produced paintings during the depression era evoking the national mindset. However, rather than depict historically specific scenes, Hopper took as his subject the more generalized theme of the overwhelming loneliness and echoing isolation of modern life in the United States. Trained as a commercial artist, Hopper studied painting and printmaking in New York and Paris before returning to the United States. He then concentrated on scenes of contemporary American city and country life, painting buildings, streets, and landscapes that are curiously muted, still, and filled with empty spaces. Motion is stopped and time suspended, as if the artist recorded the major details of a poignant personal memory. From the darkened streets outside a restaurant in *Nighthawks* (FIG. **33-76**), viewers glimpse the lighted interior through huge plate-glass windows, which lend the inner space the paradoxical sense of being both a safe refuge and a vulnerable place for the three customers and the counterman. The seeming indifference of Hopper's characters to one another and the echoing spaces that surround them evoke the pervasive loneliness of modern humans. Hopper invested works such as *Nighthawks* with the straightforward mode of representation, creating a kind of realist vision recalling that of nineteenth-century artists such as Thomas Eakins (see FIG. 29-11) and Henry Ossawa Tanner (see FIG. 29-14).

THE STRUGGLES OF AFRICAN AMERICANS

African-American artist JACOB LAWRENCE (b. 1917) found his subjects in modern history, concentrating on the culture and history of African Americans. Lawrence moved to Harlem, New York, in 1927 at about age ten. There, he came under the spell of the African art and the African-American history he found in lectures and exhibitions and in the special programs sponsored by the 135th Street New York Public Library, which had outstanding collections of African-American art and archival data. Inspired by the politically oriented art of Goya (see FIG. 28-39), Daumier (see FIG. 29-6), and Orozco (FIG. 33-80), Lawrence found his subjects in the everyday life of Harlem and his people's history. He defined his own vision of the continuing African-American struggle against discrimination.

In 1941, Lawrence began a sixty-painting series titled *The Migration of the Negro.* Unlike his earlier historical paintings depicting important figures in American history, such as Frederick Douglass, Toussaint L'Ouverture, and Harriet Tubman, this series called attention to a contemporaneous event—the ongoing exodus of black labor from the southern United States. Disillusioned with their lives in the South, hundreds of thousands of African Americans migrated north in the years following World War I, seeking improved economic opportunities and more hospitable political and social conditions. This subject had personal relevance to Lawrence. He explained: "I was part of the

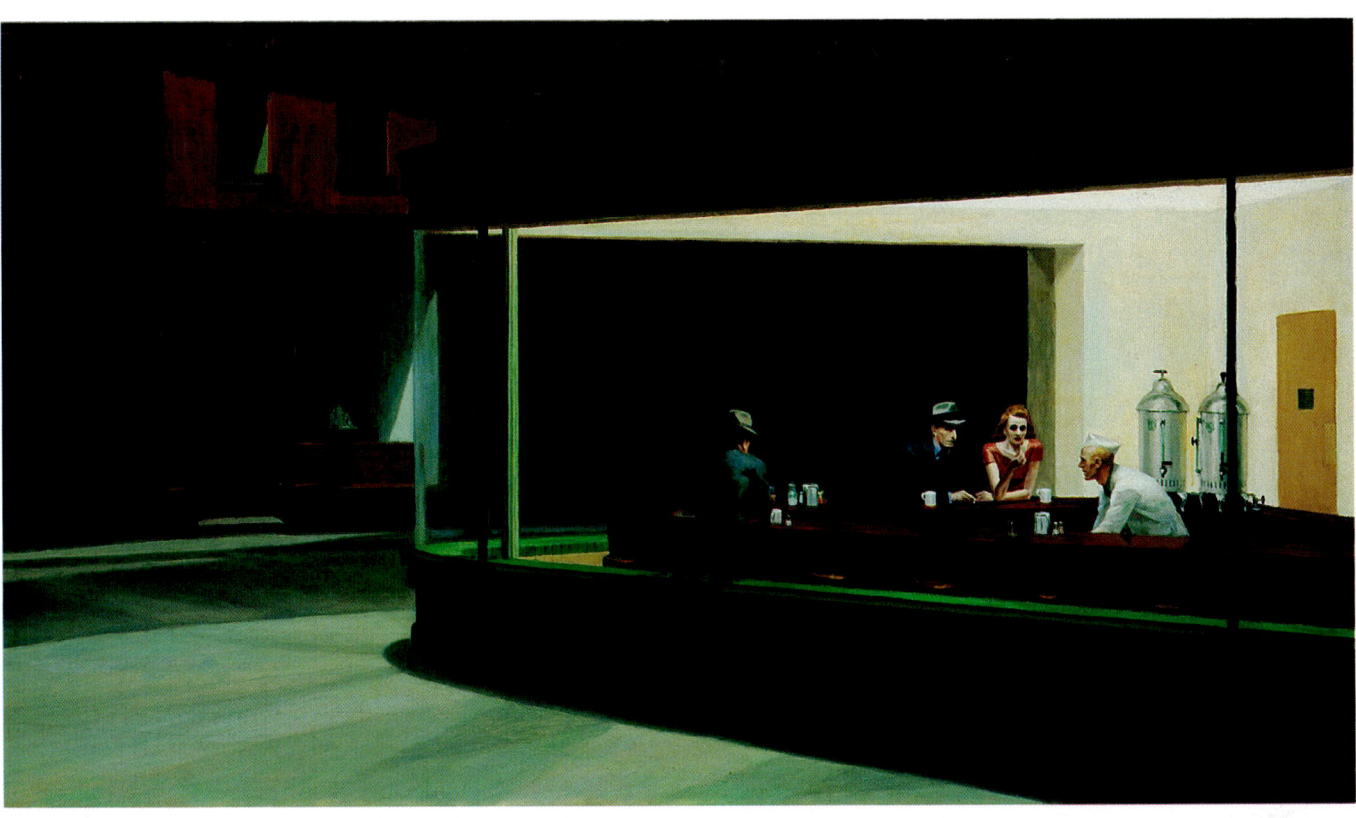

33-76 EDWARD HOPPER, *Nighthawks,* 1942. Oil on canvas, 2′ 6″ × 4′ 8$\frac{11}{16}$″. The Art Institute of Chicago, Chicago (Friends of American Art Collection).

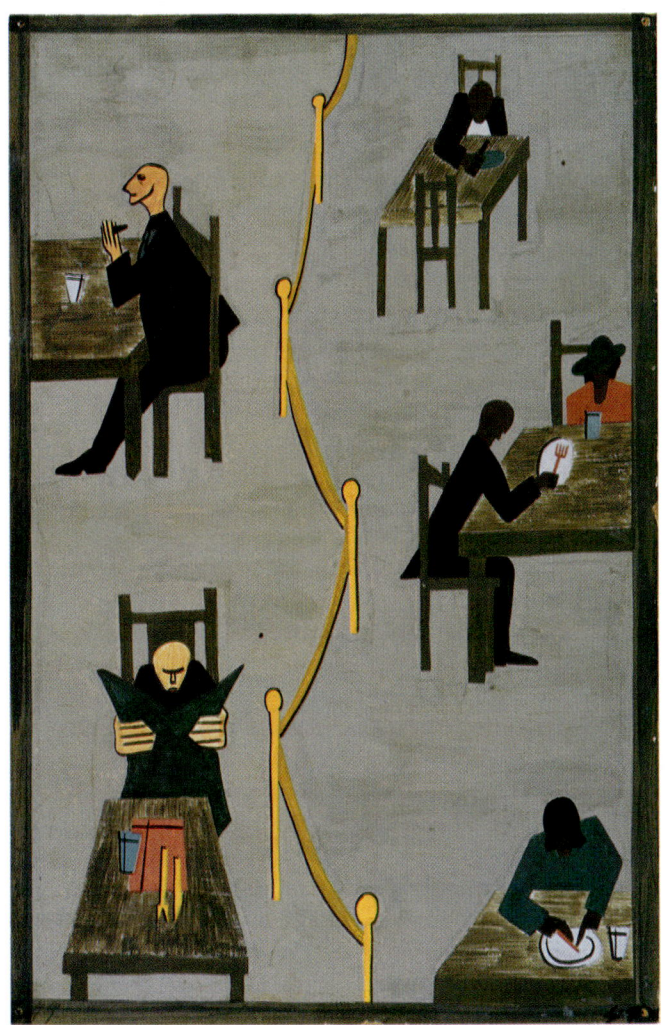

migration, as was my family, my mother, my sister, and my brother. . . . I grew up hearing tales about people 'coming up,' another family arriving. . . . I didn't realize what was happening until about the middle of the 1930s, and that's when the *Migration* series began to take form in my mind."[80]

The "documentation" of the period, such as the FSA program, ignored African Americans, and thus this major demographic shift remained largely invisible to most Americans. Of course, the conditions African Americans encountered both during their migration and in the north were often as difficult and discriminatory as those they had left behind in the South.

Lawrence's series provides numerous vignettes capturing the experiences of these migrating people. Often, a sense of bleakness and of the degradation of African-American life dominates the images. *No. 49* of this series (FIG. **33-77**) bears the caption "They also found discrimination in the North although it was much different from that which they had known in the South." The artist depicted a blatantly segregated dining room with a barrier running down the room's center separating the whites on the left from the African Americans on the right. To ensure a continuity and visual integrity among all sixty paintings, Lawrence interpreted his themes systematically in rhythmic arrangements of bold, flat, and strongly colored shapes. His style drew equally from his interest in the push-pull effects of Cubist space and his memories of the patterns made by the colored

33-77 JACOB LAWRENCE, *No. 49* from *The Migration of the Negro,* 1940–1941. Tempera on masonite, 1′ × 1′ 6″. The Phillips Collection, Washington.

scatter rugs brightening the floors of his childhood homes. Further, he unified the narrative with a consistent palette of bluish green, orange, yellow, and grayish brown throughout the entire series. Like every subject Lawrence painted during his long career, he believed this story had important lessons to teach viewers.

Regionalism

Although the city or rapidly developing technological advances enamored many American artists, such as the Precisionists (FIGS. 33-35, 33-36, and 33-37), others chose not to depict these aspects of modern life. The Regionalists, sometimes referred to as the American Scene Painters, turned their attention to rural life as America's cultural backbone. One of the Regionalists, GRANT WOOD (1891–1942), for example, published an essay titled "Revolt Against the City" in 1935. Although this movement was not formally organized, Wood acknowledged its existence in 1931, when he spoke at a conference. In his address, he announced a new movement developing in the Midwest known as Regionalism, which he described as focused on American subjects and as standing in reaction to "the abstraction of the modernists" in Europe and New York.[81]

THE APPEAL OF RURAL IOWA   Grant Wood's paintings focus on rural scenes from Iowa, where he was born and raised. The work that catapulted Wood to national prominence was *American Gothic* (FIG. 33-78), which became an American icon. The artist depicted a farmer and his spinster daughter standing in front of a neat house with a small lancet window, typically found on Gothic cathedrals. The man and woman wear traditional attire—he appears in worn overalls and she in an apron trimmed with rickrack. The dour expression on both of their faces gives the painting a severe quality, which Wood enhanced with his meticulous brushwork . When *American Gothic* was exhibited, many people enthused about the work, which they perceived as "quaint, humorous, and AMERICAN," in the words of one critic.[82] Many saw the couple as embodying "strength, dignity, fortitude, resoluteness, integrity," and were convinced Wood captured the true spirit of America.[83]

Wood's Regionalist vision involved more than his subjects, extending to a rejection of avant-garde styles in favor of a clearly readable, realist style. Surely this approach appealed to many people alienated by the increasing presence of abstraction in art. Interestingly enough, despite the accolades this painting received, it also was criticized. Not everyone saw the painting as a sympathetic portrayal of midwestern life; indeed, some in Iowa felt insulted by the depiction. In addition, despite the seemingly reportorial nature of *American Gothic,* some viewed it as a political statement—one of staunch nationalism. In light of the problematic nationalism in Germany at the time, this perceived nationalistic attitude was all the more disturbing. In other words, the discourse Regionalism was embedded in was not simply stylistic but political as well.

33-78   GRANT WOOD, *American Gothic,* 1930. Oil on beaverboard, 2′ 5⅞″ × 2′ 1⅞″. Art Institute of Chicago, Chicago (Friends of American Art Collection).

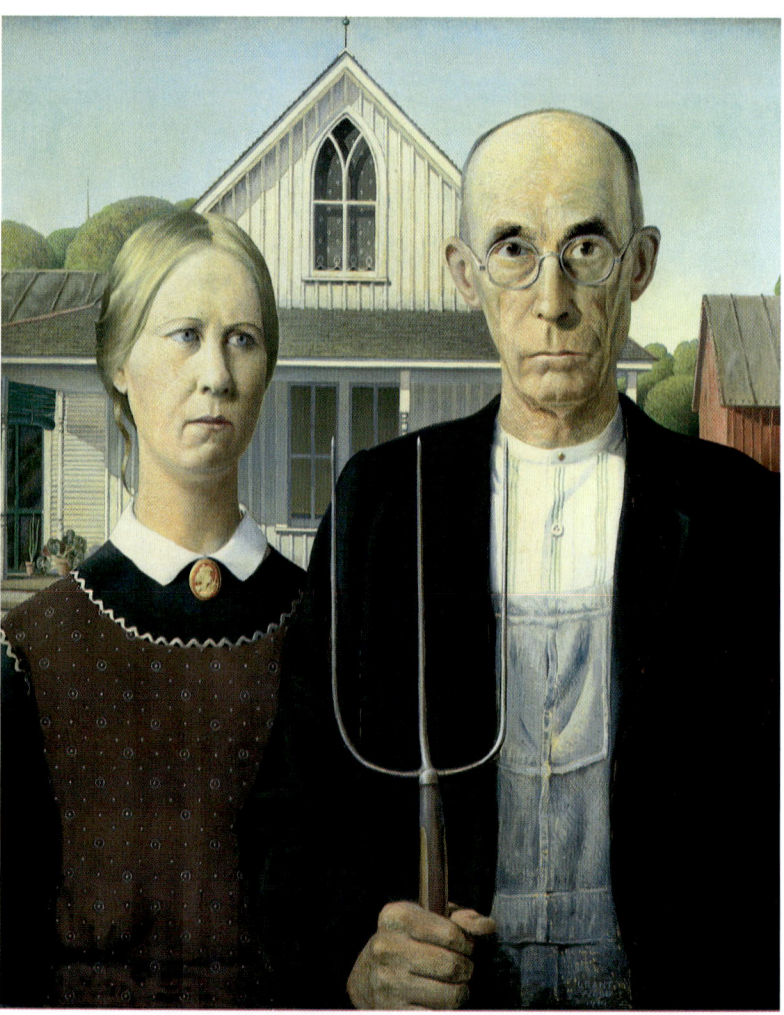

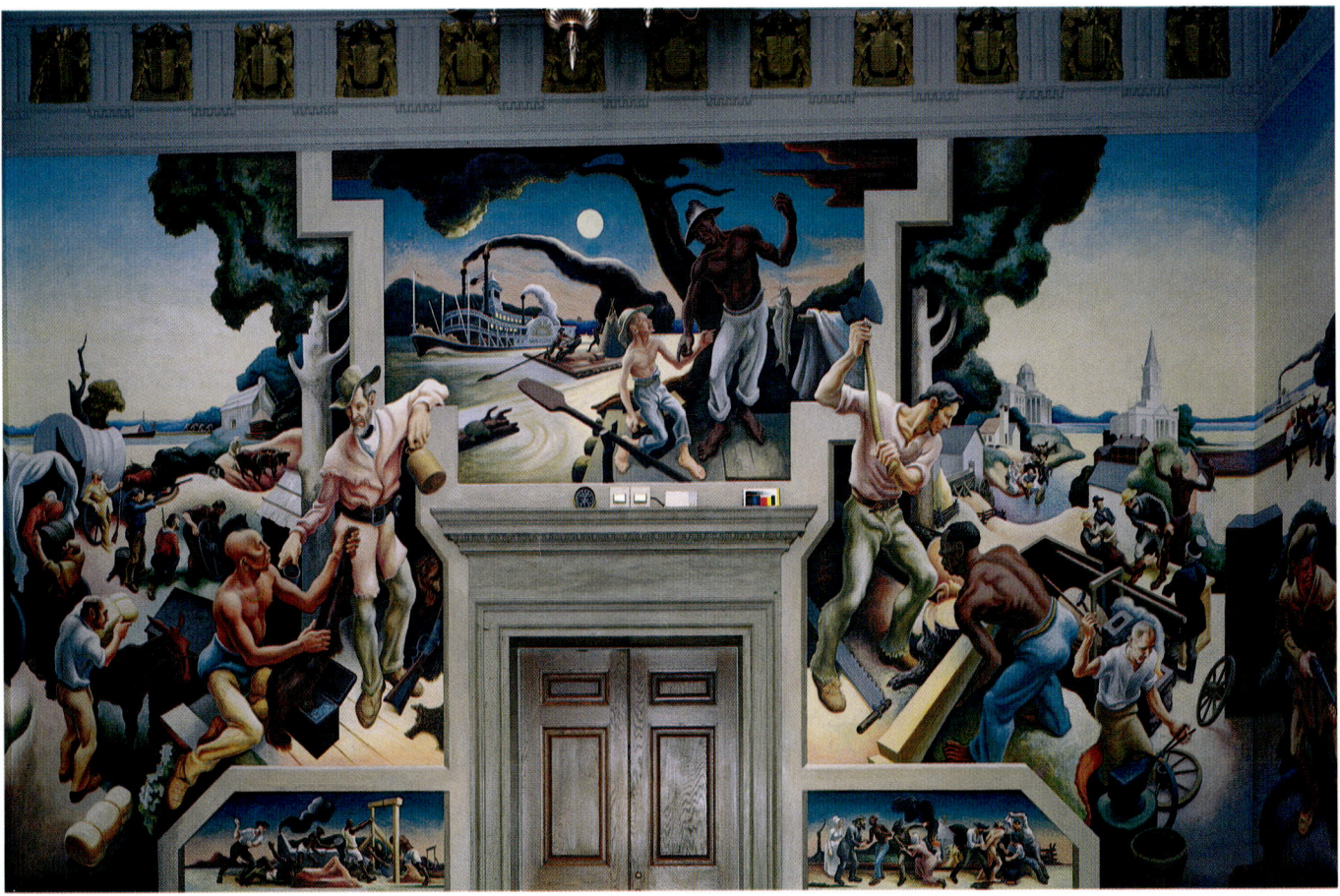

33-79   THOMAS HART BENTON, *Pioneer Days and Early Settlers,* State Capitol, Jefferson City, 1936. Mural. Copyright © T. H. Benton and R. P. Benton Testamentary Trusts/Licensed by VAGA, New York, NY.

CONSTRUCTING A HISTORY OF MISSOURI

THOMAS HART BENTON (1889–1975) was another of the major Regionalist artists. Whereas Wood focused his attention on Iowa, Benton turned to scenes from his native Missouri. Benton produced one of his major works, a series of murals titled *A Social History of the State of Missouri,* in 1936 for the Missouri State Capitol. The murals depict a collection of images from the state's true and legendary history, such as primitive agriculture, horse trading, a vigilante lynching, and an old-fashioned political meeting. Other scenes portray the mining industry, grain elevators, Native Americans, and family life. One segment, *Pioneer Days and Early Settlers* (FIG. **33-79**), shows a white man using whisky as a bartering tool with a Native American (at left), along with scenes documenting the building of Missouri. Part documentary and part imaginative, Benton's images include both positive and negative aspects of Missouri's history, as these examples illustrate. Although Regionalists were popularly perceived as dedicated to glorifying Midwestern life, that belief distorted their aims. Indeed, Grant Wood observed, "your true regionalist is not a mere eulogist; he may even be a severe critic."[84] Benton, like Wood, was committed to a visually accessible style, but he developed a highly personal aesthetic that included complex compositions, a fluidity of imagery, and simplified figures depicted in a rubbery distortion.

Not surprisingly, during the Great Depression of the 1930s, the Regionalist paintings had a popular appeal because they often projected a reassuring image of America's heartland. The public saw Regionalism as a means of coping with the national crisis through a search for cultural roots. Thus, people deemed acceptable any nostalgia implicit in Regionalist paintings or mythologies these works perpetuated because they served a larger purpose.

Mexican Muralists

VALIDATING MEXICAN HISTORY   JOSÉ CLEMENTE OROZCO (1883–1949) was one of a group of Mexican artists determined to base their art on the indigenous history and culture existing in Mexico before Europeans arrived. The movement these artists formed was part of the idealistic rethinking of society that occurred in conjunction with the Mexican Revolution (1910–1920) and the lingering political turmoil of the 1920s. Among the projects these politically motivated ar-tists undertook were vast mural cycles placed in public buildings to dramatize and validate the history of Mexico's native peoples. Orozco worked on one of the first major cycles, painted in 1922 on the walls of the National Training School in Mexico City. He carried the ideas of this mural revolution to the United States, completing many commissions for wall paintings between 1927 and 1934. From 1932 to 1934, he worked on one of his finest mural cycles in the Baker Library at Dartmouth College in New Hampshire, partly in honor of its superb collection of books in Spanish. The college let him choose the subject. Orozco depicted, in fourteen large panels and ten smaller ones, a panoramic and symbolic history of ancient and modern Mexico, from the early mythic days of the feathered-serpent god Quetzalcóatl to a contemporary and bitterly satiric vision of modern education.

The imagery in the illustrated detail, *Epic of American Civilization: Hispano-America (panel 16)* (FIG. **33-80**), revolves around the monumental figure of a heroic Mexican peasant armed to participate in the Mexican Revolution. Looming on either side of him are mounds crammed with symbolic figures of his oppressors—bankers, government soldiers, officials, gangsters, and the rich. Money-grubbers pour hoards of gold at the incorruptible peon's feet, cannons threaten him, and a bemedaled general raises a dagger to stab him in the back. Orozco's training as an architect gave him a sense of the framed wall surface, which he easily commanded, projecting his clearly defined figures onto the solid mural plane in monumental scale.

In addition, Orozco's early training as a maker of political prints and as a newspaper artist had taught him the rhetorical strength of graphic brevity, which he used here to assure that his allegory was easily read. His special merging of the graphic and mural media effects give his work an originality and force rarely seen in mural painting after the Renaissance and Baroque periods.

THE POWER OF PUBLIC ART   Diego Rivera (1886–1957), like his countryman Orozco, achieved great renown for his murals, both in Mexico and in the United States. A staunch Marxist, Rivera was committed to developing an art that served his people's needs. Toward that end, he sought to create a national Mexican style focusing on Mexico's history and also incorporating a popular, generally accessible aesthetic (in keeping with the Socialist spirit of the Mexican Revolution). Rivera produced numerous large murals in public buildings, among them a series (FIG. **33-81**) lining the staircase of the National Palace in Mexico City. In these images, painted between 1929 and 1935, he depicted scenes from Mexico's history. These scenes represent the conflicts between the indigenous people and the Spanish colonizers. Rivera included portraits of important figures in Mexican history and, in particular, in the struggle for Mexican independence. Although complex, the decorative animated murals retain the legibility of folklore—the figures consist of simple monumental shapes and areas of bold color.

ÉMIGRÉS AND EXILES: ENERGIZING AMERICAN ART AT MIDCENTURY

The Armory Show in 1913 in New York City, discussed earlier, was an important vehicle for disseminating information about developments in European art. Equally significant was the emigration of European artists around the European continent and across the Atlantic Ocean to America. The havoc Hitler and the National Socialists wreaked in the early 1930s forced artists to flee. The United States, among other countries, offered both survival and amore hospitable environment for producing their art.

Many artists gravitated to Paris and London, but when the threat of war expanded, the United States became an attractive alternative. Several artists and architects associated with the Bauhaus—Gropius, Moholy-Nagy, Albers, Breuer, Mon-

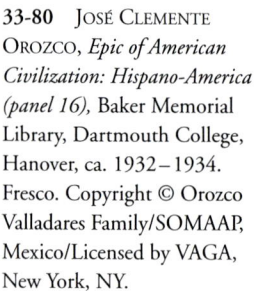
33-80 José Clemente Orozco, *Epic of American Civilization: Hispano-America (panel 16)*, Baker Memorial Library, Dartmouth College, Hanover, ca. 1932–1934. Fresco. Copyright © Orozco Valladares Family/SOMAAP, Mexico/Licensed by VAGA, New York, NY.

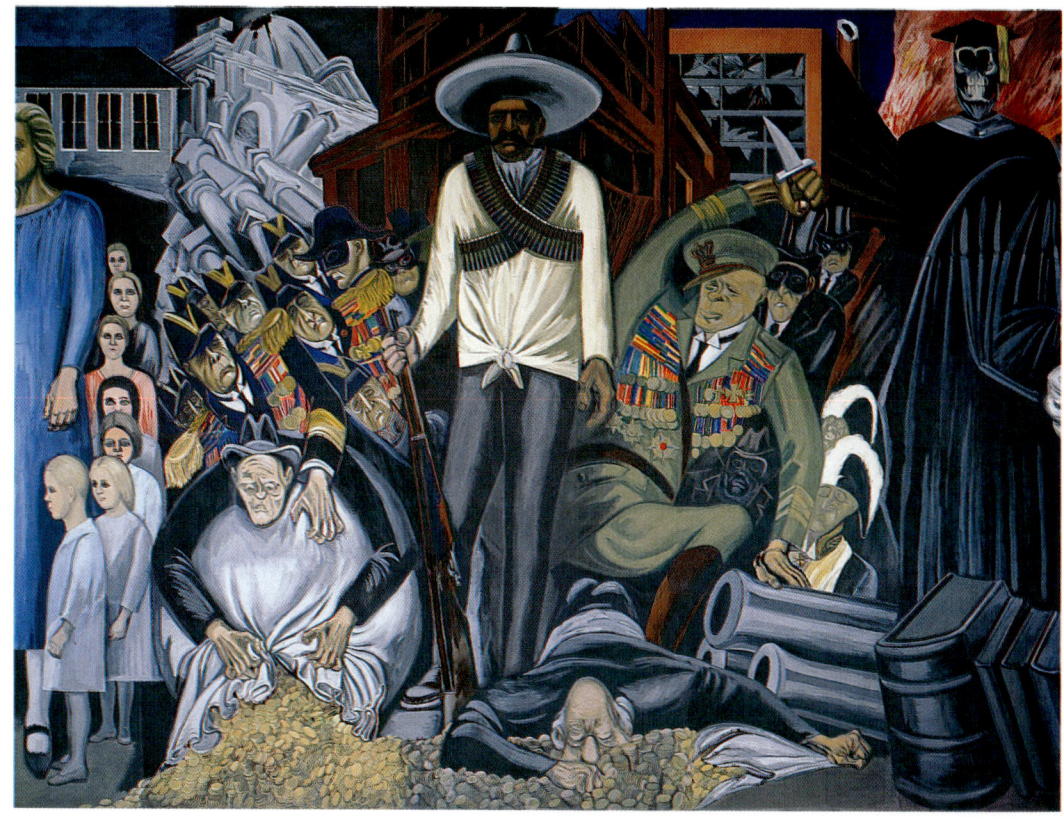

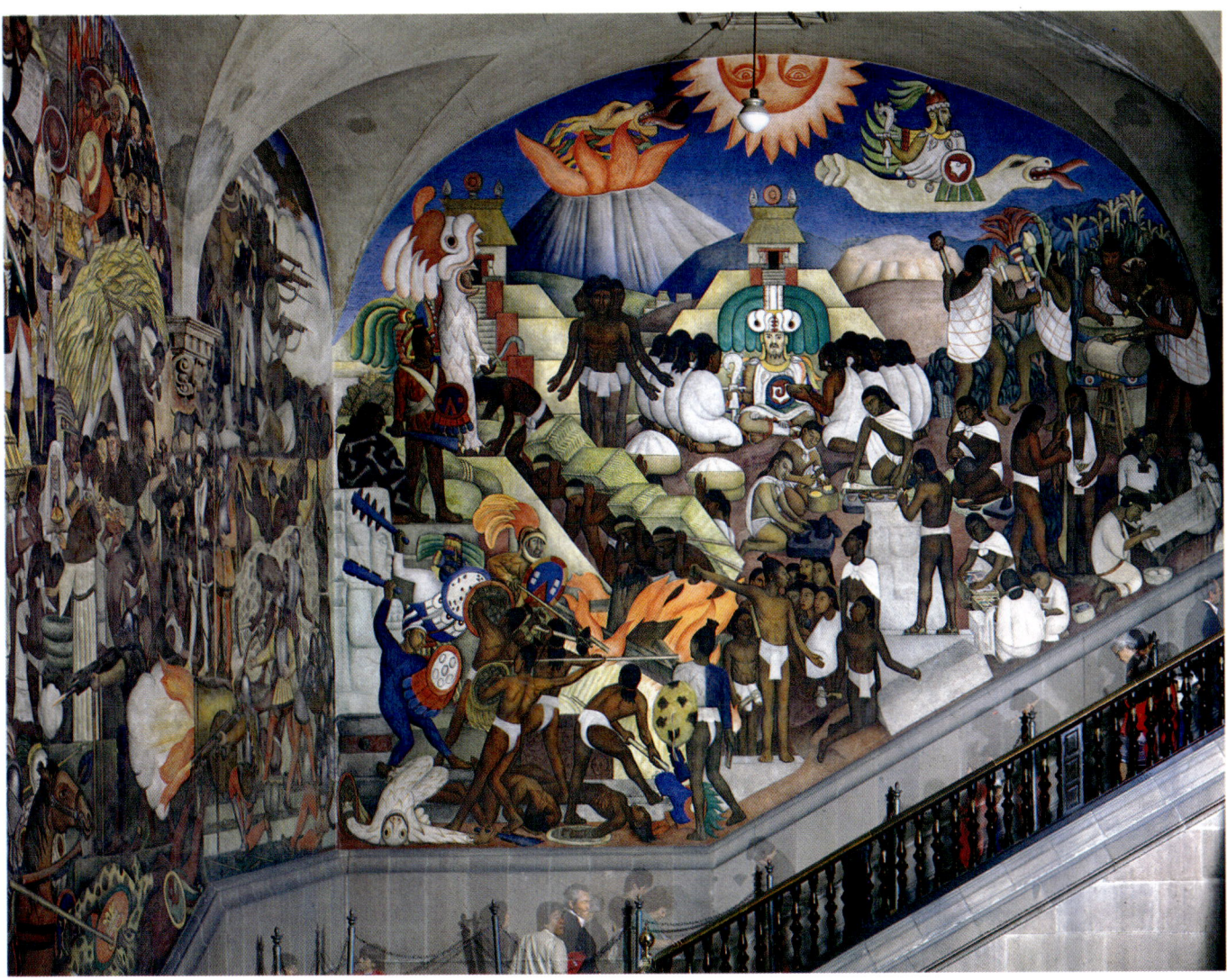

33-81 DIEGO RIVERA, *Ancient Mexico,* from the History of Mexico fresco murals, National Palace, Mexico City, 1929–1935. Fresco.

drian, and Mies van der Rohe—came to the United States. Many accepted teaching positions, providing them a means of disseminating their ideas. Artists associated with other avant-garde movements—Neue Sachlichkeit (Beckmann and Grosz), Surrealism (Ernst, Dalí, Breton, and Chagall), and Cubism (Léger and Lipchitz)—all made their way to American cities.

Museums in the United States, wanting to demonstrate their familiarity and connection with the most progressive European art, mounted exhibitions centered on the latest European artistic developments. In 1938 alone, the City Art Museum of Saint Louis in Missouri presented an exhibition of Beckmann's work, the Art Institute of Chicago organized *George Grosz: A Survey of His Art from 1918–1938,* and the Museum of Modern Art in New York offered *Bauhaus, 1919–1928.* This interest in exhibiting the work of artists persecuted and driven from their homelands also had political overtones. In the highly charged atmosphere of the late 1930s leading to the onset of World War II, people often perceived support for these artists and their work as support for freedom and democracy. In 1942, Alfred H. Barr Jr., director of the Museum of Modern Art, stated:

Among the freedoms which the Nazis have destroyed, none has been more cynically perverted, more brutally stamped upon, than the Free-

dom of Art. For not only must the artist of Nazi Germany bow to political tyranny, he must also conform to the personal taste of that great art connoisseur, Adolf Hitler. . . . But German artists of spirit and integrity have refused to conform. They have gone into exile or slipped into anxious obscurity. . . . Their paintings and sculptures, too, have been hidden or exiled. . . . But in free countries they can still be seen, can still bear witness to the survival of a free German culture.[85]

Despite this moral support for exiled artists, once the United States formally entered the war, Germany officially became the enemy. Then it was much more difficult for the art world to promote German artists, however persecuted. Many émigré artists (for example, Ernst, Dalí, Léger, and Grosz) returned to Europe after the war ended. Their collective presence in the United States until then, however, was critical for the development of American art and contributed significantly to the extensive interest in the later twentieth century of many American artists in the avant-garde.

The dialogue between American and European artists thus did much to stimulate early-twentieth-century artistic ferment and experimentation. The Armory Show and the emigration of European artists to the United States were both important catalysts for the momentum and energy in the art world that carried on into the later twentieth century.

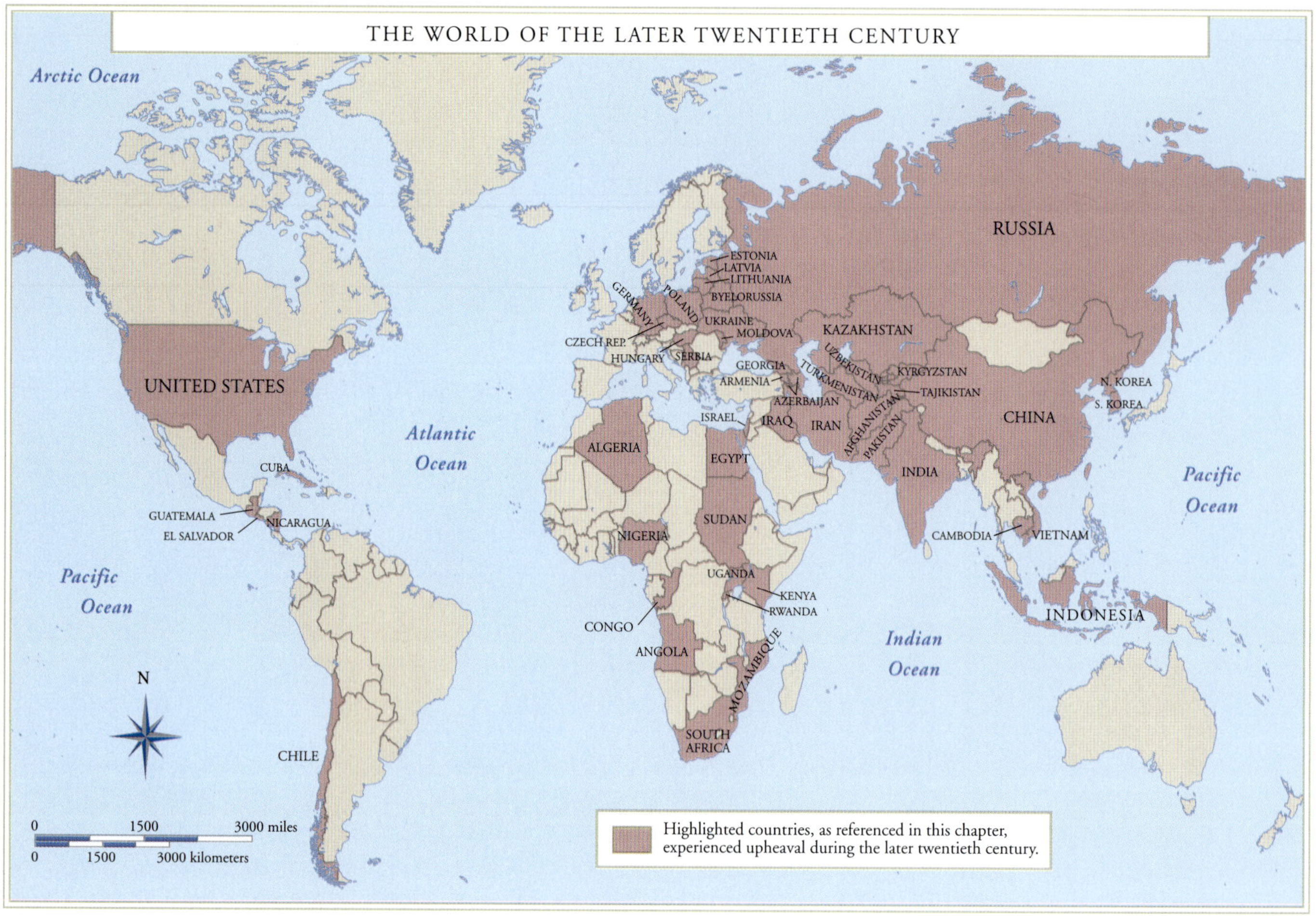

THE WORLD OF THE LATER TWENTIETH CENTURY

Arctic Ocean

RUSSIA

ESTONIA
LATVIA
LITHUANIA
BYELORUSSIA
GERMANY
POLAND
UKRAINE
CZECH REP.
HUNGARY
SERBIA
MOLDOVA
KAZAKHSTAN
GEORGIA
UZBEKISTAN
KYRGYZSTAN
ARMENIA
TURKMENISTAN
TAJIKISTAN
AZERBAIJAN
N. KOREA
S. KOREA
CHINA

UNITED STATES

Atlantic Ocean

ISRAEL
IRAQ
IRAN
AFGHANISTAN
PAKISTAN

CUBA

ALGERIA
EGYPT
INDIA

GUATEMALA
NICARAGUA
EL SALVADOR

Pacific Ocean

NIGERIA
SUDAN

CAMBODIA
VIETNAM

Pacific Ocean

UGANDA
KENYA
RWANDA

CONGO
ANGOLA
MOZAMBIQUE

INDONESIA

Indian Ocean

N

CHILE

SOUTH AFRICA

| 0 | 1500 | 3000 miles |
| 0 | 1500 | 3000 kilometers |

Highlighted countries, as referenced in this chapter, experienced upheaval during the later twentieth century.

1945   1950   1960

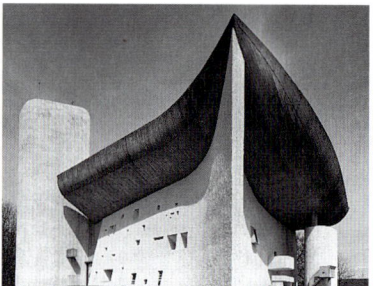

Le Corbusier
Notre Dame du Haut, 1950–1955

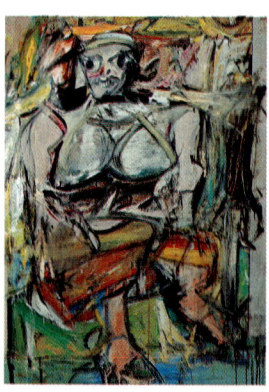

Willem de Kooning
Woman I, 1950–1952

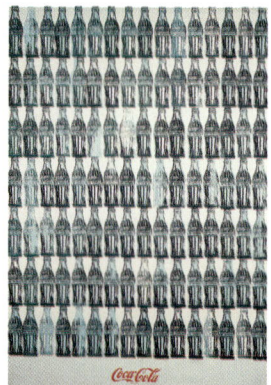

Andy Warhol
Green Coca-Cola Bottles, 1962

Existentialism, 1930–1950s

United Nations organized, 1945

Atomic bomb devastates Hiroshima and Nagasaki, 1945

Transistor invented, 1948

State of Israel created, 1948

Republic of India begun, ca. 1949

People's Republic of China established, 1949

Korean conflict, 1950–1953

Crick and Watson, Structure and function of DNA, 1954

Sputnik I launched, 1957

Computer chip invented, 1959

Lasers invented, 1960

First manned space flight, 1961

John F. Kennedy assassinated, 1963

Corporation for Public Broadcasting formed, 1967

Martin Luther King and Robert Kennedy assassinated, 1968

Moon landing, 1969

THE EMERGENCE OF POSTMODERNISM

THE LATER TWENTIETH CENTURY

1970	1980	1990

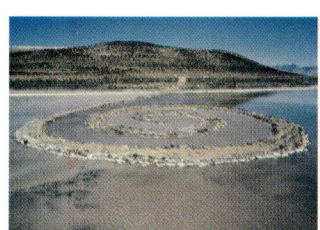

Robert Smithson
Spiral Jetty, 1970

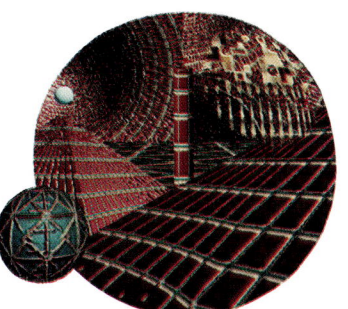

David Em
Nora, 1979

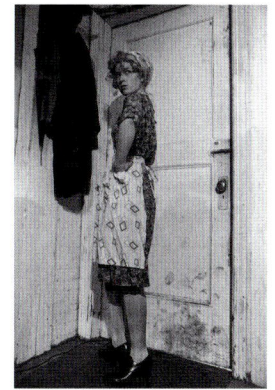

Cindy Sherman
Untitled Film Still #35, 1979

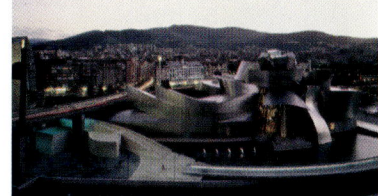

Frank Gehry
Guggenheim Museum, Bilbao, 1997

Postmodernism in art, literature, 1970s–

Watergate, 1972–1974

War in Vietnam ends, 1975

Personal computers introduced, 1975

Islamic Revolution in Iran, 1978–1979

Gorbachev comes to power
in Soviet Union, 1985

Opening of Berlin Wall, 1989,
collapse of Soviet Union

Tiananmen Square
massacre, 1989

US intervention,
Somalia, Haiti, 1990s

Gulf War, 1990s

Breakup of
Yugoslavia, 1990s

The "Cybernetic
Revolution," 1990s

WORLD WAR II AND ITS AFTERMATH

World War II was the most devastating catastrophe of the twentieth century, not only because of the destruction and extensive loss of life but also because of the long-term consequences on numerous levels—personal, cultural, political, and economic. The history of the later twentieth century, beginning with the end of World War II in 1945, is one of upheaval, change, and conflict. For much of that time, peoples of the world lived with the threat of nuclear war. The two superpowers, the United States and the Soviet Union, divided the world into spheres of influence, and each regularly intervened politically, economically, and militarily wherever and whenever it considered its interests at stake.

Disruption and Upheaval

Throughout the world, disruption and dislocation took place. In 1947, the British left India, which erupted in a murderous Hindu-Muslim war that divided the subcontinent into the new, still hostile, nations of India and Pakistan. After a catastrophic war, Communists came to power in China in 1949. North Korea tested the fledgling United Nations (UN), founded after the war, by invading South Korea in 1950 and fighting a grim war with the United States and its UN allies. The Soviets brutally suppressed uprisings in their subject nations—East Germany, Poland, Hungary, and Czechoslovakia. The United States intervened in disputes in Central and South America. Hardly had the previously colonized nations of Africa—Kenya, Uganda, Nigeria, Angola, Mozambique, the Sudan, Rwanda, and the Congo—won their independence than civil wars devastated them. In Indonesia civil war left more than a hundred thousand dead. Algeria expelled France in 1962 after a prolonged and vicious war with Algeria's Muslim natives. Following fifteen years of bitter war in Southeast Asia, the United States was defeated in Vietnam. In 1979, the Soviets invaded Afghanistan but were driven out. Arab nations, economically flourishing from oil wealth, fought wars with Israel in 1967, 1978, and the early 1980s. A revitalized Islam rose in the Arab world, inspired a fundamentalist religious revolution in Iran, and encouraged "holy war" with the West, using a new weapon—international terrorism. In 1991, West clashed with East in the Persian Gulf. South Africa formally abandoned apartheid in 1992.

Unrest continues to plague many countries worldwide. The ongoing conflict among the Serbs, Croats, and Muslims in the Balkans, the instability of the various Russian republics, and the divisive ethnic clashes in many African nations emphasize that international hostilities and political uncertainty still characterize the world situation.

This litany of worldwide upheaval reveals a fundamental characteristic of the second half of the twentieth century—change. In part because the United States emerged relatively unscathed from World War II (compared to European countries, Japan, and the Soviet Union), it could pursue its economic, political, and cultural agendas more aggressively and establish a global presence. But although North American culture seemed to take center stage during the latter part of the twentieth century, the United States was not immune from internal change and upheaval either. In the postwar years, people increasingly questioned the status quo. The struggle for civil rights for African Americans, for free speech on university campuses, and against the Vietnam War led to a rebellion of young Americans. They took to the streets in often raucous demonstrations, with violent repercussions, during the 1960s and 1970s. The prolonged ferment produced a new system of values, a "youth culture," expressed in radical rejection not only of national policies but often also of the society generating them. The young derided their elders' lifestyles and adopted unconventional dress (for that time—long hair, beards, and workers' jeans), manners, habits, and morals deliberately subversive of conventional social standards. The youth era witnessed the sexual revolution, the widespread use and abuse of drugs, and the development of rock music, then an exclusively youthful art form. Young people "dropped out" of regulated society, embraced alternative belief systems, and rejected "Western" university curricula as irrelevant.

This counterculture had considerable societal impact and widespread influence beyond its political phase. The Civil Rights movement and later the women's liberation movement reflected the spirit of rebellion, coupled with the rejection of racism and sexism. In keeping with the growing resistance to established authority, women systematically began to challenge the male-dominated culture, which they perceived as having limited their political power and economic opportunities for centuries. Feminists charged that Western society's institutions, particularly the nuclear family headed by the patriarch, perpetuated male power and subordination of women. Feminists observed that monuments of Western culture—its arts and sciences, as well as its political, social, and economic institutions—masked the realities of male power. The term "feminism," while convenient for generic usage, reflects neither the complexity of the issues involved nor the heated debate that emerged among feminists. Indeed, the term encompasses such a wide range of attitudes and ideas that its usefulness is limited.

The Dynamics of Power

Following patterns developed first in the Civil Rights movement and later in feminism, various ethnic groups and gays and lesbians all have mounted challenges to discriminatory policies and attitudes. Such groups have fought for recognition, respect, and legal protection and have battled discrimination with political action. These explorations into the politics of identity aim to increase personal and public understanding of how self-identifications, along with imposed or inherited identities, affect lives. The growing scrutiny in numerous academic fields—cultural studies, literary theory, and colonial and postcolonial studies—of the dynamics and exercise of power also have contributed to the dialogue on these issues. French philosopher-theorists, in particular Jacques Derrida and Michel Foucault, have become prominent from their publications examining the nature of the world's power structures.

THE ART WORLD'S FOCUS SHIFTS WEST

The period's emphasis on change carried over to the art world as well. The relative economic stability of the United States was a major factor in the shifting of the center of Western art from Paris to New York. This helps explain the predominance of American artists in the world markets, even while artists continued to create throughout the world. Only in the closing decades of the twentieth century, with the rising interest in multiculturalism and global economies, have countries outside the United States begun to exhibit art more broadly.

Modernism, Formalism, and Clement Greenberg

Modernism, so integral to art of the nineteenth century, shifted course in conjunction with the changing historical conditions and demands. In the postwar years, modernism increasingly became identified with a strict formalism—an emphasis on an artwork's visual elements rather than its subject—due largely to the prominence of the American Clement Greenberg (1909–1994). As an art critic who wielded considerable influence from the 1940s through the 1970s, Greenberg was instrumental in developing and articulating modernism's redefined parameters.

For Greenberg, late-twentieth-century modernist artists were those who refined the critical stance of the late-nineteenth- and early-twentieth-century modernists. This critical stance involved rejecting illusionism and exploring each artistic medium's properties. So dominant was Greenberg that scholars often refer to the general modernist tenets during this period as Greenbergian formalism. Although his complex ideas about art were modified over the years, certain basic concepts are associated with Greenbergian formalism. In particular, Greenberg promoted the idea of purity in art. He explained, "Purity in art consists in the acceptance, willing acceptance, of the limitations of the medium of the specific art."[1] In other words, he believed artists should strive for a more explicit focus on the properties exclusive to each medium—for example, two-dimensionality, or flatness in painting, and three-dimensionality in sculpture. To achieve this, artists had to eliminate illusion and embrace abstraction. Greenberg elaborated:

> It follows that a modernist work of art must try, in principle, to avoid communication with any order of experience not inherent in the most literally and essentially construed nature of its medium. Among other things, this means renouncing illusion and explicit subject matter. The arts are to achieve concreteness, "purity," by dealing solely with their respective selves—that is, by becoming "abstract" or nonfigurative.[2]

Greenberg avidly promoted the avant-garde, which he viewed as synonymous with modernism in the postwar years. Generally speaking, the spirit of rebellion and disdain for convention central to the historical avant-garde flourished in the sociopolitical upheaval and counterculture of the 1960s and 1970s. However, the acute sociopolitical dimension inherent in the avant-garde's early development had evaporated by this time (although many of the artists considered avant-garde aligned themselves with the Left). Thus the avant-garde (and modernism) became primarily an artistic endeavor. Still, the distance between progressive artists and the public widened. In his landmark 1939 article "Avant-Garde and Kitsch," Greenberg insisted on the separation of the avant-garde from kitsch (which Greenberg defined as "ersatz," or artificial, culture, such as popular commercial art and literature), thereby advocating the continued alienation of the public from avant-garde art.

The Emergence of Postmodernism

The modernists' intense criticism of the discipline and the unrelenting challenges to artistic convention eventually led to modernism's demise. To many, it seemed artistic traditions had been so completely undermined that modernism simply played itself out. From this situation emerged *postmodernism,* one of the most dramatic developments during the century. Postmodernism cannot be described as a style; it is a widespread cultural phenomenon. Many people view it as a rejection of modernist principles. Accordingly, postmodernism is far more encompassing and accepting than the more rigid confines of modernist practice. Postmodernism's ability to accommodate seemingly everything in art makes it extremely difficult to provide a clear and concrete definition of the term. In response to the elitist, uncompromising stance of modernism, postmodernism grew out of a naive and optimistic populism.

Whereas the audience for modernist art had dwindled due to the obscure meaning of abstract work, postmodern artists offer something for everyone. For example, in architecture, postmodernism's eclectic nature often surfaces in a whimsical mixture of styles and architectural elements (such as Greek columns juxtaposed with ornate Baroque decor). In other artistic media, postmodernism accommodates a wide range of styles, subjects, and formats, from traditional easel painting to video and *installation* (artwork creating an artistic environment in a room or gallery) and from the spare abstraction associated with modernism to carefully rendered illusionistic scenes. In addition, various investigations have been identified as particularly postmodern, including critiquing modernist tenets, reassessing the nature of representation, and exploring the ways in which meaning is generated. Although these inquiries are largely philosophical and theoretical, much of the art produced during the postmodern period is resolutely grounded in specific historical conditions. Thus, later in this chapter, art addressing issues of race, class, gender, sexual orientation, and ethnicity is discussed.

POSTWAR EXPRESSIONISM IN EUROPE

The end of World War II in 1945 left devastated cities, ruptured economies, and governments in chaos throughout Europe. These factors, coupled with the massive loss of life and the indelible horror of the Holocaust and Hiroshima/Nagasaki, resulted in a pervasive sense of despair, disillusionment, and skepticism. Although many (for example, the Futurists in Italy) had tried to find redemptive value in World War I, it was virtually impossible to do the same with World War II, coming as it did so closely on the heels of the war that was supposed to "end all wars." Additionally, World War I was largely a European conflict that left more than eight million people dead, while World War II was a truly global catastrophe, leaving forty-five million dead in its wake.

Existentialism: The Absurdity of Human Existence

The cynicism emerging across Europe was reflected in the popularity of existentialism (Chapter 33, page 1002), a philosophy asserting the absurdity of human existence and the impossibility of achieving certitude. Many existentialists also promoted atheism and questioned the possibility of situating God within a systematic philosophy. Existentialism's roots often are traced to the Danish theologian Søren Kierkegaard (1813–1855), and the writings of philosophers and novelists such as Friedrich Nietzsche (Chapter 33, page 1002), Martin Heidegger, Fyodor Dostoyevsky, and Franz Kafka disseminated its ideas. In the postwar period, the writings of the French author Jean-Paul Sartre (1905–1980) most clearly captured the existentialist spirit. According to Sartre, people must consider seriously the implications of atheism. If God does not exist, then individuals must constantly struggle in isolation with the anguish of making decisions in a world without absolutes or traditional values.

This spirit of pessimism and despair emerged frequently in the European art of the immediate postwar period. A brutality or roughness appropriately expressing both the artist's state of mind and the larger cultural sensibility characterized much of this art.

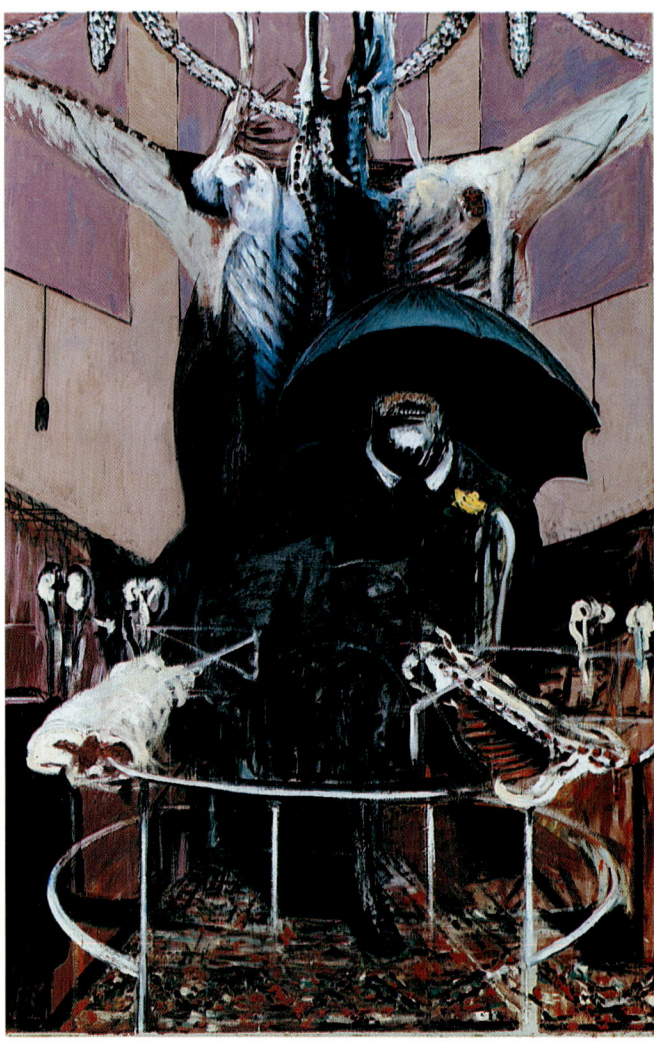

34-1 FRANCIS BACON, *Painting,* 1946. Oil and pastel on linen, 6′ 5$\frac{7}{8}$″ × 4′ 4″. Museum of Modern Art, New York (purchase).

AN INDICTMENT OF HUMANITY *Painting* (FIG. **34-1**) by British artist FRANCIS BACON (1910–1992) is a compelling and revolting image of a powerful figure who presides over a scene of slaughter. Painted in the year after World War II ended, this work can be read as an indictment of humanity and a reflection of war's butchery. The central figure is a stocky man with a gaping mouth and a vivid red stain on his upper lip, as if he were a carnivore devouring the raw meat sitting on the railing surrounding him. Bacon may have based his depiction of this central figure on news photos of Nazi leaders Joseph Goebbels and Heinrich Himmler, Benito Mussolini, or Franklin Roosevelt, which were an important part of media coverage during World War II and very familiar to the artist. The umbrella recalls wartime images of Neville Chamberlain, the British prime minister who so disastrously misjudged Hitler and was frequently photographed with an umbrella. Bacon suspended the flayed carcass hanging behind the central figure like a crucified human form, adding to the painting's visceral impact. Although the specific sources for the imagery in *Painting* may not be entirely clear, it is not difficult to see the work as "an attempt to remake the violence of reality itself" (as Francis Bacon often described his art), and the artist surely based it on what he referred to as "the brutality of fact."[3]

SCRAPED AND SMEARED CANVASES Although less specific, the works of French artist JEAN DUBUFFET (1901–1985) also express a somewhat tortured vision of the world through manipulated materials. In works such as *Vie Inquiète,* or *Uneasy Life* (FIG. **34-2**), Dubuffet presented a scene incised into thickly encrusted, parched-looking surfaces. He first built up an impasto (a layer of thickly applied pigment) of plaster, glue, sand, asphalt, or other common materials. Then, over that he painted or incised crude images of the kind children, the insane, or the scrawlers of graffiti produced. Scribblings interspersed with the images heighten the impression of smeared and gashed surfaces of crumbling walls and worn pavements marked by random individuals. Dubuffet believed the art of children, the mentally unbalanced, prisoners, and outcasts was more direct and genuine because it was unsullied by experience and untainted by conventional standards of art and aesthetic response. He promoted *Art Brut*—untaught, coarse, and rough art.

LOST IN THE WORLD'S IMMENSITY Existentialism's spirit is perhaps best expressed in the midlife sculpture of Swiss artist ALBERTO GIACOMETTI (1901–1966). Although Giacometti never claimed he pursued existentialist ideas in his art, it is hard to deny that his works capture the spirit of that

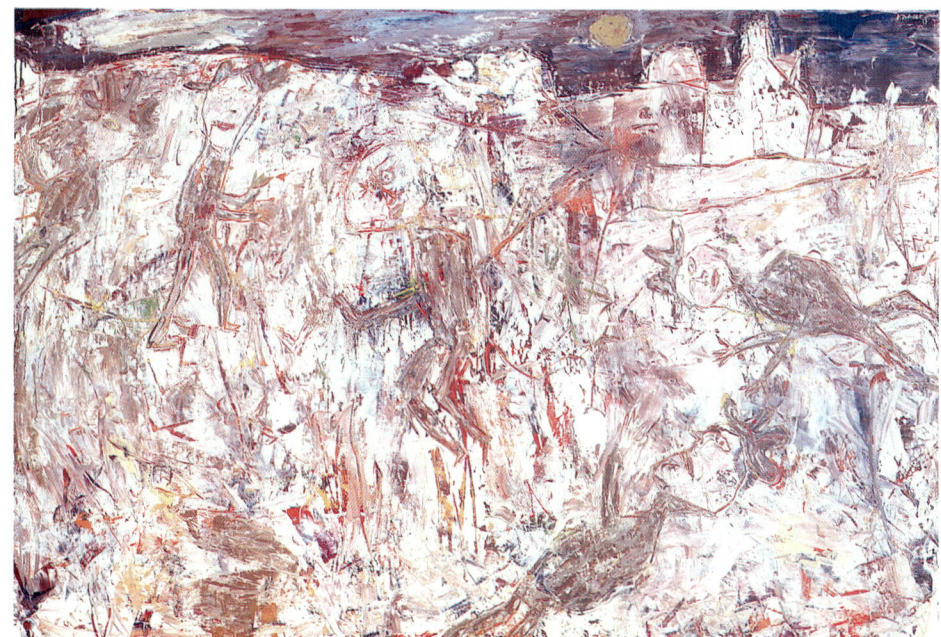

34-2 JEAN DUBUFFET, *Vie Inquiète*, 1953. Oil on canvas, approx. 4′ 3″ × 6′ 4″. Tate Gallery, London.

philosophy. Indeed, Sartre, Giacometti's friend, saw the artist's figurative sculptures as the epitome of existentialist humanity—alienated, solitary, and lost in the world's immensity. Giacometti had produced sculptures based on human models earlier in his career, but around 1940 he abandoned such direct observation and began to work from memory. His sculptures of the 1940s, such as *Man Pointing* (FIG. **34-3**), were thin, virtually featureless figures with rough, agitated surfaces. Rather than convey the solidity and mass of conventional bronze figurative sculpture, these severely attenuated figures seem swallowed up by the space surrounding them, imparting a sense of isolation and fragility. These sculptures represented quite a departure from Giacometti's earlier Surrealist-oriented work. Like much of European postwar art, Giacometti's later sculptures are evocative and moving, speaking to the pervasive despair in the aftermath of world war.

MODERNIST FORMALISM

Abstract Expressionism

As noted earlier, the center of the Western art world shifted in the 1940s from Paris to New York. This was due in large part to the devastation World War II inflicted across Europe, coupled with the influx of émigré artists escaping to the United States. American artists picked up the European avant-garde's energy, which movements such as Cubism and Dada had fostered. Interest in the avant-garde predominated much American art of the 1940s through 1970s.

Abstract Expressionism, the first major American avant-garde movement, emerged in New York (and hence is often referred to as the New York School) in the 1940s. As the name suggests, the artists associated with Abstract Expressionism produced paintings that are, for the most part, abstract but express the artist's state of mind. These artists also intended to strike emotional chords in viewers. The Abstract Expressionists tried to broaden their artistic processes to express what psychiatrist Carl Jung called the "collective

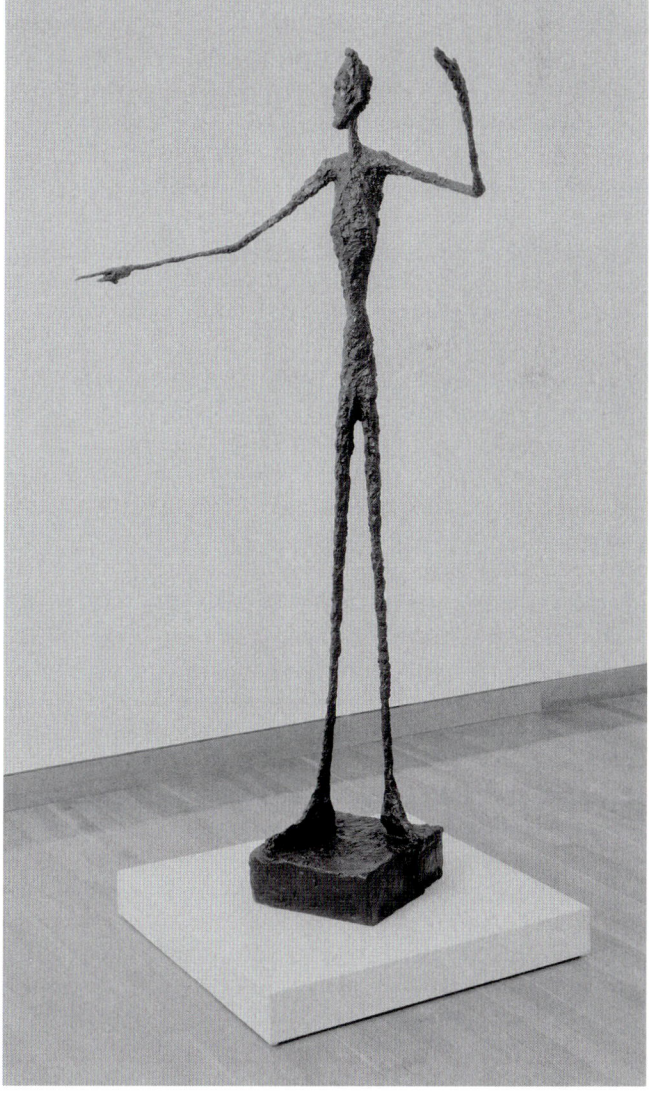

34-3 ALBERTO GIACOMETTI, *Man Pointing*, 1947. Bronze no. 5 of 6, 5′ 10″ × 3′ 1″ × 1′ 5$\frac{5}{8}$″. Nathan Emory Coffin Collection of the Des Moines Art Center, Des Moines. (Purchased with funds from the Coffin Fine Arts Trust.)

unconscious." To do so, they adopted Surrealist improvisation methods, such as "psychic automatism" (see Chapter 33, page 1037), and used their creative minds as open channels for unconscious forces to make themselves visible. These artists turned inward to create. Their works had a look of rough spontaneity and exhibited a refreshing energy. The Abstract Expressionists meant for viewers to grasp the content of their art intuitively, in a state free from structured thinking. As the artist Mark Rothko eloquently wrote:

> We assert man's absolute emotions. We don't need props or legends. We create images whose realities are self evident. Free ourselves from memory, association, nostalgia, legend, myth. Instead of making cathedrals out of Christ, man or life, we make it out of ourselves, out of our own feelings. The image we produce is understood by anyone who looks at it without nostalgic glasses of history.[4]

The Abstract Expressionist movement developed along two lines—gestural abstraction and chromatic abstraction. The gestural abstractionists relied on the expressiveness of energetically applied pigment. In contrast, the chromatic abstractionists focused on color's emotional resonance.

THE PRIMACY OF PROCESS The artist whose work best exemplifies gestural abstraction was JACKSON POLLOCK (1912–1956). Although his early work reflects the influence of his teacher, Thomas Hart Benton (see FIG. 33-79), Pollock developed his unique signature style in the mid-1940s. By 1950, Pollock had refined his technique and was producing large-scale abstract paintings such as *Number 1, 1950 (Lavender Mist)* (FIG. **34-4**). These paintings are composed of rhythmic drips, splatters, and dribbles of paint, and the mural-sized fields of energetic skeins of pigment envelop viewers, drawing them into a lacy spiderweb. The

label gestural abstraction nicely describes Pollock's working technique. Using sticks or brushes, he flung, poured, and dripped paint (not only traditional oil paints but aluminum paints and household enamels as well) onto a section of unsized canvas he simply unrolled across his studio floor (FIG. **34-5**). Responding to the image as it developed, Pollock created both spontaneous and choreographed art. His working method highlights a particularly avant-garde aspect of gestural abstraction—its emphasis on the creative process. Indeed, Pollock literally immersed himself in the painting during its creation. Pollock explained, "I feel nearer, more a part of the painting, since this way I can walk around it, work from the four sides, and literally be *in* the painting."[5] Scholars have linked the idea, as Pollock's comments suggest, that he improvised his works and drew from his subconscious to his interest in Jungian psychology and the concept of the collective unconscious. Furthermore, the Surrealists who had relied heavily on the subconscious influenced him. The improvisational nature of Pollock's work also parallels the work of Kandinsky (see FIG. 33-7), who, appropriately enough, was described as an "abstract expressionist" as early as 1919.

In addition to Pollock's unique working methods, the lack of a well-defined compositional focus in his paintings significantly departed from conventional painting. He enhanced this rejection of tradition with the expansive scale of his canvases, a resolute move away from easel painting. These avant-garde dimensions of his work earned Pollock the public's derision and the nickname "Jack the Dripper." The title of a 1949 *Life* magazine article facetiously asked: "Jackson Pollock: Is He the Greatest Living Painter in the United States?"[6] Pollock's early death in a car accident at age forty-four cut short the development of his innovative artistic vision.

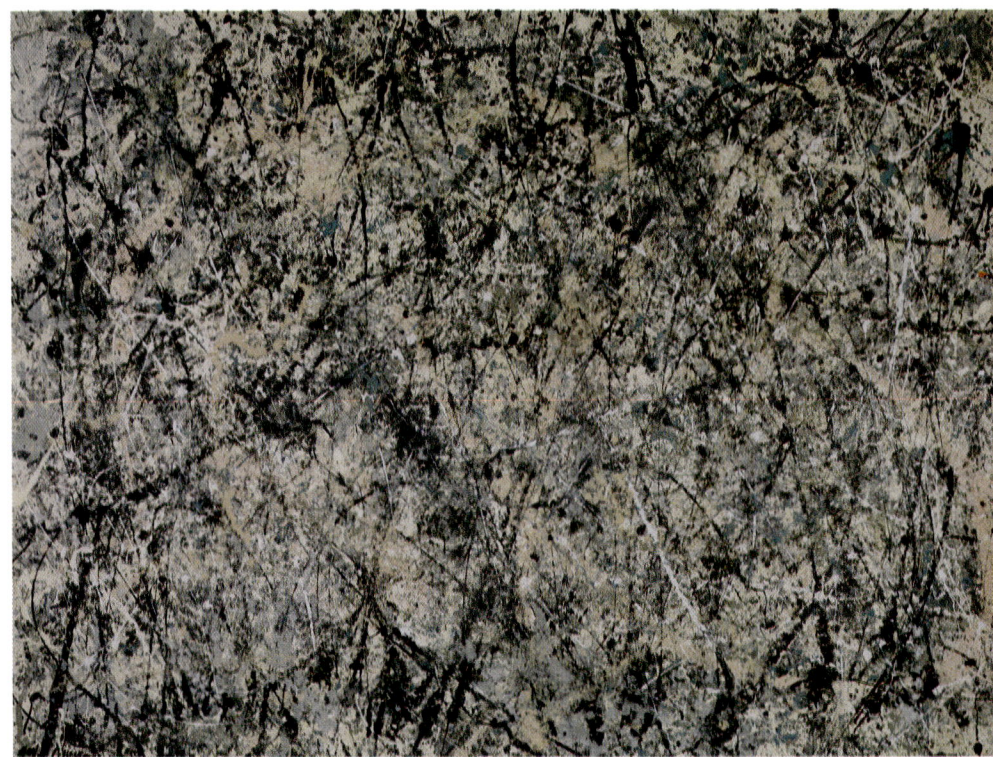

34-4 JACKSON POLLOCK, *Number 1, 1950 (Lavender Mist),* 1950. Oil, enamel, and aluminum paint on canvas, 7′ 3″ × 9′ 10″. National Gallery of Art, Washington (Ailsa Mellon Bruce Fund).

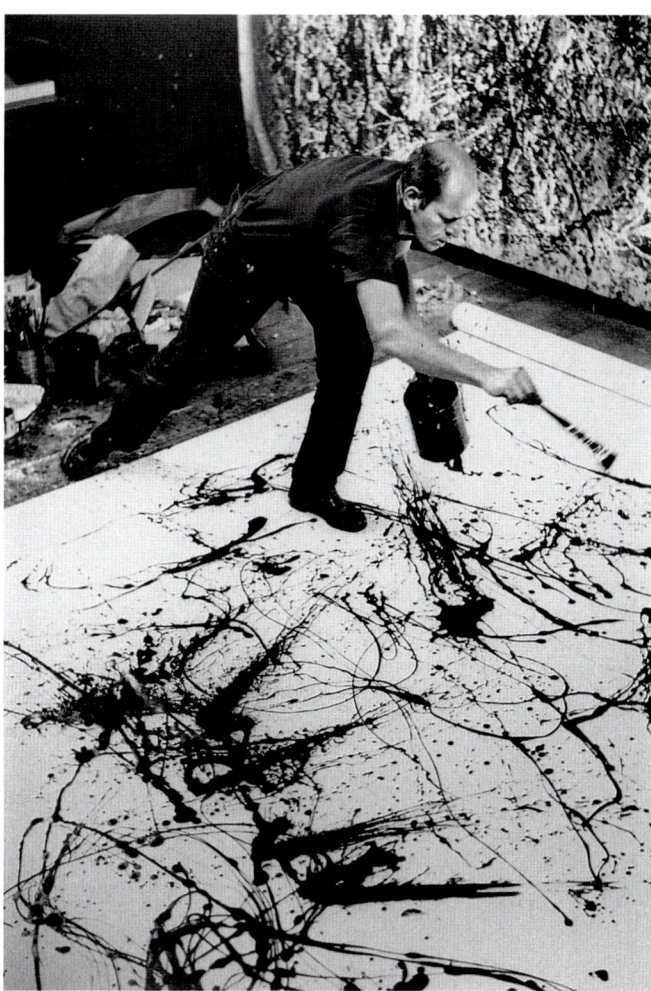

34-5 Photo of Jackson Pollock painting.

calling that de Kooning occasionally brought him paintings with ragged holes in them, the result of overly vigorous painting. Like Pollock, de Kooning was very much "in" his paintings.

People also refer to gestural painting as "action painting," a term the critic Harold Rosenberg applied first to the work of the New York School. In his influential article of 1952, "The American Action Painters," Rosenberg described the attempts of these artists to get "inside the canvas." He elaborated:

> At a certain moment the canvas began to appear to one American painter after another as an arena in which to act—rather than as a space in which to reproduce, re-design, analyze or "express" an object, actual or imagined. What was to go on the canvas was not a picture but an event. The painter no longer approached his easel with an image in his mind; he went up to it with material in his hand to do something to that other piece of material in front of him. The image would be the result of this encounter.[7]

Although many critics (Clement Greenberg among them) objected to Rosenberg's analysis of "recent" American painting, the term "action painting" was adopted and widely used.

COLOR'S ENDURING RESONANCE In contrast to the aggressively energetic images of the gestural abstractionists, the work of the chromatic abstractionists exudes a quieter aesthetic, exemplified by the work of Barnett Newman and Mark

A FEROCIOUS AND INTENSE WOMAN Despite the public's skepticism about this art, other artists enthusiastically pursued similar avenues of expression. Dutch-born WILLEM DE KOONING (1904–1997) also developed a gestural abstractionist style. Even images such as *Woman I* (FIG. 34-6), although rooted in figuration, display the sweeping gestural brushstrokes and energetic application of pigment typical of gestural abstraction. Out of the jumbled array of slashing lines and agitated patches of color appears a ferocious-looking woman with staring eyes and ponderous breasts. Her toothy smile, inspired by an ad for Camel cigarettes, seems to turn into a grimace. Female models on advertising billboards partly inspired *Woman I,* one of a series of female images, but de Kooning's female forms also suggest fertility figures and a satiric inversion of the traditional image of Venus, goddess of love.

Process was important to de Kooning, as it was for Pollock. Continually working on *Woman I* for almost two years, de Kooning painted an image and then scraped it away the next day and began anew. His wife Elaine, also a painter, estimated that he painted approximately two hundred scraped-away images of women on this canvas before settling on the final one.

In addition to this *Woman* series, de Kooning created nonrepresentational works dominated by huge swaths and splashes of pigment. His images suggest a rawness and intensity. His dealer, Sidney Janis, confirmed this impression, re-

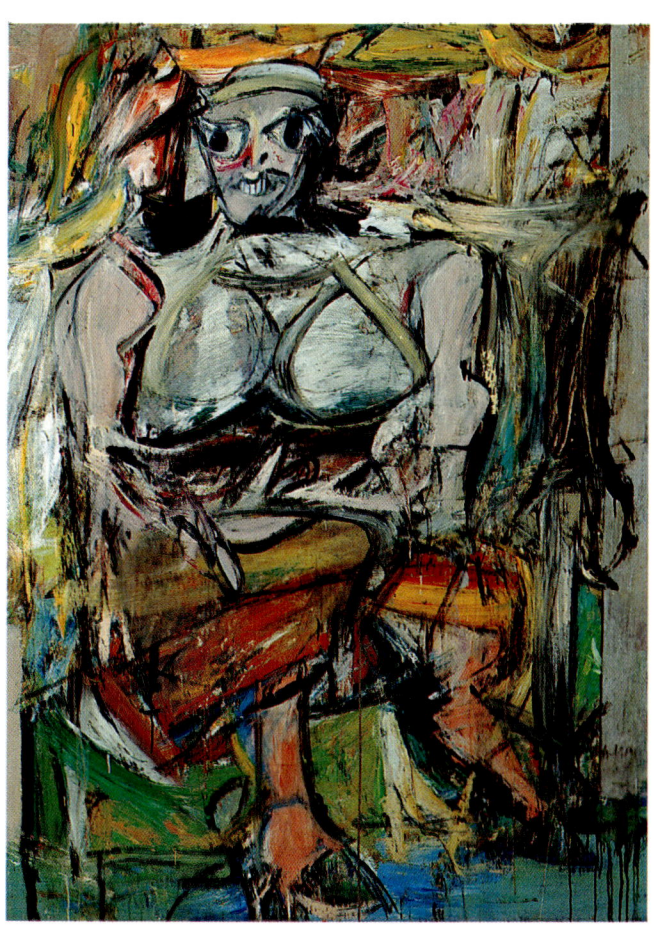

34-6 WILLEM DE KOONING, *Woman I,* 1950–1952. Oil on canvas, 6′ 3⅞″ × 4′ 10″. Museum of Modern Art, New York (purchase).

Rothko. The emotional resonance of their works derives from their eloquent use of color. In his early paintings, BARNETT NEWMAN (1905–1970) presented organic abstractions inspired by his study of biology and his fascination with Native American art. He soon simplified his compositions so that each canvas, such as *Vir Heroicus Sublimis* (*Heroic Sublime Man*; FIG. 34-7), consists of a single slightly modulated color field split by narrow bands the artist called "zips," which run from one edge of the painting to the other. As Newman explained it, "The streak was always going through an atmosphere; I kept trying to create a world around it."[8] He did not intend for viewers to perceive the zips as specific entities, separate from the ground, but as accents energizing the field and giving it scale. By simplifying his compositions, Newman increased color's capacity to communicate and to express his feelings about the tragic condition of modern life and the human struggle to survive. He claimed: "[T]he artist's problem . . . [is] the idea-complex that makes contact with mystery—of life, of men, of nature, of the hard black chaos that is death, or the grayer, softer chaos that is tragedy."[9] Confronted by one of Newman's monumental colored canvases, viewers truly feel as if they were in the presence of the epic.

"TRAGEDY, ECSTASY, DOOM"   The work of MARK ROTHKO (1903–1970) also deals with universal themes. Born in Russia, Rothko moved with his family to the United States when he was age ten. His early paintings were figurative in orientation, but he soon arrived at the belief that references to anything specific in the physical world conflicted with the sublime idea of the universal, supernatural "spirit of myth," which he saw as the core of meaning in art. In a statement cowritten with Newman and artist Adolph Gottlieb and sent to the *New York Times* critic Edward Alden Jewell, Rothko expressed his beliefs about art:

> We favor the simple expression of the complex thought. We are for the large shape because it has the impact of the unequivocal. . . . We

assert that . . . only that subject matter is valid which is tragic and timeless. That is why we profess spiritual kinship with primitive and archaic art.[10]

Rothko's paintings became compositionally simple, and he increasingly focused on color. In works such as *Untitled* (FIG. 34-8), Rothko created compelling visual experiences consisting of two or three large rectangles of pure color with hazy, brushy edges that seem to float on the canvas surface, hovering in front of a colored background. When properly lit, these paintings appear as shimmering veils of intensely luminous colors suspended in front of the canvases. Although the color juxtapositions are visually captivating, Rothko intended them as more than decorative. He saw color as a doorway to another reality, and he was convinced color could express "basic human emotions—tragedy, ecstasy, doom." He explained, "The people who weep before my pictures are having the same religious experience I had when I painted them. And if you, as you say, are moved only by their color relationships, then you miss the point."[11] Like the other Abstract Expressionists, Rothko produced highly evocative, moving paintings that relied on formal elements rather than specific representational content to raise emotions in viewers.

Post-Painterly Abstraction

Post-Painterly Abstraction, another American art movement, developed out of Abstract Expressionism. Indeed, many of the artists associated with Post-Painterly Abstraction produced Abstract Expressionist work early in their careers. Yet Post-Painterly Abstraction manifests a radically different sensibility from Abstract Expressionism. While Abstract Expressionism conveys a feeling of passion and visceral intensity, a cool, detached rationality emphasizing tighter pictorial control characterizes Post-Painterly Abstraction.

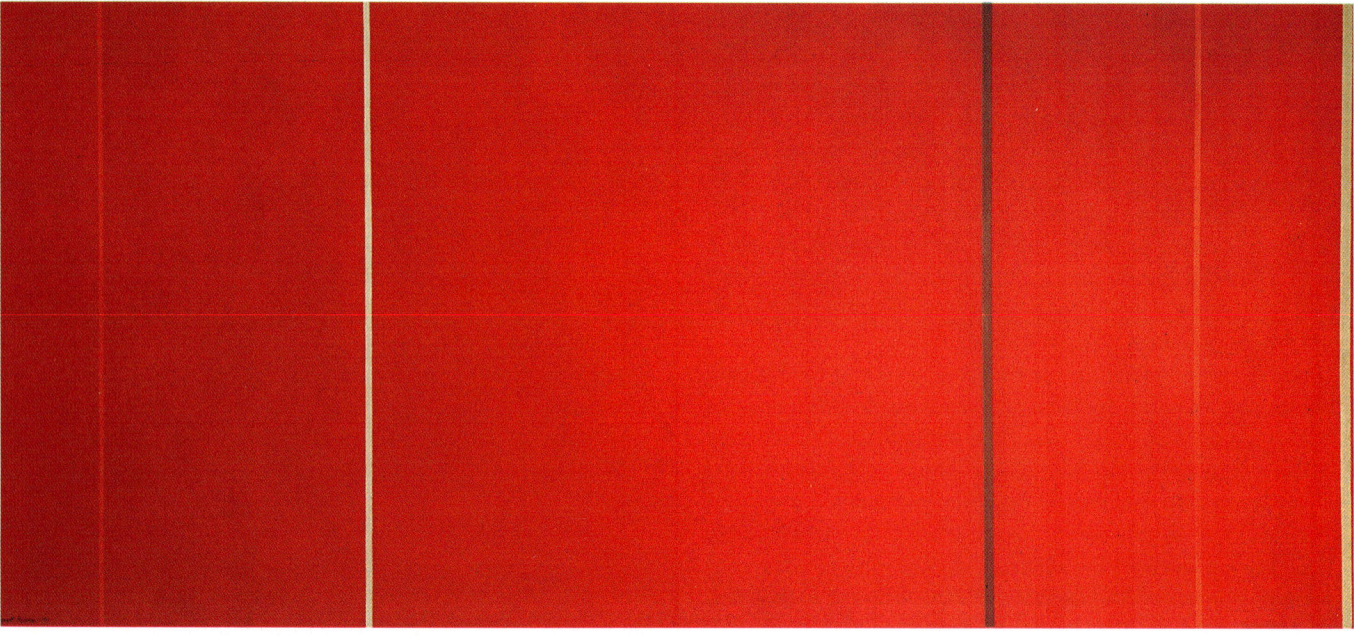

34-7   BARNETT NEWMAN, *Vir Heroicus Sublimis,* 1950–1951. Oil on canvas, 7' 11 3/8″ × 17' 9 1/4″. Museum of Modern Art, New York (gift of Mr. and Mrs. Ben Heller).

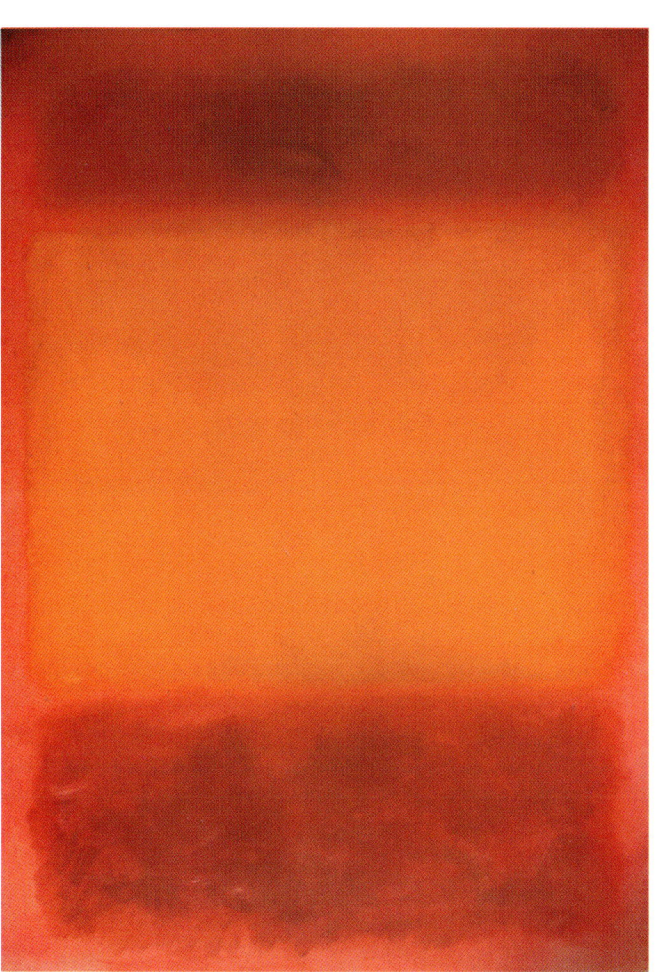

34-8 MARK ROTHKO, *Untitled*, 1961. Oil on canvas, 5′ 9″ × 4′ 2″. Collection of Mr. and Mrs. Lee V. Eastman.

The term "Post-Painterly Abstraction" was coined by the art critic Clement Greenberg, who saw this art as opposing the "painterly" concept, which refers to loose, visible pigment application. In contrast to the painterly quality of gestural abstraction, evidence of the artist's hand is conspicuously absent in Post-Painterly Abstraction. Greenberg championed this art form because it seemed to embody his idea of purity in art.

ELEMENTAL HARD-EDGE PAINTING Attempting to arrive at pure painting, the Post-Painterly Abstractionists distilled painting down to its essential elements, producing spare, elemental images. A good example of one variant of Post-Painterly Abstraction, hard-edge painting, is *Red, Blue Green* (FIG. **34-9**) by ELLSWORTH KELLY (b. 1923), with its razor-sharp edges and clearly delineated shapes. This work is, appropriately, completely abstract and extremely simple compositionally. Further, the painting contains no suggestion of the illusion of depth—the color shapes appear resolutely two-dimensional.

"WHAT YOU SEE IS WHAT YOU SEE" FRANK STELLA (b. 1936), an artist associated with the hard-edge painters, pursued similar ideas in the 1960s. In works such as

34-9 ELLSWORTH KELLY, *Red Blue Green*, 1963. Oil on canvas, 6′ 11$\frac{5}{8}$″ × 11′ 3$\frac{7}{8}$″. Collection Museum of Contemporary Art, San Diego (gift of Dr. and Mrs. Jack M. Farris).

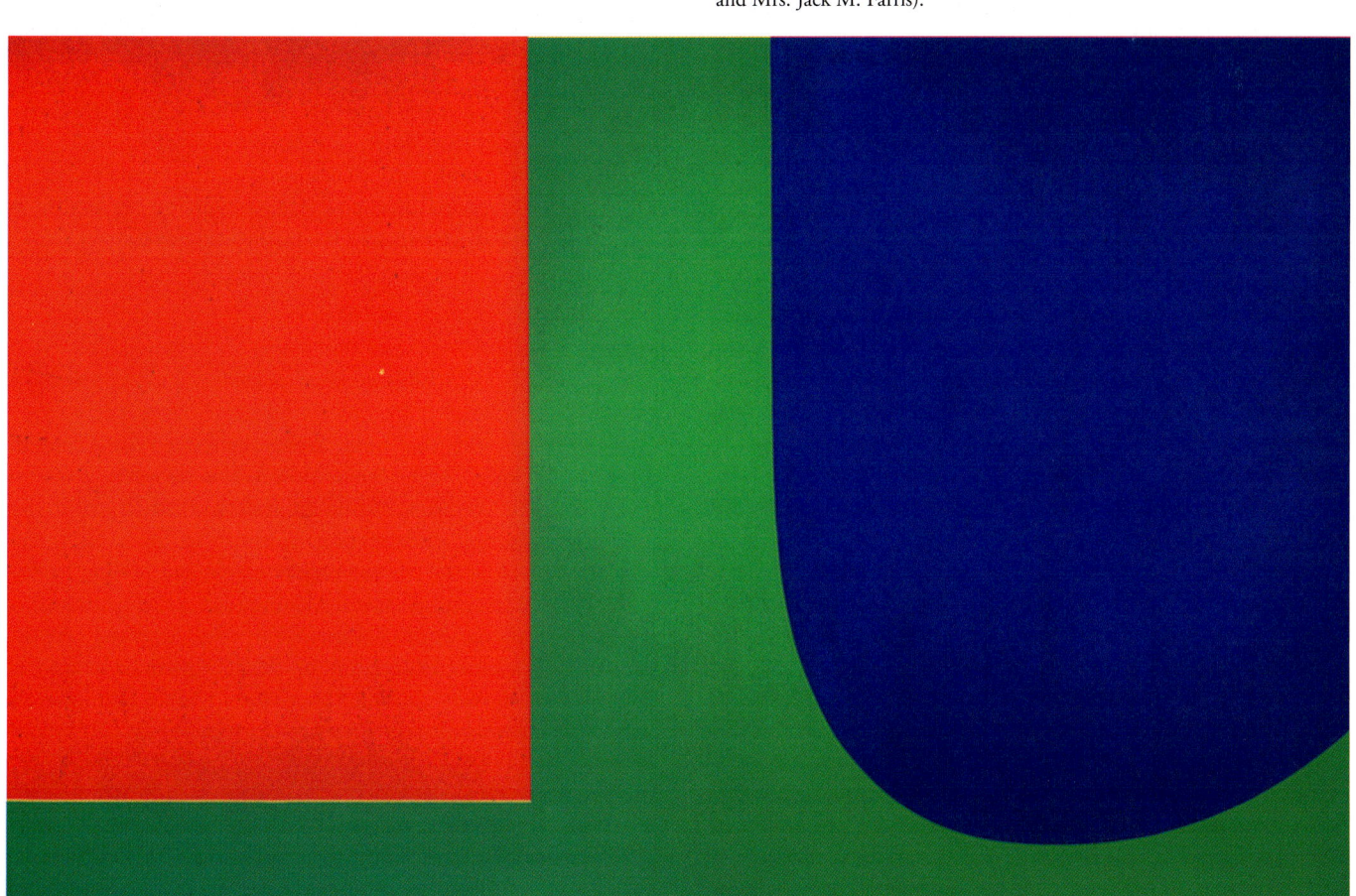

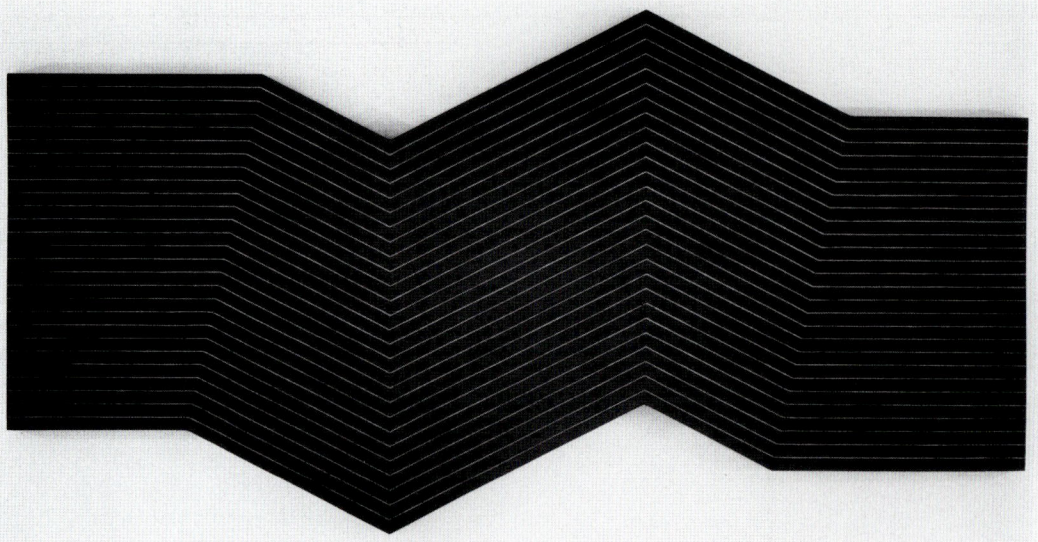

34-10 FRANK STELLA, *Nunca Pasa Nada,* 1964. Metallic powder in polymer emulsion on canvas, 9′ 2″ × 18′ 4½″. Collection Lannan Foundation.

Nunca Pasa Nada ("nothing ever happens"; FIG. **34-10**), Stella eliminated many of the variables associated with painting. His simplified images of thin, evenly spaced pinstripes on colored grounds have no central focus, no painterly or expressive elements, no surface modulation, and no tactile quality. Stella's systematic painting illustrates Greenberg's insistence on purity in art. The artist's own comment on his work, "What you see is what you see," reinforces the notions that painters interested in producing advanced art must reduce their work to its essential elements and that viewers must acknowledge that a painting is simply pigment on a flat surface.

FLAT COLOR FIELD PAINTING Color field painting, another variant of Post-Painterly Abstraction, also emphasized painting's basic properties. However, rather than produce sharp, unmodulated shapes as the hard-edge artists had done, the color field painters poured diluted paint onto unprimed canvas, allowing these pigments to soak into the fabric. It is hard to conceive another painting method that results in such literal flatness. The images created, such as *Bay Side* (FIG. **34-11**) by HELEN FRANKENTHALER (b. 1928), appear spontaneous and almost accidental. These works differ from those of Rothko and Newman in that the emotional component, so integral to their work, is here subordinated to resolving formal problems.

STAINED CANVASES Another artist who pursued color field painting was MORRIS LOUIS (1912–1962). Greenberg, who was interested in Frankenthaler's paintings, took Louis to her studio, and there she introduced him to the staining technique's possibilities. Louis used this method of pouring diluted paint onto the surface of unprimed canvas in several series of paintings. *Saraband* (FIG. **34-12**) is one of the works in Louis's *Veils* series. By holding up the canvas edges and pouring diluted acrylic resin, Louis created billowy, fluid, transparent shapes that run down the length of the canvas. Like Frankenthaler, Louis reduced painting to the concrete fact of the paint-impregnated material. Artists could go no further in their quest to reduce painting to its physical essence.

Minimal Art

Painters were not the only artists interested in Clement Greenberg's ideas. American sculptors also strove to arrive at purity in their medium. While painters worked to emphasize flatness, sculptors, understandably, chose to focus on three-dimensionality as the unique characteristic and inherent limitation of the sculptural idiom. Minimal art, or Minimalism, a predominantly sculptural movement that emerged in the 1960s, was a clear expression of this endeavor. The movement's name reveals its reductive nature; people also have referred to Minimal art as primary structures, or ABC art.

EMPHASIZING OBJECTHOOD Minimalist TONY SMITH (1912–1980) created sculptures such as *Die* (FIG. **34-13**), a simple volumetric construction like other Minimal sculptures. Difficult to describe other than as three-dimensional objects, Minimal artworks often lack identifiable sub-

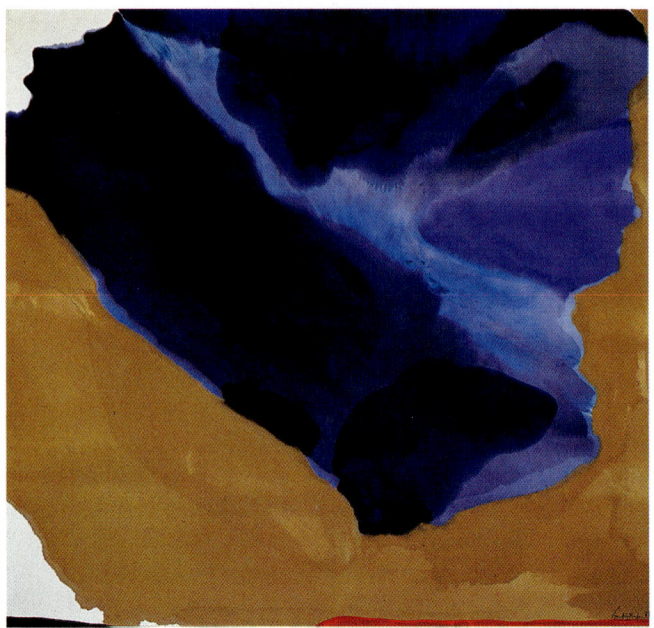

34-11 HELEN FRANKENTHALER, *Bay Side,* 1967. Acrylic on canvas, 6′ 2″ × 6′ 9″. Private Collection, New York.

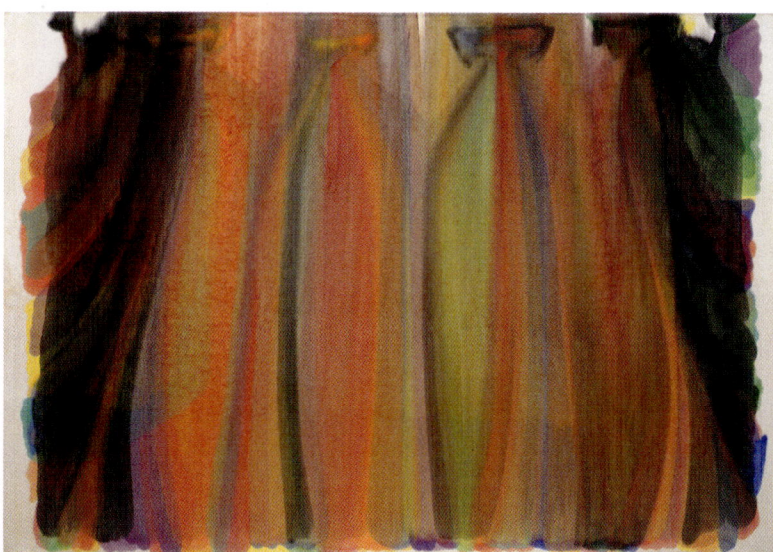

34-12 MORRIS LOUIS, *Saraband,* 1959. Acrylic resin on canvas, 8′ 5 1/8″ × 12′ 5″. Solomon R. Guggenheim Museum, New York.

jects, colors, surface textures, and narrative elements. By rejecting illusionism and reducing sculpture to basic geometric forms, Minimalists emphatically emphasized their art's "objecthood" and concrete tangibility. In so doing, they reduced experience to its most fundamental level, preventing viewers from drawing on assumptions or preconceptions when dealing with the art before them.

AN UNAMBIGUOUS VISUAL VOCABULARY

DONALD JUDD (1928–1994) sought clarity and truth in his art, which led to a spare, universal aesthetic corresponding to Minimalist tenets. Judd's determination to arrive at a visual vocabulary that avoided deception or ambiguity propelled him away from representation and toward precise and simple sculpture. For Judd, a work's power derived from its character as a whole and from the specificity of its materials. *Untitled* (FIG. **34-14**) presents basic geometric boxes constructed of brass and red plexiglass, undisguised by paint or

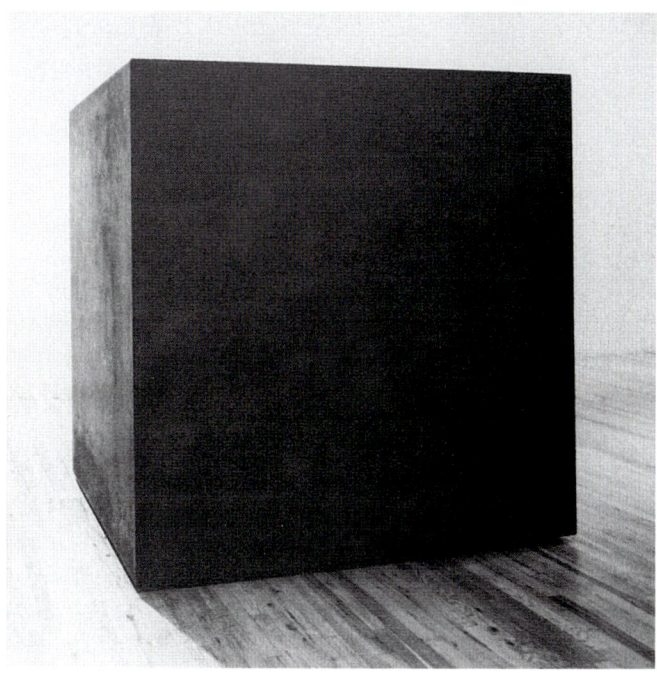

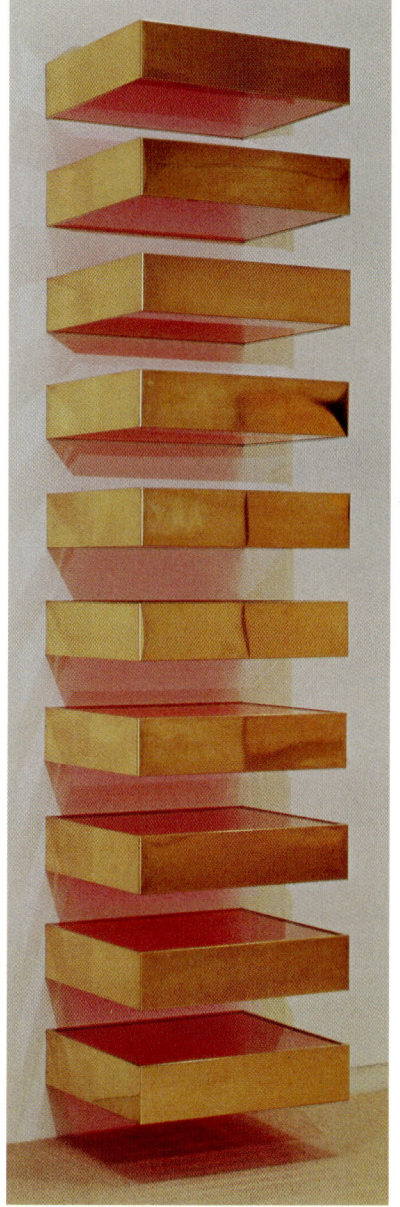

34-14 DONALD JUDD, *Untitled,* 1969. Brass and colored fluorescent plexiglass on steel brackets, ten units, 6 1/8″ × 2′ × 2′ 3″ each, with 6″ intervals. Hirshhorn Museum and Sculpture Garden, Smithsonian Institution, Washington (gift of Joseph H. Hirshhorn, 1972). Art copyright © Donald Judd Estate/Licensed by VAGA, New York, NY.

34-13 TONY SMITH, *Die,* 1962. Steel, 6′ × 6′ × 6′.

34-15   MAYA YING LIN, Vietnam Veterans Memorial, Washington, D.C., 1981–1983. Black granite, each wing 246′ long.

other materials. The artist did not intend the work to be metaphorical or symbolic but a straightforward declaration of sculpture's objecthood. In works such as this, Judd used plexiglass because its translucency allows viewers access to the interior, thereby rendering the sculpture both open and enclosed. This aspect of the design was consistent with his desire to banish ambiguity or falseness. Judd's sculptures, like those of other Minimalists, provide viewers with a unique visual experience—one both immediate and enduring.

Despite the ostensible connections between Minimalism and Greenbergian formalism, Greenberg did not embrace this direction in art. He expressed his concern:

> Minimal Art remains too much a feat of ideation [the mental forma-
> tion of ideas], and not enough anything else. Its idea remains an
> idea, something deduced instead of felt and discovered. The geo-
> metrical and modular simplicity may announce and signify the
> artistically furthest-out, but the fact that the signals are understood
> for what they want to mean betrays them artistically. There is hardly
> any aesthetic surprise in Minimal Art. . . . Aesthetic surprise hangs
> on forever—it is there in Raphael as it is in Pollock—and ideas
> alone cannot achieve it.[12]

HEALING PSYCHIC WOUNDS   A sculpture that does indeed present this enduring impact is the Vietnam Veterans Memorial (FIG. **34-15**), designed by MAYA YING LIN (b. 1960) at age twenty-one in 1981. The austere, simple memorial, a V-shaped wall constructed of polished black granite panels, begins at ground level at each end and gradually rises to a height of ten feet at the center of the V. The names of the Vietnam War's fifty-seven thousand nine hundred thirty-nine casualties (and those still missing) incised on the wall, in the order of their deaths, contribute to the work's dramatic effect. Also, Lin set the wall into the landscape, creating a feeling of descent as visitors walk along the wall toward the center.

When Lin designed this pristinely simple monument, she gave a great deal of thought to the purpose of war memorials. She concluded that a memorial "should be honest about the reality of war and be for the people who gave their lives." She decided that she "didn't want a static object that people would just look at, but something they could relate to as on a journey, or passage, that would bring each to his own conclusions. . . . I wanted to work with the land and not dominate it. I had an impulse to cut open the earth . . . an initial violence that in time would heal. The grass would grow back, but the cut would remain . . ."[13] In light of the tragedy of the war, this unpretentious memorial's allusion to a wound and long-

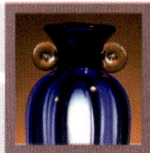

The Power of Minimalism
Maya Lin's Vietnam Veterans Memorial

Although Minimal art first seemed to many to operate only in the realm of the formal, the immediacy and physical presence of Minimalist artworks often endows the works with an enduring resonance. Maya Lin's design for the Vietnam Veterans Memorial (FIG. 34-15) is, like other Minimalist sculptures, a simple geometric form. Yet the controversy engendered when her design was first publicized and the emotional public response to the completed memorial demonstrate how some Minimalist artworks can move beyond concrete objecthood. The monument, with its serene simplicity, actively engages viewers in a psychological dialogue, rather than standing mute. This dialogue gives viewers the opportunity to explore their feelings about the Vietnam War and arrive at some sense of closure.

The history of the Vietnam Veterans Memorial provides dramatic testimony to this monument's power. In 1981, a jury of architects, sculptors, and landscape architects selected Lin's design in a blind competition for a memorial to be placed in Constitution Gardens in Washington, D.C. Conceivably, the jury not only found her design compelling but also thought its unabashed simplicity would be the least likely to provoke controversy. When the selection was made public, however, heated debate ensued. Because of the stark contrast between the monumental, vertically oriented white memorials (the Washington Monument and the Lincoln Memorial bracketing the Vietnam Veterans Memorial) and the wall, some people saw Lin's design as criticizing the Vietnam War and, by extension, the efforts of those who fought in the war. Some of these critics perceived the wall's insertion into the earth as an admission of guilt about U.S. participation in the war. The wall's color came under attack as well; one veteran charged that black is "the universal color of shame, sorrow and degradation in all races, all societies worldwide."[1]

Due to the vocal opposition, a compromise was necessary to ensure the memorial's completion. The Commission of Fine Arts, the federal group overseeing such projects, commissioned an additional memorial from artist Frederick Hart in 1983. This larger-than-life-sized realistic bronze sculpture of three soldiers, armed and in uniform, was eventually installed approximately one hundred twenty feet from the wall. More recently, a group of nurses, organized as the Vietnam Women's Memorial Project, got approval for a sculpture honoring women's service in the Vietnam War. The seven-foot-tall bronze statue by Glenna Goodacre depicts three female figures, one cradling a wounded soldier in her arms. Unveiled in 1993, the work was placed about three hundred feet south of the wall.

Despite this controversy and compromise, the wall generates dramatic responses. Commonly, visitors react very emotionally, even those who know none of the soldiers named on the monument. Many visitors leave mementos at the foot of the wall in memory of loved ones they lost in the Vietnam War or make rubbings from the incised names. It can be argued that much of this memorial's power derives from its Minimalist simplicity. Like Minimalist sculpture, it does not dictate response and therefore successfully encourages personal exploration. The polished granite surface also prompts such individual soul-searching—viewers see themselves reflected among the names.

Given the contentiousness and divided sentiments about the Vietnam War, any memorial to that conflict surely would encounter opposition. Maya Lin's wall, however, has illustrated the ability of art—even Minimalist sculpture—to elicit emotions in a diverse population and to help heal a nation.

[1] Elizabeth Hess, "A Tale of Two Memorials," *Art in America,* vol. 71, no. 4 (April 1983), 122.

---

lasting scar contributes to its communicative ability (see "The Power of Minimalism: Maya Lin's Vietnam Veterans Memorial," above).

Diverse Sculptural Directions

COMPELLING, NONTRADITIONAL MATERIALS Although Minimalism was a dominant sculptural trend in the 1960s, many sculptors pursued other styles. EVA HESSE (1936–1970), a Minimalist in the early part of her career, moved away from the severity characterizing much of Minimal art. She created sculptures that, although spare and simple, have a compelling presence. Using nontraditional sculptural materials such as fiberglass, cord, and latex, Hesse produced sculptures whose pure Minimalist forms appear to crumble, sag, and warp under the pressures of atmospheric force and gravity. Born Jewish in Hitler's Germany, the young Hesse was hidden by a Christian family when her parents and elder sister had to flee the Nazis. She was not reunited with them until the early 1940s, just before her parents divorced. Those extraordinary circumstances helped give her a lasting sense that the central conditions of modern life are strangeness and absurdity. Struggling to express these qualities in her art, she created informal sculptural arrangements with units often hung from the ceiling, leaned against the walls, or spilled out along the floor. She said she wanted her pieces to be "non art, non connotative, non anthropomorphic, non geometric, non nothing, everything, but of another kind, vision, sort."[14]

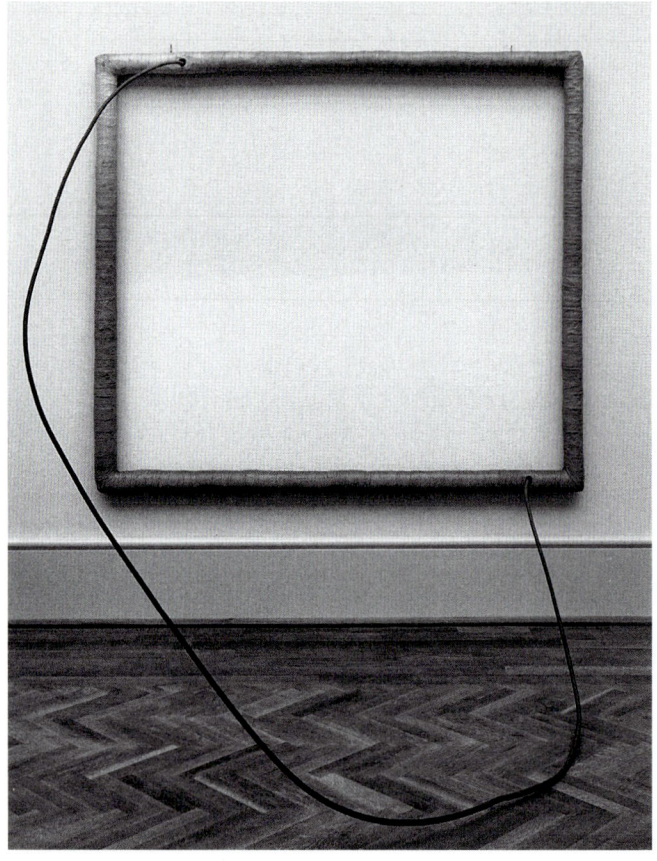

34-16 EVA HESSE, *Hang-Up,* 1965–1966. Acrylic on cloth over wood and steel, 6′ × 7′ × 6′ 6″. Art Institute of Chicago, Chicago (gift of Arthur Keating and Mr. and Mrs. Edward Morris by exchange).

Amazingly, *Hang-Up* (FIG. **34-16**) fulfills these requirements. The piece looks like a carefully made empty frame sprouting a strange feeler that extends into the room and doubles back to the frame. Hesse wrote that in this work, for the first time, her "idea of absurdity or extreme feeling came

through."[15] In her words, "[*Hang-Up*] has a kind of depth I don't always achieve and that is the kind of depth or soul or absurdity of life or meaning or feeling or intellect that I want to get."[16] The sculpture possesses a disquieting and touching presence, suggesting the fragility and grandeur of life amid the pressures of the modern age. Hesse was herself a touching and fragile presence in the art world; she died of a brain tumor at the young age of thirty-four.

MONUMENTAL METAL SCULPTURES American sculptor DAVID SMITH (1906–1965) learned to weld in an automobile plant in 1925. He later applied to his art the technical expertise in handling metals he gained from that experience. In addition, working in large scale at the factories helped him visualize the possibilities for monumental metal sculpture. Smith created the series for which he is best known, his *Cubi* series, in the early 1960s. These works, including the examples *Cubi XVIII* and Cubi *XVII* (FIG. **34-17**), consist of simple geometric forms—cubes, cylinders, and rectangular bars. Made of stainless steel, piled haphazardly on top of one another, and then welded together, these forms create imposing large-scale sculptures. Although the metal elements of these *Cubi* sculptures reproduce the basic Minimalist vocabulary, Smith composed the works in a way that suggests human characteristics. To this end, his sculptures depart from Minimalism. In addition, Smith broke with the Minimalist program by burnishing the metal with steel wool, producing swirling random-looking gestural patterns that draw attention to the two-dimensionality of the sculptural surface. This treatment, which captures the light hitting the sculpture, activates the surface and imparts a texture to these sculptures.

MULTIPLICITY OF MEANING Russian-born LOUISE NEVELSON (1899–1988) created sculpture that combines a sense of the architectural fragment with the power of Dada and Surrealist found objects to express her personal sense of

34-17 DAVID SMITH, *Cubi XVIII* and *Cubi XVII,* 1963–1964. Polished stainless steel; *Cubi XVIII,* 9′ 7¾″ high; *Cubi XVII,* 8′ 11¾″ high × 5′ 4⅜″ × 3′ 2⅛″. Museum of Fine Arts, Boston, Massachusetts (gift of Susan W. and Stephen D. Paine), and Dallas Museum of Art, Dallas (The Eugene and Margaret McDermott Fund). Copyright © Estate of David Smith/Licensed by VAGA, New York, NY.

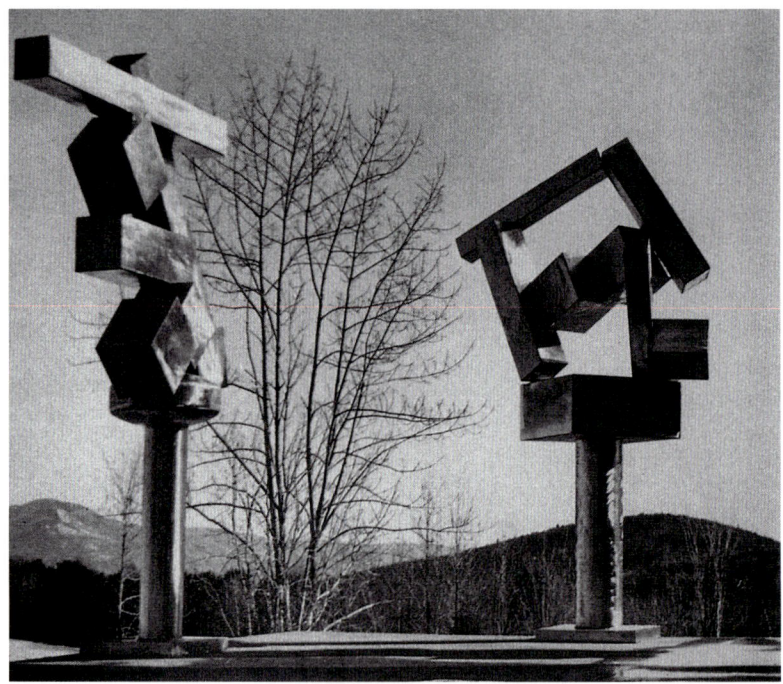

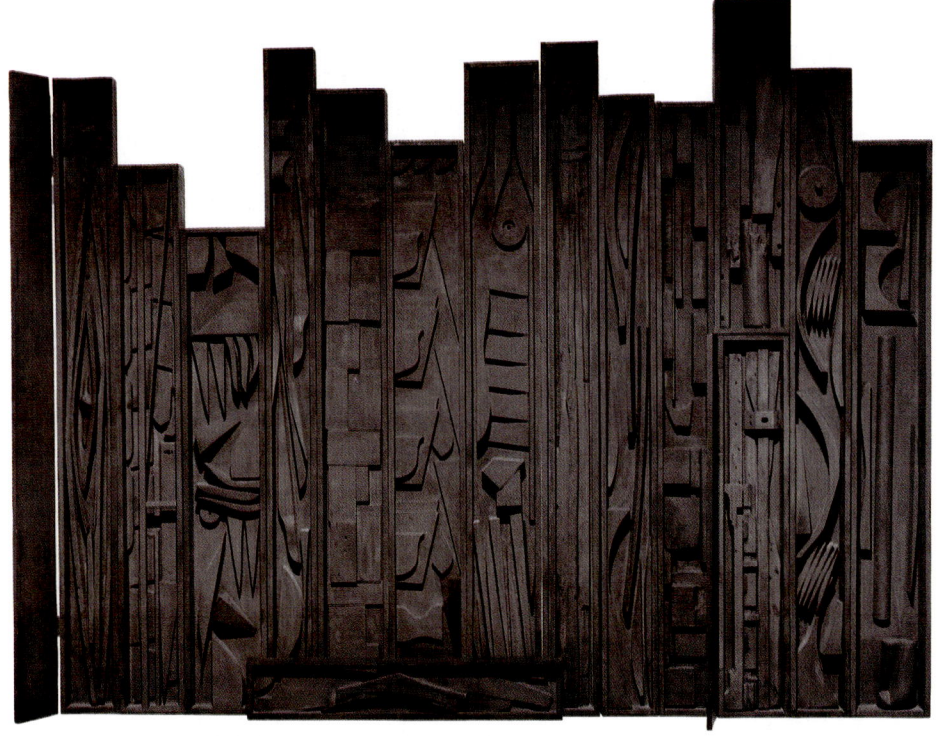

34-18 LOUISE NEVELSON, *Tropical Garden II*, 1957–1959. Wood painted black, 5′ 11½″ × 10′ 11¾″ × 1′. Musée National d'Art Moderne, Centre Georges Pompidou, Paris.

life's underlying significance. Multiplicity of meaning was important to Nevelson. She sought ". . . the in-between place. . . . The dawns and the dusks"[17]—the transitional realm between one state of being and another. By the late 1950s, she was assembling sculptures of found wooden objects and forms, enclosing small sculptural compositions in boxes of varied sizes, and joining the boxes to one another to form "walls," which she then painted in a single hue—usually black, white, or gold.

The monochromatic color scheme unifies the diverse parts of pieces such as *Tropical Garden II* (FIG. **34-18**) and creates a mysterious field of shapes and shadows. The structures suggest magical environments resembling the treasured secret hideaways dimly remembered from childhood. Yet, the boxy frames and the precision of the manufactured

found objects create a rough geometric structure that the eye roams over freely, lingering on some details. The parts of a Nevelson sculpture and their interrelation recall the *Merz* constructions of Kurt Schwitters (see FIG. 33-27). The effect is also rather like viewing an apartment building's side wall from a moving elevated train or like looking down on a city from the air.

SENSUOUS ORGANIC FORMS In contrast to the architectural nature of Nevelson's work, French-American artist LOUISE BOURGEOIS (b. 1911) often presents viewers with sensuous organic forms recalling the evocative biomorphic Surrealist forms of Joan Miró (see FIG. 33-50). She once described her sculptural subjects as "groups of objects relating to each other . . . the drama of one among many."[18] *Cumul I* (FIG. **34-19**)

34-19 LOUISE BOURGEOIS, *Cumul I*, 1969. Marble, 1′ 10⅜″ × 4′ 2″ × 4′. Musée National d'Art Moderne, Centre Georges Pompidou, Paris. Copyright © Louise Bourgeois/Licensed by VAGA, New York, NY.

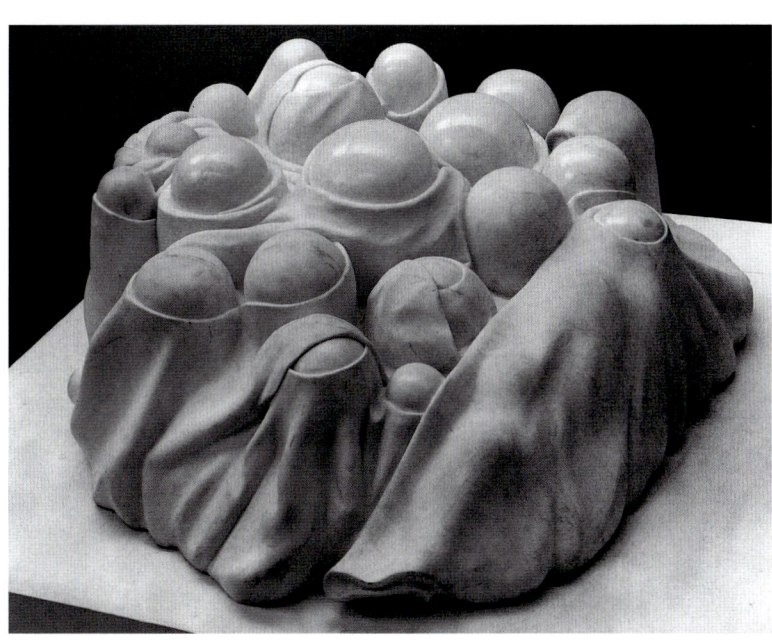

is a collection of roundheaded units huddled, with their heads protruding, within a collective cloak dotted with holes. The units differ in size, and their position within the group lends a distinctive personality to each. Although the shapes remain abstract, they refer strongly to human figures. Bourgeois uses a wide variety of materials in her works, including wood, plaster, latex, and plastics, in addition to alabaster, marble, and bronze. She exploits each material's qualities to suit the expressiveness of the piece.

In *Cumul I,* the marble's high gloss next to its matte finish increases the sensuous distinction between the group of swelling forms and the soft folds swaddling them. Like Barbara Hepworth (see FIG. 33-71), Bourgeois connects her sculpture with the body's multiple relationships to landscape: "[My pieces] are anthropomorphic and they are landscape also, since our body could be considered from a topographical point of view, as a land with mounds and valleys and caves and holes."[19] However, Bourgeois's sculptures are more personal and more openly sexual than those of Hepworth. *Cumul I* represents perfectly the allusions Bourgeois seeks: "There has always been sexual suggestiveness in my work. Sometimes I am totally concerned with female shapes—characters of breasts like clouds—but often I merge the activity—phallic breasts, male and female, active and passive."[20]

Performance Art

In the interest of challenging artistic convention, avant-garde artists in the 1960s sought innovative forms of expression. As discussed earlier, artists such as the Post-Painterly Abstractionists and the Minimalists explored the implications of two- and three-dimensionality in keeping with the modernist critique of artistic principles. Other artists produced Happenings and along with the group of Fluxus artists, both discussed later, developed the fourth dimension of time as an integral element of their artwork. These brief, temporary works eventually were categorized under the broad term Performance Art. In such work, movements, gestures, and sounds of persons communicating with an audience, whose members may or may not participate in the event, replace physical objects. Generally, the only evidence remaining after these events is the documentary photographs taken at the time. Further, the informal and spontaneous nature of much of such work using the human body as primary material pushed art outside the confines of the mainstream art institutions (for example, museums and galleries). Actions, events, and Happenings in large measure derived from the spirit characterizing Dada and Surrealist work and anticipated the rebellion and youthful exuberance of the 1960s. Initially, it appeared these artworks might serve as antidotes to the preciosity of most art objects and challenge art's function as a commodity. In the later 1960s, however, museums commissioned performances with increasing frequency, thereby neutralizing much of this art form's subversive edge.

A COMPOSER'S INFLUENCE   Many of the artists instrumental to developing Performance art were influenced by the charismatic teacher and composer JOHN CAGE (1912–1992). Cage encouraged his students at both the New School for Social Research in New York and Black Mountain College in North Carolina to link their art directly with life. He brought to music composition his interests in the thoughts of Duchamp and in Eastern philosophy. In his own work, Cage used methods such as chance to avoid the closed structures marking traditional music and, in his view, separating it from the unpredictable and multilayered qualities of daily existence. For example, the score for one of Cage's piano compositions instructs the performer to appear, sit down at the piano, raise the keyboard cover to mark the beginning of the piece, remain motionless at the instrument for four minutes and thirty-three seconds, and then close the keyboard cover, rise, and bow to signal the end of the work. The "music" would be the unplanned sounds and noises (such as coughs, whispers) emanating from the audience during the "performance."

HAPPENINGS AND FLUXUS   One of Cage's students in the 1950s was American artist ALLAN KAPROW (b. 1927). Extremely knowledgeable about art history, Kaprow was inspired by his study of music composition with Cage. Kaprow was equally committed to the intersection of art and life, and this, along with his belief that Jackson Pollock's actions when producing a painting were more important than the finished painting, led Kaprow to develop a type of event known as a Happening. He described a Happening as

> an assemblage of events performed or perceived in more than one time and place. Its material environments may be constructed, taken over directly from what is available, or altered slightly; just as its activities may be invented or commonplace. A Happening, unlike a stage play, may occur at a supermarket, driving along a highway, under a pile of rags, and in a friend's kitchen, either at once or sequentially. If sequentially, time may extend to more than a year. The Happening is performed according to plan but without rehearsal, audience or repetition. It is art but seems closer to life.[21]

Happenings were largely participatory. One Happening consisted of a constructed setting with partitions on which viewers wrote phrases, while another involved spectators walking on a pile of tires.

Other Cage students interested in the composer's search to find aesthetic potential in the nontraditional and commonplace eventually formed the Fluxus group. Eventually expanding to include European and Japanese artists, this group's performances were more theatrical than Happenings. Many of these Fluxus performances followed a compositional "score" for events and focused on single actions, such as turning a light on and off or watching falling snow—what Fluxus artist La Monte Young (b. 1935) called "the theater of the single event."[22] The artists usually executed these events on a stage separating the performers from the audience but without costumes or added decor.

PERFORMANCE AS RITUAL   German artist JOSEPH BEUYS (1921–1986) was strongly influenced by the leftist politics of the Fluxus group in the early 1960s. Drawing on Happenings and Fluxus, Beuys created actions aimed at illuminating the condition of modern humanity. He wanted to make a new kind of sculptural object that would include "Thinking Forms: how we mould our thoughts or Spoken Forms: how we shape our thoughts into words or Social

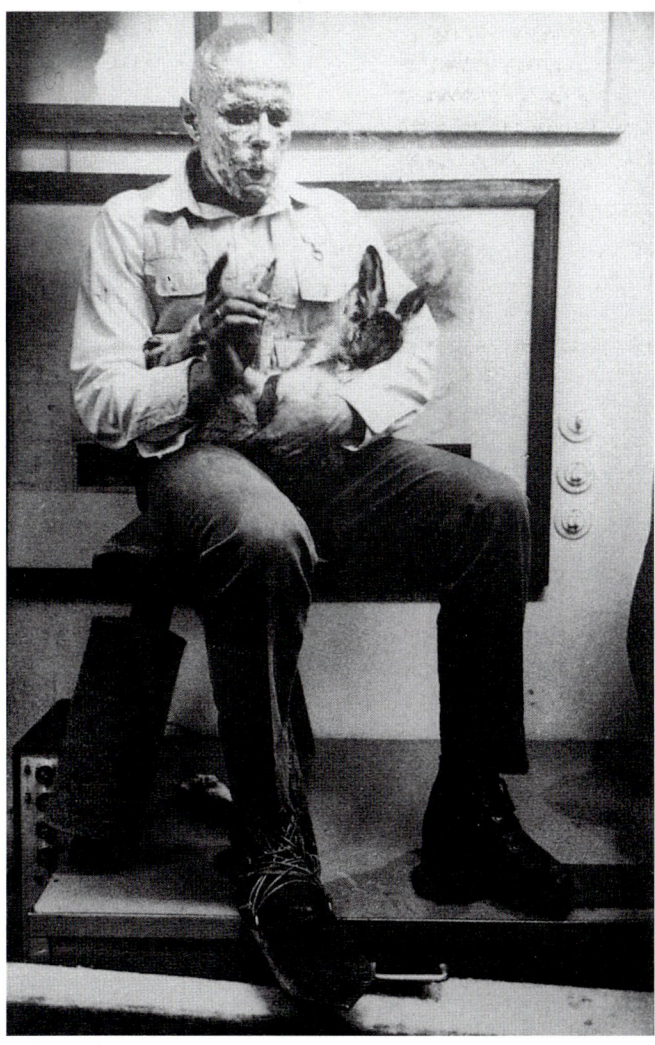

34-20   JOSEPH BEUYS, *How to Explain Pictures to a Dead Hare,* 1965. Photograph of Performance art. Schmela Gallery, Düsseldorf.

Sculpture: how we mould and shape the world in which we live."[23]

Beuys's commitment to artworks stimulating thought about art and life was partially due to his experiences during the war. While serving as a pilot, he was shot down over the Crimea, and claimed that nomadic Tatars nursed him back to health by swaddling his body in fat and felt to warm him. Fat and felt thus symbolized healing and regeneration to the artist, and he incorporated these materials into many of his sculptures and actions, such as *How to Explain Pictures to a Dead Hare* (FIG. **34-20**). This one-person event consisted of stylized actions evoking a sense of mystery and sacred ritual. Beuys appeared in a room hung with his drawings, cradling a dead hare he spoke to softly. Beuys coated his head with honey covered with gold leaf, creating a shimmering mask. In this manner, he took on the role of the shaman, an individual with special spiritual powers. As a shaman, Beuys believed he was acting to help revolutionize human thought so that each human being could become a truly free and creative person.

DESTRUCTION AS CREATION   The notion of destruction as an act of creation surfaces in a number of kinetic artworks, most notably in the sculpture of JEAN TINGUELY

(1925–1991). Trained as a painter in his native Switzerland, Tinguely's interest gravitated to motion sculpture. In the 1950s, he made a series of "metamatic" machines, motor-driven devices that produced instant abstract paintings. He programmed these metamatics electronically to act with an antimechanical unpredictability when viewers inserted felt-tipped marking pens into a pincer and pressed a button to initiate the pen's motion across a small sheet of paper clipped to an "easel." Viewers could use different colored markers in succession and could stop and start the device to achieve some degree of control over the final image. These operations created a series of small works resembling Abstract Expressionist paintings.

In 1960, Tinguely expanded the scale of his work with a kinetic piece designed to "perform" and then destroy itself in a large courtyard area at the Museum of Modern Art in New York City. He created *Homage to New York* (FIG. **34-21**) with the aid of engineer Billy Klüver, who helped him scrounge wheels and other moving objects from a dump near Manhattan. The completed structure, painted white for visibility against the dark night sky, included a player piano modified into a metamatic painting machine, a weather balloon that inflated during the performance, vials of colored smoke, and a host of gears, pulleys, wheels, and other found machine parts.

This work was premiered (and destroyed) on March 17, 1960, in the sculpture garden of the Museum of Modern Art, with New York Governor Nelson Rockefeller, an array of

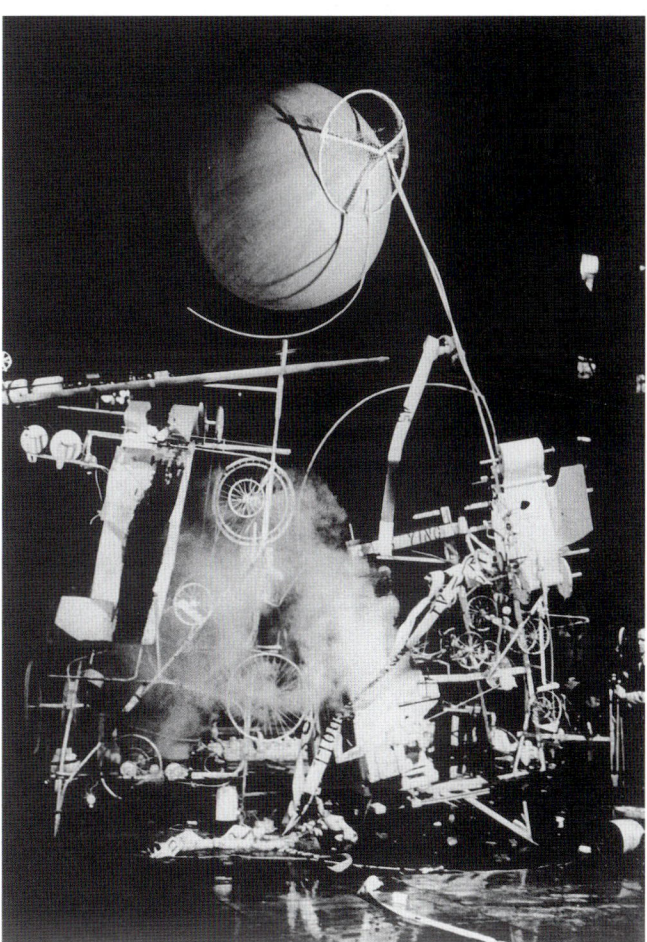

34-21   JEAN TINGUELY, *Homage to New York,* 1960, just prior to its self-destruction in the garden of the Museum of Modern Art, New York.

distinguished guests, and three television crews attending. Once the machine was turned on, smoke poured from its interior and the piano caught fire. Various parts of the machine broke off and rambled away, while one of the metamatics tried but failed to produce an abstract painting. Finally, Tinguely summoned a firefighter to extinguish the blaze and ensure the demise of *Homage to New York* with his axe. Like the artist's other kinetic sculptures, *Homage to New York* shared something of Duchamp's satiric Dadaist spirit (see FIG. 33-25) and the droll import of Klee's *Twittering Machine* (see FIG. 33-51). But Tinguely deliberately made the wacky behavior of *Homage to New York* more playful and more endearing. Having been given a "freedom" of eccentric behavior unprecedented in the mechanical world, Tinguely's creations often seem to behave with the whimsical individuality of human actors.

People first used the terms *Happening, action,* and *body art* to describe various kinds of artistic endeavors involving the body as aesthetic material. In the mid-1970s, people widely began to use the generic term *Performance art* to describe this broad range of creative activity. Extreme examples of Performance art involved artists who created various performance pieces centered on risk-taking activities with guns or broken glass. Such work dramatically challenged accepted definitions of art.

Conceptual Art

The relentless challenges to artistic convention fundamental to the historical avant-garde reached a logical conclusion with Conceptual art in the late 1960s. Conceptual artists asserted that the "artfulness" of art lay in the artist's idea, rather than in its final expression. Indeed, some Conceptual artists eliminated the object altogether. In addition, Conceptual artists rethought aesthetic issues, which long have formed the foundation of art. These artists regarded the idea, or concept, as the primary element of artistic production.

WHAT CONSTITUTES "CHAIRNESS?"   American artist JOSEPH KOSUTH (b. 1945) was a major proponent of Conceptual art. His work operates at the intersection of language and vision, dealing with the relationship between the abstract and the concrete. In a broader sense, his art explores the ways in which aesthetic meaning is generated. For example, *One and Three Chairs* (FIG. **34-22**), consists of an actual chair flanked by a full-scale photograph of the chair and a photostat of a dictionary definition of the word *chair*. Kosuth asked viewers to ponder the notion of what constitutes "chairness." He explained, "It meant you could have an art work which was that *idea* of an art work, and its formal components weren't important. I felt I had found a way to make art without formal components being confused for an expressionist composition. The expression was in the idea, not the form—the forms were only a device in the service of the idea."[24] Kosuth explored these concepts further in a series of works titled *Art as Idea as Idea*. He elaborated:

> Like every one else I inherited the idea of art as a set of *formal* problems. So when I began to re-think my ideas of art, I had to re-think that thinking process, and it begins with the making process. . . . 'Art as Idea *as Idea*' [was] intended to suggest that the real

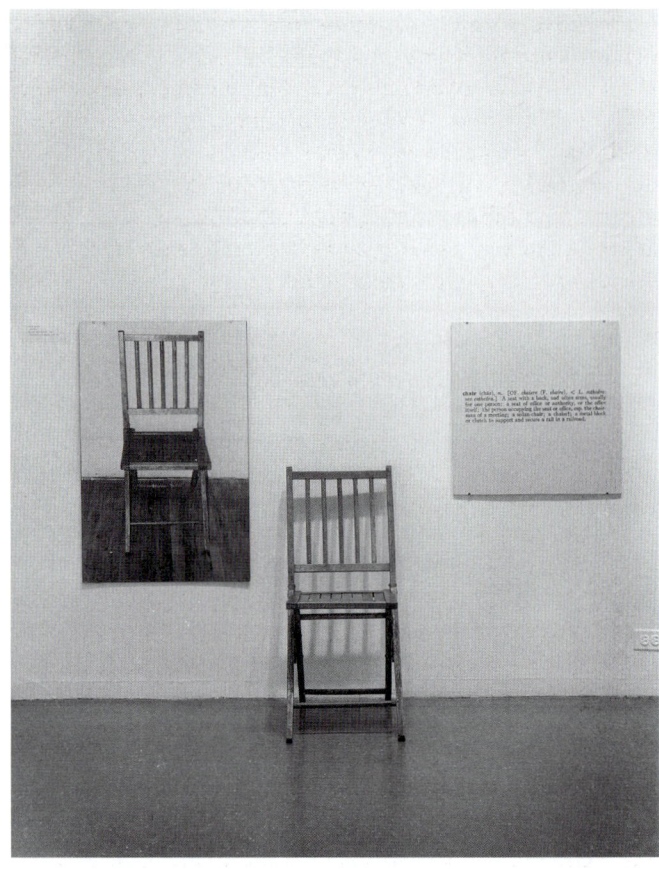

34-22   JOSEPH KOSUTH, *One and Three Chairs,* 1965. Wooden folding chair, photographic copy of a chair, and photographic enlargement of a dictionary definition of a chair; chair, $2' 8\frac{3}{8}'' \times 1' 2\frac{7}{8}'' \times 1' 8\frac{7}{8}''$; photo panel, $3' \times 2'\frac{1}{8}''$; text panel, $2' \times 2'\frac{1}{8}''$. Museum of Modern Art, New York (Larry Aldrich Foundation Fund).

creative process, and the radical shift, was in changing the idea of art itself. In other words, my idea of doing that was the real creative content.[25]

Other Conceptual artists pursued this idea that "the idea itself, even if not made visual, is as much a work of art as a product"[26] by creating works involving such invisible materials as inert gases, radioactive isotopes, or radio waves. In each case, viewers must base their understanding of the artwork on what they know about the properties of these materials, rather than on any visible empirical data, and depend on the artist's linguistic description of the work. In Conceptual artists' intellectual and aesthetic investigation of art's structure, they challenged the very foundations of art, pushing art's boundaries to a point where no concrete definition of *art* is possible.

ALTERNATIVES TO MODERNIST FORMALISM

The avant-garde provided a major directional impetus for art production in the postwar years. As seen in the work of the Abstract Expressionists, Post-Painterly Abstractionists, and Minimalists, artists most frequently expressed this interest in modernist experimental art in the vocabulary of resolute abstraction. Other artists, however, felt that the insular and introspective attitude of avant-garde artists had resulted in public alienation. These artists were committed to the communicative power of art and to reaching a wide audience with their art. This is not to suggest that they created reactionary or academic work; indeed, people easily can find avant-garde aspects in their art. However, these artists (for example, Pop artists, Superrealists, and Environmental artists) were much less committed to the single-minded focus on formal issues characteristic of the modernist mindset.

The Development of Pop Art

The prevalence of abstraction and the formal experimentation in much of postwar art had alienated the public. Pop art reintroduced all of the artistic devices—signs, symbols, metaphors, allusions, illusions, and figurative imagery—traditionally used to convey meaning in art that recent avant-garde artists, in search of purity, had purged from their abstract and often reductive works. Pop artists not only embraced representation but also produced an art resolutely grounded in consumer culture, the mass media, and popular culture, thereby making it much more accessible and understandable to the average person. Indeed, the name Pop art (credited to the British art critic Lawrence Alloway, although he is unsure of the term's initial usage) is short for *popular art* and referred to the popular mass culture and familiar imagery of the contemporary urban environment. This was an art form firmly entrenched in the sensibilities and visual language of a late-twentieth-century mass audience.

BRITISH POP: THE INDEPENDENT GROUP

Pop art's roots can be traced to a group of young British artists, architects, and writers who formed the Independent Group at the Institute of Contemporary Art in London in the early 1950s. This group's members sought to initiate fresh thinking in art, in part by sharing their fascination with the aesthetics and content of such facets of popular culture as advertising, comic books, and movies.

Discussions at the Independent Group in London probed the role and meaning of symbols from mass culture and the advertising media. In 1956, a group member, RICHARD HAMILTON (b. 1922), made a small collage, *Just What Is It That Makes Today's Homes So Different, So Appealing?* (FIG. **34-23**), that characterized many of the attitudes of British Pop art. Trained as an engineering draftsman, exhibition designer, and painter, Hamilton was very interested in the way advertising shapes public attitudes. Long intrigued by Duchamp's ideas, Hamilton consistently combined elements of popular art and fine art, seeing both as belonging to the whole world of visual communication. The Pop artist created *Just What Is It* for the poster and catalog of one section of an exhibition titled *This Is Tomorrow*—an environment/installation filled with images from Hollywood cinema, science fiction, the mass media, and one reproduction of a van Gogh painting (to represent popular fine artworks).

The fantasy interior in Hamilton's collage reflects the values of modern consumer culture through figures and objects cut from glossy magazines. *Just What Is It* reconstructs the found images into a new whole. The artist included references to the mass media (such as the television, theater marquee

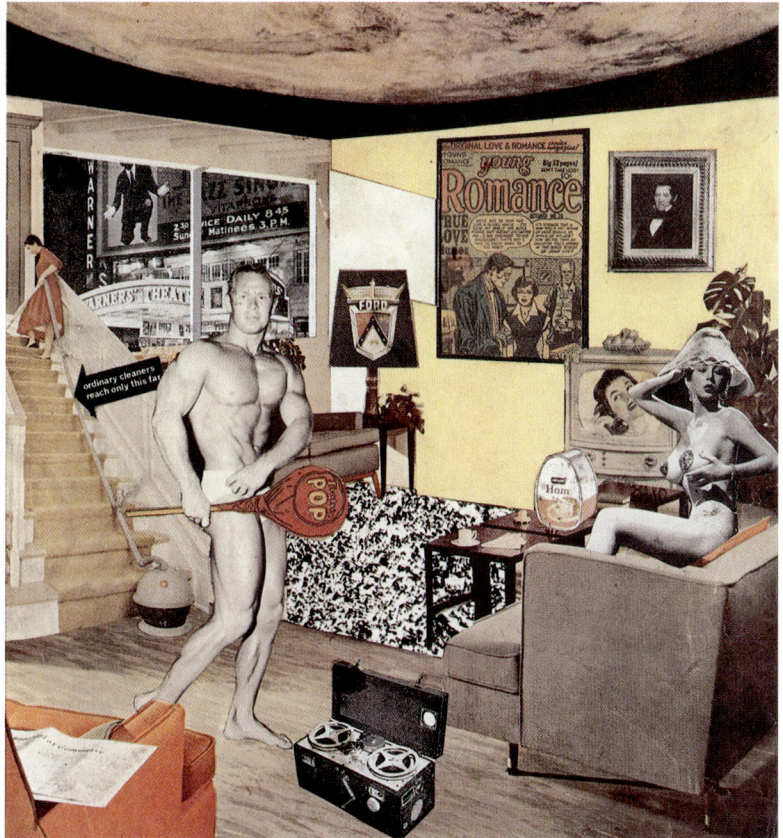

34-23 RICHARD HAMILTON, *Just What Is It That Makes Today's Homes So Different, So Appealing?*, 1956. Collage, $10\frac{1}{4}'' \times 9\frac{3}{4}''$. Kunsthalle Tübingen, Germany.

outside the window, and newspaper), to advertising (such as for Hoover vacuums, Ford cars, Armour hams, and Tootsie Pops), and to popular culture (such as the girlie magazine, Charles Atlas, and romance comic books). Scholars have written much about the possible deep meaning of this piece, and few would deny the work's sardonic effect, whether or not the artist intended to make a pointed comment. Such artworks stimulated viewers' wide-ranging speculation about society's values, and this kind of intellectual toying with mass-media meaning and imagery typified British and European Pop art.

American Pop Art and Consumer Culture

Although Pop originated in England, the movement found its greatest articulation and success in the United States, in large part because the more fully matured consumer culture provided a fertile environment in which the movement flourished through the 1960s. Indeed, Independent Group members claimed their inspiration came from Hollywood, Detroit, and Madison Avenue, New York, paying homage to America's predominance in the realms of mass media, mass production, and advertising.

Two artists pivotal to the early development of American Pop were Jasper Johns and Robert Rauschenberg. Both artists had produced earlier Abstract Expressionist work, and their forays into Pop retain the brushiness of gestural abstraction. Yet both of them introduced elements from popular culture into their art. These references add to their work's power and immediacy.

THINGS SEEN BUT NOT LOOKED AT   In his early work, JASPER JOHNS (b. 1930) was particularly interested in drawing viewers' attention to common objects in the world—what he called things "seen but not looked at."[27] To this end, he did several series of paintings of targets, flags, numbers, and alphabets. For example, *Flag* (FIG. **34-24**) is an object people view frequently but rarely scrutinize. The work's surface is highly textured due to Johns's use of encaustic, an ancient method of painting with liquid wax and dissolved pigment. First, the artist embedded a collage of newspaper scraps or photographs in wax. He then painted over them with the encaustic. Because the wax hardened quickly, Johns could work rapidly, and the translucency of the wax allows viewers to see the layered painting process.

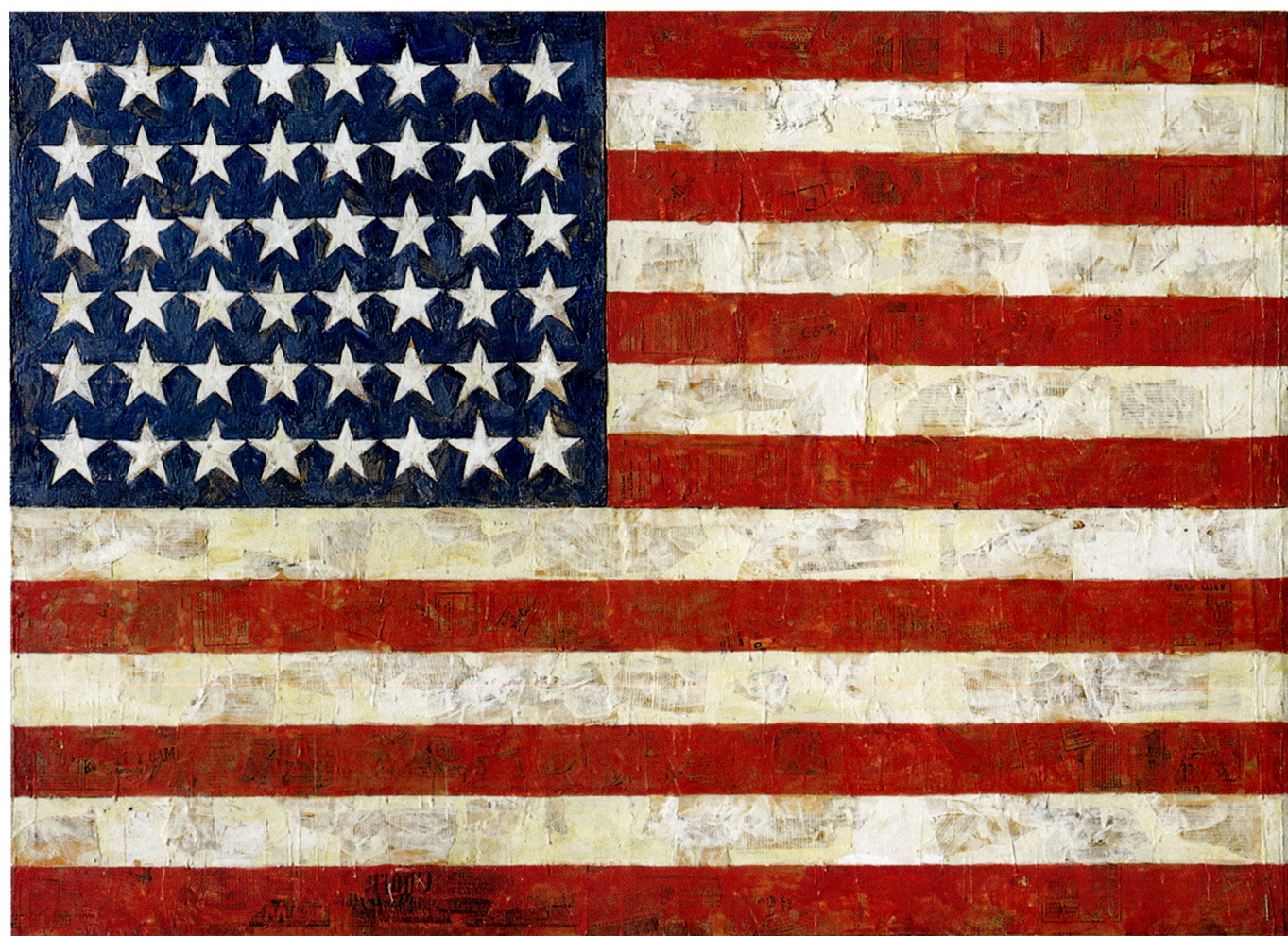

34-24 JASPER JOHNS, *Flag*, 1954–1955, dated on reverse 1954. Encaustic, oil, and collage on fabric mounted on plywood, 3′ 6¼″ × 5′ ⅝″. Museum of Modern Art, New York (gift of Philip Johnson in honor of Alfred H. Barr, Jr.). Copyright © Jasper Johns/Licensed by VAGA, New York, NY.

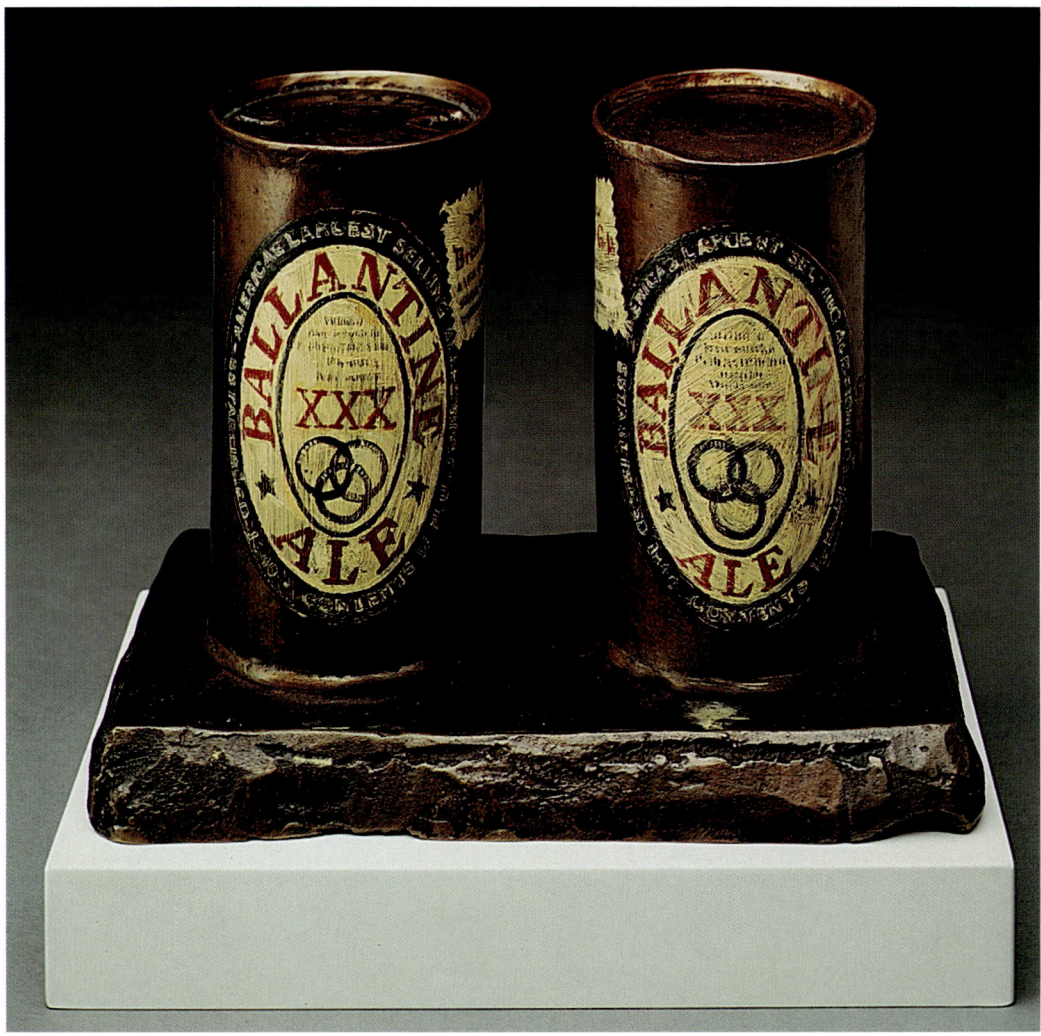

34-25 JASPER JOHNS, *Painted Bronze,* 1960. Cast bronze, paint, approx. $5\frac{1}{2}''$ high, $8''$ wide, $4\frac{3}{4}''$ deep. Museum Ludwig, Cologne. Copyright © Jasper Johns/Licensed by VAGA, New York, NY.

BEVERAGES OF BRONZE Johns's *Painted Bronze* (FIG. 34-25) also presents reassuringly familiar objects. However, by reproducing the Ballantine Ale cans in cast bronze, the artist rendered them functionless and elevated these common objects to the realm of high art, in a manner similar to Duchamp's *Fountain* (see FIG. 33-25). Because of such parallels, art scene observers in the 1960s often referred to Pop art as Neo-Dada. In *Painted Bronze,* Johns reconstituted what is customarily discarded as junk and resituated it as something worthy of the attention rarely given it. The artist solemnly exalted the banal by modeling the ale cans in plaster and then casting them in bronze, faithfully painting the commercial labels, and firmly mounting the cans upon a base. Like bronze baby shoes, the disposable container is monumentalized as a profoundly symbolic artifact of modern consumer culture.

The inspiration for *Painted Bronze* further reinforced the intersection between Pop art and consumer culture. According to Johns, he created the sculpture in response to a comment by Willem de Kooning about Johns's New York art dealer, Leo Castelli. Johns said, "Somebody told me that Bill de Kooning said that you could give that son-of-a-bitch two beer cans and he could sell them. I thought, what a wonderful idea for a sculpture."[28] The concept of art as commodity, like the ale cans themselves, is thus an integral part of this artwork. Appropriately enough, Castelli did sell the sculpture for $960.

"COMBINING" PAINTING AND SCULPTURE Johns's friend ROBERT RAUSCHENBERG (b. 1925) began using mass-media images in his work in the 1950s. Rauschenberg set out to create works that would be open and indeterminate, and he began by making "combines," which intersperse painted passages with sculptural elements. At times, these works seem to be sculptures with painting incorporated into certain sections; other combines seem to be paintings with three-dimensional objects attached to the surface. In the 1950s, such works contained an array of art reproductions, magazine and newspaper clippings, and passages painted in an Abstract Expressionist style. In the early 1960s, Rauschenberg adopted the commercial medium of silk-screen printing, first in black and white and then in color, and began filling entire canvases with appropriated news images and anonymous

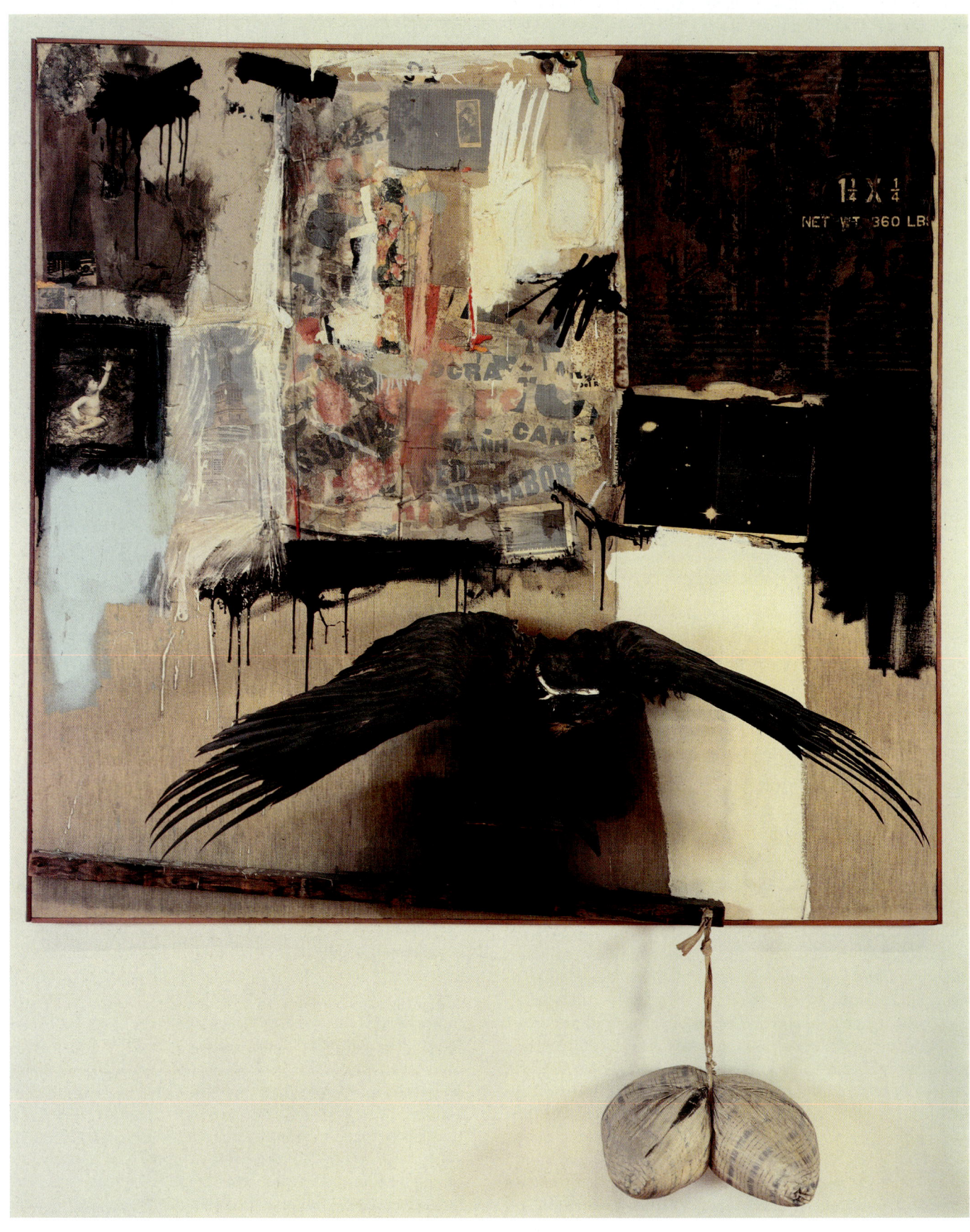

34-26 ROBERT RAUSCHENBERG, *Canyon,* 1959. Oil, pencil, paper, fabric, metal, cardboard box, printed paper, printed reproductions, photograph, wood, paint tube, and mirror on canvas, with oil on bald eagle, string, and pillow, 6′ 9¾″ × 5′ 10″ × 2′. Sonnabend Collection. Copyright © Untitled Press, Inc./Licensed by VAGA, New York.

photographs of city scenes. *Canyon* (FIG. **34-26**) is typical of his combines. Pieces of printed paper and photographs are attached to the canvas. Much of the unevenly painted surface consists of pigment roughly applied in a manner reminiscent of de Kooning's work (FIG. 34-6). A stuffed bald eagle attached to the lower part of the combine spreads its wings as if lifting off in flight toward viewers. Completing the combine, a pillow dangles from a string attached to a wood stick below the eagle. The artist presented the work's components in a jumbled fashion. He tilted or turned some of the images sideways, and each overlays or is invaded by part of another image. The compositional confusion may resemble that in a Dada collage, but the parts of Rauschenberg's combine paintings maintain their individuality more than those in a Schwitters piece (see FIG. 33-27). The various recognizable images and objects appear to be a sequence of visual non sequiturs, and it is virtually impossible to arrive at a consistent reading of a Rauschenberg combine. The eye scans a Rauschenberg canvas much as it might survey the environment on a walk through the city. As John Cage perceptively noted: "There is no more subject in a combine [by Rauschenberg] than there is in a page from a newspaper. Each thing that is there is a subject. It is a situation involving multiplicity."[29]

A "COMIC" FOCUS IN ART   As the Pop movement matured, the images became more concrete and tightly controlled. ROY LICHTENSTEIN (1923–1997) turned his attention to the comic book as a mainstay of American popular culture. In paintings such as *Hopeless* (FIG. **34-27**), Lichtenstein excerpted an image from a comic book, a form of entertainment meant to be read and discarded, and immortalized the image in monumental scale. Aside from that

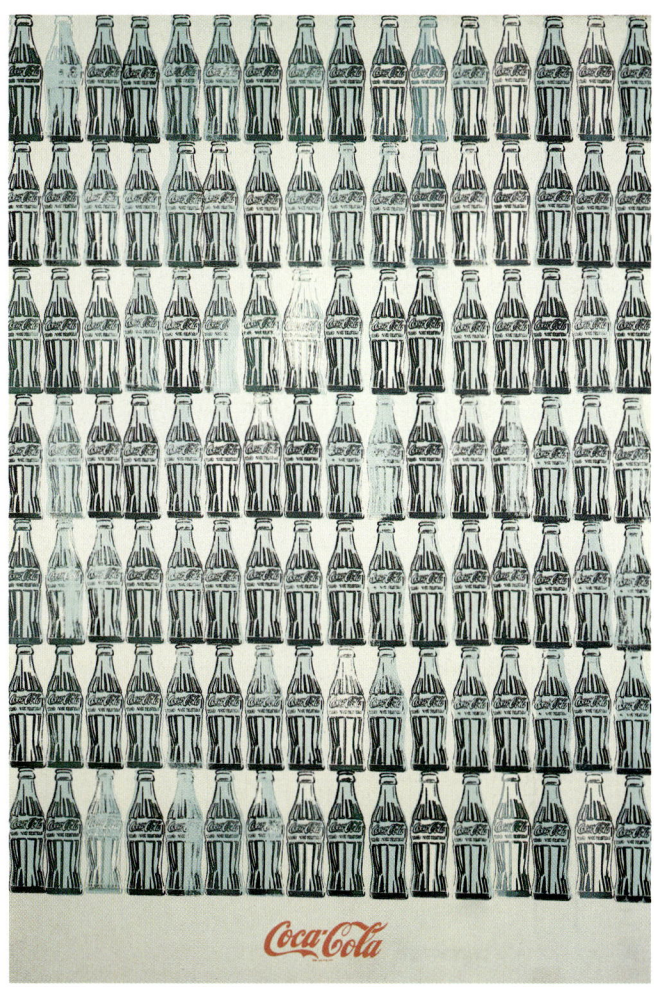

34-28   ANDY WARHOL, *Green Coca-Cola Bottles*, 1962. Oil on canvas, 6' 10½" × 4' 9". Collection of Whitney Museum of American Art, New York (purchase, with funds from the Friends of the Whitney Museum of American Art).

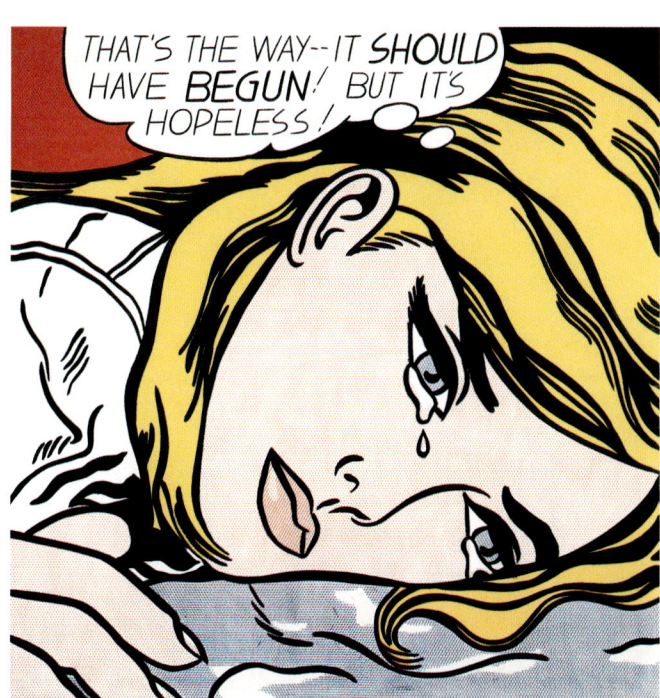

34-27   ROY LICHTENSTEIN, *Hopeless*, 1963. Oil on canvas, 3' 8" × 3' 8". Kunstmuseum, Basel (permanent loan from the Ludwig Foundation Collection).

modification, Lichtenstein was remarkably faithful to the original comic strip image. First, he selected a melodramatic scene common to the romance comic books that were exceedingly popular at the time. Second, he used the comic strip's visual vocabulary, with its dark black outlines and unmodulated color areas, and retained the familiar square dimensions. Third, Lichtenstein's printing technique, *benday dots,* calls attention to the mass-produced derivation of the image. Named after its inventor, the newspaper printer Benjamin Day, the benday dot system involves the modulation of colors through the placement and size of colored dots. Lichtenstein's work further reinforces the comic book's visual shorthand language.

THE ART OF COMMODITIES   The quintessential American Pop artist was ANDY WARHOL (1928–1987). An early successful career as a commercial artist and illustrator grounded Warhol in the sensibility and visual rhetoric of advertising and the mass media, knowledge that proved useful for his Pop art. In paintings such as *Green Coca-Cola Bottles* (FIG. **34-28**), Warhol selected an icon of mass-produced, consumer culture of the time. Despite Coca-Cola's supremacy as the best-selling cola soft drink in the early 1960s, its manufacturers felt compelled to launch a major advertising campaign to challenge the growing market share of its primary rival, Pepsi-Cola. Warhol's choice of the reassuringly familiar curved Coke bottle thus intersected with the visual imagery American consumers encountered frequently at that time. As Lichtenstein had done with his comic strip images, Warhol also used a visual vocabulary and a printing technique that reinforced the image's connections to consumer culture. The repetition and redundancy of the Coke bottle reflects the omnipresence and dominance of this product in American society. The silk-screen technique (also used by Rauschenberg) allowed Warhol to print the image endlessly. So immersed was Warhol in a culture of mass production that he not only produced numerous canvases of the same image, but he also named his studio "the Factory."

A MYTHICAL CELEBRITY   Warhol often produced images of Hollywood celebrities, such as Marilyn Monroe. Like his other paintings, these works emphasize the commodity status of the subjects depicted. Warhol created *Marilyn Diptych* (FIG. **34-29**) in the weeks following the tragic suicide of the movie star in August 1962, capitalizing on the media

frenzy her death prompted. Warhol selected a publicity photo of Monroe, one that provides no insight into the real Norma Jean Baker. Rather, all viewers see is a mask—a persona the Hollywood myth machine generated. The garish colors and the flat application of paint contribute to the image's masklike quality. Like the Coke bottles, the repetition of Monroe's face reinforces her status as a consumer product, her glamorous, haunting visage seemingly confronting viewers endlessly, as it did to the American public in the aftermath of her death. The right half of this work, with its poor registration of pigment, suggests a sequence of film stills, referencing the realm from which Monroe derived her fame.

Warhol's own ascendance to the realm of celebrity underscored his remarkable and astute understanding of mass culture's dynamics and visual language. He predicted that the age of mass media would enable everyone to become famous for fifteen minutes. His own celebrity lasted much longer, long after his death at age fifty-eight in 1987.

SUPERSIZING SCULPTURE   Pop artist Claes Oldenburg (b. 1929) has produced sculptures that have incisively commented on American consumer culture. His early works consisted of plaster reliefs of food and clothing items. Olden-

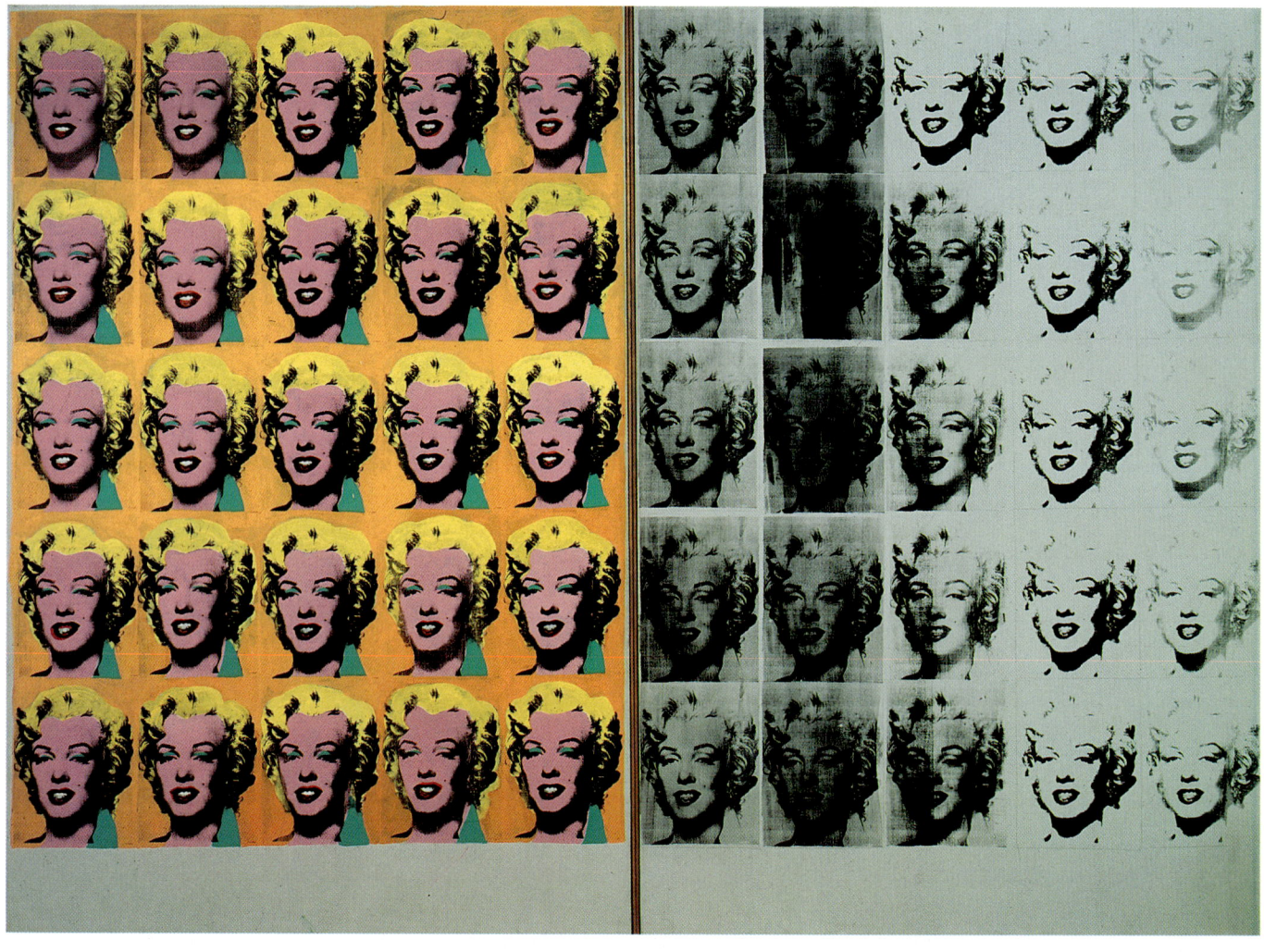

34-29   Andy Warhol, *Marilyn Diptych,* 1962. Oil, acrylic, and silk-screen enamel on canvas. Tate Gallery, London.

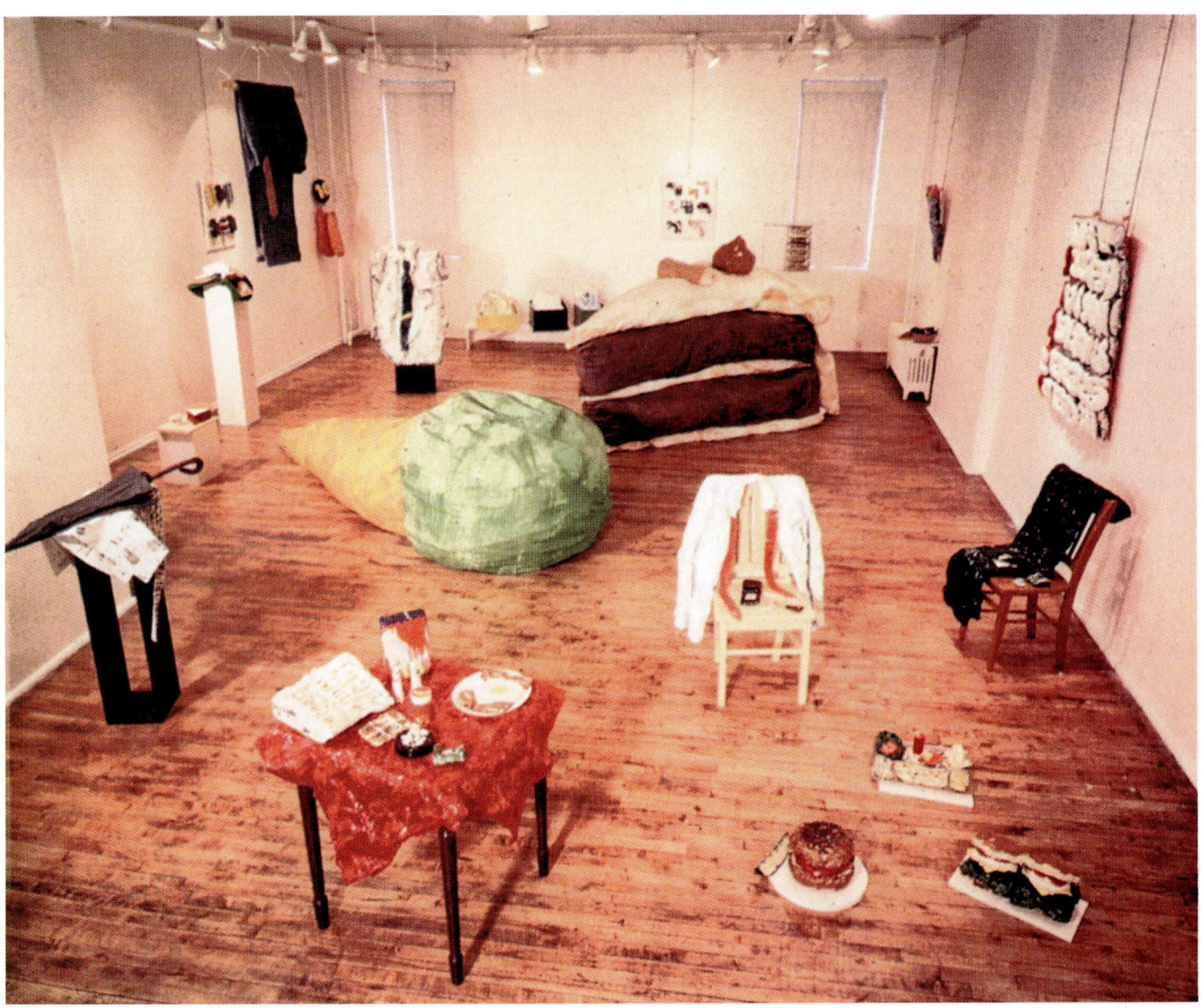

34-30 CLAES OLDENBURG, photo of one-person show at the Green Gallery, New York, 1962.

burg constructed these sculptures of plaster layered on chicken wire and muslin, painting them with cheap commercial house enamel. In later works, focused on the same subjects, he shifted to large-scale stuffed sculptures of sewn vinyl or canvas. Examples of both types of sculptures can be seen in the photograph of a one-person show (FIG. **34-30**) Oldenburg held at the Green Gallery in New York City in 1962. He had included many of the works in this exhibition in an earlier show he mounted titled *The Store. The Store,* an installation of Oldenburg's sculptures of consumer products, was an appropriate comment on art's function as a commodity in a consumer society. Over the years, Oldenburg's sculpture has become increasingly monumental. He, along with his wife and collaborator, COOSJE VAN BRUGGEN (b. 1942), are probably best known for the mammoth outdoor sculptures of familiar, commonplace objects, such as cue balls, shuttlecocks, clothespins, and torn notebooks, they have produced over the past few decades.

Superrealism

Like the Pop artists, the Superrealists were interested in finding a form of artistic communication that was more accessible to the public than the remote, unfamiliar visual language of the Abstract Expressionists or the Post-Painterly Abstractionists. The Superrealists expanded Pop's iconography in both painting and sculpture by making images in the late 1960s and 1970s involving scrupulous photographic fidelity to optical fact. Because many Superrealists used photographs as sources for their imagery, people also referred to the Superrealist painters as Photorealists. These artists reproduced in minute and unsparing detail the commonplace facts and artifacts that Pop art addressed.

EXPLORING "PHOTO-VISION" American artist AUDREY FLACK (b. 1931) was one of the movement's pioneers.

34-31 AUDREY FLACK, *Marilyn,* 1977. Oil over acrylic on canvas, 8′ × 8′. Collection of the University of Arizona Museum, Tucson (museum purchase with funds provided by the Edward J. Gallagher, Jr. Memorial Fund).

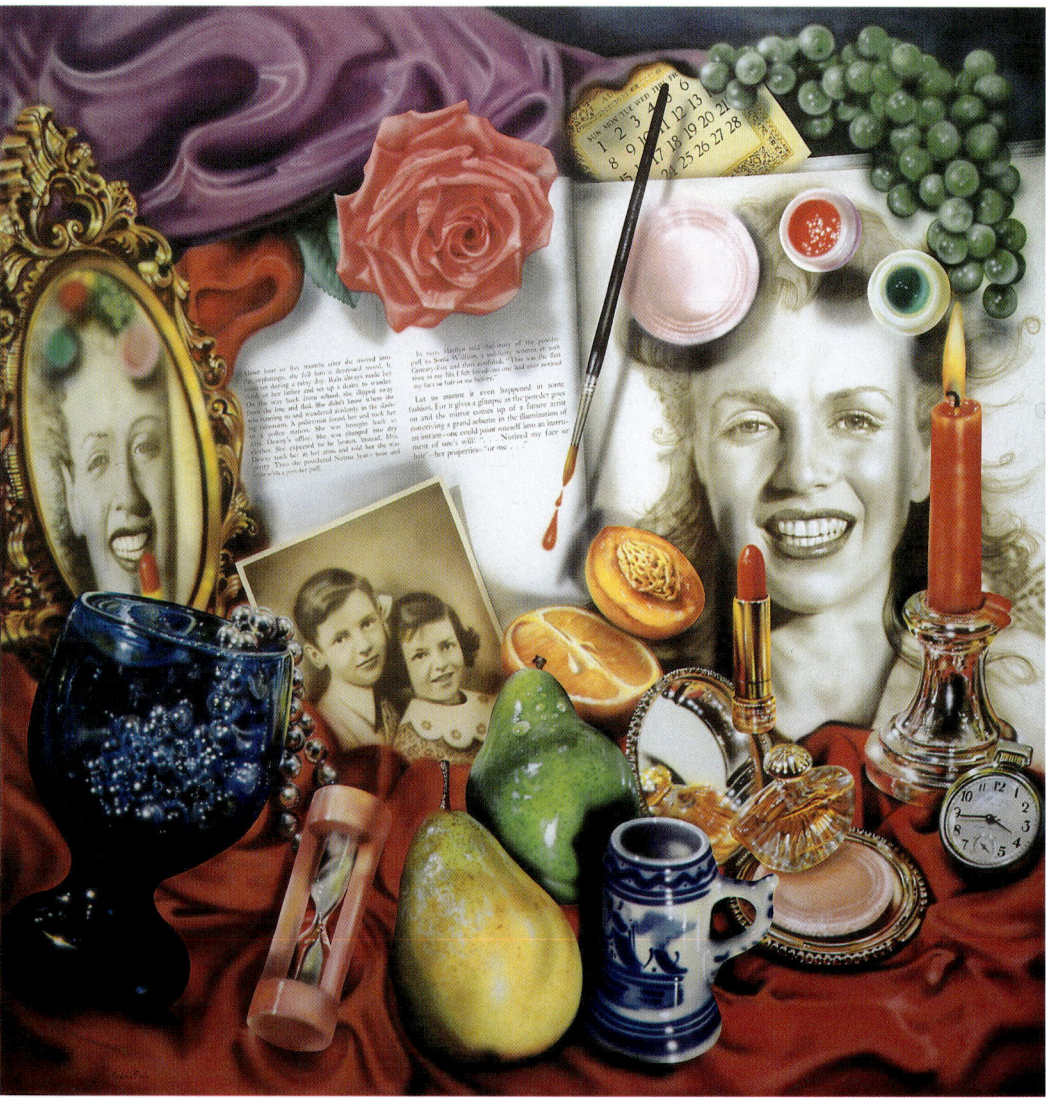

Her paintings, such as *Marilyn,* FIG. **34-31**, were not simply technical exercises but were also conceptual inquiries into the nature of photography and the extent to which photography constructs an understanding of reality. Flack noted: "[Photography is] my whole life, I studied art history, it was always photographs, I never saw the paintings, they were in Europe. . . . Look at TV and at magazines and reproductions, they're all influenced by photo-vision."[30] The photograph's formal qualities also intrigued her, and she used photographic techniques by first projecting an image in slide form onto the canvas. By next using an airbrush (a device originally designed as a photo-retouching tool), Flack could duplicate the smooth gradations of tone and color found in photographs. Her attention to detail and careful preparation resulted in paintings (mostly still lifes) that present viewers with a collection of familiar objects painted with great optical fidelity. *Marilyn* provides a different comment on the tragic death of Marilyn Monroe than does Warhol's *Marilyn Diptych* (FIG. 34-29). In Flack's still-life painting, she alludes to the traditional vanitas painting (see FIG. 24-54). As in Dutch vanitas paintings, *Marilyn* is replete with references to death. In addition to the black-and-white photographs of a youthful, smiling Monroe, fresh fruit (some of it cut), an hourglass, a burning candle, a

watch, and a calendar all refer to the passage of time and the transience of life on earth.

LARGE-SCALE PORTRAITS American artist CHUCK CLOSE (b. 1940), best known for his large-scale portraits, is another artist whose work has been associated with the Superrealist movement. However, Close felt his connection to the Photorealists was limited, because for him realism, rather than an end in itself, was actually the result of an intellectually rigorous, systematic approach to painting. He based his paintings of the late 1960s and early 1970s, such as his *Big Self-Portrait* (FIG. **34-32**), on photographs, and his main goal was to translate photographic information into painted information. Because he aimed simply to record visual information about his subject's appearance, he deliberately avoided creative compositions, flattering lighting effects, and revealing facial expressions. Close, not interested in providing great insight into the personalities of those portrayed, painted anonymous and generic people, mostly friends. By reducing the variables in his paintings (even their canvas sizes are a constant nine feet by seven feet), Close could focus on employing his methodical presentations of faces, thereby encouraging viewers to deal with his works' formal aspects. Indeed, because of the large scale of the artist's paintings, close scrutiny causes the images to dissolve into abstract patterns.

CASTS OF STEREOTYPICAL AMERICANS Super-realist sculpture has been best articulated in the work of DUANE HANSON (1925–1996). Like many of the other Superrealists, Hanson was interested in finding a visual vocabulary the public would understand. Once he perfected his casting technique, he created numerous life-size figurative sculptures. Hanson first made plaster molds from live models. He then filled the molds with polyester resin. After the resin hardened, the artist removed the outer molds and cleaned, painted with an airbrush, and decorated the sculptures with wigs, clothes, and other accessories. These works, such as *Supermarket Shopper* (FIG. **34-33**), depict stereotypical average Americans, striking chords with viewers specifically because of their familiarity. Hanson explained his choice of imagery: "The subject matter that I like best deals with the familiar lower and middle-class American types of today. To me, the resignation, emptiness and loneliness of their existence captures the true reality of life for these people. . . . I want to achieve a certain tough realism which speaks of the fascinating idiosyncracies of our time."[31] Due to Hanson's choice of imagery and careful production process, viewers often initially mistake his sculptures, when on display, for real people, accounting for his association with the Superrealist movement.

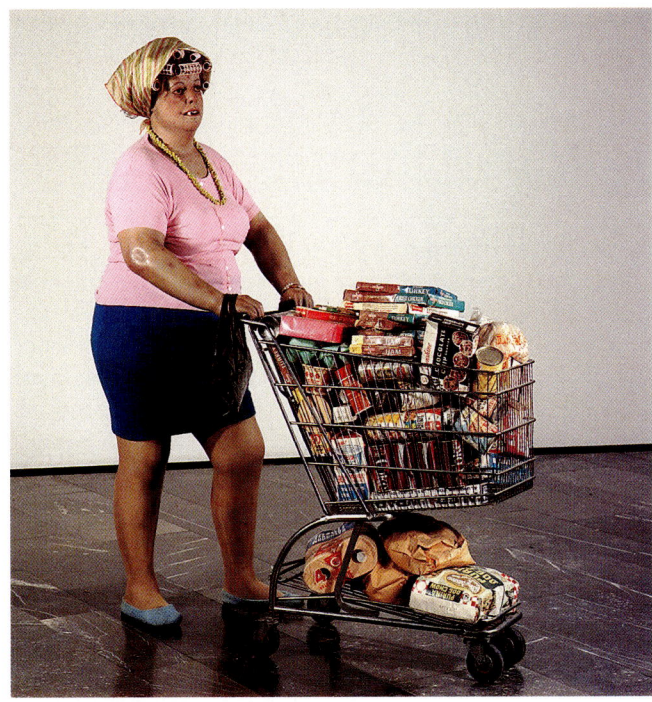

34-33 DUANE HANSON, *Supermarket Shopper,* 1970. Polyester resin and fiberglass polychromed in oil, with clothing, steel cart, and groceries, life-size. Nachfolgeinstitut, Neue Galerie, Sammlung Ludwig, Aachen.

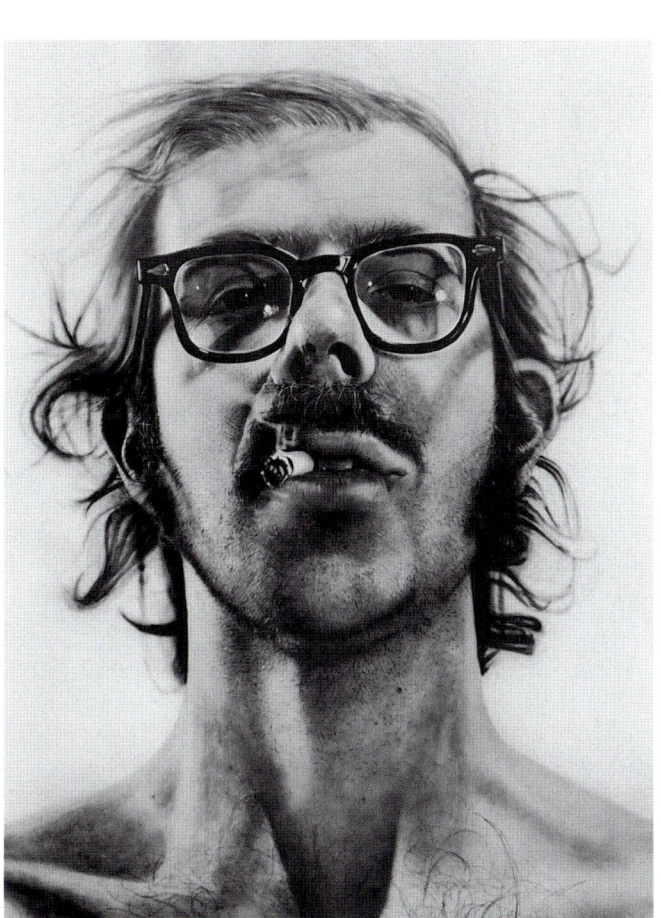

34-32 CHUCK CLOSE, *Big Self-Portrait,* 1967–1968. Acrylic on canvas, 8′ 11″ × 6′ 11″ × 2″. Collection Walker Art Center, Minneapolis (Art Center Acquisition Fund, 1969).

Site-Specific Art and Environmental Art

Environmental art, sometimes called Earth art or earthworks, emerged in the 1960s and included a wide range of artworks, most site specific and existing outdoors. Many artists associated with these sculptural projects also used natural or organic materials, including the land itself. This art form developed during a period of increased concern for the American environment. The ecology movement of the 1960s and 1970s aimed to publicize and combat escalating pollution, depletion of natural resources, and the dangers of toxic waste. The problems of public aesthetics (for example, litter, urban sprawl, and compromised scenic areas) were also at issue. Widespread concern about the environment led to the passage of the National Environmental Policy Act in 1969 and the creation of the federal Environmental Protection Agency. Environmental artists used their art to call attention to the landscape and, in so doing, were part of this national dialogue.

As an innovative art form that challenged traditional assumptions about art making and artistic models, Environmental art clearly had an avant-garde, progressive dimension. It is discussed here with the more populist art movements such as Pop and Superrealism, however, because these artists insisted on moving art out of the rarefied atmosphere of museums and galleries and into the public sphere. Most Environmental artists encouraged spectator interaction with the works. Environmental artists such as Christo and Jeanne-Claude, whose work matured in the context of Nouveaux Realisme, a European version of Pop art, made audience participation an integral part of their works. Thus these artists, like the Pop artists and Superrealists, intended their works to connect with a larger public. Ironically, the remote locations of many earthworks have limited public access.

THE ENDURING POWER OF NATURE   A leading American Environmental artist was ROBERT SMITHSON (1938–1973), who used industrial construction equipment to manipulate vast quantities of earth and rock on isolated sites. One of Smithson's best-known pieces is *Spiral Jetty* (FIG. **34-34**), a mammoth coil of black basalt, limestone rocks, and earth that extends out into Great Salt Lake in Utah. Driving by the lake one day, Smithson came across some abandoned mining equipment, left there by a company that had tried and failed to extract oil from the site. Smithson saw this as a testament to the enduring power of nature and to humankind's inability to conquer nature. He decided to create an artwork in the lake that ultimately became a monumental spiral curving out from the shoreline and running fifteen hundred linear feet into the water. Smithson insisted on designing his work in response to the location itself; he wanted to avoid the arrogance of an artist merely imposing an unrelated concept on the site. The spiral idea grew from Smithson's first impression of the location:

As I looked at the site, it reverberated out to the horizons only to suggest an immobile cyclone while flickering light made the entire landscape appear to quake. A dormant earthquake spread into the fluttering stillness, into a spinning sensation without movement. The site was a rotary that enclosed itself in an immense roundness. From that gyrating space emerged the possibility of the Spiral Jetty.[32]

The appropriateness of the spiral forms was reinforced when, while researching Great Salt Lake, Smithson discovered that the molecular structure of the salt crystals that coat the rocks at the water's edge is spiral in form. Smithson not only recorded *Spiral Jetty* in photographs, but also he filmed its construction in a movie that describes the forms and life of the whole site. The photographs and film have become increasingly important, because fluctuations in the Great Salt Lake's water level often place *Spiral Jetty* underwater.

SCULPTURE AS VOID   Although MICHAEL HEIZER (b. 1944) does not consider himself an Environmental artist, many of his sculptures do involve the landscape. One

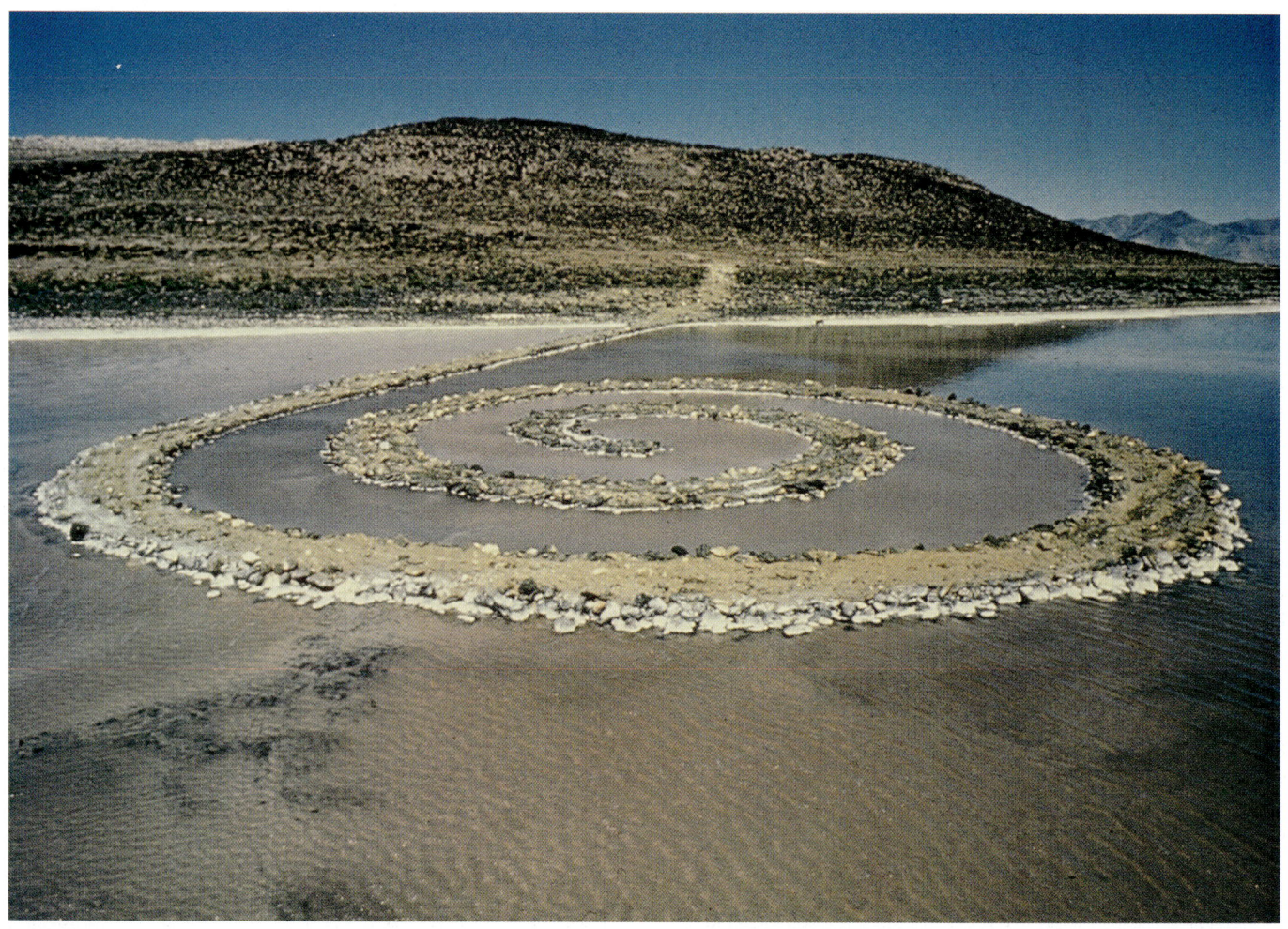

34-34   ROBERT SMITHSON, *Spiral Jetty,* 1970. Black rock, salt crystals, earth, red water (algae) at Great Salt Lake, Utah. 1,500′ × 15′ × 3½′. Estate of Robert Smithson; courtesy James Cohan Gallery, New York; collection of DIA Center for the Arts, New York.

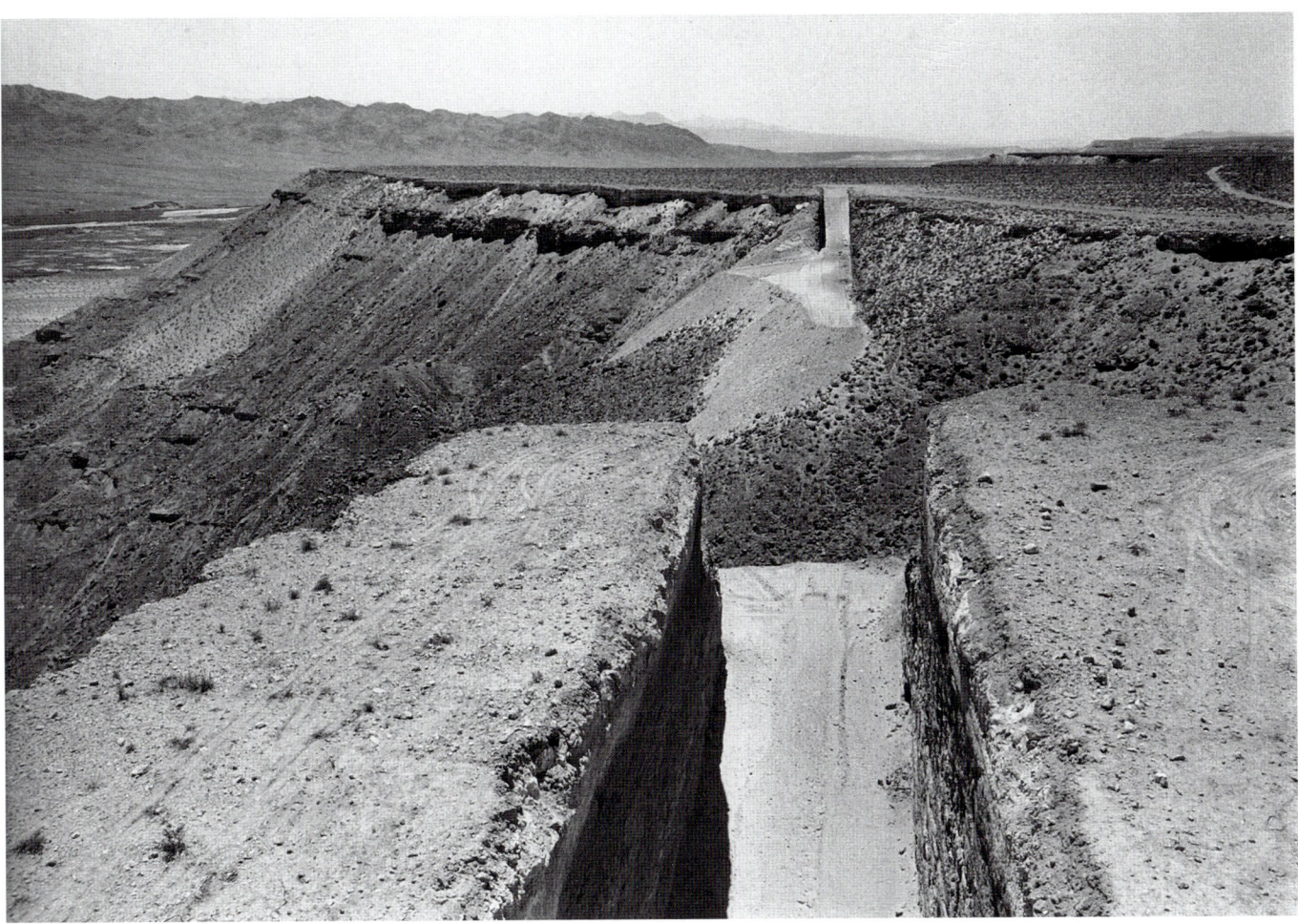

34-35 MICHAEL HEIZER, *Double Negative,* near Overton, Nevada, 1969–1970. 1,500′ × 50′ × 30′. Photo, Museum of Contemporary Art, Los Angeles.

such work, *Double Negative* (FIG. **34-35**), consists of two massive cuts in the Mormon Mesa near Overton, Nevada. Using earthmoving equipment, Heizer had each of these cuts, facing each other across a deep indentation in the cliflike ridge, excavated to a depth of fifty feet. Each cut is thirty feet wide, and the entire length of the piece is fifteen hundred feet. Thus, the sculpture exists purely as a void—space as opposed to mass or volume. While most monumental sculpture traditionally confronts viewers with a large mass, this sculpture literally allows visitors to be inside the work. Unfortunately, *Double Negative's* geographic remoteness does not permit many people to experience it; photographs in a New York gallery brought the sculpture to public attention in early 1970. Heizer, however, emphasized artistic rather than ecological issues. The conceptualization, scale, and location of this work force viewers to reconsider the nature of sculpture and to reevaluate their relationship to the land.

THE ART OF WRAPPING Like Heizer, CHRISTO JAVACHEFF and JEANNE-CLAUDE DE GUILLEBON, known as CHRISTO and JEANNE-CLAUDE (both b. 1935), intensify view-

ers' awareness of the space and features of natural and urban sites. However, rather than physically alter the land itself, as Heizer did, Christo and Jeanne-Claude prompt this awareness by modifying the landscape with cloth. Their pieces also incorporate the relationships among human sociopolitical action, art, and the environment. Christo studied art in his native Bulgaria and in Vienna. After a move to Paris, he began to encase objects in clumsy wrappings, thereby appropriating bits of the real world into the mysterious world of the unopened package whose contents can be dimly seen in silhouette under the wrap. In the 1970s, Christo and Jeanne-Claude, husband and wife, began to collaborate on large-scale projects.

Turning their attention to the environment, they created giant "air packages" in Minneapolis and Germany. Then they dealt with the land itself, carrying out projects such as wrapping more than a million square feet of Australian coast and hanging a vast curtain across a valley at Rifle Gap, Colorado. The land pieces required years of preparation, research, and scores of meetings with local authorities and interested groups of local citizens. The artists always considered the planning, the process of obtaining the numerous permits, and the visual documentation of each piece part of the artwork. These

34-36 Christo and Jeanne-Claude, *Surrounded Islands,* Biscayne Bay, Greater Miami, Florida, 1980–1983. Pink woven polypropylene fabric, $6\frac{1}{2}$ million sq. ft.

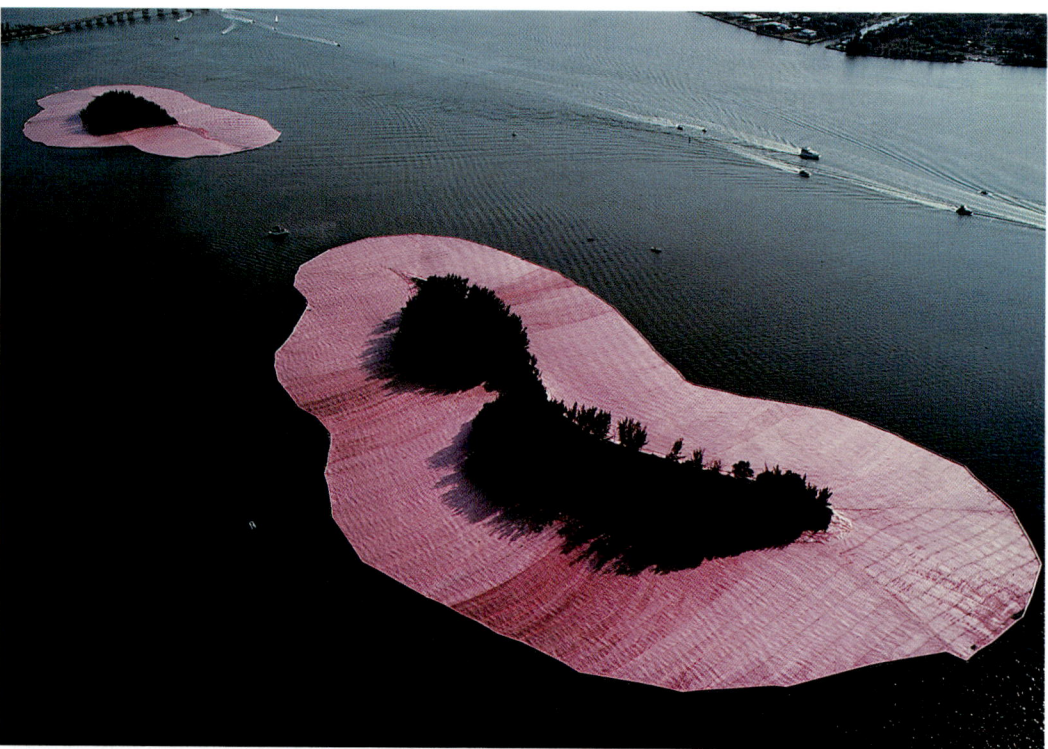

temporary works were usually on view for a few weeks. *Surrounded Islands* (FIG. 34-36), created in Biscayne Bay in Miami, Florida, for two weeks in May 1983, typified Christo and Jeanne-Claude's work. For this project, they surrounded eleven small humanmade islands in the bay (from a dredging project) with specially fabricated pink polypropylene fabric.

This Environmental art project required two years of preparation to obtain the required permissions, to assemble the necessary labor force of unskilled and professional workers, and to raise the $3.2 million cost (accomplished by selling preliminary drawings, collages, and models). Huge crowds watched as crews stripped accumulated trash from the islands (to assure maximum contrast between their dark colors, the pink of the cloth, and the blue of the bay) and then unfurled the fabric "cocoons" to form magical floating "skirts" around each tiny bit of land. Despite the brevity of its existence, *Surrounded Islands* lives on in the host of photographs, films, and books documenting the piece.

A MASSIVE WALL OF STEEL   While many works placed in the public domain (such as the Environmental artworks just discussed) sought to reawaken an appreciation of the land's power and beauty and to call attention to ecological problems, other artworks focused attention on art's role in public spaces. One sculpture that sparked national discussion about such art was *Tilted Arc* (FIG. 34-37) by American artist RICHARD SERRA (b. 1939). It was commissioned by the General Services Administration (GSA), the federal agency responsible for, among other tasks, overseeing the selection and installation of artworks for government buildings. This enormous one hundred twenty foot curved wall of Cor-Ten steel stood twelve feet high and bisected the plaza in front of the Jacob K. Javits Federal Building in lower Manhattan. Serra situated the sculpture to significantly alter the space of the open plaza and the traffic flow across the square. This site-specific sculpture, the artist explained, was intended to

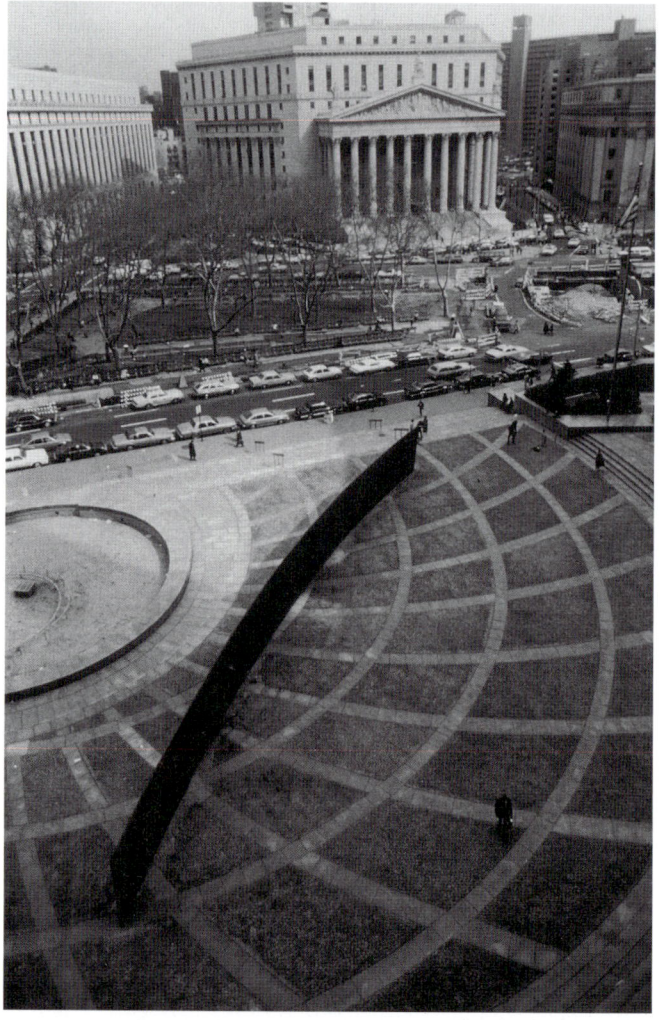

34-37   RICHARD SERRA, *Tilted Arc,* 1981. Cor-Ten steel, $12' \times 120' \times 2\frac{1}{2}''$. Installed Federal Plaza, New York City by the General Services Administration, Washington D.C. Destroyed by the U.S. Goverment 1989.

Tilted Arc and the Problems of Public Art

When *Tilted Arc* (FIG. 34-37) was installed in the plaza in front of the Jacob K. Javits Federal Building in 1981, much of the public immediately responded with hostile criticism. The chorus of complaints was prompted by the Minimalist sculpture's resolute and uncompromising presence bisecting the plaza. Many voiced the beliefs that *Tilted Arc* was ugly and attracted graffiti, that it interfered with the view across the plaza, and that it prevented using the plaza for performances or concerts. Due to the sustained barrage of protests and petitions demanding the removal of *Tilted Arc,* the GSA held a series of public hearings. Afterward, the agency decided to remove the sculpture despite its prior approval of Serra's maquette. This, understandably, infuriated Serra, who had a legally binding contract acknowledging the work's site-specific nature. "To remove the work is to destroy the work," the artist stated.[1]

This episode raised intriguing issues about the nature of public art, including the public reception of experimental art, the artist's responsibilities and rights when executing public commissions, censorship in the arts, and public art's purpose. If an artwork is placed in a public space outside the relatively private confines of a museum or gallery, do different guidelines apply? As one participant in the *Tilted Arc* saga asked, "Should an artist have the right to impose his values and taste on a public that now rejects his taste and values?"[2] One of the express functions of the historical avant-garde was to challenge convention by rejecting tradition and disrupting view-ers' complacency. Will placing experimental art in a public place always cause controversy? From Serra's statements, it is clear he intended the sculpture to challenge the public.

Another issue *Tilted Arc* presented involved the rights of the artist, who in this case accused the GSA of censorship. Serra went so far as to file a lawsuit against the government for infringement of his First Amendment rights and insisted "the artist's work must be uncensored, respected, and tolerated, although deemed abhorrent, or perceived as challenging, or experienced as threatening."[3] Did removal of the work constitute censorship? A federal district court held that it did not.

Ultimately, who should decide what artworks are appropriate for the public arena? One artist argued, "we cannot have public art by plebiscite [popular vote]."[4] But to avoid recurrences of the *Tilted Arc* controversy, the GSA changed its procedures and now solicits input from a wide range of civic and neighborhood groups before commissioning public artworks. Despite the removal of *Tilted Arc* (now languishing in storage), the sculpture maintains a powerful presence in all discussions of the aesthetics, politics, and dynamics of public art.

[1] Grace Glueck, "What Part Should the Public Play in Choosing Public Art?" *New York Times,* 3 February 1985.

[2] Calvin Tomkins, "The Art World: Tilted Arc," *New Yorker,* 20 May 1985, 98.

[3] Ibid., 98–99.

[4] Ibid., 98.

"dislocate or alter the decorative function of the plaza and actively bring people into the sculpture's context."[33] By creating such a monumental presence in this large public space, Serra succeeded in forcing viewers to reconsider the plaza's physical space as a sculptural form (see "Tilted Arc and the Problems of Public Art," above).

NEW MODELS FOR ARCHITECTURE: MODERNISM TO POSTMODERNISM

Modernism

The progressive movement toward formal abstraction in media such as painting and sculpture during the twentieth century has been chronicled. In similar fashion, modernist architects became increasingly concerned with a formalism that stressed simplicity. They articulated this in buildings that retained intriguing organic sculptural qualities, as well as in buildings that adhered to a more rigid geometry.

SCULPTING CONCRETE: THE WRIGHT STUFF

Frank Lloyd Wright, who described his architecture as "or-ganic," ended his long, productive career with his design for the Solomon R. Guggenheim Museum (FIGS. **34-38** and **34-39**), built in New York City between 1943 and 1959. Using reinforced concrete almost as a sculptor might use resilient clay, Wright designed a structure inspired by the spiral of a snail's shell.

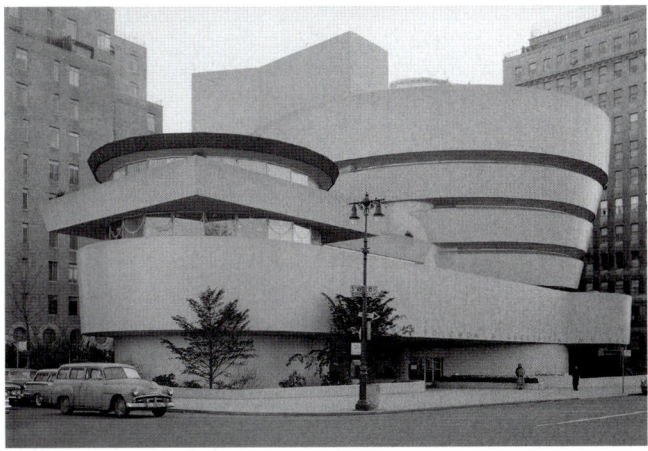

34-38 FRANK LLOYD WRIGHT, Solomon R. Guggenheim Museum (exterior view from the north), New York, 1943–1959 (photo 1962).

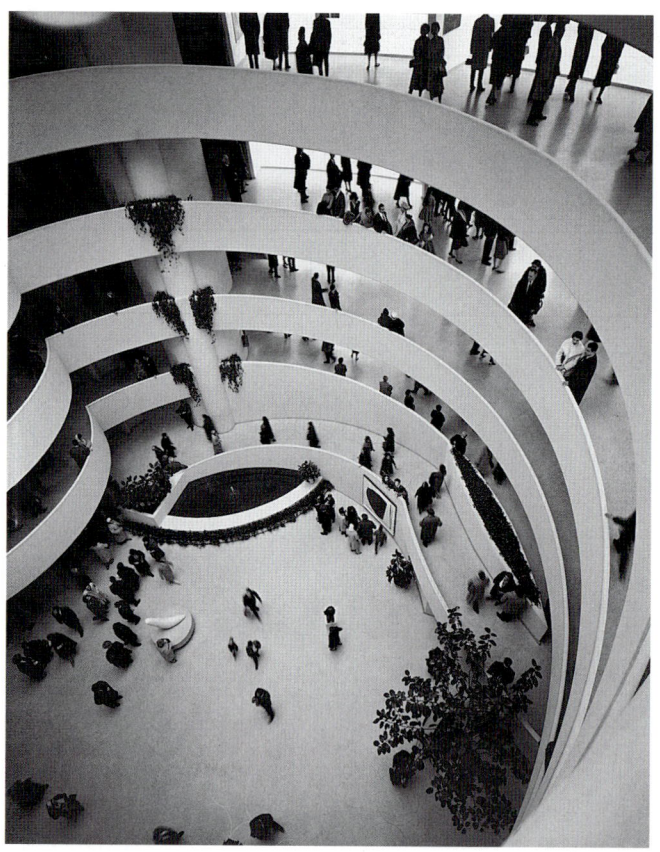

34-39 Interior of the Solomon R. Guggenheim Museum, New York, 1943–1959.

Wright had introduced curves and circles into some of his plans in the 1930s, and, as the architectural historian Peter Blake noted, "The spiral was the next logical step; it is the circle brought into the third and fourth dimensions."[34] Inside the building (FIG. 34-39), the shape of the shell expands toward the top, and a winding interior ramp spirals to connect the gallery bays, which are illuminated by a skylight strip embedded in the museum's outer wall. Visitors can stroll up the ramp or take an elevator to the top of the building and proceed down the gently inclined walkway, viewing the artworks displayed along the path. Thick walls and the solid organic shape give the building, outside and inside, the sense of turning in on itself. Moreover, the long interior viewing area opening onto a ninety-foot central well of space seems a sheltered environment, secure from the bustling city outside.

FUSING ARCHITECTURE AND SCULPTURE The startling organic forms of Le Corbusier's Notre Dame du Haut (FIGS. **34-40** and **34-41**), completed in 1955 at Ronchamp, France, present viewers with a fusion of architecture and sculpture in a single expression. The architect designed this small chapel on a pilgrimage site in the Vosges Mountains to replace a building destroyed in World War II. The monumental impression of Notre Dame du Haut seen from afar is somewhat deceptive. Although one massive exterior wall contains a pulpit facing a spacious outdoor area for large-scale open-air services on holy days, the interior holds at most two hundred people. The intimate scale, stark and

34-40 Le Corbusier, Notre Dame du Haut, Ronchamp, France, 1950–1955.

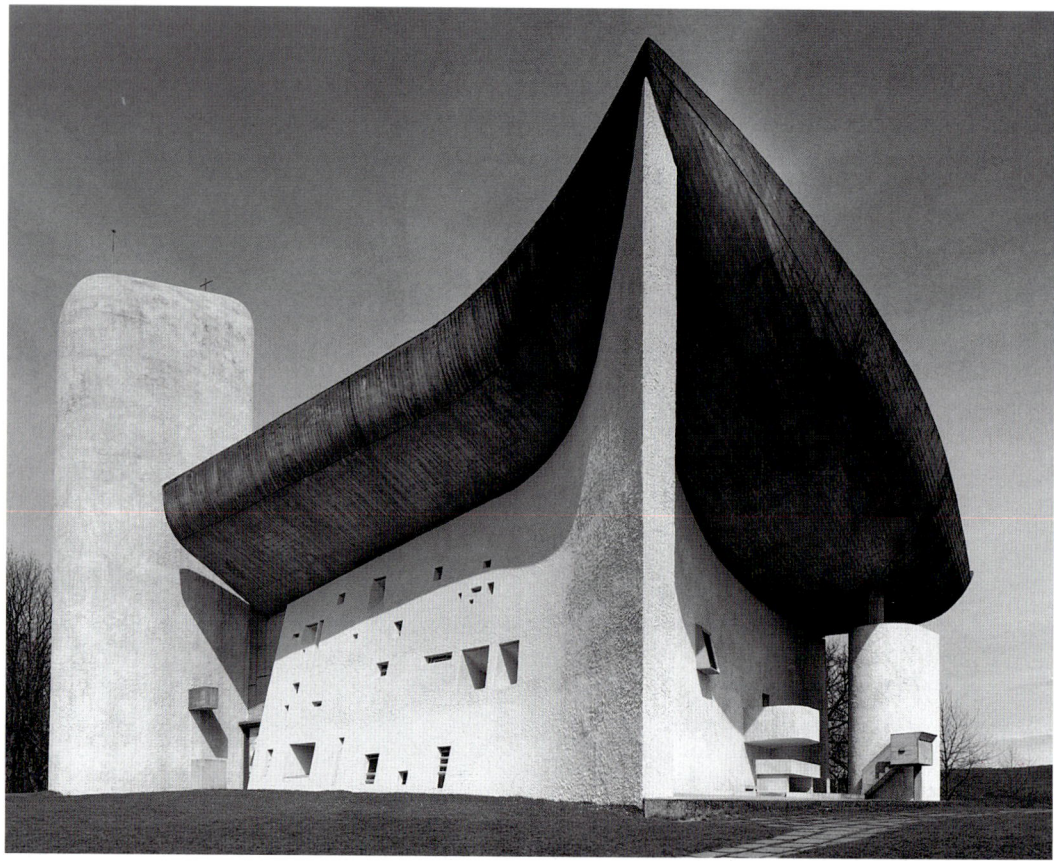

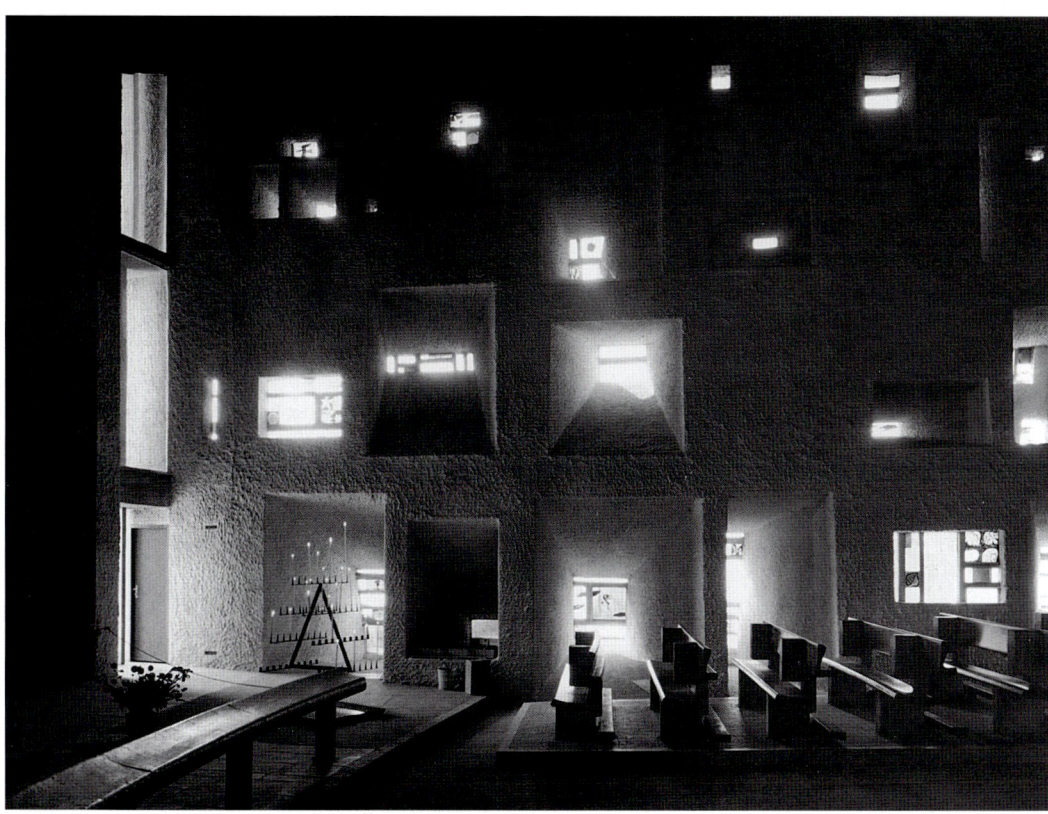

34-41 Interior of Notre Dame du Haut, Ronchamp, France, 1950–1955.

heavy walls, and mysterious illumination (jewel tones cast from the deeply recessed stained-glass windows) give this space (FIG. 34-41) an aura reminiscent of a sacred cave or a medieval monastery.

Notre Dame du Haut's structure may look free form to the untrained eye, but Le Corbusier actually based it, like the medieval cathedral, on an underlying mathematical system. The fabric was formed from a frame of steel and metal mesh, which was sprayed with concrete and painted white, except for two interior private chapel niches with colored walls and the roof, left unpainted to darken naturally with the passage of time. The roof appears to float freely above the sanctuary, intensifying the quality of mystery in the interior space. In reality, the roof is elevated above the walls on a series of nearly invisible blocks. Le Corbusier's preliminary sketches for the building indicate he linked the design with the shape of praying hands, with the wings of a dove (representing both peace and the Holy Spirit), and with the prow of a ship (a reminder that the Latin word used for the main gathering place in Christian churches is *nave,* meaning "ship"). The artist envisioned that in these powerful sculptural solids and voids, human beings could find new values—new interpretations of their sacred beliefs and of their natural environments.

SITE-SENSITIVE BUILDING METAPHORS The opera house in Sydney, Australia (FIG. **34-42**), designed by the Danish architect JOERN UTZON (b. 1918) in 1959, is a bold composition of organic forms on a colossal scale. Utzon worked briefly with Frank Lloyd Wright at Taliesin (Wright's Wisconsin residence), and the style of the Sydney Opera House resonates distantly with the Guggenheim Museum's graceful curvature. Two clusters of immense concrete shells rise from massive platforms and soar to delicate peaks. Utzon was especially taken with the platform architecture of Mesoamerica (see FIG. 14-7). Recalling at first the ogival shapes of Gothic vaults, the shells also suggest both the buoyancy of seabird wings and the sails of the tall ships that brought European settlers to Australia in the eighteenth and nineteenth centuries. These architectural metaphors are appropriate to the harbor surrounding Bennelong Point, whose bedrock foundations support the building. Utzon's matching of the structure with its site and atmosphere adds to the organic nature of this construction.

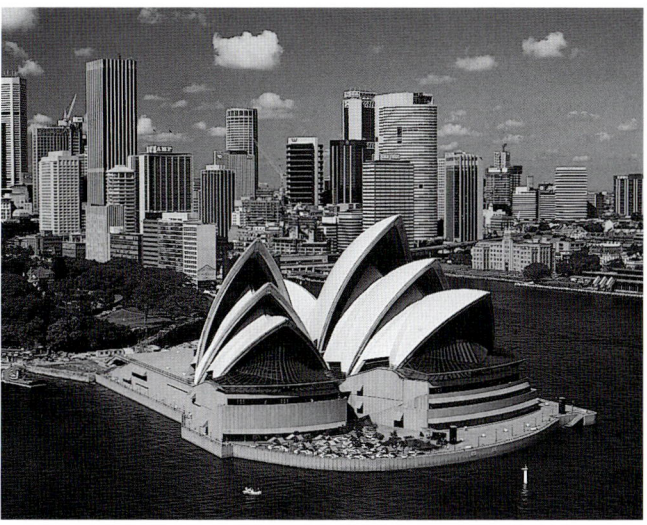

34-42 JOERN UTZON, Sydney Opera House, Sydney, Australia, 1959–1972. Reinforced concrete; height of highest shell, 200′.

34-43   Eero Saarinen, TWA terminal, Kennedy Airport, New York, 1956–1962.

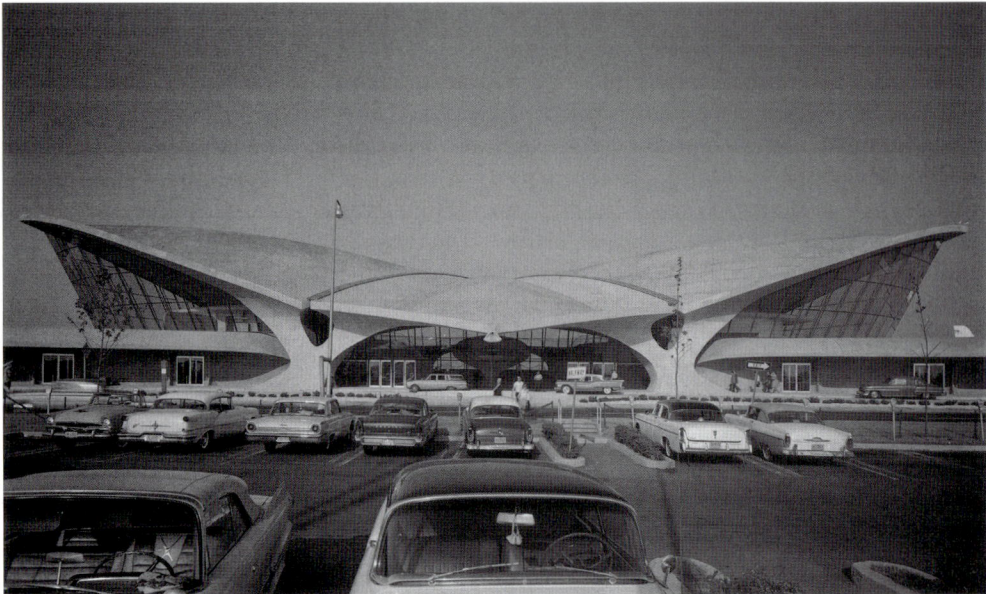

The building is not only a monument of civic pride but also functions as the city's cultural center. In addition to the opera auditorium giving the structure its name, it houses auxiliary halls and rooms for concerts, the performing arts, motion pictures, lectures, art exhibitions, conventions, and all other modern cultural activities.

Begun in 1959 and only completed in 1972, the facility took a long time to realize. From the beginning, Utzon's controversial design required unavailable constructional technology to meet the requirements of its daring innovations. Utzon left the project in 1966, and Australian architects completed it in 1972. Today it is accepted as Sydney's defining symbol.

CAPTURING MOTION IN CONCRETE Finnish-born architect EERO SAARINEN (1910–1961), responsible for selecting Utzon as the architect for the Sydney Opera House, designed his own version of the curvilinear shell building in the late 1950s. Saarinen based his design of the Trans World Airlines terminal (FIG. **34-43**) at the Kennedy Airport in New York on the theme of motion. It consists of two immense concrete shells split down the middle and slightly rotated, giving the terminal a fluid curved outline that fits its corner site. The shells immediately suggest expansive wings and flight. The architect designed everything on the interior, including the furniture, ventilation ducts, and signboards, with this same curvilinear vocabulary in mind.

From the mid-1950s through the 1970s, other architects created massive, sleek, and geometrically rigid buildings. They designed most of these structures following Mies van der Rohe's contention that "less is more," and the architecture presented pristine, authoritative faces to the public. Appropriately, such buildings and the powerful, heroic presence they exuded symbolized the monolithic corporations often inhabiting them.

A GLASS TOWER The "purest" example of these corporate skyscrapers is, undoubtedly, the rectilinear glass and bronze tower in Manhattan (FIG. **34-44**) designed for the

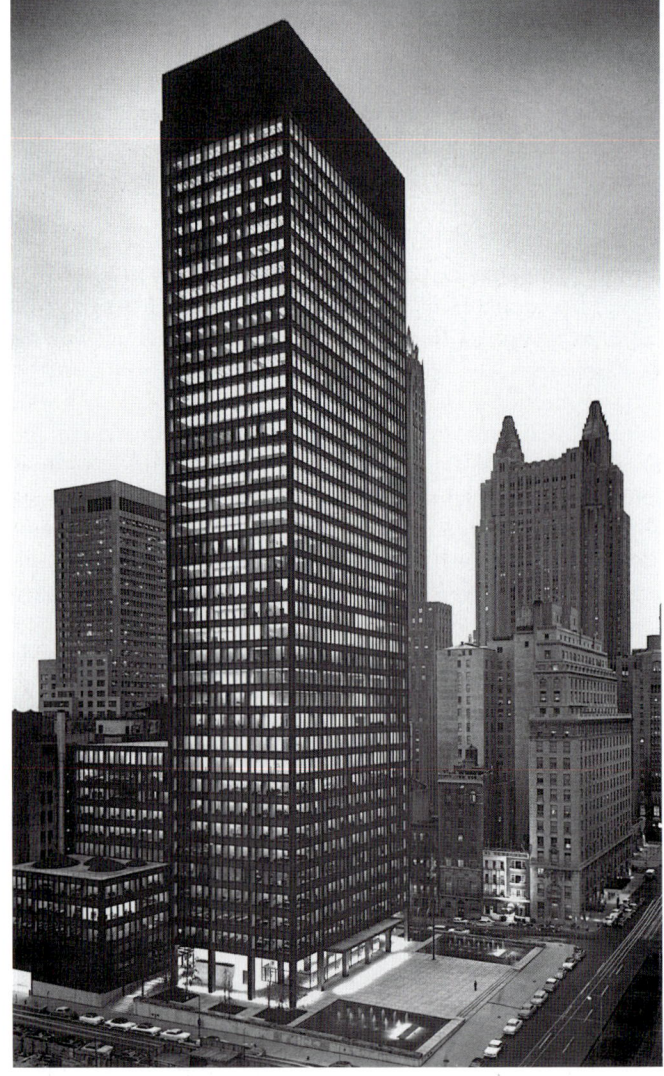

34-44   Ludwig Mies van der Rohe and Philip Johnson, Seagram Building, New York, 1956–1958.

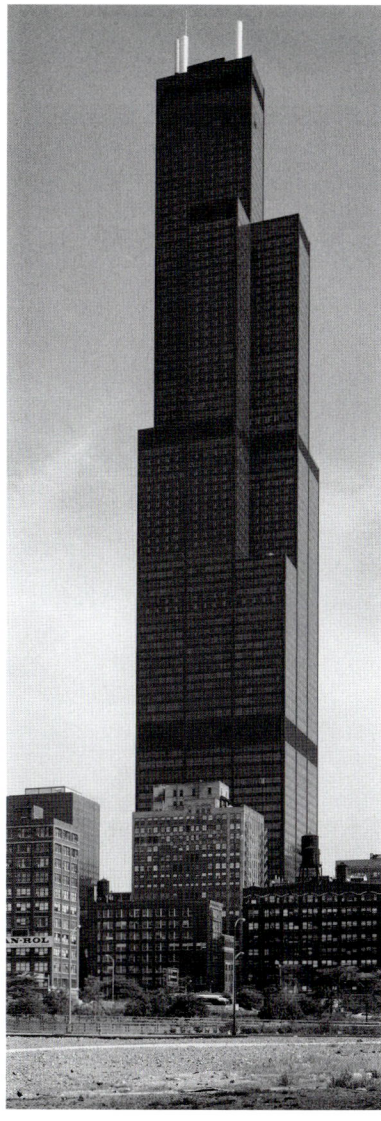

34-45 Skidmore, Owings and Merrill, Sears Tower, Chicago, 1974 (photo 1975).

ONCE THE TALLEST IN THE WORLD The architectural firm Skidmore, Owings and Merrill (SOM) can be seen as the purest proponent of Miesian-inspired structures. This firm designed a number of these simple rectilinear glass-sheathed buildings, and its growth indicates the popularity of this building type. By 1970, SOM comprised more than one thousand architects and had offices in New York, Chicago, San Francisco, Portland, and Washington, D.C. In 1974 the firm completed the Sears Tower (FIG. **34-45**), a mammoth corporate building in Chicago. Consisting of nine clustered tubes soaring vertically, this one hundred ten floor building contains enough room to support more than twelve thousand workers. Original plans called for one hundred four stories, but the architects acquiesced to Sears's insistence on making the building the tallest (measured to the structural top) in the world, a distinction it held until recently. The tower's size, coupled with the black aluminum which sheathes it and the smoked glass, give it an intimidating appearance, appropriate for the imposing image corporations were trying to project.

Postmodernism

The restrictiveness of modernist architecture and the impersonality and sterility of many of these rectilinear corporate buildings led to a rejection of modernism's authority in architecture. Along with the apparent lack of responsiveness to the unique character of the cities and neighborhoods where the structures were placed, these reactions ushered in postmodernism. In contrast to the simplicity of modernist architecture, the terms most often invoked to describe postmodern architecture are *pluralism, complexity,* and *eclecticism.* Where the modernist program was reductive, the postmodern vocabulary of the 1970s and 1980s was expansive and inclusive.

Among the first to explore this new direction in architecture were Jane Jacobs (b. 1916) and Robert Venturi (see FIG. 34-49). In their influential books *The Death and Life of Great American Cities* (Jacobs, 1961) and *Complexity and Contradiction in Architecture* (Venturi, 1966), both argued that the uniformity and anonymity of modernist architecture (in particular, the corporate skyscrapers dominating many urban skylines) are unsuited to human social interaction and that diversity is the great advantage of urban life. Postmodern architecture accepted, indeed embraced, the messy and chaotic nature of urban life.

Further, when designing these varied buildings, many postmodern architects consciously selected past architectural elements or references and juxtaposed them to contemporary elements or fashioned them of high-tech materials, thereby creating a dialogue between past and present. Postmodern architecture incorporated not only traditional architectural references but references to mass culture and popular imagery as well. This was precisely the "complexity and contradiction" Venturi referred to in the title of his book. Venturi wrote:

> Architects can no longer afford to be intimidated by the puritanically moral language of orthodox Modern architecture. . . . A valid architecture evokes many levels of meaning and combinations of focus; its space and its elements become readable and workable in several ways at once.[35]

Seagram Company by Mies van der Rohe and American architect PHILIP JOHNSON (b. 1906). By the time this structure was built (1956–1958), the concrete, steel, and glass towers, pioneered in the works of Louis Sullivan (see FIG. 29-59) and in Mies van der Rohe's own model for glass skyscrapers (see FIG. 33-63), had become a familiar sight in cities all over the world. Appealing in its structural logic and clarity, the style, although often vulgarized, was easily imitated and quickly became the norm for postwar commercial high-rise buildings. The Seagram structure's architects deliberately designed it as a thin shaft, leaving the front quarter of its midtown site as an open pedestrian plaza. The tower appears to rise from the pavement on stilts; glass walls even surround the recessed lobby. The building's recessed structural elements make it appear to have a glass skin, interrupted only by the thin strips of bronze anchoring the windows. The bronze metal and the amber glass windows give the tower a richness found in few of its neighbors. Mies van der Rohe and Johnson carefully planned every detail of the Seagram Building, inside and out, to create an elegant whole. They even planned the interior and exterior lighting to make the edifice an impressive sight both day and night.

JUXTAPOSING PAST AND PRESENT A clear example of the eclecticism and the dialogue between traditional and contemporary elements found in postmodern architecture is the Piazza d'Italia (FIG. **34-46**) by American architect CHARLES MOORE (1925–1993). Designed in the late 1970s in New Orleans, the Piazza d'Italia is an open plaza dedicated to the city's Italian American community. Appropriately, Moore selected elements relating specifically to Italian history, all the way back through ancient Roman culture.

Backed up against a contemporary high-rise and set off from urban traffic patterns, the Piazza d'Italia can be reached on foot from three sides through gateways of varied design. The approaches lead to an open circular area partially formed by short segments of colonnades arranged in staggered concentric arcs, which direct the eye to the composition's focal point—an exedra. This recessed area on a raised platform serves as a rostrum during the annual festivities of Saint Joseph's Day. Moore inlaid the Piazza's pavement with a map of Italy that centrally places Sicily, the island of origin of the Italian colony's majority. From there, the map's Italian "boot" moves in the direction of the steps that ascend the rostrum and geographically correspond to the Alps.

The Piazza's most immediate historical reference is to the Greek agora or the Roman forum (see FIG. 10-41). However, its circular form alludes to the ideal geometric figure of the Renaissance (see FIG. 22-8). The irregular placement of the concentrically arranged colonnade fragments inserts a note of instability into the design reminiscent of Mannerism (see FIG.

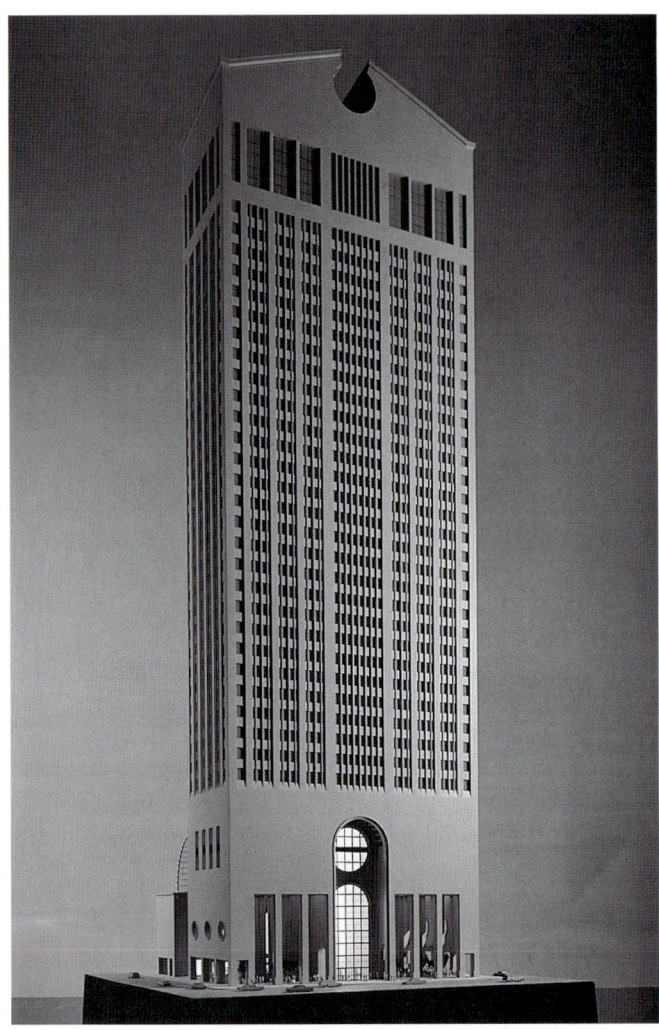

34-47 PHILIP JOHNSON and JOHN BURGEE with Simmons Architects, associated architects, a model of the AT&T Building, New York, 1978–1984.

22-26). Illusionistic devices, such as the continuation of the Piazza's pavement design (apparently through a building and out into the street), are Baroque in character (see FIG. 24-6). All of the classical orders are represented—most with whimsical modifications. Modern features, nevertheless, challenge the Piazza's historical character, such as the stainless-steel columns and capitals, neon collars around the column necks, and various parts of the exedra framed with neon lights.

In sum, Moore designed the Piazza d'Italia as a complex conglomeration of symbolic, historical, and geographic allusions—some overt and others obscure. Although the Piazza's specific purpose was to honor the Italian community of New Orleans, its more general purpose was to revitalize an urban area by becoming a focal point and an architectural setting for the social activities of neighborhood residents.

A MODERNIST EMBRACES POSTMODERNISM
Even architects instrumental in the proliferation of the modernist idiom embraced postmodernism. Philip Johnson made one of the most startling shifts of style in twentieth-century architecture, eventually moving away from the Seagram Building's severe geometric formalism to a classicizing transformation of it in his AT&T (American Telephone and Telegraph) Building in New York City (FIG. **34-47**). Architect

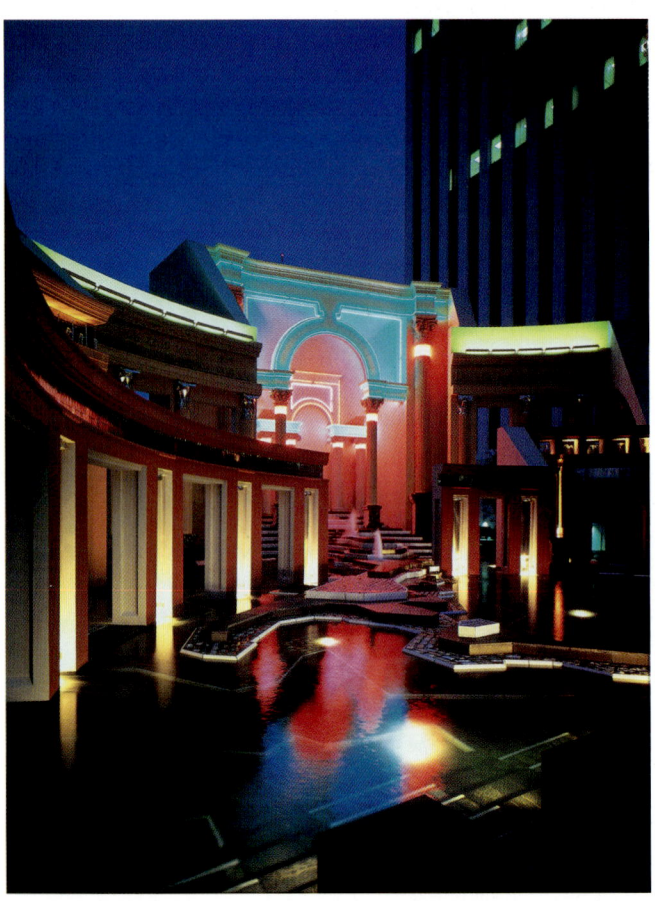

34-46 CHARLES MOORE, Piazza d'Italia, New Orleans, Louisiana, 1976–1980.

JOHN BURGEE codesigned it with assistance from Simmons Architects. This structure was influential in turning architectural taste and practice away from modernism and toward postmodernism—from organic "concrete sculpture" and the rigid "glass box" to elaborate shapes, motifs, and silhouettes freely adapted from historical styles.

The six hundred sixty foot-high slab of the AT&T Building is wrapped in granite. In contrast to the modernist glass-sheathed skyscrapers, Johnson reduced the window space to some thirty percent of the building. His design of its exterior elevation is classically tripartite, having an arcaded base and arched portal; a tall, shaftlike body segmented by slender *mullions* (vertical elements dividing a window); and a crowning pediment broken by an *orbiculum* (a disclike opening). The arrangement refers to the base/column/entablature system of ancient Greek structures and Renaissance elevations (see FIGS. 5-42 and 21-43). More specifically, the pediment, indented by the circular space, resembles the crown of a typical eighteenth-century Chippendale high chest of drawers, familiar as "colonial" in any furniture store. It rises among the monotonously flat-topped glass towers of the New York skyline as an ironic rebuke to the rigid uniformity of modernist architecture. Critics favoring modernism were not at all amused, and controversy raged over the design's legitimacy and integrity. The AT&T Building's originality and bold departure from convention, however, seem related to the much earlier, and now respected, Chrysler Building (see FIG. 33-66).

AN "ENLARGED JUKEBOX"? Philip Johnson at first endorsed, then disapproved of, a building that rode considerably farther on the wave of postmodernism than did his AT&T tower. The Portland (Oregon) Building (FIG. **34-48**), the much smaller work of American architect MICHAEL GRAVES (b. 1934), reasserts the wall's horizontality against the verticality of the tall, fenestrated shaft. Graves favored the square's solidity and stability, making it the main body of his composition (echoed in the windows), resting upon a wider base and carrying a set-back penthouse crown. Narrow vertical windows tying together seven stories open two paired facades. These support capital-like large hoods on one pair of opposite facades and a frieze of stylized Baroque roundels tied by bands on the other pair. A huge painted keystone motif joins five upper levels on one facade pair, and painted surfaces further define the building's base, body, and penthouse levels.

The assertion of the wall, the miniature square windows, and the painted polychromy define the surfaces as predominately mural and carry a rather complex symbolic program. The modernist purist surely would not welcome either ornamental wall, color painting, or symbolic reference. These features, taken together, raised an even greater storm of criticism than that which greeted the Sydney Opera House or the AT&T Building. Various critics denounced Graves's Portland Building as "an enlarged jukebox," an "oversized Christmas package," a "marzipan monstrosity," a "histrionic masquerade," and a kind of "pop surrealism." Yet others approvingly noted its classical references as constituting a "symbolic temple" and praised the building as a courageous architectural adventure. City officials and citizens joined architectural critics in commending or blaming Graves. At present, historians regard the Portland Building, like the AT&T tower, as an early marker of postmodernist innovation.

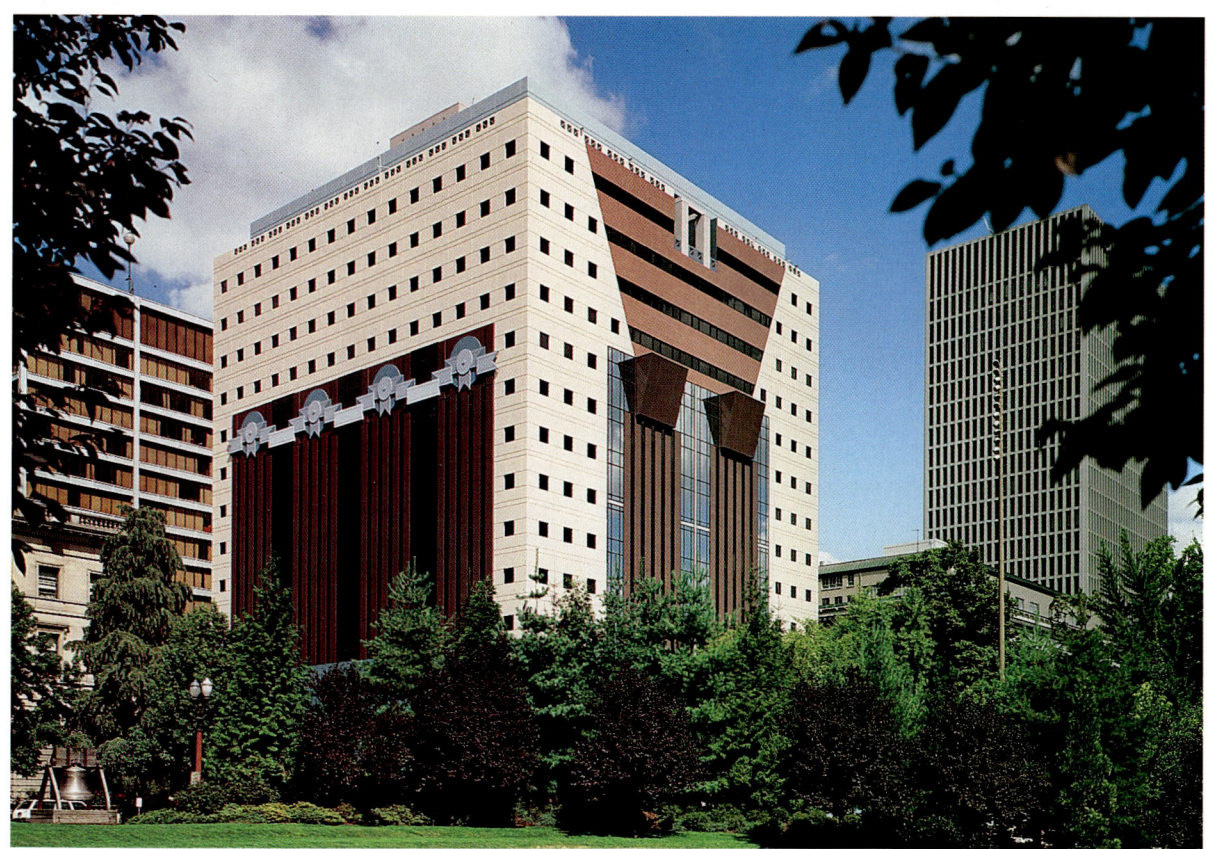

34-48 MICHAEL GRAVES, The Portland Building, Portland, 1980.

34-49 ROBERT VENTURI, JOHN RAUCH AND SCOTT BROWN house in Delaware (west elevation), 1978–1983.

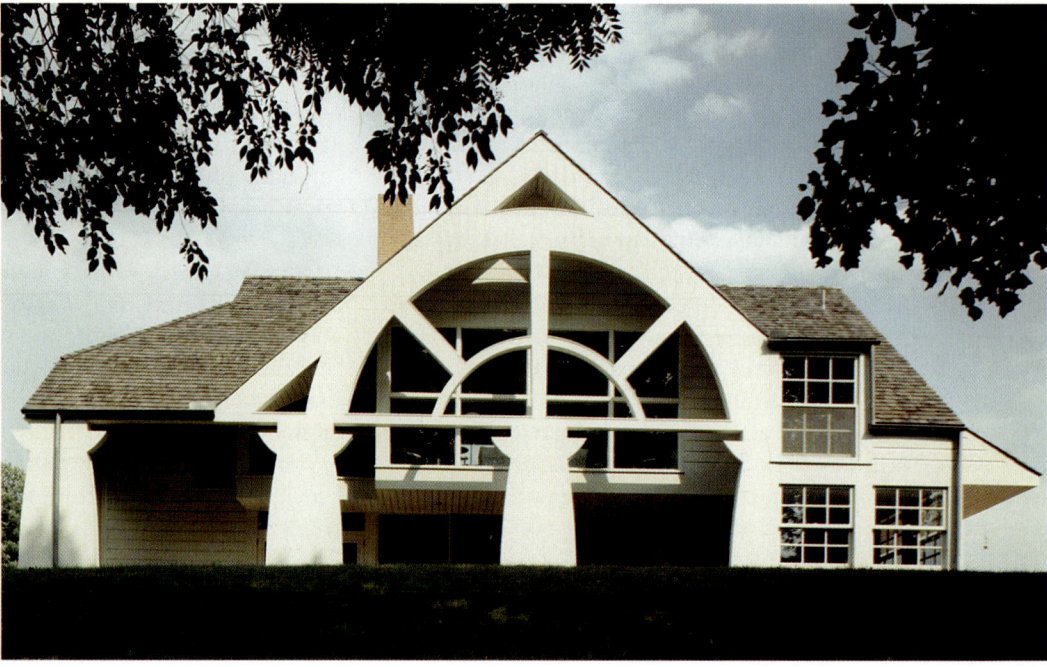

VINDICATING ARCHITECTURAL POPULISM It is important to note here the public's widening participation in the judging of new architecture, indicating an increasing awareness of the new, popular uses of the urban environment. Many observers of architectural developments have expressed the feeling that building design is none the worse for borrowing from the lively, if more-or-less garish, language of pop culture. The night-lit dazzle of entertainment sites such as Las Vegas, or the carnival colors, costumes, and fantasy of theme park props, might just as well serve as inspiration for the designers of civic architecture. ROBERT VENTURI (b. 1925) codified these ideas in his publication *Learning from Las Vegas* (1972). The Portland Building appeared to many viewers a vindication of architectural populism against the pretension of modernist elitism.

Venturi's own designs for houses show him adapting historical as well as contemporary styles to suit his symbolic and expressive purpose. A fundamental axiom of modernism is that a building's form must arise directly and logically from its function and structure. Against this rule, Venturi asserted that the form should be separate from the function and structure and that decorative and symbolic forms of everyday life should enwrap the structural core. Thus, for a Delaware residence (FIG. **34-49**) designed in 1978, with JOHN RAUCH and DENISE SCOTT BROWN, Venturi respected the countryside setting and its eighteenth-century history by recalling the stone-based barnlike, low-profile farm dwellings with their shingled roofs and double-hung multipaned windows. He fronted the house with an amusingly "cut-out" and asymmetrical parody of a Neoclassical portico. A building by Venturi is, in his own words, a kind of "decorated shed."

MAKING "METABOLISM" VISIBLE In Paris, the short-lived partnership of British architect RICHARD ROGERS (b. 1933) and Italian architect RENZO PIANO (b. 1937) involved using motifs and techniques from ordinary industrial buildings in their design for the Georges Pompidou National Center of Art and Culture, known popularly as the "Beaubourg" (FIG. **34-50**), in Paris. The anatomy of this six-level building, which opened in 1977, is fully exposed, rather like an updated version of the Crystal Palace (see FIG. 28-60). However, the architects also made visible the Pompidou Center's "metabolism." They color coded pipes, ducts, tubes, and corridors according to function (red for the movement of people, green for water, blue for air-conditioning, and yellow for electricity), much as in a sophisticated factory.

Critics who deplore the Beaubourg's vernacular qualities disparagingly refer to the complex as a "cultural supermarket" and point out that its exposed entrails require excessive maintenance to protect them from the elements. Nevertheless, the building has been popular with people since it opened. The flexible interior spaces and the colorful structural body provide a festive environment for the crowds flowing through the building enjoying its art galleries, industrial design center, library, science and music centers, conference rooms, research and archival facilities,

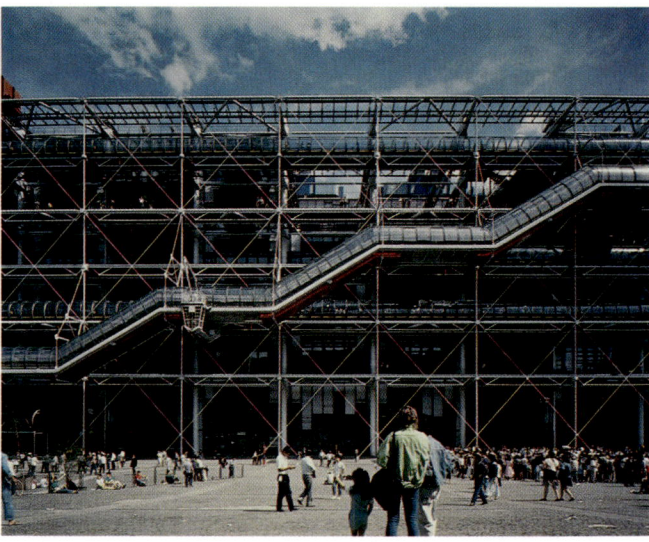

34-50 RICHARD ROGERS and RENZO PIANO, Georges Pompidou National Center of Art and Culture (the "Beaubourg"), Paris, 1977.

movie theaters, rest areas, and restaurant (which looks down and through the building to the terraces outside). The sloping plaza in front of the main entrance has become part of the local scene. Peddlers, street performers, Parisians, and tourists fill this "square" at almost all hours of the day and night. The kind of secular activity once occurring in the open spaces in front of cathedral entrances interestingly has shifted here to a center for culture and popular entertainment—perhaps the most commonly shared experiences.

Deconstructivist Architecture

In the later decades of the twentieth century, art critics (such as Clement Greenberg and Harold Rosenberg) assumed a commanding role. Indeed, their categorization of movements and their interpretation and evaluation of monuments became a kind of monitoring, gatekeeping activity that determined, as well as described, what was going on in the art world. The voluminous and influential writing these critics (along with artists and art historians) produced prompted scholars to examine the basic premises of criticism. This examination has generated a field of study known as *critical theory*. Critical theorists view art and architecture, as well as literature and the other humanities, as a culture's intellectual products or "constructs." These constructs unconsciously suppress or conceal the actual premises that inform the culture, primarily the values of those politically in control. Thus, cultural products function in an ideological capacity, obscuring, for example, racist or sexist attitudes. When revealed by analysis, the facts behind these constructs, according to critical theorists, contribute to a more substantial understanding of artworks, buildings, books, and the overall culture.

Many critical theorists use an analytical strategy called *deconstruction,* after a method developed by French intellectuals, notably Michel Foucault and Jacques Derrida, in the 1960s and 1970s. For those employing deconstruction, all cultural constructs are "texts." People can read these texts in a variety of ways, but they cannot arrive at fixed or uniform meanings. Any interpretation can be valid, and readings differ from time to time, place to place, and person to person. Further, as cultural products, how texts signify and what they signify are entirely conventional. They can refer to nothing outside of themselves, only to other texts. Thus, no extratextual reality

exists that people can reference. The enterprise of deconstruction is to reveal the contradictions and instabilities of these texts, or cultural language (written or visual).

With primarily political and social aims, deconstructive analysis has the ultimate goal of effecting political and social change. Accordingly, critical theorists who employ this approach seek to uncover, to deconstruct, the facts of power, privilege, and prejudice underlying the practices and institutions of any given culture. In so doing, deconstruction reveals the precariousness of structures and systems, such as language and cultural practices, along with the assumptions underlying them.

Critical theorists are not unified about any philosophy or analytical method, because in principle they oppose firm definitions. They do share a healthy suspicion of all traditional truth claims and value standards, all hierarchical authority and institutions. For them, deconstruction means destabilizing established meanings, definitions, and interpretations while encouraging subjectivity and individual differences.

In architecture, deconstruction as an analytical strategy emerged in the 1970s (some scholars refer to this development as Deconstructivist architecture). It proposes, above all, to disorient observers. To this end, Deconstructionist architects attempt to disrupt the conventional categories of architecture and to rupture viewers' expectations based on them. Destabilization plays a major role in Deconstructivist architecture. Disorder, dissonance, imbalance, asymmetry, unconformity, and irregularity replace their opposites—order, consistency, balance, symmetry, regularity, and clarity, as well as harmony, continuity, and completeness. The haphazard presentation of volumes, masses, planes, borders, lighting, locations, directions, spatial relations, and disguised structural facts challenge viewers' assumptions about architectural form as it relates to function. According to Deconstructivist principles, the very absence of the stability of traditional categories of architecture in a structure announces a "deconstructed" building.

DISSONANCE AS AN AESTHETIC STRATEGY British architect JAMES STIRLING (1926–1992) felt that society's current condition demands a juxtaposition of conflicting ideologies, not a resolution. Following Deconstructivist methods, Stirling explored dissonance as an aesthetic strategy in his designs. In his design for the New Staatsgalerie (New State Gallery) (FIG. **34-51**) in Stuttgart, Germany, he combined

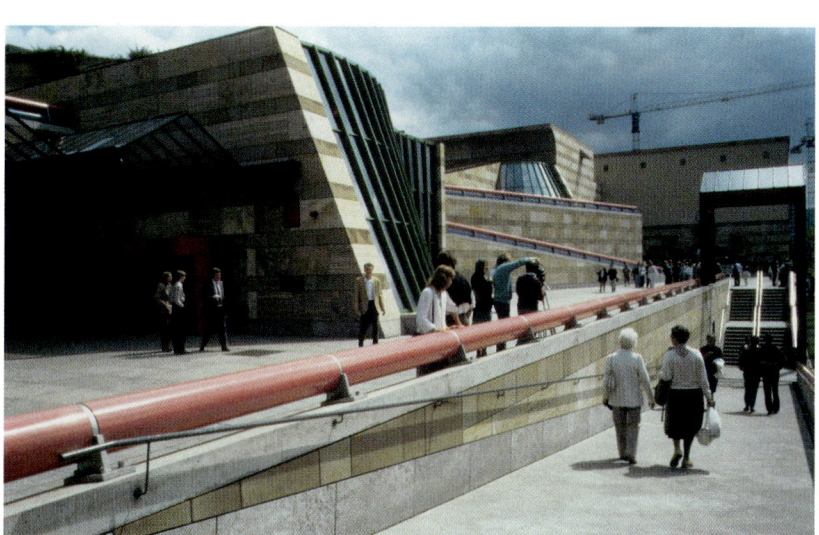

34-51 JAMES STIRLING, Neue Staatsgalerie, Stuttgart, Germany, 1977–1984.

classical forms (such as segmented arches and rustication) with bright green, pink, and blue painted elements and seemingly imbalanced lines—both straight and curvilinear—meeting at awkward and unpredictable angles. The effect is indeed disorienting, but it is also vivacious and engaging.

With deconstruction's destabilization of assumptions about architecture and examination of the premises underlying all cultural constructs, one can imagine deconstruction leading toward architectural designs incorporating the process of decay, thereby revealing deconstructive methods. When designing the air ventilation in the parking garage for the Neue Staatsgalerie, Stirling did just that. Rather than cut neat, symmetrical openings in the masonry, Stirling created irregular openings by having some of the masonry blocks removed and tossed on the ground below the vents to suggest ruins, reminiscent of those found in classical cultures.

AN ARCHITECTURE OF CHAOS   More audacious in its dissolution of form, and farther along on the path of deconstruction, is another building in Stuttgart, the Hysolar Institute Building at the University of Stuttgart (FIG. **34-52**). GÜNTER BEHNISCH (b. 1922) designed it as part of a joint

German–Saudi Arabian research project on the technology of solar energy. The architect intended to deny here the possibility of spatial enclosure altogether, and his apparently chaotic arrangement of the units defies easy analysis. The shapes of the Hysolar Institute's roof, walls, and windows seem to explode, avoiding any suggestion of clear, stable masses. Behnisch aggressively played with the whole concept of architecture and viewers' relationship to it. The disordered architectural elements that seem precariously perched and visually threaten to collapse frustrate observers' expectations of buildings.

DISORDER AND DISEQUILIBRIUM   An architect whom scholars perhaps have most identified with Deconstructivist architecture is the Canadian-born FRANK GEHRY (b. 1929). Trained in sculpture, and at different times a collaborator with Claes Oldenberg and Donald Judd, Gehry works up his designs by constructing models and then cutting them up and arranging them until he has a satisfying composition. His most recent project is the Guggenheim Museum (FIG. **34-53**) in Bilbao, Spain. The immensely dramatic building appears as a mass of asymmetrical and imbalanced forms, and the irregularity of the main masses—whose profiles change dramatically with every shift of a visitor's position—

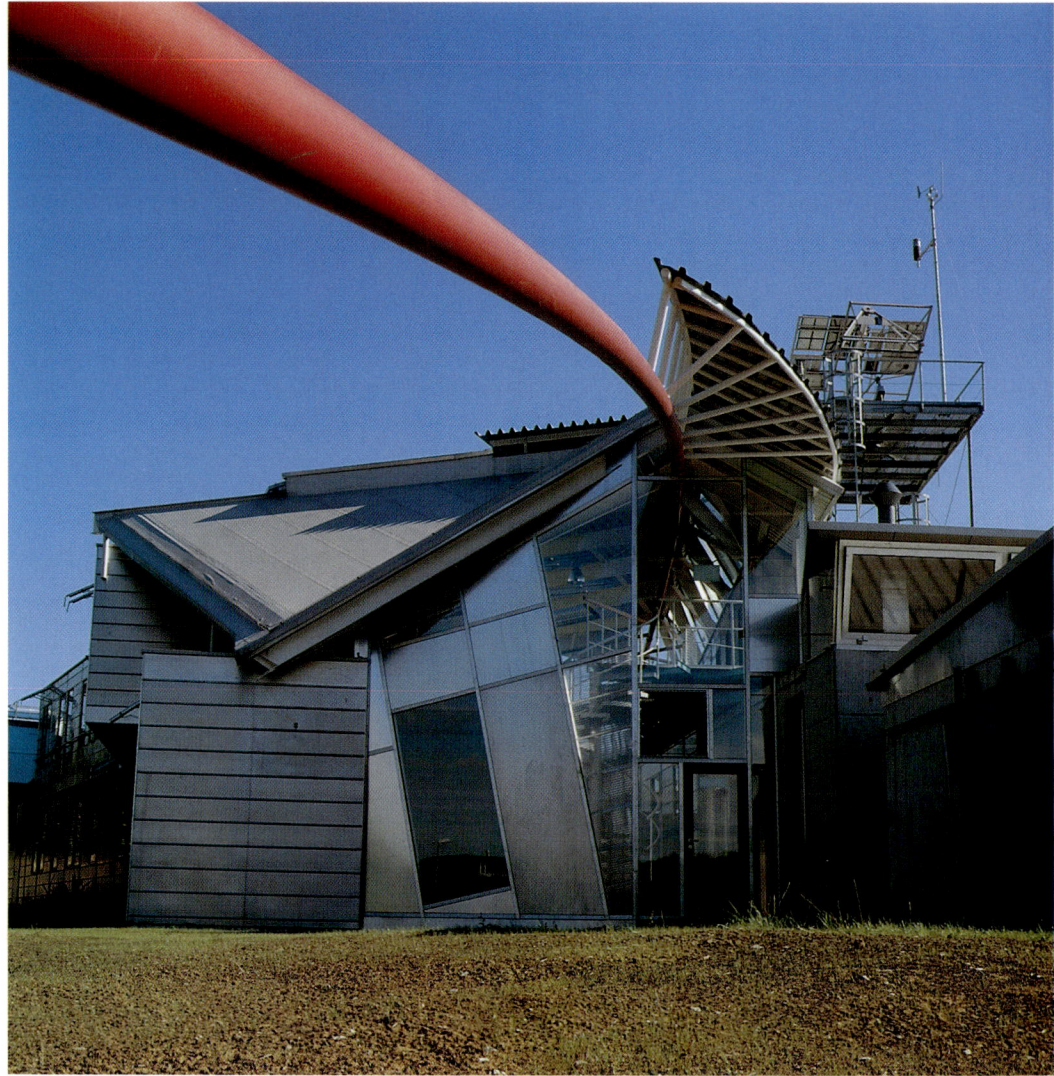

34-52 GÜNTER BEHNISCH, Hysolar Institute Building, University of Stuttgart, Stuttgart, Germany, 1987.

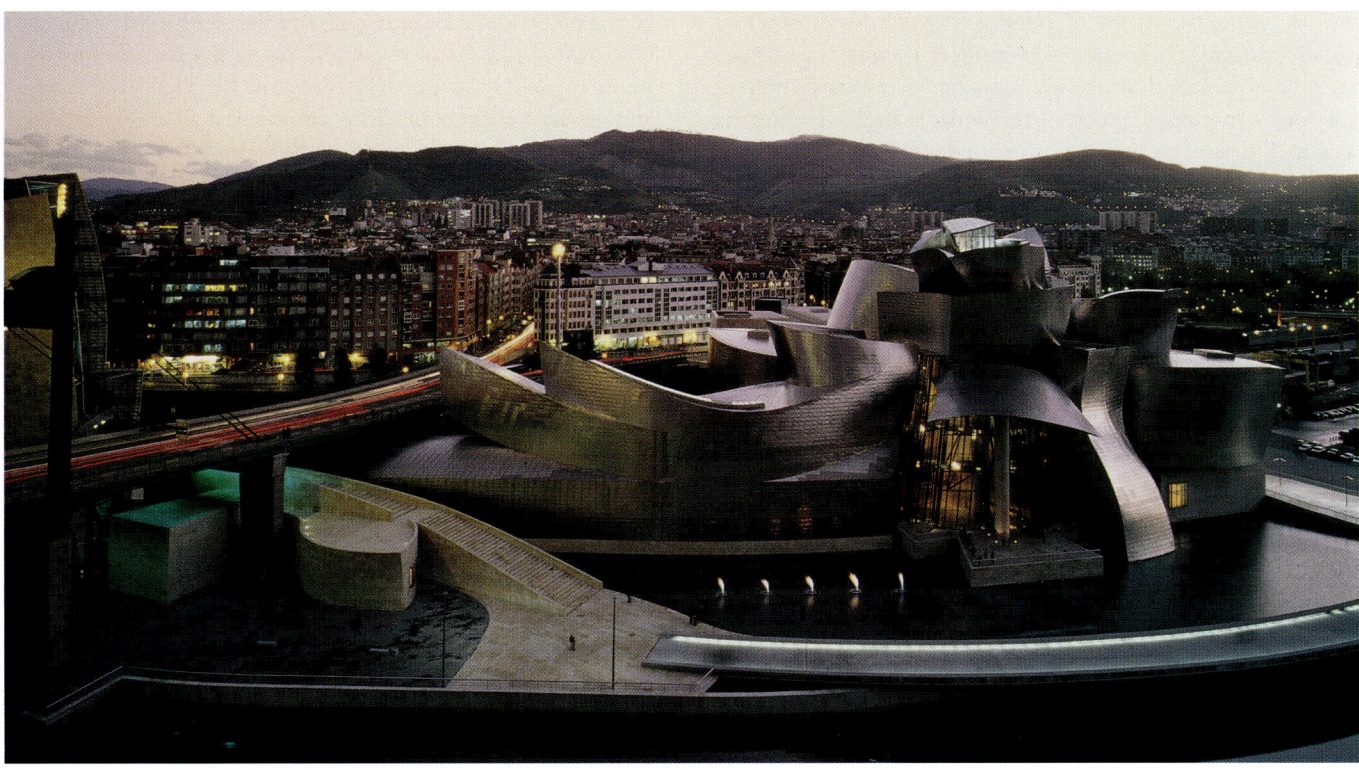

34-53   FRANK GEHRY, Guggenheim Museum, Bilbao, Spain, 1997.

seems like a collapsed or collapsing aggregate of units. The scaled limestone- and titanium-clad exterior, lends a space-age character to the building and highlights further the unique cluster effect of the many forms. A group of organic forms that Gehry refers to as a "metallic flower" tops the museum. Gehry was inspired to create the offbeat design by what he called the "surprising hardness" of the heavily industrialized city of Bilbao. The futuristic urban vision of a cold, mechanical industrial world of 2026 in Fritz Lang's film *Metropolis,* first released in 1926, also stimulated Gehry. In the museum's center, an enormous glass-walled atrium soars to one hundred sixty-five feet in height, serving as the focal point for the three levels of galleries (FIG. Intro-1) radiating from it. The seemingly weightless screens, vaults, and volumes of the interior float and flow into one another, guided only by light and dark cues. Overall, the Guggenheim at Bilbao is a profoundly compelling structure. Its disorder, its seeming randomness of design, and the disequilibrium it prompts in viewers fit nicely into postmodern and deconstructivist agendas.

POSTMODERNISM IN PAINTING, SCULPTURE, AND NEW MEDIA

The challenges to modernist doctrine that emerged in architecture have their own resolution in other artistic media. As with architecture, arriving at a concrete definition of postmodernism in other media is difficult. Historically, by the 1970s, the range of art—from abstraction to performance to figuration—was so broad that the inclusiveness central to postmodern architecture characterizes postmodern art as well. Just as postmodern architects incorporate traditional elements or historical references, many postmodern artists reveal a self-consciousness about their place in the art historical continuum. They resurrect artistic traditions to comment on and reinterpret those styles or idioms. Writings about postmodern art refer to Neo-Minimalism, Neo-Pop, and Neo-Romanticism, among others, evidencing the prevalence of this reevaluation of earlier art forms.

Beyond that, however, artists, critics, dealers, and art historians do not agree on the elements comprising the vague realm of postmodern art. Many people view postmodernism as a critique of modernism. For example, numerous postmodern artists have undertaken the task of challenging modernist principles such as the avant-garde's claim to originality. In the avant-garde's zeal to undermine traditional notions about art and to produce ever more innovative art forms, they placed a premium on originality and creativity. Postmodern artists challenge this claim by addressing issues of the copy or reproduction and the appropriation of images or ideas from others.

Other scholars, such as Frederic Jameson, assert that a major characteristic of postmodernism is the erosion between high culture and popular culture—a separation Clement Greenberg and the modernists had staunchly defended. With the appearance of Pop art, that separation became more difficult to maintain. Jameson argues that the intersection of high and mass culture is, in fact, a defining feature of the new postmodernism. He attributes postmodernism's emergence to "a new type of social life and a new economic order—what is often euphemistically called modernization, postindustrial or consumer society, the society of the media or the spectacle, or multinational capitalism."[36]

Further, the intellectual inquiries of critical theorists serving as the basis for Deconstructivist architecture also impacted the other media. For many recent artists, postmodernism involves examining the process by which meaning is generated and the negotiation or dialogue that transpires between viewers and artworks. Like the theorists using deconstructive methods to analyze "texts," or cultural products, many postmodern artists reject the notion that each artwork contains a single fixed meaning. Their work, in part, explores how viewers derive meaning from visual material.

Postmodern art, then, comprises a dizzying array of artworks. While some involve critiques of the modernist program, others present critiques of the art world, and still others incorporate elements of and provide commentary on previous art. A sampling of postmodern art in various media follows.

Neo-Expressionism

One of the first coherent movements to emerge during the postmodern era was Neo-Expressionism. This movement's name reflects postmodern artists' interest in reexamining earlier art production and connects this art to the powerful, intense works of the German Expressionists and the Abstract Expressionists, among other artists.

AN EXTENSION OF PAINT'S PHYSICALITY The art of American artist JULIAN SCHNABEL (b. 1951), in effect, forcefully restates the premises of Abstract Expressionism. When executing his works in the 1980s, however, Schnabel experimented widely with materials and supports—from fragmented china plates bonded to wood to paint on velvet and tarpaulin. He was particularly interested in the physicality

of the objects, and by attaching broken crockery, as evident in *The Walk Home* (FIG. **34-54**), he found an extension of what paint could do. Superficially, the painting recalls the work of the gestural abstractionists—the spontaneous drips of Jackson Pollock (FIG. 34-4) and the agitated brushstrokes of Willem de Kooning (FIG. 34-6). The large scale of Schnabel's works is also reminiscent of Abstract Expressionism. The thick mosaiclike texture, an amalgamation of media, brings together painting, mosaic, and low-relief sculpture. In effect, Schnabel reclaimed older media for his expressionistic method, which considerably amplifies his bold and distinctive statement.

HORSES AS METAPHORS FOR HUMANITY In the 1970s, American SUSAN ROTHENBERG (b. 1945) produced a major series of large paintings with the horse as the central image. The horse theme resonates with history and metaphor—from Roman equestrian sculpture to the paintings of German Expressionist Franz Marc. Like Marc, Rothenberg saw horses as metaphors for humanity. She stated, "The horse was a way of not doing people, yet it was a symbol of people, a self-portrait, really."[37] Rothenberg, however, distilled the image down to a ghostly outline or hazy depiction that is more poetic than descriptive. As such, her works fall in the nebulous area between representation and abstraction. In paintings such as *Tattoo* (FIG. **34-55**), the loose brushwork and agitated surface contribute to the image's expressiveness and account for Rothenberg's categorization as a Neo-Expressionist. The title, *Tattoo,* refers to the horse's head drawn within the outline of its leg—"a tattoo or memory image," according to the artist.[38]

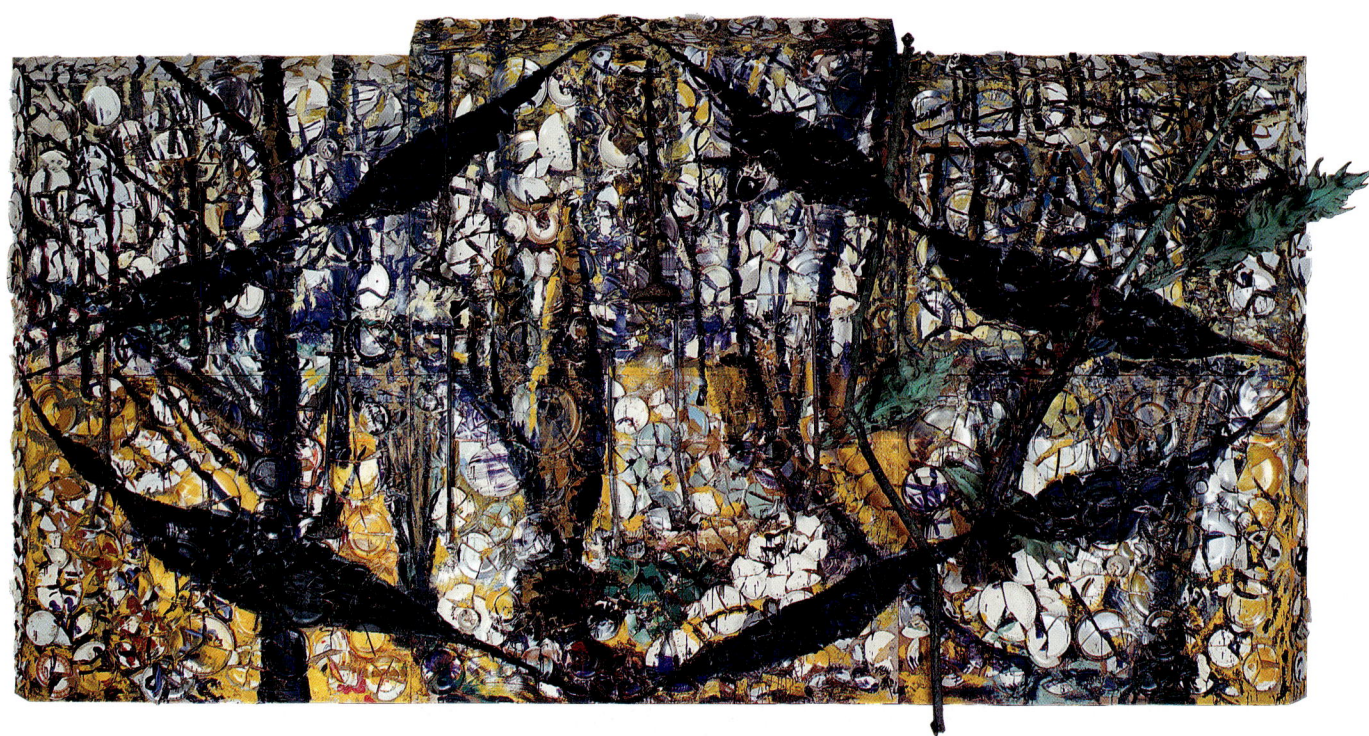

34-54 JULIAN SCHNABEL, *The Walk Home*, 1984–1985. Oil, plates, copper, bronze, fiberglass, and bondo on wood, 9′ 3″ × 19′ 4″. Eli Broad Family Foundation and the Pace Gallery, New York.

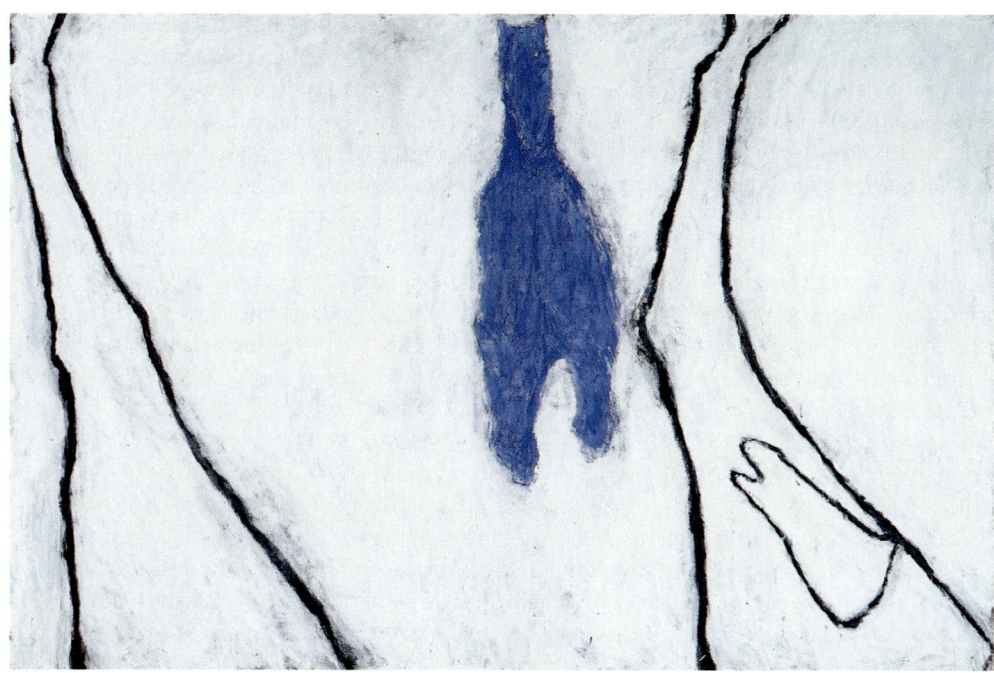

34-55 SUSAN ROTHENBERG, *Tattoo*, 1979. Acrylic, flashe on canvas, 5′ 7″ × 8′ 7$\frac{1}{8}$″ × 1$\frac{1}{4}$″. Collection Walker Art Center, Minneapolis (purchased with the aid of funds from Mr. and Mrs. Edmond R. Ruben, Mr. and Mrs. Julius E. Davis, the Art Center Acquisition Fund and the National Endowment for the Arts, 1979).

CONFRONTING GERMAN HISTORY Neo-Expressionism was by no means an American movement. The number of artists who pursued this direction in their art indicates the compelling nature of this style. German artist ANSELM KIEFER (b. 1945) has produced some of the most lyrical and engaging works of the contemporary period. His paintings, such as *Nigredo* (FIG. **34-56**), are monumental in scale, thereby commanding immediate attention. On further inspection, the works draw viewers to the agitated surface, made more complex by the addition of materials such as straw and

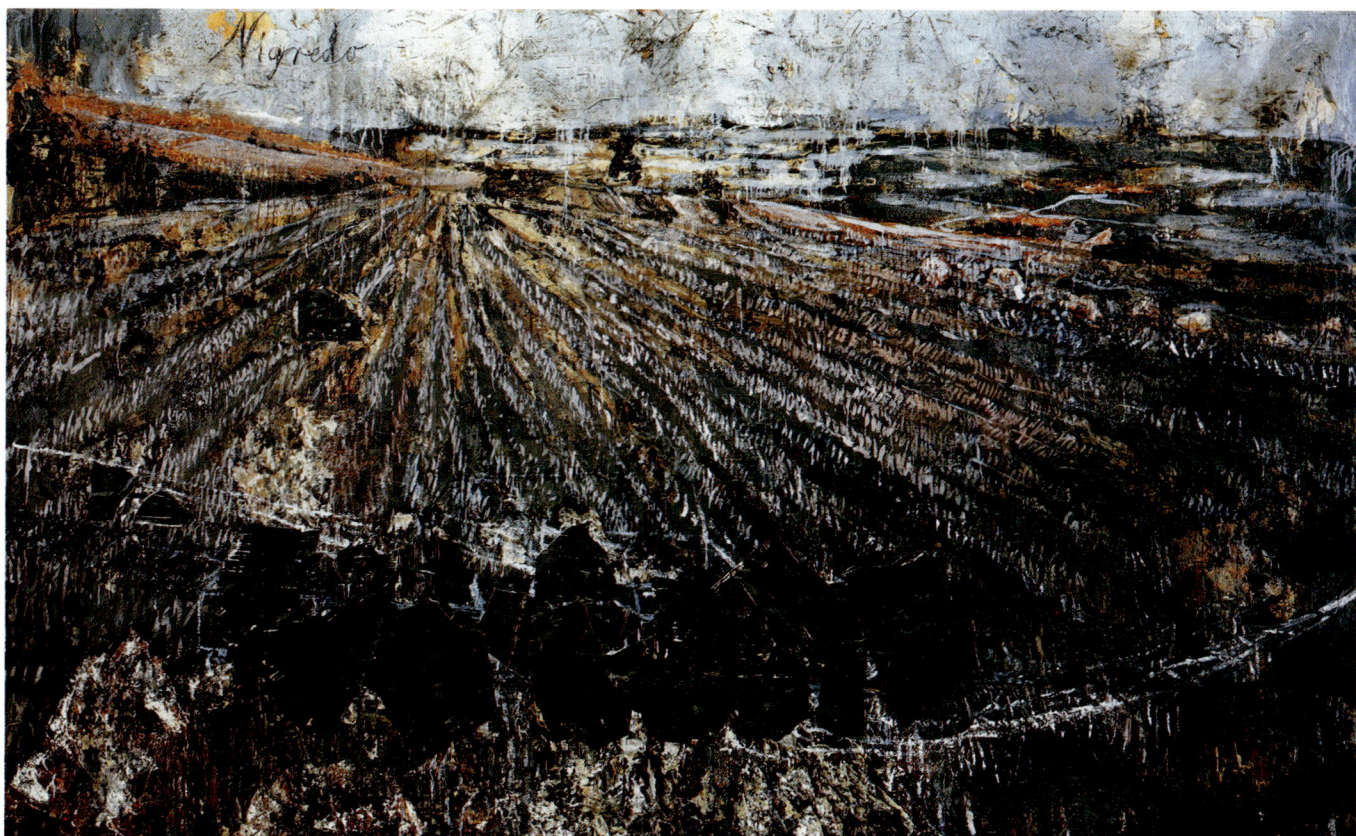

34-56 ANSELM KIEFER, *Nigredo,* 1984. Oil paint on photosensitized fabric, acrylic emulsion, straw, shellac, relief paint on paper pulled from painted wood, 11′ × 18′. Philadelphia Museum of Art, Philadelphia (gift of Friends of the Philadelphia Museum of Art).

lead. Kiefer's paintings, like those of Schnabel, have thickly encrusted surfaces. It is not just the impressive physicality of Kiefer's paintings that accounts for his work's impact, however. His images function on a mythological or metaphorical level, as well as on a historically specific one. Kiefer's works of the 1970s and 1980s often involved a reexamination of German history, particularly the painful Nazi era of 1920–1945, and evoke the feeling of despair. Kiefer believes Germany's participation in World War II and the Holocaust left permanent scars on the souls of the German people and on the souls of all humanity.

Nigredo (a word which means "black") pulls viewers into an expansive landscape depicted using Renaissance perspectival principles. This landscape, however, is far from pastoral or carefully cultivated. Rather, it appears bleak and charred. While not making specific reference to the Holocaust, this incinerated landscape does indirectly allude to the horrors of that historical event. More generally, the blackness of the landscape may refer to the notion of alchemical change or transformation, a concept of great interest to Kiefer. Black is one of the four symbolic colors of the alchemist—a color that refers both to death and to the molten, chaotic state of substances broken down by fire. The alchemist, however, focuses on the transformation of substances, and thus the emphasis on blackness is not absolute, but can also be perceived as part of a process of renewal and redemption. Kiefer thus imbued his work with a deep symbolic meaning that, when combined with the intriguing visual quality of his parched, congealed surfaces, results in powerful, moving images.

TRANSFORMING ART HISTORY LESSONS Like that of the other Neo-Expressionists, the work of Italian artist SANDRO CHIA (b. 1946) echoes with the legacies of earlier artists—the German Expressionists and, most appropriately, the Italian Futurists. *Rabbit for Dinner* (FIG. **34-57**) is one

such work. At first glance, this painting's color, energy, and power captivate viewers. Further inspection reveals the connections to previous art—the vivid colors of Ernst Ludwig Kirchner (see FIG. 33-5), the agitated brushstrokes of Emil Nolde (see FIG. 33-6), and the dissection of form reminiscent of Gino Severini's work (see FIG. 33-23). Chia believes his strength as an artist lies in his ability to absorb art history's lessons and to reinterpret those images into new contemporary visual realities. The artist explained his use of past art: "We are living in a historical period where the sensation of accumulation is very strong. The present is like the entire history of art. . . . In my opinion, we should work . . . upon this accumulation, this labyrinth of styles."[39]

Art as a Political Weapon

With the renewed interest in representation ushered in by the Pop Artists and Superrealists in the 1960s and 1970s, artists once again began to embrace the persuasive powers of art to communicate with a wide audience. In recent decades, artists have investigated more insistently the dynamics of power and privilege, especially in relation to issues of race, ethnicity, gender, and class. This section introduces artists addressing these issues, beginning with feminism.

In the 1970s, the feminist movement focused public attention on the history of women and their place in society. In art, two women—Judy Chicago and Miriam Schapiro—largely spearheaded the American feminist movement under the auspices of the Feminist Art Program. Chicago and a group of students at California State University, Fresno, founded this program, and Chicago and Schapiro coordinated it at the California Institute of the Arts in Valencia, California. In 1972, as part of this program, teachers and students joined to create projects such as Womanhouse, an abandoned house in Los Angeles they completely converted into a suite

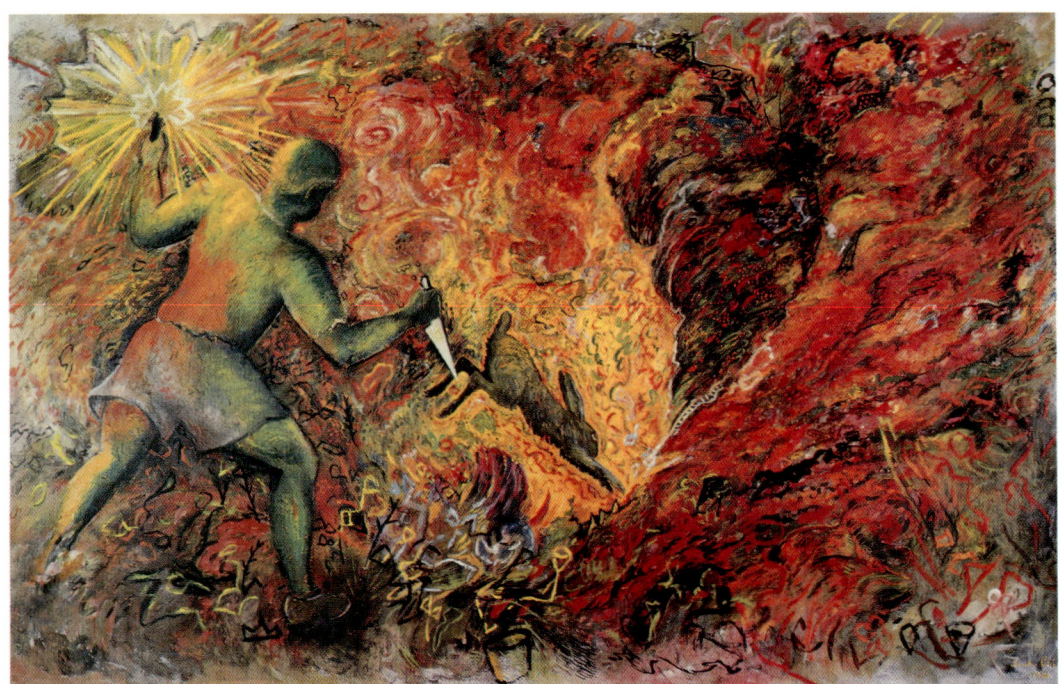

34-57 SANDRO CHIA, *Rabbit for Dinner,* 1980. Oil on canvas, 6′ 9″ × 11′ 1½″. Collection of Stedilijk Museum, Amsterdam. Copyright © Sandra Chia/ Licensed by VAGA, New York, NY.

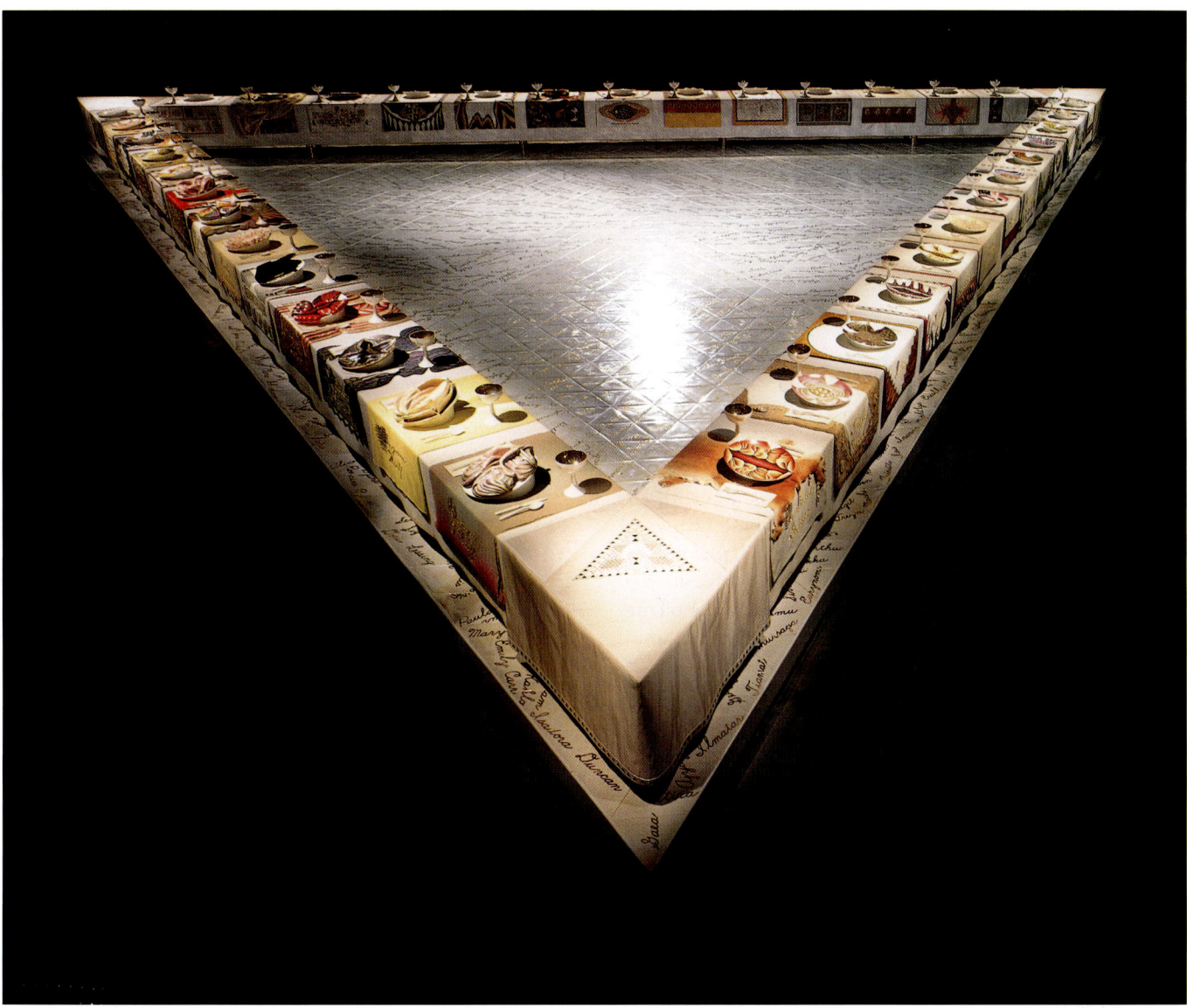

34-58 JUDY CHICAGO, *The Dinner Party,* 1979. Multimedia, including ceramics and stitchery, 48′ × 48′ × 48′ installed.

of "environments," each based on a different aspect of women's lives and fantasies.

A DINNER PARTY CELEBRATING WOMEN In her own work in the 1970s, JUDY CHICAGO (born Judy Cohen in 1939) wanted to educate viewers about women's role in history and the fine arts. She aimed to establish a respect for women and their art, to forge a new kind of art expressing women's experiences, and to find a way to make that art accessible to a large audience. Inspired early in her career by the work of Barbara Hepworth (see FIG. 33-71), Georgia O'Keeffe (see FIGS. 33-37 and Intro-4), and Nevelson (FIG. 34-18), Chicago developed a personal painting style that consciously included abstract organic vaginal images. In the early 1970s, Chicago began planning an ambitious piece, *The Dinner Party* (FIG. **34-58**), using craft techniques women traditionally practiced (such as china painting and stitchery) to celebrate the achievements and contributions women made throughout history. She originally conceived the work as a feminist Last Supper attended by thirteen women (the "honored guests"). The number thirteen also refers to the number

of women in a witches' coven. This acknowledges a religion (witchcraft) founded to encourage the worship of a female—the Mother Goddess. In the course of her research, Chicago uncovered so many worthy women that she expanded the number of guests threefold to thirty-nine and placed them around a triangular table forty-eight feet long on each side. The triangular form refers to the ancient symbol both for woman and for the Goddess. The notion of a dinner party also alludes to women's traditional role as homemakers. A team of nearly four hundred workers under Chicago's supervision assisted in the creation and assembly of the artwork to her design specifications.

The Dinner Party rests on a white tile floor inscribed with the names of nine hundred ninety-nine additional "women of achievement" to signify that the accomplishments of the thirty-nine honored guests rest on a foundation other women laid. Among the "invited" women at the table are O'Keeffe, the Egyptian pharaoh Hatshepsut, the British writer Virginia Woolf, the Native American guide Sacajawea, and the American suffragist Susan B. Anthony. Chicago acknowledged each guest with a place setting of identical eating utensils and a goblet. Each also has a unique oversized porcelain plate and a

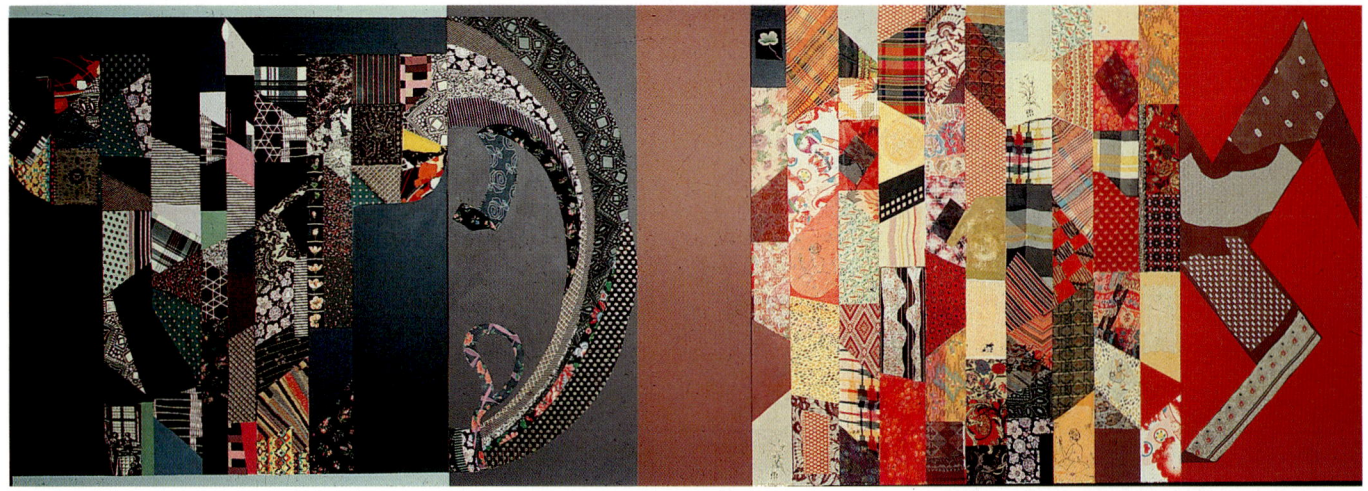

34-59 MIRIAM SCHAPIRO, *Anatomy of a Kimono* (section), 1976. Fabric and acrylic on canvas, 6′ 8″ × 8′ 6″. Collection of Bruno Bishofberger, Zurich.

long place mat or table runner filled with imagery that reflects significant facts about her life and culture. The plates range from simple concave shapes with china-painted imagery to dishes whose sculptured three-dimensional designs almost seem to struggle to free themselves. The unique designs on each plate incorporate both butterfly and vulval motifs—the butterfly as the ancient symbol of liberation and the vulva as the symbol of female sexuality. Each table runner combines traditional needlework techniques, including needlepoint, embroidery, crochet, beading, patchwork, and appliqué.

The rigorous arrangement of *The Dinner Party* and its sacramental qualities draw visitors in and let them experience the importance of forgotten details in the history of women. While the individual place settings with their carefully constructed tributes to the thirty-nine women are impressive, the entire work—both in conception and presentation—provides viewers with a powerful launching point for considering feminist concerns. This work was exhibited for nearly a decade after its completion in the United States, Canada, Australia, and Europe. Since then it has found no permanent home, although it was exhibited in 1996 in Los Angeles.

"FEMMAGES" AND THE ROOTS OF COLLAGE Pursuing a somewhat different path than that Chicago undertook, MIRIAM SCHAPIRO (b. 1923) tried in her work since the 1970s to rouse viewers to a new appreciation of the beauty in materials and techniques women artists used throughout history. Schapiro enjoyed a thriving career as a hard-edge painter when she moved to California in the late 1960s and became fascinated with the hidden metaphors for womanhood she then saw in her abstract paintings. Intrigued by the materials she had used to create a doll's house for her part in Womanhouse, Schapiro began to make huge sewn collages, assembled from fabrics, quilts, buttons, sequins, lace trim, and rickrack collected at antique shows and fairs. She called these works "femmages" to make the point that women had been doing so-called collages long before Pablo Picasso introduced them to the art world. *Anatomy of a Kimono* (FIG. **34-59**) is one of a series of monumental femmages based on the patterns of Japanese kimonos, fans, and robes. This vast composition repeats the kimono shape in a sumptuous array of fabric fragments.

FEMALE BEAUTY AND THE "MALE GAZE" Early attempts at dealing with feminist issues in art tended toward essentialism, emphasizing universal differences—either biological or experiential—between women and men. More recent discussions have gravitated toward the notion of gender as a socially constructed concept—an extremely unstable one. Identity is multifaceted and changeable, making the discussion of feminist issues more challenging. Consideration of the many variables, however, results in a more complex understanding of gender roles. American artist CINDY SHERMAN (b. 1954) addresses in her work the way much of Western art has been constructed to present female beauty for the enjoyment of the "male gaze," a primary focus of contemporary feminist theory. She produced a series of more than eighty black-and-white photographs titled *Untitled Film Stills,* which she began in 1977. Sherman considered how representation constructs reality, and this led her to rethink how her own image was conveyed. She got the idea for the *Untitled Film Stills* series when she was shown some soft-core pornography magazines and the stereotypical ways they depicted women struck her. Sherman decided to produce her own series of photographs, designing, acting in, directing, and photographing the works. In so doing, she took control of her own image and constructed her own identity. In works from the series such as *Untitled: Film Still #35* (FIG. **34-60**), Sherman appears, often in costume and wig, in a photograph that seems to be a film still. Most of the images recall popular film genres but are sufficiently generic so that viewers cannot relate them to specific movies. Sherman often reveals the constructed nature of these images with the shutter release cable (the cord runs across the floor in our illustration) she holds in her hand to take the pictures. Although she is still the object of the viewer's gaze in these images, the identity is one she has chosen to assume.

EXPLORING CULTURAL NOTIONS OF GENDER Another artist who has also explored the male gaze and the culturally constructed notion of gender in her art is BARBARA KRUGER (b. 1945), whose best-known subject has been her exploration of the strategies and techniques of contemporary mass media. Kruger's serious art career began with fiber sculpture inspired by the works of Magdalena

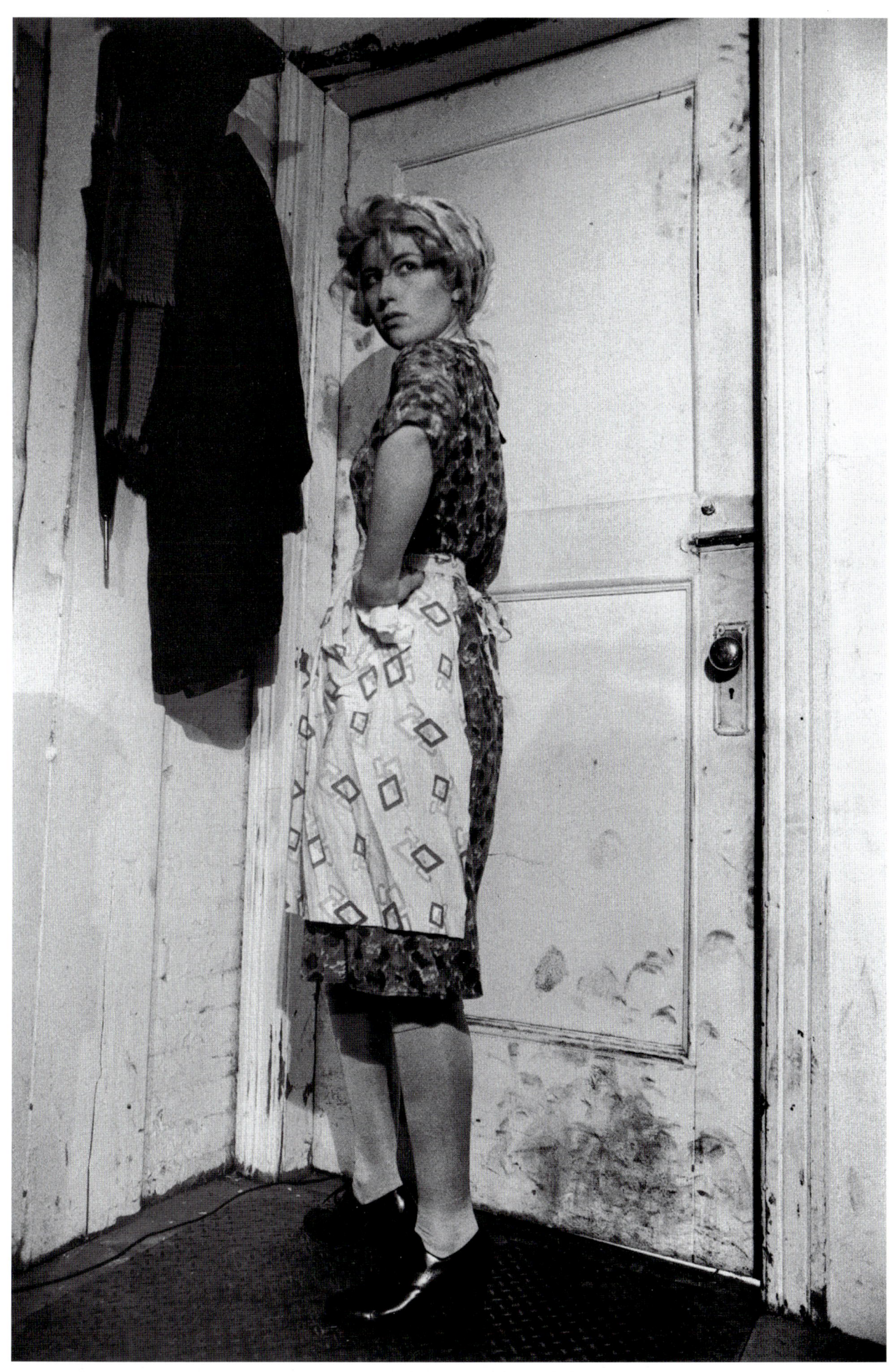

34-60 CINDY SHERMAN, *Untitled Film Still #35*, 1979. Black-and-white photograph, 10″ × 8″.

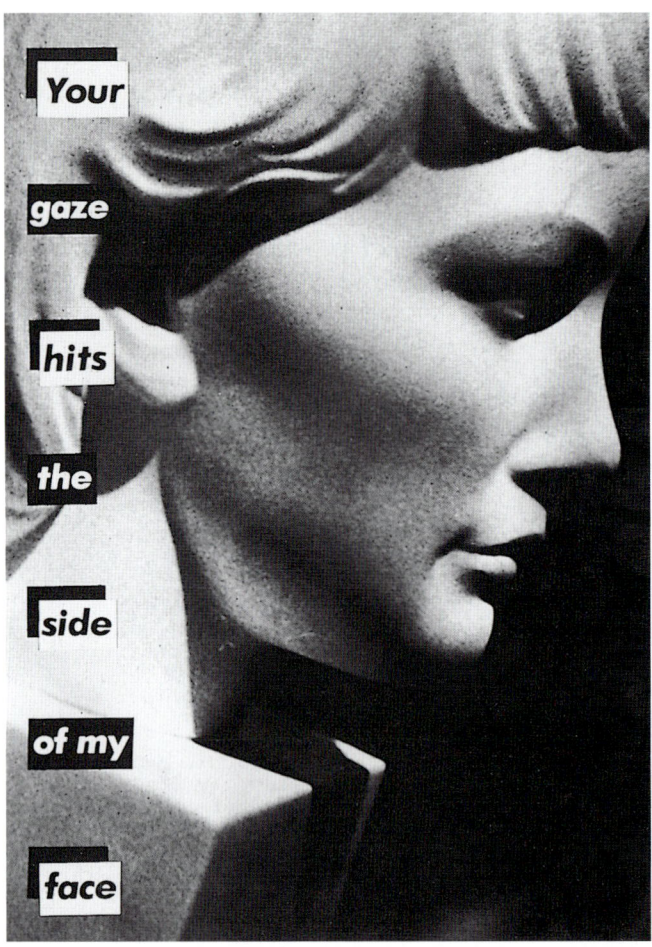

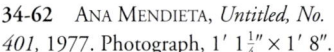

34-61   BARBARA KRUGER, *Untitled (Your Gaze Hits the Side of My Face)*, 1983. Photostat, red painted frame, 6′ 1″ × 4′ 1″.

Abakanowicz (FIG. 34-71). She soon began creating pieces that drew on her early training and work as a graphic designer for the magazine *Mademoiselle*. Mature works such as *Untitled (Your Gaze Hits the Side of My Face)*, FIG. **34-61**, incorporated layout techniques the mass media uses to sell

consumer goods. Although Kruger favored the reassuringly familiar format and look of advertising, her goal was to subvert the typical use of such imagery. Rather, she aimed to expose the deceptiveness of the media messages viewers complacently absorb. Kruger wanted to undermine the myths—particularly those about women—the media constantly reinforces. Her huge word-and-photograph collages (often four by six feet in size) challenged the cultural attitudes embedded in commercial advertising.

In *Untitled (Your Gaze Hits the Side of My Face)*, she overlaid a ready-made photograph of the head of a classically beautiful female sculpture with a vertical row of text composed of eight words selected by the artist. They cannot be taken in with a single glance. Reading them is a staccato exercise, with an overlaid cumulative quality that delays understanding and intensifies the meaning (rather like reading a series of roadside billboards from a speeding car). Kruger's use of text, of words, in her work is significant. Many cultural theorists have asserted that language is one of the most powerful vehicles for internalizing stereotypes and conditioned roles.

THE LANDSCAPE AND THE FEMALE BODY

Cuban-born artist ANA MENDIETA (1948–1985), like Sherman, used her body as a component in her artworks. Although she was concerned with gender issues, her art also dealt with issues of spirituality and cultural heritage. Mendieta's best-known series, *Silueta* (Silhouettes), consists of approximately two hundred earth and body works completed between 1973 and 1980. These works represented her attempt to carry on, as she described, "a dialogue between the landscape and the female body (based on [her] own silhouette)."[40]

Untitled, No. 401 (FIG. **34-62**) is a documentary photograph of one of the earth-body sculptures in the *Silueta* series. In this work, Mendieta outlined her body with gunpowder on a fallen log and then lit the gunpowder, creating a fiery silhouette of her body. As in Environmental art, objects and locations from the natural environment played an important role in Mendieta's art. In other works, she used flowers, clay,

34-62   ANA MENDIETA, *Untitled, No. 401*, 1977. Photograph, 1′ 1¼″ × 1′ 8″.

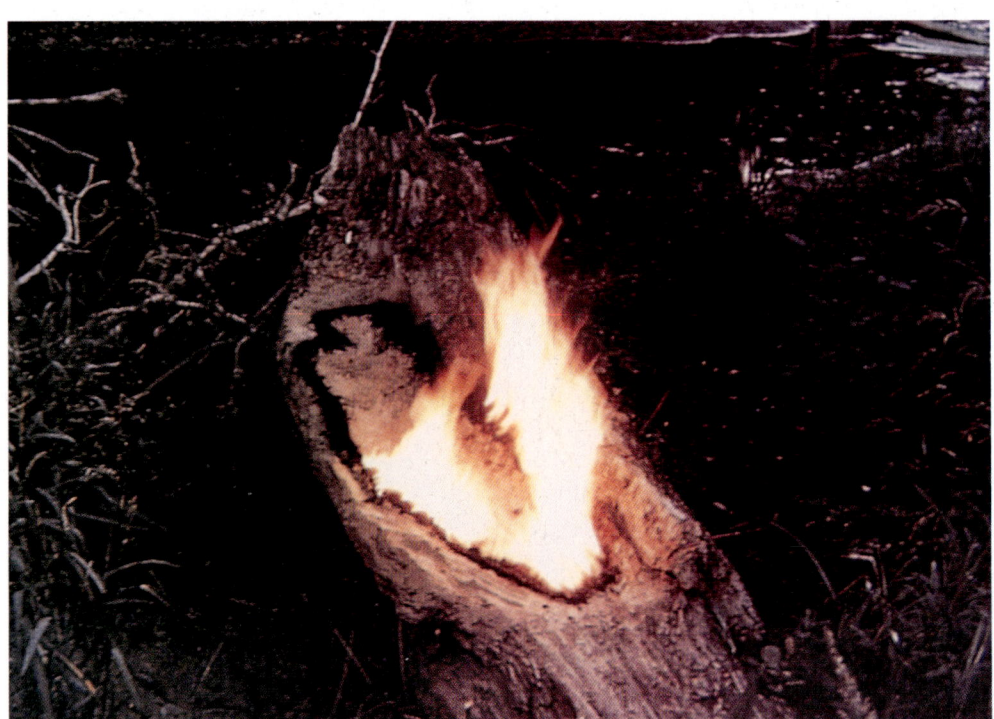

mud, and twigs. Mendieta explained the centrality of this connection to nature: "I believe this has been a direct result of my having been torn from my homeland during my adolescence. I am overwhelmed by the feeling of having been cast from the womb (nature). My art is the way I re-establish the bonds that unite me to the universe. It is a return to the maternal source. Through my earth/body sculptures I become one with the earth."[41]

The notion of burning suggests a connection to rituals of exorcism and purification, revealing the spiritual dimension of Mendieta's art. Beyond their sensual, moving presence, her works also generate a palpable spiritual force. In longing for her homeland, Mendieta sought the cultural understanding and acceptance of the spiritual powers inherent in nature that modern Western societies often seem to reject in favor of scientific and technological developments. Her art is lyrical and passionate, and operates at the intersection of cultural, spiritual, physical, and feminist concerns.

WHO CONTROLS THE BODY?   Much of the art dealing with gender issues focuses on the objectification of women and, in particular, of the human body. American KIKI SMITH (b. 1954), for example, is very interested in the issue of who controls the body. Her early work consisted of sculptures referring to bodily organs and bodily fluids. This seemingly clinical approach was due, in part, to Smith's training as an Emergency Medical Service technician in New York. Smith, however, also wants to reveal the socially constructed nature of the body, and, in her more recent art, she encourages viewers to consider how external forces, such as the media, shape people's perceptions of their bodies. In works such as *Untitled* (FIG. **34-63**), the artist presents viewers with depictions of the body that dramatically depart from conventional representations of the body, both in art and in the media. *Untitled* consists of two life-size wax figures, one male and one female. Both are nude and appear suspended from metal stands. Smith marked each of the sculptures with long white drips—bodily fluids running from the woman's breasts and down the man's leg. She commented:

Most of the functions of the body are hidden . . . from society. . . . [W]e separate our bodies from our lives. But, when people are dying, they are losing control of their bodies. That loss of function can seem

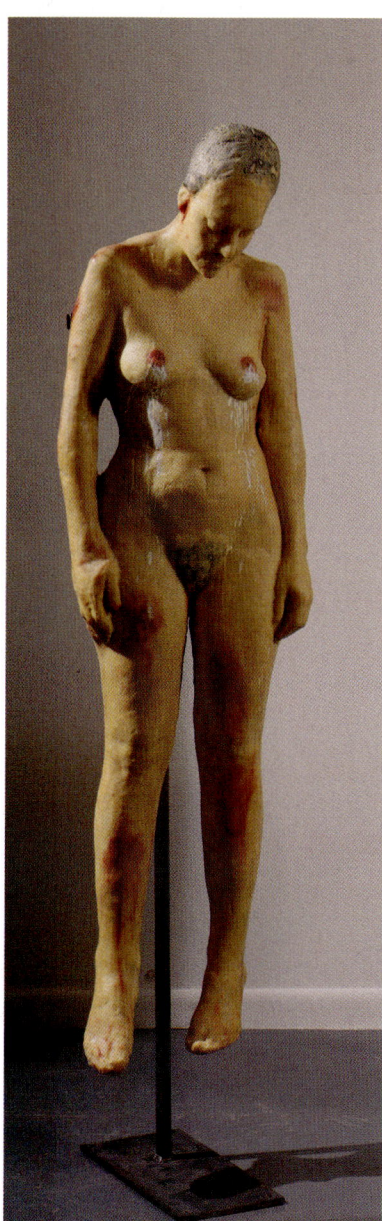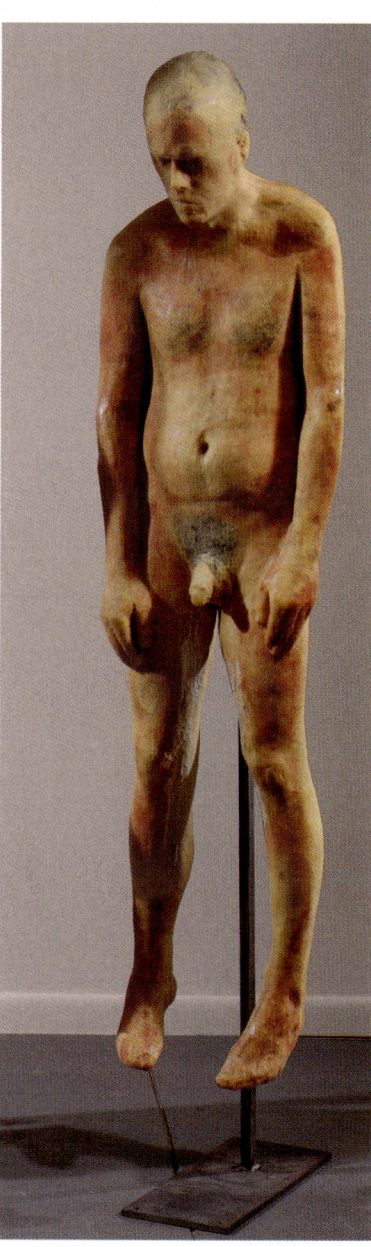

34-63   KIKI SMITH, *Untitled,* 1990. Beeswax and microcrystalline wax figures on metal stands, female figure installed height 6′ 1½″ and male figure installed height 6′ 4 15/16″. Collection Whitney Museum of American Art, New York (purchase, with funds from the Painting and Sculpture Committee).

34-64 FAITH RINGGOLD, *Who's Afraid of Aunt Jemima?*, 1983. Acrylic on canvas with fabric borders, quilted, 7′ 6″ × 6′ 8″. Private collection.

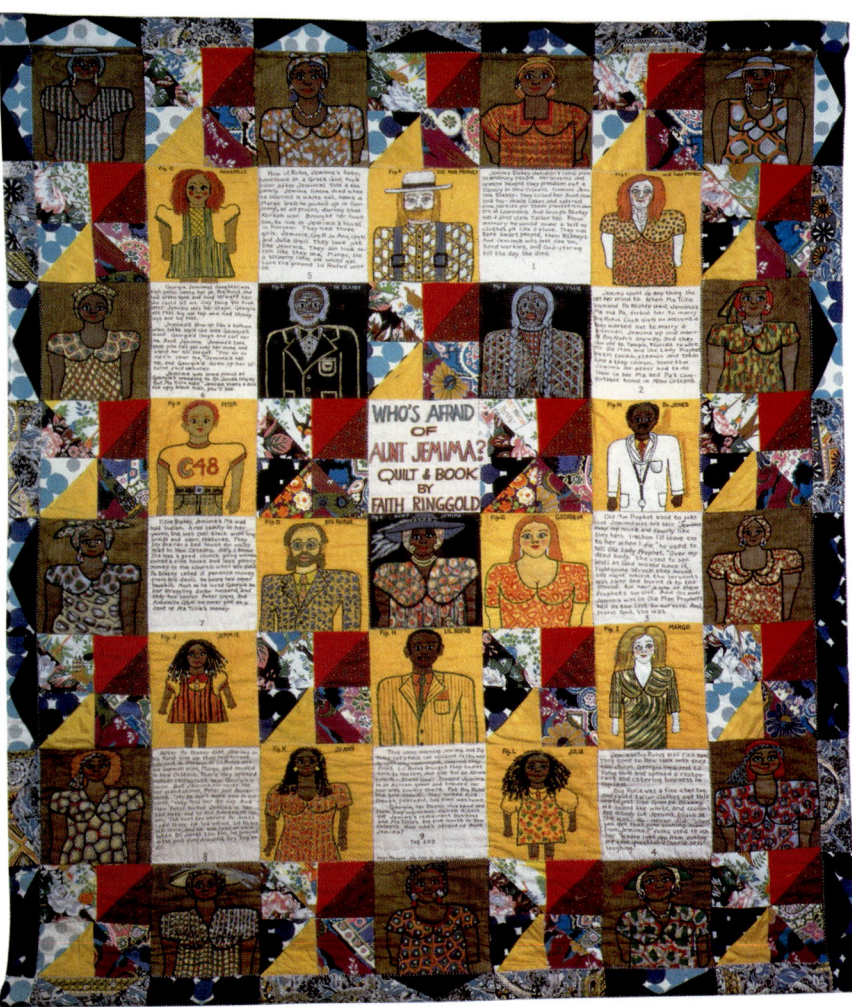

humiliating and frightening. But, on the other hand, you can look at it as a kind of liberation of the body. It seems like a nice metaphor—a way to think about the social—that people lose control despite the many agendas of different ideologies in society, which are trying to control the body(ies) . . . medicine, religion, law, etc. Just thinking about control—who has control of the body? . . . Does the mind have control of the body? Does the social?[42]

BOTH PERSONAL AND POLITICAL Faith Ringgold and Adrian Piper both use their art to explore issues associated with being African American and women in contemporary America. Inspired by the Civil Rights movement, FAITH RING-GOLD (b. 1930) produced numerous works in the 1960s that provided pointed and incisive commentary on the realities of racial prejudice. She increasingly incorporated references to gender as well and, in the 1970s, turned to fabric as the predominant material in her art. Using fabric allowed her to make more specific reference to the domestic sphere, traditionally associated with women, and to collaborate with her mother, Willi Posey, a fashion designer. After her mother's death in 1981, Ringgold created *Who's Afraid of Aunt Jemima?* (FIG. **34-64**), a quilt composed of dyed, painted, and pieced fabric. A moving tribute to her mother, this work combines the personal and the political. The quilt includes a narrative—the witty story of the family of Aunt Jemima, most familiar as the stereotypical black "mammy" but here a successful African-American businesswoman. Ringgold conveyed this narrative both through a text, written in black dialect, and embroidered portraits, all interspersed with traditional patterned squares.

This work, while resonating with personal, autobiographical references, also speaks to the larger issues of the history of African-American culture and the struggles of women to overcome oppression.

AN INSTALLATION CONFRONTING VIEWERS ADRIAN PIPER (b. 1948) has been committed to using her art to effect social change—in particular, to combat pervasive racism. Appropriately, her art is provocative and confrontational, such as the installation *Cornered* (FIG. **34-65**). This piece included a video monitor placed behind an overturned table. Piper appeared on the video monitor, literally cornered behind the table, as she spoke to viewers. Her comments sprang from her experiences as a light-skinned African-American female and from her belief that although overt racism had diminished, subtle and equally damaging forms of bigotry were still rampant. "I'm black," she announces on the sixteen-minute videotape. "Now let's deal with this social fact and the fact of my stating it together. . . . If you feel that my letting people know that I'm not white is making an unnecessary fuss, you must feel that the right and proper course of action for me to take is to pass for white. Now this kind of thinking presupposes a belief that it's inherently better to be identified as white," she continues. The directness of Piper's art forces viewers to examine their own behaviors and values.

COUNTERACTING OBJECTIFICATION The issues of racism and sexism are also central to the work of LORNA

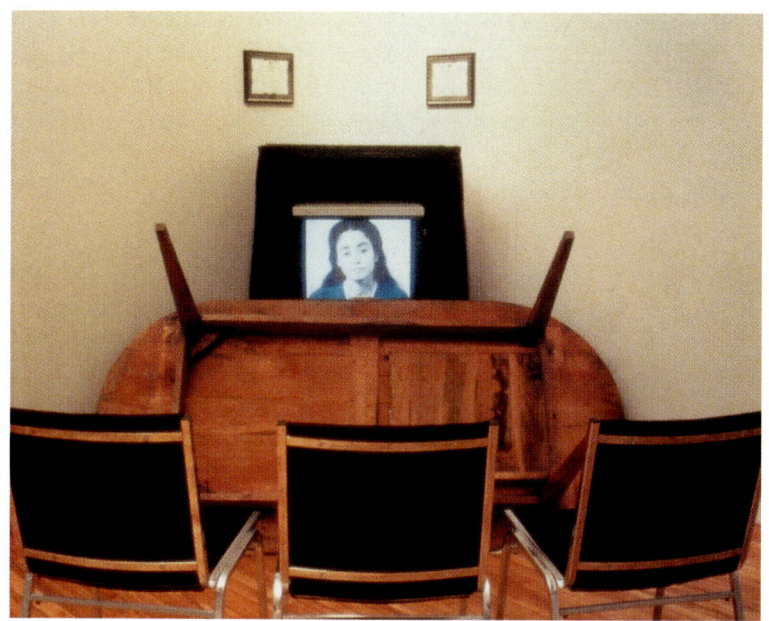

34-65 ADRIAN PIPER, *Cornered,* 1988. Mixed-media installation of variable size; video monitor, table, and birth certificates. Collection of Museum of Contemporary Art, Chicago.

SIMPSON (b. 1960). Simpson has spent much of her career producing photographs that explore feminist and African-American strategies to reveal and subvert conventional representations of gender and race. Like Sherman (FIG. 34-60), she deals with the issue of the gaze, trying to counteract the process of objectification to which both women and African Americans are subject.

In *Stereo Styles* (FIG. **34-66**), a series of Polaroids and engravings, Simpson focuses on African-American hairstyles, often used to symbolize the entire race. Hair is a physical code tied to issues of social status and position. A scholar who has studied the cultural importance of hair pointed out,

"[h]air is never a straightforward biological 'fact' because it is almost always groomed, . . . cut, . . . and generally 'worked upon' by human hands. Such practices socialize hair, making it the medium of significant 'statements' about self and society."[43] Even further, regarding race, this same scholar argues, "where race structures social relations of power, hair—as visible as skin color, but also the most tangible sign of racial difference—takes on another forcefully symbolic dimension."[44] In *Stereo Styles,* Simpson also comments on the appropriation of African-derived hairstyles as a fashion commodity, and the personality traits listed correlate with specific hairstyles.

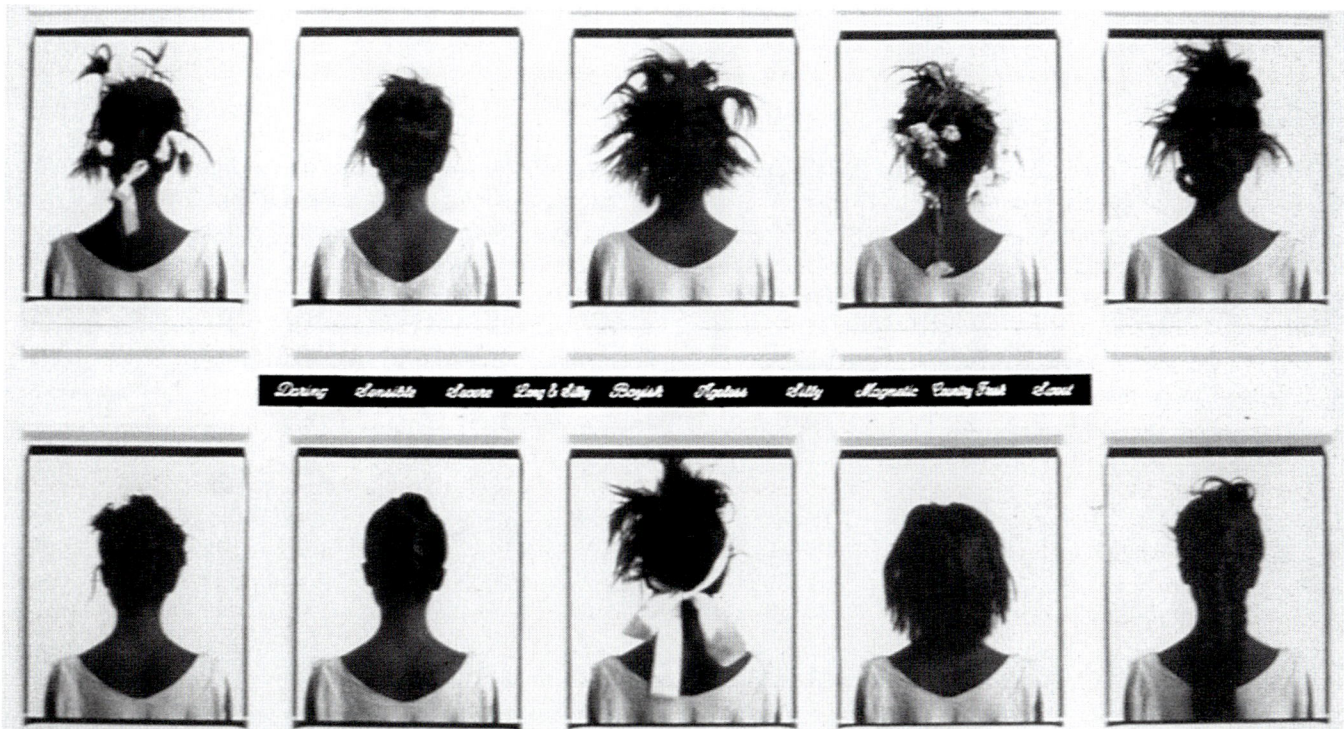

34-66 LORNA SIMPSON, *Stereo Styles,* 1988. 10 black-and-white Polaroid prints and 10 engraved plastic plaques, 5′ 4″ × 9′ 8″ overall. Collection of Raymond J. Learsy, Sharon, Connecticut.

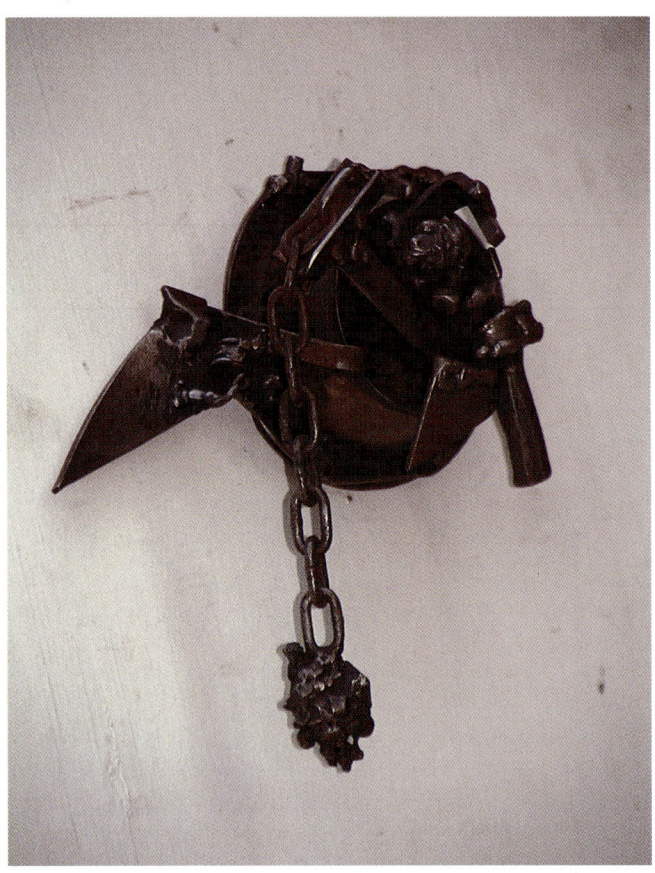

34-67 Melvin Edwards, *Some Bright Morning*, 1963. Welded steel, 1′ 2¼″ × 9¼″ × 5″. Collection of the artist.

"LYNCH FRAGMENTS" American Melvin Edwards (b. 1937) also has sought to reveal a history of collective oppression through his art. One of Edwards's major sculptural series focused on the metaphor of lynching to provoke thought about the legacy of racism. This *Lynch Fragment* series encompassed more than one hundred fifty welded-steel sculptures produced in the years after 1963. Lynching as an artistic theme prompts an immediate and visceral response, conjuring up chilling and gruesome images from the past. Edwards sought to extend this emotional resonance further and in his art explored what lynching "means metaphorically or symbolically."[45]

He constructed his relatively small welded wall-hung sculptures in this series, such as *Some Bright Morning* (FIG. **34-67**), from found metal objects—for example, chains, hooks, hammers, spikes, knife blades, and handcuffs. Although Edwards often intertwined or welded together the individual metal components so as to diminish immediate identifiability, the sculptures still retain a haunting connection to the overall theme. Regarding *Some Bright Morning*, for example, the artist noted, "The dangling ball of steel at the bottom of the chain is the plastic metaphor of hanging. [And] the piece had to hang on the wall, which furthered the metaphor. I said to myself, 'It is hanging there like a lynching.'"[46]

While these works refer to a historical act that evokes a collective memory of oppression, they are also informed by and speak to the continuing contemporary struggle for civil rights and an end to racism. Growing up in Los Angeles, Edwards was surrounded by racial conflict. He picked up some of the metal objects incorporated into his *Lynch Fragments* sculptures in the streets in the aftermath of the Watts riots in 1965, thereby imbuing these disquieting, haunting works with an even greater intensity.

34-68 David Hammons, *Public Enemy,* installation at Museum of Modern Art, New York, 1991. Photographs, balloons, sandbags, guns, and other mixed media.

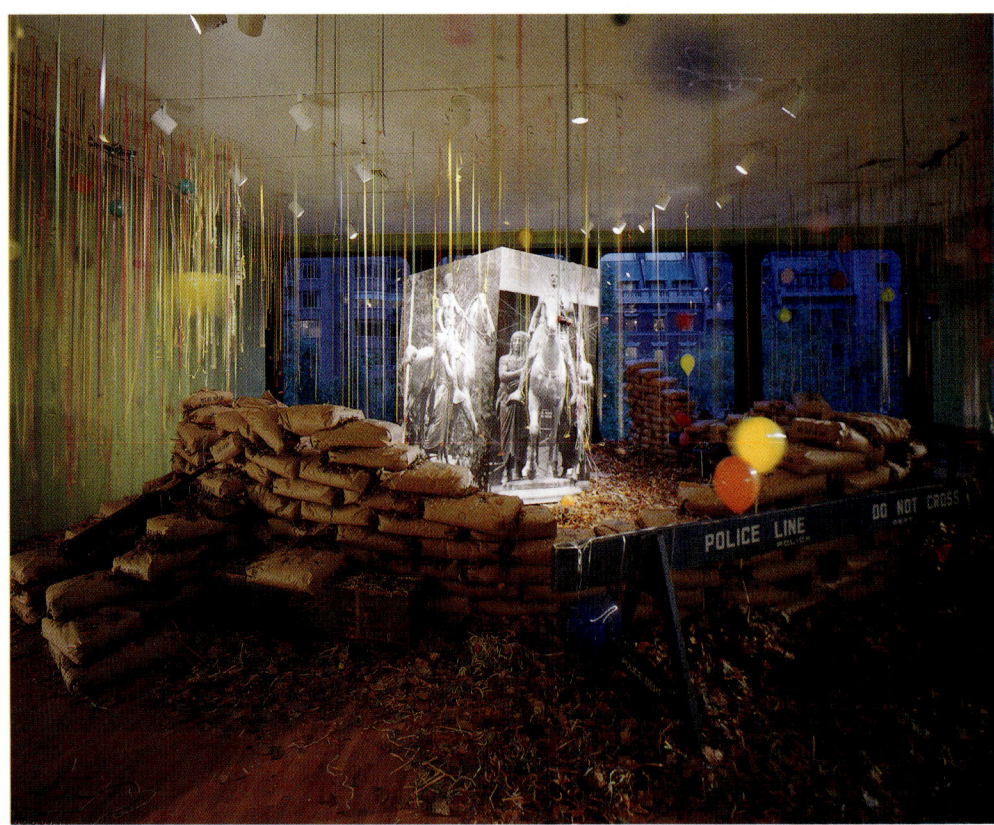

CHALLENGING CULTURAL ICONS   Nurturing viewer introspection is the driving force behind the art of DAVID HAMMONS (b. 1943). In his installations, he combines sharp social commentary with beguiling sensory elements to push viewers to confront racism in American society. He created *Public Enemy* (FIG. **34-68**) for an exhibition at the Museum of Modern Art in New York in 1991. Hammons enticed viewers to interact with the installation by scattering fragrant autumn leaves on the floor and positioning helium-filled balloons throughout the gallery. The leaves crunched underfoot, and the dangling strings of the balloons gently brushed spectators walking around the installation. Once drawn into the environment, viewers encountered the central element in *Public Enemy*—large black-and-white photographs of a public monument depicting Teddy Roosevelt triumphantly seated on a horse, flanked by an African-American man and a Native American man, both appearing in the role of servants. Around the installation's edge, circling the photographs of the monument, were piles of sandbags with both real and toy guns propped on top, aimed at the statue. By selecting evocative found objects and presenting them in a dynamic manner that encouraged viewer interaction, Hammons attracted an audience and then revealed the racism embedded in received cultural heritage and prompted reexamination of values and cultural emblems.

TRADING WITH THE WHITE MAN   Exploring the politics of identity has been an important activity for people from many different walks of life. JAUNE QUICK-TO-SEE SMITH (b. 1940) is a Native American artist descended from the Shoshone, the Salish, and the Cree tribes and raised on the Flatrock Reservation in Montana. Quick-to-See Smith's native heritage always has informed her art, and her concern for the invisibility of Native American artists has led her to organize exhibitions of their art. Yet she has acknowledged a wide range of influences in her work, including "pictogram forms from Europe, the Amur [the river between Russia and China], the Americas; color from beadwork, parfleches [hide cases], the landscape; paint application from Cobra art, New York expressionism, primitive art; composition from Kandinsky, Klee or Byzantine art."[47] She even has compared her use of tribal images to that of the Abstract Expressionists.

Despite the myriad references and visual material in Quick-to-See Smith's art, her work retains a coherence and power, and, like many other artists who have explored issues associated with identity, she challenges stereotypes and unacknowledged assumptions. *Trade (Gifts for Trading Land with White People)*, FIG. **34-69** is a large-scale painting with collage elements and attached objects, reminiscent of a Rauschenberg combine (FIG. 34-26). The painting's central image, a canoe, appears in an expansive field painted in loose Abstract Expressionist fashion and covered with clippings from Native American newspapers. Above the painting, as if hung from a clothesline, is an array of objects. These include Native American artifacts, such as beaded belts and feather headdresses, and contemporary sports memorabilia from teams with American Indian–derived names—the Cleveland Indians, Atlanta Braves, and Washington Redskins. The inclusion of these contemporary objects immediately recalls the vocal opposition to such names and to acts such as the Braves's

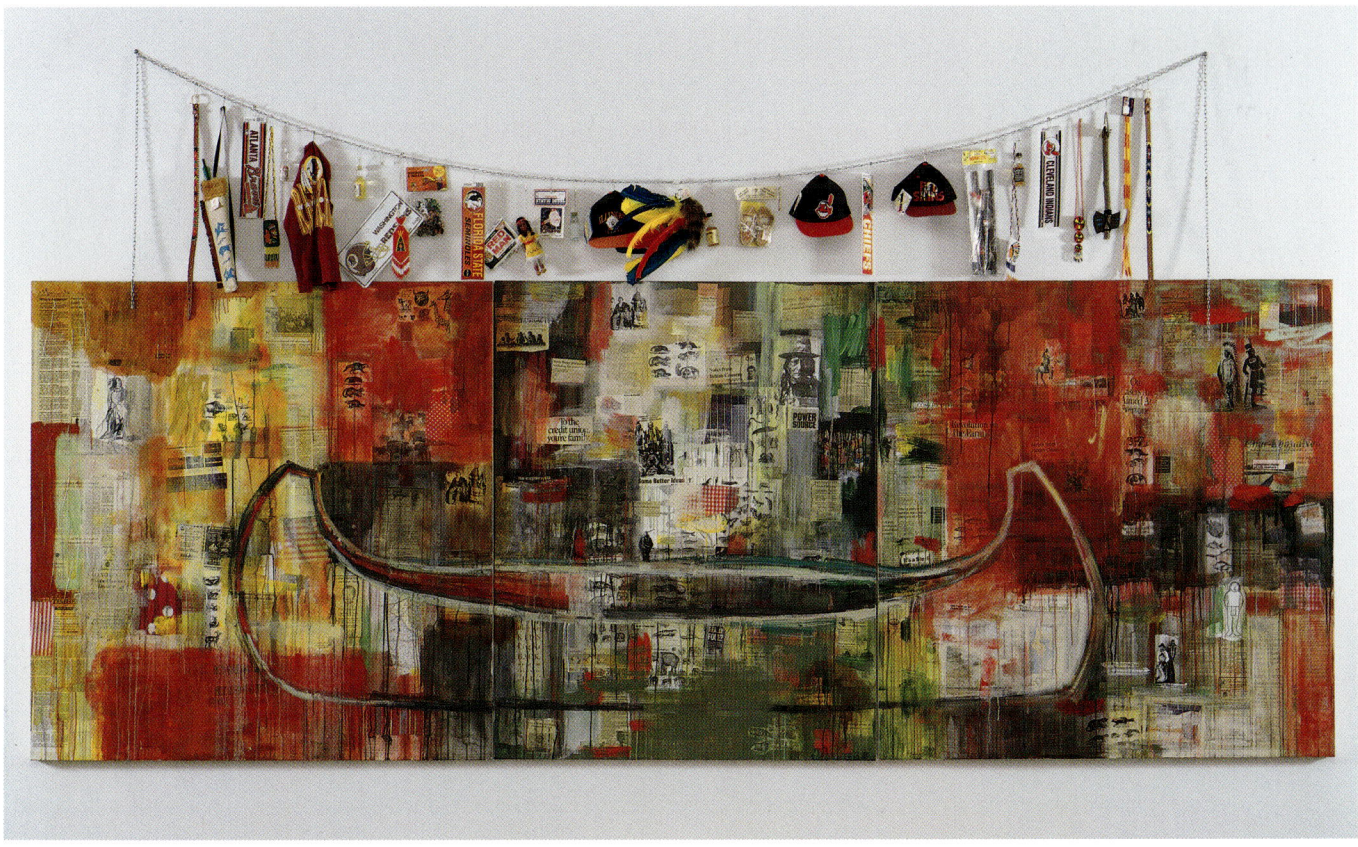

34-69   JAUNE QUICK-TO-SEE-SMITH, *Trade (Gifts for Trading Land with White People)*, 1992. Oil and mixed media on canvas, 5′ × 14′ 2″. Chrysler Museum of Art, Norfolk, Virginia (museum purchase 93.2).

"tomahawk chop." Like Edwards, Quick-to-See Smith uses the past—cultural heritage and historical references—to comment on the present.

BRUTAL VISIONS OF VIOLENT TIMES   Other artists have used their art to speak out about pressing social and political issues, sometimes in universal terms and other times with searing specificity. In his art, American artist LEON GOLUB (b. 1923) has expressed a seemingly brutal vision of contemporary life through a sophisticated reading of the news media's raw data. The work he is best known for deals with violent events of recent decades—the narratives people have learned to extract from news photos of anonymous characters participating in atrocious street violence, terrorism, and torture. Paintings in Golub's *Assassins* and *Mercenaries* series suggest not specific stories but a condition of being. As the artist said,

> Through media we are under constant, invasive bombardment of images—from all over—and we often have to take evasive action to avoid discomforting recognitions. . . . The work [of art] should have an edge, veering between what is visually and cognitively acceptable and what might stretch these limits as we encounter or try to visualize the real products of the uses of power.[48]

Mercenaries (IV), FIG. **34-70**, a huge canvas, represents a mysterious tableau of five mercenaries (tough freelance military professionals willing to fight, for a price, for any political cause). The three clustering at the right side of the canvas react with tense physical gestures to something one of the two other mercenaries standing at the far left is saying. The dark uniforms and skin tones of the four black fighters flatten their figures and make them stand out against the searing dark red background. The slightly modulated background seems to push their forms forward up against the picture plane and becomes an echoing void in the space between the two groups. The menacing figures loom over on-site viewers. Golub painted them so that these viewers' eyes are level with the mercenaries' knees, placing the men so close to the work's front plane that their feet are cut off by the painting's lower edge, thereby trapping such viewers with them in the painting's compressed space. Golub emphasized both the scarred light tones of the white mercenary's skin and the weapons. Modeled with shadow and gleaming highlights, the guns contrast with the harshly scraped, flattened surfaces of the figures. The rawness of the canvas reinforces the rawness of the imagery. Golub often dissolved certain areas with solvent after applying pigment and scraped off applied paint with, among other tools, a meat cleaver. The feeling of peril confronts viewers mercilessly. They become one with all the victims caught by today's political battles.

WEAVING AS A RECORD OF THE SOUL   The stoic, everyday toughness of the human spirit has been the subject of figurative works by the Polish fiber artist MAGDALENA ABAKANOWICZ (b. 1930). A leader in the recent exploration in sculpture of the expressive powers of weaving techniques, Abakanowicz gained fame with experimental freestanding pieces in both abstract and figurative modes. For Abakanowicz, fiber materials are deeply symbolic: "I see fiber as the basic element constructing the organic world on our planet, as the greatest mystery of our environment. It is from fiber that all living organisms are built—the tissues of plants and ourselves. . . . Fabric is our covering and our attire. Made with our hands, it is a record of our souls."[49]

To all of her work, this artist brought the experiences of her early life as a member of an aristocratic family disturbed

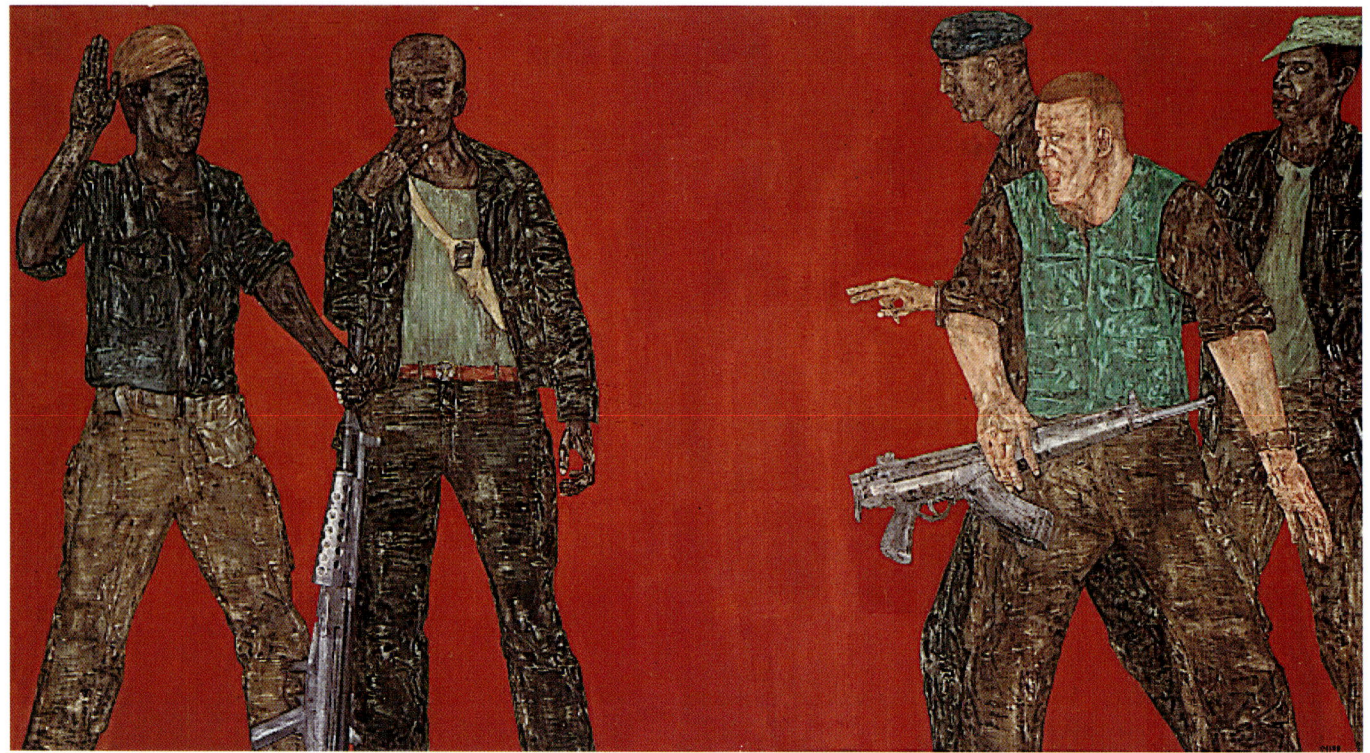

34-70   LEON GOLUB, *Mercenaries (IV)*, 1980. Acrylic on linen, 10′ × 19′ 2″. Collection Mr. and Mrs. Ulrich Meyer, Chicago.

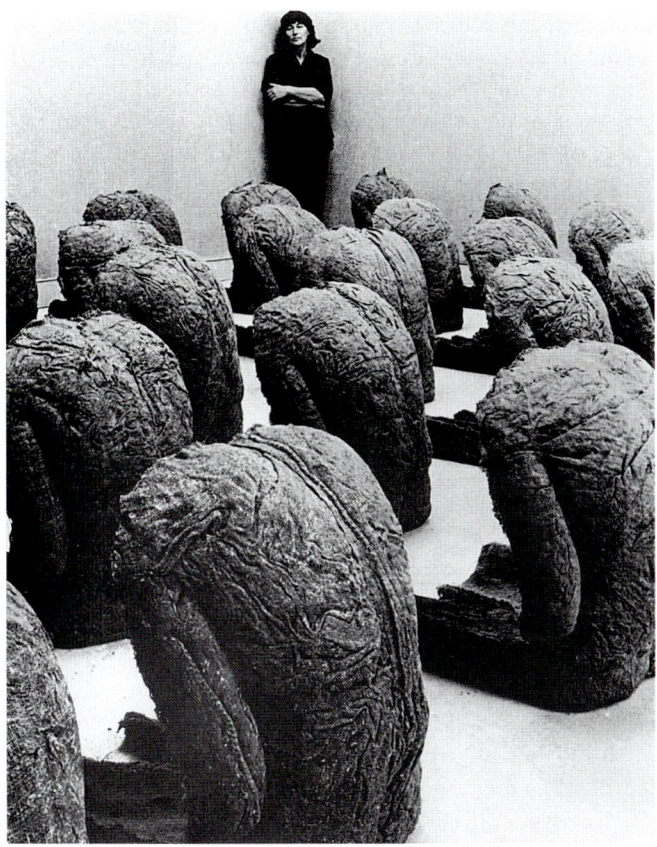

34-71 MAGDALENA ABAKANOWICZ, artist with *Backs,* at the Musée d'Art Moderne de la Ville de Paris, Paris, France, 1982. Copyright © Magdalena Abakanowicz/Licensed by VAGA, New York, NY/Marlborough Gallery, NY.

by the dislocations of World War II and its aftermath. Initially attracted to weaving as a medium that would adapt well to the small studio space she had available, Abakanowicz gradually developed huge abstract hangings she called Abakans that suggest organic spaces as well as giant pieces of clothing. She returned to a smaller scale with works based on

human forms—*Heads, Seated Figures,* and *Backs*—multiplying each type for exhibition in groups as symbols for the individual in society lost in the crowd yet retaining some distinctiveness. This impression is especially powerful in an installation of *Backs* (FIG. **34-71**). Abakanowicz made each piece by pressing layers of natural organic fibers into a plaster mold. Every sculpture depicts the slumping shoulders, back, and arms of a figure of indeterminate sex and rests legless directly on the floor. The repeated pose of the figures in *Backs* suggests meditation, submission, and anticipation. Although made from a single mold, the figures achieve a touching sense of individuality because each assumed a slightly different posture as the material dried and because the artist imprinted a different pattern of fiber texture on each.

DEALING WITH AIDS DAVID WOJNAROWICZ (1955–1992) devoted the latter part of his artistic career to producing images dealing with issues of homophobia and acquired immune deficiency syndrome (AIDS). As a gay activist and as someone who had seen many friends die of AIDS, Wojnarowicz created disturbing and eloquent works about the tragedy of this disease, such as *When I Put My Hands On Your Body* (FIG. **34-72**). In this image, the artist overlaid a photograph of a pile of skeletal remains with evenly spaced typed commentary that communicates his feelings about watching a loved one dying of AIDS. He movingly describes the effects of AIDS on the human body and soul. Wojnarowicz juxtaposed text with imagery, which, like the works of Barbara Kruger (FIG. 34-61) and Lorna Simpson (FIG. 34-66), paralleled the use of both words and images in advertising. The public's familiarity with this format ensured greater receptivity to the artist's message. Wojnarowicz's career was cut short when he also died of AIDS in 1992.

PUBLICLY EXPOSING POWER STRUCTURES When working in Canada in 1980, Polish-born artist KRZYSZTOF WODICZKO (b. 1943) developed artworks involv-

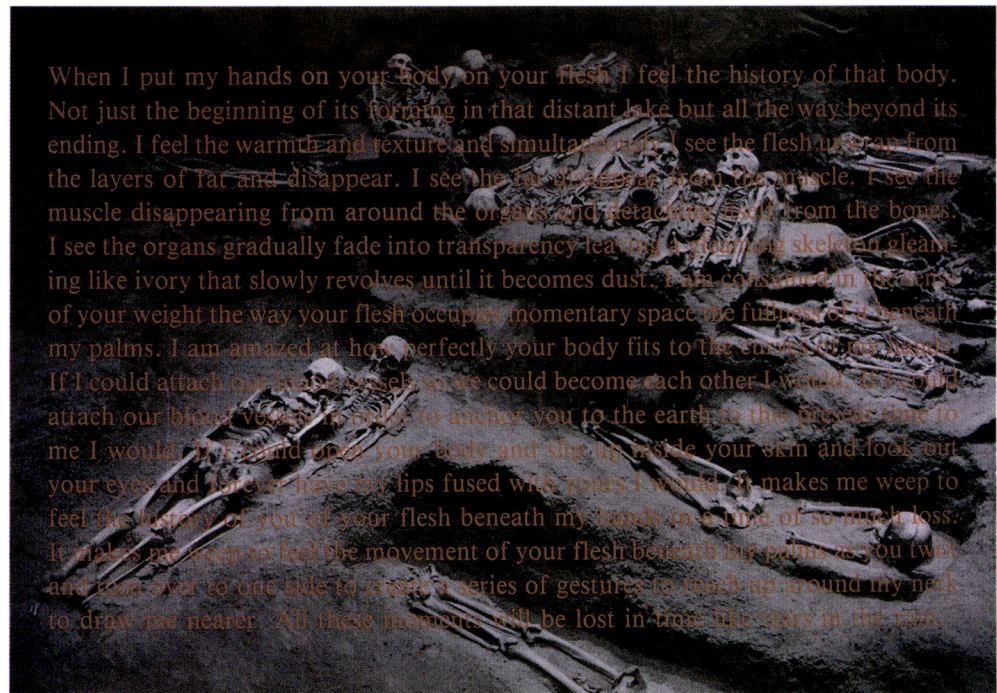

When I put my hands on your body, on your flesh, I feel the history of that body. Not just the beginning of its forming in that distant lake but all the way beyond its ending. I feel the warmth and texture and simultaneously I see the flesh uncran from the layers of fat and disappear. I see the fat disappear from the muscle. I see the muscle disappearing from around the organs and detaching itself from the bones. I see the organs gradually fade into transparency leaving a gleaming skeleton gleaming like ivory that slowly revolves until it becomes dust. I am consumed in the sense of your weight the way your flesh occupies momentary space the fullness of it beneath my palms. I am amazed at how perfectly your body fits to the curves of my hands. If I could attach our blood vessels so we could become each other I would. If I could attach our blood vessels in order to anchor you to the earth to this present time to me I would. If I could open up your body and slip up inside your skin and look out your eyes and forever have my lips fused with yours I would. It makes me weep to feel the history of you of your flesh beneath my hands in a time of so much loss. It makes me weep to feel the movement of your flesh beneath my palms as you twist and turn over to one side to create a series of gestures to reach up around my neck to draw me nearer. All these memories will be lost in time like the tears in the rain.

34-72 DAVID WOJNAROWICZ, *When I Put My Hands On Your Body,* 1990. Gelatin-silver print and silk-screened text on museum board, 2′ 2″ × 3′ 2″.

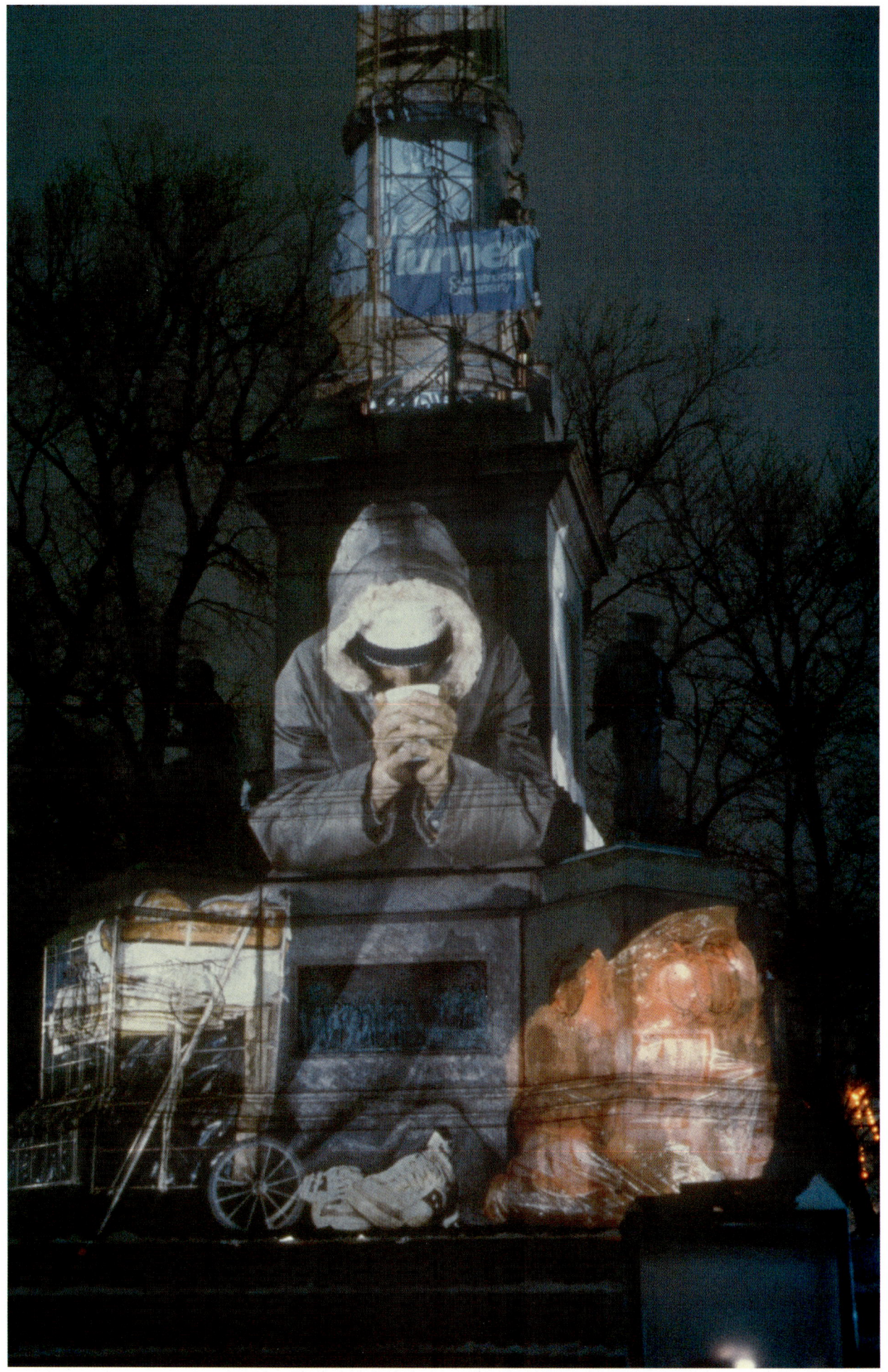

34-73 Krzysztof Wodiczko, *The Homeless Projection,* 1986–1987. Outdoor slide projection at the Soldiers and Sailors Civil War Memorial, Boston, organized by First Night, Boston..

ing outdoor slide images. He projected photographs on specific buildings to expose how civic buildings embody, legitimize, and perpetuate power. When Wodiczko moved to New York in 1983, the pervasive homelessness troubled him, and he resolved to use his art to publicize this problem. In 1987, he produced *The Homeless Projection* (FIG. **34-73**) as part of a New Year's celebration in Boston. The artist projected images of homeless people on all four sides of the Soldiers' and Sailors' Civil War Memorial on the Boston Common. In these photos, plastic bags filled with their possessions flanked those depicted. At the top of the monument Wodiczko projected a local condominium construction site, which helped viewers make a connection between urban development and homelessness.

New Technologies: Video and Digital Imagery

Initially, video was available only in commercial television studios and only was occasionally accessible to artists. In the 1960s, with the development of relatively inexpensive portable video recording equipment and of electronic devices allowing manipulation of the recorded video material, artists began to explore in earnest the particularly expressive possibilities of this new medium. In its basic form, video technology involves a special motion-picture camera that captures visible images and translates them into electronic data that can be displayed on a video monitor or television screen. Video pictures resemble photographs in the amount of detail they contain, but, like computer graphics, a video image is displayed as a series of points of light on a grid, giving the impression of soft focus. Viewers looking at television or video art are not aware of the monitor's surface. Instead, fulfilling the Renaissance ideal, they concentrate on the image and look through the glass surface, as through a window, into the "space" beyond. Video images combine the realism of photography with the sense that the subjects move in real time in a deep space "inside" the monitor.

FROM VIDEO TO COMPUTER IMAGES When video introduced the possibility of manipulating subjects in real time, artists such as the Korean-born, New York-based videographer NAM JUNE PAIK (b. 1932) were eager to work with the medium. Inspired by American composer John Cage's ideas and after studying music performance, art history, and Eastern philosophy in Korea and Japan, Paik worked with electronic music in Germany in the late 1950s. He then turned to performances using modified television sets. In 1965, after relocating to New York City, Paik acquired the first inexpensive video recorder sold in Manhattan (the Sony Porta-Pak) and immediately recorded everything he saw out the window of his taxi on the return trip to his studio downtown. Experience acquired as artist-in-residence at television stations WGBH in Boston and WNET in New York allowed him to experiment with the most advanced broadcast video technology.

A grant permitted Paik to collaborate with the gifted Japanese engineer-inventor Shuya Abe in developing a video synthesizer. This instrument allows artists to manipulate and change the electronic video information in various ways, causing images or parts of images to stretch, shrink, change color, or break up. With the synthesizer, artists also can layer images, inset one image into another, or merge images from various cameras with those from video recorders to make a single visual kaleidoscopic "time-collage." This kind of compositional freedom permitted Paik to combine his interests in the ideas of Cage, painting, music, Eastern philosophy, global politics for survival, humanized technology, and cybernetics. Paik called his video works *physical music* and said that his musical background enabled him to understand time better than video artists trained in painting or sculpture.

Paik's best-known video work, *Global Groove* (FIG. **34-74**), combines in quick succession fragmented sequences of female tap dancers, poet Allen Ginsberg reading his work, a performance of cellist Charlotte Moorman using a man's back as her instrument, Pepsi commercials from Japanese television, Korean drummers, and a shot of the Living Theatre group performing a controversial piece called *Paradise Now.* Commissioned originally for broadcast over the United Nations satellite, the cascade of imagery in *Global Groove* was intended to give viewers a glimpse of the rich worldwide television menu Paik had predicted would be available in the future.

While some new technologies were revolutionizing the way artists could work with pictorial space, other technologies, especially those of computer graphics, were transforming how artists could create and manipulate illusionistic three-dimensional forms. Computer graphics as a medium uses light to make images and, like photography, can incorporate specially recorded camera images. Computer graphics allows artists to work with wholly invented forms, as painters can.

Developed during the 1960s and 1970s, computer graphics opened up new possibilities for both abstract and figurative art. It involves electronic programs dividing the surface of the computer monitor's cathode-ray tube into a grid of tiny boxes called "picture elements" (pixels). Artists can electronically address these picture elements individually to create a design, much as knitting or weaving patterns have a gridded matrix as a guide for making a design in fabric. Once created, parts of a computer graphic design can be changed quickly through an electronic program, allowing artists to revise or duplicate shapes in the design and to manipulate at will the color, texture, size, number, and position of any desired detail.

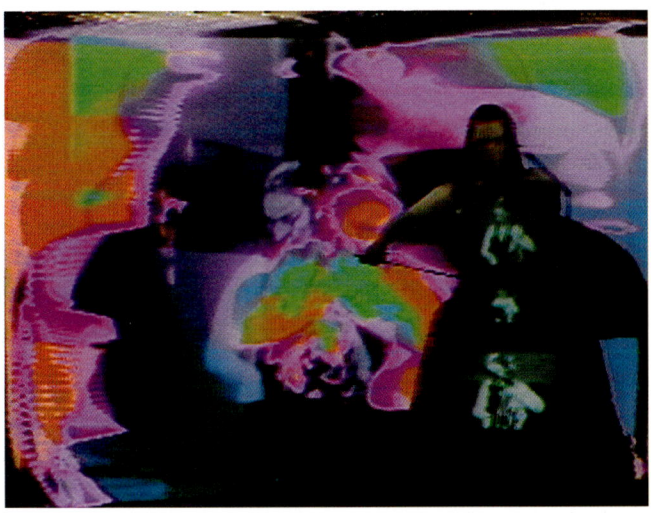

34-74 NAM JUNE PAIK, *Global Groove*, 1973. Video still.

34-75   DAVID EM, *Nora*, 1979.
Computer-generated color photograph,
1′ 5″ × 1′ 11″. Private collection.

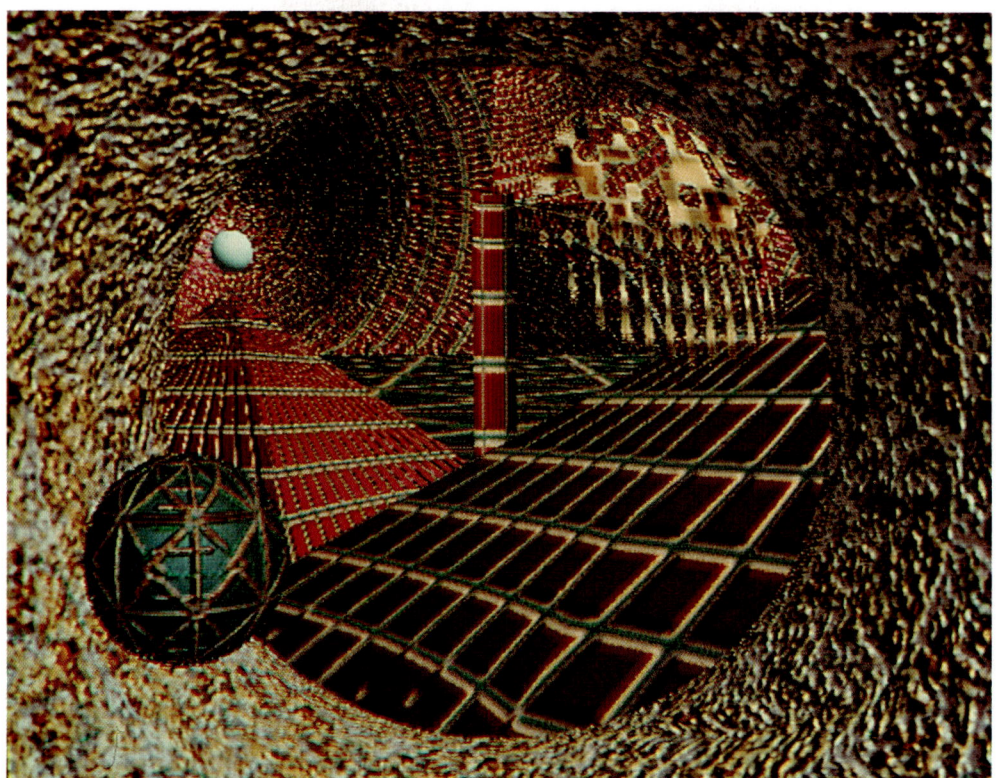

A computer graphic picture is displayed in luminous color on the cathode-ray tube. The effect suggests a view into a vast world existing inside the tube.

COMPUTER-GENERATED LANDSCAPES   One of the best-known artists working in this electronic painting mode, DAVID EM (b. 1952), uses what he terms *computer imaging* to fashion fantastic imaginary landscapes. These have an eerily believable existence within the "window" of the computer monitor. As a former artist-in-residence at the California Institute of Technology's Jet Propulsion Laboratory, Em created brilliantly colored scenes of alien worlds using the laboratory's advanced computer graphic equipment. He also had access to software programs developed to create computer graphic simulations of the National Aeronautics and Space Administration missions in outer space. Creating images with the computer allows Em great flexibility in manipulating simple geometric shapes—shrinking or enlarging them, stretching or reversing them, repeating them, adding texture to their surfaces, and creating the illusion of light and shadow. In images such as *Nora* (FIG. **34-75**), Em created futuristic geometric versions of Surrealistic dreamscapes whose forms seem familiar and strange at the same time. The illusion of space in these works is immensely vivid and seductive. It almost seems possible to wander through the tubelike foreground "frame" and up the inclined foreground plane or hop aboard the hovering globe at the lower left for a journey through the strange patterns and textures of this mysterious labyrinthine setting.

THE EFFICIENCY AND AUTHORITY OF SIGNS
In conjunction with the growing popularity of digital imagery and the expanding interest in video technology, many artists

have appropriated the mechanisms and strategies of these media. JENNY HOLZER (b. 1950) has been interested in reaching a wide audience with her art. Realizing the efficiency of signs, she created several series using electronic signs, most involving light-emitting diode (LED) technology. In 1989, Holzer did a major installation at the Guggenheim Museum in New York that included elements from her previous series and consisted of a large continuous LED display spiraling around the museum's interior ramp (FIG. **34-76**). Holzer's art focused specifically on text, and she invented sayings with an authoritative tone for her LED displays. Statements included "Protect me from what I want," "Abuse of power comes as no surprise," and "Romantic love was invented to manipulate women." The statements, which people could read from a distance, were purposefully vague and ambiguous and, in some cases, contradictory.

SUBVERTING MEDIA MESSAGES   American DARA BIRNBAUM (b. 1946) also turned from traditional painting and sculpture to video early in her career. However, rather than focus on the aesthetic capabilities of this new technology, Birnbaum made commercial television her subject. Much of her work involved analyzing the medium's structure and the ideological basis of television content. *PM Magazine* (FIG. **34-77**), a large-scale installation, centered on footage from a network magazine-format show, *PM Magazine*. The modified footage appeared on two video monitors embedded in large photographic enlargements of scenes from the videos. Birnbaum's manipulation of the video—using pauses, freeze-frames, slow motion, wipes (lines signaling transitions), and dissolves—exposed both news and entertainment as formats exploiting women.

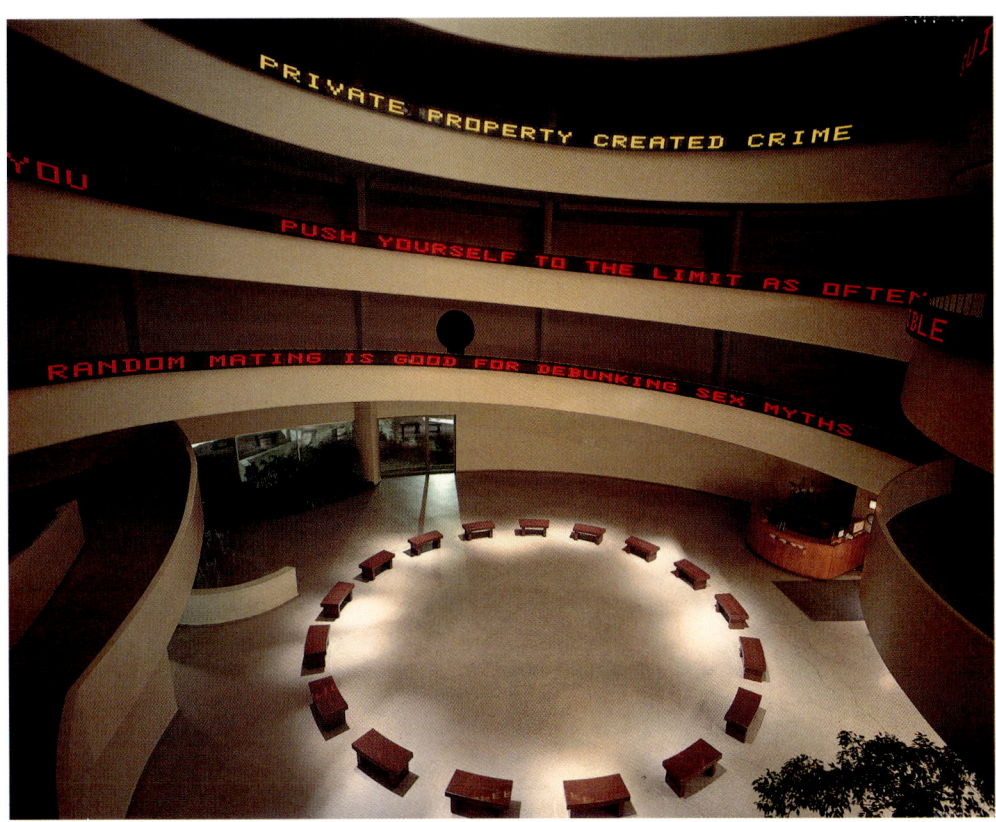

34-76 JENNY HOLZER, *Untitled* (Selections from *Truisms, Inflammatory Essays, The Living Series, The Survival Series, Under a Rock, Laments,* and *Child Text*), 1989. Extended helical tricolor LED electronic display signboard, 16″ × 162′ × 6″. Solomon R. Guggenheim Museum, New York, December 1989–February 1990 (partial gift of the artist, 1989).

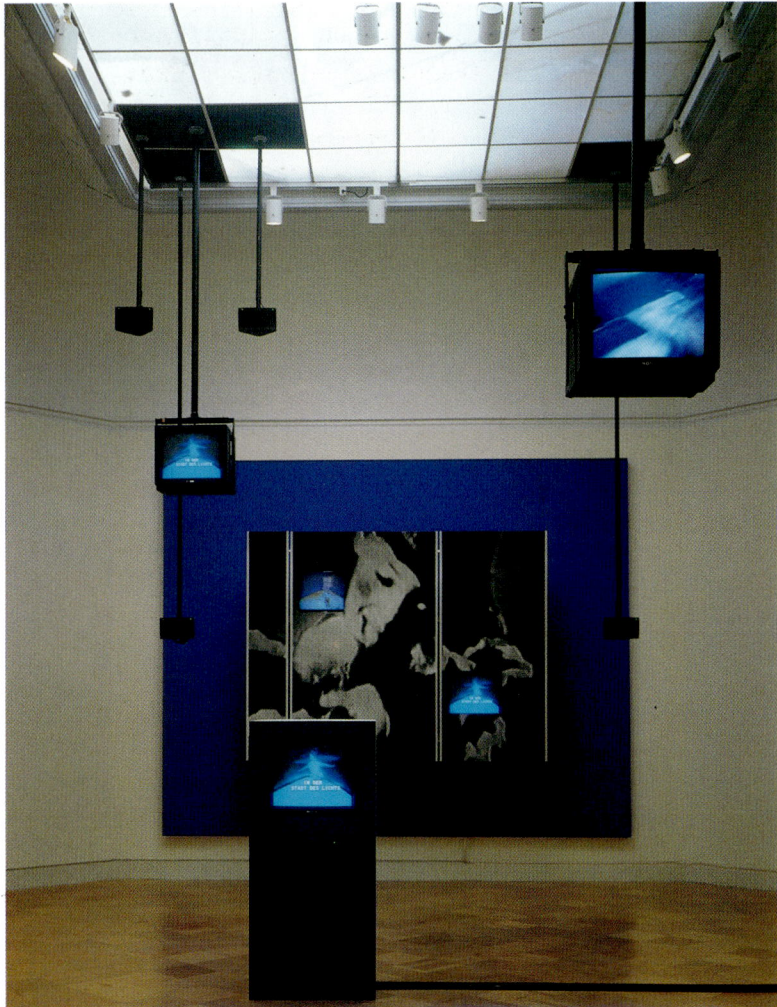

34-77 DARA BIRNBAUM, *PM Magazine,* 1982. Installation at San Francisco Museum of Modern Art, May 9–September 16, 1997. Five-channel color video and sound installation, installation panel 6′ × 8′. San Francisco Museum of Modern Art (purchased through a gift of Rena Bransten and the Accessions Committee Fund; gift of Collectors Forum, Doris and Donald G. Fisher, Evelyn and Walter Haas, Jr., Byron R. Meyer, and Norah and Norman Stone.

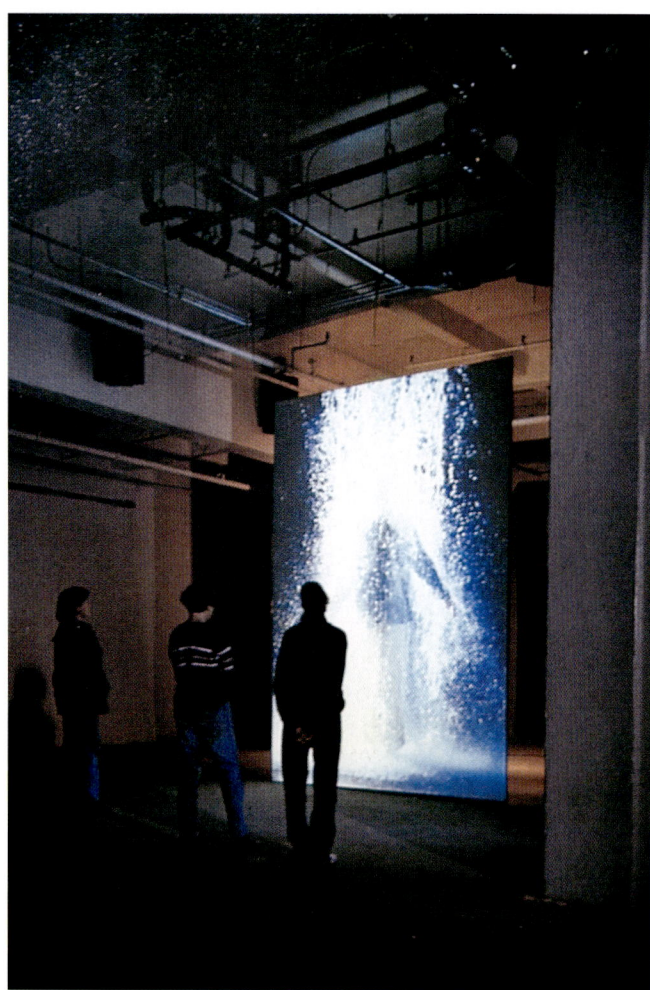

34-78   BILL VIOLA, *The Crossing,* 1996. Installation with two channels of color video projection onto 16'-high screens.

SENSORY IMPACT OF DIGITAL IMAGING BILL VIOLA (b. 1951) has spent much of his artistic career exploring the capabilities of digitized imagery, producing many video installations and single-channel works. Often focusing on sensory perception, the pieces not only heighten viewer awareness of the senses but also suggest an exploration into the spiritual realm. Viola, an American, spent years seriously studying Buddhist, Christian, Sufi, and Zen mysticism. Because he fervently believes in art's transformative power and in a spiritual view of human nature, Viola designs works encouraging spectator introspection. His recent video projects involve techniques such as extreme slow motion, contrasts in scale, shifts in focus, mirrored reflections, staccato editing, and multiple or layered screens to achieve dramatic effects.

The power of Viola's work is evident in *The Crossing* (FIG. **34-78**), an installation piece involving two color video channels projected on sixteen-foot-high screens. The artist either shows the two projections on the front and back of the same screen or on two separate screens in the same installation. In these two companion videos, shown simultaneously on the two screens, a man surrounded in darkness appears, moving closer until he fills the screen. On one screen, drops of water fall from above onto the man's head, while, on the other screen, a small fire breaks out at the man's feet. Over the next

few minutes, the water and fire increase in intensity until the man disappears in a torrent of water on one screen and flames consume the man on the other screen. The deafening roar of a raging fire and torrential downpour accompany these visual images. Eventually, everything subsides and fades into darkness. This installation's elemental nature and its presentation in a dark space immerse viewers in a pure sensory experience very much rooted in tangible reality.

Postmodernism and Commodity Culture

SYMBOLS OF EVERYTHING WRONG TODAY? In keeping with Fredric Jameson's evaluation of postmodern culture as inextricably linked to consumer society and mass culture, several postmodern artists have delved into the is-

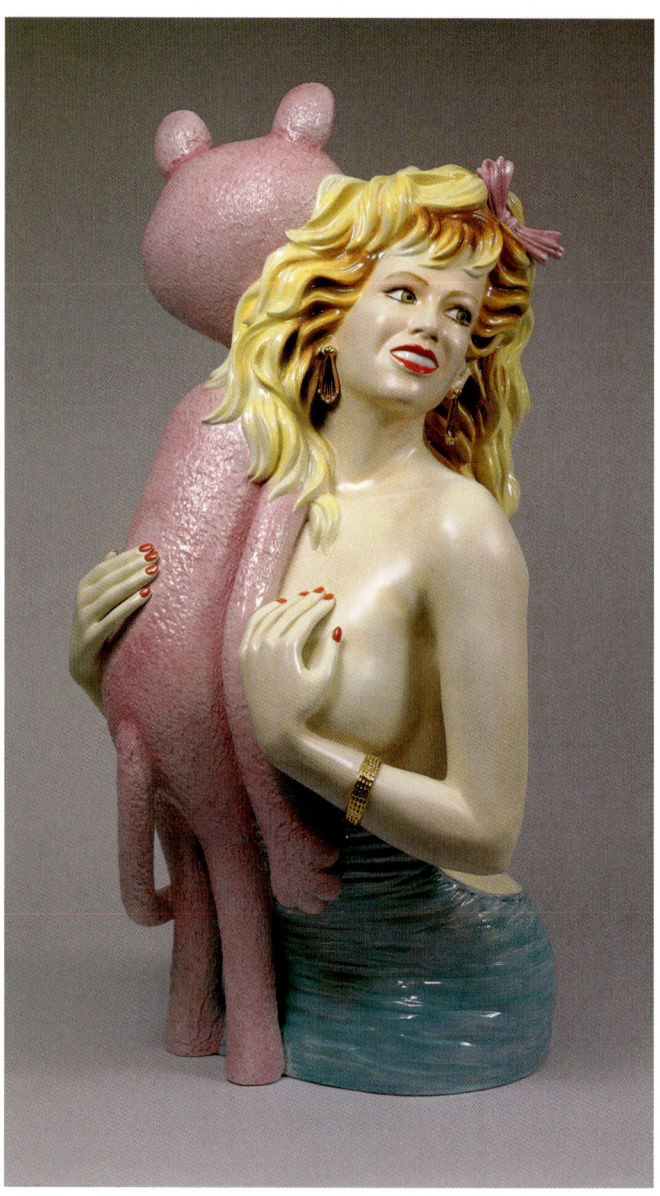

34-79   JEFF KOONS, *Pink Panther,* 1988. Porcelain, 3' 5" × 1' 8½" × 1' 7". Collection Museum of Contemporary Art, Chicago (Gerald S. Elliot Collection).

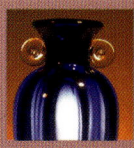

ART AND SOCIETY

The Art Market in the Later Twentieth Century

Art always has been a commodity, yet most people are reluctant to discuss it as such. Until the seventeenth century, commissions from patrons generated most art produced for public view. Because of the private nature of these arrangements, the public was not usually aware of the price of each work. Information about how much patrons paid artists traveled, rather unreliably, via word of mouth, if at all.

The growth of professions dedicated to selling art prompted the evolution of the modern art market. Art dealers, serving as intermediaries between artists and collectors or patrons, emerged in the Western art world in the seventeenth century. The auction house, although dating back to Imperial Rome, developed into a major force in the eighteenth century. With the increased participation of these "art sellers," the prices of artworks were disseminated more widely. The expansion of sophisticated communication networks—national and international newspapers and magazines, telephone systems, radio and television broadcasts, and, more recently, the Internet—has made information about artwork prices more readily available in the public domain. Further, because most buyers acquire their art from dealers who represent artists and display and sell art in galleries, the purchase of art today is often a straightforward financial transaction.

This wide dissemination of information about art prices, coupled with the allure of collecting art fostered by consumer culture, raises the issue of what, exactly, is the relationship between the price and the value of an artwork? Certainly, the value of art extends far beyond monetary worth. But the perception that cost reflects value or quality is a popular myth consumer culture perpetuates.

In recent decades, the amounts paid for art have risen dramatically. Prices for works of the Old Masters (such as Rembrandt, Leonardo, and Vélazquez) always have been high, but prices for modern artists, even contemporary living artists, also have soared. In part, the prosperity of the 1980s, a decade of corporate expansion and widespread speculative business ventures, drove this increase. Even the sobering stock market crash of October 19, 1987, known as Black Monday, did little to curb the momentum of the inflated art market. Among the works sold at auction during the early 1980s were the Gospels of Henry the Lion, purchased in 1983 by the West German government for $11.3 million. The phenomenal sale of van Gogh's *Sunflowers* a few years later in 1987 for $39.9 million stunned art lovers around the world. Some months later the sale of van Gogh's *Irises* for $53.9 million surpassed that. Eventually, the market peaked in 1989 and 1990, with the auctioning of Picasso's *Pierrette's Wedding* for $51.7 million, Renoir's *Le Moulin de la Galette* (see FIG. 29-23) for $78.1 million, and van Gogh's *Portrait of Dr. Gachet* for $82.5 million, the highest price ever paid for an artwork. Japanese collectors purchased these last three works.

The astonishing prices paid for artworks testifies to the importance of art in modern life. However, a downside exists. Higher prices for art reduce the ability of museums, on limited budgets, to purchase and insure artworks, thereby decreasing the opportunities the public has to view art. Museum directors have decried this development and now must work even harder to find ways to continue to make a wide range of art available to their audiences.

---

sues associated with commodity culture. American JEFF KOONS (b. 1955) first became prominent in the art world for a series of works in the early 1980s that involved exhibiting common purchased objects such as vacuum cleaners. Clearly following in the footsteps of artists such as Marcel Duchamp and Andy Warhol, Koons made no attempt to manipulate or alter the objects. Critics and other art world participants perceived them as representing the commodity basis of both the art world and society at large. Koons's experience as a commodities broker before turning to art and his blatant self-promotion have led to accusations that his art is market driven (see "The Art Market in the Later Twentieth Century," above).

More recently, Koons has produced several porcelain sculptures, such as *Pink Panther* (FIG. 34-79). Here, Koons continued his immersion into contemporary mass culture by intertwining a magazine centerfold nude with a well-known cartoon character. He reinforced the trite and kitschy nature of this imagery by titling the exhibition of which this work was a part *The Banality Show*. Some art critics have argued that

Koons and his work instruct viewers because both artist and work serve as the most visible symbols of everything wrong with contemporary American society. Whether or not this is true, people must acknowledge that, at the very least, Koons's prominence in the art world indicates he, like Warhol before him, has struck a chord that resonates with many viewers.

Postmodernism and the Critique of Art History

Postmodern architecture often incorporates historical forms and styles. Art world participants have cited that awareness of the past frequently as a defining characteristic of postmodernism, both in architecture and art. Such awareness, however, extends beyond mere citation. People have described it as a self-consciousness on the part of artists about their places in the continuum of art history. Not only do artists demonstrate their knowledge about past art, but they also express awareness of the mechanisms and institutions of the art

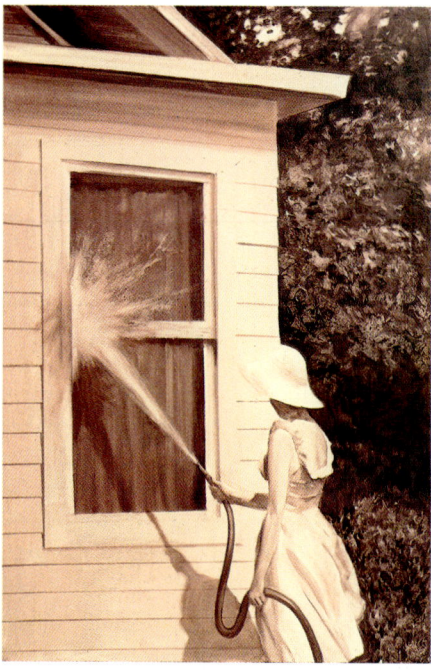 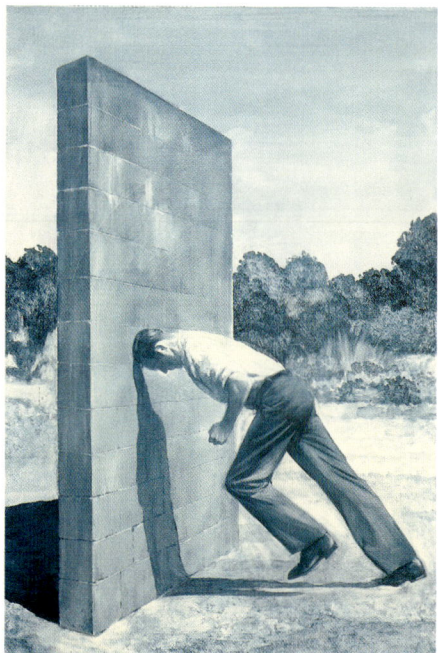 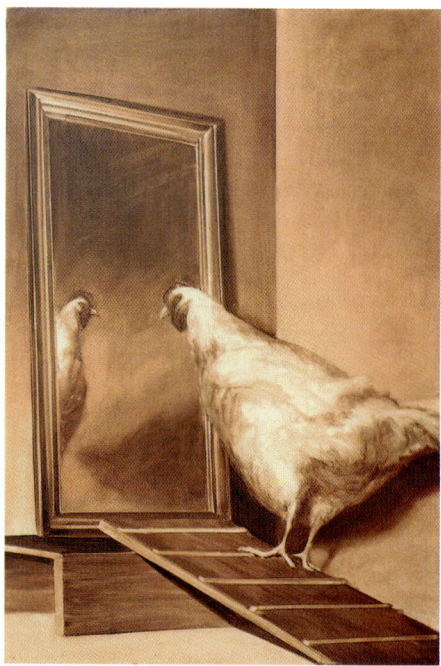

34-80   MARK TANSEY, *A Short History of Modernist Painting,* 1982. Oil on canvas, three panels, each 4′ 10″ × 3′ 4″.

world. For many postmodern artists, then, referencing the past moves beyond simple quotation from earlier works and styles and involves a critique of or commentary on fundamental art historical premises. In short, their art is about making art.

EVIDENCING ART HISTORY IN ART   In his *A Short History of Modernist Painting* (FIG. **34-80**), American artist MARK TANSEY (b. 1949) provides viewers with a summary of the various approaches to painting artists have embraced over the years. Tansey presents a sequence of three images, each visualizing a way of looking at art. At the far left, a glass window encapsulates the Renaissance ideal of viewing art as though one were looking through a window. In the center image, a man pushing his head against a solid wall visualizes the thesis central to much of modernist formalism—that the painting should be acknowledged as an object in its own right. Modernism, particularly that Clement Greenberg promoted in the 1960s and 1970s, was based on the rejection of imitation and illusion as a primary artistic goal. In the image on the right, Tansey summarizes the postmodern approach to art with a chicken pondering its reflection in the mirror. The chicken's action reveals postmodern artists' self-consciousness or awareness of their places in the art historical continuum.

SATIRICAL CERAMIC SCULPTURE   ROBERT ARNE-SON (1930–1992) has spent his life in a small town north of San Francisco, and this fact provided the impetus for his ceramic work *California Artist* (FIG. **34-81**). By then, Arneson had developed a body of work over the years of predominantly figurative ceramic sculpture, often satirical or amusing and sometimes biting. In 1981, well-known art critic Hilton Kramer published a review of an exhibition including Arneson's work. Kramer's assessment of Arneson's art was searingly negative. Arneson decided to create *California Artist* as a direct response to the critic, particularly to Kramer's derogatory comments on the provincialism of California art. This ce-

ramic sculpture, a half-length self-portrait, incorporates all of the critic's stereotypes. The artist placed the top half of his likeness on a pedestal littered with beer bottles, cigarette butts, and marijuana plants. Arneson appears clad only in a denim jacket and sunglasses, looking very defiant with his arms crossed. By creating an artwork that responded directly to an art critic's comments, Arneson revealed his comprehension of the mechanisms (for example, art criticism) people use currently to evaluate and validate art.

CHALLENGING ORIGINALITY   American artist SHERRIE LEVINE (b. 1947) has presented what is perhaps the most dramatic challenge to art's premises and legitimization. Levine appropriated well-known artworks by other artists for a series of works. For example, she produced *Untitled (After Walker Evans;* FIG. **34-82**), based on *Kitchen Corner, Tenant Farmers, Hale County, Alabama* (FIG. **34-83**) by WALKER EVANS (1903–1975). Evans took his photograph in 1936 as part of a Farm Security Administration assignment (see Chapter 33, pages 1064–1065) in Alabama during the Great Depression. Not only is Levine's version an exact duplicate, but it is also clear from her title that she wants viewers to know the source of her image. In so doing, Levine directly challenges the notions of originality and authorship. The concept of (or at least the myth of) originality was one of the bedrocks of modernism, and here the artist has announced her affiliation with postmodern theory in her rejection of modernist principles. One critic commented that Levine's photographs contain

no combinations, no transformations, no additions, no synthesis. . . . In such an undisguised theft of already existing images, Levine lays no claim to conventional notions of artistic creativity. She makes use of the images, but not to constitute a style of her own. Her appropriations have only functional value for the particular historical discourses into which they are inserted.[50]

This critical evaluation points out how Levine's work, like that of other postmodern artists, operates as part of a larger

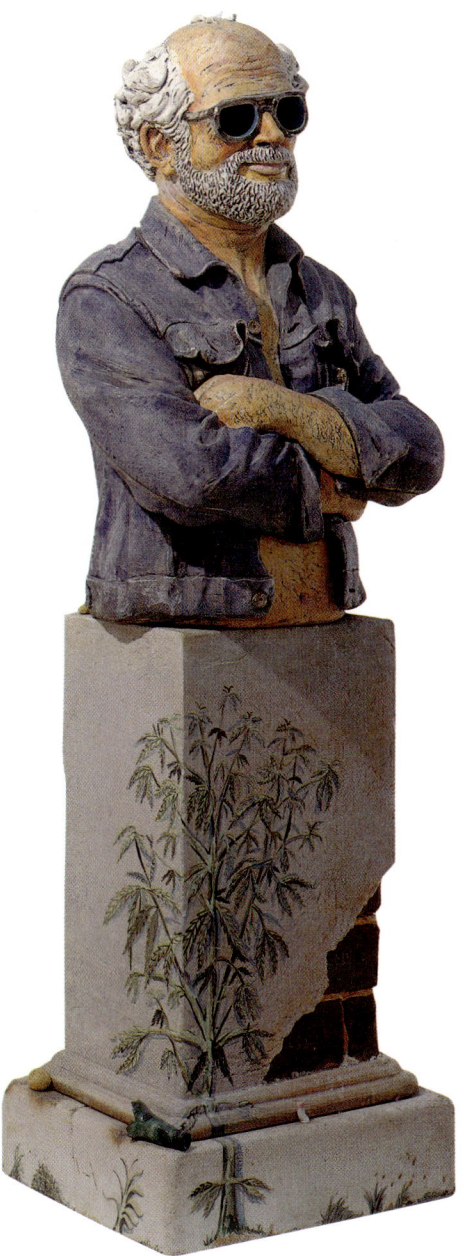

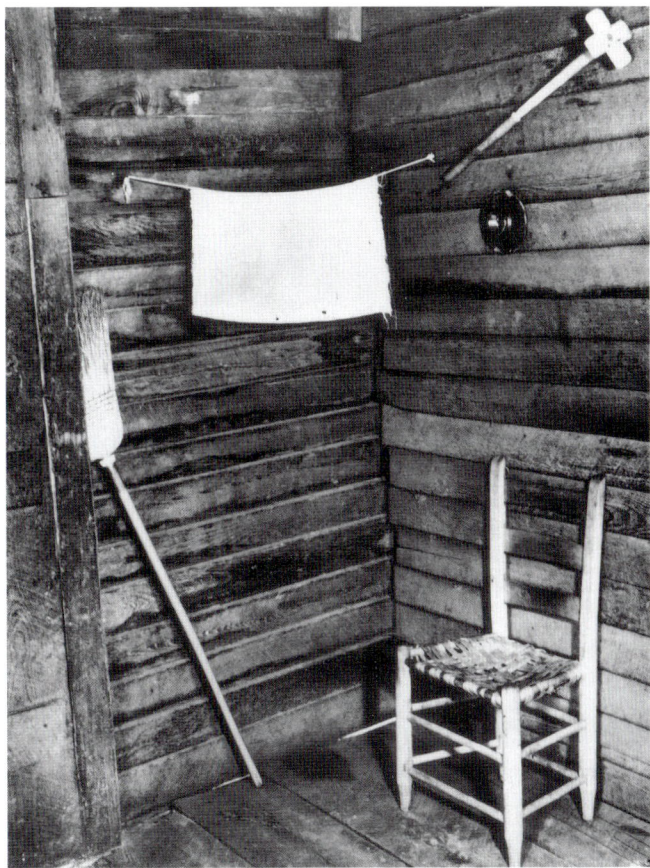

34-82   SHERRIE LEVINE, *Untitled (After Walker Evans)*, 1981. Gelatin silver print. Metropolitan Museum of Art, New York (gift of the artist, 1995).

34-81   ROBERT ARNESON, *California Artist,* 1982. Glazed stoneware, 5′ 8¼″ × 2′ 3½″ × 1′ 8¼″. San Francisco Museum of Modern Art (gift of the Modern Art Council). Copyright © Estate of Robert Arneson/Licensed by VAGA, New York, NY.

art historical discussion and that its importance can be truly understood only in that context.

Postmodernism and Art Institutions

Along with a conscious reappraisal of the processes of art historical validation, postmodern artists have turned to assessing art institutions, such as museums and galleries. Not only have such artists addressed issues associated with the role of these institutions in validating art, but also, in keeping with increased public concern about issues of race, class, gender and ethnicity, they have scrutinized the discriminatory policies and politics of these institutions.

MUSEUMS AND THE POLITICIZATION OF ART
German artist HANS HAACKE (b. 1936) has focused his atten-

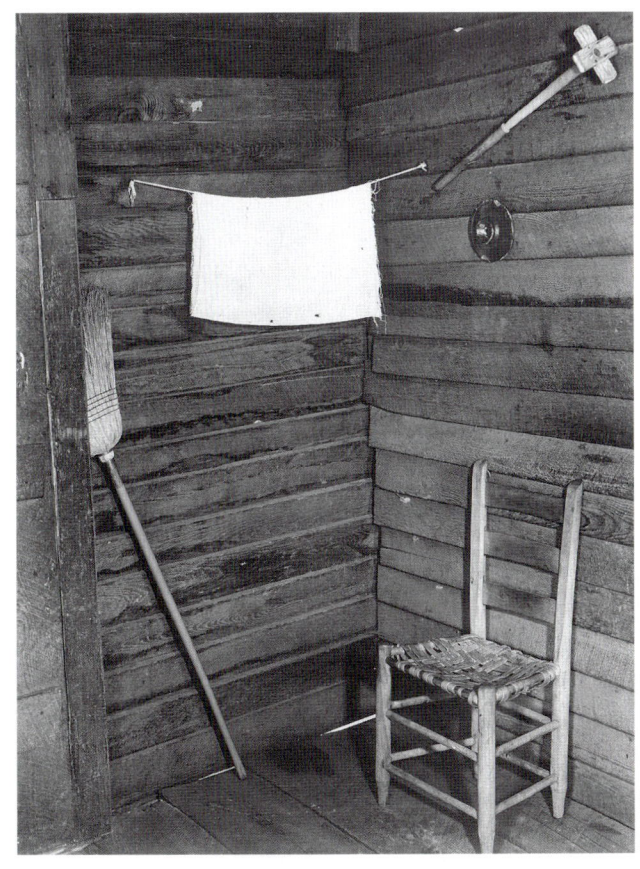

34-83   WALKER EVANS, *Kitchen Corner, Tenant Farmers, Hale County, Alabama,* 1936. Black-and-white photograph.

34-84 HANS HAACKE, *MetroMobiltan,* 1985. Fiberglass construction, three banners, and photomural, 11′ 8″ × 20′ × 5′. Collection Centre Georges Pompidou, Paris.

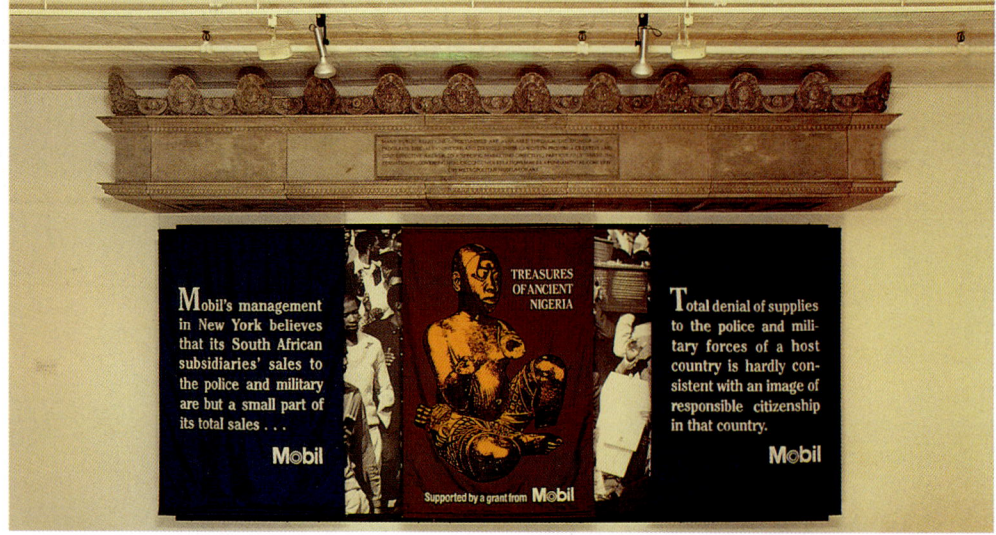

tion on the politics of art museums and how these politics affect the art exhibited and, ultimately, museum visitors' understanding of art history. The specificity of his works, based on substantial research, make them stinging indictments of the institutions whose practices he critiques. In *MetroMobiltan* (FIG. **34-84**), Haacke illustrated the connection between the realm of art (more specifically, the Metropolitan Museum of Art in New York) and the "real" world of political and economic interests. A large photomural of a funeral for South African black people provided the backdrop for a banner for the 1980 Mobil Oil–sponsored Metropolitan Museum show *Treasures of Ancient Nigeria.* In 1980, Mobil was a principal U.S. investor in South Africa, and this work suggests that their sponsorship of this exhibition was in part driven by the fact Nigeria was one of the richest oil-producing countries in Africa. In 1981, the public pressured Mobil's board of directors to stop providing

oil to the white South African military and police. Haacke provided the official corporate response to this demand on the blue banners hanging on either side of *MetroMobiltan.* He set the entire tableau in a fiberglass replica of the museum's entablature. By placing these disparate elements, both visual and textual, together, Haacke forced viewers to think about the connections among multinational corporations, political and economic conditions in South Africa, and the conflicted politics of corporate patronage of art exhibitions. The complicity of Mobil Oil and other corporations in perpetuating injustice extends to the museum world, one the public often views as exempt from political and economic concerns.

THE "CONSCIENCE OF THE ART WORLD" The New York–based GUERRILLA GIRLS, formed in 1984, bill themselves as the "conscience of the art world." This group

34-85 GUERRILLA GIRLS, *The Advantages of Being A Woman Artist,* 1988. Poster.

THE ADVANTAGES OF BEING A WOMAN ARTIST:

Working without the pressure of success.
Not having to be in shows with men.
Having an escape from the art world in your 4 free-lance jobs.
Knowing your career might pick up after you're eighty.
Being reassured that whatever kind of art you make it will be labeled feminine.
Not being stuck in a tenured teaching position.
Seeing your ideas live on in the work of others.
Having the opportunity to choose between career and motherhood.
Not having to choke on those big cigars or paint in Italian suits.
Having more time to work when your mate dumps you for someone younger.
Being included in revised versions of art history.
Not having to undergo the embarrassment of being called a genius.
Getting your picture in the art magazines wearing a gorilla suit.

A PUBLIC SERVICE MESSAGE FROM **GUERRILLA GIRLS** CONSCIENCE OF THE ART WORLD
532 LaGUARDIA PLACE, #237• NY, NY 10012
www.guerrillagirls.com

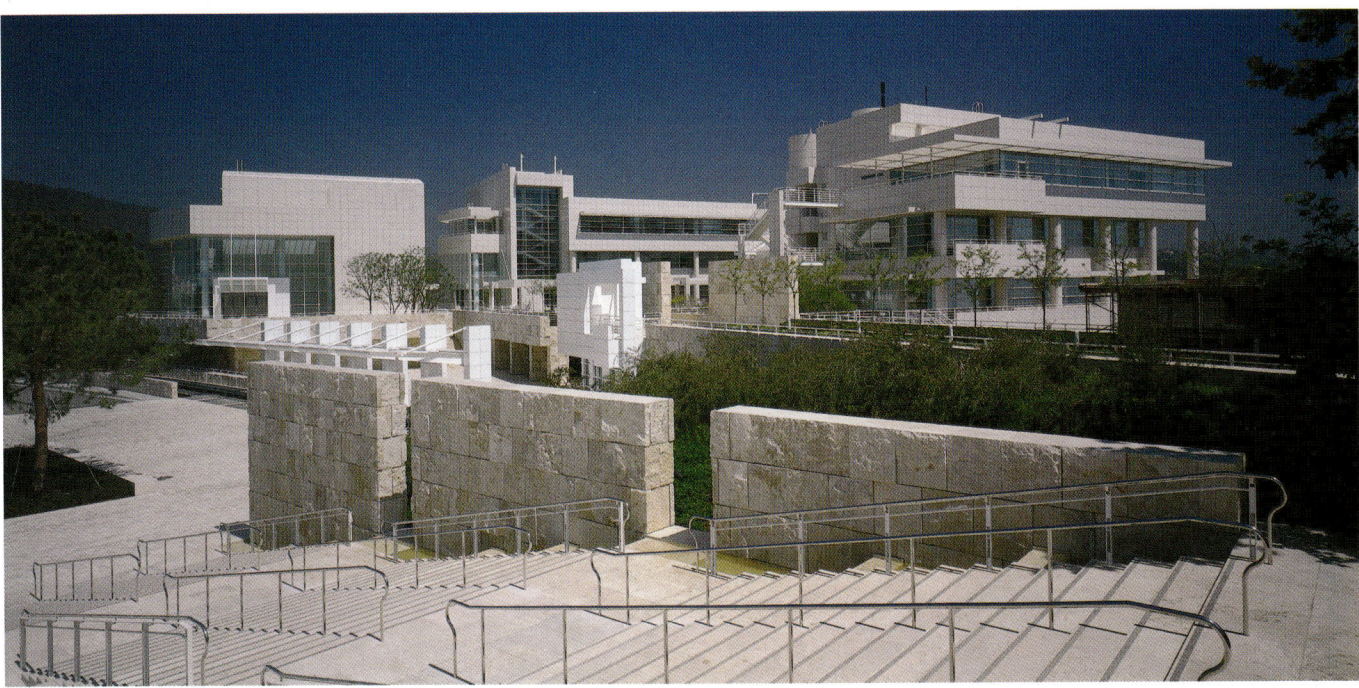

34-86 RICHARD MEIER, Getty Center, Los Angeles, 1997.

sees it as their duty to call attention to injustice in the art world, especially what they perceive as the sexist and racist orientation of the major institutions. The women who are members of the Guerrilla Girls remain anonymous at all times and protect their identities by wearing gorilla masks in public. They employ guerrilla tactics (hence their name) by putting up posters and fliers in public places. This distribution network expands the impact of their messages. One poster that reflects the Guerrilla Girls's agenda facetiously lists "the advantages of being a woman artist" (FIG. **34-85**). Actually, the list itemizes for readers the numerous obstacles women artists face in the contemporary art world. The Guerrilla Girls hope their publicizing of these obstacles will inspire improvements in the situation for women artists.

Into the Twenty-First Century: The Future of Art and Art History

At the end of the nineteenth century, a unique fin-de-siècle culture emerged, followed by the emergence in the early twentieth century of prodigious artistic talents such as Matisse, Duchamp, and Picasso. What will the twenty-first century bring? Will a similarly fertile period in art and culture arise as we usher in the new century and the new millennium, as some people anticipate? It is, of course, impossible to predict anything with any certainty. Further, with the expansive scope of postmodernism, no single approach, style, or direction dominates.

A MONIED MUSEUM'S TOTAL INVOLVEMENT
One institution that may play a significant role in the future of art and art history is the Getty Center in Los Angeles. The recently completed buildings, housing both exhibition space and offices, and gardens (designed by American artist Robert Irwin) cover twenty-four acres. The work of American architect RICHARD MEIER (b. 1934), the sprawling complex of buildings (FIG. **34-86**) incorporates both modernist and postmodern design elements. Much of the architecture recalls pristine modernism—clean lines, geometric rationality, and near-white walls. In postmodern fashion, Meier made each of the dozen pavilions on the site different from one another, creating an interesting dialogue between the architectural spaces and forms. The interior design reinforces the postmodern notion of eclecticism. Museum Director John Walsh requested traditional galleries, and Meier designed each gallery, with varying wall colors and surface treatments, to house a specific collection of artworks. He reconstructed historical rooms for some of the galleries, such as an elegantly decorative paneled room of the early eighteenth century.

The Getty Center is far more than a museum, and this aspect has many people speculating on the impact it may have on the art world in the twenty-first century. In addition to the J. Paul Getty Museum in Malibu, the new Getty Center houses five other programs—the Getty Research Institute for the History of Art and the Humanities, the Getty Conservation Institute, the Getty Education Institute, the Getty Grant Program, and the Getty Leadership Institute for Museum Management. The scope of these programs reveals the Getty's involvement in virtually every aspect of art and its presentation, including art history and art education. As such, it is positioned to have a dramatic effect on the future of art and its study. Further, the considerable funds the Getty Trust has access to (the result of J. Paul Getty's endowment of $700 million in Getty Oil stock on his death in 1976) has placed the Getty in a position to acquire art, exhibit it, study it, conserve it, and document it on a scale far beyond the means of any other museum in the world.

Appropriately enough, the Getty Center is perched high on a hill, allowing visitors to survey the expanse of Los Angeles that stretches out on every side. Only time will tell where art is headed, how scholars will reassess art history (necessitating new textbooks), and the extent of the Getty Center's influence.

NOTES

Chapter 2

1. Françoise Tallon, trans., *The Royal City of Susa,* by Prudence O. Harper et al. (New York: Metropolitan Museum of Art, 1992), 132.

Chapter 3

1. Herodotus, *Histories,* 2.35.
2. We follow the chronology proposed by John Baines and Jaromír Malék in *Atlas of Ancient Egypt* (Oxford: Oxford University Press, 1980), 36–37, and the division of kingdoms favored by, among others, Mark Lehner, *The Complete Pyramids* (New York: Thames and Hudson, 1997), 8–9, and David P. Silverman, ed., *Ancient Egypt* (New York: Oxford University Press, 1997), 20–39.

Chapter 4

1. Homer, *Iliad,* II. 466–649.

Chapter 5

1. Thucydides, *Peloponnesian War,* II.40–41.
2. Aristotle, *Politics,* I.2.15.
3. Ibid., VII. 11.1.
4. Plutarch, *Life of Pericles,* 12.
5. Pliny, *Natural History,* 34.74.
6. Ibid., 36.20.
7. Lucian, *Amores,* 13–14; *Imagines,* 6.
8. Plutarch, *Moralia,* 335A–B. Translated by J. J. Pollitt, *The Art of Ancient Greece: Sources and Documents* (New York: Cambridge University Press, 1990), 99.
9. Pliny, *Natural History,* 35.110.
10. Diodorus Siculus, *History,* XVII.117.4.

Chapter 7

1. Michael Sullivan, *The Birth of Landscape Painting in China* (Berkeley: University of California Press, 1962), 103.
2. Ibid., 105.

Chapter 10

1. J. J. Pollitt, *The Art of Rome, c. 753 B.C.–A.D. 337: Sources and Documents* (New York: Cambridge University Press, 1983), 170.
2. Livy, *History of Rome,* XXV.40.1–3.
3. Pollitt, 32.
4. Recorded by the Venerable Bede, the great English scholar, monk, and saint, who died in 735; translated by Lord Byron in *Childe Harold's Pilgrimage* (1817) IV.145.
5. Juvenal *Satires* III. 225, 232.

Chapter 12

1. Cyril Mango, trans., *The Art of the Byzantine Empire, 312–1453: Sources and Documents* (Englewood Cliffs, N.J.: Prentice-Hall, 1972), 85–86.
2. Ibid., 74.
3. Ibid., 83, 86.
4. Colm Luibheid, trans., *Pseudo-Dionysius: The Complete Works* (New York: Mahwah, 1987), 68ff.
5. Mango, 75.
6. Nina G. Garsoïan, "Later Byzantium," in *The Columbia History of the World,* ed. John A. Garraty and Peter Gay (New York: Harper and Row, 1972), 453.
7. Ibid., 460.

Chapter 16

1. Kevin Crossley-Holland, trans., *Beowulf* (New York: Farrar, Straus & Giroux, 1968), 119.
2. Ibid., 33.
3. Françoise Henry, *The Book of Kells* (New York: Alfred A. Knopf, 1974), 165.

Chapter 17

1. Quoted in Elizabeth G. Holt, *A Documentary History of Art* (New York: Doubleday Anchor Books, 1957), 1: 18.
2. Translated by Calvin B. Kendall, *The Allegory of the Church. Romanesque Portals and Their Verse Inscriptions* (Toronto: University of Toronto Press, 1998), 207.
3. Holt, 1: 20.

Chapter 18

1. Giorgio Vasari, *Introduzione alle tre arti del disegno* (1550), ch. 3. Paul Frankl, *The Gothic: Literary Sources and Interpretation through Eight Centuries* (Princeton, N.J.: Princeton University Press, 1960), 290–91, 859–60.
2. Dante, *Divine Comedy,* Purgatory, XI.81.
3. Roland Behrendt, trans., *Johannes Trithemius, In Praise of Scribes: De Laude Scriptorum* (Lawrence, Kansas: Coronado Press, 1974), 71.
4. Frankl, 55.

Chapter 19

1. Robert Gottfried, *The Black Death: Natural and Human Disaster in Medieval Europe* (New York: Free Press, 1985), xiii.

Chapter 20

1. Henry Dussart, ed., *Fragments inédits de Romboudt de Doppere: Chronique brugeoise de 1491 à 1498,* (Bruges, Belgium: L. de Plancke, 1892), 49.

2. Johan A. Huizinga, *The Waning of the Middle Ages,* (1924; reprint, New York: St. Martin's Press, 1988), 156.

Chapter 21

1. Elizabeth Gilmore Holt, ed., *Literary Sources of Art History* (Princeton, N.J.: Princeton University Press, 1947), 87–88.

2. Giorgio Vasari, *Lives of the Painters, Sculptors and Architects,* trans. Gaston du C. de Vere (New York: Alfred A. Knopf, 1996), 1:304.

3. Holt, *Literary Sources,* 90–91.

4. Vasari, 1:318

5. H.W. Janson, *The Sculpture of Donatell*o (Princeton, N.J.: Princeton University Press, 1965), 154.

Chapter 22

1. Da Vinci to Ludovico Sforza, ca. 1480–81, *Literary Sources of Art History,* ed. Elizabeth Gilmore Holt (Princeton: Princeton University Press, 1947), 170.

2. Anthony Blunt, *Artistic Theory in Italy, 1450–1600* (London: Oxford University Press, 1964), 34.

3. Heinrich Wölfflin, *Classic Art: An Introduction to the Italian Renaissance,* 4th ed. (Ithaca, N.Y.: Cornell University Press, 1980), 27.

4. Erwin Panofsky, "Artist, Scientist, Genius," in *The Renaissance,* ed. Wallace K. Ferguson (New York: Harper & Row, 1962), 147

5. Bruce Boucher, *Andrea Palladio: The Architect in His Time* (New York: Abbeville Press, 1998), 229.

6. Holt, *Literary Sources,* 240.

7. James M. Saslow, *The Poetry of Michelangelo: An Annotated Translation* (New Haven, Conn.: Yale University Press, 1991), 195.

8. Ibid., 239.

9. Ibid., 407.

10. Vasari, 2: 736.

11. Robert J. Clements, *Michelangelo's Theory of Art* (New York: New York University Press, 1961), 320.

12. Francesco Valcanover, "An Introduction to Titian," in *Titian Prince of Painters* (Venice: Marsilio Editori, S.p.A., 1990), 23–24.

13. Vasari, 1: 860.

14. Holt, *Literary Sources,* 229.

Chapter 23

1. Jackson J. Spielvogel, *Western Civilization Since 1300,* 3rd ed., (Minneapolis: West Publishing Company, 1997), 465.

2. Wolfgang Stechow, *Northern Renaissance Art 1400–1600: Sources and Documents* (Evanston, Ill.: Northwestern University Press, 1989), 111.

3. Ibid., 118.

4. Ibid., 123.

5. Vasari, 2: 863.

Chapter 24

1. Wolfgang Stechow, *Rubens and the Classical Tradition* (Cambridge: Harvard University Press, 1968), 26.

2. David G. Wilkins, Bernard Schultz, and Katheryn M. Linduff, *Art Past, Art Present,* 3rd ed. (New York: Harry N. Abrams, 1997), 365.

3. Bob Haak, *The Golden Age: Dutch Painters of the Seventeenth Century* (New York: Abrams, 1984), 75.

4. Ibid., 450.

5. Robert Goldwater and Marco Treves (eds.), *Artists on Art,* 3rd ed. (New York: Pantheon Books, 1958), 155.

6. Ibid., 155.

7. Ibid., 151–153.

8. Jonathan Brown, *Kings and Connoisseurs: Collecting Art in Seventeenth-Century Europe* (Princeton, N.J.: Princeton University Press, 1995), 207.

9. Goldwater and Treves (eds.), 157.

Chapter 25

1. Milo Beach, *The Imperial Image* (Washington, D.C.: Freer Gallery of Art, Smithsonian Institution, 1981), 169.

2. Vidya Dehejia et al., *Devi: The Great Goddess* (Washington, D.C.: The Arthur M. Sackler Gallery, Smithsonian Institution, in association with Mapin Publishing, Ahmedabad and Prestel Verlag, Munich, 1999), 260.

3. *Kamol Tassananchalee: 39 Years Retrospective* (Bangkok: National Gallery, 1999), 29.

Chapter 28

1. Thomas A. Bailey, *The American Pageant: A History of the Republic,* 2nd ed. (Boston: D.C. Heath and Company, 1961), 280.

2. *The Indispensable Rousseau,* compiled and presented by John Hope Mason (London: Quartet Books, 1979), 39.

3. Voltaire to Rousseau, 30 August 1755, *The Collected Writings of Rousseau,* Vol. 3, eds. Roger D. Masters and Christopher Kelly (Hanover, N.H.: University Press of New England, 1992), 102.

4. Elizabeth Gilmore Holt, *Literary Sources of Art History* (Princeton: Princeton University Press, 1947), 532.

5. Robert Goldwater and Marco Treves, *Artists on Art,* 3rd ed. (New York: Random House, 1958), 206.

6. Ibid., 205.

7. Ibid., 205.

8. Alexander Pope, *Epistles to Several Persons (Moral Essays),* ed. F. W. Bateson (London and New Haven: Metheun & Co. Ltd. and Yale University Press, 1961), 155.

9. Edgar Allen Poe, "To Helen" (1831).

10. Marcus Whiffen and Fredrick Koeper, *American Architecture 1607–1976* (Cambridge, MA: The MIT Press, 1981), 130.

11. Goldwater and Treves, 218.

12. Ibid., 216.

13. Gwyn A. Williams, *Goya and the Impossible Revolution* (London: Allen Lane, 1976), 175–77.

14. Walter Pach, trans., *Journal of Eugène Delacroix* (New York: Crown Publishers, 1948), 511.

15. Théophile Gautier, *Histoire de Romantisme* (Paris: Charpentier, 1874), 204.

16. Delacroix to Auguste Jal, 4 June 1832, *Art in Theory 1815–1900: An Anthology of Changing Ideas,* eds. Charles Harrison and Paul Wood with Jason Gaiger (Oxford: Blackwell Publishers Ltd., 1998), 88.

17. Théophile Silvestre, *Les Artistes Français-I: Romantiques* (Paris: Les Éditions G. Crès and C-ie, 1926). 75.

18. H. Borsch-Supan, *Caspar David Friedrich* (New York: Brazillier, 1974), 7.

19. Harrison and Wood with Gaiger, 54.

20. Brian Lukacher, "Nature Historicized: Constable, Turner, and Romantic Landscape Painting," in *Nineteenth Century Art: A Critical History,* ed. Stephen F. Eisenman (New York: Thames and Hudson, 1994), 121.

21. John W. McCoubrey, *American Art 1700–1960: Sources and Documents* (Englewood Cliffs, N.J.: Prentice-Hall, 1965), 98.

22. *The New York Weekly Tribune,* 30 September 1865.

23. Nikolai Cikovsky Jr. and Franklin Kelly, *Winslow Homer* (Washington, D.C.: National Gallery of Art, 1995), 26.

24. Holt, *Literary Sources,* 547, 548.

25. Nicholas Pevsner, *An Outline of European Architecture* (Baltimore, Md.: Penguin, 1960), 627.

26. Letter from Delaroche to François Arao, in Helmut Gernsheim, *Creative Photography* (New York: Bonanza Books, 1962), 24.

27. Naomi Rosenblum, *A World History of Photography* (New York: Abbeville Press, 1984), 69.

Chapter 29

1. Clement Greenberg, "Modernist Painting," *Art & Literature,* no. 4 (spring 1965): 193.

2. Ibid., 194.

3. Linda Nochlin, *Realism and Tradition in Art 1848–1900* (Englewood Cliffs, N.J.: Prentice-Hall, Inc., 1966), 39, 38, 42.

4. Goldwater and Treves, 295–97.

5. Comment by French critic Enault in Linda Nochlin, *The Nature of Realism* (New York: Penguin Books, 1971), 34.

6. Nochlin, *Realism and Tradition in Art,* 42.

7. In George Heard Hamilton, *Manet and His Critics* (New Haven, Conn.: Yale University Press, 1954), 45.

8. Stephen F. Eisenman, *Nineteenth Century Art: A Critical History* (London: Thames and Hudson, 1994), 242.

9. "On the Heroism of Modern Life" (the closing section of Baudelaire's *Salon of 1846,* published as a brochure in Paris in 1846).

10. Lloyd Goodrich, *Thomas Eakins, His Life and Work* (New York: Whitney Museum of American Art, 1933), 51–52.

11. In Kenneth MacGowan, *Behind the Screen* (New York: A Dell Book, Delta, 1965), 49.

12. In Robert A. Sobieszak, *Masterpieces of Photography from the George Eastman House Collection* (Rochester: International Museum of Photography, 1985), 214.

13. Linda Nochlin, *Realism* (Harmondsworth, England: Penguin Books, 1971), 28.

14. Linda Nochlin, *Impressionism and Post-Impressionism 1874–1904* (Englewood Cliffs, N J : Prentice Hall, 1966), 35.

15. Roy McMullan, *Degas: His Life, Times, and Work* (Boston: Houghton Mifflin Company, 1984), 293.

16. John McCoubrey, *American Art 1700–1960: Sources and Documents* (Englewood Cliffs, N.J.: Prentice Hall, 1965), 184.

17. Laurie Schneider Adams, *A History of Western Art,* 2nd ed. (Madison, Wis.: Brown & Benchmark, 1997), 443.

18. Goldwater and Treves, 322.

19. Van Gogh to Theo van Gogh, 3 September 1888, *Van Gogh: A Self-Portrait, Letters Revealing His Life as a Painter,* selected by W. H. Auden (New York: Dutton, 1963), 319.

20. Van Gogh to Theo van Gogh, 11 August 1888, *Van Gogh: A Self-Portrait, Letters Revealing His Life as a Painter,* 313.

21. Van Gogh to Theo van Gogh, 11 August 1888, *Van Gogh: A Self-Portrait, Letters Revealing His Life as a Painter,* 321.

22. Van Gogh to Theo van Gogh, September 1888, *The Complete Letters of Vincent van Gogh,* ed. J. van Gogh–Bonger and W. V. van Gogh (Greenwich, Conn.: 1979), 3: no. 534.

23. Van Gogh to Theo van Gogh, 8 September 1888, *Van Gogh: A Self-Portrait, Letters Revealing His Life as a Painter,* selected by W. H. Auden (New York: Dutton, 1963), 320.

24. Van Gogh to Theo van Gogh, 16 July 1888, ibid., 299.

25. Belinda Thompson, ed. *Gauguin by Himself* (Boston: Little, Brown and Company, 1993), 270–71.

26. Herschel B. Chipp, *Theories of Modern Art* (Berkeley: University of California Press, 1968), 72.

27. Maurice Denis, "The Influence of Paul Gauguin," in *Theories of Modern Art,* 103.

28. Goldwater and Treves, 375.

29. Ibid., 378.

30. Richard W. Murphy, *The World of Cézanne 1839–1906* (New York: Time-Life Books, 1968), 70.

31. Goldwater and Treves, 363.

32. Cézanne to Émile Bernard, 15 April 1904, *Theories of Modern Art,* 19.

33. Goldwater and Treves, eds., 361.

34. George Heard Hamilton, *Painting and Sculpture in Europe 1880–1940,* 6th ed. (New Haven: Yale University Press, 1993), 124.

35. V. Frisch and J.T. Shipley, *Auguste Rodin,* (New York: Stokes, 1939), 203.

36. Eileen Boris, *Art and Labor: Ruskin, Morris, and the Craftsman Ideal in America* (Philadelphia: Temple University Press, 1986), 7.

37. Siegfried Giedion, *Space, Time, and Architecture* (Cambridge, Mass.: Harvard University Press, 1965), 282.

Chapter 30

1. Alfred M. Tozzer, ed., *Landa's Relación de las cosas de Yucatán: A Translation* (Landa's account of the things of Yucatán), (Cambridge: Peabody Museum Papers, 1941; reprint, New York: Kraus Reprint Corporation, 1966), 18:169.

2. Bernal Díaz del Castillo, *The Discovery and Conquest of Mexico,* trans. A. P. Maudslay (New York: Farrar, Straus, Giroux, 1956), 218–19.

Chapter 31

1. This iconographical explanation courtesy of Meteorolgical Service of New Zealand Limited, Kelburn, Wellington.

Chapter 33

1. Benito Mussolini, "The Doctrine of Fascism," in *Italian Fascisms from Pareto to Gentile,* ed. Adrian Lyttleton, trans. Douglas Parmée (London: Cape, 1973), 42.

2. Herwarth Walden, "Kunst und Leben," *Der Sturm* (1919), 10: 2.

3. John Elderfield, *The "Wild Beasts": Fauvism and Its Affinities* (New York: Museum of Modern Art, 1976), 29.

4. John Russell and the editors of Time-Life Books, *The World of Matisse 1869–1954* (New York: Time-Life Books, 1969), 98.

5. Peter Selz, *German Expressionist Painting* (Berkeley: University of California Press, 1957), 95.

6. Chipp, 182.

7. Frederick S. Levine, *The Apocalyptic Vision: The Art of Franz Marc as German Expressionism* (New York: Harper & Row, 1979), 57.

8. Sam Hunter and John Jacobus, *Modern Art,* 3rd ed. (New York: Harry N. Abrams, 1992), 121.

9. Roland Penrose, *Picasso: His Life and Work,* rev. ed. (New York: Harper & Row, 1971), 122.

10. Hamilton, *Painting and Sculpture,* 246.

11. Edward Fry, ed., *Cubism* (London: Thames & Hudson, 1966), 112–13, 116.

12. Hamilton, *Painting and Sculpture,* 238.

13. Michael Hoog, *R. Delaunay* (New York: Crown, 1976), 49.

14. Françoise Gilot and Carlton Lake, *Life With Picasso* (New York: McGraw-Hill, 1964), 77.

15. From the *Initial Manifesto of Futurism,* first published 20 February 1909.

16. Ibid.

17. Umberto Boccioni, et al. "Futurist Painting: Technical Manifesto," *Poesia,* April 10, 1910.

18. Hans Richter, *Dada: Art and Anti-Art* (London: Thames & Hudson, 1961), 25.

19. Robert Short, *Dada and Surrealism* (London: Octopus Books, 1980), 18.

20. Robert Motherwell, ed., *The Dada Painters and Poets: An Anthology,* 2nd ed. (Cambridge, Mass.: Belknap Press of Harvard University, 1989).

21. Richter, 64–65.

22. Ibid., 57.

23. Arturo Schwarz, *The Complete Works of Marcel Duchamp* (London: Thames & Hudson, 1965), 466.

24. Charles C. Eldredge, "The Arrival of European Modernism," *Art in America* 61 (July-August 1973), 35.

25. Dorothy Norman, *Alfred Stieglitz: An American Seer* (Millerton, N.Y.: Aperture, 1973).

26. Ibid., 161.

27. Ibid., 9–10, 161.

28. Gail Stavitsky, "Reordering Reality: Precisionist Directions in American Art, 1915–1941," in *Precisionism in America 1915–1941: Reordering Reality* (New York: Harry N. Abrams, 1994), 12.

29. Carol Troyen and Erica E. Hirshler, *Charles Sheeler: Paintings and Drawings* (Boston: Museum of Fine Arts, 1987), 116.

30. Miles Orvell, "Inspired by Science and the Modern: Precisionism and American Culture," in *Precisionism in America,* 54.

31. Karen Tsujimoto, *Images of America: Precisionist Painting and Modern Photography* (Seattle: University of Washington Press, 1982), 70.

32. Matthias Eberle, *World War I and the Weimar Artists: Dix, Grosz, Beckmann, Schlemmer* (New Haven: Yale University Press, 1985), 65.

33. Ibid., 54.

34. Ibid., 22.

35. Ibid., 42.

36. William S. Rubin, *Dada, Surrealism, and Their Heritage* (New York: Museum of Modern Art, 1968), 64.

37. Hamilton, *Painting and Sculpture,* 392.

38. Richter, 155.

39. Ibid., 159.

40. Rubin, *Dada, Surrealism, and Their Heritage,* 111.

41. Hunter and Jacobus, 179.

42. William S. Rubin, *Miró in the Collection of the Museum of Modern Art* (New York: Museum of Modern Art, 1973), 32.

43. Chipp, 182–86.

44. Ibid., 341, 345.

45. Robert L. Herbert, ed., *Modern Artists on Art* (Englewood Cliffs, N.J.: Prentice Hall, 1965), 140–41, 145–46.

46. Chipp, 328, 334, 336.

47. Ibid., 332, 335.

48. Camilla Gray, *The Russian Experiment in Art 1863–1922* (New York: Harry N. Abrams, 1970), 216.

49. Ibid., 232–33.

50. Kenneth Frampton, *A Critical History of Modern Architecture* (London: Thames & Hudson, 1985), 142.

51. Ibid., 147.

52. Chipp, 349, and Michel Seuphor, *Piet Mondrian: Life and Work* (New York: Harry N. Abrams, 1956), 177.

53. Hamilton, *Painting and Sculpture,* 319.

54. Chipp, 349.

55. Ibid., 350.

56. Hans L. Jaffeé, comp., *De Stijl* (New York: Harry N. Abrams, 1971), 185–188.

57. Piet Mondrian, "Dialogue on the New Plastic," in *Art in Theory 1900–1990: An Anthology of Changing Ideas,* eds. Charles Harrison and Paul Wood (Oxford: Blackwell Publishers Ltd., 1992), 285.

58. Walter Gropius, from *The Manifesto of the Bauhaus,* April 1919.

59. Ibid.

60. Ibid.

61. László Moholy-Nagy, *Vision in Motion* (Chicago: Paul Theobald, 1969), 268.

62. Hamilton, *Painting and Sculpture,* 345.

63. Ibid.

64. *Josef Albers: Homage to the Square* (New York: Museum of Modern Art, 1964), n.p.

65. John Willett, *Art and Politics in the Weimar Period: The New Sobriety, 1917–1933,* (New York: Da Capo Press, 1978), 119.

66. Wayne Craven, *American Art: History and Culture* (Madison, Wis.: Brown and Benchmark, 1994), 403.

67. Vincent Scully, Jr., *Frank Lloyd Wright* (New York: George Braziller, Inc., 1960), 18.

68. Edgar Kauffmann, ed., *Frank Lloyd Wright, An American Architect* (New York: Horizon, 1955), 205, 208.

69. Philip Johnson, *Mies van der Rohe,* rev. ed. (New York: Museum of Modern Art, 1954), 200–201.

70. Hamilton, *Painting and Sculpture,* 462.

71. H. H. Arnason and Marla F. Prather, *History of Modern Art,* 4th ed. (Upper Saddle River, N.J.: Prentice Hall, 1998), 180.

72. Barbara Hepworth, *A Pictorial Autobiography* (London: The Tate Gallery, 1978), 9, 53.

73. Herbert, 139.

74. Herbert, 140–141, 145–146.

75. Herbert, 143.

76. Frances K. Pohl, *Ben Shahn: New Deal Artist in a Cold War Climate, 1947–1954* (Austin, Tex: University of Texas Press, 1989), 159.

77. Pablo Picasso, "Statement to Simone Téry," in *Art in Theory 1900–1990: An Anthology of Changing Ideas,* eds. Charles Harrison and Paul Wood (Oxford: Blackwell Publishers Ltd., 1992), 640.

78. Roland Penrose, *Picasso: His Life and Work,* rev. ed. (New York: Harper and Row, 1973), 311n.

79. Milton Meltzer, *Dorothea Lange: A Photographer's Life* (New York: Farrar, Strauss, Giroux, 1978), 133, 220.

80. Henry Louis Gates Jr., "New Negroes, Migration, and Cultural Exchange," in *Jacob Lawrence: The Migration Series,* ed. Elizabeth Hutton Turner (Washington, D.C.: The Phillips Collection, 1993), 20.

81. James M. Dennis, *Grant Wood: A Study in American Art and Culture* (Columbia, Mo.: University of Missouri Press, 1986), 143.

82. Wanda M. Corn, *Grant Wood: The Regionalist Vision* (New Haven: Yale University Press, 1983), 131.

83. Corn, Grant Wood, 131.

84. Matthew Baigell, *A Concise History of American Painting and Sculpture* (New York: Harper & Row, 1984), 264.

85. Vivian Endicott Barnett, "Banned German Art: Reception and Institutional Support of Modern German Art in the United States, 1933–45," in *Exiles + Emigrés: The Flight of European Artists from Hitler,* by Stephanie Barron (Los Angeles: Los Angeles County Museum of Art, 1997), 283.

Chapter 34

1. Clement Greenberg, "Toward a Newer Laocoon," *Partisan Review* 7, no. 4 (July/August 1940): 305.

2. Clement Greenberg, "Sculpture in Our Time," *Arts Magazine* 32, no. 9 (June 1956): 22.

3. Dawn Ades and Andrew Forge, *Francis Bacon* (London: Thames & Hudson, 1985), 8; and David Sylvester, *The Brutality of Fact: Interviews with Francis Bacon,* 3rd ed. (London: Thames & Hudson, 1987), 182.

4. Marcus Rothko and Adolph Gottlieb, in "The Realm of Art: A New Platform and Other Matters: 'Globalism' Pops into View," by Edward Alden Jewell, *New York Times,* 13 June 1943, x9.

5. Jackson Pollock, "My Painting," *Possibilities* 1 (Winter 1947), 79.

6. "Jackson Pollack: Is He the Greatest Living Painter in the United States?" *Life,* vol. 27 (August 8, 1949), 42–44.

7. Harold Rosenberg, *The Tradition of the New* (New York: Horizon Press, 1959), 25.

8. Thomas Hess, *Barnett Newman* (New York: Walker and Company, 1969), 51.

9. John P. O'Neill, ed., *Barnett Newman: Selected Writings and Interviews* (New York: Knopf, 1990), 108.

10. Mark Rothko, quoted in Sidney Janis, *Abstract and Surrealist Art in America* (New York: Reynal & Hitchcock, 1944), 118. Rothko and Gottlieb, in "The Realm of Art: A New Platform and Other Matters: 'Globalism' Pops into View," x9.

11. In Selden Rodman, *Conversations with Artists* (New York: Devin-Adair, 1957), 93–94.

12. Clement Greenberg, "Recentness of Sculpture," in *Minimal Art: A Critical Anthology,* ed. Gregory Battcock (New York: E. P. Dutton, 1968), 183–84.

13. Maya Lin, in *National Geographic* 167, no. 5 (May 1985): 557.

14. Lucy Lippard, *Eva Hesse* (New York: New York University Press, 1976), 165.

15. Ibid., 56.

16. Ibid., 56.

17. John Gordon, *Louise Nevelson* (New York: Frederick A. Praeger, 1967), 12.

18. Deborah Wye, *Louise Bourgeois* (New York: Museum of Modern Art, 1982), 22.

19. Ibid., 25.

20. Ibid., 22, 25, 27.

21. H. H. Arnason, *History of Modern Art,* 3rd ed., (Englewood Cliffs, N.J.: Prentice Hall, 1986), 472.

22. Barbara Haskell, *Blam! The Explosion of Pop, Minimalism, and Performance 1958–1964* (New York: Whitney Museum of American Art), 53.

23. Caroline Tisdall, *Joseph Beuys* (New York: Thames and Hudson, 1979), 6.

24. "Joseph Kosuth: Art as Idea as Idea," in *Artwords: Discourse on the 60s and 70s,* ed. Jeanne Siegel (Ann Arbor, Mich.: UMI Research Press, 1985), 225.

25. Ibid., 221.

26. Daniel Wheeler, *Art Since Mid-Century: 1945 to the Present* (Englewood Cliffs, N.J.: Prentice-Hall, 1991).247.

27. Richard Francis, *Jasper Johns* (New York: Abbeville Press, 1984), 21.

28. Ibid., 9.

29. John Cage, *Silence* (Middletown, Conn.: Wesleyan University Press, 1961), 101.

30. Christine Lindey, *Superrealist Painting and Sculpture* (London: Orbis, 1980), 50.

31. Ibid., 130.

32. Nancy Holt, ed., *The Writings of Robert Smithson* (New York: New York University Press, 1975), 111.

33. Calvin Tomkins, "The Art World: Tilted Arc," *New Yorker,* 20 May 1985, 100.

34. Peter Blake, *Frank Lloyd Wright* (Hammondsworth, England: Penguin Books, 1960), 115.

35. Robert Venturi, *Complexity and Contradiction in Architecture,* 2nd ed. (New York: Museum of Modern Art, 1977), 16.

36. Fredric Jameson, "Postmodernism and Consumer Society," in *The Anti-Aesthetic: Essays on Postmodern Culture,* ed. Hal Foster (Port Townsend, Wash.: Bay Press, 1983), 113.

37. Grace Glueck, "Susan Rothenberg: New Outlook for a Visionary Artist," *New York Times Magazine,* 22 July 1984, 20.

38. *Walker Art Center: Painting and Sculpture from the Collection* (Minneapolis: Walker Art Center, 1990), 435.

39. Gerald Marzorati, "Sandro Chia: The Last Hero," *Artnews* 82, no. 4 (April 1983): 60.

40. Susanna Torruella Leval, "Recapturing History: The (Un)official Story in Contemporary Latin American Art," *Art Journal* 51, no. 4 (Winter 1992): 74.

41. Ibid.

42. *Corporal Politics* (Cambridge: MIT List Visual Arts Center, 1993), 46.

43. Kobena Mercer, "Black Hair/Style Politics," in *Out There: Marginalization and Contemporary Culture,* ed. Russell Ferguson, Martha Gever, Trinh T. Minh-ha, and Cornel West (New York: New Museum of Contemporary Art, 1990), 248–49.

44. Ibid., 249.

45. Brooke Kamin Rapaport, "Melvin Edwards: Lynch Fragments," *Art in America* 81, no. 3 (March 1993): 62.

46. Ibid.

47. Jaune Quick-to-See Smith and Harmony Hammond, *Women of Sweetgrass: Cedar and Sage* (New York: American Indian Center, 1984), 97.

48. Richard Marshall and Robert Mapplethorpe, *50 New York Artists* (San Francisco: Chronicle Books, 1986), 448–49.

49. Mary Jane Jacob, *Magdalena Abakanowicz* (New York: Abbeville, 1982), 94.

50. Douglas Crimp, "Appropriating Appropriation," in *Image Scavengers: Photography* (Philadelphia: Institute of Contemporary Art, 1982), 30.

PRONUNCIATION GUIDE TO ARTISTS' NAMES

KEY

ŭ **a**b**u**t, **ki**tt**e**n a **co**t, c**ar**t ā b**a**ke ă b**a**ck au **ou**t
ch **ch**in e l**e**ss ē **ea**sy g **g**ift ĭ tr**i**p ī l**i**fe
j **j**oke k̲ **k**i**ck** ⁿ French vi**n** ng si**ng** o fl**aw** ō b**oa**t
ö b**i(r)**d oi **coi**n u f**oo**t ū l**oo**t ü f**ew**
y yo**y**o zh vi**si**on

Artist's Name	Phonetic Pronunciation
Abakanowicz, Magdalena	a-ba-kan-ˈo-wits, mag-dŭ-ˈlā-nŭ
Achilles Painter	ŭ-ˈkil-ēz
Aertsen, Pieter	ˈart-sen, ˈpē-tŭr
Alberti, Leon Battista	ăl-ˈber-tē, lā-ˈōn bat-ˈtēs-ta
Alexandros of Antioch-on-the-Meander	ă-lig-ˈzăn-dros *of* ˈăn-tē-ak *on the* mē-ˈăn-dŭr
Altdorfer, Albrecht	ˈalt–dor-fŭr, ˈal-brek̲t
Andokides Painter	ăn-ˈdo-kŭ-dēz
Andrea del Castagno	an-ˈdrā-ŭ del ka-ˈstan-yō
Angas, George French	ˈăng-gŭs
Angelico, Fra	an-ˈjel-li-kō, fra
Anguissola, Sofonisba	ang-gwēs-ˈsō-lŭ, sō-fō-ˈnēz-bŭ
Antelami, Benedetto	an-te-ˈla-mē, be-ne-ˈdet-tō
Anthemius of Tralles	ăn-ˈthē-mē-ŭs *of* trăl-ēz
Apollodorus of Damascus	ŭ-pal-ŭ-ˈdor-ŭs *of* dŭ-ˈmăs-kŭs
Archipenko, Aleksandr	ar-ki-ˈpeng-kō, al-ik-ˈsan-dŭr
Arnolfo di Cambio	ar-ˈnol-fō dē ˈkam-byō
Arp, Jean	arp, zhaⁿ
Asam, Egid Quirin	ˈaz–am, ā-ˈgēt kvē-ˈrēn
Athanadoros	ŭ-thă-nŭ-ˈdor-ŭs
Balla, Giacomo	ˈbal–la, ˈja-kō-mō
Barlach, Ernst	ˈbar-lak̲, ernst
Barye, Antoine-Louis	ba-ˈrē, aⁿ-ˈtwan lwē
Beckmann, Max	ˈbek-man, maks
Behnisch, Günter	ˈben-ish, ˈgun-tŭr
Bellini, Giovanni	bel-ˈlē-nē, jō-ˈvan-nē
Berlinghieri, Bonaventura	ber-ling-ˈgye-rē, bo-na-ven-ˈtū-ra
Bernini, Gianlorenzo	ber-ˈnē-nē, jan-lo-ˈren-zō
Beuys, Joseph	bois, ˈyō-zef
Bichitr	bēch-ˈhēt(-r)
Bierstadt, Albert	ˈbēr-shtat
Boccioni, Umberto	bōt-ˈchō-nē, ūm-ˈber-tō
Boffrand, Germain	bo-ˈfraⁿ, zher-ˈmăⁿ
Bonheur, Rosa	bon-ˈur, ˈrō-zŭ
Borromini, Francesco	bor-rō-ˈmē-nē, fran-ˈches-kō
Bosch, Hieronymous	bash (*or* bosh), hŭ-ˈran-ŭ-mus
Botticelli, Sandro	bot-ti-ˈchel-ē, ˈsan-drō
Boucher, François	bū-ˈshā, fraⁿ-ˈswa
Bouguereau, William	bū-gŭ-ˈrō, wēl-ˈyam
Bourgeois, Louise	bor-ˈzhwa
Bouts, Dirk	bauts, dirk
Bramante, Donato d'Angelo	bra-ˈman-tā, do-ˈna-tō ˈdan-je-lō
Brancusi, Constantin	brăn-ˈkū-zē, kon-stan-ˈtēn
Braque, Georges	brak, zhorzh
Breuer, Marcel	ˈbroi-ŭr, mar-ˈsel
Broederlam, Melchior	ˈbrū-dŭr-lam, ˈmel-kyor
Bronzino, Agnolo	bron-ˈzē-nō, ˈanʸ-o-lō
Bruegel the Elder, Pieter	ˈbroi-gŭl, ˈpē-tŭr
Brunelleschi, Filippo	brūn-ŭ-ˈles-kē, fē-ˈlēp-pō
Burgee, John	ˈbŭr-jē
Caillebotte, Gustave	ka-y(ŭ)-ˈbot, gŭ-ˈstav
Callot, Jacques	ka-ˈlō, ˈzhak

Artist's Name	Phonetic Pronunciation
Campin, Robert	kaⁿ-ˈpeⁿ, rō-ˈber
Canaletto, Antonio	ka-na-ˈlet-tō, an-ˈtōn-yō
Canova, Antonio	ka-ˈnō-va, an-ˈtōn-yō
Caradosso, Christoforo Foppa	kar-ŭ-ˈdos-sō, krē-ˈsto-fo-rō, ˈfop-pa
Caravaggio	kar-ŭ-ˈvad-jō,
Carpeaux, Jean-Baptiste	kar-ˈpō, zhaⁿ bap-ˈtēst
Carracci, Annibale	ka-ˈrat-chē, an-ˈnē-bŭ-lā
Cassatt, Mary	kŭ-ˈsat
Cavallini, Pietro	ka-va-ˈlē-nē, ˈpye-trō
Celer	ˈke-lŭr
Cellini, Benvenuto	chel-ˈlē-nē, ben-vŭ-ˈnū-tō
Cézanne, Paul	sā-ˈzan, pōl
Chagall, Marc	shŭ-ˈgal, mark
Chardin, Jean-Baptiste-Siméon	shar-ˈdăⁿ, zhaⁿ bap'tēst si-mā-ˈōⁿ
Chia, Sandro	ˈkē-ŭ, ˈsan-drō
Chirico, Giorgio de	ˈkēr-i-kō, ˈjor-jō de
Chong Son	chung son
Christo	ˈkris-tō
Christus, Petrus	ˈkris-tŭs, ˈpet-rŭs
Cimabue	chē-ma-ˈbū-ā
Clodion	klō-dē-ˈoⁿ
Clouet, Jean	klū-ˈā, zhaⁿ
Cormont, Renaud de	kor-ˈmoⁿ, rŭ-ˈnō dŭ
Cormont, Thomas de	kor-ˈmoⁿ, tō-ˈma dŭ
Corot, Jean-Baptiste-Camille	ko-ˈrō, zhaⁿ bap'tēst kŭ-ˈmēl
Correggio, Antonio Allegri da	kor-ˈred-jō, an-ˈtō-nē-ō al-leg-rē da
Courbet, Gustave	kur-ˈbā, gū-ˈstav
Coypel, Antoine	kwa-ˈpel, aⁿ-ˈtwan
Cranach the Elder, Lucas	ˈkran-ak̲, ˈlū-kŭs
Cuvilliés, François de	kyū-vē-ˈyā, fraⁿ-ˈswa dŭ
Cuyp, Aelbert	koip, ˈel-bŭrt
Daddi, Bernardo	ˈdad-dē, ber-ˈnar-dō
Daedalus	ˈdī-dŭ-lŭs
Daguerre, Louis-Jacques-Mandé	da-ˈger, lū-ˈē zhak maⁿ-ˈdā
Dai Jin	dī jin
Dali, Salvador	ˈda-lē (*or* da-ˈlē) sal-vŭ-ˈdor
Daoji	dau-jē
Daphnis of Miletos	ˈdăf-nis *of* mī-ˈlē-tŭs
Daumier, Honoré	dō-ˈmyā, o-nor-ˈā
David, Jacques-Louis	da-ˈvēd, zhak lū-ˈē
De Kooning, Willem	dŭ ˈkū-ning, ˈwil-ŭm
Degas, Edgar	dŭ-ˈga, ed-ˈgar
Delacroix, Eugène	del-ŭ-ˈk(r)wa, ö-ˈzhen
Delaunay, Robert	dŭ-lō-ˈnā, rō-ˈber
Della Robbia, Andrea	ˈdel-la ˈrō-bē-ŭ, an-ˈdrā-ŭ
Della Robbia, Giovanni	ˈdel-la ˈrō-bē-ŭ, jō-ˈvan-nē
Della Robbia, Girolamo	ˈdel-la ˈrō-bē-ŭ, jē-ro-ˈlam-ō
Della Robbia, Luca	ˈdel-la ˈrō-bē-ŭ, ˈlū-ka
Demuth, Charles	dŭ-ˈmūth
Derain, André	dŭ-ˈrăⁿ, an-ˈdrā
Donatello	do-nŭ-ˈtel-lō
Dong Qichang	dong chō-chang
Dubuffet, Jean	ˈdŭ-bŭ-fā, zhaⁿ
Duccio di Buoninsegna	ˈdūt-chō dē bwo-nin-ˈsā-nya
Duchamp, Marcel	dū – ˈshaⁿ, mar-ˈsel
Dürer, Albrecht	ˈdü-rŭr, ˈal-brek̲t
Durieu, Eugène	dūr-ˈyü, ö-ˈzhen
Eadwine the Scribe	ā-ˈad-wŭn
Eakins, Thomas	ˈā-kŭnz
Eiffel, Alexandre-Gustave	e-ˈfel, ˈal-ek-san-drŭ gū-ˈstav
El Greco	el ˈgre-kō (*or* ˈgrā-kō)

Artist's Name	Phonetic Pronunciation	Artist's Name	Phonetic Pronunciation
Epigonos	e-'pig-o-nos	Horta, Victor	'hor-tŭ, 'vēk-tor
Ergotimos	er-'go-ti-mos	Houdon, Jean-Antoine	ū-'doⁿ, zhaⁿ aⁿ-'twan
Ernst, Max	ernst, maks	Huang Binhong	hwang bēn-hung
Eulalios	yū-'lā-lē-os	Huang Gongwang	hwang gon-wang
Euphronios	yū-'frō-nē-os	Iaia of Cyzicus	ī-'ī-a *of* 'siz-ŭ-kŭs
Euthymides	yū-'thim-ŭ-dēz	Iktinos	ik-'tēn-os
Exekias	ek-'zēk-ē-ŭs	Imhotep	im-'hō-tep
Eyck, Jan van	'īk, yan văn	Ingres, Jean-Auguste Dominique	'ăⁿ(ng)grŭ, zhaⁿ o-'gūst do-mi-'nēk
Fouquet, Jean	fū-'kā, zhaⁿ		
Fragonard, Jean-Honoré	frăg-ŭ-'nar, zhaⁿ o-no-'rā	Isidorus of Miletus	iz-ŭ-'dor-ŭs *of* mī-'lē-tŭs
Frankenthaler, Helen	'frăng-kŭn-tha-lŭr	Jeanne-Claude	zhăn-klod
Friedrich, Caspar David	'frēd-ri<u>k</u>, 'kas-par 'dav-it	Jones, Inigo	jōnz, 'in-ŭ-gō
Fuseli, Henry	'fūs-lē (*or* 'fū-z(ŭ)-lē), 'hen-rē	Jouvin, Hippolyte	zhū-'vaⁿ, ēp-po-'lēt
Gabo, Naum	'gab-ō, 'na-ūm	Juvara, Filippo	yū-'var-a, fē-'lēp-pō
Gaddi, Taddeo	'gad-dē, 'tad-dā-ō	Kahlo, Frida	'ka-lō, 'frē-da
Garnier, J.L. Charles	gar-'nyā, sharl	Kalf, Willem	kalf, 'vil-ŭm
Garsia, Stephanus	gar-'sē-ŭ, 'stef-an-ŭs	Kallikrates	kal-'ē-krŭ-tēz
Gaudí, Antonio	gau-'dē, an-'tōn-ē-ō	Kallimachos	kŭ-'lim-ŭ-kŭs
Gauguin, Paul	gō-'găⁿ, pōl	Kandinsky, Vassily	kăn-'din(t)-skē, vŭs-'ēl-ē
Gaulli, Giovanni Battista	'gaul-lē, jō-'van-nē bat-'tēs-ta	Kano Eitoku	ka-no e-ē-tō-kū
Gehry, Frank	'ge-rē	Kano Motonobu	ka-nō mō-tō-nō-bū
Gelduinus, Bernardus	gel-'dwē-nŭs, bŭr-'nar-dŭs	Kaprow, Allan	'kăp-rō
Gentile da Fabriano	jen-'tē-lā da fab-rē-'an-ō	Käsebier, Gertrude	'kāz-ŭ-bēr, 'ger-trūd
Gentileschi, Artemisia	jen-ti-'les-kē, art-ŭ-'mē-zhŭ	Katsushika Hokusai	kat-sū-shē-kŭ, hō-kū-sī
Gentileschi, Orazio	jen-ti-'les-kē, o-'rat-syō	Kauffmann, Angelica	'kauf-man, an-'je-li-kŭ
Gerhard of Cologne	'gār-hard	Kei	kā-ē
Géricault, Théodore	zhe-ri-'kō, tā-ō-'dor	Kenzo Tange	ken-zō tan-ge
Ghiberti, Lorenzo	gi-'ber-tē, lo-'ren-zō	Kiefer, Anselm	'kē-fŭr, 'an-selm
Ghirlandaio, Domenico	gir-lŭn-'da-yō, do-'men-i-kō	Kimou, Owie	kē-mau, ō-wē-ā
Giacometti, Alberto	ja-ko-'met-tē, ăl-'ber-tō	Kirchner, Ernst Ludwig	'kir<u>k</u>-nŭr, ernst 'lūd-vig
Giorgione da Castelfranco	jor-'jō-nā da kas-tel-'frang-kō	Klee, Paul	klā, pōl
Giotto di Bondone	'jot-tō dē bon-'dō-nā	Kleitias	'klī-tē-ŭs
Giovanni da Bologna	jō-'van-nē da bo-'lōn-yŭ	Klimt, Gustav	klimt, 'gus-taf
Girardon, François	zhē-rar-'don, fran-'swa	Kollwitz, Käthe	'kol-vits, 'ket-ŭ
Girodet-Trioson, Anne-Louis	zhē-ro-'dā trē-ō-'zoⁿ, an-lū-'ē	Kosuth, Joseph	kō-'sūth
Gislebertus	gē-zŭl-'ber-tŭs	Kresilas	'kres-ŭ-las
Glykon of Athens	'glī-kon *of* 'ăth-ŭnz	Kwei, Kane	kwī, ka-nā
Gnosis	'nō-sŭs	L'Enfant, Pierre	laⁿ-'faⁿ, pyer
Goes, Hugo van der	gōz, 'hyū-gō văn dŭr	La Tour, Georges de	la 'tūr, zhorzh dŭ
Gogh, Vincent van	gō, vin-'sent văn	Labrouste, Henri	la-'brūst, aⁿ-'rē
Golub, Leon	'go-lŭb	Le Brun, Charles	lŭ 'brŭⁿ, sharl
González, Julio	'gon-sal-ās, 'hūl-yō	Le Corbusier	lŭ kor-b^yū-zē-'ā
Gossaert, Jan	'gos-art, yan	Le Nôtre, André	lŭ 'nōtr(ŭ), aⁿ-'drā
Goujon, Jean	gū-'zhoⁿ, zhaⁿ	Le Nain, Louis	lŭ 'năⁿ, lū-'ē
Goya y Lucientes, Francisco José de	'goi-yŭ ē lū-'syen-tās, fran-'sis-kō hō-'sā dā	Le Vau, Louis	lŭ 'vō, lū-'ē
		Léger, Fernand	lā-'zhā, fer-'naⁿ
Greenough, Horatio	'grē-nō, hŭ-'rā-shē-ō	Lehmbruck, Wilhelm	'lām-bruk, 'vil-helm
Greuze, Jean-Baptiste	grŭz (*or* gröz), zhaⁿ bap-'tēst	Lemoine, J.B.	lŭ-'mwan
Gropius, Walter	'grō-pē-us, 'wol-tŭr	Leonardo da Vinci	lē-ŭ-'nar-dō da 'vin-chē
Gros, Antoine-Jean	grō, aⁿ-'twan zhaⁿ	Lescot, Pierre	les-'kō, pyer
Grosz, George	grōs	Leyster, Judith	'lī-stŭr, 'yū-dith
Grünewald, Matthias	'grü-nŭ-valt, ma-'tē-ŭs	Libon of Elis	'lī-bŭn *of* 'e-lŭs
Gu Kaizhi	gū kī-tsi	Lichtenstein, Roy	'lik-tŭn-stīn
Guarini, Guarino	'gwar-ē-nē, 'gwar-ē-nō	Limbourg, Hennequin	'lim-burk, 'hen-ŭ-kăⁿ
Haacke, Hans	'ha-kŭ, hans	Limbourg, Herman	'lim-burk, 'her-man
Hadrian	'hā-drē-ŭn	Limbourg, Pol	'lim-burk, pol
Hagesandros	hăg-ŭ-'săn-dros	Lin, Maya Ying	lin, 'mī-ŭ yēng
Hals, Frans	hals, frants	Lipchitz, Jacques	'lip-shits, zhak
Hamada Shoji	ha-ma-da shō-jē	Lippi, Filippino	'lēp-pē, fē-lē-'pē-nō
Hardouin-Mansart, Jules	ar-'dwăⁿ -man-'sar, zhūl	Lippi, Fra Filippo	'lēp-pē, fē-'lēp-pō
Hasegawa Tohaku	has-e-ga-wa tō-ha-ku	Lochner, Stephan	'lo<u>k</u>-nŭr, 'stā-fan
Heda, Willem Claesz	'hā-da, 'vil-ŭm klas	Lorenzetti, Ambrogio	lo-rent-'set-tē, am-'brō-jō
Hemessen, Caterina van	'hā-me-sŭn, ka-te-'rē-na văn	Lorenzetti, Pietro	lo-rent-'set-tē, pē-'ā-trō
Herrera, Juan de	er-'rer-a, hwan dā	Lorrain, Claude	lŭ-'răⁿ, klōd
Hippodamos of Miletos	hip-'ad-ŭ-mŭs *of* mī-'lē-tŭs	Luzarches, Robert de	lu-'zarsh, rō-'ber dŭ
Höch, Hannah	hö<u>k</u>, 'ha-na	Lysippos of Sikyon	lī-'sip-os *of* 'sik-ē-an
Holbein, Hans the Younger	'hōl-bīn, hants	Ma Yuan	ma yū-an
Holzer, Jenny	'hōlt-zŭr	Mabuse, Jan	ma-'büz, yan
Honam Koeisu	hō-na-mē kō-et-su	Machuca, Pedro	ma-'chū-ka, 'pā-drō
Honnecourt, Villard de	on-ŭ-'kūr, vē-'lar (*or* vē-'yar) dŭ	Maderno, Carlo	ma-'der-nō, 'kar-lō
Honthorst, Gerrit van	'hont-horst, 'gher-ŭt van	Magritte, René	ma-'grēt, rŭ-'nā

Artist's Name	Phonetic Pronunciation	Artist's Name	Phonetic Pronunciation
Maiano, Giuliano da	′mī-a-nō, jū-lē-′a-nō dä	Pisano, Giovanni	pē-′zan-ō, jō-′van-nē
Maillol, Aristide	mī-′yōl, ar-ŭ-′stēd	Pisano, Nicola	pē-′zan-ō, nē′-ko-la
Maitani, Lorenzo	mī-′ta-nē, lo-′ren-zō	Pissarro, Camille	pŭ-′zar-ō, ka-′mēl (or ka-′mēy)
Malevich, Kazimir	mŭl-′yav-ich, ′kaz-ē-mēr	Piula, Trigo	pē-ū-la, trē-gō
Manet, Édouard	ma-′nā, ā-′dwar	Pollaiuolo, Antonio	pol-lī-′wō-lō an-′tō-nē-ō
Mansart, François	man-′sar, fran-′swa	Pollock, Jackson	′pal-ŭk
Mantegna, Andrea	man-′tān-yŭ, an-′drā-ŭ	Polydoros	pal-i-′dor-os
Maqsud of Kashan	mak-′sūd of ka-′shan	Polyeuktos	pal-i-′yuk-tos
Marc, Franz	mark, frants	Polygnotos of Thasos	pal-ig-′nōt-os of ′thā-sos
Marika, Mawalan	ma-rē-ka, ma-wa-lan	Polykleitos of Argos	pal-i-′klīt-os of ′ar-gos
Martini, Simone	mar-′tē-nē, sē-′mōn-ā	Pontormo, Jacopo da	pon-′tor-mō, ′ya-ko-pō da
Maruyama Okyo	ma-rū-ya-ma ō-kyō	Porta, Giacomo della	′por-ta, ′ja-ko-mō ′del-la
Masaccio	ma-′zat-chō	Poussin, Nicolas	pū-′săn, ni-kō-′la
Masolino da Panicale	ma-sō-′lē-nō da pa-nē-′ka-lā	Pozzo, Fra Andrea	′pot-tsō, fra an-′drā-ŭ
Massys, Quinten	′mat-zīs, ′kwin-tŭn	Praxiteles	prak-′sit-ŭl-ēz
Master Honoré	o-no-′rā	Primaticcio, Francesco	prē-ma-′tēt-chō, fran-′ches-kō
Master of Flemalle	flā-′mal	Pucelle, Jean	pū-′sel, zhan
Matisse, Henri	ma-′tēs, an-′rē	Puget, Pierre	pū-′zhā, pyer
Melozzo da Forlì	me-′lot-sō da for-′lē	Pugin, A.W.N.	′pyū-jin
Memling, Hans	′mem-ling, hants	Puvis de Chavannes, Pierre	pü-vē-dŭ-sha-′van, pyer
Memmi, Lippo	′mem-mē, ′lēp-pō	Quarton (or Charonton),	kar-′ton (or sha-ron-′ton),
Mendieta, Ana	men-dē-′e-ta, ′a-na	Enguerrand	an-ge-′ran
Michelangelo Buonarroti	mī-kŭ-′lăn-jŭ-lō (or mē-ke-′lan-jŭ-lō)	Quick-to-See-Smith, Jaune	jōn
	bwo-nar-′rō-tē	Rainer of Huy	rī-nŭr of wē
Michelozzo di Bartolommeo	mē-ke-′lot-tsō dē bar-tō-lōm-′mā-ō	Raphael	ra-fa-′yel (or ′rӑf-ē-ŭl)
Mies van der Rohe, Ludwig	mēz van dŭ-′rō(-ŭ) ′lud-vik	Rauch, John	rauch
Millais, John Everett	mil-′ā	Rauschenberg, Robert	′rau-shŭn-bŭrg
Millet, Jean-François	mē-′yā (or mi-′lā), zhan fran-′swa	Redon, Odilon	rŭ-′don, ō-di-′lon
Miró, Joan	mi-′rō, zhu-′an	Regnaudin, Thomas	re-nyo-′dӑn, to-′ma
Mnesikles	(m-)′nes-i-klēz	Rembrandt van Rijn	′rem-brӑnt van rīn
Moholy-Nagy, László	mō-′hō-lē ′na-zhē, ′laz-lō	Reni, Guido	′rӑ-nē, ′gwē-dō
Mondrian, Piet	mon-drē-′an, pēt	Renoir, Pierre-Auguste	ren-′war, pyer-ō-′gūst
Monet, Claude	mō-′nā, klōd	Ribera, José (Jusepe) de	rē-′be-ra, hō-′sā (jū-′se-pe) dä
Moreau, Gustave	mo-′rō, gū-′stav	Riemenschneider, Tilman	′rē-mŭn-shnī-dŭr, ′til-man
Morisot, Berthe	mo-rē-′zō, bert	Rietveld, Gerrit	′rēt-velt, ′ger-ŭt
Muhammad ibn al-Zayn	mū-′ha-mad ′ēb(ŭ)n ӑl-′zān	Rigaud, Hyacinthe	rē-′gō, ē-ŭ-′sent (or ya-′sant)
Munch, Edvard	mungk, ′ed-vard	Rivera, Diego	ri-′ve-ra, dē-′ā-gō
Muqi	mū-kē	Rodin, Auguste	rō-′dӑn(n), o-′gūst
Muybridge, Eadweard	′mī-brij, ′ed-wŭrd	Romano, Giulio	rō-′man-ō, ′jūl-yō
Nadar	na-′dar	Rossellino, Bernardo	ros-sŭl-′lē-nō, ber-′nar-dō
Nanni di Banco	′nan-nē dē ′bang-kō	Rosso Fiorentino	′ros-sō fyor-ŭn-′tē-nō
Natoire	na-′twar	Rouault, Georges	rū-′ō, zhorzh
Neumann, Balthasar	′noi-man, ′bal-tŭ-zar	Rousseau, Henri	rū-′sō, an-′rē
Niobid Painter	nī-′ō-bid	Rublyev, Andrei	rū-′blev, ′an-drā
Nolde, Emil	′nol-dŭ, ′ā-mēl	Rude, François	rüd, fran-′swa
Novios Plautios	′nō-vē-os ′plau-tē-os	Ruisdael, Jacob van	′rīz-dal, ′ya-kob van
Odo of Metz	′ō-dō of mets	Ruysch, Rachel	roish, ra̱k-ŭl
Ogata Korin	ō-ga-ta kō-rēn	Saarinen, Eero	′săr-ŭ-nŭn, ′ār-ō
Olbrich, Joseph Maria	′ōl-bri̱k, ′yō-zŭf ′ma-rē-a	Saint-Gaudens, Augustus	sānt ′god-ŭnz, ŭ-′gŭs-tŭs
Oldenberg, Claes	′ōl-dŭn-bŭrg, klas	Sangallo the Younger, Antonio da	sang-′gal-lō, an-′tō-nē-ō da
Onesimos	o-′nes-i-mos	Sansovino, Jacopo	san-sō-′vē-nō, ′ya-ko-pō
Oppenheim, Meret	′ap-ŭn-hīm, ′mer-ŭt	Schnabel, Julian	′shna-bŭl
Orcagna, Andrea	or-′kan-ya, an-′drā-ŭ	Schongauer, Martin	′shōn-gau-ŭr, ′mar-tin
Orozco, José Clemente	o-′rōs-kō, hō-′sā kle-′men-tā	Schwitters, Kurt	′shvit-ŭrs, kurt
Paik, Nam June	pīk, nam jūn	Senmut	sen-′mūt
Paionios of Ephesos	pī-′ō-nē-ŭs of ′ef-ŭ-sŭs	Sen No Rikyu	sen nō rē-kyū
Palladio, Andrea	pal-′la-dē-ō, an-′drā-ŭ	Seurat, Georges	sŭ-′ra, zhorzh
Parmigianino	par-mi-ja-′nē-nō	Severini, Gino	se-ve-′rē-nē, ′jē-nō
Patinir, Joachim	pa-ti-′nēr, ′yō-a-ke̱m	Severus	se-′vēr-ŭs
Pentewa, Otto	pen-′te-wa	Signorelli, Luca	sē-nyo-′rel-lē, ′lū-ka
Perrault, Claude	pŭ-′rō, klōd	Siloé, Gil de	sē-lō-′ā, hēl dä
Perugino	per-ŭ-′jē-nō	Sinan the Great	sŭ-′nan
Phiale Painter	fē-′a-lā	Sitani, Mele	si-ta-nē, mā-lā
Phidias	′fid-ē-ŭs	Skopas of Paros	′skō-pŭs of ′păr-os
Philoxenos of Eretria	fŭ-′lak-sŭ-nos of er-′e-trē-ŭ	Sluter, Claus	′slū-tŭr, klaus
Piano, Renzo	pē-′a-nō, ′ren-zō	Song Huizong	song hwā-tsong
Picasso, Pablo	pi-′kas-ō, ′pab-lō	Soufflot, Jacques-Germain	sū-′flō, zhak zher-′men
Piero della Francesca	′pyer-ō ′del-lŭ fran-′ches-ka	Steen, Jan	stān, yan
Pietro da Cortona	′pyā-trō da kor-′tō-na	Stieglitz, Alfred	′stēg-lits
Piranesi, Giovanni Battista	pē-ra-′nä-zē jō-′van-nē bat-′tēs-ta	Stölzl, Gunta	′shtö(l)-tsŭl, ′gun-ta
Pisano, Andrea	pē-′zan-ō, an-′drā-ŭ	Stoss, Veit	shtōs, vēt

Artist's Name	Phonetic Pronunciation	Artist's Name	Phonetic Pronunciation
Sulayman	′sū-lā-man	Venturi, Robert	ven-′tū-rē
Sultan-Muhammad	sūl-′tan (or ′sūl-tan)-mū-′ha-mad	Vermeer, Jan	vŭr-′mēr, yan
Suzuki Harunobu	sū-zū-kē ha-rū-nō-bū	Veronese, Paolo	ver-ŭ-′nā-zā, ′pau-lō
Takahashi Yuichi	ta-ka-ha-shē yū-ē-chē	Verrocchio, Andrea del	vŭr-′rok-kyō, an-′drā-ŭ del
Tanner, Henry Ossawa	ō-′sa-wa	Vigée-Lebrun, Élisabeth Louise	vē-zhā-lŭ-′brönⁿ, ā-lē-za-′bet lŭ-′ēz
Tassananchalee, Kamol	tas-san-anch-′ha-lē, ka-′mol	Vignola, Giacomo da	vē-′nyō-lŭ, ′ja-kō-mō da
Tatlin, Vladimir	′tat-lin, ′vla-di-mir	Vignon, Pierre	vin-′yonⁿ, pyer
Te Pehi Kupe	tā pā-hē kū-pā	Vitruvius	vŭ-′trū-vē-ŭs
Te Whanau-a-Apanui	tā wa-naū-a-a-pa-nū-ē	Vulca of Veii	′vŭl-ka of ′vā-ē
Ter Brugghen, Hendrick	tŭr ′brū-gŭn, ′hen-drik	Wang Wei	wang wā
Theodoros of Phokaia	thē-o-′dor-os of ′fō-kā-ŭ	Warhol, Andy	′wor-hol
Theotokópoulous, Doménikos	thā-o-to-′ko-pū-los, dō-′mā-nē-kŭs	Watteau, Antoine	wa-′tō, aⁿ-′twan
Thutmose	′thŭt-mōs-e	Weyden, Rogier van der	′vī-dŭn, ′ra-jŭr van dŭr
Tiepolo, Giambattista	tē-′ā-pŭ-lō, jam-bat-′tēs-ta	Wiligelmo	vē-lē-′gel-mō
Tinguely, Jean	′tăⁿ-glŭ, zhaⁿ	William of Sens	sanⁿ
Tintoretto	tin-tŭ-′ret-tō	Witz, Konrad	vits, ′kon-rat
Titian	′tish-ŭn	Wodiczko, Krzysztof	vō-′dētsh-kō, (k-)′shish-tof
Toledo, Juan Bautista de	tō-′lā-dō, hwan bau-′tēs-ta dā	Wojnarowicz, David	voi-na-′rō-vich
Tori Busshi	tō-rē bū-shē	Wolgemut, Michel	′vōl-gŭ-mūt, ′mik-ŭl
Tosa Mitsunobu	tō-sa mēt-sun-ō-bu	Wright of Derby, Joseph	rīt of ′dar-bē
Toulouse-Lautrec, Henri de	tū-′lūz-lō-′trek, aⁿ-′rē dŭ	Wu Zhen	ū jŭn
Tournachon, Gaspar-Félix	tūr-na-′shonⁿ, ga-′spar ′fā-lēks	Xia Gui	shya gwā
Toyo Sesshu	tō-yō ses-shu,	Xu Bing	shū bing
Uccello, Paolo	ūt-′chel-lō, ′pau-lō	Yan Liben	yan lē-bŭn
Utzon, Joern	′ut-zōn, ′yor-(ŭ)n	Yi Chae-Gwan	yē chī-gwan
Van Bruggen, Coosje	van ′brū-gŭn, ′kōs-zhŭ	Yokoyama Taikan	yō-kō-ya-ma ta-ē-kan
Van Dyck, Anthony	văn ′dīk, ′an-tŭ-nē	Yosa Buson	yō-sa bus-ōn
Vanbrugh, John	văn-′brū	Zhou Jichang	jō jē-chang
Vecelli, Tiziano	ve-′chel-ē, tēts-′ya-nō	Zong Bing	tsong bing
Velázquez, Diego	ve-′las-kez, dē-′ā-gō	Zurbarán, Francisco de	zur-ba-′ran, fran-′sis-kō dā

GLOSSARY

Italicized terms in definitions are defined elsewhere in the glossary. A pronunciation guide is now included for a select number of technical terms and uses the key provided on page 1144.

abacus—(ă-ba-ʹkŭs) The uppermost portion of the *capital* of a *column,* usually a thin slab.

Abakans—(a-baʹkanz) Abstract woven hangings suggesting organic spaces as well as giant pieces of clothing made by Magdalena Abakanowicz.

abstract—In painting and sculpture, emphasizing a derived, essential character that has only a stylized or symbolic visual reference to objects in nature.

Abstract Expressionism—Also known as the New York School. The first major American avant-garde movement, Abstract Expressionism emerged in New York City in the 1940s. The artists produced abstract paintings that expressed their state of mind and were intended to strike emotional chords in viewers. The movement developed along two lines: *Gestural Abstraction* and *Chromatic Abstraction.*

acropolis—(a-ʹkra-pŭ-lŭs) Literally, the "high city." In Greek architecture, usually the site of the city's most important temple(s).

Action Painting—Also called *Gestural Abstraction.* The kind of *Abstract Expressionism* practiced by Jackson Pollock, in which the emphasis was on the creation process, the artist's gesture in making art. Pollock stood on his canvases, pouring liquid paint in linear webs, thereby literally immersing himself in the painting during its creation.

additive—A kind of sculpture technique in which materials, e. g., clay, are built up or "added" to create form.

addorsed—Set back-to-back, especially as in heraldic design.

adobe—(a-ʹdō-bē) The clay used to make a kind of sun-dried mud brick of the same name; a building made of such brick.

aerial perspective—See *perspective.*

aesthetic properties of works of art—The visual and tactile features of an object: form, shape, line, color, mass, and volume.

aesthetics—The branch of philosophy devoted to theories about the nature of art and artistic expression. Also referring to such theories.

agora—(a-go-ʹra) An open square or space used for public meetings or business in ancient Greek cities.

aisle—The portion of a church flanking the *nave* and separated from it by a row of *columns* or *piers.*

akua ba (pl. **akua mma**)—Small wooden fertility figures carved by Asante men in Ghana (West Africa).

alabaster—A variety of gypsum or calcite of dense, fine texture, usually white, but also red, yellow, gray, and sometimes banded.

altarpiece—A panel, painted or sculpted, sit-

uated above and behind an altar. See also *retable.*

alternate-support system—In medieval church architecture, the use of alternating wall supports in the *nave,* usually *piers* and *columns* or *compound piers* of alternating form.

amalaka—(a-ma-ʹla-ka) In Hindu temple design, the large flat disk with ribbed edges surmounting the beehive-shaped tower.

amalau—(a-ma-la-ū) In the Caroline Islands of Micronesia, a spirit house that served as a communal religious structure for both men and women.

Amazonomachy—(ă-mŭ-zon-ʹa-mŭ-kē) In Greek mythology, the legendary battle between the Greeks and Amazons.

ambulatory—(ʹăm-byŭ-lŭ-to-rē) A covered walkway, outdoors (as in a *cloister*) or indoors; especially the passageway around the *apse* and the *choir* of a church.

amphiprostyle—(ăm-fi-ʹpro-stīl) The style of Greek building in which the *colonnade* was placed across both the front and back, but not along the sides.

amphitheater—Literally, a double theater. A Roman building type resembling two Greek theaters put together. The Roman *amphitheater* featured a continuous elliptical *cavea* around a central *arena.*

amphora—(ʹăm-fŭ-ra) A two-handled jar used for general storage purposes, usually to hold wine or oil.

amulet—An object worn to ward off evil or to aid the wearer.

Analytic Cubism—The first phase of *Cubism,* developed jointly by Pablo Picasso and Georges Braque, in which the artists analyzed form from every possible vantage point to combine the various views into one pictorial whole.

anamorphic image—(ăn-ŭ-ʹmor-fik) A distorted image that must be viewed by some special means (such as a mirror) to be recognized.

andron—Dining room in a Greek house.

aniconic—(ăn-ī-ʹkan-ik) Non-image representation.

animal style—A generic term for the characteristic ornamentation of artifacts worn and carried by nomadic peoples who, for almost two millennia (B.C. into A.D.) migrated between China and western Europe. The style is characterized by use of phantasms, like the dragon.

antae—(ʹăn-tī) The molded projecting ends of the walls forming the *pronaos* or *opisthodomos* of an ancient Greek temple.

apadana—(ă-pa-ʹda-na) The great audience hall in ancient Persian palaces.

apotheosis—(ŭ-path-ē-ʹō-sŭs) Elevated to the rank of gods or the ascent to heaven.

apotropaic—(ap-a-trō-ʹpā-ik) Capable of warding off evil.

apse—(ăps) A recess, usually singular and semi-circular, in the wall of a Roman *basilica* or at the east end of a Christian church.

arabesque—(ă-rŭ-ʹbesk) Literally, "Arablike." A flowing, intricate pattern derived from stylized organic motifs, usually floral, often arranged in symmetrical *palmette* designs; generally, an Islamic decorative motif.

arcade—A series of *arches* supported by *piers* or *columns.*

Arcadian (adj.)—In Renaissance and later art, depictions of an idyllic place of rural peace and simplicity. Derived from "Arcadia," an ancient district of the central Peloponnesus in southern Greece.

arch—A curved structural member that spans an opening and is generally composed of wedge-shaped blocks (*voussoirs*) that transmit the downward pressure laterally. A diaphragm arch is a transverse, wall-bearing arch that divides a *vault* or a ceiling into compartments, providing a kind of firebreak. See also *thrust.*

architrave—(ʹar-kŭ-trāv) The *lintel* or lowest division of the *entablature;* sometimes called the epistyle.

archivolt—One of a series of concentric bands on a *Romanesque* or a *Gothic* arch.

arcuated—Of arch-column construction.

arena—In a Roman *amphitheater,* the central area where bloody gladiatorial combats and other boisterous events took place.

arhat—(ʹar-hat) Also *bodhisattva.* A *Buddhist* holy person who has achieved enlightenment and *nirvana* by suppression of all desire for earthly things

Arianism—An early Christian movement, condemned by the Church as heretical, that denied the equality of the three aspects of the *Trinity* (Father, Son, and Holy Spirit).

armature—(ʹar-mŭ-chŭr) The crossed, or diagonal, arches that form the skeletal framework of a *Gothic* rib vault. In sculpture, the framework for a clay form.

arras—(ʹar-ŭs) A kind of tapestry originating in Arras, a town in northeastern France.

arrises—(ŭ-ʹrēz-sŭz) In *Doric* columns, the raised edges of the *fluting.* See also *fillets.*

Art Brut—(ar brū) A term coined by artist Jean Dubuffet to characterize art that is genuine, untaught, coarse, even brutish.

Art Deco—Descended from *Art Nouveau,* this movement of the 1920s and 1930s sought to upgrade industrial design in competition with "fine art" and to work new materials into decorative patterns that could be either machined or hand-crafted. Characterized by "streamlined" design, elongated and symmetrical.

Art Nouveau—(ar nū-ˈvō) A late nineteenth-/early twentieth-century art movement whose proponents tried to synthesize all the arts in an effort to create art based on natural forms that could be mass-produced by technologies of the industrial age.

asceticism—Self-discipline and self-denial.

ashlar masonry—(ˈash-lar) Carefully cut and regularly shaped blocks of stone used in construction, fitted together without mortar.

assemblage—(a-sem-ˈblazh) A three-dimensional composition made of various materials such as *found objects,* paper, wood, and cloth. See also *collage.*

atlantid—(ăt-ˈlăn-tid) A male figure that functions as a supporting *column.* See also *caryatid.*

atlatl—(ˈăt(-ŭ)-lăt(-ŭ)l) Spear thrower.

atmospheric or aerial perspective—See *perspective.*

atrium (pl. **atria**)—The court of a Roman house that is partly open to the sky. Also the open, colonnaded court in front of and attached to a Christian *basilica.*

attic—In architectural terminology, the uppermost story.

attribution—Assignment of a work to a maker or makers. Based on *documentary evidence* (e.g., signatures and dates on works and/or artist's own writings) and *internal evidence* (stylistic and iconographical analysis).

automatism—In painting, the process of yielding oneself to instinctive motions of the hands after establishing a set of conditions (such as size of paper or medium) within which a work is to be carried out.

avant-garde—(ˈă-vanⁿ gard) Literally, the advance guard in a platoon. Late-nineteenth- and twentieth-century artists who emphasized innovation and challenged established convention in their work. Also used as an adjective.

avatar—A manifestation of a deity incarnated in some visible form in which the deity performs a sacred function on earth. In Hinduism, an incarnation of a god.

avlu—A courtyard forming a summer extension of the *mosque* and surrounded by porticoes formed by domed squares.

axial plan—See *plan.*

backstrap loom—A simple loom used by Andean weavers and others since ancient times.

bai—(ba-ē) Elaborately painted men's ceremonial clubhouses on Belau in the Caroline Islands of Micronesia.

baldacchino—(bal-da-ˈkē-nō) A canopy on columns, frequently built over an altar. See also *ciborium.*

balustrade—(ˈbăl-us-trād) A row of vase-like supports surmounted by a railing.

baptistery—(ˈbăp-tus-trē) In Christian architecture, the building used for baptism, usually situated next to a church.

bar tracery—See *tracery.*

barays—The large reservoirs laid out around Cambodian *wats* that served as means of transportation as well as irrigation. The reservoirs were connected by a network of canals.

Baroque—A blanket designation for the art of the period 1600 to 1750.

barrel or **tunnel vault**—See *vault.*

bas-relief—(ˈba rŭ-ˈlēf) See *relief.*

base—In ancient Greek architecture, the lowest part of *Ionic* and *Corinthian* columns.

basilica—(bu-ˈsil-ŭ-kŭ) In Roman architecture, a public building for assemblies (especially tribunals), rectangular in plan with an entrance usually on a long side. In Christian architecture, a church somewhat resembling the Roman basilica, usually entered from one end and with an *apse* at the other, creating an axial *plan.*

Bauhaus—(ˈbau-haus) A school of architecture in Germany in the 1920s under the aegis of Walter Gropius, who emphasized the unity of art, architecture, and design. The Bauhaus trained students in a wide range of both arts and crafts, and was eventually closed by the National Socialists in 1933.

beehive tomb—In Mycenaean architecture, a beehive-shaped tomb covered by an earthen mound and constructed as a *corbeled vault.* See *tholos.*

ben-ben—(ˈben-ben) A pyramidal stone; a *fetish* of the Egyptian god Re.

bevel—See *chamfer.*

bhakti—In *Buddhist* thought, the adoration of a personalized deity (*bodhisattva*) as a means of achieving unity with it; love felt by the devotee for the deity. In Hinduism, the devout, selfless direction of all tasks and activities of life to the service of one god.

bi—(bē) In ancient China, jade disks carved as ritual objects for burial with the dead. They were often decorated with piercework carving extending entirely through the object.

bilingual vases—Experimental Greek vases produced for a short time in the late sixth century B.C.; one side featured decoration in *red-figure technique,* the other *black-figure technique.*

black-figure technique—In early Greek pottery, the silhouetting of dark figures against a light background of natural, reddish clay, with linear details incised through the silhouettes.

blind arcade (wall arcade)—An *arcade* having no actual openings, applied as decoration to a wall surface.

block statue—In ancient Egyptian sculpture, a cubic stone image with simplified body parts.

bo nun amuin—Composite imaginary animal masks created by Baule people of Côte d'Ivoire (West Africa). Representing the spirit power of the bush, these sacred and secret masks served a policing function in traditional Baule society.

bodhisattva—(bod-hē-sat-va) In *Buddhist* thought, one of the host of divinities provided to the *Buddha* to help him save humanity. A potential *Buddha.* See also *bhakti.*

bombé—Outwardly bowed.

bottega—(bōt-ˈtā-gŭ) A shop; the studio-shop of an Italian artist.

breviary—(brē-vē-e-rē) A Christian religious book of selected daily prayers and psalms.

brocade prints—Japanese *woodblock* prints in which the pictures are printed (not hand painted) in many colors.

Buddha (adj. **Buddhist**)—The supreme enlightened being of Buddhism; an embodiment of divine wisdom and virtue.

Buddha triad—A group of three statues with a central *Buddha* flanked on each side by a *bodhisattva.*

burin—(ˈbyū-rin) A pointed tool used for *engraving* or *incising.*

buttress—(ˈbŭt-trŭs) An exterior masonry structure that opposes the lateral thrust of an *arch* or a *vault.* A pier buttress is a solid mass of masonry; a flying buttress consists typically of an inclined member carried on an arch or a series of arches and a solid buttress to which it transmits lateral *thrust.*

bwoom—A mythical ancestor mask of the Kuba people of the Democratic Republic of Congo.

Byzantium (adj. **Byzantine**)—(biz-ˈan-te-um/ ˈbiz-un-tēn) The Christian Eastern Roman Empire, which lasted until 1453, when Constantinople was captured by the Ottoman Turks.

caduceus—(ka-ˈd(y)ū-sē-ŭs) In ancient Greek mythology, a magical rod entwined with serpents carried by Hermes (Roman, Mercury), the messenger of the gods.

caldarium—(kal-ˈdă-rē-ŭm) The hot-bath section of a Roman bathing establishment.

caliph(s)—(kā-lef *or* kal-ŭf) *Muslim* rulers, regarded as successors of Muhammad.

calligraphy—Handwriting or penmanship, especially elegant or "beautiful" writing as a decorative art. In Chinese writing, the brushing of characters in different styles.

calotype—(ˈkă-lŭ-tip) A photographic process in which a positive image is made by shining light through a negative image onto a sheet of sensitized paper.

camera lucida—(ˈkă-mŭ-rŭ lū-ˈsē-dŭ) A device in which a small lens projects the image of an object downward onto a sheet of paper. Literally, "lighted room."

camera obscura—(ˈkă-mŭ-rŭ ŭb-ˈskyū-rŭ) An ancestor of the modern camera in which a tiny pinhole, acting as a lens, projects an image on a screen, the wall of a room, or the ground-glass wall of a box; used by artists in the seventeenth, eighteenth, and early nineteenth centuries as an aid in drawing from nature. Literally, "dark room."

campaniform—Bell-shaped.

campanile—(kam-pa-ˈnē-lā) A bell tower of a church, usually, but not always, free-standing.

canon—Rule, e.g., of proportion. The ancient Greeks considered beauty to be a matter of "correct" proportion and sought a canon of proportion, in music and for the human figure.

canon law—The law system of the Roman Catholic church, as opposed to civil or secular law.

canonization—In the Roman Catholic church, the process by which a revered deceased person is declared a *saint* by the pope.

canopic jars—(kă-'nō-pik *jars*) In ancient Egypt, containers in which the organs of the deceased were placed for later burial with the mummy.

capital—The uppermost member of a *column*, serving as a transition from the *shaft* to the *lintel*. The form of the capital varies with the *order*.

Capitolium—(kă-pi-'tō-lē-ŭm) An ancient Roman temple honoring the divinities Jupiter, Juno, and Minerva.

cardo—('kar-dō) The north–south street in a Roman town, intersecting the *decumanus* at right angles

Caroline minuscule—The alphabet that *Carolingian* scribes perfected, from which our modern alphabet was developed.

Carolingian (adj.)— (kă-rō-'lin-jŭn) Pertaining to the empire of Charlemagne and his successors.

carpet pages—In early *medieval* manuscripts, decorative pages resembling textiles.

cartoon—In painting, a full-size preliminary drawing from which a painting is made.

caryatid—(kă-rē-ăt-id) A female figure that functions as a supporting *column*. See also *atlantid*.

castrum—(kăs-trŭm) A Roman military encampment, famed for the precision with which it was planned and laid out.

catacombs—(kăt-ŭ-kōmz) Subterranean networks of galleries and chambers designed as cemeteries for the burial of the dead.

catafalque—(kăt-ŭ-fălk) The framework that supports and surrounds a deceased person's body on a bier.

cathedra—(ku-thē-drŭ) Literally, the seat of the bishop, from which the word *cathedral* is derived.

cavea—(kă-vē-ŭ) The seating area in ancient Greek and Roman theaters and *amphitheaters*. Literally, a hollow place or cavity.

celadon—(sel-ŭ-dan) A Chinese–Korean pottery glaze, fired in an oxygen-deprived kiln to a characteristic gray–green or pale blue color.

cella—('se-lŭ) The chamber (Greek—*naos*) at the center of an ancient temple; in a classical temple, the room in which the cult statue usually stood.

celt—(selt) In *pre-Columbian* Mexico, Olmec ax-shaped form made of polished jade; generally a prehistoric metal or stone implement shaped like a chisel or ax head.

cement—See *concrete*.

centaur—In ancient Greek mythology, a fantastical creature, with the front or top half of a human and the back or bottom half of a horse.

centauromachy—(sen-to-'ra-mŭ-kē) In ancient Greek mythology, the battle between the Greeks and *centaurs*.

central plan—See *plan*.

cestrum—('kes-trŭm) A small spatula used in *encaustic* painting.

chaitya—(tshī-'tyŭ) An Indian rock-cut temple hall having a votive *stupa* at one end.

chakra—The wheel that sometimes marks the Buddha's feet as a supernatural sign; one of the *lakshanas* of the Buddha.

chakravartin—In India, the ideal king, the Universal Lord who ruled through goodness.

chamfer—('cham-fŭr) The surface formed by cutting off a corner of a board or post; a bevel.

Chan—See *Zen*.

chancel—The elevated area at the altar end of a church reserved for the priest and choir.

Charuns—Etruscan death demons.

chatra—('cha-tra) See *yasti*.

chevet—The east, or apsidal, end of a *Gothic* church, including *choir*, *ambulatory*, and radiating chapels.

chi-rho-iota—(kī-rō-ī-'ō-tŭ) The three initial letters of Christ's name in Greek (**XPI**), which came to serve as a monogram for Christ.

chiaroscuro—(kē-ă-rō-'skū-rō) In drawing or painting, the treatment and use of light and dark, especially the gradations of light that produce the effect of *modeling*.

chicha—Fermented maize beer consumed on numerous ceremonial and non-ceremonial occasions in the Andes.

chigi—(chē-gē) The crosspiece at the gables of Japanese shrine architecture.

chimera—(kī-mer-ŭ) A monster of Greek invention with the head and body of a lion and the tail of a serpent. A second head, that of a goat, grows out of one side of the body.

chiton—('kī-tan) A Greek tunic, the essential (and often only) garment of both men and women, the other being the *himation*, or *mantle*.

choir—The space reserved for the clergy in the church, usually east of the *transept* but, in some instances, extending into the *nave*.

Christogram—(kris-tō-grăm) See *chi-rho-iota*.

Chromatic Abstraction—A kind of *Abstract Expressionism* that focused on the emotional resonance of color, as exemplified by the work of Barnett Newman and Mark Rothko.

chryselephantine—(kris-el-ŭ-'făn-tīn) Fashioned of gold and ivory.

ciborium—(su-'bor-ē-ŭm) A canopy, often freestanding and supported by four columns, erected over an altar; also, a covered cup used in the sacraments of the Christian church. See *baldacchino*.

circumambulation—In *Buddhist* worship, walking around the *stupa* in a clockwise direction.

cire perdue—(sēr per-'dū) See *lost-wax process*.

cista—('sis-tŭ) An Etruscan cylindrical container made of sheet bronze with cast handles and feet, often with elaborately engraved bodies, used for women's toilet articles.

city-state—An independent, self-governing city that rules the surrounding countryside.

clerestory—('klēr-sto-rē) The *fenestrated* part of a building that rises above the roofs of the other parts. In Roman *basilicas* and medieval churches, the windows that form the *nave's* uppermost level below the timber ceiling or the *vaults*.

cloison—(kloi-zŭn) Literally, a partition. A cell made of metal wire or a narrow metal strip soldered edge-up to a metal base to hold enamel or other decorative materials.

cloisonné—(kloi-zŭ-nā) A process of enameling employing *cloisons*.

cloister—A monastery courtyard, usually with covered walks or *ambulatories* along its sides.

cluster pier—See *compound pier*.

codex (pl. **codices**)—(kō-deks/kō-dŭ-sēz) Separate pages of *vellum* or *parchment* bound together at one side and having a cover; the predecessor of the modern book. The *codex* superseded the *rotulus*. In *pre-Columbian Mesoamerica*, a painted and inscribed book on long sheets of bark paper or deerskin coated with fine white plaster and folded into accordion-like pleats.

coffer—A sunken panel, often ornamental, in a *soffit*, a *vault*, or a ceiling.

collage—(kō-'lazh) A composition made by combining on a flat surface various materials such as newspaper, wallpaper, printed text and illustrations, photographs, and cloth. See also *photomontage*.

colonnades—A series or row of *columns*, usually spanned by *lintels*.

colonnette—A small *column*.

colophon—('ka-lŭ-fan) An inscription, usually on the last page, giving information about a book's manufacture. In Chinese painting, written texts on attached pieces of paper or silk.

color—See *primary*, *secondary*, and *complementary colors*. The value or tonality of a color is the degree of its lightness or darkness. The intensity or saturation of a color is its purity, its brightness or dullness.

color field painters—A variant of *Post-Painterly Abstraction* whose artists sought to reduce painting to its physical essence by pouring diluted paint onto unprimed canvas, allowing these pigments to soak into the fabric. Examples include the work of Helen Frankenthaler and Morris Louis.

colorito—(ko-lo-'rē-tō) Literally, "colored" or "painted." A term used to describe the application of paint, characteristic of sixteenth-century Venetian art. It is distinguished from *disegno*, which emphasizes careful design preparation based on preliminary drawing.

column—A vertical, weight-carrying architectural member, circular in cross-*section* and consisting of a base (sometimes omitted), a *shaft*, and a *capital*.

complementary colors—Those pairs of colors, such as red and green, that together embrace the entire spectrum. The complement of one of the three *primary colors* is a mixture of the other two. In pigments, they produce a neutral gray when mixed in the right proportions.

Composite capital—A capital with an ornate combination of *Ionic* volutes and *Corinthian* acanthus leaves that became popular in Roman times.

composite view—See *twisted perspective*.

composition—The way in which an artist organizes *forms* in an art work, either by placing shapes on a flat surface or arranging forms in space.

compound pier—A *pier* with a group, or cluster, of attached *shafts*, or *responds*, especially characteristic of *Gothic* architecture.

computer imaging—A medium developed during the 1960s and 1970s that uses computer programs and electronic light to make designs and images on the surface of a computer or television screen.

conceptual approach to representation—See *descriptive approach to representation*.

Conceptual Art—An American avant-garde art trend of the 1960s that asserted that the "artfulness" of art lay in the artist's idea, rather than its final expression. A major proponent was Joseph Kosuth.

conch—(kank) Semi-circular half-dome.

concrete—A building material invented by the Romans and consisting of various proportions of lime mortar, volcanic sand, water, and small stones. From the Latin *caementa*, from which the English "cement" is derived.

condottiere—(kon-da-′tyer-ē) A professional military leader employed by the Italian city-states in the early Renaissance.

confraternities—(kon-frŭ-′tŭr-nŭ-tēz) In late medieval Europe, organizations founded by laypeople who dedicated themselves to strict religious observances.

connoisseur—(kan-ŭ-′sūr) An expert on works of art and the individual styles of artists.

Constructivism—A movement in art formulated by Naum Gabo, who built up his sculptures piece by piece in space instead of carving or modeling them in the traditional way. In this way the sculptor worked with "volume of mass" and "volume of space" as different materials.

contextuality—The causal relationships among artists, art work, and the society or culture that conditions them.

continuous narration—In painting or sculpture, the convention of the same figure appearing more than once in the same space at different stages in a story.

contour line—In art, a continuous line defining an object's outer shape.

contrapposto—(kon-trŭ-′pas-tō) The disposition of the human figure in which one part is turned in opposition to another part (usually hips and legs one way, shoulders and chest another), creating a counter-positioning of the body about its central axis. Sometimes called weight shift because the weight of the body tends to be thrown to one foot, creating tension on one side and relaxation on the other.

corbel—(′kor-bŭl) A projecting wall member used as a support for some element in the superstructure. Also, courses of stone or brick in which each course projects beyond the one beneath it. Two such structures, meeting at the topmost course, create a corbeled arch.

corbel tables—Horizontal projections resting on *corbels*.

corbeled arch—See *corbel*.

corbeled vault—A *vault* formed by the piling of stone blocks in horizontal courses, cantilevered inward until the two walls meet in a pointed arch. No mortar is used, and the vault is held in place only by the weight of the blocks themselves, with smaller stones used as wedges.

Corinthian capital—A more ornate form than *Doric* or *Ionic*; it consists of a double row of acanthus leaves from which tendrils and flowers grow, wrapped around a bell-shaped *echinus*. Although this *capital* form is often cited as the distinguishing feature of the Corinthian *order*, there is, strictly speaking, no Corinthian order, but only this style of capital used in the *Ionic* order.

cornice—The projecting, crowning member of the *entablature* framing the *pediment*; also, any crowning projection.

Cosmati—(kos-′ma-tē) A group of twelfth-to fourteenth-century craftsmen who worked in marble and mosaic, creating work (known as **Cosmato work**) characterized by inlays of gold and precious or semi-precious stones and finely cut marble in geometric patterns.

crenellation—(kren-ŭ-′lā-shŭn) Notches or indentations, usually with respect to tops of walls, as in battlements.

cromlech—(′krom-lek) A circle of *monoliths*. Also called henge.

cross vault—See *vault*

crossing—The space in a *cruciform* church formed by the intersection of the *nave* and the *transept*.

crossing square—The area in a church formed by the intersection (*crossing*) of a *nave* and a *transept* of equal width, often used as a standard measurement of interior proportion.

cruciform—Cross-shaped.

Crusades—In *medieval* Europe, armed pilgrimages aimed at recapturing the Holy Land from the Muslims.

crypt—A vaulted space under part of a building, wholly or partly underground; in *medieval* churches, normally the portion under an *apse* or a *chevet*.

cubiculum (pl. **cubicula**)—(kū-′bik-yū-lŭm) A small cubicle or bedroom that opened onto the *atrium* of a Roman house. Also, a chamber in an Early Christian catacomb that served as a mortuary chapel.

Cubism—An early twentieth-century art movement that rejected naturalistic depictions, preferring compositions of shapes and forms "abstracted" from the conventionally perceived world. See also *Analytic Cubism* and *Synthetic Cubism*.

cuerda seca—(′kwer-dŭ ′sā-kū) A type of polychrome tilework used in decorating Islamic buildings.

cuirass—(′kwēr-ăs) A breastplate. In Roman art, the emblem of a military officer.

cultural constructs—In the reconstruction of the context of a work of art, experts consult the evidence of religion, science, technology, language, philosophy, and the arts to discover the thought patterns common to artists and their audiences.

culture—The collective characteristics by which a community identifies itself and by which it expects to be recognized and respected.

cunei—(′kū-nē-ī) In ancient Greek theaters, wedge-shaped sections of stone benches separated by stairs.

cuneiform—(kyū-′nā-ŭ-form) Literally, "wedge-shaped." A system of writing used in ancient Mesopotamia, in which wedge-shaped characters were produced by pressing a stylus into a soft clay tablet, which was then baked or otherwise allowed to harden.

cupola—(′kū-pō-lŭ) An exterior architectural feature composed of *drums* with shallow caps; a dome.

cutaway—An architectural drawing that combines an exterior view with an interior view of part of a building.

Cycladic art—(sik-′lăd-ik) The pre-Greek art of the Cycladic Islands.

Cyclopean—(sī-klō-′pē-ŭn) Gigantic, vast and rough, massive. Cyclopean masonry is a method of stone construction using large, irregular blocks without mortar. The huge unhewn and roughly cut blocks of stone were used to construct Bronze Age fortifications such as Tiryns and other *Mycenaean* sites.

cylinder seal—A cylindrical piece of stone usually about an inch or so in height, decorated with a design in *intaglio* (incised), so that a raised pattern was left when the seal was rolled over soft clay. In the ancient Near East documents, storage jars, and other important possessions were signed, sealed, and identified in this way.

Dada—(′da-da) An art movement that reflected a revulsion against the absurdity and horror of World War I. Dada rejected all art, modern or traditional, as well as the civilization that had produced it, to create an art of the absurd. Foremost among the Dadaists was Marcel Duchamp.

Daedalic—Refers to a Greek *Orientalizing* style of the seventh century B.C. named after the legendary Daedalus. Characteristic of the style is the triangular flat-topped head framed by long strands of hair that form complementary triangles to that of the face.

daguerreotype—(da-ʹger-ō-tip) A photograph made by an early method on a plate of chemically treated metal; developed by Louis J. M. Daguerre.

damnatio memoriae—The Roman decree condemning those who ran afoul of the Senate. Those who suffered damnatio memoriae had their memorials demolished and their names erased from public inscriptions.

darshan—In Hindu worship, seeing images of the divinity and being seen by the divinity.

De Stijl—(du stēl) Dutch for "the style." An early twentieth-century art movement (and magazine) founded by Piet Mondrian and Theo van Doesburg, whose members promoted utopian ideals and developed a simplified geometric style.

deceptive cadence—In a horizontal scroll, the "false ending," which arrests the viewer's gaze by appearing to be the end of a narrative sequence, but which actually sets the stage for a culminating figure or scene.

deconstruction—An analytical strategy developed in the late twentieth century according to which all cultural "constructs" (art, architecture, literature) are "texts." People can read these texts in a variety of ways, but they cannot arrive at fixed or uniform meanings. Any interpretation can be valid, and readings differ from time to time, place to place, and person to person. For those employing this approach, deconstruction means destabilizing established meanings and interpretations while encouraging subjectivity and individual differences.

Deconstructivist architecture—Using *deconstruction* as an analytical strategy, Deconstructionist architects attempt to disorient observers by disrupting the conventional categories of architecture. The haphazard presentation of volumes, masses, planes, lighting, etc. challenges viewers' assumptions about form as it relates to function.

découpage—(de-kŭ-ʹpazh) A technique of decoration in which letters or images are cut out of paper or some such material and then pasted onto a surface.

decumanus—The east–west street in a Roman town, intersecting the *cardo* at right angles.

decursio—The ritual circling of a Roman funerary pyre.

demos—The Greek word meaning "the people," from which *democracy* is derived.

demotic—Late Egyptian writing.

denarius—The standard Roman silver coin from which the word *penny* ultimately derives.

descriptive approach to representation—In artistic representation, that which is "known" about an object is represented. To represent a human profile "descriptively" would require the artist to depict both eyes rather than just one.

dharma—In Buddhism, moral law based on the *Buddha's* teaching.

di sotto in sù—(dē ʹsot-tō in ʹsū) A technique of representing perspective in ceiling painting. Literally, "from below upwards."

diagonal rib—See *rib*.

diaphragm arch—See *arch*.

diorite—(ʹdì-ŭ-rīt) An extremely hard stone used in Mesopotamian and Egyptian art.

dipteral—(ʹdip-tŭr-ŭl) The term used to describe the architectural feature of double *colonnades* around Greek temples. See also *peripteral*.

diptych—(ʹdip-tik) A two-paneled painting or *altarpiece;* also, an ancient Roman, Early Christian, or Byzantine hinged writing tablet, often of ivory and carved on the external sides.

disegno—(dē-ʹzā-nyō) In Italian, "drawing" and "design." Renaissance artists considered drawing to be the external physical manifestation (*disegno esterno*) of an internal intellectual idea of design (*disegno interno*).

documentary evidence—In *attributions* of works of art, this consists of contracts, signatures, and dates on works as well as the artist's own writings.

doges—(dōzh) Rulers of *medieval* Venice and Genoa.

dolmen—Several large stones (*megaliths*) capped with a covering slab, erected in prehistoric times.

dome—A hemispheric *vault;* theoretically, an *arch* rotated on its vertical axis.

domus—(ʹdō-mŭs) A Roman private house.

Doric—(ʹdor-ik) One of the two systems (or *orders*) evolved for articulating the three units of the elevation of an ancient Greek temple—the platform, the *colonnade*, and the superstructure (*entablature*). The Doric order is characterized by, e.g., capitals with funnel-shaped *echinuses,* columns without bases, and a frieze of *triglyphs* and *metopes*. See also *Ionic*.

dotaku—(do-ta-kū) Ancient Japanese bronze ceremonial bells, usually featuring raised decoration.

dromos—The passage leading to a *beehive tomb*.

drum—The circular wall that supports a *dome;* also, one of the cylindrical stones of which a non-monolithic *shaft* of a *column* is made.

dry fresco—See *fresco*.

dry-joining—Fitting stone blocks together without mortar.

dry point—An engraving in which the design, instead of being cut into the plate with a *burin*, is scratched into the surface with a hard steel "pencil." See also *engraving, etching, intaglio*.

dukha—The *Buddha's* insight that life is pain.

earthenware—Pottery made of clay that is fired at low temperatures and that is slightly porous.

eaves—The lower part of a roof that overhangs the wall.

echinus—(ŭ-ʹkīn-ŭs) In architecture, the convex element of a *capital* directly below the *abacus*.

écorché—A figure painted or sculptured to show the muscles of the body as if without skin.

effigy mounds—Ceremonial mounds built in the shape of animals or birds by *pre-Columbian* Native American cultures.

elevation—In drawing and architecture, a geometric projection of a building on a plane perpendicular to the horizon; a vertical projection. A head-on view of an external or internal wall, showing its features and often other elements that would be visible beyond or before the wall.

emblema—(em-ʹblā-mŭ) The central section or motif of a *mosaic*.

embrasure—A *splayed* opening in a wall that enframes a doorway or a window.

embroidery—The technique of sewing threads onto a finished ground to form contrasting designs.

encaustic—(en-ʹkos-tik) A painting technique in which pigment is mixed with wax and applied to the surface while hot.

engaged column—A half-round *column* attached to a wall. See also *pilaster*.

engraving—The process of *incising* a design in hard material, often a metal plate (usually copper); also, the print or impression made from such a plate. See also *dry point, etching, intaglio*.

entablature—(in-ʹtăb-lŭ-chŭr) The part of a building above the *columns* and below the roof. The entablature has three parts: *architrave* or *epistyle, frieze,* and *pediment*.

entasis—(ʹen-tŭ-sŭs) A convex tapering (an apparent swelling) in the *shaft* of a *column*.

Environmental or **Earth Art**—An American art form that emerged in the 1960s. Often using the land itself as their material, Environmental artists constructed monuments of great scale and minimal form. Permanent or impermanent, these works transform some section of the environment, calling attention both to the land itself and to the hand of the artist.

epistyle—(ʹep-ŭ-stil) See *architrave*.

escutcheon—(ŭ-ʹskŭt-chŭn) An emblem bearing a coat of arms.

esthetic properties of works of art—The visual and tactile features of an object: form, shape, line, color, mass, and volume.

etching—A kind of *engraving* in which the design is incised in a layer of wax or varnish on a metal plate. The parts of the plate left exposed are then **etched** (slightly eaten away) by the acid in which the plate is immersed after incising. See also *dry point, engraving, intaglio.*

ethnocentrism—The tendency to explain and to judge artifacts from the perspective of one's own culture and to the detriment of other cultures.

Eucharist—('yū-ku-rist) In Christianity, the partaking of the bread and wine, which believers hold to be either Christ himself or symbolic of him.

ewer—A large pitcher.

exedra—(ek-'sē-drŭ) Recessed area, usually semi-circular.

exemplum virtutis—Example or model of virtue.

existentialism—A philosophy asserting the absurdity of human existence and the impossibility of achieving certitude.

Expressionism—Twentieth-century *modernist* art that is the result of the artist's unique inner or personal vision and that often has an emotional dimension. Expressionism contrasts with art focused on visually describing the empirical world. It is characterized by bold, vigorous brushwork, emphatic line, and bright color. Two important groups of early twentieth-century German *expressionists* were Die Brücke, in Dresden, and Der Blaue Reiter, in Munich.

extrados—(ek-'stra-das) The upper or outer surface of an arch. See *intrados.*

facade—(fŭ-'sad) Usually, the front of a building; also, the other sides when they are emphasized architecturally.

faïence—(fa-'an(t)s or fī-'aⁿs) Earthenware or pottery, especially with highly colored design (from Faenza, Italy, a site of manufacture for such ware). Glazed earthenware.

fan vault—See *vault*

fasciae—('făsh-ē-ī) In the Classical Greek *Ionic order,* the three horizontal bands that make up the *architrave.*

fauces—('fo-sēz) Literally, the throat of the house. In a Roman house, the narrow foyer leading to the *atrium.*

Fauvism—('fō-viz-ŭm) From the French word *fauves,* literally, "wild beasts." An early twentieth-century art movement led by Henri Matisse, for whom color became the formal element most responsible for pictorial coherence and the primary conveyor of meaning. The Fauves intensified color with startling contrasts of vermilion and emerald green and of cerulean blue and vivid orange, held together by sweeping brushstrokes and bold patterns.

femmage—(fem-'azh) A kind of feminist sewn collage made by Miriam Schapiro in which she assembles fabrics, quilts, buttons, sequins, lace trim, and rickrack to explore hidden metaphors for womanhood, using techniques historically associated with

women's crafts (techniques and media not elevated to the status of fine art).

fenestration—('fen-ŭ-strā-shŭn) The arrangement of the windows of a building.

fengshui—(fŭng-shwā) A Chinese notion of "wind and water," the breath of life, which is scattered by wind and must be stopped by water; thus the forces of wind and water must be adjusted for in the orientation of Chinese architecture.

fête galante—(fet ga-'laⁿ) A type of *Rococo* painting depicting the outdoor amusements of upper-class society.

fetish—('fet-ish) An object believed to possess magical powers, especially one capable of bringing to fruition its owner's plans; sometimes regarded as the abode of a supernatural power or spirit.

feudalism—The *medieval* political, social and economic system held together by the relationship of a liege-lord and vassal.

fibula—('fib-yū-lŭ) A decorative pin, usually used to fasten garments.

figura serpentinata—(fii-'gū-ra ser-pen-ti-'na-ta) In Renaissance art, a contortion or twisting of the body in contrary directions, especially characteristic of the sculpture and paintings of Michelangelo and the Mannerists.

fillets—('fil-ŭts) The flat ridges of *Ionic fluting.* See also *arrises.*

fin de siècle—(fã ⁿ-dŭ-sē-'ek-lŭ) Literally, the end of the century. A period in western cultural history from the end of the nineteenth century until just before World War I, when decadence and indulgence masked anxiety about an uncertain future.

First Style—The earliest style of Roman mural painting. Also called the masonry style, because the aim of the artist was to imitate, using painted stucco relief, the appearance of costly marble panels.

Flamboyant style—A Late *Gothic* style of architecture superseding the *Rayonnant* style and named for the flamelike appearance of its pointed bar *tracery.*

flashing—In making stained-glass windows, fusing one layer of colored glass to another to produce a greater range of colors.

flute or fluting—Vertical channeling, roughly semicircular in cross-*section* and used principally on *columns* and *pilasters.*

Fluxus—A group of American, European, and Japanese artists of the 1960s who created *Performance Art.* Their performances focused on single actions, such as turning a light on and off or watching falling snow, and were more theatrical than *Happenings.*

flying buttress—See *buttress.*

folio—A page of a manuscript or book.

foreshortening—(for-'shor-tŭ-ning) The use of *perspective* to represent in art the apparent visual contraction of an object that extends back in space at an angle to the perpendicular plane of sight.

form—In art, an object's shape and structure, either in two dimensions (a figure painted

on a surface) or in three dimensions (such as a statue).

formalism—Strict adherence to, or dependence on, stylized shapes and methods of composition. An emphasis on an artwork's visual elements rather than its subject.

forum—The public square of an ancient Roman city.

found objects—Images, materials, or objects as found in the everyday environment that are appropriated into works of art.

Fourth Style—In Roman mural painting, the Fourth Style marks a return to architectural illusionism, but the architectural vistas of the Fourth Style are irrational fantasies.

freedmen—In ancient and *medieval* society, the class of men and women who had been freed from servitude, as opposed to having been born free.

freestanding sculpture—See *sculpture in the round.*

fresco—('fres-kō) Painting on lime plaster, either dry (dry fresco or fresco secco) or wet (true or buon fresco). In the latter method, the pigments are mixed with water and become chemically bound to the freshly laid lime plaster. Also, a painting executed in either method.

fresco secco—('fres-kō 'sek-ō) See *fresco.*

fret or meander—An ornament, usually in bands but also covering broad surfaces, consisting of interlocking geometric motifs. An ornamental pattern of contiguous straight lines joined usually at right angles.

frieze—(frēz) The part of the *entablature* between the *architrave* and the *cornice;* also, any sculptured or ornamented band in a building, on furniture, etc.

frigidarium—(fri-jŭ-'dă-rē-ŭm) The cold-bath section of a Roman bathing establishment.

frottage—(frō-'tazh) A process of rubbing a crayon or other medium across paper placed over surfaces with a strong and evocative texture pattern to combine patterns.

Futurism—An early-twentieth century movement involving a militant group of Italian poets, painters, and sculptors. These artists published numerous manifestoes declaring revolution in art against all traditional tastes, values, and styles and championing the modern age of steel and speed and the cleansing virtues of violence and war.

gable—See *pediment.*

garbha griha—('garb-ha 'grē-ha) Literally, "womb chamber." In Hindu temples, this is the *cella,* the inner sanctum, for the cult image or symbol, the holiest of places in the temple.

genetrix—A legendary founding clan mother.

genii—Guardian spirits.

genre—('zhaⁿ-rŭ) A style or category of art; also, a kind of painting realistically depicting scenes from everyday life.

gesso—('jes-sō) Plaster mixed with a binding

material and used for *reliefs* and as a *ground* for painting.

Gestural Abstraction—Also known as *Action Painting.* A kind of abstract painting in which the gesture, or act of painting, is seen as the subject of art. Its most renowned proponent was Jackson Pollock. See also *Abstract Expressionism.*

gigantomachy—(jī-gŭn-'ta-mŭ-kē) In ancient Greek mythology, the battle between gods and giants.

gishes—Medicine canes belonging to *Yei.*

glaze—A vitreous coating applied to pottery to seal and decorate the surface; it may be colored, transparent, or opaque, and glossy or *matte.* In oil painting, a thin, transparent, or semitransparent layer put over a color to alter it slightly.

glazed brick—Bricks painted and then kiln fired to fuse the color with the baked clay.

glory—See *nimbus.*

Golden Mean—Also known as the Golden Rule or Golden Section, a system of measuring in which units used to construct designs are subdivided into two parts in such a way that the longer subdivision is related to the length of the whole unit in the same proportion as the shorter subdivision is related to the longer subdivision. The *esthetic* appeal of these proportions has led artists of varying periods and cultures to employ them in determining basic dimensions.

gong—In ancient China, covered vessels, often in animal forms, holding wine, water, grain, or meat for sacrificial rites.

gopuras—('gō-pū-rŭz) The massive, ornamented entrance gateway towers of South Indian temple compounds.

gorget—('gor-jŭt) Throat armor or a neck pendant.

gorgon—In ancient Greek mythology, a hideous female demon with snake hair. Medusa, the most famous gorgon, was capable of turning anyone who gazed at her into stone.

Gospels—The four New Testament books that relate the life and teachings of Jesus.

Gothic—Originally a derogatory term named after the Goths, used to describe the history, culture, and art of *medieval* western Europe in the twelfth to fourteeth centuries.

gouache—A painting technique employing pigments ground in water.

granulation—A decorative technique in which tiny metal balls, granules, are fused to a metal surface.

graver—A cutting tool used by engravers and sculptors.

Greek cross—A cross in which all the arms are the same length.

grisaille—(grŭ-'zīy) A monochrome painting done mainly in neutral grays to simulate sculpture.

groin—The edge formed by the intersection of two *vaults.*

groin or **cross vault**—Formed by the intersection at right angles of two barrel vaults

of equal size. Lighter in appearance than the barrel vault, the groin vault requires less *buttressing.* See *vault.*

ground—A coating applied to a canvas or some other surface to prepare that surface for painting; also, background.

ground line—In paintings and reliefs, a painted or carved base line on which figures appear to stand.

guilloche—(gē-'yōsh) An architectural ornament that imitates braided ribbon or that consists of interlaced, curving bands.

Hallenkirche—('hal-ŭn-kēr-ḵŭ) A hall church. A type of *Gothic* design much favored in Germany in which the *aisles* rise to the same height as the *nave.*

handscroll—In Asian art, a horizontal painted scroll that is unrolled to the left and often used to present illustrated religious texts or landscapes.

haniwa—(ha-nē-wa) Sculptured fired pottery cylinders, modeled in human, animal, or other forms and placed around early (archaic) Japanese burial mounds.

Happenings—Loosely structured performances initiated in the 1960s, whose creators were trying to suggest the dynamic and confusing qualities of everyday life; most shared qualities of unexpectedness, variety, and wonder.

hard-edge painting—A variant of *Post-Painterly Abstraction* that rigidly excluded all reference to gesture, and incorporated smooth knife-edge geometric forms to express the notion that the meaning of painting should be its form and nothing else. Ellsworth Kelly is an example.

harihara—A Hindu religious statue divided vertically into a Shiva half and a Vishnu half.

harmika—(har-'mē-ka) In *Buddhist* architecture, a stone fence or railing that encloses an area surmounting the dome of a *stupa* that represents one of the Buddhist heavens; from the center, arises the *yasti.*

hatching—A technique used in drawing, engraving, etc., in which fine lines are cut or drawn close together to achieve an effect of shading.

Hejira—See *Hijra.*

Helladic art—(hŭ-'lăd-ik *art*) The pre-Greek art of the Greek mainland (Hellas).

Hellenes (adj. **Hellenic**)—The name the ancient Greeks called themselves as the people of Hellas, to distinguish themselves from people who did not speak Greek.

Hellenistic—The term given to the culture that developed after the death of Alexander the Great in 323 B.C. and lasted almost three centuries, until the Roman conquest of Egypt in 31 B.C.

herm—A bust on a quadrangular pillar.

Hiberno-Saxon—('hi-ber-no 'sak-sŭn) An art style that flourished in the monasteries of the British Isles in the early *Middle Ages.* Also called Insular.

hierarchy of scale—An artistic convention

in which greater size indicates greater importance.

hieratic—(hī-ŭ-'ră-tik) A method of representation fixed by religious principles and ideas.

hieroglyphic—(hī-rō-'glif-ik) A system of writing using symbols or pictures.

high relief—See *relief.*

Hijra (Hejira)—The flight of Muhammad from Mecca to Medina in A.D. 622, the year from which Islam dates its beginnings.

himation—(hī-'mā-shŭn) An ancient Greek *mantle* worn by men and women over the tunic and draped in various ways.

Hippodamian plan—A city plan devised by Hippodamos of Miletos ca. 466 B.C., in which a strict grid was imposed upon a site, regardless of the terrain, so that all streets would meet at right angles. A *Hippodamian plan* also called for separate quarters for public, private, and religious functions, so that such a city was logically as well as regularly planned.

hiragana—(hē-ra-ga-na) A sound-based writing system developed in Japan from Chinese characters; it came to be the primary script for Japanese court poetry.

historiated—Ornamented with representations, such as plants, animals, or human figures, that have a narrative—as distinct from a purely decorative—function. Historiated initial letters were a popular form of manuscript decoration in the *Middle Ages.*

Holy Spirit—In Christianity, the third "person" of the *Trinity* (with the Father and the Son), often symbolized by a dove.

horror vacui—Literally, "fear of empty space," a technique of design in which an entire surface is covered with pattern.

hue—The name of a *color.* See *primary colors, secondary colors,* and *complementary colors.*

humanism—In the Renaissance, an emphasis on education and on expanding knowledge (especially of classical antiquity), the exploration of individual potential and a desire to excel, and a commitment to civic responsibility and moral duty.

hydria—('hī-drē-ŭ) An ancient Greek three-handled water pitcher.

hypaethral—(hīp-'ēth-rŭl) A building having no pediment or roof, open to the sky.

hypostyle hall—('hī-pŭ-stīl *hall*) In Egyptian architecture, a hall with a roof supported by columns. Also, in Islamic architecture, a *mosque* prayer hall with its roof supported by numerous columns.

icon—A portrait or image; especially in the Eastern Christian churches, a panel with a painting of sacred personages that are objects of veneration. In the visual arts, a painting, a piece of sculpture, or even a building regarded as an object of veneration.

iconoclasm—(ī-'kan-'ŭ-klăz(-ŭ)m) The destruction of images. In *Byzantium* the period from 726 to 843 when there was an imperial ban on images. The destroyers of images were known as iconoclasts, while those who opposed such a ban were known as iconophiles or iconodules.

iconography—(ī-kŭn-ʹa-grŭ-fē) Literally, the "writing of images." The term refers both to the content, or subject, of an art work and to the study of content in art. It also includes the study of the symbolic, often religious, meaning of objects, persons, or events depicted in works of art.

iconostasis—(ī-kŭ-ʹnas-tū-sŭs) The large icon-bearing chancel screen that shuts off the sanctuary of a *Byzantine* church from the rest of the church. In the Eastern Christian churches, a screen or a partition, with doors and many *tiers* of *icons,* separating the sanctuary from the main body of the church.

idealization—The representation of things according to a preconception of ideal form or type; a kind of *esthetic* distortion to produce idealized forms. See also *realism.*

ideogram—(ʹī-dē-ŭ-gram *or* ʹid-ē-ŭ-gram) A simple, picturelike sign filled with implicit meaning.

ikegobo—(ē-kā-gō-bō) The Benin (West African) altar of the hand or arm, symbolizing the Benin king's powers of accomplishment.

illumination—Decoration with drawings (usually in gold, silver, and bright colors), especially of *medieval* manuscript pages.

imagines (sing. **imago**)—(i-ʹma-gi-nes) In ancient Rome, wax portraits of ancestors.

imam—(i-ʹmam or i-ʹmam) In Islam, the leader of collective worship.

impasto—(im-ʹpas-tō) A style of painting in which the pigment is applied thickly or in heavy lumps, as in many paintings by Jean Dubuffet or Anselm Kiefer.

imperator—(im-pŭ-ʹra-tŭr) A Latin term meaning "commander in chief," from which the word *emperor* is derived.

impluvium—(im-ʹplū-vē-ŭm) In a Roman house, the basin located in the *atrium* that collected rainwater.

impost block—A stone with the shape of a truncated, inverted pyramid, placed between a *capital* and the *arch* that springs from it.

Impressionism—A late nineteenth-century art movement that sought to capture a fleeting moment by conveying the illusiveness and impermanence of images and conditions.

in antis—In ancient Greek architecture, between the *antae.*

in situ—(in sŭ-ʹtū) In place; in the original position.

incise—(in-ʹsīz) To cut into a surface with a sharp instrument; also, a method of decoration, especially on metal and pottery.

incrustation—Wall decoration consisting of bright panels of different colors.

india ink—A soot-based ink used in China for both writing and drawing.

inscriptions—Texts written on the same surface as the picture (such as in Chinese

paintings) or *incised* in stone (such as in ancient art). See also *colophon.*

installation—A *postmodernist* artwork creating an artistic environment in a room or gallery.

insula—(ʹin-sū-lŭ) In Roman architecture, a multistory apartment house, usually made of brick-faced *concrete;* also refers to an entire city block.

Insular—See *Hiberno-Saxon.*

intaglio—(in-ʹta-lē-ō) A graphic technique in which the design is *incised,* or scratched, on a metal plate, either manually (*engraving, dry point*) or chemically (*etching*). The incised lines of the design take the ink, making this the reverse of the *woodcut* technique.

intarsia—(in-ʹtar-sē-ŭ) Inlay work, primarily in wood and sometimes in mother-of-pearl, marble, etc.

interaxial—The distance between the center of one column drum and the center of the next.

intercolumniation—(in-ter-kŭ-lŭm-ne-ʹa-shŭn) The space or the system of spacing between *columns* in a *colonnade.*

internal evidence—In *attributions* of works of art, what can be learned by stylistic and iconographical analysis, in comparison with other works, and by analysis of the physical properties of the medium itself.

International Style—A style of fourteenth- and fifteenth-century painting begun by Simone Martini, who adapted the French *Gothic* manner to Sienese art fused with influences from the North. This style appealed to the aristocracy because of its brilliant color, lavish costume, intricate ornament, and themes involving splendid processions of knights and ladies. Also a style of twentieth-century architecture associated with Le Corbusier, whose elegance of design came to influence the look of modern office buildings and skyscrapers.

intrados—(ʹin-trū-das) The underside of an *arch* or a *vault.* See *extrados.*

Ionic—(ī-ʹan-ik) One of the two systems (or *orders*) evolved for articulating the three units of the elevation of a Greek temple, the platform, the *colonnade,* and the superstructure (*entablature*). The Ionic order is characterized by, e.g., *volutes, capitals, columns* with *bases,* and an uninterrupted *frieze.*

iron-wire lines—In ancient Chinese painting, thin brush lines suggesting tensile strength.

iwan—(ʹē-wan) In Islamic architecture, a vaulted rectangular recess opening onto a courtyard.

jamb—In architecture, the side posts of a doorway.

jataka—Tales of the past lives of, or a scriptural account of, the *Buddha.* See also *sutra.*

jihad—(ji-ʹhad) In Islam, holy war, death in which assures a faithful *Muslim* of the reward of Paradise.

jina—The Sanskrit word for "saint"; root

word for the English word "Jainism", the religion founded by Mahavira.

jipae—Among the Asmat of western New Guinea, special rites during which celebrants wear dramatic woven fiber basketry costumes to appease the spirit of a dead ancestor.

jomon—(jo-mon) A type of Japanese decorative technique characterized by rope-like markings. *Jomon* means "rope decoration."

ka—(ka) In ancient Egypt, immortal human substance; the concept approximates the Western idea of the soul.

Kaaba—(ʹka-ba) From the Arabic word for "cube." A small cubical building in Mecca, the *Muslim* world's symbolic center.

Kachina—(ku-ʹchē-nu) An art form of Native Americans of the Southwest, the Kachina doll represents benevolent supernatural spirits (kachinas) living in mountains and water sources.

kami—Shinto deities or spirits, believed in Japan to exist in nature (mountains, waterfalls) and in charismatic people.

kaolin—(ʹkā-ŭ-lin) A fine white clay used in making *porcelain.*

karma—In Vedic religions, the ethical consequence of a person's life, which determine his or her fate.

keep—A fortified tower in a castle that served as a place of last refuge.

ketos—(ʹke-tos) Greek for sea dragon.

key or **meander**—See *fret.*

keystone—The central, uppermost *voussoir* in an *arch.*

khutba—An *imam's* speech, including both a sermon and a profession of allegiance by the *Muslim* community to its leader, that takes place near the *qibla* wall.

Kinetic Art—A kind of moving art. Closely related to *Op Art* in its concern with the perception of motion by visual stimulus, it was a logical step to present objects that actually moved. Characteristic of the work of Alexander Calder and the *Constructivists.*

kiva—(ʹkē-vŭ) A large circular underground structure that is the spiritual and ceremonial center of Pueblo Indian life.

kondo—(kon-do) Literally, "golden hall." In a Japanese Buddhist temple complex, the building housing the main sculptural icons.

Koran—See *Quran.*

kore (pl. **korai**)—(ʹkor-ā/ʹkor-ī) Greek for "young woman."

kouros (pl. **kouroi**)—(ʹkūr-os/ʹkūr-oi) Greek for "young man."

krater—An ancient Greek wide-mouthed bowl for mixing wine and water.

kufic—(ʹkū-fŭk) An early form of the Arabic alphabet.

kylix—An ancient Greek shallow drinking cup with two handles and a stem.

labret—(ʹlā-brŭt) A lip plug.

lacquer—(ʹlak-ŭr) In Chinese art, a varnish-like substance made from the sap of the Asiatic sumac, used to decorate wood and other organic materials. It is often colored with mineral pigments, cures to great hardness, and has a lustrous surface.

lakshana(s)—(laksh-'ha-na) Distinguishing marks of the *Buddha*. They include the *urna* and *ushnisha*.

lalita—(la-'lē-ta) In Hindu art, the dance pose of the god Shiva, in which his multiple arms swing rhythmically in an arc.

lamassu—(la-'ma-sū) In Assyrian art, guardians in the form of man-headed winged bulls.

lancet—('lăn-sŭt) In *Gothic* architecture, tall narrow window ending in pointed arch.

landscape—A picture showing natural scenery, without narrative content.

lapis lazuli—('lă-pŭs 'lă-zhyŭ-lē) A rich, ultramarine, semiprecious stone used for carving and as a source for pigment.

lectionary—('lek-shŭn-er-ē) A book containing passages from the *Gospels*, arranged in the sequence that they were to be read during the celebration of religious services, including the *Mass,* throughout the year.

lekythos—('lek-ē-thos) A flask containing perfumed oil; lekythoi were often placed in Greek graves as offerings to the deceased.

letterpress—The technique of printing with movable type invented in Germany in the fifteenth century.

lierne—(lē-'ŭrn) A short *rib* that runs from one main rib of a *vault* to another.

linear perspective—See *perspective*.

linga—In Hindu art, the depiction of Shiva as a phallus or cosmic pillar.

lintel—('lin-tŭl) A beam used to span an opening.

literati—In China, talented amateur painters and scholars from the landed gentry whose work reached maturity during the Yuan Dynasty (A.D. 1279–1368).

loculi—('lak-yŭ-lē) Openings in the walls of *catacombs* to receive the dead.

loggia—('lo-jŭ) A gallery with an open *arcade* or a *colonnade* on one or both sides.

logogram—('la-gŭ-gram) One of the thousands of characters in the Chinese writing system, corresponding to one meaningful language unit. See also *pictograph*.

longitudinal plan—See *plan*.

lost-wax process (cire perdue)—A bronze-casting method in which a figure is modeled in wax and covered with clay; the whole is fired, melting away the wax and hardening the clay, which then becomes a mold for molten metal.

lotiform capital—A capital in the form of a lotus petal.

low relief—See *relief*.

lunette—(lŭ-'net) A semi-circular area (with the flat side down) in a wall over a door, a niche, or a window.

madrasa—(mŭ-'dra-sŭ) An Islamic theological college adjoining and often containing a *mosque*.

maebyong—(mī-byŭng) A Korean vase similar to the Chinese *meiping*.

maestà—(mī-ŭ-'sta) A depiction of the Virgin Mary as the Queen of Heaven enthroned in majesty amid choruses of angels and saints.

magi—('mă-jī) The wise men from the East who present gifts to the infant Jesus.

Mahathat—Literally, "Great Relic."

malanggan—(ma-lang-gan) A type of New Ireland (Papua New Guinea) polychrome sculpture, noted for its bewildering intricacy, created by generous use of openwork and sliverlike projections and by overpainting in minute geometric patterns that further subdivide the image, resulting in a splintered or fragmented and airy effect.

mana—('ma-na) A Polynesian concept expressing spiritual power.

mandapa—(man-'da-pa) An often-pillared, Hindu assembly hall, part of a temple.

mandorla—(măn-'dor-lŭ) An almond-shaped *nimbus,* or *glory,* surrounding the figure of Christ or other sacred figure.

Mannerism—A style of later Renaissance art that emphasized "artifice," contrived imagery not derived directly from nature. Such artworks showed a self-conscious stylization involving complexity, caprice, fantasy, and polish. Mannerist architecture tended to flout the classical rules of order, stability, and symmetry, sometimes to the point of parody.

mantle—A sleeveless, protective outer garment or cloak. See *himation*.

maqsura—(mak-'sū-ra) In some *mosques,* a screened area in front of the *mihrab* that was reserved for a ruler.

marga—The path proposed by the *Buddha* as a way to stop desire.

masjid-i jami—('măs-jid-ē-'ja-mē) The "Friday *mosque,*" large enough to accommodate an Islamic community's entire population for the Friday noonday prayer.

Masonry Style—See *First Style*.

masquerade—Among some African groups, a ritualized drama performed by several masked dancers, embodying ancestors or nature spirits.

Mass—The Catholic and *Orthodox* ritual in which believers understand that Christ's redeeming sacrifice on the cross is repeated when the priest consecrates the bread and wine in the *Eucharist*.

mastaba—(ma-'sta-ba) Arabic for "bench." An ancient Egyptian rectangular brick or stone structure with sloping sides erected over a subterranean tomb chamber connected with the outside by a shaft.

matte (also **mat**)—In painting, pottery, and photography, a dull finish.

mausoleum—A central-plan, domed structure, built as a memorial.

meander or **key**—See *fret*.

medieval—See *Middle Ages*.

medium—The substance or agency in which an artist works; also, in painting, the vehicle (usually liquid) that carries the pigment.

megalith (adj., **megalithic**)—('me-gŭ-lith/ me-gŭ-'lith-ik) Literally, "great stone"; a large, roughly hewn stone used in the construction of monumental prehistoric structures. See also *cromlech, dolmen, menhir*.

megaron—('meg-ŭ-ron) The large reception hall of the king in a Mycenaean palace, fronted by an open, two-columned porch.

meiping—(mā-ping) A Chinese vase of a high-shouldered shape; the *sgrafitto* technique was used in decorating such vases.

memento mori—(mi-'ment-ō 'mo-rē) A reminder of human mortality, usually represented by a skull.

mendicants—In *medieval* Europe, friars belonging to the Franciscan and Dominican orders, who renounced all worldly goods, lived by contributions of laypeople (the word *mendicant* literally means "beggar"), and devoted themselves to preaching, teaching, and doing good works.

menhir—('men-hir) A prehistoric *monolith,* uncut or roughly cut, standing singly or with others in rows or circles.

menorah—(mŭ-no-rŭ) The seven-branched candelabrum used in Jewish religious practices.

Mesoamerica—The region that comprises Mexico, Guatemala, Belize, Honduras, and the Pacific coast of El Salvador.

Mesolithic—(mez-ō-'lith-ik) The "middle" prehistoric period, between the *Paleolithic* and the *Neolithic* ages.

Messiah—(mŭ-'si-ŭ) The savior of the Jews prophesized in the Old Testament. Christians believe that Jesus of Nazareth was the Messiah.

metates—(mŭ-'ta-tāz) Ceremonial grinding stones, perhaps used as thrones in northern South America and various Central American regions.

metope—('met-ŭ-pē) The panel between the *triglyphs* in a *Doric frieze,* often sculptured in *relief*.

Mexica—The name used by a group of initially migratory invaders from northern Mexico to identify themselves; settling on an island in Lake Texcoco in central Mexico, they are known today as the Aztecs.

Middle Ages (adj. **medieval**)—In European history, the period of roughly a thousand years (ca. A.D. 400–1400) from the end of the Western Roman Empire to the Renaissance.

mihrab—(mi-'rab) A semi-circular niche set into the *qibla* wall of an Islamic *mosque*.

minaret—('min-ŭ-ret) A distinctive feature of Islamic *mosque* architecture, a tower from which the *muezzin* calls the faithful to worship.

minbar—('min-bar) In a *mosque,* the pulpit on which an *imam* stands.

miniatures—Small individual paintings intended by Indian painters to be held in the hand and viewed by one or two individuals at one time.

Minimalism (Minimal Art)—An American

predominantly sculptural trend of the 1960s whose works consist of a severe reduction of form to single, homogeneous units called "primary structures." Examples include the sculpture of Tony Smith and Donald Judd.

Minoan art—(Mŭ-ʹnō-ŭn *art*) The pre-Greek art of Crete, named after the legendary King Minos of Knossos.

mobile—(ʹmō-bēl) A sculpture with moving parts.

modeling—The shaping or fashioning of three-dimensional forms in a soft material, such as clay; also, the gradations of light and shade reflected from the surfaces of matter in space, or the illusion of such gradations produced by alterations of value in a drawing, painting, or print.

modern—In art, styles that break with traditional forms and techniques.

Modernism—A movement in Western art that developed in the second half of the nineteenth century and sought to capture the images and sensibilities of the age. Modernist art goes beyond simply dealing with the present and involves the artist's critical examination of the premises of art itself. After World War II modernism increasingly became identified with a strict *formalism.*

module—A basic unit of which the dimensions of the major parts of a work are multiples. The principle is used in sculpture and other art forms, but it is most often employed in architecture, where the module may be the dimensions of an important part of a building, such as a *column,* or simply some commonly accepted unit of measurement (the centimeter or the inch, or, as with Le Corbusier, the average dimensions of the human figure).

molding—In architecture, a continuous, narrow surface (projecting or recessed, plain or ornamented) designed to break up a surface, to accent, or to decorate.

mondop—In Thai architecture, brick buildings adjacent to stupas that enclose *Buddha* images.

monochromatic—(ma-nō-krō-ʹmăt-ŭk) Consisting of a single color.

monolith—A column that is all in one piece (not composed of *drums*); a large, single block or piece of stone used in *megalithic* structures.

Monophysitism—(mŭ-ʹnaf-ŭ-sit-iz-ŭm) An early Christian movement, condemned by the Church as heretical, that denied the duality of Jesus Christ's divine and human natures.

monumental—In art criticism, any work of art of grandeur and simplicity, regardless of its size.

moralized Bible—Gothic heavily illustrated Bibles, each page pairing Old and New Testament episodes with *illuminations* explaining their moral significance.

mortise-and-tenon system—(ʹmor-tŭs- and-ʹten-ŭn) See *tenon.*

mosaic—(mō-ʹzā-ŭk) Patterns or pictures made by embedding small pieces of stone or glass (*tesserae*) in cement on surfaces such as walls and floors; also, the technique of making such works.

mosaic tilework—An Islamic decorative technique in which large ceramic panels are fired, cut into smaller pieces, and set in plaster.

moschophoros—The Greek word for "calf-bearer."

moshaambwooy—A mask representing a primordial nature spirit, a mythical ancestor, of the Kuba people of the Democratic Republic of Congo. It serves social control functions and embodies the king's supernatural and political powers.

mosque—(mask) An Islamic religious building. From the Arabic word *masjid,* meaning a place for bowing down.

mudra—(ʹmŭ-drŭ, *or* ʹmū-drŭ) A stylized and symbolic hand gesture of mystical significance, usually in representations of the *Buddha* and of Hindu deities.

muezzin—(myū-ʹez-ŭn) In Islam, the crier who calls the faithful to worship.

muhaqqaq—(mū-ha-ʹkak) A style of Islamic calligraphy.

mullah—(ʹmŭ-lŭ) An Islamic teacher.

mullion—(ʹmŭl-yŭn) A vertical member that divides a window or that separates one window from another.

mummification—A technique used by ancient Egyptians to preserve human bodies so that they may serve as the eternal home of the immortal *ka.*

muqarna(s)—(mū-ʹkar-na) Stucco decorations of Islamic buildings in which "stalactite"-like forms break a structure's solidity.

mural—A wall painting; a *fresco* is a type of mural medium and technique.

Muslim—A believer in Islam.

Mycenaean—(mī-sŭ-ʹnē-ŭn) The late phase of *Helladic* art, named after the site of Mycenae.

Nabis—The Hebrew word for prophet. A group of *Symbolist* painters influenced by Paul Gauguin.

Nang-yai—(nang-yī) Thai term for shadow puppets cut from large pieces of leather and held above the heads of performers by two sticks tied to a wood frame.

naos—(ʹnā-os) See *cella.*

narrative composition—Elements in a work of art arranged in such a manner as to tell a story.

narthex—(ʹnar-theks) A porch or vestibule of a church, generally *colonnaded* or *arcaded* and preceding the *nave.*

natatio—(na-ʹta-tē-ō) In Roman baths, the swimming pool.

Naturalism—The doctrine that art should adhere as closely as possible to the appearance of the natural world. *Naturalism,*with varying degrees of fidelity to appearance, recurs in the history of Western art.

nave—The part of a church between the

chief entrance and the *choir,* demarcated from *aisles* by *piers* or *columns.*

nave arcade—In *basilica* architecture, the series of *arches* supported by *piers* separating the *nave* from the side *aisles.*

ndop—((n)dap) A male figure commemorating a living or dead king, carved by the Kuba people of the Democratic Republic of Congo.

necking—A groove at the bottom of the ancient Greek *Doric capital* between the *echinus* and the *flutes* that masks the junction of *capital* and *shaft.*

necropolis—(nŭ-ʹkrop-ŭ-lŭs) A large burial area or cemetery; literally, a city of the dead.

nemes—In ancient Egyptian statuary, the linen headdress worn by the pharaoh, with the uraeus cobra of kingship on the front.

nenfro—See *tufa.*

Neo-Expressionism—A postmodern art movement that emerged in the 1970s and that reflects the artists' interest in earlier art, notably German *Expressionism* and *Abstract Expressionism.*

Neolithic—(Nē-ō-ʹlith-ik) The "new" Stone Age, approximately 7000–3000 B.C.

Neoplasticism—A theory of art developed by Piet Mondrian to create a pure plastic art comprised of the simplest, least subjective, elements, *primary colors,* primary values, and primary directions (horizontal and vertical).

Neue Sachlichkeit (New Objectivity)—(ʹnoi-ŭ ʹsak-lik-kīt) An art movement that grew directly out of the World War I experiences of a group of German artists who sought to show the horrors of the war and its effects.

ngady amwaash—A female mythical ancestor mask of the Kuba people in the Democratic Republic of Congo, used in reenacting creation stories that also reinforce basic social values.

niello—(nē-ʹel-ō) A black metallic alloy used to fill incised designs in decorating metal objects.

nihonga—(nē-hong-ga) A nineteenth-century Japanese painting style that incorporated some Western techniques in basically Japanese-style painting, as opposed to "yoga" (Western painting).

nimbus—A halo, aureole, or *glory* appearing around the head of a holy figure to signify divinity.

nirvana—In Buddhism and Hinduism, a blissful state brought about by absorption of the individual soul or consciousness into the supreme spirit. Also called moksha.

nkisi nduda—A traditional Kongo power figure.

nkisi n'kondi—((n)kē-sē (n)kan-dē) A power figure carved by the Kongo people of the Democratic Republic of Congo. Such images embodied spirits believed to heal and give life or capable of inflicting harm or death.

nomoli—(ʹna-ma-lī) Stone figures created by the Sapi people on the Atlantic coast of West Africa in the fifteenth and sixteenth centuries.

nymphs—In classical mythology, female divinities of springs, caves, and woods.

octafoliate—Eight-leafed design.

oculus (pl., **oculi**)—(a-kyū-lus/a-kyū-lē) The round central opening or "eye" of a dome. Also, small round windows in *Gothic* cathedrals.

ogee arch—(ō-'jē) A Late *Gothic* arch made up of two double-curving lines meeting at a point.

ogive (adj., **ogival**)—(ō-'jī-vŭl) The diagonal *rib* of a *Gothic vault;* a *pointed,* or Gothic, *arch.*

oliphants—('al-ŭ-fŭnts) Ivory hunting horns carved by Sapi (West African) artists for European patrons in the late fifteenth and early sixteenth centuries.

one-point perspective—See *perspective.*

opisthodomos—(o-pis-'thad-ŭ-mŭs) In Greek architecture, a porch at the rear, set against the blank back wall of the *cella.*

Optical or **Op Art**—A kind of painting style in which precisely drafted patterns directly, even uncomfortably, affect visual perception.

optical approach to representation—In artistic representation, only that which is actually "seen" is represented, rather than what is "known" (e.g., a human profile depicted optically would reveal only one eye, whereas a profile depicted "descriptively" would feature two eyes). See *descriptive approach to representation.*

opus reticulatum—('ō-pŭs rŭ-tik-ŭ-'lat-ŭm) A method of facing concrete walls with lozenge-shaped bricks or stones to achieve a netlike ornamental surface pattern.

orant—('or-ănt) In Early Christian art, a figure represented with hands raised in prayer.

orbiculum—(or-'bik-yŭ-lŭm) A disc-like opening in a *pediment.*

orchestra—In ancient Greek theaters, the circular piece of earth with a hard and level surface on which the ancient rites took place. Literally, a dancing place.

order—In classical architecture a style represented by a characteristic design of the *columns* and *entablature.* See also *superimposed order.*

Orientalizing—The early phase of Archaic Greek art, so named because of the adoption of forms and motifs from the ancient Near East and Egypt.

orrery—A special technological model to demonstrate the theory that the universe operates like a gigantic clockwork mechanism.

Orthodox—The trinitarian Christian doctrine established in *Byzantium.*

orthogonal—(or-'thag-ŭn-ŭl) A line imagined to be behind and perpendicular to the picture plane; the *orthogonals* in a painting appear to recede toward a vanishing point on the horizon.

orthogonal plan—The imposition of a strict grid plan upon a site, regardless of the terrain, so that all streets meet at right angles. See also *Hippodamian plan.*

Ottonian (adj.)—Pertaining to the empire of Otto I and his successors.

overglaze decoration—In *porcelain* decoration, the techniques of applying paint colors over the *glaze* after the work has been fired. The overglaze colors, or enamels, fuse to the glazed surface in a second firing at a much lower temperature than the main firing. See also *underglaze decoration.*

pagan—A person who worships many gods.

pagoda—(pŭ-'gō-dŭ) A Chinese tower, usually associated with a temple, having a multiplicity of winged eaves; thought to be derived from the Indian *stupa.*

pala—In Christian churches, an altarpiece, or panel placed behind and over the altar.

Paleolithic—(pā-lē-ō-'lith-ik) The "old" Stone Age, during which humankind produced the first art objects beginning ca. 30,000 B.C.

palestra—An ancient Greek and Roman exercise area, usually framed by a *colonnade,* often found in bathing establishments.

palette—In ancient Egypt, a slate slab used for ceremonial purposes, as in the *Palette of King Narmer.* A thin board with a thumb hole at one end on which an artist lays and mixes colors; any surface so used. Also, the colors or kinds of colors characteristically used by an artist.

palmette—A conventional, decorative ornament of ancient origin composed of radiating petals springing from a cuplike base.

Pantocrator—(pan-'tak-rŭ-tŭr) In Christian art, the image of Christ as ruler and judge of heaven and earth.

papyrus—(pŭ-'pī-rŭs) A plant native to Egypt and adjacent lands used to make paperlike writing material; also, the material or any writing on it.

parapet—A low, protective wall along the edge of a balcony or roof.

parchment—Lambskin prepared as a surface for painting or writing, one of the materials which comprised the leaves of a *codex.*

parekklesion—(pă-rŭ-'klē-zŭ-an) The side chapel in a *Byzantine* church.

parinirvana—Reclining images of the *Buddha,* often viewed as representing his death.

parterres—(par-'tārz) Raised flower beds in Chinese gardens.

passage grave—A burial chamber entered through a long, tunnel-like passage.

pastels—Chalk-like crayons made of ground color pigments mixed with water and a binding medium. They lend themselves to quick execution and sketching and offer a wide range of colors and subtle variations of tone, suitable for rendering nuances of value.

patricians—Freeborn landowners of the Roman Republic.

pebble mosaics—Mosaics made of irregularly shaped stones of various colors.

pectoral—An ornament worn on the chest.

pediment—In classical architecture, the triangular space (gable) at the end of a building, formed by the ends of the sloping roof above the *colonnade;* also, an ornamental feature having this shape.

pendentive—A concave, triangular piece of masonry (a triangular section of a hemisphere), four of which provide the transition from a square area to the circular base of a covering *dome.* Although they appear to be hanging (pendant) from the dome, they in fact support it.

peplos—('pep-los) A simple long woolen belted garment worn by ancient Greek women that gives the female figure a columnar appearance.

Performance Art—An American avant-garde art trend of the 1960s that made time an integral element of art. It produced works in which movements, gestures, and sounds of persons communicating with an audience replace physical object. Documentary photographs are generally the only evidence remaining after these events. See also *Happenings.*

peripteral colonnade—(pŭ-'rip-tŭr-ŭl) A colonnade or *peristyle.* See also *dipteral.*

peristyle—('per-rŭ-stīl) In ancient Greek architecture, a *colonnade* all around the *cella* and its porch(es).

Perpendicular style—The last English *Gothic* style, also known as Tudor, characterized by a strong vertical emphasis and dense thickets of ornamental vault ribs that serve entirely decorative functions.

persistence of vision—Retention in the brain for a fraction of a second of whatever the eye has seen; it causes a rapid succession of images to merge one into the next, producing the illusion of continuous change and motion in media such as cinema.

personification—Abstract ideas codified in bodily form.

perspective—A formula for projecting an illusion of the three-dimensional world onto a two-dimensional surface. In linear (single vanishing point) perspective, the most common type, all parallel lines or lines of projection seem to converge on one, two, or three points located with reference to the eye level of the viewer (the horizon line of the picture), known as vanishing points, and associated objects are rendered smaller the farther from the viewer they are intended to seem. Atmospheric, or aerial, perspective creates the illusion of distance by the greater diminution of color intensity, the shift in color toward an almost neutral blue, and the blurring of contours as the intended distance between eye and object increases.

petroglyphs—('pet-rō-glif) *Engravings* or *incisings* in rock.

petuntse—(pŭ-'tŭnt-se) A type of feldspar, ground for mixing with clay in *porcelain.*

photomontage—(fō-tō-mon-'taj) A composition made by fitting together pictures or parts of pictures, especially photographs. See also *collage.*

Photorealists—See *Superrealism.*

physical music—A kind of video narrative made by Nam June Paik which comprises in quick succession fragmented sequences of a variety of media: dance, advertising, poetry, street scenes, etc.

pictograph—('pik-tō-grăf) A picture, usually stylized, that represents an idea; also, writing using such means; also painting on rock. See also *hieroglyphic.*

Pictorial style—An early style of photography in which photographers desired to achieve effects of painting, using centered figures, framing devices, and soft focus. Gertrude Käsebier was a noted proponent of this style of photography.

pier—A vertical, freestanding masonry support.

pier buttress—See *buttress.*

pietà—(pē-a-'ta) A painted or sculpted representation of the Virgin Mary mourning over the body of Christ.

pietra serena—(pē-'et-rŭ sŭ-'ā-nŭ) Literally, "serene stone," a type of gray stone used for its harmonious appearance when contrasted with stucco or other smooth finish in architecture.

pilaster—A flat, rectangular, vertical member projecting from a wall of which it forms a part. It usually has a *base* and a *capital* and is often *fluted.*

pillar—Usually a weight-carrying member, such as a *pier* or a *column;* sometimes an isolated, freestanding structure used for commemorative purposes.

pinakotheke—(pin-a-kō-thē-kē) The Greek word for "picture gallery."

pinnacle—In *Gothic* churches, a sharply pointed ornament capping the piers or flying buttresses; also used on church *facades.*

pittura metafisica—(pēt-'tū-ra me-ta-'fē-sē-ka) Literally, metaphysical painting. Exemplified by the work of Giorgio de Chirico, a precursor of *Surrealism.*

plan—The horizontal arrangement of the parts of a building or of the buildings and streets of a city or town, or a drawing or a diagram showing such an arrangement as a horizontal *section.* In an axial plan, the parts of a building are organized longitudinally, or along a given axis; in a central plan, the parts radiate from a central point.

plate tracery—See *tracery.*

plebeian—(pli-'be-ŭn) In the Roman Republic, the social class that included small farmers, merchants, and freed slaves.

plein-air—('plen-ār) An approach to painting much favored by the *Impressionists,* in which artists sketch outdoors to achieve a quick impression of light, air and color. The sketches were then taken to the studio for reworking into more finished works of art.

plinth—The lowest member of a *base;* also a square slab at the base of a *column.*

poesia—(pō-e-zē-ŭ) A term describing "poetic" art, notably Venetian Renaissance paintings, which emphasize the lyrical and sensual.

pointed arch—See *ogive.*

pointillism—('poin-tŭ-liz-ŭm) A system of painting that focused on color analysis, devised by the nineteenth-century French painter Georges Seurat. The artist separates color into its component parts and then applies the component colors to the canvas in tiny dots (points). The image only becomes comprehensible from a distance, when the viewer's eyes blend the pigment dots.

polis (pl. **poleis**)—Independent city-states in ancient Greece.

polychrome—('pa-lē-krōm) Done in several colors.

polyptych—An *altarpiece* made up of more than three sections.

pontifex maximus—A Latin term meaning "chief priest" of the state religion.

Pop Art—A term coined by British art critic Lawrence Alloway to refer to art, first appearing in the 1950s, that incorporated elements from popular culture, such as images from motion pictures, television, advertising, billboards, commodities, etc.

porcelains—Extremely fine, hard white ceramics. Unlike stoneware, porcelain is made from a fine white clay called *kaolin* mixed with ground *petuntse,* a type of feldspar. True porcelain is translucent and rings when struck.

porphyry—('por-fŭ-rē) Purple marble.

portico—('por-tŭ-kō) A porch with a roof supported by *columns;* an entrance porch.

post-and-lintel system—A *trabeated* system of construction in which two posts support a *lintel.*

Post-Painterly Abstraction—An American art movement that developed out of *Abstract Expressionism,* yet manifests a radically different sensibility. While Abstract Expressionist art conveys a feeling of passion and visceral intensity, a cool, detached rationality emphasizing tighter pictorial control characterizes *Post-Painterly Abstraction.* See also *color field painting* and *hard-edge painting.*

Postmodernism—A reaction against *Modernist* formalism, which is seen as elitist. Far more encompassing and accepting than the more rigid confines of modernist practice, postmodernism offers something for everyone by accommodating a wide range of styles, subjects, and formats, from traditional easel painting to *installation* and from abstraction to illusionistic scenes.

pottery—Objects (usually vessels) made of clay and hardened by firing.

prasada—In Hindu worship, food that becomes sacred by first being given to a god.

Precisionists—A group of American painters, active in the 1920s and 1930s, whose work concentrated on portraying manmade environments in a clear and concise manner to express the beauty of perfect and precise machine forms. Charles Sheeler is an example.

pre-Columbian (adj.)—The cultures that flourished in the Western Hemisphere before European contact and conquest.

predella—(prŭ-'del-lŭ) The narrow ledge on which an *altarpiece* rests on an altar.

prefiguration—In Early Christian art, the depiction of Old Testament persons and events as prophetic forerunners of Christ and New Testament events.

Pre-Raphaelite Brotherhood—A group of nineteenth-century artists, including John Everett Millais, who refused to be limited to contemporary scenes and chose instead to represent fictional, historical, and fanciful subjects using *realist* techniques.

primary colors—The colors—red, yellow, and blue—from which all other colors may be derived. *Secondary colors* result from mixing pairs of primaries.

Productivism—An art movement that emerged in the Soviet Union after the Revolution, whose members believed that artists must direct art toward creating products for the new society.

pronaos—('pro-nā-os) The space, or porch, in front of the *cella* or *naos* of an ancient Greek temple.

propylaion (pl. **propylaia**)—A gateway building leading to an open court preceding an ancient Greek or Roman temple. The monumental entrance to the Acropolis in Athens.

proscenium—(prō-'sē-nē-ŭm) The part of the stage in front of the curtain. The stage of an ancient Greek or Roman theater.

prostyle—('prō-stīl) A style of ancient Greek temple in which the *columns* stand in front of the *naos* and extend its full width.

provenance—('prō-vŭ-naⁿs) Origin or source.

psalter—('sol-tŭr) A book containing the Psalms of the Bible.

pseudoperipteral—(sū-dō-pŭ-'rip-tŭr-ŭl) In Roman architecture, a *pseudoperipteral* temple has a series of engaged columns all around the sides and back of the *cella* to give the appearance of a *peripteral colonnade.*

pueblo—('pwe-blō) Communal multistoried dwellings made of stone or *adobe* brick by the Native Americans of the Southwest; with cap. also used to reference various groups that occupied such dwellings.

purlins—('pŭr-lin) Horizontal beams in a roof structure, parallel to the *ridgepoles,* resting on the main rafters and giving support to the secondary rafters.

putto (pl. **putti**)—('pū-tō/'pū-ti) A cherubic young boy, a favorite subject in Italian painting and sculpture.

pylon—The simple and massive gateway, with sloping walls, of an Egyptian temple.

pyxides—('pik-sŭ-dēz) Small ivory boxes used in church ceremonies; crafted by Sapi (West African) artists for European patrons in the late fifteenth and early sixteenth centuries.

qibla—('kē-blŭ) In the *Muslim* religion, the direction (towards Mecca) the faithful turn when praying.

quadrant arches—Arches whose curve extends for one quarter of a circle's circumference.

quadrant vault—Half-barrel vaults. See *vault.*

quadro riportato—('kwa-drō re-por-'ta-tō) A ceiling design in which painted scenes are arranged in panels resembling framed pictures transferred to the surface of a shallow, curved *vault.*

quatrefoil—A shape or plan in which the parts assume the form of a cloverleaf.

quipu—('kē-pū) Andean record-keeping device made of fibers in which numerous knotted strings hung from a main cord recorded by position and color numbers and categories of things.

quoins—(kwoin) The large, sometimes *rusticated,* usually slightly projecting stones that often form the corners of the exterior walls of masonry buildings.

Quran—(ko-'ran) Also spelled **Koran.** Islam's sacred book, composed of *surahs* (chapters) divided into verses.

radiating chapels—In *medieval* churches, chapels for the display of *relics* that opened directly onto the *ambulatory* and the *transept.*

radiocarbon dating—Method of measuring the decay rate of carbon isotopes in organic matter to provide dates for organic materials such as wood and fiber.

raffia cloth—('răf-ē-ŭ *cloth*) Textiles made from the raffia palm by the Kuba peoples of the Democratic Republic of Congo. Elaborate geometric patterns are created by embroidery and by cut-pile stitching (producing a velvet-like surface by pulling short raffia strands through plain raffia cloth and scraping the tuft ends to spread them out).

raking cornice—The *cornice* on the sloping sides of a *pediment.*

ratha—('rat-ha) Small, freestanding Hindu temple carved from a huge boulder (found in Mahabalipuram, India).

Rayonnant—(rā-yō-'naⁿ) The "radiant" style of *Gothic* architecture, dominant in the second half of the thirteenth century and associated with the French royal court of Louis IX at Paris.

realism—The representation of things according to their appearance in visible nature (without *idealization*).

Realism—A movement that emerged in mid-nineteenth-century France. Realist artists represented the subject matter of everyday life (especially that which up until then had been considered inappropriate for depiction) in a realistic mode.

red-figure technique—In later Greek pottery, the silhouetting of red figures against a black background, with painted linear details; the reverse of the *black-figure technique.*

refectory—(rŭ-'fek-tŭ-rē) The dining hall of a Christian monastery.

Regionalism—A twentieth-century American movement that rejected avant-garde art and portrayed American rural life in a clearly readable, realist style. Major regionalists include Grant Wood and Thomas Hart Benton.

register—One of a series of superimposed bands in a pictorial narrative, or the particular levels on which motifs are placed.

relics—In Christianity, the body parts, clothing, or objects associated with a saint or with Christ himself.

relief—In sculpture, figures projecting from a background of which they are part. The degree of relief is designated high, low (*bas*), sunken (hollow), or *intaglio.* In the last, the artist cuts the design into the surface so that the image's highest projecting parts are no higher than the surface itself. See also *repoussé.*

relieving triangle—In a *corbeled arch,* the opening above the lintel that serves to lighten the weight to be carried by the *lintel* itself.

relievo—(rē-'lyā-vō) *Relief.*

reliquary—('rel-ŭ-kwe-rē) A container for keeping *relics.*

renovatio imperii Romani—Literally, "renewal of the Roman Empire," as claimed by Charlemagne, the first *Carolingian* emperor.

repoussé—(rŭ-pū-'sā) Formed in *relief* by beating a metal plate from the back, leaving the impression on the face. The metal is hammered into a hollow mold of wood or some other pliable material and finished with a *graver.* See also *relief.*

respond—An engaged *column, pilaster,* or similar element that either projects from a *compound pier* or some other supporting device or is bonded to a wall and carries one end of an *arch.*

retables—(rē-'tā-bŭlz) An architectural screen or wall above and behind an altar, usually containing painting, sculpture, carving, or other decorations. See also *altarpiece.*

revetment—(rŭ-'vet-mŭnt) In architecture, an exteral covering or facing.

rhyton—An ancient ceremonial drinking vessel, sometimes in the form of the head of an animal, a person or a mythological creature.

rib—A relatively slender, molded masonry *arch* that projects from a surface. In *Gothic* architecture, the ribs form the framework of the *vaulting.* A diagonal rib is one of the ribs that form the X of a *groin vault.* A transverse rib crosses the nave or aisle at a ninety-degree angle.

rib vault—*Vaults* in which the diagonal and transverse *ribs* compose a structural skeleton that partially supports the still fairly massive paneling between them.

ridgepole—The beam running the length of a building below the peak of the gabled roof.

Rococo—(rō-kō-'kō) A style, primarily of interior design, that appeared in France around 1700. Interiors were designed as total works of art with elegant furniture, small sculpture, ornamental mirrors and easel paintings, and tapestry complementing architecture, reliefs, and wall painting.

Romanesque—(rō-mŭ-'nesk) Literally, "Roman-like." A term used to describe the history, culture, and art of *medieval* western Europe from about 1050 to about 1200.

Romanticism—A Western cultural phenomenon, beginning around 1750 and ending about 1850, that gave precedence to feeling and imagination over reason and thought. More narrowly, the art movement that flourished from about 1800 to 1840.

roof comb—The elaborately sculpted vertical projection surmounting a Maya temple-pyramid.

rose window—A circular stained glass window.

Rosetta Stone—An Egyptian artifact that gave scholars a key to deciphering *hieroglyphic* writing.

rotulus—('rat-yū-lŭs) The long manuscript scroll used by Egyptians, Greeks, Etruscans, and Romans; predecessor of the *codex.*

roundel—See *tondo.*

rusticate—To give a rustic appearance by roughening the surfaces and beveling the edges of stone blocks to emphasize the joints between them. A technique popular during the Renaissance, especially for stone courses at the ground-floor level.

sacra conversazione—('sa-kra kno-ver-sa-tsē-o-nā) Literally, "holy conversation," a style of *altarpiece* painting popular after the middle of the fifteenth century, in which saints from different epochs are joined in a unified space and seem to be conversing either with each other or with the audience.

saint—From the Latin word *sanctus,* meaning "made holy by God." Persons who suffered and died for their Christian faith or who merited reverence for their Christian devotion while alive. In the Roman Catholic church, a worthy deceased Catholic who is *canonized* by the pope.

samsara—In Hindu belief, the rebirth of the soul into a succession of lives.

samurai—('sam-ŭ-rī) Medieval Japanese warriors.

sarcophagus (pl. **sarcophagi**)—(sar-'kof-ŭ-gŭs/sar-'kof-ŭ-gī) A coffin, usually of stone. From the Latin, "consumer of flesh."

sarsen—('sar-sŭn) A form of sandstone used for the *megaliths* at Stonehenge.

satyr—A male follower of the ancient Greek god Dionysos, represented as part human, part goat.

saz—(săz) An Ottoman Turkish design of sinuous curved leaves and blossoms.

scarification—Decorative markings made with scars on the human body.

school—A chronological and stylistic classification of works of art with a stipulation of place.

scriptoria—(skrip-′tor-ē-ŭ) The writing studios of monasteries and churches in early *medieval* Europe.

sculpture in the round—Freestanding figures, carved or modeled in three dimensions.

Second Style—In Roman mural painting, from ca. 80 to ca. 15 B.C. the aim was to dissolve the confining walls of a room and replace them with the illusion of a three-dimensional world constructed in the artist's imagination.

secondary colors—Orange, green, and purple, obtained by mixing pairs of *primary colors* (red, yellow, blue).

section—In architecture, a diagram or representation of a part of a structure or building along an imaginary plane that passes through it vertically. Drawings showing a theoretical slice across a structure's width are lateral sections. Those cutting through a building's length are longitudinal sections. See also *elevation* and *cutaway*.

senate—Literally, a council of elders. The legislative body in Roman constitutional government.

serdab—(sŭ(r)-′dab) A small concealed chamber in an Egyptian tomb (*mastaba*) for the statue of the deceased.

serpentine (line)—The "S" curve, which was regarded by Hogarth as the line of beauty.

Severe Style—The earliest phase of Classical Greek sculpture.

severies (vaulting web)—(′sev-u-rēz) In *Gothic* architecture, the masonry blocks that fill the area between the *ribs* of a *groin vault*.

sexpartite vaults—Vaults whose *ribs* spring from compound *piers*. The branching ribs divide the large rectangular vault compartment into six sections. See *vault*.

sfumato—(sfū-′ma-tō) A smokelike haziness that subtly softens outlines in painting; particularly applied to the painting of Leonardo and Correggio.

sgrafitto—(skraf-′fē-tō) A Chinese ceramic technique in which the design is incised through a colored *slip*.

shaft—The part of a *column* between the *capital* and the *base*.

shakti—In Hinduism, the female power of the deity Devi (or Goddess), which animates the matter of the cosmos.

shaman—(′sha-mŭn) Among Native Americans, a medicine man thought to have direct contact with supernatural powers, which he uses to help people.

Shiites—Muslims who believe that only direct descendants of the Prophet Muhammad are qualified for the highest political and religious leadership.

shogun—In feudal Japan, a military governor who managed the country on behalf of a figurehead emperor.

silverpoint—A *stylus* made of silver, used in

drawing in the fourteenth and fifteenth centuries because of the fine line it produced and the sharp point it maintained.

single vanishing point perspective—See *perspective*.

siren—In ancient Greek mythology, a creature that was part bird, part woman.

skene—(′skā-nā) In ancient Greek theaters, the scene building that housed dressing rooms for the actors and also formed a backdrop for the plays.

skenographia—(skā-no-gra-′fē-u) The Greek term for *perspective*, literally, "scene painting," which employed linear, or single vanishing point, perspective to create the illusion of depth.

skiagraphia—(skē-u-gra-′fē-u) The Greek term for shading, literally "shadow painting," said to have been invented by Apollodoros, an Athenian painter of the fifth century B.C.

slip—A mixture of fine clay and water used in ceramic decoration.

soak stain—A technique of painting pioneered by Helen Frankenthaler in which the artist drenches the fabric of raw canvas with fluid paint to achieve flowing, lyrical, painterly effects.

socle—(′sak-ŭl) A molded projection at the bottom of a wall or a *pier*, or beneath a pedestal or a *column base*.

soffit—The underside of an architectural member such as an *arch, lintel, cornice*, or stairway. See also *intrados*.

space—The bounded or boundless container of collections of objects.

spandrel—(′spăn-drŭl) The roughly triangular space enclosed by the curves of adjacent *arches* and a horizontal member connecting their vertexes; also, the space enclosed by the curve of an *arch* and an enclosing right angle. The area between the arch proper and the framing *columns* and *entablature*.

sphinx—(sfengks) A mythical Egyptian beast with the body of a lion and the head of a human.

splay—A large *bevel* or *chamfer*.

splayed—An opening (as in a wall) that is cut away diagonally so that the outer edges are farther apart than the inner edges. See also *embrasure*.

springing—The lowest stone of an *arch*, resting on the *impost block*. In *Gothic* vaulting, the lowest stone of a diagonal or transverse *rib*.

squinch—(skwinch) An architectural device used as a transition from a square to a polygonal or circular base for a *dome*. It may be composed of *lintels, corbels*, or *arches*.

stanze—(′stan-zā) The Italian word for "rooms."

statue column—See *atlantid* or *caryatid*.

stave—A wedge-shaped timber; vertically placed *staves* embellish the architectural features of the building.

stele—(′stē-lē) A carved stone slab used to mark graves and to commemorate historical events.

stigmata—In Christian art, the wounds that Christ received at his crucifixion that miraculously appear on the body of a saint.

still life—A picture depicting an arrangement of objects.

stoa—(′sto-ŭ) In ancient Greek architecture, an open building with a roof supported by a row of *columns* parallel to the back wall. A covered *colonnade*.

stonewear—Pottery fired at high temperatures producing a stonelike hardness and density.

strategos—An ancient Greek general.

strigil—A scraper, used by ancient Greek athletes to scrape oil from their bodies after exercising.

stringcourse—A raised horizontal *molding*, or band in masonry, ornamental but usually reflecting interior structure.

stucco—(′stŭk-kō) Fine plaster or cement used as a coating for walls or for decoration.

stupa—(′stū-pŭ) A large, mound-shaped *Buddhist* shrine.

stylobate—(′stī-lŭ-bāt) The uppermost course of the platform of a classical temple, which supports the *columns*.

stylus—(′stī-lŭs) A needlelike tool used in *engraving* and *incising*.

subtractive—A kind of sculpture technique in which materials are taken away from the original mass, i.e., carving.

sultan—A Muslim ruler.

sunken relief—In sculpture, *reliefs* created by chiseling below the stone's surface, rather than cutting back the stone around the figures to make them project from the surface.

Sunna—Collections of the Prophet Muhammad's moral sayings and descriptions of his deeds.

Sunnites—Muslims who recognize the legitimacy of the first *caliphs*, who were rulers who had been followers of Muhammad but were not directly descended from him.

superimposed orders—*Orders* of architecture that are placed one above another in an *arcaded* or *colonnaded* building, usually in the following sequence: *Doric* (the first story), *Ionic*, and *Corinthian*. Superimposed orders are found in later Greek architecture and were used widely by Roman and Renaissance builders.

superimposition—The nesting of earlier structures within later ones, a common *Mesoamerican* building trait.

Superrealism—A school of painting and sculpture of the 1960s and 1970s which emphasized making images of persons and things with scrupulous, photographic fidelity to optical fact. The Superrealist painters were also called Photorealists because many used photographs as sources for their imagery.

Suprematism—A type of art formulated by Kazimir Malevich to convey his belief that the supreme reality in the world is pure feeling, which attaches to no object and thus calls for new, nonobjective forms in art—shapes not related to objects in the visible world.

surahs—Chapters of the *Quran* (Koran), divided into verses.

Surrealism—A successor to *Dada, Surrealism* incorporated the improvisational nature of its predecessor into its exploration of the ways to express in art the world of dreams and the unconscious. Biomorphic Surrealists such as Joan Miro produced largely abstract compositions. Naturalistic Surrealists, notably Salvador Dalí, presented recognizable scenes transformed into a dream or nightmare image.

sutra—('sū-trŭ) In Buddhism, an account of a sermon by or a dialogue involving the *Buddha*. A scriptural account of the Buddha. See also *jataka.*

Symbolists—In the late nineteenth century, a group of artists and poets who shared a view that the artist was not an imitator of nature but a creator who transformed the facts of nature into a symbol of the inner experience of that fact.

symmetria—(sim-ŭ-'trē-ŭ) Commensurability of parts. Polykleitos's treatise on his *canon* of proportions summarized the principle of symmetria.

Synthetic Cubism—In 1912 *Cubism* entered a new phase during which the style no longer relied on a decipherable relation to the visible world. In this new phase, called *Synthetic Cubism,* paintings and drawings were constructed from objects and shapes cut from paper or other materials to represent parts of a subject in order to play visual games with variations on illusion and reality.

taberna—(ta-'ber-na) In Roman architecture, a single-room shop covered by a barrel *vault.*

tapa—(ta-pa) Polynesian decorative bark cloth.

tapestry—A weaving technique in which the *weft* threads are packed densely over the *warp* threads so that the designs are woven directly into the fabric.

tapu—(ta-'pŭ) A Polynesian concept, the counterpart to *mana,* and creating with mana a dynamic opposition of forces dominating social and religious practices.

tarashikomi—(ta-ra-shi-ko-mē) In Japanese art, a painting technique involving the dropping of ink and pigments onto surfaces still wet with previously applied ink and pigments.

tatami—(ta-ta-mē) The traditional woven straw mat used for floor covering in Japanese architecture.

tattoo—A Polynesian word for the permanent decoration of human bodies.

technique—The processes that artists employ to create *form,* as well as the distinctive, personal ways in which they handle their materials and tools.

tell—In Near Eastern archeology, a hill or a mound, usually an ancient site of habitation.

tempera—('tem-pŭ-rŭ) A technique of painting using pigment mixed with egg yolk, glue or casein; also the *medium* itself.

temple mounds—Complex platformed earthworks built by *pre-Columbian* North Americans.

templon—('tem-plan) The columnar screen separating the sanctuary from the main body of a *Byzantine* church.

tenebrism—('ten-ŭ-briz(-ŭ)m) Painting in the "dark manner," using violent contrasts of light and dark, as in the work of Caravaggio.

tenon—A projection on the end of a piece of wood that is inserted into a corresponding hole (mortise) in another piece of wood to form a joint.

tenoned—Attached by stone pegs.

tepidarium—(tep-ŭ-'dă-rē-ŭm) The warm bath section of a Roman bathing establishment.

terracotta—(te-rŭ-'ko-tŭ) Hard-baked clay, used for sculpture and as a building material. It may be *glazed* or painted.

tesserae—('tes-ŭ-rē) Tiny stones or pieces of glass cut to desired shape and size to use in *mosaics* to create design and composition.

tetrarchy—(tet-rark-ē) Rule by four. A type of Roman government established in the late third century A.D. by Diocletian in an attempt to share power with potential rivals.

texture—The quality of a surface (rough, smooth, hard, soft, shiny, dull) as revealed by light. In represented texture, a painter depicts an object as having a certain texture even though the paint is the actual texture.

theatron—In ancient Greek theaters, the slope overlooking the *orchestra* on which the spectators sat. Literally, the place for seeing.

Theotokos—(thē-'ō-tō-kos) In Greek, "bearer of God." In Christian art, an image of the Virgin Mary, the mother of Jesus.

thermoluminescence—A method of dating amounts of radiation found within the clay of ceramic or sculptural forms, as well as in the clay cores from metal castings.

Third Style—In Roman mural painting, the style in which delicate linear fantasies were sketched on predominantly *monochromatic* backgrounds.

tholos (pl. **tholoi**)—('thō-los/'thō-loi) A circular structure, generally in classical style; also, in Aegean architecture, a circular beehive-shaped tomb.

thrust—The outward force exerted by an *arch* or a *vault* that must be counterbalanced by *buttresses.*

tier—A series of architectural rows, layers, or ranks arranged above or behind one another.

togu na—(tō-gū na) The "head" and most important part of the Dogon (Mali, West Africa) anthropomorphized village. Literally, "house of words," *togu na* is the men's house where deliberations vital to community welfare take place.

tokonoma—(to-ko-no-ma) A shallow alcove in a Japanese teahouse which is used for a single adornment, e.g., a painting or stylized flower arrangement.

tondo—('ton-dō) A circular painting or *relief* sculpture.

Torah—The scroll containing the Pentateuch, the first five books of the Hebrew Scriptures.

torana—('to-ra-na) Gateway in the stone fence around a *stupa,* located at the cardinal points of the compass.

torque—(tork) The neck band worn by Gauls.

trabeated—('tra-bē-āt-ŭd) Of *post-and-lintel* construction. Literally, "beamed" construction.

tracery—Ornamental stonework for holding stained glass in place, characteristic of *Gothic* cathedrals. In plate tracery the glass fills only the "punched holes" in the heavy ornamental stonework. In bar tracery the stained-glass windows fill almost the entire opening and the stonework is unobtrusive.

transept—('trăn-sept) The part of a *cruciform* church with an axis that crosses the main axis at right angles.

transverse rib—See *rib.*

treasuries—In ancient Greece, small buildings set up for the safe storage of *votive offerings.*

trefoil—A cloverlike ornament or symbol with stylized leaves in groups of three.

tribune—In *Romanesque* church architecture, galleries built over the inner *aisles.*

triclinium—(tri-'klin-ē-um) The dining room of a Roman house.

trident—The three-pronged pitchfork associated with the ancient Greek sea god Poseidon (Roman, Neptune).

triforium—(tri-'for-ē-ŭm) The bank of *arcades* below the *clerestory* that occupies the space corresponding to the exterior strip of wall covered by the sloping timber roof above the galleries. In a *Gothic* cathedral, the *blind arcaded* gallery below the *clerestory;* occasionally the arcades are filled with stained glass.

triglyph—('tri-glif) A projecting, grooved member of a *Doric frieze* that alternates with *metopes.*

trilithons—('tri-lith-onz) A pair of *monoliths* topped with a *lintel;* found in *megalithic* structures.

triptych—('trip-tik) A three-paneled painting or *altarpiece.*

triumphal arch—In Roman architecture, freestanding *arches* commemorating important events such as military victories.

trompe l'œil—(tronp 'loi) A form of illusionistic painting that attempts to represent an object as existing in three dimensions at the surface of the painting; literally, "fools the eye."

true fresco—See *fresco.*

trumeau—(trū-'mō) In architecture, the *pillar* or center post supporting the *lintel* in the middle of the doorway.

tubicen—('tū-bŭ-sŭn) The Latin word for "trumpeter."

Tudor—See *perpendicular style.*

tufa—('tū-fŭ) A porous rock formed from deposits of springs.

tumulus (pl. **tumuli**)— ('tū-myū-lus/ 'tū-myū-li) Burial mound; in Etruscan architecture, tumuli cover one or more subterranean multichambered tombs cut out of the local *tufa*. Also characteristic of the Japanese Kofun period of the third and fourth centuries where they signal the rise of grand political leaders.

tunnel vaults—See *vaults.*

Tuscan column—Also known as Etruscan *column.* Resemble ancient Greek *Doric* columns, but made of wood, unfluted, and with *bases.* They were spaced more widely than were Greek columns.

Tusci—The ancient people who inhabited Etruria and gave their name to modern-day Tuscany.

twining—A nonloom technique in which the weaver twists two threads around each other to form the finished cloth.

twisted perspective—A convention of representation in which part of a figure is seen in profile and another part of the same figure frontally. Not strictly *optical* (organized from the perspective of a fixed viewpoint), but *descriptive.*

tympanum—('tim-pŭ-nŭm) The space enclosed by a *lintel* and an *arch* over a doorway.

ubosoth—(ū-bō-soth) The ordination hall of a *Buddhist* temple in Thailand.

ukiyo-e—(ū-kē-yō-ā) A style of Japanese *genre* painting ("pictures of the floating world") that influenced nineteenth-century Western art.

underglaze decoration—In *porcelain* decoration, the application of mineral colors to the surface before the main firing, followed by an application of clear *glaze.* See also *overglaze decoration.*

urna—('ŭr-nŭ) A whorl of hair, represented as a dot, between the brows of the *Buddha;* one of the *lakshanas* of the Buddha.

ushabtis—(ū-'shăb-te) In ancient Egypt, figurines placed in a tomb to act as the deceased's servants in the afterlife.

ushnisha—(ūsh-'nesh-ha) The knot of hair on the top of the *Buddha's* head; one of the *lakshanas* of the Buddha.

value—See *color.*

vanitas—('va-nē-tas) A term describing paintings that include references to death.

vault—A masonry roof or ceiling constructed on the *arch* principle. A *barrel* or tunnel vault, semicylindrical in cross-*section* is, in effect, a deep arch or an uninterrupted series of arches, one behind the other, over an oblong space. A quadrant vault is a half-*barrel* vault. A *groin* or cross vault is formed at the point at which two barrel vaults intersect at right angles. In a ribbed vault, there is a framework of *ribs* or arches under the intersections of the vaulting sections. A sexpartite vault is a rib vault with six panels. A fan vault is a development of *lierne* vaulting characteristic of English Perpendicular *Gothic,* in which radiating ribs form a fan-like pattern.

veda—('vād-u) The Sanskrit word for "knowledge."

veduta—(ve-'dū-ta) Type of naturalistic landscape and cityscape painting popular in eighteenth-century Venice. Literally, "view" painting.

velarium—(ve-'lar-ē-ŭm) In a Roman *amphitheater,* the cloth awning that could be rolled down from the top of the *cavea* to shield spectators from sun or rain.

vellum—Calfskin prepared as a surface for writing or painting, one of the materials which comprised the leaves of a *codex.*

veristic—(ver-'is-tik) True to natural appearance.

vestibule—See *portico.*

vihan—In Thai architecture, halls with walls and roof of brick, stucco, wood, and ceramic tiles that stand in front of monastery stupas.

vihara—(vē-'ha-ra) A *Buddhist* monastery, often cut into a hill.

volute—A spiral, scroll-like form characteristic of the ancient Greek *Ionic* and the Roman *Composite capital.*

votive offering—A gift of gratitude to a deity.

voussoir—(vū-'swar) A wedge-shaped block used in the construction of a true *arch.* The central voussoir, which sets the arch, is the *keystone.*

wabi—(wa-bē) A sixteenth-century Japanese art style characterized by refined rusticity.

wall rib—The *rib* at the junction of the *vault* and the wall.

warp—The vertical threads of a loom or cloth.

wat—(wat) A *Buddhist* monastery in Cambodia.

weft—The horizontal threads of a loom or cloth.

weight shift—See *contrapposto.*

westwork—The *facade* and towers at the western end of a *medieval* church, principally in Germany.

wet fresco—See *fresco.*

white-ground technique—An ancient Greek vase painting technique in which the pot was first covered with a *slip* of very fine white clay, over which black *glaze* was used to outline figures, and diluted brown, purple, red, and white were used to color them.

woodcut or **woodblock**—A wooden block on the surface of which those parts not intended to print are cut away to a slight depth, leaving the design raised; also, the printed impression made with such a block.

yaksha/yakshi—(yak-shŭ/yak-shē) Lesser local male and female *Buddhist* and Hindu divinities. Yakshas, the male equivalent of yakshis, are often represented as corpulent, powerful males. Yakshis are goddesses associated with fertility and vegetation.

yamato-e—(ya-ma-tō-ā) Also known as native-style painting, a purely Japanese style of sophisticated and depersonalized painting created for the Fujiwara nobility.

yang—In Chinese cosmology, the principle of active masculine energy, which permeates the universe in varying proportions with *ying,* the principle of passive feminine energy.

yasti—('yas-tē) In *Buddhist* architecture, the mast or pole that arises from the dome of the *stupa* and its *harmika* and symbolizes the axis of the universe; it is adorned with a series of *chatras* (stone disks) assigned various meanings.

Yei—Holy people portrayed in Navajo sand paintings.

ying—See *yang.*

yoga—See *nihonga.*

Zen—A *Buddhist* sect and its doctrine, emphasizing enlightenment through intuition and introspection rather than the study of scripture. In Chinese, Chan.

ziggurat—('zig-ŭ-rot) A monumental platform for a temple, built in ancient Mesopotamia.

zullah—Shaded area along the central court of Mohammad's house in Medina.

BIBLIOGRAPHY

This list of books is intended to be comprehensive enough to satisfy the reading interests of the beginning art history student and general reader, as well as those of more advanced readers who wish to become acquainted with fields other than their own. The resources listed range from works that are valuable primarily for their reproductions to those that are scholarly surveys of schools and periods. No entries for periodical articles appear, but some of the major periodicals that publish art-historical scholarship in English are noted.

SELECTED PERIODICALS

The following list is by no means exhaustive. Students wishing to pursue research in journals should contact their instructor, their college or university's reference librarian, or the online catalog for additional titles.

African Arts
American Indian Art
American Journal of Archaeology
Archaeology
Archives of Asian Art
Ars Orientalis
The Art Bulletin
Art History
The Art Journal
The Burlington Magazine
Journal of the Society of Architectural Historians
Journal of the Warburg and Courtauld Institutes
Latin American Antiquity

GENERAL STUDIES

Arntzen, Etta, and Robert Rainwater. *Guide to the Literature of Art History*. Chicago: American Library Association, 1981.

Bator, Paul M. *The International Trade in Art*. Chicago: University of Chicago Press, 1988.

Baxandall, Michael. *Patterns of Intention: On the Historical Explanation of Pictures*. New Haven: Yale University Press, 1985.

Bindman, David, ed. *The Thames & Hudson Encyclopedia of British Art*. London: Thames & Hudson, 1988.

Broude, Norma, and Mary D. Garrard, eds. *The Expanding Discourse: Feminism and Art History*. New York: Harper Collins, 1992.

———. *Feminism and Art History: Questioning the Litany*. New York: Harper & Row, 1982.

Bryson, Norman. *Vision and Painting: The Logic of the Gaze*. New Haven: Yale University Press, 1983.

Bryson, Norman, et al. *Visual Theory: Painting and Interpretation*. New York: Cambridge University Press, 1991.

Cahn, Walter. *Masterpieces: Chapters on the History of an Idea*. Princeton: Princeton University Press, 1979.

Chadwick, Whitney. *Women, Art, and Society*. New York: Thames & Hudson, 1990.

Cheetham, Mark A., Michael Ann Holly, and Keith Moxey, eds. *The Subjects of Art History: Historical Objects in Contemporary Perspective*. New York: Cambridge University Press, 1998.

Chilvers, Ian, and Harold Osborne, eds. *The Oxford Dictionary of Art*. Rev. ed. New York: Oxford University Press, 1997.

Cummings, P., *Dictionary of Contemporary American Artists*. 6th ed. New York: St. Martin's Press, 1994.

Derrida, Jacques. *The Truth in Painting*. Chicago: University of Chicago Press, 1987.

Deepwell, K., ed. *New Feminist Art*. Manchester: Manchester University Press, 1994.

Encyclopedia of World Art. 15 vols. New York: Publisher's Guild, 1959–1968. Supplementary vols. 16, 1983; 17, 1987.

Fielding, Mantle. *Dictionary of American Painters, Sculptors, and Engravers*. 2nd rev. and enl. ed. Poughkeepsie: Apollo, 1986.

Fleming, John, Hugh Honour, and Nikolaus Pevsner. *Penguin Dictionary of Architecture*. 4th ed. New York: Penguin, 1991.

Freedberg, David. *The Power of Images: Studies in the History and Theory of Response*. Chicago: University of Chicago Press, 1985.

Giedion, Siegfried. *Space, Time and Architecture: The Growth of a New Tradition*. 5th ed. Cambridge: Harvard University Press, 1982.

Gombrich, Ernst Hans Josef. *Art and Illusion*. 5th ed. London: Phaidon, 1977.

Haggar, Reginald G. *A Dictionary of Art Terms: Architecture, Sculpture, Painting, and the Graphic Arts*. Poole: New Orchard Editions, 1984.

Hall, James. *Dictionary of Subjects and Symbols in Art*. 2nd rev. ed. London: J. Murray, 1979.

Harris, Anne Sutherland, and Linda Nochlin. *Women Artists: 1550–1950*. Los Angeles: Los Angeles County Museum of Art; New York: Knopf, 1977.

Hauser, Arnold. *The Sociology of Art*. Chicago: University of Chicago Press, 1982.

Hind, Arthur M. *A History of Engraving and Etching from the Fifteenth Century to the Year 1914*. 3rd rev. ed. New York: Dover, 1963.

Holt, Elizabeth G., ed. *A Documentary History of Art*. 2nd ed. 2 vols. Princeton: Princeton University Press, 1981.

Hults, Linda C. *The Print in the Western World: An Introductory History*. Madison: University of Wisconsin Press, 1996.

Kostof, Spiro. *A History of Architecture: Settings and Rituals*. 2nd ed. Oxford: Oxford University Press, 1995.

Kronenberger, Louis. *Atlantic Brief Lives: A Biographical Companion to the Arts*. Boston: Little, Brown, 1971.

Kultermann, Udo. *The History of Art History*. New York: Abaris, 1993.

Lucie-Smith, Edward. *The Thames & Hudson Dictionary of Art Terms*. London: Thames & Hudson, 1984.

Murray, Peter, and Linda Murray. *A Dictionary of Art and Artists*. 5th ed. New York: Penguin, 1988.

Myers, Bernard Samuel, ed. *Encyclopedia of Painting: Painters and Painting of the World from Prehistoric Times to the Present Day*. 4th rev. ed. New York: Crown, 1979.

Myers, Bernard S., and Myers, Shirley D., eds. *Dictionary of 20th-Century Art*. New York: McGraw-Hill, 1974.

Osborne, Harold, ed. *The Oxford Companion to 20th Century Art*. New York: Oxford University Press, 1981.

Parker, Rozsika, and Griselda Pollock. *Old Mistresses: Women, Art, and Ideology*. London: Routledge & Kegan Paul, 1981.

Penny, Nicholas. *The Materials of Sculpture*. New Haven: Yale University Press, 1993.

Pevsner, Nikolaus. *A History of Building Types*. London: Thames & Hudson, 1987. Reprint of 1979 ed.

———. *An Outline of European Architecture*. 8th ed. Baltimore: Penguin, 1974.

———. *The Buildings of England*. 46 vols. Harmondsworth: Penguin, 1951–1974.

Pickover, C., ed. *Visions of the Future: Art, Technology and Computing in the Twenty-First Century*. New York: St. Martin's Press, 1994.

Pierce, James Smith. *From Abacus to Zeus: A Handbook of Art History*. Rev. 5th ed. Upper Saddle River: 1998.

Pierson, William H., Jr., and Martha Davidson. eds. *Arts of the United States, A Pictorial Survey*. 1960. Reprint. Athens: University of Georgia Press, 1975.

Placzek, Adolf K., ed. *Macmillan Encyclopedia of Architects*. 4 vols. New York: Macmillan, 1982.

Podro, Michael. *The Critical Historians of Art*. New Haven: Yale University Press, 1982.

Pollock, Griselda. *Vision and Difference: Femininity, Feminism and Histories of Art*. London: Routledge, 1988.

Preziosi, Donald, ed. *The Art of Art History: A Critical Anthology*. New York: Oxford University Press, 1998.

Read, Herbert, and Nikos Stangos. eds. *The Thames & Hudson Dictionary of Art and Artists*. Rev. ed. London: Thames & Hudson, 1988.

Reid, Jane D. *The Oxford Guide to Classical Mythology in the Arts 1300–1990s*. 2 vols. New York: Oxford University Press, 1993.

Roth, Leland M. *Understanding Architecture: Its Elements, History, and Meaning*. New York: Harper & Row, 1993.

Rosenblum, Naomi. *A World History of Photography*. New York: Abbeville, 1984.

Rubenstein, Charlotte Streifer. *American Women Artists from Early Indian Times to the Present*. Boston: G. K. Hall/Avon Books, 1982.

Slatkin, Wendy. *Women Artists in History: From Antiquity to the 20th Century*. 2nd ed. Englewood Cliffs: Prentice-Hall, 1985.

Smith, Alistair, ed. *The Larousse Dictionary of Painters*. New York: Larousse, 1981.

Smith, G. E. Kidder. *The Architecture of the United States: An Illustrated Guide to Buildings Open to the Public*. 3 vols. Garden City: Doubleday/Anchor, 1981.

Stangos, Nikos. *The Thames & Hudson Dictionary of Art and Artists*. Rev. ed. New York: Thames & Hudson, 1994.

Steer, John, and Antony White. *Atlas of Western Art History: Artists, Sites and Monuments from Ancient Greece to the Modern Age*. New York: Facts on File, 1994.

Stratton, Arthur. *The Orders of Architecture: Greek, Roman and Renaissance*. London: Studio, 1986.

Sutton, Ian. *Western Architecture: From Ancient Greece to the Present*. New York: Thames & Hudson, 1999.

Trachtenberg, Marvin, and Isabelle Hyman. *Architecture, from Prehistory to Post-Modernism*. New York: Abrams, 1986.

Tufts, Eleanor. *American Women Artists, Past and Present, A Selected Bibliographic Guide*. New York: Garland Publishers, 1984.

———. *Our Hidden Heritage, Five Centuries of Women Artists*. London: Paddington Press, 1974.

Turner, Jane, ed. *The Dictionary of Art*. 34 vols. New York: Grove Dictionaries, 1996.

Van Pelt, R., and C. Westfall. *Architectural Principles in the Age of Historicism*. New Haven: Yale University Press, 1991.

Waterhouse, Ellis. *The Dictionary of British 18th Century Painters in Oils and Crayons*. Woodbridge, England: Antique Collectors' Club, 1981.

Wilkins, David G. *Art Past, Art Present*. New York: Abrams, 1994.

Wittkower, Rudolf. *Sculpture Processes and Principles*. New York: Harper & Row, 1977.

Wölfflin, Heinrich. *The Sense of Form in Art*. New York: Chelsea, 1958.

Young, William, ed. *A Dictionary of American Artists, Sculptors, and Engravers*. Cambridge: W. Young, 1968.

ANCIENT ART, GENERAL

Boardman, John, ed. *The Oxford History of Classical Art*. New York: Oxford University Press, 1997.

Clayton, Peter A., and Martin J. Price, eds. *The Seven Wonders of the Ancient World*. New York: Routledge, 1988.

Connolly, Peter, and Hazel Dodge. *The Ancient City. Life in Classical Athens and Rome*. New York: Oxford Unversity Press, 1998.

Davies, W. Vivian, and Louise Schofield, eds. *Egypt, the Aegean and the Levant. Interconnections in the Second Millennium BC*. London: British Museum Press, 1995.

De Grummond, Nancy Thomson, ed. *An Encyclopedia of the History of Classical Archaeology*. 2 vols. Westport: Greenwood, 1996.

Dunbabin, Katherine. *Mosaics of the Greek and Roman World*. New York: Cambridge University Press, 1999.

Kampen, Natalie B. ed., *Sexuality in Ancient Art.* New York: Cambridge University Press, 1996.

Lexicon Iconographicum Mythologiae Classicae. Zurich: Artemis, 1981 –.

Ling, Roger. *Ancient Mosaics.* Princeton: Princeton University Press: 1998.

Lloyd, Seton, and Hans Wolfgang Muller. *Ancient Architecture: Mesopotamia, Egypt, Crete.* New York: Electa/Rizzoli, 1980.

Oliphant, Margaret. *The Atlas of the Ancient World: Charting the Great Civilizations of the Past.* New York: Simon & Schuster, 1992.

Onians, John. *Classical Art and the Cultures of Greece and Rome.* New Haven: Yale University Press, 1999.

Renfrew, Colin, and Bahn, Paul G.. *Archaeology: Theories, Methods, and Practices.* London: Thames & Hudson, 1991.

Saggs, H. W. F. *Civilization before Greece and Rome.* New Haven: Yale University Press, 1989.

Stillwell, Richard, et al., eds. *The Princeton Encyclopedia of Classical Sites.* Princeton: Princeton University Press, 1976.

Ward-Perkins, John B. *Cities of Ancient Greece and Italy: Planning in Classical Antiquity.* Rev. ed. New York: Braziller, 1987.

Wolf, Walther. *The Origins of Western Art: Egypt, Mesopotamia, the Aegean.* New York: Universe, 1989.

CHAPTER 1
THE BIRTH OF ART:
AFRICA, EUROPE, AND THE NEAR EAST IN THE STONE AGE

Bahn, Paul G. *The Cambridge Illustrated History of Prehistoric Art.* New York: Cambridge University Press, 1998.

Bahn, Paul G., and Jean Vertut. *Journey through the Ice Age.* Berkeley: University of California Press, 1997.

Beltrán, Antonio, ed. *The Cave of Altamira.* New York: Harry N. Abrams, 1999.

Breuil, Henri. *Four Hundred Centuries of Cave Art.* New York: Hacker, 1979. Reprint of 1952 ed.

Burl, Aubrey. *Great Stone Circles.* New Haven: Yale University Press, 1999.

Chauvet, Jean-Marie, et al. *Dawn of Art: The Chauvet Cave.* New York: Abrams, 1996.

Chippindale, Christopher. *Stonehenge Complete.* New York: Thames & Hudson, 1994.

Cunliffe, Barry, ed. *The Oxford Illustrated Prehistory of Europe.* New York: Oxford University Press, 1994.

Graziosi, Paolo. *Paleolithic Art.* New York: McGraw-Hill, 1960.

Kenyon, Kathleen M. *Digging Up Jericho.* New York: Praeger, 1974.

Leroi-Gourhan, André. *The Dawn of European Art: An Introduction to Paleolithic Cave Painting.* Cambridge: Cambridge University Press, 1982.

———. *Treasures of Prehistoric Art.* New York: Abrams, 1967.

Marshack, Alexander. *The Roots of Civilization: The Cognitive Beginnings of Man's First Art, Symbol and Notation.* 2nd ed. Wakefield: Moyer Bell, 1991.

Mellaart, James. *Çatal Hüyük: A Neolithic Town in Anatolia.* New York: McGraw-Hill, 1967.

———. *The Neolithic of the Near East.* New York: Scribner, 1975.

Piggott, Stuart. *Ancient Europe.* Chicago: Aldine, 1966.

Pfeiffer, John E. *The Creative Explosion: An Inquiry into the Origins of Art and Religion.* New York: Harper & Row, 1982.

Renfrew, Colin, ed. *British Prehistory: A New Outline.* London: Noyes Press, 1975.

Ruspoli, Mario. *The Cave of Lascaux. The Final Photographs.* New York: Abrams, 1987.

Sandars, Nancy K. *Prehistoric Art in Europe.* 2nd ed. New Haven: Yale University Press, 1985.

Scarre, Chris. *Exploring Prehistoric Europe.* New York: Oxford University Press, 1998.

Sieveking, Ann. *The Cave Artists.* London: Thames & Hudson, 1979.

Trump, David H. *The Prehistory of the Mediterranean.* New Haven: Yale University Press, 1980.

Ucko, Peter J., and Andrée Rosenfeld. *Palaeolithic Cave Art.* New York: McGraw-Hill, 1967.

Wainwright, Geoffrey. *The Henge Monuments: Ceremony and Society in Prehistoric Britain.* London: Thames & Hudson, 1990.

CHAPTER 2
THE RISE OF CIVILIZATION: THE ART OF THE ANCIENT NEAR EAST

Akurgal, Ekrem. *Art of the Hittites.* New York: Abrams, 1962.

Amiet, Pierre. *Art of the Ancient Near East.* New York: Abrams, 1980.

Collon, Dominique. *Ancient Near Eastern Art.* Berkeley: University of California Press, 1995.

———. *First Impressions. Cylinder Seals in the Ancient Near East.* 2nd ed. London: British Museum, 1993.

———. *Near Eastern Seals.* Berkeley: University of California Press, 1990.

Crawford, Harriet. *Sumer and the Sumerians.* New York: Cambridge University Press, 1991.

Curtis, John E. *Ancient Persia.* Cambridge: Harvard University Press, 1990.

Curtis, John E., and Julian E. Reade. *Art and Empire. Treasures from Assyria in the British Museum.* New York: Metropolitan Museum of Art, 1995.

Frankfort, Henri. *The Art and Architecture of the Ancient Orient.* 5th ed. New Haven: Yale University Press, 1996.

Ghirshman, Roman. *The Arts of Ancient Iran: From Its Origins to the Time of Alexander the Great.* New York: Golden Press, 1964.

———. *Persian Art, the Parthian and Sassanian Dynasties, 249 B.C.–A.D. 651.* New York: Golden Press, 1962.

Harper, Prudence O., et al. *The Royal City of Susa. Ancient Near Eastern Treasures in the Louvre.* New York: Metropolitan Museum of Art, 1992.

Kramer, Samuel N. *The Sumerians: Their History, Culture, and Character.* Chicago: University of Chicago Press, 1971.

Lloyd, Seton. *The Archaeology of Mesopotamia: From the Old Stone Age to the Persian Conquest.* London: Thames & Hudson, 1984.

———. *The Art of the Ancient Near East.* New York: Oxford University Press, 1969.

Macqueen, James G. *The Hittites and Their Contemporaries in Asia Minor.* rev. ed. New York: Thames & Hudson, 1986.

Meyers, Eric M. ed. *The Oxford Encyclopedia of Archaeology in the Near East.* New York: Oxford University Press, 1997.

Moortgat, Anton. *The Art of Ancient Mesopotamia.* New York: Phaidon, 1969.

Oates, Joan. *Babylon.* Rev. ed. London: Thames & Hudson. 1986.

Oppenheim, A. Leo. *Ancient Mesopotamia.* Rev. ed. Chicago: University of Chicago Press, 1977.

Parrot, André. *The Arts of Assyria.* New York: Golden Press, 1961.

———. *Sumer: The Dawn of Art.* New York: Golden Press, 1961.

Porada, Edith. *Man and Images in the Ancient Near East.* Wakefield: Moyer Bell, 1995.

Porada, Edith, and Robert H. Dyson. *The Art of Ancient Iran: Pre-Islamic Cultures.* Rev. ed. New York: Greystone, 1969.

Postgate, J. Nicholas. *Early Mesopotamia: Society and Economy at the Dawn of History.* London: Routledge, 1992.

———. *The First Empires.* Oxford: Elsevier-Phaidon, 1977.

Reade, Julian E. *Assyrian Sculpture.* Cambridge: Harvard University Press, 1999.

———. *Mesopotamia.* Cambridge: Harvard University Press, 1991.

Roaf, Michael. *Cultural Atlas of Mesopotamia and the Ancient Near East.* New York: Facts on File, 1990.

Russell, John M. *Sennacherib's Palace without Rival at Nineveh.* Chicago: University of Chicago Press, 1991.

Saggs, H. W. F. *Babylonians.* London, British Museum, 1995.

Sasson, Jack M., ed. *Civilizations of the Ancient Near East.* New York: Scribner, 1995.

Snell, Daniel C. *Life in the Ancient Near East. 3100–332 B.C.* New Haven: Yale University Press, 1997.

Strommenger, Eva, and Hirmer, Max. *5000 Years of the Art of Mesopotamia.* New York: Abrams, 1964.

Zettler, Richard L., and Lee Horne. *Treasures from the Royal Tombs of Ur.* Philadelphia: University of Pennsylvania Museum of Archaeology and Anthropology, 1998.

CHAPTER 3
PHARAOHS AND THE AFTERLIFE: THE ART OF ANCIENT EGYPT

Aldred, Cyril. *The Egyptians.* London: Thames & Hudson, 1987.

Arnold, Dieter. *Building in Egypt, Pharaonic Stone Masonry.* New York: Oxford University Press, 1991.

Arnold, Dorothea. *The Royal Women of Amarna.* New York: Metropolitan Museum of Art, 1996.

———. *When the Pyramids Were Built. Egyptian Art of the Old Kingdom.* New York: Rizzoli, 1999.

Arnold, Dorothea, et al. *Egyptian Art in the Age of the Pyramids.* New York: Harry N. Abrams, 1999.

Badawy, Alexander. *A History of Egyptian Architecture.* 3 vols. Berkeley: University of California Press, 1954–1968.

Baines, John, and Jaromír Málek. *Atlas of Ancient Egypt.* New York: Facts on File, 1980.

Bard, Kathryn A. ed. *Encyclopedia of the Archaeology of Ancient Egypt.* London: Routledge, 1999.

Bianchi, Robert S. *Cleopatra's Egypt: Age of the Ptolemies.* Brooklyn: Brooklyn Museum, 1988.

———. *Splendors of Ancient Egypt from the Egyptian Museum, Cairo.* London: Booth-Clibborn, 1996.

Bietak, Manfred. *Avaris, the Capital of the Hyksos.* London: British Museum Press, 1996.

Capel, Anne K., and Glenn E. Markoe, eds. *Mistress of the House, Mistress of Heaven: Women in Ancient Egypt.* New York: Hudson Hills, 1996.

D'Auria, Sue, Peter Lacovara, and Catharine H. Roehrig. *Mummies and Magic. The Funerary Arts of Ancient Egypt.* Boston: Museum of Fine Arts, 1988.

Davis, Whitney. *The Canonical Tradition in Ancient Egyptian Art.* New York: Cambridge University Press, 1989.

Grimal, Nicholas. *A History of Ancient Egypt.* Oxford: Blackwell, 1992.

Ikram, Salima, and Dodson, Aidan. *The Mummy in Ancient Egypt: Equipping the Dead for Eternity.* New York: Thames & Hudson, 1998.

Kozloff, Arielle P., and Betsy M. Bryan. *Egypt's Dazzling Sun: Amenhotep III and His World.* Cleveland: Cleveland Museum of Art, 1992.

Lange, Kurt, and Max Hirmer. *Egypt: Architecture, Sculpture and Painting in Three Thousand Years.* 4th ed. London: Phaidon, 1968.

Lehner, Mark. *The Complete Pyramids. Solving the Ancient Mysteries.* New York: Thames & Hudson, 1997.

Mahdy, Christine, ed. *The World of the Pharaohs: A Complete Guide to Ancient Egypt.* London: Thames & Hudson, 1990.

Málek, Jaromír. *Egyptian Art.* London: Phaidon, 1999.

Málek, Jaromír, ed., *Egypt. Ancient Culture, Modern Land.* Norman: University of Oklahoma Press, 1993.

Redford, Donald B. *Akhenaton, the Heretic King.* Princeton: Princeton University Press, 1984.

Reeves, C. Nicholas. *The Complete Tutankhamun: The King, the Tomb, the Royal Treasure.* London: Thames & Hudson, 1990.

Robins, Gay. *The Art of Ancient Egypt.* Cambridge: Harvard University Press, 1997.

———. *Egyptian Painting and Relief.* Aylesbury: Shire Publications, 1986.

———. *Proportion and Style in Ancient Egyptian Art.* Austin: University of Texas Press, 1994.

———. *Women in Ancient Egypt.* London: British Museum, 1993.

Romer, John. *Valley of the Kings. Exploring the Tombs of the Pharaohs.* New York: Holt, 1994.

Russmann, Edna R. *Egyptian Sculpture. Cairo and Luxor.* Austin: University of Texas Press, 1989.

Schulz, Regina, and Matthias Seidel, eds. *Egypt. The World of the Pharaohs.* Cologne: Könemann, 1999.

Schäfer, Heinrich. *Principles of Egyptian Art.* Rev. ed. Oxford: Clarendon, 1986.

Shafer, Byron E., ed. *Temples of Ancient Egypt.* Ithaca: Cornell University Press, 1997.

Shaw, Ian, and Paul Nicholson. *The Dictionary of Ancient Egypt.* London: British Museum, 1995.

Silverman, David P., ed. *Ancient Egypt.* New York: Oxford University Press, 1997.

Smith, William Stevenson, and William Kelly Simpson. *The Art and Architecture of Ancient Egypt.* Rev. ed. New Haven: Yale University Press, 1998.

Trigger, Bruce G., et al., *Ancient Egypt. A Social History.* Cambridge: Cambridge University Press, 1983.

Weeks, Kent R. *The Lost Tomb.* New York: William Morrow, 1998.

Wildung, Dietrich. *Egypt. From Prehistory to the Romans.* Cologne: Taschen, 1997.

CHAPTER 4
MINOS AND THE HEROES OF HOMER: THE ART OF THE PREHISTORIC AEGEAN

Barber, R. L. N. *The Cyclades in the Bronze Age.* Iowa City: University of Iowa Press, 1987.

Betancourt, Philip P. *A History of Minoan Pottery.* Princeton: Princeton University Press, 1965.

Cadogan, Gerald. *Palaces of Minoan Crete.* London: Methuen, 1980.

Chadwick, John. *The Mycenaean World.* New York: Cambridge University Press, 1976.

Cottrell, Arthur. *The Minoan World.* New York: Scribner, 1980.

Demargne, Pierre. *The Birth of Greek Art.* New York: Golden Press, 1964.

Dickinson, Oliver P. T. K. *The Aegean Bronze Age.* New York: Cambridge University Press, 1994.

Doumas, Christos. *Thera, Pompeii of the Ancient Aegean: Excavations at Akrotiri, 1967–1979.* New York: Thames & Hudson, 1983.

————. *The Wall-paintings of Thera.* Athens: Thera Foundation, 1992.

Fitton, J. Lesley. *Cycladic Art.* Cambridge: Harvard University Press, 1989.

Getz-Preziosi, Patricia. *Sculptors of the Cyclades. Individual and Tradition in the Third Millennium B.C.* Ann Arbor: University of Michigan Press, 1987.

Graham, James W. *The Palaces of Crete.* Princeton: Princeton University Press, 1987.

Hampe, Roland, and Erika Simon. *The Birth of Greek Art. From the Mycenaean to the Archaic Period.* New York: Oxford University Press, 1981.

Higgins, Reynold. *Minoan and Mycenaean Art.* Rev. ed. New York: Thames & Hudson, 1997.

Hood, Sinclair. *The Arts in Prehistoric Greece.* New Haven: Yale University Press, 1978.

Immerwahr, Sarah A. *Aegean Painting in the Bronze Age.* University Park: Pennsylvania State University Press, 1990.

McDonald, William A., and Carol G. Thomas. *Progress into the Past: The Rediscovery of Mycenaean Civilization.* 2nd ed. Bloomington: Indiana University Press, 1990.

Marinatos, Nanno. *Art and Religion in Thera: Reconstructing a Bronze Age Society.* Athens: Mathioulakis, 1984.

Marinatos, Spyridon, and Max Hirmer. *Crete and Mycenae.* London: Thames & Hudson, 1960.

Morgan, Lyvia. *The Miniature Wall Paintings of Thera: A Study in Aegean Culture and Iconography.* New York: Cambridge University Press, 1988.

Pendlebury, John. *The Archeology of Crete.* London: Methuen, 1967.

Preziosi, Donald, and Louise A. Hitchcock, *Aegean Art and Architecture.* New York: Oxford University Press, 1999.

Taylour, Lord William. *The Mycenaeans.* London: Thames & Hudson, 1990.

Vermeule, Emily. *Greece in the Bronze Age.* Chicago: University of Chicago Press, 1972.

Wace, Alan. *Mycenae, an Archeological History and Guide.* New York: Biblo & Tannen, 1964.

Warren, Peter. *The Aegean Civilisations from Ancient Crete to Mycenae.* 2nd ed. Oxford: Elsevier-Phaidon, 1989.

CHAPTER 5
GODS, HEROES, AND ATHLETES: THE ART OF ANCIENT GREECE

Arias, Paolo. *A History of One Thousand Years of Greek Vase Painting.* New York: Abrams, 1962.

Ashmole, Bernard. *Architect and Sculptor in Classical Greece.* New York: New York University Press, 1972.

Berve, Helmut, Gottfried Gruben, and Max Hirmer. *Greek Temples, Theatres, and Shrines.* New York: Abrams, 1963.

Biers, William. *The Archaeology of Greece: An Introduction.* 2nd ed. Ithaca: Cornell University Press, 1996.

Boardman, John. *Athenian Black Figure Vases.* Rev. ed. New York: Thames & Hudson, 1985.

————. *Athenian Red Figure Vases: The Archaic Period.* New York: Thames & Hudson, 1988.

————. *Athenian Red Figure Vases: The Classical Period.* New York: Thames & Hudson, 1989.

————. *Early Greek Vase Painting, 11th–6th centuries B.C.* New York: Thames & Hudson, 1998.

————. *Greek Sculpture: The Archaic Period.* Rev. ed. New York: Thames & Hudson, 1985.

————. *Greek Sculpture: The Classical Period.* New York: Thames & Hudson, 1987.

————. *Greek Sculpture: The Late Classical Period and Sculpture in Colonies and Overseas.* New York: Thames & Hudson, 1995.

————. *The Parthenon and Its Sculpture.* Austin: University of Texas Press, 1985.

Carpenter, Thomas H. *Art and Myth in Ancient Greece.* New York: Thames & Hudson, 1991.

Charbonneaux, Jean, Roland Martin, and François Villard. *Archaic Greek Art.* New York: Braziller, 1971.

————. *Classical Greek Art.* New York: Braziller, 1972.

————. *Hellenistic Art.* New York: Braziller, 1973.

Coldstream, J. Nicholas. *Geometric Greece.* New York: St. Martin's, 1977.

Coulton, J. J. *Ancient Greek Architects at Work.* Ithaca: Cornell University Press, 1982.

Fullerton, Mark D. *Greek Art.* New York: Cambridge University Press, 2000.

Haynes, Denys E. L. *The Technique of Greek Bronze Statuary.* Mainz: von Zabern, 1992.

Houser, Caroline. *Greek Monumental Bronze Sculpture.* New York: Vendome, 1983.

Hurwit, Jeffrey M. *The Art and Culture of Early Greece, 1100–480 B.C.* Ithaca: Cornell University Press, 1985.

————. *The Athenian Acropolis: History, Mythology, and Archaeology from the Neolithic Era to the Present.* New York: Cambridge University Press, 1999.

Jenkins, Ian. *The Parthenon Frieze.* Austin: University of Texas Press, 1994.

Langlotz, Ernst, and Max Hirmer. *The Art of Magna Graecia. Greek Art in Southern Italy and Sicily.* New York: Abrams, 1965.

Lawrence, Arnold W., and R. A. Tomlinson. *Greek Architecture.* Rev. ed. New Haven: Yale University Press, 1996.

Martin, Roland. *Greek Architecture: Architecture of Crete, Greece, and the Greek World.* New York: Electa/Rizzoli, 1988.

Mattusch, Carol C. *Classical Bronzes. The Art and Craft of Greek and Roman Statuary.* Ithaca: Cornell University Press, 1996.

————. *Greek Bronze Statuary from the Beginnings through the Fifth Century B.C.* Ithaca: Cornell University Press, 1988.

Morris, Sarah P. *Daidalos and the Origins of Greek Art.* Princeton: Princeton University Press, 1992.

Osborne, Robin. *Archaic and Classical Greek Art.* New York: Oxford University Press, 1998.

Palagia, Olga. *The Pediments of the Parthenon.* Leiden: E. J. Brill, 1993.

Palagia, Olga, and J. J. Pollitt, *Personal Styles in Greek Sculpture.* New York: Cambridge University Press, 1996.

Pedley, John Griffiths. *Greek Art and Archaeology.* 2nd ed. Upper Saddle River: Prentice Hall, 1998.

Pollitt, Jerome J. *Art and Experience in Classical Greece.* New York: Cambridge University Press, 1972.

————. *Art in the Hellenistic Age.* New York: Cambridge University Press, 1986.

————. *The Art of Ancient Greece: Sources and Documents.* 2nd ed. New York: Cambridge University Press, 1990.

Pugliese Carratelli, G. *The Greek World: Art and Civilization in Magna Graecia and Sicily.* New York: Rizzoli, 1996.

Reeder, Ellen D., ed. *Pandora. Women in Classical Greece.* Baltimore: Walters Art Gallery, 1995.

Rhodes, Robin F. *Architecture and Meaning on the Athenian Acropois.* New York: Cambridge University Press, 1995.

Richter, Gisela M. *The Portraits of the Greeks.* Rev. ed. by R. R. R. Smith. Ithaca: Cornell University Press, 1984.

Ridgway, Brunilde S. *The Archaic Style in Greek Sculpture.* 2nd ed. Chicago: Ares, 1993.

————. *Fifth Century Styles in Greek Sculpture.* Princeton: Princeton University Press, 1981.

————. *Fourth-century Styles in Greek Sculpture.* Madison: University of Wisconsin Press, 1997.

————. *Prayers in Stone. Greek Architectural Sculpture.* Berkeley: University of California Press, 1999.

————. *Roman Copies of Greek Sculpture: The Problem of the Originals.* Ann Arbor: University of Michigan Press, 1984.

————. *Hellenistic Sculpture I: The Styles of ca. 331–200 B.C.* Madison: University of Wisconsin Press, 1990.

————. *The Severe Style in Greek Sculpture.* Princeton: Princeton University Press, 1970.

Robertson, Martin. *The Art of Vase-Painting in Classical Athens.* New York: Cambridge University Press, 1992.

————. *A History of Greek Art.* 2 vols. Rev. ed. New York: Cambridge University Press, 1986.

————. *A Shorter History of Greek Art.* New York: Cambridge University Press, 1981.

Rolley, Claude. *Greek Bronzes.* London: Sotheby's, 1986.

Shapiro, H. Alan. *Art and Cult in Athens under the Tyrants.* Mainz: von Zabern, 1989.

————. *Myth into Art. Poet and Painter in Classical Greece.* New York: Routledge, 1994.

Smith, R. R. R. *Hellenistic Sculpture.* New York: Thames & Hudson, 1991.

Spivey, Nigel. *Greek Art.* London: Phaidon, 1997.

Stansbury-O'Donnell, *Pictorial Narrative in Ancient Greek Art.* New York: Cambridge University Press, 1999.

Stewart, Andrew. *Art, Desire, and the Body in Ancient Greece.* New York: Cambridge University Press, 1997.

————. *Greek Sculpture. An Exploration.* 2 vols. New Haven: Yale University Press, 1990.

Wycherley, Richard E. *How the Greeks Built Cities.* New York: Norton, 1976.

CHAPTER 6
PATHS TO ENLIGHTENMENT: THE ANCIENT ART OF SOUTH AND SOUTHEAST ASIA

Asher, Frederick M. *The Art of Eastern India, 300–800.* Minneapolis: University of Minnesota Press, 1980.

Barrett, Douglas E. *Early Chola Bronzes.* Bombay: Bhulabhai Memorial Institute, 1965.

Brown, Robert L. *The Dvaravati Wheels of the Law and the Indianization of South East Asia.* Leiden: E. J. Brill, 1996.

Chihara, Daigoro. *Hindu-Buddhist Architecture in Southeast Asia.* Leiden: E. J. Brill, 1996.

Coomaraswamy, Ananda K. *History of Indian and Indonesian Art.* New York: Dover, 1985.

Craven, Roy C. *Indian Art: A Concise History.* London: Thames & Hudson, 1985.

Dehejia, Vidya. *Early Buddhist Rock Temples.* Ithaca: Cornell University Press, 1972.

Desai, Vishakha N., and Darielle Mason. *Gods, Guardians, and Lovers: Temple Sculptures from North India A.D. 700–1200.* New York: The Asia Society Galleries, 1993.

Frederic, Louis. *Borobudur.* New York: Abbeville Press, 1996.

Gopinatha Rao, T. A. *Elements of Hindu Iconography*. 2nd ed. 4 vols. New York: Paragon, 1968.

Gray, Basil, ed. *The Arts of India*. Ithaca: Cornell University Press, 1981.

Harle, James C. *The Art and Architecture of the Indian Subcontinent*. New Haven: Yale University Press, 1992.

Huntington, Susan L. *The "Pala-Sena" School of Sculpture*. Leiden: E. J. Brill, 1984.

Huntington, Susan L., and John C. Huntington. *The Art of Ancient India: Buddhist, Hindu, Jain*. New York: Weatherhill, 1985.

Jessup, Helen Ibbitson, and Thierry Zephir, eds. *Sculpture of Angkor and Ancient Cambodia: Millenium of Glory*. Washington: National Gallery of Art, 1997.

Kramrisch, Stella. *The Hindu Temple*. 2 vols. Delhi: Motilal Banarsidass, 1991. (Original edition 1946.)

Meister, Michael W., ed. *Encyclopedia of Indian Temple Architecture*. (8 vols.) New Delhi: American Institute of Indian Studies. Philadelphia: University of Pennsylvania Press, 1983–1996.

Rawson, Phillip. *The Art of Southeast Asia*. New York: Thames & Hudson, 1990.

Rowland, Benjamin. *The Art and Architecture of India: Buddhist, Hindu, Jain*. Harmondsworth, England: Penguin, 1977.

Srinivasan, Doris Meth. *Many Heads, Arms and Eyes: Origin, Meaning and Form of Multiplicity in Indian Art*. Leiden: E. J. Brill, 1997.

Williams, Joanna Gottfried. *The Art of Gupta India: Empire and Province*. Princeton: Princeton University Press, 1982.

Zimmer, Heinrich, and Joseph Campbell, eds. *The Art of Indian Asia; Its Mythology and Transformations*. Bollingen Series 39. 2 vols. Princeton: Princeton University Press, 1983.

CHAPTER 7
DAOISM, CONFUCIANISM, AND BUDDHISM: THE ART OF EARLY CHINA AND KOREA

Barnhart, Richard M., et al. *Three Thousand Years of Chinese Painting*. New Haven: Yale University Press; Beijing: Foreign Languages Press, 1997.

Bush, Susan, and Shio-yen Shih. *Early Chinese Texts on Painting*. Cambridge: Harvard University Press, 1985.

Cahill, James. *Chinese Painting*. New York: Rizzoli, 1960.

———. *The Painter's Practice: How Artists Lived and Worked in Traditional China*. New York: Columbia University Press, 1994.

Clunas, Craig. *Art in China*. New York: Oxford University Press, 1997.

Fong, Wen. *Beyond Representation: Chinese Painting and Calligraphy, 8th–14th Century*. Princeton Monographs in Art and Archaeology, 48; New York: Metropolitan Museum of Art; New Haven: Yale University Press, 1992.

———. *The Great Bronze Age of China: An Exhibition from the People's Republic of China*. New York: Metropolitan Museum of Art, 1980.

Li, Chu-tsing, ed. *Artists and Patrons: Some Social and Economic Aspects of Chinese Painting*. Lawrence: Kress Department of Art History in cooperation with Indiana University Press, 1989.

Powers, Martin J. *Art and Political Expression in Early China*. New Haven: Yale University Press, 1991.

Rawson, Jessica. *Ancient China: Art and Archaeology*. New York, Harper & Row, 1980.

Rawson, Jessica, et al. *The British Museum Book of Chinese Art*. New York: Thames & Hudson, 1992.

Sickman, Laurence, and A. C. Soper. *The Art and Architecture of China*, 3rd ed. New Haven: Yale University Press, 1992.

Silbergeld, Jerome. *Chinese Painting Style: Media, Methods, and Principles of Form*. Seattle and London: University of Washington Press, 1982.

Sullivan, Michael. *The Arts of China*, 3rd ed. Berkeley: University of California Press, 1984.

———. *The Birth of Landscape Painting*. Berkeley: University of California Press, 1962.

Thorp, Robert L. *Son of Heaven: Imperial Arts of China*. Seattle: Son of Heaven Press, 1988.

Vainker, S. J. *Chinese Pottery and Porcelain: From Prehistory to the Present*. London: G. Braziller, 1991.

Weidner, Marsha, ed. *Flowering in the Shadows: Women in the History of Chinese and Japanese Painting*. Honolulu: University of Hawaii Press, 1990.

Whitfield, Roger, and A. Farrer. *Caves of the Thousand Buddhas: Chinese Art of the Silk Route*. London: G. Braziller, 1990.

Wu, Hung. *Monumentality in Early Chinese Art*. Stanford: Stanford University Press, 1996.

———. *The Wu Liang Shrine: The Ideology of Early Chinese Pictorial Art*. Stanford: Stanford University Press, 1989.

CHAPTER 8
SACRED STATUES AND SECULAR SCROLLS: THE ART OF EARLY JAPAN

Aikens, C. Melvin, and Takayama Higuchi. *Prehistory of Japan*. New York: Academic Press, 1982.

Akiyama, Terukazu. *Japanese Painting*. Geneva: Skira; New York: Rizzoli, 1977.

Coaldrake, William H. *Architecture and Authority in Japan*. London: Routledge, 1996.

Drexler, Arthur. *The Architecture of Japan*. New York: Museum of Modern Art, 1966.

Elisseeff, Danielle, and Vadime Elisseeff. *Art of Japan*. Trans. I. Mark Paris. New York: Abrams, 1985.

Ienaga, Saburo. *Painting in the Yamato Style*. Trans. John M. Shields. New York: Weatherhill, 1973.

Kidder, J. Edward, Jr. *Japanese Temples: Sculpture, Paintings, Gardens, and Architecture*. Tokyo: Bijutsu Shuppan-sha, n.d.

———. *Masterpieces of Japanese Sculpture*. Tokyo: Bijutsu Shuppan-sha, 1961.

———. *The Art of Japan*. New York: Park Lane, 1985.

Kurata, Bunsaku. *Horyu-ji: Temple of the Exalted Law*. Trans. W. Chie Ishibashi. New York: Japan Society, 1981.

Mason, Penelope. *History of Japanese Art*. New York: Abrams, 1993.

Nishi, Kazuo, and Kazuo Hozumi. *What Is Japanese Architecture?* Trans. H. Mack Horton. New York: Kodansha International, 1985.

Nishikawa, Kyotaro, and Emily Sano. *The Great Age of Japanese Buddhist Sculpture A.D. 600–1300*. Fort Worth: Kimbell Art Museum, 1982.

Noma, Seiroku. *The Arts of Japan*. Translated and adapted by John Rosenfield and Glenn T. Webb. Tokyo: Kodansha International, 1966.

Okudaira, Hideo. *Narrative Picture Scrolls*. Adapted by Elizabeth ten Grotenhuis. New York: Weatherhill, 1973.

Rosenfield, John M., and Elizabeth ten Grotenhuis. *Journey of the Three Jewels*. New York: Asia Society, 1979.

Rosenfield, John M., and Shujiro Shimada. *Traditions of Japanese Art: Selections from the Kimiko and John Powers Collection*. Cambridge: Fogg Art Museum, 1970.

Rosenfield, John. *Japanese Art of the Heian Period, 794–1185*. New York: Asia Society, 1967.

Stanley-Baker, Joan. *Japanese Art*. New York: Thames & Hudson, 1984.

Suzuki, Kakichi. *Early Buddhist Architecture in Japan*. Translated and adapted by Mary Neighbor Parent and Nancy Shatzman Steinhardt. New York: Kodansha International, 1980.

Swann, Peter C. *Concise History of Japanese Art*. New York: Kodansha International, 1979.

Weidner, Marsha, ed. *Flowering in the Shadows: Women in the History of Chinese and Japanese Painting*. Honolulu: University of Hawaii Press, 1990.

CHAPTER 9
ITALY BEFORE THE ROMANS: THE ART OF THE ETRUSCANS

Banti, Luisa. *The Etruscan Cities and Their Culture*. Berkeley: University of California Press, 1973.

Boethius, Axel. *Etruscan and Early Roman Architecture*. 2nd ed. New Haven: Yale University Press, 1978.

Bonfante, Larissa, ed. *Etruscan Life and Afterlife. A Handbook of Etruscan Studies*. Detroit: Wayne State University Press, 1986.

Brendel, Otto J. *Etruscan Art*. 2nd ed. New Haven: Yale University Press, 1995.

Cristofani, Mauro. *The Etruscans: A New Investigation*. London: Orbis, 1979.

Heurgon, Jacques. *Daily Life of the Etruscans*. London: Weidenfeld & Nicolson, 1964.

Pallottino, Massimo. *Etruscan Painting*. Geneva: Skira, 1953.

———. *The Etruscans*. Harmondsworth: Penguin, 1978.

Richardson, Emeline. *The Etruscans: Their Art and Civilization*. Chicago: University of Chicago Press, 1976. Reprint of 1964 ed., with corrections.

Ridgway, David, and Francesca Ridgway, eds. *Italy before the Romans*. New York: Academic Press, 1979.

Spivey, Nigel. *Etruscan Art*. New York: Thames & Hudson, 1997.

Spivey, Nigel, and Simon Stoddart, *Etruscan Italy: An Archaeological History*. London: Batsford, 1990.

Sprenger, Maja, Gilda Bartoloni, and Max Hirmer. *The Etruscans: Their History, Art, and Architecture*. New York: Abrams, 1983.

Steingräber, Stephan, ed. *Etruscan Painting: Catalogue Raisonné of Etruscan Wall Paintings*. New York: Johnson, 1986.

CHAPTER 10
FROM SEVEN HILLS TO THREE CONTINENTS: THE ART OF ANCIENT ROME

Anderson, James C., Jr. *Roman Architecture and Society*. Baltimore: Johns Hopkins University Press, 1997.

Andreae, Bernard. *The Art of Rome*. New York: Abrams, 1977.

Bianchi Bandinelli, Ranuccio. *Rome: The Center of Power. Roman Art to A.D. 200*. New York: Braziller, 1970.

———. *Rome: The Late Empire. Roman Art A.D. 200–400*. New York: Braziller, 1971.

Brendel, Otto J. *Prolegomena to the Study of Roman Art*. New Haven: Yale University Press, 1979.

Claridge, Amanda. *Rome. An Oxford Archaeological Guide*. New York: Oxford University Press, 1998.

Clarke, John R. *The Houses of Roman Italy, 100 B.C.–A.D. 250*. Berkeley: University of California Press, 1991.

Cornell, Tim, and John Matthews. *Atlas of the Roman World*. New York: Facts on File, 1982.

D'Ambra, Eve. *Roman Art*. New York: Cambridge University Press, 1998.

D'Ambra, Eve, ed. *Roman Art in Context*. Englewood Cliffs: Prentice Hall, 1994.

Elsner, Jaś. *Imperial Rome and Christian Triumph*. New York: Oxford University Press, 1998.

Gazda, Elaine K., ed., *Roman Art in the Private Sphere*. Ann Arbor: University of Michigan Press, 1991.

Grant, Michael. *Cities of Vesuvius: Pompeii and Herculaneum*. Harmondsworth: Penguin, 1976.

Hannestad, Niels. *Roman Art and Imperial Policy*. Aarhus: Aarhus University Press, 1986.

Henig, Martin, ed. *A Handbook of Roman Art*. Ithaca: Cornell University Press, 1983.

Jones, Mark Wilson. *Principles of Roman Architecture*. New Haven: Yale University Press, 1999.

Kent, John P. C., and Max Hirmer. *Roman Coins*. New York: Abrams, 1978.

Kleiner, Diana E. E. *Roman Sculpture*. New Haven: Yale University Press, 1992.

Kleiner, Diana E. E., and Susan B. Matheson, eds. *I Claudia. Women in Ancient Rome*. New Haven: Yale University Art Gallery, 1996.

———. *I Claudia II: Women in Roman Art and Society*. New Haven: Yale University Art Gallery, 2000.

Kraus, Theodor. *Pompeii and Herculaneum: The Living Cities of the Dead*. New York: Abrams, 1975.

Ling, Roger. *Roman Painting*. New York: Cambridge University Press, 1991.

L'Orange, Hans Peter. *The Roman Empire: Art Forms and Civic Life*. New York: Rizzoli, 1985.

MacCormack, Sabine G. *Art and Ceremony in Late Antiquity*. Berkeley: University of California Press, 1981.

MacDonald, William L. *The Architecture of the Roman Empire I: An Introductory Study*. Rev. ed. New Haven: Yale University Press, 1982.

———. *The Architecture of the Roman Empire II: An Urban Appraisal*. New Haven: Yale University Press, 1986.

———. *The Pantheon: Design, Meaning, and Progeny*. Cambridge: Harvard University Press, 1976.

McKay, Alexander G. *Houses, Villas, and Palaces in the Roman World*. Ithaca: Cornell University Press, 1975.

Maiuri, Amedeo. *Roman Painting*. Geneva: Skira, 1953.

Nash, Ernest. *Pictorial Dictionary of Ancient Rome*. 2 vols. 2nd ed. New York: Praeger, 1962.

Pollitt, Jerome J. *The Art of Rome, 753 B.C.–A.D. 337*. Rev. ed. New York: Cambridge University Press, 1983.

Ramage, Nancy H., and Andrew Ramage. *Roman Art: Romulus to Constantine*. 2nd ed. Englewood Cliffs: Prentice Hall, 1996.

Richardson, Lawrence, Jr. *A New Topographical Dictionary of Ancient Rome*. Baltimore: Johns Hopkins University Press, 1992.

———. *Pompeii. An Architectural History*. Baltimore: Johns Hopkins University Press, 1988.

Sear, Frank. *Roman Architecture*. Rev. ed. Ithaca: Cornell University Press, 1989.

Stambaugh, John E. *The Ancient Roman City*. Baltimore: Johns Hopkins University Press, 1988.

Strong, Donald, and Roger Ling. *Roman Art*. 2nd ed. New Haven: Yale University Press, 1988.

Toynbee, Jocelyn M. C. *Death and Burial in the Roman World*. London: Thames & Hudson, 1971.

Wallace-Hadrill, Andrew. *Houses and Society in Pompeii and Herculaneum*. Princeton: Princeton University Press, 1994.

Ward-Perkins, John B. *Roman Architecture*. New York: Electa/Rizzoli, 1988.

———. *Roman Imperial Architecture*. 2nd ed. New Haven: Yale University Press, 1981.

Wood, Susan. *Roman Portrait Sculpture A.D. 217–260*. Leiden: E. J. Brill, 1986.

Yegül, Fikret. *Baths and Bathing in Classical Antiquity*. Cambridge, MA: MIT Press, 1992.

Zanker, Paul. *Pompeii: Public and Private Life*. Cambridge: Harvard University Press, 1998.

———. *The Power of Images in the Age of Augustus*. Ann Arbor: University of Michigan Press, 1988.

MEDIEVAL ART, GENERAL

Alexander, Jonathan J. G. *Medieval Illuminators and Their Methods of Work*. New Haven: Yale University Press, 1992.

Andrews, Francis B. *The Mediaeval Builders and Their Methods*. New York: Barnes & Noble, 1993.

Binski, Paul. *Painters (Medieval Craftsmen)*. Toronto: University of Toronto Press, 1991.

Calkins, Robert G. *Illuminated Books of the Middle Ages*. Ithaca: Cornell University Press, 1983.

———. *Medieval Architecture in Western Europe: From A.D. 300 to 1500*. New York: Oxford University Press, 1998.

———. *Monuments of Medieval Art*. New York: E. P. Dutton, 1979.

Coldstream, Nicola. *Masons and Sculptors (Medieval Craftsmen)*. Toronto: University of Toronto Press, 1991.

Cross, Frank L., and Livingstone, Elizabeth A., eds. *The Oxford Dictionary of the Christian Church*. 3rd ed. New York: Oxford University Press, 1997.

De Hamel, Christopher. *Scribes and Illuminators (Medieval Craftsmen)*. Toronto: University of Toronto Press, 1992.

Focillon, Henri. *The Art of the West in the Middle Ages*. 2nd ed. 2 vols. Ithaca: Cornell University Press, 1980. Reprint of 1963 ed.

Lasko, Peter. *Ars Sacra, 800–1200*. 2nd ed. New Haven, Yale University Press, 1994.

Murray, Peter, and Linda Murray. *The Oxford Companion to Christian Art and Architecture*. New York: Oxford University Press, 1996.

Pächt, Otto. *Book Illumination in the Middle Ages: An Introduction*. London: Miller, 1986.

Pelikan, Jaroslav. *Mary through the Centuries: Her Place in the History of Culture*. New Haven: Yale University Press, 1996.

Reilly, Bernard F., et al. *The Art of Medieval Spain, A.D. 500–1200*. New York: Metropolitan Museum of Art, 1993.

Rickert, Margaret. *Painting in Britain: The Middle Ages*. 2nd ed. Harmondsworth: Penguin, 1965.

Ross, Leslie. *Medieval Art. A Topical Dictionary*. Westport: Greenwood, 1996.

Schiller, Gertrud. *Iconography of Christian Art*. 2 vols. Greenwich, CT: New York Graphic Society, 1971–1972.

Snyder, James. *Medieval Art: Painting, Sculpture, Architecture, 4th–14th Century*. New York: Abrams, 1989.

Stokstad, Marilyn. *Medieval Art*. New York: Harper & Row, 1986.

Stoddard, Whitney. *Art and Architecture in Medieval France*. New York: Harper & Row, 1966.

Tasker, Edward G. *Encyclopedia of Medieval Church Art*. London: Batsford, 1993.

Webb, Geoffrey F. *Architecture in Britain: The Middle Ages*. Harmondsworth: Penguin, 1965.

Zarnecki, George. *Art of the Medieval World: Architecture, Sculpture, Painting, the Sacred Arts*. New York: Abrams, 1975.

CHAPTER 11
PAGANS, CHRISTIANS, AND JEWS:
THE ART OF LATE ANTIQUITY

Beckwith, John. *Early Christian and Byzantine Art*. 2nd ed. New Haven: Yale University Press, 1980.

Bowersock, G. W., Peter Brown, and Oleg Grabar, eds. *Late Antiquity. A Guide to the Postclassical World.*. Cambridge: Harvard University Press, 1998.

Brown, Peter. *The World of Late Antiquity, A.D. 150–170*. London: Thames & Hudson, 1971.

Elsner, Jaś. *Art and the Roman Viewer: The Transformation of Art from the Pagan World to Christianity*. New York: Cambridge University Press, 1995.

———. *Imperial Rome and Christian Triumph*. New York: Oxford University Press, 1998.

Grabar, André. *The Beginnings of Christian Art, 200–395*. London: Thames & Hudson, 1967.

———. *Christian Iconography*. Princeton: Princeton University Press, 1980.

Gutmann, Joseph. *Sacred Images: Studies in Jewish Art from Antiquity to the Middle Ages*. Northampton: Variorum, 1989.

Hutter, Irmgard. *Early Christian and Byzantine Art*. London: Herbert, 1988.

Janes, Dominic. *God and Gold in Late Antiquity*. New York: Cambridge University Press, 1998.

Kitzinger, Ernst. *Byzantine Art in the Making*. Cambridge: Harvard University Press, 1977.

———. *Early Medieval Art*. 3rd ed. London: British Museum, 1983.

Koch, Guntram. *Early Christian Art and Architecture*. London: SCM Press, 1996.

Krautheimer, Richard. *Rome, Profile of a City: 312–1308*. Princeton: Princeton University Press, 1980.

Krautheimer, Richard, and Slobodan Curcić. *Early Christian and Byzantine Architecture*. 4th rev. ed. New Haven: Yale University Press, 1986.

Lowden, John. *Early Christian and Byzantine Art*. London: Phaidon, 1997.

Lowrie, Walter S. *Art in the Early Church*. New York: Norton, 1969.

Mathews, Thomas, P. *The Clash of Gods: A Reinterpretation of Early Christian Art*. Rev. ed. Princeton: Princeton University Press, 1999.

Milburn, Robert. *Early Christian Art and Architecture*. Berkeley: University of California Press, 1988.

Perkins, Ann Louise. *The Art of Dura-Europos*. Oxford: Clarendon, 1973.

Stevenson, James. *The Catacombs: Rediscovered Monuments of Early Christianity*. London: Thames & Hudson, 1978.

Volbach, Wolfgang. *Early Christian Mosaics, from the Fourth to the Seventh Centuries*. New York: Oxford University Press, 1946.

Volbach, Wolfgang, and Max Hirmer. *Early Christian Art*. New York: Abrams, 1962.

Webster, Leslie, and Michelle Brown, eds. *The Transformation of the Roman World, A.D. 400–900*. Berkeley: University of California Press, 1997.

Weitzmann, Kurt. *Ancient Book Illumination*. Cambridge: Harvard University Press, 1959.

———. *Late Antique and Early Christian Book Illumination*. New York: Braziller, 1977.

Weitzmann, Kurt, ed. *Age of Spirituality. Late Antique and Early Christian Art, Third to Seventh Century*. New York: Metropolitan Museum of Art, 1979.

CHAPTER 12
ROME IN THE EAST:
THE ART OF BYZANTIUM

Beckwith, John. *The Art of Constantinople: An Introduction to Byzantine Art (330–1453)*. 2nd ed. New York: Phaidon, 1968.

Borsook, Eve. *Messages in Mosaic: The Royal Programmes of Norman Sicily*. Oxford: Clarendon, 1990.

Cormack, Robin. *Painting the Soul. Icons, Death Masks, and Shrouds*. London: Reaktion, 1997.

———. *Writing in Gold: Byzantine Society and Its Icons*. New York: Oxford University Press, 1985.

Cutler, Anthony. *The Hand of the Master: Craftsmanship, Ivory, and Society in Byzantium (9th–11th Centuries)*. Princeton: Princeton University Press, 1994.

Demus, Otto. *Byzantine Art and the West*. New York: New York University Press, 1970.

———. *The Mosaic Decoration of San Marco, Venice*. Chicago: University of Chicago Press, 1990.

Evans, Helen C., and William D. Wixom, eds. *The Glory of Byzantium. Art and Culture of the Middle Byzantine Era A.D. 843–1261*. New York: Metropolitan Museum of Art, 1997.

Grabar, André. *Byzantine Painting*. New York: Rizzoli, 1979.

———. *The Golden Age of Justinian: From the Death of Theodosius to the Rise of Islam*. New York: Odyssey Press, 1967.

Grabar, André, and Manolis Chatzidakis. *Greek Mosaics of the Byzantine Period*. New York: New American Library, 1964.

Lowden, John. *Early Christian and Byzantine Art*. London: Phaidon, 1997.

Maguire, Henry. *Art and Eloquence in Byzantium*. Princeton: Princeton University Press, 1981.

———. *The Icons of Their Bodies: Saints and Their Images in Byzantium*. Princeton: Princeton University Press, 1996.

Mainstone, Rowland J. *Hagia Sophia: Architecture, Structure and Liturgy of Justinian's Great Church*. London: Thames & Hudson, 1988.

Mango, Cyril. *Art of the Byzantine Empire, 312–1453: Sources and Documents*. Toronto: University of Toronto Press, 1986. Reprint of 1972 ed.

———. *Byzantine Architecture*. New York: Electa/Rizzoli, 1985.

———. *Byzantium: The Empire of New Rome*. New York: Scribner's, 1980.

———. *Byzantium and Its Image: History and Culture of the Byzantine Empire and Its Heritage*. London: Variorum, 1984.

Mark, Robert, and Ahmet S. Cakmak, eds. *Hagia Sophia from the Age of Justinian to the Present*. New York: Cambrdige University Press, 1992.

Mathews, Thomas F. *Byzantium from Antiquity to the Renaissance*. New York: Harry N. Abrams, 1998.

Ousterhout, Robert. *Master Builders of Byzantium*. Princeton: Princeton University Press, 2000.

Pelikan, Jaroslav. *Imago Dei: The Byzantine Apologia for Icons*. Princeton: Princeton University Press, 1990.

Rodley, Lyn. *Byzantine Art and Architecture: An Introduction*. New York: Cambridge University Press, 1994.

Von Simson, Otto G. *Sacred Fortress: Byzantine Art and Statecraft in Ravenna*. Princeton: Princeton University Press, 1986.

Walter, Christopher. *Art and Ritual of the Byzantine Church.* London: Variorum, 1982.

Weitzmann, Kurt. *Ancient Book Illumination.* Cambridge: Harvard University Press, 1959.

———. *Art in the Medieval West and Its Contacts with Byzantium.* London: Variorum, 1982.

———. *The Icon.* New York: Dorset, 1987.

———. *Illustrations in Roll and Codex.* Princeton: Princeton University Press, 1970.

CHAPTER 13
MUHAMMAD AND THE MUSLIMS: ISLAMIC ART

Asher, Catherine B. *Architecture of Mughal India.* New York: Cambridge University Press, 1992.

Aslanapa, Oktay. *Turkish Art and Architecture.* London: Faber & Faber, 1971.

Atil, Esin. *The Age of Sultan Suleyman the Magnificent.* Washington: National Gallery of Art, 1987.

Baker, Patricia L. *Islamic Textiles.* London: British Museum, 1995.

Blair, Sheila S., and Jonathan Bloom. *The Art and Architecture of Islam 1250–1800.* New Haven: Yale University Press, 1994.

Bloom, Jonathan, and Sheila S. Blair. *Islamic Arts.* London: Phaidon, 1997.

Brend, Barbara. *Islamic Art.* Cambridge: Harvard University Press, 1991.

Canby, Sheila. *Persian Painting.* London: British Museum, 1993.

Creswell, Keppel A. C. *A Short Account of Early Muslim Architecture.* Rev. ed. by James W. Allan. Aldershot: Scolar, 1989.

Dodds, Jerrilynn D., ed. *Al-Andalus: The Art of Islamic Spain.* New York: Metropolitan Museum of Art, 1992.

Ettinghausen, Richard. *Arab Painting.* Geneva: Skira, 1977.

———. *From Byzantium to Sassanian Iran and the Islamic World.* Leiden: E. J. Brill, 1972.

Ettinghausen, Richard, and Oleg Grabar. *The Art and Architecture of Islam, 650–1250.* New Haven: Yale University Press, 1992.

Ferrier, Ronald W., ed. *The Arts of Persia.* New Haven: Yale University Press, 1989.

Frishman, Martin, and Hasan-Uddin Khan. *The Mosque: History, Architectural Development and Regional Diversity.* New York: Thames & Hudson, 1994.

Goodwin, Godfrey. *A History of Ottoman Architecture.* 2nd ed. New York: Thames & Hudson, 1987.

Grabar, Oleg. *The Alhambra.* Cambridge: Harvard University Press, 1978.

———. *The Formation of Islamic Art.* Rev. ed. New Haven: Yale University Press, 1987.

Grube, Ernst J. *Architecture of the Islamic World: Its History and Social Meaning.* 2nd ed. New York: Thames & Hudson, 1984.

Hillenbrand, Robert. *Islamic Architecture: Form, Function, Meaning.* Edinburgh: Edinburgh University Press, 1994.

———. *Islamic Art and Architecture.* New York: Thames & Hudson, 1999.

Hoag, John D. *Islamic Architecture.* New York: Electa/Rizzoli, 1977.

Irwin, Robert. *Islamic Art in Context: Art, Architecture, and the Literary World.* New York: Abrams, 1997.

Lings, Martin. *The Qur'anic Art of Calligraphy and Illumination.* London: World of Islam Festival Trust, 1976.

Michell, George, ed. *Architecture of the Islamic World.* New York: Thames & Hudson, 1978.

Porter, Venetia. *Islamic Tiles.* London: British Museum, 1995.

Robinson, Frank. *Atlas of the Islamic World.* Oxford: Equinox, 1982.

Schimmel, Annemarie. *Calligraphy and Islamic Culture.* New York: New York University Press, 1984.

Stierlin, Henri. *Islam I: Early Architecture from Baghdad to Cordoba.* Cologne: Taschen, 1996.

Ward, Rachel M. *Islamic Metalwork.* New York: Thames & Hudson, 1993.

Welch, Anthony. *Calligraphy in the Arts of the Islamic World.* Austin: University of Texas Press, 1979.

CHAPTER 14
FROM ALASKA TO THE ANDES: THE ARTS OF ANCIENT AMERICA
Pre-Columbian

Alva, Walter, and Christopher Donnan. *Royal Tombs of Sipán.* Los Angeles: Fowler Museum of Cultural History, 1993.

Benson, Elizabeth P., and Beatriz de la Fuente, eds. *Olmec Art of Ancient Mexico.* Washington: National Gallery of Art, 1996.

Berrin, Kathleen, ed. *The Spirit of Ancient Peru: Treasures from the Museo Arqueologico Rafael Larco Herrera.* San Francisco: The Fine Arts Museums, 1997.

Berrin, Kathleen, and Esther Pasztory, eds. *Teotihuacan: Art from the City of the Gods.* San Francisco: Thames & Hudson/The Fine Arts Museums of San Francisco, 1993.

Boone, Elizabeth, ed. *Andean Art at Dumbarton Oaks.* 2 vols. Washington: Dumbarton Oaks, 1996.

Bruhns, Karen O. *Ancient South America.* New York: Cambridge University Press, 1994.

Burger, Richard. *Chavín and the Origins of Andean Civilization.* New York: Thames & Hudson, 1992.

Coe, Michael D. *Mexico.* 4th ed. New York: Thames & Hudson, 1994.

———. *The Maya.* 6th edition. New York: Thames & Hudson, 1999.

Coe, Michael D., and Justin Kerr. *The Art of the Maya Scribe.* New York: Abrams, 1998.

Donnan, Christopher. *Ceramics of Ancient Peru.* Los Angeles: Fowler Museum of Cultural History, 1992.

Fash, William. *Scribes, Warriors, and Kings: the City of Copan and the Ancient Maya.* New York: Thames & Hudson, 1991.

Hadingham, Evan. *Lines to the Mountain Gods: Nazca and the Mysteries of Peru.* Norman: University of Oklahoma Press, 1988.

Jones, Julie, ed. *The Art of Pre-Columbian Gold: the Jan Mitchell Collection.* New York: Metropolitan Museum of Art, 1985.

Kolata, Alan. *The Tiwanaku: Portrait of an Andean Civilization.* Cambridge: Blackwell, 1993.

Kubler, George. *The Art and Architecture of Ancient America: the Mexican, Maya, and Andean Peoples.* 3rd ed. New Haven: Yale University Press, 1992.

Lapiner, Alan. *Pre-Columbian Art of South America.* New York: Abrams, 1976.

Miller, Mary E. *The Art of Mesoamerica, from Olmec to Aztec.* 2nd ed. New York: Thames & Hudson, 1996.

Miller, Mary E., and Karl Taube. *The Gods and Symbols of Ancient Mexico and the Maya: An Illustrated Dictionary of Mesoamerican Religion.* New York: Thames & Hudson, 1993.

Morris, Craig, and Adriana von Hagen. *The Inka Empire and its Andean Origins.* New York: Abbeville, 1993.

Olmecs. Special edition of *Arqueología Mexicana.* Mexico City: Editorial Raíces, 1998.

Pang, Hilda. *Pre-Columbian Art: Investigations and Insights.* Norman: University of Oklahoma Press, 1992.

Pasztory, Esther. *Pre-Columbian Art.* New York: Cambridge University Press, 1998.

Paul, Anne. *Paracas Ritual Attire. Symbols of Authority in Ancient Peru.* Norman: University of Oklahoma Press, 1990.

Schele, Linda, and Peter Mathews. *The Code of Kings: The Language of Seven Sacred Maya Temples and Tombs.* New York: Scribner, 1998.

Schele, Linda, and Mary E. Miller. *The Blood of Kings: Dynasty and Ritual in Maya Art.* Fort Worth: Kimbell Art Museum, 1986.

Schmidt, Peter, Mercedes de la Garza, and Enrique Nalda, eds. *Maya.* New York: Rizzoli, 1998.

Stone-Miller, Rebecca, ed. *To Weave for the Sun: Andean Textiles in the Museum of Fine Arts, Boston.* Boston: Museum of Fine Arts, 1992.

Stone-Miller, Rebecca. *Art of the Andes from Chavín to Inca.* New York: Thames & Hudson, 1996.

Townsend, Richard F., ed. *Art From Sacred Landscapes.* Chicago: Art Institute of Chicago, 1992.

Townsend, Richard F., ed. *Ancient West Mexico.* Chicago: Art Institute of Chicago, 1998.

Von Hagen, Adriana, and Craig Morris. *The Cities of the Ancient Andes.* New York: Thames & Hudson, 1998.

Weaver, Muriel Porter. *The Aztecs, Mayas, and Their Predecessors.* 3rd ed. San Diego: Academic Press, 1993.

Native American

Berlo, Janet C., and Ruth B. Phillips. *Native North American Art.* New York: Oxford University Press, 1998.

Brody, J. J. and Rina Swentzell. *To Touch the Past: The Painted Pottery of the Mimbres People.* New York: Hudson Hills, 1996.

Brose, David. *Ancient Art of the American Woodland Indians.* New York: Abrams, 1985.

Cordell, Linda S. *Ancient Pueblo Peoples.* Washington: Smithsonian Institution Press, 1994.

Fagan, Brian. *Ancient North America: the Archaeology of a Continent.* 2nd ed. New York: Thames & Hudson, 1995.

Feest, Christian F. *Native Arts of North America.* 2nd ed. New York: Thames & Hudson, 1992.

Fitzhugh, William W., and Aron Crowell, eds. *Crossroads of Continents: Cultures of Siberia and Alaska.* Washington: Smithsonian Institution Press, 1988.

Furst, Peter, and Jill Furst. *North American Indian Art.* New York: Rizzoli, 1982.

Mathews, Zena, and Aldona Jonaitis, eds. *Native North American Art History.* Palo Alto: Peek Publications, 1982.

Nabokov, Peter, and Robert Easton. *Native American Architecture.* New York: Oxford University Press, 1989.

O'Connor, Mallory M. *Lost Cities of the Ancient Southeast.* Gainesville: University Press of Florida, 1995.

Penney, David, and George C. Longfish. *Native American Art.* Hong Kong: Hugh Lauter Levin and Associates, Inc, 1994.

Wardwell, Allen. *Ancient Eskimo Ivories of the Bering Strait.* New York: Rizzoli, 1986.

Whiteford, Andrew H., et al. *I am Here: 2000 Years of Southwest Indian Arts and Crafts.* Santa Fe: Museum of New Mexico Press, 1989.

CHAPTER 15
SOUTH OF THE SAHARA: EARLY AFRICAN ART

Bassini, Ezio, and William Fagg. *Africa and the Renaissance: Art in Ivory.* New York: Center for African Art, 1988.

Ben-Amos, Paula. *The Art of Benin.* London: Thames & Hudson, 1980.

Bourgeois, Jean-Louis, and Carollee Pelos. *Spectacular Vernacular: The Adobe Tradition.* New York: Aperture, 1989.

Dark, Philip, J. C. *An Introduction to Benin Art and Technology.* Oxford: Clarenden Press,1973.

Eyo, Ekpo, and Frank Willett. *Treasures of Ancient Nigeria.* New York: Knopf, 1980.

Ezra, Kate. *Royal Art of Benin: The Perls Collection in the Metropolitan Museum of Art,* 1992. New York: Metropolitan Museum of Art, 1992.

Fagg, Bernard. *Nok Terracottas.* Lagos: Ethnographica, 1977.

Garlake, Peter S. *Great Zimbabwe.* London: Thames & Hudson, 1973.

Gillon, Werner. *A Short History of African Art.* New York: Facts on File Publication, 1984.

Huffman, Thomas N. *Snakes & Crocodiles. Power and Symbolism in Ancient Zimbabwe.* Johannesburg: Witwatersrand University Press, 1996.

Kaplan, Flora Edouwaya S., ed. *Queens, Queen Mothers, Priestesses, and Power. Case Studies in African Gender.* Annals of the New York Academy of Sciences. Vol. 810. New York: 1997, 73–102.

Perani, Judith, and Fred Smith. *The Visual Arts of Africa. Gender, Power, and Life-Cycle Rituals.* Upper Saddle River: Prentice Hall, 1998.

Phillips, Tom, ed. *Africa. The Art of a Continent.* New York: Prestel, 1995.

Phillipson, David W. *African Archaeology.* 2nd ed. Cambridge: Cambridge University Press, 1993.

Prussin, Labelle. *Hatumere: Islamic Design in West Africa.* Berkeley and Los Angeles: University of California Press, 1986.

Schaedler, Karl-Ferdinand, et al. *Earth and Ore: 2500 Years of African Art in Terra-Cotta and Metal.* Munich: Panterra Verlag, 1997.

Shaw, Thurstan. *Unearthing Igbo-Ukwu: Archaeological Discoveries in Eastern Nigeria.* New York: Oxford University Press, 1977.

Willett, Frank. *Ife in the History of West African Sculpture.* New York: McGraw-Hill, 1967.

CHAPTER 16
EUROPE AFTER THE FALL OF ROME: EARLY MEDIEVAL ART IN THE WEST

Alexander, Jonathan J. G. *Insular Manuscripts, Sixth to the Ninth Century.* London: Miller, 1978.

Backhouse, Janet, et al., eds. *The Golden Age of Anglo-Saxon Art, 966–1066.* Bloomington: Indiana University Press, 1984.

Barral i Altet, Xavier. *The Early Middle Ages. From Late Antiquity to A.D. 1000.* Cologne: Taschen, 1997.

Beckwith, John. *Early Medieval Art.* New York: Oxford University Press, 1964.

Collins, Roger. *Early Medieval Europe, 300–1000.* New York: St. Martin's, 1991.

Conant, Kenneth J. *Carolingian and Romanesque Architecture, 800–1200.* 4th ed. New Haven: Yale University Press, 1992.

Davis-Weyer, Caecilia. *Early Medieval Art, 300–1150: Sources and Documents.* Toronto: University of Toronto Press, 1986. Reprint of 1971 ed.

Diebold, William J. *Word and Image. An Introduction to Early Medieval Art.* Boulder: Westview Press, 2000.

Dodwell, Charles R. *Anglo-Saxon Art: A New Perspective.* Ithaca: Cornell University Press, 1982.

———. *The Pictorial Arts of the West, 800–1200.* New Haven: Yale University Press, 1993.

Grabar, André, and Carl Nordenfalk. *Early Medieval Painting from the Fourth to the Eleventh Century.* Lausanne: Skira, 1957.

Henderson, George. *Early Medieval.* New York: Penguin, 1972.

———. *From Durrow to Kells: The Insular Gospel-Books, 650–800.* London: Thames & Hudson, 1987.

Henry, Françoise. *Irish Art during the Viking Invasions, 800–1020 A.D.* Ithaca: Cornell University Press, 1967.

———. *Irish Art in the Early Christian Period, to 800 A.D.* Rev. ed. Ithaca: Cornell University Press, 1965.

Horn, Walter W., and Ernest Born. *The Plan of Saint Gall.* 3 vols. Berkeley: University of California Press, 1979.

Hubert, Jean, et al. *The Carolingian Renaissance.* New York: Braziller, 1970.

———. *Europe of the Invasions.* New York: Braziller, 1969.

Klindt-Jensen, Ole, and David M. Wilson. *Viking Art.* 2nd ed. Minneapolis: University of Minnesota Press, 1980.

Mayr-Harting, Henry. *Ottonian Book Illumination: An Historical Study.* 2 vols. London: Miller, 1991–1993.

Megaw, Ruth, and John Vincent Megaw. *Celtic Art: From Its Beginning to the Book of Kells.* New York: Thames & Hudson, 1989.

Mütherich, Florentine, and Joachim E. Gaehde. *Carolingian Painting.* New York: Braziller, 1976.

Nordenfalk, Carl. *Celtic and Anglo-Saxon Painting: Book Illumination in the British Isles, 600–800.* New York: Braziller, 1977.

Richardson, Hilary, and John Scarry. *An Introduction to Irish High Crosses.* Dublin: Mercier, 1996.

Stalley, Roger. *Early Medieval Architecture.* New York: Oxford University Press, 1999.

Wilson, David M. *Anglo-Saxon Art: From the Seventh Century to the Norman Conquest.* London: Thames & Hudson, 1984.

CHAPTER 17
THE AGE OF PILGRIMS AND CRUSADERS: ROMANESQUE ART

Armi, C. Edson. *Masons and Sculptors in Romanesque Burgundy: The New Aesthetics of Cluny III.* 2 vols. University Park: Pennsylvania State University Press, 1983.

Barral i Altet, Xavier. *The Romanesque. Towns, Cathedrals and Monasteries.* Cologne: Taschen, 1998.

Cahn, Walter. *Romanesque Bible Illumination.* Ithaca, Cornell University Press, 1982.

———. *Romanesque Manuscripts: The Twelfth Century.* 2 vols. London: Miller, 1998.

Clapham, Alfred W. *Romanesque Architecture in Western Europe.* Oxford: Clarendon, 1959.

Conant, Kenneth J. *Carolingian and Romanesque Architecture, 800–1200.* 4th ed. New Haven: Yale University Press, 1992.

Demus, Otto. *Romanesque Mural Painting.* New York: Thames & Hudson, 1970.

Dodwell, Charles R. *The Pictorial Arts of the West, 800–1200.* New Haven: Yale University Press, 1993.

Fergusson, Peter. *Architecture of Solitude: Cistercian Abbeys in Twelfth-Century Europe.* Princeton: Princeton University Press, 1984.

Forsyth, Ilene H. *The Throne of Wisdom: Wood Sculptures of the Madonna in Romanesque France.* Princeton: Princeton University Press, 1972.

Gantner, Joseph, Marcel Pobé, and Jean Roubier. *Romanesque Art in France.* London: Thames & Hudson, 1956.

Grabar, André, and Carl Nordenfalk. *Romanesque Painting.* New York: Skira, 1958.

Grape, Wolfgang. *The Bayeux Tapestry: Monument to a Norman Triumph.* New York: Prestel, 1994.

Hearn, Millard F. *Romanesque Sculpture: The Revival of Monumental Stone Sculpture in the Eleventh and Twelfth Centuries.* Ithaca: Cornell University Press, 1981.

Kahn, Deborah, ed. *The Romanesque Frieze and Its Spectator.* London: Miller, 1992.

Kauffmann, Claus M. *Romanesque Manuscripts, 1066–1190.* Boston: New York Graphic Society, 1975.

Kubach, Hans E. *Romanesque Architecture.* New York: Electa/Rizzoli, 1988.

Kunstler, Gustav, ed. *Romanesque Art in Europe.* London: Thames & Hudson, 1969.

Little, Bryan D. G. *Architecture in Norman Britain.* London: Batsford, 1985.

Male, Émile. *Religious Art in France: The Twelfth Century.* Rev. ed. Princeton: Princeton University Press, 1978.

Nichols, Stephen G. *Romanesque Signs: Early Medieval Narrative and Iconography.* New Haven, Yale University Press, 1983.

Nordenfalk, Carl. *Early Medieval Book Illumination.* New York: Rizzoli, 1988.

Petzold, Andreas. *Romanesque Art.* New York: Abrams, 1995.

Schapiro, Meyer. *Romanesque Art: Selected Papers.* New York: Braziller, 1977.

———. *The Sculpture of Moissac.* New York: Thames & Hudson, 1985.

Swarzenski, Hanns. *Monuments of Romanesque Art: The Art of Church Treasures in North-Western Europe.* 2nd ed. Chicago: University of Chicago Press, 1967.

Tate, Robert B., and Marcus Tate. *The Pilgrim Route to Santiago.* Oxford: Phaidon, 1987.

Toman, Rolf, ed. *Romanesque: Architecture, Sculpture, Painting.* Cologne: Könemann, 1997.

Zarnecki, George. *Romanesque Art.* New York: Universe, 1971.

———. *Studies in Romanesque Sculpture.* London: Dorian, 1979.

Zarnecki, George, et al. *English Romanesque Art, 1066–1200.* London: Weidenfeld & Nicolson, 1984.

CHAPTER 18
THE AGE OF THE GREAT CATHEDRALS: GOTHIC ART

Alexander, Jonathan J. G., and Paul Binski, eds. *Age of Chivalry: Art in Plantagenet England, 1200–1400.* London: Royal Academy, 1987.

Bony, Jean. *The English Decorated Style: Gothic Architecture Transformed, 1250–1350.* Ithaca: Cornell University Press, 1979.

———. *French Gothic Architecture of the Twelfth and Thirteenth Centuries.* Berkeley: University of California Press, 1983.

Branner, Robert. *Manuscript Painting in Paris during the Reign of St. Louis.* Berkeley: University of California Press, 1977.

———. *St. Louis and the Court Style in Gothic Architecture.* London: Zwemmer, 1965.

Branner, Robert, ed. *Chartres Cathedral.* New York: Norton, 1969.

Brown, Sarah, and David O'Connor. *Glass-Painters (Medieval Craftsmen).* Toronto: University of Toronto Press, 1991.

Camille, Michael. *Gothic Art: Glorious Visions.* New York: Abrams, 1996.

———. *The Gothic Idol. Ideology and Image-making in Medieval Art.* New York: Cambridge University Press, 1989.

Courtenay, Lunn T., ed. *The Engineering of Medieval Cathedrals.* Aldershot: Scolar, 1997.

Erlande-Brandenburg, Alain. *Gothic Art.* New York: Abrams, 1989.

Favier, Jean. *The World of Chartres.* New York: Abrams, 1990.

Frankl, Paul. *Gothic Architecture.* Harmondsworth: Penguin, 1962.

———. *The Gothic: Literary Sources and Interpretations during Eight Centuries.* Princeton: Princeton University Press, 1960.

Frisch, Teresa G. *Gothic Art 1140–c. 1450: Sources and Documents.* Toronto: University of Toronto Press, 1987. Reprint of 1971 ed.

Gerson, Paula, ed. *Abbot Suger and Saint-Denis.* New York: Metropolitan Museum of Art, 1986.

Gimpel, Jean. *The Cathedral Builders.* New York: Grove, 1961.

Grodecki, Louis. *Gothic Architecture.* New York: Electa/Rizzoli, 1985.

Grodecki, Louis, and Catherine Brisac. *Gothic Stained Glass, 1200–1300.* Ithaca: Cornell University Press, 1985.

Jantzen, Hans. *High Gothic: The Classic Cathedrals of Chartres, Reims, Amiens.* Princeton: Princeton University Press, 1984.

Male, Émile. *Religious Art in France: The Thirteenth Century.* rev. ed. Princeton: Princeton University Press, 1984.

Martindale, Andrew. *Gothic Art.* New York: Thames & Hudson, 1985.

Nussbaum, Norbert. *German Gothic Church Architecture.* New Haven: Yale University Press, 2000.

Panofsky, Erwin. *Abbot Suger on the Abbey Church of St. Denis and Its Art Treasures.* 2nd ed. Princeton: Princeton University Press, 1979.

———. *Gothic Architecture and Scholasticism.* New York: New American Library, 1985. Reprint of 1951 ed.

Radding, Charles M., and William W. Clark. *Medieval Architecture, Medieval Learning.* New Haven: Yale University Press, 1992.

Sauerländer, Willibald, and Max Hirmer. *Gothic Sculpture in France 1140–1270.* New York: Abrams, 1973.

Simson, Otto G. von. *The Gothic Cathedral: Origins of Gothic Architecture and the Medieval Concept of Order.* 3rd ed. Princeton: Princeton University Press, 1988.

Toman, Rolf, ed. *The Art of Gothic: Architecture, Sculpture, Painting.* Cologne: Könemann, 1999.

Williamson, Paul. *Gothic Sculpture, 1140–1300.* New Haven: Yale University Press, 1995.

Wilson, Christopher. *The Gothic Cathedral: The Architecture of the Great Church, 1130–1530.* London: Thames & Hudson, 1990.

CHAPTER 19
FROM GOTHIC TO RENAISSANCE: THE FOURTEENTH CENTURY IN ITALY

Andrés, Glenn, et al. *The Art of Florence*. 2 vols. New York: Abbeville Press, 1988.

Antal, Frederick. *Florentine Painting and Its Social Background*. London: Keegan Paul, 1948.

Bomford, David. *Art in the Making: Italian Painting before 1400*. London: National Gallery, 1989.

Borsook, Eve, and Fiorelli Superbi Gioffredi. *Italian Altarpieces 1250–1550: Function and Design*. Oxford: Clarendon Press, 1994.

Cennini, Cennino. *The Craftsman's Handbook (Il Libro dell'Arte)*. Trans. Daniel V. Thompson, Jr. New York: Dover, 1954.

Cole, Bruce. *Sienese Painting: From Its Origins to the Fifteenth Century*. New York: HarperCollins, 1987.

Cole, Bruce. *Italian Art, 1250–1550: The Relation of Renaissance Art to Life and Society*. New York: Harper & Row, 1987.

Hills, Paul. *The Light of Early Italian Painting*. New Haven: Yale University Press, 1987.

Meiss, Millard. *Painting in Florence and Siena after the Black Death*. Princeton: Princeton University Press, 1976.

Norman, Diana, ed. *Siena, Florence, and Padua: Art, Society, and Religion 1280–1400*. New Haven: Yale University Press, 1995.

Panofsky, Erwin. *Renaissance and Renascences in Western Art*. New York: HarperCollins, 1972.

Pope-Hennessy, John. *Introduction to Italian Sculpture*. 3rd. ed. 3 vols. New York: Phaidon, 1986.

———. *Italian Gothic Sculpture*. 3rd ed. Oxford: Phaidon, 1986.

Smart, Alastair. *The Dawn of Italian Painting*. Ithaca: Cornell University Press, 1978.

Stubblebine, James. *Assisi and the Rise of Vernacular Art*. New York: Harper & Row, 1985.

White, John. *Art and Architecture in Italy 1250–1400*. 3rd ed. New Haven: Yale University Press, 1993.

CHAPTER 20
OF PIETY, PASSION, AND POLITICS: FIFTEENTH-CENTURY ART IN NORTHERN EUROPE AND SPAIN

Baxendall, M. *The Limewood Sculptors of Renaissance Germany*. New Haven: Yale University Press, 1980.

Blum, Shirley Neilsen. *Early Netherlandish Triptychs: A Study in Patronage*. Berkeley: University of California Press, 1969.

Campbell, Lorne. *The Fifteenth Century Netherlandish Schools*. London: National Gallery Publications, 1998.

Chatelet, Albert. *Early Dutch Painting*. New York: W. S. Konecky, 1988.

Cuttler, Charles P. *Northern Painting from Pucelle to Bruegel*. New York: Holt, Rinehart & Winston, 1968.

Friedlander, Max J. *Early Netherlandish Painting*. 14 vols. New York: Praeger/Phaidon, 1967–1976.

———. *From Van Eyck to Bruegel*. 3rd ed. Ithaca: Cornell University Press, 1981.

Huizinga, Johan. *The Waning of the Middle Ages*. 1924. Reprint. New York: St. Martin's Press, 1988.

Jacobs, Lynn F. *Early Netherlandish Carved Altarpieces, 1380–1550: Medieval Tastes and Mass Marketing*. Cambridge: Cambridge University Press, 1998.

Lane, Barbara G. *The Altar and the Altarpiece: Sacramental Themes in Early Netherlandish Painting*. New York: Harper & Row, 1984.

Meiss, Millard. *French Painting in the Time of Jean de Berry: The Limbourgs and Their Contemporaries*. New York: Braziller, 1974.

Müller, Theodor. *Sculpture in the Netherlands, Germany, France and Spain, 1400–1500*. New Haven: Yale University Press, 1986.

Panofsky, Erwin. *Early Netherlandish Painting: Its Origins and Character*. 2 vols. Cambridge: Harvard University Press, 1966.

Prevenier, Walter, and Wim Blockmans. *The Burgundian Netherlands*. Cambridge: Cambridge University Press, 1986.

Snyder, James. *Northern Renaissance Art: Painting, Sculpture, the Graphic Arts from 1350 to 1575*. New York: Abrams, 1985.

Wolfthal, Diane. *The Beginnings of Netherlandish Canvas Painting, 1400–1530*. New York: Cambridge University Press, 1989.

CHAPTER 21
HUMANISM AND THE ALLURE OF ANTIQUITY: FIFTEENTH-CENTURY ITALIAN ART

Adams, Laurie Schneider. *Key Monuments of the Italian Renaissance*. Denver: Westview Press, 1999.

Alberti, Leon Battista. *On Painting*. Trans. J. B. Spencer, Rev. ed. New Haven: Yale University Press, 1966.

———. *Ten Books on Architecture*. Ed. J. Rykwert. Trans. J. Leoni. London: Tiranti, 1955.

Ames-Lewis, Francis. *Drawing in Early Renaissance Italy*. New Haven: Yale University Press, 1981.

Baxandall, Michael. *Painting and Experience in Fifteenth Century Italy. A Primer in the Social History of Pictorial Style*. 2nd ed. New York: Oxford University Press, 1988.

Beck, James. *Italian Renaissance Painting*. New York: HarperCollins, 1981.

Blunt, Anthony. *Artistic Theory in Italy, 1450–1600*. Oxford: Clarendon Press, 1966.

Bober, Phyllis Pray, and Ruth Rubinstein. *Renaissance Artists and Antique Sculpture: A Handbook of Sources*. Oxford: Oxford University Press, 1986.

Borsook, Eve. *The Mural Painters of Tuscany*. New York: Oxford University Press, 1981.

Burckhardt, Jacob. *The Architecture of the Italian Renaissance*. Chicago: University of Chicago Press, 1987.

———. *The Civilization of the Renaissance in Italy*. 4th ed. 1867. Reprint. London: Phaidon, 1960.

Christiansen, Keith, Laurence B. Kanter, and Carl B. Strehle, eds. *Painting in Renaissance Siena, 1420–1500*. New York: Metropolitan Museum of Art, 1988.

Cole, Alison. *Virtue and Magnificence: Art of the Italian Renaissance Courts*. New York: Harry N. Abrams, 1995.

Cole, Bruce. *Masaccio and the Art of Early Renaissance Florence*. Bloomington: Indiana University Press, 1980.

Dempsey, Charles. *The Portrayal of Love: Botticelli's Primavera and Humanist Culture at the Time of Lorenzo the Magnificent*. Princeton: Princeton University Press, 1992.

Edgerton, Samuel Y., Jr. *The Heritage of Giotto's Geometry: Art and Science on the Eve of the Scientific Revolution*. Ithaca: Cornell University Press, 1991.

———. *The Renaissance Rediscovery of Linear Perspective*. New York: Harper & Row, 1976.

Gilbert, Creighton, ed. *Italian Art 1400–1500: Sources and Documents*. Evanston: Northwestern University Press, 1992.

Goldthwaite, Richard A. *The Building of Renaissance Florence: An Economic and Social History*. Baltimore: Johns Hopkins University Press, 1980.

Gombrich, E. H. *Norm and Form: Studies in the Art of the Renaissance*. 4th ed. Oxford: Phaidon, 1985.

Hall, Marcia B. *Color and Meaning: Practice and Theory in Renaissance Painting*. Cambridge: Cambridge University Press, 1992.

Hartt, Frederick. *History of Italian Renaissance Art: Painting, Sculpture, Architecture*. 4th ed. rev. by David G. Wilkins. Englewood Cliffs: Prentice-Hall, 1994.

Heydenreich, Ludwig H., and Wolfgang Lotz. *Architecture in Italy 1400–1600*. Harmondsworth: Penguin, 1974.

Hollingsworth, Mary. *Patronage in Renaissance Italy: From 1400 to the Early Sixteenth Century*. Baltimore: Johns Hopkins University Press, 1994.

Kemp, Martin. *Behind the Picture: Art and Evidence in the Italian Renaissance*. New Haven: Yale University Press, 1997.

Kempers, Bram. *Painting, Power, and Patronage: The Rise of the Professional Artist in the Italian Renaissance*. London: Penguin, 1992.

Kent, F. W., and Patricia Simons, eds. *Patronage, Art, and Society in Renaissance Italy*. Canberra: Humanities Research Centre & Clarendon Press, 1987.

Lieberman, Ralph. *Renaissance Architecture in Venice*. New York: Abbeville Press, 1982.

McAndrew, John. *Venetian Architecture of the Early Renaissance*. Cambridge: MIT Press, 1980.

Meiss, Millard. *The Painter's Choice, Problems in the Interpretation of Renaissance Art*. New York: HarperCollins, 1977.

Murray, Peter. *The Architecture of the Italian Renaissance*. Rev. ed. New York: Schocken, 1986.

———. *Renaissance Architecture*. New York: Electa/Rizzoli (paperbound), 1985.

Murray, Peter, and Linda Murray. *The Art of the Renaissance*. London: Thames & Hudson, 1985.

Olson, Roberta J. M. *Italian Renaissance Sculpture*. London: Thames & Hudson, 1992.

Panofsky, Erwin. *Renaissance and Renascences in Western Art*. New York: HarperCollins, 1972.

Pater, Walter. *The Renaissance: Studies in Art and Poetry*. Ed. D. L. Hill. Berkeley: University of California Press, 1980.

Pope-Hennessy, John. *An Introduction to Italian Sculpture*. 3rd ed. 3 vols. New York: Phaidon, 1986.

Seymour, Charles. *Sculpture in Italy, 1400–1500*. New Haven: Yale University Press, 1966.

Thomson, David. *Renaissance Architecture: Critics, Patrons, and Luxury*. Manchester: Manchester University Press, 1993.

Turner, A. Richard. *Renaissance Florence: The Invention of a New Art*. New York: Harry N. Abrams, 1997.

Vasari, Giorgio. *The Lives of the Most Eminent Painters, Sculptors and Architects, 1550–1568*. 3 vols. New York: Abrams, 1979.

Wackernagel, Martin. *The World of the Florentine Renaissance Artist: Projects and Patrons, Workshops and Art Market*. Princeton: Princeton University Press, 1981.

Welch, Evelyn. *Art and Society in Italy 1350–1500*. Oxford: Oxford University Press, 1997.

White, John. *The Birth and Rebirth of Pictorial Space*. 3rd ed. Boston: Faber & Faber, 1987.

Wilde, Johannes. *Venetian Art from Bellini to Titian*. Oxford: Clarendon Press, 1981.

Wittkower, Rudolf. *Architectural Principles in the Age of Humanism*. 4th ed. London: Academy, 1988.

CHAPTER 22
BEAUTY, SCIENCE, AND SPIRIT IN ITALIAN ART: THE HIGH RENAISSANCE AND MANNERISM

Blunt, Anthony. *Artistic Theory in Italy, 1450–1600*. London: Oxford University Press, 1975.

Brown, Patricia Fortini. *Art and Life in Renaissance Venice*. New York: Harry N. Abrams, 1997.

Castiglione, Baldassare. *Book of the Courtier*. 1528. Reprint. New York: Viking Penguin, 1976.

Farago, Claire, ed. *Reframing the Renaissance: Visual Culture in Europe and Latin America 1450–1650*. New Haven: Yale University Press, 1995.

Freedberg, Sydney J. *Painting in Italy, 1500–1600*. 3rd ed. New Haven: Yale University Press, 1993.

———. *Painting of the High Renaissance in Rome and Florence*. Rev. ed. New York: Hacker, 1985.

Friedlaender, Walter. *Mannerism and Anti-Mannerism in Italian Painting*. New York: Schocken, 1965.

Goffen, Rona. *Piety and Patronage in Renaissance Venice: Bellini, Titian, and the Franciscans*. New Haven: Yale University Press, 1986.

Haskell, Francis, and Nicholas Penny. *Taste and the Antique: The Lure of Classical Sculpture, 1500–1900*. New Haven: Yale University Press, 1981.

Holt, Elizabeth Gilmore, ed. *A Documentary History of Art. Vol. 2, Michelangelo and the Mannerists*. Rev. ed. Princeton: Princeton University Press, 1982.

Humfry, Peter. *Painting in Renaissance Venice*. New Haven: Yale University Press, 1995.

Huse, Norbert, and Wolfgang Wolters. *The Art of Renaissance Venice: Architecture, Sculpture, and Painting*. Chicago: University of Chicago Press, 1990.

Levey, Michael. *High Renaissance*. New York: Viking Penguin, 1978.

Murray, Linda. *The High Renaissance and Mannerism*. New York: Oxford University Press, 1977.

Partner, Peter. *Renaissance Rome, 1500–1559: A Portrait of a Society*. Berkeley: University of California Press, 1977.

Partridge, Loren. *The Art of Renaissance Rome*. New York: Harry N. Abrams, 1996.

Pietrangeli, Carlo, et al. *The Sistine Chapel: The Art, the History, and the Restoration*. New York: Harmony Books, 1986.

Pope-Hennessy, John. *Italian High Renaissance and Baroque Sculpture*. 3rd ed. 3 vols. Oxford: Phaidon, 1986.

Rosand, David. *Painting in Cinquecento Venice: Titian, Veronese, Tintoretto*. New Haven: Yale University Press, 1982.

Shearman, John K. G. *Mannerism*. Baltimore: Penguin, 1978.

———. *Only Connect . . . Art and the Spectator in the Italian Renaissance*. Princeton: Princeton University Press, 1990.

Summers, David. *Michelangelo and the Language of Art*. Princeton: Princeton University Press, 1981.

Venturi, Lionello. *The Sixteenth Century: From Leonardo to El Greco*. New York: Skira, 1956.

Wölfflin, Heinrich. *The Art of the Italian Renaissance*. New York: Schocken, 1963.

———. *Classic Art: An Introduction to the Italian Renaissance*. 4th ed. Oxford: Phaidon, 1980.

CHAPTER 23
THE AGE OF REFORMATION: SIXTEENTH-CENTURY ART IN NORTHERN EUROPE AND SPAIN

Benesch, Otto. *Art of the Renaissance in Northern Europe*. Rev. ed. London: Phaidon, 1965.

———. *German Painting from Dürer to Holbein*. Geneva: Skira, 1966.

Blunt, Anthony. *Art and Architecture in France 1500–1700*. 4th ed. New Haven: Yale University Press, 1982.

Gibson, W. S. *"Mirror of the Earth": The World Landscape in Sixteenth Century Flemish Painting*. Princeton: Princeton University Press, 1989.

Harbison, Craig. *The Mirror of the Artist: Northern Renaissance Art in its Historical Context*. New York: Harry N. Abrams, 1995.

Hitchcock, Henry-Russell. *German Renaissance Architecture*. Princeton: Princeton University Press. 1981.

Landau, David, and Peter Parshall. *The Renaissance Print: 1470–1550*. New Haven: Yale University Press, 1994.

Smith, Jeffrey C. *German Sculpture of the Later Renaissance c. 1520–1580*. Princeton: Princeton University Press, 1993.

Stechow, Wolfgang. *Northern Renaissance Art, 1400–1600: Sources and Documents*. Englewood Cliffs: Prentice-Hall, 1966.

CHAPTER 24
OF POPES, PEASANTS, MONARCHS, AND MERCHANTS: BAROQUE AND ROCOCO ART

Adams, Laurie Schneider. *Key Monuments of the Baroque*. Denver: Westview Press, 1999.

The Age of Caravaggio. New York: Metropolitan Museum of Art, 1985.

Alpers, Svetlana. *The Art of Describing: Dutch Art in the Seventeenth Century*. Chicago: University of Chicago Press, 1984.

———. *Rembrandt's Enterprise: The Studio and the Market*. Chicago: University of Chicago Press, 1988.

Blunt, Anthony. *Art and Architecture in France:*

1500 to 1700. 4th ed. New Haven: Yale University Press, 1988.

Blunt, Anthony, ed. *Baroque and Rococo: Architecture and Decoration*. Cambridge: Harper & Row, 1982.

Brown, Christopher. *Scenes of Everyday Life: Dutch Genre Painting of the Seventeenth Century*. London: Faber & Faber, 1984.

Brown, Jonathan. *The Golden Age of Painting in Spain*. New Haven: Yale University Press, 1991.

———. *Kings and Connoisseurs: Collecting Art in Seventeenth-Century Europe*. Princeton: Princeton University Press, 1994.

Bryson, Norman. *Word and Image: French Painting of the Ancien Régime*. Cambridge: Cambridge University Press, 1981.

Duncan, Carol. *The Pursuit of Pleasure: The Rococo Revival in French Romantic Art*. New York: Garland, 1976.

Enggass, Robert, and Jonathan Brown. *Italy and Spain, 1600–1750: Sources and Documents*. Englewood Cliffs: Prentice Hall, 1970.

Franits, Wayne. *Looking at Seventeenth-Century Dutch Art: Realism Reconsidered*. Cambridge: Cambridge University Press, 1997.

Freedberg, Sydney J. *Circa 1600: A Revolution of Style in Italian Painting*. Cambridge: Harvard University Press, 1983.

Gerson, Horst, and E. H. ter Kuile. *Art and Architecture in Belgium 1600–1800*. Baltimore: Penguin, 1960.

Haak, Bob. *The Golden Age: Dutch Painters of the Seventeenth Century*. New York: Abrams, 1984.

Haskell, Francis. *Patrons and Painters: A Study in the Relations between Italian Art and Society in the Age of the Baroque*. Rev. ed. New Haven: Yale University Press, 1980.

Held, Julius, and Donald Posner. *17th and 18th Century Art: Baroque Painting, Sculpture, Architecture*. New York: Abrams, 1971.

Hempel, Eberhard. *Baroque Art and Architecture in Central Europe*. New York: Viking Penguin, 1977.

Hibbard, Howard. *Carlo Maderno and Roman Architecture, 1580–1630*. London: Zwemmer, 1971.

Hitchcock, Henry Russell. *Rococo Architecture in Southern Germany*. London: Phaidon, 1968.

Howard, Deborah. *The Architectural History of Venice*. London: B. T. Batsford, 1981.

Huyghe, René, ed. *Larousse Encyclopedia of Renaissance and Baroque Art*. See Reference Books.

Kahr, Madlyn Millner. *Dutch Painting in the Seventeenth Century*. New York: Harper & Row, 1978.

Kalnein, Wend, and Michael Levey. *Art and Architecture of the Eighteenth Century in France*. Harmondsworth: Penguin, 1972.

Kitson, Michael. *The Age of Baroque*. London: Hamlyn, 1976.

Krautheimer, Richard. *The Rome of Alexander VII, 1655–1677*. Princeton: Princeton University Press, 1985.

Lagerlöf, Margaretha R. *Ideal Landscape: Annibale Carracci, Nicolas Poussin and Claude Lorrain*. New Haven: Yale University Press, 1990.

Lees-Milne, James. *Baroque in Italy*. New York: Macmillan, 1960.

Levey, Michael. *Painting and Sculpture in France, 1700–1789*. New ed. New Haven: Yale University Press, 1993.

Martin, John R. *Baroque*. New York: Harper & Row, 1977.

Millon, Henry A. *Baroque and Rococo Architecture*. New York: Braziller, 1965.

Montagu, Jennifer. *Roman Baroque Sculpture: The Industry of Art*. New Haven: Yale University Press, 1989.

Muller, Sheila D., ed. *Dutch Art: An Encyclopedia*. New York: Garland Publishers, 1997.

Norberg-Schulz, Christian. *Baroque Architecture*. New York: Rizzoli, 1986.

———. *Late Baroque and Rococo Architecture*. New York: Electa/Rizzoli, 1986.

North, Michael. *Art and Commerce in the Dutch Golden Age*. New Haven: Yale University Press, 1997.

Pope-Hennessy, Sir John. *The Study and Criticism of Italian Sculpture*. New York: Metropolitan Museum, 1981.

Rosenberg, Jakob, Seymour Slive, and E. H. ter Kuile. *Dutch Art and Architecture, 1600–1800*. New Haven: Yale University Press, 1979.

Schama, Simon. *The Embarrassment of Riches: An Interpretation of Dutch Culture in the Golden Age*. Berkeley: University of California Press, 1988.

Stechow, Wolfgang. *Dutch Landscape Painting of the 17th Century*. 3rd ed. Oxford: Phaidon, 1981.

Summerson, Sir John. *Architecture in Britain: 1530–1830*. 7th rev. and enl. ed. New Haven: Yale University Press, 1983.

Varriano, John. *Italian Baroque and Rococo Architecture*. New York: Oxford University Press, 1986.

Waterhouse, Ellis Kirkham. *Baroque Painting in Rome*. London: Phaidon, 1976.

———. *Italian Baroque Painting*. 2nd ed. London: Phaidon, 1969.

———. *Painting in Britain, 1530–1790*. 4th ed. New Haven: Yale University Press, 1979.

Wittkower, Rudolf. *Art and Architecture in Italy 1600–1750*. 3rd ed. Harmondsworth: Penguin, 1982.

Wölfflin, Heinrich. *Principles of Art History: The Problem of the Development of Style in Later Art*. 7th ed. New York: Dover, 1950.

———. *Renaissance and Baroque*. London: Collins, 1984.

Wright, Christopher. *The French Painters of the 17th Century*. New York: New York Graphic Society, 1986.

BOOKS SPANNING THE FOURTEENTH THROUGH SEVENTEENTH CENTURIES

Campbell, Lorne. *Renaissance Portraits: European Portrait-Painting in the Fourteenth, Fifteenth, and Sixteenth Centuries*. New Haven: Yale University Press, 1990.

Dunkerton, Jill, Susan Foister, Dillian Gordon, and Nicholas Penny. *Giotto to Durer: Early Renaissance Painting in the National Gallery*. New Haven: Yale University Press, 1991.

Gilbert, Creighton. *History of Renaissance Art throughout Europe*. New York: Abrams, 1973.

Haskell, Francis, and Nicholas Penny. *Taste and the Antique: The Lure of Classical Sculpture 1500–1900*. New Haven: Yale University Press, 1981.

Huyghe, René. *Larousse Encyclopedia of Renaissance and Baroque Art*. See Reference Books.

Kemp, Martin. *The Science of Art: Optical Themes in Western Art From Brunelleschi to Seurat*. New Haven: Yale University Press, 1990.

Paoletti, John T,. and Gary M. Radke. *Art in Renaissance Italy*. Upper Saddle River: Prentice Hall, 1997.

CHAPTER 25
RELIGIOUS CHANGE AND COLONIAL RULE: THE LATER ART OF SOUTH AND SOUTHEAST ASIA

Beach, Milo Cleveland. *Mughal and Rajput Painting*. Cambridge: Cambridge University Press, 1992.

———. *The Imperial Image: Paintings for the Mughal Court*. Washington: Freer Gallery of Art, 1981.

Boisselier, Jean. *The Heritage of Thai Sculpture*. New York: Weatherhill, 1975.

Brand, Michael, and Glenn D. Lowry. *Akbar's India: Art from the Mughal City of Victory*. New York: The Asia Society Galleries, 1985.

Brown, Roxanna. *The Ceramics of South-East Asia: Their Dating and Identification*. 2nd ed. Singapore: Oxford University Press, 1988.

Dallapiccola, Anna Libera, ed. *Vijayanagara—City and Empire*. 2 vols. Stuttgart: Steiner Verlag Viesbaden GMBH, 1985.

Dehejia, Vidya, ed. *Devi: The Great Goddess*. Washington: Arthur M. Sackler Gallery, 1999.

Gascoigne, Bamber. *The Great Moghuls*. New York: Harper & Row, 1971.

Girard-Gestan, Maud, et al. *Art of Southeast Asia.* Trans. J. A. Underwood. New York: Harry N. Abrams, 1998.

Gosling, Betty. *Sukhothai: Its History, Culture, and Art.* Singapore: Oxford University Press, 1991.

Goswamy, B. N., and Eberhard Fischer. *Pahari Masters: Court Painters of Northern India.* Zurich: Artibus Asiae Publishers, 1992.

Jacques, Claude, and Michael Freeman. *Angkor: Cities and Temples.* Bangkok: River Books, 1997.

Michell, George. *Architecture and Art of Southern India: Vijayanagara and the Successor States, 1350–1750.* Cambridge: Cambridge University Press, 1995.

Narula, Karen Schur. *Voyage of the Emerald Buddha.* Kuala Lumpur: Oxford University Press, 1994.

Pal, Pratapaditya, ed. *Master Artists of the Imperial Mughal Court.* Bombay: Marg, 1991.

Poshyananda, Apinan. *Modern Art in Thailand: Nineteenth and Twentieth Century.* Singapore: Oxford University Press, 1992.

Stadtner, Donald M. *The Art of Burma: New Studies.* Mumbai: Marg, 1999.

Stevenson, John, and John Guy, eds. *Vietnamese Ceramics: A Separate Tradition.* Chicago: Art Media Resources, 1997.

Welch, Stuart Cary. *India: Art and Culture 1300–1900.* New York: The Metropolitan Museum of Art, 1985.

CHAPTER 26
INCURSION, RESTORATION, AND TRANSFORMATION: THE ART OF LATER CHINA AND KOREA

Andrews, Julia Frances, and Kuiyi Shen. *A Century in Crisis: Modernity and Tradition in the Art of Twentieth-Century China.* New York: Guggenheim Museum; 1998.

Barnhart, Richard M. *Painters of the Great Ming: The Imperial Court and the Zhe School.* Dallas: Dallas Museum of Art, 1993.

Barnhart, Richard M., et al. *Three Thousand Years of Chinese Painting.* New Haven: Yale University Press; Beijing: Foreign Languages Press, 1997.

Cahill, James. *Chinese Painting.* New York: Rizzoli, 1960.

——. *The Painter's Practice: How Artists Lived and Worked in Traditional China.* New York: Columbia University Press, 1994.

Clunas, Craig. *Art in China.* Oxford: Oxford University Press, 1997.

Fong, Wen C., and James C. Y. Watt. *Possessing the Past: Treasures from the National Palace Museum, Taipei.* New York: Metropolitan Museum of Art, 1996.

Lee, Sherman E., and Wai-Kam Ho. *Chinese Art under the Mongols: The Yuan Dynasty (1279–1368).* Cleveland: Cleveland Museum of Art, 1969.

Li, Chu-tsing, ed. *Artists and Patrons: Some Social and Economic Aspects of Chinese Painting.* Lawrence: Kress Department of Art History in cooperation with Indiana University Press, 1989.

Rawson, Jessica, et al. *The British Museum Book of Chinese Art.* New York: Thames & Hudson, 1992.

Sickman, Laurence, and A. C. Soper. *The Art and Architecture of China.* New Haven: Yale University Press, 1992.

Silbergeld, Jerome. *Chinese Painting Style: Media, Methods, and Principles of Form.* Seattle: University of Washington Press, 1982

Sullivan, Michael. *Art and Artists of Twentieth-Century China.* Berkeley: University of California Press, 1996.

——. *The Arts of China,* 3rd ed. Berkeley: University of California Press, 1984.

Thorp, Robert L. *Son of Heaven: Imperial Arts of China.* Seattle: Son of Heaven Press, 1988.

Vainker, S. J. *Chinese Pottery and Porcelain: From Prehistory to the Present.* London: G. Braziller, 1991.

Weidner, Marsha, ed. *Flowering in the Shadows: Women in the History of Chinese and Japanese Painting.* Honolulu: University of Hawaii Press, 1990.

CHAPTER 27
FROM THE SHOGUNS TO THE PRESENT: THE ART OF LATER JAPAN

Akiyama, Terukazu. *Japanese Painting.* Geneva: Skira, New York: Rizzoli, 1977.

Bring, Mitchell and Josse Wayembergh. *Japanese Gardens: Design and Meaning.* New York: McGraw Hill, 1981.

Cahill, James. *Scholar Painters of Japan.* New York: Asia Society, 1972.

Coaldrake, William H. *Architecture and Authority in Japan.* London: Routledge, 1996.

Drexler, Arthur. *The Architecture of Japan.* New York: Museum of Modern Art, 1966.

Edo: Art in Japan 1615–1868. Washington: National Gallery of Art, 1998.

Elisseeff, Danielle, and Vadime Elisseeff. *Art of Japan.* Trans. I. Mark Paris. New York: Abrams, 1985.

Fontein, Jan, and Money L. Hickman. *Zen Painting and Calligraphy.* Greenwich: New York: Graphic Society, 1970.

Guth, Christine. *Art of Edo Japan: The Artist and the City, 1615–1868.* New York: Abrams, 1996.

Hashimoto, Fumio. *Architecture in the Shoin Style.* Trans. and adapted by H. Mack Horton. New York: Kodansha International, 1981.

Hickman, Money L., et al. *Japan's Golden Age: Momoyama.* New Haven: Yale University Press, 1996.

Kawakita Michiaki. *Modern Currents in Japanese Art.* Trans. Charles E. Terry. New York: Weatherhill, 1974.

Kidder, J. Edward, Jr. *The Art of Japan.* New York: Park Lane, 1985.

Kurokawa, Kisho. *New Wave Japanese Architecture.* London: Academy Editions; Berlin: Ernst & Sohn; New York: St. Martin's Press, 1993.

Lane, Richard. *Images from the Floating World: The Japanese Print.* New York: Dorset, 1978.

Lee, Sherman. *Reflections of Reality in Japanese Art.* Cleveland: Cleveland Museum of Art, 1983.

Mason, Penelope. *History of Japanese Art.* New York: Abrams, 1993.

Meech-Pekarik, Julia. *The World of the Meiji Print: Impressions of a New Civilization.* New York: Weatherhill, 1986.

Mizuo, Hiroshi. *Edo Painting: Sotatsu and Korin.* Trans. John M. Shields. New York: Weatherhill, 1972.

Munroe, Alexandra. *Japanese Art after 1945: Scream against the Sky.* New York: Abrams, 1994.

Nishi, Kazuo, and Kazuo Hozumi. *What Is Japanese Architecture?* Trans. H. Mack Horton. New York: Kodansha International, 1985.

Noma, Seiroku. *The Arts of Japan.* Trans. and adapted by John Rosenfield and Glenn T. Webb. Tokyo: Kodansha International, 1966.

Rosenfield, John M., and Elizabeth ten Grotenhuis. *Journey of the Three Jewels.* New York: Asia Society, 1979.

Rosenfield, John M., and Shujiro Shimada. *Traditions of Japanese Art: Selections from the Kimiko and John Powers Collection.* Cambridge: Fogg Art Museum, 1970

Sanford, James H., William R. LaFleur, and Masatoshi Nagatomi. *Flowing Traces: Buddhism in the Literary and Visual Arts of Japan.* Princeton: Princeton University Press, 1992.

Shimizu, Yoshiaki, et al. *Japan: The Shaping of Daimyo Culture, 1185–1868.* Washington: National Gallery of Art, 1988.

Stanley-Baker, Joan. *Japanese Art.* New York: Thames & Hudson, 1984.

Stewart, David B. *The Making of a Modern Japanese Architecture, 1868 to the Present.* New York: Kodansha International, 1988.

Weidner, Marsha, ed. *Flowering in the Shadows: Women in the History of Chinese and Japanese Painting.* Honolulu: University of Hawaii Press, 1990.

Worlds Seen and Imagined: Japanese Screens from the Idemitsu Museum of Art. New York: The Asia Society, 1995.

CHAPTER 28
THE ENLIGHTENMENT AND ITS LEGACY: NEOCLASSICISM THROUGH THE MID-NINETEENTH CENTURY

Bermingham, Ann. *Landscape and Ideology: The English Rustic Tradition, 1740–1850.* Berkeley: University of California Press, 1986.

Boime, A. *Art in the Age of Bonapartism, 1800–1815.* Chicago: University of Chicago Press, 1990.

——. *Art in the Age of Revolution, 1750–1800.* Chicago: University of Chicago Press, 1987.

Braham, Allan. *The Architecture of the French Enlightenment.* Berkeley: University of California Press, 1980.

Brion, Marcel. *Art of the Romantic Era: Romanticism, Classicism, Realism.* New York: Praeger, 1966.

Bryson, Norman. *Tradition and Desire: From David to Delacroix.* New York: Cambridge University Press, 1984.

Burchard, John, and Albert Bush-Brown. *The Architecture of America: A Social and Cultural History.* Boston: Little, Brown/The American Institute of Architects, 1965.

Clark, Kenneth. *The Romantic Rebellion: Romantic versus Classic Art.* New York: Harper & Row, 1973.

Clay, Jean. *Romanticism.* New York: Phaidon, 1981.

Conisbee, Philip. *Painting in Eighteenth-Century France.* Ithaca: Phaidon/Cornell University Press, 1981.

Cooper, Wendy A. *Classical Taste in America, 1800–1840.* Baltimore: Baltimore Museum of Art, 1993.

Crow, Thomas E. *Painters and Public Life in Eighteenth-Century Paris.* New Haven: Yale University Press, 1985.

Davis, Terence. *The Gothick Taste.* Cranbury: Fairleigh Dickinson University Press, 1975.

Eitner, Lorenz. *Neoclassicism and Romanticism, 1750–1850: An Anthology of Sources and Documents.* New York: Harper & Row, 1989.

Gaunt, W. *The Great Century of British Painting: Hogarth to Turner.* New York: Phaidon, 1971.

Herrmann, Luke. *British Landscape Painting of the Eighteenth Century.* New York: Oxford University Press, 1974.

Holt, Elizabeth Gilmore, ed. *From the Classicists to the Impressionists: A Documentary History of Art and Architecture in the Nineteenth Century.* Garden City: Anchor Books/Doubleday, 1966.

Honour, Hugh. *Neo-Classicism.* Harmondsworth: Penguin, 1968.

——. *Romanticism.* New York: Harper & Row, 1979.

Kalnein, Wend Graf, and Michael Levey. *Art and Architecture of the Eighteenth Century in France.* New York: Viking/Pelican, 1973.

Kroeber, Karl. *British Romantic Art.* Berkeley: University of California Press, 1986.

Levey, Michael. *Painting in Eighteenth-Century Venice.* Ithaca: Phaidon/Cornell University Press, 1980.

——. *Rococo to Revolution: Major Trends in Eighteenth-Century Painting.* London: Thames & Hudson, 1966.

Mendelowitz, Daniel M. *A History of American Art.* 2nd ed. New York: Holt, Rinehart & Winston, 1970.

Middleton, Robin, and David Watkin. *Neoclassical and 19th Century Architecture.* 2 vols. New York: Electa/Rizzoli, 1987.

Novotny, Fritz. *Painting and Sculpture in Europe, 1780–1880.* Harmondsworth: Penguin, 1980.

Pierson, William. *American Buildings and Their Architects.* Vol. 1, *The Colonial and Neo-Classical Style.* Garden City: Doubleday, 1970.

Porterfield, Todd. *The Allure of Empire: Art in the Service of French Imperialism 1798–1836.* Princeton: Princeton University Press, 1998.

Rosenblum, Robert. *Transformations in Late Eighteenth Century Art.* Princeton: Princeton University Press, 1970.

Roston, Murray. *Changing Perspectives in Literature*

and the Visual Arts, 1650–1820. Princeton: Princeton University Press, 1990.

Rykwert, Joseph. *The First Moderns: Architects of the Eighteenth Century.* Cambridge: MIT Press, 1983.

Stillman, Damie. *English Neo-classical Architecture.* 2 vols. London: A Zwemmer, 1988.

Vaughn, William. *German Romantic Painting.* New Haven: Yale University Press, 1980.

Wilton, Andrew. *The Swagger Portrait: Grand Manner Portraiture in Britain from Van Dyck to Augustus John 1630–1930.* London: Tate Gallery, 1992.

Wolf, Bryan Jay. *Romantic Revision: Culture and Consciousness in Nineteenth-Century American Painting and Literature.* Chicago: University of Chicago Press, 1986.

CHAPTER 29
THE RISE OF MODERNISM:
THE LATER NINETEENTH CENTURY

Adams, Steven. *The Barbizon School and the Origins of Impressionism.* London: Phaidon, 1994.

Barger, M. Susan, and William B. White. *The Daguerreotype: Nineteenth-Century Technology and Modern Science.* Washington: Smithsonian Institution, 1991.

Baudelaire, Charles. *The Mirror of Art, Critical Studies.* Trans. Jonathan Mayne. Garden City: Doubleday & Co., 1956.

————. *The Painter of Modern Life, and Other Essays.* Trans. and ed. Jonathan Mayne. London: Phaidon, 1964.

Boime, Albert. *The Academy and French Painting in the 19th Century.* London: Phaidon, 1971.

Broude, Norma. *Impressionism: A Feminist Reading.* New York: Rizzoli, 1991.

Clark, Kenneth. *The Gothic Revival: An Essay in the History of Taste.* New York: Humanities Press, 1970.

Clark, T. J. *The Absolute Bourgeois: Artists and Politics in France, 1848–1851.* London: Thames & Hudson, 1973.

————. *Image of the People: Gustave Courbet and the 1848 Revolution.* London: Thames & Hudson, 1973.

————. *The Painting of Modern Life: Paris in the Art of Manet and His Followers.* Princeton: Princeton University Press, 1984.

Duncan, Alastair. *Art Nouveau.* New York: Thames & Hudson, 1994.

Eisenmann, Stephen F. *19th-Century Art: A Critical History.* New York: Thames & Hudson, 1994.

Farwell, Beatrice. *Manet and the Nude: A Study in the Iconology of the Second Empire.* New York: Garland, 1981.

Fried, Michael. *Courbet's Realism.* Chicago: University of Chicago Press, 1982.

————. *Manet's Modernism, or, The Face of Painting in the 1860s.* Chicago: The University of Chicago Press, 1996.

Friedlaender, Walter. *From David to Delacroix.* New York: Schocken Books, 1968.

Gerdts, William H. *American Impressionism.* New York: Abbeville Press, 1984.

Hamilton, George H. *Painting and Sculpture in Europe, 1880–1940.* 6th ed. New Haven: Yale University Press, 1993.

Herbert, Robert L. *Impressionism: Art, Leisure, and Parisian Society.* New Haven: Yale University Press, 1988.

Hilton, Timothy. *The Pre-Raphaelites.* New York: Oxford University Press, 1970.

Holt, Elizabeth B. *From the Classicists to the Impressionists: Art and Architecture in the Nineteenth Century.* Garden City: Doubleday/Anchor, 1966.

Holt, Elizabeth Gilmore, ed. *The Expanding World of Art 1874–1902.* New Haven: Yale University Press, 1988.

Janson, Horst W. *19th-Century Sculpture.* New York: Harry N. Abrams, 1985.

Jensen, Robert. *Marketing Modernism in Fin-de-Siècle Europe.* Princeton: Princeton University Press, 1994.

Klingender, Francis Donald and Elton, Arthur, ed. & rev. *Art and the Industrial Revolution.* London: Evelyn, Adams & MacKay, 1968.

Krell, Alain. *Manet and the Painters of Contemporary Life.* London: Thames & Hudson, 1996.

Leymarie, Jean. *French Painting in the Nineteenth Century.* Geneva: Skira, 1962.

Macaulay, James. *The Gothic Revival, 1745–1845.* Glasgow: Blackie, 1975.

Mainardi, Patricia. *Art and Politics of the Second Empire: The Universal Expositions of 1855 and 1867.* New Haven: Yale University Press, 1987.

————. *The End of the Salon: Art and the State in the Early Third Republic.* Cambridge: Cambridge University Press, 1993.

Middleton, Robin, ed. *The Beaux-Arts and Nineteenth-Century French Architecture.* Cambridge: MIT Press, 1982.

Miller, Angela L. *The Empire of the Eye: Landscape Representation and American Cultural Politics, 1825–1875.* Ithaca: Cornell University Press, 1993.

Needham, Gerald. *19th-Century Realist Art.* New York: Harper & Row, 1988.

Nochlin, Linda. *Impressionism and Post-Impressionism, 1874–1904: Sources and Documents.* Englewood Cliffs: Prentice-Hall, 1966.

————. *Realism and Tradition in Art, 1848–1900: Sources and Documents.* Englewood Cliffs: Prentice-Hall, 1966.

Novak, Barbara. *American Painting of the Nineteenth Century: Realism and the American Experience.* New York: Harper & Row, 1979.

Novotny, Fritz. *Painting and Sculpture in Europe: 1780–1880.* 2nd ed. New Haven: Yale University Press, 1978.

Pevsner, Nikolaus. *Pioneers of Modern Design.* Harmondsworth: Penguin, 1964.

Rewald, John. *The History of Impressionism.* New York: Museum of Modern Art, 1973.

————. *Post-Impressionism: From Van Gogh to Gauguin.* New York: Museum of Modern Art, 1956.

Rosen, Charles, and Henri Zerner. *Romanticism and Realism: The Mythology of Nineteenth-Century Art.* New York: Viking Press, 1984.

Rosenblum, Robert, and Horst W. Janson. *19th Century Art.* New York: Harry N. Abrams, 1984.

Schapiro, Meyer. *Modern Art: 19th & 20th Centuries.* New York: Braziller, 1978.

Schorske, Carl E. *Fin de Siècle Vienna: Politics and Culture.* New York: Alfred Knopf, 1980.

Shiff, Richard. *Cézanne and the End of Impressionism: A Study of the Theory, Technique, and Critical Evaluation of Modern Art.* Chicago: University of Chicago Press, 1984.

Silverman, Debora L. *Art Nouveau in Fin-de-Siècle France: Politics, Psychology, and Style.* Berkeley: University of California Press, 1989.

Sloane, Joseph C. *French Painting Between the Past and the Present: Artists, Critics, and Traditions from 1848 to 1870.* Princeton: Princeton University Press, 1973.

Smith, Paul. *Impressionism: Beneath the Surface.* New York: Harry N. Abrams, 1995.

Sullivan, Louis. *The Autobiography of an Idea.* New York: Dover, 1956.

Van Gogh: A Self Portrait: Letters Revealing His Life as a Painter. Selected by W. H. Auden. New York: E. P. Dutton, 1963.

Weisberg, Gabriel P. *The European Realist Tradition.* Bloomington: Indiana University Press, 1982.

Wilmerding, John, et al. *American Light: The Luminist Movement, 1850–1875: Paintings, Drawings, Photographs.* Washington: National Gallery of Art, 1980.

Wood, Christopher. *The Pre-Raphaelites.* New York: Viking Press, 1981.

CHAPTER 30
BEFORE AND AFTER THE
CONQUISTADORS: NATIVE ARTS OF
THE AMERICAS AFTER 1000
Pre-Columbian

Boone, Elizabeth, ed. *Andean Art at Dumbarton Oaks,* 2 vols., Washington: Dumbarton Oaks, 1996.

Boone, Elizabeth. *The Aztec World.* Washington: Smithsonian Institution Press, 1994.

Bruhns, Karen O. *Ancient South America.* New York: Cambridge University Press, 1994.

Coe, Michael D. *Mexico.* 4th ed. New York: Thames & Hudson, 1994.

————. *The Maya.* 6th ed. New York: Thames & Hudson, 1999.

Coe, Michael D., and Justin Kerr. *The Art of the Maya Scribe.* New York: Abrams, 1998.

Diaz, Gisele, and Alan Rodgers. *The Codex Borgia.* New York: Dover, 1993.

Donnan, Christopher. *Ceramics of Ancient Peru.* Los Angeles: Fowler Museum of Cultural History, 1992.

Gasparini, Graziano, and Luise Margolies. *Inca Architecture.* Bloomington: Indiana University Press, 1980.

Jones, Julie, ed. *The Art of Pre-Columbian Gold: the Jan Mitchell Collection,* New York: Metropolitan Museum of Art, 1985.

Kubler, George. *The Art and Architecture of Ancient America: the Mexican, Maya, and Andean Peoples.* 3rd ed. New Haven: Yale University Press, 1992.

Lapiner, Alan. *Pre-Columbian Art of South America.* New York: Abrams, 1976.

Malpass, Michael A. *Daily Life in the Inca Empire.* Westport: Greenwood Press, 1996.

Matos, Eduardo M. *The Great Temple of the Aztecs: Treasures of Tenochititlan.* New York: Thames & Hudson, 1988.

Miller, Mary E. *The Art of Mesoamerica, from Olmec to Aztec.* 2nd ed. New York: Thames & Hudson, 1996.

Miller, Mary E., and Karl Taube. *The Gods and Symbols of Ancient Mexico and the Maya: An Illustrated Dictionary of Mesoamerican Religion.* New York: Thames & Hudson, 1993.

Morris, Craig, and Adriana von Hagen. *The Inka Empire and its Andean Origins.* New York: Abbeville, 1993.

Pasztory, Esther. *Aztec Art.* New York: Abrams, 1983.

Plazas, Clemencia, Ana Maria Falchetti, and Armand J. Labbé. *Tribute to the Gods: Treasures of the Museo del Oro.* Santa Ana: Bowers Museum of Cultural Art, 1992.

Townsend, Richard F., ed. *Art From Sacred Landscapes.* Chicago: Art Institute of Chicago, 1992.

Weaver, Muriel Porter. *The Aztecs, Mayas, and Their Predecessors.* 3rd ed. San Diego: Academic Press, 1993.

Native American

Anderson, Richard, and Karen L. Field, eds., *Art in Small-Scale Societies: Contemporary Readings.* Englewood Cliffs: Prentice Hall, 1993.

Berlo, Janet C., ed. *Plains Indian Drawings 1865–1935.* New York: Abrams, 1996.

Berlo, Janet C., and Ruth B. Phillips. *Native North American Art.* New York: Oxford University Press, 1998.

Berlo, Janet C., and Lee Anne Wilson, eds., *Arts of Africa, Oceania, and the Americas: Selected Readings.* Englewood Cliffs: Prentice Hall, 1993.

Feest, Christian F. *Native Arts of North America.* 2nd ed. New York: Thames & Hudson, 1992.

Fienup-Riordan, Ann. *The Living Tradition of Yup'ik Masks.* Seattle: University of Washington Press, 1996.

Fitzhugh, William W., and Aron Crowell, eds. *Crossroads of Continents: Cultures of Siberia and Alaska.* Washington: Smithsonian Institution Press, 1988.

Furst, Peter, and Jill Furst. *North American Indian Art.* New York: Rizzoli, 1982.

Hill, Tom, and Richard W. Hill, Sr., eds. *Creation's Journey: Native American Identity and Belief.* Washington: Smithsonian Institution Press, 1994.

Jonaitis, Aldona. *From the Land of the Totem Poles: The Northwest Coast Indian Art Collection at the American Museum of Natural History.* Seattle: University of Washington Press, 1988.

MacDonald, George. *Haida Art.* Seattle: University of Washington Press, 1996.

Maurer, Evan M. *Visions of the People: a Pictorial History of Plains Indian Life.* Seattle: University of Washington Press, 1992.

Mathews, Zena, and Aldona Jonaitis, eds. *Native*

North American Art History. Palo Alto: Peek Publications, 1982.

Nabokov, Peter, and Robert Easton. *Native American Architecture.* New York: Oxford University Press, 1989.

Penney, David. *Art of the American Indian Frontier.* Seattle: University of Washington Press, 1992.

Penney, David, and George C. Longfish. *Native American Art.* Hong Kong: Hugh Lauter Levin & Associates, Inc., 1994.

Peterson, Susan. *The Living Tradition of Maria Martinez.* Tokyo: Kodansha International, 1977.

Samuel, Cheryl. *The Chilkat Dancing Blanket.* Norman: Unversity of Oklahoma Press, 1982.

Schaafsma, Polly, ed. *Kachinas in the Pueblo World.* Albuquerque: University of New Mexico Press, 1994.

Stewart, Hilary. *Looking at Totem Poles.* Seattle: University of Washington Press, 1993.

Wardwell, Allen. *Tangible Visions: Northwest Coast Indian Shamanism and its Art.* New York: Monacelli Press, 1996.

Washburn, Dorothy. *Living in Balance: The Universe of the Hopi, Zuni, Navajo, and Apache.* Philadelphia: University Museum, 1995.

Whiteford, Andrew H., et al. *I am Here: 2000 Years of Southwest Indian Arts and Crafts.* Santa Fe: Museum of New Mexico Press, 1989.

Wyman, Leland C. *Southwest Indian Drypainting.* Albuquerque: University of New Mexico Press, 1983.

CHAPTER 31
ELDERS, "BIG MEN," CHIEFS, AND KINGS: THE ARTS OF OCEANIA

Barrow, Terence. *The Art of Tahiti and the Neighboring Society, Austral and Cook Islands.* London: Thames & Hudson, 1979.

Berndt, Ronald M. et. al. *Australian Aboriginal Art.* New York: Macmillan, 1964.

Corbin, George A. *Native Arts of North America, Africa, and the South Pacific: An Introduction.* New York: HarperCollins, 1988.

Hanson, Allan, and Louise Hanson, eds. *Art and Identity in Oceania.* Honolulu: University of Hawaii Press, 1990.

Cox, J. Halley, and William H. Davenport. *Hawaiian Sculpture.* Rev. ed. Honolulu: University of Hawaii Press, 1988.

D'Alleva, Anne. *Arts of the Pacific Islands.* New York: Abrams, 1998.

Feldman, Jerome, and Donald H. Rubinstein. *The Art of Micronesia.* Honolulu: University of Hawaii Art Gallery, 1986.

Greub, Suzanne, ed. *Authority and Ornament: Art of the Sepik River, Papua New Guinea.* Basel: Tribal Art Centre, 1985.

Guiart, Jean. *Arts of the South Pacific.* New York: Golden Press, 1963.

Kaeppler, Adrienne L., Christian Kaufmann, and Douglas Newton. *Oceanic Art.* New York: Abrams, 1997.

Kooijman, Simon, *Tapa in Polynesia.* Honolulu: Bernice P. Bishop Museum Bulletin 234, 1972.

Lincoln, Louise, ed. *Assemblage of Spirits: Idea and Image in New Ireland.* New York: Braziller in association with Minneapolis Institute of Arts, 1987.

Mead, Sidney Moko, ed. *Te Maori: Maori Art from New Zealand Collections.* New York: Abrams in association with American Federation of Arts, 1984.

Rockefeller, Michael C. *The Asmat of New Guinea: The Journal of Michael Clark Rockefeller.* Greenwich: New York Graphic Society, 1967.

Schmitz, Carl A. *Oceanic Art: Myth, Man and Image in the South Seas.* New York: Abrams, 1971.

Schneebaum, Tobias. *Embodied Spirits: Ritual Carvings of the Asmat.* Salem: Peabody Museum of Salem, 1990.

Smidt, Dirk, ed. *Asmat Art: Woodcarvings of Southwest New Guinea.* New York: Braziller in association with Rijksmusum voor Volkenkunde, Leiden, 1993.

Sutton, Peter, ed. *Dreamings: The Art of Aboriginal Australia.* New York: Braziller in association with The Asia Society Galleries, 1988.

Thomas, Nicholas. *Oceanic Art.* London: Thames & Hudson, 1995.

CHAPTER 32
EXPLORATION, COLONIZATION, AND INDEPENDENCE: LATER AFRICAN ART

Abiodun, Roland, Henry J. Drewal, and John Pemberton III (eds.). *The Yoruba Artist: New Theoretical Perspectives on African Arts.* Washington: Smithsonian Institution, 1994.

Blier, Suzanne P. *The Royal Arts of Africa.* New York: Abrams, 1998.

Boone, Sylvia A. *Radiance from the Waters. Ideals of Feminine Beauty in Mende Art.* New Haven: Yale University Press, 1986.

Cole, Herbert M., ed. *I Am Not Myself: The Art of African Masquerade.* Los Angeles: Museum of Cultural History, University of California, 1985.

———. *Icons: Ideals and Power in the Art of Africa.* Washington: National Museum of African Art, Smithsonian Institution, 1989.

———. *Mbari, Art and Life among the Oweri Igbo.* Bloomington: Indiana University Press, 1982.

Cole, Herbert M., and Chike C. Aniakor. *Igbo Art. Community and Cosmos.* Los Angeles, Fowler Museum of Cultural History, 1984.

Cole, Herbert M., and Doran H. Ross. *The Arts of Ghana.* Los Angeles: Museum of Cultural History, UCLA, 1977.

Cornet, Joseph. *Art Royal Kuba.* Milan: Edizioni Sipiel, 1982.

Drewal, Henry J., and Margaret T. Drewal. *Gelede: Art and Female Power among the Yoruba.* Bloomington, Indiana University Press, 1983.

Ezra, Kate. *The Art of the Dogon: Selections from the Lester Wunderman Collection.* New York: Metropolitan Museum of Art, 1988.

———. *A Human Ideal in African Art: Bamana Figurative Sculpture.* New York: Metropolitan Museum of Art, 1986.

Fischer, Eberhard, and Hans Himmelheber. *The Arts of the Dan in West Africa.* Trans. Anne Biddle, Zurich: Museum Reitberg, 1984.

Fraser, Douglas F., and Herbert M. Cole, eds. *African Art and Leadership.* Madison: University of Wisconsin Press, 1972.

Geary, Christraud M. *Images from Bamum: German Colonial Photographs at the Court of King Njoya, Cameroon, West Africa, 1902–1915.* Washington: National Museum of African Art, Smithsonian Institution Press, 1988.

———. *Things of the Palace; A Catalogue of the Bamum Palace Museum in Foumban (Cameroon).* Weisbaden: Franz Steiner Verlag, 1983.

Glaze, Anita J. *Art and Death in a Senufo Village.* Bloomington: Indiana University Press, 1981.

Himmelheber, Hans. trans Eberhard Fischer. *Zaire 1938/39.* Zurich: Museum Reitberg, 1993.

Kasfir, Sidney L. *West African Masks and Cultural Systems.* Tervuren: Musée Royal de l'Afrique Centrale, 1988.

Kennedy, Jean. *New Currents, Ancient Rivers: Contemporary African Artists in a Generation of Change.* Washington: Smithsonian Institution Press, 1992.

Lamp, Frederick. *Art of the Baga. A Drama of Cultural Reinvention.* New York: The Museum for African Art & Prestel, 1996.

McGaffey, Wyatt, and Michael Harris. *Astonishment and Power (Kongo Art).* Washington: Smithsonian Institution Press, 1993.

McNaughton, Patrick R. *The Mande Blacksmiths: Knowledge, Power, and Art in West Africa.* Bloomington: Indiana University Press, 1988.

Nooter, Mary H. *Secrecy: African Art that Conceals and Reveals.* New York: Museum for African Art, 1993.

Perrois, Louis. trans. Francine Farr. *Ancestral Art of Gabon from the Collections of the Barbier-Mueller Museum.* Geneva: Musée Barbier-Mueller, 1985.

Phillips, Ruth B. *Representing Woman. Sande Masquerades of the Mende of Sierra Leone.* Los Angeles: UCLA Fowler Museum of Cultural History, 1995.

Roy, Christopher D. *Art and Life in Africa: Selections*

from the Stanley Collection. Iowa City: University of Iowa Museum of Art, 1992.

Sieber, Roy, and Roslyn A. Walker. *African Art in the Cycle of Life.* Washington: Smithsonian Institution Press, 1987.

Thompson, Robert F., and Joseph Cornet. *The Four Moments of the Sun: Kongo Art in Two Worlds.* Washington: National Gallery of Art, 1981.

Vansina, Jan. *The Children of Woot. A History of the Kuba Peoples.* Madison: University of Wisconsin Press, 1978.

Vinnicombe, Patricia. *People of the Eland. Rock Paintings of the Drakensberg Bushmen as a Reflection of Their Life and Thought.* Pietermaritzburg: University of Natal Press, 1976.

Vogel, Susan M., ed. *For Spirits and Kings: African Art from the Tishman Collection.* New York: Metropolitan Museum of Art, 1981.

———. ed. *Art/Artifact: African Art in Anthropology Collections.* New York: TeNeues, 1988.

———, et al. *Africa Explores: Twentieth-Century African Art.* New York: TeNeues, 1990.

———. *Baule. African Art. Western Eyes.* New Haven: Yale University Press, 1997.

CHAPTER 33
THE TRIUMPH OF MODERNIST ART: THE EARLY TWENTIETH CENTURY

Antliff, Mark. *Cultural Politics and the Parisian Avant-Garde.* Princeton: Princeton University Press, 1993.

Baigell, Matthew. *The American Scene: American Painting of the 1930s.* New York: Praeger, 1974.

Barr, Alfred H., Jr. *Cubism and Abstract Art: Painting, Sculpture, Constructions, Photography, Architecture, Industrial Arts, Theatre, Films, Posters, Typography.* Cambridge: Belknap, 1986.

———. ed. *Fantastic Art, Dada, Surrealism.* Reprint of 1936 ed. by the Museum of Modern Art. New York: Arno Press, 1969.

Barron, Stephanie, ed. *Degenerate Art: The Fate of the Avant-Garde in Nazi Germany.* Los Angeles: Los Angeles County Museum of Art, 1991.

———. *Exiles + Emigrés: The Flight of European Artists from Hitler.* Los Angeles: Los Angeles County Museum of Art, 1997.

Bayer, Herbert, Walter Gropius, and Ise Gropius. *Bauhaus, 1919–1928.* New York: Museum of Modern Art, 1975.

Bearden, Romare, and Harry Henderson. *A History of African-American Artists from 1792 to the Present.* New York: Pantheon Books, 1993.

Breton, André. *Surrealism and Painting.* New York: Harper & Row, 1972.

Brown, Milton. *Story of the Armory Show: The 1913 Exhibition That Changed American Art.* 2nd ed. New York: Abbeville, 1988.

Campbell, Mary Schmidt, David C. Driskell, David Lewis Levering, and Deborah Willis Ryan. *Harlem Renaissance: Art of Black America.* New York: The Studio Museum, Harlem/Harry N. Abrams, 1987.

Carrá, Massimo, Ewald Rathke, Caroline Tisdall, and Patrick Waldberg. *Metaphysical Art.* New York: Frederick A. Praeger, 1971.

Davidson, Abraham A. *Early American Modernist Painting, 1910–1935.* New York: Harper & Row, 1981.

Eberle, Matthias. *World War I and the Weimar Artists: Dix, Grosz, Beckmann, Schlemmer.* New Haven: Yale University Press, 1985.

Elderfield, John. *The "Wild Beasts": Fauvism and Its Affinities.* New York: The Museum of Modern Art/Oxford University Press, 1976.

Elsen, Albert. *Origins of Modern Sculpture.* New York: Braziller, 1974.

Fer, Briony, David Batchelor, and Paul Wood. *Realism, Rationalism, Surrealism: Art Between the Wars.* New Haven: Yale University Press, 1993.

Frampton, Kenneth. *A Critical History of Modern Architecture.* London: Thames & Hudson, 1985.

Friedman, Mildred, ed. *De Stijl: 1917–1931, Visions of Utopia.* Minneapolis: Walker Art Center/New York: Abbeville Press, 1982.

Fry, Edward, ed. *Cubism*. London: Thames & Hudson, 1966.

Golding, John. *Cubism: A History and an Analysis, 1907–1914*. Cambridge: Belknap, 1988.

Gordon, Donald E. *Expressionism: Art and Idea*. New Haven: Yale University Press, 1987.

Gray, Camilla. *The Russian Experiment in Art: 1863–1922*. New York: Harry N. Abrams, 1970.

Gropius, Walter. *Scope of Total Architecture*. New York: Collier Books, 1962.

Hamilton, George Heard. *Painting and Sculpture in Europe, 1880–1940*. 6th ed. New Haven: Yale University Press, 1993.

Harrison, Charles, Francis Frascina, and Gill Perry. *Primitivism, Cubism, Abstraction: The Early Twentieth Century*. New Haven: Yale University Press, 1993.

Herbert, James D. *Fauve Painting: The Making of Cultural Politics*. New Haven: Yale University Press, 1992.

Hunter, Sam. *American Art of the 20th Century*. New York: Harry N. Abrams, 1972.

Hurlburt, Laurance P. *The Mexican Muralists in the United States*. Albuquerque: University of New Mexico Press, 1989.

Jaffé, Hans L. C. *De Stijl, 1917–1931: The Dutch Contribution to Modern Art*. Cambridge: Belknap, 1986.

Kahnweiler, Daniel H. *The Rise of Cubism*. New York: Wittenborn, Schultz, 1949.

Kandinsky, Wassily. *Concerning the Spiritual in Art*. Trans. M. T. H. Sadler. New York: Dover, 1977.

Krauss, Rosalind. *The Originality of the Avant-Garde and Other Modernist Myths*. Cambridge: MIT Press, 1986.

Kuspit, Donald. *The Cult of the Avant-Garde Artist*. Cambridge: Cambridge University Press, 1993.

Le Corbusier. *The City of Tomorrow*, Cambridge: MIT Press, 1971.

Lloyd, Jill. *German Expressionism: Primitivism and Modernity*. New Haven: Yale University Press, 1991.

Lodder, Christina. *Russian Constructivism*. New Haven: Yale University Press, 1983.

Martin, Marianne W. *Futurist Art and Theory*. Oxford: Clarendon Press, 1968.

Moholy-Nagy, László. *Vision in Motion*. Chicago: Paul Theobald, 1969, first published in 1946.

Mondrian, Pieter Cornelius. *Plastic Art and Pure Plastic Art*. 3rd ed. New York: Wittenborn, Schultz, 1947.

Motherwell, Robert, ed. *The Dada Painters and Poets: An Anthology*. 2nd ed. Boston: G. K. Hall & Co., 1981.

Myers, Bernard S. *The German Expressionists: A Generation in Revolt*. New York: Frederick A. Praeger, 1956.

Osborne, Harold. *The Oxford Companion to Twentieth Century Art*. New York: Oxford University Press, 1981.

Read, Herbert, ed. *Surrealism*. New York: Frederick A. Praeger, 1971.

Richter, Hans. *Dada: Art and Anti-Art*. London: Thames & Hudson, 1961.

Rosenblum, Robert. *Cubism and Twentieth-Century Art*. Rev. ed. New York: Harry N. Abrams, 1984.

Rubin, William S. *Dada and Surrealist Art*. New York: Harry N. Abrams, 1968.

———. *Dada, Surrealism and Their Heritage*. New York: Museum of Modern Art, 1968.

Rubin, William S., ed. *Pablo Picasso: A Retrospective*. New York: Museum of Modern Art/Boston: New York Graphic Society, 1980.

———. *"Primitivism" in 20th-Century Art: Affinity of the Tribal and the Modern*. 2 vols. New York: Museum of Modern Art, 1984.

Selz, Peter. *German Expressionist Painting*. 1957. reprint. Berkeley: University of California Press, 1974.

Silver, Kenneth E. *Esprit de Corps: The Art of the Parisian Avant-Garde and the First World War, 1914–1925*. Princeton: Princeton University Press, 1989.

Steinberg, Leo. *Other Criteria: Confrontations with 20th-Century Art*. New York: Oxford University Press, 1972.

Stott, William. *Documentary Expression and Thirties America*. New York: Oxford University Press, 1973.

Taylor, Brandon. *Avant-Garde and After*. New York: Harry N. Abrams, 1995.

Taylor, Joshua C. *Futurism*. New York: Museum of Modern Art, 1961.

Tisdall, Caroline, and Angelo Bozzolla. *Futurism*. New York: Oxford University Press, 1978.

Tsujimoto, Karen. *Images of America: Precisionist Painting and Modern Photography*. Seattle: University of Washington Press, 1982.

Tucker, William. *Early Modern Sculpture*. New York: Oxford University Press, 1974.

Vogt, Paul. *Expressionism: German Painting, 1905–1920*. New York: Harry N. Abrams, 1980.

Weiss, Jeffrey S. *The Popular Culture of Modern Art: Picasso, Duchamp, and Avant-Gardism*. New Haven: Yale University Press, 1994.

Whitford, Frank. *Bauhaus*. New York: Thames & Hudson, 1984.

Wright, Frank Lloyd; Edgar Kaufmann, ed. *American Architecture*. New York: Horizon, 1955.

CHAPTER 34
THE EMERGENCE OF POSTMODERNISM: THE LATER TWENTIETH CENTURY

Alloway, Lawrence. *American Pop Art*. New York: Whitney Museum of American Art/Macmillan, 1974.

———. *Topics in American Art Since 1945*. New York: W. W. Norton, 1975.

Anfam, David. *Abstract Expressionism*. New York: Thames & Hudson, 1990.

Ashton, Dore. *American Art Since 1945*. New York: Oxford University Press, 1983.

———. *The New York School: A Cultural Reckoning*. Harmondsworth: Penguin, 1979.

Battcock, Gregory, ed. *Idea Art: A Critical Anthology*. New York: E. P. Dutton, 1973.

———. *Minimal Art: A Critical Anthology*. New York: Studio Vista, 1969.

———. *The New Art: A Critical Anthology*. New York: E. P. Dutton, 1973.

———. *New Artists Video: A Critical Anthology*. New York: E. P. Dutton, 1978.

Battcock, Gregory, and Robert Nickas, eds. *The Art of Performance: A Critical Anthology*. New York: E. P. Dutton, 1984.

Beardsley, Richard. *Earthworks and Beyond: Contemporary Art in the Landscape*. New York: Abbeville Press, 1984.

Beardsley, John, and Jane Livingston. *Hispanic Art in the United States: Thirty Contemporary Painters and Sculptors*. Houston: Museum of Fine Arts/New York: Abbeville Press, 1987.

Benthall, Jeremy. *Science and Technology in Art Today*. New York: Frederick A. Praeger, 1972.

Brion, Marcel, Sam Hunter, et al. *Art Since 1945*. New York: Harry N. Abrams, 1958.

Broude, Norma, and Mary D. Garrard. *The Power of Feminist Art: The American Movement of the 1970s, History and Impact*. New York: Abrams, 1994.

Cockcroft, Eva, John Weber, and James Cockcroft. *Toward a People's Art*. New York: E. P. Dutton, 1977.

Cook, Peter. *New Spirit in Architecture*. New York: Rizzoli, 1990.

Cummings, Paul. *Dictionary of Contemporary American Artists*. 3rd ed. New York: St. Martin's Press, 1977.

Ferguson, Russell, ed. *Discourses: Conversations in Postmodern Art and Culture*. Cambridge: MIT Press, 1990.

Frascina, Francis, ed. *Pollock and After: The Critical Debate*. New York: Harper & Row, 1985.

Geldzahler, Henry. *New York Painting and Sculpture, 1940–1970*. New York: E. P. Dutton, 1969.

Guilbaut, Serge. *How New York Stole the Idea of Modern Art*. Chicago: University of Chicago Press, 1983.

Goldberg, Rose Lee. *Performance Art: From Futurism to the Present*. Rev. ed. New York: Abrams, 1988.

Goodman, Cynthia. *Digital Visions: Computers and Art*. New York: Harry N. Abrams, 1987.

Goodyear, Frank H., Jr. *Contemporary American Realism Since 1960*. Boston: New York Graphic Society, 1981.

Green, Jonathan. *American Photography: A Critical History Since 1945 to the Present*. New York: Abrams, 1984.

Greenberg, Clement. *Clement Greenberg, The Collected Essays and Criticism*. Ed. J. O'Brien. 4 vols. Chicago: University of Chicago Press, 1986–93.

Grundberg, Andy. *Photography and Art: Interactions since 1945*. New York: Abbeville, 1987.

Hays, K. Michael, and Carol Burns, eds. *Thinking the Present: Recent American Architecture*. New York: Princeton Architectural, 1990.

Henri, Adrian. *Total Art: Environments, Happenings, and Performance*. New York: Oxford University Press, 1974.

Herbert, Robert L. *Modern Artists on Art*. Englewood Cliffs: Prentice-Hall, 1971.

Hertz, Richard, ed. *Theories of Contemporary Art*. 2nd ed. Englewood Cliffs: Prentice-Hall, 1993.

Hoffman, Katherine. *Explorations: The Visual Arts since 1945*. New York: HarperCollins, 1991.

Hughes, Robert. *The Shock of the New*. New York: Knopf, 1981.

Hunter, Sam. *An American Renaissance: Painting and Sculpture Since 1940*. New York: Abbeville, 1986.

Jacobus, John. *Twentieth-Century Architecture: The Middle Years, 1940–1964*. New York: Frederick A. Praeger, 1966.

Jencks, Charles. *Architecture 2000: Prediction and Methods*. New York: Frederick A. Praeger, 1971.

———. *The Language of Post-Modern Architecture*. 6th ed. New York: Rizzoli, 1991.

———. *What is Post-Modernism?* 3rd rev. ed. London: Academy Editions, 1989.

Johnson, Ellen H. *American Artists on Art: From 1940 to 1980*. New York: Harper & Row, 1980.

Jones, Amelia, ed. *Sexual Politics: Judy Chicago's Dinner Party in Feminist Art History*. Berkeley: University of California Press, 1996.

Kaprow, Allan. *Assemblage, Environments, and Happenings*. New York: Harry N. Abrams, 1966.

Kirby, Michael. *Happenings*. New York: E. P. Dutton, 1966.

Kramer, Hilton. *The Age of the Avant-Garde: An Art Chronicle of 1956–1972*. New York: Farrar, Straus & Giroux, 1973.

Leja, Michael. *Reframing Abstract Expressionism: Subjectivity and Painting in the 1940s*. New Haven: Yale University Press, 1993.

Lewis, Samella S. *African American Art and Artists*. Rev. ed. Berkeley: University of California Press, 1994.

Lippard, Lucy R. *Mixed Blessings: New Art in a Multicultural America*. New York: Pantheon Books, 1990.

———. *Pop Art*. New York: Frederick A. Praeger, 1966.

———, ed. *From the Center: Feminist Essays on Women's Art*. New York: E. P. Dutton, 1976.

———, ed. *Six Years: The Dematerialization of the Art Object from 1966 to 1972*. New York: Frederick A. Praeger, 1973.

Lovejoy, Margot. *Postmodern Currents: Art and Artists in the Age of the Electronic Media*. Ann Arbor: UMI Research Press, 1989.

Lucie-Smith, Edward. *Art Now*. Edison: Wellfleet Press, 1989.

———. *Movements in Art Since 1945*. new rev. ed. New York: Thames & Hudson, 1984.

Marder, Tod A. *The Critical Edge: Controversy in Recent American Architecture*. New Brunswick: Rutgers University Press, 1980.

———. *An International Survey of Recent Painting and Sculpture*. New York: Museum of Modern Art, 1984.

Meyer, Ursula. *Conceptual Art*. New York: E. P. Dutton, 1972.

Mitchell, William J. *The Reconfigured Eye: Visual Truth in the Post-Photographic Era*. Cambridge: MIT Press, 1992.

Norris, Christopher, and Andrew Benjamin. *What Is Deconstruction?* New York: St. Martin's, 1988.

Polcari, Stephen. *Abstract Expressionism and the Modern Experience*. Cambridge: Cambridge University Press, 1991.

Popper, Frank. *Origins and Development of Kinetic Art*. Trans. Stephen Bann. Greenwich: New York Graphic Society, 1968.

Price, Jonathan. *Video Visions: A Medium Discovers Itself*. New York: New American Library, 1977.

Reichardt, Jasia, ed. *Cybernetics, Art & Ideas*. Greenwich: New York Graphics Society, 1971.

Risatti, Howard, ed. *Postmodern Perspectives: Issues in Contemporary Art*. Englewood Cliffs: Prentice-Hall, 1990.

Robbins, Corinne. *The Pluralist Era: American Art, 1968–1981*. New York: Harper & Row, 1984.

Rosen, Randy, and Catherine C. Brawer, eds. *Making Their Mark: Women Artists Move into the Mainstream, 1970–1985*. New York: Abbeville, 1989.

Rosenberg, Harold. *The Tradition of the New*. New York: Horizon Press, 1959.

Russell, John, and Suzi Gablik. *Pop Art Redefined*. New York: Frederick A. Praeger, 1969.

Sandler, Irving. *Art of the Postmodern Era*. New York: HarperCollins, 1996.

———. *The Triumph of American Painting: A History of Abstract Expressionism*. New York: Frederick A. Praeger, 1970.

Sayre, Henry M. *The Object of Performance: The American Avant-Garde since 1970*. Chicago: University of Chicago Press, 1989.

Schneider, Ira, and Beryl Korot. *Video Art: An Anthology*. New York: Harcourt Brace Jovanovich, 1976.

Shapiro, David, and Cecile Shapiro. *Abstract Expressionism: A Critical Record*. New York: Cambridge University Press, 1990.

Smagula, Howard. *Currents: Contemporary Directions in the Visual Arts*. 2nd ed. Englewood Cliffs: Prentice-Hall, 1989.

Sonfist, Alan, ed. *Art in the Landscape: A Critical Anthology of Environmental Art*. New York: E. P. Dutton, 1983.

Sontag, Susan. *On Photography*. New York: Farrar, Strauss & Giroux, 1973.

Stiles, Kristine, and Peter Selz, eds. *Theories and Documents of Contemporary Art: A Sourcebook of Artists' Writings*. Berkeley: University of California Press, 1996.

Tuchman, Maurice. *American Sculpture of the Sixties*. Los Angeles: Los Angeles County Museum of Art, 1967.

Venturi, Robert, Denise Scott-Brown, and Steven Isehour. *Learning from Las Vegas*. Cambridge, MA: MIT Press, 1972.

Waldman, Diane. *Collage, Assemblage, and the Found Object*. New York: Abrams, 1992.

Wallis, Brian, ed. *Art After Modernism: Rethinking Representation*. New York: New Museum of Contemporary Art in association with David R. Godine, 1984.

Wheeler, Daniel. *Art since Mid-Century: 1945 to the Present*. Englewood Cliffs: Prentice-Hall, 1991.

Wood, Paul. *Modernism in Dispute: Art Since the Forties*. New Haven: Yale University Press, 1993.

BOOKS SPANNING THE EIGHTEENTH, NINETEENTH, AND TWENTIETH CENTURIES

Antreasian, Garo, and Clinton Adams. *The Tamarind Book of Lithography: Art and Techniques*. Los Angeles: Tamarind Workshop and New York: Harry N. Abrams, 1971.

Armstrong, John, Wayne Craven, and Norma Feder, et al. *200 Years of American Sculpture*. New York: Whitney Museum of American Art/Boston: David R. Godine, 1976.

Arnason, H. H. *History of Modern Art: Painting, Sculpture, Architecture*. 4th ed. New York: Harry N. Abrams, 1998.

Ashton, Dore. *Twentieth-Century Artists on Art*. New York: Pantheon Books, 1985.

Brown, Milton, Sam Hunter, and John Jacobus. *American Art: Painting, Sculpture, Architecture, Decorative Arts, Photography*. New York: Harry N. Abrams, 1979.

Burnham, Jack. *Beyond Modern Sculpture. The Effects of Science and Technology on the Sculpture of This Century*. New York: Braziller, 1968.

Castelman, Riva. *Prints of the 20th Century: A History*. New York: Oxford University Press, 1985.

Chipp, Herschel B. *Theories of Modern Art*. Berkeley: University of California Press, 1968.

Coke, Van Deren. *The Painter and the Photograph From Delacroix to Warhol*. Rev. and enl. ed. Albuquerque: University of New Mexico Press, 1972.

Craven, Wayne. *American Art: History and Culture*. Madison: Brown & Benchmark, 1994.

Driskell, David C. *Two Centuries of Black American Art*. Los Angeles: Los Angeles County Museum of Art/New York: Alfred A. Knopf, 1976.

Elsen, Albert. *Origins of Modern Sculpture*. New York: Braziller, 1974.

Fine, Sylvia Honig. *Women and Art: A History of Women Painters and Sculptors from the Renaissance to the 20th Century*. Montclair: Alanheld & Schram, 1978.

Flexner, James Thomas. *America's Old Masters*. New York: McGraw-Hill, 1982.

Frascina, Francis, and Charles Harrison, eds. *Modern Art and Modernism: A Critical Anthology*. New York: Harper & Row, 1982.

Giedion, Siegfried. *Space, Time and Architecture: The Growth of a New Tradition*. 4th ed. Cambridge: Harvard University Press, 1965.

Goldwater, Robert, and Marco Treves, eds. *Artists on Art*. 3rd ed. New York: Pantheon, 1958.

Greenough, Sarah, Joel Snyder, David Travis, and Colin Westerbeck. *On the Art of Fixing a Shadow: One Hundred and Fifty Years of Photography*. Washington: The National Gallery of Art/Chicago: The Art Institute of Chicago, 1989.

Hamilton, George Heard. *Nineteenth- and Twentieth-Century Art*. Englewood Cliffs: Prentice-Hall, 1972.

Herbert, Robert L., ed. *Modern Artists on Art*. Englewood Cliffs: Prentice-Hall, 1964.

Hertz, Richard, and Norman M. Klein, eds. *Twentieth-Century Art Theory: Urbanism, Politics, and Mass Culture*. Englewood Cliffs: Prentice-Hall, 1990.

Hitchcock, Henry-Russell. *Architecture: Nineteenth and Twentieth Centuries*. 4th ed. New Haven: Yale University Press, 1977.

Hunter, Sam, and John Jacobus. *Modern Art: Painting, Sculpture, and Architecture*. 3rd ed. New York: Harry N. Abrams, 1992.

Jencks, Charles. *Modern Movements in Architecture*. Garden City: Anchor Press/Doubleday, 1973.

Kaufmann, Edgar, Jr., ed. *The Rise of an American Architecture*. New York: Metropolitan Museum of Art/Frederick A. Praeger, 1970.

Krauss, Rosalind E. *The Originality of the Avant-Garde and Other Modernist Myths*. Cambridge: MIT Press, 1985.

———. *Passages in Modern Sculpture*. Cambridge, MA: MIT Press, 1981.

Licht, Fred. *Sculpture, Nineteenth and Twentieth Centuries*. Greenwich: New York Graphic Society, 1967.

Lynton, Norbert. *The Story of Modern Art*. 2nd ed. Englewood Cliffs: Prentice-Hall, 1989.

McCoubrey, John W. *American Art, 1700–1960: Sources and Documents*. Englewood Cliffs: Prentice-Hall, 1965.

Mason, Jerry, ed. *International Center of Photography Encyclopedia of Photography*. New York: Crown Publishers, 1984.

Newhall, Beaumont. *The History of Photography*. New York: The Museum of Modern Art, 1982.

Peterdi, Gabor. *Printmaking: Methods Old and New*. New York: Macmillan, 1961.

Pierson, William. *American Buildings and Their Architects: Technology and the Picturesque*. Vol. 2. Garden City: Doubleday, 1978.

Read, Herbert. *Concise History of Modern Painting*. 3rd ed. New York: Frederick A. Praeger, 1975.

———. *A Concise History of Modern Sculpture*. Rev. and enl. ed. New York: Frederick A. Praeger, 1964.

Rose, Barbara. *American Art Since 1900*. rev. ed. New York: Frederick A. Praeger, 1975.

Rosenblum, Robert. *Modern Painting and the Northern Romantic Tradition: Friedrich to Rothko*. New York: Harper & Row, 1975.

Ross, John, and Clare Romano. *The Complete Printmaker*. New York: The Free Press, 1972.

Ross, Stephen David, ed. *Art and Its Significance: An Anthology of Aesthetic Theory*. Albany: SUNY Press, 1987.

Russell, John. *The Meanings of Modern Art*. New York: Museum of Modern Art/Thames & Hudson, 1981.

Scully, Vincent. *Modern Architecture*. rev. ed. New York: Braziller, 1974.

Spalding, Francis. *British Art Since 1900*. London: Thames & Hudson, 1986.

Spencer, Harold. *American Art: Readings from the Colonial Era to the Present*. New York: Charles Scribner's Sons, 1980.

Summerson, Sir John. *Architecture in Britain: 1530–1830*. 7th rev. and enl. ed. Baltimore: Penguin, 1983.

Szarkowski, John. *Photography Until Now*. New York: Museum of Modern Art, 1989.

Tuchman, Maurice, and Judi Freeman, eds. *The Spiritual in Art: Abstract Painting, 1890–1985*. Los Angeles: Los Angeles County Art Museum/New York: Abbeville Press, 1986.

Upton, Dell. *Architecture in the United States*. Oxford: Oxford University Press, 1998.

Weaver, Mike. *The Art of Photography: 1839–1989*. New Haven: Yale University Press, 1989.

Whiffen, Marcus, and Frederick Koeper. *American Architecture, 1607–1976*. Cambridge: MIT Press, 1983.

Wilmerding, John. *American Art*. Harmondsworth, England: Penguin, 1976.

Wilson, Simon. *Holbein to Hockney: A History of British Art*. London: The Tate Gallery & The Bodley Head, 1979.

CREDITS

The authors and publisher are grateful to the proprietors and custodians of various works of art for photographs of these works and permission to reproduce them in this book. Sources not included in the captions are listed here.

Introduction—The Solomon R. Guggenheim Foundation, New York, Photo, David Heald: 1; Aerofilms Limited: 2; Scala/Art Resource, New York: 3; Copyright © 2001 The Georgia O'Keefe Foundation/Artist Rights Society (ARS), New York: 4; Copyright © 2001 Ben Shahn/Licensed by VAGA, New York: 5; Copyright © 1981 M. Sarri/Photo Vatican Museums: 7; Photo copyright © Metropolitan Museum of Art: 9; Saskia Ltd Cultural Documentation: 10; Copyright © National Gallery, London: 12; MOA Art Museum, Shizuoka-ken, Japan: 13; Joachim Blauel/Arthothek: 14; Copyright © 1983 Metropolitan Museum of Art: 15; Saskia Ltd Cultural Documentation: 17; Scala: 18.

Chapter 1—Photo: Paul G. Bahn: 1; With permission: Namibia Archaeological Trust: 2; Ulmer Museum/Thomas Stephan: 3; J.M. Arnaud/Musée d'Aquitaine: 5; Jean Dieuzaide: 6; Jean Vertut: 7, 9, 10; Cliché Mario Ruspoli/Copyright © CNMHS, Paris: 8; Hans Hinz: 11; Eurelios/French Ministry of Culture and Communication, Regional Direction for Cultural Affairs-Rhône-Alpes region-Regional department of archaeology: 12; CNMHS/SPADEM: 13; British School of Archaeology in Jerusalem: 14, 15; Arlette Mellaart: 17, 18; Pubbli Aer Foto: 19.

Chapter 2—Staatliche Museen zu Berlin: 1; Erwin Böhm: 3, 27; Hir: 4, 6, 7, 22, 25; Courtesy of The Oriental Institute of the University of Chicago: 5; University of Pennsylvania Museum (Neg.#T4-848c.): 10; Copyright © The British Museum: 11, 23, 24; Scala: 12; Saskia Ltd Cultural Documentation: 13; Erwin Böhm: 14; R.M.N.-R.G. Ojeda: 15; R.M.N.-H. Lewandowski: 16; Gir: 17, 28; photo Henri Stierlin: 18; R.M.N.-D. Chenot: 19; Saskia Ltd Cultural Documentation: 21; Klaus Göken, 1992/BPK: 26; Metropolitan Museum of Art, Fletcher Fund, 1965. (65.126) Photo copyright © 1982 By Metropolitan Museum of Art: 29; Sassoon/Robert Harding Picture Library: 30.

Chapter 3—Jürgen Liepe, Berlin: 2; Hir: 5, 6, 7, 12, 17, 27, 32; Carolyn Brown/PRI: 4; Bill Gallery, Stock, Boston: 8; Robert Harding Picture Library: 11, 25, 37, 38; Courtesy, Museum of Fine Arts, Boston. Reproduced with permission. Copyright © 2000 Museum of Fine Arts, Boston. All rights reserved: 13; R.M.N.: 14; Jean Vertut: 16; Foto Marburg/Art Resource, New York: 18, 23, 40; Photography by Egyptian Expedition, The Metropolitan Museum of Art: 19; Wim Swaan: 20; Metropolitan Museum of Art, Rogers Fund, 1929. (29.3.1) Photo by Schecter Lee. Photo copyright © 1986 Metropolitan Museum of Art: 21; John P. Stevens/AA&A: 22; Metropolitan Museum of Art, Purchase, 1890, Levi Hale Willard Bequest (90.35.1): 26; Ronald Sheridan/A&A: 28; Jürgen Liepe/BPK: 29; Copyright © The British Museum: 30, 31, 39; Margarete Büsing/BPK: 33, 34, 35; Boltin Picture Library: 36.

Chapter 4—Scala: 1; Studio Kontos: 2, 7, 26; Photo by Raymond V. Schoder, Copyright © 1987 by Bolchazy—Carducci Publishers, Inc: 3, 16; Hir: 8, 17, 23, 24; Wim Swaan: 5; Saskia Ltd Cultural Documentation: 6; Nimatallah/Art Resource, New York: 9, 13; photo Henri Stierlin: 10, 22; Hans Hinz: 11; Copyright © Michelle Jones/Ancient Art & Architecture Collection: 12; Alison Franz Collection, American School of Classical Studies at Athens: 14; Leonard von Matt: 15; Erich Lessing/

Art Resource, New York: 20; Archaeological Receipts Fund: 25.

Chapter 5—Metropolitan Museum of Art, Rogers Fund, 1914. (14.130.14) Photo copyright © 1996 Metropolitan Museum of Art: 1; Metropolitan Museum of Art, Gift of J. Pierpont Morgan, 1917. (17.190.2072). Photo copyright © 1996 Metropolitan Museum of Art: 2; Museum of Fine Arts, Boston, Francis Bartlett Collection: 3; Copyright © The British Museum: 4, 45, 46, 52; Alison Frantz: 6; R.M.N.: 7, 57; Metropolitan Museum of Art, Fletcher Fund, 1932. (32.11.1). Photo copyright © 1993 Metropolitan Museum of Art: 8; Saskia Ltd Cultural Documentation: 9, 10, 27, 28, 37, 38, 53, 54, 55, 62, 66, 71, 73, 85; Studio Kontos: 11, 12, 42, 64, 68, 77, 84; Summerfield: 13; Art Resource, New York: 15, 67; Hir: 17, 47, 48; AL: 18; Scala: 18, 34, 50, 56, 86; Photo Vatican Museums 19, 39, 60; R.M.N.-H. Lewandowski: 21; Colorphoto Hans Hinz: 22; Copyright A.C.L., Brussels: 23; photo Henri Stierlin: 24, 49; Canali: 29, 65, 69, 90; photo Paul M.R. Maeyaert: 30, 31, 32; Nimatallah/Art Resource, New York: 33, 36; Erich Lessing/Art Resource, New York: 35; Photo by Raymond V. Schoder, copyright © 1987 by Bolchazy-Carducci Publishers, Inc.: 40; DAI, Athens. Photo: G. Hellner: 48; Copyright © 1981 M. Sarri/Photo Vatican Museums: 58; Archivio I.G.D.A., Milano: 59; Archaeological Receipts Fund: 63; Photo by Raymond V. Schoder, copyright © 1987 by Bolchazy-Carducci Publishers, Inc.: 70; Vanni/AR: 72; BPK: 75, 78, 79; Photo Giovanni Lattanzi: 80; Summerfield Press Ltd.: 81; R.M.N.-G. Biot/C. Jean: 82; R.M.N.-Arnaudet; J. Schormans: 83; Ricciarini/Simion: 86 Ny Carlsberg Glyptotek: 88; Copyright © 1988 T. Okamura/Photo Vatican Museums: 89.

Chapter 6—John C. Huntington: 1, 4, 14, 15, 16; Archaeological Survey of India, Janpath, New Delhi: 2, 3, 7, 9, 11, 17, 18, 19; Robert Harding Picture Library: 5, 8, 27, 31; Douglas Dickins, FRPS: 12; Joseph Szaszfai: 13; Barnaby's Picture Library: 20; Robert L. Brown: 21, 23, 25; David Tokeley/Robert Harding Picture Library: 24; John Stevens/Ancient Art & Architecture Collection: 26; Nancy Tingley: 28; Eliot Elisofon/Life Magazine copyright © Time Inc.: 29; John Gollings Photography: 32, 33, 34; Douglas Dickins, FRPS: 35.

Chapter 7—Cultural Relics Publishing House, Beijing: 1, 3, 5, 12, 14; Asian Art Museum of San Francisco, B60 B1032: 2; Hunan Provincial Museum, Changsha City, China: 6; Chavannes: 7; Asian Art Museum of San Francisco, The Avery Brundage Collection B60 B1034: 8; Copyright © British Museum: 9; Edition d'Art, Paris: 10; Copyright © Laurence G. Liu: 11, 21; Reproduced with permission. Copyright © 2001 Museum of Fine Arts, Boston 31.643. All rights reserved: 16; The New York Public Library, Astor, Lenox and Tilden Foundations: 17; Victoria & Albert Museum, London/Art Resource, New York: 18; National Palace Museum, Taipei, Taiwan, Republic of China: 19; Reproduced with permission. Copyright © 2001 Museum of Fine Arts, Boston 33.364. All rights reserved: 20; Reproduced with permission. Copyright © 2001 Museum of Fine Arts, Boston 95.4. All rights reserved: 23; Reproduced with permission. Copyright © 2001 Museum of Fine Arts, Boston 14.61. All rights reserved: 24; Asian Art Museum of San Francisco, The Avery Brundage Collection B60 P161: 26; Photo copyright © Korea National Tourism Organization: 28, 29.

Chapter 8—Kyoryokukai: 1, 2; Courtesy of Jingu Shicho: 4; Photo: Ogawa Kozo (Askaen): 5, 6, 7, 8, 12; Robert Harding Picture Library: 10; Eisuke Ueda: 13; Reproduced with permission. Copyright © 2001 Museum of Fine Arts, Boston 11.4000. All rights reserved: 14.

Chapter 9—Hir: 1, 8, 9, 14; David Lees: 2; Canali: 3; Copyright © Mike Andrews/Ancient Art & Architecture Collection Ltd.: 4; Fototeca: 5; Archivio I.G.D.A., Milano: 7; photo Henri Stierlin:

10; Saskia Ltd Cultural Documentation: 11; Soprintendenza Archeologica per l'Etruria Meridionale: 12; AL: 13; German Archaeological Institute, Rome: 15.

Chapter 10—Photo Henri Stierlin: 1, 13, 30, 32, 50, 52; Scala: 2, 12, 15, 17, 23, 51, 58, 78; AL: 5, 35, 38, 39, 45, 55; German Archaeological Institute, Rome: 6,7; The American Numismatic Society, New York: 8; The Whittlesey Foundation/Aristide D. Caratzas, Publisher: 9; Fototeca: 11; Photo Archives Skira, Geneva, Switzerland: 14; Photo copyright © 1986 Metropolitan Museum of Art: 16; Copyright © Biblioteca Apostolica Vaticana: 19; Canali: 20, 21, 24, 41, 56, 74; Madeline Grimoldi: 22; Copyright © M. Sarri/Photo Vatican Museums: 25; Ny Carlsberg Glyptotek: 26; Saskia Ltd Cultural Documentation: 27, 28, 29, 36, 37, 80; Oliver Benn/Tony Stone Images: 31; The Image Bank/Guido Rossi: 34; Photo Alinari: 42; Photo Marcello Bertinetti/White Star: 43; Fototeca: 44; German Archaeological Institute, Rome: 46, 66, 69; Collection of Israel Antiquities Authority. Exhibited & photo copyright © Israel Museum: 47; Pubbli Aer Foto: 48; Art Resource, New York: 53; Ernani Orcorte/UTET: 54; Erich Lessing/Art Resource, New York: 56; Photo Vatican Museums: 57; De Masi/Canali: 59; German Archaeological Institute, Rome: 60, 72, 75; Canali/On license of the Ministero per i Beni Culturali ed Ambientali: 69,: 62; Peter Muscato: 63; BPK: 64; Photo copyright © 1986 Metropolitan Museum of Art: 65; Fototeca: 68; Photo copyright © 1983 Metropolitan Museum of Art: 70; G. Dagli Orti, Paris: 71; Index/Artphoto: 76; Istituto Centrale per il Catalogo e la Documentazione, (ICCD): 77; Rheinisches Landesmuseum: 81; American Numismatic Society, New York: 82; Hir: 82.

Chapter 11—The Jewish Museum, New York/Art Resource, New York: 1; Madeline Grimoldi: 3; Hir: 4, 14, 18, 20; Foto Archivio Fabbrica di San Pietro in Vaticano: 5; Saskia Ltd Cultural Documentation: 6, 8; Scala: 9, 13, 15, 16, 17; Canali: 11; Andre Held: 12; Österreichische Nationalbibliothek, Vienna: 19; Copyright © The British Museum: 21.

Chapter 12—R.M.N.-Chuzevilleh: 1; Hir: 2; Alan Oddie/PhotoEdit, Long Beach, CA: 3; photo Henri Stierlin: 5; Fotocielo, Rome: 6; Canali: 8, 10, 11; Scala: 9, 12, 24; Ronald Sheridan/AA& A: 13; Firenze, Biblioteca Medicea Laurenziana, Ms. Laur. Plut. 1.56, c. 13v Su concessione del Ministero per i beni e le attività culturali E' vietata ogni ulteriore riproduzione con qualsiasi mezzo: 14; Dumbarton Oaks, Washington, D.C.: 16; photo Paul M.R. Maeyaert: 17, 19; Studio Kontos: 20; Sostegni/Fotocielo: 21; Ricciarini/Visconti: 22; Canali/Cameraphoto: 23; Ricciarini, Milano: 25; R.M.N.: 26; Josephine Powell: 27; Sovfoto/Eastfoto: 29, 34; Studio Kontos: 30; Andre Held: 31; Hir: 33; State Historical Cultural Museum "Moscow Kremlin": 35.

Chapter 13—Yoram Lehmann, Jerusalem: 1; Erich Lessing/Art Resource, New York: 2; Aga Khan Visual Archives, MIT: 3; Photo Archives Skira, Geneva, Switzerland: 4; BPK: 6; Staatliche Museen zu Berlin: 7; Roger Wood/Continuum: 8; photo Henri Stierlin: 10, 19, 21, 23, 24, 27; Copyright © E. Simanor/Robert Harding Picture Library: 11; Saskia Ltd Cultural Documentation: 12; MAS: 13; Copyright © Adam Woolfitt/Robert Harding Picture Library: 14; Copyright © Musée Lorrain, Nancy/photo G. Mangin: 15; The State Hermitage Museum: 16; Reproduced by kind permission of the Trustees of the Chester Beatty Library, Dublin: 17; Copyright © C. Rennie/Robert Harding Picture Library: 18; Josephine Powell: 25; Photographer: Daniel McGrath: 28; Collection Prince Sadruddin Aga Khan: 29; Topkapi Palace Museum: 30; R.M.N.: 31.

Chapter 14—Copyright © Justin Kerr: 1, 8, 12; Erich Lessing/Art Resource, New York: 2; Rene Millon, 1973: 4; Lee Boltin: 5; Photo by Hillel Burger: 7, 11; Copyright © Dirk Bakker: 9, 24; Christopher

ILLUSTRATION CREDITS

INDEX

Boldfaced names refer to artists. Pages in italics refer to illustrations.